THREE GREAT HOTELS IN THREE GREAT CITIES

NEW WILLARD
WASHINGTON

WALDORF-ASTORIA
NEW YORK

BELLEVUE-STRATFORD
PHILADELPHIA

BOOMER-DUPONT PROPERTIES CORPORATION

THE
WALDORF=ASTORIA
COOKBOOK

JOHN DOHERTY with JOHN HARRISSON

PHOTOGRAPHS BY ELLEN SILVERMAN

PAGE 1: *The Waldorf=Astoria at night.*

PAGE 5: *The Waldorf=Astoria, circa 1935.*

PAGE 6–7: *Art Deco elevator doors in the lobby.*

ALL CHAPTER OPENER IMAGES: *Architectural details from the hotel.*

Bulfinch Press

Hachette Book Group USA
1271 Avenue of the Americas
New York, NY 10020
Visit our Web site at www.bulfinchpress.com

FIRST EDITION: SEPTEMBER 2006

Library of Congress Cataloging-in-Publication Data

Doherty, John.
    The Waldorf=Astoria cookbook / John Doherty with John Harrisson.
        p. cm.
    ISBN-10: 0-8212-5772-2 (hardcover)
    ISBN-13: 978-0-8212-5772-2 (hardcover)
    1. Cookery. 2. Waldorf=Astoria Hotel (New York, N.Y.) I. Harrisson,
John. II. Title.

    TX715.D6573 2006
    641.5—dc22   2005035849

Design by Joel Avirom, Jason Snyder, and Meghan Day Healey
Food styling by John Doherty

PRINTED IN SINGAPORE

To Mom, Dad,
and the Good Lord
for all I am today

CONTENTS

INTRODUCTION

Since the 1890s, the Waldorf=Astoria has represented the epitome of luxury and service in the hotel business, setting a standard that has long been admired and emulated. Over the years, it has been responsible for many historic firsts, and today its name is still synonymous with excellence and unstinting hospitality. It continues as the preferred destination for royalty, heads of state, celebrities, and leaders of every field from all over the globe, as well as for local residents and world travelers alike. Yet the Waldorf=Astoria is not simply a hotel: It enjoys landmark status as a community icon, and as a preferred setting for important and glamorous functions and occasions that define New York City. It is viewed as a magnificent institution whose attentive staff exudes warmth and helpfulness, pursuing the goal of exceeding guests' expectations whenever and wherever possible.

The history of the Waldorf=Astoria is a fascinating time capsule set within one of the most fabulous cities the world has ever seen. It is a story of wealth, imagination, and innovation—a heady mixture that changed everything. The Waldorf=Astoria not only changed people's expectations and perceptions of hotels, but it also changed the way hotels did business, and the way they were used. Before the Waldorf opened, in 1893, hotels dealt with the transient trade, mostly offering the bare necessities for travelers. No one of any standing considered holding a special event or a dinner at a hotel—the city's social elite attended dinners, balls, parties, and receptions in private homes or mansions. But with an extraordinary vision, stroke of genius, and a rather large leap of faith by the Waldorf=Astoria's founders, these habits were changed forever.

The legendary clock in the lobby of the Waldorf=Astoria.

THE RICH HISTORY OF THE WALDORF=ASTORIA:
A LEGEND IS BORN

William Waldorf Astor set plans for the Waldorf Hotel in motion shortly after inheriting the Fifth Avenue mansion and his fortune from the estate of his father, John Jacob Astor III, reputedly the richest man in America at the time of his death. He built the Waldorf on the site of that mansion, at Fifth Avenue and 33rd Street, for the then-unheard-of cost of $4 million.

Conceived from the beginning as a "home away from home" for New York's social elite, the 450-room hotel succeeded in meeting Astor's vision: a combination of European style and opulence with the comfort and familiarity of a private home. Designed by acclaimed architect Henry Hardenbergh, the Waldorf was a modern marvel—it boasted exquisitely appointed public spaces and private bathrooms in most of the guest chambers—a true innovation for that time. The thirteen-story hotel opened on March 13, 1893. Despite the inclement weather on the night of the opening, New York's crème de la crème (known as the Four Hundred) paid the enormously extravagant amount of five dollars each to attend a special charity gala thrown by the formidable Alva (Mrs. William K.) Vanderbilt to benefit St. Mary's Free Hospital for Children. Oysters, lobster, and veal were featured on the menu, and the New York Symphony provided the music.

The original Waldorf Hotel, c. 1900.

The "Unofficial Palace of New York," as it came to be known, became a gathering place for the wealthy and powerful, and several tycoons set up permanent quarters there. It quickly gained a reputation as a social headquarters and a venue to see and be seen. By the turn of the century, the Waldorf had even replaced the legendary Delmonico's restaurant as the prime location for holding special dinners and banquets.

Legend has it that Astor built the hotel at that location simply to annoy his aunt, Mrs. Caroline Schermerhorn Astor, who lived in the mansion next door and was the doyenne of New York society at the time. William was reputedly miffed at her social standing and wanted to dwarf her mansion. Whether or not that is true, once the Waldorf Hotel was built Caroline Astor did move uptown, and her son, John Jacob Astor IV (William Waldorf Astor's cousin), decided to build an equally grand hotel on the site of his mother's mansion. In November 1897, the seventeen-story Astoria Hotel (also designed by Henry Hardenbergh) opened its doors, boasting a roof garden, a ballroom, and a ground-floor "Men's Bar."

The lobby of the Waldorf Hotel.

Although the two structures were deliberately separated by thirty inches of air space (in case of a falling-out), the cousins agreed to run the two hotels, now with more than a thousand rooms, as a single entity—the Waldorf=Astoria. A three-hundred-foot-long marble corridor was built to connect the two buildings. A newspaper society editor dubbed this new promenade for the fashionably elegant "Peacock Alley" for the finery on display; as many as 15,000 onlookers daily gathered at Peacock Alley to witness the parade. The famous corridor became the enduring symbol of the combined Waldorf and Astoria hotels, represented still in the hotel logo: "Waldorf=Astoria." The saying in those days was "Meet me at the hyphen." It was immortalized in a popular song of the day whose chorus entreated, "At the Waldorf 'hyphen' Astoria/No matter who or what you are/Be sure to nod at Oscar as you enter."

For more than twenty years the hotel reigned supreme. But by the mid-1920s, Prohibition had irrevocably damaged the hotel's business, and by 1925 the overly ornate hotel was becoming outdated. Rumors began circulating of an end to the glorious run enjoyed by the Waldorf=Astoria. Closure was finally announced in December 1928, and although no plans for a new hotel had been announced, the new owner, Lucius Boomer, made clear that he had retained rights to the Waldorf=Astoria name. On Black Thursday of the Great Crash in October 1929, the final papers were signed to sell the property for $13.5 million to make way for another famous New York landmark, the 1,250-foot-high Empire State Building. The original Waldorf=Astoria closed its doors forever on May 3, 1929.

THE BUILDING AND OPENING
OF THE "NEW" WALDORF (1931)

It was the construction firm Thomson-Starrett Co. that proposed a new Waldorf=Astoria hotel to Lucius Boomer, offering their bankers' backing if he agreed to run the new venture. The site chosen was an entire city block between 49th and 50th Streets on Park Avenue (which not long before was known as the rather unfashionable Fourth Avenue). The consortium that financed the project included the New York Central Railroad and the New York, New Haven, and Hartford Railroad, over whose tracks from Grand Central Station the hotel was built. In fact, an underground railroad spur connected the rail line to a private platform two stories below ground, allowing direct access for VIPs to arrive inconspicuously in their private Pullman cars. Three buildings were demolished to make way for the new Waldorf=Astoria, including the New York Central Railroad's power plant and the central YMCA, and a budget of $28 million was established for the new building and furnishings. It was Lucius Boomer who stipulated that, just like the old Waldorf, the new hotel should feel like a "home away from home," and that no two rooms should be furnished alike.

Amazingly, the new hotel was designed over a long weekend by the architectural firm of Schultze and Weaver, who were responsible for the design of the Pierre Hotel and the Sherry-Netherland in Manhattan, and The Breakers in Palm Beach. The final drawings for the façade (including a six-foot-high rendering) and the complete interior in the Art Deco style required little change and exist to this day.

The zeppelin Hindenburg *passing over the new Waldorf=Astoria, c. 1936.*

Separate entrances on each side of the city block on which the hotel stands facilitated efficient access to different interior areas: the Main Lobby, the Grand Ballroom, Waldorf Towers, and the restaurants. The lower floors of the hotel were carefully and specifically designed to accommodate a complex of public spaces, private function rooms, and service areas. The traffic patterns anticipated and planned for seventy-five years ago have held up magnificently, and the designers' great foresight and sensibility are remarkable testaments to their genius. The drawings even detailed lighting fixtures, doorknobs, and hinges.

Site excavation began in January 1930. Sitting on 216 footings positioned between and on either side of the railroad tracks below to support the hotel's structure, the 625-foot-high building required 27,000 tons of steel, more than 3,000 cubic feet of pink granite and 80,000 cubic feet of silver-gray Indiana limestone, and 11 million bricks. One of the few items brought to the new hotel from the old was the magnificent Great Waldorf Clock made by the Goldsmith Company of London for the Chicago World's Fair of 1893. Nine feet high and weighing 2 tons, it still sits in the center of the Main Lobby, making it a popular rendezvous point.

More than 20,000 onlookers assembled outside the hotel on October 1, 1931, for the opening ceremony, as "Oscar of the Waldorf" stood at the top of the wide stairway leading into the Main Lobby, greeting familiar guests and old friends by name. The inauguration was broadcast over network radio, and President Herbert Hoover's dedication speech from the Cabinet Room of the White House was piped into the public rooms of the Waldorf and the Grand Ballroom where several thousand guests had gathered. Hoover offered congratulations on the reopening, which he viewed as a ringing endorsement of America's economic potential during the darkest days of the Great Depression.

When it opened, the new Waldorf=Astoria was the world's largest and tallest hotel, and with forty-two floors, it was also New York City's very first skyscraper hotel. It is now considered one of the finest examples of large-scale Art Deco architecture in the United States. The building simply dazzled visitors far and wide with its architectural splendor, distinctive elegance, and extraordinary luxury, just as it does today.

THE ELEGANT AFFAIRS

One of the most enduring legacies of the Waldorf=Astoria is the constant gamut of spectacular events that are hosted at the hotel. These may range from small, intimate family functions—receptions, reunions, weddings, and anniversary or birthday celebrations—to large-scale, glamorous, headline events held every year, such as the Rock and Roll Hall of Fame Dinner, the NASCAR Annual Banquet, Carnegie Hall's Opening Night Gala, a number of New York's Fashion Week events, and the Museum of the Moving Image annual dinner. Countless charitable benefits are

TOP: *Guests arriving for a Grand Ballroom event, circa 1930s.*

ABOVE: *The Grand Ballroom decorated for a recent event.*

also held at the Waldorf, and all of these high-profile events attract some of the most familiar names in the world of music, drama and entertainment, sports, and the arts. "There is definitely a 'wow' factor involved with these events," comments Tracey Brown, the Waldorf=Astoria's Director of Catering. "The Rock and Roll Hall of Fame event, attended by some of the legendary names in the business—from Elton John and the Rolling Stones to Bruce Springsteen and U2—is one of the hippest nights anywhere, anytime. There is a buzz around the hotel for days, before and after the dinner, even though our staff is used to accommodating A-list celebrities." Anton Moore, Director of Entertainment Sales, who frequently works directly with the hotel's celebrity guests, adds: "All of our events continue the peerless pedigree that has long been established. Many of our prominent guests tell us that the functions we host, in addition to the service we provide, are what put us head and shoulders above all the other properties in the city. There is no doubt that all these events keep the Waldorf in the news, contributing to the extraordinary energy and excitement of the place."

It was, after all, in 1897 that the Waldorf hosted the first grand society ball not staged in a private residence—a watershed moment in the city's history. The costume ball was thrown by Mrs. Bradley Martin and attended by nine hundred of New York's social elite. The unforgettable event cost $369,000 (several million in today's dollars), and festivities continued until breakfast time—all of which was considered scandalous by many. Still, the publicity was enormous and a precedent had been set.

"The Waldorf=Astoria has always dominated the city's market for major social events," notes Jim Blauvelt, Executive Director of Catering at the Waldorf=Astoria and its unofficial historian. "It remains the most important segment of our special events business, and the facilities and services we provide, together with our reputation for excellence, have enabled us to maintain our leading market share over the last hundred years. That's an achievement that makes us all very proud."

THE LEGACY OF COMMUNITY

The illustrious history of the Waldorf=Astoria has always, in turn, defined it and given it public perspective. Jim Blauvelt points to the unique relationship that exists between the hotel and the New York community: "There has always been a special civic connection, a feeling of public ownership and pride for what this great institution brings to the city. In our case, I think the relationship has been intensified because we are considered by many to be something of an icon. The hotel has always been connected to the social and civic agenda of New York, and we have provided a special setting for the large-scale, glamorous occasions that define the city. The hotel remains a trendsetter and a well-connected source of influence—we are a trusted landmark in our community. For all these reasons that spring from the public domain, the Waldorf=Astoria is held in a different light than most businesses."

WALDORF SERVICE—THE LEGACY OF EXCELLENCE

In the Waldorf=Astoria's kitchen is a timeworn wooden sign reminding all who tread that inner sanctum of the unofficial motto of the hotel: "The difficult immediately. The impossible takes a few minutes longer." Perhaps more than anything else, the attitude toward exemplary service at the Waldorf=Astoria is a frame of mind, and it remains an enduring asset that sets the hotel apart from its competitors.

One of the phrases that is still associated with the hotel is "Waldorf Service," a term synonymous with skilled, white-glove, tableside service that implies efficiency, sophistication, thoroughness, and excellence. Its essence is probably best summarized by the hotel's General Manager, Eric Long: "We spend a great deal of time underscoring the importance of each guest visit and interaction," he explains. "Our guest rooms and suites, our restaurants, meeting rooms, and special events venues are all in high demand, so it is important that we make each and every contact personal to our guests and validate the exceptionally high expectations they have of us."

Applying the Waldorf reputation of excellence from the marquee events and celebrity visits to individual meals enjoyed by dinner guests reflects the fact that the hotel's service philosophy is enacted by each and every member of the Food and Beverage Department. Managing high volume is one thing—a feat in itself to execute consistently well all the time—but to simultaneously succeed in maintaining and enhancing the Waldorf's reputation for fine-dining excellence and creativity on a small scale is quite another. Often, guests are surprised to learn that the Waldorf=Astoria serves over one million meals every year. Almost half of these are prepared by the Banquet and Catering Department for special events, an average of more than a thousand meals a day. At the other end of the spectrum, the exclusive Chef's Table events, held two or three times a month in the labyrinthine main kitchen, offer just thirty guests at a time the opportunity to experience the most outstanding selections from the Waldorf=Astoria's fine-dining repertoire. The award-winning Peacock Alley, the hotel's recently renovated fine-dining restaurant, likewise offers an intimate gourmet experience.

THE LEGACY AND THE FUTURE

The Waldorf=Astoria is responsible for many innovations in the hospitality industry: It was the first major hotel to offer electricity throughout, the first hotel to offer twenty-four-hour room service, and the first to host a society charity ball. At one time, the Waldorf=Astoria was the tallest and largest hotel in the world. It was the Waldorf that originated the practice of stationing assistant managers in the hotel lobby to greet guests, and it was Oscar of the Waldorf, the famous maître d', who first used the red plush rope to manage orderly lines. The hotel is famous as the birthplace of the legendary Waldorf Salad, among other classic American dishes, and for popularizing (if not necessarily inventing) numerous other favorites, including Eggs Benedict, Red Velvet Cake, Veal Oscar, Lobster Newburg, and Thousand Island Dressing. These landmark events and attributes, together with the stellar list of guests and events over the decades, have contributed to the Waldorf=Astoria's unparalleled reputation as a source of brilliant innovation and excellence.

However, resting on its past laurels is not a part of the Waldorf=Astoria's philosophy. Eric Long elaborates: "We are constantly challenging ourselves to think boldly and ensure we position this legendary hotel for the future. The expectations of today's guests are constantly evolving. We cannot allow ourselves to live in the past—we are the ones who are now creating history." This history is by no means restricted to the visits made and black tie events attended by countless heads of state, royalty, diplomats, and celebrities. It is also the history of individuals and families who come to the Waldorf to celebrate special occasions and lifetime landmarks—birthdays, anniversaries, engagements, and weddings—and the Waldorf's role in creating memories as part of that history. As Jim Blauvelt puts it, "The Waldorf=Astoria does not flaunt its social pedigree; our success and our reputation are earned every day, one event at a time."

The year was 1974, the place, Long Island, where I grew up. I was fifteen years old and pumping gas after school during the oil crisis. I remember working outside for hours in the freezing cold when a friend mentioned to me that a local restaurant, Johnny's Charcoal House, was looking for help. It turned out the position was dishwasher, but at least it got me out of the cold and away from the stressful gas lines. Soon after, I was helping prepare the food and working in the open kitchen at the front of the restaurant. I admired the owners' passions and intensity—everything was made from scratch—and the way they interacted with the customers; it was a great way to start in the business. I enjoyed the positive feedback from the owners and the customers and really took joy and pride in what I was doing. I didn't realize until later, in cooking school, how special this was.

It was my neighbor who suggested that I attend a cooking school, like the Culinary Institute of America (CIA). Once the idea was planted in my mind, I was excited and determined to pursue it. During my last year in high school, I earned cooking credits at technical school. There, Peter Berger, my Chef Instructor, picked up on my committed approach and spent a lot of time teaching me details of the trade. He provided encouragement and enrolled me in state cooking competitions and hotel shows. This was when I first thought that I wanted to work at the Waldorf=Astoria; after all, that was the epitome of luxury and excellence.

I applied to the CIA before I graduated from high school, and was accepted for enrollment in October 1976. While studying there, I had a clear goal in mind: My dream was to be good enough someday to work at the Waldorf=Astoria. As part of the curriculum at the Culinary Institute, each student served an externship between the first and second years, and although the school had placement arrangements at hotels and restaurants, the Waldorf=Astoria was not one of them. I really wanted to extern at "the greatest of them all" (to borrow Conrad Hilton's phrase), but I was on my own if I wanted to do so. I summoned up the courage to request an interview with Executive Chef Arno Schmidt. I told him I'd do whatever it took—peel potatoes, scrub floors, anything! My enthusiasm won him over and he said yes right away.

I worked at the hotel for five months on my externship, rotating through various kitchens, mostly filling in for chefs taking vacations. I got to learn the ropes in the Banqueting Department, Oscar's, Bull and Bear, and Peacock Alley. The energy of the kitchen and the challenge of learning new things was a great experience. I also learned something about professionalism from Arno Schmidt, who inspired the kitchen with his calm demeanor, neat appearance, and articulate manner. Reluctantly, I returned to school and graduated six months later, in 1978. You can imagine my pride and excitement when I was named Student Most Likely to Succeed in my forty-five-member class. Not only did the CIA ground me in the fundamentals of cooking and instill a pride in the craft, but I now understood *why* we were doing the things we were asked to do in the kitchen.

On graduating, there was only one place I wanted to work, and I was rehired on a permanent basis at the Waldorf=Astoria. The style of the food at the hotel was classic French, which was the backbone of my training at the CIA. I had been taught that the difference between a good chef and a great one was the ability to replicate classic French dishes and sauces, based on the repertoire formalized by Auguste Escoffier. It wasn't really necessary to be creative—as long as you maintained a recipe's authenticity, you were set. I loved entering this familiar world on a full-time professional level; my plan was to learn from the best and build a solid foundation through experience. Once again, I spent time rotating among different kitchen stations, and I was lucky to have been trained by real masters of haute cuisine who had been at the Waldorf for decades. They instilled in me the need to focus on detail and the importance of simplicity and flavor and, especially, hard work.

In 1981, I was appointed Chef Saucier, with overall responsibility for sauces. Although I would have preferred to gather more experience in a range of other roles, I was promoted to Sous Chef under Executive Chef Daniel Vigier in 1982. When Chef Vigier decided to promote me to Sous Chef, General Manager Eugene Scanlon sat me down to make sure I was made of the right stuff. Mr. Scanlon had come up through the ranks at the Waldorf, from kitchen apprentice to Executive Chef, Director of Food and Beverage, and finally, to General Manager. He was a huge supporter of change, and he encouraged me every step of the way. I always believed that if I worked hard and respected others, the quality of my work would speak for itself. As it turned out, it's a strategy that works in any business.

It was Chef Vigier who began changing the kitchen's philosophy in subtle ways and incorporating some influences from nouvelle cuisine as well as the food revolution that was taking root in America. He made greater use of fresh, local ingredients, introducing more creativity and contemporary ideas, while keeping true to the fundamentals of cooking. His philosophy was to make sure that the Waldorf's food was special for everyone, all the time, and this was an exciting period for me. Another helpful lesson I learned was that dramatic change or innovation was not something our clientele was looking for, so we infused our classical menu with new ideas and trends gently. Chef Vigier mentored me and helped hone my palate and creative skills; I credit him with turning me from a cook into a refined craftsman.

Doherty with Ossie Younge.

In 1983, Kurt Ermann, who had loyally served as Sous Chef at the Waldorf for thirty-five years, replaced Chef Vigier as Executive Chef, and I became Executive Sous Chef. Chef Kurt continued the process of refining our repertoire, returning authenticity to our classic dishes while supporting forward thinking and creativity. He was truly an encouraging force and has remained a firm friend. That same year, I was sent by the hotel to Europe to gain firsthand experience in some two- and three-star kitchens. During these *stages,* as the French call this style of practical training, I worked with Georges Blanc in Mâcon, in the Rhone Valley; Roger Souvereyns in Belgium; Wolf Engel in Holland; and Gerard Pangoud in Paris. These learning experiences truly inspired me and fueled my passion for cooking. The dedication and commitment of the kitchen staff were eye-opening; they confirmed my belief in what could, and should, be possible at the Waldorf=Astoria. I also realized the sheer scale of the Waldorf would mean those goals would take time and a great deal of effort, but my vision for the hotel was taking shape and I began to appreciate just what the full potential of our food-service operation might look like, and how important it would be to maintain that pinnacle of excellence. I have since returned to Europe on several occasions as a guest chef and, each time, the culture, mentality, and passion there inspire me all over again.

When Chef Kurt retired in 1985, I was appointed Executive Chef, at the age of twenty-seven. Without doubt, that was one of the greatest days in my life. Still, my tenure began inauspiciously; there was a citywide hotel strike called for June 1, the day that I started, which temporarily made things challenging. After business returned to normal a few weeks later, I found myself in charge of many of the chefs who had taught me so much. Fortunately, when I became Executive Chef, my colleague John Branda was promoted to Executive Sous Chef, and for several years was a valued partner in the kitchen. As the new Chef of this world-renowned kitchen, I knew it had great potential. The world of dining was changing rapidly. We needed to change, not just to keep up, but to become innovators, a yardstick for others to measure up to. I first created a vision for myself of what the food would look and taste like, how the chefs would conduct themselves, and how the disciplines of a great organization could accelerate positive change. In order to achieve this vision, I first set out to build a team of professionals who responded to the philosophy of excellence and were willing to put in the extra effort to achieve greatness. I have learned that the difference between good and great is effort. Greatness doesn't come easily, and even then I believed that unless you were willing to work hard, there wasn't room for you in my team. Once the team was in place, we began to set goals and objectives for dramatic change, high performance standards, and recognition for outstanding work. I learned to hone my skills of diplomacy and persuasion, and to set an example so others could follow my lead. I also learned the importance of respectfully communicating to my team new directions for the good of our business and the enjoyment of our guests. Many of the cooks and chefs who perform today were working here during this period of change.

Twenty years have come and passed since that vision of what this great kitchen could be was planted in my mind. It has taken longer than I had planned to accomplish all that has been done and I am all the wiser and stronger for it. Although we continue to raise the expectations of our performance, when I look back on all the great moments, the most gratifying element of my job is watching people recognize their own potential and helping them achieve greatness and satisfaction in their professional lives. It is the people who turn "good" into "great," a good dinner into a lifelong memory, and who uphold and surpass the legacy of this great institution.

Although I would like to consider the Waldorf as the largest boutique hotel in the world, the fact remains that the sheer volume of food served is daunting. However, growing up professionally in this environment taught me that you never need to compromise on quality to achieve quantity. It all starts with the design of the product. Of course, we use top-quality fresh ingredients and season them well, but we never try to take a dish designed for fifty people and serve it to five hundred. We respect our limits, which we push all the time.

We may serve between 3,000 and 5,000 meals a day, but they are broken up between many production areas, with the largest work group consisting of fifteen individuals. For example, each restaurant, and our twenty-four-hour Room Service operation, has its own kitchen (just like any independent restaurant does). Each kitchen is comprised of a chef, sous chef(s), and cooks. Each area in the Main Kitchen, which produces banquet food, is divided as well: a Garde Manger department for cold appetizers and hors d'oeuvres; a Pastry Shop, which operates twenty-two hours a day; a Butcher Shop, with three butchers and an assistant; a three-man sauce station; a soup kitchen with thirteen 80-gallon kettles; a Pantry staffed with five people who take care of all the fruit and cheese display platters, cut vegetables, and salads. It is the banquet crew, with two sous chefs and sixteen cooks most days, that brings all of the pieces together for service time by finishing all of the food for each party in the Banquet Kitchen. Once the basic food for each party is prepared, it is brought from the Main Kitchen to the appropriate Banquet Kitchen for finishing and service by the banquet team. There is a kitchen on the eighteenth floor for the Starlight Roof, where six hundred guests can be served, and another on the fourth floor to service smaller rooms like the Conrad Suite, the Duke of Windsor Suite, and the Louis XVI Suite. The third floor holds a kitchen that services the Grand Ballroom (capacity: 1,500 guests), while the Hilton and Empire Rooms on the Lobby level, which can each accommodate 350 guests, are serviced from the Main Kitchen on the second floor.

We have a very tightly run organization with systems that ensure quality at each step of production. The team is comprised of talented and knowledgeable people who challenge themselves and the operation each day, and of course having the proper equipment for the big parties helps us succeed every day. My job is to make sure that each chef has the tools and staff he or she needs, that they are continually looking for new ways to create memorable meals, that they are working within budget and building our business, and that we are compliant with local laws and corporate standards.

This book is a collection of recipes from recent memorable events, our restaurant menus, and personal favorites. I have chosen recipes that are challenging yet simple enough for most home cooks to reproduce with impressive results. I hope you enjoy them, together with the historical elements woven throughout the book. But this cookbook is not just a collection of great recipes; it also recognizes some great work that has been undertaken by many inspired professionals. You will learn some of their names and see their faces as you turn the pages.

I am sometimes asked to define my cooking style and palate. These were formed and underpinned, at least in part, by vivid childhood memories of my grandmother's meals. She was a fabulous cook—roast duck, fresh ham, dumplings, lots of flavorful sauces—I can still smell her cooking. My style has developed and evolved over the years to most often evoke the heart-

BREAKFAST LEMON CAKE

FOR THE LEMON CAKE

1 cup plus 3½ tablespoons
granulated sugar

1½ cups plus 1 tablespoon
all-purpose flour

1½ teaspoons baking powder

4 medium eggs

½ cup crème fraîche

3 tablespoons plus 1 teaspoon
freshly squeezed lemon juice

Zest of 3 lemons, grated

6 tablespoons butter, melted and
slightly cooled

FOR THE GLAZE

½ cup powdered sugar, sifted

Juice of 1 lemon

THIS RECIPE IS A DEFINITE in-house favorite! When I walk into the pastry shop in the morning, I usually find one of these cakes on the counter, cut into neat little pieces for kitchen staff. It is my favorite breakfast pastry because it's not too sweet and the lemony flavor is perfectly balanced. The thin hard glaze contrasts with the soft texture of the cake and, somehow, coffee never tastes so good as when it's served with this cake. We often bake a batch to present to our Chef's Table guests (see page 24) as they leave for the evening. We gift wrap them in little wooden baskets and let them know it's for the next morning's breakfast. I always wonder if these cakes ever make it home!

Preheat the oven to 350°F. Butter a 9-inch loaf pan.

TO PREPARE THE CAKE In the bowl of an electric mixer fitted with a paddle attachment, combine the sugar, flour, and baking powder on the lowest speed. Add the eggs and continue mixing until the mixture forms a smooth paste. Mix in the crème fraîche, lemon juice, lemon zest, and melted butter. Pour the batter into the buttered loaf pan and transfer to the center rack of the oven. Bake for 60 to 65 minutes or until a toothpick inserted into the center of the cake comes out clean. Let the cake cool in the pan for 5 to 10 minutes, then turn it out onto a rack to cool.

TO PREPARE THE GLAZE In a bowl, mix the powdered sugar and lemon juice until the sugar dissolves. Brush the top of the cake with the glaze while the cake is still warm.

Eggs Baked In Prosciutto with Tomato Salsa

SERVES 8

8 thin slices prosciutto

8 large eggs

1 ounce Fontina cheese, cut into
eight ½-inch cubes

2 tablespoons Pesto (page 257)

2 cups Tomato-Basil Salsa
(page 250)

THE CREATIVE SPIRIT IN OUR kitchen leads to many new and fun dishes for the brunch buffet at Oscar's, and this is one of them. I think you will love as much as I do the combination of the salty ham, creamy cheese, and the flavors of tomatoes and basil, all brought together by the soft eggs, which run a little when sliced open. To me, this is what breakfast should be about. There is even more to like about this recipe. You can cook the eggs for everybody all at once, and while the eggs are in the oven, you can tend to the toast, pour the coffee, and prepare the table. Breakfast can be hard enough without the perils of cold eggs, burned toast, and squabbling over who gets served first!

Preheat the oven to 375°F. Butter 8 cups of a muffin tin (or use nonstick muffin tins).

TO PREPARE THE PROSCIUTTO AND EGGS Line each of the 8 compartments of the muffin tin with a prosciutto slice. Crack 1 egg into each prosciutto cup. Add a cube of cheese and ¼ tablespoon of pesto to each egg. Transfer to the oven and bake until the eggs are just set, about 7 minutes; the egg yolks should still be a little runny when done. Remove from the oven and let rest for 2 or 3 minutes before carefully removing the prosciutto cups from the tins. Arrange on a serving platter (or transfer to warm serving plates) and top with salsa.

CHEF'S NOTE

◇   Be sure to use a high-quality imported prosciutto such as Parma, and make sure it is sliced paper thin.

Oscar's Crunchy Banana-Stuffed French Toast with Pineapple-Coconut Sauce

SERVES 8

FOR THE FRENCH TOAST BATTER

10 large eggs

½ cup heavy cream

Zest of ½ orange, grated

Zest of 1 lime, grated

1 tablespoon vanilla extract

¼ cup dark rum

Pinch of salt

½ cup powdered sugar

FOR THE CARAMELIZED BANANAS

3 tablespoons butter

3 ripe bananas, sliced

3 tablespoons brown sugar

FOR THE FRENCH TOAST

14 cups corn flakes, crushed
(about 8 cups crushed)

12 slices Warm Waldorf Brioche
(page 42), ½ inch thick

¼ cup melted butter

HERE IS A DELICIOUS RECIPE that will transport you to the tropics—better ask your company to sit down at the table in their aloha shirts and straw hats. We serve it at Oscar's year-round for breakfast and brunch, even when the snow is swirling. This is a perfect example of how we develop recipes at the Waldorf=Astoria as a team by experimentation. We start with an idea, and from there, we bounce around suggestions for variables based on the season, available ingredients, and our customers' preferences. In this case, we started with the idea of stuffing French toast and wound up with a tropical version that is a huge brunch seller.

TO PREPARE THE BATTER Whisk together the eggs, cream, citrus zest, vanilla extract, rum, salt, and powdered sugar in a mixing bowl. Cover and transfer to the refrigerator.

TO PREPARE THE BANANAS Heat the butter in a small skillet set over medium heat until it is completely melted. Add the bananas, sprinkle with the sugar, and toss to combine. Turn down the heat to low and let the bananas caramelize for about 5 minutes, carefully turning once or twice. Remove from heat and let cool to room temperature.

Preheat the oven to 375°F.

TO PREPARE THE FRENCH TOAST Pour the crushed corn flakes into a large shallow bowl and set aside. Heat a large, heavy skillet or griddle over medium-low heat. Lay out 6 slices of the brioche on a clean work surface. Spread each slice of brioche with the cooled, softened bananas. Place the remaining slices of brioche on top of the bananas to form a sandwich. Set each sandwich in the batter and let soak for 1 minute on each side, until the brioche absorbs the liquid, then dredge the brioche in the crushed corn flakes. Turn the brioche over and coat the other side. Melt the butter in the warm skillet and tilt, so the bottom of the skillet is well coated, and add the dredged brioche. Cook until golden brown, about 3 minutes on each side. Transfer to a cookie sheet and finish in the oven for 5 minutes.

FOR THE PINEAPPLE-
COCONUT SAUCE

2 cups pineapple juice

*¾ cup canned unsweetened
coconut milk*

*2 tablespoons Malibu
(coconut-flavored rum)*

½ tablespoon softened butter

*2 tablespoons sifted powdered sugar,
for dusting*

TO PREPARE THE PINEAPPLE-COCONUT SAUCE While the brioche is baking, pour the pineapple juice and coconut milk into a medium saucepan and set over medium heat. Continue to cook until the mixture is reduced by about half and 1½ cups remain, about 10 to 12 minutes. Stir in the Malibu rum and butter.

TO SERVE Cut each piece of French toast in half diagonally. Arrange 3 halves on each warm serving plate and sprinkle with powdered sugar. Pour some of the sauce around the plate and serve the rest at the table.

CHEF'S NOTE

◇   Use a store-bought loaf-style brioche, if you prefer.

WARM WALDORF BRIOCHE

[1 LOAF]

FOR THE BRIOCHE

¼ cup milk

1 package dry yeast

2¼ cups plus 2 tablespoons
bread flour

2 tablespoons large-grain rock
or granulated sugar

1 teaspoon salt

4 medium eggs (at room temperature)

1 cup plus 1 tablespoon butter,
slightly softened

FOR THE EGG WASH

1 medium egg plus 1 egg yolk, beaten

½ teaspoon large-grain rock sugar
or granulated sugar (optional)

A GOOD, RICH BRIOCHE—BUTTERY YET LIGHT—is hard to beat. This is the recipe we use for our breakfast and coffee service at the Waldorf, and like the Lemon Cake (page 28), it is often packaged as a parting gift for our Chef's Table guests to enjoy the next morning. We sometimes add candied orange or grapefruit confit for an added flavor dimension, and our savory variation, with caramelized onions, makes a wonderful bun for our burgers (see Chef's Note opposite).

———————————

TO PREPARE THE BRIOCHE Heat the milk in a saucepan until lukewarm. Sprinkle the yeast into the milk and let sit for 8 minutes. Combine the flour, sugar, and salt in the bowl of an electric mixer fitted with a dough hook and mix on low speed until combined. With the mixer running, add the eggs and yeast mixture and continue to mix just until the flour is moistened. Stop the mixer and scrape down the sides of the bowl with a rubber spatula, incorporating any remaining dry ingredients. Turn the mixer to medium speed and beat for 10 to 12 minutes, scraping down the sides of the bowl as needed, until the mixture comes together and pulls away from the sides of the bowl.

Reduce the mixer speed to low, add the butter, and continue mixing until completely incorporated. Transfer the dough to a floured rimmed sheet pan (or a metal bowl) and cover with plastic wrap. Let rest in a warm place (about 72°F) for 30 to 40 minutes.

Butter a loaf pan measuring 9 inches by 5 inches by 3 inches. Remove the dough from the refrigerator and shape into 10 or 12 balls about 2 inches in diameter. Place the balls, 2 across, in the bottom of the prepared loaf pan. Let the dough rise in a warm place (about 72°F) until it doubles in volume, 1 to 1½ hours.

Preheat the oven to 350°F.

Brush the top of the brioche dough with the egg wash and sprinkle the top with sugar, if desired. Transfer the loaf pan to the center rack of the oven and bake for about 25 minutes or until the brioche turns deep golden brown. Let the brioche cool in the pan for about 5 minutes, then turn out onto a rack to cool completely.

CHEF'S NOTES

◇ You can use ¾ ounce cake yeast, crumbled, instead of dry yeast.

◇ Proofing the dough on a sheet pan (rather than in a bowl) is preferable because the more surface contact the dough has, the better.

◇ This recipe will make 10 to 12 burger rolls. For this purpose, I recommend using ½ tablespoon less sugar in the dough. After shaping the dough into balls just prior to baking, space them on a baking sheet and sprinkle 1 tablespoon of caramelized onions (see recipe on page 250) on top of each dough ball. Bake as directed above.

Classic Eggs Benedict with Hollandaise

SERVES 6

FOR THE HOLLANDAISE
SAUCE

2 large egg yolks

*2 teaspoons freshly squeezed
lemon juice*

1 cup (8 ounces) melted butter

Pinch of salt

Pinch of cayenne

*12 slices (⅛ inch thick)
Canadian-style bacon*

FOR THE EGGS

3 tablespoons white vinegar

12 eggs (at room temperature)

6 English muffins, split with a fork

FOR THE GARNISH

*12 slices black winter truffle
(optional)*

ONE THEORY REGARDING THE CREATION of this timeless classic suggests that it was created at the Waldorf in 1894 for a Wall Street broker and regular patron, Lemuel Benedict, who requested a plate of toast, crispy bacon, poached eggs, and hollandaise sauce to help with his hangover. According to an account published in the *New Yorker* magazine in 1942, the legendary maitre d' of the Waldorf, Oscar Tschirky (page 98), improvised and ordered a plate for Mr. Benedict with Canadian bacon and a muffin (instead of crispy rashers and toast). The dish was a huge hit not only with Mr. Benedict but with other guests too, and it is as popular today as it ever has been. In fact, this is our single most popular brunch item at the Waldorf=Astoria, and it is the dish my wife, Donna, eats whenever she visits the hotel for breakfast or brunch—she never even opens the menu. By contrast, she has stopped ordering it anywhere else because she is always disappointed. Now, there is a recommendation!

TO PREPARE THE SAUCE Bring a saucepan of water to a simmer. In a nonreactive bowl, whisk together the egg yolks, lemon juice, and ½ tablespoon water. Place the bowl over the saucepan, making sure the bowl is not touching the water, and continue to whisk vigorously until ribbons form; be careful not to overheat the yolks or they will scramble. Remove the bowl and slowly drizzle in the melted butter, continuing to whisk until the butter is absorbed into the mixture. Add the salt and cayenne. Transfer to a ceramic serving bowl and keep on a warm place on the stove for up to 1 hour.

Preheat the broiler.

Heat a dry heavy skillet and saute the bacon over medium-high heat for 1 or 2 minutes on each side until lightly browned. Turn off the heat and cover skillet to keep bacon warm.

TO PREPARE THE EGGS Pour at least 2 inches of water into a large shallow saucepan, add the vinegar, and heat the water to 180°F (small bubbles form and the water is visibly moving). Gently crack the eggs and drop them into the water as close to the surface as possible. Poach for about 3½ minutes until the egg whites are set and the yolks are still a little soft. Remove with a slotted spoon, allowing excess water to drain, and gently blot dry with a paper towel.

TO SERVE Place the split muffins on a large cookie sheet and toast under the broiler until golden brown. Transfer the toasted muffins to warm serving plates and place one slice of the bacon on each muffin half. Place a poached egg on top of the bacon and spoon the hollandaise over each egg. Garnish each egg with a slice of truffle, if desired.

CHEF'S NOTES

◇ The secret to perfect Eggs Benedict, in addition to top-quality English muffins, Canadian bacon, and eggs, is the excellence of the hollandaise sauce. A perfect version has complete balance between the flavor and richness of the egg and butter, and the subtle acidity and piquancy of the lemon juice and cayenne pepper. If the hollandaise sauce seems too thick, whisk in a few drops of warm water.

◇ Adding vinegar to the water in which the eggs are cooking helps to keep the eggs from spreading.

◇ A nonreactive bowl is any bowl made of glass, stainless steel, ceramic, or china. Copper, silver, or aluminum pans may discolor the mixture and affect its flavor.

The Waldorf=Astoria's Room Service stays open twenty-four hours, and the busiest single meal period is breakfast. On a typical day, as many meals are prepared for breakfast in the Room Service kitchen as for lunch, dinner, and after-hours combined. With a daily average of 500 to 700 in-room meals, rising to 1,200 at busy times of the year, that's a lot of pastries, eggs, and coffee. The daily operation is directed by Room Service Chef de Cuisine Alan Ashkinaze (left with Louis Giordano), who is now on his second tour of duty at the Waldorf. Alan, a graduate of the Culinary Institute of America, was a Sous Chef at New York's Plaza Hotel and Executive Sous Chef at the Waldorf's Peacock Alley before leaving to broaden his experience on both the East and West Coasts. After an eight-year hiatus, Alan returned to the Waldorf to head up Room Service, overseeing a staff of eighteen cooks and more than sixty service personnel.

"Our motto in Room Service may apply to the whole Waldorf=Astoria kitchen," says Alan, "but we live it every day: 'The difficult immediately; the impossible takes a few minutes longer.' It's a good credo. A big part of our job is to accommodate our guests' requests, and our success in meeting those demands is what sets us apart. That's a big part of what I enjoy the most about my job—every day is different, you never know what lies ahead. It's important to prepare and anticipate as far as you can, but everything is fluid, and sometimes you have to flat-out like problem-solving. Our challenge, bottom line, is in the details—to meet the expectations of hundreds of guests by 9:00 A.M. The bacon has to be crisp, the eggs have to be soft and warm, it all needs to be done just right."

Alan's philosophy in Room Service mirrors Chef Doherty's. "Another of our biggest challenges, when it comes to breakfast, is to offer the timeless classics—ideally with an interesting twist, but that twist cannot affect the overall integrity of the flavors or the enjoyment of our guests. It's a fine line. Take Eggs Benedict, for example, a dish that is more than a hundred years old and identified with Oscar Tschirky and this hotel. Food trends come and go, tastes and products change and evolve, but Eggs Benedict in its timeless, classic form will always be on our menu. The same is true for corned beef hash or hash brown potatoes. It's what people like. There's no need to change a great piece of classical music, and some foods are just the same."

For Alan, Room Service is at its most demanding—and interesting—come September, when United Nations delegations attending the UN General Assembly in New York are headquartered at the Waldorf. Typically, up to thirty heads of state from around the world stay at the hotel during this time. "We double our in-room dining service during this time," he explains. "One or two of the delegations bring their own chefs, but most don't. Some bring us ingredients they'd like us to use, and it's fascinating to learn about some of the different traditions and food cultures from around the world, even at breakfast. Then again, every week of the year we are feeding VIPs and movers and shakers, and I am sometimes asked how we treat them differently. The truth is, and I can say this honestly, we treat every guest the same, with the common goal of an excellent product delivered with outstanding service. That's why I'm proud to be part of the Waldorf legacy. It's also why I returned without hesitation to work here—it's my favorite hotel in the country, and undoubtedly one of the best in the world."

—J.H.

Pancetta and Mozzarella Strata with Olive-Rosemary Bread

SERVES 6

2 cups finely diced pancetta

1 cup finely diced onion

1 tablespoon balsamic vinegar

16 eggs, beaten

1 cup half-and-half

1 tablespoon Roasted Garlic Purée
(page 257)

1 teaspoon salt

¼ teaspoon freshly ground
white pepper

4 cups cubed black olive bread
(about ½ large round loaf)

1 cup finely diced tomatoes

2 cups finely diced fresh
mozzarella cheese

½ tablespoon minced fresh rosemary

HERE IS ANOTHER DO-AHEAD BREAKFAST or brunch dish that is a real crowd pleaser; as long as the ratio of bread, eggs, and cream remains the same, you can get as creative as you like with the garnish. The main idea is to have fun with the ingredients. For example, you might try some combination of chicken or turkey sausage with broccoli rabe, smoked mozzarella, and Portobello mushrooms. Come to think of it, I may just have come up with tomorrow morning's strata!

Preheat the oven to 325°F. Butter a large baking dish or casserole.

Place the pancetta in a saucepan over medium-low heat. Cook until golden brown, about 8 minutes, stirring occasionally. Transfer the pancetta to a bowl, leaving the rendered fat in the pan. Add the onions to the pan and sauté until translucent, 3 or 4 minutes. Add the vinegar and deglaze the pan, stirring with a wooden spoon to loosen any solids stuck to the bottom. Transfer the mixture to the bowl with the onions and let cool to room temperature. In a separate mixing bowl, combine the eggs, half-and-half, garlic purée, salt, and pepper and set the bowl aside.

Evenly distribute the bread cubes in the buttered baking dish and top with the tomatoes and half of the mozzarella. Pour the egg mixture into the baking dish, making sure that all of the bread is immersed. Set aside to let the bread absorb the egg mixture for at least 30 minutes.

Distribute the remaining mozzarella on top of the mixture and cover with foil. Place the baking dish in the oven and bake, covered, for 30 minutes. Remove the foil and continue baking until the eggs are set in the middle, about 20 minutes. Remove from the oven, divide the strata among warm serving plates, and garnish with the rosemary.

Maple-Glazed Pecan-Orange Waffles

SERVES 8

FOR THE MAPLE GLAZE

1¾ cups pure maple syrup

6 tablespoons butter,
cut into small pieces

4 tablespoons orange marmalade

2 tablespoons freshly squeezed
orange juice

1 teaspoon finely grated orange zest

FOR THE WAFFLES

2 cups pecan pieces

2 cups all-purpose flour

1½ cups cornmeal

¼ cup sugar

4 teaspoons baking powder

1 teaspoon salt

6 large eggs, separated

3 cups milk

¾ cup melted butter

2 teaspoons finely grated orange zest

WAFFLES ARE GREAT FOR BREAKFAST, brunch, or dessert. Crunchy on the outside, moist and creamy on the inside, they lend themselves well to fruit and yogurt as a lighter alternative to maple syrup. Speaking of syrup, only pure amber maple syrup is allowed on my breakfast table at home. There is no substitute. I find natural maple flavor amazing, and it cannot be created artificially, as is claimed by many manufacturers. Our maple glaze is simply decadent on these crunchy waffles—your guests will want to know how you did it.

TO PREPARE THE MAPLE GLAZE   Pour the maple syrup into a heavy-bottomed saucepan and set over medium heat. Bring to a low boil and remove the pan from the heat. Whisk in the butter, a few pieces at a time, until thoroughly combined. Stir in the marmalade, orange juice, and orange zest and incorporate. Keep warm over low heat.

TO PREPARE THE WAFFLES   Preheat and lightly oil a waffle iron. Place the pecans in a dry skillet and set over medium-high heat. Toast, stirring frequently, until the pecans turn dark and are fragrant, 3 to 4 minutes; take care not to burn them. Transfer to a food processor and finely chop. Add the flour, cornmeal, sugar, baking powder, and salt and continue to process until the mixture forms a fine meal. Transfer to a mixing bowl and whisk in the egg yolks one at a time, then the milk, melted butter, and orange zest. In a separate bowl, beat the egg whites until stiff peaks form. With a spatula, carefully fold the egg whites into the waffle batter.

Pour the batter into the preheated waffle iron until it is level with the rim of the iron. Close the lid. Cook the waffles according to the manufacturer's instructions or until crisp and golden brown. Transfer to warm plates and serve with the warm glaze.

CHEF'S NOTE

◇   The glaze can be prepared ahead of time and refrigerated for up to 3 days. Warm over low heat, stirring constantly; if the glaze separates, remove from the heat and whisk in a little hot water.

⟞◎ THE WHEEL OF LIFE ◎⟞

In 1939, a remarkable, eighteen-foot diameter Art Deco style mosaic, composed of one hundred forty-eight thousand tiles, was installed in the floor of the Park Avenue Foyer, depicting twelve life-size figures from birth through old age. It reproduced the design of the forty-eight-foot square "Wheel of Life" rug designed by French artist Louis Rigal; the mosaic took eight months to complete. Rigal also painted the thirteen allegorical friezes located in the Main Foyer and designed the Art Deco bronze panels on the elevator doors. The mosaic and murals were covered over in the late 1940s and were restored to their former glory during extensive renovations in the early 1980s.

2

COCKTAILS AND HORS D'OEUVRES

Put cocktails and hors d'oeuvres together, add a few people, and you have yourself a party. This chapter presents some recipes for both, so now it's up to you to round up some friends! The original Waldorf=Astoria on Fifth Avenue developed quite a reputation for creating and serving innovative mixed drinks, especially at The Old Bar. Some of the best cocktails that were first mixed at the hotel are included here, with the recipe introductions providing historical background. Hotel records for the year 1912, for example, show that wine and liquor accounted for the biggest single expense in the food and beverage operation, at a cost of $245,000 (by comparison, fuel accounted for $125,000, meat for $125,000, and poultry, $121,000). Oscar Tschirky, the hotel's legendary maitre d', lamented that the saddest day of his long career at the Waldorf was June 30, 1919, the day Prohibition went into effect. Shortly afterward, a soda fountain replaced the Old Bar, an event Oscar described as "heartbreaking." When the new Waldorf=Astoria opened at its current location on Park Avenue in 1931, the Prohibition era was almost over; when it finally ended in 1933, Oscar was a happy man once more.

Hors d'oeuvres—little tempting tidbits to get things started—can serve as a prelude to a meal or, with enough variety, the food for an event, party, or even a picnic. They are the perfect icebreaker, and can also be the most challenging part of a meal for a number of reasons. First, they set the tone for the dishes that are to come. If your hors d'oeuvres selection is predictable—for example, cocktail franks, crudités, chips and dip, or shrimp cocktail—why would anyone think the dinner would be any more interesting? On the other hand, if they are light, flavorful, and creative—you get the idea.

Before I introduce these original Waldorf=Astoria hors d'oeuvres, let me touch upon those predictables I mentioned. Take cocktail franks. Many people truly like them because they find them familiar and perhaps their taste in food is not quite as adventurous as others. However, the time comes when creating something new and different is just the right thing to do. Make the effort to turn the ordinary into something extraordinary, for example, with crudités: Cut your vegetables into interesting shapes or use a crinkle-cut knife. Put each vegetable in its own dish, and pour the dip into a hollowed-out cabbage or acorn squash. Or, instead of boiled shrimp cocktail, grill the shrimp with a little garlic, lemon zest, and parsley—much tastier! How about those pigs in blankets? Making your own is very easy and considerably better tasting—and more impressive— than the frozen product. Get good-quality miniature franks from your butcher and wrap them in cut puff pastry sheets purchased frozen from the grocery store or bakery. Serve them with a good-quality mustard, perhaps one that's infused with green peppercorns or raspberries, and trust me, they will be a hit!

Whether the event is a party or a dinner, the selection of hors d'oeuvres is as important as the main event. They should be tempting, pretty, use seasonal ingredients, and should tie into your chosen theme. For instance, if your buffet or sit-down dinner is Mediterranean-inspired, keep the hors d'oeuvres tuned to that concept rather than starting with, for example, Asian-style hors d'oeuvres. Anything you like to eat can become an hors d'oeuvres; just think about classic flavor combinations (or your favorite pairings) and miniaturize them. If it can be put on a crostini or cracker, great! If not, try serving it on a spoon or in a corn tortilla cup, shot glass, or small dish. Use baskets, wood or stone surfaces, or pretty platters—be creative! A variety of presentations will create a sense of fun, bring more attention to the food, and, in the end, help make for a more memorable event.

The hors d'oeuvres I have chosen to share with you are delicious and beautiful. More important, think of them in terms of minibites. For each little dish, you can make endless variations, depending on your personal taste, your menu, your favorite style of presentation, or even the serving pieces that you have.

✇ LIGHTS! CAMERA! ACTION! ✇

It is fitting that the Waldorf=Astoria, which featured its own Oscar (see page 98), boasts its own extensive movie pedigree. Ginger Rogers, Lana Turner, and Walter Pidgeon starred in *Weekend at the Waldorf* (1945), set at the hotel. More recently, numerous movies have been filmed in or around the Waldorf. These include *Scent of a Woman, Coming To America, You've Got Mail, First Wives' Club, The Royal Tannenbaums, Maid in Manhattan, Serendipity, Mr. Deeds, Hannah and Her Sisters, Alfie,* and *Analyze This.* In many cases, the stars of these films stayed at the Waldorf during the shooting on location.

Red Velvet Cake Martini

1 COCKTAIL

2 ounces premium vodka

1 ounce Crème de Fraise
(strawberry liqueur)

1 tablespoon whipped cream,
for garnish

1 teaspoon chocolate shavings,
for garnish

THIS MARTINI CLEVERLY ECHOES THE coloration of the Red Velvet Cake (page 222), a traditional dessert at the Waldorf, thanks to legendary maitre d' Oscar Tschirky. This is a modern creation that is fun to look at and will get the conversation flowing for sure.

Pour the vodka and Crème de Fraise into a cocktail shaker; add ice, and shake vigorously for a few seconds. Pour into a martini glass, add the whipped cream, and garnish with the chocolate shavings.

The Rob Roy

1 COCKTAIL

2 ounces premium Scotch whisky

1½ ounces dry vermouth

Dash orange bitters
(see Chef's Note)

1 maraschino cherry

THIS COCKTAIL ORIGINATED AT THE old Waldorf Hotel in 1894, shortly after it opened. It was created in honor of the opening of the operetta Rob Roy, which premiered near Herald Square, just a couple of blocks away. Interesting new cocktails were a hallmark of the Gay Nineties, as that decade was known, and as this combination proves. If you prefer, make your Rob Roy with sweet vermouth instead of dry, and by all means omit the orange bitters.

Place ice cubes in a mixing glass and add all the ingredients. Stir with a cocktail spoon for several seconds and strain into a martini glass. Garnish with the cherry.

CHEF'S NOTE

 Back in the day, orange bitters, made from the peel of sour oranges marinated in alcohol and infused with spices, was a fairly common ingredient in cocktails. In fact, there were several types of herbal bitters, most of which fell out of favor after Prohibition. Nowadays, only Angostura bitters is familiar to most cocktail lovers, but the flavor is quite different from orange bitters. The good news is that there is a mail-order source for orange bitters (see page 261).

THE BRONX

1 COCKTAIL

1 ounce gin

2 ounces freshly squeezed orange juice

¼ ounce sweet vermouth

¼ ounce dry vermouth

1 slice orange peel
(use a vegetable peeler)

THIS COCKTAIL IS ANOTHER HISTORIC creation from pre-Prohibition days at the Waldorf=Astoria. The story goes that bartender Johnnie Solon was challenged by a dinner guest to make a new cocktail, and that he was inspired by the Duplex, a popular drink at the time, which contained sweet and dry vermouth and orange bitters. Apparently, Solon named it *The Bronx* after a visit he had made a day or two before to New York's Bronx Zoo. He later recollected that on that trip he had seen many beasts that he had never seen before, which reminded him of patrons of his after a few mixed drinks. Solon reported that soon after he created The Bronx cocktail, he had to order several cases of oranges a day to keep up with demand, so, if your guests should enjoy this one, be prepared!

Place ice cubes in a cocktail shaker and add the gin, orange juice, and sweet and dry vermouth. Shake vigorously for a few seconds and strain into a cocktail glass. Garnish with orange peel.

THE ROBERT BURNS

1 COCKTAIL

1½ ounces Scotch whisky

½ ounces sweet vermouth

Dash orange bitters
(see note, page 56)

Dash Pernod

HERE IS A COCKTAIL THAT also first saw the light of day (or, more likely, the dark of night) at the bar of the old Waldorf=Astoria. It would be romantic to retell of its naming for the celebrated Scottish poet, but in *The Old Waldorf=Astoria Bar Book,* published in 1931, the author and former hotel historian Albert Stevens Crockett suggests a more mundane origin. His theory is that it was named after a cigar salesman who used to frequent the hotel's Old Bar, although he does not rule out the possibility that the Burns could have been named after the poet. In the old days, by the way, the cocktail was made with absinthe rather than Pernod.

Place ice cubes in a cocktail shaker and add all the ingredients. Stir with a cocktail stick for a few seconds and strain into a cocktail glass.

People come to the Waldorf=Astoria to celebrate their weddings, receptions, and special events, which is when the champagne flows. When I asked the hotel's purchasing department about how much champagne we used, they told me the figure for a recent year was more than sixteen thousand five hundred bottles, well over three hundred bottles a week. That's a lot of bubbly!

The name *champagne* is limited not only to a specific region of France (about ninety miles northeast of Paris) but also to the wine-making process itself.

Approximately 250 million bottles of champagne are produced each year, so we have a way to go at the Waldorf before we make a serious dent in the total inventory.

Like other wine varietals, part of what makes the champagne special is the chalky soil that holds moisture well. The history of the region helps too: Vines were first planted in the region in the third century A.D., and monks cultivated grapes to make communion and table wine.

According to legend, it was in the seventeenth century that a Benedictine monk named Dom Perignon discovered the technique for making sparkling wine. After the first sip, he is said to have told his assistants, "Come quick, I'm tasting stars!"

Servers Nehemias Rodriguez and Hon Lim Chung in the Royal Suite.

All champagne grapes are hand-picked; harvesting machines are not allowed. The bubbles occur during the wine's second fermentation in the bottle.

There are several different styles of champagne. Here are some helpful terms:

NONVINTAGE—a blend of the wines from several different years

VINTAGE—the wines of one specific year only

BLANC DE BLANCS—champagne made with 100 percent Chardonnay grapes

BLANC DE NOIRS—champagne made with Pinot Noir or Pinot Meunier grapes, or a blend of the two

BRUT—bone dry

EXTRA SEC—dry

SEC—slightly sweet

DEMI-SEC—sweet

Nonvintage and blanc de blancs are perfect aperitifs and good companions for light appetizers and seafood or poultry. Old vintages are more robust and can be consumed throughout dinner. As with great Cabernets and Pinot Noirs, exceptional vintage champagnes can age for decades and, like a great Chardonnay, should be decanted in order to let all the flavors come through.

RICOTTA GNOCCHI WITH WHITE TRUFFLES AND PARMESAN CREAM

2 pounds sheep's milk ricotta cheese

FOR THE PARMESAN CREAM

1 pound Parmesan cheese rind
(see Chef's Note)

4 cups Chicken Stock (page 252)

2 sprigs fresh thyme

1 clove garlic

1 dried bay leaf

1 cup heavy cream

½ tablespoon white truffle oil

FOR THE GNOCCHI

2 large eggs

1½ cups all-purpose flour,
plus ¼ cup for dusting

1 teaspoon salt

Pinch freshly ground white pepper

Pinch cayenne

1 ounce fresh white truffle,
for garnish

I GUARANTEE THAT YOU WILL not find a lighter, more delicious gnocchi anywhere, as guests and food reviewers will attest. These particular Italian-style dumplings, developed by Executive Sous Chef Peter Daledda, were created for our Chef's Table event (see page 24) and are an elegant way to start an evening. These gnocchi are delicate and refined, so take care not to overpower them if you choose to pair them with other plates. This tasty little dish can be easily turned into an appetizer with the addition of some thinly sliced asparagus.

Place the ricotta in a fine-mesh strainer set over a bowl. Cover the strainer with foil or plastic wrap and put in the refrigerator to drain overnight.

TO PREPARE THE PARMESAN CREAM Cut the cheese rind into 2-inch pieces and place in a saucepan. Add the stock, thyme, garlic, and bay leaf and bring to a boil. Turn down the heat to medium low and simmer for 1 hour. Strain 1 cup of the liquid through a fine-mesh strainer into a clean saucepan. Stir in the heavy cream and bring to a simmer over high heat. Turn down the heat to medium and reduce the mixture until 1 cup remains, about 20 minutes. Stir in the truffle oil and keep warm.

TO PREPARE THE GNOCCHI Remove the drained ricotta from the refrigerator and place in the bowl of a food processor. Blend about 1 minute, until smooth. Transfer the ricotta to a mixing bowl and mix in the eggs using a wooden spoon. Add 1½ cups of the flour, salt, pepper, and cayenne, and mix. Return to the refrigerator and chill for 2 hours.

Sprinkle some flour on a clean work surface. Take a handful of the chilled dough and place it on the floured surface. Lightly coat your hands with flour and roll out the dough to form an even log about 1-inch thick. Use a knife dusted in flour to cut the log into 1-inch pieces; pinch each piece lightly in the center to give it an hourglass shape. Place the gnocchi on a floured cookie sheet, taking care that they do not touch one another or they will stick together. Repeat this process until all the dough has been rolled, cut, and shaped. Refrigerate the gnocchi for at least 1 hour before cooking.

Roasted Garlic Flans with Porcini Mushrooms and Tomato

(1 or 2 per person)

12 large eggs, wiped clean

1½ cups heavy cream

¼ cup Roasted Garlic Purée
(page 257)

Salt and freshly ground white pepper
to taste

1 tablespoon olive oil

1 cup finely diced porcini mushrooms

3 plum tomatoes, finely diced

2 teaspoons balsamic vinegar

2 tablespoons minced fresh parsley

1 cup pink peppercorns

1 cup green or white peppercorns

1 cup black peppercorns

I LOVE THIS DISH BECAUSE of the delicious taste, visual presentation, and versatility—the variations are endless. In this case, the rich flan is flavored with the subtle sweetness of the roasted garlic purée, countered by the acidity and earthiness of the mushroom and tomato mixture. The flan can be made with almost any purée—just use flavor combinations that are proven winners, and stick to the principle of balancing the creamy flan with a contrasting acidic garnish. We serve hors d'oeuvres made with eggs at many VIP events throughout the year, and this one is an invaluable standby.

Preheat the oven to 350°F.

Use an egg cutter or topper to remove the tops of the eggs. Over a mixing bowl, carefully pour out the contents of 5 of the eggs into a bowl, and separate the yolks from the whites. Transfer the yolks to another bowl and whisk in the cream, roasted garlic, salt, and pepper. (Use the 5 egg whites and the contents of the remaining 7 eggs for other dishes.) Pour the mixture into a creamer.

Carefully rinse the hollowed eggs under cold running water and return to the egg carton. Fill each hollowed egg halfway with the whisked egg mixture. Place the carton in a roasting pan and pour enough warm water into the pan to come halfway up the sides of the eggs. Cover the pan with foil and transfer to the oven. Cook for about 20 minutes, or until the custard is firm and does not break when touched with your finger.

While the eggs are cooking, pour the oil into a heavy skillet and set over medium-high heat. When the oil is hot and shimmering, add the mushrooms and sauté for 2 minutes. Add the tomatoes and continue to sauté until most of the liquid has evaporated. Sprinkle with vinegar, season with salt and pepper, and mix in the minced parsley.

Remove the eggs from the oven, and carefully spoon the mushroom-tomato mixture on top of the custard, inside the eggshells. To serve, arrange the three types of peppercorns in the bottom of a serving dish, platter, or basket. Set the filled eggs upright on the peppercorns and serve with demitasse spoons.

CHEF'S NOTES

◇ For this recipe, buy a dozen eggs in a cardboard carton (not polystyrene). You will need the carton not only to make assembly easier but also as a baking tray.

◇ To clean the eggs for best presentation, carefully rinse under cold running water and wipe gently with a paper towel. Egg cutters are available at most kitchen specialty stores.

Smoked Salmon and Quail Eggs on Potato Pancakes

SERVES 6

(2 per person)

FOR THE POTATO PANCAKES

1 tablespoon butter

1 large baking potato, peeled and julienned (see Chef's Note)

Salt and freshly ground black pepper to taste

FOR THE SALMON AND QUAIL EGGS

6 ounces smoked salmon

12 quail eggs

2 tablespoons finely sliced fresh chives

THIS DISH IS A PERFECT example of classic flavor combinations reduced to a single bite. Think fried eggs, smoky bacon, and hash brown potatoes; this dish has similar flavor elements but in a very different form. These little gems not only taste great but are a surefire way of getting the conversation flowing—people are drawn to them because these small bites are cute and fun. I enjoy seeing their eyes open wide with delight as they munch the crunchy crisp potato and taste the salty, smoky egg.

TO PREPARE THE POTATO PANCAKES Melt the butter in a large nonstick skillet set over high heat. Add the julienned potato and season with salt and pepper. Using a spatula, mix the potato sticks to evenly coat them with the butter, then spread them evenly and just overlapping over the bottom of the pan to form a large pancake. Sauté for about 5 minutes, or until the julienned potatoes begin to stick together; do not let them brown. To turn over, slide the pancake onto the back side of a cookie sheet. Wipe out the sauté pan with a paper towel and then invert the sauté pan over the potato pancake on the cookie sheet. Place one hand under the cookie sheet and, while holding the sauté pan over the potatoes, flip together so that the potatoes return to the sauté pan with the uncooked side down (be careful, as the sauté pan will still be hot). Cook for 5 minutes longer, then slide the cooked pancake onto a cutting board.

Using a 1¾-inch or 2-inch round cookie cutter or ring mold, cut out 12 small circles, or as many as you can, from the pancake. Carefully place the small pancakes into the sauté pan and brown them over medium heat for 3 to 4 minutes on each side or until browned and crispy. Remove the pancakes and let cool.

TO PREPARE THE SALMON Thinly slice the smoked salmon on a cutting board and cut into 1¼-inch squares. Lay a salmon square on top of each potato pancake.

TO PREPARE THE EGGS Use a serrated knife to carefully saw the top off of a quail egg. Empty the egg into a cup and repeat with the rest of the eggs (this is to expedite putting the eggs in the pan so they can be cooked simultaneously). Set the same nonstick skillet used for the pancakes over low heat and lightly coat with nonstick cooking spray or a teaspoon of butter. Carefully but quickly drop 1 egg at a time from the cup into the pan, allowing them to cook separately. When the egg whites have solidified, use a small spatula to remove the eggs from the pan and place them on the potato pancakes. Sprinkle with a little salt and the sliced chives.

CHEF'S NOTES

◇   Use a mandoline to julienne the potato into matchstick-size pieces; alternatively, use a very sharp knife. For more on mandoline slicers, see page 263.

◇   The smoked salmon can be replaced with prosciutto, but I can almost guarantee this recipe will turn anyone into a smoked salmon lover!

◇   No quail eggs? No problem! Simply substitute soft scrambled eggs made with a little cream.

Zina Oussova of the Garde Manger department.

Key Lime Cocktail with Spicy Crab Salad on Blue Corn Tortillas

SERVES 8

THIS RECIPE MATERIALIZED WHEN OUR Chef Saucier, Peter Andino, suggested an hors d'oeuvre that combined the elements of a margarita and a seafood taco. In this case, we have updated a classic by putting the cocktail in the glass and laying the crab salad with crispy tortilla across the rim—talk about fun!

TO PREPARE THE CHIPS Pour the vegetable oil into a saucepan and set over medium-high heat until the oil is hot and shimmering. Cut each tortilla into 8 wedge-shaped chips. Place the tortilla chips in the hot oil and fry until crispy, about 3 minutes. Remove with a slotted spoon and drain on paper towels. Season with salt and set aside.

TO PREPARE THE SALAD Pick through the crabmeat to remove any shell or cartilage and place the cleaned crabmeat in a mixing bowl. Add the mayonnaise, crème fraîche, cilantro, lime juice, jalapeño, and mix. Season with salt and keep chilled until ready to serve.

TO PREPARE THE COCKTAIL Place ¼ cup water and the sugar in a saucepan and bring to a boil, stirring to dissolve the sugar. Remove from the heat and let the simple syrup cool. When you are ready to serve, pour the tequila into a blender and add the simple syrup, lime juice, Grand Marnier, and ice. Purée at high speed.

TO SERVE Pick the 8 flattest tortilla chips and place ½ teaspoon of the crab-salad mixture on each (use the other chips for snacking.) Fill 8 shot glasses with the cocktail mixture and balance a crab tortilla on top of each shot glass so that it sits flat. Serve, advising your guests to first eat the crab tortilla, then chase it with the slushy shooter.

FOR THE CHIP GARNISH

1 quart vegetable oil

2 blue corn tortillas

Salt to taste

FOR THE CRAB SALAD

8 ounces fresh crabmeat (preferably blue crab)

2 teaspoons mayonnaise

1 teaspoon crème fraîche

2 teaspoons minced fresh cilantro

Juice of ½ lime (2 tablespoons), preferably Key lime

1 teaspoon seeded and minced jalapeño chile

Salt to taste

FOR THE COCKTAIL

¼ cup sugar

½ cup tequila

½ cup freshly squeezed lime juice (preferably Key limes)

½ cup Grand Marnier

2 cups ice

CHEF'S NOTE

◇ The Key lime is a subspecies of the small, round, yellow to greenish "bartender," or Mexican, lime. It is smaller than the more common thick-rind Persian lime, which is dark green and shaped like a lemon but is less juicy. Key limes have high acidity and a distinctively citrusy flavor. They were the predominant lime in the citrus groves of Florida until the great hurricane of 1926 wiped out most of the crop. Farmers mostly replanted other citrus or Persian limes, which are easier to grow and less sensitive to occasional cold weather.

POACHED QUAIL EGGS AND CAVIAR

SERVES 8

¼ cup distilled white vinegar

8 fresh quail eggs

Salt and freshly ground white pepper
to taste

2 teaspoons crème fraîche

2 teaspoons sliced fresh chives

2 teaspoons Osetra caviar

THERE ARE MANY REASONS OTHER than style that teaspoons make a great presentation for hors d'oeuvres. They are a great vehicle for any kind of salad whenever you want to make a change from the ubiquitous cracker or crostini base, and they really work if you want to ration your caviar—the spoon allows an even distribution of caviar so there's enough for everyone to enjoy. I first served this dish for President Ronald Reagan when he hosted the fortieth anniversary of the United Nations at the Waldorf. Our Chef Garde Manger at the time tied tiny bows of silk ribbon on each spoon and rested them on crushed ice served in a silver tray—a great example of understated elegance!

Prepare an ice bath (page 260). Bring 4 cups water to a boil in a saucepan, turn down the heat to a simmer, and add the vinegar. Crack the quail eggs one at a time into a coffee cup, then carefully drop them one by one into the simmering water. Poach for about 1 minute; the yolk should still be soft. Remove each egg with a slotted spoon and transfer to the ice bath to stop the cooking process. When cool, remove from the ice bath and let dry on a clean towel. Season with salt and pepper.

In a bowl, mix the crème fraîche, chives, salt, and pepper, and spoon into a sealable plastic sandwich bag. Squeeze the mixture into one corner of the bag and snip off the corner using scissors. Squeeze a small amount of the crème fraîche mixture into a teaspoon, place a quail egg on top, and add ¼ teaspoon caviar.

CHEF'S NOTES

◇ Quail eggs, available at specialty stores or online sources, are considerably smaller than chicken eggs; by volume, the ratio is about five to one. The proportion of yolk to egg white is higher for quail, making the flavor a little more intense, and the speckled shells are spectacular.

◇ This recipe calls for Osetra caviar, but if your taste and wallet prefer, you can use eggs from paddlefish or trout.

◇ The photo opposite shows this hors d'oeuvre in front of a glass of Sweet Corn Soup.

Sweet Corn Soup with Black Truffle Cream

FOR THE STOCK

8 ears fresh corn (or 3 pounds
    frozen corn kernels)

¼ cup chopped celery

¼ cup chopped onion

¼ cup chopped leek

2 tablespoons chopped garlic

2 sprigs fresh thyme

2 sprigs fresh parsley

½ tablespoon black peppercorns

4 cups Chicken Stock (page 252)

FOR THE SOUP

3 tablespoons butter

¼ cup minced shallots

2 tablespoons minced garlic

¼ cup dry white wine

¼ cup heavy cream

1 sprig fresh thyme

1 teaspoon minced black
    winter truffle

Salt and freshly ground white pepper
    to taste

THIS IS A FAVORITE RECIPE from our Chef's Table events (see page 24). At most of these special dinners, as we enjoy a selection of hors d'oeuvres and a glass of champagne to start things off, I serve shots of seasonal soup. We also serve small cups or glasses of soup at wedding receptions as the guests arrive, and it always receives a positive reaction. Little servings of soup make an excellent hors d'oeuvre—in the fall we might make a chestnut soup with apples and port; in the spring, a nice bright green ramp (wild leek) soup with balsamic-glazed mushrooms fills the bill. This one is an early summer favorite.

TO PREPARE THE STOCK Shuck the corn cobs, discard the outer husks and silky threads, and keep the stalks attached to the cobs. Stand a cob on its tip on a cutting board and holding the stalk end, cut down with a sharp knife to remove the kernels. Repeat for the remaining ears and reserve the kernels. Cut the stalks into 2-inch lengths, and transfer to a stock pot. Add the celery, onion, leek, garlic, thyme, parsley, peppercorns, and stock. Bring to a boil, then turn down the heat to medium-low and simmer for 45 minutes. Strain the liquid through a medium-mesh strainer into a clean saucepan, discarding the solids. Reduce the liquid over medium-high heat until about 3 cups remain, about 15 minutes.

MEANWHILE, PREPARE THE SOUP Heat 1 tablespoon of the butter in a large saucepan over medium-high heat. When the butter begins to foam, add the shallots and garlic and sauté for 3 to 4 minutes until softened. Add the reserved corn kernels, wine, cream, thyme, and reduced stock. Bring to a boil, turn the heat to medium low, and simmer for about 20 minutes, until the liquid is reduced to about 2 cups. Remove from the heat and let cool slightly. Transfer to a blender and purée until smooth. Strain through a fine-mesh strainer into a bowl.

Rinse the blender and return ⅓ of the purée mixture to the blender. Add the chopped truffle and blend until smooth. Set the truffle cream aside. Transfer the remaining ⅔ of the purée to a clean saucepan and bring just to a boil. Season with salt and pepper and add the remaining 2 tablespoons of butter, stirring until it is melted and incorporated.

TO SERVE Ladle the warm soup into small glasses or demitasse cups (allow about ¼ cup of soup per serving) and spoon the truffle cream on top.

Coconut-Tuna Tartare and Avocado Mousse

SERVES 8

⅓ cup sweetened shredded coconut

¼ cup chopped almond slivers, toasted

1 pound sushi-grade tuna, finely diced

1 teaspoon soy sauce

2 tablespoons freshly squeezed lime juice

1 teaspoon unseasoned rice wine vinegar

¼ cup currants

1 teaspoon minced ginger

½ teaspoon minced garlic

1 tablespoon grapeseed oil

½ teaspoon dark sesame oil

Salt and freshly ground white pepper, to taste

2 ripe avocados, cut in half and pitted

¼ teaspoon ground cumin

⅛ teaspoon cayenne

⅛ teaspoon paprika

1 tablespoon olive oil

AT THE WALDORF=ASTORIA WE SERVE several different seviches—marinated raw fish—in martini glasses, including red snapper with lime, fresh cilantro, and jalapeño chile; bay scallops with orange and mint; and sea bass with Thai chiles, coconut milk, and saba vinegar (see Chef's Note). Another big-time favorite is our tuna tartare with olive oil, lemon juice, black truffles, and sea salt. This version was recently served as an appetizer with pea soup and grilled shrimp (see photo, opposite) at a fund raiser hosted by Katie Couric. The glasses add style and make a fun presentation. These little hors d'oeuvres are not only festive but easy to eat.

Preheat the oven to 325°F.

Spread the coconut evenly on a cookie sheet and toast in the oven for 3 to 4 minutes, until just golden brown, watching it carefully to prevent it from burning. Transfer to a nonreactive mixing bowl. Place the almonds on the cookie sheet and toast for 3 to 4 minutes, until golden brown. Transfer to the bowl with the coconut and add the tuna, soy sauce, 1 tablespoon of the lime juice, rice wine vinegar, currants, ginger, garlic, grapeseed oil, and sesame oil. Mix gently to thoroughly combine, and season with salt and pepper.

Scoop out the avocado flesh from the skin and roughly chop. Place in a separate nonreactive mixing bowl and add the remaining 1 tablespoon of lime juice, cumin, cayenne, paprika, and olive oil. Mash with a fork until creamy, and season with salt and pepper. Spoon the mixture into the bottom of 8 martini glasses and smooth out. Evenly spoon the tuna mixture on top and serve immediately.

CHEF'S NOTE

◇ Saba vinegar is an Italian product made from the first pressing of balsamic grapes. It is sweeter and thicker than regular balsamic vinegar and is available at specialty food stores.

Seared Scallops with Osetra Caviar and Potato-Chive Mousseline

FRESHLY SHUCKED OR DRY-PACKED SCALLOPS are so sweet you can sample them raw to make sure they'll be good enough to cook. Of course, you need to know the source, so that you can be sure of their freshness. For a special presentation, serve these hors d'oeuvres on small scallop shells. This combination of ingredients is so succulent and elegant it starts any dinner party on the right note—it certainly did when President Bill Clinton was entertaining heads of state in the Presidential Suite in 2000.

SERVES 8

FOR THE POTATO-CHIVE MOUSSELINE

1 pound Yukon Gold potatoes, peeled and cut in half

2 teaspoons Kosher salt

¼ cup softened butter

¼ cup milk

2 tablespoons chopped fresh chives

Salt and freshly ground white pepper to taste

FOR THE SCALLOPS

8 scallops (about 8 ounces)

Salt and freshly ground white pepper to taste

1 teaspoon olive oil

Juice of 1 lemon

1 teaspoon butter

2 ounces Osetra caviar

TO PREPARE THE MOUSSELINE Put the potatoes in a saucepan, cover with cold water, and add the Kosher salt. Bring to a boil over high heat. Turn heat to medium low and simmer until soft when pierced with a fork, about 20 minutes. Drain the potatoes, using a fine-mesh sieve, and then press them through the sieve into the saucepan. (You can use a food mill or ricer, but the texture will not be as fine.) Stir in the butter and milk and reheat the potato mixture over low heat. Add the chives, salt, and pepper. Keep warm over low heat, stirring occasionally until ready to serve.

TO PREPARE THE SCALLOPS Pat the scallops dry and season with salt and pepper. Pour the oil into a heavy skillet and set over high heat until the oil is shimmering. Carefully add the scallops to the hot skillet and sauté for 2 minutes on each side until golden brown and just cooked through (do not flip). Remove the scallops and transfer to a warm plate. Turn the heat to low, add the lemon juice to the skillet, and add the butter. Stirring with a wooden spoon, deglaze the skillet to dissolve any solids. Pour the liquid through a fine mesh strainer into a gravy boat or serving cup.

TO SERVE Place 2 teaspoons of the potato purée in the center of each small plate (or use scallop shells if available). Place each scallop, browned side up, in the center of the purée and evenly distribute the caviar on top. Drizzle the lemon sauce around the potato purée.

CHEF'S NOTES

◇ Mousselines often contain whipped cream or egg whites as a lightening agent, but in this case, the sieved potatoes provide the airy texture.

◇ If you can find day-boat, or "dry," scallops for this recipe, buy them. Most commercial scallops are caught on fishing boats that stay out at sea for several days at a time, so their catch is either frozen or not as fresh as that of day boats, which put out and return the same day. Some commercial boats also soak scallops in a brine that makes them plump and heavy, but when cooked, they release the liquid, making them difficult to brown.

3

SOUPS

Whenever I conduct tours of the city-block-long Waldorf=Astoria kitchen, I make a point of stopping at our soup kitchen. We refer to this as the steam room, because everything therein is cooked by this method, whether in the steam-jacketed stock kettles or in the high-pressure stack steamer. The thirteen stainless-steel stock kettles ("cauldrons," I warn the kids), which hold up to eighty gallons, cook an average of 1,000 pounds of bones and 160 pounds of vegetables every day. It is here, too, that we poach, boil, or steam pasta, vegetables, shrimp, lobster, chicken, or any other ingredient required by Banquet Operations, Room Service, or the Main Kitchen. For those taking the kitchen tour, I joke that although the chefs in charge of the soups and stocks have to lift and empty heavy crates of ingredients and work in steamy conditions, they go home with beautiful skin that makes them look ten years younger. Of course, I make sure my crew is out of earshot so they don't growl at me!

It may get hot and humid in the soup kitchen, but the reward is the twenty gallons of savory rich broth from each eighty-gallon kettle. This is the foundation for all our soups, and a good broth is indeed the secret to great soups and sauces. At the Waldorf, as at home, anything we make will only be as good as its basic ingredients. Many, perhaps most, kitchens have long given up the art of great stock-making. For us, it is as much about professional pride as it is a passion for a wholesome product and an intense depth of flavor. I do recommend making your own stock at home if you possibly can, and I have included several stock recipes in a later chapter (see pages 252 to 256). If you prefer a shortcut, purchase the best-quality stock you can find—the extra investment will prove worthwhile.

At the Waldorf, we have a reputation for serving the best soup you can find anywhere, and in fact, soup outsells both appetizers and salads, even at Oscar's. We also put

Soup Chef David Giampiola.

a lot of effort into presentation, which includes colorful garnishes. Generally speaking, soup is the ultimate comfort food; it is just better if it is kept rustic, unless it is a classic consommé, in which the degree of clarity is one of the true tests of a cook's skill. Traditionally, soup garnishes are diced or shredded and mixed into the soup for ease of consumption, but there is no reason why a soup can't be as beautiful to look at as it is to eat. The idea is fairly simple: Take the traditional garnish for, let's say, chicken noodle soup. Instead of dicing everything as you normally would, twirl the noodles on a fork and lay them in the bowl, slice some grilled spicy chicken and fan it out, and add a baby carrot, baby beet, and some sliced celery. Present this to your guests with the broth separately, and you have brought a whole new meaning to a usually predictable dish. With other soups, serve a breadstick, Parmesan Tuile (page 121), or miniature cheese popover (page 244) on the side.

In addition to one or two classic soups that we offer year-round, such as French Onion Soup and Black Bean Soup, we rotate our soups on a daily basis, and change the whole soup menu with every season. As with other courses, one of my main recommendations when it comes to soup is to use whatever is in season. Some people think of soup as a fall or winter dish, but summer presents even more opportunities to enjoy the bounty of ingredients that are available, and this chapter includes some chilled soup recipes that are ideal summer starters. One of the best things about soup is that you can use almost any of your favorite foods. If you enjoy certain combinations of flavors and ingredients as an hors d'oeuvre or appetizer, chances are you can use those same combinations as a soup—creativity is all about thinking without boundaries.

Roasted Butternut Squash Soup with Watercress, Blue Cheese, and Spicy Pecans

SERVES 6 TO 8

5 pounds butternut squash

⅓ cup diced bacon

1 cup diced onion

¾ cup diced fennel bulb

¼ cup diced celery

3 cloves garlic, chopped

2 teaspoons minced ginger

6 cups Chicken Stock (page 252)

¼ teaspoon ground cinnamon

⅛ teaspoon ground clove

⅛ teaspoon ground nutmeg

2 tablespoons pure maple syrup

1 sprig fresh thyme

Salt and freshly ground black pepper
to taste

½ cup watercress leaves

½ cup crumbled blue cheese

Spicy Pecans (page 259)

THIS IS A NATURAL FALL and winter soup, yet it is versatile enough to be enjoyed any time that butternut squash is available. There are plenty of assertive flavors in this soup, and they combine brilliantly.

Split the squash in half, scoop out and discard the seeds, and place it cut surface down on a cookie sheet. Bake in the oven until tender, 35 to 40 minutes. Remove and let cool to room temperature. Scoop out the baked squash with a spoon and transfer to a bowl; discard the skin.

While the squash is baking, place the bacon in a saucepan set over medium heat and sauté until crispy and all the fat is rendered, about 5 minutes. Remove the bacon with a slotted spoon and drain on paper towels. Discard all but 2 teaspoons of the bacon fat. Return the bacon fat to medium-high heat and add the onion, fennel, celery, garlic, and ginger. Sauté until lightly browned and caramelized, about 5 minutes, stirring occasionally. Stir in the baked squash and chicken stock, then the cinnamon, clove, nutmeg, maple syrup, thyme, salt, and pepper. Stir again and bring to a boil. Turn down the heat to low and simmer, uncovered, for 15 minutes.

To serve, ladle the soup into bowls and sprinkle the bacon, watercress, blue cheese, and spicy pecans on top.

CHEF'S NOTE

◇ Some other garnishes we have used for this soup include duck confit and figs poached in port, and spicy grilled chicken with Roasted Red Bell Pepper Coulis (page 256).

Consommé and Carpaccio of Red Snapper with Zucchini and Browned Garlic

| SERVES 6 |

2 quarts Fish Fumet (page 254)

3 egg whites

¼ cup thinly sliced fennel bulb

¼ cup peeled and thinly sliced carrot

¼ cup thinly sliced shallots

½ cup diced tomato

1 teaspoon saffron threads

1 zucchini, unpeeled

3 tablespoons olive oil

2 cloves garlic, finely sliced

Salt and freshly ground white pepper to taste

3 pounds fresh red snapper, scaled and cleaned

WE SERVE THIS INTRIGUING DISH for parties and special events, and it is a real conversation piece. As the hot broth is poured over the finely sliced raw fish at the table, it cooks in front of the guests' eyes, changing color as well as texture. Now, that's something a little different! If you can, buy whole snapper and ask your fishmonger to fillet the fish for you, making sure he gives you the head and bones so you can make the stock. This dish echoes the Japanese technique for sukiyaki, which usually involves thinly sliced raw beef. I was inspired to create this dish by a hotel reception catered by Inagiku, the Waldorf's Japanese restaurant.

———

Pour the Fish Fumet into a large saucepan and set over medium heat. Warm through. Meanwhile, gently whisk the egg whites in a mixing bowl until frothy, 30 seconds. Add the fennel, carrot, shallot, tomato, and saffron. Stir the egg mixture into the warm stock and continue to stir until the eggs begin to coagulate and turn white. Turn the heat to low and simmer gently for 20 minutes.

Place a strainer lined with cheesecloth or a paper coffee filter over a clean saucepan. Gently ladle the broth through the strainer. Keep the consommé warm over low heat and season with salt and pepper. Just before serving, heat the consommé to almost boiling.

Using a mandoline slicer (see page 263) with a ¹⁄₁₆-inch blade and julienne comb, cut the zucchini lengthwise into long thin julienne (like spaghetti). Pour the olive oil in a small saucepan and set over medium heat. When the oil is hot and shimmering, add the sliced garlic and sauté until light golden brown, 4 or 5 minutes. Remove the garlic and drain on paper towels; set aside. Turn up the heat to medium high and add the julienned zucchini. Season with salt and pepper and quickly sauté until the zucchini wilts. Remove from the heat and drain on paper towels.

Using a very sharp chef's knife, slice the snapper filets paper thin on a bias. Arrange the snapper slices in overlapping layers on shallow soup plates and garnish with the sautéed zucchini and garlic in the center. Place the plates in front of your guests at the table. Transfer the hot consommé to a heated teapot or soup tureen, bring to the table, and pour or ladle the hot broth over the snapper. After 30 seconds or so, the sliced fish will turn from translucent to an opaque white.

CHEF'S NOTE

◇   Other fish you can use for this recipe include sea bass, grouper, or larger turbot.

Cauliflower Soup with Caramelized Onions, Apple, and Curried Shrimp

SERVES 6 TO 8

FOR THE SOUP

2 heads cauliflower

2 tablespoons butter

2 tablespoons olive oil

1½ cups diced onion

½ tablespoon minced garlic

1 cup dry white wine

1 cup brandy

3 cups Chicken Stock (page 252)

1 Bouquet Garni (page 259)

1 cup heavy cream

Salt and freshly ground white pepper
to taste

FOR THE CURRIED SHRIMP

8 shrimp (about 8 ounces), peeled
and deveined

1 teaspoon olive oil

½ teaspoon curry powder

⅛ teaspoon ground allspice

¼ teaspoon salt

Pinch of freshly ground white pepper

IF I HAD TO DESCRIBE one soup as fun, this would be it. The flavors seem to dance on one's palate—the subtle bittersweet onions, spicy shrimp, sweet-tart apple, and the earthy, creamy cauliflower that pulls all the other elements together. It is a good soup to make when you are entertaining, because you garnish the plates in the kitchen and pour the soup at the table—a finishing touch that always impresses. Best of all, it is a very straightforward soup to make.

FOR THE APPLE GARNISH

1 Granny Smith apple, peeled

¼ teaspoon cider vinegar

6 to 8 tablespoons Caramelized Onions (page 250)

TO PREPARE THE CAULIFLOWER GARNISH Remove and discard the green leaves from the cauliflower. Break off 8 small florets for garnish; standing a floret upright on a cutting board, slice downward on opposite sides of the floret to leave a flat ½-inch-thick cross section. Repeat for the remaining florets and reserve the cauliflower trimmings for the soup. Place 1 tablespoon of the butter in a sauté pan and set over medium heat. When the butter is melted and foamy, add the 8 floret cross sections and sauté gently for 4 or 5 minutes on each side until lightly caramelized. Season with salt and pepper and set aside.

TO PREPARE THE SOUP Cut the remaining cauliflower into 1- or 2-inch pieces. Pour the oil into a large saucepan, add the remaining 1 tablespoon of butter, and set over medium-high heat. When the butter is melted and foamy, add the onion and garlic and sauté until translucent, 3 to 4 minutes. Add the wine and brandy and reduce until the liquid is almost evaporated. Add the chopped cauliflower (and the trimmings from the garnish), stock, 3 cups of water, and the bouquet garni and bring to a simmer. Turn down the heat to medium low, cover the pan, and simmer for 30 minutes.

When the cauliflower is tender, transfer the mixture to a blender or food process and purée. (This should be done in small batches to prevent splashing of the hot liquid.) Return to a clean saucepan, set over medium heat, and add the cream. Bring to a boil, season with salt and pepper, and turn down the heat to keep warm. If the soup seems too thick, add a little water or stock.

Prepare the grill (or preheat the broiler to high).

TO PREPARE THE CURRIED SHRIMP Place the shrimp in a mixing bowl and add the oil, curry powder, allspice, salt, and pepper. Toss to thoroughly coat the shrimp. Grill over high heat (or broil) for 1 to 2 minutes on each side until cooked through. Transfer to an ovenproof dish, cover with foil, and place in a 180°F oven to keep warm.

TO PREPARE THE APPLE GARNISH Using a mandoline (page 263) fitted with a comb attachment, julienne the apple and transfer to a bowl (alternatively, julienne with a knife, or finely dice). Drizzle the vinegar over the apple and mix together to prevent the apple from oxidizing and turning brown.

TO SERVE Arrange the grilled shrimp, cauliflower cross sections, caramelized onions, and apple garnish in the center of warm serving bowls and transfer to the table. Pour the soup into a tureen or serving bowl and ladle the soup into the serving bowls, around the garnish, at the table.

CHEF'S NOTE

◇   For a stylish presentation, peel the apple for garnish with a Japanese spiral vegetable peeler (see photo for garnish), available at gourmet kitchen supply stores (see Sources, page 261).

Chilled Vichyssoise with Curried Tempura Oysters

SERVES 6 TO 8

FOR THE SOUP

1½ pounds Russet potatoes, peeled and chopped

2 cups chopped onions

1 cup chopped leeks (white part only)

1 dried bay leaf

3 sprigs fresh thyme

5 white peppercorns

5 cups Chicken Stock (page 252)

3 cups light cream

Salt and freshly ground white pepper to taste

FOR THE WATERCRESS PURÉE

1 cup watercress leaves

1 tablespoon extra virgin olive oil

FOR THE CURRIED TEMPURA OYSTERS

2 quarts vegetable oil, for deep-frying

1 cup all-purpose flour plus ½ cup for dredging

¼ cup cornstarch

1 teaspoon curry powder

1 teaspoon salt

1 large egg, beaten

16 to 24 oysters

VICHYSSOISE, THE FRENCH CHILLED SOUP of potatoes, leeks, and cream, has been on the Waldorf=Astoria menu since well before my time. It is usually considered to be a summer soup but I think it is great year-round, especially for lunch. Just for a change, sometimes we cut back on the cream to give the soup a thicker consistency, and float a half ounce of Osetra caviar on top.

TO PREPARE THE SOUP Place the potatoes, onions, and leeks in a stockpot. Create a bouquet garni by placing the bay leaf, thyme, and peppercorns in a square of cheesecloth and tying with kitchen twine. Add the bouquet garni and chicken stock to the pot and bring the ingredients to a boil. Turn the heat to medium low and simmer until the potatoes are tender, about 35 minutes. Strain and reserve the liquid, and discard the bouquet garni. Purée the potatoes and other solid ingredients through a food mill with a fine-hole attachment. Combine with the reserved stock, mix well, and cool the mixture in the refrigerator until chilled, about 5 hours. When ready to serve, stir in the cream and combine thoroughly; season with salt and pepper.

TO PREPARE THE WATERCRESS PURÉE Prepare an ice bath (page 260). Bring a saucepan of salted water to a boil and add the watercress leaves. Blanch for 1 minute and remove immediately with a slotted spoon. Transfer to the ice bath to stop the cooking process. When cool, transfer the leaves to a blender and add the olive oil. Purée at high speed, adding a little water if necessary to make puréeing possible. Set aside.

TO PREPARE THE OYSTERS Heat the oil in a large saucepan or deep fryer to 350° F. While the oil is heating, sift together 1 cup of the flour, cornstarch, curry powder, and salt into a bowl. In another bowl, combine the egg and 1 cup of ice water and add to the dry ingredients, mixing until the batter is smooth. Holding the oysters down on a work surface with a kitchen towel, use the tip of an oyster knife to pry them open and cut the oyster meat free. Dredge the oysters lightly in the remaining ½ cup flour and then in the batter. Using a fork, transfer the oysters to the hot oil and deep-fry until golden brown and crispy, 1 to 1½ minutes. Remove with a slotted spoon and drain on paper towels.

TO SERVE Pour the soup into individual serving bowls or cups and swirl in 1 teaspoon of watercress purée per serving. Serve the curried oysters separately.

Chilled Cavaillon Melon Soup with Spicy Calamari

SERVES 6 TO 8

FOR THE SOUP

4 Cavaillon melons (or 2 ripe cantaloupes, about 2 pounds each)

1 cup brut champagne

2 tablespoons unseasoned rice wine vinegar

Salt and freshly ground white pepper to taste

FOR THE GARNISH

1 yellow bell pepper, seeded and very finely diced

1 red bell pepper, seeded and very finely diced

2 tablespoons very finely diced red onion

2 tablespoons quartered Kalamata olives

1 tablespoon minced fresh parsley

1 tablespoon extra-virgin olive oil

Salt and freshly ground black pepper to taste

FOR THE SPICY CALAMARI

1 tablespoon extra-virgin olive oil

8 ounces calamari, sliced into ¼-inch rings

2 teaspoons minced garlic

1 tablespoon freshly squeezed lime juice

Pinch of dried red pepper flakes

Salt and freshly ground black pepper to taste

THE
WALDORF=ASTORIA
COOKBOOK

AROUND THE TIME WE WERE testing soup recipes for this chapter, we received some French Cavaillon melon at the hotel. Unfortunately, the melon season is all too short, but Sous Chef Daniel Bendix tried puréeing some of it with champagne, an inspired choice! It was so good that we developed the combination further and put this soup on our Chef's Table menu (see page 24), garnished with sautéed calamari, olives, and peppers. After all, if the combination of salty prosciutto and melon can stand the test of time, why not salty olives, vinegary peppers, and tender calamari? Well, if it was good enough to lure everyone into the kitchen for a taste or three, into the cookbook it goes. Now, we can't wait for next summer.

———

TO PREPARE THE SOUP Cut the melons in half, scoop out the seeds, and cut off the rind. Chop the melon flesh and transfer to a blender. Add the champagne and vinegar and purée until completely smooth, about 3 minutes. Season with salt and white pepper, and strain through a fine-mesh sieve into a mixing bowl. Transfer to the refrigerator and keep chilled until ready to serve.

TO PREPARE THE GARNISH Place the yellow and red bell peppers, onion, olives, and parsley in a mixing bowl. Add the olive oil and mix well. Season with salt and pepper and chill the mixture in the refrigerator for at least 2 hours.

TO PREPARE THE CALAMARI Heat the olive oil in a large skillet and set over medium-high heat. When the oil is hot and shimmering, add the calamari and sauté for about 30 seconds. Add the garlic and continue to sauté for 30 seconds longer. Add the lime juice and red pepper flakes, sauté for 1 minute longer, and season with salt and pepper. Remove from the heat and add the cooked calamari to the chilled garnish mixture and combine thoroughly. Let chill in the refrigerator for at least 1 hour.

TO SERVE Ladle the chilled soup into soup plates, and spoon the calamari garnish in the center of the soup.

Summer White Gazpacho with Lobster Brochettes

SERVES 8

FOR THE SOUP

2 or 3 cucumbers, peeled

3 cups sliced almonds

3 cups fresh white breadcrumbs

1½ cups green seedless grapes

¾ cup white verjus (see page 263)

¼ cup extra-virgin olive oil

2 teaspoons sherry vinegar

Dash of almond extract

FOR THE LOBSTER BROCHETTES

3 live lobsters, about 1½ pounds each

1 teaspoon olive oil

½ teaspoon minced lemon zest

Salt and freshly ground white pepper to taste

Dash of cayenne

FOR THE GARNISH

3 tablespoons chopped fresh chives

24 green grapes, split in half

¼ cup finely diced red bell pepper

WHEN EXECUTIVE SOUS CHEF PETER DALEDDA first made this gazpacho made with bread, almonds, verjus, and grapes and proposed we put it on our menu, I was skeptical. It was a Spanish classic, Peter reassured me; he has never steered me wrong, so I kept an open mind. It was a hit! We do a number of versions at the Waldorf, serving it with grilled spicy shrimp as an appetizer, and in a small glass with lobster as a cocktail hour canapé.

TO PREPARE THE SOUP Run the cucumbers through a juicer and reserve ¾ cup juice. (Alternatively, purée in a blender and strain.) Place the almonds and 2½ cups water in a food processor and purée until the mixture is milky in appearance, about 3 minutes (process in batches if necessary). Add the breadcrumbs, the reserved cucumber juice, grapes, verjus, oil, vinegar, and almond extract and blend for 1 minute longer (again, in batches if necessary). Strain through a fine-mesh strainer into a mixing bowl and let chill in the refrigerator for at least 4 hours.

Preheat the grill.

TO PREPARE THE BROCHETTES Bring a stockpot of salted water to a boil and plunge the lobsters in head first (cook 1 or 2 at a time if they don't all fit). Blanch for 2 to 3 minutes, remove with tongs, and let cool for 5 minutes. Twist off the tails and squeeze the tail shells until they crack and can be pulled apart and the meat can be removed. Remove the intestinal tract from the tails. Cut the tail meat in half lengthwise, then into ½-inch slices. In a mixing bowl, combine the oil, lemon zest, salt, pepper, and cayenne. Add the lobster slices, combine to season well, and thread 3 lobster slices onto each of 8 five-inch wooden skewers. Grill the skewers over medium heat for 2 to 3 minutes or until the lobster is cooked and firm in texture but not dried out.

TO SERVE Pour the chilled soup into bowls and garnish with the chives, grapes, and bell pepper. Lay the lobster brochettes across the bowls.

The affable Oscar Tschirky, maître d' and unofficial ambassador of the Waldorf=Astoria for fifty years, became as much a New York institution as the hotel itself. His name is permanently associated with the preparation of epicurean foods and the art of fine dining, and it is Oscar who is remembered for several classic recipes, due to his genius at recognizing and promoting innovative dishes such as the Waldorf Salad, Eggs Benedict, Thousand Island Dressing, and Veal Oscar. Part of Oscar's talent also lay in befriending guests and cultivating relationships, becoming a confidant and guide in the enjoyment of fine dining, and in the delicate and successful management of the hundreds of personalities and temperaments in the food-service realm of the hotel.

An émigré from Switzerland, Oscar began his career at New York's renowned Hoffman House hotel, where he became a popular waiter, learning how to discreetly accommodate a discerning clientele. He moved on to the landmark Delmonico's restaurant, then, helped by impressive recommendations, he was hired in 1893 as head waiter by George Boldt, the Waldorf's first manager. Oscar quickly became known as "Oscar of the Waldorf," or, to subordinates, "Mr. Oscar." Oscar defined the art of hospitality in New York City and was considered a resident arbiter of taste. It was Oscar who first devised the use of a red plush rope to maintain orderly lines for the hotel restaurants. After his wife died in 1939, Oscar took up residence at the hotel. "At long last the Waldorf=Astoria is actually my home: it is my life now, utter and complete," he wrote wistfully. Oscar finally retired in 1943, after fifty years of service, and died in 1950.

In 1949, Conrad N. Hilton, founder and president of Hilton Hotels Corporation, had "dared to dream," as he put it, patiently bided his time, and realized a lifelong ambition by acquiring the Holy Grail of hotels, the Waldorf=Astoria. A born entrepreneur, Hilton began his career in rural New Mexico as a merchant and trader. After enlisting in World War I and serving in France, he moved to Texas to seek his fortune during an oil boom. Spotting an opportunity, he entered the hotel business in 1919, running and later buying the forty-room Mobley Hotel in Cisco, Texas. (The town's Web site banner proudly proclaims Cisco as "Home of Hilton's First Hotel.") He acquired and managed several other hotel properties in Texas before building his first Hilton Hotel in downtown Dallas in 1925; other Hilton Hotels followed across the state.

Like a great many businessmen, Conrad Hilton was rocked by the Depression that followed the Great Crash of 1929. Staring bankruptcy in the face, Hilton came across a newspaper account of the reopening of the Waldorf=Astoria on Park Avenue in 1931. As he recalled in his autobiography, *Be My Guest* (Prentice Hall, 1957), he read about the Art Deco Valhalla. "It was a presumptuous, an outrageous time to dream. Still, I cut out that picture of the Waldorf and wrote across it 'The Greatest of Them All.' As soon as I had won back a desk of my own I slipped the dog-eared clipping under the glass top. From then on it was always in front of me." To Hilton, the Waldorf=Astoria represented what could be done in the face of adversity.

Little by little, Conrad Hilton restored the health of his hotel empire and began making significant acquisitions across the country, including the Plaza Hotel in New York. By the 1940s, the Hilton Hotel network became the first coast-to-coast hotel chain in the country. Hilton began purchasing stock in the Waldorf=Astoria Corporation and, by 1949, he had acquired 68 percent of the stock for about $3 million; that October, he took over management. In 1977, Hilton's son, Barron, completed his father's dream when he purchased the land on which the hotel stood from the bankrupt Penn Central Railroad for $36 million. Conrad Hilton lived just long enough to appreciate the transaction, as he died two years later at the age of ninety-one. The Waldorf=Astoria has remained the jewel in the crown of the Hilton Hotels Corporation ever since.

Whether I am planning a meal for my friends or family at home, a formal dinner in the Presidential Suite at the Waldorf, or making a recommendation to a guest at the Bull and Bear Steakhouse, I have two goals in mind when it comes to appetizers: Pick something that will thrill the guests, and make sure it is light enough that it does not spoil their appetites. The course should both take the edge off an appetite and make you want to eat more once it is finished.

People's eating habits have changed over the years, and one of the biggest changes, in New York City in particular, has been the trend toward smaller, lighter portions. It is acceptable, even fashionable, to order two or three appetizers rather than an appetizer and main course. The advantage to this style of grazing through a menu is that it offers the diner a wider range of flavors and an opportunity to sample more of the menu.

Mushroom purveyor Atef Boulaabi.

At the Waldorf=Astoria, schedules are another huge factor in appetizer design. For example, restaurant dining at lunchtime is no longer a two-hour event; these days, most people barely have an hour away from the office. For banquets, the timing is very tight and, sometimes, if the event goes too long, people just get up and leave! So the format and style of appetizers are shaped by these wider food trends and typical time constraints. This has led us to develop a lighter repertoire of nutritionally balanced appetizers with an intense flavor impact. At the same time, the dishes are compatible with our need to both prepare ahead and keep them as simple as possible to allow for last-minute plating, making us more efficient. When cooking at home, for the same reasons, these recipes allow you to spend more time with your guests and less time fussing over last-minute details.

When it comes to preparing appetizers at home, I encourage you to bear a few things in mind, even if your dinner consists of your own recipes: Keep the appetizers seasonal, simple, and small. Aim to make the flavors bright and light by using ingredients such as spices and lemon juice or a good-quality vinegar. Finally, plan the meal so the appetizers preface larger, bolder flavors with the main course.

Maine Lobster with Mango-Cilantro Salsa and Crispy Ginger

FOR THE LOBSTER

8 live lobsters, 1 to 1½ pounds each,
or 4 lobsters, 2 pounds each

2½ tablespoons olive oil

¼ cup brandy

½ cup crushed and sliced lemongrass

1 cup sliced red onion

¼ cup peeled and minced ginger

1 tablespoon minced garlic

¼ cup tomato paste

1 teaspoon red Thai curry paste

¼ cup freshly squeezed lime juice

5 cups canned unsweetened
coconut milk

1 dried bay leaf

3 sprigs fresh thyme

Salt and freshly ground white pepper
to taste

Mango-Cilantro Salsa (page 251)

FOR THE CRISPY GINGER

½ cup sugar

4 teaspoons finely julienned ginger

2 cups vegetable oil

¼ cup fresh basil, julienned

WHAT COULD BE MORE DECADENT than lobster, with its rich texture and delicate flavor? Whenever I am assisting our guests in planning an event for a special occasion, I usually recommend lobster as a starter, for many reasons. There are virtually limitless combinations of compatible ingredients, lobster is considered by most people to be a luxury and, most important of all, we can make it both beautiful and delicious for groups of any size. This recipe uses the technique of poaching lobster—a useful addition to your repertoire and a change from the traditional methods of boiling or broiling.

TO PREPARE THE LOBSTER AND SAUCE Place a live lobster on a cutting board and, using a cleaver or sharp chef's knife, cut down through the middle of the lobster head. If the lobster is female, this will reveal the dark green egg sac (coral); carefully remove it and reserve. Remove and discard the remaining innards from the head. Use the cleaver or knife to separate the claws, claw joints, and tail from the body. Chop the claws and body into 2- to 3-inch pieces; leave the tail whole. Repeat for the remaining lobsters.

Pour 1½ tablespoons of the olive oil into a saucepan and set over medium-high heat. When the oil is hot and shimmering, add the chopped lobster pieces and shells. Cook the lobster until the shells turn bright red, 8 to 10 minutes. Remove the shells and set them aside in a large bowl. Let cool, remove the meat from the shells. Reserve the meat and shells separately.

Add the brandy to the saucepan and set over medium heat. Using a wooden spoon, deglaze the pan by scraping the solids on the bottom to loosen. Cook for 1 to 2 minutes longer, then pour the brandy reduction into the bowl with the chopped lobster shell. Add the remaining 1 tablespoon of olive oil to the saucepan and set over medium-high heat. Add the lemongrass and onion and sauté until translucent, 4 or 5 minutes. Add the ginger and garlic and sauté for 2 minutes more. Add the tomato paste and curry paste and sauté for another 2 minutes. Add the lime juice, coconut milk, 5 cups of water, the bay leaf, thyme, reserved lobster shells, and brandy reduction (but not the lobster meat). Bring the mixture to a boil, turn the heat to medium low, and simmer for 45 minutes. Strain the sauce into a bowl and season with salt and pepper; discard the solids. Let cool.

Assistant Chef Saucier Will Lustberg.

Prepare the Mango-Cilantro Salsa.

TO PREPARE THE CRISPY GINGER Place the sugar and 2 tablespoons of water in a saucepan and set over medium heat, stirring to dissolve the sugar. Bring to a simmer, add the julienned ginger, and cook until tender, 5 minutes. Strain the ginger and blot dry with paper towels. In a saucepan, heat the vegetable oil to 350°F. Add the ginger and fry until golden brown and crispy, 1 to 2 minutes. Remove the ginger with a slotted spoon, drain on paper towels, and let cool.

TO SERVE Spoon the mango salsa onto the middle of serving plates. Slice the reserved lobster tail meat into ¼-inch slices and arrange on top of the salsa. Sprinkle the fried ginger and basil on top of the lobster, drizzle with the sauce, and garnish with the claw meat.

Wine Recommendation Austrian Riesling (well-balanced and rich with peach and mineral flavors).

Five-Spice Duck Breast with Citrus-Fennel Salad

SERVES 8

FOR THE DUCK

3 duck breasts, about 10 ounces each (preferably Long Island duck)

1½ teaspoons Chinese five-spice powder

Salt and freshly ground white pepper to taste

FOR THE FENNEL SALAD

2 fennel bulbs, cut paper thin

24 orange sections (page 260), from 3 oranges

1 teaspoon sliced fresh chives

2 tablespoons extra-virgin olive oil

1 teaspoon Pernod

Salt and freshly ground white pepper to taste

½ cup Blood Orange Sauce (page 166)

IN ADDITION TO MAKING A wonderful year-round appetizer, this dish can also be served as a summertime main course—at the Waldorf, we use it for both. Because this dish is served at room temperature, it makes a great choice for entertaining—what preparation there is can be done ahead, long before your guests arrive. Make sure you cook the duck breast to no more than 130°F, which will bring it to medium rare by the time it has rested for a few minutes. Any higher temperature and your duck will turn out dry. It is also important to slice the breast thinly—this helps give it a tender texture.

Preheat the oven to 325°F.

TO PREPARE THE DUCK Trim any excess fat from the top of the duck breasts, leaving a ¼-inch layer. Using a sharp knife, score the fat side of the ducks to form a lattice pattern. Season the duck breasts evenly with the five-spice powder, salt, and pepper. Set a dry nonstick pan over medium-high heat for 2 minutes. Place a duck breast, fat side down, in the hot pan and sear until golden brown, 3 to 4 minutes; watch carefully that the fat does not burn. Turn over and sear the other side for 3 to 4 minutes and transfer to a baking sheet. Repeat with the remaining duck breasts. Roast in the oven until the internal temperature reaches 120°F, about 8 minutes, for medium rare. Remove the breasts from the oven and let them rest for about 10 minutes.

TO PREPARE THE FENNEL SALAD Place the fennel in a mixing bowl and add the orange sections, chives, oil, and Pernod. Mix well so the ingredients are thoroughly combined and season with salt and pepper.

TO SERVE Slice the duck breasts very thin, on a bias. Arrange the fennel salad on serving plates, fan out the duck slices on top of the salad, and drizzle with the blood orange sauce.

Wine Recommendation New Zealand Sauvignon Blanc (intense flavors of citrus and grass, with a long finish).

Steamed Dover Sole with Champagne Sauce and Caviar

SERVES 8

THIS DISH WAS CREATED FOR a 1998 State Dinner hosted by President Bill Clinton for a group of foreign dignitaries. It calls for simply steaming the sole filets over a fumet, or stock, made with the bones, fish trimmings, and vegetables. Then, the sauce is made with the reduced fumet and cream, finished with American sturgeon caviar, trout caviar, and chives. Simple perfection! The sauce goes very well with most steamed white fish, especially halibut or turbot.

FOR THE FISH

3 Dover sole, about 1 to 1¼ pounds each, each cut into 4 filets (see Chef's Note)

1 tablespoon softened butter

¼ cup Fish Fumet (page 254), made with brut champagne or dry white wine

Juice of ½ lemon

Salt and freshly ground white pepper to taste

FOR THE CHAMPAGNE SAUCE

1 cup heavy cream

1 cup Fish Fumet (page 254)

2 teaspoons American sturgeon caviar (or sevruga)

2 teaspoons salmon or trout caviar

2 teaspoons chopped fresh chives

Salt and freshly ground white pepper to taste

FOR THE GARNISH

8 pinches sea salt

4 sprigs fresh chervil

Preheat the oven to 350°F.

TO PREPARE THE FISH Cut each filet in half crosswise, to make 24 pieces. Lightly butter a baking sheet or a large cookie sheet with a rim and arrange the sole on the sheet, skin side down. Sprinkle the filets with the Fish Fumet and lemon juice and season with salt and pepper. Cover with aluminum foil and transfer to the oven. After about 8 minutes, lift the foil and check on the fish; it is done when it is no longer translucent (depending on the thickness of the fish, this may take 10 to 12 minutes). Remove the baking sheet from the oven and set aside in a warm place (on the stove top or in a 150°F oven) until ready to serve.

TO PREPARE THE CHAMPAGNE SAUCE Stir together the cream and Fish Fumet in a small saucepan and set over medium-high heat. Reduce the mixture by half, until about 1 cup remains. Spoon half of the broth from the baking sheet containing the cooked fish and strain into the sauce. Add both types of caviar and the chives. Season with salt and pepper and stir well to thoroughly incorporate.

TO SERVE Place 3 pieces of fish in the center of each warm serving plate. Spoon the sauce over the fish and garnish with a pinch of sea salt and the chervil.

Wine Recommendation Brut champagne (maturing flavors of brioche, hazelnut, ginger, and mineral).

CHEF'S NOTES

◇   At the Waldorf, our fresh Dover sole is flown in twice a week from Europe. Some commercially available Dover sole is frozen, which tends to dry out when cooked, so I recommend buying fresh lemon sole or grey sole if you cannot get fresh Dover sole.

◇   If American sturgeon caviar is not available, hackleback, paddlefish, or imported sevruga will do. These alternatives may be a bit saltier than sturgeon, so season the sauce after adding the caviar.

TO PREPARE THE FOIE GRAS Generously season the slices of foie gras with salt and pepper. Set a dry, heavy skillet over high heat for 2 to 3 minutes. When the skillet is hot, add the foie gras and sear on the first side until browned, about 2 minutes. Turn over and sear the other side for 2 minutes longer; remove and set aside to drain on paper towels.

TO SERVE Place a slice of the caramelized apple on each warm serving plate and arrange a piece of foie gras on top. Garnish the foie gras with the apple salad and drizzle the sauce over and around the plate.

Wine Recommendation Sancerre (rich texture, with notes of green apple).

CHEF'S NOTES

◇ Apples and foie gras are natural partners—the mild acidity and crunchy texture of the fruit cuts the richness and soft texture of the goose liver. At the same time, the sweet yet acidic caramelized apple brings out the subtleties of the foie gras.

◇ No butter or oil is needed to cook foie gras in the skillet—just make sure the pan is sufficiently hot to sear it.

Growing up in Alsace and Montpelier in the South of France, Cedric Tovar always knew he was destined for a professional kitchen. At age six, he was making bread pudding and stews and helping out with the backyard grill. By the time he was ten years old, he had made his first mayonnaise, a landmark moment. Whenever his grandmother came to visit in the summer, Cedric would shadow her so that he could learn something of her kitchen skills.

Cedric began his formal training at age sixteen, when he moved to Paris and into the kitchen of acclaimed chef Jean-Paul Duquesnoy to begin his apprenticeship. After completing studies at cooking school, Cedric took his first professional position, at Joël Robuchon's Restaurant Laurent, off the Champs Elysées. As part of his national military service, he was assigned to cook for Prime Minister Michel Rocard. "It was a unique opportunity and a great experience for me," he remarks. Then, after spells at the legendary Fauchon and Tour d'Argent, and another stint with Robuchon, Cedric was recruited by the world-class Plaza Athénée Hotel to work with the legendary Alain Ducasse.

There are few of us who can claim a career-changing move resulting from a truffle-hunting weekend in the South of France, but Cedric is one. After meeting American chef/restaurateur Geoffrey Zakarian there, he was offered a Sous Chef position in New York to open Zakarian's new restaurant, Town, becoming Executive Chef shortly afterward. Following subsequent spells at Theo and Django, Cedric was appointed by the Waldorf=Astoria in 2005 to reopen the prestigious Peacock Alley dining room.

"Appetizers are often my guests' first impression," says Cedric, "so, as a chef, it is important to pay special attention to them. My style is to focus on a central character on the plate—what I call 'the star of the show.' I choose seasonal products I like, and I prefer simple presentations with clean, bright flavors. Often, I will return to my training and my personal food memories and give a traditional recipe a novel twist and a special touch. My travels have also played an important role in my food choices; I found Vietnam and Southeast Asia particularly inspiring." Cedric clearly respects traditional cuisine and enjoys reviving classic dishes, rephrasing them in a modern idiom while maintaining respect for their authenticity.

"I care a lot about where my ingredients come from and how they are grown," says Cedric. "I like to buy from farmers who enjoy what they do because it shows in their product. When I first came to America, I assumed it would be hard to find suppliers like that, but the reverse is true. There are a lot of people here who put in a huge amount of effort and commitment, and that inspires me even further. For the home cook, I recommend scouting out farmers' markets and taking the growers into account too."

—J.H.

115

APPETIZERS

Caramelized Onion and Tomato Tart with Goat Cheese and Fennel Salad

SERVES 8

THE
WALDORF=ASTORIA
COOKBOOK

FOR THE TART SHELL

3 tablespoons fennel seeds

1 sheet pie dough (page 248)

FOR THE GOAT CHEESE
MIXTURE

¾ cup goat cheese

3 tablespoons minced Kalamata olives

1 teaspoon rinsed and minced capers

½ teaspoon grated lemon zest

FOR THE ONIONS

1 tablespoon olive oil

1 tablespoon butter

*3 Vidalia or other sweet onions, sliced
(about 3 cups)*

2 tablespoons sherry vinegar

½ teaspoon minced anchovy

Tomato Confit (page 257)

THIS ELEGANT VEGETARIAN DINNER APPETIZER is very versatile—it also works well as an excellent light lunch entrée or brunch or buffet item. Occasionally we serve this with Grilled Spicy Shrimp (page 121) or grilled chicken or beef as a salad entrée. It became a star when it was introduced at the Rock and Roll Hall of Fame dinner. You can prepare all the ingredients hours ahead of time and simply plate it whenever your guests are ready to sit down to dinner.

Preheat the oven to 350°F.

TO PREPARE THE TART SHELL Place the fennel seeds in a dry sauté pan set over medium heat. Toast the seeds until golden brown, 3 to 4 minutes. Using a spice grinder or sharp knife, chop the seeds until they are coarse but not too fine.

Roll out the pie dough until it is about 10 inches square and ⅛-inch thick. Using a cookie cutter, mold, or knife, cut the dough into eight 3-inch-diameter circles. Place the circles on a large cookie sheet lined with parchment paper and sprinkle each circle with the toasted fennel seeds. Cover the circles with a second piece of parchment paper and another cookie sheet or roasting pan. Bake the pie dough in the oven for about 15 minutes, or until golden brown. Remove and let cool. Turn the oven to 275°F.

FOR THE GOAT CHEESE MIXTURE Place the goat cheese in an ovenproof dish and soften in the oven for about 5 minutes. Remove from the oven and add the olives, capers, and lemon zest. Mix thoroughly and let cool.

FOR THE ONIONS Put the olive oil and butter in a large sauté pan and set over medium-high heat. When the oil is hot and the butter is melted, add the onions and sauté, stirring frequently, until they turn a rich brown color, 8 to 10 minutes. Add the vinegar and continue cooking until the liquid is just evaporated, about 2 minutes. Remove the pan from the heat and let cool; mix in the anchovy.

FOR THE FENNEL SALAD

½ *fennel bulb*

1 tablespoon extra-virgin olive oil

1 teaspoon Pernod

Pinch of salt

TO PREPARE THE TOMATO CONFIT   After baking the tomatoes, remove them from the oil, peel and discard the skins, and set the oil and 2 tomato halves aside for the sauce. Roughly chop the remaining 14 tomato halves and set aside. In a blender or food processor, purée the reserved tomatoes and oil and reserve for sauce.

TO ASSEMBLE THE TARTS   Place the baked pie dough circles inside 3-inch molds or 3-inch cookie cutters (these will help the tarts retain their shape). Using a spoon, evenly spread the goat cheese mixture on top of the dough and arrange the onion mixture on top. Add a layer of the chopped tomatoes, then remove the molds.

FOR THE FENNEL SALAD   Using a mandoline (see page 263), shave the fennel very finely and transfer to a small mixing bowl. Add the oil, Pernod, and salt, and thoroughly combine.

TO SERVE   Place the tarts on serving plates, garnish the tops with the fennel salad, and drizzle with the reserved tomato sauce.

Wine Recommendation   Côtes de Provence Rosé (bone dry, fragrant, flavorful).

CHEF'S NOTE

◇   If you do not already own a couple of 3-inch ring molds or cookie cutters, this would be a good time to invest in some—they are ideal for making this recipe. They will also be useful in many other ways.

Bacon-Wrapped Rabbit Loin with Chanterelle Mushrooms and Pumpkin Purée

SERVES 8

FOR THE BALSAMIC REDUCTION

3 rabbit saddles (bone-in loins)

2 tablespoons vegetable oil

2 cups sliced onions

1 cup peeled and sliced carrots

1 cup sliced celery

2 cloves garlic

2½ cups balsamic vinegar

3 sprigs fresh thyme

1 dried bay leaf

Butternut Squash Purée (page 246)

FOR THE CHANTERELLE MUSHROOMS

1 teaspoon olive oil

1 tablespoon butter

2 cups chanterelle mushrooms

1 tablespoon minced shallot

2 teaspoons sherry vinegar

Salt and freshly ground black pepper to taste

¼ cup fresh parsley leaves

RABBIT IS AN INGREDIENT THAT is so misunderstood by so many. I think most people feel a little squeamish about ordering it because they have encountered cuddly domesticated or pet rabbits. Wild rabbit is a different matter, and has been hunted and enjoyed for dinner for centuries. For others, reluctance may be the result of the unremarkable flavor. Once you put those prejudices aside, you will find that this preparation is spectacular! I like to serve this dish in between a fish course and the entrée, as I did for President George W. Bush at a state dinner in 2002.

Preheat the oven to 400°F.

TO PREPARE THE BALSAMIC REDUCTION Using a sharp boning knife, carefully cut along each rabbit saddle bone to remove both loins and transfer to the refrigerator. Trim any excess meat from the bones; place the rabbit trimmings and bones in a roasting pan and drizzle with the vegetable oil. Transfer to the oven and roast for about 1 hour, until golden brown. Add the onions, carrots, celery, and garlic to the roasting pan and continue roasting for 20 to 25 minutes more.

Remove the pan from the oven and add the balsamic vinegar. With a wooden spoon, deglaze the pan by scraping any solids that are stuck to the pan and stirring the liquid to absorb them. Transfer the contents of the roasting pan to a large saucepan, add the thyme, bay leaf, and 3 cups of water, and bring to a boil over medium-high heat. Turn the heat to medium-low and simmer for 60 minutes. Strain the liquid through a fine-mesh sieve into a clean saucepan and discard the trimmings, bones, and vegetables. Continue to reduce the liquid until it reaches a syrupy consistency and about ⅓ cup remains. Remove from heat and cover. Reheat when ready to serve.

Prepare the Butternut Squash Purée.

TO PREPARE THE CHANTERELLES Place the olive oil and butter in a large sauté pan or skillet and set over high heat until the butter is melted and stops crackling. Add the mushrooms and sauté until the mushrooms release their juice, 3 or 4 minutes. Stir in the shallot and cook for 2 minutes longer. Add the sherry, season with salt and pepper, and continue cooking until all of the juice has evaporated. Remove from the heat and stir in the parsley.

FOR THE RABBIT

2 tablespoons Garlic Confit
(page 257)

2 tablespoons Dijon mustard

2 teaspoons minced fresh thyme

8 thin slices bacon

TO PREPARE THE RABBIT   Place the reserved rabbit loins on a plate and season with the garlic confit, mustard, and thyme. Place a 12-inch-long piece of plastic wrap on a clean counter surface. With the cut end of the plastic wrap closest to you, lay out 4 pieces of the bacon, overlapping slightly from left to right. Lay 2 of the rabbit loins across the bacon at the end nearest you, then place a third loin on top of the other two to form a little pyramid. Lift the plastic wrap end closest to you and begin to roll the package, so that the bacon starts to wrap around the rabbit loins (avoid wrapping the plastic wrap inside the package). Apply pressure so that the bacon wraps tightly about 1½ times around the loins, then cut off any extra bacon. Use butcher's twine to keep the bacon from unraveling during cooking by tying the twine at 4 points along the log; starting at the left end, tie after ¾ inch, then at 2¼ inches, 3¾ inches, and 5¼ inches. Cut through the log between the knots, creating 4 tournedos (see photo). Repeat with the remaining rabbit loins and bacon.

The Mushroom Conundrum: Sweetbread and Mushroom Casserole

4 cups milk

1¼ pounds veal sweetbreads

1 Bouquet Garni (page 259)

1 cup dry white wine

2 cups port wine

2 cups Veal Stock (page 253)
or Chicken Stock (page 252)

3 tablespoons butter

5 thick slices bacon,
cut into 1-inch pieces

2 tablespoons olive oil

8 cups sliced assorted mushrooms

2 shallots, minced

6 ounces fresh sea beans
(see Chef's Note)

½ cup halved green seedless grapes,
cut lengthwise

¼ cup fresh parsley leaves

THIS DISH STARRED ON THE Waldorf=Astoria episode of the TV series *At the Chef's Table* on PBS. On screen, I jokingly asked Alex Boylan, the host, to come up with a name for the dish by the time he'd finished prepping it with me. "Make it a pretty name," I said, and when he dubbed it "The Mushroom Conundrum," I told him, simply, "no." Then a guest at the dinner, chef and author Roseanne Gold, proclaimed on air that she loved the name and, I must admit, it's grown on me and does make a great talking point! The earthy mushrooms, sweet grapes, salty, crisp sea beans, and soft, rich sweetbreads make a truly memorable combination.

Pour the milk into a large dish or shallow bowl and add the sweetbreads. Cover with plastic wrap and let soak overnight in the refrigerator.

Preheat the oven to 375°F. Prepare an ice bath (page 260).

Put 2 quarts of salted water in a large saucepan and add the Bouquet Garni and wine. Bring this court bouillon to a boil, drain the sweetbreads and, and using a large spoon, lower them into the boiling court bouillon. Return to a boil and simmer for 2 minutes. Remove the sweetbreads with a slotted spoon and transfer to the ice bath to stop the cooking process. When cool, remove the thin outer membrane with a sharp knife. Cut into large (¾-inch) cubes and set aside (the sweetbreads will be rare in the middle).

Pour the port and stock into a large saucepan and bring to a boil over high heat. Turn down the heat to medium high and reduce the liquid until ¼ cup remains, 10 to 12 minutes. Remove from the heat and whisk in 2 tablespoons butter. Keep warm over low heat.

Place the bacon in a sauté pan and set over medium heat. Sauté for 5 or 6 minutes, until the bacon pieces are almost crisp. Reserve the cooked bacon and the bacon fat separately. Pour 1 tablespoon of the hot bacon fat into a large clean skillet or sauté pan. Add 1 tablespoon of the olive oil and set over medium-high heat. When the oil and bacon fat is hot and shimmering, add 4 cups of the mushrooms and sauté for 3 to 4 minutes, stirring frequently. Add half of the shallots and continue to cook for 2 minutes longer. Set aside and repeat for the remaining bacon fat, olive oil, mushrooms, and shallots.

Refresh the ice bath. Bring a saucepan of lightly salted water to a boil and blanch the sea beans for about 1 minute. Remove with a slotted spoon and transfer immediately to the ice bath to stop the cooking process. When cool, drain.

Place the remaining 1 tablespoon of butter in a sauté pan and set over medium heat. When it is melted and has stopped crackling, add the diced sweetbreads and sauté until brown, about 3 minutes. Add the sautéed mushrooms, bacon, and blanched sea beans and continue to sauté for 2 minutes longer. Stir in the port wine reduction, grapes, and parsley, and adjust the seasonings with salt and pepper. Serve immediately.

Wine Recommendation Carneros (CA) Chardonnay (mature flavors of figs, lemon meringue, and exotic spices, with floral scents).

CHEF'S NOTES

◇ Sweetbreads, beloved by many, are the thymus glands found in the neck of veal calves or lamb; typically, they are white and elongated in shape. Round sweetbreads, also called *heart sweetbreads,* are derived from the animals' pancreas, and are marginally preferable because they slice more evenly. Either way, it is very important to buy sweetbreads from a reputable source as freshness is key—they are particularly perishable. Note that the sweetbreads must be soaked overnight before cooking.

◇ I recommended using 4 different kinds of seasonal mushrooms—2 cups of each variety, such as chanterelle, oyster, lobster, hen-of-the-woods, or black trumpet mushrooms. You will need about 6 ounces of each type to yield 2 cups sliced or cut-up mushrooms.

◇ Fresh sea beans, also called *samphire, salicornia,* or *pousse pied,* are harvested from both Pacific and Atlantic coasts and are mostly available in summer and fall. Blanched haricots verts (steamed for 6 or 7 minutes) or julienned uncooked snow peas can be substituted for these salty, crisp, and delicate sea beans.

The most famous Waldorf suites are located in the Waldorf Towers, an exclusive hotel-within-a-hotel located on the twenty-sixth to forty-second floors of the Waldorf=Astoria. In all, the Waldorf Towers, which has been described as "the world's most exclusive boutique hotel," features 119 commodious one-to four-bedroom deluxe suites and ninety-one executive guest rooms. Some of the luxurious, ultraprivate suites are occupied by permanent or long-term residents. The Towers has its own dedicated street entrance, lobby, and elevators, and the exclusive white-glove service enjoyed by guests helps create an environment of maximum luxury and complete privacy. Each of the Towers suites is distinctively and individually designed with antiques and antique reproduction furnishings; no two suites are decorated the same way.

THE PRESIDENTIAL SUITE This four-bedroom suite on the thirty-fifth floor of the Waldorf Towers—at 3,100 square feet, the largest in the hotel—has accomodated not only presidents, but royalty and heads of state as well. Since the Waldorf=Astoria opened on Park Avenue in 1931, all thirteen U.S. presidents have stayed in the suite. The suite contains General MacArthur's desk, Jimmy Carter's Eagle desk set, and John F. Kennedy's rocking chair. Other signature items donated by past presidents include a gold oval mirror and eagle-base table in the foyer, given by Ronald Reagan, and a pair of eagle wall sconces provided by Lyndon B. Johnson. All the paintings in the suite are by American artists. The suite was recently renovated at a cost of $9 million, and although the U.S. State Department has first call on the apartment for visiting dignitaries, it can be rented by private individuals for $10,000 per night.

THE ROYAL SUITE When Queen Elizabeth II and her husband, Prince Philip, the Duke of Edinburgh, arrived for a state visit in October 1957, their scheduled stay in the Presidential Suite was preempted by the unexpectedly extended presence of King Faisal of Saudi Arabia due to illness. Another suitable suite on the penthouse level, extending the length of the East 50th Street block on the forty-second floor, with commanding, unobstructed views of the city was prepared instead. It was lavishly furnished with antiques and period furniture and duly renamed the Royal Suite. Following the queen's visit, the Duke and Duchess of Windsor moved from their permanent residence on the twenty-eighth floor and adopted this suite as their New York home for the next decade. There was a touch of delightful irony in this turn of events, given the dynamic of the British royal family and the strained relations between the queen and the duke, her uncle, who had abdicated the British throne (as King Edward VIII) in 1937 to marry Wallis Simpson, who became the Duchess of Windsor. The suite, which can accommodate fifty-five guests for a seated dinner or one hundred guests for a reception, underwent a $1 million renovation in 2004, with inspiration drawn from the Windsors' decorative style, using their estate outside Paris as a design model. The suite can be privately rented for $10,000 per night.

THE MacARTHUR SUITE In 1946, representatives of the United States, Britain, France, and Russia formally met in suite 37A at the Waldorf to sign a peace treaty that shaped the post-World War II world. After returning from Korea in 1952, General MacArthur (below) and his wife, Jean, became permanent residents of the suite. Jean MacArthur moved into a smaller suite following her husband's death, living there until 2000. Suite 37A is used today to host political dignitaries and VIPs. In the 1990s, Madeleine Albright held the negotiations in the suite with Yasser Arafat and Benjamin Netanyahu that formed the basis of the Wye Plantation Middle East peace talks, and a series of meetings there formed the foundation of the Irish Peace Accords. Treaties dealing with Italy, Hungary, Bulgaria, Yugoslavia, and Finland have all been agreed upon in this celebrated suite, which can be rented for $7,000 per night.

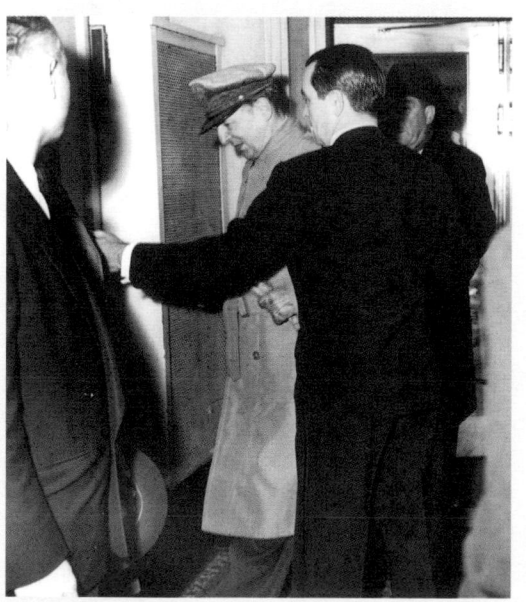

THE COLE PORTER SUITE Composer Cole Porter (above, with Elsa Maxwell) wrote many of his most famous lyrics and melodies while a resident of this suite, which he called home for twenty-five years, until his death in 1964. We like to think he was inspired by the beautiful floral print Steinway grand piano given to him by the hotel! Porter's piano now resides in the Cocktail Terrace in the lobby, where it is played nightly. Frank Sinatra and his fourth wife, Barbara, later lived in the suite until 1987. The apartment still features the Sinatras' monogrammed shower stalls, and guests may soak in the ambience (or in the shower stalls) for $7,000 per night.

THE SUITE OF THE U.S. AMBASSADOR TO THE UNITED NATIONS When the United Nations was created after World War II and headquartered in New York, the Waldorf Towers was chosen as the site for the official residence of the U.S. Ambassador to the United Nations. To this day, the Waldorf=Astoria is the only hotel in the world to house an ambassadorial residence.

As lighter and healthier eating habits have become the general rule over the last thirty years or so, dating back at least to the advent of California cuisine, chefs everywhere have become increasingly creative when it comes to salads. Nowadays, whether eating out or cooking for guests at home, it is typical to see a salad taking a prominent place as an appetizer. The same is true for the majority of the special events we do at the Waldorf=Astoria. Years ago, the salad course was eaten with cheese after the main course, and I still see it served that way when we have a classic gourmet dinner. Of course, it is fine to enjoy your salad in this style if you prefer, but the change in the role that salads play has probably been more profound than any other development in contemporary American cuisine.

In this chapter, you will find a selection of salad-type appetizers we serve at the Waldorf that present well, are easy to prepare, and are definite crowd pleasers. They can all be made in larger quantities for a lunch entrée, or can be adapted as a side course with the main meal, in lieu of a vegetable. In talking to guests who love to cook at home, as well as to caterers and party planners, I have come to realize that a common concern is that a salad served as an appetizer might be insufficient to satisfy hungry guests; at the same time, you don't want your guests leaving and complaining they were too full and uncomfortable or that the food was unstylishly heavy. These recipes fill the bill on all counts.

When following one of these recipes or preparing a classic mixed green salad at home, I suggest you look for as much produce as possible at your local farmers' market. The greens are usually picked within a day or two and have not been transported vast distances, as much store-bought produce has. If in doubt, look at the stem end of the lettuce; if it is brown and dry, you can be sure the head is old and will be dry. If the leaves are torn and bruised, you will have to discard them. When it comes to the oil I use for the dressing, my preference is for extra-virgin olive oil or grapeseed oil; there is a wide range of price and quality on the market. Remember, expensive doesn't necessarily mean better. Bear in mind that just like wines, the same brand of extra-virgin olive oil can vary in quality from year to year. Choose one that is fragrant and has a balance of fruitiness and acidity, as well as a pleasant olive and peppery aftertaste. Do not feel compelled to use extra-virgin olive oil every time; when you want to cut back on the assertive flavor and seek a neutral taste, I recommend grapeseed oil, or a blend of both. As for vinegar, the quality is only as good as the wine used to make it; good vinegars generally do cost more. You do not always have to use vinegar to dress a salad—there are times when freshly squeezed lemon juice is all the acidity fresh greens need.

Waldorf Salad with Truffles and Candied Walnuts

FOR THE CANDIED WALNUTS

2 quarts vegetable oil

2 cups apple juice

½ cup honey

¼ cup dark molasses

¼ cup maple syrup

2 cups walnut halves

FOR THE DRESSING

½ cup crème fraîche

½ cup plain yogurt

3 teaspoons freshly squeezed lemon juice

¼ cup walnut oil

Salt and freshly ground white pepper to taste

1½ tablespoons minced black winter truffles

FOR THE WALDORF SALAD

2 large Granny Smith apples (unpeeled)

2 large Gala apples (or Braeburn, Empire, or other crisp red apples), unpeeled

½ cup peeled and julienned celeriac

½ cup celery leaves (from 1 bunch celery)

IT MAY NOT SURPRISE YOU to hear that this is the single most frequently requested recipe at the Waldorf=Astoria from people around the world. There is just one tiny problem—I can't bring myself to eat the original version of apples and mayonnaise, which dates back to the 1890s and the early days of the original Waldorf Hotel (the walnuts were added a bit later). It may have been fashionable once, but most people these days steer a wide berth around mayonnaise in a salad. On top of that, other people's versions were often made incorrectly. Our recipe has been a little revamped over the years, and this is my favorite version—it is light, refreshing, and the truffles give it that special touch. In fact, it is more popular now than it has ever been; we serve it at Oscar's American Brasserie, on our Room Service menu, at Bull and Bear, and for special events. Oh, and by the way (I am often asked), I now actually like it!

TO PREPARE THE CANDIED WALNUTS Pour the oil into a large saucepan and set over medium-low heat until a thermometer reads 375°F. Meanwhile, in a small saucepan set over medium heat, warm the apple juice, honey, molasses, and maple syrup. Bring to a strong simmer, add the walnuts, then turn the heat to medium low. Continue to simmer for 15 minutes. Remove the pan from the heat and strain the nuts, discarding the liquid. Carefully add the nuts to the hot oil in batches and fry for about 20 seconds, or until they are mahogany in color; be careful not to overfry the nuts, as they will burn quickly. Remove the nuts from the oil with a slotted spoon and spread out on a cookie sheet lined with parchment paper to cool. When room temperature, chop the walnuts. Store in the refrigerator in an airtight container.

TO PREPARE THE DRESSING Combine the crème fraîche, yogurt, and lemon juice in a mixing bowl. Whisk in the walnut oil and season with salt and pepper. Fold in half of the truffles.

TO PREPARE THE SALAD Using a mandoline (see page 263) on the fine comb setting, julienne the Granny Smith and Gala apples into matchstick-size strips, being careful to avoid the seeds in the core; transfer to a mixing bowl. Add the julienned celeriac to the apples. Gently fold the dressing into the apple mixture until well combined. Divide the salad between chilled serving plates and garnish the top of each salad with some celery leaves and the remaining truffles. Scatter the candied walnuts around each plate.

Wine Recommendation Chilean Sauvignon Blanc (rich, with lemon zest and grapefruit tones and a balanced finish).

CHEF'S NOTES

◇ At the Waldorf, we have successfully paired this famous salad with game dishes such as venison or smoked duck breast with black currant sauce, as well as roasted chicken and Veal Oscar (page 198).

◇ Celeriac is the root of the celery plant. If unavailable, you may substitute regular peeled celery.

◇ The nuts can be made ahead and stored in an airtight container. For a shortcut, use store-bought candied walnuts.

Oscar's Spicy Asian Chicken Salad with Cashews and Ginger-Chive Dressing

SERVES 8

FOR THE CHICKEN

8 boneless, skinless chicken breasts, about 6 ounces each

1 cup Asian Spice Rub for Chicken (page 258)

FOR THE GINGER-CHIVE DRESSING

¼ cup chopped fresh ginger

½ cup chopped fresh chives

1 tablespoon pickled ginger

1 clove garlic

¼ cup unseasoned rice wine vinegar

2 tablespoons soy sauce

1 large egg yolk

1 cup canola oil

¼ cup dark sesame oil

½ cup Spicy Cashews (page 259)

WHENEVER I WALK THROUGH OSCAR'S and stop by tables to greet our guests, I usually ask them if they have decided what they're going to eat. Many times, with their heads hung apologetically, they say, "the spicy chicken salad," or "I know I should try something new, but I just love that Asian chicken salad." No need to apologize—to me, that just shows good taste! This salad was first introduced by former Oscar's chef Robert Trainor. Before coming to the Waldorf, Robert was the original chef of Manhattan's famed Asia de Cuba restaurant. We adapted this version for Oscar's and it has been a hit ever since. Thank you, Robert!

Preheat the oven to 375°F.

TO PREPARE THE CHICKEN Coat the chicken with the spice rub and place in a resealable plastic bag. Transfer to the refrigerator and let sit for 30 minutes. Place the chicken on a baking sheet or in a roasting pan and roast in the oven until cooked through, 15 to 20 minutes. Remove and let cool in the refrigerator; when chilled, cut into large (¾-inch) cubes.

TO PREPARE THE DRESSING Place the ginger, chives, pickled ginger, garlic, ¼ cup of water, vinegar, soy sauce, and egg yolk in a blender or food processor. Purée the ingredients until smooth, and with the blender running, slowly drizzle in the canola oil and sesame oil until thoroughly incorporated. If dressing becomes too thick, add a little cold water.

Prepare the Spicy Cashews.

TO PREPARE THE SALAD In a large mixing bowl, combine the cabbage and watercress. Add the diced chicken, cashews, and orange sections. Neatly cut the cheese into ½-inch long diamonds and add to the salad. Mix until evenly blended.

TO SERVE Add 2 cups of the dressing and toss to combine. Evenly distribute the salad into 8 bowls. Sprinkle each salad with a pinch of the togarashi spice (this is the spicy ingredient in this salad, so be careful not to overdo it).

FOR THE SALAD

6 cups sliced Napa cabbage,
cut lengthwise and then into
½-inch thick strips

3 cups stemmed watercress

1½ cups orange sections (page 260)

2 ounces Manchego cheese,
thinly sliced

Pinch of shichimi togarashi,
or to taste (see Chef's Note)

Beverage Recommendation Japanese Sapporo beer (smooth, elegant flavor, clean finish).

CHEF'S NOTES

◇ *Shichimi togarashi* spice mix, available in Asian markets, is a Japanese spice blend containing Szechwan peppercorns, black and white sesame seeds, poppy seeds, dried orange peel, dried seaweed (nori), and crushed chile peppers.

◇ Those with health concerns should note that the dressing contains raw egg yolk.

Niçoise Salad, Asian Chicken Salad, and Tuna Panini (l–r), served at Oscar's by Sameh Sasa.

Roasted Figs Wrapped in Prosciutto with Portobellos, Arugula, and Fontina Crostini

SERVES 8

FOR THE ROASTED MUSHROOMS

2 portobello mushrooms

2 tablespoons extra-virgin olive oil

2 tablespoons balsamic vinegar

½ teaspoon minced garlic

1 teaspoon minced fresh thyme

FOR THE FIGS

4 slices of prosciutto, cut paper thin

8 fresh figs

FOR THE DRESSING AND SALAD

2 tablespoons freshly squeezed lemon juice

1 teaspoon Dijon mustard

⅓ cup extra-virgin olive oil

½ teaspoon finely grated lemon zest

½ teaspoon sugar

Salt and freshly ground black pepper to taste

8 cups baby arugula

THIS DISH IS A POPULAR appetizer in Oscar's American Brasserie, and we sometimes feature the roasted figs for our special events. If we can pull off roasted figs perfectly for one thousand people during a Grand Ballroom event, I am confident you can create it for eight dinner guests (remember, all these recipes were tested under home conditions). The sweet and salty combination of the figs and prosciutto creates conversation at the table every time, and the recipe is just too tempting to pass up!

Preheat the oven to 350°F.

TO PREPARE THE MUSHROOMS Combine the portobellos, oil, vinegar, garlic, and thyme in a nonreactive mixing bowl. Marinate for 20 to 30 minutes. Transfer the mushrooms to a roasting pan and roast in the oven for 15 minutes. Remove and set aside to cool.

TO PREPARE THE FIGS Cut the prosciutto slices lengthwise into 1½-inch-wide strips. Wrap each fig twice around with a prosciutto strip. Transfer to a cookie sheet or roasting pan and roast in the oven for 8 minutes. Remove and let cool.

Preheat the broiler.

TO PREPARE THE DRESSING In a small nonreactive mixing bowl, combine the lemon juice and Dijon mustard. Slowly whisk in the olive oil until thoroughly incorporated. Stir in the lemon zest and sugar until the sugar dissolves, and season with salt and pepper. Set aside. When ready to serve, place the arugula in a mixing bowl and toss with the dressing.

TO PREPARE THE CROSTINI Place the slices of bread on a large cookie sheet and toast on both sides under the broiler. Remove and rub each piece of bread with the garlic. Place 1 piece of Fontina cheese on each slice of bread; return to the oven and broil until melted, 2 or 3 minutes.

FOR THE CROSTINI

*4 slices rustic sourdough bread,
cut in half crosswise, or 8 small slices*

2 cloves garlic

*10 ounces Fontina cheese,
cut into 8 thin slices*

*¼ cup Balsamic Glaze (page 258),
for garnish*

TO SERVE Cut each of the reserved roasted mushrooms on the bias into 8 slices and arrange 2 mushroom slices on each serving plate. Place a crostini next to the mushroom and arrange the tossed arugula on top of the mushroom slices. Drizzle the Balsamic Glaze around each plate.

On the busiest days of the year, Oscar's Brasserie at the Waldorf=Astoria might serve fifteen hundred guests for breakfast, lunch, and dinner, and we can count on a lot of those diners ordering one of the restaurant's specialties—salads. Michael Bourquin, Chef de Cuisine at Oscar's (right, with Neil Joiner), makes sure every day there are at least five salads on hand for the lunch buffet and several others available for the dinner menu. "I enjoy taking a classic salad and having fun with it," says Michael. "Take the Cobb salad, for example, which started life at the Brown Derby Restaurant in Los Angeles back in 1937. Instead of the traditional chopped salad arranged in neat little piles, I paired the same components, unchopped, with spinach greens. Then, I substituted pancetta for the bacon, pickled red onions for the raw onion, and a slice of goat cheese instead of crumbled blue cheese. Salads seem to encourage creativity, and our guests really appreciate that. We even have fun with the names sometimes. Recently, we put together a Greek salad, made it a little differently, but called it, after the movie hit, "My Big Fat Greek Salad." A lot of customers ordered it out of curiosity and ended up raving about it. My advice for preparing salads at home is the same as I tell my staff here 'Keep it simple. Go with seasonal ingredients. Make sure combinations work—use tried and true pairings. And, most of all, have fun.'

Like Executive Chef John Doherty, Michael Bourquin studied at the Culinary Institute of America ("the other CIA," jokes Michael) and interned at the Waldorf while in school.

He rotated through the hotel's kitchens, as a banquet chef, at Peacock Alley, in Garde Manger, and as Room Service Sous Chef before taking over Oscar's. As he heads toward his twenty-year anniversary at the Waldorf, Michael still enjoys the challenges his work involves. "The biggest single issue is sheer volume some days," he concedes. "Sometimes, we start the day serving nine hundred guests breakfast.

For every one of those diners, we need to provide consistently excellent food and service, and everything needs to be in sync. When I began at the Waldorf, I was awestruck by the scale, and by the quality. One of my first assignments was in the Garde Manger station, preparing a thousand salads for The Rock and Roll Hall of Fame dinner. They all went out perfectly—of course! One of the things I enjoy the most is the size of this place. It's like a city within a building. It took me weeks just to figure out where everything was, even in the kitchen—it's huge! But it also means you learn different things from a lot of people very fast, and you never get stuck in a rut."

I had to ask Michael for his take on the famous Waldorf Salad. At Oscar's, he serves the revamped version (page 128) that brings an old favorite into the twenty-first century; he also offers a curried Waldorf Salad. These two are easily the best sellers on his menu, and Michael is proud of their popularity. I confess I am not, by any means, what you would describe as a salad person, but I would walk many a mile to track these babies down!

—J.H.

Bibb and Endive Salad with Candied Pecans, Goat Cheese Brulée, and Orange-Balsamic Vinaigrette

SERVES 8

1 cup Spicy Pecans (page 259)

FOR THE ORANGE-BALSAMIC
VINAIGRETTE

1 cup freshly squeezed orange juice

1 teaspoon light brown sugar

2 tablespoons balsamic vinegar

*½ cup plus 2 tablespoons
extra-virgin olive oil*

FOR THE SALAD

3 heads Bibb lettuce

2 heads endive

1 bunch watercress, stemmed

16 orange sections (page 260)

*Salt and freshly ground white pepper
to taste*

FOR THE GOAT CHEESE
BRULÉE

8 ounces herbed goat cheese

4 teaspoons granulated sugar

I CAME UP WITH THE idea for this salad one summer night when having friends over for a barbecue. I find it very refreshing and balanced, and everyone enjoyed it so much that I served it for the first time at the Waldorf=Astoria for a NASCAR dinner, one of our biggest annual events, and it took off from there! In the fall, I add julienned or roasted pears; otherwise I like to use fresh citrus sections and, when we can get them, fresh hearts of palm.

Prepare the Spicy Pecans.

TO PREPARE THE VINAIGRETTE Pour the orange juice into a nonreactive saucepan set over medium heat. Add the brown sugar, stirring to dissolve, and reduce the liquid until 2 tablespoons remain, about 5 minutes. Transfer to a nonreactive bowl and let cool. Once cooled, add the balsamic vinegar and gradually whisk in the olive oil until thoroughly incorporated. Season with salt and pepper.

TO PREPARE THE SALAD Reserve 8 attractive leaves of the Bibb lettuce for the base of the salad. Cut the remaining Bibb lettuce hearts into 1-inch squares and transfer to a nonreactive mixing bowl. Slice the endive crosswise into ¼-inch strips and add to the bowl. Add the watercress, orange sections, Spicy Pecans, and 6 tablespoons of the vinaigrette. Toss the salad well and season with salt and pepper.

Preheat the broiler.

TO PREPARE THE GOAT CHEESE BRULÉE Cut the goat cheese into 8 equal slices and place on a lightly buttered cookie sheet. Sprinkle each slice with ½ teaspoon of granulated sugar and transfer to the broiler. Slowly brown the goat cheese under a broiler until brown; watch carefully so the sugar does not burn.

TO SERVE Place the reserved Bibb leaves in the middle of chilled serving plates and drizzle each plate with the remaining vinaigrette. Add the salad mixture and place a slice of the goat cheese brulée next to the salad.

Wine Recommendation South African Chenin Blanc (white peach, almond, and citrus flavors).

Bull and Bear Maine Lobster Salad with Mango, Corn, and Citrus-Chile Vinaigrette

SERVES 6

FOR THE CITRUS-CHILE VINAIGRETTE

¼ red onion, chopped

½ mango, peeled and chopped

½ cup freshly squeezed orange juice

¼ cup freshly squeezed lime juice

¼ cup sherry vinegar

1 canned chipotle chile in adobo sauce

2 tablespoons honey

2 tablespoons Dijon mustard

1 cup olive oil

Salt and freshly ground white pepper to taste

FOR THE LOBSTERS, POTATOES, AND PEAS

6 live lobsters, about 1½ pounds each

12 small purple Peruvian potatoes, or Red Bliss new potatoes

12 sugar snap peas

WHEN THIS DISH WAS FIRST created by the Bull and Bear Steakhouse kitchen team I have to confess I was a little skeptical. It sounded as though there were too many different flavors, but I was pleasantly surprised by just how well they worked together, and the variety of textures and colors made an outstanding presentation. Our Bull and Bear regulars loved it from the get-go, and they'd be sure to let me know about it if I ever tried to change it.

FOR THE MANGO SALAD

6 ears fresh corn or 3 cups frozen kernels, thawed

4 mangoes, cut in half, pitted, peeled, and diced

½ red onion, finely minced

3 tablespoons roughly chopped cilantro leaves, or to taste

2 avocados, cut in half, pitted, peeled, and diced

Salt and freshly ground white pepper to taste

1 tablespoon finely sliced fresh chives

TO PREPARE THE VINAIGRETTE In a blender or food processor, blend the onion, mango, orange juice, lime juice, vinegar, chipotle, honey, and mustard. Slowly add the olive oil in a steady stream and continue to blend until thoroughly incorporated. Add salt and pepper to taste and set aside in the refrigerator.

TO PREPARE THE LOBSTERS Bring a large stockpot of salted water to a boil and plunge the lobsters in head first (cook 1 or 2 at a time if they don't all fit). Cook for 7 minutes, remove with tongs, and let cool. Twist off the tails and squeeze the tail shells until they crack and can be pulled apart and the tail meat can be removed. Using a sharp paring knife, remove the intestinal tract from the top side of the lobster tails. Slice the tail meat. Use lobster crackers to crack the claws and remove the claw meat. Keep the lobster meat refrigerated until ready to serve.

While the lobsters are cooking, bring a large saucepan of water to a boil and add the potatoes. Cook until tender, about 20 minutes. Drain, let cool, then chill in the refrigerator.

Prepare an ice bath (page 260). Bring a saucepan of salted water to a boil and blanch the sugar snap peas for 1 minute; drain and transfer to the ice bath to stop the cooking process. When cool, drain and reserve.

TO PREPARE THE MANGO SALAD Bring a large saucepan of water to boil and add the corn. Cook until tender, about 5 minutes. Remove and let cool; then cut the kernels from the cobs. Transfer to a mixing bowl and when ready to serve, add the diced mango, onion, cilantro, avocado, snap peas, and 1½ cups of the vinaigrette. Season with salt and pepper; add more vinaigrette if needed.

TO SERVE Slice the potatoes into rounds and arrange the slices in a circle around the center of each plate. Place the mango salad in the middle of the plate, inside the circle of potatoes. Arrange the lobster tail meat on top of the mango salad and place the meat from 2 claws on each plate leaning up on either side of the salad. Drizzle the plates with additional vinaigrette and sprinkle with the sliced chives.

Wine Recommendation Columbia Valley (WA) Semillon (smooth, generous, aromas of fig, black pepper, and citrus).

CHEF'S NOTE

◇ The vinaigrette will keep, refrigerated in an airtight container, for up to 1 week.

Roasted Beet and Goat Cheese Timbales with Apples and Walnut Vinaigrette

FOR THE WALNUT DRESSING

¼ cup sherry vinegar

1 teaspoon Dijon mustard

½ cup vegetable oil

¼ cup walnut oil

½ teaspoon sugar

Salt and freshly ground black pepper
to taste

FOR THE SALAD

3 large red beets, about 1½ pounds,
cut into ⅜-inch dice

½ cup olive oil

Salt and freshly ground black pepper
to taste

2 Granny Smith apples, peeled

½ teaspoon minced fresh parsley

½ teaspoon sliced fresh chives

½ teaspoon minced fresh tarragon

2 tablespoons sherry vinegar

4 ounces aged goat cheese,
crumbled and divided into 8 portions

1 cup frisée

½ cup toasted walnut pieces

WHEN YOU THINK OF BEETS, you may not think of roasting them, and I would be willing to bet you will love them with goat cheese. In contrast, apples, cheese, and walnuts are a classic combination, so this appetizer provides plenty of interest. This is another meatless first course that is very popular just as it is, especially for today's lighter palates, but is also spectacular with the addition of a little rich and slightly salty duck confit.

Preheat the oven to 350°F.

TO PREPARE THE DRESSING Combine the vinegar and mustard in a nonreactive mixing bowl and while continuously whisking, slowly pour in the vegetable oil and the walnut oil. Still whisking, add the sugar until it dissolves and is thoroughly combined (use a little more sugar if the dressing tastes too acidic.) Season with salt and pepper and set aside.

TO PREPARE THE SALAD Toss the beets in 2 tablespoons of the olive oil and season with salt and pepper. Place the beets on a well-oiled cookie sheet and transfer to the oven. Roast until the beets are soft but not mushy, 12 to 15 minutes. Cut 1 of the peeled apples into ⅜-inch cubes and transfer to a nonreactive mixing bowl. Add the beets, parsley, chives, tarragon, remaining olive oil, and sherry vinegar. Mix well and season with salt and pepper. Separate the beet salad into 8 equal portions. Create a timbale for each portion using a 3½-inch-diameter mold or cookie cutter. Place the mold on a serving plate, spoon a portion of the salad into the mold and press lightly to make even. Sprinkle with a portion of the goat cheese.

Julienne the remaining apple into matchstick lengths and put in a nonreactive mixing bowl. Add the frisée and 3 tablespoons of the walnut dressing. Season with salt and pepper and toss together. Place some of this salad on top of the goat cheese in the mold. Sprinkle with the toasted walnuts and drizzle with additional walnut dressing to taste. Repeat for the remaining ingredients and serve.

Wine Recommendation Spanish Albarino (round wine with flavors of peaches and pears and herbal notes).

Peacock Alley Cured Sardine and Heirloom Tomato Salad

SERVES 8

FOR THE MARINADE AND SARDINES

¼ cup extra-virgin olive oil

⅔ teaspoon sea salt

Pinch of dried red pepper flakes

1 tablespoon fresh thyme leaves

1 clove garlic, sliced

12 sardines

FOR THE LEMON

1 lemon, very thinly sliced

Pinch of salt

Pinch of sugar

2 tablespoons extra-virgin olive oil

FOR THE TOMATOES

1 sheet gelatin

6 red heirloom tomatoes

Pinch of celery salt

4 green heirloom tomatoes, cut into 1-inch wedges

4 yellow heirloom tomatoes, cut into 1-inch wedges

4 scallions (white part only), cut crosswise into 4 lengths

2 teaspoons extra-virgin olive oil

Sea salt and freshly ground white pepper to taste

2 teaspoons aged balsamic vinegar

IN SUMMERTIME, WHEN FRESH SARDINES are available, Chef Cedric Tovar likes to put this recipe on the Peacock Alley menu. Avoid the common mistake of grilling sardines, which just dries them out. Here, we cure, then briefly broil them, which gives them a delicious buttery tenderness. Paired with intensely tasty heirloom tomatoes—varieties that have been passed down over the generations—this dish offers an explosion of flavors that you won't soon forget.

TO PREPARE THE MARINADE AND SARDINES Combine ¼ cup olive oil, sea salt, red pepper flakes, thyme, and garlic in a shallow dish. Clean and scale the sardines. Remove the heads and cut 2 filets from each fish. Add the sardine filets to the marinade, cover, and let sit overnight in the refrigerator.

TO PREPARE THE LEMON Place the lemon slices in a separate bowl and season with a pinch of salt, a pinch of sugar, and the olive oil. Cover and let sit overnight in the refrigerator.

TO PREPARE THE TOMATOES Prepare an ice bath (page 260). Pour 2 cups cold water into a bowl, add the gelatin, and let rest for 10 minutes to let it bloom. Meanwhile, chop 2 of the red heirloom tomatoes and place in a blender or food processor. Purée and pass through a fine mesh strainer into a small metal bowl. Transfer 1 tablespoon of the tomato purée to a small saucepan and set over low heat. Stir in the bloomed gelatin and cook until the gelatin is melted. Remove from the heat and stir into the remaining tomato purée. Set the bowl over the ice bath and whisk continuously until the mixture becomes a white tomato mousse. Season with a pinch of celery salt and refrigerate until ready to serve.

Cut each of the remaining 4 red tomatoes into 1-inch wedges and place in a mixing bowl with the green and yellow tomato wedges. Add the scallions and season with olive oil, sea salt, and pepper. Sprinkle with the balsamic vinegar.

TO SERVE Place the tomato salad in the center of each serving plate. Top with 3 sardine filets and season with red pepper flakes and sea salt. Sprinkle with the celery leaves and 2 slices of marinated lemon on each plate. Garnish with a spoon of the reserved tomato mousse and, if desired, drizzle a little balsamic vinegar and olive oil around each plate.

FOR THE GARNISH

Dried red pepper flakes to taste

Sea salt to taste

1 cup celery leaves
(from 1 or 2 bunches of celery)

Wine Recommendation New Zealand (Marlborough) Sauvignon Blanc (tart and juicy with a Granny Smith apple finish).

CHEF'S NOTE

◇ Sardines are small saltwater fish that are part of the herring family; they school in summer time, when they are most easily found in markets. They are sometimes marketed as sprats, young herring, or young pilchards. Sardines are similar in flavor and texture to mackerel, or you can substitute mackerel or branzino filets (see page 151), trimmed small.

GRILLED VEGETABLE TIMBALES

SERVES 8

1½ cups Israeli couscous

2 yellow squash

2 zucchini

1 Italian eggplant

½ cup plus 1 teaspoon extra-virgin olive oil

Salt and freshly ground black pepper

1 tablespoon white balsamic vinegar

1½ tablespoons Pesto (page 257)

¼ cup balsamic vinegar

4 sprigs fresh thyme, finely chopped

Tomato Confit (page 257), roughly chopped

1 cup arugula

⅓ cup shaved Parmesan cheese

2 tablespoons Balsamic Glaze (page 258)

A TIMBALE IS A METAL or ceramic mold, typically used when cooking savory ingredients such as meat and/or vegetables. The term is also used to describe the finished dish prepared this way. This salad timbale recipe uses a mold, but only for shaping the final presentation. This versatile dish is very popular with our special-event dinner coordinators because it is beautiful, delicious, and light, which is a hard combination to beat! Our chefs also like it for the same reasons, plus it is relatively easy to prepare and a consistent crowd pleaser.

Prepare the grill. (See Chef's Note.)

In a small saucepan, bring 4 cups of lightly salted water to a boil. Add the couscous and cook for 8 to 10 minutes. Strain the couscous, transfer to a mixing bowl, and let cool.

Meanwhile, cut each squash and zucchini on the bias into 8 slices, about ¼-inch thick, and place in a mixing bowl. Cut 8 slices (not on a bias) from the eggplant, about ¼-inch thick, and add to the bowl. Pour in the ½ cup of olive oil, season with salt and pepper, and toss. Transfer the vegetables to the grill and cook over high heat until just tender, 1 or 2 minutes per side. Place the grilled vegetables on a cookie sheet and let cool to room temperature.

Combine the white balsamic vinegar and the couscous in a bowl and slowly mix in the pesto to taste. Drizzle the ¼ cup of balsamic vinegar over the vegetables and sprinkle with thyme. Season with salt and pepper.

Using a 3½-inch diameter mold or cookie cutter, prepare the timbale on each serving plate by layering the vegetables. Place a slice of the eggplant in the bottom of the mold and then add 2 slices of yellow squash and 2 slices of zucchini. Add ¼ cup couscous and press lightly to make even. Top with the tomato confit and carefully remove the mold. Repeat until you have 8 timbales. Toss the arugula in a bowl with the Parmesan and the remaining 1 teaspoon of olive oil and place on top of each timbale. Drizzle the timbales with the Balsamic Glaze and serve.

Wine Recommendation Sancerre Rosé (light body, dry, with dark fruit aromas).

CHEF'S NOTES

◇ Why Israeli couscous? It has a texture that is more like pasta, which is perfect for this dish. If unavailable, use orzo, cooked al dente according to the instructions on the package.

◇ The vegetables can be broiled rather than grilled, if you prefer.

Edamame Salad with Miso Dressing

SERVES 8

FOR THE DRESSING

1 teaspoon light (yellow) miso paste

¼ cup unseasoned rice wine vinegar

1 large egg yolk

1 tablespoon pickled ginger

1 teaspoon soy sauce

½ cup vegetable oil

½ teaspoon dark sesame oil

Salt and freshly ground white pepper to taste

FOR THE SALAD

2 cups frozen shelled edamame (soy beans)

1 tablespoon olive oil

¾ cup shiitake mushrooms, finely diced

1 tablespoon sesame seeds

½ cup shredded Napa cabbage

½ cup finely diced red bell pepper

½ cup finely diced yellow bell pepper

AS OUR GUESTS HAVE BECOME increasingly health conscious, they have become more focused on their diets and exercise routines. As a result, Peter Betz, our Chef Garde Manger (see page 63) has been approached on more than one occasion with a request for edamame, the Japanese name for soy beans harvested in their green or immature stage (also called vegetable soy beans). They are a very healthy food because they are easy to digest and high in protein, fiber, vitamin A, and amino acids. Peter was familiar with the ingredient because his wife Moriko is of Japanese heritage, and, as it turns out, her dad is quite the cook. Peter has found his passion for Japanese cuisine inspiring, and came up with this salad as an accompaniment for spicy ginger chicken at a dinner held for 1,200 guests by The Asia Society. I just loved it, and so did our guests!

TO PREPARE THE DRESSING Place the miso paste in a blender and add the vinegar, egg yolk, ginger, and soy sauce. Blend until smooth and with the motor running, slowly add the vegetable oil and sesame oil in a steady stream until completely incorporated. Season with salt and pepper.

TO PREPARE THE SALAD Prepare an ice bath (page 260). Bring a saucepan of salted water to a boil and blanch the edamame for 2 minutes. Remove with a slotted spoon and transfer to the ice bath to stop the cooking process.

Pour the olive oil into a large, heavy skillet and set over high heat. When the oil is hot and shimmering, add the mushrooms and sauté until slightly soft, about 3 minutes. Remove from the heat and let cool. Place the sesame seeds in a small dry sauté pan set over medium heat and toast for about 3 minutes, until golden brown. Transfer to a mixing bowl and add the sautéed mushrooms, cabbage, and the red and yellow bell pepper. Drain the edamame, add to the bowl, and gently toss.

TO SERVE Add ½ cup of the dressing to the salad mixture and season to taste, adding more dressing if desired. Divide the dressed salad between 8 chilled serving plates.

Beverage Recommendation A good-quality, crisp, dry sake, served cold to retain its delicate flavors.

Mixed Green Salad on a Potato–Blue-Cheese Galette with Roasted Pears and Spicy Pecans

SERVES 6 TO 8

FOR THE POTATO–BLUE-CHEESE GALETTE

½ tablespoon olive oil

¾ cup sliced onion

2 pounds Russet potatoes, peeled and thinly sliced (1/16-inch thick)

1 tablespoon minced fresh thyme

3 cups Chicken Stock (page 252)

Salt and freshly ground white pepper to taste

2 cups crumbled blue cheese

FOR THE ROASTED PEARS

2 Bosc pears (unpeeled), cored and each cut into 8 wedges

1 teaspoon sugar

½ cup balsamic vinegar

½ cup olive oil

Salt and freshly ground white pepper to taste

½ cup Spicy Pecans (page 259)

THE BEST THING ABOUT MIXED salad greens is that you can play with the different textures and flavors, especially if you take the trouble to blend your own and add highlights such as fresh herbs, shaved fennel, or endive. Many people find a mixed salad too ordinary or insubstantial for a special meal or when entertaining. This salad is the perfect antidote for anyone with mixed salad fears! The potato and blue cheese galette lends substance and full flavor, the roasted pears provide sweetness, and the spicy nuts give the dish a little kick. The earthy mixed greens pull it all together perfectly.

———————

Preheat the oven to 350°F. Lightly butter a 9- by 11-inch rimmed baking sheet or a roasting pan.

TO PREPARE THE GALETTE Pour the olive oil into a sauté pan and set over medium-high heat. When the oil is hot and shimmering, add the onion and sauté until brown and caramelized, about 8 minutes. Transfer to a mixing bowl, add the sliced potatoes and thyme, and mix until well combined. Place the potato and onion mixture on the prepared baking sheet and spread out evenly. Add the stock (there should be enough to reach the top of the potatoes, without covering them) and season with salt and pepper. Cover the baking sheet with foil and transfer to the oven. Roast for about 45 minutes or until tender when pierced with a knife. Remove from the oven and let cool on the baking sheet to room temperature.

Preheat the broiler.

Cut the potato mixture into 8 equal squares and top evenly with the blue cheese. Place under the broiler for 2 to 3 minutes, until the cheese is melted. Let cool to room temperature.

Turn the oven to 350°F.

TO PREPARE THE ROASTED PEARS Lightly butter a rimmed cookie or baking sheet. Place the pears in a mixing bowl and add the sugar, balsamic vinegar, and olive oil. Toss well to combine, season with salt and pepper, and transfer to the sheet. Bake in the oven until golden brown, 12 to 15 minutes.

FOR THE DRESSING AND SALAD

½ cup sherry vinegar

1 clove garlic, minced

1 teaspoon minced shallot

½ teaspoon minced fresh thyme

1½ cups extra-virgin olive oil

Salt and freshly ground white pepper to taste

6 cups mesclun salad mix

Prepare the Spicy Pecans.

TO PREPARE THE DRESSING AND SALAD Place the sherry vinegar, garlic, shallot, and thyme in a mixing bowl and slowly whisk in the extra-virgin olive oil. Place the mesclun mix in a separate bowl and toss with some of the dressing; season with salt and pepper. Place a square of potato galette off-center on each serving plate. Arrange the dressed greens so some are over the galette, and the rest are in the center of each plate. Lean the pear wedges against the salad, sprinkle with the pecans and drizzle additional dressing around each plate.

Wine Recommendation Napa Valley late harvest Semillon (tropical fruit tones with rich, round texture).

☜ ⊚ THOUSAND ISLAND DRESSING ⊚ ☞

ABOUT 1¼ CUPS

¾ cup mayonnaise

¼ cup bottled chile sauce

2 tablespoons tomato ketchup

1½ tablespoons minced onion

2 teaspoons sweet pickle relish

½ large hard-boiled egg, pushed through a sieve or finely chopped

¼ teaspoon Kosher salt, or to taste

Freshly ground black pepper to taste

THE WALDORF=ASTORIA popularized the classic Thousand Island Salad Dressing that has been a perennial American favorite since the early days of the twentieth century. The famous dressing, made with a base of mayonnaise and ketchup or chile sauce, and typically combined with finely minced onion and olives, and minced hard-cooked egg, derives its name from the Thousand Island resort area in upstate New York, where Sophia LaLonde, the wife of a popular fishing guide, George LaLonde Jr., created it for shore dinners she helped prepare for her husband's fishing parties. One of LaLonde's visiting clientele, a well-known New York City actress (and cookbook author) of the day, May Irwin, asked for the recipe which the LaLondes willingly gave her. Miss Irwin gave the dressing its famous name and in turn passed on the recipe to George Boldt, manager of the Waldorf=Astoria and frequent summer visitor to the Thousand Islands region. Boldt suggested to Maitre d' Oscar Tschirky that the dressing might be added to the hotel menu. Oscar recognized its potential and it immediately proved a big hit with guests, who in turn credited the famous "Oscar of the Waldorf" for introducing a classic to an appreciative dining public.

In a small mixing bowl, whisk the mayonnaise, chile sauce, ketchup, onion, relish, and egg until thoroughly combined. Season with salt and pepper.

Cooking fish is the true litmus test of any chef, whether in the professional kitchen or at home, not because it is so hard to cook (it's not), but because it is just too easy to ruin. To prepare a fish dish to perfection—conversation-stopping, eyes-rolling-back perfection—can be difficult. The most important step in preparing great fish is freshness. If you are not the fisherman, you may not really know for sure how old the fish is, but there are ways to tell how fresh it is: Check the overall appearance of whole fish, which should be intact, unblemished, and shiny; check the eyes, which should appear clear, not cloudy, and not sunken; check the gills, which should be bright red; check the firmness of the flesh, which should spring back after pressing it with your finger; and check the odor, which should smell like the sea, not fishy.

Ideally, buy fish from a reputable fishmonger, or track down a source you can trust. Do not be afraid to ask questions about the source of the fish, how long it has been out of the water, and about the type of fish itself, if you are unfamiliar with it. If the fish store is busy, you can be pretty sure the product will turn over quickly. If you can examine the whole fish, do so; if the fish is cut into portions, beware of dried and discolored edges, or coloration that is not uniform. Even if the fish is packaged, give it a sniff before buying it. Avoid buying frozen fish if you can, because the process changes the delicate structure of the flesh and alters its natural moisture content. This way too, you will avoid fish of uncertain vintage and fish that has been refrozen.

Once you have brought your fresh fish home, use it as soon as possible. If you are not cooking it immediately, wrap it in a damp cloth or damp paper towels and place in the coldest part of the refrigerator. When you are ready to prepare the fish, the only thing you can do to mess it up is to overcook or overseason it, both of which are common mistakes. The key is to focus on details when preparing fish, and the most important detail is to constantly monitor its degree of doneness as it cooks. Do not leave it untended, as leaving it to cook for just a little too long can bring dry and unappetizing results. Thickness of fish varies considerably, so cooking times are often approximate. Follow all this advice, and you are well on your way to seeing a big difference in your fish.

Some of the dishes in this chapter are main courses taken from our dining-room menus at the Waldorf=Astoria; others have been adapted from special event menus. For these events, the fish course follows the classical tradition of falling between the appetizer and the meat entrée. In this case, we have adjusted the portion size and added or recommended side dishes so these recipes can be prepared as a main course. In either case, the fish is the star of the plate, and we usually aim to let its natural qualities—its flavor, texture, and richness—speak for itself.

Warm Smoked Copper River Salmon with Fresh Lentils and Tomatoes

SERVES 8

FOR THE TOMATO-BASIL
SALAD

*1 clove garlic, crushed with a knife
(see Chef's Note)*

*8 ounces grape (oval) or cherry
tomatoes, cut in half*

1 teaspoon balsamic vinegar

1 teaspoon extra-virgin olive oil

3 large basil leaves, julienned

*Pinch of salt and freshly ground black
pepper, or to taste*

FOR THE LENTILS

¼ cup diced bacon

½ cup diced onion

¼ cup peeled and diced carrot

¼ cup diced celery

3 cloves garlic, minced

1 cup green (or brown) lentils

5 cups Chicken Stock (page 252)

*Salt and freshly ground black pepper
to taste*

WARM SMOKING IS A COMPLETELY different process from cold smoking, the traditional method for curing salmon, and it yields equally different results when it comes to flavor and texture. Cold smoking uses a salt and sugar brine to cure the fish over a period of several hours; the salmon is then smoked slowly for hours at a cool temperature of 70° to 90°F. In this recipe, the salmon is not cured at all. Instead, it is smoked over hot wood chips for just a few minutes, then finished in the oven until still slightly pink in the center. The results highlight the salmon's natural taste and texture, enhanced with a delicate, smoky flavor.

TO PREPARE THE SALAD   Rub the inside of a mixing bowl with the crushed garlic to provide flavor for the salad; discard the garlic. Place the tomatoes, vinegar, olive oil, and basil in the mixing bowl and toss to thoroughly combine. Season with salt and pepper.

TO PREPARE THE LENTILS   Place the bacon in a large saucepan and set over medium heat. Cook for 5 or 6 minutes, until the bacon is almost crispy and most of the fat is rendered. Remove the bacon from the saucepan and reserve, discarding all but 1 tablespoon of the bacon fat. Add the onion to the pan and cook over medium heat until translucent, about 4 or 5 minutes. Add the carrot, celery, and garlic, and cook for 4 minutes longer. Add the lentils and the chicken stock. Bring to a boil, turn the heat to medium low, and simmer until the lentils are tender, about 25 to 30 minutes. Season with salt and pepper, and keep warm over low heat.

Prepare the smoker (See Chef's Notes for an alternative to a smoker). Preheat the oven to 350°F.

FOR THE SALMON

*1 cup fruit wood chips
(such as apple or cherry)*

*8 skinless salmon filets,
about 6 ounces each*

1 tablespoon grapeseed or olive oil

*Salt and freshly ground white pepper
to taste*

TO PREPARE THE SALMON Soak the wood chips for about 20 minutes in cold water. Set the salmon filets on a plate and coat with the oil, salt, and pepper. Place the salmon in the smoker and smoke for 7 to 10 minutes. Remove the salmon and transfer to a roasting pan. Finish in the oven until cooked through, about 5 to 7 minutes, depending on the thickness of the fish.

TO SERVE Spoon the lentils in the center of warm serving plates. Arrange the salmon filets on top of the lentils and serve with the tomato-basil salad.

Wine Recommendation Chilean Chardonnay (pear, fig, and pineapple tones with moderate toastiness).

CHEF'S NOTES

◇ If you do not have a stovetop smoker, you can make one using a roasting pan. Place a sheet of aluminum foil on the bottom of the pan. Roll 4 more sheets of aluminum foil each into the size of golf balls, and place one ball in each corner of the roasting pan. Drain the wood chips and spread them evenly over the center area of the roasting pan where the stove will heat them directly. Set the roasting pan on top of the stove over medium-high heat. Arrange the salmon filets on a wire rack that will fit evenly over the foil balls. When the wood chips begin to smoke, place the rack of fish on the foil balls over the wood chips and turn the heat to low. Cover the whole pan with aluminum foil or another inverted roasting pan of the same size and let the chips smoke for 7 to 10 minutes, until the edges of the salmon begin to turn yellow. Remove the roasting pan from the heat and discard the wood chips. Finish cooking the salmon in the oven, uncovered, for 5 to 7 minutes longer, depending on the thickness of the fish.

◇ To crush garlic, place the clove of garlic on a cutting board. Rest the side of a large heavy chef's knife on top of the garlic clove, and with the butt of your hand, carefully press down on the flat side of the knife, crushing the garlic. Remove the peel.

Grilled Branzino with Arugula Salad and Lemon-Caper Vinaigrette

SERVES 8

FOR THE MARINADE AND FISH

2 lemons, zested and juiced

1½ cups olive oil

4 tablespoons finely minced garlic (about 1 head of garlic)

1 teaspoon dried red pepper flakes

8 branzini, about 1½ pounds each, cleaned and boned

Salt and freshly ground white pepper to taste

FOR THE ARUGULA SALAD

1 pound baby arugula

1 red tomato, seeded and julienned

1 yellow tomato, seeded and julienned

½ fennel bulb, shaved finely

2 teaspoons capers, rinsed and drained

Juice of 1 lemon

1 cup olive oil

Salt and freshly ground black pepper to taste

BRANZINO IS THE ITALIAN NAME for Mediterranean striped sea bass; it is a hallmark of Venetian cooking in particular. It is particularly prized for grilling and roasting. For this recipe, I recommend branzini (the plural of branzino) weighing between one and two pounds, as they will remain moist through the cooking process.

TO PREPARE THE MARINADE Mince the lemon zest and set aside separately from the juice. Pour the oil into a large sauté pan and set over medium-low heat. When the oil is hot, add the garlic and sauté until golden brown, 8 to 10 minutes, stirring often so the garlic does not stick to the pan. Remove from the heat, stir in the lemon zest and red pepper flakes, and transfer the garlic oil mixture to a measuring cup with a lip or another container that makes it easy to pour; let cool.

Place the reserved lemon juice in a bowl and whisk in the cooled garlic oil to create a marinade. Place the branzini in a large dish and pour the marinade over the fish. Transfer to the refrigerator and marinate for at least 4 hours, preferably overnight.

Prepare the grill.

TO PREPARE THE SALAD Mix the arugula, tomatoes, fennel, and capers in a bowl. In a mixing bowl, whisk together the lemon juice and olive oil and season with salt and pepper. When ready to serve, pour the dressing over the salad.

TO COOK THE FISH Lightly oil the bars of the grill so that the fish does not stick. Remove the fish from the marinade and transfer to the grill over high heat. Grill for about 3 or 4 minutes on each side, turning only once.

TO SERVE Place a grilled fish on each warm serving plate. Arrange the salad over the cooked fish (or to the side) and serve immediately.

Wine Recommendation Sonoma Valley Sauvignon Blanc (rich and concentrated with ripe melon, green apple, and lemon peel flavors).

CHEF'S NOTES

◇ Ask your fishmonger to scale, clean, and debone the fish for you.

◇ Oiling the grill bars and then grilling over high heat helps prevent the fish from sticking. Turning it only once, using a spatula, also minimizes the chances of the fish sticking and breaking up.

Poppadom-Crusted Salmon with Grapefruit Sauce and Avocado

SERVES 6

FOR THE GRAPEFRUIT SAUCE

3 raspberries

2 cups pink grapefruit juice

½ cup Fish Fumet (page 254) or Chicken Stock (page 252)

1 teaspoon minced ginger

1½ teaspoons honey

6 cardamom pods, crushed

1 tablespoon coriander seeds, crushed

4 cloves

2 star anise

Small pinch dried red pepper flakes

2 tablespoons butter

Salt and freshly ground white pepper to taste

FOR THE GARNISH

1 lime

½ cup sugar

1 avocado, cut in half and pitted

INSPIRED BY THE WONDERFUL FLAVORS of India, this dish is not timid. Poppadoms are flat, paper-thin, circular wafers made from lentil flour; they are used like flatbread and break very easily. Here, we crumble them as a coating for the salmon. The grapefruit sauce has a perfect balance of flavorful spices; I have been asked by guests to bottle it! If your fishmonger has whole salmon, ask to take a look at the fish and check that the eyes are clear and the gills are red. With a really fresh salmon, when you open its belly and inhale, you will smell the sea and a pleasant aroma that's like sweet melon. Serve this dish with Coconut Sticky Rice (page 244) or long-grain basmati rice, if you like.

TO PREPARE THE SAUCE Place the raspberries in a saucepan and crush with a fork. Add the grapefruit juice and Fish Fumet in a saucepan; then add the ginger, honey, cardamom, coriander, cloves, star anise, and red pepper flakes. Set over medium heat and bring to a boil. Continue to cook for 10 to 12 minutes longer, reducing the liquid to 1 cup. Whisk in the butter and adjust the seasonings. Strain the sauce through a fine mesh strainer into a clean small saucepan and keep warm over low heat.

TO PREPARE THE GARNISH Use a vegetable peeler to remove strips of zest from the lime. Use a sharp knife to remove any bitter white pith from the zest and cut the lime strips into julienne. Juice the lime and reserve. Place the lime zest in a small saucepan with the sugar and ½ cup water. Set over medium heat and bring to a boil. Continue to simmer the mixture until the zest is coated with the sugar glaze, 4 or 5 minutes. Remove from the heat and set aside. Use a melon baller or small scoop to make small avocado balls, or dice the avocado with a knife. Transfer the avocado to a small bowl and mix with the reserved lime juice to prevent it from browning.

Preheat the oven to 300°F.

FOR THE CRUST AND SALMON

½ cup all-purpose flour

1 large egg

Salt and freshly ground white pepper
to taste

3 plain poppadoms

6 skinless salmon filets,
about 6 ounces each

3 tablespoons olive oil

TO PREPARE THE CRUST AND SALMON Place the flour on a plate. In a shallow bowl, beat together the egg and 1 tablespoon of water and season with salt and pepper. Break the poppadoms into small pieces, place in a food processor, and pulse for about 30 seconds, until coarse crumbs form. Transfer the poppadom crumbs to a separate plate. Season the salmon with salt and white pepper and crust the fish by dipping the cut side first into the flour, then into the egg wash, and finally into the poppadom crumbs.

Place half of the olive oil in a large skillet or sauté pan and set over medium-high heat. When the oil is hot and shimmering, add 3 of the salmon filets, crust side down, and sauté until browned, about 4 to 5 minutes. Remove the fish with a spatula and transfer to a baking sheet. Repeat the process for the remaining filets. Place the baking sheet into the oven and roast until the fish is just cooked and still a little rosy in the center, about 6 to 8 minutes, depending on the thickness of the filets.

TO SERVE Place the filets on warm serving plates. Drizzle 2 tablespoons of the sauce around each serving and arrange some of the sugared lime zest on top. Sprinkle the avocado around the fish.

Wine Recommendation Loire Valley Cabernet Franc (ripe and supple with currant flavors and firm tannins).

CHEF'S NOTES

◇ Crusting fish (as well as meat) has become a popular technique over the last few years. It provides additional flavor, texture, and color, and helps seal in the natural moisture. Minced nuts and herbs, sliced potatoes, plain or seasoned breadcrumbs, and Japanese-style breadcrumbs (panko) all make excellent crusts.

◇ I prefer wild salmon to farmed because the flavor is more intense. There are several types of wild salmon that vary in appearance and flavor; even similar species may differ depending on the waters they come from, the time of year, and upon what the salmon feeds.

Grilled Yellowfin Tuna Panini on Olive Bread

SERVES 6

6 tablespoons Pickled Slivered Onions
(page 250)

FOR THE LEMON-CAPER
AÏOLI

2 teaspoons capers, rinsed and drained

1 canned anchovy filet

1 tablespoon Kalamata olives, pitted

1 tablespoon Garlic Confit (page 257)

1 tablespoon roughly chopped
fresh parsley

2 teaspoons finely grated lemon zest

½ teaspoon Tabasco Sauce

1 large egg yolk

1 cup canola oil

Salt and freshly ground black pepper
to taste

FOR THE TUNA

3 tablespoons vegetable oil

3 yellowfin tuna steaks,
about 8 ounces each

Salt and freshly ground white pepper
to taste

FOR THE SANDWICH

12 slices crusty olive bread, ½-inch thick

1 red bell pepper, roasted, seeded, peeled,
and cut into thin strips (page 260)

3 cups arugula

4 tablespoons softened butter

IF SALADS ARE A SPECIALTY at Oscar's (page 134), then sandwiches run a close second. In addition to the best burger you will ever try (see page 184), Chef Michael Bourquin and his team consistently come up with the best sandwiches. One day, I walked into the kitchen and found a huddle of chefs surrounding a sandwich on a plate—the prototype of this panini. I got the impression they were daring me to try the sandwich, and my first reaction was to think, "It may look great, but maybe there is something odd about it." I took a bite. "Michael," I said, "you could get famous with something like this!" It is a sublime sandwich and is still a personal favorite of mine—it is not coming off the menu any time soon!

Prepare the Pickled Onions.

TO PREPARE THE AÏOLI Place the capers, anchovy, olives, garlic, and parsley in a blender or food processor and pulse until coarsely chopped. Add the lemon zest, Tabasco, and egg yolk, and pulse again. Slowly add the oil while blending and season with salt and pepper. Cover and refrigerate until needed.

TO PREPARE THE TUNA Pour the oil into a large, dry skillet and set over medium-high heat. Season the tuna steaks with salt and pepper and when the oil is hot and shimmering, add the tuna to the pan. Cook on each side until seared on the outside but still rare in the middle, 2 to 3 minutes. Remove from the pan and slice on a bias to make ¼-inch-thick slices.

TO PREPARE THE SANDWICHES Heat a griddle or set a large, dry skillet over medium heat. Lay out the bread slices on a clean work surface and spread evenly with the aïoli. Arrange 4 or 5 tuna slices on each of the 6 slices of bread and add 1 tablespoon each of the pickled onions and roasted pepper strips. Top with the arugula and the remaining 6 slices of bread. Spread about 1 teaspoon of softened butter on each side of the sandwiches and transfer them to the griddle or skillet. Toast the sandwiches until golden brown, about 3 minutes per side.

Wine Recommendation Central Coast (CA) Chardonnay (rich and opulent, honey texture with mouth-filling aftertaste).

RICE-FLAKED HALIBUT WITH COCONUT RICE, LONG BEAN SALAD, AND PASSION FRUIT SAUCE

SERVES 8

Long Bean Salad (page 247)

Coconut Sticky Rice (page 244)

FOR THE PASSION FRUIT SAUCE

2 teaspoons light sesame oil

1½ tablespoons minced shallots

1½ tablespoons minced ginger

½ tablespoon minced garlic

½ cup passion fruit purée (see Chef's Note)

Pinch of dried red pepper flakes

1 tablespoon butter

Salt to taste

FROM TIME TO TIME, I experiment with Asian ingredients. There are so many flavors that can play off each other yet work so well together. A dish that contains elements that are sweet, sour, and spicy can be very exciting on the palate if the balance is right. The origin of this dish was a crispy soft-shell crab with coconut rice and passion fruit sauce that I made for a Chef's Table dinner (see page 24), but after the all-too-brief soft shell crab season, I decided to continue the wonderful flavor and texture profile by using crispy rice flakes to crust the fish.

FOR THE HALIBUT

*8 skinless halibut filets,
about 6 ounces each*

*Salt and freshly ground white pepper
to taste*

½ cup all-purpose flour

1 large egg, beaten

*¾ cup Asian rice flakes or ground
poppadoms (see page 154)*

3 tablespoons peanut oil

Prepare the Long Bean Salad and the Coconut Rice.

TO PREPARE THE PASSION FRUIT SAUCE Pour the oil into a small saucepan and set over medium-high heat for 1 minute until hot. Add the shallots, ginger, and garlic and sauté for 2 minutes. Add the passion fruit purée and the red pepper flakes and bring the mixture to a simmer. Turn the heat to medium low and simmer for 3 minutes; then whisk in the butter and season with salt. Strain the sauce into a clean saucepan and keep warm over low heat.

Preheat the oven to 325°F.

TO PREPARE THE HALIBUT Season both sides of the halibut filets with salt and white pepper. Place the flour, egg, and rice flakes in 3 separate shallow bowls for the breading process. Dip the cut side of the fish only (not the skin side) first into the flour, then the egg, and finally into the rice flakes. Let the coated filets rest on a plate, coated side up. Pour the peanut oil into a large, heavy skillet or sauté pan and set over medium-high heat. When the oil is hot and shimmering, add the fish, coated side down, and cook until golden brown, about 3 to 4 minutes (cook in 2 batches if necessary). Transfer the partially cooked fish to a baking sheet or roasting pan and place in the oven. Roast for 4 or 5 minutes, or until the fish is firm to the touch.

TO SERVE Spoon a serving of the Coconut Rice on one side of each warm serving plate. Place a halibut filet on top of the rice and drizzle the passion fruit sauce around the fish. Place a serving of the Long Bean Salad next to the fish.

Wine Recommendation South African Stellenbosch Chardonnay (flavors of plum, pear, and toast with a lengthy finish).

CHEF'S NOTES

◇ Sea bass can be substituted for the halibut.

◇ We use peanut oil to sauté the halibut as it has a high smoking point and a neutral flavor.

◇ Rice flakes can be purchased at Asian markets.

◇ Frozen passion fruit purée can be purchased in the frozen section of gourmet markets. To make your own, purchase 6 to 8 fresh passion fruit, cut in half, and scoop out the pulp. Press the juice through a fine-mesh strainer, pressing down on the pulp with the back of a spoon.

◇ The bean salad, rice, and sauce may all be prepared up to 5 hours in advance.

Slow-Roasted Monkfish with Baby Carrots, Zucchini Blossoms, and Verjus Emulsion

SERVES 8

FOR THE BABY CARROTS

3 bunches baby carrots, stemmed and unpeeled (about 4 cups)

½ tablespoon butter

FOR THE VERJUS EMULSION

4 cups green seedless grapes

3 tablespoons verjus (see page 263)

1 tablespoon butter

FOR THE ZUCCHINI BLOSSOM TEMPURA

4 cups canola oil

¼ cup all-purpose flour

1 tablespoon cornstarch

¼ teaspoon salt

½ tablespoon beaten egg

8 fresh zucchini blossoms

Salt and freshly ground white pepper to taste

MONKFISH, ALSO KNOWN AS *poor man's lobster,* is one of the ugliest fish in the ocean. It feeds on the sea floor from northern Atlantic waters down to the Carolinas. It also happens to be one of the tastiest fish, provided it is cooked correctly. Trust me when I tell you that Chef Cedric Tovar cooks monkfish the right way! By roasting it in the oven at a very low temperature, and cooking it on the bone, the fish's natural moisture and flavor is retained. This is one of the first dishes Cedric created for the new Peacock Alley and it has been a favorite of mine from the very beginning.

———————

TO PREPARE THE CARROTS Prepare an ice bath (page 260). Bring a saucepan of salted water to a boil. Add ⅔ of the carrots and blanch for 2 minutes. Remove the carrots with a slotted spoon and transfer to the ice bath to stop the cooking process. When cool, drain and remove the skin with your fingers. Run the remaining carrots through a juicer, transfer the juice to a saucepan, and set over medium-high heat. Reduce the liquid by one-third, 4 to 5 minutes. Stir in ½ tablespoon of butter. Stir or lightly whisk until the sauce has emulsified. Add the blanched carrots and remove the pan from the heat. Reheat when ready to serve.

TO PREPARE THE VERJUS EMULSION Place 10 of the grapes in a small saucepan and crush with the back of a fork. Add the verjus and bring to a boil over medium heat. Remove from the heat and strain through a fine mesh strainer into a clean saucepan, pressing hard on the crushed grapes to extract as much juice as possible. Add 1 tablespoon of butter to the strained liquid and stir or lightly whisk until the sauce has emulsified. Set aside and let cool. Cut the remaining grapes in half and set aside at room temperature until ready to serve.

Preheat the oven to 250°F.

TO PREPARE THE ZUCCHINI BLOSSOM TEMPURA Pour the canola oil into a deep fryer or large saucepan and heat to 340°F. While the oil is heating, sift the flour, cornstarch, and salt into a bowl and mix together. In a small bowl, combine the egg with ¼ cup ice water, then add to the dry ingredients, mixing until the batter is smooth; the consistency should be like room-temperature honey. Cut each of the zucchini blossoms lengthwise into 3 strips and coat lightly in the tempura batter, shaking off any excess. Carefully place the blossom strips in the hot oil and deep-fry until they are crispy but not browned, about 1 to 1½ minutes. Remove with a slotted spoon, drain on paper towels, and season with salt.

FOR THE MONKFISH

4 monkfish tails, about 2 pounds each, skin removed and bone in

Sea salt and freshly ground black pepper to taste

1 tablespoon butter

3 cloves garlic

1 sprig fresh thyme

FOR ASSEMBLY

2 cups mâche salad, or baby spinach

2 tablespoons extra-virgin olive oil

Salt and freshly ground white pepper to taste

TO PREPARE THE FISH Season the monkfish with sea salt and black pepper. Place 1 tablespoon of butter in an ovenproof skillet or sauté pan and set over medium-high heat. When the butter has melted, add the monkfish tails and sear until browned, 3 to 4 minutes on each side. Add the garlic cloves and thyme to the skillet and transfer to the oven. Roast the monkfish for 25 minutes, or until cooked through, with an internal temperature of 130°F. Remove the skillet from the oven and let the monkfish rest at room temperature for 10 minutes.

TO SERVE In a bowl, toss the mâche salad with the olive oil and season with salt and pepper. Cut the monkfish from the bone and place a filet on each serving plate, cut side up. Spoon the carrots and sauce onto the plates and arrange the mâche salad next to the monkfish. Garnish the fish with the zucchini blossom strips, and spoon the grapes and a drizzle of the verjus emulsion around the fish. Season with a sprinkling of sea salt and pepper.

Wine Recommendation South African Central Coast Chenin Blanc (firm wine with lots of butter and apple notes, and a long, creamy finish).

CHEF'S NOTES

◇ Cooked squash blossoms are a traditional summer preparation in the south of France; interestingly, they also feature in Mexican and Southwestern cooking. Look for squash blossoms at your local farmers' market in the summer.

◇ Mâche is better known in some parts of the United States as corn salad or field salad. In its native Europe, where it grows wild, it is called lamb's lettuce. It is an early spring green with velvety leaves and it has a sweet, nutty flavor.

If you think you have a problem cooking fish at home, consider Peter Daledda's task here at the Waldorf=Astoria, when he must serve perfectly cooked fish to fifteen hundred guests at a prestigious event in the Grand Ballroom, or when a big event for four thousand is taking up every banquet room in the hotel. "Just recently," says Peter, the Waldorf's Executive Sous Chef (right), "we served branzini, or Mediterranean sea bass, en papillote for eight hundred guests at the Carnegie Hall Opening Night dinner held in the Grand Ballroom, by special request. This technique calls for baking the fish inside a parchment paper bag so it steams as it roasts. The logistics involved were interesting. A team of banquet cooks prepared and wrapped the fish all afternoon. Then, at the signal from a sous chef

watching for us in the ballroom, we had to wait until the last minute to roast all the bags at the same time for exactly eight minutes. Then, with military precision, we transported the bags from our main kitchen one flight up to the ballroom in warmers and served them immediately. It was ambitious all right, but it went off without a hitch." Just another average day at the Waldorf=Astoria!

Peter Daledda, whom Executive Chef John Doherty describes as "my right-hand man," has spent fifteen years at the Waldorf in two spells, gaining additional experience at landmark New York restaurants such as Le Cirque and Picholine in the intervening years. In addition to managing the schedules of 160 kitchen staff, his prime responsibility now is the Banquet Department, supervising fifty-five cooks. "Typically, we use more Chilean sea bass and Atlantic salmon than any other type of fish," says Peter. All of the hotel's fish is cut and prepared in house. "There's the old rule that says to avoid eating fish on Sundays and Mondays because the fish markets are closed on the weekends, but here in New York, and with our volume and the reputation of our suppliers, you can enjoy fish at the Waldorf seven days a week and know it's fresh, no problem. That's one of the advantages of working in New York at an institution with our history and reputation—our suppliers take special care of us and provide us with the best product. I am proud of that integrity and it's important in keeping up with the everchanging demands of our guests. As their expectations increase, partly reflecting the exciting and vibrant food culture we're in, we need to meet and exceed those expectations. That's a key part of the Waldorf=Astoria philosophy."

—J.H.

163

FISH AND SEAFOOD

Seared Sea Bass with Basil Mashed Potatoes, Tomato Confit, and Red Wine Glaze

THE WALDORF=ASTORIA COOKBOOK

SERVES 8

Tomato Confit (page 257)

FOR THE RED WINE GLAZE

3 pounds fish bones (see Chef's Note)

2 cups thinly sliced onions

¾ cup peeled and thinly sliced carrots

¾ cup thinly sliced celery

¾ cup thinly sliced fennel bulb

1 dried bay leaf

4 sprigs fresh thyme

1 bottle (750 ml) red wine, preferably Burgundy or Pinot Noir

1 cup port wine

2 tablespoons butter

Salt and freshly ground white pepper to taste

Basil Mashed Potatoes (page 242)

I FIRST MADE THIS DISH when I was invited to cook for a ten-day stint in the new Conrad Hotel in Brussels, Belgium. One evening, a very distinguished guest at the Conrad summoned me into the dining room to tell me that he had just concluded a dining tour of several two- and three-star Michelin restaurants throughout Europe, and this was the best fish dish he had tasted anywhere. This made me realize I might be onto something! I have used it ever since for important occasions, weddings, receptions, and other events, and it always gets a tremendous response.

———————

Prepare the Tomato Confit.

TO PREPARE THE RED WINE GLAZE Combine the fish bones, onions, carrots, celery, fennel, bay leaf, thyme, red wine, and port in a stock pot and set over medium-high heat. Bring to a boil, turn the heat to medium low, and continue to simmer, uncovered, for 45 minutes. Strain the liquid through a fine-mesh strainer into a large, clean saucepan; discard the bones and solids. Bring to a boil and reduce the liquid at a strong simmer until the liquid has reduced to about ¾ cup, about 45 minutes. Whisk in the butter and season with salt and pepper. Strain the liquid again through a fine-mesh strainer into a clean pan and keep warm over low heat.

Prepare the Basil Mashed Potatoes.

Preheat the oven to 325°F.

TO PREPARE THE SEA BASS Place 1 tablespoon of the butter and 1 teaspoon of the olive oil in a large, heavy skillet or sauté pan and set over medium-high heat. Season the sea bass filets with salt and pepper, and when the butter stops crackling, add half of the fish to the pan, skin side down. Add half of the garlic, the thyme, and lemon peel to the pan and cook for 6 to 7 minutes, basting the sea bass with the butter and oil from the pan until the skin is browned and crisp. While the fish is cooking, use a spatula to hold down the filets to prevent them from curling. Transfer the fish, skin side up, to a baking sheet or roasting pan and repeat the process for the remaining filets. Transfer the baking sheet to the oven and roast for 3 to 4 minutes, or until the sea bass is cooked through.

FOR THE SEA BASS

2 tablespoons butter

2 teaspoons olive oil

8 sea bass filets, about 6 ounces each

*Salt and freshly ground black pepper
to taste*

2 cloves garlic, quartered

8 sprigs fresh thyme

*2 strips lemon peel (cut with
a vegetable peeler)*

TO SERVE Spoon the Basil Mashed Potatoes onto warm serving plates. Lean a sea bass filet on the potatoes, and spoon the Tomato Confit and red wine glaze around each plate.

Wine Recommendation Willamette Valley (OR) Pinot Noir (silky texture, palate of ripe blackberry and currant fruit).

CHEF'S NOTES

◇ When purchasing fish bones for this recipe, ask your fishmonger for five pounds of bones from lean white fish such as sea bass, sole, or turbot. Rinse the bones under cold water to make sure all blood is washed away.

◇ This dish also pairs well with steamed haricot verts or fennel salad (page 105).

Brown-Butter-Bathed Lobster with Parsley Risotto and Blood Orange Sauce

SERVES 8

FOR THE LOBSTERS

*8 female lobsters, about 1½ to
2 pounds each (see Chef's Note)*

FOR THE BLOOD ORANGE
SAUCE

*2 cups blood orange juice
(from 6 blood oranges)*

¼ cup extra-virgin olive oil

Parsley Risotto (page 245)

TO FINISH THE DISH

¼ cup butter

*½ cup minced fresh chervil
or parsley, for garnish*

THIS RECIPE PLAYS OFF THE classic, tried-and-true combination of boiled lobster served with clarified butter. Lobster has a naturally sweet flavor but a dry texture due to its lack of natural fat, so the fat in butter transports the flavor of the lobster to our palates. Add a spritz of lemon juice to cut all that richness, and you're in business! There is just one problem: Boiling a lobster for several minutes causes the meat fibers to contract, making it chewy and occasionally downright tough. The technique of bathing the lobster slowly in butter, on the other hand, keeps it tender and moist. The browned butter also adds an interesting nutty flavor. The bonus of this dish is the beautiful bright orange color provided by the cooked lobster roe, which coats the lobster meat. Together with the earthy, creamy Parsley Risotto and the acidic, fruity sauce, this is one of our most popular dishes.

TO PREPARE THE LOBSTERS Bring a stockpot of salted water to a boil and plunge the lobsters in head first (cook 1 or 2 at a time if they do not all fit). Blanch for 2 minutes, remove with tongs, and let cool for 5 minutes. Twist off the tails and squeeze the tail shells until they crack and can be pulled apart and the meat can be removed. Using a sharp paring knife, remove the intestinal tract from the top side of the tails. Use lobster crackers to crack the claws and remove the claw meat. (The lobster meat will still be rare to raw.) Transfer the lobster meat, covered, to the refrigerator. Reserve the lobster shells for making lobster stock. Remove the dark green egg sack from each lobster body cavity, press the roe through a strainer into a bowl, and reserve in the refrigerator.

TO PREPARE THE SAUCE Pour the orange juice into a saucepan and reduce over medium-high heat until ½ cup remains, about 10 minutes. Whisk in the olive oil and season with salt and pepper. Set aside and let cool.

Prepare the Parsley Risotto.

TO FINISH THE DISH Coat the reserved lobster meat in the green lobster roe. Melt the butter in a sauté pan set over high heat; when it foams, then begins to brown, add the lobster meat and remove the pan from the heat. Use a spoon to baste the lobster with the butter and return the pan to low heat. Baste until the lobster is just cooked, about 3 minutes. Remove the lobster from the pan and reserve.

TO SERVE Spoon the risotto into warm soup plates. Arrange a cooked lobster tail and a claw on top of the risotto and drizzle with the butter from the pan. Spoon the blood orange sauce around each plate and garnish the lobster with the chervil.

Wine Recommendation Sonoma Valley Chardonnay (bright, round in texture, with a touch of cream to finish).

CHEF'S NOTES

◇ You want female lobsters for the roe. How can you tell the difference between a male and female lobster? Of course, the easiest way is to ask your lobster purveyor, but here's how you can distinguish them: Turn the lobster over, and if the two fins between the tail and the body are thin and flexible and almost feathery, it is a female. If the fins are hard and enlarged, it is a male.

◇ When removing the meat from the lobster shells and claws, you may find it easier if you use a kitchen towel and kitchen shears.

◇ You can use regular oranges instead of blood oranges if necessary, or use frozen blood orange purée. The sauce may be made several hours ahead and stored, covered, in the refrigerator.

Herb-Crusted Cod with Brandade and Tomato Coulis

SERVES 8

FOR THE BRANDADE

1 pound salt cod

¼ cup olive oil

4 cloves garlic, minced

1 cup heavy cream

2 tablespoons extra-virgin olive oil

Salt and freshly ground white pepper to taste

Tomato Coulis (page 256)

FOR THE HERB CRUST

2 tablespoons olive oil

1 tablespoon minced shallot

½ tablespoon minced garlic

1 cup fresh parsley leaves

2 tablespoons fresh tarragon leaves

1 tablespoon fresh thyme leaves

¼ cup sliced fresh chives

½ teaspoon grated lemon zest

¾ cup panko (Japanese breadcrumbs)

Salt and freshly ground white pepper to taste

IF YOU LOOK UP THE word *brandade* in classical French cookbooks, you will probably find many different preparations for salt cod—typically, with garlic, olive oil, and cream. Most of these preparations will tell you to beat the salt cod to the consistency of whipped potatoes. An entirely separate recipe, *Brandade Lyonnaise,* does call for the addition of potatoes; it was created at a time when salt cod had become very expensive and potatoes were used to stretch the ingredients. This recipe echoes the original brandade, adding fresh cod and a simple fresh tomato sauce, with well-balanced and attractive results.

TO PREPARE THE BRANDADE Place the salt cod in a large bowl or dish and cover with cold water. Soak overnight in the refrigerator. The next day, remove the cod and rinse under cold running water for 1 minute. Bring a saucepan of water to a boil and add the rinsed cod. Simmer for 3 minutes. Drain the cod and discard the water. Repeat this process two more times.

Pour the olive oil into a saucepan and set over medium-high heat. When it is hot and shimmering, add the garlic and the cod and break up with a wooden spoon until it is finely shredded. Add the cream and extra-virgin olive oil gradually, until the mixture has a consistency of potato purée. Season with salt and pepper. Cover and remove from the heat. Reheat just before you are ready to serve (the brandade can be prepared 1 day ahead up to this point).

Prepare the Tomato Coulis and keep warm.

TO PREPARE THE HERB CRUST Pour the oil into a sauté pan and set over high heat. When the oil is hot and shimmering, add the shallot and garlic, turn the heat to medium, and sauté until translucent, 3 or 4 minutes. Transfer to a food processor and add the parsley, tarragon, thyme, chives, and lemon zest. Process until the herbs are finely minced. Add the panko, salt, and pepper, and continue to process for 2 minutes until thoroughly blended. Keep refrigerated if not using immediately.

Preheat the oven to 325°F.

FOR THE COD

8 cod filets, about 6 ounces each

*1 tablespoon olive oil, plus 4 teaspoons
for garnish*

*Salt and freshly ground white pepper
to taste*

TO PREPARE THE COD   Place the filets on a cookie sheet so they are not touching. Brush with 1 tablespoon of olive oil and season with salt and pepper. Evenly distribute the herb crust on top of the filets, creating a coating about ¼-inch thick. Transfer the cookie sheet to the oven and roast until the cod is cooked through and feels firm when squeezed at the sides, 12 to 15 minutes (exact cooking time will depend on the thickness of the filets).

TO SERVE   Spoon some of the coulis onto warm serving plates and place about ¼ cup of the brandade in the middle. Arrange the cod on top of the brandade, and drizzle ½ teaspoon of olive oil around the coulis on each plate.

Wine Recommendation   Napa Valley Chardonnay (supple and generous with spicy berry and currant flavors).

CHEF'S NOTES

◇   Note that the brandade must be started the day before you plan on serving this dish. Served with crusty bread or toast points, the brandade makes a great hors d'oeuvre.

◇   Pepperade (page 251) makes a good accompaniment for this dish.

Poached Turbot with Asparagus and Black Truffle Sauce

SERVES 8

FOR THE SAUCE

1½ cups heavy cream

1 tablespoon olive oil

½ teaspoon minced shallot

¼ teaspoon minced garlic

1 tablespoon dry white wine

1 ounce black winter truffle

1 cup Fish Fumet (page 254)

Salt and freshly ground black pepper to taste

FOR THE FISH

8 skinless turbot filets, 6 to 7 ounces each

½ cup Fish Fumet (page 254)

Juice from ½ lemon

Salt and freshly ground white pepper to taste

FOR THE ASPARAGUS

32 jumbo asparagus spears, trimmed to top 5 inches only

Salt and freshly ground black pepper to taste

8 sprigs fresh chervil, for garnish

TURBOT IS PROBABLY MY FAVORITE fish, which is the main reason it ends up on many of the menus I create for memorable events, when it is time to pull out all the stops. European turbot happens to be very expensive, but the Canadian variety is much more affordable; unfortunately, it does not have the same elegant texture. If you are buying from a reputable fishmonger, be sure to ask about the source, because it does matter. This fish is so outstanding on its own that anything you do to it may be too much, which is why my favorite pairing is sweet, juicy, fresh asparagus and earthy black truffles blended right into a turbot fish fumet with reduced cream—my idea of heaven!

Preheat the oven to 350°F.

TO PREPARE THE SAUCE Pour the cream into a small saucepan, set over medium-high heat, and reduce the cream until ½ cup remains, about 10 minutes. Meanwhile, pour the olive oil into a separate saucepan and set over medium heat. When it is hot and shimmering, add the shallot and garlic and sauté for 2 to 3 minutes, until translucent. Add the wine, truffle, and Fish Fumet and simmer until the mixture is reduced by half, about 5 minutes. Remove the sauce from the heat and transfer to a blender or food processor. Purée, and add the reduced cream. Add half of the broth from the roasting pan containing the cooked fish and blend all the ingredients again. Using a fine-mesh sieve, strain into a small saucepan. When ready to serve, warm over low heat, adding salt and pepper to taste.

TO PREPARE THE TURBOT Butter a 9- by 13-inch rimmed cookie sheet or roasting pan and evenly arrange the fish in a single layer. Add the Fish Fumet and lemon juice to the pan and season the fish with salt and pepper. Cover the pan with aluminum foil and transfer to the oven. After about 8 minutes, lift the foil and check the fish; it is done when it is no longer translucent and the fish separates or flakes when gently pressed with your finger (depending on the thickness of the fish, this may take up to 12 minutes). Remove the pan from the oven and set aside in a warm place such as the stove top until ready to serve. Turn the oven temperature to 200°F.

TO PREPARE THE ASPARAGUS Prepare an ice bath (page 260). Using a vegetable peeler, peel each asparagus spear from just below the tips to the end. Using cooking twine, tie the asparagus into 4 bundles. Bring a large saucepan of salted water to a boil, add the asparagus bundles, and cook until tender yet still firm, about 6 or 7 minutes (cook in batches if necessary). Using tongs, lift out the bundles and plunge into the ice bath to stop the cooking process.

TO SERVE Return the turbot to the oven for 3 or 4 minutes to reheat. Warm the sauce and reheat the asparagus by warming in a microwave oven, or dipping into hot water and draining; season with salt and pepper. Evenly space 4 asparagus spears, parallel to each other, on each warm serving plate and arrange a piece of fish on top. Spoon the sauce around the plate and garnish the turbot with the chervil.

Wine Recommendation Puligny Montrachet (smoky style with aromas of toasted bread, honey, and minerals).

CHEF'S NOTE

◇ You may substitute halibut or sole for the turbot.

WHOLE ROASTED RED SNAPPER WITH SAFFRON POTATOES

SERVES 6 TO 8

1 red snapper (or 2 small snapper),
6 to 8 pounds

Salt and freshly ground white pepper
to taste

5 cloves garlic, minced

1 teaspoon minced fresh rosemary

1 teaspoon minced fresh thyme

3 tablespoons minced fresh parsley

2 tablespoons minced fresh tarragon

½ teaspoon grated orange zest

½ teaspoon dried red pepper flakes

½ teaspoon minced ginger

½ cup olive oil

Saffron Potatoes (page 242)

HERE IS A SPECTACULAR WAY to present a delicious fish! There is something about the presentation of whole fish that appeals to most people with the added benefit of retaining more moisture and flavor. In addition, it connects us to the source, the ingredient, more than is usually the case. At the Waldorf=Astoria, we serve this dish for many of our Mediterranean buffets; occasionally, we change the flavorings to include garlic, ginger, cilantro, and orange for our Asian buffets. I first served this dish at a holiday dinner I was preparing for friends. I still vividly remember how beautiful and tasty it was and how much everyone enjoyed it. It is extremely easy to prepare and a lot of fun to serve.

Preheat the oven to 500°F.

TO PREPARE THE SNAPPER Once the oven is hot, place a roasting pan on the top rack and let it heat for 10 minutes. Meanwhile, remove the gills from the snapper with a pair of kitchen scissors. Remove the scales completely using a dull knife or the backside of a sharp knife. Score both sides of the fish 5 times, about ¾-inch deep, and season both sides with salt and pepper. In a mixing bowl, combine the garlic, rosemary, thyme, parsley, tarragon, orange zest, red pepper flakes, and ginger. Rub the mixture onto both sides of the fish. Pour ¼ cup of the olive oil into the hot roasting pan; add the fish. Drizzle the remaining ¼ cup of oil over the snapper and return to the oven. Roast until cooked through, about 40 minutes (if using two smaller fish, roast about 30 minutes). Use 2 spatulas to carefully remove the fish from the roasting pan and transfer to a serving platter. Serve with the Saffron Potatoes.

Wine Recommendation Long Island (NY) Merlot (berry fruit, some sweet toast, with bell pepper finish; quite dry).

CHEF'S NOTE

◇   The fennel salad that accompanies the duck recipe on page 105 makes a perfect foil for the snapper and potatoes.

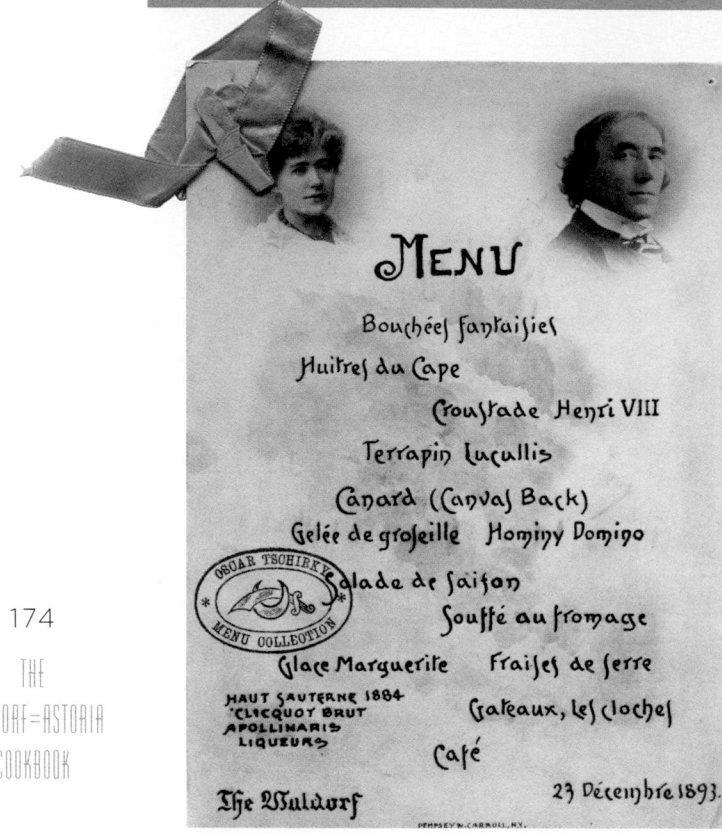

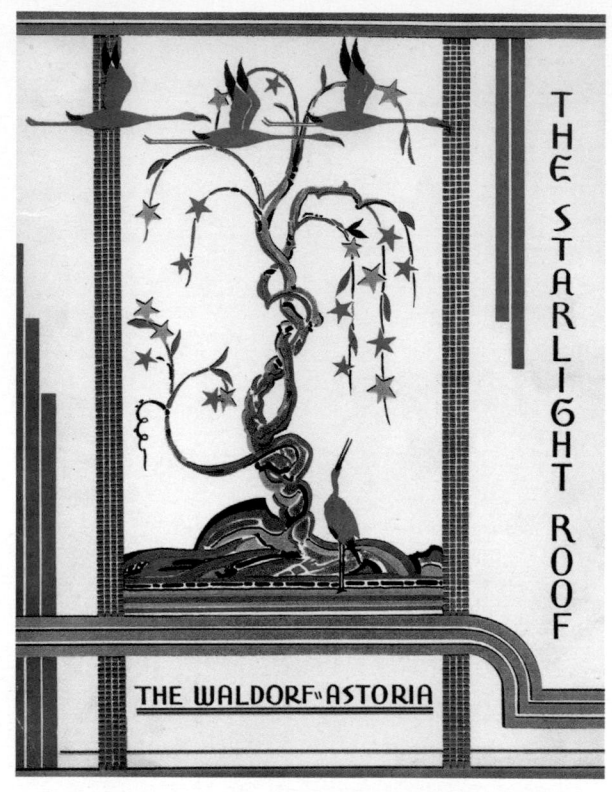

A tribute to
Mr. and Mrs. Oscar Tschirky
on their
Fiftieth Wedding Anniversary
September 18, 1937

On the occasion of the Fiftieth Wedding Anniversary of Mr. and Mrs. Oscar Tschirky we desire to express our congratulations and our esteem.

We and innumerable other friends of Oscar and Mrs. Tschirky throughout the world recognize that their Anniversary symbolizes the most perfect of all human relationships— the abiding devotion of two people for one another.

We rejoice with them at this golden hour and wish them many anniversaries of continued peace and happiness together.

Americans love their meat and, despite the enormous increase in popularity over recent years of fish, chicken, and vegetarian dishes, nothing is as popular as beef. Most fine-dining establishments use USDA Prime or Choice grade beef, so when entertaining and designing a menu, bear in mind that top-quality beef is king! Whenever I am entertaining for friends, I usually lean toward beef—sirloin, tenderloin, or rib eye. Filet mignon happens to be the most popular item we sell at our Bull and Bear Steakhouse and at our catered affairs. At the Waldorf=Astoria, with one million guests per year, we purchase two hundred sixty-three thousand pounds of beef, of which one hundred fourteen thousand pounds is beef tenderloin, served by our Banquet department. Perhaps, these days, it is better to be a dairy cow.

Then there is chicken. Americans have come to know three main types of chicken: Dry, overcooked chicken, lovingly referred to as "rubber chicken"; crispy, fatty, fried chicken pumped full of salted, additive-laden water; and the style I call Chicken Nondescript—underseasoned and uninteresting. The truth is, it is harder to make chicken taste great than most other foods. If the heat is not high enough, it won't get crispy, and if you cook it too long to try and crisp it, it can become too dry. If you do not season it well enough, it will taste bland because, on its own, chicken does not have a whole lot of flavor. That is why I recommend organic, free-range chicken, which has more flavor, is better for you, and is worth the extra cost.

Regardless of the kind of meat you are cooking, I have five pointers that will turn good results into great ones and make you look like a true professional.

First, *use high-quality meat.* A reputable butcher will help you determine which particular cut is best for the dish you want to prepare. Avoid butcher shops that are not busy, where turnover is probably low, perhaps because of that shop's reputation. If you are selecting meat yourself, make sure the meat looks fresh and is not oxidized and brownish in color.

Second, *use the proper methods.* It is important to understand why the little things matter in cooking, such as temperature, time, and the size of the cooking vessel.

Third, *learn how to determine doneness* when it comes to meat. There is nothing more disappointing than serving underdone burger meat or overcooked grilled or roasted meat. I recommend purchasing a good quality meat thermometer and using it every time.

Fourth, *let meat rest.* If you do everything else right but do not let meat rest after you've cooked it, the natural juices will not have time to seep back into the center of the meat, which can make it dry and tough.

Fifth, *learn how to slice meat the right way.* Always slice against the grain, which cuts the meat fibers into very small pieces, making the meat much more tender.

Filet Mignon with Blue Cheese Crust, Bull and Bear Popover, Port Wine Sauce, and Béarnaise

SERVES 6

FOR THE PORT WINE SAUCE

2 cups port wine

1 cup Veal Jus (page 254), made without the 2 tablespoons butter

2 tablespoons butter

FOR THE BÉARNAISE SAUCE

3 tablespoons dried tarragon

⅛ teaspoon freshly ground white pepper

¼ cup dry white wine

¼ cup white wine vinegar

1 tablespoon Veal Jus (page 254)

3 large egg yolks

2 tablespoons freshly squeezed lemon juice

2 cups melted butter

1 teaspoon salt

⅛ teaspoon cayenne

Bull and Bear Popovers (page 244)

FILET MIGNON, WHICH IS CUT from the tenderloin section that runs along the steer's back, is not a heavily used muscle, which is why it is so tender. For that matter, it can also be dry and somewhat bland because it has less marbling (internal fat). However, I cannot argue with all the people who just love it because of its tenderness and delicate flavor. The Angus Prime filet we use is far more flavorful than comparable cuts because of its marbling. But Angus or no Angus, I readily admit that the addition of blue cheese balanced with the port wine sauce and béarnaise makes for one awesome dinner! You will love the popovers too, which are an excellent accompaniment for any beef dish.

———

TO PREPARE THE PORT WINE SAUCE Pour the port into a saucepan and set over medium heat. Reduce to ¼ cup, about 15 minutes, taking care to avoid a flare-up as the alcohol burns off. Add the Veal Jus (do not add the butter at the end of the Veal Jus recipe). Simmer for 1 minute, season with salt and pepper, then stir in 2 tablespoons butter. Keep warm over low heat.

TO PREPARE THE BÉARNAISE SAUCE Place the tarragon and pepper in a small saucepan, add the wine and vinegar, and set over medium heat. Bring to a boil and continue to cook until the liquid has almost evaporated but the ingredients are still moist, 4 to 5 minutes. Add the Veal Jus, return to a boil, and remove from the heat. Set aside.

In a stainless steel bowl set over a saucepan of simmering water, whisk the yolks, lemon juice, and 2 tablespoons of water until cooked (about 140°F), thick, and aerated 4 to 5 minutes. Slowly whisk in the melted butter and season with salt and cayenne. Add the reserved tarragon reduction, stir to thoroughly incorporate, and keep warm over low heat.

Prepare the grill.

Prepare the Bull and Bear Popovers.

(Recipe continues on page 180)

FOR THE STEAKS AND CRUST

6 ounces Stilton cheese

6 filet mignon steaks, about 8 ounces each

1 tablespoon canola oil

Salt and freshly ground black pepper to taste

FOR THE WATERCRESS GARNISH

1 cup watercress leaves

1 teaspoon extra-virgin olive oil

Pinch of salt

TO PREPARE THE STEAKS Form the cheese into 6 balls and flatten each ball to the size of a steak. Season the filets with oil, salt, and pepper and transfer to the hot grill. Grill the filets until medium-rare to medium, or to the desired doneness, about 9 to 10 minutes on each side. Place the cheese on top of the steaks during the last 2 to 3 minutes of cooking time to let it melt.

TO SERVE In a bowl, toss the watercress with the oil and salt. Place 1½ tablespoons of the béarnaise sauce in the center of each warm serving plate. Drizzle 1½ tablespoons of the port wine sauce around the béarnaise. Place a filet in the center of the sauce and top with the tossed watercress.

Wine Recommendation Napa Valley Cabernet Sauvignon (spicy mocha and chocolate-oak aromas, ripe and rich finish).

CHEF'S NOTE

◇ Béarnaise sauce traditionally contains egg yolks that are not fully cooked—an issue for some with immunity concerns. For food safety reasons, discard the sauce after 2 hours.

Bull and Bear Marinated Rib Eye Steak with Chimichurri, Creamed Spinach, and Garlic Mashed Potatoes

SERVES 6

FOR THE CHIMICHURRI SAUCE

¼ cup red wine vinegar

¼ cup minced red onion

1 teaspoon minced garlic

¼ cup Veal Jus (page 254)

¼ cup olive oil

2 tablespoons minced fresh cilantro

2 tablespoons minced fresh parsley

1 teaspoon dried oregano

1 teaspoon dried red pepper flakes

1 teaspoon sugar

Salt to taste

FOR THE STEAK

¾ cup Spice Rub for Beef (page 258)

1 cup olive oil

6 rib eye steaks, about 14 ounces each

Garlic Mashed Potatoes (page 242)

Creamed Spinach (page 243)

THIS RECIPE IS DELICIOUS WITH any steak. I wanted to create something flavorful with interesting accompaniments, but nothing that would compete with the naturally great taste of the high-quality meat.

TO PREPARE THE CHIMICHURRI Combine the vinegar, red onion, and garlic in a mixing bowl. Whisk in the veal jus and the olive oil. Season with cilantro, parsley, oregano, red pepper flakes, sugar, and salt and mix thoroughly.

TO PREPARE THE STEAK Place the spice rub in a large glass dish or shallow bowl. Add the oil and whisk to combine. Add the steaks, cover with plastic wrap, and marinate in the refrigerator for 3 to 5 hours or overnight, turning once or twice.

Prepare the Garlic Mashed Potatoes and the Creamed Spinach.

Preheat the grill.

Remove the steaks from the marinade and wipe off any excess. Grill the steaks over medium-high heat until the steak is cooked to the desired doneness, 7 or 8 minutes per side. Serve with the potatoes, spinach, and chimichurri sauce.

Wine Recommendation: Australian (New South Wales) Syrah (big, rich, and concentrated, with peppery, black cherry, and plum tones).

CHEF'S NOTE

◇ Chimichurri sauce is a popular Argentinean condiment that is a traditional accompaniment for steak. It also perks up other grilled meats and egg dishes, and makes a great marinade. The sauce may be prepared 1 day in advance.

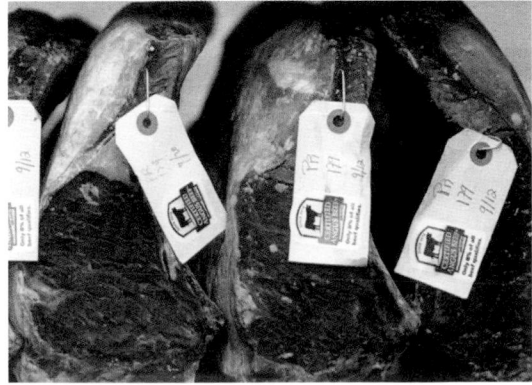

Crispy Organic Chicken with Red Grape Salad and Potato Pancakes

SERVES 8

THE
WALDORF=ASTORIA
COOKBOOK

FOR THE CRISPY CHICKEN

1 tablespoon Kosher salt

4 cloves garlic, minced

3 shallots, minced

2 teaspoons minced fresh thyme

1 teaspoon coarsely ground
black pepper

8 chicken thighs, 5 or 6 ounces each

4 cups Brown Chicken Stock
(page 253)

FOR THE RED GRAPE
SALAD

1½ cups halved red seedless grapes,
cut lengthwise

¼ cup packed fresh parsley leaves

½ teaspoon sherry vinegar

1 teaspoon honey

2 teaspoons minced
black winter truffle

¼ teaspoon extra-virgin olive oil

Pinch of salt

Potato Pancakes (page 66)

1 tablespoon butter

THIS DISH WAS INSPIRED BY Chef Laurent Manrique, former chef at Peacock Alley. Laurent is from Gascony, a region of France that has a well-deserved reputation for gastronomy; he is a fabulous cook. I have built on the technique he used at the Waldorf=Astoria for crisping chicken; here, I use skin-on chicken thighs that have enough natural fat to keep the meat deliciously moist. The chicken is marinated overnight so the flavors have time to permeate the skin; the finished product is perfectly balanced in flavor and texture by the grape salad and potato.

TO PREPARE THE CHICKEN: In a shallow bowl, combine the salt, garlic, shallots, thyme, and pepper. Toss the chicken thighs in the mixture and place in a plastic resealable bag. Transfer to the refrigerator and let sit overnight.

Remove the chicken from the refrigerator and wipe off the marinade. Place the chicken in a dry, heavy cast-iron skillet, skin side down, and set over medium heat; adjust the heat if necessary so you can hear the chicken sizzling gently. Cook for about 20 to 25 minutes without turning; the skin should be brown and crisp, but the chicken should be barely cooked through, with the uppermost meat almost raw. Remove the thighs from the skillet and transfer to a roasting pan, skin side up.

Preheat the oven to 400°F.

Place the chicken stock in a saucepan and set over medium-high heat. Reduce the stock by half, so that about 2 cups remain, about 10 minutes. Pour the reduced stock into the roasting pan with the chicken; the stock should reach about one-third of the way up the side of the chicken. Place the roasting pan in the oven and cook for 15 minutes. When cooked, transfer the chicken to a platter; reserve the pan juices. Set chicken aside on the stove top to keep warm.

While the chicken is cooking, prepare the Potato Pancakes, making each pancake 4″ in diameter.

TO PREPARE THE SALAD: Place the grapes and parsley in a mixing bowl. Add the vinegar, honey, truffle, oil, and salt. Combine all the ingredients and toss.

TO SERVE: Place the pancakes on warm serving plates and arrange the chicken on top. Garnish the chicken with the red grape salad and the pan juices.

Wine Recommendation: New Zealand Pinot Noir (light in color, orange scented, cherry flavors).

CHEF'S NOTE

◇   The chicken should be marinated overnight before cooking. If you know your guests will bring hearty appetites, double the number of chicken thighs and the amount of coating.

Oscar's Prime Angus Burger on Onion Brioche with Seasoned Hand-Cut Fries

SERVES 6

Seasoned Hand-Cut Fries (page 243)

3 pounds prime ground beef
(preferably 80 percent lean)

Salt and freshly ground black pepper
to taste

6 slices sharp Cheddar cheese
(about ⅛-inch thick and
4 inches square)

6 brioche buns (page 42),
cut in half horizontally

6 lettuce leaves

6 slices of tomato, ½-inch thick

¾ cup Caramelized Onions
(page 250)

I COULD NEVER BRING MYSELF to eat a fast-food burger. I just did not get it: tasteless meat pounded way too thin, griddled in its own fat, and placed on a bun that seemed more substantial than the meat itself. And that was before I ever knew anything about food! Oscar's burger is the best in town simply because it is made with Certified Angus prime grade beef. There is a big difference between a good burger and a great burger. The main thing is to go and find great ground beef. Ask your butcher if he can order USDA prime chuck for grinding. If not, combining choice grade sirloin and chuck that is 80 percent lean will taste great, too.

Prepare the grill.

Prepare the Seasoned Hand-Cut Fries up to the cold water bath then refrigerate until ready to use (may be made up to this point 1 day in advance).

TO PREPARE THE BURGERS Divide the ground beef into 6 portions of 8 ounces each and form into patties; compact the meat lightly so that the burgers do not fall apart on the grill. Season the patties with salt and pepper. When the grill is hot, add the patties and grill on the first side for 3 minutes. Turn them 90 degrees (on the same side) and grill for 3 minutes longer until grill marks form. Flip the patties over and cook on the other side for 3 minutes. Then add a slice of cheese to each patty and turn them 90 degrees. Continue to grill for 3 more minutes. The burger should be medium rare after 12 minutes of total cooking time and reach medium doneness after 15 minutes (depending on the heat of your grill.) Transfer the burgers to a platter and let them rest for about 5 minutes; this will allow the burgers to better retain their juiciness. While the burgers are resting, finish the Seasoned Hand-Cut Fries according to the instructions on page 243. Set aside. Lightly toast the brioche buns on the grill for 1 or 2 minutes, or toast the buns under the broiler.

TO SERVE Place the lettuce and tomato on the bottom half of each toasted brioche bun. Add cheeseburgers and top each with 2 tablespoons of the Caramelized Onions. Close the burgers with the top half of the brioche buns, and serve with the seasoned fries.

For many people, comfort food means a juicy steak, tender broiled lobster, a crisp salad, or a thick, meaty chop. The appeal of perfectly cooked, familiar food served in elegant surroundings is a large part of the appeal of the Bull and Bear Steakhouse at the Waldorf=Astoria. The restaurant's reputation places it in the top echelon of the city's steakhouse league, and Marc A. Melillo, Chef de Cuisine (right with Osei Adjapong), took over the reins in 2005. Marc is now on his second tour of duty at the hotel, with more than ten years of service. After starting work in the restaurant business at the age of fifteen and graduating from the Culinary Institute of America, Marc rose through the Waldorf ranks, including periods as Sous Chef at Peacock Alley and as Room Service Chef de Cuisine.

"I enjoy focusing on serving tried and true combinations, using the very best product," explains Marc. "At Bull and Bear, our plate compositions offer a contemporary twist on traditional dishes, and our aim is to perfect the classics, offering excellence with a touch of flair. For example, we utilize custom spice rubs and marinades for secondary cuts, and incorporate seasonal offerings such as stone crabs, Hawaiian hearts of palm, soft-shelled crabs, and Florida pompano. When you use the very best product, such as Aged Certified Angus Prime steak, Nantucket Bay scallops, or our fresh lump crabmeat, you want to nurture it and let it speak for itself rather than confusing or obscuring its natural qualities. Our guests, many of whom are regulars, have a familiarity with the main ingredients, and the comfortable ambience of Bull and Bear further enhances the dining experience. I often hear our guests say, 'This was the best steak I have ever tasted.' It is really inspiring when they tell me how memorable their meal was.

"Two of the topics I am asked about most when it comes to steak," says Marc, "are aging and marbling. We are proud of the quality of our product, especially our Aged Angus Prime steak, and it is in such limited supply that we are the only restaurant on the East Coast to carry it. The fact is, many authentic steakhouses, if asked, will tell you their meat is aged. However, most wet-age their steaks, which involves putting the steak on a shelf in a vacuum-sealed plastic bag. This allows the enzymes to naturally tenderize the meat but will do nothing to develop flavor. Dry-aging meat means letting it sit on shelves in a low-humidity refrigerated room with ultraviolet light and constantly blowing fans. This process actually evaporates the water from the meat, creating a more concentrated steak flavor.

"Marbling—the pattern of fat contained in the interior of the steak—is another important consideration. If the meat is not heavily marbled, with high fat content, the aging process will leave you with a dry, tasteless steak. The marbling in our Aged Certified Angus Prime is so exquisite that we can dry-age the meat for four full weeks, which is another reason the steak at Bull and Bear is the best in the city!"

—J.H.

BBQ Pulled Pork with Macaroni and Cheese

SERVES 6 TO 8

FOR THE PORK

3 pounds pork butt, trimmed of fat

Spice Rub for Pork (page 258)

FOR THE BBQ SAUCE

¼ cup olive oil

1 large onion, diced

1 tablespoon minced garlic

1 teaspoon dried oregano

1 teaspoon dried thyme

1 tablespoon smoked paprika
(see Chef's Note)

1 cup tomato paste

¼ cup brandy

¼ cup sherry vinegar

1 tablespoon puréed chipotle
(from canned chipotle chiles)

Salt and freshly ground white pepper
to taste

ONE OF THE ADVANTAGES OF directing the various Waldorf=Astoria kitchens with their diverse concepts—Peacock Alley, Oscar's, Room Service, Banqueting, Bull and Bear Steakhouse, and special events—is the cross-fertilization of ideas. We serve this dish at Oscar's from time to time, but we first introduced it at a wedding cocktail party when the client requested something "down home." We got together in the kitchen to plan the event and discussed what we like to eat, and this was one idea, served with great elegance in a cocktail glass! The enthusiastic line of guests at the party, waiting their turn to try it, told us we had a hit on our hands, and onto the menu it went. Personally, I think the clincher is the pickled cucumber that adds a refreshing lightness to the rich combination of pork and macaroni and cheese.

TO PREPARE THE PORK Place the pork butt in an ovenproof dish or roasting pan and massage thoroughly with the spice rub. Cover the pork with foil and refrigerate overnight.

Remove the pork from the refrigerator and let sit at room temperature for 1 hour. Preheat the oven to 250°F. Transfer the pork (still covered with foil) to the oven and cook for 4 to 5 hours, or until the meat shreds easily when pulled with a fork. Remove the pork from the oven, lift it from the roasting dish, and set aside in a clean dish or pan. Skim any fat from the juices left in the dish or roasting pan and discard. Drizzle the remaining cooking juices over the cooked pork and let cool to room temperature. When cooled, use a fork to shred the pork; transfer to a dish and keep refrigerated until ready to serve.

TO PREPARE THE BBQ SAUCE Pour the oil into a large saucepan and set over medium heat. When the oil is hot and shimmering, add the onion and sauté until translucent, 3 to 4 minutes, then add the garlic and sauté for about 2 minutes longer. Add the oregano, thyme, and paprika, and cook for 2 more minutes. Add the tomato paste, cook for another 2 minutes, and then add the brandy, vinegar, 5 cups of water, chipotle purée, salt, and pepper. Bring to a boil, turn the heat to medium-low, and simmer until the sauce has thickened to a ketchuplike consistency, about 30 minutes (there should be about 3 cups of sauce).

FOR THE MACARONI
AND CHEESE

2 tablespoons olive oil

½ large onion, diced

¾ cup dry white wine

1 quart (4 cups) milk

2 tablespoons Dijon mustard

2 tablespoons Worcestershire sauce

⅛ teaspoon cayenne

4 ounces Gruyère cheese,
grated (about ⅔ cup)

4 ounces Monterey Jack cheese,
grated (about ⅔ cup)

4 ounces Cheddar cheese,
grated (about ⅔ cup)

4 ounces Taleggio cheese,
grated (about ⅔ cup)

3 tablespoons cornstarch

1½ pounds elbow macaroni

FOR THE TOPPING

1 cup panko (Japanese breadcrumbs)

1 tablespoon olive oil

½ cup grated Parmesan cheese

3 tablespoons minced fresh parsley

Salt and freshly ground white pepper
to taste

1 cup Pickled Cucumbers (page 250)

12 to 18 large flour tortillas, warmed

TO PREPARE THE MACARONI AND CHEESE Pour the oil into a large saucepan and set over medium heat. When the oil is hot and shimmering, add the onion and sauté until translucent, 3 to 4 minutes. Add the wine and cook for about 5 minutes or until the liquid has reduced by one-third. Add the milk, mustard, Worcestershire sauce, and cayenne, and bring to a simmer. Meanwhile, in a mixing bowl, combine the grated cheeses and cornstarch. While constantly stirring the milk mixture, add the grated cheese, a little at a time. Simmer the sauce for 15 minutes, stirring occasionally. Remove from the heat and keep warm over low heat.

Preheat the oven to 375°F. Butter a 9- by 11-inch baking dish. Bring a large saucepan of salted water to a boil, add the pasta, and cook until al dente, about 7 minutes. Drain the pasta, add to the cheese mixture, and mix well. Pour the macaroni into the buttered baking dish.

TO PREPARE THE TOPPING In a bowl, combine the panko, oil, Parmesan, parsley, salt, and pepper, and sprinkle on top of the macaroni.

TO ASSEMBLE Bake the macaroni in the oven until the topping is golden brown, about 12 to 15 minutes. Heat the shredded pork in a microwave oven until warm, about 2 minutes. Add 1 cup of the BBQ sauce, and mix gently. Heat again in the microwave until the pork is hot, about 2 minutes longer. Heat the remaining BBQ sauce in the microwave until it is hot, 2 to 3 minutes.

TO SERVE Arrange the pork in a mound on warm serving plates and garnish with the pickled cucumber. Place the tortillas between 2 damp paper towels and heat for 1 to 2 minutes in the microwave. Spoon the macaroni and cheese next to the pork and serve with the warm tortillas.

Wine Recommendation Napa Valley Syrah (ripe, rich, and deeply flavored with spice scents).

CHEF'S NOTES

◇ Note that the pork should be marinated overnight before cooking. The BBQ sauce may also be prepared 1 day in advance.

◇ For notes on Taleggio cheese, see page 112; for notes on panko, see page 154.

◇ Smoked paprika, with its subtle, complex flavor, is available at spice stores or specialty food markets. By all means, substitute regular paprika.

Parmesan-Crusted Chicken with Asparagus Morel Risotto and Tomato Confit

SERVES 8

Tomato Confit (page 257)

FOR THE CHICKEN

2 cups all-purpose flour

4 large eggs

3 cups grated Parmesan cheese

1 cup plain breadcrumbs

8 boneless, skinless chicken breasts, about 6 ounces each

Salt and freshly ground black pepper to taste

1 tablespoon butter

1 tablespoon olive oil

Asparagus and Morel Mushroom Risotto (page 246)

ONE DAY, AS I WAS casually flipping through a food magazine, I came across a photograph of a beautifully browned crusted chicken breast. Before I even checked out the description or the recipe, I figured it was crusted in Parmesan cheese, and thought, "What a great idea!" I quickly turned to the recipe only to find out there wasn't a speck of cheese in it—so much for jumping to conclusions. So, I cannot say this recipe is a completely original idea, exactly, but it is close enough. This has become the most popular and longest-running chicken dish on our menus and is also a dish I make at home for my family.

Prepare 4 plum tomatoes (8 halves) using the tomato confit recipe. Set aside on the stove top to keep warm.

Preheat oven to 350°F.

TO PREPARE THE CHICKEN Set up 3 shallow bowls for the breading procedure. Place the flour in the first bowl, beat together the eggs and ¼ cup of water in the second bowl, mix together the grated cheese and breadcrumbs in the third bowl. Season the chicken breasts with salt and pepper. To bread the chicken, first evenly coat each chicken breast in the flour, then dip in the egg wash, then thoroughly coat with the cheese and breadcrumb mixture. Set aside on a large plate or platter.

Place ½ tablespoon each of the butter and oil in a large sauté pan and set over medium-high heat. When the butter stops crackling, add 4 of the coated chicken breasts and cook on one side until golden brown, 4 or 5 minutes. Turn each piece over and cook the second side for another 4 or 5 minutes (the chicken will still be undercooked in the center). Transfer the chicken to a cookie sheet. Add the remaining butter and olive oil to the pan and repeat for the remaining chicken breasts. Transfer the cookie sheet with the chicken breasts to the oven and cook until the chicken is thoroughly cooked through and no longer pink in the center, about 5 minutes. Keep warm.

Prepare the Asparagus and Morel Mushroom Risotto.

TO SERVE   Spoon the risotto on warm serving plates and arrange the chicken on top. Place a tomato confit half next to the chicken.

Wine Recommendation: Italian Barolo (full-bodied, velvety tannins, flavors of crushed berries and plums).

CHEF'S NOTES

◇   Make sure you use good quality, freshly grated Parmesan cheese.

◇   Although you only need 4 plum tomatoes cooked in the confit method, it is worth making the whole recipe and using the remaining tomatoes for another purpose, or live life to the fullest and serve 2 per person!

Thai Braised Short Ribs with Plum Chutney and Rice Noodles

SERVES 8

2 tablespoons canola oil

12 pounds beef short ribs

Salt and freshly ground black pepper
to taste

2 onions, chopped

1 celery stalk, chopped

1 carrot, peeled and chopped

1 Gala or other crisp red apple (unpeeled),
cored and chopped

¼ pineapple, peeled, cored, and chopped

1 banana, peeled and chopped

3 tablespoons minced ginger

1 tablespoon sliced lemongrass

1 tablespoon minced garlic

1 tablespoon Thai red curry paste

¼ cup Indian curry powder

1 cup carrot juice

1 cup apple juice

½ cup unseasoned rice wine vinegar

2 bottles (750 ml. each) dry red wine

½ cup soy sauce

8 cups Veal Stock (page 253)

½ cup canned unsweetened coconut milk

40 snow peas, for garnish

2 pounds dried Asian rice noodles

Plum Chutney (page 251)

IF YOU ARE LIKE ME, and enjoy tender, braised cuts of meat, you will make this dish over and over again. This recipe calls for Thai curry, which is quite different from Indian curry. Braised beef short ribs have become very popular in New York City (and beyond) because they are so flavorful and match up with so many homey foods. At the Waldorf, we have figured out a way to prepare these ribs for large parties. For example, recently we smothered them with a terrific chile barbecue sauce for the annual NASCAR dinner with 1,250 invited guests—and they loved it! This particular version has become my favorite preparation; the ribs taste even better when made a day or two ahead and reheated. The bonus is that you can spend more time with your guests and less time in the kitchen.

Preheat the oven to 350°F.

TO PREPARE THE RIBS Pour the oil into a large, heavy-bottomed ovenproof saucepan or casserole and set over high heat until the oil is hot and shimmering. Season the short ribs with salt and pepper, add to the pan, and sear the meat on all sides until browned, 3 to 4 minutes on each side. Remove the ribs and set aside. Add the onions, celery, and carrot to the pan and cook until the vegetables are browned and caramelized, 4 to 5 minutes. Add the apple, pineapple, banana, ginger, lemongrass, and garlic and continue to cook for 3 to 4 minutes, making sure the vegetables do not burn. Add the curry paste and curry powder, and cook for 2 or 3 minutes longer, stirring often.

Stir in the carrot juice and apple juice and continue to cook until the liquid is reduced and almost evaporated, 7 or 8 minutes; then add the vinegar, red wine, and soy sauce and cook until the liquid is reduced by half, 10 to 12 minutes. Return the ribs to the pan and cover with the stock. Cover the pot with foil, transfer to the oven, and cook for 3 to 4 hours, or until the meat is very tender when pierced with a skewer.

When the meat is cooked, gently remove the ribs from the pan and keep warm. Use a ladle to remove and discard any fat that is floating on top of the sauce. Strain the sauce into a clean saucepan, reserving the solids and transferring them to a blender. Add the coconut milk to the blender and purée. Stir the purée into the sauce and bring to a boil. Turn the heat to a simmer and adjust the seasonings. Cook for 2 to 3 minutes. Turn the heat to low and keep warm until ready to serve.

TO PREPARE THE SNOW PEA GARNISH   Prepare an ice bath (page 260). Bring a saucepan of salted water to a boil, add the snow peas, and blanch for 2 or 3 minutes. Remove with a slotted spoon and transfer to the ice bath to stop the cooking process. Drain and set aside.

TO PREPARE THE NOODLES   Bring a large saucepan of salted water to a boil, add the rice noodles, and cook for 2 or 3 minutes until tender. Strain the noodles and transfer to a bowl. Add 1½ cups of the sauce and toss together to coat the noodles.

TO SERVE   Place the noodles in warm serving bowls and top with the short ribs. Spoon the remaining sauce over the ribs. Garnish with a heaping tablespoon of Plum Chutney and the blanched snow peas.

Wine Recommendation   South African Pinotage (ripe with fruit-driven plum and toast notes).

CHEF'S NOTE

◇   Both the short ribs and Plum Chutney may be prepared 1 day ahead, making this a great dish for entertaining.

Chile-Crusted Venison with Chocolate Sauce, Red Cabbage, and Spaetzle

SERVES 8

FOR THE CHOCOLATE SAUCE

¼ cup diced bacon

6 ounces venison scraps

1 clove garlic, crushed

½ cup thinly sliced shallots

2 cups dry red wine

2 quarts Venison Stock (page 256)

1 dried bay leaf

2 fresh thyme sprigs

Salt and freshly ground black pepper to taste

¾ ounce semisweet chocolate, melted (about 2 tablespoons)

½ tablespoon butter

FOR THE PARSNIP GARNISH

2 cups canola oil

1 parsnip, peeled

I AM ALWAYS SURPRISED HOW popular venison is, even in the summer months. I was also surprised to learn that venison has less fat per ounce than chicken. USDA regulations ensure that all venison sold in restaurants and markets is farm raised. Most of these farms let the deer run free on large, fenced properties, where they enjoy a natural diet of grains, berries, tree bark, and the like. The controlled environment of farm-raised venison has a definite impact on the flavor of the meat—it is milder and not really gamey at all, which is the quality most often raised as an objection to trying venison. So, reconsider venison if you have been reluctant until now. In this recipe, I have taken the proven flavor combination of chile and chocolate (perfected in ancient Mexico) and paired it with the venison. Of course, we are not talking about using leftover hot fudge from last night's dessert, just enough chocolate to take the bite out of the chile.

TO PREPARE THE SAUCE Place the bacon in a large saucepan and set over medium-high heat. Sauté for 4 to 5 minutes, or until almost crisp. Add the venison scraps and cook until well caramelized, about 10 minutes. Add the garlic and shallots and cook until caramelized, about 5 minutes longer. Add the wine, stock, bay leaf, and thyme. Bring to a boil and turn the heat to medium low. Reduce the liquid until about 1 cup remains, about 35 minutes. Strain through a fine-mesh sieve into a clean saucepan, discard the solids, and season with salt and pepper. Whisk in the chocolate and butter and set aside. Warm the sauce just before serving.

Preheat the oven to 350°F.

TO PREPARE THE PARSNIP GARNISH Pour the oil into a saucepan and heat to 350°F. Using a vegetable peeler, cut long strips from the length of the parsnip and add to the hot oil. Fry for 2 to 3 minutes, or until golden brown. Remove with a slotted spoon and drain on paper towels.

FOR THE CABBAGE

¼ cup diced bacon

1 cup diced onion

16 cups shredded red cabbage

2 cups dry red wine

¼ cup red wine vinegar

3 tablespoons sugar

½ stick cinnamon

4 cloves

10 black peppercorns

4 sprigs fresh thyme

1 dried bay leaf

2 Granny Smith apples, peeled, cored,
and diced

Herbed Spaetzle (page 247)

FOR THE VENISON

4 dried serrano chiles

1 teaspoon dried oregano

3 pounds venison loin, boned and
silverskin trimmed (reserve scraps)

2 tablespoons butter

Salt and freshly ground black pepper
to taste

TO PREPARE THE CABBAGE Place the bacon in a large saucepan and set over medium heat. Sauté until almost crisp, about 5 minutes. Remove and reserve the bacon; pour off all but 1 tablespoon of fat. Add the onion and sauté until soft, about 5 minutes. Add the cabbage, wine, vinegar, sugar, and the reserved bacon. Place the cinnamon, cloves, peppercorns, thyme, and bay leaf in a piece of cheesecloth and secure it with butcher's twine. Add to the saucepan, mix well, and bring to a simmer. Continue to cook, uncovered, for 20 minutes. Add the apples and cook for 15 minutes longer. Remove the bouquet garni.

While the cabbage is cooking, prepare the Herbed Spaetzle.

TO PREPARE THE VENISON Place the chiles and oregano in a spice grinder or blender and pulse until they form a powder. Sprinkle this powder evenly over the venison. Use butcher's twine to tie the loin every 2 inches to help it cook evenly and to give it a better appearance. Melt the butter in a large, heavy skillet set over medium-high heat. When the butter stops crackling, add the venison and season with salt and pepper. Sear the meat, maintaining an even temperature so it browns but the butter does not burn. Brown the venison well on all sides, about 10 minutes, and transfer the meat to a roasting pan. Roast in the oven, uncovered, to an internal temperature of 125°F, 25 to 30 minutes. Remove the meat from the oven, and let rest for about 10 minutes before slicing.

TO SERVE Spoon the cabbage onto warm serving plates. Carve the venison into ½-inch-thick slices and arrange on top of the cabbage. Spoon some spaetzle and sauce next to the cabbage and meat. Garnish with the fried parsnip ribbons.

Wine Recommendation Napa Valley Zinfandel (Firm and concentrated with complex raspberry and wild berry flavors).

CHEF'S NOTES

◇ If you must bone the venison yourself, use a sharp boning knife and follow along the bones until they are separated from the meat. Save any bones and trimmings for the sauce.

◇ If you purchase the venison from a butcher, make sure that you are given the scraps from the trimming.

◇ The sauce may be prepared up to 5 hours in advance; the venison can also be seared ahead of time. The parsnip garnish and cabbage may be held for 1 hour and reheated before serving.

Veal Oscar

SERVES 8

FOR THE TARRAGON VINAIGRETTE

1 teaspoon minced shallot

½ teaspoon minced garlic

1 large egg yolk

1 teaspoon Dijon mustard

¼ cup tarragon vinegar

3 tablespoons fresh tarragon leaves

1 cup canola oil

Salt and freshly ground white pepper to taste

8 Crispy Crab Cakes (page 106)

FOR THE VEAL OSCAR

32 jumbo asparagus spears, trimmed and peeled

16 veal scaloppine, about 3 ounces each, pounded thin

Salt and freshly ground white pepper to taste

½ cup canola oil

¼ cup butter

1 teaspoon white truffle oil

2 tablespoons minced shallot

1 cup seeded and diced tomatoes

SOME SAY THAT VEAL OSCAR was named for King Oscar II of Sweden who ruled at the end of the nineteenth century and into the twentieth. We like to think it was another culinary coup orchestrated by the celebrated "Oscar of the Waldorf" (page 98). The traditional Veal Oscar was a little on the heavy side, calling for sautéed veal medallions with Alaskan crab legs, asparagus, and béarnaise sauce. For today's palates, we have lightened the dish by replacing the béarnaise with tarragon vinaigrette, and simplified it by using miniature crab cakes instead of the traditional legs. We have also switched the veal from medallions to scaloppine, making it more economical as well as easier and quicker to cook. This is the number-one-selling entrée on the menu at Oscar's and, if you look at the recipe, it really is not an intimidating dish to put together.

TO PREPARE THE VINAIGRETTE Combine the shallot, garlic, egg yolk, mustard, and tarragon vinegar in a blender and blend until incorporated. With the blender running, add the tarragon leaves and slowly add the oil in a steady stream. Continue to blend until thoroughly incorporated. Season with salt and pepper. Transfer to a bowl and keep refrigerated.

Prepare the Crispy Crab Cakes. Finish in the oven as described in the recipe, then turn down the oven to 250°F.

TO PREPARE THE ASPARAGUS AND VEAL Prepare an ice bath (page 260). Bring a large saucepan of salted water to a boil and add the asparagus. Cook until tender, 6 or 7 minutes, then transfer the asparagus to the ice bath to stop the cooking process. Slice 8 of the spears into ¼-inch lengths and set aside. Season both sides of the veal scaloppine with salt and pepper. Pour ¼ cup of the oil into a large, heavy skillet and set over medium-high heat. When the oil is hot and shimmering, add the veal in batches and cook until golden brown, about 2 minutes per side; use the remaining oil as needed. Transfer the scaloppine to a platter and keep warm in the oven.

In the same pan in which the veal was sautéed, add the butter and melt over low heat. When melted, add the 24 reserved asparagus spears and sauté for 3 to 4 minutes, until heated through. Season with salt and pepper and set aside. Still using the same pan, pour in the truffle oil and set over medium heat. When the oil is hot and shimmering, add the shallot and sauté for 1 minute. Add the cooked asparagus and the tomatoes and sauté for 1 minute longer. Season with salt and pepper and transfer to a serving bowl.

TO SERVE Place the veal scaloppine on warm serving plates. Neatly arrange 3 asparagus spears, pointing in the same direction, on top of the veal. Place another scaloppine on top of the asparagus and spoon the asparagus-tomato mixture over the scaloppini. Top with a crab cake and drizzle ¼ cup of the tarragon vinaigrette around each plate; serve the remaining vinaigrette at the table.

Wine Recommendation Santa Barbara (CA) Pinot Noir (elegant and intense, with blackberry jam fruit on the palate and light oak).

CHEF'S NOTES

◇　Those with health concerns should note that there is raw egg in the vinaigrette.

◇　I rarely use truffle oil, which is available at most specialty food stores, as I do not think it imparts the same flavor quality as fresh truffles, but it is ideal for this recipe.

◇　The crab cakes may be prepared 1 day in advance and cooked just before you are ready to serve. The vinaigrette may be made up to 2 hours in advance.

Herb-Crusted Rack of Lamb with Eggplant, Tomato, and Goat Cheese Tarts and Rosemary Sauce

SERVES 6 TO 8

FOR THE ROSEMARY SAUCE

1 tablespoon olive oil

6 ounces lamb scraps

1 clove garlic, crushed

⅓ cup thinly sliced shallots

1 dried bay leaf

2 sprigs fresh thyme

2 sprigs fresh rosemary

2 quarts Lamb Stock (page 255)

Salt and freshly ground black pepper
to taste

2 tablespoons butter

Eggplant, Tomato, and
Goat Cheese Tarts (page 248)

WE OFTEN SERVE RACK OF lamb for our grand galas. There are so many different ways to prepare it; one of my personal favorites is the classic preparation called *persillade,* with parsley. In this method, minced shallots are sautéed in butter and combined with breadcrumbs and lots of fresh parsley, which adds a refreshing taste. The herb crust we use here is made in a similar fashion; it is healthy and bright in color and makes an attractive presentation. Alongside it, we serve the Eggplant, Tomato, and Goat Cheese Tart with Moroccan spices, dried apricots, and olives. It is a fabulous combination.

————————

TO PREPARE THE ROSEMARY SAUCE Pour the oil into a large saucepan and set over medium-high heat. When the oil is hot and shimmering, add the lamb scraps and brown on all sides, about 10 minutes, stirring to ensure even caramelization. Add the garlic and shallots and cook until they are caramelized, about 5 minutes longer. Add the bay leaf, thyme, rosemary, and stock, deglazing the pan by scraping the bottom with a wooden spoon to dislodge the cooked solids. Bring to a boil, turn the heat to medium low, and simmer until the liquid has reduced to 1 cup, about 1½ hours. Strain the liquid into a clean saucepan, discarding the solids, and season with salt and pepper. Set aside. When ready to serve, warm the sauce through and whisk in the butter.

While the sauce is reducing, prepare the Eggplant, Tomato, and Goat Cheese Tarts. Preheat the oven to 350°F.

TO PREPARE THE LAMB Rub the lamb racks vigorously with the crushed garlic. Evenly rub the Dijon mustard over the lamb and season with salt and pepper. Place the butter in a large skillet and set over medium-high heat. When the butter stops crackling, add the lamb racks and the rosemary sprigs to the skillet. Sear the lamb on both sides while basting with the butter, about 10 minutes; maintain an even temperature so the meat browns but the butter does not burn.

Transfer the seared lamb racks to a large roasting pan and evenly distribute the herbed crust over the top. Roast in the oven until the internal temperature reaches 130°F, 12 to 15 minutes; begin checking the temperature after about 10 minutes. Remove the meat from the oven and let it rest 8 to 10 minutes before serving.

FOR THE LAMB

3 lamb racks (8 bones per rack), preferably Colorado lamb, trimmed of fat and frenched (see Chef's Note)

4 cloves garlic, lightly crushed

1½ teaspoons Dijon mustard

Salt and freshly ground black pepper to taste

2 tablespoons butter

2 sprigs fresh rosemary

¾ cup Herb Crust (page 168)

TO SERVE If necessary, warm the eggplant tarts in the oven for 2 to 3 minutes. Slice each lamb rack into 8 even chops and serve 3 or 4 chops on each warm serving plate. Spoon the sauce next to the lamb and serve with the tarts.

Wine Recommendation Spanish Rioja (light and fresh, with berry and rhubarb flavors and vanilla-tobacco scents).

CHEF'S NOTE

◇ *Frenching* a lamb rack refers to cutting the meat from in between the bones to expose them and improve the presentation. This takes a little skill and may mean some nicked fingers before you master the technique, so please be careful if you attempt this at home, and always cut away from your hand. The best bet is to ask your butcher to do it for you.

Slow-Roasted Shoulder of Lamb with Artichoke and Tomato Fricassee

SERVES 8

FOR THE LAMB SHOULDER

1 carrot, peeled and chopped into
1-inch lengths

1 stalk celery, chopped into 1-inch lengths

1 large onion, chopped

6 cloves garlic, unpeeled

1 cup Garlic Confit (page 257)

½ cup Dijon mustard

2 tablespoons chopped fresh thyme

Salt and freshly ground black pepper
to taste

1 lamb shoulder, 5 to 6 pounds, boned,
trimmed, and butterflied (see Chef's Note)

1 cup Lamb Stock (page 255)

1 cup Chicken Stock (page 252)

Artichoke, Tomato, and Garlic Fricassee
(page 248)

FOR THE ARTICHOKE AND PARMESAN SALAD

4 baby artichokes

¼ cup shaved Parmesan cheese
(see Chef's Note)

Juice of ½ lemon

1 tablespoon extra-virgin olive oil

Pinch of salt

I CREATED THIS DO-AHEAD DISH for a family gathering and, even though it sounded like a good idea at the time, just how good it turned out to be took me totally by surprise. Now I serve it for special private gourmet dinners such as for Waldorf=Astoria Distinguished Alumni, former executives who have made their mark in other prestigious organizations. It is a particular favorite of mine and a few of the other chefs at the Waldorf. The fragrant flavors of the browned garlic, rosemary, and lamb are simply intoxicating and the contrasting textures of the tender lamb and the al dente artichokes is hard to beat. The good news for entertaining is that this dish is best when made the day before, because once it is finished cooking for 5 hours, the boneless shoulder is actually too tender to slice. After it has refrigerated overnight, you can slice the cold meat and reheat it with the sauce whenever you are ready to serve it.

Preheat the oven to 275°F.

TO PREPARE THE LAMB Place the carrot, celery, onion, and garlic in the bottom of a roasting pan. In a bowl, mix together the Garlic Confit, mustard, and thyme, and season with salt and pepper. Season the inside of the lamb shoulder with salt and pepper before rubbing with the Garlic Confit–mustard mixture. Roll up the lamb shoulder from either end and tie firmly using butcher's twine. Season the outside of the lamb shoulder with salt and pepper. Place the lamb on top of the vegetables in the roasting pan and pour the Lamb Stock and Chicken Stock into the pan until the liquid comes about one-third of the way up the sides of the lamb. Cover the pan with foil and transfer to the oven. Roast the lamb for 3½ hours, turning the meat over every hour. Remove the foil and cook in the oven for 1½ hours longer, turning the lamb over every 30 minutes, until the meat is fork tender. Remove the pan from the oven and gently transfer to a baking dish. Strain the braising liquid through a fine-mesh sieve over the lamb and let cool. Cover and let rest in the refrigerator overnight.

The next day, preheat the oven to 350°F.

TO FINISH THE LAMB Remove the lamb from the congealed sauce in the baking dish and cut the strings securing the meat. Transfer the sauce to a saucepan and set over medium heat. Carve 8 lamb slices, 1 inch thick, and lay in a single layer on a rimmed baking sheet or in a roasting pan. Bring the sauce to a boil, remove from the heat, and spoon half of it over the lamb. Cover the lamb with foil and transfer to the oven. Roast for 20 minutes. Keep the remaining sauce in the saucepan warm over low heat.

While the lamb is roasting, prepare the Artichoke and Tomato Fricassee.

TO PREPARE THE ARTICHOKE SALAD Use a paring knife to trim all the green leaves from the artichokes; trim any green parts from the stem. Cut out the fuzzy choke from the center of each artichoke and discard. Slice the artichokes thin on a mandoline slicer (page 263), or with a very sharp knife, and transfer to a mixing bowl. Add the cheese, lemon juice, and oil, and season with salt. Set aside in the refrigerator.

TO SERVE Spoon the fricassee on warm serving plates and place a lamb slice on top. Spoon about 2 tablespoons of the remaining sauce over the lamb and top with the artichoke salad.

Wine Recommendation Willamette Valley (OR) Pinot Noir (ripe, plush, and zesty with red fruit tones).

CHEF'S NOTES

◇ The easiest way to bone, trim, and butterfly the lamb shoulder is to ask your butcher to do it for you. Better yet, buy the lamb shoulder already boned.

◇ The best way to shave Parmesan cheese is to use a vegetable peeler to slice it into thin strips.

WILD PEPPER PORK WITH PARSNIP PURÉE

SERVES 8

FOR THE WILD PEPPER PORK

4 shallots, roughly sliced

½ carrot, peeled and roughly sliced

3 teaspoons wild black peppercorns (see Chef's Note)

1 sprig fresh thyme

1 dried bay leaf

1 stalk lemongrass, pounded with a mallet and chopped

1-inch piece ginger, sliced

¼ cup olive oil

¼ cup Thai basil leaves (or green basil, snipped with scissors)

8 large cloves garlic, peeled and crushed

2 racks pork (preferably organic), about 6 pounds each (see Chef's Note)

Sea salt to taste

1 tablespoon butter

FOR THE PARSNIP PURÉE

1 pound parsnips, peeled and chopped

1¼ cups milk

Sea salt to taste

2 tablespoons butter

IN APRIL 2005, PEACOCK ALLEY Executive Chef Cedric Tovar journeyed to Vietnam to join other culinarians helping orphaned children there. It was during these travels that he discovered wild peppercorns and, when he returned to New York, Cedric paired them with organic Colorado pork. You will be pleased to know that he has simplified his recipe for the home cook because, at the Waldorf, Cedric marinates pork loin every day and seals it in a plastic vacuum pouch—not a common technique in the average home kitchen. He then cooks the pork slowly in the pouch, submerged in water at 145°F for 1¼ hours, until it is just medium rare. He then sears it gently on the stove top so the pork is the epitome of tenderness and juiciness when sliced. Well worth the price of admission!

TO PREPARE THE PORK Place the shallots and carrot in a large shallow dish and add 1 teaspoon of the peppercorns, the thyme, bay leaf, lemongrass, ginger, olive oil, half of the basil, and 5 of the crushed cloves of garlic. Mix well. Remove the pork loins from the bone and rub them with this mixture. Cover the dish and transfer to the refrigerator to marinate overnight.

Preheat the oven to 225°F.

Cut the remaining 3 garlic cloves in half and reserve. Remove the pork from the refrigerator; wipe off the pork, and reserve the marinade. Season the pork with sea salt and 1 teaspoon of the crushed wild pepper. Set a roasting pan over medium heat on the stove top and add 1 tablespoon of butter. When the butter has melted, add the pork loins and brown on all sides until nicely caramelized, 10 to 12 minutes. Add the chopped pork bones (see Chef's Note), the reserved marinade, and the halved garlic cloves to the pan. Transfer to the oven and roast the pork, uncovered, until it reaches an internal temperature of 135°F for medium doneness, about 1 hour. Turn the oven off and let the pork rest in the oven for a few minutes until you are ready to serve.

TO PREPARE THE PARSNIP PURÉE While the pork is roasting, place the chopped parsnips in a large saucepan, add 1 cup of the milk, 2 cups water, and salt, and set over high heat. Bring to a boil and turn down the heat to a simmer; cook until tender, about 30 minutes. Drain the parsnips, chop, and transfer to a food processor. Add 2 tablespoons of butter and the remaining ¼ cup of milk. Process the parsnips until they are smooth. Return to a clean saucepan and keep warm.

TO ASSEMBLE Skim the fat from the pork juices in the roasting pan and reserve. Strain the juices into a small saucepan and add the remaining basil leaves. Let this *jus* sit for 15 minutes; remove the basil leaves before serving. Carve each pork loin into 12 slices and rub them with the reserved fat skimmed from the cooking juices. Season the sliced pork with the remaining 1 teaspoon of crushed wild peppercorns, and sea salt.

TO SERVE Divide the parsnip purée among warm serving plates. Arrange 3 slices of pork over the parsnip, spoon the *jus* around the plate, and garnish to taste with a sprinkling of sea salt and black pepper.

Wine Recommendation French Cahors (mouth filling and gamey with a good concentration of currant and berry).

CHEF'S NOTES

⬧ Wild black peppercorns are available in specialty food stores or ethnic markets (and see Sources, page 261). You can substitute Szechwan peppercorns.

⬧ Ask your butcher to remove the pork loin meat from the bone and to chop the bones into small pieces so you can use them for the pork jus. If you have trouble finding racks of pork, buy loin meat and pork bones separately and use them as directed in the recipe. Note that the pork must be marinated overnight before cooking.

8

DESSERTS

love to brag about the Waldorf's pastry department. What impresses me most about our pastry kitchen team is the consistently high quality of the desserts they produce, day after day. Consistency is the single most difficult element to manage in any handcrafted food operation, in which meals are made entirely from scratch. The integrity of the dessert recipes we use is outstanding, and the ingredients and raw products used to make all our guests' endings sweet are the best available, whether it is fresh fruit, chocolate, or vanilla. All that means nothing, however, without strong leadership and team focus.

What I like least about the hotel's dessert and pastry operaton is the ventilation system, clearly designed and maintained by an invisible enemy force that wafts tempting, mouth-watering aromas from the pastry kitchen into my office, next door. As I am conducting an interview or holding a team meeting, the delicious yeasty scent of freshly baking brioche seeps in; sometimes, it's the aroma of melting chocolate from the assembly of soufflés, or fresh raspberry sauce. Soon the conversation turns to what is being whipped up *today* by Jean-Claude Perennou and his staff,

and our attention starts to wander. It is around about then that I realize my willpower is being tested to the limit as I consider making another "quality-control" check. Sometimes I tell myself that the effort of walking all the way to the pastry kitchen will cancel out the calories involved in my food testing. Hey, it's what I'm supposed to do—I'm the chef!

When considering which recipes to include in this chapter, I was reminded of the answers I sometimes give when asked about what makes our desserts so special: attention to detail, commitment to quality, respect for tradition, and a passion for innovation. I am proud to say these are also hallmarks of the entire Waldorf=Astoria kitchen, but it is especially true of the pastry kitchen and exemplified by this selection of desserts.

Caramelized Pineapple, Piña Colada Milkshake, and Coconut Ice Cream

SERVES 6

FOR THE COCONUT ICE CREAM

2 cups milk

*1 can (15 fl. oz.) Coco Lopez
(cream of coconut)*

FOR THE CARAMELIZED PINEAPPLE

¼ cup butter

½ pineapple, peeled, cored, and diced

3 tablespoons granulated sugar

*1 vanilla bean, split lengthwise
and seeds scraped
(or 1 teaspoon vanilla extract)*

FOR THE PIÑA COLADA MILKSHAKE

*½ cup canned Coco Lopez
(cream of coconut)*

½ cup pineapple juice

*⅓ cup Malibu rum
(or other coconut-flavored rum)*

2 cups crushed ice

JEAN-CLAUDE PUT TOGETHER THIS FUN dessert using ideas from one of his Peacock Alley creations and a presentation for a Chef's Table event (see page 24). It is nothing if not tropical, and is a great combination of sweet and tart, hot and cold, fruity and creamy. If you are making this dessert for a dinner that includes children or teenagers, make sure you serve them a virgin colada milkshake!

TO PREPARE THE ICE CREAM Combine the milk and the Coco Lopez in a mixing bowl. Pour the mixture into an ice-cream maker and freeze according to the manufacturer's directions. Store tightly covered in the freezer.

Preheat the oven to 200°F.

TO PREPARE THE PINEAPPLE Melt the butter in a sauté pan set over medium heat. When the butter starts to crackle, add the diced pineapple and sprinkle with the sugar. Add the vanilla seeds and bean and sauté the mixture, stirring continuously, until the pineapple turns golden brown, 3 to 4 minutes. Remove the pineapple and transfer to a cookie sheet. Spread it out in a single layer and let cool; reserve the cooking juices. Remove the split vanilla bean from the pineapple mixture and place the bean on a cookie sheet or in a small roasting pan. Transfer the vanilla bean to the oven and turn the oven off. Leave the vanilla bean in the oven until it is dried out, about 45 minutes. Cut each half of the vanilla bean lengthwise into 3 pieces and reserve for garnish.

TO PREPARE THE MILKSHAKE Place the Coco Lopez, pineapple juice, rum, and ice in a blender and purée until smooth.

TO SERVE Spoon some of the caramelized pineapple on each chilled serving plate, piling it slightly. Drizzle the pineapple with the reserved cooking juices. Pour the milkshake into small juice glasses or sherry glasses and place a glass on each serving plate with the pineapple; garnish the glass with a piece of the reserved dried vanilla bean. Place a small scoop of coconut ice cream on the plate next to the pineapple and serve.

CHEF'S NOTE

◇   The ice cream recipe yields almost 2 pints.

Pumpkin Pie with a Demitasse of Hot Chocolate

SERVES 8 TO 10

(one 9-inch pie)

FOR THE PUMPKIN

1 cheese or other baking pumpkin (5 to 6 pounds)

FOR THE PIE CRUST

1¼ cups all-purpose flour

½ teaspoon salt

½ cup plus 3 tablespoons very cold butter

FOR THE FILLING

2 medium eggs, beaten

6 tablespoons granulated sugar

1 tablespoon ground cinnamon

¾ teaspoon salt

¼ teaspoon nutmeg

1⅓ cups heavy cream

3 tablespoons cognac

1 tablespoon melted butter

FOR THE HOT CHOCOLATE

3 ounces milk chocolate, preferably Valrhona, chopped

2¾ ounces bittersweet chocolate, preferably Valrhona, chopped

2½ cups milk

½ teaspoon vanilla extract

FOR THE SWEETENED WHIPPED CREAM

1 cup heavy cream

2 tablespoons sugar

HAVING GROWN UP IN THE Brittany region of France and being classically trained as a pastry chef, Jean-Claude Perennou had a tough time appreciating some of America's finer pastry traditions, such as angel food cake, puddings, fruit pies, and, yes, the all-American pumpkin pie. In his first Thanksgiving as the Waldorf's pastry chef, he asked for a recipe for pumpkin pie, then refused to make it because it called for canned pumpkin. I admired his commitment to quality, but to make pumpkin pie from scratch for the Waldorf=Astoria, we needed eight hundred pounds of pumpkin! Fast! Jean-Claude was not deterred; he and his team went on a mission to create the perfect pumpkin pie, and now it is the only pumpkin pie I will eat.

Preheat the oven to 325°F.

TO PREPARE THE PUMPKIN Cut the pumpkin in half crosswise (horizontally) and place cut side down on a baking sheet or in a roasting pan. Transfer to the oven and bake until the skin of the pumpkin is soft and a knife or fork easily penetrates it, about 1 hour. Remove and let cool completely. Scrape out the seeds with a spoon and discard. Scoop out the pumpkin meat and place in a colander over a bowl or pan. Cover with plastic wrap and let drain in the refrigerator overnight.

TO PREPARE THE PIE CRUST Sift together the flour and salt into a mixing bowl. Using a pastry blender or fork, cut the butter into the flour and salt, until the mixture combines to form small pieces the size of peas. Add ¼ cup ice water and stir the dough with a fork until the mixture combines to form a ball, being careful not to overmix. Flatten the ball and wrap it in plastic wrap, then refrigerate the dough for 1 hour.

On a clean, lightly floured work surface, roll out the dough into a circle about ⅛-inch thick and 12 inches in diameter. Place the dough on a cookie sheet (to easily move the dough, roll it around the rolling pin and then unroll on the sheet) and chill in the refrigerator for 1 hour longer. When chilled, place the dough into a 9-inch pie pan and trim the excess dough, leaving a ½-inch edge. Fold the edge under and, using your index fingers, crimp the edge. Refrigerate for at least 30 minutes.

Preheat the oven to 375°F.

Line the pie shell with parchment paper or foil and fill the shell with pie weights, dried peas, or beans to prevent the dough from shrinking. Bake the crust for 6 to 7 minutes until the edges start to turn a golden brown. Remove the foil and weights, peas, or beans, and return the crust to the oven. Continue to bake until the crust is golden, 2 or 3 minutes longer (if the center puffs up part way through baking, gently push it down with the back of a spoon). Remove the pie crust and let cool completely on a wire rack.

Turn the oven temperature to 325°F.

TO PREPARE THE FILLING Whisk together the eggs and 1½ cups of the roasted pumpkin in a mixing bowl. In a separate bowl, combine the sugar, cinnamon, salt, and nutmeg. Stir the dry ingredients into the pumpkin mixture until thoroughly combined. Stir in the cream, cognac, and melted butter. Using a handheld immersion blender, or an electric beater, blend the mixture to a smooth and creamy consistency; the filling should be quite liquid in appearance. Pour the filling into the prepared pie crust and transfer to the center rack of the oven. Bake until the center of the pie is set, 45 to 50 minutes. Remove from the oven and let cool completely on a wire rack.

TO PREPARE THE HOT CHOCOLATE Place the milk chocolate and bittersweet chocolate in a small mixing bowl. In a small saucepan, scald the milk (bring to just below boiling point). Pour the scalded milk over the chocolate and stir until the chocolate is completely melted, then stir in the vanilla. Pour into demitasse cups.

Place the chopped chocolate in a small bowl. Pour the remaining ½ cup of cream in a saucepan and bring to a boil. Carefully pour the hot cream over the chopped chocolate and, using a hand whisk, mix to a smooth consistency. Using a spatula, fold the egg yolk mixture into the chocolate mixture. Then fold in the refrigerated whipped cream mixture in 3 or 4 increments.

Preheat the oven to 350°F.

TO PREPARE THE CANDIED ALMONDS   Pour ½ cup water into a small saucepan, add the sugar, and set over medium heat, stirring to dissolve the sugar. Bring to a boil and cook for 1 minute. Remove the pan from the heat, pour the simple syrup into a mixing bowl and let cool for 15 minutes. Add the almond slices to the syrup, stirring to ensure they are completely coated. Using a slotted spoon, remove the almonds from the syrup and transfer to a rimmed baking sheet lined with parchment paper. Bake in the oven, stirring the nuts every few minutes to ensure even color, until the nuts are golden brown, 6 to 8 minutes. Remove and let the almonds cool completely.

TO ASSEMBLE   Scoop a serving of hazelnut pot de crème into the bottom of a large martini glass. Fit a pastry bag with an 11 mm. (medium) round flat tip. Fill the bag with the chocolate mousse and squeeze a serving of mousse on top of the hazelnut pot de crème. Sprinkle a few caramelized almond slices and chocolate shavings over the mousse and serve immediately.

CHEF'S NOTES

◇   Hazelnut paste is available at specialty baking stores and gourmet markets.

◇   If you do not own a pastry bag, fill a freezer bag with some of the mousse, seal, and snip off a corner of the bag so you can pipe the mousse out. Refill the bag as needed.

Red Velvet Cake

FOR THE CAKE

3 ounces unsweetened chocolate, chopped

2 cups granulated sugar

4 large eggs

1½ cups vegetable oil

1½ teaspoons vanilla extract

2 cups all-purpose flour

2¼ teaspoons baking soda

¼ teaspoon salt

1½ pounds canned beets, drained and puréed

1 teaspoon red food coloring

FOR THE ICING

2 cups heavy cream

12 ounces cream cheese, at room temperature

12 ounces mascarpone cheese

½ teaspoon vanilla extract

1½ cups powdered sugar, sifted

THIS IS A STRIKING-LOOKING DESSERT, with a red interior and creamy white frosting. Many people think that Red Velvet Cake is a Southern invention and, although it has gained popularity there, it actually started out as a signature dessert at the Waldorf=Astoria in the 1920s. You may have heard the urban legend that the landmark department store Neiman-Marcus charges big bucks for their chocolate-chip cookie recipe—a rumor that is completely unfounded. Back in the 1940s, a similar urban legend surrounded this cake and the recipe, which explains why it is also known as *$100 Cake.* But the myth is just that—a complete fairy tale. In any event, here is an updated recipe, and it is absolutely free!

Pastry Cook Michael Ottomanelli.

Preheat the oven to 350°F. Butter three 9-inch round cake pans and line them with parchment paper or waxed paper.

TO PREPARE THE CAKE   Melt the chocolate in a metal bowl set over a saucepan of boiling water or in the top of a double boiler (or melt in a microwave for 20 to 25 seconds). Meanwhile, place the sugar, eggs, oil, and vanilla in the bowl of an electric mixer fitted with a paddle attachment and mix on low speed for 2 minutes. In a mixing bowl, sift together the flour, baking soda, and salt. Add the dry ingredients to the egg mixture and continue to mix on low speed, scraping down the sides of the bowl with a spatula so everything is well incorporated. Add the melted chocolate to this mixture and continue to mix on low speed. Add the puréed beets and food coloring. Continue to mix on low speed until everything is thoroughly combined. Evenly divide the batter between the 3 prepared pans and bake in the middle of the oven for 20 to 25 minutes or until the center of the cake springs back when touched, or when an inserted toothpick comes out clean. Remove the pans from the oven and transfer to a cooling rack. Let cool for 10 minutes in the pans, then turn the layers out onto the rack and let cool completely.

TO PREPARE THE ICING   Pour the cream into a small bowl and whip to soft peaks. Set aside in the refrigerator. Place the cream cheese in the bowl of an electric mixer fitted with a paddle attachment and mix on low speed until it is soft and smooth. Add the mascarpone and continue to mix on low speed until the cheeses are well combined. Add the vanilla and powdered sugar and mix until everything is just combined. Turn off the mixer and fold in the whipped cream by hand with a spatula. Keep refrigerated until ready to assemble.

TO ASSEMBLE   Using a serrated knife, trim the top of each layer of cake so that it is flat. Place the first layer on a cake plate or serving platter and top with some of the icing. Repeat until all the layers are covered with icing, then ice the top and sides of the cake. Store the cake in the refrigerator until ready to serve.

CHEF'S NOTES

◇   This is a great cake to serve for special occasions like Valentine's Day and Christmas, when red plays a big part in the color scheme.

◇   Sliced canned beets are easier to work with in this recipe than whole beets.

On a clean, lightly floured work surface, roll out the chilled dough into a rectangle, about 11 inches by 6 inches and ⅓ inch thick. Transfer the dough to an unbuttered cookie sheet (to easily move the dough, roll it around the rolling pin and then unroll on the cookie sheet). Transfer to the oven and bake until golden brown, 25 to 30 minutes. Remove from the oven and let cool completely.

Increase the oven temperature to 400°F.

TO PREPARE THE PEACHES Cut each (unpeeled) peach half into 4 wedges and place the slices on a buttered jelly-roll pan or a rimmed cookie sheet. Sprinkle the peach slices with the sugar and bake in the oven until the peaches are glazed, 5 or 6 minutes. Remove from the oven and let cool; reserve the juice from the pan separately.

TO ASSEMBLE THE TART Neatly cut the baked crust into 8 strips, 5 inches by 1¼ inches, and place each strip on a serving plate. Place 3 or 4 peach slices on the dough strip, peel side down, so the fruit curves upward. Drizzle the reserved peach juice around each portion and serve with a scoop of the vanilla ice cream.

CHEF'S NOTES

◇ Note that the tart dough must be chilled overnight before baking.

◇ Hazelnut flour, like almond flour, is available from specialty baking stores or gourmet stores. If unavailable, substitute additional almond flour, although this will eliminate the subtle hazelnut flavor it contributes to the tart dough.

◇ Because this is fresh ice cream, without preservatives and stabilizers, the creamy consistency will not hold for more than 24 hours. Of course, a good quality store-bought ice cream is a suitable substitute, but it will not be close to this delicious! For best results, the custard can be made up to 2 days in advance and placed in the ice-cream maker an hour or two before service.

Lemon Balm with Tropical Fruit and Passion Fruit Sorbet

SERVES 6 TO 8

THIS IS ONE OF EXECUTIVE Pastry Chef Jean-Claude Perennou's favorite recipes. "It's light, it has a great flavor, and the broth is wonderfully aromatic," he explains. For my money, it also wins the Waldorf award for most refreshing dessert. It is not only a favorite of ours—the rest of the chefs love it as well. Jean-Claude always needs to make extra because after a long day in a hot kitchen, I am good for a double portion. Sometimes we use this as a predessert before serving something richer, or it may be the only dessert when the menu calls for something light. Either way, it's truly delicious and easy to make.

FOR THE PASSION FRUIT SORBET

¾ cup granulated sugar

1 cup passion fruit purée

1 tablespoon light corn syrup

FOR THE LEMON BALM

⅓ cup granulated sugar

1 vanilla bean, split lengthwise and seeds scraped

4 white cardamom seeds

10 black peppercorns

½ stalk lemongrass, cut in half lengthwise

Juice and peel of ½ lemon

Juice and peel of ½ orange

½ bunch fresh mint, ends trimmed

FOR THE TROPICAL FRUIT

¼ pineapple, peeled, cored, and very finely diced

½ fresh mango, cut in half, pitted, peeled, and very finely diced

½ fresh papaya, cut in half, seeded, peeled, and very finely diced

TO PREPARE THE SORBET Combine ¾ cup plus 2 tablespoons water and the sugar in a small saucepan and set over medium heat. Stir until the sugar dissolves, then bring to a boil. Add the passion fruit purée and the corn syrup and stir to combine. Bring to a boil and remove from the heat. Let the mixture cool, then place in your ice-cream maker and freeze according to the manufacturer's directions.

TO PREPARE THE LEMON BALM Place 2 cups of water and the sugar in a small saucepan. Add the vanilla, cardamom, peppercorns, lemongrass, lemon, orange, and mint and bring to a simmer over medium-high heat, stirring occasionally so the sugar dissolves. Remove the pan from the heat and let cool. Strain the broth, reserving the lemongrass and cutting it lengthwise into slivers for garnish. Chill the broth in the refrigerator.

TO PREPARE THE TROPICAL FRUIT Place the pineapple, mango, and papaya in a mixing bowl, and toss gently to combine. Chill in the refrigerator until ready to serve.

TO SERVE Place 1 heaping tablespoon of the diced fruit in the center of each chilled shallow serving bowl. Place a small scoop of the sorbet on top of the fruit, and spoon ¼ cup of the lemon balm around the fruit and sorbet. Garnish by arranging slivers of the lemongrass across the top of the sorbet.

CHEF'S NOTE

◇ White cardamom, the aromatic seed of a plant in the ginger family, can be purchased at gourmet stores. Regular cardamom can be used, but the flavor will not be quite as intense.

Peanut Caramel Sundae with Tapioca

FOR THE PEANUT BUTTER ICE CREAM

1 pint Vanilla Ice Cream (page 227), slightly softened

⅓ cup smooth peanut butter

FOR THE TAPIOCA

2½ cups milk

⅓ cup small tapioca pearls

½ teaspoon vanilla extract

FOR THE CARAMEL SAUCE

½ cup light corn syrup

11 tablespoons (½ cup plus 3 tablespoons) granulated sugar

3 tablespoons butter

1 cup plus 1½ tablespoons heavy cream

2 teaspoons sea salt

FOR THE CARAMEL RICE KRISPIES

1½ tablespoons granulated sugar

1 small box Rice Krispies (25 grams, or about 1 cup)

THIS RECIPE WAS DEVELOPED BY former Peacock Alley Sous Chef Michael Rispe. We still use it today, because it happens to be Jean-Claude's favorite. It is the only dessert you'll find him eating—which is different from tasting! It also happens to be my daughter Jenna's favorite dessert; you can find it on the menu at Oscar's.

TO PREPARE THE PEANUT BUTTER ICE CREAM Prepare the vanilla ice-cream recipe to the point at which the custard is cooling over the water bath (before transferring it to an ice-cream maker). Warm the peanut butter slightly in the microwave oven and swirl it into the custard. Transfer to an ice-cream maker and freeze according to the manufacturer's directions. (Alternatively, place 1 pint of slightly softened store-bought vanilla ice cream in a bowl and stir in the warmed peanut butter.)

TO PREPARE THE TAPIOCA Pour 2¼ cups of the milk into a small saucepan and add the tapioca pearls and vanilla. Set over medium-high heat and bring the mixture to a boil. Turn the heat to medium low and simmer the tapioca, stirring constantly, until soft, 5 to 6 minutes. Transfer the pudding to a bowl and let cool to room temperature. When the tapioca has cooled, stir in the remaining ¼ cup of milk, to give the pudding a creamy consistency.

TO PREPARE THE CARAMEL SAUCE Pour the corn syrup and sugar into a small saucepan and stir. Set over medium heat and cook (without stirring) until the mixture turns a medium caramel color, 3 or 4 minutes. Remove the pan from the heat and carefully add the butter, cream, and salt. Avoid splashing yourself with the mixture as it will be very hot. Return the mixture to medium heat and bring to a boil, stirring constantly. Remove from the heat and let cool to room temperature.

TO PREPARE THE CARAMEL RICE KRISPIES Butter a cookie sheet and set aside. Pour 1½ tablespoons of water into a small saucepan, stir in the sugar, and set over medium-high heat until the mixture reaches the soft ball stage, about 248°F on a candy thermometer. Add the Rice Krispies and, stirring constantly, continue cooking the mixture until the sugar has caramelized and the Rice Krispies are thoroughly coated. Pour the mixture onto the cookie sheet and spread out with a spatula. Let cool completely. When ready to serve, carefully crumble into small chunks.

With a spatula, fold a small amount of the refrigerated whipped cream into the warm chocolate, working quickly to prevent lumps from forming. Fold in the egg yolk and gelatin mixture, and fold in the remaining whipped cream. Transfer to the refrigerator.

FOR ASSEMBLY Lightly butter the bottom and sides of a 10-inch springform pan. Cut a circle slightly less than 10 inches in diameter from a clean piece of cardboard and, using this template, cut two 10-inch circles from the baked puff pastry. Place 1 of the puff pastry circles, flat side down, on the bottom of the springform pan. Spread a thin layer of the strawberry jam over the puff pastry. Line the inside of the pan with the strawberry halves, with the flat (cut) sides against the rim of the pan and the tips pointing up. Place half of the white chocolate mousse on top of the jam layer. Arrange the sliced strawberries evenly over the mousse, pressing them down into the mousse. Add the remaining mousse on top of the strawberry slices, spreading it evenly to the sides of the pan. Place the second puff pastry circle on top of the mousse with the flat side up, and press it down gently. Refrigerate for at least 3 hours before serving.

TO SERVE Release the clamp on the springform pan and remove the rim. Carefully transfer the Napoleon to a serving plate, dust the top with the powdered sugar, and serve.

CHEF'S NOTES

◇ This dessert is most easily cut with a serrated knife.

◇ Pectin and gelatin sheets are available at specialty baking or gourmet stores (and see Sources, page 261). Frozen puff pastry is available at most supermarkets.

◇ For a shortcut, use the best-quality prepared strawberry jam you can find.

CREAMY CHURROS

FOR THE CHURRO DOUGH

1 cup plus 3 tablespoons bread flour

1 teaspoon salt

2 teaspoons granulated sugar

½ cup milk

½ cup butter, chopped

3 large eggs

FOR THE COATING AND FRYING

2 cups granulated sugar

1½ teaspoons ground cinnamon

Vegetable oil, for frying

CHURROS ARE THE MEXICAN EQUIVALENT of doughnuts, and our pastry team has perfected the art form. They are delightfully crunchy on the outside and creamy soft on the inside. Enjoy with a nice foamy capuccino or, for authenticity, a cafe con leche!

TO PREPARE THE DOUGH Combine the flour, salt, and sugar in a mixing bowl and set aside. In a saucepan, combine ½ cup of water with the milk and butter, set over medium-high heat, and bring to a boil. Immediately remove from the heat and add the flour mixture. Using a wooden spoon, stir the mixture until it forms a ball; it should appear very smooth. Transfer the dough to the bowl of an electric mixer fitted with a paddle attachment. Mix on low speed to start the cooling process.

While mixing, crack the eggs one at a time into a cup, remove any shell, and add each egg to the dough as it mixes, one at a time. Make sure each egg is well incorporated before adding the next one. When all the eggs have been mixed in, cover the bowl with plastic wrap and set aside at room temperature.

TO FRY THE CHURROS Line 2 cookie sheets with paper towels. Combine the sugar and cinnamon in a large shallow bowl. Place one-third of the dough into a pastry bag fitted with a #6 star tip. Pour the vegetable oil into large, heavy saucepan (ideally about 11 inches across by 7 inches high) until it reaches 3 or 4 inches up the sides. Set over medium heat and bring the oil to a temperature of 350°F. Carefully squeeze the dough from the pastry bag in 4-inch-long pieces into the hot oil, using the edge of the saucepan to separate the dough from the end of the star tip. Fry in batches of 4 or 5 pieces at a time, and cook for about 2½ minutes per side, turning with tongs 2 or 3 times.

Carefully remove the churros from the oil with the tongs or a slotted spoon and transfer to the paper-towel-lined cookie sheets to drain. While the churros are still warm, toss them in the cinnamon-sugar mixture to coat. Serve immediately; churros are best enjoyed while still warm.

CHEF'S NOTE

 As you cook the churros in the hot oil, try to maintain an even temperature; you may need to adjust the heat frequently to achieve this.

Chocolate-Apricot Nut Bars

FOR THE CRUST

4½ tablespoons powdered sugar, sifted

5 tablespoons butter, melted

1½ tablespoons honey

1¾ cups graham cracker crumbs

FOR THE FILLING

¾ cup sweetened shredded coconut

¾ cup semisweet chocolate chips

¾ cup chopped walnuts

¾ cup dried apricots, chopped

¾ cup slivered almonds

¾ cup chopped hazelnuts

¾ cup chopped pecans

6 tablespoons muesli

1⅔ cups canned condensed milk

¾ teaspoon vanilla extract

THESE CHEWY, DELICIOUS BARS BEGAN their eminent career as sustenance for our kitchen meeting coffee breaks. They made a healthier alternative to packaged granola bars and sweet cookies; due to popular acclaim, we have made wider use of their versatility. Now we serve these at the Waldorf=Astoria for holiday buffets, morning coffee, and afternoon tea-time snacks, and, sometimes, as a base for fruit tarts and chocolate cheesecake.

Preheat the oven to 350°F. Lightly butter a rimmed baking sheet or cookie sheet measuring about 15 inches by 10 inches (or use 2 smaller sheets).

TO PREPARE THE CRUST

In a small bowl, combine the sugar, melted butter, honey, and graham cracker crumbs. Pat the mixture onto the buttered baking sheet and transfer to the oven. Bake until golden brown, 5 or 6 minutes. Remove and let cool completely.

Increase the oven temperature to 400°F.

TO PREPARE THE FILLING

In a large mixing bowl, thoroughly combine the coconut, chocolate chips, walnuts, dried apricots, almonds, hazelnuts, pecans, and muesli. Distribute this mixture evenly onto the baked crust. In a separate mixing bowl, combine the condensed milk and vanilla. Starting along the outside edge, pour the liquid over the nut mixture, working in a circular motion toward the center as you pour. Try to distribute the liquid as evenly as possible. Transfer the pan to the middle rack of the oven and immediately turn the heat to 325°F. Bake for 25 to 30 minutes or until the top is slightly browned and the inside still soft. Let cool and cut into 24 bars.

Double Chocolate Cherry Cookies

SERVES 6 TO 12

(12 large cookies)

4 ounces bittersweet chocolate (preferably Valrhona), chopped

1½ ounces unsweetened chocolate, chopped

2 tablespoons butter

2 tablespoons crème fraîche

1½ teaspoons vanilla extract

1 teaspoon instant espresso powder

2 medium eggs

⅓ cup dark brown sugar

2½ tablespoons granulated sugar

½ cup all-purpose flour

¼ teaspoon baking soda

¼ teaspoon salt

6 ounces semisweet chocolate chips (preferably Valrhona)

¾ cup lightly toasted walnuts, chopped

¾ cup dried cherries

LET'S HEAR IT FOR MARY Ellen Miller of our pastry kitchen team! She helped adapt and test the recipes in this chapter for home consumption, which was no small feat. She is also responsible for this, our most popular Waldorf=Astoria cookie, which she developed years ago. (By the way, if you choose to hold your wedding reception at the hotel, it will be Mary Ellen who decorates your cake!) Thank you, Mary Ellen.

Preheat the oven to 350°F. Lightly butter a cookie sheet and set aside.

In the top of a double boiler (or in a metal bowl set over a small saucepan of simmering water), melt together the bittersweet chocolate, unsweetened chocolate, butter, and crème fraîche. Set aside and keep warm. In a separate bowl, combine the vanilla and espresso powder, whisking together to dissolve the espresso. Stir this mixture into the warm chocolate mixture and set aside in a warm place, being careful not to let it set.

In another metal bowl, whisk together the eggs, dark brown sugar, and granulated sugar. Place the bowl over a large saucepan of simmering water and whisk the mixture constantly until it is warm. Using an electric mixer, beat on high speed until the mixture is pale, 4 to 5 minutes. Fold the warm chocolate mixture into the egg mixture.

Sift together the flour, baking soda, and salt, and fold into the chocolate mixture. Stir in the chocolate chips, toasted walnuts, and dried cherries. Using a size 16 ice cream scoop (available at most kitchen supply stores) or a ⅓-cup measure, scoop the cookie dough onto the cookie sheet. Bake in the oven for 9 to 12 minutes, being careful not to overbake. These cookies are best served warm or the same day they are baked.

S ide dishes are the supporting cast for the star of the show—the main course. If the side is not well chosen, or if it contains assertive flavors, the main course can seem unexciting or overpowered. In my experience, home cooks have their favorite side dishes or accompaniments that are part of their familiar repertoire and do not understand why, sometimes, they just do not work. Forget for a moment what you like, and think instead about the main recipe you have chosen—its flavor profile, how it is cooked, its richness and degree of assertiveness. The goal should be to create a balance of flavors and textures that complement each other. For example, if you are serving something rich, such as steak, foie gras, or a protein with cream sauce, match it with a side dish that has some acidity, crispness, and a refreshing edge to it, such as blanched vegetables or greens sprinkled with a little vinegar or citrus juice.

If you are serving chicken or fish, which are low in fat and can dry out during the cooking process, plan on matching it with a side dish that is creamy or has a rich texture. Likewise, soft foods should be paired with something crispy. The same principle applies to contrasting flavors. Spicy foods can be matched with sweet ones, sweet foods with sour flavors, and salty dishes with earthy ones, for example. You can also play with differences in temperature, so that hot main dishes can be served with cold or room temperature sides or accompaniments. If you think about classic food combinations that work—bacon and eggs, steak and salad, sweet and sour pork, peanut butter and jelly sandwiches, warm apple pie and ice cream—each side of the equation complements and contrasts with the other, and neither partner overshadows or overwhelms. This is the thinking behind the food combinations that we serve here at the Waldorf=Astoria, and it explains many of the sides in this chapter. These side dishes may not be stars, but they play a vital supporting role in rounding out the plate as a whole.

Assistant Chef Saucier Tommy Thothongkum.

We do not actually offer peanut butter and jelly sandwiches on the Waldorf menus (although we would make you one if you asked). But if we did offer them, I would probably use superchunky and creamy peanut butter and a good-quality strawberry preserve on whole-grain toast. That would be a great combination of sweetness, saltiness, crunchiness, earthiness, and toasty goodness. Then again, I may have said too much and just given away my secret late-night indulgence!

GARLIC MASHED POTATOES

SERVES 6 TO 8

2 pounds Russet potatoes, peeled and quartered

2 tablespoons extra-virgin olive oil

¼ cup Chicken Stock (page 252)

¾ cup butter

3 tablespoons Roasted Garlic Purée (page 257)

Salt and freshly ground white pepper to taste

THERE IS NO BETTER MATCH with grilled or roasted chicken than this. The mellow roasted garlic and extra-virgin olive oil give these classic mashers a real flavor edge. I prefer Russet baking potatoes for mashed potato recipes because they are starchier, giving better texture, and are full of flavor.

Place the potatoes in a large saucepan, cover with salted water, and set over high heat. Bring to a boil, turn the heat to medium, and cook until tender, 25 to 30 minutes. Drain the potatoes and pass them through a ricer or a food mill into a large bowl (or mash by hand). Return the potatoes to the saucepan, set over low heat, and add the oil, stock, and butter. Mix in the garlic purée and season with salt and pepper. Cover the pan and keep warm over low heat until ready to serve.

BASIL MASHED POTATOES

SERVES 6 TO 8

2 pounds Idaho potatoes, peeled and quartered

3 cups packed fresh basil leaves

1 tablespoon Garlic Confit (page 257)

2 tablespoons extra-virgin olive oil

¼ cup Chicken Stock (page 252)

¾ cup butter

Salt and freshly ground white pepper to taste

COLORFUL AND DELICIOUS, THESE MASHED potatoes go wonderfully well with chicken, fish, or veal. Try serving a tomato salad or Tomato Confit (page 257) alongside.

Place the potatoes in a large saucepan, cover with salted water, and set over high heat. Bring to a boil, turn the heat to medium low, and cook until tender, 25 to 30 minutes.

While the potatoes are cooking, prepare the basil purée. Prepare an ice bath (page 260). Bring a saucepan of salted water to a boil, add the basil leaves, and blanch for 3 to 4 minutes until tender. Drain the basil and transfer to the ice bath to stop the cooking process.

When cool, transfer the basil leaves to a blender, add about ¼ cup of the ice water, and purée until smooth (there should be about ½ cup of purée).

Drain the potatoes and pass them through a ricer or a food mill into a large bowl (or mash by hand.) Return the potatoes to the saucepan, set over low heat, and add the garlic confit, oil, stock, and butter. Stir in the basil purée and season with salt and pepper. Cover the pan and keep warm over low heat until ready to serve.

SAFFRON POTATOES

SERVES 8

2 quarts Chicken Stock (page 252)

1½ teaspoons saffron threads

Salt and freshly ground white pepper to taste

2 pounds Red Bliss potatoes, peeled

THESE COLORFUL AND DISTINCTIVELY flavored potatoes match well with any chicken or fish dish that contains such Mediterranean ingredients as garlic, tomatoes, fennel, and fresh herbs. We have paired them with the Whole Roasted Red Snapper (page 173). Try cooking cauliflower florets the same way.

Place the stock, saffron, salt, and pepper in a large saucepan, set over medium heat, and bring to a simmer. Cut the potatoes into wedges (quarter them if the potatoes are small, or cut into sixths if they are large) and add to the stock. Return to a simmer and cook until fork tender, 20 to 22 minutes. Drain the potatoes and serve.

SEASONED HAND-CUT FRIES

[SERVES 8]

FOR THE SEASONING SALT

⅓ cup Kosher salt

½ tablespoon paprika

½ teaspoon dried oregano

⅛ teaspoon cayenne

⅛ teaspoon freshly ground white pepper

FOR THE FRIES

2 quarts vegetable oil, for deep-frying

3 large Idaho potatoes, about 6 inches long, unpeeled

2 teaspoons minced fresh parsley

AT THE WALDORF WE SERVE our fries wrapped in white butcher paper and placed inside a conical metal holder, but, believe me, they taste just as good on a plate! They are best known at the Waldorf=Astoria as the drop-dead accompaniment for our acclaimed burgers (page 184), but they will enhance most main course dishes. These fries may seem like a lot of trouble, but they are well worth it. One taste and you will realize what French fries should have tasted like all along.

Preheat oven to 350°F.

TO PREPARE THE SEASONING SALT Spread the Kosher salt onto a cookie sheet and bake in oven for 30 minutes (this will prevent the mixture from caking). Transfer to a small mixing bowl and add the paprika, oregano, cayenne, and pepper. Mix thoroughly and store in an airtight container.

Heat the oil in a deep fryer to 250°F; alternatively, use a large, deep saucepan or stockpot.

TO PREPARE THE FRIES Scrub the potatoes under cold running water and cut lengthwise into ¼-inch slices. Lay each slice flat on a cutting board and cut it into ¼-inch wide strips (the potato strips should be 4 to 6 inches long and ¼-inch thick). Place the potato strips in a bowl of cold water until you are ready to fry them.

Drain the potatoes and dry completely with paper towels. Carefully add to the hot oil in small batches, being careful not to splatter yourself. Cook the fries for about 15 minutes, then remove them with a slotted spoon and drain on paper towels; the fries should *not* be browned at this point. When all of the fries have been cooked, raise the oil temperature to 375°F. Cook the fries again in small batches for 4 to 5 minutes, or until they are golden brown and crispy. Remove with a slotted spoon and drain on paper towels lining a shallow bowl. Season the fries while still hot with about ½ tablespoon of the seasoned salt and the parsley.

CHEF'S NOTES

◇ The seasoned salt recipe yields about 6 tablespoons (you will need about ½ tablespoon for the fries). Store the rest in an airtight container and use whenever you feel the need for a seasoning that is a little different.

◇ Adding the fries to the hot oil in small batches ensures that the temperature of the oil does not drop too much, which keeps the fries crisp, not soggy.

CREAMED SPINACH

[SERVES 8]

4 cups heavy cream

2 tablespoons butter

Salt and freshly ground black pepper to taste

Pinch of nutmeg

2 pounds chopped frozen spinach, thawed and gently squeezed dry

SOMEHOW, NOTHING GOES WITH A steak quite like creamed spinach. This dish has been a staple at Bull and Bear for longer than I can remember. It is so simple and so good, it is one side dish that I have never had to change or take off the menu.

Pour the cream into a large saucepan and set over medium-high heat. Bring to a boil and reduce the cream by half, until 2 cups remain, about 10 minutes. Add the butter, salt, pepper, and nutmeg. Add the spinach and cook, stirring frequently, until it is warmed through. Adjust the seasonings and keep warm over low heat.

BULL AND BEAR POPOVERS

| SERVES 6 |

½ cup grated Romano cheese

8 large eggs

3 cups milk

Pinch of nutmeg

Salt and freshly ground white pepper to taste

2 cups all-purpose flour

¾ cup shredded Gruyère cheese

THIS IS A SIGNATURE SIDE dish at our Bull and Bear Steakhouse. What we call a *popover* is known as Yorkshire Pudding (or more colloquially, *Yorkie Pud*) in England, where it is indispensable with roast beef of all kinds. Of course, over there, cheese would not be found in authentic recipes—which, sadly, is their loss, because it provides a terrific twist on a classic.

———————

Preheat the oven to 400°F. Butter the inside of six 7-ounce ramekins (or a large-muffin tin) and sprinkle with some of the Romano cheese to coat; shake out and reserve the excess.

Break the eggs into a mixing bowl, add the milk, nutmeg, salt, and pepper, and whisk together. Slowly whisk in the flour. Pass the mixture through a fine-mesh strainer into a clean bowl. Place the prepared ramekins on a baking sheet and half fill each one with the batter. Sprinkle 1 tablespoon of the Romano cheese on top of the batter and add more of the batter until each ramekin is three-quarters full.

Transfer to the oven and bake for 10 minutes. Turn the oven to 350°F and bake for 50 minutes longer. Spoon the Gruyère cheese over the tops of each popover and bake for 10 minutes to melt the cheese. Remove from oven and let cool slightly. Remove the popovers from the ramekins and serve immediately. Alternatively, keep warm in a low oven (180°) or rewarm in a 250° oven.

COCONUT STICKY RICE

| SERVES 8 |

2 cups Calrose rice

2 cups canned unsweetened coconut milk

1-inch piece ginger, minced

1 stalk lemongrass, about 8 inches long

3 tablespoons unseasoned rice wine vinegar

½ tablespoon salt

THE IMPORTANT THING ABOUT THIS dish is to use the medium-grain (also called short-grain) rice, sometimes marketed as *sushi rice*. When cooked, it is stickier than long-grain rice, as the grains plump up and cling together, which is an ideal quality if you are making sushi or some other item that involves molding. It is also satisfying served as a side dish, especially when flavored with tantalizing Asian ingredients. It also pairs well with sea scallops or soft-shell crabs.

———————

Place the rice in a saucepan, add 2 cups of cold water, and bring to a boil over medium-high heat. As soon as the rice reaches a boil, stir in the coconut milk, ginger, and lemongrass, and turn the heat to low. Cover the pan and cook for about 20 minutes, or until the liquid has been completely absorbed by the rice; stir occasionally so that it does not stick to the sides of the pan. Remove from the heat and season with the vinegar and salt. Let sit, covered, for 10 to 15 minutes before serving.

CHEF'S NOTE

◊ You can make this side dish ahead; Pour it about ½-inch thick onto a rimmed cookie sheet, and refrigerate it overnight. The next day, cut out round, square, or diamond shapes, cover with foil, and heat slowly in the oven at 350° for 10 minutes.

PARSLEY RISOTTO

SERVES 8

FOR THE PARSLEY PURÉE
3 cups packed fresh parsley leaves
½ teaspoon salt

FOR THE RISOTTO
2 tablespoons olive oil
½ cup finely diced onion
¼ teaspoon minced garlic
1 cup Arborio rice
4½ cups Chicken Stock (page 252)
3 tablespoons mascarpone cheese
¼ cup grated Parmesan cheese
Juice of ½ lemon
Salt and freshly ground white pepper to taste

THE CREAMY, HERBAL QUALITY OF this risotto matches the Brown-Butter–Bathed Lobster dish on page 166 perfectly. Serve it with other shellfish or delicately flavored fish. You can also serve it on its own as an appetizer.

Prepare an ice bath (page 260). Place the parsley leaves in a saucepan of boiling salted water and blanch for 1 minute. Remove with a slotted spoon and transfer to the ice bath to stop the cooking process. When cool, drain the parsley and transfer to a blender. Add 3 tablespoons of the ice water and the salt, and purée at high speed (add a little more water if necessary). Set aside.

Pour the olive oil into a large sauté pan and set over medium-high heat. When the oil is hot and shimmering, add the onion and garlic and sauté until translucent, 3 or 4 minutes. Add the rice and stir with a wooden spoon to coat. Add ½ cup of the stock, bring to a simmer, and stir until the rice absorbs the liquid. Continue to add the stock in 1 cup increments, or enough to cover the rice, stirring until the rice absorbs the liquid each time before adding another cup. When all the stock is absorbed and the rice is al dente, add the mascarpone, Parmesan, and lemon juice. Season with salt and pepper and stir in the parsley purée. Serve immediately.

CORN RISOTTO

SERVES 8

4 large ears fresh sweet corn
7 cups Chicken Stock (page 252)
Salt and freshly ground white pepper to taste
¼ cup butter
½ cup minced onion
2 cups Arborio rice
2 cups dry white wine
½ cup mascarpone cheese

OSCAR'S CHEF MICHAEL BOURQUIN AND his team pair this side dish with grouper (page 158), and I have made it at home for guests to accompany the Brown-Butter–Bathed Lobster (page 166). Either way, it is delicious.

Cut the kernels from the ears of corn (there should be about 3 cups); reserve the cobs. Place 2 cups of the corn kernels in a saucepan and add about 2 cups of the stock, or enough to just cover the corn. Season with salt and pepper, set over medium-high heat, and bring to a boil. Turn down the heat to medium and simmer for 15 minutes. Strain the corn, reserving the liquid, and return the corn to the pan. Using a hand-held immersion blender (or use a blender or food processor), blend the corn to a porridgelike consistency; add a little more stock if necessary. Adjust the seasoning and strain through a fine mesh strainer into a clean saucepan. Keep warm over low heat.

Pour the remaining 5 cups of stock into a saucepan and add the reserved corn cobs. Bring to a boil, then turn down the heat and simmer for 15 minutes. Meanwhile, melt the butter in a separate saucepan set over medium-low heat. Add the onion to the butter and sauté until translucent, about 6 minutes. Add the rice and continue to sauté, stirring frequently with a wooden spoon, about 3 minutes. Add the wine, and season the rice with salt and pepper. Bring to a simmer and stir the rice constantly until most of the liquid has been absorbed, 5 or 6 minutes. Continue to add the hot stock in 1 cup increments, or enough to cover the rice, stirring until the rice absorbs the liquid each time before adding another cup. When all the stock is absorbed and the rice is al dente, about 18 to 20 minutes, add the reserved corn purée and remaining 1 cup of corn kernels and season with salt and pepper. Stir in the mascarpone and serve immediately.

BUTTERNUT SQUASH PURÉE

SERVES 6 TO 8

3½ pounds butternut squash (1 or 2),
cut in half lengthwise and seeded

2 tablespoons mascarpone cheese

Salt and freshly ground white pepper to taste

THIS SIMPLE RECIPE MAKES A great fall side dish—we pair it with rabbit (page 118). We also use this purée as a base for a ravioli filling and drizzle the ravioli with browned butter, prosciutto, and grated Parmesan cheese—a terrific combination.

Preheat the oven to 375°F.

Place both halves of the squash on a baking sheet, cut side down. Transfer to the oven and roast until tender when poked with a skewer, about 45 minutes. Remove from the oven and let cool. Using a spoon, scoop out the flesh and pass through a food mill or ricer. Transfer to a saucepan, set over medium heat, and cook until any liquid or moisture is evaporated, 8 to 10 minutes. Stir in the mascarpone, season with salt and pepper, and serve.

ASPARAGUS AND MOREL MUSHROOM RISOTTO

SERVES 8

FOR THE RISOTTO

1½ pounds asparagus

1 tablespoon butter

16 fresh morel mushrooms, cut in half lengthwise

Salt and freshly ground white pepper to taste

2 tablespoons olive oil

½ cup diced white onion

2 cups Arborio rice

¼ cup dry white wine

4 cups warm Chicken Stock (page 252)

¼ teaspoon grated lemon zest

2 tablespoons mascarpone cheese

3 tablespoons grated Parmesan cheese

THE CREAMY TEXTURE AND EARTHY flavor of this risotto is contrasted with the crispy Parmesan-Crusted Chicken recipe on page 190, and it also makes a great match with a firm, white-fleshed fish such as halibut or striped bass, as well as roasted loin of veal or pork.

Prepare an ice bath (page 260). Cut the tips and the white bottoms from each asparagus spear. Reserve the tips and stems and discard the bottoms. In a large saucepan, bring 2 quarts of salted water to a boil and add the asparagus tips. Cook until al dente, 3 to 4 minutes. Remove with a slotted spoon and transfer to the ice bath to stop the cooking process. When cool, drain and set aside. Add the asparagus stems to the boiling water and cook until tender, about 7 minutes. Remove the stems with a slotted spoon (reserve the cooking water), and transfer to the ice bath. When cool, place the asparagus stems in a blender, add about ¼ cup of the cooking water, and purée until smooth. Set aside.

Place the butter in a large sauté pan or skillet and melt over medium-high heat. When the butter melts and stops crackling, add the morels and season with salt and pepper. Sauté until the mushrooms are soft, about 4 minutes, and set aside.

Pour the olive oil into a saucepan and set over medium heat. When the oil is hot and shimmering, add the onion and sauté until translucent, 3 or 4 minutes. Add the rice and stir with a wooden spoon to coat. Add the wine and ½ cup of chicken stock. Bring to a simmer and stir until the rice absorbs the liquid. Continue to add the stock in 1 cup increments, stirring until the rice absorbs the liquid each time before adding another cup. When all the stock is absorbed and the rice is al dente, add the lemon zest, mascarpone, and cheese. Stir in 1 cup of the reserved asparagus purée; when warmed through, gently stir in the reserved asparagus tips and morels. Adjust the seasoning with salt and pepper. Serve immediately.

HERBED SPAETZLE

SERVES 8

5 large eggs
1½ cups all-purpose flour
1 teaspoon whole-grain mustard
2 teaspoons minced fresh tarragon
2 teaspoons minced fresh parsley
2 teaspoons finely sliced chives
1 teaspoon minced fresh thyme
½ teaspoon salt
Pinch of freshly ground white pepper

SPAETZLE IS A TRADITIONAL GERMAN side dish of tiny dumplings made from flour and eggs. The dough can be rolled out and cut into slivers, or pressed through a colander or sieve into boiling water, as in this recipe. Typically, spaetzle is served as a side dish instead of potatoes or rice. It is easy to make and highly versatile, and is also good made a day ahead then sautéed in butter, which gives it a deliciously nutty flavor.

In a mixing bowl, whisk the eggs until well beaten. Whisk in the flour and continue whisking until there are no lumps. Add the mustard, minced herbs, salt, and pepper, and set aside. In a large saucepan, bring 4 quarts of salted water to a boil. Set a colander over the pan and, with one hand, carefully pour a small amount of batter into the colander. With a rubber spatula in the other hand, scrape the batter through the colander; small drops of batter will fall through into the boiling water to form tiny dumplings. Cook the spaetzle for 3 to 4 minutes. When all the batter has passed through the colander, rinse the colander and use it to strain the spaetzle from the boiling water. Run cold water over the spaetzle to stop the cooking process and let drain.

LONG BEAN SALAD

SERVES 8

1 pound Chinese long beans, cut into 2- or 3-inch lengths
½ cup peeled and julienned carrots
1 tablespoon peanut oil
2 cloves garlic, minced
4 shiitake mushrooms, sliced
3 tablespoons soy sauce
2 tablespoons Thai chile sauce
3 tablespoons unseasoned rice wine vinegar
1 teaspoon hoisin sauce
2 teaspoons dark sesame oil
2 scallions, sliced
1 tablespoon toasted sesame seeds
¼ cup Crispy Ginger (page 103)

CHINESE LONG BEANS ARE ALSO called *yardlong beans* because of their size—they can grow to two feet or more in length. They are a popular ingredient in Southeast Asia, and are becoming increasingly available in the United States. The long green pods are crisp and tender with a great flavor when cooked correctly. We pair this dish, containing Asian flavors, with the halibut that is influenced by ingredients from the same region (page 156).

Prepare an ice bath (page 260).

Bring a large saucepan of salted water to a boil. Add the long beans and cook for 5 minutes. Add the carrots and cook until the long beans are tender but still firm, 2 minutes longer. Drain the beans and carrots and plunge them into the ice bath to stop the cooking process. When cool, drain and set aside in a bowl.

Pour the peanut oil into a small skillet or sauté pan and set over medium-high heat. When the oil is hot and shimmering, add the garlic and sauté for 1 minute. Add the mushrooms and sauté until the mushrooms are soft, 2 minutes longer. Transfer the mushroom mixture to the bowl containing the long beans and carrots.

In a separate bowl, whisk together the soy sauce, chile sauce, vinegar, hoisin sauce, and sesame oil until thoroughly combined. Pour the mixture over the cooked vegetables and toss well. Sprinkle with the scallions, sesame seeds, and crispy ginger.

ARTICHOKE, TOMATO, AND GARLIC FRICASSÉE

SERVES 6 TO 8

Juice of 1 lemon

20 baby artichokes, peeled and cut in half

3 tablespoons olive oil

3 cloves garlic, sliced

1 cup heavy cream

1 cup diced tomatoes

¼ cup minced fresh parsley

Salt and freshly ground white pepper to taste

CELEBRATE ARTICHOKE SEASON BY MAKING this wonderful side dish. We have matched it with lamb, but it will be equally tasty with any simple steak or chicken dish. If only large artichokes are available, buy eight and cut them into quarters.

Place 1 quart of water and the lemon juice in a large bowl. Use a paring knife to trim all the green leaves from the artichokes; trim any green parts from the stem. Cut out the fuzzy choke from the center of each artichoke. Cut the artichokes in half and transfer to the lemon water to prevent them from oxidizing and turning brown.

Pour the olive oil into a large skillet or sauté pan and set over medium heat. When the oil is hot and shimmering, add the garlic and sauté, continuously moving the pan, until the garlic turns golden brown, 4 or 5 minutes. Remove the garlic with a slotted spoon and reserve. Turn the heat to medium high. Drain the artichokes, add to the skillet, and sauté until they begin to turn brown, 3 to 4 minutes. Add the cream and the reserved browned garlic and cook until the cream is reduced and coats the artichokes, 3 or 4 minutes longer. Add the tomatoes and simmer until the liquid is thick enough to coat the back of a spoon, 3 or 4 minutes. Add the parsley and season with salt and pepper. Keep warm over low heat.

EGGPLANT, TOMATO, AND GOAT CHEESE TARTS

SERVES 8

FOR THE PIE CRUST

½ cup all-purpose flour

5 tablespoons cold butter, cut into small pieces

½ tablespoon salt

2 teaspoons fennel seeds

1 teaspoon sea salt

FOR THE FILLING

2 tablespoons olive oil

2 cups diced eggplant

1 teaspoon minced shallot

1 teaspoon minced garlic

2 tablespoons pitted Kalamata olives

3 large dried figs, diced

2 teaspoons minced fresh cilantro leaves

2 teaspoons minced fresh parsley leaves

1 teaspoon sherry vinegar

½ teaspoon honey

Salt and freshly ground black pepper to taste

5 ounces fresh goat cheese, cut into 8 slices

4 plum tomatoes, sliced crosswise

2 teaspoons sugar

MAKE THESE TARTS A LITTLE bigger and you have a terrific vegetarian appetizer. Leave as they are, or add 2 or 3 grilled Lemon-Thyme–Scented Shrimp (page 121) and you have an even more spectacular appetizer. Our guests love these, and yours will too.

Preheat the oven to 375°F.

TO PREPARE THE PIE CRUST Place the flour, butter, and salt in the bowl of a food processor and process for about 30 seconds or until the butter has broken into small pieces. With the machine running, add ¼ cup of cold water and continue to mix until the dough comes together and pulls away from the sides of the bowl, about 30 seconds longer. Remove the dough from the bowl and transfer to a floured work surface. Sprinkle a little flour on the top of the dough and roll out to a ¼-inch thickness.

Toast the fennel seeds in a dry sauté pan over high heat until the seeds are fragrant, 3 or 4 minutes. Remove from the heat and sprinkle the seeds and sea salt over the dough, pressing in with your fingertips. Cut the dough into 16 rectangles, about 2 inches by 3 inches, and place on a large cookie sheet lined with parchment paper. Bake in the oven until lightly browned, about 8 minutes. Remove and let cool.

TO PREPARE THE FILLING Pour the oil into a large skillet or sauté pan and set over high heat. When the oil is hot and shimmering, add the eggplant and cook for 3 or 4 minutes. Add the shallot and garlic and continue cooking, 3 minutes longer. Add the olives, figs, cilantro, parsley, vinegar, and honey, mix well, and remove the skillet from the heat. Season with salt and pepper.

Preheat the broiler.

TO ASSEMBLE Lay out 8 pieces of crust on a clean work surface and place a slice of goat cheese on each one. Evenly distribute the eggplant mixture on top of the goat cheese and cover with a second piece of crust. Arrange the sliced tomatoes in overlapping shingles over the top crust and sprinkle each tart with ¼ teaspoon of the sugar. Place the tarts under the broiler for 2 to 3 minutes, until the sugar bubbles and is caramelized. Serve the tarts warm or at room temperature.

CHEF'S NOTE

◇ To cut the goat cheese more easily, use a length of unwaxed dental floss.

SWEET-AND-SOUR EGGPLANT

SERVES 8

2 tablespoons olive oil

2 cloves garlic, minced

2 plum tomatoes, blanched, peeled, seeded,
and chopped (page 260)

1 large Italian eggplant, about 1 pound, diced

Pinch of ground cardamom

Pinch of ground turmeric

Pinch of ground cinnamon

Pinch of ground cumin

Pinch of cayenne

Pinch of paprika

2 tablespoons sherry vinegar

¼ cup honey

Salt and freshly ground black pepper to taste

1 tablespoon chopped fresh parsley

WE PAIR THIS WONDERFUL SIDE dish with the flavors of Moroccan lamb (page 75). It was created by Chef Saucier Peter Andino, who was inspired by similar Spanish and Turkish eggplant dishes. His version is also akin to dishes you might find in North African cooking. It can be served hot, cold, or at room temperature, and goes well with chicken breast, lamb chops, or leg of lamb, or even with the Lemon-Thyme–Scented Shrimp (page 121) instead of the Pepperade.

Pour the olive oil into a skillet and set over medium-high heat. When the oil is hot and shimmering, add the garlic and sauté for 1 minute. Add the tomatoes and sauté for 2 minutes longer. Add the eggplant and spices, and sauté for 3 minutes longer. Add the vinegar, honey, salt, and pepper, and simmer gently until the eggplant is tender, 2 to 3 minutes longer. Stir in the parsley, remove the mixture from the heat, and let cool.

CARAMELIZED ONIONS

ABOUT 2 CUPS

1 tablespoon olive oil

1 tablespoon butter

3 cups sliced Vidalia or other sweet onions

2 tablespoons sherry vinegar

Salt and freshly ground black pepper to taste

SERVE WITH GRILLED MEAT OF any kind— among several other uses, we top our burgers with them. For a fabulous soup, just add chicken stock to these onions, purée, and serve with toasted bread with some melted Gruyère cheese on top.

———————

Place the olive oil and butter in a large sauté pan and set over medium-high heat. When the oil is hot and the butter is melted, add the onions and sauté, stirring frequently, until they turn rich brown in color, 8 to 10 minutes. Add the vinegar and continue cooking until the liquid is just evaporated, about 2 minutes. Season with salt and pepper. Remove the pan from the heat and let cool.

PICKLED SLIVERED ONIONS

ABOUT 2 CUPS

2 small red onions, about 8 ounces each, thinly sliced

½ cup white wine vinegar

¼ cup unseasoned rice wine vinegar

1 dried bay leaf

6 juniper berries

THESE PRETTY PINK ONIONS BRIGHTEN any dish or salad. Serve them on top of a filet mignon or grilled chicken, and you may be surprised at just how good they taste.

———————

Place the onions in a nonreactive bowl. Pour the white wine vinegar and rice wine vinegar into a saucepan, add ¾ cup water, and bring to a boil. Pour the liquid into the bowl containing the onions and add the bay leaf and juniper berries. Cover with plastic wrap, let cool to room temperature, and refrigerate overnight.

PICKLED CUCUMBERS

ABOUT 1½ CUPS

1 English cucumber, rinsed well and sliced very thin

4 tablespoons unseasoned rice wine vinegar

2 teaspoons sugar

Pinch of dried red pepper flakes

Salt to taste

ENGLISH OR HOTHOUSE CUCUMBERS, the ones that often come wrapped in plastic to prevent water loss, are thin, long, very sweet, and have a firm, crisp texture. They are unwaxed, so they do not have to be peeled. Avoid cucumbers that are soft, wrinkled, or beginning to turn yellow.

———————

Place the sliced cucumber, vinegar, sugar and 1 tablespoon of water in a bowl and let sit in the refrigerator for at least 20 minutes and no more than 1 hour. Season with red pepper flakes and salt to taste.

TOMATO-BASIL SALSA

ABOUT 2 CUPS

2 large tomatoes, seeded and finely diced

1 tablespoon minced shallot

1 clove garlic, minced

1 teaspoon finely grated lemon zest

1 tablespoon julienned fresh basil

3 tablespoons finely diced ricotta salata (see Chef's Note)

3 tablespoons extra-virgin olive oil

1 tablespoon sherry vinegar

Tabasco sauce to taste

Salt and freshly ground black pepper to taste

THIS CLASSIC NEEDS NO MESSING with. We use it with eggs and prosciutto (page 34) and warm smoked salmon (page 66), which shows its versatility. At home, I like to put it on fresh mozzarella, and it is great in sandwiches or simply tossed with pasta.

———————

Place the tomatoes in a mixing bowl and add the shallot, garlic, lemon zest, basil, and ricotta. Toss gently until evenly mixed. Add the oil, vinegar, Tabasco, salt, and pepper. Keep refrigerated until ready to serve.

◇ Ricotta salata (in English, *salted ricotta*), a specialty Italian sheep milk cheese, is a firm, dry ricotta with a tangy yet mild flavor. Any Spanish Manchego cheese or feta make good substitutes.

MANGO-CILANTRO SALSA

ABOUT 2 CUPS

2 cups diced mango (from 2 or 3 mangoes)

2 tablespoons unseasoned rice wine vinegar

¼ cup olive oil

½ teaspoon minced fresh cilantro

Salt and freshly ground white pepper to taste

THIS STRAIGHTFORWARD TROPICAL accompaniment puts a refreshing twist on any grilled chicken or shrimp. We have paired it to good effect with lobster (page 103), and it will perk up any salad.

In a mixing bowl, combine the mango, vinegar, oil, and cilantro and season with salt and pepper. Serve at room temperature or chilled.

PEPPERADE

ABOUT 1¼ CUPS

2 tablespoons olive oil

2 tablespoons diced red onion

2 teaspoons minced garlic

½ cup seeded and diced yellow bell pepper

½ cup seeded and diced red bell pepper

3 tablespoons diced fennel bulb

2 tablespoons chopped black olives

1 tablespoon sherry vinegar

¼ teaspoon grated lemon zest

1 tablespoon freshly squeezed lemon juice

2 teaspoons minced fresh parsley

Salt and freshly ground black pepper to taste

THIS SIDE WORKS WITH JUST about everything— beef, lamb, chicken, calamari, shrimp, vegetables, even cheese. It is a great condiment to have on hand in the refrigerator.

Pour the oil into a large, heavy skillet and set over medium-high heat. When the oil is hot and shimmering, add the onion and sauté for 2 minutes. Add the garlic and sauté for 2 minutes longer. Add the yellow and red bell peppers and fennel and cook for 2 minutes longer. Add the olives, vinegar, lemon zest, lemon juice, and parsley, and season with salt and pepper. Keep warm until ready to serve (the pepperade can also be served at room temperature if preferred). It will keep for up to 4 days, covered, in the refrigerator.

PLUM CHUTNEY

ABOUT 2 CUPS

1 teaspoon butter

1 tablespoon minced onion

1½ teaspoons minced garlic

1½ teaspoons minced ginger

4 teaspoons sugar

¼ cup unseasoned rice wine vinegar

4 large red plums, pitted and diced

MAKE THIS CHUTNEY THE NEXT time you roast duck or sauté foie gras—its sweetness and acidity works magic with their richness. Chutneys can also be made with this recipe using peaches, pears, or even kumquats instead of the plums.

Melt the butter in a saucepan set over medium heat. When the butter stops crackling, add the onion and sauté for 2 minutes. Add the garlic and ginger and sauté for 2 minutes longer. Add the sugar, vinegar, and ¼ cup water, and bring to a boil. Turn down the heat to medium low and simmer the mixture until thickened, 3 to 4 minutes. Add the plums and continue to cook until the juice from the plums reduces to a syrup, 3 to 4 minutes longer. Let the mixture cool to room temperature and serve, or store in the refrigerator, covered, for up to 1 week.

251

SIDE DISHES, CONDIMENTS, AND BASIC RECIPES

GRILLED PINEAPPLE SALSA

[ABOUT 4 CUPS]

½ pineapple, peeled, cored, and sliced into ¼-inch rounds

1 ear fresh corn, husked

½ red bell pepper, seeded and finely diced

½ green bell pepper, seeded and finely diced

½ yellow bell pepper, seeded and finely diced

½ red onion, minced

½ jalapeño chile, seeded and minced

¼ cup minced fresh cilantro

¼ cup freshly squeezed lime juice

¼ cup olive oil

Salt and freshly ground white pepper to taste

THIS VERY COLORFUL SALSA WILL also brighten up fish or grilled chicken with its refreshing, zesty flavors. You can vary the spiciness by adding more (or less) jalapeño. If you are feeling brave, and you know your guests are tolerant of spicy foods, use a whole minced chile.

———

Prepare the grill or preheat broiler.

Place the pineapple slices on the grill or in the broiler, and cook over medium-high heat until grill marks are apparent, 2 to 3 minutes on each side. Remove the slices, finely dice, and transfer to a mixing bowl. Put the corn on the grill and cook until golden brown, about 10 minutes, turning often. Cut the corn kernels from the cobs and add to the mixing bowl. Add the red, green, and yellow bell peppers, the red onion, and jalapeño. Stir in the cilantro, lime juice, olive oil, salt, and pepper. Adjust the seasonings and serve immediately or cover and reserve at room temperature for up to 2 hours.

FENNEL-ORANGE MARMALADE

[ABOUT 1 CUP]

½ teaspoon fennel seeds

1 fennel bulb, sliced ¼-inch thick

1 cup freshly squeezed orange juice

½ cup Pernod

½ cup dry white wine

½ cup Chicken Stock (this page)

THIS SWEET AND FLORAL MARMALADE has a thick, saucelike consistency and pairs very well with sautéed scallops or shrimp. Add chicken stock and purée to make a magnificent soup.

———

Place the fennel seeds in a dry saucepan set over medium-high heat. Toast until fragrant, 3 to 4 minutes, shaking the pan frequently. Add the fennel bulb, orange juice, Pernod, wine, and stock, and bring to a simmer. Turn the heat to medium low and continue to simmer until most of the liquid is evaporated and the fennel is tender, 1 hour.

CHICKEN STOCK

[ABOUT 3 QUARTS]

(12 cups)

5 pounds chicken bones and necks

2 cups chopped onions

¾ cup peeled and chopped carrots

½ cup chopped celery

4 cloves garlic

10 sprigs fresh thyme

5 sprigs fresh parsley

1 dried bay leaf

6 black peppercorns

CHICKEN STOCK IS AN ESSENTIAL element in the cuisine at the Waldorf=Astoria. We use it not only in our soups and sauces, but also for our risottos, polenta, vinaigrettes, and some vegetable dishes. A well-made chicken stock should be clear from the slow cooking of clean bones, sweet from fresh vegetables, and aromatic from fresh herbs. At home, I freeze chicken bones whenever I am done with carcasses or cooked chicken pieces and make a stock when I have saved enough. After I have reduced it, I freeze the concentrated stock in ice-cube trays and transfer it to freezer bags; this process makes thawing out small quantities easy.

———

Wash the chicken bones and necks under cold running water (this process cleans the bones of any blood, making for a clearer stock). Transfer to a large stockpot. Add the onions, carrots, celery, garlic, thyme, parsley, bay leaf, peppercorns, and 5 quarts of water, using more or less water to just cover the ingredients. Set over medium heat and bring slowly to a boil. Immediately turn the heat to low and simmer the stock for 3 hours, skimming frequently to remove any impurities or fat.

Prepare an ice bath (page 260). With a ladle, pass the stock through a fine-mesh strainer lined with a double layer of cheesecloth, then into a large bowl placed over the ice bath. Do not ladle out any stock at the bottom of the stockpot that contains impurities. Discard the bones and vegetables.

Use the stock immediately or refrigerate for up to 3 days. The stock can be frozen for up to 1 month.

BROWN CHICKEN STOCK

ABOUT 3 QUARTS

(12 cups)

5 pounds chicken bones and necks
4 tablespoons vegetable oil
2 cups chopped onions
1 cup peeled and chopped carrots
1 cup chopped celery
1 head garlic, cut in half
½ cup tomato paste
4 sprigs fresh thyme
8 sprigs fresh parsley
1 dried bay leaf
6 black peppercorns
3 quarts Chicken Stock (page 252)

WITH MOST SAUCES, REGULAR CHICKEN stock works fine, but there are times when dishes such as sautéed or roasted chicken cry out for a sauce with a more complex stock base, which is when this recipe comes in handy. Like the Veal Jus (page 254), this stock is a reduction made from caramelized bones and vegetables.

Preheat the oven to 350°F.

Spread out the chicken bones and necks in a large roasting pan and mix them thoroughly with 2 tablespoons of the vegetable oil. Transfer the roasting pan to the oven and roast for 45 minutes.

Pour the remaining 2 tablespoons of vegetable oil into a large stockpot and set over medium-high heat. Add the onions, carrots, celery, and garlic, and sauté until browned, about 15 minutes, stirring continuously. Stir in the tomato paste and cook for 1 minute longer. Add the roasted bones and necks, thyme, parsley, bay leaf, peppercorns, stock, and enough water to just cover the bones (about 5 cups). Pour 1 cup of water into the empty roasting pan and deglaze by scraping the cooked solids off the bottom of the pan with a wooden spoon; add to the stockpot. Bring to a boil and immediately turn down the heat to low and simmer the stock for 4½ hours, skimming frequently to remove any impurities or fat.

Prepare an ice bath (page 260). With a ladle, pass the stock through a fine mesh strainer lined with a double layer of cheesecloth, then into a large bowl placed over the ice bath. Do not ladle out any stock at the bottom of the stockpot that contains impurities. Discard the bones and vegetables.

Use the stock immediately or refrigerate for up to 3 days. The stock can be frozen for up to 1 month.

VEAL STOCK

ABOUT 2 QUARTS

(8 cups)

5 pounds veal bones
4 tablespoons vegetable oil
2 cups chopped onions
1 cup peeled and chopped carrots
1 cup chopped celery
1 head garlic, cut in half
½ cup tomato paste
¾ cup chopped plum tomatoes
15 sprigs fresh thyme
12 sprigs fresh parsley
2 dried bay leaves
10 black peppercorns

VEAL STOCK IS THE FOUNDATION for most brown sauces and is something that we take pride in doing the traditional way at the Waldorf=Astoria. There is no shortcut to quality, and there is no such thing as a great sauce without a great stock. We lightly roast our veal bones (250 pounds per day, by the way), which brings a slightly sweeter stock with a more pronounced veal flavor than fully roasted bones. Not roasting the bones at all is another option, but further reduction is required to get as rich a flavor.

———

Preheat the oven to 350°F.

Spread out the veal bones in a large roasting pan and mix them thoroughly with 2 tablespoons of vegetable oil. Transfer the roasting pan to the oven and roast for 45 minutes.

Pour the remaining 2 tablespoons of vegetable oil into a large stockpot and set over medium-high heat. Add the onions, carrots, celery, and garlic, and sauté for about 15 minutes, stirring continuously until browned. Stir in the tomato paste and cook 1 minute longer. Add the roasted bones, tomatoes, thyme, parsley, bay leaves, peppercorns, and just enough water to cover the bones (about 5 quarts). Pour 1 cup of water into the empty roasting pan and deglaze by scraping the cooked solids off the bottom of the pan with a wooden spoon; add to the stockpot. Bring to a boil and immediately turn down the heat to low and simmer the stock for 4½ hours, skimming the top frequently to remove any impurities or fat.

Prepare an ice bath (page 260). With a ladle, pass the stock through a fine mesh strainer lined with a double layer of cheesecloth, then into a large bowl placed over the ice bath. Do not ladle out any stock at the bottom of the stockpot that contains impurities. Discard the bones and vegetables.

Use the stock immediately or refrigerate for up to 3 days. The stock can be frozen for up to 1 month.

VEAL JUS

ABOUT 1 CUP

1 tablespoon vegetable oil

6 ounces veal or beef scraps

1 clove garlic, crushed

½ cup thinly sliced shallots

1 dried bay leaf

2 sprigs fresh thyme

8 cups Veal Stock (page 253)

Salt and freshly ground black pepper to taste

2 tablespoons butter

THIS IS A WONDERFUL CONCENTRATED stock that we use as the base for many sauces at the Waldorf.

———

Pour the oil into a large saucepan and set over medium-high heat. When the oil is hot and shimmering, add the meat scraps and brown on all sides, about 10 minutes, stirring to ensure they are evenly caramelized. Add the garlic and shallots and sauté until caramelized, about 5 minutes. Add the bay leaf, thyme, and veal stock. Deglaze the pan by scraping the cooked solids off the bottom of the pan with a wooden spoon. Bring to a boil, turn the heat to medium low and simmer until the liquid is reduced to about 1 cup, about 1½ hours. Strain the liquid into a clean saucepan, discarding the solids, and season with salt and pepper. Keep warm; whisk in the butter when ready to serve.

FISH FUMET

ABOUT 2½ TO 3 CUPS

1 pound fish bones, thoroughly rinsed

1½ cups thinly sliced button mushrooms

2 or 3 shallots, thinly sliced

¼ bulb fennel, thinly sliced

½ stick celery, thinly sliced

1 clove garlic, peeled and crushed

½ teaspoon black peppercorns

2 bay leaves

5 sprigs fresh thyme

1 bottle (750 ml.) brut champagne or dry white wine

THE TERM FUMET REFERS TO a concentrated fish stock typically used for flavoring sauces, soups, or other dishes. The same word is occasionally used also for a mushroom stock.

———

Place the fish bones in a stockpot and add the mushrooms, shallots, fennel, celery, garlic, peppercorns, bay leaves, and thyme. Add enough champagne or wine to just cover the ingredients; if necessary, add some water. Bring the liquid to a boil and reduce the heat to medium low. Simmer for 50 minutes, strain, and let cool.

LOBSTER STOCK

2 tablespoons vegetable oil

3 pounds lobster shells

½ cup chopped celery

¾ cup chopped fennel

1½ cups button mushrooms

2 plum tomatoes, chopped

3 cloves garlic

1 dried bay leaf

5 sprigs fresh thyme

12 black peppercorns

1 cup dry vermouth

THIS FLAVORFUL STOCK IS IDEAL for making sauces to accompany lobster, shellfish, or fish. It can also be used to make seafood risottos or other rice dishes. Ask your fishmonger for frozen lobster shells; they are much cheaper than buying whole lobster and really do the trick.

Pour the vegetable oil into a stockpot and set over medium-high heat. Add the lobster shells and cook until bright red. Add the celery, fennel, mushrooms, tomatoes, and garlic and stir until softened. Add the bay leaf, thyme, peppercorns, vermouth, and 6 cups of water; add more or less water to just cover the ingredients. Bring to a boil, then turn the heat to low. Simmer for 50 minutes to 1 hour. Strain the stock and discard the solids.

Use the stock immediately or refrigerate for up to 3 days. The stock can be frozen for up to 1 month.

LAMB STOCK

5 pounds lamb bones

4 tablespoons vegetable oil

2 cups chopped onions

1 cup peeled and chopped carrots

1 cup chopped celery

1 head garlic, cut in half

¼ cup tomato paste

¾ cup chopped plum tomatoes

8 sprigs fresh thyme

5 sprigs fresh parsley

3 dried bay leaves

10 black peppercorns

USE THIS STOCK TO MAKE sauces with lamb dishes, or for braising less tender cuts, such as lamb shoulder (see page 203).

Preheat the oven to 350°F.

Spread the lamb bones in a large roasting pan and mix them thoroughly with 2 tablespoons of the vegetable oil. Transfer the roasting pan to the oven and roast for 45 minutes.

Pour the remaining 2 tablespoons of vegetable oil into a large stockpot and set over medium-high heat. Add the onions, carrots, celery, and garlic, and sauté, stirring continuously, until browned, about 15 minutes. Stir in the tomato paste and cook 1 minute longer. Add the roasted bones, tomatoes, thyme, parsley, bay leaves, peppercorns, and just enough water to cover the bones (about 5 quarts). Pour 1 cup of water into the empty roasting pan and deglaze by scraping the cooked solids off the bottom of the pan with a wooden spoon; add to the stockpot. Bring to a boil, then immediately turn the heat to low and simmer the stock for 3 hours, skimming the top frequently to remove any impurities or fat.

Prepare an ice bath (page 260). With a ladle, pass the stock through a fine mesh strainer lined with a double layer of cheesecloth, then into a large bowl placed over the ice bath. Do not ladle out any stock at the bottom of the stockpot that contains impurities. Discard the bones and vegetables.

Use the stock immediately or refrigerate for up to 3 days. The stock can be frozen for up to 1 month.

VENISON STOCK

ABOUT 2 QUARTS

5 pounds venison bones

4 tablespoons vegetable oil

2 cups chopped onions

1 cup peeled and chopped carrots

1 cup chopped celery

1 head garlic, cut in half

½ cup tomato paste

¾ cup chopped plum tomatoes

15 sprigs fresh thyme

12 sprigs fresh parsley

2 dried bay leaves

10 black peppercorns

Preheat the oven to 350°F.

Spread out the venison bones in a large roasting pan and mix them thoroughly with 2 tablespoons of the vegetable oil. Transfer the roasting pan to the oven and roast for 45 minutes.

Pour the remaining 2 tablespoons of vegetable oil into a large stockpot and set over medium-high heat. Add the onions, carrots, celery, and garlic, and sauté for about 15 minutes, stirring continuously, until browned. Stir in the tomato paste and cook for 1 minute longer. Add the roasted bones, tomatoes, thyme, parsley, bay leaves, peppercorns, and enough water to just cover the bones (about 5 quarts). Pour 1 cup of water into the empty roasting pan and deglaze by scraping the cooked solids off the bottom of the pan with a wooden spoon; add to the stockpot. Bring to a boil, then immediately turn down the heat to low and simmer the stock for 3½ hours, skimming the top frequently to remove any impurities or fat.

Prepare an ice bath (page 260). With a ladle, pass the stock through a fine mesh strainer lined with a double layer of cheesecloth, then into a large bowl placed over the ice bath. Do not ladle out any stock at the bottom of the stockpot that contains impurities. Discard the bones and vegetables.

Use the stock immediately or refrigerate for up to 3 days. The stock can be frozen for up to 1 month.

TOMATO COULIS

ABOUT 3 CUPS

2 tablespoons olive oil

¼ cup minced shallots

2 teaspoons minced garlic

8 plum tomatoes, cored, seeded, and diced (about 3 cups)

Pinch of dried red pepper flakes

½ teaspoon sherry vinegar

2 tablespoons extra-virgin olive oil

Salt and freshly ground black pepper to taste

THIS COULIS (SIMPLE PURÉE) IS a versatile, multipurpose sauce that can be paired with many fish or chicken dishes, or with vegetables and pasta.

———

Pour the olive oil into a saucepan and set over medium-high heat. When the oil is hot and shimmering, add the shallots and garlic and cook until translucent, 2 to 3 minutes. Add the tomatoes and red pepper flakes and continue cooking for 15 minutes, stirring occasionally. Carefully transfer the tomato mixture to a blender and purée until smooth. Add the vinegar and extra-virgin olive oil, season with salt and pepper, and purée again. Return to a clean saucepan and reheat when ready to serve.

ROASTED RED BELL PEPPER COULIS

ABOUT ½ CUP

1 large red bell pepper, roasted, peeled, seeded, and chopped (page 260)

3 tablespoons hot Chicken Stock (page 252)

1 teaspoon olive oil

1 clove garlic

Salt and freshly ground white pepper to taste

½ teaspoon Tabasco sauce, or to taste, optional

THIS IS ANOTHER VERSATILE SAUCE that can be used with chicken and fish dishes (for example, the grouper on page 158). Roasting the bell pepper gives it satisfyingly complex flavors; you may omit the Tabasco Sauce.

———

Place the roasted bell pepper in a food processor or blender and add the stock, oil, and garlic. Purée until smooth. Strain into a saucepan and warm the coulis. Season with salt, pepper, and Tabasco, if using.

ROASTED GARLIC PURÉE

ABOUT ⅓ CUP

3 heads fresh garlic

1 tablespoon butter

6 sprigs fresh thyme

1 tablespoon olive oil

Salt and freshly ground white pepper to taste

Preheat the oven to 375°F.

Standing each head of garlic on its side, carefully use a sharp knife to cut about one-half-inch off the top (or pointed) end to expose the cloves. Discard the tops and set the heads of garlic in a baking dish, cut side up. Evenly arrange the butter, thyme, and olive oil over the garlic, and season with salt and pepper. Cover the dish with aluminum foil and bake in the oven for about 1¾ hours.

Remove the garlic and let cool. Pour out any excess olive oil into a small bowl. Separate the heads of garlic into cloves and push them through a strainer into the bowl of olive oil, using a spoon to press down on the garlic and to scrape the cloves through the strainer. Mix the garlic and oil well and store in an airtight container in the refrigerator for up to 1 week.

GARLIC CONFIT

ABOUT 2 CUPS

2 cups garlic cloves, peeled

2 cups vegetable oil

2 sprigs fresh thyme

Preheat oven to 300°F.

Combine the garlic, vegetable oil, and thyme in a roasting pan or ovenproof dish. Cover with foil and transfer to the oven for 1 hour. Remove the pan from the oven and let cool.

Mash the garlic in the oil with a fork: store in an airtight container in the refrigerator for up to 1 week.

TOMATO CONFIT

ABOUT 3 CUPS

8 plum tomatoes, cut lengthwise and seeded

4 cloves garlic, finely sliced

1 tablespoon fresh thyme leaves (from 6 sprigs)

2 cups extra-virgin olive oil

THESE SLOWLY ROASTED TOMATOES ARE infused with flavor and really add a new dimension to dishes such as the Grilled Vegetable Timbales (page 142) and Parmesan-Crusted Chicken (page 190). The oil used to roast the tomatoes is also deliciously flavorful and can be used for vinaigrettes.

Preheat the oven to 300°F.

Place the tomatoes, cut side up, in a 2-inch-deep lasagna pan or similar size roasting pan. Arrange the garlic on top of the tomatoes and sprinkle with the thyme leaves. Drizzle with the oil, cover the pan with foil, and transfer to the oven. Roast for 2 hours, then remove from the oven and let cool. Remove the tomatoes from the oil, peel, and discard the skins. Use whole, or roughly chop, according to the recipe.

PESTO

ABOUT 1 CUP

1 tablespoon pine nuts

1 cup fresh basil leaves

1 clove garlic, chopped

¼ cup grated Parmesan cheese

¼ cup extra-virgin olive oil

Salt and freshly ground black pepper to taste

THIS IS A GREAT CONDIMENT to have on hand in the fridge or freezer. Use it on grilled bread for crostini, as a pasta sauce, or with eggs.

Preheat the oven to 350°F.

Place the pine nuts in a roasting pan and transfer to the middle rack of the oven. Roast for 6 or 7 minutes or until golden brown; watch closely as the nuts will burn easily if overcooked. Transfer the toasted nuts to a blender and add the basil, garlic, and cheese. Add the oil to the blender while pulsing. Blend until coarse, then season with salt and pepper. Keep refrigerated.

ACKNOWLEDGMENTS

There are a multitude of individuals I would like to thank for helping me produce this labor of love and influencing my career.

For the book itself, I thank my literary agent, David Hale Smith, for persuading us all to get the project underway, bringing the best in the cookbook business to my doorstep, and for his patience throughout the process.

Leigh Mastriani, my assistant, was instrumental in translating my handwriting into English and the recipes into a workable form. Her diligence and hard work helped turn the material into a book in just a few short months.

John Harrisson, my coauthor, brought his knowledge, expertise, and experience to bear on the entire process; his calm style and cool head meant the book came together beautifully in record time, all while he juggled his sons' pee-wee soccer careers.

I want to express my gratitude to the team at Bulfinch Press for making this book a reality. In particular, thanks to publisher Jill Cohen, for seeing the value in this project; associate publisher Karen Murgolo, for her support and expertise, and our editor, Karyn Gerhard, for her enthusiasm, eye for detail, gracious patience, and keeping John and me on track.

One glance through the pages of this book should be enough to explain why I am so grateful to photographer Ellen Silverman and her team. Ellen is a superb photographer and a consummate professional. Her assistant Christina Holmes provided lighting expertise that made all the difference, and prop stylist Marina Malchin brought her creativity and good taste to the images.

At the Waldorf=Astoria, thanks go to Eric Long, General Manager, for his support in getting this project off the ground and approved; Ed Russo, Operations Analyst, for his help in ironing out all the contractual details that can make or break a project, and for his belief in me; Matt Zolbe, Director of Marketing, who gave his usual support and enthusiasm, and helped with my coauthor's logistics; Grady Colin, Director of Food and Beverage, for his everyday partnership and support; and Jim Blauvelt, Director of Catering, for his time, his expertise, and his extraordinary knowledge of the history of the hotel. I would also like to thank Karen Krugel,

our public relations guru, and vice president at Lou Hammond & Associates, for her tireless support and belief in who we are.

When it came to contributing recipes for this book, a number of our culinary team stepped up in a big way: Peter Daledda, Executive Sous Chef; Jean-Claude Perennou, Executive Pastry Chef; Peter Betz, Chef Garde Manger; Michael Bourquin, Chef de Cuisine, Oscar's; Marc Melillo, Chef de Cuisine, Bull and Bear; and Cedric Tovar, Chef de Cuisine, Peacock Alley. Thank you all for your dedication to the Waldorf legacy, for your passion toward your craft, and your daily support toward our common goals.

Several other individuals participated when the time came to fine-tune and test the recipes in this book. Thank you, Dan Bendix, Sous Chef; Peter Andino, Chef Saucier; Tommy Thothongkum, Assistant Chef Saucier; and Jorge Valencia, Butcher. Special thanks are also due to Mary Ellen Miller, Pastry Assistant. Beyond these individuals, my sincere thanks go to the entire Waldorf=Astoria culinary team, especially Sous Chefs Ryan Alday, Joshua Bierman, Joe Bixel, Kenneth Braun, Dominick DiNapoli, Louis Giordano, Paul Hoti, Neil Joiner, Esteban Matos, Ian Wilson, and Pastry Sous Chefs Charlie Romano and Gnanasam (Samba) Sabaratnam. Without them we would have nothing to write about. These professionals work with such fervor and focus, I'm proud to be associated with them.

I would be remiss if I did not express my gratitude and appreciation to two previous Executive Chefs at the Waldorf=Astoria: Arno Schmidt (Executive Chef, 1970–80), the epitome of professionalism and who also possessed the wisdom to hire a certain young cook out of culinary school named John Doherty; and Kurt Ermann (Executive Chef, 1982–85), for preparing me for the humbling task as chef of this great institution.

Several other Waldorf=Astoria staff members contributed in various ways to the book: Stephane Dartois, Beverage Manager; Christophe Orlarei, Bull and Bear Manager; Evelyn Hsu of Peacock Alley; and Louis Quagliana, Assistant Director of Purchasing.

I have great faith in our purveyors and suppliers here at the Waldorf, and for this project, my particular thanks go to Atef Boulaabi of SOS; Marc Sarrazin of De Bragga & Spitler; and Barry Slavin of M. Slavin & Sons.

My thanks go also to Hilton Hotels leadership: Ted Ratcliff, senior vice-president, Hilton/Doubletree Operations East; Paul Keeler, vice president, Food & Beverage Operations; Gregory Dillon, vice chairman and director emeritus, Hilton Hotels; Carl Mottek, director emeritus, past president, Hilton Hotels Corporation; Jorgen Hansen, retired senior vice president, Hilton Hotels Corporation; Fred Kleisner, for having enough faith in me to appoint me as chef of this great hotel; and the late Eugene Scanlon, former Chef then general manager of the Waldorf=Astoria, for always believing in me.

On a personal note, my thanks to Chef Roger Souvereyns, for the years of friendship and inspiration; the late Chef Peter Berger, for taking me under his wing and giving me a head start; Bob Berenson, retired vice chairman and general manager of Grey Global Group, for his professional guidance and friendship; and Dr. Tim Ryan, president of the CIA, for keeping me involved with the development of young culinarians.

John Harrisson and I would also like to acknowledge the advice and contributions made by food writers Bryan Miller, Arthur Schwartz, and Michael Batterberry.

Finally, and most important, I wish to thank my wife, Donna, for all her support and for raising three wonderful children and putting in the long hours without me, and my children, Jenna, Patrick, and Evan, for the never-ending source of love that makes it all worthwhile.

DICTIONNAIRE

FRANÇAIS ANGLAIS

COLLECTION SATURNE

par Marguerite-Marie Dubois
Docteur ès lettres
professeur à l'université de Paris-IV

AVEC LA COLLABORATION DE
Charles Cestre †
professeur honoraire à la Sorbonne

Barbara Shuey
M.A. (University of California)

Denis J. Keen
M.A. (Cantab.)
Maître-assistant à l'université de Paris-III

W. Ian James
B.A. Hons. (London)
Licencié ès lettres
Senior Modern Languages Master
King Edward VI Grammar School Chelmsford

RÉVISEUR GÉNÉRAL
William Maxwell Landers
B.A., Ph. D.
Sub Dean. King's College. London.

RÉVISEURS ASSISTANTS
Roger Shattuck
B.A. (Yale)
Society of Fellows (Harvard),
Associate Professor of Romance Languages
University of Texas

Margaret G. Cobb
Editorial Consultant (New York)

nouvelle édition
augmentée
de 10 000 termes

Michèle Beaucourt
Jacqueline Blériot
David Jones

REED HIGH SCHOOL LIBRARY

LIBRAIRIE LAROUSSE

17, rue du Montparnasse, 75006 Paris.

GUIDE D'EMPLOI

ORDRE DES MOTS

a) Les mots-souches se présentent toujours dans l'ordre alphabétique. Toutefois, si deux mots-souches ont le même sens et des orthographes très voisines, ils peuvent être groupés (ex. : **autonomic** et **autonomous**). S'ils possèdent une double forme, la partie variable du mot peut être placée entre parenthèses : [**rhythmic(al)** signifie qu'on emploie *rhythmic* ou *rhythmical*]. Si deux mots-souches homonymes ont des étymologies différentes, ils font l'objet d'articles différents (ex. : **perche** [poisson] et **perche** [gaule]).

b) Les mots composés écrits avec un trait d'union sont traités à la fin du mot simple dont ils dérivent (ainsi **couvre-chef** est à chercher à **couvre**; **axle-arm** à **axle**). Les « mots composés » écrits en un seul mot sont à leur ordre alphabétique (ainsi **adman** est à son ordre, il n'est pas avec **ad**). Étant donné le flottement dans l'usage orthographique anglais concernant l'emploi du trait d'union, on aura intérêt, quand on aura cherché en vain un terme composé sous son premier élément, à se reporter à l'ordre alphabétique.

c) Les verbes français accidentellement pronominaux, dépendant d'un verbe simple, sont donnés à la suite du verbe simple (cherchez **se perdre** à **perdre**). Les verbes français essentiellement pronominaux, ne dépendant d'aucun verbe simple, sont traités comme des mots-souches à l'ordre alphabétique du verbe (cherchez *s'évanouir* à **évanouir [s']**).

d) Les verbes anglais suivis d'une postposition, présentant des sens qui les différencient du verbe simple, sont traités à la suite de ce verbe simple (cherchez **to go about** à **go**).

PRONONCIATION FIGURÉE

La prononciation figurée, placée entre crochets à la suite du mot-souche, est indiquée selon la méthode universellement connue de l'Association phonétique internationale. (Pour son utilisation pratique, consultez les tableaux détaillés I et II, p. XIII-XIV.)

INDICATIONS GRAMMATICALES

a) La nature morphologique du mot-souche est indiquée par une abréviation très claire. (Voir la liste I, p. VI.) Notez que n. (noun) désigne tous les substantifs anglais généralement neutres, alors qu'en français m., f., s. correspondent au masculin, au féminin, aux deux genres. L'emploi du précis grammatical (pour le français voir I, p. VII et pour l'anglais, II, p. VII) rend inutile l'indication des variantes régulières de genre et de nombre pour les mots-souches français. C'est pourquoi le masculin singulier du substantif est seul indiqué lorsque le féminin et le pluriel sont réguliers (**voleur** suppose le féminin *voleuse*; **cheval** suppose le pluriel *chevaux*). En revanche, le féminin et le pluriel irréguliers sont toujours mentionnés (*directrice, chacals*). Toutefois, afin de faciliter la tâche des lecteurs les moins avertis, le double genre des adjectifs français a été uniformément signalé. De même, on a précisé avec soin le genre des mots français traduisant des mots-souches anglais.

b) Le pluriel régulier des mots composés français, c'est-à-dire portant sur les deux termes (ex. : *des petits-enfants*), n'est jamais indiqué. En revanche, des précisions sont fournies pour les emplois irréguliers (ex. : **en-tête**, pl. **en-têtes**).

USERS' GUIDE

WORD-ORDER

a) Words are given in strictly alphabetical order. Head-words having the same meaning and closely related spellings may be found grouped under the same entry (e.g. : **autonomic** and **autonomous**). If they exist in two forms, the variable part of the word is, wherever possible, placed between brackets : thus **rhythmic(al)** means that the forms *rhythmic* and *rhythmical* are both found. If two head-words spelt identically differ in etymology, they are glossed as separate entries (e.g. : **perche** [fish] and **perche** [pole]).

b) Hyphenated compound words will be found entered alphabetically under their first element (thus **couvre-chef** is to be found under **couvre** and **axle-arm** under **axle**). Compounds written as one word are treated as headwords and will be found at their alphabetical place (thus **adman** is not under **ad**). However, as English usage varies considerably as to whether the two elements of a compound are hyphenated or merged into a single word, if a compound word is not to be found under its first element, it is advisable to look it up in its alphabetical place.

c) French pronominal (reflexive) verbs used also in a simple, non-pronominal form, are glossed after their simple verb forms (e.g. : **se perdre** is to be found under **perdre**). Exclusively pronominal French verbs are entered in the alphabetical order of the simple verb (e.g. : *s'évanouir* is to be found under **évanouir [s']**).

d) English verbs, followed by postpositions and differing in meaning from the simple verb, are glossed after the simple verb entry (e.g. : **to go about** is to be found under **go**).

PHONETIC TRANSCRIPTION

The pronunciation, shown between square brackets immediately after the head-word, is given in the phonetic transcription of the International Phonetic Association. (See I et II, p.XIII-XIV, for explanatory tables.)

GRAMMATICAL INFORMATION

a) The grammatical function of the head-word is made clear by an abbreviation placed after it. (See list on I, p. VI.) Note that n. (noun) is used for all the generally neuter English nouns, whereas, in the case of French nouns, m. corresponds to the masculine, f. to the feminine, and s. to both masculine and feminine genders. The inclusion of a grammatical summary (see I, p. VII for the French, and II, p. VII for the English sections) has made it unnecessary to show regular variations in gender and number in French head-words. For this reason only the masculine singular of the noun is given when the feminine and plural forms are regular (thus **voleur** presupposes the feminine *voleuse*; **cheval** presupposes the plural *chevaux*. On the other hand, irregular feminine and plural forms are always given (e.g. : *directrice, chacals*). However, to simplify matters for the less experienced, both masculine and feminine forms of adjectives in the French-English part have been indicated. Similarly we have shown the genders of French words translating English head-words.

b) The regular plural of French compound nouns, i.e. when both elements are affected (e.g. : *des petits-enfants*), is not given. On the other hand, irregular forms are indicated in the text (e.g. **en-tête**, pl. **en-têtes**).

c) Quand le même mot-souche revêt plusieurs formes grammaticales, ces différentes formes sont traitées dans le même article en alinéas distincts (à **personne** on trouve le substantif, puis le pronom; à **personnel**, l'adjectif, puis le nom).

d) La conjugaison des verbes français et anglais est indiquée par un numéro, placé entre parenthèses à la suite de l'abréviation d'ordre morphologique [**faire**, v. tr. (50); **cast**, v. tr. (32)]. Ces numéros renvoient aux indications grammaticales complètes, contenues, I, p. VIII pour le français, et II, p. VIII pour l'anglais.

c) When the same head-word has several grammatical functions, they are treated under the same entry in separate paragraphs (e.g. : under **personne**, the noun is followed by the pronoun; under **personnel**, the adjective is followed by the noun).

d) The conjugations of French and English verbs are given by a bracketed number placed after the abbreviation showing their grammatical function (e.g. : **faire**, v. tr. [50] ; **cast**, v. tr. [32]). These numbers refer back to the appropriate section of the grammatical summary. (See I, p. VIII for the French section, II, p. VIII for the English section.)

DISTINCTION DES SENS

Les traductions sont groupées par acception, les groupes étant séparés par le signe ‖. Ces acceptions sont très nettement différenciées, de façon que le lecteur puisse aisément trouver la nuance souhaitée, sans être obligé de lire l'article dans son entier. Si un terme présente des significations multiples, un tableau récapitulatif des sens numérotés est placé en tête de l'article (v. **faire**). Les sens courants sont traités les premiers. Viennent ensuite les sens dépendant des principales rubriques (en voir la liste, I, p. VI), puis les sens figurés et familiers, enfin les locutions. Les trois degrés de familiarité du langage ont été distingués pour éviter l'emploi de termes peu convenables. FAM. correspond à « familier mais admis », POP. à « populaire et vulgaire », ARGOT à « très vulgaire ou même indécent ». Afin de conserver à la version le ton juste, on s'est efforcé de traduire toute expression familière par un équivalent familier. Il convient de noter que l'abréviation FAM., précédant la traduction, s'applique au mot-souche traduit (par ex. : à **chap**, la rubrique « FAM. type » signifie que le mot-souche *chap* est familier); quand elle la suit, elle s'applique à la traduction elle-même [ex. : à **individual**, dont l'équivalent est « individu », la mention « type (fam.) » signifie que « type » est un mot français familier pouvant traduire *individual*].

DIFFERENTIATION OF MEANINGS

Translations are grouped according to meaning, the groups being separated by the sign ‖. Each acceptation is carefully distinguished, so that the user may readily find the desired shade of meaning without having to read through the whole entry. If a word has a great variety of meanings, a table with numbered references summarizing the meanings is inserted at the beginning of the entry (see **faire**). The usual meanings are given first, followed by those classified under abbreviations (see list on p. VI); figurative and familiar meanings are then listed, and finally, expressions. We have distinguished three categories of familiar speech, in order to guard against the use of unsuitable expressions in translation. FAM. corresponds to "familiar but accepted", POP. to "popular and vulgar", and ARGOT to "very vulgar or even indecent". For stylistic reasons, familiar expressions have, as far as possible, been translated by a familiar equivalent. It is to be noted that the abbreviation FAM., preceding the translation, applies to the head-word used in that sense (e.g. under **chap**, the translation "FAM. type" means that *chap* is an English familiar word); but when (fam.) follows the translation, it applies solely to the translation [e.g. under **individual**, the equivalent of which is "individu", the translation "type (fam.)" means that "type" is a familiar French word which can be used to translate *individual*].

ÉCLAIRCISSEMENT DES SENS

Afin que le texte soit aisément compris et que tout lecteur puisse choisir sans erreur la traduction juste, les nuances de sens ont été précisées par des mots d'éclaircissement, placés entre parenthèses à la suite des versions proposées [à **pernicieux**, correspondent : pernicious (action); noxious (effet); baneful (influence), etc.]. Le choix du lecteur se trouve ainsi facilité et les risques de contresens aussi réduits que possible.

CLARIFICATION OF MEANINGS

For the sake of easy and accurate reference, shades of meaning are made clear by words, illustrating usage, placed in brackets immediately after the proposed translations; thus under **pernicieux** are to be found : pernicious (action); noxious (effect); baneful (influence), etc. Such examples of usage help the user in his choice of words, and reduce the risks of mistranslation to a minimum.

EXEMPLES

Les exemples, rangés par ordre alphabétique, sont brefs et donnés le plus souvent sous une forme idiomatique, afin d'offrir au chercheur un florilège d'expressions toutes faites et de formules courantes. Quand le choix existe entre plusieurs termes, l'emploi de l'indication (ou) dans la section française et de (or) dans la partie anglaise permet d'éviter la répétition d'un membre de phrase [*to look ill* (ou) *unwell* signifie qu'on peut dire *to look ill* ou *to look unwell*]. Dans le même ordre d'idées, au lieu de refaire un exemple pour chaque mot, on a groupé les formes similaires (*marché aux fleurs, au poisson, à la volaille*, « flower, fish, poultry market », signifie que *marché au poisson* se traduit par « fish market »).

EXAMPLES

The examples, arranged in alphabetical order, are short, and generally given in an idiomatic form so as to offer the user a wide range of ready-made expressions and common phrases. When there is a choice of several terms, the indications (ou) in the French-English part, and (or) in the English-French part, save unnecessary repetition of a phrase : thus *to look ill* (ou) *unwell* means that one may use *to look ill* or *to look unwell*. In the same way, similar forms have been grouped together : thus *marché aux fleurs, au poisson, à la volaille*, "flower, fish, poultry market", means that *marché au poisson* is translated by "fish market".

AMÉRICANISMES

Le développement de l'américain en tant que langue indépendante nous a conduits à introduire dans cet ouvrage les formes propres à l'anglais d'Amérique. Les américanismes sont précédés de la mention U. S., dans la mesure où ils ne sont pas encore entièrement adoptés par l'anglais insulaire. Les variantes orthographiques américaines font l'objet d'un paragraphe général, II, p. XII ; certaines sont indiquées à l'intérieur du dictionnaire, quand elles sont très éloignées, dans l'ordre alphabétique, de la forme anglaise correspondante.

AMERICANISMS

The growth of American as an independent language has led to the inclusion in this work of characteristic forms of American English. Americanisms are preceded by the abbreviation U. S., wherever they have not been completely adopted by British English. Variations in American spelling are dealt with in general terms on II. p. XII; variants are included in the dictionary when their alphabetical place is too far from that of the corresponding English form.

ABRÉVIATIONS ET SIGLES

Les abréviations et sigles les plus usuels ont été classés à leur ordre alphabétique. Dans la partie française, on a indiqué leur genre (ainsi **H. L. M.** est noté « *m.* ou *f.* »). La transcription phonétique indique s'ils se prononcent en un seul mot (comme **U. N. E. S. C. O.** [ju'neskou]) ou en détachant chaque lettre.

ABBREVIATIONS AND ACRONYMS

The most common abbreviations and acronyms are included in their alphabetical place. In the French section their gender is shown (thus **H. L. M.** is followed by the mention « *m.* or *f.* »). The phonetic transcription indicates whether they are pronounced as a single word (as with **U. N. E. S. C. O.** [ju'neskou]) or whether each letter is pronounced separately.

TABLEAUX

Des tableaux hors texte offrent au lecteur soucieux de synthèse de vastes centres d'intérêt où se trouvent groupés les principaux éléments du vocabulaire concernant une notion maîtresse (telle que automobile, machine).

WORD-LISTS

Full-page word-lists group together the essential vocabulary of a number of specialized subjects, e.g. car and machines. (Cf. p. XVI.)

ILLUSTRATIONS

Des illustrations, effectuées avec le plus grand soin, permettent enfin d'associer l'image au mot et constituent le plus heureux des moyens mnémotechniques.

ILLUSTRATIONS

Accurate illustrations provide the user with an effective and interesting method of associating words and images, and of enlarging his vocabulary.

———

Ma reconnaissance la plus vive va tout d'abord à mes collaborateurs anglais, américains et français qui ont rédigé une partie de cet ouvrage dans un inappréciable esprit d'équipe et dont la haute compétence confère à ce volume un caractère de sérieux et de sécurité. A cet égard, l'apport du Dr Landers, qui a revu l'ensemble du travail, apparaît comme primordial, tandis qu'au professeur R. Shattuck, à Miss Shuey et à Mrs. Cobb est dû plus particulièrement l'aspect américain du dictionnaire. L'expérience du regretté M. Cestre, la subtilité de Mr. Keen, la précision de Mr. James ont abouti à des pages denses et nuancées. Je remercie également les nombreux professeurs et étudiants qui m'ont apporté leur concours sur leurs suggestions, tout spécialement le Dr. King, professeur à l'Université de Londres et Mr. J. C. Palmes, Librarian of the Royal Institute of British Architects.

M.-M. DUBOIS

———

My warmest thanks are due in the first place to my English, American and French colleagues who have shown the very greatest spirit of co-operation in composing part of the text, and whose competence and scholarship have made this dictionary a sound and reliable work of reference. In this respect, special mention must be made of the invaluable contribution of Dr. Landers who has read through the entire work both in manuscript- and proof-form; while for the American side of the dictionary we are particularly indebted to Prof. R. Shattuck, to Miss Shuey and to Mrs. Cobb. The long experience of M. Cestre, the subtle mind of Mr. Keen, and Mr. James's predilection for accuracy, have helped to make this work one filled with useful linguistic information, and rich in shades of meaning. I also wish to thank a very large number of teachers and students for their assistance and suggestions, especially Dr. King, of London University and Mr. J. C. Palmes, Librarian of the Royal Institute of British Architects.

M.-M. DUBOIS

ABBREVIATIONS

abrév.	abréviation	abbreviation	n.	nom anglais	noun
adj.	adjectif	adjective	pers.	personnel	personal
adv.	adverbe	adverb	pl.	pluriel	plural
art.	article	article	poss.	possessif	possessive
aux.	auxiliaire	auxiliary	p.p.	participe passé	past participle
comp.	comparatif	comparative	p.pr.	participe présent	present participle
cond.	conditionnel	conditional	pr.	présent	present
conj.	conjonction	conjunction	préf.	préfixe	prefix
déf.	défini	definite	prép.	préposition	preposition
défect.	défectif	defective	pron.	pronom, pronominal	pronoun, pronominal
démonstr.	démonstratif	demonstrative	prop.	propre	proper, literal
dimin.	diminutif	diminutive	qqch.	quelque chose	something
f.	féminin	feminine	qqn	quelqu'un	someone
imp.	imparfait	imperfect	réfl.	réfléchi	reflexive
imper.	impératif	imperative	rel.	relatif	relative
impers.	impersonnel	impersonal	s.	substantif français masculin ou féminin	substantive
ind.	indicatif	indicative			
indéf.	indéfini	indefinite	s.o.	quelqu'un	someone
interj.	interjection	interjection	sth.	quelque chose	something
interrog.	interrogation	interrogation	sup.	superlatif	superlative
intr.	intransitif	intransitive	tr.	transitif	transitive
invar.	invariable	invariable	U.S.	Etats-Unis	United States
m.	masculin	masculine	v.	verbe	verb

LABELS

AGRIC.	Agriculture, économie rurale.	Agriculture, husbandry.	GRAMM.	Grammaire, linguistique.	Grammar, linguistics.
ARCHIT.	Architecture, construction.	Architecture, building.	INFORM.	Informatique.	Data processing.
ARGOT	Argot, termes indécents.	Slang; not in decent use.	JUR.	Jurisprudence, administration, politique, sociologie.	Jurisprudence, administration, politics, sociology.
ARTS	Arts.	Arts.			
ASTRON.	Astronomie.	Astronomy.	LOC.	Locution.	Phrase.
ASTRONAUT.	Astronautique.	Astronautics.	MATH.	Mathématiques.	Mathematics.
AUTOM.	Automobilisme.	Automobilism.	MÉD.	Médecine, biologie, hygiène, pharmacie, art vétérinaire.	Medicine, biology, hygiene, pharmacy, veterinary science.
AVIAT.	Aviation, aéronautique.	Aviation, aeronautics.			
BLAS.	Blason.	Heraldry.	MILIT.	Militaire.	Military.
BOT.	Botanique.	Botany.	MUS.	Musique.	Music.
CH. DE F.	Chemin de fer.	Railways.	NAUT.	Art nautique, marine.	Nautical, navy.
CHIM.	Chimie.	Chemistry.	PHILOS.	Philosophie.	Philosophy.
CINEM.	Cinématographie.	Cinematography.	PHYS.	Physique.	Physics.
COMM.	Commerce.	Commerce, trade.	POP.	Populaire.	Popular.
CULIN.	Art culinaire, nourriture.	Culinary.	PSYCH.	Psychologie, psychiatrie, psychanalyse.	Psychology, psychiatry, psychoanalysis.
ECCLES.	Église, religion.	Ecclesiastical.	RADIO.	Radiophonie, télévision.	Radiophony, television.
ELECTR.	Électricité, électronique.	Electricity, electronics.	SPORTS	Sports, jeux.	Sports, games.
FAM.	Familier.	Familiar, colloquial.	TECHN.	Technologie, mécanique, industrie.	Technology, mechanics, industry.
FIG.	Figuré.	Figuratively.			
FIN.	Finances.	Finance.	THEATR.	Théâtre.	Theatre.
GEOGR.	Géographie.	Geography.	†	Vieux. Histoire.	Archaism. History.
GÉOL.	Géologie.	Geology.	ZOOL.	Zoologie.	Zoology.

THE ESSENTIALS OF FRENCH GRAMMAR

SENTENCE-BUILDING

Interrogation. — When the subject is a pronoun, place it after the verb, and in compound tenses, between the auxiliary and the verb. Ex. : Do you speak?, *parlez-vous?*; did you speak?, *avez-vous parlé?* With verb ending in a vowel, put an euphonic *t* before a third person pronoun. Ex. : Did he speak?, *a-t-il parlé?*; does he speak?, *parle-t-il?* When the subject is a noun, add a pronoun. Ex. : Does Paul speak?, *Paul parle-t-il?*

A handy way of putting questions is merely to place *est-ce que* before the positive sentence. Ex. : Does he write?, *est-ce qu'il écrit?*

Objective pronouns. — They are placed after the verb only in the imperative of reflexive verbs : sit down, *asseyez-vous*. They come before the verb even in compound tenses : he had said it to me, *il me l'avait dit*. The verb should be separated from its auxiliary only by an adverb, or by a pronoun subject in an interrogative sentence. Ex. : *il a bien fait; avez-vous mangé?*

THE ARTICLE

The **definite article** is *le* (m.), *la* (f.), *les* (m. f. pl.). Ex. : the dog, *le chien;* the girl, *la fille;* the cats, *les chats. Le, la* are shortened to *l'* before a vowel or a mute *h*. Ex. : the man, *l'homme;* the soul, *l'âme* (but *le héros*). The **indefinite article** is *un, une*. Ex. : a boy, *un garçon;* a woman, *une femme*.

The **partitive article,** *du* (m.), *de la* (f.), *des* (pl.), is used in sentences like : take some bread, *prenez du pain;* here are pears, *voici des poires*.

THE NOUN

Plural. — The plural is generally formed in s, as in English.

Nouns in s, x and z do not change in the plural.

Nouns in **au** and **eu** (except *bleu*) and some in **ou** (*bijou, caillou, chou, genou, hibou, joujou, pou*) form their plural in **x**. Ex. : *chou* (cabbage), *choux; jeu* (game), *jeux*.

Nouns in **al** and **ail** form their plural in **aux**. Ex. : *cheval* (horse), *chevaux; travail* (work), *travaux*.

Aïeul, ciel and *œil* become *aïeux, cieux, yeux* in the ordinary meaning.

Gender of nouns. — There are no neuter nouns in French. Nearly all nouns ending in a mute e are feminine, except those in **isme, age,** generally masculine, and **iste** (the latter being often either m. or f.). — Nearly all nouns ending in a consonant or a vowel other than a mute **e** are masculine, except nouns in **ion** and **té** (*été, pâté* are m.).

Feminine. — The feminine is generally formed by adding e to the masculine. Ex. : *parent* (relative), *parente; ami* (friend), *amie*.

Nouns in **er** form their feminine in **ère.** Ex. : *laitier* (milkman), *laitière*. Nouns in **en, on** form their feminine in **enne, onne.** Ex. : *chien* (dog), *chienne; lion, lionne*. Nouns in **eur** form their feminine in **euse,** except those in **ateur,** which give **atrice.** Ex. : *acheteur, acheteuse; admirateur, admiratrice*. A few words in e form their feminine in **esse** : *maître, maîtresse*.

N. B. — Only irregular forms of the plural or of the feminine are given in the dictionary.

THE ADJECTIVE

Plural. — The plural is generally formed in s.

Adjectives in s or x do not change. Adjectives in **al** form their plural in **aux** (except *bancal, fatal, final, glacial, natal, naval* which take an s). Ex. : *principal, principaux; naval, navals*.

Feminine. — The feminine is generally formed by adding **e** to the masculine form. Ex. : *élégant, élégante; poli, polie.* Adjectives in f change f into **ve.** Ex. : *Vif, vive.* Those in x change x into **se.** Ex. : *heureux, heureuse* (except : *doux, douce; faux, fausse; roux, rousse;* and *vieux, vieille*). — Adjectives in **er** form their feminine in **ère.** Ex. : *amer, amère.* — Those in **el, eil, en, et, on** double the final consonant before adding e. Ex. : *bel, belle; bon, bonne; ancien, ancienne*.

N. B. — Only irregular forms of the plural or of the feminine are given in the dictionary.

Comparative. — « More » or the ending « -er » of adjective should be translated by *plus*, « less » by *moins*, and « than » by *que*. Ex. : More sincere, *plus sincère;* stronger, *plus fort;* less good than, *moins bon, moins bonne que.* « As... as » should be translated by *aussi... que;* « as much... as » and « as many... as » by *autant... que;* « not so... as » by *pas si... que;* « not so much (many)... as » by *pas tant... que*.

Superlative. — « The most » or the ending « -est » should be translated by *le plus.* Ex. : The poorest, *le plus pauvre;* the most charming, *le plus charmant.* « Most » is in French *très.* Ex. : Most happy, *très heureux*.

Irregular forms. — Better, *meilleur;* the best, *le meilleur;* smaller, *moindre;* the least, *le moindre;* worse, *pire;* the worst, *le pire*.

Cardinal numbers. — *Un, deux, trois, quatre, cinq, six, sept, huit, neuf, dix, onze, douze, treize, quatorze, quinze, seize, dix-sept, dix-huit, dix-neuf, vingt, vingt et un, vingt-deux; trente et un; quarante, cinquante, soixante; soixante-dix, quatre vingts, quatre-vingt-dix; cent, cent un, cent deux; deux cents, trois cents; mille, un million, un milliard*.

Vingt and *cent* are invariable when immediately followed by another number. Ex. : *Quatre-vingt-trois ans; deux cent douze francs*.

Mille is invariable (in dates, it is written *mil*).

Ordinal numbers. — *Premier, deuxième, troisième, quatrième, cinquième, sixième, septième, huitième, neuvième, dixième, onzième, douzième, treizième, quatorzième, quinzième, seizième, dix-septième, dix-huitième, dix-neuvième; vingtième, vingt et unième, vingt-deuxième; trentième, quarantième; centième, deux centième; millième; millionième*

Demonstrative adjectives. — « This » and « that » are generally translated by *ce*, *cet* (m.), *cette* (f.), *ces* (pl.) [*ce* before a masc. noun beginning with a consonant or an aspirate *h*; *cet* before a masc. word beginning with a vowel or a mute *h*]. The opposition between « this » and « that » may be emphasized by adding -*ci* or -*là*. Ex. : this book, *ce livre-ci*; those men, *ces hommes-là*.

« That of » should be translated by *celui* (f. *celle*; pl. *ceux*, *celles*) *de*; « he who », « the one which », « those or they who » by *celui* (*celle*, *ceux*, *celles*) *qui*.

Possessive adjectives. — « My » is in French *mon* (m.), *ma* (f.), *mes* (pl.). « Your » (for « thy ») is *ton*, *ta*, *tes*; « his », « her », « its » are *son*, *sa*, *ses* (agreeing with the following noun). « Our » is *notre* (m. f.), *nos* (pl.) ; « your » is *votre*, *vos*; « their » is *leur* (m. f.), *leurs* (pl.). Ex. : His king, *son roi*; his sister, *sa sœur*; his books, *ses livres*; her father, *son père*; her mother, *sa mère*.

THE PRONOUN

Personal pronouns (subject). — *Je*, *tu*, *il*, *elle* (f.) ; pl. *nous*, *vous*, *ils*, *elles* (f.). Ex. : You speak, *tu parles* (*vous parlez*) ; she says, *elle dit*.

The second person singular (*tu*, *toi*, *ton*, *ta*, *tes*, *le tien*, etc.) indicating intimacy, is used between members of the same family, at school, between soldiers and close friends.

Personal pronouns (direct object). — *Me*, *te*, *le*, *la* (f.) ; pl. *nous*, *vous*, *les*. Ex. : I see her, *je la vois*; I see him, *je le vois*; I see it, *je le vois* (the same pronoun is used for masculine and neuter in most cases).

Personal pronouns (indirect object; dative). — *Me*, *te*, *lui* (m. f.) ; pl. *nous*, *vous*, *leur*. Ex. : He speaks to her, *il lui parle*.

Personal pronouns (after a preposition). — *Moi*, *toi*, *lui*, *elle* (f.) ; pl. *nous*, *vous*, *eux*. They are also used emphatically : I think, *moi je pense*.

Reflexive pronouns. — *Me*, *te*, *se*; pl. *nous*, *vous*, *se*. Ex. : they flatter each other, *ils se flattent*.

Possessive pronouns. — *Le mien* (f. *la mienne*; pl. *les miens*, *les miennes*) ; *le tien* (f. *la tienne*; pl. *les tiens*, *les tiennes*) ; *le sien* (f. *la sienne*; pl. *les siens*, *les siennes*) ; *le nôtre* (f. *la nôtre*; pl. *les nôtres*) ; *le vôtre* (f. *la vôtre*; pl. *les vôtres*) ; *le leur* (f. *la leur*; pl. *les leurs*). Ex. : I have lost my watch, lend me yours, *j'ai perdu ma montre*, *prêtez-moi la vôtre*.

N. B. — This book is mine, his, hers... *Ce livre est à moi*, *à toi* (*à vous*), *à lui*, *à elle*... See Personal pronouns (after a preposition).

Relative pronouns. — « Who » is translated by *qui*; « whom » by *que* (*qui* after a preposition) ; « whose » by *dont*; « which » by *qui* (subject) or *que* (object). Ex. : The man who comes, *l'homme qui vient*; the girl whom I see, *la fille que je vois*; the author whose book I read, *l'auteur dont je lis le livre*; the books which (or that) I read, *les livres que je lis*.

N. B. — After a preposition « which » should be translated by *lequel* (m.), *laquelle* (f.), *lesquels* (m. pl.), *lesquelles* (f. pl.) ; « of which » by *duquel*, *de laquelle*, *desquels*, *desquelles*; « to which » by *auquel*, *à laquelle*, *auxquels*, *auxquelles*.

Interrogative pronouns. — « Who », « whom » are translated by *qui*; « what » by *que* (object). « What », when adjective, should be translated by *que*, *quelle*, *quels*, *quelles*; when subject by *qu'est-ce qui*. Ex. : Who came?, *qui est venu?*; what do you say?, *que dis-tu?*; what time is it?, *quelle heure est-il?*; what happened?, *qu'est-ce qui est arrivé?*

THE ADVERBS

Most French adverbs are formed by adding **ment** to the feminine form of the corresponding adjective. Ex. : happily, *heureusement*.

Adjectives in **ant** form their adverbs in **amment**, and those in **ent** in **emment**. Ex. : abundantly, *abondamment*; patiently, *patiemment*.

Negative adverbs and pronouns. — « Not » should be translated by *ne... personne*, « nothing » by *ne... rien*, « nowhere » by *ne... nulle part*. Ex. : I do not speak, *je ne parle pas*; he never comes, *il ne vient jamais*. « Nobody », when subject, should be translated by *personne ne*, and « nothing » by *rien ne*. Ex. : Nobody laughs, *personne ne rit*; nothing stirred, *rien n'a bougé*.

THE VERBS

French regular verbs are generally grouped in four classes or conjugations ending in **er**, **ir**, **oir**, and **re**.

Compound tenses are conjugated with the auxiliary *avoir* and the past participle, except reflexive verbs and the most usual intransitive verbs (like *aller*, *arriver*, *devenir*, *partir*, *rester*, *retourner*, *sortir*, *tomber*, *venir*, etc.) which are conjugated with *être*. Ex. : He spoke, *il a parlé*; he came, *il est venu*.

The French past participle. — It always agrees with the noun to which it is either an attribute or an adjective. Ex. : The boy was punished, *le petit garçon fut puni*; the broken tables, *les tables brisées*.

It agrees with the object of a verb conjugated with *avoir*, only when the object comes before it. Ex. : He broke the plates, *il a cassé les assiettes*; the plates he broke, *les assiettes qu'il a cassées*.

1. *First conjugation.* — **Aimer**, to love.   **2.** *Second conjugation.* — **Finir**, to end.

INDICATIVE

Present.	Past tense.	Present.	Past tense.
J'aime.	J'aimai.	Je finis.	Je finis.
Tu aimes.	Tu aimas.	Tu finis.	Tu finis.
Il aime.	Il aima.	Il finit.	Il finit.
Nous aimons.	Nous aimâmes.	Nous finissons.	Nous finîmes.
Vous aimez.	Vous aimâtes.	Vous finissez.	Vous finîtes.
Ils aiment.	Ils aimèrent.	Ils finissent.	Ils finirent.

Imperfect.	Future.	Imperfect.	Future.
J'aimais.	J'aimerai.	Je finissais.	Je finirai.
Tu aimais.	Tu aimeras.	Tu finissais.	Tu finiras.
Il aimait.	Il aimera.	Il finissait.	Il finira.
Nous aimions.	Nous aimerons.	Nous finissions.	Nous finirons.
Vous aimiez.	Vous aimerez.	Vous finissiez.	Vous finirez.
Ils aimaient.	Ils aimeront.	Ils finissaient.	Ils finiront.

CONDITIONAL		CONDITIONAL	
J'aimerais.	Nous aimerions.	Je finirais.	Nous finirions.
Tu aimerais.	Vous aimeriez.	Tu finirais.	Vous finiriez.
Il aimerait.	Ils aimeraient.	Il finirait.	Ils finiraient.

IMPERATIVE			IMPERATIVE		
Aime.	Aimons.	Aimez.	Finis.	Finissons.	Finissez

SUBJUNCTIVE		SUBJUNCTIVE	
Present.	*Imperfect.*	*Present.*	*Imperfect.*
Que j'aime.	Que j'aimasse.	Que je finisse.	Que je finisse.
Que tu aimes.	Que tu aimasses.	Que tu finisses.	Que tu finisses.
Qu'il aime.	Qu'il aimât.	Qu'il finisse.	Qu'il finît.
Que nous aimions.	Que nous aimassions.	Que nous finissions.	Que nous finissions.
Que vous aimiez.	Que vous aimassiez.	Que vous finissiez.	Que vous finissiez.
Qu'ils aiment.	Qu'ils aimassent.	Qu'ils finissent.	Qu'ils finissent.

PRES. PARTICIPLE	PAST PARTICIPLE	PRES. PARTICIPLE	PAST PARTICIPLE
Aimant.	Aimé, ée, és, ées.	Finissant.	Fini, ie, is, ies.

3. *Third conjugation.* — **Recevoir**, to receive.   **4.** *Fourth conjugation.* — **Rompre**, to break.

INDICATIVE		INDICATIVE	
Present.	*Past tense.*	*Present.*	*Past tense.*
Je reçois.	Je reçus.	Je romps.	Je rompis.
Tu reçois.	Tu reçus.	Tu romps.	Tu rompis.
Il reçoit.	Il reçut.	Il rompt.	Il rompit.
Nous recevons.	Nous reçûmes.	Nous rompons.	Nous rompîmes.
Vous recevez.	Vous reçûtes.	Vous rompez.	Vous rompîtes.
Ils reçoivent.	Ils reçurent.	Ils rompent.	Ils rompirent.

Imperfect.	*Future.*	*Imperfect.*	*Future.*
Je recevais.	Je recevrai.	Je rompais.	Je romprai.
Tu recevais.	Tu recevras.	Tu rompais.	Tu rompras.
Il recevait.	Il recevra.	Il rompait.	Il rompra.
Nous recevions.	Nous recevrons.	Nous rompions.	Nous romprons.
Vous receviez.	Vous recevrez.	Vous rompiez.	Vous romprez.
Ils recevaient.	Ils recevront.	Ils rompaient.	Ils rompront.

CONDITIONAL		CONDITIONAL	
Je recevrais.	Nous recevrions.	Je romprais.	Nous romprions.
Tu recevrais.	Vous recevriez.	Tu romprais.	Vous rompriez.
Il recevrait.	Ils recevraient.	Il romprait.	Ils rompraient.

IMPERATIVE			IMPERATIVE		
Reçois.	Recevons.	Recevez.	Romps.	Rompons.	Rompez.

SUBJUNCTIVE		SUBJUNCTIVE	
Present.	*Imperfect.*	*Present.*	*Imperfect.*
Que je reçoive.	Que je reçusse.	Que je rompe.	Que je rompisse.
Que tu reçoives.	Que tu reçusses.	Que tu rompes.	Que tu rompisses.
Qu'il reçoive.	Qu'il reçût.	Qu'il rompe.	Qu'il rompît.
Que nous recevions.	Que nous reçussions.	Que nous rompions.	Que nous rompissions.
Que vous receviez.	Que vous reçussiez.	Que vous rompiez.	Que vous rompissiez.
Qu'ils reçoivent.	Qu'ils reçussent.	Qu'ils rompent.	Qu'ils rompissent.

PRES. PARTICIPLE	PAST PARTICIPLE	PRES. PARTICIPLE	PAST PARTICIPLE
Recevant.	Reçu, ue, us, ues.	Rompant.	Rompu, ue, us, ues.

N. B. — Note the use of the over-compound tenses : *il a eu fini; elle avait eu reçu*, etc.

5. Verbs, having a mute e or closed é in the last syllable but one of the present infinitive, change the mute **e** or closed é to open **è** before a mute syllable (except in the future and conditional). Ex. : *espérer, j'espère, il espérera, il espérerait*.

Note that, in the interrogative form *soulevé-je*, the final é is not mute; hence the stem vowel e is unchanged.

6. Verbs in **cer** take ç before endings in *a, o*. Ex. : *percer, je perçais, nous perçons*.

7. Verbs in **ger** add **e** before endings in *a, o*. Ex. : *manger; je mangeais; nous mangeons*.

8. *a)* Verbs in **eler, eter** double the l or t before a mute e. Ex. : *appeler, j'appelle; jeter, je jette*.

b) The following verbs do not follow this rule and only take *è* : *acheter, agneler, bégueter, celer, ciseler, congeler, corseter, crocheter, déceler, dégeler, démanteler, écarteler, fureter, geler, haleter, harceler, marteler, modeler, peler, racheter, receler, regeler*.

Ex. : *agneler, agnèle*.

9. *a)* Verbs in **yer** change y into i before a mute e. They require a y and an i in the first two persons plural of the imperf. ind. and of the pres. subj. Ex. : *ployer, je ploie, vous ployiez*.

b) Verbs in **ayer** may keep the y or change it to an i before a mute e. Ex. : *payer, je paie, je paye*.

c) Verbs in **eyer** keep the y throughout the conjugation. Ex. : *grasseyer, je grasseye, nous grasseyions*.

10. Absoudre. Pr. ind. : *absous, absous, absout, absolvons, absolvez, absolvent*. Imp. : *absolvais, absolvions*. Fut. : *absoudrai, absoudrons*. Condit. : *absoudrais, absoudrions*. Imper. : *absous, absolvons, absolvez*. Pr. subj. : *absolve, absolvions*. Pr. part. : *absolvant*. Past part. : *absous, absoute*. No past tense; no imp. subj.

11. Abstraire. Pr. ind. : *abstrais, abstrayons.* Imp. : *abstrayais, abstrayions.* Fut. : *abstrairai, abstrairons.* Condit. : *abstrairais, abstrairions.* Imper. : *abstrais, abstrayons, abstrayez.* Pr. subj. : *abstraie, abstrayions.* Pr. part. : *abstrayant.* Past part. : *abstrait.* No past tense ; no imp. subj.

12. Accroire is used only in the infinitive and always with the verb *faire.*

13. Acquérir. Pr. ind. : *acquiers, acquiers, acquiert, acquérons, acquérez, acquièrent.* Imp. : *acquérais, acquérions.* Past tense : *acquis, acquîmes.* Fut. : *acquerrai.* Pr. subj. : *acquière, acquières, acquière, acquérions, acquériez, acquièrent.* Pr. part. : *acquérant.* Past part. : *acquis.*

14. Advenir. Only used in the third person. Pr. ind. : *advint.* Imp. : *advenait.* Fut. : *adviendra.* Condit. : *adviendrait.* Pr. subj. : *advienne.* Imp. subj. : *advînt.*

15. Aller. Pr. ind. : *vais, vas, va, vont.* Imp. : *allais, allais, allait, allions, alliez, allaient.* Fut. : *irai, iras, ira, irons, irez, iront.* Condit. : *irais, irions.* Imper. : *va, (vas-y), allons, allez.* Pr. subj. : *aille, ailles, aille, allions, alliez, aillent.* Imp. subj. : *allasse, allasses, allât, allassions, allassiez, allassent.* Pr. part. : *allant.* Past part. : *allé.*

16. Apparoir is used as a law term only in the third person : *appert.*

17. Assaillir. Pr. ind. : *assaille, assaillons.* Imp. : *assaillais, assaillions.* Past tense : *assaillis, assaillîmes.* Fut. : *assaillirai, assaillirons.* Condit. : *assaillirais, assaillirions.* Imper. : *assaille, assaillons, assaillez.* Pr. subj. : *assaille, assaillions.* Imp. subj. : *assaillisse, assaillissions.* Pr. part. : *assaillant.* Past part. : *assailli.*

18. Asseoir. Pr. ind. : *assieds, assieds, assied, asseyons, asseyez, asseyent.* Imp. : *asseyais, asseyions.* Past tense : *assis, assîmes.* Fut. : *assiérai, assiérons.* Condit. : *assiérais, assiérions.* Imper. : *assieds, asseyons, asseyez.* Pres. subj. : *asseye, asseyions.* Pr. part. : *asseyant.* Past part : *assis.* In the figurative meaning, pr. ind. : *assois, assoyons.* Fut. : *assoirai, assoirons.* Imper. : *assois.* Pr. subj. : *assoie, assoyions.*

19. Avoir. Pr. ind. : *ai, as, a, avons, avez, ont.* Imp. : *avais, avais, avait, avions, aviez, avaient.* Past tense : *eus, eûmes.* Fut. : *aurai, aurons.* Condit. : *aurais, aurions.* Imper. : *aie, ayons, ayez.* Pres. subj. : *aie, ayons.* Imper. subj. : *eusse, eussions.* Pr. part. : *ayant.* Past part. : *eu.*

20. Battre. Pr. ind. : *bats, battons.* Imp. : *battais, battions.* Past tense : *battis, battîmes.* Fut. : *battrai, battrons.* Condit. : *battrais, battrions.* Imper. : *bats, battons, battez.* Pr. subj. : *batte, battons.* Imp. subj. : *battisse, battît.* Pr. part. : *battant.* Past part. : *battu.*

21. Boire. Pr. ind. : *bois, bois, boit, buvons, buvez, boivent.* Imp. : *buvais, buvions.* Past tense : *bus, but, bûmes.* Fut. : *boirai, boirons.* Condit. : *boirais, boirions.* Imper. : *bois, buvons, buvez.* Pr. subj. : *boive, buvions.* Imp. subj. : *busse, bût.* Pr. part. : *buvant.* Past part. : *bu.*

22. Bouillir. Pr. ind. : *bous, bous, bout, bouillons, bouillez, bouillent.* Imp. : *bouillais, bouillions.* Past tense : *bouillis, bouillîmes.* Fut. : *bouillirai, bouillirons.* Condit. : *bouillirais, bouillirions.* Imper. : *bous, bouillons, bouillez.* Pr. subj. : *bouille, bouillions.* Imp. subj. : *bouillisse.* Pr. part. : *bouillant.* Past part. : *bouilli.*

23. Braire. Only used in the third pers. Pr. ind. : *brait, braient.* Fut. : *braira, brairont.*

24. Bruire. Only used in the third pers. Pr. ind. : *bruit, bruissent.* Imp. : *bruissait, bruissaient.* Pr. part. : *bruissant.*

25. Choir. Pr. ind. : (only used in) *chois, chois, choit.* Past tense : *chus, chûmes.* Fut. : *choirai* (or) *cherrai, choirons* (or) *cherrons.* Condit. : *choirais, choirions.* Past part. : *chu.* Generally used only in the infinitive and past tense.

26. Circoncire. Pr. ind. : *circoncis, circoncisons.* Imp. : *circoncisais, circoncisions.* Past tense : *circoncis, circoncîmes.* Fut. : *circoncirai.* Condit. : *circoncirais, circoncirions.* Imper. : *circoncis, circoncisons, circoncisez.* Pr. subj. : *circoncise.* Pr. part. : *circoncisant.* Past part. : *circoncis.*

27. Clore. Only used in the following tense. Pr. ind. : *clos, clos, clôt* (no plural). Fut. : *clorai, clorons.* Condit. : *clorais, clorions.* Pres. subj. : *close, closions.* Past part. : *clos.*

28. Comparoir. Only used in the infinitive and pr. part. : *comparant.*

29. Conclure. Pr. ind. : *conclus, conclus, conclut, concluons, concluez, concluent.* Imp. : *concluais, concluions.* Past tense : *conclus, conclûmes.* Fut. : *conclurai.* Condit. : *conclurais.* Imper. : *conclus, concluons, concluez.* Pr. subj. : *conclue, concluions.* Imp. subj. : *conclusse, conclût.* Pr. part. : *concluant.* Past part. : *conclu.*

30. Confire. Pr. ind. : *confis, confisons.* Imp. : *confisais.* Past tense : *confis, confîmes.* Fut. : *confirai, confirons.* Condit. : *confirais, confirions.* Imper. : *confis, confisons, confisez.* Pr. subj. : *confise, confisions.* Pr. part. : *confisant.* Past part. : *confit.*

31. Coudre. Pr. ind. : *couds, cousons.* Imp. : *cousais, cousions.* Fut. : *coudrai, coudrons.* Imper. : *couds, cousons, cousez.* Pr. subj. : *couse, cousions.* Pr. part. : *cousant.* Past part. : *cousu.*

32. Courir. Pr. ind. : *cours, courons.* Imp. : *courais, courions.* Past tense : *courus, courûmes.* Fut. : *courrai, courront.* Condit. : *courrais, courrions.* Imper. : *cours, courons, courez.* Pr. subj. : *coure, courions.* Imp. subj. : *courusse, courût.* Pr. part. : *courant.* Past part. : *couru.*

33. Croire. Pr. ind. : *crois, croyons.* Imp. : *croyais, croyions.* Past tense : *crus, crûmes.* Fut. : *croirai, croirons.* Condit. : *croirais, croirions.* Pr. subj. : *croie, croyions.* Imp. subj. : *crusse, crût, crussions.* Pr. part. : *croyant.* Past part. : *cru.*

34. Croître. Pr. ind. : *croîs, croîs, croît, croissons, croissez, croissent.* Imp. : *croissais, croissions.* Past tense : *crûs, crûmes.* Fut. : *croîtrai, croîtrons.* Condit. : *croîtrais, croîtrions.* Imper. : *croîs, croissons, croissez.* Pr. subj. : *croisse, croissions.* Imp. subj. : *crûsse, crût, crussions.* Pr. part. : *croissant.* Past part. : *crû, crue.*

35. Cueillir. Pr. ind. *cueille, cueillons.* Imp. : *cueillais, cueillions.* Past tense : *cueillis, cueillîmes.* Fut. : *cueillerai, cueillerons.* Condit. : *cueillerais, cueillerions.* Imper. : *cueille, cueillons, cueillez.* Pr. subj. : *cueille, cueillions.* Imp. subj. : *cueillisse, cueillît.* Pr. part. : *cueillant.* Past part. : *cueilli.*

36. Déchoir. Pr. ind. : *déchois, déchois, déchoit, déchoyons, déchoyez, déchoient.* Past tense : *déchus, déchûmes.* Fut. : *décherrai, décherrons.* Condit. : *décherrais, décherrions.* Pr. subj. : *déchoie, déchoyions.* Imp. subj. : *déchusse, déchût.* Past part. : *déchu.* No imp., no pr. part.

37. Déconfire. Only used in the infinitive and past part. : *déconfit.*

38. Défaillir. Pr. ind. : *défaus, défaus, défaut* (†) ; *défaillons, défaillez, défaillent.* Imp. : *défaillais.* Past tense : *défaillis.* Pr. part. : *défaillant.* The other tenses are wanting.

39. Devoir. Pr. ind. : *dois, dois, doit, devons, devez, doivent.* Imp. : *devais, devions.* Past tense : *dus, dûmes.* Fut. : *devrai, devrons.* Condit. : *devrais, devrions.* Imper. : *dois, devons, devez.* Pr. subj. : *doive, devions.* Imp. subj. : *dusse, dût, dussions.* Pr. part. : *devant.* Past part. : *dû, due, dus.*

40. Dire. Pr. ind. : *dis, dis, dit, disons, dites, disent.* Imp. : *disais, disions.* Past tense : *dis, dîmes.* Fut. : *dirai, dirons.* Condit. : *dirais, dirions.* Imper. : *dis, disons, dites.* Pres. subj. : *dise, disions.* Imp. subj. : *disse, dît.* Pr. part. : *disant.* Past part. : *dit.*

41. Dormir. Pr. ind. : *dors, dormons.* Imp. : *dormais, dormions.* Past tense : *dormis, dormîmes.* Fut. : *dormirai, dormirons.* Condit. : *dormirais, dormirions.* Imper. : *dors, dormons, dormez.* Pres. subj. : *dorme, dormions.* Imp. subj. : *dormisse, dormît.* Pr. part. : *dormant.* Past part. : *dormi.*

42. Échoir. Only used in the third person. Pr. ind. : *échoit ; échoient.* Imp. : *échéait.* Past tense : *échut, échurent.* Fut. : *écherra, écherront.* Condit. : *écherrait, écherraient.* Pr. subj. : *échée, échéent.* Imp. subj. : *échût, échussent.* Pr. part. : *échéant.* Past part. : *échu.*

43. Éclore. Only used in the third person. Pr. ind. : *éclôt, éclosent.* Fut. : *éclora, écloront.* Condit. : *éclorait, écloraient.* Pr. subj. : *éclose, éclosent.* Past part. : *éclos.*

44. Écrire. Pr. ind. : *écris, écrivons.* Imp. : *écrivais, écrivions.* Past tense : *écrivis, écrivîmes.* Fut. : *écrirai, écrirons.* Condit. : *écrirais, écririons.* Imper. : *écris, écrivons, écrivez.* Pres. subj. : *écrivisse, écrivît.* Pr. part. : *écrivant.* Past part. : *écrit.*

45. Ensuivre (s'). Only used in the third person. Pr. ind. : *s'ensuit, s'ensuivent.* Imp. : *s'ensuivait, s'ensuivaient.* Past tense : *s'ensuivit, s'ensuivirent.* Fut. : *s'ensuivra, s'ensuivront.* Pr. subj. : *s'ensuive, s'ensuivent;* Pr. part. : *ensuivant.* Past part. : *ensuivi.*

46. Envoyer. Pr. ind. : *envoie, envoyons.* Imp. : *envoyais, envoyions.* Fut. : *enverrai, enverrons.* Condit. : *enverrais, enverrions.* Pr. subj. : *envoie, envoyions.* Pr. part. : *envoyant.* Past part. : *envoyé.*

47. Éprendre (s'). Conjugated like *prendre,* but especially used in the past part. *épris.*

48. Être. Pr. ind. : *suis, es, est, sommes, êtes, sont.* Imp. : *étais, étions.* Past tense : *fus, fûmes.* Fut. : *serai, serons.* Condit. : *serais, serions.* Imper. : *sois, soyons, soyez.* Pr. subj. : *sois, soyons.* Imp. subj. : *fusse, fût, fussions.* Pr. part. : *étant.* Past part. : *été. Eté* is invariable.

49. Faillir. Only used in the following tenses. Past tense : *faillis, faillîmes.* Fut. : *faudrai (or) faillirai.* Condit. : *faudrais (or) faillirais.* Pr. part. : *faillant.* Past part. : *failli.*

50. Faire. Pr. ind. : *fais, fais, fait, faisons, faites, font.* Imp. : *faisais, faisions.* Past tense : *fis, fîmes.* Fut. : *ferai, ferons.* Condit. : *ferais, ferions.* Imper. : *fais, faisons, faites.* Pr. subj. : *fasse, fassions.* Imp. subj. : *fisse, fît, fissions.* Pr. part. : *faisant.* Past part. : *fait.*

51. Falloir. Only used in the third person. Pr. ind. : *faut.* Imp. : *fallait.* Past tense : *fallut.* Fut. : *faudra.* Condit. : *faudrait.* Pr. subj. : *faille.* Imp. subj. : *fallût.* Past part. : *fallu.*

52. Férir. The infinitive is only used in the phrase *sans coup férir.* The past part. *féru* is only adjective.

53. Fleurir. Pr. ind. : *fleuris, fleurissons.* Imp. : *fleurissais, fleurissions.* Past tense : *fleuris, fleurîmes.* Fut. : *fleurirai, fleurirons.* Condit. : *fleurirait, fleuriraient.* Pr. subj. : *fleurisse, fleurissions.* Imp. subj. : *fleurisse, fleurît.* Pr. part. : *fleurissant.* Past part. : *fleuri.* In the figurative meaning, note the imp. : *florissais,* and pr. part. : *florissant.*

54. Forfaire. Only used in the infinitive and compound tenses.

55. Frire. Only used in the following tenses. Pr. ind. : *fris, fris, frit.* Fut. : *frirai, frirons.* The verb *faire* is used with *frire* to supply the persons and tenses that are wanting : as *nous faisons frire.*

56. Fuir. Pr. ind. : *fuis, fuyons.* Imp. : *fuyais, fuyions.* Past tense : *fuis, fuîmes.* Fut. : *fuirai, fuirons.* Condit. : *fuirais, fuirions.* Imp. : *fuis, fuyons, fuyez.* Pr. subj. : *fuie, fuyions.* Pr. part. : *fuyant.* Past part. : *fui.*

57. Gésir. Only used in the following tenses. Pr. ind. : *gît, gisons, gisez, gisent.* Imp. : *gisais, gisions.* Pr. part. : *gisant.*

58. Haïr. Pr. ind. : *hais, hais, hait, haïssons, haïssez, haïssent.* Imp. : *haïssais, haïssions.* Past tense : *haïs, haïmes.* Fut. : *haïrai, haïrons.* Condit. : *haïrais, haïrions.* Pr. subj. : *haïsse, haïssions.* Pr. part. : *haïssant.* Past part. : *haï.*

59. Joindre. Pr. ind. : *joins, joins, joint, joignons, joignez, joignent.* Imp. : *joignais, joignions.* Past tense : *joignis.* Fut. : *joindrai, joindrons.* Condit. : *joindrais, joindrions.* Pr. subj. : *joigne, joignions.* Pr. part. : *joignant.* Past part. : *joint.*

60. Lire. Pr. ind. : *lis, lisons.* Imp. : *lisais, lisions.* Past tense : *lus, lûmes.* Fut. : *lirai, lirons.* Condit. : *lirais, lirions.* Imper. : *lis, lisons, lisez.* Pr. subj. : *lise, lisions.* Imp. subj. : *lusse, lût, lussions.* Pr. part. : *lisant.* Past part. : *lu.*

61. Luire. Pr. ind. : *luis, luisons.* Imp. : *luisais, luisions.* Fut. : *luirai, luirons.* Condit. : *luirais, luirions.* Pres. subj. : *luise, luisions.* Pr. part. : *luisant.* Past part. : *lui.* No past tense; no imp. subj. The past part. *lui* has no feminine.

62. Maudire. Pr. ind. : *maudis, maudit, maudissons, maudissez, maudissent.* Imp. : *maudissais, maudissions.* Past tense : *maudis, maudîmes.* Fut. : *maudirai, maudirons.* Condit. : *maudirais, maudirions.* Pr. subj. : *maudisse, maudissions.* Imper. : *maudis, maudissons, maudissez.* Pr. part. : *maudissant.* Past part. : *maudit.*

63. Médire is conjugated like *dire,* except pr. ind. and imper. *médisez.*

64. Mettre. Pr. ind. : *mets, mettons.* Imp. : *mettais, mettions.* Past tense : *mis, mîmes.* Fut. : *mettrai, mettrons.* Condit. : *mettrais, mettrions.* Imper. : *mets, mettons, mettez.* Pr. subj. : *mette, mettions.* Imp. subj. : *misse, mît, missions.* Pr. part. : *mettant.* Past part. : *mis.*

65. Moudre. Pr. ind. : *mouds, mouds, moud, moulons, moulez, moulent.* Imp. : *moulais, moulions.* Past tense : *moulus, moulûmes.* Fut. : *moudrai, moudrons.* Condit. : *moudrais, moudrions.* Imper. : *mouds, moulons, moulez.* Pr. subj. : *moule, moulions.* Imp. subj. : *moulusse, moulût.* Pr. part. : *moulant.* Past part. : *moulu.*

66. Mourir. Pr. ind. : *meurs, meurs, meurt, mourons, mourez, meurent.* Imp. : *mourais, mourions.* Past tense : *mourus, mourûmes.* Fut. : *mourrai, mourrons.* Condit. : *mourrais, mourrions.* Imp. subj. : *mourusse, mourût.* Pr. subj. : *meure, mourions.* Pr. part. : *mourant.* Past part. : *mort.*

67. Mouvoir. Pr. ind. : *meus, meus, meut, mouvons, mouvez, meuvent.* Imp. : *mouvais, mouvions.* Past tense : *mus, mûmes.* Fut. : *mouvrai, mouvrons.* Condit. : *mouvrais, mouvrions.* Imper. : *meus, mouvons, mouvez.* Pr. subj. : *meuve, mouvions.* Imp. subj. : *musse, mût.* Pr. part. : *mouvant.* Past part. : *mû (f. mue).*

68. Naître. Pr. ind. : *nais, nais, naît, naissons, naissez, naissent.* Imp. : *naissais, naissions.* Past tense : *naquis, naquîmes.* Fut. : *naîtrai, naîtrons.* Condit. : *naîtrais, naîtrions.* Imper. : *nais, naissons, naissez.* Pr. subj. : *naisse, naissions.* Imp. subj. : *naquisse, naquît.* Pr. part. : *naissant.* Past part. : *né.* The auxiliary is *être.*

69. Nuire is conjugated like *luire.* Note the past tense : *nuisis, nuisîmes.* Imp. subj. : *nuisisse, nuisît, nuisissions.*

70. Oindre is conjugated like *craindre* but seldom used other than in the past part. *oint,* in the imp. *oignais, oignait,* and in the well-known slogan : *oignez vilain, il vous poindra.*

71. Ouïr is now seldom used other than in the infinitive *ouïr,* in the pr. *oyez,* in the past part. *ouï* and in the compound tenses. The auxiliary is *avoir.*

72. Ouvrir. Pr. ind. : *ouvre, ouvrons.* Imp. : *ouvrais, ouvrions.* Past tense : *ouvris, ouvrîmes.* Fut. : *ouvrirai, ouvrirons.* Condit. : *ouvrirais, ouvririons.* Imper. : *ouvre, ouvrons, ouvrez.* Pr. subj. : *ouvre, ouvrions.* Imp. subj. : *ouvrisse, ouvrît.* Pr. part. : *ouvrant.* Past part. : *ouvert.*

73. Paître. Pr. ind. : *pais, paît, paissons.* Imp. : *paissais, paissions.* Fut. : *paîtrai, paîtrons.* Condit. : *paîtrais, paîtrions.* Imper. : *pais, paissons, paissez.* Pr. subj. : *paisse, paissions.* Pr. part. : *paissant.* No past tense; no imp. subj.; no past part.

74. Paraître. Pr. ind. : *parais, paraissons.* Imp. : *paraissais, paraissions.* Past tense : *parus, parûmes.* Fut. : *paraîtrai, paraîtrons.* Condit. : *paraîtrais, paraîtrions.* Imper. : *parais, paraissons, paraissez.* Pr. subj. : *paraisse, paraissions.* Imp. subj. : *parusse, parût, parussions.* Pr. part. : *paraissant.* Past part. : *paru.*

75. Plaire. Pr. ind. : *plais, plaisons.* Imp. : *plaisais, plaisions.* Past. tense : *plus, plûmes.* Fut. : *plairai, plairons.* Condit. : *plairais, plairions.* Imper. : *plais, plaisons, plaisez.* Pr. subj. : *plaise, plaisions.* Imp. subj. : *plusse, plût, plussions.* Pr. part. : *plaisant.* Past part. : *plu.*

76. Pleuvoir. Only used in the third person sg. Pr. ind. : *pleut.* Imp. : *pleuvait.* Past tense : *plut.* Fut. : *pleuvra.* Condit. : *pleuvrait.* Pr. subj. : *pleuve.* Pr. part. : *pleuvant.* Past part. : *plu.*

77. Poindre. Only used now in the third person. Pr. ind. : *point.* Fut. : *poindra, poindront.* Condit. : *poindrait, poindraient.* Pr. part. : *poignant.* Past part. : *point.* Note the old form *poignez.*

78. Pourvoir. Pr. ind. : *pourvois, pourvoyons.* Imp. : *pourvoyais, pourvoyions.* Past tense : *pourvus, pourvûmes.* Fut. : *pourvoirai, pourvoirons.* Condit. : *pourvoirais, pourvoiririons.* Imp. : *pourvois, pourvoyons, pourvoyez.* Pr. subj. : *pourvoie, pourvoyions.* Imp. subj. : *pourvusse, pourvût, pourvussions.* Pr. part. : *pourvoyant.* Past part. : *pourvu.*

79. Pouvoir. Pr. ind. : *peux (or) puis, peux, peut, pouvons, pouvez, peuvent.* Imp. : *pouvais, pouvions.* Past tense : *pus, pûmes.* Fut. : *pourrai, pourrons.* Condit. : *pourrais, pourrions.* Pr. subj. : *puisse, puissions.* Imp. subj. : *pusse, pût, pussions.* Pr. part. : *pouvant.* Past part. : *pu.* No imper.

80. Prendre. Pr. ind. : *prends, prenons.* Imp. : *prenais, prenions.* Past tense : *pris, prîmes.* Fut. : *prendrai, prendrons.* Condit. : *prendrais, prendrions.* Imper. : *prends, prenons, prenez.* Pr. subj. : *prisse, prît, prissions.* Pr. part. : *prenant.* Past part. : *pris.*

81. Prévaloir is conjugated like *valoir,* except in the pr. subj. : *prévale, prévalions.*

82. Prévoir is conjugated like *voir* except in fut. : *prévoirai, prévoirons,* and condit. : *prévoirais, prévoirions.*

83. Promouvoir is conjugated like *mouvoir* but used especially in infinitive, compound tenses, past part. *promu* and occasionally in past tense : *promut, promurent.*

84. Quérir is used only in the infinitive after the verbs *aller, venir, envoyer.*

85. Réduire. Pr. ind. : *réduis, réduisons.* Imp. : *réduisais, réduisions.* Past tense : *réduisis, réduisîmes.* Fut. : *réduirai, réduirons.* Condit. : *réduirais, réduirions.* Imper. : *réduis, réduisons, réduisez.* Pr. subj. : *réduise, réduisions.* Imp. subj. : *réduisisse, réduisît.* Pr. part. : *réduisant.* Past part. : *réduit.*

86. Repaître is conjugated like *paître,* but has the past tense : *repus, repûmes,* the imp. subj. : *repusse, repût,* the past part. : *repu.*

87. Résoudre. Pr. ind. : *résous, résolvons.* Imp. : *résolvais, résolvions.* Past tense : *résolus, résolûmes.* Fut. : *résoudrai, résoudrons.* Condit. : *résoudrais, résoudrions.* Imper. : *résous, résolvons, résolvez.* Pr. subj. : *résolve, résolvions.* Imp. subj. : *résolusse, résolût, résolussions.* Pr. part. : *résolvant.* Past part. : *résolu.* In chemistry, note the past part. *résous* (only m.).

88. Ressortir is conjugated like *sortir,* but like *finir,* when used as a law term : pr. ind. : *ressortit;* imp. : *ressortissait;* past part. : *ressortissant.*

89. Rire. Pr. ind. : *ris, rions.* Imp. : *riais, riions.* Past tense : *ris, rîmes.* Fut. : *rirai, rirons.* Condit. : *rirais, ririons.* Imper. : *ris, rions, riez.* Pr. subj. : *rie, riions.* Imp. subj. : *risse, rît, rissions.* Pr. part. : *riant.* Past part. : *ri.*

90. Rompre (fourth conjugation) takes a *t* in the third pers. of the sg.

91. Saillir is used only in the third person. Pr. ind. : *saille, saillent.* Fut. : *saillera, sailleront.* Condit. : *saillerait, sailleraient.* Pr. subj. : *saille, saillent.* Imp. subj. : *saillisse, saillît.* Pr. part. : *saillant.* Past part. : *sailli.* When it means « to gush » or « to serve a mare », it is conjugated like *finir.*

92. Savoir. Pr. ind. : *sais, savons.* Imp. : *savais, savions.* Past tense : *sus, sûmes.* Fut. : *saurai, saurons.* Condit. : *saurais, saurions.* Imper. : *sache, sachons, sachez.* Pr. subj. : *sache, sachions.* Imp. subj. : *susse, sût, sussions.* Pr. part. : *sachant.* Past part. : *su.*

93. Sentir. Pr. ind. : *sens, sentons.* Imp. : *sentais, sentions.* Past tense : *sentis, sentîmes.* Fut. : *sentirai, sentirons.* Condit. : *sentirais, sentirions.* Impers. : *sens, sentons, sentez.* Pr. subj. : *sente, sentions.* Imp. subj. : *sentisse, sentît.* Pr. part. : *sentant.* Past part. : *senti.*

94. Seoir (to sit) is used in the participles only. Pr. part. : *séant.* Past part. : *sis.*

Seoir (to suit) is used only in the following forms. Pr. part. : *seyant.* Pr. ind. : *sied, siéent.* Imp. : *seyait, seyaient.* Fut. : *siéra, siéront.*

95. Servir. Pr. ind. : *sers, servons.* Imp. : *servais, servions.* Past tense : *servis, servîmes.* Fut. : *servirai, servirons.* Condit. : *servirais, servirions.* Imper. : *sers, servons, servez.* Pr. subj. : *serve, servions.* Imp. subj. : *servisse, servît.* Pr. part. : *servant.* Past part. : *servi.*

96. Sourdre. Only used in the infinitive and in the third person of the pr. ind. : *sourd, sourdent.*

97. Suffire. Pr. ind. : *suffis, suffisons.* Imp. : *suffisais, suffisions.* Past tense : *suffis, suffîmes.* Fut. : *suffirai, suffirons.* Condit. : *suffirais, suffirions.* Imper. : *suffis, suffisons, suffisez.* Pr. subj. : *suffise, suffisions.* Imp. subj. : *suffisse, suffît.* Pr. part. : *suffisant.* Past part. : *suffi.*

98. Suivre. Pr. ind. : *suis, suivons.* Imp. : *suivais, suivions.* Past tense : *suivis, suivîmes.* Fut. : *suivrai, suivrons.* Condit. : *suivrais, suivrions.* Imper. : *suis, suivons, suivez.* Pr. subj. : *suive, suivions.* Imp. subj. : *suivisse, suivît.* Pr. part. : *suivant.* Past part. : *suivi.*

99. Surgir. Pr. ind. : *surgis, surgissons.* Imp. : *surgissais, surgissions.* Past tense : *surgis, surgîmes.* Fut. : *surgirai, surgirons.* Condit. : *surgirais, surgirions.* Imper. : *surgis, surgissons, surgissent.* Imp. subj. : *surgisse, surgît.* Pr. part. : *surgissant.* Past part. : *surgi.*

100. Surseoir. Pr. ind. : *sursois, sursoyons.* Imp. : *sursoyais, sursoyions.* Past tense : *sursis, sursîmes.* Fut. : *surseoirai, surseoirons.* Condit. : *surseoirais, surseoirions.* Imper. : *sursois, sursoyons, sursoyez.* Pr. subj. : *sursoie, sursoyions.* Imp. subj. : *sursisse, sursît.* Pr. part. : *sursoyant.* Past part. : *sursis.*

101. Tenir. Pr. ind. : *tiens, tenons.* Imp. : *tenais, tenions.* Past tense : *tins, tînmes.* Fut. : *tiendrai, tiendrons.* Condit. : *tiendrais, tiendrions.* Imper. : *tiens, tenons, tenez.* Pr. subj. : *tienne, tenions.* Imp. subj. : *tinsse, tînt, tinssions.* Pr. part. : *tenant.* Past part. : *tenu.*

102. Vaincre. Pr. ind. : *vaincs, vaincs, vainc, vainquons, vainquez, vainquent.* Imp. : *vainquais, vainquions.* Past tense : *vainquis, vainquîmes.* Fut. : *vaincrai, vaincrons.* Condit. : *vaincrais, vaincrions.* Imper. : *vaincs, vainquons, vainquez.* Pr. subj. : *vainque, vainquions.* Imp. subj. : *vainquisse, vainquît.* Pr. part. : *vainquant.* Past part. : *vaincu.*

103. Valoir. Pr. ind. : *vaux, vaux, vaut, valons, valez, valent.* Imp. : *valais, valions.* Past tense : *valus, valûmes.* Fut. : *vaudrai, vaudrons.* Condit. : *vaudrais, vaudrions.* Imper. : *vaux, valons, valez.* Pr. subj. : *vaille, valions.* Imp. subj. : *valusse, valût, valussions.* Pr. part. : *valant.* Past part. : *valu.*

104. Vêtir. Pr. ind. : *vêts, vêts, vêt, vêtons, vêtez, vêtent.* Imp. : *vêtais, vêtions.* Past tense : *vêtis, vêtîmes.* Fut. : *vêtirai, vêtirons.* Condit. : *vêtirais, vêtirions.* Imper. : *vêts, vêtons, vêtez.* Pr. subj. : *vête, vêtions.* Imp. subj. : *vêtisse, vêtît.* Pr. part. : *vêtant.* Past part. : *vêtu.*

105. Vivre. Pr. ind. : *vis, vis, vit, vivons, vivez, vivent.* Imp. : *vivais, vivions.* Past tense : *vécus, vécûmes.* Fut. : *vivrai, vivrons.* Condit. : *vivrais, vivrions.* Imper. : *vis, vivons, vivez.* Pr. subj. : *vive, vivions.* Imp. subj. : *vécusse, vécût.* Pr. part. : *vivant.* Past part. : *vécu.*

106. Voir. Pr. ind. : *vois, vois, voit, voyons, voyez, voient.* Imp. : *voyais, voyions.* Past tense : *vis, vîmes.* Fut. : *verrai, verrons.* Condit. : *verrais, verrions.* Imper. : *vois, voyons, voyez.* Pr. subj. : *voie, voyions.* Imp. subj. : *visse, vît.* Pr. part. : *voyant.* Past part. : *vu.*

107. Vouloir. Pr. ind. : *veux, veux, veut, voulons, voulez, veulent.* Imp. : *voulais, voulions.* Past tense : *voulus, voulûmes.* Fut. : *voudrai, voudrons.* Condit. : *voudrais, voudrions.* Imper. : *veux, voulons, voulez* (or) *veuille, veuillons, veuillez.* Pr. subj. : *veuille, voulions.* Imp. subj. : *voulusse, voulût.* Pr. part. : *voulant.* Past part. : *voulu.*

TABLE OF PHONETIC SYMBOLS

Symbols. The symbols used are those of the International Phonetic Alphabet, according to the method of A. Barbeau and E. Rodhe.

Stress. The stress is not indicated in the French-English part. It generally falls on the last sounded syllable of the word.

« Liaison ». In most cases, when a word begins with a vowel or a mute *h,* it is joined with the last consonant of the preceding word, even when the consonant is followed by a mute *e.* Ex. : *Sept heures* [sɛtœ:r], *cette âme* [sɛtɑ:m]. In such cases, final *c* and *g* are pronounced as *k* (*avec elle* [avɛkɛl]; *sang impur* [sɑ̃kɛ̃pyr]; final *s* and *x* as *z* (*sise à* [siza]; *six années* [sizane]); final *d* as *t* (*grand homme* [grɑ̃tɔm]). The liaison only occurs when the two words are intimately connected and pronounced with one breath.

XIII

FRENCH SOUNDS

CONSONANTS

SYMBOLS	KEY WORDS
[b]	bas [bɑ]
[d]	dame [dam]
[dʒ]	djinn [dʒin], bridge [bridʒ]
[f]	fin [fɛ̃], aphte [aft]
[g]	gris [gri], guerre [gɛːr], ghetto [gɛto], aggraver [agrave], second [.səgɔ̃]
[gn]	gnome [gnom]
[ɲ]	pagne [paɲ]
[gw]	lingual [lɛ̃gwal]
[gɥ]	linguiste [lɛ̃gɥist]
[gz]	exempt [egzɑ̃], eczéma [egzema]
[ʒ]	jaspe [ʒasp], genêt [ʒənɛ], geai [ʒɛ]
[*]	héros [*ero]
[k]	caduc [kadyk], kaki [kaki], khédive [keːdiːv], écho [eko], ecchymose [ɛkimoːz], queue [kø], becqueter [bɛkte]
[ks]	équinoxe [ekinɔks], coccyx [kɔksis]
[kw]	quartz [kwarts]
[l]	lent [lɑ̃], bacille [basil]
[m]	mime [mim], gemme [ʒɛm]
[n]	nef [nɛf], bonne [bɔn], automne [otɔn]
[p]	part [par], appel [apɛl]
[r]	roi [rwa], terre [tɛːr], arrhes [aːr]
[s]	lis, lice [lis], ceci [səsi], scie [si], facétie [fasesi], garçon [garsɔ̃]
[ʃ]	chat [ʃa], schisme [ʃism], shampooing [ʃɑ̃pwɛ̃]
[sk]	scandale [skɑ̃dal], ski [ski], schizophrène [skizofrɛn]
[skw]	squame [skwam]
[t]	taupe [toːp], thé [te], sotte [sɔt]
[tʃ]	tchèque [tʃɛk]
[v]	vent [vɑ̃], wagon [vagɔ̃]
[z]	zèle [zɛːl], rose [roːz]

VOWELS

SYMBOLS	KEY WORDS
[a]	bague [bag], tabac [taba], surah [syra], drap [dra], plat [pla], orgeat [orʒa], femme [fam]
[aː]	tard [taːr]
[ɑ]	ras, raz [rɑ], bât [bɑ]
[ɑː]	sable [sɑːbl], âge [ɑʒ]
[e]	été [ete], pied [pje], bouchée [buʃe], crier [krije], volontiers [vɔlɔ̃tje], nez [ne]
[ɛ]	freiner [frɛne], legs [lɛg], sept [sɛt], abcès [absɛ], est [ɛ], archet [arʃe], rets [rɛ], bey [bɛ], vrai [vrɛ], laid, lait [lɛ], sagaie [sagɛ], rabais [rabɛ], faix [fɛ]
[ɛː]	treize [trɛːz], hêtre [*ɛːtr], paire [pɛːr], mère [mɛːr]
[i]	ni, nid [ni], lubie [lybi], fusil [fyzi], habit [abi], pris, prix [pri], riz [ri], jury [ʒyri], abbaye [abɛi], pays [pei]
[iː]	rire [riːr], abîme [abiːm], lyre [liːr]
[o]	franco [frɑ̃ko], accroc [akro], galop [galo], chaos [kao], sabot [sabo], au, eau, aulx [o], chaud, chaux [ʃo], haut [*o]
[oː]	aube [oːb], heaume [*oːm], rose [roːz], côte [koːt]
[ɔ]	tonne [tɔn], oignon [ɔɲɔ̃]
[ɔː]	éloge [elɔːʒ], mors [mɔːr]
[ø]	bleu [blø], queue [kø], nœud [nø], émeut [emø], œufs, eux [ø]
[øː]	veule [vøːl], jeûne [ʒøːn]
[œ]	seul [sœl], œuf [œf], cueillir [kœjiːr]
[œː]	peur [pœːr], œuvre [œːvr]
[u]	cou, coud, coût, coup [ku], boue, bout [bu], joug [ʒu], août [u], pouls [pu], goût [gu], houx [*u], remous [rəmu], saoul, sou, sous [su]
[uː]	rouge [ruːʒ], bourg [buːr]
[y]	cru, crû, crue [kry], rude [ryd], jus [ʒy], début [deby], flux [fly], ciguë [sigy], eu [y]
[yː]	ruse [ryːz], usure [yzyːr], bûche [byːʃ], gageure [gaʒyːr]
[ə]	le [lə], regard [rəgaːr], benêt [bənɛ]

SEMI-VOWELS

SYMBOLS	KEY WORDS
[j]	pieu [pjø], pléiade [plejad], joyeux [ʒwajø], grillon [grijɔ̃], maillon [majɔ̃]
[w]	wallon [walɔ̃], ouate [wat], quadruple [kwadrypl], jaguar [ʒagwaːr] (cf. [kw], [gw])

CLUSTERS
SEMI-VOWELS AND VOWELS

SYMBOLS	KEY WORDS
[wa]	loi [lwa], froid [frwa], poids [pwa], proie [prwa], fois [fwa], doigt, doit [dwa], choix [ʃwa], ouate [wat]
[waː]	loir [lwaːr]
[ɥi]	nuit [nɥi], muid [mɥi], pluie [plɥi], buis [bɥi], fruit [frɥi], puy [pɥi]
[ɥe]	arguer [argɥe]
[aːj]	bail [baːj], cobaye [kɔbaːj], maille [maːj]
[ɑːj]	bâiller [bɑːje]
[ɛj]	grasseyer [grasɛje], balayer [balɛje]
[ɛːj]	soleil [sɔlɛːj], veille [vɛːj], paye [pɛːj], asseye [asɛːj]
[ij]	pillage [pijaːʒ]

CLUSTERS	
SYMBOLS	KEY WORDS
[i:j]	fille [fi:j]
[œj]	œillet [œjɛ], cueillette [kœjɛt]
[œ:j]	seuil [sœ:j], œil [œ:j]
[øj]	feuillet [føjɛ]
[ø:j]	feuille [fø:j]

NASALS

SYMBOLS	KEY WORDS
[ɑ̃]	camper [kɑ̃pe], ancien [ɑ̃sjɛ̃], banc [bɑ̃], marchand [marʃɑ̃], sang [sɑ̃], céans [seɑ̃], paon [pɑ̃], tremblant [trɑ̃blɑ̃], fend [fɑ̃], encens [ɑ̃sɑ̃], tourment [turmɑ̃], empan [ɑ̃pɑ̃], temps [tɑ̃], exempt [egzɑ̃]

[ɑ̃:]	ange [ɑ̃:ʒ], ample [ɑ̃:pl], encre [ɑ̃:kr], semble [sɑ̃:bl]
[ɛ̃]	instinct [ɛ̃stɛ̃], vingt, vin, vain, vainc [vɛ̃], quint [kɛ̃], impie [ɛ̃pi], thym, tain [tɛ̃], saint, sein, seing, ceint [sɛ̃], essaim [esɛ̃], examen [egzamɛ̃], appendice [apɛ̃dis], viens [vjɛ̃]
[ɛ̃:]	linge [lɛ̃:j], crainte [krɛ̃:t], geindre [ʒɛ̃:dr]
[ɔ̃]	non, nom [nɔ̃], plomb [plɔ̃], romps, rond [rɔ̃], prompt [prɔ̃], jonc [ʒɔ̃], bond [bɔ̃], long [lɔ̃], répons [repɔ̃], mont [mɔ̃], fonts [fɔ̃], lumbago [lɔ̃bago]
[ɔ̃:]	onde [ɔ̃:d], ombre [ɔ̃:br], jungle [ʒɔ̃:gl]
[œ̃]	alun [alœ̃], parfum [parfœ̃], jeun [ʒœ̃], emprunt [ɑ̃prœ̃]
[œ̃:]	défunte [defœ̃:t], humble [œ̃:bl]

FRENCH ALPHABET

FRENCH TYPE upper and lower case	PRONUNCIATION		
A, a	[a]	N, n	[ɛn]
B, b	[be]	O, o	[o]
C, c	[se]	P, p	[pe]
D, d	[de]	Q, q	[ky]
E, e	[ə]	R, r	[ɛr]
F, f	[ɛf]	S, s	[ɛs]
G, g	[ʒe]	T, t	[te]
H, h	[aʃ]	U, u	[y]
I, i	[i]	V, v	[ve]
J, j	[ʒi]	W, w	[dubləve]
K, k	[ka]	X, x	[iks]
L, l	[ɛl]	Y, y	[igrɛk]
M, m	[ɛm]	Z, z	[zɛd]

SEPARATION OF SYLLABLES IN FRENCH WORDS

1. As a rule French words may be divided between syllables : *arche-vêque, ex-com-mu-nier, ré-u-nir, domp-teur.*

2. A word is never divided :
   a) before a mute syllable : not *vendan-ge,* but *ven-dange ;* not *servi-ce,* but *ser-vice ;*
   b) before or after *x* or *y* coming between two vowels : not *di-x-ième, fra-y-eur,* but *dixième, frayeur ;* but a word may be divided after those letters when they are followed by a consonant : *tex-tile, pay-san.*

3. A sigla must not be divided : *U. R. S. S., O. N. U., U. N. E. S. C. O.*

4. The initials of a person's name are never separated : not *M. H. - Durand,* but *M. H. Durand.*

5. A word is never separated from a figure accompanying it : not *Henri - IV,* but *Henri IV ;* not *le 5 - avril,* but *le 5 avril.*

XV

FRENCH CURRENCY, WEIGHTS AND MEASURES

Currency.

1 franc = 100 centimes.
Coins: 5 centimes. 10 centimes. 20 centimes. 1/2 F. 1 F. 2 F. 5 F. 10 F. 50 F.
Banknotes: 10 F. 50 F. 100 F. 500 F.

Metric weights.

Milligramme	1 thousandth of a gramme.	0.015 grain.
Centigramme	1 hundredth of a gramme.	0.154 grain.
Décigramme	1 tenth of a gramme.	1.543 grain.
Gramme	1 cub. centim. of pure water.	5.432 grains.
Décagramme	10 grammes.	6. 43 pennweight.
Hectogramme	100 grammes.	3.527 oz. avoir.
Kilogramme	1 000 grammes.	2.204 pounds.
Quintal métrique	100 kilogrammes.	220.46 pounds.
Tonne	1 000 kilogrammes.	19 cwts 2 grs 23 lb.

Metric lineal measures.

Millimètre	1 thousandth of a mètre.	0.039 inch.
Centimètre	1 hundredth of a mètre.	0.393 inch.
Décimètre	1 tenth of a mètre.	3.937 inches.
Mètre	1 mètre.	1.0936 yard.
Décamètre	10 mètres.	32.7 ft., 10.9 yards.
Hectomètre	100 mètres.	109.3 yards.
Kilomètre	1 000 mètres.	1,093 yards.

Metric square and cubic measures.

Centiare	1 square mètre.	1.196 square yard.
Are	100 square mètres.	about 4 poles.
Hectare	100 ares.	about 2 1/2 acres.

Metric fluid and corn measures.

Centilitre	1 hundredth of a litre.	0.017 pint.
Décilitre	1 tenth of a litre.	0.176 pint.
Litre	Litre.	1.76 pint.
Décalitre	10 litres.	2.2 gallons.
Hectolitre	100 litres.	22.01 gallons.

— N. B. American usage is to use the plural for any unit over 1.00.

Thermometer.

0⁰ Celsius = 32⁰ Fahrenheit.
100⁰ Celsius = 212⁰ Fahrenheit.
To convert Fahrenheit degrees into Celsius, deduct 32, multiply by 5 and divide by 9.
Pour convertir les degrés Celsius en degrés Fahrenheit, multiplier par 9, diviser par 5 et ajouter 32.

TABLEAUX ET ILLUSTRATIONS

Les mots suivis du signe ● sont illustrés; le chiffre romain I désigne la partie fran-
çais-anglais, II la partie anglais-français; les chiffres arabes renvoient aux pages.

FRANÇAIS-ANGLAIS

A

a [α] m. A, a; *des a minuscules,* small a's; *ne savoir ni A ni B,* not to know A from B; not to know chalk from cheese (fam.); *prouver par a plus b,* to prove mathematically. ‖ ELECTR. A., ampere.

a [α] V. AVOIR.

à [a] prép. At (sans mouvement); *à dix milles de distance,* at a distance of ten miles; *assise à son travail,* sitting at her work; *retenu à la maison,* kept at home. ‖ To (en direction); *le coup le jeta à terre,* the blow felled (ou) struck him to the ground; *le dos au feu,* with one's back to the fire; *plein à déborder,* full to overflowing. ‖ By (manière, mesure, moyen); *à la livre,* by the pound; *fait à la main,* made by hand; *prendre à la gorge,* to take by the throat. ‖ For (attribution, échange, espace); *à dix milles à la ronde,* for ten miles around; *ce n'est pas à nous de critiquer,* it's not for us to criticize; *vendu à un prix élevé,* sold at a high price. ‖ From (extraction); *arracher, emprunter à,* to tear, to borrow from; *à partir de maintenant,* from now on. ‖ In (manière, résidence, temps); *à voix basse,* in a low voice; *chacun à sa manière,* each in his own way; *habile à voler,* expert in stealing; *le plus grand au monde,* the biggest in the world; *paysages à l'huile,* landscapes in oil. ‖ Into (pénétration); *pénétrer au cœur des choses par la réflexion,* to think one's way into the heart of things. ‖ Of (appartenance, attribut); *un ami à moi,* a friend of mine; *une jeune femme à la mise modeste,* a plainly dressed young woman. ‖ On (moment, position); *à cette occasion,* on this occasion; *à certaines conditions,* on certain conditions; *à cheval ou à pied,* on horseback or on foot; *au moment de partir,* on starting. ‖ With (attribut, instrument, relation); *combattre à la baïonnette,* to fight with the bayonet; *l'homme à la longue barbe,* the man with the long beard. ‖ Loc. *A bride abattue,* full tilt; *à qui est ce livre?,* whose book is this?, *il est à moi, à mon frère,* it is mine, my brother's; *une tasse à thé,* a tea-cup.

abaissant, ante [abɛsɑ̃, ɑ̃:t] adj. Lowering.

abaisse [abɛ:s] f. CULIN. Thin layer of pastry, undercrust. ‖ **Abaisse-langue,** m. invar. MÉD. Tongue-depressor.

abaissement [-mɑ̃] m. Lowering; dip, fall, falling; abatement; depression. ‖ Subsidence (des eaux); lowering of the height (d'un mur); *abaissement de la température,* fall in temperature. ‖ COMM. Dropping (des prix). ‖ JUR. *Abaissement des barrières douanières,* lowering of tariff walls. ‖ MÉD. Couching (de la cataracte); prolapse (d'un organe). ‖ FIG. Abasement. (V. DÉCLIN.)

abaisser [-se] v. tr. (1). To lower, to bring down; *abaisser les yeux,* to look down; *abaisser un store,* to pull down a blind. ‖ MATH. To bring down (un chiffre); to drop (une perpendiculaire). ‖ FIN. To lower (le niveau de vie, les prix); to bring down (la valeur). ‖ MÉD. To couch (une cataracte). ‖ MILIT. To reduce (un intervalle). ‖ FIG. To humiliate, to humble.
— v. pr. **S'abaisser,** to fall away, to slope downward, to sink; to decline; *les eaux se sont abaissées,* the waters have subsided. ‖ FIG. To humble (ou) to demean oneself; *s'abaisser à,* to condescend to, to stoop to; *s'abaisser devant,* to humble oneself before, to cringe to; *s'abaisser jusqu'à,* to abase oneself so far as to.

abaisseur, euse [-sœ:r, ø:z] adj., m. MÉD. Depressor.

abandon [abɑ̃dɔ̃] m. Surrender; renunciation; relinquishment; abandonment; *faire abandon de qqch. à qqn,* to make over (ou) to resign sth. to s.o. ‖ Neglect; *laisser à l'abandon,* to let run wild (un enfant); to leave uncared for (ou) at random (qqch.). ‖ Unreserve, unaffectedness; *parler avec abandon,* to speak unrestrainedly (ou) freely. ‖ NAUT. *A l'abandon,* derelict (navire). ‖ AVIAT. *Abandon du bord en vol,* bailing out. ‖ MILIT. Desertion (de poste). ‖ JUR. Renunciation (de droits); abandonment (de domicile, de famille).

abandonné, ée [-dɔne] adj. Abandoned (enfant); deserted (femme, maison); forsaken (personne); *petit abandonné,* little waif. ‖ Untidy (allure). ‖ NAUT. Derelict (navire). ‖ MÉD. *Abandonné par les médecins,* given up by the doctors.
— m. *Les abandonnés,* the forsaken; waifs and strays (enfants).

abandonner [-dɔne] v. tr. (1). To forsake (ses amis, un idéal); to leave, to quit (un emploi); to abandon (un espoir); to leave (le pays); *abandonner à,* to give up to, to yield to, to entrust to. ‖ MILIT. To desert (son poste). ‖ NAUT. To abandon (un navire). ‖ JUR. To relinquish, to renounce, to surrender (ses droits, ses prétentions). ‖ SPORTS. To retire, to give up (la course, la lutte). ‖ FIG. To forsake, to leave, to give up, to fail; *ses forces l'abandonnent,* his strength is failing him. ‖ FAM. *Abandonner la partie,* to throw up the sponge, to throw in the towel.
— v. pr. **S'abandonner,** to neglect oneself, to let oneself go (se laisser aller); to lose heart (perdre courage); *s'abandonner à,* to give way to (une émotion, un sentiment); to give oneself up to, to become addicted to, to indulge (un plaisir, un vice); to commit oneself to, to put oneself in the hands of (la Providence, qqn); *s'abandonner au hasard,* to trust to fortune.

abaque [abak] m. Abacus. ‖ Counting-table, calculating frame. ‖ Graph, diagram, chart, scale. ‖ MILIT. *Abaque de tir,* graphic range table.

abasourdir [abazurdi:r] v. tr. (2). To stun, to

daze. ‖ Fam. To amaze, to bewilder, to nonplus, to dumbfound, to flabbergast.

abasourdissant, ante [-disᾰ, ᾰ:t] adj. Stunning (bruit). ‖ Fam. Amazing, bewildering, astounding.

abasourdissement [-dismᾰ] m. Deafening. ‖ Fam. Amazement, stupor, bewilderment.

abat [aba] m. Slaughtering. ‖ Culin. Pl. Offal, giblets. ‖ **Abat-jour**, m. invar. Sun-blind (auvent); lamp-shade (réflecteur); eye-shade (visière). ‖ **Abat-son**, m. invar. Archit. Louvre-board. ‖ **Abat-vent**, m. invar. Archit. Chimney-cowl; louvre boarding.

abâtardi, ie [abɑtardi] adj. Degenerate.

abâtardir [-di:r] v. tr. (2). To mongrelize; to cause to degenerate; to debase. ‖ Fig. To weaken, to mar, to spoil. (V. avilir.)

— v. pr. **S'abâtardir**, to degenerate, to deteriorate.

abâtardissement [-dismᾰ] m. Degeneracy. (V. dégénérescence.) ‖ Retrogression; debasement.

abattage [abata:ʒ] m. Slaughtering (des animaux); felling, cutting down (des arbres); pulling down, knocking down (d'un édifice). ‖ Sports. *Grand abattage de gibier*, heavy bag of game. ‖ Milit. Abatage, anchoring. ‖ Techn. Extracting; quarrying. ‖ Fam. Blowing up, rating, dressing down. (V. savon.)

abattant [abatᾰ] m. Flap (de comptoir); leaf (de porte); *siège abattant*, tilting seat.

abattement [-tmᾰ] m. Dejection, lowness of spirits, despondency; *tomber dans l'abattement*, to be down in the dumps, U. S. to be feeling blue. (V. accablement, dépression.) ‖ Méd. Prostration. ‖ Fin. *Abattement à la base*, basic abatement, preliminary deduction, personal allowance.

abatteur [-tœ:r] m. Slaughterer (d'animaux); wood-cutter (de bois). ‖ Fig. Slogger, U. S. plugger (de besogne).

abattis [abati] m. Heap, pile, mass (d'arbres); felling, clearing (de bois); killing, slaughter (de gibier). ‖ Milit. Abatis; abattis. ‖ Culin. Offal (d'animal); giblets (de volaille). ‖ Fam. Fins, wings (bras); stumps, pegs (jambes); *numérote tes abattis*, I am going to break every bone in your body.

abattoir [-twa:r] m. Slaughter-house.

abattre [abatr] v. tr. (20). To cut down, to fell, to clear (des arbres); to pull down, to demolish (un bâtiment); to lop off (des branches); to strike (une tente); *abattu par le vent*, blown down by the wind (arbre); flattened by the wind (blé). ‖ To kill (un animal dangereux); to slaughter (les animaux de boucherie); to destroy (un cheval); to shoot down, to bring down (le gibier). ‖ To overthrow, to defeat, to lay low, to down (un adversaire). ‖ To cover (des kilomètres). ‖ Naut. *Abattre à la côte*, to drift on shore; *abattre sur bâbord*, to cast to port. ‖ Aviat. To bring down, U. S. to down (un avion). ‖ Techn. To round, to blunt (un angle); to clinch (un rivet). ‖ Fig. To subdue (la colère); to depress, to cast down (le courage); to dash, to damp (l'enthousiasme); to weaken, to pull down (les forces); to humble, to lower (l'orgueil); *ne pas se laisser abattre par*, to bear up against; *se laisser abattre*, to grow disheartened, to become depressed. ‖ Fam. *Abattre de la besogne*, to get through (ou) U. S. to knock out a lot of work. ‖ Loc. *Abattre son jeu*, to lay one's cards on the table.

— v. pr. **S'abattre**, to fall, to collapse; to die down (vent); *s'abattre sur*, to swoop down on (oiseau de proie); to sweep down on (orage). ‖ Méd. To abate (fièvre). ‖ Aviat. To come down, to crash, to crack up (avion).

abattu, ue [abaty] adj. Thrown down, overthrown, felled. ‖ Méd. Prostrate, limp. ‖ Fig. Downcast, despondent, dejected, dispirited.

abbatial, ale [abasjal] adj. Ecclés. Abbatial;

dignité abbatiale, abbacy; *église abbatiale*, minster, abbey.

abbatiale [-sja:l] f. Ecclés. Abbey.

abbaye [abɛi] f. Ecclés. Abbey, monastery. ‖ Fam. *L'abbaye de Thélème*, Liberty Hall.

abbé [abe] m. Ecclés. Abbot (de monastère). Roman Catholic priest (prêtre); curate (vicaire); *Monsieur l'abbé X*, Father X.

abbesse [-ɛs] f. Ecclés. Abbess.

A. B. C. [abese] m. A B C, alphabet. ‖ Spelling-book; primer (livre élémentaire). ‖ Fig. Rudiments, basic elements.

abcès [absɛ] m. Méd. Abscess (en général); gumboil (aux gencives). ‖ Fig. *Crever l'abcès*, to bring the situation to a head.

abdicataire [abdikatɛ:r] adj. Abdicant, abdicated.

— m. Abdicator.

abdication [-kasjɔ̃] f. Abdication (de la couronne). ‖ Renunciation (aux droits, plaisirs, prétentions); *faire abdication de*, to renounce, to surrender, to waive, to give up.

abdiquer [-ke] v. tr. (1). To abdicate (la couronne, le pouvoir). ‖ To renounce (ses droits); to resign (ses fonctions).

— v. intr. To abdicate.

abdomen [abdɔmen] m. Méd. Abdomen.

abdominal, ale [-minal] adj. Méd. Abdominal.

— m. pl. Abdominal muscles.

abducteur [abdyktœ:r] adj. Méd. Abducent (muscle).

— m. Méd. Abductor (muscle). ‖ Chim. Delivery tube.

abduction [-sjɔ̃] f. Abduction.

abécédaire [abesedɛ:r] adj. Abecedarian. ‖ Elementary, rudimentary.

— m. Primer, spelling-book. (V. alphabet.)

abée [abe] f. Leat (de moulin); flume (voie d'eau).

abeille [abɛ:j] f. Zool. Bee, honey-bee; *abeille mâle*, drone; *reine des abeilles*, queen bee. ‖ *Nid d'abeille*, smocking (en couture); honeycomb (tissu).

aber [abɛ:r] m. Géogr. Aber, valley estuary in Brittany.

aberrance [-abɛrrᾰs] f. Aberrance.

aberrant, ante [-rᾰ, ᾰ:t] adj. Aberrant, deviating.

aberration [-rasjɔ̃] f. Techn. Aberration. ‖ Fig. Aberration, mental lapse, mental derangement.

abêtir [abɛ:ti:r] v. tr. (2). To stupefy. (V. abrutir.) ‖ To besot (par l'alcool).

— v. pr. **S'abêtir**, to become dull, to grow stupid.

abêtissement [-tismᾰ] m. Dullness, stupor, stupidity.

abhorrer [abɔre] v. tr. (1). To abhor, to loathe.

abîme [abi:m] m. Abyss, abysm; chasm; bottomless pit, unfathomable gulf; *précipiter dans un abîme*, to hurl into an abyss. ‖ Ocean depths, deep (mer). ‖ Fig. Abyss (de honte); extremity (de malheur); abyss, infinity (de temps); *un abîme d'ignorance*, an unfathomable ignorance; *il y a un abîme entre*, there is a gulf between.

abîmer [-me] v. tr. (1). † To engulf, to overthrow. ‖ Fam. To spoil, to ruin, to damage. (V. détériorer.) ‖ Fam. To run down, to slate (critiquer). ‖ Pop. *Abîmer le portrait à qqn*, to push s.o.'s face in, U. S. to shove s.o.'s mug in.

— v. pr. **S'abîmer**, to be engulfed (ou) swallowed up; *s'abîmer dans les eaux*, to be swallowed up by the waters; *s'abîmer dans les flammes*, to crash down into the flames. ‖ To spoil, to get spoiled, to go bad (se gâter); *un fruit mûr s'abîme vite*, a ripe fruit is soon rotten; *s'abîmer la vue*, to spoil one's eyes. ‖ Fig. To sink (dans, into) [un songe].

ab intestat [abɛ̃tɛsta] loc. adv. Jur. Ab intestate; *héritier ab intestat*, heir in intestancy, next of kin; *succession ab intestat*, intestate succession.

abismal, ale [abismal] adj. Abysmal, fathomless.

abject, ecte [abʒɛkt] adj. Abject, wretched. (V. MISÉRABLE.) ‖ Degraded, base. (V. BAS, MÉPRISABLE, VIL.)

abjection [-ʒɛksjɔ̃] f. Abjection, abasement, degradation (déchéance). ‖ Abjectness, vileness (vilenie).

abjuration [abʒyrasjɔ̃] f. Abjuration, forswearing. ‖ Recantation (des opinions); *faire abjuration de*, to abjure.

abjurer [-re] v. tr. (1). ECCLÉS. To abjure, to forswear (sa foi). ‖ FIG. To recant; to retract; to abjure, to give up (ses opinions).

ablactation [ablaktasjɔ̃] f. MÉD. Ablactation.

ablatif, ive [ablatif, i:v] adj., m. GRAMM. Ablative; *à l'ablatif*, in the ablative.

ablation [-sjɔ̃] f. Ablation, removal. ‖ MÉD. Excision. ‖ GÉOL. Wearing away, ablation.

ablette [ablɛt] f. Zool. Bleak, ablet, ablen.

ablution [ablysjɔ̃] f. ECCLÉS. Ablution. ‖ FAM. Washing; *faire ses ablutions*, to wash oneself.

abnégation [abnegasjɔ̃] f. Abnegation, renunciation; giving-up; *faire abnégation de*, to renounce. ‖ Self-denial, self-sacrifice; *faire abnégation de soi*, to sacrifice oneself.

aboi [abwa] m. Bark, barking; yelp, yelping; bay, baying. ‖ FIG. *Aux abois*, at bay, cornered, hard pressed, up against it, with one's back to the wall.

aboiement [-mɑ̃] m. Bark, barking; yelp, yelping; bay, baying; *pousser un aboiement*, to give a bark. ‖ FIG. Cry (du camelot); yelping (de la presse).

abolir [abɔli:r] v. tr. (2). To abolish; to suppress, to do away with, to put an end to. ‖ JUR. To cancel (une dette). [V. ABROGER.]

abolissement [-lismɑ̃] m. Abolishment.

abolition [-lisjɔ̃] f. Abolition, abolishing, suppression. ‖ JUR. Annulment, abrogation, rescission (d'un décret); cancelling (d'une dette). ‖ MÉD. Obliteration, annihilation (de la sensibilité).

abolitionnisme [-lisjɔnism] m. Abolitionism.

abolitionniste [-lisjɔnist] m. Abolitionist. ‖ Free-trader.

abominable [abɔminabl] adj. Abominable; vile; loathsome. ‖ Odious (acte); heinous (crime, offense). ‖ FAM. Disagreeable, nasty (v. DÉTESTABLE); *goût abominable*, abominable taste; *temps abominable*, horrible weather.

abominablement [-nabləmɑ̃] adv. Abominably.

abomination [-nasjɔ̃] f. Abomination. ‖ Abhorrence, detestation (v. EXÉCRATION); *avoir en abomination*, to abominate; *être en abomination à*, to be abominated by, to be an abomination to. ‖ FAM. *Cette sauce est une abomination*, this sauce is filthy stuff.

abominer [-ine] v. tr. (1). To abominate.

abondamment [abɔdamɑ̃] adv. Abundantly, plentifully, profusely; *peu abondamment*, scantily, sparely.

abondance [-dɑ̃:s] f. Abundance, plenty, plenteousness; *une année d'abondance*, a year of plenty. ‖ Prosperity, opulence; *corne d'abondance*, horn of abundance (ou) of plenty. ‖ Wealth, affluence (de détails); effusion, flow (de paroles); exuberance (de style); *parler d'abondance*, to extemporize, to speak impromptu, to hold forth, to speechify. ‖ FIG. Abundance (du cœur).

abondant, ante [-dɑ̃, ɑ̃:t] adj. Abundant (en, in); plentiful. ‖ AGRIC. Luxuriant (feuillage); bounteous (moisson); copious (récolte). ‖ CULIN. Hearty (repas). ‖ MÉD. Profuse (hémorragie). ‖ FIG. Prolific (auteur); profuse (excuses, paroles); abundant (preuve); rich (sujet, vocabulaire);

abondant en détails, teeming with (ou) abounding in details.

abonder [-de] v. intr. (1). To abound, to be plentiful (ou) wealthy (*en*, in). ‖ To be filled, to be well stocked (*en*, in); to teem (*en*, with). ‖ FIG. *Abonder dans le sens de X*, to be entirely of X's opinion, to chime in (ou) to agree with X.

abonné [abɔne] s. Subscriber (à un journal, au théâtre); consumer (au gaz). ‖ CH. DE FER. Season-ticket holder; U. S. commuter.

abonnement [-nmɑ̃] m. Subscription; *prendre un abonnement à*, to subscribe to. ‖ Telephone rate (au téléphone); *payer par abonnement*, to pay by instalments (acompte). ‖ CH. DE FER. Season-ticket; U. S. commutation ticket. ‖ JUR. *Abonnement au timbre*, composition for stamp duty.

abonner [-ne] v. tr. (1). To take out a subscription for (à, to); *être abonné à*, to subscribe to.
— v. pr. **S'abonner à**, to subscribe to (un journal); *s'abonner à l'électricité, au gaz*, to have electricity, gas, installed (ou) laid on. ‖ CH. DE FER. To take a season-ticket; U. S. to commute. ‖ JUR. To compound for.

abord [abɔ:r] m. Access, approach (*de*, to); *d'un abord difficile*, difficult of access. ‖ NAUT. Landing. ‖ FIG. Address, aspect, bearing; *d'un abord facile*, accessible, approachable, easy to approach. ‖ Pl. Approaches, surroundings, outskirts (*de*, of); *abords couverts*, covered approaches; *aux abords de*, on the outskirts of. ‖ Loc. *Au premier abord*, at first sight; *d'abord*, at first; *d'abord et avant tout*, first and foremost; *de prime abord*, offhand; *dès l'abord*, from the start, from the outset.

abordable [-dabl] adj. Accessible; easy to approach (lieu). ‖ COMM. Reasonable (prix). ‖ FIG. Accessible (v. ACCESSIBLE); *peu abordable*, aloof, stand-offish (personne).

abordage [-da:ʒ] m. NAUT. Boarding (acte de guerre); fouling, collision (par accident); coming alongside (manœuvre d'accostage); berthing (à quai); *monter à l'abordage*, to board a ship.

aborder [-de] v. tr. (1). To reach (un lieu); to accost, to address (une personne); to approach (une position). ‖ FIG. To meet, to attack (une difficulté); to deal with, to grapple with, to tackle (un problème, une question); to take up, to enter upon (un sujet). ‖ NAUT. To come alongside (accoster); to board (à l'abordage); to collide with, to run foul of, to run into (par collision). ‖ MILIT. To attack, to engage.
— v. intr. NAUT. To berth (à quai); to touch land, to arrive; to go ashore (à terre); *aborder à un port*, to reach a port.
— v. récipr. **S'aborder**, to meet.

aborigène [abɔriʒɛn] adj. Aboriginal, indigenous, native; *aborigène de l'Amérique du Sud*, indigenous to South America.
— m. pl. Aborigines; natives; autochtones.

abortif, ive [abɔrtif, i:v] adj. Abortive; *manœuvres abortives*, means to procure abortion. ‖ JUR. Abortive.
— m. MÉD. Abortifacient.

abouchement [abuʃmɑ̃] m. Interview (de personnes). ‖ TECHN. Junction, butt-joining, butting. ‖ MÉD. Anastomosis.

aboucher [-ʃe] v. tr. (1). To bring together for an interview. ‖ TECHN. To butt, to join together end to end.
— v. pr. **S'aboucher**, to confer, to have an interview, to get in touch (*avec*, with). ‖ MÉD. To inosculate, to connect.

abouler [abule] v. tr. (1). POP. To fork out, to hand over (objet, argent); to ante up (argent).
— v. pr. **S'abouler**, POP. To get a move on.

aboulie [abuli] f. MÉD. Aboulia.

aboulique [-lik] adj. MÉD. Aboulic.

about [abu] m. TECHN. Butt-end; junction.

aboutement [-tmɑ̃] m. TECHN. Butting; abutment.

abouter [-te] v. tr. (1). TECHN. To join end to end, to butt. ‖ NAUT. To bend.

aboutir [abutir] v. intr. (2). To end (*à*, at, in); to come, to lead (*à*, to) [chemin]; to abut (*à*, on) [terrain]. ‖ MÉD. To burst, to come to a head (abcès). ‖ FIG. To succeed, to materialize, to come off (plan, projet); *aboutir à*, to result in, to lead to, to end in; *aboutir à qqch*, to bring sth. about; *faire aboutir*, to bring to a successful conclusion, to bring off; *ne pas aboutir*, to fail, to fall through, to come to nothing.

aboutissant, ante [-tisɑ̃, ɑ̃:t] adj. Abutting (*à*, on).
— m. pl. JUR. Abuttals (d'une affaire, d'une terre); circumstances (d'une question).

aboutissement [-tismɑ̃] m. Issue, outcome, result, effect (des désirs, efforts). ‖ Materialization (d'un plan, projet). ‖ MÉD. Festering, coming to a head (d'un abcès).

aboyer [abwaʃe] v. intr. (9 *a*). To bark, to bay, to yelp, to give tongue; *aboyer après*, to yelp after. ‖ FIG. To clamour (*après*, *contre*, against); to snarl (*après*, at).

aboyeur, euse [-jœ:r, ø:z] adj. Barking. ‖ FIG. Abusive, carping.
— m. FIG. Barker (camelot); dun (créancier); carper (critique). ‖ SPORTS. Tout (aux courses).

abracadabrant, ante [abrakadabrɑ̃, ɑ̃:t] adj. Stunning, amazing, preposterous. ‖ Wild (propos); *une histoire abracadabrante*, a fantastic yarn, a cock-and-bull story.

abrasif, ive [abrazif, i:v] adj. Abrasive.
abrasion [-zjɔ̃] f. Abrasion.
abréaction [abreaksjɔ̃] f. PHILOS., MÉD. Abreaction.

abrégé [abreʒe] m. Epitome (bref aperçu); abridgment, precis (condensé); digest (digeste); synopsis (plan); miniature (reproduction en abrégé); compendium, abstract, brief (résumé); summary (sommaire); *abrégé pour*, short for; *écrire en abrégé*, to abbreviate, to shorten, to write in an abridged form; *en abrégé*, in brief, in a few words, in a nutshell.

abrègement [abrɛʒmɑ̃] m. Abridgment; condensation; curtailment; epitomizing. ‖ GRAMM. Shortening.

abréger [abreʒe] v. tr. (5, 7). To shorten (dans la durée); to curtail, to cut short (brusquement); to abridge, to condense, to sum up, to epitomize, to boil down (en conservant l'essentiel); *abréger une visite*, to cut a call short, to shorten a visit; *abréger un livre*, to condense a book. ‖ GRAMM. To shorten (une syllabe). ‖ LOC. *Pour abréger*, for short, to be brief, to make a long story short.
— v. pr. **S'abréger**, to shorten; to grow shorter.

abreuvage [abrœva:ʒ] m. Watering (des bestiaux). ‖ TECHN. Priming (d'une pompe).

abreuver [-ve] v. tr. (1). To water (les bestiaux); to irrigate, to flood (les terres). ‖ TECHN. To prime (une pompe); to season (un tonneau). ‖ FIG. *Abreuver de*, to saturate with, to drench with, to steep in; *abreuver d'outrages*, to heap insults on; *abreuver de peines*, to overburden with sorrows; *abreuvé de sang*, drenched (ou) sated with blood.
— v. pr. **S'abreuver**, to drink (bestiaux); to quench (ou) slake one's thirst (personnes).

abreuvoir [-vwa:r] m. Watering-place; horse pond (étang). ‖ Watering- (ou) drinking-trough (auge); *mener les chevaux à l'abreuvoir*, to take the horses to water.

abréviation [abrevjasjɔ̃] f. Abbreviation, shortening; *par abréviation*, for short.

abri [abri] m. Shelter, covering; *sans abri*, homeless, roofless; *les sans-abri*, the homeless. ‖ Windscreen (contre le vent). ‖ MILIT. Shelter, dug-out; air-raid shelter; *gagner les abris*, to go to the shelters. ‖ NAUT. Harbourage, berthage. ‖ FIG. Defence, protection; haven, screen. ‖ LOC. *A l'abri*, sheltered, under cover; *à l'abri de*, under shelter (ou) cover of, safe from, secure from; *à l'abri du besoin*, secure from want; *à l'abri du danger*, in safety; *chercher un abri sous*, to seek shelter under; *mettre à l'abri*, to shelter, to house, to screen, to hide, to secure (*de*, from); *se mettre à l'abri*, to take shelter (ou) cover (ou) refuge (*de*, from); *offrir un abri*, to give cover.

Abribus [-bys] m. (nom déposé). Bus-shelter.

abricot [abriko] m. Apricot.
— adj. Apricot-coloured.
abricoté, ée [-kɔte] adj. *Pêche abricotée*, yellow peach.

abricotier [-tje] m. BOT. Apricot-tree.

abriter [abrite] v. tr. (1). To shelter, to house, to put under cover (en général); to screen (contre le vent). ‖ To shelter, to cover, to harbour, to put under cover, to shield (contre un danger). ‖ To hide (cacher); to shadow (ombrager).
— v. pr. **S'abriter**, to take cover (ou) shelter (*de*, from).

abrogatif, ive [abrɔgatif, i:v] adj. Abrogative.
abrogation [sjɔ̃] f. JUR. Abrogation, cancellation, abolition. ‖ JUR. Rescission (d'un décret); repeal (d'une loi).
abrogatoire [-twa:r] adj. JUR. Abrogatory.
abrogeable [abrɔʒabl] adj. JUR. Repealable.
abroger [-ʒe] v. tr. (7). To rescind (un ordre). ‖ JUR. To abrogate, to repeal (une loi).

abrupt, upte [abrypt] adj. Steep (colline); precipitous (hauteur); sheer (falaise); abrupt (pente). ‖ FIG. Abrupt, sudden, hasty, precipitate (départ); gruff, brusque (manières, parole); jerky, disconnected (style).
— m. Steep slope, precipice.

abruptement [-mɑ̃] adv. Abruptly, steeply, sheerly. ‖ Suddenly (soudain). ‖ Abruptly, bluntly, gruffly (avec brusquerie).

abruti [abryti] m. Dolt, dullard; sot (par l'alcool); *quel abruti!*, what a clod (ou) boor!

abrutir [-ti:r] v. tr. (2). To brutalize, to bestialize, to brutify. (V. ABÊTIR.) ‖ To besot (par l'alcool); *abruti par l'alcool*, drink-sodden. ‖ FAM. To tire out (par la fatigue); to stupefy, to stun, to daze (par la surprise). [V. HÉBÉTER.]
— v. pr. **S'abrutir**, to besot oneself (en buvant); to grow stupid; to become doltish; to moulder (dans l'inaction).

abrutissant, ante [-tisɑ̃, ɑ̃:t] adj. Stupefying, brutifying. ‖ FAM. Dull, deadening; *besogne abrutissante*, drudgery, plod.

abrutissement [-tismɑ̃] m. Degradation. ‖ Brutishness, sottishness.

abscisse [absis] f. MATH. Abscissa; co-ordinate.
abscons, onse [abskɔ̃, ɔ̃s] adj. Recondite. (V. ABSTRUS.)

absence [absɑ̃:s] f. Absence (*de*, from); non-attendance (à l'école, à une réunion); *en l'absence de*, in the absence of; *pendant mon absence*, in my absence; *revenu d'une longue absence*, back from a long absence. ‖ Absence, want, lack (manque); *absence de soin*, carelessness. ‖ Absence of mind, absent-mindedness, abstraction (distraction); *il a des absences*, his mind wanders; *un moment d'absence*, a fit of abstraction. ‖ MILIT. *Absence irrégulière*, absence without leave. ‖ JUR. *Absence de testament*, intestacy.

absent, ente [-sɑ̃, ɑ̃:t] adj. Absent (non présent). ‖ Away, away from home (parti). ‖ Wanting (marquant). ‖ FIG. Wool-gathering, distraught, absent-minded, abstracted. (V. DISTRAIT.)
— s. Absent person; absentee. ‖ Pl. The absent.

absentéisme [-teism] m. Absenteeism; *absentéisme scolaire*, truancy.

absentéiste [-teist] m. Absentee.

absenter (s') [sabsɑ̃te] v. pr. (1). To absent oneself (*from*, de); to go away, to be (ou) stay away.

absidal, ale [absidal], **absidial, ale** [-djal] adj. Apsidal.

abside [absi:d] f. ARCHIT. Apse.

absidiole [-djɔl] f. ARCHIT. Apsidal chapel.

absinthe [absɛ̃:t] f. BOT. Wormwood. ‖ COMM. Absinth, absinthe (boisson).

absolu, ue [absɔly] adj. Absolute; *ablatif absolu,* ablative absolute; *majorité absolue,* absolute majority; *plafond, zéro absolu,* absolute ceiling, zero. ‖ Perfect; complete, total; *confiance absolue,* sheer (ou) utter confidence. ‖ Pure; *alcool absolu,* absolute alcohol. ‖ Positive, certain, real; *preuve absolue,* positive proof. ‖ Unrestricted, autocratic (v. DICTATORIAL); *caractère absolu,* imperious character; *monarchie absolue,* absolute monarchy; *refus absolu,* flat refusal; *règle absolue,* hard and fast (ou) strict rule.
— m. PHIL. Absolute.

absolument [-mɑ̃] adv. Absolutely. ‖ Completely, perfectly. ‖ Purely. ‖ Positively, really. ‖ Without fail, strictly, utterly. ‖ LOC. *Absolument rien à ajouter,* nothing whatever to add; *il faut absolument que je parte,* I really must go; *il n'y a absolument aucune raison pour que,* there is no reason on earth why; *il le veut absolument,* he insists upon it.

absolution [-sjɔ̃] f. ECCLÉS. Absolution (*de,* from). ‖ JUR. Discharge.

absolutisme [-tism] m. Absolutism.

absolutiste [-tist] m. Absolutist.

absolutoire [-twa:r] adj. Absolutory, absolving. ‖ JUR. *Jugement absolutoire,* legal acquittal.

absorbable [absɔrbabl] adj. Absorbable.

absorbant, ante [-bɑ̃, ɑ̃:t] adj. Absorptive (fonction); absorbent (substance, tissu). ‖ FIG. Absorbing, engrossing (travail).
— m. Absorbent.

absorbé, ée [-be] adj. Absorbed in thought; *absorbé par,* absorbed in.

absorber [-be] v. tr. (1). To drink (une boisson); to consume (la nourriture). ‖ To absorb, to soak in (ou) up (la chaleur, un liquide, la lumière); to occlude (un gaz). ‖ FIN. To swallow up (les bénéfices). ‖ FIG. To absorb, to engross (l'attention); to engulf, to swallow up (une fortune); to take up (le temps).
— v. pr. **S'absorber dans,** to be absorbed in, to be swallowed up by. ‖ FIG. To be engrossed (ou) lost (ou) buried in.

absorption [absɔrpsjɔ̃] f. Absorption.

absoudre [absudr] v. tr.(10). ECCLÉS. To absolve, to forgive (un pénitent). ‖ JUR. To acquit (pour manque de preuve); to exonerate, to pardon (exempter de peinc). ‖ FIG. *Absoudre qqn de qqch.,* to forgive (ou) to pardon s.o. sth.; to absolve s.o. from sth.

absoute [-sut] f. ECCLÉS. Absolution.

abstenir (s') [sabstəni:r] v. pr. (101). To stand aside (ou) aloof; *s'abstenir de,* to abstain (ou) refrain (ou) forbear from, to forgo. ‖ FAM. To abstain from voting (électeur). ‖ LOC. *Dans le doute, abstiens-toi,* when in doubt, don't.

abstention [abstɑ̃sjɔ̃] f. Abstention, abstaining. ‖ JUR. Withdrawal, self-challenge (de juge).

abstentionnisme [-sjɔnism] m. Abstentionism, refusal to vote.

abstentionniste [-sjɔnist] m. Abstentionist.

abstinence [ɔbstinɑ̃:s] f. Abstinence; abstemiousness; *faire abstinence de,* to abstain from. ‖ FIG. Abstention, refraining (de, from).

abstinent, ente [-nɑ̃, ɑ̃:t] adj. Abstinent, abstemious.
— s. Total abstainer; teetotaller.

abstraction [abstraksjɔ̃] f. Abstraction; *faire*

abstraction de, to disregard, to set aside, to exclude, to leave out of account; *abstraction faite de,* apart from, setting aside, not taking into consideration. ‖ Abstract question.

abstractionnisme [-sjɔnism] m. ARTS. Abstractionism.

abstraire [abstrɛ:r] v. tr. (11). To abstract, to separate. ‖ To dissociate, to isolate, to detach (*de,* from).
— v. pr. **S'abstraire,** to become absorbed (ou) wrapped (*dans,* in); to withdraw oneself (*de,* from).

abstrait, aite [-strɛ, ɛt] adj. Abstruse, abstract (argument, théorie); abstract (idée). ‖ MATH., ARTS, GRAMM., Abstract.
— m. PHILOS. Abstract. ‖ ARTS. Abstract art; abstract painter.

abstraitement [-təmɑ̃] adv. Abstractedly, in the abstract.

abstrus, use [abstry, yz] adj. Abstruse.

absurde [absyrd] adj. Foolish, silly, senseless, nonsensical (conclusion, propos); ludicrous (expression); absurd (hypothèse); preposterous (revendication). [V. DÉRAISONNABLE, INSENSÉ.]
— m. Absurdity; *par l'absurde,* ad absurdum.

absurdement [-dəmɑ̃] adv. Absurdly, senselessly.

absurdité [-dite] f. Absurdity, foolishness, nonsense. ‖ Drivel, twaddle (en paroles).

abus [aby] m. Misuse, abuse (*de,* of); *abus de pouvoir,* abuse of power, misuse of authority. ‖ Breach, violation, infringement; *abus de confiance,* breach of trust, embezzlement. ‖ Immoderate use, excess (*de,* of); over-indulgence (*de,* in). ‖ Perversion, corrupt practice. ‖ Pl. Abuses.

abuser [-ze] v. tr. (1). To abuse, to deceive.
— v. intr. *Abuser de,* to misuse, to waste (un bien). ‖ To presume (ou) to impose upon (l'amabilité); to deceive (la confiance); to overstep the limits of (ses droits); to overstrain (ses forces); to indulge in (un plaisir); to take advantage of (qqn); to trespass (ou) to encroach upon (temps de qqn). ‖ To seduce, to dishonour (une femme).
— v. pr. **S'abuser,** to deceive oneself, to be mistaken.

abusif, ive [-zif, i:v] adj. Excessive, undue. ‖ Unauthorized (réquisition). ‖ GRAMM. Improper, wrong (sens).

abusivement [-zivmɑ̃] adv. Abusively.

abuter [abyte] v. intr. (1). To abut.

abyssal, ale [abissal] adj. Abyssal (faune, flore). ‖ FIG. Unfathomable.

abysse [abis] m. Abyss, ocean depths.

acabit [akabi] m. FAM. Stamp; *du même acabit,* of a feather, of the same kidney, tarred with the same brush. (V. ESPÈCE.)

acacia [akasja] m. BOT. Acacia; locust-tree.

académicien [akademisjɛ̃] m. Academician.

académie [-mi] f. Academy (grecque, universitaire, savante). ‖ ARTS. School (école); nude, academy-figure (nu). ‖ FAM. Anatomy.

académique [-mik] adj. Academic, academical. ‖ Speculative, theoretical (discussion); classic (pose); scholarly (style).

académiquement [-mik·mɑ̃] adv. Academically.

académisme [-mism] m. ARTS. Conventionalism, lack of originality, adherence to classical convention.

acagnarder [akaɲarde] v. tr. (1). To make lazy.
— v. pr. **S'acagnarder,** to grow lazy; to laze (paresser). ‖ To keep snug, to lounge, to snuggle (au coin du feu, dans un fauteuil).

acajou [akaʒu] m. Mahogany; *noix d'acajou,* cashew nut.
— adj. Dark auburn (cheveux).

acanthe [akɑ̃:t] f. BOT., ARCHIT. Acanthus.

acare [akar] m. MÉD. Acarus.

acariâtre [akarjɑ:tr] adj. Crabbed, cantankerous, cross, nagging, peevish; shrewish.

acariâtreté [-trəte] f. Cantankerousness.
acarien [akarjɛ̃] m. ZOOL. Acarid.
acarpe [akarp] adj. BOT. Acarpous.
acatène [akatɛ:n] adj. Chainless.
acaule [ako:l] adj. BOT. Acaulous.
accablant, ante [akablɑ̃, ɑ̃t] adj. Overwhelming (chagrin); oppressive, sweltering (chaleur); crushing (charge). ‖ JUR. Overwhelming (preuve); damning (témoignage).
accablé, ée [-ble] adj. Overpowered, weighed down. ‖ Overcome (de chaleur); worn out (de fatigue); overwhelmed (de travail). ‖ MÉD. Prostrate.
accablement [-bləmɑ̃] m. Depression (fatigue). [V. ABATTEMENT.] ‖ MÉD. Prostration. ‖ COMM. Pressure (des affaires).
accabler [-ble] v. tr. (1). To overpower, to crush, to weigh down; accabler de, to overcharge with, to overburden with (charges, impôts, honneurs); to harass with (questions); to load with (reproches). ‖ To inveigh against (critiquer). ‖ To overcome (un adversaire).
accalmie [akalmi] f. Calm (en mer); lull (du vent). ‖ MÉD. Intermission (d'une fièvre). ‖ COMM. Slack period (des affaires).
accaparement [akaparmɑ̃] m. Buying up, cornering, hoarding, forestalling, monopolizing. ‖ JUR. Coemption.
accaparer [-re] v. tr. (1). To corner, to garner, to hoard, to abroach (des denrées). ‖ COMM. To capture (le marché); to buy up; to stockpile (des stocks). ‖ FIG. To monopolize (la conversation); to buttonhole (qqn); to absorb (le temps).
accapareur, euse [-rœ:r, ø:z] s. Grasper. ‖ Monopolist, monopolizer.
— adj. Possessive.
accéder [aksede] v. intr. (5). To have access (à, to) [un lieu]; to accede (à, to) [un poste]. ‖ FIG. To assent, to accede, to yield (à, to); to comply (à, with).
accélérateur [akseleratœ:r] adj. Accelerating, accelerative.
— m. AUTOM. Accelerator.
accélération [-rasjɔ̃] f. Acceleration; pédale d'accélération, accelerator pedal. ‖ Hastening, speeding up (du travail, du rythme).
accéléré, ée [-re] adj. Accelerated, speeded up; fast, rapid; au pas accéléré, in quick time.
— m. CINÉM. Quick motion.
accélérer [-re] v. tr. (5). To accelerate; to speed up (le mouvement); to hurry (le travail).
— v. pr. S'accélérer, to accelerate.
accent [aksɑ̃] m. Accent; emphasis (oratoire); stress (tonique). ‖ Accent, pronunciation; twang (américain); brogue (irlandais). ‖ Tone, intonation. ‖ Pl. Accents, strains. ‖ GRAMM. Accent.
accentuation [-tyasjɔ̃] f. GRAMM., FIG. Accentuation.
accentué, ée [-tye] adj. Stressed; accentuated, pronounced. ‖ FIG. Marked (traits).
accentuer [-tye] v. tr. (1). To stress, to emphasize, to accentuate. ‖ GRAMM. To accent. ‖ FIG. To increase.
— v. pr. S'accentuer, to become accentuated, to increase, to grow stronger.
acceptable [aksɛptabl] adj. Acceptable, satisfactory, agreeable. ‖ Reasonable, fair. ‖ Decent, possible, passable.
acceptablement [-mɑ̃] adv. Acceptably.
acceptant [-tɑ̃] m. COMM. Acceptor; drawee.
acceptation [-tasjɔ̃] f. Acceptance (d'un poste). ‖ COMM. Acceptance; revêtu de l'acceptation, duly accepted.
accepter [-te] v. tr. (1). To accept (un cadeau, une invitation, une proposition); to agree to, to acquiesce in (une condition, une décision); to take up (un défi, un pari); to admit (des excuses);

to take (un risque). ‖ COMM. To accept, to honour (une traite); ne pas accepter, to dishonour.
accepteur [-tœ:r] m. COMM. Acceptor, drawee.
acception [-sjɔ̃] f. Acceptation (v. SIGNIFICATION); dans toute l'acception du terme, in the full acceptation of the word. ‖ Acceptance (considération); sans acception de personnes, without respect of persons.
accès [aksɛ] n. Access, approach; admittance; d'un accès facile, accessible; donner accès à, to give access to; trouver accès auprès, to gain admission to. ‖ MÉD. Attack, fit. ‖ FIG. Outburst, fit, huff (de colère); fit (de désespoir); burst (d'enthousiasme); ecstasy (de gaieté); pet (d'humeur).
accessibilité [-sibilite] f. Accessibility; get-at-ableness.
accessible [-sibl] adj. Accessible, open (à, to); available (à, for); accessible à la flatterie, susceptible to flattery. ‖ Attainable (à la portée) [à, by]. ‖ Obtainable (procurable). ‖ Approachable.
accession [-sjɔ̃] f. Accession (au pouvoir). Adherence, adhesion (à un contrat, à un parti).
accessit [aksɛsit] m. Accessit.
accessoire [aksɛswa:r] adj. Accessory. (V. SECONDAIRE.) ‖ Subsidiary, incidental (frais); droit accessoire, appurtenance; garantie accessoire, collateral security.
— m. Accessory, adjunct, appurtenance; corollary. ‖ Pl. Accessories, appliances. ‖ COMM. Outfit (de réparation); fitting; requisites (de toilette). ‖ AUTOM. Motor (ou) U. S. automobile accessories. ‖ THÉÂTR. Properties; props (fam.); magasin des accessoires, property room, prop-room (fam.).
accessoirement [-rmɑ̃] adv. Accessorily.
accessoiriste [-rist] m. THÉÂTR. Property man.
accident [aksidɑ̃] m. Accident, mishap; fortuitous event; accident d'auto (ou) de la circulation, motor-car (ou) traffic (ou) road accident, smash; accident d'avion, air crash; accident de personne, casualty; accident du travail, injury to workmen, industrial injury; sans accident, safely. ‖ Accident, unevenness; accidents du terrain, irregularities of the ground. ‖ MUS. Accidental. ‖ PHILOS. Accident. ‖ LOC. Par accident, accidentally, by chance.
accidenté, ée [-te] adj. Hilly (paysage); uneven, broken, rough (terrain); eventful, chequered (vie).
— m. Casualty, victim.
accidentel, elle [-tɛl] adj. Incidental, casual, accidental; adventitious; haphazard. (V. FORTUIT, INATTENDU.) ‖ MUS. Accidental.
accidentellement [-tɛlmɑ̃] adv. Accidentally, by accident.
accidenter [-te] v. tr. (1). To render uneven (un terrain). ‖ To vary (le style). ‖ To cause an accident to (qqn).
accise [aksi:z] f. FIN. Excise; inland revenue.
acclamateur [aklamatœ:r] m. Acclaimer.
acclamation [-masjɔ̃] f. Acclamation; cheering.
acclamer [-me] v. tr. (1). To acclaim, to cheer, to hail.
acclimatable [aklimatabl] adj. Acclimatizable.
acclimatation [-tasjɔ̃] f. Acclimatization; U. S. acclimation.
acclimatement [-tmɑ̃] m. Acclimatation.
acclimater [-te] v. tr. (1). To acclimatize (à, to); U. S. to acclimate. ‖ FIG. To season; to adapt.
— v. pr. S'acclimater, to become (ou) to get acclimatized. ‖ FIG. To get used (choses); to become inured (à, to) [personnes].
accointance [akwɛ̃tɑ̃s] f. Association, intimacy, intercourse. ‖ Pl. Dealings, connections, relations.
accointer (s') [sakwɛ̃te] v. pr. (1). FAM. To take up (avec, with).
accolade [akɔlad] f. Accolade (à l'épée). ‖

Embrace, hug (embrassement). ‖ Brace (en typographie). ‖ Mus. Accolade.

accolement [-lmã] m. Joining, uniting. ‖ Coupling. ‖ Milit. In line abreast.

accoler [-le] v. tr. (1). To embrace (embrasser). ‖ To couple; to place side by side (réunir). ‖ To bracket (en typographie). ‖ Agric. To tie up. ‖ Milit. To put in line abreast.

accommodable [akɔmɔdabl] adj. Adjustable. ‖ Culin. That can be dressed (à, with).

accommodage [-da:ʒ] m. Culin. Dressing, cooking, preparing.

accommodant, ante [-dã, ã:t] adj. Accommodating, compliant. (V. conciliant.)

accommodation [-dasjɔ̃] f. Accommodation, adaptation. ‖ Méd. Accommodation.

accommodement [-dmã] m. Adjustment, amicable settlement (v. arrangement, compromis); *en venir à un accommodement avec,* to come to terms with. ‖ Composition (avec des créanciers).

accommoder [-de] v. tr. (1). To be convenient to; to suit (qqn). ‖ To accommodate (de, with). ‖ To adjust (un différend); to reconcile (des adversaires); to arrange, to dispose (des meubles). ‖ To arrange, to trim, to attire (parer). ‖ Culin. To cook, to dress, to season, to do up. ‖ Fig. To slander, to criticize (critiquer); to beat up (rosser). — v. pr. **S'accommoder,** to make oneself comfortable; to become reconciled (adversaires); to be arranged (différend); *s'accommoder à,* to accommodate oneself to, to conform to; to comply with; *s'accommoder avec,* to compromise, to compound with (créanciers); to consort with, to agree with (qqn); *s'accommoder de,* to make do with, to make the best of, to put up with.

accompagnateur, trice [akɔ̃paɲatœ:r, tris] s. Mus. Accompanist.

accompagnement [-ɲmã] m. Accompanying; escorting; attendance. ‖ Mus. Accompaniment; obbligato; *sans accompagnement,* unaccompanied. ‖ Culin. Sauce, trimmings. ‖ Milit. *Tir d'accompagnement,* supporting fire.

accompagner [-ɲe] v. tr. (1). To accompany, to go along with; *accompagner qqn à la porte,* to see s.o. off (ou) to the door. ‖ To escort; to attend (qqn); to chaperon (une jeune fille); to squire (une femme). ‖ To follow from, to arise from (découler de). ‖ To go with, to match, to suit (s'assortir). ‖ Mus. To accompany. ‖ *Accompagner de,* to follow up with, to accompany by. — v. pr. **S'accompagner,** to be accompanied (de, by); to be attended (de, with). ‖ Mus. *S'accompagner au piano,* to accompany oneself on the piano.

accompli, ie [akɔ̃pli] adj. Completed, ended, achieved; *fait accompli,* accomplished fact; *il a vingt ans accomplis,* he has turned twenty. ‖ Accomplished. — m. Gramm. Perfective.

accomplir [-pli:r] v. tr. (2). To carry out (un dessein, un projet); to perform (son devoir, un travail); to carry through (une entreprise); to achieve (un exploit); to accomplish (une mission, une prophétie, un sauvetage); to execute (un ordre); to fulfil (une promesse); to effect (une réforme); *accomplir des merveilles,* to work wonders. ‖ To complete, to conclude (achever). ‖ Milit. To do (on service militaire). — v. pr. **S'accomplir,** to happen, to take place (arriver). ‖ To be accomplished (ou) performed (ou) fulfilled (se réaliser).

accomplissement [-plismã] m. Satisfaction (d'une condition); accomplishment, performance, carrying out (du devoir, d'une œuvre); fulfilment (d'une promesse). ‖ Jur. Completion (d'un contrat).

accord [akɔ:r] m. Agreement, consent; *d'un commun accord,* with one accord. ‖ Concord, harmony; union, concert; *d'accord!,* agreed!, quite so!, U. S. O. K., check!; *d'accord avec,* in agreement (ou) conformity with; *en accord parfait avec,* perfectly atuned to; *en accord avec soi-même,* consistent, true to oneself; *être d'accord avec,* to agree (ou) to concur (ou) to chime in with; *mettre d'accord,* to harmonize, to reconcile; *se mettre d'accord,* to come to an agreement (ou) to an understanding. ‖ Jur. Grant. ‖ Radio. Tuning. ‖ Mus. Tune (d'un instrument); pl. Strains (notes); *accord parfait,* perfect chord. ‖ Gramm. Agreement; *règles d'accord,* concords.

accordable [-dabl] adj. Reconcilable. ‖ Allowable, grantable. ‖ Mus. Tunable.

accordage [-da:ʒ] m. Mus. Tuning.

accordailles [-da:j] f. pl. † Betrothal.

accordéon [-deɔ̃] m. Mus. Accordion; concertina. ‖ Fig. *En accordéon,* accordion pleated (pli); concertinaed, crumpled up (voiture).

accordéoniste [-deonist] m. Mus. Accordionist, concertina player.

accorder [-de] v. tr. (1). To grant (une audience, une autorisation, son attention); to concede, to bestow (une faveur); to confer (un privilège); *accorder avec,* to harmonize with, to adjust to; *accorder que,* to agree (ou) to admit (ou) to grant that. ‖ To reconcile (des adversaires); to adjust, to arrange, to settle (un différend); to bestow (en mariage); to give (sa main). ‖ Jur. To adjudge, to award (des dommages). ‖ Arts. To harmonize (en peinture). ‖ Mus. To tune (des accents); to key (un piano); to string (un violon). ‖ Electr. To tune (la radio). ‖ Gramm. To make agree. — v. pr. **S'accorder,** to be on good terms, to get on well, U. S. to hit it off (fam.) [s'entendre]; to agree, to come to terms (se mettre d'accord); to become reconciled (se réconcilier). ‖ To harmonize, to match, to tally (avec, with). ‖ To be granted (ou) awarded (ou) bestowed (être accordé) [à, to]. ‖ Mus. To tune up. ‖ Gramm. To agree.

accordeur [-dœ:r] m. Mus. Tuner.

accordoir [-dwa:r] m. Mus. Tuning-hammer.

accore [akɔ:r] m. Naut. Shore, prop (de construction); edge (d'écueil). — adj. Sheer; bluff.

accorer [-re] v. tr. (1). Naut. To shore up.

accorte [akɔ:rt] adj. f. Sprightly, trim, engaging.

accostable [akɔstabl] adj. Approachable; accessible.

accostage [-ta:ʒ] m. Naut. Coming alongside (de, of). ‖ Fig. Approaching, accosting (d'une personne).

accoster [-te] v. tr. (1). Naut. To come alongside; to berth, to moor (à quai). ‖ Naut. To board (à l'abordage). ‖ Fig. To accost, to approach (qqn).

accotement [akɔtmã] m. Side-path, sidewalk, roadside. ‖ Ch. de f. Side space.

accoter [-te] v. tr. (1). To shore up (un bateau); to stay (un mur). — v. pr. **S'accoter,** to lean (contre, against).

accotoir [-twa:r] m. Arm-rest. (V. accoudoir.)

accouchée [akuʃe] f. Woman in childbed.

accouchement [-ʃmã] m. Méd. Childbirth; confinement; parturition, accouchement.

accoucher [-ʃe] v. intr. (1). Méd. To be confined, to lie in, to be delivered, to accouche; *accoucher de,* to give birth to. ‖ Fam. To bring forth; to spit it out, to cough it up; *allons, accouche!,* out with it! — v. tr. Méd. To deliver.

accoucheur [-ʃœ:r] m. Méd. Accoucheur, obstetrician.

accoucheuse [-ʃœ:z] f. Méd. Accoucheuse, midwife.

accoudement [akudmɑ̃] m. Leaning on one's elbows.

accouder (s') [sakude] v. pr. (1). To lean on (ou) to rest on one's elbows (sur, on).

accoudoir [akudwa:r] m. Arm-rest, elbow-rest.

accouple [akupl] f. Leash.

accouplement [-pləmɑ̃] m. Coupling. ‖ Pairing, mating; accouplement consanguin, in-breeding. ‖ TECHN. Joining, linking, coupling; bielle d'accouplement, connecting rod. ‖ ELECTR. Connection; linkage (électro-magnétique) ‖ RADIO. Coupling.

accoupler [-ple] v. tr. (1). To couple; to pair, to mate. ‖ To yoke (des bœufs). ‖ TECHN. To join, to couple up. ‖ ELECTR. To group, to connect; hauts parleurs accouplés, dual loud-speakers. ‖ FIG. To match.
— v. pr. S'accoupler, to couple; to mate, to pair; to copulate.

accourir [akuri:r] v. intr. (32). To run up, to hasten up.

accoutrement [akutrəmɑ̃] m. Accoutrement, attire. ‖ FAM. Get-up, rig-out, duds, togs.

accoutrer [-tre] v. tr. (1). To accoutre, to equip, to attire. ‖ FAM. To get up, to rig out, to perk up, to tog up, to trick out, U.S. to outfit.
— v. pr. S'accoutrer, to rig oneself out, to get oneself up (de, in).

accoutumance [akutymɑ̃:s] f. Familiarisation (à, with); inurement (à, to). ‖ Habit, use, practice (habitude).

accoutumé, ée [-me] adj. Accustomed, usual, customary (habituel). ‖ Accustomed, used, inured (à, to). ‖ LOC. A l'accoutumée, usually, as usual.
— m. Regular customer (usager); customary caller (visiteur).

accoutumer [-me] v. tr. (1). To accustom, to habituate (à, to); to familiarize (à, with). ‖ To inure (aguerrir) [à, to].
— v. intr. † Avoir accoutumé de, to be used to, to be wont to.
— v. pr. S'accoutumer, to get used to, to become accustomed (à, to).

accouvage [akuva:ʒ] m. Artificial incubation.

accrédité, ée [akredite] adj. Accredited (diplomate). ‖ Of good standing.
— m. Accredited agent (ou) party; payee.

accréditer [-te] v. tr. (1). To accredit (un diplomate) [auprès de, to]. ‖ To cause to be believed, to sanction, to give support to (une idée). ‖ FIN. To open a credit to.
— v. pr. S'accréditer, to gain currency (opinion); to gain favour (personne).

accréditeur [-tœ:r] m. FIN. Guarantor, surety.

accréditif, ive [-tif, i:v] n. FIN. Letter of credit, credential; credit.

accroc [akro] m. Tear, rent (à, in). [V. DÉCHIRURE.] ‖ Scrap (morceau arraché). ‖ FIG. Snag, hitch. (V. COMPLICATION.)

accrochage [-ʃa:ʒ] m. Hanging up (d'un tableau). ‖ ELECTR. Picking up (d'un poste, à la radio). ‖ SPORTS. Clinch (à la boxe); hooking (à la pêche). ‖ CH. DE F. Hitching on (d'un wagon). ‖ AUTOM. Collision, grazing. ‖ NAUT. Running foul. ‖ MILIT. Engagement, brush, encounter. ‖ FAM. Squabble, wrangle, set-to (dispute).

accroche [akroʃ] m. Hanger. ‖ **Accroche-cœur**, m. invar. Love-lock, kiss-curl. ‖ **Accroche-plat**, m. invar. Plate-hanger.

accrocher [-ʃe] v. tr. (1). To hang up (suspendre) [à, on, from]. ‖ To hook (avec un crochet, un hameçon); to catch (à une ronce). ‖ RADIO. To pick up (un poste). ‖ SPORTS. To catch (un poisson). ‖ CH. DE F. To couple, to hitch (un wagon). ‖ AUTOM. To run into. ‖ NAUT. To grapple. ‖ MILIT. To engage, to come to grips with. ‖ FAM. To stop (arrêter); to buttonhole (cramponner).

— v. intr. FAM. To come to a standstill; to run into difficulties; to be held up.
— v. pr. S'accrocher, to be clasped (ou) hooked; s'accrocher à, to catch on, to get caught on (une ronce). ‖ SPORTS. To cling (à la boxe). ‖ FIG. To cling (à, to) [un espoir]. ‖ FAM. To wrangle (se disputer); to stick (à, to) [cramponner].

accrocheur, euse [-ʃœ:r, ʃø:z] adj. Dogged, tenacious (combatif, tenace); il est accrocheur, he is a sticker. ‖ Inviting, enticing (racoleur).

accroire [akrwa:r] v. tr. (12). En faire accroire à, to impose upon, to delude, to humbug; s'en faire accroire, to fancy oneself, to overestimate oneself, to get a swollen head.

accroissement [akrwasmɑ̃] m. AGRIC. Growth. ‖ FIN. Accumulation (du capital); increase (des revenus). ‖ JUR. Accretion (d'héritage). ‖ MATH. Increment.

accroître [akrwa:tr] v. tr. (34). COMM. To enlarge (une affaire). ‖ FIN. To increase (une dette); to augment (son revenu). ‖ FIG. To add to (la confusion); to heighten (la gloire); to increase (le pouvoir); to enhance (la réputation).
— v. pr. S'accroître, to increase, to grow.

accroupi, ie [akrupi] adj. Squatting, crouching. ‖ BLAS. Couchant.

accroupir (s') [sakrupi:r] v. pr. (2). To squat, to crouch; to cower.

accroupissement [akrupismɑ̃] m. Squatting, crouching.

accru, ue [akry] p. p. V. ACCROÎTRE.
— m. BOT. Sucker.

accrue f. Alluvion (fluviale); increase (de forêt); accretion (de terre).

accu [aky] m. ELECTR., AUTOM. Accumulator, battery (V. ACCUMULATEUR); recharger ses accus, to recharge one's batteries (prop., fig.).

accueil [akœ:j] m. Reception; welcome (bienvenue); accueil défavorable, hostile reception; faire bon accueil à, to welcome (qqn); to accede to (une requête); to honour (une traite); recevoir un accueil chaleureux, to meet with a warm response (demande).

accueillant, ante [-jɑ̃, ɑ̃:t] adj. Hospitable, welcoming.

accueillir [-ji:r] v. tr. (35). To receive (en général); to welcome, to greet (aimablement). ‖ To subscribe to (une doctrine); to entertain, to give ear to, to accede to (une requête); to credit (une rumeur). ‖ FIN. To honour (une traite).

acculer [akyle] v. tr. (1). To bring to bay (un animal); to corner, to tree, to drive to the wall (qqn).
— v. intr. NAUT. To pitch by the stern, to pitch astern.

acculturation [akyltyrasjɔ̃] f. Acculturation.

accumulateur, trice [akymylatœ:r, tris] adj. Accumulative, acquisitive.
— m. ELECTR. Accumulator, storage battery.

accumulation [-lasjɔ̃] f. Accumulation; collection. ‖ Heap (d'objets). ‖ FIN. Hoarding (de capitaux). ‖ FIG. Storage (d'énergie).

accumuler [-le] v. tr. (1). To accumulate.
— v. intr. To hoard.
— v. pr. S'accumuler, to accumulate, to accrue.

accusable [akysabl] adj. Accusable (de, of); chargeable (de, with).

accusateur, trice [-tœ:r, tris] adj. Accusing, accusatory.
— s. Accuser, indicter. ‖ JUR. Accusateur public, Public prosecutor.

accusatif [-tif] m. GRAMM. Accusative.

accusation [-sjɔ̃] f. Accusation, charge. ‖ JUR. Indictment; arraignment, impeachment (de haute trahison); prosecution, case for the prosecution (partie plaignante); accusation calomnieuse, defamation; chef d'accusation, charge, specification of charges; mise en accusation, indictment, committal for trial; *porter une accusation,* to bring (ou) to lodge a charge.

accusatoire [-twa:r] adj. JUR. Accusatory, accusatorial.

accusé, ée [akyse] adj. Marked, prominent, pronounced, bold (traits).
— m. JUR. Accused; defendant, prisoner at the bar. (V. INCULPÉ.) ‖ COMM. *Accusé de réception,* acknowledgment of receipt.

accuser v. tr. (1). To accuse, to blame (qqch.). ‖ To exhibit, to show (un résultat). ‖ To accuse, to arraign, to proffer (ou) bring charges against (qqn); *accuser de,* to accuse of, to charge with, to indict for, to impeach for (haute trahison); to tax with (ingratitude). ‖ To bring out, to reveal, to set off (faire ressortir). ‖ COMM. *Accuser réception,* to acknowledge receipt. ‖ SPORTS. To acknowledge (un coup).
— v. pr. *S'accuser,* to be marked (défaut, trait). ‖ To accuse oneself (personne) [*de,* of].

acéphale [asefal] adj. Acephalous.

acerbe [asɛrb] adj. Sour, bitter, acrid (goût); biting, sharp, caustic (remarque, ton).

acerbité [-bite] f. Acerbity, bitterness, sharpness. ‖ Bitterness, sourness (au goût).

acéré, ée [asere] adj. Sharp-edged (lame); biting, cutting, stinging (langue, trait); keen (pointe).

acérer v. tr. (5). To sharpen, to point, to edge (un tranchant). ‖ TECHN. To steel. ‖ FIG. To sharpen, to give point to, to give a sting to.

acescent, ente [asɛsɑ̃, ɑ̃:t] adj. Acescent.

acétabule [asetabyl] m. Acetabulum.

acétamide [-tamid] m. CHIM. Acetamide.

acétate [-tat] m. CHIM. Acetate.

acéteux, euse [-tø, ø:z] adj. CHIM. Acetous.

acétification [-tifikasjɔ̃] f. Acetification; acetifying.

acétifier [-tifje] v. tr. (1). To acetify.
— v. pr. *S'acétifier,* to turn sour.

acétique [-tik] adj. CHIM. Acetic.

acétone [-tɔn] f. CHIM. Acetone.

acétylcholine [-tilkɔlin] f. MÉD. Acetylcholine.

acétylène [-tilɛ:n] m. CHIM. Acetylene.

achalandé, ée [aʃalɑ̃de] adj. *Bien achalandé,* well stocked.

acharné, ée [aʃarne] adj. Inveterate (joueur); hot, relentless (poursuite); *acharné à,* set upon, bent on. ‖ COMM. *Concurrence acharnée,* keen competition. ‖ MILIT. Stiff, stubborn, desperate, furious (combat); fierce, bitter (ennemi).

acharnement [-nəmɑ̃] m. Fury; animosity; obstinacy; *avec acharnement,* eagerly, fiercely, furiously, desperately; like mad (fam.).

acharner [-ne] v. tr. (1). To flesh (un chien); to bait (un leurre).
— v. pr. *S'acharner,* to set (*sur,* upon) [une proie]; to be dead set (*sur,* against); to have one's teeth (*sur,* in); U. S. to light (*sur,* into) [qqn]. ‖ *S'acharner à,* to hammer away at, to persist in, to slog at (un travail).

achat [aʃa] m. Buying (action); purchase (objet); *aller faire ses achats,* to go shopping; *pouvoir d'achat,* purchasing power. ‖ COMM. *Achat à terme,* credit purchase. ‖ FIN. *Achat à terme,* purchase for the settlement.

acheminement [aʃminmɑ̃] m. Step, course, advancement, progression (*vers,* towards). ‖ Dispatching, routing (des colis); forwarding (du matériel).

acheminer [-ne] v. tr. (1). To direct, to dispatch (qqn) [*sur, vers,* towards]; to route, to forward (qqch.) [*sur,* to].
— v. pr. *S'acheminer,* to proceed, to be on the way, to move; to progress.

achetable [aʃtabl] adj. Buyable, purchasable.

acheter [-te] v. tr. (8 *b*). To buy, to purchase (à,

from; *pour,* for; *au prix de,* at, for); *j'en ai acheté pour dix mille francs,* I bought ten thousand francs' worth; *acheter un chapeau cinq cents francs,* to buy a hat for five hundred francs. ‖ FIG. To buy, to bribe (qqn). ‖ FAM. To kid, to take in (berner).

acheteur [-ʃtœ:r] s. Purchaser, buyer. ‖ COMM. Buyer; shopper. ‖ JUR. Vendee.

achevé, ée [aʃve] adj. Ended, finished; over. ‖ FIG. Accomplished; absolute, utter (v. ACCOMPLI); *le type achevé de,* the model of; *menteur achevé,* consummate liar.

achèvement [aʃɛvmɑ̃] m. Ending; conclusion; *en voie d'achèvement,* in process of completion.

achever [aʃve] v. tr. (5). To conclude (un discours); to end, to finish, to terminate, to bring to a close (une entreprise); to complete; to put the finishing touch to, to polish off (un travail). [V. FINIR.] ‖ To finish off, to dispatch. (V. TUER.) ‖ FAM. *La perte de son fils l'a achevé,* his son's death was the end of him.
— v. intr. To end, to finish; *achever de faire,* to finish doing; *il achevait de dîner,* he was just finishing dinner.
— v. pr. *S'achever,* to end, to close, to come to an end, to be fulfilled.

achoppement [aʃɔpmɑ̃] m. Knock; stumble; obstacle. ‖ FIG. *Pierre d'achoppement,* stumbling-block.

achopper [-pe] v. intr. (1). To trip up; to stumble (*contre,* over). ‖ FIG. To stumble.

achromatique [akrɔmatik] adj. Achromatic.

achromatisme [-tism] m. Achromatism.

achromatopsie [-tɔpsi] f. MÉD. Achromatopsy.

acide [asid] adj. Acid. ‖ FIG. Tart.
— m. CHIM. Acid.

acidifiable [-difiabl] adj. Acidifiable.

acidifiant, ante [-difjɑ̃, ɑ̃:t] adj. Acidifying.
— m. Acidifier.

acidification [-difikasjɔ̃] f. Acidification.

acidifier [-difje] v. tr. (1). To acidify.
— v. pr. *S'acidifier,* to turn sour; to become acid.

acidité [-dite] f. Acidity, sourness.

acido-basique [-dobazik] adj. MÉD. *Equilibre acido-basique,* acid-base equilibrium.

acidose [-dɔ:z] f. Acidosis, autointoxication.

acidulé, ée [-dyle] adj. Acidulated, acidulous; *bonbons acidulés,* acid drops, U. S. sour balls.

aciduler [-dyle] v. tr. (1). To acidulate.
— v. pr. *S'aciduler,* to turn acid.

acier [asje] m. Steel; *lame d'acier,* steel blade. ‖ FIG. Sword, dagger (arme); *regard d'acier,* steely glance.

aciérage [-ra:ʒ] m. Steeling; acierage; case-hardening.

aciérer [-re] v. tr. (5). TECHN. To steel, to case-harden.

aciérie [-ri] f. Steel-works.

aciériste [-rist] m. Steel-worker.

aclinique [aklinik] adj. PHYS. Aclinic.

acmé [akme] f. Acme, apogee.

acné [akne] f. MÉD. Acne.

acolyte [akɔlit] m. ECCLÉS. Acolyte. ‖ FAM. Attendant, assistant (aide); accomplice, confederate (complice).

acompte [akɔ̃:t] m. COMM. Instalment (v. PROVISION); *verser un acompte de dix mille francs sur,* to pay ten thousand francs on account of. ‖ FIN. Cover, margin (en bourse).

aconit [akɔnit] m. BOT. Aconite; monkshood.

a contrario [akɔ̃trarjo] adv. *Raisonnement a contrario,* argumentation by antithesis.

acoquiner (s') [sakɔkine] v. pr. To become attached (à, to) [un lieu]; to become debased (*auprès de,* by contact with).

Açores [asɔ:r] f. pl. GÉOGR. Azores.

à-côté [akote] m. Aside (remarque). ‖ Pl. Byways,

sidelights (de l'histoire); side-issues (de la question). ‖ FAM. Extras, perquisites, U. S. kick-back (en argent).

à-coup [aku] m. Jerk, jolt, jar; *par à-coups*, by fits and starts; *sans à-coups*, smoothly, without a hitch. ‖ Sudden halt (ou) stop (arrêt). ‖ MILIT. Check. ‖ ELECTR. Surge. ‖ FAM. *Il a eu beaucoup d'à-coups dans sa vie,* he has taken a lot of knocks in his life.

acoustique [akustik] adj. Acoustic (nerf); acoustical (science); *cornet acoustique,* ear-trumpet.
— f. Acoustics (qualité de sonorisation, science).

acquéreur [akerœ:r] m. COMM. Buyer, purchaser. ‖ JUR. Vendee.

acquérir [-ri:r] v. tr. (13). To buy, to purchase (acheter); to obtain (obtenir); to acquire (recevoir). ‖ FIG. To gain (de l'expérience); to win (de l'estime); to get into (une habitude).
— v. intr. To improve (s'améliorer).
— v. pr. **S'acquérir,** to accrue; to be gained (ou) obtained.

acquêt [akɛ] m. JUR. Acquest; *communauté réduite aux acquêts,* joint estate.

acquiert [akjɛr] indic. prés. V. ACQUÉRIR (13).

acquiescement [akjɛsmɑ̃] m. Acquiescence (à, in). ‖ JUR. Acceptance (d'un jugement).

acquiescer [-se] v. intr. (1). To agree, to assent, to consent (à, to); to acquiesce (à, in); to comply (à, with).

acquis [aki] adj. COMM. Bought. ‖ FIG. Obtained; acquired (connaissance); vested (droit); established (fait); indisputable, admitted (vérité); *acquis à;* devoted to; *bien mal acquis,* ill-gotten goods; *je vous suis tout acquis,* I am all yours.
— m. Acquirements, experience; learning.

acquisitif, ive [akizitif, i:v] adj. Acquisitive.

acquisition [-sjɔ̃] f. Acquisition (v. ACHAT); purchase (objet); *faire l'acquisition de,* to acquire. ‖ FIG. Attainments (de l'esprit).

acquit [aki] m. Receipt, acquittance (de paiement); *pour acquit,* received with thanks. ‖ Discharge, release (d'engagements). ‖ FIG. *Par acquit de conscience,* for conscience sake. ‖ **Acquit-à-caution,** m. Permit.

acquittement [akitmɑ̃] m. JUR. Acquittal; *verdict d'acquittement,* verdict of not guilty. ‖ COMM. Discharge, payment, settlement (de dette); clearing (d'une créance).

acquitter [-te] v. tr. (1). To acquit, to pay off, to discharge (une dette); to receipt (une facture). ‖ JUR. To acquit, to declare not guilty (un accusé); *acquitter de,* to acquit of, to absolve from, to release from.
— v. pr. **S'acquitter,** to return obligations; *comment m'acquitter envers vous?* how can I acknowledge (ou) repay your kindness? ‖ *S'acquitter de,* to clear, to pay (ses dettes); to perform (un devoir); to discharge (une fonction); to fulfil (une obligation); to execute (une tâche); to carry out, to do (un travail).

acre [akr] f. Acre.

âcre [ɑ:kr] adj. Acrid, bitter (acide); pungent; sharp (piquant). ‖ FIG. Acrimonious; cutting.

âcreté [ɑkrəte] f. Pungency (de la fumée); acridity, bitterness (du goût). ‖ FIG. Acrimoniousness.

acridien [akridjɛ̃] m. ZOOL. Locust.

acrimonie [akrimɔni] f. Acrimony, acridness, bitterness, harshness, asperity.

acrimonieux, euse [-njø, ø:z] adj. Acrimonious.

acrobate [akrobat] m. Acrobat, tumbler; stunt man. ‖ Tightrope walker.

acrobatie [-basi] f. Acrobatism, acrobatics. ‖ Pl. Acrobatic tricks (ou) stunts. ‖ AVIAT. Aerobatics, stunts; *faire des acrobaties,* to stunt. ‖ FIG. Pl. Acrobatics.

acrobatique [-batik] adj. Acrobatic.

acropole [akrɔpɔl] f. ARCHIT. Acropolis.

acrostiche [akrɔstiʃ] m. Acrostic.

acrylique [akrilik] adj., m. CHIM. Acrylic.

acte [akt] m. Act, action; deed; *acte de courage,* courageous (ou) brilliant deed; *acte dommageable,* nuisance. ‖ Rolls, records (documents); transactions, proceedings (d'un congrès); bill, act (du Parlement). ‖ THÉÂTR. Act. ‖ MILIT. *Acte de guerre,* act of war. ‖ ECCLÉS. Acts (des apôtres); act (de foi). ‖ NAUT. *Acte de nationalité,* certificate of registry. ‖ COMM. Bill, bond, contract; *acte de vente,* bill of sale, conveyance. ‖ JUR. Deed, legal instrument; *acte d'accusation,* bill of indictment; *acte de décès, de mariage, de naissance,* death, marriage, birth certificate. ‖ LOC. *Donner acte de,* to acknowledge officially; *faire acte de,* to show, to give evidence of; *faire acte de présence,* to put in an appearance; *prendre acte de,* to record formally, to make note of.

acteur [-tœ:r] m. THÉÂTR. Actor; player; performer (v. ACTRICE); *acteur de troisième ordre,* ham actor; *se faire acteur,* to go on the stage. ‖ FIG. Actor.

actif, ive [-tif, i:v] adj. Busy, alert, brisk, sprightly (personne); active, busy (vie). ‖ MÉD. Active (remède). ‖ MILIT. Regular (armée). ‖ FIN. Active, lively (marché); *dettes actives,* book debts. ‖ COMM. Working (associé).
— m. COMM. Credit (d'un compte); assets (capitaux); *actif susceptible d'accroissement,* dependencies. ‖ FIG. *A son actif,* to his credit.
— f. MILIT. Active army.

actinie [aktini] f. ZOOL. Actinia.

actinique [-nik] adj. PHYS. Actinic.

actinisme [-nism] m. PHYS. Actinism.

actinium [-njɔm] m. CHIM. Actinium.

actinomètre [-nɔmɛtr] m. Actinometer.

action [aksjɔ̃] f. Act, action (en général); deed, feat (haut fait); *action d'éclat,* brilliant feat. ‖ Action, activity. ‖ Action, effect, influence (sur, on; upon); *action toxique,* toxic effect. ‖ Action; gestures (attitude). ‖ THÉÂTR. Action, plot. ‖ MILIT. Engagement; *action d'éclat,* brilliant feat of arms; *action combinée,* combined operation; *entrer en action,* to go into action. ‖ JUR. Action-at-law, lawsuit, trial (procès); *action civile,* civil suit; *action criminelle,* criminal proceedings; *action en justice,* judicial process; *action juridique,* legal action; *intenter une action,* to prosecute, to sue. ‖ FIN. Share, stock; *société par actions,* joint-stock company. ‖ TECHN. Action, operation, working; *machine à simple action,* single-acting engine. ‖ ECCLÉS. *Action de grâces,* thanksgiving.

actionnable [aksjɔnabl] adj. JUR. Actionable.

actionnaire [-nɛ:r] m. FIN. Shareholder.

actionnariat [-narja] m. Shareholders (personnes); shareholding (système).

actionner [-ne] v. tr. (1). JUR. To bring an action against, to proceed against, to prosecute; *actionner en dommages et intérêts,* to sue for damages. ‖ TECHN. To set in motion, to actuate, to work.

activation [aktivasjɔ̃] f. Activation. ‖ PHYS. *Activation nucléaire,* nuclear activation.

activement [aktivmɑ̃] adv. Actively; diligently; energetically.

activer [-ve] v. tr. (1). To expedite (une affaire); to stir up, to fan (le feu); to hasten (la marche). [V. ACCÉLÉRER.] ‖ MÉD. To activate (la digestion); *boue activée,* radio-active mud. ‖ PHYS. To activate. ‖ FAM. To rouse (qqn).
— v. pr. **S'activer,** to be busy; to bustle about; *s'activer à,* to press on with, to be busily engaged in, to busy oneself with.

activisme [-vism] m. Activism.

activiste [-vist] m. Activist.
— adj. Activist, activistic.

activité [-vite] f. Activity, diligence; briskness; *activités politiques*, political activities; *débordant d'activité*, full of go; *en pleine activité*, in full swing. ‖ JUR. Active employment (d'un fonctionnaire). ‖ COMM. *Période de grande activité*, busy time. ‖ MILIT. Active service; *en activité*, on the active list.

actrice [aktris] f. THÉÂTR. Actress. (V. ACTEUR.)

actuaire [aktɥɛːr] m. JUR. Actuary.

actualisation [aktɥalizasjɔ̃] f. Actualization.

actualiser [-ze] v. tr. (1). To actualize.

actualité [-te] f. Actuality, matter of present interest, reality; *d'actualité*, topical. ‖ Pl. Current news, topics of the day (dans un journal). ‖ CINÉM. Newsreel. ‖ FIG. *Au premier plan de l'actualité*, in the limelight.

actuariel, elle [aktɥarjɛl] adj. FIN. Actuarial.

actuel, elle [aktɥɛl] adj. Present, real, current; *à l'heure actuelle*, at the present time. ‖ PHILOS., THÉOL. Actual.

actuellement [-mɑ̃] adv. Now, at the present time.

acuité [akɥite] f. Sharpness (d'un clou). ‖ MÉD. Acuteness (d'une douleur); keenness (de la vue). ‖ FIG. Shrillness (d'un bruit); acuity (de la pensée).

acuminé, ée [akymine] adj. BOT. Acuminate.

acuponcteur [akypɔ̃ktœːr] m. MÉD. Acupunctor.

acuponcture [akypɔ̃ktyːr] f. MÉD. Acupuncture.

acutangle [akytɑ̃ːgl] adj. MATH. Acute-angled.

acyclique [asiklik] adj. Acyclic.

A. D. [ɑde] abrév. de *Anno Domini*, A. D.

adage [adaːʒ] m. Adage.

Adam [adɑ̃] m. Adam; *ne connaître ni d'Eve ni d'Adam*, not to know from Adam. ‖ MÉD. *Pomme d'Adam*, Adam's apple.

adamantin [adamɑ̃tɛ̃] adj. Adamantine.

adaptabilité [adaptabilite] f. Adaptibility.

adaptable [adaptabl] adj. Adaptable.

adaptateur, trice [-tatœːr, tris] s. Adapter.

adaptation [-tasjɔ̃] f. Adaptation; adjustment; *faculté d'adaptation*, adaptability. ‖ RADIO. Matching. ‖ CINÉM. Treatment.

adapter [-te] v. tr. (1). To adapt, to accommodate, to conform; *adapter un roman de*, to adapt a novel from. ‖ To adapt, to fit, to suit (à, to). ‖ RADIO. To match.
— v. pr. **S'adapter**, to fit, to hook (à, on). ‖ FIG. To adapt (ou) to adjust oneself (à, to) [des circonstances]; to conform oneself (à, to) [des nécessités].

addenda [adɛ̃da] m. Addendum.

additif, ive [additif, iːv] adj. Additive.
— m. Additional clause; rider.

addition [-sjɔ̃] f. Addition (v. AUGMENTATION); *additions progressives*, accretion. ‖ MATH. Adding up; totting up (action); addition (résultat); *faire une addition*, to sum up, to add up, to tot up. ‖ FAM. Bill, check (note).

additionnel, elle [-sjɔnɛl] adj. Additional; extra. ‖ FIN. *Centimes additionnels*, extra centimes. ‖ JUR. *Clause additionnelle*, rider.

additionner [-sjɔne] v. tr. (1). MATH. To add up, to reckon up, to tot up; to sum up. ‖ FIG. To admix (mêler); *additionner de*, to mix with; to lace with (alcool); to dilute with (eau).

additionneuse [-sjɔnøːz] f. TECHN. Adding-machine; totalizer.

adducteur [addyktœːr] adj. MÉD. Adducent. ‖ TECHN. Feeding.
— m. MÉD. Adductor. ‖ TECHN. Supply-main.

adduction [-sjɔ̃] f. MÉD. Adduction. ‖ TECHN. Conveying (d'eau).

adénite [adenit] f. MÉD. Adenitis.

adénoïde [adenɔid] adj. MÉD. Adenoid, adenoidal; *végétations adénoïdes*, adenoids.

adénome [adeno:m] m. MÉD. Adenoma.

adent [adɑ̃] m. TECHN. Joggle; dovetail; dent.

adenter [-te] v. tr. (1). TECHN. To indent.

adepte [adɛpt] m. Adept.

adéquat [adekwa] adj. Adequate. ‖ Equivalent.

adéquation [-sjɔ̃] f. Balance.

adhérence [aderɑ̃ːs] f. Adherence, adhesion. ‖ Tackiness (de la colle). ‖ AUTOM. Grip, traction (des roues). ‖ MÉD. Adhesion.

adhérent, ente [-rɑ̃, ɑ̃ːt] adj. Adherent. ‖ Adhesive, tacky, sticky (collant).
— m. Adherent, supporter, follower, member.

adhérer [-re] v. intr. (5). To adhere, to cling, to stick (à, to). ‖ AUTOM. *Adhérer à la route*, to grip the ground. ‖ FIG. To adhere, to cleave (à, to); *adhérer à un parti*, to join a party (ou) to become a member of a party.

adhésif, ive [-zif, iːv] adj., m. Adhesive.

adhésion [-zjɔ̃] f. Sticking. ‖ FIG. Adhesion; adherence; accession (à, to); *donner son adhésion à*, to signify one's adhesion to.

adhésivité [-zivite] f. Adhesiveness.

ad hoc [adɔk] loc. adv. Ad hoc; *comité ad hoc*, ad hoc committee; *l'homme ad hoc*, the right man.

ad hominem [adɔminɛm] adj. *Argument ad hominem*, ad hominem argument.

adiabatique [adjabatik] adj. PHYS. Adiabatic.

adieu [adjø] interj., adv. Adieu, farewell.
— m. pl. Farewell, adieu; *baiser d'adieux*, farewell kiss; *faire ses adieux à*, to take one's leave of; *sans adieu*, good-bye for the present.

adipeux, euse [adipø, øːz] adj. Adipose.

adiposité [-pozite] f. Adiposity.

adjacence [adʒasɑ̃ːs] f. MATH. Adjacency.

adjacent, ente [-sɑ̃, ɑ̃ːt] adj. Adjoining (pièces); contiguous (propriétés); conterminous (à, to). ‖ MATH. Adjacent (angles).

adjectif, ive [adʒɛktif, iːv] adj. Adjectival.
— m. GRAMM. Adjective.

adjectivement [-tivmɑ̃] adv. Adjectively, U. S. adjectivally.

adjoindre [adʒwɛ̃ːdr] v. tr. (59). To appoint as assistant (qqn). ‖ To associate; to incorporate; to unite (unir) [à, with].
— v. pr. **S'adjoindre**, to engage, to secure, to take as assistant; *s'adjoindre à*, to join with, to associate with.

adjoint, ointe [-ʒwɛ̃, wɛ̃ːt] adj. Assistant.
— s. Assistant; *adjoint au maire*, deputy-mayor; *commissaire adjoint*, joint-commissioner; *professeur adjoint*, assistant-master, lecturer.

adjonction [-ʒɔ̃ksjɔ̃] f. Adjunction (à, to).

adjudant [adʒydɑ̃] m. MILIT. Warrant officer, Company (ou) Battery Serjeant-Major. ‖ NAUT. *Adjudant principal*, chief boatswain. ‖ ZOOL. Adjudant-bird. ‖ **Adjudant-chef**, m. MILIT. Senior warrant officer, Regimental Sergeant-Major.

adjudicataire [adʒydikatɛːr] m. Contractor, contracting party, successful tender (d'un contrat); successful bidder (aux enchères).

adjudicateur, trice [-tœːr, tris] s. Adjudicator, awarder (de contrats); auctioneer (aux enchères).

adjudication [-sjɔ̃] f. JUR. Sale by auction (vente); *adjudication au rabais*, allocation to lowest tender, Dutch auction. ‖ JUR. Awarding of contract (attribution); *mettre en adjudication*, to invite tenders (ou) bids for; *par voie d'adjudication*, by auction, by tender.

adjuger [adʒyʒe] v. tr. (7). To award (les dépens); *adjuger les dépens*, to award costs. ‖ To knock down (aux enchères); *une fois, deux fois, trois fois, adjugé!*, going, going, gone! ‖ To accept a tender for; to give out a contract, to appropriate (par contrat). ‖ FAM. To adjudge (un prix).
— v. pr. **S'adjuger**, to appropriate, to take to oneself. (V. APPROPRIER [s'].)

adjuration [adʒyrasjɔ̃] f. Adjuration; entreaty.

adjurer [-re] v. tr. (1). To adjure; to beseech, to entreat; to charge on oath. ‖ ECCLÉS. To exorcise.

adjuvant, ante [adʒyvɑ̃, ɑ̃:t] adj., m. Adjuvant.

ad libitum [adlibitɔm] adv. Ad libitum, ad lib.

admettre [admɛtr] v. tr. (64). To accept, to grant, to allow, to entertain (accorder); to concede, to assume, to take for granted (concéder); to acknowledge, to admit, to confess (reconnaître); to admit, to receive, to allow in, to let in (recevoir).

administrateur, trice [administratœ:r, trice] s. Director, manager (de société); trustee, administrator (de succession); *administrateur judiciaire*, administrator, receiver.

administratif, ive [-tif, i:v] adj. Administrative.

administration [-sjɔ̃] f. Administration, management (gestion); authorities (membres). ‖ MÉD. Application, dispensation (d'un remède). ‖ JUR. Production, advancing (d'une preuve). ‖ MILIT. *Officier d'administration*, accountant officer.

administrativement [-tivmɑ̃] adv. Administratively.

administré [administre] m. Person under a jurisdiction (ou) an administration.

administrer v. tr. (1). To direct, to manage, to govern (une entreprise); to rule (un pays). ‖ JUR. To administer, to dispense (la justice); to adduce, to produce, to bring forward (une preuve). ‖ ECCLÉS. To dispense, to administer (les sacrements). ‖ FAM. To deal (un coup); *administrer une raclée à qqn*, to give s.o. a good hiding.

admirable [admirabl] adj. Admirable, wonderful. ‖ Excellent.

admirablement [-blǝmɑ̃] adv. Wonderfully; marvellously.

admirateur, trice [-tœ:r, tris] s. Admirer. ‖ FAM. Fan; *jeune admiratrice*, bobby-soxer. — adj. Admiring.

admiratif, ive [-tif, iv] adj. Admiring.

admiration [-sjɔ̃] f. Admiration; wonder; *en admiration devant*, standing speechless before; *faire l'admiration de*, to excite the admiration of.

admirativement [-tivmɑ̃] adv. Admiringly.

admiré [admi:e] p. p. adj. Admired (*de, par*, by).

admirer v. tr. (1). To admire, to wonder at.

admis, ise [admi, iz] adj. Admitted.

admissibilité [-sibilite] f. Admissibility. ‖ Qualification for the oral examination.

admissible [-sibl] adj. Admittable (en un lieu). ‖ Admissible, allowable, permissible. ‖ Acceptable, warrantable (excuse, preuve). ‖ Eligible (*à*, to). ‖ Who has qualified for a « viva » (candidat). ‖ JUR. *Admissible en droit*, admissible, legally responsible.

admission [-jɔ̃] f. Admission, admittance (*à*, to). ‖ TECHN. Intake; *admission d'air*, accession of air; *avance à l'admission*, preadmission, intake-advance; *soupape d'admission*, inlet-valve.

admittance [admitɑ̃:s] f. ELECTR. Admittance.

admixtion [admikstjɔ̃] f. MÉD. Admixture.

admonestation [admɔnɛstasjɔ̃] f. Admonition, admonishment.

admonester [-te] v. tr. (1). To admonish.

admoniteur, trice [admɔnitœ:r, tris] s. Admonisher.

admonition [-sjɔ̃] f. Admonition.

A.D.N. [ɑdeɛn] m. Abrév. de *acide désoxyribonucléique*, DNA, deoxyribonucleic acid.

adolescence [adɔlɛssɑ̃:s] f. Adolescence.

adolescent, ente [-sɑ̃, ɑ̃:t] adj. Adolescent. — s. Adolescent; teenager (fam.).

Adonis [adɔnis] m. Adonis. ‖ BOT. Adonis. ‖ FAM. Beau.

adoniser [-nize] v. tr. (1). To smarten up. — v. pr. **S'adoniser**, to titivate, to spruce oneself up, U. S. to doll up.

adonné, ée [adɔne] adj. Given, addicted (*à*, to). ‖ Devoted (*à*, to).

adonner (s') [sadɔne] v. pr. To give oneself up to, to devote oneself to, to take up, to go in for; to cultivate. ‖ To indulge in, to become addicted to (in vice).

adoptable [adɔptabl] adj. Adoptable.

adoptant, ante [-tɑ̃, ɑ̃:t] s. Adopter.

adopté, ée [-te] adj. Adopted, adoptive (enfant). — s. Adoptee.

adopter [-te] v. tr. (1). JUR. To adopt (un enfant); to pass (une loi); to assume (un nom); to approve (un procès-verbal); to carry (une proposition); to accept (un rapport). ‖ GRAMM. To naturalize (un mot). ‖ FIG. To embrace (une cause); to borrow (une idée); to follow (la mode); to take up (une opinion).

adoptif, ive [-tif, i:v] adj. Adoptive.

adoption [-sjɔ̃] f. Adoption (d'un enfant, d'un nom, d'une mode); carrying, passage (d'une loi). ‖ Borrowing (d'une idée); acceptance (d'une opinion); *pays d'adoption*, adopted country.

adorable [adɔrabl] adj. Adorable. ‖ FAM. Charming, delightful, divine.

adorablement [-blǝmɑ̃] adv. Adorably.

adorateur, trice [-tœ:r, tris] s. Worshipper; adorer. ‖ FAM. Adorer, warm admirer; fan (fam.).

adoration [-sjɔ̃] f. ECCLÉS. Adoration, worship. ‖ FAM. Adoration, idolization.

adorer [adɔre] v. tr. (1). ECCLÉS. To worship, to adore. ‖ FAM. To dote upon, to be mad about, to be passionately fond of (qqch., qqn); to adore, to idolize (qqn); *il adore chanter*, he is terribly keen on singing (ou) crazy about singing.

ados [ado] m. Banked up bed; ridge.

adossement [adɔsmɑ̃] m. Leaning, backing.

adosser [-se] v. tr. (1). To back (*à*, against). ‖ ARCHIT. To build (*à*, against) [un mur]. — v. pr. **S'adosser**, to lean one's back (*à*, against).

adoubement [adubmɑ̃] m. Knighting. ‖ Coat of mail.

adouber [adube] v. tr. (1). To dub (un chevalier); to adjust (au jeu d'échecs).

adoucir [adusi:r] v. tr. (2). To sweeten (une boisson). ‖ To round off (un contour); to subdue (la lumière); to tone down (une teinte). ‖ To milden (la température). ‖ TECHN. To smooth (l'acier, le bois); to soften (la fonte); to rough-polish (le verre). ‖ FIG. To assuage, to temper, to alleviate, to allay, to soothe (une douleur, une souffrance); to tone down (une expression); to appease, to mollify, to temper (l'irritation); to refine (les manières); to mitigate (une peine); to soften (la physionomie, les sentiments, le ton); to make smoother (la vie). — v. pr. **S'adoucir**, to grow milder (temps). ‖ To mellow (caractère); to lessen (douleur); to grow softer, to soften (voix).

adoucissement [-sismɑ̃] m. Sweetening (d'une acidité, d'une amertume). ‖ Softening (des contours, de la lumière); rise (de la température). ‖ TECHN. Smoothing (de l'acier); softening (de la fonte); rough-polishing (du verre). ‖ FIG. Pacifying, mollifying (du caractère, de la colère); relief, alleviation, assuagement, easing (d'une douleur); qualification (des paroles); mitigation (d'une peine); softening (du ton).

adoucisseur [-sisœ:r] m. Water-softener.

ad patres [adpatrɛs] adv. FAM. *Aller ad patres*, to give up the ghost; *envoyer qqn ad patres*, to send s.o. to meet his maker.

adragante [adragɑ̃:t] adj. f. *Gomme adragante*, tragacanth, gum dragon.

adrénaline [adrenalin] f. MÉD. Adrenalin.

adrénergique [-nɛrʒik] adj. MÉD. Adrenergic.

adressage [adrɛsa:ʒ] m. INFORM. Addressing.

adresse [adrɛs] f. Address (sur une lettre); destination; *à l'adresse de*, for, addressed to, directed to. ‖ Address, domicile. ‖ Address (allocution, supplique). ‖ Skill, adroitness, dexterity (habileté); *tour d'adresse*, trick of sleight-of-hand, feat of skill. ‖ Adroitness (vivacité d'esprit); craftiness, artfulness, cunning (ruse).

adresser [-se] v. tr. (1). To address, to send (une lettre, un paquet). ‖ To put up, to offer up (une prière) [à, to]; to administer (des reproches); to send in (une requête); to give (un sourire). ‖ To introduce, to recommend, to refer (qqn) [à, to].
— v. pr. **S'adresser**, to apply (à, at) [un endroit donné]; to apply (à, to) [qqn]. ‖ *S'adresser à*, to be meant for, to be addressed to (être destiné à); to appeal to (faire appel à); to address, to speak to (parler à).

adret [adrɛ] m. GÉOGR. Adret, side of hill receiving the maximum sunshine.

Adriatique [adriatik] adj. f. GÉOGR. Adriatic.

adroit, oite [adrwa, wa:t] adj. Skilful, dexterous, adroit, deft (v. HABILE); *adroit de ses mains*, clever with his hands. ‖ FIG. Clever, shrewd.

adroitement [-tmɑ̃] adv. Skilfully; cleverly; shrewdly; artfully.

absorber [adsɔrbe] v. tr. (1). PHYS. To adsorb.

adulateur, trice [adylatœ:r, tris] adj. Adulatory, fawning.
— s. Adulator; sycophant; toady.

adulation [-sjɔ̃] f. Adulation.

aduler [adyle] v. tr. (1). To adulate, to fawn upon. (V. FLATTER.)

adulte [adylt] adj., s. Adult, grown-up.

adultération [adyltɛrasjɔ̃] f. Adulteration.

adultère [adyltɛ:r] adj. Adulterous.
— s. Adultery (acte). ‖ JUR. Criminal conversation. ‖ Adulteress (femme); adulterer (mari); *complice d'adultère*, co-respondent.

adultérer [adyltere] v. tr. (5). To adulterate.

adultérin, ine [adylterɛ̃, in] adj., s. Adulterine.

aduste [adyst] adj. Adust, sunburnt.

advenir [advəni:r] v. intr. (14). To occur, to happen; to come about; to chance; to befall, to turn out; to come to pass.
— v. imp. *Il advint que*, it came to pass that; *il m'advient de*, I happen to; *on ne sait ce qu'il en adviendra*, nobody knows what will come of it; *qu'est-il advenu d'elle?*, what has become of her?; *quoi qu'il advienne, advienne que pourra*, come what may.

adventice [advɑ̃tis] adj. Adventitious. ‖ BOT. Self-sown.

adventiste [advɑ̃tist] adj., s. ECCLÉS. Adventist.

adverbe [advɛrb] m. GRAMM. Adverb.

adverbial, ale [-bjal] adj. GRAMM. Adverbial.

adverbialement [-bjalmɑ̃] adv. Adverbially.

adversaire [advɛrsɛ:r] m. Adversary, opponent.

adversatif, ive [adversatif, i:v] adj. GRAMM. Adversative.

adverse [advɛrs] adj. Adverse, opposite; *fortune adverse*, adversity.

adversité [-site] f. Adversity.

adynamie [adinami] f. MÉD. Adynamia.

aède [aɛ:d] m. Greek epic poet.

aérage [aera:ʒ] m. TECHN. Airing, ventilation (dans les mines).

aérateur [aeratœ:r] m. Adjustable louvres (ou) ventilators.

aération [aerasjɔ̃] f. Airing; ventilation. ‖ Aeration (de l'eau).

aéré, ée [aere] adj. Airy, ventilated (pièce); *centre aéré*, outdoor day centre. ‖ TECHN. Aerated (béton).

aérer [aere] v. tr. (5). To air, to ventilate. ‖ To aerate (l'eau).

aérien, enne [aerjɛ̃, ɛn] adj. Aerial, atmospheric (phénomène, région). ‖ Overhead (câble); aerial (échelle). ‖ CH. DE F. Elevated (métro). ‖ AVIAT. Air (arme, espace, flotte, ligne, poste); aerial (torpille). ‖ FIG. Airy (allure, marche).
— m. RADIO. Aerial.

aérifère [aerifɛ:r] adj. Aeriferous.

aérifier [-fje] v. tr. (1). To aerify.

aérium [aerjɔm] m. MÉD. Aerium.

aérobie [aerɔbi] m. MÉD. Aerobe.

aérocartographie [aerɔkartɔgrafi] f. AVIAT. Aerocartography, aerial cartography.

aérochimique [-ʃimik] adj. MILIT. *Guerre aérochimique*, chemical warfare from the air.

aéro-club [-klyb] m. AVIAT. Flying-club.

aérodrome [-drɔ:m] m. AVIAT. Aerodrome; U. S. airdrome.

aérodynamique [-dinamik] adj. Aerodynamic; *tunnel aérodynamique*, wind-tunnel. ‖ AUTOM. Streamlined.
— f. Aerodynamics.

aérodyne [-di:n] m. AVIAT. Aerodyne.

aérofrein [-frɛ̃] m. TECHN. Air-brake.

aérogare [-ga:r] f. AVIAT. Airport, air terminal.

aéroglisseur [-glisœ:r] m. TECHN. Hovercraft (sur terre ou sur mer); hovertrain (sur terre).

aérogramme [-gram] m. Air-mail letter, aerogram.

aérographe [-gra:f] m. ARTS. Sprayer, air-brush. (V. PISTOLET.) ‖ AVIAT. Aerograph.

aérolithe [-lit] m. ASTRON. Aerolite, meteorite.

aérologie [-lɔʒi] f. AVIAT. Aerology.

aéromaritime [-maritim] adj. Aeromarine.

aéromètre [-mɛtr] m. Aerometer.

aéromodélisme [-mɔdelism] m. AVIAT. Aeromodelling.

aéromoteur [-mɔtœ:r] m. Wind-engine.

aéronaute [-no:t] m. AVIAT. Aeronaut.

aéronautique [-notik] adj. Aeronautical.
— f. AVIAT. Aeronautics; *aéronautique navale*, Fleet Air Arm; U. S. Naval Air Service.

aéronaval [-naval] adj. AVIAT. Aeronaval; *forces aéronavales*, air and sea forces.

aéronavale [-nava:l] f. AVIAT. Fleet Air Arm, Naval Aviation; U. S. Naval Air Service.

aéronef [-nɛf] m. AVIAT. Airship, aircraft.

aérophagie [-faʒi] f. MÉD. Aerophagia.

aérophare [-fa:r] m. Air-beacon.

aérophotographie [-fɔtɔgrafi] f. Aerophotography, aerial photography.

aéroplane [-plan] m. AVIAT. Aeroplane, airplane; plane (fam.).

aéroport [-pɔ:r] m. AVIAT. Air-port; air-station.

aéroportable [-pɔrtabl] adj. AVIAT. Transportable by air.

aéroporté, ée [-pɔrte] adj. AVIAT. Airborne.

aéropostal, ale [-pɔstal] adj. Air-mail.

aéroroute [-ru:t] r. Air-route; airway.

aérosol [-sɔl] m. Aerosol.

aérospatial, ale [-spasjal] adj. Aerospace.

aérostat [-sta] m. AVIAT. Aerostat; lighter-than-air-craft. (V. BALLON.)

aérostation [-stasjɔ̃] f. Aerostation; *aérostation d'observation*, observation balloon service.

aérostatique [-statik] adj. Aerostatic.
— f. Aerostatics.

aérostier [-stje] m. AVIAT. Aeronaut, balloonist; *corps d'aérostiers militaires*, balloon corps.

aérotechnique [-teknik] f. Aerotechnics.

Aérotrain [-trɛ̃] m. (nom déposé). CH. DE F. Aerotrain, hovertrain.

affabilité [afabilite] f. Affability.

affable [afa:bl] adj. Affable; kindly. (V. AIMABLE.)

affabulation [afabylasjɔ̃] f. Plot (intrigue d'un roman). ‖ Story-telling, fabrication, fantasy (mensonge).

affabuler [-le] v. intr. (1). To tell (ou) make up stories, to fantasize.

affadir [afadi:r] v. tr. (2). To make insipid (ou) tasteless. ‖ Fig. To make dull; to take all the pep out of (fam.)
— v. pr. **S'affadir**, to lose flavour; to become dull (ou) insipid.

affadissant, ante [-disɑ̃, disɑ̃:t] adj. Reducing savour (ou) vigour.

affadissement [-dismɑ̃] m. Loss of flavour. ‖ Fig. Dulling; cloying.

affaiblir [afebli:r] v. tr. (2). To weaken, to enfeeble. ‖ To lighten (une couleur); to dim, to dull (la lumière). ‖ Fin. To debase (la monnaie). ‖ Méd. To lay low (un malade); to impair, to debilitate (la santé); to attenuate (un virus). ‖ Techn. To plane down (une planche). ‖ Fig. To reduce (l'ardeur); to weaken (un sentiment).
— v. pr. **S'affaiblir**, to grow fainter (bruit); to grow dim (lumière); to grow weaker; to lose one's strength (personne); to fail (yeux). ‖ Fig. To decay, to weaken (facultés).

affaiblissement [-blismɑ̃] m. Weakening, enfeeblement (des forces). ‖ Fin. Debasement (de la monnaie). ‖ Méd. Debility. ‖ Fig. Sinking, decay.

affaire [afɛ:r] f. Affair; business, matter, job; *affaire de cœur*, love affair, affaire; *affaire d'honneur*, duel; *affaire de goût*, matter of taste; *avoir affaire à*, to deal with, to have business with; *avoir affaire avec*, to do business with; *être à son affaire*, to be in one's element; to be wrapped up in one's work; *ce n'est pas une affaire*, there is nothing in it; *ce n'est pas une petite affaire*, it's a large order; *c'est une autre affaire*, it is another story; *ça ne fait pas l'affaire*, it won't do, it does not suit; *connaître son affaire*, to know one's business, to know the ropes; *en faire son affaire*, to deal with the matter, to take it upon oneself; *faire l'affaire de*, to serve the purpose of; *faire son affaire à*, to do for, to settle the hash of; *ne pas être à son affaire*, not to feel up to the mark; *se tirer d'affaire*, to get out of a scrape (ou) out of the wood; *tirer d'affaire*, to get out of difficulty. ‖ Jur. Cause, case, suit; *affaire civile*, civil action. ‖ Milit. Engagement, action. ‖ Comm. Business, concern; deal; bargain, transaction (marché); venture (finances); *une bonne affaire*, a sound transaction, a bargain; U. S. a good buy; *faire une mauvaise affaire*, to make a bad bargain; *régler une affaire*, to settle a deal; *traiter une affaire avec*, to do (ou) to transact business with. ‖ Pl. Affairs, business (affaires publiques); *l'expérience des affaires*, practical (ou) official experience; *Affaires étrangères*, Foreign Affairs; *ministère des Affaires étrangères*, Foreign Office, U. S. State Department. ‖ Pl. Business (affaires privées); *occupez-vous de vos affaires*, mind your own business; *personne qui s'occupe des affaires d'autrui*, busybody, meddler; *raconter ses affaires*, to open one's heart. ‖ Pl. Things, belongings (objets); *serrer ses affaires*, to put away one's things. ‖ Jur. *Homme d'affaires*, lawyer. ‖ Comm. Business; *dans les affaires*, in business; *brasseur d'affaires*, big business man; *cabinet d'affaires*, general agency; *homme d'affaires*, businessman; *faire des affaires*, to do business; *faire de bonnes affaires*, to do well, to work at a profit; *faire de mauvaises affaires*, to do badly, to work at a loss; *parler d'affaires*, to talk business.

affairé, ée [-re] adj. Busy; bustling.

affairement [-rmɑ̃] m. Fuss, bustle.

affairer (s') [safɛre] v. pr. (1). To bustle about, to fuss.

affairisme [afɛrism] m. Intrusion of business into every aspect of life.

affairiste [afɛrist] m. Shark; wide boy.

affaissement [afɛsmɑ̃] m. Sagging (d'une poutre); sinking, subsidence (du terrain); collapse (du toit). ‖ Fin. Sinking (des prix). ‖ Méd. Prostra-

tion (d'un malade); flabbiness (des muscles); depression (des nerfs).

affaisser [-se] v. tr. (1). To make sag, to weigh down (faire ployer); to make sink (tasser). ‖ Fig. To depress, to dispirit, to discourage (abattre).
— v. pr. **S'affaisser**, to sag, to give way (ployer); to sink, to subside (se tasser); to sink down (*dans*, into). ‖ Méd. To become depressed (malade); to break up (santé).

affaler [afale] v. tr. (1). Naut. To haul down.
— v. pr. **S'affaler**. Naut. To slide down. ‖ Fam. To fall, to drop, to slouch, to subside.

affamé, ée [afame] adj. Hungry (*de*, for); starving, famished, ravenous. ‖ Fig. Eager, greedy.

affamer v. tr. (1). To starve (qqn, une ville).

affameur [-mœ:r] s. Starver.

affect [afɛkt] m. Psych. Affect.

affectable [afɛktabl] adj. Impressionable. ‖ Jur. Mortgageable.

affectation [-tasjɔ̃] f. Affectation, show, pretence. ‖ Mannerism, pomposity, artificiality, stiltedness (afféterie). ‖ Assignment (à un poste); allotment (à un usage). ‖ Comm. Application, appropriation, charging (de crédits). ‖ Jur. *Affectation hypothécaire*, mortgage charge. ‖ Milit. *Affectation spéciale*, reserved occupation.

affecté, ée [-te] adj. Affected, concerned, moved (ému); assumed, feigned (feint); exaggerated (outré). ‖ Conceited, foppish, fussy, theatrical (v. Maniéré); *un sourire affecté*, a simper.
— m. Milit. *Affecté spécial*, man in a reserved occupation.

affecter [-te] v. tr. (1). To affect (v. Émouvoir); to influence (influencer). ‖ To pretend, to affect, to put on. (V. Feindre.) ‖ To affect, to hurt, to harm (nuire à). ‖ To assume, to take on (revêtir). ‖ To assign, to allocate, to appropriate (*à*, to). ‖ Comm. To apply, to appropriate, to earmark (des crédits). ‖ Jur. To apply; *affecté d'hypothèque*, mortgaged. ‖ Milit. To post; to draft, to detail.
— v. pr. **S'affecter**, to be affected (ou) grieved.

affectif, ive [-tif, i:v] adj. Affective; emotional.

affection [-sjɔ̃] f. Affection, liking (v. Attachement, tendresse); *prendre en affection, se prendre d'affection pour*, to become fond of, to conceive a liking for, to take a liking to. ‖ Méd. Affection.

affectionné, ée [-sjɔne] adj. Affectionate, loving.

affectionner [-sjɔne] v. tr. (1). To be fond of, to become attached to, to take a fancy to; to delight in.

affectivité [-tivite] f. Philos. Affectivity.

affectueusement [-tɥøzmɑ̃] adv. Affectionately; fondly.

affectueux, euse [-tɥø, ø:z] adj. Affectionate, fond. (V. Aimant.)

afférent, ente [aferɑ̃, ɑ̃:t] adj. Concerning, pertaining, relating (*à*, to); *portion afférente à*, portion accruing to. ‖ Méd. Afferent.

affermable [afɛrmabl] adj. Leasable, rentable. ‖ Fin. Farmable (impôts).

affermage [-ma:ʒ] m. Letting, leasing. ‖ Agric. Renting (de la terre). ‖ Comm. Contracting (d'une entreprise). ‖ Fin. Farming out (des impôts).

affermer [-me] v. tr. (1). To let; to lease; to rent. ‖ Comm. To contract. ‖ Fin. To farm out.

affermir [afɛrmi:r] v. tr. (2). To harden (durcir); to strengthen (fortifier); to steady, to fix (stabiliser); ‖ Fig. To consolidate; to establish; to confirm; to make firm.
— v. pr. **S'affermir**, to harden; to become stronger (se renforcer). ‖ To take root, to persist (s'ancrer).

affermissement [-mismɑ̃] m. Strengthening; hardening; steadying. (V. Consolidation.)

affété, ée [afete] adj. V. Affecté (maniéré).

afféterie [-tri] f. V. Affectation.

affichage [afiʃa:ʒ] m. Bill-sticking, bill-posting; placarding; *tableau d'affichage,* notice-board; telegraph board; U. S. bulletin- (ou) bill-board. ‖ Fig. Display, flaunting (de ses idées); publicity.

affiche [afiʃ] f. Bill, poster, placard; picture poster (illustrée); *annoncer par voie d'affiches,* to placard; *colleur d'affiches,* bill-poster (ou) -sticker; *poser une affiche,* to stick up a bill. ‖ Théâtr. Play-bill; *tenir l'affiche,* to run, to have a long run.

afficher [-ʃe] v. tr. (1). To placard, to post up, to stick up, to affix (une affiche); *défense d'afficher,* stick (ou) post no bills. ‖ Théâtr. To bill. ‖ Fig. To display, to air, to parade, to flaunt. — v. pr. **S'afficher,** to flaunt oneself; to attract notice. ‖ To be seen everywhere (avec, with).

affichette [-ʃɛt] f. Small notice.

afficheur [-ʃœ:r] m. Bill-sticker, bill-poster.

affichiste [-ʃist] m. Poster-designer.

affidé [afide] m. Confederate.

affilage [afila:ʒ] m. Whetting (d'une faux); sharpening (d'une lame); setting (d'une scie).

affilé, ée [afile] adj. Sharp (lame, langue).

affilée (d') [dafile] loc. adv. At a stretch.

affiler [afile] v. tr. (1). To whet (un couteau, une faux); to sharpen (une épée); to hone, to strop (un rasoir); to set (une scie). ‖ To wiredraw (l'argent, l'or).

affileur [-lœ:r] m. Sharpener.

affiliation [afiljasjɔ̃] f. Affiliation.

affilié, ée [-lie] adj. Affiliated. — s. Affiliated member.

affilier [-lie] v. tr. (1). To affiliate (à, to, with). — v. pr. **S'affilier,** to affiliate oneself (à, to); to become affiliated (à, with).

affiloir [afilwa:r] m. Sharpener, whetstone (pierre). ‖ Strop, hone (de rasoir).

affinage [afina:ʒ] m. Pointing (d'une aiguille); thinning (d'une planche); refining (de l'or). ‖ Culin. Ripening, maturing (du fromage).

affinement [-nmã] m. Sharpening (de l'esprit); refinement, polishing (des manières). ‖ Techn. *Affinement aérodynamique,* streamlining.

affiner [-ne] v. tr. (1). Techn. To refine (l'acier, l'or); to point (les aiguilles, les clous); to thin (le bois); to sift (le ciment); to hatchel, to heckle (le chanvre); to calender (le papier). ‖ Fig. To refine, to polish. — v. pr. **S'affiner.** Culin. To ripen, to mature (fromage, vin). ‖ Fig. To improve (goût); to become more refined (manières).

affineur [-nœ:r] m. Techn. Metal refiner.

affinité [afinite] f. Affinity; relationship (par alliance). ‖ Chim. Affinity. ‖ Fig. Connection (des choses); congeniality, attraction, affinity (des personnes).

affirmatif, ive [afirmatif, i:v] adj. Affirmative; *signe affirmatif,* nod. ‖ Assertive (personne). — f. Affirmative.

affirmation [-masjɔ̃] f. Affirmation, assertion, asseveration, assurance; statement. ‖ Philos. Predication. ‖ Jur. *Affirmation sous serment,* affidavit, statement on (ou) under oath.

affirmativement [-tivmã] adv. Affirmatively; in the affirmative.

affirmer [-me] v. tr. (1). To affirm, to assert, to state positively, to aver, to avouch. ‖ To allege, to warrant, to maintain, to contend (prétendre). ‖ To enforce, to make felt (son autorité). ‖ Philos. To predicate. — v. pr. **S'affirmer.** To assert one's authority; to take one's place (comme, as). ‖ Fam. To assert itself (défaut, qualité).

affixe [afiks] adj. Affixed. — m. Gramm. Affix.

affleurage [aflœra:ʒ] m. Techn. Soaking, hydration.

affleurement [-rmã] m. Levelling. ‖ Géol. Outcrop, basset. ‖ Philos. Outcropping.

affleurer [-re] v. tr. (1). To level (niveler). ‖ To make flush with (les bords). — v. intr. To be even (ou) flush. ‖ Géol. To crop out.

afflictif, ive [afliktif, i:v] adj. Jur. Bodily, corporal; *peine afflictive,* personal punishment.

affliction [-sjɔ̃] f. Affliction.

affligé, ée [afliʒe] adj. Afflicted; grieved (par, at). ‖ Fig. Afflicted, burdened, troubled (de, with).

affligeant, ante [afliʒã, ã:t] adj. Distressing, saddening, sad (nouvelle); painful, lamentable, pitiful (état).

affliger [afliʒe] v. tr. (7). To afflict, to distress, to grieve. (V. attrister.) ‖ To plague, to strike, to smite (frapper). — v. pr. **S'affliger,** to be afflicted (ou) distressed (ou) sorrowful; *s'affliger de,* to sorrow about, to grieve at, to mourn (ou) sorrow over.

afflouer [aflue] v. tr. (1). Naut. To refloat.

affluence [aflɥã:s] f. Affluence, confluence, concourse, influx; *heures d'affluence,* rush hours. ‖ Affluence. (V. abondance.) ‖ Flow, flood (d'eau).

affluent, ente [-ã, ã:t] adj. Géogr. Tributary. ‖ Méd. Affluent. — m. Géogr. Affluent, tributary. ‖ Techn. Feeder.

affluer [-e] v. intr. (1). To flow (eau); to crowd, to flock (personnes); to abound (richesse).

afflux [afly] m. V. affluence. ‖ Méd. Afflux, rush (de sang).

affolant, ante [afolã, ã:t] adj. Maddening; distracting, bewildering.

affolé, ée [-le] adj. Bewildered, distracted, alarmed, frantic, scared (personne). ‖ Techn. Spinning (boussole); racing (machine).

affolement [-lmã] m. Bewilderment, distraction, flap, panic. ‖ Techn. Spinning, unsteadiness (de la boussole); racing (d'un moteur).

affoler [-le] v. tr. (1). To madden (d'amour); to distract, to bewilder; to drive crazy (de peur, de soucis). ‖ Techn. To disturb (la boussole); to race (un moteur); *boussole affolée,* defective compass. — v. pr. **S'affoler,** to become bewildered, to fly into a panic; to get frantic (isolément); to stampede (en groupe). ‖ Techn. To spin (boussole); to begin to race (moteur).

afforestation [afɔrɛstasjɔ̃] f. Afforestation.

affouillement [afujmã] m. Géogr. Undermining; underwashing.

affouiller [-je] v. tr. (1). Géogr. To undermine.

affourager [afuraʒe] v. tr. (7). Agric. To fodder.

affourche [afurʃ] f. Naut. Mooring tackle.

affourcher [-ʃe] v. tr. (1). Naut. To moor.

affranchi, ie [afrã̃ʃi] adj. Emancipated, freed, manumitted (esclave); Prepaid, stamped (lettre). ‖ Fig. Relieved, free (de, of). ‖ Pop. In the know. — m. Freedman. ‖ Pop. Person in the know. **affranchie** f. Freedwoman (esclave).

affranchir [-ʃi:r] v. tr. (2). To emancipate, to liberate, to manumit (un esclave). ‖ To stamp, to prepay (un envoi, une lettre). ‖ To clear, to unblock (aux cartes). ‖ Fin. To discharge (de, of); to exempt (de, from) [impôts]. ‖ Techn. To season (un tonneau). ‖ Fig. To free, to emancipate (l'esprit). ‖ Pop. To let in the know. — v. pr. **S'affranchir,** to free (ou) to emancipate oneself; *s'affranchir de,* to get rid of, to break away from.

affranchissement [-ʃismã] m. Enfranchisement, manumission. ‖ Emancipation, liberation, freeing. ‖ Postage, U. S. mailing; carriage (d'un colis); stamping, postmark (d'une lettre). ‖ Fin. Discharge, exemption (d'un impôt). ‖ Fig. Releasing, relief (de l'esprit).

affres [afr] f. pl. Throes, pangs.
affrètement [afrɛtəmɑ̃] m. NAUT. Chartering, freighting.
affréter [-te] v. tr. (5). NAUT. To charter, to freight.
affréteur [-tœ:r] m. NAUT. Charterer, freighter.
affreusement [afrøzmɑ̃] adv. Dreadfully, frightfully. ‖ Shockingly.
affreux, euse [afrø, ø:z] adj. Hideous, ugly (laid); dreadful, horrid, frightful, ghastly (terrifiant). [V. HORRIBLE.] ‖ Shocking; abominable. ‖ FAM. Wretched, horrible (temps).
affriander [afriɑ̃de] v. tr. (1). To entice, to tempt, to allure.
affriolant, ante [afriɔlɑ̃, ɑ̃:t] adj. Appetizing. ‖ FIG. Alluring.
affrioler [-le] v. tr. (1). To entice, to tempt. ‖ FIG. To allure.
affriqué, ée [afrike] adj. GRAMM. Affricative.
— f. GRAMM. Affricate.
affront [afrɔ̃] m. Affront, slight, snub; *faire un affront à*, to insult, to slight.
affronté, ée [-te] adj. BLAS. Affrontee.
affrontement [-tmɑ̃] m. Confrontation, clash, encounter.
affronter [-te] v. tr. (1). To face, to confront, to meet face to face. ‖ TECHN. To join face to face (ou) edge to edge; to bring together. ‖ MÉD. To set. ‖ FIG. To brave; to face.
— v. pr. **S'affronter**, to face each other, to meet face to face.
affublement [afyblǝmɑ̃] m. Rig-out, get-up.
affubler [-ble] v. tr. (1). To deck out; to rig out (de, in). [V. ACCOUTRER.]
— v. pr. **S'affubler**, to masquerade; to rig oneself out (de, in). ‖ FIG. *S'affubler de*, to assume (un faux nom); to encumber oneself with (une femme).
affusion [afyzjɔ̃] f. MÉD. Affusion.
affût [afy] m. MILIT. Gun-carriage; *affût de canon*, mount. ‖ SPORTS. Lurking-place; *chasser à l'affût*, to stalk. ‖ FIG. *Etre à l'affût de*, to lie in wait for, to be on the watch (ou) look-out for.
affûtage [-ta:ʒ] m. Sharpening, grinding. ‖ MILIT. Mounting.
affûter [-te] v. tr. (1). To sharpen. (V. AFFILER.)
affûteur [-tœ:r] m. Grinder, sharpener (d'outils). ‖ Stalker (chasseur).
affûteuse [-tø:z] f. Sharpener, grinding machine.
affûtiau [afytjo] m. FAM. Bauble (bagatelle); trinket (fanfreluche).
afghan, ane [afgɑ̃, an] adj., s. GÉOGR. Afghan, afghani.
— m. GRAMM. Afghan, afghani (langue).
Afghanistan [afganistɑ̃] m. GÉOGR. Afghanistan.
afin de [afɛ̃də] loc. prép. In order to, so as to; to.
afin que [afɛ̃kə] loc. conj. In order that; so that; that.
a fortiori [aforsjori] adv. A fortiori.
africain [afrikɛ̃] adj., s. GÉOGR. African.
africanisation [-kanizasjɔ̃] f. Africanization.
africaniste [-kanist] s. Africanist.
afrikaans [-kɑ̃:s] m. GRAMM. Afrikaans.
afrikaner [-kanɛr] s. Afrikaner.
Afrique [afrik] f. GÉOGR. Africa. ‖ **Afrique du Sud**, f. GÉOGR. South Africa.
afro- [afro] préf. Afro-. ‖ **Afro-américain**, adj., s. Afro-American. ‖ **Afro-asiatique**, adj., s. Afro-Asian.
after-shave [aftœrʃɛv] m. After-shave.
agaçant, ante [agasɑ̃, ɑ̃:t] adj. Irritating. ‖ Provoking; provocative, alluring (sourire).
agacement [agasmɑ̃] m. Irritation. (V. IMPATIENCE.) ‖ Setting on edge (des dents, des nerfs).

agacer [agase] v. tr. (5). To vex, to irritate, to annoy, to provoke (v. ÉNERVER); *agacer les dents*, to set one's teeth on edge; *agacer les nerfs de qqn*, to get on (ou) to jump s.o.'s nerves; *sa voix m'agace*, her voice grates on me. ‖ To tease (un chien); to rouse, to excite (qqn).
— v. pr. **S'agacer**, to get annoyed, to become irritated. (V. ÉNERVER [s'].)
agaceries [agasri] f. pl. Provocation, rousing, flirting. ‖ Teasing (taquinerie).
agame [agam] adj. BOT., ZOOL. Agamic (reproduction).
agape [agap] f. ECCLÉS. Agape, love-feast. ‖ FAM. Pl. Banquet.
agar-agar [agaraga:r] m. Agar-agar.
agate [agat] f. Agate (bille, pierre, outil).
agave [agav] m. BOT. Agave.
âge [ɑ:ʒ] m. Age; *âge légal*, full age, majority; *âge de raison*, years of discretion; *avant l'âge*, prematurely; *bas âge*, early childhood; *d'un certain âge*, elderly; *entre deux âges*, of doubtful age; *dans la force de l'âge*, in the prime of life; *paraître son âge*, to look one's age; *premier âge*, infancy; *quand j'avais son âge*, when I was his age; *quel âge avez-vous?* how old are you? ‖ Age (époque); *d'un autre âge*, of another generation; *âge du bronze, du fer, de pierre, de la pierre polie*, bronze, iron, stone, neolithic age; *âge d'or*, golden age; *Moyen Age*, Middle Ages.
âgé, ée [ɑʒe] adj. Aged; old; elderly (v. VIEUX); *âgé de trente ans*, aged thirty years; *il est âgé de trente ans*, he is thirty years old (ou) of age; *le plus âgé des deux*, the elder of the two; *plus âgé que*, older than.
agence [aʒɑ̃:s] f. Agency, office (bureau); agency (entreprise); branch office (succursale). ‖ NAUT. *Agence maritime*, shipping agency.
agencement [-smɑ̃] m. Adjustment, arrangement, disposition. ‖ Furnishing (d'une maison). ‖ Construction (d'une phrase). ‖ Pl. Fittings, fixtures (d'une maison, d'un magasin).
agencer [-se] v. tr. (6). To arrange, to dispose, to set up. ‖ To equip, to fit up, to furnish (un local). ‖ ARTS. To harmonize (des couleurs). ‖ GRAMM. To balance, to construct (une phrase). ‖ TECHN. To adjust (une mécanique).
agenda [aʒɛ̃da] m. Memorandum book (ou) pad; diary.
agenouillé, ée [aʒnuje] adj. Kneeling.
agenouillement [-jmɑ̃] m. Kneeling.
agenouiller [-je] v. tr. (1). To make kneel down.
— v. pr. **S'agenouiller**, to kneel, to kneel down.
agenouilloir [-jwa:r] m. Hassock; kneeling-stool.
agent [aʒɑ̃] m. Agent, broker; representative; middleman; *agent d'affaires*, business agent; *agent d'assurances*, insurance broker; *agent de change*, stockbroker; *agent comptable*, accountant; *agent diplomatique*, diplomatic agent; *agent électoral*, canvasser; *agent de liaison*, liaison agent; *agent de location*, house agent; *agent de police*, policeman; *agent provocateur*, professional agitator, « agent provocateur »; *agent secret*, secret agent. ‖ Agent, factor, medium; *agent chimique mortel*, lethal chemical agent. ‖ **Agent voyer**, n. Road surveyor (ou) inspector.
agglomérant [aglɔmerɑ̃] m. TECHN. Binding material.
agglomérat [-ra] m. Conglomerate.
agglomération [-sjɔ̃] f. Agglomeration, conglomeration. ‖ Cluster (d'arbres, d'îles, de maisons). ‖ Caking (de charbon); packing (de neige). ‖ Crowd, concourse (de personnes). ‖ Centre of population, urban district (ville).
aggloméré, ée [-re] adj. Agglomerate.
— m. GÉOL. Conglomerate. ‖ COMM. Compressed fuel, briquette (charbon). ‖ ARCHIT. Adobe.
agglomérer [-re] v. tr. (5). To agglomerate.

— v. pr. S'**agglomérer**, to agglomerate; to mass. || To cake (charbon).

agglutinant, ante [aglytinᾱ, ᾱ:t] adj. Agglutinant. || GRAMM. Agglutinate (langue).
— m. Agglutinant. || Med*i*um (en peinture). || Bond (pour aggloméré).

agglutination [-nasjɔ̃] f. Agglutination. || Binding (des agglomérés); caking (du charbon).

agglutiner [-ne] v. tr. (1). To agglutinate.
— v. pr. S'**agglutiner**, to agglutinate. || To bind (agglomérés); to cake (charbon). || FIG. To congregate (personnes).

agglutinine [-nin] f. MÉD. Agglutinin.

agglutinogène [-nɔʒɛn] adj. MÉD. Agglutinogen.

aggravant, ante [agravᾱ, ᾱ:t] adj. Aggravating.

aggravation [-vasjɔ̃] f. Aggravation. || JUR. Increase (de la peine).

aggraver [-ve] v. tr. (1). To aggravate, to make worse, to worsen (empirer). || To augment, to increase (accroître); to intensify (intensifier).
— v. pr. S'**aggraver**, to grow worse; to worsen, to become aggravated.

agile [aʒil] adj. Agile, nimble. || Light-footed (à la course); nimble-fingered (de ses doigts). || FIG. Prompt, quick-minded (de l'esprit).

agilement [-lmᾱ] adv. Nimbly, quickly.

agilité [lite] f. Agility, nimbleness. || Quickness.

agio [aʒjo] m. FIN. Agio, premium; discount charges (frais); speculation (fam.).

agiotage [-ta:ʒ] m. FIN. Agiotage, stock-jobbing.

agioter [-te] v. intr. (1). FIN. To deal in stocks.

agioteur [-tœ:r] m. FIN. Stock-jobber, U. S. stockbroker; speculator, gambler.

agir [aʒi:r] v. intr. (2). To act, to do; *faire agir,* to call into action (qqch.), to set in motion, to actuate, to set to work (qqn). || To behave (*envers,* towards); *agir loyalement,* to play fair; *bien, mal agir,* to behave well, badly; *façon d'agir,* behaviour, goings-on. || MÉD. To operate, to take effect, to work (remède); *agir sur,* to act upon; to bear upon, to influence. || JUR. *Agir contre,* to take action against; to sue (au civil); to prosecute (au criminel); *faire agir la loi,* to set the law in motion. || MILIT. *Agir en action retardatrice,* to fight a delaying action. || FIN. *Agir sur le marché,* to rig the market.
— v. impers. *De quoi s'agit-il?,* what's up?, what is it about?; *il s'agit de Jean,* it is about John, it concerns John; *il ne s'agit pas de ça,* that's not the question; *il s'agit de son avenir,* his future is at stake; *il s'agit de savoir si,* the question is whether; *il ne s'agit que de moi,* I alone am concerned; *il s'agit de travailler,* it's a matter of getting down to work; *voici ce dont il s'agit,* the thing is this.

agissant, ante [aʒisᾱ, ᾱ:t] adj. Active; efficient; efficacious.

agissements [-smᾱ] m. pl. Doings, dealings.

agitant, ante [-tᾱ, ᾱ:t] adj. Agitating; excitative; stimulating.

agitateur, trice [-tatœ:r, tris] s. Agitator. || m. CHIM. Stirrer, glass-rod.

agitation [-tasjɔ̃] f. Agitation; restlessness; fidgetiness; fidgets. || Commotion, ferment, unrest, convulsion, agitation (troubles sociaux). || MÉD. Jactitation, tossing, twitching, titubation. || FIG. Disturbance, excitement, flurry, flutter, hurry.

agité, ée [-te] adj. Boisterous, riotous, tumultuous (foule); restless, excited, fidgety (personne). || Troublous, unsettled, stirring (époque); eventful, roving (vie). || Boisterous, choppy, wild (mer). || MÉD. Perturbed, troubled, excited (esprit); feverish, fidgety (malade); restless, sleepless (nuit); broken, fitful (sommeil).
— s. Fidgety (ou) restless person.

agiter [-ɕe] v. tr. (1). To flap, to flutter (les ailes); to fan, to stir (l'air); to rock, to sway (les branches); to wave (les bras); to flutter (un éventail); to stir (les feuilles); to agitate, to shake, to stir (un liquide); to wave (un mouchoir); to agitate, to whisk (la queue). || To rouse, to work up, to stir up (une foule); to rouse (la mer). || MÉD. To agitate, to excite (un malade). || FIG. To excite, to agitate, to disturb, to flurry (l'esprit); to discuss (un projet, une question).
— v. pr. S'**agiter**, to move about, to bustle, to be in a flurry, to hurry (s'activer); to fidget (nerveusement); to toss (dans son sommeil). || To ferment, to stir (pensées, population). || To rise (mer).

agneau [aɲo] m. ZOOL. Lamb.

agnelage [aɲəla:ʒ] m. Lambing, yeaning (acte); lambing-season (époque).

agnelée [-le] f. Fall of lambs.

agneler [-le] v. intr. (8b). To lamb.

agnelet [-lɛ] m. ZOOL. Lambkin.

agneline [-lin] f. Lamb's-wool.

agnelle [aɲɛl] f. ZOOL. Ewe-lamb.

agnosticisme [agnɔstisism] m. Agnosticism.

agnostique [-tik] adj., s. Agnostic.

agonie [agɔni] f. Death agony, agonies of death; pangs of death; *entrer en agonie,* to begin one's death struggle; *être à l'agonie,* to be at the point of death (ou) at one's last gasp. || FIG. Anguish.

agonir [-ni:r] v. tr. (2). To blackguard; to revile; *agonir d'injures,* to call names, to load with abuse, to insult right and left.

agonisant, ante [-nizᾱ, ᾱ:t] adj. Dying, at death's door, at the point of death.
— s. Dying person. || Pl. Dying.

agoniser [-nize] v. intr. (1). To be dying, to be at the point of death (ou) at one's last gasp. || FIG. To be in decay (empire).

agoraphobie [agɔrafɔbi] f. MÉD. Agoraphobia.

agouti [aguti] m. ZOOL. Agouti.

agrafage [agrafa:ʒ] m. Stapling (d'une brochure); buckling (d'une ceinture); clipping (de papiers); hooking on, fastening (d'un vêtement). || ARCHIT. Bracing, clamping cramping. || TECHN. Welting, welted seam.

agrafe [agraf] f. Clasp (de broche); buckle (de ceinture); snap (de fermoir); clip, U. S. staple (de papiers); hook, fastening (de robe); *agrafe et porte,* hook and eye. || ARCHIT. Brace, clamp; cramp. || MÉD. Agraffe. || MILIT. Coupling pin. || TECHN. Welt.

agrafer [-fe] v. tr. (1). To clasp (une broche); to staple (une brochure); to buckle (une ceinture); to clip (des papiers); to hook, to fasten (une robe). || ARCHIT. To brace, to clamp; to cramp.
— v. pr. S'**agrafer**, to hook up; to cling.

agrafeuse [-fø:z] f. Stapler.

agraire [agrɛ:r] adj. Agrarian; *mesures agraires,* land-measures.

agrammatical, ale [agrammatikal] adj. Ungrammatical.

agrandir [agrᾱdi:r] v. tr. (2). To add to (un bâtiment); to expand (un empire); to enlarge (un jardin, une maison, un trou); to magnify (un objet); to enlarge (une photo). || FIG. To ennoble, to elevate (l'âme).
— v. pr. S'**agrandir**, to augment (augmenter); to grow larger; to widen (s'élargir); to extend, to expand (s'étendre). || COMM. To extend one's premises (magasin).

agrandissement [-dismᾱ] m. Extension (d'un local); enlargement (d'une maison, d'un territoire); magnification (d'un objet); enlargement (d'une photo). || Aggrandizement (du pouvoir).

agrandisseur [-disœ:r] m. Enlarger (de photo).

agraphie [agrafi] f. PSYCH. Agraphia.

agrarien [agrarjɛ̃, ɛn] adj., m. Agrarian.

agréable [agreabl] adj. Agreeable; nice; enjoyable. (V. AIMABLE, PLAISANT.) || Grateful (chaleur);

gratifying (expérience, nouvelle); prepossessing, winsome (manières, physionomie); comfortable (position); enjoyable (promenade); *agréable au goût, à l'odorat, à la vue*, palatable, savoury, sightly; *être agréable à*, to please, to be acceptable to; *pour lui être agréable*, to oblige him; *se rendre agréable à*, to make oneself agreeable to, to ingratiate oneself with.
— m. Agreeable; *joindre l'utile à l'agréable*, to combine the useful and the agreeable (ou) business with pleasure.

agréablement [-blǝmã] adv. Agreeably; pleasantly; nicely.

agréé [agree] adj. Approved.
— m. JUR. Attorney; counsel (ou) solicitor before a Commercial Court.

agréer v. tr. (1). To accept; to agree to, to recognize; *agréez mes excuses*, accept my apologies; *agréez l'expression de mes sentiments distingués*, yours truly (ou) faithfully.
— v. intr. *Agréer à*, to please, to suit, to be agreeable to.

agrégat [agrega] m. BOT., CHIM. Aggregate.

agrégatif, ive [-gatif, i:v] adj. CHIM. Aggregative.

agrégation [-gasjõ] f. Aggregation, combining. ‖ Agglomeration, conglomeration. ‖ Admission. ‖ Competitive examination qualifying successful candidates to hold teaching posts in Lycées.

agrégé, ée [-ʒe] adj. Aggregate. ‖ GÉOL. Clastic.
— s. Person who has been successful at the « agrégation ».

agréger [-ʒe] v. tr. (7). To aggregate (*à*, to).
— v. pr. **S'agréger**, to aggregate, to unite; *s'agréger à*, to join.

agrément [agremã] m. Approbation, approval. (V. ACQUIESCEMENT.) ‖ Attractiveness, pleasantness. (V. CHARME.) ‖ Pleasure, delight; *jardin d'agrément*, pleasure-grounds; *voyage d'agrément*, pleasure-trip. ‖ Pl. Ornaments, embellishments, trimmings (d'une robe); flourishes, embellishments (du style). ‖ JUR. Amenities (avantages locatifs). ‖ MUS. Grace-notes.

agrémenter [-te] v. tr. (1). To ornament.

agrès [agrɛ] m. pl. NAUT. Rigging, tackle. ‖ AVIAT. Tackle. ‖ Fittings, apparatus (de gymnastique).

agresser [agrɛse] v. tr. (1). To attack (un pays, une personne), to assault (une personne); *se faire agresser*, to get mugged (dans la rue, dans le métro).

agresseur [agrɛsœ:r] m. Aggressor.

agressif, ive [-sif, i:v] adj. Aggressive.

agressivement [-sivmã] adv. Aggressively.

agression [-sjõ] f. JUR., MILIT. Aggression.

agressivité [-sivite] f. Aggressiveness.

agreste [agrɛst] adj. AGRIC. Rural, rustic. ‖ FAM. Countrified.

agricole [agrikɔl] adj. AGRIC. Agricultural; *grande exploitation agricole*, large-scale farming.

agriculteur [-kyltœ:r] m. AGRIC. Farmer, agriculturist.

agriculture [-kylty:r] f. Agriculture; farming; husbandry; tillage.

agriffer (s') [sagrife] v. pr. (1). To claw (*à*, at); to cling (*à*, to).

agripper [agripe] v. tr. (1). To clutch, to grab, to snatch.
— v. pr. **S'agripper**, to clutch, to grab (*à*, at); to cling (*à*, to).

agro-alimentaire [agroalimãtɛr] adj. Food-processing (industries, techniques).

agrologie [agrɔlɔʒi] f. AGRIC. Agrology.

agronome [-nom] m. AGRIC. Agronomist; agricultural expert.

agronomie [-nomi] f. Agronomy; agronomics.

agronomique [-nomik] adj. AGRIC. Agronomic, agronomical.

agrumes [agry:m] m. pl. Citrus fruit.

aguerri, ie [agɛri] adj. Seasoned, hardened (endurci); trained (entraîné).

aguerrir [-ri:r] v. tr. (2). To inure; to harden, to season (*à*, to).
— v. pr. **S'aguerrir**, to become seasoned (ou) hardened (ou) inured (*à*, to); *s'aguerrir contre*, to steel oneself against; to inure oneself to.

aguerrissement [-rismã] m. Hardening, seasoning, inurement; training. ‖ Hardened condition.

aguets [agɛ] m. pl. Watch, watching; *aux aguets*, on the look-out, on the watch.

aguichant, ante [agiʃã, ã:t] adj. Alluring, seductive (femme); enticing (sourire).

aguicher [-ʃe] v. tr. (1). FAM. To allure, to entice, to ogle; to give the glad eye to (fam.); U. S. to give the come-on to (fam.).

aguicheuse [-ʃø:z] f. Alluring woman; vamp.

ah [α] interj. Ah, aha!; oh!

ahan [ahã] m. (†) Great effort, groan.

ahaner [ahane] v. intr. (1). To pant (haleter); to toil (trimer).

ahuri, ie [ayri] adj. Bewildered, dumbfounded, dazed, amazed, confused, taken aback, flummoxed.
— s. Blockhead, dolt.

ahurir [ayri:r] v. tr. (2). To bewilder, to dumbfound, to daze, to confuse, to flabbergast.

ahurissant, ante [ayrisã, ã:t] adj. Bewildering, flabbergasting.

ahurissement [-smã] m. Bewilderment, stupefaction.

ai [ɛ]. V. AVOIR.

aï [αi] m. ZOOL. Ai.

aiche [ɛʃ] f. SPORTS. Bait.

aide [ɛ:d] f. Aid, help (assistance); rescue (sauvetage); succour (secours); *à l'aide de*, by the aid of, with the help of; *crier à l'aide*, to shout (ou) to call for help; *sans aide*, without help, singlehanded, unassisted; *venir à l'aide de*, to come to the aid of; *venir en aide à*, to help, to assist. ‖ FIN. Grant-in-aid, relief, subsidy (en argent). ‖ Pl. Aids. ‖ MÉD. *Aide médicale à domicile*, home care.
— s. Assistant, helper, aide. (V. AUXILIAIRE.) ‖ **Aide-comptable**, s. Accounting (ou) accounts clerk. ‖ MILIT. *Aide de camp*, aide-de-camp. ‖ **Aide-maçon**, m. Hodman, builder's labourer. ‖ **Aide-mémoire**, m. invar. Handbook, aide-mémoire.

aider [ɛde] v. tr. (1). To help, to aid (v. ASSISTER); *aidez-le à mettre son habit*, help him on with his coat; *aider à avancer, à descendre, à sortir, à traverser*, to help forward, down, out, through (ou) across; *se faire aider*, to get assistance (ou) help. ‖ To succour. (V. SECOURIR.)
— v. intr. *Aider à*, to help on, to promote (qqch.); to help, to assist (qqn).
— v. pr. **S'aider**, to help oneself. ‖ To make use (de, of).
— v. récipr. **S'aider**, to help one another.

aïe! [ai] interj. Oh! oo!

aïeul [ajœl] m. Grandfather.

aïeule [ajœ:l] f. Grandmother.

aïeux [ajø] m. pl. Forefathers, ancestors; ancestry.

aigle [ɛgl] m. ZOOL. Eagle. ‖ Eagle (décoration, monnaie); elephant (format); lectern (lutrin). ‖ ‖ ASTRON. Aquila. ‖ FIG. Genius, intellect, master mind (v. PHÉNIX); *à l'œil d'aigle*, eagle-eyed.

aigle f. ZOOL. Female eagle. ‖ Eagle (en héraldique). ‖ Pl. MILIT. Eagles (enseignes).

aiglefin [ɛglǝfɛ̃] m. ZOOL. Haddock.

aiglette [ɛglɛt] f. BLAS. Eaglet.

aiglon [ɛglõ] m. ZOOL. Eaglet. ‖ FIG. Duke of Reichstadt.

aigre [ɛ:gr] adj. Sour, tart. (V. ACIDE.) ‖ Harsh,

grating (bruit); sour (goût, odeur); sharp, shrill (son, ton); bitter, biting (vent). ‖ TECHN. Short. ‖ FIG. Crabbed, peevish, sour, snappish, surly (caractère); *aigre-doux*, bitter-sweet.
— m. *Sentir l'aigre*, to smell sour. ‖ FAM. *Tourner à l'aigre*, to become acrimonious.

aigrefin [ɛgrəfɛ̃] m. Sharper, shark. (V. ESCROC.)

aigrelet, ette [ɛgrəlɛ, ɛt] adj. Sourish, acidulous, tart.

aigrement [ɛgrəmã] adv. Sourly, bitterly.

aigrette [ɛgrɛt] f. Egret, aigrette, tuft, crest (d'oiseau). ‖ Plume (de casque); osprey, egret-plume (de chapeau); aigrette, spray (de diamants). ‖ TECHN. Aigrette.

aigreur [ɛgrœːr] f. Sourness, bitterness, tartness (d'un fruit); bitterness (du vent). ‖ MÉD. Heartburn, water brash (d'estomac). ‖ TECHN. Shortness. ‖ FIG. Crabbedness, sourness, peevishness (du caractère).

aigri, ie [ɛgri] adj. Turned sour. ‖ FIG. Embittered, soured.

aigrir [ɛgriːr] v. tr. (2). To turn (le lait); to sour, to turn sour (le vin). ‖ FIG. To sour, to embitter.
— v. intr. To turn sour.
— v. pr. S'aigrir, to turn sour (lait, vin). ‖ FIG. To become embittered, to grow sour (caractère).

aigrissement [ɛgrismã] m. Souring; sourness. ‖ FIG. Embittering.

aigu, uë [egy] adj. Sharp, pointed (pointu). ‖ Piercing, shrill (cri); treble, screaming, shrill (voix). ‖ Fierce (conflit); critical (danger); keen, penetrating (esprit); keen, piercing, penetrating (regard). ‖ MATH., MÉD., GRAMM. Acute.
— m. MUS., RADIO. Treble.

aigue-marine [ɛgmarin] f. Aquamarine.

aiguière [egjɛːr] f. Ewer.

aiguillage [egɥija:ʒ] m. CH. DE F. Shunting, U. S. switching.

aiguille [egɥiːj] f. Needle; *aiguille à coudre, à repriser, à tricoter*, sewing-, darning-, knitting-needle; *aiguille de tapissier*, upholsterer's needle; *travaux d'aiguille*, needle-work. ‖ Needle (de boussole, de pin, de montagne); spire (de clocher); pointer (de balance); needle, pointer (de manomètre); point (d'obélisque, de pyramide); needle (de tourne-disque); *talon aiguille*, stiletto heel. ‖ Hand (d'horloge); *petite aiguille*, hour hand. ‖ MÉD. *Aiguille à injection, à suture*, hypodermic, suture needle. ‖ MILIT. Firing-pin. ‖ CH. DE F. Points, U. S. switch. ‖ LOC. *Dans le sens (ou) dans le sens inverse des aiguilles d'une montre*, clockwise, counter-clockwise; *en forme d'aiguille*, needle-shaped, acerous, acicular.

aiguillée [egɥije] f. Needleful (de fil).

aiguiller v. tr. (1). TECHN. To shunt, to switch. ‖ FIG. To shunt (ou) switch on (sur, to); *aiguiller sur une autre voie*, to divert (la conversation).
— v. pr. S'aiguiller, to be switched (sur, to).

aiguilleter [-jte] v. tr. (8a). To tag (ferrer).

aiguillette [-jɛt] f. Aiguillette, aglet (de costume, de lacet); shoulder-knot (d'épaulette). ‖ CULIN. Slice of duck.

aiguilleur [-jœːr] m. CH. DE F. Pointsman, U. S. switchman; *poste d'aiguilleur*, signal-box, U. S. block station.

aiguillier [-jie] m. Needle-case.

aiguillon [-jɔ̃] m. Goad, prod (de bouvier). ‖ ZOOL. Sting (dard). ‖ BOT. Prickle, thorn. ‖ FIG. Sting (de la douleur); spur, stimulus, incentive (de l'orgueil); thorn, pricks (du remords).

aiguillonnement [-jɔnmã] m. Goading; pricking. ‖ FIG. Incitement.

aiguillonner [-jɔne] v. tr. (1). To goad, to prod. ‖ FIG. To stimulate, to spurn on. (V. PIQUER, STIMULER.)

aiguillot [egijo] m. NAUT. Pintle.

aiguisage [egɥiza:ʒ (or) egiza:ʒ] m. V. AFFÛTAGE.

aiguiser [-ze] v. tr. (1). To whet, to sharpen; to point (en pointe); to file up (à la lime); *pierre à aiguiser*, whetstone. ‖ FIG. To whet (l'appétit); to sharpen (l'esprit); to stimulate, to stir up (un sentiment).
— v. pr. S'aiguiser, to be sharpened.

aiguiseur [-zœːr] m. Knife-grinder, sharpener.

aiguisoir [-zwa:r] m. Sharpener. (V. AFFILOIR.)

ail [a:j] (pl. ails) m. BOT. Allium. ‖ (Pl. aulx [o].) CULIN. Garlic.

aile [ɛl] f. Wing (d'insecte, d'oiseau); *avoir du plomb dans l'aile*, to be winged (oiseau); *battre des ailes*, to flutter, to flap the wings; *bout d'aile*, wing-tip; *bruit d'ailes*, whir; *coup d'aile*, wing beat; *couper les ailes à*, to clip the wings of. ‖ Brim (de chapeau). ‖ ECCLÉS. Wing (d'ange); aisle (d'église). ‖ ARCHIT. Wing, U. S. ell (de bâtiment); wing, sail, vane (de moulin à vent). ‖ MILIT. Wing (d'armée). ‖ AVIAT. Wing (d'avion); blade (d'hélice). ‖ AUTOM. Wing, mudguard; U. S. fender. ‖ MÉD. Wing (du nez). ‖ FIG. Wing (du vent); wing (protection); *voler de ses propres ailes*, to stand on one's own feet. ‖ FAM. Wing, fin, flipper (bras).

ailé, ée [ɛle] adj. Winged; *la gent ailée*, the feathered tribe.

aileron [ɛlrɔ̃] m. Pinion (d'oiseau); flipper (de pingouin); fin (de requin). ‖ Paddle (de roue de moulin). ‖ AVIAT. Aileron, wing-flap.

ailette [ɛlɛt] f. Winglet. ‖ TECHN. Wing (d'écrou); blade (de turbine, de ventilateur); lug, vane, paddle (de divers mécanismes); flange, fin, gill (de radiateur). ‖ MILIT. Fin (de bombe). ‖ AVIAT. Rib, fin.

ailier [ɛlje] m. SPORT. Winger.

aillade [ajad] f. CULIN. Garlic sauce.

aille [a:j]. V. ALLER (15).

ailler [aje] v. tr. (1). CULIN. To flavour with garlic (rôti); to rub with garlic (croûton de pain).

ailleurs [ajœːr] adv. Elsewhere; somewhere else; *l'esprit ailleurs*, absent-minded; *nulle part ailleurs*, nowhere else; *partout ailleurs*, everywhere else. ‖ D'ailleurs, besides, moreover (en outre); otherwise (d'un autre point de vue). ‖ Par ailleurs, otherwise, in other respects; besides.

ailloli [ajɔli] m. CULIN. Garlic mayonnaise.

aimable [ɛmabl] adj. Lovable (digne d'amour). ‖ Friendly (amical); amiable, pleasant. ‖ Nice, kind (v. AFFABLE); *aimable envers*, nice to (ou) with; *c'est très aimable à vous*, it is very kind of you; *voulez-vous être assez aimable pour*, will you be so kind as to.

aimablement [-bləmã] adv. Pleasantly, kindly.

aimant, ante [ɛmã, ã:t] adj. Loving.

aimant [ɛmã] m. Magnet (artificiel); loadstone (naturel). ‖ FIG. Magnet.

aimantation [-tasjɔ̃] f. Magnetization.

aimanter [-te] v. tr. (1). To magnetize; *aiguille aimantée*, magnetic needle.

aimé, ée [ɛme] adj. Loved (de, by).
— s. Beloved (de, of).

aimer v. tr. (1). To love (d'affection, d'amour); to be fond of (d'affection, d'amitié); to be in love with (d'amour); to dote on (d'engouement); to like (de sympathie); *se faire aimer de*, to win the love (ou) the affection of. ‖ To care for, to enjoy (la campagne, son métier); to be fond of, to like; to relish, to have a taste for (les gâteaux). ‖ *Aimer à faire*, to like doing (ou) to do; to be fond of doing; *il n'aime pas qu'on le fasse attendre*, he does not like being kept waiting. ‖ Aimer autant, to be as fond of; to have just as soon; *j'aime autant vous dire*, I may as well tell you; *j'aime autant le miel que le sucre*, I like honey just as well as sugar; *j'aime autant venir*, I would just as soon come; *j'aime autant qu'elle ne vienne pas,* I would just as soon she didn't come. ‖ **Aimer mieux que,** to like better than, to prefer; *j'aimerais beaucoup mieux ne pas en parler,* I would much rather not talk about it.

aine [ɛn] f. Méd. Groin.

aîné, ée [ɛne] adj. Elder, senior (de deux); eldest, first-born (de plusieurs); *la branche aînée,* the elder branch.
— s. Senior (au regard des frères); first-born (au regard des parents); *il est notre aîné de cinq ans,* he is five years older than we are (ou) five years our senior. ‖ Pl. Elders, betters.

aînesse [ɛnes] f. Primogeniture (par la naissance); *droit d'aînesse,* birth-right. ‖ Seniority (par l'âge).

ainsi [ɛ̃si] adv. Thus (dans cet état); like that, in this way (de cette façon); so, thus (de la façon indiquée); thus, as follows (de la façon suivante); *ainsi soit-il,* so be it, amen; *et ainsi de suite,* and so forth (ou) on; *les choses étant ainsi,* this being the case; *pour ainsi dire,* as it were, so to speak; *s'il en est ainsi,* if so.
— conj. So, and so (donc, en conséquence); *ainsi que,* as (comme, de la façon dont); like, as well as (de même que); *ainsi qu'il s'y attendait,* just as he expected; *ainsi que ses frères,* as well as (ou) likewise his brothers.

air [ɛːr] m. Air; *au grand air, en plein air,* in the open air, outdoors; *courant d'air,* draught (ou) U. S. draft; *dans les airs, en l'air,* in the air; *donner de l'air à (ou) mettre à l'air,* to air; *prendre l'air,* to take the air (ou) a breath of fresh air, to got out for a walk (ou) outdoors; *sans air,* stuffy. ‖ Wind; *il fait de l'air,* it is windy. ‖ Techn. *Admission, conduite, sortie d'air,* air intake, duct, outlet. ‖ Fig. Atmosphere. ‖ Loc. *En l'air,* current, prevalent (actuel); topsy-turvy (bouleversé); idle, imaginary (imaginaire); *up in the air* (non décidé); *mettre tout en l'air,* to upset everything; *regarder en l'air,* to look up.

air [ɛːr] m. Air, appearance, aspect (aspect); *avoir l'air à son aise,* to look comfortable; *ça en a tout l'air,* it looks very much like it; *cela lui donne l'air d'un imbécile,* it makes him look a fool; *elle a l'air d'être votre amie,* she seems to be your friend; *elle a l'air de vous attendre,* she looks as if she were waiting for you. ‖ Countenance; bearing, carriage (comportement); manner, look (manières); mien (mine); *à l'air intelligent,* intelligent-looking; *avoir un air de famille,* to bear a family likeness; *de grand air,* aristocratic, distinguished; *un air noble,* a stately bearing; *un drôle d'air,* an odd look; *prendre un air satisfait,* to put on a satisfied (ou) smug look; *se donner des airs,* to put on airs. ‖ Mus. Air.

airain [ɛrɛ̃] m. Bronze, brass; *airain sonore,* bell; *d'airain,* brazen.

aire [ɛːr] f. Barn-floor, threshing-floor (d'une grange). ‖ Math., Archit. Area. ‖ Eyrie (d'un aigle). ‖ Naut. Wind direction; point of the compass; rhumb. ‖ Techn. Face (d'un marteau); roadway (d'un pont). ‖ Aviat. Area; *aire de manœuvre,* apron.

airelle [ɛrɛl] f. Bot. Bilberry, whortleberry; U. S. huckleberry, blueberry.

ais [ɛ] m. † Plank, board.

aisance [ɛzɑ̃ːs] f. Ease, facility (facilité); easiness, freedom, unconstraint (liberté); room (place). ‖ Easement, right of way (servitude de voisinage). ‖ Comforts, competency, competence, easy circumstances, sufficiency (fortune).

aise [ɛːz] f. Joy, satisfaction, pleasure; *comblé d'aise,* overjoyed. ‖ Ease; *à votre aise,* as you wish (ou) like; *en prendre à son aise,* to take it easy; *en prendre à son aise avec,* not to bother with (qqch.); to pay little heed to (qqn); *mettez-vous à l'aise,* take off your things; *mettre qqn à*

l'aise, to put s.o. at his ease; *se sentir à l'aise,* to feel comfortable (ou) at ease (ou) at home; *se sentir mal à l'aise,* to feel uncomfortable (ou) awkward (ou) unwell. ‖ Pl. Comfort; *aimer ses aises,* to be fond of one's creature comforts. ‖ Easy circumstances (fortune); *être à son aise,* to be quite well off.
— adj. Glad, content; *bien aise,* delighted, well pleased.

aisé, ée [ɛze] adj. Easy, effortless. (V. FACILE.) ‖ Free; natural. ‖ Comfortable. ‖ Well-to-do, well off, in easy circumstances (fortuné); U. S. on easy street (fam.).

aisément [-mɑ̃] adv. Easily. (V. FACILEMENT.)

aisselle [ɛsɛl] f. Méd. Armpit.

aîtres [ɛːtr] m. pl. Ins and outs.

ajointer [aʒwɛ̃te] v. tr. (1). Techn. To join up.

ajonc [aʒɔ̃] m. Bot. Furze, gorse; *couvert d'ajoncs,* furzy, furze-covered.

ajour [aʒuːr] m. Aperture, light (dans un mur); openwork (dans une sculpture). ‖ Hemstitch (dans une lingerie).

ajouré, ée [-re] adj. Pierced (sculpture); *travail ajouré,* fretwork. ‖ Open-work (linge).

ajourer [-re] v. tr. (1). To perforate (le métal). ‖ To hemstitch (le linge).

ajournable [aʒurnabl] adj. Adjournable, postponable.

ajournement [-nəmɑ̃] m. Postponement, putting off (de décision); adjournment (de réunion). ‖ Failing, reference (à un examen). ‖ Jur. Summons; *décret d'ajournement,* writ of subpoena. ‖ Milit. Deferment.

ajourner [-ne] v. tr. (1). To stay, to delay (une décision); to adjourn (une réunion); to postpone, to put off (un travail) [v. REMETTRE]. ‖ To fail, to refer (un candidat). ‖ Milit. To defer. ‖ Jur. To prorogue (la Chambre); to table (la discussion d'un projet de loi); to suspend (une sentence); *ajourner sine die,* to shelve.
— v. pr. **S'ajourner,** to adjourn.

ajout [aʒu] m. Addition (action), thing added (chose ajoutée); insertion (dans un manuscrit).

ajouté [aʒute] m. Addition, rider.

ajouter v. tr. (1). To add; to join. ‖ To append (un appendice); to annex (un codicille); to put in, to add (un détail). ‖ To say further, to go on to say, to add (en paroles). ‖ Loc. *Ajouter foi à,* to give credit to, to trust in.
— v. intr. *Ajouter à,* to add to; to increase.
— v. pr. **S'ajouter,** to be added (à, to), to come on top (à, of).

ajustable [aʒystabl] adj. Adjustable.

ajustage [-tɑ:ʒ] m. Techn. Adjustment; fitting.

ajusté, ée [-te] adj. Close-fitting (habit).

ajustement [-təmɑ̃] m. Adjustment. ‖ Dress, attire (habit).

ajuster [-te] v. tr. (1). To adjust, to set (des outils). ‖ To arrange, to adjust (ses vêtements); to fit (à, sur, on). ‖ To aim (un coup); to aim at (qqn). ‖ Techn. To true up, to finish (une pièce).
— v. pr. **S'ajuster,** to fit; to tally.

ajusteur [-tœːr] m. Techn. Adjuster, fitter.

ajustoir [-twaːr] m. Assay balance, trebuchet.

ajut [aʒy] m. Naut. Carrick bend.

alacrité [alakrite] f. Alacrity.

alaire [alɛːr] adj. Aviat. Alar; *charge alaire,* wing-load.

alaise [alɛːz] f. Méd. Draw-sheet.

alambic [alɑ̃bik] m. Phys. Still, alembic.

alambiqué, ée [-bike] adj. Fam. Alembicated, oversubtle, supersubtle, oversubtilized.

alambiquer [-bike] v. tr. (1). Fam. To over-refine; to subtilize.

alangui, ie [alɑ̃gi] adj. Languid; languishing.

alanguir [-giːr] v. tr. (2). To weaken, to make

languid; *alanguir son regard,* to cast a languishing look.
— v. pr. **S'alanguir,** to grow languid, to languish, to flag, to droop.
alanguissement [-gismᾶ] m. Languor, languidness, droopiness.
alarmant, ante [alarmᾶ, ᾶ:t] adj. Alarming, frightening, disquieting.
alarme [alarm] f. Alarm; *donner, jeter, sonner l'alarme,* to give, to spread, to sound the alarm; *sonnette d'alarme,* alarm-bell, communication cord. ‖ Fear; anxiety (crainte).
alarmer [-me] v. tr. (1). To alarm; to frighten.
— v. pr. **S'alarmer,** to take fright; to be alarmed (ou) frightened (ou) apprehensive.
alarmiste [-mist] m. Alarmist; jitterbug (fam.)
albanais, aise [albanɛ, ɛ:z] adj., s. GÉOGR. Albanian.
Albanie [-ni] f. GÉOGR. Albania.
albâtre [alba:tr] m. Alabaster; *d'albâtre,* alabaster.
albatros [albatrɔs] m. ZOOL. Albatross.
alberge [albɛrʒ] f. BOT. Clingstone peach (ou) apricot.
albigeois, oise [albiʒwa, waz] adj. GÉOGR. Of (ou) from Albi. ‖ ECCLÉS. Relating to the Albigenses.
— s. GÉOGR. Inhabitant (ou) native of Albi. ‖ ECCLÉS. Albigenses (pl.).
albinisme [albinism] m. MÉD. Albinism.
albinos [albinɔ:s] adj., s. Albino.
album [albɔm] m. Scrap-book (de découpures); picture-book (d'images); album (à photos). ‖ ARTS. Sketch-book (à croquis). ‖ COMM. Sample-book (d'échantillons). [V. CATALOGUE.]
albumen [albymɛn] m. MÉD., BOT. Albumen.
albumine [albymin] f. MÉD. Albumin.
albumineux, euse [-nø, ø:z] adj. MÉD. Albuminous.
albuminoïde [-nɔid] adj., m. CHIM. Albuminoid.
albuminurie [-nyri] f. MÉD. Albuminuria.
alcade [alkad] m. Alcade.
alcaïque [alkaik] adj. Alcaic (vers, strophe).
alcalescent, ente [alkalessᾶ, ᾶ:t] adj. CHIM. Alkalescent.
alcali [alkalɪ] m. CHIM. Alkali.
alcalin, ine [-lɛ̃, in] adj. CHIM. Alkaline.
alcaliniser [-linize] v. tr. (1). CHIM. To alkalify.
alcalinité [-linite] f. CHIM. Alkalinity.
alcaloïde [-lɔid] adj., m. CHIM. Alkaloid.
alcarazas [alkarazas] m. Alcarraza.
alchimie [alʃimi] f. Alchemy.
alchimique [-mik] adj. Alchemic, alchemical.
alchimiste [-mist] m. Alchemist.
alcool [alkɔl] m. Alcohol; *alcool à brûler (ou) dénaturé,* methylated spirit, U. S. denatured alcohol; *alcool carburant,* motor spirit; *lampe à alcool,* spirit-lamp, U. S. alcohol lamp; *moteur à alcool,* spirit fuel engine. ‖ Spirits (boisson); U. S. hard liquor.
alcoolat [alkɔɔla] m. CHIM. Alcoholate.
alcoolémie [alkɔlemi] f. MÉD. *Taux d'alcoolémie,* blood-alcohol level.
alcoolique [alkɔlik] adj., s. Alcoholic.
alcoolisation [-lizasjɔ̃] f. Alcoholization.
alcoolisé, ée [-lize] adj. Alcoholic (boissons).
alcooliser [-lize] v. tr. (1). To alcoholize (qqn). ‖ To load, to fortify (le vin).
— v. pr. **S'alcooliser,** to become alcoholic.
alcoolisme [-lism] m. Alcoholism.
alcoomètre [-mɛtr] m. Alcoholometer.
alcootest [-tɛst] m. Breathalyser (appareil), breath test (examen); *faire passer un alcootest,* to breathalyse.
alcôve [alko:v] f. Alcove (renfoncement). ‖ Bedchamber (chambre). ‖ FIG. Sexual intimacy.
alcyon [alsjɔ̃] m. ZOOL. Halcyon.
aldéhyde [aldeid] m. CHIM. Aldehyde.

aléa [alea] m. Hazard, risk, chance.
aléatoire [-twa:r] adj. Risky, hazardous, contingent; chancy (fam.) ‖ JUR. Aleatory.
alémanique[alemanik]adj.GÉOGR.Alemannian; *Suisse alémanique,* German Switzerland.
alène [alɛn] f. Awl.
alentour [alᾶtu:r] adv. About, around, round about; *d'alentour,* neighbouring.
— m. pl. Surroundings. (V. ENVIRONS, VOISINAGE.)
alérion [alerjɔ̃] m. BLAS. Allerion.
alerte [alɛrt] adj. Alert, brisk, nimble (personne); spry (vieillard). ‖ Crisp (style).
— f. Alarm; *à la première alerte,* at the first alarm; *donner l'alerte,* to give the alarm; *fausse alerte,* false alarm. ‖ Alert; *se tenir en alerte,* to keep on the alert; *tenir l'ennemi en alerte,* to harass the enemy. ‖ AVIAT. Air-raid warning, alert; *fin d'alerte,* « all clear ».
— interj. MILIT. To arms! ‖ FAM. Look out!
alertement [-tmᾶ] adv. Alertly, briskly, nimbly.
alerter [-te] v. tr. (1). To give the alarm to; to alert. ‖ To warn, to send a warning to (avertir); to inform (informer).
alésage [aleza:ʒ] m. TECHN. Boring; drilling; reaming; cylinder bore.
alèse, alèze [alɛz] V. ALAISE.
aléser [aleze] v. tr. (5). TECHN. To drill, to bore; to ream.
aléseuse [-zø:z] f., **alésoir** [-zwa:r] m. TECHN. Boring-machine; reamer.
alevin [alvɛ̃] m. ZOOL. Alevin, fry, young fish.
alevinage [alvina:ʒ] m. Stocking with fry.
aleviner [-nə] v. tr. (1). To stock with fry.
alevinier [-nje] m. Nursery, breeding-pond.
alexandrin [alɛksᾶdrɛ̃] adj., m. Alexandrine.
alezan, ane [alzᾶ, an] adj., m. Chestnut, sorrel; *alezan roux,* red bay.
alèze [alɛz] V. ALAISE.
alfa [alfa] m. BOT. Alfa; esparto-grass.
algarade [algarad] f. Quarrel (querelle); rating (remontrance). ‖ Prank. (V. INCARTADE.)
algèbre [alʒɛbr] f. MATH. Algebra; *par l'algèbre,* algebraically.
algébrique [-brik] adj. MATH. Algebraic.
algébriquement [-brikmᾶ] adv. MATH. Algebraically.
algébriste [-brist] s. MATH. Algebraist.
Alger [alʒe] f. GÉOGR. Algiers.
Algérie [-ri] f. GÉOGR. Algeria.
algérien, enne [-rjɛ̃, ɛn] adj., s., GÉOGR. Algerian.
algérois, oise [-wa, wa:z] adj. Pertaining to Algiers.
— s. Native of Algiers.
algésie [alʒezi] f. MÉD. Algesia.
algide [alʒid] adj. MÉD. Algid.
algol [algɔl] m. INFORM. Algol.
algorithme [algɔritm] m. MATH. Algorithm.
algorithmique [-ritmik] adj. MATH. Algorithmic.
algue [alg] f. BOT. Seaweed, alga. ‖ Pl. Algae, seaweed.
alias [aljas] adv. Alias.
alibi [alibi] m. Alibi; *fournir, invoquer un alibi,* to produce, to plead an alibi.
aliboron [alibɔrɔ̃] m. FAM. Ass, donkey (âne); jackass (nigaud).
aliénabilité [aljenabilite] f. Alienability.
aliénable [aljenabl] adj. Alienable, transferable.
aliénant, ante [-nᾶ, ᾶ:t] adj. Alienating.
aliénataire [-natɛ:r] m. JUR. Alienee.
aliénateur, trice [-nat:œr, tris] s. JUR. Alienator.
aliénation [-nasjɔ̃] f. JUR. Alienation, conveyance, transfer (de biens). ‖ MÉD. Insanity, lunacy, mental derangement. (V. FOLIE.)
aliéné, ée [-ne] adj. Insane.

— m. MÉD. Lunatic, madman; insane person. (V. FOU.)

aliéner [-ne] v. tr. (5). To alienate, to convey, to transfer (des biens, une terre, un titre). ‖ MÉD. To derange (l'esprit). ‖ FIG. To lose, to estrange (la sympathie).
— v. pr. **S'aliéner**, to lose (la sympathie).

aliéniste [-nist] adj., m. MÉD. Alienist.

alignement [aliɲmɑ̃] m. Alignment (en général); building-line (des maisons); *dépasser l'alignement*, to overstep the building-line; *frapper d'alignement*, to instruct to conform to the building-line. ‖ Alignment (en typographie). ‖ COMM. Adjustment; *alignement des comptes*, balancing of accounts. ‖ MILIT. Dressing.

aligner [-ɲe] v. tr. (1). To align; to aline; to line up; to set in line. ‖ To bring into alignment (des maisons). ‖ FIN. To balance, to adjust (des comptes). ‖ MILIT. To dress, to draw up, to marshal.
— v. pr. **S'aligner**, to dress, to fall into line, to pick up the dressing. ‖ FAM. *S'aligner avec*, to take on.

aliment [alimɑ̃] m. Food, aliment, nutriment, nourishment; *aliment complet*, complete food. ‖ JUR. Interest, risk, value (d'assurance); inducement (en droit maritime); alimony, maintenance (pour pension). ‖ FIG. Support, sustenance.

alimentaire [-tɛr] adj. Alimentary (v. NUTRITIF); *conserves alimentaires*, tinned (ou) U. S. canned food; *pâtes alimentaires*, Italian pasta. ‖ MÉD. *Bol alimentaire*, bolus. ‖ JUR. Alimentary; *pension alimentaire*, alimony, allowance.

alimentation [-tasjɔ̃] f. Alimentation, food, feeding, nutrition (v. NOURRITURE); *alimentation défectueuse*, malnutrition. ‖ COMM. Provisioning, supply; *rayon de l'alimentation*, food department. ‖ TECH. Feeding (en, with); feed; *alimentation en combustible*, fuel supply; *tuyau d'alimentation*, feed pipe.

alimenter [-te] v. tr. (1). To feed (nourrir); to maintain, to support (soutenir). ‖ To feed (un foyer); to supply (une machine); *alimenter en*, to serve with. ‖ JUR. To provide alimony.
— v. pr. **S'alimenter**, to eat; to keep oneself. ‖ To live, to subsist (de, on). ‖ TECHN. *S'alimenter en combustible*, to lay in fuel.

alinéa [alinea] m. Indented line (ligne); paragraph (passage).

aliquote [alikɔt] adj., f. MATH. Aliquot.

alise [ali:z] f. BOT. Sorb.

alisier [-zje] m. BOT. Service-tree.

alité, ée [alite] adj. Confined to bed, laid up.

aliter v. tr. (1). To confine to bed; to keep in bed.
— v. pr. **S'aliter**, to take to one's bed.

alizés [alize] m. pl. Trade winds.

allaitement [alɛtmɑ̃] m. Bottle-feeding (au biberon); lactation, nursing, suckling (au sein).

allaiter [-te] v. tr. (1). To suckle, to feed.

allant, ante [alɑ̃, ɑ̃:t] adj. Alert, active, lively, spry.
— m. Dash, buoyancy, go, liveliness (v. ENTRAIN); *avoir beaucoup d'allant*, to have plenty of drive.

alléchant, ante [aleʃɑ̃, ɑ̃:t] adj. Attractive; tempting, appetizing.

allèchement [alɛʃmɑ̃] m. Attraction, allurement, enticement.

allécher [aleʃe] v. tr. (5). To entice.

allée [ale] f. Narrow road; lane; alley. ‖ Avenue, path, ride (d'un bois); walk (d'un jardin, d'un parc); *allée carrossable*, drive.

allégation [alegasjɔ̃] f. Allegation, averment.

allège [alɛ:ʒ] f. NAUT. Lighter, tender; *frais d'allège*, lighterage. ‖ ARCHIT. Window-breast.

allégeance [aleʒɑ̃:s] f. † Allegiance.

allégement [aleʒmɑ̃] m. Lightening (d'un poids). ‖ FIN. Reduction (d'un impôt). ‖ JUR. Mitigation

(d'une peine). ‖ FIG. Relief (de, from); alleviation (de, of) [une douleur]; relief (de, from) [un souci].

alléger [-ʒe] v. tr. (5-7). To lighten (un fardeau). ‖ JUR. To mitigate (une peine). ‖ FIG. To alleviate (une douleur); to relieve (un souci).
— v. pr. **S'alléger**, to grow lighter (poids). ‖ FIG. To grow lighter, to lighten.

allégorie [allegɔri} f. Allegory.

allégorique [-rik] adj. Allegorical.

allégoriquement [-rikmɑ̃] adv. Allegorically.

allégoriste [-rist] m. Allegorist.

allègre [allɛ:gr] adj. Brisk. (V. ALERTE.) ‖ Buoyant, blithe (gai).

allégrement [-egrəmɑ̃] adv. Briskly; buoyantly.

allégresse [-grɛs] f. Gladness, cheerfulness.

alléguer [allege] v. tr. (5). To advance, to bring forward, to offer (une excuse); to adduce, to produce (une preuve); to allege, to plead (une raison); to cite, to quote (un texte).

alléluia [allelyja] m., interj. ECCLÉS. Alleluia.

Allemagne [almaɲ] f. GÉOGR. Germany; *l'ambassadeur d'Allemagne*, the German ambassador.

allemand, ande [almɑ̃, ɑ̃:d] adj., s., German; *le bas allemand*, Low German.

allemande [-ɑ̃:d] f. MUS. Allemande.

aller [ale] v. intr. (15).

---

1. Se mouvoir. — 2. Conduire. — 3. S'étendre. — 4. Fonctionner. — 5. Se sentir. — 6. S'ajuster, s'assortir. — 7. Convenir. — 8. Etre admissible. — 9. Durer. — 10. Aller suivi de l'infinitif. — 11. Etre sur le point de. — 12. Se monter à. — 13. Etre attribué à. — 14. MILIT. — 15. NAUT. — 16. LOC.

---

1. To go (*à*, to) [se mouvoir]; *aller en autobus, en bateau, à bicyclette, à cheval, à pied, en traîneau, en voiture*, to go by bus, to boat, to cycle, to ride, to walk (ou) to go on foot, to sledge, to drive; *aller son chemin*, to go one's way; *aller à grands pas*, to stride along; *aller au trot*, to trot (cheval); *aller et venir*, to come and go, to ply. ‖ 2. To go, to lead, to run (*à*, to). [route]. ‖ 3. To go, to stretch, to extend (s'étendre). ‖ 4. To go, to work (fonctionner); *aller comme sur des roulettes*, to go like clockwork; *cette montre ne va pas*, this watch isn't going. ‖ 5. To do, to go, to be going; to get on (se sentir); *comment allez-vous?, ça va, ça va mieux, ça ne va pas*, how are you?, I am all right, I am better, I am not too well (ou) not up to the mark; *ça ne peut manquer d'aller*, it cannot fail to go. ‖ 6. To fit, to sit, to suit (s'ajuster); *aller avec*, to go with, to match (s'assortir); *ce chapeau ne va pas bien*, this hat doesn't sit well; *cette robe vous va bien*, this dress fits you well. ‖ 7. To suit, to be becoming (convenir); *le blanc me va bien*, white is becoming to me (ou) suits me well; *ce climat ne lui va pas*, this climate doesn't agree with him. ‖ 8. To do (être admissible); *ça ne peut pas aller*, that won't do. ‖ 9. To go, to last (durer); *ce manteau n'ira pas loin*, this coat won't last long. ‖ 10. To go, to go and; *aller chercher*, to fetch, to go for; *aller se coucher*, to go to bed; *allez le voir*, go and see him. ‖ 11. To be going, to be about, to be on the point of (être sur le point de); *elle va chanter*, she is going to sing, she will sing. ‖ 12. To amount, to come (*à*, to) [se monter à]. ‖ 13. To go, to be allotted, to fall (*à*, to) [être attribué à]. ‖ 14. MILIT. *Aller au feu*, to go into action. ‖ 15. NAUT. *Aller au fond*, to sink, to go to the bottom. ‖ 16. LOC. *Aller au-devant du malheur*, to forestall misfortune; *aller jusqu'au bout*, to see it through; *allons!* come!, well!, now!; *allons*

bon!, well!, confound it!; *allons donc!*, go along
with you!; *ça va!* right! (bon); agreed!, U. S.
O. K. (d'accord); that's enough (il suffit!); *cela
va de soi*, it is a matter of course; *on y va!*,
coming!; *y aller doucement*, to go about it gently;
y aller de bon cœur, to go at it, to pitch in; *il y va
de sa vie*, his life is at stake; *il y va de la vie*,
it is a matter of life and death; *il en va de même
pour vous*, it's the same with you.
— v. pr. **S'en aller**, to go away, to get away, to
depart, to leave, to withdraw; to retire. ‖ To
remove, U. S. to move (déménager); to pass
away, to disappear, to go off, to be dying, to die
(disparaître, mourir); to come off, to wash off
(partir au nettoyage); *s'en aller furtivement*, to
steal away.
— m. Outward journey; *à l'aller*, on the way
there. ‖ Сн. DE F. Single ticket (billet); *aller et
retour*, return ticket, U. S. round trip ticket. ‖
Loc. *Pis-aller*, makeshift; *au pis aller*, at the
worst. (V. PIS.)
allergène [alɛrʒɛn] m. MÉD. Allergen.
allergie [-ʒi] f. MÉD. Allergy.
allergique [-ʒik] adj. MÉD. Allergic.
alleu [alø] m. † Allodium, U. S. alodium.
alliable [aljabl] adj. Miscible. ‖ FIG. Compatible.
alliacé, ée [aljase] adj. BOT. Alliaceous.
alliage [alja:ʒ] m. Alloy; *sans alliage*, unalloyed.
alliance [aljã:s] f. Alliance, union (internationale). ‖ Union, marriage; relationship (par
mariage); *parent par alliance*, relative by marriage. ‖ Wedding ring (bague). ‖ Combination;
association, blending.
allié, ée [alje] adj. Allied (en politique). ‖
Connected, related (par mariage).
— s. Ally (nation). ‖ Relative, connection
(parent); *allié par le sang*, blood relation.
allier v. tr. (1). To ally (par traité). ‖ To ally, to
connect (par mariage) [à, with]. ‖ To blend, to
match (des couleurs); to alloy (des métaux); to
mix (avec, with). ‖ FIG. To ally, to combine.
— v. pr. **S'allier**, to ally, to become allies, to
confederate (par traité). ‖ To unite; to marry;
to be connected by marriage (à, with). ‖ To
blend (couleurs); to alloy (métaux).
alligator [aligato:r] m. ZOOL. Alligator.
allitération [alliterasjɔ̃] f. GRAMM. Alliteration.
allitérer [-re] v. tr. (5). GRAMM. To alliterate.
allô [alo] interj. Hallo, U. S. hello (au téléphone).
allocataire [alɔkatɛ:r] s. Allocatee.
allocation [-sjɔ̃] f. Allotment (d'actions); allocation, apportionment, assignment (de crédits).
‖ Dole, unemployment benefit (de chômage);
allocations familiales, family allowance, child
benefit. ‖ Allowance, award, compensation
(indemnité); grant, allowance, subsidy (somme
allouée).
allocution [allɔkysjɔ̃] f. Address, speech, allocution.
allomorphe [allɔmɔrf] m. GRAMM. Allomorph.
allonge [alɔ̃:ʒ] f. Extension piece. ‖ Meat-hook
(de boucherie). ‖ Leaf (de table). ‖ JUR. Rider.
‖ NAUT. Stanchion. ‖ SPORTS. Reach (à la boxe).
allongé, ée [alɔ̃ʒe] adj. Long; lengthened; elongated. ‖ Oblong. ‖ Strung out (étiré). ‖ SPORTS.
Smart (trot).
allongement [-ʒmɑ̃] m. Lengthening; extension;
elongation, prolonging. ‖ JUR. Prolongation, protraction. ‖ AVIAT. Aspect ratio. ‖ GRAMM. *Allongement compensatoire*, compensatory lengthening.
allonger [-ʒe] v. tr. (7). To lengthen. ‖ To crane
(le cou); to stretch out (le bras); to hold out
(la main); to draw out (un fil de métal); to make
longer (une robe); to cast (une ombre); *allonger
le pas*, to stride, to step out. ‖ CULIN. To eke

out (le repas); to thin (une sauce). ‖ JUR. To
prolong, to protract. ‖ MILIT. *Allonger le tir*, to
lengthen the range. ‖ FAM. To fork out (de l'argent); to aim (un coup); *allonger à qqn un bon
pourboire*, to slip s.o. a handsome tip; *allonger
une gifle à qqn*, to give s.o. a slap across the
face; *allonger la sauce*, to spin it out.
— v. intr. *Les jours allongent*, the days are getting
longer.
— v. pr. **S'allonger**, to lengthen, to stretch out,
to grow longer. ‖ To stretch oneself out (se coucher); *s'allonger pendant une heure*, to lie down
for an hour. ‖ FIG. To draw out (jours). ‖ FAM.
To fall (visage).
allopathe [allɔpat] adj. MÉD. Allopathic.
— s. MÉD. Allopath, allopathist.
allopathie [-ti] f. MÉD. Allopathy.
allophone [-fɔn] m. GRAMM. Allophone.
allotropie [allɔtrɔpi] f. CHIM. Allotropy.
allotropique [-pik] adj. CHIM. Allotropic, allotropical.
allouable [alwabl] adj. Allowable, grantable.
allouer [alwe] v. tr. (1). To allot, to assign (une
part); to allow, to apportion (une portion); to
allocate (une somme). [V. ATTRIBUER.] ‖ To
award, to grant. (V. ASSIGNER.)
allumage [alyma:ʒ] m. Kindling (d'un feu);
lighting (d'une lampe). ‖ MILIT. Firing (d'une
mine). ‖ TECHN. Ignition; *couper l'allumage*, to
switch off the ignition.
allume [alym] V. ALLUMER. ‖ **Allume-cigares**,
m. invar. Cigar-lighter. ‖ **Allume-feu**, m. invar.
Fire-lighter. ‖ **Allume-gaz**, m. invar. Gas-lighter.
allumé, ée [-me] adj. Burning, lighted (feu);
alight (lampe). ‖ FIG. Gleaming, lustful, randy
(regard); glowing, fiery (teint).
allumer [-me] v. tr. (1). To light (une cigarette,
le gaz, une lampe); to switch on (l'électricité);
to kindle (le feu). ‖ MILIT. To fire (une mine). ‖
FIG. To kindle (une guerre, une passion); to
inflame, to arouse, to excite (le désir).
— v. intr. To light the lamp, to light up, to
switch on the light, to switch on. ‖ To light up
(fumeur).
— v. pr. **S'allumer**, to catch fire, to take fire
(combustible); to kindle (feu). ‖ FIG. To break
out (guerre); to take fire, to flare up (personne);
to light up (regard).
allumette [-mɛt] f. Match. ‖ CULIN. *Allumettes
au fromage*, cheese straws. ‖ **Allumette-bougie**,
f. Wax-vesta. ‖ **Allumette-tison**, f. Fusee.
allumeur [-mœ:r] m. Lighter; *allumeur de réverbères*, lamp-lighter.
allumeuse [-mø:z] f. FAM. Vamp, tease.
allumoir [-mwa:r] m. Lighter.
allure [aly:r] f. Rhythm, speed (régime de marche);
speed, pace (v. TRAIN, VITESSE); *allonger, régler
l'allure*, to increase, to set the pace; *à toute
allure*, at full tilt, at full (ou) top speed; *à
vive allure*, at a brisk pace. ‖ Gait, walk
(démarche); *allure chancelante*, staggering gait. ‖
Air, aspect, bearing, behaviour, manners, ways
(façons); *d'allures libres*, fast; *d'allure louche*,
suspicious- (ou) unsavoury-looking. ‖ Aspect, air,
look (apparence); style (distinction); *avoir l'allure
d'un clochard*, to look like a tramp. ‖ FIN. Aspect
(du marché). ‖ FIG. Turn (des événements).
allusif, ive [allyzif, i:v] adj. Allusive.
allusion [-zjɔ̃] f. Allusion, hint, innuendo; *allusion peu voilée, vague*, broad, dark hint; *faire
allusion à*, to hint at, to refer to, to allude to.
alluvial, ale [allyvjal], **alluvionnaire** [-vjɔnɛr]
adj. GÉOGR. Alluvial.
alluvion [-vjɔ̃] f. GÉOGR. Alluvion; *terrains d'alluvion*, alluvium.
alluvionnement [-vjɔnmɑ̃] m. GÉOGR. Alluviation.

almanach [almana] m. Almanac.
almée [alme] f. Almah.
aloès [alɔɛs] m. Bot. Aloe. ‖ Méd. Bitter aloes.
aloi [alwa] m. Alloy, degree of fineness; *de bon aloi*, sterling, genuine; *monnaie de mauvais aloi*, base coin. ‖ Fig. Quality, standing; *de bon aloi*, sound (argument).
alopécie [alɔpesi] f. Méd. Alopecia.
alors [alɔ:r] adv. Then (à ce moment-là); *jusqu'alors*, till then; *le roi d'alors*, the then king. ‖ So, and so (ainsi, donc); then, therefore, in such a case (dans ce cas, par conséquent); then, next, after that (ensuite, sur ce); *alors que*, when (quand); whereas, while (tandis que); *alors même que*, even when, even though; *et alors?*, so what? (fam.); *et puis alors?*, what then?
alose [alo:z] f. Zool. Alosa, shad.
alouette [alwɛt] f. Zool. Lark, skylark.
alourdi, ie [alurdi] adj. Heavy. (V. lourd.) ‖ Fig. Dull (esprit).
alourdir [-di:r] v. tr. (2). To make heavy (ou) heavier (fardeau); to weigh down, to burden (qqn). ‖ Fig. To dull (l'esprit).
— v. pr. **S'alourdir**, to become heavy (ou) heavier (fardeau, taille). ‖ Fig. To become burdensome (charges, soucis); to become dull (esprit).
alourdissement [-dismã] m. Heaviness. ‖ Fig. Dullness.
aloyau [alwajo] m. Culin. Sirloin of beef.
alpaga [alpaga] m. Zool., Comm. Alpaca (animal, tissu).
alpage [alpa:ʒ] m. Mountain pasture.
alpaguer [alpage] v. tr. (1). Arg. To nick, to pinch (arrêter qqn).
alpe [alp] f. Géogr. Alp.
alpenstock [alpɛnstɔk] m. Alpenstock. (V. piolet.)
alpestre [-pɛstr] adj. Alpine.
alpha [alfa] m. Alpha. ‖ Phys. *Rayons alpha*, alpha rays.
alphabet [alfabɛ] m. Alphabet. ‖ Spelling-book, U. S. speller (livre).
alphabétique [-betik] adj. Alphabetical.
alphabétiquement [-tikmã] adv. Alphabetically.
alphabétisation [-tizasjɔ̃] f. Alphabetization.
alphabétiser [-tize] v. tr. (1). To alphabetize.
alpin, ine [alpɛ̃, in] adj. Géogr., Milit. Alpine.
alpinisme [alpinism] m. Sports. Mountaineering; *faire de l'alpinisme*, to mountaineer, to go in for climbing.
alpiniste [-nist] s. Sports. Alpinist, mountaineer.
Alsace [alzas] f. Géogr. Alsace.
alsacien, enne [-sjɛ̃, ɛn] adj., s. Géogr. Alsatian.
altérabilité [alterabilite] f. Liability to deterioration.
altérable [-rabl] adj. Liable to deterioration.
altérant, ante [-rã, ã:t] adj. Thirst-provoking, parching.
— m. Méd. Alterative.
altération [-rasjɔ̃] f. Comm. Adulteration, falsification (de produits). ‖ Fin. Debasement (de la monnaie). ‖ Méd. Impairing, impairment (de la santé); change (du visage); break (de la voix). ‖ Mus. Inflecting. ‖ Fig. Misrepresentation (des faits, de la vérité); falsification (des textes).
altercation [altɛrkasjɔ̃] f. Altercation.
altéré, ée [altere] adj. Comm. Adulterated (produit). ‖ Fin. Debased (monnaie). ‖ Méd. Impaired (santé); drawn, perturbed (visage); broken (voix). ‖ Fig. Misrepresented (fait, vérité); falsified (texte).
altéré, ée adj. Thirsty. (V. assoiffé.) ‖ Fig. *Altéré de sang*, bloodthirsty.
alter ego [altɛrego] m. Alter ego.
altérer v. tr. (5). Comm. To adulterate (un produit). ‖ Fin. To debase (la monnaie). ‖ Méd. To impair (la santé); to distort (le visage). ‖ Fig.

To alloy (le bonheur); to misrepresent (les faits); to corrupt, to falsify, to tamper with (un texte); to twist (la vérité).
— v. pr. **S'altérer**, to deteriorate; to spoil, to decay (denrée). ‖ To be impaired (santé); to change (visage); to break, to falter (voix).
altérer v. tr. (5). To make thirsty.
— v. intr. To provoke thirst, to parch the mouth.
altérité [alterite] f. Philos. Alterity.
alternance [altɛrnã:s] f. Alternation.
alternant, ante [-nã, ã:t] adj. Alternating. ‖ Agric. Rotating (culture). ‖ Géol. Alternant (couches).
alternateur [-natœ:r] m. Electr. Alternator.
alternatif, ive [-natif, i:v] adj. Alternative. ‖ Electr. Alternating. ‖ Techn. Reciprocating.
alternative [-nati:v] f. Interchange, alternation (succession). ‖ Alternative (choix).
alternativement [-nativmã] adv. Alternatively.
alterne [altɛrn] adj. Math. Alternate (angles).
alterné, ée [-ne] adj. Alternate. ‖ Agric. *Culture alternée*, rotation of crops.
alterner [-ne] v. tr. (1). Agric. To rotate (les cultures).
— v. intr. To alternate (avec, with). ‖ To take turns; to exchange places.
altesse [altɛs] f. Highness (titre).
altier, ère [altje, ɛr] adj. Haughty; lofty. (V. hautain.)
altimètre [altimɛtr] m. Aviat. Altimeter.
altiport [-pɔ:r] m. Aviat. Mountain airport.
altiste [altist] s. Mus. Viola player.
altitude [-tyd] f. Altitude, height, elevation. ‖ Aviat. *Altitude d'utilisation*, cruising altitude; *cote d'altitude*, map elevation; *prendre de l'altitude*, to gain altitude (ou) to climb. ‖ Méd. *Cure d'altitude*, mountain cure.
alto [alto] m. Mus. Viola, tenor (instrument); alto, contralto (voix de femme); counter-tenor (voix d'homme).
altocumulus [altokymylys] m. Altocumulus.
altostratus [-stratys] m. Altostratus.
altruisme [altrɥism] m. Altruism.
altruiste [-ist] adj. Altruistic.
— s. Altruist.
aluminate [alyminat] m. Chim. Aluminate.
alumine [-min] f. Chim. Alumina.
aluminium [-minjɔm] m. Aluminium, U. S. aluminum.
alun [alœ̃] m. Chim. Alum.
alundum [alœ̃dɔm] m. Chim. Alundum.
aluner [alyne] v. tr. (1). Chim. To alum.
alunir v. intr. To land on the moon.
alunissage m. Landing on the moon.
alunite [-nit] f. Alunite, alum-stone.
alvéolaire [alveɔlɛ:r] adj. Alveolar; honeycomb (formation).
alvéole [-ɔl] m. Alveolus; cell (d'abeille). ‖ Small cavity, pocket, pit. ‖ Méd. Socket (de dent).
alvéolé, ée [-ɔle] adj. Alveolate; honeycombed. ‖ Full of small cavities.
amabilité [amabilite] f. Amiability, amiableness, kindliness. ‖ Pl. Civilities; attentions.
amadou [amadu] m. Amadou, touchwood; tinder; U. S. punk.
amadouer [amadwe] v. tr. (1). To coax, to wheedle. (V. cajoler.) ‖ To soften (adoucir).
amaigrir [amɛgri:r] v. tr. (2). To make thin; to emaciate (qqn). [V. amincir.]
— v. pr. **S'amaigrir**, to grow thin, to lose flesh, U. S. to reduce; *s'amaigrir terriblement*, to become emaciated, to grow appallingly thin.
amaigrissant, ante [-grisã, ã:t] adj. Reducing, thinning.
amaigrissement [-grismã] m. Wasting away, losing of flesh. (V. dépérissement, émaciation.)
amalgamation [amalgamasjɔ̃] f. Chim., Jur.

Amalgamation. ‖ Fin. Combination, merging (de capitaux).

amalgame [amalgam] m. Amalgam. (V. MÉLANGE.) ‖ Fig. Mixture.

amalgamer [-me] v. tr. (1). To amalgamate. (V. MÉLANGER.) ‖ Jur. To consolidate; to merge. — v. pr. **S'amalgamer**, to amalgamate. ‖ To blend (couleurs).

aman [amã] m. Mercy; *demander l'aman*, to cry for quarter, to beg for mercy.

amande [amã:d] f. Almond (fruit); kernel (d'un noyau); *en amande*, almond-shaped.

amandier [-dje] m. Bot. Almond-tree.

amanite [amanit] f. Bot. Amanita (vénéneuse).

amant [amã] m. Lover; paramour. (V. AMOUREUX.) ‖ Fig. Lover, devotee.

amante [amã:t] f. Mistress. ‖ † Lady-love.

amarante [amarã:t] Bot. Amaranth. — adj. invar. Amaranth, dark purple (couleur).

amarinage [amarina:ʒ] f. Naut. Seasoning (d'un marin); manning (d'un vaisseau).

amariner [-ne] v. tr. (1). Naut. To season (un matelot); to place a prize crew on board, to man (un vaisseau). — v. pr. **S'amariner**, to find one's sea-legs.

amarrage [amara:ʒ] m. Naut. Mooring, berthing, berth (d'un bateau); lashing (d'un cordage); lanyard (du couteau).

amarre [ama:r] f. Naut. Mooring rope; cable; hawser; guide rope (de touage); *rompre ses amarres*, to part cables, to break adrift.

amarrer [amare] v. tr. (1). Naut. To moor, to berth (à quai); to secure (un canot); to lash (un cordage). — v. pr. **S'amarrer**, to moor. ‖ Fig. To make fast.

amas [ama] m. Mass, heap; accumulation; *amas de neige*, snow-drift. ‖ Astron. *Amas stellaire*, stardust.

amasser [-se] v. tr. (1). To heap up, to pile up (empiler); to amass, to hoard, to lay by, to save up (thésauriser). [V. ACCUMULER.] —v. pr. **S'amasser**, to heap (ou) pile up, to gather. ‖ Méd. To fester; to gather (fam.).

amasseur [-sœ:r] m. Hoarder, collector.

amateur [amatœ:r] m. Lover, devotee; enthusiast; fan (fam.); *amateur de cinéma*, film-fan, U. S. movie-fan; *amateur d'oiseaux*, bird fancier. ‖ Amateur; dabbler; *dessin d'amateur*, amateurish drawing (péj.); *faire de la peinture en amateur*, to dabble in painting; *travailler en amateur*, to work for the fun of it (ou) in dilettante fashion. ‖ Comm. Buyer, taker (acheteur); bidder (enchérisseur).

amateurisme [-tørism] m. Amateurism.

amatir [amati:r] v. tr. (2). To mat.

amaurose [amoro:z] f. Méd. Amaurosis.

amazone [amazo:n] f. † Amazon. ‖ Horsewoman (cavalière); riding-habit (costume); *monter en amazone*, to ride side-saddle.

ambages [ãba:ʒ] f. pl. Circumlocutions, ambages; *sans ambages*, plainly, straight out, without beating about the bush.

ambassade [ãbasad] f. Embassy. ‖ Fam. Errand, mission; *envoyer qqn en ambassade*, to send s.o. as an intermediary.

ambassadeur [-dœ:r] m. Ambassador (*auprès de*, to). ‖ Fam. Messenger.

ambassadrice [-dris] f. Ambassadress.

ambiance [ãbjã:s] f. Environment; milieu. ‖ Atmosphere, spirit, tone; *ambiance générale*, prevailing atmosphere (ou) mood (ou) feeling.

ambiant, ante [ãbjã, ã:t] adj. Ambient, surrounding; *air ambiant*, atmosphere.

ambidextre [ãbidɛkstr] adj. Ambidextrous. — s. Ambidexter.

ambigu, uë [ãbigy] adj. Cryptic (avertissement);

doubtful, shady (caractère); ambiguous (expression); equivocal (réponse).

ambiguïté [-gɥite] f. Ambiguity.

ambitieusement [-sjøzmã] adv. Ambitiously.

ambitieux [ãbisjø] adj. Ambitious; aspiring; thirsting; eager for. ‖ Pretentious, showy (allures); studied (style). — m. Ambitious person; careerist; go-getter (fam.). [V. ARRIVISTE.]

ambition [-sjɔ̃] f. Ambition; *mettre son ambition à*, to make it one's ambition to, to set one's heart on.

ambitionner [-sjɔne] v. tr. (1). To aspire to, to be eager for, to hanker after, to aim at.

ambivalence [ãbivalã:s] f. Ambivalence.

ambivalent, ente [-lã, ã:t] adj. Ambivalent.

amble [ã:bl] m. Amble; *aller l'amble*, to amble.

ambler [-ble] v. tr. (1). To amble.

ambon [ãbɔ̃] m. Archit. Ambo. ‖ Méd. Ambon.

ambre [ã:br] m. Ambergris (gris); amber (jaune). ‖ Fam. *Fin comme l'ambre*, as sharp as a needle.

ambré, ée [ãbre] adj. Amber-coloured (couleur); perfumed with amber (parfum).

ambrer v. tr. (1). To amber.

ambroisie [ãbrwazi] f. Ambrosia; *d'ambroisie*, ambrosial.

ambrosiaque [ãbrɔzjak] adj. Ambrosial.

ambulance [ãbylã:s] f. Ambulance. ‖ Autom. Motor ambulance. ‖ Milit. Field hospital; *ambulance de campagne*, field ambulance.

ambulancier [-lãsje] m. Milit. Medical orderly; stretcher-bearer.

ambulancière [-lãsjɛ:r] f. Milit. Ambulance nurse.

ambulant, ante [-lã, ã:t] adj. Itinerant; strolling; *marchand ambulant*, hawker, pedlar, U. S. peddler. (V. NOMADE.) ‖ Théâtr. *Comédiens ambulants*, strolling players. — m. Travelling post-office employee.

ambulatoire [-latwa:r] adj. Ambulatory. ‖ Méd. Ambulant.

âme [ã:m] f. Soul (principe spirituel et vital); *à fendre l'âme*, heart-breaking; *âme damnée de*, tool (ou) stooge of; *comme une âme en peine*, like a lost soul; *conservateur dans l'âme*, conservative to the backbone; *de toute son âme*, with all his soul; *en mon âme et conscience*, to the best of my knowledge and belief; *état d'âme*, mood, frame of mind; *une grande âme*, a noble soul; *rendre l'âme*, to give up the ghost, to breathe one's last. ‖ Soul, living person (individu, habitant); *une âme sœur*, a kindred spirit; *pas âme qui vive*, not a living soul; *une population de cent mille âmes*, a population of a hundred thousand souls. ‖ Soul (émotion, sentiment); *avec âme*, with feeling, soulfully. ‖ Mus. Sound-post (de violon). ‖ Techn. Bore (d'armes à feu); core (de câble). ‖ Fig. Soul, essence, life (d'une entreprise, de la résistance, de la révolte).

améliorable [ameljɔrabl] adj. Improvable.

améliorant, ante [-rã, rã:t] adj. Bot., Agric. *Plante améliorante*, regenerative crop.

améliorateur, trice [-ratœ:r, ratris] adj. Ameliorative.

amélioration [-rasjɔ̃] f. Amelioration, betterment, improvement.

améliorer [-re] v. tr. (1). To ameliorate; to improve, to better; *améliorer sa condition*, to better oneself. — v. pr. **S'améliorer**, to ameliorate; to improve; to grow better. ‖ To clear up (temps). ‖ Méd. To mend (santé).

amen [amɛn] interj., m. Amen.

amenage [amna:ʒ] m. Conveyance, transport (de marchandises). ‖ Techn. Feed.

aménagement [amena3mã] m. Fitting up (ou) out, appointment, arrangement (de local); U. S.

set-up; *aménagements locatifs*, fittings, fixtures. ‖ Harnessing (de chute d'eau). ‖ Agric. Parcelling out (de forêt); preparation (de terrain). ‖ Ch. de f. Grading (d'une voie). ‖ Fin. Adjustment (des impôts). ‖ Techn. Feeding (d'une machine).

aménager [-ʒe] v. tr. (7). To fit up (ou) out, to arrange (un local); to plan (une ville). ‖ To harness (une chute d'eau). ‖ Agric. To prepare (un terrain); to parcel out (une forêt). ‖ Ch. de f. To grade (une voie). ‖ Fin. To adjust (des impôts). ‖ Techn. To feed (une machine).

amendable [amɑ̃dabl] adj. Agric. Improvable.

amende [amɑ̃d] f. Amends, apology; *faire amende honorable*, to make amends, to apologize. ‖ Fine, penalty; *amende de principe*, nominal fine; *être mis à l'amende*, to have to pay a forfeit (au jeu); *mettre à l'amende*, to fine.

amendement [amɑ̃dmɑ̃] m. Improvement. ‖ Jur. Amendment; *déposer un amendement*, to move (ou) to propose an amendment.

amender [-de] v. tr. (1). To amend (qqch.). ‖ Agric. To improve (la terre). ‖ Jur. To amend (un projet de loi). ‖ Fig. *Amender sa conduite*, to mend one's ways, to reform.
— v. pr. **S'amender**, to improve (conduite); to mend one's ways (personne).

amène [amɛn] adj. Mild (caractère); pleasant, agreeable (lieu).

amenée [amne] f. Leading; intake; *conduite d'amenée*, delivery pipe.

amener v. tr. (5). To bring, to lead (un animal); to bring, to lead, to conduct (qqn); *amener à*, to lead to; *amener à pied d'œuvre*, to bring to the site (ou) the working site. ‖ To bring, to convey (l'eau, le gaz). ‖ To throw (aux dés). ‖ Naut. To lower (une embarcation, les voiles); *amener pavillon*, to strike the colours. ‖ Jur. *Mandat d'amener*, warrant of arrest. ‖ Fig. To bring round (la conversation) [*sur*, to]; to lead up to (un dénouement); to bring, to cause, to lead to, to bring about (des ennuis); to introduce (un sujet); *amener à*, to induce to, to win over to (pousser).
— v. pr. **S'amener**, Fam. To come along, to turn up, to roll up.

aménité [amenite] f. Amenity, attractiveness. ‖ Pl. Civilities, compliments (sens ironique).

amenuisement [amənɥizmɑ̃] m. Reduction, decrease.

amenuiser [amənɥize] v. tr. (1). To thin down (une chose). ‖ To reduce (amaigrir).
— v. pr. **S'amenuiser**, to grow thin. ‖ To become sharpened (traits).

amer [amɛ:r] m. Naut. Sea-mark.

amer [amɛ:r] adj. Bitter. ‖ Fig. Sharp, keen (douleur); galling (expérience); biting (ironie).
— m. Bitters (boisson). ‖ Zool. Gall (fiel).

amèrement [amɛrmɑ̃] adv. Bitterly; sharply.

américain, aine [amerikɛ̃, ɛn] adj. American.
— s. Géogr. American; Yankee, Yank (fam.).

américanisation [amerikanizasjɔ̃] f. Americanization.

américaniser [-kanize] v. tr. (1). To Americanize.
— v. pr. **S'américaniser,** to become Americanized.

américanisme [-kanism] m. Americanism.

américaniste [-kanist] s. Americanist.

américium [amerisjɔm] m. Chim. Americium.

amérindien [amerĩdjɛ̃] m. Géogr. Amerind, Amerindian, American Indian.

Amérique [amerik] f. Géogr. America.

amerlo [amɛrlo], **amerloque** [-lɔk] s. Pop. American, Yank, Yankee.

amerrir [amerir] v. intr. (2). Aviat. To alight on the water.

amerrissage [-risa:ʒ] m. Aviat. Alighting on the water.

amertume [amɛrtym] f. Bitterness. ‖ Fig. Pl. Bitters, gall.

améthyste [ametist] f. Amethyst.

ameublement [amøbləmɑ̃] m. Furnishing (action); furniture (meubles); upholstery (tapisserie).

ameublir [amøbli:r] v. tr. (2). Jur. To convert realty into personalty. ‖ Agric. To break up.

ameuter [amøte] v. tr. (1). Sports. To form into a pack (des chiens). ‖ Fig. To set (des ennemis) [*contre*, upon]; to rouse, to stir up, to muster (une foule) [*contre*, against].
— v. pr. **S'ameuter**, to rise, to mutiny; *s'ameuter autour*, to mob.

ami, ie [ami] s. Friend (*de*, of); *ami d'enfance*, childhood friend, lifelong friend, old playmate; *en ami*, in a friendly way, as a friend; *mon ami*, my dear fellow (ou) boy (à un égal); my good man (ou) fellow (à un inférieur); *parents et amis*, kith and kin; *se faire un ami*, to make a friend. ‖ Boy-friend; girl-friend (flirt). ‖ Lover (amant); mistress (maîtresse). ‖ Fan (amateur); patron (mécène); supporter (partisan).
— adj. Friendly, kindly.

amiable [amjabl] adj. Amicable, friendly; *arrangement à l'amiable*, settlement out of court, amicable settlement, private agreement; *vente à l'amiable*, sale by private contract (ou) by mutual agreement.

amiante [amjɑ̃:t] f. Asbestos, amianthus. ‖ **Amiante-ciment,** m. Asbestos cement.

amibe [amib] f. Méd. Amœba.

amibiase [-bja:z] f. Méd. Amœbiasis.

amibien, enne [-bjɛ̃, ɛn] adj. Méd. Amœbic.

amical, ale [amikal] adj. Amicable, friendly; *peu amical*, unfriendly.

amicale [-ka:l] f. Friendly society (ou) association.

amicalement [-kalmɑ̃] adv. In a friendly way, amicably; like a friend.

amict [ami] m. Ecclés. Amice.

amidon [amidɔ̃] m. Starch.

amidonnage [-dɔna:ʒ] m. Starching.

amidonner [-dɔne] v. tr. (1). To starch.

amincir [amɛ̃si:r] v. tr. (2). To make thinner (ou) slimmer. ‖ To thin down (le bois). ‖ To slim down, U. S. to slenderize (qqn, une silhouette).
— v. pr. **S'amincir**, to grow thinner.(ou) slimmer.

amincissant, ante [-sisɑ̃, ɑ̃:t] adj. Slimming; U. S. slenderizing.

amincissement [-sismɑ̃] m. Slimming, reducing.

amine [ami:n] f. Chim. Amine.

aminé, ée [amine] adj. Chim. *Acide aminé*, amino-acid.

amiral [amiral] m. Naut. Admiral (personne); *vaisseau amiral*, flagship.

amirale f. Admiral's wife.

amirauté [-rote] f. Naut. Admiralty.

amiralat [-rala] m. Naut. Admiralship.

amitié [amitje] f. Friendship; *se prendre d'amitié pour*, to take a liking to. ‖ Kindness, favour; *faites-moi l'amitié de*, do me the favour of, give me the pleasure of. ‖ Pl. Compliments; *amitiés à tous*, love (ou) kind regards to all. ‖ Pl. Demonstrations, effusions.

ammoniac [amɔnjak] m. Chim. Ammonia.

ammoniac, aque adj. Chim. Ammoniac.

ammoniacal [-njakal] adj. Chim. Ammoniacal.

ammoniacé, ée [-njase] adj. Chim. Ammoniated.

ammoniaque [-njak] f. Chim. Ammonia.

ammonite [amɔnit] f. Zool. Ammonite.

ammonium [amɔnjɔm] m. Chim. Ammonium.

amnésie [amnezi] f. Méd. Amnesia.

amnésique [-zik] adj. Méd. Amnesic.

amniotique [amnjɔtik] adj. Zool., Méd. Amniotic (liquide, membrane); *poche amniotique*, amnion.

amnistie [amnisti] f. Amnesty, general pardon;

loi d'amnistie, act of grace (ou) oblivion, amnesty ordinance.
amnistier [-tje] v. tr. (1). To amnesty, to grant amnesty.
amocher [amɔʃe] v. tr. (1). FAM. To damage. (V. ABÎMER.) ‖ POP. To hit in the face, to bash, to knock about; to beat up (frapper).
amodier [amɔdje] v. tr. (1). AGRIC. To farm out, to lease for a rent usually paid in kind.
amoindrir [amwɛ̃driːr] v. tr. (2). To reduce, to lessen; to belittle. ‖ FIG. To mitigate.
— v. pr. **S'amoindrir,** to grow less, to decrease, to diminish.
amoindrissement [-drismɑ̃] m. Lessening, decrease.
amollir [amɔliːr] v. tr. (2). To soften; to mollify. ‖ FIG. To enervate, to weaken (affaiblir); to melt, to soften (attendrir).
— v. pr. **S'amollir,** to soften, to weaken. ‖ To melt (fondre).
amollissant, ante [-isɑ̃, ɑ̃ːt] adj. Softening. ‖ FIG. Enervating.
amollissement [-lismɑ̃] m. Softening. ‖ FIG. Weakening, softening; enervation.
amonceler [amɔ̃sle] v. tr. (8a). To heap up, to pile up. (V. ACCUMULER.)
— v. pr. **S'amonceler,** to pile up; to accumulate. ‖ To drift (neige); to bank up (nuages).
amont [amɔ̃] m. Upstream water; head waters; *en amont,* upstream, upriver; *en amont de,* above.
amoral, ale [amɔral] adj. Amoral.
amorçage [amɔrsaːʒ] m. Priming (d'une pompe). ‖ SPORTS. Baiting (à la pêche). ‖ MILIT. Priming (d'un fusil); fusing (d'une mine); capping (d'un obus). ‖ ELECTR. Starting; excitation. ‖ FIG. Alluring (aguichage); starting up, setting going (mise en train).
amorce [amɔrs] f. Priming (de pompe). ‖ SPORTS. Bait (de pêcheur). ‖ MILIT. Cap (de fusil); amorce (de pistolet d'enfant). ‖ ELECTR. Fuse; *tube d'amorce,* fuse casing. ‖ THÉÂTR. Leader; trailer, U. S. teaser (au cinéma). ‖ FIG. Lure, allurement, starting, beginning.
amorcer [-se] v. tr. (6). To prime (une pompe). ‖ SPORTS. To bait (un poisson, une ligne). ‖ MILIT. To prime (un fusil); to fuse (une mine); to cap (un obus). ‖ ELECTR. To start; to energize. ‖ FIG. To allure, to inveigle (aguicher); to initiate, to start, to set going, to put into motion (mettre en train).
— v. pr. **S'amorcer,** TECHN. To prime; to energize. ‖ FIG. To start, to begin.
amorçoir [-swaːr] m. TECHN. Boring-bit.
amorphe [amɔrf] adj. Amorphous. ‖ FIG. Lumpish; flabby; spineless; lackadaisical. (V. MOU.)
amorphisme [-fism] m. Amorphism.
amorti, ie [amɔrti] adj. Deadened; amortized; made less violent. ‖ NAUT. Neaped, grounded, aground. ‖ ELECTR. Damped (onde).
— m. SPORTS. Drop shot (au tennis).
amortir [-tir] v. tr. (2). To muffle, to stifle (un bruit, un son); to absorb, to deaden (un choc); to break (une chute). ‖ To subdue (la lumière); to damp (une onde); to slacken (la vitesse). ‖ FIN. To amortize, to extinguish (une dette); to redeem, to sink, to buy up (la dette publique); to pay off (une hypothèque); to allow for depreciation, to depreciate, to write off (une installation, du matériel); to alienate (un terrain). ‖ MÉD. To assuage (la douleur). ‖ FIG. To weaken (l'ardeur).
— v. pr. **S'amortir,** FIN. To be redeemed (dette). ‖ PHYS. To grow less (oscillations). ‖ MÉD. To be assuaged (douleur). ‖ FIG. To cool (passion).
amortissable [-tisabl] adj. FIN. Redeemable.
amortissement [-tismɑ̃] m. Deadening (d'un bruit); absorbing (d'un choc); breaking (d'une

chute); sound-proofing (du son). ‖ ELECTR. Damping (des oscillations). ‖ FIN. Amortization, extinction (d'une dette); redemption, buying up, sinking (de la Dette publique); absorption of depreciation amounts written off (de matériel); *aliénation* (d'un terrain); *fonds* (ou) *caisse d'amortissement,* sinking fund.
amortisseur [-tisœːr] m. AUTOM. Shock-absorber. ‖ NAUT. Fender. ‖ ELECTR. Damper.
amour [amur] m. Love; *amour intéressé,* cupboard love; *chagrin d'amour,* heartbreak, love-trouble; *l'amour de l'argent,* love of money; *mariage d'amour,* love-match. ‖ Liking (attrait); *amour des affaires,* liking for business. ‖ Pl. ARTS. Cupids, loves. ‖ FAM. *Un amour d'enfant,* a little darling; *un amour de petit sac,* a lovely (ou) sweet little handbag; *vous êtes un amour,* you are a dear (ou) darling.
— pl. f. Love, love-making (commerce amoureux); amours (intrigue galante); *amours déréglées,* loose amours. ‖ Object of love; *une de mes anciennes amours,* an old flame of mine; *la musique et la peinture, voilà mes seules amours,* music and painting are my only passions. ‖ **Amour-propre,** m. Self-pride; self-esteem; self-respect; amour-propre.
amouracher [-raʃe] v. tr. (1). To enamour.
— v. pr. **S'amouracher,** to fall in love, to be infatuated (de, with); to lose one's heart (de, to).
amourette [-rɛt] f. Amourette, love-affair (amour passager); calf-love, puppy love (premier amour).
amoureuse [-rœːz] f. Girl-friend, sweetheart.
amoureusement [-røzmɑ̃] adv. Lovingly; amorously.
amoureux, euse [-rø, ø:z] adj. In love (de, with); enamoured (de, of); infatuated (de, with); *tomber amoureux de,* to fall in love with, to fall for. ‖ Amatory (lettre); amorous, loving (regard); amorous (tempérament).
— m. Lover; boy-friend. (V. BÉGUIN, GALANT, SOUPIRANT.)
amovibilité [amɔvibilite] f. Detachableness (d'une chose); liability to withdrawal (d'un droit); removability (d'un fonctionnaire).
amovible [-vibl] adj. Detachable, removable (chose); revocable at pleasure (droit); removable (fonctionnaire).
ampérage [ɑ̃peraːʒ] m. ELECTR. Amperage.
ampère [-ɑ̃pɛːr] m. ELECTR. Ampere.
ampèreheure [-rœːr] m. ELECTR. Ampere-hour.
ampèremètre [-mɛtr] m. ELECTR. Ammeter.
amphétamine [ɑ̃fetamin] f. CHIM., MÉD. Amphetamine.
amphi [ɑ̃fi] m. FAM. Lecture-theatre, lecture-room.
amphibie [ɑ̃fibi] adj. Amphibious. ‖ MILIT. Land and sea (opération); *camion amphibie,* amphibious truck; duck (fam.).
— m. ZOOL., MILIT., AVIAT. Amphibian.
amphibien [-bjɛ̃] m. ZOOL. Amphibian.
amphibologie [ɑ̃fibɔlɔʒi] f. GRAMM. Amphibology, ambiguity.
amphibologique [-ʒik] adj. Amphibological.
amphigouri [ɑ̃figuri] m. Amphigouri, amphigory; nonsensical writing.
amphigourique [ɑ̃figurik] adj. Nonsensical; rambling; obscure (style).
amphithéâtre [ɑ̃fiteaːtr] m. Amphitheatre, U. S. amphitheater (arène). ‖ Lecture-room (salle).
amphitryon [ɑ̃fitrjɔ̃] m. Amphitryon. (V. HÔTE.)
amphore [ɑ̃fɔːr] f. Amphora.
ample [ɑ̃ːpl] adj. Ample, copious, abundant, plentiful (abondant); spacious, roomy (vaste). ‖ Broad, loose, full (habit); full (forme, style, voix). ‖ LOC. *Pour plus ample informé,* for further details.
amplement [-pləmɑ̃] adv. Amply, fully.

ampleur [-plœ:r] f. Width, breadth, spaciousness, extensiveness (étendue). ‖ Ampleness; amplitude. ‖ Importance. ‖ Fullness (plénitude).

ampli [-pli] m. ELECTR., FAM. Amp (amplificateur).

ampliatif, ive [ãpljatif, i:v] adj. JUR. Ampliative; duplicate.

ampliation [-sjɔ̃] f. JUR. Certified (ou) true copy; office copy; exemplification; *pour ampliation,* certified true copy.

amplificateur, trice [ãplifikatœ-r, tris] adj. Magnifying. ‖ FIG. Given to exaggeration.
— m. ELECTR. Amplifier; *amplificateur de tension,* voltage amplifier. ‖ TECHN. Enlarger (de photo).

amplification [-sjɔ̃] f. Amplification, development. ‖ PHYS. Magnification (en optique); enlarging (en photo). ‖ RADIO. Amplification. ‖ FIG. Exaggeration.

amplifier [ãplifje] v. tr. (1). To amplify, to enlarge, to develop. ‖ PHYS. To magnify (en optique); to enlarge (une photo). ‖ RADIO. To amplify. ‖ FIG. To embroider, to magnify.

amplitude [ãplityd] f. Amplitude, vastness (de l'espace); *mouvement de faible amplitude,* limited movement. ‖ PHYS., ASTRON. Amplitude.

ampoule [ãpul] f. Phial (fiole). ‖ MÉD. Ampulla (anatomique); ampoule (pour injections); blister, bleb (sur la peau). ‖ ELECTR. Bulb.

ampoulé, ée [-le] adj. Bombastic (v. BOURSOUFLÉ, ENFLÉ); *langage ampoulé,* bombast.

amputation [ãpytasjɔ̃] f. JUR. Reduction, curtailment. ‖ MÉD. Amputation. ‖ FIG. Cutting-down (de, of); cut (de, in) [dans un texte].

amputer [-te] v. tr. (1). MÉD. To amputate; *il est amputé d'un bras,* he has lost an arm. ‖ JUR. To curtail. ‖ FIG. To cut down.

amuïr (s') [samчir] v. pr. GRAMM. To disappear.

amuïssement [amчismã] m. GRAMM. Disappearance (d'un son).

amulette [amylɛt] f. Amulet.

amunitionner [amynisjɔne] v. tr. (1). MILIT. To supply.

amure [amyr] f. NAUT. Tack of sail.

amurer [-re] v. tr. (1). NAUT. To board the tack of, to brace to windward.

amusant, ante [amyzã, ã:t] adj. Amusing. (V. DIVERTISSANT.) ‖ Funny. (V. COMIQUE.)

amuse-gueule [amyz-gœ:l] m. pl. CULIN. Cocktail-snack.

amusement [amyzmã] m. Amusement, entertainment. (V. DISTRACTION.) ‖ Game (jeu).

amuser [-ze] v. tr. (1). To amuse, to entertain. ‖ To delude, to beguile (duper).
— v. pr. S'amuser, to play (enfants); to sow one's wild oats, to have one's fling (jeunes gens). ‖ To take one's pleasure, to enjoy oneself, to have a good time, to have fun (se divertir); *pour s'amuser,* by way of joke, in sport. ‖ To waste one's time; to loiter; dawdle (flâner). ‖ S'amuser à, to divert oneself by, to while away the time by. ‖ S'amuser avec, to toy (ou) play with. ‖ S'amuser de, to make fun of (rire de); to play fast and loose with (jouer avec, leurrer).

amusette [-zɛt] f. Plaything; diversion. ‖ FAM. Child's play.

amuseur [-zœ:r] s. Amuser, entertainer.

amygdale [amigdal] f. MÉD. Tonsil.

amygdalite [-dalit] f. MÉD. Tonsillitis.

amylacé, ée [amilase] adj. CHIM. Amylaceous.

amylase [-la:z] f. CHIM. Amylase.

amyle [amil] m. CHIM. Amyl.

amylique [amilik] adj. CHIM. Amylic (alcool).

an [ã] m. Year; *bon an mal an,* taking one year with another; year in year out; *elle n'a pas encore vingt ans,* she is still under twenty (ou) in her teens; *il a trente ans,* he is thirty years old; *par an,* a year; *un ami de dix ans,* a friend of ten

years' standing; *qui a lieu tous les deux ans,* biennial; *tous les ans,* every year; *tous les deux ans,* every other year.

ana [ana] m. invar. Ana.

anabaptiste [anabatist] s. Anabaptist.

anabolisme [anabɔlism] m. Anabolism.

anacarde [anakard] m. BOT. Anacard, cashew-nut.

anacardier [-dje] m. BOT. Cashew-tree.

anachorète [anakɔrɛt] m. Anchorite, anchoret.

anachronique [anakrɔnik] adj. Anachronic.

anachronisme [-nism] m. Anachronism.

anacoluthe [anakɔlyt] f. GRAMM. Anacoluthon.

anaconda [anakɔ̃da] m. ZOOL. Anaconda.

anacrouse [-krus] f. MUS., GRAMM. Anacrusis.

anaérobie [anaerɔbi] adj. MÉD. Anaerobic.
— m. MÉD. Anaerobe.

anagramme [anagram] f. Anagram.

anal, ale [anal] adj. MÉD. Anal.

analectes [analekt] m. pl. Analects, analecta.

analeptique [analɛptik] adj., m. MÉD. Analeptic.

analgésie [analʒezi] f. MÉD. Analgesia.

analgésique [-zik] adj., m. MÉD. Analgesic.

analogie [analɔʒi] f. Analogy.

analogique [-ʒik] adj. Analogical.

analogiquement [-ʒikmã] adj. Analogically.

analogue [analɔg] adj. Analogous (à, to).
— m. Analogue, counterpart.

analphabète [analfabɛt] adj., s. Illiterate.

analphabétisme [-betism] m. Illiteracy, analphabetism.

analysable [analizabl] adj. Analysable.

analyse [-li:z] f. GRAMM. *Analyse grammaticale,* parsing; *analyse logique,* sentence analysis. ‖ ELECTR., PHYS., MATH. Analysis; *analyse électrolytique,* electro-analysis; *analyse spectrale,* spectrum analysis. ‖ FIG. *L'esprit d'analyse,* the (ou) an analytical mind; *en dernière analyse,* in the final analysis, when all is said and done.

analyser [-lize] v. tr. (1). To analyse. ‖ GRAMM. To parse (grammaticalement); to analyse (logiquement).

analyste [-list] s. CHIM., PHILOS. Analyst.

analytique [-litik] adj. MATH. Analytic. ‖ GRAMM., PHILOS. Analytical.

ananas [anana] m. BOT. Pineapple, ananas.

anapeste [anapɛst] m. GRAMM. Anapaest.

anaphore [anafɔːr] m. GRAMM. Anaphora.

anaphorique [-fɔrik] adj. GRAMM. Anaphoric.

anaphylactique [anafilaktik] adj. MÉD. Anaphylactic.

anaphylaxie [-si] f. MÉD. Anaphylaxis.

anaplastie [anaplasti] f. MÉD. Anaplasty.

anar [anar] s. FAM. Anarchist.

anarchie [anarʃi] f. Anarchy, disorder.

anarchique [-ʃik] adj. Anarchic.

anarchiquement [-ʃikmã] adv. Anarchically.

anarchisme [-ʃism] m. Anarchism.

anarchiste [-ʃist] adj., s. Anarchist.

anarcho- [-ko] préf. Anarcho-. ‖ **Anarcho-syndicalisme,** m. Anarcho-syndicalism. ‖ **Anarcho-syndicaliste,** s., adj. Anarcho-syndicalist.

Anastasie [anastazi] f. Anastasia. ‖ FAM. « Dora », the censorship.

anastigmat [anastigmat] m. PHYS. Anastigmat, anastigmatic lens (photo).

anastigmatique [-tik] adj. PHYS. Anastigmatic.

anastomose [anastɔmoz] f. MÉD., BOT. Anastomosis.

anastrophe [anastrɔf] f. GRAMM. Anastrophe.

anathématiser [anatɛmatize] v. tr. (1). ECCLÉS. To anathematize.

anathème [anatɛm] m. ECCLÉS. Anathema (excommunication, personne). ‖ FAM. Curse.
— adj. Accursed; anathema. ‖ ECCLÉS. Pronouncing the anathema (bulle).

anatife [anatif] m. ZOOL. Barnacle.

anatomie [anatɔmi] f. Méd. Anatomy; *pièce d'anatomie*, anatomical figure. || Fam. Anatomy.
anatomique [-mik] adj. Méd. Anatomical.
anatomiquement [-mikmɑ̃] adv. Anatomically.
anatomiser [-mize] v. tr. (1). Méd. To anatomize.
anatomiste [-mist] m. Méd. Anatomist.
ancestral, ale [ɑ̃sɛstral] adj. Ancestral.
ancêtre [ɑ̃sɛtr] m. Ancestor; forefather. || Pl. Ancestry, ancestors. || Fig. Ancestor.
anche [ɑ:ʃ] m. Mus. Reed.
anchois [ɑ̃ʃwa] m. Zool. Anchovy. || Culin. Anchovy; *beurre d'anchois*, anchovy-paste.
ancien, enne [ɑ̃sjɛ̃, ɛn] adj. Antiquated (décor); ancient (histoire); antique (meuble); early, bygone, past (temps); *Pline l'Ancien*, Pliny the Elder. || Former, previous, old (adresse); former, previous (mari); retired (commerçant); former, ex (ministre); *ancien élève*, old boy, U. S. alumnus. || Milit. *Ancien combattant*, ex-serviceman, U. S. veteran; *l'officier le plus ancien*, the senior officer. || Fig. Old (habitude); pristine (gloire).
— m. Senior (plus ancien); old man (vieillard). || Pl. Ancients.
anciennement [ɑ̃sjɛnmɑ̃] adj. Formerly, in days gone by, in days of yore (ou) of old; anciently.
ancienneté [-te] f. Ancientness, antiquity. || Length of service (d'emploi); seniority (de grade); *à l'ancienneté*, by seniority.
ancillaire [ɑ̃sillɛr] adj. Ancillary.
ancolie [ɑ̃kɔli] f. Bot. Columbine.
ancrage [ɑ̃kra:ʒ] m. Naut., Archit. Anchorage; anchoring.
ancre [ɑ̃:kr] f. Naut. Anchor; *ancre d'amarrage*, mooring anchor; *être à l'ancre*, to ride (ou) lie at anchor; *jeter, mouiller l'ancre*, to drop, to cast anchor; *lever l'ancre*, to weigh anchor. || Archit. Anchor, brace; cramp-iron. || Techn. Anchor, lever (d'horlogerie). || Fig. Anchor, sheet-anchor.
ancrer [ɑ̃kre] v. tr. (1). Naut. To anchor. || Archit. To brace, to stay, to cram. || Fig. *Ancré dans*, rooted in.
— v. pr. S'ancrer, Naut. To anchor. || Fig. To anchor oneself, to establish oneself, to become rooted (dans, in).
ancrure [ɑ̃kry:r] f. Naut. Anchor. || Archit. Cramp, brace.
andain [ɑ̃dɛ̃] m. Agric. Swath.
andalou, oue [ɑ̃dalu] adj., s. Géogr. Andalusian.
andin, ine [ɑ̃dɛ̃, in] adj. Géogr. Andean, andine.
Andorre [-dɔ:r] f. Géogr. Andorra.
andouille [ɑ̃du:j] f. Culin. Chitterlings. || Pop. Duffer, mutt, twerp, twirp, U. S. sap; *bougre d'andouille*, you B. F.! (= bloody fool.)
andouiller [ɑ̃duje] m. Tine (du cerf).
andouillette [ɑ̃dujɛt] f. Culin. Small sausage made of chitterlings.
androgène [ɑ̃drɔʒɛn] adj. Méd. Androgenic.
— m. Méd. Androgen.
androgyne [ɑ̃drɔʒin] adj. Méd., Bot. Androgynous.
— s. Androgyne. (V. hermaphrodite.)
androïde [ɑ̃drɔi:d] m. Android.
âne [ɑ:n] m. Ass, jackass, donkey (v. baudet, bourricot); onager (sauvage); *promenade à âne*, donkey ride. || *Chaussée en dos d'âne*, cambered road. || Fig. Jackass, blockhead.
anéantir [aneɑ̃ti:r] v. tr. (2). To reduce to nothing; to annihilate, to destroy, to wipe out. || To blast (souffler). || To overpower (accabler); *to stun* (stupéfier). || Jur. To annul (un contrat); to suppress (un droit). || Fam. To exhaust; *je suis anéanti*, I am done, I'm beat.
— v. pr. S'anéantir, to be annihilated, to be destroyed. || Fig. To prostrate oneself.
anéantissement [-tismɑ̃] m. Annihilation, des-

truction. || Fig. Exhaustion (fatigue); dejection (prostration); self-humiliation.
anecdote [anɛkdɔt] f. Anecdote.
anecdotier [-dɔtje] s. Anecdotist.
anecdotique [-dɔtik] adj. Anecdotic, anecdotal.
ânée [ɑ̃ne] f. Donkey-load.
anémie [anemi] f. Méd. Anaemia.
anémié, ée [-mje] adj. Méd. Anaemic.
anémier [-mje] v. tr. (1). To make anaemic. || Fig. To impoverish, to debilitate.
— v. pr. S'anémier, to become anaemic. || Fig. To weaken.
anémique [-mik] adj. Méd. Anaemic.
anémomètre [anemɔmɛtr] m. Anemometer.
anémone [anemɔn] f. Bot. Anemone, windflower. || Zool. Actinia, sea-anemone.
ânerie [ɑ:nri] f. Asininity; stupidity; absurdity (sottise). || Tomfoolery, nonsense (faute).
anéroïde [anerɔid] adj., m. Phys. Aneroid.
ânesse [ɑ:nɛs] f. Zool. She-ass.
anesthésiant, ante [anɛstezjɑ̃, ɑ̃:t] adj., m. Méd. Anaesthetic.
anesthésie [anɛstezi] f. Méd. Anaesthesia; etherization.
anesthésier [-zje] v. tr. (1). Méd. To anaesthetize.
anesthésique [-zik] adj., m. Méd. Anaesthetic.
anesthésiste [-zist] s. Méd. Anaesthetist.
anévrisme [anevrism] m. Méd. Aneurism.
anfractuosité [ɑ̃fraktyɔzite] f. Anfractuosity. || Pl. Ruggedness, crags (des rochers); windings (de la route); rugged outlines (du terrain). || Méd. Pl. Anfractuosities (du cerveau).
ange [ɑ̃:ʒ] m. Ecclés. Angel; *ange gardien*, guardian angel. || Sports. *Saut de l'ange*, swallowdive, U. S. swan dive. || Loc. *Être aux anges*, to be highly delighted, to walk on air; *faiseuse d'anges*, abortionist; *le mauvais ange de qqn*, s.o.'s evil genius; *rire aux anges*, to wear a beatific smile. || Fam. *Mon ange*, my sweet.
angélique [-ʒelik] adj. Angelic.
— f. Bot., Culin. Angelica.
angéliquement [-likmɑ̃] adv. Angelically, in a cherublike way.
angélisme [-lism] m. Other-worldliness.
angelot [ɑ̃ʒlo] m. Angelot. || Arts. Cherub.
angélus [ɑ̃ʒely:s] m. Ecclés. Angelus (prière, sonnerie); ave-bell (sonnerie).
angevin, ine [ɑ̃ʒvɛ̃, in] adj., s. Géogr. Angevin.
angine [ɑ̃ʒin] f. Méd. Quinsy, tonsillitis (aux amygdales); angina (surtout au cœur); *angine de Vincent*, Vincent's tonsillitis (ou) angina; *angine de poitrine*, angina pectoris.
angineux, euse [-nø, nø:z] adj. Méd. Anginal.
angiographie [ɑ̃ʒjografi] f. Méd. Angiography.
angiologie [ɑ̃ʒjolɔʒi] f. Méd. Angiology.
angiosperme [ɑ̃ʒjospɛrm] f. Bot. Angiosperm.
anglais, aise [ɑ̃glɛ, ɛ:z] adj. British (armée); English (langue, peuple). || Britannia (métal); fisherman's (nœud).
— m. Géogr. Englishman; *les Anglais*, the English. || Gramm. English, the English language; *mauvais anglais*, broken English.
anglaise [ɑ̃glɛ:z] f. Géogr. Englishwoman. || Pl. Ringlets (boucles). || Italian hand (écriture). || Fam. *Filer à l'anglaise*, to take French leave.
anglaiser [ɑ̃glɛze] v. tr. (1). To nick; *cheval anglaisé*, cocktail.
angle [ɑ̃:gl] m. Angle; *angle limite*, critical angle; *angle de la rue*, corner of the street; *angle visuel*, angle of vision. || Math. Angle; *à angle droit*, at right angles; *relever un angle*, to take an angle. || Aviat. *Angle d'assiette, d'attaque*, angle of trim, of attack; *angle de bombardement, de planement*, range, gliding angle. || Milit. *Angle de chute, de divergence, de hausse, de tir*, angle of

ANATOMIE HUMAINE — HUMAN ANATOMY

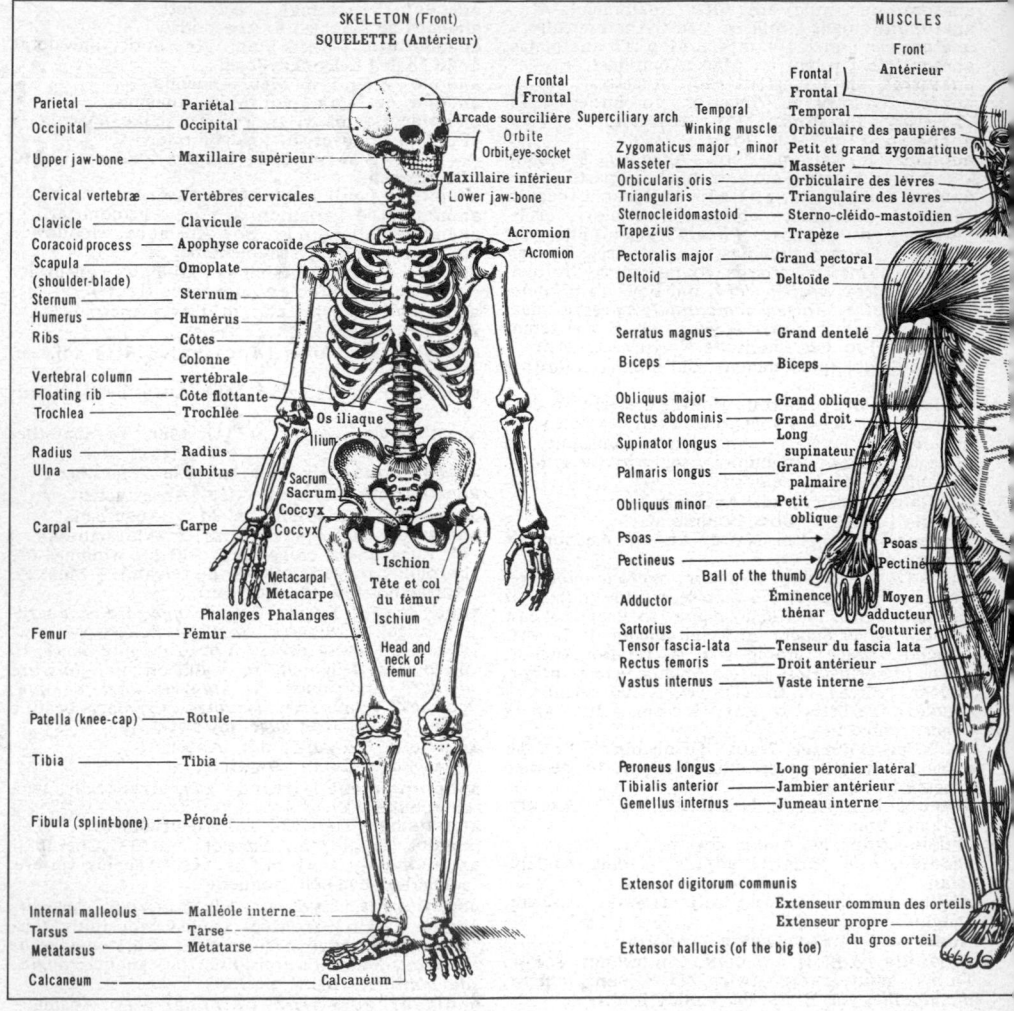

SKELETON (Front) / SQUELETTE (Antérieur) — MUSCLES Front / Antérieur

impact, of distribution, of elevation, of departure. ‖ RADIO. *Angle de déphasage,* angle of phase difference (radio); *angle de vision,* viewing angle (télévision). ‖ FIG. Point of view; angle; *arrondir les angles,* to round off the corners.

Angleterre [ɑ̃glətɛːr] f. GÉOGR. England.

anglican, ane [ɑ̃glikɑ̃, an] adj. ECCLÉS. Anglican (dogme); *l'Eglise anglicane,* the Church of England.
— s. ECCLÉS. Anglican.

anglicanisme [-kanism] m. Anglicanism.

anglicisant, ante [-sizɑ̃, ɑ̃:t] s. Student of English.

angliciser [-size] v. tr. (1). To Anglicize; to Anglify.
— v. pr. **S'angliciser,** to adopt English ways.

anglicisme [-sism] m. Anglicism.

angliciste [-sist] s. Student of (ou) authority on English language and literature.

anglo [ɑ̃glɔ] préf. Anglo-. ‖ **Anglo-arabe,** m. ZOOL. Anglo-Arab. ‖ **Anglo-catholique,** adj.

ECCLÉS. Anglo-Catholic. ‖ **Anglo-Normand,** adj. Anglo-Norman; *les iles Anglo-Normandes,* the Channel Islands. ‖ **Anglo-Saxon,** adj., s. Anglo-Saxon.

anglomanie [ɑ̃glɔmani] f. Anglomania.

anglophile [-fil] adj., s. Anglophile.

anglophilie [-fili] f. Pro-English feeling, U. S. Anglophilia.

anglophobe [-fɔb] adj., s. Anglophobe.

anglophobie [-fɔbi] f. Anglophobia.

anglophone [-fɔn] adj. English-speaking, anglophone.
— s. English-speaking person, anglophone.

angoissant, ante [ɑ̃gwasɑ̃, ɑ̃:t] adj. Distressing; agonizing.

angoisse [ɑ̃gwas] f. Distress, anguish, agony; anxiety. ‖ MÉD. Anguish (en général); pangs (de la mort). ‖ LOC. *Poire d'angoisse,* choke-pear.

angoissé, ée [-se] adj. Agonized, distressed, anguished; anxious.

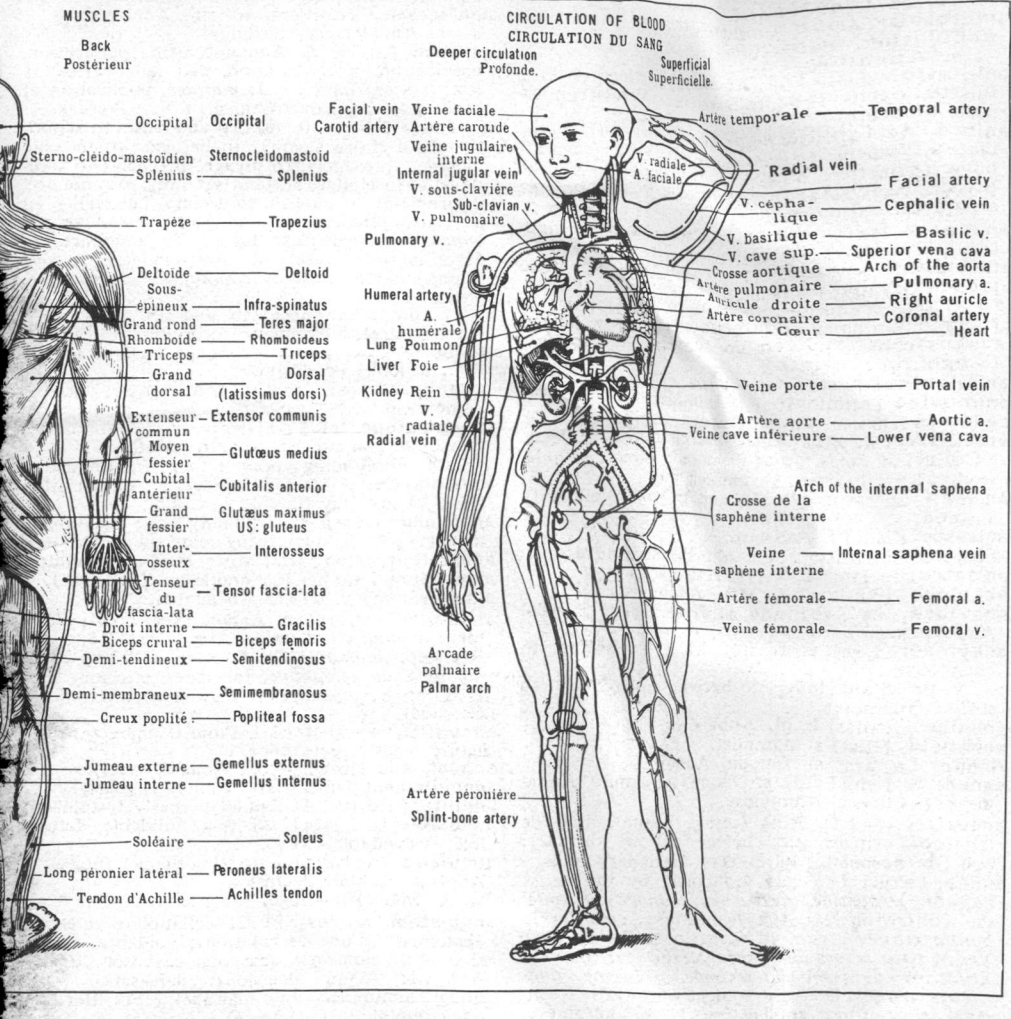

MUSCLES

Back
Postérieur

CIRCULATION OF BLOOD
CIRCULATION DU SANG

Deeper circulation
Profonde.

Superficial
Superficielle.

Occipital — Occipital

Sterno-cléido-mastoïdien — Sternocleidomastoid
Splénius — Splenius

Trapèze — Trapezius

Deltoïde — Deltoid
Sous-épineux — Infra-spinatus
Grand rond — Teres major
Rhomboïde — Rhomboideus
Triceps — Triceps
Grand dorsal — Dorsal (latissimus dorsi)
Extenseur commun — Extensor communis
Moyen fessier — Glutœus medius
Cubital antérieur — Cubitalis anterior
Grand fessier — Glutœus maximus US: gluteus
Inter-osseux — Interosseus
Tenseur du fascia-lata — Tensor fascia-lata
Droit interne — Gracilis
Biceps crural — Biceps femoris
Demi-tendineux — Semitendinosus
Demi-membraneux — Semimembranosus
Creux poplité — Popliteal fossa

Jumeau externe — Gemellus externus
Jumeau interne — Gemellus internus

Soléaire — Soleus
Long péronier latéral — Peroneus lateralis
Tendon d'Achille — Achilles tendon

Facial vein — Veine faciale
Carotid artery — Artère carotide
Veine jugulaire interne — Internal jugular vein
V. sous-clavière — Sub-clavian v.
V. pulmonaire — Pulmonary v.

Humeral artery — Artère carotide
A. humérale — Lung Poumon
Liver Foie
Kidney Rein
V. radiale — Radial vein

Arcade palmaire — Palmar arch

Artère péronière — Splint-bone artery

Artère temporale — Temporal artery
V radiale — Radial vein
A. faciale
Facial artery
V. céphalique — Cephalic vein
V. basilique — Basilic v.
V. cave sup. — Superior vena cava
Crosse aortique — Arch of the aorta
Artère pulmonaire — Pulmonary a.
Auricule droite — Right auricle
Artère coronaire — Coronal artery
Cœur — Heart

Veine porte — Portal vein

Artère aorte — Aortic a.
Veine cave inférieure — Lower vena cava

Arch of the internal saphena
Crosse de la saphène interne

Veine saphène interne — Internal saphena vein

Artère fémorale — Femoral a.
Veine fémorale — Femoral v.

---

angoisser [-se] v. tr. (1). To anguish, to distress.
Angola [ãgɔla] m. Géogr. Angola.
angora [ãgɔra] adj., m. Zool., Comm. Angora.
angstrœm [ãgstrœm] m. Phys. Angstrom.
anguiforme [ãgiform] adj. Anguine, snake-like.
anguille [ãgi:j] f. Zool. Eel; *anguille de mer*, conger-eel. ‖ Loc. *Fuyant comme une anguille*, slippery as an eel; *il y a anguille sous roche*, there is a snake in the grass, there's sth. fishy going on.
anguillère [ãgijɛ:r] f. Eel-pond.
angulaire [ãgylɛ:r] adj. Angular; *pierre angulaire*, corner-stone, headstone.
anguleux, euse [-lø, ø:z] adj. Angular (distance). ‖ Fig. Stiff, angular (caractère). ‖ Fam. Angular, gaunt (personne); angular (traits).
angusture [ãgysty:r] f. Bot. *Écorce d'angusture*, angostura bark; *fausse angusture*, bark of poison nut.

anharmonique [anarmɔnik] adj. Math. Anharmonic.
anhéler [anele] v. intr. (5). To pant; to gasp.
anhydre [anidr] adj. Chim. Anhydrous.
anhydride [-drid] m. Chim. Anhydride; *anhydride carbonique, sulfureux, sulfurique*, carbon-dioxide, sulphur-dioxide, sulphur-trioxide.
anicroche [anikrɔʃ] f. Hitch, snag (v. Compli-cation); *se passer sans anicroche*, to go off smoothly (ou) without a hitch.
ânier [anje] m. Donkey-driver.
aniline [anilin] f. Chim. Aniline.
animal [animal] m. Zool. Animal. (V. bête.) ‖ Fam. Beast, blighter, rotter.
— adj. Animal. ‖ Brutish, bestial.
animalcule [-malkyl] m. Zool. Animalcule.
animalier [-malje] m. Arts. Animalist; animal painter.

animaliser [-malize] v. tr. (1). To animalize, to brutify.

animalité [-malite] f. Animality.

animateur, trice [-matœ:r, tris] adj. Animating, stimulating, inspiriting.
— s. Animator.

animation [-sjɔ̃] f. Animation, liveliness (vie). ‖ Bustle, excitement (affairement). ‖ Vivacity, briskness (entrain).

animé, ée [anime] adj. Animate (vivant). ‖ Animated, warm (discussion); sparkling (regard); busy (quartier, vie); heightened (teint). ‖ Fin. Brisk, lively (marché). ‖ Théâtr. Dessins animés, animated cartoons.

animer v. tr. (1). To animate, to quicken; to vitalize; to vivify. ‖ To enliven, to stir up; to kindle, to inflame (enflammer). ‖ To incite, to impel, to propel (inciter, pousser).
— v. pr. S'animer, to come to life (chose); to become animated (conversation); to grow heated (discussion); to liven up, to warm (personne); to light up (regard).

animisme [-mism] m. Philos. Animism.

animosité [animɔzite] f. Animosity.

anion [anjɔ̃] m. Chim., Electr. Anion.

anis [ani] m. Bot. Anise; graine d'anis, aniseed. ‖ Culin. A l'anis, anise-flavoured; gâteau à l'anis, seed-cake; un anis, an aniseed ball.

aniser [-ze] v. tr. (1). To anisate, to flavour with aniseed.

anisette [-zɛt] f. Anisette.

anisotrope [anizɔtrɔp] adj. Phys. Anisotropic.

anisotropie [-pi] f. Phys. Anisotropy.

ankylose [ãkilo:z] f. Méd. Anchylosis.

ankylosé, ée [-ze] adj. Stiff, stiffened. ‖ Méd. Anchylosed.

ankyloser [-ze] v. tr. (1). Méd. To stiffen, to anchylose.
— v. pr. S'ankyloser, to become stiff (corps); to stiffen (membre).

annales [annal] f. pl. Annals.

annaliste [-list] s. Annalist.

Annam [anam] m. Géogr. Annam.

annamite [-mit] adj., s. Géogr. Annamite, Annamese. ‖ Gramm. Annamese.

anneau [ano] m. Ring (cercle, bague); link (de chaîne); ringlet (de cheveux); bow (de clé); coil (de serpent). ‖ Pl. Sports. Stationary rings.

année [ane] f. Year; à l'année, by the year; l'année prochaine, next year; l'année suivante, the following year, the year after; souhaiter la bonne année à qqn, to wish s.o. a Happy New Year; tout le long de l'année, all the year round. ‖ Etudiant de première, seconde, troisième, quatrième année, first-year student (ou) U. S. freshman, second-year student (ou) U. S. sophomore, third-year student (ou) U. S. junior, fourth-year student (ou) U. S. senior. ‖ Année-lumière ou de lumière f. Light-year.

annelé, ée [anle] adj. Archit. Ringed (colonne). ‖ Zool. Annulate, annulose.

annélides [anelid] m. pl. Zool. Annelida.

annexe [annɛks] f. Annex, appendage (à un local). ‖ Schedule (à un document); enclosure (à une lettre); supplement (à un rapport); appendix (à un texte); lettre annexe, covering letter. ‖ Jur. Rider (à un projet de loi). ‖ Méd. Appendage (d'un organe).
— adj. Subsidiary; annexed.

annexer [-se] v. tr. (1). To annex (un pays). ‖ To append, to annex (un document); to enclose (une pièce à une lettre).

annexion [-sjɔ̃] f. Annexation.

annexionnisme [-sjɔnism] m. Annexationism.

annexionniste [-sjɔnist] adj., s. Annexationist.

annihilable [anniilabl] adj. Annihilable. ‖ Jur. Annullable.

annihilation [-lasjɔ̃] f. Annihilation.

annihiler [-le] v. tr. (1). To annihilate, to wipe out. (V. détruire.) ‖ Jur. To annul.

anniversaire [anivɛrsɛ:r] adj. Anniversary.
— m. Anniversary; birthday.

annonce [anɔ̃s] f. Announcement, publication, notification. ‖ Declaration, call (aux cartes). ‖ Jur. Notice; annonce de mariage, publication of bans. ‖ Comm. Advertisement. ‖ Fig. Presage.

annoncer [-se] v. tr. (6). To announce, to report, to herald (faire savoir); to betoken, to indicate (dénoter, présager); to preach (prêcher); to forebode, to foretell, to portend (prédire); to announce, to proclaim, to publish, to declare (publier). ‖ To advertise (mettre une annonce); demander par annonce, to advertise for. ‖ To announce, to usher in (introduire); se faire annoncer, to give in one's name; qui dois-je annoncer?, what name please?
— v. pr. S'annoncer, to give in one's na (s'introduire). ‖ To augur, to promise, to bid f to be (augurer); cela s'annonce bien, it aug' well, it looks promising.

annonceur [-sœ:r] m. Comm. Advertiser. ‖ Rad Announcer.

annonciateur, trice [-sjatœ:r, tris] s. Announc (personne); annunciator-board (tableau).
— adj. Foreboding; premonitory; forerunner.

Annonciation [-sjasjɔ̃] f. Ecclés. Annunciation (fête); Lady Day (jour).

annoncier [-sje] m. Publicity (ou) advertising manager; U. S. advertising man, ad-man (fam.'

annotateur, trice [anɔtatœ:r, tris] s. Annotato

annotation [-tasjɔ̃] f. Annotation. (V. note.)

annoter [-te] v. tr. (1). To annotate.

annuaire [anɥɛ:r] m. Annual; year-book; dir tory; annuaire de l'armée, Army List, U. S. A Register; annuaire de la Marine, Navy annuaire du téléphone, telephone directory U. S. book; annuaire de l'Université, Univer Calendar.

annualité [anɥalite] f. Annual characte: nature, yearly recurrence.

annuel, elle [anɥɛl] adj. Annual, yearly.

annuellement [-mã] adv. Annually, yearly.

annuité [anɥite] f. Annuity, yearly instalmᵉ

annulable [anɥlabl] adj. Jur. Voidable, defe. ible, rescindable.

annulaire [anɥlɛ:r] adj. Ring-shaped (objet). Astron. Annular (éclipse).
— m. Méd. Ring-finger (doigt).

annulation [anɥlasjɔ̃] f. Cancellation (d'un acte abatement (d'une assignation); voidance, rᵉ sion (d'un contrat); quashing, cassation, rᵉ reversion (d'une décision); defeasance droit); annulment (d'un mariage). ‖ Fin. Revᵉ (en comptabilité).

annuler [-le] v. tr. (1). To cancel (un actᵉ quash, to repeal, to reverse (une décision); aside (un décret, un testament); to defea droit); to annul, to nullify (un mariage). cancel (une commande); to rescind (un ordᵉ to call off (un rendez-vous).
— v. récipr. S'annuler, to counterbalance (oᵗ to cancel each other.

anobli, ie [anɔbli] adj., s. Ennobled.

anoblir [-blir] v. tr. (2). To ennoble. ‖ To raise to the peerage (en Angleterre).

anoblissement [-blismã] m. Ennoblement. ‖ Raising to the peerage (en Angleterre).

anode [anɔd] f. Electr. Anode.

anodin, ine [anɔdɛ̃, in] adj. Méd. Anodyne. ‖ Fig. Inoffensive, harmless.
— m. Méd. Anodyne (calmant).

anodique [anɔdik] adj. Electr. Anodic.

anodiser [-dize] v. tr. (1). Techn. To anodize.

anomal, ale [anɔmal] adj. Anomalous.

anomalie [anɔmali] f. Anomaly.

anomie [anɔmi] f. Anomy, anomie.

ânon [ɑːnɔ̃] m. Zool. Ass's foal. ‖ Fam. Dunce.

anone [anɔn] f. Bot. Anona (arbre); custard-apple (fruit).

ânonnement [anɔnmɑ̃] m. Stumbling way of speaking or reading, humming and hawing.

ânonner [-ne] v. tr. (1). To drone out, to speak (ou) read in a stumbling way; *ânonner sa leçon*, to falter (ou) stumble through one's lesson.
— v. intr. To hum and haw, U.S. to hem and haw.

anonymat [anɔnima] m. Anonymity; *garder l'anonymat*, to remain anonymous.

anonyme [-nim] adj. Anonymous (lettre, ouvrage); nameless, unnamed (personne). ‖ Jur. *Société anonyme*, limited company.
— m. Anonym (personne). ‖ Anonymous writer (écrivain).

anonymement [-nimmɑ̃] adv. Anonymously.

anophèle [anɔfɛːl] m. Zool. Anopheles.

anorak [anɔrak] m. Anorak, wind-jacket, wind-cheater.

anordir [anɔrdiːr] v. intr. (2). To veer to the north.

anorexie [anɔrɛksi] f. Méd. Anorexia.

anormal, ale [anɔrmal] adj. Abnormal. ‖ Unnatural; unusual; irregular. ‖ Méd. Mentally deficient (ou) retarded (enfant).
— s. Méd. Mentally deficient person; *psychologie des anormaux*, abnormal psychology.

anormalement [-mɑ̃] adv. Abnormally; unusually.

anse [ɑ̃ːs] f. Ear (d'une cruche, d'un pot); handle (d'un panier). ‖ Shackle (d'un cadenas); loop, bight (d'une corde); bow (d'une montre). ‖ Méd. Flexure (de l'intestin). ‖ Géogr. Bight, cove. ‖ *Faire danser l'anse du panier*, to get pickings (ou) a rake-off (fam.).

anspect [ɑ̃spɛk] m. Naut. † Handspike.

antagonique [ɑ̃tagɔnik] adj. Antagonistic.

antagonisme [-nism] m. Antagonism.

antagoniste [-nist] adj., s. Antagonist.

antalgique [ɑ̃talʒik] adj. Méd. Antalgic.
— m. Méd. Anodyne.

antan (d') [dɑ̃tɑ̃] adj. Of yester-year, of yore.

antarctique [ɑ̃tarktik] adj. Géogr. Antarctic.

ante [ɑ̃ːt] f. Archit. Anta.

antebois [ɑ̃tbwa] m. Archit. Chair-rail.

antécédent [ɑ̃tesedɑ̃] adj. m. Math., Gramm., Philos., Méd., Fig. Antecedent. ‖ Fig., Méd. Pl. Family background.

antéchrist [-krist] m. Antichrist.

antédiluvien, enne [-dilyvjɛ̃, ɛn] adj. Antediluvian.

antenne [ɑ̃tɛn] f. Zool. Antenna, feeler. ‖ Naut. Lateen yard. ‖ Radio. Aerial, antenna; *antenne à cadre*, loop (ou) frame aerial; *antenne dirigée, (ou) (visée*, directional, fish-pole aerial; *antenne radar*, radar scanner. ‖ Fig. *Personne qui a des antennes, « sensitive »*. ‖ **Antenne-parapluie**, f. Radio. Umbrella-aerial.

antépénultième [ɑ̃tepenyltjɛm] adj., f. Gramm. Antepenultimate, last but two.

antéposé, ée [ɑ̃tepoze] adj. Gramm. Prepositive.

antérieur, eure [ɑ̃terjœːr] adj. Former. ‖ Previous, prior, anterior (à, to). ‖ Méd. *Membre antérieur*, forelimb. ‖ Gramm. *Futur, passé antérieur*, future, past perfect.

antérieurement [-mɑ̃] adv. Anteriorly; previously. ‖ Prior (à, to).

antériorité [ɑ̃terjɔrite] f. Anteriority.

anthère [ɑ̃tɛːr] f. Bot. Anther.

anthologie [ɑ̃tɔlɔʒi] f. Anthology.

anthozoaires [ɑ̃tozɔɛːr] m. pl. Zool. Anthozoa.

anthracène [ɑ̃trasɛn] m. Chim. Anthracene.

anthracite [ɑ̃trasit] m. Anthracite, U.S. hard coal.

anthrax [ɑ̃traks] m. Méd. Carbuncle, anthrax.

anthropocentrisme [ɑ̃trɔpɔsɑ̃trism] m. Philos. Anthropocentrism.

anthropoïde [-id] adj., m. Zool. Anthropoid.

anthropologie [-lɔʒi] f. Anthropology.

anthropologue [-lɔg], anthropologiste [-lɔ-ʒist] m. Anthropologist.

anthropométrie [-metri] f. Anthropometry.

anthropométrique [-metrik] adj. Anthropometric, anthropometrical.

anthropomorphe [-mɔrf] adj. Anthropomorphous.
— m. Anthropoid.

anthropomorphisme [-mɔrfism] m. Anthropomorphism.

anthroponymie [-nimi] f. Anthroponymy.

anthropophage [-faːʒ] adj. Anthropophagous, cannibalistic.
— m. Cannibal.

anthropophagie [-faʒi] f. Anthropophagy.

anthropopithèque [-pitɛk] m. Anthropopithecus.

antiaérien, enne [ɑ̃tiaerjɛ̃, ɛn] adj. Anti-aircraft; *feu antiaérien*, ack-ack, flak.

antialcoolique [-alkɔlik] adj. Anti-alcoholic.
— s. Anti-alcoholist, teetotaller; U.S. prohibitionist, dry (fam.).

antialcoolisme [-alkɔlism] m. Teetotalism; U.S. prohibitionism.

antiatomique [-atomik] adj. Phys. Anti-atomic.

antiaveuglant [-avøglɑ̃] adj. Méd. Anti-dazzle, anti-glare.

antibiotique [-biɔtik] m. Méd. Antibiotic.

antibrouillard [-brujar] m. invar. Fog-dispersing apparatus. ‖ Autom. De-mister (désembueur); fog-lamp, U.S. fog light (phare). ‖ Milit., Aviat. Fido.

antibruit [-brɥi] adj. invar. Sound-proof (mur); noise abatement (campagne), antinoise (mesure).

anticancéreux [-kɑ̃serø] adj. Méd. *Sérum anticancéreux*, cancer-serum.

anticasseurs [-kasœːr] adj. invar. Jur. *Loi anticasseurs*, French law intended to limit damage in demonstrations.

anticathode [-katɔd] f. Electr. Anticathode.

antichambre [-ʃɑ̃br] f. Anteroom, antechamber, waiting-room; *faire antichambre chez*, to dance attendance on.

antichar [-ʃar] adj. Anti-tank.

anticipation [ɑ̃tisipaʃjɔ̃] f. Anticipation; *par anticipation*, in advance, beforehand, in anticipation. ‖ Jur. Encroachment (sur des droits).

anticipé, ée [-pe] adj. Anticipatory, before due date; *versement anticipé*, advance payment.

anticiper [-pe] v. intr. (1). To anticipate; to forestall; to encroach (sur, upon).
— v. tr. To anticipate; to prevent (l'avenir); to forestall (une difficulté).

anticlérical, ale [ɑ̃tiklerikal] adj. Anticlerical.

anticléricalisme [-klerikalism] m. Anticlericalism.

anticoagulant, ante [-kɔagylɑ̃] m. Méd. Anti-coagulant.

anticolonialisme [-kɔlɔnjalism] m. Anticolonialism.

anticolonialiste [-kɔlɔnjalist] m. Anticolonialist.

anticommunisme [-kɔmynism] m. Anticommunism.

anticonceptionnel [-kɔ̃sɛpsjɔnɛl] adj. Contraceptive.

anticonformisme [-kɔ̃fɔrmism] m. Non-conformism, non-conformity.

anticonformiste [-kɔ̃fɔrmist] adj., n. Non-conformist.

anticonstitutionnel, elle [-kɔ̃stitysjɔnɛl] adj. Anticonstitutional.

anticorps [-kɔr] m. Méd. Antibody.

anticyclone [-siklɔːn] m. Anticyclone.

antidater [-date] v. tr. (1). To antedate.

antidémocratique [-demɔkratik] adj. Antidemocratic.

antidérapant [-derapã] adj. AUTOM. Non-skidding, non-skid.
— m. AUTOM. Non-skid tyre (ou) U. S. tire.
antidétonant, ante [-detɔnɑ̃, ɑ̃:t] adj. AUTOM. Anti-knock, knock-free.
antidiphtérique [-difterik] adj. MÉD. Diphtheria (sérum, piqûre).
antidoping [-dɔpiŋ], **antidopage** [-dɔpa:ʒ] adj. invar. SPORTS. Intended to curb the use of illicit stimulants (test, mesures, loi).
antidote [ɑ̃tidɔt] m. MÉD. Antidote (à, de, for, to, against).
antiéconomique [-ekɔnɔmik] adj. Against the economic interests of the country.
antiémétique [-emetik] adj., m. MÉD. Antiemetic.
antienne [ɑ̃tjɛn] f. ECCLÉS. Antiphon; anthem. ‖ FIG. Chanter toujours la même antienne, to be always harping on the same string.
antiesclavagiste [ɑ̃tiɛsklavagist] adj. Antislavery.
— s. Abolitionist.
antifading [-fediŋ] adj. RADIO. Antifading.
antifébrile [-febril] adj., m. MÉD. Antifebrile, antipyretic.
antifongique [-fɔʒik] adj. ZOOL., MÉD. Antifungal.
antifriction [-friksjɔ̃] f. TECHN. Antifriction.
anti-g [-ʒe] adj. invar. ASTRONAUT. Anti-gravity, anti-g.
antigang [-gɑ̃g] adj. invar. Brigade antigang, special police squad set up to fight organized crime.
antigel [-ʒɛl] m. AUTOM. Anti-freeze.
antigène [-ʒɛn] m. MÉD. Antigen.
antigivre [-ʒivr] m. AUTOM. De-icer, anti-icer; de-icing, anti-icing.
antigouvernemental, ale [-guvɛrnmɑ̃tal] adj. Anti-government.
antigrippal [-gripal] adj. MÉD. Anti-flu.
antihalo [-alo] adj. invar. Non-halation.
— m. Backing.
antihéros [-hero] m. Anti-hero.
antihistaminique [-istaminik] m. MÉD. Antihistamine.
antihygiénique [-iʒjenik] adj. Insanitary.
anti-inflationniste [-ɛ̃flasjɔnist] adj. FIN. Anti-inflation.
antilibéral, ale [-libɛral] adj. Antiliberal.
antillais, aise [ɑ̃tijɛ, ɛ:z] adj., s. GÉOGR. West Indian.
Antilles [ɑ̃ti:j] f. pl. GÉOGR. West Indies; mer des Antilles, Caribbean Sea.
antilogarithme [ɑ̃tilɔgaritm] m. MATH. Antilogarithm.
antilogie [ɑ̃tilɔʒi] f. GRAMM. Antilogy.
antilope [ɑ̃tilɔp] f. ZOOL. Antelope.
antimagnétique [ɑ̃timaɲetik] adj. Antimagnetic.
antimatière [-matjɛ:r] f. PHYS. Antimatter.
antimilitarisme [-ɑ̃timilitarism] m. Antimilitarism.
antimilitariste [-rist] s. Antimilitarist.
antimissile [-misil] adj. MILIT. Antimissile.
antimite [ɑ̃timit] m. Moth-killer.
antimoine [ɑ̃timwan] m. CHIM. Antimony.
antimonarchiste [ɑ̃timɔnarʃist] adj., s. Antimonarchist.
antinational, ale [-nasjɔnal] adj. Antinational.
antinévralgique [-nevralʒik] adj., m. MÉD. Antineuralgic.
antinomie [ɑ̃tinɔmi] f. Antinomy.
antinomique [-nɔmik] adj. Antinomic, antinomical.
antinucléaire [-nyklеɛ:r] adj. Antinuclear.
— s. Person opposed to nuclear energy.
antipape [ɑ̃tipap] m. Anti-pope.
antiparasite [-parazit] m. RADIO. Suppressor.
antiparasiter [-parazite] v. tr. (1). RADIO. To fit a suppressor to.

antiparlementaire [-parləmɑ̃tɛ:r] adj., n. Antiparliamentarian.
antiparlementarisme [-parləmɑ̃tarism] m. Antiparliamentarianism.
antiparticule [-partiky:l] n. PHYS. Antiparticule.
antipathie [ɑ̃tipati] f. Antipathy (contre, against, to); aversion (contre, for, to).
antipathique [-tik] adj. Antipathetic; antipathetical (à, to).
antipatriotique [ɑ̃tipatriɔtik] adj. Antipatriotic.
antipéristaltique [-pɛristaltik] adj. MÉD. Antiperistaltic; contractions antipéristaltiques, antiperistalsis; reversed peristalsis.
antipersonnel [-pɛrsɔnɛl] adj. MILIT. Antipersonel (bombe, mine).
antiphlogistique [-flɔʒistik] adj. MÉD. Antiphlogistic.
antiphonaire [ɑ̃tifɔnɛ:r] m. ECCLÉS. Antiphonary.
antiphrase [ɑ̃tifrɑ:z] f. GRAMM. Antiphrasis.
antipode [ɑ̃tipɔd] m. GÉOGR. Antipode; des antipodes, antipodal. ‖ FIG. Exact opposite.
antipoison [-pwazɔ̃] adj. invar. Centre antipoison, emergency center for poison cases.
antipoliomyélitique [-pɔljɔmjelitik] adj. MÉD. Polio (vaccin, piqûre).
antiprohibitionniste [ɑ̃tiprɔibisjɔnist] adj., s. Antiprohibitionist.
antiprotectionniste [-nist] adj. Antiprotectionist.
— s. Free-trader.
antiproton [ɑ̃tiprɔtɔ̃] n. ELECTR. Anti-proton.
antipsychiatrie [-psikjatri] f. PSYCH. Antipsychiatry.
antipyrétique [-piretik] adj. MÉD. Antipyretic.
antipyrine [ɑ̃tipirin] f. MÉD. Antipyrine.
antiquaille [ɑ̃tikɑ:j] f. Antique. ‖ Pl. Lumber.
antiquaire [-kɛ:r] s. COMM. Antiquarian; curio dealer (fam.). ‖ † Antiquary (archéologue).
antique [ɑ̃tik] adj. Antique (v. ANCIEN). ‖ Old-fashioned; antiquated, out-of-date (démodé).
— s. Antique.
antiquité [-kite] f. Antiquity (période, qualité); ancientness. ‖ Pl. Antiquities (objets); magasin d'antiquités, old curiosity shop.
antirachitique [ɑ̃tiraʃitik] adj., m. MÉD. Antirachitic.
antiraciste [-rasist] adj., s. Antiracialist, antiracist.
antiradar [-radar] adj. MILIT. Antiradar.
antirationnel [-rasjɔnel] adj. Antirational.
antireflet [-rəflɛ] adj. PHYS. Antireflection.
antireligieux [-rəliʒjø] adj. Antireligious.
antirépublicain, aine [-repyblikɛ̃, ɛn] adj., s. Antirepublican.
antirévolutionnaire [-revɔlysjɔnɛ:r] adj., s. Antirevolutionary.
antirides [-rid] adj. Anti-wrinkle.
— m. invar. Anti-wrinkle cream (ou) lotion.
antirouille [-ru:j] m. Anti-rust.
antiroulis [-ruli] adj. NAUT., AUTOM. Anti-roll.
antiscorbutique [-skɔrbytik] adj., m. MÉD. Antiscorbutic.
antiségrégationniste [-segregasjɔnist] adj., s. Antisegregationist.
antisémite [-semit] adj. Anti-Semitic.
— s. Anti-Semite.
antisémitisme [-semitism] m. Anti-Semitism.
antisepsie [-sɛpsi] f. MÉD. Antisepsis.
antiseptique [-sɛptik] adj. Antiseptic.
— m. MÉD. Germicide; antiseptic.
antisérum [-serɔm] m. MÉD. Antiserum.
antisocial, ale [-sɔsjal] adj. Antisocial.
antispasmodique [-spasmɔdik] adj., m. MÉD. Antispasmodic.
antisportif, ive [-spɔrtif, i:v] adj. Unsporting, unsportsmanlike.

antistatique [-statik] adj. Antistatic.
— m. Antistatic product.
antitank [-tăk] adj., m. MILIT. Antitank.
antitétanique [-tetanik] adj. MÉD. Antitetanic.
antithèse [-tɛ:z] f. GRAMM. Antithesis. ‖ FIG. Contrast.
antithétique [-tɛtik] adj. Antithetical.
antitoxine [-tɔksin] f. MÉD. Antitoxin.
antitoxique [-tɔksik] adj. MÉD. Antitoxic.
antitrust [-trœst] adj. invar. FIN. Antitrust.
antituberculeux, euse [-tybɛrkylǿ, ǿ:z] adj. MÉD. Antitubercular.
antitype [-ti:p] m. Antitype.
antivariolique [-varjɔlik] adj. MÉD. Smallpox (vaccin, piqûre).
antivénéneux, euse [-venenǿ, ǿ:z] adj. Alexipharmic, antidotal.
antivenimeux, euse [-vənimǿ, ǿ:z] adj. MÉD. Antivenin.
antivirus [-virys] m. MÉD. Antivirus.
antivol [-vol] adj. invar. Anti-theft (chaîne).
Antoine [ătwan] n. pr. m. Anthony, Antony; Tony.
antonomase [ătɔnɔma:z] f. Antonomasia (en rhétorique).
antonyme [ătɔnim] m. GRAMM. Antonym.
antonymie [ătɔnimi] f. GRAMM. Antonymy.
antre [ă:tr] m. Cave, cavern; antre (en poésie). ‖ Lair, den (d'un lion). ‖ MÉD. Antrum (sinus). ‖ FAM. Den, snuggery (studio).
anucléaire [anyklɛɛ:r] adj. Anuclear.
anurie [anyri] f. MÉD. Anuria.
anus [anys] m. MÉD. Anus; anus artificiel, artificial anal opening.
anxiété [ăksjete] f. Anxiety; concern; avec anxiété, anxiously.
anxieusement [ăksjøzmă] adv. Anxiously.
anxieux, euse [ăksjø, ø:z] adj. Anxious (de, to, for); troubled. ‖ Eager (avide) [de, to].
anxiogène [-sjɔʒɛn] adj. Anxiety-producing, angst-forming.
aoriste [aɔrist] m. GRAMM. Aorist.
aorte [aort] f. MÉD. Aorta.
aortique [-tik] adj. MÉD. Aortic.
août [u] m. August (mois).
aoûtat [auta] m. ZOOL. Harvest-bug (ou) -louse.
aoûtien, enne [ausjě, ɛn] s. August holidaymaker.
apache [apaʃ] m. Apache (Indien). ‖ Hooligan, thug, apache, U.S. tough (bandit).
apagogie [apagɔʒi] f. PHILOS., MATH. Apagoge.
apaisant, ante [apɛză, ă:t] adj. Soothing, consoling.
apaisement [apɛzmă] m. Appeasement; pacification, pacifying, quieting (de qqn); subsiding, abatement (du vent). ‖ Appeasing, allaying (de la faim); assuaging, quenching (de la soif); assuaging, alleviation (de la souffrance). ‖ FIG. Pl. Satisfactory assurances.
apaiser [-ze] v. tr. (1). To propitiate (une divinité); to placate, to pacify, to mollify (qqn). ‖ To appease, to satisfy (la faim); to quench, to assuage (la soif). ‖ To lull (la tempête); to quell (une querelle, une révolte). ‖ To salve (la conscience); to alleviate (la douleur).
— v. pr. S'apaiser, to be appeased. ‖ To subside (orage). ‖ To be appeased (ou) satisfied (faim); to be quenched (soif). ‖ FIG. To quieten down, to be soothed (douleur); to abate (excitation); to calm down, to soften, to be mollified (personne).
apanage [apana:ʒ] m. Appanage, apanage.
aparté [aparte] m. THÉÂTR. Aside, stage-whisper; en aparté, aside. ‖ FAM. Private conversation.
apartheid [apartɛd] m. Apartheid.
apathie [apati] f. Apathy, torpidity.
apathique [-tik] adj. Apathetic; torpid.
apatride [apatriʒ] adj. Stateless.
— s. Stateless person.

Apennins [apennɛ̃] m. pl. GÉOGR. Apennines.
aperception [apɛrsɛpsjɔ̃] f. PHILOS. Apperception.
apercevable [apɛrsəvabl] adj. Perceivable, visible; perceptible.
apercevoir [-səvwa:r] v. tr. (3). To perceive, to see (voir). ‖ To notice (remarquer).
— v. pr. S'apercevoir, to perceive; to notice, to realize; to become aware of; sans s'en apercevoir, unwittingly, unawares.
aperçu [-sy] m. Aperçu, glance, glimpse; insight, hint (notion). ‖ Rough estimate (estimation); sketch, aperçu, outline, summary, conspectus (exposé). ‖ View (appréciation).
apériodique [aperjɔdik] adj. ELECTR. Aperiodic.
apéritif, ive [aperitif, i:v] adj. Appetizing. ‖ MÉD. Opening.
— m. Appetizer, apéritif; heure de l'apéritif, cocktail time.
apéro [-ro] m. FAM. Drink (apéritif).
aperture [apɛrty:r] f. GRAMM. Opening.
apesanteur [apazătœ:r] f. Weightlessness, zero gravity.
apétale [apetal] adj. BOT. Apetalous.
à-peu-près [apøprɛ] m. Approximation.
apeuré, ée [apøre] adj. Scared, frightened. ‖ Timid (animal).
apex [apɛks] m. invar. MÉD., ASTRON. Apex.
aphasie [afazi] f. MÉD. Aphasia.
aphasique [-zik] adj. MÉD. Aphasic.
— s. MÉD. Aphasiac.
aphélie [afeli] f. ASTRON. Aphelion.
aphérèse [afɛrɛz] f. GRAMM. Apheresis.
aphidiens [afidjě] m. pl. ZOOL. Aphides.
aphlogistique [aflɔʒistik] adj. Fireproof.
aphone [afɔn] adj. MÉD. Aphonic, voiceless.
aphonie [-ni] f. MÉD. Aphonia.
aphorisme [afɔrism] m. Aphorism.
aphrodisiaque [afrɔdizjak] adj., m. Aphrodisiac.
aphte [aft] m. MÉD. Aphtha (pl. aphthae).
aphteux, euse [-tø, ø:z] adj. Aphthous; fièvre aphteuse, foot-and-mouth disease.
api [api] m. AGRIC. Pomme d'api, lady-apple.
à-pic [apik] m. 'nvar. Precipice, steep drop.
apical, ale [api al] adj. MÉD., GRAMM. Apical.
— f. GRAMM. Apical.
apicole [apikɔl] adj. Apiarian, bee-keeping.
apiculteur [-kyltœ:r] m. AGRIC. Apiarist, beekeeper.
apiculture [-kylty:r] f. AGRIC. Apiculture; beekeeping.
apidés [apide] m. pl. ZOOL. Apidae.
apiquer [apike] v. tr. (1). NAUT. To peak.
apitoiement [apitwamă] m. Pitying, compassion.
apitoyant, ante [-jă, ă:t] adj. Piteous; pitiful (lamentable). ‖ Pitiable (pitoyable).
apitoyer [-je] v. tr. (9 a). To touch, to move (ou) to incite to pity.
— v. pr. S'apitoyer, to be moved to pity, to feel compassion; s'apitoyer sur, to pity, to feel compassion for, to commiserate with, to condole with.
aplaigner [aplɛɲe] v. tr. (1). TECHN. To teasel.
aplanir [aplani:r] v. tr. (2). To plane (du bois); to planish (du métal); to level (une route); to float (du plâtre). ‖ FIG. To smooth; to smooth down, to remove, to iron out (les difficultés).
— v. pr. S'aplanir, to become level; to grow easier (route). ‖ FIG. To disappear, to be ironed out (difficultés).
aplanissement [-nismă] m. Planing; levelling; planishing; floating. ‖ FIG. Removal; ironing out.
aplat [apla] m. ARTS. Flat-wash (d'un tableau). ‖ TECHN. Flat-tint (d'une impression).
aplati, ie [aplati] adj. Flat, flattened, squashed flat.
aplatir [aplati:r] v. tr. (2). To level (une surface).

‖ To flatten (une couture); to flat (du métal); to flatten, to squash (un objet); to hammer down (un rivet). ‖ FAM. To lay out flat; to flatten, to squash (qqn).
— v. pr. **S'aplatir,** to collapse (ballon); to go flat (pneu). ‖ FAM. To lie down flat on the ground (tomber); *s'aplatir devant,* to grovel before.
aplatissement [-tismã] m. Levelling; flattening; flatting; squashing. ‖ FIG. Humiliation; truckling (*devant,* to).
aplatissoir [-tiswa:r] m. TECHN. Flatter, flatting-hammer (ou) mill.
aplomb [aplɔ̃] m. Perpendicularity; equilibrium; balance; uprightness; stand (d'un cheval); *à l'aplomb de,* plumb with; *d'aplomb,* plumb, steady; *hors d'aplomb,* out of plumb, unsteady. ‖ FAM. Aplomb, self-possession (v. ASSURANCE); cheek, nerve (v. TOUPET); *qui a de l'aplomb,* self-assured; *remettre d'aplomb,* to set up, to buck up.
apnée [apne] f. MÉD. Apnoea, U. S. apnea.
apocalypse [apɔkalips] f. ECCLÉS. Apocalypse (événement, livre); Revelation (livre).
apocalyptique [-liptik] adj. ECCLÉS. Apocalyptic. ‖ FIG. Cryptic (style).
apocope [apɔkɔp] f. GRAMM. Apocope.
apocryphe [apɔkrif] adj. ECCLÉS. Apocryphal; uncanonical. ‖ FIG. Spurious (document).
— m. ECCLÉS. Apocrypha (invar. au pl.).
apode [apɔd] adj. ZOOL. Apodal.
— m. ZOOL. Apod.
apodictique [apɔdiktik] adj. PHILOS. Apodictic, apodeictic, apodeictical.
apogée [apɔʒe] m. ASTRON. Apogee. ‖ FIG. Acme, climax, apex.
apolitique [apɔlitik] adj. Apolitical, non-political.
apolitisme [-tism] m. Lack of interest in politics, apoliticism.
Apollon [apɔlɔ̃] m. Apollo (dieu). ‖ FIG. Apollo.
apologétique [apɔlɔʒetik] adj. Apologetic.
— f. Apologetics.
apologie [apɔlɔʒi] f. Apologia; justification, vindication; *faire l'apologie de,* to vindicate.
apologiste [-ʒist] m. Apologist.
apologue [apɔlɔg] m. Apologue.
aponévrose [apɔnevro:z] f. MÉD. Aponeurosis.
apophonie [apɔfɔni] f. GRAMM. Apophony.
apophtegme [apɔftɛgm] m. Apophthegm.
apophyse [apɔfi:z] f. MÉD. Apophysis.
apoplectique [apɔplɛktik] adj., m. MÉD. Apoplectic.
apoplexie [-si] f. MÉD. Apoplexy.
apostasie [apɔstazi] f. ECCLÉS. Apostasy.
apostasier [-tasje] v. intr. (1). ECCLÉS. To apostatize.
apostat [-ta] adj., s. ECCLÉS. Apostate.
a posteriori [apɔsterjɔri] adv., adj. A posteriori.
apostille [apɔsti:j] f. Apostil, apostille (note); commendatory note (recommandation).
apostiller [apɔstije] v. tr. (1). JUR. To add a commendatory note to.
apostolat [apɔstɔla] m. ECCLÉS., FIG. Apostolate.
apostolique [-lik] adj. ECCLÉS. Apostolic.
apostrophe [apɔstrɔf] m. Apostrophe.
apostropher [-fe] v. tr. (1). To apostrophize.
apothème [apɔtɛm] m. MATH. Apothem.
apothéose [apɔteo:z] f. Apotheosis. ‖ Glorification. ‖ THÉÂTR. Finale.
apothicaire [apɔtikɛ:r] m. MÉD. Apothecary. ‖ LOC. *Compte d'apothicaire,* exorbitant bill.
apôtre [apo:tr] m. ECCLÉS. Apostle. ‖ FIG. Apostle; *faire le bon apôtre,* to sham the honest man, to play the saint.
Appalaches [apalaʃ] f. pl. GÉOGR. Appalachians, Appalachian mountains.

apparaître [aparɛ:tr] v. intr. (74). To appear; to come into sight. ‖ FIG. To become visible (ou) patent (ou) understood (ou) evident.
apparat [apara] m. State, display; *d'apparat,* formal, ceremonial.
apparatchik [aparatʃik] m. Apparatchik.
apparaux [aparo] m. pl. NAUT. Gear, tackle.
appareil [aparɛ:j] m. Array, show, display (apparat); apparatus, gear (préparatifs). ‖ Attire, garb, apparel (vêtement); *dans le plus simple appareil,* in one's birthday suit. ‖ Apparatus; *appareil critique (ou) scientifique,* critical apparatus. ‖ TECHN. Machinery, appliance; contrivance, device, machine (en général); *appareils électroménagers,* home appliances; *appareil frigorifique, photographique,* refrigerator, camera. ‖ ÉLECTR. Set (de radio); instrument (téléphone); *qui est à l'appareil?,* who is speaking? ‖ AVIAT. Plane, machine (avion); *appareil d'oxygène,* oxygen-equipment. ‖ NAUT. *Appareil de sauvetage,* life-saving apparatus. ‖ MÉD. *Appareil digestif,* alimentary canal; *appareil chirurgical,* surgical appliance; *appareil prothétique,* artificial limb; *appareil respiratoire,* breathing (ou) respiratory apparatus; respirator. ‖ ARCHIT. Height (des pierres); bond (système).
appareillage [-rɛja:ʒ] m. Preparation, fitting up. ‖ Equipment; outfit. ‖ Accessories, fixtures. ‖ NAUT. Getting under way; sailing.
appareiller [-rɛje] v. tr. (1). To prepare; to bond (des pierres). ‖ NAUT. To rig, to fit out.
— v. intr. NAUT. To set sail, to get under way.
appareiller [-rɛje] v. tr. (1). To pair, to mate (accoupler); to match (assortir).
apparemment [aparamã] adv. Apparently.
apparence [-rã:s] f. Appearance, look (aspect); sign, mark (marque); pretence, semblance (semblant); *sous l'apparence de,* in the guise (ou) form of; *en apparence,* outwardly, in appearance, seemingly; *contre toute apparence,* contrary to all appearances; *juger d'après les apparences,* to judge by appearances; *se fier aux apparences,* to trust to appearances; *sauver les apparences,* to keep up appearances, to save face.
apparent, ente [-rã, ã:t] adj. Apparent; visible. ‖ Conspicuous (manifeste); noticeable, evident; *héritier apparent,* heir-apparent; *prétexte apparent,* ostensible reason.
apparentement [aparãtmã] m. Electoral alliance. ‖ Pl. Pooling (ou) linking arrangements (en politique).
apparenter [-te] v. tr. (1). To connect, to relate by marriage.
— v. pr. **S'apparenter,** to become connected (*à,* with).
appariement [aparimã] m. Matching, pairing.
apparier [aparje] v. tr. (1). To pair, to mate, to couple (accoupler); to match, to pair (assortir).
— v. pr. **S'apparier,** to pair, to mate.
appariteur [aparitœ:r] m. Apparitor (à la cour); porter, beadle, U. S. attendant (à l'université). ‖ Mace-bearer, usher (huissier).
apparition [aparisjɔ̃] f. Apparition (action, fantôme); ghost (fantôme). ‖ Appearance; *faire une apparition à,* to put in an appearance at. ‖ Publication, appearance (d'un livre).
appartement [apartmã] m. Flat, suite of rooms, suite; U. S. apartment.
appartenance [apartənã:s] f. Appurtenance.
appartenant, ante [-nã, ã:t] adj. Appertaining, belonging (*à,* to).
appartenir [-ni:r] v. intr. (101). *Appartenir à,* to be connected with (par alliance); to appertain to, to lie (ou) rest with (par privilège); to belong to (par propriété). ‖ To appertain to, to form a part of (faire partie de). ‖ To fit, to suit, to

concern (dépendre de); *il lui appartient de,* it behoves (ou) U. S. behooves him to.
— v. pr. **S'appartenir,** to be one's own master, to be independent.

appas [apa] m. pl. Charms (en général); bust (d'une femme). ‖ Attractions, allurements.

appât [apα] m. Bait, lure (prop. et fig.); *appât corrupteur,* bribe.

appâter [-te] v. tr. (1). To lure with a bait (le poisson); to fatten (les oies). ‖ FAM. To allure (qqn). [V. AMORCER.]

appauvrir [apovri:r] v. tr. (2). To impoverish (une langue, qqn, un terrain). ‖ MÉD. To thin (le sang); to weaken; to exhaust (le tempérament).
— v. pr. **S'appauvrir,** to become poor, to grow poorer (personne). ‖ To become impoverished (langue). ‖ AGRIC. To become sterile (terrain). ‖ MÉD. To degenerate (race); to thin (sang).

appauvrissement [-vrismα] m. Impoverishment (d'une langue, d'une personne, d'un terrain). ‖ MÉD. Degeneration (d'une race); thinning (du sang); impoverishment (de la santé).

appeau [apo] m. Decoy-bird; bird-call.

appel [apεl] m. Call; summons; *appel à la prière,* call to prayer; *appel au secours,* cry for help; *appel téléphonique,* telephone call. ‖ Appeal; *appel au calme,* appeal for calm; *faire appel à,* to appeal to, to call in, to call upon (ou) on. ‖ MILIT. Roll call, muster (au quartier); calling up (d'une classe); *battre l'appel,* to sound the fall-in; *faire l'appel,* to call the roll; *feuille d'appel,* mobilization papers; *manquer à l'appel,* to be absent from roll-call. ‖ NAUT. Lead (d'un cordage); *faire l'appel,* to muster the hands. ‖ COMM. *Appel de fonds,* call for funds. ‖ JUR. Appeal; *cour d'appel,* Court of Appeal, U. S. Appellate Court; *juger en appel,* to hear an appeal; *sans appel,* non-appealable (ou) final (jugement). ‖ TECHN. *Appel d'air,* indraught.

appelant, ante [aplα, α:t] adj. JUR. Appellant.
— s. JUR. Party appealing, appellant. ‖ Decoy (oiseau).

appelé [aple] m. MILIT. Conscript, man called up for service. ‖ JUR. Second legatee. ‖ ECCLÉS. *Il y a beaucoup d'appelés, mais peu d'élus,* many are called, but few are chosen.

appeler v. tr. (8). To call, to hail (héler); *appeler un taxi,* to hail a taxi (ou) a cab; *appeller au travail,* to summon to work; *appeler qqn au secours,* to call to s.o. for help; *appeler le médecin,* to send for the doctor; *appeler au téléphone,* to ring up. ‖ To call; to name; to address (v. NOMMER); *on l'a appelée Marguerite,* they have called her Margaret; *il l'a appelé imbécile,* he called him a fool; *il l'a appelé M. X,* he addressed him as Mr. X.; *voilà ce que j'appelle une gracieuseté,* that's what I call a kindness. ‖ To call, to appoint, to designate (destiner à); *appelé au commandement,* appointed to the command; *appelé à la notoriété,* destined (ou) marked out for fame. ‖ To call for, to require (exiger); *les affaires m'appellent à Bordeaux,* business calls me away to Bordeaux; *appeler un châtiment,* to call for punishment; *l'heure m'appelle,* it is time for me to go. ‖ To call, to call forth, to provoke (attirer); *on a appelé notre attention sur,* our attention has been drawn to; *le mensonge appelle le mensonge,* lies beget lies. ‖ To appeal to, to call on, to invoke (invoquer); *appeler la bénédiction du ciel sur,* to call down the blessings of Heaven on. ‖ MILIT. To call up (une classe); *appeler sous les drapeaux,* to call to the colours. ‖ JUR. To call (une affaire); to call over (une liste de noms); to sue, to summon (en justice); to cite; to subpoena (un témoin); *appeler en témoignage,* to call to witness; *être appelé,* to come up (affaire).

— v. intr. To call, to cry; *en appeler à, de,* to appeal to, against. ‖ To call, to declare (aux cartes).
— v. pr. **S'appeler,** to be called (ou) named; *comment s'appelle-t-elle?,* what is her name?, what is she called?; *elle s'appelle Marie,* her name is Mary, she is called Mary; *comment s'appelle cet outil?* what do you call this tool?, what is the name of this tool? ‖ To be termed; *voilà ce qui s'appelle génie,* that really can be termed genius; *voilà ce qui s'appelle neiger,* that is something like snow.

appellation [apεllasjɔ̃] f. Appellation (v. DÉNOMINATION, NOM); *appellation injurieuse,* term of abuse. ‖ COMM. Trade name.

appendice [apε̃dis] m. Appendage; annex (à un local); appendix (pl. appendixes, appendices) [à un livre]; *petit appendice,* appendicle. ‖ MÉD. Appendix (pl. appendixes).

appendicite [-disit] f. MÉD. Appendicitis.

appendiculaire [-dikylε:r] adj. MÉD. Appendicular.

appentis [apα̃ti] m. Penthouse, outhouse (bâtiment); lean-to roof (toit).

appert (il) [ilapε:r] v. impers. JUR. It appears (de, from; que, that).

appesantir [apəzα̃tir] v. tr. (2). To weigh down; to make heavy. ‖ FIG. To bring down heavily (la colère); to dull (l'esprit).
— v. pr. **S'appesantir,** to become heavy; *s'appesantir sur,* to weigh heavy on; to fall heavily on (frapper); to over-insist on, to dwell at too great a length on (insister).

appesantissement [-tismα̃] m. Heaviness; dullness.

appétence [apetα̃s] f. Appetence, appetency (pour, for, of, after).

appétissant, ante [-tisα̃, α̃:t] adj. Appetizing; savoury. ‖ FIG. Alluring.

appétit [-ti] m. Appetite; *aiguiser l'appétit* (ou) *mettre en appétit,* to whet the appetite; *couper l'appétit à qqn,* to spoil s.o.'s appetite; *émousser l'appétit,* to take the edge off the appetite; *manger avec appétit,* to eat with relish. ‖ FIG. Appetite, longing, craving; *maîtriser ses appétits,* to curb one's appetites; *mettre en appétit,* to whet the desire (ou) appetite of.

applaudir [aplodi:r] v. tr. (2). To applaud, to clap. ‖ FIG. To applaud. (V. ACCLAMER, LOUER.)
— v. intr. To approve (à, of).
— v. pr. **S'applaudir,** to congratulate oneself (de, on).

applaudissement [-dismα̃] m. Applause, clapping (v. ACCLAMATION); *l'applaudissement des foules,* popular applause. ‖ FIG. Approval, applause.

applaudisseur [-disœ:r] m. Applauder.

applicabilité [aplikabilite] f. Applicability.

applicable [-kabl] adj. Applicable; appropriate (à, to); *règlement applicable à dater du,* rule to take effect from; *être applicable à,* to apply to. ‖ JUR. Chargeable (à, against). ‖ FIN. Assignable.

application [-kasjɔ̃] f. Applying; application; *mettre en application,* to apply, to administer. ‖ Plaster (emplâtre). ‖ Appliqué (broderie). ‖ Application, relevance (à, to). ‖ Application, exertion, assiduous attention; *avec application,* studiously, assiduously. ‖ JUR. Enforcement, U. S. administration (d'une mesure); infliction (d'une peine); *en application de,* in pursuance of. ‖ FIN. Appropriation (de crédits).

applique [aplik] f. Applique (broderie). ‖ ELECTR. Wall bracket; sconce.

appliqué, ée [aplike] adj. Painstaking, studious, assiduous (élève). ‖ Applied (arts, sciences).

appliquer [-ke] v. tr. (1). To apply (à, contre, sur, to); to put, to lay (à, contre, sur, on); *appliquer de la colle forte sur,* to apply glue to; *appliquer* *une échelle contre,* to set up (ou) to lean a ladder against. ‖ MÉD. To administer (un remède). ‖ JUR. To enforce (une loi, une mesure); to inflict (une peine). ‖ FIN. To appropriate (des crédits). ‖ FIG. To apply, to bend, to exercise (son attention, son esprit); to bestow, to direct (son énergie); to put to use, to put into practice (une invention, des théories); to apply (un texte). ‖ FAM. To give (un baiser); to deal (un coup); *un coup bien appliqué,* a well-planted blow. — v. pr. **S'appliquer,** to take pains, to give one's full attention (être attentif); *s'appliquer à,* to apply oneself to, to bend (ou) put one's mind to, to work hard at (apporter son attention à); to employ oneself in, to do one's utmost to (s'employer à). [V. S'ADONNER.] ‖ To apply, to hold good (citation, remarque); to be applied (ou) employed (méthode); to be laid on (peinture). ‖ MÉD. To be applied (sangsue).

appogiature [apɔʒjaty:r] f. MUS. Appoggiatura.

appoint [apwɛ̃] m. FIN. Odd money, balance; small change (monnaie); *faire l'appoint,* to make up the even money, to tender the exact amount. ‖ FIG. Addition; contribution.

appointage [-taʒ] m. Pointing.

appointé, ée [-te] adj. Salaried (employé). ‖ JUR. Referred (cause). ‖ BLAS. Appointé.

appointements [-tmɑ̃] m. pl. Emoluments.

appointer [-te] v. tr. (1). To give a salary to.

appointer [-te] v. tr. (1). To point (aiguiser).

appontage [apɔ̃taʒ] m. AVIAT. Landing on an aircraft-carrier.

appontement [-tmɑ̃] m. NAUT. Pier; landing stage; flying bridge.

apponter [-te] v. intr. (1). AVIAT. To land on an aircraft-carrier; to deck-land.

apport [apɔ:r] m. Bringing in, thing brought; contribution. ‖ Alluvion, sediment, alluvial deposit (alluvion). ‖ JUR. Adduction (de preuve); *apport dotal,* wife's dowry. ‖ FIN. *Action d'apport,* founder's share; *capital d'apport,* initial capital; *apport de capitaux,* assignment of assets.

apporter [-te] v. tr. (1). To bring, to bear (des nouvelles); to bring (des objets). ‖ FIN. To contribute, to provide, to supply (des fonds); to bring in (du profit). ‖ JUR. To adduce, to produce (des preuves). ‖ FIG. To apply (de l'énergie); to cause, to bring (des ennuis); to make (des modifications); to raise (des obstacles); to exercise (des soins).

apposer [apoze] v. tr. (1). To post, to stick up (une affiche); to affix, to append (un sceau); to append, to put (une signature); to stick (un timbre). ‖ JUR. To add, to insert (une clause); *apposer les scellés,* to seal up, to put under seals.

appositif, ive [-zitif, i:v] adj. GRAMM. Appositive.

apposition [-zisjɔ̃] f. Apposition, placing; affixing, appending (d'un sceau, d'une signature). ‖ JUR. Addition, insertion (d'une clause); *apposition des scellés sur,* sealing. ‖ GRAMM. Apposition; *en apposition,* appositive, in apposition.

appréciable [apresjabl] adj. Appreciable. ‖ Noticeable, appreciable, palpable.

appréciateur, trice [-jatœ:r, tris] adj. Appreciative, appreciatory. — s. Appreciator. ‖ COMM. Valuer, appraiser.

appréciatif, ive [-sjatif, i:v] adj. Appreciatory (regard). ‖ COMM. *Devis appréciatif,* estimate; *état appréciatif,* valuation.

appréciation [-sjasjɔ̃] f. Appreciation, estimate; *appréciation des distances,* judgment of distance. ‖ Appraisal, appraisement. (V. ESTIMATION, ÉVALUATION.) ‖ Judgment (jugement).

apprécier [-sje] v. tr. (1). To appraise; to estimate; to evaluate (évaluer). ‖ To value; to prize; to esteem; to rate; to judge (estimer); *ne pas apprécier à sa juste valeur,* to fail to appreciate.

‖ To enjoy, to appreciate (aimer). ‖ LOC. *Apprécier court,* to underestimate the range.

appréhender [apreɑ̃de] v. tr. (1). To fear, to dread (craindre). ‖ To apprehend, to seize (arrêter).

appréhensif, ive [apreɑ̃sif, iv] adj. Apprehensive, anxious, uneasy.

appréhension [-sjɔ̃] f. Apprehension (v. CRAINTE); *avoir l'appréhension que,* to be filled with apprehension lest; *plein d'appréhension,* apprehensive. ‖ PHILOS. Apprehension.

apprendre [aprɑ̃:dr] v. tr. (80). To learn (v. ÉTUDIER); to acquire (une langue); *apprendre à écrire,* to learn to write; *apprendre par cœur,* to learn by heart. ‖ To hear, to hear of, to be informed, to find (être informé); *apprendre quelque chose à qqn,* to inform s.o. of sth.; *je l'ai appris de source autorisée,* I have it on good authority. ‖ To teach, to instruct, to school (v. ENSEIGNER); *apprendre qqch. à qqn,* to teach s.o. sth. ‖ FAM. *Ça vous apprendra!,* serve(s) you right; *je vous apprendrai à m'insulter,* I'll teach you to insult me. — v. pr. **S'apprendre,** to teach oneself (à, to); to instruct oneself (à, in).

apprenti, ie [aprɑ̃ti] s. Apprentice, prentice (ouvrier). ‖ FAM. Novice, tyro.

apprentissage [-sa:ʒ] m. Apprenticeship; *contrat d'apprentissage,* indenture; articles of apprenticeship; *faire son apprentissage chez,* to serve one's apprenticeship with; *mettre en apprentissage chez,* to apprentice to; *prendre en apprentissage,* to indenture. ‖ FIG. Experience, experiment; *faire l'apprentissage de,* to become acquainted with, to learn by experience.

apprêt [aprɛ] m. Priming (du bois); stiffening (des cuirs); dressing (d'une étoffe); sizing, glazing (du papier). ‖ Pl. Preparations (préparatifs). ‖ CULIN. Dressing (d'un plat). ‖ FIG. Affectation; *sans apprêt,* unaffectedly.

apprêtage [-ta:ʒ] m. Dressing; stiffening; glazing; priming.

apprêté, ée [-te] adj. Boiled, stiff-fronted (chemise); dressed (tissu). ‖ CULIN. Cooked (viande). ‖ FIG. Affected (manières, style, ton).

apprêter [-te] v. tr. (1). To prepare, to get ready (ses bagages). ‖ CULIN. To cook, to prepare (un repas). ‖ TECHN. To prime (du bois); to starch (une chemise); to stiffen (des cuirs); to dress (une étoffe); to glaze (du papier). — v. pr. **S'apprêter,** to prepare, to get ready (se préparer). ‖ To be brewing (être imminent). ‖ To dress (s'habiller); to attire, to titivate (se parer).

apprêteur [-tœ:r] m. Dresser (d'étoffes). ‖ Pointer (sur verre).

apprêteuse [-tø:z] f. Trimmer.

apprivoisable [aprivwazabl] adj. Tam(e)able.

apprivoisé, ée [-ze] adj. Tame, domesticated.

apprivoisement [-zmɑ̃] m. Taming.

apprivoiser [-ze] v. tr. (1). To tame (un animal). [V. DOMESTIQUER.] ‖ FIG. To make tractable, to get round (un enfant); to make sociable (une personne). — v. pr. **S'apprivoiser,** to become tame (animal). ‖ To become sociable (personne); *s'apprivoiser avec,* to become familiar with.

approbateur, trice [aprɔbatœ:r, tris] adj. Approving; of approval (v. APPROBATIF); *sourire approbateur,* smile of approval. — s. Approver; applauder; yes-man (fam.).

approbatif, ive [-tif, i:v] adj. Approbative, approbatory.

approbation [-sjɔ̃] f. Approbation, approval. ‖ Commendation, approbation (louange). ‖ Consent, assent (assentiment). ‖ FIN. Certifying, passing (de comptes).

approbativement [-tivmɑ̃] adj. Approvingly.

approchable [aprɔʃabl] adj. Accessible, approachable (pr. et fig.).

approchant, ante [-ʃɑ̃, ɑ̃:t] adj. Approaching, similar; approximate; approximative; *qqch. d'approchant*, something similar; *rien d'approchant*, nothing like it.

approche [aprɔʃ] f. Approach; oncoming; advance; *à son approche*, on his approach (ou) drawing near; *l'approche de l'hiver*, the oncoming of winter; *à l'approche du jour*, at daybreak. ‖ Pl. Approaches, surroundings (abords); *aux approches de la cinquantaine*, nearly fifty. ‖ Math. Approximations. ‖ Phys. *Lunette d'approche*, spy-glass. ‖ Milit. *Marche d'approche*, approach march. ‖ Fig. *Travaux d'approche*, approach works.

approché, ée [-ʃe] adj. Approximate.

approcher [-ʃe] v. tr. (1). To bring near, to draw near (qqch.) [*de*, to]; to have access (*de*, to;) *difficile à approcher*, difficult of access. ‖ To approach (qqn). [V. aborder.]
— v. intr. To approach, to draw near; *approcher de*, to come near, to get near (arriver auprès de); to approximate to (atteindre presque); to border on (être à la limite de); to resemble (ressembler à); *approcher de la perfection*, to approach to perfection.
— v. pr. **S'approcher**, to approach, to come nearer; *s'approcher de*, to approach, to go near, to go up to, to step up to; *approchez-vous*, come closer (ou) nearer; *ne vous approchez pas de*, keep at a distance from.

approfondi, ie [aprɔfɔ̃di] adj. Full, thorough; elaborate (étude); extensive (travaux).

approfondir [-di:r] v. tr. (2). To deepen, to excavate. ‖ Fig To go deeply into, to examine thoroughly, to get to the core of, to fathom.

approfondissement [-dismɑ̃] m. Deepening. ‖ Fig. Thorough analysis (ou) study.

appropriable [aprɔpriabl] adj. Appropriable.

appropriation [-priasjɔ̃] f. Appropriation; *appropriation illicite de fonds*, embezzlement. ‖ Adaptation (*à*, to; *de*, of).

approprié, ée [-prije] adj. Appropriate, fitting, proper (*à*, to); suitable (*à*, to, for).

approprier [-prije] v. tr. (1). To fit, to adapt (*à*, to); to make fit (*à*, for). ‖ To clean (nettoyer).
— v. pr. **S'approprier**, to appropriate, to possess oneself of, to adopt (légitimement); to embezzle, to usurp, to take unlawful possession of (malhonnêtement).

approuvé [apruve] m. Jur. Form of approval; countersignature.

approuver v. tr. (1). To approve of, to assent to (consentir); to confirm; to sanction (sanctionner). ‖ To authorize; to subscribe to, to agree to (souscrire à); *approuver qqn*, to agree with s.o.; *approuver qqn de faire qqch.*, to approve of s.o.'s doing sth. ‖ Jur. *Approuvé l'écriture ci-dessus*, examined and found correct; *lu et approuvé*, read and approved. ‖ Comm. To pass (les comptes, une facture).

approvisionnement [aprɔvizjɔnmɑ̃] m. Provisioning, stocking (action); stock, store, supply (provisions). ‖ Pl. Supplies. ‖ Milit. Army supplies. ‖ Naut. Victualling; *approvisionnement en charbon*, coaling.

approvisionner [-ne] v. tr. (1). To provision, to victual; to supply (*en*, with); *bien approvisionné*, well-stocked.
— v. pr. **S'approvisionner**, to lay in supplies (ou) stores. ‖ To get one's supplies (*chez*, from).

approvisionneur [-nœ:r] s. Purveyor; victualler; supplier; caterer. (V. ravitailleur.)

approximatif, ive [aprɔksimatif, i:v] adj. Approximate; rough (calcul).

approximation [-sjɔ̃] f. Approximation; close estimate; near likeness.

approximativement [-tivmɑ̃] adv. Approxi-

mately; nearly; roughly (v. environ, presque); *dans une heure approximativement*, in an hour or so; *trois livres approximativement*, three pounds or thereabouts.

appui [apɥi] m. Support, prop, rest, shore; *appui de fenêtre*, window-sill; *à hauteur d'appui*, breast-high; *barre d'appui*, hand-rail. ‖ Ch. de f. Foot (d'un rail). ‖ Fig. Support, stay, prop, aid, protection (v. soutien); *recevoir un appui de*, to receive support from; *sans appui*, friendless, unprotected, unsupported; *trouver un appui auprès de*, to find a supporter (ou) protector in; *venir à l'appui de*, to support. ‖ Jur. *A l'appui de*, in support of, backing up; *avec documents à l'appui*, with documents annexed, with supporting documents; *pièce à l'appui*, voucher. ‖ Techn. Bearing; *point d'appui*, fulcrum. ‖ Milit. Appui; *appui de tir*, firing rest; *point d'appui*, point of appui. ‖ Mus., Gramm. Stress. ‖ **Appui-bras**, m. Arm-rest. ‖ **Appui-livre**, m. Book-rest. ‖ **Appui-main**, m. Maulstick. ‖ **Appui-tête**, m. Head-rest.

appuyer [-je] v. tr. (9a). To prop, to shore up, to support (soutenir). ‖ To lay, to rest (poser) [*sur*, on]; to lean, to prop (poser) [*contre*, against]; to press, to set (presser) [*sur*, upon, on]. ‖ Archit. To build up (une maison) [*contre*, against]. ‖ Milit. To support. ‖ Naut. To haul taut (les boulines); to enforce (un signal); *appuyer la chasse*, to keep up a running fight. ‖ Sports. To passage (un cheval) [à l'équitation]; to urge on (les chiens) [à la chasse]; to dwell on (la botte) [à l'escrime]. ‖ Fig. To second, to back, to support (aider); to back up, to patronize, to recommend; to speak of favourably (recommander); *appuyer une demande*, to support (ou) second a petition (ou) a request.
— v. intr. To bear, to press (*sur*, on, upon); *appuyer sur le bouton*, to press the button, to touch the bell; *appuyer sur un mot*, to lay emphasis upon (ou) to emphasize a word; *appuyer sur une note*, to sustain a note; *appuyer sur une syllabe*, to stress a syllable. ‖ Milit. *Appuyez à droite*, right close. ‖ Fig. To dwell, to insist (*sur*, upon); to emphasize.
— v. pr. **S'appuyer**, to lean, to rest (*contre*, against; *sur*, on). ‖ Fig. To take one's stand (*sur*, upon) [un argument]; to be grounded (ou) based (*sur*, on, upon) [une idée]; to rely (*sur*, on) [qqn]. ‖ Fam. *S'appuyer une corvée*, to have to drudge it (ou) U. S. to slave at it; *s'appuyer un bon dîner*, to treat oneself to a good dinner.

âpre [ɑ:pr] adj. Harsh; rough, tart (goût); sour (fruit); rough (vin). ‖ Biting, sharp (froid); raw (temps); keen, sharp (vent). ‖ Comm. Keen (concurrence). ‖ Fig. Crabbed, bitter (caractère); scathing (ironie); greedy, grasping (personne avide); scathing, bitter, cutting (remarque); acrimonious (ton); rasping (voix).

âprement [-mɑ̃] adv. Harshly, roughly (rudement). ‖ Bitingly, bitterly (amèrement). ‖ Greedily (avidement).

après [aprɛ] prop. After (en général); *après cinq heures*, after five; *après avoir lu ce livre*, after reading this book; *après vous, Madame!*, after you, Madam! *courir après l'autobus*, to run after the bus. ‖ Next (ensuite); *que feront-ils après?*, what will they do next? ‖ From (de retour de); *revenu après une longue absence*, back from a long absence. ‖ Behind (derrière); *marcher après qqn*, to walk behind s.o. ‖ At (contre); *aboyer après qqn*, to bark at s.o.; *après qui en a-t-il?*, who is he getting at? (fam.). ‖ Loc. *Après tout*, after all; *après quoi*, whereupon, after which; *aussitôt après*, immediately after (ou) afterwards; *après que*, after. ‖ **Après-demain**, adv. The day after to-morrow. ‖ **Après-dîner**, m. Afternoon; evening. ‖ **Après-guerre**, m. After-war period (ou) years. ‖ **Après-midi**, m. Afternoon; *au début*

de l'après-midi, early in the afternoon; *à deux heures de l'après-midi,* at two p.m., at two in the afternoon. ‖ **Après-rasage,** adj. invar. *Lotion après-rasage,* after-shave lotion. ‖ **Après-ski,** m. invar. Footwear put on after skiing. ‖ **Après-vente,** adj. invar. After-sales (service).
— adv. After, behind (derrière); next (ensuite); afterwards, later, after (plus tard); *et puis après?,* and then?, what then?; *peu après,* a short time after, presently; *quelques jours après,* a few days later.
— loc. prép., adv. **D'après,** after, from; *d'après nature,* from nature. ‖ According to; by; from; *d'après le calendrier,* by the calendar; *d'après ce que je sais,* from what I know; *d'après lui,* according to him; *l'année d'après,* the following year; *l'instant d'après,* the next moment.
âpreté [αprəte] f. Harshness; tartness, sourness (acidité). ‖ FIG. Greediness (avidité); harshness, roughness (rudesse).
a priori [apriɔri] adj. A priori.
— adv. A priori, at first sight.
— m. A priori reasoning (ou) judgement, presumption.
aprioriste [apriɔrist] s. Apriorist.
apriorisme [-rism] m. Apriorism, apriority.
à-propos [aprɔpɔ] m. Appropriateness, aptness, pertinence, relevance, opportuneness; *l'esprit d'à-propos,* the knack of saying the right thing; *manque d'à-propos,* irrelevancy; *manquer d'à-propos,* to be inopportune, to have no sense of timing.
apside [apsid] f. ASTRON. Apsis.
apte [apt] adj. Qualified; fit; apt, suited; *apte à apprendre,* quick to learn; *apte à faire un roi,* fit to be a king, fit for a king; *apte à enseigner,* qualified to teach; *apte à occuper cette fonction,* fitted for this function. ‖ JUR. Capable of; *être apte à tester,* to be sui juris; *apte à hériter,* entitled to inherit. ‖ MILIT. *Apte au service,* fit for military service.
aptère [aptɛ:r] adj. ZOOL. Apterous (sans ailes). ‖ ARCHIT. Apteral (sans colonnades latérales).
aptéryx [-teriks] m. ZOOL. Apteryx.
aptitude [-tityd] f. Aptitude, fitness; tendency, inclination; ability, capacity (v. TALENT); *certificat d'aptitude,* teacher's diploma (ou) U. S. certificate. ‖ Pl. Qualifications, gifts, abilities. ‖ JUR. Capacity, qualification.
apurement [apyrmᾶ] m. FIN. Auditing, checking. ‖ FAM. Wiping off (nettoyage).
apurer [-re] v. tr. (1). FIN. To audit (les comptes); to wipe off (une dette); to check (un solde).
apyrétique [apiretik] adj. MÉD. Antipyretic (médicament); apyretic (personne).
aquaculture [akwakylty:r], **aquiculture** [akwikylty:r] f. Aquaculture.
aquafortiste [akwafɔrtist] s. ARTS. Aquafortist, etcher.
aquaplane [-plan] m. SPORTS. Surf-board, aquaplane.
aquaplaning [-planiŋ], **aquaplanage** [-plana:3] m. AUTOM. Aquaplaning.
aquarelle [-rɛl] f. ARTS. Aquarelle, water-colour; *peindre à l'aquarelle,* to paint in water colours.
aquarelliste [-rɛlist] s. ARTS. Aquarellist, water colourist.
aquarium [-rjɔm] m. Aquarium.
aquatile [-til] adj. BOT. Aquatic.
aquatinte [-tɛ̃t] f. ARTS. Aquatint.
aquatintiste [-tɛ̃tist] s. ARTS. Aquatinter.
aquatique [-tik] adj. Aquatic (plante); *fête aquatique,* water festival, U. S. aquacade; *sports aquatiques,* aquatics.
aqueduc [akdyk] m. Aqueduct; conduit.

aqueux, euse [akø, ø:z] adj. MÉD., CHIM. Aqueous. ‖ FAM. Watery (fruit); water-logged (terrain).
aquiculture [akwikylty:r] f. V. AQUACULTURE.
aquifère [akwifɛ:r] adj. Aquiferous, water-bearing; *tuyau aquifère,* water-conduit.
aquilin, ine [akilɛ̃, in] adj. Aquiline, Roman.
aquilon [akilɔ̃] m. North wind.
ara [ara] m. ZOOL. Macaw.
arabe [arab] adj. Arabic (langue); Arab, Arabian (peuple); *chiffres arabes,* arabic numerals; *cheval arabe,* Arab.
— s. Arabic (langue); Arab, Arabian (personne).
arabesque [arabɛsk] adj., f. Arabesque.
Arabie [arabi] f. GÉOGR. Arabia; *le désert de l'Arabie,* the Arabian Desert. ‖ **Arabie Saoudite,** f. GÉOGR. Saudi Arabia.
arabique [-bik] adj. Arabic; Arabian; *le golfe Arabique,* the Arabian Gulf; *la gomme arabique,* gum arabic.
arabisant, ante [-bizᾶ, ᾶ:t] s. Arabist.
arabisation [-bizasjɔ̃] f. Arabization.
arabiser [-bize] v. tr. (1). To arabize.
arable [arabl] adj. AGRIC. Arable, tillable.
arachide [araʃid] f. BOT. Arachis, peanut, groundnut; *huile d'arachide,* peanut oil.
arachnéen, enne [araknéɛ̃, ɛn] adj. Arachnoid; gossamer, filmy, cobweb-like.
arachnide [araknid] m. ZOOL. Arachnid.
arachnoïde [araknɔid] f. MÉD. Arachnoid.
arachnoïdien, ienne [-djɛ̃, ɛn] adj. MÉD. Arachnoid.
arack [arak] m. Arrack.
araignée [arɛɲe] f. ZOOL. Spider; *toile d'araignée,* spider's web, cobweb; *araignée de mer,* sea-spider, spider-crab; weever. ‖ MILIT. Araignée. ‖ NAUT. Hammock-clew (crochet); gill-net (filet). ‖ TECHN. Grapnel, drag; spider-support. ‖ FAM. *Avoir une araignée au plafond,* to have bats in the belfry, to have a screw loose.
araire [arɛ:r] m. AGRIC. Swing-plough.
araméen, enne [araméɛ̃, ɛn] adj. Aramean (coutumes); Aramaic (langue).
— s. Aramaic.
arasement [arazmᾶ] m. ARCHIT. Levelling. ‖ TECHN. Tonguing, shoulder.
araser [-ze] v. tr. (1). To level (un mur); to plane down (une planche); to make flush (des pierres); *une cuillerée arasée,* a level spoonful.
aratoire [aratwa:r] adj. AGRIC. Ploughing; *instruments aratoires,* agricultural implements.
araucaria [arokaria] m. BOT. Araucaria, monkey-puzzle.
arbalète [arbalɛt] f. Crossbow, arbalest.
arbalétrier [-letrje] m. Crossbow-man.
arbitrage [arbitra:3] m. Arbitration, arbitrament (décision); *arbitrage des conflits du travail,* labour arbitrations; *conseil d'arbitrage,* conciliation board; *mettre en arbitrage,* to refer to arbitration. ‖ COMM. Hedging. ‖ FIN. Arbitrage; jobbing.
arbitraire [arbitrɛ:r] adj. Arbitrary (choix, quantité); discretionary (peine); *détention arbitraire,* false imprisonment; *procédé arbitraire,* high-handed proceeding. ‖ Capricious, despotic.
— m. Arbitrariness. ‖ High-handedness; capriciousness; *laissé à l'arbitraire de,* left to the discretion of.
arbitrairement [-mᾶ] adv. Arbitrarily.
arbitral, ale [arbitral] adj. Arbitral; *commission arbitrale,* board of referees; *jugement arbitral, sentence arbitrale,* arbitrator's award.
arbitralement [-tralmᾶ] adv. By arbitration.
arbitre [arbitr] m. Arbitrator, arbiter. ‖ JUR. Arbitrator; *tiers arbitre,* umpire, adjudicator. ‖ SPORTS. Umpire (au baseball, au cricket); referee (au basketball, à la boxe, au football, au rugby); judge (au tennis). ‖ PHILOS. *Libre arbitre,* free will. ‖ FIG. Master, disposer, arbiter; *arbitre des élégances,* arbiter elegantiarum.

arbitrer [-tre] v. tr. (1). To arbitrate; *arbitrer un différend*, to settle a difference. ‖ SPORTS. To umpire, to referee.

arborer [arbore] v. tr. (1). To hoist, to fly (un drapeau). ‖ To bear, to raise, to set up (porter). ‖ To sport (un habit voyant). ‖ NAUT. To step (un mât).

arborescence [arbɔrɛssɑ̃:s] f. BOT. Arborescence.

arborescent, ente [-sɑ̃, ɑ̃:t] adj. BOT. Arborescent; *fougère arborescente*, tree-fern.

arboricole [arbɔrikɔl] adj. ZOOL. Arboreal, tree-dwelling (faune). ‖ AGRIC. Arboricultural, relating to arboriculture (productions, techniques).

arboriculteur [arbɔrikyltœ:r] m. AGRIC. Arboriculturist.

arboriculture [-kyltyr] f. AGRIC. Arboriculture.

arborisation [-zasjɔ̃] f. Arborization.

arbouse [arbu:z] f. BOT. Arbutus-berry.

arbousier [-zje] m. BOT. Arbutus, strawberry-tree.

arbre [arbr] m. BOT. Tree; *arbre de haute futaie*, forest tree; *arbre de plein vent*, standard; *arbre vert*, evergreen; *jeune arbre*, sapling. ‖ JUR. *Arbre généalogique*, pedigree, family tree. ‖ TECHN. Arbor, shaft, axle, spindle; *arbre à cames (ou) de distribution*, camshaft; *arbre de couche*, driving shaft; *arbre coudé*, crankshaft; *arbre de direction*, steering post; *arbre de transmission*, propeller shaft. ‖ AVIAT. *Arbre porte-hélice*, propeller shaft.

arbrisseau [-briso] m. BOT. Shrubby tree.

arbuste [-byst] m. BOT. Shrub.

arc [ark] m. Bow; *tir à l'arc*, archery; *tirer à l'arc*, to shoot with a bow. ‖ ARCH. Arch; *arc de triomphe*, triumphal arch. ‖ MATH. Arc (de cercle). ‖ NAUT. Sagging; hogging. ‖ ELECTR. Electric (ou) voltaic arc. ‖ TECHN. *Arc denté*, curved rack. ‖ FIG. *Avoir plusieurs cordes à son arc*, to have several strings to one's bow. ‖ **Arc-en-ciel,** n. Rainbow. ‖ **Arc-rampant,** m. ARCHIT. Rampant arch.

arcade [arkad] f. Arcade, passageway (d'une rue). ‖ ARCHIT. Arcade; arching. ‖ MÉD. *Arcade sourcilière*, superciliary arch.

arcane [arkan] m. Arcanum (alchimie, secret). ‖ FIG. Pl. Secrets, mysteries, arcana.

arcature [arkaty:r] f. ARCHIT. Arcature.

arc-boutant [arkbutɑ̃] m. ARCHIT. Flying buttress; strut, spur, stay; *pilier d'arc-boutant*, buttress. ‖ FIG. Mainstay.

arc-bouter [-te] v. tr. (1). ARCHIT. To buttress; to prop up. ‖ FIG. To buttress, to support.
— v. pr. **S'arc-bouter,** to lean (*contre*, against); to set one's back (*contre*, against); to brace up.

arceau [arso] m. Ball (de voiture). ‖ ARCHIT. Arch. ‖ MÉD. Cradle. ‖ SPORTS. Hoop (au croquet); *passer l'arceau*, to run the hoop.

archaïque [arkaik] adj. Archaic.

archaïsant, ante [-izɑ̃, ɑ̃:t] adj. Archaistic.
— n. Archaist, archaiser.

archaïsme [-ism] m. Archaism.

archange [arkɑ̃:ʒ] m. ECCLÉS. Archangel.

arche [arʃ] f. ARCHIT. Arch. ‖ SPORTS. Hoop.

arche f. Ark; *l'arche d'alliance*, the Ark of the Covenant; *l'arche de Noé*, Noah's Ark.

archéologie [arkeɔlɔʒi] f. Archaeology.

archéologique [-lɔʒik] adj. Archaeological.

archéologue [-lɔg] m. Archaeologist.

archer [arʃe] m. Archer, bowman.

archet [arʃɛ] m. MUS. Bow (de violon). ‖ TECHN. Bow.

archétype [arketip] adj. Archetypal.
— m. Archetype.

archevêché [arʃəvɛʃe] m. ECCLÉS. Archbishopric, archdiocese. ‖ ARCHIT. Archbishop's house.

archevêque [arʃvɛ:k] m. ECCLÉS. Archbishop.

archibondé [arʃibɔ̃de] adj. Overcrowded, full-up.

archicomble [-kɔ̃bl] adj. Packed, filled to the rafters.

archiconfrérie [-kɔ̃frɛri] f. ECCLÉS. Archconfraternity.

archidiaconat [-djakɔna] m. ECCLÉS. Archdeaconship.

archidiaconé [-jakɔne] m. ECCLÉS. Archdeaconry.

archidiacre [-djakr] m. ECCLÉS. Archdeacon.

archidiocèse [-djɔsɛ:z] m. ECCLÉS. Archbishopric, archdiocese, archsee.

archiduc [-ɔ̃yk] m. Archduke.

archiducal [-dykal] adj. Archducal.

archiduché [-dyʃe] m. Archduchy.

archiduchesse [-dyʃɛs] f. Archduchess.

archiépiscopal, ale [arkiepiskɔpal] adj. ECCLÉS. Archiepiscopal.

archiépiscopat [-pa] m. ECCLÉS. Archiepiscopate.

archifou, olle [arʃifu, ɔl] adj. FAM. Frantic, scatty, loopy, U. S. goofy.

archimandrite [-mɑ̃drit] m. ECCLÉS. Archimandrite.

archimillionnaire [-miljɔnɛ:r] s. Multimillionaire.

archipel [arʃipɛl] m. GÉOGR. Archipelago.

archipompe [arʃipɔ̃:p] f. NAUT. Well; pumpwell.

archiprêtre [arʃiprɛ:tr] m. ECCLÉS. Arch-priest.

architecte [arʃitɛkt] m. Architect (pr. et fig.)

architectonique [-tɛktɔnik] adj. Architectonic.
— f. ARCHIT. Architectonics.

architectural, ale [-tɛktyral] adj. ARCHIT. Architectural; *d'une façon architecturale, du point de vue architectural*, architecturally.

architecture [-tɛkty:r] f. ARCHIT., FIG. Architecture.

architrave [-tra:v] f. ARCHIT. Architrave.

architravée [-trave] adj. ARCHIT. Architraved.
— f. ARCHIT. Architraved cornice.

archiver [arʃive] v. tr. (1). To archive.

archives [arʃi:v] f. pl. Archives; records, public records; *archives nationales*, national archives. ‖ Record Office (local).

archiviste [-vist] m. Archivist; *archiviste-paléographe*, palaeographer.

archivolte [arʃivɔlt] f. ARCHIT. Archivolt.

arçon [arsɔ̃] m. Saddle-bow (ou) -tree; *arme d'arçon*, holster pistol; *bande d'arçon*, side-bar of saddle; *vider les arçons*, to be thrown, to be unhorsed. ‖ TECHN. Bow (à textile).

arctique [arktik] adj. GÉOGR. Arctic.

arcure [arky:r] f. TECHN. Bending; arching.

ardélion [ardeljɔ̃] m. Busybody.

ardemment [ardamɑ̃] adv. Ardently, warmly; eagerly; zealously.

ardent, ente [ardɑ̃, ɑ̃:t] adj. Burning (buisson, miroir); hot (chaleur); fiery (fournaise); burning, scorching, blazing (feu); scorching, boiling (soleil); *charbons ardents*, live coals. ‖ Mettlesome (cheval); fiery (couleur); ardent, glowing (regard, yeux); parching (soif). ‖ NAUT. Griping. ‖ MÉD. Burning, raging (fièvre). ‖ FIG. Passionate (amour, colère); earnest (désir); ardent (étude); eager (espoir); burning (foi, haine); keen (joueur, sportif); zealous, enthusiastic (partisan); impassioned (plaidoyer); fervent (prière).
— m. MÉD. *Mal des ardents*, ergotism.

ardeur [-dœ:r] f. Heat, warmth (chaleur). ‖ FIG. Ardour; fieriness; eagerness; strenuousness; *avec ardeur*, eagerly, strenuously, fervently. (V. ENTHOUSIASME, FEU, ZÈLE.)

ardillon [ardijɔ̃] m. Tongue (de boucle).

ardoise [ardwa:z] f. Slate; *couvrir en ardoise*, to slate; *gris ardoise*, slate-grey. ‖ Debt; *avoir une ardoise chez*, to have credit with, to be able to chalk it up at, U. S. to buy it on the cuff at; *liquider une vieille ardoise*, to pay off an old score.

ardoisé, ée [-ze] adj. Slate-coloured.
ardoisier [-zje] m. Slate-quarryman.
ardoisière [-zjɛ:r] f. Slate-quarry.
ardu, ue [ardy] adj. Arduous, steep (pente). ‖ Intricate (matière); hard (problème); difficult (question); uphill (travail).
are [a:r] m. Are (mesure); 100 square metres; 119.6 square yards.
arec [arek] m. Bot. Areca.
arénacé, ée [arenase] adj. Géol. Arenaceous.
arène [arɛ:n] f. Arena; amphitheatre. ‖ Sports. Bull-ring (en tauromachie); ring. ‖ Fig. Arena; *descendre dans l'arène,* to enter the fray.
aréole [areɔl] f. Bot., Méd. Areole.
aréomètre [areɔmɛtr] m. Phys., Chim. Areometer, hydrometer.
aréopage [areɔpa:ʒ] m. Areopagus.
aréopagite [-paʒit] m. Areopagite.
arête [arɛ:t] f. Fish-bone (de poisson); backbone (grande arête); *enlever les arêtes,* to bone; *plein d'arêtes,* bony. ‖ Bridge (du nez). ‖ Géogr. Arête, ridge. ‖ Archit. Arris (de colonne); chamfer (de moulure); angle of intersection (de deux surfaces); groin (de voûte); *à arêtes,* groined. ‖ Milit. Ridge (de baïonnette). ‖ Aviat. Crown line (du fuselage). ‖ Bot. Beard (d'épi).
argent [arʒã] m. Silver (métal, pièces); *argent en feuille,* silverfoil; *d'argent,* silver, silvery; *en argent,* silver; *pièce d'argent,* silver coin. ‖ Money; *argent comptant,* cash; *argent de poche,* pocket money; *avoir peu d'argent disponible,* to have little available money; *coûter de l'argent,* to cost money; *envoi d'argent,* remittance; *en avoir pour son argent,* to get one's money's worth, to get good value for one's money; *un homme d'argent,* a money-grubber; *voir la couleur de l'argent de qqn,* to see the colour of s.o.'s money. ‖ Blas. Argent.
argentan [-tã] m. Nickel silver. (V. MAILLECHORT.)
argenté, ée [-te] adj. Silvery, silver (couleur). ‖ Silver-plated. ‖ Comm. Silver (renard). ‖ Fam. Flush, moneyed, monied, U. S. well-heeled.
argenter [-te] v. tr. (1). To silver-plate. ‖ Fig. To silver.
argenterie [-tri] f. Silver-plate, plate; silverware; table silver, U. S. flatware.
argenteur [-tœ:r] m. Techn. Silver-plater.
argentier [-tje] m. Techn. Silversmith. ‖ Fin. Treasurer; banker.
argentifère [-tifɛ:r] adj. Argentiferous.
argentin, ine [-tɛ̃, in] adj. Tinkling (son); silvery (voix). ‖ Argentine.
argentin, ine [-tɛ̃, in] adj., s. Géogr. Argentine; *la république Argentine,* the Argentine Republic, Argentina.
argenture [arʒãty:r] f. Silvering (glace); silver-plating.
argile [arʒil] f. Kaolin (blanche); clay (ordinaire); fire-clay (réfractaire).
argileux, euse [-lø, ø:z] adj. Argillaceous, clayey.
argon [argɔ̃] m. Chim. Argon.
argonaute [argɔnо:t] m. Argonaut.
argot [argo] m. Slang (familier); jargon (de métier).
argotique [-tik] adj. Slangy.
argotisme [-tism] m. Gramm. Slang word (ou) expression.
argousin [arguzɛ̃] m. Warder (surveillant). ‖ Fam. Bobby, U. S. cop (flic); lubber, booby (sot).
arguer [argɥe] v. tr. (1). To infer, to deduce, to conclude (conclure); to deduce (*de,* from). ‖ Jur. To assert; *arguer une pièce de faux,* to assert that a document is spurious.
— v. intr. To argue, to plead (invoquer); *arguer de qqch.,* to put sth. forward as a reason.

argument [argymã] m. Argument; support (*en faveur de,* for). ‖ Evidence, proof (preuve); *tirer argument de,* to ground oneself upon, to adduce as proof, to argue from. ‖ Case (ensemble des arguments favorables); *trouver des arguments pour justifier qqn,* to make out a case for s.o. ‖ Argument (sommaire). ‖ Math. Argument.
argumentateur, trice [-tatœ:r, tris] s. Arguer, wrangler.
argumentation [-tasjɔ̃] f. Argumentation.
argumenter [-te] v. intr. (1). To argue (*à propos de,* about; *contre,* against).
argus [argy:s] m. Zool. Argus. ‖ Argus, argus-eyed person; *Argus de la presse,* press-cutting agency, U. S. clipping bureau (ou) service. ‖ Spy (espion).
argutie [argysi] f. Cavil, quibble, quirk.
argyronète [argirɔnɛt] f. Zool. Water-spider.
aria [arja] m. Fam. Fuss; trouble.
aria f. Mus. Aria.
Ariane [arjan] n. pr. f. Ariadne; *fil d'Ariane,* Ariadne's clew.
arianisme [arjanism] m. Ecclés. Arianism.
aride [arid] adj. Arid, dry, barren (pr. et fig.).
aridité [-dite] f. Aridity; dryness; barrenness. ‖ Dullness (ennui).
arien, enne [arjɛ̃, ɛn] adj., s. Arian.
ariette [arjɛt] f. Mus. Arietta, ariette.
Aristarque [aristark] n. pr. m. Aristarchus. ‖ Fig. Severe critic.
aristo [aristo] f. Fam. Swell, knob, toff.
aristocrate [-crat] s. Aristocrat.
aristocratie [-crasi] f. Aristocracy.
aristocratique [-cratik] adj. Aristocratic.
aristocratiquement [-kratikmã] adj. Aristocratically.
Aristote [aristɔt] m. Aristotle.
aristotélicien, enne [-tɔtelisjɛ̃, ɛn] adj., s. Aristotelian.
arithméticien, enne [aritmetisjɛ̃, ɛn] s. Arithmetician.
arithmétique [aritmetik] f. Math. Arithmetic-book (livre); arithmetic (science).
— adj. Math. Arithmetical, U. S. arithmetic.
arithmétiquement [-metikmã] adv. Math. Arithmetically.
arithmographe [-mɔgraf] arithmomètre [-mɔmɛtr] m. Arithmometer; comptometer.
arlequin [arləkɛ̃] m. Harlequin; *en arlequin,* in motley. ‖ Fig. Weathercock.
arlequinade [-kinad] f. Harlequinade.
arlésien, enne [arlezjɛ̃, ɛn] adj. Of (ou) from Arles.
— s. Native (ou) inhabitant of Arles.
armada [armada] f. † *L'invincible Armada,* the (Spanish) Armada. ‖ Fig. Armada, hordes of, heaps of (grand nombre de).
armagnac [armaɲak] m. Armagnac brandy.
armateur [armatœ:r] m. Naut. Ship-owner; fitter-out.
armature [-ty:r] f. Armature; brace; truss; reinforcement. ‖ Mus. Key-signature. ‖ Electr. Armature; condenser plate; sheathing (de câble). ‖ Fig. Structure, framework.
arme [arm] f. Milit. Arm, weapon (moyen de défense); arm, branch of the service (partie de l'armée); *arme à feu,* firearm; *arme de guerre,* military weapon; *carrière des armes,* military profession; *être sous les armes,* to be under arms; *faire ses premières armes,* to be on one's first campaign; *maniement des armes,* weapon training (ou) exercise; *mettre l'arme à la bretelle,* to sling arms; *mettre l'arme sur l'épaule,* to slope arms; *passer par les armes,* to execute by shooting, to shoot; *place d'armes,* parade ground; *port d'armes prohibées,* illegal carrying of weapons; *porter les armes,* to bear arms; *portez*

armes!, slope (ou) U. S. shoulder arms!; *prendre les armes*, to take up arms; *présenter les armes*, to present arms; *prise d'armes*, ceremonial parade, U. S. military review; *sans armes*, unarmed; *sous les armes*, under arms. || Sports. *Faire des armes*, to fence; *maître d'armes*, fencing-master; *salle d'armes*, fencing-school (à l'escrime). || Blas. Arms; *aux armes de*, bearing the arms of. || Fig. *A armes égales*, on equal terms. || Fam. *Avec armes et bagages*, lock, stock and barrel; *faire ses premières armes*, to make one's début, to have one's first experience; *passer l'arme à gauche*, to kick the bucket, to go west, U. S. to croak.

armé, ée [-me] adj. Armed, with arms (personne). || Reinforced (béton, ciment); armoured (câble). || Naut. Commissioned. || Blas. Armed.
— m. Cock (d'une arme à feu).

armée [-me] f. Milit. Army; field army; forces; *armée de l'air*, air force; *armée de terre*, land forces; *armée d'occupation*, army of occupation; *armée du Rhin*, Army of the Rhine; *Armée du Salut*, Salvation Army. || Fig. Crowd, host, army.

armement [-məmɑ̃] m. Arming; equipping (d'une armée); cocking (d'une arme). || Armament; equipment. || Naut. Commissioning; outfitting; manning. || Comm. Shipping.

arménien, enne [armenjɛ̃, ɛn] adj., s. Géogr. Armenian.

armer [arme] v. tr. (1). To arm; to equip (qqn). || To cock (une arme à feu). || Techn. To set (un appareil); to arm (un aimant, une fusée); to reinforce (du béton); to sheathe (un câble); to wind (une dynamo); to set (un frein); to mount (une machine); to truss (une poutre). || Naut. To ship (les avirons); to man, to commission (un navire). || Mus. To put the signature in. || † *Armer qqn chevalier*, to dub s.o. a knight.
— v. intr. To arm. || Naut. To commission; to fit out; to man.
— v. pr. **S'armer**, to arm oneself (*de*, with); *s'armer de courage*, to take one's courage in one's hands; *s'armer de patience*, to have patience.

armillaire [armillɛ:r] adj. Armillary.

armistice [armistis] m. Armistice.

armoire [armwa:r] f. Wardrobe, cabinet, clothes-press, U. S. closet (à vêtements). || Chest (à pharmacie); cupboard, cabinet (à provisions, à vaisselle).

armoiries [armwari] f. pl. Blas. Arms; armorial bearings.

armoise [armwa:z] f. Bot. Artemisia, mugwort.

armorial, ale [armɔrjal] adj., m. Blas. Armorial.

armoricain, aine [armɔrikɛ̃, ɛn] adj., s. Géogr. Armorican.

armorier [-rje] v. tr. (1). Blas. To emblazon.

armure [army:r] f. Armour. || Tree-guard (d'arbre); plate (de construction); weave (de tissu). || Mus. Signature.

armurerie [-ri] f. Armoury (dépôt); arms factory (fabrique); gunsmith's shop (magasin).

armurier [-rje] m. Armourer; gunsmith.

A.R.N. [aɛrɛn] abrév. de *Acide ribonucléique*, RNA, ribonucleic acid.

arnaque [arnak] f. Pop. Con trick, rip-off, sting.

arnaquer [-ke] v. tr. (1). Pop. To con, to rip off, to sting (escroquer). || Pop. To cop, to nab, to pinch (arrêter).

arnaqueur [-kœ:r] m. Pop. Con man, rip-off artist.

arnica [arnika] f. Bot., Méd. Arnica.

aromate [arɔmat] m. Aromatic substance.

aromatique [-tik] adj. Aromatic, aromatical.

aromatiser [-tize] v. tr. (1). To aromatize, to flavour.

arôme [aro:m] m. Aroma, flavour; fragrance. (V. PARFUM.)

aronde [arɔ̃:d] f. Techn. *Queue-d'aronde*, dovetail; *assembler en queue d'aronde*, to dovetail.

arpège [arpɛ:ʒ] m. Mus. Arpeggio.

arpéger [-peʒe] v. intr. (7). Mus. To play in arpeggios (ou) broken chords.
— v. tr. Mus. To arpeggiate.

arpent [arpɑ̃] m. Arpent; about an acre.

arpentage [arpɑ̃ta:ʒ] m. Land-surveying; land-measuring.

arpenter [-te] v. tr. (1). To survey, to measure. || Fig. To stride along, to tramp up and down, to pace.

arpenteur [-tœ:r] m. Land-surveyor.

arpenteuse [-tø:z] f. Zool. Span-worm; looping caterpillar; measuring worm; U. S. inch-worm.

arpète [arpɛt] f. Milliner's apprentice.

arqué, ée [arke] adj. Bowed. || Arched (sourcils); *aux jambes arquées*, bow-legged. || Naut. Hogged (navire).

arquebuse [arkəby:z] f. Arquebus, harquebus.

arquebusier [-zje] m. Arquebusier, harquebusier.

arquer [arke] v. tr. intr. (1). To arch, to bend, to curve, to camber.
— v. pr. **S'arquer**, to arch, to curve; to be bowed.

arrachage [araʃa:ʒ] m. Wrenching (d'un clou). || Agric. Pulling up, uprooting (d'une plante). || Méd. Extraction, pulling out (d'une dent).

arrache [araʃ] f. V. ARRACHER. || **Arrache-clou**, m. Nail-wrench (ou) extractor. || **Arrache-pied (d')**, loc. adv. Steadily; *quatre heures d'arrache-pied*, four hours at a stretch (ou) non-stop.

arraché [-ʃe] m. Sports. Snatch (en haltérophilie). || Fig. *Victoire à l'arraché*, hard-won victory; *obtenir qqch. à l'arraché*, to snatch sth.

arrachement [-ʃmɑ̃] m. Fig. Wrench.

arracher [-ʃe] v. tr. (1). To uproot, to root up (un arbre); to pull up (des légumes, des mauvaises herbes); to dig up, to lift (des pommes de terre). || To draw (un bouchon); to pull out, to wrench out, to twist out, to screw out (un clou, une vis). || To tear off, to strip off (la peau); to pluck (des plumes); to tear out, to claw out (les yeux). || To tear off (du tissu); *arracher qqch. des mains de qqn*, to snatch sth. out of s.o.'s hands. || Méd. To extract, U. S. to pull (une dent). || Fig. To extort (de l'argent); to wrest, to wring (un aveu); to break (le cœur); to draw forth (des compliments); to wring (des larmes); to drag, to wrench, to snatch, to force (la vérité); *arracher à*, to wrest from (une destinée); to rescue (ou) to save from (la mort); to rouse from (un rêve).
— v. pr. **S'arracher**, to tear out; *s'arracher les cheveux*, to pluck at (ou) to tear one's hair. || To struggle for; *on se l'arrache*, he is all the rage, he is in great demand; *on s'arrache ce livre*, there is a scramble for this book. || *S'arracher à*, to wrench oneself free from (une étreinte); to break off (ou) away from (un rêve); to tear oneself away from (des sollicitations).

arracheur [-ʃœ:r] m. Puller; *arracheur de dents*, tooth-drawer (ou) U. S. -puller. || Fam. *Mentir comme un arracheur de dents*, to lie like a trooper.

arracheuse [-ʃø:z] f. Agric. Grubber; *arracheuse de pommes de terre*, potato-lifter.

arrachis [-ʃi] m. Uprooting (arrachage); clearing (terre défrichée); bedding plant (plante).

arrachoir [-ʃwa:r] m. V. ARRACHEUSE.

arraisonnement [arɛzɔnmɑ̃] m. Naut. Boarding, visiting (acte); examination of ship's bill of health (examen).

arraisonner [-ne] v. tr. (1). Naut. To hail (ou) to stop and examine; to visit (un navire).

arraisonneur [-nœ:r] m. NAUT. Examination-vessel.
— adj. Hailing (navire).

arrangeant, ante [arɑ̃ʒɑ̃, ɑ̃:t] adj. Accommodat-ing, obliging. (V. CONCILIANT.)

arrangement [-ʒmɑ̃] m. Arrangement, disposi-tion, ordering (disposition); order; putting in order (mise en ordre). ‖ Repairing, mending (rac-commodage). ‖ Agreement (accord); arrangement, accommodation, settlement, adjustment (conci-liation); composition (avec des créanciers). ‖ Pl. Arrangements, preparations, plans (mesures); *prendre ses arrangements*, to take measures. ‖ Pl. Arrangements, terms (avec des créanciers); *prendre des arrangements avec*, to come to terms with, to compound with, to make arrangements with. ‖ MUS. Arrangement; adaptation; *écrire des arrangements*, to arrange.

arranger [-ʒe] v. tr. (7). To arrange, to place, to dispose, to put in order, to tidy up (mettre en ordre). ‖ To hatch, to get up (un complot); to adjust, to settle (un différend); to arrange (un mariage); to organize (une réunion); *arranger l'affaire*, to straighten (ou) to mend matters. ‖ To overhaul (examiner pour réparations); to adjust, to mend, to put right, to touch up, to alter (raccommoder). ‖ To accommodate, to oblige; to suit; *ça m'arrange*, it suits me. ‖ MUS. To arrange. ‖ FAM. *Je t'arrangerai!*, I'll fix you!
— v. pr. **S'arranger**, to settle down, to settle oneself (s'installer). ‖ To dress, to get oneself up (se parer). ‖ To come to an agreement (s'en-tendre); *s'arranger avec*, to come to an agreement with, to arrange with (s'entendre); to settle with, to compound with, to compose with (transiger); *s'arranger pour le paiement d'une dette*, to compound for a debt. ‖ To manage, to contrive, to make shift (trouver le moyen); *arrangez-vous au mieux*, manage as best you can; *il s'est arrangé pour venir*, he made it convenient to come. ‖ To make do, to put up (se contenter) [*avec, de*, with]; *s'arranger de tout*, to be very adaptable (ou) content with anything. ‖ To be adjusted (se terminer par un compromis); to come (ou) to go right, to be straightened out (se terminer favora-blement); *ça s'arrangera*, that will turn out all right; *si tout s'arrange*, if everything goes right.

arrangeur [-ʒœ:r] m. MUS. Arranger, adapter.

arrérages [arera:ʒ] m. pl. FIN. Arrears; back-interest.

arrestation [arɛstasjɔ̃] f. JUR. Apprehension, arrest; *en état d'arrestation*, under arrest; *mettre en état d'arrestation*, to take into custody.

arrêt [arɛ] m. Stop, stopping, halt (halte); standstill (immobilisation); intermission (inter-ruption, repos); stopping-place (point d'arrêt); pause (temps d'arrêt); *arrêt au cours d'un voyage*, break in a journey; *marquer un temps d'arrêt*, to pause, to halt, to mark time; *trois minutes d'ar-rêt*, three minutes' stop. ‖ TECHN. Stoppage, blockage, lock, jam (blocage). ‖ AUTOM. *Arrêt facultatif*, request stop. ‖ RADIO. *Arrêt d'émis-sion*, breakdown, interruption of transmission. ‖ SPORTS. *Chien d'arrêt*, pointer, setter; *coup d'arrêt*, counter (à la boxe); stop-thrust (à l'es-crime); *tomber en arrêt*, to point (à la chasse). ‖ MILIT. *Arrêts simples, de rigueur*, open, close arrest; *garder les arrêts*, to remain under arrest; *lever les arrêts de*, to release from arrest; *mettre aux arrêts*, to put under arrest. ‖ JUR. Arrest. ‖ JUR. Adjudication, decree, judgment, sentence (en général); decision (de la Cour d'appel); *arrêt de mort*, death sentence; *rendre un arrêt*, to pass sentence, to deliver judgment. ‖ JUR. Attachment, distraint, seizure, impounding; *faire arrêt sur*, to seize, to impound. ‖ NAUT. *Mettre arrêt sur*, to put an embargo upon, to order the detention of.

arrêté, ée [arɛte] adj. Standing; at a standstill. ‖ Decided, fixed, settled, determined, steady (idée, intention, opinion, résolution). ‖ SPORTS. Stand-ing (départ).
— m. Decision, order; *arrêté ministériel*, decree, Order in Council; *arrêté de police*, police ordi-nance; *prendre un arrêté*, to pass a decree. ‖ COMM. Closing; settlement (de comptes).

arrêter [-te] v. tr. (1). To stop; to check, to stay. ‖ To pull up (un cheval); to fasten, to fix, to secure (un point, un volet); to detain, to keep back (qqn qui veut partir). ‖ To engage (un domestique). ‖ MÉD. To stunt (la croissance); to stop, to check (une hémorragie). ‖ JUR. To arrest, to apprehend (un malfaiteur); *faire arrêter qqn*, to have s.o. arrested. ‖ FIN. To close, to settle, to balance (un compte). ‖ SPORTS. To save, to stop (au football). ‖ FIG. To determine, to fix, to settle (un choix, un plan, une résolution); to impede, to hinder, to delay, to hold up (le développe-ment); to plan, to decide upon (un projet, un système); *arrêter que*, to decide (ou) to order (ou) to decree that.
— v. intr. To hold up (malfaiteur). ‖ SPORTS. To point (chien d'arrêt). ‖ JUR. To decree, to order. ‖ FAM. To stop, to cease; *elle n'arrête pas de pleurer*, she keeps on crying.
— v. pr. **S'arrêter**, to halt, to pause, to make a pause; *s'arrêter en marchant*, to stand. ‖ To come to a stop (ou) to a standstill. ‖ To cease (bruit); to pull up (cavalier, voiture); to stop (montre). ‖ CH. DE F. To stop. ‖ NAUT. To touch, to call. ‖ *S'arrêter chez*, to call at; *s'arrêter de*, to desist from, to leave off; *s'arrêter pour*, to stay to; *s'arrêter sur*, to fall on (choix); to pause (ou) to dwell (ou) to insist upon (pensée); to rest (ou) to fix (ou) to fasten on (regard); *ne pas s'ar-rêter sur*, to pass over.

arrêtoir [-twa:r] m. TECHN. Stop; catch; pawl. ‖ Keeper (de chaîne).

arrhes [a:r] f. pl. Earnest money; deposit, hand-sel; arles (token (ou) down payment (v. ACOMPTE); *verser trois cents francs d'arrhes*, to pay a deposit of three hundred francs, to leave three hundred francs as a deposit.

arriération [arjerasjɔ̃] f. MÉD. *Arriération men-tale*, feeble-mindedness, backwardness.

arrière [arjɛ:r] interj. Back!; *arrière les médi-sants!*, enough scandalmongering!
— adv. TECHN. *Feu arrière*, rear light; *faire machine en arrière*, to reverse the engines; *marche arrière*, reverse motion, reversing; *faire marche arrière*, to reverse; *entrer, sortir en marche arrière*, to back in, out; *roue arrière*, rear (ou) back wheel; *siège arrière de moto*, pillion-seat. ‖ NAUT. *Point arrière*, back-stitch (en couture). ‖ NAUT. *Cale arrière*, afterhold; *vent arrière*, before the wind; *vitesse arrière*, astern speed. ‖ FIG. *Faire marche arrière*, to back; to go into reverse (fam.)
— m. Back; rear; back part (d'une voiture). ‖ MILIT. Rear (de l'armée); home front (les civils). ‖ NAUT. Stern (du navire); *à l'arrière*, aft; *sur l'arrière de la passerelle*, aft of (ou) abaft the bridge. ‖ SPORTS. Back (au football); full back (au rugby); *arrière droit, gauche*, right, left full back.
— loc. adv. **En arrière**, back, backwards, behind; *aller en arrière*, to back; *cinquante ans en arrière*, fifty years back; *faire un pas en arrière*, to take a step backwards; *jeter un regard en arrière*, to cast a glance behind; *rester en arrière*, to stay (ou) to drop (ou) to fall behind; *revenir en arrière*, to go back; *voyager en arrière*, to travel with one's back to the engine. ‖ NAUT. Astern; *en arrière toute!*, full speed astern!
— loc. prépos. **En arrière de**, behind; *en arrière de sa classe*, behind the rest of the form; U. S.

at the foot of the class; *en arrière de son temps,* behind the times.
— adj. **Arrière-ban,** m. Arrière-ban, rear vassals; *le ban et l'arrière-ban,* the whole clan. ‖ **Arrière-bouche,** f. Back of the mouth. ‖ **Arrière-boutique,** f. Back-shop. ‖ **Arrière-corps,** m. inv. Rear premises. ‖ **Arrière-cour,** f. Back-yard. ‖ **Arrière-cuisine,** f. Back-kitchen; scullery. ‖ **Arrière-garde,** f. Rear guard. ‖ **Arrière-gorge,** f. MÉD. Back of the throat. ‖ **Arrière-goût,** m. Aftertaste; smack. ‖ **Arrière-grand-mère,** f. Great-grandmother. ‖ **Arrière-grand-oncle,** m. Great-grand-uncle. ‖ **Arrière-grand-père,** m. Great-grandfather. ‖ **Arrière-grand-tante,** f Great-grand-aunt. ‖ **Arrière-main,** f. Back of the hand (main); hindquarters (du cheval). ‖ **Arrière-neveu,** m. Grand-nephew. ‖ **Arrière-nièce,** f. Grand-niece. ‖ **Arrière-pays,** m. GÉOGR. Hinterland. ‖ **Arrière-pensée,** f. Ulterior (ou) hidden motive. ‖ **Arrière-petit-fils,** m. Great-grandson. ‖ **Arrière-petite-fille,** f. Great-granddaughter. ‖ **Arrière-petits-enfants,** m. pl. Great-grandchildren. ‖ **Arrière-plan,** m. Background; FIG. *A l'arrière-plan,* of secondary importance. ‖ **Arrière-port,** m. Inner harbour. ‖ **Arrière-saison,** f. Late season (ou) autumn; FIG. Evening of life, last period. ‖ **Arrière-salle,** f. Back-room. ‖ **Arrière-train,** m. Hindquarters (d'un animal); rear part (d'un véhicule).
arriéré, ée [-re] adj. Outstanding, overdue; owing (paiement). ‖ Backward (enfant); old-fashioned, outmoded, antiquated (idée, goût); benighted (mentalité, peuple).
— m. COMM. Arrears. ‖ MÉD. Backward child.
arriérer [-re] v. tr. (5). COMM. To let fall into arrears; to defer.
— v. pr. **S'arriérer,** to fall into arrears (paiement); to fall behind (personne).
arrimage [arima:ʒ] m. AVIAT. Stowage, packing. ‖ NAUT. Stowage, stowing, trimming (de la cargaison); trim (du navire); *bois d'arrimage,* dunnage, stowage; *changement d'arrimage,* cargo shifting, rummage.
arrimer [-me] v. tr. (1). NAUT. To stow, to trim, to pack. ‖ AVIAT. To pack, to trim. ‖ To secure.
arrimeur [-mœ:r] m. Stevedore; stower; trimmer; packer.
arrivage [ariva:ʒ] m. Arrival (des marchandises, des personnes).
arrivant [-vɑ̃] m. Comer, arrival.
arrivée [-ve] f. Arrival, coming. (V. AVÈNEMENT, VENUE.) ‖ SPORTS. Finish; *franchir la ligne d'arrivée,* to breast the tape. ‖ NAUT. Falling off, lee lurch. ‖ TECHN. Intake; inlet; *arrivée d'eau,* water-supply; *tuyau d'arrivée,* delivery pipe.
arriver [-ve] v. intr. (1). To arrive, to come; *arriver à,* to arrive at, to reach; *arrivé à destination,* arrived at one's destination; *arriver à Paris,* to get to Paris; *arrivez vite,* hurry up; *j'arrive juste à temps pour,* I am just in time to; *elle arrivera trop tard,* she will be too late; *ils arriveront chez eux vers dix heures,* they will get home about ten; *cette lettre m'est arrivée hier,* this letter reached me yesterday; *le train doit arriver à quatre heures,* the train is due at four. ‖ To succeed, to do well; to make one's way; to get on (réussir); *il n'arrivera jamais à rien,* he will never achieve anything, he will never get anywhere. ‖ To happen, to occur, to take place, to come to pass (survenir); *arriver à,* to happen to, to befall, to come to (advenir); *cela n'arrive qu'à moi,* it would happen to me, just my luck; *des choses qui arrivent tous les jours,* everyday things, things of daily occurrence; *que cela ne vous arrive plus,* don't let that occur again; *les enfants jouissent du présent, ce qui ne nous arrive guère,* children enjoy the present, which very few

of us do. ‖ SPORTS. To come in. ‖ **Arriver à,** to achieve, to reach (atteindre); to succeed in, to manage to (réussir à); *arriver à ses fins,* to achieve one's ends; *arriver à un grand âge,* to reach a great age; *arriver à un rang éminent,* to attain to eminence; *comment y arriver?,* how is it to be managed?; *il n'arrive pas à comprendre,* he simply can't understand. ‖ **En arriver à,** to get, to reach; to come to, to end by; *en arriver aux coups,* to come to blows; *en arriver à mourir de faim,* to be reduced to starvation; *il n'en est pas arrivé là,* he has not got so far, he has not come to that. ‖ **Faire arriver,** to bring on, to bring about, to bring to pass; to cause, to be responsible for.
— v. impers. *Il est arrivé un accident,* an accident occurred; *il ne lui était jamais arrivé de voir,* he had never happened (ou) chanced to see; *il m'arrive souvent de m'enrhumer,* I often catch a cold; *il lui arrive souvent de se tromper,* he is apt (ou) it is common with him to make mistakes; *il lui arrivera malheur,* he will come to grief; *quoi qu'il arrive,* happen what may, whatever may happen; *s'il vous arrive de trouver,* if you happen to find, if you ever find.
arrivisme [-vism] m. Place-seeking; art of getting on; go-getting (fam.). [V. AMBITION.]
arriviste [-vist] s. Careerist, climber, thruster, go-getter; arriviste. (V. INTRIGANT.)
arrogamment [arɔgamɑ̃] adv. Arrogantly, haughtily, superciliously.
arrogance [arɔgɑ̃:s] f. Arrogance. (V. HAUTEUR.)
arrogant, ante [-gɑ̃, ɑ̃:t] adj. Arrogant, overbearing. (V. HAUTAIN.)
arroger (s') [sarɔʒe] v. tr. pr. (7). To arrogate to oneself (v. APPROPRIER [s']); *les Anglais s'arrogent l'empire des mers,* the English claim command of the sea.
arrondi, ie [arɔ̃di] adj. Rounded, round. ‖ FIG. Well-rounded (phrase).
— m. Round, rounded outline; curve (courbe). ‖ AVIAT. Flattening-out.
arrondir [-di:r] v. tr. (2). To round; to round off; to make round. ‖ To hump (le dos). ‖ NAUT. To round (ou) double (un cap). ‖ FIG. To increase; to round off (les angles, une somme).
— v. pr. **S'arrondir,** to become (ou) to grow round. ‖ To increase (domaine, fortune).
arrondissement [-dismɑ̃] m. Rounding off, making round (action); roundness (état). ‖ Increase (d'une fortune); rounding (d'une terre). ‖ Arrondissement, district (d'un département); ward; borough (d'une ville).
arrosage [arɔza:ʒ] m. Watering, sprinkling, spraying (des fleurs); irrigation (des prés); watering (des rues); *voiture d'arrosage,* watering-cart; *tuyau d'arrosage,* hose. ‖ CULIN. Basting (d'un rôti). ‖ MILIT. Sweeping, plastering. ‖ FIG. Bribing (concussion). ‖ FAM. Wetting (célébration).
arroser [-ze] v. tr. (1). To water, to sprinkle, to spray (les fleurs, les pelouses); to irrigate (les prés); to water (les rues). ‖ CULIN. To water (le lait, le vin); to wash down (un repas); to baste (un rôti); *arroser d'alcool,* to lace (son café). ‖ MILIT. To sweep, to plaster; to strafe (fam.). ‖ FIG. To bribe (corrompre). ‖ FAM. To wet (un marché, un succès).
arroseur [-zœ:r] m. Waterer, sprayer.
arroseuse [-zø:z] f. Sprinkler (des jardins); watering-cart (des rues).
arrosoir [-zwa:r] m. Watering-can (ou) pot; sprinkling can.
arrow-root [arorut] m. BOT. Arrowroot.
arsenal [arsənal] m. MILIT. Arsenal; armoury; *arsenal d'artillerie,* gun factory, gunshop; *arsenal de construction,* workshop. ‖ NAUT. Naval yard; dockyard. ‖ FIG. Arsenal; storehouse; repository; apparatus.

arséniate [arsenyat] m. CHIM. Arseniate.
arsenic [arsənik] m. CHIM. Arsenic; *arsenic sulfuré rouge,* realgar.
arsenical, ale [-nikal] adj. CHIM. Arsenical.
arsénieux, euse [arsenjø, ø:z] adj. CHIM. Arsenious.
arsénique [-nik] adj. CHIM. Arsenic.
arsénite [-nit] m. CHIM. Arsenite.
arséniure [-njy:r] m. CHIM. Arsenide.
arsine [arsi:n] f. CHIM. Arsine.
arsonvalisation [arsɔvalizasjɔ] f. MÉD. Treatment by diathermy.
arsouille [arsu:j] s. POP. Blackguard.
art [ar] m. Art; *l'art de la danse, de la guerre,* the art of dancing, of war; *l'art pour l'art,* art for art's sake; *une œuvre d'art,* a work of art; *un ouvrage d'art,* an engineering work, an artificial (ou) man-made feature. ‖ Art, craft, profession; *l'art dramatique,* dramatic art; *l'art de gouverner,* statesmanship; *l'art de l'ingénieur,* engineering; *l'art militaire,* the military art, soldiering. ‖ Art, skill, artfulness, knack (habileté); *avoir l'art de,* to have the art (ou) knack of. ‖ Pl. Arts; *arts d'agrément,* accomplishments; *arts ménagers,* domestic arts; *beaux-arts,* fine arts.
artefact [artefakt] m. Artefact, artifact (phénomène artificiel ou accidentel).
artère [artɛ:r] f. MÉD. Artery. ‖ ELECTR. Feeder. ‖ FIG. Thoroughfare, arterial road (rue).
artérialiser [-rjalize] v. tr. (1). MÉD. To arterialize.
artériel, elle [-riɛl] adj. MÉD. Arterial.
artériole [-rjɔl] f. MÉD. Arteriole.
artériosclérose [-rjɔsclero:z] f. MÉD. Arteriosclerosis.
artérite [-rit] f. MÉD. Arteritis.
artésien, enne [artezjɛ̃, ɛn] adj. Pertaining to Artois (ou) Arras. ‖ Artesian (puits).
— s. Artesian.
arthrite [artrit] f. MÉD. Arthritis.
arthritique [-tik] adj., s. MÉD. Arthritic.
arthritisme [-tism] m. MÉD. Arthritism.
arthropodes [artropo:d] m. pl. ZOOL. Arthropods.
arthrose [artro:z] f. MÉD. Arthrosis.
artichaut [artiʃo] m. BOT., CULIN. Artichoke. ‖ Spikes in clusters; spiked barrier. ‖ FAM. *Avoir un cœur d'artichaut,* to be fickle-hearted.
article [artikl] m. JUR. Item, entry, point (de compte); clause, stipulation, provision (de contrat, de traité); section (de loi); *faits et articles,* circumstances and facts. ‖ COMM. Article, commodity; pl. goods, wares; *articles de Paris,* fancy goods; *articles de bureau,* writing-materials; *faire l'article,* to puff one's goods, to boost a product, U. S. to plug an item. ‖ Article, contribution (de journal); *article de fond,* feature article; *article de tête,* editorial, leading article, leader; *petit article,* paragraph. ‖ Article, matter, point (sujet). ‖ GRAMM. Article. ‖ BOT., ZOOL. Joint. ‖ ECCLÉS. Article (de foi); *à l'article de la mort,* at the point of death. ‖ Article-réclame, m. COMM. Leader.
articulaire [artikulɛ:r] adj. MÉD. Articular; *douleur articulaire,* arthrodynia, arthralgia.
articulation [-lasjɔ̃] f. MÉD. Knuckle (des doigts); articulation, joint (des membres); articulation, utterance (de la parole). ‖ JUR. Enumeration, formulation, statement (des faits). ‖ TECHN. Joint, connection. ‖ MILIT. Deployment, breaking into groups. ‖ BOT. Node.
articulé, ée [-le] adj. MÉD. Articulate (membre, parole). ‖ TECHN. Jointed; articulated.
— m. pl. ZOOL. Articulata.
articuler [-le] v. tr. (1). To articulate. (V. PRONONCER.) ‖ JUR. To set forth (une accusation); to enumerate, to state fully and precisely (des faits); *articuler des preuves,* to detail the evidence. ‖ TECHN. To joint, to link, to hinge. ‖ MILIT. To subdivide, to divide up, to break into groups.
— v. intr. To articulate well, to enunciate, to speak distinctly.
— v. pr. S'**articuler,** to be connected (ou) linked (ou) jointed, to hinge. ‖ MILIT. *S'articuler en largeur,* to spread out in width; *s'articuler en profondeur,* to echelon in depth.
artifice [artifis] m. Artifice; skill, ingenuity; trickery, craft (habileté). ‖ Clever expedient; artful device; trick, guile; stratagem; *artifice de guerre,* artifice of war. ‖ Pyrotechnic display; *tirer un feu d'artifice,* to let off fireworks. ‖ FIG. *Feu d'artifice,* flash of wit, sparkling wit.
artificiel, elle [-sjel] adj. Artificial (fleur). ‖ ELECTR. Artificial (lumière). ‖ COMM. Artificial (produit). ‖ MÉD. False (dent); artificial (insémination). AGRIC. Artificial (prairie). ‖ PHYS. Manmade (satellite). ‖ FIG. Affected (attitude); fictitious (caractère); strained (gaieté); artificial, unnatural (style, vie).
artificiellement [-sjɛlmɑ̃] adv. Artificially.
artificier [-sje] m. Pyrotechnist. ‖ MILIT. Artificer.
artificieusement [-sjøzmɑ̃] adv. Artfully, craftily, cunningly.
artificieux, euse [-sjø, ø:z] adj. Artful, crafty, cunning, wily.
artillerie [artijri] f. MILIT. Artillery, ordnance; mounted guns (armes); gunnery (science); *artillerie de campagne, de montagne,* field, mountain artillery. ‖ FIG. Batteries, guns, artillery.
artilleur [artijœ:r] m. MILIT. Artilleryman, gunner.
artimon [artimɔ̃] m. NAUT. Mizzen-mast.
artisan [artizɑ̃] m. Craftsman, artisan. ‖ FIG. Architect; builder, maker; *artisan de son sort,* architect of one's own destiny, master of one's fate.
artisanal, ale [-zanal] adj. In the style of cottage industry, by craftsmen; *bombe artisanale,* home-made bomb.
artisanalement [-zanalmɑ̃] adv. Following oldfashioned cottage industry techniques, by craftsmen.
artisanat [-zana] m. Handicraft, manual trade; cottage industry. ‖ Artisan class.
artiste [artist] s. Artist; *artiste capillaire,* tonsorial artist. ‖ Performer. ‖ THÉÂTR. Artiste; actor, actress; *entrée des artistes,* stage-entrance. ‖ ARTS. Artist; *artiste peintre,* painter. ‖ MUS. Artist, artiste.
— adj. Artistic.
artistement [-tmɑ̃] adv. Artistically; finely.
artistique [-tik] adj. Artistic; *qualité (ou) talent artistique,* artistry.
artistiquement [-tikmɑ̃] adv. Artistically.
arum [arɔm] m. BOT. Arum.
aruspice [aryspis] m. Haruspex.
aryen, enne [arjɛ̃, ɛn] adj., s. Aryan.
arythmie [aritmi] f. MÉD. Arrhythmia, irregularity of pulse.
arythmique [aritmik] adj. Arrhythmic.
as [ɑ:s] m. As (mesure). ‖ Ace (jeu); *as de pique,* ace of spades. ‖ AVIAT. Ace. ‖ SPORTS. Crack, star. ‖ FIG. Ace, first-rater. ‖ FAM. *Fichu comme l'as de pique,* tricked out like a guy (personne); botched (travail); *passer à l'as,* to juggle away; *il est plein aux as,* he's got bags of lolly, U. S. he's got wads of dough.
asbeste [azbɛst] m. Asbestos.
ascaris [askaris] m. MÉD. Ascarid.
ascendance [asɑ̃dɑ̃:s] f. Ancestry, lineage. ‖ ASTRON. Ascent.
ascendant, ante [-dɑ̃, ɑ̃:t] adj. Rising, ascending, upward, climbing. ‖ MATH. Increasing.
— m. Ascendency (v. INFLUENCE); *prendre de*

l'ascendant sur, to gain a hold on. ‖ ASTRON. Ascendant. ‖ Pl. Ancestors, ancestry.

ascenseur [asɑ̃sœ:r] m. Lift; U. S. elevator; *maison sans ascenseur*, house without a lift, U. S. walk-up (fam.). ‖ Hoist (de marchandises).

ascension [-sjɔ̃] f. Ascension, ascent; rising. ‖ SPORTS. Climb, climbing; *faire l'ascension de*, to climb. ‖ AVIAT. Climb. ‖ ASTRON. Ascension. ‖ ECCLÉS. Ascension (fête); Ascension Day (jour).

ascensionnel, elle [-sjɔnɛl] adj. Ascensional; lifting, elevating (force); upward (mouvement).

ascensionniste [-sjɔnist] s. Climber, mountaineer.

ascèse [asɛz] f. Asceticism.

ascète [asɛt] s. Ascetic.

ascétique [assetik] adj. Ascetic.

ascétisme [-tism] m. Asceticism.

ascidie [assidi] f. BOT. Ascidium.

ascorbique [askɔrbik] adj. MÉD. *Acide ascorbique*, ascorbic acid.

asdic [asdik] m. NAUT. Asdic.

asepsie [asɛpsi] f. MÉD. Asepsis.

aseptique [-tik] adj., m. MÉD. Aseptic.

aseptisation [-tizasjɔ̃] f. MÉD. Sterilization.

aseptiser [-tize] v. tr. (1). To sterilize.

asexué, ée [asɛksɥe] adj. Asexual, sexless.

Asiate [azjat] s. GÉOGR. Asiatic.

asiatique [azjatik] adj. Asiatic; Asian.
— s. GÉOGR. Asiatic.

Asie [azi] f. GÉOGR. Asia; *l'Asie Mineure*, Asia Minor.

asile [azil] m. Asylum; *asile d'aliénés*, lunatic asylum, mental hospital; *asile des indigents*, workhouse, poor-house, almshouse; *asile de nuit*, night-shelter; doss-house, U. S. flop-house; *asile des vieillards*, home for the aged, old people's home. ‖ Shelter, home, refuge (v. ABRI); *droit d'asile*, right of sanctuary; *sans asile*, homeless. ‖ FIG. Harbour, haven.

asine [azin] adj., f. ZOOL. Asinine.

asocial, ale [asɔsjal] adj. Asocial, antisocial.

asparagus [asparagys] m. BOT. Asparagus fern.

aspect [aspɛ] m. Sight, view (vue); *au premier aspect*, at first sight. ‖ Aspect, look, appearance; likeness (v. APPARENCE); *changer d'aspect*, to look different; *d'un aspect singulier*, queer- (ou) odd-looking; *d'aspect tranquille*, quiet-looking. ‖ Aspect, face; point of view, viewpoint; *l'aspect de l'affaire*, the look of the matter; *prendre un facheux aspect*, to be shaping badly; *sous tous ses aspects*, in all its aspects; from all angles; *sous un autre aspect*, from another point of view. ‖ ASTRON., GRAMM. Aspect.

asperge [aspɛrʒ] f. BOT. Asparagus (invar.). ‖ FAM. Maypole, lamp-post, U. S. string bean (personne).

asperger [aspɛrʒe] v. tr. (7). To spray; to sprinkle (de, with).

aspérité [asperite] f. Asperity; jaggedness. ‖ FIG. Roughness; harshness.

aspersion [aspɛrsjɔ̃] f. Aspersion, sprinkling, spraying.

aspersoir [-swa:r] m. Holy-water sprinkler, aspergillum (goupillon); rose (d'arrosoir).

asphaltage [asfaltaʒ] m. Asphalting.

asphalte [asfalt] m. Asphalt, asphaltum. (V. BITUME.) ‖ Pavement (trottoir).

asphalter [-te] v. tr. (1). To asphalt.

asphalteur [-tje] m. Asphalter.

asphodèle [asfɔdɛl] m. BOT. Asphodel.

asphyxiant, ante [asfiksjɑ̃, ɑ̃:t] adj. Asphyxiating. ‖ Poison (gaz).

asphyxie [-si] f. MÉD. Asphyxia; asphyxiation.

asphyxier [-sje] v. tr. (1). To asphyxiate, to gas.
— v. pr. S'**asphyxier**, to asphyxiate oneself, to gas oneself.

aspic [aspik] m. ZOOL. Asp, aspic (vipère). ‖

BOT. Aspic (lavande). ‖ CULIN. Aspic (plat en gelée).

aspidistra [aspidistra] m. BOT. Aspidistra.

aspirant, ante [aspirɑ̃, ɑ̃:t] adj. Sucking; *pompe aspirante*, suction-pump.
— s. Aspirant. (V. CANDIDAT.) ‖ NAUT. Midshipman. ‖ MILIT. Officer cadet. ·

aspirateur, trice [-ratœ:r, tris] adj. Aspiratory.
— m. Vacuum cleaner (à poussière). ‖ TECHN. Aspirator, exhauster.

aspiration [-rasjɔ̃] f. MÉD. Inspiration, breath, inhaling. ‖ TECHN. Suction; intake; *aspiration d'air*, air suction; *clapet d'aspiration*, intake valve; *temps d'aspiration*, suction stroke. ‖ GRAMM. Aspiration. ‖ FIG. Aspiration (à, to); yearning (à, after).

aspiré, ée [-re] adj. GRAMM. Aspirate.

aspirer [-re] v. intr. (1). MÉD. To breathe in, to inhale. (V. INSPIRER.) ‖ FIG. To aspire (à, to, after); to long (à, for); *aspirer à la députation*, to be aiming at a seat in Parliament.
— v. tr. To inhale, to breathe in (de l'air); to suck up, to draw up (un liquide). ‖ GRAMM. To aspirate, to breathe; *ne pas aspirer les « h »*, to drop one's *h*'s.

aspirine [aspirin] f. MÉD. Aspirin; *un comprimé d'aspirine*, an aspirin (tablet).

aspiro-batteur [aspirobatœ:r] m. Double action vacuum cleaner.

assagir [asaʒi:r] v. tr. (2). To make wiser, to sober down, to knock sense into.
— v. pr. S'**assagir**, to sober down, to settle down, to become reasonable.

assagissement [-ʒismɑ̃] m. Mellowing, settling down.

assaillant, ante [asajɑ̃, ɑ̃:t] adj. Attacking.
— s. Assailant, attacker, assaulter. (V AGRESSEUR.)

assaillir [-ji:r] v. tr. (17). To assail, to assault, to attack, to storm, to set upon. ‖ FIG. To beset (*with*, de) [craintes]; to assail (de, with) [reproches]; to bombard (de, with) [questions].

assainir [asɛni:r] v. tr. (2). To decontaminate; to make wholesome. (V. DÉSINFECTER, PURIFIER.) ‖ AGRIC. To sweeten (le terrain). ‖ FIG. To purge; to clean up; to reform.
— v. pr. S'**assainir**, to become healthy (ou) healthier.

assainissement [-nismɑ̃] m. Sanitation; decontamination; drainage. (V. DÉSINFECTION, PURIFICATION.) ‖ FIN. Rehabilitation (des finances). ‖ FIG. Reform, reorganization.

assaisonnement [asɛzɔnmɑ̃] m. CULIN. Seasoning, flavouring (en général); dressing (de la salade); condiment, spice, relish (ingrédient). ‖ FIG. Spice, zest, piquancy.

assaisonner [-zɔne] v. tr. (1). CULIN. To season, to flavour; to give relish to (un plat); to dress (la salade). ‖ FIG. To season, to give zest to.

assassin, ine [asasɛ̃, in] adj. Murderous; bloodthirsty. ‖ FAM. Provocative, killing.
— m. Assassin, murderer; *femme assassin*, murderess.

assassinat [-sina] m. Assassination, murder; wilful manslaughter; *assassinat légal*, judicial murder.

assassiner [-sine] v. tr. (1). To assassinate (un grand personnage); to murder (un individu ordinaire). ‖ FAM. To worry to death (ennuyer) [de, with]; to murder, to ruin, to harm (maltraiter).

assaut [aso] m. MILIT. Assault, attack; storming; *donner l'assaut*, to attack, to charge; *monter à l'assaut*, to charge, to go over the top; *enlever (ou) prendre d'assaut*, to take (ou) capture by storm; *repousser un assaut*, to beat off an attack. ‖ SPORTS. Contest, bout, match; *assaut de boxe*, sparring match; *faire assaut avec*, to fence with (à l'escrime. ‖ Fig. Attack, onslaught (des vagues); *faire assaut d'amabilités avec*, to vie in civilities with; *faire assaut d'esprit*, to thrust and parry.

assèchement [asɛ∫mɑ̃] m. Drying. (V. DRAINAGE.)

assécher [ase∫e] v. tr. (5). To dry. (V. DRAINER.)

assemblage [asɑ̃bla:ʒ] m. Assemblage, assembling; gathering; collecting (action). ‖ Assemblage, collection; concourse (de gens); collocation, combination (d'idées). ‖ TECHN. Assembling, joining (en général); bond (en maçonnerie); coupling, connection, joint (en mécanique); gathering (en typographie); *tige d'assemblage*, link. ‖ ELECTR. Connection.

assemblée [-ble] f. Assembly (corps constituant). ‖ Company, gathering, assembly (groupe). ‖ Meeting; conference (reunion); *assemblée générale*, general meeting. ‖ ECCLÉS. *Assemblée des fidèles*, congregation.

assembler [-ble] v. tr. (1). To gather, to collect, to heap up (des choses); to assemble, to summon (ou) bring together (des personnes). ‖ JUR. To convene (un comité, une société). ‖ MILIT. To muster (des soldats). ‖ TECHN. To joint, to join (en général); to couple, to fit together (en mécanique); to gather (en typographie).
— v. pr. **S'assembler**, to assemble, to meet, to gather. (V. ATTROUPER [s'].) ‖ TECHN. To be joined (ou) assembled.

assembleur [-blœ:r] m. Assembler. ‖ TECHN. Fitter (en mécanique); gatherer (en typographie).

assener [asəne] v. tr. (5). To strike; *bien assené*, telling (coup).

assentiment [asɑ̃timɑ̃] m. Assent, consent (v. ACQUIESCEMENT); *donner son assentiment à*, to agree to, to acquiesce in, to subscribe to.

asseoir [aswa:r] v. tr. (18). To seat, to sit (qqn). ‖ To pitch (un camp, une tente); to lay (des fondations); to place, to set (qqch.). ‖ FIN. To base, to assess (un impôt). ‖ AVIAT. To pancake. ‖ FIG. To base, to ground (un jugement, une opinion); to establish, to strengthen (sa réputation). ‖ POP. To sit on, to take aback, to make sit up (qqn).
— v. pr. **S'asseoir**, to sit down; *asseyez-vous*, sit down, take (ou) U. S. have a seat. ‖ To settle (maison). ‖ AVIAT. To pancake.

assermenté, ée [asɛrmɑ̃te] adj. Sworn-in (fonctionnaire); juror (prêtre); on oath (témoin).

assermenter v. tr. (1). To swear in; to administer the oath to.

assertion [asɛrsjɔ̃] f. Assertion.

asservi, ie [asɛrvi] adj. Enslaved; servile.

asservir [-vi:r] v. tr. (2). To enslave (à, to) [prop. et fig.]. ‖ FIG. To subjugate, to subdue; to tie down (à, to). [V. OPPRIMER.]
— v. pr. **S'asservir**, to enslave oneself, to submit (à, to).

asservissant, ante [-visɑ̃, ɑ̃:t] adj. Enslaving; servile.

asservissement [-vismɑ̃] m. State of bondage; enslavement. (V. SERVITUDE.) ‖ FIG. Subjection, subservience.

assesseur [asɛsœ:r] m. JUR. Assessor; assistant (ou) puisne judge.

assez [ase] adv. Enough, sufficiently, sufficient (suffisamment); *assez grand, vite*, large, fast enough; *il dort bien assez*, he sleeps quite enough; *il a assez travaillé*, he has worked long enough. ‖ Enough, fairly, rather, pretty, somewhat (plutôt); *elle parle assez bien le français*, she speaks fairly good French; *il est assez fatigué*, he is rather tired; *il va assez bien*, he is pretty well; *il a assez de jugement*, he has plenty of judgment; *il est assez en retard*, he is somewhat (ou) rather late. ‖ FAM. *J'en ai assez*, I'm sick of it. ‖ **Assez de**, enough, sufficient; *j'ai assez d'argent*, I have enough money; *il a assez de mille francs*, he has enough with a thousand francs; *elle avait assez*

de lui, she had had enough of him; *il avait assez de la vie*, he was sick (ou) tired of life; *on ne put trouver assez de lits*, not enough beds were to be found. ‖ **Assez pour**, enough for; *avoir assez pour vivre*, to have sufficient money (ou) enough to live on; *il n'est pas assez vieux pour mourir*, he is not old enough to die; *vous n'êtes pas assez sot pour le croire*, you are not so stupid (ou) such a fool as to believe it. ‖ **Assez pour que**, enough to; *pas assez jolie pour qu'on l'admire*, not pretty enough to be admired.
— interj. That will do!, enough!, stop!.

assidu, ue [asidy] adj. Attentive (*auprès de*, to). ‖ Assiduous; regular (à, in); diligent (à, at); *assidu au cours*, attending the lecture regularly.

assiduité [-dɥite] f. Regular (ou) constant attendance (à, to, at). ‖ Assiduity, assiduousness; constant application (à, to). ‖ Pl. Assiduities.

assidûment [-dymɑ̃] adv. Assiduously, diligently.

assied [asje]. V. ASSEOIR (18).

assiégé, ée [asjeʒe] adj., s. MILIT. Besieged.

assiégeant, ante [-ʒɑ̃, ɑ̃:t] adj. MILIT. Besieging.
— m. MILIT. Besieger.

assiéger [-ʒe] v. tr. (5-7). MILIT. To besiege, to lay siege to, to beleaguer, to beset (une ville). ‖ FAM. To crowd (ou) to throng round, to besiege, to beset, to mob, to surround, to throng round (qqch., qqn); to assail; to harry, to harass (qqn) [de, by, with]. ‖ FAM. To dun (un débiteur); to haunt (l'esprit).

assiette [asjɛt] f. Plate; *assiette creuse* (ou) *à soupe, à dessert*, soup, dessert plate; *assiette plate*, plate; *manger dans une assiette*, to eat from a plate. ‖ Plateful (assiettée). ‖ Seat (à cheval); *perdre son assiette*, to lose one's seat. ‖ Situation, stable position; *assiette matérielle*, material position. ‖ ARCHIT. Set (d'une poutre); situation, site (d'une maison). ‖ TECHN. Bed, support (d'une machine). ‖ FIN. Basis (de l'impôt). ‖ NAUT. Trim. ‖ FIG. Condition, state; *ne pas se sentir dans son assiette*, not to be up to the mark, to be out of sorts, not to be in good form. ‖ FAM. *L'assiette au beurre*, cushy job, jobs-for-the-boys; U. S. soft job, gravy train.

assiettée [-te] f. Plateful, plate.

assignable [asiɲabl] adj. Assignable. ‖ JUR. Suable, sueable.

assignat [asiɲa] m. † Assignat, paper money issued during French Revolution.

assignation [-ɲasjɔ̃] f. JUR. Subpoena, summons, writ; *envoyer* (ou) *remettre une assignation à*, to serve a writ on. ‖ FIN. Assignment (de crédits); allotment (de parts) .

assigner [-ɲe] v. tr. (1). JUR. To summon, to subpoena, to issue a writ against (v. CITER); *assigner qqn en justice*, to sue s.o. at law. ‖ FIN. To earmark (des crédits); to allocate, to assign (une somme). ‖ FIG. To ascribe, to allot (affecter); to assign (à, to); to fix, to appoint (fixer).

assimilable [asimilabl] adj. Assimilable.

assimilateur, trice [-latœ:r, tris] adj. Absorptive, assimilatory, digestive (facilitant la digestion). ‖ Integrating (favorisant l'intégration sociale).

assimilation [-lasjɔ̃] f. Assimilation (pr. et fig.). ‖ Comparison. ‖ Correlation of ranks. ‖ GRAMM. Assimilation.

assimilé [-le] m. Civilian (ou) serviceman attached to fighting unit (dans l'armée); employee with similar status (dans la fonction publique, les entreprises).

assimiler [-le] v. tr. (1). To assimilate; to rank together (des fonctions diverses). ‖ To assimilate, to liken (à, to). ‖ GRAMM., MÉD. To assimilate.
— v. pr. **S'assimiler**, to assimilate, to digest (pr. et fig.). ‖ To become alike; *s'assimiler à*, to be likened to, to liken oneself to.

assis, ise [asi, i:z] adj. Seated; sitting; *être assis à table*, to sit at table; *rester assis*, to remain

seated, to keep one's seat; *place assise,* seat. ‖
ARCHIT. Situated, set (bâtiment). ‖ JUR. *La magistrature assise,* the judiciary, the Bench. ‖ FIG.
Based, resting; established (réputation); solid
(fortune); sound (entreprise). ‖ FAM. Stunned with
surprise.

assise [asi:z] f. Seating (des fondations, d'un
véhicule). ‖ Seat (à cheval). ‖ ARCHIT. Course,
row, layer. ‖ GÉOL. Bed, stratum. ‖ Pl. FIG.
Foundations, groundwork. (V. BASE.) ‖ JUR. Pl.
Assizes; Assize Court (cour); sessions, sittings,
meetings (séances); *envoyer aux assises,* to commit
for trial; *tenir ses assises,* to hold one's meetings.

assistanat [asistana] m. Assistant lectureship.

assistance [asistɑ̃:s] f. Assistance, help, relief;
attendance (aide); *prêter assistance à,* to assist,
to help, to lend one's aid to. ‖ Audience; bystanders; spectators; onlookers; assembly (assemblée); *toute l'assistance,* all present. ‖ Attendance,
presence; *l'assistance au cours,* attendance at
the lecture. ‖ Champerty (complicité). ‖ JUR.
Assistance judiciaire, legal aid, assistance of the
Court; *avec l'assistance judiciaire,* in forma
pauperis; *assistance sociale,* social welfare work;
assistance à l'enfance, child care. ‖ ECCLÉS. Congregation.

assistant, ante [-tɑ̃, ɑ̃:t] adj. Assistant.
— s. Assistant, helper (aide); assistant, U. S.
instructor (professeur); *poste d'assistant,* assistant
instructorship. ‖ *Assistante sociale,* social welfare
worker; *assistante familiale,* case-worker. ‖ Bystander, onlooker, spectator; *les assistants,* those
present.

assisté, ée [-te] adj. Attended; helped; relieved.
— s. Person relieved; U. S. person on relief;
enfants assistés, children in the care of local
authorities, foundlings.

assister [-te] v. tr. (1). To assist, to help (v. AIDER,
SECOURIR); *assister de,* to help with. ‖ To minister
to (les blessés, les malades, les mourants).
— v. intr. **Assister à,** to witness (un accident);
to attend, to assist at (une réunion).

associable [asɔsjabl] adj. Associable.

associatif, ive [-sjatif, i:v] adj. Associative.

association [-sjasjɔ̃] f. Association (pr. et fig.). ‖
Gang (de malfaiteurs). ‖ COMM. Partnership,
society, company, association; *association de
bienfaisance,* charitable organization. ‖ ELECTR.
Connection.

associationnisme [-sjasjɔnism] m. PHILOS.
Associationism.

associé, ée [-sje] adj. Associated; associate (d'une
société savante). ‖ AGRIC. *Cultures associées,*
companion crops.
— m. Associate (d'une société savante). ‖ COMM.
Partner; *prendre comme associé,* to take into
partnership.

associer [-sje] v. tr. (1). To associate; to join;
to unite; *associer qqch. à,* to associate (ou) to
connect sth. with; *associer qqn à,* to make s.o.
share, to make s.o. a party to. ‖ ELECTR. To
connect.
— v. pr. **S'associer,** to associate; *s'associer qqn,*
to take s.o. as a partner (ou) as a helper. ‖
S'associer à (ou) *avec,* to go (ou) to enter into
partnership with, to form a partnership with, to
associate (ou) to combine with, to mix with, to
take up with (un honnête homme); to mix with,
to consort (un mauvais sujet). ‖ *S'associer à,* to
take part in, to attach oneself to, to share (qqch.);
to join in (ou) to become a party to, to participate
in (qqch.); *je m'associe à votre douleur,* I share
your grief; *il s'associe à votre opinion,* he sympathizes with you.

assoiffé, ée [aswafe] adj. Thirsty. (V. ALTÉRÉ.)
‖ FIG. Eager, thirsty (de, for).

assoiffer v. tr. (1). To make thirsty.

assois [aswa]. V. ASSEOIR (18).

assolement [asɔlmɑ̃] m. AGRIC. Rotation.

assoler [-le] v. tr. (1). AGRIC. To rotate the crops
on (une terre).

assombri, ie [asɔ̃bri] adj. Darkened. ‖ Cloudy,
overcast (ciel). ‖ FIG. Gloomy (visage).

assombrir [-bri:r] v. tr. (2). To darken. ‖ FIG.
To make gloomy, to cloud.
— v. pr. **S'assombrir,** to darken. ‖ To become
cloudy (ciel). ‖ FIG. To become gloomy, to cloud
over (visage).

assombrissement [-brismɑ̃] m. Darkening. ‖
Gloominess.

assommant, ante [asɔmɑ̃, ɑ̃:t] adj. Overwhelming (argument); stunning (coup). ‖ Deadly dull,
dull as ditch water, soporific, somniferous
(endormant); boring (ennuyeux, importun);
tedious, wearisome (ennuyeux); tiresome, plaguy
(insupportable); *type assommant,* deadly bore.

assommer [-me] v. tr. (1). To fell, to knock down,
to stun. ‖ FIG. To stun, to stupefy (stupéfier);
assommé par, sodden with (la boisson); overcome
with (la chaleur). ‖ FAM. To bore, to plague; to
pester. (V. EMBÊTER, ENNUYER.)

assommeur [-mœ:r] m. Slaughterer (de bétail).
Ruffian, thug; U. S. tough (bandit). ‖ FAM. Bore.

assommoir [-mwa:r] m. Bludgeon, club, cosh,
U. S. blackjack (gourdin); *coup d'assommoir,*
knock-out blow. ‖ Grog-shop, gin palace, low
pub, U. S. dive (caboulot). ‖ Deadfall (trappe).

Assomption [asɔ̃psjɔ̃] f. PHILOS., ECCLÉS.
Assumption. ‖ GÉOGR. Asunción.

assonance [asɔnɑ̃:s] f. GRAMM. Assonance.

assonant, ante [-nɑ̃, ɑ̃:t] adj. Assonant.

assorti, ie [asɔrti] adj. Assorted, mixed (bonbons, gâteaux). ‖ Matched, suited, paired; *couple
bien assorti,* well-matched couple; *union bien
assortie,* very suitable match; *des nuances assorties,* shades to match; *une robe et des souliers
assortis,* a dress with shoes to match (ou) to go
with it. ‖ COMM. Stocked, well stocked (ou)
furnished (approvisionné).

assortiment [-timɑ̃] m. Assortment, choice,
variety, collection, set. ‖ Matching, harmony,
suitability; *mauvais assortiment,* mismatchment. ‖
COMM. Assortment.

assortir [-ti:r] v. tr. (2). To match, to harmonize,
to pair, to sort, to assort (à, with) [une couleur,
une étoffe]; *mal assortir,* to mismatch (des
époux). ‖ To suit (à, to); to associate (à, with). ‖
COMM. To assort, to stock, to furnish.
— v. intr. To match, to go well together; to suit.
— v. pr. **S'assortir,** to assort, to match, to suit
one another, to harmonize; *s'assortir bien* (ou)
mal, to go well (ou) badly together. ‖ COMM. To
stock a variety of goods. ‖ FIG. To agree, to tally
with, to get on well (moralement).

assortissant, ante [-tisɑ̃, ɑ̃:t] adj. Suiting, matching (à, with).

assoupir [asupi:r] v. tr. (2). To make sleepy
(ou) drowsy. ‖ FIG. To assuage, to deaden.
— v. pr. **S'assoupir,** to doze off, to fall into a
light sleep, to nap, to begin to nod. ‖ FIG. To
subside; to abate; to deaden.

assoupissant, ante [-pisɑ̃, ɑ̃:t] adj. Causing
sleep; soporific; somniferous, somnific.

assoupissement [-pismɑ̃] m. Somnolence; drowsiness; sleepiness (torpeur). ‖ Nap, doze (court
sommeil). ‖ FIG. Apathy, sluggishness (apathie);
inertness (inertie); torpor (torpeur).

assouplir [asupli:r] v. tr. (2). To make supple,
to supple (pr. et fig.); to break in.
— v. pr. **S'assouplir,** to become supple. ‖ FIG.
To become more tractable.

assouplissement [-plismɑ̃] m. Making supple
(pr. et fig.); *exercices d'assouplissement,* suppling
(ou) warming-up exercises, Swedish drill.

assourdir [asurdiːr] v. tr. (2). To deafen (pr. et fig.). ‖ To subdue, to tone down (les couleurs, la lumière); to muffle, to damp, to deaden (un son). ‖ Mus. To mute (un violon). ‖ Gramm. To unvoice (une consonne).
— v. pr. **S'assourdir,** to grow duller (ou) fainter, to fade (couleur, son); to decrease (douleur). ‖ Gramm. To become unvoiced (consonne).
assourdissant, ante [-disɑ̃, ɑ̃ːt] adj. Deafening.
assourdissement [-dismɑ̃] m. Deafening. ‖ Muffling, damping, deadening (d'une couleur, d'un son). ‖ Gramm. Unvoicing (d'une consonne). ‖ Méd. Dullness of hearing.
assouvir [asuviːr] v. tr. (2). To satiate, to sate, to satisfy (sa faim); to slake, to quench (sa soif). ‖ Comm. To glut (le marché). ‖ Fig. To satisfy, to gratify, to slake (ses passions); assouvir sa haine, to satisfy one's hatred to the full.
— v. pr. **S'assouvir,** to sate (ou) to satiate oneself; to gratify oneself; to become surfeited (ou) sated (de, with).
assouvissement [-vismɑ̃] m. Satiation, sating, satisfying (action). ‖ Satiety.
assuétude [asɥetyd] f. Méd. Dependency; qui crée une assuétude, habit-forming.
assujetti, ie [asyʒeti] adj. Fixed, fastened (attaché). ‖ Subject, liable, tied down (à, to).
assujettir [-tiːr] v. tr. (2). To fix, to fasten (fixer). ‖ To subdue, to subjugate. (V. opprimer.) ‖ To subject, to bind, to compel, to force, to make liable (à, to) [forcer]. ‖ To tie down, to absorb (absorber). ‖ Fig. To curb (ses passions).
— v. pr. **S'assujettir,** to submit (ou) to subject oneself; to bend, to yield (à, to).
assujettissant, ante [-tisɑ̃, ɑ̃ːt] adj. Absorbing, tying, demanding (travail).
assujettissement [-tismɑ̃] m. Fixing, fastening (action). ‖ Subjection, dependence, constraint (contrainte). ‖ Fin. Assujettissement à l'impôt, tax liability.
assumer [asyme] v. tr. (1). To assume, to take upon oneself.
assurable [asyrabl] adj. Insurable, assurable.
assurance [-rɑ̃ːs] f. Assurance (v. certitude); avoir la parfaite assurance, to be perfectly sure. ‖ Assurance; self-confidence, self-assurance, self-reliance (confiance en soi); manquer d'assurance, to lack confidence. ‖ Cheek, effrontery. (V. aplomb.) ‖ Assurance, safety (sécurité). ‖ Assurance, proof, ground; pledge, guarantee (garantie). ‖ Assurance (v. affirmation, promesse); donner l'assurance formelle, to give a solemn assurance, to promise solemnly. ‖ Jur. Assurance. ‖ Insurance; assurance contre les accidents, personal accident insurance; assurance contre les accidents du travail, employer's liability insurance, U. S. workmen's compensation insurance; assurance contre l'incendie, fire-insurance; assurance maladie, sickness insurance; assurance maritime, marine insurance; assurances sociales, social security scheme; assurance sur la vie, life-assurance; assurance vieillesse, old age insurance; passer un contrat d'assurance, to effect (ou) to take out an insurance policy.
assuré, ée [-re] adj. Confident (air); firm (démarche); steady (main, voix); bold (regard, parole); guaranteed (service); secure (situation, travail); certain, sure (succès); assuré du succès, confident of success; une liaison assurée par, a connection insured by; mal assuré, unsteady (pas); rien d'assuré, nothing fixed. ‖ Insured (biens); assured (vie).
— s. Jur. Insurant, policy-holder; assuré social, person paying national insurance contributions.
assurément [-remɑ̃] adv. Assuredly.
assurer [-re] v. tr. (1). To fix, to fasten, to secure, to make steady (fixer, stabiliser). ‖ To assure, to

certify, to warrant, to vouch for. (V. affirmer.) ‖ To guarantee, to ensure (à, to) [garantir]; assurer le service, to ensure good service. ‖ To insure (qqch., qqn); to assure (la vie de qqn).
— v. pr. **S'assurer,** to ascertain, to make certain, to assure, to see, to satisfy oneself (que, that); to make sure, to assure oneself (de, of). ‖ S'assurer l'accès à, to obtain access to. ‖ S'assurer de la personne de qqn, to seize s.o., to apprehend s.o.; s'assurer de la protection de qqn, to secure s.o's protection. ‖ Jur. To insure oneself; s'assurer sur la vie, to have one's life assured; s'assurer contre, to insure (ou) to get insured against.
assureur [-rœːr] m. Jur. Insurer, insurance-broker; assureur maritime, underwriter.
assyrien, enne [asirjɛ̃, ɛn] adj., s. Géogr. Assyrian.
assyriologie [-rjɔlɔʒi] f. Assyriology.
astate [astat] m. Chim. Astatine.
astatique [astatik] adj. Phys. Astatic.
aster [astɛːr] m. Bot. Aster, Michaelmas daisy. ‖ Méd. Aster (d'une cellule).
astérie [asteri] f. Zool. Starfish.
astérisque [-risk] m. Asterisk.
astéroïde [-rɔid] m. Astron. Asteroid.
asthénie [asteni] f. Méd. Asthenia.
asthénique [-nik] adj., s. Méd. Asthenic.
asthmatique [asmatik] adj., s. Méd. Asthmatic.
asthme [asm] m. Méd. Asthma.
asticot [astiko] m. Maggot (ver); cheese-hopper (fam.) [du fromage]; gentle (pour la pêche). ‖ Fam. Chap, guy, johnny, cove.
asticoter [-kɔte] v. tr. (1). Fam. To harass, to tease; to nag.
astigmate [astigmat] adj. Méd. Astigmatic.
astigmatisme [-tism] m. Méd. Astigmatism.
astiquage [astika:ʒ] m. Polishing, furbishing.
astiquer [-ke] v. tr. (1). To polish; to scour. (V. briquer, fourbir.)
— v. pr. **S'astiquer,** Fam. To titivate.
astragale [astragal] m. Archit., Milit., Astragal. ‖ Bot., Méd. Astragalus.
astrakan [astrakɑ̃] m. Zool., Comm. Astrakhan.
astral, ale [astral] adj. Astron. Astral.
astre [astr] m. Astron. Star, heavenly body; l'astre du jour, the sun. ‖ Fig. Star.
astreignant, ante [astrɛɲɑ̃, ɑ̃ːt] adj. Exacting. ‖ Tying; absorbing (travail).
astreindre [astrɛ̃ːdr] v. tr. (59). To compel, to force, to subject, to tie down (à, to). [V. obliger.]
— v. pr. **S'astreindre,** to force oneself, to tie oneself down; to bind oneself.
astreint, einte [astrɛ̃, ɛ̃ːt] adj. Bound; compelled (obligé); subjected (soumis) [à, to]. ‖ Liable (assujetti) [à, to].
astreinte [astrɛ̃ːt] f. Jur. Compulsion; fine.
astrictif, ive [astriktif, iːv] adj. Méd. Astrictive.
astriction [-jɔ̃] f. Astriction.
astringence [astrɛ̃ʒɑ̃ːs] f. Astringency.
astringent, ente [-ʒɑ̃, ɑ̃ːt] adj., m. Astringent. ‖ Méd. Styptic (anti-hémorragique).
astrobiologie [astrɔbjɔlɔʒi] f. Astrobiology.
astrolabe [astrɔlab] m. Astron. Astrolabe.
astrologie [-lɔʒi] f. Astron. Astrology.
astrologique [-lɔʒik] adj. Astrological.
astrologue [-lɔg] s. Astrologer.
astronaute [-noːt] m. Astronaut.
astronautique [-notik] f. Astronautics.
astronef [-nɛf] m. Aviat. Space-ship.
astronome [-nɔm] m. Astronomer.
astronomie [-nɔmi] f. Astronomy.
astronomique [-nɔmik] adj. Astronomical (année, jour, unité). ‖ Fam. Astronomical (prix).
astronomiquement [-nɔmikmɑ̃] adv. Astronomically.
astrophysicien [-fizisjɛ̃] m. Astrophysicist.
astrophysique [-fizik] f. Astrophysics.

astuce [astys] f. Astuteness, wiliness; foxiness (ruse). ‖ Wile; trick (tour). ‖ FAM. Pun; witticism (plaisanterie).

astucieusement [-sjøzmɑ̃] adv. Astutely, cunningly, artfully.

astucieux, euse [-sjø, ø:z] adj. Astute; wily (flatterie); foxy, cunning, artful (personne); cunning (plan).

asymétrie [asimetri] f. Asymmetry.

asymétrique [-trik] adj. Asymmetrical, unsymmetrical.

asymptote [asɛ̃ptɔt] f. MATH. Asymptote.

asymptotique [-tɔtik] adj. MATH. Asymptotic, asymptotical.

asynchrone [asɛ̃kron] adj. PHYS. Asynchronous.

asyndète [asɛ̃dɛt] f. GRAMM. Asyndeton.

ataraxie [ataraksi] f. PHILOS., MÉD. Ataraxia.

atavique [atavik] adj. Atavistic.

atavisme [-vism] m. Atavism.

ataxie [ataksi] f. MÉD. Ataxy, ataxia.

ataxique [-sik] adj. MÉD. Ataxic.
— s. Person suffering from ataxia.

atèle [atɛl] m. ZOOL. Spider-monkey.

atelier [atəlje] m. Studio, atelier (d'artiste); workroom (de couture); workshop (d'ouvriers); studio (de photographe); *atelier d'ajustage, d'assemblage, de réparations,* fitting, assembly, repair shop. ‖ MILIT. Working party; *atelier d'artificiers,* military workshop. ‖ ARTS. School (école); students (élèves).

atemporel, elle [atɑ̃pɔrɛl] adj. Timeless.

atermoiement [atɛrmwamɑ̃] m. Delay, procrastination, putting off. ‖ JUR. Deferment of payment; arrangement with creditors.

atermoyer [-je] v. tr. (9a). To put off, defer.
— v. intr. To delay; to procrastinate; to dally.
— v. pr. **S'atermoyer,** to obtain extra time (*avec, from*).

athée [ate] s. Atheist, nullifidian.
— adj. Atheistic.

athéisme [-ism] m. Atheism.

athénée [atene] m. Athenaeum.

Athènes [atɛ:n] f. GÉOGR. Athens.

athénien, enne [atenjɛ̃, ɛn] adj., s. GÉOGR. Athenian.

athermane [atɛrman] adj. PHYS. Athermanous.

athlète [atlɛt] m. SPORTS. Athlete.

athlétique [atletik] adj. SPORTS. Athletic.

athlétisme [-tism] m. SPORTS. Athleticism (qualité); athletics (sport).

atlante [atlɑ̃:t] m. ARCHIT. Telamon. ‖ GÉOGR. Atlantean.

atlantique [atlɑ̃tik] adj., m. GÉOGR. Atlantic.

atlas [atla:s] m. GÉOGR., MÉD. Atlas.

atmosphère [atmosfɛ:r] f. PHYS., FIG. Atmosphere.

atmosphérique [-ferik] adj. Atmospheric.

atoll [atɔl] m. GÉOGR. Atoll, coral island.

atome [ato:m] m. CHIM., PHYS. Atom. ‖ FIG. Atom, particle, jot.

atomicité [atɔmisite] f. CHIM. Atomicity.

atomique [-mik] adj. Atomic (énergie, nombre, poids, théorie, volume); *bombe atomique,* atomic (ou) atom bomb; *attaquer, détruire à la bombe atomique,* to atom-bomb.

atomisation [-mizasjɔ̃] f. Atomization (destruction, pulvérisation). ‖ Atomization, split (éclatement d'un groupe, d'un tout).

atomiser [-mize] v. tr. (1). To atomize, to pulverize (pulvériser). ‖ To atomize (détruire).

atomiseur [-mizœ:r] m. Atomizer.

atomisme [-mism] m. PHILOS. Atomism.

atomiste [-mist] m. PHILOS. Atomist. ‖ PHYS. Atomic scientist (ou) physicist.

atomistique [-mistik] adj. PHILOS. Atomistic.
— f. PHYS. Atomic theory.

atonal, ale [atɔnal] adj. MUS. Atonal.

atonalité [atɔnalite] f. MUS. Atonality.

atone [aton] adj. GRAMM. Unaccented, unstressed, atonic. ‖ MÉD. Atonic. ‖ FIG. Lustreless; lifeless; vacant, lack-lustre (regard); dull, drab (vie); flat, colourless (voix).

atonie [atɔni] f. MÉD. Atony. (V. APATHIE.)

atonique [-nik] adj. MÉD. Atonic.

atour [atu:r] m. Attire, finery, apparel; *dans ses plus beaux atours,* dressed up to the nines, dressed fit to kill, in full fig (fam.).

atout [atu] m. Trump (au jeu); *jouer atout,* to play trumps (ou) a trump; *prendre avec un atout,* to trump. ‖ FIG. *Avoir tous les atouts en main,* to hold all the winning cards; *un atout dans sa manche (ou) en réserve,* an ace up one's sleeve; *un gros atout,* a great asset. ‖ FAM. Knock, blow, smash (coup).

A. T. P. [atepe] abrév. de *Adénosine triphosphate,* ATP, adenosine triphosphate.

atrabilaire [atrabilɛ:r] adj. Atrabilious.

âtre [a:tr] m. Hearth, fireplace.

atroce [atrɔs] adj. Atrocious (en général); heinous (crime); abominable, atrocious (goût, odeur); exquisite, agonizing (souffrance); monstrous (vice).

atrocement [-smɑ̃] adv. Atrociously, outrageously. ‖ Dreadfully.

atrocité [-site] f. Atrocity; atrociousness. ‖ FAM. Atrocity, shameful (ou) tasteless thing.

atrophie [atrɔfi] f. MÉD. Atrophy; *dû à l'atrophie,* atrophic. ‖ FIG. Withering.

atrophié, ée [-fje] adj. MÉD., FIG. Atrophied.

atrophier [-fje] v. tr. (1). MÉD., FIG. To atrophy.
— v. pr. **S'atrophier,** to atrophy (pr. et fig.).

atropine [atrɔpin] f. CHIM., MÉD. Atropine.

attabler (s') [satable] v. pr. (1). To sit down to table; to settle down at the table.

attachant, ante [ataʃɑ̃, ɑ̃:t] adj. Attractive; fascinating. ‖ Arresting, interesting (livre).

attache [ataʃ] f. Fastening, tie. ‖ Cord, guy (corde); chain, leash (laisse); rope, tether (longe); clip, paper-clip, paper-fastener (trombone); *à l'attache,* on a leash. (chien); *piquet d'attache,* tethering-stake. ‖ TECHN. Binder; coupling; connection, brace. ‖ MÉD. Joint; ankle (cheville); wrist (poignet). ‖ Pl. FIG. Ties, links; connection; attachment; *sans attaches,* unconnected, unattached. ‖ FIG. *Être toujours à l'attache,* to be tied down to one's work, to be always at it.

attaché, ée [-ʃe] adj. Fastened, tied-up, bound, chained (lié). ‖ Attached, bound, devoted (à, to) [qqn]. ‖ Tenacious (à, of); wedded (à, to) [qqch.]; *être attaché à,* to adhere to, to cling to. ‖ Incident, attaching (à, to) [une fonction].
— m. Attaché. ‖ **Attaché-case,** m. Attaché case, brief-case.

attachement [-ʃmɑ̃] m. Attachment. (V. AFFECTION.) ‖ Adherence, devotedness, adhesion.

attacher [-ʃe] v. tr. (1). To attach; to fasten; to tie (lier). ‖ To rope (avec une corde); to tether (avec une longe). ‖ To chain; to tie up (un chien). ‖ FIG. To attach (associer); to attract (attirer); to affix, to assign, to attribute (attribuer); to link, to bind (unir); *attacher de l'importance à,* to attach importance to; *attacher du prix à,* to set value upon; *attacher un sens à,* to attach (ou) to attribute a meaning to.
— v. intr. CULIN. To stick, to catch.
— v. pr. **S'attacher,** to fasten (se boutonner); to be tied (se lier); to stick (se coller); to cling (se cramponner) [à, to]; *s'attacher aux pas de,* to follow, to dog. ‖ FIG. *S'attacher à,* to stick to (adhérer à); to become attached (ou) devoted to (aimer); to attach to, to belong to, to appertain to (appartenir à); to apply oneself to, to make a point of, to aim at (s'appliquer à); to pay particular attention to, to cling to, to stick to (s'intéresser à).

attaquable [atakabl] adj. Open to attack; attackable. ‖ Assailable, challengeable, contestable (décision, testament); doubtful, questionable (réputation).

attaquant, ante [-kɑ̃, ɑ̃:t] adj. Attacking.
— s. Assailant, attacker.

attaque [atak] f. MILIT. Attack, onslaught. (V. ASSAUT.) ‖ AVIAT. *Attaque aérienne,* air raid (ou) attack. ‖ MÉD. Attack (de goutte, de grippe); *attaque d'apoplexie,* apoplectic stroke. ‖ JUR. Attack, assault. ‖ TECHN. Drive. ‖ MUS. Attack. ‖ FIG. Attack, thrust, criticism. ‖ FAM. *Etre d'attaque,* to feel fit, to be in fine condition.

attaquer [-ke] v. tr. (1). To attack, to assault. (V. ASSAILLIR.) ‖ To attack, to erode, to eat, to corrode (ronger); to wear away (user). ‖ To attack, to go to work on, to begin upon, to tackle, to start on (entamer). ‖ MÉD. To attack, to affect. ‖ JUR. To attack, to contest (un acte); to prosecute, to sue, to bring an action against (qqn en justice). ‖ MUS. To attack, to strike up. ‖ TECHN. To drive, to engage with. ‖ SPORTS. To address (la balle). ‖ FIG. To attack, to criticize, to go for (qqn); to impugn, to impeach (la véracité).
— v. intr. To attack.
— v. pr. **S'attaquer à,** to assail, to assault, to attack. ‖ FIG. To attack, to tackle, to grapple with (une difficulté); *s'attaquer à une tâche,* to get down to a task (ou) U. S. to a job.

attardé, ée [atarde] adj. Belated. ‖ FIG. Benighted; behind the times (retardataire); backward, mentally retarded (arriéré).

attarder v. tr. (1). To delay; to keep late.
— v. pr. **S'attarder,** to tarry, to stay up late; to linger, to dawdle (flâner); to dally (lambiner); to loiter (traîner). ‖ To dally, to linger (à, sur, over).

atteindre [-atɛ̃:dr] v. tr. (59). To reach, to attain. ‖ To strike, to hit (frapper, toucher). ‖ MILIT. To overtake. ‖ COMM. To rise to (un chiffre); to reach (un prix); to fetch, U. S. to bring (un prix aux enchères). ‖ MÉD. To affect; to impair; *être atteint de,* to suffer from. ‖ TECHN. To attain (une vitesse). ‖ FIG. To reach, to arrive at (un âge); to accomplish, to achieve, to effect, to attain (un but); to reach (un sommet); *atteindre qqn dans son honneur,* to wound s.o. in his honour.
— v. intr. *Atteindre à,* to reach. ‖ FIG. To attain.

atteinte [atɛ̃:t] f. Reach; *hors d'atteinte,* beyond (ou) out of reach. ‖ Contact, touch (contact); blow, stroke, shock (coup). ‖ MÉD. Attack, fit (de, of); inroads (à, on). ‖ FIG. Outrage, harm, damage; *porter atteinte à,* to injure, to impair, to violate, to infringe, to damage.

attelage [atla:ʒ] m. Harnessing (action). ‖ Yoke (de bœufs); team (de chevaux); *attelage à quatre,* four-in-hand; *attelage en flèche,* tandem team. ‖ Turn-out (équipage). ‖ TECHN. Coupling.

atteler [atle] v. tr. (8a). To yoke (des bœufs); to harness (des chevaux); to put horses to (une voiture); *atteler ensemble,* to team up. ‖ TECHN. To couple (des wagons). ‖ FIG. *Etre attelé à,* to be harnessed (ou) tied to.
— v. pr. **S'atteler,** to harness oneself (prop.). ‖ FAM. *S'atteler à,* to get down (ou) to settle down to, to tackle (ou) to buckle to.

attelle [atɛl] f. Hame (harnais). ‖ MÉD. Splint.

attenant, ante [atnɑ̃, ɑ̃:t] adj. Adjoining; abutting, bordering (à, on). [V. ADJACENT.]

attendre [atɑ̃:dr] v. tr. (4). To await, to wait for; *aller attendre,* to go to (ou) and meet; *attendre avec impatience,* to long for; *faire attendre qqch. à qqn,* to keep s.o. waiting for sth.; *la réponse ne se fit pas attendre,* the answer was not long in coming; *elle se fait attendre,* she is late. ‖ To wait, to stay, to stop; *attendez que j'ouvre la porte,* wait till I open the door, wait for me to open the door; *elle n'attend pas la réponse,* she

does not pause for an answer; *il attend son heure,* he is biding his time. ‖ To expect, to look for; *on l'attend d'une minute à l'autre,* he is expected any minute; *qu'attendre d'un pareil froussard?,* what can you expect from such a cur? ‖ To await, to be in store for (être réservé à); *un bel avenir vous attend,* you have a fine future before you; *le dîner nous attend,* dinner is ready. ‖ **En attendant,** meanwhile, meantime, in the meantime; *en attendant le dîner,* till dinner-time; while waiting for dinner; *en attendant qu'il revienne,* till he comes back; pending his return.
— v. intr. To be delayed; *cela peut attendre,* it can be delayed, it can wait, it can lie over; there is no need for haste.
— v. pr. **S'attendre,** to look out, to be prepared (à, for); *s'attendre à,* to expect; to anticipate; to look forward to; *il ne s'attendait pas à la voir, à ce qu'elle le vît,* he did not expect to see her, her to see him; *il faut vous attendre à tout,* you must be prepared for the worst, you must expect anything to happen.

attendri, ie [atɑ̃dri] adj. Compassionate; melting.

attendrir [atɑ̃dri:r] v. tr. (2). To make tender. ‖ FIG. To touch, to melt, to mollify.
— v. pr. **S'attendrir,** to become tender. ‖ FIG. To soften, to be moved.

attendrissant, ante [-drisɑ̃, ɑ̃:t] adj. Moving, affecting, touching.

attendrissement [-drismɑ̃] m. Pity; emotion.

attendrisseur [-drisœ:r] m. Meat tenderizer.

attendu [atɑ̃dy] prép. Considering, seeing, owing to, because of, on account of.
— loc. conj. **Attendu que,** considering that, seeing that. ‖ JUR. Whereas, inasmuch as.
— m. JUR. Argument, item. ‖ Pl. « Whereas » clauses, reasons adduced.
— p.p. V. ATTENDRE.

attenir [atni:r] v. intr. (2). To adjoin; to be adjacent (ou) contiguous, to join on (à, to); to border (à, on).

attentat [atɑ̃ta] m. Attempt (contre, upon) [la vie]; outrage; offence; *attentat à l'ordre public,* riot; *attentat à la pudeur,* indecent assault (ou) exposure; *attentat contre la sûreté de l'Etat,* treason, felony.

attentatoire [-twa:r] adj. JUR. Damaging, prejudicial, detrimental (à, to).

attente [atɑ̃:t] f. Wait, waiting; *salle d'attente,* waiting-room. ‖ Expectation; *contre toute attente,* contrary to all expectations; *dans l'attente de,* waiting for, awaiting, looking forward to.

attenter [atɑ̃te] v. intr. (1). To make an attempt (à, on, against); *attenter à ses jours,* to attempt suicide.

attentif, ive [atɑ̃tif, i:ve] adj. Attentive (à, to); heedful, regardful, mindful (à, of). ‖ Careful, close (examen); thoughtful (personne); earnest, watchful (regard). ‖ Attentive, considerate, courteous (prévenant).

attention [-sjɔ̃] f. Attention, observing; heed, notice; *avec attention,* attentively; *attirer l'attention sur,* to attract notice to; to call (ou) to draw attention to; *défaut d'attention,* inattention, inattentiveness; *faire attention à,* to pay attention to; to mind; to take heed of; to beware of. ‖ Thoughtfulness; attentions; care (soins).
— interj. Look out!, take care!, caution!; *attention aux marches,* mind the step.

attentionné, ée [-sjɔne] adj. Attentive, considerate.

attentisme [-tism] m. Wait-and-see (ou) sitting-on-the-fence policy.

attentiste [-tist] adj. *Politique attentiste,* waiting (ou) « wait-and-see » policy.
— n. One who practises a policy of « wait and see ».

attentivement [-tivmã] adv. Attentively; mindfully; assiduously.

atténuant, ante [atenɥ$\tilde{a}$, $\tilde{a}$:t] adj. Extenuatory, palliating. ‖ JUR. Extenuating, mitigating (circonstances).

atténuation [-nɥasjɔ̃] f. Subduing (d'une couleur). ‖ Attenuation (d'une affirmation); lessening, abatement (d'une douleur); toning down (des faits); extenuation, palliation (d'une faute); mitigation (d'une peine). ‖ MÉD. Attenuation.

atténuer [-nɥe] v. tr. (1). To subdue (une couleur, une lumière); to soften (un son). ‖ To gloss over (les défauts); to abate, to alleviate (la douleur); to tone down (des faits); to palliate, to extenuate (une faute) to mitigate (une peine); to reduce (les risques); *atténuer ses exigences concernant,* to soft-pedal one's demands regarding. — v. pr. **S'atténuer,** to soften, to decrease, to die down (bruit); to lessen (douleur); to be palliated (faute).

atterrage [atɛra:ʒ] m. NAUT. Approach; shoaling (action); landing conditions (conditions); landing place (lieu). ‖ Landfall (atterrissage).

atterrer [-re] v. tr. (1). To astound, to stun; *être atterré,* to be dismayed (ou) thunderstruck (ou) bowled over.

atterrir [-ri:r] v. intr. (2). AVIAT. To alight, to land (avion); to ground (ballon); *atterrir en vol plané,* to glide down to land; *atterrir en catastrophe,* to crash-land. ‖ NAUT. To make a landfall. ‖ FAM. To land-up.

atterrissage [-risa:ʒ] m. AVIAT. Alighting, landing; *atterrissage forcé,* forced (ou) emergency landing; *baisser, relever le train d'atterrissage,* to lower, to raise the under-carriage. ‖ NAUT Landfall; grounding.

atterrisseur [-risœ:r] m. AVIAT. Landing gear, undercarriage.

attestation [atɛstasjɔ̃] f. Attestation (en général); certificate, character, testimonial (certificat); affidavit (déposition). ‖ Testimony, attestation (témoignage).

attester [-te] v. tr. (1). To attest, to certify (certifier); to bear witness to, to testify to, to vouch for (témoigner). ‖ To call to witness (prendre à témoin).

attiédir [atjedi:r] v. tr. (2). To cool (le chaud); to warm (le froid). ‖ FIG. To damp (l'ardeur). — v. pr. **S'attiédir,** to become lukewarm. ‖ FIG. To cool off (ou) down.

attiédissement [-dismã] m. Cooling, cooling off.

attifement [atifmã] m. Rigging out (action); get-up, rig-out (vêtement).

attifer [-fe] v. tr. (1). To deck out; to rig out (v. ACCOUTRER); to spruce up, to titivate (parer). — v. pr. **S'attifer,** to deck oneself out (s'endimancher); to titivate oneself (se parer).

attiger [atiʒe] v. intr. (7). FAM. To come it strong, to go a bit too far. (V. EXAGÉRER.)

attique [attik] adj., m. Attic.

attique m. ARCHIT. Attic.

attirail [atira:j] m. Finery, pomp, display. ‖ Paraphernalia, stuff (péj.). ‖ TECHN. Apparatus; implements; gear; outfit, tackle.

attirance [atirã:s] f. Attraction (vers, to). ‖ Fascination, allurement, lure.

attirant, ante [-rã, ã:t] adj. Attractive; inviting.

attirer [-re] v. tr. (1). To draw (vers, towards). ‖ To bring down, to draw down (sur, on). ‖ FIG. To decoy, to entice, to lure (allécher); to attract, to allure, to win (séduire). — v. pr. **S'attirer,** to bring upon oneself.

attiser [atize] v. tr. (1). To poke, to stir (le feu). ‖ FIG. To arouse, to rouse, to stir up (la haine, les passions). [V. EXCITER.]

attisoir [-zwa:r] m. Poker.

attitré, ée [atitre] adj. Appointed, regular, recognized. ‖ COMM. *Fournisseur attitré de,* purveyor by appointment to, regular supplier of.

attitrer v. tr. (1). To accredit, to appoint.

attitude [atityd] f. Attitude (pr. et fig.) [*envers,* towards].

attouchement [atuʃmã] m. Touch; *guérir par attouchement,* to touch for.

attractif, ive [atraktif, iv] adj. PHYS. Attractive; gravitational.

attraction [-sjɔ̃] f. PHYS. Attraction; *attraction universelle,* gravitation, attraction of gravity. ‖ FIG. Attraction, attractiveness. ‖ Pl. Attractions; *parc des attractions,* amusement park, fun fair.

attrait [atrɛ] m. Attraction (v. ATTIRANCE); charm (v. CHARME, SÉDUCTION); *plein d'attraits,* attractive. ‖ Enticement, lure (péj.). ‖ Inclination, liking (*pour,* for).

attrapade [atrapad] f. Talking-to, telling-off, rebuke, row.

attrape [atrap] f. Snare (piège). ‖ NAUT. Lifeline. ‖ FAM. Take-in, trick, catch, joke. ‖ **Attrape-mouches,** m. invar. Fly-paper. ‖ **Attrape-nigaud,** m. Booby-trap.

attraper [-pe] v. tr. (1). To catch, to get (en général). ‖ To snare, to trap (prendre au piège); to pick up (recueillir); to take, to seize, to catch hold of (saisir); *attraper la ressemblance,* to catch the likeness. ‖ To come on, to take by surprise (surprendre); ‖ To take in, to have on (mystifier, tromper); *il s'est fait attraper,* he has been had, he got bitten. ‖ MÉD. To catch (une maladie). ‖ FAM. To slate, to come down on, to drop on (enguirlander); *se faire attraper,* to get a good talking-to, to catch it (*par,* from). ‖ POP. To get, to catch; *attrape!,* take that!; *en attraper pour cinq ans,* to get five years. — v. pr. **S'attraper,** to stick, to cling (s'accrocher); to be acquired (s'acquérir); to stick (coller). ‖ MÉD. To be infectious (ou) catching. ‖ FAM. To bicker, to wrangle (avec, with).

attrayant, ante [atrɛjã, ã:t] adj. Attractive; engaging. (V. ATTIRANT.)

attribuable [atribyabl] adj. Ascribable, allotable, attribuable. ‖ Imputable, traceable (à, to).

attribuer [-bɥe] v. tr. (1). To attribute. (V. ALLOUER, DÉCERNER.) ‖ *Attribuer à,* to ascribe to, to attribute to (un acte, une œuvre, un résultat); to put down to, to refer to, to trace to (un effet); to impute to (une faute); to confer on, to assign to, to award to, to allot to, to apportion to (une part); to attach to (des privilèges); *attribuer une qualité à qqn,* to credit s.o. with a quality. — v. pr. **S'attribuer,** to appropriate; to usurp.

attribut [-by] m. Attribute (caractéristique, symbole). ‖ GRAMM. Predicate. ‖ MILIT. Badge.

attributaire [-bytɛ:r] s. FIN. Allottee. ‖ JUR. Assignee.

attributif, ive [bytif, i:v] adj. Attributive. ‖ GRAMM. Predicative. ‖ JUR. Of assignment.

attribution [-bysjɔ̃] f. Attribution (action); allotment, allocation, assignment; ascription. ‖ Attributions, duties (v. FONCTIONS); competence; *rentrer dans le cadre des attributions de qqn,* to lie within the scope of s.o.'s duties. ‖ GRAMM. Predication.

attristant, ante [atristã, ã:t] adj. Saddening.

attristé, e [-te] adj. Sad, sorrowful, dejected.

attrister [-te] v. tr. (1). To darken, to cast a gloom on, to overcloud (obscurcir). ‖ To sadden. — v. pr. **S'attrister,** to become sad; to mope, to grow despondent, to feel blue (personne). ‖ To cloud over; to lour (ciel, visage).

attrition [atrisjɔ̃] f. ECCLÉS., TECHN. Attrition.

attroupement [atrupmã] m. Mob (foule); unlawful (ou) riotous assembly. (V. RASSEMBLEMENT.) ‖ Gathering (assemblage).

attrouper [-pe] v. tr. (1). To gather.
— v. pr. S'attrouper, to crowd; to flock together.
atypique [atipik] adj. Atypical.
au [o] art. contract. V. à, le.
aubade [obad] f. Aubade, dawn song. || Charivari, noisy demonstration.
aubaine [obɛn] f. Godsend, windfall, stroke of good luck. (V. chance.)
aube [o:b] f. Dawn, daybreak. || Ecclés. Alb.
aube [o:b] f. Naut. Paddle. || Techn. Vane, blade.
aubépine [obepin] f. Bot. Hawthorn (arbre); may (fleurs).
auberge [obɛrʒ] f. Inn, tavern; auberge de la jeunesse, youth hostel.
aubergine [obɛrʒi:n] f. Bot. Aubergine, brinjal; U. S. egg-plant.
— adj. Modena (couleur).
aubergiste [obɛrʒist] m. Innkeeper; landlord, host.
— f. Landlady, hostess.
aubier [obje] m. Bot. Alburnum, sap-wood.
auburn [oboœ:rn] adj. Auburn.
aucuba [okyba] m. Bot. Aucuba.
aucun [okœ̃] adj. Any (dans une proposition affirmative ou interrogative); a-t-elle aucun espoir de revenir?, has she any hope of coming back?; sans aucune exception, without any exception. || No, not any (dans une proposition négative); il n'a aucun don, he has no gift; ne prononcez aucun nom, don't mention any names.
— pron. Any (dans une proposition dubitative); je me demande si aucun de nous réussira, I wonder whether any of us will succeed. || Not any, none (dans une proposition négative); je n'aime aucun d'eux, I don't like any of them; aucun n'a travaillé, none of them worked. || No one, no man, nobody (personne); aucun n'est content de son sort, nobody is content with his lot. || Loc. D'aucuns, some, some people.
aucunement [okynmɑ̃] adv. At all, in any way, in any degree (dans une proposition dubitative ou interrogative). || Not at all, in no way, in no degree, not in any way, by no means, in no wise (dans une proposition négative).
audace [odas] f. Boldness; daring; audacity. (V. hardiesse.) || Front, cheek, face (v. effronterie); presumption; avoir l'audace de, to dare to; payer d'audace, to brazen it out, to face the music.
audacieusement [-sjøzmɑ̃] adv. Audaciously, boldly, daringly.
audacieux, euse [-sjø, ø:z] adj. Audacious. (V. hardi.) || Cheeky, audacious. (V. effronté.)
au-deçà [odəsa] adv. On this side.
au-dedans [odədɑ̃] adj. Within, inside.
— loc. prép. Au-dedans de, within, inside.
au-dehors [odəor] adv. Outside. || Abroad (à l'étranger).
au-delà [odəla] adv. More, still more (davantage); on the other side (en face); longer (plus longtemps); beyond (plus loin).
— loc. prép. Au-delà de, beyond, over. || Fig. Beyond, above, past; au-delà de ses espérances, beyond his hopes; au-delà du tolérable, past endurance, beyond bearing.
— m. Beyond; de l'au-delà, from beyond the grave.
au-dessous [odəsu] adv. Below; underneath; l'étage au-dessous, the floor below; trois ans et au-dessous, three years and under; pourri au-dessous, rotten underneath.
— loc. prép. Au-dessous de, below, lower down than; beneath; underneath; au-dessous de la rivière, under the river; au-dessous de vingt ans, under twenty; au-dessous de lui, beneath him; au-dessous de tout, beneath contempt; au-dessous de sa tâche, unequal to his task; au-dessous

de la moyenne, below average (mesure, qualité, quantité); below the pass-mark (note).
au-dessus [odəsy] adv. Above; over; overhead; upwards; une glace au-dessus, a mirror above; vingt ans et au-dessus, twenty years and upwards.
— loc. prép. Au-dessus de, above; higher up than; over; au-dessus de la mer, de la vallée, over the sea, the valley; au-dessus du rang de lieutenant, above the rank of lieutenant; au-dessus de vingt ans, over twenty; au-dessus de zéro, above zero; il est au-dessus de ça, he is above it.
au-devant [odəvɑ̃] adv. Aller au-devant, to go to meet sth.; Fig. to anticipate sth.
— loc. prép. Aller au-devant de, to go to meet (qqch., qqn). || Fig. To anticipate (désirs); to court, to head for (échec); to forestall (objections, difficultés).
audibilité [odibilite] f. Audibility.
audible [odibl] adj. Audible.
audience [odjɑ̃:s] f. Audience; hearing; solliciter une audience, to request an audience. || Jur. Sitting, session; en audience publique, in open court; l'audience est reprise, the case is resumed; tenir audience, to hold a court.
audiencier [-sje] adj., m. Jur. Usher, court-crier.
audiofréquence [odjofrekɑ̃:s] f. Audiofrequency.
audiomètre [odjomɛtr] m. Audiometer.
audiovisuel, elle [odjovizɥɛl] adj. Audiovisual.
— m. Audio-visual techniques (ou) methods, television and films.
auditeur, trice [oditœ:r, tris] s. Listener; hearer; les auditeurs, the audience. || Jur. Auditor; auditeur au Conseil d'Etat, probationary member of the Council of State; auditeur à la Cour des Comptes, probationary auditor to the Exchequer and Audit Office.
auditif, ive [-tif, i:v] adj. Auditory.
audition [-sjɔ̃] f. Audition. || Jur. Hearing, examination (de témoins); nouvelle audition, re-hearing. || Fin. Auditing, audition (de comptes). || Mus. Performance, recital (d'un morceau); audition (d'un musicien).
auditionner [-sjɔne] v. tr. (1). Théâtr., Mus. To audition (faire passer une audition).
— v. intr. Théâtr., Mus. To audition (passer en audition).
auditoire [-twa:r] m. Audience, attendance, hearers. || Jur. Court-room.
auditorium [-tɔrjɔm] m. Auditorium, auditory.
auge [o:ʒ] f. Watering (ou) drinking trough (abreuvoir); trough, feeding trough, manger (mangeoire); || Techn. Trough (de maçon); bucket (de roue à eau).
auget [oʒe] m. Seed-trough, water-trough (de cage à oiseaux). || Milit. Feeder; cartridge carrier; feed plate; rear casing. || Techn. Hopper (de moulin); bucket (de roue à eau).
augment [ogmɑ̃] m. Gramm. Augment.
augmentatif, ive [-tatif, i:v] adj., m. Gramm. Augmentative.
augmentation [-tasjɔ̃] f. Augmentation; increase, rise (de prix, de valeur); augmentation de salaire, rise (ou) U. S. raise in wages (ou) in pay. || Increment (accroissement). || Single over (au tricot). || Fin. Increase (de capital).
augmenter [-te] v. tr. (1). To enlarge (ses affaires, une édition); to increase (ses dettes, son poids, la vitesse). || Fin. To raise, to put up (le prix); to augment (ses revenus). || Fig. To increase (les difficultés); to aggravate (la douleur); to heighten (l'intérêt).
— v. intr. To augment; to increase. || To make one (ou) a stitch (au tricot). || Fin. To grow dearer, to mount up (prix).
augural, ale [ogyral] adj. Augural.

augure [ogy:r] m. Augur (devin). ‖ Augury;
portent; omen (v. PRÉSAGE); *de bon augure,* auspicious, of good omen; *de mauvais augure,*
ominous, of ill omen.
augurer [ogyre] v. intr. (1). To augur (*de,* of);
to anticipate (*de,* from).
— v. tr. To foresee, to forecast (l'avenir).
auguste [ogyst] adj. August; majestic.
augustin [ogystɛ̃] m. ECCLÉS. Augustine.
augustinien, enne [-tinjɛ̃, ɛn] adj., s. ECCLÉS.,
PHILOS. Augustinian.
aujourd'hui [oʒurdɥi] adv. Today (ce jour);
nowadays (de nos jours); *d'aujourd'hui en huit,*
a week today, today week; *la jeunesse d'aujourd'hui,* young people of today.
aulnaie [o:nɛ] f. V. AUNAIE.
aulne [o:n] m. BOT. Alder.
aulx [o:] m. pl. V. AIL.
aumône [omo:n] f. Alms; charity; *demander
l'aumône,* to beg, to ask for alms; *faire l'aumône,*
to give alms; *vivre d'aumônes,* to live on charity.
aumônerie [omonri] f. ECCLÉS. Chaplaincy, chaplainship (charge); chaplain's house (résidence).
aumônier [-nje] m. Almoner (faiseur d'aumônes).
‖ ECCLÉS. Chaplain; *aumônier militaire,* army
chaplain; padre (fam.).
aumônière [-njɛ:r] f. †. Alms-purse. ‖ Mesh-bag,
Dorothy bag.
aumusse [omys] f. ECCLÉS. Amice.
aunaie, aulnaie [onɛ] f. Alder-plantation.
aune [o:n] m. BOT. Alder.
aune f. Ell. ‖ LOC. *Une figure longue d'une aune,*
a face as long as a fiddle; *mesurer les autres à
son aune,* to judge others by oneself.
aunée [one] f. Ell.
auner v. tr. (1). To measure by the ell.
auparavant [oparavã] adv. Before, beforehand;
previously (préalablement). [V. AVANT.]
auprès [oprɛ] adv. Close to, close by, near.
— loc. prép. **Auprès de,** close to, close by, beside,
near (à côté de); compared with, in comparison
with (en comparaison de); with (dans l'esprit de);
ambassadeur auprès de la Cour de Saint-James,
ambassador to the Court of Saint James's; *appelé
auprès de son frère mourant,* called to his dying
brother; *être de service auprès de,* to attend on
(ou) upon; *intercéder auprès de,* to intercede
with; *se tenir en sentinelle auprès de,* to stand
sentry over.
auquel [okɛl]. V. LEQUEL.
aura [ora]. V. AVOIR (19).
aura [ora] f. MÉD. Aura.
auréole [oreol] f. ECCLÉS. Aureola, aureole, halo,
glory. ‖ ASTR. Aureole, corona, halo. ‖ PHYS.
Halation (en photo). ‖ FIG. Prestige; radiance;
crown.
auréolé, ée [-le] adj. Haloed.
auréoler [-le] v. tr. (1). To halo.
auréomycine [oreomisi:n] f. MÉD. Aureomycine.
aureux [orø] adj. CHIM. Aurous.
auriculaire [orikylɛ:r] adj. MÉD., ECCLÉS. Auricular. ‖ JUR. *Témoin auriculaire,* ear-witness.
— m. Little finger (doigt).
auricule [-kyl] f. MÉD. Auricle. ‖ BOT., ZOOL.
Auricula.
aurifère [orifɛ:r] adj. Auriferous, gold-bearing.
aurification [-fikasjɔ̃] f. MÉD. Filling (ou) stopping with gold.
aurifier [-fje] v. tr. (1). MÉD. To fill (ou) stop
with gold.
aurique [orik] adj. NAUT. Fore-and-aft. ‖ CHIM.
Auric.
— f. NAUT. Fore-and-aft sail.
auriste [orist] m. MÉD. Aurist, otologist.
aurochs [orɔks] m. ZOOL. Aurochs.
aurore [orɔ:r] f. Dawn, daybreak (v. AUBE); east
(poét.); *aurore australe, boréale,* aurora aus-

tralis, borealis; southern, northern lights. ‖
ECCLÉS. Aurora. ‖ FIG. Dawn.
— adj. Golden yellow.
auscultation [oskyltasjɔ̃] f. MÉD. Auscultation;
sounding.
ausculter [-te] v. tr. (1). MÉD. To auscultate; to
sound.
auspice [ospis] m. Auspex (devin); auspice (présage); *sous d'heureux auspices,* auspiciously. ‖
Pl. Auspices. (V. PATRONAGE.)
aussi [osi] adv. Also, too, as well, so, likewise
(pareillement); *elle aussi l'a vu,* she saw it also;
vient-il aussi?, is he coming too?; *il m'en faut
aussi,* I want some as well; *elle vient et moi aussi,*
she is coming and so am I; she comes and so do I.
‖ Also, too, as well, again (de plus); *rappelez-
vous aussi que,* remember too that. ‖ Such (si,
tellement); *dans une situation aussi désespérée,*
in such a desperate condition. ‖ As (autant);
aussi... que, as... as; *il est aussi grand que son
frère,* he is as tall as his brother; *est-il aussi grand
que vous?,* is he as tall as you?; **pas aussi... que,**
not so... as, not such... as (dans une proposition
négative); not as... as (dans une proposition
interro-négative); *il n'est pas aussi avancé que
notre ami,* he is not so proficient as our friend;
vous n'avez pas d'aussi beaux livres qu'eux, you
have not such fine books as they; *n'êtes-vous pas
aussi capable de le faire que moi?,* are you not
as capable of doing it as I? ‖ Then (alors); *aussi,
qu'aviez-vous besoin d'aller lui dire ça!,* why
should you go and say that to him then!
— conj. Therefore; consequently; and so; *la
vie est chère, aussi faut-il économiser,* living is
dear, therefore (ou) and so one has to save. ‖
Aussi bien (d'ailleurs), besides, moreover and
indeed; *aussi bien que,* as well as; *pas aussi bien
que,* not so well as. ‖ **Aussi longtemps que,** as
long as; *pas aussi longtemps que,* not so long as.
aussitôt [-to] adv. At once, immediately, forthwith, directly; *aussitôt après,* immediately after.
— loc. conj. **Aussitôt que,** as soon as; *aussitôt
que possible,* as soon as possible; *aussitôt après
son retour,* as soon as he comes back, immediately
on his return.
austère [ostɛ:r] adj. Austere, stern. (V. SÉVÈRE.) ‖
Austere, abstinent. (V. ASCÉTIQUE.) ‖ Austere,
grave, sober (visage). ‖ Austere, plain, lacking
ornament (dépouillé).
austèrement [-tɛrmã] adv. Austerely, sternly,
severely.
austérité [osterite] f. Austerity. ‖ Pl. Austerities;
asceticism.
austral, ale [ostral] adj. Austral, southern;
southerly.
Australasie [ostralazi] f. GÉOGR. Australasia.
Australie [ostrali] f. GÉOGR. Australia.
australien, enne [-ljɛ̃, ɛn] adj., s. Australian.
autan [otɑ̃] m. South wind.
autant [otɑ̃] adv. The same, as much, so much,
as soon; *c'est autant de fait,* it is so much to
the good; *cela valait autant,* it was just as well;
elle en fera autant, she will do the same; *elle
en a fait autant pour lui,* she has done as much
for him; *il ne vous en donnera pas autant,* he
will not give you so much; *j'aimerais autant lire,*
I would just as soon read; *il ne peut en dire
autant,* he cannot say the same. ‖ **Autant de...
que,** as much... as, as many... as; *pas autant de...
que,* not so much... as, not so many... as; *j'ai
autant de courage que lui,* I have as much courage
as he; *il n'a pas autant de chances que moi,* he
has not so many chances as I. ‖ **Autant que,** as
far as; as much as, as near as; *autant que je le
sache,* as far as I know, to the best of my knowledge; *autant que s'étendaient ses connaissances,*
so far as his knowledge went; *je ne le ferai*

qu'autant que vous n'y verrez pas d'inconvénients, I shall do it only in so far as you don't object. ‖ **Autant... autant,** as... as; so much... so much; *autant d'argent vous lui donnerez, autant il en dépensera,* the more money you give him, the more he will spend; *autant vous êtes bonne, autant elle est belle,* she is as beautiful as you are good. ‖ **D'autant,** by so much, in proportion, proportionally. ‖ **D'autant que,** the more so as, all the more so because. ‖ **D'autant plus que,** all the more... as; doubly so... as; *d'autant plus fier,* all the prouder ; *d'autant plus puissant que,* the more powerful because (ou) as; *je suis d'autant plus inquiète que,* I am all the more anxious because (ou) as. ‖ **D'autant moins... que,** all the less... because (ou) as. ‖ **Pour autant que,** as far as, so long as.

autarcie [otarsi] f. Autarky.

autarcique [-sik] adj. Autarkic, autarkical.

autel [otel] m. ECCLÉS. Altar; *maître autel,* high altar; *mettre sur les autels,* to canonize; *pierre d'autel,* altar-stone.

auteur [otœːr] m. Author, writer, composer; *femme auteur,* authoress; *droits d'auteur,* royalties. ‖ Cause, party at fault (d'un accident); perpetrator, author (d'un crime); maker (d'une découverte); sponsor, original mover (d'une motion); contriver, promoter, originator (d'un projet); *l'auteur de mes jours,* my father.

authenticité [otɑ̃tisite] f. Authenticity, genuineness.

authentifier [-tifje], **authentiquer** [-tike] v. tr. (1). To authenticate; to make valid; *inventaire authentifié,* certified inventory.

authentique [-tik] adj. Authentic, genuine, true; authoritative. ‖ JUR. Legal, authentic (acte); certified, exemplified (copie).

authentiquement [-tikmɑ̃] adv. Authentically.

autisme [otism] m. PSYCH. Autism.

autiste [otist], **autistique** [otistik] adj. PSYCH. Autistic.

auto [oto] f. AUTOM. Motor-car, car, motor; U.S. auto; *faire de l'auto,* to motor, to drive.

auto- [oto] préf. Auto-, self-; AUTOM. car. ‖ **Auto-adhésif, ive** adj. Self-sticking, self-adhesive. ‖ **Auto-allumage,** m. Self- (ou) pre-ignition. ‖ **Auto-couchettes,** adj. invar. AUTOM., CH. DE F. *Train auto-couchettes,* car sleeper. ‖ **Auto-école,** f. AUTOM. Driving school. ‖ **Auto-érotique,** adj. Autoerotic. ‖ **Auto-érotisme,** m. Autoerotism, autoeroticism. ‖ **Auto-immune,** adj. MÉD. *Maladies auto-immunes,* autoimmune diseases. ‖ **Auto-immunitaire,** adj. MÉD. Autoimmune (processus, mécanismes). ‖ **Auto-induction,** f. ELECTR. Self-induction. ‖ **Auto-intoxication,** f. MÉD. Auto-intoxication, autotoxaemia. ‖ **Auto-stop,** m. AUTOM. Hitch-hiking, hitching (fam.); *faire de l'auto-stop,* to hitch-hike, to hitch, to thumb a lift. ‖ **Auto-stoppeur, euse,** s. AUTOM. Hitch-hiker, hitcher (fam.).

autoberge [otobɛrʒ] f. Car track on river bank.

autobiographe [otobiɔgraf] s. Autobiographer.

autobiographie [-fi] f. Autobiography.

autobiographique [-fik] adj. Autobiographic.

autobus [otobyːs] m. AUTOM. Motor-bus, bus, omnibus; *monter en autobus,* to embus.

autocar [-kaːr] m. AUTOM. Motor coach, charabanc, autocar.

autocensure [-sɑ̃syːr] f. Act (ou) practice of censoring oneself.

autochenille [-ʃniːj] f. MILIT. Caterpillar-tractor; half-track vehicle.

autochir [-ʃiːr] f. MILIT. Motor surgical ambulance.

autochtone [otɔktɔn] adj. Autochthonous.
— s. Autochthon.

autoclave [otoklaːv] adj. Autoclave; steam-tight.

— m. CHIM. Autoclave. ‖ MÉD. Sterilizer. ‖ CULIN. Pressure-cooker, U. S. autoclave.

autocoat [-kot] m. Driving coat.

autocollant, ante [-kɔlɑ̃, ɑ̃:t] adj. Self-sticking, self-adhesive.
— m. Sticker.

autocrate [-krat] m. Autocrat.

autocratie [-krasi] f. Autocracy.

autocratique [-kratik] adj. Autocratic.

autocritique [-kritik] f. Autocriticism, self-criticism.

autocuiseur [-kɥizœːr] m. CULIN. Self-cooker.

autodafé [-dafe] m. Auto-da-fé. ‖ Bonfire (feu de joie).

autodéfense [-defɑ̃:s] f. Self-defence.

autodestructeur, trice [-dɛstryktœːr, tris] adj. Self-destructive.

autodestruction [-dɛstryksjɔ̃] f. Self-destruction.

autodétermination [-detɛrminasjɔ̃] f. JUR. Self-determination (en politique).

autodidacte [-didakt] adj. Self-taught, self-educated.
— s. Autodidact.

autodiscipline [-disiplin] f. Self-discipline.

autodrome [-dro:m] m. Motor-racing track; speedway; autodrome.

autofécondation [-fekɔ̃dasjɔ̃] f. Self-fecondation (ou) -fertilization.

autofinancement [-finɑ̃smɑ̃] m. COMM., FIN. Self-financing.

autofinancer (s') [-finɑ̃se] v. pr. (6). FIN. To finance (ou) fund oneself.

autogène [-ʒɛ:n] adj. MÉD. Autogenous (vaccin). ‖ TECHN. Oxy-acetylene (soudure).

autogéré, ée [-ʒere] adj. Controlled (ou) run by workers.

autogestion [-ʒɛstjɔ̃] f. Worker management, control of business by workers, workers' control.

autogire [-ʒi:r] m. AVIAT. Autogiro.

autographe [-graf] adj. Autographic; handwritten.
— m. Autograph.

autographie [-grafi] f. Autography, autolithography.

autographier [-grafje] v. tr. (1). To autograph.

autographique [-grafik] adj. Autographic; *encre autographique,* transfer-ink.

autoguidage [-gida:ʒ] m. Self-steering.

autoguidé, ée [-gide] adj. Self-directional (ou) -steering.

autolubrifiant, ante [-lybrifjɑ̃, ɑ̃:t] adj. Self-lubricating.

automate [-mat] m. Automaton, robot.

automaticité [-matisite] f. Automaticity.

automation [-masjɔ̃] f. Automation.

automatique [-matik] adj. Automatic (appareil, arme, machine, téléphone, revolver). ‖ CH. DE F. Automatic, self-closing (portillon).
— m. Automatic (revolver). ‖ TECHN. Automation (science).

automatiquement [-matikmɑ̃] adv. Automatically.

automatisation [-matizasjɔ̃] f. Automation.

automatisme [-matism] m. Automatism.

automédon [-medɔ̃] m. Cabby, Jehu.

automitrailleuse [-mitrajøz] f. MILIT. Bren carrier; light armoured car.

automnal, ale [otɔmnal] adj. Autumnal.

automne [otɔn] m. Autumn; U. S. fall. ‖ FIG. Autumn.

automobile [otomɔbil] adj. Self-propelling; auto-kinetic; automobile, automotive.
— f. AUTOM. Motor-car; U. S. automobile, car; *automobile volante,* helicab.

automobiliste [-mɔbilist] s. AUTOM. Motorist.

automoteur, trice [-mɔtœːr, tris] adj. Self-propelling, motor, automobile.

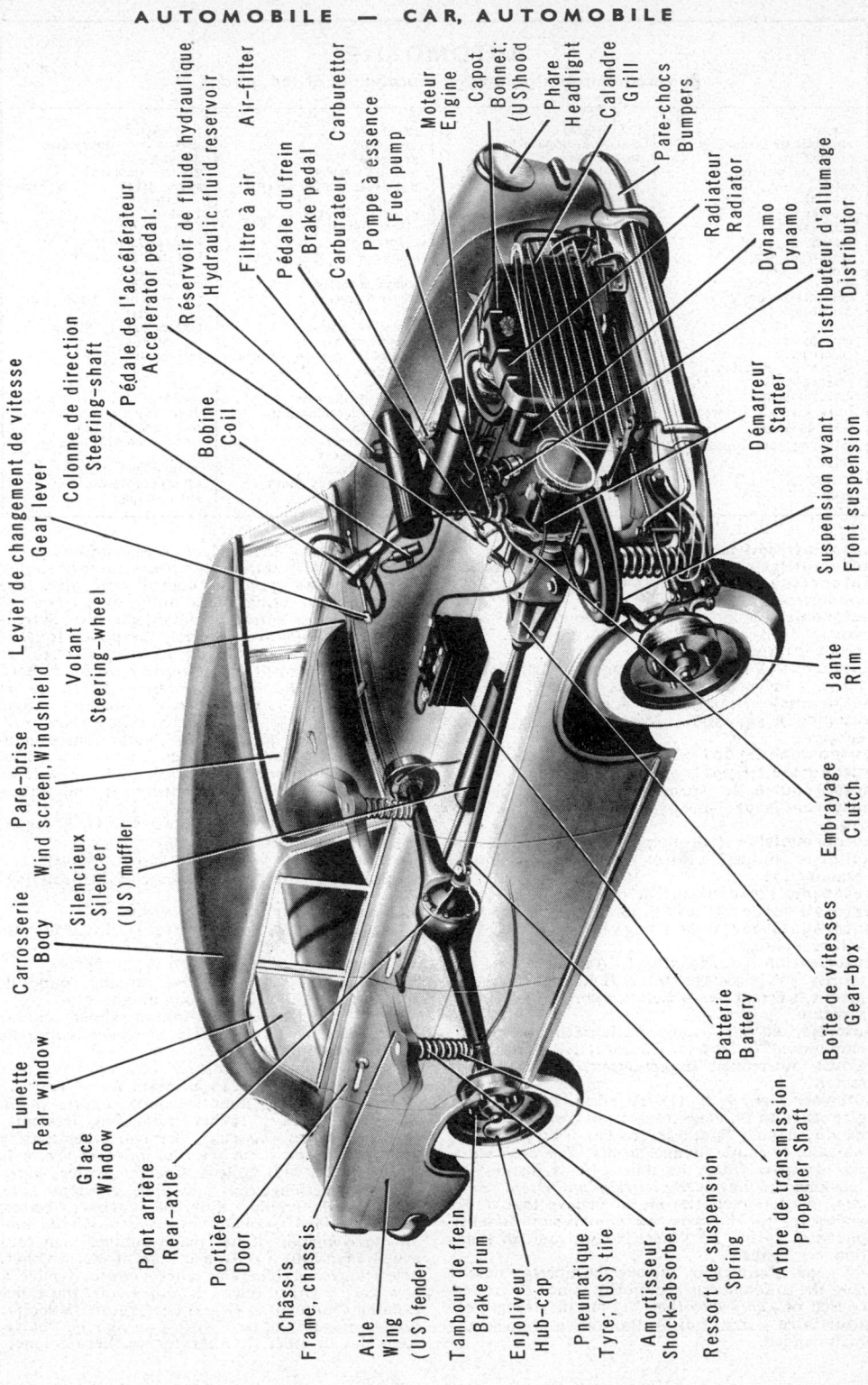

Réservoir de fluide hydraulique
Hydraulic fluid reservoir

Filtre à air   Air-filter

Pédale du frein
Brake pedal

Carburateur   Carburettor

Pompe à essence
Fuel pump

Moteur
Engine

Capot
Bonnet;
(US)hood

Phare
Headlight

Calandre
Grill

Pare-chocs
Bumpers

Radiateur
Radiator

Distributeur d'allumage
Distributor

Dynamo
Dynamo

Pédale de l'accélérateur
Accelerator pedal.

Bobine
Coil

Colonne de direction
Steering-shaft

Levier de changement de vitesse
Gear lever

Volant
Steering-wheel

Démarreur
Starter

Suspension avant
Front suspension

Pare-brise
Wind screen, Windshield

Silencieux
Silencer
(US) muffler

Carrosserie
Body

Jante
Rim

Embrayage
Clutch

Lunette
Rear window

Glace
Window

Pont arrière
Rear-axle

Portière
Door

Châssis
Frame, chassis

Aile
Wing
(US) fender

Tambour de frein
Brake drum

Enjoliveur
Hub-cap

Pneumatique
Tyre; (US) tire

Amortisseur
Shock-absorber

Ressort de suspension
Spring

Arbre de transmission
Propeller Shaft

Batterie
Battery

Boîte de vitesses
Gear-box

AUTOMOBILE
Vocabulaire du garage. — Vocabulary of the garage.

à plat	flat (-tyre)	graissage	lubrication
appareil de levage	hoisting apparatus	graisseur	grease-cup, lubricator
bloquer	to jam on	grippage	seizing
boîte de vitesses	gear-box	marche arrière	reverse (motion)
caler	to stall	pas assez gonflé (pneu)	slack (tyre) ; U. S. soft
camion	lorry, U. S. truck		(tire)
capoter	to upset, to overturn	patiner, déraper	to skid
carburant	fuel	pièces détachées	spare parts
cogner	to knock	point mort	neutral gear
crevaison	puncture	pompe à air	tyre inflator pump; U. S.
crevé, à plat	punctured, flat		air pump
cric	(lifting) jack	pompe à graisse	grease gun
démonte-pneu	tyre-lever, U. S. tire-iron	poste d'essence	petrol pump, U. S. gaso-
démonter	to remove (un pneu)		line station
éclater	to burst, U. S. to blow out	première vitesse	bottom (ou) U. S. low gear
endommagé	damaged	quatrième vitesse	top gear
enjoliveur	hub-cap	queue de poisson (déra-	tail-wobble
entrer en collision	to collide	page)	
essence	petrol, U. S. gasoline	ratés	misfires
être tamponné	to be bumped into	retour de flamme	backfire
faire marche arrière	to back	robinet de vidange	drain tap
faire le plein	to refuel, to fill up	serrer (boulons)	to tighten (bolts)
faire un tête-à-queue	to swing tail-end first	supprimer le jeu	to take up the play
fuite	leak	tamponnement	smash
garage	garage	traction avant	front-wheel drive
gonfler	to inflate	traction toutes roues	all-wheel drive
		vulcanisation	vulcanizing

---

automotrice [-mɔtris] f. CH. DE. F. Railcar.

automutilation [-mytilasjɔ̃] f. Self-mutilation.

autonettoyant, ante [-netwajɑ̃, ɑ̃:t] adj. *Four autonettoyant*, self-cleaning oven.

autonome [otono:m] adj. Autonomous, autonomic; self-governing. ‖ Self-contained, independent (groupe, unité).

autonomie [-nɔmi] f. Autonomy; self-government. ‖ Independence. ‖ AVIAT. Range.

autonomiste [-nɔmist] s. Autonomist.

autoplastie [-plasti] f. MÉD. Autoplasty; plastic surgery.

autopompe [-pɔ̃p] f. Fire engine.

autoportrait [-pɔrtrɛ] m. Self-portrait.

autopropulsé, ée [-prɔpylse] adj. Self-propelled.

autopropulseur [-prɔpylsœ:r] adj. Self-propelling.

autopropulsion [-prɔpylsjɔ̃] f. Self-propulsion.

autopsie [otɔpsi] f. MÉD. Autopsy; post-mortem examination.

autoradio [-radjo] m. Car radio.

autorail [otora:j] m. CH. DE F. Railcar.

autorégulateur, trice [-regylatœ:r, tris] adj. Self-regulating.

autorisation [otɔrizasjɔ̃] f. Authorization, authority. (V. PERMISSSION.) ‖ JUR. Leave, license, permit, warrant; *autorisation maritale*, husband's sanction.

autorisé, ée [-ze] adj. Authorized; permitted, empowered (à, to). ‖ Authoritative (source). ‖ COMM. Accredited (représentant). ‖ JUR. Legal (acte).

autoriser [-ze] v. tr. (1). To allow, to permit, to give leave to (v. PERMETTRE); *nul n'est autorisé à mentir*, nobody is allowed to lie. ‖ To justify, to warrant, to entitle (donner droit); *il se croit autorisé à parler franc*, he thinks he is justified in speaking candidly; *cette lettre m'autorise à croire que*, this letter entitles me to believe that. ‖ To authorize, to empower, to commission (donner pouvoir). ‖ JUR. To license, to warrant, to sanction, to legalize.

— v. pr. **S'autoriser**, to take the liberty; *s'autoriser de*, to found one's authority upon; to ground oneself on; *en s'autorisant de*, on the strength of.

autoritaire [-tɛ:r] adj. Authoritative (v. ABSOLU); high-handed.

autoritarisme [-tarism] m. Authoritarianism.

autorité [-te] f. Authority; *avoir autorité sur*, to have authority upon (ou) control over; *faire acte d'autorité*, to bring one's authority to bear. ‖ Authority; *les autorités civiles*, the civil authorities; *les agents de l'autorité*, the police force. ‖ Authority, influence; *avoir de l'autorité sur*, to have influence over; *faire autorité*, to be authoritative; *faire autorité en matière de*, to be an authority on; *sans autorité*, unauthoritative, unwarranted. ‖ Authoritativeness; *d'autorité*, authoritatively; *air d'autorité*, authoritative manner. ‖ MILIT. *Autorité militaire*, military control. ‖ JUR. *Par autorité de justice*, under a writ of execution. ‖ Pl. *Citer ses autorités*, to quote one's authorities.

autoroute [otorut] f. Motorway; U. S. superhighway, turnpike, expressway.

autoroutier, ère [-rutje, ɛ:r] adj. Motorway.

autosatisfaction [-satisfaksjɔ̃] f. Self-satisfaction.

autostrade [-strad] f. Motorway.

autosuggestion [-sygʒɛstjɔ̃] f. Autosuggestion.

autotrophe [-trɔf] adj. BOT. Autotrophic.

autour [otu:r] adv. Around; about; round it; *tout autour*, all around, round about.

— loc. prép. **Autour de**, round, about; *autour de la table*, round the table; *regarder autour de soi*, to look about one.

autour m. ZOOL. Accipiter.

autovaccin [otovaksɛ̃] m. MÉD. Auto-vaccine.

autre [o:tr] adj. Other (second); *l'autre main*, the other hand. ‖ Other, remaining (restant); *ses deux autres chapeaux*, her two other hats. ‖ Other, different; *c'est une tout autre affaire*, it is quite another (ou) quite a different matter; *autre chose*, something (ou) anything different; *pas autre chose*, nothing different. ‖ Other, better, new, reformed (transformé); *cela a fait de moi un autre homme*, it has made another man (ou) a new man (ou) a reformed man of me. ‖ Other, new (nouveau); *j'ai une autre voiture*, I have a new car. ‖ Other (passé); *l'autre soir*, the other evening (ou) night. ‖ Other, next, future (à venir); *l'autre monde*, the next world; *un jour ou l'autre*, some day or other. ‖ Other, far, farther (éloigné);

de l'autre côté de la rue, on the other side of the street, across the street; *vers l'autre rive,* towards the farther bank. ‖ Other, second (pareil); *un autre moi-même,* a second self, my alter ego. ‖ Else, other, more (en plus); *encore un autre,* one more, still (ou) yet another; *aucune autre personne n'est venue,* nobody else called; *en quel autre lieu?,* where else?; *autre chose,* something (ou) anything else; not only that but, and furthermore; *pas autre chose,* nothing else. ‖ *Nous autres, vous autres,* we, you (sujet); us, you (complément); *l'un et l'autre (les deux),* both.
— pron. Other; *l'autre,* the other; *un autre,* another. ‖ *Les autres,* the others, other men; *les deux autres,* the other two, the two others; *quelques autres,* some (ou) a few others. ‖ *D'autres,* others, other people; *à d'autres!* tell that to the marines!; *il n'en fait pas d'autres,* he always makes the same mistakes; *il en a vu d'autres,* he has been through worse; *parler de choses et d'autres,* to speak of this, that and the other. ‖ *D'autres,* else; *aller de côté et d'autre,* to go here and there; *qui d'autre?,* who else?; *quelqu'un d'autre,* somebody else; *que voulez-vous d'autre?* what else do you want?; *quoi que ce soit d'autre,* anything else. ‖ *Autre que,* other than; *aucun autre que lui,* none other but he; *il n'a pas pu aller à d'autre école que celle-ci,* he could not go to any other school than this; *qui d'autre que mon frère peut le faire?,* who else but my brother can do it? ‖ *L'un ou l'autre,* one or the other, either; *lequel voulez-vous?, l'un ou l'autre,* which will you have?, either. ‖ *Les uns ou les autres,* some or others, some; *il nous faut rester les uns ou les autres,* some of us have to stay. ‖ *L'un et l'autre,* both (réunis); either (séparés); *l'un et l'autre ont été tués,* both were killed; *ce qu'il y avait de ridicule ou d'odieux en l'un et l'autre augmentait le mépris général pour tous les deux,* whatever was ridiculous or odious in either increased public scorn for both of them. ‖ *Ni l'un ni l'autre,* neither; *ni les uns ni les autres,* none of them; *ni l'un ni l'autre n'est français,* neither is French; *je n'ai écrit ni les uns ni les autres,* I have written none of them. ‖ *L'un l'autre, les uns les autres,* each other, one another; *ils s'aident l'un l'autre,* they are helping one another; *ils sont très dévoués l'un à l'autre,* they are very devoted to each other; *elles sont très affectueuses les unes pour les autres,* they are very fond of one another. ‖ *L'un... l'autre,* one... the other; *les uns... les autres,* some... others, some... some; *les uns sont des rêveurs, les autres des hommes d'action,* some are dreamers, some are men of action; *des différends les ont séparés l'un de l'autre,* differences have estranged one from the other; *ils sont arrivés l'un après l'autre,* they arrived one after the other; *ils sont arrivés l'un par l'autre,* they have reached high positions through each other; *l'un dans l'autre,* taking one with the other. ‖ Loc. *Comme dit l'autre,* as they say; *de temps à autre,* from time to time; *d'un moment à l'autre,* any time, any minute; *une idée comme une autre,* not a bad idea; *tout l'un ou tout l'autre,* this or that.
autrefois [otrəfwa] adv. Formerly, of old; in the past. ‖ In olden days, of yore, in days of old; *d'autrefois,* ancient, bygone, old-time.
autrement [-mɑ̃] adv. More, far more (davantage); differently, otherwise (différemment); particularly, much (particulièrement); else, otherwise (sinon); otherwise, in other respects (sous d'autres rapports); *il n'y a pas moyen de faire autrement,* there is no help for it; *elle ne pouvait faire autrement que de le voir,* she could not help (ou) avoid seeing him.
Autriche [otriʃ] f. GÉOGR. Austria.
autrichien, enne [-ʃjɛ̃, ɛn] adj., s. Austrian.

autruche [otryʃ] f. ZOOL. Ostrich; *plume d'autruche,* ostrich-feather (ou) plume.
autrui [otrɥi] pron. Others, other people; *les enfants d'autrui,* other people's children.
— m. Neighbour (prochain).
auvent [ovɑ̃] m. ARCHIT. Penthouse (toit); porch-roof (de porte). ‖ AGRIC. Screen, matting (d'espalier). ‖ AUTOM. Bonnet (ou) U. S. hood louvre (de capot).
auvergnat, ate [overɲa, at] adj., s. Pertaining to Auvergne.
aux [o] art. V. À, LE.
auxiliaire [oksiljɛ:r] adj. Auxiliary; subsidiary; *bureau auxiliaire,* sub-office. ‖ MILIT. *Services auxiliaires de l'armée,* non-combatant services.
— m. Auxiliary. (V. AIDE.) ‖ GRAMM. Auxiliary. ‖ MILIT. Non-combatant services (service); auxiliaries (troupes).
auxiliairement [-ljɛrmɑ̃] adv. Accessorily, secondarily.
auxquels [okel] art. V. LEQUEL.
avachi, ie [avaʃi] adj. Out of shape, shapeless (chaussures). ‖ FAM. Flabby, sloppy (personne).
avachir [-ʃi:r] v. tr. (2). To soften (le cuir). ‖ FAM. To make flabby, to enervate (les gens).
— v. pr. **S'avachir,** to lose shape (chaussure, habit); to become slack (tissu). ‖ FAM. To become flabby (ou) sloppy (ou) limp (personne).
avachissement [-ʃismɑ̃] m. Deterioration. ‖ Sloppiness, flabbiness.
aval [aval] m. COMM. Backing, endorsement; *donner son aval à,* to endorse.
aval m. Downstream direction; lower course; *en aval,* downstream; *en aval de,* below.
avalage [-la:ʒ] m. Cellaring, lowering (d'une pièce de vin). ‖ NAUT. Going downstream (d'un bateau).
avalanche [avalɑ̃:ʃ] f. Avalanche. ‖ FAM. Shower, avalanche (pluie).
avalancheux, euse [-lɑ̃ʃø, ø:z] adj. Subject to avalanches, avalanche-prone.
avalement [avalmɑ̃] m. Swallowing.
avaler [-le] v. tr. (1). To swallow (v. ENGLOUTIR, INGURGITER); *avaler gloutonnement,* to guzzle (boisson); to wolf, to gorge (nourriture); *avaler rapidement,* to bolt, to gulp down, to gobble up; *avaler d'un trait,* to swig off. ‖ To lower (un tonneau). ‖ FIG. To pocket, to swallow, to stomach (un affront); *dur à avaler,* bitter (pilule). ‖ FAM. To swallow; to take in (une histoire). ‖ FAM. To bite s.o.'s head off (qqn); *avaler des yeux,* to devour with one's eyes.
— v. pr. **S'avaler,** to go down, to sag.
avaleur [-lœ:r] s. Swallower; *avaleur de sabres,* sword-swallower. ‖ Glutton (goulu).
avaliser [avalize] v. tr. (1). COMM. To back, to endorse, to guarantee.
avaliste [-list] m. COMM. Backer, endorser, guarantor.
à-valoir [avalwar] m. FIN. Instalment.
avance [avɑ̃:s] f. Advance, progress, progression. ‖ Lead, start; *avoir une sérieuse avance sur,* to have a substantial lead over; *prendre de l'avance sur,* to get the start of. ‖ Gaining (d'une pendule); *ma montre est en avance,* my watch is fast; *elle a dix minutes d'avance,* it is ten minutes fast. ‖ Pl. Advances, overtures, approaches; *faire des avances à,* to make up to; *répondre aux avances de,* to meet the advances of. ‖ FIN. Loan, advance (de fonds); *des avances provisoires,* deficiency bills. ‖ AUTOM. *Avance à l'allumage,* advance of the spark, advanced ignition, ignition advance. ‖ SPORTS. Start; U. S. headstart; *il m'a accordé cinq minutes d'avance,* he allowed me a start of five minutes (ou) five minutes' start. ‖ TECHN. Lead (d'échappement, d'admission); travel (d'outil). ‖ ELECTR. Lead (de, in) [la phase]. ‖ FAM. *La belle avance!,* a lot of good that will do

you! ‖ **A l'avance, d'avance, par avance,** beforehand; in advance; in anticipation; before the time; *arranger d'avance,* to prearrange; *escompter à l'avance,* to anticipate; *huit jours d'avance,* a week beforehand; *jouir d'avance de,* to look forward to; *payé d'avance,* prepaid. ‖ **En avance,** before time; early; *être en avance,* to be before one's time; *arriver en avance,* to arrive early.

avancé, ée [-se] adj. Advanced (âge, civilisation, heure); late, far gone, far advanced (heure, jour, saison); *à une heure peu avancée de la soirée,* early on in the evening. ‖ Forward (élève); advanced (idée, opinion). ‖ Advanced; *n'être pas plus avancé,* to be no further forward, not to be much the wiser, to be no better off. ‖ CULIN. Ripe (fromage); over-ripe (fruit); high (gibier); bad, going bad (poisson); tainted, high (viande). ‖ FIN. Advanced (argent). ‖ MILIT. Advanced (poste). ‖ CH. DE F. Distant (signal).

avancée [-se] f. Projection, salient; *avancée en profondeur,* underthrust. ‖ MILIT. Advance post.

avancement [-s̜mɑ̃] m. Projection, jutting out (saillie). ‖ Advancing, putting forward (de l'heure, d'un pion). ‖ Progress (des études, des recherches); advancement (des sciences). ‖ Promotion, preferment; *avancement au choix,* promotion by selection; *recevoir de l'avancement,* to be promoted; *tableau d'avancement,* promotion list.

avancer [-se] v. tr. (5). To hold out (la main); to stretch forward (le pied); to set, to put forward (un siège). ‖ To advance (un pion). ‖ To hasten (le départ, la mort); to put on (une pendule); to bring forward (une réunion). ‖ AGRIC. To help on (la végétation). ‖ FIN. To advance, to lend (de l'argent). ‖ FIG. To forward, to further, to better (une affaire); to promote (la science); to hurry on, to speed up (des travaux). ‖ FIG. To advance, to put forward (une idée); to allege, to adduce, to set forth (des raisons); to set up, to put forth (une théorie). ‖ FAM. To profit (qqn); *cela ne nous avance pas beaucoup,* this does not get us much farther forward.
— v. intr. To advance, to go (ou) move (ou) step forward; to proceed, to progress, to go on; *continuer à avancer,* to continue; *faire avancer,* to advance, to urge on, to bring up. ‖ To protrude, to project, to jut out (saillie). ‖ To be fast, gain, to go too fast (montre). ‖ To be promoted (fonctionnaire). ‖ FIG. To advance, to make progress, to get on (affaires, civilisation, travail).
— v. pr. **S'avancer,** to advance; to move (ou) to come forward; to approach; to progress. ‖ To get on (journée). ‖ To jut out, to push out, to project; to run out (faire saillie). ‖ To go too far (s'engager).

avanie [avani] f. V. AFFRONT.

avant [avɑ̃] prép. Before (dans la distance, l'ordre, le temps); *avant peu,* before long. ‖ Above (dans le choix); *avant tout,* above everything else (au-dessus de tout); above all (surtout); first of all (tout d'abord). ‖ For, within (dans la durée); *ils ne chanteront pas avant une demi-heure,* they will not sing for half an hour yet.
— adv. Before (auparavant); *trois jours avant,* three days before. ‖ Late, far (tard); *bien avant dans la nuit,* far into the night. ‖ Deep (profondément); *très avant dans les chairs,* deep into the flesh. ‖ Far (loin); *très avant dans le bois,* very far into the forest; *plus avant,* further.
— loc. prép. **Avant de,** before.
— loc. conj. **Avant que,** before (dans les propositions affirmatives). ‖ **Pas avant que,** not until; *elle ne chantera pas avant que vous ne le lui demandiez,* she will not sing till you ask her.
— m. Forepart, front. ‖ NAUT. Bow (proue); steerage (avant-carré); *de l'avant à l'arrière,* fore and aft. ‖ AVIAT. Nose. ‖ AUTOM. *Roue avant,* front wheel. ‖ SPORTS. Forward (footballer). ‖ FIG.

Aller de l'avant, to go ahead. ‖ LOC. **D'avant,** previous, before; *la nuit d'avant,* the previous night, the night before. ‖ **En avant,** forward, ahead, in advance; *se précipiter en avant,* to rush forward; *faire un pas en avant,* to go a step forward, to advance a step; *mettre en avant,* to put forward, to allege, to advance; *se mettre en avant,* to push oneself forward. ‖ **En avant de,** ahead of, in front of, in advance of. ‖ **Avant-bec,** m. Cutwater. ‖ **Avant-bras,** m. Forearm. ‖ **Avant-carré,** m. NAUT. Steerage. ‖ **Avant-centre,** m. SPORTS. Centre-forward. ‖ **Avant-corps,** m. Fore-part. ‖ **Avant-cour,** m. Forecourt. ‖ **Avant-coureur, avant-courrier** adj. Precursory; s. forerunner. ‖ **Avant-dernier,** adj., s. Last but one, next to the last. ‖ **Avant-garde,** f. Vanguard; advance guard. ‖ **Avant-goût,** m. Foretaste; anticipation (fig.). ‖ **Avant-guerre,** m. Pre-war period. ‖ **Avant-hier,** adv. The day before yesterday. ‖ **Avant-port,** m. NAUT. Outer harbour. ‖ **Avant-poste,** m. MILIT. Outpost. ‖ **Avant-première,** f. THÉÂTR. Dress rehearsal. ‖ **Avant-projet,** m. Rough draft, preliminary plan. ‖ **Avant-propos,** m. Foreword. ‖ **Avant-scène,** f. THÉÂTR. Proscenium, forestage; stage-box (loge). ‖ **Avant-toit,** m. Eaves. ‖ **Avant-train,** m. Forehand (d'un cheval); forecarriage (d'un véhicule); MILIT. Limber (d'un canon). ‖ **Avant-veille,** f. Two days before.

avantage [avɑ̃ta:ʒ] m. Advantage, benefit, profit; *avantage pécuniaire,* monetary gain; *tirer avantage de,* to derive advantage from, to benefit from, to make a profit from; *trouver son avantage dans,* to find one's account in. ‖ Superiority, advantage; odds (v. DESSUS); *ils avaient l'avantage,* the odds were in their favour; *prendre l'avantage sur,* to get an advantage over; *remporter l'avantage sur,* to get the better of. ‖ Pleasure, honour; *l'avantage de vous connaître,* the honour of knowing you. ‖ Better; *changer à son avantage,* to change for the better; *être à son avantage,* to look one's best. ‖ MILIT. Upper hand, temporary superiority. ‖ JUR. Donation; *à titre d'avantage,* as a gift.

avantager [-ʒe] v. tr. (7). To favour, to benefit, to give an advantage to (favoriser); to flatter (flatter). ‖ To become (aller bien à).

avantageux, euse [-ʒø, ø:z] adj. Advantageous; profitable (marché); popular (prix); *être très avantageux,* to be very good value. ‖ Favourable, flattering (portrait); becoming (robe). ‖ Conceited, supercilious (ton).

avantageusement [-ʒøzmɑ̃] adv. Advantageously; favourably.

avare [ava:r] adj. Miserly; close-fisted, stingy. (V. AVARICIEUX.) ‖ FIG. Sparing, chary (de, of).
— s. Miser; niggard. (V. LADRE.)

avariable [avarjabl] adj. Damageable.

avarice [avaris] f. Avarice, niggardliness, stinginess; tightness (fam.).

avaricieux, euse [-risjø, ø:z] adj. Avaricious.

avarie [avari] f. Deterioration (de marchandises); *subir une avarie,* to be damaged, to break down. ‖ NAUT. Damage, injury; average. ‖ TECHN. Breakdown.

avarié, ée [-rje] adj. Over-ripe (fruit); damaged (marchandises); tainted (viande).

avarier (s') [savarje] v. pr. (1). To be damaged, to spoil (marchandises); to go bad (viande).

avatar [avata:r] m. Avatar. ‖ Metamorphosis, transformation; phase. ‖ Misadventure; Pl. Ups and downs.

Ave [ave], **Ave Maria** [avemarja] m. invar. ECCLÉS. Ave, Ave Maria.

avec [avɛk] prép. With (accord, collaboration, comparaison, manière, moyen, possession, union, réciprocité, relativité); *avec son grand nez,* with his long nose; *avec l'intention de,* with the aim of; *avec une plume,* with a pen; *avec patience,* with patience. ‖ With, in (temps); *avec le temps,* with (ou) in time. ‖ For, in spite of, with (malgré); *avec toute sa gloire il n'est pas heureux,* with (ou) in spite of (ou) for all his fame he is not happy. ‖ To (ressemblant à); *offrir une ressemblance avec,* to show a resemblance to. ‖ With, by, under (grâce à); *avec l'aide de Dieu,* with (ou) by God's help. ‖ Under, from (sous l'égide de); *avec lui j'ai trouvé le latin facile,* under him I found Latin easy. ‖ With, by (sous l'effet de); *blanchir avec l'âge,* to turn grey with age. ‖ From, of, out of (extraction); *se faire entièrement avec du vinaigre,* to be made entirely of vinegar; *combustible fait avec du charbon,* fuel produced from coal. ‖ From (différence); *distinguer le bleu d'avec le vert,* to distinguish the blue from the green. ‖ Loc. *Avec ça,* into the bargain; *et avec ça?,* what next?, and now?; *et avec ça, Madame?,* anything else, Madam?; *avec ça!* nonsense!; *avec ça que...!,* as if...!

aveline [avlin] f. Bot. Filbert, hazel-nut.

aven [avɛn] m. Géogr., Géol. Sink-hole, pothole.

avenant, ante [avnɑ̃, ɑ̃:t] adj. Gracious; comely; pleasant. (V. AIMABLE.)
— m. *A l'avenant,* of a piece, to suit, in keeping; in conformity (de, with).

avenant m. Jur. Additional clause; rider.

avènement [avɛnmɑ̃] m. Advent. (V. ARRIVÉE, VENUE.) ‖ Accession (à, to).

avenir [avni:r] m. Future; *à l'avenir,* in the future, hereafter, in time to come. ‖ Fig. Future, destiny; *un bel avenir devant soi,* a fine future (ou) fine prospects before one; *un garçon d'avenir,* a young man with a future.

avenir, à-venir, m. invar. Jur. Summons served by one solicitor on another, citation.

Avent [avɑ̃] m. Ecclés. Advent.

aventure [avɑ̃ty:r] f. Adventure; venture, enterprise; experience (v. PÉRIPÉTIE); *chercher aventure,* to seek adventures. ‖ Love affair, intrigue (amoureuse). ‖ Fortune; *dire la bonne aventure,* to tell fortunes; *diseuse de bonne aventure,* fortune-teller. ‖ Chance (hasard); *à l'aventure,* at random; aimlessly; rovingly; haphazard; *d'aventure,* by chance. ‖ Comm. *Prêt à la grosse aventure,* bottomry bond.

aventuré, ée [avɑ̃tyre] adj. Adventurous, risky (v. RISQUÉ).

aventurer [-re] v. tr. (1). To venture, to risk.
— v. pr. **S'aventurer,** to venture; to hazard oneself, to take risks.

aventureux, euse [-rø, ø:z] adj. Adventurous. (V. AUDACIEUX, ENTREPRENANT.) ‖ Hazardous. (V. HASARDEUX.)

aventureusement [-røzmɑ̃] adv. Adventurously; daringly; recklessly.

aventurier [-rje] m. Adventurer.

aventurière [-rjɛ:r] f. Adventuress.

aventurine [avɑ̃tyrin] f. Aventurine.

aventurisme [avɑ̃tyrism] m. Adventurism, foolhardiness (en politique).

avenu, ue [avny] adj. *Non avenu,* cancelled, nonexistent; *nul et non avenu,* null and void.

avenue [avny] f. Avenue (allée plantée d'arbres). ‖ Drive (allée carrossable). ‖ Fig. Avenue.

avéré, ée [avere] adj. Authenticated (v. CONFIRMÉ, ÉTABLI, NOTOIRE); arrant, out-and-out (péj.). ‖ Patent (crime); proved (fait). ‖ Known (criminel); professed (doctrinaire); avowed (ennemi).

avérer v. tr. (5). To establish; to prove; to verify. ‖ Jur. To aver.

avers [avɛr] m. Obverse (d'une pièce).

averse [avɛrs] f. Shower; downpour. ‖ Fig. Flood, deluge, shower.

aversion [avɛrsjɔ̃] f. Aversion (pour, to, for);

dislike (pour, to, for, of) [qqn]. ‖ Distaste (pour, for); repugnance (pour, to) [qqch.]; *prendre en aversion,* to take a dislike to.

averti, ie [avɛrti] adj. Informed, experienced. ‖ Forewarned, forearmed (prévenu); *se tenir pour averti,* to take the warning.

avertir [-ti:r] v. tr. (2). To notify; to give notice to (aviser); to inform (de, of) [informer]. ‖ To warn (de, of); to caution (de, against) [mettre en garde].

avertissement [-tismɑ̃] m. Warning, notice (acte). ‖ Caution, warning (avis). ‖ Admonition (blâme). ‖ Foreword (préface). ‖ Fin. Demand note.

avertisseur [-tisœ:r] m. Annunciator, warner (personne). ‖ Warning signal; alarm; call-bell; *avertisseur d'incendie,* fire-alarm. ‖ Autom. Motor-horn, hooter. ‖ Théâtr. Call-boy.
— adj. Warning, premonitory.

aveu [avø] m. Acknowledgment (d'une dette, d'un état); avowal, admission, confession (d'une faute); *de son propre aveu,* by his own admission; *faire l'aveu de,* to confess, to acknowledge; *passer des aveux complets,* to make a clean breast of it. ‖ Agreement, assent (v. APPROBATION); *de l'aveu général,* admittedly, by common consent; *sans l'aveu de son père,* without his father's consent. ‖ Loc. *Individu sans aveu,* disreputable character.

aveuglant, ante [avøglɑ̃, ɑ̃:t] adj. Blinding, dazzling; glaring (soleil). ‖ Fig. Overpowering; categorical, indubitable.

aveugle [avøgl] adj. Blind, sightless; *aveugle de naissance,* blind from birth. ‖ Archit. Blind (fenêtre). ‖ Fig. Blind (amour, force, hasard, zèle); blind, implicit (confiance); blind, unreasoning (haine); blind, unquestioning (obéissance).
— s. *Les aveugles,* the blind; *un aveugle,* a blind man; *une aveugle,* a blind woman. ‖ Loc. *En aveugle,* blindly, blindfold, in the dark.

aveuglement [avøgləmɑ̃] m. Blinding (action); blindness (résultat). ‖ Fig. Blindness. ‖ Naut. Fothering (d'une fuite).

aveuglément [-glemɑ̃] adv. Blindly; unquestioningly; implicitly; recklessly.

aveugler [-gle] v. tr. (1). To blind (qqn). ‖ To dazzle (éblouir). ‖ Naut. To fother, to stop (une voie d'eau). ‖ Fig. To blind, to hoodwink (qqn); to blind, to obscure (la raison).
— v. pr. **S'aveugler,** to blind oneself. ‖ Fig. To be blind, to shut one's eyes (sur, to).

aveuglette (à l') [alavøglɛt] loc. adv. Blindly.

aveulir [avøli:r] v. tr. (2). To enervate, to make limp (qqn); to deaden (les sentiments).
— v. pr. **S'aveulir,** to become limp (ou) enervated (ou) indifferent.

aveulissement [-lismɑ̃] m. Enervation, limpness.

aviateur [avjatœ:r] m. Aviat. Aviator, airman, flier, flying man.

aviation [-sjɔ̃] f. Aviat. Aviation; flying. ‖ Air force, aircraft; *aviation embarquée,* carrier-based aircraft.

aviatrice [-tris] f. Aviat. Airwoman; aviatrix.

avicole [avikɔl] adj. Poultry.

aviculteur [avikyltœ:r] m. Poultry-farmer; bird-fancier.

aviculture [-ty:r] f. Aviculture; poultry farming; bird-fancying.

avide [avid] adj. Hungry (affamé); voracious. (V. GLOUTON.) ‖ Fig. *Avide de,* greedy for (argent); covetous of (argent, bien d'autrui); eager for (étude, plaisir); greedy for (honneurs); avid for (pouvoir); keen on (succès); *très avide d'argent,* very grasping.

avidement [-dmɑ̃] adv. Hungrily. ‖ Covetously; eagerly.

avidité [-dite] f. Avidity, voracity (pour la nourriture). ‖ Fig. Greediness, graspingness (pour l'argent); eagerness, keenness (pour l'étude).

avilir [avili:r] v. tr. (2). To debase, to degrade; to lower; to vilify; to dishonour. ‖ COMM. To lower, to depreciate.
— v. pr. **S'avilir,** to debase (ou) to demean oneself. ‖ COMM. To depreciate, to fall off.

avilissant, ante [-lisɑ̃, ɑ̃:t] adj. Debasing; degrading, depraving.

avilissement [-lismɑ̃] m. Debasement, depravation, depravity, degradation. ‖ COMM. Depreciation.

aviné, ée [avine] adj. Inebriated, in liquor; drunk.

aviner v. tr. (1). To season (un fût).
— v. pr. **S'aviner.** FAM. To liquor up, to booze, to soak, to swill.

avion [avjɔ̃] m. AVIAT. Aeroplane, plane, avion; U. S. airplane; *avion de bombardement,* bomber; *avion de guerre,* military plane, war plane; *avion à réaction,* jet, jet-propelled aircraft; *avion de reconnaissance, de transport, de tourisme,* reconnaissance, transport, private aeroplane; *par avion,* by airmail (poste); by air (voyage). ‖ **Avioncargo,** m. Freight plane. ‖ **Avion-cible,** m. Target plane; «Queen Bee». ‖ **Avion-citerne,** m. Air tanker. ‖ **Avion-école,** m. Training (ou) trainer plane.

avionnette [avjɔnɛt] f. AVIAT. Light plane; U. S. flivver.

aviron [avirɔ̃] m. NAUT. Oar; *faire de l'aviron,* to row, to go boating.

avis [avi] m. Judgment, opinion, view; U. S. guess (fam.); *à mon avis,* in my opinion, to my mind; *être d'avis que,* to be of opinion that. ‖ Advice, counsel; consultation; *un avis,* a piece of advice; *l'avis des juges,* the decision of the court; *prendre, suivre l'avis de qqn,* to take, to follow s.o.'s advice; *profiter d'un avis,* to profit from (ou) by a piece of advice. ‖ Notice; warning (avertissement); information; announcement (notification); *lettre d'avis,* advice note; *jusqu'à nouvel avis,* until further notice; *sauf avis contraire,* unless I (ou) we (ou) you hear to the contrary; *sans avis préalable,* without warning; *suivant avis de,* as per advice from.

avisé, ée [-ze] adj. Wary, cautious, discerning (v. JUDICIEUX, PRUDENT); *bien, mal avisé,* well-, ill-advised.

aviser [-ze] v. tr. (1). To notice, to perceive, to catch sight of, to glimpse (apercevoir). ‖ To advise (de, of); to notify. (V. AVERTIR, INFORMER, PRÉVENIR.)
— v. intr. To consider; to think about it; to look into the matter; *aviser à,* to see about (ou) to, to see that, to think of (ou) how to; *aviser aux moyens de,* to consider how to; *j'y aviserai,* I shall see to it, I shall deal with it, I shall take the necessary steps.
— v. pr. **S'aviser,** to take into one's head (de, to) [avoir l'idée]; to venture, to dare (de, to) [oser]; to bethink oneself (de, of) [penser]; to find a way (de, to) [trouver le moyen].

aviso [avizo] m. NAUT. Aviso, dispatch-boat; sloop (colonial).

avitaminose [avitamino:z] f. MÉD. Vitamin-deficiency, avitaminosis.

aviver [avive] v. tr. (1). To quicken; to revive (la combustion, une couleur, le tirage); to fan, to stir up (le feu); to repolish (un métal). ‖ To sharpen (l'appétit, une souffrance); to stimulate, to stir up (la colère); to brighten (le regard). ‖ MÉD. To refresh (les bords d'une cicatrice); to irritate (une plaie).
— v. pr. **S'aviver,** to revive, to quicken. ‖ FIG. To become keener (ou) more acute.

avocaillon [avɔkajɔ̃] m. JUR. Petty lawyer, briefless barrister.

avocasserie [avɔkasri] f. † Pettifogging, chicanery, pettiness.

avocassier, ère [avɔkasje, ɛr] adj. JUR. Pettifogging.
— m. JUR. Pettifogger.

avocat [avɔka] m. JUR. Counsel, practising barrister; advocate (en Ecosse); U. S. trial lawyer; *avocat conseil,* counsel; *avocat consultant,* consulting barrister, chamber-counsel; *avocat général,* advocate general, procurator fiscal; *avocat de la partie adverse,* opposing counsel; *avocat d'office,* counsel suing in forma pauperis; *membre du Conseil de l'Ordre des avocats,* bencher. ‖ FIG. Advocate; *se faire l'avocat de,* to plead in favour of, to advocate.

avocat [avɔka] m. BOT. Avocado- (ou) alligator-pear.

avocate [avɔkat] f. JUR. Lady advocate; woman barrister; U. S. woman lawyer.

avocatier [avɔkatje] m. BOT. Avocado (arbre).

avoine [avwan] f. BOT. Oat, oats; *farine d'avoine,* oatmeal; *folle avoine,* wild oats.

avoir [avwar] v. tr. (19). To have (posséder); *avoir de l'argent,* to have money; *avoir un bon fils,* to have a good son; *avoir du crédit,* to have credit; *avoir les yeux bleus,* to have blue eyes; *ne pas avoir de volonté,* to be weak-willed, to lack will-power. ‖ To be (éprouver); *avoir chaud, faim, froid, peur, soif,* to be warm, hungry, cold, afraid, thirsty. ‖ To be (atteindre); *avoir vingt ans,* to be twenty years old. ‖ To keep (entretenir); *avoir plusieurs voitures,* to keep several cars. ‖ To have, to conceive; *avoir des préventions contre,* to have a prejudice against. ‖ To have, to hold (entretenir); *avoir une opinion,* to hold an opinion; *avoir des relations avec,* to have dealings with. ‖ To hold (tenir); *avoir en haute estime,* to hold in high esteem. ‖ To pay, to show (manifester); *avoir des amabilités pour,* to pay attentions to; *avoir de l'intérêt pour,* to show an interest in. ‖ To get; to reach (atteindre); to obtain (obtenir); to procure (procurer); *il aura une réponse,* he will get an answer; *elle m'aura cet emploi,* she will get me this job; *l'arbre est haut, pouvez-vous avoir la pomme?,* the tree is high, can you reach the apple?; *je n'ai pas pu l'avoir,* I couldn't get through to him (au téléphone); *on a la B.B.C. facilement,* we get the B.B.C. easily; *vous l'avez,* you are through (ou) U. S. connected (au téléphone). ‖ To give, to make (émettre, faire); *il eut un rire bref,* he gave a short laugh; *il eut un geste de désespoir,* he made a gesture of despair; *elle eut une grimace de douleur,* she winced. ‖ To wear, to have on (porter); *elle avait un manteau de sport,* she wore a sports coat. ‖ FAM. To have, to get, to do; U. S. to take (tromper); *on vous a eu,* you've been had (ou) U. S. taken. ‖ FAM. To beat; to get the better of (vaincre); *on les aura,* we'll beat them yet, we'll get them. ‖ LOC. **Avoir à,** to have to, to have got to; *en avoir à* (ou) *contre,* to be angry with, to have a grudge against; *en avoir assez pour,* to have enough for; *j'en ai pour une heure,* it will take me an hour; *j'en ai assez,* I am sick of it; *il en a eu pour vingt francs,* he had to pay twenty francs; *n'avoir qu'à,* to have nothing to do but, to have only to.
— v. impers. **Y avoir,** to be; *il y a un doute,* there is a doubt; *il y avait plusieurs livres,* there were several books; *il y a loin,* it is far; *il ne doit pas y avoir de retard,* there must be no delay; *il ne peut y avoir de doute,* there can be no doubt. ‖ Ago, since, before (temps écoulé depuis une action achevée); *mon frère était soldat il y a trois ans,* my brother was a soldier three years ago; *elle était partie en Amérique il y avait deux ans,* she had gone to America two years before (ou) previously; *il y a une douzaine d'années,* a dozen years back; *il y a deux mois que j'ai*

passé mon examen, I took my exam two months ago, it is two months since I took my exam. ‖ For (temps écoulé depuis une action non achevée); *il y a deux jours que je l'attends,* I have been expecting him for two days; *il y a trop longtemps que ça dure,* it has lasted too long; *il y avait vingt minutes qu'il nageait,* he had been swimming for twenty minutes. ‖ Loc. *Il doit y avoir quelque chose,* there must be something the matter; *il n'y a rien de grave,* there is nothing much the matter; *il n'y a rien,* there is nothing wrong; *il y a un instant,* just now; *il y a à peine quelques mois,* within the last few months; *il n'y a rien à faire,* there is nothing doing; *il n'y a pas de quoi,* don't mention it; *qu'y a-t-il?* what's the matter?, what's up?
— v. aux. To have.
— m. Possession; property. ‖ Fin. Fortune; holding; assets; *avoirs étrangers,* foreign resources (ou) assets. ‖ Comm. Credit, credit side.
avoisinant, ante [[avwazinɑ̃, ɑ̃:t] adj. Neighbouring; nearby. (V. ADJACENT.)
avoisiner [-ne] v. tr. (1). To be near, to be close (ou) adjacent to.
avorté, ée [avɔrte] adj. Abortive (pr. et fig.).
avortement [-təmɑ̃] m. Méd. Abortion.
avorter [-te] v. intr. (1). Méd. To abort; to miscarry; *faire avorter,* to procure abortion, to bring on a miscarriage; *se faire avorter,* to cause oneself to miscarry. ‖ Zool. To slink, to slip (animal). ‖ Bot. To abort (plante). ‖ Fig. To fail, to miscarry, to come to nothing, to fizzle out; *faire avorter,* to frustrate.
avorteur, euse [-tœ:r, ø:z] s. Abortionist.
avorton [-tɔ̃] m. Abortion. ‖ Bot. Stunted plant. ‖ Fig. Abortion, squit (fam.).
avouable [avwabl] adj. Avowable.
avoué [avwe] m. Jur. Solicitor, attorney-at-law.
avoué, ée adj. Avowed. (V. ADMIS, CONFESSÉ.)
avouer v. tr. (1). To approve, to ratify, to endorse (un acte); to recognize, to acknowledge (une dette, un fait); to admit, to confess, to own to (une faute); *avouez donc!,* own up!
— v. pr. **S'avouer,** to be confessed (faute); *s'avouer coupable,* to acknowledge (ou) to own oneself guilty, to plead guilty.
avril [avril] m. April; *le premier avril,* All (ou) U. S. April Fools' Day; *poisson d'avril,* April fool hoax.
avulsion [avylsjɔ̃] f. Méd. Extraction. ‖ Jur. Avulsion.
avunculaire [avɔ̃kylɛ:r] adj. Avuncular.

axe [aks] m. Math., Phys. Axis. ‖ Techn. Axle, spindle, pin; *axe de piston,* gudgeon pin; *axe de pompe,* pump spindle. ‖ Aviat. Line; *axe de descente,* line of descent, glide path. ‖ Fig. Axis (en politique).
axer [-se] v. tr. Fam. To centre; *axer un roman sur une intrigue,* to build (ou) centre a novel round a plot.
axial, ale [aksjal] adj. Axial.
axillaire [aksillɛ:r] adj. Méd. Axillary.
axiomatique [aksjɔmatik] adj. Math. Axiomatic, axiomatical.
— f. Math. Axiomatics.
axiome [aksjo:m] m. Axiom.
axiomètre [aksjɔmɛtr] m. Naut. Telltale; steering indicator.
axis [aksis] m. Méd. Axis.
axone [akson] m. Méd. Axon.
axonge [aksɔ̃:ʒ] f. Lard. ‖ Milit. Rifle grease.
ayant [ɛjɑ̃]. V. AVOIR. ‖ **Ayant cause,** m. Jur. Assign, assignee; cessionary; trustee, executor. ‖ **Ayant droit,** m. Jur. Rightful owner (ou) claimant; beneficiary; interested party, recipient.
ayons [ɛjɔ̃]. V. AVOIR (19).
azalée [azale] f. Bot. Azalea.
azimut [azimyt] m. Astron. Azimuth.
azimutal, ale [-tal] adj. Astron. Azimuth(al).
— m. Azimuthal compass.
azoïque [azɔik] adj. Chim. Aniline. ‖ Géol. Azoic.
azotate [azɔtat] m. Chim. Nitrate; *azotate de potassium,* nitre; U. S. niter, saltpeter.
azote [azɔt] m. Chim. Nitrogen, azote.
azoté, ée [-te] adj. Chim. Nitrogenous.
azoter [-te] v. tr. Chim. To azotize, to nitrogenize.
azoteux, euse [-tø, ø:z] adj. Chim. Nitrous, azotous.
azotique [-tik] adj. Chim. Nitric, azotic.
azotite [-tit] m. Chim. Nitrite.
azoture [-ty:r] m. Chim. Nitride.
aztèque [aztɛk] adj., s. Géogr. Aztec. ‖ Fam. Little squit, shrimp.
azur [azy:r] m. Azure; *d'azur,* azure; *la Côte d'Azur,* the Riviera.
— adj. Azure. (V. BLEU, CÉRULÉEN.)
azuré, ée [-re] adj. Azure, blue, sky-blue.
azurer v. tr. (1). To blue, to azure.
azurine [-rin] f. Azurine.
azurite [-rit] f. Azurite.
azygos [azigɔs] adj. Méd. Azygous.
azyme [azim] adj. Unleavened.
— m. Unleavened bread.

B

b [b] m. B, b.
B. A. [bea] f. Abrév. de *bonne action,* good deed; *faire une B. A.,* to do a good deed.
baba [baba] m. Culin. Baba.
baba adj. Fam. Flabbergasted; open-mouthed; agape; wide-eyed; *en rester baba,* to be struck dumb with astonishment.
babeurre [babœ:r] m. Culin. Buttermilk.
babil [babil] m. Babble, prattle (d'enfant). ‖ Chatter, twittering (d'oiseaux); babble, murmur (de ruisseau).

babillage [babija:ʒ] m. Babbling (d'enfant, de ruisseau); twittering, chattering (d'oiseaux). ‖ Babble, natter (de bavard).
babillard, arde [-ja:r, ard] adj. Talkative (personne); babbling (ruisseau).
— s. Babbler. (V. BAVARD.)
babiller [-je] v. intr. (1). To babble, to prattle (enfant); to chatter (personne); to babble (ruisseau). [V. BAVARDER.]
babine [babin] f. Pendulous lip. ‖ Pl. Chops (d'un

chien); flews (d'un dogue). ‖ FAM. Lips, chops (d'une personne).
babiole [babjɔl] f. Bauble, gewgaw, knick-knack, gimcrack. (V. BROUTILLE.) ‖ Toy (jouet).
bâbord [babɔ:r] m. NAUT. Port.
babouche [babuʃ] f. Babouche, Turkish slipper.
babouin [babwɛ̃] m. ZOOL. Baboon. ‖ MÉD. Pimple on the lip, fever blister.
baby-foot [babifut] m. invar. Table football.
Babylone [babilɔn] f. Babylon (pr. et fig.).
babylonien, enne [-njɛ̃, ɛn] adj., s. Babylonian.
baby-sitter [bebisitɛ:r] s. Baby-sitter.
bac [bak] m. Tub (baquet); tank, vat (réservoir). ‖ Sink (d'évier). ‖ NAUT. Ferry, ferryboat; *bac transbordeur*, train ferry; *passer qqn en bac*, to ferry s.o. over.
bacantes [bakɑ̃:t] f. pl. V. BACCHANTES.
baccalauréat [bakalorea] (abrév. **bac**) m. Baccalauréat, secondary school leaving; *baccalauréat ès lettres, ès sciences*, matriculation; General Certificate of Education (Advanced Level). ‖ JUR. *Baccalauréat en droit*, bachelorship in Law.
baccara [bakara] m. Baccarat (jeu).
baccarat [bakara] m. Baccarat crystal.
bacchanale [bakana:l] f. FAM. Bacchanal (danse, débauche). ‖ Pl. Bacchanalia.
bacchante [-kɑ̃:t] f. Bacchante.
bacchantes f. pl. POP. Whiskers, moustache.
bâchage [bɑʃa:ʒ] m. Covering with a tarpaulin. ‖ TECHN. Casing.
bâche [bɑ:ʃ] f. Coarse canvas cover; awning; tilt; *bâche goudronnée*, tarpaulin. ‖ Drag-net (filet). ‖ AGRIC. Frame. ‖ TECHN. Tank cistern; casing (en mécanique).
bachelier, ère [baʃlje, ɛr] s. Student who has taken his « baccalauréat ». ‖ † Squire.
bâcher [bɑʃe] v. tr. (1). To cover, to sheet; to tilt. ‖ To case.
bachique [baʃik] adj. Bacchic; bacchanalian.
bachot [baʃo] m. NAUT. Punt, wherry. (V. BAC.)
bachot m. FAM. V. BACCALAURÉAT; *boîte à bachot*, cramming school, crammer's (fam.).
bachotage [-ta:ʒ] m. FAM. Cramming.
bachoter [-te] v. intr. (1). FAM. To cram.
bachoteur [-tœ:r] m. NAUT. Wherryman.
bachoteur [-tœ:r] m. FAM. Crammer; swot.
bacillaire [basilɛ:r] adj. MÉD. Bacillary.
bacille [basil] m. MÉD. Bacillus (pl. bacilli); *porteur de bacilles*, germ-carrier.
bacillose [basilo:z] f. MÉD. Bacillary infection.
bâclage [bakla:ʒ] m. Scamping; botching, messing. ‖ NAUT. Blocking up.
bâcle [bɑ:k] f. Bar.
bâclé [-kle] adj. Scamped, slap-dash, botched, bungled. ‖ NAUT. Blocked (port).
bâcler [-kle] v. tr. (1). To scamp, to botch, to patch up (un ouvrage); to hurry over (sa toilette). ‖ To patch up (la paix). ‖ To bar (la porte). ‖ NAUT. To block.
bâcleur, euse [-klœ:r, ø:z] s. Patcher-up, scamper, botcher; slap-dash worker, bungler. (V. BOUSILLEUR.)
bacon [bekœn] m. CULIN. Bacon.
bactéricide [bakterisid] adj. MÉD. Bactericide.
bactérie [-ri] f. MÉD. Bacterium (pl. bacteria).
bactérien, enne [-rjɛ̃, ɛn] adj. MÉD. Bacterial.
bactériologie [-rjɔlɔʒi] f. MÉD. Bacteriology.
bactériologique [-rjɔlɔʒik] adj. MÉD. Bacteriological.
bactériologiste [-rjɔlɔʒist] s. MÉD. Bacteriologist.
bactériophage [-rjɔfa:ʒ] m. MÉD. Bacteriophage.
badaud [bado] s. Gaper; U. S. rubber-necker.
badauder [-de] v. intr. (1). To lounge; U. S. to rubber-neck (v. FLÂNER); *badauder dans les rues*, to go gaping about the streets. ‖ To gape (*devant*, at).

badauderie [-dri] f. Rubbernecking, gaping.
baderne [badɛrn] f. NAUT. Mat, fender. ‖ FAM. *Vieille baderne*, old fogy; back number.
badiane [badjan] f. BOT. Anise.
badigeon [badiʒɔ̃] m. Whitewash (blanc); distemper (de couleur). ‖ TECHN. Badigeon. ‖ FAM. Make-up (maquillage).
badigeonnage [-ʒɔna:ʒ] m. Whitewashing; distempering. ‖ MÉD. Application; painting.
badigeonner [-ʒɔne] v. tr. (1). To whitewash (en blanc); to colour-wash, to distemper (en couleur). ‖ TECHN. To apply badigeon to. ‖ MÉD. To paint, to coat. ‖ FAM. To make up, to paint.
badigeonneur [-ʒɔnœ:r] m. Whitewasher. ‖ FAM. Dauber. (V. BARBOUILLEUR, RAPIN.)
badin, ine [badɛ̃, in] adj. Playful.
badin m. AVIAT. Air-speed indicator.
badinage [badina:ʒ] m. Badinage, banter, jesting; teasing.
badine [badin] f. Switch, light stick.
badiner [badine] v. intr. (1). To sport, to toy (jouer) [*avec*, with]; to joke, to trifle (plaisanter) [*avec*, with]; to banter, to tease (taquiner); *en badinant*, jokingly, sportively, in fun.
badinerie [-nri] f. Banter; joking; bit of fun.
badminton [badmintɔn] m. SPORTS. Badminton.
baffe [baf] f. POP. Clout, sock, smack.
baffle [bafl] m. TECHN. Baffle-board. ‖ FAM. Speaker, loudspeaker.
bafouer [bafwe] v. tr. (1). To scoff at; to gibe at, to flout. (V. RAILLER.)
bafouillage [bafuja:ʒ] m. FAM. Spluttering, stammering.
bafouille [bafu:j] f. POP. Epistle.
bafouiller [-je] v. tr. (1). FAM. To splutter out, to stammer out.
— v. intr. To splutter, to stammer.
bafouilleur [-jœ:r] s. FAM. Splutterer, stammerer.
bâfrer [bɑ:fre] v. intr. (1). POP. To tuck in, to gorge, to gobble, to guzzle, to gormandise.
— v. tr. To gobble, to guzzle, to stuff oneself with, to wolf (la nourriture).
bâfreur, euse [-frœ:r, ɸ:z] s. POP. Guzzler.
bagage [baga:ʒ] m. Luggage, U. S. baggage; *menus bagages*, hand-luggage; U. S. light baggage. ‖ MILIT. Baggage. ‖ FIG. Stock of knowledge (connaissances); works (œuvres). ‖ LOC. *Plier bagage*, to pack up and be off.
bagagiste [-gaʒist] m. Porter, luggage handler; U.S. bell boy (dans un hôtel).
bagarre [baga:r] f. Affray; scuffle, brawl; free-for-all. (V. RIXE.) ‖ FAM. Quarrel.
bagarrer (se) [səbagare] v. pr. (1). FAM. To scuffle (se battre) [*avec*, with]; to stand up to (tenir tête à) [*avec*, with].
bagarreur, euse [bagarœ:r, ɸ:z] adj. Scrappy, aggressive.
— s. One for a good fight.
bagatelle [bagatɛl] f. Bagatelle; trifle, trinket; knick-knack; gewgaw; whimwham (v. BRICOLE); *pour une bagatelle*, for a mere trifle, for a song. ‖ Love-making; *porté sur la bagatelle*, amorous, randy (pop.).
bagnard [baɲa:r] m. Convict.
bagne [baɲ] m. JUR. Penal servitude (peine); convict prison (pénitencier).
bagnole [baɲɔl] f. Rickety car; ramshackle carriage. ‖ FAM. Crock, U.S. jalopy, flivver.
bagou(t) [bagu] m. Gab; glibness; *avoir du bagout*, to have the gift of the gab (ou) U. S. the gift of gab.
baguage [baga:ʒ] m. ZOOL., BOT. Ringing.
bague [bag] f. Ring (de doigt). ‖ Band (de cigare); clip (de stylo). ‖ BOT. Annulus (de champignon). ‖ TECHN. Collar, sleeve, ring.

baguenaude [bagno:d] f. Bot. Bladder-nut.
baguenauder [-de] v. intr. (1). To fiddle-faddle, to moon about (muser); to footle about, to fribble, to fool around (s'amuser).
baguenaudier [-dje] m. Loafer, fribbler (personne). ‖ Ring-puzzle (jeu). ‖ Bot. Bladder-senna, bladder-nut tree.
baguer [bage] v. tr. (1). To put a ring (ou) a band on. ‖ To ring (un arbre, un oiseau); to band (un pigeon). ‖ To baste, to tack (une couture). ‖ Techn. To collar, to ferrule.
baguette [bagɛt] f. Rod, switch; wand; *baguette de démonstration, de laboratoire*, pointer, stirrer; *baguette de fée*, magic wand; *baguette de sourcier*, dowsing rod. ‖ Clock (sur un bas); stitching (sur un gant). ‖ Culin. Vienna loaf (pain). ‖ Milit. *Baguette de fusil*, rocket stick. ‖ Archit. Fillet; moulding. ‖ Mus. Baton (de chef d'orchestre); *baguette de tambour*, drumstick. ‖ Fam. *Faire marcher à la baguette*, to rule with a rod of iron.
baguier [bagje] m. Ring-box (ou) -case.
bah [bɑ] interj. Bah!; really?
Bahamas [bahama] f. pl. Géogr. Bahamas, Bahama Islands.
Bahrein [barɛjn] m. Géogr. Bahrain.
bahut [bay] m. Cabinet, chest. ‖ Archit. Saddleback coping. ‖ Pop. School, lycée.
bai, ie [bɛ] adj., m. Zool. Bay (cheval).
baie f. Géogr. Bay. ‖ Archit. Bay; bay-window.
baie f. Bot. Berry.
baignade [bɛɲad] f. Bathe (bain); bathing-place (lieu). ‖ Watering (des chevaux).
baignage [-ɲa:ʒ] m. Bathing; soaking.
baigner [-ɲe] v. tr. (1). To bathe (le corps); to bath (un enfant). ‖ To wash (la côte); to water (une région); *baigné de larmes*, suffused with tears.
— v. intr. To soak, to steep; *faire baigner dans*, to soak in. ‖ Fig. *Baigner dans son sang*, to welter in one's blood.
— v. pr. Se **baigner**, to take a bath (dans une baignoire); to bathe (dans la mer).
baigneur [-ɲœ:r] m. Bath-keeper ‖ Water-drinker, bather (aux eaux); bather (à la mer). ‖ Bath (ou) bathing attendant (employé des bains). ‖ Celluloid doll (poupée). ‖ Culin. Small china doll (fève du gâteau des rois).
baigneuse [-ɲœ:z] f. Bath-attendant (employée); bathing-wrap, U. S. bath-robe (peignoir).
baignoire [-ɲwa:r] f. Bath, bath-tub. ‖ Théâtr. Baignoire. ‖ Naut. Conning-tower (fam.).
bail [ba:j] (pl. **baux**) m. Lease; *donner à bail*, to lease; *faire, passer, résilier un bail*, to execute, to draw up, to cancel a lease; *prendre à bail*, to lease. ‖ Agric. *Bail à ferme*, farming lease.
baille [ba:j] f. Naut. Tub; *la baille* (arg.), the drink.
bâillement [bɑjmɑ̃] m. Yawning; yawn; gaping, gape.
bailler [baje] v. tr. (1). †. To give; *vous me la baillez belle!*, tell it to the marines!, you are pulling my leg!, tell me another!
bâiller [bɑ:je] v. tr. (1). To yawn; *bâiller à se décrocher la mâchoire*, to yawn one's head off. ‖ To gape (chaussure, couture); to stand ajar (porte).
bailleur, eresse [-jœ:r, rɛ:s] m. Lessor. ‖ Fin. *Bailleur de fonds*, sleeping partner, financial backer (commanditaire); money-lender (prêteur).
bâilleur, euse [bɑjœ:r, ∅:z] s. Yawner.
bailli [baji] m. † Bailiff.
bailliage [baja:ʒ] m. † Bailiff's court (tribunal); bailiwick (juridiction).
bâillon [bɑjɔ̃] m. Gag.
bâillonnement [-jɔnmɑ̃] m. Gagging, putting a gag on. ‖ Fig. Muzzling.
bâillonner [-jɔne] v. tr. (1). To gag. ‖ Fig. To muzzle.

bain [bɛ̃] m. Bath (dans une baignoire); bathe (dans la mer ou une rivière); *bain de boue, de pieds, de siège, de soleil, de vapeur*, mud-bath, foot-bath, hip-bath (ou) sitz-bath, sun-bath, steam-bath; *bains de mer*, sea-bathing, sea-baths; *établissement de bains*, public baths, U. S. bath-house; *faire prendre, prendre un bain* (v. Baigner, Baigner [se]); *peignoir de bain*, bathing-wrap, U. S. bath-robe; *salle de bain*, bathroom. ‖ Techn. Bath; *bain de fixage*, fixing-bath. ‖ Fam. *Envoyer qqn au bain*, to send s.o. packing, to tell s.o. where to get off; *être dans le bain*, to be in the know. ‖ Loc. *L'ordre du Bain*, the Order of the Bath. ‖ **Bain-douche**, m. Shower-bath. ‖ **Bain-marie**, m. Kitchen-range boiler, jacketed-saucepan, bain-marie, double boiler.
baïonnette [bajɔnɛt] f. Milit. Bayonet; *baïonnette au canon*, fixed bayonet; *charge à la baïonnette*, bayonet charge; *enlever à la baïonnette*, to take at the bayonet's point.
baise-en-ville [bɛzɑ̃vil] m. invar. Pop. Overnight bag (ou) case.
baisemain [bɛzmɛ̃] m. Hand-kissing.
baisement [-mɑ̃] m. Ecclés. Kissing.
baiser [bɛze] v. tr. (1). To kiss (qqch.) [v. Embrasser]; *baiser la main d'une femme*, to kiss a lady's hand. ‖ Arg. To fuck, to screw, to lay (faire l'amour). ‖ Arg. To screw, to do (duper).
— m. Kiss; *baiser de paix*, kiss of peace; *donner un baiser à*, to kiss; *gros baiser*, smack.
baisoter [bɛzɔte] v. tr. (1). Fam. To peck at.
baisse [bɛ:s] f. Decrease; subsidence (des eaux); ebb (de la marée); fall (de la température, du potentiel). ‖ Sinking (des forces, de la voix); failing (de la vue). ‖ Fin. Fall, drop (des valeurs); *baisse rapide*, slump, falling off; *en baisse*, falling (actions); *jouer à la baisse*, to bear.
baissé, ée [bɛse] adj. Pulled down (rideau). ‖ Bent down, downcast, on the ground (yeux); *tête baissée*, blindly (à l'aveuglette); full tilt, headlong (impétueusement).
baisser v. tr. (1). To lower, to drop (le rideau); to let down, to pull down (un store, une vitre). ‖ To lower, to reduce the height of (un mur, une séparation). ‖ To lower (la main, un objet, la voix); to hang (la tête); to cast down (les yeux); *elle baissa les yeux*, she looked down; *faire baisser les yeux à*, to outstare. ‖ Comm. To lower, to bring down (les prix). ‖ Mus. To lower (un morceau, un ton). ‖ Autom. To dim (les phares).
— v. intr. To subside, to sink (eaux); to ebb (marée). ‖ To dip (balance). ‖ To burn down (ou) low, to sink (feu, flamme); to decline, to fade (lumière); to sink (soleil); to fall (température). ‖ To run low (réserves). ‖ To decline (forces, influence, moral); to fail (mémoire, vue); to fall off, to degenerate (moralité); to sink, to weaken (voix); *baisser dans l'estime de*, to sink in the esteem (ou) estimation of. ‖ Comm. To fall, to decline, to drop; to sag; to go down, U. S. to dip (prix); *faire baisser*, to lower; *empêcher de baisser*, to keep up. ‖ Méd. To decline (malade, santé); *qqn qui a beaucoup baissé*, U. S. a has-been.
— v. pr. Se **baisser**, to stoop, to bend down; *se baisser brusquement*, to duck.
— m. Théâtr. Drop, fall (du rideau).
baissier [-sje] m. Fin. Bear; U. S. short.
baissière [-sjɛ:r] f. Agric. Hollow. ‖ Lees.
bajoue [baʒu] f. Chap, chop; flabby (ou) baggy cheek.
Bakélite [bakelit] f. (nom déposé). Chim. Bakelite.
bakhchich [bakʃiʃ] m. Baksheesh.
bal [bal] m. Ball.
balade [balad] f. Fam. Outing; stroll, ramble (à pied). ‖ Run, drive (en auto).
balader [-de] v. tr. (1). Fam. To push around (qqch.); to take for a walk (qqn); *envoyer bala-*

der qqch., to chuck sth. away; *envoyer balader qqn*, to send s.o. packing.

— v. pr. **Se balader.** FAM. To stroll, to saunter; *aller se balader*, to go out for a stroll.

baladeur, euse [-dœ:r, ø:z] adj. Strolling. ‖ AUTOM. *Train baladeur*, sliding gear.

baladeuse [-dø:z] f. Costermonger's barrow, hand-cart (de marchand ambulant). ‖ ELECTR. Inspection lamp, U. S. trouble lamp.

baladin [baladɛ̃] m. Mountebank. ‖ FIG. Clown.

balafre [balafr] f. Slash, gash (au visage). ‖ Scar (cicatrice).

balafrer [-fre] v. tr. (1). To gash, to slash; to scar.

balai [balɛ] m. Broom (en général); besom (en bouleau, chiendent, genêt); hair broom (de crin); mop (à franges); *balai mécanique*, carpet-sweeper; *donner un coup de balai à une pièce*, to sweep out a room. ‖ FAM. *Donner un coup de balai à*, to make a clean sweep of; *un bon coup de balai*, a good clean-out.

balaise [balɛ:z] adj., s. V. BALÈZE.

balalaïka [balalaika] f. MUS. Balalaika.

balance [balɑ̃:s] f. Balance, scales. ‖ Automatic scales (automatique); shop-scales (à plateaux); weighing-machine (bascule); beam-scales (commune); analytical balance (de précision); steel-yard (romaine). ‖ SPORTS. Hoop-net (pour la pêche). ‖ ASTRON. The Balance, the Scales, Libra. ‖ FIN. Balance; *établir une balance*, to balance an account (ou) the books; *faire la balance*, to strike the balance. ‖ FIG. *Etre en balance*, to hang in the balance; *faire pencher la balance*, to turn the scales; *jeter dans la balance*, to throw into the balance; *mettre en balance*, to compare; *tenir en balance*, to keep in suspense; *tenir la balance égale entre*, to hold the balance even between.

balancé, ée [-se] adj. Balanced. ‖ POP. *Bien balancé*, curvaceous (femme), beefy, brawny (homme).

balancelle [-sɛl] f. Garden swing, swing.

balancement [-smɑ̃] m. Swinging, swaying, rocking; balancing. ‖ FIG. Harmony (de la phrase). ‖ FIG. Indecision, wavering.

balancer [-se] v. tr. (6). To rock, to swing, to sway (qqch., qqn). [V. BERCER.] ‖ FIN. To balance (un compte). ‖ FIG. To compare (comparer); to counter-balance, to make up for (compenser); to hesitate, to waver (hésiter); to balance, to weigh (soupeser). ‖ FAM. To chuck away (qqch.); to sack, to fire (qqn).

— v. intr. To balance, to waver, to hesitate, to demur, to falter (hésiter); to swing, to oscillate, to dangle (osciller).

— v. pr. **Se balancer,** to sway, to swing (sur une balançoire); to rock (sur une chaise à bascule). ‖ To waddle (se dandiner). ‖ FIN. To balance. ‖ FAM. *Je m'en balance*, I don't care a rap!, I couldn't care less!

balancier [-sje] m. Balance wheel (de montre); pendulum (de pendule). ‖ Balancing-pole (d'équilibriste). ‖ COMM. Scale-manufacturer (fabricant). ‖ TECHN. Beam (de machine).

balancine [-sin] f. NAUT. Lift.

balançoire [-swa:r] f. See-saw, U. S. teeter-totter (bascule); swing (escarpolette). ‖ FAM. Humbug. ‖ POP. *Envoyer à la balançoire*, to send to blazes.

balayage [balɛja:ʒ] m. Sweeping (de la maison); scavenging (de la rue). ‖ Sweeping (des mines). ‖ RADIO. *Balayage de l'écran*, scanning.

balayer [-je] v. tr. (9 b). To sweep, to sweep away (qqch.); to sweep out (une pièce); to scavenge (une rue). ‖ ELECTR. To scan. ‖ FIG. To sweep away (enlever); to mow (faucher). ‖ FAM. To make a clean sweep of (un bureau); to fire, to sack (le personnel).

balayette [-jɛt] s. Small broom; brush.

balayeur [-jœ:r] m. Road-sweeper, scavenger.

balayeuse [-jø:z] f. Mechanical street-sweeper (de rues); carpet-sweeper (de tapis).

balayures [-jy:r] f. pl. Sweepings.

balbutiant, ante [balbysjɑ̃, ɑ̃:t] adj. Stammering, stuttering.

balbutiement [-simɑ̃] m. Stammering, stuttering.

balbutier [-sje] v. tr. (1). To stammer out, to stutter out.

— v. intr. To stammer, to stutter; to mumble.

balcon [balkɔ̃] m. Balcony. ‖ THÉÂTR. Dress-circle. ‖ NAUT. Pulpit.

balconnet [-kɔnɛ] m. Half-cup bra.

baldaquin [baldakɛ̃] m. Tester (de lit); *lit à baldaquin*, tester bed. ‖ Baldaquin, canopy (dais).

bale [bal] f. Chaff, husk.

baleine [balɛ:n] f. ZOOL. Whale; *graisse de baleine*, blubber; *huile de baleine*, whale-oil; *pêcher la baleine*, to whale. ‖ COMM. Baleen, whalebone (en fanon de baleine); steel (en acier); *baleine de corset*, corset-steel (ou) -stay (ou) U. S. -bone; *baleine de parapluie*, umbrella-rib.

baleiné, ée [-ne] adj. Whaleboned, stiffened with whalebone.

baleineau [-no] m. ZOOL. Whale-calf.

baleiner [-ne] v. tr. (1). To bone; to steel; to rib; to stiffen.

baleinier, ère [-nje, ɛ:r] adj. Whaling.

— m. NAUT. Whaler (homme et navire).

baleinière [-njɛ:r] f. NAUT. Whale-boat.

balèze ou **balaise** [balɛ:z] adj. POP. Beefy, hefty.

— s. POP. Beefy (ou) hefty person; *il est balèze*, he is six foot of solid muscle.

balisage [baliza:ʒ] m. NAUT. Beaconage; buoying, signalling. ‖ AVIAT. Beaconing, ground-lighting; *balisage général de route*, course lights.

balise [bali:z] f. NAUT. Beacon. ‖ AVIAT. Ground-beacon. (V. BOUÉE.)

baliser [-ze] v. tr. (1). NAUT. To beacon, to buoy. ‖ AVIAT. To mark out (la route); to provide with ground-lights (le terrain); *axe balisé*, aural radio-range course; *piste balisée*, flare-path.

baliseur [-zœ:r] m. NAUT. Buoy-keeper (personne); ship in charge of servicing buoys.

balistique [balistik] adj. Ballistic.

— f. MILIT. Ballistics; gunnery.

baliveau [balivo] m. MILIT. Staddle. ‖ ARCHIT. Scaffold-pole.

baliverne [balivɛrn] f. Twaddle, piffle, bosh; U. S. flapdoodle, hooey. ‖ Pl. Balderdash, gammon, rubbish, bunkum, twaddle, bosh.

baliverner [balivɛrne] v. tr. (1). To talk rubbish, to blether.

balkanique [balkanik] adj. GÉOGR. Balkan.

Balkans [-kɑ̃] m. pl. GÉOGR. Balkans.

ballade [balad] f. Ballad (légende en vers); ballade (petit poème).

ballant [balɑ̃] adj. Swinging, dangling; *les bras ballants*, with his arms swinging, dangling his arms.

— m. Swing. ‖ NAUT. Slack.

ballast [balast] m. Ballast. ‖ NAUT. Water-ballast.

ballaster [-te] v. tr. (1). To ballast.

balle [bal] f. BOT. Chaff, husk.

balle f. SPORTS. Ball; *balle de cricket, de tennis*, cricket-, tennis-ball; *balle au camp*, rounders; *balle au mur*, fives; *faire des balles*, to have a knock-up; *jouer à la balle*, to play ball. ‖ MILIT. Bullet; *à l'épreuve des balles*, bullet-proof; *tirer à balle*, to fire ball cartridge. ‖ COMM. Bale (de coton); bale, pack (de laine); *mettre en balle*, to bale. ‖ FIG. *Enfant de la balle*, born into the profession; *renvoyer la balle*, to return the compliment; *se renvoyer la balle*, to bandy jokes; to let s.o. have it back; to pass the baby (ou) the buck (fam.). ‖ FAM. Dial, mug, U. S. map (figure). ‖ POP. Franc; *peau de balle!*, nix!

baller [bale] v. intr. (1). To rock, to hang loosely.
ballerine [balrin] f. THÉÂTR. Ballerina.
ballet [balɛ] m. THÉÂTR. Ballet; *corps de ballet*, corps de ballet, ballet.
ballon [balɔ̃] m. Ball, football (à jouer). ‖ Balloon glass (verre à dégustation); *manches ballon*, balloon sleeves. ‖ AUTOM. *Pneu ballon*, balloon tyre. ‖ NAUT. Ball. ‖ CHIM. Balloon; flask, bag (d'oxygène). ‖ GÉOGR. Ballon. ‖ AVIAT. Balloon; *ballon d'observation, de protection*, observation-, barrage balloon; *ballon d'essai*, pilot balloon. ‖ FIG. *Ballon d'essai*, feeler. ‖ **Ballon-cigare**, m. Cigar-shaped balloon. ‖ **Ballon-pilote**, m. Pilot-balloon. ‖ **Ballon-réclame**, m. Advertising balloon. ‖ **Ballon-sonde**, m. Sounding balloon.
ballonnement [balɔnmɑ̃] m. Ballooning, swelling. ‖ MÉD. Hoove, U. S. bloat (des animaux); distension, flatulence (des personnes).
ballonner [balɔne] v. tr. (1). To distend, to swell. ‖ To puff out (une manche).
— v. intr. To balloon out (manche).
— v. pr. Se **ballonner**, MÉD. To distend, to swell.
ballonnet [balɔnɛ] m. AVIAT. Ballonet, small balloon; *ballonnet de bout d'aile*, wing float; *ballonnet d'hydravion*, stub-wing stabilizer.
ballonnier [-nje] m. Toy-balloon maker (ou) seller.
ballot [balo] m. Bale; bundle. ‖ Pack (de colporteur). ‖ POP. Boob, simp; ninny; U. S. sucker.
ballottage [balɔta:ʒ] m. Jolting. ‖ Second ballot (en Angleterre); ballotage (en France); *il y a ballottage*, a second ballot (ou) poll will be necessary.
ballottement [balɔtmɑ̃] m. Jolting (d'une voiture). ‖ Shaking about (d'une pièce desserrée). ‖ NAUT. Tossing.
ballotter [balɔte] v. tr. (1). To shake about (un objet). ‖ To jolt (voiture). ‖ NAUT. To toss. ‖ FIG. To put off (qqn).
— v. intr. To toss about (bateau); to shake about (objet); to wobble (table). ‖ FIG. To toss.
ballottine [balɔtin] f. CULIN. Ballottine.
ball-trap [baltrap] m. SPORTS. Trap (appareil); clay-pigeon shooting, trap-shooting (tir).
balluchon [balyʃɔ̃] m. FAM. Bundle.
balmoral [balmɔral] m. Balmoral.
balnéaire [balneɛ:r] adj. Bathing; *station balnéaire*, watering-place, spa (aux eaux); seaside resort (à la mer).
balnéation [-asjɔ̃] f. MÉD. Taking of curative (ou) medicinal baths.
balnéothérapie [balneoterapi] f. MÉD. Balneotherapy.
balourd, ourde [balu:r, u:rd] adj. Dense, doltish.
— m. Duffer, block-head; lout, clod-hopper. (V. LOURDAUD.) ‖ TECHN. Unbalance.
balourdise [balurdi:z] f. Doltishness; loutishness (sottise). ‖ Blunder, bloomer, boner (gaffe).
balsa [balsa] m. BOT. Balsa.
balsamier [balzamje] m. BOT. Balsam, balsam fir.
balsamine [balzamin] f. BOT. Balsamine, balsam.
balsamique [-mik] adj. Balsamic, balmy.
balte [balt] adj. GÉOGR. Baltic.
— s. GÉOGR. Balt.
— m. GRAMM. Baltic (langue).
balthazar [baltaza:r] m. Belshazzar. ‖ FAM. Banquet, blow-out.
baltique [baltik] adj. Baltic.
— f. Baltic Sea.
baluchon [balyʃɔ̃] m. V. BALLUCHON.
balustrade [balystrad] f. Balustrade; railing.
balustre [balystr] m. Baluster; banister.
balzacien, enne [balzasjɛ̃, ɛn] adj. Balzacian, relating to Honoré de Balzac.
balzan, ane [balzɑ̃, an] adj. White-stockinged.
balzane [balzɑn] f. White stocking.

bambin [bɑ̃bɛ̃] m. Urchin; tiny tot. (V. GOSSE.)
bambochade [bɑ̃bɔʃad] f. ARTS. Bambocciade.
bambochard, arde [bɑ̃bɔʃa:r, ard] adj. FAM. Revelling, pleasure-seeking.
— s. FAM. Reveller, pleasure-seeker. (V. BAMBOCHEUR.)
bamboche [bɑ̃bɔʃ] f. FAM. Spree, high jinks, binge, U. S. jag. (V. BOMBE.) ‖ Marionnette. ‖ BOT. Bamboo-shoot. ‖ FAM. Little runt (personne).
bambocher [-ʃe] v. intr. (1). FAM. To carouse; to go on the razzle (ou) on a binge. (V. NOCER.)
bambocheur [-ʃœ:r] s. FAM. Carouser; reveller. (V. NOCEUR.)
bambou [bɑ̃bu] m. BOT. Bamboo. ‖ FAM. *Coup de bambou*, sunstroke; *il a reçu un coup de bambou*, his mind is wandering.
bamboula [bɑ̃bula] f. FAM. *Faire la bamboula*, to go on a binge.
ban [bɑ̃] m. † Ban; *le ban et l'arrière-ban*, all one's supporters, the whole clan, every man Jack. ‖ Announcement, proclamation; *publier les bans*, to publish (ou) to put up the bans. ‖ Round of applause; *battre un ban*, to applaud, to clap rhythmically. ‖ MILIT. Roll of drum. ‖ JUR. Ban; sentence of outlawing; *mettre au ban*, to outlaw, to banish; *rupture de ban*, breaking of bounds (ou) ticket-of-leave. ‖ FIG. *Etre au ban de*, to be banned by.
banal, ale [banal] adj. Communal (moulin); village (pressoir). ‖ Commonplace; banal; trite (v. COMMUN); *peu banal*, unusual, exceptional; *phrase banale*, hackneyed sentence. ‖ Unimportant.
banalement [-lmɑ̃] adv. In a banal manner, tritely.
banalisation [-lizasjɔ̃] f. Making commonplace. ‖ Popularization. ‖ Disguising (d'une voiture de police). ‖ Removal of special rights from (d'un campus universitaire).
banaliser [-lize] v. tr. (1). To make commonplace (ou) trite. ‖ To vulgarize, to popularize. ‖ To disguise (une voiture de police); *voiture de police banalisée*, unmarked police car. ‖ To remove special rights from (un campus universitaire).
banalité [-lite] f. Banality, triviality; triteness (caractère). ‖ Truism; commonplace (chose); *dire des banalités*, to platitudinize; *sans banalité*, unhackneyed, fresh (langage).
banane [banan] f. BOT. Banana. ‖ ELECTR. Plug. ‖ AUTOM. Over-rider.
bananeraie [-nrɛ] f. BOT. Banana-plantation.
bananier [-nje] m. BOT. Banana-tree, banana.
banc [bɑ̃] m. Bench, form; *banc d'église*, pew; *banc de jardin*, garden-seat. ‖ JUR. Dock (des accusés); jury-box (des jurés); *banc des ministres*, front bench. ‖ GÉOL. Layer, stratum; shelf, ledge; *banc de corail*, coral-reef; *banc de glace*, ice-floe; *banc de rochers*, reef; *banc de sable*, sand-bank. ‖ School, shoal (de poissons); *banc d'huîtres*, oyster-bed. ‖ NAUT. *Banc de brume*, fog-bank. ‖ TECHN. *Banc d'essai, d'étirage, de montage*, testing, drawing, assembly-bench.
bancable [bɑ̃kabl] adj. FIN. Bankable.
bancaire [-kɛ:r] adj. FIN. Bank, banking.
bancal, ale, als [bɑ̃kal] adj. Bandy (jambe); bandy-legged, bow-legged (personne). ‖ Wobbly (meuble).
— s. Bandy-legged person. (V. BOITEUX.)
banco [bɑ̃ko] adj. inv. *Faire banco*, to go banco.
bandage [bɑ̃da:ʒ] m. MÉD. Bandaging (action); belt (ceinture); bandage (pansement); *bandage de corps*, binder; *bandage herniaire*, truss. ‖ TECHN. Hoop; band. ‖ AUTOM. Tyre, U. S. tire.
bandagiste [-ʒist] m. MÉD. Truss-maker.
bande [bɑ̃:d] f. Band (d'étoffe, de papier, de métal); stretch, belt, strip (de terre, de terrain); *bande dessinée*, comics; *bande de journal*, news-

paper wrapper; *bande de pantalon,* trouser stripe. ‖ Cushion (de billard). ‖ COMM. *Bande publicitaire,* avertising streamer (sur autobus). ‖ MILIT. *Bande de mitrailleuse,* loading belt. ‖ NAUT. Heel, list; *donner de la bande,* to heel, to list; *mettre à la bande,* to cant. ‖ AUTOM. *Bande de frein,* brake band (ou) strap. ‖ BLAS. Bend. ‖ MÉD. Bandage. ‖ ELECTR. Bar (de distribution). ‖ RADIO. *Bande de fréquences,* frequency band. ‖ CINÉM. Strip (des images); reel (du film); *bande sonore,* sound track. ‖ **Bande-annonce,** f. Trailer. ‖ **Bande-chargeur,** f. MILIT. Cartridge belt. ‖ **Bande-image,** f. Picture-film. ‖ **Bande-son,** f. Sound-track. ‖ **Bande-texte,** f. Film-strip.

bande [bɑ̃:d] f. Rout (de fêtards); bevy (de jeunes filles); band, troop, throng, clique (de personnes). ‖ Gang, pack (de voleurs). ‖ Wedge (de cygnes); swarm (de fourmis); pride (de lions); pack (de loups); gaggle (d'oies); flock, flight (d'oiseaux); shoal, school (de poissons); skulk (de renards).

bandeau [bɑ̃do] m. Headband, bandeau; diadem (de tête). ‖ Bandage (sur la mâchoire, les yeux). ‖ ARCHIT. Band, fillet. ‖ FIG. *Avoir un bandeau sur les yeux,* to have a film over one's eyes, to be hoodwinked.

bandelette [bɑ̃dlɛt] f. Strip; wrapping (de momie).

bander [-de] v. tr. (1). To draw, to bend (un arc); to stretch, to strain (un câble); to tighten (un ressort). ‖ AUTOM. To tyre (une roue). ‖ MÉD. To bandage, to tie up. ‖ FIG. To bend (l'esprit); to strain (les nerfs); to blindfold (les yeux); *bander les yeux à,* to hoodwink.
— v. intr. POP. To have a hard-on.
— v. pr. **Se bander,** to be bent (arc). ‖ *Se bander les yeux,* to blindfold one's eyes.

banderille [bɑ̃deri:j] f. Banderilla.

banderole [bɑ̃drɔl] f. Banderole. ‖ Pennant.

bandit [bɑ̃di] m. Bandit; gangster; *bandit de grand chemin,* highwayman, highway-robber. ‖ FAM. Scoundrel, ruffian, U. S. hijacker.

banditisme [-tism] m. Banditry.

bandoulière [bɑ̃duljɛ:r] f. Bandoleer; shoulder-belt (ou) -sash (ou) -strap; *en bandoulière,* over the shoulder; *sac à bandoulière,* shoulder-bag.

bang [bɑ̃g] m. AVIAT. Sonic boom.

Bangladesh [bɑ̃gladɛʃ] m. GÉOGR. Bangladesh.

banian [banjã] m. BOT. Banyan-tree.

banjo [bɑ̃jo] m. MUS. Banjo.

banlieue [bɑ̃ljø] f. Suburb (localité); *la banlieue,* the suburbs, the city outskirts, Suburbia (péj.); *de banlieue,* suburban.

banlieusard, arde [-za:r, ard] s. Suburbanite (fam.); commuter (travaillant en ville).

banne [ban] f. Coal cart (à charbon). ‖ Hamper, skep (panier). ‖ Tilt, tarpaulin. (V. BÂCHE.)

banneret [banərɛ] adj. m. Banneret.

banneton [bantɔ̃] m. Bread-basket. ‖ Corf (à poisson).

banni, ie [bani] adj. Exiled, banished, outlawed. — s. Exile, outlaw. (V. EXILÉ.)

bannière [banjɛ:r] f. MILIT., ECCLÉS. Banner. ‖ FIG. *Se ranger sous la bannière de,* to side with, to join the party (ou) the banner of. ‖ FAM. Shirt-tail.

bannir [bani:r] v. tr. (2). To banish, to exile (de, from); to outlaw.

bannissement [banismã] m. Banishment. (V. EXIL.)

banque [bɑ̃:k] f. FIN. Bank; *banque de dépôt, d'escompte,* deposit, discount bank; *banque d'émission,* bank of issue; *carnet de banque,* bank-book; *employé de banque,* bank clerk. ‖ Bank; *faire sauter la banque,* to break the bank (au jeu). ‖ MÉD. *Banque du sang, des yeux,* blood, eye bank.

banqueroute [bɑ̃krut] f. JUR. Fraudulent bankruptcy. ‖ FIG. Failure.

banqueroutier [-tje] s. Fraudulent bankrupt; bankrupt trader. (V. FAILLI.)

banquet [bɑ̃kɛ] m. Banquet; public dinner.

banqueter [bɑ̃kte] v. intr. (8 a). To banquet.

banquette [bɑ̃kɛt] f. Bench (banc). ‖ Seat (d'autobus, de train); wall-sofa (de restaurant). ‖ MUS. Duet-stool (de piano). ‖ ARCHIT. Window-sill (de fenêtre); railings (de jardin). ‖ MILIT. *Banquette de tir,* banquette, fire-step. ‖ SPORTS. Bunker (au golf).

banquier [bɑ̃kje] m. FIN. Banker.

banquise [bɑ̃ki:z] f. Ice-field, ice-floe, ice-pack.

bantou [bɑ̃tu] m. GRAMM. Bantu (langue).

baobab [baɔbab] m. BOT. Baobab.

baptême [batɛ:m] m. ECCLÉS. Baptism; christening; *baptême d'une cloche,* blessing of a bell; *nom de baptême,* Christian name; *recevoir le baptême,* to be baptised (ou) christened; *robe de baptême,* christening dress. ‖ NAUT. Christening (d'un navire); *baptême de la ligne,* « crossing the line » ducking ceremony. ‖ AVIAT. *Baptême de l'air,* first flight. ‖ MILIT. *Baptême du feu,* baptism of fire.

baptiser [-tize] v. tr. (1). To christen (qqch.); to baptise, to christen (qqn). ‖ To name (nommer); to nickname, to dub (surnommer). ‖ FAM. To water down (le lait, le vin).

baptismal, e, aux [-tismal, o] adj. ECCLÉS. Baptismal; *fonts baptismaux,* font.

baptisme [-tism] m. ECCLÉS. Baptist doctrine.

Baptiste [-tist] m. Baptist; *Jean-Baptiste,* John the Baptist.

baptistère [-tistɛ:r] m. ECCLÉS. Baptistry.

baquet [bakɛ] m. Tub; bucket. ‖ Trough (abreuvoir). ‖ AUTOM. Bucket-seat. ‖ AVIAT. Well seat.

bar [ba:r] m. ZOOL. Bar; sea-dace; bass.

bar m. PHYS. Bar.

bar m. Bar (v. BUVETTE); *au bar,* in the bar; *dans un bar,* in a pub.

baragouin [baragwɛ̃] m. Gibberish; jabber.

baragouinage [-gwina:ʒ] m. Jabbering (acte); gibberish (résultat).

baragouiner [-gwine] v. intr. (1). To jabber, to gibber. (V. BALBUTIER.)
— v. tr. To jabber, to talk gibberish; *baragouiner l'anglais,* to talk broken English.

baragouineur, euse [-gwinœ:r, ø:z] s. FAM. Jabberer, person who talks gibberish.

baraka [baraka] f. FAM. Luck; *avoir la baraka,* to be lucky.

baraque [barak] f. FAM. Hut, shanty. (V. BICOQUE.) ‖ Booth (de foire). ‖ FAM. Hovel.

baraqué, ée [-ke] adj. POP. Hefty, beefy.

baraquement [-kmã] m. Hutting; hutments.

baraquer [-ke] v. tr., intr. (1). MILIT. To hut.

baraterie [baratri] f. NAUT. Barratry.

baratin [baratɛ̃] m. POP. Patter, empty talk; U. S. spiel, line, ballyhoo.

baratiner [baratine] v. intr. (1). POP. To speechify; U. S. to gas.

baratineur, euse [-nœ:r, nø:z] s. POP. Smooth talker (bonimenteur); gasbag, windbag (discoureur).

barattage [barata:ʒ] m. Churning (du lait).

baratte [barat] f. Churn.

baratter [-te] v. tr. (1). To churn.

barbacane [barbakan] f. †. Barbican; loop-hole. ‖ ARCHIT. Weeper, weep-hole.

Barbade (la) [labarbad] f. GÉOGR. Barbados.

barbant, ante [barbɑ̃, ɑ̃:t] adj. FAM. Boring.

barbaque [barbak] f. FAM. Third-rate meat.

barbare [barba:r] adj. Barbarous; uncivilized; cruel. ‖ Barbaric (art, conception, costume, mœurs); *acte barbare,* barbarity.
— m. Barbarian.

barbaresque [-resk] adj., s. † Barbaresque.
barbarie [-ri] f. Barbarism (manque de culture). ‖ Barbarousness, barbarity (cruauté).
barbarisme [-rism] m. GRAMM. Barbarism.
barbe [barb] adj., m. ZOOL. Barb (cheval).
barbe f. Beard (d'homme); goatee (bouc); Newgate frill (collier); *barbe de deux jours*, stubble; *se faire la barbe*, to shave; *plat à barbe*, shaving-basin; *porter toute sa barbe*, to wear a full beard. ‖ Whiskers (de chat); beard (de chèvre, de comète, d'épi); wattle (d'oiseau, de poisson); barb (de plume, de papier). ‖ NAUT. *Tirer en barbe*, to fire in barb (ou) barbette. ‖ FIG. *A la barbe de qqn*, under s.o.'s nose; *rire dans sa barbe*, to laugh up one's sleeve. ‖ FAM. Bother, bore; *la barbe!*, dry up! ‖ **Barbe-de-capucin** (pl. *barbes-de-capucin*), f. BOT. Wild chicory.
barbeau [barbo] m. ZOOL. Barbel. ‖ BOT. Corn-flower. ‖ POP. Pimp (souteneur).
barbecue [barbəkju] m. Barbecue.
barbelé, ée [barbəle] adj. Barbed; *fil de fer barbelé*, barbed wire.
— m. pl. Barbed-wire entanglements.
barber [barbe] v. tr. (1). FAM. To bore stiff.
— v. pr. **Se barber**, to be bored; to be cheesed (ou) browned off (ou) fed up. (V. S'EMBÊTER.)
barbet [barbɛ] m. ZOOL. Barbet.
barbette [barbɛt] f. ECCLÉS. Wimple (guimpe). ‖ MILIT. Barbette.
barbiche [barbiʃ] f. Goatee.
barbichette [-biʃɛt] f. Small goatee.
barbier [-bje] m. Barber.
barbifier [-bifje] v. tr. (1). FAM. To shave.
barbillon [barbijɔ̃] m. Barb (d'hameçon, de flèche). ‖ ZOOL. Barber. ‖ Pl. Barbs.
barbiturique [barbityrik] adj. CHIM. Barbituric.
— n. CHIM. Barbiturate.
barbon [barbɔ̃] m. Greybeard, old fogey.
barbotage [barbɔta:ʒ] m. Paddling. ‖ AGRIC. Bran mash. ‖ FAM. Stammering (bafouillage); filching, pinching, stealing, lifting (vol).
barboter [-te] v. intr. (1). To dabble (canard); to paddle, to splash (personne). ‖ FAM. To filch.
barboteur, euse [-tœ:r, ø:z] s. Paddler. ‖ Floun-derer (pataugeur). ‖ FAM. Filcher, pilferer.
barboteuse [-tø:z] f. Rompers (d'enfant). ‖ Washing-machine.
barbouillage [barbuja:ʒ] m. Blurring, blur. ‖ Scribble, scrawl. (V. GRIBOUILLAGE.) ‖ Daubing; daub (en peinture).
barbouillé, ée [-je] adj. Smutty, grimy (visage); *barbouillé d'encre, de suie*, inky (ou) inkstained, smutty. ‖ FAM. Sick, squeamish (nauséeux).
barbouiller [-je] v. tr. (1). To blot. ‖ To scribble, to smudge (en écrivant); to daub (en peignant). ‖ To smear, to grime, to begrime; *barbouiller d'encre, de suie*, to ink, to smut. ‖ FAM. To upset; *barbouiller le cœur*, to turn one's stomach.
— v. intr. To daub (en peinture).
— v. pr. **Se barbouiller**, to smear (ou) to dirty one's face. ‖ FAM. To make up.
barbouilleur, euse [-jœ:r, ø:z] s. FAM. Scribbler, pen-pusher, ink-slinger (écrivain); dauber (peintre).
barbouillis [-ji] m. V. BARBOUILLAGE.
barbouze [barbu:z] m. ou f. POP. Unofficial secret policeman, undercover policeman, spy.
barbu, ue [barby] adj. Bearded. ‖ BOT. Barbate.
— m. Bearded man.
barbue f. ZOOL. Brill.
barcarolle [barkarɔl] f. MUS. Barcarole.
barcasse [barka:s] f. Lighter, tender.
bard [ba:r] m. Wheel-less hand-barrow.
barda [barda] m. MILIT. Full kit. ‖ FAM. Things, luggage; kit.
bardane [bardan] f. BOT. Burdock.
barde [bard] m. Bard (poète).
barde f. Bard (de fer). ‖ CULIN. Bard.

bardé, ée [-de] adj. Barded; *bardé de fer*, steel-clad. ‖ CULIN. Barded.
bardeau [-do] m. ARCHIT. Shingle; weather-boarding, U. S. clap-boarding.
barder [-de] v. tr. (1). To carry on a barrow.
— v. intr. FAM. To go strong (v. CHAUFFER); *ça barde pour son matricule*, he is going through it; *ça va barder*, there's trouble brewing (ou) tough going ahead.
barder [-de] v. tr. (1). To bard (de fer). ‖ CULIN. To bard. ‖ FAM. To cover [de, with].
bardis [-di] m. NAUT. Shifting-board.
bardot [-do] m. ZOOL. Hinny.
barème [barɛm] m. Scale, schedule (des impôts, des prix). ‖ Ready reckoner; graph; graphic table.
bareter [barete] v. intr. (8 b). [V. BARRIR.]
barge [barʒ] f. NAUT. Barge, lighter. ‖ AGRIC. Haystack.
barge f. ZOOL. Godwit.
barguignage [bargiɲa:ʒ] m. FAM. Dilly-dallying, shilly-shallying.
barguigner [-ɲe] v. intr. (1). To shilly-shally, to dilly-dally (v. HÉSITER); to wait to see which way the cat jumps.
barguigneur, euse [-ɲœ:r, ø:z] s. Shilly-shallyer.
baricaut [bariko] m. Keg.
baril [bari] m. Keg, cask. (V. TONNEAU.)
barillet [-jɛ] m. Small keg. ‖ TECHN. Barrel. ‖ MÉD. Middle-ear.
bariolage [barjɔla:ʒ] m. Variegation; varie-gating; medley (de couleurs). [V. BIGARRURE.]
bariolé, ée [-le] adj. Motley; variegated; many-hued; many-coloured. ‖ Gaudy.
barioler [-le] v. tr. (1). To variegate. (V. BIGAR-RER.) ‖ To paint in gaudy colours.
bariolure [-ly:r] f. Motley (ou) clashing (ou) gaudy colours.
barmaid [-med] f. Barmaid.
barman [barman] (pl. **barmen**) m. Barman, U. S. bartender.
bar-mitsva [barmitsva] f. ECCLÉS. Bar mitzvah.
barnacle [barnakl] f. ZOOL. Barnacle.
barnum [barnɔm] m. Showman (personne). ‖ FAM. Clatter, shindy, U. S. callithump (éclat).
barographe [-graf] m. PHYS. Barograph.
baromètre [-mɛtr] m. PHYS. Barometer; glass; *baromètre enregistreur*, barograph.
barométrique [-metrik] adj. PHYS. Barometric.
baron [barɔ̃] m. Baron.
baronnage [barona:ʒ] m. Baronage.
baronne [baron] f. Baroness.
baronnet [barɔnɛ] m. Baronet.
baronnie [-ni] f. Barony (seigneurie); baronage (titre).
baroque [barɔk] adj. Baroque (perle, style). ‖ Queer, quaint, whimsical. (V. BIZARRE.)
— m. Baroque (style). ‖ Oddness, quaintness, queerness (bizarrerie).
baroscope [barɔskɔp] m. PHYS. Baroscope.
baroud [barud] m. FAM. Scrap, set-to; *baroud d'honneur*, last stand.
baroudeur [-dœ:r] m. FAM. Scrapper.
barouf [baruf] m. POP. Row, rumpus, racket.
barque [bark] f. NAUT. Barge, small boat (grande); barque, bark (petite). ‖ FIG. *Bien mener sa barque*, to manage one's affairs well, to have things well in hand (ou) under control.
barquette [-kɛt] f. NAUT. Skiff. ‖ CULIN. Small boat-shaped tart.
barracuda [barakuda] m. ZOOL. Barracuda.
barrage [bara:ʒ] m. Barrage, dam, weir (de rivière); road-block (de route). ‖ Barrier, fence (barrière). ‖ NAUT. Boom. ‖ MILIT. Barrage; *barrage aérien*, anti-aircraft barrage; *effectuer un barrage*, to lay down a barrage; *tir de barrage*,

barrage (ou) curtain fire. ‖ Fig. Obstruction, barrier.

barre [baːr] f. Bar, U. S. cake (de chocolat, de fer, de savon); bar, ingot (de métal précieux). ‖ Bar (de fermeture). ‖ Bar (de gymnastique); *barre fixe*, horizontal bar. ‖ Stripe (de couleur). ‖ Line, dash, stroke (d'écriture); cross-stroke (d'un t). ‖ Mus. Bar. ‖ Techn. Bar. ‖ Autom. *Barre de connection*, tie (ou) connecting-rod. ‖ Jur. Bar; *barre des témoins*, witness box; *se présenter à la barre*, to appear at the bar. ‖ Naut. Helm, tiller (de gouvernail); *donner un coup de barre*, to put the helm over; *homme de barre*, helmsman. ‖ Pl. Prisoner's base (jeu); *toucher barre*, to make a brief stop. ‖ Fig. *Avoir barre sur*, to have the pull on (ou) an advantage over; *donner un coup de barre*, to veer round, to change course.

barré, ée [-re] adj. Crossed; *mot barré*, crossed out (ou) cancelled word; *rue barrée*, no thoroughfare, road blocked. ‖ Fin. Crossed (chèque); *non barré*, open. ‖ Méd. Locked (dent). ‖ Naut. Crossjack (vergue). ‖ Blas. Barry.

barreau [-ro] m. Cross-bar (de chaise); rung (d'échelle); bar (de fenêtre, de prison). ‖ Jur. Bar; barrister's bench; *entrer au barreau*, to become a member of the bar; U. S. to be admitted to the bar; *être inscrit au barreau*, to be called to the bar; *rayer du barreau*, to disbar.

barrement [-rmɑ̃] m. Fin. Crossing (d'un chèque).

barrer [-re] v. tr. (1). To cancel, to cross (ou) strike out (un mot, une phrase). [V. biffer.] ‖ To cross (un t). ‖ To dam (une rivière); to block up (une rue); to bar (une porte). ‖ To bar, to obstruct (le chemin). ‖ Naut. To steer. ‖ Fin. To cross (un chèque).
— v. intr. Naut. To steer.
— v. pr. **Se barrer**, Pop. To buzz off.

barrette [-rɛt] f. Ecclés. Biretta.

barrette [-rɛt] f. Small bar. ‖ Bar (de broderie); hair-slide (ou) grip, U. S. barrette (de cheveux); ankle-strap (de chaussure); spray (de diamants).

barricade [barikad] f. Barricade.

barricader [-de] v. tr. (1). To barricade.

barrière [barjɛːr] f. Fence (clôture); barrier; gate (de ville). ‖ Jur. *Barrières douanières*, tariff walls; *barrière d'octroi*, toll-gate. ‖ Ch. de f. Gate (de passage à niveau). ‖ Fig. Barrier (*contre*, against).

barrique [barik] f. Cask, hogshead, butt. (V. tonneau.) ‖ Aviat. Barrel roll.

barrir [bariːr] v. intr. (2). Zool. To trumpet.

barrissement [barismɑ̃] m. Trumpeting.

barrot [baro] m. Naut. Beam, cross-beam, girder.

bartavelle [bartavɛːl] f. Zool. Red-legged partridge.

Barthélemy [bartelmi] m. Bartholomew; *le massacre de la Saint-Barthélemy*, the massacre of St Bartholomew's Eve.

barye [bari] f. Phys. Barye.

barymétrie [-metri] f. Estimation of weight from dimensions.

baryon [barjɔ̃] m. Phys. Baryon.

baryton [baritɔ̃] adj., m. Mus., Gramm. Barytone.

baryum [barjɔm] m. Chim. Barium.

bas, basse [bɑ, bɑːs] adj. Low (front, mer, mur, niveau, plafond, pression, rivière, siège, soleil, température, voix); *tête basse*, with a hang-dog look. ‖ Low; *le bas allemand*, low German. ‖ Lower (par comparaison avec une idée de hauteur); *les basses classes*, the lower classes; *la Chambre basse*, the lower House; *le bas Rhin*, the lower Rhine. ‖ Ecclés. Low (messe). ‖ Comm. Low (prix); *les prix les plus bas*, rock-bottom prices. ‖ Sports. Below the belt (coup). ‖ Fig. Degrading (affaire); vile (action); servile, degrading (besogne); base, mean, disgraceful (conduite); lowly (extrac-

tion); contemptible (motif); low (naissance); overcast (temps); *bas âge*, infancy, early childhood; *au bas mot*, at the very least, at the lowest estimate; *à la vue basse*, short-sighted; *en ce bas monde*, here below. ‖ **Bas-côté**, m. Aisle (d'église); roadside (de route). ‖ **Bas-fond**, m. Bottom, low-lying ground (terrain); scum (de la société). ‖ **Bas-mât**, n. Naut. Lower-mast. ‖ **Bas-relief**, m. Arts. Low- (ou) bas-relief. ‖ **Bas-ventre**, m. Lower abdomen; Fam. guts; *un coup dans le bas-ventre*, a kick in the groin.
— adv. Low; *bien bas*, at death's door (mourant); *bas les pattes!*, keep your paws off (fam.)!; *chapeaux bas*, hats off; *mettre bas*, to bring forth; to foal (ânesse, jument); to lamb (brebis); to kitten (chatte); to kid (chèvre); to pup, to whelp (chienne); to cub (lionne, louve); to pig (truie); *mettre bas les armes*, to lay down one's arms; *parler bas*, to speak in an undertone; *parler tout bas*, to speak in a whisper (ou) under one's breath; *partir de bien bas*, to start from nothing; to start on a shoestring; *tomber bien bas*, to fall very low.
— loc. adv. **A bas**, down; *à bas le tyran!*, down with the tyrant!; *mettre à bas*, to overthrow, to lay low, to ruin; *sauter au bas du lit*, to jump out of bed. ‖ **En bas**, downstairs (à un étage inférieur); hereafter (ci-dessous); below (plus bas); *de bas en haut*, upward; *de haut en bas*, downward, from top to bottom; *par en bas*, towards the lower part. ‖ **Là-bas**, yonder, over there, down there.
— m. Bottom, foot (d'une lettre, d'une page, d'une rue); bottom (du visage); small (de la jambe); *au (ou) en bas de*, at the bottom (ou) foot of. ‖ Fig. Outside (du pavé); *les hauts et les bas de*, the ups and downs of.

bas [bɑ] m. Stocking; *bas de soie*, silk stockings; *bas en Nylon*, nylons. ‖ Fig. *Bas de laine*, savings. ‖ **Bas-bleu**, m. Blue-stocking.

basal, e [bazal] adj. Méd. Basal; *membrane basale*, basal membrane.

basalte [bazalt] m. Basalt.

basaltique [-tik] adj. Basaltic.

basane [bazan] f. Sheepskin, basan.

basané, ée [-ne] adj. Sunburnt, tanned.

basaner [-ne] v. tr. (1). To sunburn, to tan.

basculaire [baskylɛːr] adj. Seesaw (mouvement).

basculant, ante [-lɑ̃, ɑ̃:t] adj. Tilting, tipping; *benne basculante*, tipping-bucket; *pont basculant*, draw-bridge; *siège basculant*, tip-up seat.

bascule [baskyl] f. Bascule; rocker (de berceau, de fauteuil); *fauteuil à bascule*, rocking chair. ‖ See-saw (balançoire). ‖ Lever (de fusil). ‖ Weighing machine; platform scales (balance).

basculer [-le] v. intr. (1). To seesaw; to rock; U. S. to teeter (balancer); to topple, to tilt up (culbuter); *faire basculer*, to tip up, to dip.
— v. tr. To tip up; to topple over.

basculeur [-lœ:r] m. Tilter. ‖ Techn. Rocker-arm; dipper (de phares).

base [bɑːz] f. Base; basis; foundation; bottom (fond); foot (pied). ‖ Base, chief ingredient; *la base de l'alimentation*, staple food; *de base*, basic (livre, salaire, vocabulaire). ‖ Méd., Bot., Math., Milit., Chim. Base; *de base*, parent (métal). ‖ Naut. Naval base; *base d'essai*, measured mile. ‖ Aviat. Air base; *base d'hydravion*, sea-plane station. ‖ Fig. Basis, ground; *base de comparaison*, basis for comparison; *jeter les bases de*, to lay the foundations of; *former la base de*, to do the groundwork of (ou) for.

base-ball [bɛsbɔl] m. Sports. Base-ball.

baser [baze] v. tr. (1). To base; to ground; to found [*sur*, on].

basidiomycète [bazidjɔmisɛt] m. Bot. Basidiomycete.

Basile [bazil] m. Basil.
basilic [bazilik] m. Basilisk, cockatrice. ‖ BOT. Basil.
basilique f. ARCHIT. Basilica.
— adj. ECCLÉS. Basilican.
basique [bazik] adj. CHIM. Basic.
basket [baskɛt] m. SPORTS. Basketball.
basketteur, euse [-tœ:r, ø:z] s. SPORTS. Basketball player.
basoche [bazɔʃ] f. FAM. The bar, lawyers, the legal profession.
basochien, enne [-ʃjɛ̃, ɛn] adj. FAM. Pertaining to the bar.
— s. FAM. Lawyer.
Basquaise [baskɛ:z] f. Basque woman.
basque [bask] adj., m. GÉOGR. Basque. ‖ MUS. *Tambour de basque*, tambourine.
basque f. Tail, skirt (d'habit).
basse [ba:s] f. MUS. Cellist (artiste); bass (chanteur); bass-viol, cello (instrument); bass (voix). ‖ NAUT. Shoal, reef. ‖ **Basse-contre**, f. (pl. *basses-contre*). MUS. Deep bass, basso-profundo, ‖ **Basse-cour**, f. Farmyard, poultry yard, fowlrun, U. S. chicken-yard. ‖ **Basse-fosse**, f. Dungeon. ‖ **Basse-taille**, f. MUS. Bass-barytone.
bassement [basmɑ̃] adv. Basely, vilely, meanly.
bassesse [basɛs] f. Baseness, lowness (situation). ‖ Base (ou) low action (action); *faire des bassesses*, to stoop to some humiliating expedient. ‖ Vulgarity (d'une expression). ‖ Baseness, ignobleness (du caractère, des sentiments).
basset [basɛ] m. ZOOL. Basset hound (chien). ‖ MUS. *Cor de basset*, basset-horn.
bassin [basɛ̃] m. Basin; bowl; water-basin (cuvette). ‖ Pond, artificial lake (pièce d'eau). ‖ MÉD. Pan, bed-pan (récipient); pelvis (partie du corps). ‖ ECCLÉS. Collection-plate, alms basin. ‖ TECHN. Basin; pit; tank; reservoir. ‖ NAUT. Dock; *bassin de radoub*, dry dock. ‖ GÉOGR. *Bassin d'un fleuve*, river basin; *bassin houiller*, coal field.
bassinage [basina:ʒ] m. Warming (du lit). ‖ MÉD. Bathing (d'une plaie). ‖ AGRIC. Sprinkling (des semis).
bassine [-sin] f. Copper pan; *bassine à confitures*, preserving-pan. ‖ Basin (cuvette).
bassiner [-sine] v. tr. (1). To warm (le lit). ‖ MÉD. To bathe (une plaie). ‖ AGRIC. To spray (les semis). ‖ FAM. To plague, to bore. (V. BARBER.)
bassinet [-sinɛ] m. Bowl, small basin. ‖ ECCLÉS. Collection plate. ‖ † Basinet, basnet (casque). ‖ FAM. *Cracher au bassinet*, to pay up, to cough up.
bassinoire [-sinwa:r] f. Warming-pan. ‖ POP. Bore. (V. RASEUR.)
bassiste [basist] m. MUS. Cellist; tuba-player, saxhorn-player.
basson [basɔ̃] m. MUS. Bassoonist (artiste); bassoon (instrument).
bassoniste [-sɔnist] s. MUS. Bassoonist, bassoon-player. (V. BASSON.)
basta [basta] interj. That's enough!, stop!
baste f. Basket (panier). ‖ Basto (quadrille).
bastide [bastid] f. Bastide (ville forte). ‖ Small country-house (maison).
bastille [basti:j] f. †. Bastille. ‖ FAM. Fortress.
bastillé, ée [-je] adj. BLAS. Embattled.
bastingage [bastɛ̃ga:ʒ] m. NAUT. Bulwarks; topsides; rails.
bastion [bastjɔ̃] m. MILIT. Bastion. ‖ FIG. Stronghold, bastion (de la liberté).
bastionner [-tjɔne] v. tr. (1). To bastion.
bastonnade [bastɔnad] f. Bastinado.
bastringue [bastrɛ̃:g] m. POP. Popular dancehall, U. S. honky-tonk joint (bal); shindy, row, racket (bruit); kit (fourniment).
bât [bɑ] m. Pack; pack load (charge); pack-

saddle (selle); *cheval de bât*, pack-horse. ‖ MILIT. Pack. ‖ FIG. *Savoir où le bât le blesse*, to know where the shoe pinches.
bataclan [bataklɑ̃] m. FAM. *Tout le bataclan*, the whole caboodle (ou) jolly lot (ou) bang shoot.
bataille [batɑ:j] f. MILIT. Battle; *bataille navale*, sea-fight, naval engagement; *engager la bataille*, to engage; *en ordre de bataille*, in battle order. ‖ FAM. Fight, quarrel, scrap (v. BAGARRE, LUTTE); *les cheveux en bataille*, dishevelled. ‖ Beggar-my-neighbour (aux cartes).
batailler [-je] v. intr. (1). To fight, to battle (contre, against). ‖ FIG. To fight, to battle.
batailleur, euse [-jœ:r, ø:z] adj. Quarrelsome; pugnacious.
— s. Fighter; pugnacious person.
bataillon [-jɔ̃] m. MILIT. Battalion; *chef de bataillon*, major, battalion commander.
bâtard, arde [bɑta:r, ard] adj. Bastard, mongrel (animal); bastard, natural, illegitimate (enfant); degenerate (race). ‖ Bastard (format); hybrid (solution).
— s. Mongrel (chien); bastard (enfant). ‖ CULIN. Loaf of bread (pain).
bâtarde [bɑtard] f. Slanting round-hand.
batardeau [-do] m. TECHN. Embankment, dam.
bâtardise [-di:z] f. Bastardy.
batave [bata:v] adj., s. GÉOGR. Batavian.
batavia [batavja] f. AGRIC. Web lettuce.
batayole [batajɔl] f. NAUT. Stanchion.
bâté, ée [bɑte] adj. Bearing a pack-saddle; loaded. ‖ FIG. *Un âne bâté*, a regular ass.
bateau [bato] m. NAUT. Boat; ship; *bateau à moteur, à voiles*, motor, sailing boat; *bateau à vapeur*, steamer; *bateau de pêche, de plaisance*, fishing-, pleasure-boat. ‖ NAUT. Ship-load, boat-load; shipment, cargo (chargement). ‖ FAM. Hoax (mystification); *monter un bateau à qqn*, to pull s.o.'s leg. *Être du dernier bateau*, to be in the latest fashion. ‖ Pl. POP. Beetle-crushers, boats, U. S. gunboats (chaussures). ‖ **Bateau-citerne**, m. NAUT. Tanker. ‖ **Bateau-école**, m. NAUT. Training-ship. ‖ **Bateau-feu**, m. NAUT. Lightship. ‖ **Bateau-hôpital**, m. MÉD. Hospital-ship. ‖ **Bateau-mouche**, m. NAUT. Water-bus, passenger-steamer. ‖ **Bateau-pêcheur**, m. NAUT. Fishing-boat. ‖ **Bateau-phare**, m. NAUT. Lightship. ‖ **Bateau-pilote**, m. NAUT. Pilot boat.
batelée [batle] f. NAUT. Boatload.
bateler v. tr. (8 a). NAUT. To transport in lighters.
batelet [batlɛ] m. NAUT. Small boat.
bateleur, euse [batlœ:r, ø:z] s. Juggler, tumbler, mountebank. ‖ Buffoon.
batelier [batəlje] m. NAUT. Boatman; bargee. ‖ Lighterman, ferryman (passeur).
batellerie [batɛlri] f. NAUT. Lighterage. ‖ River boats, small craft. ‖ Inland navigation.
bâter [bɑte] v. tr. (1). To put a packsaddle on, to load (un âne).
bat-flanc [baflɑ̃] m. Bail; swinging bail.
bath [bat] adj. POP. First rate, posh, tip-top.
bathymètre [batimɛtr] m. NAUT. Bathometer, bathymeter.
bathymétrie [-metri] f. NAUT. Bathometry, bathymetry.
bathymétrique [-metrik] adj. NAUT. Bathometric, bathometrical, bathymetric, bathymetrical.
bathyscaphe [batiskaf] m. NAUT. Bathyscaphe.
bathysphère [-sfɛr] f. NAUT. Bathysphere.
bathysphériste [-sfɛrist] m. Deep-sea observer; bathyspherist.
bâti [bati] m. TECHN. Frame; structure; stand; rack; *bâti moteur*, engine mount.
bâti m. Basting together (action); tacking- (ou) basting-thread (fil); *point de bâti*, tack.
bâti, ie adj. Built (maison); *bien bâti*, well-built.

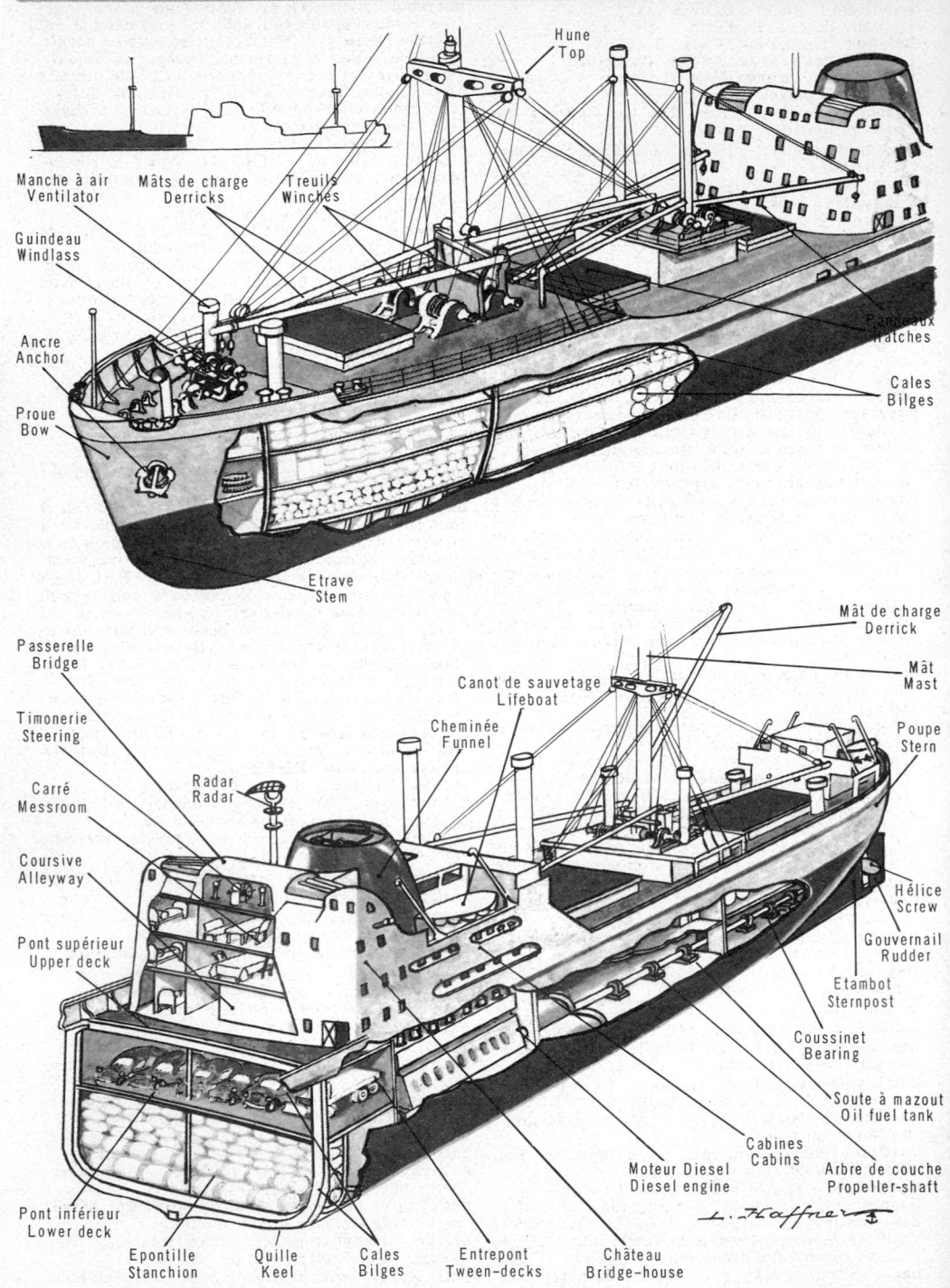

Hune
Top

Manche à air
Ventilator

Mâts de charge
Derricks

Treuils
Winches

Guindeau
Windlass

Ancre
Anchor

Proue
Bow

Panneaux
Hatches

Cales
Bilges

Etrave
Stem

Passerelle
Bridge

Canot de sauvetage
Lifeboat

Mât de charge
Derrick

Timonerie
Steering

Cheminée
Funnel

Mât
Mast

Carré
Messroom

Radar
Radar

Poupe
Stern

Coursive
Alleyway

Hélice
Screw

Pont supérieur
Upper deck

Gouvernail
Rudder

Etambot
Sternpost

Coussinet
Bearing

Soute à mazout
Oil fuel tank

Pont inférieur
Lower deck

Cabines
Cabins

Arbre de couche
Propeller-shaft

Epontille
Stanchion

Quille
Keel

Cales
Bilges

Entrepont
Tween-decks

Château
Bridge-house

Moteur Diesel
Diesel engine

L. Haffner

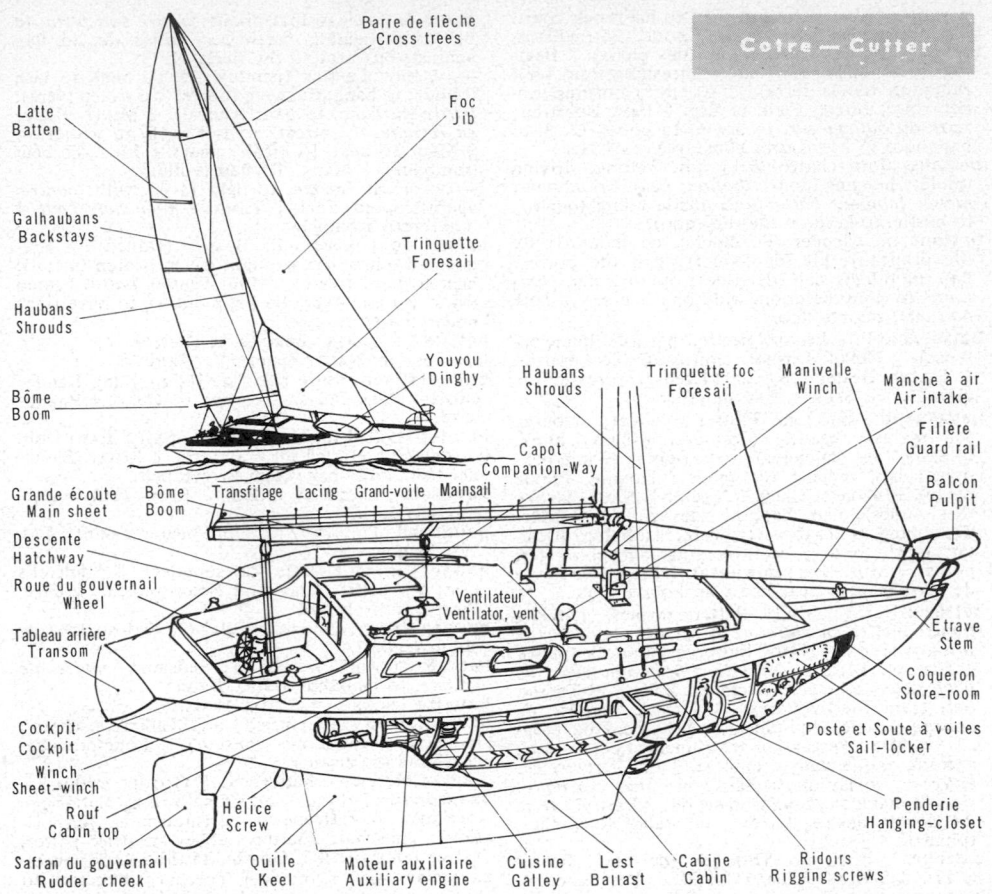

Barre de flèche / Cross trees
Foc / Jib
Latte / Batten
Galhaubans / Backstays
Trinquette / Foresail
Haubans / Shrouds
Youyou / Dinghy
Haubans / Shrouds
Trinquette foc / Foresail
Manivelle / Winch
Manche à air / Air intake
Bôme / Boom
Filière / Guard rail
Capot / Companion-Way
Balcon / Pulpit
Grande écoute / Main sheet
Bôme / Boom
Transfilage / Lacing
Grand-voile / Mainsail
Descente / Hatchway
Roue du gouvernail / Wheel
Ventilateur / Ventilator, vent
Etrave / Stem
Tableau arrière / Transom
Coqueron / Store-room
Cockpit / Cockpit
Poste et Soute à voiles / Sail-locker
Winch / Sheet-winch
Rouf / Cabin top
Hélice / Screw
Penderie / Hanging-closet
Safran du gouvernail / Rudder cheek
Quille / Keel
Moteur auxiliaire / Auxiliary engine
Cuisine / Galley
Lest / Ballast
Cabine / Cabin
Ridoirs / Rigging screws

‖ FAM. *Bien bâti*, well-built; *il est drôlement bâti*, he is a funny-looking sort of chap.

batifolage [batifɔla:ʒ] m. Frolicking. ‖ Cuddling, U. S. necking, petting.

batifoler [-le] v. intr. (1). To frolic, to romp. ‖ *Batifoler avec une femme*, to cuddle (ou) to rumple a woman.

batifoleur [-lœ:r] m. Frolicker, romper. ‖ Womaniser.

batik [batik] m. Batik.

bâtiment [batimã] m. Building, edifice. ‖ Building trade (industrie). ‖ FAM. *Etre du bâtiment*, to belong to the trade. ‖ NAUT. Ship (v. BATEAU); *bâtiment de ligne*, capital ship. ‖ **Bâtiment-balise**, m. NAUT. Lightship.

bâtir [bati:r] v. tr. (2). To build. (V. CONSTRUIRE.) ‖ FIG. To build up (une réputation); to construct (un roman, une scène). — v. intr. To build (pr. et fig.); *terrain à bâtir*, building land. ‖ LOC. *Bâtir en l'air*, to build castles in the air. — v. pr. Se bâtir, to be built; *la maison se bâtit*, the house is building (ou) is being built.

bâtir v. tr. (2). To baste, to tack (un vêtement); *fil à bâtir*, tacking-thread, basting-thread.

bâtisse [-tis] f. Masonry. ‖ FAM. Building.

bâtisseur [-sœ:r] m. Builder (pr. et fig.). ‖ FAM. Person who has a craze for building.

batiste [batist] f. Batiste, cambric.

bâton [batɔ̃] m. Stick, rod (bâton léger); pole (bâton long); staff (bourdon); cudgel, bludgeon (gros bâton); pikestaff, alpenstock (bâton ferré); *coup de bâton*, blow (ou) rap with a stick; *volée de coups de bâton*, cudgeling. ‖ Truncheon, U. S. night stick (d'agent de police). ‖ Stretcher, crossbar (de chaise). ‖ Lipstick (de rouge à lèvres). ‖ Stroke (d'écriture); *faire des bâtons*, to make pothooks. ‖ MUS. Baton (de chef d'orchestre). ‖ MILIT. Baton (de maréchal). ‖ NAUT. *Bâton de pavillon*, flagstaff. ‖ BLAS. Baton. ‖ ARCHIT. Rollmoulding. ‖ FIG. *Bâton de vieillesse*, staff (ou) prop of one's old age; *à bâtons rompus*, in snatches, by fits and starts, spasmodically; *chercher le bâton pour se faire battre*, to cut a club to knock one's own brain out; *mettre les bâtons dans les roues*, to put a spoke in one's wheel, to throw a spanner (ou) U. S. monkey-wrench in the works; *vie de bâton de chaise*, fast (ou) rollicking life.

bâtonnat [batɔna] m. JUR. Presidency of the local corporation of French barristers.

bâtonner [-ne] v. tr. (1). To cudgel.

bâtonnet [-nɛ] m. Small stick. ‖ Chopstick (à riz). ‖ Tip-cat, kitty-cat (jeu). ‖ Square ruler (règle). ‖ MÉD. Rod-bacterium.

bâtonnier [-nje] m. JUR. President of the cor-

poration of barristers attached to a French court.
batraciens [batrasjɛ̃] m. pl. ZOOL. Batrachians.
battage [bata:ʒ] m. Driving (des pieux). ‖ Beating (des tapis). ‖ AGRIC. Threshing (du blé);
ramming (de la terre). ‖ CULIN. Churning (du
beurre). ‖ MILIT. Field of fire. ‖ FAM. Boosting;
faire du battage sur, to boom, to boost, U. S. to
ballyhoo. (V. RÉCLAME, PUBLICITÉ, TAM-TAM.)
battant, ante [batɑ̃, ɑ̃:t] adj. Pelting, driving
(pluie); hanging (door); *battant neuf,* brand-new;
mener tambour battant, to hustle along (qqch.);
to bustle, to keep on the run (qqn).
battant m. Clapper (de cloche, de moulin); fly
(de drapeau); lift (de loquet); leaf (de porte);
flap (de table); slab (de voile); *ouvrir à deux battants,* to fling the doors wide open; *porte à deux
battants,* double door.
batte [bat] f. Beater, beetle, bat (de blanchisseuse). ‖ CULIN. Dasher, churnstaff (de baratte).
‖ TECHN. Beater (de blanchisseuse); dresser (de
plombier). ‖ SPORTS. Bat (de cricket).
battement [-tmɑ̃] m. Flutter (d'ailes); clapping
(de mains); beating (des oscillations); blink,
blinking (des paupières); tick, ticking (d'une pendule); tap, tapping (de pieds); banging (d'une
porte). ‖ SPORTS. Clash (d'épée). ‖ NAUT. Stroke
(des rames); flap, flapping (des voiles). ‖ MÉD.
Throbbing (d'un abcès); throb, throbbing, palpitation (du cœur); beat, beating, throbbing (du
pouls). ‖ MUS. Beat; downbeat. ‖ FAM. *Une heure
de battement,* a clear hour, an hour's wait.
batterie [-tri] f. MILIT. Battery (armes); gun-site
(lieu); *mettre en batterie,* to set up a gun in the
firing position. ‖ NAUT. Battery; gun-deck (pont).
‖ ELECTR. Battery; *batterie d'accumulateurs, de
projecteurs,* storage, searchlight battery. ‖ TECHN.
Set, train (de cylindres). ‖ CULIN. *Batterie de
cuisine,* kitchen equipment, set of cooking utensils. ‖ MUS. Percussion instruments, percussion;
batterie de tambour, drumbeat. ‖ FIG. *Dresser ses
batteries,* to lay one's plans; *masquer ses batteries,* to make one's plans in secret. ‖ FAM. *Batterie
de cuisine,* gongs, U. S. fruit salad (médailles,
rubans).
batteur [-tœ:r] m. Thresher (de blé); beater
(d'or). ‖ SPORTS. Batsman. ‖ MUS. Percussionist.
batteuse [-tø:z] f. AGRIC. Threshing-machine,
thresher. ‖ TECHN. Driver (de pieux); beater
(d'or). ‖ CULIN. Egg-whisk (ou) -beater.
battitures [-tity:r] f. pl. TECHN. Hammer- (ou)
forge-scales.
battoir [-twa:r] m. Bat, beater, beetle, paddle (de
blanchisseuse). ‖ SPORTS. Bat, racquet. ‖ FAM.
Flipper; *avoir des mains comme des battoirs,* to
be ham-fisted.
battre [batr] v. tr. (20). To beat, to thrash; to
strike (V. FRAPPER, ROSSER); *battre comme plâtre,*
to beat to a pulp (ou) to a jelly; to beat black and
blue. ‖ To flail, to thresh (le blé); to card (le
coton); to hammer (une faux, le fer); to beat (le
linge, l'or, un tapis); to drive (un pieu); to ram
down (la terre). ‖ To beat (l'air, les bois, les
buissons); to scour (la campagne); to hunt, to
scour (la ville). ‖ To shuffle (les cartes). ‖ To flap,
to flutter (des ailes); to clap (des mains). ‖ FIN.
To mint, to coin (monnaie). ‖ CULIN. To churn
(le beurre); to whip, to whisk (des œufs); to beat
(la viande). ‖ MUS. *Battre la mesure,* to beat
time; *battre du tambour,* to beat a drum. ‖ MILIT.
To beat, to defeat (vaincre); *battre à plate couture,* to rout; to beat hollow; *battre en brèche,*
to batter. ‖ MILIT. To batter; to sweep with fire
(canonner); to sound (l'alarme, l'appel, la charge);
to cover (un objectif); *battre la campagne,* to
scour the country; *battre le réveil,* to sound
reveille. ‖ NAUT. *Battre pavillon,* to fly a flag. ‖
LOC. *Battre froid,* to turn the cold shoulder;

battre le pavé, to loaf about; *battre son plein,* to
be at its height; *battre les talons de,* to flap
against (ou) around the heels of.
— v. intr. To tick (pendule). ‖ To beat, to lash
(pluie); to bang, to swing (porte); to sweep (vent);
battre du flanc, to pant (cheval). ‖ MILIT. *Battre
en retraite,* to retreat; to fall back, to withdraw.
‖ MÉD. To beat, to throb (cœur). ‖ MUS. To beat
(tambour). ‖ NAUT. To flap (voile).
— v. pr. Se **battre,** to fight [*avec,* with; *contre,*
against; *pour,* for]. ‖ FAM. *Je m'en bats l'œil,* I
don't care a hang.
battu, ue [baty] adj. Beaten (vaincu). ‖ Frequented (chemin); wrought (fer); beaten (métal);
beaten, hard (terre). ‖ FIG. *Sentier battu,* beaten
track. ‖ FAM. *Avoir les yeux battus,* to have rings
under the eyes.
battue f. SPORTS. Beat (à la chasse).
bau [bo] m. NAUT. Beam. (V. BARROT.)
baudelairien, enne [bodlɛrjɛ̃, ɛn] adj. Baude-
lairean, Baudelairian, relating to Charles Baude-
laire.
baudet [bodɛ] m. Donkey. (V. ÂNE.) ‖ FAM. Dolt.
baudrier [bodrije] m. † Baldric. ‖ MILIT. Shoulder-belt; cross-belt; Sam Brown belt.
baudroie [bodrwa] f. ZOOL. Frog- (ou) angler-
fish, sea-devil.
baudruche [bodry:ʃ] f. Gold-beater's skin. ‖ FIG.
Windbag.
bauge [bo:ʒ] f. Lair (de sanglier). ‖ Squirrel's
nest. ‖ ARCHIT. Clay and straw mortar. ‖ FAM.
Pigsty, filthy hovel.
bauger (se) [səboʒe] v. pr. (7). To go into its
lair (sanglier).
baume [bo:m] m. Balm; balsam; *oindre de
baume,* to embalm. ‖ FIG. Balm.
bauxite [boksit] f. CHIM. Bauxite.
bavard, arde [bava:r, ard] adj. Talkative, chatty,
loquacious, garrulous (causeur). ‖ Long-tongued,
gossiping (médisant).
— s. Chatterer, chatterbox. ‖ Gossip, tattler.
bavardage [-da:ʒ] m. Chattering, jabbering
(action); talkativeness, garrulousness (disposition); chit-chat, chatter, jabber, prattle, patter,
natter (entretien). ‖ Gossip, tattling (médisance).
bavarder [-de] v. intr. (1). To chat, to chatter, to
natter, to yatter, to prattle. ‖ To tattle (médire).
bavarois, oise [bavarwa, wa:z] adj., s. GÉOGR.
Bavarian.
bavaroise [-rwa:z] f. CULIN. Bavarian cream.
bavasser [bavase] v. intr. (1). FAM. To natter,
to rattle on, to gas, to gossip.
bave [ba:v] f. Slobber (de chien); spittle (de
crapaud); slime (d'escargot, de limace); dribble
(de personne); *couvrir de bave,* to slaver, to
beslaver, to slime, to beslime. ‖ FIG. Venom.
baver [bave] v. intr. (1). To slaver (chien); to
smudge (encre); to run (plume); to slobber, to
dribble, to slaver (personne); to blob (stylo) [*sur,*
on]. ‖ FIG. *Baver sur,* to blemish, to smudge,
beslaver. ‖ FAM. *En baver,* to sweat blood; *baver
de colère,* to foam at the mouth.
— v. tr. To drivel, U. S. to drool. ‖ To vomit (des
insultes).
bavette [bavɛt] f. Bib (d'enfant, de tablier). ‖
CULIN. Top of the sirloin. ‖ FIG. *Tailler une
bavette,* to chat.
baveux, euse [bavø, ø:z] adj. Slavery, U. S.
drooling (bouche, enfant). ‖ Blurred (lettres). ‖
CULIN. Moist, juicy. ‖ MÉD. Weeping (plaie).
bavochure [bavɔʃy:r] f. Blur; mackle.
bavoir [bavwa:r] m. Bib.
bavolet [bavɔlɛ] m Bonnet, coif. ‖ Flap (de sac);
à bavolet, flapped. ‖ AUTOM. Side-apron.
bavure [bavy:r] f. Smudge (d'encre, de plume).
‖ TECHN. Bur, burr.

bayadère [bajadɛ:r] f. Indian dancing-girl.
— adj. Bayadere (tissu).
bayer [baje] v. intr. (9 b). To gape; *bayer aux corneilles*, to star-gaze, to stand open-mouthed.
bayou [baju] m. GÉOGR. Bayou.
bazar [baza:r] m. Emporium, stores (grand magasin); cheap stores, U. S. five-and-ten (magasin à prix réduit). ‖ Bazaar (en Orient). ‖ FAM. *Tout le bazar*, all the stuff. (V. BATACLAN.)
bazarder [-de] v. tr. (1). POP. To discard, to drop all idea of (rejeter); to sell off (vendre).
bazooka [bazuka] m. MILIT. Bazooka.
B. C. G. [beseʒe] m. MÉD. BCG, BCG vaccine.
B.D. [bede] f. FAM. Abrév. de *bande dessinée*, comic strips.
béant, ante [beã, ã:t] adj. Gaping (bouche); yawning (gouffre); wide open (porte). ‖ MÉD. Gaping (plaie).
béarnais, aise [bearnɛ, ɛ:z] adj. GÉOGR. Of (ou) from Béarn. ‖ CULIN. *Sauce béarnaise*, Béarnaise sauce.
— s. Native (ou) inhabitant of Béarn.
béat, ate [bea, at] adj. Sanctimonious, smug (air); smug (optimisme).
béatement [-tmã] adv. Sanctimoniously.
béatification [beatifikasjõ] f. ECCLÉS. Beatification.
béatifier [-fje] v. tr. (1). ECCLÉS. To beatify.
béatifique [-fik] adj. ECCLÉS. Beatific (vision).
béatitude [-tyd] f. Beatitude. ‖ Bliss; blessedness.
beatnik [bitnik] m. Beatnik.
beau [bo], **bel** [bɛl] (f. **belle** [bɛ:l]) adj. Fine; fine-looking; handsome; beautiful; pretty (v. JOLI); *le beau sexe*, the fair sex; *un fort beau visage*, a face of great beauty. ‖ Fine (champ, collection, désordre, écriture, fleur, machine, paysage, récolte, statue, yeux). ‖ Calm (mer); fine, fair (temps); *il fait beau*, it is fine. ‖ Smart, stylish; *se faire beau*, to dress up, to titivate. ‖ Splendid (appétit); good, grand, great, favourable (occasion); fair (paroles). ‖ MÉD. Excellent (santé). ‖ FIN. Fine, large, comfortable (bénéfices, fortune, salaire). ‖ FIG. Noble (âme); chivalrous, honourable (attitude); glorious, honoured (nom); lofty (pensées); fine (projet, rêve). ‖ LOC. *La belle affaire!*, what of it?, so what? (fam.); *le bel âge*, youth; *un bel âge*, a ripe old age; *le beau côté*, the sunny (ou) bright side; *beau joueur*, good loser, good sport; *les beaux jours*, summer days; *dans ses beaux jours*, in his heyday; *au beau milieu de*, in the very middle of, right in the middle of; *le beau monde*, fashionable society, the smart set; *un beau parleur*, a smooth tongue, a glib talker; *il y a beau temps* (ou) *belle lurette que*, it's a long time since; *pour les beaux yeux de*, for the love of; *tout cela est bel et bon*, that's all very well; *en faire de belles*, to be up to one's old tricks; to make bad blunders; to do mischief; *en faire voir de belles à qqn*, to give s.o. an unholy time; *en raconter de belles sur*, to tell some pretty tales about; *de la belle façon* (ou) *manière*, severely; in the good old-fashioned way; *de plus belle*, more and more; harder than ever; *une belle peur*, a fearful fright. ‖ **Beau-fils**, m. Son-in-law (gendre); stepson (par remariage). ‖ **Beau-frère**, m. Brother-in-law. ‖ **Beau-père**, m. Father-in-law (par mariage); stepfather (parâtre). ‖ **Beaux-arts**, m. ARTS. Fine arts. ‖ **Beaux-parents**, m. Parents-in-law; in-laws (fam.). ‖ **Belle-de-jour**, (pl. *belles-de-jour*) f. BOT. Bindweed. ‖ **Belle-de-nuit** (pl. *belles-de-nuit*) f. BOT. Marvel of Peru; U. S. four-o'clock. ‖ **Belle-famille**, f. In-laws. ‖ **Belle-fille**, f. Daughter-in-law (bru); step-daughter (par remariage). ‖ **Belles-lettres**, f. pl. Belles lettres. ‖ **Belle-mère**, f. Mother-in-law (par mariage); step-mother (marâtre). ‖ **Belle-sœur**, f. Sister-in-law.

— m. Beau, dandy. ‖ FIG. *Le beau*, the beautiful. ‖ LOC. *Faire le beau*, to beg, to sit up (chien); to show off (personne); *le plus beau de l'affaire*, the best of the story; *le temps est au beau fixe*, the weather is set fair.
— f. V. BELLE.
— adv. **Avoir beau**; *j'ai beau essayer*, try as I may; *elle a eu beau faire, elle n'a pas pu*, do what she would, she could not; *il a beau dire*, in spite of all he says. ‖ **Faire beau**; *il ferait beau voir que*, it would be a fine thing if. ‖ FAM. *Elle fait beau*, she is fuming.
— loc. adv. *Voir tout en beau*, to see the sunny side of everything. ‖ **Tout beau!**, gently!, softly!, stop! ‖ **Bel et bien**, actually, entirely, indeed.
beauceron, onne [bosrõ, ɔn] adj. GÉOGR. Of (ou) from Beauce.
— s. Native (ou) inhabitant of Beauce.
beaucoup [boku] adv. Much; a great deal; far; *beaucoup plus jeune que*, much younger than; *beaucoup trop orgueilleux*, much (ou) far too proud; *boire beaucoup*, to drink a great deal; *compter pour beaucoup*, to count for much; *se sentir beaucoup mieux*, to feel a great deal better. ‖ Much; widely; greatly; extensively; largely (largement); *différer beaucoup de*, to differ much (ou) greatly from; *être pour beaucoup dans*, to contribute largely to; *se servir beaucoup de*, to use extensively; *voyager beaucoup*, to travel widely. ‖ Many, a great many; a large number, a lot; *beaucoup l'ont vu*, many have seen him; *il n'y en a pas beaucoup comme vous*, there are not many like you. ‖ **Beaucoup de**, much (au sg.); many (au pl.); a great deal of (quand on ne peut pas compter); *beaucoup d'entre eux*, many of them; *beaucoup plus de*, much (ou) many more than; *elle lui a fait beaucoup de compliments*, she paid him many compliments; *il y a beaucoup d'autos dans les rues*, there are a great many cars (ou) a lot of cars in the street; *il y a beaucoup de blé à vendre*, there is a great deal of wheat to be sold; *il y a beaucoup de fleurs*, there are plenty of flowers. ‖ **De beaucoup**, by far, by a great deal, greatly; *de beaucoup la meilleure solution*, by far the best solution; *je préférerais de beaucoup*, I should far prefer, I'd much rather; *il s'en faut de beaucoup que je sois aussi riche*, I am far from being so rich; *je ne suis pas aussi riche à beaucoup près*, I am nothing like (ou) near so rich; *à beaucoup près*, by far.
Beaufort [bofɔ:r] GÉOGR. *Echelle de Beaufort*, Beaufort scale.
beaujolais [boʒolɛ] m. AGRIC. Beaujolais (vin).
beaupré [bopre] m. NAUT. Bowsprit.
beauté [-te] f. Beauty (le beau). ‖ Beauty, beauteousness, fairness, pulchritude, handsomeness, loveliness, comeliness; *en beauté*, looking fine, looking one's best; *de toute beauté*, splendid, magnificent; *finir en beauté*, to end in a blaze of glory, to make a dignified end. ‖ Beauty, belle (person); *une vrai beauté*, quite a beauty, U. S. a real looker (fam.).
bébé [bebe] m. Baby (enfant). ‖ Doll (poupée). ‖ **Bébé-trott** (nom déposé), m. FAM. Go-cart.
be-bop [bibɔp] m. Be-bop.
bec [bɛk] m. Bill, beak (d'oiseau); snout, nose (de pieuvre, de poisson, de tortue); *à bec crochu*, hook-beaked; *à bec de canard*, duck-billed; *coup de bec*, peck; *donner des coups de bec*, to peck. ‖ Lip (de cruche); beak, horn (d'enclume); burner, jet (de gaz); jib (de grue); burner (de lampe); nose (d'outil); nib (de plume); cutwater (de pont); peak (de selle de bicyclette); nozzle (de tuyau); spout (de verseuse); *bec Auer*, incandescent burner; *bec de gaz*, lamp-post; *bec vaporisateur*, spray nozzle. ‖ MUS. Mouthpiece (de flûte). ‖ NAUT. Bill (d'ancre); prow (de navire). ‖

Aviat. *Bec d'aile,* wing tip. ‖ Milit. *Bec de crosse,* toe of the butt. ‖ Loc. *Bec et ongles,* tooth and nail; *avoir bec et ongles,* to know how to defend oneself; *avoir bon bec,* to have the gift of the gab (ou) a sharp tongue; *le bec dans l'eau,* in the lurch, on a string; *claquer du bec,* to live on thin air, to clem; *clore le bec à qqn,* to shut s.o. up; *prise de bec,* bicker, tiff, squabble; *sans ouvrir le bec,* without opening one's mouth; *se rincer le bec,* to wet one's whistle; *tomber sur un bec,* to catch a Tartar, U. S. to hit a bad snag. ‖ **Bec-d'âne, bédane,** m. Techn. Framing-chisel, mortise-chisel. ‖ **Bec-de-cane,** m. Flat-nosed pliers (outil); lever-handle (poignée). ‖ **Bec-de-corbeau,** m. Wire-nippers. ‖ **Bec-de-corbin,** m. Techn. Claw; Méd. crow-bill. ‖ **Bec-de-lièvre,** m. Méd. Hare-lip. ‖ **Bec-fin,** m. Warbler (oiseau); epicure, gourmet (personne).
bécane [bekan] f. Fam. Bike.
bécarre [beka:r] m., adj. Mus. Natural.
bécasse [bekas] f. Zool. Woodcock. ‖ Fam. Goose.
bécasseau [-so] m. Zool. Young woodcock. ‖ Sandpiper.
bécassine [-sin] f. Zool. Snipe. ‖ Fam. Little goose (ou) silly.
becfigue [bɛkfig] m. Zool. Beccafico, garden warbler, blackcap, pipit.
béchage [bɛʃa:ʒ] m. Digging up. ‖ Fam. Backbiting.
béchamel [beʃamɛ:l] f. Culin. Bechamel.
bêche [bɛ:ʃ] f. Agric., Milit. Spade.
bêche-de-mer [-dəmɛ:r] f. (pl. *bêches-de-mer*). Zool. Bêche-de-mer; U. S. trepang. ‖ Gramm. Beach-la-mar, bêche-de-mer.
bêcher [bɛʃe] v. tr., intr. (1). Agric. To dig, to dig up (la terre). ‖ Fam. To backbite (qqn).
bêcheur [-ʃœ:r] m. Digger. ‖ Fam. Backbiter.
bêchoir [-ʃwa:r] m. Agric. Broad hoe.
bécot [beko] m. Fam. Kiss, peck; *gros bécot,* smack, big kiss.
bécoter [-te] v. tr. (1). Fam. To peck, to kiss.
— v. pr. **Se bécoter,** to bill and coo, U. S. to smooch.
becquée [bɛke] f. Beakful; *donner la becquée à,* to feed (un oiseau).
becquetage [bɛkta:ʒ] m. Pecking.
becqueter [-te] v. tr. (8b). To pick up (des miettes); to peck at (un autre oiseau).
— v. pr. **Se becqueter,** to bill, to beak.
bectance [bɛktɑ̃:s] f. Pop. Nosh, grub.
becter [bɛkte] v. intr. (1). Pop. To eat, to nosh; *qu'est-ce qu'il y a à becter,* what's for grub.
bedaine [bədɛn] f., **bedon** [bədɔ̃] m. Fam. Paunch, corporation, bread-basket, U. S. pot (panse); pot-belly (personne).
bedeau [bədo] m. Ecclés. Beadle, verger.
bedon [bədɔ̃] m. Fam. Pot-belly, pot, paunch.
bedonnant, ante [bədɔnɑ̃, ɑ̃:t] adj. Fam. Paunchy, tubby, portly, pot-bellied.
bedonner [-ne] v. intr. (1). Fam. To grow paunchy (ou) pot-bellied, to develop a corporation.
bédouin [bedwɛ̃] adj., s. Géogr. Bedouin.
bée [be] adj. Gaping; *bouche bée,* agape, open-mouthed, gaping.
béer. V. bayer.
beffroi [bɛfrwa] m. Alarm-bell (cloche); belfry (clocher).
bégaiement [begɛmɑ̃] m. Stammering, stuttering. ‖ Lisping (d'un enfant).
bégayer [-je] v. tr. (9b). To stammer, to stutter, to falter out.
— v. intr. To stammer, to stutter. ‖ To lisp (enfant). ‖ To falter (balbutier); to gabble, to mumble (bredouiller).
bégayeur [-jœ:r] m. Stammerer.

bégonia [begɔnja] m. Bot. Begonia.
bègue [bɛg] adj. Stammering, stuttering.
— s. Stammerer, stutterer.
bégueter [begte] v. intr. (8b). To bleat.
bégueule [begœl] adj. Prudish, priggish, puritanical, U. S. prissy.
— f. Prig, Mrs Grundy. (V. prude.)
bégueulerie [begœlri] f. Fam. Prudery, priggishness, over-fastidiousness.
béguin [begɛ̃] m. Bonnet; mob-cap. ‖ Fam. Lady-love, sweetheart, girl-friend (femme); sweetheart, boy-friend (homme); mash (personne); infatuation (v. toquade); *avoir le béguin pour,* to be gone (ou) soft on, to take a fancy to, to be sweet upon, to have a crush on.
béguinage [begina:ʒ] m. Ecclés. Beguinage.
béguine [begin] f. Ecclés. Beguine.
behaviorisme [beavjɔrism] m. Philos. Behaviourism.
beige [bɛ:ʒ] adj., m. Beige.
beigne [bɛɲ] f. Pop. Biff, cuff.
beignet [bɛɲɛ] m. Culin. Beignet; fritter, U. S. doughnut.
béjaune [beʒo:n] m. Zool. Young bird. ‖ Fam. Greenhorn; tyro.
bel [bɛl] V. beau.
bel canto [bɛlkɑ̃to] m. Mus. Bel canto.
bêlement [bɛlmɑ̃] m. Bleating; bleat.
bêler [bɛle] v. tr. (1). To bleat, U. S. to blat.
belette [bəlɛt] f. Zool. Weasel.
belge [bɛlʒ] adj., m. Géogr. Belgian.
Belgique [-ʒik] f. Géogr. Belgium.
bélier [belje] m. Zool. Ram. ‖ Astron. Aries, the Ram. ‖ Milit. Battering ram. ‖ Techn. *Bélier hydraulique,* hydraulic ram.
bélinogramme [belinɔgram] m. Telephotograph.
bélître [belitr] m. Knave, scoundrel. ‖ Pedant.
belladone [bɛlladɔn] f. Bot. Belladonna.
bellâtre [bɛlɑ:tr] m. Pop. Beau.
belle [bɛ:l] adj. V. beau.
belle [bɛ:l] f. Belle, beauty, U. S. flossy. ‖ Mistress. ‖ Rubber game (aux cartes). ‖ Sports. Final set (au tennis).
bellement [-mɑ̃] adv. Nicely, gently, fairly.
bellicisme [bɛllisism] m. Warmongering.
belliciste [-sist] m. Warmonger.
belligérance [-ʒerɑ̃:s] f. Milit. Belligerency.
belligérant, ante [-ʒerɑ̃, ɑ̃:t] adj., m. Milit. Belligerent.
belliqueux, euse [-kø, ø:z] adj. Warlike; bellicose. (V. guerroyeur.) ‖ Pugnacious, quarrelsome. (V. batailleur.)
bellot, otte [bɛlo, ot] adj. Fam. Pretty.
belluaire [bɛlɥɛ:r] m. Wild-beast tamer.
belon [bəlɔ̃] f. Zool., Culin. Belon oyster, round flat oyster from the Belon in Brittany.
belote [bəlɔt] f. Belote (jeu).
belvédère [bɛlvede:r] m. Belvedere.
bémol [bemɔl] adj., m. Mus. Flat.
bémoliser [-lize] v. tr. (1). Mus. To flatten.
bénarde [benard] adj. Techn. Pin-key.
bénédicité [benedisite] m. Ecclés. Grace, benedicite; *dire, réciter le bénédicité,* to say grace.
bénédictin [benediktɛ̃] adj., m. Ecclés. Benedictine.
bénédictine [-tin] f. Ecclés., Comm. Benedictine.
bénédiction [-sjɔ̃] f. Ecclés. Benediction (en général); consecration (d'une église, du drapeau); *bénédiction nuptiale,* marriage ceremony. ‖ Benediction, blessing; *donner sa bénédiction à,* to give one's blessing to, to bless. ‖ Fam. Blessing, godsend, windfall (chance); *c'est une bénédiction qu'il soit venu,* his coming is a blessing (ou) a stroke of luck; *il pleut que c'est une bénédiction,* it is raining with a vengeance.
bénef [benɛf] m. Pop. Profit, perk.

bénéfice [benefis] m. COMM. Profit, gain; earnings (v. GAIN); *petits bénéfices*, perquisites. ‖ JUR. Privilege (de l'âge); benefit (du doute); *sous bénéfice d'inventaire*, conditionally, with reservations. ‖ ECCLÉS. Benefice, living.

bénéficiaire [-sjɛ:r] adj. Showing a profit; *solde bénéficiaire*, profit balance.
— m. Beneficiary. ‖ FIN. Payee, recipient.

bénéficier [-sje] v. intr. (1). To make a profit, to profit, to benefit (de, by); *faire bénéficier qqn d'une expérience*, to give s.o. the benefit of one's experience. ‖ JUR. *Bénéficier d'un non-lieu*, to be discharged; *faire bénéficier qqn d'une remise*, to allow s.o. a discount.

bénéfique [benefik] adj. Benefic, beneficent.

Benelux [bənəlyks] m. GÉOGR. Benelux.

benêt [bənɛ] adj. Silly, simple.
— m. Noodle, booby, U. S. sap. (V. NIAIS.)

bénévolat [benevɔla] m. Voluntary (ou) unpaid work (ou) help (ou) service.

bénévole [benevɔl] adj. Gentle, kind (aimable); gratuitous; unpaid (gratis); voluntary (volontaire).

bénévolement [-mɑ̃] adv. Kindly; gratuitously; voluntarily.

Bengale [bɛ̃gal] m. GÉOGR. Bengal. ‖ *Feu de Bengale*, bengal light, flare.

bengali [-li] m. GÉOGR. Bengali, Bengalese. ‖ GRAMM. Bengali (langue). ‖ ZOOL. Waxbill.

bénignité [beniɲite] f. Benignity; benevolence; benignency. ‖ MÉD. Mildness.

bénin [benɛ̃] (f. **bénigne** [beniɲ]) adj. Benign, benignant. ‖ MÉD. Mild, benign, non-malignant.

Bénin [benɛ̃] m. GÉOGR. Benin.

béni-oui-oui [beniwiwi] m. invar. FAM. Yes-man.

bénir [beni:r] v. tr. (2). To bless (qqn). ‖ To bless, to glorify; *Dieu soit béni!*, God be praised!; *bénir le ciel de*, to thank God for. ‖ ECCLÉS. To consecrate (l'eau, le pain, une église); to solemnize (un mariage).

bénit [beni] adj. Consecrated (cierge, église, pain, drapeau); holy (eau, médaille). ‖ LOC. *Eau bénite de cour*, court holy-water, fair promises, soft-talk, just so many words, blarney; *c'est pain bénit!*, it serves him right!

bénitier [-tje] m. ECCLÉS. Holy-water basin; stoup. ‖ ZOOL. Giant clam. ‖ FAM. *Se démener comme un diable dans un bénitier*, to jump about like a cat on hot bricks (ou) U.S. on a hot tin roof.

benjamin [bɛ̃ʒamɛ̃] m. Junior (moins âgé); youngest child (le plus jeune). ‖ Darling (chéri).

benjoin [bɛ̃ʒwɛ̃] m. BOT. Benjamin; benzoin.

benne [bɛn] f. AGRIC. Hamper; pannier (à vendanges). ‖ TECHN. Bucket (de drague); bucket, truck, corf (de mine). ‖ AUTOM. *Camion à benne basculante*, tip-lorry, U. S. dump truck.

benoît [bənwa] m. Benedict.
— adj. † Blessed. ‖ Gentle. ‖ Sanctimonious; mealy-mouthed (patelin).

benoîtement [-tmɑ̃] adv. In a mealy-mouthed way, ingratiatingly.

benthique [bɛ̃tik] adj. BOT., ZOOL. Benthic.

bentonite [bɛ̃tɔnit] f. Bentonite.

benzène [bɛ̃zɛn] m. CHIM. Benzene.

benzine [bɛ̃zin] f. CHIM. Benzine.

benzoïque [bɛ̃zɔi:k] adj. CHIM. Benzoic.

benzol [bɛ̃zɔl] m. CHIM. Benzol.

béotien, enne [beɔsjɛ̃, ɛn] adj., s. Beotian. ‖ FIG. Barbarian, philistine.

B.E.P.C. [beəpese] m. Abrév. de *Brevet d'études du premier cycle*, exam taken at end of 4th year of secondary school.

béquillard [bekija:r] m. FAM. Cripple; person walking on crutches.

béquille [beki:j] f. Crutch; *marcher avec des béquilles*, to walk on crutches. ‖ AUTOM. Stand (de moto). ‖ TECHN. Lever-handle. ‖ NAUT. Prop, leg. ‖ AVIAT. *Patin de béquille*, tail skid.

béquiller [bekije] v. tr. (1). To shore, to shore up (un bateau).

béquillon [bekijɔ̃] m. Crutch-handled walking-stick.

ber [bɛ:r] m. NAUT. Cradle.

berbère [bɛrbɛ:r] adj., s. GÉOGR. Berber.

berbéris [bɛrberis] m. BOT. Berberis, barberry.

bercail [bɛrka:j] m. Sheep-fold. (V. BERGERIE.) ‖ FIG. Fold; *rentrer au bercail*, to return to the fold.

berceau [bɛrso] m. Cradle, cot (d'enfant); bassinet (en osier). ‖ Arbour, bower (tonnelle). ‖ ARCHIT. Barrel (de voûte). ‖ NAUT. Cradle. ‖ MILIT. Bed. ‖ AVIAT. *Berceau à bombes*, bomb rack. ‖ FIG. Infancy; *dès le berceau*, from birth; *encore au berceau*, still in infancy. ‖ FIG. Birthplace, cradle (de la civilisation, d'une race).

bercelonnette [-səlɔnɛt] f. Swing-cot.

bercement [-səmɑ̃] m. Rocking; lulling.

bercer [bɛrse] v. tr. (5). To rock (dans un berceau); to nurse (dans les bras); to dandle (sur les genoux). ‖ FIG. To lull (une douleur); to nurse (un espoir); to delude (qqn, d'illusions).
— v. pr. **Se bercer**, to rock, to swing. ‖ FIG. *Se bercer de*, to delude oneself with, to indulge in.

berceur, euse [-sœ:r, ø:3] adj. Rocking. ‖ FIG. Lulling.

berceuse [-sø:z] f. Swing-cot (bercelonnette). ‖ Rocking-chair. ‖ MUS. Lullaby, berceuse (chant).

béret [berɛ] m. Beret (basque); tam-o'-shanter (écossais).

bergamasque [bɛrgamask] f. MUS. Bergamasque.

bergamote [bɛrgamɔt] f. BOT. Bergamot (fruit, essence).

bergamotier [-mɔtje] m. BOT. Bergamot (arbre).

berge [bɛr3] f. Bank, steep river bank (d'une rivière). ‖ CH. DE F. Banked edge. ‖ MILIT. Slope; rampart; parapet.

berger [bɛr3e] m. Shepherd (v. PÂTRE); *chien de berger*, sheep-dog; *étoile du berger*, evening star. ‖ FIG. Pastor, shepherd. (V. PASTEUR.)

bergère [-3ɛ:r] f. Shepherdess (femme). ‖ Easy-chair (siège).

bergerie [-3əri] f. Sheep-fold, pen; *enfermer le loup dans la bergerie*, to set the fox to mind the geese. ‖ Pastoral (poème, tableau).

bergeronnette [-3ərɔnɛt] f. ZOOL. Wagtail.

bergsonisme [bɛrgsɔnism] m. PHILOS. Bergsonism.

béribéri [beriberi] m. MÉD. Beriberi.

berkélium [bɛrkeljɔm] m. CHIM. Berkelium.

berline [bɛrlin] f. AUTOM. Berline, four-door saloon (ou) U. S. sedan. ‖ TECHN. Tub, truck (de mines).

berlingot [bɛrlɛ̃go] m. CULIN. Burnt-sugar, caramel; U. S. caramel candy.

berlinois, oise [bɛrlinwa, wa:z] adj. GÉOGR. Of (ou) from Berlin.
— s. Berliner.

berlue [bɛrly] f. MÉD. Fallacy of vision; deceptio visus; optical illusion. ‖ FIG. *Avoir la berlue*, not to see straight, to be mistaken.

berme [bɛrm] f. Berm.

bermuda [bɛrmyda] m. Bermuda shorts, Bermudas.

bernacle [bɛrnakl] f. ZOOL. Barnacle.

Bernard [bɛrna:r] m. Bernard. ‖ **Bernard-l'ermite**, m. ZOOL. Hermit-crab.

bernardin [bɛrnardɛ̃] m. ECCLÉS. Bernardine.

berne [bɛrn] f. NAUT. *En berne*, half-mast; *mettre le pavillon en berne*, to half-mast the flag. ‖ MILIT. Furled and craped.

berner [bɛrne] v. tr. (1). To toss in a blanket (faire sauter). ‖ To fool, to hoodwink. (V. DUPER.)

bernique [bɛrnik] interj. FAM. No go!, nothing doing!

bernois, oise [bɛrnwa, wa:z] adj., s. GÉOGR. Bernese.

berrichon, onne [beriʃɔ̃, ɔn] adj. GÉOGR. Of (ou) from Berry.
— s. Native (ou) inhabitant of Berry.

berthe [bɛrt] f. Bertha (collerette). ‖ Milk-can (de laitier).

berthon [bɛrtɔ̃] m. NAUT. Berthon collapsible boat.

bertillonnage [bɛrti:jɔna:ʒ] m. JUR. Bertillon system; anthropometry.

béryl [beril] m. Beryl.

béryllium [beriljɔm] m. CHIM. Beryllium.

besace [bəzas] f. Scrip. (V. BISSAC.)

bésef [bezɛf] adv. V. BÉZEF.

besicles [bəzikl] f. pl. FAM. Specs, giglamps, U. S. cheaters. (V. LUNETTES.)

bésigue [bezig] m. Bezique (jeu).

besogne [bəzɔɲ] f. Work, labour, toil; piece of work; *aller trop vite en besogne,* to scamp one's work; to rush the job (pop.); *être attelé à la besogne,* to be (ou) to live in harness; *faire de la bonne besogne,* to do a good piece of work; *ce n'est pas une petite besogne,* it is no easy matter; *une sale besogne,* a nasty job.

besogner [-ne] v. intr. (1). To labour, to drudge.

besogneux, euse [-ɲø, ø:z] adj. Needy; short of money; *écrivain besogneux,* pot-boiler.

besoin [bəzwɛ̃] m. Want, need, requirement (de l'existence). ‖ Want, need, necessity (v. NÉCESSITÉ); occasion; *au besoin, en cas de besoin,* at need, in case of need, on occasion. ‖ Needs (de la nature); *faire ses (petits) besoins,* to relieve oneself (ou) nature. ‖ Needs; neediness; want; reduced circumstances (v. IMPÉCUNIOSITÉ); *se mettre à l'abri du besoin,* to keep the wolf from the door. ‖ FIG. Urge, impulse, craving (de, for). ‖ **Avoir besoin de,** to need, to have need of; to be in need of, to have necessity for (qqch., qqn); *il n'a pas besoin de s'inquiéter,* he has no occasion to be alarmed; *j'ai grand besoin d'argent,* I am in urgent need of money; *personne n'a besoin de lui,* nobody wants him; *j'ai besoin qu'on me prête ce livre,* I want s.o. to lend me this book. ‖ Etre besoin; *si besoin est,* if need be; *il n'est pas besoin de,* there is no need to; *toutes les fois que de besoin,* whenever necessary; *en tant que de besoin,* to the extent that it may be required.

bessemer [bɛsmɛr] m. TECHN. Bessemer converter.

bestiaire [bɛstjɛ:r] m. Bestiarius (gladiateur); bestiary (livre).

bestial, ale [-tjal] adj. Bestial, beastly, brutish. ‖ MÉD. Theroid.

bestialement [-tjalmɑ̃] adv. Bestially, brutishly.

bestialiser [-tjalize] v. tr. (1). To brutify, to bestialize.

bestialité [-tjalite] f. Bestiality, brutishness; beastliness.

bestiaux [-tjo] m. pl. ZOOL. Cattle, livestock.

bestiole [-tjɔl] f. ZOOL. Tiny beast (ou) creature.

best-seller [bɛstsɛlœ:r] m. Best-seller.

bêta [bɛta] (f. **bêtasse** [-s]) adj. Dull, doltish, wet (fam.). [V. SOT.]
— m. Simpleton, booby, zany, U. S. sap.

bêta m. Beta. ‖ PHYS. *Rayons bêta,* beta rays.

bétail [beta:j] m. AGRIC. Cattle; livestock; grazing stock; *bétail sur pied,* cattle on the hoof.

bétaillère [-tajɛ:r] f. Cattle- (ou) sheep-truck.

bêtatron [betatrɔ̃] m. PHYS. Betatron.

bête [bɛ:t] f. ZOOL. Animal, beast; *bête à bon Dieu,* lady-bird. ‖ FIG. Dunce, fool; *faire la bête,* to play the fool. ‖ FAM. *Bête noire,* pet aversion, bête noire; *bonne bête,* good sort, good-natured simpleton; *chercher la petite bête,* to see spots in the sun; to be captious (ou) hypercritical (ou)

fussy; *reprendre du poil de la bête,* to buck up, to have another go (ou) try.
— adj. Foolish, asinine, stupid (v. SOT); *bête comme chou,* a child's play; *qu'il est bête!,* what a fool he is!, U. S. what a sap he is!

bétel [betɛl] m. BOT. Betel.

bêtement [bɛtmɑ̃] adv. Foolishly.

bêtifiant, ante [betifjɑ̃, ɑ̃:t] adj. Childish, idiotic.

bêtifier [betifje] v. intr. (1). To play the fool; to make an ass of oneself.

bêtise [beti:z] f. Silliness; foolishness; folly; foolery (v. SOTTISE, STUPIDITÉ); *bêtise noire,* stupidity, obtuseness. ‖ Nonsense, rubbish, piffle, bunkum, rot, bosh; *dire des bêtises,* to talk nonsense. ‖ Mistake (erreur); blunder (v. BOURDE); mischief (gaminerie). ‖ Trifle (motif futile); *se disputer pour une bêtise,* to quarrel about a mere trifle. ‖ Gewgaw (babiole); flea-bite, pinch of snuff (broutille, rien).

béton [betɔ̃] m. ARCHIT. Concrete.

bétonnage [betɔna:ʒ] m. ARCHIT. Concreting.

bétonner [-ne] v. tr. (1). ARCHIT. To concrete.

bétonnière [-njɛ:r] f. ARCHIT. Concrete-mixer.

bette [bɛt] f. BOT., CULIN. White beet. ‖ NAUT. Flat-bottomed boat, lighter.

betterave [bɛtra:v] f. BOT. Beetroot; U. S. beet; *betterave fourragère,* mangel-wurzel; *betterave sucrière,* sugar-beet.

betteravier, ère [-vje, ɛr] adj. Beet (industrie).
— m. Beet-grower (ou) worker.

beuglant, ante [bøglɑ̃, ɑ̃:t] m. POP. Penny gaff, cheap café-concert. (V. BOUI-BOUI.)
— f. POP. Yell of protest. ‖ POP. Rowdy song.

beuglement [-gləmɑ̃] m. Lowing (d'une vache); bellowing (d'un taureau). ‖ FAM. Bawling, howling (d'une personne).

beugler [-gle] v. intr. (1). To bellow (taureau); to low (vache). ‖ FAM. To bawl (personne).

beurre [bœ:r] m. CULIN. Butter (de lait); *beurre d'anchois,* anchovy paste; *beurre de cacao,* cocoa-butter; *petit beurre,* butter-biscuit. ‖ FAM. *Comme dans du beurre,* quite easily; *faire son beurre,* to feather one's nest, to make one's pile; *main de beurre,* butter-fingers; *mettre du beurre dans les épinards,* to oil the wheels; *la tartine tombe toujours du côté du beurre,* the bread always falls butter side down.
— adj. Butter-coloured (couleur). ‖ Butter (haricot, papier).

beurré [bœre] m. BOT. Butter-pear.

beurrée f. CULIN. Slice of bread and butter.

beurrer v. tr. (1). To butter.

beurrerie [bœrri] f. Butter-factory.

beurrier, ère [bœrje, ɛr] adj. Butter (industrie); butter-producing (région).
— m. COMM. Butter-maker (ou) -man (fabricant). ‖ CULIN. Butter-dish; *beurrier rafraîchisseur,* butter-cooler.

beuverie [bøvri] f. Drinking bout; soak.

bévatron [bevatˈɔ̃] m. PHYS. Bevatron.

bévue [bevy] f. Blunder, U. S. boner; *commettre une bévue,* to make a mistake (ou) a slip (ou) a howler; to drop a brick, U. S. to pull a boner.

bey [bɛ] m. Bey.

beylical, ale [belikal] adj. Beylic, Beylical.

bézef [bezef] adv. POP. Muckle; a lot.

biais, aise [bjɛ, ɛ:z] adj. Skew (pont).
— m. Skew, slant; *de biais, en biais,* slantwise, aslant, askew, slantly; *regarder de biais,* to look askance at. ‖ Bias; *couper dans le biais,* to cut on the cross (ou) bias. ‖ FIG. Expedient, shift (v. DÉTOUR); *de biais,* indirectly, in a round-about way.

biaiser [-ze] v. tr. (1). To skew, to slant. ‖ FIG. To shuffle; to use shifts. (V. LOUVOYER.)

biaural, e [bioral] adj. V. BINAURAL.

bibasique [bibazik] adj. Снім. Bibasic, dibasic.
bibelot [biblo] m. Trinket, knick-knack, curio, bibelot. ‖ Trifle; gewgaw.
bibeloter [-blɔte] v. intr. (1). To buy (ou) to collect knick-knacks. ‖ To do odd jobs, to potter, U. S. to putter.
biberon [bibrɔ̃] m. Bottle, feeding bottle; être élevé au biberon, to be bottle-fed. ‖ FAM. Service-biberon, baby-sitting.
biberonner [-brɔne] v. intr. (1). FAM. To tipple, to soak, to booze, U. S. to liquor up.
bibi [bibi] m. POP. I, myself, number one. ‖ FAM. Tile. (V. GALURIN.)
bibine [bibin] f. FAM. Gnat's piss, plonk.
bible [bibl] f. Bible; papier bible, Bible paper.
bibliobus [bibliɔbys] m. Mobile library, U. S. bookmobile.
bibliographe [-graf] s. Bibliographer.
bibliographie [-grafi] f. Bibliography.
bibliographique [-grafik] adj. Bibliographical.
bibliomanie [-mani] f. Bibliomania.
bibliophile [-fil] s. Bibliophile; book-collector (ou) -lover.
bibliophilie [-fili] f. Bibliophilism.
bibliothécaire [-tekɛ:r] s. Librarian.
bibliothèque [-tɛk] f. Library; reading-room (collection, salle); bookstall (de gare); bookcase, book-shelves (meuble).
biblique [biblik] adj. Biblical.
bicamérisme [bikamerism] m. Bicameral system.
bicarbonate [bikarbɔnat] m. Снім. Bicarbonate; bicarbonate de soude, bicarbonate of soda, sodium bicarbonate, U. S. saleratus.
bicarré, ée [bikare] adj. MATH. Biquadratic.
bicentenaire [bisãtnɛ:r] adj. 200-year-old, bicentenary, bicentennial.
— m. Bicentenary, bicentennial.
bicéphale [bisefal] adj. Bicephalous.
biceps [bisɛps] m., adj. MÉD. Biceps. ‖ FAM. Avoir du biceps, to be muscular (ou) sinewy (ou) stalwart.
biche [biʃ] f. ZOOL. Doe, hind; ventre-de-biche, light fawn, reddish white, skewbald (couleur).
bicher [biʃe] v. intr. (1). POP. To get on well; to hit it off well.
bichlorure [biklɔry:r] f. Снім. Bichloride.
bichon [biʃɔ̃] m. ZOOL. Maltese dog. ‖ TECHN. Valvet pad. ‖ FAM. Darling.
bichonner [-ʃɔne] v. tr. (1). To curl (friser); to titivate, to doll up (parer).
— v. pr. Se **bichonner**, to spruce oneself, to titivate, to doll up.
bichromate [bikrɔmat] m. Снім. Bichromate, dichromate.
bicolore [bikɔlɔ:r] adj. Two-coloured, bicoloured.
biconcave [bikɔ̃ka:v] adj. Biconcave, double-concave.
biconvexe [-vɛks] adj. Biconvex, double-convex.
bicoque [bikɔk] f. FAM. Shanty. (V. BARAQUE.)
bicorne [bikɔrn] adj. Two-cornered.
— m. Cocked hat.
bicot [biko] m. ZOOL., FAM. Kid. ‖ FAM. Arab.
bicycle [bisikl] m. Velocipede; penny-farthing.
bicyclette [-klɛt] f. AUTOM. Bicycle, cycle; bike (fam.); aller à bicyclette, to bicycle, to cycle. ‖ SPORTS. Cycling; faire de la bicyclette, to cycle.
bidasse [bida:s] m. POP. Soldier, squaddy.
bide [bid] m. POP. Belly (ventre), paunch (bedaine). ‖ POP. Flop, fiasco (échec); faire un bide, to flop.
bident [bidã] m. AGRIC. Two-pronged pitchfork.
bidenté, ée [-te] adj. Bidentate, double-toothed.
bidet [bidɛ] m. ZOOL. Nag. (V. CANASSON.) ‖ Bidet (appareil hygiénique).
bidoche [bidɔʃ] m. POP. Meat.
bidon [bidɔ̃] m. Can, tin; jerrycan; bidon à

essence, à huile, à lait, petrol- (ou) U. S. gasoline-, oil-, milkcan. ‖ Balaam (en langage journalistique). ‖ MILIT. Canteen; water-bottle. ‖ POP. Belly, paunch (ventre); fake (chiqué).
bidonnant, ante [bidɔnã, ã:t] adj. POP. Killing (v. CREVANT); c'est bidonnant, it's a scream.
bidonner (se) [səbidɔne] v. pr. POP. To split one's sides. (V. RIGOLER.)
bidonville [bidɔ̃vil] m. Shanty-town.
bidule [bidyl] m. Gadget, U. S. doodad.
bief [bjɛf] m. Level (de canal); mill-race, sluice (de moulin).
bielle [bjɛl] f. TECHN. Crank arm; push rod; bielle d'accouplement, connecting rod; bielle maîtresse, motrice, main, driving rod. ‖ AUTOM. Big-end. ‖ ARCHIT. Brace, strut (de construction).
biélorusse [bjelorys] adj., s. GÉOGR. Belorussian, Byelorussian.
— m. GRAMM. Belorussian, Byelorussian (langue).
bien [bjɛ̃] adv.

1. Absolument. — 2. Avantageusement. — 3. A vrai dire. — 4. Beaucoup. — 5. Cependant. — 6. Certainement. — 7. Convenablement. — 8. Correctement. — 9. Habilement. — 10. Loyalement. — 11. Solidement. — 12. Volontiers. — 13. Employé comme attribut. — 14. Emphatique. ‖ 15. Aussi bien. — 16. Aussi bien que. — 17. Bien du. — 18. Bien plus. — 19. Bien que. — 20. Si bien que. — 21. Ou bien. — 22. Loc.

1. Well, just; exactly; quite (absolument, tout à fait); c'est bien cela, just so; bien se rappeler, to remember exactly (ou) well; bien mort, quite dead; être bien d'accord, to agree entirely (ou) thoroughly; bien à vous, yours sincerely. ‖ 2. Well; fair; right (avantageusement, sagement); s'en trouver bien, to find it to one's advantage; se passer bien, to go off well, to come out right; faire bien de, to do right to. ‖ 3. Indeed (à vrai dire, en fait); je l'ai bien vu, indeed, I saw him; I did see him. ‖ 4. Well; much; far; a lot (beaucoup); bien nourri, well-fed; bien plus grand que moi, much (ou) a lot taller than I; bien trop tard, far too late. ‖ 5. However, yet (cependant); nous arriverons bien à le convaincre, we shall convince him yet. ‖ 6. Well, certainly (certainement); savoir bien que, to know well that. ‖ 7. Well, duly (convenablement); bien balayé, swept clean; bien caché, securely hidden; bien reçu, duly received; faire bien les choses, to do things well. ‖ 8. Rightly, right; properly (correctement); bien parler anglais, to speak good English; si je comprends bien, if I understand well (ou) rightly. ‖ 9. Skilfully, well (habilement); chanter bien, to sing well; s'y prendre bien, to set about sth. properly; viser bien, to aim carefully. ‖ 10. Fairly; rightly, well (loyalement); bien agir, to behave well, to act fairly. ‖ 11. Fast (solidement); bien fixé, fixed fast; être bien ajusté, to fit tight. ‖ Very, much (très); bien heureux, very happy; bien obligé, much obliged. ‖ 12. Willingly, with pleasure (volontiers); j'irais bien si, I would willingly go if, I would like to go if. ‖ 13. Well (employé comme attribut avec valeur adjectivale); êtes-vous bien?, are you comfortable? (à l'aise); are you well? (en bonne santé); elle était très bien jadis, she was formerly very beautiful; nous ne sommes pas très bien, we are not on good terms (ou) right. ‖ 14. (Sens emphatique); il faut bien que je, I really must; qu'est-ce que cela peut bien être?, what on earth can that be?; quand bien même, even though. ‖ 15. Aussi bien, anyway, anyhow; in any case (de toute manière). ‖

16. Aussi **bien que**, as well as (de même que). ‖
17. **Bien du, bien de la**, much (beaucoup); **bien des**, many; *bien des fois*, many times; *bien du mal*, much ado, a lot of trouble. ‖ 18. **Bien plus**, what's more. ‖ 19. **Bien que**, although, though (quoique). ‖ 20. **Si bien que**, however well (si parfaitement que); so, so that (de sorte que). ‖ 21. **Ou bien**, or else. ‖ 22. Loc. *Bien lui en a pris*, it was a good thing for him; *mener à bien*, to carry through, to achieve; *ni bien ni mal*, so, so; *quelqu'un de très bien*, a man of good position (ou) breeding (ou) education; *quelque chose de bien*, something good (de bonne qualité); *tant bien que mal*, after a fashion, as well as possible, somehow or other; *se trouver bien de*, to be the better for; to derive benefit from; *vous tombez bien*, you have come just in the nick of time (ou) at the right moment.

— interj. **Bien!** all right! good! ‖ **Eh bien!**, well!, why!, now! ‖ **Eh bien?**, well? ‖ **Très bien!**, very good!, very well!

— m. Good; righteousness (vertu); *ramener au bien*, to reclaim; *rendre le bien pour le mal*, to return good for evil. ‖ Good, blessing, boon (avantage); *bien inestimable*, priceless boon; *un bien pour un mal*, a blessing in disguise; *faire du bien*, to do good; to benefit; to mend; *plus de mal que de bien*, more harm than good; *pour son bien*, for his own good. ‖ Good, welfare, profit; *le bien public*, the public good; the common welfare (ou) weal; *grand bien lui fasse*, much good may it do him; *vouloir du bien*, to wish well. ‖ Praise; *dire du bien de*, to speak well of, to say a good word for; to praise. ‖ Property, estate, possessions; goods and chattels; belongings (v. DOMAINE, PATRIMOINE, PROPRIÉTÉ); *bien de famille*, family estate; ancestral acres (fam.). ‖ **Bien-aimé**, adj. Beloved, darling. ‖ **Bien-être**, m. Well-being, comfort, cosiness. ‖ **Bien-fondé**, m. JUR. Cogency, conclusiveness; merits [de, of]; grounds [de, for]. ‖ **Bien-fonds** (pl. **biens-fonds**), m. Real estate, landed property. ‖ **Bien-jugé**, m. JUR. Legally valid decision. ‖ **Bien-pensant**, adj. Conformist, right-thinking, priggish; s. conformist, right-thinking person, prig.

bienfaisance [-fɛzɑ̃:s] f. Beneficence; charity; benevolence.

bienfaisant, ante [-fɛzɑ̃, ɑ̃:t] adj. Benevolent, charitable. ‖ Beneficial, benignant.

bienfait [-fɛ] m. Benefit, act of kindness; charity. ‖ FIG. Blessing, boon (de la civilisation).

bienfaiteur [-fɛtœ:r] m. Benefactor.

bienfaitrice [-fɛtris] f. Benefactress.

bienheureux, euse [bjɛ̃nørø, ø:z] adj. ECCLÉS. Blessed. ‖ FAM. Blessed, blissful.

— m. pl. Blessed, blest.

biennal, ale [biɛnal] adj. Biennial.

— f. Biennial (festival).

bienséance [bjɛ̃seɑ̃:s] f. Decency, propriety, seemliness; decorum.

bienséant, ante [-seɑ̃, ɑ̃:t] adj. Becoming, proper, seemly; decorous.

bientôt [-to] adv. Soon; shortly; before long; *à bientôt*, so long; *c'est bientôt dit*, it is easy to say.

bienveillance [-vɛjɑ̃:s] f. Benevolence, kindness; goodwill; *avec bienveillance*, favourably.

bienveillant [-jɑ̃] adj. Benevolent.

bienvenir [-vni:r] v. tr. (2). *Se faire bienvenir*, to curry favour, to ingratiate oneself (de, with).

bienvenu, ue [-vəny] adj., m. Welcome (à, to).

bienvenue [-vəny] f. Welcome; *souhaiter la bienvenue à qqn*, to welcome s.o., to wish s.o. welcome. ‖ FAM. *Payer sa bienvenue*, to pay one's footing.

bière [bjɛ:r] f. Coffin. (V. CERCUEIL.)

bière f. Beer. ‖ FAM. *Ce n'est pas de la petite bière,*

ce type-là, not a bad chap, that; *ne pas se prendre pour de la petite bière*, to think no small beer. (ou) potatoes of oneself.

biffage [bifa:ʒ] m. Erasure, crossing-out.

biffer [-fe] v. tr. (1). To cross (ou) strike out; to cross off.

biffin [bifɛ̃] m. Rag-and-bone man; rag-picker, rag-man, U. S. junkman. ‖ MILIT., FAM. Footslogger.

biffure [bify:r] f. Crossing-out, erasure.

bifocal, ale [bifɔkal] adj. PHYS. Bifocal.

bifteck [biftɛk] m. CULIN. Beefsteak.

bifurcation [bifyrkasjɔ̃] f. Bifurcation; embranchment (de rivière); branching, forking (de route, de tronc d'arbre); road fork (de route). ‖ ELECTR. Shunt. ‖ CH. DE F. Junction.

bifurquer [-ke] v. intr. (1). To fork, to bifurcate, to branch off.

bigame [bigam] adj. Bigamous.

— m. Bigamist.

bigamie [-mi] f. Bigamy.

bigarré, ée [bigare] adj. Variegated, motley.

bigarreau [bigaro] m. BOT. Bigaroon (cerise).

bigarrer [bigare] v. tr. (1). To variegate, to chequer, to mottle, to speckle. (V. BARIOLER.)

bigarrure [-ry:r] f. Variegation; motley.

bigle [bigl] adj. MÉD. Squint (œil); squint-eyed, cock-eyed (fam.) [personne].

bigler [bigle] v. intr. (1). To squint, to be cross-eyed.

— v. tr. FAM. To squint at, to have a squint (ou) a butcher's at.

bigleux, euse [-glø, ∅:z] adj. FAM. Half-blind, as blind as a bat (myope); cock-eyed, cross-eyed (qui louche).

bigophone [bigɔfɔn] m. POP. Phone, blower; *passer un coup de bigophone*, to give s.o. a buzz.

bigorne [bigɔrn] f. TECHN. Two-beaked anvil.

bigorneau [-no] m. TECHN. Beak-iron. ‖ ZOOL. Winkle (coquillage).

bigorner [bigɔrne] v. tr. (1). POP. To mess up, to ruin (une voiture, etc.); to clout, to sock (une personne).

— v. pr. **Se bigorner**, POP. To scrap, to have a scrap.

bigot [bigɔ] m. AGRIC. Mattock.

bigot, ote adj. Sanctimonious; churchy; priest-ridden; pietistical.

— m. Pietist; religious bigot. (V. CAGOT.)

bigoterie [-tri] f. Religious bigotry.

bigoudi [bigudi] m. Hair-curler, curling-pin.

bigre [bigr] interj. By Jove!, Heavens!, Gosh!

bigrement [-grəmɑ̃] adv. Jolly; awfully; devilishly.

bigrille [bigri:j] adj. ELECTR. Double-grid.

bigue [big] f. TECHN. Sheers.

bihebdomadaire [biɛbdɔmadɛ:r] adj. Twice-weekly, bi-weekly.

bijection [biʒɛksjɔ̃] f. MATH. Bijection.

bijou [biʒu] (pl. **bijoux**) m. Jewel; *coffret à bijoux*, jewel-case. (V. JOYAU.) ‖ FIG. Jewel, gem (chose précieuse); darling, beauty (être aimé).

bijouterie [-tri] f. Jeweller's art (ou) shop (ou) trade (art, boutique, commerce). ‖ Jewelry, jewellery (bijoux).

bijoutier [-tje] m. Jeweller, U. S. jeweler.

bikini [bikini] m. Bikini.

bilabial, ale [bilabjal] adj. GRAMM. Bilabial.

— f. GRAMM. Bilabial.

bilame [bila:m] adj. Two-bladed.

bilan [bilɑ̃] m. FIN. Balance-sheet (déclaration); statement of affairs, schedule (de liquidation); balance (d'un compte); *déposer son bilan*, to file one's petition; *dresser le bilan*, to draw up the balance-sheet, to strike a balance. ‖ MILIT. *Bilan d'une opération militaire*, result of an operation

81

with regard to achievements and casualties. ‖ *Bilan énergétique*, energy demand.

bilatéral, ale [bilateral] adj. Bilateral. ‖ Two-sided (convention).

bilboquet [bilbɔkɛ] m. Cup-and-ball (jouet).

bile [bi:l] f. MÉD. Bile, gall. ‖ FIG. Bad temper; anger (colère); worry (souci); *se faire de la bile*, to worry, to fret.

biler (se) [səbile] v. pr. (1). FAM. To worry oneself, to fret, to get worked up; *il ne se bile pas*, he takes it easy.

bileux, euse [bilø, ø:z] adj. FAM. Easily upset; worrying; fretting; care-laden. (V. INQUIET.)

bilharzie [bilarzi] f. ZOOL., MÉD. Bilharzia.

biliaire [-ljɛ:r] adj. MÉD. Biliary; *calcul biliaire*, gall-stone.

bilieux, euse [-ljø, øz] adj. MÉD. Bilious, jaundiced (teint). ‖ FAM. Cross; choleric.

bilingue [bilɛ̃:g] adj. Bilingual.

bilinguisme [-gɥism] m. Bilingualism.

billard [bija:r] m. Billiards (jeu); billiard-room (salle); billiard-table (table); *billard russe*, snookerette; *joueur de billard*, billiards-player. ‖ FAM. *Passer sur le billard*, to undergo an operation.

bille [bi:j] f. Billiard-ball (de billard). ‖ Marble; *jouer aux billes*, to play at marbles. ‖ Block, log (de bois). ‖ TECHN. Ball; *roulement à billes*, ball bearing; *stylo à bille*, ball-point pen. ‖ CH. DE F. Sleeper. ‖ FAM. Phiz, dial, mug, U. S. map, pan (tête).

billet [bijɛ] m. Note; *billet doux*, love letter, billet doux; *billet d'invitation*, invitation-card. ‖ CH. DE F. Ticket; *billet d'aller et retour*, return ticket; U. S. round-trip ticket; *billet de correspondance, de quai*, transfer, platform ticket; *billet simple*, single ticket, single. ‖ THÉÂTR. Ticket. ‖ MILIT. Billet; *billet de logement*, billeting-order. ‖ MÉD. *Billet d'entrée, de sortie*, admission order, order of discharge (à l'hôpital). ‖ COMM. Bill, note; *billet à ordre*, promissory note; *billet à vue*, demand bill. ‖ FIN. Note; *billet de banque*, banknote; U. S. bank-bill, bank-note. ‖ FAM. *Billet de parterre*, cropper, purler; *je vous en fiche mon billet*, I am in for it.

billette [bijɛt] f. Billet (bois). ‖ ARCHIT., BLAS. Billet.

billetterie [bijɛtri] f. Ticket issuing (ou) distribution, ticketing; ticket-office. ‖ A. T. M., Automatic teller machine.

billevesée [bilvəze] f. Rubbish; U. S. hooey. (V. BALIVERNE.)

billion [biljɔ̃] m. Billion (10¹²); U.S. trillion. ‖ (before 1948) Milliard (10⁹); U. S. billion.

billot [bijo] m. Block (de bois, de boucher, d'échafaud); stock (d'enclume); drag (de roue).

bilobé, ée [bilɔbe] adj. Bilobate, bilobed.

bimane [biman] adj. Bimanous, bimanal; two-handed.
— m. Bimane.

bimbeloterie [bɛ̃bəlɔtri] f. Toy-trade; « bazaar » trade (commerce); toys, fancy goods, novelties (objets).

bimbelotier [-tje] m. Toy-dealer; dealer in fancy goods.

bimensuel, elle [bimɑ̃sɥɛl] adj. Twice-monthly, fortnightly.

bimestriel, elle [bimɛstrjel] adj. Bimonthly; every other month (fam.).

bimétal [bimetal] m. Bimetal.

bimétallique [-lik] adj. Bimetallic.

bimétallisme [-lism] m. Bimetallism.

bimoteur [bimɔtœ:r] m. AVIAT. Twin-engine (ou) bimotored plane.

binage [bina:ʒ] m. AGRIC. Hoeing; second dressing (ou) ploughing. ‖ ECCLÉS. Celebration of two masses in one day.

binaire [binɛ:r] adj. Binary.

binard [bina:r] m. Dray.

binaural, e [binɔral] adj. Binaural.

biner [bine] v. tr. (1). AGRIC. To hoe; to dress a second time.
— v. intr. ECCLÉS. To celebrate two masses in one day.

binette [binɛt] f. AGRIC. Hoe; weeder. ‖ FAM., Phiz, U. S. map. (V. BILLE.)

biniou [binju] m. MUS. Breton bag-pipes.

binoclard, arde [binɔkla:r, ard] adj. FAM. Wearing specs (ou) goggles.
— s. Four-eyes.

binocle [binɔkl] m. Lorgnette (face à main); pince-nez, eye-glasses (lorgnon). ‖ Pl. FAM. Specs, goggles.

binoculaire [-kylɛ:r] adj. Binocular.

binôme [bino:m] adj., m. MATH. Binomial.

binucléaire [binyklee:r] adj. PHYS. Binuclear.

biochimie [biɔʃimi] f. Biochemistry.

biochimique [-ʃimik] adj. Biochemical.

biochimiste [-ʃimist] s. Biochemist.

biodégradable [-degradabl] adj. Biodegradable.

biogenèse [-ʒənɛ:z] f. MÉD. Biogenesis.

biographe [-graf] s. Biographer.

biographie [-grafi] f. Biography.

biographique [-grafik] adj. Biographical.

biologie [-lɔʒi] f. Biology.

biologique [-lɔʒik] adj. Biological.

biologiste [-lɔʒist] m. Biologist.

biométrie [-metri] f. Biometrics; biometry.

bion [bjɔ̃] m. BOT. Shoot, sucker.

bionique [bjɔnik] f. Bionics.

biophysique [biɔfisik] f. PHYS. Biophysics.

biopsie [-psi] f. MÉD. Biopsy.

biosphère [-sfɛ:r] f. Biosphere.

biosynthèse [-sɛ̃tɛ:z] f. Biosynthesis.

biothérapie [-terapi] f. MÉD. Biotherapy.

biotique [-tik] adj. Biotic.

biotope [-tɔp] m. Biotope.

bioxyde [biɔksid] m. CHIM. Dioxide.

bipale [bipa:l] adj. AVIAT. Two-bladed.

biparti, e [biparti] adj. Bipartite (feuille, organe). ‖ Bipartite, bilateral (alliance, traité). ‖ Bipartisan, two-party (gouvernement, comité).

bipartisme [-tism] m. Two-party system, bipartisan government.

bipartite [-tit] adj. invar. V. BIPARTI.

bipède [bipɛd] adj. ZOOL. Biped.
— m. ZOOL. Biped. ‖ FAM. Bloke, chap.

biplace [biplas] adj., m. AVIAT., AUTOM. Two-seater.

biplan [biplɑ̃] m. AVIAT. Biplane.

bipolaire [bipɔlɛ:r] adj. GÉOGR., ELECTR. Bipolar.

bipolarité [-larite] f. Bipolarity.

bipoutre [biputr] adj. AVIAT. Twin-boom.

bique [bik] f. FAM. Nanny-goat. ‖ FAM. Hag.

biquet [-kɛ] s. FAM. Kid (chevreau).

biquotidien, enne [bikɔtidjɛ̃, ɛn] adj. Twice daily, taking place twice a day.

birbe [birb] m. FAM. Greybeard.

biréacteur [bireaktœ:r] m. AVIAT. Twin-jet aircraft.

biréfringence [birefrɛ̃ʒɑ̃:s] adj. PHYS. Birefringence, double refraction.

biréfringent [-ʒɑ̃] adj. PHYS. Birefringent, doubly-refractive.

birman [birmɑ̃] adj., m. GÉOGR. Burmese.

Birmanie [-mani] f. GÉOGR. Burma.

biroute [birut] f. AVIAT. Sleeve, wind sock (fam.).

bis [bi] adj. Greyish-brown (couleur); brown, wholemeal, U. S. whole wheat (pain); unbleached (toile).

bis [bis] adv. Twice; once more. ‖ Repeat (reprise). ‖ A (numéro); *11 bis*, 11 A.
— interj. Encore!

— m. Encore; *crier bis,* to encore.
bisaïeul [bizajœl] m. Great-grandfather.
bisaïeule [-jœ:l] f. Great-grandmother.
bisannuel, elle [-nɥɛl] adj., m. Biennial; bi-annual.
bisbille [bisbi:j] f. FAM. Set-to, bickering, tiff; *en bisbille avec,* at loggerheads with. (V. CHICANE.)
Biscaye [biska:j] f. GÉOGR. Biscay.
biscornu, ue [biskɔrny] adj. Crooked, misshapen (chose, personne); irregular (edifice); cranky, crotchety (esprit); bizarre, queer, distorted (idée); illogical (raisonnement).
biscotin [biskɔtɛ̃] m. CULIN. Crisp biscuit.
biscotte [biskɔt] f. CULIN. Rusk, U. S. Melba toast.
biscuit [biskɥi] m. CULIN. Biscuit, U. S. cracker; *biscuit de mer,* hard tack; ship's biscuit; *biscuit à la cuiller,* sponge-finger, U. S. lady-finger; *biscuit de Savoie,* sponge-cake. ‖ COMM. Biscuit, bisque (porcelaine).
biscuiterie [-tri] f. COMM. Biscuit factory (ou) trade.
bise [bi:z] f. Bise, north wind. ‖ FIG. Winter; the wintry blast.
bise f. FAM. Kiss, smack.
biseau [bizo] m. Bevel; chamfer; bevelled (ou) chamfered edge (bord). ‖ Skew-chisel (outil).
biseautage [-ta:ʒ] m. Bevelling, chamfering. ‖ Marking (des cartes).
biseauter [-te] v. tr. (1). To bevel, to chamfer; to mark (cartes).
biser v. intr. (1). To darken, to blacken (noircir). ‖ To redye (teindre).
biser v. tr. (1). FAM. To kiss.
bisexué, ée [bisɛksɥe] adj. Bisexual.
bismuth [bismyt] m. CHIM. Bismuth.
bison [bizɔ̃] m. ZOOL. Bison, U. S. buffalo.
bisou [bizu] m. FAM. Smacker, kiss.
bisquant, ante [-kɑ̃, ɑ̃:t] adj. FAM. Vᴏꭓing, irritating, teasing. (V. AGAÇANT.)
bisque [bisk] f. SPORTS. Bisque (jeu). ‖ CULIN. Bisk; U. S. bisque. ‖ FAM. Pet; ill-humour.
bisquer [-ske] v. intr. (1). FAM. To be riled; *faire bisquer,* to rile. (V. RÂLER.)
bissac [bisak] m. Double bag; scrip (†). (V. BESACE.) ‖ MILIT. Ammunition bag.
bissecter [bisɛkte] v. tr. (1). MATH. To bisect.
bissecteur [-tœ:r] adj. Bisecting.
bissectrice [-tris] f. Bisector, bisectrix.
bisser [bise] v. tr. (1). To encore (un acteur); to repeat (une chanson).
bissextile [bisɛktil] adj. *Année bissextile,* leap-year.
bis(s)exué, ée [bisɛksɥe]. **bis(s)exuel, elle** [bisɛksɥɛl] adj. V. BISEXUÉ.
bissoc [bisɔk] m. AGRIC. Double-furrow plough.
bistorte [bistɔrt] f. BOT. Bistort.
bistouri [bisturi] m. MÉD. Lancet, knife.
bistre [bistr] adj. Bistre; dark-brown (couleur); sepia (papier).
— m. Bistre.
bistré, ée [-stre] adj. Browned, swarthy.
bistro(t) [bistro] m. POP. Pub (café); publican (cafetier); *le bistrot du coin,* the local.
bisulfite [bisylfit] m. CHIM. Bisulphite.
bisulfure [-fyr] m. CHIM. Disulphide, bisulphide.
B. I. T. [beite] m. Abrév. de *Bureau international du travail,* International Labour Organization, ILO.
bit [bit] m. INFORM. Bit.
bitension [bitɑ̃sjɔ̃] f. ELECTR. Dual voltage.
biterrois, oise [biterwa, wa:z] adj. GÉOGR. Of (ou) from Béziers.
— s. Native (ou) inhabitant of Béziers.
bitord [bitɔ:r] m. NAUT. Spun yarn.
bitte [bit] f. NAUT. Bollard, bitt. ‖ POP. Cock, prick, tool.
bitter [bitɛr] m. Bitters.

bitumage [bityma:ʒ] m. Asphalting.
bitume [bitym] m. Bitumen. (V. ASPHALTE.)
bitumé, ée [-me] adj. Tarred (carton, trottoir).
bitumer [-me] v. tr. (1). To bitumate, to bituminize (la route).
bitumineux, euse [-minø, ø:z] adj. Bituminous.
biture [bity:r] f. POP. Binge; *tenir une biture,* to be pissed (ou) sloshed.
biturer (se) [səbityre] v. pr. POP. To get pissed (ou) sloshed.
biunivoque [biynivɔk] adj. MATH. One-to-one.
bivalent, ente [bivalɑ̃] adj. CHIM. Bivalent, divalent.
bivalve [bivalv] adj., m. Bivalve.
bivouac [bivwak] m. MILIT. Bivouac.
bivouaquer [-ke] v. intr. (1). MILIT. To bivouac.
bizarre [biza:r] adj. Bizarre; odd; queer; peculiar; quaint.
bizarrement [-mɑ̃] adv. Oddly, queerly, quaintly.
bizarrerie [-ri] f. Oddness; quaintness (étrangeté). ‖ Whimsicality (de caractère). ‖ Pl. Peculiarities; queer ways.
bizarroïde [-rɔid] adj. FAM. Sort of weird, rum.
bizou [bizu] m. V. BISOU.
bizut [bizy] m. FAM. Fresher, freshman.
bizutage [-ta:ʒ] m. FAM. Ragging of freshmen.
bizuter [-te] v. tr. (1). FAM. To rag.
bla-bla-bla [blablabla] m. FAM. Claptrap, blah, bunkum, bunk, hot air, U. S. baloney.
blackboulage [blakbula:ʒ] m. Blackballing.
blackbouler [-le] v. tr. (1). To blackball; to turn down (par un vote). ‖ FAM. To plough, U. S. to flunk (à un examen).
black-out [blakaut] m. Black-out. ‖ FIG. *Faire le black-out sur,* to hush up, to keep dark.
blafard, arde [blafa:r, rd] adj. Pallid; lurid; wan; lambent. (V. BLÊME.) ‖ Lambency, faint, pale (lueur).
blague [blag] f. Tobacco-pouch (à tabac). ‖ FAM. Hoax, trick (tour); *sale blague,* dirty trick. ‖ FAM. Fib; humbug; bunk; flummery; spoof; taradiddle (v. BALIVERNE, BOBARD); *blague à part,* joking apart; *sans blague,* no kidding!, no fooling!
blaguer [-ge] v. intr. (1). To take in; to hoax; to fool (attraper). ‖ FAM. To natter, to gas (bavarder); to fool about (avec, with).
— v. tr. FAM. To chaff; to kid.
blagueur, euse [blagœ:r, ø:z] adj. Ironical, bantering.
— m. Humbug; joker; leg-puller; taradiddler (plaisantin); scoffer, spoofer (railleur).
blair [blɛ:r] m. POP. Snout (nez).
blaireau [blɛro] m. ZOOL. Badger. ‖ Shaving-brush (à barbe).
blairer [blɛre] v. tr. (1). POP. To stand (s.o.); to sniff at (sth.).
blâmable [blɑmabl] adj. Blamable; blame-worthy; censurable.
blâme [blɑ:m] m. Censure, disapproval (désapprobation); reproof, reprimand, reprehension (reproche); *voter un blâme à,* to pass a vote of censure on.
blâmer [-me] v. tr. (1). To blame, to censure.
blanc, anche [blɑ̃, ɑ̃ʃ] adj. White (en général); white, hoary (cheveux); blank, empty, plain (page); colourless (verre); *bois blanc,* deal, white wood; *blanc comme la neige,* snow-white, snowy. ‖ Milled (riz); white (sauce, viande, vin). ‖ ZOOL. White (merle, vers); polar (ours); Arctic (renard). ‖ AGRIC. *Gelée blanche,* hoar frost. ‖ MILIT. *Arme blanche,* cutting weapon, side-arm; *à l'arme blanche,* with cold steel. ‖ JUR. Blank (bulletin); unconsummated (mariage). ‖ MÉD. Coated (langue); sleepless (nuit); pale, white (teint). ‖ FIG. Pure, stainless, innocent (âme); blank (vers); toneless (voix); *carte blanche,* full powers, carte blanche, free hand.

— m. White (couleur, pâleur). ‖ White, linen drapery (linge); ducks (vêtements blancs); *articles de blanc,* white goods; *exposition de blanc,* linen show, white sale. ‖ White, white man (homme); *les blancs,* the whites. ‖ FIN. Blank; *chèque en blanc,* blank cheque; *en blanc,* in blank. ‖ MÉD. White (de l'œil). ‖ CULIN. White (d'œuf); breast (de volaille). ‖ MILIT. Bull's-eye (d'une cible); *mettre dans le blanc,* to score a bull's-eye. ‖ TECHN. Space (en typo); *blanc de baleine,* spermaceti; *blanc de céruse,* white lead; *blanc de chaux,* whitewash; *blanc d'Espagne,* whiting, Spanish white. ‖ FAM. *Regarder qqn dans le blanc des yeux,* to look s.o. square in the face. ‖ **A blanc;** *chauffé à blanc,* white-hot; *chauffer à blanc,* to raise to white heat; *cartouche à blanc,* blank cartridge; *saigner qqn à blanc,* to bleed s.o. white; *tir à blanc,* blank shot. ‖ **Blanc-bec,** m. Greenhorn. ‖ **Blanc-manger,** m. CULIN. Blancmange. ‖ **Blanc-seing,** m. Blank signature; *donner blanc-seing à qqn,* to give s.o. full powers.

blanchaille [-ʃɑ:j] f. Whitebait.

blanchâtre [-ʃɑ:tr] adj. Whitish.

blanche [blɑ̃:ʃ] f. White ball (boule); white woman (femme). ‖ MUS. Minim, half-note.

blancheur [blɑ̃ʃœ:r] f. Whiteness (couleur); paleness. (V. PÂLEUR.) ‖ FIG. Purity, innocence.

blanchiment [-ʃimɑ̃] m. Washing (de l'argent); whitening (du ciel, des cheveux, du linge, du teint); whitewashing (d'un mur); bleaching (des os, de la toile). ‖ CULIN. Blanching (des châtaignes). ‖ FIG. Whitewashing (d'un criminel, de la réputation).

blanchir [-ʃi:r] v. tr. (2). To whiten (les cheveux, le linge, le teint); to turn grey (les cheveux); to wash (le linge, qqn); to clean up, to blanch (un métal); to whitewash, U. S. to calcimine (un mur à la chaux); to space out (un texte); to bleach (de la toile, des os). ‖ FIG. To whitewash (qqn, une réputation). [V. DISCULPER, LAVER.] — v. intr. To whiten; to become (ou) grow white; to become (ou) go (ou) turn pale. ‖ To become hoary; to turn grey (cheveux, personne); to fade, to pale (couleur); to bleach (toile, os). ‖ CULIN. *Faire blanchir,* to scald. — v. pr. **Se blanchir,** to be bleached (toile). ‖ FIG. To exculpate oneself. (V. DISCULPER [SE].)

blanchissage [-ʃisa:ʒ] m. Washing; wash; laundering; *envoyer au blanchissage,* to send to the wash. ‖ Refining (du sucre). ‖ Whitewashing (d'un mur).

blanchissement [-ʃismɑ̃] m. Whitening.

blanchisserie [-ʃisri] f. Laundering (acte); laundry (lieu). ‖ Bleachery, bleaching-house (de toiles).

blanchisseuse [-ʃisø:z] f. Laundress, laundryhand, washerwoman. (V. LAVEUSE.)

blanquette [blɑ̃kɛt] f. CULIN. Blanquette (ragoût, vin). ‖ BOT. White grape, white fig, white pear.

blase [bla:z] m. ARG. Conk, hooter, snout (nez). ‖ Moniker, name (nom).

blasé, ée [blaze] adj. Blasé. (V. INDIFFÉRENT.) ‖ Satiated. (V. RASSASIÉ.)

blaser v. tr. (1). To sate, to saturate; to pall; to cloy (les sens). — v. pr. **Se blaser,** to become indifferent [*de,* to]; to grow weary (*de,* of); to be surfeited (*de,* with) [v. LASSER (SE)]; *on se blase de tout,* everything palls.

blason [blazɔ̃] m. BLAS. Coat of arms; blazon; armorial bearing; escutcheon (armoiries); heraldry (science).

blasphémateur, trice [blasfematœ:r, tris] adj. Blaspheming; blasphemous, profane. — s. Blasphemer.

blasphématoire [-twa:r] adj. Blasphemous, profane.

blasphème [blasfɛ:m] m. Blasphemy. (V. JURON.)

blasphémer [-feme] v. tr., intr. (5). To blaspheme.

blastoderme [blastɔdɛrm] m. MÉD. Blastoderm.

blatte [blat] f. ZOOL. Cockroach; blackbeetle.

blaze [bla:z] m. V. BLASE.

blazer [blaze:r] m. Blazer.

blé [ble] m. Corn; U. S. wheat; *blé à moudre,* grist; *blé d'Espagne,* maize, U. S. corn; *blé en herbe,* corn in the blade; *blé noir,* buckwheat; *terre à blé,* wheat-growing land.

bled [blɛd] m. Rolling country. ‖ FAM. The back of beyond.

blême [blɛ:m] adj. Livid; ghastly; sallow. (V. LIVIDE.) ‖ Wan. (V. BLAFARD.)

blêmir [-mi:r] v. intr. (2). To blanch, to turn livid (personne). ‖ To grow wan (lumière).

blêmissement [-mismɑ̃] m. Paling, blanching.

blende [blɑ̃:d] f. Blende.

blennorragie [blɛnɔraʒi] f. MÉD. Blennorrhagia.

blépharite [blefarit] f. MÉD. Blepharitis.

blèse [blɛ:z] adj. Lisping, with a lisp. — m. Lisper.

blèsement [-zmɑ̃] m. Lisping, lisp.

bléser [-ze] v. intr. (5). To lisp. (V. ZÉZAYER.)

blessant, ante [blɛsɑ̃, ɑ̃:t] adj. Wounding, cutting (parole).

blessé, ée [-se] adj. Wounded; hurt; injured. ‖ FIG. Offended, wounded. — m. Wounded (ou) injured person. ‖ MILIT. Wounded soldier; casualty; *les blessés,* the wounded; *grands blessés,* serious cases, severely wounded.

blesser [-se] v. tr. (1). To wound (au combat); to injure (par accident); to hurt, to pinch (par pincement); to chafe (par frottement). ‖ FIG. To offend (les convenances, la modestie, la vue); to hurt (les intérêts); to jar upon (l'oreille); to wound, to hurt (qqn). — v. intr. To wound, to offend; *il n'y a que la vérité qui blesse,* truth alone wounds. — v. pr. **Se blesser,** to wound (ou) injure oneself. ‖ FIG. To take offence (ou) U. S. offense (*de,* at).

blessure [-sy:r] f. Wound (au combat); hurt, injury (par accident); sore, gall (par frottement). ‖ FIG. Wound; injury (*à,* to); pain, pangs.

blet, ette [blet, ɛt] adj. Over-ripe, soft (fruit).

blette [blɛt] f. BOT. White beet.

blettir [-tir] v. intr. (2). To become overripe (fruit).

blettissement [-tismɑ̃] m. Overripeness.

bleu, eue [blø] adj. Blue. (V. AZUR, CÉRULÉEN.) ‖ MÉD. *Enfant bleu,* blue baby. ‖ FIG. Blue; *conte bleu,* fairy tale (ou) story; *peur bleue,* blue funk. ‖ FAM. Flabbergasted (stupéfié). — m. Blue; blue colour, blueness; *bleu ciel,* sky-blue, azure; *bleu de Prusse,* Prussian blue. ‖ Laundry-blue; U. S. bluing; *passer au bleu,* to blue (le linge). ‖ MÉD. Bruise (v. CONTUSION); *couvert de bleus,* all black and blue. ‖ MILIT., FAM. Recruit, conscript, rookie. ‖ AVIAT. Sprog. ‖ Pl. Blue-jeans; overalls, dungarees (combinaison de travail). ‖ TECHN. Blueprint (dessin). ‖ CULIN. Blue cheese (fromage); blue mould (moisissure); wine sauce (pour poissons). ‖ FIG. Rawhand, tyro. (V. NOVICE.) ‖ FAM. *N'y voir que du bleu,* to be blind to sth., to be blissfully unaware of sth.; *passer qqch. au bleu,* to hush sth. up. — f. *La grande bleue,* the briny, the Mediterranean, the blue, blue water.

bleuâtre [-ɑ:tr] adj. Bluish.

bleuet [-ɛ] m. BOT. Cornflower.

bleuir [-i:r] v. tr. (2). To blue. — v. intr. To turn blue; to look blue.

bleuissage [-isa:ʒ] m. Blueing, U. S. bluing.

bleuissement [-ismɑ̃] m. Turning blue.

bleuté, ée [-te] adj. Bluish; steely blue. ‖ Blued (verre).

bleuter [-te] v. tr. (1). To give a blue tinge to. ‖ To blue (le linge).

blindage [blɛ̃da:ʒ] m. MILIT. Armour; armour plate. ‖ TECHN. Timbering (de galerie de mines); sheeting (de tranchée). ‖ ELECTR. Screening; shrouding.

blindé, ée [-de] adj. Strong (chambre). ‖ MILIT. Bombproof (abri); armoured (division, navire, train). ‖ TECHN. Timbered; sheeted. ‖ ELECTR. Armoured; screened; shrouded. ‖ FIG. Proof (contre, against).
— **m.** MILIT. Armoured car; les blindés, the armour.

blinder [-de] v. tr. (1). MILIT. To armour-plate; to render bombproof. ‖ TECHN. To timber; to sheet. ‖ ELECTR. To screen, to shroud.

blizzard [bliza:r] m. Blizzard.

bloc [blɔk] m. Block; lump. ‖ Bloc (groupement politique). [V. COALITION.] ‖ Writing-pad, U. S. tablet (pour correspondance); memorandum-block, desk-pad, U. S. tablet (pour notes). ‖ TECHN. Bloc d'alimentation, feed block. ‖ Bloc sonore, sound unit (ou) set. ‖ FIG. Faire bloc contre, to unite against; former bloc, to form one unit, to constitute a bloc. ‖ POP. Lock-up; quod, clink, jug. (V. BOÎTE, TAULE.) ‖ LOC. À bloc, home, tight, close; en bloc, in a lump, wholesale; as a whole. ‖ Bloc-cuisine, m. Kitchen unit. ‖ Bloc-moteur, m. TECHN. Engine block, motor unit. ‖ Bloc-notes, m. Scribbling-block, U. S. scratch-pad.

blocage [blɔka:ʒ] m. Blocking (de la circulation). ‖ Blockading (d'un port, d'une ville). ‖ FIN. Freezing (d'une dette). ‖ TECHN. Locking (d'un écrou, des roues); jamming (on des freins); turn (d'une lettre, d'un mot); jamming, sticking (du piston). ‖ COMM. Impounding (du vin).

blocaille [blɔkɑ:j] f. Rubble; hardcore.

blockhaus [blɔko:s] m. MILIT. Block-house, pillbox. ‖ NAUT. Conning tower.

block-système [blɔksistɛm] m. CH. DE F. Block-system.

blocus [blɔky:s] m. Blockade. ‖ JUR. Blocus continental, Continental System.

blond, onde [blɔ̃, ɔ̃:d] adj. Fair, blond, flaxen, straw-coloured, yellowish-brown (cheveux); fair-haired, fair (personne); blond ardent, cendré, doré, vénitien, auburn, ash-, (ou) silvery, golden, Titian-red (ou) Venitian. ‖ Golden, yellow (blé, épi); pale (bière).
— **m.** Blond (couleur, homme).

blondasse [-das] adj. Flaxen, washed out (cheveux); flaxen-haired, tow-headed (personne).

blonde [blɔ̃:d] f. Blonde (femme); blonde évaporée, dizzy blonde; blonde platinée, platinum blonde. ‖ Blond (dentelle).

blondeur [-dœ:r] f. Fairness, blondness (des personnes). ‖ Gold (des blés).

blondin [-dɛ̃] m. AVIAT. Aerial cable railway.

blondin, ine [-dɛ̃, din], **blondinet, ette** [-dinɛ, dinɛt] adj. Blond, blonde, fair-haired.
— **s.** Little blond (ou) blonde.

blondir [-di:r] v. intr. (2). To turn blond (cheveux). ‖ To become yellow; to put on a golden hue (blé).
— **v. tr.** To dye blond (les cheveux).

bloom [blum] m. TECHN. Bloom.

bloquer [blɔke] v. tr. (1). To block, to block up (une route); bloqué par la neige, snow-bound. ‖ To shut in (ou) up (qqn). ‖ To pocket, to jam (une bille, un billard). ‖ COMM. To impound (une denrée). ‖ TECHN. To jam on (les freins); to turn (une lettre d'imprimerie); to jam (une porte); to lock (une roue). ‖ MILIT. To blockade. ‖ FIN.

To block (un compte, des crédits); to freeze (les salaires). ‖ ARCHIT. To fill in with rubble. " SPORTS. To trap, to block (le ballon). ‖ FIG. To obstruct, to block (une initiative, un projet de loi); to close in (la vue).
— **v. pr.** Se bloquer, to jam, to catch; to stick; l'ascenseur s'est bloqué, the lift (ou) U. S. elevator has stuck.

blottir (se) [səblɔti:r] v. pr. (2). To crouch down (s'accroupir); to nestle down, to huddle up (se pelotonner); blotti dans un fauteuil, curled up in an armchair; blotti dans la verdure, nestling (ou) embowered in trees; se blottir dans les bras de qqn, to snuggle in s.o's arms.

blouse [blu:z] f. SPORTS. Pocket (de billard).

blouse f. Overall (d'écolier); blouse, U. S. shirt-waist (de femme); smock-frock (de paysan). ‖ Blouse-tablier, f. Smock.

blouser [-ze] v. tr. (1). SPORTS. To pocket (au billard). ‖ FAM. To gull, to take in (qqn).

blouser [-ze] v. intr. (1). To blouse; to drape loosely; to gather in the waistline.

blouson [-zɔ̃] m. MILIT. Battle-dress blouse. ‖ COMM. Lumber-jacket; wind-cheater, U. S. wind-breaker; blouson chemisier, chemise blouse.

blue-jean [bludʒin] m. Jeans, blue-jeans.

blues [blu:z] m. MUS. Blues.

bluet [blyɛ] m. BOT. Cornflower.

bluette [blyɛt] f. Novelette; trivial short story.

bluff [blœf] m. Bluff.

bluffer [-fe] v. intr. (1). To bluff.
— **v. tr.** To bluff; to try it on.

bluffeur [-fœ:r] m. Bluffer.

blutage [blyta:ʒ] m. Bolting. (V. TAMISAGE.)

bluter [-te] v. tr. (1). To bolt. (V. TAMISER.)

bluterie [-tri] f. Bolting-mill.

blutoir [-twa:r] m. Bolter.

B.N. [beɛn] f. Abrév. de Bibliothèque nationale, French national library in Paris.

boa [bɔa] m. Boa (fourrure, serpent).

bob [bɔb] m. SPORTS. Bob-sleigh, bobsled.

bobard [bɔba:r] m. FAM. Claptrap; bunk; bunkum, U. S. baloney, hooey (v. BLAGUE); monter un bobard, to put up a yarn, to shoot a line.

bobby-soxer [bɔbisɔksœ:r] f. FAM. Bobby-soxer.

bobèche [bɔbɛ:ʃ] f. Candle-ring; socket.

bobinage [bɔbina:ʒ] m. Reeling, winding. ‖ ELECTR. Coiling.

bobine [bɔbin] f. Bobbin. ‖ Reel, spool (de coton, de fil); drum (de câble, de fil de fer); reel (de film); spool (de pellicule). ‖ ELECTR. Coil; bobine de self, inductor. ‖ FAM. Phiz, mug, U. S. map.

bobiner [-ne] v. tr. (1). To reel, to wind, to spool. ‖ ELECTR. To coil.

bobinette [-nɛt] f. Latch, wooden latch.

bobineur [-nœ:r] m. Winder.

bobineuse [-nø:z] f., **bobinoir** [-nwa:r] m. TECHN. Winding-machine.

bobo [bɔbo] m. FAM. Pain, sore.

bobsleigh [bɔbslɛg] m. SPORTS. Bob-sleigh, bobsled.

bocage [bɔka:ʒ] m. Grove; boscage. ‖ Wooded district.

bocager, ère [-kaʒe, ɛ:r] adj. Hedged.

bocal [bɔkal] m. Glass jar (à conserve); mettre en bocal, to bottle. ‖ Globe, fish-bowl (à poissons rouges).

bocarder [bɔkarde] v. tr. (1). To crush, to stamp.

Boccace [bɔkas] m. Boccacio.

boche [bɔʃ] adj. FAM. Boche.
— **m.** FAM. Hun; jerry; goon.

bock [bɔk] m. Beer-glass (verre). ‖ Glass of beer (verre plein). ‖ MÉD. Enema; douche.

Boer [bɔɛr, bu:r] m. GÉOGR. Boer.

bœuf [bœf] (pl. bœufs [bø]) m. ZOOL. Ox (pl. oxen); bullock; bœufs à l'engrais, beeves, U. S. beefs. ‖ CULIN. Beef (viande); bœuf en conserve,

corned beef. ‖ FAM. *Travailler comme un bœuf,* to work like a Trojan.
— adj. inv. POP. Tremendous, U. S. bully.

B.O.F. [beɔɛf] m. FAM. Spiv, black marketeer.

bof! [bɔf] interj. Pff, exclamation expressing lack of enthusiasm.

boghei, boguet [bɔgɛ] m. Gig, U. S. buggy.

bog(g)ie [bɔʒi] m. CH. DE F. Bogie; U. S. truck.

bogue [bɔg] f. BOT. Chestnut-husk. ‖ TECHN. Mud-shovel.

Bohême [bɔɛ:m] f. GÉOGR. Bohemia.

bohème adj. Bohemian.
— m. Bohemian (artiste); impoverished writer (écrivain).
— f. Bohemia (monde); bohemianism (vie); *vie de bohème,* Bohemian life.

bohémien, enne [-mjɛ̃, ɛn] adj., s. Bohemian (de Bohême); gipsy, Romany (romanichel).

boire [bwa:r] v. tr. (21). To drink, to sip (à petits coups); to swill (avidement); to swig off (d'un trait); to quaff, to swig (à longs traits); *boire un coup,* to take (ou) have a drink; *boire une bouteille,* to crack (ou) to drain a bottle; *boire sa paie,* to drink one's wages away. ‖ To absorb, to drink up, to suck up, to imbibe (l'encre, la pluie, la rosée). ‖ FIG. To pocket, to swallow (une insulte); to drink in (les paroles).
— v. intr. To drink; *boire à sa soif,* to drink one's fill; *faire boire les chevaux,* to water the horses; *payer à boire à qqn,* to stand s.o. a drink. ‖ To drink, to bib, to soak (s'enivrer); *il a bu,* he is in his cups. ‖ To suck up; to blot (papier).
— m. Drinking; *le boire et le manger,* food and drink.

bois [bwɑ] m. Wood; timber; *bois de charpente,* timber; *bois de chauffage,* firewood; *bois de rose,* rosewood; *en bois,* wood, wooden; *menu bois,* brushwood. ‖ Wood (forêt); spinney, copse, holt (petit bois); *bois de hêtres,* beech-grove (ou) wood; *sous-bois,* undergrowth; *sous bois,* in the woods. ‖ Framework (de chaise); stock (de fusil); shaft (de lance); *bois de justice,* scaffold; *bois de lit,* bedstead. ‖ Pl. Horns (du cerf). ‖ ARTS. Woodblock (bois); woodcut (gravure); *graveur sur bois,* wood-engraver. ‖ MUS. Les bois, the wood-wind. ‖ AVIAT. *Casser du bois,* to go for a Burton, to crash. ‖ FIG. Stuff, mettle (étoffe); *de bois,* insensible, case-hardened; *tête de bois,* blockhead.

boisage [-za:ʒ] m. Timbering, tubbing.

boisé, ée [-ze] adj. Woody; wooded; *pays boisé,* woodland, wooded country.

boisement [-zəmɑ̃] m. Afforestation, tree-planting.

boiser [-ze] v. tr. (1). To afforest (une contrée); to timber, to tub (une mine); to wainscot, to panel (une pièce).

boiserie [-zri] f. Woodwork; wainscot; wainscoting, panelling (d'une pièce).

boisseau [bwasɔ] m. Bushel (mesure). ‖ Draintile (de cheminée); dome casing (de robinet). ‖ FIG. *Mettre la lumière sous le boisseau,* to hide one's light under a bushel.

boisson [bwasɔ̃] f. Drink (v. BREUVAGE); liquor (alcoolique, fermentée); stimulant (forte); *pris de boisson,* in liquor, intoxicated.

boîte [bwa:t] f. Box (en général); tin, can (en fer blanc); *boîte à lait,* milk-can; *boîte d'allumettes,* match-box; *boîte de chocolats,* box of chocolates; *boîte de conserve,* tin, can; *boîte aux lettres,* letter-box, pillar-box, U. S. mailbox; *boîte à ordures,* dustbin, U. S. garbage can; *boîte à thé,* tea-caddy; *boîte postale,* post-office box. ‖ MUS. *Boîte à musique,* musical-box, U. S.

music-box; *boîte à violon,* violin-case. ‖ TECHN. *Boîte à engrenages,* gear-box; *boîte de vitesses,* gear box. ‖ AVIAT., CH. DE F. Box. ‖ MILIT. *Boîte d'amorce,* primer box; *boîte à culasse,* breech casing. ‖ ELECTR. *Boîte de `distribution,* switchboard. ‖ FAM. *Une sale boîte,* a rotten hole; *boîte de nuit,* night club, cabaret; *mettre qqn en boîte,* to pull s.o.'s leg. ‖ POP. Clink (bloc).

boitement [bwatmɑ̃] m. MÉD. Limping (d'une personne). ‖ TECHN. Jerky action (d'une machine).

boiter [-te] v. intr. (1). To limp; to be (ou) to walk lame.

boiterie [-tri] f. MED. Lameness.

boiteux, euse [-tø, ø:z] adj. MÉD. Lame, limping (personne). ‖ FIG. Rickety (chaise). ‖ FIG. Patched-up (accord, paix); halting (esprit, vers); ill-assorted (mariage, union); lame (raisonnement).
— m. Cripple, lame person. (V. BANCAL.)

boîtier [bwatje] m. Case; *boîtier de montre,* watch-case. ‖ Box-maker (fabricant). ‖ Postman clearing letter-boxes (ou) U. S. mailboxes (postier).

boitiller [bwatije] v. intr. (1). To hobble.

bol [bɔl] m. Bowl, basin (contenant, contenu). ‖ MÉD. Bolus (alimentaire). ‖ *Bol d'Arménie,* Armenian bole. ‖ POP. Luck; *avoir du bol,* to be lucky (ou) jammy. ‖ V. aussi RAS-LE-BOL.

bolchevique, bolchevik [bɔlʃəvik] adj., s. Bolshevik.

bolchevisme [-vism] m. Bolshevism.

bolcheviste [-vist] adj., m. Bolshevik.

bolduc [bɔldyk] m. Tape, coloured ribbon.

bolée [bɔle] f. Bowlful.

boléro [bɔlero] m. Bolero (danse, veste).

bolet [bɔlɛ] m. BOT. Boletus.

bolide [bɔlid] m. ASTRON. Bolide. (V. MÉTÉORE.) ‖ U. S. Hot-shot (véhicule). ‖ FIG. Thunderbolt.

Bolivie [bɔlivi] f. GÉOGR. Bolivia.

bolivien, enne [bɔlivjɛ̃, ɛn] adj., s. GÉOGR. Bolivian.

bollard [bɔla:r] m. NAUT. Bollard.

bolomètre [bɔlomɛtr] m. PHYS. Bolometer.

bombance [bɔ̃bɑ̃:s] f. Revelling; blow-out; *faire bombance,* to carouse, to feast.

bombarde [bɔ̃bard] f. MILIT. † Bombard.

bombardement [bɔ̃bardəmɑ̃] m. MILIT. Bombing; bombardment, shelling; strafe, blitz. ‖ PHYS. Bombardment (électronique).

bombarder [-de] v. tr. (1). MILIT. To bomb; to bombard; to shell. ‖ PHYS. To bombard. ‖ FIG. *Bombarder de,* to pelt with (pierres); to bombard (ou) to assail with (questions). ‖ FAM. To pitchfork (nommer); *bombarder qqn ministre,* to boot s.o. into the Ministry.

bombardier [-je] m. MILIT. Bombardier. ‖ AVIAT. Bomber, bomb-aimer; bombardier (aviateur); bomber (avion).

bombardon [bɔ̃bardɔ̃] m. MUS. Bombardon.

bombe [bɔ̃:b] f. MILIT. Bomb; block-buster (grosse bombe); mortar shell; *à l'épreuve des bombes,* bomb-proof. ‖ CULIN. *Bombe glacée,* bombe glacée. ‖ FIG. Spree, U. S. binge, jag; *faire la bombe,* to go on the spree, U. S. to make whoopee.

bombé, ée [-be] adj. Swelling outward (boîte); rounded (dos); bulging, jutting (front); thrown-out (poitrine); *chaussée bombée,* barrel-road.

bombement [-bmɑ̃] m. Camber (d'une route, d'une aile d'avion); bulge (du front, d'une boîte).

bomber [-be] v. tr. (1). To cause to bulge; to make convex; to camber (une route). ‖ To round (le dos); to stick out (la poitrine). ‖ FIG. *Bomber le torse,* to stick out one's chest.
— v. intr. To bulge out.

bombyx [bɔ̃biks] m. ZOOL. Bombyx.

bon [bɔ̃] (f. **bonne** [bɔn]) adj.

1. Agréable. — 2. Aimable. — 3. Amusant. — 4. Apte. — 5. Avantageux. — 6. Bienveillant. 7. Charitable. — 8. Confortable. — 9. Convenable. — 10. Cordial. — 11. Distingué. — 12. Favorable. — 13. Grand. — 14. Habile. — 15. Heureux. — 16. Long. — 17. Lucratif. — 18. Propice. — 19. Rapide. — 20. Sain. — 21. Sérieux. — 22. Valable. — 23. Vertueux. — 24. Vigoureux. — 25. Sports. — 26. Techn. 27. Loc. — 28. Fam.

1. Good, nice, pleasant (agréable); *bonne odeur,* nice smell; *bonne soirée,* pleasant evening; *trouver bon,* to like, to relish. ‖ 2. Good, kind (aimable); *elle est très bonne pour moi,* she is very kind to me. ‖ 3. Good, amusing (amusant); *bonne histoire,* good story; *bon mot,* witticism, witty saying, U. S. wisecrack. ‖ 4. Good, fit (apte); *bon à manger,* fit to eat, eatable; *bon à rien,* good for nothing. ‖ 5. Good, profitable (avantageux); *bonne affaire,* fine stroke of business; *bon à savoir,* worth knowing. ‖ 6. Good; benevolent; gracious (bienveillant); *notre bon roi,* our gracious king. ‖ 7. Good, charitable, generous, open-handed (charitable); *qui a bon cœur,* kind-hearted. ‖ 8. Comfortable; snug (confortable); *un bon fauteuil,* a comfortable easy-chair. ‖ 9. Good, proper, right (convenable); *bon état,* proper condition; *bon usage,* good (ou) right use; *au bon moment,* at the right time. ‖ 10. Good, hearty (cordial); *un bon baiser,* a hearty kiss. ‖ 11. Good, honourable; high (distingué, élevé); *de bonne famille,* of good family, with a good background); ‖ 12. Good, fair, favourable (favorable); *de bons renseignements,* a favourable report. ‖ 13. Large (grand, gros); *un bon morceau de pain,* a large piece of bread. ‖ 14. Good, clever, expert, skilful (habile); *bon musicien,* fine musician; *bon en latin,* proficient in (ou) good at Latin. ‖ 15. Good, happy (heureux); *la bonne année,* a happy New Year; *à bonne fin,* to a happy issue. ‖ 16. Good, long (long); *un bon bout de temps,* quite a long while; *à une bonne distance,* a long way off; *une bonne heure,* a full hour. ‖ 17. Good, lucrative, paying (lucratif); *un bon emploi,* a well-paid job. ‖ 18. Good, propitious (propice); *une bonne étoile,* a lucky star. ‖ 19. Good, tidy (rapide); *à bonne allure,* at a good pace. ‖ 20. Good, wholesome (sain); *une bonne alimentation,* wholesome food. ‖ 21. Good, sound (sérieux); *une bonne maison,* a sound firm. ‖ 22. Good, sound, valid, sterling (valable); *un bon argument,* a sound (ou) valid argument; *une bonne monnaie,* a sound currency. ‖ 23. Good, dutiful, virtuous (vertueux); *bonne pensée,* good thought; *bon fils,* good (ou) dutiful son. ‖ 24. Good, severe (vigoureux); *bonne raclée,* severe thrashing, good hiding. ‖ 25. Sports. In, not out (balle de tennis). ‖ 26. Techn. Stet (en typogr.); *bon à tirer,* ready for press. ‖ 27. Loc. *Une bonne fois,* once for all; *bon premier,* an easy first; *le bon vieux temps,* the good old days; *à quoi bon?,* what's the use?; *bon!, c'est bon!,* well!, all right!; *comme bon lui semble,* as he thinks best, as he prefers; *il est bon de,* it is well to; *quand bon vous semblera,* when you please; *trouver bon,* to think fit; to allow. ‖ 28. Fam. *Je suis bon pour,* I am due for; I am in for.

— m. Good (bien, qualité); *les bons,* the good; *le bon et le beau,* the good and the beautiful; *le bon de l'histoire,* the best of the story. ‖ Bond, coupon; order; ticket; voucher; *bon de caisse,* cash voucher, deposit receipt; *bon de commande, de livraison,* order-slip, delivery-slip; *bon d'épargne,* savings certificate; *bon de poste,*

postal order; *bon du Trésor,* Treasury bond. ‖ **Bon-bec,** m. Chatterbox; spitfire. ‖ **Bon-papa,** m. Grand-dad. ‖ **Bon-prime,** m. Free-gift coupon. ‖ **Bonne-Espérance,** m. Géogr. Good-Hope (cap). ‖ **Bonne-femme,** f. Simple-minded woman; old woman; *remède de bonne femme,* old wives' remedy; *vieille bonne femme,* old body. ‖ **Bonne-maman,** f. Grand-mama, granny.

— adv. Nice (agréablement); *sentir bon,* to smell nice. ‖ Fast (solidement); *tenir bon,* to hold fast; to stand firm; to hold one's ground. ‖ *Pour de bon, tout de bon,* in earnest, for good, seriously.

bonace [bɔnas] f. Calm.
bonapartisme [bɔnapartism] m. Bonapartism.
bonapartiste [bɔnapartist] adj., s. Bonapartist.
bonasse [bɔnas] adj. Pliable, easy-going.
bonbon [bɔ̃bɔ̃] m. Sweet; bonbon; comfit; U. S. candy; *bonbons anglais,* acid drops.
bonbonne [-bɔn] f. Carboy (d'acide); demijohn (d'alcool, de vin).
bonbonnière [-bɔnjɛ:r] f. Sweet-box, U. S. candy box. ‖ Fig. Nice little house.
bond [bɔ̃] m. Bounce, rebound (rebondissement); bound, jump, leap, spring (saut, sursaut); *entrer (ou) sortir d'un bond,* to jump in (ou) out; *faire un bond,* to bounce (balle); to give a jump, to take a leap (personne); *faire un bond en arrière,* to jump (ou) spring back; *se lever d'un bond,* to jump up, to stand up with a start, to leap from one's seat. ‖ Fin. Jump (des prix, des valeurs); *faire un bond,* to jump up. ‖ Fig. *Faire faux bond à,* to let down; *saisir la balle au bond,* to jump at the opportunity.
bonde [bɔ̃d] f. Plug (de baignoire, d'évier); sluice, shut-off (d'étang); bung, bung-hole (de tonneau).
bondé, ée [bɔ̃de] adj. Teeming, thronged (rue); crammed, packed (salle, voiture). [V. comble.]
bonder v. tr. (1). To overcrowd, to cram.
bondieuserie [bɔ̃djøzri] f. Fam. Pietism. ‖ Pl. Church ornaments.
bondir [bɔ̃di:r] v. intr. (2). To jump, to bound, to leap; to spring, to bounce. ‖ To gambol, to caper, to frisk (gambader). ‖ Fig. To burst out, to explode; *faire bondir,* to make wild.
bondissement [bɔ̃dismɑ̃] m. Leaping, bounding. ‖ Frisking.
bondon [bɔ̃dɔ̃] m. Bung (de tonneau).
bonheur [bɔnœ:r] m. Happiness; bliss (v. béatitude, félicité, plaisir); *c'est un bonheur que d'être mère,* it is a blessed thing to be a mother; *faire le bonheur de qqn,* to make s.o. happy; *s'exprimer avec bonheur,* to express oneself felicitously. ‖ Luck, good fortune, luckiness (chance); *au petit bonheur,* in a haphazard (ou) happy-go-lucky manner; *par bonheur,* fortunately, happily; *porter bonheur à,* to bring luck to. ‖ **Bonheur-du-jour** (pl. *bonheurs-du-jour*) m. Escritoire.
bonhomie [bɔnɔmi] f. Geniality; bonhomie, good-nature; joviality.
bonhomme [bɔnɔm] (pl. **bonshommes** [bɔ̃zɔm]) m. Simple-minded man; old fellow; *air bonhomme,* bland appearance; *faux bonhomme,* hypocrite; *petit bonhomme,* little chap; *vieux bonhomme,* old body. ‖ Man, mannikin; *bonhomme de neige,* snowman; *bonhomme en pain d'épice,* gingerbread mannikin; *dessiner des bonshommes,* to draw funny faces. ‖ Techn. Bolt. ‖ Loc. *Aller son petit bonhomme de chemin,* to jog along.
boni [bɔni] m. Profit, bonus (bénéfice); allowance, rebate (escompte); bonus (gratification); surplus (revenant bon). ‖ Milit. Ration savings.
bonification [-fikasjɔ̃] f. Improvement (des terres, du vin). ‖ Comm. Allowance, rebate, discount.
bonifier [-fje] v. tr. (1). To better, to improve. (V. améliorer.) ‖ Comm. To make good.
— v. pr. Se **bonifier,** to improve.

boniment [bɔnimɑ̃] m. Patter (de camelot), sales pitch (de vendeur). ‖ Claptrap (bla-bla-bla). ‖ Compliments ; *faire du boniment à*, to cajole, to pay court to.

bonjour [bɔ̃ʒuːr] m. Good morning (le matin) ; good day (en général) ; good afternoon (l'après-midi) ; how do you do? ; *dites bonjour à*, my kind regards to. ‖ Loc. *Simple comme bonjour*, as easy as ABC (ou) as falling off a log.

bonne [bɔn] f. Maid, servant, girl ; waitress (de restaurant) ; *bonne à tout faire*, general help (ou) servant, U. S. general houseworker ; *bonne d'enfant*, children's nurse.

bonnement [-mɑ̃] adv. *Tout bonnement*, simply ; naively ; plainly.

bonnet [bɔnɛ] m. Cap ; hood (d'enfant) ; busby (de hussard) ; coif (de paysanne) ; *bonnet à poil*, bearskin ; *bonnet d'âne*, dunce's cap ; *bonnet de bain*, bathing cap ; *bonnet de nuit*, night-cap ; *bonnet de police*, garrison (ou) overseas (ou) forage cap. ‖ Loc. *Blanc bonnet et bonnet blanc*, much of a muchness ; *gros bonnet*, bigwig, big pot, big bug, U. S. big wheel, shot ; *opiner du bonnet*, to nod assent ; *prendre sous son bonnet de*, to take into one's own hands to ; *la tête près du bonnet*, hot-headed ; *triste comme un bonnet de nuit*, dull as ditch-water.

bonneterie [bɔntri] f. Hosiery.

bonnetier [-tje] m. Hosier.

bonnette [bɔnɛt] f. Bonnet (d'enfant). ‖ TECHN. Supplementary lens (photo). ‖ NAUT. Studding-sail. ‖ MILIT. Bonnet (de fortification).

bonniche [bɔniʃ] f. POP. Slavey, skivvy.

bonnichon [-ʃɔ̃] m. Child's cap.

bonsoir [bɔ̃swaːr] m. Good evening, good night.

bonté [bɔ̃te] f. Goodness ; kindness ; benevolence ; benignancy ; kind-heartedness (bienveillance). ‖ Kindness (amabilité) ; *ayez la bonté de*, be so kind as to. ‖ Goodness (qualité) ; *la bonté du terrain*, the goodness of the soil ; *la bonté d'une cause*, the justice of a cause. ‖ Pl. Kindness, favours. ‖ Loc. *Bonté divine!*, Good gracious!

bonus [bɔnyːs] m. FIN. No-claim (ou) no-claims bonus.

bonze [bɔ̃ːz] m. Buddhist priest, bonze. ‖ FAM. *Vieux bonze*, old duffer.

bonzerie [-ri] f. Bonzery.

bonzesse [bɔ̃zɛs] f. Buddhist priestess.

boogie-woogie [bugiwugi] m. Boogie-woogie.

bookmaker [bukmekœːr] m. Bookmaker.

boom [bum] m. FIN. Boom.

boomerang [bumrɑ̃g] m. Boomerang (prop., fig.).

boqueteau [bɔkto] m. Copse, spinney.

borate [bɔrat] m. CHIM. Borate.

borax [bɔraks] m. CHIM. Borax.

borborygme [bɔrbɔrigm] m. MÉD. Rumbling in the bowels ; borborygmus.

bord [bɔr] m. Border. ‖ Brink (d'un abîme, d'un précipice) ; border, edge (d'un champ) ; brim (d'un chapeau) ; edge (de l'eau, d'un précipice, d'une surface, d'une table) ; outskirts (d'une forêt) ; margin (d'un lac) ; seaside, shore (de la mer) ; bank (d'une rivière) ; side (d'une route) ; rim (du soleil) ; kerb, kerbstone, U. S. curb, curbstone (du trottoir) ; brim, rim (d'un verre) ; hem (d'un vêtement) ; *au bord de la rivière*, on the river-side ; *au bord de la route*, by the roadside (ou) wayside ; *bord à bord*, side by side. ‖ MÉD. Lip (d'une plaie). ‖ NAUT. Tack (bordée) ; board (navire) ; side (du navire) ; *à bord*, aboard, on board ; *à mon bord*, on board my ship ; *virer de bord*, to turn. ‖ AVIAT. *Bord d'attaque*, leading edge ; *bord de parachute*, parachute skirt. ‖ FIG. Borders (de la conscience) ; brink (du désastre) ; margin (de l'erreur) ; verge (de la ruine) ; *du même bord que*, of the same opinion (ou) party as.

bordage [-daːʒ] m. Bordering ; edging ; hemming. ‖ TECHN. Flanging. ‖ NAUT. Planking ; sheathing.

bordé [-de] m. Braid. ‖ NAUT. Planking ; plating.

bordeaux [bɔrdo] m. COMM. Bordeaux ; *bordeaux rouge*, claret. ‖ GÉOGR. Bordeaux.

bordée [bɔrde] f. NAUT. Board, tack (louvoyage) ; watch (quart) ; broadside (tir) ; *lâcher une bordée*, to fire a broadside ; *tirer une bordée*, to tack (en mer) ; to go on the spree (à terre). ‖ FAM. Volley (de jurons).

bordel [bɔrdɛl] m. Brothel ; bawdy-house ; knocking-shop (pop.) ; U. S. cat-house (pop.). ‖ POP. Bloody mess.

bordelais, aise [bɔrdəlɛ, ɛz] adj., s. Pertaining to Bordeaux.

bordelaise [-lɛːz] f. Bordeaux bottle.

bordélique [bɔrdelik] adj. POP. Messy (personne, maison) ; slovenly (personne).

border [bɔrde] v. tr. (1). To border ; to edge ; to line ; to skirt ; to fringe. ‖ To hem, to border (un vêtement) ; *border de*, to edge with. ‖ To tuck in (un lit, qqn). ‖ NAUT. To skirt (la côte).

bordereau [bɔdəro] m. Memorandum ; statement (de compte) ; docket, bordereau ; list, schedule (de pièces) ; *bordereau d'achat*, purchase contract ; *bordereau d'expédition*, consignment (ou) dispatch note ; *bordereau de versement*, paying-in slip. ‖ FIN. Note (en banque).

bordure [bɔrdyːr] f. Skirt (du bois) ; border, edge (de fleurs) ; border (de papier à lettres) ; binding (de tapis) ; kerb, U. S. curb (de trottoir) ; *en bordure de*, running along, on the skirts of, bordering on. ‖ NAUT. Foot. ‖ BLAS. Bordure.

bore [bɔːr] CHIM. Boron.

boréal, ale [bɔreal] adj. Boreal ; *aurore boréale*, aurora borealis, the northern lights.

borgne [bɔrɲ] adj. One-eyed. ‖ Suspicious ; disreputable ; shady ; fishy (compte) ; shady, evil-looking (hôtel) ; *rue borgne*, blind alley.

borique [bɔrik] adj. CHIM. Boric, boracic.

boriqué, ée [-ke] adj. MÉD. Borated ; *onguent boriqué*, boracic (ou) boric ointment.

bornage [bɔrnaːʒ] m. Setting of boundaries ; demarcation ; stating. ‖ NAUT. Coastal navigation.

borne [bɔrn] f. Landmark, boundary-stone (de champ) ; road-sign (de signalisation) ; *borne d'essence*, petrol (ou) U. S. gasoline pump ; *borne postale*, pillar- (ou) U. S. mail-box ; *borne routière*, milestone. ‖ ELECTR. Terminal. ‖ FAM. Post, block of wood (personne). ‖ FIG. Pl. Bounds, limits (v. CONFINS, LIMITE) ; *dépasser les bornes*, to pass all bounds ; *franchir les bornes de*, to overstep (ou) overleap the bounds of ; *sans bornes*, boundless, beyond all bounds. ‖ **Borne-fontaine**, f. Street-fountain.

borné, ée [bɔrne] adj. Narrow (esprit) ; limited, narrow-minded (personne) ; cramped, narrow (vie) ; limited (vues).

borner v. tr. (1). To limit, to mark out the boundaries of ; to set up the boundary-stones of (un champ) ; *borné par*, bounded by (pays). ‖ FIG. To confine (ses besoins) ; to set bounds to (ses désirs) ; to limit (sa puissance). [V. LIMITER.] — v. pr. **Se borner**, to restrict (ou) to limit oneself (à, to) ; to restrain oneself (se restreindre) ; *se borner à*, to content oneself with.

Borromées [bɔrome] f. pl. GÉOGR. *Iles Borromées*, Borromean Islands.

boscot, otte [bɔsko, ɔt] adj. Hunchbacked. — m. Hunchback. (V. BOSSU.)

bosniaque [bɔsnjak], **bosnien, enne** [bɔsnjɛ̃, ɛn] adj., s. GÉOGR. Bosnian.

boson [bɔzɔ̃] m. PHYS. Boson.

Bosphore [bɔsfɔːr] m. GÉOGR. Bosphorus.

bosquet [bɔskɛ] m. Grove, thicket, bosket (bocage); arbour (charmille).

bossage [bɔsa:ʒ] m. Relief; embossment; bossage. ‖ TECHN. Boss.

bosse [bɔs] f. Hunch, hump (d'un bossu); hump (du chameau); bump (du crâne, d'un chemin); lump (du front); relief (d'une sculpture); bulge, bump, knob (d'une surface). ‖ MÉD. Bump (après un coup). ‖ NAUT. Stopper. ‖ FIG. Bump; *avoir la bosse de*, to have a gift for. ‖ LOC. *Rouler sa bosse*, to knock about, to be a rolling stone.

bosselage [-la:ʒ] m. Embossment, embossing.

bosseler [-le] v. tr. (8a). To emboss (travailler en bosse). ‖ FAM. To batter (cabosser).
— v. pr. **Se bosseler**, to become battered (objet); to become uneven (ou) bumpy (route).

bossellement [bɔsɛlmɑ̃] m., **bosselure** [bɔsly:r] f. Denting. ‖ Embossment.

bosser [bɔse] v. tr. (1). NAUT. To stopper.
— v. intr. POP. To plod (ou) peg away, to keep one's nose to the grindstone. (V. TRIMER.)

bossette [bɔsɛt] f. Boss (du mors).

bosseur, euse [bɔsœ:r, ø:z] adj. FAM. Hard-working.
— s. FAM. Hard-worker, slogger.

bossoir [bɔswa:r] m. NAUT. Davit; bow; cathead.

bossu, ue [bɔsy] adj. Gibbous, humped (en général). ‖ Hump-backed, hunchbacked; round-shouldered (du dos); pigeon-chested (de la poitrine).
— m. Hunchback, humpback.

bossuer [bɔsɥe] v. tr. (1). To batter.

Boston [bɔstɔ̃] m. GÉOGR. Boston. ‖ Hesitation waltz (danse); boston (jeu).

bot, ote [bo, ɔt] adj. MÉD. *Pied bot*, club-foot.

botanique [bɔtanik] adj. BOT. Botanical.
— f. BOT. Botany.

botaniser [-nize] v. intr. (1). To botanize.

botaniste [-nist] m. Botanist.

Botswana [bɔtswana] m. GÉOGR. Botswana.

botte [bɔt] f. SPORTS. Thrust, pass (d'escrime); *porter une botte à*, to make a thrust at.

botte f. Boot, Wellington boot; *botte allemande*, jackboot; *bottes de caoutchouc*, Wellingtons, U.S. rubber boots; *bottes à l'écuyère*, riding-boots; *bottes d'égoutier*, waders. ‖ FIG. *A propos de bottes*, talking of boots, à propos of nothing at all, without rhyme or reason.

botte f. Bunch (de carottes, de fleurs). ‖ AGRIC. Truss, bundle (de foin).

botteler [-le] v. tr. (8 a). To tie in bunches (des fleurs). ‖ AGRIC. To truss (du foin).

botteleuse [-lø:z] f. AGRIC. Binder, bundling-machine.

botter [bɔte] v. tr. (1). To supply with boots. ‖ To put boots on. ‖ FAM. To kick (le ballon, un but, le derrière). ‖ POP. To fit, to suit (convenir).
— v. pr. **Se botter**, to put on one's boots.

bottier [bɔtje] m. Bootmaker.

bottillon [bɔtijɔ̃] m. Bootee.

Bottin [bɔtɛ̃] m. (nom déposé). French directory; U. S. social register.

bottine [bɔtin] f. Ankle-boot; button-boots.

botulisme [bɔtylism] m. MÉD. Botulism.

bouc [buk] m. He-goat (animal); billy-goat beard, goatee (barbe); stinker (personne sale). ‖ FIG. *Bouc émissaire*, scapegoat, U. S. fall guy.

boucan [bukɑ̃] m. FAM. Racket, rumpus, shindy, row; *faire un boucan de tous les diables*, to kick up (ou) to make an infernal racket.

boucan [bukɑ̃] m. CULIN. Buccan (gril); barbecue (viande).

boucanage [bukana:ʒ] m. CULIN. Buccaning.

boucaner [-ne] v. tr. (1). CULIN. To buccan (la viande). ‖ FAM. To tan, to brown (la peau).
— v. intr. To be smoke-dried.

boucanier [-nje] m. Buccaneer.

bouchage [buʃa:ʒ] m. Corking; plugging (acte). ‖ Cork; plug (objet).

bouche [bu:ʃ] V. BOUCHER. ‖ **Bouche-bouteilles**, m. invar. Bottle-corker. ‖ **Bouche-trou** (pl. *bouche-trous*), n. THÉÂTR. Super; FAM. stop-gap, substitute.

bouche [bu:ʃ] f. Mouth (de l'homme, des animaux); *faire la bouche en cœur*, to simper; *mauvaise bouche*, a bad taste in the mouth. ‖ Mouth, tongue, lips; *avoir qqch. constamment à la bouche*, to keep on repeating sth.; *fermer la bouche à qqn*, to shut s.o. up, to stop s.o.'s mouth; *dans toutes les bouches*, on everybody's lips; *ne pas ouvrir la bouche*, not to say a word; *parler par la bouche de*, to speak out of the mouth of. ‖ Mouth; *bouche inutile*, useless mouth; *faire la petite bouche*, to be dainty (ou) fastidious (ou) finicky; *fine bouche*, sweet tooth. ‖ Orifice, vent, opening; slot; *bouche d'aération, de chaleur*, air-, hot-air vent; *bouche d'égout*, man-hole; *bouche d'incendie*, hydrant; *bouche de métro*, underground entrance (ou) U. S. subway. ‖ GÉOGR. Pl. Mouths. ‖ MILIT. *Bouche à feu*, piece of artillery. ‖ **Bouche-à-bouche**, m. invar. Kiss of life, mouth-to-mouth resuscitation; *pratiquer le bouche-à-bouche*, to give the kiss of life.

bouché, ée [buʃe] adj. Corked (bouteille); blocked (ouverture); blocked, clogged (passage); choked (pipe, tuyau); thick, foggy (temps); stopped (trou); bottled (vin); *bouché à l'émeri*, stoppered. ‖ FIG. Dense, obtuse. (V. BORNÉ.)

bouchée f. Mouthful; morsel; gulp; bit; *d'une bouchée*, at a mouthful, at a gulp; *mettre les bouchées doubles*, to wolf one's food. ‖ CULIN. *Bouchée à la reine*, patty. ‖ FIG. *Mettre les bouchées doubles*, to work at double speed; *pour une bouchée de pain*, for a song.

boucher v. tr. (1). To cork (une bouteille); to overcrowd (une carrière); to clog (un conduit); to nail up (une fenêtre); to obturate (un orifice); to block up, to obstruct (le passage); to occlude, to block up, to close (les pores); to wall up (une porte); to bung (un tonneau); to stop, to fill up (un trou); to choke up (un tuyau); to block, to cut off (la vue); *boucher hermétiquement*, to cork tightly; *boucher avec une cheville*, to plug. ‖ FIG. *Boucher les yeux à qqn*, to pull the wool over somebody's eyes.
— v. pr. **Se boucher**, to become obstructed (ou) choked up (ou) clogged up (ou) filled up; *le temps se bouche*, it is becoming foggy. ‖ *Se boucher le nez*, to hold one's nose; *se boucher les oreilles*, to hold one's hands over one's ears.

boucher m. Butcher (pr. et fig.).

bouchère [buʃɛ:r] f. Butcher's wife; woman-butcher.

boucherie [buʃri] f. Butcher's shop (boutique); butcher's trade (commerce). ‖ FIG. Butchery, slaughter; *scène de boucherie*, shambles.

bouchon [buʃɔ̃] m. Cork (de bouteille); tampion (de canon); stopper (de carafe); cork, float, bob (de ligne); wad, wisp (de paille); cap (de radiateur, de valve); bung (de tonneau); *bouchon à vis, en bois*, screw, wooden plug; *bouchon à l'émeri*, ground-glass stopper; *sentir le bouchon*, to be corked (ou) Cork-penny (jeu). ‖ ELECTR. *Bouchon fusible*, safety plug. ‖ FAM. Pub (cabaret). ‖ FAM., AUTOM. Traffic jam, hold-up (embouteillage).

bouchonner [-ʃɔne] v. tr. (1). To rub down.
— v. intr. AUTOM. To form a traffic jam, to cause a hold-up.

bouchot [buʃo] m. Mussel-bed (ou) -scalp.

bouclage [bukla:ʒ] m. Buckling, fastening (d'une ceinture); curling, curls (des cheveux); ringing (d'un taureau, d'un porc); sealing off (d'une rue, d'un quartier).

boucle [bukl] f. Buckle (de ceinture); lock, curl (de cheveux); bight, eye (de corde); loop (de cours d'eau, de nœud); ring (de rideau); bow (de ruban); buckle (de soulier); *boucle d'oreilles*, earring. ‖ AVIAT. *Boucler la boucle*, to loop the loop. ‖ CH. DE F. Loop (de voie ferrée).

bouclé, ée [bukle] adj. Buckled (ceinture, soulier); curly (cheveux); looped (étoffe); worsted, knop (laine).
— m. Bouclé (tissu).

boucler v. tr. (1). To buckle (une ceinture); to loop (une corde, un ruban). ‖ To curl (les cheveux). [V. FRISER.] ‖ To ring (un porc, un taureau). ‖ To lock (les malles); to strap (une valise). ‖ To seal (ou) cordon off (une rue, un quartier). ‖ FAM. To lock up (v. COFFRER); *la boucle!*, stop it! cut the clack!; *la boucler*, to pipe down, U. S. to clam up.
— v. intr. To curl (cheveux).

bouclette [-klɛt] f. Ringlet.

bouclier [buklje] m. Buckler; shield. ‖ MILIT. *Bouclier articulé*, apron shield. ‖ FIG. *Levée de boucliers*, public protest, general outcry.

bouddha [buda] m. Buddha.

bouddhique [-dik] adj. Buddhistic.

bouddhisme [-dism] m. Buddhism.

bouddhiste [-dist] adj., s. Buddhist.

bouder [bude] v. intr. (1). To sulk; to pout.
— v. tr. To be sulky with, to be cool towards.

bouderie [-dri] f. Sulks, sulking, pouting.

boudeur, euse [-dœ:r, ø:z] adj. Moody, sulky, pouting, sullen, U. S. ponty.
— m. Sulky person.

boudeuse [-dø:z] f. Back-to-back settee.

boudin [budɛ̃] m. CULIN. Black-pudding; U. S. blood sausage. ‖ Roll (d'étoffe); sausage (de mine); roll, torus (moulure); flange (de roue); twist, roll (de tabac); *à boudin*, spiral (ressort).

boudiné, ée ⌊budine] adj. Sausage-shaped, podgy (partie du corps). ‖ *Boudiné dans*, squeezed into, bursting out of (personne).

boudiner [budine] v. tr. (1). To rove (du fil). ‖ FAM. To dress in close-fitting garments (qqn).

boudineuse [-nø:z] f. Roving-frame.

boudoir [budwa:r] m. Boudoir.

boue [bu] f. Mud; slime; mire; slush. (V. FANGE.) ‖ Mud, sediment. ‖ MÉD. Mud. ‖ FIG. Mud, mire; *traîner dans la boue*, to drag through the mire.

bouée [bue] f. Buoy; *bouée de sauvetage*, lifebuoy; *bouée lumineuse, sonore*, light, bell buoy.

boueur [buœ:r] m. Scavenger; street cleaner; U. S. garbageman, garbage collector.

boueux, euse [buø, ø:z] adj. Muddy (route, soulier); sloppy, spongy, squashy (terrain). [V. BOURBEUX.]
— m. Scavenger. (V. BOUEUR, ÉBOUEUR.)

bouffant, ante [bufɑ̃, ɑ̃:t] adj. Fluffy, wavy, baggy (culotte); puffed (manche); feather-weight (papier); puffed out, full (robe). ‖ Wavy, padded (cheveux).
— m. Puff.

bouffarde [bufard] f. FAM. Cutty, stubby pipe.

bouffe [buf] adj. Comic. ‖ THÉÂTR. *Opéra bouffe*, musical comedy.

bouffe f. POP. Grub, scoff (nourriture); nosh-up (repas).

bouffée [bufe] f. Rush (d'air); puff (de cigarette, de fumée, de vent); whiff (de parfum). ‖ MÉD. *Bouffée de chaleur*, hot flush. ‖ FIG. Fit, gust, outburst (de colère, d'éloquence, d'orgueil).

bouffer v. intr. (1). To fluff out, to be fluffy (cheveux); to puff (manche); *faire bouffer une manche*, to full (ou) to puff a sleeve. ‖ POP. To tuck in, to guzzle.
— v. tr. POP. To scoff, to wolf (de la nourriture). ‖ To blue, to run through (de l'argent).
— v. pr. **Se bouffer**, POP. *Se bouffer le nez*, to

bicker, to squabble, to scratch each other's eyes out.

bouffetance [buftɑ̃:s] f. V. BOUFFE.

bouffette [bufɛt] f. Rosette, tassel.

bouffi, ie [bufi] adj. Puffy, overfed, bloated (corps); chubby (joue); swollen (yeux). ‖ FIG. Bloated, puffed up, swollen (de, with) [orgueil].

bouffir [-fi:r] v. tr. (2). To bloat, to puff up.
— v. intr. To swell, to become bloated.

bouffissure [-fisy:r] f. Puffiness (du corps). ‖ FIG. Turgidity (du style). ‖ FAM. Swollen head (vanité).

bouffon [bufɔ̃] m. Jester, fool (du roi). ‖ Buffoon, clown, prankster, droll. (V. FARCEUR.)
— adj. Farcical; ludicrous, droll, jocular.

bouffonnerie [-fɔnri] f. Buffoonery, clownery. ‖ Farce, tomfoolery.

bougainvillée [bugɛ̃vile], **bougainvillier** [bugɛ̃vilje] m. BOT. Bougainvillaea.

bouge [bu:ʒ] m. Hovel, sty, slum. ‖ NAUT. Camber.

bougeoir [buʒwa:r] m. Flat candlestick. ‖ ECCLÉS. Taper-stand.

bougeotte [buʒɔt] f. *Avoir la bougeotte*, to have the fidgets.

bouger [buʒe] v. tr. (7). FAM. To move. (V. DÉPLACER.) ‖ FAM. To shift (un meuble).
— v. intr. To move, to budge, to stir (v. REMUER); to go out. (V. SORTIR.) ‖ FIG. To make a move, to act (agir).

bougie [buʒi] f. Candle (chandelle); candle-light (éclairage); *bougie nouvelle*, cand, candela. ‖ ELECTR. Candle-power (intensité). ‖ AUTOM. Sparking-plug; U. S. spark-plug. ‖ MÉD. Bougie.

bougnat [buɲa] m. FAM. Coalman.

bougon [bugɔ̃] adj. Grumbling, grousing, grouchy, grumpy.
— m. Grumbler, grouser, croaker.

bougonnement [-gɔnmɑ̃] m. Grumbling, grumble, grousing, muttering.

bougonner [-gɔne] v. intr. (1). To grumble, to grouse, to croak, to grunt.

bougre [bugr] m. POP. Chap, fellow, guy; *pauvre bougre*, poor devil; *sale bougre*, nasty fellow; *bougre d'idiot!*, you blooming idiot!
— interj. By Jove!

bougrement [-grəmɑ̃] adv. POP. Devilishly, awfully; *bougrement mauvais*, darned bad.

bougresse [-grɛs] f. POP. Jade, doxy.

boui-boui [bwibwi] m. POP. Penny gaff; U. S. honky-tonk. (V. BEUGLANT.)

bouif [bwif] m. POP. Cobbler.

bouillabaisse [bujabɛs] f. CULIN. Bouillabaisse, U. S. fish chowder.

bouillant, ante [bujɑ̃, ɑ̃:t] adj. Boiling. ‖ FIG. Boiling, seething (de, with).

bouille [bu:j] f. POP. Face, mug, kisser; *une bonne bouille*, a pleasant face.

bouilleur [-jœ:r] m. Distiller; *bouilleur de cru*, private distiller. ‖ TECHN. Boiler-tube. ‖ PHYS. *Bouilleur atomique*, nuclear reactor, atomic furnace.

bouilli [-ji] m. CULIN. Boiled beef.

bouillie f. Pap, gruel (pour enfant); porridge, U. S. oat meal (d'avoine); *réduire en bouillie*, to boil to rags, to reduce to a mash. ‖ Pulp (pâte à papier). ‖ AGRIC. Wash, Bordeaux mixture. ‖ FAM. *Réduire en bouillie*, to beat to a jelly (ou) to a pulp.

bouillir [-ji:r] v. intr. (22). To boil; *faire bouillir*, to boil. ‖ FIG. To boil, to seethe (de, with); to hanker, to be itching (de, to). ‖ FAM. *Bouillir de la cafetière*, to have bats in the belfry.

bouilloire [-jwa:r] f. Kettle, U. S. teakettle.

bouillon [-jɔ̃] m. CULIN. Broth (bouillon, légumes) [v. CONSOMMÉ]; *bouillon cube*, bouillon cube; *bouillon gras*, beef-tea; *bouillon de légumes, de viande*, vegetable, meat soup. ‖ Bubble; *bouillir* *à gros bouillons,* to boil furiously; *jaillir à gros bouillons,* to gush out; *faire donner un bouillon,* to bring well to the boil. || Puff, bouillon (bouffant); bullion (torsade). || Returns, unsold copies (invendus). || MÉD. *Bouillon de culture,* culture medium (ou) fluid. || FAM. Shower, soak (averse); *boire un bouillon,* to meet with a loss; *bouillon d'onze heures,* poison.

bouillonnant, ante [-jɔnɑ̃, ɑ̃:t] adj. Foaming. || FIG. Seething, boiling, bubbling (*de,* with).

bouillonné [-jɔne] m. Shirring (en couture).

bouillonnement [-jɔnmɑ̃] m. Bubbling; boiling; seething. || Foaming, frothing. || FIG. Effervescence, heat.

bouillonner [-jɔne] v. intr. (1). To bubble, to boil, to seethe (liquide); to foam, to froth (vagues). || FIG. To seethe, to boil (*de,* with).
— v. tr. To shirr (du tissu).

bouillotte [-jɔt] f. Hot-water bottle (en caoutchouc); foot-warmer (chaufferette). [V. CRUCHON.]

bouillotter [-jɔte] v. intr. (1). To simmer.

boulange [bulɑ̃:ʒ] f. Bakery, baker's trade.

boulanger [-ʒe] v. intr. (7). To make bread, to bake.
— v. tr. To bake (la farine, le pain).

boulanger m. Baker.

boulangère [-ʒɛ:r] f. Baker's wife. || AUTOM. Van, U. S. truck. || Old dance.

boulangerie [-ʒəri] f. Baker's shop (boutique); bakery trade (commerce); bread-making (fabrication).

boulant, ante [bulɑ̃, ɑ̃:t] adj. *Sables boulants,* quicksands. || ZOOL. *Pigeon boulant,* pouter.

boule [bul] f. Ball (de billard, de croquet, de loto, de quille); boule (de casino); wood, bowl (de jeu de boules); *jeu de boules,* U. S. bowling alley (allée); bowling-green (boulingrin); bowls (jeu). || Sphere (de mappemonde); knob (de tringle); *boule de neige,* snowball. || MÉD. Drop (de gomme); *boule d'eau chaude,* hot-water bottle; *boule Quies,* ear-plug. || AGRIC. *En boule,* bushy-topped (arbre). || FAM. *En boule,* on edge (irrité); *perdre la boule,* to go dotty (ou) off one's head; U. S. to go nuts; *se mettre en boule,* to get spiky (se fâcher); to curl up (se pelotonner). || **Boule-de-neige,** f. BOT. Guelder-rose.

bouleau [bulo] m. BOT. Birch-tree (arbre); birchwood (bois).

bouledogue [buldɔg] m. ZOOL. Bulldog (chien); bull-bitch (chienne).

bouler [bule] v. intr. (1). To roll along. || FAM. *Envoyer bouler,* to send packing.

boulet [bulɛ] m. MILIT. Shot; shell; cannon ball. || Fetlock (de cheval). || Round briquette (de charbon). || Ball (de forçat). || FIG. Drag (*pour,* on); millstone (*pour,* round the neck of).

boulette [bulɛt] f. Pellet (de mie, de pain, de papier); *boulette empoisonnée,* bolus, poison ball. || CULIN. Ball (de viande). || FIG. Bloomer, U. S. boner. [V. BÉVUE, GAFFE.]

boulevard [bulva:r] m. Boulevard. (V. AVENUE.) || Bulwark.

boulevardier [-dje] adj. Fashionable.
— m. Man-about-town.

bouleversant, ante [bulvɛrsɑ̃, ɑ̃:t] adj. Upsetting; staggering.

bouleversé, ée [-se] adj. Turned upside down (maison). || FIG. Upset (esprit); distressed (visage); *bouleversé par l'émotion,* in a tumult of feeling.

bouleversement [-səmɑ̃] m. Overthrow; disorder; upset. || FIG. Consternation; upheaval.

bouleverser [-se] v. tr. (1). To overthrow; to upset; to disrupt; to turn topsy-turvy. || FIG. To upset, to bowl over.

boulier [bulje] m. Abacus (abaque); scoring-board (de billard).

boulimie [bulimi] f. MÉD. Bulimia.

boulimique [-mik] adj. Bulimic, voracious, insatiable.
— s. Compulsive eater, person suffering from bulimia; *boulimique de lecture,* compulsive reader.

boulin [bulɛ̃] m. Putlog, putlog-hole (de maçonnerie); pigeon-hole (de pigeonnier).

bouline [bulin] f. NAUT. Bowline.

bouliner [-ne] v. tr. (1). NAUT. To haul.
— v. intr. NAUT. To sail close-hauled.

boulingrin [bulɛ̃grɛ̃] m. SPORTS. Bowling-green.

bouliste [bulist] s. Boule player, bowls player.

boulle [bul] m. Buhl (meuble).

boulocher [bulɔʃe] v. intr. (1). To go (ou) become fluffy, to fluff.

boulodrome [bulodro:m] m. Court for playing boule, bowling pitch.

boulon [bulɔ̃] m. TECHN. Bolt; pin.

boulonnage [bulɔna:ʒ] m. Bolting.

boulonner [-ne] v. tr. (1). To bolt.
— v. intr. FAM. To grind. (V. TRIMER.)

boulot, otte [bulo, ot] adj. FAM. Squab, chunky, dumpy, podgy, fubsy, tubby, roly-poly (v. RONDELET); *pain boulot,* long cylindrical loaf.

boulot m. FAM. Job (emploi); grind, chore (travail); *quel boulot!,* what a sweat!

boulotter [bulote] v. tr. (1). POP. To blue (l'argent); to scoff, to bolt (la nourriture).
— v. intr. POP. To tuck in, to stuff (manger); to jog along (vivoter). [V. BOUFFER.]

boum [bum] interj. Bang!

boum m. Bang. || FAM. Hit, smash-hit (pièce, film, etc.); *en plein boum,* busy, hard at it.
— f. FAM. Party.

boumerang [bumrɑ̃g] m. V. BOOMERANG.

bouquet [bukɛ] m. Clump, cluster (d'arbres); cluster (de feuilles); bunch, nosegay, posy (de fleurs); tuft (de plumes). || CULIN. Bunch (de fruits, de persil, de thym); bouquet (du vin). || Final display (de feu d'artifice). || FIG. Finale; climax; *c'est le bouquet!,* that beats the band!, that's the last straw!, that takes the cake!

bouquet m. ZOOL. Prawn (crevette). || ZOOL. Buckhare, buck-rabbit.

bouquetière [buktjɛ:r] f. Flower-girl.

bouquetin [buktɛ̃] m. ZOOL. Ibex.

bouquin [bukɛ̃] m. ZOOL. Old he-goat.

bouquin m. FAM. Book.

bouquiner [bukine] v. intr. (1). To hunt for (ou) to pore over books; to browse among bookstalls (ou) in bookshops.

bouquiniste [-nist] m. Second-hand bookseller.

bourbe [burb] f. Mire, slime. (V. BOUE, VASE.)

bourbeux, euse [-bø, ø:z] adj. Muddy, miry, oozy. (V. BOUEUX.)

bourbier [-bje] m. Slough, quagmire. || FIG. Sink of iniquity, morass of depravity. || FAM. Mess, fix (difficulté); scrape (embarras). [V. PÉTRIN.]

bourbillon [burbijɔ̃] m. MÉD. Head, core.

bourbonien, enne [burbɔnjɛ̃, ɛn] adj. Bourbon.

bourcet [burse] m. NAUT. Lug.

bourde [burd] f. Blob; clanger; blunder, U. S. boner (bévue); thumper (énormité); fib (invention); nonsense (sottise).

bourdon [burdɔ̃] m. TECHN. Omission.

bourdon m. Pilgrim's staff (bâton).

bourdon m. Great bell (cloche). || ZOOL. Humble-bee, bumble-bee; *faux bourdon,* drone. || MUS. Drone (de cornemuse); bourdon stop (d'orgue).

bourdonnement [burdɔnmɑ̃] m. Buzz, buzzing, hum, humming (d'abeilles); drone (de bourdon); boom (de cloches, d'insectes, de foule); hum (de la rue); buzz (de voix). || MÉD. Head-noises, singing (d'oreilles).

bourdonner [-ne] v. intr. (1). To hum, to buzz, to boom (abeilles, insectes); to sound (cloches); to murmur (foule). || MÉD. To sing (oreilles).

bourg [buːr] m. Borough; market-town.

bourgade [burgad] f. Large village.

bourgeois, oise [burʒwa, ʒwaz] s. † Burgess. ‖ Citizen; middle-class person. ‖ Civilian (civil); *en bourgeois*, in mufti; in plain clothes. ‖ Philistine, bourgeois, lowbrow (d'esprit bourgeois). ‖ Capitalist. ‖ Pop. Boss (patron); missis (femme). — adj. Common, homely, plain, simple (esprit, goût); middle-class (famille); private (maison, pension); comfortable (ordinaire); bourgeois, narrow-minded, smug (opinion, préjugé); residential (quartier); humdrum (train-train). ‖ CULIN. Good plain, home (cuisine). ‖ JUR. *Caution bourgeoise,* good security.

bourgeoisement [-ʒwasmɑ̃] adv. In a simple (ou) plain (ou) humdrum way; comfortably; unimaginatively. ‖ As a private house (habité, loué); in civilian (ou) plain clothes (vêtu).

bourgeoisie [-ʒwazi] f. Burgesses; citizenship (privilèges). ‖ Middle-class; *haute, petite bourgeoisie,* upper, lower middle-class.

bourgeon [burʒɔ̃] m. BOT. Bud; burgeon (de plante); shoot (de vigne); *couvert de bourgeons,* budded. ‖ Grog-blossom, carbuncle (au nez d'un ivrogne).

bourgeonnement [-ʒɔnmɑ̃] m. BOT. Budding, sprouting.

bourgeonner [-ʒɔne] v. intr. (1). BOT. To bud, to burgeon; to sprout, to shoot (vigne). ‖ MÉD. To granulate. ‖ FAM. To be grog-blossomed (ou) carbuncled (nez d'un ivrogne); to become pimply, to break out in pimples (visage d'adolescent).

bourgeron [burʒərɔ̃] m. Blouse, overall (d'ouvrier). ‖ MILIT. Fatigue dress. ‖ NAUT. Jumper.

bourgmestre [burgmɛstr] m. Burgomaster.

Bourgogne [burgɔɲ] f. GÉOGR. Burgundy.

bourgogne m. Burgundy (vin).

bourguignon, onne [burgiɲɔ̃, ɔn] adj., s. Burgundian.

bourlinguer [burlɛ̃ge] v. tr. (1). NAUT. To make heavy weather. ‖ FAM. To navigate, to sail (naviguer); to knock about (rouler sa bosse); to make heavy weather (ou) going (travailler).

bourrache [buraʃ] f. BOT. Borage.

bourrade [burad] f. Blow; slap; thump; *qui aime donner des bourrades,* back-slapper.

bourrage [buraːʒ] m. Cramming (d'un poêle); filling-in (d'un trou). ‖ Padding, stuffing (d'une broderie). ‖ Tamping (d'armes); charge (d'explosif); charging, tamping (de mine). ‖ Packing (de piston). ‖ FAM. Cramming, swotting (des études); *bourrage de crâne,* baloney, eyewash, bluff, U. S. ballyhoo.

bourrasque [burask] f. Squall, flurry (de neige); gust (de vent).

bourratif, ive [buratif, iːv] adj. FAM. Stodgy, filling.

bourre [buːr] f. Fluff (d'étoffe); flock (de laine); floss (de soie). ‖ Wad (de fusil); packing, tamping (de mine). ‖ Hair (d'animal); down (de bourgeon). ‖ Stuffing (matelassure). ‖ POP. *Etre à la bourre,* to be late; to be in a rush. ‖ POP. *De première bourre,* first-rate.

bourre m. ARG. Cop, flatfoot.

bourreau [buro] m. Executioner (en général); headsman (pour décapitation); hangman (pour pendaison). ‖ FIG. Tormentor; *bourreau d'argent,* spendthrift; *bourreau des cœurs,* lady-killer; *bourreau de travail,* slogger, U. S. plugger.

bourrée [bure] f. MUS. Bourrée.

bourreler [burle] v. tr. (8 b). To torment; to rack; *bourrelé de remords,* tortured by remorse.

bourrelet [burlɛ] m. Weather-strip, draught excluder (de fenêtre, de porte); pad, cushion (de siège). ‖ Padded cap (d'enfant). ‖ Swelling, bulge (de chair); roll (de graisse); spare tyre (fam.)

[à la taille]. ‖ Swell (de fusil). ‖ Bead (de pneu); rim, flange (de roue).

bourrelier [burlje] m. Harness-maker, saddler.

bourrer [bure] v. tr. (1). To pack tight (une armoire). ‖ To stuff (un coussin, un matelas); to pad (un siège). ‖ To stuff (l'estomac); to fill (une pipe). ‖ MILIT. To ram home (ou) down (un canon); to tamp (une mine). ‖ SPORTS. To snap at (le gibier). ‖ FIG. To cram (l'esprit); to load (la mémoire). ‖ FAM. *Bourrer de coups,* to pummel, to thrash, to batter, U. S. to slug; *bourrer le crâne à,* to stuff up, to humbug. — v. pr. Se **bourrer,** FAM. to stuff oneself (s'empiffrer). — v. récipr. Se **bourrer.** FAM. To slog (ou) to biff (ou) U. S. to slug one another (se battre).

bourrette [-rɛt] f. Floss silk.

bourreur [-rœːr] m. FAM. *Bourreur de crânes,* opiate-monger.

bourriche [buriʃ] f. Hamper (contenant); hamperful (contenu).

bourrichon [-ʃɔ̃] m. FAM. Mug, cranium; *monter le bourrichon à qqn,* to work s.o. up.

bourricot [buriko] m. ZOOL. Donkey; cuddy.

bourrin [burɛ̃] m. FAM. Donkey; nag.

bourrique [burik] f. ZOOL. She-ass. ‖ FAM. Dunce, donkey.

bourru, ue [bury] adj. Shaggy (étoffe); rough (fil); unfermented (vin). ‖ BOT. Villous, vilose. ‖ FIG. Grumpy, surly (personne, ton); rugged (personne). — m. Curmudgeon, bear, John Blunt.

bourse [burs] f. Money, funds (argent); purse (sac). ‖ Scholarship, fellowship (d'études). ‖ ECCLÉS. Bag (de quête). ‖ SPORTS. Bag-net (de chasse). ‖ MÉD. Bursa. ‖ ZOOL. Pouch. ‖ JUR. Royal Exchange (du commerce); Labour Exchange (du travail); Stock Exchange (des valeurs). ‖ LOC. *La bourse ou la vie,* stand and deliver; your money or your life!; *sans bourse délier,* without expense.

boursicot [-siko] m. FAM. Small purse (bourse); nest-egg (économiser).

boursicoter [-sikɔte] v. intr. (1). FAM. To save little by little (économiser); to dabble in stocks (spéculer).

boursier, ère [-sje, ɛːr] adj. *Etudiant boursier,* scholarship- (ou) grant-holder. ‖ FIN. Stock Market, Stock Exchange. — s. Scholar (d'une public school); scholarship- (ou) grant-holder (d'une université). ‖ FIN. Speculator.

boursouflé, ée [bursufle] adj. Puffy, swollen (visage, etc.); blistered (peinture). ‖ FIG. Bombastic, pompous (style, personnage).

boursouflement [bursufləmɑ̃] m. V. BOURSOUFLURE.

boursoufler [-fle] v. tr. (1). To puff up (de bouffissure); to swell (d'enflure); to bloat (de graisse). ‖ To blister (la peinture). ‖ FIG. To inflate (V. AMPOULER). — v. pr. Se **boursoufler,** to become puffed up; to swell; to become bloated. ‖ FIG. To blister; to become turgid.

boursouflure [-flyːr] f. Puffiness (bouffissure); swelling (enflure); bloatedness (graisse). ‖ Blister (de la peinture); cockle (du papier). ‖ FIG. Bombast, turgidity (du style).

bousculade [buskylad] f. Crush, jostling, pushing about (cohue); scramble, scrimmage (mêlée); hustle, rush (précipitation).

bousculer [-le] v. tr. (1). To tumble, to turn upside down (bouleverser); to manhandle, to knock about (malmener); to rout (mettre en fuite); to hustle, to jostle, to shove (pousser); to hustle, to bustle, to rush, to hurry (presser); to rate, to bully (rudoyer); to upset (secouer). — v. pr. Se **bousculer,** to scramble, to push

about (se pousser); to hurry (se presser). ‖ To scuffle, to have a scuffle with (se colleter).
bouse [bu:z] f. Cow-dung.
bouseux [buzø] m. FAM. Peasant, yokel.
bousier [-zje] m. ZOOL. Dung-beetle.
bousillage [busija:ʒ] m. ARCHIT. Cob; mud-walling. ‖ AUTOM. Smashing, smashing-up (d'une voiture). ‖ FAM. Botching, bungling (du travail).
bousiller [-je] v. tr. (1). ARCHIT. To build with cob. ‖ AUTOM., FAM. To smash (sa voiture). ‖ AVIAT., FAM. To prang (un avion). ‖ FAM. To botch, U. S. to louse up (un travail). ‖ FAM., TECHN. U. S. To gum up.
bousilleur [-jœ:r] m. ARCHIT. Builder in cob. ‖ FAM. Botcher. (V. BÂCLEUR.)
boussole [busɔl] f. Compass; *boussole marine*, mariner's compass; *marcher à la boussole*, to march on a compass bearing. ‖ ELECTR. Galvanometer (des tangentes). ‖ FAM. *Perdre la boussole*, to be all at sea (être désorienté); to be off one's rocker (être fou).
boustifaille [bustifa:j] f. POP. Grub, chuck, chow, prog.
bout [bu] m. End (v. EXTRÉMITÉ); muzzle (d'une arme à feu); toe (d'un bas); ferrule (d'une canne); end (d'une chaîne, d'une maison, du monde, d'un objet, de la rue, de la ville); toe-cap (d'une chaussure); tip (d'une cigarette); chape (de fourreau); shoe (de lance); nose (d'outil); mouthpiece (d'une pipe); nib (d'une plume); nozzle (d'un tuyau); *bout à bout*, end to end, abutting, conterminous; *de bout en bout, d'un bout à l'autre*, from start to finish, from beginning to end, through; *du bout des lèvres*, in a forced manner; *joindre les deux bouts*, to make both ends meet, to make buckle and tongue meet; *jusqu'au bout*, throughout, to the last, to the bitter end; *sur le bout du doigt*, at one's finger-tips. ‖ Bit, piece, fragment (v. MORCEAU); patch (de ciel, de terrain); fag-end, butt (de cigarette); length (de corde); stump (de crayon, de cigare); scrap (d'étoffe, de ruban, de tapis, de terrain); piece, bit (de ficelle); fragment (de livre, de papier); particle (de métal); scraps (de papier); *un bout de*, a bit of; *un petit bout d'homme*, a little wisp of a man. ‖ End (v. FIN, TERME); end (des difficultés, de la patience, des soucis); *à bout*, tired out, done, worn out, knocked up (fatigué); exasperated (énervé); *à bout de bras*, at arm's length; *à bout de patience, de souffle*, out of patience, of breath; *à bout de ressources*, at the end of one's resources; *venir à bout de*, to get outside (achever de manger); to achieve, to manage (effectuer); to overcome, to get the better of (maîtriser); to get over, to cope with (surmonter); *à bout portant*, point-blank; *au bout du compte*, after all; *au bout d'un mois*, after (ou) in a month; *au bout de son rouleau*, at the end of one's tether (ou) rope; *à tout bout de champ*, at every turn; *tout le bout du monde*, the utmost. ‖ ECCLÉS. *Bout de l'an*, year's end mass. ‖ CULIN. Scraps (de fromage, de pain); end (d'un œuf). ‖ MÉD. Tip (du doigt, de la langue, du nez); nipple (du sein). ‖ FAM. *Tenir le bon bout*, to keep the upper hand; to get the whip-hand; *tenir son bout*, to keep one's end. ‖
Bout-dehors, m. NAUT. Jib-boom (de foc), studding-sail-boom (de bonnette). ‖ **Bouts-rimés**, m. pl. Bouts-rimés.
bout [bu]. V. BOUILLIR (22).
boutade [butad] f. Whim, fit (caprice); sally, quip (répartie).
boute-en-train [butãtrɛ̃] m. inv. Teaser (étalon). ‖ Life and soul of the party (personne).
bouteille [butɛ:j] f. Bottle; *boire à la bouteille*, to drink from the bottle's mouth (ou) straight from the bottle; *bouteille à gaz*, gas cylinder;

mettre en bouteille, to bottle; *vert bouteille*, bottle-green. ‖ ELECTR. *Bouteille de Leyde*, Leyden jar. ‖ FAM. *Bouteille à l'encre*, drivel, hopeless muddle; *caresser la bouteille*, to be fond of the bottle; *prendre de la bouteille*, to age.
bouteillon [-jɔ̃] m. MILIT. Dixie.
bouter [bute] v. tr. (1). † To oust, to cast out.
bouterolle [butrɔl] f. TECHN. Rivet-snap. ‖ ‖ Fishing-net. ‖ Ward (de clef, de serrure); chape (de fourreau).
bouteroue [butru] f. Guard-stone; spur-stone.
boute-selle [butsɛl] m. MILIT. Boot and saddle.
boutique [butik] f. Shop; U. S. store. (V. MAGASIN.) ‖ Booth (de foire); stall (de marché); boutique (de maison de couture); corf (de pêcheurs). ‖ Workshop (atelier); set of tools (outils). ‖ LOC. *Fermer boutique*, to shut up shop; to wind up; *parler boutique*, to talk shop. ‖ FAM. *Quelle boutique!*, what a beastly place!
boutiquier [-kje] s. Shopkeeper.
boutoir [butwa:r] m. TECHN. Paring-knife (de corroyeur); butteris (de maréchal); bulldozer. ‖ Snout (de sanglier). ‖ FIG. *Coup de boutoir*, sly hit, cutting remark.
bouton [butɔ̃] m. Stud, U. S. button (de col); bud (de fleur); button (de fleuret, d'habit); link (de manchette); knob (de porte); press-button, snap-fastener (à pression); bell-push, push-button, (de sonnette). ‖ MÉD. Pimple (bouton); weal (papule); boil (furoncle); nipple (de sein); couvert de boutons, pimply. ‖ MILIT. Sight (de fusil). ‖ RADIO. Knob; *bouton de mise en marche*, motor switch (de radio-phono); *bouton de puissance*, volume control. ‖ ELECTR. Switch (d'éclairage); *tourner le bouton*, to switch the light on (ou) off (pour allumer ou pour éteindre). ‖ **Bouton-arrêtoir**, n. Stop. ‖ **Bouton-d'or** (pl. *boutons-d'or*), m. BOT. Buttercup. ‖ **Bouton-pression**, m. Snap-fastener, press-stud, popper.
boutonnage [butɔna:ʒ] m. Buttoning (action); buttons (manière).
boutonner [butɔne] v. intr. (1). To button (habit); to bud (plante).
— v. tr. To button (un habit). ‖ SPORTS. To button (un fleuret); to touch (qqn à l'escrime).
— v. pr. Se boutonner, to button (habit); to button up one's clothes, to button oneself up (personne).
boutonnerie [-nri] f. Button factory (ou) trade.
boutonneux, euse [-nø, ø:z] adj. Pimply.
boutonnier [-nje] m. COMM. Button-maker.
boutonnière [-njɛ:r] f. Buttonhole (fente, fleur); U. S. Corsage, boutonniere (fleur).
bouturage [butyra:ʒ] m. AGRIC. Propagation by (ou) planting of cuttings.
bouture [buty:r] f. AGRIC. Cutting, slip.
bouturer [-re] v. tr. (1). AGRIC. To plant cuttings; to propagate.
— v. intr. To shoot suckers.
bouvet [buvɛ] m. TECHN. Grooving-plane; tonguing-plane, plough-plane.
bouvier [buvje] m. Cowherd; drover (toucheur).
bouvillon [buvijɔ̃] m. ZOOL. Steer, young bullock.
bouvreuil [buvrœ:j] m. ZOOL. Bullfinch.
bovidé [bɔvide] m. ZOOL. Bovid (pl. bovidae).
bovin, ine [bɔvɛ̃, in] adj., m. ZOOL. Bovine.
bowling [buliŋ] m. Bowling (jeu); bowling-alley (lieu).
bow-spring [bospriŋ] m. TECHN. Bow-spring.
box [bɔks] m. Cubicle (de dortoir). ‖ AGRIC. Loose-box, U. S. box stall (d'écurie); stall (de porcherie). ‖ JUR. Dock (des accusés); box, U. S. stand (des témoins). ‖ AUTOM. Lock-up, U. S. lock-up stall (de garage). ‖ COMM. Box-calf.
boxe f. SPORTS. Boxing; pugilism (de combat); sparring (de démonstration).
boxer [-se] v. intr. (1). SPORTS. To box : *boxer amicalement avec*, to spar with.

— v. tr. FAM. To strike; *faire mine de vouloir boxer qqn*, to spar up to s. o.

boxer [-sɛr] m. ZOOL. Boxer.

boxeur [-sœ:r] m. SPORTS. Boxer; *partenaire d'un boxeur*, sparring partner.

boy [bɔj] m. Houseboy, boy (domestique). ‖ Chorus boy (au music-hall).

boyard [bɔja:r] m. † Boyar.

boyau [bwajo] m. MÉD. Bowel, gut; *corde à boyau*, cat-gut. ‖ TECHN. Gut (passage); hose-pipe (tuyau). ‖ AUTOM. Inner tube; *boyau pour bicyclette*, bicycle tyre. ‖ MILIT. Trench, communication trench. ‖ CULIN. Casing.

boycottage [bɔjkɔta:ʒ], **boycott** [bɔjkɔt] m. Boycott.

boycotter [-te] v. tr. (1). To boycott.

boy-scout [bɔjskut] m. V. SCOUT.

brabançon, onne [brabɑ̃sɔ̃, ɔn] adj. GÉOGR. Of (ou) from Brabant; *la Brabançonne*, the Brabançonne (hymne national belge).
— s. Native (ou) inhabitant of Brabant.

brabant [brabɑ̃] m. AGRIC. Plough, U. S. plow.

bracelet [braslɛ] m. Bracelet (en général); anklet (à la cheville); armlet (au-dessus du coude); bangle (en cercle); watch-strap (en cuir pour montre). ‖ MÉD. Wrist-band (pour poignet). ‖ **Bracelet-montre**, m. Wrist-watch.

brachial, ale [brakjal] adj. MÉD. Brachial.

brachiopode [brakjɔpɔd] m. ZOOL. Brachiopod.

brachycéphale [brakisefal] adj. Brachycephalic.

brachygraphie [-grafi] f. Brachygraphy.

braconnage [brakɔna:ʒ] m. Poaching.

braconner [-ne] v. intr. (1). To poach.

braconnier [-nje] m. Poacher.

brader [brade] v. tr. (1). To sell off; to undersell.

braderie [-dri] f. Clearance-sale, jumble-sale, U. S. rummage sale.

braguette [bragɛt] f. Fly, flies (de pantalon).

brahmane [braman] m. Brahman, Brahmin.

brahmanique [-nik] adj. Brahminic, Brahminical.

brahmanisme [-nism] m. Brahmanism, Brahminism.

brahmine [bramin] m. Brahmin.

brai [brɛ] m. Pitch; tar; rosin (goudron).

braies f. pl. Breeches.

braillard, arde [braɑja:r, ard] adj. Clamorous, vociferous, brawling. ‖ Squalling (enfant).
— m. Brawler; babbler (chien); squaller (enfant).

Braille [bra:j] m. Braille.

braillement [brɑjmɑ̃] m. Bawling; squalling (d'enfant).

brailler [-je] v. intr. (1). To bawl, to squall, to brawl.
— v. tr. To howl out (une chanson, des injures); to bawl out (des insultes).

brailleur, euse [-jœ:r, ø:z] adj., s. V. BRAILLARD.

braiment [brɛmɑ̃] m. Bray; braying; hee-haw.

brainstorming [brɛnstɔrmiŋ] m. Brainstorming.

brain-trust [-trœst] m. Brains trust, think-tank.

braire [brɛ:r] v. intr. (23). To bray (âne). ‖ FAM. To boohoo (personne).

braise [brɛ:z] f. Live charcoal; glowing embers. ‖ POP. Oof. (V. GALETTE.)

braiser [-ze] v. tr. (1). CULIN. To braise.

bramement [brammɑ̃] m. Belling, troating.

bramer [brɑme] v. intr. (1). To bell, to troat (cerf, daim). ‖ FAM. To boohoo (personne).

bran [brɑ̃] m. Sawdust (de bois); bran (de son).

brancard [brɑ̃ka:r] m. Stretcher (civière). ‖ Shaft (de voiture).

brancardier [-dje] m. Stretcher-bearer.

branchage [brɑ̃ʃa:ʒ] m. Branches, boughs, U. S. branchery.

branche [brɑ̃:ʃ] f. BOT. Branch, bough (d'arbre);

spray (d'arbre en fleur). [V. RAMEAU.] ‖ TECHN. Branch (d'une chandelier, d'une rivière, d'une trajectoire); stem (de clé); leg (de compas); prong (de fourche); side (de lunettes); cheek (de mors). ‖ COMM. *Branche commerciale*, line of business. ‖ FIG. Branch (d'une famille, d'une science); *branche de connaissances*, branch (or) department of learning. ‖ FAM. Aristocratic bearing; *il a de la branche*, his breeding does tell. ‖ POP. *Vieille branche*, old chap.

branchement [-ʃmɑ̃] m. ELECTR. Tapping, lead; connection. ‖ TECHN. Service pipe (d'eau, de gaz); branch (de tuyau). ‖ CH. DE F. Junction.

brancher [-ʃe] v. tr. (1). ELECTR. To branch; to connect; *brancher sur*, to tap, to run off. ‖ RADIO. To plug in, to switch on to a line (au téléphone). ‖ FAM. To hang (pendre).
— v. pr. Se brancher, to perch, to roost (oiseau). ‖ TECHN. To connect up (sur, with).

branchette [-ʃɛt] f. Branchlet, twig.

branchial, ale [-ʃial] adj. ZOOL. Branchial.

branchies [-ʃi] f. pl. ZOOL. Branchiae, gills; *sans branchies*, abranchial.

branchiopode [-kjɔpɔd] m. ZOOL. Branchiopod.

branchu, ue [-ʃy] adj. Branchy.

brandade [brɑ̃dad] f. CULIN. Brandade.

brande [brɑ̃d] f. Heath, brush (végétation); heathland (terrain).

brandebourg [brɑ̃dbu:r] m. Frog; *garni de brandebourgs*, frogged.

brandiller [brɑ̃dije] v. tr., intr. (1). To dangle.

brandir [brɑ̃di:r] v. tr. (2). To flourish (un bâton, une canne); to wave (un chapeau, un journal); to brandish (une épée).

brandon [brɑ̃dɔ̃] m. Fire-brand, brandon. ‖ JUR. *Saisie-brandon*, seizure of growing crops. ‖ FIG. *Brandon de discorde*, fire-brand, mischief-maker.

branlant, ante [brɑ̃lɑ̃, ɑ̃:t] adj. Tumbledown (bâtiment); shaky (meuble); tottering (mur); rocking (pierre); unsteady (table). ‖ Tottering (démarche); unsteady, weaving (pas). ‖ MÉD. Loose (dent). ‖ CINÉM. Unsteady (image). ‖ FIG. Tottering (dynastie, empire).

branle [brɑ̃:l] m. Swing (d'une cloche). ‖ NAUT. Hammock. ‖ FIG. Impulse; *donner le branle à*, to give impetus to; to set going, to start; *mener le branle*, to lead the dance; *mettre en branle*, to set in motion. ‖ **Branle-bas**, m. NAUT. Quarters, FIG. bustle, commotion, disturbance; *branle-bas de combat*, clearing for action.

branlement [-lmɑ̃] m. Swinging (d'une cloche); wagging (de la tête).

branler [-le] v. tr. (1). To wag (la tête).
— v. intr. To shake (couteau). ‖ MÉD. To be loose (dent). ‖ FIG. *Branler dans le manche*, to be shaky (ou) precarious, to be in jeopardy.

branloire [-lwa:r] f. See-saw (balançoire); hanging box (caisse).

braquage [braka:ʒ] m. MILIT. Aiming (d'un fusil); laying (d'un canon). ‖ AVIAT. Deflection (de l'aileron, du gouvernail). ‖ AUTOM. Steering; *angle de braquage*, steering-lock; *braquage maximum*, steering range; *rayon de braquage*, turning circle.

braque [brak] m. ZOOL. Brach, pointer (chien). ‖ FAM. Feather-brain.

braquer [brake] v. tr. (1). MILIT. To lay, to level (un canon); to aim (un fusil) [sur, at]. ‖ AVIAT. To deflect. ‖ AUTOM. To steer; to deflect. ‖ CH. DE F. To swivel (un bogie). ‖ LOC. *Braquer une longue-vue sur*, to train a telescope on; *braquer son regard sur*, to stare at.
— v. pr. Se braquer, FAM. To refuse stubbornly, to dig one's heels in; *se braquer contre*, to be dead set against.

bras [bra] m. Arm (de l'homme, du singe); *à plein bras*, with both arms; *donner le bras à qqn*, to give s.o. one's arm; *lever les bras au ciel*, to hold up one's hands; *un parapluie au bras,* an umbrella on one's arm. ‖ Pl. Arms, hands; *manquer de bras,* to be short-handed. ‖ Arm (d'ancre); shaft (d'aviron, de voiture); limb (de croix); arm (de fauteuil); jib (de grue); crank arm (de manivelle); sail arm (de moulin); handle (d'outil, de pompe). ‖ GÉOGR. Arm (de mer); branch (de rivière). ‖ LOC. *A bras le corps,* round the waist; *avoir le bras long,* to have a long arm (ou) reach; *avoir sur les bras,* to have on one's hands; *bras dessus, bras dessous,* arm-in-arm; *le bras droit de qqn,* s.o.'s right-hand man; *les bras m'en tombent,* 1 don't know whether I am standing on my head or my heels; I can't get over it; *couper bras et jambes,* to prey on the mind, to dishearten; *livrer au bras séculier,* to hand over to the secular arm; *rester les bras croisés,* to twirl one's thumbs; *voiture à bras,* hand-cart.

braser [braze] v. tr. (1). TECHN. To braze, to hard-solder; to copper-solder.

brasero [brazero] m. Brazier, charcoal-pan.

brasier [-zje] m. Glowing coals; blazing mass.

brasiller [-zilje] v. tr. (1). To grill, to broil. — v. intr. To glimmer. (V. SCINTILLER.) ‖ CULIN. To sizzle.

brasque [brask] f. TECHN. Brasque.

brassage [brasa:ʒ] m. Handling (des affaires); brewing (de la bière); mixing (d'un mélange).

brassard [brasa:r] m. Brassard (d'armure); *mourning-band* (de crêpe); armlet (de communiant); arm badge, armband (d'insigne).

brasse [bras] f. Span of the arms (dimension). ‖ NAUT. Fathom (mesure). ‖ SPORTS. Breast-stroke (à la nage). ‖ TECHN. Pitch-stirrer.

brassée [brase] f. Armful. ‖ SPORTS. Stroke.

brasser v. tr. (1). To brew (la bière); to stir up (l'eau, un liquide); to churn (du lait); to mix (un mélange). ‖ To puddle (de la fonte). ‖ COMM., FIN. To put through, to handle (des affaires); to handle, to turn over (des capitaux). ‖ FIG. To hatch (une intrigue). [V. OURDIR.] — v. pr. **Se brasser,** to mix, to go into the melting pot (races, idées, etc.), to interbreed (races).

brasser v. tr., intr. (1). NAUT. To brace.

brasserie [brasri] f. Brasserie; public-house, beer-garden, beer-house (débit); beer-making (fabrication); brewery (fabrique). ‖ Restaurant.

brasseur [-sœ:r] m. Brewer (de bière); puddler (de fonte); *brasseur d'affaires,* big business-man; tycoon (fam.).

brassière [brasjɛ:r] f. Child's bodice (ou) vest. ‖ Shoulder-strap (bandoulière). ‖ NAUT. *Brassière de sauvetage,* life-jacket.

brassin [brasɛ̃] m. Gyle.

brasure [brazy:r] f. TECHN. Brazing (soudure); brazing metal.

bravache [bravaʃ] m. Bravo, bully, braggart. — adj. Braggart, bullying.

bravade [bravad] f. Bravado.

brave [bra:v] adj. Brave (v. COURAGEUX); honest, good, decent (bon, honnête); *homme brave,* brave man; *brave homme,* worthy (ou) good man. ‖ Nice, smart (beau, élégant). — m. Brave man; good fellow.

bravement [-vmɑ̃] adv. Bravely.

braver [-ve] v. tr. (1). To brave, to affront, to face (le danger). ‖ To brave (qqn). [V. DÉFIER.]

bravo [bravo] interj. Bravo!, hear, hear!, well said!, well done! — m. pl. Applause; cheers.

bravo m. Bravo (spadassin).

bravoure [bravu:r] f. Bravery, gallantry, fearlessness. (V. COURAGE.)

brayer [brɛje] v. tr. (9b). NAUT. To pitch.

brayer m. Thong (de cloche); bucket (de hampe); sling (pour soulever). ‖ MÉD. Hernia-truss.

break [brɛk] m. Break; estate (ou) shooting brake; U. S. station wagon.

brebis [brəbi] f. ZOOL. Ewe. ‖ FIG. Sheep, lamb; *brebis galeuse,* black sheep.

brèche [brɛ:ʃ] f. Breach, gap, break (à une clôture, un mur); notch, nick (à une lame). ‖ MILIT. Breach (à un rempart); *battre en brèche,* to batter; *ouvrir une brèche,* to open a breach, to break through. ‖ NAUT. Hole (à un navire). ‖ FIG. *Battre en brèche,* to disparage (qqn); *être sur la brèche,* to be hard at it; *une brèche à sa fortune,* a hole in one's capital. ‖ **Brèche-dent** (pl. *brèche-dents*) m. Gap-toothed.

brèche f. GÉOL. Breccia.

bréchet [breʃɛ] m. Breast-bone.

bredouillage [brəduja:ʒ] m. Gabbling, spluttering.

bredouille [brədu:j] adj. Empty-handed; with an empty bag.

bredouillement [-dujmɑ̃] m. V. BREDOUILLAGE.

bredouiller [-je] v. tr. (1). To stammer out, to jabber out. — v. intr. To gabble, to splutter. (V. BALBUTIER.)

bredouillis [-ji] m. V. BREDOUILLAGE.

bref [brɛf] (f. **brève** [brɛ:v]) adj. Brief, short (durée); curt, sharp (parole); concise (style). ‖ GRAMM. Short (syllabe, voyelle). — adv. In short, in a few words, succinctly (en un mot); in fine (en conclusion); curtly (impérativement). — m. ECCLÉS. Papal brief. ‖ JUR. Brief, summary of facts. (V. BRÈVE.)

bréhaigne [breɛɲ] adj. Barren, sterile.

breitschwanz [bretʃwɑ̃:ts] m. COMM. Broadtail.

brelan [brəlɑ̃] m. Pair-royal (coup); brelan (jeu); gambling-den (tripot).

breloque [brələk] f. Charm, trinket, breloque (bijou). ‖ NAUT. Dismiss; *battre la breloque,* to sound the dismiss. ‖ FAM. *Battre la breloque,* to go pit-a-pat (cœur); to go badly (pendule); to have a screw loose (personne).

brème [brɛm] f. ZOOL. Bream (poisson).

Brême [brɛm] m. GÉOGR. Bremen.

Brésil [brezil] m. GÉOGR. Brazil.

brésilien [breziljɛ̃] adj., s. Brazilian.

bressan, ane [brɛsɑ̃, an] adj. GÉOGR. Of (ou) from Bresse. — s. Native (ou) inhabitant of Bresse.

Bretagne [brətaɲ] f. GÉOGR. Brittany; *Grande-Bretagne,* Great Britain.

bretelle [brətɛl] f. Shoulder-strap (de chemise); sling (de fusil); braces, U. S. suspenders (de pantalon); strap (de sac).

bretessé, ée [brətese] adj. BLAS. Bretessy.

breton, onne [brətɔ̃, on] adj., m. Breton. ‖ NAUT. *En breton,* aburton.

bretonnant, ante [-tɔnɑ̃, ɑ̃:t] adj. Breton-speaking.

bretteler [brɛtle] v. tr. (8a). To notch; to score.

bretteur [brɛtœ:r] m. Swashbuckler.

bretzel [brɛtsɛl] m., f. Pretzel.

breuil [brœ:j] m. Coppice, spinney.

breuvage [brœva:ʒ] m. Beverage. (V. BOISSON.) ‖ Drench (buvée).

brève [brɛ:v] f. Dot (en morse). ‖ GRAMM. Short syllable. ‖ MUS. Breve.

brevet [brəvɛ] m. Diploma, certificate; *brevet simple* (ou) *élémentaire, supérieur,* elementary, school leaving certificates. ‖ Badge (de scout). ‖ MILIT. Commission; *brevet d'officier d'état-major,* Staff College certificate. ‖ AVIAT. Licence (de pilote). ‖ JUR. *Brevet d'apprentissage,* articles, indentures; *brevet d'invention,* letters patent; *prendre un brevet,* to take out a patent.

brevetable [-vtabl] adj. Patentable, liable to be patented.

breveté, ée [-vte] adj. Certificated, graduate (étudiant); holding letters patent (inventeur); patented (invention); qualified (spécialiste).

breveter [-vte] v. tr. (8 a). To patent (une invention); to issue (ou) grant a patent to (un inventeur); to license (qqn); *faire breveter,* to take out a patent for. ‖ MILIT. To commission (un officier).

bréviaire [brevjɛ:r] m. ECCLÉS. Breviary.

briard, arde [brija:r, ard] adj. GÉOGR. Of (ou) from Brie.
— s. Native (ou) inhabitant of Brie.

bribes [b˘ib] f. pl. Scraps, bits (de pain, de papier, de repas); odds and ends (d'objets divers, de repas); driblets (de provisions). ‖ Scraps (de conversation); smattering, scraps (de connaissances); snippets (de lectures).

bric [brik] m. De bric et de broc, by hook or by crook. ‖ **Bric-à-brac,** old curiosity shop (boutique); curio dealer, broker (brocanteur); bric-à-brac, curios (objets).

brick m. NAUT. Brig.

bricolage [brikɔla:ʒ] m. Tinkering, pottering (ou) U. S. puttering about.

bricole [brikɔl] f. Stroke off the cushion (au billard). ‖ Toils (de chasse); double-hook (de pêche). ‖ Breast-harness (de cheval). ‖ Hoist-strap (de portefaix); window-strap (de portière). ‖ Pl. FAM. Odd jobs, odds and ends, trifles.

bricoler [brikɔle] v. intr. (1). FAM. To potter, to tinker, U. S. to putter.
— v. tr. To wangle, to fiddle, U. S. to finagle (une affaire).

bricoleur [-lœ:r] m. Handy-man, potterer, U. S. putterer, tinker.

bride [brid] f. Bridle, rein (de cheval); *lâcher la bride à,* to give rein to (ou the bridle to; *serrer la bride,* to rein in; *tourner bride,* to turn back. ‖ Bar, loop (de boutonnière); bridle (de dentelle); string (de chapeau); strap (d'épaulette). ‖ MÉD. Bride, U. S. adhesion. ‖ CULIN. String. ‖ TECHN. Strap (de bielle); clamp (de serrage); flange (de tuyau). ‖ FIG. *A bride abattue,* at full gallop (ou) tilt; *lâcher la bride à,* to let loose; to give free rein to; *laisser la bride sur le cou à qqn,* to give s.o. rope; *serrer la bride à,* to bridle, to curb; *tourner bride,* to turn back.

bridé, ée [-de] adj. Slanting, slant (œil).

brider [-de] v. tr. (1). To bridle (un cheval). ‖ To bind (une boutonnière). ‖ CULIN. To truss. ‖ NAUT. To lash (les cordages); to swift in (les haubans). ‖ TECHN. To flange, to clamp. ‖ FIG. To check, to restrain, to curb (la colère, la curiosité, les passions); to rein in (qqn).; *être bridé aux entournures,* to be ill-at-ease.

bridge [bridʒ] m. Bridge (dentier, jeu).

bridger [-dʒe] v. intr. (7). To play bridge.

bridgeur, euse [-dʒœ:r, ø:z] s. Bridger, bridge-player.

bridon [bridɔ̃] m. Snaffle, bridoon.

Brie [bri] f. GÉOGR. Brie.

brie m. CULIN. Brie cheese (fromage).

briefing [brifiŋ] m. AVIAT. Briefing.

brièvement [briɛvmɑ̃] adj. Briefly, concisely.

brièveté [briɛvte] f. Brevity, briefness, shortness (de durée). ‖ Brevity, terseness, succinctness; télégraphese (fam.) [d'expression].

briffer [brife] v. tr., intr. (1). POP. To tuck in, U. S. to stow away. (V. CROÛTER.)

brigade [brigad] f. Squad (de gendarmes); gang (d'ouvriers); force (de policiers). ‖ MILIT. Brigade.

brigadier [-dje] m. MILIT. Corporal (dans l'armée); sergeant (dans la police).

brigand [brigɑ̃] m. Brigand, robber. ‖ FAM. Rascal, rogue, scamp.

brigandage [-da:ʒ] m. Brigandage.

brigantin [brigɑ̃tɛ̃] m. NAUT. Brigantine.

brigantine [-tin] f. NAUT. Spanker.

brigue [brig] f. Intrigue.

briguer [-ge] v. tr. (1). To court (l'alliance, l'amitié, les faveurs); to intrigue for (un emploi); to solicit (un honneur); to canvass for (des suffrages). [V. AMBITIONNER.]
— v. intr. To intrigue.

brillamment [brijamɑ̃] adv. Brilliantly.

brillance [-jɑ̃:s] f. Brilliance, brightness. ‖ PHYS. Luminance.

brillant [-jɑ̃] adj. Bright, shining, brilliant (acier, astre, lumière, yeux); gay, bright, vivid (couleur); glittering (lumière, yeux); radiant (lumière); lustrous (soie). ‖ FIG. Brilliant, talented, prominent (artiste, écrivain, orateur); bright (avenir, époque); brilliant (combat, esprit, intelligence); sparkling (conversation); vivid (description, imagination); splendid (espérance, spectacle); shining (exemple); dashing (joueur); flourishing (santé); brilliant, prosperous (situation); dazzling (succès). ‖ FAM. *Pas brillant, ça!,* not too good!
— m. Sheen (des cheveux, de l'eau, d'une étoffe, des plumes, de la soie); shine, polish (du cirage, du vernis); brilliance, brilliancy (d'une couleur, de l'esprit, de la musique, du style); glaze (du cuir); sparkle (du diamant, des yeux); sparkling (des étoiles); gloss (de la glace, du satin); glossiness (du papier). ‖ Diamond, brilliant (diamant); *monté en brillant,* mounted as a brilliant; *taillé en brillant,* diamond-cut; *brillant faux,* imitation diamond, Rhinestone.

brillanté, ée [-jɑ̃te] adj. Bright-silk, glazed (coton); glossed (surface).

brillanter [-jɑ̃te] v. tr. (1). To gloss, to glaze (du coton, du fil). ‖ To cut as a brilliant (une pierre). ‖ FIG. To tinsel (son style).

brillantine [-jɑ̃tin] f. Brilliantine, bandoline (pour cheveux); lustrine (pour tissu).

briller [-je] v. intr. (1). To shine (en général); to glisten, to glint (comme l'acier); to glimmer (comme une bougie, de l'eau); to glitter, to sparkle, to twinkle (comme les étoiles); to blaze (comme les flammes); to shimmer (comme la lune, le satin); to glitter, to glisten (comme l'or); to glare (comme des phares aveuglants); to gleam (comme le soleil levant); to glow (comme des tisons). ‖ FIG. To be conspicuous (par l'absence ou l'intelligence); to shine (dans la conversation); *faire briller qqn,* to draw s.o. out, to show s.o. off.

brimade [brimad] f. Bullying, U. S. hazing (à l'école). ‖ Rough joke; ragging. ‖ FIG. Vexation.

brimbale [brɛ̃bal] f. Handle, rocker-arm.

brimbaler [-le] v. intr. (1). To dangle, to wobble.
— v. tr. To swing (des cloches); to carry about, U. S. to tote about (un paquet).

brimborion [brɛ̃bɔrjɔ̃] m. Bauble, knick-knack.

brimer [brime] v. tr. (1). To rag, to bully, U. S. to haze.

brin [brɛ̃] m. Blade (de blé, d'herbe); shoot (de bois); sprig (de bruyère); spray (de mimosa, de muguet); bit, wisp (de paille). ‖ Staple (de chanvre, de lin); strand (de corde, de ficelle); yarn, fibre (de fil); ply (de laine). ‖ Dash (d'alcool); scrap, crumb (de pain); modicum, drop (de vin); drop (de vinaigre). ‖ Breath (d'air); dash (de couleur); Rib (d'éventail). ‖ ELECTR. Wire (d'antenne). ‖ FIG. Atom (de bon sens); touch (de folie, d'impatience); particle (de méchanceté); shade (of regret). ‖ LOC. *Un brin de causette,* a bit of a chat; *un beau brin de fille,* a fine figure of a girl; *un brin plus bas,* a shade lower; *brin à brin,* bit by bit.

brindille [brɛ̃di:j] f. Twig, sprig.

bringue [brɛ̃:g] f. *Une grande bringue,* a lamp-post, a maypole. ‖ FAM. Spree, U. S. binge; *faire la bringue,* to make a night of it. (V. BOMBE.)

bringuebaler [brɛ̃gbale]. V. BRIMBALER.

brio [briɔ] m. Brio, spirit, dash, pep.

brioche [brijɔʃ] f. CULIN. Brioche.

brioché, ée [-ʃe] adj. CULIN. Brioche-like; brioché (pain).

brique [brik] f. Brick; *en brique,* brick. ‖ Bar, cake (de savon). — adj. Brick-red (rouge).

briquer [-ke] v. tr. (1). NAUT. To holystone. ‖ FAM. To furbish. (V. ASTIQUER.)

briquet [brikɛ] m. Tinder-box (à amadou); lighter (à essence); *battre le briquet,* to strike a light.

briquet m. ZOOL. Beagle (chien).

briquetage [brikta:ʒ] m. ARCHIT. Brickwork.

briqueter [brikte] v. tr. (8a). ARCHIT. To brick, to brick up. ‖ To paint in imitation brickwork.

briqueterie [briktri] f. Brick-making (fabrication); brickyard (lieu).

briqueteur [briktœ:r] m. Bricklayer.

briquetier [briktje] m. Brick-maker.

briquette [brikɛt] f. Briquette, briquet, compressed slack.

bris [bri] m. Breaking (de verre). ‖ JUR. Breach (de clôture); breaking (de scellés). ‖ NAUT. Break-up (de navire).

brisance [brizɑ̃:s] n. PHYS. Brisance (fission nucléaire).

brisant [brizɑ̃] adj. MILIT. Disruptive (explosif); high-explosive (obus). — m. Reef (récif); breaker (vague déferlante). ‖ Pl. Surf (sur les côtes).

briscard [briska:r] m. MILIT. Veteran.

brise [bri:z] f. Breeze; *brise légère,* breath of wind; *forte brise,* gale, stiff breeze.

brise. V. BRISER. ‖ **Brise-bise,** m. invar. Brise-bise, window-curtain. ‖ **Brise-circuit,** m. invar. ELECTR. Cut-out, interrupter, circuit-breaker. ‖ **Brise-fer,** m. invar. Bull in a china-shop, butter-fingers. ‖ **Brise-glace,** m. invar. Ice-beam, ice-plough (éperon); ice-breaker (navire); ice-apron (de pont). ‖ **Brise-jet,** m. invar. Anti-splash tap-nozzle. ‖ **Brise-lames,** m. invar. Breakwater, groyne. ‖ **Brise-mottes,** m. invar. Clod-crusher. ‖ **Brise-tout,** s. invar. FAM. Breaker, wrecker. ‖ **Brise-vent,** m. invar. Wind-screen; U. S. wind-break.

brisé, ée [brize] adj. Broken (objet, verre). ‖ Folding (volet). ‖ GÉOM. Broken (ligne). ‖ CULIN. Short (pâte). ‖ FIG. Broken (cœur, voix). ‖ FAM. Tired out, stiff all over. (V. ROMPU.)

brisées f. pl. SPORTS. Broken branches (à la chasse). ‖ FIG. *Marcher sur les brisées de qqn,* to encroach (ou) trespass s.o.'s preserves; *suivre les brisées de qqn,* to follow in s.o.'s tracks, to take a leaf out of s.o.'s book.

brisement [-zmɑ̃] m. V. BRIS.

briser [-ze] v. tr. (1). To break (sens général); to break (un bâton, des chaînes, une corde, le roc, un verre); to snap (un bâton, une canne, une corde); to shatter (une glace, du verre); to burst (des liens, une porte). [V. CASSER.] ‖ To break (le chanvre, le lin); to crush (la terre). ‖ To break (une grève). ‖ MILIT. To smash, to subdue (un ennemi). ‖ MÉD. To ruin, to shatter (la santé). ‖ FIG. To ruin (l'avenir); to break (le cœur, une puissance, une résistance); to cut short (une conversation); to shatter, to smash, to blight (des espérances); to exhaust (les forces); to overcome (un obstacle, une résistance); to crush (une opposition); to quell, to suppress (une révolte). ‖ FAM. To tire out (qqn de fatigue). — v. intr. To break (avec, with); *brisons là,* let's leave it at that. — v. pr. Se briser, to break (sens général); to snap (canne); to shatter (verre). ‖ FIG. To break (cœur, voix).

briseur [-zœ:r] m. *Briseur de grève,* strike-breaker.

brisquard [briska:r] m. V. BRISCARD.

brisque [brisk] f. MILIT. Stripe, chevron.

bristol [bristɔl] m. Visiting-card (carte); pasteboard, Bristol-board (carton).

brisure [brizy:r] f. Break; crack. ‖ Folding-joint (de volet). ‖ CULIN. *Brisures de riz,* broken rice. ‖ BLAS. Brisure.

britannique [britanik] adj. British (citoyen, îles); Britannic (majesté). — s. Briton, U. S. Britisher; *les Britanniques,* the British.

broc [bro] m. Pitcher (à vin); jug, water-jug (de toilette).

brocante [brokɑ̃:t] m. Bartering; broking; second-hand dealing. ‖ Odd job.

brocanter [-te] v. tr. (1). To buy and sell; to barter. — v. intr. To deal in second-hand goods.

brocanteur [-tœ:r] m. Second-hand dealer.

brocard [broka:r] m. ZOOL. Brocket.

brocard m. Squib, lampoon. (V. RAILLERIE.)

brocarder [-de] v. tr. (1). To squib, to lampoon.

brocart [broka:r] m. Brocade, broché.

brochage [broʃa:ʒ] m. Sewing, stitching (d'un livre); brocading (d'un tissu).

brochant, ante [-ʃɑ̃, ɑ̃:t] adj. BLAS. Brochant, overlying. ‖ LOC. *Brochant sur le tout,* to cap it all.

broche [broʃ] f. Brooch, U. S. breastpin (bijou). ‖ Skewer (de boucherie). ‖ Pin (de charnière); spike-nail (de menuiserie); spigot (de tonneau). ‖ Brog (de cordonnier); spit (d'imprimeur); spindle (de filateur). ‖ Bar (de manœuvre); key (de roue); brooch, pin (de serrure); peg (de tente). ‖ ZOOL. Tusk (de sanglier). ‖ MILIT. Pin (de cartouche). ‖ ELECTR. Pin (de prise de courant); *fiche à deux broches,* two-pin plug. ‖ CULIN. Spit, broach, skewer (de cuisine); spit (de harengs); *mettre à la broche,* to spit. ‖ FIN. Sheaf of small bills (monnaie). ‖ FAM. Knitting-needle (à tricoter).

broché, ée [-ʃe] adj. Sewn, paper-bound (livre); brocaded (tissu). — m. Brocading (procédé); brocade, broché (tissu).

brochée [-ʃe] f. CULIN. Spitful.

brocher [-ʃe] v. tr. (1). To sew, to stitch (un livre); to brocade (une étoffe).

brochet [broʃɛ] m. ZOOL. Pike (poisson).

brochette [broʃɛt] f. CULIN. Small skewer, brochette (broche); spitful (brochée). ‖ FAM. Row (de décorations); brochette (de médailles).

brocheur, euse [broʃœ:r, ø:z] s. Sewer, stitcher (de livres).

brocheuse [-ʃø:z] f. TECHN. Stapling-machine.

brochoir [-swa:r] m. Shoeing-hammer (à ferrer).

brochure [-ʃy:r] f. Brochure, pamphlet, tract. (V. OPUSCULE.) ‖ Stitching (de livres); inwoven pattern (de tissus).

brocoli [brokɔli] m. BOT. Broccoli.

brodequin [brɔdkɛ̃] m. Half-boot (de femme). ‖ THÉÂTR. Sock, buskin (de comédie). ‖ MILIT. Ammunition-boot (de soldat). ‖ † Boot (de torture).

broder [brɔde] v. tr. (1). To embroider. ‖ FIG. To embroider, to embellish.

broderie [-dri] f. Embroidery (sur le linge); gold (ou) silver lace (sur un uniforme); *broderie anglaise,* broderie anglaise, U. S. eyelet embroidery. ‖ MUS. Pl. Graces; grace-notes. ‖ FIG. Embroidery, embellishment.

brodeur [-dœ:r] m. Embroiderer.

brodeuse [-dø:z] f. Embroideress (femme); embroidering machine (machine).

broiement [brwamɑ̃] m. V. BROYAGE.

bromate [brɔmat] m. CHIM. Bromate.

brome [bro:m] m. CHIM. Bromine.

bromhydrate [brɔmidrat] m. CHIM. Hydrobromide.

bromhydrique [-drik] adj. CHIM. Hydrobromic.

bromique [brɔmik] adj. CHIM. Bromic.

bromure [-my:r] m. CHIM. Bromide.

bronche [brɔ̃:ʃ] f. MÉD. Bronchus (pl. bronchi, bronchia); wind-pipe.

broncher [brɔ̃ʃe] v. intr. (1). To budge, to stir (remuèr); to stumble (trébucher). ‖ To flinch, to blench, to wince (sourciller); *sans broncher*, without flinching (ou) blenching, without turning a hair (fam.).

bronchial, ale [brɔ̃ʃial] adj. MÉD. Bronchial.

bronchiole [-ʃiɔl] f. MÉD. Bronchiole.

bronchique [-ʃik] adj. MÉD. Bronchial.

bronchite [-ʃit] f. MÉD. Bronchitis; *bronchite capillaire*, suffocative catarrh, bronchiolitis.

bronchitique [-ʃitik] adj., s. MÉD. Bronchitic.

broncho-pneumonie [brɔ̃kopnømɔni] f. MÉD. Broncho-pneumonia.

brondir [brɔ̃dir] ·v. intr. (2). To hum.

brondissement [brɔ̃dismɑ̃] m. Humming (d'un moteur, d'une toupie).

brontosaure [brɔ̃tozo:r] m. ZOOL. Brontosaurus.

bronzage [brɔ̃za:ʒ] m. Tan, sun-tan.

bronze [brɔ̃:z] m. Bronze (métal, statue) [v. AIRAIN]; *bronze d'aluminium*, aluminium (ou) U. S. aluminum bronze. ‖ FIG. *Cœur de bronze*, heart of steel.

bronzé, ée [-ze] adj. Bronze, bronzy, bronze-coloured. ‖ Bronzed, tanned, sunburnt, brown (peau). [V. HÂLÉ.]

bronzer [-ze] v. tr. (1). To tan, to sunburn (la peau). ‖ To blue (l'acier); to bronze (une statue). ‖ FIG. To steel, to harden (le cœur).
— v. pr. Se bronzer, to tan, to bronze (peau). ‖ FIG. To harden (cœur).

bronzeur [-zœ:r], **bronzier** [brɔ̃zje] m. Bronze founder.

broquette [brɔkɛt] f. Tack (clou).

brosse [brɔs] f. Brush; *brosse à chapeau, à cheveux, à chaussures, à dents, à habits, à ongles, à reluire*, hat-, hair-, shoe-, tooth-, clothes-, nail-, polishing-brush; *brosse à parquets*, floor-polisher; *brosse en chiendent*, scrubbing-brush; *brosse métallique*, wire brush; *brosse de peintre*, sweep-brush (à coller); paint-brush (à peindre); *coup de brosse*, brush, brushing, brush-up; *être coiffé en brosse*, to wear a crew-cut. ‖ Pl. Brushwood.

brossée [-se] f. FAM. Drubbing. (V. RACLÉE.)

brosser v. tr. (1). To brush away (la boue, la poussière); to brush (un chapeau, des vêtements); to scrub (la cuisine, le pont d'un navire); to brush up (les miettes); to brush down (ou) up (qqn). ‖ To paint (un décor, une toile); to brush in (les draperies, le fond); *brosser un tableau de*, to give an outline of, to draw a picture of. ‖ FAM. To thrash. (V. ROSSER.)
— v. pr. Se brosser, to brush, to brush out (les cheveux); to brush oneself, to give oneself a brush-up (les vêtements); *se faire brosser*, to have a brush-up. ‖ FAM. To go without it; *tu peux te brosser!*, you can whistle for it!

brosserie [-sri] f. Brush-trade (commerce); brush-factory (fabrique).

brossier [-sje] m. Brush-maker (fabricant); brush-dealer (vendeur).

brou [bru] m. Husk; U. S. shuck; *brou de noix*, walnut-liqueur (liqueur); walnut-stain (teinture).

brouet [bruɛ] m. CULIN. Gruel, skilly (bouillie); caudle (chaudeau).

brouette [bruɛt] f. Wheelbarrow; *brouette porte-brancard*, wheeled stretcher-carrier.

brouettée [bruɛte] f. Wheelbarrow-load; barrow-ful, barrow-load.

brouetter v. tr. (1). To barrow, to wheel in a barrow.

brouhaha [bruaa] m. Hubbub. (V. TAPAGE.)

brouillage [bruja:ʒ] m. ÉLECTR. Interference (accidentel); jamming (voulu) [à la radio].

brouillamini [brujamini] m. FIG. Tangle, muddle.

brouillard [bruja:r] m. Fog; dense fog (brouillard épais); smog (brouillard fumeux); haze (brouillasse); mist (brume); *faire du brouillard*, to be foggy; *perdu dans le brouillard*, fog-bound. ‖ *Papier-brouillard*, blotting-paper. ‖ COMM. Waste-book, counter cash book. ‖ FAM. *Dans le brouillard*, hazy, in a mist, a little fogged.

brouillasse [-jas] f. Mist (brume); drizzle (pluie).

brouillasser [-jase] v. impers. (1). To be misty; to be drizzling.

brouille [bru:j] f. Falling-out, estrangement; *semer la brouille dans*, to disunite, to bring division into.

brouillé, ée [bruje] adj. Shuffled (cartes). ‖ Murky (ciel); blurred (image, photo); blotchy, muddy (teint); bedimmed (yeux). ‖ On bad terms, estranged (personnes). ‖ CULIN. Scrambled (œufs). ‖ FIG. Confused (idées).

brouiller v. tr. (1). To shuffle (les cartes); to mix up (des documents, des papiers). ‖ To blur (une image, un miroir, une photo, la vue); to make muddy (le teint). ‖ To embroil (une affaire). ‖ To jam, to interfere with (une émission); to hamper (une serrure). ‖ To estrange, to set at variance (des personnes). ‖ CULIN. To scramble (des œufs). ‖ FIG. To addle (le cerveau); to confuse (les idées). ‖ FAM. *Brouiller les cartes*, to cloud the issue; to sow discord; to spread confusion.
— v. pr. Se brouiller, to become overcast (ciel); to break up (temps). ‖ To get mixed up (documents, papiers). ‖ To grow dim (yeux). ‖ To fall out (personnes). ‖ To become confused (idées).

brouillerie [-jri] f. Tiff.

brouillon [brujɔ̃] adj. Harum-scarum (esprit); untidy, muddle-headed (personne).
— m. Muddle-head, muddler (personne).

brouillon m. Scribbling-pad, U. S. scratch pad (cahier); scribbling-paper (papier); rough copy (ou) U. S. draft (texte). ‖ JUR. Draft.

brouillonner [-jɔne] v. tr. (1). To write the rough copy (ou) draft of.

brouir [bru:ir] v. tr. (1). To blight.

brouissure [-isy:r] f. Frost-nip; withering.

broussaille [brusɑ:j] f. Brushwood; undergrowth, underbrush.

broussailleux, euse [-jø, ø:z] adj. Bushy (terrain). ‖ Shaggy, bushy (barbe, sourcils).

brousse [brus] f. Bush (pr. et fig.).

broutage [bruta:ʒ], **broutement** [-tmɑ̃] m. TECHN. Chattering. ‖ ZOOL. Browsing.

brouter [brute] v. tr. (1). ZOOL. To browse, to graze (de l'herbe); to nibble at (du fromage). ‖ FAM. To nibble at (un gâteau).
— v. intr. To browse (bétail); to nibble (rongeur). ‖ TECHN. To jump, to chatter (frein, outils).

broutille [-ti:j] f. Twig, sprig. ‖ FIG. Trifle.

brownien [braunjɛ̃] adj. m. *Mouvement brownien*, Brownian movement.

browning [brauniŋ] m. Browning (arme).

broyage [brwaja:ʒ] m. Braking (du chanvre); powdering (du charbon); grinding (des couleurs); crushing (des pierres, de la terre).

broyer [-je] v. tr. (9 a). To crunch (des aliments); to brake (du chanvre); to pulverise (du charbon); to grind, to bray (des couleurs); to mill (du grain); to pound (des pierres, des pommes, du sucre, la terre); to crush (la pierre, le sucre, la terre); to crush (qqn). ‖ FAM. *Broyer du noir*, to be down in the dumps, to have the blues, to wear the willow.

broyeur, euse [-jœ:r, ø:z] adj. Crushing, grinding (moulin).
— m. Crusher, grinder (machine, personne). ‖ FAM. *Un broyeur de noir*, a dismal Jimmy, U. S. a sad sack.

broyeuse [-jø:z] f. TECHN. Brake.

brrr! [br] interj. Brr!
bru [bry] f. Daughter-in-law.
brucelles [brysɛl] f. pl. Tweezers.
brucellose [brysɛlo:z] f. MÉD. Brucellosis.
brugnon [bryɲɔ̃] m. BOT. Nectarine.
brugnonier [-ɲɔnje] m. BOT. Nectarine tree.
bruine [brɥin] f. Drizzle, mizzle.
bruiner [-ne] v. impers. (1). To drizzle, to mizzle.
bruineux, euse [-nø, ø:z] adj. Drizzly, mizzly.
bruire [brɥi:r] v. intr. (24). To rustle (feuilles); to buzz (insectes); to hum (machine); to splash (mer); to plash (pluie); to murmur (ruisseau); to whisper (vent).
bruissant [-sɑ̃] part. prés. V. BRUIRE.
bruissement [-smɑ̃] m. Noise (d'une aiguille, de pick-up); rustle, rustling (des feuilles); buzz, buzzing (des insectes); hum, humming (d'une machine); murmur, murmuring (d'un ruisseau); whisper, whispering (du vent).
bruit [brɥi] m. Noise (sens général). ‖ Whir (d'ailes); roar (d'auto, de canon, de feu qui ronfle, de la mer, d'un orage); zip (de balle qui siffle, de déchirure); din (de la bataille, d'une machine assourdissante, des sirènes); snap (d'une boîte, d'un bouton-pression qu'on ferme, des dents, des doigts ou d'un fouet qui claquent); pop (d'un bouchon qui saute); crack (de branches qu'on casse, de coups de fusil, de craquements); scrunch, crunch (de broiement); boom (du canon); splash (d'une cascade); clang, clanging, clanking (de chaînes); rumble (de chariot, de tonnerre); swish (de cinglée); clangour (des cloches); clash (des cloches, des épées, des verres); clatter (de conversation, de fourchettes, de sabots, de vaisselle); swash (de corps qui tombe à l'eau); bang, crack, ping (de coups de feu); click (de couteau qu'on ferme); wash (des flots); uproar (de foule, de multitude); sizzle (de friture); patter (de grêle); rattle (de grelots, de roues); hammering (de marteau); thud (d'objet qui tombe sur un tapis, de vagues lointaines); roll (d'orgue, de tambour, de tonnerre); footfall (de pas); tramp (de pas lourds); tread (de piétinement); plop (de pierre qui tombe à l'eau); pattering (de pluie); creak (de porte qui grince); blare (de trompette); clink (de verres heurtés); sound (de voix); *faire du bruit*, to make a noise; *sans bruit*, noiselessly, silently. ‖ FIG. Turmoil (agitation, trouble); stir (éclat, émoi); disturbance (émeute, tapage); sensation (événement); noise, report, rumour, bruit, whisper (rumeur); *beaucoup de bruit pour rien*, much ado about nothing; *faire du bruit*, to create a sensation, to cause an uproar; *il fait plus de bruit que de mal*, his bark is worse than his bite; *sans bruit*, quietly.
bruitage [-ta:ʒ] m. THÉÂTR. Sound effects.
bruiter [-te] v. intr. (1). To make sound effects.
bruiteur [-tœ:r] m. THÉÂTR. Sound effects man.
brûlage [bryla:ʒ] m. Roasting (du café); singeing (des cheveux); burning (des détritus, des herbes); *faire un brûlage à qqn*, to singe s.o.'s hair.
brûlant, ante [-lɑ̃, ɑ̃:t] adj. Burning-hot (en général). ‖ Broiling (atmosphère); blazing (feu, soleil); fiery (fournaise, soleil); scorching hot (journée); burning (sable). ‖ CULIN. Steaming (ou) piping hot (café, thé); biting (goût); scalding (liquide). ‖ CHIM. Corrosive (produit). ‖ MÉD. Burning (fièvre); feverish (malade). ‖ BOT. Stinging (plante). ‖ FIG. Ardent, eager, fervent (désir, zèle); burning (désir, question); fervid (sentiment); ticklish (sujet); dangerous (terrain); *brûlant de*, impatient to, anxious to.
brûle [bryl]. V. BRÛLER. ‖ **Brûle-gueule**, m. invar. Cutty, nose-warmer. ‖ **Brûle-parfum**, m. invar. Perfume-burner (ou) brazier, cassolette. ‖ **Brûle-pourpoint (à)**, loc. Point-blank. ‖ **Brûle-tout**, m. invar. Save-all.

brûlé, ée [bryle] adj. Burnt (en général); sunburnt (teint). ‖ FIG. *Tête brûlée*, dare-devil. ‖ POP. Done for (fini); given away (trahi). ‖ LOC. *Politique de la terre brûlée*, scorched earth policy.
— m. Burnt taste (goût); smell of burning (odeur). [V. ROUSSI.]
brûler v. tr. (1). To burn (en général). ‖ To scald (par l'eau bouillante); to singe (les cheveux); to singe, to scorch (le linge). ‖ To cremate (un mort); to char (des os); *brûler vif*, to burn alive. ‖ To use, to consume (de l'électricité, du gaz). ‖ CULIN. To roast, to torrefy (du café); to bite (par les épices). ‖ AGRIC. To nip, to sear (par le gel); to parch, to blast, to shrivel (par le soleil). ‖ CHIM. To corrode (par un acide). ‖ MÉD. To sear, to cauterize (une plaie). ‖ SPORTS. To run past (un concurrent). ‖ MILIT. *Brûler une étape*, to continue non-stop. ‖ CH. DE F. *Brûler une station*, not to stop at a station, to pass a station. ‖ AUTOM. *Brûler la route*, to burn up the road; *brûler un signal*, to overrun a signal, to over-shoot the traffic lights, U. S. to run through a red light. ‖ THÉÂTR. *Brûler les planches*, to give a spirited performance. ‖ FIG. To inflame (le sang); *brûler les étapes*, to make rapid progress; *brûler la politesse à*, to take short leave of; *brûler ses vaisseaux*, to burn one's boats. ‖ POP. To nose out, to spot (qqn).
— v. intr. To burn (en général); to burn, to be burning (combustible, feu, maison). ‖ To burn, to be alight (lumière). ‖ CULIN. To burn, to get scorched (aliment); to catch (lait). ‖ MÉD. To be feverish (corps); to smart (peau irritée). ‖ FIG. *Brûler de*, to be eager (ou) impatient to; to burn with; *brûler d'amour*, to be madly in love; *brûler d'envie de*, to be dying to.
brûlerie [-lri] f. Brandy-distillery.
brûleur [-lœ:r] m. Incendiary. ‖ CULIN. Roaster (de café); burner (de réchaud).
brûloir [-lwa:r] m. Coffee-roaster.
brûlot [-lo] m. † Fire-ship. ‖ Burnt-brandy. ‖ AVIAT. Flare. ‖ FIG. Fire-brand.
brûlure [-ly:r] f. Sore, burn (par un acide); scald (par l'eau bouillante ou la vapeur); burn (par le feu). ‖ Hole (dans un tissu). ‖ AGRIC. Blight, nip (des plantes). ‖ MÉD. Heartburn (d'estomac).
brumaille [bryma:j] f. Mist.
brumaire [brymɛ:r] m. Brumaire, second month in French Republican calendar, October-November.
brumasser [-mase] v. impers. (1). To be hazy (ou) misty (ou) foggy.
brume [brym] f. Mist. ‖ NAUT. Fog; *par temps de brume*, in foggy weather; *signal de brume*, fog-horn. ‖ FIG. Mist.
brumeux, euse [-mø, ø:z] adj. Misty, hazy, foggy.
brun, une [brœ̃, yn] adj. Brown; *brun fauve*, fawn; *brun foncé*, dun, fuscous, dark-brown. ‖ Dark (cheveux); dark-haired (personne); bronzed, swarthy, sunburnt, tanned (teint). ‖ Brown (bière).
— m. Brown (couleur); dark man, U. S. brunet (homme).
brunâtre [brynɑ:tr] adj. Brownish, darkish.
brune [bry:n] f. Nightfall, dusk (crépuscule). ‖ Brunette (femme).
brunet, ette [-nɛ, ɛt] adj. Brownish.
brunette [-nɛt] f. Love-song (chanson); small brunette (jeune fille).
bruni [-ni] m. Burnished part.
— adj. Burnished (métal). ‖ Sunburnt, tanned (teint). [V. HÂLÉ.]
brunir [-ni:r] v. tr. (2). To burnish, to polish (le métal). ‖ To tan (le teint).
— v. intr. To darken, to brown.

brunissage [-nisa:ʒ] m. TECHN. Burnishing.
brunissement [-nismɑ̃] m. Darkening (des cheveux); browning (du teint).
brunisseur [-nisœ:r] m. Burnisher (ouvrier).
brunissoir [-niswa:r] m. TECHN. Burnisher, polisher (outil).
brunissure [-nisy:r] f. Burnishing (art); burnish (poli). ‖ AGRIC. Potato-rot (ou) -blight (de la pomme de terre); brown rust (de la vigne).
brushing [brœʃiŋ] m. Brush-drying; se faire faire un brushing, to have one's hair brush-dried.
brusque [brysk] adj. Sudden (attaque, changement); short, sharp (caractère); brusque, gruff, rough (matière); bluff, blunt (personne); hasty (soupçon); abrupt, brusque (ton); sharp (tournant, transition).
brusqué, ée [-ske] adj. Sudden; attaque brusquée, surprise attack.
brusquement [-skəmɑ̃] adv. Abruptly, suddenly, bluntly.
brusquer [-ske] v. tr. (1). To precipitate (les choses, un départ); to hurry (le dénouement); to handle roughly, to be blunt with (qqn).
brusquerie [-skəri] f. Brusqueness, bluntness.
brut [bryt] adj. Brute (bête). ‖ Natural, unsweetened (champagne). ‖ Lumber (bois); uncut, rough (diamant); rough, raw (matière); crude (minerai, pétrole); undressed, rough (pierre); primary (produit); unrefined, raw (sucre); à l'état brut, in the rough. ‖ Unfinished (travail). ‖ Gross (poids). ‖ FIN. Gross (bénéfice, valeur).
— m. Crude, crude oil (pétrole).
— adv. COMM., FIN. Gross. (V. NET.)
brutal, ale [brytal] adj. Savage (coup); jeu brutal, horse play. ‖ Rough, crude (façons); brute (force); brutal (instinct); brutal, rough (personne). ‖ Rude (exposé); brutal (fait); coarse, rude (langage); plain-spoken (personne); plain, brute (vérité). ‖ MÉD. Rough (remède).
— m. Brute, bully.
brutalement [-lmɑ̃] adv. Brutally, roughly (avec rudesse); bluntly (sans ménagements).
brutaliser [-lize] v. tr. (1). To brutalize; to bully.
brutalité [-lite] f. Brutality; coarseness; roughness. ‖ Savagery.
brute [bryt] f. Brute (pr. et fig.).
Bruxelles [brysɛl] f. GÉOGR. Brussels.
bruyamment [bryjamɑ̃] adv. Noisily; boisterously. ‖ Loudly; clamorously.
bruyant, ante [-jɑ̃, ɑ̃:t] adj. Loud, clamorous (applaudissements); noisy (conversation, enfant, foule); rompish (jeu); vociferous, riotous, loud-talking (personne); uproarious, rollicking (réunion); noisy, bustling (rue). ‖ Boisterous (gaieté); uproarious (rire); loud (son, voix). ‖ FIG. Resounding (succès).
bruyère [bryjɛ:r] f. BOT. Heath, heather (plante); moor, moorland (terrain); couvert de bruyère, heathy; terre de bruyère, heath-mould. ‖ ZOOL. Coq de bruyère, grouse, moorcock.
buanderie [bɥɑ̃dri] f. Wash-house, laundry-room.
buandier [-dje] m. Blcacher.
buandière [-djɛ:r] f. † Washerwoman; laundrywoman.
bubon [bybɔ̃] m. MÉD. Bubo.
bubonique [-bɔnik] adj. MÉD. Bubonic.
buccal, ale [bykkal] adj. MÉD. Buccal.
buccin [byksɛ̃] m. MUS. Trumpet. ‖ ZOOL. Trumpet-conch.
bucco-dentaire [bykodɑ̃tɛ:r] adj. Mouth and dental (hygiène); congrès bucco-dentaire, dental surgeons' congress.
bûche [by:ʃ] f. Log; bûche de Noël, Yule-log. ‖ CULIN. Swiss roll. ‖ FAM. Cropper (chute); blockhead (personne); ramasser une bûche, to have (ou) take a spill, to come a cropper.

bûcher [-ʃe] m. Wood-pile (bois); wood-shed (lieu). ‖ Pyre (funéraire); stake (supplice).
bûcher [-ʃe] v. tr. (1). To rough-hew (un' bloc de bois). ‖ FAM. To plod away at, to swot up, U. S. to bone up on.
— v. intr. FAM. To cram, to swot, U. S. to dig, to slug, to bone.
bûcheron [-ʃrɔ̃] m. Woodcutter, woodman; U. S. lumberjack, lumberman.
bûchette [-ʃɛt] f. Stick.
bûcheur [-sœ:r] m. FAM. Plodder, swot, swotter; U. S. digger, slugger; grub.
bucolique [bykɔlik] adj., f. Bucolic, pastoral.
budget [bydʒɛ] m. FIN. Budget (de l'état et des particuliers); estimates (des services armés); boucler son budget, to make ends meet.
budgétaire [-ʒetɛ:r] adj. FIN. Budgetary; année budgétaire, financial (ou) fiscal year; prévisions budgétaires, budget estimates.
budgétisation [-ʒetizasjɔ̃] f. FIN. Inclusion in the budget.
budgétiser [-ʒetize] v. tr. (1). FIN. To include in the budget.
buée [bɥe] f. Steam (d'eau bouillante); haze (d'évaporation); blur (de respiration); mist (sur une glace); reek, moisture, vapour (sur une vitre); enlever la buée de, to demist.
buffet [byfɛ] m. Kitchen dresser (de cuisine); side-board, buffet (de salle à manger). ‖ Refreshment-table, supper-table, U. S. buffet, sandwich-counter (de réception). ‖ CH. DE F. Buffet, refreshment-room (ou) stand (de gare). ‖ MUS. Casing, organ-case (d'orgue).
buffetier [byftje] m. Buffet manager.
buffle [byfl] m. ZOOL. Buffalo; peau de buffle, buffalo-hide.
bufflonne [byflɔn] f. ZOOL. Cow-buffalo.
buggy [bœge] m. V. BOGHEI.
bugle [bygl] m. MUS. Key-bugle (à clefs); saxhorn (grand bugle).
buglosse [byglɔs] f. BOT. Bugloss.
buire [bɥi:r] f. Ewer.
buis [bɥi] m. BOT. Box-tree (arbre); box-wood (bois); box (branche). ‖ ECCLÉS. Buis bénit, palm.
buisson [bɥisɔ̃] m. Bush, shrub (arbuste); thicket (fourré); hedge (haie); copse (taillis). ‖ BOT. Buisson ardent, pyracanth. ‖ ECCLÉS. Buisson ardent, burning bush.
buissonneux, euse [-sɔnø, ø:z] adj. Bushy.
buissonnier [-sɔnje] adj. ZOOL. Lapin buissonnier, thicket-rabbit; grive buissonnière, hedge-thrush. ‖ LOC. Faire l'école buissonnière, to play truant, U. S. to play hookey.
bulbe [bylb] m. BOT., MÉD., ARCHIT. Bulb.
bulbeux, euse [-bø, ø:z] adj. Bulbous. ‖ BOT. Bulbaceous; bulbed.
bulgare [bylga:r] adj., s. Bulgarian.
Bulgarie [bylgari] f. GÉOGR. Bulgaria.
bulldozer [buldɔzɛr] m. Bulldozer.
bulle [byl] f. Bull (acte, sceau). ‖ Bubble; bulle de savon, soap-bubble. ‖ MÉD. Blister. ‖ Papier bulle, Manila paper.
bulletin [byltɛ̃] m. Bulletin; gazette; report; list; bulletin d'actualités, news bulletin; bulletin officiel, official bulletin (ou) report. ‖ Bulletin; report; bulletin météorologique, de santé, weather, health report; bulletin de souscription, application form; bulletin de vote, ballot-paper, voting-paper. ‖ COMM. Bulletin de commande, order form; bulletin de dépôt, deposit receipt, certificate of delivery; bulletin d'envoi, despatch note; bulletin de vente, sale-note. ‖ FIN. Bulletin des cours, stock-market reports. ‖ CH. DE F. Bulletin de bagages, luggage-ticket, U. S. baggage check; bulletin de consigne, cloak-room ticket, U. S. check; bulletin d'expédition, waybill.
buna [byna] m. Buna.

bungalow [bɛ̃galo] m. Bungalow (habitation indienne). ‖ Chalet (à la montagne, à la mer, d'hôtel).

bunker [bunkœ:r] m. MILIT. Bunker.

buraliste [byralist] m. Clerk (poste); receiver (régie); tobacconist (tabac).
— adj. *Receveur buraliste.* V. BURALISTE.

bure [by:r] f. Frieze, homespun (étoffe). ‖ ECCLÉS. Frock (robe). ‖ FIG. Sackcloth.

bure [by:r] f. Shaft (de mine).

bureau [byro] m. Bureau; roll-top desk (américain); writing-desk (écolier); knee-hole desk (ministre); writing-table (table). ‖ Department (d'une administration); office (du directeur, des employés); committee, board (membres de la direction); *bureau de bienfaisance,* relief committee, National Assistance Board; *bureau du courrier,* message centre; *bureau de location,* box-office; *bureau de tabac,* tobacconist's, U. S. cigar store; *à bureau ouvert,* on demand, on presentation. ‖ MILIT. *Deuxième bureau,* Intelligence Department; M.I. 5, Military Intelligence, Section 5.

bureaucrate [-krat] m. Bureaucrat.

bureaucratie [-krasi] f. Bureaucracy, officialdom (fonction); red-tapism, red-tape, beadledom (péj.).

bureaucratique [-kratik] adj. Bureaucratic.

bureaucratisation [-kratizasjɔ̃] f. Bureaucratization.

bureaucratiser [-kratize] v. tr. (1). To bureaucratize.

burèle, burelle [byrɛl] f. BLAS. Barrulet.

burette [byrɛt] f. Cruet (d'église, de table); oilcan, oiler (de graissage). ‖ CHIM. Burette.

burgrave [byrgra:v] m. Burgrave.

burin [byrɛ̃] m. Chipping chisel (à couper); graver, burin (à graver).

buriné, ée [byrine] adj. Engraved (gravure); clear-cut, strongly marked (traits).

buriner v. tr. (1). ARTS. To engrave. ‖ FIG. To mark. ‖ FAM. To swot. (V. TRIMER.)

burineur [-nœ:r] m. Engraver (artiste, outil). ‖ FAM. Plodder. (V. BÛCHEUR.)

burlesque [byrlɛsk] adj., m. Burlesque.

burnous [byrnu] m. Burnous, U. S. burnoose.

bus [bys] m. Abrév. de *autobus,* bus.

busard [byza:r] m. ZOOL. Buzzard.

busc [bysk] m. Busk, whalebone (de corset); mitre-sill (d'écluse); shoulder (de fusil).

buse [by:z] f. ZOOL. Buzzard. ‖ FAM. Nitwit.

buse f. TECHN. Air-shaft (de mine); flume (de moulin); nozzle nose (de tuyère).

business [biznɛs] m. POP. Work, job (travail). ‖ Pretty kettle of fish, hell of a job (affaire compliquée). ‖ Shady job, racket (affaire louche). ‖ Thingummy, whatsit (truc).

busqué, ée [byske] adj. Aquiline, hooked (nez).

busquer v. tr. (1). To busk (un corset). ‖ To curve.

buste [byst] m. Bust (corps et statue); *en buste,* half-length; *au buste court,* short-waisted.

bustier [bystje] m. Strapless brassiere (ou) blouse.

but [byt, by] m. Mark, target, objective (cible); *but à éclipses,* disappearing target. ‖ SPORTS. Home, winning-post (aux courses); tee (au curling); goal (au football). ‖ FIG. Aim (v. DESSEIN, FIN, OBJECTIF, OBJET, PROPOS, VISÉE, VUES); *atteindre son but,* to gain (ou) attain (ou) reach one's ends; to achieve one's purpose; *dans ce but,* with this end in view; *dans le but de,* for the

purpose of; with the aim of, with a view to; *loin du but,* wide of the mark; *quel est votre but?,* what are you aiming at?, what is your object?; *sans but,* aimless, aimlessly. ‖ FIG. Point; *aller droit au but,* to go straight to the point. ‖ LOC. *De but en blanc,* point-blank, bluntly; slap-bang (fam.).

but [by]. V. BOIRE (21).

butadiène [bytadjɛ:n] n. CHIM. Butadiene.

butane [bytan] m. CHIM. Butane.

buté, ée [byte] adj. FAM. Dead set. (V. TÊTU.)

butée f. ARCHIT. Abutment. ‖ TECHN. Block stop; thrust bearing.

butène [bytɛn] m. V. BUTYLÈNE.

buter v. intr. (1). To abut (s'appuyer) [*contre,* against]; to knock (se heurter) [*contre,* against]; to stumble (trébucher) [*contre,* against, over]. — v. tr. To prop up, to buttress (un mur). ‖ POP. To bump off (tuer). — v. pr. **Se buter,** to dig one's heels in; to lean (s'appuyer) [*contre,* against]. ‖ To bump (se heurter) [*contre,* into]. ‖ FIG. To be bent (*à,* on).

buteur [bytœ:r] m. SPORTS. Goal-scorer.

butin [bytɛ̃] m. Booty, spoils, plunder, loot. ‖ FIG. Harvest.

butiner [bytine] v. tr. (1). To pilfer, to glean, to pick up; to gather. — v. intr. To plunder, to loot, to pillage. ‖ To gather honey (abeilles).

butoir [bytwa:r] m. Stop (de porte). ‖ CH. DE F. Buffer-stop. (V. HEURTOIR.) ‖ TECHN. Catch, stop. ‖ MILIT. Seating-pin.

butor [bytɔ:r] m. ZOOL. Bittern.

butor m. Lout, oaf, churl, boor.

buttage [byta:ʒ] m. AGRIC. Earthing-up; ridging.

butte [byt] f. Knoll, hillock, mound; U. S. butte, mesa. (V. MAMELON, TERTRE.) ‖ MILIT. Butts. ‖ FIG. Butt; *en butte à,* exposed to.

butter [byte] v. tr. (1). AGRIC. To earth up (les plantes); to ridge (la terre).

buttoir [-twa:r] m. AGRIC. Ridge-plough.

butyle [bytil] m. CHIM. Butyl.

butylène [-lɛ:n] m. CHIM. Butylene.

butylique [-lik] adj. CHIM. Butylic.

butyreux, euse [bytirø, ø:z] adj. Butyrous, buttery.

butyrine [-rin] f. CHIM. Butyrin.

butyrique [-rik] adj. Butyric.

butyromètre [-rɔmɛtr] m. Butyrometer.

buvable [byvabl] adj. Drinkable, potable. ‖ POP. Acceptable.

buvard [byva:r] m. Blotter (bloc); blotting-paper (papier); blotting-pad (sous-main). — adj. Blotting.

buvarder [-de] v. tr. (1). FAM. To blot.

buvée [byve] f. Drench.

buvetier [byvtje] m. Bar-keeper, publican.

buvette [-vɛt] f. Refreshment-bar (ou) -stand (de gare); pump-room, well-room (de station thermale); U. S. soda-fountain. (V. BAR.)

buveur, euse [-vœ:r, ø:z] s. Drinker; *buveur d'eau,* teetotaler, water-drinker. ‖ Bibber, tippler (ivrogne).

buvons [byvɔ̃]. V. BOIRE (21).

buvoter [-vɔte] v. tr., intr. (1). To sip.

byronien, enne [bajrɔnjɛ̃, ɛn] adj. Byronic.

Byzance [bizɑ̃:s] f. GÉOGR. Byzantium.

byzantin, ine [bizɑ̃tɛ̃, in] adj., s. Byzantine.

byzantinisme [-tinism] m. Byzantinism.

byzantiniste [-tinist], **byzantinologue** [-tinɔlɔg] s. Byzantinist.

C

c [se] m. C, c; *ressort en C*, C-spring.
ça [sa] pron. démonstr. V. CELA.
— m. PSYCH. Id.
çà [sa] adv. Hither; *çà et là*, here and there; about.
— interj. *Ah çà!*, now then!, why!
cab [kab] m. Hansom cab.
cabale [kabal] f. Cabala (science, tradition). ‖ Intrigue, cabal. ‖ Cabal, faction, junto, clique.
cabaliste [-list] m. Cabalist.
cabalistique [-listik] adj. Cabalistic.
caban [kabɑ̃] m. NAUT. Greatcoat.
cabane [kaban] f. Hut, shanty (v. CAHUTE, HUTTE); *cabane à lapins*, rabbit-hutch. ‖ NAUT. Cabin (de péniche). ‖ AVIAT. Wing pylon (ou) canopy.
cabanon [-nɔ̃] m. Hut, cabin (cabane); bungalow (maison). ‖ Dark cell (de criminels); padded cell (de fous).
cabaret [kabarɛ] m. Tavern, pot-house, pub; ale-house, wine-shop; U. S. public bar, saloon, bar-room (bistrot). ‖ Cabaret (restaurant). ‖ Liqueur service, cabaret (service).
cabaretier [-rtje] m. Publican.
cabas [kabɑ] m. Frail, basket (à fruits); shopping-basket, market-bag (de ménagère); bass (d'ouvrier).
cabêche [kabɛːʃ] f. FAM. Noddle (tête).
cabestan [kabɛstɑ̃] m. NAUT. Capstan.
cabillaud [kabijo] m. Fresh cod, codfish.
cabillot m. NAUT. Toggle pin.
cabine [kabin] f. NAUT. Cabin; *cabine de luxe*, state-room. ‖ Signal-box (d'aiguilleur); car (d'ascenseur); bathing-hut (ou) -box (de bain); cab (de grue, de locomotive); call-box, telephone kiosk (ou) booth (de téléphone). ‖ AVIAT. *Cabine étanche*, pressure cabin. ‖ CINÉM. *Cabine de projection*, projection booth.
cabinet [kabinɛ] m. Closet; small room; *cabinet d'aisance, cabinets*, water-closet, w.c., toilet; *cabinet noir*, dark room (pour photo); *cabinet particulier*, private dining-room; *cabinet de toilette*, dressing-room. ‖ Business agency (d'affaires); chambers (d'avocat, de magistrat); office (d'avoué, de notaire); surgery (de dentiste); reading-room, lending-library (de lecture); consulting-room (de médecin); room, collection (de musée); study (de travail). ‖ Clientele, connexion (clientèle en général); practice (clientèle d'architecte, d'avocat, de médecin). ‖ Cabinet (meuble); Departmental staff (entourage d'un ministre); cabinet, ministry (ministère); government (en politique étrangère); *membre du cabinet*, cabinet-minister (ou) U. S. member.
câblage [kɑblaːʒ] m. Wiring; cabling.
câble [kɑːbl] m. Cable, rope; *câble de halage, de remorque*, draw, towing line. ‖ Cable (câblogramme). ‖ NAUT., ARCHIT. Cable. ‖ ELECTR. Cable. ‖ AVIAT. *Câble d'amarrage*, mooring line.
câbler [-ble] v. tr., intr. (1). To cable.
câblerie [-bləri] f. TECHN. Cable manufacture. ‖ Cable-manufacturing plant (usine).
câblier [-blije] m. NAUT. Cable-ship.
câblogramme [-blɔgram] m. Cablegram.
cabochard, arde [kabɔʃaːr, ard] adj. Pig-headed.
caboche [kabɔʃ] f. Hob-nail (clou). ‖ FAM. Noddle. (V. CABÊCHE.)
cabochon [-ʃɔ̃] m. Stud-nail, brass-nail (clou); cabochon (pierre). ‖ FAM. Noddle.

cabosse [kabɔs] f. BOT. Cacao-pod. ‖ FAM. Bump.
cabosser [kabɔse] v. tr. (1). To dent (l'argenterie); to bash in (un chapeau); *casserole cabossée*, battered saucepan.
cabot [kabo] m. ZOOL. Bull-head. ‖ FAM. Ham actor (acteur); corporal (caporal); tyke (chien).
cabotage [kabɔtaːʒ] m. NAUT. Coasting; coastal navigation (ou) shipping; coastal trade.
caboter [-te] v. intr. (1). NAUT. To coast.
caboteur [-tœːr] m. NAUT. Coaster (bâtiment, marin); coasting-vessel (navire).
cabotin, ine [kabɔtɛ̃, in] m. THÉÂTR. Ham-actor; busker, mummer. ‖ FAM. Stagey (ou) histrionic person.
cabotinage [-tina:ʒ] m. Barn-storming (d'acteur). ‖ Quackery, histrionics (de sot). ‖ Self-advertisement (battage).
cabotiner [-tine] v. intr. (1). To busk. ‖ FAM. To play to the gallery.
caboulot [kabulo] m. FAM. Low pub, U. S. dive.
cabrer [kɑbre] v. tr. (1). AVIAT. To nose up, to hoick, to buck.
— v. pr. Se cabrer, to rear (cheval). ‖ To kick, to jib (personne) [*contre*, at]. ‖ AVIAT. To nose up.
cabri [kabri] m. FAM. Kid.
cabriole [kabrijɔl] f. Capriole.(du cheval); caper (d'une personne); *faire des cabrioles*, to cavort (cheval); to turn somersaults. (V. GAMBADE.)
cabrioler [-le] v. intr. (1). To caper about, to cut capers, to cavort.
cabriolet [kabrijɔlɛ] m. Cabriolet.
cabus [kaby] adj. Headed (chou).
caca [kaka] m. POP. Cack. ‖ *Caca d'oie*, gosling green (couleur).
cacahouète [kakauɛt] f. Peanut.
cacao [kakao] m. CULIN. Cocoa. ‖ BOT. Cacao.
cacaoté, ée [-te] adj. CULIN. Cocoa-flavoured.
cacaoyer [-je] m. BOT. Cacao-tree.
cacarder [kakarde] v. tr. (1). To cackle (oie).
cacatoès [kakatɔɛs] m. ZOOL. Cockatoo.
cacatois [kakatwa] m. NAUT. Royal; *grand, petit cacatois*, main-, fore-royal.
cachalot [kaʃalo] m. ZOOL. Sperm-whale, cachalot.
cache [kaʃ] f. Hiding-place.
— m. Mask (à photo). ‖ Cache-cache, m. Hide-and-seek. ‖ Cache-col, m. Scarf. ‖ Cache-entrée, m. Keyhole-plate. ‖ Cache-flamme, m. Flash concealer (ou) hider. ‖ Cache-nez, m. Muffler. ‖ Cache-pot, m. Flower-pot cover, jardinière. ‖ Cache-poussière, m. Dust-coat, U. S. duster (vêtement); TECHN. cover (en mécanique). ‖ Cache-sexe, m. Slip; bikini; briefs, panties. ‖ Cache-tampon, m. Hide-the-handkerchief.
cachectique [kaʃɛktik] adj. MÉD. Cachectic.
cachemire [kaʃmiːr] m. Cashmere (châle, tissu).
cacher [kaʃe] v. tr. (1). To hide (sens général). ‖ To hide, to conceal; to screen; to dissemble (celer); to bury (enfouir); to hide, to cloak, to mask, to disguise (masquer); to cover, to cloak, to mantle (recouvrir); to withhold, to keep back, to hold back, to keep in, to bottle up (taire, tenir secret); *cacher son jeu*, to hide one's cards.
— v. pr. Se cacher, to hide (sens général). ‖ To act secretly (agir en secret); to hide (ou) bury (ou) secrete oneself (se dissimuler); to skulk (s'em-

busquer); to abscond (fuir la justice); to hide (ou) conceal from oneself (se leurrer sur); to hide, to lurk (se tapir); to keep quiet (se tenir coi). || *Se cacher de*, to make a secret of (qqch.); to conceal one's actions from, to act unknown to (qqn). || Loc. *En se cachant*, secretly, on the sly; *sans se cacher*, openly, overtly.

cacher [kaʃɛːr] adj. V. KASHER.

cachet [kaʃɛ] m. Mark, stamp (marque); seal (sceau); *cachet de la poste*, post-mark. || † *Lettre de cachet*, order bearing the king's seal. || Fee (d'artiste, de professeur); *courir le cachet*, to give tuition. || MÉD. Cachet, wafer (en général); dose (d'aspirine). || FIG. Air (de distinction); stamp (du génie); character (d'une œuvre); style, chic (d'un vêtement); *qui a du cachet*, stylish.

cachetage [kaʃtaːʒ] m. Sealing.

cacheter [-te] v. tr. (8a). To seal up; *vin cacheté*, vintage wine.

cachette [kaʃɛt] f. Hiding-place; lurking-place; place of concealment; cache; *en cachette*, secretly, furtively, stealthily, sneakingly.

cachexie [kaʃɛksi] f. MÉD. Cachexy, cachexia.

cachot [kaʃo] m. Cell; prison.

cachotterie [kaʃɔtri] f. Mysterious ways; secrecy.

cachottier, ère [-tje, ɛr] adj. Secretive.
— s. Secretive person.

cachou [kaʃu] m. Cachou (bonbon); catechu (colorant).

cacique [kasik] m. Cacique (chef indien). || FAM. Bigwig; *les caciques*, the top brass. || Student who gets first place in a competitive exam.

cacochyme [kakoʃim] adj. MÉD. Cacochymic.

cacodylate [kakɔdilat] m. MÉD. Cacodylate.

cacophonie [kakɔfɔni] f. Cacophony.

cacophonique [-fɔnik] adj. Cacophonous.

cactacée [kaktase], **cactée** [kakte] f. BOT. Cactaceous plant.

cactus [kakty:s] m. BOT. Cactus.

cacuminal [kakyminal] adj. GRAMM. Cerebral.

c.-à-d. [seɑde] abrév. de *c'est-à-dire*, namely, i.e.

cadastral, ale [kadastral] adj. Cadastral; *matrice cadastrale*, land register.

cadastre [kadastr] m. Cadastre; land registry; Ordnance Survey.

cadastrer [-stre] v. tr. (1). To draw up a land survey; to register in the land-register.

cadavéreux, euse [kadaverø, øːz] adj. Cadaverous (teint).

cadavérique [-rik] adj. Cadaveric; *rigidité cadavérique*, rigor mortis.

cadavre [kadɑːvr] m. Corpse, dead body, cadaver. || Carcass, carcase (d'animal).

caddie [kadi] m. Caddie, caddy (au golf).

caddy m. Shopping cart, trolley (de supermarché).

cade [kad] m. BOT. Cade; *huile de cade*, cade oil.

cadeau [kado] m. Gift, present (v. DON); *cadeau de noces*, wedding-present; *cadeau de Noël*, Christmas-box; *faire cadeau de qqch. à qqn*, to make a present of sth. to s.o.; *j'aimerais mieux en faire cadeau*, I would rather give it away.

cadenas [kadnɑ] m. Padlock.

cadenasser [-se] v. tr. (1). To padlock (la porte). || FIG. To close (les lèvres). || FAM. *Cadenassé*, close-tongued, tight-lipped, buttoned-up.
— v. pr. **Se cadenasser.** FAM. To seal one's lips.

cadence [kadɑ̃ːs] f. Cadence. (V. RYTHME.) || Cyclic rate; gait (allure, vitesse).

cadencé, ée [-se] adj. Measured (pas); swinging (rythme); rhythmic (vers); *au pas cadencé*, in step.

cadence [kadɑ̃ːs] f. Cadence. (V. RYTHME.) || ARTS. To lead up to a cadence.

cadencer [-dɑ̃se] v. tr. (6). To balance (phrase), to make rhythmic (vers); *cadencer son pas*, to walk (ou) get in step.

cadet [kadɛ] adj. Younger; youngest; junior.
— m. Younger son (fils); younger brother (frère); youngest (dernier-né). || Junior; *mon cadet de deux ans*, my junior by two years. || MILIT. Cadet. || SPORTS. Caddie (golf). || FAM. *Le cadet de mes soucis*, the least of my worries.

cadette [kadɛt] f. Younger daughter (fille); younger sister (sœur). || Junior. || Half-butt (au billard). || Flagstone (pavage).

cadmium [kadmjɔm] m. CHIM. Cadmium.

cadogan [kadɔgɑ̃] m. V. CATOGAN.

cadrage [kadra:ʒ] m. Centring, centering.

cadran [kadrɑ̃] m. Dial (de radio, de téléphone); face (d'horloge); *cadran solaire*, sundial.

cadrat [kadra] m. Quadrat.

cadratin [-tɛ̃] f. Em-quad.

cadrature [-ty:r] f. Dial-work.

cadre [kɑːdr] m. Frame (de bicyclette, de broderie, de châssis, de porte, de ruche, de tableau); packing-case (d'emballage); set, casing (de mines); casing (de panneau); border (de sous-verre). || ELECTR. Frame aerial, coil (ou) loop antenna (de radio). || FIG. Setting (d'une action); plan, outline (d'un ouvrage); surroundings (d'une personne); *dans le cadre de ses fonctions*, within his activities. || NAUT. Cot (couchette); Navy List (officiers). || MILIT. Cadre; skeleton; nucleus; *rajeunir les cadres*, to reduce the age of retirement. || COMM. Manager, executive (dans une entreprise); *cadres dirigeants (ou) supérieurs*, top management; *cadres moyens*, middle management.

cadrer [kadre] v. intr. (1). To square, to agree, to tally, to fit in (*avec*, in). || CINÉM. To centre the film image.

cadreur [-drœːr] m. CINÉM. Cameraman.

caduc, uque [kadyk] adj. Declining (âge); ruinous, dilapidated (bâtiment); insecure, precarious, transitory (biens, richesses); shattered, frail (santé). || JUR. Null and void (accord, contrat); unclaimed, barred by limitation (dette); obsolescent (legs); lapsed (police d'assurance); statute barred (testament). || BOT. Caducous (feuille). || MÉD. *Mal caduc*, epilepsy.

caducée [kadyse] m. Caduceus, Mercury's wand.

caducité [kadysite] f. Caducity (de l'âge, des biens, de la vie); decay, ruinous state (d'un bâtiment). || JUR. Caducity, lapsing (d'un legs); nullity (d'un testament). || BOT. Caducity.

cæcal [sekal] adj. MÉD. Caecal.

cæcum [-kɔm] m. MÉD. Caecum.

cæsium [seziɔm] m. CHIM. Caesium, cesium.

cafard [kafaːr] m. ZOOL. Cockroach. || FAM. Hump; *avoir le cafard*, to be in the dumps; to have the blues; to be browned off (fam.).

cafard adj. Sanctimonious.
— m. FAM. Sneak, squealer (rapporteur); humbug, Pecksniff (tartufe).

cafardage [-da:ʒ] m. Talebearing.

cafarder [-de] v. intr. (1). To be sanctimonious. || FAM. To carry tales; to let on.

cafardeur, euse [-dœːr, øːz] s. FAM. Tell-tale, sneak.

cafardeux, euse [-dø, øːz] adj. FAM. In the dumps, cheesed (ou) browned off.

café [kafe] m. Coffee; *café au lait*, coffee with milk; *café crème, en poudre*, white, ground coffee. || Coffee-house, café (établissement). || Coffee-room (salle d'hôtel). || **Café-concert**, m. Café providing entertainments, cabaret. || **Café-filtre**, m. V. FILTRE. || **Café-théâtre**, m. Small theatre, experimental theatre, theatre workshop. || **Café-restaurant**, m. Café-restaurant.
— adj. invar. Coffee-coloured; *café-au-lait*, café-au-lait, pale brown (couleur).

caféier [kafeje] m. BOT. Coffee-tree.

caféière [-jɛ:r] f. BOT. Coffee-plantation.

caféine [-in] f. CHIM. Caffeine.

cafetan [kaftɑ̃] m. Caftan.

cafétéria [kafeterja] m. Cafeteria.

cafetier [kaftje] m. Coffee-house keeper, café-owner, U. S. saloonkeeper.

cafetière [-tjɛ:r] f. Coffee-pot. ‖ POP. Noddle.

cafouillage [kafuja:ʒ], **cafouillis** [-ji] m. FAM. Blunder (bourde) ; botch-up, bungle, muddle, shambles (gâchis).

cafouiller [-je] v. intr. (1). FAM. To blunder, to make a botch-up (personne) ; to go wrong (ou) haywire (appareil).

cafouilleux, euse [-jø, ø:z], **cafouilleur, euse** [-jœːr, ø:z] adj. Haywire, jumbled, messy.
— s. Botcher, bungler.

cafre [kɑ:fr] adj., m. Kaffir.

cage [ka:ʒ] f. Cage (d'animaux) ; hutch (à lapins) ; bird-cage (à oiseaux) ; coop (à volaille) ; *mettre en cage*, to cage. ‖ Shaft (d'ascenseur) ; well (d'escalier) ; shell (de maison) ; cage (de mines). ‖ FAM. *Cage à poules*, doll's house ; *mettre un voleur en cage*, to lock up (ou) to cage a thief.

cageot [kaʒo] m. Hamper (à fruits).

cagibi [kaʒibi] m. FAM. Lumber-room, den.

cagna [kaɲa] f. MILIT. Dug-out. ‖ FAM. Hut ; room, den.

cagneux, euse [kaɲø, ø:z] adj. Pigeon-toed (cheval) ; bent-in (jambe) ; knock-kneed (personne).

cagnotte [kaɲɔt] f. Kitty.

cagot [kago] m. Pecksniff. (V. BIGOT.)
— adj. Sanctimonious, canting.

cagoterie [kagɔtri] f. Sanctimoniousness.

cagoule [kagul] f. Cowl (de moine) ; hood (de pénitent).

cahier [kaje] m. Copy-book, exercise-book, cahier ; paper book. ‖ JUR. *Cahier des charges*, conditions of contract (marché) ; specifications (travaux) ; particulars of sale (vente). ‖ MILIT. *Cahier de punitions*, defaulters' book. ‖ MÉD. *Cahier de visites*, hospital record.

cahin-caha [kaɛ̃kaa] adv. Haltingly (en boitillant) ; so-so (couçi-couça) ; anyhow (sans méthode).

cahot [kao] m. Jolt ; bump. ‖ FIG. Ups and downs.

cahotant, ante [-ɔtɑ̃, ɑ̃:t] adj. Bumpy (chemin) ; jolting (voiture).

cahotement [-tmɑ̃] m. Jolt.

cahoter [-te] v. tr. (1). To jolt ; to jog ; to bump along. ‖ FIG. To toss about.
— v. intr. To jolt.

cahoteux, euse [-tø, ø:z] adj. Bumpy (route).

cahute [kayt] f. Hut. (V. CABANE.)

caïd [kaid] m. Kaid, North African magistrate. ‖ POP. Big boss, ring leader, big shot.

caillage [kaja:ʒ] m. Curdling, clotting.

caillasse [kajas] f. FAM. Stones, pebbles. ‖ TECHN. Shingle.

caille [ka:j] f. ZOOL. Quail.

caillé [kaje] m., **caillebotte** [kajbɔt] f. Curds ; U. S. bonnyclabber.

caillebotis [kajbɔti] m. NAUT. Gratings. ‖ MILIT. Duckboards.

caillebotter [-te] v. tr., intr. (1). To curdle.
— v. pr. Se *caillebotter*, to curdle, to clot.

caillement [kajmɑ̃] m. Curdling, clotting.

cailler [kaje] v. tr. (1). To curdle (du lait) ; to cake (du sang) ; *lait caillé*, curds.
— v. pr. Se *cailler*, to curdle (lait) ; to coagulate, to clot (sang).

caillette [-jɛt] f. CULIN. Rennet. ‖ ZOOL. Abomasum.

caillot [-jo] m. Clot (de lait, de sang).

caillou [kaju] (pl. **cailloux**) m. Pebble (pierre ordinaire [ou] précieuse) ; stone (pierre vulgaire). ‖ Flint (caillou dur) ; boulder (caillou rond) ; cobble (d'empierrement). ‖ FAM. Bald head ; *il n'a plus un poil sur le caillou*, he has lost his thatch.

cailloutage [-ta:ʒ] m. Metalling (d'une route) ; pebble-paving (du sol).

caillouter [-te] v. tr. (1). To gravel (une allée) ; to metal (une route).

caillouteux, euse [-tø, ø:z] adj. Shingly, pebbly (plage) ; flinty, stony (route).

caillloutis [-ti] m. Gravel (d'allée) ; road-metal.

caïman [kaimɑ̃] m. ZOOL. Cayman, caïman.

Caire (Le) [ləkɛ:r] m. GÉOGR. Cairo.

cairn [kɛrn] m. Cairn.

caisse [kɛ:s] f. Chest, box, case (boîte, coffre) ; crate (cageot) ; packing-case (d'emballage) ; tank (à eau) ; window-box, tub (à fleurs, à plantes) ; cistern (à huile) ; case (d'horloge, de piano) ; box (de locomotive) ; shell (de poulie). ‖ AUTOM. Body (carrosserie). ‖ MÉD. Drum (du tympan). ‖ MUS. Drum ; *grosse caisse*, bass-drummer (artiste) ; bass drum, big drum (instrument). ‖ COMM., FIN. Cash-box (coffre) ; cashier's desk, pay desk, pay office (comptoir, guichet) ; bank, office (établissement) ; funds, treasury, cash (fonds) ; fund (fonds spéciaux) ; till (tiroir) ; *caisse noire*, graft ; *les caisses de l'Etat*, the coffers of the State ; *argent en caisse*, cash in hand, money on hand (ou) in the till ; *faire sa caisse*, to make up one's cash, to balance the cash ; *filer avec la caisse*, to run off with the cash ; U. S. to skip with the kitty ; *passer à la caisse*, to be paid (paiement) ; to be paid off (renvoi) ; *tenir la caisse*, to keep the cash.

caissette [-sɛt] f. Small box (ou) case.

caissier, ère [-sje, ɛr] s. Cashier, teller (de banque) ; cash-clerk (de magasin).

caisson [-sɔ̃] m. ARCHIT. Coffer ; caisson ; panel. ‖ MILIT. Caisson ; ammunition-waggon. ‖ NAUT. Locker ; bin. ‖ AUTOM. Seat-box, boot, U. S. trunk. ‖ FAM. *Se faire sauter le caisson*, to blow one's brains out.

cajoler [kaʒɔle] v. tr. (1). To cajole ; to coax ; to wheedle ; to blarney ; U. S. to baby.

cajolerie [-lri] f. Cajolery, coaxing.

cajoleur [-lœːr] adj. Cajoling, coaxing.
— m. Cajoler, coaxer.

cajou [kaʒu] m. BOT. Cashew-nut.

cajun [kaʒœ̃] adj., s. GÉOGR. Cajun, Cajan.

cake [kɛk] m. CULIN. Fruit-cake.

cal [kal] (pl. **cals**) m. BOT., MÉD. Callus. ‖ Callosity.

calage [kala:ʒ] m. Wedging, steadying (d'un meuble) ; chocking (de roue, de tonneau) ; scotching (d'une roue). ‖ TECHN. Keying (coinçage) ; propping (étaiement) ; fixing (fixage) ; cottering (goupillage). ‖ AUTOM. Stalling (du moteur). ‖ ELECTR. Adjustment. ‖ AVIAT. Chocking.

calamar [kalama:r] m. V. CALMAR.

calamine [kalamin] f. CHIM. Calamine. ‖ TECHN. Carbon deposit (de moteur).

calaminer (se) [səkalamine] v. pr. (1). AUTOM. To carbon up, to coke up.

calamistré, ée [kalamistre] adj. Brilliantined, oiled.

calamité [kalamite] f. Calamity. (V. CATASTROPHE.) ‖ FAM. Infliction.

calamiteux, euse [-tø, ø:z] adj. Calamitous. ‖ FAM. Wretched ; rotten ; broken-down.

calandrage [kalɑ̃dra:ʒ] m. Mangling (du linge) ; calendering (du papier).

calandre [kalɑ̃:dr] f. Mangle (pour linge) ; calender (pour papier). ‖ AUTOM. Shell ; radiator grill.

calandrer [-dre] v. tr. (1). To mangle (le linge) ; to calender (le papier).

calanque [kalɑ̃:k] f. Creek.

calcaire [kalkɛ:r] adj. Calcareous ; chalky ; *eau calcaire*, hard water.
— m. Limestone.

calcanéum [kalkaneɔm] m. MÉD. Calcaneum.

calcédoine [kalsedwan] f. Chalcedony.

calcification [kalsifikasjɔ̃] f. Calcification.
calcifier [-fje] v. tr. (1). To calcify.
— v. pr. Se calcifier, to calcify.
calcination [kalsinasjɔ̃] f. Calcination; calcining.
calciner [-ne] v. tr. (1). CHIM. To calcine. ‖ To char, to calcine, to burn to a cinder. (V. BRÛLER.)
— v. pr. Se calciner, to calcine.
calcique [kalsik] adj. CHIM. Calcic.
calcite [kalsit] f. CHIM. Calcite.
calcium [kalsjɔm] m. CHIM. Calcium.
calcul [kalkyl] m. Calculus (différentiel); arithmetic (général, mental); très faible en calcul, very bad at sums (ou) arithmetic. ‖ Computation, reckoning, calculation; calcul faux, miscalculation. ‖ FIG. Calculations; selfish motives; self-interest; faux calcul, error of judgment.
calcul m. MÉD. Calculus, stone.
calculable [-labl] adj. Computable, calculable.
calculateur, trice [-latœːr, -tris] adj. MATH. Calculating.
— m. MATH. Reckoner, calculator. ‖ TECHN. Computer (électronique). ‖ FIG. Calculator.
calculatrice [-tris] f. TECHN. Calculator, pocket calculator.
calculé, ée [-le] adj. MATH. Calculated. ‖ FIG. Premeditated. (V. DÉLIBÉRÉ, INTENTIONNEL.)
calculer [-le] v. tr. (1). MATH. To reckon, to compute, to count, to calculate (compter). ‖ FIG. To plan, to concoct, to think out (une affaire); to weigh (les conséquences); to time (ses coups); to regulate (ses dépenses); to calculate (ses effets); to measure (ses efforts); to judge (son élan); to work out (les intérêts, le prix).
— v. intr. MATH. To reckon; to calculate; calculer vite, to be quick at figures. ‖ FIG. To calculate, to weigh things up (combiner). ‖ FAM. To prove parsimonious (ou) sparing.
calculeux, euse [-lø, ø:z] adj. MÉD. Calculous.
cale [kal] f. NAUT. Hold (de cargaison); yard, stocks (de construction); shipway, slipway (de lancement); cale de radoub, graving dock; cale sèche, dry dock; fond de cale, bilge; sur cale, on the slips. ‖ FIG. A fond de cale, on the rocks, on one's last legs.
cale f. Wedge (de meuble); scotch (de roue). ‖ AVIAT. Chock. ‖ TECHN. Liner (de bourrage); key (de coinçage); shim (d'épaisseur); needle (d'étai); quoin (de typographie). ‖ Cale-pied (pl. cale-pieds) m. SPORTS. Toe-clip.
calé, ée [-le] adj. Steady (d'aplomb); propped up (appuyé); jammed, stalled (bloqué). ‖ FAM. Difficult (difficile); well-to-do (fortuné); full up (rassasié). ‖ FAM. Well up (en, in).
calebasse [kalbas] f. Calabash.
calebassier [-sje] m. BOT. Calabash-tree.
calèche [kalɛʃ] f. Calash, calèche.
caleçon [kalsɔ̃] m. Drawers, pants, shorts; caleçons de bain, bathing slip, U. S. trunks.
calédonien, enne [kaledɔnjɛ̃, ɛn] adj., s. GÉOGR. Caledonian. ‖ GÉOL. Plissement calédonien, Caledonian orogeny.
calembour [kalɑ̃buːr] m. Pun.
calembredaine [kalɑ̃brədɛn] f. Nonsense; bosh.
calendes [kalɑ̃ːd] f. pl. Calends. ‖ FAM. Aux calendes grecques, when pigs fly.
calendrier [kalɑ̃drje] m. Calendar.
calepin [kalpɛ̃] m. Note-book.
caler [kale] v. intr. (1). NAUT. To draw.
caler v. tr. (1). To steady with a wedge (un meuble); to scotch, to wedge (une roue). ‖ TECHN. To stall (un moteur); to key (une poulie); to shim (un rail); to jam (une soupape); to clamp (un télescope). ‖ AVIAT. To chock (un avion).
— v. intr. To stall (moteur). ‖ POP. To back out (caner); to balk (devant, at).

— v. pr. Se caler, to stall (moteur); to get wedged (roue). ‖ To prop oneself (personne) [contre, against]. ‖ FAM. Se caler les côtes, to stoke up.
calfat [kalfa] m. Caulker.
calfatage [-taːʒ] m. Caulking.
calfater [-te] v. tr. (1). To caulk.
calfeutrage [kalføtraːʒ] m. Listing, weather-stripping (d'une fenêtre, d'une porte); stopping-up (d'une fissure).
calfeutrer [-tre] v. tr. (1). To list; to make draught-proof (ou) air-tight, to weather-strip (une fenêtre, une porte); to stop up (une fissure).
— v. pr. Se calfeutrer, to shut oneself up.
calibrage [kalibraːʒ] m. Calibrating, calibration. ‖ Grading, trimming (en photo).
calibre [-br] m. Calibre, caliber (d'une arme à feu); diameter, size (d'une balle, d'un boulet); diameter (d'une colonne); gauge (d'un écrou); former (d'une forme). ‖ Gauge (jauge, mesure); template (gabarit, modèle). ‖ FIG. Calibre, stamp.
calibrer [-bre] v. tr. (1). To gauge (un mécanisme); to trim (une photo); to calibrate (un thermomètre).
calice [kalis] m. BOT. Calyx. ‖ ECCLÉS. Chalice. ‖ MÉD. Calix. ‖ FIG. Cup of bitterness.
calicot [kaliko] m. Calico; U. S. unbleached muslin. ‖ FAM. Counter-jumper (commis).
califat [kalifa] m. Caliphate.
calife [kalif] m. Caliph.
Californie [kalifɔrni] f. GÉOGR. California.
californien [-njɛ̃] adj., s. Californian.
californium [kalifɔrnjɔm] m. CHIM. Californium.
califourchon (à) [akalifurʃɔ̃] loc. adv. Astride, astraddle; s'asseoir à califourchon sur, to bestride, to straddle.
câlin, ine [kalɛ̃, iːn] adj. Wheedling, caressing.
— m. Wheedler, coaxer.
câliner [kɑline] v. tr. (1). To wheedle, to coax; to fondle; se faire câliner, to be petted.
— v. pr. Se câliner, to coddle oneself.
— v. récipr. Se câliner, to cuddle; to fondle each other.
câlinerie [-nri] f. Wheedling, coaxing; fondling; caress.
calisson [kalisɔ̃] m. CULIN. Lozenge-shaped marzipan sweet from Aix-en-Provence.
calleux, euse [kalø, ø:z] adj. Callous, horny. ‖ BOT. Callous. ‖ Corps calleux, corpus callosum.
call-girl [kɔlgərl] f. Call-girl.
calligraphe [kalligraf] s. Calligrapher, calligraphist.
calligraphie [kalligrafi] f. Calligraphy, penmanship.
calligraphier [-fje] v. tr., intr. (1). To calligraph; to write beautifully.
callosité [kalɔsite] f. Callus, callosity.
calmant [kalmɑ̃] adj. MÉD. Sedative; anodyne; calmative; abirritant. ‖ FIG. Soothing (apaisant).
— m. MÉD. Sedative, anodyne.
calmar [kalmaːr] m. ZOOL., CULIN. Squid.
calme [kalm] m. Peace, order (ordre); peace, peacefulness (paix); calm, quiet, quietness (quiétude); calmness, composure, self-possession, coolness, placidity (sang-froid); repose, placidity (sérénité); stillness, calm (silence). ‖ NAUT. Calm; calme plat, dead calm. ‖ FIG. Calme avant l'orage, hush.
— adj. Still (air); calm (atmosphère); serene (ciel); smooth, calm, unruffled (mer). ‖ Calm, composed, cool (froid); dispassionate, self-possessed (imperturbable); sedate, sober (posé); serene, quiet (serein); flat, slack, even, uneventful (uni).
calmement [kalməmɑ̃] adv. Calmly, quietly.
calmer [kalme] v. tr. (1). To calm, to quiet (sens général). [V. APAISER.] ‖ To assuage, to allay, to

appease (l'appétit, la faim); to damp, to cool (l'ardeur); to pacify, to smooth down, to cool, to soothe, to allay, to mollify (la colère); to allay, to still (la crainte); to silence (les cris); to assuage (le désir); to allay, to smooth down (une dispute); to assuage, to allay, to soothe, to mitigate (la douleur); to still (une émeute); to pacify (un enfant, une foule); to calm, to soothe, to lay at rest (l'esprit); to sober, to quieten (l'excitation); to allay, to abate (la fièvre); to lull (l'inquiétude); to smooth down, to lull (la mer); to settle, to appease (les passions); to quench (la soif); to lull, to allay (la tempête); to still, to lull (le vent).
— v. pr. **Se calmer,** to calm (ou) to quieten down (sens général). ‖ To abate (activité, zèle); to smooth down (colère, mer); to wear off, to abate, to remit, to be soothed (douleur); to subside (excitation, tempête, tumulte, vent); to abate, to subside (fièvre, orage, peur); to cool, to quieten, down, to compose oneself (personne).

calmir [kalmi:r] v. intr. (9). NAUT. To abate, to calm down, to lull (mer); to subside, to drop, to die down (vent).

calomel [kalɔmɛl] m. MÉD. Calomel.

calomniateur, trice [kalɔmnjatœ:r, -tris] adj. Slanderous.
— m. Calumniator, slanderer, traducer.

calomnie [kalɔmni] f. Calumny; calumniation; slander; aspersion; *répandre des calomnies sur,* to cast aspersions upon. ‖ Libel (par écrit).

calomnier [-nje] v. tr., intr. (1). To calumniate, to slander, to malign.

calomnieusement [-njøzmɑ̃] adv. Slanderously.

calomnieux, euse [-njø, ø:z] adj. Calumnious, calumniatory; slanderous. ‖ Libellous (écrit).

caloricité [kalɔrisite] f. Caloricity.

calorie [kalɔri] f. PHYS. Calory, U. S. calorie; *grande, petite calorie,* major, lesser calory; U. S. large, small calorie.

calorifère [-fɛ:r] adj. Heat-conveying.
— m. Central heating apparatus (ou) installation.

calorifique [-fik] adj. Calorific.

calorifuge [-fy:ʒ] adj. Heat-insulating; fire-proof.
— m. Heat-insulator; non-conductor.

calorifugeage [fyʒa:ʒ] m. Heat-insulation.

calorifuger [-fyʒe] v. tr. (7). To insulate.

calorimètre [-mɛtr] m. PHYS. Calorimeter.

calorimétrie [-metri] f. PHYS. Calorimetry.

calorique [-rik] adj. Heating (pouvoir).
— m. Caloric, heat.

calorisation [-zasjɔ̃] f. Calorizing, calorization.

calot [kalo] m. MILIT. Forage-cap; U. S. garrison-cap.

calot m. Large marble.

calotin [kalɔtɛ̃] m. Churchy person.

calotte [kalɔt] f. Cap (de bouton); crown (de chapeau); case (de montre). ‖ ECCLÉS. Calotte, skull-cap (bonnet); parsondom (clergé); clerical party (parti). ‖ MÉD. Crown (crânienne). ‖ GÉOGR. Vault, dome (des cieux); *calotte glacière,* ice-cap. ‖ MATH. *Calotte sphérique,* portion of a sphere. ‖ FAM. Cuff. (V. GIFLE.)

calotter [-te] v. tr. (1). To cuff.

calquage [kalka:ʒ] m. Tracing. ‖ FIG. Copy.

calque [kalk] m. Tracing, transfer; U. S. counter-drawing. ‖ Tracing-paper (papier). ‖ GRAMM. Calque.

calquer [-ke] v. tr. (1). To trace (sur, from). ‖ FIG. To copy closely.

calquoir [-kwa:r] m. Tracer.

calter [kalte] v. intr., **se calter** [səkalte] v. pr. (1). To buzz off, to scram, to clear out; *se calter avec l'argent,* to do a bunk with the money.

calumet [kalymɛ] m. Calumet. ‖ FIG. Pipe (de la paix).

calvados [kalvadɔs] m. Calvados, cider-brandy.

calvaire [kalvɛ:r] m. ECCLÉS. Calvary. ‖ ARCHIT. Wayside cross. ‖ FIG. Cross.

calvinisme [kalvinism] m. Calvinism.

calviniste [-nist] adj. Calvinistic.
— s. Calvinist.

calvitie [kalvisi] f. Baldness.

camaïeu [kamajø] m. Camaieu (peinture, pierre). ‖ FIG. Trash.

camail [kama:j] m. ECCLÉS. Camail.

camarade [kamarad] s. Companion; partner; *camarade de jeu,* playmate; *bon camarade,* good pal, boon companion. ‖ MILIT. Comrade; *camarade de chambrée,* room-mate; *camarade de régiment,* army chum; *faire camarade,* to throw up one's hands.

camaraderie [-dri] f. Comradeship; camaraderie; good fellowship. ‖ Cliquism, clannishness, U. S. cliquishness (esprit de corps).

camard, arde [kama:r, ard] adj., s. V. CAMUS. ‖ FIG. *La camarde,* Death.

cambiste [kɑ̃bist] m. FIN. Cambist.

Cambodge [kɑ̃bɔdʒ] m. GÉOGR. Cambodia.

cambodgien, enne [-dʒjɛ̃, ɛn] adj., s. GÉOGR. Cambodian.

cambouis [kɑ̃bwi] m. Dirty oil, cart-grease.

cambrage [kɑ̃bra:ʒ] m. Cambering.

cambré, ée [kɑ̃bre] adj. Bow-legged (cheval); arched (pied); cambered (poutre); shapely (taille).

cambrer v. tr. (1). To arch (le pied); to camber (une poutre); *cambrer la taille,* to throw out one's chest, to brace oneself up.
— v. pr. **Se cambrer,** to camber (poutre); to throw out one's chest (personne).

cambrien [kɑ̃brjɛ̃] adj., m. GÉOL. Cambrian.

cambriolage [kɑ̃brjɔla:ʒ] m. House-breaking (le jour); burglary (la nuit).

cambrioler [-le] v. tr. (1). To break into; to burgle.

cambrioleur [-lœ:r] m. Housebreaker; burglar; cracksman; U. S. yegg (pop.).

cambrousse [kɑ̃brus] f. FAM. Country; *au fin fond de la cambrousse,* in the middle of nowhere, at the back of beyond.

cambrure [kɑ̃bry:r] f. Arch (du pied); camber (d'une poutre); curve (de la taille).

cambuse [kɑ̃by:z] f. NAUT. Store-room. ‖ Canteen (de chantier). ‖ FAM. Low pub (boui-boui); hovel (turne).

cambusier [-zje] m. NAUT. Steward. ‖ Canteen-keeper. (V. CANTINIER.)

came [kam] f. TECHN. Cam; lifter; wiper.

came f. POP. Dope, drugs, junk.

camé, ée [kame] adj. POP. Doped, drugged, on drugs.
— s. POP. Junkie, dope-fiend.

camée [kame] m. Cameo.

caméléon [kameleɔ̃] m. ZOOL. Chameleon. ‖ FIG. Chameleon; turncoat, trimmer.

camélia [kamelja] m. BOT. Camelia.

camelot [kamlo] m. Cheapjack, street-hawker. ‖ *Camelots du roi,* supporters of the royalist party.

camelote [kamlɔt] f. Trash (sens général); shoddy (marchandise); junk (rossignols); frippery (tissu). ‖ FAM. *Vendre sa camelote,* to sell one's stuff.

camembert [kamɑ̃bɛ:r] m. CULIN. Camembert.

caméra [kamera] f. Cine-camera.

cameraman [-man] m. Camera-man.

camérier [kamerje] m. Chamberlain.

camériste [-rist] f. Maid of honour. ‖ Chamber-maid (femme de chambre).

camerlingue [kamɛrlɛ̃:g] m. ECCLÉS. Cardinal camerlingo.

Cameroun [kamrun] m. GÉOGR. Cameroon.

camerounais, aise [-runɛ, ɛ:z] adj., s. GÉOGR. Cameroonian.

camion [kamjɔ̃] m. Dray; waggon (voiture). ‖ Paint-pot (de peintre). ‖ Autom. Lorry; U. S. truck; *camion automobile*, motor lorry; U. S. autotruck, motor truck. ‖ **Camion-citerne**, m. Tank waggon, petrol lorry, U. S. tank truck. ‖ **Camion-plate-forme**, m. Platform waggon, U. S. platform truck.

camionnage [kamjɔna:ʒ] m. Carriage (frais); cartage, haulage, U. S. trucking (transport).

camionner [-ne] v. tr. (1). To cart.

camionnette [-nɛt] f. Light motor-lorry, delivery van, U. S. light (ou) delivery truck; *camionnette de police*, police van.

camionneur [-nœ:r] m. Carter, carrier, carman, drayman (voiturier). ‖ Autom. Lorry-driver, U. S. truck driver.

camisole [kamizɔl] f. Camisole, loose jacket. ‖ Méd. *Camisole de force*, strait-jacket.

camomille [kamɔmi:j] f. Bot. Camomile. ‖ Méd. Camomile tea (tisane).

camouflage [kamufla:ʒ] m. Milit. Camouflage; *camouflage des lumières*, black-out; *camouflage partiel des lumières*, partial black-out, U. S. dim-out. ‖ Fig. Disguising.

camoufler [kamufle] v. tr. (1). To camouflage; *camoufler les lumières*, to black out. ‖ Fig. To disguise. (V. cacher.)

camouflet [kamuflɛ] m. Milit. Camouflet. ‖ Fam. Snub.

camp [kɑ̃] m. Faction, party (de partisans); *changer de camp*, to change sides. ‖ Milit. Camp. ‖ Sports. Camp (de campement); side (de joueurs); *camp de vacances*, holiday camp. ‖ Fam. *Ficher le camp*, to clear off, U. S. to scram.

campagnard [kɑ̃paɲa:r] m. Countryman; rustic. — adj. Rustic (manières); country (personne).

campagne [kɑ̃paɲ] f. Country residence (maison); country, fields (pays); countryside (population et région); *en pleine* (ou) *rase campagne*, in the open country; *les gens de la campagne*, country people; *la vie à la campagne*, country life. ‖ Campaign, season (époque des travaux). ‖ Campaign, drive (effort, propagande); *campagne électorale*, electoral drive, canvassing; *campagne de presse, de publicité*, press, publicity campaign; *faire campagne contre*, to campaign against; *se mettre en campagne pour*, to set to work on behalf of, to busy oneself in the interests of. ‖ Milit. Campaign; *battre la campagne*, to scout, to comb the country; *en campagne*, in the field; *entrer en campagne*, to take the field. ‖ Fig. *Battre la campagne*, to be off one's head, to rave.

campagnol [-ɲɔl] m. Zool. Vole.

campanile [kɑ̃panil] m. Archit. Campanile.

campanule [kɑ̃panyl] f. Bot. Campanula.

campé, ée [kɑ̃pe] adj. Milit. Encamped. ‖ Drawn, presented (personnage); set-up (personne); *bien campé sur ses jambes*, firmly fixed on one's legs.

campêche [kɑ̃pɛ:ʃ] m. Campeachy; *bois de campêche*, camwood.

campement [kɑ̃pmɑ̃] m. Encamping, camping (action); camp, encampment, camping ground (lieu); billeting party (personnes).

camper [kɑ̃pe] v. intr. (1). Milit. To encamp, to camp; to set up (ou) to pitch camp. ‖ Sports. To camp out. ‖ Fam. To camp.
— v. tr. Milit. To encamp, to camp (une armée). ‖ To draw, to bring out (un personnage); to fix, to set up (qqch.).
— v. pr. *Se camper*, Milit. To encamp, to camp (armée). ‖ Fam. To plant oneself (personne).

campeur [kɑ̃pœ:r] m. Sports. Camper.

camphre [kɑ̃:fr] m. Chim. Camphor.

camphrer [-fre] v. tr. (1). To camphorate.

camphrier [-frije] m. Bot. Camphor-tree.

camping [kɑ̃piŋ] m. Sports. Camping; *art du camping*, camp-craft; *faire du camping*, to go camping, to camp out.

campos [kɑ̃po] m. Fam. Holiday; day off; *avoir campos l'après-midi*, to have an afternoon off.

campus [kɑ̃pys] m. Campus.

camus [kamy] adj. Snub, pug, flat (nez); snub-nosed, pug-nosed, flat-nosed (personne).

Canaan [kanaɑ̃] m. Canaan.

Canada [kanada] m. Géogr. Canada.

canadianisme [-djanism] m. Gramm. Canadianism.

canadien, enne [-djɛ̃, ɛn] adj., s. Géogr. Canadian.

canadienne [-djɛn] f. Sheepskin jacket (vêtement). ‖ Estate car, U. S. station wagon (voiture).

canaille [kanɑ:j] f. Rabble, riff-raff (populace); scum (racaille). ‖ Scoundrel, blackguard, scab, bad lot (filou); shyster, spiv (homme d'affaires véreux); U. S. heel. [V. vaurien.]
— adj. Vulgar, coarse (air, voix); dirty, crooked, caddish (conduite).

canaillerie [-ri] f. Rascality, roguery; improbity (malhonnêteté). ‖ Caddishness (goujaterie). ‖ Dirty trick (sale tour).

canal [kanal] m. Canal (artificiel); channel (bras de mer). ‖ Géogr. *Canal de Panama, de Suez*, Panama, Suez Canal; *Canal de Mozambique*, Mozambique Channel. ‖ Techn. Conduit, pipe, tube (en général); flue (d'aérage); feeder (d'amenée); ditch (d'irrigation). ‖ Méd. Canal (alimentaire, médullaire); duct (biliaire, pancréatique, salivaire); meatus (urinaire). ‖ Fig. Medium, channel. (V. intermédiaire.)

canalisation [-lizasjɔ̃] f. Canalization (action); mains (à l'extérieur); pipes (à l'intérieur). ‖ Wiring (d'électricité); pipe-line (de pétrole).

canaliser [-lize] v. tr. (1). To make navigable (un cours d'eau); to canalize (une région, une rivière); to pipe (le pétrole). ‖ Fig. To canalize (les énergies); to restrain (la foule).

cananéen, enne [kananeɛ̃, ɛn] adj. Canaanitish, Canaanitic.
— s. Canaanite.

canapé [kanape] m. Sofa, settee; U. S. davenport. ‖ Culin. Canapé. ‖ **Canapé-lit**, m. Sofa-bed.

canard [kana:r] m. Zool. Duck; *canard mâle*, drake; *canard sauvage*, wild duck. ‖ Fam. Nag, jade (cheval); squawk (fausse note); hoax, false report (ou) news, canard (fausse nouvelle); rag (journal); lump of sugar dipped in brandy or coffee (sucre); *marcher comme un canard*, to waddle. (V. dandiner [se].)

canardeau [-do] m. Zool. Duckling.

canarder [-de] v. tr. (1). Milit. To fire at, to pepper, to snipe at.
— v. intr. Naut. To pitch. ‖ Fam. To quack.

canardière [-djɛ:r] f. Duck-pond (mare). ‖ Punt-gun (arme).

canari [kanari] m. Zool. Canary.

canasson [kanasɔ̃] m. Fam. Jade, hack, nag.

canasta [kanasta] m. Canasta (jeu).

cancan [kɑ̃kɑ̃] m. Cancan (danse). ‖ Gossip, tittle-tattle; *faire des cancans*, to tattle.

cancanage [kɑ̃kana:ʒ] m. Gossiping, tittle-tattle.

cancaner [-ne] v. intr. (1). To gossip, to tattle.

cancanier, ère [-nje, ɛr] adj. Gossipy, tale-bearing.
— s. Tattler, tale-bearer (ou) teller.

cancer [kɑ̃sɛ:r] m. Méd. Cancer; *cancer du sang*, leukaemia. ‖ Astron. Cancer.

cancéreux, euse [-rø, ø:z] adj. Méd. Cancerous.
— s. Cancer patient.

cancériforme [-rifɔrm] adj. Méd. Cancroid.

cancérigène [-riʒɛ:n] adj. Carcinogenic, cancer-producing.

cancérologie [-rɔlɔʒi] f. Méd. Cancerology.

cancérologue [-rɔlɔg] s. Méd. Cancerologist.

cancre [kɑ̃:kr] m. Dunce, dud (écolier).
cancrelat [kɑ̃krəla] m. ZOOL. Cockroach.
cancroïde [kɑ̃krɔid] m. MÉD. Cancroid.
candela [kɑ̃dela] f. PHYS. Candela.
candélabre [kɑ̃delabr] m. Candelabrum, branched candlestick.
candeur [kɑ̃dœ:r] f. Ingenuousness, guilelessness (ingénuité); innocence, naivety.
candi [kɑ̃di] adj. Candied; sucre candi, candy.
candidat [kɑ̃dida] m. Candidate, examinee (à un examen); candidate (à une fonction); applicant (à un poste); candidat à la députation, standing (ou) running for Parliament.
candidature [-ty:r] f. Candidature, U. S. candidacy; poser sa candidature à, to apply for.
candide [kɑ̃did] adj. Ingenuous, guileless (ingénu); innocent, naive.
candidement [-mɑ̃] adv. Ingenuously; innocently.
candir (se) [səkɑ̃di:r] v. pr. To candy.
cane [kan] f. ZOOL. Duck.
caner [kane] v. intr. (1). POP. To funk it, to cave in; U. S. to chicken out. (V. CALER.)
caneton [kantɔ̃] m. ZOOL. Duckling.
canette [kanɛt] f. Can (de bière); spool (de machine à coudre).
canette f. ZOOL. Female duckling, duckling.
canevas [kanvɑ] m. Canvas. || TECHN. Skeleton map (ou) triangulation. || FIG. Groundwork, outline; broder sur un canevas, to fill in a sketch.
cangue [kɑ̃:g] f. Cangue.
caniche [kaniʃ] m. ZOOL. Poodle.
caniculaire [kanikylɛ:r] adj. Canicular; les jours caniculaires, dog-days. || Sultry, stifling (chaleur).
canicule [-kyl] f. Canicule, dog-days.
canif [kanif] m. Penknife, pocket-knife.
canin, ine [kanɛ̃, in] adj. Canine (dent, espèce).
canine [kanin] f. MÉD. Canine, eyetooth.
canisse [kanis] f. V. CANNISSE.
caniveau [kanivo] m. Gutter (de rue). || TECHN. Conduit.
cannabis [kanabis] m. Cannabis, hemp, Indian hemp.
cannage [kana:ʒ] m. Cane-bottoming (action); cane-bottom (fond).
cannaie [kanɛ] f. Cane-plantation.
canne [kan] f. Cane, stick; donner des coups de canne à, to cane. || SPORTS. Canne à pêche, fishing-rod. || BOT. Canne à sucre, cane, sugar-cane. || FIG. Avaler sa canne, to stand straight.
canné, ée [kane] adj. Cane-bottomed.
cannelé, ée [kanle] adj. Grooved; fluted.
canneler v. tr. (8a). To groove; to flute; to striate; to corrugate.
cannelle [kanɛl] f. BOT. Cinnamon; canella.
cannelle f. Tap (robinet).
cannelure [kanly:r] f. Groove; corrugation. || GÉOL. Fault-fissure. || ARCHIT. Fluting.
canner [kane] v. tr. (1). To cane-bottom.
canneur [kanœ:r] m. Caner.
cannibale [kanibal] adj. Cannibalistic (coutumes); cannibal (peuplade).
— s. Cannibal. (V. ANTHROPOPHAGE.)
cannibalisme [kanibalism] m. Cannibalism.
can(n)isse [kanis] f. Rush fence.
canoë [kanɔe] m. Canoe; faire du canoë, to canoe.
canoéiste [-eist] s. Canoeist.
canon [kanɔ̃] m. MILIT. Cannon, gun; à portée de canon, within cannon range; canon court, howitzer; canon lance-torpilles, torpedo-launching tube; canon-mitrailleuse, pompom. || NAUT. Canon de marine, naval gun; canon de chasse, de retraite, bow-chaser, stern-chaser. || Barrel (d'arme à feu); à deux canons, double-barreled. || ELECTR. Canon à électrons, electron gun. || TECHN. Spout (d'arrosoir); pipe (de clé); barrel (de montre, de stylo). || Cannon bone, shank (de cheval). || Cannions (de dentelle). || Glass (de vin).
|| Canon-char, m. MILIT. Self-propelled gun.
canon m. ARTS, FIG. Canon. || ECCLÉS. Canon; droit canon, canon law.
cañon [kaɲɔ̃] m. GÉOGR. Cañon, canyon.
canonial, ale [kanɔnjal] adj. ECCLÉS. Canonical; maison canoniale, chapter house.
canonicat [-nika] m. ECCLÉS. Canonry.
canonique [-nik] adj. Canonical (âge, livre, peine); canon (droit).
canonisation [-nizasjɔ̃] f. ECCLÉS. Canonization.
canoniser [-nize] v. tr. (1). ECCLÉS. To canonize.
canoniste [-nist] m. ECCLÉS. Canonist.
canonnade [kanɔnad] f. MILIT. Cannonade.
canonnage [-na:ʒ] m. MILIT. Gunnery.
canonner [-ne] v. tr. (1). MILIT. To cannonade, to shell, to batter.
canonnier [-nje] m. MILIT. Gunner.
canonnière [-njɛ:r] f. NAUT. Gunboat. || Pop-gun (d'enfant).
Canossa [kanɔsa] m. GÉOGR. Canossa. || LOC. Aller à Canossa, to eat humble pie.
canot [kano] m. Boat; cutter, dinghy; barge (de l'amiral); pinnace (grand canot); gig, jolly-boat (petit canot); canot automobile, motor boat; canot à voile, sailing-boat; canot pneumatique, inflatable dinghy; canot de sauvetage, lifeboat; faire une partie de canot, to go boating. || Canot-cible, m. NAUT. Target-boat.
canotage [kanɔta:ʒ] m. Boating; rowing (à l'aviron); sailing (à la voile); partie de canotage, row.
canoter [-te] v. intr. (1). To boat; to row (à la rame); to sail (à la voile).
canotier [-nɔtje] m. Boater, straw-hat (chapeau). || NAUT. Rower, oarsman.
cantaloup [kɑ̃talu] m. BOT. Cantaloup.
cantate [kɑ̃tat] f. MUS. Cantata.
cantatrice [kɑ̃tatris] f. MUS. Cantatrice.
cantharide [kɑ̃tarid] f. ZOOL. Cantharis.
cantilène [kɑ̃tilɛ:n] f. Cantilena.
cantine [kɑ̃tin] f. MILIT. Uniform (ou) equipment-case (malle); canteen (restaurant); cantine tractée, U. S. chow wagon. || School-canteen, lunch-room (à l'école).
cantinier, ère [-nje, ɛ:r] s. MILIT. Canteen-keeper; sutler.
cantique [kɑ̃tik] m. ECCLÉS. Canticle; Cantique des Cantiques, Song of Solomon, Song of Songs.
canton [kɑ̃tɔ̃] m. Canton, district, U. S. township (d'arrondissement); section (de forêt, de route). || CH. DE F. Section, block. || GÉOGR. Canton (en Suisse). || BLAS. Canton.
cantonade [kɑ̃tɔnad] f. THÉÂTR. Wings; à la cantonade, off the stage; off, off-stage.
cantonais [kɑ̃tɔnɛ] m. GRAMM. Cantonese (langue).
cantonal [kɑ̃tɔnal] adj. Cantonal.
cantonnement [-nmɑ̃] m. MILIT. Cantonment; billeting; quartering (action); cantonment, billets, quarters (locaux); répartir le cantonnement, to allot billets. || Area; section; delimitation of boundaries. || Confinement; confining (isolement). || CH. DE F. Block-section.
cantonner [-ne] v. tr. (1). MILIT. To billet, to quarter, to canton. || To confine, to isolate (isoler); to entrench (renfermer). || JUR. To pay into court, to earmark (une somme).
. — v. intr. MILIT. To be billeted (ou) quartered (ou) stationed; to canton.
— v. pr. Se cantonner, MILIT. To canton. || FIG. To isolate oneself; to withdraw; se cantonner dans, to confine oneself to, to keep within, to immure oneself in.
cantonnier [kɑ̃tɔnje] m. Roadman, roadmender.
cantonnière [kɑ̃tɔnjɛ:r] f. Valance.

canulant, ante [kanylã, ã:t] adj. Pop. Boring.
canular [-la:r] m. Fam. Canard, hoax, leg-pull.
canularesque [-laresk] adj. Farcical.
canule [kanyl] f. Méd. Nozzle, cannula. ‖ Pop. Nuisance.
canuler [-le] v. tr. (1). Pop. To plague.
canut, use [kany, y:z] s. Silk-worker.
canyon [kaɲɔ̃] m. V. cañon.

caoutchouc [kautʃu] m. India rubber, rubber, elastic gum; *caoutchouc durci*, hard rubber, vulcanite; *caoutchouc mousse*, sponge-rubber (pour balles); foam-rubber (pour coussins); *caoutchouc synthétique*, synthetic rubber, buna. ‖ Rubber band (anneau); elastic (élastique); rubber (rondelle). ‖ Rain-coat, waterproof (vêtement). ‖ Pl. Rubber overshoes, galoshes, U. S. rubbers (chaussures). ‖ Fin. Rubber-shares (en Bourse).
caoutchouter [-te] v. tr. (1). To rubberize.
caoutchouteux, euse [-tø, ø:z] adj. Rubbery.

cap [kap] m. Géogr. Cape; foreland; headland; *le cap Horn*, Cape Horn; *doubler un cap*, to round a cape. ‖ Naut. Head; heading; *cap au vent*, head on to the wind; *changement de cap*, change of direction; *franchir un cap*, to weather a cape; *mettre le cap sur*, to head for, to steer for. ‖ Aviat. Course; *conservateur de cap*, directional gyro. ‖ Loc. *Avoir doublé le cap de la cinquantaine*, to be on the wrong (ou) shady side of fifty; *de pied en cap*, from head to foot, cap-à-pie.
C. A. P. [seape] m. Abrév. de *Certificat d'aptitude professionnelle*, technical diploma taken by apprentices. ‖ Abrév. de *Certificat d'aptitude pédagogique*, diploma for teaching in primary schools.
capable [kapabl] adj. Capable, able, competent, efficient (v. apte, qualifié); *capable de*, able to, capable of, fitted for (compétent pour, susceptible de); fit to (propre à); liable to (sujet à); *ce deuil est capable de la tuer*, this bereavement is enough to kill her; *être capable de tout*, to be capable of sticking at nothing. ‖ Géom. Containing. ‖ Jur. Legally competent; *rendre capable de*, to enable.
capacité [kapasite] f. Ability, faculty, power (possibilité); *capacité d'attaque*, power of attack; *capacité de marche*, mobility; *capacité manœuvrière*, manœuvrability. ‖ Capacity, capaciousness (contenance, mesure); scope (étendue, portée); *capacité de charge*, load capacity; *la capacité de l'esprit*, the scope of the intellect. ‖ Radio. Condenser. ‖ Électr. *Capacité électrostatique*, capacitance. ‖ Naut. Tonnage (de chargement); burden, carrying capacity (du vaisseau). ‖ Jur. Capacity; legal competency; *priver de capacité*, to incapacitate; *capacité en droit*, lower legal diploma. ‖ Inform. Storage capacity, capacity (d'une mémoire). ‖ Fig. Ability, capability (v. compétence). ‖ Pl. Abilities, capabilities, talents.
caparaçon [kaparasɔ̃] m. Caparison, trappings.
caparaçonner [kaparasɔne] v. tr. (1). To caparison.
cape [kap] f. Cloak, cape; *de cape et d'épée*, cloak and dagger (roman); *rire sous cape*, to laugh in (ou) up one's sleeve. ‖ Coke, bowler hat, U. S. derby (chapeau). ‖ Naut. *Être à la cape*, to be hove to; *mettre à la cape*, to heave to.
capelage [kapla:ʒ] n. Naut. Rigging.
capeler [kaple] v. tr. (8a). To rig.
capeline [kaplin] f. Broad-brimmed sun-hat.
C. A. P. E. S. [kapɛs] m. Abrév. de *Certificat d'aptitude pédagogique à l'enseignement secondaire*, postgraduate diploma for teaching in secondary schools.
capésien, enne [-pezjɛ̃, ɛn] s. Holder of C. A. P. E. S.
capharnaüm [kafarnaɔm] m. Lumber-room.
cap-hornier [kapɔrnje] m. Naut. Cape-horner.

capillaire [kapillɛ:r] adj. Méd. Capillary.
— m. Méd. Capillary. ‖ Bot. Maidenhair; adiantum.
capillarité [kapillarite] f. Capillarity.
capilliculteur [kapillikyltœ:r] m. Hair-stylist, coiffeur.
capilotade (en) [kapilɔtad] Loc. Crushed to a jelly (ou) to a pulp, smashed to smithereens.
capitaine [kapitɛn] m. Milit. Captain. ‖ Naut. Master mariner, deep-sea captain, captain of ocean-going merchantman (ou) ship (au long cours); lieutenant-commander (de corvette); commander (de frégate); harbour-master (de port); captain (de vaisseau); skipper, master (d'un vaisseau marchand). ‖ Sports. Captain, skipper. ‖ Fig. Chief, captain, leader.
capital, ale [kapital] adj. Capital, outstanding (dominant); capital, essential, fundamental (essentiel); chief, major (primordial); principal, main (principal). ‖ Jur. Capital; *peine capitale*, capital punishment, death penalty. ‖ Ecclés. Deadly (péché).
— m. Fin. Capital, funds, stocks; *capital social*, assets, joint stock; *se procurer des capitaux*, to raise money; *manque de capitaux*, lack of capital (ou) finance; *capitaux flottants*, floating assets (ou) capital.
capitale [kapita:l] f. Capital (lettre). ‖ Capital; *la capitale de la France*, the French capital.
capitalisable [kapitalizabl] adj. Fin. Which can be capitalized.
capitalisation [kapitalizasjɔ̃] f. Fin. Capitalization.
capitaliser [-ze] v. tr. (1). Fin. To capitalize.
— v. intr. To save.
capitalisme [-lism] m. Fin. Capitalism.
capitaliste [-list] m. Fin. Capitalist.
— adj. Capitalistic.
capitation [kapitasjɔ̃] f. Jur. Capitation, head-money.
capiteux, euse [kapitø, ø:z] adj. Sensuous (beauté); exciting, sexy (femme); heady (vin).
Capitole [kapitɔl] m. Capitol.
capiton [kapitɔ̃] m. Padding, wadding.
capitonnage [kapitɔna:ʒ] m. Upholstering (action); upholstery (rembourrage).
capitonner [-ne] v. tr. (1). To upholster, to pad.
capitulaire [kapitylɛ:r] adj. Ecclés. Capitular.
— m. Jur. Capitulary.
capitulard, arde [kapityla:r, ard] adj. Defeatist, faint-hearted.
— s. Defeatist, faint-heart.
capitulation [kapitylasjɔ̃] f. Capitulation, surrender. (V. reddition.) ‖ Fig. Abandonment; yielding.
capituler [-le] v. intr. (1). Milit. To capitulate, to surrender. ‖ Fig. To yield.
capoc [kapɔk] m. Kapok.
capon, onne [kapɔ̃, ɔn] adj. Cowardly, chicken-hearted, white-livered, U. S. yellow.
— m. Coward, dastard. (V. poltron.)
caporal [kapɔral] m. Milit. Corporal; *caporal d'ordinaire*, mess corporal. ‖ Comm. Caporal (tabac). ‖ **Caporal-chef**, m. Milit. Senior corporal in the French army.
caporaliser [-lize] v. tr. (1). To Prussianize.
caporalisme [-lism] m. Militarism.
capot [kapo] m. Autom. Bonnet, U. S. hood. ‖ Techn. Cap (d'essieu). ‖ Naut. Cover (de canon); cowl (de cheminée); companion-way (de cotre); conning tower (de sous-marin). ‖ Aviat. Cowl, cowling.
capot m. Capot (jeu).
— adj. *Être capot*, to have lost all the tricks; *faire capot*, to take all the tricks. ‖ Fig. Abashed.
capotage [kapɔta:ʒ] m. Naut. Capsizing. ‖

Aviat. Somersault, overturn. ‖ Autom. Upset, overturn, overturning (retournement).

capote [kapɔt] f. Capote (manteau). ‖ Autom. Hood, U. S. top. ‖ Milit. Greatcoat, overcoat. ‖ Naut. Watch-coat. ‖ Pop. *Capote anglaise,* French letter.

capoter [-te] v. intr. (1). Naut. To capsize, to turn turtle. ‖ Aviat. To turn a somersault. ‖ Autom. To upset, to turn over, to overturn. — v. tr. To hood (une voiture).

câpre [kɑ:pr] f. Bot. Caper.

capricant, ante [kaprikɑ̃, ɑ̃:t] adj. Leaping, jerky (allure). ‖ Méd. Caprisant (pouls).

caprice [kapris] m. Caprice, whim, fancy (d'enfant); vagary (de la mode); fancy, caprice (de personne amoureuse); caprice, capriciousness, wantonness, impulse (de personne inconstante); freak (du sort); *par caprice,* on impulse.

capricieux, euse [-sjø, ø:z] adj. Capricious, changeful, wayward, irregular, uncertain (chose, humeur). ‖ Capricious, fanciful, freakish, moody, whimsical (fantaisiste); capricious, flighty, skittish (inconstant).

capricieusement [-sjøzmɑ̃] adv. Capriciously; whimsically.

Capricorne [kaprikɔrn] m. Capricorn.

câprier [kɑprije] m. Bot. Caper-bush.

caprin, ine [kaprɛ̃, in] adj. Zool. Caprine. ‖ Fam. Goat-like. — m. Zool. Caprid.

capsulage [kapsyla:ʒ] m. Capsuling, capping.

capsulaire [-lɛ:r] adj. Capsular.

capsule [kapsyl] f. Capsule, cap, seal (de bouteille). ‖ Méd., Bot., Chim. Capsule. ‖ Milit. Capsule; primer. ‖ Astronaut. *Capsule spatiale,* space capsule.

capsuler [-le] v. tr. (1). To capsule, to cap.

captage [kapta:ʒ] m. Harnessing, tapping, piping, water-catchment (d'eau, de source). ‖ Electr. Picking-up (de courant).

captateur, trice [kaptatœ:r, tris] s. Jur. Inveigler; *captateur de successions,* legacy-hunter.

captation [-sjɔ̃] f. Jur. Captation, inveiglement; *captation d'héritage,* legacy-hunting. (V. captage.)

captatoire [-twa:r] adj. Jur. Inveigling; legacy-securing.

capter [kapte] v. tr. (1). Techn. To recover (des déchets de fabrication); to collect, to canalize, to catch, to drain off (l'eau, une source). ‖ Electr. To tap (le courant). ‖ Radio. To intercept (une conversation, un message); to tune in to (les ondes); to pick up (un poste). ‖ Jur. To obtain by undue influence. ‖ Fig. To win by insidious means; to rivet (l'attention); to capture (la confiance); to capture, to nobble (des suffrages).

capteur [kaptœ:r] m. Techn. Sensor, detector.

captieux, euse [kapsjø, ø:z] adj. Captious.

captif, ive [kaptif, iv] adj., s. Captive.

captivant, ante [-tivɑ̃, ɑ̃:t] adj. Bewitching, winsome (femme); absorbing, fascinating (lecture); charming, winning (manières, physionomie, sourire); captivating.

captiver [-tive] v. tr. (1). To absorb, to fascinate; to captivate, to bewitch; to enthrall.

captivité [-tivite] f. Captivity, bondage. ‖ Confinement (emprisonnement). ‖ Fig. Subjection.

capture [kapty:r] f. Arrest (arrestation). ‖ Naut. Capture (prise).

capturer [kaptyre] v. tr. (1). To seize, to arrest. ‖ Milit., Naut. To capture.

capuce [kapys] m. Ecclés. Capuche.

capuche [kapyʃ] f. Ecclés. Capuchin; hood.

capuchon [-ʃɔ̃] m. Cowl, hood (de cheminée); hood (d'imperméable); cap (de stylo). ‖ Ecclés. Hood, cowl. ‖ Zool., Bot. Hood.

capucin [-sɛ̃] m. Ecclés. Capuchin. ‖ Fam. Hare.

capucin m. Zool. Capuchin monkey, capuchin.

capucine [-sin] f. Bot. Nasturtium. ‖ Milit. Band.

capulet [-lɛ] m. Woman's hood.

caque [kak] f. Keg, herring-barrel.

caquelon [kaklɔ̃] m. Culin. Earthenware (ou) cast iron pot.

caquet [kakɛ] m. Chatter (de pie); cackle (de poule). ‖ Fam. Chatter, gossip; *rabattre le caquet à qqn,* to take s.o. down a peg, to make s.o. sing small.

caquetage [kakta:ʒ] m. Chattering (de pie); cackling, cackle (de poule). ‖ Fam. Tittle-tattle, chitter-chatter.

caqueter [-te] v. intr. (8a). To chatter (pie); to cackle (poule). ‖ To clack (moulin). ‖ To babble, to prattle, to chatter, to jaw (personne).

caqueteur [-tœ:r] m. Gossip, tattler.

car [ka:r] conj. For, because. — m. invar. Reason why; *accumuler les mais, les si et les car,* to beat about the bush.

car m. Motor-coach, motor charabanc; U. S. bus, stagecoach; *car de luxe,* motor saloon coach; *car de police,* police van; *car de radio-reportage,* outside broadcasting van; *car sonore,* talkie-van.

carabe [karab] m. Zool. Carabus.

carabin [karabɛ̃] m. Fam. Medical student.

carabine [karabin] f. Milit. Carbine.

carabiné, ée [-ne] adj. Stiff (histoire, note); raging (fièvre); violent, heavy (rhume).

carabinier [-nje] m. Milit. Carabineer. ‖ Jur. Custom-house officer (en Espagne); constable (en Italie).

caraco [karako] m. Camisole; jacket.

caracole [karakɔl] f. Caracole.

caracoler [-le] v. intr. (1). To caracole, to prance (cheval); to caper about (enfant); to galumph (personne).

caractère [karaktɛ:r] m. Characteristic, feature (caractéristique); *caractère accidentel, arbitraire,* accidentality, arbitrariness; *caractères acquis,* negative eugenics; ‖ Character, fortitude, firmness, moral strength (fermeté); *avoir du caractère,* to have character (ou) backbone; *sans caractère,* spiritless, weak-hearted; ‖ Character, complexion, nature (genre, nature); *caractère de gravité,* alarming nature, serious complexion; *caractère officiel,* official nature. ‖ Temper, nature, disposition, composition (humeur, tempérament); *avoir bon (ou) mauvais caractère,* to have a good (ou) bad temper, to be good- (ou) bad-tempered; *d'un caractère facile,* easy-going; *d'un caractère jaloux,* of a jealous disposition; *un caractère mal fait,* a warped (ou) twisted nature. ‖ Character, expression; individuality, personality; originality (originalité); *comédie, danse de caractère,* character comedy, dance; *un caractère,* a case (un original). ‖ Capacity, authority, character (qualité, titre); *avoir caractère pour,* to be entitled to. ‖ Math. Symbol. ‖ Techn. Character (v. lettre); type (d'imprimerie; *petit caractère,* small print; *écrivez en caractères d'imprimerie, s.v.p.,* please use block letters, U. S. please print. ‖ Méd. Pl. Eugenics.

caractériel, elle [-rjɛl] adj. Temperamental. — s. Méd. Psychopath.

caractérisation [-rizasjɔ̃] f. Characterization.

caractérisé, ée [-rize] adj. Marked, determined.

caractériser [-rize] v. tr. (1). To characterize; to particularize; to mark; to be characteristic of. — v. pr. Se **caractériser,** to be characterized (ou) distinguished (*par,* by).

caractéristique [-ristik] adj. Characteristic, distinctive, typical, specific. — f. Characteristic.

caracul [karakyl] m. Caracul.

carafe [karaf] f. Water-bottle, carafe (à eau);

decanter (à vin). ‖ Fam. *Rester en carafe*, to be left in the lurch; to be stuck.
carafon [-fɔ̃] m. Small decanter.
caraïbe [karaib] adj. Caribbean.
— s. Carib, Caribbee; *mer des Caraïbes*, Caribbean Sea.
carambolage [karɑ̃bɔla:z] m. Cannon (au billard). ‖ Fam. Collision.
caramboler [-le] v. intr. (1). To cannon; U. S. to carom, to make a carom shot.
— v. tr. Fam. To run into, to collide with.
carambouillage [karɑ̃buja:ʒ] m. Jur. Fraudulent sale for cash of goods bought on credit.
carambouilleur [-jœ:r] m. Jur. Swindler who buys on credit and sells for cash.
caramel [karamɛl] m. Caramel; butter-scotch, toffee, U. S. taffy; stick-jaw (fam.) [bonbon]. ‖ Culin. Caramel, burnt-sugar.
caramélisation [-melizasjɔ̃] f. Culin. Caramelization.
caraméliser [-melize] v. tr., intr. (1). To caramelize. ‖ Culin. To colour with caramel; *crème caramélisée*, caramel custard.
carapace [karapas] f. Carapace, shell.
carapater (se) [sakarapate] v. pr. (1). Pop. To clear off, to split, to do a bunk.
carat [kara] m. Carat.
caravane [karavan] f. Caravan; U. S. trailer; *voyageur en caravane*, caravanner, caravanist. ‖ Conducted tour (ou) party (de touristes).
caravanier [-nje] m. Caravaneer.
caravaning [-niŋ] m. Caravanning, caravan holidays; *faire du caravaning*, to go on a caravan holiday.
caravansérail [karavɑ̃sera:j] m. Caravanserai.
caravelle [karavɛl] f. Naut. Caravel, carvel.
carbochimie [karboʃimi] f. Chim. Chemistry of coal derivatives.
carbonade [karbɔnad] f. Culin. Carbonade.
carbonate [karbɔnat] m. Chim. Carbonate; *carbonate de soude*, sodium carbonate, washing soda.
carbone [karbɔn] m. Chim. Carbon. ‖ Comm. Carbon paper (papier).
carboné, ée [-ne] adj. Chim. Carbonaceous, carburetted.
carbonifère [-nifɛ:r] adj. Chim., Géol. Carboniferous.
— m. Géol. Carboniferous.
carbonique [-nik] adj. Chim. Carbonic; *acide carbonique*, carbonic acid, carbon dioxide; *neige carbonique*, carbon dioxide snow.
carbonisation [-nizasjɔ̃] f. Carbonization.
carboniser [-nize] v. tr. (1). Chim. To carbonize. ‖ Fam. To char. (V. brûler.)
carbonnade [karbɔnad] f. V. carbonade.
carbonyle [-nil] m. Chim. Carbonyl.
Carborundum [-rœ̃dɔm] m. Chim. Carborundum.
carboxyle [karbɔksil] m. Chim. Carboxyl.
carburant [karbyrɑ̃] m. Autom. Motor-fuel.
— adj. Techn. *Mélange carburant*, air-petrol mixture, mixture.
carburateur [-ratœ:r] m. Carburettor, U. S. carburetor.
carburation [-rasjɔ̃] f. Chim. Carburetting. ‖ Techn. Carburization. ‖ Autom. Vaporization; internal combustion.
carbure [karby:r] m. Chim. Carbide.
carburé, ée [-re] adj. Chim. Carbonaceous, carburetted.
carburer [-re] v. tr. (1). Chim. To carburet. ‖ Techn. To carburize. ‖ Autom. To vaporize. ‖ Fam. To go strong; to fag.
carcailler [karkaje] v. intr. (1). To call (caille).
carcajou [karkaʒu] m. Zool. Carcajou, wolverine.
carcan [karkɑ̃] m. Iron collar, carcan. ‖ Pop. Jade (cheval); gawk (femme).

carcasse [karkas] f. Carcass, carcase (d'animal); shape (de chapeau); framework (de parapluie). ‖ Archit. Shell, skeleton (de maison). ‖ Techn. Carcase (de moteur). ‖ Naut. Carcase, hulk (de navire). ‖ Autom. Casing (de pneu). ‖ Fam. Carcass (d'homme).
carcéral, ale [karseral] adj. Prison, jail.
carcinogène [karsinɔʒen] adj. V. cancérigène.
carcinologie [-lɔʒi] f. V. cancérologie.
carcinome [karsino:m] m. Méd. Carcinoma.
cardage [karda:ʒ] m. Carding.
cardan [kardɑ̃] m. Autom. Universal (ou) cardan joint.
carde [kard] f. Techn. Card; teasel. ‖ Bot. Chard.
carder [-de] v. tr. (1). Techn. To teasel (le drap); to card (la laine); to comb out (un matelas).
cardeur [-dœ:r] s. Carder.
cardeuse [-dø:z] f. Techn. Carder, carding-machine.
cardia [kardja] m. Méd. Cardia.
cardialgie [-djalʒi] f. Méd. Cardialgia.
cardiaque [-djak] adj. Méd. Cardiac; *crise cardiaque*, heart attack; *remède cardiaque*, cardiac.
— s. Méd. Heart-patient; heart-case.
cardigan [kardigɑ̃] m. Cardigan.
cardinal, ale [kardinal] adj., m. Math., Zool., Ecclés. Cardinal.
cardinalat [-la] m. Ecclés. Cardinalate, cardinalship.
cardinalice [-lis] adj. Ecclés. Of a cardinal; *pourpre cardinalice*, cardinalate purple.
cardiogramme [kardiɔgram] m. Méd. Cardiogram.
cardiographe [-graf] m. Méd. Cardiograph.
cardiographie [-grafi] f. Méd. Cardiography.
cardiologie [-lɔʒi] f. Méd. Cardiology.
cardiologue [-lɔg] s. Méd. Cardiologist.
cardio-vasculaire [kardjovaskylɛ:r] adj. Méd. Cardio-vascular.
cardite [kardit] f. Méd. Carditis.
cardon [kardɔ̃] m. Bot. Cardoon.
carême [karɛ:m] m. Ecclés. Lent (période): lenten sermons (sermons). ‖ Loc. *Face de carême*, gloomy face; *comme mars en carême*, unfailingly. ‖ **Carême-prenant**, m. Shrovetide reveller (masque); Shrovetide (temps).
carénage [karena:ʒ] m. Naut. Careenage. ‖ Aviat. Fairing (d'atterrisseur, de roue); covering (de fuselage).
carence [karɑ̃:s] f. Defaulting; slackness; avoiding of responsibilities; *la carence des pouvoirs publics*, the inefficiency (ou) indifference of public authorities. ‖ Jur. Non-existence of assets; *procès-verbal de carence*, report of insolvency. ‖ Méd. Deficiency; *maladie par carence*, deficiency disease.
carène [karɛn] f. Naut. Hull, bottom. ‖ Aviat. Body, hull.
caréner [-rene] v. tr. (5). Naut. To careen. ‖ Aviat. To streamline.
caressant, ante [karɛsɑ̃, ɑ̃:t] adj. Caressing, affectionate (enfant); tender, wheedling (geste, parole, voix); soft (vent).
caresse [-rɛs] f. Caress, endearment (d'enfant); light touch (du vent). ‖ Pat, stroke (à un animal). ‖ Pl. Love-making, U. S. petting, necking (d'amoureux); cajolery (de flatteur).
caresser [-rɛse] v. tr. (1). To stroke, to pat (un animal); to fondle, to play with (les cheveux); to caress, to wheedle, to fondle, to dandle (un enfant); to caress, to cuddle (un être aimé); to kiss (les feuilles, le rivage). ‖ Fig. To cherish, to indulge (un espoir); to dally with (une idée). ‖ Fam. To cajole, to fawn upon (flatter).

cargaison [kargɛzɔ̃] f. NAUT. Cargo, freight; lading. ‖ Shipload.

cargo [kargo] m. NAUT. Cargo-boat; tramp; freighter; *cargo mixte,* mixed cargo and passenger vessel.

cargue [karg] f. NAUT. Brail.

carguer [-ge] v. tr. (1). To take in, to clew (ou) brail up.

cari, cary [kari] m. CULIN. Curry.

cariatide [karjatid] f. ARCHIT. Caryatid.

caribou [karibu] m. ZOOL. Caribou.

caricatural, ale [karikatyral] adj. Caricatural.

caricature [-ty:r] f. Caricature, cartoon (dessin). ‖ FIG. Caricature, parody, travesty. ‖ FAM. Fright, figure of fun (personne).

caricaturer [-tyre] v. tr. (1). To caricature, to take off.

caricaturiste [-tyrist] m. Caricaturist, cartoonist.

carie [kari] f. MÉD. Decay, caries (des dents); caries (des os). ‖ BOT. Blight (des arbres); rot (du bois); bunt, smut (du froment).

carier [-rje] v. tr. (1). MÉD. To decay. ‖ BOT. To rot (un arbre); to smut (du froment).
— v. pr. **Se carier,** to decay (dent). ‖ BOT. To rot (arbre); to smut (froment).

carillon [karijɔ̃] m. Carillon; chimes, peal (cloches, sonnerie); bob (sonnerie). ‖ Chiming-clock (pendule).

carillonnement [-jɔnmɑ̃] m. Chiming; jingling.

carillonner [-jɔne] v. tr. (1). To chime out (un air); to chime (les cloches, l'heure); to ring for (une fête); *fête carillonnée,* High (ou) Grand Feast-day.
— v. intr. To carillon; to chime the bells, to ring the changes (carillonneur); to chime, to jingle (cloches).

carillonneur [-jɔnœ:r] m. Bell-ringer, carillonneur, carillon player, change-ringer.

carlin [karlɛ̃] m. ZOOL. Pug, pug-dog.

carlingue [karlɛ̃:g] f. NAUT. Keelson. ‖ AVIAT. Cockpit, cabin.

carliste [karlist] adj., s. Carlist.

carmagnole [karmaɲɔl] f. Carmagnole.

carme [karm] m. ECCLÉS. Carmelite; white friar.

carmélite [karmelit] f. ECCLÉS. Carmelite.

carmin [karmɛ̃] adj., m. Carmine.

carminé, ée [karmine] adj. Carmine, purplish-red, crimson.

carminer v. tr. (1). To dye with carmine.

carnage [karna:ʒ] m. Slaughter, carnage (v. MASSACRE). ‖ Raw meat (pâture).

carnassier, ère [karnasje, ɛr] adj. Carnivorous (animal); meat-eating (personne).
— m. Carnivore. ‖ ZOOL. Pl. Carnivora.

carnassière [-sjɛ:r] f. Game-bag.

carnation [-sjɔ̃] f. Complexion (v. TEINT). ‖ ARTS. Pl. Flesh tints.

carnaval [-val] m. Shrove Tuesday (mardi gras); Carnival, Shrovetide (jours gras). ‖ King Carnival (mannequin). ‖ FAM. Scarecrow, guy (personne).

carnavalesque [-valɛsk] adj. Carnivalesque.

carne [karn] f. POP. Nag, jade (cheval); brute (homme); slut (femme); tough meat (viande).

carné, ée [-ne] adj. MÉD. *Régime carné,* meat diet. ‖ BOT. Flesh-coloured.

carnet [karnɛ] m. Note-book, memorandum book; *carnet d'alimentation,* ration book; *carnet de bal,* dance card (ou) programme; *carnet de dépenses,* housekeeping book. ‖ FIN. *Carnet de chèques,* cheque book, U. S. checkbook; *carnet à souches,* counterfoil book, U. S. stub book. ‖ MILIT. *Carnet de tir,* firing record. ‖ **Carnet-répertoire,** n. Address-book.

carnier [karnje] m. Game-bag.

carnivore [-nivɔr] adj., m. V. CARNASSIER.

carolingien, ienne [karɔlɛ̃ʒjɛ̃, -jɛn] adj. Carolingian.

carotène [karɔtɛn] m. Carotene.

carotide [karɔtid] adj., f. MÉD. Carotid.

carottage [karɔta:ʒ] m. FAM. Cadging; wangling.

carotte [karɔt] f. BOT. Carrot. ‖ Tobacco-shop sign (de bureau de tabac); plug (de chiqueur). ‖ SPORTS. Drop-shot (au tennis). ‖ FAM. Hoax, swindle, take-in.
— adj. invar. Carrotty (couleur); *Poil de carotte,* Ginger, Carrots.

carotter [-te] v. tr. (1). To diddle; *carotter qqch. à qqn,* to do (ou) U. S. to gyp s.o. out of sth. ‖ FAM. To wangle (une permission).

carotteur [-tœ:r], **carottier** [-tje] m. Wangler; diddler; U. S. gyp.

caroube [karub], **carouge** [-ru:ʒ] f. BOT. Carob.

caroubier [-bje] m. BOT. Carob- (ou) locust-tree.

carpe [karp] m. MÉD. Carpus.

carpe f. ZOOL. Carp (poisson).

carpeau [-po] f. ZOOL. Young carp.

carpette [karpɛt] f. Rug.

carpien, enne [karpjɛ̃, ɛn] adj. MÉD. Carpal.

carquois [karkwa] m. Quiver.

carrare [kara:r] m. GÉOGR. Carrara. ‖ COMM. Carrara marble (marbre).

carre [ka:r] f. Crown (d'un chapeau); edge (d'un patin); thickness (d'une planche); square-toe (d'un soulier).

carré, ée [kare] adj. Square (décolleté, épaules, forme, mot, pièce, table, voile). ‖ MATH. Square (mètre, nombre, racine). ‖ FIG. Square; frank; outspoken; downright, forthright, straightforward (personne); square, plain, blunt, straight (réponse).
— m. Square; *carré magique,* magic square. ‖ Landing (d'escalier); patch (de jardin); square piece (de tissu). ‖ MATH. Square; *élever au carré,* to square. ‖ NAUT. Wardroom; mess-room. ‖ MILIT. Square.

carreau [-ro] m. Quarrel (d'arbalète); diamonds (aux cartes); tile, flagstone (de cuisine, de pavage); pillow (de dentellière); pane (d'étoffe, de fenêtre); market-floor (des halles); glass, eye (de lunettes); pit-head (de mine); wall-tile (de revêtement); goose, seam-presser (de tailleur); *à carreaux bleus,* blue-checkered; *orner de carreaux,* to chequer, to checker; *tablier à carreaux,* chequed-apron. ‖ FAM. *Rester sur le carreau,* to lie dead; to be crocked; to be left out of the running; *se tenir à carreau,* to keep one's weather eye open.

carrée [-re] f. Frame (de lit). ‖ MILIT. Barrack-room. ‖ FAM. Digs (logis).

carrefour [karfu:r] m. Cross-roads, intersection (de route); square, circus (en ville).

carrelage [karla:ʒ] m. Tiling (action); tiled floor, flagstone-pavement (pavage).

carreler [-le] v. tr. (8 a). To pave (la cour); to tile, to floor (la cuisine); to chequer, to checker (une étoffe); to square (du papier).

carrelet [karlɛ] m. Sewing awl (de bourrelier); square ruler (de dessinateur); packing-needle (d'emballeur); square dipping-net (de pêcheur); sail-needle (de voilier).

carreleur [karlœ:r] m. Tile-layer, paviour.

carrément [karemɑ̃] adv. Square, at right angles. ‖ FIG. Squarely; straight out; bluntly; in no uncertain terms; *y aller carrément,* to make no bones about it.

carrer [kare] v. tr. (1). To square (un cercle, un nombre, une pierre).
— v. pr. **Se carrer,** to swagger, to swank, to put on airs (se pavaner); to loll, to loll back, to recline (se prélasser).

carrier [karje] m. Quarrier, quarryman.

carrière [-rjɛ:r] f. Quarry.

carrière [-rjɛ:r] f. Career, course of life; *à la fin de sa carrière*, at the end of one's life. ‖ Career (v. PROFESSION); *la Carrière*, the Diplomatic Service; *diplomate de carrière*, career diplomat; *magistrat de carrière*, professional judge; *officier de carrière*, regular officer. ‖ FIG. *Donner carrière à*, to give free play (ou) full scope (ou) vent to; *se donner carrière*, to let oneself go.

carriériste [-rjerist] s. Careerist.

carriole [karjɔl] f. Light cart. ‖ FAM. Old crock, U. S. jalopy.

carrossable [karɔsabl] adj. Carriageable; *avenue, route, voie carrossable*, carriage-drive (ou) -road (ou) -way.

carrosse [karɔs] m. State-coach; *rouler carrosse*, to live in style.

carrossée [-se] f. FAM. Carriageful.

carrosser v. tr. (1). AUTOM. To fit a body to.

carrosserie [-sri] f. AUTOM. Body, coachwork; U. S. panel body. ‖ Coachbuilding (construction).

carrossier [-sje] m. AUTOM. Coach- (ou) body-builder.

carrousel [karuzɛl] m. MILIT. Carrousel.

carrure [kary:r] f. Breadth of shoulders, *d'une forte carrure*, burly.

cartable [kartabl] m. Drawing portfolio (à dessin); satchel (d'écolier).

carte [kart] f. Card (carton); *carte d'alimentation*, ration card; *carte d'échantillons*, show-card; *carte d'entrée*, admission ticket; *carte d'immatriculation, d'invitation*, registration, invitation card; *carte à jouer*, card, playing card; *carte de Noël*, Christmas card; *carte de restaurant*, bill of fare, menu; *carte de textile*, clothing-coupon book; *carte des vins*, wine-list; *carte de visite*, card, visiting-card, U. S. calling card; *carte postale*, postcard; *à la carte*, à la carte (menu). ‖ AUTOM. *Carte grise*, car-licence; *carte rose*, driving licence. ‖ CH. DE F. *Carte d'abonnement*, season ticket; *carte de circulation*, free pass, U. S. railroad pass. ‖ GÉOGR. Map; *carte d'état-major, du ciel*, ordnance (ou) official, astronomical map; *faire une carte de*, to map. ‖ NAUT. Chart; *porter sur la carte*, to chart; *sans carte*, chartless. ‖ AVIAT. Aeronautical (ou) air (ou) aviation map. ‖ AUTOM. *Carte routière*, road map. ‖ LOC. *Carte blanche*, carte blanche, full powers, free hand; *jouer cartes sur table*, to be above-board; *femme en carte*, registered prostitute; *perdre la carte*, to go off one's head; ‖ **Carte-lettre**, f. Letter-card.

cartel [kartɛl] m. † Cartel, coalition (en politique). ‖ Hanging wall-clock (pendule). ‖ MILIT., NAUT. Cartel. ‖ COMM. Cartel, trust, ring, combine.

carter [kartɛr] m. TECHN. Gear-case, chain-guard (de bicyclette); crankcase (d'engrenage); housing (de réducteur). ‖ AUTOM. Sump.

cartésianisme [kartezjanism] m. PHILOS. Cartesianism.

cartésien [-zjɛ̃] adj., s. PHILOS. Cartesian.

carthaginois, oise [kartaʒinwa, wa:z] adj., s. Carthaginian.

cartilage [kartila:ʒ] m. MÉD. Cartilage.

cartilagineux, euse [kartilaʒinø, ø:z] adj. MÉD. Cartilaginous. ‖ Gristly (fam.).

cartographe [kartɔgraf] s. Cartographer, chartographer.

cartographie [-grafi] f. Cartography, chartography; map drawing, mapping.

cartographique [-grafik] adj. Cartographic, chartographic.

cartomancie [-mɑ̃si] f. Cartomancy.

cartomancien, enne [-mɑ̃sjɛ̃, ɛn] s. Fortune-teller (by cards).

carton [kartɔ̃] m. Carton (boîte); pasteboard, cardboard (matière). ‖ Filing-case (de bureau); satchel (d'écolier); invitation-card (pour invitation); bandbox (de modiste); board, millboard (pour reliure); *carton à chapeau*, hat box. ‖ ARTS. Cartoon (d'artiste); *carton à dessin*, drawing portfolio. ‖ MILIT. Miniature target, U. S. carton; *faire un carton*, to fill a target. ‖ TECHN. Mount (photo). ‖ FIG. *Maison de carton*, jerry-built house. ‖ **Carton-pâte** (ou) **-pierre**, m. Papier mâché.

cartonnage [kartɔna:ʒ] m. Cardboard-box making. ‖ Boarding (action); boards (reliure).

cartonné, ée [-ne] adj. In boards.

cartonner [-ne] v. tr. (1). To bind in boards.

cartonnerie [-nri] f. Cardboard manufactory (ou) trade.

cartonneur [-nœ:r] s. Binder in boards.

cartonnier [-nje] m. Filing-cabinet; set of filing cases (casier). ‖ Cardboard-maker (ouvrier).

cartouche [kartuʃ] m. ARCHIT. Cartouche.

cartouche f. MILIT. Cartridge (de fusil); canister (de masque à gaz). ‖ Refill (pour stylo).

cartoucherie [-ʃri] f. Cartridge-factory.

cartouchière [-ʃjɛ:r] f. Cartridge-belt (ceinture); cartridge-pouch (sac).

cartulaire [kartylɛ:r] m. ECCLÉS. C(h)artulary.

cary [kari] m. V. CARI.

caryatide [karjatid] f. V. CARIATIDE.

caryotype [karjɔtip] m. MÉD. Karyotype.

cas [ka] m. Case, matter (affaire); *se faire un cas de conscience de*, to make a point of. ‖ Case, circumstance, chance, event (circonstance); *cas de force majeure*, case of absolute necessity (ou) of unforeseen circumstances, uncontrollable matter; *cas urgent*, emergency; *au cas où*, in the event of; *au cas que*, supposing, if; *dans ce cas, en ce cas*, in that case, if so; *dans tous les cas, en tout cas*, in any case, at all events, at any rate; *en cas de*, in case of, in the event of; *en aucun cas*, in no case, under no circumstances; *en pareil cas*, in such a case; *le cas ou jamais*, a case of now or never; *selon le cas*, as the case may be. ‖ Case, position, situation (état); *un mauvais cas*, a bad position; *dans un mauvais cas*, in a sorry plight. ‖ Case, instance (exemple); *c'est votre cas*, it is the case with you; *dans le premier cas*, in the first instance. ‖ Value, account (importance); *faire cas de*, to make much account of, to set value on, to think highly of (ou) much of; *faire peu de cas de, ne pas faire grand cas de*, to make little account of, to make light of, to think little of, to attach little importance to, to hold cheap, to set small store by; *ne faire aucun cas de*, to take no account of, to count for nothing. ‖ JUR. Case; *cas de divorce*, grounds for divorce; *cas d'espèce*, concrete (ou) individual case. ‖ MÉD. Case (malade, maladie). ‖ GRAMM. Case.

casanier, ère [kazanje, ɛr] adj. Stay-at-home.
— s. Home-bird, stay-at-home; U. S. homebody.

casaque [kazak] f. Casaque; jumper; U. S. blouse (de femme); jacket (de jockey). ‖ FIG. *Tourner casaque*, to turn one's coat.

casaquin [-kɛ̃] m. Jumper. ‖ FAM. *Tomber sur le casaquin à qqn*, to give s.o. a good hiding.

casbah [kazba] f. Citadel, kasba. ‖ FAM. Den.

cascade [kaskad] f. Cascade, waterfall; *cascade d'un glacier*, icefall. ‖ FIG. Cascade, shower (pluie); succession (suite); *cascade de rires*, peals of laughter.

cascader [-de] v. intr. (1). To cascade (eau). ‖ FAM. To lead a loose life, to go the pace.

cascadeur, euse [-dœr, ø:z] adj. Loose, disorderly, fast.
— m. Rip; reveller. ‖ CINÉM. Stunt man.

cascatelle [-tɛl] f. Small cascade.

case [kɑːz] f. Pigeon-hole (de bureau, de lettres); box (à la poste); locker (d'élève, d'employé). ‖ Square (d'échiquier); point (de trictrac). ‖ Cabin (v. CABANE, PAILLOTE); *la Case de l'oncle Tom*, Uncle Tom's Cabin. ‖ MÉD. Division (du cerveau). ‖ FAM. *Avoir une case vide*, to have rooms to let (ou) U. S. to rent.

caséeux, euse [kazeø, øːz] adj. Caseous.

caséifier [-ifje] v. tr. (1). To produce casein.

caséine [-in] f. Casein.

casemate [kazmat] f. MILIT. Casemate.

casematé, ée [-te] adj. Casemated.

caser [kɑze] v. tr. (1). To place, to stow (qqch.); to accommodate (qqn). ‖ FIG. To marry off (marier); to provide for, to find a berth for (qqn); *il est bien casé*, he has a good billet.
— v. pr. Se caser, to settle down (s'établir); to marry (se marier); to find a home (trouver une habitation) [*chez*, with]; to find an employment (trouver un emploi); *arriver à se caser*, to find a berth; *tous ses enfants se sont casés*, all his children are married off.

caserne [kazɛrn] f. MILIT. Barracks; *caserne de pompiers*, fire-station; *à la caserne*, in barracks. ‖ FIG. Barrack, spacious building.

casernement [kazɛrnəmɑ̃] m. MILIT. Barracking (action); barrack buildings (bâtiments); *officier de casernement*, barrack-master.

caserner [kazɛrne] v. tr. (1). MILIT. To barrack.
— v. intr. To live in barracks.

casernier [kazɛrnje] m. MILIT. Barrack-warden.

cash [kaʃ] adv. Cash down.

casher [kaʃeːr] adj. V. KASHER.

cash-flow [kaʃflo] m. inv. FIN. Cash flow.

casier [kazje] m. *Casier à bouteilles*, wine-bin, bottle-rack; *casier à lettres*, mail box, pigeon-hole for letters; *casier de malle*, tray of trunk; *casier à musique*, music-cabinet, canterbury; *casier à papiers*, pigeon-hole. ‖ JUR. *Casier judiciaire*, record of convictions; police (ou) judicial record; *casier vierge*, no record; *extrait du casier judiciaire*, copy of police record.

casino [kazino] m. Casino.

casoar [kazɔaːr] m. ZOOL. Cassowary. ‖ Plume (plumet).

Caspienne [kaspjɛn] adj. f. GÉOGR. Caspian; *la mer Caspienne*, the Caspian Sea.

casque [kask] m. Casque, helmet (d'armure). ‖ MILIT. Helmet, metal helmet; battle bowler (fam.); *casque colonial*, sun-helmet, topee; *casque à pointe*, spiked helmet. ‖ AUTOM. Crash-helmet. ‖ RADIO. *Casque téléphonique*, head-phones (ou) -set. ‖ BOT., BLAS. Helmet. ‖ FAM. Headache.

casqué, ée [-ke] adj. BLAS., ZOOL. Helmeted.

casquer [-ke] v. intr. (1). FAM. To fork out, to foot the bill.

casquette [-kɛt] f. Cap.

cassable [kɑsabl] adj. Breakable.

cassage [-saːʒ] m. Breaking. ‖ Crushing.

Cassandre [kasɑ̃dr] f. Cassandra; U. S. Calamity Jane; *jouer les Cassandre*, to be a prophesier of evil.
— m. Cassandra. ‖ FAM. Greybeard.

cassant, ante [kasɑ̃, ɑ̃ːt] adj. Short (acier); crisp (biscuit, gâteau); brittle (porcelaine, verre). ‖ FIG. Abrupt, short (abord, manières); peremptory, self-assertive (personne); sharp, curt, imperious, trenchant (ton).

cassate [kasat] f. Cassata.

cassation [kasasjɔ̃] f. JUR. Cassation; annulment; quashing; *Cour de cassation*, Supreme Court of Appeal. ‖ MILIT. Cashiering (d'un officier); reduction to the ranks (d'un sous-officier).

casse [kɑːs] f. Case; *bas de casse*, lower case.

casse f. BOT. Cassia. ‖ MÉD. Senna.

casse m. ARG. Robbery, break-in, job.

casse f. Breaking (action); breakage, damage (dommage); breakages (objets cassés); *payer la casse*, to pay for the damage. ‖ MILIT. Losses, casualties; *limiter la casse*, to keep down casualties. ‖ FAM. Row, bickering, squabble (dispute). ‖ **Casse-cou**, m. invar. Dangerous spot (endroit); dare-devil, reckless driver, stuntman (personne); *crier casse-cou à qqn*, to warn s.o. of a danger. ‖ **Casse-croûte**, m. invar. Snack, U. S. lunch. ‖ **Casse-noisettes, casse-noix**, m. invar. Nutcrackers. ‖ **Casse-pattes**, m. invar. Rotgut, U. S. Mickey Finn (alcool). ‖ **Casse-pieds**, m. invar. Bore, bind. ‖ **Casse-pierres**, m. invar. Stonebreaker (machine); stone-breaker's hammer (marteau). ‖ **Casse-pipes**, m. invar. FAM. Shooting-range. ‖ **Casse-tête**, m. invar. Club (arme); loaded stick, truncheon (bâton, matraque); rumpus (boucan); puzzle (énigme); headache (problème); care (souci); *casse-tête chinois*, chinese puzzle.

cassé, ée [-se] adj. Creasy (étoffe); broken (objet). ‖ Wing (col). ‖ Broken off (mariage). ‖ Broken down (vieillard); cracked, broken (voix). ‖ Dismissed (fonctionnaire). ‖ JUR. Quashed. ‖ MILIT. Degraded; cashiered. ‖ LOC. *Qu'est-ce qu'il y a de cassé?*, what's the trouble?

cassement [-smɑ̃] m. *Cassement de tête*, headache, puzzle (énigme); worry (souci).

casser [-se] v. tr. (1). To break (sens général); To snap (un bâton, une branche); to chop (du bois); to break, to fracture (un membre); to crush (des pierres); to crack (la voix); *casser en mille morceaux*, to break in pieces, to smash to pieces, to shatter; *casser net*, to snap. ‖ JUR. To discharge, to dismiss (un fonctionnaire); to annul, to quash, to reverse (un jugement); to rescind, to declare null (un testament). ‖ MILIT. To degrade; to cashier (un officier); to reduce to the ranks (un sous-officier); U. S. to break. ‖ LOC. *Casser bras et jambes à*, to bowl over (déconcerter); to dishearten, to prey on the mind of (décourager); to tie s.o.'s hands (entraver); *casser la figure à qqn*, to punch s.o.'s head; *casser les oreilles*, to pierce (ou) split the ears; *casser sa pipe*, to kick the bucket; *casser les vitres*, to cause a rumpus, to make a scene; *ça ne casse rien*, it's not up to much; *à tout casser*, high-sounding.
— v. intr. To break, to part.
— v. pr. Se casser, to break (sens général); *se casser net*, to snap. ‖ To break up (personne, vieillard); to crack (voix). ‖ LOC. *Se casser le nez*, to find nobody at home; *se casser la tête*, to rack one's brains; *se casser la tête contre le mur*, to run one's head into a wall; *ne rien se casser*, to take it easy.

casserole [kasrɔl] f. CULIN. Saucepan, stew-pan. ‖ CHIM. Casserole. ‖ FAM. Old crock, U. S. jalopy (auto); tin-kettle (piano).

casserolée [-le] f. Panful.

cassette [kasɛt] f. Casket, money box; *la cassette du roi*, the king's privy purse.

casseur [kasœːr] m. Breaker (de pierres). ‖ Demonstrator who damages property. ‖ AUTOM. Scrap dealer. ‖ ARG. Burglar.

cassis [kasis] m. BOT. Black-currant bush (arbuste); black-currant (fruit). ‖ COMM. Black-currant liqueur (liqueur).

cassis [kasi] m. AUTOM. Water-bar, furrow-drain across the road.

cassolette [kasɔlɛt] f. Casolette, perfume-pan.

cassonade [kasɔnad] f. Brown sugar.

cassoulet [kasulɛ] m. CULIN. Cassoulet, ragout of goose, pork, mutton and beans; U. S. sort of casserole-dish.

cassure [kɑsyːr] f. Break (fracture). ‖ Broken edge (bord); broken fragment (morceau). ‖ Crease-edge (du col, du revers); crease (d'une étoffe). ‖ GÉOL. *Cassure avec rejet,* fault.

castagnettes [kastaɲɛt] f. pl. Castanets; *joueur de castagnettes,* castanet-player.

caste [kast] f. Caste; *esprit de caste,* class-consciousness; *hors caste,* outcaste.

castel [kastɛl] m. Manor; castle.

castillan, ane [kastijɑ̃, an] adj., s. Castilian.

Castille [-ti:j] f. GÉOGR. Castile.

castor [kastɔ:r] m. ZOOL. Beaver; *castor du Chili,* coypu. ‖ COMM. Beaver-hat, beaver (chapeau); beaver (fourrure); *castor du Chili,* nutria.

castorette [-stɔrɛt] f. COMM. Beaverette.

castorine [-stɔrin] f. Beaver, castor (tissu).

castrat [kastra] m. Eunuch, castrated man. ‖ MUS. Castrato.

castration [-sjɔ̃] f. Gelding (d'un animal); castration (en général).

castrer [kastre] v. tr. (1). To geld; to castrate; to neuter. ‖ To emasculate.

castriste [kastrist] adj., s. Castroist, Castroite.

casuel, elle [kazɥɛl] adj. Accidental, casual, fortuitous. ‖ JUR. Contingent (condition); *revenus casuels,* fees, perquisites. ‖ GRAMM. *Désinences casuelles,* case-endings.
— m. ECCLÉS. Surplice-fees.

casuiste [kazɥist] m. ECCLÉS. Casuist. ‖ FAM. Quibbler, sophist, casuist.

casuistique [-tik] f. ECCLÉS. Casuistry. ‖ FAM. Sophistry; quibbling.

casus belli [kazysbelli] m. inv. Casus belli.

catabolisme [katabɔlism] m. MÉD. Catabolism.

catachrèse [katakrɛ:z] f. GRAMM. Catachresis.

cataclysmal, ale [kataklismal], **cataclysmique** [-mik] adj. Cataclysmal, cataclysmic.

cataclysme [kataklism] m. Cataclysm (v. CATASTROPHE); *de cataclysme,* cataclysmic.

catacombes [katakɔ̃:b] f. pl. Catacombs.

catadioptre [katadiɔptr] m. Reflector.

catafalque [katafalk] m. Catafalque.

catalan, ane [katalɑ̃, an] adj., s. Catalan.

catalepsie [katalɛpsi] f. MÉD. Catalepsy.

cataleptique [-tik] adj., s. MÉD. Cataleptic.

Catalogne [-lɔɲ] f. GÉOGR. Catalonia.

catalogue [katalɔg] m. Catalogue; *faire le catalogue de,* to catalogue. ‖ COMM. Price-list; trade-catalogue; *prix de catalogue,* list price.

cataloguer [-ge] v. tr. (1). To catalogue. ‖ To categorize. ‖ FAM. To size up (qqn).

catalpa [katalpa] m. BOT. Catalpa.

catalyse [katali:z] f. CHIM. Catalysis.

catalyser [-lize] v. tr. (1). CHIM. To catalyse. ‖ FAM. To be the catalyst of, to trigger off, to precipitate.

catalyseur [-zœ:r] m. CHIM. Catalyser.

catalytique [katalitik] adj. CHIM. Catalytic.

catamaran [katamarɑ̃] m. NAUT. Catamaran.

Cataphote [katafɔt] m. AUTOM. Cat's-eye; U. S. reflector.

cataplasme [kataplasm] m. MÉD. Cataplasm, poultice; *cataplasme électrique,* electric pad; *cataplasme sinapisé,* mustard plaster; *mettre un cataplasme sur,* to poultice.

cataplexie [kataplɛksi] f. MÉD. Cataplexy.

catapultable [katapyltabl] adj. Catapult-launched.

catapultage [-ta:ʒ] m. AVIAT. Catapulting, catapult-launching; catapult start.

catapulte [katapylt] f. Catapult.

catapulter [-te] v. tr. (1). AVIAT. To catapult, to catapult off. ‖ FAM. To hurl.

cataracte [katarakt] f. Waterfall, cataract. ‖ MÉD. Cataract. ‖ FIG. Flood, deluge.

catarrhal, ale [kataral] adj. MÉD. Catarrhal.

catarrhe [kata:r] m. MÉD. Catarrh.

catarrheux, euse [-rø, ø:z] adj. Catarrhous.

catastrophe [katastrɔf] f. Catastrophe.

catastrophé [-fe] adj. FAM. Wrecked, come to grief, sore at heart.

catastropher [-fe] v. tr. (1). FAM. To shatter, to bowl over, to shake up.

catastrophique [-fik] adj. Catastrophic.

catatonie [katatɔni] f. MÉD. Catatony.

catch [katʃ] m. SPORTS. Catch-as-catch-can; all-in wrestling.

catcheur [katʃœ:r] m. SPORTS. All-in wrestler.

catéchèse [kateʃɛ:z] f. ECCLÉS. Catechizing, catechesis.

catéchisation [-ʃizasjɔ̃] f. Teaching the gospel, catechization. ‖ FIG. Indoctrination.

catéchiser [-ʃize] v. tr. ECCLÉS. To catechize. ‖ FIG. To preach to; to indoctrinate (endoctriner); to coach (seriner). ‖ FAM. To lecture (sermonner).

catéchisme [-ʃism] m. Catechism.

catéchiste [-ʃist] s. ECCLÉS. Catechist.

catéchumène [-kymɛn] m. ECCLÉS. Catechumen.

catégorie [kategɔri] f. Class, category, division, sort, type; *de la même catégorie,* of the same stamp (fam.); *de dernière catégorie,* of poor quality; *ranger par catégorie,* to categorize.

catégoriel, elle [-rjɛl] adj. Concerning job status; *conflit catégoriel,* differential dispute. ‖ GRAMM. Categorial.

catégorique [-rik] adj. Categorical; square; declaratory; *refus catégorique,* flat refusal. ‖ PHILOS. Categorical.

catégoriquement [-rikmɑ̃] adv. Categorically.

catégorisation [-rizasjɔ̃] f. Categorization.

catégoriser [-rize] v. tr. (1). To categorize.

caténaire [katenɛ:r] adj. CH. DE F. Catenary.

catgut [katgyt] m. MÉD. Catgut.

catharsis [katarsis] f. PHILOS., PSYCH. Catharsis.

cathédrale [katedral] adj., f. Cathedral.

Catherine [katrin] f. Catherine (dimin. : Cathy, Kat, Kit, Kitty). ‖ LOC. *Coiffer sainte Catherine,* to be twenty-five and not yet married.

Catherinette [-nɛt] f. Twenty-five-year-old girl (ou) milliner still unmarried.

cathéter [katetɛ:r] m. MÉD. Catheter.

cathétérisme [-terism] m. MÉD. Catheterism.

cathétomètre [-tɔmɛtr] m. PHYS. Cathetometer.

cathode [katɔd] f. ELECTR. Cathode.

cathodique [-dik] adj. ELECTR. Cathodic (faisceau); cathode (rayons).

catholicisme [katɔlisism] m. ECCLÉS. Roman Catholicism.

catholicité [-lisite] f. ECCLÉS. Catholicity (doctrine); Catholics, Roman Catholics (fidèles).

catholique [-lik] adj. ECCLÉS. Roman Catholic. ‖ FAM. Orthodox, genuine, ship-shape; *pas catholique,* equivocal, suspicious.

cati [kati] m. Gloss, lustre, sheen (du tissu).

catimini (en) [ɑ̃katimini] loc. adv. On the sly, under the rose, stealthily.

catin [katɛ̃] f. POP. Whore, tart, wench, strumpet.

cation [katjɔ̃] m. PHYS. Cation.

catir [kati:r] v. tr. (2). To gloss (une étoffe); to press (du papier).

catogan [katɔgɑ̃] m. Cadogan, catogan.

catoptrique [katɔptrik] adj. PHYS. Catoptric.
— f. PHYS. Catoptrics.

Caucase [koka:z] m. GÉOGR. Caucasus.

caucasien, enne [-zjɛ̃, ɛn] adj., s. Caucasian.

cauchemar [koʃma:r] m. Nightmare. ‖ FIG. Nightmare, bugbear, pet aversion.

cauchemardesque [-dɛsk] adj. Nightmarish.

caudal, ale [kodal] adj. ZOOL. Caudal.

caudataire [kodatɛ:r] m. ECCLÉS. Train-bearer.

caulescent, ente [kolɛsɑ̃, ɑ̃:t] adj. BOT. Caulescent.

causal, ale [kozal] adj. Causal.

causalité [-lite] f. PHILOS. Causality.
causant, ante [kozɑ̃, ɑ̃:t] adj. Talkative
(v. LOQUACE); *il n'est pas très causant,* he is a man
of few words.
causatif, ive [kozatif, iv] adj. GRAMM. Causative.
cause [ko:z] f. Cause, reason, consideration,
motive, ground (v. MOTIF); *à cause de,* on account
of (en considération de); by reason of (en raison
de); through, on account of, because of, owing to
(par suite de); *et pour cause,* and for a good
reason; *pour cause de,* on account of; from;
pour quelle cause? for what reason?, why?;
sans cause, without reason, causeless, groundless.
‖ Cause (origine, principe); *cause première,* prime
cause (ou) mover, originator; *être la cause de,*
to be the cause of; to occasion; *c'est vous qui
en êtes cause,* this is your doing (ou) fault. ‖
Cause, side (parti); *épouser la cause de, prendre
fait et cause pour,* to espouse the cause of; to
take up the cudgels on behalf of; *faire cause
commune avec,* to make common cause with,
to side with; *gagner qqn à sa cause,* to win s.o.
over. ‖ JUR. Case, suit, cause (à juger); brief (à
plaider); *cause célèbre,* famous trial; *avocat sans
cause,* briefless barrister; *avoir gain de cause,*
to carry the cause, to gain one's point; *donner
gain de cause à qqn,* to decide in s.o.'s favour;
être en cause, to be a party to the suit; to be
concerned; *hors de cause,* irrelevant (questions);
mettre en cause, to question, to reflect upon
(qqch.); to implicate (qqn); *mettre hors de cause,*
to absolve, to clear, to exonerate. ‖ Loc. *En
connaissance de cause,* knowingly; *en tout état
de cause,* at all events.
causer [-ze] v. tr. (1). To cause; to bring about;
to lead to (v. OCCASIONNER); *causer de la peine,
du plaisir à qqn,* to give s.o. grief, pleasure. ‖
JUR. To state the considerations of.
causer [-ze] v. intr. (1). To talk, to converse, to
chat; *causer avec,* to talk with, to have a talk
with; *causer de,* to talk of (ou) about. ‖ To
gossip; to blab; *faire causer,* to set tongues
waggings (soulever les commentaires); to pump
(ou) to worm secrets out of (tirer les vers du nez).
causerie [-zri] f. Causerie (en général); informal
talk (ou) lecture (à la radio). ‖ Chat (causette).
causette [-zɛt] f. Chit-chat; *faire la causette avec,*
to have a chat with.
causeur, euse [-zœ:r, ø:z] adj. Talkative, chatty
(bavard); conversational, conversable (sociable).
— s. Talker; tattler (bavard). ‖ Conversation-
alist (de bonne conversation).
causeuse [-zø:z] f. Settee, U. S. love seat.
causse [ko:s] m. GÉOGR. Causse, limestone plateau in central and southern France.
causticité [kostisite] f. Causticity (pr. et fig.).
caustique [-tik] adj. Caustic. ‖ FIG. Cutting.
— m. CHIM. Caustic.
— f. PHYS. Caustic; *caustique par réflexion, par
réfraction,* catacaustic, diacaustic.
caustiquement [-tikmɑ̃] adv. Caustically.
cautèle [kotɛl] f. Cunning, guile.
cauteleux, euse [-tlø, ø:z] adj. Wily, sly, crafty
(rusé); mealy-mouthed, fawning (servile).
cautère [kotɛ:r] m. MÉD. Cautery. ‖ FAM. *Un
cautère sur une jambe de bois,* a poultice on a
wooden leg.
cautérisation [koterizasjɔ̃] f. Cauterization.
cautériser [-ze] v. tr. (1). MÉD. To cauterize.
caution [kosjɔ̃] f. JUR. Bail; guarantee, surety,
security (v. GARANTIE); *donner caution,* to give
security, to furnish bail; *mettre en liberté sous
caution,* to let out on bail; *sujet à caution,*
unreliable, untrustworthy, requiring confirmation.
‖ JUR. Guarantor; surety (garant); *se porter caution pour,* to go bail for, to stand surety for, to

become guarantee for; to warrant the truth of. ‖
COMM. Deposit (somme).
cautionné [kosjɔne] m. JUR. Guarantee.
cautionnement [-nmɑ̃] m. Guarantee; surety-
bond (contrat); caution money, security, deposit
(somme).
cautionner [-ne] v. tr. To guarantee, to stand
surety for. ‖ JUR. To go bail for. ‖ FIG. To answer
for, to guarantee.
cautionneur [-nœ:r] m. Guarantor.
cavaillon [kavajɔ̃] m. Melon from Cavaillon. ‖
Narrow strip of land between two vine plants that
cannot be reached by plough.
cavalcade [kavalkad] f. † Cavalcade (réunion).
‖ Stampede (course).
cavalcader [-kade] v. intr. (1). To career, to
stampede, to hurtle.
cavale [kaval] f. ZOOL. Mare. ‖ FAM. Gawk of a
woman.
cavaler [-le] v. intr. POP. To leg it; *cavaler chez
l'épicier,* to pop over to the grocer's.
— v. tr. POP. To bore stiff.
— v. pr. POP. Se cavaler, to scoot, to hop it.
cavalerie [-lri] f. MILIT. Cavalry; horse; *officier
de cavalerie,* cavalry officer.
cavaleur, euse [-lœ:r, ɸ:z] adj. Randy.
— m. FAM. A bit of a lad, philanderer.
— f. FAM. Nympho, hussy.
cavalier [-lje] m. † Gentleman; *un beau cavalier,*
a dashing young man. ‖ Cavalier, escort (suivant); *servir de cavalier à,* to escort. ‖ Partner
(danseur). ‖ Knight (aux échecs). ‖ Staple (clou).
‖ SPORTS. Rider, horseman; equestrian. ‖ MILIT.
Horseman, trooper, cavalryman (homme); cavalier (ouvrage); *dix mille cavaliers,* ten thousand
horse.
— adj. Riding; *allée cavalière,* ride; *chemin
cavalier,* bridle-path. ‖ Cavalier, jaunty (air);
flippant (attitude, remarque); off-hand, cavalier
(manière); high-handed, cavalier (procédé).
cavalière [-ljɛ:r] f. Horsewoman (amazone). ‖
Partner (danseuse).
cavalièrement [-ljɛrmɑ̃] adv. Cavalierly.
cavatine [kavati:n] f. MUS. Cavatina.
cave [ka:v] adj. Hollow, gaunt (joues); sunken
(yeux). ‖ MÉD. *Veine cave,* vena cava.
cave f. Cellar; vault; *cave à vin,* wine-cellar. ‖
Cellar (vins); *avoir une bonne cave,* to keep a good
cellar. ‖ Cellaret; liqueur cabinet (à liqueurs).
cave m. ARG. Person outside the underworld;
mug, sucker (dupe).
caveau [kavo] m. Small cellar (cave). ‖ Tomb,
sepulchral vault; *caveau de famille,* family vault.
caveçon [kavsɔ̃] m. Cavesson. ‖ FIG. *Donner un
coup de caveçon à qqn,* to take s.o. down a peg.
caver [kave] v. tr. (1). To hollow (la pierre).
caverne [kavɛrn] f. Cave, cavern; *homme des
cavernes,* cave-man. ‖ Den (repaire). ‖ MÉD.
Cavity.
caverneux, euse [-nø, ø:z] adj. Cavernous (montagne, rocher); sepulchral (voix).
cavernicole [-nikɔl] adj. ZOOL. Cavernicolous.
— m. ZOOL. Cavernicolous animal.
caviar [kavja:r] m. CULIN. Caviar, caviare.
caviarder [kavjarde] v. tr. (1). To caviare.
caviste [kavist] m. Cellarman.
cavitation [kavitasjɔ̃] f. AVIAT., NAUT. Cavitation.
cavité [-te] f. Cavity; pit. (V. EXCAVATION, TROU.)
‖ MÉD. Cavity; *cavité articulaire,* socket.
C.C.P. [sesepe] m. Abrév. de *compte courant
postal,* post-office (ou) giro account.
C.D. [cede] Abrév. de *corps diplomatique,* Corps
diplomatique.
C.E. [ceə] m. Abrév. de *comité d'entreprise,*

works council concerned with certain aspects of management and employees' welfare.

ce [sə] pr. dém. † *Ce faisant*, so doing; *ce me semble*, it seems to me, methinks; *pour ce faire*, in order to do this. ‖ This; these (désignant un objet); *ce n'est pas mon chapeau*, this (ou) it is not my hat; *ce sont mes livres*, these (ou) they are my books. ‖ He, she, it, they (désignant une personne déterminée); *c'est mon ami*, he is my friend; *c'est une institutrice*, she is a schoolmistress; *ce sont des marins*, they are sailors. ‖ It (désignant une personne indéterminée); *ce doit être mon cousin*, it must be my cousin; *ce sont mes sœurs qui*, it is my sisters who; *est-ce vous, Marie?*, is that you, Mary? ‖ **C'est** (dans les réponses) *qui est-ce?*, *c'est moi*, who is it? it is I; *qui l'a battu?*, *c'est lui*, who has beaten him?, he has; *qui les a vus?*, *c'est elle*, who saw them?, she did; *à qui est ce chapeau?*, *c'est à mon frère*, whose hat is this?, my brother's. ‖ **C'est** (dans les locutions); *c'est pourquoi*, that's why; *c'est-à-dire*, that is to say, i.e.; *qu'est-ce que c'est?*, what is it?; *qu'est-ce à dire?*, what does that mean?; *si ce n'est*, except; *voilà ce que c'est que mentir*, that's what comes of lying. ‖ **Ce... de;** *c'est difficile de plaire à tout le monde*, it's hard to please everybody; *c'est à vous de parler*, it is your turn (ou) your duty to speak; *c'était à lui d'y veiller*, it was for him (ou) it was his business to see to it. ‖ **Ce... que;** *ce ne pouvait être que vous*, it could only be you; *ce doit être elle qui est venue*, it must be she who has come; *c'est lui qui me l'a dit*, it was he who told me; *ce serait folie que de se fier à lui*, it would be madness to trust him; *s'il n'a pas répondu, c'est qu'il n'a pas reçu votre lettre*, he didn't answer, probably because he hasn't got your letter; *ce n'est pas que je tienne beaucoup à y aller*, it is not that I am very keen on going; *c'est que...*, you see... (hésitation). ‖ **Ce qui, ce que** (la chose qui, que); *ils se conformèrent aux règlements, ce qui était juste*, they conformed to the rules, which was correct; *il aurait fallu qu'il fût intelligent, ce qu'il n'est pas*, he would have had to be intelligent, which he is not. ‖ **Ce qui, ce que** (la chose qui, que), what; *vous voyez ce qui est arrivé*, you see what happened; *vous ignorez ce qu'est la vie*, you do not know what life is. ‖ **Tout ce qui, tout ce que** (toutes les choses qui, que), all that, everything that; *tout ce qui brille n'est pas or*, all that glitters is not gold; *c'est tout ce que je sais*, this is all I know. ‖ **Ce que** (combien), what, how, how much; *j'ignore ce que ça coûte*, I don't know how much it is (ou) what it will cost; *ce que c'est difficile!* how difficult it is!; *ce que ça m'a coûté d'ennuis!*, what trouble it has given me! ‖ **Ce à quoi** (chose à laquelle), which; *il s'est suicidé, ce à quoi personne ne s'attendait*, he committed suicide, which nobody expected. ‖ **Ce à quoi** (la chose à laquelle), what; *je vois ce à quoi vous faites allusion*, I see what you are alluding to. ‖ **Ce qui... ce**, what; *ce qui me plaît en elle, c'est sa gentillesse*, what I like in her is her kind nature. ‖ **A ce que;** *il ne s'attendait pas à ce qu'elle s'en défendît*, he did not expect her to deny it; *à ce qu'on dit*, according to what they say. ‖ **Pour ce qui** (quant à), as to, as for, as regards, with respect to; *pour ce qui est de moi*, as for me, for my part.

ce, cet [sə, sɛt] (f. **cette** [sɛt]; pl. **ces** [sɛ]) adj. fém. This, that (au sg.); these, those (au pl.). ‖ **Ce, ce... ci**, this; *cette petite fille est ma sœur*, this little girl is my sister; *répondez à ces questions*, answer these questions; *ce mois-ci a été beau*, this month has been fair. ‖ **Ce, ce... là**, that; *prenez cette chaise* (ou) *cette chaise-là*, sit on that chair; *cet individu n'a jamais été votre ami*, that

fellow has never been your friend. ‖ **Ce** (marquant le temps); *ce matin*, this morning; *cette nuit*, last night (passée); *ce soir*, to-night (actuellement [ou] à venir); *ce jour-là*, that day; *un de ces jours*, one of these days. ‖ **Ce** (intensif); *ce dernier*, the latter; *un de ces arguments sans réplique*, one of those unanswerable arguments; *peut-il avoir cette délicatesse?*, is he tactful enough to do so? ‖ **Ce** (exclamatif, intensif); *oh! cette idée!*, what an idea!; *cette raison!*, what a reason to give!; *cette bonne Marie!*, dear kindhearted Mary!; *il a de ces expressions!*, he uses such expressions!; *une de ces frousses!*, a devil of a fright! ‖ **Ce** (interrogatif); *et ce bras, comment va-t-il?*, well, how's your arm?; *et ce livre, est-il écrit?*, what about that book? is it written? ‖ **Ce** (de politesse); *que désirent ces dames?*, what can I show you, ladies?; *ces dames sont parties faire des courses*, the ladies went shopping.

céans [seã] adv. † Here; in this house; *le maître de céans*, the master of the house.

ceci [səsi] pr. dém. This; *ceci est mon sang*, this is my blood; *ce qui arrivera, c'est ceci*, what will happen is this; *l'affaire offre ceci de spécial que*, the case is particular in that.

cécité [sesite] f. Cecity, blindness, ablepsy; *frappé de cécité*, struck blind.

cédant, ante [sedã, ã:t] adj. JUR. Assigning, transferring, granting.
— m. JUR. Assignor, grantor, transferor.

céder [sede] v. tr. (5). To yield, to cede; to give up (à, to); *céder le haut du pavé à qqn*, to let s.o. walk on the inside; *céder le pas à*, to give way to; *céder la place à*, to give place to; *céder sa place à*, to give up one's seat to; *céder ses possessions à*, to surrender one's possessions to; *céder du terrain*, to give ground; *ne le céder à personne*, to be second to none, to yield to nobody. ‖ JUR. To make over, to hand over, to convey, to transfer (ses biens) [à, to]. ‖ COMM. To dispose of, to part with, to let, to sell; *céder à bail*, to lease; *céder son fonds*, to dispose of one's business.
— v. intr. To yield, to give way (fléchir); to cave in (s'enfoncer); *la porte a cédé*, the door has given way. ‖ MÉD. To yield (à, to). ‖ FIG. *Céder à*, to yield to, to give way to, to submit to, to knuckle down to (qqn); to yield to (sollicitations, terreur, vœux); to succumb to (sommeil, tentation); to yield to, to bow to (volonté); *contraindre à céder*, to bring to terms.

cédétiste [sedetist] adj. Pertaining to the C. F. D. T. (Confédération française démocratique du travail).
— s. Member of the C. F. D. T., trade-unionist.

cedex [sedɛks] m. Abrév. de *courrier d'entreprise à distribution exceptionnelle*, PO box.

cédille [sedi:j] f. GRAMM. Cedilla.

cédraie [sedrɛ] f. Cedar-grove.

cédrat [sedra] m. BOT. Citron-tree (arbre); citron (fruit).

cèdre [sɛ:dr] m. BOT. Cedar, cedar-tree (arbre); cedar, cedar-wood (bois).

cédulaire [sedylɛ:r] adj. JUR. Schedular, scheduled (impôts).

cédule [-dyl] f. Script, note. ‖ JUR. Summons (de citations); schedule (d'impôts).

C. E. E. [seəə] f. Abrév. de *Communauté économique européenne*, EEC, European Economic Community.

cégétiste [seʒetist] m. Member of the C.G.T. (Confédération générale du travail); trade-unionist.
— adj. Pertaining to the C. G. T. (= *T. U. C.* [Trades Union Congress]; U. S. *C. I. O.* [Con-

gress of Industrial Organizations]; *A.F.L.* [American Federation of Labor]).

ceindre [sɛ:dr] v. tr. (59). To put on, to assume (la couronne); to gird on (une écharpe); to belt on, to gird on, to buckle on (une épée); to bind up, to wreathe (la tête); to encompass, to begird, to surround (une ville); *ceindre de,* to gird with. — v. pr. **Se ceindre,** to gird oneself; *se ceindre les reins,* to gird up one's loins.

ceintrage [sɛ̃tra:ʒ] m. TECHN. Bending. ‖ NAUT. Swifting.

ceintre [sɛ̃:tr] m. NAUT. Swifter.

ceintrer [-tre] v. tr. (1). NAUT. To swift.

ceinture [sɛ̃ty:r] f. Girdle (de corde); belt (de cuir); sash (d'étoffe); waistband (de jupe, de pantalon); zone, cincture (en poésie); *ceinture de natation,* swimming-belt; *ceinture de sauvetage,* life-belt, life-saving jacket; *ceinture de sauvetage pneumatique,* inflatable rubber life-belt; Mae West (pop.). ‖ Waist, middle (du corps); *nu jusqu'à la ceinture,* stripped to the waist; *il avait de l'eau jusqu'à la ceinture,* he was waist-deep in the water. ‖ CH. DE F: Circle; *grande, petite ceinture,* outer, inner circle. ‖ SPORTS. Waistlock (à la lutte). ‖ MÉD. *Ceinture pelvienne,* pelvic (ou) hip girdle. ‖ MILIT. Belt (de fortifications); band (de projectiles). ‖ AVIAT. *Ceinture de fixation,* safety belt. ‖ NAUT. Swifter (de bateau); fender (de navire). ‖ ECCLÉS. Surcingle (de soutane). ‖ FIG. Belt (d'arbres, de collines); girdle (de murs). ‖ FAM. *Se mettre la ceinture,* to tighten one's belt, to do without.

ceinturer [-re] v. tr. (1). To girdle, to belt (qqn); to belt, to surround, to encircle (qqch.). ‖ SPORTS. To tackle low (au rugby); to grip round the waist (à la lutte).

ceinturon [-rɔ̃] m. Uniform belt (dans l'armée, etc.); wide belt.

cela [səla], **ça** [sa] pr. dém. That (opposé à *ceci*); *ceci et cela,* this and that. ‖ This (sens de *ceci*); *c'est ça votre chien?* is this your dog? ‖ It (sujet apparent); *cela m'amuse de vous aider,* it amuses me to help you; *cela semble parfaitement naturel qu'elle ait réussi,* that she was successful seems perfectly natural. ‖ That (sens général); *à cela près,* except on that point, with that one exception; *ah ça, non!,* no indeed!, no, I tell you!; *après ça,* after that, next; *et avec cela,* and besides all that; *et avec ça, Madame?,* anything else, Madam?; *avec ça!* tell that to the marines!, tell me another!; *ça y est,* that's that!; *c'est cela,* that's it, quite so; *c'est comme ça!* that's how it is!; *c'est pour cela que,* that's why; *ce n'est plus ça,* it's no longer what it was, there is something amiss; *comment ça?,* how so?; *comment ça va?,* how are you?; *comme ci, comme ça,* so-so, middling; *et comme ça,* and so; *il est comme ça,* he is like that, that's the sort of man he is; *dix ans de cela,* ten years ago; *il n'y a que ça pour,* there is nothing like it for; *il ne manquerait plus que ça!,* that would be the last straw!; *malgré tout cela,* for all that; *n'est-ce que cela?,* is that all?; *où ça,* where?; *pas de ça ici!,* that won't do here!, none of that!; *pour ça oui!,* yes rather!, bless you, yes!; *pour cela même que,* for no other reason than; *que dites-vous de ça?,* what do you say of that?; *qu'est-ce que c'est que ça?,* what's that?; *qu'est-ce que ça signifie?,* what does that mean?; *sans cela,* otherwise (autrement); or else (sinon); *il ira parce que sans cela...* he'll go because if he didn't...

céladon [sɛladɔ̃] m., adj. Celadon.

célébrant [selebrɑ̃] m. ECCLÉS. Celebrant.

célébration [-brasjɔ̃] f. Celebration.

célèbre [selɛbr] adj. Celebrated, noted [*par,* for]. (V. ILLUSTRE.) ‖ Famous, noted (lieu); noted, well-publicized (produit).

célébrer [selebre] v. tr. (1). To celebrate, to observe (une fête, une tradition). ‖ To sing (les exploits); to celebrate, to extol, to glorify (qqn). ‖ ECCLÉS. To celebrate, to solemnize (un mariage); to celebrate (la messe); to perform (un rite).

célébrité [-brite] f. Celebrity. (V. RÉPUTATION.) ‖ Celebrity, notability, man of mark, very important person (V.I.P.) [personne].

celer [səle] v. tr. (8 b). To conceal.

céleri [selri] m. BOT. Celery. ‖ CULIN. *Céleri rémoulade,* celery salad. ‖ **Céleri-rave** m. BOT. Celeriac.

célérité [selerite] f. Celerity; swiftness. (V. VITESSE.) ‖ Alacrity (empressement).

célesta [selɛsta] m. MUS. Celesta.

céleste [selɛst] adj. Heavenly (beauté, corps, musique); divine (don); celestial (esprit, globe, pole, sphère); *bleu céleste,* sky-blue; *voûte céleste,* vault of heaven. ‖ GÉOGR. Celestial (empire).

célibat [seliba] m. Celibacy (en général); spinsterhood (de femme); bachelorhood (d'homme); *vivre dans le célibat,* to lead a single life.

célibataire [-tɛ:r] m. Celibate (en général); spinster (femme); bachelor (homme); *mener la joyeuse vie des célibataires,* to live in single blessedness; *vivre en célibataire,* U. S. to bach it. — adj. Unmarried, single.

celle [sɛl] V. CELUI.

cellérier [selerje] m. ECCLÉS. Cellarer.

cellier [selje] m. Store-room (à provisions); wine-cellar (à vins).

celloïdine [sɛlɔidin] f. Celloidin.

Cellophane [sɛlɔfan] f. (nom déposé). Cellophane.

cellulaire [sɛlylɛ:r] adj. MÉD. Cellular (tissu). ‖ JUR. *Régime cellulaire,* solitary confinement; *voiture cellulaire,* prison-van; Black Maria (fam.); U. S. paddy wagon.

cellule [selyl] f. ZOOL., MÉD., ELECTR., JUR. Cell. ‖ BOT. Cellule. ‖ AVIAT. Air-frame. ‖ MILIT. Cells; *trois jours de cellule,* three days' cells.

cellulite [-lit] f. MÉD. Cellulitis.

celluleux, euse [-lø, ø:z] adj. Cellulous.

Celluloïd [-lɔid] m. (nom déposé). Celluloid.

cellulose [-lo:z] f. CHIM. Cellulose.

cellulosique [-lɔzik] adj. Cellulosic.

celte [sɛlt] s. Celt, Kelt. — adj. Celtic, Keltic.

celtique [-tik] adj., s. Celtic.

celtisant [-tizɑ̃] m. Celtologist.

celtium [sɛltjɔm] m. CHIM. Celtium.

celui [səlɥi] (f. **celle** [sɛl]; pl. **ceux** [sø], **celles** [sɛl]) pr. dém. **Celui de, celle de,** that of, 's; **ceux de, celles de,** those of, 's, ones; *celles d'autrefois,* those of long ago; *celui de mon ami,* my friend's, that of my friend; *ceux d'il y a cent ans,* those of a hundred years ago; *les casseroles d'aluminium et celles de cuivre,* aluminium saucepans and copper ones. ‖ **Celui qui, celui que** (personne), he who (ou) that, the one that (sujet); him whom (compl.); **celle qui, celle que,** she who, she that (sujet); her whom (compl.); *celui qui vous a dit cela est un sot,* he who told you that is a fool; *celui de mes amis que je préfère,* of all my friends the one I like best; *je connais celle que vous estimez tant,* I know her whom you regard so highly. ‖ **Ceux qui, ceux que; celles qui, celles que** (personne), those who, those that, those whom, such as; *ceux qui lisent ces livres,* those who read these books; *secourez ceux pour qui le destin est dur,* help those to whom Fate is unkind. ‖ **Tous ceux qui, toutes celles qui,** all those who, all who; *tous ceux qui ont des oreilles comprennent ceci,* all who have ears understand this. ‖ **Celui qui, celui que; celle qui, celle que** (chose), that which, the one which; *parmi de nombreux mots, celui qu'il fallait se rappeler,* among many words, the one which had to be remembered. || **Ceux qui, ceux que; celles qui, celles que** (chose), those (ou) the ones which; *regardez ces poulets, ceux que j'ai achetés hier,* look at the chickens, those that I bought yesterday; *ces fenêtres sont celles qui donnent sur la rue,* these windows are the ones which (ou) that look into the street. || **Tout ce qui, tout ce que,** all that, everything that; *tout ce qui vous amuse m'ennuie,* all that amuses you wearies me. || **Celui-ci,** this one, this; the latter; **celui-là,** that one, that; the former; *celui-ci est mon meilleur élève,* this is my best pupil; *ce livre-ci est à vous, celui-là est à moi,* this book is yours, that one is mine; *celui-ci est à vous, celui-là est à moi,* the latter is yours, the former is mine. || **Ce...là** (mis pour *cela*); *c'est là ce que je pensais,* that was what I thought; *ce n'était pas là mon avis,* such was not my opinion.

cément [semɑ̃] m. Méd., Techn. Cement.

cémentation [-tasjɔ̃] f. Techn. Cementation; case-hardening.

cémenter [semɑ̃te] v. tr. (1). Techn. To cement; to case-harden.

cénacle [senakl] m. Ecclés. Upper Room. || †. Cenacle, supping room. || Fig. Coterie, group.

cendre [sɑ̃:dr] f. Ash; cinders; *cendres rouges,* embers; *couleur de cendre,* ashen, cinereous, ashy grey; *réduire en cendres,* to burn to ashes (ou) cinders, to cinder. || Ashes (des morts); *renaître de ses cendres,* to rise again from one's ashes. || Ecclés. *Mercredi des Cendres,* Ash-Wednesday.

cendré, ée [sɑ̃dre] adj. Ash-coloured, ashen, ashy, ash-grey; cinereous; *blond cendré,* ash-blond.

cendrée f. Sports. Dust-shot (de chasse); cinder-track (de course).

cendrer v. tr. (1). To colour ash-grey (un mur); to cinder (une piste). || Techn. To ash.

cendreux, euse [sɑ̃drø, ø:z] adj. Full of ashes. || Techn. Flawy. || V. cendré.

cendrier [-drje] m. Ash-tray (de fumeur); ash-pan (de poêle). || Techn. Ash-pit (de haut fourneau); ash-box (de locomotive).

Cendrillon [-drijɔ̃] f. Cinderella. || Fig. Sit-by-the-fire, Cinderella.

Cène [sɛn] f. Ecclés. Last Supper (du Christ); Communion (du culte protestant).

cénesthésie [senɛstezi] f. Méd. Coenesthesia, cenesthesia.

cénesthésique [-zik] adj. Méd. Coenesthetic, cenesthetic.

cénobite [senɔbit] m. Ecclés., Fig. Coenobite.

cénobitique [senɔbitik] adj. Coenobitic. || Fig. Austere, coenobitic.

cénobitisme [senɔbitism] m. Coenobitism.

cénotaphe [senɔtaf] m. Cenotaph.

cénozoïque [senɔzɔik] adj., m. Géol. Cenozoic, cainozoic.

cens [sɑ̃:s] m. †. Census. || Jur. Quit-rent; payment in kind. || Fin. Rating; *cens électoral,* property qualification, U. S. poll tax.

censé, ée [sɑ̃se] adj. Deemed, considered, regarded (v. réputé, supposé); *il est censé l'ignorer,* he is not supposed to know it; *être censé ignorer la loi,* to be presumed to ignore the law.

censément [-mɑ̃] adv. Supposedly. || Practically.

censeur [sɑ̃sœ:r] m. †. Censor. || Censor (de la presse, du théâtre). || Vice-principal (de lycée). || Fin. Auditor. || Fig. Censurer, critic.

censitaire [sɑ̃sitɛ:r] adj. † *Suffrage censitaire,* vote based on property qualification.
— m. † Citizen paying *cens* (= tax entitling him to vote or be elected).

censurable [sɑ̃syrabl] adj. Censurable.

censure [sɑ̃sy:r] f. Censorship, censor (de la presse, des spectacles); *contrôlé par la censure,* passed by the censor. || Fin. Audit (des comptes). || Ecclés. Pl. Censure. || Fig. Censure, blame.

censurer [-re] v. tr. (1). To censor (un film). || Fig. To censure.

cent [sɑ̃] adj. num. Hundred; a hundred, one hundred; *cinq pour cent,* five per cent; *deux cent douze,* two hundred and twelve; *page quatre cent,* page four hundred; *mil neuf cent dix-sept (1917),* nineteen hundred and seventeen, nineteen seventeen; *un tant pour cent,* a percentage; a commission (de courtier). || Sports. *Cent mètres.*
— m. Hundred; *un cent de clous,* a hundred nails; *un cent au billard,* a hundred up at billiards; *avoir des mille et des cents,* to be rolling in money.

cent [sɛnt] m. Fin. Cent (monnaie).

centaine [sɑ̃tɛn] f. About a hundred; *par centaines,* in (ou) by hundreds; *plusieurs centaines d'enfants,* several hundred children; *des centaines d'années,* hundreds of years.

centaure [sɑ̃tɔ:r] m. Centaur.

centaurée [-re] f. Bot. Centaury.

centenaire [sɑ̃tnɛ:r] adj. Centenary, century-old; a hundred years old.
— m. Centenary (anniversaire); centenary celebrations (fêtes); centenarian (personne).

centenier [-tənje] m. Centurion.

centennal, ale [-tɛnnal] adj. Centennial.

centésimal, ale [-tezimal] adj. Math. Centesimal.

centiare [-tja:r] m. Math. One square metre; centiare.

centième [-tjɛm] adj., m. Math. Hundredth.
— f. Théâtr. Hundredth performance.

centigrade [sɑ̃tigrad] adj. Centigrade.

centigramme [-gram] m. Centigramme.

centilitre [-litr] m. Centilitre.

centime [sɑ̃tim] m. Centime.

centimètre [-mɛtr] m. Centimetre.

centimétrique [-metrik] adj. Centimetric.

centrafricain, aine [sɑ̃trafrikɛ̃, ɛn] adj. Géogr. Central African.

centrage [sɑ̃tra:ʒ] m. Centring, centering.

central, ale [sɑ̃tral] adj. Central (chauffage). || Central, principal, head, chief (administration, bureau); central, middle (lieu, partie, point); *École centrale,* School of Civil Engineering. || Jur. *Maison centrale,* prison, gaol, U. Ş. jail.
— m. *Central téléphonique,* telephone exchange, U. S. central.

centrale [sɑ̃tra:l] f. Techn. Generating station (ou) plant, power station. || *Centrale syndicale,* group of affiliated trade unions, national union.

centralien, enne [sɑ̃traljɛ̃, ɛn] s. Student (ou) former student of the École centrale.

centralisateur, trice [sɑ̃tralizatœ:r, tris] adj. Centralizing.
— s. Centralizer.

centralisation [-zasjɔ̃] f. Centralization; centralizing.

centraliser [-lize] v. tr. (1). To centralize.
— v. pr. Se centraliser, to centralize.

centralisme [-lism] m. Centralism.

centraliste [-list] m. Centralist.

centre [sɑ̃:tr] m. Centre; U. S. center; central (ou) focal point (v. milieu); *centre de dépression,* storm centre. || Centre (des affaires, d'un cercle, de la politique, d'une roue, de la terre); *le parti du centre,* the Centre Party. || Centre; *centre d'accueil,* rest-centre; *centre d'études,* college; *centre industriel,* manufacturing centre; *centre touristique,* holiday resort; *les grands centres,* the great urban centres. || Math. Centre. || Phys. *Centre de gravité,* centre of gravity; *centre de poussée,* centre of pressure (ou) of buoyancy. ||

CH. DE F. *Centre de triage*, railway yard. ‖ MILIT. Centre (d'une armée, de résistance). ‖ NAUT. *Centre de carène*, centre of buoyancy. ‖ AVIAT. *Centre d'aviation*, air station. ‖ MÉD. *Centre nerveux*, nerve centre; *centre hospitalier*, hospital centre; *centre de récupération*, convalescent hospital. ‖ SPORTS. Centre (au basket-ball, au football, au hockey); *avant centre*, centre-forward.

centrer [sᾶtre] v. tr. (1). TECHN. To centre, to adjust. ‖ SPORTS. To centre (le ballon). ‖ FIG. To centre, to focus, to concentrate (l'attention, la discussion, l'observation).

centrifugation [sᾶtrifygasjɔ̃] f. Centrifugation.

centrifuge [sᾶtrify:ʒ] adj. Centrifugal.

centrifuger [-fyʒe] v. tr. (7). To centrifugalize, to centrifuge.

centrifugeur, euse [-fyʒœ:r, ø:z] adj. Centrifugal.
— f., m. Centrifuge.

centripète [-pɛt] adj. Centripetal.

centrisme [sᾶtrism] m. Centrism.

centriste [-trist] adj., s. Centrist.

centuple [sᾶtypl] adj. Centuple; hundredfold.
— m. Centuple, U. S. centuplicate; *au centuple*, a hundredfold; a hundred times as much (ou) as many.

centupler [-ple] v. tr. (1). To centuple, to centuplicate, to increase a hundredfold.

centurie [sᾶtyri] f. † Centuria, century.

centurion [-rjɔ̃] m. † Centurion.

cep [sɛp] m. BOT. Vine-stock. ‖ Pl. Fetters, stocks.

cépage [sɛpa:ʒ] m. BOT. Vine-plant.

cèpe [sɛp] m. BOT. Flap mushroom, edible fungus.

cependant [səpᾶdᾶ] adv. Meanwhile, in the meantime.
— conj. However, yet, nevertheless, still; *cependant nous essaierons de le persuader demain*, however, we shall try to persuade him to-morrow; *cependant il est si obstiné qu'il peut refuser*, still he is so obstinate that he may refuse; *il reste cependant une chance de*, yet there remains a bare chance of.

céphalalgie [sefalalʒi] f. MÉD. Cephalalgy.

céphalée [seꜰale] f. MÉD. Headache.

céphalique [sefalik] adj. MÉD. ZOOL. Cephalic.

céphalopode [sefalɔpɔd] m. ZOOL. Cephalopod.

céphalo-rachidien, enne [sefaloraʃidjɛ̃, ɛn] adj. MÉD. Cerebro-spinal; *liquide céphalo-rachidien*, cerebro-spinal fluid.

céphéide [sefeid] f. ASTRON. Cepheid.

céramique [seramik] adj. Ceramic.
— f. ARTS. Ceramics.

céramiste [seramist] s. ARTS. Ceramist.

cérat [se a] m. MÉD. Cerate.

cerbère [sɛrbɛr] m. Cerberus (pr. et fig.); *de Cerbère*, Cerberean.

cerceau [sɛrso] m. Hoop (d'enfant, de fût, de robe); *jouer au cerceau*, to trundle a hoop. ‖ Half-hoop (de capote). ‖ MÉD. Cradle (de lit).

cerclage [sɛrkla:ʒ] m. Hooping (de fût); tyring, binding (de roue).

cercle [sɛrkl] m. MATH. Circle; *quart de cercle*, quadrant. ‖ ASTR. *Cercle polaire*, polar circle. ‖ Ring, band (anneau). ‖ Tyre, U. S. tire (de roue); flesh-hoop (de tambour); hoop (de tonneau). ‖ Set, circle, club (d'amis); circle (de connaissances); circle, society (d'études); club (de jeu); coterie (de partisans); *cercle littéraire*, literary circle; *cercle militaire*, officers' club; *faire cercle autour*, to gather in a circle round. ‖ FIG. Circle, sphere (d'activités); range, field (de connaissances intellectuelles); round (de travaux); *cercle vicieux*, vicious circle; *tourner dans un cercle vicieux*, to argue in a circle.

cercler [-kle] v. tr. (1). To encircle, to ring (d'un anneau). ‖ To tyre, U. S. to tire (une roue); to hoop (un tonneau).

cercleux [-klø] m. FAM. Clubman.

cercueil [sɛrkœ:j] m. Coffin (en bois); shell (en plomb).

céréale [sereal] f. BOT. Cereal.

céréaliculture [-likylty:r] f. AGRIC. Cereal (ou) grain growing.

céréalier, ère [-lje, ɛ:r] adj. Cereal.

céréalier m. NAUT. Grain-carrier (ou) grain-carrying ship.

cérébelleux, euse [serebɛllø, ø:z] adj. MÉD. Cerebellar.

cérébral, ale [serebral] adj. MÉD. Cerebral; *fatigue, fièvre cérébrale*, brain-fag, -fever.
— m. Brain-worker.

cérébro-spinal, ale [serebrospinal] adj. MÉD. Cerebro-spinal.

cérémonial [seremɔnjal] m. invar. ECCLÉS. Ceremonial. ‖ JUR. Etiquette.

cérémonie [-ni] f. Ceremony (solennité); *maître des cérémonies*, master of ceremonies. ‖ Ceremony, formality; form; *faire des cérémonies*, to make a fuss (ou) a to-do; *sans cérémonie*, informally, in a homely (ou) U. S. homelike way.

cérémoniel, elle [-njɛl] adj. Ceremonial.

cérémonieusement [-njøzmᾶ] adv. Ceremoniously.

cérémonieux, euse [-njø, ø:z] adj. Ceremonious; formal; *façons cérémonieuses*, ceremoniousness.

cerf [sɛ:r] m. ZOOL. Hart, stag, red deer; *jeune cerf*, staggard. ‖ **Cerf-volant**, m. Stag-beetle (insecte); kite (jouet); signal kite (signalisation); *jouer au cerf-volant*, to fly a kite.

cerfeuil [sɛrfœ:j] m. BOT. Chervil.

cerisaie [sərizɛ] f. Cherry-orchard.

cerise [səri:z] f. BOT. Cherry; *cerises à l'eau de vie*, brandied cherries; *eau-de-vie de cerises*, cherry-brandy.
— adj. invar. Cerise, cherry-red.

cerisier [sərizje] m. BOT. Cherry-tree (arbre); cherry-wood (bois).

cérite [serit] f. CHIM. Cerite.

cérium [serjɔm] m. CHIM. Cerium.

cerne [sɛrn] m. Ring (d'une blessure, de la lune, d'une tache, des yeux). ‖ BOT. Ring (d'un arbre).

cerneau [sɛrno] m. Green walnut.

cerner [sɛrne] v. tr. (1). To make a ring round (une blessure, une tache, les yeux); *avoir les yeux cernés*, to have rings (ou) circles under the eyes. ‖ MILIT. To hem in (v. ASSIÉGER, INVESTIR); to besiege (l'ennemi); to surround, to encircle (une maison, une ville). ‖ AGRIC. To girdle, to ring; to dig around (un arbre); to shell (des noix).

cernure [sɛrny:r] f. Ring (d'une tache); blue (ou) dark ring (des yeux).

certain, aine [sɛrtɛ̃, ɛn] adj. Certain, fixed, determined, undisputed, legal (date); certain, assured (fait); sure, certain, positive, clear, confident (personne); unquestionable, positive (preuve); sure (signe); *certain de réussir*, sure of succeeding; *je n'en suis pas bien certain*, I am not so sure; *je veux en être tout à fait certain*, I want to be quite clear on that point; *on peut considérer comme certain que*, it may be taken as certain that; *une chose certaine*, a certainty; *sûr et certain*, absolutely certain. ‖ PHILOS. Apodictic.
— adj. indéf. Certain, some; *certaines personnes*, some people; *une certaine somme*, a certain sum; *jusqu'à un certain point*, up to a point, in some measure; *dans un certain sens*, in a way. ‖ One, certain; *un certain M. D.*, one Mr. D., a Mr. D., a certain Mr. D.
— pron. indéf. Some, some people; *certains pensent*, some think.

— m. Certainty; sure thing. ‖ FIN. *Donner le certain,* to quote certain.

certainement [-tɛnmᾶ] adv. Certainly. (V. ASSURÉMENT.) ‖ Of course; U. S. surely, sure (fam.) [dans les réponses].

certes [sɛrt] adv. Most certainly, surely; to be sure; *non certes,* no indeed!

certifiable [sɛrtifjabl] adj. Certifiable.

certificat [sɛrtifika] m. Character testimonial (d'employeur). ‖ Diploma. ‖ MÉD. Certificate (de médecin). ‖ JUR. *Certificat de bonne vie et mœurs,* certificate of good character. ‖ FIN. Certificate (de dépôt); *certificat provisoire,* scrip. ‖ COMM. Certificate (d'origine). ‖ NAUT. *Certificat de chargement,* certificate of receipt. ‖ FIG. Guarantee (de longévité, de santé).

certificateur [-tœ:r] m. Certifier, guarantor.

certificatif, ive [-tif, i:v] adj. Certificatory.

certification [-sjɔ̃] f. JUR. Certification; guaranteeing (de caution); witnessing (de signature).

certifié, ée [sɛrtifje] adj. Who holds C. A. P. E. S., qualified.
— s. Holder of C. A. P. E. S., qualified teacher.

certifier [sɛrtifje] v. tr. (1). To certify, to assure (v. AFFIRMER); *certifier qqch. à qqn,* to certify s.o. of sth. ‖ JUR. To certify, to guarantee (une caution); to authenticate, to witness (une signature). ‖ FIN. To certify (un chèque).

certitude [-tyd] f. Certainty (d'un fait); certitude, conviction, sureness (d'une personne); *avoir la certitude de,* to be sure of; *avec certitude,* with certainty.

céruléen, enne [serylēɛ̃, ɛn] adj. Cerulean, sky-blue, azure.

cérumen [serymɛn] m. MÉD. Cerumen, ear-wax.

céruse [sery:z] f. Ceruse.

cerveau [sɛrvo] m. MÉD. Brain; *cervéau antérieur, moyen, postérieur,* forebrain, midbrain, hindbrain; *malade du cerveau,* brain-sick; *rhume de cerveau,* cold in the head; *tumeur au cerveau,* tumour on the brain. ‖ Brains, wits, mind, intelligence; *cerveau brûlé,* hot-head; *cerveau creux,* dreamer; *au cerveau fêlé,* crack-brained; *au cerveau d'oiseau,* scatter- (ou) hare-brained; *une cervelle d'oiseau,* a feather-brain; *se torturer le cerveau,* to beat (ou) rack one's brain.

cervelas [-vəla] m. CULIN. Saveloy, cervelat.

cervelet [-vəlɛ] m. MÉD. Cerebellum.

cervelle [-vɛl] f. MÉD. Brain. ‖ CULIN. Brains. ‖ ‖ LOC. Brains; *se brûler* (ou) *se faire sauter la cervelle,* to blow one's brains out; *se creuser la cervelle,* to rack (ou) cudgel one's brains; *sans cervelle,* brainless.

cervical, ale [-vikal] adj. MÉD. Cervical.

cervidé [sɛrvide] m. ZOOL. Deer; pl. Cervid.

cervin, ine [sɛrvɛ̃, in] adj. ZOOL. Cervine. ‖ GÉOGR. *Le mont Cervin,* the Matterhorn.

cervoise [sɛrvwa:z] f. † Barley-beer.

ces [sɛ]. V. CE.

C.E.S. [seəɛs] m. Abrév. de *collège d'enseignement secondaire,* comprehensive school, school for pupils aged 11 to 15.

césarien, enne [sezarjɛ̃, ɛn] adj. † Caesarean, caesarian.

césarienne f. MÉD. Caesarean, caesarian.

césarisme [sɛzarism] m. Cæsarism.

césium [sezjɔm] m. CHIM. Cæsium; U. S. cesium.

cessant, ante [sɛsᾶ, ᾶ:t] adj. Ceasing, suspending; *toute affaire cessante,* straight away, to the exclusion of all other business, immediately.

cessation [sɛsasjɔ̃] f. Closure (de contrat); discontinuance (des études, de fabrication, de travaux); cessation, suspension (des hostilités); suspension, stoppage (de paiements); breach (des relations).

cesse [sɛs] f. Cease, ceasing; *n'avoir de cesse*

que, not to rest till; *pas de cesse,* no respite; *sans cesse,* ceaselessly, incessantly, unceasingly, constantly.

cesser [-se] v. tr. (1). To cease (ses efforts); to stop, to cease from, to leave off (le travail); *cesser de boire,* to break off drinking; *cesser de parler,* to stop talking; *cesser de se voir,* to cease seeing each other; *ne pas cesser de dire,* to say again and again. ‖ MILIT. *Cesser le feu,* to cease fire (ou) firing. ‖ COMM. *Cesser ses paiements,* to stop payment.
— v. intr. To stop (bruit); to cease, to stop (pluie); *faire cesser,* to put down (des abus); to put a stop to (qqch.).

cessez-le-feu [seselfø] m. inv. Cease-fire.

cessibilité [-sibilite] f. JUR. Transferability (de propriétés). ‖ FIN. Negotiability (de titres).

cessible [-sibl] adj. JUR. Transferable, assignable. ‖ FIN. Negotiable.

cession [-sjɔ̃] f. JUR. Transfer (de bail, de créances); cession, conveyance, transfer (de biens); assignment, surrender (de droits); *faire cession de,* to convey, to transfer. ‖ **Cession-transport,** f. JUR. Transfer of claim.

cessionnaire [-jɔnɛ:r] m. JUR. Assignee; cessionary. ‖ FIN. Transferee.

c'est-à-dire [sɛtadi:r] loc. conj. That is to say; i.e. (= id est).

cestode [sɛstɔd] m. ZOOL. Cestode.

césure [sezy:r] f. Cæsura.

cet, cette [sɛt] V. CE.

C.E.T. [seəte] m. Abrév. de *collège d'enseignement technique,* technical school for pupils aged 11 to 15.

cétacé, ée [setase] adj. ZOOL. Cetacean, cetaceous.
— m. ZOOL. Cetacean.

cétane [setan] m. CHIM. Cetane; *indice de cétane,* cetane number.

cétoine [setwan] f. ZOOL. Cetonia; *cétoine dorée,* rose-beetle.

cétone [setɔn] f. CHIM. Ketone.

ceux [sø]. V. CELUI.

cévenol, ole [sevnɔl] adj. GÉOGR. Of (ou) from Cévennes.
— s. Native (ou) inhabitant of Cévennes.

Ceylan [sɛlᾶ] m. GÉOGR. Ceylon.

cf [seɛf] abrév. de *confer,* cf.

C.F.A. [seɛfα] abrév. de *Communauté financière africaine; franc C.F.A.,* franc in use in former French colonies, franc CFA.

C.F.D.T. [seɛfdete] f. Abrév. de *Confédération française démocratique du travail,* trade-union CFDT.

C.G.S. [seʒeɛs] abrév. de *centimètre, gramme, seconde,* CGS.

C.G.T. [seʒete] f. Abrév. de *Confédération générale du travail,* trade-union CGT.

chablis [ʃabli] m. Chablis (vin). ‖ Windfall (bois).

chabot [ʃabo] m. ZOOL. Bull-head, miller's thumb.

chabraque [ʃabrak] f. MILIT. Shabrack.

chacal [ʃakal] m. (pl. *chacals*). ZOOL. Jackal.

chaco(n)ne [ʃakɔn] f. MUS. Chaconne.

chacun, une [ʃakœ, yn] pr. indéf. Each (individuellement); everyone, everybody (collectivement); *chacun de ces deux vers a cinq pieds,* each of these two verses has five feet; *chacun sait que,* everybody knows that; *chacun pour soi,* every man for himself; *chacun son goût,* every man to his taste; *chacun avait sa chacune,* every Jack has his Jill. ‖ FAM. *Tout un chacun,* everyone, every Tom, Dick and Harry.

chadouf [ʃaduf] m. Shadoof.

chafouin, ine [ʃafwɛ̃, in] adj. Weasel-faced; *à la mine chafouine,* sly-looking.
— s. Weasel-faced person.

chagrin [ʃagrɛ̃] m. Shagreen (cuir); *peau de chagrin*, shagreen.

chagrin, ine adj. Sorrowful, sorry, sad; gloomy. ‖ Troubled, distressed (*de*, at). ‖ Fretful (irritable); *humeur chagrine*, fretfulness.

chagrin m. Sorrow, grief, affliction; trouble; *avoir du chagrin*, to be in sorrow; *faire du chagrin à*, to grieve, to distress; *usé par le chagrin*, grief-worn (ou) -consumed.

chagrinant, ante [ʃagrinã, ã:t] adj. Afflicting, distressing. ‖ Annoying, vexing.

chagriné, ée [ʃagrine] adj. Aggrieved, distressed; *être chagriné*, to feel aggrieved.

chagriné, ée adj. Shagreened (cuir); granulated (papier).

chagriner v. tr. (1). To grieve, to distress (affliger); to annoy, to vex (ennuyer).

chagriner v. tr. (1). To shagreen (le cuir).

chah [ʃa] m. Shah.

chahut [ʃay] m. Din, uproar, rowdyism (bruit); *faire du chahut*, to kick up a shindy, to raise Cain. ‖ Rag (d'étudiants).

chahuter [-te] v. intr. (1). To kick up a shindy; to be rowdy (faire du bruit). ‖ To rag (étudiants); to barrack, to boo (spectateurs).
— v. tr. To boo (des artistes); to rag (un professeur). ‖ SPORTS. To barrack, to jeer (des sportifs). ‖ FAM. To upset (qqch.).

chahuteur, euse [-tœ:r, ø:z] adj. Rumbustious, rowdy; U. S. rambunctious.
— s. High-kicker, ragger.

chai [ʃɛ] m. Wine-store.

chaînage [ʃɛna:ʒ] m. Chaining. ‖ Clamping.

chaîne [ʃɛ:n] f. Chain (de chien); *mettre un chien à la chaîne*, to chain up a dog, to put a dog on the chain. ‖ Chain; *chaîne de montre*, watch-chain; *chaîne de porte*, safety-chain. ‖ Chain; *chaîne d'arpenteur*, surveyor's chain, measuring chain; *chaîne d'huissier*, usher's chain of office. ‖ Chain; *chaîne de bicyclette*, bicycle-chain; *chaîne antivol*, chain-lock. ‖ Warp (d'un tissu). ‖ Chain-letter (circulaire). ‖ Pl. Chains, irons, shackles, fetters (de prisonnier). ‖ MILIT. Line (de tirailleurs). ‖ NAUT. Cable (d'ancre); boom (de port); *chaîne d'ancrage*, anchor chain. ‖ GÉOGR. *Chaîne de montagnes*, chain of mountains, mountain range. ‖ ARCHIT. Tie (barre); pier (pile). ‖ CHIM. *Réaction en chaîne*, chain of reactions, chain reaction; *chaîne fermée d'atomes*, closed chain of atoms. ‖ CH. DE F. *Chaîne d'attelage*, chain-coupling. ‖ TECHN. *Chaîne de montage*, assembly line; *chaîne de transmission*, driving chain. ‖ TECHN. Chain, line (de personnes); *faire la chaîne*, to make (ou) form a chain; *travail à la chaîne*, chain-work, assembly line work, serial production, gang work; *travailler à la chaîne*, to form a chain, to pass from hand to hand. ‖ RADIO. Network (à la T. V.); *transmettre en chaîne*, to transmit over a network. ‖ FIG. Link, bond, bondage, chain (lien); *rivé à la chaîne*, in hopeless bondage; *rompre ses chaînes*, to escape from bondage. ‖ FIG. Sequence (d'événements); series (de faits).

chaîner [ʃɛne] v. tr. (1). To chain (mesurer); to tie (relier).

chaînette [-nɛt] f. Chainlet. ‖ *Point de chaînette*, chain-stitch; *coudre au point de chaînette*, to chain-stitch. ‖ MATH. *En chaînette*, catenary (arc).

chaînon [-nɔ̃] m. Link (d'une chaîne). ‖ GÉOGR. Secondary range (de montagnes).

chair [ʃɛ:r] f. Flesh; *chair de poule*, gooseflesh; *donner la chair de poule à qqn*, to make s.o.'s flesh creep (ou) crawl; *bien en chair*, plump; *en chair et en os*, in the flesh; *ni chair ni poisson*, neither flesh, fowl, nor good red herring; *pénétrer dans les chairs*, to go deep into the flesh. ‖ CULIN. Flesh; meat (viande); *chair à saucisses*, sausage-meat. ‖ BOT. Flesh, pulp (de fruit). ‖ MILIT. *Chair à canon*, cannon fodder, U. S. bullet bait. ‖ ARTS. Pl. Flesh-tints. ‖ FIG. Flesh; *la chair est faible*, the flesh is weak.
— adj. invar. Flesh-coloured; *maillot chair*, flesh-tights.

chaire f. Chair, professorship (de professeur de faculté); lectureship (de maître de conférences); *titulaire d'une chaire de*, holder of a chair in. ‖ Chair (meuble). ‖ ECCLÉS. Throne (d'un évêque); chair (du pape); pulpit (d'un prédicateur); *du haut de la chaire*, from the pulpit; *monter en chaire*, to ascend the pulpit. ‖ FIG. *L'éloquence de la chaire*, pulpit eloquence.

chaise [ʃɛ:z] f. Chair; *chaise électrique*, electric chair, the chair; *chaise longue*, lounge-chair, reclining chair, chaise-longue; *chaise percée*, commode; *chaise pliante*, folding chair; *chaise à porteurs*, sedan chair; *chaise de poste*, post-chaise; *chaise roulante*, Bath-chair; *il est obligé de faire de la chaise longue*, he is obliged to lie down every day. ‖ TECHN. Support, bracket. ‖ CH. DE F. Chair. ‖ NAUT. Rope sling. ‖ FAM. *Rester le derrière entre deux chaises*, to fall between two stools.

chaisier [ʃɛzje] m. Chair-maker.

chaisière [ʃɛzjɛ:r] f. Pew-opener (à l'église); chair-attendant (à l'église, dans les jardins).

chaland [ʃalã] m. COMM. Customer. (V. CLIENT.)

chaland m. NAUT. Barge, lighter; *transport par chaland*, lighterage.

chalazion [kalazjɔ̃] m. MÉD. Chalazion, sty, hordeolum.

chalcographe [kalkɔgraf] m. ARTS. Chalcographer.

chalcographie [kalkɔgrafi] f. ARTS. Chalcography.

chalcolithique [kalkɔlitik] adj. Chalcolithic.
— m. The Chalcolithic Age.

chalcopyrite [kalkɔpirit] f. GÉOL. Chalcopyrite.

chalcosine [kalkɔzin], **chalcosite** [-zit] f. GÉOL. Chalcocite.

chaldaïque [kaldaik] adj. Chaldaic.

Chaldée [kalde] f. GÉOGR. Chaldea.

chaldéen, enne [kaldeɛ̃, ɛn] adj., s. GÉOGR. Chaldean, Chaldee.

châle [ʃɑ:l] m. Shawl.

chalet [ʃalɛ] m. Swiss chalet. ‖ Chalet (maison); *chalet de nécessité*, street lavatory, public convenience.

chaleur [ʃalœ:r] f. Heat; *les grandes chaleurs*, the hot season (ou) weather (ou) days; *qui absorbe la chaleur*, heat-absorbing. ‖ Warmth; *une agréable sensation de chaleur*, a glow, a pleasant sense of warmth. ‖ *En chaleur*, in heat (animal). ‖ COMM. *Craint la chaleur*, to be kept in a cool place. ‖ PHYS. Heat. ‖ ARTS. Warmth (d'une couleur). ‖ FIG. Warmth (d'un accueil, de la discussion, d'une recommandation); heat (du combat, de la composition, de la discussion, du moment, des passions); glow (de l'enthousiasme, de la jeunesse, du teint); *chaleur communicative des banquets*, convivial expansiveness.

chaleureusement [ʃalørøzmã] adv. Warmly; cordially; impetuously.

chaleureux, euse [-rø, ø:z] adj. Warm, hearty (accueil, compliments, remerciements); cordial (accueil); warm (applaudissements, recommandation); glowing (couleur, termes); fiery (imagination); *en termes chaleureux*, glowingly.

châlit [ʃali] m. Bedstead.

challenge [ʃalã:ʒ] m. SPORTS. Challenge trophy (épreuve); trophy (coupe).

challenger [ʃalɛndʒœ:r] m. SPORTS. Challenger.

chaloir [ʃalwa:r] v. tr. impers. (3). † *Peu me chaut*, little do I care.

chaloupe [ʃalup] f. NAUT. Launch; sloop.
chalouper [-pe] v. intr. (1). To walk with a roll.
chalumeau [ʃalymo] m. Straw (pour boire). ‖ MUS. Pipe, chalumeau. ‖ TECHN. Blowpipe, blowlamp; découpage au chalumeau, oxy-acetylene cutting-out.
chalut [ʃaly] m. Trawl-net, trawl.
chalutier [-tje] m. NAUT. Trawler (bateau, pêcheur).
chamade [ʃamad] f. † MILIT. Chamade. ‖ FIG. Battre la chamade, to beat wildly (cœur).
chamaille [ʃama:j] f. V. CHAMAILLERIE.
chamailler [ʃamɑje] v. tr. (1). To squabble with, to wrangle with.
— v. pr. Se chamailler, to bicker, to squabble.
chamaillerie [-jri] f. Wrangle; bickering.
chamailleur, euse [-jœ:r, ø:z] adj. Quarrelsome, wrangling.
— s. Bickerer, squabbler.
chamanisme [ʃamanism] m. Shamanism.
chamarré, ée [ʃamare] adj. Chamarré de, plastered over, glittering with (personnage); ablaze with, bedecked with (uniforme); bedizened with (style); chamarré d'or, gold-laced.
chamarrer v. tr. (1). To bedeck; to bedizen.
chamarrure [-ry:r] f. Bedizenment, bedizening.
chambard [ʃɑ̃:bar] m. Din, row, racket.
chambardement [-dəmɑ̃] m. Upheaval; upset.
chambarder [-de] v. tr. (1). To upset, to turn upside down. (V. BOULEVERSER.) ‖ FIG. To upset (les plans, les projets).
chambellan [ʃɑ̃bɛllɑ̃] m. Chamberlain.
chambertin [ʃɑ̃bɛrtɛ̃] m. COMM. Chambertin (vin).
chambouler [ʃɑ̃bule] v. tr. (1). To upset, to turn upside down; tout chambouler dans la maison, to turn the house upside down. ‖ FAM. Ça l'a rudement chamboulé, it gave him a nasty turn.
chambranle [ʃɑ̃brɑ̃:l] m. Mantelpiece (de cheminée); frame, casing (de fenêtre); frame, jamblining, U. S. trim (de porte).
chambre [ʃɑ̃:br] f. Room, bedroom; chambre d'ami, spare room, guest-room; chambre à coucher, bedroom; chambre d'enfants, nursery; chambre à un lit, à deux lits, single room, double room; garder la chambre, to keep to one's room; to be confined to one's room; faire une chambre, to clean out (ou) to do a room; faire chambre à part, to sleep in separate rooms; ouvrier en chambre, cottage labourer, garret-craftsman; stratège en chambre, armchair strategist. ‖ Set of bedroom furniture (meubles). ‖ Room; chambre froide, cold storage. ‖ Chamber, House (assemblée); Chambre de commerce, Chamber of Commerce; U. S. Board of Trade; Chambre des députés, House of Representatives (en Amérique); House of Commons (en Angleterre); Chamber of Deputies (en France). ‖ JUR. Court-room, court, chamber; section (du tribunal). ‖ MILIT. Chamber (de revolver). ‖ NAUT. Cabin, room; chambre des machines, engine-room. ‖ MÉD. Chamber (de l'œil). ‖ AUTOM. Chambre à air, inner tube; chambre d'explosion, combustion-chamber; sans chambre, tubeless (pneu). ‖ TECHN. Chamber (d'une écluse, d'une mine); camera (en photographie); chambre d'agrandissement, enlarging camera; chambre claire, noire, camera lucida, obscura. ‖ MUS. Musique de chambre, chamber music.
chambrée [-bre] f. MILIT. Barrack-room (pièce); roomful (soldats).
chambrer v. tr. (1). To lock up (enfermer); to closet (prendre à part). ‖ To take the chill off, to bring to room temperature (du vin).
chambrette [-brɛt] f. Small room.

chambrière [-brjɛ:r] f. Lunging whip (fouet). ‖ Prop (de voiture).
chameau [ʃamo] m. ZOOL. Camel. ‖ NAUT. Camel. ‖ CH. DE F. Dolly. ‖ FAM. Shrew, scold, bitch (femme); beast, dirty dog (homme).
chamelier [ʃaməlje] m. Cameleer.
chamelle [ʃamɛl] f. ZOOL. She-camel.
chamito-sémitique [kamitosemitik] adj., m. Hamito-Semitic.
chamois [ʃamwa] m. Chamois (animal); peau de chamois, chamois- (ou) shammy-leather, washleather.
— adj. Chamois, fawn-coloured.
chamoiser [-ze] v. tr. (1). To chamois.
chamoniard, arde [ʃamɔnja:r, ard] adj. GÉOGR. Of (ou) from Chamonix.
— s. Native (ou) inhabitant of Chamonix.
champ [ʃɑ̃] m. De champ, v. CHANT.
champ m. AGRIC. Field (terre labourable); champ de blé, field of corn, corn-field. ‖ Pl. Country, fields (campagne); à travers champs, across the fields, across country. ‖ Ground, field (terrain); champ clos, lists, tilt-yard; champ de courses, racecourse, U. S. race track; champ de foire, fair-ground; champ de neige, snow-field. ‖ MILIT. Champ de bataille, battlefield; champ d'honneur, field of honour; champ de manœuvre, parade ground; champ de mines, minefield; champ de tir, rifle range; practice ground; field of fire. ‖ SPORTS., ELECTR., PHYS. Field. ‖ MÉD. Champ opératoire, operative field; champ visuel, field (ou) range of vision. ‖ ARTS. Field, ground (de tableau). ‖ BLAS. Field. ‖ CINÉM. Dans le champ, in the shot. ‖ FIG. Field, sphere (d'action); range (d'hypothèses, d'observations); compass (de la littérature); champ de recherches, field for inquiry; avoir du champ, to have elbow-room; ouvrir le champ à, to open a wide field for (ou) to; prendre du champ, to give oneself room; laisser le champ libre à, to give a clear field to, to make room for. ‖ LOC. A tout bout de champ, at every turn; sur-le-champ, on the spot, at once.
champagne [ʃɑ̃paɲ] f. GÉOGR. Champagne. ‖ COMM. Fine champagne, liqueur brandy.
— m. COMM. Champagne (vin); champagne brut, nature, mousseux, d'origine, extra-dry, still, sparkling, vintage champagne.
champagnisation [-ɲizasjɔ̃] f. AGRIC. Processing of wine following the method used for champagne.
champagniser [-ɲize] v. tr. (1). To aerate, to give sparkle to (le vin).
champenois, oise [ʃɑ̃pənwa, a:z] adj. GÉOGR. Of (ou) from Champagne.
— s. Native (ou) inhabitant of Champagne.
champêtre [ʃɑ̃pɛ:tr] adj. Rustic (banc, écriture); village (fête); rustic, rural (mœurs); rural (pittoresque); pastoral (poésie); country (vie).
champignon [ʃɑ̃piɲɔ̃] m. BOT., CULIN. Mushroom, champignon (comestible); toadstool, fungus (vénéneux); champignon de couche, cultivated mushroom; pousser comme un champignon, to spring up like a mushroom, to mushroom; sauce aux champignons, mushroom ketchup (ou) sauce. ‖ Hat-stand (à chapeaux); round-headed peg (à vêtements). ‖ MÉD. Fungus. ‖ FAM., AUTOM. Accelerator pedal; appuyer sur le champignon, to step on it, U. S. to gun it.
champignonnière [-ɲɔnjɛ:r] f. Mushroom-bed.
champion [ʃɑ̃pjɔ̃] m. Champion, supporter (v. DÉFENSEUR); se faire le champion de, to champion. ‖ SPORTS. Champion. ‖ FAM. C'est champion, that takes the cake.
championnat [-pjɔna] m. SPORTS. Championship.
champlever [ʃɑ̃ləve] v. tr. (1). ARTS. To chase out (un émail); to gouge out (une gravure).

chançard, arde [ʃɑ̃sa:r, ard] adj. Lucky.
— FAM. Lucky person (v. VEINARD).
chance [ʃɑ̃:s] f. Chance, luck (v. VEINE); *avoir de la chance*, to be lucky; *avoir la chance de faire*, to have the luck to do; to have the good fortune of doing; *bonne chance!* good luck!; *pas de chance!*, hard luck!; *porter chance à qqn*, to bring s.o. good luck; *tenter sa chance*, to try one's luck, to chance it. ‖ Piece of luck; godsend, blessing (v. AUBAINE); *quelle chance!*, what a blessing! ‖ Chance, fortune, risk; *courir la chance de*, to run the risk of. ‖ Chance, possibility, probability; *avoir des chances égales*, to have an even chance; *avoir toutes les chances contre soi*, to have all the odds against oneself; *n'avoir pas l'ombre d'une chance*, not to have an earthly chance; *donner sa chance à qqn*, to give s.o. a chance; *il y a une chance*, it is just possible; *il y a de grandes chances que*, the chances are that; *il n'y a pas de chance que*, it is unlikely to; *une vague chance que*, an off chance of.
chancelant, ante [ʃɑ̃slɑ̃, ɑ̃:t] adj. Shaky (affaires, meuble, position, santé); faltering, wavering (courage, mémoire, résolution); unsteady (démarche, position, raison); tottering (dynastie, pouvoir); tottering, staggering, faltering (pas); tottering staggering (personne).
chancelariat [ʃɑ̃slarja] m. Chancellorship.
chanceler [ʃɑ̃sle] v. intr. (8 a). To reel, to stagger (v. FLAGEOLER); *chanceler sur ses jambes*, to be shaky on one's legs, U. S. to weave (ivrogne). ‖ FIG. To falter (courage, mémoire, résolution); to totter (dynastie, pouvoir); to waver (vertu).
chancelier [ʃɑ̃səlje] m. Chancellor; *Chancelier de l'Echiquier*, Chancellor of the Exchequer. ‖ Secretary (d'ambassade).
chancelière [-ljɛ:r] f. Foot-muff.
chancellerie [ʃɑ̃sɛlri] f. Chancellery; Chancellor's office. ‖ Secretaryship (diplomatique); chancery (de légation).
chanceux, euse [ʃɑ̃sø, ø:z] adj. Risky, hazardous (affaire, entreprise); uncertain (avenir, résultat); lucky (personne).
chancre [ʃɑ̃kr] m. MÉD. Canker; chancre. ‖ BOT. Canker; blister.
chancreux, euse [ʃɑ̃krø, ø:z] adj. MÉD. Cankerous; chancrous; cankered. ‖ BOT. Cankered.
chancroïde [ʃɑ̃krɔid] m. MÉD. Chancroid.
chandail [ʃɑ̃da:j] m. Sweater.
— SYN. : MAILLOT, PULL-OVER.
Chandeleur [ʃɑ̃dlœ:r] f. ECCLÉS. Candlemas.
chandelier [ʃɑ̃dəlje] m. Candlestick (objet). ‖ Candle-maker (fabricant).
chandelle [ʃɑ̃dɛl] f. Candle, tallow candle (bougie); taper (cierge); *à la chandelle*, by candle-light; *bout de chandelle*, candle-end; *fabrication des chandelles*, tallow-chandlery. ‖ AVIAT. *Monter en chandelle*, to zoom, to shoot up like a rocket. ‖ SPORTS. Lob, skyer (au tennis); *faire une chandelle*, to sky a ball. ‖ ARCHIT. Prop; pillar. ‖ FAM. Icicle (glaçon). ‖ POP. Snot (mcrvc). ‖ LOC. *Brûler la chandelle par les deux bouts*, to burn the candle at both ends; *devoir une fière chandelle à*, to owe a debt of gratitude to; *économie de bouts de chandelle*, cheese-paring economy; *le jeu n'en vaut pas la chandelle*, the game is not worth the candle; *s'éteindre comme une chandelle*, to go out like a light; *tenir la chandelle*, to hold a candle to the devil; *voir trente-six chandelles*, to see stars.
chanfrein [ʃɑ̃frɛ̃] m. Chamfrain (d'armure); forchcad (de cheval).
chanfrein m. TECHN. Chamfer, bevelled edge.
chanfreiner [-frɛne] v. tr. (1). To chamfer.
change [ʃɑ̃:ʒ] m. FIN. Exchange (en général); agio (bénéfice); change (monnaie); *bureau de change*, foreign exchange office; *change élevé*,

hard currency; *lettre de change*, bill. ‖ Exchange, barter (troc); *gagner au change*, to gain by the exchange. ‖ SPORTS. Wrong scent (à la chasse). ‖ FIG. *Donner le change à*, to side-track, to mislead.
changeable [-ʒabl] adj. Changeable, alterable. ‖ Exchangeable.
changeant [-ʒɑ̃] adj. Unsteady (affection); fickle, capricious, unstable, unsettled, unsteady (caractère); changeable, iridescent (couleur); uneven, fickle (humeur); changeable, mercurial, fitful, wayward (personne); shifting (relations, scène); shot (soie); variable, unsettled (temps).
changement [-ʒmɑ̃] m. Change (d'air, de domicile, d'idée, de ministère, de nom, d'occupation); *changement de temps*, change in the weather; *un changement complet s'est produit dans son existence*, his whole life has been changed. ‖ Alteration (changement partiel); *de légers changements*, some slight alterations. ‖ Mutation, transfer (de classe, de poste); *demander son changement*, to apply for a transfer. ‖ MILIT. Conversion. ‖ AUTOM. *Changement de vitesse*, gear-change, change of gear (action); change-speed-gear (dispositif). ‖ CH. DE F. *Changement de voie*, turn-off. ‖ THÉÂTR. *Changement à vue*, transformation scene; *changement de décor*, change of scenery. ‖ LOC. « *Changement de propriétaire* », « Under New Ownership ».
changer [-ʒe] v. tr. (7). To change (remplacer); *changer la nappe, un pneu*, to change the table-cloth, a tyre. ‖ To change, to move, to shift (déplacer); *changer qqch. de place*, to change the place of sth. ‖ To change, to turn (transformer) [en, into]; *changer qqn en loup*, to turn s.o. into a wolf. ‖ To change, to alter (modifier); *cela le change beaucoup*, that makes him look very different, that alters him much. ‖ To divert (distraire); *cela me change fort*, it's a great change for me; *cela me change les idées*, it makes a change for me, it turns my thoughts in another direction, it takes my mind off my work (ou) my sorrows. ‖ To exchange, to barter (échanger); *changer une chose pour une autre*, to change one thing for another; *changer de place avec*, to change places with. ‖ To change the clothes of; *changer un enfant*, to change a child's napkin (ou) U. S. diaper. ‖ FIN. To change (un billet de banque). ‖ THÉÂTR. To shift (les décors). ‖ NAUT. To shift (une voile). ‖ FAM. *Changer son fusil d'épaule*, to change one's line of conduct.
— v. intr. To alter (choses, événements); to vary (opinion); to change (personne, temps); to shift, to veer (vent); *il a beaucoup changé*, he is greatly altered. ‖ *Changer de chaussures, de vêtements*, to change one's shoes, one's clothes; *changer de peau*, to shed one's skin. ‖ *Changer de cours*, to shift one's course (rivière); *changer de domicile*, to move, to shift one's quarters; *changer de place*, to shift round, to make a shift; to change one's place; to change one's seat; *changer de position*, to shift one's position; *changer de route*, to take another road. ‖ THÉÂTR. To shift (décor, scène). ‖ CH. DE F. *Changer de train, de voiture*, to change trains, carriages. ‖ MILIT. *Changer de front*, to change front. ‖ AUTOM. *Changer de vitesse*, to change gear. ‖ FIG. *Changer d'avis, de condition, de ton*, to change one's mind, condition, tune; *changer de couleur, de main, de parti*, to change colours, hands, parties; *changer de sujet*, to change the subject.
— v. pr. Se changer, to change, to change one's clothes. ‖ *Se changer en*, to turn into, to change into.
changeur [-ʒœ:r] m. FIN. Money-changer. ‖ RADIO. *Changeur d'ondes*, waveband change switch.
chanlat(t)e [ʃɑ̃lat] f. ARCHIT. Eaves-board, chantlate.

chanoine [ʃanwan] m. ECCLÉS. Canon.

chanoinesse [-nɛs] f. Canoness.

chanson [ʃɑ̃sɔ̃] f. MUS. Song (v. CHANT); song (d'oiseaux); singing (du vent); *chanson à boire*, drinking song; *chanson d'amour*, love-song; *chanson de bord, de marin*, chanty; *chanson de geste*, chanson de geste, gest; *chanson à plusieurs parties*, glee, part-song; *chanson de route*, marching song. ‖ FAM. Chansons!, rubbish!, fiddlesticks!, fiddlededee!, nonsense!. ‖ LOC. *C'est une autre chanson*, that's another story; *chanter toujours la même chanson*, to sing the same old song, to harp always on the same string, to go over the same ground; *il en a l'air et la chanson*, his appearance is full of truth; *finir par des chansons*, to end in songs.

chansonner [ʃɑ̃sɔne] v. tr. (1). To lampoon.

chansonnette [-nɛt] f. MUS. Canzonet. ‖ Comic-song.

chansonnier [-nje] m. MUS. Song-writer, chansonnier. ‖ Song-book (recueil).

chant [ʃɑ̃] m. MUS. Singing (action); song (chanson); *chant de Noël*, Christmas carol; *chant de guerre*, battle-song, war-song; *des leçons de chant*, singing lessons. ‖ Carol, song (de l'alouette); chirp (de la cigale, du grillon); crowing (du coq); song, woodnote (des oiseaux); song, jug-jug (du rossignol); *au chant du coq*, at cockcrow. ‖ Canto (d'un poème); epics (d'un poète épique); song, lay (d'un poète lyrique). ‖ ECCLÉS. *Chant grégorien*, Gregorian chant. ‖ MÉD. *Chant du coq*, whoop, whooping (coqueluche). ‖ FIG. *Chant du cygne*, swan-song.

chant m. *De chant*, on edge, edgeways, edgewise.

chantable [-tabl] adj. Singable.

chantage [-ta:ʒ] m. Blackmail, blackmailing; *faire du chantage auprès de*, to blackmail.

chantant, ante [-tɑ̃, ɑ̃:t] adj. Sing-song, lilting (accent, voix); melodious (air, musique); musical (soirée, vers); *café chantant*, café, music-hall.

chanteau [ʃɑ̃to] m. Cutting (d'étoffe); hunch, chunk (de pain).

Chanteclair [ʃɑ̃tklɛ:r] m. Chanticleer.

chantepleure [ʃɑ̃tplœ:r] f. Sprayer (arrosoir); colander (entonnoir); tap (robinet). ‖ Weeper (dans un mur).

chanter [ʃɑ̃te] v. intr. (1). To sing (en général); to carol (avec gaieté); to lilt, to sing-song (en parlant); *chanter en s'accompagnant de la guitare*, to sing to the guitar; *chanter pour endormir un enfant*, to sing a child to sleep. ‖ To carol (alouette); to chirp (cigale, grillon); to crow (coq); to sing (oiseaux); to cackle (poule); to jug (rossignol); to coo (tourterelle). ‖ To sing (eau qui bout); to hiss (eau qui va bouillir); to sizzle (friture); to creak (porte grinçante). ‖ ECCLÉS. To descant (en déchant); to chant (en psalmodiant). ‖ FIG. To pay hush-money; *faire chanter*, to blackmail. ‖ FAM. *Si ça vous chante*, if it suits you, if you like the idea of it. — v. tr. MUS. To sing (une chanson, un opéra); to keen (une mélopée funèbre). ‖ ECCLÉS. To sing (une cantique, la messe, les vêpres). ‖ FIG. To sing, to celebrate (l'amour, la nature); to sing, to chant, to sound (les louanges); *chanter victoire*, to sing victory, to crow. ‖ FAM. To tell a fairy-tale; *qu'est-ce que vous chantez là?*, what are you talking about?; *chanter qqch. sur tous les tons*, to ring the changes on the subject.

chanterelle [ʃɑ̃trɛl] f. BOT. Chanterelle.

chanterelle f. SPORTS. Decoy-bird (à la chasse). ‖ ARTS. Highest (ou) E string (du violon). ‖ FAM. *Appuyer sur la chanterelle*, to rub it in, to hammer it home.

chanteur [-tœ:r] m. MUS. Singer, vocalist (personne); *chanteur des rues*, street singer. ‖ ZOOL. Song-bird; songster (oiseau). — adj. Singing; *oiseau chanteur*, song-bird.

chanteuse [-tø:z] f. MUS. Woman singer, vocalist, U. S. chanteuse. (V. CANTATRICE).

chantier [ʃɑ̃tje] m. Yard; « *chantier* »,· « work in progress », « men at work ». ‖ ARCHIT. Building yard (de construction). ‖ TECHN. Open-cast workings (de mines à ciel ouvert); gantry, barrel-horse (pour tonneaux). ‖ NAUT. Yard; *chantier de construction navale*, ship-yard; *mettre un navire en chantier*, to lay a ship on the stocks (ou) slips. ‖ FIG. *Avoir un ouvrage sur le chantier*, to have a piece of work in hand, to have sth. on.

chantilly [ʃɑ̃tiji] f. CULIN. Whipped cream, chantilly.

chantonnement [ʃɑ̃tɔnmɑ̃] m. Humming.

chantonner [ʃɑ̃tɔne] v. tr., intr. (1). To hum.

chantoung [ʃɑ̃tung] m. Shantung (tissu).

chantourner [ʃɑ̃turne] v. tr. (1). To jig-saw, to whip-saw.

chantre [ʃɑ̃tr] m. ECCLÉS. Chanter; cantor; chorister (à la maîtrise); *premier chantre*, precentor; *sous-chantre*, succentor. ‖ FIG. Bard, songster (poète).

chanvre [ʃɑ̃vr] m. BOT. Hemp; *chanvre de Manille*, Manila hemp, abaca; *chanvre indien*, Indian hemp, hemp.

chanvrier [-vrje] s. Hemp-grower; hemp-dresser. — adj. Hemp (industrie).

chaos [kao] m. Chaos (pr. et fig.); *dans le chaos*, in a state of chaos.

chaotique [kaɔtik] adj. Chaotic.

chapardage [ʃaparda:ʒ] m. Pilfering, pinching, scrounging.

chaparder [-de] v. tr. (1). To pilfer, to pinch, to scrounge, to sneak, to filch.

chapardeur, euse [ʃapardœ:r, ø:z] s. Filferer, filcher, sneak-thief. — adj. Pilfering, pinching, filching.

chape [ʃap] f. ECCLÉS. Cope. ‖ AUTOM. Tread (de pneu). ‖ ARCHIT. Cope (de moule de sculpture); coating (de voûte). ‖ TECHN. Shell, fork (de poulie). ‖ BLAS. Chape.

chapeau [ʃapo] m. Hat (de femme, d'homme); *chapeau de chasse*, deerstalker; *chapeau mou*, soft (ou) felt hat, trilby; U. S. fedora; *chapeau de paille*, straw-hat; *chapeau de paille d'Italie*, Leghorn-hat; *chapeau de soleil*, sun-hat; *chapeau pointu*, sugar-loaf hat; *chapeau bas*, cap in hand; *le chapeau sur la tête*, with his hat on; *donner un coup de chapeau à*, tirer son chapeau à, to take off one's hat to (pr. et fig.); *mettre son chapeau sur l'oreille*, to cock one's hat; *porter la main à son chapeau*, to touch one's hat. ‖ Heading, lead-in, U. S. caption (d'article); cap (de stylo). ‖ ECCLÉS. *Chapeau de cardinal*, cardinal's hat; *chapeau d'ecclésiastique*, shovel-hat. ‖ ARCHIT. Cowl, hood (de cheminée); bolster (de pilier). ‖ CULIN. Hat (de vol-au-vent). ‖ AUTOM. *Chapeau de roue*, hub cap. ‖ TECHN. Head (d'alambic); cap (de soupape); cap-sill (de vanne). ‖ NAUT. Funnel bonnet (de cheminée). ‖ MUS. *Chapeau chinois*, Chinese pavilion. ‖ FAM. *Travailler du chapeau*, to have a screw loose.

chapeauté, ée [-pɔte] adj. FAM. With a hat on; *bien chapeautée*, wearing a lovely hat.

chapeauter [-pɔte] v. tr. (1). To be at the head of, to supervise.

chapelain [ʃaplɛ̃] m. ECCLÉS. Chaplain.

chapelet [ʃaplɛ] m. ECCLÉS. Beads, chaplet, rosary; *dire son chapelet*, to tell one's beads. ‖ CULIN. String (d'oignons). ‖ MILIT. Stick (de bombes). ‖ GÉOGR. Chain (de collines, de rochers); string (d'îlots). ‖ ELECTR. Chain (d'isolateurs); *en chapelet*, in series. ‖ FIG. String (de décorations, d'injures); chain (d'événements); *débiter un chapelet de vers*, to reel off verses.

chapelier [ʃaplje] m. Hatter. — adj. Hat (industrie).

chapelière [-ljɛ:r] f. Saratoga (ou) hat trunk.
chapelle [ʃapɛl] f. ECCLÉS. Chapel (ensemble, partie); *chapelle de la Sainte Vierge*, Lady chapel; *chapelle de secours*, chapel of ease. ‖ MUS. Choir; *maître de chapelle*, choir master. ‖ TECHN. Case, box. ‖ FIG. Literary set (ou) clique (en littérature). ‖ LOC. *Chapelle ardente*, mortuary chamber, chapelle ardente.
chapellenie [-ni] f. ECCLÉS. Chaplaincy.
chapellerie [ʃapɛlri] f. Hat-industry. ‖ Hat-trade (commerce); hatter's shop (magasin).
chapelure [ʃaply:r] f. CULIN. Bread-crumb topping, bread crumbs.
chaperon [ʃaprɔ̃] m. † Hood (de faucon, d'homme); *le Petit Chaperon rouge*, Little Red Riding Hood. ‖ ARCHIT. Coping (de mur). ‖ FIG. Chaperon; *servir de chaperon à*, to chaperon.
chaperonner [ʃaprɔne] v. tr. (1). To hood (un faucon); to cope (un mur). ‖ To chaperon (qqn); *le fait de chaperonner*, chaperonage.
chapiteau [ʃapito] m. Cornice (d'armoire, de buffet). ‖ Head (d'alambic, de fusée). ‖ Top, big top (de cirque). ‖ ARCHIT. Capital.
chapitre [ʃapitr] m. Chapter (d'un livre); *chapitre un*, Chapter One. ‖ COMM. Head, heading, item (des dépenses). ‖ ECCLÉS. Chapter (de chanoines); *salle du chapitre*, chapter-house. ‖ FIG. Subject, matter, head, point, score (sujet); *assez sur ce chapitre*, enough on that subject; *avoir voix au chapitre*, to have a say in the matter; *commencer un nouveau chapitre de sa vie*, to turn over a new leaf.
chapitrer [-tre] v. tr. (1). To admonish.
chapon [ʃapɔ̃] m. ZOOL. Capon (coq). ‖ CULIN. Crust rubbed with garlic.
chaponner [ʃapɔne] v. tr. (1). To caponize.
chapska [ʃapska] m. Schapska, polish cap.
chaptalisation [ʃaptalizasjɔ̃] f. AGRIC. Chaptalization (du vin).
chaptaliser [-lize] v. tr. (1). AGRIC. To chaptalize (le vin).
chaque [ʃak] adj. invar. Every (collectivement); each (séparément); either, both (s'il s'agit de deux); *chaque élève a sa grammaire*, every pupil has his grammar (tous l'ont); *une place pour chaque chose*, a place for everything; *on a donné à chaque élève un sujet de composition différent*, each pupil was given a different subject for an essay; *chaque rive*, either bank (ou) side of the river; *une fleur à chaque main*, a flower in both hands. ‖ LOC. *A chaque instant*, at every moment.
char [ʃa:r] m. † Chariot (de course). ‖ Car (de défilé, de triomphe). ‖ Waggon; U. S. wagon (voiture); *char à banc*, horse-charabanc; *char funèbre*, hearse. ‖ AGRIC. Ox-cart. ‖ MILIT. Tank; *char d'assaut* (ou) *de combat*, tank; *chef de char*, tank commander. ‖ FIG. *Le char de l'Etat*, the Ship of State; *le char de Phébus*, Apollo's chariot.
charabia [ʃarabja] m. FAM. Gibberish, U. S. gobbledegook. (V. GALIMATIAS.)
charade [ʃarad] f. Charade. ‖ FIG. Puzzle.
charançon [ʃarɑ̃sɔ̃] m. ZOOL. Weevil.
charançonné, ée [-sɔne] adj. AGRIC. Weevilled, weevil-eaten, weevilly (blé).
charasse [ʃara:s] f. Crate, skeleton case.
charbon [ʃarbɔ̃] m. Coal, coals, U. S. soft coal (combustible); coal (minerai); *charbon activé*, activated charcoal; *charbon animal*, animal charcoal, char; *charbon de bois*, charcoal; *réduire en charbon*, to burn to a cinder. ‖ AGRIC. Blight, black rust, smut (des céréales). ‖ ARTS. *Agrandissement au charbon*, carbon enlargement. ‖ TECHN. *Charbon de cornue*, gas carbon. ‖ ELECTR. *A filament de charbon*, carbon filament (lampe). ‖ MÉD. Anthrax (des animaux); anthrax, carbuncle

(de l'homme). ‖ FIG. *Etre sur des charbons ardents*, to be on pins and needles (ou) on tenterhooks, U. S. to be on the anxious seat.
charbonnage [ʃarbɔna:ʒ] m. Coal-mining (exploitation); coal-mine, colliery (houillère).
charbonner [-ne] v. tr. (1). To char, to carbonize, to burn to a cinder (brûler). ‖ To blacken with charcoal (noircir). ‖ NAUT. To coal. ‖ ARTS. To draw with charcoal (dessiner).
— v. intr. To char, to carbonize. ‖ NAUT. To take in coal.
— v. pr. **Se charbonner**, to black (ou) to grime one's face.
charbonnerie [-nri] f. Coal depot.
charbonneux, euse [-nø, ø:z] adj. Coaly, carbonaceous; sooty. ‖ MÉD. Carbuncled (malade); anthrax-carrying (mouche).
charbonnier, ère [-nje, ɛr] adj. *Centre charbonnier*, coal-field; *industrie charbonnière*, coal-mining industry.
— m. Charcoal-burner (fabricant de charbon de bois); coal-heaver (déchargeur); coal-merchant, coal-dealer, coalman (marchand). ‖ Coal-cellar, coal-hole (cave). ‖ NAUT. Coaler, coaling-boat, collier (navire). ‖ LOC. *Charbonnier est maître chez soi*, a man's house is his castle; *la foi du charbonnier*, a simple faith.
charbonnière [-njɛ:r] f. Coal-scuttle (seau). ‖ NAUT. Coal-lighter. ‖ ZOOL. Coal-tit (mésange).
charouter [ʃarkyte] v. tr. (1). To hack, to mangle (un poulet, de la viande). ‖ FAM. To knife, to butcher (un opéré).
charcuterie [-tri] f. COMM. Pork-butcher's shop (boutique); pork-butcher's trade (commerce); pork-butcher's meat, delicatessen (produits).
charcutier, ière [-tje, ɛr] s. COMM. Pork-butcher. ‖ FAM. Sawbones (chirurgien).
chardon [ʃardɔ̃] m. BOT. Thistle. ‖ Pl. Spikes (de grille, de mur).
chardonneret [ʃardɔnrɛ] m. ZOOL. Goldfinch.
charentais, aise [ʃarɑ̃tɛ, ɛ:z] adj., s. Pertaining to Charentes.
charentaise [-tɛ:z] f. Felt and leather slipper.
Charenton [-tɔ̃] m. GÉOGR. Charenton. ‖ FAM. Bedlam, madhouse (asile).
charge [ʃarʒ] f. Load, burden (v. FARDEAU); weight, strain (poids); *charge d'un cheval, d'une charrette*, horse-load, cart-load; *charge à vide*, weight empty; *en avoir sa charge*, to have as much as one can carry. ‖ NAUT. Lading, loading (d'un navire). ‖ MILIT. Charge (d'une arme, de la cavalerie). ‖ AVIAT. *Charge alaire*, wing load; *charge du palier*, bearing stress. ‖ ELECTR. Charge (d'un accu); *en charge*, live (fil, rail). ‖ FIN. Charge, expenses, costs, encumbrances (frais); *charges de famille*, dependents; *charges fiscales*, fiscal (ou) tax burden; *à charge*, dependent (enfant); *grevés de charge*, onerous (biens); *les frais sont à la charge de*, the costs are to be paid by (ou) chargeable to; *ma mère est à ma charge*, my mother is dependent on me. ‖ Pl. Incidental charges (de location); Office, duties, mandate, trust (fonctions); *charge d'avoué*, solicitor's (ou) attorney's practice; *charge de notaire*, notary's office and goodwill; *charges publiques*, public offices; *charge de surveillant*, overseership; *il a la charge de*, his office is to, he is in charge of; *se démettre de sa charge*, to resign one's functions. ‖ JUR. Charge, indictment; *relever des charges contre*, to bring charges against; *témoin à charge*, witness for the prosecution. ‖ ARTS. Caricature, cartoon; *faire la charge de*, to caricature. ‖ THÉÂTR. Over-acting (d'un rôle). ‖ FIG. Charge, burden, drag (fardeau, entrave); *être à charge à*, to be a burden to (ou) a drag on; *la vie m'est à charge*, life is a burden to me, life hangs heavy on my hands. ‖ FIG. Trust, care,

responsibility (responsabilité); *charge d'âmes*, cure of souls; *les enfants confiés à ma charge*, children in my care; *prendre en charge*, to assume responsibility for. ‖ Fig. Onus, charge, obligation (obligation); *à charge de revanche*, on condition of reciprocity; *à charge pour vous de payer*, on condition you pay; *avoir la charge de*, to have the onus of; *prendre en charge*, to take charge of. ‖ Fam. Charge (attaque); *faire une charge à fond de train contre*, to fall upon; *revenir à la charge*, to return to the charge.

chargé, ée [-ʒe] adj. Heavy, cloudy, overcast (ciel, temps); full (emploi du temps); heavy, full, busy (journée); insured, registered (lettre, paquet); *chargé de*, full of (admiration, ans, honneurs, tristesse); heavy with (parfums); pregnant with (sens). ‖ Fin. *Chargé des comptes*, in charge of the accounts; *chargé d'impôts*, heavily taxed. ‖ Naut. Laden (navire). ‖ Milit. Loaded (arme); live (obus). ‖ Méd. Tainted (hérédité); coated, furred (langue); cloudy (urine). ‖ Fig. Burdened (conscience); *avoir un passé chargé*, to have a past.
— m. *Chargé d'affaires*, chargé d'affaires, envoy; *chargé de cours*, assistant (ou) deputy (ou) temporary lecturer.

chargement [-ʒmɑ̃] m. Loading (d'un appareil photographique, d'une voiture). ‖ Registering, registration (d'une lettre, d'un paquet). ‖ Electr. Charging (d'un accu). ‖ Milit. Loading (d'une arme); filling (d'une cartouche, d'un obus). ‖ Naut. Shipping, shipment (des marchandises); lading (du navire); freight, cargo, shipment, ship-load (cargaison). ‖ Ch. de f. *Chargement d'un wagon*, waggon-load, U. S. car-load.

charger [-ʒe] v. tr. (7). To load (un cheval, une voiture) [*de*, with]; to fire (une chaudière); to feed, to stoke (le feu, le poêle); *charger sa mémoire*, to burden one's memory; *charger qqn de paquets*, to encumber (ou) to load s.o. with parcels; *charger la table de plats*, to pile the table with dishes. ‖ To load, to heap (un fardeau) [*sur*, on]; *charger une caisse sur son épaule*, to heave up a case on one's shoulder. ‖ To pick up, to load (un client, un passager, un voyageur). ‖ To overcast (le ciel, le temps). ‖ Techn. To load (un appareil photographique, une soupape). ‖ Electr. To charge (un accu). ‖ Milit. To load (une arme); to charge (l'ennemi). ‖ Naut. To ship (une cargaison); *charger de*, to lade with; *charger sur*, to ship on. ‖ Méd. To lie heavy on (l'estomac); to coat, to fur (la langue). ‖ Comm. To overvalue (l'actif); to swell, to inflate (les comptes). ‖ Jur. To charge, to indict (un prévenu); *charger qqn d'un crime*, to charge s.o. with a crime, to charge a crime upon s.o. ‖ Fig. To accuse, to charge (un adversaire); *charger de louanges*, to overwhelm with praises; *charger de malédictions*, to heap curses on; *il l'a chargé de ses propres méfaits*, he saddled him with his own misdeeds. ‖ Fig. *Charger de*, to charge with (une commission); to entrust with (une mission, un travail); *charger qqn de faire qqch.*, to commission (ou) direct (ou) instruct s.o. to do sth. ‖ Fig. To overcolour (ou) to overstate, to overdraw (un incident, un récit); to overdraw, to overcharge, to make a caricature of (un portrait); to overact (un rôle); to overdecorate (le style).
— v. intr. Milit. To charge. ‖ Naut. To load. ‖ Fig. *Charger à fond contre*, to fall upon.
— v. pr. Se charger, to be loaded (arme, appareil photographique); to grow cloudy (ou) overcast (ciel). ‖ Méd. To fur (langue). ‖ *Se charger de qqch.*, to take charge of sth., to charge oneself with sth., to attend to sth., to take sth. in hand; *se charger de qqn*, to take charge (ou) care of s.o.; *se charger de faire qqch.*, to make it

one's business (ou) to take it upon oneself (ou) to undertake to do sth.; *se charger d'une question*, to take up a question; *je m'en charge*, I'll see to it.
— v. récipr. Se charger, to charge one another.

chargeur [-ʒœːr] m. Stoker, fireman (de chaudière, de fourneau). ‖ Cassette, film-holder (d'appareil photographique). ‖ Naut. Loader, shipper, freighter, shipping agent. ‖ Milit. Loading clip, cartridge clip (d'arme); loader (canonnier). ‖ Electr. Charger (d'accu).

chariot [ʃarjo] m. Agric. Wain (†); waggon; U. S. wagon. ‖ Base-board (de chambre noire); go-cart, U. S. baby-walker (d'enfant); carriage (de machine à écrire); truck (de porteur); shopping cart (pour le marché). ‖ Techn. Trolley, runner. ‖ Aviat. Undercarriage (d'atterrissage); *chariot de queue*, conveyor. ‖ Milit. Cradle (d'artillerie); *chariot de manutention de bombes*, bomb-carrying trolley. ‖ Astron. *Le Chariot*, Charles's Wain, U. S. the Big Dipper.

charisme [karism] m. Charisma, charism.

charitable [ʃaritabl] adj. Charitable (acte, fondation, personne); benevolent (association, intention, personne) [*envers, to*].

charitablement [-tabləmɑ̃] adv. Charitably.

charité [-te] f. Charity (vertu); *charité bien ordonnée commence par soi-même*, charity begins at home; *dame de charité*, lady visitor; *sœur de charité*, Sister of Charity; *par pure charité*, out of mere charity, for charity's sake. ‖ Charity, act of charity, kindness (acte); *ce serait une charité que de lui écrire*, it would be a kindness to write to him. ‖ Alms, alms-giving (aumône); *demander la charité*, to beg; *faire la charité*, to give alms; *vivre de charités*, to live on charity.

charivari [ʃarivari] m. Charivari. ‖ Fig. Din.

charlatan [ʃarlatɑ̃] m. Charlatan, mountebank; impostor, humbug (imposteur); quack (médicastre); political mountebank (politicien); *remède de charlatan*, nostrum, quack remedy.

charlatanerie [-tanri] f. Charlatanry.

charlatanesque [-tanɛsk] adj. Charlatanical, quackish.

charlatanisme [-tanism] m. Charlatanism, quackery.

Charlemagne [ʃarləmaɲ] m. Charlemagne; *faire Charlemagne*, to leave the game when winning, to quit while the going is good.

Charles [ʃarl] m. Charles, Charley, Charlie, Carl.

charleston [ʃarlɛstɔn] m. Charleston.

charlotte [ʃarlɔt] f. Charlotte, Lottie, Lotty. ‖ Culin. Charlotte, apple-charlotte; *charlotte russe*, charlotte russe.

charmant, ante [ʃarmɑ̃, ɑ̃ːt] adj. Charming (jeune fille, personne, prince); sweet (jeune fille, manières, vieille dame); winsome (jeune fille, physionomie); bewitching (femme); lovely (heure, personne, scène); winning (manières, sourire); delightful (spectacle, ville, voix).

charme [ʃarm] m. Bot. Yoke-elm, hornbeam.

charme m. Spell, charm, enchantment (v. SORTILÈGE); *exercer un charme*, to wield (ou) to exercise a charm; *jeter un charme sur*, to put a spell on, to cast a spell over; *rompre un charme*, to break a charm (ou) a spell; *sous un charme*, under a spell. ‖ Fig. Charm, fascination, seduction (en général); winsomeness (d'un enfant, d'une jeune fille); glamour (d'une femme, de la jeunesse); witchery, bewitchment (des mots, du regard, du sourire); attraction, charm (de la nouveauté); *donner du charme à*, to add charm to; *tenir sous le charme*, to fascinate, to hold spellbound; *tomber sous le charme de*, to fall under the spell of, to fall a victim to the charms of. ‖ Pl. Charms, physical attractions (appas). ‖ Loc. *Se porter comme un charme,* to be in the pink of condition, to be hale and hearty, to be as fit as a fiddle.

charmé, ée [-me] adj. Bewitched, fascinated, spellbound. ‖ Fam. Delighted, pleased, charmed.

charmer v. tr. (1). To charm, to enchant, to bewitch, to fascinate (en général). ‖ To charm (les serpents). ‖ Fig. To captivate (les cœurs); to appeal to (l'imagination); to beguile, to charm (les loisirs); to charm (les oreilles); to charm away (la peine, les soucis); to charm, to allure, to bewitch (qqn); to delight (le regard).

charmeur, euse [-mœ:r, ø:z] adj. Bewitching, fascinating, winning, alluring, engaging.
— m. Charmer; enchanter; *charmeur de serpents,* snake-charmer. ‖ Fig. Charmer.

charmeuse [-mø:z] f. Charmer (d'oiseaux). ‖ Charmeuse (soie). ‖ Fig. Charmer, fascinating girl (ou) woman; witch (fam.).

charmille [ʃarmi:j] f. Arbour, bower.

charnel, elle [ʃarnɛl] adj. Carnal, fleshly (désir, plaisir); carnal, sensual (personne).

charnellement [-mã] adv. Carnally; sensually.

charnier [ʃarnje] m. Charnel-house. (V. ossuaire.) ‖ Naut. Scuttle-butt.

charnière [ʃarnjɛ:r] f. Techn. Hinge; *à charnière,* hinged; *charnière de timbre-poste,* stamp-hinge. ‖ Méd., Zool. Hinge. ‖ Milit. Pivot. ‖ Fig. Hinge (d'une affaire).

charnu, ue [ʃarny] adj. Fleshy; beefy (fam.). ‖ Fleshy, pulpy (fruit).

charognard [-ɲa:r] m. Zool. Vulture. ‖ Fam. Vulture, ghoul.

charogne [ʃarɔɲ] f. Carrion. ‖ Pop. Slut (femme); scoundrel, swine (homme).

charolais, aise [ʃarɔlɛ, ɛ:z] adj. Géogr. Of (ou) from Charolais. ‖ Agric. Charol(l)ais.
— s. Géogr. Native (ou) inhabitant of Charolais. ‖ Agric. Charol(l)ais.

charpentage [ʃarpãta:ʒ] m. Timbering.

charpente [ʃarpãt] f. Timbering, woodwork (d'un bâtiment); skeleton (d'un bâtiment, d'un navire); scaffolding (d'un échafaudage); framework (d'un pont, d'un toit); *charpente en fer,* iron-work. ‖ Méd. Build, frame (du corps); skeleton (ossature). ‖ Fig. Framework, structure (d'un ouvrage).

charpenté, ée [-te] adj. Framed, constructed. ‖ Well-built (ou) -knit, strapping, burly (personne). ‖ Fig. Well-constructed, well-knit (ouvrage).

charpenter v. tr. (1). To cut, to square (du bois). ‖ Fig. To construct, to frame (un ouvrage).

charpenterie [-tri] f. Carpentry; carpenter's work; *charpenterie en fer,* iron-work.

charpentier [-tje] m. Carpenter. ‖ Naut. Shipwright.

charpie [ʃarpi] f. Lint (étoffe); *mettre en charpie,* to shred (le linge); to cook to shreds (la viande). ‖ Fig. *Mettre qqn en charpie,* to pound s.o. into a jelly.

charretée [ʃarte] f. Cartful, cart-load.

charretier [-tje] m. Carter, carrier, carman. ‖ Loc. *Langage de charretier,* Billingsgate; *jurer comme un charretier,* to swear like a trooper.
— adj. Carriageable; *voie charretière,* cart-road.

charreton [-tɔ̃] m. Small cart.

charrette [ʃarɛt] f. Cart; *charrette à bras,* hand-cart, push-cart, barrow; *charrette anglaise,* dog-cart. ‖ Tumbril (des condamnés).

charriage [ʃarjaʒ] m. Carriage, cartage. ‖ Drifting (des glaçons).

charrier [-rje] v. tr. (1). To cart (en charrette); to carry, to transport (en voiture). ‖ To wash down, to carry along (par eau). ‖ Fam. To chaff. — v. intr. To drift ice. ‖ Fam. To draw the long bow.

charroi [ʃarwa] m. Cartage.

charron [ʃarɔ̃] m. Cartwright, wheelwright.

charronnage [ʃarona:ʒ] m. Cartwright's work.

charroyer [ʃarwaje] v. tr. (1). To cart.

charroyeur [-jœ:r] m. Carter.

charrue [ʃary] f. Agric. Plough, U. S. plow. ‖ Loc. *Mettre la charrue devant les bœufs,* to put the cart before the horse, to bridle the horse by the tail. ‖ **Charrue-balance,** f. Agric. Balance (ou) throw-over plough. ‖ **Charrue-semoir,** f. Agric. Seeding plough.

charte [ʃart] f. Charter; *charte de l'Atlantique,* Atlantic Charter; *accorder une charte à,* to charter; *à charte,* charted (compagnie); *l'école des Chartes,* the School of Paleography; *la Grande Charte,* Magna Carta. ‖ **Charte-partie,** f. Naut. Charter-party.

charter [ʃartɛ:r] m. Aviat. Charter, charter plane.

chartisme [ʃartism] m. Chartism (en Angleterre).

chartiste [-tist] m. Chartist (en Angleterre); student at the School of Paleography (en France).

chartreuse [ʃartrø:z] f. Ecclés. Carthusian monastery (couvent). ‖ Comm. Chartreuse (liqueur). ‖ Fig. Solitude.

chartreux [-trø] m. Ecclés. Carthusian.

chartrier [ʃartrje] m. Keeper of charters (archiviste); cartulary (recueil); charter-room (salle).

Charybde [karibd] m. Charybdis; *tomber de Charybde en Scylla,* to fall out of the frying-pan into the fire (ou) out of the briars into the thorns.

chas [ʃa] m. Eye; *ouvrier qui fait les chas d'aiguille,* eyer.

chasse [ʃas] f. Stalking (à l'affût); hunting, chase (à courre); sticking (à l'épieu); hawking (au faucon); ferreting (au furet); shooting (au fusil); coursing (au lévrier); trapping (au piège); *chasse en barque,* punt shooting; *chasse au chevreuil, aux lapins, au renard, au sanglier,* deer-stalking, rabbit-shooting (ou) rabbiting, fox-hunting, pig-sticking; *chasse aux champignons, aux papillons,* mushroom hunt (ou) mushrooming, butterfly chase; *chasse aux rats, aux souris,* rat-catching, mousing; *aller à la chasse,* to go shooting (ou) hunting. ‖ Hunting-song (air de chasse). ‖ Hunt, chase (chasseurs); *suivre la chasse,* to follow the hunt. ‖ Game, bag (gibier); *faire bonne chasse,* to get a good bag. ‖ Shooting-season (saison); *la chasse est fermée, ouverte,* the shooting-season has ended, begun. ‖ Chase; shoot; hunt; hunting-ground (terrain); *chasse gardée,* game-preserves; *« chasse réservée »,* « private shooting rights »; *louer une chasse,* to rent a shoot. ‖ Naut. Chase; *donner la chasse,* to chase; *navire qui donne la chasse,* chaser. ‖ Aviat. *Avion de chasse,* fighter (ou) pursuit plane; *chasse adverse,* pursuit by the enemy. ‖ Techn. Play, clearance (jeu); *chasse d'air,* air blast; *chasse d'eau,* flush, cistern; *tirer la chasse,* to pull the lavatory chain. ‖ Fig. *La chasse aux appartements, aux bibelots* (ou) *curiosités, aux maris,* house-, curio-, husband-hunting; *chasse à l'homme,* man-hunt; *faire la chasse à un voleur,* to hunt (ou) to pursue a thief. ‖ **Chasse-clous,** m. invar. Nail-punch. ‖ **Chasse-goupille** (pl. *chasse-goupilles*), m. Pin-drift. ‖ **Chasse-mouches,** m. invar. Fly-swatter (balai); fly-net (pour chevaux). ‖ **Chasse-neige,** m. invar. Snow-plough. ‖ Sports. stem (au ski); *virage en chasse-neige,* stem-turn. ‖ **Chasse-pierres,** m. invar. Cow-catcher; track-clearer. ‖ **Chasse-roue(s),** m. invar. Guard-stone, fender.

châsse [ʃɑ:s] f. Ecclés. Shrine, reliquary. ‖ Techn. Mounting (de bijou); frame (de lunette). ‖ Fam. *Couverte de bijoux comme une châsse,* loaded with jewellery like an idol.

chassé [ʃase] m. Chassé; *danser le chassé,* to

chassé. ‖ **Chassé-croisé**, m. Chassé-croisé (danse); cross-fire (paroles); general post (remaniement).

chasselas [ʃasla] m. Chasselas.

chassepot [ʃaspo] m. MILIT. Chassepot (fusil).

chasser [ʃase] v. tr. (1). To stalk (à couvert, à l'affût); to hunt (à courre); to hawk (au faucon); to net (au filet); to shoot (au fusil); to ferret (au furet); to snare, to catch (au lacet, au collet); to course (au lévrier); to trap (au piège). ‖ *Chasser les champignons*, to go mushrooming; *chasser les papillons*, to chase butterflies. ‖ To prey on, to hunt (animal); *le chat chasse les souris*, the cat mouses. ‖ To brush away, to flap away, to swat (les mouches, une poussière). ‖ To dispel (le brouillard); to blow away (les nuages); to drive (la pluie). ‖ To eject (une cartouche); to drive out, to punch out (un clou); to expel (un corps étranger, un liquide). ‖ To eject (un agitateur, un fonctionnaire, un locataire); to sack, U.S. to fire (un domestique); to turn out (un domestique, un employé, un locataire); to expel (un élève); to beat off, to drive out (un ennemi); to get rid of (un gêneur). ‖ ECCLÉS. To cast out (les démons). ‖ FIG. To banish (la crainte); to dismiss (une idée); to drive away (les soucis). ‖ LOC. *Un clou chasse l'autre*, one fire drives out another.

— v. intr. To hunt (à courre); to go shooting (au fusil). ‖ To scud, to drive (nuages); to drive (pluie); to blow (vent). ‖ NAUT. To drag (ancre); *chasser sur l'ancre*, to drag. ‖ AUTOM. To spin (roue). ‖ TECHN. To drive out (en typographie).

chasseresse [ʃasrɛs] adj., f. Huntress.

châsses [ʃɑːs] m. pl. ARG. Eyes, peepers.

chasseur [ʃasœːr] m. Stalker (à l'affût); hunter, huntsman (à courre); gun (au fusil); ferreter (au furet); trapper (au piège). ‖ Page-boy, messenger-boy, commissionaire; U. S. chasseur, bellboy, bellhop (d'hôtel). ‖ NAUT. Chaser. ‖ MILIT. *Chasseurs alpins*, Alpine troops; *chasseur alpin*, mountain light infantryman. ‖ AVIAT. Fighter, pursuit plane. ‖ **Chasseur-fusée**, m. AVIAT. Rocket fighter.

chassie [ʃasi] f. MÉD. Gum, rheum.

chassieux, euse [-sjø, øːz] adj. MÉD. Rheumy, gummy (œil); gummy-eyed (personne).

châssis [ʃɑsi] m. Frame (dormant); casement (à gonds); sash (à guillotine); *châssis de fenêtre, de porte*, window-frame, door-frame. ‖ Leaf (de paravent); frame, canvas-stretcher (de tableau). ‖ TECHN. Flask (de fonderie); chase (d'imprimerie); set, frame (de mine); casting (ou) moulding box (de moulage); slide, holder (de photo). ‖ MILIT. Slide, chassis. ‖ AVIAT. Chassis, undercarriage. ‖ AUTOM., RADIO. Chassis. ‖ AGRIC. Forcing-frame, glass-frame. ‖ FAM. Build, frame. ‖ **Châssis-presse**, m. Printing frame.

chaste [ʃast] adj. Chaste. (V. CONTINENT, PUR.)

chastement [-təmɑ̃] adv. Chastely.

chasteté [-təte] f. Chastity; *ceinture de chasteté*, chastity belt.

chasuble [ʃazybl] f. ECCLÉS. Chasuble.

chat [ʃa] (f. v. CHATTE) m. Cat, tomcat; puss, pussy (fam.); *chat de gouttière*, tile (ou) U.S. alley cat; *chat sauvage*, wildcat; *petit chat*, kitten; *Chat botté*, Puss in Boots. ‖ *Chat coupé*, crosstag; *chat perché*, long tag (jeux). ‖ NAUT. *Chat à neuf queues*, cat-o'nine-tails. ‖ BOT. *Herbe aux chats*, catmint. ‖ LOC. *Acheter chat en poche*, to buy a pig in a poke; *à bon chat bon rat*, tit for tat; *appeler un chat un chat*, to call a spade a spade; *avoir un chat dans la gorge*, to have a frog in the throat; *chat fourré*, gentleman of the long robe; *s'entendre comme chien et chat*, to live a cat-and-dog life; *mon petit chat*, pet; *pas un chat*, not a soul. ‖ **Chat-huant**, m. ZOOL. Screech-owl. ‖ **Chat-tigre**, m. ZOOL. Tiger-cat.

châtaigne [ʃatɛːɲ] f. Chestnut.

châtaigneraie [-nrɛ] f. Chestnut-grove.

châtaignier [-ɲje] m. BOT. Chestnut-tree (arbre); chestnut-wood (bois).

châtain, aine [ʃatɛ̃, ɛn] adj. Chestnut-brown (cheveux); brown-haired (personne); *châtain clair*, auburn.

château [ʃato] m. Castle (féodal); stronghold, citadel, fortified castle (fort); palace (royal); hall, manor, country seat, country mansion (de grand propriétaire); château (de vignoble). ‖ *Château d'eau*, water-tower. ‖ NAUT. Bridge-house. ‖ LOC. *Château en Espagne*, castle in the air, Cloud-Cuckoo-Land; *s'effondrer comme un château de cartes*, to fall down like a house of cards; *mener la vie de château*, to live like a lord. ‖ **Château-la-pompe**, m. FAM. Adam's ale.

chateaubriand [-brijɑ̃] m. CULIN. Chateaubriand; double tenderloin.

châtelain [ʃatlɛ̃] m. † Castellan. ‖ Squire; lord of the manor; landowner.

châtelaine [-lɛn] f. † Castellan's wife. ‖ Lady of the manor; landowner's wife. ‖ Chatelaine (chaîne).

châtelet [ʃatlɛ] m. Small castle.

châtier [ʃatje] v. tr. (1). To chastise, to castigate. ‖ FIG. To chasten, to improve (le style).

chatière [ʃatjɛːr] f. Ventilation-hole (d'aération); cat-hole (passage). ‖ Cat-trap (piège).

châtiment [ʃatimɑ̃] m. Punishment, chastisement (de, for). ‖ FIG. Infliction. (V. PUNITION.)

chatoiement [ʃatwamɑ̃] m. Play, shimmer, lustre (des couleurs); sheen (d'une étoffe); glistening, sparkling (d'une pierre).

chaton [ʃatɔ̃] m. ZOOL. Kitten. ‖ BOT. Catkin.

chaton m. Bezel, setting. ‖ Stone (gemme).

chatouille [ʃatuːj] f. Tickle; *craindre la chatouille*, to be ticklish; *fait de craindre la chatouille*, ticklishness.

chatouillement [-jmɑ̃] m. Tickling, titillation; tickle (dans, in). ‖ FIG. Titillation.

chatouiller [-je] v. tr. (1). To tickle, to titillate (qqn). ‖ FIG. To tickle (l'amour-propre); to stir up (la curiosité); to greet (l'oreille); to titillate (le palais, les sens). ‖ FAM. *Chatouiller les côtes à qqn*, to give s.o. a good licking.

chatouilleux, euse [-jø, øːz] adj. Ticklish. ‖ FIG. Ticklish, delicate (affaire); punctilious (honneur); testy, thin-skinned, touchy (personne).

chatoyant, ante [ʃatwajɑ̃, ɑ̃ːt] adj. Iridescent (écaille, plumage); shot (étoffe); chatoyant (pierre, soie).

chatoyer [-je] v. intr. (1). To shimmer, to play (couleurs); to shimmer (étoffe); to glisten, to sparkle (pierres).

châtrer [ʃatre] v. tr. (1). To castrate, to geld; to emasculate. ‖ AGRIC. To prune. ‖ FIG. To expurgate, to bowdlerize, to mutilate.

châtreur [-trœːr] m. Castrator, gelder.

chatte [ʃat] f. ZOOL. She-cat, cat.

— adj. Feline, coaxing (manière, personne).

chattemite [-mit] f. FAM. Toady; *celle-là, c'est une chattemite*, butter wouldn't melt in her mouth.

chattepelouse [-pluːz] f. ZOOL. Processionary caterpillar.

chatterie [-tri] f. Coaxing. ‖ Pl. Delicacies.

chatterton [ʃatɛrtɔn] m. ELECTR. Insulating tape, Chatterton's compound.

chaud, aude [ʃo, oːd] adj. Hot (air, liquide, temps); warm (climat, corps, couverture, vêtement); hot, mulled (vin); *avoir chaud*, to be warm, to feel warm; *il fait chaud, très chaud*, it is warm, very hot; *tout chaud*, steaming-hot, piping-hot. ‖ FIG. Warm (accueil, cœur, coloris, partisan, piste); sharp, furious (affaire, engagement); passionate,

impassioned (discours, éloquence); animated, warm (discussion); violent (dispute); bitter (larmes); hot, passionate (nature); amorous, hot (tempérament); *au sang chaud*, hot-blooded; *à la tête chaude*, hot-headed, hot-tempered; *jouer à la main chaude*, to play hot cockles; *pleurer à chaudes larmes*, to cry one's eyes out. ‖ FAM. *Il a eu chaud*, he had a narrow escape.
— adv. Warm; *tenir chaud*, to keep warm. ‖ CULIN. *Manger chaud*, to eat warm food; *servir chaud*, to serve up hot. ‖ FAM. *Coûter chaud*, to cost a pretty penny.
— m. Hot; *être bien au chaud*, to be snug and warm; *rester* (ou) *tenir au chaud*, to keep in a warm room (ou) place. ‖ MÉD. *A chaud*, in the acute stage; *chaud et froid*, chill; *opération à chaud*, emergency operation. ‖ CULIN. *Tenir un plat au chaud*, to keep a dish hot. ‖ FAM. *Ni chaud ni froid*, no difference, all one; *souffler le chaud et le froid*, to blow hot and cold. ‖ **Chaud-froid**, m. CULIN. Chaud-froid. ‖ **Chaude-pisse**, f. POP. Clap.

chaude [ʃoːd] f. TECHN. Heat.

chaudeau [-do] m. CULIN. Caudle (chabrol); egg-nog (lait de poule).

chaudement [-dmɑ̃] adv. Warmly.

chaudière [-djɛːr] f. Boiler.

chaudron [ʃodrɔ̃] m. Cauldron. ‖ FAM. Tin-kettle (piano).

chaudronnerie [ʃodrɔnri] f. Brazier (ou) copper wares (marchandises); coppersmith's (ou) tin-smith's trade, braziery (métier).

chaudronnier [-nje] m. Coppersmith, tinsmith, brazier. ‖ Tinker (ambulant).

chauffage [ʃofaːʒ] m. Heating (d'une chaudière, d'une pièce, d'un plat); firing (d'un four); warming (d'un plat); *chauffage à l'air chaud, à la vapeur*, hot-air, steam heating; *chauffage central*, central heating; *centrale de chauffage urbain*, central heating station of a town. ‖ FAM. Cramming (d'un candidat).

chauffant, ante [-fɑ̃, ɑ̃ːt] adj. Electric (couverture); heating (résistance); electrically heated (tapis).

chauffard [ʃofaːr] m. FAM. Road-hog, speedster; U. S. hit-and-run driver (avec délit de fuite).

chauffe [ʃoːf] f. Heating, warming, firing; *surface de chauffe*, heating surface. ‖ Fire-box, fire-chamber (lieu). ‖ Distillation. ‖ **Chauffe-assiette**, m. Plate-warmer. ‖ **Chauffe-bain**, m. Geyser; U. S. water-heater. ‖ **Chauffe-biberon**, m. Bottle warmer. ‖ **Chauffe-eau**, m. inv. Boiler; water-heater. ‖ **Chauffe-pieds**, m. inv. Foot-warmer. ‖ **Chauffe-plat**, m. inv. Dish-warmer, chafing-dish.

chauffer [ʃofe] v. tr. (1). To warm (le corps, l'eau, un lit, une pièce); to heat (l'eau, le métal, une pièce); to stoke up fire (une machine). ‖ AGRIC. To force. ‖ SPORTS. *Chauffer ses muscles*, to limber up. ‖ FIG. To cram (un candidat). ‖ POP. To pinch (v. CHAPARDER); *se faire chauffer*, to get pinched.
— v. intr. To heat (eau, pièce); to get up steam (machine); to run hot (moteur, roue). ‖ LOC. *Ça va chauffer*, we are in for a hot time. (V. BARDER.)
— v. pr. **Se chauffer**, to warm oneself (personne); *se chauffer au soleil*, to bask in the sun, to sun-bathe, to sun oneself. ‖ To get warm (ou) hot (maison, pièce). ‖ LOC. *De quel bois je me chauffe*, what stuff I am made of.

chaufferette [-frɛt] f. Foot-warmer. ‖ AUTOM. Car-heater.

chaufferie [-fri] f. Chafery. ‖ Boiler-house (d'usine). ‖ NAUT. Stokehold.

chauffeur [-fœːr] m. TECHN. Stoker, fireman. ‖ AUTOM. Chauffeur, driver; *chauffeur de taxi*, taxi-driver, taximan.

chauffeuse [-føːz] f. Fireside chair.

chaulage [ʃolaːʒ] m. AGRIC. Liming.

chauler [-le] v. tr. (1). AGRIC. To limewash (des arbres); to lime (un terrain).

chaume [ʃoːm] m. Stubble (champ); thatch (toit); *couvrir de chaume*, to thatch. ‖ BOT. Culm.

chaumer [-me] v. tr. (1). AGRIC. To stubble.

chaumière [-mjɛːr] f. Thatched cottage. ‖ LOC. *Une chaumière et un cœur*, love in a cottage.

chaumine [-min] f. Cot.

chaussant, ante [ʃosɑ̃, ɑ̃ːt] adj. That fits well.

chaussé, ée adj. *Chaussé de ses éperons*, spurred; *chaussé de ses bas*, in stockinged-feet; *chaussé de ses pantoufles*, wearing her slippers; *bien chaussé*, well-shod.

chaussée [ʃose] f. Highway, paved road, roadway, carriageway (route); causeway (surélevée). ‖ Embankment (de rivière). ‖ NAUT. Reef.

chausse-pied m. Shoe-horn. ‖ **Chausse-trape**, f. Trap. ‖ MILIT. Caltrop. ‖ FIG. Trick.

chausser v. tr. (1). To put on (ses lunettes, ses souliers); *chausser qqn*, to shoe s.o., to provide s.o. with shoes, to make s.o.'s shoes (faire les souliers de); to put s.o.'s shoes on (mettre les souliers à). ‖ To wear (ou) to take a size; *combien chaussez-vous?*, what size do you take in shoes? ‖ To fit; *une chaussure qui chausse bien*, a shoe that fits well. ‖ AGRIC. To earth up (un arbre).
— v. pr. **Se chausser**, to put on one's shoes; *se chausser chez*, to get one's shoes from, to buy one's shoes at.

chausses [ʃoːs] f. pl. † Hose.

chaussette [-sɛt] f. Sock. ‖ COMM. Half-hose.

chausseur [-søːr] m. Bootmaker, shoemaker; footwear specialist.

chausson [-sɔ̃] m. Slipper (pantoufle); bootee, slipper (d'enfant). ‖ ARTS. Sandal (de danse). ‖ SPORTS. Boxing-shoe (de boxe); fencing-shoe (d'escrime). ‖ CULIN. *Chausson aux pommes*, apple-turnover.

chaussure [-syːr] f. Footwear, footgear; shoe; boot; *chaussures d'appartement* (ou) *d'intérieur*, house-shoes; *chaussures de fatigue* (ou) *de sport*, walking-shoes; *chaussures habillées*, fine shoes; *fabricant de chaussures*, boot and shoe manufacturer. ‖ FAM. *Trouver chaussure à son pied*, to find one's match; to find what suits one's convenience; *pas digne de dénouer les cordons de ses chaussures*, not fit to black his boots.

chaut [ʃo]. V. CHALOIR.

chauve [ʃoːv] adj. Bald. ‖ FIG. Bare (mont). ‖ **Chauve-souris**, f. ZOOL. Bat.
— m. Bald-head.

chauvin, ine [ʃovɛ̃, in] adj. Chauvinistic, jingoistic.
— s. Chauvinist; jingo; U. S. hundredpercenter.

chauvinisme [ʃovinism] m. Chauvinism, jingoism; U. S. spread-eagleism.

chaux [ʃo] f. Lime; *chaux sulfatée*, gypsum; *chaux vive*, quicklime. ‖ FAM. *Bâti à chaux et à sable*, made of iron, strong as a horse.

chavirement [ʃavirmɑ̃] m. Capsizing, overturning.

chavirer [-re] v. intr. (1). To tip over, to upset (véhicule). ‖ NAUT. To capsize, to turn turtle.
— v. tr. FAM. To bowl over, to upset (qqn); *le regard chaviré*, showing the whites of one's eyes.

chéchia [ʃeʃja] f. Chechia, tarboosh.

check-list [ʃɛklist] m. Check list.

check-up [ʃɛkœp] m. inv. MÉD. Check-up.

chef [ʃɛf] m. † Head. ‖ Chieftain (de brigands); principal (de division); head (de l'État, de famille); captain (d'industrie); leader (de parti); chief, headman (de tribu); *chef d'atelier*, shop-foreman; *chef de bureau*, chief clerk, head of a department; *chef de cabinet*, principal private secretary; *chef de la comptabilité*, chief accountant; *chef d'équipe*, ganger, foreman, chargeman (ouvrier); *chef de famille*, householder; *chef d'une grande famille*, head of a noble family; *chef de file*, party leader; *chef de patrouille*, scout-master, patrol-leader (scout); *chef de rayon*, shopwalker, U. S. floor-walker; *chef de service*, departmental manager; *en chef*, in chief; *commandement en chef*, general command. ‖ MILIT. *Chef de bataillon*, battalion commander; *chef de corps*, commanding officer; *chef d'escadron*, major; *chef d'état-major*, chief of staff; *chef de file*, front-rank man, file leader; *chef de musique*, bandmaster; *chef de pièce*, number 1 of a gun. ‖ AVIAT. *Chef d'escadrille*, squadron commander. ‖ NAUT. *Chef de file*, leading ship; *chef de pièce*, captain of a gun. ‖ CH. DE F. *Chef de gare*, station-master; *chef de train*, guard, U. S. conductor; *chef du service des ateliers*, works manager; *chef du service des signaux*, signal superintendent. ‖ SPORTS. *Chef d'équipe*, captain. ‖ MUS. *Chef d'orchestre*, orchestra leader, conductor. ‖ CULIN. Chef. ‖ BLAS. Chief. ‖ JUR. *Chef d'accusation*, count of indictment, charge; *chef des jurés*, foreman of the jury; *au premier chef*, in the highest degree; *du chef de sa femme*, in his wife's right. ‖ FIG. Count, point, heading (point, question); *au premier chef*, essentially; *il importe au premier chef que*, it is of the highest importance that; *rangé sous plusieurs chefs*, classified under several main heads. ‖ FIG. Authority; *agir de son propre chef*, to act on one's own authority. ‖ **Chef-d'œuvre** (pl. *chefs-d'œuvre*) m. Masterpiece. ‖ **Chef-lieu** (pl. *chefs-lieux*) m. County town (en Angleterre); county seat (aux Etats-Unis); chief town (en France).

chefferie [-ri] f. Chieftaincy, chieftainship.

cheftaine [-tɛn] f. Scout-mistress.

cheik [ʃɛk] m. Sheik.

chelem [ʃlɛm] m. Slam; *être chelem*, to lose all the tricks; *faire chelem*, to slam.

chélidoine [kelidwan] f. BOT. Celandine.

chéloïde [keloid] f. MÉD. Cheloid, keloid.
— adj. MÉD. Cheloidal, keloidal.

chemin [ʃəmɛ̃] m. Path, track; way; *chemin de halage*, towpath; *chemin pour piétons*, foot path; *chemin de rondins*, corduroy road; *chemin de terre*, farm-road, cart-track; *grand chemin*, highway; *le chemin de*, the way to; *chemin faisant*, on the road; *à mi-chemin*, half-way; *en chemin*, on the way; *le bon chemin*, the right road; *un bout de chemin*, a little way; *un bon bout de chemin*, a good distance; *continuer*, *suivre son chemin*, to proceed, to continue on one's way; *demander son chemin*, to ask one's way; *passer son chemin*, to go one's way; *passez votre chemin*, move along; *prendre par le plus court chemin*, to go the shortest way; *reprendre le chemin de la maison*, to set off home again; *se mettre en chemin*, to set off, to start out; *sur le chemin de l'autobus*, on the bus route; *sur votre chemin*, on your way; *toujours par les chemins*, always on the move. ‖ ECCLÉS. *Chemin de croix*, Way of the Cross. ‖ NAUT. Way; *chemin nord*, northing; *chemin parcouru*, day's run; *faire du chemin*, to make way. ‖ CH. DE F. *Chemin de fer*, railway, train; U. S. railroad; *chemin de fer à crémaillère*, rack railway; *chemin de fer d'intérêt local*, local line; *par chemin de fer*, by train, by rail. ‖ CINÉM. *Chemin de défilement*, film-channel (ou) -track. ‖ FIG. *Le chemin des écoliers*, un *chemin détourné*, a roundabout way; *le chemin de la gloire*, the road to glory; *le chemin de l'honneur*, the path of honour; *un chemin de table*, a table-runner; *s'arrêter à mi-chemin*, to stop half-way; *faire son chemin*, to gain ground (idée); to work one's way up,

to rise in the world (personne); *ne pas y aller par quatre chemins*, not to beat about the bush; *prendre un bon chemin*, to make a good start; *suivre son petit bonhomme de chemin*, to go quietly one's own way.

chemineau [ʃəmino] m. Tramp; U. S. hobo.

cheminée [ʃəmine] f. Fireplace (âtre); fireside (coin du feu); chimney-piece, mantelpiece (manteau); chimney, flue (tuyau); chimney-stack (ou) -top, stalk (sur le toit); *cheminée électrique*, electric fire. ‖ Funnel, smoke-stack (de bateau, de locomotive); chimney (de lampe); gas-duct (de réacteur); smoke-stack (d'usine). ‖ GÉOL. Chimney.

cheminement [ʃəminmɑ̃] m. Walking, trudging (marche). ‖ CINÉM. *Cheminement d'un film*, film-run. ‖ MILIT. Covered approach. ‖ FIG. Advance along avenues of approach; progress (d'une idée).

cheminer [-ne] v. intr. (1). To walk; to amble along; *cheminer péniblement*, to trudge, to plod on. ‖ MILIT. To approach. ‖ FIG. To progress.

cheminot [-no] m. CH. DE F. Railwayman.

chemisage [ʃəmiza:ʒ] m. TECHN. Lining, casing.

chemise [ʃəmiz] f. Chemise, shift (†). ‖ Shirt; *chemise de nuit*, night-dress (ou) -gown (de femme); night-shirt (d'homme); ‖ Folder, wrapper (de dossier); dust-jacket (de livre); *chemise de carton*, cardboard (ou) U. S. manila folder. ‖ *Chemises brunes*, brown shirts. ‖ TECHN. Case, casing (d'arbre, de projectile). ‖ **Chemise-culotte**, f. Cami-knickers, combinations.

chemiser [-ze] v. tr. (1). TECHN. To case, to jacket; to line. ‖ ELECTR. To cover.

chemiserie [-zri] f. Shirt-making (fabrication); haberdasher's shop (magasin).

chemisette [-zɛt] f. Front, chemisette (blouse); dickey (plastron).

chemisier [-zje] m. Shirt-maker (fabricant); haberdasher (marchand). ‖ Tailored blouse, shirt (ou) sports blouse, U. S. shirtwaist (blouse).

chênaie [ʃɛ:nɛ] f. Oak-plantation.

chenal [ʃənal] m. Mill-race (de moulin). ‖ NAUT. Channel, fairway.

chenapan [ʃənapɑ̃] m. Rascal, scamp.

chêne [ʃɛ:n] m. BOT. Oak; *chêne vert*, holm, ilex; *de chêne*, oaken. ‖ **Chêne-liège**, m. BOT. Cork-oak.

chéneau [ʃeno] m. Gutter.

chenet [ʃənɛ] m. Fire-dog, andiron.

chènevière [ʃɛnvjɛ:r] f. Hempfield.

chènevis [-vi] m. BOT. Hemp-seed.

chenil [ʃəni] m. Kennel.

chenille [ʃəni:j] f. ZOOL. Caterpillar. ‖ COMM. Chenille (de soie). ‖ AUTOM. Track, caterpillar (de véhicule). ‖ FAM. Slow-coach, U. S. slow-poke; *marcher comme une chenille*, to go at a snail's pace.

chenillé, ée [-je] adj. MILIT. Tracked.

chenillette [-jɛt] f. MILIT. Bren-gun carrier, whippet, full-track (ou) cross-country cargo carrier.

chenu, ue [ʃəny] adj. Snowy (mont); hoary (personne, tête).

cheptel [ʃɛptɛl, ʃətɛl] m. Cattle, live-stock; *cheptel mort*, implements and buildings.

chèque [ʃɛk] m. FIN. Cheque, U. S. check (de, for); *chèque de voyage*, traveller's cheque. ‖ **Chèque-essence**, m. Petrol-voucher, U. S. gasoline coupon.

chéquier [ʃekje] m. FIN. Cheque-book, U. S. check-book.

cher, ère [ʃɛ:r] adj. Dear (à, to); beloved (à, by); *se rendre cher à*, to endear oneself to. ‖ FIN. Dear, expensive, costly (marchandise); dear (marchand); high (prix); expensive (restaurant); *c'était trop cher pour lui*, he could not afford it; *la vie chère*, the high cost of living, high prices;

moins cher, cheaper. ‖ Fɪɢ. Dear, cherished (désir, espoir, vœu).

— s. *Mon cher,* my dear friend, my dear fellow; *ma chère,* my dear.

— adv. *Acheter cher,* to buy at a high price (ou) figure; *payer cher,* to pay a high price for; *payer trop cher,* to pay too high; *il prend cher pour ses leçons,* his terms for lessons are high; *cela se vend cher,* that fetches a high price; *vendre cher,* to sell dear. ‖ Fɪɢ. *Elle vous le fera payer cher,* she will make you pay for it; *vous me le paierez cher,* you shall smart for this; *ne pas valoir cher,* not to be worth much, not to be up to much; *ça ne vaut pas cher,* it's no great catch.

chercher [ʃɛrʃe] v. tr. (1). To seek (un abri, une aide, l'amitié, l'approbation, l'aventure, la cause, un conseil, un emploi, un objet perdu, le repos, la solitude); to seek after (la gloire, le succès, la vérité). ‖ To look for (chercher du regard); to look for (un emploi, des ennuis, une excuse, qqn, qqch., la sortie); to look up (un mot, l'heure d'un train). ‖ To search for, to search after, to fumble for (en fouillant); to fumble for (ses mots, le trou de la serrure); to search for (une nouveauté, qqn, qqch.); to search after (une solution, la vérité); *chercher dans tout le dictionnaire pour trouver un mot,* to search through the dictionary for a word. ‖ To grope for (en tâtonnant); *chercher son chemin à l'aveuglette,* to grope one's way; *chercher un mouchoir dans sa poche,* to grope in one's pocket for a handkerchief. ‖ To feel for (en tâtant); *chercher son chemin en tâtant le terrain,* to feel one's way. ‖ To pursue, to hunt for, to hunt after (en poursuivant); to pursue (le bonheur, son intérêt, le plaisir); to hunt for (un évadé, un voleur, qqch., qqn); to hunt after (la gloire, la fortune). ‖ To court (en sollicitant); to court (l'alliance, l'amitié, le danger, les éloges, la faveur, la mort, la popularité). ‖ To turn to (ou) toward (en se tournant); to turn toward (la lumière, le soleil). ‖ To try to find, to cast about for (en essayant de trouver); to try to find (sa route, une solution); to cast about for (une excuse, une faveur, un moyen). ‖ To seek out, to find out (en trouvant); to seek out (un criminel, un objet caché); to find out (le défaut, le point faible, la vérité). ‖ **Chercher à,** to attempt to (faire, résister); to endeavour to (faire, satisfaire); to try to (comprendre, fuir, tromper). ‖ **Aller chercher,** to go for, to fetch, to go and get (qqch., qqn); to go to meet (aller au-devant de); *aller chercher du vin,* to go for some wine; *allez la chercher,* go and fetch her; *aller chercher qqn à la gare,* to go to meet s.o. at the station; *aller chercher qqn,* to go for s.o. (chercher noise); *aller chercher les ennuis,* to meet trouble half-way; *ça va chercher dans les 300 francs,* that will fetch about 300 francs. ‖ *Envoyer* (ou) *faire chercher,* to send for (qqch., qqn); *venir chercher,* to call for (qqn, qqch.).

— v. intr. To seek; to look.

— v. récipr. **Se chercher,** to look for one another.

— v. pr. **Se chercher.** Fɪɢ. To try to find one's feet; to feel one's way.

chercheur [-ʃœːr] m. Seeker (en général); inquirer, investigator (enquêteur); searcher (perquisiteur); research worker (savant); *chercheur d'or,* gold-seeker, gold-digger. ‖ Tᴇᴄʜɴ. Finder (de télescope); *chercheur focimétrique,* viewfinder (photo). ‖ Rᴀᴅɪᴏ. Cat's whisker.

— adj. Inquiring (esprit); searching (regard, tête).

chère [ʃɛːr] f. † Countenance; welcome. ‖ Cheer, fare, living; *aimer la bonne chère,* to be fond of good fare (ou) living (ou) eating; *faire bonne, maigre chère,* to fare well, badly.

chèrement [-mɑ̃] adv. Dearly, tenderly (affectueusement); dear, dearly, at a high price (cher).

chéri, e [ʃeri] adj., s. Dear, darling.

chérif [ʃerif] m. Sherif.

chérifien [-fjɛ̃] adj. Pertaining to the Sherif. ‖ Moroccan.

chérir [ʃerir] v. tr. (2). To cherish, to love (qqn). ‖ To cherish, to attach great value to (une chose, une espérance, un souvenir).

chérot [ʃero] adj. m. Fᴀᴍ. Pricey, pricy.

cherry [ʃɛri] m. Cherry brandy.

cherté [ʃɛrte] f. Costliness, high price.

chérubin [ʃerybɛ̃] m. Cherub (prop. et fig.).

chester [ʃɛsteːr] m. Cᴜʟɪɴ. Cheshire cheese.

chétif, ive [ʃetif, iːv] adj. Puny (arbuste, enfant); stunted (arbuste); weak (corps, mémoire, santé); sickly (enfant, mine, plante); poor (mine, récolte); paltry, puny (personne); paltry (raison).

chétivement [ʃetivmɑ̃] adj. Weakly; poorly.

chevaine [ʃəvɛn] m. Zᴏᴏʟ. Chub.

cheval [ʃəval] m. Horse; steed (coursier); *cheval de course, de fiacre, de labour, de manège, de renfort, de selle, de trait,* race-, cab-, plough-, school-, trace-, saddle-, draught- (ou) cart-horse; *à cheval,* on horseback; *à cheval!,* to horse!; *être à cheval sur,* to sit astride (à califourchon); to overlap, to straddle (enjamber); *homme de cheval,* horse-lover, horsy man; *se tenir à cheval,* to sit a horse; *une voiture à quatre chevaux,* a four-in-hand. ‖ *Cheval à bascule,* rocking-horse; *chevaux de bois,* merry-go-round, whirligig; *petits chevaux,* petits chevaux (jeu). ‖ Mɪʟɪᴛ. *Cheval de bataille,* charger; *cheval de troupe,* troop-horse; *chevaux de frise,* chevaux-de-frise. ‖ Aᴜᴛᴏᴍ. Horse-power; *une quatre chevaux,* a four-horse-power car. ‖ Zᴏᴏʟ. *Cheval marin,* hippocampus (hippocampe); sea-horse (morse). ‖ Fɪɢ. *Son cheval de bataille,* his pet subject, his favourite topic; *cheval de retour,* old lag; *être à cheval sur,* to be a stickler for, to cling tightly to; *monter sur ses grands chevaux,* to ride one's high horse; *un remède de cheval,* a drastic remedy. ‖ **Cheval-vapeur,** m. Aᴜᴛᴏᴍ. Horse-power.

chevalement [ʃəvalmɑ̃] m. Tᴇᴄʜɴ. Shoring, scaffolding (d'une construction); pit-head gear, head frame, gallows, frame (d'une mine).

chevaler [-le] v. tr. (1). To shore up (un mur).

chevaleresque [-lrɛsk] adj. Chivalrous, knightly; *conduite chevaleresque,* chivalry, chivalrousness.

chevalerie [-lri] f. Chivalrousness (conduite); knighthood (corps, qualité); chivalry (institution).

chevalet [-lɛ] m. † Rack (de torture). ‖ Aʀᴛs. Easel (de peintre). ‖ Mᴜs. Bridge (de violon). ‖ Tᴇᴄʜɴ. Wooden-horse (de montage); saw-horse (de scieur). ‖ Aʀᴄʜɪᴛ. Trestle (de ponton).

chevalier [-lje] m. Knight; *chevalier errant,* knight-errant. ‖ Knight, knight-companion (d'un ordre); *faire chevalier,* to knight. ‖ Zᴏᴏʟ. Sandpiper. ‖ Fɪɢ. *Chevalier d'industrie,* adventurer, crook, swindler, sharper.

chevalière [-ljɛːr] f. Signet-ring (bague).

chevalin, ine [-lɛ̃, in] adj. Equine (race); *boucherie chevaline,* horse-butcher's shop.

chevauchant, ante [ʃəvoʃɑ̃, ɑ̃ːt] adj. Overlapping.

chevauchée [ʃəvoʃe] f. Ride.

chevauchement [-ʃmɑ̃] m. Riding (d'un cheval). ‖ Crossing (de fils); overlapping (de tuiles). ‖ Mᴇᴅ. Overlapping (des dents).

chevaucher [-ʃe] v. tr. (1). To ride (un cheval); to sit astride (un banc). ‖ To span (une rivière).

— v. intr. To ride (à cheval); *chevaucher sur,* to sit astride. ‖ To overlap (tuiles). ‖ To fall out of place (lettres); *caractères d'imprimerie chevauchant,* squabbled type. ‖ To overlap (dents).

— v. pr. **Se chevaucher,** to overlap.

CHEVAL — HORSE

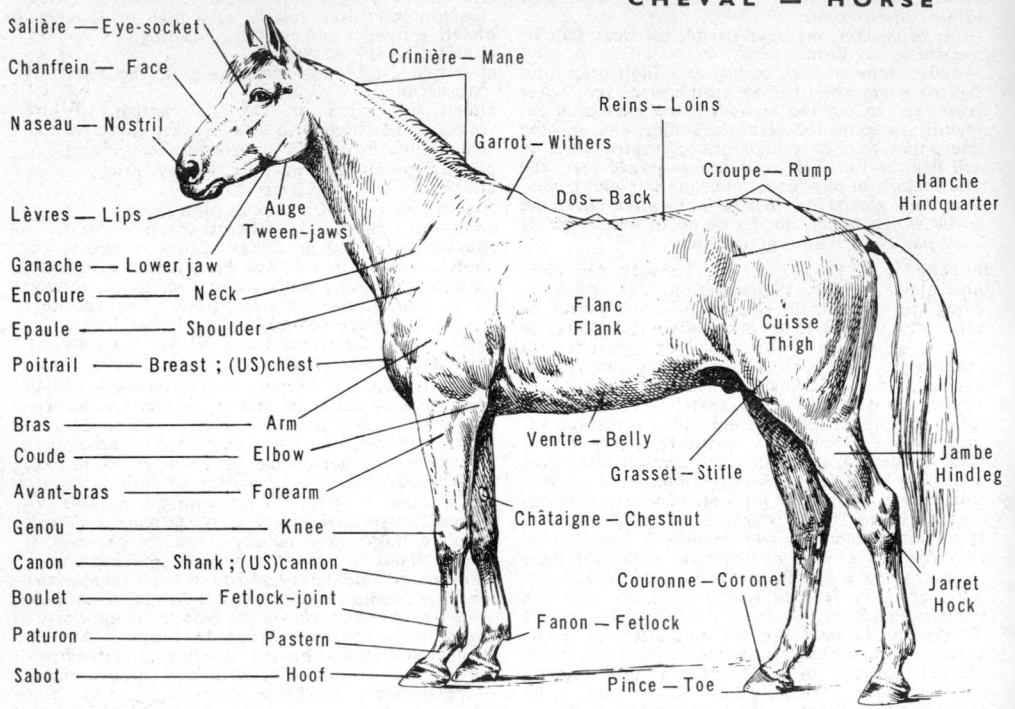

Salière — Eye-socket
Chanfrein — Face
Crinière — Mane
Naseau — Nostril
Reins — Loins
Garrot — Withers
Croupe — Rump
Hanche Hindquarter
Dos — Back
Lèvres — Lips
Auge Tween-jaws
Ganache — Lower jaw
Encolure — Neck
Epaule — Shoulder
Poitrail — Breast ; (US)chest
Flanc Flank
Cuisse Thigh
Bras — Arm
Coude — Elbow
Ventre — Belly
Jambe Hindleg
Avant-bras — Forearm
Grasset — Stifle
Genou — Knee
Châtaigne — Chestnut
Canon — Shank ; (US)cannon
Boulet — Fetlock-joint
Couronne — Coronet
Jarret Hock
Paturon — Pastern
Fanon — Fetlock
Sabot — Hoof
Pince — Toe

chevau-léger [ʃəvoleʒe] m. † Light horseman; *les chevau-légers*, the light horse.

chevelu, ue [ʃəvəly] adj. Hairy (personne); long-haired (tête). ‖ FIG. Wooded (montagne).

chevelure [-ly:r] f. Hair, head of hair; scalp. ‖ BOT. Coma. ‖ ASTRON. Coma, tail.

chevesne [ʃəvɛn] m. V. CHEVAINE.

chevet [ʃəvɛ] m. Head, bedhead (de lit); bedside (d'un malade); *lampe, table de chevet*, bedside lamp, table; *livre de chevet*, bedside book; *le médecin qui sait le mieux se comporter au chevet d'un malade*, the doctor with the best bedside manner. ‖ ARCHIT. Chevet (d'église).

cheveu [ʃəvø] m. Hair (sg. et pl.); *sortir en cheveux*, to go out bare-headed. ‖ LOC. *Ne tenir qu'à un cheveu*, to be hanging by a hair; *saisir l'occasion par les cheveux*, to take time by the forelock; *s'en falloir (ou) s'en manquer de l'épaisseur d'un cheveu*, to be within a hair's breadth of, to be within an inch of. ‖ FAM. *Avoir mal aux cheveux*, to have a hang-over; *comme des cheveux sur la soupe*, like mustard after dinner; *se faire des cheveux*, to worry oneself grey; *se prendre aux cheveux*, to come to blows; *tiré par les cheveux*, far-fetched; *un cheveu*, a hitch, a fly in the ointment.

cheville [ʃəvi:j] f. Peg (en bois); bolt (en fer); pin (d'accouplage); bolt (d'assemblage). ‖ ELECTR. *Cheville d'interrupteur*, switch contactor. ‖ MUS. Peg (de violon). ‖ MÉD. Ankle (du pied). ‖ FIG. Padding (de phrase); stopgap (de vers); *cheville ouvrière*, mainspring, linchpin; *être en cheville avec qqn*, to play ball; *ne pas monter à la cheville de*, not to be named in the same breath with.

cheviller [-je] v. tr. (1). To peg; to bolt, to pin. ‖ FIG. To pad out (des vers); *avoir l'âme chevillée au corps*, to be hard to kill.

chèvre [ʃɛ:vr] f. ZOOL. Goat, she-goat; nanny-goat (fam.). ‖ TECHN. Saw-horse (pour scier); gin (pour soulever). ‖ FIG. *Ménager la chèvre et le chou*, to run with the hare and hunt with the hounds.

chevreau [ʃəvro] m. ZOOL. Kid. ‖ Kid, kid-skin; kid-leather (peau); *en chevreau*, kid.

chèvrefeuille [ʃɛvrəfœ:j] m. BOT. Honeysuckle.

chevrette [ʃəvrɛt] f. ZOOL. Female kid, young she-goat (jeune chèvre); roe, doe (chevreuil femelle); shrimp (crevette).

chevreuil [ʃəvrœ:j] m. ZOOL. Roebuck, roe-deer.

chevrier [ʃəvrije] m. Goat-herd.

chevrier m. BOT. White haricot bean.

chevron [ʃəvrɔ̃] m. ARCHIT. Rafter. ‖ MILIT. Chevron; service stripe. ‖ BLAS. Chevron.

chevronné, ée [ʃəvrɔne] adj. MILIT. Wearing stripes. ‖ FIG. Experienced, practised; in the know.

chevrotant, ante [ʃəvrɔtã, ã:t] adj. Quavering, quavery.

chevrotement [ʃəvrɔtmã] m. Quaver, quavering, tremulousness.

chevroter [-te] v. intr. (1). To kid (mettre bas). ‖ To bleat (chèvre). ‖ To quaver (personne).

chevrotine [-tin] f. Buck-shot.

chewing-gum [ʃwingɔm] m. Chewing-gum.

chez [ʃe] prép. To (avec mouvement; suivi d'un substantif ou d'un pronom non sujet de la proposition); *il allait chez le docteur*, he was going to the doctor's; *nous les avons envoyés chez vous*, we sent them to your house; *venez chez moi*, come to my house. ‖ Home (avec mouvement; suivi du pronom sujet de la proposition);

elle va chez elle, she is going home; *il suivit Jean jusque chez lui,* he followed John home. ‖ At (sans mouvement; suivi d'un substantif); *nous sommes ici chez Mrs. Brown,* we are here at Mrs. Brown's. ‖ At home (sans mouvement; suivi du pronom sujet de la proposition); *il est retenu chez lui par un rhume,* he is kept at home by a cold. ‖ At... house (sans mouvement; suivi d'un pronom non sujet de la proposition); *elle a séjourné un mois chez lui,* she spent a month at his house (ou) at his place. ‖ With (avec, auprès de); *il habite chez son oncle,* he lives with his uncle. ‖ Care of, c/o (sur une adresse); *adressé chez M. Brown,* sent care of Mr. Brown. ‖ In (ou) to the country of (pays); *beaucoup d'Italiens se sont établis chez nous,* many Italians have settled in our country. ‖ De chez; *je n'ai pas de nouvelles de chez moi,* I've no news from home; *loin de chez lui,* far from his house; *près de chez elle,* near her house. ‖ Devant chez; *devant chez moi,* in front of my house; *devant chez le boucher,* in front of the butcher's. ‖ Pour chez; *il part pour chez son frère,* he is off to his brother's. ‖ Chez qui, in (ou) to whose home, with whom, where; *les gens chez qui je prenais pension,* the people at whose house I boarded; *l'ami chez qui il voulait aller,* the friend to whose house he wished to go; *chez qui allez-vous?,* where are you going?; *de chez qui venez-vous?,* from whose house are you coming?. ‖ Chez soi; *faire comme chez soi,* to make oneself at home; *rester chez soi,* to stay at home; *rien ne vaut son chez soi,* there's no place like home. ‖ Fig. With, in, among; *chez lui, c'est une méthode.* it is systematic with him; *chez un enfant bien élevé,* in a well-bred child; *chez les Grecs,* among the Greeks.

chiader [ʃjade] v. tr. (1). Pop. To swot up (ou) for (examen); to make a thorough job of, to take pains over (travail); *un problème chiadé,* a tough problem.
— v. intr. Pop. To slog away, to work hard.

chiadeur, euse [-dœ:r, ø:z] adj. Pop. Slogging, studious.
— s. Pop. Swot, slogger.

chialer [ʃjale] v. intr. (1). Pop. To blubber.

chialeur, euse [-lœ:r, ø:z] adj. Pop. Whining, snivelling, blubbering.
— s. Pop. Cry-baby, sniveller, blubberer.

chiant, ante [ʃjɑ̃, ɑ̃:t] adj. Pop. Draggy, boring; *c'est chiant,* it's a drag.

chianti [kjɑ̃ti] m. Comm. Chianti (vin).

chiasma [kjasma] m. Méd. Chiasma, chiasm.

chiasme [kjasm] m. Gramm. Chiasmus.

chiasse [ʃjas] f. Techn. Dross. ‖ Argot. Squitters, U. S. runs.

chic [ʃik] m. Knack (habileté); *avoir le chic pour,* to have the knack of. ‖ Style, chic (élégance); *avoir du chic,* to be chic, to have smartness (ou) style; *robe qui a du chic,* stylish dress; *ça manque de chic,* there is no style about it. ‖ Arts. *De chic,* without a model. ‖ Fig. *De chic,* off-hand.
— adj. Chic, stylish, smart (élégant); fashionable, swell (en vogue); slap-up, bang-up (de premier ordre); *ça fait chic,* it looks smart; *les gens chics,* the smart set, the fashionable world. ‖ Decent, square, nice (généreux); *un chic type,* a good sort, a sport, a decent chap; *c'est très chic de votre part,* it's awfully decent of you.
— interj. Fam. *Chic alors!,* Fine!, grand!

chicane [ʃikan] f. Jur. Chicanery, pettifoggery (procès); pettifoggers, lawyers (gens du Palais). ‖ Quarrel, quibbling (dispute); *chercher chicane à,* to pick a quarrel with. ‖ Milit. Zig-zag trench. ‖ Techn. Baffle, baffler, baffle-plate; staggered deflector. ‖ Sports. Obstacle (à skis).

chicaner [-ne] v. intr. (1). To chicane, to quibble,

to wrangle, to cavil. ‖ To quibble (*sur,* over).
— v. tr. To wrangle (ou) squabble with (qqn).

chicanerie [-nri] f. Quibbling, hassle.

chicaneur, euse [-nœ:r, ø:z] s. Jur. Barrator, pettifogger. ‖ Quibbler, caviller, carper.
— adj. Cavilling, carping; argumentative.

chicanier, ère [-nje, ɛ:r] adj. Quibbling.
— s. V. chicaneur.

chiche [ʃiʃ] adj. Stingy, tight-fisted (v. rapiat); *chiche de,* sparing of, selfish about, stingy with. ‖ Scanty, poor (chose).

chiche adj. Bot. *Pois chiche,* chick pea.
— interj. *Chiche!,* I dare you!; bet you can't!; bet you I will!; *chiche que* I bet you that.

chichement [-mɑ̃] adv. Niggardly, stingily.

chichi [ʃiʃi] m. False hair (cheveux); frill (parure). ‖ Fam. Fuss, frills (manières). [V. façons.]

chichiteur, euse [-tœ:r, ø:z] s. Fam. Poser, prig.

chicorée [ʃikɔre] f. Endive (frisée); chicory (sauvage, torréfiée).

chicot [ʃikɔ] m. Méd. Stump, stub (de dent).

chicotin [ʃikɔtɛ̃] m. Loc. *Amer comme chicotin,* as bitter as aloes.

chiée [ʃje] f. Pop. Loads, bags (*de,* of).

chien [ʃjɛ̃] m. Zool. Dog; *chien de berger, de chasse,* sheep, hound (ou) hunting (ou) sporting dog; *chien de garde, de salon, de traîneau,* watch- (ou) house-, lap-, sledge-dog; *jeune chien,* pup, puppy. ‖ Fringe (frange); *être coiffée à la chien,* to wear a fringe (ou) a bang. ‖ Milit. Cock, hammer (d'arme, de fusil); *sans chien,* hammerless. ‖ Zool. *Chien de mer,* dog- (ou) hound-fish. ‖ Fam. Glamour; *avoir du chien,* to be alluring (ou) sexy. ‖ Fam. Cur, dirty dog, swine (triste individu); *chien couchant,* fawner, back-scratcher, lick-spittle, U. S. apple-polisher. ‖ De chien : *caractère de chien,* beastly temper; *d'une humeur de chien,* out of humour, as cross as two sticks; *un métier de chien,* a brute of a job; *temps de chien,* filthy weather; *vie de chien, chienne de vie,* dog's life. ‖ Loc. *Bon à jeter aux chiens,* fit for the dogs, currish; *comme un chien dans un jeu de quilles,* as a dog on a putting green; *coup de chien,* squall; *garder un chien de sa chienne pour,* to have a rod in pickle for; to have a grudge against; *entre chien et loup,* at nightfall; *ne pas valoir les quatre fers d'un chien,* not to be worth a button (ou) a bean; *regarder en chien de faïence,* to stare like a stuck pig; *rompre les chiens,* to cut short; *se coucher en chien de fusil,* to curl up in bed. ‖ Chien-loup, m. Zool. Wolf-dog, U. S. police dog.
— adj. Close-fisted, stingy. (V. rapiat.)

chiendent [ʃjɛ̃dɑ̃] m. Bot. Twitch, scutch-grass. ‖ Fam. Rub, snag.

chienlit [ʃjɑ̃li] f. † Carnival mask, disguise. ‖ Fam. Havoc, hullaballoo.

chienne [ʃjɛn] f. Zool. Bitch, dog. ‖ Pop. Bitch.

chier [ʃje] v. intr., tr. Argot. To shit; *il me fait chier,* he puts years on me.

chiffe [ʃif] f. Fig. Weakling; *sé sentir mou comme une chiffe,* to feel like a rag.

chiffon [ʃifɔ̃] m. Rag (étoffe). ‖ Scrap (de papier). ‖ Pl. Frills; *parler chiffons,* to talk dress.

chiffonnage [ʃifɔna:ʒ] m. Rumpling (d'une étoffe); crumpling (du papier).

chiffonné [ʃifɔne] adj. Rumpled (étoffe); crumpled (papier). ‖ Fig. Piquant (mine). ‖ Fam. Worried (inquiet).

chiffonner v. tr. (1). To rumple, to crease, to ruffle (une étoffe); to crumple (du papier). [V. froisser.] ‖ Fam. To rile (qqn).
— v. pr. Se chiffonner, to rumple (étoffe); to crumple (papier).

chiffonnier [-nje] m. Rag-picker, ragman, U. S. junkman. ‖ Chiffonnier, U. S. dresser (meuble).

chiffrable [ʃifrabl] adj. Calculable; *difficilement chiffrable*, difficult to estimate.
chiffrage [ʃifra:ʒ] m. Calculation. ‖ Coding (d'un message). ‖ Stamping (du papier à lettres).
chiffre [ʃifr] m. MATH. Figure, number, cipher, numeral; *un nombre de dix chiffres*, a ten-figure number. ‖ FIN. Amount, total (montant); *en chiffres ronds*, in round figures; *chiffre d'affaires*, turnover. ‖ Monogram (initiales); figure-stamp (poinçon). ‖ Code, cipher (code); *officier du chiffre*, cipher officer. ‖ FIG. *Un zéro en chiffre*, a mere cipher, a nobody.
chiffrement [-frəmɑ̃] m. Encoding, enciphering.
chiffrer [-fre] v. tr. (1). To calculate, to figure out (un montant). ‖ To mark (du linge). ‖ To code, to cipher (un message).
— v. intr. To calculate, to reckon, to cipher (calculer). ‖ To reach a high figure (monter).
— v. pr. Se chiffrer, to amount, to tot up (*à*, to); *se chiffrer par*, to work out at, to number.
chiffreur [-frœ:r] m. Encoder.
chignole [ʃiɲɔl] f. TECHN. Hand-drill, breast-drill. ‖ FAM. Old rock, U. S. flivver (voiture).
chignon [ʃiɲɔ̃] m. Chignon; bun (fam.); *en chignon*, coiled up.
chi'isme [ʃiism] m. ECCLÉS. Shiism.
chi'ite [ʃiit] adj. ECCLÉS. Shiitic.
— s. ECCLÉS. Shiite.
Chili [ʃili] m. GÉOGR. Chile.
chilien, enne [-ljɛ̃, ɛn] adj., s. Chilean, Chilian.
chimère [ʃimɛ:r] f. Chimera. ‖ FIG. Idle dream; day-dream.
chimérique [-merik] adj. Chimerical, visionary (esprit, personne); airy, chimerical, fantastic (projet, rêve); *lieu chimérique*, cloud-castle, castle in the air.
chimie [ʃimi] f. CHIM. Chemistry; *chimie biologique*, bio-chemistry.
chimiosynthèse [ʃimjosɛ̃tɛ:z] f. Chemosynthesis.
chimiothérapie [ʃimjoterapi] n. MÉD. Chemotherapy.
chimique [ʃimik] adj. CHIM. Chemical; *produit chimique*, chemical. ‖ PHYS. Actinic (rayon). ‖ MILIT. Chemical (guerre).
chimiquement [-mɑ̃] adv. CHIM. Chemically.
chimisme [ʃimism] m. Chemism.
chimiste [-mist] m. CHIM. Chemist.
chimpanzé [ʃɛ̃pɑ̃ze] m. ZOOL. Chimpanzee.
chinchilla [ʃɛ̃ʃilla] m. ZOOL. Chinchilla.
Chine [ʃin] f. GÉOGR. China.
chine m. China (matière); china object (vase, bibelot).
chiné, ée [ʃine] adj. Mottled, clouded, chiné.
— m. Chiné.
chiner v. tr. (1). To cloud, to mottle (un tissu). ‖ FAM. To chaff; U. S. to josh (qqn). [V. BLAGUER.]
chinetoque [ʃintok] s. POP. Chinee, Chink.
chinois, oise [ʃinwa, wa:z] adj. GÉOGR. Chinese. ‖ FAM. Punctilious.
— m. Chinese, Chinaman. ‖ Chinese (langue).
Chinoise [ʃinwa:z] f. Chinese woman.
chinoiserie [-ri] f. Chinese curio (bibelot). ‖ FAM. Fuss; *chinoiseries administratives*, red tape.
chintz [ʃints] m. Chintz.
chiot [ʃjo] m. ZOOL. Whelp, pup, puppy.
chiottes [ʃjɔt] f. pl. ARGOT. Bog, shit-house.
chiourme [ʃjurm] f. † Crew of galley-rowers. ‖ Gang of convicts; chain-gang.
chiper [ʃipe] v. tr. (1). FAM. To pinch, to swipe.
chipeur, euse [-pœ:r, ø:z] s. FAM. Pilferer.
chipie [ʃipi] f. FAM. Sour-puss.
chipolata [ʃipolata] m. CULIN. Chipolata.
chipotage [ʃipɔta:ʒ] m. FAM. Fussiness, fastidiousness (en mangeant). ‖ FAM. Cavilling, quibbling (ergoterie).

chipoter [ʃipɔte] v. intr. (1). FAM. To nibble at one's food; to be finicky in eating; to pick and choose. ‖ FAM. To cavil (ergoter); to haggle (marchander).
chipoteur, euse [-tœ:r, ø:z] adj. Fastidious (en mangeant). ‖ Cavilling (ergoteur).
— s. Fastidious person. ‖ Caviller; haggler.
chips [ʃip] m. pl. CULIN. Potato crisps (ou) chips.
chique [ʃik] f. Quid, chew (de tabac). ‖ ZOOL. Chigger, chigoe, jigger, redbug.
chiqué [ʃike] m. MILIT. Bull. ‖ FAM. Sham, fake, make-believe (faux-semblant); eye-wash (tromperie); *le faire au chiqué*, to make believe. ‖ FAM. Fuss; to do (manières); *faire du chiqué*, to show off; to bluff.
chiquement [ʃikmɑ̃] adv. Smartly. ‖ Decently.
chiquenaude [ʃikno:d] f. Fillip, flick, flip; *donner une chiquenaude à*, to flick; *faire tomber d'une chiquenaude*, to flick off.
chiquer [ʃike] v. tr. To chew (du tabac).
— v. intr. To chew tobacco.
chiqueur [-kœ:r] m. Chewer.
chiromancie [kirɔmɑ̃si] f. Chiromancy, palmistry.
chiromancien [-mɑ̃sjɛ̃] s. Chiromancer, palmist.
chiropracteur [kirɔpraktœ:r] m. MÉD. Chiropractor.
chiropractie [-prakti], **chiropraxie** [-praksi] f. MÉD. Chiropractic.
chiroptère [-ptɛ:r] m. ZOOL. Cheiropteran.
chirurgical, ale [ʃiryrʒikal] adj. MÉD. Surgical; *ventre chirurgical*, acute abdomen.
chirurgie [-ʒi] f. MÉD. Surgery.
chirurgien, enne [-ʒjɛ̃, ɛn] s. MÉD. Surgeon; *chirurgien esthétique*, plastic surgeon; *chirurgien militaire*, army surgeon. ‖ **Chirurgien-dentiste**, m. MÉD. Dental surgeon.
chitine [kitin] f. ZOOL. Chitin.
chiure [ʃjy:r] f. ARGOT. Fly-speck (de mouches).
chlamyde [klamid] f. † Chlamys.
chleuh, e [ʃlø] adj., s. FAM. Hun, kraut.
chloral [klɔral] (pl. **chlorals**) m. CHIM. Chloral.
chlorate [klɔrat] m. CHIM. Chlorate.
chlore [klɔ:r] m. CHIM. Chlorine.
chloré, ée [klɔre] adj. CHIM. Chlorinated.
chlorhydrate [-ridrat] m. CHIM. Chlorhydrate.
chlorhydrique [-ridrik] adj. CHIM. Hydrochloric.
chlorique [-rik] adj. CHIM. Chloric.
chloroforme [-rɔfɔrm] m. Chloroform.
chloroformer [-rɔfɔrme] v. tr. MÉD. To chloroform.
chloromycétine [-rɔmisetin] f. MÉD. Chloromycetine.
chlorophylle [-fil] f. BOT. Chlorophyll.
chlorophyllien, enne [-filjɛ̃, ɛn] adj. BOT. Chlorophyllous, chlorophyllose.
chloropicrine [-pikrin] f. CHIM. Trichlornitromethane; chloropicrin; nitrochloroform.
chlorose [klɔro:z] f. MÉD., BOT. Chlorosis.
chlorotique [klɔrɔtik] adj. MÉD. Chlorotic.
chloruration [klɔryrasjɔ̃] f. CHIM. Chlorination.
chlorure [klɔry:r] m. CHIM. Chloride; *chlorure de sodium*, sodium chloride.
chlorurer [-ryre] v. tr. (1). CHIM. To chlorinize, to chlorinate.
chnouf [ʃnuf] f. ARGOT. Snow, heroin.
choc [ʃɔk] m. Shock (en général); clash (des armées, de la foule); brunt, onslaught (de l'attaque); clink (des épées, des verres); impact (d'un projectile); jar (d'une secousse); bump (d'une voiture cahotante); collision (de deux voitures); *choc sourd*, dull thud, bump; *choc violent et sonore*, clash; *gare au choc en retour*, look out for the come-back (fam.). ‖ MILIT. Shock, encounter; *action, troupes de choc*, shock action, troops. ‖ AVIAT. *Choc d'atterrissage*, impact load.

‖ MÉD. Shock; *choc électrique, opératoire,* electric, surgical shock; *choc nerveux,* jar to the nerves. ‖ FIG. Conflict (des idées); clash (des intérêts); *choc en retour,* boomerang.
— adj. inv. Shock (prix).

chochotte [ʃɔʃɔt] f. FAM. Fussy (ou) squeamish woman.

chocolat [ʃɔkɔla] m. Chocolat (barre, boisson, bonbon); U. S. chocolate candy (bonbon).
— adj. Chocolate, reddish-brown. ‖ POP. *Etre chocolat,* to be diddled, to be done brown; *rester chocolat,* to be stranded.

chocolaté, ée [-te] adj. Flavoured with chocolate; U. S. chocolate.

chocolaterie [-tri] f. Chocolate-factory.

chocolatier, ière [-tje, tjɛr] s. Chocolate-maker (fabricant); chocolate-seller (marchand).

chocolatière [-tjɛːr] f. Chocolate pot.

chocottes [ʃɔkɔt] f. pl. ARG. *Avoir les chocottes,* to have the jitters (ou) the willies, to be in a funk, to be in a blue funk.

chœur [kœːr] m. ARTS. Chorus (de chants, de chanteurs, de la tragédie antique); *en chœur,* in chorus; *faire partie des chœurs,* to go on in the chorus; *tous en chœur!,* all together! ‖ ECCLÉS. Choir (maîtrise); choir, chancel (de l'autel).

choir [ʃwaːr] v. intr. (25). To fall.

choisi, ie [ʃwazi] adj. Choice (articles, termes); chosen (auditeurs); selected (fruits, morceaux); picked (invités); appropriate (nom); select (public, société); *choisi comme chef du parti,* chosen (ou) appointed leader of the party; *choisi parmi des milliers,* singled out from among thousands.

choisir [-zir] v. tr. (2). To choose, to make choice of (sens général); to choose (entre deux possibilités); to single out (distinguer); to fix on (fixer son choix sur); to select (sélectionner); to pick out (trier). [V. OPTER.]
— v. intr. *Choisir entre,* to choose between, to take one's choice of; *le droit de choisir,* the power of choice, the choice.

choix [ʃwa] m. Choice (v. OPTION, SÉLECTION); *au choix,* at choice (par goût); by selection (par promotion); *de mon choix,* of my choosing; *arrêter son choix sur,* to fix on; *faire choix de,* to make choice of; *faire son choix parmi,* to take one's choice from; *laisser à aan le choix entre,* to give s.o. his choice of; *l'embarras du choix,* too much to choose from, embarrassment of riches; *n'avoir pas le choix,* to have no choice (ou) alternative. ‖ Range (de couleurs, d'échantillons, de sujets); selection (d'exemples, de morceaux, de poèmes); collection (de tissus). ‖ COMM. *De choix,* choice; *de premier choix,* prime, first class; of the highest quality; *avoir du choix,* to have plenty to choose from; *il n'y avait pas grand choix,* there was little to choose, there wasn't must choice.

cholédoque [kɔledɔk] adj., m. MÉD. Choledoch.

cholémie [-mi] f. MÉD. Cholaemia.

choléra [kɔlera] m. MÉD. Cholera.

cholérine [-rin] f. MÉD. Cholerine, bilious (ou) sporadic cholera.

cholérique [-rik] adj. MÉD. Choleraic.
— s. Cholera patient.

cholérique adj. Bilious. (V. ATRABILAIRE.)

cholestérol [kɔlɛsterɔl] m. MÉD. Cholesterol.

cholinergique [kɔlinɛrʒik] adj. MÉD. Cholinergic.

chômage [ʃomaːʒ] m. Work stoppage, closing (des jours fériés); unemployment (des ouvriers); shutting down (d'une usine); *en chômage,* out of work, unemployed; *s'inscrire au chômage,* to register as unemployed; to go on the dole (fam.).

chômer [-me] v. intr. (1). To abstain from work (les jours fériés); *jour chômé,* day off. ‖ To be unemployed (ou) idle, to be out of work (ou) off

work (ouvriers). ‖ To be (ou) to lie idle (machine, usine); to stop work, to shut down (usine).
— v. tr. To keep (une fête).

chômeur, euse [-mœːr, øːz] s. Unemployed worker. ‖ Pl. The unemployed.
— adj. Out-of-work, unemployed.

chondriosome [kɔ̃drijɔzoːm] m. MÉD. Chondriosome.

chope [ʃɔp] f. Tankard, beer mug.

choper [ʃɔpe] v. tr. (1). SPORTS. To chop (tennis). ‖ FAM. To pinch; *se faire choper,* to get nabbed.

chopin [ʃɔpɛ̃] m. POP. Windfall, godsend.

chopine [ʃɔpin] f. Half-litre mug. ‖ CANADA, pint. ‖ POP. Bottle.

choquant, ante [ʃɔkɑ̃, ɑ̃ːt] adj. Shocking.

choquer [-ke] v. tr. (1). To knock against (qqch., qqn); *choquer les verres,* to clink glasses. ‖ FIG. To grate on (l'amour-propre, l'oreille); to outrage (la bienséance, le bon sens); to jar on (l'esprit, l'oreille, les sentiments); to shock (l'oreille, qqn); to scandalize (qqn); to offend (qqn, les regards, la vue); to hurt (les sentiments). [V. HEURTER.]
— v. pr. Se choquer, to strike against each other, to collide with each other; to clash (avec fracas). ‖ FIG. To take offence (de, at); to be offended (se froisser).

choral [kɔral] (pl. **chorals**) m. MUS. Choral, chorale.
— adj. Choral.

chorale [kɔraːl] f. MUS. Choral society; choir.

chordé [kɔrde] m. ZOOL. V. CORDÉ.

chorégraphe [kɔregraf] s. Choregrapher.

chorégraphie [kɔregrafi] f. Choreography.

chorégraphique [-fik] adj. Choreographic.

choreute [kɔrøːt] m. Choreutes, member of chorus (dans la Grèce antique).

choriste [kɔrist] s. THÉÂTR. Chorist. ‖ ECCLÉS. Chorister.

chorographie [kɔrɔgrafi] f. GÉOGR. Chorography.

choroïde [kɔrɔid] f. MÉD. Choroid.

chorus [kɔryːs] m. *Faire chorus,* to chime in.

chose [ʃoːz] f. Thing (sens général, indéfini); *avoir autre chose à faire,* to have something else to do; *c'est la même chose,* it is the same thing, it is all one, it comes to the same thing; *ce n'est pas chose facile,* it is not an easy matter; *chose étrange,* strange to say; *ne pas faire grand-chose,* not to do much, to do little; *parler de chose et autre,* to talk of one thing and another; *peu de chose,* a trifle; *si peu de chose,* so small a matter. ‖ Pl. Things, affairs, matters; *les choses vont mal,* things are going badly; *l'état actuel des choses,* the present state of affairs; *ce sont des choses qui arrivent,* it's just one of those things; *dans l'état actuel des choses,* as things stand; *dites bien des choses à,* remember me kindly to, kind regards to; *en mettant les choses au mieux,* at best; *faire bien les choses,* to spare no expense; *par la force des choses,* through force of circumstance; *un type qui prend les choses comme elles viennent,* a happy-go-lucky fellow. ‖ Property, chattel; *être la chose de qqn,* to be the slave of (ou) a mere tool in the hands of s.o. ‖ JUR. Thing, case, matter, affair; *la chose jugée,* res judicata; *la chose publique,* the common weal. ‖ FAM. *Monsieur Chose,* Mr. What-d'you-call-him, Mr. What's-his-name, Mr. So-and-So; *le petit Chose,* Little Thingummy.
— adj. invar. FAM. Queer (bizarre); out of sorts, uncomfortable (malade); *tout chose,* queer, troubled, disturbed.

chosifier [ʃozifje] v. tr. (1). PHILOS. To reify. ‖ FAM. To treat (ou) consider as a mere object.

chou [ʃu] m. (pl. **choux**). BOT. Cabbage; *chou de Bruxelles,* Brussels sprouts. ‖ CULIN. *Chou à la crème,* cream puff. ‖ COMM. Cabbage-knot, rosette (de ruban). ‖ FAM. *Etre dans les choux,* to be in the soup; *faire chou blanc,* to draw a blank; *faire ses choux gras,* to feather one's nest; *feuille de chou,* rag (journal); *mon petit chou,* darling, honey, sweet; *rentrer dans le chou à,* to make a set at. ‖ **Chou-fleur** (pl. *choux-fleurs*) m. BOT. Cauliflower. ‖ **Chou-palmiste** (pl. *choux-palmistes*) m. BOT. Cabbage-palm. ‖ **Chou-rave** (pl. *choux-raves*) m. BOT. Kohlrabi.

chouan [ʃwɑ̃] m. Chouan.

chouannerie [ʃwanri] f. Chouan rising (ou) partisans.

choucas [ʃuka] m. ZOOL. Jackdaw.

chouchou, oute [ʃuʃu, ut] m. FAM. Pet, cosset; blue-eyed boy. (V. FAVORI.)

chouchoutage [-ta:ʒ] m. FAM. Favouritism (à l'école).

chouchouter [-te] v. tr. (1). FAM. To pet, to cosset, to dandle, to coddle.
— v. pr. **Se chouchouter,** FAM. To coddle oneself; to have a cushy time.

choucroute [ʃukrut] f. CULIN. Sauerkraut.

chouette [ʃwɛt] f. ZOOL. Barn-owl; wood-owl.

chouette adj. FAM. Grand, U. S. swell.
— interj. *Chouette alors!,* what luck!; U. S. oh boy!

chouia [ʃuja] m. ARG. Wee bit, spot, mite.

chouque [ʃuk] m. NAUT. Cap.

chouriner [ʃurine] v. tr. V. SURINER.

chow-chow [ʃuʃu] n. ZOOL. Chow (chien).

choyer [ʃwaje] v. tr. (9a). To fondle, to coddle.

chrême [krɛ:m] m. ECCLÉS. Chrism.

chrémeau [-mo] m. ECCLÉS. Chrismal, chrisom.

chrestomathie [krɛstomati] f. Chrestomathy.

chrétien, enne [kretjɛ̃, ɛn] adj., s. ECCLÉS. Christian.

chrétiennement [-tjɛnmɑ̃] adv. In a Christian manner; Christianly.

chrétienté [-tjɛ̃te] f. ECCLÉS. Christendom.

Chris-craft [kriskraft] m. (nom déposé). NAUT. Speed-boat.

Christ [krist] m. ECCLÉS. Christ. ‖ Crucifix.

christiania [kristjanja] m. SPORTS. Christiania, Christie.

christianisation [kristjanizasjɔ̃] f. ECCLÉS. Christianization.

christianiser [-tjanize] v. tr. (1). ECCLÉS. To Christianize.

christianisme [-tjanism] m. ECCLÉS. Christianity.

Christmas [-mas] m. Christmas-card.

chromage [krɔma:ʒ] m. Chromium plating.

chromate [krɔmat] m. CHIM. Chromate.

chromatine [-tin] f. MÉD. Chromatin.

chromatique [-tik] adj. ARTS, MUS. Chromatic. ‖ MÉD. Chromosomal.

chromatisme [-tism] m. Chromatism (couleur). ‖ MUS. Chromaticism.

chromatographie [-tɔgrafi] f. CHIM. Chromatography.

chrome [kro:m] m. CHIM. Chromium. ‖ COMM. Chrome.

chromé, ée [krome] adj. Chrome (acier).

chromer v. tr. (1). To chrome.

chromo [kromo] m. ARTS. Chromo.

chromolithographie [-litografi] f. ARTS. Chromolithograph (épreuve); chromolithography (procédé).

chromophotographie [-fɔtɔgrafi] f. Chromophotograph (épreuve); chromophotography (procédé).

chromosome [-zom] m. MÉD. Chromosome.

chromosomique [-zɔmik] adj. MÉD. Chromosomal.

chronicité [krɔnisite] f. MÉD. Chronicity.

chronique [-nik] adj. MÉD. Chronic.

chronique f. Chronicle (annales). ‖ News, reports, article; *chronique dramatique,* review of theatrical productions; *chronique financière,* financial news; *chronique juridique,* law reports; *chro-*

nique littéraire, literary intelligence; *chronique scandaleuse,* scandalous gossip.

chroniqueur [-nikœ:r] m. Chronicler (historien). ‖ Writer of news pars (ou) reports, newswriter; *chroniqueur financier,* financial editor.

chrono [krɔno] m. FAM. V. CHRONOMÈTRE.

chronographe [krɔnɔgraf] m. Chronograph.

chronologie [-lɔʒi] f. Chronology.

chronologique [-lɔʒik] adj. Chronological.

chronologiquement [-lɔʒikmɑ̃] adv. Chronologically.

chronométrage [-metra:ʒ] m. SPORTS. Timing, time-keeping.

chronomètre [-mɛ:tr] m. Chronometer; stop watch. (V. MONTRE.)

chronométrer [-metre] v. tr. (1). To time.

chronométreur [-metrœ:r] m. Time-keeper.

chronométrie [-metri] f. Chronometry, time-measurement.

chronométrique [-metrik] adj. Chronometric.

chrysalide [krizalid] f. ZOOL. Chrysalid, chrysalis.

chrysanthème [krizɑ̃tɛ:m] m. BOT. Chrysanthemum.

chrysocale [krizɔkal] m. Pinchbeck.

chrysolithe [krizɔlit] f. Chrysolite.

chrysoprase [-prɑ:z] f. Chrysoprase.

cht(h)onien, enne [ktɔnjɛ̃, ɛn] adj. Chthonic.

C.H.U. [seaʃy] m. Abrév. de *centre hospitalo-universitaire,* teaching hospital.

chu, chut [ʃy]. V. CHOIR (25).

chuchotement [ʃyʃɔtmɑ̃] m. Whispering.

chuchoter [-te] v. tr., intr. (1). To whisper.

chuchoterie [-tri] f. FAM. Whispering, gossip.

chuchoteur, euse [-tœ:r, ø:z] s. Whisperer.

chuchotis [-ti] m. V. CHUCHOTEMENT.

chuintant, ante [ʃɥɛ̃tɑ̃, ɑ̃:t] adj. GRAMM. Tongue-and-after-gum (consonne); hushing (son).

chuintement [ʃɥɛ̃tmɑ̃] m. Hissing (d'un gaz, d'un liquide). ‖ GRAMM. Hushing (d'une consonne). ‖ ZOOL. Hooting (de la chouette).

chuinter [-te] v. intr. (1). ZOOL. To hoot (chouette). ‖ GRAMM. To utter hushing sounds.

chut! [ʃyt] interj. Hush!

chute f. Fall (en général); fall (d'un corps, des feuilles, de neige, du rideau); *faire une chute,* to have a fall; *faire une chute de cheval,* to fall off one's horse. ‖ Fall, hang (d'une robe, d'un tissu). ‖ Fall (du baromètre, de la température). ‖ Drop (de terrain). ‖ *Chute d'eau,* fall, waterfall, chute, cascade, cataract. ‖ Pl. Cuttings (de bois); parings (de papier); clippings (de tissu). ‖ ARCHIT. Pitch (d'un toit). ‖ ECCLÉS. Fall; lapse; *la chute de l'homme,* the Fall of Man. ‖ FIN. Collapse (des cours); *la chute des prix,* fall (ou) drop in prices. ‖ ELECTR. *Chute de potentiel,* voltage drop; *chute de tension,* drop of potential. ‖ MÉD. *La chute des reins,* the small of the back. ‖ AVIAT. Fall. ‖ FIG. Downfall (d'un empire); overthrow (d'un empire, d'un ministère); fall (d'un souverain, d'une ville). ‖ FIG. Close (d'un discours, d'un sonnet); rounding off (d'une phrase); cadence (de la voix). ‖ FIG. Downfall (des espérances); overthrow (des projets); fall, ruin, downfall (de qqn).

chuter [-te] v. intr. (1). POP. To tumble. ‖ FIG. To slip (femme); to blot one's copy-book (fam.).

chyle [ʃi:l] m. MÉD. Chyle.

chyme [ʃi:m] m. MÉD. Chyme.

Chypre [ʃipr] m. GÉOGR. Cyprus. ‖ COMM. Cyprian wine (vin).

chypriote [-prijɔt] adj., s. V. CYPRIOTE.

ci [si]. V. CECI.

ci adv. Here; *ci-gît,* here lies; *de-ci de-là, par-ci par-là,* here and there. ‖ *Ci-après,* hereafter, below. ‖ *Ci-contre,* opposite. ‖ *Ci-dessous,* hereunder, below. ‖ *Ci-dessus,* above, above-mentioned. ‖ *Ci-devant,* formerly; one-time;

quondam; ci-devant. ‖ **Ci-inclus,** herein; herewith enclosed; included. ‖ **Ci-joint,** hereto attached; subjoined; accompanying.
cibiche [sibiʃ] f. Fam. Gasper, coffin-nail, U. S. weed.
cible [sibl] f. Target; *cible parlante,* self-recording target. ‖ Fig. Butt; *prendre pour cible,* to aim one's shafts at; *servir de cible,* to be a butt for. ‖ **Cible-paysage,** f. Landscape target. ‖ **Cible-silhouette,** f. Silhouette target.
ciboire [sibwa:r] m. Ecclés. Ciborium, pyx.
ciboule [sibul] f. Bot. Welsh onion, scallion.
ciboulette [-lɛt] f. Bot. Chives.
ciboulot [-lo] m. Fam. Pate, brain-pan. (V. cabêche.)
cicatrice [sikatris] f. Méd. Cicatrice; scar (balafre); seam (couture).
cicatriciel, elle [-sjɛl] adj. Méd. Cicatricial (marque); *tissu cicatriciel,* scar tissue.
cicatrisant, ante [-zɑ̃, ɑ̃:t] adj. Cicatrizing.
— m. Méd. Cicatrizant.
cicatrisation [-zasjɔ̃] f. Méd. Cicatrization; skinning over.
cicatriser [-ze] v. tr. (1). To cicatrize, to scar (une blessure). ‖ Fig. To heal (une douleur).
— v. pr. **Se cicatriser,** to cicatrize, to heal up, to scar over, to skin over.
cicéro [sisero] m. Pica (en typo).
cicerone [siserɔn] m. Cicerone.
cidre [sidr] m. Cider; *cidre doux,* sweet cider.
cidrerie [-drəri] f. Cider-house.
cidrier [-drje] adj. Cider.
— m. Cider-maker.
ciel [sjɛl] (pl. **cieux**) m. Heaven, sky; welkin (poétique) [v. firmament]; *entre ciel et terre,* between heaven and earth; *en plein ciel,* in mid air. ‖ Sky, climate; *sous des cieux étrangers,* under foreign skies, in foreign climes. ‖ Ecclés. Heaven (v. paradis); *aller au ciel,* to go to paradise, U. S. to climb the golden stairs (fam.); *au septième ciel,* in the seventh heaven; *du haut du ciel,* from on high; *plût au ciel que,* would to God that; *tomber du ciel,* to come as a godsend. — interj. *Ciel!,* good heavens!, good gracious!
ciel (pl. **ciels**) m. Tester (de lit); roof (de carrière, de casemate). ‖ Arts. Sky (des paysagistes). ‖ Géogr., Aviat. Climate.
cierge [sjɛrʒ] m. Ecclés. Taper, candle.
cigale [sigal] f. Zool. Cicada.
cigare [siga:r] m. Cigar; weed (fam.).
cigarette [sigarɛt] f. Cigarette; fag, U. S. coffin-nail, weed (pop.).
cigarière [-rjɛ:r] f. Cigar-maker.
cigarillo [-rillɔ] m. Whiff.
cigogne [sigɔɲ] f. Zool. Stork.
ciguë [sigy] f. Bot. Hemlock (plante et poison).
cil [sil] m. Méd. Eye-lash, lash. ‖ Bot. Cilium (pl. cilia).
ciliaire [siljɛ:r] adj. Méd. Ciliary.
cilice [silis] m. Cilice, hair-shirt.
cillement [sijmɑ̃] m. Blinking, nictitation.
ciller [-je] v. tr. et intr. (1). To blink, to wink. ‖ Fig. *On n'ose pas ciller devant lui,* nobody dares move a muscle before him.
cimaise [simɛ:z] f. Archit. Cyma. ‖ Arts. Line.
cime [si:m] f. Top (d'un arbre); top, summit (d'une montagne). [V. sommet.]
ciment [simɑ̃] m. Cement; *ciment armé,* reinforced concrete; *ciment non broyé,* clinker; *lait de ciment,* grout, thin mortar. ‖ Fig. Cement.
cimenter [-te] v. tr. (1). To cement. ‖ Fig. To cement. (V. consolider, sceller.)
cimenterie [-tri] f. Techn. Cement works (ou) plant.
cimentier [-tje] m. Cement-maker (fabricant); cement-worker (ouvrier).
cimeterre [simtɛ:r] m. Scimitar.

cimetière [simtjɛ:r] m. Cemetery, graveyard, burial-ground; churchyard (près de l'église).
cimier [simje] m. Crest. ‖ Blas. Crest. ‖ Culin. Haunch of venison.
cinabre [sina:br] m. Chim. Cinnabar; vermilion.
cinchonine [sɛ̃kɔnin] f. Chim. Cinchonine.
ciné [sine]. V. cinéma. ‖ **Ciné-caméra,** f. Motion-camera. ‖ **Ciné-club,** m. Cine-club, film-society. ‖ **Ciné-comédie,** f. Comedy film. ‖ **Ciné-film,** m. Cine-film. ‖ **Ciné-journal,** m. Newsreel. ‖ **Ciné-roman,** m. Film-story.
cinéaste [sineast] m. Film-producer; cinematographer (producteur); scenario-writer (scénariste).
cinéma [sinema] m. Théâtr. Cinema (art, édifice, film); cinematics (art); pictures, flicks (fam.); U. S. movies, flickers (film); picture palace, U. S. motion-picture theater, movie-house (théâtre); *faire du cinéma,* to act for the films, to be in films; U. S. to be in the movies.
Cinémascope [-skɔp] m. Cinemascope.
cinémathèque [-tɛk] f. Film-store, film-library.
cinématique [-tik] adj. Kinematic, kinematical.
— f. Kinematics.
cinématographe [-tɔgraf] m. Cinematograph.
cinématographie [-tɔgrafi] f. Cinematography.
cinématographier [-tɔgrafje] v. tr. (1). To cinematize, to cinematograph; to film.
cinématographique [-tɔgrafik] adj. Cinematographic.
cinémodérivomètre [sinemɔderivomɛtr] m. Aviat. Ground speed meter.
cinémomètre [sinemɔmɛtr] m. Kinemometer.
cinéphile [sinefil] s. Film-fan, cinema-goer, movie-goer, film-goer; U. S. film-buff.
cinéraire [sinerɛ:r] adj. Cinerary (urne).
— f. Bot. Cineraria.
Cinérama [sinerama] m. Cinerama.
cinétique [-tik] adj. Phys. Kinetic (énergie).
— f. Phys. Kinetics.
cing(h)alais, aise [sɛ̃galɛ, ɛ:z] adj., s. Géogr. Sinhalese, cingalese (†).
cinglage [sɛ̃gla:ʒ] m. Naut. Day's run.
cinglant, ante [-glɑ̃, ɑ̃:t] adj. Keen, bitter, biting (froid); driving, lashing (pluie); cutting, biting (vent). ‖ Fig. Slashing (ironie); scathing, stinging, cutting (remarque); *adresser à qqn des reproches cinglants,* to lash s.o. with one's tongue.
cinglé [-gle] adj. Fam. Batty; barmy; daft, dotty; U. S. slap-happy, nutty, nuts, goofy, loco; *être cinglé,* to be off one's nut, U. S. to be off one's rocker.
cingler v. intr. (1). Naut. To steer (vers, to); to make (vers, for); to scud along.
cingler v. tr. (1). To swish through (l'air); to lash (qqn). ‖ Fig. To lash.
cinname [sinnam] m. Bot. Cinnamon.
cinnamique [-mik] adj. Chim. Cinnamic.
cinoche [sinɔʃ] m. Pop. Flicks, pictures.
cinq [sɛ̃k, sɛ̃] adj. num. invar. Five; *cinq doigts,* five fingers; *page cinq,* page five. ‖ Fifth; *Henry Cinq,* Henry the Fifth; *le cinq janvier,* the fifth of January, January the fifth; *au chapitre cinq,* in the fifth chapter. ‖ Loc. *Il est moins cinq,* it is five to (heure); *il était moins cinq,* it was a narrow escape (danger).
— m. invar. Cinque (aux cartes, aux dés). ‖ Fin., Math. Five.
cinquantaine [sɛ̃kɑ̃tɛn] f. About fifty; fifty or so; *une cinquantaine de poires,* about fifty pears. ‖ Fifty (âge); *friser la cinquantaine,* to be getting on for fifty, U. S. to be pushing fifty.
cinquante [sɛ̃kɑ̃:t] adj. num. invar. Fifty; *elle a dépassé cinquante ans,* she is over fifty.
cinquantenaire [-tnɛ:r] adj. Fifty-year-old.
— s. Fifty-year-old (quinquagénaire).
— m. Fiftieth anniversary.

cinquantième [-tjɛm] adj. num. Fiftieth.

cinquième [sɛ̃kjɛm] adj. num. Fifth.
— m. Fifth floor (étage); fifth (rang, partie).
— f. Second form (classe).

cinquièmement [-mɑ̃] adv. Fifthly.

cintrage [sɛ̃tra:ʒ] m. Cent(e)ring (des arches); bending (des tôles).

cintre [sɛ̃tr] m. ARCHIT. Curve of an arch; curvature, soffit; de plein cintre, round, semi-circular. ‖ COMM. Coat-hanger (pour habits).

cintré, ée [-tre] adj. Curved, arched. ‖ Waisted, fitted (vêtement).

cintrer [-tre] v. tr. To take in at the waist (un vêtement). ‖ TECHN. To bend; to camber. ‖ ARCHIT. To centre (une arche); to arch (une fenêtre).

Cipaye [sipa:j] s. Sepoy; la révolte des Cipayes, the Indian Mutiny.

cippe [sip] m. ARCHIT. Cippus.

cirage [sira:ʒ] m. Polishing, blacking (des chaussures); polishing, waxing (du parquet). ‖ Shoepolish; cirage noir, blacking; cirage-crème, shoecream. ‖ FAM. Mess, fix.

circadien, enne [sirkadjɛ̃, ɛn] adj. Circadian.

circoncire [sirkɔ̃si:r] v. tr. (26). To circumcise.

circoncision [-sizjɔ̃] f. Circumcision.

circonférence [-ferɑ̃:s] f. Girth (d'un arbre); outline, perimeter (d'une propriété, d'une ville). ‖ MATH. Circumference. ‖ FAM. Il a une de ces circonférences!, he is of an ample girth.

circonflexe [-flɛks] adj., m. Circumflex.

circonlocution [-lɔkysjɔ̃] f. Circumlocution.

circonscription [-skripsjɔ̃] f. Division (administrative); district, circumscription (militaire); circonscription électorale, constituency, electoral (ou) voting district. ‖ MATH. Circumscribing.

circonscrire [-skri:r] v. tr. (44). MATH. To circumscribe (à, about). ‖ FIG. To limit, to bound; l'incendie était circonscrit, the fire was under control.
— v. pr. Se circonscrire, to limit oneself. ‖ To centre (autour de, on).

circonspect, ecte [sirkɔ̃spɛ, ɛkt] adj. Circumspect, wary. (V. PRUDENT.)

circonspection [-spɛksjɔ̃] f. Circumspection, cautiousness, wariness.

circonstance [sirkɔ̃stɑ̃:s] f. Circumstance, occurrence, event (événement); occasion; circonstance fortuite, mere chance; dans cette circonstance, on this occasion; de circonstance, occasional; appropriate, suitable; special; suited to the occasion; en pareille circonstance, in such a case, under such circumstances; pour la circonstance, for the occasion. ‖ Pl. Circumstances; dans les circonstances présentes, under existing circumstances; faire la part des circonstances, to take circumstances into account; profiter des circonstances, to take the opportunity, to take advantage of the occasion; se montrer à la hauteur des circonstances, to rise to the emergency (ou) occasion; suite de circonstances, train of circumstances. ‖ JUR. Pl. Attendant facts; adjuncts (faits); circumstances (particularités); circonstances atténuantes, extenuating circumstances; circonstances et dépendances, appurtenances.

circonstancié, ée [-sje] adj. Detailed.

circonstanciel, elle [-sjɛl] adj. Circumstantial. ‖ GRAMM. Adverbial (complément).

circonvallation [sirkɔ̃valasjɔ̃] f. Circumvallation.

circonvenir [-vni:r] v. tr. (101). To circumvent; to get round.

circonvoisin, ine [-vwazɛ̃, in] adj. Circumjacent.

circonvolution [-vɔlysjɔ̃] f. Circumvolution. ‖ Windings (d'une rivière). ‖ MÉD. Convolution (du cerveau).

circuit [sirkɥi] m. Circuit, circumference (pourtour). ‖ Circuit, roundabout way, detour; faire un long circuit, to make a long circuit (détour). ‖ SPORTS. Circuit; circuit touristique, organized tour; boucler le circuit, to lap the course; faire un circuit en Suisse, to tour Switzerland. ‖ ELECTR. Circuit; ouvrir le circuit, to switch on. ‖ AUTOM. Circuit d'allumage, ignition wiring (ou) circuit. ‖ FIN. Circuity (d'actions). ‖ FIG. Mettre qqn hors de circuit, to cut s.o. out.

circulaire [sirkylɛ:r] adj. Circular (lettre, mouvement, surface, voyage). ‖ CH. DE F. Billet circulaire, circular tour ticket, tourist ticket.
— f. Circular (lettre). ‖ Memorandum, note (instructions).

circulant, ante [-lɑ̃, ɑ̃:t] adj. Circulating, mobile (bibliothèque); current, in circulation (monnaie).

circulation [-lasjɔ̃] f. MÉD. Circulation. ‖ Circulation (de l'eau, des nouvelles, de la sève); mettre en circulation, to put into circulation, to circulate; retirer de la circulation, to withdraw from circulation, to call in. ‖ Traffic (des gens, des voitures); rétablir la circulation, to start the traffic again. ‖ AVIAT. Circulation aérienne, air traffic. ‖ CH. DE F. Running (des trains). ‖ FIN. Currency, circulation (de la monnaie).

circulatoire [-latwa:r] adj. MÉD. Circulatory.

circuler [-le] v. intr. (1). To circulate (choses, livres); to move on (foule); to go about, to flow (personnes); circuler dans les rues, to go about the streets; faire circuler, to circulate (l'air, l'argent); to move on (la foule); to pass round (un plateau); to hand about (une photographie). ‖ FIN. To circulate (argent). ‖ CH. DE F. To run (trains). ‖ BOT. To flow (sève). ‖ ELECTR. To flow (courant). ‖ MÉD. To circulate (sang). ‖ FIG. To go about, to circulate (bruit, nouvelles); faire circuler, to spread, to circulate (un bruit).

circumlunaire [sirkɔmlynɛ:r] adj. Circumlunar.

circumnavigation [sirkɔmnavigasjɔ̃] f. NAUT. Circumnavigation.

circumpolaire [-pɔlɛ:r] adj. Circumpolar.

circumsolaire [-sɔlɛ:r] adj. Circumsolar.

circumstellaire [-stɛllɛ:r] adj. Circumstellar.

circumterrestre [-tɛrɛstr] adj. Circumterrestrial.

cire [si:r] f. Wax; cire à cacheter, sealing wax. ‖ MÉD. Earwax (cérumen). ‖ FIG. C'est une cire molle, he is yielding as wax (ou) soft as putty; teint de cire, waxy complexion.

ciré, ée [sire] adj. Waxed (plancher); polished; blacked (souliers); toile cirée, oilcloth.
— m. Oilskins (imperméable).

cirer v. tr. (1). To wax, to polish, U. S. to shine (le plancher, les souliers); cirer au cirage noir, to black. ‖ FAM. Cirer toujours le même bouton, to be always harping on the same string.

cireur [-rœ:r] m. Polisher (de plancher); shoeblack, bootblack (de souliers).

cireuse [-rø:z] f. Floor-polisher, U. S. waxer.

cireux, euse [-irø, ø:z] adj. Waxy, waxen.

ciron [sirɔ̃] m. ZOOL. Mite.

cirque [sirk] m. Circus. ‖ GÉOGR. Cirque.

cirrhose [sirro:z] f. MÉD. Cirrhosis.

cirro-cumulus [sirokymylys] m. Cirro-cumulus.

cirro-stratus [-straty:s] m. inv. Cirro-stratus.

cirrus [sirys] m. Cirrus; mare's tail.

cisaillement [sizɑjmɑ̃] m. Shearing, scissoring.

cisailler [-je] v. tr. (1). To shear, to nip; to scissor.

cisailles [sizɑ:j] f. pl. Shears; wire-cutter.

cisalpin [sizalpɛ̃] adj. GÉOGR. Cisalpine.

ciseau [sizo] m. ARTS. Chisel (de sculpteur). ‖ Pl. Scissors (de couturière); clippers, shears (de jardinier); ciseaux de manucure, cuticle scissors.

nail-scissors; *coup de ciseaux*, snip; *travailler à coups de ciseaux*, to work with scissors and paste. ‖ Fig. Shears (d'Atropos).

cisèlement [sizɛlmɑ̃], **ciselage** [sizla:ʒ] m. Chiselling, chasing.

ciseler [sizle] v. tr. (8 b). To chisel; to chase. ‖ Fig. To chisel.

ciseleur [-lœ:r] m. Engraver.

ciselure [-ly:r] f. Chiseling, chasing, delicate carving.

Cisjordanie [sisʒɔrdani] f. Géogr. The West Bank of the Jordan.

cistercien [sistɛrsjɛ̃] adj., m. Ecclés. Cistercian.

cistre [sistr] m. Mus. Cithern, cittern.

citadelle [sitadɛl] f. Citadel.

citadin, ine [sitadɛ̃, in] adj. City (vie), city-dwelling (population), urban (pratiques, habitudes), citified (air, allure).
— s. City-dweller; townsman (homme), townswoman (femme).

citation [sitasjɔ̃] f. Quotation; *citation incorrecte*, misquotation. ‖ Jur. Summons (à comparaître); subpoena (de témoins). ‖ Milit. *Citation à l'ordre du jour*, mention in general orders (ou) in despatches.

cité [site] f. City, large town (ville); *droit de cité*, freedom of a city; *donner droit de cité à*, to enfranchise. ‖ Group of dwellings, U. S. housing development (agglomération); block of tenements, workers' flats (ouvrière); students' hostels (universitaire), citified (air, allure). ‖ Cité-dortoir, f. Dormitory suburb, overspill town. ‖ Cité-jardin, f. Garden-city.

citer v. tr. (1). To quote (un auteur, une autorité, un fait, une preuve, un texte); to cite (un auteur, une autorité, un passage); to adduce (une autorité, des preuves); to allege (un exemple); to mention (un fait, des noms); *citer qqch. comme exemple*, to mention sth. as an instance; *citer qqn en exemple*, to quote s. o. as an example. ‖ Jur. To summon (en justice); to subpoena (un témoin); *citer à comparaître*, to accite. ‖ Milit. *Citer à l'ordre du jour*, to mention in general orders (ou) in despatches.

citerne [sitɛrn] f. Underground cistern; tank. ‖ Naut. Tanker. ‖ Ch. de F. Tank-car.

cithare [sita:r] f. Mus. Cithara (ancienne); cither, zither (moderne).

cithariste [-tarist] s. Mus. Citharist; zitherist.

citoyen [sitwajɛ̃] s. Citizen; *citoyen d'honneur d'une ville*, freeman of a city. ‖ Fam. Bloke, fellow, U. S. guy.

citoyenneté [-jɛnte] f. Citizenship.

citrate [sitrat] m. Chim. Citrate.

citrin, ine [sitrɛ̃, in] adj. Citrine.

citrique [sitrik] adj. Chim. Citric.

citron [sitrɔ̃] m. Lemon; lime; *citron pressé*, lemon squash, fresh lemonade; *essence de citron*, lemon oil. ‖ Fam. Nut, U. S. noodle.
— adj. invar. Lemon-coloured.

citronnade [sitrɔnad] f. Lemon-squash, still lemonade.

citronnelle [-nɛl] f. Bot. Citronella; lemon balm.

citronnier [-nje] m. Bot. Lemon-tree (arbre); citron-wood (bois).

citrouille [sitru:j] f. Pumpkin.

cive [si:v], **civette** [-vɛt] f. Bot. Chives.

civet [sivɛ] m. Culin. Stew; *civet de lapin, de lièvre*, jugged rabbit, hare; U.S. rabbit, hare stew.

civette [sivɛt] f. Zool. Civet-cat. ‖ Comm. Civet.

civière [sivjɛ:r] f. Stretcher, litter (pour blessés); handbarrow, barrow (de chargement).

civil, ile [sivil] adj. Civil. ‖ Milit. Civil (guerre). ‖ Jur. Legal, calendar (année); civil (droit, liste, mariage, vie); *chambre civile*, nisi prius court; *état civil*, civil status; *la partie civile*, the plaintiff. ‖ Fig. Civil. (V. courtois.)
— m. Layman (laïc); civilian (non militaire);

en civil, in plain clothes; in mufti, U. S. in civvies (fam.) [militaire]; *dans le civil*, in private life, in Civvy Street (fam.)

civilement [-lmɑ̃] adv. Jur. Civilly; *civilement responsable*, legally responsible; *se marier civilement*, to marry before the civil authorities, to contract a civil marriage. ‖ Fig. Courteously.

civilisable [-lizable] adj. Civilizable.

civilisateur, trice [-lizatœ:r, tris] adj. Civilizing.
— m. Civilizer.

civilisation [-lizasjɔ̃] f. Civilization.

civiliser [-lize] v. tr. (1). To civilize. ‖ Fam. To polish, to rub the corners off. [V. policer.]
— v. pr. Se civiliser, to become civilized. ‖ Fam. To become more polished.

civiliste [-list] m. Jur. Common lawyer.

civilité [-lite] f. Civility. (V. courtoisie, politesse.) ‖ Pl. Civilities; regards. (V. compliments.)

civique [sivik] adj. Civic (centre, droits, garde, vertus); civil (droits, libertés).

civisme [-vism] m. Civism.

clabaud [klabo] m. Zool. Babbler (chien).

clabaudage [-da:ʒ] m. Babbling. ‖ Fig. Tittle-tattle (bavardage); bawling (braillement).

clabauder [-de] v. intr. (1). To babble (chien). ‖ Fig. To babble, to bawl (crier); to chatter (potiner); *clabauder contre qqn*, to run s.o. down.

clabauderie [-dri] f. Slandering, muck-raking.

claboter [klabɔte] v. intr. (1). Pop. To snuff it, to kick the bucket, to croak.

clac! [klak] interj. Slam, bang.

clafoutis [klafuti] m. Culin. Tart, fruit flan.

claie [klɛ] f. Tray (à fruits). ‖ Screen (crible). ‖ Hurdle (barrière, clôture, supplice).

clair, e [klɛ:r] adj. Light (couleur, pièce, robe, son); clear (eau, feu, œil, son, teint, temps, voix); limpid (eau, liquide); bright (feu, temps); *bleu clair*, pale (ou) light blue. ‖ Thin (barbe). ‖ Agric. Thin (blé). ‖ Culin. Thin (potage, sauce). ‖ Fig. Explicit (déclaration); distinct (élocution, souvenir); lucid (esprit, explication); pellucid (esprit, style); clear (idée, image, perception, personne, style, vision); *pas clair*, suspicious (attitude); *voilà qui est clair*, that's clear enough. ‖ Fig. Plain, obvious, evident (devoir, preuve); *il est clair que j'ai raison*, I am obviously right. ‖ Loc. *Le plus clair de*, the best part of, most of.
— adv. Clear, clearly, distinctly; *faire clair*, to be daylight (ou) day (à l'aube); to be light (dans une pièce); *parler clair*, to speak out (ou) clearly; *pour parler clair*, to put it plainly; *voir clair*, to see distinctly (avoir bonne vue); to be clear-sighted (être clairvoyant); to see through (pénétrer); to see one's way (savoir se conduire). ‖ Clair-obscur, m. Arts. Chiaroscuro. ‖ Claire-voie, f. Lattice-work; *à claire-voie*, open-work; *caisse à claire-voie*, crate; *claire-voie d'église*, clerestory.
— m. *Clair de lune*, moonlight; *au clair de la lune*, in the moonlight. ‖ *En clair*, in clear (ou) plain language; *sabre au clair*, with drawn sword; *tirer au clair*, to clear up, to unravel. ‖ Pl. Thin places (d'une étoffe). ‖ Arts. Highlights.

clairaudience [rodjɑ̃:s] f. Clairaudience.

clairement [-rmɑ̃] adv. Clearly; obviously.

clairet, ette [-rɛ, ɛt] adj. Light-red (vin).
— m. Light-red wine.

clairette [-rɛt] f. Light sparkling wine (vin).

clairière [-rjɛ:r] f. Glade, clearing (d'un bois). ‖ Thin place (d'un tissu).

clairon [klɛrɔ̃] m. Bugle, clarion (instrument); bugler (joueur).

claironnant, ante [klɛrɔnɑ̃, ɑ̃:t] adj. Brassy (son); trumpet-like (voix); *à la voix claironnante*, clarion-voiced.

claironner [-ne] v. tr. (1). To trumpet, to clarion forth (les nouvelles).
— v. intr. To trumpet.

clairsemé, ée [klɛrsəme] adj. Sparse (arbres, cheveux, population); scattered (maison, population); thin (barbe, blé).

clairvoyance [klɛrvwajɑ̃:s] f. Clearsightedness. (V. PERSPICACITÉ.) || Clairvoyance (seconde vue).

clairvoyant, ante [-jɑ̃, ɑ̃:t] adj. Clearsighted. (V. PERSPICACE.) || Clairvoyant (voyant).

clam [klam] m. ZOOL. Clam.

clameau [klamo] m. ARCHIT. Clamp.

clamer [klame] v. tr. (1). To shout, to cry out; clamer son innocence, to protest one's innocence.

clameur [-mœ:r] f. Outcry, clamour, shout. || FIG. Roaring (de la mer, de la tempête, du vent).

clampin [klɑ̃pɛ̃] m. FAM. Slow-coach, loafer. || MILIT. Straggler.

clamser [klamse] v. intr. (1). POP. To pop off, to kick the bucket; U. S. to croak. (V. CLAQUER.)

clan [klɑ̃] m. Clan. || FIG. Clan. (V. CLIQUE.)

clandé [klɑ̃de] m. ARG. Clandestine brothel, cathouse.

clandestin, ine [klɑ̃dɛstɛ̃, i:n] adj. Clandestine; underhand, stealthy (agissements, manœuvres); illicit (commerce, débit, pari); secret (mariage); underground (presse). || NAUT. Passager clandestin, stowaway. || MILIT. Covert (ennemi); armée clandestine, underground forces.

clandestinement [-tinmɑ̃] adv. Clandestinely; in an underhand manner; sub rosa.

clandestinité [-tinite] f. Underground movement. || Clandestineness.

clapet [klapɛ] m. TECHN. Valve; clapper. || ELECTR. Rectifier.

clapier [-pje] m. Hutch (de ferme); burrow (de garenne).

clapir [-pi:r] v. intr. (2). To squeal (lapin).
— v. pr. Se clapir, to squat in a burrow.

clapotant, ante [klapɔtɑ̃, ɑ̃:t] adj. V. CLAPOTEUX.

clapotement [klapɔtmɑ̃], clapotis [-pɔti] m. Squelch (de la boue foulée); lapping, chopping, swashing (de la mer); plashing (de la pluie).

clapoter [-pɔte] v. intr. (1). To squelch (boue foulée); to plash (liquide secoué, pluie); to lap, to splash (mer, vagues).

clapoteux, euse [-pɔtø, øz] adj. Plashy (bruit); choppy (mer).

clappement [klapmɑ̃] m. Smack, smacking (de langue). || GRAMM. Click.

clapper [-pe] v. intr. (1). To smack. || GRAMM. To click.

claquage [klaka:ʒ] m. MÉD. Strain (d'un muscle); Claquage sportif, strained heart.

claquant, ante [klakɑ̃, ɑ̃:t] adj. POP. Backbreaking, killing.

claque [klak] f. Slap; crack (ou) rap on the head; box in the ear (v. GIFLE); donner une claque à, to slap, to smack. || THÉÂTR. Claque, paid clappers. || LOC. En avoir sa claque, to be on one's last legs.
— m. Opera-hat; crush-hat (fam.).

claqué, ée [-ke] adj. MÉD. Strained (cœur); strained, snapped (tendon). || FAM. Hamstrung (cheval); done in, jaded, dead-beat (personne).

claquement [-kmɑ̃] m. Crack (de branches cassées, de coup de feu, de fouet, d'os brisé); flick (de chiquenaude, de fouet); snap (de ciseaux, de couvercle, de dents qui mordent, de doigts, de fouet); clack (de claquet); ping (de coup de feu); smack (de coup de feu, de fouet); bang (de coup de feu, de porte, de volet qui bat); slamming (de couvercle, de fenêtre, de porte); click (de déclic, de talons); chatter (de dents heurtées, de machine); flap, flapping (de drapeau qui bat);

rattle (de fusillade, de grêle, de porte en fer); click, tchick, smack (de langue); clatter (de machine, de sabots); clapping (de mains).

claquemurer [-kmyre] v. tr. (1). To wall in, to immure; to coop up, to mew up.
— v. pr. Se claquemurer, to shut oneself up; to immure oneself; to closet oneself.

claquer [-ke] v. intr. (1). To crack (branches, coup de feu, fouet, os); to snap (ciseaux, couvercle, dents qui mordent, doigts, fouet); to clack (claquet); to clap to (ou) on (couvercle); to smack (coup de feu, fouet); to bang (coup de feu, porte, volet); to slam (couvercle, fenêtre, porte); to click (déclic, talons); to chatter (dents qui se heurtent, machine); to flap (drapeau qui bat); to rattle (fusillade, grêle, porte en fer); to smack, to click (langue); to clatter (machine, sabots); to clap (mains); elle claquait des dents, her teeth were chattering; claquer des mains, to clap, to applaud; claquer des talons, to click one's heels; la porte claqua, the door closed with a slam; faire claquer, to snap (ses doigts); to smack (sa langue). || FAM. To pop off, to peg out, to snuff it, to kick the bucket, U. S. to croak; claquer du bec, to clem, to be famished; l'affaire a claqué, the business fell through.
— v. tr. To smack, to slap the face of. (V. GIFLER.) || To slam, to bang (la porte). || THÉÂTR. To clap for (un acteur). || FAM. To crock; to jade (un cheval); to blue, U. S. to blow (une fortune); to strain (un muscle, un nerf); to overwork, to fag, to jade (qqn).
— v. pr. Se claquer, FAM. To die of overwork. || To overtask one's strength; to tire oneself out.

claquet [klakɛ] m. Clapper.

claquette [-kɛt] f. Clapper (claquoir). || Pl. Tapdancing.

claquoir [-kwa:r] m. Clapper.

clarifiant, ante [klarifjɑ̃, ɑ̃:t] adj. Clarifying.

clarification [-fikasjɔ̃] f. Clarification.

clarifier [-fje] v. tr. (1). To clarify (le beurre, le sirop, le vin); to settle, to purify (un liquide). || MÉD. To purify (le sang). || FIG. To clarify (l'esprit, la vision).
— v. pr. Se clarifier, to clarify; to purify.

clarine [klarin] f. Cattle- ou cow-bell.

clarinette [-nɛt] f. Clarinet (instrument); clarinetist (joueur).

clarinettiste [-nɛtist] s. Clarinet(t)ist.

Clarisse [klaris] f. Clarissa (prénom). || ECCLÉS. Clare (religieuse).

clarté [klarte] f. Clearness, limpidity (limpidité); light, brightness, luminousness, luminosity (lumière); transparency (transparence). || FIG. Clearness, clarity, lucidity (netteté). || FIG. Pl. Lights; ideas, notions.

classe [klɑ:s] f. Class, category, sort (v. CATÉGORIE); class, rank (v. POSITION, RANG); de première classe, first-rate, A-1. || BOT., ZOOL. Class. || CH. DE F. Première classe, first-class (compartiment); voyager en première, to travel first class. || MILIT. Class; age-group; annual contingent of recruits; soldat de première classe, de deuxième classe, lance-corporal, private. || Standard (dans l'enseignement primaire); form (dans le secondaire); U. S. grade (division); class (élèves); class, lesson (enseignement); studies (études); class- (ou) school-room (pièce); aller en classe, to go to school; avant la classe, before school; de la même classe que, in the same class with; faire la classe, to take a class.

classement [klasmɑ̃] m. Classification; sorting (par catégorie, triage); grading (par difficulté, qualité); rating (par évaluation, grade); rank (par mérite); sizing (par ordre de grandeur, taille). || Filing (de papiers). || JUR. Shelving (d'une affaire).

classer [-se] v. tr. (1). To class (par classe, cote) ; to classify (par classification). ‖ To sort (par catégorie, triage) ; to grade (par difficulté, qualité) ; to rate (par évaluation, grade) ; to rank (par mérite) ; to size (par ordre de grandeur, taille). ‖ To file (des papiers). ‖ JUR. To shelve (une affaire). ‖ ARCHIT. To schedule, U. S. to classify (un monument).
— v. pr. **Se classer**, to be classed (candidat) ; *se classer dans*, to fall into ; *se classer comme, parmi*, to rank as, among.

classeur [-sœ:r] m. Card-index, file (à fiches) ; letter-file (à lettres) ; rack (à lettres, à musique) ; file (à papiers) ; filing-cabinet (meuble). ‖ TECHN. Classifier ; sorter ; sizer.

classicisme [klasisism] m. Classicism.
classificateur [-fikatœ:r] m. Classifier.
classification [-fikasjɔ̃] f. Classification.
classifier [-fje] v. tr. (1). To classify.
classique [klasik] adj. Classic (auteur, beauté, littérature, musique, peinture) ; classical (études) ; standing (excuse, plaisanterie) ; recognized (expressions, manières) ; orthodox (méthode) ; standard (modèle, ouvrage) ; straight (plongeon) ; *coup classique*, old trick ; *livre classique*, school-book.
— m. Classic (auteur de l'Antiquité ou de la période classique) ; classicist (partisan du genre classique). ‖ Standard author (ou) book (ou) edition (ou) work. ‖ ARTS. Classical art (ou) literature (ou) music (ou) painting (ou) poetry.
classiquement [-sikmɑ̃] adv. Classically.
claudicant, ante [klodikɑ̃, ɑ̃:t] adj. Limping, halting.
claudication [-kasjɔ̃] f. Lameness ; halting.
claudiquer [-ke] v. intr. (1). To limp, to have a slight limp.
clause [klo:z] f. JUR. Clause, stipulation (en général) ; provision (de contrat).
claustral [klostral] adj. Claustral.
claustration [-trasjɔ̃] f. Confinement, seclusion.
claustrer [-tre] v. tr. (1). To cloister, to immure. ‖ FIG. To confine, to coop up.
— v. pr. **Se claustrer**, to confine oneself, to shut oneself up.
claustrophobe [-trɔfɔb] adj., s. PSYCH. Claustrophobic.
claustrophobie [-trɔfɔbi] f. PSYCH. Claustrophobia.
claveau [klavo] m. ARCHIT. Arch-stone.
clavecin [klavsɛ̃] m. MUS. Harpsichord, clavichord.
claveciniste [-sinist] s. MUS. Harpsichordist.
clavelée [klavle] f. Sheep-pox.
claveter [klavte] v. tr. (8a). To key, to pin.
clavette [klavɛt] f. TECHN. Key, peg, pin, catch, latch ; forelock (de boulon).
clavicorde [klavikɔrd] m. MUS. Clavichord.
clavicule [klavikyl] f. MÉD. Clavicle.
clavier [klavje] m. Keyboard, fingerboard (de machine à écrire, de piano). ‖ MUS. Range (d'un instrument à vent) ; manual (d'orgue).
clayère [klɛjɛ:r] f. Oyster-park ; U. S. oyster-bed.
clayette [klɛjɛt] f. Rack, wire shelf.
clayon [klɛjɔ̃] m. Wicker-tray (à fromages) ; wire pastry-stand (à pâtisserie). ‖ Wattle enclosure (clôture).
clayonnage [klɛjɔna:ʒ] m. Wattle, wattling ; *en clayonnage*, wattled, wattle-and-daub (mur).
clayonner [-ne] v. tr. (1). To wattle.
clearing [kli:riŋ] m. FIN. Clearing.
clebs [klɛbs] m. POP. Tyke, U. S. mutt, pooch.
clef, clé [kle] f. Key (en général) ; latch-key (de porte) ; *clef de montre*, watch-key ; *clef de tuyau de poêle*, damper ; *sous clé*, under lock and key. ‖ TECHN. *Clef anglaise*, crescent-type wrench, monkey-wrench, monkey-spanner ; *clef univer-*

selle, screw-monkey-wrench ; *clef pour roue*, wheel-brace. ‖ ELECTR. Switch-key. ‖ ARCHIT. *Clef de voûte*, keystone. ‖ ECCLÉS. *Pouvoir des clefs*, power of the keys. ‖ MUS. Clef ; key-signature (armature) ; *à la clef*, in the signature ; *clef de sol*, G (ou) treble clef ; *clef d'accordeur*, wrest (harpe) ; tuning-hammer (piano) ; *clef de violon*, pin. ‖ FIN. Key (d'accès, de message chiffré, du mystère, d'une position, du problème) ; clue (d'une énigme) ; *la clef de*, the key (ou) clue to ; *la clef de voûte de*, the keystone of ; *industrie clef*, key-industry ; *roman à clef*, roman a clef. ‖ FAM. *Mettre la clef sous la porte*, to do a moonlight flit ; *prendre la clé des champs*, to take to the open, to do a bunk, to slip the collar ; *qqch. à la clef*, sth. tacked on to it.
clématite [klematit] f. BOT. Clematis.
clémence [klemɑ̃:s] f. Clemency. (V. MISÉRICORDE.) ‖ Mildness (des éléments, du temps).
clément [-mɑ̃] adj. Clement (personne) ; clement, mild (temps) ; *ciel clément*, mild climate.
clémentine [-mɑ̃tin] f. Clementine, U. S. tangerine (mandarine).
clenche [klɑ̃:ʃ] f. Door-latch.
clepsydre [klɛpsidr] f. † Clepsydra, water-clock.
cleptomane [klɛptɔman] s. MÉD. Kleptomaniac.
cleptomanie [-mani] f. MÉD. Kleptomania.
clerc [klɛ:r] m. JUR. Clerk (d'avoué, de notaire) ; *principal clerc*, managing clerk. ‖ ECCLÉS. Cleric ; clergyman (ecclésiastique) ; *grand clerc*, altaryouth. ‖ FIG. Scholar, clerk (savant). ‖ Loc. *Pas de clerc*, untimely step.
clergé [-ʒe] m. ECCLÉS. Clergy ; priests. ‖ FIG. The cloth.
clergie [-ʒi] f. † Clergy.
clérical, ale [klerikal] adj. ECCLÉS. Clerical. ‖ FAM. Churchy (calotin).
— m. Clerical.
cléricalisme [-lism] m. Clericalism.
cléricature [-ty:r] f. ECCLÉS. Minor orders. ‖ JUR. Clerkship.
clic [klik] interj., m. Click. ‖ **Clic-clac**, m. Clatter.
clichage [kliʃa:ʒ] m. Stereotyping.
cliché [-ʃe] m. Wax-stencil (de dactylographie) ; stereotype, plate, cliché (d'imprimerie) ; negative (de photographie) ; *prendre un cliché*, to make an exposure. ‖ FIG. Cliché, stock phrase.
clicher [-ʃe] v. tr. (1). To stereotype, to plate.
clicheur [-ʃœ:r] m. Stereotyper.
client [klijɑ̃] m. † Client (dans l'Antiquité). ‖ JUR. Client (d'un avocat, d'un notaire). ‖ AUTOM. Fare (d'un chauffeur de taxi). ‖ COMM. Customer, patron (d'un commerçant) ; visitor (d'un hôtel). ‖ MÉD. Patient (d'un médecin). ‖ ARTS. Sitter (d'un portraitiste). ‖ FAM. *Un drôle de client*, a queer customer (ou) chap.
clientèle [-tɛl] f. † Clientage. ‖ Patronage (d'un acheteur) ; *donner sa clientèle à*, to patronize. ‖ Practice, clientèle (d'avocat, d'homme de loi) ; customers, custom (de commerçant) ; clientèle (de commerçant, de médecin, de théâtre) ; practice (de médecin). ‖ Goodwill ; connection ; *une belle clientèle*, a wide connection ; *acheter la clientèle de*, to purchase the goodwill of.
clignement [kliɲmɑ̃] m. Blinking, winking.
cligner [-ɲe] v. tr. (1). *Cligner les yeux*, to screw up one's eyes.
— v. intr. To blink, to wink ; to wince ; *cligner de l'œil à*, to cock one's eye at, to wink at ; *regarder en clignant des yeux*, to blink at.
clignotant, ante [-ɲɔtɑ̃, ɑ̃:t] adj. Twinkling (astre) ; flickering (feu) ; blinking (œil). ‖ ZOOL. Nictitating (membrane). ‖ ELECTR. Flickering.
— m. AUTOM. Winker, winking-light direction indicator (ou) trafficator, intermittent signal ; blinker ; U. S. turn indicator, direction light.

clignotement [-ɲɔtmα] m. Twinkling (d'un astre); flickering (d'un feu); blinking (de l'œil); twitching (des paupières). ‖ ELECTR. Flickering. (de l'arc).

clignoter [-ɲɔte] v. intr. (1). To twinkle (astre); to flicker (feu); to blink (œil); to twitch (paupière). ‖ ELECTR. To flicker (arc, lumière).

climat [klima] m. Climate (conditions atmosphériques); clime (poét.); region, climate (région). ‖ FIG. Mood, state of mind; atmosphere.

climatérique [klimaterik] adj. Climacteric (année). — f. Grand climacteric.

climatique [-tik] adj. Climatic; *station climatique*, health-resort.

climatisation [-tizasjɔ̃] f. Air-conditioning.

climatiser [-tize] v. tr. (1). To air-condition.

climatiseur [-tizœ:r] m. Air-conditioner.

climatologie [-tɔlɔʒi] f. Climatology.

climatologique [-tɔlɔʒik] adj. Climatological.

climatothérapie [-tɔterapi] f. MÉD. Climatotherapy.

clin [klɛ̃] m. *Clin d'œil*, wink; *en un clin d'œil*, in a trice, in the twinkling of an eye, in a flash; *faire un clin d'œil à*, to wink at.

clinfoc [klɛ̃fɔk] m. NAUT. Flying jib.

clinicien [klinisjɛ̃] m. MÉD. Clinician.

clinique [-nik] adj. MÉD. Clinic; clinical (leçons). — f. MÉD. Clinic, bedside class; *le chef de clinique*, the professor. ‖ Nursing-home, clinic (établissement).

clinker [kliŋkœ:r] m. Clinker.

clinomètre [klinɔmɛtr] m. Clinometer. ‖ AVIAT. Bank indicator. ‖ NAUT. Water-level.

clinquant, ante [klɛ̃kα̃, α̃:t] adj. Flashy, garish, gaudy, tawdry. — m. Foil (lamelle); tinsel (paillettes). ‖ FIG. Flashiness, tawdriness, tinsel (du style).

clip [klip] m. Clip (bijou).

clipper [-pœ:r] m. NAUT., AVIAT. Clipper.

clique [klik] f. MILIT. Drum and bugle band. ‖ FAM. *Prendre ses cliques et ses claques*, to clear off with bag and baggage. ‖ FAM. Clique (v. COTERIE); *toute la clique*, all the rest of it.

cliquet [klikɛ] m. TECHN. Pawl, claw, click (de roue dentée). ‖ Catch (fermoir).

cliquètement [klikɛtmα̃] m. V. CLIQUETIS.

cliqueter [klikte] v. intr. (8a). To clash (armes, cymbales); to rattle (chaînes, ferraille); to jingle (clefs, grelots, monnaie, verres); to clatter (fourchettes); to pink (moteur); to clink (verres).

cliquetis [-ti] m. Clash (des armes, des cymbales); rattle (de chaînes, de ferraille); jingle (de clefs, de grelots, de monnaie, de verres); clatter (de fourchettes, de vaisselle); pinking, U. S. pink (de moteur); clink, clinking (de verres).

cliquette [-kɛt] f. Castanets. ‖ Sinker (de filet).

clissage [klisa:ʒ] m. Wickering (de bouteilles). ‖ MÉD. Splinting.

clisse [klis] f. Wicker tray (à fromages). ‖ Wicker covering (à bouteilles). ‖ MÉD. Splint.

clisser [-se] v. tr. (1). To wicker (les bouteilles). ‖ MÉD. To splint.

clitoridien, enne [klitɔridjɛ̃, ɛn] adj. MÉD. Clitorial, clitoral.

clitoris [-ris] m. MÉD. Clitoris.

clivage [kliva:ʒ] m. Cleaving (d'un cristal); cleavage (des minéraux).

cliver [-ve] v. tr. (1). To cleave.

cloaque [klɔak] m. Cesspool. ‖ FIG. Sink, cesspool.

clochard [klɔʃa:r] m. FAM. Tramp; U. S. hobo.

cloche [klɔʃ] f. Bell; *cloche de brouillard*, fogbell; *cloche à plongeur*, diving-bell; *en forme de cloche*, bell-shaped. ‖ Cloche-hat (chapeau). ‖ TECHN. Bell (de gazomètre); receiver (de machine pneumatique). ‖ CULIN. Cheese-cover (à fromage); dish-cover (à plat). ‖ AGRIC. Bell-glass;

cloche. ‖ FAM. *Sonner les cloches à qqn*, to haul s.o. over the coals. ‖ POP. Dope. ‖ LOC. *Un autre son de cloche*, another account; *qui n'entend qu'une cloche n'entend qu'un son*, he hears but half who hears one side only.

clochement [klɔʃmα̃] m. Limping.

cloche-pied (à) [aklɔʃpje] loc. adv. Hop; *sauter à cloche-pied*, to hop along.

clocher [klɔʃe] m. ARCHIT. Bell-tower; church-tower, steeple (v. BEFFROI, CAMPANILE); *course au clocher*, steeple-chase. ‖ FIG. *Esprit de clocher*, parochialism; *politique de clocher*, parish-pump politics; *rivalités de clocher*, local bickering.

clocher v. intr. (1). To limp, to hobble. ‖ FIG. *Quelque chose cloche*, there is something not quite right; *vers qui clochent*, halting lines.

clocheton [-ʃtɔ̃] m. ARCHIT. Pinnacle, bell-turret.

clochette [-ʃɛt] f. Small bell; hand bell (à main); bell (de collier). ‖ BOT. Bell-flower.

clodo [klɔdo] m. POP. Tramp, dosser, bum.

cloison [klwazɔ̃] f. ARCHIT. Partition, partition-wall; *séparer qqch. par une cloison*, to partition sth. off. ‖ MÉD., BOT. Septum (pl. septa). ‖ NAUT. Bulkhead. ‖ AUTOM. Baffle-plate. ‖ FIG. *Cloison étanche*, watertight compartment.

cloisonnage [klwazɔna:ʒ] m. Partitioning (action); partitionment (dispositif). ‖ AUTOM. Baffle-plating.

cloisonné, ée [-ne] adj. ARCHIT. Partitioned. ‖ BOT. Septated. ‖ TECHN. Tube-plate (chaudière). ‖ ARTS. Cloisonné (émail). — m. Cloisonné enamel.

cloisonnement [-nmα̃] m. ARCHIT. Partitioning. ‖ BOT. Septation. ‖ FIG. Compartmentation.

cloisonner [-ne] v. tr. (1). To partition off.

cloître [klwα:tr] m. ARCHIT. Cloister. ‖ ECCLÉS. Cloister, monastery, convent (couvent). ‖ FIG. Cloister; *vie du cloître*, monastic life.

cloîtré [klwatre] adj. ECCLÉS. Cloistered; enclosed, immured (religieuses). ‖ FIG. Retired, secluded.

cloîtrer v. tr. (1). ECCLÉS. To cloister, to immure (les religieux). ‖ FIG. To confine (qqn). — v. pr. **Se cloîtrer**, ECCLÉS. To enter a convent; to retire from the world. ‖ FIG. To live retired (ou) secluded; to confine oneself.

clone [klon] m. BOT., MÉD. Clone.

clope [klɔp] m. POP. Cig, ciggy, fag (cigarette); dog-end, butt (mégot).

clopin-clopant [klɔpɛ̃klɔpα̃] loc. adv. Limpingly; *aller clopin-clopant*, to hobble along. ‖ FIG. So-so.

clopiner [klɔpine] v. intr. (1). To limp, to hobble.

clopinettes [klɔpinɛt] f. pl. FAM. Peanuts, damn all; *je l'ai eu pour des clopinettes*, I got it for peanuts (ou) damn all.

cloporte [klɔpɔrt] m. ZOOL. Wood-louse, U. S. sow-bug, pill-bug.

cloque [klɔk] f. Blister (sur la peinture). ‖ BOT. Blight, curl. ‖ MÉD. Blister (ampoule).

cloqué [klɔke] m. Cloque, cloqué (tissu); *cloqué de soie*, rippled-silk fabric.

cloquer v. intr. (1). To blister.

clore [klɔ:r] v. tr. (27). To close (un parc, les portes); to shut (une porte) [v. FERMER]; *clore de murs*, to enclose with walls. ‖ AGRIC. To enclose (un champ). ‖ FIN. To close (un compte). ‖ FIG. To terminate (une amitié); to close, to closure, to disjourn (les débats); to end (un discours, une discussion). — v. pr. **Se clore**, to end (discours, discussion).

clos, ose [klo, o:z] adj. Closed, shut (porte); enclosed (terrain); *clos de murs*, walled-in; *champ clos*, tilt-yard. ‖ JUR. *A huis clos*, in camera, behind locked doors, U. S. in secret session. ‖ FIN. Closed (compte). ‖ FIG. Closed (débat, crise, session) : *à la nuit close*, after dark; *demeurer*

lettre close pour, to be a closed book to. ‖ Loc.
Maison close, brothel.
clos m. Plot, enclosure (enclos); orchard (verger);
vineyard (vignoble).
closerie [klɔzri] f. Little close. ‖ Pleasure garden
(en ville). ‖ Agric. Croft.
clôture [kloty:r] f. Enclosure; hedgerow (d'arbustes, de haies); fence (claie, palissade); wire
fence (en fil de fer); grating (en grillage ou
treillis); boarding (en planches). ‖ Ecclés. Screen
(du chœur); enclosure (des religieux). ‖ Fin.
Closing, winding up (de compte). ‖ Jur. Closure
(des débats); termination (de faillite); adjournment (de séance); *demander la clôture d'un débat,*
to move the closure.
clôturer [-tyre] v. tr. (1). To enclose, to close in;
to fence in; to wall in. ‖ Jur. To close (un
compte, une faillite); to conclude (une session).
clou [klu] m. Nail (en général); hobnail (à
chaussures) : bullen-nail, upholsterer's nail (de
tapissier); clout (ou) spike nail (à tête plate);
brad, sprig (sans tête); hook-nail (à piton); tack
(semence); stud (de siège). ‖ Pl. Pedestrian crossing; U. S. crosswalk; *traverser dans les clous,*
to cross at a pedestrian crossing. ‖ Méd. Boil.
(V. furoncle.) ‖ Culin. *Clou de girofle,* clove.
‖ Fig. Great show, star-turn; chief attraction,
clou; U. S. high spot (d'un spectacle); *comme
clou à la fête,* as a climax to the entertainment. ‖
Fam. Pawnshop, U. S. hock shop (mont-de-piété);
mettre au clou, to pop, U. S. to hock. ‖ Fam.
Vieux clou, old crock, U. S. jalopy (voiturɛ); *ça
lui a rivé son clou,* that was a clincher for him;
river son clou à qqn, to shut s.o. up. ‖ Pop. Jug,
U. S. cooler (prison).
clouage [-a:ʒ] m. Nailing.
clouer [-e] v. tr. (1). To nail up (une caisse); to
tack down, to nail down (un couvercle); to pin
(du papier avec des punaises); to nail (une
planche); to nail on (une semelle); to tack up
(une tenture); *tapis cloué,* fitted carpet. ‖ Milit.
Clouer au sol, to pin down. ‖ Fam. To shut up
(qqn). ‖ Fig. *Cloué au lit,* confined to one's bed;
cloué sur place, nailed to the spot.
clouté, ée [-te] adj. Studded (cuir, siège); hob-
nailed, bradded (souliers); *passage clouté,* pedestrian crossing, street- (ou) zebra-crossing; U.S.
pedestrian crosswalk.
clouter v. tr. (1). To stud.
clouterie [-tri] f. Nail-trade (commerce); nail-
making (fabrication); nail-factory (fabrique).
cloutier [-tje] m. Nail-dealer (commerçant); nail-
maker (fabricant).
cloutière [-tjɛ:r] f. Nail-box (boîte); nail-making
machine (instrument).
clovisse [klɔvis] f. Zool. Cockle.
clown [klun] m. Théâtr. Clown. ‖ Fam. Funny
man.
clownerie [-ri] f. Clowning.
clownesque [klunɛsk] adj. Clownish,
clownlike.
club [klœb] m. Club. ‖ Sports. Club (de golf).
clubman [-man] m. Clubman.
cluse [kly:z] f. Géogr. Cluse, transverse valley.
clystère [klistɛ:r] m. Méd. Clyster, enema.
C.N.P.F. [seɛnpeɛf] m. Abrév. de *Conseil national du patronat français,* French employers' federation, equivalent of Confederation of British
Industry (CBI).
C.N.R.S. [seɛnɛrɛs] m. Abrév. de *Centre national de la recherche scientifique,* French organization for the promotion and coordination of scientific research.
c/o [seo] abrév. de *care of,* c/o.
coaccusé, ée [koakyze] s. Jur. Co-defendant.
coacquéreur [koakerœ:r] m. Joint-Purchaser.
coactif, ive [koaktif, i:v] adj. Coercive, compulsory, co-active.

coaction [-sjɔ̃] f. Coercion, compulsion, co-action.
coadjuteur [koadʒytœ:r] m. Ecclés. Coadjutor.
coadministrateur [koadministratœ:r] m. Comm.
Co-director. ‖ Jur. Co-trustee.
coagulable [koagylabl] adj. Coagulable.
coagulant, ante [-lɑ̃, ɑ̃:t] adj., m. Coagulant.
coagulateur, trice [-latœ:r, tris] adj. Coagu-
lative.
coagulation [-lasjɔ̃] f. Coagulating (action);
coagulation (résultat).
coaguler [-le] v. tr. (1). To congeal (la confiture,
la gelée, l'huile, le sang); to coagulate, to curdle
(le lait).
— v. pr. Se coaguler, to congeal; to coagulate;
to curdle.
coalisé, ée [koalize] adj. Allied (nation).
— m. Coalitionist.
coaliser v. tr. (1). To unite in a coalition.
— v. pr. Se coaliser, to form a coalition.
coalition [-sjɔ̃] f. Coalition; fusion. ‖ Fig.
Combine, combination, ring (d'intérêts).
coaltar [koaltar] m. Tar, coal-tar.
coassement [koasmɑ̃] m. Croaking.
coasser [-se] v. intr. (1). To croak (grenouille).
coassociation [-sjasjɔ̃] f. Co-partnership.
coassocié, ée [koasɔsje] s. Co- (ou) joint-
partner.
coassurance [koasyrɑ̃:s] f. Fin. Co-insurance.
coauteur [kootœ:r] m. Co-author, joint author.
‖ Jur. Accessory (d'un crime); abettor, accomplice (d'un criminel).
coaxial, ale [koaksjal] adj. Math. Coaxial.
cobalt [kobalt] m. Chim. Cobalt.
cobaye [kɔba:j] m. Zool. Guinea-pig.
cobelligérant, ante [kobɛlliʒɛrɑ̃, ɑ̃:t] adj., s.
Milit. Co-belligerent.
cobol [kɔbɔl] m. Inform. Cobol.
cobra [kɔbra] m. Zool. Cobra.
coca [kɔka] f. Bot. Coca. ‖ **Coca-Cola,** s. Coca-
Cola; coke (fam.).
cocagne [kɔkaɲ] f. Plenty; *mât de cocagne,*
greasy pole; *pays de Cocagne,* Cockaigne, Never-
Never Land.
cocaïne [kɔkain] f. Cocaine. ‖ Méd. *Anesthésier
à la cocaïne,* to cocainize.
cocaïnomane [-nɔman] s. Cocaine addict, cocain-
ist, cocainomaniac.
cocarde [kɔkard] f. Cockade. ‖ Aviat. *Cocarde
de la R. A. F.,* Air force roundel.
cocardier, ière [-dje, -jɛr] adj. Flag-waving.
cocasse [kɔkas] adj. Funny, droll, quizzical.
cocasserie [-ri] f. Drollness. (V. drôlerie.)
coccinelle [kɔksinɛl] f. Zool. Ladybird.
coccyx [kɔksis] m. Méd. Coccyx.
coche [kɔʃ] m. Stage-coach. ‖ Fig. *Manquer le
coche,* to miss the bus (ou) boat.
coche f. Notch, score; *faire une coche,* to notch.
cochenille [kɔʃni:j] f. Chim. Cochineal.
cocher [kɔʃe] m. Coachman; *cocher de fiacre,*
cabman, cab-driver.
cocher v. tr. (1). To notch; to score (par entaille);
to check, to tick off (au crayon, au stylo).
cochère [kɔʃɛ:r] adj. f. *Porte cochère,* carriage-
entrance (ou) gateway.
cochet [kɔʃɛ] m. Zool. Cockerel.
Cochinchine [kɔʃɛ̃ʃin] f. Géogr. Cochin-China.
cochinchinois, oise [-nwa, waz] adj., s. Géogr.
Cochin-Chinese.
cochon [kɔʃɔ̃] m. Pig, hog, swine; *les cochons,*
swine; *cochon de lait,* suckling pig. ‖ Culin.
Pork. ‖ Zool. *Cochon d'Inde,* guinea-pig; *cochon
de mer,* porpoise, sea-hog.
— m. Fig. Dirty pig, swine; *amis comme
cochons,* as thick as pickpockets in a fair; *le
cochon de payant,* the mug, U. S. the sucker; *se
conduire comme un cochon,* to behave like a pig
(ou) swine; *tour de cochon,* dirty trick.

— adj. Dirty, filthy, swinish (sale). ‖ Smutty, bawdy (grivois).

cochonnaille [kɔʃɔnaːj] f. FAM. Delicatessen.

cochonne [kɔʃɔn] f. FAM. Slut.

cochonner [-ne] v. intr. (1). To farrow, to pig (truie).
— v. tr. FAM. To bungle (un travail).

cochonnerie [-nri] f. Filth, filthiness (saleté). ‖ Nasty stuff (nourriture); trash (objet); smut (propos); lousy trick (tour).

cochonnet [-nɛ] m. Piglet (petit cochon). ‖ Jack (au jeu de boules).

cocker [kɔkɛr] m. ZOOL. Cocker spaniel, cocker.

cockpit [kɔkpit] m. AVIAT., NAUT. Cockpit.

cocktail [kɔktɛl] m. Cocktail (boisson); cocktail party (réunion); robe de cocktail, cocktail dress. ‖ Cocktail Molotov, Molotov cocktail.

coco [kɔko] m. BOT. Coconut; lait de coco, coconut milk. ‖ CULIN. Liquorice water (boisson). ‖ FAM. Bread-basket (estomac); egg (œuf); chap, guy (type); un joli coco, a dirty dog; un drôle de coco, a queer stick; mon coco, my darling.
— f. POP. Snow (cocaïne).

cocon [kɔkɔ̃] m. Cocoon.

cocorico [kɔkɔriko] m. Cock-a-doodle-do.

cocose [kɔkoːz] f. Cocose, butter substitute.

cocotier [kɔkɔtje] m. BOT. Coconut palm.

cocotte [kɔkɔt] f. CULIN. Stew-pan, U. S. saucepan. ‖ FAM. Chickabiddy (poule); paper hen (en papier); ma cocotte, my little chick. ‖ FAM. Cocotte, U. S. floozy (fille). ‖ **Cocotte Minute** (nom déposé), f. Pressure cooker.

cocu [kɔky] m., adj. Cuckold.

cocuage [kɔkɥaːʒ] m. Cuckoldom.

cocufier [kɔkyfje] v. tr. (1). To cuckold.

coda [kɔda] m. MUS. Coda.

codage [kɔdaːʒ] m. Coding, encoding.

code [kɔd] m. Code (chiffré, télégraphique). ‖ JUR. Code, laws; statute-book (livre); code civil, civil law; code de commerce, commercial law; code de justice militaire, articles of war. ‖ AUTOM. Code de la route, rule of the road; se mettre en code, to dim one's lights. ‖ FIG. Code (de l'honneur).

codébiteur [kodebitœːr] m. Joint-debtor.

codéine [kodein] f. CHIM., MÉD. Codeine.

coder [kɔde] v. tr. (1). To code.

codétenu, ue [kodetny] s. Fellow-prisoner.

codex [kɔdɛks] m. MÉD. Codex.

codicillaire [-silɛːr] adj. JUR. Codicillary.

codicille [kɔdisil] m. JUR. Codicil; rider.

codificateur, trice [kɔdifikatœːr, tris] adj. Codifying.
— s. Codifier.

codification [kɔdifikasjɔ̃] f. JUR. Codification.

codifier [kɔdifje] v. tr. (1). To codify.

codirecteur [kodirɛktœːr] m. Co-director; joint-manager.

codirectrice [-tris] f. Co-directress; joint-manageress.

codonataire [kodɔnatɛːr] m. Joint-donee.

coefficient [koefisjɑ̃] m. Coefficient; coefficient de sécurité, safety factor.

cœlacanthe [selakɑ̃t] m. ZOOL. Cœlacanth.

cœlentérés [selɑ̃tere] m. pl. ZOOL. Cœlenterata.

cœlioscopie [seljɔskɔpi] f. MÉD. Laparoscopy.

cœnesthésie [senɛstezi] f. MÉD. Cœnesthesia, cenesthesia.

coéquation [koekwasjɔ̃] f. Proportional assessment.

coéquipier [koekipje] m. SPORTS. Team-mate.

coercible [kɔɛrsibl] adj. Coercible.

coercitif [-sitif] adj. Coercive.

coercition [-sisjɔ̃] f. Coercion.

coéternel [koetɛrnɛl] adj. Coeternal.

cœur [kœːr] m. MÉD. Heart (organe). ‖ Heart; en forme de cœur, heart-shaped. ‖ Stomach (esto-

mac); avoir mal au cœur, to feel seasick (ou) squeamish. ‖ Heart, bosom, breast (poitrine); serrer sur son cœur, to clasp to one's heart (ou) breast. ‖ Heart, mind (confiance); à cœur ouvert, unreservedly, freely; dire ce qu'on a sur le cœur, to get sth. off one's chest. ‖ Heart, conscience, mind (conscience); au cœur noble, high-minded, great-hearted; au fond du cœur, in one's heart; jusqu'au fond du cœur, to the heart's core. ‖ Heart, spirit, courage (courage); avoir du cœur au ventre, to have guts; donner du cœur à, to put new heart into, to put fresh spunk into; n'avoir pas le cœur de, not to have the heart to. ‖ Heart, mood (disposition); avoir à cœur, to have one's heart set on; avoir le cœur à, to be in the mood for; avoir le cœur de, to find it in one's heart to; de gaieté de cœur, light-heartedly; de tout cœur, with heart and hand; prendre à cœur, to take (ou) lay to heart, to set one's heart on. ‖ Heart; mind (esprit); en avoir le cœur net, to clear the matter up, to have it out. ‖ Heart, kindness (générosité); avoir le cœur sur la main, to be free-handed; de bon cœur, heartily. ‖ Mind, liking (gré); à contrecœur, reluctantly; de bon cœur, willingly; si le cœur vous en dit, if you so desire, if it appeals to you. ‖ Heart (mémoire); par cœur, by heart, by rote. ‖ Mind (rancune); avoir sur le cœur, to resent; rester sur le cœur, to rankle in one's mind; ça m'est resté sur le cœur, it stuck in my throat. ‖ Heart, affection (sentiment); aller au cœur, to touch to the heart; bon cœur, kind-heartedness, good nature; de cœur avec vous, with you in spirit; du fond du cœur, from the bottom of my heart; de tout mon cœur, with all my heart; le cœur gros, with a heavy heart; donner son cœur à, to lose one's heart to; faire le joli cœur, to play the swell; U. S. to put on the dog; joli cœur, sissy; manque de cœur, heartlessness; porter dans son cœur, to take to one's bosom; sans cœur, heartless; s'en donner à cœur joie, to indulge to one's heart's content. ‖ ECCLÉS. Sacré-Cœur, Sacred Heart. ‖ BLAS. Heart; heartpoint. ‖ Hearts (aux cartes). TECHN. Cœur de la pile, core of the reactor. ‖ AGRIC., CULIN. Heart (d'un arbre, d'artichaut, de chou, de la forêt); loaf (de chou pommé, de salade); core (d'un fruit). ‖ FIG. Kernel (d'une affaire); height (de l'été); depth (de l'hiver); core (d'une ville).

coexécuteur [koɛgzekytœːr] m. Coexecutor.

coexécutrice [-tris] f. Coexecutrix.

coexistant, ante [koɛgzistɑ̃, ɑ̃ːt] adj. Coexistent.

coexistence [-tɑ̃ːs] f. Coexistence.

coexister [-te] v. intr. (1). To coexist.

cofferdam [kɔfɛrdam] m. NAUT. Cofferdam.

coffrage [kɔfraːʒ] m. Framing (pour béton); coffering (pour tranchées).

coffre [kɔfr] m. Bin (à grain); chest (à outils). ‖ FIN. Coffer, safe; les coffres de l'Etat, the Treasury. ‖ MUS. Case (de piano). ‖ ELECTR. Cabinet (de poste de radio). ‖ MILIT. Coffre à munitions, ammunition chest. ‖ NAUT. Mooring buoy. ‖ AUTOM. Boot. ‖ CH. DE F. Ballast bed. ‖ FAM. Il a bon coffre, he is sound in wind and limb (poitrine). ‖ **Coffre-fort**, m. Safe; strong-box.

coffrer [kɔfre] v. tr. (1). To coffer. ‖ FAM. To jug.

coffret [kɔfrɛ] m. Small box (ou) chest : coffret à outils, toolbox. ‖ Casket (à bijoux).

codéfendeur [kɔfidejɛsɔ̃ːr] m. JUR. Co-surety.

cogérant, ante [koʒerɑ̃, ɑ̃ːt] s. Joint-manager. ‖ JUR. Joint administration.

cogestion [koʒɛstjɔ̃] f. Workers' participation.

cogitation [kɔʒitasjɔ̃] f. FAM. Pondering, rumination.

cogiter [-te] v. intr. (1). FAM. To ruminate, to ponder.

cognac [kɔɲak] m. Cognac.

cognassier [kɔɲasje] m. Bot. Quince tree.
cogne [kɔɲ] m. Argot. Copper, U. S. cop.
cognée [kɔɲe] f. Axe.
cognement [kɔɲmɑ̃] m. Hammering, thumping, striking, knocking. ‖ Autom. Knocking, pinking.
cogner v. tr. (1). To drive in, to hammer in (un clou). ‖ To strike, to thump, to bump, to pound (qqn, qqch.).
— v. intr. To knock; *cogner à la porte*, to knock at the door, to beat (ou) rap on the door; *cogner sur la table*, to thump the table. ‖ Méd. To beat, to thump (cœur). ‖ Techn. To knock (moteur).
— v. pr. Se **cogner**, to strike; to knock, to bump (à, contre, against); *se cogner la tête contre*, to knock one's head against.
— v. récipr. Se **cogner**, to jostle (se bousculer); to come to grips (se colleter).
cognitif, ive [kɔgnitif, i:v] adj. Cognitive.
cognition [kɔ̃gnisjɔ̃] f. Philos. Cognition.
cohabitation [koabitasjɔ̃] f. Cohabitation.
cohabiter [-te] v. intr. To cohabit.
cohérence [kɔerɑ̃:s] f. Coherence.
cohérent [-rɑ̃] adj. Coherent.
cohéreur [-rœ:r] m. Electr. Coherer.
cohériter [koerite] v. intr. (1). To inherit jointly.
cohéritier [-tje] m. Co-heir, joint-heir. ‖ Coparcener (indivisaire).
cohéritière [-tjɛ:r] f. Co-heiress, joint-heiress.
cohésif, ive [koezif, i:v] adj. Cohesive.
cohésion [-zjɔ̃] f. Cohesion, cohesiveness.
cohorte [kɔɔrt] f. Cohort. ‖ Fam. Band.
cohue [kɔy] f. Crush, throng, press. (V. foule.)
coi, oite [kwa, wat] adj. Quiet; *rester coi*, to be nonplussed; *se tenir coi*, to keep silent.
coiffe [kwaf] f. Lining (de chapeau); cover (de képi); coif, head-dress (de paysanne). ‖ Caul (de nouveau-né). ‖ Milit. Cover (de culasse); cap (de fusée); guard (d'obturateur).
coiffé, ée [-fe] adj. Arranged, dressed (chevelure); *être coiffé*, to have done one's hair; *être bien coiffé*, to have well-dressed hair; *être coiffé à la Jeanne d'Arc*, to wear one's hair bobbed; *coiffé d'une casquette*, wearing a cap. ‖ Fig. *Coiffé de qqn*, infatuated with s.o.; *né coiffé*, born with a silver spoon in one's mouth.
coiffer v. tr. (1). To put on (un chapeau); to dress (la chevelure); to put a hat on, to cover (la tête); *coiffer qqn*, to put a hat on s.o.'s head (chapeauter); to do s.o.'s hair (peigner). ‖ To cap (une bouteille, une fusée); *coiffer qqch. de*, to cover sth. with. ‖ Milit. To cover (le but); to reach (l'objectif). ‖ Naut. To gybe, U. S. to jibe. ‖ Sports. *Coiffer d'une courte tête*, to win by a short head.
— v. pr. Se **coiffer**, to do (ou) dress one's hair; to put on one's hat. ‖ Fig. *Se coiffer de*, to be smitten with, to become infatuated with, to fall for (qqn).
coiffeur [-fœ:r] m. Hairdresser, coiffeur.
coiffeuse [-fø:z] f. Hairdresser. ‖ Dressing-table, coiffeuse (meuble).
coiffure [-fy:r] f. Head-gear (chapeau). ‖ Hair-dressing (art); hair-style, headdress (genre).
coin [kwɛ̃] m. Corner (d'un angle, de la bouche, d'un livre, d'une maison, d'un mouchoir, de l'œil, de rue); place, nook, spot (à la campagne); patch (de ciel); nook (d'une salle); patch, plot, piece of ground, bit of land (de terre); *coin du feu*, fireside, chimney corner, ingle-nook; *coins et recoins*, nooks and corners, ins and outs; *les quatre coins*, puss-in-the-corner (jeu); *les quatre coins du monde*, the four corners of the earth; *la maison du coin*, the corner house; *mettre au coin*, to put in the corner; *en tournant au coin de la rue*, round the corner. ‖ Wedge, quoin (à caler); wedge (à fendre); *enfoncer comme un coin*, to wedge in. ‖ Ch. de f. Corner; *place de coin*, corner seat. ‖ Milit., Aviat. Chock. ‖ Techn., Fig. Stamp (à frapper); *frappé*

au coin du génie, bearing the stamp of genius. ‖ Fam. *Ça vous en bouche un coin!*, that knocks you! that's a corker!; *il la connaît dans les coins*, you can't tell him a thing about it. ‖ **Coin-repas**, n. Breakfast recess (ou) U. S. nook.
coinçage [-sa:ʒ] m. Wedging.
coincement [-smɑ̃] m. Jamming.
coincer [-se] v. tr. (6). To wedge (avec un coin). ‖ To jam (une machine). ‖ To wedge, to corner (qqn dans un coin); *coincé entre*, caught between. ‖ Fam. To pinch; *se faire coincer*, to get nabbed.
— v. pr. Se **coincer**, to jam, to stick.
coïncidence [kɔɛ̃sidɑ̃:s] f. Coincidence.
coïncident, ente [-dɑ̃, ɑ̃:t] adj. Coincident.
coïncider [-de] v. intr. (1). To coincide; to fall in (avec, with).
coin-coin [kwɛ̃kwɛ̃] m. invar. Quack (du canard). ‖ Autom. Blaring; honking, honk-honk.
coïnculpé, ée [koɛ̃kylpe] s. Jur. Co-defendant.
coing [kwɛ̃] m. Bot. Quince.
cointéressé, ée [koɛ̃terese] s. Partner, sharer. ‖ Naut. Co-adventurer.
coït [kɔit] m. Coition, copulation.
coke [kɔk] m. Coke; charred coal.
cokéfaction [kɔkefaksjɔ̃] f. Techn. Coking.
cokerie [kɔkri] f. Techn. Coking plant.
col [kɔl] m. Neck (cou). ‖ Neck (d'une bouteille, d'un vase). ‖ Collar (de vêtement); *col Claudine*, lady's Eton collar; *col Danton*, Byron collar; open neck; *chemise à col Danton*, open-necked shirt; *faux col*, detachable collar. ‖ Géogr. Pass, col. ‖ Méd. Neck. ‖ Fam. *Faux col*, head (de la bière). ‖ Techn. *Col-de-cygne*, swan-neck. ‖ **Col-bleu**, m. Fam., Naut. Bluejacket. ‖ **Col-cravate**, m. Stock.
cola [kɔla] m. Bot. Cola.
colback [kɔlbak] m. Milit. Busby.
colchique [kɔlʃik] m. Bot. Colchicum.
cold-cream [kɔldkri:m] m. Cold cream.
colégataire [kolegatɛ:r] m. Co-legatee, joint legatee.
coléoptère [kɔleɔptɛ:r] m. Zool. Coleopter (pl. coleoptera).
colère [kɔlɛ:r] f. Anger, passion; *accès de colère*, fit of anger; *avec colère*, angrily; *colère noire*, white rage; *être en colère*, to be angry; *mettre qqn en colère*, to make s.o. angry; *se mettre en colère*, to fly into a passion; *passer sa colère sur*, to vent one's anger on. ‖ Ecclés. *Jour de colère*, day of wrath.
— adj. Irascible, fiery. (V. rageur.)
coléreux, euse [kɔlerø, øz] adj. Irascible, fiery; peppery (fam.).
colérique [-lerik] adj. Choleric.
colibacille [kɔlibasil] m. Méd. Colon bacillus.
colibacillose [kɔlibasilo:z] f. Méd. Colibacillosis, infection caused by Escherichia coli.
colibri [kɔlibri] m. Zool. Colibri, humming-bird.
colicitant [kɔlisitɑ̃] m. Jur. Co-vendor.
colifichet [kɔlifiʃɛ] m. Fal-lal, gew-gaw. (V. babiole.) ‖ Bird-cake (pain d'oiseau). ‖ Comm. Fancy-goods.
colimaçon [kɔlimasɔ̃] m. Zool. Snail. ‖ *Escalier en colimaçon*, spiral-stairs; staircase.
colin [kɔlɛ̃] m. Zool. Hake.
colin-maillard [kɔlɛ̃maja:r] m. Blind-man's-buff.
colinot [kɔlino] m. Zool. Small hake.
colique [kɔlik] f. Méd. Colic (hépatique, intestinale, néphrétique). ‖ Fam. Stomach-ache, belly-ache; *des coliques*, collywobbles, gripes; *avoir la colique*, to have an attack of colic; *sujet à la colique*, colicky.
colis [kɔli] m. Parcel, package; *colis postal*, postal parcel; *par colis postal*, by parcel post. ‖ Pl. Luggage, articles (bagages).
colistier [kɔlistje] m. Fellow candidate.

colite [kɔlit] f. MÉD. Colitis.

collaborateur, trice [kɔlaboratœːr, tris] s. Collaborator, colleague, fellow-worker (de bureau); fellow-author (co-auteur); contributor (journaliste). ‖ Collaborationist, collaborator (pendant la guerre).

collaboration [-sjɔ̃] f. Collaboration; contribution (à un journal). ‖ Collaboration (en politique).

collaborationnisme [-sjɔnism] m. Collaboration.

collaborationniste [-sjɔnist] m. Collaborationist.

collaborer [kɔlabɔre] v. intr. (1). To cooperate, to collaborate (à, in). ‖ To write (à, for); to contribute (à, to) [un journal]. ‖ To collaborate (en politique).

collage [kɔla:ʒ] m. Gluing (à la colle forte); pasting (à la colle de pâte); sticking, gumming (à la gomme); collage des papiers peints, paperhanging. ‖ Fining (du vin). ‖ ARTS. Collage. ‖ FAM. Liaison, companionate marriage.

collagène [kɔlaʒɛn] m. Collagen.

collant, ante [-lɑ̃, ɑ̃:t] adj. Sticky, gluey; adhesive; tacky. ‖ Close-fitting, tight (vêtement). ‖ FAM. Etre collant, to stick like a leech.
— m. pl. Tights, pantihose (bas); leotard (de danse).

collante [-lɑ̃:t] f. FAM. Notification; recevoir sa collante, to be notified (of the date of an exam).

collapsus [kɔlapsys] m. MÉD. Shock (circulatoire).

collargol [kɔlargɔl] m. CHIM., MÉD. Collargol.

collatéral, ale [kɔllateral] adj. JUR. Collateral.
— m. JUR. Collateral. ‖ ECCLÉS. Side-aisle.

collatéralement [-mɑ̃] adv. JUR. Collaterally.

collation [kɔllasjɔ̃] f. Collation (d'une copie, de documents); checking (des épreuves). ‖ Collation (repas). ‖ ECCLÉS. Advowson (de bénéfice).

collationnement [kɔllasjɔnmɑ̃] m. Collation; collating.

collationner [kɔllasjɔne] v. tr. (1). To collate, to compare, to check (une copie, des documents); télégramme collationné, repetition paid telegram.
— v. intr. To have a collation (ou) snack.

colle [kɔl] f. Glue (colle forte); gum (colle de gomme); paste (colle de pâte); size (colle à empois, à peinture); peinture à la colle, size paint, distemper. ‖ FAM. Sticker, poser, teaser, puzzler (question); ploughing, U. S. flunking (recalage); keeping-in (retenue).

collé, ée [-le] adj. Clotted (par le sang). ‖ FIG. Collé à, glued to, pressed against, stuck to. ‖ FAM. Ploughed, U. S. flunked (recalé); kept-in (puni).

collecte [kɔlɛkt] f. Collection (quête); collecting (ramassage). ‖ ECCLÉS. Collect.

collecter [-te] v. tr. (1). To collect.

collecteur [-tœːr] m. Collector (personne). ‖ ‖ Main sewer (égout). ‖ NAUT. Collecteur d'incendie, fire mains. ‖ AUTOM. Manifold. ‖ ELECTR. Collector. ‖ RADIO. Collecteur d'ondes, aerial.

collectif, ive [-tif, i:v] adj. Collective (acte, contrat). ‖ MÉD. Mass (radiographie).
— m. GRAMM. Collective noun.

collection [-sjɔ̃] f. Collecting; faire collection de, to collect. ‖ Line (d'échantillons); file (de journaux); full set (d'ouvrages du même auteur); series (d'ouvrages du même genre); collection (de médailles, de plantes, de tableaux, de timbres); cabinet (de papillons); back numbers (de revue); présentation de collections, fashion parade (ou) U. S. show. ‖ MÉD. Collection, gathering of pus.

collectionner [-sjɔne] v. tr. (1). To collect.

collectionneur [-sjɔnœːr] s. Collector.

collectivement [kɔlɛktivmɑ̃] adv. Collectively.

collectivisation [-vizasjɔ̃] f. Collectivization.

collectiviser [-vize] v. tr. (1). To collectivize.

collectivisme [-vism] m. Collectivism.

collectiviste [-vist] s. Collectivist.

collectivité [-vite] f. Collectivity.

collège [kɔlɛʒ] m. College; collège électoral, body of electors, U. S. electoral college. ‖ Secondary grammar school, high school (école). ‖ ECCLÉS. Sacré Collège, Sacred College, College of Cardinals.

collégial, ale [kɔlɛʒjal] adj. Collegiate, collegial.
— f. ECCLÉS. Collegiate church.

collégialité [-ʒjalite] f. Collegiality.

collégien [-ʒjɛ̃] m. Schoolboy; college student.

collégienne [-ʒjɛn] f. Schoolgirl, U. S. co-ed.

collègue [kɔllɛg] s. Colleague.

coller [kɔle] v. tr. (1). To glue (à la colle forte); to gum (à la colle de gomme); to paste (à la colle de pâte). ‖ To paste up (une affiche); to stick down (une enveloppe); to glue on (un morceau cassé); to size (du papier); to hang (du papier peint); to gum (du papier, du tissu, de la toile); to stick on (un timbre). ‖ To clarify (le vin). ‖ CULIN. To stick (à, to). ‖ FIG. To stick; coller son œil au trou de la serrure, to glue one's eye to the key-hole. ‖ FAM. To keep in (consigner); to stick like a leech (cramponner); to stump, to floor (embarrasser); to plough, to pip, to flunk (recaler); collez ça n'importe où, stick that down anywhere; coller la responsabilité à qqn, to shove the responsibility on to s.o.; coller son poing sur la figure de qqn, to biff s.o. in the face.
— v. intr. To stick, to adhere; coller au corps, to cling to the figure (vêtement); coller derrière, to stick close to. ‖ AUTOM. Coller à la route, to cling to the road. ‖ FAM. Ça colle!, Right-o! ; O. K.; ça colle?, all right? ; ça ne colle pas, it doesn't work; on ne colle pas avec lui, I can't get on with him, we don't pull together.
— v. pr. Se coller, to stick; se coller au palais, to cleave to one's palate; se coller contre la porte, to stand close to the door; se coller contre qqn, to cling close to s.o. ‖ FAM. To cohabit; to live (ou) U. S. to shack up (pop.) [avec, with].

collerette [kɔlrɛt] f. Collarette, lace collar. ‖ BOT. Annulus, ring (de champignon). ‖ TECHN. Flange (de tuyau).

collet [kɔlɛ] m. Collar (de vêtement); prendre au collet, to collar, to seize by the collar. ‖ Cape (pèlerine); collet de fourrure, tippet. ‖ Snare, springe (rets); prendre au collet, to snare, to springe. ‖ CULIN. Neck (d'animal de boucherie). ‖ MÉD. Neck (de dent). ‖ BOT. Collar. ‖ TECHN. Flange; collar. ‖ FIG. Collet monté, stiff-necked, up-stage, U. S. prissy.

colleter [kɔlte] v. tr. (8a). To collar.
— v. intr. To set snares (ou) springes.
— v. pr. Se colleter, to scrap, to collar each other; se colleter avec, to come to grips with.

colleur [kɔlœːr] m. Sticker, gluer; paster; colleur d'affiches, bill-sticker; colleur de papiers peints, paper-hanger. ‖ FAM. Examiner.

collier [kɔlje] m. Collar (de cheval, de chien, de certains oiseaux); necklace (de femme). ‖ Newgate frill (barbe). ‖ NAUT. Collar ‖ TECHN. Collar, ring clamp. ‖ ELECTR. Coup de collier, sudden overload. ‖ FAM. Donner un coup de collier, to put one's back into it; reprendre le collier, to be back in harness (ou) U. S. back to the chain-gang.

colliger [kɔlliʒe] v. tr. (7). To collect, to check.

collimateur [kɔlimatœːr] m. PHYS. Collimator. ‖ MILIT. Sights. ‖ FAM. Avoir qqn dans le collimateur, to be after s.o. for his scalp.

colline [kɔlin] f. Hill; petite colline, hillock.

collision [kɔlizjɔ̃] f. Collision (d'autos, de navires, de trains, de troupes); shock (de troupes); entrer en collision avec, to collide with, to run foul of. ‖ FIG. Collision, clash, conflict (d'intérêts).

collocation [kɔllokasjɔ̃] f. JUR. Collocation.

collodion [kɔllɔdjɔ̃] m. CHIM. Collodion.

colloïdal, ale [kɔllɔidal] adj. CHIM. Colloidal.

colloïde [kɔllɔid] m. CHIM. Colloid.
colloque [kɔllɔk] m. Colloquy ; *tenir un colloque,* to confab (fam.). ‖ Symposium (congrès).
colloquer [kɔllɔke] v. tr. (1). JUR. To collocate.
collusion [kɔllyzjɔ̃] f. Collusion. (V. COMPLICITÉ.)
collusoire [kɔllyzwa:r] m. JUR. Collusive.
collutoire [kɔllytwa:r] m. MÉD. Mouth-wash (pour bain de bouche) ; gargle (pour gargarisme).
collyre [kɔlli:r] m. MÉD. Eye-wash ; collyrium.
colmatage [kɔlmata:ʒ] m. Sealing (d'une fissure) ; filling in (des trous) ; choking (d'un tuyau). ‖ MILIT. Stopping up (d'une brèche) ; consolidation (d'une position). ‖ AGRIC. Warping (d'une terre).
colmater [-te] v. tr. (1). To seal (une fissure) ; to clog (un filtre) ; to fill in (des trous) ; to choke (un tuyau). ‖ MILIT. To stop up (une brèche). ‖ AGRIC. To warp.
— v. pr. **Se colmater,** to clog, to choke up.
colocataire [kɔlɔkatɛ:r] m. Joint tenant.
Colomb [kɔlɔ̃] m. *Christophe Colomb,* Christopher Columbus.
colombage [kɔlɔ̃ba:ʒ] m. Half-timbering ; *maison à colombage,* half-timbered house.
colombe [kɔlɔ̃:b] f. Cooper's plane (outil).
colombe f. ZOOL. Dove.
Colombie [kɔlɔ̃bi] f. GÉOGR. Colombia.
colombien, enne [-bjɛ̃, ɛn] adj., s. GÉOGR. Colombian.
colombier [kɔlɔ̃bje] m. Dove-cot. ‖ Colombier (format).
colombin [-bɛ̃] adj. Dove-coloured.
— m. Pigeon-dung.
colombine [-bin] f. Columbine.
colombophile [-bɔfil] adj. Pigeon-fancier.
colombophilie [-bɔfili] f. Pigeon-fancying.
colon [kɔlɔ̃] m. Colonist, settler, planter.
côlon [kɔlɔ̃] m. MÉD. Colon.
colonel [kɔlɔnɛl] m. MILIT. Colonel.
colonelle [-nɛ:l] f. Colonel's wife.
colonial, ale [-njal] adj., s. Colonial.
coloniale [-nja:l] f. MILIT. Colonial troops.
colonialisme [-njalism] m. Imperialism.
colonialiste [-njalist] adj., m. Imperialist.
colonie [kɔlɔni] f. Colony (à l'étranger) ; *ministère des Colonies,* Colonial Office. ‖ Colony (population) ; *la colonie irlandaise à Paris,* the Irish colony in Paris. ‖ Settlement (groupe) ; *colonie de vacances,* holiday camp.
colonisateur, trice [-zatœ:r, tris] adj. Colonizing.
— s. Colonizer.
colonisation [-zasjɔ̃] f. Colonization.
coloniser [-ze] v. tr. (1). To colonize, to settle.
colonnade [kɔlɔnad] f. ARCHIT. Colonnade; *à colonnade,* colonnaded.
colonne [kɔlɔn] f. Column (d'air, de chiffres, d'eau, de journal, de fumée, de mercure). ‖ ARCHIT. Column, pillar. ‖ MÉD. Column ; *colonne vertébrale,* spine, backbone, spinal column. ‖ ‖ MILIT. Column; *colonne par trois,* column of threes ; *cinquième colonne,* fifth column.
colonnette [-nɛt] f. Small column.
colophane [kɔlɔfan] f. Colophony, rosin.
colophaner [-fane] v. tr. (1). To rosin.
coloquinte [kɔlɔkɛ̃:t] f. BOT. Colocynth, bitter-apple. ‖ FAM. Noddle.
colorant, ante [kɔlɔrɑ̃, ɑ̃:t] adj. Colouring.
— m. Colouring ; stainer. (V. TEINTURE.)
coloration [-rasjɔ̃] f. Colouring (action) ; colouration (ton).
coloré, ée [-re] adj. Coloured (objet) ; ruddy, florid (teint). ‖ FIG. Florid, highly coloured.
colorer [-re] v. tr. (1). To colour, to tint, to tinge. ‖ FIG. To colour (une description, le style).
— v. pr. **Se colorer,** to colour (objet); to grow ruddy (teint).

coloriage [-rja:ʒ] m. Colouring.
colorier [-rje] v. tr. (1). To colour.
colorimètre [-rimɛtr] m. Colorimeter.
coloris [-ri] m. Colouring. ‖ ARTS. Colour; colour scheme. ‖ FIG. Brightness, floridness, colour.
coloriste [-rist] s. ARTS. Colourist. ‖ Colourer (de cartes postales).
colossal, ale [kɔlɔsal] adj. Colossal.
colossalement [kɔlɔsalmɑ̃] adv. Colossally.
colosse [kɔlɔs] m. Colossus. (V. GÉANT.)
colportage [kɔlpɔrta:ʒ] m. Hawking, peddling.
colporter [-te] v. tr. (1). To hawk, to peddle. ‖ FIG. To spread, to retail (une nouvelle).
colporteur, euse [-tœ:r, -tøz] s. Hawker, peddlar ; U. S. peddler. ‖ FIG. Newsmonger.
colt [kɔlt] m. Pistol.
coltinage [kɔltina:ʒ] m. Porterage, carrying.
coltiner [-ne] v. tr. (1). To porter.
— v. pr. **Se coltiner,** to lug (une lourde charge) ; to take on, to be (ou) get landed with (un travail, une corvée).
coltineur [-nœ:r] m. Porter.
columbarium [kɔlɔ̃barjɔm] m. Columbarium.
colza [kɔlza] m. BOT. Colza ; rape ; coleseed ; *huile de colza,* colza oil, rape oil.
coma [kɔma] m. MÉD. Coma ; *dans le coma,* in a coma.
comateux, euse [-tø, ø:z] adj. MÉD. Comatose.
combat [kɔ̃ba] m. Fight, struggle ; *combat de coqs,* cock-fight ; *combat d'ours et de chiens,* bear-baiting ; *combat singulier,* single combat ; *hors de combat,* knocked out, disabled, out of the fight (personne). ‖ MILIT. Combat, battle, engagement ; fight ; fighting ; *aller au combat,* to take the field. ‖ NAUT. *Combat naval,* sea fight, naval action. ‖ AVIAT. *Combat aérien,* aerial combat. ‖ SPORTS. Fight (boxe). ‖ FIG. Contest, conflict ; struggle.
combatif, ive [-tif, i:v] adj. Combative, pugnacious.
combativité [-tivite] f. Combativeness, pugnaciousness.
combattant, ante [-tɑ̃, ɑ̃:t] adj. Fighting.
— m. MILIT. Fighter, combatant. ‖ SPORTS. Fighting-cock (coq).
combattre [kɔ̃batr] v. tr. (20). To fight with (un ennemi) ; to fight (un ennemi, un incendie) ; to struggle against, to wrestle with (qqn à la lutte). ‖ FIG. To war against (les abus, un adversaire, une doctrine) ; to contend with, to wrestle with (les difficultés, ses passions) ; to combat, to fight (la maladie, le sommeil) ; to oppose (des projets) ; to impugn (une proposition) ; to contend against, to oppose, to stand against (qqn en discutant).
— v. intr. To fight (*contre,* against ; *pour,* for). ‖ FIG. To contend (*contre,* against).
combe [kɔ̃:b] f. GÉOGR. Coomb, combe, dale.
combien [kɔ̃bjɛ̃] adv. How, how much (degré) ; *combien de dérangement je vous cause!,* what trouble I give you! ; *combien il dit vrai!,* how right he is! ; *combien elle désire vous revoir!,* how much she wishes to see you again! ; *je vois combien elle est aimable,* I see how kind she is. ‖ How far (distance) ; *combien y a-t-il d'ici à Bordeaux?,* how far is it to Bordeaux? ‖ How many (nombre) ; *combien de fois?,* how many times?, how often? ; *combien de livres avez-vous?,* how many books have you? ; *combien pensent que,* how many people think that. ‖ How much (prix) ; *combien ce chou-fleur?,* how much is this cauliflower? ; *combien croyez-vous que ça vaille?,* what price do you put upon it? ; *à combien est-ce?,* how much is it? ‖ How much (quantité) ; *dites-moi combien de vin il vous faut,* tell me how much wine you want. ‖ How long (temps) ; *combien vous a-t-il fallu pour venir?,* how long did it take you to come? ; *pour combien de temps en*

avez-vous encore?, how much longer will you be? ‖ Loc. *Combien peu*, how little (au sing.); how few (au plur.); *je ne sais combien de fois, de gens, de temps*, ever so often, ever so many people, ever so long.
— m. inv. Fam. *Tu étais le combien à la composition?*, where did you come in the test?; *nous sommes le combien aujourd'hui?*, what's the date today?; *tous les combien?*, how often?

combientième [kɔ̃bjɛ̃tjɛm] adj. Fam. *C'est la combientième fois?*, how many times does that make?
— s. Fam. *La combientième étais-tu à l'examen?*, where did you come in the test?; *il est le combientième?*, where was he placed?

combinaison [kɔ̃binɛzɔ̃] f. Scheme (de couleur, de rimes); combination (d'éléments); assemblage (de matériaux, de pièces). ‖ One-piece flying suit (d'aviateur); slip (de femme); dungarees, overalls (de mécanicien, d'ouvrier). ‖ Chim., Math. Combination. ‖ Fig. Contrivance (artifice, manigance); device (expédient); scheme, intrigue (machination); plan.

combinard, arde [kɔ̃binar, ard] s. Pop. Racketeer, grafter, spiv; schemer.

combinat [kɔ̃bina] m. Industrial complex, kombinat.

combinatoire [kɔ̃binatwa:r] adj. Combinative, combinatory, combinatorial. ‖ Math. *Analyse combinatoire*, combinatorial analysis.

combine [kɔ̃bin] f. Fam. Racket, scheme; fiddle, fiddling.

combiné [kɔ̃bine] m. Chim. Compound. ‖ Sports. All-round test (au ski). ‖ Combined set, combined hand microphone and receiver (téléphone). ‖ Radio. *Combiné radio-pick-up*, radiogram.

combiner [-ne] v. tr. (1). To unite (deux armées, deux parties, deux sociétés); to combine (des mots); to compound (des éléments). ‖ Chim. To combine. ‖ Fig. To plan (une attaque, une évasion, un projet); to combine (ses efforts); to devise, to concert, to think out (un plan); *combiner de faire qqch.*, to plan to do sth.
— v. pr. *Se combiner*, to combine. ‖ To unite (avec, with).

comble [kɔ̃bl] m. Archit. Attic, garret (grenier); roof, roofing (toit); *de fond en comble*, from top to bottom. ‖ Heaped measure, overmeasure (surplus). ‖ Fig. Summit (du bonheur, des honneurs); depth (du désespoir); acme (de la gloire); height (de la joie, de la sottise); *à son comble*, at its peak; *c'est le comble*, that beats all, that's the last straw, that takes the cake; *mettre le comble à*, to cap, to add the finishing touch to; *pour comble de malheur*, to crown (ou) complete the misfortune.
— adj. Heaped up (mesure); crowded, packed (salle); full to the brim (verre). ‖ Théâtr. *Faire salle comble*, to draw full houses. ‖ Fig. *La mesure est comble*, that's the limit.

comblement [-bləmɑ̃] m. Filling in (ou) up (d'une excavation, d'un trou). ‖ Géol. Aggradation (d'une vallée). ‖ Fin. Making up (ou) good (d'un déficit). ‖ Fig. Fulfilment (d'un désir).

combler [-ble] v. tr. (1). To fill up (une mesure). ‖ To fill in, to fill up (une excavation, un trou). ‖ Géol. To aggrade (une vallée). ‖ Fin. To make up (un déficit). ‖ Fig. To fulfil, to satisfy, to gratify (un désir); to fill (une lacune, la mesure, un vide); to load (qqn) [*de*, with].

comburant, ante [kɔ̃byrɑ̃, ɑ̃:t] adj. Combustive.

combustibilité [kɔ̃bystibilite] f. Combustibility, combustibleness.

combustible [kɔ̃bystibl] adj. Combustible.
— m. Fuel.

combustion [-tjɔ̃] f. Combustion; *moteur à combustion interne*, internal combustion engine.

comédie [kɔmedi] f. Théâtr. Comedy (genre); play (pièce); performance (représentation); *comédie de salon*, private theatricals. ‖ Fig. Farce, play; *c'est une vraie comédie*, it's as good as a play. ‖ Fig. Acting, sham, make-believe (feinte).

comédien [-djɛ̃] m. Théâtr. Comedian. ‖ Fig. Shammer, poseur.

comédienne [-djɛn] f. Théâtr. Comedienne, comedy actress. ‖ Fig. Shammer, poseuse.

comédon [kɔmedɔ̃] m. Comedo, blackhead.

comestible [kɔmɛstibl] adj. Eatable, edible.
— m. Comestible. ‖ Pl. Foodstuffs, victuals.

comète [kɔmɛt] f. Astron. Comet. ‖ *Vin de la comète*, comet-wine.

comices [kɔmis] m. pl. † Comitia. ‖ Meeting; *comice agricole*, agricultural show.

comique [kɔmik] adj. Théâtr. Comic (acteur, opéra). ‖ Comical, comic, funny, droll, ludicrous.
— m. Théâtr. Comic actor (acteur); comedian (acteur, auteur); comic (genre). ‖ Funny part (aspect); humour (sens).

comiquement [-mɑ̃] adv. Comically.

comité [kɔmite] m. Committee, board. ‖ Loc. *En petit comité*, in a small group, in a little friendly meeting (amical); *se réunir en petit comité*, to hold an informal meeting (politique).

comma [kɔma] m. Mus. Comma.

commandant [kɔmɑ̃dɑ̃] m. Milit. Commandant, commanding officer (fonction); major (grade); *commandant en chef*, commander-in-chief. ‖ Aviat. Squadron-leader (grade). ‖ Naut. Captain (grade); *oui, mon commandant*, yes, sir.

commande [kɔmɑ̃d] f. Comm. Order; *commande en double expédition*, indent; *ouvrage composé sur commande*, work commissioned by the publisher; *sur commande*, to order. ‖ Techn. Drive; *levier de commande*, operating lever. ‖ Autom. Drive, lever; U. S. control; *tableau des commandes*, dashboard. ‖ Naut. Fox. ‖ Aviat. Control. ‖ Fig. *De commande*, forced, feigned (artificiel); obligatory, compulsory (obligatoire).

commandement [-dmɑ̃] m. Order, command (ordre). ‖ Milit. Command; *haut commandement*, High Command; *prendre le commandement*, to assume command. ‖ Ecclés. Commandment (de Dieu). ‖ Jur. Summons to pay (par huissier).

commander [-de] v. tr. (1). To order, to command (qqch., qqn); *commander qqch. à qqn*, to order sth. from s.o.; to give s.o. an order for sth. ‖ To order, to call for (une consommation); to order (un repas). ‖ To dominate, to command (une position); *commander l'accès à*, to give access to. ‖ To commission (un livre, un tableau). ‖ Milit. To command (une armée); to lead (une expédition). ‖ Techn. To control; to drive. ‖ Comm. To order. ‖ Fig. To demand, to require; *commander le respect*, to command (ou) compel respect.
— v. intr. To order, to give orders; *il aime à commander*, he is fond of ordering people about; *commander à qqn de faire qqch.*, to order s.o. to do sth.; *commander à qqn de descendre, d'entrer, de monter, de partir, de revenir, de s'éloigner, de sortir*, to order s.o. to come down, come in, come up, go away, come back, go off, go out; *commander à ses nerfs*, to control one's nerves. ‖ *Commander de*, to order, to command; *commander d'apporter un siège*, to order a seat to be brought.
— v. pr. *Se commander*, to control oneself. ‖ To be beyond control; *cela ne se commande pas*, it does not depend upon your will.
— v. récipr. *Se commander*, to command each other (ou) one another (personnes); to lead into each other (ou) one another (pièces).

commandeur [-dœ:r] m. Commander.

commanditaire [-ditɛ:r] s. Comm. Sleeping (ou) limited (ou) U. S. silent partner. ‖ Théâtr. Backer, U. S. angel.

commandite [-dit] f. Limited partnership (fait); capital invested by sleeping partners (fonds); commandite (société).

commandité [kɔmɑ̃dite] m. Active and responsible partner.
— adj. Financed, supported.

commanditer [kɔmɑ̃dite] v. tr. (1). Comm. To finance, to provide capital; U. S. to stake. ‖ Théâtr. To finance, U. S. to angel.

commando [kɔmɑ̃dɔ] m. Milit. Commando.

comme [kɔm] conj. et adv. As (ainsi que); *balancés comme dans un bateau,* rocked as in a boat; *comme je m'y attendais,* as I expected; *piqué comme par une guêpe,* stung as if by a wasp. ‖ As, just as (alors que, tandis que); *il sortait comme vous entriez,* he went out just as you entered; *comme nous allions notre chemin, il se mit à pleuvoir,* as we went on, it began to rain. ‖ Like (à la manière de); *courir comme un dératé,* to run like a hare; *se conduire comme un galant homme,* to behave like a gentleman. ‖ As (à mesure que); *comme il avançait, je reculais,* as he advanced, I drew back. ‖ As, for (à titre de, en tant que); *comme contribuable, je proteste,* as a tax-payer, I protest; *fameux comme orateur,* famous as an orator; *prendre comme ami,* to make a friend of; *vendue comme esclave,* sold as a slave. ‖ As (autant que); *intelligent comme il paraît l'être,* intelligent as he seems; *elle est loin d'être aimable comme vous,* she is nothing like so kind as you. ‖ How, how much (combien); *comme votre père est bon!,* how kind a man your father is! ‖ How (comment); *Dieu sait comme!,* Heaven knows how! ‖ As (de la façon dont); *comme il vous plaira,* as you please, as you like it; *comme vous pourrez,* as best you can. ‖ As (de même que); *comme je vous ai aidé, vous devriez aider mon fils,* as I helped you, so you ought to help my son; *ici c'est comme ailleurs,* here it is as elsewhere. ‖ In the way of, as regards, for (en fait de); *c'est tout ce que vous avez comme fleurs?,* is that all you have in the way of flowers? ; *comme intelligence il n'est pas remarquable,* he is not remarkable for brains. ‖ Like (pareil à); *je pense comme vous,* I think like you; *il m'aimait comme un fils,* he loved me like a son; *tout comme un autre,* just like anybody else. ‖ Like, such as (tel que); *des gens comme vous et moi,* people like you and me, such men as you and I; *des philosophes comme Bergson,* philosophers such as Bergson. ‖ As, since (parce que, puisque); *comme j'étais très pris par mon travail, je n'ai pu vous recevoir,* as I was very much taken up by my work, I could not entertain you; *comme il est mineur, il ne peut tester,* since he is not of age, he cannot make a will. ‖ Loc. *Comme ci, comme ça,* so-so (fam.); *comme ceci,* thus, in this way; *comme si,* as if; *et comme ça vous allez bien?,* and so you're quite well then?; *été comme hiver,* summer and winter alike; *c'est comme si c'était fait,* it is as good as done; *c'est tout comme,* it comes to the same thing; *il est comme ça,* it is his way; *il est comme mort,* he is almost dead.

commémoraison [kɔmmemɔrɛzɔ̃] f. Ecclés. Commemoration (d'un saint).

commémoratif, ive [-ratif, i:v] adj. Commemorative; memorial (service).

commémoration [-rasjɔ̃] f. Commemoration.

commémorer [-re] v. tr. (1). To commemorate.

commençant, ante [kɔmɑ̃sɑ̃, ɑ̃:t] adj. Beginning.
— m. Beginner.

commencement [-smɑ̃] m. Beginning (v. début); *au commencement,* in the beginning; *dès le commencement,* from the beginning (ou) outset; *du commencement à la fin,* from beginning to end, from first to last.

commencer [-se] v. tr. (6). To begin (sens général); to commence, to embark upon (une carrière); to open (une conversation, un débat, des négociations); to start (une conversation, des négociations, une guerre, un travail); to begin (un récit). ‖ Fam. To ground (un élève).
— v. intr. To begin (sens général); *la nuit commence,* night is setting in; *pour commencer,* to begin with. ‖ **Commencer à,** to begin to; *commencer à faire,* to begin (ou) commence doing (ou) to do; to start to do (qqch.); *il commence à grisonner,* his hair is turning grey. ‖ **Commencer par,** to begin with, to commence by; *commencer par faire,* to begin (ou) commence by doing (qqch.); *commencer par le commencement,* to begin at the beginning. ‖ Comm. *Commencer à courir,* to attach.

commende [kɔmɑ̃d] f. Ecclés. Commendam.

commensal, ale [kɔmɑ̃sal] m. Commensal, messmate; table-companion; fellow boarder. ‖ Guest (invité).

commensalisme [-lism] m. Zool. Commensalism.

commensurabilité [kɔmɑ̃syrabilite] f. Commensurability.

commensurable [-rabl] adj. Commensurable (avec, with).

comment [kɔmɑ̃] adv. How (cause); *comment se fait-il que?,* how is it that? ‖ How (état); *comment va-t-il?,* how is he?; *comment est-elle, cette jeune fille?* what sort of girl is she?, what is this girl like? ‖ How, what (manière); *comment faire?* what is to be done?, what can I do?; *je ne sais comment cela arriva,* I don't know how it happened; *comment s'écrit ce mot?,* how do you spell this word? ‖ How (moyen); *comment a-t-il découvert le pot aux roses?,* how did he find out all about it? ‖ What (nom); *comment vous appelez-vous?,* what's your name? what are you called? ‖ How?, what? (surprise); *comment cela?* how so?
— interj. What! how!; *comment donc!* of course!, by all means!, to be sure!; *et comment!,* and how!, not half!
— m. *Les comment et les pourquoi,* the whys and the wherefores.

commentaire [kɔmɑ̃tɛ:r] m. Commentary, note (en littérature). ‖ Pl. Commentaries (de César). ‖ Fig. Remark, comment; *faire des commentaires sur,* to comment upon; *se passer de commentaire,* to speak for itself.

commentateur, trice [-tatœ:r, tris] s. Commentator.

commenter [-te] v. tr. (1). To comment on.

commérage [kɔmera:ʒ] m. Gossiping, gossip. ‖ Pl. Tittle-tattle.

commerçant, ante [kɔmɛrsɑ̃, ɑ̃:t] adj. Mercantile (nation); business, shopping (quartier); shopping (rue); trading, commercial (ville).
— s. Comm. Tradesman, trader (v. marchand); *commerçant en gros,* merchant, wholesale dealer. ‖ Pl. Tradespeople, tradesfolk.

commerce [kɔmɛrs] m. Comm. Trade (intérieur); commerce (international); *commerce du charbon,* coal trade; *commerce des chevaux,* horse dealing; *dans le commerce,* on sale (objet); in business (personne); *faire du commerce,* to trade (avec, with); *faire le commerce de,* to deal (ou) trade in; *gros, petit commerce,* large, small business; *hors commerce,* for private circulation (livre); *maison de commerce,* firm, concern. ‖ Comm. Dealers (commerçants); *le grand commerce,* big dealers, merchants; *le petit commerce,* shopkeepers, small tradespeople. ‖ Jur. *Commerce* *sexuel,* intercourse. ‖ Fig. Intercourse, interchange; relationship; dealing (rapports); *commerce avec l'ennemi,* intercourse with the enemy; *le commerce des livres,* reading; *d'un commerce agréable,* pleasant to deal with.

commercer [-se] v. intr. (6). Comm. To trade (ou) deal (*avec,* with). ‖ Fig. To have relations, to hold intercourse (*avec,* with).

commercial, ale [-sjal] adj. Comm. Commercial; *directeur commercial,* business (ou) sales manager; *droit commercial,* law merchant; *société commerciale,* trading company.

commerciale f. Autom. Van, utility vehicle.

commercialement [-sjalmã] adv. Commercially.

commercialisation [-sjalizasjõ] f. Commercialization.

commercialiser [-sjalize] v. tr. (1). To commercialize.

commère [komɛ:r] f. Ecclés. Fellow-sponsor at baptism. ‖ Fam. Gossip, tattler (bavarde).

commérer [-mere] v. intr. (5). Fam. To gossip, to tattle, to prattle.

commettant [komɛtã] m. Jur. Principal.

commettre [komɛtr] v. tr. (64). To commit, to perpetrate (une action criminelle); to make (une erreur). ‖ To commit, to entrust (confier). ‖ To appoint, to nominate (désigner). ‖ To commit, to compromise, to imperil, to endanger (risquer). — v. pr. *Se commettre,* to commit oneself; to throw in one's lot (*avec,* with).

commis [komi] m. Clerk (aux écritures); salesman (à la vente). ‖ Naut. *Commis aux vivres,* ship's steward. ‖ Comm. *Commis voyageur,* commercial traveller, representative, travelling salesman.

commise [-miz] f. Comm. Shop-assistant, saleswoman; shop-girl.

commisération [komizerasjõ] f. Commiseration; *témoigner de la commisération à,* to commiserate with.

commissaire [komisɛ:r] m. Commissary (délégué); steward (ordonnateur). ‖ Jur. Commissioner; *commissaire du gouvernement,* governmental commissioner; *commissaire de police,* superintendent of police, U. S. police commissioner, U. S. chief of police; *haut-commissaire,* High Commissioner. ‖ Milit. *Commissaire du gouvernement,* prosecutor (au conseil de guerre). ‖ Naut. *Commissaire d'avarie,* average-surveyor; *commissaire de la marine d'Etat, de la marine marchande,* paymaster, purser. ‖ **Commissaire-priseur,** m. Auctioneer.

commissariat [-sarʃa] m. Police-station (bureau, local). ‖ Jur. Superintendence (fonction). ‖ Comm. Auditorship. ‖ Naut. Paymastership; pursership.

commission [-sjõ] f. Errand (course); message; *faire une commission,* to do an errand; to deliver a message; *faire des commissions,* to run errands. ‖ Comm. Commission, factorage (courtage); *à la commission,* on commission. ‖ Fin. Brokerage, percentage (à la Bourse). ‖ Jur. Commission, charge; warrant (mission). ‖ Committee, commission, board (dans l'administration); *commission du Budget,* Budget Committee; *commission d'enquête,* board of enquiry (ou) U. S. of investigation; *commission mixte d'enquête industrielle,* working party; *commission d'examen,* examination board.

commissionnaire [komisjonɛ:r] m. Errand-boy. (V. messager, porteur.) ‖ Forwarding agent (de transport); common carrier, carter (de roulage). ‖ Comm. Commission-agent (en général); factor (en gros).

commissionner [-sjone] v. tr. (1). Jur., Comm. To commission. ‖ Milit. To re-enlist.

commissure [komisy:r] f. Méd. Commissure; corner of the lips.

commode [komɔd] adj. Convenient (accès, heure); handy (outil); suitable (plan); easy (route); comfortable (siège, vêtement). [V. aisé, facile.] ‖ Fig. Accommodating (morale); easy (ouvrage, tâche, vie); easy-going, compliant (personne); *il n'est pas commode,* he is a tough customer. — f. Chest of drawers, commode, U. S. bureau, dresser, lowboy; *commode haute,* tallboy, U. S. highboy.

commodément [komɔdemã] adv. Conveniently; comfortably.

commodité [-dite] f. Convenience (en général); comfort (d'un local, d'un vêtement). ‖ Pl. Conveniences (de la vie). ‖ Pl. Water-closet.

commodore [komɔdɔr] m. Naut. Commodore.

commotion [komɔsjõ] f. Commotion. ‖ Méd. Concussion (au cerveau); shock (électrique); shell-shock (par éclatement d'obus). ‖ Fig. Commotion, disturbance.

commotionner [-sjone] v. tr. (1). Méd. To concuss; to shock.

commuable [komyabl] adj. Jur. Commutable.

commuer [komye] v. tr. (1). Jur. To commute (*en,* into).

commun, une [komœ̃, yn] adj. Common (à plusieurs); *amis communs,* mutual friends; *salle commune,* common room. ‖ Common, joint (conjoint); *à frais communs,* sharing expenses; U. S. Dutch treat; *d'un commun accord,* with one accord. ‖ Common, general; *bien commun,* public interest; *faute commune,* general fault; *sens commun,* common sense. ‖ Usual, ordinary, common (v. banal, habituel); *peu commun,* unusual. ‖ Vulgar, commonplace (vulgaire); *expression commune,* vulgar expression. ‖ Math. Common (diviseur). ‖ Gramm. Common (nom). — m. Common people; *le commun des mortels,* ordinary mortals, the common run of humanity. ‖ Commonplace, banality; *hors du commun,* out of the common. ‖ Fin. Common funds; *en commun,* in common; jointly; *mettre en commun,* to pool. ‖ Archit. Pl. Outbuildings, outhouses, offices, appurtenances (d'une maison).

communal, ale [komynal] adj. Communal (conseil, forêt); parish (école, fête); *chemin communal,* by-road, U. S. back road.

communale f. Fam. Primary school.

communaliste [-nalist] s. Communalist.

communard, arde [komyna:r, ard] adj. † Of the Paris Commune of 1871. — s. † Communard, partisan of the Paris Commune of 1871.

communautaire [komynotɛ:r] adj. Of the community; *centre communautaire,* community centre.

communauté [-te] f. Community, commonalty, society (société). ‖ Ecclés. Community. ‖ Jur. Community, joint possession; *communauté de biens,* co-ownership (entre époux); *communauté conjugale,* communal estate. ‖ Fig. Community (des idées, des intérêts).

commune [komyn] f. Parish (division); parishioners (membres). ‖ Pl. House of Commons (Chambre). ‖ *La Commune,* the Commune.

communément [-nemã] adv. Commonly.

communiant [komynjã] s. Ecclés. Communicant.

communicable [komynikabl] adv. Communicable. ‖ Méd. Catching, communicable (maladie). ‖ Jur. Transferable (droit).

communicant [-kã] adj. Communicating.

communicateur, trice [-katœ:r, tris] adj. Connecting.

communicatif, ive [-katif, i:v] adj. Catching (rire). ‖ Communicative (v. expansif); *peu communicatif,* uncommunicative, reticent.

communication [-kasjɔ̃] f. Communication, information; *donner communication de qqch. à qqn*, to communicate sth. to s. o.; *faire une communication à*, to read a paper to (une société savante). ‖ Communication, intercourse (commerce) [*avec*, with]. ‖ Communication, call (au téléphone); *avoir la communication*, to be through; *mettre en communication avec*, to connect with, to put through to. ‖ Communication (contact); *mettre en communication avec*, to put in touch with; *porte de communication*, communicating door; *voie de communication*, thoroughfare. ‖ Communication (de papiers, de projets); *envoyé en communication*, sent for perusal (document).

communier [kɔmynje] v. intr. (1). ECCLÉS. To communicate, to take Holy Communion. ‖ FIG. To be in intimate converse (avec, with).
— v. tr. ECCLÉS. To communicate, to administer Holy Communion to (qqn).

communion [-njɔ̃] f. ECCLÉS. Communion, persuasion (croyance, église); communion (réception du sacrement). ‖ FIG. Communion; *être en communion d'idées avec*, to be intellectually in harmony with.

communiqué [kɔmynike] m. Communiqué, bulletin, official intimation (ou) report; *communiqué à la presse*, official statement to the press; *communiqué de presse*, press release; *communiqué publié conjointement*, joint communiqué.

communiquer v. tr. (1). To communicate, to impart (un mouvement); to circulate (un objet à la ronde). ‖ MÉD. To transmit (une maladie); *communiquer une maladie à qqn*, to infect s.o. with a disease. ‖ FIG. To communicate, to impart, to make known (des idées, une nouvelle, un plan).
— v. intr. To communicate; to be in connection; *communiquer avec*, to communicate with, to open into (pièces, porte). ‖ To communicate, to hold communication (ou) intercourse (*avec qqn*, with s. o.).
— v. pr. **Se communiquer**, to spread.

communisant, ante [kɔmynizɑ̃, ɑ̃:t] adj. Communistic.
— s. Fellow-traveller, Communist sympathizer.

communisme [-nism] m. Communism.

communiste [-nist] adj., m. Communist.

commutateur [kɔmytatœ:r] m. ELECTR. Commutator, switch.

commutatif, ive [kɔmmytatif, i:v] adj. JUR. Commutative.

commutation [kɔmmytasjɔ̃] f. JUR., ELECTR. Commutation.

commutatrice [-tris] f. ELECTR. Rotary converter.

commuter [-myte] v. tr. ELECTR. To commutate.

Comores [kɔmɔ:r] f. pl. GÉOGR. Comoro Islands.

compacité [kɔ̃pasite] f. Compactness.

compact, acte [kɔ̃pakt] adj. Compact. (V. DENSE.)

compagne [kɔ̃paɲ] f. Companion (en général); schoolmate (en classe). ‖ Helpmate, U. S. helpmeet, wife (épouse); mistress (maîtresse). ‖ FIG. Attendant (*de*, upon).

compagnie [-ɲi] f. Company (fréquentation); *ce n'est pas une compagnie pour vous*, he is no fit company for you; *mauvaises compagnies*, bad company. ‖ Company (réunion); *nombreuse compagnie*, large gathering (ou) company (ou) party. ‖ Company (présence); *aller de compagnie*, to keep company together; *en compagnie de*, in company with; *fausser compagnie à qqn*, to give s.o. the slip; *tenir compagnie à qqn*, to bear (ou) keep s.o. company; *par désir de compagnie*, for the sake of companionship. ‖ ZOOL. Bevy (d'alouettes, de cailles); covey (de coqs de bruyères, de perdrix). ‖ COMM. Company; Co. ‖

MILIT. Company; *compagnie de débarquement*, landing party. ‖ NAUT. Division. ‖ ECCLÉS. Society.

compagnon [-ɲɔ̃] m. Companion; fellow; mate; *compagnon de jeu*, playmate; *compagnon d'infortune*, companion in misfortune, fellow-sufferer; *compagnon de route* (ou) *de voyage*, fellow traveller. ‖ Helpmate, consort, husband (époux). ‖ Workman; journeyman (ouvrier). ‖ MILIT. *Compagnon d'armes*, comrade in arms, fellow-soldier, brother officer. ‖ FIG. Attendant (*de*, on); companion (*de*, of). ‖ FAM. Fellow; *un joyeux compagnon*, a jolly fellow; *un drôle de compagnon*, a queer chap.

compagnonnage [-ɲɔna:ʒ] m. † Trade-guild.

comparable [kɔ̃parabl] adj. Comparable (*à*, with, to); *nul ne lui est comparable*, nobody can compare with him.

comparaison [kɔ̃parɛzɔ̃] f. Comparison (*entre*, between); *en comparaison de*, in comparison with, compared to; *par comparaison avec*, comparatively to; *sans comparaison*, beyond all comparison. ‖ GRAMM. Simile (figure); *degrés de comparaison*, degrees of comparison.

comparaître [kɔ̃parɛ:tr] v. intr. (74). JUR. To appear; *faire comparaître devant*, to bring before.

comparatif, ive [kɔ̃paratif, i:v] adj. Comparative.
— m. GRAMM. Comparative; *au comparatif*, in the comparative.

comparatiste [-tist] s. Comparatist.

comparativement [-tivmɑ̃] adv. Comparatively (*à*, to, with).

comparé, ée [kɔ̃pare] adj. Comparative (anatomie, littérature).

comparer v. tr. (1). To compare (*à*, to; *avec*, with); to liken (*à*, to).
— v. pr. **Se comparer**, to compare (*à*. with).

comparoir [-rwa:r] v. intr. (28). JUR. To appear.

comparse [kɔ̃pars] s. THÉÂTR. Supernumerary, super. ‖ FIG. Confederate.

compartiment [kɔ̃partimɑ̃] m. Square (d'un damier); compartment (d'un meuble, d'un tiroir). ‖ CH. DE F. Compartment; *compartiment de fumeurs*, smoking compartment. ‖ NAUT. *Compartiment du fret*, cargo compartment.

compartimentage [-ta:ʒ] m. Partitioning; division into compartments. ‖ Subdividing (du terrain). ‖ NAUT. Compartmentation, subdivision.

compartimentation [-tasjɔ̃] f. V. COMPARTIMENTAGE.

compartimenter [-te] v. tr. (1). To compart; to divide into compartments; U. S. to compartmentalize.

comparution [kɔ̃parysjɔ̃] f. JUR. Appearance; *non comparution*, non appearance, default.

compas [kɔ̃pa] m. Compasses; *compas à pointes sèches*, dividers; *compas à quart de cercle*, wing compasses; *compas de calibre*, calipers. ‖ NAUT. Compass; *quart de compas*, point of compass; *rose de compas*, compass card. ‖ FAM. *Allonger le compas*, to step out; *avoir le compas dans l'œil*, to have an accurate eye.

compassé, ée [-se] adj. Formal, starched, starchy.

compasser v. tr. (1). TECHN. To measure with compasses. ‖ FIG. To make formal (ou) stilted.

compassion [kɔ̃pasjɔ̃] f. Compassion (v. PITIÉ); *avec compassion*, compassionately.

compatibilité [kɔ̃patibilite] f. Compatibility.

compatible [-tibl] adj. Compatible, consistent (*avec*, with).

compatir [-ti:r] v. intr. (2). To take pity (*à*, on); to commiserate (*aux malheurs de*, with).

compatissant, ante [-tisɑ̃, ɑ̃:t] adj. Compassionate; commiserative, sympathetic.

compatriote [-triɔt] s. Compatriot; fellow-countrywoman (femme), fellow-countryman (homme).

compendieusement [kɔ̃pɑ̃djøzmɑ̃] adv. Compendiously, concisely.

compendieux, euse [-djø, ø:z] adj. Compendious.
compendium [-djɔm] m. Compendium.
compensateur, trice [kɔ̃pɑ̃satœ:r, tris] adj. Compensating.
— m. ELECTR., PHYS. Compensator. ‖ AVIAT. Trimming tab, trimmer.
compensation [-sasjɔ̃] f. Compensation, offset, making up (de, for) [v. DÉDOMMAGEMENT]; faire compensation, to make up for it. ‖ COMM. Clearing; accord de compensation, barter agreement. ‖ FIN. Chambre de compensation, clearing-house; caisse de compensation, equalizing fund; cours de compensation, making-up price. ‖ TECHN. Compensation, balancing (des forces).
compensatoire [-satwa:r] adj. Compensatory, compensating.
compensé, ée [-se] adj. A semelles compensées, wedge-heeled (chaussures).
compenser v. tr. (1). To compensate for, to make up for; to offset; to counterbalance. ‖ TECHN. To balance, to compensate. ‖ FIN. To clear. ‖ NAUT. To balance. ‖ JUR. To balance, to set off; compenser les dépens, to order each party to pay its own costs.
— v. récipr. Se **compenser**, to balance; to neutralize each other (ou) one another.
compère [kɔ̃pɛr] m. ECCLÉS. Fellow sponsor. ‖ Confederate (d'un filou); associate (dans un tour); puffer (dans une vente). ‖ FAM. Crony; fellow; rusé compère, sly dog. ‖ **Compère-loriot**, m. MÉD. Stye (orgelet).
compétence [kɔ̃petɑ̃:s] f. Competence, ability, efficiency (v. CAPACITÉ). ‖ JUR. Ability, legal capacity, qualification (d'une personne); competence, powers, jurisdiction (d'un tribunal). ‖ FIG. Province, scope. (V. RAYON.)
compétent, ente [-tɑ̃, ɑ̃:t] adj. Competent, efficient (v. QUALIFIÉ); compétent en matière de, conversant with. ‖ JUR. Having jurisdiction (juge); competent; qualified (tribunal); la juridiction compétente, the court of competent jurisdiction.
compéter [-te] v. intr. (1). JUR. To come within the competency (à, of). ‖ FAM. To belong by right to.
compétiteur, trice [kɔ̃petitœ:r, tris] s. Competitor. (V. RIVAL.)
compétitif, ive [-tif, ti:v] adj. Competitive.
compétition [-sjɔ̃] f. Competition. (V. RIVALITÉ.) ‖ SPORT. Match, meeting.
compétitivité [-tivite] f. Competitiveness.
compilateur, trice [kɔ̃pilatœ:r, tris] s. Compiler.
compilation [-sjɔ̃] f. Compiling (action); compilation (texte).
compiler [kɔ̃pile] v. tr. (1). To compile.
complainte [kɔ̃plɛ̃:t] f. Plaintive ballad (ou) song. ‖ JUR. Complaint. ‖ FAM. Lament.
complaire [kɔ̃plɛ:r] v. intr. (75). Complaire à, to please, to gratify.
— v. pr. Se **complaire**, to delight (ou) to take pleasure (à, in).
complaisamment [kɔ̃plɛzamɑ̃] adv. Obligingly, complacently.
complaisance [-zɑ̃:s] f. Kindness (acte); accommodativeness (esprit accommodant); complaisance, willingness, obligingness (obligeance); par complaisance, out of kindness, obligingly. ‖ Complacency, complacence, self-flattery, self-satisfaction (vanité); avec complaisance, complacently. ‖ Pl. Compliances, servility. ‖ COMM. Billet de complaisance, accommodation bill; kite (fam.).
complaisant, ante [-zɑ̃, ɑ̃:t] adj. Accommodative (accommodant); kind (aimable); obliging (obligeant); un mari complaisant, a complaisant husband; une oreille complaisante, a sympathetic (ou) ready (ou) willing ear. ‖ Complacent, self-satisfied (content de soi). ‖ Servile.

complément [kɔ̃plemɑ̃] m. Complement.
complémentaire [-tɛ:r] adj. Complementary; pour renseignements complémentaires, for further information. ‖ Cours complémentaire, continuation classes.
complémentarité [-tarite] f. Complementarity.
complet, ète [kɔ̃plɛ, ɛt] adj. Complete, entire, whole (entier); full (plein); absolute, total, comprehensive (total). ‖ CULIN. Complete (aliment); whole-meal, U. S. whole-wheat (pain); café complet, coffee and rolls. ‖ AUTOM. Full up! (dans l'autobus). ‖ FAM. C'est complet!, that caps all! — m. Completeness; au grand complet, in full strength (ou) force (personnes); filled to capacity, having its full complement (véhicule). ‖ COMM. Suit of clothes; lounge suit (vêtement). ‖ **Complet-veston**, n. Lounge suit, U. S. business suit.
complètement [kɔ̃pletmɑ̃] adv. Completely; fully; thoroughly; complètement fou, stark raving mad; complètement ruiné, utterly ruined.
compléter [-te] v. tr. (5). To complete; to supplement; to make up (une somme).
— v. pr. Se **compléter**, to come together, to become complete (devenir complet). ‖ To complement each other, to match (s'accorder).
complétif, ive [-tif, i:v] adj. GRAMM. Subordinate; proposition complétive, object clause.
complexe [kɔ̃plɛks] adj. Complicated (affaire, situation); complex (caractère, phrase, quantité); compound (nombre, phrase); many-sided (question); intricate (problème); d'une manière complexe, complexly.
— m. MÉD., PHILOS. Complex; complexe d'Œdipe, d'infériorité, Œdipus, inferiority complex.
complexer [-se] v. tr. (1). FAM. To give complexes (ou) hang-ups to; être complexé, to have hang-ups.
complexion [-sjɔ̃] f. Constitution.
complexité [-site] f. Complexity.
complication [kɔ̃plikasjɔ̃] f. TECHN. Complexity (d'un mécanisme). ‖ MÉD. Complication. ‖ FIG. Complication (diplomatique); intricacy (d'un problème, d'une question). [V. ANICROCHE.]
complice [kɔ̃plis] m. Accomplice, confederate. ‖ JUR. Abettor, accomplice (de, of); accessory, party (de, to) [d'un délit]; co-respondent (en adultère).
— adj. Accessory, abetting; knowing (regard).
complicité [-site] f. Complicity; de complicité avec, in collusion with. ‖ JUR. Abetment, aiding and abetting.
complies [kɔ̃pli] f. pl. ECCLÉS. Compline, complin.
compliment [kɔ̃plimɑ̃] m. Compliment; débiter son compliment, to say one's party piece; réciter un compliment, to pay a well-prepared compliment. ‖ Congratulation; faire des compliments à, to congratulate; sans compliment, without flattery. ‖ Pl. Regards, compliments.
complimenter [-te] v. tr. (1). To compliment, to congratulate (sur, on).
complimenteur, euse [-tœ:r, ø:z] adj. Complimentary.
— m. Flatterer; toady; eulogist.
compliqué, ée [kɔ̃plike] adj. Complicated (affaire, situation); intricate (affaire, question); complex (caractère); involved (style). ‖ MÉD. Compound (fracture).
compliquer v. tr. (1). To complicate.
— Se **compliquer**, to become complicated (ou) intricate. ‖ MÉD. La maladie se complique, complications are setting in.
complot [kɔ̃plo] m. Plot (v. CONJURATION, CONSPIRATION); complot contre la sûreté de l'Etat, treason-felony.
comploter [-te] v. tr. (1). To plot, to scheme. (V. MACHINER.) ‖ FAM. To be up to (qqch.).

comploteur [-tœ:r] m. Plotter. (V. CONSPIRA-TEUR.) ‖ FAM. Schemer.

complu, ue [kɔ̃ply] p.p. V. COMPLAIRE.

componction [kɔ̃pɔ̃ksjɔ̃] f. ECCLÉS. Compunction. ‖ FAM. Gravity.

comporte [kɔ̃pɔrt] f. AGRIC. Tub ; cowl.

comportement [kɔ̃pɔrtmɑ̃] m. Comportment, behaviour. (V. ATTITUDE.)

comporter [-te] v. tr. (1). To allow, to admit of (admettre) ; to involve, to entail, to bring about, to occasion (entraîner) ; to require, to demand, to imply (impliquer) ; to comprise, to include (inclure).
— v. pr. Se **comporter**, to behave, to bear oneself (v. CONDUIRE [SE]) ; se comporter mal, to misbehave. ‖ To act (vis-à-vis de, envers, towards). ‖ To stand, to look (se présenter).

composant, ante [kɔ̃pɔzɑ̃, ɑ̃:t] adj., s. Component.

composé, ée [-ze] adj. Compound ; compacted (de, of). ‖ CHIM. Compound. ‖ TECHN. Compound (mouvement); built-up (poutre) ; combined (résistance). ‖ MATH. Compound (intérêts). ‖ BOT. Composite (fleur, fruit). ‖ MUS. Mesure composée, compound time. ‖ GRAMM. Compound (mot, temps). ‖ FIG. Impassive, stiff (attitude).
— m. CHIM. Compound. ‖ FIG. Composition.

composée f. BOT. Composite.

composer [-ze] v. tr. (1). To compose, to constitute (former). ‖ To compose, to make up (de, of). ‖ To set (une ligne d'impression); to dial (un numéro téléphonique). ‖ To compose, to write, to indite (écrire). ‖ ARTS, MUS. To compose. ‖ CHIM. To compound (de, of). ‖ THÉÂTR. To personate (un rôle). ‖ FIG. To compose ; composer son visage, to compose one's countenance.
— v. intr. To compound, to compromise, to come to terms, to make a composition (avec, with). [V. TRANSIGER.] ‖ To write an examination paper (en classe). ‖ MUS. To compose.
— v. pr. Se **composer**, to be composed (ou) compounded (de, of). ‖ To assume (une attitude).

composite [-zit] adj. ARCHIT., FIG. Composite.
— m. ARCHIT. Composite order.

compositeur, trice [kɔ̃pɔzitœ:r, tris] s. MUS. composer. ‖ Type-setter, compositor (en typogr.). ‖ JUR. Arbitrator.

composition [-sjɔ̃] f. Composition, constitution (action) ; composition, compound, mixture (résultat). ‖ Type-setting, composition (en typogr.). ‖ Composition, essay, U. S. theme (en classe) ; examination paper (à l'examen). ‖ ARTS, TECHN. Composition; composition radiophonique, feature programme. ‖ THÉÂTR. Rôle de composition, character part. ‖ FIG. Composition, terms (v. COMPROMIS) ; amener, venir à composition, to bring, to come to terms ; entrer en composition avec, to enter into a composition with.

compost [kɔ̃pɔst] m. AGRIC. Compost.

compostage [-ta:ʒ] m. Dating, stamping (de feuillets) ; punching (d'un ticket).

composter [-te] v. tr. (1). AGRIC. To compost.

composter v. tr. (1). To date, to stamp (des feuillets) ; to punch (un ticket).

composteur [-tœr] m. Dater, dating stamp (à dater). ‖ Setting-stick, composing-stick (en typogr.).

compote [kɔ̃pɔt] f. CULIN. Compote (de fruits); compote de pommes, stewed apples, apple sauce. ‖ FAM. En compote, crushed to pulp.

compotier [-tje] m. Fruit-dish (ou) -stand.

compound [kɔ̃pund] adj., f. TECHN., ELECTR. Compound.

compréhensibilité [kɔ̃preɑ̃sibilite] f. Comprehensibility.

compréhensible [-sibl] adj. Comprehensible, understandable (v. INTELLIGIBLE).

compréhensif, ive [-sif, i:v] adj. Understanding.

compréhension [-sjɔ̃] f. Comprehension, under-standing (entendement). ‖ Apprehension, realization, grasp (d'une idée). ‖ PHILOS. Connotation.

comprendre [kɔ̃prɑ̃dr] v. tr. (80). To compre-hend, to comprise, to cover (v. INCLURE). ‖ To understand, to make out, to grasp, to catch, to make sense of (v. SAISIR) ; à n'y rien comprendre, beyond understanding ; je comprends!, I see!, I think so! ; je n'y comprends rien, I can't under-stand it ; il comprend la plaisanterie, he enters into the joke ; faire comprendre à qqn que, to make it clear to s.o. that ; faire comprendre qqch., to hint at sth. (suggérer); se faire comprendre, to make oneself clear. ‖ To admit (une attitude) ; je le comprends!, I don't blame him.
— v. pr. Se **comprendre**, to be understood (idée) ; ça se comprend, of course ; ça ne se comprend pas, there is no accounting for it.
— v. récipr. Se **comprendre**, to understand each other (personnes).

comprenette [kɔ̃prənɛt] f. FAM. Uptake ; avoir la comprenette lente, to be slow on the uptake.

compresse [kɔ̃pres] f. MÉD. Compress.

compresser [-se] v. tr. (1). FAM. To pack.

compresseur [-sœ:r] adj. Compressing; rouleau compresseur, steam- (ou) road-roller.
— m. TECHN. Compressor ; blower. ‖ AUTOM. Supercharger.

compressibilité [-sibilite] f. Compressibility.

compressible [-sibl] adj. Compressible.

compressif, ive [-sif, i:v] adj. Compressive. ‖ FIG. Restrictive (mesure).

compression [-sjɔ̃] f. Compression, crushing ; squeezing. ‖ FIN. Reduction (des dépenses). ‖ AUTOM. Compression. ‖ FIG. Repression, con-straint ; restriction.

comprimable [kɔ̃primabl] adj. Compressible.

comprimé, ée [-me] adj. TECHN. Compressed.
— m. MÉD. Tablet, tabloid, lozenge.

comprimer v. tr. (1). To compress. ‖ FIN. To cut down (les dépenses). ‖ FIG. To restrain, to check, to curb (ses passions).

compris [kɔ̃pri] adj. Non compris, exclusive of, not included (ou) counted ; jusques et y compris, up to and including ; tout compris, all inclusive, all in ; prix tout compris, inclusive terms.

compromettant, ante [kɔ̃prɔmɛtɑ̃, ɑ̃:t] adj. Compromising.

compromettre [-mɛtr] v. tr. (64). To impair (l'autorité); to compromise (qqn, sa réputation). ‖ To jeopardize, to endanger, to imperil. (V. EXPO-SER.) ‖ To implicate, to involve, to mix up (impli-quer). ‖ MÉD. To impair (sa santé).
— v. pr. Se **compromettre**, to compromise one-self. ‖ To commit oneself ; ne pas se compro-mettre, U. S. to pussyfoot.

compromis, ise [-mi, iz] adj. Implicated, involved, mixed up (dans, in). ‖ Jeopardized (affaires, hon-neur); impaired (autorité, fortune, santé) ; imper-illed (espérances, réputation).
— m. Compromise. (V. ARRANGEMENT, COMPOSI-TION.) ‖ Compromis d'arbitrage, compromise.

compromission [-misjɔ̃] f. Compromising with conscience.

comptabilisation [kɔ̃tabilizasjɔ̃] f. FIN. Enter-ing into the books, posting.

comptabiliser [kɔ̃tabilize] v. tr. (1). FIN. To enter into the books.

comptabilité [-te] f. FIN. Accounts (comptes); accountant's department, U. S. counting room (bureau) ; accountancy, accountantship (profes-sion); book-keeping, U. S. accountability (tenue des livres) ; comptabilité en partie double, simple, double-, single-entry book-keeping ; comptabilité publique, public accountancy ; tenir la compta-bilité de, to keep the books of. ‖ **Comptabilité-**

deniers, f. Fɪɴ. Book-keeping for funds. ‖
Comptabilité-matières, f. Fɪɴ. Book-keeping for property.

comptable [kɔ̃tabl] adj. Fɪɴ. Relating to book-keeping; *pièce comptable,* voucher. ‖ Accountable (d'une dette) [*de,* for; *envers,* to]. ‖ Fɪɢ. Responsible, accountable (*de,* for; *envers,* to).
— m. Cᴏᴍᴍ. Accountant, book-keeper.

comptage [kɔ̃ta:ʒ] m. Counting.

comptant, ante [kɔ̃tɑ̃, ɑ̃:t] adj. Ready, spot.
— adv. Cash; *payer comptant,* to pay cash.
— m. Cash, ready money; *au comptant,* cash down; *paiement au comptant,* cash payment.

compte [kɔ̃t] m. Count, reckoning (calcul); *erreur n'est pas compte,* mistakes don't count; *faire le compte de,* to reckon up, to add up, to tot up; *faire un compte rond,* to make a round sum; *inclure dans un compte,* to count in; *se tromper dans ses comptes,* to be out in one's reckoning. ‖ Charge, expense (charge); *à mon compte,* chargeable to me. ‖ Accounts (comptabilité); *arrêter un compte,* to strike a balance; *comptes matières,* property accounts; *faire ses comptes,* to make up (ou) to cast up one's accounts. ‖ Due (dû); *avoir son compte,* to get one's due. ‖ Advantage, account, profit (intérêt, profit); *de compte à demi,* on joint account; *pour le compte de qqn,* on s.o.'s account (ou) behalf; *trouver son compte à,* to profit by, to find it to one's advantage. ‖ Cᴏᴍᴍ. Account; bill (facture); *à bon compte,* cheap, at small cost; *donner son compte à,* to pay off (renvoyer); *être en compte,* to have an account running; *laisser pour compte,* to leave on the seller's hands; *pour solde de tout compte,* for full settlement; *s'établir à son compte,* to set up on one's own account (ou) for oneself; *suivant compte remis,* as per account rendered. ‖ Fɪɴ. Account (en banque); *compte de frais,* bill of costs; *porter au compte créditeur de qqn,* to place to s.o.'s credit; *porter au compte débiteur de qqn,* to charge to s.o.'s account. ‖ Sᴘᴏʀᴛs. *Aller à terre pour le compte,* to be counted out. ‖ Fɪɢ. *Au bout du compte,* when all is said and done; *avoir un compte à régler avec,* to have an old score to pay off with; *avoir son compte,* to be done for (être épuisé); to be plastered (être ivre); *il a son compte,* he's had it; *demander à qqn compte de,* to call on s.o. to account for; *en fin de compte,* all told; *en ligne de compte,* into account (ou) consideration; *être quitte à bon compte,* to get off lightly; *faire le compte de,* to suit (convenir à); *faire son compte,* to manage; *faire rendre compte,* to call to account; *jour du règlement de comptes,* day of reckoning; *loin de compte,* wide of the mark; *mettre sur le compte de,* to impute (ou) attribute (ou) ascribe to; *n'avoir pas de compte à rendre à,* not to be accountable to; *ne pas entrer en ligne de compte,* to have nothing to do with; *ne pas tenir compte de,* to disregard, to ignore, to take no notice of; *régler son compte à qqn,* to cook s.o.'s goose, to settle s.o.'s hash; *rendre compte de,* to account for (ses actes); to review (un livre); to report (un rapport). ‖ **Compte(-)chèques, m.** Fɪɴ. Current account, U.S. checking account. ‖ **Compte-fils,** m. invar. Linen-prover. ‖ **Compte-gouttes,** m. invar. Drip-feed lubricator (en mécanique); dropper (en pharmacie); filler (pour stylo); *au compte-gouttes,* in driblets. ‖ **Compte-tours,** m. invar. Tᴇᴄʜɴ. Revolution counter, tachometer. ‖ **Compte(-)rendu,** m. Transactions (de congrès); review (de livre); report (de mission, de renseignements); *compte-rendu de lecture,* precis writing; *donner le compte-rendu de,* to give an account of; *faire le compte-rendu de,* to review (un livre, une pièce); to report upon (une mission, une séance).

compter [kɔ̃te] v. tr. (1). To reckon, to count, to compute, to calculate (calculer); *à pas comptés,* with measured steps; *compter jusqu'à mille,* to count up to a thousand; *mal compter,* to miscount, to misreckon; *tout compté,* all told. ‖ To number, to count, to reckon (dénombrer); *compter les jours,* to count the days; *en la comptant,* including her; *ne pas compter d'ennemis,* to be no one's enemy; *ne pas compter qqn,* to leave s.o. out of account; *ne plus se compter,* to be innumerable; *sans la compter,* besides her, without counting her; *ses jours sont comptés,* his days are numbered. ‖ To charge (facturer); *compter qqch. trop cher,* to overcharge for sth.; *il me l'a compté cinquante francs,* he charged me fifty francs for it. ‖ To count (figurer); *compter au nombre de, parmi,* to count (ou) to number among. ‖ To count out, to pay (payer); *compter trois cents francs à qqn,* to pay s.o. three hundred francs. ‖ To expect, to hope, to count on, to think of, to intend to (espérer, se proposer de); *compter faire qqch.,* to expect to do sth.; *je comptais qu'il viendrait,* I expected him to come; *il compte venir demain,* he intends to come (ou) coming tomorrow. ‖ To consider, to regard (estimer); *compter comme,* to count as; *compter pour rien,* to take little account of; *compter sa vie pour rien,* to hold one's life of no account. ‖ To count, to mention (mentionner); *sans compter,* to say nothing of, exclusive of, not counting; *sans compter que,* besides the fact that, without mentioning that.
— v. intr. To count, to reckon (v. ᴄᴀʟᴄᴜʟᴇʀ); *à compter de,* reckoning from; *donner sans compter,* to give generously; *dépenser sans compter,* to spend one's money unsparingly. ‖ To count (dater); *à compter de demain,* counting from tomorrow. ‖ Fɪɢ. To rely, to depend (avoir confiance); *comptez sur moi,* rely on me; *puis-je y compter?,* may I depend upon it? ‖ To be counted (être considéré); *ça ne compte pas,* that doesn't count, that goes for nothing; *n'être compté pour rien,* to stand for nothing. ‖ Fɪɢ. To reckon (prendre garde); *compter avec,* to reckon with, to take into consideration.

compteur [kɔ̃tœ:r] m. Counter, checker. ‖ Tᴇᴄʜɴ. Meter; *compteur à eau, à électricité, à gaz,* water, gas, electric-light meter. ‖ Aᴜᴛᴏᴍ. *Compteur kilométrique,* cyclometer; *compteur de taxi,* trip-recorder; *compteur de vitesse,* speedometer. ‖ Nᴀᴜᴛ. Deck chronometer; hack-watch.

comptine [-tin] f. Nursery rhyme, counting-out rhyme.

comptoir [kɔ̃twa:r] m. Cᴏᴍᴍ. Agency, factory (agence); counter (meuble); bar (de café); department (de grand magasin). ‖ Fɪɴ. Bank (banque); branch (succursale); *comptoir d'escompte,* discount bank.

compulser [kɔ̃pylse] v. tr. (1). To examine, to go through, to look into.

compulsif, ive [kɔ̃pylsif, i:v] adj. Psʏᴄʜ. Compulsive.

compulsion [-sjɔ̃] f. Psʏᴄʜ. Compulsion.

comput [kɔ̃pyt] m. Eᴄᴄʟᴇ́s. Computation.

computer [-te] v. tr. (1). To compute.

comtal [kɔ̃tal] adj. Pertaining to a count.

comte [kɔ̃t] m. Earl (en Angleterre); count.

comté [kɔ̃te] m. Gᴇ́ᴏɢʀ. County, shire.

comtesse [kɔ̃tɛs] f. Countess.

comtois [kɔ̃twa] adj. Of Franche-Comté.

comtoise [kɔ̃twa:z] f. Grandfather clock.

con [kɔ̃] m. Aʀɢᴏᴛ. Twerp; U. S. juk.

concassage [kɔ̃kasa:ʒ] m. Crushing (des céréales); breaking (des pierres); grinding (du poivre).

concasser [kɔ̃kɑse] v. tr. (1). To crush (des

céréales); to break (des pierres); to grind (du poivre); *sucre concassé,* nub (ou) crushed sugar.
concasseur [-sœ:r] m. TECHN. Crusher, breaker; disintegrator.
concaténation [kɔkatenasjɔ̃] f. GRAMM. Concatenation.
concave [kɔka:v] adj. Concave.
concavité [kɔkavite] f. Concavity.
concéder [kɔsede] v. tr. (5). To concede, to cede (un droit, un privilège). ‖ To grant (un point).
concentration [kɔsɑ̃trasjɔ̃] f. Concentration; *camp, point de concentration,* concentration camp, point.
concentrationnaire [sjɔnɛ:r] adj. Of concentration camps.
concentré, ée [kɔsɑ̃tre] adj. CHIM. Concentrated. ‖ FIG. Absorbed (absorbé); uncommunicative (renfermé). ‖ *Lait concentré,* condensed milk.
— m. CULIN. Concentrate; *concentré de viande,* meat extract.
concentrer v. tr. (1). CHIM., MILIT. To concentrate. ‖ To concentrate (son attention); to contain (sa colère); to concentrate, to centre (ses efforts); to focus (l'observation, les rayons, les sons).
— v. pr. Se **concentrer,** to be concentrated, to concentrate. ‖ ‖ FIG. To focus (attention, observation, rayons, sons); to concentrate, to centre (efforts); to concentrate (personne); *se concentrer autour, sur,* to centre round, in (ou) on.
concentrique [-trik] adj. Concentric.
concept [kɔsɛpt] m. PHILOS. Concept.
concepteur, trice [-tœ:r, tris] s. Copy-writer (en publicité).
conceptif, ive [-tif, i:v] adj. PHILOS. Conceptive.
conception [-sjɔ̃] f. MÉD. Conception. ‖ FIG. Conception, comprehension (faculté); idea, notion (idée). ‖ FAM. *C'est une conception,* that's one way of looking at it, it's a point of view.
conceptualisation [-tɥalizasjɔ̃] f. Conceptualization.
conceptualiser [-tɥalize] v. tr. (1). To conceptualize.
conceptuel, elle [-tɥɛl] adj. PHILOS. Conceptual.
concernant [kɔsɛrnɑ̃] prép. Concerning, regarding; about; with regard (ou) respect to; relating to; dealing with.
concerner [-ne] v. tr. (1). To affect (les intérêts); to interest, to concern (qqn); *en ce qui concerne,* with regard (ou) respect to, concerning; *en ce qui me concerne,* as for me, for my part, as far as I am concerned.
concert [kɔsɛ:r] m. MUS. Concert; *concert spirituel,* sacred concert; *salle de concert,* concert-hall (ou) -room. ‖ FIG. Concert, concord, harmony (entente); chorus (de louanges). ‖ LOC. *De concert avec,* in agreement with.
concertant, ante [-tɑ̃, ɑ̃:t] adj. MUS. Concertante (partie); concerted (symphonie).
concertation [-tasjɔ̃] f. Dialogue, concerted policy.
concerté, ée [-te] adj. Concerted (action); studied (manière).
concerter v. tr. (1). To concert, to devise.
— v. pr. Se **concerter,** to concert (ou) work together; tò take counsel together; to connive. ‖ To discuss the matter (*avec,* with).
concertina [-tina] f. MUS. Concertina.
concertino [-tino] m. MUS. Concertino.
concertiste [-tist] s. MUS. Concert performer.
concerto [-to] m. MUS. Concerto.
concesseur [kɔsɛsœ:r] m. JUR. Grantor.
concessible [-sibl] adj. JUR. Concessible.
concessif, ive [-sif, i:v] adj. GRAMM. *Proposition concessive,* concessive clause.
concession [-sjɔ̃] f. Plot (terrain); *concession à perpétuité,* grant in perpetuity. ‖ JUR. Concession, grant. ‖ FIG. Concession; *faire des concessions à,*

to make concessions to; *faire des concessions de principe,* to make a surrender of principle.
concessionnaire [-sjɔnɛ:r] adj. Concessionary.
— m. JUR. Grantee, licence-holder, patentee; concessionaire, U. S. concessionary.
concetti [kɔsetti] m. pl. Conceits, concetti.
concevable [kɔsvabl] adj. Conceivable.
concevoir [kɔsəvwa:r] v. tr. (3). MÉD. To conceive. ‖ FIG. To conceive (de l'amitié, de l'amour, un dessein, une espérance, un projet); to form (des doutes, une idée); to realize (un fait); to devise (un moyen); to view (une question). ‖ To imagine, to conceive (l'éternité, l'infini). ‖ To express; *ainsi conçu,* worded (ou) conceived as follows; *être ainsi conçu,* to read as follows, to run in these words.
conchoïde [kɔkɔid] f. MATH. Conchoid.
conchyliologie [kɔkiljɔlɔʒi] f. ZOOL. Conchology.
concierge [kɔsjɛ:rʒ] s. House-porter, door-keeper, caretaker, U. S. janitor. ‖ Concierge (en France). ‖ Lodge-keeper (de château); keeper (de prison).
conciergerie [-ʒəri] f. Porter's lodge (loge). ‖ Conciergerie (prison).
concile [kɔsil] m. ECCLÉS. Council.
conciliable [-ljabl] adj. Reconcilable.
conciliabule [-ljabyl] m. Confabulation (entretien). ‖ Secret meeting (assemblée). ‖ ECCLÉS. Conciliabule.
conciliaire [-ljɛ:r] adj. Conciliar.
conciliant, ante [-ljɑ̃, ɑ̃:t] adj. Conciliating, conciliatory, conciliative.
conciliateur, trice [-ljatœ:r, tris] adj. Conciliatory.
— s. Conciliator, peace-maker, appeaser.
conciliation [-ljasjɔ̃] f. Conciliation; *de conciliation,* conciliatory (esprit); appeasement (politique). ‖ JUR. Conciliation, friendly settlement (de deux personnes); reconciliation (de deux textes).
conciliatoire [-ljatwa:r] adj. Conciliatory, conciliative.
concilier [-lje] v. tr. (1). To reconcile, to conciliate (des adversaires, des intérêts opposés, des textes); to adjust, to settle (un différend); to reconcile (des théories). ‖ To conciliate, to win (la bienveillance, la confiance).
— v. pr. Se **concilier,** to come into agreement; *se concilier avec,* to agree with, to chime in with, to fit in with. ‖ To gain (la sympathie); *se concilier la faveur de,* to ingratiate oneself with; *se concilier qqn,* to gain s.o.'s goodwill.
concis, e [kɔsi, i:z] adj. Concise (écrivain); brief, short (récit); concise, succinct (style).
concision [-zjɔ̃] f. Concision, conciseness (v. BRIÈVETÉ); succinctness; terseness; *avec concision,* concisely, tersely.
concitoyen [kɔsitwajɛ̃] s. Fellow-citizen.
conclave [kɔklav] m. ECCLÉS. Conclave.
concluant, ante [kɔklyɑ̃, ɑ̃:t] adj. Conclusive.
conclure [kɔkly:r] v. tr. (29). To come to (un accord); to conclude (une affaire, la paix, un traité, to close (un marché). ‖ To wind up (les débats, un discours); to conclude, to end (un discours, un ouvrage); to close (une série). ‖ To conclude, to deduce, to infer (déduire); *en conclure que,* to infer therefrom that, to conclude from this that. ‖ JUR. *Son avocat a conclu que,* his counsel moved that.
— v. intr. To conclude, to end (achever). ‖ To conclude (décider); *conclure à,* to conclude in favour of, to decide upon. ‖ To conclude, to come to the conclusion, to draw an inference (inférer); to infer (de, from).
conclusif, ive [kɔklyzif, i:v] adj. Conclusive.
conclusion [-zjɔ̃] f. Conclusion, decision. ‖ Conclusion, settlement (établissement). ‖ Conclusion,

close (fin). ‖ Conclusion, inference (déduction); *tirer la conclusion*, to draw the conclusion; *tirer une conclusion*, to draw an inference. ‖ JUR. Findings (du jury); opinion (du ministère public); *déposer des conclusions*, to deliver a statement.

concocter [kɔkɔkte] v. tr. (1). FAM. To concoct, to brew up, to hatch.

concombre [kɔkɔ̃br] m. BOT. Cucumber.

concomitance [kɔkɔmitɑ̃:s] f. Concomitance.

concomitant, ante [-tɑ̃, ɑ̃:t] adj. Concomitant (*de*, with).

concordance [kɔkɔrdɑ̃:s] f. Concordance; correspondence (*avec*, with; *entre*, between). ‖ JUR. *Concordance des témoignages*, agreement of evidence. ‖ ECCLÉS. Concordance (de la Bible). ‖ GRAMM. Sequence (des temps).

concordant, ante [-dɑ̃, ɑ̃:t] adj. Concordant, agreeing, corroborative.

concordat [-dɑ] m. ECCLÉS. Concordat. ‖ COMM. Bankrupt's certificate; *accorder un concordat*, to certificate.

concordataire [-datɛ:r] adj. COMM., JUR. Certificated.

concorde [kɔkɔrd] f. Concord.

concorder [-de] v. intr. (1). To agree, to tally (*avec*, with).

concourant, ante [kɔkurɑ̃, ɑ̃:t] adj. MATH. Converging, concurrent.

concourir [kɔkuri:r] v. intr. (32). To cooperate, to concur (v. CONTRIBUER); *tout concourt à prouver*, everything combines to prove. ‖ To compete (*avec*, with; *pour*, for). ‖ PHYS., MATH. To converge.

concours [kɔku:r] m. Concourse, gathering (de personnes). ‖ Concurrence, conjunction, combination, concatenation (de circonstances). ‖ Co-operation, assistance, instrumentality (assistance); *avec le concours de*, with the assistance of, assisted by; *prêter son concours*, to give assistance, to lend one's aid. ‖ Competitive examination, competition (examen); *concours d'admission*, entrance examination. ‖ Show (exposition, parade); *concours agricole, hippique*, agricultural, horse show; *concours d'élégance*, rally. ‖ MILIT. *Concours de tir*, rifle match. ‖ AVIAT. *Concours d'aviation*, aviation contest, flying-show. ‖ MATH., PHYS. Convergence.

concret, ète [kɔkrɛ, ɛt] adj. Actual (cas); concrete (nombre, terme); concrete, solid (substance).

concrètement [kɔkrɛtmɑ̃] adv. In practice, in reality, concretely.

concréter [kɔkrete] v. tr. (5). To concrete.

concrétion [-sjɔ] f. Concretion, concrescence (action); concretion, concrete mass (amas).

concrétisation [-tizasjɔ] f. Idea (ou) principle put in a concrete form.

concrétiser [-tize] v. tr. (1). To put in concrete form, U. S. to concretize.
— v. pr. Se **concrétiser**, to materialize; *se concrétiser par*, to result in, to bring about in practice.

concubin, ine [kɔkybɛ̃, in] adj. Concubinary.

concubinage [kɔkybina:ʒ] m. Concubinage; *vivre en concubinage*, to live as husband and wife, to live together.

concubinaire [-nɛ:r] s. Concubinary.

concubine [kɔkybin] f. Concubine.

concupiscence [kɔkypisɑ̃:s] f. Concupiscence.

concupiscent, ente [-sɑ̃, ɑ̃:t] adj. Concupiscent.

concurremment [kɔkyramɑ̃] adv. Competitively (en compétition); concurrently (en conjonction) [*avec*, with].

concurrence [-rɑ̃:s] f. Competition [*avec*, with]. (V. RIVALITÉ.) ‖ COMM. Competition; *faire concurrence à*, to compete with; *jusqu'à concur-*

rence de , up to, to the amount of, not exceeding. ‖ JUR. Equality of rights (entre créanciers).

concurrencer [-rɑse] v. tr. (6). To compete with.

concurrent, ente [-rɑ̃, ɑ̃:t] adj. Rival, competing, competitive (maisons). ‖ Co-operative (actions).
— s. Competitor; *les concurrents*, the candidates.

concurrente [-rɑ̃:t] f. Competitress; candidate.

concurrentiel, elle [-rɑ̃sjɛl] adj. Competitive.

concussion [kɔkysjɔ] f. Peculation.

concussionnaire [-sjɔnɛ:r] adj. Guilty of extortion.
— m. Extortioner, peculator.

condamnable [kɔdanabl] adj. Condemnable.

condamnation [-nasjɔ] f. JUR. Condemnation; sentence; *condamnation à mort*, sentence of death; *prononcer une condamnation*, to sentence, to pass judgment; *subir une condamnation*, to serve a prison sentence. ‖ ARCHIT. Blocking up, sealing off (d'une fenêtre, d'une porte). ‖ FIG. Blame, censure (blâme); condemnation.

condamnatoire [-natwa:r] adj. Condemnatory.

condamné, ée [-ne] adj. JUR. Condemned, sentenced (personne). ‖ FIG. Doomed; fated (à, to). ‖ FAM. Out-of-repair, unfit for service, out of order (objet).
— s. JUR. Condemned person; convict.

condamner v. tr. (1). JUR. To convict, to sentence, to pass judgment on, to pronounce guilty; *condamné aux dépens*, ordered to pay costs. ‖ To block up, to close up (une fenêtre, une porte); *condamner sa porte*, to be « not at home » to visitors. ‖ MÉD. To give up (un malade). ‖ FIG. To condemn, to doom (astreindre); to condemn, to censure, to blame (blâmer); to proscribe (prohiber).

condé [kɔde] m. ARG. Plain clothes man.

condensable [kɔdɑ̃sabl] adj. Condensable.

condensateur, trice [-tœ:r, tris] adj. Condensing.
— m. Condenser.

condensation [-sjɔ] f. Condensation.

condensé, ée [-se] adj. Condensed (lait).
— m. Digest.

condenser v. tr. (1). To condense.
— v. pr. Se **condenser**, to condense.

condenseur [-sœ:r] m. TECHN., PHYS. Condenser.

condescendance [kɔdɛsɑdɑ̃:s] f. Condescension.

condescendant, ante [-sɑdɑ̃, ɑ̃:t] adj. Condescending.

condescendre [-sɑ̃:dr] v. intr. (4). To condescend (à, to) [s'abaisser]. ‖ To comply (à, with) [consentir].

condiment [kɔdimɑ̃] m. CULIN. Condiment. (V. ASSAISONNEMENT.) ‖ FIG. Spice.

condisciple [kɔdisipl] m. Schoolmate, classmate, fellow-student.

condition [kɔdisjɔ] f. Condition (base essentielle, qualité); *conditions requises*, requirements, requisites, essentials, qualifications; *répondant aux conditions requises*, eligible (candidat). ‖ Condition, case, circumstance (circonstances); *conditions de travail*, working conditions; *dans ces conditions*, under these circumstances. ‖ Condition, stipulation (clause); *à condition de* (ou) *que*, on condition that, providing that; *sans condition*, unconditionally; *sous condition*, conditionally. ‖ Condition, state (état); *en bonne condition*, in good condition (ou) fettle. ‖ Condition, class, rank, position, station (v. RANG); *de condition modeste*, in humble circumstances; *personne de condition*, person of quality. ‖ COMM. Terms (tarif); *acheter à condition*, to buy on approval (ou) on sale or return; *aux conditions que vous fixerez vous-même*, on your own terms; *faire ses conditions*, to make (ou) name one's own terms. ‖ † Service (chez, with).

conditionné, ée [-ne] adj. Made (fabriqué). ‖ PHILOS., MÉD. Conditioned.

conditionnel, elle [-nɛl] adj., m. Conditional.

conditionnement [-nmã] m. Conditioning (de l'air, du blé, de la laine). ‖ COMM. Wrapping (emballage).

conditionner [-ne] v. tr. (1). To condition (la température, les textiles). ‖ COMM. To wrap up. ‖ JUR., FAM. To condition.

conditionneur [-nœ:r] m. Conditioner; *conditionneur d'air,* air-conditioner.

condoléances [kɔ̃dɔleã:s] f. pl. Condolence; *mes sincères condoléances,* my deepest sympathy.

condominium [kɔ̃dɔminjɔm] m. Condominium.

condor [kɔ̃dɔr] m. ZOOL. Condor.

condottiere [kɔ̃dɔtjɛ:re] m. Condottiere.

conductance [kɔ̃dyktã:s] f. ELECTR. Conductance.

conducteur, trice [-tœ:r, tris] adj. Driving. ‖ ELECTR. Conductive; *bon conducteur,* conducting; *mauvais conducteur,* non-conducting. ‖ FIG. Guiding; *fil conducteur,* clue.
— s. Driver, drover (de bestiaux); leader (d'hommes); driver (de véhicule); conductor (de visiteurs). ‖ TECHN. Clerk (de travaux). ‖ CH. DE F. Guard (de train). ‖ AUTOM. Driver. ‖ ELECTR. Conductor, lead, main.

conductibilité [-tibilite] f. PHYS. Conductibility.

conductible [-tibl] adj. PHYS. Conductible.

conduction [-sjɔ̃] f. PHYS., ELECTR. Conduction; *de conduction,* conductive. ‖ JUR. Renting.

conductivité [-tivite] f. ELECTR. Conductivity, specific conductance.

conduire [kɔ̃dɥi:r] v. tr. (85). To accompany (accompagner); to conduct, to guide (guider); to show in (ou) into (introduire); to lead, to take (mener); to drive, to carry (transporter); to lead, to bring (à, to); *conduire qqn à la gare, à la porte,* to see s.o. off, out; *conduire en prison,* to march off to gaol (ou) U. S. jail. ‖ To lead (une armée, un cheval par la bride, un chien en laisse); to drive (un cheval attelé, un troupeau, un véhicule); to ride (un cheval de selle); to wheel (une voiture d'infirme). ‖ NAUT. To row, to steer, to sail, to manage (un bateau). ‖ MUS. To conduct (un orchestre). ‖ ELECTR. To conduct. ‖ TECHN. To convey. ‖ FIG. To manage (une affaire, un commerce); to conduct (des opérations, des pourparlers); *conduire qqn à penser que,* to lead s o. to think that; *conduire qqn à sa perte,* to bring s.o. to his ruin.
— v. intr. To lead (chemin); to drive (conducteur). ‖ FIG. To lead, to conduce (à, to) [un résultat].
— v. pr. **Se conduire,** to find one's way (se diriger). ‖ FIG. To behave, to conduct oneself (v. SE COMPORTER); *se mal conduire,* to misbehave, to misdemean oneself. ‖ FIG. To look after oneself, to take care of oneself (se suffire).

conduit [kɔ̃dɥi] p.p. V. CONDUIRE.

conduit m. TECHN. Conduit, pipe, channel; *conduit à air,* air passage (ou) duct, ventilation shaft; *conduit à gaz,* gas pipe; *conduit d'alimentation,* feed pipe, feeder. ‖ MÉD. Canal, duct.

conduite [kɔ̃dɥit] f. Conduct, guidance; *sous la conduite de,* under the guidance of, escorted by. ‖ Send-off (de qqn qui part). ‖ Direction, control, management, work (d'une affaire, d'une maison); treatment, conduct (d'un ouvrage, d'une pièce); superintendence (des travaux); driving (d'un véhicule). ‖ AUTOM. Drive; *conduite à droite,* right-hand drive; *conduite intérieure,* saloon (ou) closed car; U. S. sedan. ‖ MILIT. Conduct (de la guerre); command (des troupes). ‖ AVIAT. *Conduite intérieure,* enclosed cockpit, closed cabin. ‖ NAUT. Sailing (d'un bateau). ‖

TECHN. Pipe, piping, main; *conduite d'eau,* water-main; *conduite montante,* rising main. ‖ FIG. Behaviour, conduct; *changer de conduite,* to mend one's ways, to turn over a new leaf; *mauvaise conduite,* misbehaviour, misdemeanour.

condyle [kɔ̃dil] m. MÉD. Condyle.

cône [ko:n] m. MATH. Cone. ‖ GÉOL., BOT., ASTRON. Cone; *cône lumineux,* cone of light. ‖ MILIT. *Cône d'éclatement,* cone of dispersion. ‖ NAUT. Storm cone (ou) signal. ‖ TECHN. Cone, cone pulley; *en forme de cône,* cone-shaped.

confection [kɔ̃fɛksjɔ̃] f. Mixing (d'un cocktail); drawing up (d'une liste); elaboration (d'un livre); making, making up (d'un plat, d'un vêtement); manufacturing (de vêtements); *de ma confection,* of my own making. ‖ COMM. Ready-made clothes (habits); ready-made shop (magasin); ready-made department (rayon); *de confection,* ready-made, ready-to-wear.

confectionner [-sjɔne] v. tr. (1). To make; to make up.

confectionneur [-sjɔnœ:r] m. COMM. Ready-made outfitter; clothier.

confédératif [kɔ̃federatif] adj. Confederative.

confédération [-rasjɔ̃] f. Confederation (action, nations); confederacy (ligue, nations); *Confédération Générale du Travail* (C. G. T.), Trades Union Congress. (V. CÉGÉTISTE.)

confédéré, ée [-re] adj. Confederate (nations). ‖ Associated (personnes); *non confédéré,* non-affiliated (syndicat).
— m. Confederate.

confédérer [-re] v. tr. (1). To confederate.
— v. pr. **Se confédérer,** to confederate.

conférence [kɔ̃ferã:s] f. Conference (de diplomates, de personnalités); *conférence de presse,* press conference. ‖ Lecture; *faire une conférence,* to deliver (ou) give a lecture. ‖ MÉD. Consultation (de médecins).

conférencier, ère [-sje, ɛ:r] s. Lecturer.

conférer [kɔ̃fere] v. tr. (5). To compare (des documents). ‖ To confer, to bestow (un grade, un privilège) [à, on].
— v. intr. To confer (avec, with); *conférer de qqch.,* to talk sth. over.

confesse [kɔ̃fɛs] f. ECCLÉS. Confession.

confesser [-se] v. tr. (1). To confess; to own up to (un crime); to own to (une erreur); to avow (une faute); to admit (ses torts). ‖ ECCLÉS. To confess (ses péchés, un pénitent). ‖ FAM. To get the truth out of, to pump (qqn).
— v. intr. ECCLÉS. To confess.
— v. pr. **Se confesser,** to confess one's sins; to confess oneself (à, to); *se confesser de qqch.,* to confess to having done sth.

confesseur [-sœ:r] m. ECCLÉS. Confessor.

confession [-sjɔ̃] f. Confession. (V. AVEU.) ‖ ECCLÉS. Confession (de foi, des péchés); confessing (d'un pénitent); *sous le secret de la confession,* under the seal of the confessional. ‖ Pl. ECCLÉS. Communities, confessions (religions).

confessionnal [-sjɔnal] m. ECCLÉS. Confessional.

confessionnel, elle [-sjɔnɛl] adj. ECCLÉS. Confessional; *école confessionnelle,* denominational (ou) U. S. parochial school.

confetti [kɔ̃fɛtti] m. pl. Confetti.

confiance [kɔ̃fjã:s] f. Confidence, reliance, trust; *avoir confiance en qqn, faire confiance à qqn,* to trust s.o.; *de confiance,* confidential (homme); trustworthy (maison); reliable (personne); of trust, confidential (poste); *de confiance, en toute confiance,* confidently, on trust, trustfully; *en confiance,* safely, freely; *y aller de confiance,* to go confidently ahead. ‖ Sanguineness (espoir, optimisme); *avoir confiance en l'avenir,* to have confidence in (ou) to feel sanguine about the future. ‖ Confidence; *confiance en soi,* self-confidence, self-reliance, self-assurance; *avoir confiance en soi*, to be self-confident. || Public confidence; *poser la question de confiance*, to ask for a vote of confidence.

confiant, ante [-fjɑ̃, ɑ̃:t] adj. Confiding, trusting (*dans*, in). || Self-confident (assuré); sanguine (optimiste); trustful, confiding (ouvert).

confidence [kɔ̃fidɑ̃:s] f. Confidence; *faire des confidences à*, to be confidential with, to confide secrets to; *mettre dans la confidence*, to let into the secret.

confident [-dɑ̃] m. Confidant. || Sociable (siège).

confidente [-dɑ̃:t] f. Confidante.

confidentiel, elle [-dɑ̃sjɛl] adj. Confidential.

confidentiellement [-dɑ̃sjɛlmɑ̃] adv. Confidentially; in confidence.

confier [-fje] v. tr. (1). To trust, to entrust (un dépôt); to confide, to impart (un secret) [*à*, to]. || *Confier à*, to put into the hands of (une affaire); to commit to the care of (qqn); *confier à la mémoire*, to commit to memory.
— v. pr. **Se confier à**, to trust to, to put faith in, to rely on (se fier à); to confide in (s'ouvrir à). || **Se confier dans**, to rely on, to rest on.

configuration [kɔ̃figyrasjɔ̃] f. Configuration, outline; shape; *configuration du terrain*, lie of the land.

confiné, ée [kɔ̃fine] adj. Confined (air); *les gens confinés chez eux*, the stay-at-homes.

confiner v. tr. (1). To confine, to shut up, to keep shut up (*dans*, in).
— v. intr. To border (*à*, on); to be contiguous (*à*, to). || FIG. To verge, to border (*à*, on).
— v. pr. **Se confiner**, to seclude oneself, to shut oneself up. || FIG. To confine oneself (*dans*, to).

confins [kɔ̃fɛ̃] m. pl. Confines, borders. || FIG. Confines. (V. BORNE.)

confire [kɔ̃fi:r] v. tr. (30). CULIN. To pickle (des cornichons); to preserve, to candy (des fruits); to pot (une oie).

confirmand [kɔ̃firmɑ̃] m. ECCLÉS. Confirmand.

confirmatif, ive [-matif, i:v] adj. Confirmative.

confirmation [-masjɔ̃] f. Corroboration (de faits); confirmation, ratification (de jugement); ratification (de traité). || JUR. Verification. || ECCLÉS. Confirmation.

confirmatoire [-matwa:r] adj. Confirmatory.

confirmer [-me] v. tr. (1). To support (une accusation); to uphold (une décision, un verdict); to confirm (un fait, une nouvelle); to ratify (un jugement, un traité); to bear out, to corroborate (un témoignage). || To confirm (ou) establish (qqn) [*dans*, in]. || ECCLÉS. To confirm.
— v. pr. **Se confirmer**, to be confirmed (nouvelle); to be corroborated (témoignage). || To be confirmed (*dans*, in) [une opinion].

confiscable [kɔ̃fiskabl] adj. Confiscable.

confiscation [-kasjɔ̃] f. Confiscation; forfeiture (d'un bien). || JUR. Seizure.

confiserie [kɔ̃fizri] f. Preserving (action, art); confectioner's shop, sweet-shop, U. S. candy shop (boutique); confectionery, sweets (marchandises). || Sardine-curing (des sardines).

confiseur [-zœ:r] s. Confectioner.

confisquer [kɔ̃fiske] v. tr. (1). To confiscate (un bien); to take away (un livre). || JUR. To seize.

confit [kɔ̃fi] adj. Preserved, candied (fruits). || FIG. Steeped (*dans*, in); *confit en dévotion*, pietistical, steeped in piety.
— m. CULIN. Preserve (d'oie).

confiture [-ty:r] f. CULIN. Jam, preserves. || FAM. Soft soap. || FAM. *De la confiture aux chiens*, caviar for the general.

confiturerie [-tyrri] f. Jam factory.

confiturier [-tyrje] m. Jam-maker (fabricant); jam-pot (pot).

conflagration [kɔ̃flagrasjɔ̃] f. Conflagration.

conflictuel, elle [kɔ̃fliktɥɛl] adj. Of conflict, of dispute. || PSYCH. Conflictful.

conflit [kɔ̃fli] m. Conflict, dispute; *conflit du travail*, trade dispute. || MILIT. Conflict, fight. || JUR. Conflict. || FIG. Conflict, clash, collision; *entrer en conflit avec*, to conflict with, to come into collision with, to be at strife with; *en conflit*, conflicting (théories).

confluence [kɔ̃flyɑ̃:s] f. MÉD. Confluence.

confluent [-flyɑ̃] adj. BOT., MÉD. Confluent.
— m. Confluence (de cours d'eau); confluent, influx (de deux rivières en une seule). || FIG. Junction, meeting.

confluer [-flye] v. intr. (1). To meet; to fall (*avec*, into).

confondre [kɔ̃fɔ̃:dr] v. tr. (4). To confound (faire échouer); to confound, to mingle (mêler); to confound, to confuse (ne pas distinguer); to mistake for (prendre pour); to confound, to abash, to confuse (rendre confus); to overwhelm (rendre reconnaissant); to disconcert, to astound, to bewilder, to dumbfound (stupéfier).
— v. pr. **Se confondre**, to become confused (ou) blurred (se brouiller); to become identical (ou) one (s'identifier); to mingle, to merge, to blend (se mêler); *se confondre en remerciements*, to overflow with gratitude, to be profuse (ou) effusive in one's thanks.

confondu, ue [kɔ̃fɔ̃dy] adj. Abashed; disconcerted; dumbfounded (*de*, at). || Overwhelmed (*de*, by) [reconnaissant].

conformation [kɔ̃formasjɔ̃] f. Conformation.

conforme [kɔ̃form] adj. Conformable, true (*à*, to). || JUR. Certified (copie); *conforme au règlement*, in order; *pour copie conforme*, certified true copy. || COMM. *Conforme à l'échantillon*, up to standard; *écriture conforme*, corresponding entry. || FIG. *Conforme à*, consonant with; in conformity (ou) unison with, corresponding with; consistent with.

conformé, ée [-me] adj. Formed, shaped; *mal conformé*, misshapen.

conformément [-memɑ̃] adv. *Conformément à*, according to, suitably to; in accordance (ou) conformity with; in application of.

conformer [-me] v. tr. (1). To form, to shape. || FIG. To conform, to shape (*à*, to).
— v. pr. **Se conformer**, to conform oneself (*à*, to) [s'adapter]; to comply (*à*, with), to abide (*à*, by) [se soumettre].

conformisme [-mism] m. Conventionalism; U. S. conformity. || Orthodoxy (en politique). || ECCLÉS. Conformity.

conformiste [-mist] m. Formalist, conventionalist; U. S. conformist. || ECCLÉS. Conformist.

conformité [-mite] f. Harmony, accordance, agreement (*avec*, with) [accord]. || Conformity (*avec*, with) [ressemblance]. || Conformity, submission (*à*, to) [soumission].

confort [kɔ̃for] m. Comfort; *de très grand confort*, outstandingly comfortable; *posséder tout le confort*, to have every modern convenience. || AUTOM. *Pneus confort*, balloon tyres.

confortable [-tabl] adj. Comfortable; easy (fauteuil); snug (maison); cosy (pièce); *peu confortable*, uncomfortable.

confortablement [-tablemɑ̃] adv. Comfortably.

conforter [kɔ̃forte] v. tr. (1). To corroborate, to strengthen, to reinforce.

confraternel, elle [kɔ̃fratɛrnɛl] adj. Brotherly, fraternal.

confraternité [-nite] f. Brotherhood, confraternity.

confrère [kɔ̃frɛ:r] m. Confrère, colleague (d'une même profession); fellow-member, colleague

(d'une même société). ‖ Contemporary (entre journaux). ‖ Jur. *Mon cher confrère,* my learned friend.
confrérie [kɔ̃freri] f. Confraternity. ‖ Guild.
confrontation [kɔ̃frɔ̃tasjɔ̃] f. Collation (de textes). ‖ Jur. Confrontation, confronting.
confronter [-te] v. tr. (1). To coliate, to compare (des textes). ‖ Jur. To confront.
confucianisme [kɔ̃fysjanism] m. Confucianism.
confus, use [kɔ̃fy, yz] adj. Confused (amas, discours, souvenir); obscure (argument, rôle, style); indistinct (bruit, souvenir); confused, foggy (esprit); faint (idée); vague (impression, souvenir); dim (intelligence, mémoire). ‖ Confused, embarrassed, at a loss (embarrassé); mortified, ashamed (honteux); *je suis confus de vos bontés,* I am overwhelmed by your kindness.
confusément [-zemɑ̃] adv. Confusedly; indistinctly; vaguely.
confusion [-zjɔ̃] f. Confusion, disorder (désordre); confusion, mingling (mélange). ‖ Confusion, indistinctness (manque de netteté). ‖ Indistinction (manque de discernement); confusion, misunderstanding, mistake (méprise). ‖ Confusion, abashment; shame (embarras, honte); *remplir de confusion,* to confuse; *sans la moindre confusion,* unabashed. ‖ Jur. Merger (de droits); extinguishment (d'obligations); concurrency (de peines).
congé [kɔ̃ʒe] m. Leave; leave of absence; *congé de maladie,* sick leave; *congé payé,* holidays with pay; *donner, prendre un congé,* to grant, to take leave; *être en congé,* to be on leave; *prendre un petit congé à la campagne,* to pop down to the country (fam.). ‖ Holiday (des classes). ‖ Notice (donné par un domestique, un employeur); dismissal (donné par un employeur); notice to leave (donné par un locataire); notice to quit (donné par un propriétaire); *demander son congé,* to ask to be relieved of one's duties; *donner congé,* to give notice; *prendre congé de,* to take leave of. ‖ Milit. Leave, furlough. ‖ Naut. *Congé maritime,* clearance. ‖ Archit. Congé. ‖ Jur. Permit; *congé pour le transport des vins,* release of wine from bond.
congédiable [kɔ̃ʒedjabl] adj. Milit. Due for discharge.
congédiement [-dimɑ̃] m. Dismissal (d'un domestique, d'un employé). ‖ Milit. Discharging. ‖ Naut. Paying off (de l'équipage).
congédier [-dje] v. tr. (1). To dismiss (une assemblée, un domestique, un employé); to lay off (des ouvriers); to send away, to dismiss (un visiteur). ‖ Milit. To discharge. ‖ Naut. To pay off.
congelable [kɔ̃ʒlabl] adj. Congealable, freezable.
congélateur [kɔ̃ʒelatœ:r] m. Deep-freeze.
congélation [kɔ̃ʒelasjɔ̃] f. Congelation; freezing, icing (de l'eau); solidification (de l'huile); freezing (de la viande); *point de congélation,* freeze point.
congeler [kɔ̃ʒle] v. tr. (8b). To congeal; to freeze, to ice (l'eau); to coagulate, to solidify (l'huile); to freeze (la viande).
— v. pr. Se **congeler,** to congeal, to freeze. ‖ To coagulate; to become solidified.
congénère [kɔ̃ʒenɛ:r] adj. Méd. Congenerous (muscle). ‖ Bot. Congeneric (plante). ‖ Gramm. Cognate (mot).
— s. Congener. ‖ Fam. Like, equal, fellow.
congénital, ale [kɔ̃ʒenital] adj. Méd. Congenital, connate.
congère [kɔ̃ʒɛ:r] f. Snowdrift.
congestif, ive [kɔ̃ʒɛstif, i:v] adj. Méd. Congestive.
congestion [-tjɔ̃] f. Méd. Congestion; *congestion cérébrale,* stroke, apoplexy; *congestion pulmonaire,* pneumonia.
congestionné, ée [-tjɔne] adj. Flushed.

congestionner v. tr. (1). Méd. To congest. ‖ To flush (le visage). ‖ Fam. To congest (une rue).
— v. pr. Se **congestionner,** Méd. To become congested. ‖ To turn purple in the face, to have a flushed face (personne); to flush up (visage).
conglomérat [kɔ̃glɔmera] m. Conglomerate.
conglomération [-rasjɔ̃] f. Conglomeration.
conglomérer [-re] v. tr. (5). To conglomerate.
— v. pr. Se **conglomérer,** to conglomerate.
conglutiner [kɔ̃glytine] v. tr. (1). To conglutinate.
— v. pr. Se **conglutiner,** to conglutinate.
Congo [kɔ̃go] m. Géogr. Congo (fleuve, État).
congolais, aise [kɔ̃gɔlɛ, ɛ:z] adj., s. Géogr. Congolese.
congratulateur, trice [kɔ̃gratylatœ:r, tris] adj. Congratulatory.
— s. Congratulator.
congratulation [-sjɔ̃] f. Congratulation.
congratulatoire [-twa:r] adj. Congratulatory.
congratuler [-tyle] v. tr. (1). To congratulate.
— v. pr. Se **congratuler,** to congratulate oneself.
— v. récipr. Se **congratuler,** to congratulate each other (ou) one another.
congre [kɔ̃:gr] m. Zool. Conger.
congréganiste [kɔ̃greganist] adj., m. Ecclés. Congreganist.
congrégation [-sjɔ̃] f. Ecclés. Congregation.
congrégationalisme [-sjɔnalism] m. Ecclés. Congregationalism.
congrégationaliste [-sjɔnalist] s. Ecclés. Congregationalist.
congrès [kɔ̃grɛ] m. Congress (politique, scientifique); *du congrès,* congressional; *membre du Congrès (des Etats-Unis),* Congressman, Congresswoman.
congressiste [kɔ̃grɛsist] m. Member of a congress.
congru, ue [kɔ̃gry] adj. Adequate, fitting (v. Approprié); *portion congrue,* bare living, scanty portion; *réduire à la portion congrue,* to put on short commons. ‖ Ecclés. Congruous (grâce). ‖ Math. Congruent (nombre).
congruence [kɔ̃gryɑ̃:s] f. Math. Congruence.
congruent [-ɑ̃] adj. Math. Congruent (à, with).
congruité [kɔ̃gryite] f. Congruity.
congrûment [kɔ̃grymɑ̃] adv. Appropriately; adequately; pertinently.
conicité [kɔnisite] f. Conicalness, conicity.
conifère [kɔnifɛ:r] adj. Bot. Coniferous.
— m. Bot. Conifer.
conine [kɔnin] f. Chim. Conine, conicine.
conique [kɔnik] adj. Math. Conic (projection, section). ‖ Conical; coniform.
— m. pl. Math. Conics.
conirostre [kɔnirɔstr] adj. Zool. Conirostral.
— m. Zool. Coniroster (pl. conirostres).
conjecturable [kɔ̃ʒɛktyrabl] adj. Conjecturable.
conjectural, ale [-ral] adj. Conjectural.
conjecture [kɔ̃ʒɛktyr] f. Conjecture, surmise (v. Supposition); *par conjecture,* conjecturally, as a guess; *se livrer à des conjectures,* to indulge in speculation.
conjecturer [-re] v. tr. (1). To conjecture, to surmise, to guess.
conjoindre [kɔ̃ʒwɛ̃:dr] v. tr. (59). To join in marriage. ‖ To conjoin.
conjoint, ointe [kɔ̃ʒwɛ̃, wɛ̃:t] adj. Conjoined, conjunct, joint. (V. Uni.) ‖ Married. ‖ Jur. *Conjoint et solidaire,* joint and several.
— s. Spouse; conjunct; *les conjoints,* husband and wife; *les futurs conjoints,* the bride and bridegroom, the fiancés.
conjointement [kɔ̃ʒwɛ̃tmɑ̃] adv. Jointly; conjunctively.
conjoncteur [kɔ̃ʒɔ̃ktœ:r] m. Électr. Circuit-closer; cut-in. ‖ **Conjoncteur-disjoncteur,** m.

ELECTR. Self-closing circuit-breaker, cut-out make-and-break key.

conjonctif, ive [-tif, i:v] adj. MÉD., GRAMM. Conjunctive.

conjonction [-sjɔ̃] f. Conjunction, connection, union. ‖ ASTR., GRAMM. Conjunction.

conjonctive [-ti:v] f. MÉD. Conjunctiva.

conjonctivite [-tivit] f. MÉD. Conjunctivitis.

conjoncture [-ty:r] f. Conjuncture; *dans cette conjoncture,* at this juncture, in these circumstances.

conjoncturel, elle [-tyrɛl] adj. Of (ou) to do with the current economic situation.

conjugable [kɔ̃ʒygabl] adj. That can be conjugated.

conjugaison [kɔ̃ʒygɛzɔ̃] f. GRAMM. Conjugation. ‖ MILIT. Pairing (d'armes); combining (de hausses).

conjugal, ale [-gal] adj. Conjugal; connubial, matrimonial; *domicile conjugal,* home; *état conjugal,* conjugality; *lien, lit conjugal,* marriage bond, bed; *vie conjugale,* married life.

conjugalement [-galmɑ̃] adv. Conjugally.

conjugué, ée [-ge] adj. BOT., MÉD., MATH., PHYS., GRAMM. Conjugate. ‖ TECHN. Paired (machines). ‖ MILIT. Combined (hausses). ‖ AVIAT. Interconnected (commandes). ‖ AUTOM. Coupled (freins). ‖ FIG. Combined (efforts).

conjuguer v. tr. (1). GRAMM. To conjugate. ‖ TECHN. To couple. ‖ MILIT., FIG. To combine.

conjungo [kɔ̃ʒɔ̃go] m. FAM. Marriage, wedlock; conjugality; married life. (V. MARIAGE.)

conjuration [kɔ̃ʒyrasjɔ̃] f. Conspiracy. (V. COMPLOT.) ‖ Conjuration. (V. INCANTATION.) ‖ Pl. Entreaties. (V. SUPPLICATION.)

conjuré [-re] s. Conspirator.

conjurer v. tr. (1). To entreat, to beseech, to adjure (supplier). ‖ ECCLÉS. To exorcise (le démon). ‖ FIG. To avert, to ward off (le danger); to stave off (le désastre, la ruine).
— v. intr. To conspire (*contre,* against).

connaissable [kɔnɛsabl] adj. Knowable. ‖ PHILOS. Cognizable, cognoscible.

connaissance [-sɑ̃:s] f. Knowledge, understanding; *à ma connaissance,* to my knowledge, so far as I know; *avoir connaissance de,* to know of, to have knowledge of, to be aware of; *connaissance de soi,* self-knowledge, autognosis; *donner connaissance à qqn de, porter à la connaissance de qqn,* to acquaint s.o. with, to inform s.o. of; *en connaissance de cause,* with knowledge of the facts; on good grounds; advisedly; purposely; *prendre connaissance de,* to look into (ou) through. ‖ Knowledge, command, learning (savoir); *connaissance des affaires,* experience in business; *connaissance étendue de l'anglais,* wide command of English; *connaissance superficielle de,* superficial knowledge of, smattering of, nodding acquaintance with. ‖ Pl. Knowledge, learning; attainment, acquirement; *niveau des connaissances,* standard of attainment; *quelques connaissances en droit,* some acquaintance with the law; *ses connaissances sont considérables,* he is a man of considerable learning. ‖ Acquaintance (relation); *chercher à faire connaissance avec,* to seek acquaintance with; to try to scrape acquaintance with (sens péjoratif); *faire, refaire connaissance,* to make, to renew acquaintance; *faire la connaissance de qqn,* to become acquainted with s.o., to make s.o.'s acquaintance; *faire faire connaissance à deux personnes,* to make two people acquainted, to bring two people together; *en pays de connaissance,* among familiar faces; on familiar ground; *qqn de ma connaissance,* somebody I know; a person of my acquaintances; *vieille connaissance,* old acquaintance. ‖ MÉD. Consciousness (conscience); *conserver sa connais-*

sance jusqu'à la fin, to be conscious to the end; *faire reprendre connaissance à qqn,* to bring s.o. round; *reprendre connaissance,* to recover one's senses, to come to; *perdre connaissance,* to faint; *sans connaissance,* unconscious, senseless, insensible. ‖ PHILOS. Cognition.

connaissement [kɔnɛsmɑ̃] m. NAUT. Bill of lading; shipping bill.

connaisseur, euse [kɔnɛsœ:r, ø:z] adj. Expert; critical (œil).
— s. Connoisseur. (V. AMATEUR.) ‖ Expert.

connaître [kɔnɛ:tr] v. tr. (74). To know, to be acquainted with, to be aware of (qqch.); *connaître Rome,* to know Rome; *connaître la route,* to be familiar with the road; *je ne vous connaissais pas ce chapeau,* I didn't know you had this hat. ‖ To know, to be acquainted with (qqn); *connaître de vue,* to know by sight; *elle l'a connu à Londres,* she met him in London; *si je le connais!, je ne connais que lui!,* don't I know him!; *je le lui ai fait connaître,* I made her acquainted with him, I introduced him to her; *ils ne se connaissent plus,* they have become estranged. ‖ To know, to appreciate, to understand (apprécier); *gagner à être connu,* to improve on acquaintance. ‖ To perceive, to distinguish, to discern (discerner); *connaître le bien du mal,* to know good from evil; *je ne lui connais pas de défauts,* I see no fault in him. ‖ To know, to feel, to experience (expérimenter); *connaître l'amour, la vie,* to know what love (ou) life is. ‖ To know, to acknowledge; *ne pas connaître de bornes,* to know no bounds. ‖ To know, to recognize (reconnaître); *connaître qqn à la voix,* to know s.o. by his voice. ‖ To know, to be acquainted with, to be versed in (être versé); *connaître à fond,* to have a thorough knowledge of, to be intimately acquainted with; *je n'y connais rien,* I know nothing about it; *il n'y connaît rien de rien,* he doesn't know how many beans make five; *faire connaître qqch. à qqn,* to notify s.o. of sth., to let s.o. know sth.; *faire connaître qqn,* to make s.o. known, to bring s.o. into the public eye; *se faire connaître,* to reveal oneself, to make oneself known. ‖ FAM., LOC. *Ça me connaît,* you can't teach me anything about that; *la connaître dans les coins,* to be up to every move (en général); to know it backwards (spécialement).
— v. intr. JUR. To take cognizance (*de,* of); to have jurisdiction (*de,* on).
— v. pr. Se connaître, to know oneself; *il ne se connaît plus,* he is beside himself. ‖ To be a judge (ou) an expert; *je ne m'y connais pas,* I know nothing about it; *il s'y connaît,* he knows what's what, he knows his onions.
— v. récipr. Se connaître, to know each other (ou) one another, to be acquainted; *il se vante que nous nous connaissions,* he claims acquaintance with me; *nous nous connaissons un peu,* we are slightly acquainted.

connecter [kɔnɛkte] v. tr. (1). To connect.

connecteur [-tœ:r] m. ELECTR. Connector.

connectif, ive [-tif, i:v] adj. MÉD. Connective.

connerie [kɔnri] f. ARGOT. Bloody nonsense; bunkum. ‖ Asinine behaviour.

connétable [kɔnetabl] m. High Constable.

connexe [kɔnɛks] adj. Connected (*de,* with). ‖ Allied (service).

connexion [-sjɔ̃] f. Connection; *en connexion avec,* connected with.

connexité [-site] f. Connexity, relatedness. ‖ PHILOS. Relationship.

connivence [kɔnivɑ̃:s] f. Connivance (v. COMPLICITÉ); *de connivence avec qqn,* in connivance (ou) cahoots with s.o., with s.o.'s connivance.

connotation [kɔnɔtasjɔ̃] f. GRAMM. Connotation.

connoter [-te] v. tr. (1). GRAMM. To connote.

connu, ue [kɔny] adj. Known, well known (fait); well known, noted, of note (personne); *être connu sous le nom de*, to go by the name of. — m. PHILOS. Known.

conoïdal, ale [kɔnɔidal] adj. Conoidal.

conopée [kɔnɔpe] m. ECCLÉS. Canopy.

conque [kɔ̃:k] f. ZOOL., MÉD. Conch.

conquérant, ante [kɔ̃keʀɑ̃, ɑ̃:t] adj. Conquering. ‖ Swaggering (air). — m. Conqueror.

conquérir [-riʀ] v. tr. (13). To conquer (un pays). ‖ FIG. To win (l'affection, l'estime).

conquête [kɔ̃kɛ:t] f. MILIT. Conquest. ‖ FIG. Conquest; *faire la conquête de qqn*, to make a conquest of s.o., to gain s.o.'s esteem (ou) sympathy, to win s.o.'s heart (ou) favour.

conquis [kɔ̃ki] p. p. de CONQUÉRIR; *comme en pays conquis*, as if they were at home.

conquistador [kɔ̃kistadɔʀ] m. Conquistador. ‖ FAM. Lady-killer.

consacré, ée [kɔ̃sakre] adj. Accepted, recognized, usual (terme); established, time-honoured (usage); *consacré par l'usage*, sanctioned by usage (expression); *expression consacrée*, stock phrase, cliché. ‖ ECCLÉS. Consecrated, sacred (lieu, vase); hallowed (terre). ‖ FIG. Devoted, consecrated, given up (à, to).

consacrer v. tr. (1). To ratify (un droit); to sanction (une erreur); to confirm (un privilège); to establish (une réputation). ‖ ECCLÉS. To consecrate. ‖ FIG. To devote, to consecrate, to give up, to dedicate (à, to). — v. pr. **Se consacrer**, to consecrate (ou) devote (ou) dedicate oneself (à, to) [v. S'ADONNER].

consanguin, ine [kɔ̃sɑ̃gɛ̃, in] adj. Consanguinean, consanguineous; *frère consanguin*, half-brother; *mariages consanguins*, inbreeding.

consanguinité [-gɥinite] f. Consanguinity, agnation. ‖ Inbreeding.

consciemment [kɔ̃sjamɑ̃] adv. Consciously; knowingly.

conscience [kɔ̃sjɑ̃:s] f. Consciousness (connaissance); *avoir conscience de*, to be aware (ou) conscious (ou) sensible of; *la conscience de soi-même*, self-awareness; *prendre conscience de*, to awake to the consciousness of; to realize; *j'en ai pris conscience*, it came home to me. ‖ Conscience (sens moral); *affaire* (ou) *cas de conscience*, matter of conscience; *avoir sur la conscience*, to have on one's conscience; *n'avoir pas la conscience tranquille*, to have an uneasy conscience (ou) twinges of conscience; *par acquit de conscience*, for conscience's sake; *sans conscience*, conscienceless. ‖ Conscience (sincérité); *dire ce qu'on a sur la conscience*, to speak one's mind; *en conscience*, in all conscience; *en mon âme et conscience*, with all my heart and soul; solemnly and sincerely. ‖ Conscientiousness, scrupulousness (scrupulosité); *avoir beaucoup de conscience*, to be very scrupulous (ou) conscientious; *manque de conscience*, unscrupulousness; *travailler en conscience*, to work conscientiously. ‖ MÉD. *Perdre conscience*, to faint, to lose consciousness. ‖ FAM. *Ça m'est resté sur la conscience*, it's lying on my stomach (repas copieux).

consciencieusement [-sjœzmɑ̃] adv. Conscientiously.

consciencieux, euse [-sjø, ø:z] adj. Conscientious. ‖ Careful (soigneux).

conscient, ente [kɔ̃sjɑ̃, ɑ̃:t] adj. Conscious, aware, sensible (de, of). ‖ PHILOS. Conscious, sentient. — m. PHILOS. Conscious.

conscription [kɔ̃skripsjɔ̃] f. MILIT. Conscription, U. S. draft.

conscrit [kɔ̃skri] m. MILIT. Conscript, U. S. draftee. — adj. † Conscript (Pères).

consécration [kɔ̃sekrasjɔ̃] f. Devotion, dedication (de soi-même). ‖ Ratification (d'une idée, d'un usage). ‖ ECCLÉS. Consecration.

consécutif, ive [kɔ̃sekytif, i:v] adj. Consecutive; *dix jours consécutifs*, ten days running; *pendant trois jours consécutifs*, for three consecutive days, three days in a row. ‖ Consecutive, due (à, to); resulting (à, from); following, consequent (à, upon). ‖ GRAMM. Consecutive.

consécutivement [-tivmɑ̃] adv. Consecutively.

consécutrice [-tʀis] adj. PHILOS. *Image consécutrice*, after-sensation.

conseil [kɔ̃sɛ:j] m. Counsel, advice; piece of advice; *un bon conseil*, a sound piece of advice; *demander conseil à*, *prendre conseil de qqn*, to take (ou) seek s.o.'s advice; *donner un conseil à qqn*, to give s.o. advice, to advice s.o.; *sur le conseil de*, on the advice of. ‖ Pl. Hints (suggestions); *conseils pour les ménagères*, hints for housewives; *conseils pour l'entretien d'un appareil*, *pour la conduite d'une voiture*, maintenance, driving hints. ‖ Council (assemblée); meeting (réunion); *conseil général, municipal, privé*, County, Town, Privy Council; *Conseil d'Etat*, Council of State; *conseil des ministres*, Cabinet (en Angleterre); Council of Ministers (en France); *Conseil de la République*, Upper House of French Parliament; *Conseil de sécurité*, Security Council. ‖ COMM. *Conseil d'administration*, board of directors. ‖ ECCLÉS. *Conseil de fabrique*, parish council, vestry. ‖ MILIT. *Conseil de guerre*, war council (pour la conduite de la guerre); court martial (pour les jugements); *conseil de révision*, recruiting (ou) U. S. draft board; *Conseil supérieur de l'Air, de la Guerre, de la Marine*, Air Council, Army Council, Board of Admiralty (ou) U. S. Navy Council; *Conseil supérieur interallié*, Allied War Council; *passer en conseil de guerre*, to be court-martialled. ‖ JUR. Counsel (avocat); *conseil judiciaire*, administrator, guardian; *conseil de famille*, family council, board of guardians. ‖ TECHN. *Ingénieur-conseil*, consulting engineer.

conseiller [kɔ̃sɛje] v. tr. (1). To advise, to counsel, to give advice to (qqn); *conseiller qqch. à qqn*, to recommend sth. to s.o.; *conseiller à qqn de faire qqch.*, to advise s. o. to do sth.

conseiller m. Counsellor, adviser, U. S. advisor (de qqn). ‖ Councillor; *conseiller général, municipal*, county-, town-councillor; *conseiller d'ambassade*, Counsellor; *conseiller d'Etat*, Councillor of State; *conseiller à la Cour*, judge at the Court. ‖ JUR. *Conseiller juridique*, legal adviser.

conseilleur [-jœ:r] m. Adviser, U. S. advisor.

consensus [kɔ̃sɛsy:s] m. Consensus.

consentant, ante [kɔ̃sɑ̃tɑ̃, ɑ̃:t] adj. Willing, agreeable. ‖ JUR. Consenting.

consentement [-tmɑ̃] m. Consent, assent; *du consentement de tous*, by universal assent.

consenti, ie [-ti] adj. COMM. Current (prêt); *librement consenti*, voluntary.

consentir [-ti:r] v. intr. (93). To consent, to agree (à, to). — v. tr. To allow, to grant (autoriser).

conséquemment [kɔ̃sekamɑ̃] adv. Consequently. ‖ Consistently.

conséquence [-kɑ̃:s] f. Consequence, inference (conclusion); *tirer les conséquences de*, to draw inferences from. ‖ Consequence, result (effet, résultat); *en conséquence*, accordingly, as a result. ‖ Importance; *ne pas tirer à conséquence*, to be of no importance; *sans conséquence*, of no importance. ‖ PHILOS. Consistence.

conséquent, ente [-kɑ̃, ɑ̃:t] adj. Logical (esprit). ‖ Consistent (avec, with). ‖ PHYS. Consequent.

‖ Fam. Handsome, sizeable (considérable); important (important); *personnage conséquent*, bigwig. — m. Philos., Math. Consequent. — loc. conj. *Par conséquent*, therefore, consequently; accordingly.

conservable [kɔsɛrvabl] adj. Conservable.

conservateur, trice [-tœ:r, tris] adj. Conservative; preservative. — m. Deep-freeze, freezer (réfrigérateur). ‖ Preservative (produit chimique). — s. Warden (des eaux et forêts); registrar (des hypothèques); curator, keeper (de musée). ‖ Conservative (en politique).

conservation [-sjɔ̃] f. Conservation, preservation; *instinct de conservation*, self-preservation, self-defence, U. S. self-defense. ‖ Comm. Preserving, canning. ‖ Jur. Conservancy (des eaux et forêts); registry (des hypothèques).

conservatisme [-tism] m. Conservatism.

conservatoire [-twa:r] adj. Jur. Conservatory, protective; *saisie conservatoire*, seizure for security. — m. Museum (des Arts et Métiers). ‖ Mus. Academy, conservatoire, U. S. conservatory.

conserve [kɔsɛrv] f. Culin. Preserve; *conserves en bocal, en boîte, en pot*, bottled, tinned (ou) U. S. canned, potted foods; *conserves au vinaigre*, pickles; *fabricant, fabrique de conserves*, canner, cannery; *faire des conserves de*, to preserve. ‖ Naut. Consort; *de conserve*, in company (ou) consort. ‖ Pl. Preserves, coloured glasses (lunettes). ‖ Fig. *De conserve*, in company, together; hand in hand; concordantly; in agreement.

conserver [-ve] v. tr. (1). To preserve; to bottle (en bocal); to can, to tin (en boîtes); to pot (en pot); to pickle (dans du vinaigre); to keep (des denrées périssables). ‖ To preserve (un bâtiment, un monument); to keep, to retain (un bien). ‖ Fig. To maintain (son allure, des relations, la santé, le silence, son sang-froid); to keep (ses amis); to preserve (une coutume, le souvenir); to entertain (un doute, un espoir); to retain (ses facultés, un usage, un souvenir, une qualité); to cling to (ses opinions). — v. pr. Se conserver, to keep (denrées); to preserve oneself (personnes); *bien conservé*, well preserved (personne).

conserverie [-vri] f. Canning industry (ou) factory; cannery.

conserveur, euse [-vœ:r, vøz] s. Canner.

considérable [kɔsiderabl] adj. Substantial (aide, différence, progrès); considerable (différence, nombre, personnage); wide (écart, expérience, influence); ample (fortune, loisirs, ressources); powerful (influence); notable (personnage); heavy (perte); large, considerable (somme); extensive (rôle, usage).

considérablement [-bləmɑ̃] adv. Substantially, considerably, widely, largely.

considérant [kɔsiderɑ̃] m. Jur. Grounds (de jugement); preamble (de loi). — loc. conj. *Considérant que*, considering that, whereas.

considération [-rasjɔ̃] f. Consideration; *prendre en considération*, to consider, to take into consideration (ou) account. ‖ Consideration, reason; *en considération de*, on account of. ‖ Consideration, regard (pour, for); *agréez l'expression de ma considération distinguée*, yours truly; *par considération pour*, out of regard for. ‖ Pl. Reflections, reflexions, remarks (sur, on).

considérer [-re] v. tr. (5). To consider, to esteem; to reckon; *on le considère fort*, he is highly thought of. ‖ To regard, to look upon, to consider, to take (comme, as); *considérer qqn comme étant*, to consider (ou) to hold s.o. to be.

‖ To consider, to examine, to take into account; *tout bien considéré*, all things considered. ‖ To consider, to look at, to gaze on (regarder). — v. pr. Se considérer, to look at oneself (se contempler). ‖ Fig. *Se considérer comme lié par serment*, to consider (ou) to hold oneself bound by an oath.

consignataire [kɔsiɲatɛ:r] m. Comm. Consignee. ‖ Jur. Depositary, trustee.

consignateur, trice [-tœ:r, tris] s. Comm. Consignor; shipper.

consignation [-sjɔ̃] f. Comm. Consignment (de marchandises); consignation, deposit (somme). ‖ Fin. Deposit (somme). ‖ Fig. Mention, registration, entry (de faits).

consigne [kɔsiɲ] f. Detention (punition scolaire). ‖ Milit. Orders, instructions (ordres); confinement to barracks (punition). ‖ Ch. de f. Cloakroom; U. S. baggage-room, check-room. ‖ Comm. *En consigne à la douane*, held up at the custom-house. ‖ Comm. Deposit (somme en dépôt).

consigner [-ɲe] v. tr. (1). Milit. To confine to barracks (un soldat); to keep in barracks (les troupes): to put out of bounds (un lieu à la troupe). ‖ To keep in (un élève). ‖ Comm. To deposit (de l'argent); to consign (des marchandises); *consigner à la douane*, to stop at the custom-house. ‖ Ch. de f. To leave at the cloakroom; U. S. to check. ‖ Fig. To enter, to record, to write down (des faits). [V. citer.] ‖ Loc. *Consigner sa porte*, to be at home to no one; to refuse admittance (à, to).

consistance [kɔsistɑ̃:s] f. Consistency (d'un liquide, d'une substance); *sans consistance*, flabby (chairs); loose (sol); flimsy (tissu). ‖ Jur. Area (d'un domaine); amount (d'une succession). ‖ Fig. Firmness (du caractère); *sans consistance*, spineless, lax, weak (personne). ‖ Fig. Credit; *sans consistance*, unfounded (bruit).

consistant, ante [-tɑ̃, ɑ̃:t] adj. Firm (chair, étoffe, gelée, terrain); solid (chair); heavy, stiff, set (graisse fondue); substantial (repas); consistent (sirop). ‖ Fig. Well-grounded (ou) -founded (bruit); solid, firm (caractère); consistent (personne).

consister [-te] v. intr. (1). To consist, to be composed (de, of). ‖ To be composed (en, of). ‖ To consist, to lie (dans, in).

consistoire [-twa:r] m. Ecclés. Consistory.

consistorial, ale [-tɔrjal] adj. Ecclés. Consistorial.

consœur [kɔsœ:r] f. Colleague, sister-member.

consolable [kɔsɔlabl] adj. Consolable.

consolant, ante [-lɑ̃, ɑ̃:t] adj. Comforting.

consolateur, trice [-latœ:r, tris] m. Comforter, consoler. — adj. Comforting, consoling, consolatory.

consolation [-lasjɔ̃] f. Consolation, comfort, solace; *adresser des paroles de consolation à*, to speak words of comfort to; *chercher une consolation dans*, to turn for consolation to; *trouver une consolation à faire*, to find comfort in doing.

console [kɔsɔl] f. Console-table (meuble). ‖ Archit., Mus. Console.

consoler [kɔsɔle] v. tr. (1). To comfort (de, for); to console, to solace. — v. pr. Se consoler, to console oneself (de, for); to be comforted. — v. récipr. Se consoler, to console (ou) comfort each other (ou) one another.

consolidation [kɔsɔlidasjɔ̃] f. Bracing (d'une construction); consolidation, strengthening (en général). ‖ Fin. Consolidation; *de consolidation*, funding (emprunt). ‖ Jur. Merger (d'usufruit). ‖ Milit. Strengthening (du front, des positions). ‖ Méd. Building up (de la santé).

consolidé, ée [-de] adj. Consolidated. ‖ Fin.

Funded (dette, fonds); *non consolidé*, floating; *rentes consolidées*, consols (fam.).

consolider [-de] v. tr. (1). To consolidate, to strengthen (sens général). ‖ ARCHIT. To brace (une construction). ‖ FIN. To fund (une dette). ‖ JUR. To merge (l'usufruit). ‖ MILIT. To strengthen (le front, les positions). ‖ MÉD. To unite, to heal up (une fracture); to build up (la santé).
— v. pr. Se **consolider**, to grow firm, to solidify. ‖ MÉD. To unite, to heal (blessure, fracture); to improve (santé).

consommable [kɔsɔmabl] adj. Consumable.

consommateur, trice [-tœ:r, tris] s. Consumer (de denrées); customer (au café, au restaurant).

consommation [-asjɔ̃] f. Completion (achèvement). ‖ Perpetration (d'un crime); consummation (du mariage). ‖ Consumption (de denrées, de produits); drink (au café); *denrées de consommation*, consumer goods; *marchandises non destinées à la consommation*, capital goods; *taxe à la consommation*, purchase tax. ‖ AUTOM. Consumption (d'essence); *concours de consommation*, economy run. ‖ MILIT. Expenditure (du matériel).

consommé, ée [kɔsɔme] adj. Consumed, used up (denrée); used (électricité, gaz). ‖ JUR. Consummated (mariage). ‖ ÉLECTR. *Energie consommée*, power consumption. ‖ FIG. Consummate. (V. ACCOMPLI.)
— m. CULIN. Consommé, clear soup, beef-tea; stock. (V. BOUILLON.)

consommer v. tr. (1). To consummate, to complete, to achieve (achever). ‖ To perpetrate (un crime); to consummate (le mariage, un sacrifice). ‖ To consume, to use up (une denrée); to use (du gaz, de l'électricité).
— v. intr. To have a drink, to drink (au café).
— ◆v. pr. Se **consommer**, to be consummated (ou) perpetrated (crime); to be consummated (mariage). ‖ To be consumed (denrées); to be used (produits). ‖ CULIN. To boil down (bouillon).

consomptible [kɔsɔptibl] adj. Consumable.

consomption [-sjɔ̃] f. MÉD. Wasting, decline.

consonance [kɔsɔnɑ̃:s] f. Consonance; *aux consonances étrangères*, foreign-sounding.

consonant, ante [-nɑ̃, ɑ̃:t] adj. Consonant.

consonantique [-nɑ̃tik] adj. Consonantal.

consonantisme [-nɑ̃tism] m. GRAMM. Consonant system.

consonne [kɔsɔn] f. Consonant.

consort [kɔsɔ:r] adj. m. Consort (prince).
— m. pl. JUR. Partners. ‖ FAM. Associates, fellow-plotters, confederates.

consortium [kɔsɔrsjɔm] m. Consortium.

conspirateur, trice [kɔspiratœ:r, tris] adj. Conspiring.
— m. Conspirator, plotter. (V. CONJURÉ.)

conspiration [kɔspirasjɔ̃] f. Conspiracy.

conspiratrice [-tris] f. Conspiratress.

conspirer [-re] v. intr. (1). To conspire, to plot (contre, against). [V. COMPLOTER.] ‖ To conspire, to concur (à, to). [V. CONCOURIR.]
— v. tr. To conspire, to conspire to do (qqch.).

conspuer [kɔspye] v. tr. (1). To conspue, to run down (en général); *conspuez Un tel!*, down with So-and-So! ; U. S. to razz. ‖ SPORTS. To barrack; U. S. to razz. ‖ THÉÂTR. To boo, to boo at. [V. HUER.]

constamment [kɔstamɑ̃] adv. Constantly (continuellement); steadfastly (avec persévérance).

constance [-tɑ̃:s] f. Constancy, steadfastness (fermeté); constancy (fidélité, persévérance); constancy, invariability (stabilité). ‖ ÉLECTR. Constancy.

constant, ante [-tɑ̃, ɑ̃:t] adj. Constant, continual, incessant (continuel); constant, steadfast, firm, unshaken (ferme); established, patent, certain (patent); persevering, unremitting (persévérant); constant, changeless, unchanging (stable).

constante [-tɑ̃:t] f. PHYS., MATH. Constant.

constat [kɔsta] m. JUR. Constat, official statement, certified report; *constat d'huissier*, affidavit made by a process-server. ‖ Established fact.

constatation [-tasjɔ̃] f. Ascertainment, establishment (d'un fait). ‖ Investigation; notice; *faire une constatation*, to note. ‖ JUR. Proof (de décès, d'identité); findings (d'une enquête); *constatations d'usage*, routine inquiry.

constater [kɔstate] v. tr. (1). To ascertain, to establish, to record, to verify (un fait)). ‖ To notice, to remark, to observe; to aver; to discover, to find (que, that). ‖ FIN. *Valeur constatée*, registered value.

constellation [kɔstɛlasjɔ̃] f. ASTRON. Constellation.

constellé, ée [kɔstelle] adj. Constellated, star-spangled. ‖ FIG. Starred, bespangled (de, with).

consteller v. tr. (1). To constellate, to spangle. ‖ FIG. To star.

consternant, ante [kɔstɛrnɑ̃, ɑ̃:t] adj. Dismaying, dumbfounding.

consternation [kɔstɛrnasjɔ̃] f. Consternation, dismay (atterrement). ‖ Affliction, grief (peine).

consterné, ée [-ne] adj. Dismayed (de, at); in dismay. ‖ Very sorry, grieved.

consterner v. tr. (1). To dismay (atterrer). ‖ To afflict. (V. ATTRISTER, CONTRISTER.)

constipant, ante [kɔstipɑ̃, ɑ̃:t] adj. MÉD. Constipating; binding.

constipation [-pasjɔ̃] f. MÉD. Constipation, costiveness.

constipé, ée [-pe] adj. MÉD. Constipated, costive. ‖ FAM. Cramped.

constiper v. tr. (1). MÉD. To constipate.
— v. intr. To bind the bowels.

constituant, ante [kɔstituɑ̃, ɑ̃:t] adj. Constituent (assemblée, élément); component, integral (partie).
— m. Component part. ‖ JUR. Constituent (d'un mandataire); grantor (de rente).

constituante [-ɑ̃:t] f. † Constituent Assembly.

constitué, ée [-e] adj. Constituted (par, by); composed (par, of). ‖ MÉD. *Bien constitué*, of sound constitution. ‖ JUR. Constituted (autorités); briefed (avocat); *corps constitués*, corporate bodies, public authorities.

constituer v. tr. (1). To constitute, to compose, to make up. ‖ JUR. To appoint, to brief (avocat); to instruct (avoué); to set up (un comité); to constitute (un délit); to settle (une dot); to empanel (un jury); to form, to constitute (un ministère); *constituer qqn son héritier*, to appoint s.o. one's heir.
— v. pr. Se **constituer**, to constitute oneself. ‖ COMM. To form (en, in). ‖ JUR. *Se constituer partie civile*, to bring in a civil action; *se constituer prisonnier*, to give oneself up.

constitutif, ive [kɔstitytif, i:v] adj. Constitutive, basic; *acte constitutif*, title deed.

constitution [-sjɔ̃] f. Constitution (sens général et politique). ‖ MÉD. Constitution. ‖ CHIM. Composition. ‖ JUR. Briefing (d'avocat); instructing (d'avoué); settlement (de dot, de rente); formation (de société); *constitution en société*, incorporation.

constitutionnaliser [-sjɔnalize] v. tr. (1). To constitutionalize.

constitutionnalité [-sjɔnalite] f. Constitutionality.

constitutionnel, elle [-sjɔnɛl] adj. Constitutional; *rendre constitutionnel*, to constitutionalize.

constitutionnellement [-sjɔnɛlmɑ̃] adv. Constitutionally.

constricteur [kɔstriktœ:r] adj., m. MÉD., ZOOL. Constrictor.

constrictif, ive [-tif, i:v] adj. Constrictive.

constriction [-sjɔ̃] f. Constriction.

constringent, ente [kɔ̃strɛ̃ʒɑ̃, ɑ̃:t] adj. MÉD. Constringent.

constructeur, trice [kɔ̃stryktœ:r, tris] adj. Manufacturing, building, constructing. ‖ FIG. Constructive.
— m. Manufacturer (d'automobiles, de chaudières); builder (de bâtiments, de bateaux); constructor (de machines).

constructif, ive [-tif, i:v] adj. Constructive.

construction [-sjɔ̃] f. Construction, building (action, édifice); boîte (ou) jeu de constructions, constructional set; de construction, building (matériaux). ‖ Build; de construction française, French-built. ‖ PHILOS. Construct (de l'esprit). ‖ MATH. Figure. ‖ GRAMM. Construction; faire la construction, to construe. ‖ FIG. Construction, composition.

constructivisme [-tivism] m. ARTS. Constructivism.

construire [kɔ̃strɥi:r] v. tr. (85). To construct (une auto, un barrage, une machine); to build (une maison, un navire, un pont, une route). ‖ MATH. To construct. ‖ GRAMM. To construct; to construe. ‖ FIG. To compose (une œuvre); to build up (une théorie).
— v. pr. Se construire, to be built; to be building. ‖ GRAMM. To be construed (avec, with).

consubstantialité [kɔ̃sybstɑ̃sjalite] f. ECCLÉS. Consubstantiality.

consubstantiation [-sjasjɔ̃] f. ECCLÉS. Consubstantiation.

consubstantiel, elle [-sjɛl] adj. ECCLÉS. Consubstantial (à, with).

consul [kɔ̃syl] m. Consul; consul général, consul general; consul de France, French consul.

consulaire [-lɛ:r] adj. Consular. ‖ COMM., JUR. Commercial (tribunal); droits consulaires, consulages; personnage consulaire, statesman.

consulat [-la] m. Consulate (bureaux); consulship (fonction).

consultable [kɔ̃syltabl] adj. That can be consulted.

consultant, ante [kɔ̃syltɑ̃, ɑ̃:t] adj. Consulting. ‖ MÉD. Médecin consultant, consultant.

consultatif, ive [-tatif, i:v] adj. Advisory; à titre consultatif, in an advisory capacity; comité consultatif, business advisory committee.

consultation [-tasjɔ̃] f. Consultation (action, avis); expert advice (avis). ‖ MÉD. Consultation; consultation externe, out-patients department; consultation de nourrissons, infant welfare centre. ‖ JUR. Consultation d'avocat, counsel's opinion; consultation électorale, general election.

consulter [-te] v. tr. (1). To consult, to refer to (un ouvrage); to consult, to seek (ou) to take the advice of (qqn); to appeal to (le pays). ‖ FIG. To take stock of (ses forces, ses intérêts).
— v. intr. MÉD. To hold a consultation; consulter avec, to consult with.
— v. pr. Se consulter, to consider, to deliberate; se consulter au sujet de, to reflect upon, to think over.
— v. récipr. Se consulter, to consult (ou) to take counsel together.

consumé, ée [kɔ̃syme] adj. Consumed. ‖ FIG. Consumé par, eaten (ou) burnt up by (l'ambition); burnt up by, consumed with (le désir, la jalousie, la soif); burnt up by (le feu); harassed by, worn out (ou) away by (les soucis).

consumer v. tr. (1). To consume, to burn up. (V. BRÛLER.) ‖ FIG. To consume, to burn up; to eat up; to harass, to wear out (ou) away.
— v. pr. Se consumer, to burn out (combustible). ‖ FIG. To be consumed, to waste away (énergie, fortune, vie); se consumer de chagrin, to eat one's heart out, to pine away with grief.

consumérisme [kɔ̃symerism] m. Consumerism.

contact [kɔ̃takt] m. Contact, touch; entrer en contact (ou) prendre contact avec, to come (ou) to get into touch with; prise de contact officielle, preliminary contacts (ou) talks. ‖ ÉLECTR. Switch; contact; contact de terre, ground connection; couper, mettre le contact, to switch off, on. ‖ AUTOM. Clef de contact, ignition key. ‖ MILIT. Contact (avec, with). ‖ MÉD. Verre de contact, contact lens. ‖ MATH. Contact. ‖ AVIAT. Vol de contact, contact flying.

contacter [-te] v. tr. (1). FAM. To contact.

contacteur [-tœ:r] m. ÉLECTR. Switch; contact maker. ‖ AUTOM. Switch contactor.

contagieux, euse [kɔ̃taʒjø, ø:z] adj. MÉD. Contagious, infectious, catching. ‖ FIG. Contagious, catching.
— s. MÉD. Contagious person.

contagion [-ʒjɔ̃] f. MÉD. Contagion.

contagiosité [-ʒjozite] f. MÉD. Contagiousness.

container [kɔ̃tɛnɛ:r] m. Container.

contamination [kɔ̃taminasjɔ̃] f. MÉD. Contamination. ‖ Pollution.

contaminer [-ne] v. tr. (1). MÉD. To contaminate, to infect.

conte [kɔ̃:t] m. Tale, story; conte de fées, fairytale. ‖ FAM. Story, yarn, fib; conte à dormir debout, cock-and-bull story, baloney.

contemplateur, trice [kɔ̃tɑ̃platœ:r, tris] s. Contemplator.

contemplatif, ive [-tif, i:v] adj., s. ECCLÉS. Contemplative.

contemplation [-sjɔ̃] f. Contemplation. ‖ FAM. Gazing.

contempler [kɔ̃tɑ̃ple] v. tr. (1). To contemplate; to meditate upon (méditer). ‖ To contemplate, to behold, to gaze on (ou) at (regarder); du haut de ces pyramides quarante siècles vous contemplent, from these pyramids forty centuries look down upon you.

contemporain, aine [kɔ̃tɑ̃pɔrɛ̃, ɛn] adj. Contemporaneous; contemporary; coeval (de, with). ‖ Present-day, contemporary (actuel).
— s. Contemporary.

contempteur, trice [kɔ̃tɑ̃ptœ:r, tris] adj. Contemptuous.
— s. Contemner.

contenance [kɔ̃tnɑ̃:s] f. Burden (d'un navire); capacity (d'un fût); area (d'un terrain). ‖ FIG. Countenance, bearing; faire bonne contenance, to carry it off, to put a good face on it, to keep smiling; faire perdre contenance à qqn, to put s.o. out of countenance; se donner une contenance, to keep oneself in countenance.

contenant, ante [-nɑ̃, ɑ̃:t] adj. Containing.
— m. Container.

conteneur [-nœ:r] m. V. CONTAINER.

contenir [kɔ̃tni:r] v. tr. (101). To contain, to hold (en capacité). ‖ To contain, to include, to enclose. (V. RENFERMER.) ‖ To contain, to keep in, to restrain (retenir). ‖ FIG. To control, to repress (ses passions).
— v. pr. Se contenir, to control oneself, to hold oneself in, to command one's temper.

content, ente [kɔ̃tɑ̃, ɑ̃:t] adj. Content (de, with) [v. SATISFAIT]; content de soi, self-satisfied, smug. ‖ Glad, happy, pleased (joyeux).
— m. Fill; avoir son content de, to have enough of (ou) one's fill of.

contentement [-tmɑ̃] m. Content (suffisance). ‖ Satisfaction; contentement de soi, self-content, complacency. ‖ Joy, gladness (bonheur).

contenter [-te] v. tr. (1). To content, to please (qqn). [V. SATISFAIRE.] ‖ To suit (les besoins); to gratify (la curiosité).

— v. pr. **Se contenter,** to satisfy oneself; to indulge oneself. ‖ To content oneself, to be content, to put up (*de,* with); *elle se contenta de sourire,* she merely smiled, her only answer was to smile.

contentieux, euse [kɔ̃tɑ̃sjø, ø:z] adj. † Quarrelsome. ‖ Jur. Contentious.
— m. Jur. Contentious matters, contested cases, matters in dispute; legal business; *service du contentieux,* legal (ou) claims department.

contention [kɔ̃tɑ̃sjɔ̃] f. Application. ‖ Contention. (V. DISPUTE.)

contenu, ue [kɔ̃tny] adj. Reserved (caractère); stifled (rire); restrained (passion, style).
— m. Contents.

conter [kɔ̃te] v. tr. (1). To tell, to relate (v. NARRER); *en conter à,* to humbug, to take in; *en conter de belles sur,* to tell tall stories about.

contestable [kɔ̃tɛstabl] adj. Contestable, questionable, debatable.

contestataire [-tatɛ:r] adj. Dissentient, rebellious.
— s. Dissentient, rebel.

contestation [-tasjɔ̃] f. Contestation (v. DIFFÉREND); *contestations sans fondement,* groundless arguments; *en contestation avec,* at variance (ou) issue with; *sans contestation,* beyond all question. ‖ Rebelliousness, protest (en politique).

conteste [kɔ̃tɛst] f. *Sans conteste,* indisputably.

contester [-te] v. tr. (1). To challenge, to dispute (une affirmation); to contest (une question); to impeach, to impugn (la véracité). ‖ Jur. To contest (une dette, un droit); to impeach, to impugn (un témoignage); to challenge (des titres, un juré).
— v. intr. To protest.

conteur [kɔ̃tœ:r] m. Writer of short stories (écrivain); teller, narrator (narrateur). ‖ Fam. *Conteur de fariboles,* fibber, story-teller.

contexte [kɔ̃tɛkst] m. Context. ‖ Jur. Text.

contexture [-ty:r] f. Contexture. ‖ Méd. Texture (des muscles, des os). ‖ Fig. Contexture; composition; framework (d'un récit).

contigu, uë [kɔ̃tigy] adj. Contiguous (*à,* to).

contiguïté [kɔ̃tiguite] f. Contiguity; adjacency.

continence [kɔ̃tinɑ̃:s] f. Continence.

continent, ente [-nɑ̃, ɑ̃:t] adj. Continent.

continent [kɔ̃tinɑ̃] m. Géogr. Continent, mainland; *le Nouveau Continent,* the New World; *voyage sur le Continent,* continental tour.

continental, ale [-tal] adj. Continental.

contingence [kɔ̃tɛ̃ʒɑ̃:s] f. Contingency.

contingent [-ʒɑ̃] adj. Philos. Contingent.
— m. Contingent; quota. ‖ Ration, allowance, allocation. ‖ Milit. Contingent; intake; call-up (d'une classe); unit (troupe).

contingentement [-ʒɑ̃tmɑ̃] m. Quota system; fixing of quotas; application of the quota system. ‖ Apportioning.

contingenter [-ʒɑ̃te] v. tr. (1). To establish quotas for. ‖ To allocate; to apportion.

continu, ue [kɔ̃tiny] adj. Unceasing (effort, travail); continued (proportion); unbroken (silence); continuous (suite). ‖ Math. Continuous (fonction); continued (fraction). ‖ Méd. Continued (fièvre). ‖ Ch. de F. Continuous (freins). ‖ Électr. Continuous, direct (courant).
— m. Philos. Continuum. ‖ Électr. Direct current.

continuateur, trice [-nɥatœ:r, tris] s. Continuator.

continuation [-nɥasjɔ̃] f. Continuation.

continuel, elle [-nɥɛl] adj. Continual, ceaseless.

continuellement [-nɥɛlmɑ̃] adv. Continually, ceaselessly. (V. CONSTAMMENT.)

continuer [kɔ̃tinɥe] v. tr. (1). To pursue, to continue, to proceed on (v. POURSUIVRE); *conti-*

nuer sa course, son travail, son vol, son voyage, to run on, to work on, to fly on, to journey on. ‖ To keep on with, to go on with (ses efforts, ses études); to carry on (la tradition). ‖ Ch. de F. To extend, to prolong (une ligne).
— v. intr. To continue; to go on, to keep on; *continuez!,* go on!, go ahead!; *continuer à chanter, à dormir, à nager, à peiner,* to sing on, to sleep on, to swim on, to toil on; *continuer à faire,* to continue to do, to go on doing. ‖ To keep on (durer); to continue, to run on, to extend (se prolonger).
— v. pr. **Se continuer,** to continue, to keep on.

continuité [kɔ̃tinɥite] f. Continuity; *solution de continuité,* solution of continuity. ‖ Naut. *Continuité du voyage,* continuous voyage.

continuum [-nɥɔm] m. Continuum; *continuum spatio-temporel,* space-time continuum, space-time.

contondant, ante [kɔ̃tɔ̃dɑ̃, ɑ̃:t] adj. Bruising, contusive.

contorsion [kɔ̃tɔrsjɔ̃] f. Contortion.

contorsionner [-sjɔne] v. tr. (1). To contort, to distort.
— v. pr. **Se contorsionner,** to contort oneself; to writhe.

contorsionniste [-sjɔnist] m. Contortionist.

contour [kɔ̃tu:r] m. Contour (d'une colonne, d'un objet); outline (de l'horizon, d'un monument); line (d'une statue); circuit, circumference (d'une ville).

contourné, ée [kɔ̃turne] adj. Twisted, distorted, crooked (membre). ‖ Blas. Contourné, reguardant. ‖ Fig. Tortuous, intricate (style).

contourner v. tr. (1). To shape (modeler). ‖ To distort, to contort (contorsionner). ‖ To move around; to skirt (une forêt); to go round (une montagne); to turn (un obstacle). ‖ Jur. To evade (la loi).

contraceptif, ive [kɔ̃trasɛptif, i:v] adj., m. Contraceptive.

contraception [-sɛpsjɔ̃] f. Contraception.

contractant, ante [kɔ̃traktɑ̃, ɑ̃:t] adj. Contracting (partie).
— s. Jur. Contracting party.

contracte [kɔ̃trakt] adj. Gramm. Contracted.

contracté, ée [-te] adj. Pursed (lèvres); contorted (visage); *contracté par la douleur,* drawn with pain; *les mâchoires contractées,* with jaws set. ‖ Gramm. Contracted (article).

contracter v. tr. (1). To form (une alliance); to enter into (un engagement); to contract, to acquire (une habitude); to contract, to enter into (mariage); to incur, to undertake, to lay oneself under (une obligation). ‖ Fin. To contract (une dette); to raise (un emprunt). ‖ Jur. To take out (une assurance); to take (un bail). ‖ Méd. To contract (une maladie); to catch (un rhume).

contracter v. tr. (1). To contract (un métal); to constrict. ‖ To contract, to contort (les traits). ‖ Gramm. To contract (un mot).
— v. pr. **Se contracter,** to contract (traits); to shrink, to narrow; to shrivel. ‖ Gramm. To contract (mot).

contractile [-til] adj. Contractible.

contraction [-sjɔ̃] f. Contraction.

contractuel, elle [-tɥɛl] adj. Jur. Contractual; granted by contract; *main-d'œuvre contractuelle,* contract labour.
— s. Person on contract, contract employee. ‖ Autom. Traffic warden; meter maid (femme).

contracture [-ty:r] f. Méd. Contracture.

contradicteur, trice [kɔ̃tradiktœ:r, tris] m. Contradictor.

contradiction [-sjɔ̃] f. Contradiction; *esprit de contradiction,* contrariness, contradictiousness; *en contradiction avec qqn,* at variance (ou) issue with s.o. ‖ Inconsistency ; *en contradiction avec qqch.*, inconsistent with sth.

contradictoire [-twa:r] adj. Contradictory ; conflicting ; inconsistent ; *conférence contradictoire,* public discussion, debate ; *société de conférences contradictoires,* debating society. ‖ JUR. After trial (jugement) ; *les débats sont contradictoires,* both sides are given a full hearing ; *examen contradictoire,* cross-examination.
— m. pl. Contradictory terms.

contradictoirement [-twarmɑ̃] adv. Contradictorily. ‖ JUR. *Arrêt rendu contradictoirement,* judgment given after hearing both sides.

contraignant, ante [kɔ̃trɛɲɑ̃, ɑ̃:t] adj. Exacting, demanding (travail), cramping (horaire).

contraindre [kɔ̃trɛ̃:dr] v. tr. (59). To constrain, to restrain, to curb (qqn, ses sentiments). ‖ To constrain, to compel, to force (à, to) ; to coerce (à, into) [v. OBLIGER] ; *contraindre à avancer, à descendre, à entrer, à monter, à reculer, à sortir,* to force on, down, in, up, back, out. ‖ JUR. *Contraindre par corps,* to arrest.
— v. pr. **Se contraindre,** to restrain oneself (se contenir). ‖ To force (ou) compel oneself to (se forcer).

contraint, ainte [kɔ̃trɛ̃, trɛ̃:t] adj. Forced, constrained.

contrainte [kɔ̃trɛ̃:t] f. Constraint, fetters (entrave) ; restraint (retenue) ; *sans contrainte,* freely. ‖ Constraint, compulsion (v. COERCITION, PRESSION) ; *par contrainte,* under compulsion (ou) duress. ‖ JUR. Distraint, seizure ; *contrainte par corps,* arrest, constraint.

contraire [kɔ̃trɛ:r] adj. Contrary, opposed ; conflicting ; adverse (adverse) ; contrary, opposite (opposé). ‖ Unsuitable, injurious, prejudicial (nuisible). ‖ JUR. Cross (action). ‖ NAUT. Cross (mer) ; contrary (vent).
— m. Contrary ; *au contraire,* on the contrary ; *au contraire de,* unlike, contrary to, counter to. ‖ JUR. *Défense au contraire,* counter-claim.

contrairement [kɔ̃trɛrmɑ̃] adv. Contrarily, contrary (à, to).

contralto [kɔ̃traltɔ] m. MUS. Contralto.

contrapontiste, contrapuntiste [kɔ̃trapɔ̃tist] s. MUS. Contrapuntist.

contrariant, ante [kɔ̃trarjɑ̃, ɑ̃:t] adj. Trying, vexatious ; tiresome (chose) ; provoking ; contradictious (personne).

contrarié, ée [-rje] adj. Annoyed, vexed ; sorry. ‖ Upset (*de*, at) ; *être contrarié dans ses projets,* to have one's plans upset.

contrarier v. tr. (1). To vex, to annoy, to provoke, to upset, to spite (dépiter). ‖ To impede ; to hinder, to check, to hamper (entraver). ‖ To thwart, to cross, to interfere with (s'opposer à). ‖ To contrast (des couleurs).
— v. pr. **Se contrarier,** to be vexed (ou) annoyed. ‖ To be in contrast, to contrast (couleurs).
— v. récipr. **Se contrarier,** to vex each other ; to be at cross purposes.

contrariété [jete] f. Annoyance, vexation, nuisance ; *il se décourage à la moindre contrariété,* if anything crosses him ever so little, he loses heart. ‖ Opposition, clashing (des couleurs). ‖ Hindrance (entrave). ‖ Chagrin. (V. DÉSAPPOINTEMENT.)

contrastant, ante [kɔ̃trastɑ̃, ɑ̃:t] adj. Contrasting.

contraste [kɔ̃trast] m. Contrast (opposition) ; *mettre en contraste,* to contrast.

contrasté, ée [-te] adj. Contrasting (caractères, couleurs) ; with a lot of contrast (photo).

contraster [-te] v. intr. (1). To contrast.

contrat [kɔ̃tra] m. Contract ; agreement (en général) ; deed (d'association) ; *contrat de mariage,* marriage settlement (ou) articles (ou) contract ; *contrat social,* social contract (ou) compact.

contravention [kɔ̃travɑ̃sjɔ̃] f. Contravention,

transgression, infringement ; petty offence. ‖ JUR. Minor infraction ; *dresser contravention à qqn,* to take s.o's name and address, U. S. to give s.o. a ticket ; *être en contravention avec,* to act in contravention of.

contravis [kɔ̃travi] m. Counter-advice.

contre [kɔ:tr] prép. Against ; at (opposition) ; *contre son gré,* against his will ; *contre toute attente,* contrary to expectation ; *jurer contre qqn,* to swear at s.o. ‖ To (proportion) ; *dix contre un,* ten to one. ‖ Against, close to (proximité) ; *contre la grille,* against (ou) close to the gate. ‖ For, in exchange for (échange) ; *échanger contre,* to exchange for. ‖ JUR., SPORTS. Versus. ‖ LOC. *Envers et contre tous,* in spite of everyone.
— adv. Against ; *contre à contre,* alongside ; *pour et contre,* for and against ; *par contre,* on the other hand, but.
— m. *Le pour et le contre,* the pros and cons. ‖ SPORTS. Counter (à l'escrime). ‖ **Contre-alizé,** m. Anti-trade (vent). ‖ **Contre-allée,** f. Sidewalk. ‖ **Contre-amiral,** m. NAUT. Rear-admiral. ‖ **Contre-appel,** m. MILIT. Check roll-call. ‖ **Contre-approches,** f. pl. MILIT. Counter-approaches. ‖ **Contre-assurance,** f. JUR. Reinsurance. ‖ **Contre-attaque,** f. MILIT. Counter-attack. ‖ **Contre-attaquer,** v. tr. MILIT. To counter-attack. ‖ **Contre-boutant,** m. ARCHIT. Shore, buttress, countefort. ‖ **Contre-chant,** m. MUS. Countermelody. ‖ **Contre-courant,** m. Counter-current ; *à contre-courant,* up-stream. ‖ **Contre-culture,** f. Counterculture. ‖ **Contre-digue,** f. Strengthening dyke. ‖ **Contre-échange (en),** adv. In exchange (ou) return. ‖ **Contre-écrou,** m. Counter-nut, lock-nut, check-nut, set screw. ‖ **Contre-électromotrice,** adj. f. Impedance (force). ‖ **Contre-enquête,** f. JUR. Counter-enquiry. ‖ **Contre-épreuve,** f. Counter-proof ; second test. ‖ **Contre-espionnage,** m. MILIT. Counter-espionnage, U. S. counter-intelligence. ‖ **Contre-essai,** m. Check-test. ‖ **Contre-examiner,** v. tr. To cross-examine, to cross-question. ‖ **Contre-expertise,** f. Counter-valuation. ‖ **Contre-feu,** m. Counter-fire. ‖ **Contre-fiche,** f. ARCHIT. Truss, strut, brace. ‖ **Contre-fil,** m. *A contre-fil,* the wrong way (gén.) ; against the grain (d'un bois, d'une étoffe) ; against the current (d'une rivière). ‖ **Contre-filet,** m. CULIN. Sirloin. ‖ **Contre-fugue,** f. MUS. Counter-fugue. ‖ **Contre-haut (en),** adv. At a higher level, up above. ‖ **Contre-hermine,** f. BLAS. Ermines. ‖ **Contre-indication,** f. MÉD. Contra-indication. ‖ **Contre-indiquer,** v. tr. To advise (ou) to warn against ; MÉD. to contra-indicate ; *médicament contre-indiqué à,* medicine not to be taken by. ‖ **Contre-interrogatoire,** m. JUR. Cross-examination. ‖ **Contre-interroger,** v. tr. JUR. To cross-examine. ‖ **Contre-jour,** m. Half-light ; *à contre-jour,* against the light, with one's back to the light. ‖ **Contre-manifestant,** m. Counter-demonstrator. ‖ **Contre-manifestation,** f. Counter-demonstration. ‖ **Contre-manifester,** v. intr. To hold (ou) go on a counter-demonstration. ‖ **Contre-manœuvre,** f. Counter-manœuvre. ‖ **Contre-mesure,** f. Countermeasure. ‖ **Contre-miner,** v. tr. MILIT. To countermine. ‖ **Contre-offensive,** f. MILIT. Counter-offensive. ‖ **Contre-pas,** m. MILIT. Half-step. ‖ **Contre-pente,** f. Reverse slope. ‖ **Contre-performance,** f. SPORTS., FIG. Poor performance. ‖ **Contre-pied,** m. SPORTS. Backscent (à la chasse) ; wrong foot (au tennis). ‖ FIG. *Prendre le contre-pied de,* to take the opposite course to, to run counter to. ‖ **Contre-plaçage,** m. Plywood construction. ‖ **Contre-plaqué,** m. Plywood. ‖ **Contre-plongée,** f. CINÉM. Low-angle shot. ‖ **Contre-poil (à),** adv. Against the hair (d'un animal), against the nap (d'un textile) ; *prendre qqn à contre-poil,* to rub s.o. up the wrong way. ‖ **Contre-porte,** f. Inside of a refrigerator door, inner door. ‖ **Contre-préparation,** f. MILIT.

Counter-preparation. ‖ **Contre-projet,** m. Counter-project. ‖ **Contre-propagande,** f. Counter-propaganda. ‖ **Contre-proposition,** f. Counter-proposition, alternative proposal. ‖ **Contre-rail,** m. CH. DE F. Guard-rail. ‖ **Contre-Réforme,** f. ECCLÉS. Counter-Reformation. ‖ **Contre-révolution,** f. Counter-revolution. ‖ **Contre-révolutionnaire,** adj., s. Counter-revolutionary. ‖ **Contre-terrorisme,** m. Counterterrorism. ‖ **Contre-terroriste,** adj., s. Counterterrorist. ‖ **Contre-torpilleur,** m. NAUT. Destroyer, light cruiser. ‖ **Contre-ut,** m. MUS. C in alt. ‖ **Contre-valeur,** f. FIN. Exchange value. ‖ **Contre-visite,** f. MÉD. Check inspection (ou) examination. ‖ **Contre-voie,** f. CH. DE F. Wrong side of the train; *à contre-voie,* up the down track, down the up track.

contrebalancer [kɔ̃trəbalɑ̃se] v. tr. (1). To counterbalance; to compensate.
— v. pr. **Se contrebalancer,** FAM. *S'en contrebalancer,* not to give (ou) care a damn.

contrebande [-bɑ̃:d] f. Contraband, smuggling (acte); smuggled goods (produit); *faire de la contrebande,* to smuggle.

contrebandier [-bɑ̃dje] s. Smuggler.

contrebas [-ba] m. *En contrebas,* lower down.

contrebasse [-bɑ:s] f. MUS. Double-bass, contra-bass (instrument); double-bass player (musicien).

contrebassiste [-bɑsist] s. MUS. Contrabassist, double-bass player.

contrebasson [-bɑsɔ̃] m. MUS. Contrabassoon, double bassoon.

contrebatterie [-batri] f. MILIT. Counter-battery.

contrebattre [-batr] v. tr. (20). MILIT. To counterbatter.

contrecarrer [-kare] v. tr. (1). To counteract, to oppose (des plans); to cross, to thwart (qqn).

contrechamp [-ʃɑ̃:] m. Reverse shot (au cinéma).

contrechâssis [-ʃɑsi] m. Outside window; double sash. ‖ TECHN. Top-flask.

contrecœur [-kœ:r] m. *A contrecœur,* unwillingly, reluctantly.

contrecœur m. Back-plate (de cheminée). ‖ CH. DE F. Guard-rail, wing-rail.

contrecoup [-ku] m. Rebound (d'une balle); jar (d'un coup); backlash (d'une explosion). ‖ FIG. After-effect; *par contrecoup,* on the rebound.

contredanse [-dɑ̃:s] f. Country dance; quadrille. ‖ FAM. Police officer's report.

contredire [-di:r] v. tr. (63). To gainsay, to deny (un propos); to contradict (qqn). ‖ To be contrary to, to be inconsistent (ou) at variance with (qqch.).
— v. pr. **Se contredire,** to contradict oneself.
— v. récipr. **Se contredire,** to contradict each other (ou) one another.

contredisant, ante [-dizɑ̃, ɑ̃:t] adj. Contradictious; contentious.
— s. JUR. Opposing party.

contredit [-di] m. Contradiction; *sans contredit,* unquestionably. ‖ JUR. Rejoinder.

contrée [kɔ̃tre] f. Region, district. (V. PAYS.)

contrefaçon [kɔ̃trəfasɔ̃] f. Counterfeiting, forging (action); counterfeit, forgery (résultat); *de contrefaçon,* spurious. ‖ JUR. Infringement.

contrefacteur [-faktœ:r] m. Counterfeiter, forger. ‖ JUR. Infringer (de brevet).

contrefaction [-faksjɔ̃] f. Forgery (d'effets); counterfeiting (de monnaies).

contrefaire [-fɛ:r] v. tr. (50). To mimic, to ape, to imitate (une allure); to disguise (son écriture, sa voix); to pirate (un livre); to imitate, to mock (qqn). ‖ JUR. To forge (un billet); to falsify, to forge (un document); to counterfeit (la monnaie); to infringe (un objet breveté). ‖ FIG. To feign, to fake, to counterfeit (l'émotion).

contrefait, aite [-fɛ, ɛt] adj. Disguised (écriture, voix); pirated (édition); deformed (personne). ‖

JUR. Forged (billet, document); counterfeit, spurious (monnaie). ‖ FIG. Feigned.

contreficher (se) [səkɔ̃trafiʃe] v. pr. (1). POP. *Je m'en contrefiche,* I don't care a hang; U. S. I don't give a rap.

contrefort [-fɔ:r] m. Stiffening, counter (de chaussures). ‖ ARCHIT. Buttress, counterfort. ‖ GÉOGR. Counterfort, spur; pl. foothills.

contremaître [-mɛ:tr] m. Foreman, overseer, ganger. ‖ NAUT. Boatswain's mate.

contremaîtresse [-mɛtrɛs] f. Forewoman.

contremandement [-mɑ̃dmɑ̃] m. Cancelling, countermanding.

contremander [-mɑ̃de] v. tr. (1). To countermand, to cancel, to revoke (une invitation, un ordre); to call off, to cancel (une réunion).

contremarche [-marʃ] f. MILIT. Countermarch. ‖ ARCHIT. Riser.

contremarque [-mark] f. COMM. Countermark. ‖ THÉÂTR. Pass-out ticket, check.

contrepartie [-parti] f. COMM. Counterpart, duplicate, contra (document); *en contrepartie,* per contra. ‖ JUR. Other side (ou) party. ‖ FIN. Consideration (valeur) [*en, in*]. ‖ MUS. Counterpart. ‖ FIG. Compensation; *en contrepartie,* as against this.

contrepèterie [-pɛtri] f. Spoonerism.

contrepoids [-pwɑ] m. Counterweight, counterpoise, counterbalance; *faire contrepoids à,* to counterbalance. ‖ Balancing-pole (de danseur de corde); counterbalance (d'horloge).

contrepoint [-pwɛ̃] m. MUS. Counterpoint.

contrepoison [-pwazɔ̃] m. MÉD. Antidote, counter-poison.

contrer [kɔ̃tre] v. tr. (1). SPORTS. To counter (à la boxe). ‖ To double (aux cartes). ‖ FAM. To cross, to thwart, to interfere with (qqn).

contrescarpe [kɔ̃trɛskarp] f. Counterscarp.

contreseing [kɔ̃trəsɛ̃] m. JUR. Counter-signature.

contresens [-sɑ̃:s] m. Wrong way, wrong direction; opposite direction. ‖ Misconception (des mots, d'un passage); misconstruction (d'une phrase); misinterpretation (du sens); mistranslation (du texte); *faire un contresens,* to misunderstand (ou) to mistranslate a sentence. ‖ Absurdity.

contresigner [-siɲe] v. tr. (1). To countersign.

contretemps [kɔ̃trətɑ̃] m. Disappointment (déception); inconvenience (embarras); contretemps, mishap, hitch (mésaventure); *à contretemps,* unseasonably, inopportunely. ‖ MUS. Contra tempo; syncopation.

contretype [-tip] m. TECHN. Duplicate, dupe (en photographie, au cinéma).

contrevallation [-vallasjɔ̃] m. Contravallation.

contrevenant [-vənɑ̃] s. JUR. Contravener, infringer, offender; delinquent.

contrevenir [-vəni:r] v. intr. (101). *Contrevenir à,* to contravene, to infringe, to transgress.

contrevent [-vɑ̃] m. Outside shutter (volet). ‖ ARCHIT. Wind-brace.

contrevérité [-verite] f. Untruth, misstatement.

contribuable [kɔ̃tribɥabl] s. Taxpayer.

contribuant, ante [-bɥɑ̃, ɑ̃:t] adj. Contributing.
— m. Contributor.

contribuer [-bɥe] v. intr. (1). To contribute (à, to); *contribuer aux dépenses,* to pay one's share of the expenses. ‖ To contribute, to conduce (à, to) [v. CONCOURIR]; to play a part (à, in).

contributaire [-bɥtɛ:r] adj., s. Contributory.

contributif, ive [-bɥtif, i:v] adj. Taxpaying.

contribution [-bɥsjɔ̃] f. FIN. Duty; rate; tax (impôt); *contributions directes,* direct taxation; *contributions indirectes,* excise revenue, indirect taxation. ‖ FIG. Contribution (participation); *mettre à contribution,* to lay under contribution, to press into service.

contristant, ante [kɔ̃tristɑ̃, ɑ̃:t] adj. Afflicting, saddening.

contrister [-te] v. tr. (1). To afflict, to sadden.

contrit, ite [kɔ̃tri, it] adj. Contrite.

contrition [-sjɔ̃] f. Contrition; *avec contrition,* contritely.

contrôlable [kɔ̃trolabl] adj. Verifiable.

contrôle [kɔ̃trɔ:l] m. Verification; checking; supervision. ‖ Hall-marking (des métaux précieux); assaying (de la monnaie); hall-mark (poinçon). ‖ FIN. Control (des changes); auditing (des comptes). ‖ MILIT. Roll, muster roll; roster. ‖ FIG. *Contrôle de soi,* self-control.

contrôlé, ée [kɔ̃trole] adj. Hall-marked (bijoux); *appellation contrôlée,* guaranteed vintage (des vins).

contrôler v. tr. (1). To verify, to check; to supervize; to inspect. ‖ To hall-mark (des métaux précieux); to assay (la monnaie). ‖ FIN. To audit (les comptes). ‖ THÉÂTR. To check (les billets). ‖ CH. DE F. To inspect (les billets).
— v. pr. **Se contrôler,** to control oneself.

contrôleur [-lœ:r] s. Inspector, supervisor. ‖ Inspector (de magasin); time-keeper, time-clerk (d'usine). ‖ FIN. Auditor (des comptes); inspector (des contributions); controller, comptroller (de la monnaie). ‖ CH. DE F. Ticket-collector. ‖ Ticket-inspector, U. S. conductor (d'autobus, de métro). ‖ THÉÂTR. Check-taker, U. S. ticket-taker (de billets). ‖ NAUT. Controller. ‖ AVIAT. *Contrôleur de vol,* flight indicator. ‖ AUTOM. *Contrôleur de vitesse,* speedometer.

controller [-lœ:r] m. ELECTR. Controls.

contrordre [kɔ̃trɔrdr] m. Counter-order.

controuvé, ée [kɔ̃truve] adj. Forged, spurious.

controversable [kɔ̃trɔvɛrsabl] adj. Controversial; controvertible.

controverse [-vɛ:rs] f. Controversy; *matière à controverse,* debating (ou) talking point.

controversé, ée [-vɛrse] adj. Debated (question).

controverser v. tr. (1). To controvert; to discuss.

controversiste [-vɛrsist] m. Controversialist, controvertist.

contumace [kɔ̃tymas] f. JUR. Contumacy; *par contumace,* in absentia, by default.

contumax [kɔ̃tymaks] adj. JUR. Contumacious.
— s. JUR. Absconder, defaulter.

contus, use [kjɔ̃ty, yz] adj. Contused; *plaie contuse,* bruise.

contusion [-zjɔ̃] f. Contusion, bruise. (V. BLEU.)

contusionner [-zjɔne] v. tr. (1). To contuse.

conurbation [kɔnyrbasjɔ̃] f. Conurbation.

convaincant, ante [kɔ̃vɛ̃kɑ̃, ɑ̃:t] adj. Convincing *(de,* of).

convaincre [kɔ̃vɛ̃:kr] v. tr. (102). To convince, to persuade *(de,* of); *se laisser convaincre,* to let oneself be persuaded. ‖ JUR. To convict, to prove guilty *(de,* of).
— v. pr. **Se convaincre,** to convince oneself.

convaincu, ue [kɔ̃vɛ̃ky] adj. Convinced, persuaded *(de,* of); *non convaincu,* unsatisfied. ‖ Convinced, earnest; *un conservateur convaincu,* a dyed-in-the-wool Conservative. ‖ JUR. Convicted; *convaincu de trahison,* accused of treason.

convalescence [kɔ̃valɛsɑ̃:s] f. MÉD. Convalescence; *être en convalescence,* to convalesce.

convalescent, ente [-sɑ̃, ɑ̃:t] adj., s. MÉD. Convalescent.

convection [kɔ̃vɛksjɔ̃] f. PHYS. Convection; *de convection,* convectional.

convenable [kɔ̃vənabl] adj. Decent, passable, fair (acceptable); fit, fitting, suitable, proper (v. APPROPRIÉ); decent, decorous, correct; respectable, well-behaved (correct); *peu convenable,* improper, indecorous, unseemly.

convenablement [-bləmɑ̃] adv. Decently; suitably, fitly; correctly; decorously.

convenance [kɔ̃vənɑ̃:s] f. Conformity, accordance, harmony (accord). ‖ Appropriateness, convenience, fitness (commodité); *mariage de convenance,* marriage of convenience; *raisons de convenance,* grounds of expediency. ‖ Pl. Good manners, decency, proprieties; social conventions; rule of decorum; *sauvegarder les convenances,* to observe the proprieties.

convenir [-ni:r] v. intr. (101). *Convenir à,* to please, to suit (agréer); to fit, to suit; to become, to befit; to be suitable (ou) adapted to (être approprié). ‖ *Convenir de,* to agree on (ou) about (qqch.); *convenir de faire qqch.,* to agree to do sth. ‖ *Convenir que,* to agree (ou) to acknowledge (ou) to admit (ou) to confess that.
— v. impers. *Il convient de, que,* it is fitting (ou) proper (ou) advisable to, that; *comme il convient,* suitably to the occasion.

conventicule [kɔ̃vɑ̃tikyl] m. Conventicle.

convention [-sjɔ̃] f. Agreement (accord); covenant (clause); convention, contract (contrat); convention (internationalement); *convention syndicale,* underwriting contract; *convention tacite,* tacit understanding; *sauf convention contraire,* unless otherwise provided, unless there be any clause to the contrary. ‖ Convention, rule, standard (règle); *de convention,* conventional.

conventionné, ée [-sjɔne] adj. MÉD. *Médecin conventionné, clinique conventionnée,* doctor, clinic operating within the French National Health Service.

conventionnel, elle [-sjɔnɛl] adj. Conventional. ‖ JUR. Conventionary; by agreement; *obligations conventionnelles,* contractual obligations.
— m. † Member of the Convention, 1792-1795.

conventionnellement [-sjɔnɛlmɑ̃] adv. Conventionally.

conventionnement [-sjɔnmɑ̃] m. MÉD. Agreement between doctors and the French National Health Service.

conventuel, elle [kɔ̃vɑ̃tɥɛl] adj. ECCLÉS. Conventual.

convenu, ue [kɔ̃vəny] adj. Agreed; admitted; *c'est convenu,* right-o, U. S. O. K! ‖ Conventional (langage); stipulated, agreed upon (lieu).

convergence [kɔ̃vɛrʒɑ̃:s] f. Convergence, convergency.

convergent, ente [-ʒɑ̃, ɑ̃:t] adj. Convergent, converging. ‖ MILIT. Concentrated (feu).

converger [-ʒe] v. intr. (7). To converge. ‖ MILIT. *Faire converger,* to concentrate.

convers, erse [kɔ̃vɛ:r, ɛrs] adj. ECCLÉS. Lay.

conversation [kɔ̃vɛrsasjɔ̃] f. Conversation, talk (de vive voix); call (au téléphone); *changer de conversation,* to change the subject, to turn the conversation; *engager la conversation avec qqn,* to engage s.o. in conversation, to enter into conversation with s.o.; *faire les frais de la conversation,* to do all the talking; *langage de la conversation,* colloquial language.

converse [kɔ̃vɛrs] adj., f. PHILOS. Converse.

converser [-se] v. intr. (1). To talk, to converse.

conversion [-sjɔ̃] f. ECCLÉS., FIN., MATH., PHILOS. Conversion. ‖ MILIT. Wheeling; chance of direction (ou) front. ‖ SPORTS. *Conversion en descente,* down-hill turn (au ski).

converti, ie [-ti] adj. Converted.
— s. ECCLÉS. Convert. ‖ FIG. *Prêcher un converti,* to preach to the converted.

convertibilité [-tibilite] f. Convertibility.

convertible [-tibl] adj. Convertible.
— m. Bed settee. ‖ AVIAT. Convertiplane.

convertir [-ti:r] v. tr. (2). To convert, to bring over *(à,* to); to convert, to change *(en,* into). ‖ FIN., MATH., TECHN., CHIM., ECCLÉS., PHILOS. To convert.

— v. pr. **Se convertir**, to become converted; to reform; *se convertir en*, to turn into, to be converted into.

convertissable [-tisabl] adj. Convertible; transformable.

convertissage [-tisa:ʒ] m. Techn. Converting, conversion.

convertissement [-tismɑ̃] m. Fin. Conversion.

convertisseur [-tisœ:r] m. Electr. Transformer. ‖ Techn. Converter.

convexe [kɔ̃vɛks] adj. Convex.

convexité [-site] f. Convexity.

convict [kɔ̃vikt] m. Convict.

conviction [kɔ̃viksjɔ̃] f. Conviction, firm belief (v. certitude); *avoir la conviction que*, to be convinced that; *emporter la conviction*, to carry conviction. ‖ Ecclés. Pl. Convictions. ‖ Jur. Proof of guilt; *pièce à conviction*, exhibit.

convié, ée [kɔ̃vje] adj. Invited.
— s. Guest; person invited.

convier v. tr. (1). To invite (*à*, to) [pr. et fig.].

convive [kɔ̃vi:v] s. Guest.

convivialité [-vivjalite] f. Conviviality.

convocation [kɔ̃vɔkasjɔ̃] f. Convocation; call. ‖ Jur. Summons, notice. ‖ Milit. Calling up.

convoi [kɔ̃vwa] m. Funeral procession (cortège funèbre). ‖ Ch. de f. Train. ‖ Milit., Naut. Convoy, protecting escort. ‖ Autom. *Convoi automobile*, motor transport column, motor train. ‖ Fam. *Du même convoi*, in the same boat.

convoiement [-mɑ̃] m. V. convoyage.

convoitable [kɔ̃vwatabl] adj. Covetable.

convoiter [-te] v. tr. (1). To covet, to lust after; to hanker after (fam.).

convoitise [-ti:z] f. Covetousness; lust; longing; *regard de convoitise*, covetous look.

convoler [kɔ̃vɔle] v. intr. (1). To marry.

convoquer [kɔ̃vɔke] v. tr. (1). To summon, to convoke. ‖ To notify (un candidat). ‖ Jur. To convene (une assemblée); to summon (le Parlement). ‖ Milit. To call up.

convoyage [kɔ̃vwaja:ʒ] m. Conveyance.

convoyer [-je] v. tr. (9 *a*). Milit., Naut. To convoy; to escort.

convoyeur [-jœ:r] m. Naut. Convoy (bateau); convoying officer (officier). ‖ Techn. Conveyor. ‖ Aviat. *Pilote convoyeur*, ferry pilot. ‖ Ch. de f. *Convoyeur des postes*, railway mail sorter.

convulser [kɔ̃vylse] v. tr. (1). To convulse.

convulsif, ive [-tif, i:v] adj. Convulsive.

convulsion [-sjɔ̃] f. Convulsion (pr. et fig.).

convulsionnaire [-sjɔnɛ:r] s. Convulsionary.

convulsionner [-sjɔne] v. tr. (1). To convulse. ‖ Fig. To upset, to convulse.

convulsivement [-sivmɑ̃] adv. Convulsively.

coobligation [kɔɔbligɑsjɔ̃] f. Jur. Joint obligation.

coobligé, ée [-ʒe] s. Jur. Co-obligor, joint obligor.

cooccupant [kɔɔkypɑ̃] s. Jur. Joint occupier.

cooccurrence [kɔɔkyrɑ̃:s] f. Gramm. Co-occurrence.

coolie [kuli] m. Coolie.

coopérant [kɔɔperɑ̃] m. Young man doing his military service in Service de la coopération.

coopérateur, trice [kɔɔperatœ:r, tris] adj. Co-operating.
— s. Co-operator.

coopératif, ive [-tif, tiv] adj. Co-operative.

oooopération [-sjɔ̃] f. Co-operation; support. ‖ *Service de la coopération*, form of military service in which young men work as cultural or technical advisers abroad (similar to USO or Peace Corps).

coopératisme [-tism] m. Cooperation, cooperative movement.

coopérative [-tiv] f. Co-operative; co-op (fam.).

coopérer [kɔɔpere] v. intr. (5). To co-operate, to contribute (*à*, to); to co-operate (*avec*, with).

cooptation [kɔɔptasjɔ̃] f. Co-optation.

coopter [-te] v. tr. (1). To co-opt.

coordination [kɔɔrdinasjɔ̃] f. Co-ordination.

coordonnateur, trice [kɔɔrdɔnatœ:r, tris] adj. Co-ordinating.

coordonné, ée [-ne] adj. Co-ordinated (mouvements). ‖ Gramm. Co-ordinate.
— m. pl. Co-ordinates, separates (dans l'habillement).

coordonnée f. Math. Co-ordinate. ‖ Pl. Fig. Personal details, particulars; *je n'ai pas ses coordonnées*, I don't know how to get in touch with him.

coordonner v. tr. (1). To co-ordinate.

copain [kɔpɛ̃] m. Fam. Mate, pal, chum; U. S buddy; *être bons copains*, to be pally.

copal [kɔpal] m. Copal.

copartage [kɔparta:ʒ] m. Jur. Coparcenary.

copartageant [-ʒɑ̃] s. Jur. Coparcener.

copartager [-ʒe] v. tr. (7). Jur. To be coparceners.

coparticipant [kɔpartisipɑ̃] s. Jur. Co-partner.

coparticipation [-pasjɔ̃] f. Co-partnership; *coparticipation aux bénéfices*, profit-sharing.

copeau [kɔpo] m. Shaving (de bois, au rabot); chip (de bois, de métal); turnings (de métal).

copiage [kɔpja:ʒ] m. Copying, cribbing (d'un devoir). ‖ Copying, reproducing (d'un modèle).

copie [kɔpi] f. Copy, transcript (à la main); carbon copy (à la machine); *copie au net*, fair copy. ‖ Copy, imitation. ‖ Print (au cinéma, en photographie). ‖ Paper (de candidat); exercise, task (d'écolier); copy (de journaliste). ‖ Arts. Copy, reproduction; replica. ‖ **Copie-lettres**, m. Comm. Copy letter book.

copier [kɔpje] v. tr. (1). To copy, to imitate (imiter); to copy, to reproduce (reproduire); to copy, to make a copy of, to transcribe (transcrire). ‖ To crib (un devoir) [*sur*, from]. ‖ Fig. To mimic, to ape (qqn).

copieur, euse [kɔpjœ:r, ø:z] s. Copy-cat, cribber.

copieusement [kɔpjøzmɑ̃] adv. Copiously.

copieux, euse [kɔpjø, ø:z] adj. Copious, plentiful. ‖ Substantial (repas).

copilote [kɔpilɔt] m. Aviat. Second pilot, U. S. co-pilot.

copinage [kɔpina:ʒ] m. Fam. Favouritism (dans le milieu professionnel).

copine [kɔpin] f. Fam. Girl chum. (V. copain.)

copiner [-ne] v. intr. (1). Fam. To pal up (ou) chum up with, to make friends with.

copinerie [-nri] f. Fam. Matiness, chumminess, palliness.

copiste [kɔpist] s. Copyist.

coposséder [kɔpɔsede] v. tr. (5). To possess (ou) own jointly.

copossesseur [kɔpɔsɛsœ:r] m. Co-tenant, joint owner.

copossession [-sjɔ̃] f. Co-tenancy.

copra [kɔpra] m. Copra.

copreneur [kɔprənœ:r] m. Jur. Co-lessee.

coproduction [kɔprɔdyksjɔ̃] f. Ciném. Coproduction.

coprophagie [kɔprɔfaʒi] f. Coprophagy.

copropriétaire [kɔprɔprjetɛ:r] s. Jur. Co-proprietor, joint tenant. ‖ Fin. Part-owner.

copropriété [-te] f. Joint ownership.

coprospérité [kɔprɔsperite] f. Mutual prosperity.

copte [kɔpt] s. Copt.
— m., adj. Coptic (langue).

copulatif, ive [kɔpylatif, i:v] adj. Gramm. Copulative.

copulation [-sjɔ̃] f. Copulation.

copule [kɔpyl] f. Gramm. Copula.

copyright [kɔpirait] m. Copyright.

coq [kɔk] m. Cock, cockerel; rooster; *coq de bruyère*, grouse, capercaillie; *coq de combat*, game-cock; *coq de roche*, cock-of-the-rock. ‖ ARCHIT. *Coq de clocher*, weather-cock. ‖ FIG. *Coq de village*, cock of the walk; *comme un coq en pâte*, in clover, like a fighting cock. ‖ LOC. *Sauter du coq à l'âne*, to have a butterfly mind, to jump from one thing to another. ‖ **Coq-à-l'âne**, m. invar. Cock-and-bull story.

coq m. NAUT. Cook.

coquart, coquard [kɔka:r] m. POP. Black eye, shiner.

coque [kɔk] f. Shell; *coque de noix*, nutshell; *coque d'œuf*, eggshell. ‖ Kink (de corde); loop (de ruban). ‖ NAUT., AVIAT. Hull. ‖ ZOOL. Cockle. ‖ CULIN. *Œuf à la coque*, boiled egg.

coquebin [kɔkbɛ̃] m. Greenhorn.

coquelet [kɔklɛ] m. CULIN. Cockerel.

coquelicot [kɔkliko] m. BOT. Poppy.

coqueluche [kɔklyʃ] f. MÉD. Whooping- (ou) hooping-cough. ‖ FAM. Idol, favourite; cynosure.

coquemar [kɔkma:r] m. CULIN. Kettle.

coquerie [kɔkri] f. NAUT. Galley.

coqueriquer [kɔkrike] v. intr. To crow (coq).

coquet, ette [kɔkɛ, ɛt] adj. Coquettish (aguichant). ‖ Spruce, smart (bien habillé). ‖ Stylish (ameublement, chapeau, robe); natty, U. S. sharp (fam.) [vêtement]. ‖ Trim, neat (jardin, ville). ‖ FAM. Generous (salaire); tidy (somme).

coqueter [kɔkte] v. tr. (8a). To coquet.

coquetier [kɔktje] m. CULIN. Egg-cup. ‖ COMM. Egg-merchant. ‖ SPORTS. Cup, pot. ‖ FAM. *Gagner le coquetier*, to win the prize.

coquetière [-tjɛ:r] f. CULIN. Egg-boiler.

coquette [kɔkɛt] f. Coquette, flirt.

coquettement [-tmɑ̃] adv. Smartly; stylishly.

coquetterie [-tri] f. Love of dress (goût de la toilette). ‖ Stylishness, smartness (du vêtement). ‖ Coquetry; *la coquetterie est le fond de l'humeur des femmes*, all women are fundamentally coquettes. ‖ Pl. Advances. ‖ Affectation, mannerism (minauderie); ostentation, pride (orgueil).

coquillage [kɔkija:ʒ] m. Shell (coquille); shellfish (mollusque).

coquille [kɔki:j] f. Shell (d'escargot, de fruit, de mollusque, d'œuf). ‖ Misprint, printer's (ou) typographical error (en typogr.). ‖ MILIT. Baskethilt, hand-guard (d'épée). ‖ BLAS. Escallop. ‖ TECHN. Chill-mould; casing. ‖ CULIN. Scallop; *coquilles de beurre*, butter-pats, flakes of butter; *coquilles Saint-Jacques*, scallops in shells.

coquiller [kɔkıje] v. tr. (1). To cockle (une étoffe); to chill (un métal); to blister (le pain).

coquillette [kɔkıjɛt] f. CULIN. Pasta.

coquillier, ère [kɔkıje, ɛ:r] adj. GÉOL. Conchitic, shelly.

coquin [kɔkɛ̃] m. Rascal, rogue, scoundrel. (V. FRIPON.) ‖ FAM. Rascal, beggar; *heureux coquin*, lucky dog.
— adj. Roguish.

coquine [kɔkin] f. Jade, hussy. ‖ FAM. Hussy, minx (maligne).

coquinerie [ri] f. Knavish trick, knavery, roguery (acte); knavishness (caractère).

cór [kɔr] m. MUS. Horn (instrument); hornplayer (musicien); *cor anglais*, tenor oboe. ‖ FIG. *Demander à cor et à cri*, to clamour for; *poursuivre à cor et à cri*, to pursue with hue and cry.

cor m. Corn (au pied); *emplâtre pour les cors*, corn-plaster.

cor m. ZOOL. Tine, point (de cerf); *un dix-cors*, a hart of ten; a deer with ten points.

corail [kɔra:j] (pl. **coraux** [kɔro]) m. Coral.
— adj. Coral-red, coralline.

corallien, enne [-ljɛ, ɛn] adj. Coral; *récif corallien*, coral-reef, cay.

coralligène [-liʒɛ:n] adj. GÉOL. Coralligenous; *calcaire coralligène*, coral limestone.

corallin [-lɛ̃] adj. Coralline.

coralline [-lin] f. Coralline.

Coran [kɔrɑ̃] m. Koran.

coranique [-ranik] adj. Koranic.

corbeau [kɔrbo] m. ZOOL. Raven, crow. ‖ ARCHIT. Corbel. ‖ NAUT. Grappling-iron.

corbeille [kɔrbɛ:j] f. Basket; *corbeille à ouvrage*, *à pain, à papier*, work-, bread-, paper- (ou) waste-paper-basket; *corbeille de mariage*, wedding-presents; *corbeille des affaires à examiner, des affaires terminées*, in-, out-tray. ‖ AGRIC. Flower-bed. ‖ THÉÂTR. Dress-circle. ‖ ARCHIT. Basket, corbeil.

corbeillée [-bɛje] f. Basketful.

corbillard [kɔrbija:r] m. Hearse.

corbillon [-jɔ̃] m. Small basket. ‖ Crambo (jeu).

corbleu [kɔrblø] interj. By Jove!

cordage [kɔrda:ʒ] m. Cordage, rope. ‖ NAUT. Rigging.

corde [kɔrd] f. Rope, cord; *corde à nœuds*, knotted climbing rope; *corde raide*, tight-rope. ‖ Thread (de tissu); *usé jusqu'à la corde*, threadbare. ‖ Cord (mesure de bois). ‖ MUS. Wire, string (de piano); string (de violon); *à cordes*, stringed (instrument); *les cordes*, the strings. ‖ MÉD. *Cordes vocales*, vocal cords. ‖ SPORTS. Rails (aux courses); string (de raquette). ‖ AUTOM. *Prendre un virage à la corde*, to cut a corner close. ‖ LOC. *Avoir plusieurs cordes à son arc*, to have several strings to one's bow, to have several irons in the fire; *c'est tout à fait dans mes cordes*, that's just in my line, that's right up my street; *être à la corde*, to be at the end of one's tether; to be on the rocks; *il pleut* (ou) *tombe des cordes*, the rain is coming down in sheets; *ne pas valoir la corde pour le pendre*, not to be worth the rope to hang him, not worth the powder to blow him up; *se mettre la corde au cou*, to put one's neck into the noose, U. S. to ball-and-chain it; *toucher la corde sensible*, to touch the right key. ‖ **Corde-signal**, f. Signal-rope.

cordé [kɔrde] m. ZOOL. Chordate.

cordeau [kɔrdo] m. Tracing-line; U. S. tracing-tape; *tiré au cordeau*, in a straight line. ‖ Match; fuze, U. S. fuse (de mines).

cordée [kɔrde] f. SPORTS. Line, rope, roped party (d'alpinistes); *premier de cordée*, leader. ‖ TECHN. Hoist (de mine).

cordeler [kɔrdəle] v. tr. (8a). To twist into a rope.

cordelette [-lɛt] f. Small cord.

cordelier [-lje] m. ECCLÉS. Franciscan friar.

cordelière [-ljɛ:r] f. Girdle, cord. ‖ ARCHIT. Twisted fillet.

corder [kɔrde] v. tr. (1). To cord (du bois). ‖ To cord (un colis); to string (une raquette).

corderie [-dəri] f. Rope-trade (commerce); rope-making (fabrication).

cordial, ale [kɔrdjal] adj. Cordial, hearty, warm.
— m. MÉD. Cordial.

cordialement [-lmɑ̃] adv. Cordially, heartily.

cordialité [-lite] f. Cordiality, heartiness.

cordier [kɔrdje] m. Rope-maker. ‖ MUS. Tail-piece.

cordillère [kɔrdijɛ:r] f. GÉOGR. Cordillera.

cordite [kɔrdit] f. MILIT. Cordite.

cordon [kɔrdɔ̃] m. Cord; string; tape; *cordons de la bourse*, purse-strings; *cordon de porte, de sonnette*, door-, bell-pull. ‖ Cordon (décoration). ‖ Cordon (de police); *établir un cordon autour*, to cordon off. ‖ MILIT. Cordon, cord; *cordon de postes*, chain of posts. ‖ MÉD. *Cordon médullaire*, spinal cord; *cordon ombilical*, umbilical cord,

navel string; *cordon sanitaire*, sanitary cordon, U. S. quarantine line. ‖ ARCHIT. Cordon. ‖ Cordon-bleu, m. CULIN. First-rate cook, cordon-bleu.
cordonner [-dɔne] v. tr. (1). To twist.
cordonnerie [-dɔnri] f. Shoemaker's shop (boutique); shoemaking (travail).
cordonnet [-dɔne] m. Braid, lace.
cordonnier [-dɔnje] m. Shoemaker, bootmaker; cobbler.
cordouan, ane [kɔrdwɑ̃, an] adj., s. GÉOGR. Cordovan.
Cordoue [kɔrdu] f. GÉOGR. Cordova; *cuir de Cordoue*, cordovan.
Corée [kɔre] f. GÉOGR. Korea.
coréen, enne [kɔreɛ̃, ɛn] adj., s. Korean.
— m. GRAMM. Korean (langue).
coreligionnaire [kɔreliʒjɔnɛ:r] s. ECCLÉS. Coreligionist.
coriace [kɔrjas] adj. Tough (pr. et fig.).
coriandre [kɔrjɑ̃:dr] f. BOT. Coriander.
coricide [kɔrisid] m. MÉD. Corn-killer (ou) -plaster.
corindon [kɔrɛ̃dɔ̃] m. Corundum.
corinthien, enne [kɔrɛ̃tjɛ̃, ɛn] adj., s. GÉOGR. Corinthian.
corion [kɔrjɔ̃] m. MÉD. Corium.
cormier [kɔrmje] m. BOT. Service tree, service.
cormoran [kɔrmɔrɑ̃] m. ZOOL. Cormorant.
cornac [kɔrnak] m. Mahout, elephant-keeper. Bear-leader (pour l'ours).
cornage [kɔrna:ʒ] m. ZOOL. Roaring. ‖ MÉD. Death rattle.
cornaline [kɔrnalin] f. Cornelian.
cornard [kɔrna:r] adj. FAM. Deceived (mari).
— m. FAM. Cuckold.
corne [kɔrn] f. Horn (d'animal); *bêtes à cornes*, horned cattle; *coup de corne*, butt, thrust; *corne de cerf*, antler; *donner un coup de corne à*, to gore. ‖ Horn (matière); *à monture de corne*, horn-rimmed (lunettes); *corne à chaussure*, shoehorn. ‖ Dog-ear (à un livre); horn (de la lune); *chapeau à cornes*, cocked hat. ‖ NAUT. *Corne de brume*, fog-horn. ‖ AUTOM. Hooter, horn. ‖ FIG. *Corne d'abondance*, cornucopia, horn of plenty. ‖ FAM. *Faire les cornes à*, to jeer at; *porter des cornes*, to be deceived (mari).
corné, ée [-ne] adj. Horny; corneous.
cornée f. MÉD. Cornea.
cornéen, enne [kɔrneɛ̃, ɛn] adj. MÉD. Corneal; *lentilles cornéennes*, contact lenses.
corneille [kɔrnɛ:j] f. ZOOL. Crow.
cornélien, enne [kɔrneljɛ̃, ɛn] adj. Relating to Pierre Corneille. ‖ FIG. *Choix cornélien*, impossible choice; *être dans une situation cornélienne*, to be in a quandary.
cornemuse [-my:z] f. MUS. Bagpipe.
cornemuseur [-myzœ:r], **cornemuseux** [-mysø] m. MUS. Piper.
corner [kɔrne] v. intr. (1). AUTOM. To hoot, to sound one's horn, to honk. ‖ MÉD. To buzz, to ring (oreilles). ‖ FIG. *Les oreilles lui cornent*, his ears are burning.
— v. tr. To turn down the corner of (une carte); to dog-ear (un livre). ‖ To horn, to gore, to butt (qqn). ‖ MUS. To blow a horn (artiste); to cipher (orgue). ‖ FAM. To trumpet, to proclaim, to shout, to blare forth (qqch.).
corner [kɔrnɛ:r] m. SPORTS. Corner, corner kick.
cornet [kɔrnɛ] m. *Cornet à dés*, dice-box; *cornet de papier*, screw of paper. ‖ MUS. Cornet (d'orgue); *cornet à pistons*, cornet. ‖ MÉD. Turbinate bone (du nez); *cornet acoustique*, eartrumpet. ‖ CULIN. *Cornet de glace*, ice-cream cone (or) cornet; *cornet de pâtisserie*, pastry

horn. ‖ TECHN. Cornet (d'essai); mouthpiece (de micro); receiver (de téléphone).
cornette [kɔrnɛt] f. ECCLÉS. Cornet, cornette, coif. ‖ MILIT. Cornet.
— m. MILIT. Cornet.
cornettiste [-tist] m. MUS. Cornetist.
corneur [kɔrnœ:r] adj. ZOOL. Roarer (cheval).
corniaud [kɔrnjo] m. Mongrel, cur (chien).
corniche [kɔrniʃ] f. ARCHIT. Cornice; *route en corniche*, cliff-road.
cornichon [kɔrniʃɔ̃] m. BOT. Gherkin. ‖ CULIN. Pickled gherkins, pickles. ‖ FAM. Ninny, noodle; U. S. dope, drip.
cornière [kɔrnjɛ:r] f. ARCHIT. Valley. ‖ TECHN. Angle-iron. ‖ AVIAT. T-piece.
cornique [kɔrnik] adj. GÉOGR. Cornish.
— m. GRAMM. Cornish.
corniste [kɔrnist] m. MUS. Horn-player.
Cornouaille [kɔrnwa:j] f. GÉOGR. Cornwall.
cornouille [kɔrnu:j] f. BOT. Cornel-berry, dogberry.
cornouiller [-je] m. BOT. Cornel-tree (arbre); dogwood (bois).
cornu, ue [kɔrny] adj. Horned. ‖ PHILOS. *Argument cornu*, cornutus, horned question. ‖ FIG. Preposterous, absurd (idée).
cornue f. CHIM. Retort.
corollaire [kɔrɔllɛ:r] m. Corollary. ‖ FIG. Consequence, inference.
corolle [kɔrɔl] f. BOT. Corolla.
coron [kɔrɔ̃] m. Mining village.
coronaire [kɔrɔnɛ:r] adj., f. MÉD. Coronary.
coronal, ale [-nal] adj. MÉD. Coronal.
coroner [kɔrɔnœ:r] m. JUR. Coroner.
corozo [kɔrozo] m. Corozo; vegetable ivory.
corporal [kɔrpɔral] m. ECCLÉS. Corporal.
corporatif, ive [kɔrpɔratif, i:v] adj. Corporate, corporative.
corporation [-sjɔ̃] f. Guild. ‖ JUR. Corporation.
corporatisme [-tism] m. Corporatism.
corporéité [kɔrpɔreite] f. Corporality; corporeity.
corporel, elle [-rɛl] adj. Corporeal. ‖ Corporal (châtiment). ‖ MÉD. Bodily (lésion).
corporellement [-rɛlmɑ] adv. Corporeally, corporally, bodily.
corps [kɔ:r] m. MÉD. Body; *à mi-corps*, up to the waist; *saisir à bras le corps*, to seize around the waist. ‖ Corpse, dead body (cadavre). ‖ Main building (de bâtiment); frame (de bicyclette); part (d'un meuble); body (d'une étoffe, d'un vêtement, du vin); housing (d'une lanterne à projection); barrel (d'une pompe). ‖ Corpus (recueil). ‖ Body (groupement); *corps diplomatique, législatif*, diplomatic, legislative body; *corps enseignant, médical*, teaching, medical profession; *corps de métiers*, guild, trade association; *esprit de corps*, esprit de corps. ‖ Body (en typographie). ‖ PHYS., CHIM. Body. ‖ MILIT. Corps; arm; force; *corps d'armée*, corps; *corps expéditionnaire*, expeditionary force; *corps franc*, commando, volunteer corps; *corps de garde*, guardroom (ou) house; *corps de sapeurs-pompiers*, fire brigade; *corps à corps*, hand-to-hand fighting, fighting at close quarters. ‖ JUR. *Corps du délit*, corpus delicti; *prise de corps*, arrest. ‖ THÉÂTR. *Corps de ballet*, corps de ballet. ‖ SPORTS. *Corps à corps*, clinch, in-fighting (à la boxe). ‖ NAUT. *Corps mort*, moorings; *perdu corps et biens*, lost with all hands on board. ‖ LOC. *A corps perdu*, neck and crop; *à son corps défendant*, in self-defence; reluctantly; *donner corps à*, to embody; *drôle de corps*, odd fish, queer chap, U. S. strange guy; *faire corps avec*, to form one body with; *passer sur le corps à qqn*, to run s.o. over; *prendre corps*, to materialize.

corpulence [kɔrpylɑ̃:s] f. Corpulent, stoutness.
corpulent, ente [-lɑ̃, ɑ̃:t] adj. Corpulent, stout ; bulky.
corpus [kɔrpys] m. JUR. Corpus.
corpusculaire [-kylɛ:r] adj. MÉD. Corpuscular.
corpuscule [-kyl] m. MÉD. Corpuscle.
corral [kɔral] m. Corral.
correct, ecte [kɔrɛkt] adj. Correct (conduite, personne); proper (emploi, langue); accurate (récit); pure (style); *il est très correct*, he has perfect manners. ‖ AVIAT. Smooth (atterrissage).
correctement [-tmɑ̃] adv. Correctly.
correcteur, trice [-tœ:r, tris] s. Corrector. ‖ Proof-reader (d'imprimerie). ‖ MILIT. Corrector.
— adj. *Verres correcteurs*, corrective lenses.
correctif, ive [-tif, i:v] adj., m. Corrective.
correction [-sjɔ̃] f. Correcting, correction. (V. RECTIFICATION.) ‖ Reading (des épreuves); emmendation (d'un texte). ‖ Correctness, properness (de la conduite); accuracy (d'un dessin, d'un récit); correction (du style). ‖ PHYS., MATH. Correction. ‖ Beating; whipping, flogging (punition corporelle). ‖ JUR. *Maison de correction*, Borstal school, reformatory, house of correction.
correctionnaliser [-sjɔnalize] v. tr. (1). JUR. To reduce to a misdemeanour (un crime).
correctionnel, elle [-sjɔnɛl] adj. JUR. Relating to misdemeanours; *délit correctionnel*, minor offence, misdemeanour ; *tribunal correctionnel*, court of petty sessions ; U. S. police court.
corrélatif, ive [kɔrrelatif, i:v] adj., m. Correlative.
corrélation [-sjɔ̃] f. Correlation ; *être* (ou) *mettre en corrélation avec*, to correlate with.
correspondance [kɔrɛspɔ̃dɑ̃:s] f. Correspondence, correlation (entre les choses); communication (entre les lieux); correspondence, intercourse (entre les personnes). ‖ Correspondence, letters; mail ; *faire sa correspondance*, to write some letters. ‖ CH. DE F. Connection, U.S. transfer, transfer point ; *assurer la correspondance avec*, to connect with.
correspondancier [-dɑ̃sje] s. COMM. Correspondence-clerk.
correspondant, ante [-dɑ̃, ɑ̃:t] adj. Corresponding. ‖ Equivalent; analogous.
— s. Correspondent ; *correspondant de guerre*, war (ou) military correspondent (*auprès de*, with). ‖ Corresponding member (de société savante). ‖ FAM. Pen-friend, U. S. pen-pal.
correspondre [kɔrɛspɔ̃:dr] v. intr. (4). To communicate (lieux, pièces); to correspond (*avec*, with) [personne]. ‖ CH. DE F. To run in connection, U. S. to connect (*avec*, with). ‖ *Correspondre à*, to correspond to, to agree to; to answer to.
corrida [kɔrida] f. Corrida, bullfight. ‖ FAM. Free-for-all, battle.
corridor [kɔridɔ:r] m. Corridor. (V. PASSAGE.)
corrigé [kɔriʒe] m. Correct version; key, crib.
corriger v. tr. (7). To correct (un abus, un devoir, une erreur, une faute, un texte) ; to correct, to read (des épreuves). ‖ To mend, to reform (un défaut, sa conduite). ‖ To modify, to rectify (un goût, le sort). ‖ To correct, to chastise ; to beat ; *corriger qqn de*, to break (ou) to cure (ou) to wean s.o. of. ‖ PHYS., CHIM., ASTRON. To correct.
— v. pr. Se corriger, to mend one's ways. (V. S'AMENDER.) ‖ To break oneself (*de*, of).
corrigeur, euse [-ʒœ:r, ø:z] s. TECHN. Corrector.
corrigible [-ʒibl] adj. Corrigible.
corroborant, ante [kɔrobɔrɑ̃, ɑ̃:t] adj. Corroborative, corrobating.
— m. MÉD. Corroborant.
corroboratif, ive [-ratif, i:v] adj., m. Corroborative. (V. CONFIRMATOIRE.)
corroboration [-rasjɔ̃] f. Corroboration.

corroborer [-re] v. tr. (1). To corroborate.
corrodant, ante [kɔrodɑ̃, ɑ̃:t] adj., m. Corrosive.
corroder [-de] v. tr. (1). To corrode, to erode.
corroi [kɔrwa] m. Currying (du cuir).
corroierie [-ri] f. TECHN. Curriery.
corrompre [kɔrɔ̃:pr] v. tr. (90). To corrupt, to spoil, to taint (la nourriture). ‖ To corrupt (la langue); to falsify, to vitiate (un texte). ‖ To taint (l'esprit, les mœurs); to pervert, to corrupt (qqn). ‖ To suborn (un fonctionnaire) ; to corrupt, to bribe, to buy (qqn) [v. ACHETER, SUBORNER, SOUDOYER] ; *esayer de corrompre un témoin*, to tamper with a witness.
— v. pr. Se corrompre, to spoil, to putrefy (nourriture). ‖ To become corrupt (langue). ‖ To become corrupt (ou) depraved (mœurs, personne).
corrompu, ue [kɔrɔpy] adj. Tainted, putrefied (nourriture). ‖ Corrupt (langue). ‖ Corrupt, depraved (mœurs, personne). ‖ Suborned (juge); bribed (témoin).
corrosif, ive [kɔrozif, i:v] adj., m. Corrosive.
corrosion [-zjɔ̃] f. Corrosion.
corrosivité [-zivite] f. Corrosiveness.
corroyage [kɔrwaja:ʒ] m. Currying, dressing (du cuir); welding (du fer).
corroyer [-je] v. tr. (9a). To curry, to dress (le cuir); to weld (le fer).
corroyeur [-jœ:r] s. Currier, leather dresser.
corrupteur, trice [kɔryptœ:r, tris] adj. Corrupting.
— m. Corrupter, debaucher, perverter (des mœurs); corrupter (d'un texte). ‖ Briber (de qqn).
— f. Corruptress.
corruptibilité [-tibilite] f. Corruptibility.
corruptible [-tibl] adj. Corruptible.
corruption [-sjɔ̃] f. Corruption, putrefaction; putridity (de la nourriture). ‖ Corruption, adulteration (de la langue, d'un texte). ‖ Corruption, depravation; depravity (des mœurs). ‖ Bribery, corruption (de fonctionnaire).
corsage [kɔrsa:ʒ] m. Bust (de femme); bodice, corsage (de robe); blouse, U. S. waist (blouse).
corsaire [kɔrsɛ:r] m. NAUT. Corsair. ‖ Pants, slacks (pantalon); calf-length jeans, U. S. clam-diggers, pedal-pushers.
Corse [kɔrs] f. GÉOGR. Corsica.
corse adj., s. GÉOGR. Corsican.
corsé, ée [kɔrse] adj. Spicy (goût, propos, sauce) ; thick (tissu) ; full-bodied (vin).
corselet [kɔrsəlɛ] m. Corselet. ‖ ZOOL. Corslet.
corser [kɔrse] v. tr. (1). To spice (les aliments); to stiffen (le tissu) ; to give body to (le vin). ‖ To intensify (une action); to spice (une conversation, des propos); to enliven (un récit).
— v. pr. Se corser, FAM. To get serious ; *ça se corse*, the plot thickens.
corset [kɔrsɛ] m. Corset, stays.
corseter [-səte] v. tr. (8 b). To corset.
corsetière [-sətjɛ:r] f. Corset-maker.
corso [kɔrso] m. *Corso fleuri*, procession of flower-decked floats.
cortège [kɔrtɛ:ʒ] m. Retinue, suite, train, attendance (d'un personnage). ‖ Procession ; *cortège funèbre, nuptial*, burial, bridal procession ; *cortège historique*, pageant; *fermer le cortège*, to bring up the rear. ‖ FIG. Appurtenances, inevitable accompaniment.
cortex [kɔrtɛks] m. MÉD. Cortex ; *cortex cérébral*, cerebral cortex.
cortical, ale [kɔrtikal] adj. MÉD., BOT. Cortical; *substance corticale*, cortex.
corticostéroïde [-kosteroïd] m. MÉD. Corticosteroid.
cortico-surrénal, ale [-kosyrrenal] adj. MÉD. Adrenocortical.
— f. MÉD. Adrenal cortex.
cortine [kɔrtin] f. MÉD. Cortine.

cortisone [kɔrtizɔn] f. Méd. Cortisone.
corvéable [kɔrveabl] adj. † Liable to statute labour.
corvée [-ve] f. † Statute labour. ‖ Milit. Fatigue; fatigue-duty (travail); fatigue-party (travailleurs); *de corvée*, on fatigue-duty; *homme de corvée*, fatigue-man. ‖ Fam. Drudgery; fag; irksome task; thankless job.
corvette [kɔrvɛt] f. Naut. Corvette, sloop.
coryphée [kɔrife] m. † Coryphaeus. ‖ Théâtr. Coryphée, principal dancer.
coryza [kɔriza] m. Méd. Coryza. (V. rhume.)
cosaque [kɔzak] adj., m. Cossack.
cosécante [kɔsekɑ̃:t] f. Math. Cosecant.
cosignataire [kɔsiɲatɛ:r] s. Co-signatory.
cosinus [kɔsinys] m. Math. Cosine.
cosmétique [kɔsmetik] adj., m. Cosmetic.
cosmétologie [-tɔlɔʒi] f. Cosmetology.
cosmétologue [-tɔlɔg] s. Cosmetician, cosmetologist.
cosmique [kɔsmik] adj. Cosmic.
cosmogonie [kɔsmɔgɔni] f. Philos. Cosmogony.
cosmogonique [-nik] adj. Cosmogonic.
cosmographe [kɔsmɔgraf] m. Cosmographer.
cosmographie [-fi] f. Cosmography.
cosmographique [-fik] adj. Cosmographic.
cosmologie [kɔsmɔlɔʒi] f. Cosmology.
cosmologique [-ʒik] adj. Cosmological.
cosmonaute [kɔsmono:t] s. Cosmonaut.
cosmopolite [kɔsmɔpɔlit] adj., s. Cosmopolitan.
cosmopolitisme [-tism] m. Cosmopolitanism.
cosmos [kɔsmɔs] m. Cosmos.
cossard [kɔsa:r] adj. Sluggish. (V. flemmard.)
— s. Fam. Sluggard, lazybones, never-sweat.
cosse [kɔs] f. Pod, hull, husk (de légumes). ‖ Electr. Spade terminal.
cosse f. Pop. Sluggishness, laziness; *j'ai la cosse*, I feel lazy, I can't be bothered.
cosser [kɔse] v. tr. (1). To butt.
cossu, ue [kɔsy] adj. Fam. Well-off, moneyed (personne); rich (habit); U. S. brownstone (immeuble).
costal, ale [kɔstal] adj. Méd. Costal.
costard [kɔsta:r] m. Arg. Suit.
Costa Rica [kɔstarika] m. Géogr. Costa Rica.
costaud, aude [kɔsto, o:d] adj. Fam. Hefty, beefy, stalwart, U. S. husky.
— m. Tough guy, muscleman.
costume [kɔsty:m] m. Costume; dress; suit; wearing apparel; *costume de bain*, bathing-costume (ou) U. S. suit; *costume civil*, mufti, civvies; *costume de golf*, plus-fours; *costume marin*, sailor suit; *costume militaire*, military uniform; *costume de sport, de ville*, sports, town-suit; *costume tailleur*, tailor-made costume; *costume zazou*, Teddy-boy suit, U. S. zoot-suit; *grand costume*, full dress. ‖ Théâtr. *Répétition en costume*, dress rehearsal.
costumé, ée [-me] adj. Fancy-dress (bal); in fancy dress (personne).
costumer v. tr. (1). To dress; to costume.
— v. pr. Se costumer, to dress up (*en*, as).
costumier [-mje] m. Costumier. ‖ Théâtr. Wardrobe-keeper.
cosy [kɔzi] m. Divan with shelves attached.
cotangente [kɔtɑ̃ʒɑ̃:t] f. Math. Cotangent.
cotation [kɔtasjɔ̃] f. Fin. Quotation, quoting.
cote [kɔt] f. Fin., Jur. Assessment, rating; *cote en Bourse*, quotation; *cote mobilière*, assessment on income. ‖ Height; altitude; reading; *cote de niveau*, bench-mark, spot level; *cote 648*, hill 648. ‖ Mark (note); mark, number, letter, reference, shelf-mark, call-number (d'un livre). ‖ Sports. Odds, betting (*de*, on) [aux courses]. ‖ Naut. Character, classification. ‖ Fig. *Cote mal taillée*, rough compromise. ‖ Fam. *Avoir une grosse cote*, to be highly thought of.

coté, ée [kɔte] adj. Fin. *Coté en Bourse*, listed. ‖ Arts. Dimensioned (dessin). ‖ Sports. Well-backed (cheval). ‖ Fig. Esteemed, respected.
côte [ko:t] f. Rib (d'animal); *côte d'aloyau, de porc*, wingrib, sparerib; *côte première*, loin-chop; *fausses côtes*, small ribs. ‖ Rib (d'un homme); *côte à côte*, side by side. ‖ Rib (de fruit); midrib (de feuille). ‖ Rib (d'étoffe); *à côtes*, ribbed, corded. ‖ Hill (v. montée); *à mi-côte*, halfway up; *vitesse en côte*, speed uphill. ‖ Coast, shore (rivage); *la Côte d'Azur*, the Riviera; *le long de la côte*, coastwise; *à la côte*, aground, ashore (navire). ‖ Fig. *A la côte*, on the rocks, stony-broke, flat broke. ‖ Fam. *Avoir les côtes en long*, to be a lazybones; *se tenir les côtes*, to hold (ou) to split one's sides. ‖ **Côte-d'Ivoire**, f. Géogr. The Ivory Coast.
côté [kote] m. Side (du corps, d'une étoffe, d'une route, d'un terrain); *à côté*, near; *à côté de*, near, close to, next to, beside; *de ce côté-ci*, on this side; *de l'autre côté de*, on the other side of, across; *le jardin à côté*, the next garden; *la maison d'à côté*, the house next door. ‖ Side, quarter, way (direction); *de côté*, sideways (démarche); sidelong (regard); *de ce côté*, this way; *de divers côtés*, from several quarters; *de tous les côtés*, in all directions, all over the place, everywhere, on every side; *du côté de*, towards; *de côté de chez Durand*, out toward Durand's; *chacun de son côté*, everyone his own way; *laisser de côté*, to leave out, to lay aside; *mettre de côté*, to save, to lay (ou) put by (de l'argent); to set apart (un objet); *passer (ou) toucher à côté*, to miss the mark (ou) the point; *se tenir de côté*, to stand apart. ‖ Side (aspect, point de vue); *à côté de*, compared with, on a level with; *bon côté*, sunny side; *côté faible*, weak side; *côté finances*, as regards financial resources; *d'un autre côté*, on the other side, on the other hand; *de mon côté*, for my part; *par certains côtés*, in some ways; *prendre qqch. du bon côté*, to take sth. in good part. ‖ Side (parenté); *du côté maternel*, on the distaff-side; *côté paternel*, male (ou) sword side. ‖ Side (parti); *du côté de*, in sympathy with; *mettre les rieurs de son côté*, to get all the laughter on one's side; *se mettre du côté de*, to side with. ‖ Math., Naut. Side. ‖ Pl. Neighbourhood (parages).
coteau [kɔto] m. Hill, knoll, hillock (colline). ‖ Vineyard (vignoble).
côtelé, ée [kotle] adj. Ribbed, corded; *velours côtelé*, corduroy.
côtelette [kotlɛt] f. Cutlet, chop (de mouton); chop (de porc); cutlet (de veau). ‖ Pl. Side-boards, side-whiskers, mutton chops.
coter [kɔte] v. tr. (1). To mark (un devoir); to number, to letter, to mark (un document, un livre). ‖ Fin. To assess; to quote. ‖ Arts. To dimension. ‖ Fig. To esteem (qqn).
— v. intr. To give marks.
coterie [kɔtri] f. Coterie.
cothurne [kɔtyrn] m. Buskin; cothurnus.
côtier, ière [kotje, jɛr] adj. Coastal (défense); coasting (navigation, pilote); inshore (pêche).
— m. Naut. Coaster.
cotillon [kɔtijɔ̃] m. Petticoat (jupe). ‖ Cotillon (danse).
cotisant, ante [kɔtizɑ̃, ɑ̃:t] s. Subscriber.
cotisation [-zasjɔ̃] f. Contribution (à une assurance); subscription (à une société).
cotiser [-ze] v. intr. (1). To assess, to rate. ‖ To subscribe.
— v. pr. Se cotiser, to club together.
côtoiement [kotwamɑ̃] m. Contiguity, coexistence (de choses); frequentation (de personnes).
coton [kɔtɔ̃] m. Cotton; *coton à coudre, à broder, à repriser*, sewing-, embroidery-, darning-cotton; *coton perlé*, crochet wool, corded cotton. ‖ Cot-

ton; *tissu laine et coton*, linsey-woolsey. ‖ Fluff (de drap); cotton, down (de plantes). ‖ Méd. *Coton hydrophile*, absorbent cotton-wool. ‖ Fig. *Elever dans du coton*, to coddle; *filer un mauvais coton*, to be in a bad way. ‖ **Coton-poudre**, m. Gun-cotton.

cotonnade [kɔtɔnad] f. Cotton fabric; cotton goods.

cotonner [-ne] v. tr. (1). To pad.
— v. pr. Se cotonner, to become cottony.

cotonnerie [-nri] f. Cotton-plantation (lieu); cotton-mill (usine).

cotonneux, euse [-nø, øːz] adj. Cottony, downy (feuille); woolly (fruit); fleecy (nuage).

cotonnier, ère [-nje, ɛːr] adj. Cotton.
— m. Bot. Cotton plant. ‖ Techn. Cotton worker.

côtoyer [kotwaje] v. tr. (9 a). To skirt (une forêt); to walk (ou) travel alongside (une rivière). ‖ To rub elbows with, to frequent (des gens). ‖ Naut. To coast (le rivage). ‖ Fig. To border on (la vérité).

cotre [kɔtr] m. Naut. Cutter.

cotriade [kɔtrijad] f. Culin. Chowder.

cottage [kɔtɛdʒ] m. Cottage.

cotte [kɔt] f. Petticoat (de paysanne); overalls (de travailleur). ‖ *Cotte de mailles*, coat of mail.

cotutelle [kɔtytɛːl] f. Jur. Joint guardianship.

cotuteur, trice [-tœːr, tris] s. Jur. Joint guardian.

cotyle [kɔtil] f. Méd. Acetabulum; socket.

cotylédon [kɔtiledɔ̃] m. Bot. Cotyledon.

cotylédoné, ée [-dɔne] adj. Bot. Cotyledonous.

cou [ku] m. Neck; *couper le cou à*, to behead; *jusqu'au cou*, up to the elbows (ou) eyes (ou) ears; *prendre ses jambes à son cou*, to take to one's heels, to show a clean pair of heels; *rentrer le cou dans les épaules*, to make oneself small; *sauter au cou de qqn*, to fall on s.o.'s neck. ‖ **Cou-de-pied** (pl. *cous-de-pied*) m. Méd. Instep.

couac [kwak] m. Mus. Squawk.

couard, arde [kwaːr, ard] adj. Cowardly.
— s. Coward. (V. LÂCHE, PEUREUX.)

couardise [kwardiːz] f. Cowardice.

couchage [kuʃaːʒ] m. Lying in bed (action); bedding (literie); night's lodging (logement).

couchant, ante [kuʃɑ̃, ɑ̃ːt] adj. Setting (soleil). ‖ Blas. Couchant. ‖ Fig. *Chien couchant*, lickspittle; fawner.
— n.. Sunset (coucher de soleil); west (occident). ‖ Fig. Wane, decline.

couche [kuːʃ] f. Couch, bed (lit). ‖ Coat (de goudron); layer (de poussière). ‖ Méd. Confinement, lying-in (de l'accouchée); childbirth (naissance); napkin, U. S. diaper (linge du nouveau-né); *fausse couche*, miscarriage. ‖ Arts. Wash (de couleur); coat, coating (de peinture). ‖ Géol. Bed, seam (de charbon); layer (de sable); layer, stratum (de terrain); *couche de quartz, de roche*, ledge, sill. ‖ Bot. Ring (de bois). ‖ Agric. *Couche arable*, topsoil; *couche de fumier*, hot bed, forcing bed; *semer sur couche*, to sow in heat. ‖ Culin. *Gâteau disposé en couches*, layer-cake. ‖ Fig. Class; *couches sociales*, social strata, classes of society; *la nouvelle couche*, the rising generation. ‖ Fam. *Il en a une couche!*, he is wood from the neck up! ‖ **Couche-culotte**, m. Pilch.

couché, ée [kuʃe] adj. Lying; in bed (personne); recumbent (position). ‖ Slanting, sloping (lettres); couched, art (papier). ‖ Fam. *Couché!*, down! (à un chien). ‖ Loc. *Être couché et nourri*, to live in; *le soleil est couché*, the sun is down.

coucher v. tr. (1). To lay, to lay down (un accidenté); to put to bed (un enfant); to put up (un voyageur). ‖ Agric. To lodge, to beat down (les blés); to lay (des branches). ‖ To slant (l'écriture). ‖ Arts. To lay on (un enduit, une peinture). ‖ Milit. *Coucher en joue*, to aim at. ‖ Loc. *Cou-*

cher par écrit, to write down; *coucher sur son testament*, to mention in one's will.
— v. intr. To sleep, to pass the night; to lodge (loger); *envoyer coucher un enfant*, to pack a child off to bed; *je ne veux pas vous faire coucher tard*, I don't want to keep you up. ‖ To sleep (avec, with). ‖ Fam. *Envoyer coucher qqn*, to send s.o packing.
— v. pr. Se coucher, to go to bed (s'aliter); to lie down (s'étendre); *l'heure de se coucher*, bedtime; *se préparer à se coucher*, to prepare for bed. ‖ To set, to sink (soleil). ‖ Naut. To heel over. ‖ Sports. *Se coucher sur les avirons*, to throw one's weight on the oars. ‖ Fam. *Va te coucher!*, hop it!, U. S. beat it!
— m. Going to bed (action); bedding (literie); *le coucher et la nourriture*, board and lodging. ‖ Setting (du soleil); *coucher de soleil*, sunset, U. S. sundown.

coucherie [kuʃri] f. Fam. Sex, screwing.

couchette [kuʃɛt] f. Cot (d'enfant). ‖ Ch. de f. Berth. ‖ Naut. Bunk.

coucheur [-ʃœːr] s. Bedfellow. ‖ Fam. *Mauvais coucheur*, spiky individual.

couci-couça [kusikusa] adv. Fam. So-so.

coucou [kuku] m. Cuckoo-clock (pendule). ‖ Zool. Cuckoo. ‖ Bot. Cowslip. ‖ Aviat., Fam. Crate. (V. zinc.)
— interj. Cuckoo! ‖ Peek-a-boo!, peep-bo!

coude [kud] m. Elbow (d'homme, de vêtement); *coude à coude*, side by side; in sympathy; *coup de coude dans les côtes*, poke in the ribs; *jouer des coudes*, to elbow one's way; *pousser du coude*, to nudge. ‖ Bend, turn (d'une rivière, d'une route). ‖ Techn. Elbow (de barre); knee (de tuyau). ‖ Fam. *Huile de coude*, elbow-grease; *lever le coude*, to lift one's elbow.

coudé, ée [kude] adj. Techn. Cranked, bent, kneed; *essieu coudé*, crank-axle.

coudée f. Cubit (mesure); *à cent coudées au-dessus de*, highly superior to. ‖ Loc. *Avoir ses coudées franches*, to have elbow-room (ou) free scope.

couder v. tr. (1). To crank; to bend; to knee.
— v. pr. Se couder, to bend.

coudoiement [kudwamɑ̃] m. Elbowing. ‖ Fig. Close contact.

coudoyer [-je] v. tr. (9 a). To elbow. ‖ Fig. To rub shoulders with, to hobnob with.

coudraie [kudrɛ] f. Hazel-grove.

coudre [kudr] v. tr. (31). To sew; to sew on (un bouton); to stitch (du cuir, un vêtement); to sew up (un ourlet). ‖ Méd. To sew, to stitch.
— v. intr. To sew.

coudrier [kudrie] m. Bot. Hazel, hazel-tree.

couenne [kwan] f. Pork-rind, rind. ‖ Culin. Crackling. ‖ Méd. Membrane.

couenneux, euse [kwanø, øz] adj. Méd. *Angine couenneuse*, diphtheria.

couette [kwɛt] f. Feather-bed. ‖ Techn. Bearing. ‖ Naut. Slipway.

couette f. Fam. Scut (de lapin).

couffin [kufɛ̃] m. Shopping basket (à provisions); carrycot (pour bébés).

cougouar [kugwaːr] m. Zool. Cougar.

couic [kwik] m. Fam. Squeak (cri); *faire couic*, to snuff it.

couille [kuːj] f. Pop. Ball, bollock.

couillon [kujɔ̃] m. Pop. Twerp; U. S. jerk.

couillonnade [kujɔnad], **couillonnerie** [-nri] f. Pop. Rot; screw-up; U. S. baloney.

couillonner [kujɔne] v. tr. (1). Pop. To swindle, to con, to take for a ride.

couinement [kuinmɑ̃] m. Squeaking.

couiner [kuine] v. intr. (1). To squeak (lapin). ‖ Techn. To send morse signals.

coulage [kulaːʒ] m. Guttering (d'une bougie); leaking (d'un liquide). ‖ Techn. Casting (d'un métal). ‖ NAUT. Sinking, scuttling (d'un navire). ‖ FIG. Waste, leakage (gaspillage).

coulant, ante [kulɑ̃, ɑ̃:t] adj. Flowing (liquide); running slip (nœud). ‖ FIG. Easy, accommodating (personne); fluent, easy, smooth (style). — m. Sliding ring. ‖ Keeper (de ceinture).

coule [kul] f. ECCLÉS. Cowl, hood.

coule f. FAM. *Etre à la coule*, to know the ropes.

coulé, ée [kule] adj. Cast (métal). ‖ NAUT. Sunk. ‖ FAM. Gone under, U.S. sunk; dished; wiped out. — m. MUS. Portamento; slide; slur. ‖ SPORTS. Follow (au billard).

coulée f. Outflow (de lave); pouring, casting, tapping (de métal). ‖ Running hand (écriture).

coulemelle [kulmɛl] f. BOT. Parasol mushroom.

couler v. tr. (1). To cast, to tap (du métal). ‖ To strain. (V. FILTRER.) ‖ MUS. To slur. ‖ NAUT. To sink, to send to the bottom (immerger); to scuttle (saborder). ‖ AUTOM. To run (une bielle). ‖ FIG. *Couler qqn*, to do for (ou) to dish s.o.; *couler un regard*, to cast a glance; *se la couler douce*, to have an easy (ou) a cushy time. — v. intr. To flow, to run (eau, larmes); to flow, to glide, to stream (rivière); to flow (sang); to trickle (sueur); *faire couler de l'eau*, to turn the water on. ‖ To slip (nœud). ‖ To gutter (bougie). ‖ To leak (stylo, tonneau). ‖ MÉD. To run (nez). ‖ CULIN. To run (fromage, glace). ‖ NAUT. To sink, to founder. ‖ SPORTS. *Couler à pic*, to sink and to drown (nageur). ‖ FIG. To glide by (années, temps); to flow (vers). — v. pr. *Se couler*, to glide, to slip, to creep, to slide. ‖ FAM. To do for oneself (se discréditer).

couleur [kulœ:r] f. Colour, tint, hue (teinte); *de couleur*, coloured (linge); *en couleur*, colour (impression, photographie). ‖ Colour, paint (produit); *couleurs à l'aquarelle, à l'huile*, water-colours; *marchand de couleurs*, colour-man, chandler, dry-salter. ‖ Colour, complexion (teint); *avoir des couleurs*, to be rosy-complexioned (ou) high-coloured; *fraîches couleurs de la jeunesse*, bloom of youth; *homme de couleur*, coloured man. ‖ Suit (aux cartes). ‖ MILIT. Pl. Colours, flag (drapeau); *amener, hisser les drapeaux*, to haul down, to hoist the colours. ‖ CINÉM. *Film en couleurs*, colour film. ‖ SPORTS. Pl. Colours (d'un jockey). ‖ FIG. Colour, opinion (en politique); FIG. Colour, dye, hue (aspect); *couleur locale*, local colour; *peindre sous les plus vives couleurs*, to paint in the liveliest colours; *présenter sous de fausses couleurs*, to misrepresent. ‖ FIG. Colour (prétexte); *sous couleur de*, under colour of, under the pretence of. ‖ FAM. *En dire de toutes les couleurs à qqn*, to give s.o. the rough edge of one's tongue; *en voir de toutes couleurs*, to be up to the neck in trouble.

couleur m. TECHN. Caster.

couleuvre [kulœ:vr] f. ZOOL. Grass-snake.

couleuvrine [kulœvrin] f. MILIT. † Culverin.

coulis [kuli] adj. *Vent coulis*, draught. — m. CULIN. Cullis; strong clear broth; *coulis de tomate*, tomato sauce.

coulissant, ante [kulisɑ̃, ɑ̃:t] adj. Sliding (porte).

coulisse [kulis] f. Slider, slide, sliding panel (pièce mobile); groove, slideway (rainure); *à coulisse*, sliding. ‖ TECHN. Slot. ‖ FIN. Outside market; curb exchange. ‖ THÉÂTR. Wings, U. S. backstage; *dans les coulisses*, behind the scenes. ‖ Loc. *Regard en coulisse*, side-glance, U. S. sidelong glance; *travailler dans les coulisses*, to pull the strings; U. S. to use one's drag.

coulisseau [-so] m. TECHN. Slide, slide-block, guide-block. ‖ Runner (de tiroir).

coulisser [-se] v. tr. (1). To provide with slides.

‖ To run up (une couture). — v. intr. To slide.

coulissier [-sje] m. FIN. Outside-broker.

couloir [kulwa:r] m. Passage; passageway. ‖ Lobby (au Parlement); *faire les couloirs*, to lobby. ‖ CH. DE F. Corridor. ‖ AUTOM. Gangway, U. S. aisle (de l'autobus). ‖ GÉOL. Gully. ‖ GÉOGR. Couloir; channel. ‖ NAUT. Chute.

coulomb [kulɔ̃] m. ELECTR. Coulomb.

coulommiers [kulɔmje] m. CULIN. Coulommiers cheese.

coulpe [kulp] f. † Guilt. ‖ Loc. *Battre sa coulpe*, to beat one's breast.

coulure [kuly:r] f. TECHN. Run-out, break-out.

coup [ku] m.

---

1. Avec un instrument. — 2. Avec une partie du corps. — 3. Appel. — 4. Explosion. — 5. Action. — 6. Mus. — 7. Arts. — 8. Naut. — 9. Méd. — 10. Milit. — 11. Sports. — 12. Jur. — 13. Fig. — 14. Fam. — 15. Loc.

---

1. Blow (en général); *coup de bâton, du bout d'une canne, de caillou, de canne, d'épée, de fouet, de hache, de marteau, de poignard, de sabre*, whack, poke, hit, cut, thrust, lash (ou) flick, chop, stroke, stab, slash; *donner un coup de bâton, de canne, de lanière, de règle*, to cudgel, to cane, to strap, to rap; *enfoncer à coups de marteau*, to hammer in; *sans coup férir*, without striking a blow; *tué sur le coup*, killed outright (ou) on the spot. ‖ 2. *Coup d'aile, de bec, de corne, de coude, de dent, de doigt, de griffe, de langue, d'ongle, de pied, de poing, de queue, de tête*, wing-stroke (ou) wing-flap, peck, thrust (ou) butt, nudge (ou) poke, snap (ou) nip (ou) bite, tap (ou) rap, scratch, lick, kick, cuff (ou) blow (ou) punch, flick, butt; *coup violent*, violent blow, bash (fam.); *donner des coups de corne, de coude, de dent, de griffe (ou) d'ongle, de pied, de poing*, to gore, to nudge, to bite (ou) to snap, to scratch, to kick, to punch; *faire descendre l'escalier à coups de pied*, to kick downstairs; *se donner un coup contre*, to knock against; *tuer à coups de bec*, to peck to death. ‖ 3. *Coup de cloche (ou) de sonnette, de sifflet*, ring (ou) peal, whistle; *coup de l'heure*, stroke; *coup à la porte*, knock, rap, tap; *coup de téléphone*, telephone call; *donner un coup de téléphone à qqn*, to call up s.o. on the phone, to ring s.o.? ‖ 4. *Coup de grisou*, firedamp explosion; *coup de tonnerre*, thunderclap. ‖ 5. *Coup de balai, de brosse, de ciseau*, sweep-out, brush-up, snip; *donner un coup de fer à*, to press (ou) iron up. ‖ 6. MUS. *Coup d'archet*, bowing, stroke. ‖ 7. ARTS. *Coup de crayon*, pencil stroke; *coup de pinceau*, stroke, touch. ‖ 8. NAUT. *Coup de filet*, haul; *coup de mer, de roulis, de tangage*, heavy sea, lurch (ou) roll, pitch; *coup de semonce*, warning shot; *coup de sonde*, cast with the lead; *coup de vent*, gale, gust, blast. ‖ 9. MÉD. Bruise (meurtrissure); *coup au cœur*, stab; *coup de chaleur, de froid*, heat-stroke, cold (ou) chill; *coup de fouet*, tearing of a ligament; *coup de sang*, apoplectic stroke; *coup de soleil*, insolation, sunstroke, sunburn; *couvert de coups*, covered with bruises. ‖ 10. MILIT. *Coup court, long*, short, over; *coup de canon*, gun- (ou) cannon-shot; *coup de fusil*, rifle-shot, gun-shot (action); report of a shot (bruit); *coup de feu*, shot; *coup de grâce*, coup de grâce, mercy (ou) finishing stroke; *coup de main*, surprise attack, raid, foray; *coup de revolver*, revolver-shot; *à deux coups*, double-barrelled (fusil); *faire le coup de feu*, to fire one's shot. ‖ 11. SPORTS. Stroke, shot (au billard); blow (à la boxe); throw (de dés); move (aux dames, échecs);

kick (au football); stroke (au tennis); *coup de crosse*, hit (au hockey); *coup de fer*, iron shot (au golf); *coup franc, placé*, free-, place-kick (au football). ‖ **12.** Jur. *Coup d'Etat*, coup; *faire le coup du père François*, to throttle; *réussir un coup*, to pull off a coup, to make a scoop; *tomber sous le coup de la loi*, to come under the law, to fall with the provisions of the law. ‖ **13.** Fig. Blow, shock, turn; *coup de chien, de torchon*, rioting, dust-up; *coup de collier*, pull tug; *coup d'essai*, first go, attempt; *coup de dents*, snarl; *coup droit*, home thrust; *coup dur*, staggering blow, hard stroke; *coup de fouet*, stimulus, boost (fam.); *coup de fusil*, overcharging (dans un restaurant); *coup de gueule*, shout, brawling; *coup de hasard*, mere chance, fluke; *coup de langue*, cutting remark; *coup de main*, helping hand (aide); know-how (habileté); *coup de maître*, master-stroke; *coup de massue*, crusher, floorer; *coup d'œil*, glance, glimpse, U. S. peek (regard); sight (spectacle); *coup de patte*, fling; *coup de sonde*, sounding; *coup du sort*, buffet of fate; *coup de tête*, rash impulse, freak; *attraper le coup de main*, to get the swing of it. ‖ **14.** Fam. Draught, drink (à boire); *coup de l'étrier*, stirrup-cup; *boire un coup*, to have a drink; *boire à petits coups*, to sip. ‖ **15.** Loc. *A coups de*, with the help of; *à coup sûr*, surely; securely; *après coup*, after the event; *aux cent coups*, in sheer desperation, mad with grief, beside oneself with worry; *à tout coup*, every time; *beau coup*, pretty piece of business, nice work; *coup sur coup*, blow after blow (pr.); uninterruptedly, in close succession (fig.); *donner un coup de main*, to lend a hand; *d'un seul coup*, at once; *du premier coup*, at the first go; *encore un coup*, once more; *en mettre un coup*, to buckle to it, to put some vim into it; *faire d'une pierre deux coups*, to kill two birds with one stone; *faire les quatre cents coups*, to plunge into dissipation; *faire un sale coup à*, to do the dirty on s.o., to do s.o. dirt; *frapper un grand coup*, to strike hard; *jeter un coup d'œil*, to cast a glance; *jeter un coup d'œil scrutateur sur qqch.*, to look sth. over, U. S. to give sth. the once-over; *manquer son coup*, to miss the mark; *porter un coup à*, to deal a heavy blow to (fig.); *pour le coup*, this time; *réussir son coup*, to bring it off; *risquer le coup*, to take one's chance; *sous le coup de*, under the influence of; *sur le coup*, on the spot; *tenir le coup*, to take it, to keep one's chin up, to keep a stiff upper lip; *tout à coup*, suddenly, all of a sudden; *tout d'un coup*, at one go. ‖ **Coup-de-poing**, m. Pocket-pistol (revolver); *coup-de-poing américain*, knuckleduster.

coupable [kupabl] adj. Culpable (négligence); guilty (personne) [*de*, of].
— s. Culprit. ‖ Jur. Delinquent; offender.

coupablement [-bləmɑ̃] adv. Guiltily.

coupage [kupa:3] m. Cutting. ‖ Blending (du vin).

coupailler [kupɑje] v. tr. (1). To whittle.

coupant, ante [kupɑ̃, ɑ̃:t] adj. Cutting; edged. ‖ Fig. Sharp, cutting.
— m. Edge. (V. TRANCHANT.)

coupe [kup] f. Cup, beaker (à boire); bowl (à fruits); *coupe à champagne*, champagne glass. ‖ Sports. Cup (athlétisme); plate (hippisme). ‖ Fig. Cup (d'amertume, des plaisirs).

coupe f. Cutting (en général). ‖ Coupe, cutting, felling (d'arbres); *coupe de cheveux*, haircut. ‖ Bolt (de drap); cut (d'étoffe); length (de soie); cut (d'un vêtement). ‖ Outline (du visage). ‖ Division (d'un vers). ‖ Section; *coupe transversale*, cross-section; *coupe verticale*, sectional elevation. ‖ Cut (aux cartes). ‖ Sports. Coupe, trophy, cup. ‖ Fig. *Etre sous la coupe de qqn*, to be under s.o.'s thumb; *faire des coupes dans*, to weed out; *faire des coupes sombres*, to carry out a purge; *mettre en coupe réglée*, to fleece; *sous la coupe des Allemands*, under German control; *tenir sous sa coupe*, to keep under one's thumb. ‖ **Coupe-chou**, m. Short sword. ‖ **Coupe-cigares**, m. invar. Cigar-cutter. ‖ **Coupe-circuit**, m. invar. Electr. Cut-out, circuit-breaker. ‖ **Coupe-coupe**, m. invar. Machete. ‖ **Coupe-feu**, m. invar. Fire-break. ‖ **Coupefile**, m. invar. Police pass. ‖ **Coupe-gorge**, m. invar. Cutthroat locality, death-trap. ‖ **Coupe-jarret**, m. Cutthroat, thug, ruffian. ‖ **Coupe-légumes**, m. invar. Culin. Vegetable-cutter. ‖ **Coupe-pâte**, m. invar. Pastry-cutter. ‖ **Coupe-papier**, m. invar. Paper-knife. ‖ **Coupe-racines**, m. invar. Agric. Cutter, chopper. ‖ **Coupe-vent**, m. invar. Wind-cutter, cutter.

coupé, ée [kupe] adj. Broken (sommeil). ‖ Diluted (vin).
— m. Brougham, coupé (voiture). ‖ Blas. Coupé.

coupée f. Naut. Gangway.

coupelle [kupɛl] f. Chim. Cupel.

couper [kupe] v. tr. (1). To cut (sens général); to clip (les ailes); to cut down, to fell (les arbres); to chop, to chip (du bois); to cut, to crop (les cheveux); to cut off (un échantillon); to clip, to trim (une haie); to pare (les ongles); to crop (les oreilles d'un chien); to dock (la queue d'un cheval); to cut off (la tête); to cut out (un vêtement); *couper d'un coup de ciseaux* (ou) *de dents*, to snip (ou) snick off; *couper en lanières, en morceaux, en tranches*, to shred, to cut up, to slice; *couper net*, to snap off; *se faire couper les cheveux*, to have one's hair cut. ‖ To cut off, to turn off (l'eau, le gaz); *couper la communication*, to ring off, to cut off (au téléphone). ‖ To cut (un animal). ‖ To dilute, to water (le vin). ‖ Agric. To reap (le blé); to mow (le foin). ‖ Archit. To partition up (une pièce). ‖ Méd. To take away (l'appétit); to bring down (la fièvre). ‖ Sports. To cut in (aux courses); to cross (au polo); to cut (au tennis). ‖ Techn. To shut off (la vapeur). ‖ Electr. To break (le circuit); to switch (ou) turn off (la lumière). ‖ Autom. To cut off (l'allumage). ‖ Milit. To cut off (la retraite). ‖ Fig. To cut up (la journée); *couper les cheveux en quatre*, to split hairs; *couper l'herbe sous le pied de qqn*, to cut s.o. out; *couper la parole à*, to interrupt; *couper les vivres*, to cut off supplies. ‖ Fam. *Ça te la coupe!*, that's a knock for you!, U. S. top that!
— v. intr. To cut (sens général). ‖ To cut across; *couper au plus court*, to take a short cut. ‖ To cut, to trump (aux cartes). ‖ Fig. *Couper court à*, to cut short. ‖ Fam. *Couper à*, to dodge.
— v. pr. **Se couper**, to cut oneself; *se couper le doigt*, to cut one's finger. ‖ To intersect (lignes); to chafe, to crack (peau); to cut, to split (soie). ‖ Fam. To give oneself away (se contredire).

couperet [kuprɛ] m. Chopper; cleaver. ‖ Knife, blade (de la guillotine).

couperose [kupro:z] f. Méd. Acne rosacea. ‖ Chim. Copperas.

couperosé, ée [kupəroze] adj. Méd. Blotched (personne); blotchy (teint).

couperoser v. tr. Méd. To blotch; to make blotchy.

coupeur [kupœ:r] s. Cutter (de vêtements).

couplage [kupla:3] m. Coupling. ‖ Electr. Coupling, connection.

couple [kupl] m. Pair (d'animaux); yoke (de bœufs); couple, pair (de personnes). ‖ Techn. Torque, couple. ‖ Aviat. *Couple redresseur*, restoring torque. ‖ Electr. Cell; *couple d'induit*, armature torque. ‖ Naut. Frame; *aviron à couple*, double-scull.
— f. Couple, brace, pair.

couplement [kupləmɑ̃] m. Techn. Coupling.

coupler [-ple] v. tr. (1). To couple; to yoke. ‖ Techn., Electr. To couple.

couplet [kuplɛ] m. Verse. ‖ TECHN. Strap-hinge. ‖ FAM. Tirade.

coupole [kupɔl] f. ARCHIT. Cupola, dome. ‖ MILIT. Revolving gun turret. ‖ AVIAT. Astrodome. ‖ LOC. *Sous la Coupole*, before the Académie française.

coupon [kupɔ̃] m. Remnant; short length (de tissu). ‖ FIN. Coupon; *coupon attaché, détaché*, cum-coupon, ex-dividend. ‖ CH. DE F., THÉÂTR. Ticket. ‖ **Coupon-réponse**, m. International reply-coupon.

coupure [kupy:r] f. Crack (gerçure); cut, gash (incision). ‖ Cutting (de presse); cut (dans un texte, dans un tissu). ‖ FIN. Small banknote (billet). ‖ ELECTR. *Coupure de courant*, electricity (ou) power cut; U. S. outage of electric current.

cour [ku:r] f. Court (du roi); *à la cour*, at Court; *bien en cour*, in high favour. ‖ Courtship; love-making; *faire la cour à*, to court, to woo, to make advances (ou) love to. ‖ Courtyard, court, yard; *cour de collège*, quadrangle; *cour d'honneur*, great courtyard; *cour de récréation*, playground; *sur cour*, giving on to the backyard. ‖ THÉÂTR. Opposite prompt side. ‖ JUR. Court of Justice; *cour de justice*, law court. ‖ ARCHIT. *Cour de cloître*, cloistered quadrangle.

courage [kura:ʒ] m. Courage (v. BRAVOURE, VAILLANCE, VALEUR); heart (cœur); go, grit, guts (cran); fortitude (force d'âme); *avoir le courage de*, to have the courage (ou) grit to; *rassembler tout son courage*, to screw one's courage to the sticking point; *reprendre courage*, to regain one's courage; *se sentir le courage de*, to feel up to. ‖ FAM. *Bon courage!*, keep your chin up!

courageusement [kuraʒøzmɑ̃] adv. Courageously; gallantly; pluckily.

courageux, euse [-ʒø, ø:z] adj. Courageous, gallant (v. BRAVE); plucky (fam.). ‖ Spirited, full of go; *courageux au travail*, hard-working.

courailler [kurɑje] v. intr. (1). FAM. To gad about. ‖ To gallivant, to wench.

couramment [kuramɑ̃] adv. Fluently, readily, easily (facilement); currently, generally, usually (habituellement).

courant, ante [kurɑ̃, ɑ̃:t] adj. Running (eau, écriture); usual (expression, pratique); current, common (opinion); routine (renseignement, service, travail); general (usage); everyday (vie); *titre courant*, running headline. ‖ Current, present (année, mois); *daté du 5 courant*, dated 5th instant. ‖ COMM. Routine (affaire); standard (marque, taille); ready (vente). ‖ FIN. Current (compte, monnaie); running (dépenses); floating (dette). ‖ ZOOL. *Chien courant*, hound.

— m. Current, stream; tide (d'eau); *en remontant, en suivant le courant*, upstream, downstream. ‖ Current (atmosphérique); *courant d'air*, draught, U. S. draft; air current (en météo). ‖ Course (des affaires, des événements, de la journée); *dans le courant de*, in the course of. ‖ Inflow (d'immigration); wave (d'opinion). ‖ COMM. *Au courant*, posted up (livre comptable). ‖ FIN. *Le courant du marché*, current market prices. ‖ ELECTR. Current. ‖ LOC., FIG. *Ecrire au courant de la plume*, to let one's pen run on; *être au courant*, to be up to date (ouvrage); to know all about it (personne); to know the ropes, U. S. to be on the ball (fam.); *mettre au courant de*, to be conversant with; *mettre au courant de*, to tell all about it; *nager dans le courant*, to struggle against circumstances; *se mettre au courant de*, to keep abreast of; *suivre au courant*, to go with the stream; *tenir au courant*, to keep informed.

courante [-ɑ̃:t] f. MUS. Courante. ‖ POP. Shits, U. S. runs.

courbatu, ue [kurbaty] adj. Foundered (cheval); stiff in the joints, aching all over (personne).

courbature [-ty:r] f. Founder (d'un cheval); stiffness (d'une personne).

courbaturé, ée [-tyre] adj. Stiff, aching all over.

courbaturer [-tyre] v. tr. (1). To make stiff, to cause to ache all over.

courbe [kurb] adj. Curved.

— f. Bend (de la rivière); curb, sweep (de la route). ‖ Curve, graph; *courbe de débit*, hydrograph; *courbe de justesse*, accuracy curve (en balistique); *courbe de niveau*, contour line. ‖ MÉD. *Courbe de température*, temperature-chart. ‖ NAUT. Knee; rib. ‖ MILIT. *Courbe de tir*, range table. ‖ AUTOM. *Courbe de consommation*, consumption curve.

courbé, ée [kurbe] adj. Curved, bent. ‖ Bent, bowed (dos); *courbé en deux*, bent double.

courber v. tr. (1). To curve, to bend (le bois, le fer). ‖ To bow (le dos); *courber la tête*, to hang one's head.

— v. pr. **Se courber**, to bend, to bow, to stoop. ‖ FIG. To bow, to truckle (*devant*, to).

courbette [kurbɛt] f. Curvet (du cheval). ‖ FIG. *Faire des courbettes*, to bow and scrape; to kowtow (*à*, to).

courbure [-by:r] f. Curvature. ‖ Curve (d'un arc, d'un tuyau); camber (d'une chaussée, d'une poutre). ‖ ARCHIT. Sweep (d'une arche). ‖ MÉD. Curve. ‖ AVIAT. Camber.

courette [kurɛt] f. Small courtyard.

coureur [-rœ:r] m. SPORTS. Runner, racer; *coureur à pied, de fond, de vitesse*, runner, stayer, sprinter. ‖ MILIT. Runner. ‖ FAM. Philanderer, U. S. wolf; *coureur de cotillons*, skirt-hunter, U. S. petticoat-chaser; *coureur de dot*, fortune- (ou) heiress-hunter. ‖ FAM. Rover, gallivanter, gadabout; *coureur de spectacles*, haunter of theatres.

coureuse [-rø:z] f. FAM. Slut, trollop.

courge [kurʒ] f. BOT. Gourd.

courgette [-ʒɛt] f. BOT., CULIN. Courgette; U. S. zucchini.

courir [kuri:r] v. intr. (32). To run (*après*, after); *descendre, entrer, sortir en courant*, to run down, in, out; *se mettre à courir*, to break into a run. ‖ To run, to hasten, to hurry (se dépêcher). ‖ To gad about, to rove, to wander (errant). ‖ To run after women, to wench (débauché). ‖ To glide, to scud (nuages). ‖ THÉÂTR. *Faire courir*, to draw. ‖ FIN. To accrue (intérêts). ‖ SPORTS. To run, to race; *faire courir*, to keep racehorses; *faire courir un cheval*, to run a horse. ‖ AUTOM. To race (pour, for). ‖ MILIT. *Courir aux armes*, to fly to arms. ‖ NAUT. To sail; *courir de l'avant*, to forge ahead. ‖ AVIAT. *Courir sur le redan*, to skim along the water (hydravion). ‖ MÉD. To prevail (épidémie); to run, to course (sang). ‖ FIG. To circulate (bruit); to lie, to stretch (chemin, piste); to run, to fly (temps); *le bruit court que*, there is a rumour that; *faire courir un bruit*, to spread a rumour; *les temps qui courent*, the times we live in; *par les temps qui courent*, as things are. ‖ FIG. *Courir à une déception, à un échec, au-devant du danger*, to court disappointment, disaster, danger.

— v. tr. To course (le lièvre); to hunt (le renard). ‖ To rove (les bois); *courir les bistros, les magasins*, to go pub-crawling, shopping; *courir le monde*, to roam the world over. ‖ To run after (les femmes); *courir la gueuse*, to wench. ‖ SPORTS. *Courir une course*, to run a race. ‖ NAUT. *Courir des bords*, to tack. ‖ FIG. To run after (les honneurs); to run (un risque); *courir sa chance*, to take one's chance.

courlis [kurli] m. ZOOL. Curlew.

couronne [kurɔn] f. Wreath (de fleurs); crown (de lauriers). ‖ Coronet (de duc, de comte); crown (de roi); *les diamants de la couronne*, the

Crown Jewels. ‖ Crown (royauté) ; *le discours de la Couronne*, the Speech from the Throne, the Queen's (ou) the King's Speech. ‖ Ring-shaped bread (pain). ‖ TECHN. Crown work (fortification) ; ring (de piston) ; rim (de roue). ‖ MÉD. Corona, crown (de dent). ‖ FIN., FIG. Crown.

couronné, ée [kurɔne] adj. Rewarded (élève) ; prize (ouvrage) ; crowned (souverain, tête) ; *couronné de fleurs*, wreathed with flowers ; *couronné de neige*, snow-capped. ‖ Broken-kneed (cheval). ‖ FIG. *Couronné de succès*, crowned with success.

couronnement [-nmᾶ] m. Coronation (du roi). ‖ ARCHIT. Capping, coping. ‖ FIG. Crowning-piece. ‖ FAM. Finishing stroke, last straw.

couronner [-ne] v. tr. (1). To crown (qqn, un roi) [de, with]. ‖ To wreathe, to garland. ‖ To laureate (un auteur) ; to award a prize to (un animal exposé, un auteur, un ouvrage) ; to reward (un écolier) ; *couronner un élève*, to award a pupil a prize. ‖ *Couronner un cheval*, to let a horse down on its knees. ‖ ARCHIT. To cape, to cope. ‖ MILIT. To occupy (une hauteur). ‖ FIG. To crown, to grant (les désirs) ; to put the finishing touch to (une œuvre).
— v. pr. Se couronner, to break its knees (cheval). ‖ FAM. *Se couronner en jouant au football*, to get a knee from football.

courre [ku:r] v. intr. † *Chasse à courre*, hunting ; *laisser courre*, to lay on, to slip (les chiens).

courrier [kurje] m. Courier, messenger. (V. MESSAGER.) ‖ Post ; mail ; letters ; *faire son courrier*, to write one's letters ; *l'heure du courrier*, posttime, U. S. mail time ; *par retour du courrier*, by return of post, U. S. by return mail. ‖ Correspondence section (bureau). ‖ News, report ; par (fam.) ; *courrier mondain*, gossip column.

courriériste [kurjerist] s. Columnist ; par writer.

courroie [kurwa] f. Strap ; *courroie porte-paquets*, luggage-strap ; *courroie de portière*, door-strap ; *attacher avec une courroie*, to strap up. ‖ TECHN. Belt. ‖ **Courroie-support**, f. Bearing (ou) supporting strap.

courroucé, ée [kuruse] adj. Wrathful, incensed.
courroucer v. tr. (6). To incense, to enrage.
— v. pr. Se courroucer, to become angry.

courroux [kuru] m. Wrath, ire.

cours [ku:r] m. Course, flow (d'un fleuve) ; *cours d'eau*, stream. ‖ ASTRON. Course (d'un astre). ‖ FIN. Circulation, currency (de l'argent) ; current price (de la rente) ; *au cours*, at market price ; *cours de la Bourse*, market prices ; *cours du change*, rate of exchange ; *cours de clôture*, closing price ; *cours légal*, legal tender ; *qui n'a plus cours*, out of circulation (monnaie). ‖ NAUT. *Capitaine, navire au long cours*, sea-going captain, ship ; *voyage au long cours*, ocean voyage. ‖ MÉD. Course, progress (d'une maladie). ‖ Walk, mall (promenade). ‖ Class, school (classe) ; lesson, lecture (enseignement) ; handbook, manual (ouvrage) ; *cours d'adultes*, continuation school ; U. S. adult education courses ; *cours de danse*, dancing-school ; *cours de vacances*, holiday course ; *continuer à suivre des cours tout en travaillant*, to continue as a part-time student ; *faire des cours*, to lecture ; *suivre les cours de*, to attend the lectures of, to study under. ‖ FIG. Course, run, train, process (des choses) ; currency, train (des idées, des pensées) ; course (des réflexions, du temps) ; currency (d'un terme) ; *avoir cours, n'avoir plus cours*, to be current, to be out of use (ou) obsolete (expression) ; *donner libre cours à*, to give full vent (ou) free rein to. ‖ LOC. *Au cours de*, in the course of ; *en cours*, in hand (affaire) ; current (année, mois) ; in process (construction) ; *en cours de*, in the course (ou) process of ; *en cours de route*, on the way.

course [kurs] f. Running (action) ; *au pas de course*, at a run ; at the double. ‖ Walk ; drive ; run, distance (trajet) ; journey (de taxi) ; *prix de la course*, fare. ‖ Errand (commission) ; *faire une course*, to go on an errand ; *faire des courses*, to run errands ; to go shopping. ‖ SPORTS. Race ; race-meeting ; *course d'autos*, au clocher, de chevaux, de haies, d'obstacles, à pied, de vitesse*, motor-race, steeplechase, horse-race, hurdle-race, obstacle-race, foot-race, sprint ; *voiture de course*, racing car. ‖ NAUT. Privateering (expédition) ; privateer (navire). ‖ MILIT. Flight (d'une balle, d'un obus). ‖ ASTRON. Course (d'un astre). ‖ TECHN. Stroke (du piston) ; lift (d'une soupape) ; *course de manivelle*, crank throw. ‖ AUTOM. *Course de l'embrayage*, clutch travel.

courser [kurse] v. tr. (1). FAM. To run after, to chase after.

coursier [kursje] m. Courser, steed (cheval). ‖ Flume (canal). ‖ COMM. Errand-boy (garçon).

coursière [-sjɛ:r] f. COMM. Errand-girl.

coursive [-si:v] f. NAUT. Alleyway. ‖ AVIAT. Runway ; gangway ; catwalk.

court [ku:r] m. SPORTS. Court (de tennis).

court, ourte [ku:r, u:rt] adj. Short (en durée, longueur et taille) ; insufficient (prix) ; limited (savoir) ; *à la vue courte*, short-sighted ; *c'est plus court de passer par le jardin*, it is quicker to go through the garden. ‖ SPORTS, RADIO. Short.
— adv. Short ; *couper court à*, to cut short ; *rester court*, to stop short ; *tourner court*, to turn sharply ; to change suddenly ; *tout court*, simply and nothing else ; *Jean tout court*, plain John.
— loc. adv. *De court*, short ; *prendre qqn de court*, to leave s.o. little time ; *tenir qqn de court*, to keep a tight hold on s.o.
— loc. prép. *A court d'argent*, short of money ; *être à court de*, to run out of.
— m. Quickest (ou) shortest way ; *prendre au plus court*, to take a short cut. ‖ **Court-bouillon**, m. CULIN. Spiced water in which fish is cooked. ‖ **Court-circuit**, m. ELECTR. Short-circuit. ‖ **Court-circuiter**, v. tr. ELECTR. To short-circuit ; FAM. To bypass. ‖ **Court-jus**, m. POP. Shortcircuit, short. ‖ **Court métrage**, m. CINÉM. Short. ‖ **Court-vêtu**, adj. Short-skirted.

courtage [kurta:ʒ] m. Brokerage ; broking. ‖ Commission.

courtaud, aude [-to, o:d] adj. Dumpy, stocky.
— s. Stocky person.

courtepointe [-təpwɛ̃:t] f. Counterpane, quilt.

courtier [kurtje] s. Broker ; *courtier en diamants*, diamond-broker ; *courtier électoral*, canvasser. ‖ FIN. *Courtier marron*, stag, outside broker. ‖ NAUT. *Courtier maritime*, ship-broker.

courtilière [kurtiljɛ:r] f. ZOOL. Mole-cricket.

courtine [kurtin] f. Bed curtain. ‖ MILIT. Curtain.

courtisan [kurtizᾶ] m. Courtier. ‖ Toady, flunkey (flatteur).

courtisane [-zan] f. Courtesan, lady of the town.

courtiser [-ze] v. tr. (1). To court, to pay court to, to woo (une femme). ‖ To fawn upon, to toady to (flatter).

courtois, oise [kurtwa, az] adj. Courteous (envers, to) ; urbane. (V. POLI.)

courtoisement [-zmᾶ] adv. Courteously.

courtoisie [-zi] f. Courtesy, courteousness.

couru, ue [kuru] adj. Popular, favourite (personnage) ; competed for (poste) ; well attended (réunion, spectacle). ‖ FIN. Accrued (intérêts).

cousai [kuze]. V. COUDRE (31).

couscous [kuskus] m. CULIN. Couscous.

cousette [kuzɛt] f. Dressmaker's assistant.

couseuse [-sø:z] f. Sewer, seamstress. ‖ TECHN. Stitcher.

cousin, ine [kuzɛ̃, in] s. Cousin. ‖ FAM. *Ils ne*

sont pas cousins, they don't get on together; *le roi n'est pas son cousin,* he is as pleased as Punch (joyeux) [ou] as proud as a peacock (orgueilleux).
cousin m. ZOOL. Gnat, midge.
cousinage [-zina:ʒ] m. Cousinship; cousinhood.
cousiner [-zine] v. intr. (1). FAM. To get on well together.
— v. tr. FAM. To call cousins with.
coussin [kusɛ̃] m. Cushion (d'ameublement); pillow (de dentelière). ‖ AUTOM. Squab.
coussinet [kusinɛ] m. Small cushion. ‖ TECHN. Bearing.
cousu, ue [kuzy] adj. Sewn. ‖ FIG. *Cousu de,* covered with (boutons); *cousu d'or,* wallowing in wealth, rich as Croesus, rolling in riches, U. S. well-heeled; *bouche cousue!,* hold your tongue!, mum's the word! ‖ **Cousu-machine,** adj. Machine-stitched. ‖ **Cousu-main,** adj. Hand-sewn.
coût [ku] m. Cost, expense. (V. PRIX.)
coûtant, ante [kutɑ̃, ɑ̃:t] adj. *A prix coûtant,* at cost price.
couteau [kuto] m. Knife; *couteau de cuisine, à découper, à dessert, à éplucher, de guerre, de poche, de table,* kitchen-, carving-, dessert-, potato-, commando-, clasp-, table-knife. ‖ MÉD. *Couteau interosseux,* catling. ‖ ELECTR. *Couteau de commutateur,* switch blade. ‖ FIG. *A couteaux tirés,* at daggers drawn, at loggerheads; *le couteau sur la gorge,* with the knife at one's throat; *figure en lame de couteau,* hatchet face. ‖ **Couteau-scie,** m. Knife with serrated edge, bread knife.
coutelas [-tlɑ] m. Cook's (ou) butcher's knife. ‖ NAUT. Cutlass.
coutelier [-tlje] s. Cutler.
coutellerie [-tɛlri] f. Cutlery (commerce, marchandise); cutler's shop (magasin).
coûter [kute] v. intr. (1). FIN. To cost (pr. et fig.); *cela coûte cher,* it is expensive; *cela coûte joliment cher,* it costs a pretty penny; *cela me coûte,* it costs me an effort; *coûte que coûte,* at any cost (ou) price.
— v. impers. FIG. *Il me coûte de,* it grieves (ou) pains me to; *il lui en a coûté la vie,* it cost him his life.
— v. tr. FIN. To cost; *coûter cent francs à qqn,* to cost s.o. a hundred francs. ‖ FIG. *Coûter la vie à qqn,* to cost s.o. his life. ‖ FAM. *Pour ce que ça vous coûte!,* a fat lot of difference it makes to you!
coûteusement [-tøzmɑ̃] adv. Expensively, dearly.
coûteux, euse [-tø, ø:z] adj. Costly, expensive.
coutil [kuti] m. Ticking (à matelas); duck (à vêtements).
coutre [kutr] m. AGRIC. Coulter.
coutume [kutym] f. Custom, use, wont, practice, habit (des gens); usage, custom (d'un pays); *avoir coutume de,* to be in the habit of, to be accustomed (ou) wont to, to use to; *comme de coutume,* as usual. ‖ JUR. Usage; customary law.
coutumier, ère [-mje, ɛr] adj. Customary, usual, ordinary (habituel). ‖ *Coutumier de,* wont to, in the habit of; *être coutumier du fait,* to be an old hand at the trick. ‖ JUR. Customary, common, unwritten (droit).
— m. JUR. Customary.
couture [kuty:r] f. Sewing (action); seam (résultat); needlework (travaux); *couture à la machine,* machine-sewing; *couture en baguette,* welted seam; *toute la couture de la maison,* all the needlework of the household. ‖ Dressmaking (métier); *haute couture,* haute couture, high-class dressmaking; *maison de couture,* couture house. ‖ MÉD. Scar (cicatrice); suture (suture). ‖ TECHN. Rivet seam. ‖ NAUT. Seam. ‖ FIG. *A plate couture,* to a jelly; *sur toutes les coutures,* from every angle.

couturé, ée [kutyre] adj. Scarred, covered with scars.
couturier [-rje] m. Couturier, ladies' tailor.
couturière [-rjɛ:r] f. Dressmaker; couturière. ‖ THÉÂTR. Dress rehearsal.
couvain [kuvɛ̃] m. ZOOL. Brood (œufs); honey comb (rayon).
couvaison [kuvɛzɔ̃] f. Brooding, sitting.
couvée [kuve] f. Clutch, sitting (d'œufs); brood, hatch (de poussins). ‖ FIG. Brood (d'enfants).
couvent [kuvɑ̃] m. ECCLÉS. Convent (en général); nunnery (de femmes); monastery (d'hommes); *entrer au couvent,* to go into a convent. ‖ Convent-school (école).
couventine [-tin] f. Convent-educated girl. ‖ ECCLÉS. Nun.
couver [kuve] v. tr. (1). To sit on, to hatch (des œufs). ‖ MÉD. To be sickening for, to be getting (une maladie). ‖ FIG. To brood over (le feu, un projet); to hatch (un complot); to mollycoddle [un enfant]; *couver du regard,* to gloat over; to gaze longingly at; to look fondly at.
— v. intr. To brood, to sit (poule); *faire couver,* to set. ‖ FIG. To smoulder (feu, passion); to brew (orage).
couvercle [kuvɛrkl] m. Lid, cover (de boîte, de pot); *couvercle à vis,* screw-cap. ‖ TECHN. Cover.
couvert [kuvɛ:r] adj. Covered [de, with] (sens général); *couvert d'une croûte,* crusted over; *couvert d'herbe,* overgrown with grass; *couvert de neige,* snow-covered. ‖ Wearing one's hat (chapeauté); clad (vêtu); *restez couvert,* keep your hat on. ‖ Shady (allée); overcast, cloudy (ciel); *chemin couvert,* covered way. ‖ ARCHIT. Roofed; *couvert de chaume,* thatched, thatch-roofed. ‖ FIG. *A mots couverts,* covertly; *laisser entendre à mots couverts,* to hint.
— m. Cover; knife, fork and spoon; *acheter des couverts,* to buy cutlery; *mettre, ôter le couvert,* to lay, to clear the table; *mettre trois couverts,* to lay the table for three; *vous aurez toujours votre couvert mis,* there will always be a meal for you, you will always have your place at our table. ‖ House-charge, cover-charge (prix au restaurant); *le gîte et le couvert,* board and lodging. ‖ Cover, shelter (abri); *être à couvert,* to be under cover (ou) shelter; *se mettre à couvert,* to take cover. ‖ FIN. Cover; *être à couvert,* to be covered; *mettre ses intérêts à couvert,* to safeguard one's interests; *vendre à couvert,* to sell for delivery. ‖ FIG. *Sous le couvert de,* under cover (ou) pretence (ou) pretext of.
couverte [kuvɛrt] f. ARTS. Glaze (de faïence). ‖ FAM. Blanket.
couverture [-ty:r] f. Blanket, coverlet (au lit); *couverture de cheval,* horse-cloth; *couverture piquée,* quilt; *couverture de voyage,* travelling-rug. ‖ Cover, wrapper (de livre); *couverture de livre en papier imitation reliure,* duxeen, U. S. fabrikoid; *couverture de parapluie,* umbrella-covering. ‖ ARCHIT. Roofing (de maison); *couverture de tuiles,* tiled roof. ‖ COMM. Cover. ‖ MILIT. Cover; protection; *de couverture,* covering (troupes). ‖ FIN. Margin (en banque). ‖ FIG. *Tirer la couverture à soi,* to take the lion's share.
couveuse [kuvø:z] f. Incubator (appareil); brooder, hatcher, brood-hen (poule).
couvi [kuvi] adj. Addled (œuf).
couvre [kuvr] v. V. COUVRIR. ‖ **Couvre-amorce,** m. MILIT. Primer-cover. ‖ **Couvre-bouche,** m. MILIT. Muzzle-cover. ‖ **Couvre-chef,** m. Headgear. ‖ **Couvre-culasse,** m. MILIT. Breech-cover. ‖ **Couvre-feu,** m. Curfew. ‖ **Couvre-joint,** m. TECHN. Covering-plate; butt-strap; welt. ‖ **Couvre-lit,** m. Bed-spread. ‖ **Couvre-livre,** m. Wrapper, jacket. ‖ **Couvre-nuque,** m. Flap. ‖

Couvre-œil, m. Eye patch. ‖ **Couvre-pieds,** m. Quilt; U. S. foot blanket; *couvre-pieds piqué,* wadded quilt, U. S. comfort, comfortable. ‖ **Couvre-plat,** m. Dish-cover. ‖ **Couvre-radiateur,** m. AUTOM. Radiator-muff. ‖ **Couvre-théière,** m. Tea-cosy.

couvreur [kuvrœ:r] m. Slater (en ardoises); thatcher (en chaume); tiler (en tuiles). ‖ SPORTS. Cover-point (au cricket); *couvreur arrière,* extra-cover.

couvrir [-vri:r] v. tr. (72). To cover [*de,* with] (sens général); *couvrir de baisers,* to shower kisses on; *couvrir de bave,* to beslaver; *couvrir d'une croûte,* to crust. ‖ To cover, to muffle, to wrap up (vêtir); *couvrez-vous bien,* put warm clothes on. ‖ To cover (un animal). ‖ ARCHIT. To roof (la maison); to overlay (un mur); *couvrir d'ardoises, de chaume, de tuile,* to slate, to thatch, to tile. ‖ MILIT. To cover (ses derrières). ‖ COMM. To cover, to defray (les dépenses); to cover (les risques); *couvrir les frais d'envoi,* to refund the postage (ou) the carriage; *couvrir une enchère,* to make a higher bid. ‖ SPORTS. To cover. ‖ FIG. To cover, to drown (le bruit); to cover (une distance); to hide, to conceal (ses intentions); to screen (ses subordonnés); *couvrir de confusion, d'honneurs,* to cover with confusion, honours.
— v. pr. Se couvrir, to cover oneself (sens général); to put one's hat on (se coiffer); to clothe oneself warmly (s'habiller chaudement). ‖ To become overcast (ou) cloudy (ciel, temps). ‖ SPORTS. To cover up, to guard oneself (à la boxe, à l'escrime). ‖ BOT. *Se couvrir de feuilles,* to come into leaf. ‖ FIG. To screen oneself; *se couvrir de,* to cover oneself with (gloire).

covalence [kovalɑ̃:s] f. CHIM. Covalency.

cover-girl [kɔvœrgœrl] f. Cover-girl.

cow-boy [kɔbo:j] m. Cowboy.

coxal, ale [kɔksal] adj. MÉD. Coxal.

coxalgie [-ʒi] f. MÉD. Coxalgia.

coyote [kɔjɔt] m. ZOOL. Coyote.

C.Q.F.D. [sekyɛfde] abrév. de *ce qu'il fallait démontrer,* Q. E. D., quod erat demonstrandum.

crabe [kra:b] m. ZOOL. Crab.

crac [krak] interj. Crack!

crachat [kraʃa] m. Spittle. ‖ MÉD. Sputum. ‖ FAM. Star (décoration). ‖ FAM. *Se noyer dans un crachat,* to be drowned in a puddle.

craché, ée [-ʃe] adj. FAM. *C'est son père tout craché,* he is the spit of his father.

crachement [-ʃmɑ̃] m. Spitting; *crachement de sang,* hemoptysis. ‖ ELECTR. Sparking. ‖ TECHN. Fizzing (de vapeur). ‖ MILIT. Backfiring (de fusil). ‖ FAM. Rattle (d'un haut-parleur); sputtering (de la radio); frying (du téléphone).

cracher [-ʃe] v. intr. (1). To spit. (V. EXPECTORER.) ‖ To splutter (plume); to splash (robinet). ‖ ELECTR. To spark. ‖ MILIT. To backfire. ‖ FAM. To rattle (haut-parleur); to splutter (radio). ‖ FAM. To cough up (payer); *cracher sur qqch.,* to turn one's nose up at sth.
— v. tr. To spit, to spit out (de la salive, du sang). ‖ MILIT. To vomit, to belch out (le feu). ‖ FIG. To spit out (des injures). ‖ FAM. To fork out, to cough up (de l'argent).

cracheur, euse [-ʃœ:r, ø:z] s. Spitter.

crachin [-ʃɛ̃] m. Mizzle, drizzle.

crachiner [-ʃine] v. impers. (1). To drizzle.

crachoir [-ʃwa:r] m. Spittoon. ‖ FAM. *Tenir le crachoir à,* to talk up to.

crachotement [-ʃɔtmɑ̃] m. Sputtering. ‖ FAM. V. CRACHEMENT.

crachoter [-ʃɔte] v. intr. (1). To sputter.

crack [krak] m. SPORTS. Crack horse. ‖ FAM. Star, ace, champion, U. S. crackerjack (as).

cracker [krakœr] m. Cracker (biscuit salé).

cracking [krakiŋ] m. CHIM. Cracking.

Cracovie [krakɔvi] f. GÉOGR. Cracow.

craie [krɛ] f. Chalk; *écrire à la craie,* to chalk.

craindre [krɛ̃:dr] v. tr. (59). To fear, to dread, to be afraid of (v. APPRÉHENDER, REDOUTER); *craindre sa mère,* to be afraid of one's mother; *craignez-vous d'oublier?,* are you afraid of forgetting?; *je crains qu'il ne vienne,* I fear he will come; *il y a lieu de craindre que,* it is to be feared that. ‖ To be sensitive to; to shrink from; « *craint la chaleur* », « to be kept cool »; *craindre la gelée,* not to stand the frost.
— v. intr. To be anxious (*pour,* for) [*sa sécurité*]; *craindre pour sa vie,* to go in fear of one's life; *il m'a fait craindre pour ma vie,* he put me in terror of my life.

crainte [krɛ̃:t] f. Fear, dread (v. PEUR); *avoir des craintes au sujet de,* to be fearful of; *crainte respectueuse,* awe; *sans crainte,* fearless; *soyez sans crainte,* never fear, don't you fear.
— loc. conj. *De crainte de,* for fear of; *de crainte qu'il ne pleuve,* for fear (ou) lest it should rain.

craintif, ive [krɛ̃tif, i:v] adj. Fearful; apprehensive. (V. TIMORÉ.)

craintivement [-tivmɑ̃] adv. Fearfully, timorously. (V. PEUREUSEMENT.)

cramer [krame] v. tr., v. intr. (1). POP. To burn.

cramoisi, ie [kramwazi] adj. Crimson; *cramoisi de colère,* crimson with rage; *devenir cramoisi,* to blush scarlet.
— m. Crimson.

crampe [krɑ̃:p] f. MÉD. Cramp.

crampon [krɑ̃pɔ̃] m. Crampon, cramp; staple. ‖ Calk (d'un fer à cheval); *crampon à glace,* crampon, frost nail. ‖ ARCHIT. Cramp. ‖ CH. DE F. Dog (ou) track spike. ‖ BOT. Clinging root (du lierre); tendril (de la vigne). ‖ FAM. Clinging vine; bore, clinger.

cramponner [krɑ̃pɔne] v. tr. (1). ARCHIT. To cramp, to clamp. ‖ To calk (un fer à cheval). ‖ FAM. To buttonhole, to stick to (qqn).
— v. pr. Se cramponner, to cling, to hang on (*à,* to). ‖ FIG. To hold on (*à,* to).

cran [krɑ̃] m. Notch (entaille); hole (trou); *baisser, monter d'un cran,* to take down, to go up a peg; *serrer sa ceinture d'un cran,* to draw one's belt a hole tighter, to tighten one's belt another hole. ‖ Ridge (de cheveux); step, notch (de tissu). ‖ Peg (degré); *baisser d'un cran,* to come down a peg. ‖ MILIT. Notch; *cran d'arrêt, de mire, de sûreté,* stop, sight, safety-catch. ‖ FAM. Pluck, guts; *avoir du cran,* to be plucky, to have guts; *être à cran,* to be on edge.

crâne [krɑ:n] m. MÉD. Skull, cranium; brain-pan. ‖ SPORTS. Header.

crâne adj. Jaunty (allure); plucky (conduite, personne).

crânement [krɑnmɑ̃] adv. Jauntily; pluckily.

crâner [-ne] v. intr. FAM. To swagger, to swank. (V. POSER.) ‖ To brazen it out (fanfaronner).

crânerie [-n:ri] f. Pluck, gameness, daring.

crâneur [-nœ:r] s. FAM. Swaggerer, swanker.

crânien, enne [krɑnjɛ̃, ɛn] adj. MÉD. Cranial.

cranter [krɑ̃te] v. tr. (1). To notch.

crapahuter [krapayte] v. intr. (1). ARG. To foot it, to trek.

crapaud [krapo] m. ZOOL. Toad. ‖ Flaw, blemish (dans une pierre précieuse). ‖ Tub easy-chair (fauteuil). ‖ MUS. Baby-grand (piano). ‖ NAUT. Mooring-clamp. ‖ FAM. Brat (gosse).

crapaudine [krapodin] f. Toad-stone (pierre). ‖ Waste hole (de baignoire); socket (de gond); grating (de tuyau). ‖ TECHN. Step-bearing.

crapouillot [krapujo] m. MILIT. Trench mortar.

crapule [krapyl] f. † Crapulence (débauche). ‖ Scum of the earth, riff-raff (gens); regular scoundrel, blackguard (individu).

crapulerie [-lri] f. Scoundrelly trick.
crapuleux, euse [-lø, ø:z] adj. Filthy, foul (crime); crapulous, scoundrelly (individu).
craquage [kraka:ʒ] m. V. CRACKING.
craque [krak] f. FAM. Fib, crammer, cracker.
craquelé, ée [krakle] adj. Crackled.
— m. Crackled-china (porcelaine).
craquèlement [krakɛlmɑ̃] m. Crackle, crazing.
craqueler v. tr. (8 a). To crackle.
— v. pr. Se craqueler, to crackle.
craquelin [kraklɛ̃] m. CULIN. Cracknel.
craquelure [-ly:r] f. Crack.
craquement [-mɑ̃] m. Crack, cracking. ‖ Crackling (des feuilles sèches); crunching (de la neige); creaking, squeaking (des souliers).
craquer [-ke] v. intr. (1). To crack (en général); to split (bois, couture); to snap (branche); to crackle (cailloux, neige); to creak, to squeak (souliers); faire craquer, to start (une couture); to crack (ses doigts). ‖ NAUT. To spring (mât). ‖ FIG. To give way, to crack, to totter.
— v. tr. To strike (une allumette).
craqueter [-kte] v. intr. (8 a). To crackle. ‖ To chirp (cigale); to clatter (cigogne).
craqueur [-kœ:r] s. Fibber.
crash [kraʃ] m. AVIAT. Crash-landing.
crasse [kras] f. Dirt; filth. ‖ TECHN. Dross, scum, slag. ‖ MILIT. Fouling (des armes). ‖ FAM. Dirty trick; faire une crasse à, to play a dirty trick on.
crasse adj. f. Crass (ignorance).
crasseux, euse [-sø, ø:z] adj. Dirty, filthy.
crassier [-sje] m. TECHN. Slag-heap.
cratère [kratɛ:r] m. GÉOL., ELECTR. Crater. ‖ MILIT. Shell-hole, crater.
cravache [kravaʃ] f. Horse- (ou) riding-whip; hunting-crop.
cravacher [-ʃe] v. tr. (1). To flog (un cheval); to horse-whip (une personne). ‖ FIG. To spur on, to goad on.
cravate [kravat] f. Neck-tie, tie (d'homme). ‖ Scarf, cravat (fichu); cravate de fourrure, fur tie. ‖ Scarf (décoration). ‖ NAUT. Sling. ‖ SPORTS. Neck-hold (à la lutte).
cravater [-te] v. tr. (1). To put a tie on (qqn). ‖ SPORTS. To collar, to hold round the neck.
— v. pr. Se cravater, to put one's tie on.
crawl [kro:l] m. SPORTS. Crawl; crawl-stroke.
crawler [-le] v. intr. (1). SPORTS. To do (ou) swim the crawl; dos crawlé, back crawl.
crawleur [-lœ:r] s. SPORTS. Crawl-swimmer.
crayeux, euse [krɛjø, ø:z] adj. Chalky. ‖ FIG. Pâleur crayeuse, chalkiness.
crayon [krɛjɔ̃] m. Pencil; crayon à dessin, drawing-pencil; crayon à encre indélébile, indelible pencil; fine écriture au crayon, faint pencilled writing; marquer au crayon, to pencil. ‖ Crayon à cils, à lèvres, eyebrow pencil, lipstick. ‖ ARTS. Crayon: sketch.
crayonner [-jɔne] v. tr. (1). To pencil; to jot down (des notes). ‖ ARTS. To sketch, to make a pencil-sketch.
créance [kreɑ̃:s] f. Faith; credence; credit; ajouter créance à, to give credence to; donner créance, to give credit. ‖ Lettres de créance, credentials (d'un ambassadeur). ‖ JUR. Debt (en général); claim (par hypothèque).
créancier, ère [-sje, ɛr] s. Creditor; créancier hypothécaire, mortgager.
créateur, trice [kreatœ:r, tris] adj. Creative.
— m. ECCLÉS. Creator.
— s. Creator, maker, inventor.
créatine [-tin] f. MÉD. Creatine.
création [-sjɔ̃] f. ECCLÉS. Creation (acte, résultat). ‖ Creation; production; work (œuvre). ‖ Creation, invention. ‖ Appointment, establishment, setting up (d'un comité, d'un établissement); foundation (d'un hôpital); creation, found-

ing, formation (d'une société). ‖ THÉÂTR. Creation (d'un rôle).
créativité [-tivite] f. Creativity, creativeness.
créature [-ty:r] f. Creature, created being. ‖ † Tart, U. S. broad (prostituée). ‖ FIG. Creature, tool (de qqn). ‖ FAM. Drôle de créature, queer fellow.
crécelle [kresɛl] f. Rattle. ‖ LOC. Voix de crécelle, grating (ou) corn-crake voice.
crèche [krɛ:ʃ] f. AGRIC. Manger, crib. ‖ ECCLÉS. Crib. ‖ Crèche, day-nursery (pour enfants).
crécher [kreʃe] v. intr. (5). POP. To live, to hang out (en permanence); to crash (provisoirement).
crédence [kredɑ̃:s] f. ECCLÉS. Credence. ‖ Sideboard, credenza (meuble).
crédibilité [kredibilite] f. Credibility.
crédit [kredi] m. Credit; prestige; influence (auprès de, with). ‖ Credence (confiance). ‖ Credit, reputation of solvency (d'un individu, d'une maison). ‖ COMM. Credit, trust; à crédit, on credit; établissement de crédit, loan society; faire crédit à qqn, to give s.o. credit. ‖ FIN. Credit; credit account (en banque); creditor side (en comptabilité); Crédit foncier, land bank; crédit municipal, municipal pawn-office. ‖ Pl. Crédits budgétaires, estimates, supplies. ‖ **Crédit-bail**, m. FIN. Leasing.
créditer [-te] v. tr. (1). FIN. To credit (un compte, qqn); créditer qqn de, to give s.o. credit for.
créditeur, trice [-tœ:r, tris] adj. Creditor; compte, solde créditeur, credit account, balance.
— s. Creditor.
credo [kredo] m. ECCLÉS. Creed.
crédule [kredyl] adj. Credulous, trusting (confiant); gullible (gobeur).
crédulité [-lite] f. Credulity.
créer [kree] v. tr. (1). ECCLÉS. To create. ‖ To open (un emploi); to create, to found (une chaire, un hôpital); to establish, to set up (un établissement, une société); to invent (une machine, un mot); to create (une mode); to create, to cause (des ennuis). ‖ MILIT. To form (une armée); to open (un deuxième front).
— v. pr. Se créer, to form; se créer une clientèle, to build up a connection; se créer une excuse, to trump up an excuse.
crémaillère [kremajɛ:r] f. Pot-hook, pot-hanger; chimney-hook; pendaison de crémaillère, house-warming. ‖ TECHN. Rack. ‖ MILIT. Traversing rack. ‖ CH. DE F. Cog-rail, rack; rack-railway. ‖ AUTOM. Direction à crémaillère, rack-and-pinion steering.
crémant [kremɑ̃] adj. AGRIC. Slightly sparkling.
— m. AGRIC. Slightly sparkling wine.
crémation [kremasjɔ̃] f. Cremation.
crématoire [-twa:r] adj. Crematory; four crématoire, crematorium.
crème [krɛm] f. Cream (de lait). ‖ Cream (de beauté); polish, cream (à chaussures). ‖ Crème (liqueur). ‖ CULIN. Cream. ‖ FIG. Cream; la crème des honnêtes gens, the pick of the bunch.
— adj. Cream-coloured, cream.
crémer [kreme] v. intr. (5). To cream (lait).
crémer [kreme] v. tr. (5). To cremate (incinérer).
crémerie [krɛmri] f. Dairy, creamery, milk-shop (boutique). ‖ Tea-shop, buttery, dairy (restaurant).
crémeux, euse [kremø, ø:z] adj. Creamy.
crémier [kremje] m. Dairyman; dairy-keeper (personne). ‖ Cream-jug; U. S. cream pitcher, creamer (pot).
crémière [-mjɛ:r] f. Dairywoman.
crémone [kremɔn] f. Casement bolt.
créneau [kreno] m. † Crenel; battlement. ‖ MILIT. Loophole; créneau de visée, aiming slit.
crénelage [krenla:ʒ] m. Milling (d'une pièce de monnaie).
crénelé, ée [krenle] adj. Crenellated, embattled,

battlemented (mur). ‖ Bot. Crenate. ‖ Blas. Embattled.

créneler v. tr. (8a). To crenellate. ‖ Milit. To loophole. ‖ Techn. To tooth; to notch.

crénelure [-ly:r] f. Indentation, crenellation. ‖ Bot. Crenelling.

crénom! [krenõ] interj. Damn it, confound it; *crénom de Dieu,* God damn.

créole [kreɔl] adj., s. Creole.

créosol [kreɔzɔl] m. Chim. Creosol.

créosote [-zɔt] f. Chim. Creosote.

créosoter [-zɔte] v. tr. (1). To creosote.

crêpage [krɛpa:ʒ] m. Crimping, crisping (des cheveux, des tissus). ‖ Fam. *Crêpage de chignon,* fight (ou) set-to between women.

crêpe [krɛ:p] m. Crape; *crêpe de Chine,* crêpe de Chine; *crêpe satin,* satin crepe. ‖ Crape band, mourning band (brassard); mourning crape (voile). ‖ Crepe, crepe-rubber (pour semelle). ‖ Crepe- (ou) crinkled paper (papier).

crêpe f. Culin. Pancake. ‖ Fam. *Aplati comme une crêpe,* as flat as a pancake.

crêpelé, ée [krɛple] adj. Crimped (cheveux).

crêpelure [krɛply:r] f. Fuzziness, frizziness.

crêper [krɛpe] v. tr. (1). To crimp, to frizz (les cheveux); to crimp, to crape (tissu). ‖ Fam. *Se crêper le chignon,* to tear each other's hair.

crêperie [krɛpri] f. Pancake shop (ou) restaurant.

crépi [krepi] adj. Rough-cast, pebble-dashed.
— m. Archit. Rough-cast, pebble-dash.

crépine [krepin] f. Fringe. ‖ Techn. Strainer (de tuyau). ‖ Culin. Caul (de mouton).

crépinette [-inɛt] f. Culin. Flat sausage.

crépins [krepɛ̃] m. pl. Grindery (de cordonnier).

crépir [krepi:r] v. tr. (2). Archit. To rough-cast; to parget; to pebble-dash.

crépissage [krepisa:ʒ] m. Archit. Rough-casting; pebble-dashing.

crépissure [-sy:r] f. Archit. Rough-cast.

crépitation [krepitasjõ] f. Crackling; sputtering. ‖ Méd. Crepitation.

crépitement [-tmɑ̃] m. Crackling, sputtering.

crépiter [-te] v. intr. (1). To crackle (coups de feu, étincelles); to sputter (friture); to patter (pluie). ‖ Méd. To crepitate.

crépon [krepõ] m. Crépon (tissu). ‖ Hair-pad.

crépu, ue [krepy] adj. Frizzy, crisp; woolly (cheveux). ‖ Bot. Crinkled (feuille).

crépusculaire [krepyskylɛ:r] adj. Crepuscular, twilight. ‖ Zool. Crepuscular. ‖ Fig. Dim; on the wane.

crépuscule [-kyl] m. Twilight; dusk.

crescendo [kreʃɛndo] m., adv. Mus. Crescendo. ‖ Fig. *Aller crescendo,* to be on the increase.

crésol [krezɔl] m. Chim. Cresol.

cresson [krɛsõ] m. Bot. Cress, watercress; nasturtium; *cresson des prés,* lady's smock.

cressonnière [-sɔnjɛ:r] f. Watercress bed.

Crésus [krezy:s] m. Croesus; *riche comme Crésus,* as rich as Croesus, rolling in money.

crétacé, ée [kretase] adj. Géol. Cretaceous.

crête [krɛ:t] f. Comb (de coq); crest (d'oiseau). ‖ Crest, crown (d'un barrage); crest (d'une montagne, d'une vague); coping (d'une muraille); ridge (d'un toit). ‖ Méd., Milit. Crest. ‖ Fam. *La crête basse,* crest-fallen. ‖ **Crête-de-coq** (pl. *crêtes-de-coq*) m. Bot. Cockscomb.

Crête f. Géogr. Crete.

crêté, ée [krɛte] adj. Zool. Crested, tufted.

crételer [krɛtle] v. intr. (8a). To cackle (poule).

crétin [kretɛ̃] s. Méd. Cretin. ‖ Fam. Idiot, twerp, U. S. dope, drip.
— adj. Idiotic, asinine; U. S. dopey.

crétinerie [-tinri] f. Fam. Stupidity, idiocy; *faire une crétinerie,* to do a stupid thing.

crétinisme [-tinism] m. Méd. Cretinism.

crétois, oise [kretwa, wa:z] adj., s. Géogr. Cretan.

cretonne [krətɔn] f. Cretonne (tissu).

creusage [krøza:ʒ] m. Hollowing (du bois); digging (d'une fosse); sinking (d'un puits).

creuser [krøze] v. tr. (1). To hollow out (le bois); to groove (le bois, le métal); to cut (un canal); to sink, to bore (un puits); to plough (un sillon); to burrow (un souterrain, un terrier); to scoop out, to dig out (la terre). ‖ To hollow (les joues); to wear (les marches); *creusé de rides,* furrowed with wrinkles. ‖ Fig. To open up (un abîme); to go thoroughly into (une question). ‖ Loc. *Creuser l'estomac,* to whet the appetite; *se creuser la tête,* to rack one's brains.
— v. pr. Se creuser, to grow hollow. ‖ To grow gaunt (joues).

creuset [krøzɛ] m. Crucible. ‖ Fig. Crucible, trial, test. ‖ Fig. Alambic (de l'imagination).

creux, euse [krø, ø:z] adj. Hollow (arbre); hollow, sunken (chemin); deep (vallée). ‖ Hollow (dent, joue, toux, voix); hollow, sunken (joue); deep (voix); sunken, deep-set (yeux); *avoir le ventre creux,* to feel hollow (ou) empty. ‖ Box, inverted (pli). ‖ Fin. Sagging (marché). ‖ Fig. Shallow (esprit, tête); slack (heures); barren, futile (idées); empty (mots); *à la tête creuse,* empty-headed. ‖ Fam. *Avoir le nez creux,* to have a gift for nosing things out.
— adv. Hollow; *sonner creux,* to sound hollow.
— m. Trough (d'une courbe); cavity (d'un rocher); hollow, hole (du terrain); lap, bottom (de la vallée). ‖ Méd. Pit (de l'estomac); hollow (de la main); *creux de l'aisselle,* armpit; *creux des reins,* small of the back. ‖ Naut. Trough (des lames); belly (d'une voile). ‖ Techn. Depth (d'une roue dentée); groove (d'une vis). ‖ Mus. Deep voice. ‖ Arts. Mould; *gravure en creux,* intaglio.

crevaison [krəvɛzõ] f. Autom. Puncture, U. S. blow-out. ‖ Bursting (d'un tuyau). ‖ Fam. Exhaustion (fatigue); death, U. S. croaking (mort).

crevant, ante [-vɑ̃, ɑ̃:t] adj. Fam. Killing, side-splitting, farcical (drôle). ‖ Fagging, back-breaking (éreintant).

crevard [-va:r] m. Pop. Weed, weakling.

crevasse [krəvas] f. Crevasse (de glacier); chink, cleft, crack, crevice, cranny, fissure (du terrain). ‖ Méd. Chap (de la peau); fissure (du sein).

crevasser [-se] v. tr. (1). To crack. ‖ Méd. To chap (la peau).
— v. pr. Se crevasser, to crack. ‖ Méd. To chap.

crevé, ée [krəve] adj. Burst, holed. ‖ Autom. Punctured, flat (pneu). ‖ Fam. Done up, tired out, fagged (éreinté); gone west, croaked (mort).
— m. Slash (aux manches). ‖ Fam. *Un petit crevé,* a Teddy Boy, U. S. a candy kid.

crève [krɛ:v] f. Fam. Death; *attraper la crève,* to catch one's death.

crève. V. crever. ‖ **Crève-cœur,** m. invar. Heart-rending affair; heartbreak. ‖ **Crève-la-faim,** m. invar. Fam. Down-and-out.

crever [krəve] v. tr. (5). To burst (une balle, une bulle); to burst, to break through (une digue); to put out (les yeux). ‖ Méd. To open (un abcès). ‖ Autom. To puncture (un pneu). ‖ Fig. *Crever le cœur à qqn,* to rend s.o.'s heart. ‖ Fam. *Ça crève les yeux,* it's as plain as the nose on one's face, it stands out a mile, it stares you in the face. ‖ Fam. To ride to death (un cheval); to overwork (qqn); *la crever,* to be starving.
— v. intr. To burst (sens général). ‖ To die (animal). ‖ Autom. To burst (pneu); *j'ai crevé,* I have got a puncture, U. S. I have a flat tire. ‖ Fam. To pop off, to snuff it, to peg out, U. S. to croak (v. claquer); *crever d'ennui,* to be bored to tears; *crever d'envie de faire qqch.,* to itch to do sth.;

crever de faim, to be starving; *crever de jalousie,* to burst with envy.
— v. pr. **Se crever,** FAM. To kill oneself, to overwork oneself.

crevette [krəvɛt] f. Shrimp (grise); prawn (rose).

crevettier [krəvɛtje] m. NAUT. Shrimping net (filet); shrimping boat (bateau).

cri [kri] m. Cry (sens général); scream, screech, squeal, shriek (aigu, perçant); cheer (d'acclamations); call, halloo (d'appel); bawl, yell, howl, roar (de colère); bellow, howl, yell, cry (de douleur); *demander à grands cris,* to clamour for, to call out for; *pousser un cri,* to give (ou) to set up (ou) to utter a cry. ‖ Cry (des rues); *cri de guerre,* war-cry. ‖ Bump (du butor); quack (du canard); gobble (du dindon); gaggle, honk (de l'oie); squawk (du perroquet); grunt (du porc); squeak (de la souris). ‖ Squeak (des freins); crackling (du papier froissé); creak (de la porte); rasp (de la râpe); screech (de la scie). ‖ Loc. *Des cravates dernier cri,* the latest thing in ties; *le tout dernier cri,* the latest thing out.

criaillement [kriɑjmɑ̃] m. Squalling; nagging.

criailler [-je] v. intr. (1). To squall; to nag.

criaillerie [-jri] f. Squalling; nagging.

criailleur, euse [-jœ:r, ø:z] s. Squaller, nagger.

criant, ante [kriɑ, ɑ̃:t] adj. FIG. Crying; flagrant.

criard, arde [kria:r, a:rd] adj. Crying, squalling (enfant); shrewish, scolding (femme); screeching (oiseau); bawling (personne); high-pitched, shrill, grating (voix). ‖ Loud, gaudy (couleur); showy, flashy (luxe, vêtements). ‖ Dunning (créancier); pressing (dette).
— m. Squaller, bawler.

criarde [-ard] f. Shrew; scold.

criblage [kribla:ʒ] m. Sifting (du grain); screening, jigging (du minerai).

crible [-bl] m. Sieve, riddle (à grain). ‖ Screen (à charbon); jigger (à minerai). ‖ FIG. *Passer au crible,* to sift.

cribler [-ble] v. tr. (1). To sieve, to riddle, to sift (du grain). [V. TAMISER.] ‖ To screen (du charbon); to jig (du minerai). ‖ FIG. To riddle, to pepper, to pelt (*de,* with); *cribler de,* to riddle with (balles); to bombard with (questions); *criblé de dettes,* up to the ears in debt.

cribleur [-blœ:r] m. TECHN. Sifting machine, sifter.

criblures [-bly:r] f. pl. Siftings (de grain). ‖ Screenings (de minerai).

cric [kri] m. AUTOM. Jack, lifting jack; *cric à main,* hand jack; *cric à vis,* screwjack; *mettre sur cric,* to jack, to jack up. ‖ TECHN. *Cric tenseur,* pulling jack; wire-strainer.

cric [krik] interj. Crack!

cricket [krikɛt] m. SPORTS. Cricket; *joueur de cricket,* cricketer; *match international de cricket,* test-match.

cricoïde [krikɔid] adj. MÉD. Cricoid.

cricri [krikri] m. FAM. Cricket.

criée [krije] f. Auction; *à la criée,* by auction.

crier v. intr. (1). To cry (sens général); to scream, to screech, to squeal, to shriek (d'un cri aigu); to squall (d'un cri discordant); to cheer (pour acclamer); to call, to halloo (pour appeler); to bawl, to yell, to howl, to roar (avec colère); to bellow, to howl, to yell, to cry (de douleur); to shout, to clamour (à tue-tête). ‖ To bump (butor); to quack (canard); to gobble (dindon); to gaggle, to honk (oie); to squawk (perroquet); to grunt (porc); to squeak (souris). ‖ To squeak (frein); to crackle (papier); to creak (plancher, porte); to rasp (râpe); to screech (scie); to squeak (soulier). ‖ To scold, to storm (se fâcher); *crier contre,* to cry out against; to rail at, to nag at.
— v. tr. To cry, to shout (des injures, un ordre). ‖ To cry, to call, to proclaim; *crier son inno-*

cence, to proclaim oneself innocent; *crier qqch. sur les toits,* to cry sth. from the house-tops; *crier vengeance,* to call aloud for vengeance. ‖ To cry, to hawk (un journal, une marchandise).

crieur [krijœ:r] s. Hawker; *crieur de journaux,* news boy; *crieur public,* town-crier. ‖ Auctioneer.

crime [krim] m. Crime; *crime d'Etat,* treason; *le crime fait la honte et non pas l'échafaud,* the shame is in the crime, not in the punishment. ‖ JUR. Felony. ‖ FAM. Sin, shame; crime; *ne m'en faites pas un crime,* don't hold it against me.

Crimée [krime] f. GÉOGR. Crimea; *de Crimée,* Crimean.

criminaliser [kriminalize] v. tr. (1). JUR. To transfer from civil to criminal proceedings.

criminaliste [-list] m. Criminalist, criminologist, criminal jurist.

criminalité [-lite] f. Criminality.

criminel, elle [kriminɛl, ɛ:l] adj. Criminal, felonious (acte); criminal, guilty of crime (personne); *droit criminel,* criminal law; *rapports criminels,* criminal conversation (ou) connection. ‖ FAM. Shameful (honteux); *c'est criminel d'agir ainsi,* that's a shameful thing to do.
— m. Criminal, felon. ‖ JUR. Penal action; *avocat au criminel,* criminal lawyer; *juger au criminel,* to try according to criminal law; *poursuivre au criminel,* to take criminal proceedings against.

criminellement [-nɛlmɑ̃] adv. Criminally. ‖ JUR. Criminally, according to criminal law.

criminologie [-nɔlɔʒi] f. Criminology.

criminologiste [-nɔlɔʒist] m. Criminologist.

crin [krɛ̃] m. Hair; *crin de cheval,* horsehair; *crin végétal,* vegetable fibre. ‖ *Crin de Florence,* silkworm gut (pour la pêche). ‖ FAM. *A tous crins,* out-and-out, thorough-going; *comme un crin,* tetchy (ou) testy, like touchwood or tinder.

crincrin [krɛ̃krɛ̃] m. FAM. Bad fiddle (violon); scraper (violoniste).

crinière [krinjɛ:r] f. Mane (d'animal); horse tail, tail (de casque). ‖ FAM. Mane, crop of hair.

crinoline [krinɔlin] f. Crinoline.

crique [krik] f. Creek, cove, bight.

criquet [krikɛ] m. ZOOL. Locust; cricket.

crise [kri:z] f. MÉD. Attack, fit (v. ACCÈS, ATTAQUE); *crise d'épilepsie,* epileptic fit; *crise de foie,* liver attack; *crise de goutte, de rhumatisme,* attack of gout, of rheumatism; *crise de nerfs,* attack of nerves, fit of hysterics. ‖ Crisis; *crise des affaires,* slump in business; *crise économique,* trade depression; *crise ministérielle,* cabinet crisis; *crise du papier,* paper shortage; *état de crise,* state of emergency; *traverser une crise,* to go through a critical time. ‖ FIG. Paroxysm (de désespoir); fit (de paresse). ‖ FAM. Burst (de colère, de larmes); *piquer une crise,* to fly into a passion (colère); to throw a fit (nerfs).

crispant, ante [krispɑ, ɑ̃:t] adj. Irritating, maddening, nerve-grating.

crispation [krispasjɔ̃] f. Crispation, shrivelling up (du cuir); cockling (du papier). ‖ Wince (de douleur); twitching (des mains, du visage). ‖ FAM. Fidgets, exasperation.

crisper [-pe] v. tr. (1). To contract, to distort (les traits, le visage). ‖ FAM. *Cela me crispe,* that gets on my nerves; *il est crispé,* he is on edge.
— v. pr. **Se crisper,** to crisp; to move convulsively; to clench (doigts); to wince (visage).

crispin [krispɛ̃] m. *Gant à crispin,* gauntlet.

criss [kris] m. Kris, creese (poignard).

crissement [krismɑ̃] m. Grinding (des dents); squeaking (des freins); crunching (du gravier, de la neige); grating (d'une scie); rustling (du taffetas).

crisser [-se] v. intr. (1). To grind (dents); to

squeak (freins); to crunch (gravier, neige); to grate (scie); to rustle (taffetas).

cristal [kristal] m. Crystal; *cristal de roche, de quartz*, rock-, quartz-crystal. ‖ Crystal, cut glass; *les cristaux*, glass-ware (verrerie). ‖ Fig. Transparence; pellucidity. ‖ Fam. Pl. Washing-soda (carbonate de soude).

cristallerie [-lri] f. Glass-works; crystal-glass making.

cristallin, ine [-lɛ̃. in] adj. Crystalline.
— m. Méd. Crystalline lens (de l'œil).

cristallisation [-lizasjɔ̃] f. Crystallization.

cristallisé, ée [-lize] adj. Crystallized; granulated (sucre). ‖ Frosted (émail).

cristalliser v. tr., intr. (1). To crystallize.
— v. pr. **Se cristalliser**, to crystallize.

cristallisoir [-lizwa:r] m. Crystallizing vessel.

cristallographie [-lɔgrafi] f. Crystallography.

cristallomancie [-lɔmɑ̃si] f. Crystal-gazing.

critère [kritɛ:r], **critérium** [-tɛrjɔm] m. Criterion; test; *cas servant de critère*, test-case. ‖ Jur. *Critère juridique*, legal assumption. ‖ Sports. Selection-match.

critiquable [kritikabl] adj. Criticizable, open to criticism.

critique [-tik] adj. Critical (dissertation, examen, note); critical, carping, fault-finding (personne); *esprit critique*, spirit of criticism; *sens critique*, critical faculty. ‖ Critical, crucial, decisive (moment, période, point); critical, dangerous, ticklish, trying (situation); *circonstance critique*, emergency. ‖ Méd. Critical; *âge critique*, change of life.
— m. Critic (personne).
— f. Criticism (art); review (compte rendu); critique, criticism (examen); *faire la critique.d'un livre*, to review a book. ‖ Censure, criticism, animadversion (blâme).

critiquer [-tike] v. tr. (1). To criticize, to review (un ouvrage). ‖ To criticize, to blame, to find fault with (qqch., qqn). [V. Censurer, Éreinter.]

critiqueur [-tikœ:r] s. Criticizer, fault-finder.

croassement [krɔasmɑ̃] m. Cawing; croaking.

croasser [-se] v. intr. (1). To croak (corbeau); to caw (corneille).

croate [krɔat] adj. Géogr. Croatian.
— s. Géogr. Croat, Croatian.

croc [kro] m. Fang (de chien, de loup). ‖ Hook; *croc de boucherie*, butcher's hook. ‖ Naut. Boathook, gaff-hook. ‖ Fam. *En croc*, curled-up (moustache). ‖ **Croc-en-jambe** (pl. *crocs-en-jambe*) m. Trip; *faire un croc-en-jambe à qqn*, to trip s.o. up.

croche [krɔʃ] f. Mus. Quaver; U. S. eighth note. ‖ Techn. Pl. Crook-bit tongs.

crochet [krɔʃɛ] m. Hook (en général); catch (de boîte, de volet); spiked stick (de chiffonnier); clasp (de fermoir); crochet (de portefaix); *crochet d'arrêt*, pawl, catch; *crochet d'attelage*. trace-hook; *crochet à bottines*, button hook ; *crochet de cycliste*, trouser clip; *crochet de serrurier*, picklock. ‖ Crochet-needle (à tricoter); *au crochet*, crocheted; *faire du crochet*, to crochet; *ouvrage au crochet*, crochet-work. ‖ Square brackets (en typographie). ‖ Ch. de f. *Crochet d'attelage*, draw-hook (ou) -bar. ‖ Milit. Lanyard hook; swivel (pour carabine); extractor (pour cartouches). ‖ Naut. Stanchion hook. ‖ Sports. Hook (à la boxe); *crochet du gauche*, left hook. ‖ Mus. Hook (de croche). ‖ Archit. Crocket. ‖ Autom. Turn (de la route); *crochet du capot*, bonnet (ou) U. S. hood fastener; *faire un crochet*, to swerve, to go out of one's way; *faire un crochet par*, to go via. ‖ Fig. *Vivre aux crochets de qqn*, to live at s.o.'s expense, to sponge on s.o.

crochetable [-tabl] adj. That can be picked.

crochetage [-ta:ʒ] m. Lock-picking.

crocheter [-te] v. tr. (8 *b*). To force (une porte); to pick (une serrure). ‖ To crochet (le fil, la laine). ‖ To hook in (en typogr.).

crocheteur [-tœ:r] m. Picklock, housebreaker (cambrioleur). ‖ Porter, carrier (portefaix).

crochu, ue [-y] adj. Crooked; hooked (bec); beaked, hooked (nez). ‖ Fam. *Aux doigts crochus*, close-fisted (avare); light-fingered (voleur).

crocodile [krɔkɔdil] m. Zool. Crocodile. ‖ Ch. de f. Automatic stop. ‖ Fam. *Larmes de crocodile*, crocodile tears.

crocodilien [-ljɛ̃] m. Zool. Crocodilian.

crocus [krɔky:s] m. Bot. Crocus.

croire [krwa:r] v. tr. (33). To believe; *à l'en croire*, if he is to be believed; *croire vaguement que*, to have a vague belief that; *en croire ses yeux*, to believe one's eyes; *être porté à croire*, to be inclined to believe; *faire croire*, to make believe; *je n'en crois rien*, I don't believe it (ou) a word of it; *il est à croire que*, it is to be believed that; *il m'aurait fallu le voir pour le croire*, this I must have seen to have believed. ‖ To believe, to fancy, to imagine, to suppose, to think (imaginer, penser); *c'est à croire que*, one might think that; *croire de son devoir de*, to think it incumbent on oneself to; *croire bien faire*, to think one is doing the right thing; *je crois bien que vous avez raison*, I really think you are right; *je crois que non*, I don't think so; *je crois que oui*, I think so; *j'ai cru voir*, I thought I saw; *je ne croyais pas si bien dire*, I didn't think I was so near the truth; *je ne suis pas éloigné de croire que*, I am inclined to think that; *je vous croyais plus sage*, I thought you wiser; *il croit être généreux*, he thinks himself generous; *elle le croyait avec son père*, she thought he was with her father; *on le croyait parti*, he was thought to have gone; *vous ne sauriez croire combien*, you can't imagine how, you have no idea how. ‖ To believe, to trust, to rely upon (se fier à); *croyez-m'en*, take my word for it; *vous pouvez m'en croire*, you may take it from me. ‖ To take for (prendre pour); *je ne suis pas celle que vous croyez*, I am not that kind of girl (ou) the girl you take me for. ‖ To expect (attendre); *je ne croyais pas ça de vous*, I should not have expected that of you. ‖ To hope (espérer); *j'aime à croire*, I hope, I hope and trust. ‖ To be afraid (craindre); *je crois bien qu'il est mort*, I am afraid he is dead. ‖ Loc. *Je vous crois!*, you bet!, certainly!, rather!
— v. intr. To believe (à, in); *je ne crois pas à son innocence*, I don't believe in his innocence. ‖ To rely (en, upon); *je ne crois pas en ses promesses*, I have no faith (ou) confidence in his promises. ‖ To think; *on a cru à une congestion pulmonaire*, they thought it was pneumonia. ‖ Ecclés. To believe (en, in). ‖ Loc. *C'est à n'y pas croire*, it passes (ou) is beyond belief.
— v. pr. **Se croire**, to be believed (être cru). ‖ To think oneself; *elle se croit belle*, she thinks herself (ou) she is pretty. ‖ Fam. To be self-conceited; to have no mean opinion of oneself.

croisade [krwazad] f. Crusade; *en croisade*, on a crusade.

croisé [krwaze] m. Crusader. ‖ Twill (tissu).

croisé, ée adj. Cross, crossed; folded; *les bras croisés*, with folded arms; *les jambes croisées*, cross-legged. ‖ Alternate (rime). ‖ Twilled (étoffe); double-breasted, button-over (vêtement). ‖ *Race croisée*, cross-breed; *de race croisée*, half-bred. ‖ *Mots croisés*, cross words; *faire un mot croisé*, to do a crossword puzzle. ‖ Milit. *Feux croisés*, cross-fire. ‖ Théâtr. *Feux croisés*, cross-lighting. ‖ Sports. Over-arm (au tennis).

croisée f. Casement-window (fenêtre). ‖ *Croisée*

des chemins, cross-roads. ‖ ARCHIT. *Croisée d'ogives*, intersection ribs.

croisement [-zmɑ̃] m. Folding (des bras); crossing (d'épées, de fils, de lignes); meeting (de véhicules). ‖ AUTOM. Cross-road, crossway; intersection. ‖ CH. DE F. Crossing. ‖ ZOOL. Interbreeding, crossing; cross-breed, cross (de races); *faire des croisements de races*, to cross breeds, to cross-breed.

croiser [-ze] v. tr. (1). To fold (les bras); to cross (les jambes, les fils, les lignes, qqn). ‖ To fold (un fichu); to twill (les fils d'un tissu). ‖ AUTOM. To cut across (la route); to meet (qqn, un véhicule). ‖ MILIT. *Croiser la baïonnette*, to charge bayonets; *croiser le fer*, to cross swords. ‖ ZOOL. To cross (des races). ‖ FIG. *Croiser le fer avec*, to cross swords with (discuter).
— v. intr. To lap, to fold over (vêtement). ‖ NAUT. To cruise.
— v. pr. Se **croiser**, to cross, to meet (lettres, personnes, routes); *ma lettre s'est croisée avec la vôtre*, our letters have crossed. ‖ †. To take the cross (partir à la croisade). ‖ FIG. *Se croiser les bras*, to fold one's arms.

croiseté, re [-zte] adj. BLAS. Crossleted.

croisette [-zɛt] f. Small cross. ‖ BLAS. Crosslet.

croiseur [krwazœ:r] m. NAUT. Cruiser; *croiseur de course*, raider.

croisière [-zjɛ:r] f. NAUT. Cruise; *en croisière*, on a cruise; *guerre de croisière*, commerce-destroying war; *vitesse de croisière*, cruising speed. ‖ Cruise; round trip (fam.); *faire une croisière*, to go on a cruise. ‖ AUTOM. Journey.

croisillon [krwazijɔ̃] m. Cross-bar, cross-arm, cross-piece; *croisillons d'une fenêtre*, window bars. ‖ ARCHIT. Lattice. ‖ AUTOM. Pl. Centre-bracing, cross-bars.

croissait [-sɛ], **croissant** [-sɑ̃]. V. CROÎTRE (34).

croissance [krwasɑ̃:s] f. Growth; *à croissance rapide*, quick growing; *arrêté dans sa croissance*, stunted.

croissant [-sɑ̃] m. Crescent (de la lune, des Turcs). ‖ AGRIC. Pruning-hook, bill-hook. ‖ AVIAT. *Aile en croissant*, crescent-wing. ‖ CULIN. *Croissant*, crescent-roll, horseshoe-shaped roll. ‖ BLAS. Moon.

croisure [krwazy:r] f. Alternating, alternation (des rimes); twilling (de la trame).

croître [krwa:tr] v. intr. (34). To increase (bruit, difficultés, nombre, vitesse); to lengthen, to get longer (jours); to wax (lune); to grow (plantes, personnes); rise (rivière, vent, vitesse); *croître dans l'estime de qqn*, to rise in s.o's esteem. ‖ FAM. *Croître et embellir*, to keep growing bigger and better (en bien); to go from bad to worse (en mal).

croix [krwa] f. ECCLÉS. Cross; *mise en croix*, crucifixion. ‖ Cross (d'un ordre); *croix de guerre*, Military Cross; *croix de la Légion d'honneur*, cross of the Legion of Honour. ‖ *Croix ancrée, fleuretée, potencée, tréflée*, cross moline, fleury (ou) flory, potent, botonny; *croix égyptienne, grecque, latine*, Egyptian, Greek, Latin cross; *croix gammée*, swastika; *croix de Malte*, Maltese cross, cross patée; *croix de Lorraine*, cross of Lorraine; *croix de Saint-André*, St Andrew's cross; *croix en tau*, Tau cross; *en croix*, crosswise, crossways. ‖ *Point de croix*, cross-stitch (en couture). ‖ Dagger, obelisk (en typographie). ‖ Badge (à l'école). ‖ BLAS. Saltire. ‖ MÉD. *Croix-Rouge*, Red Cross. ‖ ASTRON. *La Croix du Sud*, the Southern Cross. ‖ FIG. Cross, trial. ‖ FAM. *Il a fallu la croix et la bannière pour*, it took the very devil to.

cromesquis [krɔmɛski] m. CULIN. Kromesky.

cromlech [krɔmlɛk] m. Cromlech.

crooner [krunər] m. Crooner.

croquant, ante [krɔkɑ̃, ɑ̃:t] adj. Crisp, crunchy; *pâte croquante*, short pastry.
— m. CULIN. Gristle.

croquant m. FAM. Chawbacon; boor.

croque [krɔk]. V. CROQUER. ‖ **A la croque-au-sel**, CULIN., LOC. With salt only. ‖ **Croque-mitaine**, m. Bogey. ‖ **Croque-madame**, m. invar. CULIN. Toasted ham and cheese sandwich with an egg on top. ‖ **Croque-monsieur**, m. invar. CULIN. Toasted ham and cheese sandwich. ‖ **Croque-mort**, m. FAM. Undertaker's assistant, U. S. mortician.

croquembouche [-kɑ̃buʃ] f. CULIN. Crisp sweetmeat.

croquenot [-kno] m. POP. Shoe, beetle-crusher.

croquer [-ke] v. tr. (1). To crunch, to munch (manger une chose croquante). ‖ To eat up, to gobble (dévorer). ‖ ARTS. To sketch; *gentille à croquer*, lovely, charming. ‖ SPORTS. To tight-croquet (la boule). ‖ FAM. *Croquer le marmot*, to kick one's heels, to dance attendance.
— v. intr. To crunch.

croquet [krɔkɛ] m. SPORTS. Croquet (jeu).

croquette [-kɛt] f. CULIN. Croquette, rissole.

croqueur, euse [-kœ:r, ø:z] s. Great eater. ‖ FIG. Squanderer; *croqueuse de diamants*, gold-digger.

croquignole [-kiɲɔl] f. CULIN. Cracknel; short-bread.

croquignolet, ette [-kiɲɔlɛ, ɛt] adj. FAM. Cute, dainty, dinky.

croquis [krɔki] m. ARTS. Sketch; croquis; *cahier de croquis*, sketch-book; *faire un croquis de*, to sketch. ‖ MILIT. *Croquis d'objectifs*, plan of targets; *croquis de repérage*, range card. ‖ Outline (en littérature). ‖ **Croquis-calque**, m. Skeleton-tracing.

crosne [kro:n] m. BOT. Chinese artichoke.

cross [krɔs], **cross-country** [-kuntri] m. SPORTS. Cross-country running.

crosse [krɔs] f. ECCLÉS. Crozier, staff (d'abbé mitré, d'évêque). ‖ SPORTS. Golf-club (au golf); hockey-stick (au hockey). ‖ MUS. Scroll (de violon). ‖ MÉD. Arch (de l'aorte). ‖ MILIT. Trail (d'affût); butt, butt end, butt stock (de fusil, de mitrailleuse); grip (de revolver). ‖ TECHN. Cross-head (de piston). ‖ BOT. Crosier (de fougère).

crossé, ée [-se] adj. ECCLÉS. Croziered.

crossée f. SPORTS. Drive (au golf).

crosser v. tr. (1). SPORTS. To hit, to strike (la balle). ‖ FAM. To rebuke (qqn).

crossman [krɔsman] (pl. **crossmen**) m. SPORTS. Cross-country runner.

crotale [krɔtal] m. ZOOL. Rattlesnake; U. S. rattler.

crotte [krɔt] f. Dung, dropping (excrément). ‖ Mud, dirt (boue). ‖ CULIN. Chocolate. ‖ AVIAT., POP. Bomb.
— interj. POP. Bother!, blow!

crotté, ée [-te] adj. Dirty; mud-bespattered, mud-died, splashed with mud.

crotter v. tr. (1). To dirty, to soil.
— v. pr. Se **crotter**, to get bespattered with mud.

crottin [-tɛ̃] m. Horse-dung.

croulant, ante [krulɑ̃, ɑ̃:t] adj. Ruinous, tottering, tumble-down. ‖ FIG. Crumbling, ramshackle, tottering. ‖ FAM. *Vieux croulant*, old fossil.

crouler [-le] v. intr. To totter, to collapse (s'affaisser); to tumble (ou) crumble down; to fall in; to fall with a crash (s'effondrer); *faire crouler*, to bring down. ‖ FIG. To crumble away (influence); to crumble, to collapse (projet); *faire crouler la salle sous les applaudissements*, to bring down the house.

croup [krup] m. MÉD. Croup.

croupe f. Croup, crupper, hindquarters (du cheval); *monter en croupe,* to ride pillion (pour une femme); to ride behind (pour un homme). ‖ Géogr. Ridge, brow (d'une montagne). ‖ Archit. Hip. ‖ Fam. Rump, backside, rear-end.

croupetons (à) [akruptɔ̃] loc. adv. Squatting, crouching; on one's hunkers (fam.).

croupi, ie [krupi] adj. Stagnant, still, foul (eau).

croupier [krupje] m. Croupier (de jeux). ‖ Jur. Backer (d'agent de change).

croupière [krupjɛ:r] f. Crupper (harnais). ‖ Fam. *Tailler des croupières à qqn,* to take the wind out of s.o.'s sails.

croupion [krupjɔ̃] m. Zool. Rump (d'oiseau). ‖ Culin. Parson's (ou) U. S. pope's nose (de volaille). ‖ Méd. Coccyx.

croupir [krupi:r] v. intr. (2). To stagnate (eau). ‖ Fig. *Croupir dans,* to wallow in (la fange, le vice); to be sunk in (l'ignorance); to stagnate in (un lieu).

croupissant, ante [-pisɑ̃, ɑ̃:t] adj. Stagnating, putrid (eau).

croustade [krustad] f. Culin. Croustade, pastry case.

croustillant, ante [krustijɑ̃, ɑ̃:t] adj. Culin. Crisp, crusty, scrunchy, short. ‖ Fig. Glamorous; sexy (femme).

croustiller [-tije] v. intr. Culin. To crunch.

croustilleux, euse [krustijø, ø:z] adj. Fig. Spicy, broad.

croûte [krut] f. Crust (de pain, de pâté, de la terre, de tartre); rind (de fromage); *faire croûte,* to crust, to cake. ‖ Culin. Case (de bouchée, de vol-au-vent). ‖ Méd. Scab; *croûtes de lait,* milk-crust; *faire croûte,* to scab. ‖ Arts. Daub (peinture). ‖ Fam. *Casser la croûte,* to have a snack; *casse-croûte,* snack, U. S. quick lunch; *comme une croûte derrière une malle,* left to shift for oneself; *gagner sa croûte,* to earn one's bread and butter (ou) an honest crust, to bring home the bacon.

croûter [-te] v. intr. Fam. To grub (v. bouffer, briffer); *est-ce que ça nous donnera de quoi croûter?,* will it bake bread?

croûteux, euse [-tø, ø:z] adj. Culin. Crusty (gâteau, pain). ‖ Méd. Scabby (peau, personne).

croûton [-tɔ̃] m. Crusty end, U. S. heel (du pain); chunk (de pain). ‖ Culin. Sippet.

crown-glass [kraunglas] m. Crown-glass; *lentille en crown-glass,* crown-lens.

croyable [krwajabl] adj. Believable, credible (chose); trustworthy (personne).

croyance [-jɑ̃:s] f. Belief, credit (à, en, in). ‖ Ecclés. Faith; confession.

croyant, ante [-jɑ̃, ɑ̃:t] adj. Believing. — s. Ecclés. Believer (chrétien). ‖ Pl. The faithful (musulmans).

croyons [-jɔ̃]. V. croire (33).

C. R. S. [sɛɛrɛs] m. Riot policeman, member of a Compagnie républicaine de sécurité (= special security corps).

cru [kry] m. Agric. Vintage; wine (vin). ‖ Loc. *Du cru,* of the country, local. ‖ Fig. *De son cru,* of his own invention; *de mon cru,* of my own.

cru adj. Culin. Raw, crude, uncooked. ‖ Unvarnished (bois); sunbaked (brique); unbaked (céramique); undressed, raw (cuir); hard (eau); crude (minerai); raw (soie). ‖ Crude (couleur); glaring, garish (lumière); *jour cru,* broad daylight. ‖ Fig. Crude, unpolished (idée); coarse, spicy (histoire); plain (termes); plain, brute (vérité). — m. Culin. Raw meat (ou) food. ‖ Loc. *Monter à cru,* to ride bareback.

cru p. p. V. croire (33).

crû p. p. V. croître (34).

cruauté [kryote] f. Ferocity (des animaux); cruelty, ferociousness, mercilessness (des hommes).

‖ Act of cruelty; *se livrer à des cruautés,* to perpetrate acts of cruelty (ou) cruelties. ‖ Fig. Cruelty, harshness (du destin).

cruche [kryʃ] f. Pitcher, jug. ‖ Fam. Dolt; duffer, dunce.

cruchon [-ʃɔ̃] m. Pot; small jug. ‖ Stoneware hot-water bottle (bouillotte); pig (en grès). ‖ Fam. Dolt; duffer.

crucial [krysjal] adj. Cross-shaped (en croix). ‖ Philos., Fam. Crucial.

crucifère [krysifɛ:r] adj. Bot., Archit. Cruciferous. — f. pl. Bot. Crucifers.

crucifiement [-fimɑ̃] m. Crucifixion.

crucifier [-fje] v. tr. (1). To crucify (pr. et fig.).

crucifix [-fi] m. Ecclés. Crucifix.

crucifixion [-fiksjɔ̃] f. Crucifixion.

cruciforme [-fɔrm] adj. Cruciform, cross-shaped. ‖ Zool., Bot. Cruciate. ‖ Méd. Crucial.

cruciverbiste [-vɛrbist] s. Crossword addict.

crudité [krydite] f. Culin. Rawness (état); raw fruit, raw vegetables (fruits, légumes non cuits); ‖ Crudeness (des couleurs); glare (de la lumière). ‖ Fig. Coarseness (du langage, des termes).

crue [kry] f. Swelling (d'un cours d'eau); flood, freshet (flot montant); *en crue,* in spate.

cruel, elle [kryɛl] adj. Cruel (acte, personne); sad (déception); sore (épreuve); bitter (expérience); hard (hiver); harsh, cruel (mots); grievous (perte); acute (remords); unkind, hard (sort). — s. Cruel (ou) unkind person.

cruelle [kryɛ:l] f. Virtuous woman; *il ne trouvait pas de cruelles,* no woman could resist him.

cruellement [kryɛlmɑ̃] adv. Cruelly (avec cruauté); cruelly; bitterly; sorely (avec douleur).

crûment [krymɑ̃] adv. Crudely, bluntly (sans ménagement). ‖ Coarsely (grossièrement).

crural, ale [kryral] adj. Méd. Crural.

crustacé [krystase] adj. Zool. Crustaceous, crustacean. — m. Zool. Crustacean; shell-fish (fam.).

cryolithe [kriolit] f. Cryolite.

cryologie [kriolɔʒi] f. Phys. Cryogenics.

cryothérapie [kriotɛrapi] f. Méd. Treatment by cold.

crypte [kript] f. Archit., Méd., Bot. Crypt.

cryptique [-tik] adj. Cryptic.

cryptocommuniste [kriptɔkɔmynist] adj., s. Crypto-Communist.

cryptogame [kriptɔgam] adj. Bot. Cryptogamous. — m. Bot. Cryptogam.

cryptogramme [kriptɔgram] m. Cryptogram, cipher message.

cryptographe [-graf] m. Cryptographer.

cryptographie [-grafi] f. Cryptography.

crypton [kriptɔ̃] m. Chim. Krypton.

cubage [kyba:ʒ] m. Cubage, cubature. ‖ Cubic content; *cubage d'air,* air-space.

cubain, aine [kybɛ̃, ɛn] adj., s. Géogr. Cuban.

cubature [kybaty:r] f. Math. Cubature.

cube [kyb] adj. Cubic (centimètre, mètre). — m. Math. Cube. ‖ Pl. Building blocks (jeu). ‖ Culin. Cube, bouillon cube.

cuber [-be] v. tr. (1). Math. To cube (un nombre). ‖ Techn. To cube, to gauge (un réservoir). — v. intr. To have a cubical content of.

cubique [-bik] adj. Cubic. ‖ Math. *Racine cubique,* cube root.

cubique f. Math. Cubic curve.

cubisme [-bism] m. Arts. Cubism.

cubiste [-bist] s. Arts. Cubist.

cubital, ale [kybital] adj. Méd. Cubital.

cubitus [-ty:s] m. Méd. Ulna, cubitus.

cucul [kyky] adj. inv. Pop. Wet, twee.

cucurbitacées [kykyrbitase] f. pl. Bot. Cucurbitaceae.

cucurbite [-bit] f. CHIM. Cucurbit.

cueillaison [kœjɛzɔ̃], cueillette [-jɛt] f. Gathering; picking; *cueillette du houblon*, hop-picking.

cueilleur [-jœːˑ] s. Gatherer, picker.

cueillir [-jiːr] v. tr. (35). To gather, to pick, to pluck, to cull (des fleurs, des fruits); to pick (le houblon). ‖ SPORTS. To gather (le ballon). ‖ FIG. To snatch, to steal (un baiser); to reap (les bénéfices); to win (des lauriers). ‖ FAM. To nab, to pick up (qqn).

cueilloir [-jwaːr] m. AGRIC. Fruit-picker (outil); fruit-basket (panier).

cuiller, cuillère [kɥijɛːr] f. Spoon; *cuiller à bouche* (ou) *à soupe, à café, à dessert, à sel,* table-, tea-, dessert-, salt-spoon; *cuiller à pot,* ladle. ‖ TECHN. Ladle (de coulée); scoop, bucket (de drague). ‖ SPORTS. Spoon-bait, trolling-spoon (de pêcheur). ‖ FAM. *Il n'y va pas avec le dos de la cuiller,* he makes no bones about it.

cuillerée [-jre] f. Spoonful; *cuillerée à soupe,* table-spoonful.

cuir [kɥiːr] m. Hide (d'animal); *cuir brut,* raw hide. ‖ COMM. Leather; *cuir à rasoir,* razor strop; *cuir de Russie,* Russia leather; *ceinture en cuir,* leather belt. ‖ AVIAT. Leather flying suit (combinaison). ‖ MÉD. *Cuir chevelu,* scalp. ‖ GRAMM. Incorrect liaison; *faire un cuir,* to drop a brick (fam.). ‖ FAM. *Tanner le cuir à qqn,* to give s.o. a tanning, to tan s.o.'s hide.

cuirasse [kɥiras] f. Cuirass. ‖ NAUT. Armour. ‖ MILIT. Breast-plate; cuirass. ‖ ZOOL. Buckler.

cuirassé, ée [-se] adj. Armour-plated. ‖ TECHN. Shielded. ‖ FIG. Hardened, proof (contre, against). — m. NAUT. Battleship, armoured vessel; *cuirassé de croisière,* armoured cruiser; *cuirassé de poche,* pocket battleship.

cuirassement [-smã] m. Armouring (action); armour, armour-plating (cuirasse).

cuirasser [-se] v. tr. MILIT. To cuirass (un soldat); to armour (un véhicule). ‖ NAUT. To armour, to armour-plate. ‖ TECHN. To shield. ‖ FIG. To steel; to harden. — v. pr. Se cuirasser, MILIT. To put on one's cuirass. ‖ FIG. To steel oneself, to harden one's heart (contre, against).

cuirassier [-sje] m. MILIT. Cuirassier.

cuire [kɥiːr] v. tr. (85). CULIN. To cook (en général); *faire cuire,* to cook; *faire cuire à l'eau, au four, sur le gril, en ragoût, à petit feu, à la poêle,* to boil, to bake (ou) to roast, to grill, to stew, to simmer, to fry; *faire trop cuire,* to overdo; *ne pas faire cuire assez,* to underdo. ‖ TECHN. To kiln; to bake, to fire; to burn, to calcine. — v. intr. CULIN. To cook (en général); to bake (pain). ‖ TECHN. To bake. ‖ MÉD. To tingle, to smart (peau); to burn, to smart (yeux). ‖ LOC. *On cuit ici,* it is boiling hot here; *il vous en cuira,* you'll smart for it, you'll hear more of it.

cuisage [-zaːʒ] m. Charring (du bois).

cuisant, ante [-zã, ã:t] adj. Hot, pungent (assaisonnement). ‖ FIG. Bitter (déception); sharp (défaite); keen, smart, burning (douleur); biting (froid); bitter, keen (regrets).

cuiseur [-zœːr] m. Pressure cooker.

cuisinage [-zina:ʒ] m. JUR. Grilling.

cuisine [-zin] f. Kitchen (pièce). ‖ CULIN. Cookery (art); cooking (préparation); food (plats cuisinés); *faire la cuisine,* to do the cooking, to cook. ‖ MILIT. *Cuisine roulante,* field kitchen. ‖ NAUT. Galley. ‖ FIG. Wangling; underhand manœuvre (intrigue); cooking, faking (tripatouillage); *cuisine électorale,* gerrymandering.

cuisiné, ée [-zine] adj. Cooked; *plat cuisiné,* takeaway meal.

cuisiner [-zine] v. tr. (1). CULIN. To cook (un plat). ‖ FIG. To manipulate, to wangle, to cook (une affaire); to gerrymander (une élection). ‖ FAM. To grill (un accusé); to pump (qqn). — v. intr. CULIN. To cook; *elle cuisine bien,* she is a good cook.

cuisinier [-zinje] m. CULIN. Cook, chef.

cuisinière [-zinjɛːr] f. CULIN. Range, kitchen range (ou) stove (appareil); cooker (personne); *cuisinière à gaz,* gas cooker (ou) U. S. range.

cuissard [kɥisaːr] m. † Cuisse. ‖ MÉD. Socket.

cuissardes [kɥisard] f. pl. Waders (de pêcheurs); thigh-boots.

cuisse [kɥis] f. Thigh (d'animal, de personne). ‖ CULIN. *Cuisse de poulet,* chicken leg. ‖ FAM. *Il se croit sorti de la cuisse de Jupiter,* he thinks he is the Lord God Almighty.

cuisseau [-so] m. CULIN. Haunch, fillet of the leg (de veau).

cuisson [kɥisɔ̃] f. CULIN. Cooking (en général); baking (du pain). ‖ TECHN. Firing, burning (des poteries); calcining, calcination. ‖ MÉD. Burning (ou) smarting pain.

cuissot [kɥiso] m. CULIN. Haunch, quarter (de chevreuil).

cuistance [kɥistãːs] f. POP. Cooking; *faire la cuistance,* to make the grub.

cuistot [kɥisto] m. FAM. Cook.

cuistre [kɥistr] m. Pedant; prig.

cuistrerie [-trəri] f. Pedantry; pose.

cuit [kɥi] adj. CULIN. Cooked (en général); baked (pain); *cuit à point,* done to a turn; U. S. well done; *pas assez cuit,* underdone; *trop cuit,* overdone. ‖ POP. Sozzled, U. S. high, stewed (ivre); finished, done for (fichu); *il est cuit,* he's had it; *c'est du tout cuit,* it's all settled, it's a cinch.

cuite [kɥit] f. Baking (du pain). ‖ TECHN. Firing, burning. ‖ FAM. *Prendre une cuite,* to have one over the eight (ou) one too many; *tenir une cuite,* to be three sheets in the wind.

cuiter (se) [səkɥite] v. pr. (1). POP. To get sloshed (ou) pissed.

cuivrage [kɥivra:ʒ] m. Coppering.

cuivre [kɥiːvr] m. Brass (jaune); copper (rouge). ‖ Pl. Brass (ornements); *faire les cuivres,* to do the brass; *produit d'entretien pour les cuivres,* liquid metal polish. ‖ MUS. *Les cuivres,* the brass (instruments). ‖ ARTS. Copperplate; *gravure sur cuivre,* copperplate engraving.

cuivré, ée [-vre] adj. Coppery, copper-coloured. ‖ Reddish-brown, auburn (cheveux); lurid (ciel); copper (peau); bronzed, sunburnt (teint). ‖ Blaring, brazen, brassy (son); metallic (voix).

cuivrer v. tr. (1). To copper, to copperplate (un métal). ‖ To make copper-coloured (teinter). ‖ MUS. To make blaring (ou) brassy (un son); to make metallic (la voix). — v. pr. Se cuivrer, to turn coppery (objet). ‖ To grow metallic (voix).

cuivreux, euse [-vrø, ø:z] adj. Coppery; *couleur cuivreuse,* copper-colour; *sulfure cuivreux,* copper-glance, chalcocite. ‖ CHIM. Cuprous (oxyde).

cul [ky] m. ARGOT. Rump, haunches (des animaux); arse, bum, U. S. ass (de l'homme); *cul de plomb,* clot, clod; *cul-terreux,* clod-hopper; *cul par-dessus tête,* arse over tip (pop.), head over heels; *faire la bouche en cul de poule,* to purse one's lips. ‖ Bottom (de bouteille, d'un sac); tail (de charrette). ‖ MILIT. *Cul de chaudron,* bottom of mine crater. ‖ **Cul-blanc** (pl. *culs-blancs*), m. ZOOL. White-tail. ‖ **Cul-de-basse-fosse,** m. Dungeon. ‖ **Cul-de-jatte,** m. Legless cripple. **Cul-de-lampe,** m. ARCHIT. Cul-de-lampe; ARTS. Tailpiece. ‖ **Cul-de-sac,** m. Blind alley, cul-de-sac, dead end; CH. DE F. Blind siding; FIG. Blind alley. ‖ **Cul-terreux,** m. FAM. Peasant, clodhopper, hick.

culasse [kylas] f. MILIT. Breech (armes à feu) ; *boîte de culasse,* breech casing ; *culasse mobile,* movable breech-block. ‖ TECHN. Cylinder head. ‖ ELECTR. Yoke (d'aimant, de transformateur) ; heel-piece (d'électro-aimant). ‖ AUTOM. *Joint de culasse,* gasket.

culbutant [kylbytɑ̃] m. ZOOL. Tumbler-pigeon.

culbute [-byt] f. Somersault (v. CABRIOLE) ; *faire la culbute,* to turn a somersault. ‖ Tumble, cropper (chute). ‖ FAM. *Faire la culbute,* to fail (failli) ; to fall (ministère).

culbuter [-byte] v. intr. (1). To turn a somersault (cabrioler) ; to topple (ou) tumble over (tomber). ‖ NAUT. To pitch over. ‖ FIG. To come a cropper. — v. tr. To turn topsy-turvy (bouleverser) ; to dump, to shoot (déverser) ; to overthrow (renverser) ; to tip, to tilt (retourner). ‖ To knock over (qqn). ‖ MILIT. To overwhelm (l'adversaire).

culbuteur [-bytœːr] m. TECHN. Rocker-arm (de moteur) ; tipper, tumbler (de récipient, de voiture). ‖ ELECTR. *Interrupteur à culbuteur,* tumbler-switch. ‖ Tumbler (jouet).

culée [kyle] f. ARCHIT. Abutment ; *culée mobile,* movable bay (d'un pont). ‖ NAUT. Stern-way.

culer v. intr. (1). NAUT. To make stern-way, to drop astern. ‖ To veer astern (vent).

culinaire [kylinɛːr] adj. CULIN. Culinary.

culminant, ante [kylminɑ̃, ɑ̃ːt] adj. ASTRON. Culminant (point). ‖ FIG. Highest, culminating ; *point culminant de la gloire,* climax of glory.

culmination [-nasjɔ̃] f. ASTRON. Culmination.

culminer [-ne] v. intr. (1). To culminate, to reach the highest point.

culot [kylo] m. MILIT. Bottom (d'obus). ‖ AUTOM. *Culot de bougie,* sparking-plug body (ou) shell. ‖ ELECTR. Base (d'ampoule). ‖ Punt, kick (de bouteille) ; bottom (de lampe) ; dottle (de pipe). ‖ AGRIC. Last born. ‖ FAM. Nerve, cheek (audace) ; *avoir du culot,* to have a lot of cheek (ou) a nerve.

culottage [kylota:3] m. Seasoning (d'une pipe).

culotte [kylɔt] f. Bloomers, drawers, knickers, U.S. panties (de femme) ; knee-breeches (d'homme) ; *culotte bouffante,* knickerbockers, knickers ; *culotte de cheval,* riding breeches ; *culotte courte,* knee-breeches ; *des culottes,* trousers, U. S. pants ; *une paire de culottes,* a pair of breeches. ‖ SPORTS. *Culotte de golf,* plus-fours ; *culotte de sport,* shorts. ‖ CULIN. Rump (de bœuf). ‖ FAM. Loss (au jeu) ; *prendre une culotte,* to lose heavily. ‖ FAM. *Porter la culotte,* to wear the breeches ; *vieille culotte de peau,* old sweat (ou) ex-ranker.

culotté, ée [-te] adj. Soiled (objet) ; seasoned (pipe). ‖ FAM. Cheeky, brassy.

culotter [-te] v. tr. To breech, to put breeches on (un enfant). ‖ To season (une pipe). — v. pr. Se culotter, to put on one's breeches (ou) trousers. ‖ To season, to colour (pipe).

culottier [-tje] s. Breeches-maker.

culpabiliser [kylpabilize] v. tr. (1). To give a guilty conscience to.

culpabilité [kylpabilite] f. Guilt, guiltiness, culpability ; *sentiment de culpabilité,* sense of guilt.

culte [kylt] m. ECCLÉS. Worship (adoration) ; cult, service (cérémonie) ; religion (secte) ; *culte catholique,* Roman Catholic religion ; *culte du feu,* fire-worship ; *liberté du culte,* freedom of worship ; *rendre un culte à,* to worship. ‖ FIG. Cult, worship, adoration ; *avoir un culte pour qqn,* to worship s.o. ; *avoir le culte de,* to be devotedly attached to, to make a fetish of (qqch.).

cultivable [kyltivabl] adj. Cultivable.

cultivateur, trice [-tœːr, tris] adj. Agricultural. — s. AGRIC. Cultivator, agriculturist ; farmer. — m. AGRIC. Cultivator (charrue).

cultivé, ée [kyltive] adj. AGRIC. Cultivated. ‖ FIG. Cultivated, cultured ; well educated, well (ou) widely read.

cultiver v. tr. (1). AGRIC. To cultivate, to raise, to grow (des céréales, des plantes) ; to cultivate, to farm, to till (la terre). ‖ FIG. To cultivate (une amitié, les arts, qqn) ; to improve (son esprit) ; to nurse (une relation).

cultuel, elle [kytɥɛl] adj. ECCLÉS. Cultual.

cultural, ale [kyltyral] adj. AGRIC. Cultural.

culture [kyltyːr] f. AGRIC. Agriculture, husbandry (agriculture) ; cultivation, culture, growing (des céréales, des plantes) ; cultivation, farming, tillage, tilling (de la terre) ; *grande, petite culture,* farming on a large, small scale. ‖ Pl. Crops (récoltes) ; cultivated lands ; plantations. ‖ Breeding, culture (des abeilles, du poisson). ‖ SPORTS. *Culture physique,* physical training (ou) culture. ‖ MÉD. Culture ; *tube à culture,* culture tube. ‖ FIG. Cultivation (des arts, des sciences) ; culture, improvement (de l'esprit) ; *culture générale,* general background (ou) culture ; *la culture de son esprit,* his cultivated (ou) cultured mind ; *de haute culture,* highly cultured.

culturel, elle [-tyrɛl] adj. Cultural.

culturisme [-tyrism] m. SPORTS. Body-building.

cumin [kymɛ̃] m. BOT. Cumin.

cumul [kymyl] m. JUR. Lumping ; *cumul de fonctions,* plurality of offices, pluralism ; *cumul de peines,* cumulation (ou) non-concurrence of sentences. ‖ FIG. Accumulation.

cumulable [-labl] adj. That can be held simultaneously (responsabilités) ; that can be received simultaneously (rémunérations).

cumulard [-la:r] m. FAM. Pluralist.

cumulatif, ive [-latif, i:v] adj. Cumulative.

cumulation [-lasjɔ̃] f. JUR. Cumulation.

cumuler [-le] v. intr. (1). To hold a plurality of offices ; to pluralize. — v. tr. To pluralize (des fonctions). ‖ JUR. To cumulate (des actions, des peines, des preuves).

cumulo-nimbus [kymylonɛ̃by:s] m. Cumulo-nimbus.

cumulus [kymyly:s] m. Cumulus, cloud-rack.

cunéiforme [kyneifɔrm] adj. Cuneiform (écriture). ‖ Wedge-shaped, cuneal (en forme de coin). — m. MÉD. Cuneiform, cuneiform bone.

cupide [kypid] adj. Covetous, greedy, grasping.

cupidement [-dmɑ̃] adv. Covetously, greedily.

cupidité [-dite] f. Cupidity, covetousness, greed, greediness (avidité) ; graspingness (rapacité).

Cupidon [kypidɔ̃] m. Cupid.

cuprifère [kyprifɛːr] adj. CHIM. Cupriferous, copper-bearing.

cuprique [kyprik] adj. CHIM. Cupric.

cupro-ammoniacal [kyprɔamɔnjakal] adj. CHIM. Cupro-ammoniacal ; *liqueur cupro-ammoniacale,* cuprammonium.

cupule [kypyl] f. BOT. Cupule, acorn-cup.

curabilité [kyrabilite] f. Curability, curableness.

curable [kyrabl] adj. MÉD. Curable.

curaçao [kyraso] m. Curaçoa, curaçao (liqueur).

curage [kyra:3] m. Cleansing, flushing (d'un égout) ; clearing, cleaning out (d'un fossé, d'un puits) ; dredging (d'une rivière).

curare [kyra:r] m. Curare (poison).

curatelle [kyratɛl] f. JUR. Guardianship.

curateur [-tœːr] m. JUR. Committee (d'aliéné) ; curator (d'incapable) ; administrator (de faillite, de succession vacante) ; curator (de mineur) ; guardian (de mineur émancipé) ; *curateur au ventre,* administrator to child unborn.

curatif, ive [-tif, i:v] adj., m. MÉD. Curative.

curatrice [-tris] f. JUR. Curatrix.

cure [ky:r] f. Care ; *n'en avoir cure,* to take no notice, to pay no heed. ‖ ECCLÉS. Cure, vicarship (fonction) ; vicarage, rectory (résidence d'un clergyman) ; presbytery (résidence d'un curé). ‖ MÉD.

Cure, treatment; *cure d'air*, open-air (ou) high-altitude treatment; *cure de fruits*, fruit cure; *faire une cure à*, to take the cure at.

cure. V. CURER. ‖ **Cure-dents**, m. invar. Tooth-pick. ‖ **Cure-ongles**, m. invar. Nail-cleaner. ‖ **Cure-oreille**, m. Ear-pick. ‖ **Cure-pied**, m. Hoof-pick. ‖ **Cure-pipe**, m. Pipe-cleaner.

curé [kyre] m. ECCLÉS. Vicar, rector (anglican, protestant); curé, parish priest (catholique).

curée f. SPORTS. Quarry (à la chasse). ‖ FIG. Rush, scramble; *se ruer à la curée*, to fling oneself into the scramble, to join in the mad rush.

curer v. tr. To cleanse, to flush (un égout); to clear, to clean out (un fossé, un puits); to dredge (une rivière); *se curer les dents*, to pick one's teeth; *se curer les ongles*, to clean one's nails.

curetage [kyrta:ʒ] m. MÉD. Curetting; curettage; *faire un curetage de*, to curette.

cureter [kyrte] v. tr. (8a). MÉD. To curette.

curette [kyrɛt] f. MÉD. Curette. ‖ TECHN. Scraper.

cureur [-rœ:r] m. Cleaner (de fossé, de puits); dredger (de rivière).

curial, ale [kyrjal] adj. ECCLÉS. *Conseil curial*, select vestry. ‖ † Curial (assemblée).

curie [kyri] f. † ECCLÉS. Curia.

curie f. PHYS. Curie.

curieusement [kyrjøzmɑ̃] adv. Curiously (avec curiosité); oddly, quaintly (avec étrangeté); inquisitively (avec indiscrétion); interestedly (avec intérêt); carefully (avec minutie et soin); *curieusement ouvré*, curiously wrought.

curieux, euse [-rjø, ø:z] adj. Curious, inquisitive; meddlesome; prying (indiscret); *trop curieux*, over-inquisitive. ‖ Curious, interested, inquiring, eager to learn (intéressé); *esprit curieux*, inquiring mind; *curieux de savoir*, curious to know. ‖ Curious, odd, peculiar, strange (étrange); *chose curieuse*, curiously enough, oddly enough, strange to say; *chose curieuse à voir*, odd (ou) quaint sight; *objet curieux*, curious-looking object. ‖ FAM. *Bête curieuse*, strange beast.
— s. Curious (ou) inquisitive person. ‖ Gazer, spectator, sightseer, bystander (spectateur); *venir en curieux*, to come to have a look.
— m. Odd (ou) strange thing, odd part (particularité). ‖ POP. Examining magistrate.

curiosité [-rjɔzite] f. Curiosity, inquisitiveness, meddlesomeness (indiscrétion); *mourir de curiosité*, to be dying of curiosity; *par curiosité*, out of (ou) from curiosity. ‖ Curiosity (intérêt); *la curiosité le prit de*, he felt curious to; *elle eut la curiosité de*, she was curious enough to. ‖ Curiosity, oddness, peculiarity, strangeness (étrangeté); curiosity, curio (objet); curiosity, place of interest, sight (spectacle). ‖ Pl. Sights, curiosities (d'une ville); *visite des curiosités*, sight-seeing.

curiste [kyrist] m. One who takes a water cure.

curium [kyrjɔm] m PHYS. Curium.

curling [kərliŋ] m. SPORTS. Curling.

curriculum vitae [kyrikylɔmvite] m. Curriculum vitae; U.S. résumé.

curry [kyri] m. CULIN. Curry; curry powder.

curseur [kyrsœ:r] m. TECHN. Slider, cursor, runner, traveller; *curseur de marge*, marginal stop (de machine à écrire). ‖ MILIT. Tangent scale; *curseur à rallonge*, extension slide of a sight. ‖ ELECTR. Slide contact.

cursif, ive [-sif, i:v] adj. Cursive, running.

cursive [-si:v] f. Running hand; cursive.

cursus [kyrsy:s] m. Cursus.

curule [kyryl] adj. † Curule (chaise).

curvigraphe [kyrvigraf] m. MATH. Curve-tracer.

curviligne [-liɲ] adj. Rounded (talus). ‖ MATH. Curvilinear.

curvimètre [-mɛtr] m. Opisometer.

cuscute [kyskyt] f. BOT. Dodder.

cuspide [kyspid] f. BOT. Cusp.

cuspidé, ée [-de] adj. BOT. Cuspidate.

custode [kystɔd] f. ECCLÉS. Altar-curtain (d'autel); pyx-cloth (du ciboire); custodial (ostensoir). ‖ AUTOM. *Custode arrière*, rear-window.

cutané, ée [kytane] adj. MÉD. Cutaneous; *maladie cutanée*, skin disease.

cuticule [kytikyl] f. MÉD., BOT. Cuticle.

cuti-réaction [kytireaksjɔ̃] f. MÉD. Skin-test.

cutter [køtœ:r] m. NAUT. Cutter.

cuvage [kyva:ʒ] m. Cuvage, vatting (du vin).

cuve [kyv] f. Cistern, tank (à eau). ‖ Copper, wash-tub (de blanchisseur); tun (de brasseur); vat (de papetier, de teinturier, de viticulteur); tank (de photographe, de tanneur).

cuvée [-ve] f. Vatful (contenu); vintage (vinée).

cuvelage [-vla:ʒ] m. TECHN. Tubbing; lining.

cuver [-ve] v. intr. (1). To ferment (raisin).
— v. tr. FAM. *Cuver son vin*, to sleep it off, to sleep oneself sober.

cuvette [-vɛt] f. Wash-bowl (de lavabo); wash-basin (de toilette). ‖ Bowl (des cabinets). ‖ TECHN. Cap (de montre); dish (de photographe); race (de roulement à billes); bulb (de thermomètre). ‖ GÉOGR. Basin, hollow; punch-bowl (fam.). ‖ **Cuvette-rotule**, f. Ball-cup, ball-socket.

cuvier [-vje] m. Washing-tub, wash-tub.

CV [seve] abrév. de *cheval-vapeur*, AUTOM., FIN. Horsepower, h.p.

cyanamide [sjanamid] m., f. CHIM. Cyanamide.

cyanhydrique [sjanhidrik] adj. CHIM. Cyan-hydric, hydrocyanic; prussic (acide).

cyanose [-no:z] f. Chalcanthite, cyanosite. ‖ MÉD. Cyanosis.

cyanure [-ny:r] m. CHIM. Cyanide.

cybernéticien, enne [sibɛrnetisjɛ̃, ɛn] adj. Cybernetic.
— s. Cybernetician, cyberneticist.

cybernétique [sibɛrnetik] f. Cybernetics.

cyclable [siklabl] adj. Passable for cyclists; *piste cyclable*, cycle-path.

cyclamen [siklamɛn] m. BOT. Cyclamen.

cycle [sikl] m. Cycle (bicyclette). ‖ Cycle; *le cycle des affaires*, the business cycle; *le cycle de Charlemagne*, the Charlemagne cycle. ‖ Course (des études). ‖ ASTRON., BOT., ELECTR. Cycle.

cyclecar [sikləkar] m. AUTOM. Cycle-car.

cyclique [siklik] adj. Cyclic(al).

cyclisme [-klism] m. Cycling.

cycliste [-klist] s. Cyclist.
— adj. Cycling (course).

cyclo-cross [siklɔcrɔs] m. SPORTS. Cyclo-cross.

cyclographe [-graf] m. Cyclograph.

cycloïdal, ale [-idal] adj. MATH. Cycloidal.

cycloïde [-id] f. MATH. Cycloid.

cyclomoteur [-motœ:r] m. Moped.

cyclomotoriste [-mɔtɔrist] s. Moped rider.

cyclonal, ale [siklonal], **cyclonique** [-nik] adj. GÉOGR. Cyclonic, cyclonical.

cyclone [siklon] m. Cyclone; *abri anticyclone*, U.S. cyclone-cellar.

cyclope [siklɔp] m. Cyclops.

cyclopéen, enne [siklopeɛ̃, ɛn] adj. Cyclopean.

cyclothymique [siklɔtimik] adj., s. MÉD. Cyclothymic.

cyclotourisme [-turism] m. Touring on bicycles.

cyclotouriste [-turist] s. Cycling tourist.

cyclotron [siklɔtrɔ̃] m. ELECTR. Cyclotron.

cygne [siɲ] m. ZOOL. Swan; *cygne mâle*, cob; *jeune cygne*, cygnet.

cylindrage [silɛ̃dra:ʒ] m. Calendering (d'une étoffe); rolling (d'une route).

cylindre [silɛ̃:dr] m. TECHN. Steam-roller (compresseur); cylinder (d'imprimerie); roller (de laminoir); *cylindre à ailettes*, ribbed cylinder; *cylindre cannelé*, grooved roller; *réaléser un cylindre*, to rebore a cylinder. ‖ MILIT. Gauge.

‖ Autom., Math. Cylinder. ‖ **Cylindre-frein,** n. Recoil-checking cylinder.
cylindrée [silɛ̃dre] f. Techn. Cylinder capacity (ou) displacement (ou) charge.
cylindrer v. tr. To calender (une étoffe); to roll (une route).
cylindrique [-drik] adj. Cylindric, cylindrical.
cylindroïde [-drɔid] adj. Cylindroid.
cymaise [simɛ:z] f. V. cimaise.
cymbale [sɛ̃bal] f. Mus. Cymbal.
cymbalier [-lje], **cymbaliste** [-list] m. Mus. Cymbalist.
cymbalum [-lɔm] m. Mus. Cymbalo, dulcimer.
cynégétique [sineʒetik] adj. Cynegetic.
— f. Cynegetics.
cynique [sinik] adj. Philos. Cynic. ‖ Fig. Quite brazen (impudent); sneering, sarcastic (railleur); cynical (sceptique).
cyniquement [-nikmɑ̃] adv. Shamelessly.
cynisme [-nism] m. Philos. Cynicism. ‖ Fig. Shamelessness (impudence); cynical expression (raillerie).

cynocéphale [sinɔsefal] m. Zool. Cynocephalus.
cynodrome [-drɔ:m] m. Sports. Greyhound track (ou) stadium.
cyphose [sifo:z] f. Méd. Cyphosis.
cyprès [siprɛ] m. Bot. Cypress.
cyprin [siprɛ̃] m. Zool. Cyprinoid fish; *cyprin doré,* goldfish.
cypriote [siprjɔt] adj., s. Géogr. Cypriot.
cyrillique [sirilik] adj. Cyrillic.
cystite [sistit] f. Méd. Cystitis.
cystographie [-tɔgrafi] f. Méd. Cystography.
cystotomie [-tɔtɔmi] f. Méd. Cystotomy.
cytise [siti:z] m. Bot. Cytisus; laburnum.
cytologie [sitɔlɔʒi] f. Méd. Cytology.
cytoplasme [-plasm] m. Méd. Cytoplasm.
czar [tsa:r] m. Czar, tsar.
czardas [ksardas] f. Czardas (danse).
czarevitch [ksarevitʃ] m. Czarevitch, tsarevitch.
czarine [-ri:n] f. Czarina, tsarina.
czimbalum [tsimbalɔm] m. V. cymbalum.

D

d [de] m. D, d.
da [da] adv. *Oui-da!,* yes indeed!
dacquois, oise [dakwa, wa:z] adj. Géogr. Of (ou) from Dax.
— s. Native (ou) inhabitant of Dax.
Dacron [dakrɔ̃] m. Dacron (tissu).
dactyle [daktil] m. Dactyl (en métrique).
dactylique [-lik] adj. Dactylic (en métrique).
dactylo [-lo] f. Fam. Typist (personne); typing (travail). ‖ **Dactylo-facturière,** f. Typist invoice-clerk.
dactylographe [-lɔgraf] f. Typist.
dactylographie [-lɔgrafi] f. Typing, typewriting.
dactylographier [-lɔgrafje] v. tr. (1). To type, to typewrite.
dactylographique [-lɔgrafik] adj. Typing.
dada [dada] m. Gee-gee (cheval); hobby-horse (jouet). ‖ Fig. Hobby, fad, pet subject; *le tennis n'est pas son dada,* tennis is not his cup of tea.
dada m., adj. inv. Arts. Dada.
dadais [dadɛ] m. Fam. Ninny, booby, Tony Lumpkin, U. S. goof. (V. niais.)
dadaïsme [-daism] m. Arts. Dadaism.
dadaïste [dadaist] s. Arts. Dadaist.
dague [dag] f. Dagger; dirk (en Ecosse). ‖ Naut. Dirk. ‖ Zool. Dag, sɛ̃em, spike (de cerf).
daguerréotype [dagɛreɔtip] m. Daguerreotype.
daguet [dagɛ] m. Zool. Brocket.
dahlia [dalja] m. Bot. Dahlia.
dahoméen, enne [daɔmeɛ̃, ɛn] adj., s. Géogr. Dahomean, Dahomeyan.
Dahomey [daɔmɛ] m. Géogr. Dahomey (v. Bénin).
daigner [dɛɲe] v. tr. (1). To deign, to vouchsafe, to condescend; *il n'a pas daigné envisager mon offre,* he wouldn't even consider my offer.
daim [dɛ̃] m. Zool. Deer, buck. ‖ Buck-skin (cuir); suede (peau); *en daim,* suede (gants); buckskin (souliers). ‖ Fam. Booby, mug, U.S. sap.
daine [dɛn] f. Zool. Doe.

dais [dɛ] m. Canopy (d'autel, de trône); dais (d'estrade); *recouvrir d'un dais,* to canopy. ‖ Canopy (de feuillage).
dallage [dala:ʒ] m. Paving, slabbing, flagging (action); pavement, flags, flagstones (dalles).
dalle [dal] f. Flag, flagstone, floor-tile, paving-stone (en général); slab (de marbre); pavement light (de verre); *dalle funéraire,* ledger, flatstone. ‖ Fam. *Se rincer la dalle,* to wet one's whistle.
daller [-le] v. tr. (1). To tile (un parquet); to pave (un sol, un trottoir).
dalleur [-lœ:r] m. Pavior, flag-layer.
dalmate [dalmat] adj., s. Géogr. Dalmatian.
Dalmatie [-masi] f. Géogr. Dalmatia.
dalmatien, enne [-masjɛ̃, ɛn] s. Zool. Dalmatian.
dalmatique [dalmatik] f. Ecclés. Dalmatic.
daltonien, enne [daltɔnjɛ̃, ɛn] adj. Daltonian, colour-blind.
— s. Méd. Daltonian, colour-blind person.
daltonisme [-nism] m. Méd. Daltonism, colour-blindness.
dam [dɑ̃] m. Ecclés. Damnation. ‖ † Damage, prejudice (détriment); great displeasure (ennui).
Damas [damɑ] m. Géogr. Damascus ‖ Comm. Damask (tissu). ‖ Bot. Damson (prune). ‖ Ecclés. *Chemin de Damas,* road to Damascus.
damasquinage [damaskina:ʒ] m. Damascening.
damasquiner [-ne] v. tr. (1). To damascene.
damassé, ée [damase] adj. Damascus (acier); damask (linge).
— m. Damask linen; diaper (tissu).
damasser [damase] v. tr. (1). To damascene (l'acier); to damask (un tissu).
dame [dam] f. † Dame; *Dame Belette,* Dame Weasel; *la dame de ses pensées,* his lady-love. ‖ Lady; *dame de compagnie,* lady-companion; *dame d'honneur,* lady-in-waiting; *demoiselle d'honneur,* maid-of-honour. ‖ Queen (aux cartes, aux échecs); king (aux dames); piece (au jacquet);

aller à dame, to make a king (aux dames); to queen (aux échecs); *dame troisième,* guarded queen (aux cartes). ‖ Pl. Draughts, U. S. checkers (jeu); *jouer aux dames,* to play at draughts, U. S. to play checkers. ‖ Mus. *La Dame blanche,* the White Lady. ‖ Ch. de F. *Dames seules,* ladies only. ‖ Techn. Paving beetle; earth rammer. ‖ Fam. *Faire la dame,* to queen it. ‖ **Dame-jeanne,** f. Demijohn.

— interj. Well; *dame oui,* oh yes, yes of course; *vous le pensez? ; dame!,* do you think so? ; what else can I think?

dame [dam] f. Techn. Dam-stone.

damer [-me] v. tr. (1). To crown (un pion). ‖ Techn. To ram (la terre). ‖ Fam. *Damer le pion à,* to checkmate, to outdo, to outwit.

damier [-mje] m. Draught-board, U. S. checker-board (de jeu). ‖ Check (d'étoffe); *à damier,* check-patterned, checked, chequered.

damnable [danabl] adj. Damnable. ‖ Fam. Outrageous; rotten, frightful.

damnation [-sjɔ̃] f. Ecclés. Damnation.
— interj. Hang it!, Damnation!

damné, ée [dane] adj. Ecclés. Damned. ‖ Fam. Confounded.
— s. Ecclés. Damned, soul in torment. ‖ Fam. *Souffrir comme un damné,* to suffer the tortures of the damned.

damner v. tr. (1). Ecclés. To damn. ‖ Fam. *Faire damner qqn,* to drive s.o. mad.
— v. pr. **Se damner,** to incur damnation.

damoiseau [damwazo] m. † Damoiseau.
damoiselle [-zɛl] f. † Damsel, damozel.
dan [dan] m. Sports. Dan (au judo).
Danaïdes [danaid] f. pl. Danaides.
dancing [dɑ̃siŋ] m. Public dance-hall, palais de danse; U. S. public ballroom.
dandinement [dɑ̃dinmɑ̃] m. Waddling (d'un déhanché); swaying; wiggle (fam.) [d'une femme provocante]; rolling (d'un marin).
dandiner [-ne] v. tr. (1). To dandle.
— v. pr. **Se dandiner,** to waddle (canard); to sway, to slouch along, to waddle (personne).
dandy [dɑ̃di] m. Dandy.
dandysme [-dism] m. Dandysm.
Danemark [danmark] m. Géogr. Denmark.
danger [dɑ̃ʒe] m. Danger [*pour,* to] (v. péril); risk, jeopardy (v. risque); *en cas de danger,* in case of emergency; *en danger de mort,* in peril of death, in danger of one's life; *hors de danger,* out of danger; *il n'y a pas de danger!,* no fear!; *mettre en danger,* to endanger, to jeopardize, to hazard; *n'offrir aucun danger,* to be quite safe; *sans danger,* without danger; safely, securely.
dangereusement [dɑ̃ʒrøzmɑ̃] adv. Dangerously. ‖ Méd. Critically, seriously, dangerously.
dangereux, euse [dɑ̃ʒrø, ø:z] adj. Dangerous; perilous; unsafe. ‖ Critical (position). ‖ Méd. Critical, serious (maladie). ‖ Milit. *Zone dangereuse,* danger zone.
danois, oise [danwa, wa:z] adj. Danish.
— s. Géogr. Dane.
— m. Danish (langue). ‖ Zool. Great Dane.
dans [dɑ̃] prép. In (lieu, sans mouvement); *dans une bouteille,* in a bottle; *dans la haute société,* in Society; *dans votre pays,* in your country; *dans la politique,* in politics; *dans Shakespeare,* in Shakespeare. ‖ Within (dans les limites de); *dans les murs de la ville,* within the walls of the town; *dans un rayon de trente kilomètres,* within a radius of thirty kilometres. ‖ Into (avec mouvement de pénétration); *entrer dans un magasin,* to go into a shop; *sombrer dans un profond sommeil,* to sink into a heavy sleep. ‖ From, off, out of (avec mouvement d'extraction); *apprendre dans les livres,* to learn from books; *manger dans*

de la vaisselle d'or, to eat from (ou) off gold plate; *prendre du tabac dans sa tabatière,* to take snuff out of one's box. ‖ Under (circonstances); *dans ces circonstances,* under these circumstances; *dans ces conditions,* under these conditions. ‖ In, into (condition, état); *dans l'armée,* in the army; *dans une grande inquiétude,* in great anxiety; *tomber dans l'erreur,* to fall into error. ‖ In, during; on; within (durée); *dans l'après-midi,* in (ou) during the afternoon; *dans le courant de la nuit,* in the course of the night; *dans une semaine au plus,* within a week. ‖ In, with, to (manière); *dans les formes,* in due form; *dans la meilleure intention,* with the best of intentions; *faire qqch. dans la perfection,* to do sth. to perfection. ‖ Through (à travers); *marcher dans les rues,* to walk through the streets; *regarder dans un télescope,* to look through a telescope. ‖ About (environ); *dans les 200 francs,* about 200 francs; *avoir dans les trente ans,* to be about thirty. ‖ Among (parmi); *dans la foule,* among the crowd. ‖ (Non traduit); *entrer dans le hangar,* to enter the shed; *descendre, monter dans la cheminée,* to come down, to go (ou) climb up the chimney.

dansant, ante [dɑ̃sɑ̃, ɑ̃:t] adj. Dancing; *soirée dansante,* dance; dancing-party; hop (fam.). ‖ Lively, dancing; easy to dance to (air, musique). ‖ Springy (démarche).

danse [dɑ̃:s] f. Dancing (action); dance (air, mouvements). ‖ *aimer la danse,* to be fond of dancing. ‖ Méd. *Danse de Saint-Guy,* St Vitus's dance. ‖ Fig. *Ouvrir la danse,* to set the ball rolling, to open the ball. ‖ Fam. Thrashing (raclée).

danser [dɑ̃se] v. intr. (1). Mus. To dance; *façon de danser,* style of dancing, dancing; *faire danser qqn,* to dance with s.o. ‖ To dance, to ship (gambader); *danser de joie,* to dance (ou) to skip with (ou) for joy; *faire danser un enfant,* to dandle a child. ‖ To caper (animal); to prance (cheval). ‖ To bob (bouchon flottant); to dance, to flicker (ombre). ‖ Naut. To pitch and toss. ‖ Fam. *Danser devant le buffet,* to go hungry; *faire danser l'anse du panier,* to get a rake-off; *ne pas savoir sur quel pied danser,* to be in a quandary.
— v. tr. To dance (un tango, une valse).
— v. pr. Se danser, to be danced (danse).

danseur [-sœ:r] s. Dancer (qui danse); partner (avec qui on danse). ‖ *Danseur de corde,* tight-rope dancer. ‖ Sports. *Pédaler en danseuse,* to stand up on one's pedals. ‖ Théâtr. Ballet-dancer.

dantesque [dɑ̃tɛsk] adj. Dantesque, Dantean.

Danube [danyb] m. Géogr. Danube. ‖ Fig. *Paysan du Danube,* country bumpkin.

danubien, enne [-jɛ̃, ɛn] adj. Géogr. Danubian.

dard [da:r] m. † Dart. ‖ Burning ray (du soleil). ‖ Zool. Sting (d'insecte); forked tongue (de serpent). ‖ Bot. Pistil. ‖ Fig. Sting, dart. ‖ Fam. *Filer comme un dard,* to be off like a shot.

darder [darde] v. tr. (1). To dart out (ou) forth (son aiguillon, sa langue). ‖ To dart (ses rayons). ‖ Fig. To shoot. to flash (un regard) [*sur,* at].

dare–dare [darda:r] adv. Fam. Post-haste, full tilt.

dariole [darjɔl] f. Culin. Custard tart.

darne [darn] f. Steak (de poisson).

dartre [dartr] f. Méd. Dartre, tetter; scurf. ‖ Archit. Patch of decay.

dartreux, euse [-trø, ø:z] adj. Méd. Dartrous, tetterous; scurfy.

darwinien, enne [darwinjɛ̃, ɛn] adj. Darwinian.

darwinisme [-nism] m. Darwinism.

datable [databl] adj. Datable.

datation [datasjɔ̃] f. Dating.

datcha [datʃa] f. Dacha.

date [dat] f. Date; *de fraîche, de longue date,*

recent, long-standing; *en date du 5 avril,* dated April 5th; *erreur de date,* misdating; *faire date,* to mark an epoch (ou) a date; *qui fait date,* epoch-making; *le dernier, le premier en date,* the later, the earlier; *prendre date avec,* to make an appointment with; *prendre date pour,* to fix a date for; *sans date,* undated (non daté); dateless (non déterminé). ‖ *Date limite,* deadline.

daté, ée [date] adj. Dated; *daté de Bordeaux,* dated from Bordeaux; *daté du 5 avril,* dated April 5th; *non daté,* undated.

dater v. tr. (1). To date (une lettre).
— v. intr. To date (*de,* from); *à dater d'aujourd'hui,* from today on; *dater de loin,* to be of long standing (durer depuis longtemps); to go back a long time, to date from years before, to go a long way back (remonter à une date lointaine); *mal dater,* to misdate. ‖ To date, to be out of date (mode, vêtement).

dateur [datœ:r] m. Date-marker, date-stamp.

datif, ive [datif, i:v] adj. JUR. Dative.
— m. GRAMM. Dative.

datte [dat] f. BOT. Date. ‖ FAM. *Des dattes!,* nothing doing!, U. S. nope!, no sirree!

dattier [-tje] m. BOT. Date-palm, date-tree.

daube [do:b] f. CULIN. Daubed (ou) braised meat.

dauber [dobe] v. tr. (1). CULIN. To braise.

dauber v. intr. (1). *Dauber sur,* to backbite.

daubière [dobjɛ:r] f. CULIN. Casserole, braising-pan.

dauphin [dofɛ̃] m. ZOOL. Dolphin. ‖ ARCHIT. Gargoyle. ‖ † Dauphin (prince).

dauphine [dofin] f. Dauphiness.

dauphinois, oise [dofinwa, wa:z] adj. GÉOGR. Of (ou) from Dauphiné. ‖ CULIN. *Gratin dauphinois,* potato gratin.
— s. Native (ou) inhabitant of Dauphiné.

daurade [dorad] f. ZOOL. Gilt-head.

davantage [davãta:ʒ] adv. More (en quantité); *en demander davantage,* to ask for more. ‖ More; over; further (plus); *les enfants de sept ans et davantage,* children of seven and over; *ne pas en savoir davantage,* not to know anything more; *s'approcher davantage,* to draw nearer; *se reculer davantage,* to draw further back. ‖ Longer (plus longtemps); *ne pas dormir davantage,* not to sleep any longer, to sleep no longer. ‖ More and more (de plus en plus); *tous les jours davantage,* more and more every day.

davier [davje] m. MÉD. Forceps. ‖ TECHN. Cramp (du menuisier); dog (du tonnelier).

D.B. [debe] f. MILIT. Abrév. de *division blindée,* armoured division.

D.C.A. [desea] (abrév. : Défense contre avions) f. MILIT. A. A.; ack-ack. ‖ NAUT. *Navire de D.C.A.,* flak-ship.

D.D.T. [dedete] m. CHIM. D.D.T. (dichloro-diphényl-*t*richloro-éthane).

de [də] prép.

1. Dépendance, possession. — 2. Agent. — 3. Cause, motif. — 4. Destination, utilisation. — 5. Direction. — 6. Distance. — 7. Instrument. — 8. Lieu. — 9. Manière. — 10. Matière. — 11. Mesure, quantité. — 12. Nature, qualité. — 13. Objet. — 14. Origine. — 15. Prix.— 16. Temps.— 17. Explétif. — 18. Loc.

1. Of, 's (dépendance, possession); *le chapeau de ma sœur,* my sister's hat; *le dossier de la chaise,* the back of the chair; *un membre du Parlement,* a Member of Parliament; *les œuvres de Voltaire,* Voltaire's works; *un porteur de bacilles,* a germ-carrier. ‖ **2.** By, with (agent); *aimé de tous,* loved by all; *couvert de sang,* covered with blood. ‖ **3.** Of, for (cause, motif); *mourir de faim,* to die

of hunger; *pleurer de joie,* to weep for (ou) with joy. ‖ **4.** Of, for (destination, utilisation); *député de Langres,* M. P. for Langres; *matériaux de construction,* building materials; *porte de communication,* communicating-door; *le train de Londres,* the train for London; the London train; *des vêtements d'hommes,* men's clothing. ‖ **5.** To (direction); *le chemin de l'église,* the way to the church. ‖ **6.** Of, from (distance); *à deux milles de distance,* at a distance of two miles; *de Paris à Londres,* from Paris to London; *loin de la ville,* far from the town; *un voyage de cinquante milles,* a fifty miles' (ou) U. S. mile journey. ‖ **7.** Of, with, at (instrument); *d'un coup de son épée,* with a stroke of his sword; *montrer du doigt,* to point at; *toucher du doigt,* to touch with the finger. ‖ **8.** Of, to, at, in (lieu); *l'exposition de Paris,* the Paris Exhibition; *habitant des villes,* town- (ou) city-dweller; *rues de Paris,* streets of Paris; *un professeur de Londres,* a London professor; *tout près du jardin,* close to the garden. ‖ **9.** With, on, in (manière); *de quelle façon?* in what way (ou) manner?; *d'un pas vif,* with a quick step; *roi de nom seulement,* a king in name only; *vivre de charités,* to live on charity. ‖ **10.** In (matière); *bas de soie,* silk stockings; *collier d'or,* gold necklace; *de bois,* wooden; *robe de velours noir,* dress in black-velvet. ‖ **11.** In, of (mesure, quantité); *bâtiment haut de huit étages,* building eight stories high, eight-storied building; *de beaucoup;* by far; *de vingt à trente,* between twenty and thirty; *plus de dix,* more than ten; *plus petit de dix centimètres,* smaller by four inches; *un terrain de 2 hectares,* a field of nearly five acres. ‖ **12.** Of, to (nature, qualité); *un dîner de roi,* a dinner fit for a king; *d'esprit lourd,* dull-witted; *homme de génie,* man of genius; *prêtresse de Diane,* priestess to Diana. ‖ **13.** Of, for, in (objet); *amour de la patrie,* love of country (ou) for one's native land; *amoureux de,* in love with; *expérience des affaires,* business experience; *trafic d'armes,* traffic in arms; *traité de morale,* treatise on ethics. ‖ **14.** From, out of, by (origine); *cette idée est de lui,* the idea is his own; *la route de Brest,* the Brest road; *saigner du nez,* to bleed from the nose; to have a nose-bleed; *venir de la gare,* to come from the station; *vinaigre de vin,* wine vinegar. ‖ **15.** (Prix); *billet de cinq livres,* five-pound note; *chèque de cinq livres,* cheque for five pounds; *dix du cent,* ten per cent; *un mouchoir de soixante francs,* a sixty-franc hand-kerchief. ‖ **16.** In, by, 's (temps); *dans un délai de huit jours,* at a week's notice; *de lundi à samedi,* from Monday to Saturday; *deux heures de l'après-midi,* two in the afternoon, two p. m.; *il ne l'avait pas vue de dix ans,* he had not seen her for (ou) in ten years; *journée de huit heures,* eight-hour day; *voyager de jour,* to travel by day. ‖ **17.** (Explétif); *une bonne chose de faite,* a good thing done; *ce que c'est que de nous!,* what poor creatures we are!; *et chacun de pleurer,* and everyone began to cry; *un drôle de type,* a queer chap; *si j'étais de lui,* if I were he; *trois, de plus,* three more. ‖ **18.** LOC. *De deux à cinq,* between two and five; *de mal en pis,* from bad to worse.

— art. part. (m. **de, du** [dy]; f. **de la** [dəla]; pl. **des** [dɛ]); some, any (quantité); *avez-vous du pain?,* have you any bread?; *donnez-moi du pain,* give me some bread; *je n'ai pas de pain,* I have no bread; *n'avez-vous pas de pain?,* haven't you any bread? ‖ (Non traduit) *boire de la bière,* to drink beer; *des gens comme ça,* people like that; *faire des fautes,* to make mistakes.

— particule. De (noblesse).

dé [de] m. Thimble (à coudre). ‖ Thimbleful

[*de,* of] (plein dé). ‖ FAM. *Tenir dans un dé à coudre,* to lie on a sixpence, to go into a nutshell.

dé m. Die (pl. dice) ; *jouer aux dés,* to play dice. ‖ ARCHIT. Dado.

déambulatoire [deɑ̃bylatwa:r] m. ECCLÉS. Ambulatory.

déambuler [-le] v. intr. (1). To stroll about ; to promenade ; to saunter ; *déambuler le long de la grand-rue,* to pace the « High » (à Oxford).

débâcle [debɑ:kl] f. Breaking up, break (des glaces). ‖ FIN. Crash, smash. ‖ FIG. Collapse, downfall (chute); debacle, rout, stampede (déroute).

débâcler [debɑkle] v. tr. (1). NAUT. To clear out (un port).
— v. intr. To break up (glaces) ; to get clear (rivière).

déballage [debala:ʒ] m. Unpacking (acte). ‖ COMM. Spread, display (étalage) ; clearance (ou) rummage (ou) jumble sale (vente). ‖ FAM. Showdown.

déballer [-le] v. tr. (1). To unpack (des marchandises, un paquet). ‖ FAM. To ʻdisplay ; to give vent to (sa mauvaise humeur) ; *déballer ce qu'on a sur le cœur,* to get it off one's chest.
— v. intr. To unpack.

déballeur [-lœ:r] s. Street-hawker (camelot) ; salesman at clearance-sale (marchand).

débandade [debɑ̃dad] f. MILIT. Rout, stampede ; *à la débandade,* in disorder, in confusion.

débander [-de] v. tr. (1). MÉD. To unbandage. ‖ To unbend, to unstring (un arc). ‖ FIG. To unbend, to relax.
— v. pr. Se **débander,** MILIT. To disband ; to break into a rout.

débaptiser [debatize] v. tr. (1). To change the name of ; to rename (qqn, une rue).

débarbouillage [debarbuja:ʒ] m. Washing (du visage). ‖ FAM. Cleaning (nettoyage).

débarbouiller [-je] v. tr. (1). To wash the face of (qqn). ‖ FAM. To clean (qqch.).
— v. pr. Se **débarbouiller,** to wash one's face. ‖ FAM. To shift for oneself (se débrouiller).

débarcadère [debarkade:r] m. NAUT. Landing-stage, wharf. ‖ CH. DE F. Arrival platform.

débardage [-da:ʒ] m. Unloading, discharging.

débarder [-de] v. tr. (1). To carry to the rail-head (du bois). ‖ NAUT. To unload, to discharge.

débardeur [-dœ:r] m. Docker, stevedore.

débarqué [debarke] m. Fresh (ou) new arrival (personne) ; Landing ; arrival (arrivée) ; *au débarqué,* on arrival.

débarquement [-kəmɑ̃] m. NAUT. Landing (des marchandises, des troupes) ; unloading, discharging (des marchandises) ; disembarkation (des personnes) ; *troupes de débarquement,* landing force. ‖ CH. DE F. Detraining. ‖ FAM. Arrival.

débarquer [-ke] v. tr. (1). To land (des marchandises, des troupes) ; to unload, to discharge (des marchandises) ; to disembark (des personnes). ‖ CH. DE F. To detrain (des troupes). ‖ AUTOM. To set down (des voyageurs en autobus). ‖ FAM. To get rid of (qqn).
— v. intr. NAUT. To go ashore, to land. ‖ CH. DE F. To detrain (troupes) ; to alight (voyageurs).

débarras [debara] m. Clearing, disencumbering (action) ; *bon débarras!,* good riddance! ‖ Lumber-room ; U. S. store-room, catch-all (pièce).

débarrassé, ée [-se] adj. *Débarrassé de,* clear (ou) cleared of (qqch.) ; rid of (qqn) ; relieved (ou) divested (ou) disencumbered of (un vêtement). ‖ FIG. Relieved of (un souci).

débarrasser [-se] v. tr. (1). To clear [*de,* of] (une pièce, la table, le terrain) ; to disencumber (qqch.) ; *débarrasser le cerveau,* to clear the head. ‖ To relieve (*de,* of) [un vêtement]. ‖ To rid (*de,* of) [ses ennemis] ; *débarrasser qqn d'une mau-*

vaise habitude, to wean s. o. from a bad habit. ‖ FIG. To relieve (*de,* of) [qqn]. ‖ FAM. *Débarrassez le plancher!,* clear out!
— v. intr. To clear away (desservir).
— v. pr. Se **débarrasser de,** to get rid (ou) clear of, to extricate oneself from (qqch.) ; to get rid of, to shake off (qqn). ‖ FIG. To shake off (ses préjugés). [V. DÉFAIRE (SE).]

débat [deba] m. Discussion, debate. ‖ Dispute ; contest ; *trancher un débat,* to settle a dispute. ‖ Pl. Debates (en politique) ; proceedings (d'une société) ; *grand débat,* full-dress debate (fam.). ‖ JUR. Proceedings ; trial ; *accepter le débat,* to join issue.

débâtir [debɑtir] v. tr. (2). To unpick the tacking (ou) basting in, to untack.

débattable [debatabl] adj. Debatable.

débattement [-tmɑ̃] m. AUTOM. Wheel-clearance.

débattre [debatr] v. tr. (20). To debate, to discuss, to dispute ; to argue (une affaire, une question) ; to discuss (des intérêts) ; to haggle over (un prix) ; *prix à débattre,* price to be agreed upon.
— v. pr. Se **débattre,** to struggle ; *se débattre dans l'eau,* to flounder in the water. ‖ FIG. To struggle (*contre,* against) ; to grapple (*au milieu de, contre, dans,* with) ; *se débattre avec une traduction,* to flounder through a translation.

débattu, ue [-ty] adj. Debatable (contestable) ; debated (étudié).

débauchage [deboʃa:ʒ] m. Enticing away from work (détournement) ; discharging (renvoi).

débauche [deboʃ] f. Debauchery, crapulence, profligacy, rakishness (v. DÉVERGONDAGE); debauch (v. ORGIE) ; revel, spree (partie fine) ; *vie de débauche,* fast life. ‖ JUR. *Incitation à la débauche,* incitement to vice. ‖ FIG. Riot (de couleur).

débauché [deboʃe] adj., m. Debauched, profligate.

débauchée f. Wanton, tart.

débaucher v. tr. (1). To debauch, to seduce, to ruin (une femme) ; to debauch, to incite to vice (qqn). ‖ To induce, to strike (inciter à la grève) ; to discharge, to lay off, to turn off (renvoyer).
— v. intr. To reduce one's staff.
— v. pr. Se **débaucher,** to go astray, to turn to debauchery.

débaucheur [-ʃœ:r] s. Debaucher, corrupter ; seducer (de femmes). ‖ Picket (gréviste).

débecter [debɛkte] v. tr. (1). POP. To make sick.

débet [debɛ] m. FIN. Debit ; balance due.

débile [debil] adj. Weakened (intelligence) ; weakly, puny (personne) ; frail, weak (santé).
— s. MÉD. *Débile mental,* mental defective.

débilitant, ante [debilitɑ̃, ɑ̃:t] adj. Debilitating.
— m. Debilitant.

débilité [-te] f. MÉD. Debility (v. FAIBLESSE) ; *débilité mentale,* mental deficiency.
— adj. Debilitated.

débiliter [-te] v. tr. (1). To debilitate (qqn). [V. AFFAIBLIR.] ‖ MÉD. To undermine (la santé).

débinage [debina:ʒ] m. FAM. Running down, crabbing, disparagement.

débine [debin] f. POP. Want ; *dans la débine,* without a bean ; down on one's luck.

débiner [-ne] v. tr. (1). FAM. To run down, to carp at, to crab (V. DÉNIGRER.)
— v. récipr. Se **débiner,** FAM. To run each other down (se dénigrer).
— v. pr. Se **débiner,** POP. To hop it, to make off ; U. S. To scram. (V. DÉCAMPER.)

débineur, euse [-nœ:r, ø:z] s. POP. Faultfinder, backbiter, mudslinger.

débit [debi] m. COMM. Demand (demande) ; sale by retail (vente) ; *cet article a peu de débit,* there is small demand for this line ; *avoir un gros, un petit débit,* to be in great, little demand ; *de bon* *débit*, saleable, of ready sale. ‖ Comm. Retail-shop, licensed-shop (magasin); *débit de boissons*, public house, U. S. saloon; *débit de tabac*, tobacconist's shop, U. S. tobacco (ou) cigar store. ‖ Fin. Debit, debit side (en comptabilité); *porté au débit*, debited; in the red (fam.). ‖ Techn. Delivery (de courant, d'eau); output (d'une machine); flow, outflow (d'une pompe); flow (d'une rivière); yield (d'un puits); discharge (d'un tuyau). ‖ Autom. Traffic capacity (d'un pont); *débit du courant de circulation*, volume of traffic. ‖ Milit. Rate (ou) intensity of fire. ‖ Fig. Delivery (d'un orateur); *avoir un débit facile*, to be a fluent speaker.

débitage [-ta:ʒ] m. Cutting up, sawing up.

débitant [-tɑ̃] s. Comm. Retailer (de, of); *débitant de boissons*, publican; U. S. bartender; *débitant de tabac*, tabacconist.

débiter [-te] v. tr. (1). Comm. To retail, to sell (des marchandises). ‖ To cut up, to saw up (du bois). ‖ To discharge, to yield (de l'eau). ‖ Fin. To debit (de, with) [un compte]. ‖ Electr. To deliver (du courant). ‖ Techn. To turn out (machine). ‖ Théâtr. To recite (un rôle). ‖ Fig. To retail (des calomnies); to deliver (un discours); to utter (des mensonges); to reel off (des vers); *débiter des injures à*, to shout abuse at.

débiteur [-tœ:r] m. Comm. Retailer (de marchandises). ‖ Utterer (de paroles).

débiteur (f. **débitrice** [-tris]) m. Fin. Debtor. ‖ Fig. *Être le débiteur de qqn*, to be indebted to s.o., to be s.o.'s debtor.
— adj. Fin. Debit (compte, solde).

débiteuse [-tø:z] f. Comm. Saleswoman (ou) shop-assistant who shows customers to the pay-desk.

débitrice [-tris] f. Fin. Debtor. ‖ Techn. Feeding device (machine). ‖ Ciném. Top sprocket wheel.
— adj. Théâtr. *Bobine débitrice*, top (ou) delivery spool (au cinéma).

déblai [deblɛ] m. Clearing (action); excavation (travail). ‖ Pl. Spoil (terre). ‖ Ch. de f. Cut, cutting.

déblaiement [-mɑ̃] m. Clearing out (d'un endroit); cleaning out (d'une pièce); clearing, grubbing up (d'un terrain). ‖ Excavating (déblai).

déblatérer [deblatere] v. tr. (5). To utter, to shout (injures); to bluster out (des menaces).
— v. intr. To hurl abuse (contre, at); to rail (contre, against).

déblayer [deblɛje] v. tr. (9 b). To clear (un endroit); to clean out (une pièce); to clear (un terrain). ‖ To clear away (des détritus); to shovel (ou) sweep away (la neige). ‖ Ch. de f. To clear (la voie). ‖ Fig. *Déblayer le terrain*, to clear the ground; to prepare the way; to do the spade-work on a project.

déblocage [deblɔka:ʒ] m. Comm. Releasing (de denrées). ‖ Autom. Taking off (freins).

débloquer [-ke] v. tr. (1). Comm. To free, to release (des denrées). ‖ Milit. To relieve (une place). ‖ Techn. To unlock (un écrou); to unclamp (un étau). ‖ Autom. To take off (des freins).

déboires [debwa:r] m. pl. Disappointments, failures (échecs, déceptions); troubles (ennuis).

déboisement [debwazmɑ̃] m. Deforestation (d'un pays); clearing (d'un terrain).

déboiser [-ze] v. tr. (1). To deforest (un pays); to clear of trees (un terrain). ‖ Techn. To untimber (une mine).

déboîtement [debwatmɑ̃] m. Méd. Dislocation.

déboîter [-te] v. tr. (1). Méd. To dislocate (un membre). ‖ Techn. *Déboîter une montre*, to remove a watch from its case.
— v. intr. Autom. To filter. ‖ Milit. To break out of column.
— v. pr. **Se déboîter**. Méd. To come out of

joint (membre); *se déboîter un membre*, to twist (ou) put out a limb.

débonder [debɔde] v. tr. (1). To open the sluice-gates of (un réservoir); to unbung (un tonneau). ‖ Fig. To relieve (son cœur).
— v. intr. To rush, to gush out (eau, source).
— v. pr. **Se débonder**. Fam. To pour out one's heart.

débonnaire [debɔnɛ:r] adj. Meek, mild (doux). ‖ Good-natured, easy-going (complaisant). ‖ Debonair †; affable, genial.

débonnairement [-nɛrmɑ̃] adv. Mildly; complaisantly; in an easy-going fashion.

débonnaireté [-nɛrəte] f. Good temper; easy-going nature.

débordant [debɔrdɑ̃] adj. Overflowing, brimming over (liquide). ‖ Protruding, projecting (rocher). ‖ Milit. Outflanking (mouvement). ‖ Fig. Overflowing (enthousiasme); gushing, boisterous, exuberant (gaieté); *débordant de*, bursting with (joie, santé).

débordé, ée [-de] adj. Fig. Overwrought, overtired (surmené); *débordé de travail*, overwhelmed with work; *débordé par les visites*, snowed under with callers. ‖ Milit. Outflanked. ‖ Comm. Hard pressed, rushed.

débordement [-dmɑ̃] m. Overflowing (d'une rivière). ‖ Milit. Outflanking, envelopment. ‖ Fig. Explosion (de colère); outburst (d'insultes); outbreak (de rage). ‖ Pl. Dissoluteness, licentiousness; debauchery; wild life (débauche).

déborder [-de] v. intr. (1). To boil over (liquide bouillant); to bubble over (mousse de champagne); to run over, to brim over (récipient); to overflow (rivière). ‖ To project, to protrude, to jut out (faire saillie); to stretch out, to spread out, to overflow (s'étendre). ‖ Fig. To overflow (cœur); *déborder de*, to boil over with (colère); to bubble over with (gaieté, vie); to overflow with (richesses); to burst with (santé). ‖ Loc. *La goutte d'eau qui fait déborder le vase*, the straw that breaks the camel's back.
— v. tr. To overflow, to run over (les bords, les rives). ‖ To extend (ou) to grow beyond (les limites, en s'étalant); to project (ou) jut out beyond (en surplombant). ‖ To untuck (un lit); to cut off the border of (un vêtement). ‖ Milit. To outflank (l'ennemi). ‖ Naut. To fend off (une embarcation).

débotté [debɔte] m. Arrival; *au débotté*, immediately after arriving (ou) on arrival.

débotter v. tr. (1). To unboot.
— v. pr. **Se débotter**, to take (ou) pull off one's boots.

débouchage [debuʃa:ʒ] m. Uncorking (d'une bouteille); unstoppering (d'un flacon). ‖ Milit. Setting, cutting (d'une fusée).

débouché [-ʃe] m. Exit (d'un bâtiment); outlet (d'un égout, d'un tuyau); opening, issue (d'un passage, d'une rue, d'une vallée). ‖ Milit. Debouch. ‖ Comm. Opening, outlet, market (de marchandises); demand (pour, for); *créer un nouveau débouché pour*, to open up a new channel (ou) market for. ‖ Fig. Opening, opportunity (pour une carrière).

déboucher v. tr. (1). To uncork, to open (une bouteille); to unstop (une carafe); to unstopper (un flacon). ‖ To clear, to clean out, to unstop (un conduit). ‖ Milit. To set (une fusée); *déboucher à zéro*, to fire over open sights. ‖ Fam. To awaken (l'esprit).
— v. intr. To emerge, to step out, to debouch (gens); to open (route, rue); *déboucher sur*, to open on, to run into. ‖ Milit. To debouch, to issue forth.
— v. pr. **Se déboucher**, to uncork (bouteille); to clear (conduit). ‖ Fam. To wake up (esprit).

débouchoir [-ʃwa:r] m. Opener (décapsulateur) ; cork-drawer (tire-bouchon). ‖ MILIT. Fuse-borer.

déboucler [debukle] v. tr. (1). To unbuckle (une ceinture). ‖ To uncurl (les cheveux).
— v. pr. **Se déboucler**, to become unbuckled (ceinture). ‖ To uncurl, to become uncurled (cheveux).

déboulé [debule] m. *Au déboulé*, on breaking cover.

débouler v. intr. (1). SPORTS. To bolt (gibier). ‖ FAM. To tumble down (tomber).

déboulonnage [debulɔna:ʒ] m. TECHN. Unbolting ; unriveting. ‖ FAM. Debunking, bringing down.

déboulonner [-ne] v. tr. (1). TECHN. To unbolt ; to unrivet. ‖ FAM. To debunk (qqn) ; to topple (*de*, from).

débouquer [debuke] v. intr. NAUT. To disembogue.

débourber [deburbe] v. tr. (1). To clear, to clean out, to clean, to sluice (un égout, un fossé) ; to dredge (une rivière). ‖ To put into clean water (le poisson). ‖ To wash (un minerai).

débourrage [debura:ʒ] m. Cleaning (d'une carde) ; unhairing, scraping (d'une peau). ‖ Untamping (d'une mine).

débourrer [-re] v. tr. (1). To clean (la carde) ; to unhair (une peau). ‖ To remove the stuffing from (un fauteuil) ; to clean out, to remove the tobacco from (une pipe). ‖ MILIT. To extract the wad from (un fusil) ; to untamp (une mine).

débours [debu:r] m. pl. COMM. Expenses ; outlay ; outgoings.

déboursement [debursmɑ̃] m. Disbursement ; expenditure.

débourser [-se] v. tr. (1). To disburse, to lay out, to pay out.
— v. intr. FAM. To fork out, to put one's hand down. (V. DÉCAISSER.)

déboussoler [debusole] v. tr. (1). FAM. To dumbfound, to stun, to stagger.

debout [debu] adv. On its hind legs (chien) ; upright (chose) ; on end (œuf) ; erect, standing (personne) [dressé] ; *aidez-la à se mettre debout*, help her to her feet ; *rester debout*, to remain standing ; *se mettre debout*, to stand up, to get on to one's feet ; *se tenir debout*, to stand, to be on one's feet ; *si bas qu'on ne peut se tenir debout*, so low that it is impossible to stand upright. ‖ Standing (chose) ; standing, lIving (personne) [en équilibre] ; *je l'ai tellement fait marcher qu'elle ne tient plus debout*, I walked her off her legs ; *voilà de quoi vous remettre debout*, that will buck you up (ou) put you right. ‖ Up, out of bed (levé) ; *rester debout*, to stay up. ‖ NAUT. *Vent debout*, head wind. ‖ FAM. *A dormir debout*, cock-and-bull, lame (histoire) ; *théorie qui ne tient pas debout*, theory that does not hold water ; *mettre les choses debout*, to put things straight (ou) in order.

débouté [debute] m. JUR. Nonsuit, dismissal.
— adj. JUR. Nonsuited.

déboutement [-tmɑ̃] m. JUR. Nonsuiting.

débouter [-te] v. tr. (1). JUR. To nonsuit.

déboutonner [debutɔne] v. tr. (1). To unbutton.
— v. pr. **Se déboutonner**, to unbutton oneself (personne) ; to come unbuttoned (vêtement). ‖ FAM. To unbosom oneself.

débraillé, ée [debrɑje] adj. Loose (manières) ; unbuttoned, disarrayed, half-dressed (personne) ; loose (propos) ; untidy, slovenly (tenue).
— m. Untidiness, disarray. ‖ FIG. Slovenliness.

débrailler (se) [sədebrɑje] v. pr. (1). To show one's breast. ‖ FIG. To become coarse (ou) vulgar.

débranchement [debrɑ̃ʃmɑ̃] m. CH. DE F. Shunting. ‖ ELECTR. Disconnecting, switching-off.

débrancher [debrɑ̃ʃe] v. tr. (1). ELECTR. To disconnect.

débrayage [debrɛja:ʒ] m. AUTOM., TECHN. Disengaging, declutching, uncoupling (action) ; clutch-pedal (pédale). ‖ FAM. Sit-down strike (grève).

débrayer [-je] v. tr. (9b). TECHN. To disengage ; to throw out of gear. ‖ AUTOM. To declutch, to put the clutch out. ‖ FAM. To go on strike ; to knock off (ouvriers).

débridé, ée [debride] adj. Unbridled (pr. et fig.).

débridement [debridmɑ̃] m. Unbridling (d'un cheval). ‖ MÉD. Incision, lancing. ‖ FIG. Unbridling, letting loose (des instincts, des mœurs).

débrider v. tr. (1). To unbridle (un cheval). ‖ CULIN. To untruss (une volaille). ‖ MÉD. To incise (une plaie). ‖ FAM. *Sans débrider*, without stopping, at a stretch, all day long.

débris [debri] m. pl. Debris, remains, fragments (bouts, restes) ; waste (v. DÉCHET) ; wreckage (décombres, épaves) ; rubbish (détritus).

débrocher [debrɔʃe] v. tr. (1). To unstitch, to strip (un livre). ‖ CULIN. To unspit (une volaille).

débrouillard, arde [debruja:r, ard] adj. FAM. Resourceful ; smart.
— s. Smart customer ; go-getter, hustler.

débrouillardise [debrujardi:z], **débrouille** [debru:j] f. FAM. Wangling, resourcefulness.

débrouiller [-je] v. tr. (1). To unravel, to disentangle (un écheveau) ; to sort out (des papiers). ‖ FIG. To clear out (une affaire) ; to straighten out (des comptes).
— v. pr. **Se débrouiller**, to manage, to shift for oneself, to see it through (personne) ; *se débrouiller pour avoir*, to wangle, U. S. to finagle. ‖ To clear up (affaire, temps).

débroussaillement [debrusajmɑ̃] m. Clearing. ‖ FIG. Preliminary work (ou) study, spadework.

débroussailler [debrusɑje] v. tr. (1). To clear of brushwood (un terrain). ‖ FIG. To clear the way ; to do the spade-work on (un sujet).

débucher [debyʃe] v. intr. (1). SPORTS. To break cover ; *faire débucher*, to start.
— v. tr. SPORTS. To start (le gibier).
— m. SPORTS. Breaking cover (du gibier). ‖ Gone away (sonnerie).

débusquer [debyske] v. tr. (1). To dislodge, to drive out, to hunt out. ‖ FAM. To oust (qqn).

début [deby] m. Beginning, start, outset (v. COMMENCEMENT) ; *au début*, at the beginning (ou) outset (ou) start, at first ; *au début de l'année*, in the first days of the year ; early in the year ; *au début de la matinée*, in the early morning ; *dès le début*, from the very first, from the beginning (ou) outset, at the very start. ‖ First steps (dans, in) [une carrière] ; start (dans, in) [la vie] ; *débuts dans le monde*, debut. ‖ THÉÂTR. Debut ; first appearance. ‖ String (au billard) ; lead (aux cartes) ; first throw (ou) cast (aux dés).

débutant [-tɑ̃] m. Beginner, novice, tyro. ‖ THÉÂTR. Debutant.

débutante [-tɑ:t] f. Beginner. ‖ THÉÂTR. Debutante.

débuter [-te] v. intr. (1). To begin, to commence, to start, to open (par, with) ; *rien pour débuter*, nothing to begin with. ‖ To start (dans, in) ; to enter (dans, on, upon) ; to take (ou) make one's first steps (dans, in) ; *bien débuter*, to make a good start ; *quand il débuta dans les affaires*, when he first went into business ; *débuter dans le monde*, to come out (jeune fille). ‖ THÉÂTR. To make one's first appearance on the stage. ‖ To string (au billard) ; to lead (aux cartes) ; to throw first (aux dés) ; to play first (à un jeu).
— v. tr. To start, to begin.

deçà [dəsa] adv. On this side ; *deçà delà*, here and there ; to and fro ; in every direction, on all sides ; *en deçà de*, on this side of. ‖ FIG. *Rester en deçà de la vérité*, to be well within the truth.

décachetage [dekaʃta:ʒ] m. Unsealing, opening.

décacheter [-te] v. tr. (1). To unseal, to open, to break (ou) rip open (une lettre).

décade [dekad] f. Decade (série de dix). ‖ Period of ten years, decade (dix ans); period of ten days (dix jours). ‖ FAM. Tobacco ration.

décadence [dekadᾱ:s] f. Decadence (en art, civilisation, littérature); decay, decline (déclin).

décadent, ente [-dᾱ, ᾱ:t] adj., s. Decadent.

décaèdre [dekaɛdr] m. MATH. Decahedron.

décaféiné, ée [dekafeine] adj. Decaffeinated, caffeine-free.

décagonal [dekagɔnal] adj. MATH. Decagonal.

décagone [-gon] m. MATH. Decagon.

décagramme [-gram] m. Decagramme.

décaissement [dekɛsmᾱ] m. FIN. Disbursement, paying out.

décaisser [-se] v. tr. (1). To unpack, to uncase, to uncrate (un objet). ‖ AGRIC. To untub, to plant out. ‖ FIN. To pay out, to disburse.

décalage [dekala:ʒ] m. Altering; shifting (de l'heure); displacement (d'un objet); lag (entre deux opérations). ‖ TECHN. Unwedging (des pistons); unscotching (des roues). ‖ AVIAT. Decalage, stagger (des ailes). ‖ ELECTR. Lag (des balais); difference (de phase).

décalaminage [dekalamina:ʒ] m. Decarbonization, decoking, decoke.

décalaminant, ante [dekalaminᾱ, ᾱ:t] adj. AUTOM. Carbon-preventive; decarbonizing.

décalaminer [-ne] v. tr. (1). To decarbonize.

décalcification [dekalsifikasjɔ̃] f. MÉD. Decalcification.

décalcifier [-fje] v. tr. (1). MÉD. To decalcify.
— v. pr. **Se décalcifier**. MÉD. To become decalcified.

décalcomanie [dekalkɔmani] f. Transfer, decalcomania.

décaler [dekale] v. tr. (1). To alter, to shift (l'heure); *décaler de deux heures*, to shift two hours forward (en avant) [ou] back (en arrière). ‖ To shift, to displace; to unbalance (un objet); *décalé vers la droite*, offset to the right. ‖ TECHN. To unwedge (des pistons, une roue). ‖ AVIAT. To stagger (les ailes). ‖ ELECTR. *Etre décalé*, to lag.

décalitre [dekalitr] m. Decalitre.

décalogue [dekalɔg] m. ECCLÉS. Decalogue.

décaloter [dekalɔte] v. tr. (1). To take the top off (un œuf).

décalquage [dekalka:ʒ] m. Transferring; tracing; calking.

décalque [dekalk] m. Transfer; trace; calk.

décalquer [-ke] v. tr. (1). To transfer; to calk; *papier à décalquer*, transfer-paper. ‖ To trace off, to draw from (faire un calque). ‖ FAM. *C'est décalqué*, that was cast in the same mould; *c'est son père tout décalqué*, he is the living image of his father, he's a chip off the old block.

décamètre [dekamɛtr] m. Decametre.

décamper [dekᾱpe] v. tr. (1). MILIT. To break camp, to decamp. ‖ FAM. To scoot, to clear out, to scuttle away, to scamper off, to skedaddle, U. S. to take a powder, to beat it.

décan [dekᾱ] m. ECCLÉS., ASTRON. Decan.

décanal, ale [dekanal] adj. Decanal.

décanat [dekana] m. Deanship.

décaniller [dekanije] v. tr. (1). V. DÉCAMPER.

décantage [dekᾱta:ʒ] m. Decanting, decantation.

décanter [-te] v. tr. (1). To decant (le vin).

décanteur [-tœ:r] m. TECHN. Decanter.

décapage [dekapa:ʒ] m. Cleaning, scraping, scouring (d'un métal); pickling (à l'acide).

décapant [dekapᾱ] m. Pickle (acide); scouring solution (pour métaux); paint remover (pour peintures). ‖ Nail-varnish (ou) U. S. polish remover (pour ongles); varnish remover (pour vernis).

décapeler [dekaple] v. tr. (8 a). NAUT. To cast off (un câble); to unrig (une vergue).

décaper [dekape] v. tr. (1). To pickle (à l'acide); to scour (à la machine). ‖ To remove (la peinture, le vernis).

décapeuse [-pø:z] f. TECHN. Scouring machine.

décapitation [dekapitasjɔ̃] f. Decapitation, beheading. (V. DÉCOLLATION.)

décapiter [-te] v. tr. (1). To decapitate, to behead (qqn). ‖ FIG. To behead; to deprive of the leader. ‖ FAM. To cut the head off (qqch.).

décapode [dekapɔd] m. ZOOL. Decapod.

décapotable [dekapɔtabl] adj. AUTOM. Convertible, drop-head; *non décapotable*, fixed-head, U. S. hard top.

décapoter [-te] v. tr. (1). To open (ou) fold back the hood of.

décapsuler [-le] v. tr. (1). To open, to remove the crown cork of (une bouteille).

décapsuleur [-lœ:r] m. Bottle-opener.

décarburant, ante [dekarbyrᾱ, ᾱ:t] adj. Decarbonizing.
— m. Decarbonizer, decarburizer.

décarburer [-re] v. tr. (1). To decarbonize.

décarcasser (se) [sədekarkase] v. pr. (1). FAM. To wear oneself out. (V. DÉMANCHER [SE].)

décarreler [dekarle] v. tr. (8a). To remove the tiles from.

décasyllabe [dekasillab] adj. Decasyllabic.
— s. Decasyllable.

décasyllabique [-bik] adj. Decasyllabic.

décathlon [dekatlɔ̃] m. SPORTS. Decathlon.

décati, ie [dekati] adj. Sponged (tissu). ‖ FAM. Old and worn out; decrepit; *un vieux décati*, an old crock, a back-number.

décatir [-ti:r] v. tr. (2). To sponge, to take the gloss off (une étoffe).
— v. pr. **Se décatir**, FAM. To decay; to age; to wrinkle.

décavé, ée [dekave] adj. FAM. Broke, stony-broke, cleaned-out; skint (pop.).

décédé, ée [desede] adj., s. Deceased.

décéder v. intr. (5). To decease, to pass away.

décelable [deslabl] adj. Detectable, discernible, noticeable.

déceler [-le] v. tr. (8b). To detect, to discern (découvrir, remarquer). ‖ To reveal, to betray (trahir).

décélération [deselerasjɔ̃] f. Slowing-down.

décembre [desᾱ:br] m. December.

décemment [desamᾱ] adv. Decently, with decency, properly, with propriety (selon la bienséance); decently, modestly (selon la décence).

décence [desᾱ:s] f. Decency, propriety, seemliness (bienséance). ‖ Decency, modesty, respectability (dignité, modestie).

décennal, ale [desɛnal] adj. Decennial, decennary.

décennie [-ni] f. Decade.

décent, ente [desᾱ, ᾱ:t] adj. Decent, seemly, proper, decorous (bienséant); decent, modest (convenable).

décentrage [desᾱtra:ʒ] m. Putting out of center. ‖ PHYS. Decentration (d'une lentille).

décentralisateur, trice [desᾱtralizatœ:r, tris] adj. Decentralizing.
— s. Advocate of decentralization.

décentralisation [-zasjɔ̃] f. Decentralization.

décentraliser [-ze] v. tr. (1). To decentralize.

décentré, ée [desᾱtre] adj. Out of centre (objet); out of true (roue).

décentrement [-trəmᾱ] m. PHYS. V. DÉCENTRAGE.

décentrer v. tr. (1). PHYS. To decentre. ‖ TECHN. To put out of centre.
— v. pr. **Se décentrer**, to run out of true.

déception [desɛpsjɔ̃] f. Disappointment, setback; let-down (fam.).

décérébrer [deserebre] v. tr. (5). To decerebrate ; *chien décérébré*, decerebrate dog.

décerner [desɛrne] v. tr. (1). To award, to bestow, to grant. ‖ Jur. To issue (un mandat d'arrêt).

décès [desɛ] m. Decease. (V. MORT). ‖ Jur. Demise.

décevant, ante [desvɑ̃, ɑ̃:t] adj. Disappointing (désappointant) ; fallacious, misleading (fallacieux) ; deceptive, delusive (trompeur).

décevoir [desəvwa:r] v. tr. (3). To disappoint (désappointer) ; to deceive, to delude (tromper).

déchaîné, ée [deʃɛne] adj. Raging, furious, wild, unleashed (éléments, personnes).

déchaînement [-nmɑ̃] m. Bursting, outburst (explosion) ; unbridling, letting loose, unleashing (libération) ; fury, rage (rage).

déchaîner [-ne] v. tr. (1). To unchain, to untie (un chien) ; to unbind, to unfetter (un prisonnier). ‖ Fig. To unleash (la guerre, les passions) ; *déchaîner l'hilarité*, to raise a storm of laughter. — v. pr. Se **déchaîner**, to break loose (chien). ‖ Fig. To explode, to break loose (colère) ; to break (orage) ; to break (ou) fly out (*contre*, against) [personne] ; to rage (vent).

déchanter [deʃɑ̃te] v. intr. (1). FAM. To sing a different tune ; to sing small.

déchaper (se) [sədeʃape] v. pr. (1). AUTOM. To peel (pneu).

décharge [deʃarʒ] f. Unloading (d'une voiture). ‖ Relief, lightening (soulagement). ‖ FIN. Release (d'une dette) ; relief, rebate (d'impôt) ; *donner décharge de*, to release from. ‖ Jur. Discharge, dismissal, acquittal, release (d'un accusé) ; exculpation, favourable evidence (en faveur d'un accusé) ; *à la décharge de*, to the discharge of, in favour of, in excuse for, exonerating ; *témoin à décharge*, witness for the defence. ‖ COMM. Receipt (*de*, for). ‖ NAUT. Unlading (d'un navire). ‖ MILIT. Discharge (des armes). ‖ ELECTR. Discharge ; *en décharge*, discharging. ‖ TECHN. Discharge, outlet ; *tuyau de décharge*, waste-pipe. ‖ Lumber-room (pièce) ; store-room (resserre) ; dump (terrain).

déchargement [-ʒəmɑ̃] m. Unloading (d'une arme, d'une voiture). ‖ NAUT. Unlading.

décharger [-ʒe] v. tr. (7). To tip out, to dump (le contenu d'une voiture basculante) ; to discharge (des marchandises) ; to empty (un réservoir) ; to unload (une voiture). ‖ To unburden (un animal, une chose, une personne, d'un poids). ‖ FIG. To vent (sa bile, sa colère) ; to unburden (son cœur) ; to relieve, to disburden, to ease (sa conscience) ; *décharger de*, to acquit of, to clear of (une accusation) ; to release from (une dette) ; to exempt from (un impôt) ; to discharge of (une obligation) ; to relieve of, to let off (un travail) ; *décharger qqn de qqch.*, to disburden s.o. of sth. ‖ Jur. To clear of a charge, to discharge, to exonerate (un accusé). ‖ COMM. To receipt. ‖ ELECTR. To discharge (des accus). ‖ MILIT. To unload (en enlevant la charge) ; to discharge, to let off, to fire (en tirant) ; to remove the charge from (une cartouche, une mine). — v. intr. To discharge (couleur). — v. pr. Se **décharger**, to disburden oneself (*de*, of) [se débarrasser d'un poids] ; to flow, to discharge (*dans*, into) [se déverser]. ‖ ELECTR. To discharge, to run down (accus). ‖ MILIT. To discharge, to go off (arme). ‖ FIG. To discharge (ou) to vent oneself (*sur*, on) [colère] ; *se décharger de*, to put (ou) lay down (un fardeau) ; to carry out (une obligation) ; to get rid of (qqch, qqn) ; *se décharger sur qqn de la responsabilité de qqch.*, to make s.o. responsible for sth., to shift the responsibility of sth. on to s.o.

déchargeur [-ʒœ:r] m. Porter (aux Halles). ‖ NAUT. Docker, dock labourer. ‖ ELECTR. Arrester.

décharné, ée [deʃarne] adj. Skinny, fleshless, gaunt, scraggy, scrawny.

décharner v. tr. (1). To strip the flesh off (un os). ‖ FIG. To emaciate (qqn). — v. pr. Se **décharner**, to become emaciated (ou) scrawny.

déchaussé, ée [deʃose] adj. Barefooted (personne). ‖ MÉD. Loose (dent).

déchaussement [-smɑ̃] m. Removal of one's shoes (d'une personne). ‖ MÉD. Loosening.

déchausser [-se] v. tr. (1). To remove (ou) take off the shoes of (qqn). ‖ MÉD. To loosen (une dent). ‖ AGRIC. To bare the roots of (un arbre). — v. pr. Se **déchausser**, to take off one's shoes. ‖ MÉD. To become loose (ou) bare (dent) ; *avoir les dents qui se déchaussent*, to have receding gums.

déchaux [deʃo] adj. m. ECCLÉS. Discalced, discalceate.

dèche [dɛʃ] f. FAM. Straits (v. MOUISE) ; *dans la dèche*, broke to the wide, dead broke.

déchéance [deʃeɑ̃:s] f. Decline (de la civilisation, d'un pays) ; downfall (d'un haut personnage) ; dethronement, deposition (d'un souverain). ‖ ECCLÉS. Fall (d'une âme, de l'homme). ‖ Jur. Forfeiture (de brevet, de droits) ; disqualification (d'un mandataire) ; expiration (d'une police d'assurance) ; lapse (de propriété littéraire). ‖ FIG. Moral decay, degradation, decline.

déchet [deʃɛ] m. Waste, loss (perte) ; *déchet de route*, loss in transit. ‖ Pl. Waste, refuse (v. DÉBRIS, DÉTRITUS) ; *déchets de métal*, scrap metal ; *déchets de toison*, abb : *déchets de viande*, scraps. ‖ FIG. *Les déchets de la société*, the dregs of society. ‖ FAM. *Vieux déchet*, back-number.

déchiffonner [deʃifɔne] v. tr. (1). To smooth out. — v. pr. Se **déchiffonner**, to smooth out.

déchiffrable [deʃifrabl] adj. Legible, readable (écriture) ; decodable (message chiffré) ; decipherable (texte).

déchiffrage [-fra:ʒ] m. Reading (d'une écriture) ; deciphering (d'une inscription) ; decoding (d'un message chiffré). ‖ MUS. Sight-reading.

déchiffrer [-fre] v. tr. (1). To read, to make out, to spell out, to decipher (une écriture, un manuscrit) ; to decipher (une inscription) ; to decode (un message chiffré) ; to interpret (des signaux). ‖ MUS. To read at sight ; to sight-read.

déchiffreur, euse [-frœ:r, ø:z] s. Decipherer (de manuscrits) ; decoder (de message chiffré) ; *déchiffreur de radar*, radar scanner. ‖ MUS. Reader at sight, sight-reader.

déchiqueté, ée [deʃikte] adj. Jagged (bord) ; mangled (corps) ; shredded, torn to shreds, cut to pieces (objet). ‖ GÉOGR. Indented (côte). ‖ BOT. Laciniate (feuille).

déchiqueter v. tr. (8a). To mangle (un corps) ; to slash, to tear into shreds (ou) strips (une étoffe). ‖ CULIN. To shred (du poisson, de la viande).

déchiqueture [-ty:r] f. Laciniation (de bordure) ; slash, cut (de tissu). ‖ GÉOGR. Indentation.

déchirant, ante [deʃirɑ̃, ɑ̃:t] adj. Heart-rending, agonizing (cri, scène) ; excruciating (douleur) ; anguishing (moment) ; harrowing (récit, scène).

déchiré, ée [-re] adj. Torn, rent (objet, vêtement) ; tattered, in tatters, in rags (personne). ‖ FIG. *Déchiré par*, torn with (l'angoisse) ; vilified by (la calomnie) ; *déchiré par la guerre*, war-ravaged.

déchirement [deʃirmɑ̃] m. Tearing, rending (du tissu). ‖ MÉD. Tearing (d'un muscle). ‖ FIG. Wrench (de la séparation) ; *déchirement du cœur*, heartbreak. ‖ Pl. Convulsions, disturbances (en politique).

déchirer [-re] v. tr. (1). To lacerate, to mangle (un corps) ; to tear, to rend, to rip (le papier, le tissu) ; *déchirer en deux*, to tear asunder (ou) in

two (ou) in half ; *déchirer en lambeaux, en petits morceaux*, to tear to pieces, to tear up. ‖ To tear off (une bande de journal) ; to tear open (une enveloppe) ; *déchirer une page d'un livre*, to tear a page out of a book (pour la détacher) ; *ouvrir en déchirant*, to tear open. ‖ FIG. To rend (l'air, le cœur, les nuages) ; to tear, to harrow (l'âme) ; to split (les oreilles) ; *qui déchire le cœur, les oreilles*, heart-rending, ear-splitting. ‖ FIG. *Déchirer qqn à belles dents*, to tear s.o.'s character to shreds, to tear s.o. to pieces.
— v. pr. Se déchirer, to tear (tissu). ‖ FIG. To rend (cœur).
— v. récipr. Se déchirer, to tear each other to pieces ; to pick holes in each other.

déchirure [-ry:r] f. Tear, rent. ‖ MÉD. Laceration.

déchloruré, ée [dekloryre] adj. MÉD. Salt-free.

déchoir [deʃwa:r] v. intr. (36). To fall, to come (ou) go down (d'un état) ; to lower oneself, to lose caste (ou) prestige (d'un rang). ‖ To fall (*dans*, in) [l'estime] ; to fall (*de*, from) [sa position]. ‖ To decay, to decline (décliner).

déchristianisation [dekristjanizasjɔ̃] f. Dechristianization.

déchristianiser [dekristjanize] v. tr. (1). To dechristianize.

déchu, ue [deʃy] adj. Fallen (ange, personne) ; fallen, dethroned (souverain) ; *maison déchue de sa splendeur*, house whose glory has departed, house of broken fortunes. ‖ JUR. Forfeited ; *déchu de ses droits*, having forfeited one's rights. (V. DÉCHOIR.)

décibel [desibɛl] m. PHYS. Decibel.

décidé, ée [deside] adj. Settled (affaire, question) ; firm, decided, determined, resolute (personne) ; *ceci une fois décidé*, this being resolved upon. ‖ Determined, resolved, having made up one's mind (à, to).

décidément [-mɑ̃] adv. Decidedly, definitely (définitivement) ; firmly, resolutely (résolument) ; all things considered (tout considéré).

décider [deside] v. tr. (1). To decide, to settle (*que*, that) [régler]. ‖ To arrange, to fix (v. ARRÊTER) ; to determine (v. DÉTERMINER) ; to decide on, to resolve on (v. RÉSOUDRE) ; *qu'a-t-elle décidé?*, what decision has she come to ? ‖ To determine, to get (déterminer) ; to induce, to entice (inciter) ; to persuade (persuader) ; to move (*à*, to) [pousser]. ‖ JUR. To find (*en faveur de*, for).
— v. intr. To decide ; to judge ; *décider de qqch.*, to decide (ou) to determine sth. ; *droit de décider de soi-même*, right of self-determination.
— v. pr. Se décider, to be decided (ou) settled (affaire) ; to decide, to make up one's mind, to resolve (personne) ; *décidez-vous*, make up your mind ; *se décider à*, to decide on, to bring oneself to ; *se décider pour*, to decide for (qqch.) ; to decide on (ou) in favour of (qqn).

décidu, e [desidy] adj. BOT. Deciduous.

décigramme [desigram] m. Decigramme.

décilitre [-litr] m. Decilitre.

décimal, ale [-mal] adj. Decimal.

décimale f. Decimal.

décimalisation [-malizasjɔ̃] f. Decimalization.

décimaliser [-malize] v. tr. (1). To decimalize.

décimation [-masjɔ̃] f. Decimation.

décime [desim] m. Decime (monnaie ancienne). ‖ JUR. *Décime additionnel*, additional tenth.

décimer [-me] v. tr. (1). To decimate, to thin out ; to deplete ; *décimer les rangs de l'ennemi*, to take heavy toll of the enemy.

décimètre [-mɛtr] m. Decimetre ; *double décimètre*, rule, ruler.

décintrer [desɛ̃tre] v. tr. (1). ARCHIT. To discentre.

décisif, ive [desizif, i:v] adj. Clinching (argument) ; decisive (bataille) ; critical, crucial (moment) ; conclusive (preuve) ; peremptory (ton).

décision [-zjɔ̃] f. Decision, determination ; resolution ; *prendre une décision*, to come to (ou) to make a decision ; *s'en tenir à sa décision*, to abide by one's decision. ‖ JUR. Conclusion, settlement (d'une affaire) ; decision (d'une commission) ; *décision arbitrale*, award, ruling ; *décision du jury*, verdict ; *rendre une décision*, to make an award. ‖ FIG. Decision, resolution, determination (fermeté) ; *avec décision*, decisively, resolutely ; *esprit de décision*, decidedness, decisiveness.

déclamateur, trice [deklamatœ:r, tris] s. Declaimer ; elocutionist (récitant). ‖ Mouther, ranter, spouter, tub-thumper (orateur).

déclamation [-sjɔ̃] f. Declamation (art) ; harangue (texte). ‖ FAM. Mouthing, ranting, spouting (verbiage pompeux).

déclamatoire [-twa:r] adj. Declamatory, elocutionary. ‖ Bombastic, high-flown, turgid (style) ; grandiloquent, ranting, high-falutin (ton).

déclamer [deklame] v. tr. (1). To declaim (un discours) ; to recite (un poème). ‖ To harangue, to mouth, to rant (pompeusement).

déclarable [deklarabl] adj. JUR. Dutiable.

déclarant, ante [-rɑ̃, ɑ̃:t] s. JUR. Declarant ; informant. ‖ Affirmant, avowant (en douane).

déclaratif, ive [-ratif, i:v] adj. JUR. Declarative.

déclaration [-rasjɔ̃] f. Declaration, statement (énonciation). ‖ Declaration, proclamation. ‖ Declaration (d'amour) ; *faire sa déclaration*, to propose, to declare oneself ; to pop the question (fam.). ‖ JUR. Registration (de décès, de naissance) ; *fausse déclaration*, wilful mis-statement. ‖ MILIT. Declaration (de guerre). ‖ COMM. *Déclaration d'entrée, de sortie en douane*, clearance inwards, outwards ; *déclaration d'expédition*, invoice. ‖ FIN. *Déclaration de revenus*, declaration of income, U. S. income tax return. ‖ NAUT. *Déclaration d'avaries*, protest.

déclaratoire [-ratwa:r] adj. JUR. Declaratory.

déclaré, ée [-re] adj. Declared (en général) ; avowed, professed, declared (ennemi) ; open (guerre) ; declared, open (intention). ‖ FIN. Certified (transfert).

déclarer [-re] v. tr. (1). To declare, to state, to assert (assurer) ; to declare, to disclose, to make known (faire savoir) ; to declare, to announce, to proclaim, to make public (proclamer) ; to declare, to profess (professer) ; *déclarer son amour*, to declare one's love. ‖ To declare (au jeu). ‖ JUR. To notify, to register (une naissance) ; *déclarer coupable*, to find guilty ; *déclarer à la douane*, to declare. ‖ FIN. *Déclarer ses revenus*, to send in one's return of income. ‖ NAUT. To manifest (une cargaison) ; to report (un navire). ‖ MILIT. To declare (à, upon) [la guerre].
— v. pr. Se déclarer, to declare one's love. ‖ To declare (ou) to profess oneself ; to declare (*contre*, against ; *pour*, for) ; *se déclarer l'auteur d'un crime*, to confess to (ou) to own up to a crime. ‖ To break out (incendie). ‖ MILIT. To break out (guerre). ‖ MÉD. To break out (épidémie) ; to declare itself (maladie).

déclassé, ée [deklɑse] adj. Déclassé, lowered in social status. ‖ FIN. Displaced (valeurs). ‖ NAUT. Obsolete (navire).
— s. Declassé.

déclassement [-smɑ̃] m. Coming down in the world, lowering of one's social status. ‖ NAUT. Striking off the list (d'un navire). ‖ CH. DE F. Change of class (des voyageurs).

déclasser [-se] v. tr. (1). To lower the social status of, to bring down in the world (qqn). ‖ NAUT. To disrate (un marin) ; to strike off the list (un navire). ‖ Ch. de f. To change the class of (un voyageur).

déclenche [deklɑ̃:ʃ] f. Techn. Release device. ‖ **Déclenche-marge**, m. Margin-release.

déclenchement [-ʃmɑ̃] m. Techn. Release. ‖ Milit. Launching (d'une attaque); opening (du tir). ‖ Fig. Setting into motion (des forces).

déclencher [-ʃe] v. tr. (1). Techn. To release, to disconnect; to unlatch. ‖ Milit. To deliver (ou) launch (une attaque); to open (le feu). ‖ Fin. To start (la hausse). ‖ Fig. To start, to set in motion, to launch (la grève).
— v. pr. **Se déclencher**, to be set off, to begin, to start. ‖ Techn. To become unlatched (porte).

déclencheur [-ʃœ:r] m. Techn. Release.

déclic [deklik] m. Pawl, trip, click, trigger.

déclin [deklɛ̃] m. Astron. Wane, waning (de la lune). ‖ Fall (de l'année); wane (de la beauté, de la gloire); decline, decay (des forces); decline, close (du jour, de la vie); falling-off (de la popularité, des recettes, du talent); *au déclin de la vie*, in one's declining years.

déclinable [deklinabl] adj. Gramm. Declinable.

déclinaison [-nɛzɔ̃] f. Gramm. Declension. ‖ Phys., Astron. Declination; *déclinaison magnétique*, magnetic variation.

déclinant, ante [-nɑ̃, nɑ̃:t] adj. Waning, failing, declining, deteriorating.

décliner [-ne] v. intr. (1). Astron. To decline (étoile); to wane (lune); to sink (soleil). ‖ Méd. To abate (fièvre); to be failing (santé). ‖ Fig. To fall off (beauté, gloire); to decline (crédit, influence); to decline, to decay, to fail (forces); to decline, to be on the wane (jour); to fail (mémoire).
— v. tr. To state (son nom). ‖ To decline, to refuse (une invitation); to decline (une responsabilité). ‖ Gramm. To decline. ‖ Jur. Not to acknowledge (la compétence du tribunal).

déclinomètre [-nɔmɛtr] m. Phys. Declinometer.

déclive [dekli:v] adj. Declivous, sloping.
— f. Slope; *en déclive*, sloping.

déclivité [-vite] f. Declivity, slope, gradient.

déclore [deklɔ:r] v. tr. (27). To open.

déclouer [deklue] v. tr. (1). To unnail (une caisse); to take down, to unhang (un tableau).

décocher [dekɔʃe] v. tr. (1). To deal (un coup de poing); to shoot, to let fly, to let off (une flèche); to let fly, to fling out (une ruade). ‖ Fig. To fire off (une épigramme); to fling (des insultes); to shoot (un regard); to dart (des sarcasmes); to flash (un sourire).

décoction [dekɔksjɔ̃] f. Decoction.

décodage [dekɔda:ʒ] m. Decoding, deciphering.

décoder [-de] v. tr. (1). To decode, to decipher.

décodeur [-dœ:r] m. Decoder, decipherer.

décoiffer [dekwafe] v. tr. (1). *Décoiffer qqn*, to undo (ou) ruffle s.o.'s hair (dépeigner); to remove s.o.'s headgear (ou) hat (enlever la coiffure); *un coup de vent l'a décoiffée*, the wind has blown her hat off. ‖ To uncork (une bouteille); to uncap (une fusée). ‖ Phys. To remove the cover-glass from (une préparation).
— v. pr. **Se décoiffer**, to disarrange one's hair (accidentellement); to take one's hair down (volontairement). ‖ To remove one's headgear (ou) hat (enlever son chapeau).

décoincement [dekwɛ̃smɑ̃] m. Unwedging, loosening, unjamming.

décoincer [dekwɛ̃se] v. tr. (6). To unwedge (décaler); to loosen (dégager).

décolérer [dekɔlere] v. intr. (5). Fam. To cool down; *il ne décolère pas*, he is always boiling over.

décollage [dekɔla:ʒ] m. Unsticking, ungluing. ‖ Aviat. Taking-off, take-off; U. S. hop-off (fam.).

décollation [dekɔlasjɔ̃] f. † Decollation.

décollé, ée [-le] adj. Unstuck (papier, timbre). ‖ Méd. Protruding (omoplate); projecting, standing out, sticking out (oreille).

décollement [-lmɑ̃] m. Unsticking, ungluing. ‖ Méd. Detachment (de la rétine).

décoller [-le] v. tr. (1). To unstick, to unglue (un objet collé); to loosen, to detach (des objets serrés); to disengage (des rouages); to space (un texte trop serré). ‖ Méd. To detach, to separate (des adhérences). ‖ Fam. To tear away (*de*, from).
— v. intr. Aviat. To take off. ‖ Sports. To drop behind. ‖ Fam. To clear out; *elle ne décolle pas*, she sticks like a leech. ‖ Pop. To go to (ou) to become skin and bones (maigrir).
— v. pr. **Se décoller**, to come unstuck (ou) unglued (objets collés); to come (ou) work loose (objets en contact); to disengage (objets engrenés). ‖ Sports. To draw ahead.

décolletage [dekɔlta:ʒ] m. Décolletage; décolleté; low-cut neck, plunging neckline (d'une robe). ‖ Agric. Cutting off the tops. ‖ Techn. Screw-cutting.

décolleté, ée [-te] adj. Court (escarpin); wearing a low dress, décolleté (femme); low-necked, low-cut, décolleté (robe); *décolletée dans le dos*, cut low in the back (robe).
— m. Neckline, décolleté, decolletage (de robe); *en grand décolleté*, in a low-cut evening dress. ‖ Bare neck and shoulders (épaules); *elle a un fort joli décolleté*, she has fine shoulders.

décolleter v. tr. (8 *b*). To cut out (ou) to slope out the neck of (une robe). ‖ Agric. To cut the tops of. ‖ Techn. To cut.
— v. pr. **Se décolleter**, to wear a low-necked dress.

décolonisation [dekɔlɔnizasjɔ̃] f. Decolonization.

décoloniser [-ze] v. tr. (1). To decolonize.

décolorant, ante [dekɔlɔrɑ̃, ɑ̃:t] adj. Decolourizing; bleaching; peroxiding.
— m. Chim. Bleaching agent; peroxide; decolourizer.

décoloration [-rasjɔ̃] f. Discolouration; decolourization. ‖ Bleaching, peroxiding (des cheveux); fading (d'une couleur, d'une étoffe).

décoloré, ée [-re] adj. Bleached (cheveux); washed-out (étoffe); colourless, pale; washed-out (fam.) [teint]; *elle est décolorée*, her hair is bleached.

décolorer v. tr. (1). To decolourize, to discolour. ‖ To bleach (les cheveux); to fade (étoffe, ton). ‖ Fig. To make colourless (style).
— v. pr. **Se décolorer**, to discolour, to lose one's colour; to fade (étoffe); to grow pale (teint); *se décolorer au lavage*, to wash out.

décombres [dekɔ̃:br] m. pl. Débris, wreckage, rubbish. (V. ruines.)

décommander [dekɔmɑ̃de] v. tr. (1). Comm. To countermand. ‖ Fig. To cancel (un dîner, un rendez-vous); *décommander les invités*, to cancel the invitations.

décompensation [dekɔ̃pɑ̃sasjɔ̃] f. Aviat. Decompression.

décomposable [dekɔ̃pozabl] adj. Decomposable.

décomposé, ée [-ze] adj. Decomposed, rotten. ‖ Bot. Decomposed, decomposite. ‖ Fig. Convulsed, distorted (visage).

décomposer v. tr. (1). To decompose, to rot (une substance). ‖ Chim. To decompose (l'air). ‖ Phys. To resolve (une force); to split (la lumière). ‖ Math. To split up (une fraction). ‖ Gramm. To split up (une phrase). ‖ Milit. *En décomposant*, by numbers. ‖ Fig. To convulse, to distort (les traits).
— v. pr. **Se décomposer**, to decompose, to rot (pourrir). ‖ Phys. To resolve (des forces). ‖ Gramm. To split up (phrase). ‖ Chim. To be

decomposed. ‖ Fig. To become distorted (traits).
décomposition [dekɔpozisjɔ̃] f. Decomposition, rotting (corruption). ‖ Phys. Resolution (des forces). ‖ Math. Factoring, factorizing (d'un nombre). ‖ Chim. Decomposition (d'un corps). ‖ Gramm. Construing (d'une phrase). ‖ Fig. Convulsion, discomposure (des traits).
décompresseur [dekɔprɛsœ:r] m. Techn. Relief-cock; exhaust-lifter. ‖ Autom. Decompressor.
décompression [-sjɔ̃] f. Decompression.
décomprimer [dekɔprime] v. tr. (1). To decompress. ‖ To depressurize.
décompte [dekɔ̃:t] m. Fin. Detailed account (compte); abatement, deduction (déduction).
décompter [-te] v. tr. (1). To work out, to reckon up, to calculate (calculer); to deduct (déduire).
déconcentrer [dekɔ̃sɑ̃tre] v. tr. (1). To decentralize (disperser). ‖ To distract (distraire).
— v. pr. **Se déconcentrer,** to lose one's concentration, to be distracted.
déconcertant, ante [dekɔ̃sɛrtɑ̃, ɑ̃:t] adj. Disconcerting, perplexing.
déconcerté, ée [-te] adj. Disconcerted, confounded, bewildered, taken aback.
déconcerter [dekɔ̃sɛrte] v. tr. (1). To disconcert, to embarrass, to abash; to shake (fam.).
— v. pr. **Se déconcerter,** to become disconcerted (ou) abashed.
déconfire [dekɔ̃fi:r] v. tr. (37). † To discomfit. ‖ Fig. To nonplus, to disconcert.
déconfit, ite [dekɔ̃fi, it]. adj. Crest-fallen, nonplussed.
déconfiture [-ty:r] f. † Discomfiture (défaite). ‖ Collapse, downfall (chute). ‖ Fin. Failure, insolvency; *être en déconfiture,* to have gone bankrupt.
décongélation [dekɔ̃ʒelasjɔ̃] f. Defrosting, unfreezing.
décongeler [-ʒle] v. tr. (8b). To defrost, to unfreeze (un surgelé).
décongestionner [dekɔ̃ʒɛstjone] v. tr. (1). Méd. To relieve congestion. ‖ Fig. To clear (une salle trop pleine).
déconnecter [dekɔnɛkte] v. tr. (1). Electr. To disconnect.
déconner [dekɔne] v. intr. (1). Argot. To shoot off one's mouth, to talk rot.
déconseiller [dekɔ̃sɛje] v. tr. (1). To advise (ou) to warn against (qqch.); *déconseiller qqch. à qqn,* to advise s.o. against sth.; to dissuade s.o. from sth.
déconsidération [dekɔ̃siderasjɔ̃] f. Discredit, disrepute.
déconsidérer [-re] v. tr. (5). To discredit, to slur, to run down (qqn).
— v. pr. **Se déconsidérer,** to fall into discredit, to belittle oneself.
déconsigner [dekɔ̃siɲe] v. tr. (1). To release from barracks (soldats). ‖ To withdraw from the left-luggage office (ou) U. S. checkroom (une valise). ‖ To refund the deposit on (une bouteille, un emballage).
décontenancé, ée [dekɔ̃tnɑ̃se] adj. Abashed, put out, out of countenance. (V. déconcerté.)
décontenancer [dekɔ̃tnɑ̃se] v. tr. (6). To put out of countenance, to abash, to disconcert.
— v. pr. **Se décontenancer,** to lose countenance.
décontracté, ée [dekɔ̃trakte] adj. Relaxed, cool, U. S. laid-back.
décontracter [dekɔ̃trakte] v. tr. To relax.
— v. pr. **Se décontracter,** to relax, to unwind.
décontraction [-sjɔ̃] f. Relaxation.
déconvenue [dekɔ̃vny] f. Disappointment, blighted hope, frustration (déception); mishap (désagrément); discomfiture (échec).
décor [dekɔr] m. Decoration (d'une maison). ‖ Scenery, scene, landscape (paysage). ‖ Théâtr.

Décor; scene, set; pl. settings, scenery; *changer un décor,* to shift a scene. ‖ Fam., Autom. *Rentrer dans le décor,* to run into a tree (ou) a wall.
décorateur, trice [dekɔratœ:r, tris] s. Arts. Decorator (d'appartements). ‖ Théâtr. Scene-painter, stage- (ou) set-designer.
décoratif ive [-tif, i:v] adj. Decorative, ornamental. ‖ Arts. Decorative (arts). ‖ Fig. Stately.
décoration ⌐-sjɔ̃] f. Arts. Decoration, ornamentation (de l'appartement). ‖ Decoration, medal, order, insignia; *remise de décorations,* investiture.
décoré, ée [dekɔre] adj. Decorated, ornamented (appartement, objet). ‖ Decorated, wearing an order (personne).
— s. Holder of a decoration.
décorer v. tr. (1). To decorate. (V. orner.) ‖ To decorate, to confer an order on (qqn). ‖ Fam. *Décorer qqch. du titre de,* to dignify sth. with the name of.
décorner [dekɔrne] v. tr. (1). To dehorn (bétail); *un vent à décorner les bœufs,* a howling wind. ‖ To smooth out (ou) remove the dog-ears from (page, livre).
décorticage [dekɔrtika:ʒ] m. Decortication (en général); peeling (des amandes, des noisettes); scraping, barking (des arbres); hulling (de l'avoine); husking (du maïs, de l'orge, du riz); shelling (des noix, des petits pois).
décortiquer [-ke] v. tr. (1). To decorticate (en général); to peel (des amandes, des noisettes); to disbark (des arbres); to hull (de l'avoine); to husk (du maïs, de l'orge, du riz); to shell (des noix, des petits pois).
décorum [dekɔrɔm] m. Decorum; decency; *conserver le décorum,* to observe the proprieties.
décote [dekɔt] f. Rebate.
découcher [dekuʃe] v. intr. (1). Fam. To sleep out; to stay out all night.
découdre [dekudr] v. tr. (31). To unsew, to rip up (une couture); to unstitch (un vêtement). ‖ To tusk; to gore (un animal, qqn). ‖ Fig. *En découdre,* to fight it out.
— v. pr. **Se découdre,** to come unstitched (ou) unsewn.
découler [dekule] v. intr. (1). To flow, to stream (couler); to trickle (dégoutter). ‖ Fig. To spring,. to flow, to proceed, to arise, to derive (de, from) [résulter]; *les maux qui découlent de la guerre,* the evils that follow in the train of war.
découpage [dekupa:ʒ] m. Punching (du cuir); cutting up (d'un gâteau, du papier); cutting out (d'un patron); carving (de la viande). ‖ Théâtr. Continuity, cutting (au cinéma).
découpe [dekup] f. Scallop (en couture).
découper [-pe] v. tr. (1). To punch out (du cuir, du métal); to cut up (un gâteau, du papier); to cut out (des images, un patron); to carve (de la viande); to carve, to cut up (une volaille). ‖ To cut (*dans,* out of); *découper en dentelant, en tranches,* to indent, to slice up. ‖ To outline, to stand out (profiler).
— v. pr. **Se découper,** to cut out (papier); to carve (viande, volaille). ‖ To be outlined, to stand out (*sur,* against).
découpeur [-pœ:r] m. Culin. Carver. ‖ Techn. Puncher.
découpeuse [-pøz] f. Techn. Cutting-machine.
découplé, ée [dekuple] adj. Well set up, strongly built, strapping (personne).
découpler v. tr. (1). To uncouple.
découpoir [dekupwa:r] m. Pinking-iron (pour tissu). ‖ Techn. Cutter.
découpure [-py:r] f. Fret-work (de bois); punching (de cuir); cutting out, scrap (de papier). ‖ Géogr. Indentation (de la côte). ‖ Bot. Denticulation (d'une feuille).

décourageant, ante [dekuraʒɑ̃, ɑ̃:t] adj. Discouraging, disheartening.

découragé, ée [-ʒe] adj. Discouraged, disheartened, downhearted; dejected.

découragement [-ʒmɑ̃] m. Discouragement, dejection, despondency, lowness of spirits, depression. (V. DÉMORALISATION.)

décourager [-ʒe] v. tr. (7). To discourage, to dishearten, to depress, to dispirit, to lower (déprimer). ‖ To discourage, to dissuade (dissuader) [*de*, from].
— v. pr. **Se décourager**, to become discouraged, to lose heart; *ne pas se décourager*, to keep up one's spirits, to keep one's chin up.

découronner [dekurɔne] v. tr. To uncrown, to discrown (un roi). ‖ AGRIC. To pollard (un arbre). ‖ FAM. To debunk (qqn).

décours [dekur] m. ASTRON. Waning, wane (de la lune). ‖ MÉD. Decline (d'une maladie).

décousu, ue [dekuzy] adj. Unsewn, unstitched (couture). ‖ FIG. Incoherent (idées, termes); loose (idées, style); desultory, snatchy (lecture); disconnected, scrappy (propos); desultory, rambling (remarques); unmethodical (travail); *travailler d'une façon décousue*, to work in snatches.
— m. Desultoriness (de la conversation, des lectures); looseness (des idées, du style).

découvert, erte [dekuvɛ:r, ɛ:rt] adj. Uncovered (en général). ‖ Uncovered, bareheaded (tête nue). ‖ Open; unshaded (terrain). ‖ AUTOM. Open (virage, voiture). ‖ MILIT. Open (pays); unsupported (troupes); exposed, unprotected (ville). ‖ NAUT. Undecked (bateau). ‖ FIN. Overdrawn (compte). ‖ LOC. *A visage découvert*, openly, overtly.
— m. Open space (lieu). ‖ FIN. Uncovered margin (dans une assurance); overdraft (en banque); bears, shorts (en Bourse); deficit, shortage (dans le budget).
— loc. adv. **A découvert**, uncovered (sens général); bare (cou, épaules); openly, overtly (ouvertement); in open view (visiblement). ‖ MILIT. Unprotected, exposed, open; *se battre à découvert*, to fight unprotected by trenches. ‖ FIN. Uncovered, unsecured, unprovided; *crédit à découvert*, open credit; *être à découvert*, to be caught short; *vendre à découvert*, to bear the market, to sell short.

découverte [-vɛrt] f. Discovery, detection (d'un crime, d'un complot, d'un secret); discovery (d'un pays). ‖ Discovery, invention. ‖ MILIT. Reconnaissance.
— loc. adv. **A la découverte**, discovering, prospecting; *aller à la découverte*, to go prospecting, to explore. ‖ MILIT. *Marcher à la découverte*, to reconnoitre, to scout.

découvreur [-vrœ:r] m. Discoverer.

découvrir [-vri:r] v. tr. (72). To uncover; to take the lid off (une casserole); to uncover, to lay bare (le corps); to unveil (une statue); to bare (sa tête). ‖ To discover (une invention, un pays); to find (un trésor). ‖ To expose, to lay down (son jeu, aux cartes). ‖ To discern, to perceive, to have a glimpse of (apercevoir). ‖ ARCHIT. To unroof, to untile (une maison). ‖ MILIT. To expose (ses arrières). ‖ NAUT. To sight (la terre). ‖ JUR. To bring to light (un crime); to detect (un criminel, une fraude); *difficile à découvrir*, difficult of detection; *découvrir par son flair, en fouillant, en repérant, en suivant une piste*, to smell (ou) nose out, to rummage out, to pick out, to track down. ‖ MÉD. To discover (la cause); to diagnose (le mal); to locate (le siège). ‖ FIG. To discover (une cause); to discover, to find out (un complot); to detect (une erreur); to unmask (un imposteur); to discern (un mobile); to find out (un moyen, un secret); to penetrate, to disclose

(un secret); to ferret out, to sift out (la vérité); *découvrir par la ruse les secrets de qqn*, to fish secrets out of s.o. ‖ LOC. *Découvrir saint Pierre pour couvrir saint Paul*, to rob Peter to pay Paul.
— v. pr. **Se découvrir**, to uncover, to remove one's headgear, to bare one's head, to take off one's hat (enlever son chapeau); to take off one's warm clothing (enlever ses vêtements); to throw off one's bed-clothes (rejeter ses couvertures). ‖ To become visible, to come into sight (se discerner). ‖ To clear up (ciel, temps). ‖ SPORTS. To lower one's guard (à l'escrime). ‖ FIG. To come out, to come to light (crime, secret, vérité); *le secret est découvert*, the secret is out.

décrassage [dekrasa:ʒ] m. Scouring (d'une casserole, d'un fossé, du plancher); cleaning (du linge); cleansing (de la peau). ‖ TECHN. Scaling, cleaning (d'une chaudière); scraping (d'un métal); decarbonizing (d'un moteur). ‖ FIG. Polishing-up (d'un balourd).

décrasser [-se] v. tr. (1). To scour (une casserole, un fossé, le plancher); to clean (le linge); to cleanse (la peau). ‖ TECHN. To scale, to clean (une chaudière); to scrape (du métal); to decarbonize (un moteur). ‖ FIG. To polish up (un balourd). [V. DÉGROSSIR.]
— v. pr. **Se décrasser**, to clean oneself. ‖ FIG. To take on polish.

décrément [dekremɑ̃] m. MATH. Decrement.

décrépi, ie [dekrepi] adj. Unplastered (non crépi); peeling (perdant son crépi).

décrépir [-pi:r] v. tr. (2). To take the rough-cast off (un mur).
— v. pr. **Se décrépir**, to peel (mur). ‖ FIG. To become decrepit; to grow old and worn out.

décrépit, ite [-pi, it] adj. Decrepit, broken down, old and worn out. (V. DÉCATI.)

décrépitude [-pityd] f. Dilapidation (d'un bâtiment); decrepitude (d'une personne); *tomber en décrépitude*, to fall into decay. ‖ FIG. Decrepitude.

decrescendo [dekreʃɛndo] adv., m. inv. Decrescendo. ‖ FIG. *Aller decrescendo*, to be on the wane.

décret [dekrɛ] m. Enactment (général); decree (spécial), U. S. executive order; *décret ministériel*, ordinance. ‖ JUR. Writ, warrant. ‖ *Décret-loi*, m. Order-in-Council, U. S. executive order.

décrétale [dekretal] f. ECCLÉS., JUR. Decretal.

décréter [-te] v. tr. (5) To decree, to enact, to ordain. ‖ JUR. To issue a writ against.

décrier [dekrije] v. tr. (1). COMM., FIN. To decry (une marchandise, une monnaie). ‖ FIG. To decry, to disparage, to run down (v. DISCRÉDITER); *décrier sa famille*, to defile one's own nest.

décrire [dekri:r] v. tr. (44). To describe (v. DÉPEINDRE); *on ne saurait le décrire*, it is indescribable, it beggars all description. ‖ To trace; *décrire une courbe autour*, to curve (ou) to sweep around; *décrire un demi-cercle*, to sweep in a semicircle. ‖ MATH. To describe, to trace.

décrochage [dekrɔʃa:ʒ] m. Unhooking (d'une agrafe, d'un manteau); unhanging (d'un tableau); taking down (du téléphone). ‖ CH. DE F. Uncoupling (d'un wagon). ‖ MILIT. Disengagement; *effectuer un décrochage*, to disengage one's troops.

décrocher [-ʃe] v. tr. (1). To unhook (une agrafe, un manteau); to unsling (un hamac); to unhang (un tableau); to take down (le téléphone). ‖ CH. DE F. To uncouple (un wagon). ‖ NAUT. To unsling (un hamac). ‖ FAM. To pull down (une augmentation); *décrocher des galons*, to get stripes; *décrocher le gros lot*, to win the first prize; *décrocher une bonne place*, to land a cushy job. ‖ **Décrochez-moi-ça**, m. invar. Reach-me-downs; U. S. hand-me-downs.
— v. intr. MILIT. To lose touch. ‖ AVIAT. To stall. ‖ FAM. To lift the receiver (au téléphone).

— v. pr. **Se décrocher,** to come unhooked (agrafe). ‖ MILIT. To disengage one's troops; to detach oneself from the enemy. ‖ MÉD. To come out of joint (mâchoire); *se décrocher la mâchoire,* to dislocate one's jaw.

décroiser [dekrwaze] v. tr. (1). To uncross.

décroissance [dekrwasɑ̃:s] f. ASTRON. Wane, waning (de la lune). ‖ MÉD. Abatement (de la fièvre). ‖ Decrease, diminution (en général); falling off, slackening (de la vitesse); *être en décroissance,* to be decreasing.

décroissant, ante [-sɑ̃, ɑ̃:t] adj. Decreasing, diminishing (en général); slackening (vitesse). ‖ MATH. Descending.

décroît [dekrwa] m. ASTRON. Wane, waning.

décroître [dekrwa:tr] v. intr. (34). To decrease, to diminish (en général); to grow fainter, to fade away (bruit); to abate, to subside (colère); to subside (crue); to fail, to decline (forces); to shorten, to grow shorter (jour). ‖ FIN. To fall, to go down (prix). ‖ ASTRON. To wane (lune). ‖ MÉD. To abate, to subside (fièvre).

décrottage [dekrɔta:ʒ] m. Cleaning.

décrotter [-te] v. tr. (1). To clean (les chaussures). ‖ FAM. To polish up (un lourdaud).

décrotteur [-tœ:r] m. Shoe-black; shoe-shine boy. ‖ Boots (dans un hôtel).

décrotteuse [-tø:z] f. Shoe-brush (brosse).

décrottoir [-twa:r] m. Door-scraper, shoe-scraper (gratte-pieds); wire-mat (paillasson métallique). ‖ TECHN. Mud-scraper.

décrue [dekry] f. Subsidence, fall (des eaux).

décryptage [dekripta:ʒ], **décryptement** [-ptəmɑ̃] m. Deciphering.

décrypter [dekripte] v. tr. (1). To decipher, to decryptograph.

déçu, ue [desy] adj. Disappointed.

décubitus [dekybitys] m. MÉD. Decubitus (attitude); bed-sore (plaie).

déculotter [dekylɔte] v. tr. (1). To take off the breeches (ou) trousers of; to unbreech.
— v. pr. **Se déculotter,** to take off (ou) to let down one's breeches (ou) trousers. ‖ POP. To grass (vendre la mèche); to grovel (s'humilier); to lose one's nerve (perdre son aplomb).

décuple [dekypl] adj., m. Tenfold.

décuplement [dekypləmɑ̃] m. Decupling, tenfold increase.

décupler [dekyple] v. tr. (1). To decuple; to increase (ou) multiply tenfold; *décupler les forces de qqn,* to give s.o. the strength of ten.
— v. pr. **Se décupler,** to increase tenfold.

décuver [dekyve] v. tr. (1). To rack off (le vin).

dédaignable [dedɛɲabl] adj. Despicable (méprisable). ‖ Paltry (offre); trifling; *non dédaignable,* not to be sneezed at.

dédaigner [-ɲe] v. tr. (1). To disdain, to slight, to disregard (faire peu de cas de); to sniff at, to sneeze at, to turn one's nose up at; to pooh-pooh (fam.). ‖ To despise, to scorn. (V. MÉPRISER.) ‖ Not to deign, not to condescend (ne pas daigner).

dédaigneusement [-ɲøzmɑ̃] adv. Disdainfully; contemptuously, scornfully.

dédaigneux, euse [-ɲø, ø:z] adj. Disdainful; contemptuous, scornful (de, of); sniffy (fam.). ‖ Haughty, supercilious, lordly, arrogant (hautain); *la lèvre dédaigneuse,* with a curl of the lip.

dédain [dedɛ̃] m. Disdain, scorn (de, of); disregard, contempt (pour, for).

dédale [dedal] m. Labyrinth, maze. ‖ FIG. Intricacy.

dedans [dədɑ̃] adv. Inside; in it, in them; within; *entrer dedans,* to go inside; *prenez cette boîte, il n'y a rien dedans,* take this box, there is nothing in it. ‖ FAM. *Mettre dedans,* to put in quod (emprisonner); to bamboozle, to do, to humbug (trom-

per); *mettre les pieds dedans,* to put one's foot in it.
— loc. adv. **Au-dedans,** inside, within; *au-dedans et au-dehors,* inside and out; within and without. ‖ **De dedans,** from the inside; *de dedans une voix m'appela,* a voice within called to me. ‖ **En dedans,** on the inside; inside; *en dedans de la maison,* within the house; *la fourrure en dedans,* with the fur inside; *marcher en dedans,* to turn one's toes in; *trembler en dedans,* to shake within oneself. ‖ **Par-dedans,** inside; through the inside.
— m. Inside, interior (intérieur); home (pays). ‖ SPORTS. Inside edge (au patinage).

dédicace [dedikas] f. ECCLÉS. Dedication, consecration. ‖ Dedication (d'un livre).

dédicacer [-se] v. tr. (6). To dedicate, to autograph.

dédicatoire [-twa:r] adj. Dedicatory.

dédier [dedje] v. tr. (1). To inscribe, to dedicate (un livre). ‖ ECCLÉS. To dedicate, to consecrate. ‖ FIG. To dedicate, to devote.

dédire [dedi:r] v. tr. (63). To gainsay; to disown.
— v. pr. **Se dédire,** to withdraw, to retract, to unsay; to cancel, to take back; *se dédire de ce qu'on a dit,* to unsay (ou) to retract what one has said; *se dédire de sa promesse,* to go back on one's word; to back out (ou) down (fam.).

dédit [dedi] m. Disavowal (désaveu); retractation, withdrawal, renunciation (rétractation); retraction (retrait); breaking (rupture). ‖ COMM. Forfeit, penalty (somme à payer).

dédommagement [dedɔmaʒmɑ̃] m. Compensation, indemnification (indemnisation); indemnity, damages (indemnité).

dédommager [-ʒe] v. tr. (7). To compensate, to indemnify, to make up (de, for); *dédommager qqn de sa peine,* to repay s.o. for his trouble; to make it up to s.o. (fam.); *dédommager qqn d'une perte,* to make good a loss to s.o.
— v. pr. **Se dédommager,** to recoup oneself (de, for).

dédorer [dedɔre] v. tr. (1). To remove the gilt from.
— v. pr. **Se dédorer,** to tarnish, to lose its gilt.

dédouanage [dedwana:ʒ] m. Clearance, clearing.

dédouaner [-ne] v. tr. (1). To clear through the Customs.
— v. pr. **Se dédouaner,** FAM. To get out of a jam.

dédoublage [dedubla:ʒ] m. Unlining (d'un vêtement). ‖ CHIM. Dilution (de l'alcool).

dédoublement [-bləmɑ̃] m. Undoubling (d'une étoffe repliée). ‖ Dividing (ou) splitting (ou) division in two (partage). ‖ CHIM. Double decomposition. ‖ PHYS. Duplication (d'une image). ‖ CH. DE F. Running in two parts (d'un train). ‖ MÉD., PHILOS. *Dédoublement de la personnalité,* dual (ou) split personality.

dédoubler [-ble] v. tr. (1). To undouble, to unfold (une étoffe pliée). ‖ To cut (ou) to split (ou) to divide into two (séparer en deux). ‖ To unline (un vêtement). ‖ CHIM. To dilute (l'alcool); to split up (un corps); to decompose (une substance). ‖ PHYS. To duplicate (une image). ‖ CH. DE F. To run in two parts (un train). ‖ NAUT. To unsheathe (un navire).
— v. pr. **Se dédoubler,** to unfold (se déplier); to split (ou) divide into two (se partager).

dédramatiser [dedramatize] v. tr. (1). To defuse, to take the heat out of; *dédramatiser une situation,* to pour oil on troubled waters.

déductible [dedyktibl] adj. Deductible.

déductif, ive [dedyktif, i:v] adj. PHILOS. Deductive.

déduction [-sjɔ̃] f. PHILOS. Deduction, inference.

‖ Comm. Deduction; abatement; allowance; *déduction faite de,* after deduction of, after allowing for; *entrer en déduction de,* to be deducted from; *sous déduction de,* less, minus. ‖ Jur. *Déductions pour charges de famille,* personal allowances.

déduire [dedɥiːr] v. tr. (85). Philos. To deduce, to infer, to gather (des conséquences, un résultat) [*de,* from]. ‖ Comm., Math. To deduct, to abate, to allow, to take off (une somme); *frais déduits,* after allowing for charges (ou) costs.

déesse [deɛs] f. Goddess.

de facto [defakto] adv. Jur. De facto.

défaillance [defajãːs] f. Failure, breakdown (des forces); *moment de défaillance,* weak moment. ‖ Méd. Faint, swoon (évanouissement); *être pris de défaillance,* to feel faint. ‖ Fin. Sagging (du marché, de la monnaie). ‖ Electr. Power (ou) current failure. ‖ Jur. Default, non-appearance (d'un témoin). ‖ Fig. Failing, weakness (de l'énergie); lapse (de la mémoire); shortcomings (points faibles); *sans défaillance,* without flinching.

défaillant, ante [-jã, ãːt] adj. Sinking (cœur); fainting (courage, voix); feeble (main); failing (mémoire, santé, vue); faltering (pas); faint (personne) [*de,* with]. ‖ Fin. Sagging (marché, prix). ‖ Jur. Defaulting (partie).
— m. Jur. Defaulting party; defaulter.

défaillir [-jiːr] v. intr. (38). To become feeble, to weaken, to lose strength (s'affaiblir); to fail, to flag (forces). ‖ To fail, to flinch (faillir); to sink, to falter, to give way (courage). ‖ Méd. To faint, to faint away, to swoon (s'évanouir); to feel faint (cœur, personne) [*de,* with]. ‖ Jur. To fail to appear.

défaire [defɛːr] v. tr. (50). To undo (une agrafe, un bouton, ses cheveux, son corset, un paquet, sa robe, ses souliers, un tricot); to unfasten, to unhook (une agrafe); to unlace (son corset, ses souliers); to unstitch, to rip up (une couture); to untie (une ficelle, un nœud, un paquet, des souliers); to strip (le lit); to unpack (une malle); to unwrap (un paquet); to unknit, to ravel (un tricot). ‖ To break off (un mariage); to upset, to undo (des plans); to cancel, to annul (un traité). ‖ To defeat, to overcome (un adversaire); to defeat, to rout, to overthrow (une armée). ‖ To distort (le visage). ‖ To free, to rid (libérer); *défaire qqn de,* to cure s.o. of (une habitude); to rid s.o. of (qqch.).
— v. pr. Se **défaire,** to come undone (sens général); to unhook (agrafe); to come down (cheveux); to come unlaced (corset, souliers); to come unsewn (couture); to come untied (ficelle, nœud, souliers); to come to pieces (paquet); to come unhooked (robe). ‖ To become discomposed (ou) wasted (traits, visage). ‖ To undo one's clothes (se déshabiller). ‖ *Se défaire de,* to get rid of (se débarrasser de); to part with (se séparer de); to sell off (vendre); *se défaire d'une habitude,* to break off a habit.

défait, e [defɛ, ɛːt] adj. Unhooked (agrafe); unsewn, unstitched (couture); loose (nœud); unwrapped (paquet); *les cheveux défaits,* dishevelled. ‖ Discomposed, wasted (traits); drawn (visage). ‖ Milit. Defeated (armée).

défaite [defɛt] f. Milit. Defeat; *essuyer une défaite,* to suffer a defeat. ‖ Fig. Failure (échec). ‖ Fam. Evasion, pretence, shift, specious excuse; *trouver une défaite,* to find a way out.

défaitisme [-tism] m. Defeatism.

défaitiste [-tist] m. Defeatist.

défalcation [defalkasjɔ̃] f. Deduction; *avec défalcation de tous frais,* all expenses deducted.

défalquer [-ke] v. tr. (1). To deduct, to write off.

défatiguer [defatige] v. tr. (1). To refresh.

défausser [defose] v. tr. (1). To straighten, to true.
— v. pr. Se **défausser,** to discard (aux cartes); to get rid (de, of).

défaut [defo] m. Lack, want; failure (manque); *défaut d'attention, d'équilibre,* inattention, unbalance; *défaut de jugement,* lack of judgment; *à défaut de,* in default of, for want of, in the absence of; *faire défaut,* to be wanting (ou) lacking, to fail. ‖ Defect (défectuosité); deficiency (déficience); blemish (imperfection); insufficiency (insuffisance); shortcoming (point faible); *défaut de construction,* constructional defect; *défaut de la cuirasse,* joint in the harness, heel of Achilles, vulnerable point; *défaut de prononciation,* defect in pronunciation; *mémoire en défaut,* memory at fault. ‖ Failing (faiblesse); fault (faute, travers); *la colère est mon défaut,* quick temper is a failing of mine; *mettre la sagacité de qqn en défaut,* to outwit s.o.; *prendre qqn en défaut,* to catch s.o. at fault; *sans défaut,* faultless. ‖ Comm. *Défaut de paiement,* failure to pay. ‖ Fin. *Défaut de provision,* no funds. ‖ Jur. Default, non-appearance; *faire défaut,* to default, to fail to appear. ‖ Méd. *Défaut de l'épaule,* shoulder joint. ‖ Techn. Flaw (dans le bois, le diamant, le métal); *plein de défauts,* flawy; *sans défaut,* flawless. ‖ Sports. En *défaut,* off the scent (chiens de chasse).

défaveur [defavœːr] f. Disfavour (*auprès de,* with).

défavorable [defavɔrabl] adj. Unfavourable; contrary (v. hostile); disadvantageous (peu avantageux); unencouraging (peu encourageant); unpropitious (peu propice); *se montrer défavorable à un projet,* to discountenance a project. ‖ Fin. *Balance défavorable,* adverse trade balance.

défavorablement [-rabləmã] adv. Unfavourably.

défavoriser [-rize] v. tr. (1). To be unfair to; to disadvantage.

défécation [defekasjɔ̃] f. Méd. Defecation.

défectible [defɛktibl] adj. Fallible. ‖ Fin. Wasting.

défectif, ive [-tif, iːv] adj. Gramm. Defective. ‖ Math. Deficient (hyperbole).

défection [-sjɔ̃] f. Defection (*de,* from); desertion (*à,* of); falling away (*à,* from); *faire défection,* to fall away. ‖ Default (défaillance). ‖ Pl. Absentees (personnes).

défectivité [defɛktivite] f. Gramm. Defectiveness.

défectueusement [-tɥøzmã] adv. Defectively.

défectueux, euse [-tɥø, øːz] adj. Defective, incomplete (incomplet); defective, imperfect, faulty (imparfait); inadequate (inadéquat); unsatisfactory (peu satisfaisant).

défectuosité [-tɥozite] f. Defectiveness, faultiness (imperfection). ‖ Defect, flaw (défaut).

défendable [defãdabl] adj. Justifiable (cause, opinion); defensible (position). ‖ Milit. Tenable, defensible (forteresse).

défendant, ante [-dã, ãːt] adj. *A mon corps défendant,* in self-defence (en état de légitime défense); reluctantly, unwillingly (involontairement); under coercion (ou) compulsion, over my dead body (sous contrainte).

défendeur, eresse [-dœːr, ərɛs] s. Jur. Defendant (en général); respondent (en cas de divorce).

défendre [defãːdr] v. tr. (4). To defend (sens général) [*contre,* against]. ‖ To screen, to defend, to keep off (abriter) [*de,* from]. ‖ To vindicate, to assert, to stand on (faire valoir) [ses droits]. ‖ To hold, to maintain (maintenir); *défendre son opinion,* to stand by one's opinion. ‖ To defend, to advocate, to support, to champion, to vindicate, to stand by, to stand up for (prendre le parti de, soutenir). ‖ To defend, to shield; to protect (protéger) [*contre,* from]. ‖ To forbid,

to interdict, to prohibit (interdire); *défendre qqch. à qqn*, to forbid s.o. sth.; *défendre à qqn de faire qqch.*, to forbid s.o. to do sth.; *défendre sa porte à qqn*, to forbid s.o. the house, to refuse admittance to s.o.; *on lui défend de fumer*, he is forbidden (ou) not allowed to smoke, he is prohibited from smoking; *on lui défend le sucre*, he is forbidden to eat sugar. ‖ JUR. To defend (un accusé); to defend, to maintain, to uphold (une cause). ‖ MILIT. To defend; to hold (une forteresse).
— v. pr. **Se défendre**, to defend oneself (sens général) [*contre*, from, against]; *ne pas se défendre*, to make no defence. ‖ To stand up for oneself, to fight one's own battle, to stand fast, to hold one's own (résister); *il s'est bien défendu*, he held (ou) stood his ground well (il a été ferme dans la discussion); he stood up to it (il a tenu bon); *elle se défend bien*, she wears her age well (elle ne porte pas son âge). ‖ To protect oneself, to shield oneself (se protéger) [*de*, from]. ‖ To deny, to protest (nier, protester); *il se défend d'être jaloux*, he denies being jealous, he does not admit that he is jealous; *il ne se défend pas d'avoir menti*, he owns he was lying; *se défendre d'avoir pris part à*, to disclaim any participation in. ‖ To deny oneself (ne pas se permettre); *se défendre de fumer*, to cut out smoking. ‖ To refrain (*de*, from); to keep from, to help (s'empêcher); *il ne peut se défendre de fumer*, he can't keep from smoking; *elle ne pouvait se défendre de rire*, she couldn't help laughing.

défenestration [defənɛstrasjɔ̃] f. Defenestration.
défenestrer [-tre] v. tr. (1). To defenestrate.
défense [defɑ̃:s] f. Defence, U. S. defense (sens général); protection; *prendre la défense de qqn*, to stand up for s.o.; *sans défense*, defenceless. ‖ Prohibition, interdiction; *défense d'afficher*, stick (ou) U. S. post no bills; *défense de fumer, de traverser*, no smoking, no thoroughfare. ‖ MILIT. Defence; pl. defences, fortifications, defensive works; *sans défense*, unprotected, undefended. ‖ NAUT. Fender (de coque); *eaux intéressant la défense des Etats-Unis*, United States defence (ou) defensive waters. ‖ JUR. Defence, plea; *assurer la défense de qqn*, to conduct s.o.'s case; *cas de légitime défense*, case of legitimate self-defence (ou) of self-preservation; *cité par la défense*, called by the defendant; *pour sa défense*, in (ou) for his own defence. ‖ ZOOL. Tusk (d'éléphant). ‖ FAM. *Avoir de la défense*, to know how to stand up for oneself.
défenseur [defɑ̃sœ:r] m. Champion, supporter (d'une cause, de qqn). ‖ MILIT. Defender. ‖ JUR. Counsel for the defence (avocat); protector (de l'enfance).
défensif, ive [-sif, i:v] adj. MILIT. Defensive; *ouvrages défensifs*, defences, U. S. defenses.
défensive [-si:v] f. Defensive; *se mettre sur la défensive*, to assume the defensive. ‖ MILIT. *Défensive stratégique*, offensive-defensive.
défensivement [-sivmɑ̃] adv. Defensively.
déféquer [defeke] v. intr. (5). To defecate.
déférence [deferɑ̃:s] f. Deference, consideration, regard, respect (*pour*, for); *avec déférence*, deferentially, respectfully; *par déférence pour*, out of (ou) in deference to, out of regard for.
déférent, ente [-rɑ̃, ɑ̃:t] adj. Deferential.
déférent, ente adj. MÉD., ASTR. Deferent.
déférer [-re] v. intr. (5). To defer, to accede (*à*, to); *déférer à*, to defer to (une opinion); to accede to (une requête).
— v. tr. JUR. To refer, to remove, to submit (une cause); to hand over to justice (un coupable); to administer (le serment).
déferlement [defɛrləmɑ̃] m. NAUT. Breaking

(des vagues); unfurling (des voiles). ‖ FIG. Outpouring.
déferler [-le] v. intr. (1). To break (vague).
— v. tr. NAUT. To unfurl (les voiles).
déferré [defɛre] adj. Unshod (cheval).
déferrer v. tr. (1). To unshoe (un cheval); to take the tags off (un lacet). ‖ NAUT. *Déferrer un navire*, to slip the anchor. ‖ FAM. To flummox, to put out (qqn).
— v. pr. **Se déferrer**, to cast (ou) U. S. to lose a shoe (cheval); to lose its tag (lacet). ‖ FAM. To get flummoxed, to be put out.
défet [defɛ] m. Odd (ou) waste leaf (de livre).
défeuillaison [defœjɛzɔ̃] f. Defoliation.
défeuiller [-je] v. tr. (1). To strip the leaves off (un arbre); to defoliate (un arbuste).
— v. pr. **Se défeuiller**, to lose its leaves.
défi [defi] m. Challenge (provocation); *lancer un défi à*, to challenge; *relever un défi*, to take up a challenge. ‖ Defiance (bravade); *d'un air de défi*, defiantly; *mettre au défi de*, to defy (ou) to dare to.
défiance [defjɑ̃:s] f. Distrust, mistrust, suspicion; *avec défiance*, distrustfully, suspiciously, diffidently; *défiance de soi-même*, diffidence, lack of self-confidence, self-distrust; *sans défiance*, unsuspectingly, trustingly.
défiant, ante [defjɑ̃, ɑ̃:t] adj. Distrustful, suspicious; *défiant à l'égard de soi-même*, self-distrustful, diffident. ‖ Wary, cautious (circonspect).
déficeler [defisle] v. tr. (8 a). To untie, to take the string off (un paquet).
— v. pr. **Se déficeler**, to come untied.
déficience [defisjɑ̃:s] f. Deficiency.
déficient, ente [defisjɑ̃, ɑ̃:t] adj. Deficient.
— s. MÉD. Deficient, mental defective.
déficit [defisit] m. FIN. Deficit; *déficit de caisse*, cash short; *être en déficit*, to show a deficit. ‖ COMM. Shortage (de poids).
déficitaire [-tɛ:r] adj. FIN. Showing a deficit. ‖ AGRIC. Lean (année); short (récolte).
défier [defje] v. tr. (1). To challenge, to defy, to bid defiance to (provoquer). ‖ To defy, to brave, to face, to set at defiance, to be defiant to (v. BRAVER); *défier du regard*, to look defiantly at. ‖ To defy, to dare (mettre au défi). ‖ NAUT. To bear off (la terre).
— v. intr. NAUT. To dodge; *défier de la lame*, to dodge a sea; *défiez du vent*, don't let her shake.
— v. pr. **Se défier**, to be on one's guard. ‖ *Se défier de*, to distrust, to mistrust, not to believe in; *se défier de soi-même*, to be diffident.
défiger [defiʒe] v. tr. (7). To melt, to thaw. ‖ FIG. To put some life into (qqn).
défigurer [defigyre] v. tr. (1). To disfigure (qqch., qqn); to deface (qqch.). ‖ FIG. To distort (la vérité).
défilade [defilad] f. FAM. Procession, succession.
défilé [-le] m. Procession; parade; *défilé par deux*, crocodile (de pensionnaires). ‖ MILIT. March past. ‖ AVIAT. *Défilé aérien*, fly-past. ‖ AUTOM. *Défilé automobile*, rally; U. S. motorcade. ‖ GÉOGR. Defile, gorge, mountain pass.
défilement [-lmɑ̃] m. MILIT. Defilade. ‖ RADIO. Movement (en télévision).
défiler [-le] v. tr. (1). To unthread (une aiguille); to unstring (un collier).
— v. intr. To walk in procession. ‖ MILIT. To march past (en parade); to defile, to fire off (en rangs); *défiler devant le roi*, to march past the King.
— v. pr. **Se défiler**, to come unthreaded (aiguille); to come unstrung (collier). ‖ FAM. To shirk, to dodge the column, U. S. to goldbrick (esquiver le travail); to clear out, to make off, to slip

away (filer); *se défiler par des circonlocutions,* to put up a smoke-screen of words.

défini [defini] adj. Definite, precise, determined, settled (but); formed, well-established (conviction); definite, determined (idée); definite, clearly defined (raison). ‖ GRAMM. Definite (article); *passé défini,* preterite, past definite (ou) historic, literary past.

définir [-niːr] v. tr. (2). To define (un mot). ‖ To determine, to fix (des conditions); to describe, to portray (qqn).
— v. pr. Se **définir,** to become clear.

définissable [-nisabl] adj. Definable.

définitif, ive [-nitif, iːv] adj. Conclusive (argument); final (choix); ultimate (destination); standard (édition, œuvre); permanent (fonction, installation); final (réponse, résultat); definitive (réponse, résolution); decisive (preuve); *à titre définitif,* permanently.

définition [-nisjɔ̃] f. Definition (en général); clue (de mots croisés). ‖ RADIO. *Définition d'une image,* definition.

définitive [-nitiːv] f. *En définitive,* finally, in short, in a word, after all.

définitivement [-nitivmɑ̃] adv. Definitively, finally; for good and all. ‖ Definitely (avec précision).

déflagrant, ante [deflagrɑ̃, ɑ̃ːt] adj. Deflagrable.

déflagrateur [-gratœːr] m. Deflagrator. ‖ ELECTR. Spark-gap.

déflagration [-grasjɔ̃] f. Deflagration.

déflagrer [-gre] v. intr. (1). To deflagrate.

déflation [deflasjɔ̃] f. FIN. Deflation.

déflationniste [-sjɔnist] adj. FIN. Deflationary, deflationist.

déflecteur [deflɛktœːr] m. TECHN. Deflector; baffle-plate. ‖ AUTOM. Ventilator.

défleuraison [deflœrɛzɔ̃] f. BOT. Fall of blossom.

défleurir [-riːr] v. intr. (2). BOT. To lose its blossom.
— v. tr. To strip of its blooms. ‖ FIG. To wither.
— v. pr. Se **défleurir,** to lose its blossom.

déflexion [deflɛksjɔ̃] f. PHYS., TECHN. Deflection, deflexion.

défloraison [deflɔrɛzɔ̃] f. BOT. Defloration.

défloration [-rasjɔ̃] f. JUR. Defloration.

défloré, ée [deflɔre] adj. Deflowered (jeune fille); stale (nouvelles). ‖ BOT. Deflorate.

déflorer v. tr. (1). FIG. To deflower (une fille); to take the freshness off, to stale, to spoil (une nouvelle, un sujet).

défoliant [-ljɑ̃] adj., m. Defoliant.

défoliation [defɔljasjɔ̃] f. BOT. Defoliation.

défonçage [defɔ̃saːʒ], **défoncement** [-smɑ̃] m. Smashing in (d'un boîte, d'une caisse); breaking down (d'une clôture). ‖ Breaking up (d'un terrain). ‖ AGRIC. Digging up (d'un champ). ‖ NAUT. Staving in (d'un bateau).

défoncé, ée [defɔ̃se] adj. Smashed in (boîte, caisse); battered, bashed-in (chapeau); broken down (clôture); furrowed, rutted, bumpy (route). ‖ AGRIC. Ploughed up, dug up (champ).

défoncer v. tr. (6). To smash in (une boîte, une caisse); to batter, to bash (un chapeau); to break down (une clôture); to break up (une route); to break up, to open, to trench (un terrain). ‖ AGRIC. To plough up, to dig up (un champ). ‖ NAUT. To bilge (un bateau); to blow away (une voile). ‖ MILIT. To rout (une armée).
— v. pr. Se **défoncer,** FAM. To sweat blood, to break one's neck (s'escrimer). ‖ To get stoned (se droguer).

défonceuse [defɔ̃søːz] f. AGRIC. Trenching plough.

déformable [defɔrmabl] adj. Liable to be put out of shape.

déformant [-mɑ̃] adj. Distorting, deforming.

déformation [-masjɔ̃] f. Deformation. ‖ TECHN. Warping (du bois). ‖ PHYS., MATH. Distortion. ‖ FIG. Twist, kink (de l'esprit); *déformation professionnelle,* professional (ou) vocational bias (ou) idiosyncrasy (ou) kink.

déformer [-me] v. tr. (1). To put out of shape (un chapeau, une robe); to deform (le corps); to distort (le visage). ‖ TECHN. To warp, to strain, to buckle. ‖ PHYS. To distort (une image); to deform (une onde). ‖ FIG. To warp (l'esprit); to distort (les faits, les paroles); to spoil (le goût); to adulterate, to distort (une langue); to twist (un sens); to mangle, to torture (un texte).
— v. pr. Se **déformer,** to go out of shape; to become deformed (ou) distorted. ‖ TECHN. To warp (bois); to buckle (métal).

défoulement [defulmɑ̃] m. FAM. Letting off steam, unwinding.

défouler (se) [sədefule] v. pr. (1). FAM. To let off steam, to unwind.

défourner [defurne] v. tr. (1). To take out of the oven (le pain). ‖ TECHN. To draw out of the kiln (des poteries).

défrai [defrɛ] m. FIN. Defrayal, defrayment.

défraîchi, ie [defrɛʃi] adj. Faded (fleur, tissu). ‖ COMM. Soiled, shop-soiled, shop-worn (article). ‖ FIG. Faded (beauté, visage).

défraîchir [-ʃiːr] v. tr. (2). To take away the freshness of.
— v. pr. Se **défraîchir,** to get soiled; to fade. ‖ FIG. To fade, to lose one's bloom.

défrayer [defrɛje] v. tr. (9 b). FIN. To defray (ou) to pay the expenses of (qqn); *être défrayé,* to have one's expenses paid. ‖ FIG. *Défrayer la chronique,* to be in the news (ou) the talk of the town; *défrayer la conversation,* to be the theme (ou) topic of conversation.

défrichable [defriʃabl] adj. AGRIC. That can be cleared.

défrichage [-ʃaː3] m. AGRIC. Clearing, grubbing (action); cleared patch (terrain). ‖ FIG. Spade-work *(de,* on) [un sujet].

défricher [-ʃe] v. tr. (1). AGRIC. To clear, to grub (un champ); to break up (un terrain). ‖ FIG. To do the spade-work (on un sujet).

défricheur [-ʃœːr] m. AGRIC. Clearer. ‖ FIG. Pioneer *(de,* in); explorer *(de,* of).

défriper [defripe] v. tr. (1). To smooth out.

défriser [defrize] v. tr. (1). To put out of curl (la chevelure); to uncurl (les cheveux); *toute défrisée,* all out of curl. ‖ FAM. To put out, to put the damper on (qqn); *cette nouvelle l'a défrisé,* he was greatly dashed at the news; *il a l'air défrisé,* he looks down in the mouth.
— v. pr. Se **défriser,** to uncurl, to come out of curl (chevelure); to uncurl one's hair (personne). ‖ FAM. To lose heart; *il se défrise vite,* he's easily dashed (ou) crushed.

défroisser [defrwase] v. tr. (1). To smooth out.

défroque [defrɔk] f. Cast-off clothing. ‖ FAM. Togs; cast-offs.

défroqué, ée [-ke] adj. ECCLÉS. Unfrocked.
— m. ECCLÉS. Unfrocked priest; ex-priest; ex-monk.

défroquer [-ke] v. tr. (1). ECCLÉS. To unfrock, to defrock.
— v. pr. Se **défroquer,** to give up the frock.

défruiter [defrɥite] v. tr. (1). To strip the fruit off (un arbre). ‖ To deodorize (l'huile d'olive).

défunt, unte [defœ̃, œ̃ːt] adj. Defunct.
— s. Deceased, departed, decedent.

défunter [-te] v. intr. FAM. To pop off, to peg out, to snuff it, to croak.

dégagé, ée [dega3e] adj. Clear (ciel, route); private (escalier); open (espace, site, vue). ‖ FIG. Cavalier, jaunty, perky (air); airy, easy (allure); swinging (démarche); unbiassed (esprit); easy, casual, off-hand (manières); free (mouvements, propos); *d'un air dégagé*, off-hand, airily, casually, flippantly.

dégagement [-ʒmɑ̃] m. Disengagement (sens général); emission, liberation (de chaleur); release (de vapeur). ‖ Clearing (d'une route). ‖ Redeeming, redemption (d'un gage). ‖ Fin. Release (de titres). ‖ Milit. Extrication (des troupes); relief (d'une ville). ‖ Chim. Escape, emanation (d'un gaz); disengagement (d'hydrogène, d'oxygène). ‖ Sports. Disengagement (à l'escrime); clearance (au football). ‖ Autom. Release (des freins). ‖ Techn. Clearance (d'un outil); *dégagement du chariot*, carriage release (à la machine à écrire). ‖ Archit. Exit passage, corridor (couloir). ‖ Méd. Loosening (de l'intestin, de la toux). ‖ Fig. Disengagement, detachment (*de*, from).

dégager [-ʒe] v. tr. (7). To disengage (sens général); to emit (de la chaleur, une odeur, de la vapeur); to radiate (de la chaleur, de la lumière); to give off, to exhale (une odeur); to release (de la vapeur). ‖ To bare (le cou); to set off (la taille). ‖ To withdraw, to release (son bras, sa main); *dégager qqn des décombres*, to extricate s.o. from under the debris. ‖ To free (une pièce); to clear (la route, la voie); to disencumber (la table). ‖ To redeem, to take out of pawn (un objet en gage). ‖ Fin. To release (des titres). ‖ Milit. To extricate (des troupes); to relieve (une ville). ‖ Chim. To disengage (un gaz). ‖ Électr. To generate (de l'électricité). ‖ Naut. To clear (les pièces, le pont). ‖ Math. *Dégager l'inconnue*, to isolate the unknown quantity. ‖ Sports. To disengage (le fer à l'escrime). ‖ Autom. To release (les freins). ‖ Techn. To loosen (un écrou); to clear, to back off (un outil). ‖ Archit. To open (la vue). ‖ Méd. To relieve the congestion in (le cerveau, les poumons); to loosen (l'intestin, la toux). ‖ Fig. To draw (des conclusions); to radiate (de l'enthousiasme, de la vie); to define (ses impressions); to clear oneself of (sa responsabilité); to elucidate (le sens); to evolve (une théorie); to sift out (la vérité); *dégager qqn de*, to absolve from (une contrainte); to acquit of, to free from (une obligation, une tâche); to release from (une promesse); to relieve of (une responsabilité). ‖ Fam. *Dégager le cerveau*, to clear the head.
— v. intr. Sports. To clear (au football). ‖ Ch. de f. *Dégagez!*, mind your backs!, clear the way! ‖ Autom. *Dégagez!*, gangway! (dans l'autobus).
— v. pr. Se **dégager**, to disengage oneself (sens général) [*de*, from]; to extricate oneself (se dépêtrer) [*de*, from]; to get free, to free oneself (se libérer) [*de*, from]; to wrench (ou) to shake oneself free (se libérer par la force) [*de*, from]; to rise (ou) to emerge (sortir) [*de*, from]; to get clear (se tirer d'affaire) [*de*, of]. ‖ To clear (ciel, temps). ‖ To be given off (ou) emitted, to emanate (chaleur, odeur); to arise (fumée). ‖ Chim. To evolve (gaz). ‖ Électr. To be generated. ‖ Milit. To disengage, to extricate oneself. ‖ Naut. To get clear. ‖ Méd. To be relieved (organes). ‖ Comm. *Se dégager de*, to withdraw from (une affaire); to back out of (un marché). ‖ Fig. To become apparent, to be revealed, to come out; *se dégager de*, to clear oneself of (une accusation, un soupçon); to get clear of (une dette); to free oneself from (une invitation, une préoccupation); to clear one's mind of (des préjugés); to go back on (une promesse); to break away from (des règlements); to extricate oneself from (une situation critique).

dégaine [degɛ:n] f. Fam. Awkward gait; ungainliness.

dégainer [degɛne] v. tr. (1). To unsheathe.
— v. intr. To draw.

déganter [degɑ̃te] v. tr. (1). To unglove (la main).
— v. pr. Se **déganter**, to take off one's gloves.

dégarni, ie [degarni] adj. Bare (armoire, arbre, buffet); bald (front); unfurnished, bare of furniture (maison); stripped, bare (mur); untrimmed (robe); bald, open (terrain). ‖ Comm. Bare (comptoir); short of (ou) out of stock (magasin).

dégarnir [-ni:r] v. tr. (2). To clear out (une armoire, un buffet); to dismantle, to take the furniture out of (une maison); to strip (un mur); to untrim (une robe); to clear of trees (un terrain). ‖ To uncover (une pièce aux échecs). ‖ Naut. To unrig (un navire). ‖ Milit. To unman (une forteresse).
— v. pr. Se **dégarnir**, to lose its leaves (arbre); to empty (comptoir, salle); to grow bald (tête).

dégât [degɑ] m. Damage, havoc; *faire des dégâts dans*, to devastate. ‖ Jur. Waste. ‖ Fam. Mess.

dégauchir [degoʃi:r] v. tr. (2). To rough-plane, to surface (du bois).

dégazer [degɑze] v. tr. (1). Techn. To degas, to degasify.
— v. intr. Naut. To clean out its tanks.

dégel [deʒel] m. Thaw.

dégelée [deʒəle] f. Fam. Hail (ou) shower of blows. (V. RACLÉE.)

dégeler v. tr. (8 *b*). To thaw.
— v. impers. To be thawing.
— v. pr. Se **dégeler**, Fam. To thaw (personne).

dégénéré, ée [-re] adj., s. Degenerate.

dégénérer v. intr. (5). To degenerate (s'abâtardir); to lose caste (déroger). ‖ To degenerate (*de*, from; *en*, into). ‖ Méd. To degenerate; to develop (*en*, into).

dégénérescence [-resɑ̃:s] f. Méd. *Dégénérescence graisseuse*, fatty degeneration; *maladies de dégénérescence*, diseases consequent on degeneration, U. S. degenerative diseases.

dégénérescent, ente [-resɑ̃, ɑ̃:t] adj. Méd. Degenerating, degenerative.

dégermer [deʒerme] v. tr. (1). Agric. To strip (ou) rub the eyes off (les pommes de terre).

dégingandé, ée [deʒɛ̃gɑ̃de] adj. Lanky, gangling, ungainly.

dégivrage [deʒivra:ʒ] m. De-icing.

dégivrer [-vre] v. tr. Aviat., Autom. To de-ice.

dégivreur [-vrœ:r] m. Aviat., Autom. De-icer.

déglaçage [deglasa:ʒ], **déglacement** [-smɑ̃] m. De-icing, removal of ice (d'un bassin). ‖ Techn. Removal of glaze (d'un papier). ‖ Culin. Deglazing (d'un jus de viande).

déglacer [-se] v. tr. (6). To de-ice, to remove the ice from (un bassin). ‖ Techn. To remove the glaze from (un papier). ‖ Culin. To pour liquid in the dish to make gravy, to deglaze (un jus de viande).

déglinguer [deglɛ̃ge] v. tr. (1). Fam. To dislocate, to put out of order.
— v. pr. Se **déglinguer**, Fam. To become dislocated.

déglutir [deglyti:r] v. tr. (2). Méd. To swallow.

déglutition [-tisjɔ̃] f. Méd. Deglutition.

dégobiller [degɔbije] v. tr. (1). Pop. To bring up, to spew.
— v. intr. To spew, to spue, to cat, to puke; *avoir envie de dégobiller*, to feel queasy.

dégoiser [degwaze] v. tr. Fam. To spout, to rattle off, to reel off.
— v. intr. Fam. To rattle on, to talk nineteen to the dozen, to jaw.

dégommage [degɔma:ʒ] m. Ungumming. ‖ Fam. Sacking (renvoi).

dégommer [-me] v. tr. (1). To ungum. ‖ Fam. To sack; to debunk (qqn); *se faire dégommer*, to get the sack.

dégonflement [deʒɔ̃fləmɑ̃] m. Deflating, deflation (d'un ballon). ‖ Méd. Reducing, going down (d'une enflure). ‖ AUTOM. Deflation; collapse (d'un pneu). ‖ FAM. Backing (ou) climbing down.

dégonflé, ée [degɔ̃fle] adj. AUTOM. Flat, soft, down (pneu).
— m. FAM. Funk; yellow-belly (pop.).

dégonfler v. tr. (1). To deflate (un ballon). ‖ MÉD. To bring down, to reduce (une enflure). ‖ AUTOM. To deflate (un pneu). ‖ FAM. To debunk (qqn).
— v. pr. **Se dégonfler,** AUTOM. To collapse, to go flat. ‖ MÉD. To go down. ‖ FAM. To funk it; to climb down.

dégorgement [degɔrʒmɑ̃] m. Disgorging. ‖ Clearing, unstopping (d'une conduite). ‖ Discharge (des eaux, d'un égout); outlet (d'un réservoir). ‖ Purifying (de la laine).

dégorgeoir [-ʒwa:r] m. Disgorger (pour poisson). ‖ Overflow pipe (réservoir).

dégorger [-ʒe] v. tr. (7). To disgorge (vomir). ‖ To purge (des sangsues); *faire dégorger du poisson,* to purge fish. ‖ To discharge (des eaux). ‖ To clear, to unstop (un conduit bouché). ‖ To discharge (du cuir, une étoffe). ‖ FIG. To discharge, to disgorge, to pour out (une foule). ‖ MÉD. To discharge (abcès).

dégot(t)er [degɔte] v. tr. (1). FAM. To get, to pick up; to ferret out, to unearth.

dégoudronner [degudrɔne] v. tr. To remove the tar from.

dégouliner [deguline] v. intr. (1). To trickle.

dégoupiller [degupije] v. tr. (1). To remove (ou) pull out the pin of.

dégourdi, ie [degurdi] adj. Wide-awake, sharp (personne); *mal dégourdi,* stick-in-the-mud.
— s. Brisk person; live wire (actif); cute (ou) sharp person (intelligent).

dégourdir [-di:r] v. tr. (2). To take the numbness off (un membre). ‖ To take the chill off (un liquide). ‖ FAM. To smarten up, to sharpen the wits of (un niais); to stir up, to ginger up, to shake up (un paresseux).
— v. pr. **Se dégourdir,** to become more alert; to feel warmer; *se dégourdir les jambes,* to stretch one's legs. ‖ FAM. To learn the ropes, U. S. to wise up, to get hep (se déniaiser); *elle s'est bien dégourdie,* she's been around.

dégoût [degu] m. Disgust, loathing (pour les aliments); *éprouver du dégoût pour,* to loathe. ‖ FIG. Disgust, aversion, repugnance; *inspirer du dégoût à qqn,* to fill s.o. with disgust; *prendre qqn en dégoût,* to take a strong dislike to s.o.

dégoûtant, ante [-tɑ̃, ɑ̃:t] adj. Disgusting, loathsome, sickening, nauseating, repulsive (nauséeux, répugnant); offensive, nasty (nauséabond); filthy (sale); *un temps dégoûtant,* rotten weather; *d'une façon dégoûtante,* nauseously, disgustingly; *un vieux dégoûtant.* an old buck, a dirty old man.

dégoûtation [-tasjɔ̃] f. FAM. Revolting thing.

dégoûté, ée [-te] adj. Disgusted, nauseated, queasy (nauséeux). ‖ Fastidious, finicky, squeamish (chipoteur); finicky, picky (délicat). ‖ Sick (de, of); fed up (de, with). ‖ FIG. Weary, sick (de, of) [blasé, lassé]. ‖ FAM. *Vous n'êtes pas dégoûté,* you are not overnice (difficile); you don't want much (exigeant).
— s. FAM. *Faire le dégoûté,* to be pernickety (pour la nourriture); to turn up one's nose (être méprisant).

dégoûter v. tr. (1). To disgust, to nauseate, to sicken, to turn the stomach of (donner la nausée). ‖ To disgust (de, with); *dégoûter qqn de faire qqch.,* to give s.o. a dislike for doing sth.; *dégoûter qqn de la vie,* to make s.o. sick of life.
— v. pr. **Se dégoûter,** to grow disgusted (de, of); *se dégoûter des œufs,* to turn against eggs; *on ne*

s'en dégoûte jamais, it never palls on you, you are never tired of it. ‖ FIG. *Se dégoûter de,* to grow sick and tired of (son métier); to take a dislike to (qqn).

dégouttant, ante [deʒutɑ̃, ɑ̃:t] adj. Dripping, (de, with).

dégouttement [-mɑ̃] m. Dripping, trickling.

dégoutter [-te-] v. intr. (1). To trickle (de, from) [arbres, toit]. ‖ To be dripping (de, with) [sueur].

dégradant, ante [degradɑ̃, ɑ̃:t] adj. Degrading, lowering, debasing. (V. ABAISSANT.)

dégradation [-dasjɔ̃] f. Damage (dégât); defacement, deterioration, dilapidation (d'immeubles); wear (de la route). ‖ JUR. *Dégradation nationale,* loss of civil rights. ‖ MILIT. Dismissal from the service (en général); reduction to the ranks (d'un gradé); cashiering (d'un officier). ‖ MÉD. Decline. ‖ ARTS. Gradation, shading off (des couleurs). ‖ PHYS. Degradation. ‖ FIG. Degradation, debasement.

dégradé [-de] m. Range of colours.

dégrader v. tr. (1). To damage, to deface, to deteriorate, to dilapidate (v. DÉTÉRIORER); to undermine (les fondations, un mur); to wear (la route). ‖ MILIT. To reduce to the ranks (un gradé); to cashier (un officier). ‖ PHYS., GÉOL. To degrade. ‖ To vignette (en photographie). ‖ ARTS. To gradate, to shade off, to tone down (les couleurs). ‖ FIG. To degrade, to debase.
— v. pr. **Se dégrader,** to dilapidate, to fall in ruins. ‖ FIG. To degrade, to debase oneself; to sink into vice.

dégrafer [degrafe] v. tr. (1). To unhook, to unfasten, to undo (une agrafe, sa robe); to unclasp (un bracelet, une ceinture); *dégrafer qqn,* to unfasten (ou) undo s.o.'s dress.
— v. pr. **Se dégrafer,** to come unhooked (ou) unfastened (agrafe, robe); to come unclasped (bracelet, ceinture); to undo one's clothing (personne).

dégraissage [degrɛsa:ʒ] m. Degreasing (du cuir); scouring (de la laine); dry-cleaning (des vêtements). ‖ CULIN. Skimming (du bouillon).

dégraissant, ante [-sɑ̃] adj. Degreasing.
— m. Degreaser.

dégraisser [-se] v. tr. (1). To degrease, to kill (le cuir, la peau); to scour (la laine); to clean (les vêtements). ‖ CULIN. To skim (le bouillon). ‖ AGRIC. To impoverish (une terre).

dégraisseur [-sœ:r] m. Scourer (de laine); cleaner (de vêtements) [personne]. ‖ TECHN. Grease extractor (de cuir); scouring machine (de laine) [machine]; cleaner (de vêtements) [produit].

degré [dəgre] m. Rank (de la hiérarchie). ‖ Degree (de parenté); *cousins au second degré,* second cousins; *cousins au troisième degré,* cousins thrice removed. ‖ Degree (grade universitaire); *enseignement du second degré,* secondary education. ‖ Degree, pitch, point; *au dernier degré,* to the last degree; *au plus haut* (ou) *suprême degré,* in the highest degree, to a degree, supremely, superlatively, eminently; to the highest pitch; *jusqu'à un certain degré,* to a certain extent (en étendue); *par degrés,* by degrees, progressively. ‖ Stair, step (d'escalier). ‖ ECCLÉS. Step (de l'autel). ‖ PHYS. Degree (du baromètre, du thermomètre); *marquer 10 degrés,* to stand at (ou) to register 10 degrees. ‖ GÉOGR. Degree (de latitude); *par 3⁰20 de longitude nord,* in longitude 3⁰20 North. ‖ MATH. Degree (d'angle); *du premier, du second degré,* simple, quadratic (équation). ‖ CHIM. Percentage of alcohol (de, in); *vin de 10 degrés,* wine having ten per cent of alcohol. ‖ MUS. Degree. ‖ JUR. *Degré de juridiction,* resort, stage; *le troisième degré,* the third degree. ‖ MÉD. Stage (d'une maladie). ‖ GRAMM. Degree (de comparaison).

dégréer [degree] v. tr. (5). NAUT. To unrig (un mât) ; to dismantle (un navire).

dégressif, ive [degrɛsif, i:v] adj. FIN. Regressive, U S. degressive.

dégression [-sjɔ̃] f. FIN. Regression, U. S. degression.

dégrèvement [degrɛvmɑ̃] m. FIN. Abatement, relief, reduction, deduction (d'impôt). ‖ JUR. Disencumbrance (d'hypothèque).

dégrever [degrɑve] v. tr. (5). FIN. To disencumber, to reduce the assessment on (un bien, un immeuble) ; to derate (une industrie) ; to reduce the tax on (une marchandise) ; to relieve of a tax (qqn).

dégringolade [degrɛ̃gɔlad] f. FAM. Purler, cropper (chute) ; come-down (déchéance). ‖ FIN. Downfall (d'un financier) ; slump (d'une monnaie).

dégringoler [-le] v. intr. (1). FAM. To come a purler (ou) a cropper (tomber) ; to take a header ; *dégringoler d'une échelle,* to fall off a ladder ;| *faire dégringoler qqch.,* to topple sth. over (ou) down. ‖ To fall (un ministère). ‖ FIN. To slump (prix, monnaie). ‖ FIG. To come down, to go down, to decline, to lose caste (déchoir).
— v. tr. FAM. To come down ; *dégringoler l'escalier à toute vitesse,* to rush down the stairs. ‖ FAM. To debunk. (V. DÉBOULONNER.)

dégrisement [degrizmɑ̃] m. Sobering. ‖ FIG. Disillusionment ; subsiding (d'une passion).

dégriser [-ze] v. tr. (1). FIG. To sober. ‖ FIG. To sober down (calmer) ; to disillusion (désillusionner).
— v. pr. **Se dégriser,** to sober down (pr. et fig.).

dégrossi, ie [degrosi] adj. Licked into shape ; *mal dégrossi,* raw, rough.
— s. *Un mal dégrossi,* a boor, a lout ; U. S. a rough-neck.

dégrossir [-si:r] v. tr. (2). To rough down (du bois) ; to rough-hew (la pierre) ; to rough-plane (une planche). ‖ FIG. To rough out ; to do the spade-work on (un sujet). ‖ FAM. To polish up, to lick into shape (qqn).

dégrossissage [degrosisa:ʒ] m. Roughing, trimming (du bois) ; scabbling (de la pierre) ; rough-planing (d'une planche). ‖ FIG. Roughing out (d'un plan). ‖ FAM. Spade-work (défrichage).

dégrouiller (se) [sədegruje] v. pr. (1). POP. To get a move on, to get weaving.

déguenillé, ée [degnije] adj. Ragged, tattered, in rags ; in tatters.
— s. Ragamuffin.

déguerpir [degɛrpi:r] v. intr. (2). FAM. To clear off (ou) out, to scoot, to skedaddle, to hop it, U. S. to scram (v. DÉCAMPER) ; *faire déguerpir,* to send packing. ‖ JUR. To abandon, to give up.

déguerpissement [-pismɑ̃] m. Clearing off, skedaddling.

dégueulasse [degœlas] adj. POP. Disgusting.

déguisé, ée [degize] adj. Disguised, in disguise ; masquerading. ‖ FIG. Veiled, covert ; *non déguisé,* overt.
— s. Masquerader.

déguisement [-zmɑ̃] m. Disguise, disguising (état) ; disguise, fancy dress (habit). ‖ FIG. Disguise, cloak, concealment ; *sans déguisement,* overtly.

déguiser [-ze] v. tr. (1). To disguise (l'écriture, une personne). ‖ FIG. To disguise, to cloak (ses pensées, ses sentiments).
— v. pr. **Se déguiser,** to disguise oneself (*en, as*) ; to put on a fancy dress, to masquerade.

dégustateur, trice [degystatœ:r, tris] s. Taster.

dégustation [-tasjɔ̃] f. Tasting, sampling.

déguster [-te] v. tr. (1). To taste, to sample (goûter) ; to sip, to relish, to degustate (savourer).

déhaler [deɑle] v. tr. (1). NAUT. To warp out.
— v. pr. **Se déhaler,** NAUT. To haul off.

déhâler v. tr. (1). To whiten, to remove sunburn from (le visage).

déhanché, ée [deɑ̃ʃe] adj. Hip-shot (cheval) ; hip-swaying (femme provocante) ; lop-sided (infirme) ; waddling (personne qui se dandine).

déhanchement [-ʃmɑ̃] m. Swaying from the hips ; lop-sidedness ; waddling gait. ‖ MÉD. Dislocation of the hip.

déhancher (se) [sədeɑ̃ʃe] v. pr. (1). To dislocate its hip (cheval). ‖ To sway one's hips, to wiggle (femme provocante) ; to waddle along, to roll in one's walk (personne qui se dandine).

déharnacher ldearnaʃe] v. tr. (1). To unharness.

dehors [dəɔ:r] adv. Out, outside, without ; *dedans et dehors,* within and without ; *dîner dehors,* dine out ; *laisser dehors,* to leave outside ; *mettre dehors,* to turn out, to oust (faire sortir) ; to sack (renvoyer) ; *mettre dehors à coups de pieds,* to boot out, to kick out.
— interj. Out !, Out with you !, get out !
— loc. adv. **Au-dehors,** outside, without (hors de la maison) ; abroad (hors du pays). ‖ **De dehors,** from outside. ‖ **En dehors,** outside ; *marcher en dehors,* to turn one's toes out in walking ; *ouvrir en dehors,* to open to the outside (ou) outwards. ‖ **Par-dehors,** by the outside.
— loc. prép. **En dehors de,** beside (à côté de) ; beyond (au-delà de) ; outside, out of (hors de) ; beyond, apart from (outre) ; *en dehors de mon action,* beyond my control ; *en dehors de mes cordes,* out of my line ; *en dehors de mes intentions,* beside my purpose ; *en dehors de moi,* without my knowledge (à mon insu) ; without my having any hand in it (sans ma participation) ; *en dehors de ces motifs,* apart from these reasons ; *en dehors de la question,* beside (ou) outside the question.
— m. Outside, exterior (d'une maison) ; *des dehors plaisants,* a pleasant exterior ; *ouvrir du dehors,* to open from the outside. ‖ Abroad (étranger). ‖ *affaires du dehors,* external (ou) foreign affairs. ‖ SPORTS. Outside edge (au patinage). ‖ FIG. Pl. Appearances, externals (v. EXTÉRIEUR) ; *des dehors trompeurs,* deceitful appearances ; *sous les dehors de la vertu,* under the cloak of virtue.

déicide [deisid] m. ECCLÉS. Deicide.

déification [-fikasjɔ̃] f. Deification.

déifier [-fje] v. tr. (1). To deify. (V. DIVINISER.)

déisme [deism] m. Deism.

déiste [deist] m. Deist.
— adj. Deistic, deistical.

déité [deite] f. Deity.

déjà [deʒa] adv. Already, previously, before (auparavant, autrefois) ; *il l'aurait déjà écrit si,* he would have written it before if ; *j'ai déjà pris un engagement,* I have already committed myself. ‖ Already, even then (dès ce moment passé) ; *déjà au Xᵉ siècle,* as early as (ou) as far back as the Xth century ; *déjà il était mortellement atteint,* even then he was mortally stricken. ‖ Already, even now (dès le moment présent) ; *mon chapeau est déjà démodé,* my hat is already out of fashion ; *elle sent déjà venir l'hiver,* even now she can feel winter coming. ‖ As it is, as it was (comme cela) ; *il a déjà assez de travail,* he has work enough, as it is. ‖ FAM. *C'est déjà vieux,* that's stale news indeed ; *qu'a-t-elle dit déjà ?,* what did she say now ? ; *comment s'appelle-t-il déjà ?,* what's his name again ?

déjaler [deʒale] v. tr. NAUT. To unstock.

déjantage [deʒɑ̃ta:ʒ] m. AUTOM. Blow-out.

déjanter [-te] v. tr. AUTOM. To blow out of the beaded rim (un pneu).

déjauger [deʒoʒe] v. intr. (7). NAUT. To sew up. ‖ AVIAT. To take off.

déjection [deʒɛksjɔ̃] f. MÉD. Dejection. ‖ GÉOGR., MÉD. Dejecta.

déjeté, ée [deʒte] adj. Crooked, awry, atwist, distorted, off the straight (membre); crooked, old and worn out (personne); *il est bien déjeté,* he has aged before his years. ‖ TECHN. Warped (bois); buckled (métal).

déjeter v. tr. (8a). To twist, to distort, to make awry. ‖ To warp (le bois); to buckle (le métal).
— v. pr. **Se déjeter,** to grow crooked (ou) awry, to become distorted (corps). ‖ TECHN. To warp (le bois); to buckle (métal).

déjeuner [deʒœne] m. Breakfast (petit déjeuner); *petit déjeuner à l'anglaise,* substantial (ou) knife-and-fork (ou) U.S. American breakfast; *petit déjeuner à la française,* continental breakfast. ‖ Lunch (repas de midi); *prendre son déjeuner,* to have (ou) to take one's lunch. ‖ Breakfast service (ou) set (vaisselle). ‖ FIG. *C'est un déjeuner de soleil,* it will soon fade.
— v. tr. (1). To breakfast (le matin); *déjeuner avec du chocolat,* to have chocolate for breakfast; *déjeuner d'une tasse de thé,* to breakfast off a cup of tea; *en train de déjeuner,* at breakfast. ‖ To lunch (à midi); *déjeuner au restaurant,* to lunch at a restaurant; *donner à déjeuner à qqn, offrir un déjeuner à qqn,* to invite s.o. to lunch, to take s.o. out to lunch. ‖ FAM. *Il a trop bien déjeuné,* he is slightly fuddled.

déjouer [deʒue] v. tr. (1). To baffle (les calculs, les projets, les recherches); to foil, to frustrate (un complot); to baulk (les desseins, les projets); to frustrate (les efforts); to thwart (les menées, les projets); *déjouer les menées de,* to outwit, to outmanœuvre; *déjouer les projets de qqn,* to bring s.o.'s plans to nought.
— v. intr. To take back a move (aux échecs).

déjucher [deʒyʃe] v. intr. (1). To come off the perch.
— v. tr. To unroost.

déjuger (se) [sədeʒyʒe] v. tr. (7). To reverse one's judgment, to recant one's opinion.

de jure [deʒyre] adv. De jure.

delà [dela] adv. *De-ci de-là,* here and there, on all sides, in every direction.
— loc. adv. **Au-delà,** more, still more (davantage); beyond, farther, on the other side (plus loin); longer, further (plus longtemps) [v. AU-DELÀ]. ‖ **De delà,** from beyond. ‖ **En delà,** farther away, farther on. ‖ **Par-delà,** beyond, on the other side, farther on.
— loc. prép. **Au-delà de,** beyond, above, past; *au-delà de toute compréhension,* past all understanding; *aller au-delà des bornes,* to exceed the limits; *aller au-delà de ses forces,* to overexert oneself. (V. AU-DELÀ.) ‖ **Par-delà,** beyond; *par-delà les océans,* beyond the seas.

délabré, ée [delabre] adj. Dilapidated, ruinous, falling into disrepair (immeuble); battered (mobilier); crumbling, tumbledown (mur); shabby (pièce). ‖ MÉD. Impaired, broken (santé).

délabrement [-brəmã] m. Dilapidation, decay, falling to pieces, disrepair (des choses); decay, decrepitude (des personnes). ‖ MÉD. Impairment, breakdown (de la santé).

délabrer [-bre] v. tr. (1). To dilapidate (une maison). ‖ FIG. To impair, to ruin (sa santé).
— v. pr. **Se délabrer,** to fall to pieces (ou) into disrepair, to go to rack and ruin. ‖ MÉD. To become impaired (ou) shattered; *sa santé se délabre,* his health is not what it was, he is breaking up.

délacer [delase] v. tr. (6). To undo (les chaussures); to unlace (un corsage, un corset); to unlace (qqn).
— v. pr. **Se délacer,** to come undone (chaussures); to come unlaced (corset). ‖ To unlace oneself; to undo one's shoes; to unlace one's corset (personne).

délai [delɛ] m. Delay (retard); *sans délai,* immediately, promptly, forthwith, without delay, without any loss of time. ‖ Respite (v. RÉPIT); term (de paiement); *délai de grâce,* days of grace, respite of debt; *délai supplémentaire,* extension of time. ‖ Time-limit (limite de temps); *à bref délai,* at short notice, in the near future; *dans le plus bref délai,* in the shortest time, as soon as possible; *dans un délai de quinze jours,* at a fortnight's notice; *dans un délai de trois mois,* within three months; *sans délai,* without any time-limit. ‖ COMM. *Délai de livraison,* time-limit for delivery; *délai de livraison : huit jours,* delivery within a week. ‖ CH. DE F. *Délai de transport,* time allowed for carriage. ‖ JUR. *Délai d'appel,* time allowed for making an appeal. ‖ MILIT. *Délai de route,* travelling (ou) U.S. travel time. ‖ *User de délais,* to procrastinate. ‖ **Délai-congé,** m. Term of notice.

délainage [delɛna:ʒ] m. TECHN. Unhairing (des peaux de mouton).

délainer [-ne] v. tr. (1). TECHN. To unhair (des peaux de mouton).

délaissé, ée [delɛse] adj. Abandoned; forlorn (enfant, lieu); deserted, neglected (épouse); cast-off (maîtresse). ‖ AGRIC. Fallow, waste (terrain).

délaissement [-smã] m. Abandonment, friendlessness (isolement); *vivre dans un complet délaissement,* to be abandoned by all. ‖ NAUT. Abandonment (en assurance maritime). ‖ JUR. Relinquishment, renunciation (de droit); desertion; neglect (de famille).

délaisser [-se] v. tr. (1). To abandon (un enfant); to give up (ses amis, son travail); to desert, to forsake, to neglect (sa famille). ‖ JUR. To relinquish, to forego, to renounce (un droit, une succession); to abandon (des poursuites). ‖ NAUT. To abandon (un navire).

délarder [delarde] v. tr. (1). To remove the fat from (un porc). ‖ TECHN. To thin down (du bois); to bevel (un coin). ‖ CULIN. To unlard (un rôti).

délassant, ante [delasã, ã:t] adj. Refreshing, relaxing. ‖ FIG. Recreating, diverting.

délassement [-smã] m. Relaxation, refreshment (détente); divertissement, distraction, diversion, recreation, pastime (divertissement); rest (repos); *prendre une heure de délassement,* to relax for an hour.

délasser [-se] v. tr. (1). To relax, to refresh (détendre); to divert (distraire).
— v. pr. **Se délasser,** to refresh oneself, to relax (se détendre); to take a rest (se reposer); *chanter pour se délasser,* to seek relaxation in singing.

délateur, trice [delatœ:r, tris] s. Delator, informer, detractor. (V. DÉNONCIATEUR.)

délation [-sjɔ̃] f. Delation, denunciation.

délavage [delava:ʒ] m. Washing out (d'une couleur). ‖ CULIN. Wateriness (d'un plat).

délavé, ée [-ve] adj. Washed out, faded, washy (couleur, tissu). ‖ CULIN. Diluted (boisson); wishy-washy (nourriture). ‖ AGRIC. Wet, waterlogged (terrain).

délaver v. tr. (1). To water down, to wash out (une couleur); to make faint in colour, to fade (un tissu).

délayage [delɛja:ʒ] m. Diluting, thinning down (ou) out (d'une couleur). ‖ CULIN. Mixing (de la farine). ‖ FIG. Padding, verbiage.

délayé, ée [-je] adj. Watery (couleur). ‖ FIG. Wordy, long-drawn-out.

délayer v. tr. (1). To water down, to thin (une couleur). ‖ CULIN. To mix (de la farine) [*dans,* with]. ‖ FIG. To spin out, to pad. (V. DILUER.)

Delco [delko] m. AUTOM. Distributor.

deleatur [deleaty:r] m. Delete, dele.

délectable [delɛktabl] adj. Delectable.

délectation [-sjɔ̃] f. Delectation, delight; relish; *manger avec délectation*, to eat with gusto.

délecter (se) [sədelɛkte] v. pr. (1).· To take delight, to revel (*à, dans*, in). [V. RÉGALER (SE).]

délégataire [delegatɛːr] s. JUR. Delegatee.

délégation [delegasjɔ̃] f. Delegation, delegacy; delegates (groupe). ‖ Delegation, deputing (acte). ‖ JUR. Assignment (de créance); commission, delegation, empowerment (de pouvoirs); allotment (de traitement). ‖ FIN., COMM. Delegation. ‖ MILIT. Allotment (de solde).

délégué, ée [delege] adj. Managing (administrateur); deputy (fonctionnaire, juge); acting, deputy (professeur). ‖ Delegated (pouvoirs); allotted (traitement).
— s. Delegate; deputy (d'un fonctionnaire); proxy (mandataire); *délégué syndical*, shop steward. ‖ FIN. Delegated debtor.

déléguer [delege] v. tr. (5). To delegate (des pouvoirs) [to, à]. ‖ To delegate, to depute (v. MANDATER); *déléguer à une fonction*, to commission; *délégué par intérim à la place de*, deputized for. ‖ JUR. To assign, to transfer (une créance); to allot (un traitement). ‖ MILIT. To allot (une solde).

délestage [delɛstaːʒ] m. NAUT., AVIAT. Unballasting. ‖ ÉLECTR. Load-shedding. ‖ AUTOM. *Itinéraire de délestage*, relief road.

délester [-te] v. tr. (1). NAUT., AVIAT. To unballast. ‖ ÉLECTR. To shed the load. ‖ FAM. To relieve (*de*, of); *se faire délester de son porte-monnaie*, to get relieved of one's purse.
— v. pr. **Se délester**, NAUT. To throw out ballast; *se délester de la cargaison*, to jettison the cargo. ‖ AVIAT. To throw out ballast; *se délester de ses bombes*, to jettison one's bombs. ‖ FAM. To unburden oneself (ou) one's heart.

délesteur [-tœːr] m. Ballast-heaver.

délétère [-deletɛːr] adj. Deleterious (en général); offensive (odeur). ‖ CHIM. Noxious, poisonous (gaz). ‖ FIG. Pernicious, poisonous (doctrine).

délibérant [delibeˑrɑ̃] adj. Deliberative.

délibératif, ive [-ratif, iːv] adj. Deliberative.

délibération [-rasjɔ̃] f. Deliberation, discussion, debate (débat) [*sur*, on]. ‖ Deliberation, consideration, reflection; *après mûre délibération*, after due reflection, after the fullest deliberation; *en délibération*, in hand, under consideration. ‖ Decision, resolution. ‖ MÉD. Consultation.

délibéré, ée [-re] adj. Deliberate, purposeful, purposive, intentional (voulu); *de propos délibéré*, deliberately, of set purpose, of deliberate choice. ‖ Resolute, unhesitating, determined, purposive (résolu); *d'un air délibéré*, with an air of determination.
— m. JUR. Consultation; in camera sitting; *en délibéré*, under consideration.

délibérément [-remɑ̃] adv. Deliberately; resolutely; intentionally.

délibérer [-re] v. intr. (5). To deliberate (*avec*, with; *sur*, on); to debate; to confer, to converse; to consult together (conférer); *délibérer sur la question*, to talk the matter over, to discuss the matter. ‖ To deliberate, to reflect, to ponder (réfléchir); *délibérer au sujet de qqch.*, to think sth. over, to turn sth. over in one's mind. ‖ JUR. To confer, to consult together (jury).

délicat, ate [delika, at] adj. Tactful (allusion, comportement); delicate (attentions); delicate, fine, nice, refined (sentiment). ‖ Scrupulous (conscience), scrupulous, punctilious, touchy (personne); *peu délicat*, unscrupulous, dishonest. ‖ Discerning, refined, aesthetic (goût). ‖ Delicate, fine, subtle (nuance). ‖ Sensitive, fine (oreille). ‖ Delicate, tender (peau, teint); delicate, refined (traits). ‖ Delicate, embarrassing, ticklish (question, sujet); awkward, critical (situation); delicate;

tricky (fam.) [travail]. ‖ TECHN. Delicate (mécanisme). ‖ ARTS. Delicate, soft (coloris); light (toucher). ‖ CULIN. Dainty, delicious, delicate (mets); dainty, fastidious, finicky, squeamish (personne difficile). ‖ MÉD. Delicate (opération); delicate; weak, frail (santé); fragile, sickly, delicate (personne fragile).
— s. Finicky (ou) squeamish person; *faire le délicat*, to be over-nice, to pick at one's food.

délicatement [-tmɑ̃] adv. Delicately (avec art, délicatesse); softly, gently, tenderly (avec douceur); daintily (avec friandise, raffinement); finely (avec goût); tactfully (avec tact).

délicatesse [-tɛs] f. Tactfulness, delicacy (du comportement); delicacy, considerateness (des sentiments); *manque de délicatesse*, want of tact. ‖ Tenderness, scrupulousness (de la conscience). ‖ Refinement, nicety, delicacy (du goût). ‖ Subtleness (d'une nuance, d'un raisonnement); nicety (du style). ‖ Delicacy (de l'oreille). ‖ Tenderness (de la peau, du teint); delicacy (des traits). ‖ Delicateness, difficulty (d'une question, d'un sujet); awkwardness, difficulty (d'une situation); trickiness (d'un travail). ‖ TECHN. Trickiness (d'un mécanisme). ‖ ARTS. Softness, delicacy (d'un coloris); lightness (du toucher). ‖ CULIN. Daintiness (des mets); fastidiousness (des personnes difficiles). ‖ MÉD. Frailty, weakness, fragility.

délice [delis] m. sing. Delight; source of joy; *c'est un délice*, it is delightful (ou) a pure delight.

délices f. pl. Delights, delight; pleasures, deliciousness; *faire ses délices de*, to revel (ou) to delight (ou) to take delight in; *faire les délices de qqn*, to be s.o.'s delight.

délicieusement [-sjøzmɑ̃] adv. Deliciously, delightfully.

délicieux, euse [-sjø, ø:z] adj. Delicious (parfum); charming, lovely (personne); delightful, sweet (spectacle, voix). ‖ CULIN. Delicious (mets).

délictueux, euse [deliktɥø, ø:z] adj. Malicious, felonious. ‖ JUR. Punishable; *acte délictueux*, offence, misdemeanour.

délié, ée [delje] adj. Nimble (agile); slender, slim, thin, slight (effilé); sharp, subtle (subtil); *doigts déliés*, nimble fingers; *langue déliée*, glib (ou) garrulous tongue.
— m. Upstroke (de l'écriture).

délier v. tr. (1). To unbind, to untie, to undo (un paquet); to unfetter, to unbind (un prisonnier). ‖ FIG. To loosen (la langue); *délier la langue à qqn*, to draw s.o. out, to make s.o. open up. ‖ FIG. To release (*de*, from) [une promesse]. ‖ ECCLÉS. To absolve, to lose.

délimitation [delimitasjɔ̃] f. Demarcation, delimitation. ‖ Determination (de frontières). ‖ FIG. Determination, definition (des pouvoirs).

délimiter [-te] v. tr. (1). To delimit, to demarcate; *délimiter les frontières*, to mark the boundaries. ‖ FIG. To define (les pouvoirs).

délinéer [delinee] v. tr. (1). To delineate.

délinquance [-kɑ̃:s] f. Delinquency.

délinquant, ante [-delɛ̃kɑ̃, ɑ̃:t] adj. *La jeunesse délinquante*, juvenile delinquents (ou) offenders.
— s. JUR. Offender, delinquent.

déliquescence [delikɛsɑ̃:s] f. Deliquescence (pr. et fig.); *en déliquescence*, in a state of deliquescence; *tomber en déliquescence*, to deliquesce.

déliquescent, ente [-sɑ̃, ɑ̃:t] adj. Deliquescent.

délirant, ante [delirɑ̃, ɑ̃:t] adj. MÉD. Delirious; raving. ‖ FIG. Delirious, frenzied (imagination, joie); rapturous, ecstatic (personne); *délirant de joie*, delirious with joy.
— s. MÉD. Delirious person.

délire [deliːr] m. MÉD. Delirium; *avoir le délire*, to be delirious, to wander, to rave. ‖ MÉD.

Dementia (démence); phrenitis (frénésie). ‖ Fig. Frenzy (de douleur); ecstasy, transport (de joie).
délirer [delire] v. intr. (1). Méd. To be delirious, to rave, to wander. ‖ Fig. To be raving (ou) wild (de, with); to be in ecstasy.
delirium tremens [delirjɔmtremɛ̃:s] m. Méd. Delirium tremens; the horrors; the D.T.'s (fam.).
délit [deli] m. Jur. Misdemeanour, offence; commettre un délit, to offend against the law.
délit [deli] m. Joint, rift (d'ardoise). ‖ Archit. Side against the grain (d'une pierre).
déliter [delite] v. tr. (1). To exfoliate (des pierres). Archit. To surbed.
délitescence [delitɛsɑ̃:s] f. Chim. Efflorescence. ‖ Méd. Delitescence.
délitescent, ente [-sɑ̃, ɑ̃:t] adj. Chim. Efflorescent.
délivrance [delivrɑ̃:s] f. Deliverance, delivery; release, rescue (libération). ‖ Méd. Delivery; child-birth. ‖ Jur. Service (d'exploit); issue (de passeport); delivery (de pièces). ‖ Ch. de f. Issue (des billets).
délivrer [-vre] v. tr. (1). To deliver, to free, to set free, to rescue (libérer); délivrer qqn de ses liens, to loose s.o. from his bonds. ‖ Fig. To deliver, to set free, to free (de, from); to relieve, to rid (de, of) [débarrasser]. ‖ Comm. To deliver. ‖ Jur. To issue (un passeport); to deliver (des pièces). ‖ Méd. To deliver (une accouchée).
— Se délivrer, to deliver (ou) to free oneself (de, from); to get rid (de, of).
déloger [delɔʒe] v. intr. (7). To remove, to move out (déménager). ‖ To go off, to make off, to go out, to get away (partir); faire déloger, to clear out, to oust.
— v. tr. To eject, to evict (un locataire). ‖ To turn out, to drive out, to expel (qqn).
délover [delɔve] v. tr. (1). Naut. To uncoil.
— v. pr. Se délover, to uncoil (cordage, serpent).
déloyal [delwajal] adj. Disloyal, false, faithless, perfidious (individu); dishonest, unfair (procédé). Comm. Unfair (concurrence). ‖ Sports. Foul (jeu).
déloyalement [-jalmɑ̃] adv. Disloyally; unfairly.
déloyauté [-jote] f. Disloyalty, faithlessness; unfairness. ‖ Disloyal act.
delta [dɛlta] m. Géogr. Delta; delta renversé, shingle-spit. ‖ **Delta-plane,** m. (nom déposé). Sports. Hang-glider.
deltoïde [deltɔid] adj., m. Méd. Deltoid.
déluge [dely:ʒ] m. Deluge, flood (inondation); deluge, downpour (pluie); déluge de feu, fiery deluge. ‖ Ecclés. Deluge, flood. ‖ Fig. Torrent, flood (de larmes, de maux). ‖ Loc. Remonter au déluge, to be as old as Adam (date); to go back before the Flood (recul).
déluré, ée [delyre] adj. Wide-awake; cute (fam.).
délurer v. tr. (1). To smarten up, to knock the corners off. (V. dégourdir.)
— v. pr. Se délurer, to lose one's shyness.
délustrer [delystre] v. tr. (1). To take the sheen (ou) gloss off (une étoffe).
— v. pr. Se délustrer, to lose its gloss (étoffe).
démagnétisation [demaɲetizasjɔ̃] f. Phys. Demagnetization.
démagogie [demagɔʒi] f. Demagogy.
démagogique [-gɔʒik] adj. Demagogic.
démagogue [-gɔg] m. Demagogue.
démailler [demaje] v. tr. (1). To make a ladder (ou) U. S. run in (les bas); to unshackle (une chaîne); to undo the meshes of (un filet); to unknit (un tricot), to ravel (un tricot).
— v. pr. Se démailler, to run, to ladder (bas); to ravel (tricot).
démailloter [demajɔte] v. tr. (1). To unswaddle.
demain [demɛ̃] adv. Tomorrow; à demain!, good-bye till tomorrow!, demain matin soir, to-

morrow morning, evening; demain en huit, en quinze, tomorrow week, fortnight; a week, two weeks from tomorrow; après-demain, the day after tomorrow; jusqu'à demain, till tomorrow; le travail de demain, tomorrow's work.
démanché, ée [demɑ̃ʃe] adj. Loose in the handle (branlant); without a handle (sans manche). ‖ Fam. Out of joint (bras); rickety (meuble); ungainly, hulking (personne).
démancher v. tr. (1). To take off the handle of, to unhaft (un outil). ‖ Fam. To dislocate (un membre); to make rickety (un meuble).
— v. intr. Mus. To shift (au violon).
— v. pr. Se démancher, to work loose in the handle (branler); to lose its handle (perdre son manche). ‖ Fam. To come out of joint (membre); to get rickety (meuble); se démancher le genou, to put one's knee out of joint. ‖ Fam. Se démancher pour, to put oneself out to.
demandable [demɑ̃dabl] adj. Jur. Claimable.
demande [demɑ̃:d] f. Question; inquiry; la belle demande!, what a question! ‖ Application, request (v. requête); à la demande générale, by general (ou) public request; à la demande de qqn, at s.o.'s request; demande de, request for (argent); application for (emploi); demande en mariage, proposal; faire une demande à, to apply to; faire une demande de, to apply for, to indent for; sur demande, on application, on request. ‖ Comm. Order (commande); l'offre et la demande, supply and demand; sur demande, on call, at sight, according to order. ‖ Jur. Claim, action.
demander [demɑ̃de] v. tr. (1).

1. Solliciter. — 2. Désirer. — 3. Exiger. — 4. S'enquérir de. — 5. Souhaiter voir. — 6. Milit. — 7. Ecclés. — 8. Jur. — 9. Comm. — 10. Loc.

1. To ask, to ask for, to apply for, to request, to solicit, to entreat (solliciter); demander qqch., to ask for sth.; demander qqch. à qqn, to ask s.o. for sth., to ask sth. of s.o., to call on s.o. for sth.; demander à faire qqch., to ask to do sth.; demander à qqn de faire qqch., demander que qqn fasse qqch., to ask (ou) to want (ou) to beg s.o. to do sth.; demander à dîner à qqn, to invite oneself to dine with s.o.; demander à manger, to ask for something to eat; demander à être interrogé en chimie, to call for a question on chemistry, to ask to be questioned on chemistry; demander assistance, to call for help; demander audience, to solicit an audience; demander l'autorisation, to request permission, to ask leave; demander la charité, to beg for alms; demander grâce, to cry for mercy; demander une grâce à qqn, to ask s.o. a favour; demander l'indulgence de qqn, to entreat s.o.'s indulgence; demander justice à qqn, to seek redress at s.o.'s hands; demander en mariage, to propose to, to offer marriage to; demander pardon à qqn, to beg s.o.'s pardon; demander la parole, to ask permission to speak; demander par voie d'annonce, to advertise for; il n'y a qu'à demander, it is to be had for asking; puis-je vous demander la moutarde?, may I trouble you for the mustard? ‖2. To ask, to want (désirer); ne demander qu'à, ne pas mieux demander que, to ask nothing better than; to be willing enough to; to ask only for; to be quite ready to; to entertain no objection to. ‖ 3. To call for, to take, to need, to require (exiger); demander à être résolu, to call for a solution, to require settling, to need to be resolved; demander beaucoup de temps, to take a long time; demander un effort, to call for an effort; demander l'impossible à qqn, to expect of (ou)

to require s.o. to do impossibilities ; *demander la lune*, to ask for the moon ; *demander de la persévérance*, to require perseverance ; *demander réflexion*, to want consideration, to need thinking over ; to want (ou) need to be carefully considered ; *en demander trop à qqn*, to ask s.o. more than he can say (au-delà de ses connaissances) ; to expect from s.o. more than he can do (au-delà de ses possibilités). ‖ 4. To ask (s'enquérir de) ; *demander après qqn*, to ask after s.o. ; *demander l'heure, sa route*, to ask the time, one's way. ‖ 5. To ask for, to want (souhaiter voir) ; *demander à voir qqn, demander qqn*, to ask for s.o. ; *demander qqn au téléphone*, to call (ou) to ring s.o. up ; *faire demander qqn*, to send for s.o. ; *on vous demande*, s.o. wants to see you, you are wanted. ‖ To ask for (des cartes). ‖ 6. Milit. To sue for (la paix) ; to call for (des volontaires). ‖ 7. Ecclés. To call for (un prêtre). ‖ 8. Jur. To apply for, to claim, to bring an action (en justice) ; *demander le divorce*, to apply for a divorce ; *demander une indemnisation*, to claim damages. ‖ 9. Comm. To charge ; *combien demandez-vous pour?* how much do you charge for? ; *j'en demande trois cents francs*, I want (ou) I ask three hundred francs for it ; *on demande beaucoup cet article*, there is a great demand for this item ; *on demande une petite-main*, dressmaker's apprentice wanted. ‖ 10. Loc. *Je demande à voir*, I want to think it over ; *je vous demande un peu!*, I ask you! ; what has possessed him? (quelle idée a-t-il eue?) ; it's amazing! (c'est stupéfiant!).
— v. pr. **Se demander,** to wonder, to ask oneself (avec curiosité) ; to doubt, to wonder (avec incertitude) ; to think, to consider (avec réflexion) ; *je me demande si elle viendra*, I wonder whether she will come ; *je me demande bien pourquoi*, I can't think why ; *elle se demande comment faire*, she wonders how she is going to manage ; *on peut se demander si*, it may be asked whether. ‖ To be asked for (question) ; *cela ne se demande pas*, it's obvious (ou) evident.
demandeur, eresse [-dœːr, ərɛs] s. Jur. Plaintiff ; pursuer (en Ecosse).
demandeur [-dœːr] s. Asker ; petitioner (solliciteur). ‖ Caller (au téléphone). ‖ Déclarer (aux cartes). ‖ Comm. Demander.
démangeaison [demɑ̃ʒɛzɔ̃] f. Méd. Itching, itch ; *avoir des démangeaisons*, to itch. ‖ Fig. Itch, itching, pruriency ; *avoir la démangeaison de parler*, to be itching to give tongue (ou) to talk.
démanger [-ʒe] v. tr. (7). Méd. To itch (ou) to tickle ; *le dos me démange*, my back is itching. ‖ Fig. To itch, to tingle ; *la langue lui démange*, he is dying to give tongue (ou) to talk ; *la main me démange*, my hand is itching to box his ears.
démantèlement [demɑ̃tɛlmɑ̃] m. Dismantling.
démanteler [-tle] v. tr. (5). To dismantle.
démantibuler [demɑ̃tibyle] v. tr. (1). Méd. To dislocate, to put out of joint (la mâchoire). ‖ Autom. To smash up (une voiture). ‖ Fam. To put out of order (ou) of gear (un mécanisme).
— v.pr. **Se démantibuler,** to get out of joint (mâchoire). ‖ Fam. To get out of order (ou) of gear ; to come to pieces (mécanisme).
démaquillage [demakijaːʒ] m. *Crème de démaquillage*, cleansing cream.
démaquillant, ante [-jɑ̃, jɑ̃ːt] adj. Make-up removing.
— m. Make-up remover, cleanser.
démaquiller [-je] v. tr. (1). To take the paint (ou) the make-up off (le visage).
— v. pr. **Se démaquiller,** to take off one's make-up.
démarcatif, ive [demarkatif, iːv] adj. Demarcating.

démarcation [demarkasjɔ̃] f. Demarcation ; *ligne de démarcation*, boundary (ou) dividing line, line of demarcation.
démarchage [demarʃaːʒ] m. Comm. Door-to-door selling.
démarche [demarʃ] f. Gait, walk, step (allure). ‖ Fig. Step (en général) ; approaches (avances) ; representation (exposé, instances) ; proceeding (manœuvre) ; application, canvassing (requête) ; *démarche collective*, joint representation ; *démarches louches*, suspicious proceedings ; *faire une démarche*, to take a step, to make representations ; *tenter une démarche auprès de X en faveur de Z*, to apply to (ou) to approach X in favour of Z (ou) on Z's behalf ; *faire des démarches pour soutenir qqn aux élections*, to canvass (ou) U. S. to campaign for s.o., U. S. to tout for votes.
démarcheur, euse [-ʃœːr, øːz] s. Comm. Door-to-door salesman (ou) saleswoman, hawker.
démarier [demarje] v. tr. To unmarry. ‖ Agric. To thin (les betteraves).
démarquage [demarkaːʒ] m. Unmarking (du linge). ‖ Fig. Plagiarism ; pirating, lifting (fam.) [d'un texte].
démarque [demark] f. Comm. Marking down.
démarquer [-ke] v. tr. (1). To unmark (du linge) ; to remove the marker from (un livre) [ôter la marque]. ‖ Comm. To mark down (solder). ‖ Fig. To plagiarize, to pirate, to lift (plagier).
— v. intr. To lose mark of mouth (cheval).
— v. pr. **Se démarquer,** to set oneself apart, to dissociate oneself. ‖ Sports. To become unmarked, to throw off one's marker.
démarrage [demaraːʒ] m. Naut. Unmooring. ‖ Ch. de f., Autom., Aviat. Start, starting ; *démarrage automatique*, self-starting. ‖ Milit. Going over the top. ‖ Sports. Start, get-away (à la course). ‖ Fig. Start ; *prendre un bon démarrage dans la vie*, to get a good start in life.
démarrer [-re] v. tr. (1). Naut. To untie (un cordage) ; to unmoor (un navire).
— v. intr. Naut. To cast off. ‖ Ch. de f., Aviat., Autom. To start, to start off, to get away. ‖ Sports. To spurt (à la course). ‖ Fam. *Il ne démarre pas*, he plods away all day long (bûcher) ; he sticks there for hours (s'incruster).
démarreur [-rœːr] m. Autom. Starter ; *démarreur à manivelle, à pédale, automatique*, crank-, kick-, self-starter. ‖ Aviat. Starter ; *démarreur de bord*, cockpit starter.
démasquer [demaske] v. tr. (1). To unmask (son visage). ‖ Naut. To show (un feu). ‖ Milit. To unmask (une position). ‖ Fig. To denounce ; to expose ; to show up (qqn) ; *démasquer ses batteries*, to show one's hand.
— v. pr. **Se démasquer,** to unmask (personne). ‖ Fig. To drop the mask (personne) ; to come to light (vérité).
démâter [demɑte] v. tr. (1). Naut. To dismast, to unmast (le navire).
— v. intr. Naut. To lose her masts.
démêlage [demɛlaːʒ] m. Combing out (des cheveux) ; disentangling (d'un écheveau) ; teasing out (de la laine).
démêlé [-le] m. Contention, quarrel (v. Contestation) ; *avoir des démêlés avec la justice*, to run foul of the law ; *avoir des démêlés avec qqn*, to be at cross-purposes with s.o., to have unpleasant dealings with s.o.
démêler [-le] v. tr. (1). To comb out (les cheveux) ; to disentangle, to unravel (un écheveau) ; to tease out (la laine). ‖ Fig. To clear up, to unravel, to straighten out (une affaire) ; to elucidate (une question). ‖ To discern, to make out ; to distinguish (d'avec, from) ; *démêler le bien du mal*, to

tell right from wrong. ‖ To contest ; *avoir qqch. à démêler avec*, to have a bone to pick with.
— v. pr. **Se démêler**, to be combed out (cheveux) ; to comb out one's hair (personne). ‖ To become disentangled, to unravel (écheveau); to become teased out (laine). ‖ FIG. To unravel (intrigue) ; to come out (vérité).

démêloir [-lwa:r] m. Large-toothed comb.

démêlures [-ly:r] f. pl. Combings.

démembrement [demãbrəmã] m. Dismembering (du corps). ‖ FIG. Dismemberment, breaking-up.

démembrer [-bre] v. tr. (1). To dismember (un corps). ‖ To dismember, to break up (un royaume).
— v. pr. **Se démembrer**, to break up (royaume).

déménagement [demenaʒmã] m. Removal ; *déménagement à la cloche de bois*, moonlight flit ; *faire un déménagement*, to remove, U. S. to move ; *faire le déménagement de ses meubles*, to have one's furniture removed ; *voiture de déménagement*, furniture (ou) pantechnicon (ou) U. S. moving van. ‖ FAM. Jumble, hugger-mugger (désordre).

déménager [-ʒe] v. tr. (7). To remove the furniture from (une maison); to remove, to move out (des meubles dans une autre maison); to move to another place (des meubles dans la même maison). ‖ FAM. *Déménager la maison*, to strip the house bare (cambrioleurs).
— v. intr. To remove, to move out, to move house, to flit ; *déménager à la cloche de bois*, to do a moonlight flit ; to skip. ‖ FAM. To clear off (déguerpir) ; *faire déménager qqn*, to chuck s.o. out. ‖ FAM. To have a screw loose (déraisonner).

déménageur [-ʒœ:r] m. Furniture remover (ou) U. S. mover.

démence [demã:s] f. Madness, insanity, lunacy (folie). ‖ MÉD. Dementia, alienation. ‖ FIG. Incoherence, folly ; *ce serait de la démence*, it would be pure folly (ou) sheer madness.

démener (se) [sədemne] v. pr. (5). To throw oneself about ; to struggle ; to jostle ; to fidget (s'agiter) ; *se démener comme un diable dans un bénitier*, to dance about like a pea on a drum. ‖ To bestir oneself ; to get a move on ; to toss about ; to lay oneself out. (V. DÉMANCHER [SE].)

dément [demã] adj. Insane, mad, demented.
— s. MÉD. Lunatic, maniac. (V. FOU.)

démente [-mã:t] f. MÉD. Madwoman.

démenti [demãti] m. Contradiction, denial, refutation ; *donner un démenti à*, to give the lie to, to belie ; *opposer un démenti à*, to deny, to contradict. ‖ FAM. Failure (échec).

démentiel, elle [-sjɛl] adj. Pertaining to madness.

démentir [-ti:r] v. tr. (93). To give the lie to, to belie (qqch., qqn) ; to contradict, to refute (qqch.). ‖ To refute (une assertion) ; to deny (une évidence, un fait). ‖ To go against (sa conduite, sa parole) ; to belie (des craintes, des promesses) ; to disappoint (un espoir). ‖ To falsify ; *la réalisation dément la prophétie*, the prophecy is falsified by the event.
— v. pr. **Se démentir**, to give oneself the lie, to contradict oneself (se contredire). ‖ To act inconsistently ; *ses principes ne se démentent pas*, he holds to the same principles. ‖ To fail (cesser de se manifester) ; *un zèle qui ne se dément jamais*, an unfailing zeal.

démerder (se) [sədemɛrde] v. pr. (1). ARGOT. To shift for oneself ; to muddle through.

démérite [demerit] m. Demerit, fault.

démériter [-te] v. tr. (1). To be blameworthy (être blâmable) ; *ne pas démériter*, not to prove blameworthy. ‖ To lose the favour of, to forfeit the esteem, to lose favour (de, of).

démesure [deməzy:r] f. Disproportion ; excessiveness.

démesuré, ée [-zyre] adj. Beyond measure, out of proportion ; excessive (ambition, zèle) ; immod-

erate (appétit) ; inordinate (longueur, orgueil) ; unbounded (orgueil).

démesurément [-zyremã] adv. Beyond measure ; excessively ; immoderately ; inordinately.

démettre [demɛtr] v. tr. (64). MÉD. To dislocate, to put out of joint (un membre).
— v. pr. **Se démettre**, to be dislocated (membre) ; *se démettre l'épaule*, to put one's shoulder out.

démettre v. tr. (64). † To dismiss ; to deprive (de, of) [un poste]. ‖ JUR. *Démettre de*, to dismiss (un appel) ; to nonsuit (une demande).
— v. pr. **Se démettre de**, to give up, to resign.

démeubler [demœble] v. tr. (1). To unfurnish.

demeurant, ante [demœrã, ã:t] adj. JUR. Living, residing (habitant).
— m. JUR. Resident (résidant).
— loc. adv. **Au demeurant**, after all (après tout) ; on the whole (à tout prendre) ; howbeit (quoi qu'il en soit).

demeure [demœ:r] f. Dwelling, residence, habitation, abode (domicile) ; *à demeure*, fixed, permanently installed ; *dernière demeure*, grave, last home (ou) resting-place. ‖ † Delay ; tarrying ; *il n'y a pas péril en la demeure*, it can lie over, it can be delayed, the case is not pressing. ‖ JUR. *Mettre en demeure*, to put in suit, to give an injunction to ; to summon, to call upon ; *mise en demeure*, formal notice, summons.

demeuré, ée [demœre] adj., s. FAM. Mentally deficient ; retarded.

demeurer v. intr. (1). To live, to dwell, to reside (habiter) ; *demeurer à l'hôtel*, to stay at a hotel. ‖ To remain, to stay (rester) ; *demeurer absent*, to remain away ; *demeurer couché*, to stay in bed ; *demeurer en repos*, to keep still. ‖ To be left ; *demeurer en route*, to be left on the road ; *les biens du père demeurent aux enfants*, the father's estate is left to the children, the children inherit their father's estate. ‖ JUR. *Demeurer en fonctions*, to hold the office. ‖ MILIT. *Demeurer sur le terrain*, to be killed on the spot ; *la victoire nous demeure*, the victory remains with us. ‖ FIG. To remain, to stay ; to stop ; *demeurer court*, to stop short ; *demeurer fidèle à*, to remain faithful to ; *demeurer valable*, to hold good ; *il n'en demeure pas moins vrai que*, the fact remains that.

demi, ie [dəmi] adj. Half ; *une demi-heure*, half an hour, a half-hour ; *trois heures et demie*, three hours and a half (durée); half-past three (heure) ; *toutes les demi-heures*, half-hourly.
— m. MATH. Half ; *deux demis*, two halves. ‖ SPORTS. Half ; *les demis*, the halves ; *demi aile*, wing-half ; *demi droit*, right half-back ; *demi de mêlée*, scrum-half ; *demi d'ouverture*, stand-off half. ‖ COMM. Large glass (de bière).
— loc. adv. *A demi*, half, semi ; *à demi barbare*, *conscient*, semi-barbarous, -conscious ; *à demi cuit*, half-cooked ; *à demi-journée*, half-time ; *à demi mort*, half-dead, half-alive ; *à demi nu*, semi-nude ; half-naked ; *à demi ouvert*, half-closed ; *à demi-tarif*, half-fare ; *comprendre à demi-mot*, to take the hint ; *faire à demi*, to half-do, to do by halves. ‖ **Demi-axe**, m. MATH. Semi-axis. ‖ **Demi-bain**, m. Hip-bath. ‖ **Demi-barbare**, s. Semi-barbarian, semi-barbarous. ‖ **Demi-bas**, m. Halfhose. ‖ **Demi-bastion**, m. MILIT. Demi-bastion. ‖ **Demi-botte**, f. Half-boot. ‖ **Demi-bouteille**, f. Half-bottle. ‖ **Demi-cercle**, m. Semi-circle, demi-circle. ‖ **Demi-circulaire**, adj. Semi-circular. ‖ **Demi-clef**, f. NAUT. Half-hitch. ‖ **Demi-colonne**, f. ARCHIT. Engaged column. ‖ **Demi-couronne**, f. Half-crown. ‖ **Demi-deuil**, m. Half-mourning. ‖ **Demi-diamètre**, m. MATH. Semi-diameter. ‖ **Demi-dieu**, m. Demi-god. ‖ **Demi-douzaine**, f. Half-dozen. ‖ **Demi-fin**, adj. Medium. ‖ **Demi-finale**, f. SPORTS. Semifinal. ‖ **Demi-fina-**

liste, s. SPORTS. Semifinalist. ‖ **Demi-fond**, m. SPORTS. Medium distance. ‖ **Demi-frère**, m. Half-brother. ‖ **Demi-gros**, m. COMM. Retailwholesale. ‖ **Demi-heure**, f. Half-hour, half an hour. ‖ **Demi-jour**, m. Half-light, semi-darkness, dim light; morning twilight; ARTS. Twilight effect. ‖ **Demi-journée**, f. Half-time (ou) part-time work; *faire des demi-journées*, to do part-time work; *travailler à la demi-journée*, to work half-time. ‖ **Demi-litre**, m. Half-liter; *un demi-litre de*, half a liter of. ‖ **Demi-longueur**, f. SPORTS. Half-length. ‖ **Demi-lune**, f. Half-moon; MILIT. Semi-lune, demi-lune, ravelin. ‖ **Demi-mal**, m. Small harm. ‖ **Demi-mesure**, f. Half-measure. ‖ **Demi-mondaine**, f. Demi-mondaine, demi-rep. ‖ **Demi-monde**, m. Demi-monde. ‖ **Demi-mort**, adj. Half-dead. ‖ **Demi-obscurité**, f. Semi-obscurity. ‖ **Demi-onde**, f. PHYS. Half-wave. ‖ **Demi-pause**, f. MUS. Minim rest; U. S. half rest. ‖ **Demi-pension**, f. Partial board. ‖ **Demi-pensionnaire**, s. Day-boarder, U. S. day pupil (à l'école). ‖ **Demi-pièce**, f. Half-piece (d'étoffe); half-hogshead (de vin). ‖ **Demi-place**, f. CH. DE F. Half-fare. ‖ **Demi-portion**, f. FAM. Weakling, puny person. ‖ **Demi-quart**, m. NAUT. Half-point (au compas). ‖ **Demi-queue**, m. Semi-grand, cottage grand, half grand, U. S. baby grand (piano). ‖ **Demi-reliure**, f. Quarter binding. ‖ **Demi-ronde**, f. TECHN. Half-round file. ‖ **Demi-saison**, f. Between-season, mid-season; *de demi-saison*, between-season, in-between-season. ‖ **Demi-sang**, m. Half-breed. ‖ **Demi-savant**, m. Sciolist. ‖ **Demi-sel**, m. CULIN. Demi-sel; POP. Small-time crook. ‖ **Demi-sœur**, f. Half-sister. ‖ **Demi-solde**, f. MILIT. Half-pay; m. MILIT. Officier on half-pay. ‖ **Demi-sommeil**, m. Drowsiness, somnolence, torpor. ‖ **Demi-soupir**, m. MUS. Quaver rest; U. S. eighth rest. ‖ **Demi-tarif**, m. Half fare. ‖ **Demi-tasse**, f. Half-cup. ‖ **Demi-teinte**, f. ARTS. Half-tone, half-tint. ‖ **Demi-ton**, m. MUS. Semi-tone. ‖ **Demi-tonneau**, m. AVIAT. Half-roll. ‖ **Demi-tour**, m. Half-turn; *faire demi-tour*, to turn back; MILIT. About-turn; *faire demi-tour*, to turn about, to about-face. ‖ **Demi-vérité**, f. Half-truth. ‖ **Demi-vie**, f. PHYS. Half-life. ‖ **Demi-volée**, f. SPORTS. Half-volley. ‖ **Demi-watt**, f. ELECTR. Half-watt lamp.

demie f. Half. ‖ Half-hour; *pendule qui sonne les demies*, clock that strikes the half-hours.

démieller [demjɛle] v. tr. (1). To remove the honey from. ‖ POP. To extricate (qqn).
— v. pr. **Se démieller**, POP. To muddle through.

démilitarisation [demilitarizasjɔ̃] f. Demilitarization.

démilitariser [demilitarize] v. tr. (1). To demilitarize.

déminage [demina:ʒ] m. MILIT. Mine clearance.

déminer [-ne] v. tr. (1). To clear of mines.

démineur [-nœ:r] m. MILIT. Mine-clearer.

déminéralisation [demineralizasjɔ̃] f. MÉD. Demineralization.

déminéraliser [-ze] v. tr. (1). To demineralize.

démis [demi] adj. MÉD. Dislocated, out of joint.

démission [demisjɔ̃] f. Resignation; *donner sa démission*, to resign.

démissionnaire [-sjɔnɛ:r] adj. Resigning; outgoing.
— s. Resigner.

démissionner [-sjɔne] v. intr. (1). To resign (d'une fonction); to vacate one's seat (du Parlement); to strike one's name off the books (d'une société). ‖ MILIT. To send in one's papers, to resign one's commission.

démiurge [demjyrʒ] m. Demiurge.

démobilisation [demɔbilizasjɔ̃] f. MILIT. Demobilization; service release.

démobilisé [-ze] m. MILIT. Demobilized serviceman (ou) officer.

démobiliser [-ze] v. tr. (1). MILIT. To demobilize; to discharge.

démocrate [demɔkrat] adj. Democratic. ‖ **Démocrate-chrétien**, adj. Christian Democratic.
— s. Democrat. ‖ **Démocrate-chrétien**, s. Christian Democrat.

démocratie [-si] f. Democracy.

démocratique [-tik] adj. Democratic.

démocratiquement [-tikmɑ̃] adv. Democratically.

démocratisation [-tizasjɔ̃] f. Democratization.

démocratiser [-tize] v. tr. (1). To democratize.
— v. pr. **Se démocratiser**, to become democratized.

démodé, ée [demɔde] adj. Out of date; out of fashion; old-fashioned; outmoded; U. S. outdated. ‖ FIG. Antiquated, obsolete (conception).

démoder v. tr. (1). To send out of fashion.
— v. pr. **Se démoder**, to go out of fashion. ‖ FIG. To become antiquated (ou) obsolete.

démographe [demɔgraf] s. Demographer.

démographie [-fi] f. Demography.

démographique [-fik] adj. Demographic; *accroissement démographique*, increase in population.

demoiselle [demwazɛl] f. † Damsel. ‖ Girl, young lady (jeune fille); spinster, single (ou) unmarried woman (vieille fille); *ces demoiselles*, the young ladies; *les demoiselles X*, the Misses X; *demoiselle de compagnie*, lady companion; *demoiselle d'honneur*, bridesmaid (de la mariée); maid of honour (de la reine). ‖ COMM. *Demoiselle de magasin*, shopgirl. ‖ ZOOL. Dragonfly (libellule); *demoiselle de Numidie*, crowned crane (grue). ‖ TECHN. Beetle, rammer. (V. HIE.)

démolir [demɔli:r] v. tr. (2). To demolish, to pull down, to do away with (un bâtiment); to batter down (un mur); to break (un objet). ‖ NAUT. To break up (un navire). ‖ MILIT. To smash (une armée). ‖ AVIAT. To prang (un avion). ‖ AUTOM. To wreck, to smash up (une voiture). ‖ MÉD. To ruin, to spoil, to weaken (la santé); to wreck (les nerfs). ‖ FIG. To annihilate, to reduce to nothing, to demolish (un argument, des objections); to knock out (un candidat); to smash, to bring down (le crédit, l'influence); to overthrow (une institution); to blast (la réputation); *démolir qqn*, to run s.o. down (critiquer); to beat s.o. up (rosser); to do away with s.o. (supprimer).
— v. pr. **Se démolir**, to break up, to go to pieces.

démolissage [-lisa:ʒ] m. Pulling down. ‖ FAM. Slating (critique).

démolisseur [-lisœ:r] s. TECHN. House-breaker. ‖ FIG. Demolisher.

démolition [-lisjɔ̃] f. Demolition, pulling down (d'un bâtiment); *chantier de démolition*, house-breaker's (ou) U. S. wrecker's yard. ‖ Pl. Old materials, scraps, rubble (de constructions); salvaged material (après un incendie).

démon [demɔ̃] m. Daemon, genius (des mythologies); demon, devil, fiend (des religions). ‖ FIG. Demon, imp (enfant); devil (homme); *le démon de midi*, the emotional disturbances of the middle-aged; the difficult age.

démonétisation [demɔnetizasjɔ̃] f. FIN. Demonetization. ‖ FAM. Discrediting.

démonétiser [-ze] v. tr. (1). FIN. To demonetize. ‖ FAM. To discredit (qqn).

démoniaque [demɔnjak] adj. Demoniac(al).
— s. Demoniac; devil-possessed person.

démonologie [-nɔlɔʒi] f. Demonology.

démonstrateur, trice [demɔ̃stratœ:r, tris] s. Demonstrator.

démonstratif, ive [-tif, i:v] adj. Demonstrative, conclusive (raison). ‖ Demonstrative, expansive, effusive; back-slapper (fam.); *peu démonstratif*, undemonstrative. ‖ GRAMM. Demonstrative.
— m. GRAMM. Demonstrative.

démonstration [-sjɔ̃] f. Demonstration; conclusive experiment (expérience); demonstration (leçon). ‖ Demonstration, mass meeting (du peuple). ‖ Math. Proof; *faire une démonstration*, to demonstrate. ‖ Milit. Demonstration, show of force; *faire une démonstration*, to make a demonstration. ‖ Comm. Demonstration, explanation; *appareil, voiture de démonstration*, demonstration model, car. ‖ Sports. Match, exhibition; sparring match (de boxe). ‖ Fig. Demonstration, effusion; *faire beaucoup de démonstrations*, to be effusive (ou) demonstrative, to make a great display of affection.

démonstrativement [-tivmã] adv. Demonstratively; conclusively.

démontable [demõtabl] adj. Naut. Collapsible (canot). ‖ Archit. Portable, sectional (construction). ‖ Techn. That can be taken to pieces, dismountable, U. S. knock-down (machine); detachable (pièce).

démontage [-ta:ʒ] m. Naut. Unshipping (du gouvernail). ‖ Archit. Taking to pieces, dismantling, taking down (d'une construction). ‖ Techn. Taking to pieces; stripping; dismounting; disassembling (d'une machine). ‖ Milit. Dismounting (d'un canon).

démonté, ée [-te] adj. Dismounted (cavalier). ‖ Stormy, wild, raging, heavy (mer). ‖ Techn. Dismantled (machine); stripped (moteur). ‖ Fam. Flummoxed; put out.

démonte–pneu [-tpnø] m. Autom. Tyre-lever, U. S. tire iron.

démonter [-te] v. tr. (1). To dismount, to unhorse (un cavalier). ‖ To unset, to unmount (un diamant, une pierre); to unhinge (une porte); to unstitch (un vêtement). ‖ Naut. To unship (le gouvernail). ‖ Milit. To dismount (un canon). ‖ Autom. To remove (un pneu). ‖ Archit. To take down (une construction). ‖ Techn. To disassemble, to dismount, to dismantle (une machine); to strip (un moteur). ‖ Fam. To flummox, to put out; *se laisser démonter*, to get flurried (ou) flustered.
— v. pr. **se démonter**. Techn. To take to pieces (se désassembler); to go (ou) get out of order (se détraquer). ‖ Fam. To be put out (ou) upset (ou) flummoxed, to lose one's self-assurance, to lose countenance.

démontrable [demõtrabl] adj. Demonstrable.

démontrer [-tre] v. tr. (1). To demonstrate (en général). ‖ Math. To prove. ‖ Comm. To demonstrate, to give practical instruction in. ‖ Fig. To betoken, to reveal, to prove (manifester).
— v. pr. **se démontrer**, to be demonstrated (ou) proved; *ne pas se démontrer*, to be unprovable.

démoralisant [demɔralizã] adj. Demoralizing.

démoralisateur, trice [-zatœ:r, tris] adj. Demoralizing.
— s. Demoralizer.

démoralisation [-zasjõ] f. Demoralization.

démoraliser [-ze] v. tr. To demoralize.
— v. pr. **Se démoraliser**, to become demoralized.

démordre [demɔrdr] v. intr. (4). To let go, to give in; to depart (de, from); *ne pas en démordre*, to stand pat; to stick to it (ou) to one's guns.

démotique [demɔtik] adj. Gramm. Demotic.

démoulage [demula:ʒ] m. Arts. Unmoulding. ‖ Techn. Stripping. ‖ Culin. Turning out.

démouler [-le] v. tr. Arts. To lift (une céramique); to unmould (une statue). ‖ Techn. To strip. ‖ Culin. To turn out (un gâteau).

démoustication [demustikasjõ] f. Clearing of mosquitoes.

démoustiquer [-ke] v. tr. (1). To clear of mosquitoes.

démultiplicateur, trice [demyltiplikatœ:r, tris] adj. Techn. Reducing, gearing-down, demultiplying. ‖ Electr. Slow-motion (bouton).

— m. Techn. Reducing gear. ‖ Electr. Vernier attachment.

démultiplication [-sjõ] f. Techn. Gearing down; reduction ratio.

démultiplier [demyltiplje] v. tr. (1). Techn. To gear down, to reduce.

démuni, ie [demyni] adj. Unprovided (de, with); dispossessed (de, of); *démuni d'argent*, moneyless. ‖ Comm. Sold out of stock.

démunir [demyni:r] v. tr. (2). To deprive (de, of); *démunir les arbres de leurs feuilles*, to strip the trees of their leaves; *démunir le pays de ses richesses*, to plunder the country of its treasures. ‖ Comm. To clear out of stock (un magasin).
— v. pr. **Se démunir**, to part (de, with); to deprive oneself (de, of). ‖ Comm. To run short (de, of).

démurer [demyre] v. tr. (1). To open up, to unblock.

démuseler [demyzle] v. tr. (8a). To unmuzzle (un chien). ‖ Fig. To loose, to unleash.

démystification [demistifikasjõ] f. Demystification, disabusing.

démystifier [-fje] v. tr. (1). To demystify, to disabuse.

démythifier [demitifje] v. tr. (1). To demythologize, to demythicize.

dénantir [denãti:r] v. tr. (2). Jur. To deprive of securities.
— v. pr. **Se dénantir**, Jur. To part with one's securities.

dénasalisation [denazalizasjõ] f. Gramm. Denasalization.

dénasaliser [-lize] v. tr. (1). Gramm. To denasalize.

dénatalité [denatalite] f. Fall in the birth-rate.

dénationalisation [denasjɔnalizasjõ] f. Denationalization.

dénationaliser [denasjɔnalize] v. tr. (1). To denationalize.

dénatter [denate] v. tr. (1). To unplait, to unbraid.

dénaturaliser [-ze] v. tr. (1). To denaturalize.

dénaturant, ante [denatyrã, ã:t] adj. Denaturing.
— m. Chim. Denaturant.

dénaturation [-rasjõ] f. Falsification, misrepresentation, distortion; perversion (des faits, des paroles); denaturation, adulteration (d'une substance). ‖ Chim. Denaturing (de l'alcool). ‖ Jur. Conversion of realty into personalty.

dénaturé, ée [-re] adj. Falsified, misrepresented, altered (fait). ‖ Unnatural (enfant, parent). ‖ Perverted (goût). ‖ Chim. *Alcool dénaturé*, methylated spirit, U. S. denatured alcohol.

dénaturer [denatyre] v. tr. (1). To adulterate (un goût, une substance). ‖ Chim. To methylate, to denature. ‖ Fig. To pervert (l'âme), to garble, to falsify, to misrepresent (des faits); to distort, to alter (des paroles); to make unnatural (qqn).

dénazification [denazifikasjõ] f. Denazification.

dénazifier [-fje] v. tr. (1). To denazify.

dendrite [dãdrit] f. Géol., Méd. Dendrite.

dénégateur, trice [denegatœ:r, tris] s. Denier.

dénégation [-sjõ] f. Denial. ‖ Jur. Traverse.

déneigement [denɛʒmã] m. Snow clearing.

déneiger [-ʒe] v. tr. (7). To clear of snow.

dengue [dã:g] f. Méd. Dengue.

déni [deni] m. Denial, refusal. ‖ Jur. Denial (de justice).

déniaisé, ée [denjɛze] adj. Smartened up, U. S. on the ball (fam.). ‖ Who has lost his (ou) her innocence.

déniaiser v. tr. (1). To smarten up, to sharpen the wits of, to smarten up, U. S. to wise up (dégourdir). ‖ To show a bit of life to (apprendre la vie).
— v. pr. **Se déniaiser**, to smarten up (se débrouiller). ‖ To learn a thing or two, to learn

about life; U. S. to wise up (fam.), to get hep (pop.) [se dégourdir].

dénicher [deniʃe] v. tr. (1). To take from the nest; *dénicher des oiseaux,* to birds'-nest. ‖ Fam. To dislogse, to oust (déloger). ‖ Fam. To ferret out, to rummage out, to pick up, to unearth, to grub out (un objet); to pull down (une situation). — v. intr. To fly away (oiseau). ‖ Fam. To move off, to fly out (personne).

dénicheur, euse [-ʃœ:r, ø:z] s. Birds'-nester. ‖ Fam. Searcher, grubber-out, digger-up; curio-hunter.

dénicotiniser [denikɔtinize] v. tr. (1). To remove nicotine from; *cigarette dénicotinisée,* low nicotine (ou) nicotine-free cigarette.

denier [dənje] m. Denier (pour les bas).

denier m. † Denier (en France); denarius (à Rome). ‖ Farthing, penny; *denier à Dieu,* God's penny, key-money, gratuity. ‖ Money; *un joli denier,* a nice little sum; *de mes propres deniers,* with my own money; *les deniers publics,* public funds. ‖ Ecclés. *Le denier de saint Pierre,* Peter's pence; *le denier de la veuve,* the widow's mite.

dénier [denje] v. tr. (1). To deny (en général); to repudiate (une dette); to refuse to admit (un droit); to disclaim (une responsabilité); *dénier qqch. à qqn,* to deny (ou) to refuse s.o. sth.

dénigrement [denigrəmã] m. Disparagement, denigration, running down.

dénigrer [-gre] v. tr. (1). To backbite, to denigrate; to disparage; to pooh-pooh.

dénigreur [-grœ:r] s. Disparager, denigrator.

dénitrifier [denitrifje] v. tr. (1). Chim. To denitrate.

déniveler [denivle] v. tr. (8a). To put out of level, to make uneven (le sol). ‖ To contour (en topographie).
— v. pr. Se **déniveler,** to subside, to sink.

dénivellation [denivellasjõ] f., **dénivellement** [denivɛlmã] m. Fall of level; difference of level. ‖ Subsidence; settling (chute de terrain). ‖ Gradient of a slope (en topographie).

dénombrable [denõbrabl] adj. Countable, enumerable. ‖ Math. Denumerable, enumerable.

dénombrement [denõbrəmã] m. Counting, enumeration (des objets, des personnes); capitation, census (de la population).

dénombrer [-bre] v. tr. (1). To number, to count (des objets, des personnes); to take a census of (la population); to tell over (les voix).

dénominateur [denɔminatœ:r] m. Math. Denominator.

dénominatif, ive [-tif, i:v] adj. Denominative.

dénomination [-sjõ] f. Denomination, name; *connu sous la dénomination de,* known as.

dénommé, ée [denɔme] adj. Named (appelé); specified (spécifié). ‖ Jur. *Personne dénommée,* nominee.

dénommer v. tr. (1). To denominate, to name.

dénoncer [denõse] v. tr. (1). † To proclaim; to declare (la guerre). ‖ To declare off (un accord entre particuliers); to denounce (un accord, un traité, une trêve). ‖ To denounce; to give away (qqn); to split (ou) tell (ou) squeal on (à l'école). ‖ Fig. To denote, to reveal.
— v. pr. Se **dénoncer,** to give oneself up.

dénonciateur, trice [-sjatœ:r, tris] adj. Accusatory, tell-tale.
— s. Informer, denouncer. ‖ Tale-carrier, tattle-tale (à l'école).

dénonciation [-sjasjõ] f. Denouncement, denunciation (d'un accord, d'un traité). ‖ Denunciation; information (de, against). ‖ Tale-bearing, tattling.

dénotation [denɔtasjõ] f. Philos. Denotation.

dénoter [-te] v. tr. (1). To denote, to mark (v. INDIQUER); *dénoter l'énergie,* to express energy.

dénouement [denumã] m. Solution (d'une affaire délicate); end (d'une aventure); issue, outcome (d'un événement); ending, wind-up (d'une histoire). ‖ Théâtr. Denouement, ending (d'une pièce). ‖ Méd. Crisis, critical phase.

dénouer [denue] v. tr. (1). To untie, to undo, to unknot, to unloose (les objets noués); to let down, to undo (ses cheveux). ‖ Méd. To make supple (les membres). ‖ Fig. To bring to an end (une amitié, une crise, une liaison); to clear up, to unravel (une intrigue, une situation obscure).
— v. pr. Se **dénouer,** to come untied (ou) undone (nœud). ‖ Fig. To come to an end (crise, intrigue); to end, to wind up (histoire, pièce).

dénoyauter [denwajote] v. tr. To stone; U. S. to pit.

dénoyauteur [-tœ:r] m. Stoner, pitter.

denrée [dãre] f. Commodity; *denrées alimentaires,* foodstuffs; *denrées coloniales,* colonial produce.

dense [dã:s] adj. Thick, dense (atmosphère, brouillard); compact (formation); dense, crowded (foule, réunion); close (grain, pluie, texture); dense (population). ‖ Phys. Dense. ‖ Fig. Full of matter, rich (ouvrage, texte).

densimètre [dãsimɛtr] m. Chim. Densimeter; hydrometer.

densité [dãsite] f. Thickness, density (de l'atmosphère); compactness (d'une masse); density (de la population). ‖ Phys. Density. ‖ Milit. Density, compactness (de l'objectif); density (de tir). ‖ Fig. Fullness, substance (d'un ouvrage).

dent [dã] f. Tooth; *dents de lait, de sagesse,* milk, wisdom teeth; *d'un coup de dent,* at one bite; *faire ses dents,* to cut one's teeth, to teethe; *grosse dent,* molar; grinder (fam.); *sans dents,* toothless. ‖ Jag, scallop (de broderie, de dentelle); prong (de fourchette); tooth (de peigne). ‖ Agric. Prong (de fourche); tine (de fourche, de herse); tooth (de râteau). ‖ Bot. Tooth, serration (de feuille). ‖ Zool. Tusk (d'éléphant). ‖ Géogr. Indentation (de la côte); jagged peak (de montagne); jag (du rocher). ‖ Techn. Ward (de clé); cog, notch (de roue); tooth (de scie); *en dents de scie,* saw-toothed, serrated. ‖ Loc. *A belles dents,* with an appetite; *avoir la dent,* to be pincned with hunger, to feel peckish; *avoir une dent contre qqn,* to have a grudge against (ou) a down on s.o.; to bear s.o. a grudge; *avoir la dent dure,* to be mordant; *avoir les dents longues,* to have an itching palm; *dent pour dent,* tooth for tooth; *être sur les dents,* to be knocked up (ou) fagged out; *grommeler entre ses dents,* to grumble; *juste de quoi remplir une dent creuse,* hardly a toothful; *manger du bout des dents,* to peck; *montrer les dents,* to show one's teeth; to bristle; to set up one's back; *ne pas desserrer les dents,* not to open one's mouth, not to say (ou) speak a word; *quand les poules auront des dents,* when the cows come home; *se mettre qqch. sous la dent,* to have sth. to peck at, to have a bite or two; *serrer les dents,* to set one's teeth. ‖ **Dent-de-lion,** f. (pl. *dents-de-lion*). Bot. Dandelion. ‖ **Dent-de-loup,** f. (pl. *dents-de-loup*). Autom. Ratchet-tooth.

dentaire [dãtɛ:r] adj. Méd. Dentary (arcade); dental (chirurgie); *art dentaire,* dentistry.

dental, ale [dãtal] adj. Gramm. Dental.

dentale f. Gramm. Dental.

denté, ée [dãte] adj. Techn. Toothed, cogged, serrated; *roue dentée,* cogwheel. ‖ Bot. Serrate.

dentelé, ée [dãtle] adj. Denticulate; indented (bord); jagged (bord, contour, étoffe). ‖ Géogr. Indented (littoral); jagged (rocher). ‖ Bot. Serrate, dentate (feuille). ‖ Blas. Dantellé, dancetté.
— m. Méd. Serratus (muscle).

denteler v. tr. (8a). To indent (le bord); to jag (un contour, une étoffe); to scallop (une étoffe).

dentelle [dãtɛl] f. Lace; *dentelle à l'aiguille,*

au fuseau, à la machine, needle-, bobbin- (ou) pillow-, machine-made lace; *dentelle d'Alençon, de Malines,* French-point, Mechlin lace. ‖ ARCHIT. Wrought ironwork. ‖ TECHN. Dentelle (en reliure).

dentellerie [-lri] f. Lace-making (fabrication); lace-work (objets).

dentellier, ère [dɑ̃təlje, ɛ:r] adj. *Industrie dentellière,* lace-manufacturing.
— m. Lace-maker.

dentellière [dɑ̃təljɛ:r] f. Lacewoman.

dentelure [dɑ̃tly:r] f. Indentation, jag (d'un bord); scallop (d'une étoffe); perforation (des timbres). ‖ GÉOGR. Indentation (du littoral); jagged line (des montagnes, des rochers). ‖ BOT. Serration (d'une feuille). ‖ TECHN. Dog-tooth.

denter [dɑ̃te] v. tr. (1). TECHN. To tooth, to cog.

dentier [dɑ̃tje] m. MÉD. Denture; set of false teeth.

dentifrice [dɑ̃tifris] m. Dentifrice; tooth-paste.
— adj. *Eau dentifrice,* mouth-wash; *pâte dentifrice,* tooth-paste; *poudre dentifrice,* tooth-powder.

dentine [dɑ̃tin] f. MÉD. Dentine.

dentiste [dɑ̃tist] m. MÉD. Dentist.

dentition [dɑ̃tisjɔ̃] f. MÉD. Dentition, teething.

denture [dɑ̃ty:r] f. MÉD. Set of teeth. ‖ TECHN. Teeth, cogs.

dénucléarisation [denyklearizasjɔ̃] f. PHYS. Nuclear disengagement.

dénucléarisé, ée [-ze] adj. Atom-free.

dénudation [denydasjɔ̃] f. Denudation. ‖ THÉÂTR. *Dénudation progressive,* strip-tease.

dénudé, ée [-de] adj. Leafless (arbre); bare (arbre, os, racine, paysage, pièce); denuded (arbre, montagne); bald (crâne, montagne); naked (personne). ‖ ELECTR. Bare (fil).

dénuder v. tr. (1). To denude, to strip (un arbre); to make bald (un crâne, une montagne); to lay bare (un os, une racine, une personne); to strip of furniture, to unfurnish (une pièce). ‖ ELECTR. To strip (un fil).
— v. pr. **Se dénuder,** to grow bare (arbre, crâne, os, montagne); to strip to the skin, to strip naked (personne).

dénué, ée [denɥe] adj. Free (libre) [*de,* of]; deprived, devoid (privé) [*de,* of]; *dénué de fondement, de raison, de valeur,* groundless, senseless; valueless; *dénué de ressources,* destitute; *dénué de soucis,* devoid of cares, care-free.

dénuement [denymɑ̃] m. Destitution; want; penury; *dans un dénuement total,* utterly destitute.

dénuer [-e] v. tr. (1). To deprive (*de,* of).
— v. pr. **Se dénuer,** to strip oneself bare; to divest oneself (*de,* of); to part (*de,* with).

dénutrition [denytrisjɔ̃] f. MÉD. Denutrition.

déodorant [deɔdɔrɑ̃] adj., m. Deodorant, antiperspirant.

déontologie [deɔ̃tɔlɔʒi] f. Deontology; *déontologie médicale,* medical code (ou) ethics.

déontologique [-ʒik] adj. Deontological.

dépaillé, ée [depɑje] adj. Seatless (siège).

dépailler v. tr. (1). To remove straw from.

dépannage [depana:ʒ] m. Emergency repairing; breakdown service; *équipe de dépannage,* breakdown (ou) U. S. wrecking gang. ‖ AUTOM. Road repairs (sur route).

dépanner [-ne] v. tr. (1). To repair on the spot, to put into working order (un véhicule). ‖ AUTOM. *Dépanner une auto,* to get a car going again; *dépanner qqn,* to put s.o.'s car into running order. ‖ FAM. *Dépanner un canard boiteux,* to help a lame dog over a stile; *dépanner qqn,* to give s.o. a lift (ou) a leg-up; *cette somme va me dépanner,* this sum will tide me over.

dépanneur [-nœ:r] m. TECHN. Repair (ou) breakdown mechanic (mécanicien); U. S. wrecker,

trouble-hunter (ou) -shooter. ‖ MILIT. Maintenance fitter (de tank).

dépanneuse [-nø:z] f. AUTOM. Wrecking (ou) break-down lorry, U. S. wrecking truck.

depaqueter [depakte] v. tr. (8a). To unpack.

dépareillé, ée [deparɛje] adj. Incomplete (collection); odd, unmatched (objets); odd (volumes). ‖ COMM. *Articles dépareillés.* oddments.

dépareiller v. tr. (1). To break (une collection, un ensemble); to split (une paire).

déparer [depare] v. tr. (1). To mar; to spoil the beauty (ou) the effect of.

déparié, ée [deparje] adj. Odd; split; unassorted.

déparier v. tr. (1). To split (deux objets). ‖ FIG. To separate (des couples).

départ [depar] m. Departure, start, starting; *signal du départ,* starting signal. ‖ ARCHIT. Foot (d'escalier). ‖ COMM. *Prix de départ,* upset price; *produit de départ,* original material. ‖ MILIT. Discharge (d'un fusil); *avis de départ,* notification of departure; *ordre de départ,* marching orders. ‖ NAUT. Sailing (d'un navire); *sur le départ,* outward-bound (navire). ‖ AVIAT. Taking off, start, sortie (d'un avion). ‖ CH. DE F. Departure (d'un train); *gare, voie de départ,* departure station, platform. ‖ SPORTS. Throw-off (de la chasse); start (d'une course); *faux départ,* false start; *manquer le départ,* to be left at the post (aux courses); *position de départ,* balk (au croquet). ‖ ELECTR. *Ligne de départ,* lead. ‖ TECHN. Carrying off (des eaux). ‖ CHIM. Onset (d'une réaction). ‖ FIG. Lead-off (d'une discussion); start (dans la vie); *faire un bon départ,* to make (ou) to get a good start; *point de départ,* starting-point.

départ m. Separation, discrimination, distinction; *faire le départ entre une chose et une autre,* to distinguish (ou) to sort out sth. from sth. else, to discriminate between sth. and sth. else.

départager [departaʒe] v. tr. (7). To decide between (des avis); to settle between (des personnes); *départager les voix,* to give the casting vote.

département [departmɑ̃] m. Department (de bibliothèque). ‖ Ministry, U. S. department (ministère). ‖ GÉOGR. Department. ‖ FIG. Province (rayon); competence (ressort).

départemental, ale [-tal] adj. Departmental; provincial; *route départementale,* secondary road. ‖ CH. DE F. Local (chemin de fer).

départir [departi:r] v. tr. (93). To distribute, to dispense, to assign (distribuer); to divide, to separate (diviser).
— v. pr. **Se départir,** to depart, to swerve (*de,* from); *se départir de ses habitudes,* to break with one's habits; *se départir de toute contrainte,* to fling aside all restraint.

dépassant [depasɑ̃] m. Edging.

dépassement [-smɑ̃] m. Overstepping (d'une limite). ‖ JUR. Excess (de crédits). ‖ AUTOM. Overtaking and passing (d'une voiture).

dépasser [-se] v. tr. (1). To protrude, to project, to overhang (saillir); *dépasser l'alignement,* to project beyond the building line; *dépasser le mur,* to extend beyond the wall. ‖ To exceed, to transgress (excéder); *dépasser en nombre,* to outnumber; *dépasser un prix donné,* to cost more than a given price; *dépasser en poids, en taille,* to overweigh, to overtop; *avoir dépassé la cinquantaine,* to have turned fifty, to be over fifty. ‖ To be (ou) go (ou) move beyond, to pass (devancer); *dépasser une rue, qqn,* to go past a street, s.o.; *dépasser au vol,* to outfly. ‖ BOT. *Dépasser en hauteur,* to outgrow (une plante). ‖ TECHN. *Dépasser en rendement,* to outwork, to outstrip. ‖ NAUT. To outsail (un navire). ‖ SPORTS. To outmatch (ses concurrents); to outdrive (au golf); *dépasser à cheval,* to ride past; *dépasser à*

la course, to outrun, to outstrip, to outpace. ‖ MILIT. To overshoot (le but) ; to outmarch (l'ennemi) ; *dépasser à la lutte, en tactique*, to outfight, to outgeneral. ‖ FIG. To surpass (l'attente, les prévisions) ; to be beyond (la compétence, l'entendement) ; to overstep (les instructions) ; to exceed (les limites) ; *dépasser les bornes de la plaisanterie*, to go beyond a joke ; U. S. to run a joke into the ground ; *dépasser ses forces*, to overtax one's strength, to overexert (ou) overstrain oneself ; *dépasser l'imagination*, to be past all imagining ; *dépasser en bêtise, en finesse, en influence, en réputation*, to outfool, to outwit, to outweigh, to outshine ; *cela dépasse mes moyens*, it is beyond my means. ‖ FAM. *Cela me dépasse*, that's beyond me ! ; *dépassé*, outmoded, out-of-date (ouvrage).
— v. intr. To overlap ; *une couverture de livre qui dépasse*, a cover that overlaps ; *sa combinaison dépasse*, her slip is showing. ‖ AUTOM. To overtake, U. S. to pass (doubler).
— v. pr. **Se dépasser**, to surpass oneself.

dépassionner [depasjɔne] v. tr. (1). To calm, to take the edge off.

dépatouiller (se) [sədepatuje] v. pr. (1). FAM. To shift for oneself ; to get out of a mess.

dépaver [depave] v. tr. To unpave (une rue).

dépaysé, ée [depɛize] adj. Strange, uprooted, not at home, out of one's element, like a fish out of water ; *se sentir dépaysé*, to feel strange.

dépaysement [-zmɑ̃] m. Uprooting (action) ; strangeness (sentiment).

dépayser [-ze] v. tr. (1). To remove s.o. from his own country (ou) from his usual surroundings. ‖ FIG. To remove from one's element.

dépeçage [depəsa:ʒ] m. Cutting up (d'un animal). ‖ CULIN. Carving (d'une volaille). ‖ NAUT. Breaking up (d'un navire). ‖ FIG. Carving up (d'une nation) ; taking to pieces (d'un ouvrage).

dépecer [-se] v. tr. (6). To cut up (un animal) ; to tear up (sa proie). ‖ CULIN. To carve (une volaille). ‖ NAUT. To break up (un navire). ‖ FIG. To dismember (une nation) ; to dissect, to take to pieces (un ouvrage).

dépeceur, euse [-sœ:r, ø:z] s. Cutter-up. ‖ NAUT. Ship-breaker.

dépêche [depɛ:ʃ] f. Telegram ; wire (fam.). ‖ Dispatch (lettre officielle). ‖ COMM. Letter.

dépêcher [-ʃe] v. tr. (1). To expedite (une affaire) ; to dispatch, to hurry over (un travail) ; *dépêcher son déjeuner*, to polish off (ou) to dispose of one's lunch. ‖ To dispatch (un messager). ‖ FAM. To dispatch, to make away with, U. S. to bump off, to rub out ; *dépêcher dans l'autre monde*, to launch into eternity.
— v. pr. **Se dépêcher**, to hasten (*de*, to) ; to hurry, to make haste, to be quick ; to press on ; to hustle ; *dépêchez-vous !*, hurry up !, be quick !, U. S. hustle ! ; *se dépêcher d'entrer*, to hurry in.

dépeigné, ée [depɛɲe] adj. Dishevelled ; unkempt ; with tousled hair.

dépeigner v. tr. (1). To make untidy (les cheveux) ; to ruffle (qqn).

dépeindre [depɛ̃:dr] v. tr. (59). To depict, to paint ; to describe.

dépenaillé, ée [depnɑje] adj. FAM. In rags (ou) tatters ; dressed like a scarecrow. (V. DÉGUENILLÉ.)

dépendance [depɑ̃dɑ̃:s] f. Dependence, depending, inter-dependence (entre les choses) ; dependency (entre les Etats) ; dependence, subordination, subjection (entre les personnes) ; *dans la dépendance de*, dependent on ; subject to, under the domination (ou) the sway (ou) the thumb of. ‖ Pl. Outbuildings, appurtenances, appendages, annexes (d'une maison).

dépendant, ante [-dɑ̃, ɑ̃:t] adj. Dependent (*de*,

on) ; subject (*de*, to) [soumis]. ‖ Belonging (ou) appertaining (*de*, to) [appartenant].

dépendre [depɑ̃:dr] v. tr. (4). To take down.

dépendre v. tr. (4). To be dependent (*de*, on) ; to be subordinate (ou) subject (*de*, to) [v. RELEVER] ; *dépendre directement de qqn*, to be directly responsible to s.o. ; *ne dépendre que de soi-même*, to be one's own master. ‖ To belong (ou) appertain (*de*, to) [appartenir]. ‖ FIG. To depend, to hang (*de*, on) ; to be within the control (*de*, of) ; to be conditioned (*de*, by) ; to lie, to rest (*de*, with) ; *cela ne dépend que de vous*, it rests (ou) lies entirely with you ; *ces circonstances ne dépendent pas de nous*, these circumstances are beyond our control ; *dépendre des progrès de la science*, to be conditioned by the progress of science ; *dépendre de circonstances minimes*, to turn upon very small circumstances.
— v. intr. To depend ; *cela dépend*, that depends.
— v. impers. *Il dépend de vous de*, it rests (ou) lies with you to ; it lies within your own discretion to.

dépens [depɑ̃] m. pl. Cost, expense ; *aux dépens de qqch.*, at the sacrifice of sth. ; *aux dépens de sa santé*, to the detriment of one's health ; *aux dépens de qqn*, at s.o.'s expense ; *à mes dépens*, to my own prejudices, to my cost. ‖ JUR. Costs ; *condamné aux dépens*, ordered to pay costs.

dépense [depɑ̃:s] f. Expense, expenditure ; charge, cost ; outlay ; *au prix de grosses dépenses*, at great cost ; *dépenses de l'Etat*, national expenditure ; *faire de la dépense*, to go to expense ; *faire de grosses dépenses*, to incur heavy expense, to spend a great deal of money ; *faire la dépense de*, to go to the expense of ; *faire faire des dépenses à qqn*, to put s.o. to expense. ‖ Pantry, storeroom (réserve). ‖ FIN. Outgoings, expenses (sorties). ‖ MÉD. Dispensary (d'hôpital). ‖ FIG. Consumption (de charbon, de gaz) ; discharge (d'eau) ; expenditure, waste (de temps).

dépenser [depɑ̃se] v. tr. (1). To spend, to expend, to lay out ; *dépenser sottement*, to fool away one's money (fam.). ‖ To consume (du charbon) ; to use (du gaz, de l'électricité). ‖ FIG. To waste (son énergie) ; to spend (son temps).
— v. intr. To spend ; *aimer à dépenser*, to be a natural spendthrift.
— v. pr. **Se dépenser**, to take exercise (se remuer) ; to overexert oneself (se surmener) ; *se dépenser pour*, to devote oneself to (se dévouer) ; to lay oneself out of (se mettre en frais).

dépensier, ère [-sje, ɛ:r] adj. Thriftless, unthrifty, lavish, extravagant.
— s. Spendthrift, waster, prodigal, squanderer.

déperdition [depɛrdisjɔ̃] f. Waste (de chaleur) ; loss (d'essence) ; escape (de gaz). ‖ ELECTR. Leakage. ‖ FIG. Waste, loss (d'énergie) ; wasting away (de forces).

dépérir [deperi:r] v. intr. (2). To waste away, to pine away. ‖ MÉD. To decline, to fail (santé). ‖ BOT. To wither, to fade away (plante). ‖ JUR. To fall into decay (biens). ‖ COMM. To fall off, to dwindle (industrie).

dépérissement [-rismɑ̃] m. Wasting away, pining. MÉD. Declining. ‖ BOT. Withering, fading. ‖ JUR. Decay (de biens) ; dwindling (de capitaux) ; growing loss of validity (de preuves).

dépersonnalisation [depɛrsɔnalizasjɔ̃] f. Depersonalization.

dépersonnaliser [-ze] v. tr. (1). To depersonalize.

dépêtrer [depɛtre] v. tr. (1). To get out, to free, to extricate (qqn) ; *dépêtrer qqn de qqch.*, to disentangle s.o. from sth. ; *dépêtrer qqn de qqn*, to rid s.o. of s.o. ; to take s.o. off s.o.'s hands.
— v. pr. **Se dépêtrer**, to shift for oneself (se

débrouiller); to get out of a mess (se tirer du pétrin); *se dépêtrer de qqn*, to get rid of s.o.

dépeuplement [depœpləmɑ̃] m. Depopulation (d'un pays). ‖ Clearing (d'une forêt); unstocking (d'une rivière).

dépeupler [-ple] v. tr. (1). To depopulate, to dispeople (un pays, une région). ‖ To clear (une forêt); to unstock (une rivière).
— v. pr. **Se dépeupler**, to lose population, to become depopulated.

déphasage [defɑza:ʒ] m. ELECTR. Dephasing.

déphasé, ée [defɑze] adj. ELECTR. Out of phase. ‖ FAM. Out of step, out of touch, disorientated.

déphaser [-ze] v. tr. (1). ELECTR. To dephase.

déphosphoration [defɔsfɔrasjɔ̃] f. CHIM. Dephosphorization.

déphosphorer [-re] v. tr. (1). To dephosphorize.

dépiauter [depjote] v. tr. (1). FAM. To skin, to flay (écorcher). ‖ FAM. To dissect (un livre).

dépilation [depilasjɔ̃] f. Depilation.

dépilatoire [-twa:r] adj., m. Depilatory.

dépiler [depile] v. tr. (1). MÉD. To cause s.o.'s. hair to fall out. ‖ TECHN. To unhair (en tannerie).

dépiquage [depika:ʒ] m. AGRIC. Treading out (du blé); transplanting (d'une plante, de la vigne).

dépiquer [-ke] v. tr. (1). AGRIC. To tread out (le blé); to transplant (une plante, la vigne).

dépistage [depista:ʒ] m. Tracking down (du gibier, d'un criminel). ‖ Detection (d'une maladie).

dépister [depiste] v. tr. (1). To put (ou) throw off the scent (un chien); to track down (le gibier). ‖ FAM. To nose out, to smell out (un bandit); to unearth (un objet rare); to baffle (la police).

dépit [depi] m. Spite, vexation; grudge, resentment, chagrin; *avec dépit*, spitefully; resentfully; *par dépit*, out of vexation; *plein de dépit*, spiteful. — loc. prép. **En dépit de**, in spite of, in defiance of, in the face of, despite, notwithstanding; *en dépit du bon sens*, against all sense; *en dépit de ce que*, in spite of the fact that, although, though.

dépiter [-te] v. tr. (1). To vex, to spite.
— v. pr. **Se dépiter**, to be vexed (ou) annoyed (ou) disappointed (de, at).

déplacé, ée [deplase] adj. Displaced (chose); *personnes déplacées*, displaced persons; refugees and deportees. ‖ FIG. Out of one's place (personne); in bad taste, out of place, misplaced, uncalled-for (propos).

déplacement [-smɑ̃] m. Displacement; removing; shifting (changement de place); travelling, journeying (voyage); *les déplacements de la cour*, the movements of the court; *frais de déplacements*, travelling expenses. ‖ NAUT. Displacement (d'un navire). ‖ MILIT. Switching (du tir); movement (des troupes). ‖ JUR. Transfer (d'un fonctionnaire); transference, swing-over (des voix aux élections). ‖ FIN. Shift (des cours); displacement, shift, shifting (des fonds). ‖ TECHN. Travel.

déplacer [-se] v. tr. (6). To displace, to move, to remove, to shift (qqch.); to displace, to dislodge, to oust (qqn). ‖ NAUT. To displace (un navire). ‖ MILIT. To transfer, to move (les troupes). ‖ JUR. To transfer (un fonctionnaire). ‖ FIN. To displace (des fonds). ‖ FIG. To change (un rendez-vous); to shift (la responsabilité).
— v. pr. **Se déplacer**, to move (chose); to change place, to shift, to move (personne); to move about, to travel (voyager). ‖ MILIT. To execute a movement.

déplaire [deplɛ:r] v. intr. (75). To displease (à, to); *ses façons me déplaisent*, I don't like his manners; *elle me déplaît*, I dislike her; *elle a peur de me déplaire*, she fears to offend me.
— N. B. The past part. *déplu* is invariable.
— v. impers. *Il lui déplaît de*, he does not like

to; *ne vous déplaise*, with your leave, if you have no objection; with all due respect to you.
— v. pr. **Se déplaire**, to dislike (à, in); *il se déplaît à la campagne*, he does not like country life.
— v. récipr. **Se déplaire**, to dislike each other.

déplaisant, ante [deplɛzɑ̃, ɑ̃:t] adj. Offensive, shocking (attitude); unpleasant (obligation, temps); unpleasing, disagreeable (personne).

déplaisir [-zi:r] m. Displeasure, dissatisfaction.

déplantage [deplɑ̃ta:ʒ] m. AGRIC. Lifting, unplanting.

déplanter [deplɑ̃te] v. tr. AGRIC. To unplant.

déplantoir [-twa:r] m. AGRIC. Transplanter; garden trowel.

déplâtrage [deplɑtra:ʒ] m. ARCHIT. Removal of the plaster. ‖ MÉD. Taking out of plaster.

déplâtrer [-tre] v. tr. (1). ARCHIT. To remove the plaster from. ‖ MÉD. To take out of plaster.

déplétion [deplesjɔ̃] f. TECHN., PHYS. Depletion.

dépliage [deplija:ʒ] m. Unfolding (d'un objet plié); opening (d'un journal).

dépliant [deplijɑ̃] m. Folder.

déplier [-je] v. tr. (1). To unfold (un objet plié). ‖ To open out, to spread out (un journal).
— v. pr. **Se déplier**, to unfold, to open out.

déplissage [deplisa:ʒ] m. Unpleating.

déplisser [-se] v. tr. (1). To unpleat.
— v. pr. **Se déplisser**, to come unpleated (ou) out of pleats.

déploiement [deplwamɑ̃] m. Unfolding (d'une étoffe, d'un journal); stretching (des bras). ‖ MILIT. Unfurling (du drapeau); deployment (des troupes). ‖ NAUT. Unfurling (d'un pavillon). ‖ FIG. Display (de courage, de forces); show (de faste); exertion (d'un talent).

déplombage [deplɔ̃ba:ʒ] m. Unsealing (par la douane). ‖ MÉD. Unstopping, U. S. removal of a filling.

déplombé, ée [-be] adj. FAM. Unbalanced (esprit).

déplomber v. tr. (1). To unseal. ‖ MÉD. To unstop, U. S. to remove fillings from (les dents).

déplorable [deplɔrabl] adj. Deplorable; lamentable(fâcheux); pitiable, pitiful, piteous(pitoyable).

déplorablement [-blemɑ̃] adv. Deplorably, lamentably; piteously, pitiably.

déplorer [-re] v. tr. (1). To deplore, to lament (en général); to mourn, to grieve over (une mort). ‖ To lament for, to sigh over, to regret (regretter); to complain of (se plaindre de).

déployé, ée [deplwaje] adj. Unfolded, spread (ailes); unfolded, open, opened out (journal). ‖ MILIT. Flying, unfurled (drapeau); deployed (troupes). ‖ NAUT. Unfurled (pavillon). ‖ TECHN. Expanded (métal). ‖ LOC. *Rire à gorge déployée*, to split one's sides, to roar with laughter.

déployer v. tr. (9 a). To unfold, to spread, to stretch (ses ailes); to stretch out (les bras); to unfold, to open out (un journal); to stretch (une tente). ‖ MILIT. To fly, to hang out (un drapeau); to deploy (des troupes). ‖ NAUT. To unfurl, to fly (un pavillon); to unfurl, to set, to spread (les voiles). ‖ FIG. To show (de l'audace); to display (du courage, de la patience); to make use of (son éloquence); to put forth (sa force); to exert (son influence, son talent); to wreak (sa vengeance).
— v. pr. **Se déployer**, to spread, to unfold (ailes); to stretch away, to extend (étendue); to spread (éventail); to open out, to unfold (journal). ‖ MILIT. To fly (drapeau); to deploy (troupes). ‖ NAUT. To unfurl (pavillon, voiles). ‖ FIG. To spread (idées, renommée).

déplumé, ée [deplyme] adj. Plucked, featherless (oiseau). ‖ FAM. Hairless, bald (crâne); *il est entièrement déplumé*, he has lost his thatch.
— m. FAM. Bald-pate, bald-head (chauve).

déplumer v. tr. (1). To pluck (un oiseau). ‖ FAM. To make bald.
— v. pr. **Se déplumer**, to lose its feathers, to moult (oiseau). ‖ FAM. To grow bald, to lose one's hair (personne).

dépoétiser [depɔetize] v. tr. (1). To depoetize.

dépoiler [depwale] v. tr. (1). To grain (une peau).

dépoitraillé, ée [depwat.rɑje] adj. All unbuttoned ; hardly decent.

dépolarisant, ante [depɔlarizɑ̃, ɑ̃:t] adj. PHYS. Depolarizing.
— m. PHYS. Depolarizer.

dépolarisation [-zasjɔ̃] PHYS. Depolarization.

dépolariser [-ze] v. tr. PHYS. To depolarize.

dépoli, ie [depɔli] adj. Ground, frosted (verre).

dépolir [-li:r] v. tr. (1). To take the polish off (un meuble) ; to grind, to frost (le verre).
— v. pr. **Se dépolir**, to lose its polish.

dépolissage [-lisa:ʒ] m. Taking off the polish (d'un meuble) ; grinding, frosting (du verre).

dépolitisation [depɔlitizasjɔ̃] f. Depoliticization.

dépolitiser [-ze] v. tr. (1). To depoliticize, to make unpolitical.

déponent, ente [depɔnɑ̃, ɑ̃:t] adj., m. GRAMM. Deponent.

dépopulation [depɔpylasjɔ̃] f. Depopulation.

déport [depɔr] m. FIN. Backwardation. ‖ JUR. Self-challenge.

déportation [depɔrtasjɔ̃] f. JUR. Transportation (pénale) ; deportation (politique).

déporté, ée [-te] adj. JUR. Transported (condamné de droit commun) ; deported, displaced (condamné politique).
— s. Deportee (condamné politique) ; transport, convict (forçat).

déportement [-təmɑ̃] m. AUTOM. Swerve, lurch. ‖ Pl. † Excesses, misconduct, wild life.

déporter [-te] v. tr. (1). To shift, to carry (vers, to). ‖ JUR. To transport (les bagnards) ; to deport (les condamnés politiques). ‖ TECHN. To offset.
— v. intr. AVIAT., AUTOM. To drift (dévier).

déposant, ante [depɔzɑ̃, ɑ̃:t] adj. FIN. Depositing. ‖ JUR. Deposing.
— s. FIN. Depositor (de fonds). ‖ JUR. Bailor (de biens) ; deponent, witness (témoin).

dépose [depo:z] f. Taking-out (ou) -down (d'un lavabo) ; taking-down (d'un lustre, d'une tenture) ; taking-up (des rails, d'un tapis).

déposé, ée [depoze] adj. Deposed (roi). ‖ FIN. Deposited (somme). ‖ JUR. Lodged (plainte) ; brought in (projet de loi). ‖ COMM. *Marque déposée*, registered trade-mark.

déposer v. tr. (1). To deposit, to lay down, to set down (poser) ; to leave (sa carte, son parapluie) ; to hand in (un colis, un télégramme) ; to lay down (un fardeau) ; to dump, to shoot (des ordures) ; to lodge (des provisions en réserve). ‖ To lay aside (la couronne) ; to depose (un roi). ‖ To copyright, to enter at Stationers' Hall (un livre). ‖ To deposit (de la lie, du sable). ‖ FIN. To deposit (une somme). ‖ CH. DE F. To deposit, U. S. to check (à la consigne). ‖ COMM. To register (une marque). ‖ JUR. To file (une demande, des conclusions) ; to lodge (une plainte) ; to introduce, to bring in (un projet de loi) ; to send in (un rapport) ; *déposer que*, to depose that (témoigner). ‖ AUTOM. To discharge, to drop, to set down (un voyageur). ‖ MILIT. To lay down (les armes). ‖ FIG. To impress, to give, to drop (un baiser) ; to lay aside, to put off (le masque) ; to confide (un secret).
— v. intr. To settle (liquide). ‖ JUR. To testify, to depose, to give evidence (témoin).
— v. pr. **Se déposer**, to settle (lie, sédiment).

dépositaire [-zitɛ:r] s. Depositary ; trustee. ‖ JUR.

Bailee, nominee. ‖ COMM. Agent (*de*, for) ; *dépositaire de journaux*, news-agent, U. S. newsdealer.

déposition [-zisjɔ̃] f. Deposition, deposing (d'un roi). ‖ JUR. Deposition, evidence, testimony ; *déposition sous serment*, affidavit ; *faire une déposition*, to give evidence. ‖ ECCLÉS. Deposition (de croix).

déposséder [depɔsede] v. tr. (5). To dispossess (*de*, from) [dépouiller]. ‖ To supplant, to oust (évincer). ‖ JUR. To disseize (*de*, of). ‖ FIG. To strip, to deprive (*de*, of).

dépossession [-sjɔ̃] f. Dispossession. ‖ JUR. Eviction, disseizin.

dépôt [depo] m. Depositing (action) ; deposit (chose) ; *avoir en dépôt*, to hold in trust ; *confier en dépôt à*, to entrust with a deposit. ‖ Copyrighting (d'un livre) ; *dépôt légal*, entering at Stationers' Hall, U. S. registering of copyright. ‖ Crust (de la lie, du tanin) ; settlings (d'un liquide) ; silt (du limon, du sable) ; fur (de tartre). ‖ TECHN. Scale (dans une chaudière). ‖ FIN. Lodgment (d'argent en banque) ; deposition (d'argent en garantie) ; deposit (somme) ; *Caisse des dépôts et consignations*, Deposit and Consignment Office ; *effectuer un dépôt*, to deposit ; *en dépôt*, on deposit, in safe custody ; *mettre en dépôt à la banque*, to deposit with the Bank ; *récépissé de dépôt*, safe-custody receipt. ‖ JUR. Bailment (caution) ; custody, lock-up, prison (prison). ‖ COMM. Bailment (de marchandises) ; registering (d'une marque) ; depot, store, depository ; warehouse (entrepôt) ; *en dépôt*, in stock. ‖ CH. DE F. *Dépôt de gare*, railway station ; *dépôt de marchandises*, goods depot (ou) station, U. S. freight depot ; *dépôt de matériel roulant*, railway sheds. ‖ AUTOM. *Dépôt d'essence*, filling station, U. S. gasoline station. ‖ MILIT. Depot ; *dépôt d'approvisionnement*, supply depot ; *dépôt de munitions*, ammunition dump ; *dépôt par parachute*, dropping. ‖ FIG. *Dépôt sacré*, sacred trust.

dépotage [depɔta:ʒ], **dépotement** [-tmɑ̃] m. AGRIC. Unpotting. ‖ Decanting (d'un liquide).

dépoter [-te] v. tr. AGRIC. To unpot (changer de pot) ; to plant out (transplanter). ‖ To decant (changer de vase).

dépotoir [depɔtwa:r] m. Dumping-ground, rubbish-shoot, dump. ‖ FIG. Dump, dumping-ground.

dépoudrer [depudre] v. tr. (1). To take the powder off (le visage). ‖ To dust (un vêtement).

dépouille [depu:j] f. Skin, hide (d'animal) ; slough (de serpent). ‖ Corpse (d'homme) ; *dépouille mortelle*, mortal remains. ‖ Pl. Clothes (d'un mort). ‖ Pl. Spoils, booty (butin). ‖ ARTS. Demi-intaglio. ‖ FIG. *Dépouille des bois*, dead leaves. ‖ FAM. Pl. Duds, togs (habits).

dépouillé, ée [depuje] adj. Flayed (animal) ; bare, stripped (arbre). ‖ FIG. Fleeced (personne) ; *être dépouillé de tout*, to be left without a shirt. ‖ FIG. Reduced to essentials, unadorned (style).

dépouillement [-jmɑ̃] m. Skinning, flaying (d'un animal). ‖ Opening (du courrier) ; pulling to pieces, dissection, analysis (d'un ouvrage). ‖ FIN. Abstract, sifting (d'un compte). ‖ COMM. Analysis, précis (d'un inventaire). ‖ JUR. Counting (du scrutin).

dépouiller [-je] v. tr. (1). To skin, to flay (un animal). ‖ To cast off, to shed, to exuviate (sa peau) ; to put off, to throw off (un vêtement). ‖ To strip, to denude (les arbres, la campagne). ‖ To open, to read (le courrier) ; to dissect, to go through (un ouvrage). ‖ To plunder, to despoil (un pays) ; to rob, to fleece, to skin (qqn) ; *dépouiller de*, to strip of, to deprive of (sa fortune, ses trésors). ‖ FIN. To examine, to sift, to make an abstract (un compte). ‖ COMM. To analyse (un inventaire). ‖ JUR. To count (le scrutin). ‖ ARTS. To engrave in demi-entaglio. ‖ ELECTR.

To strip (un câble, un fil). ‖ Méd. To lay bare (un membre). ‖ Fig. To put (ou) cast aside, to cast off (un sentiment); to strip of ornaments (son style).
— v. pr. **Se dépouiller,** to become bare (ou) denuded (arbre, campagne); to slough (serpent); to settle (vin). ‖ To strip, to undress (personne); *se dépouiller de ses vêtements,* to take off one's clothes. ‖ To deprive, to divest oneself (*de,* of) [ses biens]. ‖ Fig. *Se dépouiller de,* to cast aside (ou) off [ses préjugés].

dépourvoir [depurvwa:r] v. tr. (78). To deprive (*de,* of).

dépourvu, ue [-vy] adj. Devoid, destitute, bereft (*de,* of); unprovided (*de,* with); *dépourvu d'argent, de sens,* moneyless, senseless; *dépourvu de courage,* wanting in courage.
— loc. adv. **Au dépourvu,** off one's guard, unawares; *pris au dépourvu,* caught napping (ou) unawares; taken by surprise.

dépoussiérage [depusjɛra:ʒ] m. Vacuum-cleaning. ‖ Filtering, cleaning (de l'air).

dépoussiérer [-re] v. tr. To dust.

dépoussiéreur [-rœ:r] m. Vacuum-cleaner.

dépravant, ante [depravã, ã:t] adj. Depraving.

dépravateur, trice [-vatœ:r, tris] adj. Depraving.
— s. Depraver.

dépravation [-vasjɔ̃] f. Depravation (détérioration). ‖ Fig. Depravity (corruption); *dépravation du goût,* depravation of taste.

dépravé, ée [-ve] adj. Depraved (goût); corrupt, depraved (mœurs); depraved, profligate (personne).

dépraver v. tr. (1). To poison (l'esprit); to deprave (le goût); to corrupt, to deprave (les mœurs); to debauch, to corrupt, to pervert (qqn).
— v. pr. **Se dépraver,** to become depraved.

déprécatif, ive [deprekatif, i:v] adj. Ecclés. Deprecative.

dépréciateur, trice [depresjatœ:r, tris] adj. Depreciative, depreciatory; belittling, disparaging.
— s. Fin. Depreciator (de la monnaie). ‖ Fig. Disparager (dénigreur).

dépréciatif, ive [-tif, i:v] adj. Gramm. Depreciatory, depreciative.

dépréciation [-sjɔ̃] f. Depreciation, wear and tear (du matériel). ‖ Fin. Fall in value (de la monnaie); *dépréciation frauduleuse de la monnaie,* defacing. ‖ Comm. Depreciation, fall in price. ‖ Fig. Disparagement, denigration (de qqn).

déprécier [depresje] v. tr. (1). Comm., Fin. To depreciate. ‖ Fig. To disparage, to belittle; to underrate, to undervalue (qqn).
— v. pr. **Se déprécier,** Fin., Comm. To depreciate. ‖ Fig. To cheapen oneself, to make oneself cheap.

déprédateur, trice [depredatœ:r, tris] adj. Depredatory.
— s. Depredator.

déprédation [-sjɔ̃] f. Depredation, plundering (pillage). ‖ Pl. Depredations, damages, havoc (dégâts). ‖ Fin. Misappropriation, peculation.

déprendre [deprã:dr] v. tr. (80). To unstick (décoller); to melt (dégeler).
— v. pr. **Se déprendre,** to come unstuck (se décoller); to melt, to run (se dégeler); to get free (ou) loose (se libérer). ‖ Fig. To detach oneself (*de,* from).

dépressif, ive [deprɛsif, i:v] adj. Depressive. ‖ Fig. Depressing, lowering.

dépression [-sjɔ̃] f. Depression (de l'atmosphère); depression, dip (de l'horizon). ‖ Géogr. Flattening (des pôles); depression (du sol). ‖ Phys. Depression (barométrique). ‖ Méd. Flattening (du crâne); prostration (morale); *dépression nerveuse,* nervous breakdown. ‖ Fin. Depres-

sion; slump; *dépression économique,* business depression. ‖ Fig. Depression, dejection, low spirits, dejectedness. (V. abattement.)

dépressionnaire [-sjɔnɛ:r] adj. Of low pressure.

dépressuriser [deprɛsyrize] v. tr. (1). Aviat. To depressurize.

déprimant, ante [deprimã, ã:t] adj. Lowering, depressing, preying upon the mind.

déprime [deprim] f. Fam. Depression, the blues; *être en pleine déprime,* to be in the doldrums, down in the dumps.

déprimé, ée [-me] adj. Flat (arc); flat, flattened (surface). ‖ Fin. Depressed (marché). ‖ Méd. Weak (malade); feeble (pouls). ‖ Fig. Depressed, downcast. (V. découragé.)

déprimer v. tr. (1). To depress, to flatten (enfoncer). ‖ To weaken (les forces). ‖ Fig. To lower (le moral); to discourage, to dishearten, to dispirit (qqn).
— v. pr. **Se déprimer,** to get dispirited.

de profundis [deprɔfɔ̃dis] m. Ecclés. De profundis.

dépuceler [depysle] v. tr. (8 a). Pop. To deflower.

depuis [depɥi] prép. For (au cours de, pendant); *depuis peu,* for a short time, of late; *depuis quelques années,* for the last few years; *il est mort depuis trois ans,* he died three years ago, he has been dead for three years. ‖ Since (à partir d'une date); *depuis bien des années,* for many years, many years since; *depuis combien de temps* (ou) *depuis quand êtes-vous ici?,* how long (ou) since when have you been here?; *depuis longtemps,* long since; *depuis lors,* since then, ever since. ‖ From (à partir d'une date jusqu'à une autre date exprimée ou non); *depuis son enfance,* from his childhood; *depuis le matin jusqu'au soir,* from morning till night; *je le sais depuis longtemps,* I know it from of old. ‖ From (à partir d'un point, d'un prix); *depuis cinquante francs,* from (ou) starting at fifty francs; *depuis la gare jusqu'à l'église,* from the station to the church.
— adv. Since, since then; *il est malade depuis,* he has been sick ever since (ou) since then. ‖ Later; later on (ultérieurement); *c'est arrivé depuis,* this happened later on.
— loc. prép. **Depuis que,** since; *depuis que je lui ai parlé,* since I spoke to him.

dépuratif, ive [depyratif, i:v] adj. Méd. Depurative.
— m. Méd. Depurative, depurant; blood-cleanser.

dépuration [-sjɔ̃] f. Méd. Depuration; blood-cleansing.

dépurer [depyre] v. tr. (1). Méd. To depurate. ‖ Techn. To purify.

députation [depytasjɔ̃] f. Deputing, deputation (envoi); deputation, delegation (groupe). ‖ Membership (au Parlement); *être candidat* (ou) *se présenter à la députation,* to be a candidate for the membership (ou) a Parliamentary candidate; to stand for Parliament, U. S. to run for Congress.

député [-te] m. Deputy, delegate, representative (délégué). ‖ Representative (en Amérique); Member of Parliament, M. P. (en Angleterre); deputy (en France); *élu député de,* elected member for.

députer v. tr. (1). To depute, to delegate (à, to).

déquiller [dekije] v. tr. To knock out of bounds.

der [dɛr] adj. Fam. *La der des der,* the war to end all wars.

déracinable [derasinabl] adj. Eradicable.

déraciné, ée [-ne] adj. Agric. Uprooted. ‖ Fig. Uprooted, out of one's element, withdrawn from one's customary surroundings, like a fish out of water (personne); eradicated (préjugé).

déracinement [-nmɑ̃] m. AGRIC. Rooting up, uprooting, deracination. ‖ FIG. Eradication, uprootal, extirpation.

déraciner [-ne] v. tr. (1). AGRIC. To uproot, to deracinate. ‖ MÉD. To extract (une dent). ‖ FIG. To uproot (qqn); to eradicate, to extirpate (un préjugé, un vice).

déracineur [-nœːr] s. Uprooter.

déraidir [deːɛdiːr] v. tr. (2). To unstiffen, to take the stiffness out of. ‖ FIG., FAM. To unstarch, to unbend.
— v. pr. **Se déraidir**, to unbend, to lose one's stiffness. ‖ FAM. To become supple (ou) more tractable.

déraillement [derɑjmɑ̃] m. CH. DE F. Derailment.

dérailler [-je] v. intr. (1). CH. DE F. To be derailed, to run off the metals, to jump the rails; *faire dérailler*, to derail; *ne pas dérailler*, to keep to the rails. ‖ TECHN. To leave the groove (aiguille de tourne-disque). ‖ FAM. To go astray, to be all adrift (dévier); to be unhinged (s'égarer).

dérailleur [-jœːr] m. TECHN. Derailleur, three-speed gear, U. S. gearshift (de bicyclette). ‖ CH. DE F. Shifting track.

déraison [derɛzɔ̃] f. Unreasonableness; unreason; foolishness.

déraisonnable [-zɔnabl] adj. Unreasonable; foolish, senseless (v. INSENSÉ); unwise (peu sage).

déraisonnablement [-zɔnabləmɑ̃] adv. Unreasonably; foolishly; unwisely.

déraisonner [-zɔne] v. intr. (1). To talk nonsense. (V. DIVAGUER.) ‖ MÉD. To rave.

dérangé, ée [derɑ̃ʒe] adj. MÉD. Upset (estomac); loose (intestin). ‖ TECHN. Out of order, out of gear, broken down, not working (machine). ‖ ASTRON. Unsettled (temps). ‖ FIG. Unbalanced, deranged (esprit); crazy, cracked (personne).

dérangement [-ʒmɑ̃] m. Disarrangement, displacement, disorder, upset (désordre). ‖ Trouble, inconvenience, derangement (peine); *causer du dérangement à qqn*, to give s.o. trouble; to disturb s.o., to intrude upon s.o. ‖ Disturbance, perturbation (du temps). ‖ MÉD. Upset (du corps); looseness (de l'intestin); derangement (de l'esprit). ‖ TECHN. Putting out of order, throwing out of gear (d'une machine). ‖ ELECTR. Fault; *en dérangement*, out of order (téléphone).

déranger [-ʒe] v. tr. (7). To disarrange, to misarrange, to misplace; to disorder, to jumble, to tumble (qqch.). ‖ To trouble, to inconvenience, to disturb, to intrude upon, to put out (qqn); *excusez-moi de vous déranger*, I'm sorry to bother you; *j'espère que cela ne vous dérange pas*, I hope it will not put you to any inconvenience; *je ne veux pas vous déranger plus longtemps*, I will intrude no longer; *je ne veux pas vous déranger*, I won't take you out of your way (de votre chemin) [ou] disturb you (de votre place [ou] travail). ‖ MÉD. To upset (l'estomac); to loosen (l'intestin); to unbalance, to derange (l'esprit). ‖ TECHN. To put out of order (une machine). ‖ ASTRON. To unsettle, to upset (le temps). ‖ FIG. To upset, to cross (des plans).
— v. pr. **Se déranger**, to move from one's place (se déplacer); *je ne me dérangerai pas pour lui*, I won't go out of my way to oblige him; *ne vous dérangez pas*, don't move, don't stir. ‖ To inconvenience oneself, to put oneself out, to give oneself trouble (se donner du mal). ‖ MÉD. To get upset (estomac); to become deranged (esprit). ‖ TECHN. To get out of order (machine). ‖ FIG. To run wild, to live fast, to dissipate (personne).

dérapage [derapaːʒ] m. AUTOM. Skid, skidding. ‖ NAUT. Dragging.

déraper [-pe] v. intr. (1). AUTOM. To skid (voiture). ‖ NAUT. To drag (ancre).
— v. tr. NAUT. To drag (l'ancre).

dératé [derate] m. *Courir comme un dératé*, to run like mad (ou) like the wind.
— adj. Spleened.

dérater v. tr. (1). To spleen.

dératisation [-tizasjɔ̃] f. Deratization.

dératiser [-tize] v. tr. (1). To exterminate rats.

derby [dɛrbi] m. SPORTS. Derby (course de chevaux); local Derby (match).

derechef [dərəʃɛf] adv. Once more, again, a second time.

déréglé, ée [deregle] adj. TECHN. Out of order (boussole, machine, pendule). ‖ MILIT. Inaccurate (tir). ‖ MÉD. Immoderate (appétit); disordered (estomac); deranged (esprit); irregular (pouls). ‖ FIG. Immoderate (désirs); wild (imagination); unruly (passions); disorderly, dissolute (vie).

dérèglement [derɛgləmɑ̃] m. TECHN. Disordered state, maladjusment. ‖ MILIT. Inaccuracy (du tir). ‖ MÉD. Derangement (de l'esprit); irregularity (du pouls). ‖ FIG. Immoderateness (des désirs); profligacy, dissoluteness (de la vie).

dérégler [-gle] v. tr. (5). TECHN. To put out of order (une boussole, une machine, une montre). ‖ MÉD. To unsettle (l'estomac). ‖ FIG. To disturb, to upset (les habitudes); to render profligate (ou) dissolute (la vie).
— v. pr. **Se dérégler**, TECHN. To get out of order. ‖ FIG. To lead an abandoned life, to run wild.

dérider [deride] v. tr. (1). To unwrinkle (le visage). ‖ FIG. To cheer up, to enliven (qqn).
— v. pr. **Se dérider**, to lose its wrinkles (visage). ‖ FIG. To cheer up, to brighten up, to begin to smile.

dérision [deːizsjɔ̃] f. Derision, mockery; *objet de dérision*, laughing-stock; *par dérision*, in mockery, deridingly, derisively; *tourner en dérision*, to deride, to hold up to ridicule, to make a laughing stock of. ‖ FAM. Derisive thing.

dérisoire [-zwaːr] adj. Derisory, ridiculous. ‖ Petty (frais); absurdly low, preposterous (somme); *d'un prix dérisoire*, dirt cheap (fam.).

dérisoirement [-zwarmɑ̃] adv. Ridiculously.

dérivateur [derivatœːr] m. ELECTR. Shunter, shunting device.

dérivatif, ive [-tif, iːv] adj. Derivative.
— m. GRAMM. Derivative. ‖ FIG. Distraction; diversion (à, from); *trouver un dérivatif à son chagrin*, to find relief from one's sorrow.

dérivation [-sjɔ̃] f. Diversion, tapping (d'un cours d'eau). ‖ MÉD., MATH., GRAMM. Derivation. ‖ ELECTR. Shunt; *monter en dérivation*, to shunt. ‖ CH. DE F. Loop. ‖ MILIT. Windage; drift. ‖ NAUT. Deflection, drift.

dérive [deriːv] f. NAUT. Leeway, drift; *à la dérive*, adrift. ‖ NAUT. Centre-board (quille). ‖ MILIT. Deflection. ‖ AVIAT. Leeway (déviation); fin (gouvernail). ‖ CH. DE F. Running back; *aller à la dérive*, to run back. ‖ FIG. *A la dérive*, adrift; *laisser tout aller à la dérive*, to let everything slide (ou) drift (ou) go to rack and ruin.

dérivé, ée [derive] adj. GRAMM., MATH. Derived. ‖ ELECTR. Shunted (courant); branch (fil). ‖ CHIM. *Produit dérivé*, by-product.
— m. GRAMM. Derivative. ‖ CHIM. By-product.

dérivée f. MATH. Derivative.

dériver v. tr. (1). To divert, to deflect, to turn aside (un cours d'eau); to branch off (une route). ‖ ELECTR. To shunt (un courant; to branch (un fil). ‖ GRAMM., MATH. To derive. ‖ NAUT. To surge (un câble).
— v. intr. To be diverted (rivière) [de, from]. ‖ GRAMM. To be derived (de, from). ‖ FIG. To derive, to issue, to spring, to proceed, to stem [de, from]. (V. DÉCOULER.)

dériver v. intr. (1). NAUT. To drift; *dériver sur son ancre*, to club; *dériver à la côte*, to drive ashore. ‖ AVIAT., MILIT. To drift.

dériver v. intr. (1). NAUT. To leave the shore.
— v. tr. To free from the bank.
dériver v. tr. (1); **dériveter** [derivte] v. tr.
(8 *a*). TECHN. To unrivet.
dériveur [-vœ:r] m. NAUT. Storm-sail (voile);
sailing dinghy, yacht with centre-board (bateau).
dérivomètre [-vɔmɛtr] m. AVIAT. Drift-indicator.
dermatite [dɛrmati:t] f. MÉD. Dermatitis.
dermatologie [-tɔlɔʒi] f. MÉD. Dermatology.
dermatologiste [-lɔʒist], **dermatologue**
[-lɔg] s. MÉD. Dermatologist.
dermatose [-to:z] f. MÉD. Dermatosis.
derme [dɛrm] m. MÉD. Derm, U. S. derma.
dermique [-mik] adj. MÉD. Dermic, dermal.
dermite [-mit] f. MÉD. Dermatitis.
dernier, ère [dɛrnje, ɛ:r] adj. Last (v. ULTIME);
avoir le dernier mot, to have the last word; *dernier chapitre*, last chapter; *dernier jour pour les inscriptions*, closing date for registrations; *en dernier ressort*, in the last resort; *jusqu'au dernier sou*, to the last farthing, U. S. to the bottom dollar. ‖ Rear (le plus en arrière); *le dernier rang*, the rear rank. ‖ Last, lowest, undermost, bottom (le plus bas); *la dernière assiette de la pile*, the undermost plate in the pile; *la dernière classe*, the lowest form; *le dernier élève de la classe*, the bottom boy of the class; *la dernière marche de l'escalier*, the bottom stair. ‖ Top, highest (le plus haut); *au dernier degré*, in the highest degree (d'excellence); *dernier enchérisseur*, highest bidder; *dernier étage*, top floor; *dernière marche*, top stair. ‖ Late, later, latest (le plus récent); *durant ces dernières années*, in recent years; *les derniers événements*, later events; *la dernière guerre*, the late war; *la dernière mode*, the latest (ou) newest fashion; *les dernières nouveautés*, the latest novelties, news; *les dernières pluies*, the late rains; *ces derniers temps*, these latter days, latterly. ‖ Worst (le pire); *la dernière chose à faire*, the last (ou) worst thing to do; *le dernier métier*, the worst trade. ‖ Later; latest, closing, dying (entourant la mort); *les dernières années*, *les derniers jours de sa vie*, the closing years, the last days of his life; *ses dernières paroles*, his dying words. ‖ Last, utmost, ultimate (extrême); *au dernier degré de la misère*, in the utmost (ou) direst poverty, in the extremity of wretchedness; *avec les derniers détails*, in the fullest detail, with the minutest details; *de la dernière importance*, of the utmost importance; *les dernières limites du monde*, the ultimate bounds (ou) the utmost ends of the world. ‖ Last, final (définitif); *dernier effort*, final effort; *dernier mot d'une lettre*, final word of a letter; *mettre la dernière main à*, to put the finishing touches to; *la raison dernière de*, the final justification for. ‖ Last, past (précédent); *ces dernières années*, the past few years; *en juin dernier*, last June; *la semaine dernière*, last week. ‖ FIN. *Les derniers cours*, closing prices; *dernier versement*, final instalment. ‖ COMM. *Le dernier délai*, final date; *mon dernier prix*, my lowest price.
— s. The last (l'ultime); *arriver en dernier*, to arrive last, to be the last to arrive; *jusqu'au dernier*, to the last man; *la dernière est une fille*, the last is a girl; *les deux derniers*, the last two. ‖ The least (le moindre); *le dernier de mes soucis*, the least of my worries. ‖ The vilest, the meanest (le pire); *le dernier des derniers*, the lowest of the low, the vilest of men; *traité avec le dernier mépris*, treated with the greatest scorn. ‖ *Ce dernier*, the latter, this last. ‖ **Dernier-né**, s. Last-born child.
dernièrement [-njɛrmɑ̃] adv. Of late, lately, latterly, recently, newly.
dérobade [derɔbad] f. Balking, swerve (du cheval). ‖ FIG. Escape, escaping, elusion; evading; evasion, avoidance (*devant*, of).

dérobé, ée [-be] adj. Secret, hidden (escalier, porte); *vue dérobée*, hidden light. ‖ ARCHIT. *Porte dérobée*, jib-door.
— loc. adv. **A la dérobée**, stealthily, furtively; secretly, on the sly; *entrer, sortir à la dérobée*, to steal in, to slip out.
dérober v. tr. (1). To steal, to filch, to pick, to pilfer (voler); *dérober qqch. à qqn*, to rob s.o. of sth., to filch sth. from s.o.; *dérober un baiser*, to steal a kiss. ‖ To hide, to conceal (cacher); *dérober ses intentions*, to hide one's intentions; *dérober qqch. à la vue*, to screen (ou) to hide sth. from sight. ‖ To save, to abstract (*à*, from) [soustraire]; *dérober qqn à la mort*, to rescue s.o. from death; *dérober quelques instants à sa lecture*, to steal a few moments from one's reading.
— v. pr. **Se dérober**, to swerve, to balk (cheval). ‖ To give way (*sous*, under) [fléchir]; *se dérober sous ses pieds*, to give way under his feet; *sa mémoire se déroba*, his memory failed him. ‖ To hide, to be concealed (ou) hidden (être caché); *se dérober aux regards*, to hide from sight. ‖ To slip away (*de*, from) [s'esquiver]. ‖ To elude, to evade, to escape (*à*, from) [se soustraire]; *se dérober à*, to elude (la curiosité); to fail to answer (une invitation); to shirk (une obligation); to shuffle out of (ses responsabilités); *se dérober toujours*, to take avoiding action (ne pas agir); to beat about the bush (tergiverser).
dérobeur, euse [-bœ:r, ø:z] s. Robber (voleur). ‖ Swerver, skittish horse (cheval).
dérogation [derɔgasjɔ̃] f. JUR. Derogation (*à*, from); exception; *faire dérogation à*, to depart from, to make a departure from; *par dérogation à*, in derogation of.
dérogatoire [-twa:r] adj. JUR. Derogatory.
déroger [derɔʒe] v. intr. (7). To derogate, to lose caste (*en*, by); *sans déroger à*, without derogation from. ‖ To derogate, to descend, to fall (*à*, from) [son rang]. ‖ JUR. To depart, to deviate, to diverge (*à*, from) [la loi, l'usage].
dérouillée [deruje] f. POP. Thrashing, walloping.
dérouiller [-je] v. tr. (1). To remove the rust from, to rub the rust off (un objet). ‖ FIG. To polish up, to brush up (ses connaissances); to jog (la mémoire). ‖ POP. To thrash, to beat up (qqn).
— v. intr. POP. To get beaten up (ou) thrashed (être battu); to really go through it (peiner, en baver).
— v. pr. **Se dérouiller**, to lose its rust (objet). ‖ FIG. To rub the rust off (se mettre au courant); *se dérouiller la mémoire*, to refresh one's memory. ‖ FAM. To hurry up; to be nippy about it (se dépêcher); *dérouille-toi!*, stir your stumps!
déroulage [derula:ʒ] m. Unreeling, U. S. unwinding (d'une bobine); unrolling (d'une carte, d'un rouleau de tissu); uncoiling (de cordages); unwinding (d'une pelote). ‖ TECHN. Wood-peeling.
déroulement [-lmɑ̃] m. Passing (d'un cortège). ‖ FIG. Unfolding, march (des événements); unfolding, development (d'une intrigue).
dérouler [-le] v. tr. (1). To unreel, U. S. to unwind (une bobine, un film); to unroll (une carte, un rouleau de tissu); to uncoil (ses cheveux, des cordages); to unwind (une pelote); *dérouler ses anneaux*, to uncoil itself (serpent); *dérouler ses vagues*, to roll on (ou) along (mer). ‖ MATH. To describe the evolute of (une courbe). ‖ FIG. To unfold (ses plans).
— v. pr. **Se dérouler**, to unreel, U. S. to unwind (bobine, film); to unroll (carte, drapeau, étoffe); to tumble down (cheveux); to uncoil (cordage, serpent); to unwind (pelote). ‖ FIG. To extend, to unfold, to stretch out (campagne, paysage); to pass by (cortège); to develop (crise); to march by (défilé); to take place (événement, expérience); to pass off (manifestation); to unfold (pensées,

réflexions) ; to proceed (repas) ; *laisser se dérouler les événements*, to let things develop ; *la réunion s'est déroulée dans le calme*, the proceedings were orderly.

déroutage [deruta:ʒ] m. Diverting, diversion (d'un avion, d'un bateau).

déroutant, ante [de.utɑ̃, ɑ̃:t] adj. Misleading ; disconcerting.

déroute [derut] f. MILIT. Rout ; *en pleine déroute*, in full flight ; *mettre en déroute*, to rout, to put to flight (ou) rout. ‖ FIG. Disorder, upset ; ruin.

déroutement [-tmɑ̃] m. V. DÉROUTAGE.

dérouter [-te] v. tr. (1). To put on the wrong road, to misdirect, to lead astray (un promeneur, un voyageur). ‖ NAUT., CH. DE F. To divert. ‖ FIG. To put off, to put out, to disconcert, to non-plus (un candidat) ; to turn away (la curiosité) ; to baffle (l'esprit, les recherches, les soupçons) ; to give the slip to, to throw off the track, to baffle (la police) ; to avert (les soupçons) ; *ce garçon me déroute*, this boy is a real puzzle to me. — v. pr. **Se dérouter**, to go astray, to lose the way (faire fausse route) ; to deviate from one's way (s'écarter de sa route). ‖ FIG. To be non-plussed (ou) puzzled (ou) flurried (se troubler).

derrick [de·ik] m. Derrick.

derrière [derjɛ:r] prép. Behind ; U. S. back of ; *derrière le mur*, behind the wall ; *de derrière le mur*, from behind the wall ; *marcher derrière la charrette*, to walk at the tail of the cart. ‖ NAUT. Abaft (un mât) ; astern of (un navire). ‖ FIG. At the back of, behind ; *avoir des partisans derrière soi*, to have supporters behind one (ou) at one's back ; *être derrière qqn*, to back s.o. up ; *laisser des enfants derrière soi*, to leave children behind one ; *laisser ses concurrents derrière soi*, to outrun (ou) to outdistance one's competitors. — adv. Behind ; *le mur derrière*, the wall behind ; *laisser qqn derrière*, to leave s.o. behind. ‖ NAUT. Astern. ‖ FIG. Behind ; *qu'y a-t-il derrière?*, what is behind all this ? ‖ **Devant-derrière**, wrong side foremost, hind side before. ‖ **De derrière** ; *jardin, porte de derrière*, back-garden, back-door ; *pattes de derrière*, hind legs. ‖ **Par derrière**, behind, from behind ; *les cheveux coupés par derrière*, with her hair cropped behind ; *dire du mal de qqn par derrière*, to disparage s.o. behind his back ; *poussé par derrière*, pushed on from behind ; *qqn est par derrière*, s.o. is pulling the wires (ou) strings. ‖ MILIT. *Attaquer par derrière*, to attack from (ou) in the rear. — m. Back, backside, rear (d'une chose) ; *le derrière de la charrette*, the tail of the cart ; *le derrière du piano*, the back of the piano ; *loger au troisième sur le derrière*, to lodge on the third floor back ; *sur le derrière de la maison*, at the back (ou) the rear of the house. ‖ Buttocks, haunches, hindquarters (d'un animal) ; *assis sur son derrière*, sitting on its haunches (chien). ‖ Behind, bottom, buttocks, backside, rump (de l'homme).

derviche [dɛrviʃ] m. Dervish.

des [dɛ] art. V. DE, LE, UN.

dès prép. As long ago as, as far back as (une date éloignée) ; as early as (une heure donnée) ; *dès le IIIᵉ siècle*, as far back as the third century ; *dès trois heures*, as early as three o'clock. ‖ Immediately after, as soon as (aussitôt) ; *dès son arrivée*, immediately after his arrival, as soon as he comes, the minute he arrives ; *dès avant, lors, maintenant*, even before, then, now ; *dès cette époque*, even then ; *dès le matin*, first thing in the morning ; *dès que possible*, as soon as possible ; *dès la sortie des classes*, as soon as school is over. ‖ From, since (depuis) ; *dès aujourd'hui*, this very day (aujourd'hui) ; from this day on (à partir d'aujourd'hui) ; *dès à présent*, already now,

right now (maintenant) ; from now on, henceforth (à partir de maintenant) ; *dès le début*, from the beginning. — loc. conj. **Dès lors que**, since, seeing that (puisque). ‖ **Dès que**, as soon as ; *dès qu'il eut achevé, il s'en fut*, no sooner had he finished than he went away ; *dès que vient la nuit*, as soon as night comes.

désabonnement [dezabɔnmɑ̃] m. Cancelling (ou) cancellation of subscription.

désabonner [-bɔne] v. tr. (1). To strike off the list of subscribers. — v. pr. **Se désabonner**, to cancel (ou) withdraw one's subscription (à, to).

désabusé, ée [dezabyze] adj. Blasé ; disillusioned, disappointed (déçu) ; undeceived, disabused (détrompé).

désabusement [-zmɑ̃] m. Disillusioning, disabusing (action) ; disillusionment, disenchantment, disappointment (résultat).

désabuser [-ze] v. tr. (1). To disillusion, to disappoint (désillusionner) ; to undeceive (de, with regard to) ; to disabuse (de, of) [détromper]. — v. pr. **Se désabuser**, to be disillusioned (ou) disappointed (être déçu) ; to open one's eyes, U. S. to wise up, to get wise (se détromper).

désaccord [desakɔ:r] m. Discordance, variance, discrepancy (entre, between) ; *désaccord entre deux comptes rendus*, discrepancy between two statements ; *désaccord d'opinions*, discordance of opinions. ‖ Disagreement, dissension ; discord, difference (mésintelligence) ; *être en désaccord avec*, to disagree with, to have a difference with, to be at variance with (ne pas s'entendre) ; to clash with (se heurter). ‖ COMM. Clash (d'intérêts). ‖ MUS. Discord (des notes, des voix) ; discordance (des sons).

désaccordé, ée [dezakɔrde] adj. MUS. Out of tune.

désaccorder v. tr. (1). MUS. To untune ; to put out of tune. ‖ FIG. To set at variance. — v. pr. **Se désaccorder**, MUS. To get out of tune.

désaccoupler [dezakuple] v. tr. (1). To uncouple ; to unpair.

désaccoutumance [dezakutymɑ̃:s] f. Loss of habit.

désaccoutumer [-me] v. tr. (1). To disaccustom (de, of) ; *désaccoutumer qqn de fumer*, to break s.o. of the habit of smoking. — v. pr. **Se désaccoutumer**, to lose the habit (de, of) ; *se désaccoutumer de fumer*, to break oneself of the habit of smoking ; *se désaccoutumer du latin*, to lose one's Latin.

désacralisation [desakralizasjɔ̃] f. Desacralization.

désacraliser [-ze] v. tr. (1). To desacralize.

désadaptation [dezadaptasjɔ̃] f. Loss of adaptability (ou) adaptation.

désadapter [-te] v. tr. (1). TECHN. To disconnect. — v. pr. **Se désadapter**, to lose adaptability.

désaffectation [dezafɛktasjɔ̃] f. ECCLÉS. Secularization, deconsecration (d'une église). ‖ MILIT. Discharge, transfer (d'un militaire). ‖ JUR. Release ; putting to another purpose (d'un immeuble).

désaffecter [-te] v. tr. (1). ECCLÉS. To secularize, to deconsecrate (une église). ‖ MILIT. To discharge, to transfer (un soldat). ‖ JUR. To release ; to put to another purpose (un immeuble).

désaffection [dezafɛksjɔ̃] f. Disaffection, disaffectedness (envers, to).

désaffectionner [-sjɔne] v. tr. (1). To disaffect. — v. pr. **Se désaffectionner**, to lose one's affection (de, for).

désagréable [dezagreabl] adj. Disagreeable, unpleasant (sens général) ; grating, rasping, harsh (bruit) ; distasteful, unpalatable (goût) ; offensive, nasty (odeur) ; uncomfortable (position) ; unsightly (spectacle). ‖ Forbidding, unprepossessing (aspect, physionomie) ; rough, forbidding, grumpy, surly (caractère) ; unpleasant, shocking, disagreeable (manières) ; unwelcome, unpleasant (nouvelle) ; disagreeable, bad-tempered, peevish, huffy, pettish, grumpy, surly (personne).

désagréablement [-bləmɑ̃] adv. Disagreeably ; unpleasantly ; nastily, peevishly.

désagrégation [dezagregasjɔ̃] f. Disaggregation. ‖ GÉOL. Weathering (des pierres). ‖ FIG. Breaking up, dissociation.

désagréger [-ʒe] v. tr. (7). To disaggregate. ‖ GÉOL. To weather (les pierres). ‖ FIG. To dissociate.
— v. pr. **Se désagréger**, to be disaggregated. ‖ GÉOL. To weather. ‖ FIG. To break up.

désagrément [dezagremɑ̃] m. Inconvenience ; discomfort ; nuisance. ‖ Pl. Trouble (avec, with) [qqn] ; les petits désagréments de la vie, the petty annoyances of life.

désaimantation [dezɛmɑ̃tasjɔ̃] f. PHYS. Demagnetizing (action) ; demagnetization (résultat). ‖ NAUT. Degaussing.

désaimanter [-te] v. tr. (1). PHYS. To demagnetize. ‖ NAUT. To degauss.
— v. pr. **Se désaimanter**, PHYS. To become demagnetized.

désajuster [dezaʒyste] v. tr. (1). To disarrange. ‖ TECHN. To put out of gear.
— v. pr. **Se désajuster**, to fall out of adjustment ; to become disarranged. ‖ TECHN. To get out of gear.

désaltérant [dezalterɑ̃] adj. Thirst-quenching.

désaltérer [-re] v. tr. (1). To refresh, to quench the thirst of (qqn).
— v. pr. **Se désaltérer**, to quench (ou) slake one's thirst (de, for).

désamarrer [dezamare] v. tr. (1). NAUT. To unmoor.

désamorçage [dezamɔrsa:ʒ] m. Unpriming (d'une arme, d'une pompe) ; defusing (d'un obus). ‖ FIG. Defusing (d'un conflit).

désamorcer [-se] v. tr. (6). To unprime (une arme, une pompe) ; to uncap (une fusée). ‖ FIG. To defuse (un conflit).

désapparier [dezaparje] v. tr. V. DÉPARIER.

désappointement [dezapwɛtmɑ̃] m. Disappointment. (V. DÉCEPTION.)

désappointer [-te] v. tr. (1). To disappoint (at, de).

désapprendre [dezaprɑ̃:dr] v. tr. (80). To unlearn ; to forget how to.

désapprobateur, trice [dezaprɔbatœ:r, tris] adj. Disapproving, disapprobatory, disapprobative. ‖ Of disapproval (regard).
— s. Disapprover (de, of).

désapprobation [-sjɔ̃] f. Disapproval, disapprobation.

désapproprier [dezaprɔprje] v. tr. (1). JUR. To disappropriate, to dispossess.
— v. pr. **Se désapproprier**, JUR. To renounce one's property.

désapprouver [dezapruve] v. tr. (1). To disapprove ; to disapprove of ; to disagree with.

désapprovisionner [dezaprɔvizjɔne] v. tr. (1). COMM. To unstock. ‖ MILIT. To deprive of supplies.

désarçonner [dezarsɔne] v. tr. (1). To unseat, to throw, to unsaddle (un cavalier) ; être désarçonné, to be unhorsed (ou) thrown. ‖ FIG. To put out, to dumbfound, to floor, to flabbergast (qqn).

désargenté, ée [dezarʒɑ̃te] adj. With its silver rubbed off (métal). ‖ FAM. Broke, down and out, penniless, U. S. strapped. (V. DÉCAVÉ.)

désargenter [dezarʒɑ̃te] v. tr. (1). TECHN. To desilver (le métal) ; to desilverize (le minerai). ‖ FAM. To clean out (qqn).

désarmant, ante [dezarmɑ̃, ɑ̃:t] adj. Disarming.

désarmé, ée [-me] adj. MILIT. Unloaded (fusil) ; disarmed (homme). ‖ NAUT. Laid up, out of commission. ‖ FIG. Unarmed ; defenceless.

désarmement [-məmɑ̃] m. MILIT. Disarming (d'un homme) ; disarmament (d'une nation). ‖ NAUT. Unshipping (des avirons) ; laying up, putting out of commission, U. S. decommissioning (d'un navire).

désarmer [-me] v. tr. (1). MILIT. To unload (un canon) ; to uncock (un fusil) ; to disarm (un homme). ‖ NAUT. To lay up ; to put out of commission ; U. S. to decommission (un navire). ‖ FIG. To disarm (la critique, qqn).
— v. intr. MILIT. To disarm (nation). ‖ NAUT. To be laid up, to be put out of commission (navire). ‖ FIG. To yield ; ne pas désarmer, to refuse to be mollified.

désarrimage [dezarima:ʒ] m. Shifting (d'une cargaison).

désarrimer [-me] v. tr. (1). NAUT. To break ; to shift (la cargaison) ; to put out of trim (le navire).
— v. pr. **Se désarrimer**, to shift (cargaison) ; to be out of trim (navire).

désarroi [dezarwa] m. Disarray, disorder, muddle, confusion. ‖ FIG. Distress, anguish.

désarticulation [dezartikylasjɔ̃] f. MÉD. Disarticulation.

désarticulé, ée [-le] adj. MÉD. Out of joint, dislocated ; disjointed.

désarticuler v. tr. (1). MÉD. To disarticulate.

désassembler [dezasɑ̃ble] v. tr. (1). To disjoin ; to disassemble ; to disengage ; to disconnect.

désassorti, ie [dezasɔrti] adj. Made up of odd pieces ; unmatched, unpaired (dépareillé).

désassortir [-ti:r] v. tr. (2). To spoil, to break up (un ensemble). ‖ COMM. To put out of stock (un magasin).

désastre [dezastr] m. Disaster, tragedy, calamity, catastrophe. ‖ FIN. Crash.

désastreusement [-trøzmɑ̃] adv. Disastrously.

désastreux, euse [-trø, ø:z] adj. Disastrous, calamitous, catastrophic. ‖ FAM. Sorry, unfortunate, untoward (malencontreux) ; pernicious (néfaste).

désavantage [dezavɑ̃ta:ʒ] m. Disadvantage, inferiority (infériorité) ; avoir le désavantage du nombre, to be at a numerical disadvantage, to have the odds against one. ‖ Disadvantage, detriment, prejudice (préjudice) ; au désavantage de, to the prejudice of ; paraître à son désavantage, to show oneself in a bad light ; to show oneself much below par. ‖ Handicap ; compenser un désavantage, to overcome a handicap. ‖ Drawback, inconvenience (inconvénient) [de, of] ; sa venue offre quelques désavantages, there are drawbacks to his coming. ‖ MILIT. Le désavantage du terrain, the worse ground. ‖ NAUT. Le désavantage du vent, lee-gauge.

désavantager [-taʒe] v. tr. (7). To disadvantage, to handicap (handicaper) ; to disadvantage, to injure, to prejudice, to wrong (porter tort à) ; être désavantagé par qqch., to be at a disadvantage owing to sth. ‖ JUR. To leave less than his normal share to (un héritier).

désavantageusement [-taʒøzmɑ̃] adv. Disadvantageously.

désavantageux, euse [taʒø, ø:z] adj. Disadvantageous, unfavourable ; être vu sous un jour désavantageux, to be seen at a disadvantage ; travailler dans des conditions très désavantageuses, to labour under defavourable conditions (ou) at a great disadvantage. ‖ Prejudicial, detrimental ; désavantageux pour qqn, prejudicial (ou) detrimental to s.o.'s interests.

désaveu [dezavø] m. Retractation, disavowal (d'un aveu, d'une parole) ; recanting, recantation (d'une doctrine); disclaimer (d'une œuvre); repudiation (d'une opinion); disowning (de qqn). ‖ Jur. Repudiation (de paternité).

désavouer [-vue] v. tr. (1). To disavow (une action); to retract (un aveu); to recant (une doctrine); to disclaim (une œuvre); to repudiate (une opinion); to disown (qqn). ‖ Jur. To disown (un enfant).
— v. pr. Se **désavouer**, to go back on one's word (revenir sur sa parole); to give oneself the lie (se démentir); to retract (se rétracter).

désaxé, ée [dezakse] adj. Techn. Out of true, désaxé, offset. ‖ Fig., Fam. Unbalanced, unsettled, at sea (esprit, personne); out of joint (vie).

désaxer v. tr. (1). Techn. To set over, to throw out of true. ‖ Fig. To unbalance, to unsettle.

descellement [desɛlmɑ̃] m. Jur. Unsealing. ‖ Techn. Loosening.

desceller [-le] v. tr. (1). Jur. To unseal. ‖ Techn. To loosen.

descendance [desɑ̃dɑ̃:s] f. Descent, lineage (filiation); progeny, descendants, issue (postérité).

descendant, ante [-dɑ̃, ɑ̃:t] adj. Downward (mouvement, sentier). ‖ Math., Astron., Méd. Descending. ‖ Naut. Outgoing (marée). ‖ Mus. Falling (gamme). ‖ Ch. de f. *Quai, train descendant,* up-platform, -train.
— s. Descendant. ‖ Pl. Issue, progeny.

descendeur, euse [-dœ:r, ø:z] s. Sports. Downhill racer, downhiller.

descendre [desɑ̃:dr] v. intr. (4).

> 1. Sens général. — 2. Baisser. — 3. Etre en pente. — 4. Loger. — 5. S'arrêter. — 6. Tirer son origine. — 7. Autom. — 8. Ch. de f. — 9. Aviat. — 10. Naut. — 11. Milit. — 12. Jur. — 13. Méd. — 14. Mus. — 15. Fig. S'abaisser. — 16. Fig. Condescendre. — 17. Fam. Se digérer.

1. To descend (sens général) [*de*, from]; to come down, to go down (*dans*, into); *descendre d'un arbre,* to come (ou) climb down a tree; *descendre de cheval,* to alight from horseback, to dismount (ou) to get off one's horse; *descendre en coulant, en courant,* to flow, to run down; *descendre d'un tabouret haut,* to get off a high stool; *descendre de voiture,* to get out (ou) to come out (ou) to step out (ou) to alight from a car; *faire descendre,* to call down (appeler en bas); to send down (envoyer en bas); to take (ou) to get down (décrocher); *on descend dans la cave par quelques marches,* the cellar is reached by some steps. ‖ **2.** To go down (baisser) [eau]; to ebb (marée); to fall (température); *le baromètre descend,* the barometer is falling. ‖ **3.** To fall, to sink, to slope down (être en pente); *descendre en pente brusque,* to sink abruptly, to fall away rapidly; *descendre en pente douce,* to slope down gently; *descendre en tournant,* to wind down, to curve down. ‖ **4.** To put up (loger); *descendre à l'hôtel,* to put up (ou) to stop at a hotel; *descendre chez qqn,* to stay (ou) to stop at s.o.'s house (ou) with s.o. ‖ **5.** To reach (s'arrêter); *descendre au genou,* to reach to the knees; *descendre aux talons,* to come down to the heels. ‖ **6.** To issue, to be descended (tirer son origine); *descendre d'une bonne famille,* to come of (ou) to spring from (ou) to issue from a good family. ‖ **7.** Autom. To get off (d'un autobus); *vous descendez à la prochaine?,* are you getting out at the next station? ‖ **8.** Ch. de f. To get out; U. S. to get off; *tout le monde descend!,* all change! ‖ **9.** Aviat. *Descendre en spirale, en vol plané,* to spiral down, to glide down. ‖ **10.** Naut. To disembark, to land (personne); to back (vent). ‖ **11.** Milit. To descend (*sur,* upon). ‖ **12.** Jur. To make a descent

(*sur,* on); *descendre sur les lieux,* to visit the scene, to execute a search warrant. ‖ **13.** Méd. To drop, to prolapse (organe). ‖ **14.** Mus. To descend, to go down the scale. ‖ **15.** Fig. To descend (s'abaisser); *descendre à, jusqu'à,* to stoop to, so low as to; *descendre en soi-même,* to examine one's conscience. ‖ **16.** Fig. To deign, to condescend (condescendre). ‖ **17.** Fam. To go down (se digérer); *aller se promener pour faire descendre son déjeuner,* to walk off one's lunch; *boire un verre d'eau pour faire descendre le vin,* to have a glass of water to wash the wine down; *boire un alcool pour faire descendre son dîner,* to take a liqueur to settle one's dinner; *ça ne descend pas,* it won't go down; it lies heavy on my stomach.
— v. tr. To descend; to come down, to go down; to bring down; *descendre un arbre,* to cut down a tree; *descendre l'escalier,* to come downstairs; *descendre un livre d'un rayon,* to reach (ou) to lift (ou) to get a book down from a shelf; *descendre une malle du grenier,* to carry (ou) to bring a trunk down from the attic; *descendre qqn de cheval,* to lift s.o. down from his horse; *descendre la rivière en flottant,* to float down the river; *descendre la rue,* to go (ou) to walk down the street; *descendre un store,* to let (ou) put down a blind (ou) U. S. a shade; *descendre un tableau,* to take down a picture. ‖ Mus. To loosen (une corde); to run down (la gamme); to lower (le ton). ‖ Sports. To bring down, to knock out, to down (son adversaire); to shoot (un canard sauvage). ‖ Aviat. To bring down, to shoot down (un avion). ‖ Fam. *Descendre qqn,* to debunk (s.o.) (déboulonner); to make away with s.o., U. S. to bump off (ou) rub out s.o. (tuer); *descendre un verre,* to down a drink.

descente [desɑ̃:t] f. Coming down, going down, descent (*dans,* into); *descente de cheval,* alighting from horseback, dismounting; *descente d'un tableau,* taking down of a picture; *descente de voiture,* alighting from a car, getting (ou) stepping out of a car. ‖ Descending stairs (escalier); *descente de cave,* cellar stairs (ou) steps. ‖ Sinking, subsidence (des eaux); ebb (de la marée); falling (de la température). ‖ Descent, declivity, slope down, downward gradient; *descente douce, rapide,* gentle, steep slope. ‖ Putting up (logement); *descente à l'hôtel,* putting up at a(n) hotel. ‖ Autom. Getting off (d'un autobus). ‖ Ch. de f. Getting out, U. S. getting off (du train); downward gradient (de la voie); *à la descente du train,* on alighting from the train. ‖ Aviat. *Descente en feuille morte,* falling-leaf roll; *descente en parachute,* parachute descent (ou) drop; *descente planée,* glide; *descente à plat,* pancake; *descente en tire-bouchon,* corkscrew spin. ‖ Naut. Landing. ‖ Milit. Incursion, descent (*sur,* on). ‖ Jur. *Descente de police,* police raid, search; *descente sur les lieux,* visit to the scene; *faire une descente de police dans,* to raid. ‖ Méd. Prolapse (d'un organe). ‖ Sports. Dash, run, rush down (au football). ‖ Techn. Downstroke (de piston); down pipe (tuyau). ‖ Electr. Download (en radio). ‖ Fin. *Descente des prix,* fall (ou) drop (ou) decline in prices. ‖ Ecclés. *Descente aux enfers,* descent into Hell; *descente de Croix,* deposition from the Cross. ‖ Comm. *Descente de bain,* bath mat; *descente de lit,* bedside rug.

descriptible [dɛskriptibl] adj. Describable.

descriptif, ive [-tif, i:v] adj. Descriptive.
— m. Descriptive leaflet (ou) brochure.

description [-sjɔ̃] f. Description; *faire une description de,* to describe. ‖ Jur. Specification.

déséchouer [dezeʃwe] v. tr. (1). Naut. To refloat, to float off.
— v. pr. Se **déséchouer,** to get afloat.

déségrégation [desegregasjɔ̃] f. Desegregation.

désembourber [dezãburbe] v. tr. (1). To extricate from (ou) to get out of the mud.

désembourgeoiser [dezãburʒwaze] v. tr. (1). To rid of suburban ideas (qqn).

désembouteiller [dezãbutɛje] v. tr. (1). To unblock, to clear of traffic.

désemparé, ée [dezãpare] adj. NAUT. Crippled, disabled. ‖ AVIAT. Out of control. ‖ FIG. Helpless, at a loss, at sea. (V. DÉCONCERTÉ.)

désemparer v. tr. (1). NAUT. To cripple, to disable. — v. intr. To quit a place; *sans désemparer*, without stopping (or) intermission.

désemplir [dezãpli:r] v. tr. (2). To empty; *ne pas désemplir*, to be always full.

désemprisonner [dezãprizɔne] v. tr. (1). To release from prison.

désenchaîner [dezãʃɛne] v. tr. (1). To unchain, to unfetter.

désenchanté, ée [dezãʃãte] adj. Disillusioned, sadder and wiser.

désenchantement [-tmã] m. Disenchantment. ‖ FIG. Disillusion.

désenchanter [-te] v. tr. (1). To disenchant.

désencombrement [dezãkɔ̃brəmã] m. Clearing, disencumbering.

désencombrer [dezãkɔ̃bre] v. tr. (1). To clear out (le passage); to disencumber (qqch., qqn).

désencroûter [dezãkrute] v. tr. (1). TECHN. To scale. ‖ FAM. To lift out of the rut (qqn). — v. pr. **Se désencroûter**, FAM. To get out of the rut.

désenfiler [dezãfile] v. tr. (1). To unthread (une aiguille); to unstring (des perles). — v. pr. **Se désenfiler**, to come unthreaded (aiguille); to come unstrung (perles).

désenflammer [dezãflame] v. tr. (1). MÉD. To reduce the inflammation.

désenfler [dezãfle] v. tr. (1). To reduce the swelling of. — v. intr. To go down, to become less swollen. — v. pr. **Se désenfler**, to go down, to become less swollen.

désenfourner [dezãfurne] v. tr. (1). To draw out of the oven (le pain).

désenfumé, ée [dezãfyme] adj. Smoke-free.

désenfumer v. tr. (1). To clear of smoke.

désengagement [dezãgaʒmã] m. Withdrawal, disengagement.

désengager [dezãgaʒe] v. tr. (7). To free from an engagement. ‖ TECHN. To disengage, to ungear. — v. pr. **Se désengager**, to withdraw (de, from); to break one's commitments (de, to).

désengorger [dezãgɔrʒe] v. tr. (7). To unblock.

désengrener [dezãgrəne] v. tr. (5). TECHN. To disengage; to disconnect; to ungear.

désenivrer [dezãnivre] v. tr. (1). To sober (qqn). — v. pr. **Se désenivrer**, to grow sober, to sober off (ou) up.

désennuyer [dezãnɥije] v. tr. (9 a). To divert, to cure of boredom; to rouse from dullness (qqn). — v. pr. **Se désennuyer**, to divert oneself (à, in); to seek diversion (de, from).

désensabler [dezãsable] v. tr. (1). To clear of sand, to dredge (un port, un chenal). ‖ To dig out of the sand (un véhicule).

désensibilisateur, trice [desãsibilizatœ:r, tris] adj. Desensitizing. — m. Desensitizer (en photo).

désensibiliser [-ze] v. tr. (1). To desensitize.

désensorceler [dezãsɔrsəle] v. tr. (8 a). To disenchant.

désentoiler [dezãtwale] v. tr. (1). ARTS. To remove the canvas from (un tableau). ‖ AVIAT. To remove the fabric from (les ailes).

désentortiller [dezãtɔrtije] v. tr. (1). To unravel, to disentangle.

désentraver [dezãtrave] v. tr. (1). To unshackle. ‖ FIG. To set free.

désenvaser [dezãvaze] v. tr. (1). To clear of mud (ou) silt, to dredge (un port, une rivière). ‖ To dig out of the mud, to dredge up (un véhicule).

désenvenimer [dezãvnime] v. tr. (1). MÉD. To remove the poison from. ‖ FIG. To take the sting (ou) bitterness out of.

déséquilibre [dezekilibr] m. Want of balance. ‖ FIG. Lack of balance; maladjustment.

déséquilibré, ée [-bre] adj. Unbalanced, off balance (pr. et fig.). — s. Unbalanced person.

déséquilibrer [-bre] v. tr. (1). To unbalance.

déséquiper [dezekipe] v. tr. (1). NAUT. To lay up (un navire). ‖ MILIT. To remove the outfit of (un homme).

désert, erte [dezɛr, ɛrt] adj. Desert, unfrequented, uninhabited (non fréquenté ou habité). ‖ Deserted, forsaken (abandonné). — m. Waste, wilderness, desert. ‖ GÉOGR. Desert. ‖ FIG. Wilderness; *prêcher dans le désert*, to talk to the wind, to preach to deaf ears.

déserté, ée [-te] adj. Deserted, forsaken, abandoned.

déserter v. tr. (1). To desert (un lieu, un poste); to give up, to abandon, to forsake (qqn). — v. intr. MILIT. To desert; *déserter à l'ennemi*, to go over to the enemy.

déserteur [-tœ:r] m. MILIT. Deserter.

désertification [dezɛrtifikasjɔ̃] f. Extension of desertlike conditions, desertification. ‖ FIG. Abandonment, population drain.

désertion [-sjɔ̃] f. MILIT. Desertion (à, devant, to, before).

désertique [-tik] adj. Desert, barren.

désescalade [dezɛskalad] f. De-escalation.

désespérance [dezɛsperã:s] f. Despair, hopelessness.

désespérant, ante [-rã, ã:t] adj. Heartbreaking, disheartening (nouvelle); hopeless (personne). ‖ FIG. Discouraging.

désespéré, ée [-re] adj. Despairing (marquant le désespoir); heartbroken, in despair, despondent (réduit au désespoir). ‖ Hopeless (cas); desperate, past hope (situation). ‖ MÉD. Hopeless (état); whose life is despaired of (malade); desperate (remède); *être dans un état désespéré*, to be past recovery (ou) cure. ‖ MILIT. Desperate (combat); forlorn (entreprise). — s. Desperate person.

désespérément [-remã] adv. Despairingly, hopelessly (sans espoir). ‖ Desperately, eagerly, furiously (avec acharnement); desperately, frantically (éperdument). ‖ MILIT. Desperately.

désespérer [-re] v. intr. (5). To despair (de, of); to lose hope, to be hopeless; *je ne désespère pas qu'il puisse réussir*, I am not hopeless of his being able to succeed (ou) of his success (ou) of his succeeding; *il ne faut désespérer de rien*, there is no reason for despair, there is nothing to despair about; *il ne faut jamais désespérer*, never say die. ‖ MÉD. *Désespérer de sauver qqn*, to give s.o. up, to lose all hope of s.o.'s recovery. — v. tr. To drive to despair (qqn). — v. pr. **Se désespérer**, to abandon oneself to despair, to be in despair, to lose hope. ‖ FAM. To worry, to be dreadfully worried (se tourmenter).

désespoir [dezɛspwa:r] m. Despair, hopelessness (désespérance); despair, grief (peine cruelle); *désespoir d'amour*, disappointed love; *être au désespoir*, to be in despair. ‖ Desperation (résolution désespérée); *en désespoir de cause*, in desperation, as a desperate shift (ou) measure, as a last resource (ou) resort; *réduire au désespoir,* to drive to desperation. ‖ Despair (objet de désespoir); *faire le désespoir de sa mère*, to be one's mother's despair. ‖ FAM. Regret; *être au désespoir de*, to be dreadfully (ou) desperately sorry to. ‖ **Désespoir-du-peintre** (pl. *désespoirs-du-peintre*) m. BOT. London pride.

déshabillage [dezabija:ʒ] m. Taking off one's clothes. ‖ THÉÂTR. Strip-tease (sur scène).

déshabillé, ée [-je] adj. Undressed.
— m. Undress (tenue négligée); déshabillé (vêtement); *en déshabillé*, in dishabille (ou) undress.

déshabiller [-je] v. tr. (1). To undress, to strip (qqn). ‖ JUR. To unrobe (un homme de robe). ‖ NAUT. To strip (un mât).
— v. pr. **Se déshabiller**, to undress, to take off one's clothes; to strip (à nu). ‖ To change one's clothes (se changer). ‖ JUR. To disrobe (homme de robe).

déshabituer [dezabitɥe] v. tr. (1). To disaccustom (*de*, to); to break (ou) to rid of the habit (*de*, of); *déshabituer qqn de fumer*, to get s.o. out of the habit of smoking.
— v. pr. **Se déshabituer**, to rid (ou) to break oneself of the habit (*de*, of); to grow unused (*de*, to).

désherbage [dezɛrba:ʒ] m. AGRIC. Weeding.

désherbant, ante [dezɛrbɑ̃, ɑ̃:t] adj. Weedkilling; *produit désherbant*, weed-killer.
— m. Weed-killer.

désherber [dezɛrbe] v. tr. AGRIC. To weed.

déshérence [dezerɑ̃:s] f. JUR. Escheat, abeyance; *biens en déshérence*, escheated property; *tomber en déshérence*, to escheat.

déshérité, ée [dezerite] adj. JUR. Disinherited. ‖ FAM. Plain, ill-favoured, U. S. homely (laid).
— s. JUR. Disinherited person. ‖ FIG. *Les déshérités de ce monde*, the underprivileged.

déshériter v. tr. (1). JUR. To disinherit, to disherit.

déshonnête [dezɔnɛ:t] adj. Improper, immodest; shameless.

déshonnêteté [-nɛtte] f. Impropriety, immodesty. ‖ Caddishness (goujaterie).

déshonneur [-nœ:r] m. Dishonour; ignominy; *considérer comme un déshonneur de*, to think it dishonourable to. ‖ Disgrace, shame, discredit (honte); *faire le déshonneur de qqn*, to disgrace s.o.; *c'est le déshonneur de la famille*, he is the shame (ou) disgrace of his family, he brings dishonour on his family, he disgraces his family.

déshonorant, ante [-nɔrɑ̃, ɑ̃:t] adj. Dishonourable, discreditable (action); *caractère déshonorant*, dishonourable nature, dishonourableness (d'une action). ‖ FAM. Shameful, disgraceful.

déshonorer [-nɔre] v. tr. To dishonour, to bring dishonour on (enlever l'honneur de). ‖ To disgrace, to be a discredit to, to bring shame upon (faire honte à). ‖ To defile (une jeune fille).
— v. pr. **Se déshonorer**, to dishonour oneself, to lose one's honour. ‖ To disgrace oneself, to cover oneself with shame.

déshumaniser [dezymanize] v. tr. (1). To dehumanize.

déshydratation [dezidratasjɔ̃] f. CHIM. Dehydration.

déshydrater [-te] v. tr. (1). CHIM. To dehydrate.

déshydrogénation [dezidrɔʒenasjɔ̃] f. CHIM. Dehydrogenation.

déshydrogéner [-ne] v. tr. (1). CHIM. To dehydrogenate.

déshypothéquer [dezipɔteke] v. tr. (1). JUR. To disencumber.

desiderata [deziderata] m. pl. Desiderata.

désidératif, ive [dezideratif, i:v] adj. GRAMM. Desiderative.

design [dizajn] m. Design, contemporary design, industrial design.

désignation [deziɲasjɔ̃] f. Designation; pointing out. ‖ Description. ‖ JUR. Designation, appointment, nomination (*au poste de*, as).

désigné, ée [-ɲe] adj. Specified (condition); appointed (endroit, heure); assigned (motif); *désigné pour*, marked out for; *désigné sous le titre de duc*, styled duke. ‖ COMM. Described (marchandise). ‖ ECCLÉS. Designate (évêque).

désigner v. tr. (1). To designate, to indicate (indiquer); to mark out (marquer); to point out (signaler); to specify (spécifier); *désigner du doigt*, to point at (qqch.); *désigner qqch. du doigt à qqn*, to point out sth. to s.o. ‖ To fix, to assign (assigner); *à l'heure désignée*, at the appointed time. ‖ To designate, to select (choisir); to appoint, to designate, to nominate (nommer); to appoint (*comme*, as). ‖ JUR. To describe (des titres de propriété). ‖ SPORTS. *Désigner d'avance*, to spot (le gagnant).
— v. pr. **Se désigner**, to designate oneself; *se désigner à l'attention de qqn*, to draw s.o.'s attention, to arrest (ou) to hold s.o.'s attention.

désillusion [dezillyzjɔ̃] f. Disillusion.

désillusionnement [-zjɔnmɑ̃] m. Disillusionment.

désillusionner [-zjɔne] v. tr. To disilluzion(ize).

désincarnation [dezɛ̃karnasjɔ̃] f. Disincarnation.

désincarné, ée [-ne] adj. Disincarnate.

désincarner (se) [sədezɛ̃karne] v. pr. (1). To leave the body, to become disembodied.

désincorporation [dezɛ̃kɔrpɔrasjɔ̃] f. Disembodiment.

désincorporer [-re] v. tr. (1). JUR. To disincorporate (une terre). ‖ MILIT. To demobilize (un homme); to dissolve (un régiment).
— v. pr. **Se désincorporer**, to disembody.

désincruster [dezɛ̃kryste] v. tr. (1). To scale.

désinculper [dezɛ̃kylpe] v. tr. (1). To exculpate.

désinence [dezinɑ̃:s] f. GRAMM. Ending.

désinfectant [dezɛ̃fɛktɑ̃] adj., m. Disinfectant.

désinfecter [-te] v. tr. (1). To disinfect; to decontaminate. ‖ To fumigate.

désinfection [-sjɔ̃] f. Disinfection; decontamination.

désintégration [dezɛ̃tegrasjɔ̃] f. Disintegration. ‖ PHYS. Splitting, fission (de l'atome).

désintégrer [-gre] v. tr. (5). To disintegrate. ‖ PHYS. To split (l'atome).
— v. pr. **Se désintégrer**, to disintegrate.

désintéressé, ée [dezɛ̃terɛse] adj. Not interested (ou) implicated (*dans*, in) [non engagé]. ‖ Disinterested, unbiased, unprejudiced (avis); unselfish (motif); unselfish, disinterested (personne).

désintéressement [-smɑ̃] m. Disinterestedness, unselfishness. ‖ JUR. Buying out (d'un associé); paying off (d'un créancier).

désintéresser [-se] v. tr. (1). To indemnify, to reimburse (qqn). ‖ JUR. To buy out (un associé); to pay off (un créancier). ‖ FIG. To alienate, to detach.
— v. pr. **Se désintéresser**, to take no further interest (*de*, in); to dissociate oneself (*de*, from); *je m'en désintéresse*, I give it up.

désintoxication [dezɛ̃tɔksikasjɔ̃] f. MÉD. Detoxication.

désintoxiquer [-ke] v. tr. (1). MÉD. To detoxicate.

désinviter [dezɛ̃vite] v. tr. (1). To cancel an invitation to.

désinvolte [dezɛ̃vɔlt] adj. Free; off-hand, casual, airy. (V. CAVALIER, DÉTACHÉ.)

désinvolture [-ty:r] f. Ease of manners (aisance); pertness (effronterie); unconstraint, freedom (liberté); off-handedness, casually (sans façon); *avec désinvolture*, airily; without further ado.

désir [dezi:r] m. Desire; wish; wishing; *désir ardent de*, longing (ou) yearning for; *désir insatiable de*, craving for; *désir d'apprendre*, eagerness for knowledge; *désir de gloire*, thirst (ou) hunger for glory; *désir de plaire*, desire (ou) wish to please; *c'est prendre ses désirs pour des réalités*, it's a piece of wishful thinking; *sur votre désir*, by your wish. ‖ Desire; *désir charnel*, desire; *désir malsain*, lust.

désirable [-rabl] adj. Desirable; *peu désirable*, undesirable. ‖ Desirable, exciting (femme).

désirer [-re] v. tr. (1). To desire, to wish, to want; *désirer ardemment, violemment, vivement*, to long (ou) to yearn (ou) to sigh, to crave, to be eager (ou) anxious for; *désirer beaucoup*, to want very much, to desire eagerly; *désirer faire*, to desire (ou) to wish to do, to be desirous of doing; *désirer qqch.*, to wish for (ou) to desire sth.; *désirer que qqch. se fasse*, to wish for sth. to be done, to wish sth. done; *il est à désirer que*, it is desirable that; *je désirerais être*, I wish I were; I should like to be; *je désire que vous parliez*, I want you to speak; *laisser à désirer*, to leave much to be desired; *n'avoir plus rien à désirer*, to have nothing left to wish for; *que désirez-vous?*, what would you like?; *que désirez-vous de moi?*, what do you want of me?; *se faire désirer*, to make oneself wanted. ‖ COMM. *Monsieur désire?*, what can I show you, sir?

désireux, euse [-rø, ø:z] adj. Desirous, wishful, solicitous (*de*, of); anxious, eager (*de*, for); *désireux de faire*, desirous of doing, anxious (ou) eager to do.

désistement [dezistəmã] m. Standing down, withdrawal (d'un candidat); desistance (*de*, from) [de qqn]. ‖ JUR. Waiver (d'une demande, d'un droit); withdrawal (d'une plainte); non-suit, relinquishment (de poursuite).

désister (se) [sədeziste] v. pr. (1). To stand down, to withdraw (candidat) [*en faveur de*, in favour of]. ‖ JUR. *Se désister de*, to surrender, to claim (une demande); to relinquish, to withdraw (une poursuite).

désobéir [dezɔbeiːr] v. intr. (2). To disobey; *désobéir à*, to disobey; *on a désobéi à mes ordres*, my orders have been disobeyed.

désobéissance [-sãːs] f. Disobedience (*à*, tɔ).

désobéissant, ante [-isã, ãːt] adj. Disobedient.

désobligeamment [-ʒamã] adv. Disobligingly, ungraciously.

désobligeance [dezɔbliʒãːs] f. Disobligingness. ‖ Disagreeableness.

désobligeant, ante [-ʒã, ãːt] adj. Disagreeable, unkind (attitude, paroles); disobliging, ungracious, uncivil, unfriendly (personne).

désobliger [-ʒe] v. tr. (7). To disoblige; to displease (déplaire à); to offend (offenser).

désobstruer [dezɔbstr̩ye] v. tr. (1). To clear (ou) to clean out. ‖ MÉD. To deoppilate.

désodorisant [dezɔdɔrizã] m. Deodorant.

désodorisation [-zasjɔ̃] f. Deodorization.

désodoriser [-ze] v. tr. (1). To deodorize.

désœuvré, ée [dezœvre] adj. Unoccupied, unemployed, inactive, idle; at a loose end.
— s. Idler; *les désœuvrés*, people of leisure.

désœuvrement [-vrəmã] m. Inaction, idleness; leisure.

désolant, ante [dezɔlã, ãːt] adj. Distressing, dispiriting, heart-rending (affligeant); provoking, troublesome (contrariant).

désolation [-lasjɔ̃] f. Desolation, devastation, destruction (action); desolation, desolateness (état). ‖ Desolation, grief, distress (affliction).

désolé, ée [-le] adj. Desolate, barren, waste, wild (désert); desolated, devastated (dévasté). ‖ Disconsolate, heart-broken, distressed, grieved (affligé). ‖ Very sorry (contrarié); *j'en suis absolument désolé*, I am terribly sorry for that (ou) about it (fam.).

désoler v. tr. (1). To desolate, to devastate, to lay waste (dévaster). ‖ To distress, to desolate, to

grieve, to afflict (affliger); *cela me désole*, it breaks my heart. ‖ To annoy (ennuyer).
— v. pr. **Se désoler**, to grieve, to sorrow (*de*, at, about, over); *ne vous désolez pas ainsi*, don't be so cut up about it.

désolidariser [desɔlidarize] v. tr. (1). To disunite.
— v. pr. **Se désolidariser**, to break (*de*, with); to disassociate oneself (*de*, from); *se désolidariser d'un parti*, to withdraw from a party.

désopilant, ante [dezɔpilã, ãːt] adj. FAM. Side-splitting, killing, screaming.

désopiler [-le] v. tr. (1). MÉD. To deoppilate. ‖ FAM. To set in a roar; *désopiler toute l'assemblée*, to convulse the whole audience.
— v. pr. **Se désopiler**, FAM. To split one's sides.

désordonné, ée [dezɔrdɔne] adj. Untidy, messy (lieu, pièce); disorderly, untidy (personne) [sans ordre]. ‖ Immoderate (appétit); reckless, extravagant (dépenses); ill-regulated; wild, disorderly (existence); unmethodical, unsystematic (esprit).
— s. Untidy person.

désordre [dezɔrdr] m. Disorder, confusion (défaut d'ordre); disordered state, untidiness (état désordonné); muddle, jumble, tangle (fouillis); *en désordre*, untidy; in disorder, out of order, in confusion, disorderly; *mettre le désordre dans*, to disorder, to throw into disorder. ‖ Confusion; *fuir en désordre*, to run away in confusion; *jeter le désordre*, to spread confusion. ‖ Pl. Disturbances, disorder, riot (troubles). ‖ MÉD. Disorder, discomposure (de l'esprit); disorder (d'un organe). ‖ FIG. Licentiousness, disorderliness, dissoluteness, dissipation; *vivre dans le désordre*, to lead a wild life.

désorganisateur, trice [dezɔrganizatœːr, tris] adj. Disorganizing.
— s. Disorganizer.

désorganisation [-zasjɔ̃] f. Disorganization.

désorganiser [-ze] v. tr. (1). To disorganize, to disorder. ‖ FIG. To upset (bouleverser).
— v. pr. **Se désorganiser**, to become disorganized.

désorientation [dezɔrjãtasjɔ̃] f. Disorientation.

désorienté, ée [dezɔrjãte] adj. Disorientated. ‖ FIG. At a loss, all at sea, puzzled, flummoxed; out of joint. (V. DÉCONCERTÉ.)

désorienter v. tr. (1). To disorientate, to cause to lose one's bearings (une personne). ‖ FIG. To confuse, to puzzle, to bewilder, to flummox, to put out.
— v. pr. **Se désorienter**, to lose one's bearings. ‖ FIG. To be flummoxed (ou) flurried; to be confused (ou) puzzled.

désormais [dezɔrmɛ] adv. Even now, already, now (dès maintenant); henceforth, henceforward, from now on (dorénavant).

désossé, ée [dezɔse] adj. Boned (viande). ‖ FIG. Boneless (personne).

désossement [-mã] m. Boning.

désosser [-se] v. tr. (1). To bone (une volaille). ‖ To disarticulate, to dislocate (désarticuler).
— v. pr. **Se désosser**, to be boned (viande). ‖ FIG. To become boneless (personne).

désoxydant, ante [dezɔksidã, ãːt] adj. CHIM. Deoxidizing.
— m. CHIM. Deoxidizer.

désoxyder [-de] v. tr. (1). CHIM. To deoxidate, to deoxidize.

désoxygénation [dezɔksiʒenasjɔ̃] f. CHIM. Deoxygenation.

désoxygéner [-ne] v. tr. (5). To deoxygenate.

désoxyribonucléique [dezɔksiribonykleik] adj. MÉD. *Acide désoxyribonucléique*, deoxyribonucleic acid.

despote [dɛspɔt] m. Despot.
— adj. Despotic.

despotique [-tik] adj. Despotic.

despotiquement [-tikmã] adv. Despotically.

despotisme [-tism] m. Despotism.

desquamation [dɛskwamasjɔ̃] f. MÉD. Desquamation, peeling.

desquamer [-me] v. tr. (1). MÉD. To desquamate. — v. pr. Se desquamer, to desquamate, to peel.

desquels [dekɛl]. V. LEQUEL.

dessabler [desable] v. tr. (1). To clear of sand.

dessaisir [desɛzi:r] v. tr. (2). JUR. To disseize; to dispossess; dessaisir d'une affaire, to remove a case from. || NAUT. To unlash. — v. pr. Se dessaisir, to part (de, with); se dessaisir de, to give up, to relinquish. || JUR. Se dessaisir d'une affaire, to relinquish a case, to decline to proceed to judgment.

dessaisissement [-zismã] m. Giving up. || JUR. Disseizin, dispossession; dessaisissement d'une affaire, removal of a case.

dessalage [desala:ʒ] m. V. DESSALEMENT.

dessalé, ée [-le] adj. Free of salt, unsalted. || FAM. Knowing, cute. (V. DÉGOURDI.) — s. Knowing (ou) cute person; person who has been around.

dessalement [desalmã] m. Desalination, desalting (de l'eau de mer, du sol). || CULIN. Desalting, soaking. || NAUT., FAM. Turning turtle, capsizal.

dessaler [-le] v. tr. (1). To unsalt, to soak. || FAM. To put up to a thing or two, to give lessons in love, to teach life to (qqn). — v. intr. NAUT., FAM. To turn turtle, to capsize. — v. pr. Se dessaler, to get freed of salt. || FAM. To learn a thing or two, U. S. to wise up, to get ôn the ball.

dessangler [dɛsãgle] v. tr. (1). To ungirth.

desséchant, ante [dɛseʃã, ã:t] adj. Drying; desiccating. || Parching; withering (flétrissant).

desséché, ée [-ʃe] adj. Dry (puits, ruisseau). || Parched (langue); shrivelled, emaciated, wizened (personne). || BOT. Sapless, withered (branche); sear (feuille); dry, withered (plante). || MÉD. Withered (membre). || FIG. Hardened, seared (cœur, conscience).

dessèchement [-ʃmã] m. Draining, reclaiming (d'un marais); drying-up (d'un puits); drying (de la viande). || AGRIC. Desiccation (du blé); drying (du bois). || BOT. Withering (des plantes). || MÉD. Emaciation (du corps); withering (des membres). || FIG. Hardening (du cœur).

dessécher [-ʃe] v. tr. (5). To drain (un marais); to dry up (un puits); to dry, to desiccate (de la viande). || AGRIC. To desiccate (le blé), to dry (le bois); to parch (la terre). || MÉD. To emaciate (le corps); to parch (la langue); to wither (un membre); to dry (la peau). || FIG. To harden, to steel (le cœur); to sear (la conscience). — v. pr. Se dessécher, to go dry, to dry up (puits, terrain); to dry (viande). || To dry, to become dry (bois); to get parched (ou) baked (terre). || BOT. To wither (feuille, plante). || MÉD. To become wizened (ou) emaciated (corps); to wither (membre). || FIG. To become seared, to harden (cœur).

dessein [desɛ̃] m. Design, project, plan. (V. PROJET.) || Purpose, aim, intention, object (v. INTENTION); à dessein, on purpose, intentionally, purposely, advisedly; avoir le dessein de, to intend to; dans le dessein de, with the intention of, for the purpose of; fait à dessein, intentional; sans dessein, unintentionally.

desseller [desɛle] v. tr. (1). To unsaddle.

desserrage [desɛra:ʒ] m. Slackening (d'une ceinture); loosening, untying (d'un nœud). || TECHN. Unscrewing (d'un boulon); unclamping (d'un étau); releasing, taking off (d'un frein); loosening (d'une vis).

desserré, ée [-re] adj. Slack (ceinture); loose (nœud, vis).

desserrer v. tr. (1). To slacken (une ceinture); to unclench (les dents, les poings); to relax (une étreinte); to loosen, to untie (un nœud). || TECHN. To unscrew (un boulon); to unclamp (un étau); to release, to take off (un frein); to loosen (une vis). || FIG. Sans desserrer les dents, without opening one's mouth. — v. pr. Se desserrer, to open (dents, poings); to relax (étreinte); to loosen, to work loose (vis).

dessert [desɛ:r] m. CULIN. Dessert, sweet.

desserte [desɛrt] f. Sideboard, side-table (meuble); dinner-wagon, dumb-waiter (table).

desserte f. Service (par des transports en commun). || ECCLÉS. Religious service.

dessertir [desɛrti:r] v. tr. (1). To unset. — v. pr. Se dessertir, to come unset.

desservant [desɛrvã] m. ECCLÉS. Priest in charge of a chapel (ou) a church.

desservir [-vi:r] v. tr. (95). ECCLÉS. To serve, to minister to. || CH. DE F. To serve, to ply between, to connect up. || NAUT. To call at. || ELECTR. To supply.

desservir v. tr. (95). To clear (la table). || FIG. To wrong, to do harm to, to tell against (qqn); desservir qqn auprès de, to disserve s.o. with. — v. intr. To clear the table.

dessiccatif, ive [dɛsikatif, i:v] adj. Desiccative.

dessiccation [-sjɔ] f. Desiccation.

dessiller [desije] v. tr. (1). FIG. Dessiller les yeux de qqn, to undeceive s.o., to open s.o.'s eyes. — v. pr. Se dessiller, to open (yeux); mes yeux se sont dessillés, the scales fell from my eyes.

dessin [desɛ̃] m. ARTS. Drawing, sketching (art); drawing, sketch (réalisation); dessin industriel, draughtsmanship, mechanical drawing, U. S. draftsmanship; dessin à main levée, au trait, free-hand, outline drawing; dessin en perspective, landscape sketching; dessin à la plume, pen-and-ink sketch. || Pattern, design (ornement). || Dessin pied-de-poule, broken check design; dessin au pochoir, stencilled pattern; à dessins imprimés, figured, illustrated. || Outline (du paysage, du visage). || THÉÂTR. Dessin animé, animated cartoon. || FAM. Faire des petits dessins, to doodle (en griffonnant).

dessinateur [-inatœ:r] m. Sketcher, drawer; dessinateur à l'encre, black-and-white artist; dessinateur de journal, cartoonist; dessinateur de modes, dress-designer. || TECHN. Draughtsman, U. S. draftsman. || THÉÂTR. Dessinateur de dessins animés, cartoonist.

dessinatrice [-natris] f. V. DESSINATEUR. || TECHN. Draughtswoman; U. S. draftswoman.

dessiner [-ne] v. tr. (1). To draw, to sketch; dessiner au crayon, au pochoir, aux traits, to pencil, to stencil, to delineate; dessiner à grands traits, to outline, to rough in, to block out; dessiner très vite, to dash off. || To show off, to bring out (les formes); to outline (un profil). || TECHN. To lay out (un jardin); to design, to trace (un modèle, un plan); to design (un papier peint, un tissu). || FIG. To draw, to depict (un caractère, une scène). — v. pr. Se dessiner, to stand out, to take form (se montrer); to be outlined (se profiler) [contre, against; sur, on]; to take shape (prendre forme); to loom up (s'estomper).

dessouder [desude] v. tr. (1). To unsolder.

dessouler [desule] v. intr. (1). FAM. To sober up; dessouler en dormant, to sleep it off; il ne dessoule pas, he is never sober. — v. tr. FAM. To sober (qqn). — v. pr. Se dessouler, FAM. To sober up.

dessous [dəsu] prép. † Under. — adv. Under, underneath, below, beneath; dessus dessous, face downwards, upside down;

mettez un papier dessous, put a paper beneath
(ou) under it.
— loc. adv. **De dessous,** underneath; *les pièces
de dessous,* the lower rooms; *vêtements de dessous,* underclothing, underclothes. ‖ **En dessous,**
underhand (personne); underneath (position);
agir en dessous, to act in a underhand way;
regarder en dessous, to slide a glance towards,
to squint at. ‖ **Par-dessous,** under; *passer par-
dessous la table,* to crawl through under the table.
— loc. prép. **De dessous,** from under (qqch.). ‖
En dessous de, below.
— m. Underpart, under side, lower part, bottom
(d'un objet); *dessous de bouteille, de plat,* bottle-,
table-mat; *dessous de carafe,* decanter stand. ‖
Wrong side (envers); *le dessous d'un tissu,* the
wrong side of a material. ‖ Flat (ou) floor below
(étage, local); *le voisin du dessous,* the neighbour
on the floor below. ‖ Pl. Underclothing, underwear; underclothes (vêtements); *dessous de bras,*
dress preservers (ou) shields; *dessous de robe,*
slip, underslip. ‖ FIG. Defeat (défaite); *avoir le
dessous,* to be overthrown, to go under. ‖ FIG.
Mystery; *le dessous des cartes,* what goes on
behind the scenes; *les dessous,* the seamy side. ‖
FAM. *Dessous de table,* back-hander; *dans le
trente-sixième dessous,* down-and-out.
dessus [dəsy] prép. † Upon, on.
— adv. Above, on the top; on (ou) upon (ou)
over it; *dessus et dessous,* above and below; *j'ai
failli lui marcher dessus,* I nearly trod on his
toes; *mettre un papier dessus,* to put a paper over
it. ‖ NAUT. *Avoir le vent dessus,* to be aback. ‖
FIG. *Compter dessus,* to count (ou) to rely on it;
mettre le doigt dessus, to hit the nail on the head,
to touch the spot; *mettre la main dessus,* to lay
hands on it.
— loc. adv. **De dessus;** *les pièces de dessus,* the
upper rooms. ‖ **En dessus,** at (ou) on the top, on
top, above, overhead (position).
— loc. prép. **De dessus,** from off, off; *enlever
qqch. de dessus l'étagère,* to take sth. from off the
shelf; *tomber de dessus un arbre,* to fall off a
tree. ‖ **En dessus de,** on the top of, above; *en
dessus de nos têtes,* overhead, above us. ‖ **Par-
dessus,** above, over; on top of; *par-dessus le
marché,* into the bargain; *par-dessus la rivière,
mon veston,* over the river, my jacket; *par-dessus
tout,* above all; *par-dessus tout cela,* on top of
it all.
— m. Top, upper part (d'un objet); *dessus de
buffet, de table,* sideboard, table-cover; *dessus
de lit,* coverlet, bedspread; *dessus de plateau,*
tray-cloth; *les pierres du dessus,* the top stones.
‖ Right side (d'une étoffe); back (de la main). ‖
Flat (ou) floor above (étage, local); *le voisin du
dessus,* the neighbour on the floor above. ‖
ARCHIT. *Dessus de cheminée, de porte,* mantelpiece, overdoor. ‖ THÉÂTR. Pl. Rigging-loft; flies.
‖ MÉD. *Prendre le dessus,* to get over it, to recover
one's health. ‖ FIG. *Avoir le dessus,* to have the
upper hand (ou) the best of it; to be top dog
(fam.); *le dessus du panier,* the pick of the basket
(ou) bunch; the cream of society; *prendre le
dessus,* to overcome one's grief (sur sa douleur);
prendre le dessus sur qqn, to get the upper hand
of (ou) the advantage over s.o.
déstalinisation [destalinizasjɔ̃] f. Destalini-
zation.
destin [dɛstɛ̃] m. Destiny, Fate, Fortune. ‖ Destiny, fate, lot (sort); *se plaindre de son destin,*
to complain of one's lot.
destinataire [dɛstinatɛ:r] m. Addressee (d'une
lettre); payee (d'un mandat); consignee (de marchandises).
destination [-sjɔ̃] f. Destination, intended purpose
(but); *à destination pratique,* intended for

practical purposes; *savez-vous à quelle destination cette pièce est affectée?,* do you know what
this room is meant for? ‖ Destination (lieu d'arrivée). ‖ FIN. Earmarking (d'une somme). ‖
CH. DE F. *A destination de,* addressed to (colis);
for consignment to (marchandises); running to
(train); for, going to (voyageurs). ‖ NAUT. *A destination de,* bound for (navire). ‖ AVIAT. *Ligne à
destination de l'Irlande,* air-line to Ireland.
destiné, ée [dɛstine] adj. pp. Destined; fated;
destiné au malheur, destined to be unhappy;
destiné à mourir, fated to die. ‖ Designed,
intended, meant; *destiné à des fins pratiques,*
destined for practical purposes; *destiné au grand
public,* intended for the general reader; *destiné
à servir de resserre,* meant for a store-room. ‖
Addressed (lettre) [à, to]. ‖ FIN. Assigned, earmarked, allotted (somme) [à, for].
destinée f. Destiny, Fate, Fortune (personnification). ‖ Destiny, fate, fortune; lot, portion; *être
l'artisan de sa destinée,* to work out one's destiny;
maître de sa destinée, master of one's fate; *unir
sa destinée à celle de,* to throw in one's lot with.
destiner v. tr. (1). To destine, to design, to intend
(à un sort); *destiner qqn à qqch.,* to destine s.o.
for sth., to design (ou) to intend s.o. for sth.;
destiner qqn à faire qqch., to destine (ou) to
design (ou) to intend s.o. to do sth. ‖ To intend,
to mean (à un usage); *destiner à qqn,* to intend
for s.o. ‖ FIN. To earmark, to assign, to allot
(une somme); *destiner des fonds à,* to appropriate
(ou) to earmark funds for.
— v. pr. **Se destiner à,** to intend to take up (ou)
to enter (une profession).
destituable [dɛstituabl] adj. Dismissible.
destituer [-tɥe] v. tr. (1). To dismiss, to remove
from office.
destitution [-tysjɔ̃] f. Dismissal, removal from
office.
destrier [dɛstrje] m. † Steed, charger, war-horse.
destroyer [dɛstrwajœ:r] m. NAUT. Destroyer.
destructeur, trice [dɛstryktœ:r, tris] adj.
Destroying; destructive.
— s. Destroyer, destructor.
destructible [-tibl] adj. Destructible.
destructif, ive [-tif, i:v] adj. Destructive.
destruction [-sjɔ̃] f. Destruction. ‖ MILIT. Pl.
Demolitions (actes préventifs).
destructivité [-tivite] f. Destructiveness.
désuet, ète [desɥɛ, ɛt] adj. Out-of-date, antiquated, old-fashioned. ‖ GRAMM. Obsolete (terme).
désuétude [-etyd] f. Desuetude, disuse. ‖ JUR.
Tomber en désuétude, to fall into disuse; to lapse
(droit); to fall into abeyance (loi). ‖ GRAMM.
Tomber en désuétude, to become obsolete.
désuni, ie [dezyni] adj. Disunited; at variance.
désunion [-njɔ̃] f. Disunion, dissension (désaccord); disunion, disconnection (séparation).
désunir [-ni:r] v. tr. (2). To disunite, to estrange,
to divide; to set at variance (mettre en désaccord).
‖ To disunite, to disjoin, to dissociate (séparer).
— v. pr. **Se désunir,** to divide, to disagree, to
become disunited; to fall out (se brouiller); to
separate; to become disconnected (ou) disjointed;
to come apart (se disjoindre).
détachable [detaʃabl] adj. Detachable, removable.
détachage [detaʃa:ʒ] m. Removal of stains (de,
from).
détachant [detaʃɑ̃] adj. m. Stain-removing; *produit détachant,* stain-remover.
— m. Stain-remover.
détaché, ée [-ʃe] adj. Undone (cheveux); unteth-
ered (cheval); unchained, loose (chien); undone,
loose (ficelle, lacet); undone, untied (nœud);
loose, separate (page); undone, unbuttoned (vête-

ment). ‖ Isolated (maison). ‖ Detached for temporary service, temporarily attached, seconded (fonctionnaire) [à, to; auprès de, with]. ‖ MILIT. Detached, seconded (officier, soldat); detached, on detachment (troupes). ‖ FIN. Coupon détaché, ex-dividend. ‖ SPORTS. Ahead (coureur). ‖ MUS. Staccato (note). ‖ FIG. Estranged (désaffectionné) [de, from]; drawn away, weaned (détourné) [de, from]; detached, unconcerned (indifférent).
— m. MUS. Staccato.

détachement [-ʃmɑ̃] m. Detaching, unloosing, loosening (action). ‖ Detachment for temporary service (d'un fonctionnaire). ‖ MILIT. Detachment; party; detail. ‖ NAUT. Detachment. ‖ FIG. Unconcern; detachment (de, from); indifference (de, to); détachement des biens de ce monde, unworldliness, other-worldliness.

détacher [-ʃe] v. tr. (1). To unfasten (une boucle); to unbind, to loose, to undo (les cheveux). ‖ To untether (un cheval); to unloose, to loose (un chien, un lacet); to undo, to untie (un nœud); to unbind (un prisonnier); to unhang (un rideau); to unhitch, to unhook, to take down (un tableau); to unfasten, to unbutton (des vêtements); détacher en cassant, en coupant, en mordant, en sciant, en tirant, to break off, to cut off (ou) out, to bite off, to saw off, to pull (ou) break off. ‖ To pluck, to pick (une fleur); to bring out, to give full value to (les mots); to detach, to extract, to separate (une page, un passage). ‖ To detach for temporary service (un fonctionnaire) [auprès de, with]. ‖ MILIT. To detach, to detail, to draft. ‖ NAUT. To unmoor, to unlash, to unfasten (un bateau). ‖ CH. DE F. To uncouple (un wagon). ‖ FIN. To tear out (un chèque); to detach (un coupon) [de, from]. ‖ ARTS. To bring out (un dessin, une silhouette). ‖ MUS. To detach (une note). ‖ FIG. To estrange, to detach, to alienate (désaffectionner) [de, from]; to draw (ou) to turn (ou) to wean away (détourner) [de, from]; détacher son regard de, to detach (ou) keep (ou) take one's eyes from; détacher qqn d'une mauvaise habitude, to wean s.o. from a bad habit. ‖ FAM. To deliver, to deal (décocher).
— v. pr. Se détacher, to come unfastened (boucle); to come undone (cheveux). ‖ To break off (branche); to get loose (chien); to flake off (écaille); to come off, to strip (écorce); to fall out (fond); to come undone (ou) untied (nœud); to come out (page); to flake off (peinture); to fall down (pierre); to come off (roue); to come unhooked (tableau); to work loose (vis); se détacher du rang, to step forward from the ranks; se détacher par petits groupes, to straggle off. ‖ To be clearly uttered (mot, phrase). ‖ To stand out, to be outlined (se profiler) [sur, against]. ‖ MUS. To be detached, to sound clear (note). ‖ SPORTS. To draw ahead, to break away (coureur). ‖ FIG. To turn away (pensée, regard) [de, from]; se détacher de, to withdraw from (une affaire, un parti); to break (ses chaînes); to separate from (un groupe); to detach oneself from (ce monde); to fall out with, to break away from, to become alienated from, to disaffect (qqn).

détacher v. tr. (1). To remove stains from.

détail [deta:j] m. Detail, circumstance, particular; les détails de la vie, the circumstances of life; en détail, circumstantially, in detail; pour plus de détails, s'adresser à, for further particulars apply to; questions de détail, points of detail; raconter en détail, to detail; se perdre dans les détails, not to see the wood for the trees; tous les détails, all the details, all the ins and outs, full particulars. ‖ ARTS. Detail (d'un tableau). ‖ FIN. Item (d'un compte). ‖ COMM. Retail (commerce, vente); cutting up (coupe); de détail, retail (prix); vendre

au détail, to retail. ‖ MILIT. Routine duties. ‖ LOC. C'est un détail, it doesn't matter!

détaillant [detajɑ̃] s. COMM. Retailer, retail dealer.

détaillé, ée [-je] adj. Detailed, circumstantial, minute. ‖ FIN. Detailed, itemized (compte).

détailler v. tr. (1). To detail, to enumerate (énumérer); to particularize, to relate in detail (raconter). ‖ COMM. To cut up (à la coupe); to retail (au détail). ‖ FIN. To detail, to itemize (un compte). ‖ THÉÂTR. To bring out (les mots).

détaler [detale] v. intr. (1). FAM. To make (ou) scoot (ou) scurry off, to scamper away.

détartrage [detartra:ʒ] m. TECHN., MÉD. Scaling.

détartrant, ante [-trɑ̃, ɑ̃:t] adj. Scale-removing.

détartrer [detartre] v. tr. (1). To scale, to fur.

détaxe [detaks] f. Remission of tax; de-controlling.

détaxer [-se] v. tr. (1). To take the tax off, to decontrol (une denrée).

détecter [detɛkte] v. tr. (1). To detect.

détecteur, trice [detɛktœ:r, tris] adj. Detecting.
— m. ÉLECTR. Detector; détecteur au son, sound detector; détecteur de fuites, fault-finder. ‖ MILIT. Détecteur de mines, mine-detector.

détection [-sjɔ̃] f. Detection; appareil de détection électromagnétique, radio direction-finder.

détective [-ti:v] m. Detective; tec (fam.); U. S. dick (fam.). ‖ Box-camera (appareil de photo).

détectrice [-tris] f. ÉLECTR. Detecting-valve.

déteindre [detɛ̃:dr] v. tr. (59). To remove the colour from (un tissu).
— v. intr. To wash out, to run, to bleed (couleur); to lose colour, to fade (étoffe); to come off (sur, on). ‖ FIG. To leave a mark (sur, on); to have effects (ou) repercussions (sur, on); déteindre sur qqn, to influence s.o.

dételage [detɛla:ʒ] m. Unyoking (des bœufs); unhitching, unharnessing (des chevaux). ‖ CH. DE F. Uncoupling (des wagons).

dételer [detle] v. tr. (8a). To unyoke (les bœufs); to unhitch, to unharness (les chevaux). ‖ CH. DE F. To uncouple (les wagons).
— v. intr. To unharness. ‖ FAM. To unyoke, to ease off (cesser le travail); to say good-bye to romance (renoncer à l'amour); sans dételer, at a stretch, without stopping.

détendeur [detɑ̃dœ:r] m. Pressure-reducer.

détendre [detɑ̃:dr] v. tr. (4). To unbend (un arc); to loosen, to relax, to slacken (une corde); to relax (le corps); to release, to let down (un ressort). ‖ To take down the curtains (ou) the hangings (ou) the draperies of (une pièce); to uncover (un siège); to strike (une tente); to unhang (des tentures). ‖ TECHN. To expand (la vapeur). ‖ FIG. To relax, to unbend, to divert (l'esprit, qqn); to steady, to soothe (les nerfs); to reduce the strain of, to make less strained (les relations); to make less tense (la situation).
— v. pr. Se détendre, to unbend (arc); to slacken (corde); to run down (ressort). ‖ To relax (corps); to calm down (nerfs); to unbend, to relax, to light up (visage). ‖ FIG. To relax (esprit); to become less strained (relations); to ease (situation).

détendu, ue [detɑ̃dy] adj. Unbent (arc); slack (corde); run down, weakened (ressort). ‖ Relaxed (corps, esprit, visage).

détenir [detəni:r] v. tr. (101). To hold (une charge, le pouvoir). ‖ To possess (des biens à soi); to detain, to retain possession of (les biens d'autrui). ‖ JUR. To detain (un prisonnier). ‖ SPORTS. To hold (un record).

détente [detɑ̃:t] f. Slackening (d'une corde); unbending (d'un ressort). ‖ Relaxing (des nerfs, des muscles). ‖ Lunge (mouvement brusque en avant); spring (saut); d'une détente il fut au bas *de l'escalier,* with one bound he was down the stairs. || TECHN. Warning-piece (d'horloge) ; power stroke (du moteur) ; expansion (de la vapeur). || MILIT. Pull-off (action) ; trigger (pièce du fusil) ; *détente dure,* hard pull-off ; *appuyer sur la détente,* to press the trigger ; *permission de détente,* leave. || FIN. *Marquer une détente,* to be easier (cours). || FIG. Relaxation, recreation, diversion (de l'esprit) ; improvement (des relations) ; détente, easing (de la situation) ; *aboutir à une détente,* to lead to an easing of tension ; *détente internationale,* international slackening of tension ; *une détente s'est produite,* the situation has eased. || FAM. *Dur à la détente,* close-fisted.

détenteur, trice [detɑ̃tœ:r, tris] s. Holder (d'une charge, du pouvoir). || Owner, possessor (de biens à soi) ; detainer, withholder (des biens d'autrui). || SPORTS. Holder (d'un record). || FIN. *Détenteur de titres,* shareholder.

détention [-sjɔ̃] f. Holding, possession (de ses biens) ; withholding, detainer (des biens d'autrui) ; *détention illégale,* unlawful possession. || JUR. Detention, confinement, detainment (emprisonnement). || NAUT. Detainment (de navire).

détenu, ue [detny] m. Prisoner.

détergent [detɛrʒɑ̃] adj., m. Detergent.

détérioration [deterjɔrasjɔ̃] f. Deterioration, damaging (action) ; deterioration, impairment (de la chaussée) ; dilapidation (d'un immeuble). || Pl. Dilapidations, damages to property.

détériorer [-re] v. tr. (1). To deteriorate, to damage, to impair, to deface ; to make worse. || JUR. To waste (une propriété).
— v. pr. **Se détériorer,** to deteriorate ; to spoil.

déterminable [detɛrminabl] adj. Determinable.

déterminant, ante [-nɑ̃, ɑ̃:t] adj. Determinant, determinative, determining.
— m. MATH. Determinant.

déterminatif, ive [-natif, i:v] adj., m. GRAMM. Determinative.

détermination [-nasjɔ̃] f. Determination, marking out, fixing, settling (fixation). || Determination, resolution, resolve (décision) ; *prendre une détermination,* to come to a decision. || Determination, resoluteness, firmness (caractère résolu).

déterminé, ée [-ne] adj. Well-defined (air, image) ; definite, specific, particular (but) ; appointed, fixed, settled, precise (heure, moment) ; definite, precise (intention) ; stated (jour, époque) ; given (nombre, temps) ; determinate (sens). || Resolute (personne) ; determined, resolved (à, to).

déterminer [-ne] v. tr. (1). To determine (la conduite, les dimensions, la distance, la valeur) ; to decide (les habitudes) ; to fix, to settle, to determine (une heure) ; to define (les pouvoirs, le sens) ; *déterminer l'emplacement, les limites,* to locate, to delimit. || To determine, to cause, to bring about (un accident, une maladie) ; to cause, to lead to (un événement). || To induce, to decide, to move (qqn) [à, to].
— v. pr. **Se déterminer,** to determine, to resolve, to decide (à, to).

déterminisme [-nism] m. PHILOS. Determinism.

déterministe [-nist] m. PHILOS. Determinist.

déterré, ée [detɛre] adj. Disinterred (corps). || FAM. Unearthed, routed out (objet rare, trésor).
— m. Disinterred (ou) exhumed body. || FAM. *Avoir une mine de déterré,* to look death-like (ou) ghastly ; to have a cadaverous face.

déterrer v. tr. (1). To disinter, to exhume, to untomb (un corps). || To unearth, to dig out (ou) up (un trésor, des tubercules). || FAM. To unearth, to rout out, to ferret out (un objet rare).

déterreur [-rœ:r] m. Exhumer (de cadavre). || FIG. Discoverer, ferreter-out.

détersif, ive [detɛrsif, i:v] adj. Cleansing, detergent, detersive.
— m. Detergent, cleansing product.

détersion [-sjɔ̃] f. Cleansing. || MÉD. Detersion.

détestable [detɛstabl] adj. Loathsome, vile, nauseating, nauseous, nasty (mets) ; execrable (nature, travail) ; detestable, hateful (personne) ; vile, wretched (temps).

détestablement [-bləmɑ̃] adv. Detestably.

détestation [-sjɔ̃] f. Detestation.

détester [detɛste] v. tr. (1). To nauseate (un plat) ; to detest, to hate (qqch., qqn) ; *détester être seul,* to hate to be alone.

détonant, ante [detɔnɑ̃, ɑ̃:t] adj. Detonating, explosive.
— m. Explosive.

détonateur [-natœ:r] m. Detonator.

détonation [-nasjɔ̃] f. Detonation, explosion. || Report, bang, crack (d'une arme à feu).

détoner [-ne] v. intr. To detonate ; to explode ; *faire détoner,* to detonate.

détonner v. intr. To jar, to clash (couleur) ; to be out of place (expression, parure). || MUS. To jar (note) ; to sing (ou) to play out of tune (musicien).

détordre [detɔrdr] v. tr. (4). To untwist.
— v. pr. **Se détordre,** to untwine, to untwist.

détortiller [detɔrtije] v. tr. (1). To disentangle (désenchevêtrer) ; to untwine, to untwist (détordre).
— v. pr. **Se détortiller,** to disentangle oneself (se désenchevêtrer) ; to untwist (se détordre).

détour [detu:r] m. Detour, deviation, circuit, roundabout way ; *faire un détour,* to make a detour (ou) circuit ; *faire un grand détour,* to go a long way round ; *faire un détour de deux kilomètres pour aller voir qqn,* to go two kilometres out of one's way to see s.o. || Pl. Windings, meanders, meanderings (d'une rivière) ; turns, windings (d'une route) ; *faire des détours,* to wind. || FIG. Indirect manner ; roundabout means (v. BIAIS) ; *aborder en prenant un détour,* to approach in a roundabout way ; *prendre un détour,* to work round ; *sans détour,* straightforwardly. || FIG. Pl. Intricacies (dédale) ; dodges (subterfuge).

détourné, ée [deturne] adj. Circuitous, roundabout (chemin) ; out-of-the-way (lieu) ; *chemin détourné,* by-way, side-road, by-road. || FIG. Circuitous, roundabout, oblique, indirect ; *moyens détournés,* oblique (ou) indirect means ; *voie détournée,* circuitous course.

détournement [-nəmɑ̃] m. Diversion, diverting, turning aside (de rivière). || JUR. Fraudulent abstraction (de documents) ; embezzlement, misappropriation (de fonds) ; abduction (de mineur). || AVIAT. *Détournement d'avion,* hijack, hijacking, skyjacking.

détourner [-ne] v. tr. (1). To divert (la circulation) ; to divert, to turn aside (une rivière), to turn out of one's way (un voyageur). || To turn aside, to divert, to ward off (un coup) ; to turn away (la tête) ; *détourner les yeux,* to avert one's eyes, to look away. || To abstract fraudulently (des documents) ; to embezzle, to misappropriate, to defalcate (des fonds). || To lead astray, to ruin (une jeune fille) ; to abduct (un mineur). || To divert, to draw off, to distract (l'attention) ; to turn away (la colère) ; to turn, to change, to divert, to shunt (la conversation) ; to stave off (le danger, les ennuis) ; to avert (les soupçons) ; *détourner qqn de,* to alienate from (désaffectionner) ; to dissuade (ou) to discourage (ou) to deter s.o. from, to put s.o. off (dissuader) ; to turn (ou) to divert (ou) to call s.o. off (ou) to wean s.o. from (faire renoncer à) ; *détourner par les avertissements,* to warn off ; *détourner par la séduction,* to entice (ou) to seduce (ou) to allure from. || To hijack, to skyjack (un avion) ; to hijack (un bus, un train).
— v. pr. **Se détourner,** to turn away ; *se détour-*

ner de son chemin, to deviate from one's way. ‖ Fig. To turn away, to deviate (*de,* from); *se détourner du droit chemin,* to go astray.

détracteur, trice [detraktœ:r, tris] s. Detractor, disparager.

détraqué, ée [detrake] adj. Techn. Out of order; U. S. on the blink (fam.). ‖ Méd. Out of order (estomac); broken down, deficient, shaky (santé). ‖ Fam. Crazy, unhinged, unbalanced, cracked (personne); unsettled (temps).
— s. Fam. Crank; crazy person; U. S. queer.

détraquement [-kmã] m. Techn. Putting out of order (ou) of gear (ou) out of action. ‖ Méd. Upsetting (de l'estomac); breakdown (de la santé). ‖ Fam. Derangement (de l'esprit).

détraquer [-ke] v. tr. (1). Techn. To put out of order (ou) of gear (ou) of action; U. S. to put on the blink (fam.). ‖ Méd. To upset (l'estomac); to derange (la santé). ‖ Fam. To derange, to unhinge (le cerveau); to craze, to turn the brain of (qqn); to unsettle (le temps).
— v. pr. Se détraquer. Techn. To get out of order (ou) of gear (ou) of action; U. S. to be on the blink (ou) on the bum (fam.). ‖ Méd. To be upset (estomac); to break down (santé); *se détraquer les nerfs,* to wreck one's nerves. ‖ Fam. To become unhinged (esprit); to go off one's rocker (personne).

détrempe [detrã:p] f. Techn. Annealing. ‖ Arts. Distemper.

détrempé, ée [detrãpe] adj. Waterlogged, sodden, soppy (terrain); soaking (ou) wringing wet (vêtements). ‖ Techn. Untempered, annealed (acier).

détremper v. tr. (1). To soak, to dilute. ‖ Techn. To soften.

détresse [detrɛs] f. Distress, anguish (angoisse); misery, wretchedness (misère morale); poverty, want (pauvreté). ‖ Distress, danger (péril); *signal de détresse,* distress signal, S.O.S.

détresser [detrɛse] v. tr. (1). To unbraid (les cheveux); to unravel (une corde).

détriment [detrimã] m. Detriment; prejudice; *tourner au détriment de,* to prove detrimental to.

détritique [detritik] adj. Géol. Detrital.

détritus [detrity:s] m. Rubbish; offal; refuse. ‖ Géol. Detritus.

détroit [detrwa] m. Géogr. Strait, straits.

détromper [detrɔpe] v. tr. (1). To undeceive.
— v. pr. Se détromper, to have one's eyes opened; *détrompez-vous!,* don't you believe it!

détrônement [detronmã] m. Dethronement.

détrôner [-ne] v. tr. (1). To dethrone, to depose. ‖ Fam. To oust (une méthode); to debunk (qqn).

détrousser [detruse] v. tr. (1). To rob.

détrousseur [-sœ:r] s. Robber, highwayman.

détruire [detrɥi:r] v. tr. (85). To overthrow (un empire); to destroy, to demolish, to wreck, to pull down (un édifice); to exterminate (des insectes, une population). ‖ Milit. To destroy (une armée). ‖ Aviat. *Deux appareils ont été détruits,* two machines were lost (ou) written off (fam.). ‖ Naut., Autom. To wreck. ‖ Agric. To ruin (une récolte). ‖ Méd. To ruin (la santé). ‖ Fig. To disprove (une affirmation); to ruin (l'ambition, une idée, un sentiment); to demolish (un argument); to blast (l'avenir, le bonheur); to dash (l'enthousiasme); to blast, to destroy, to dash, to wreck (l'espérance); to overthrow (un projet); to ruin, to blast (la réputation).
— v. pr. Se détruire, to kill oneself, to make (ou) to do away with oneself (se suicider).
— v. récipr. Se détruire, to neutralize each other (s'annuler).

dette [dɛt] f. Debt; *dette d'honneur,* debt of honour; *dette de jeu,* gambling debt; *avoir des dettes, être dans les dettes,* to be in debt; *faire des dettes,* to run into debt; *n'avoir pas* (ou) *plus de dettes,* to be out of debt. ‖ Fig. *Payer sa dette à la nature,* to pay the debt of nature.

deuil [dœ:j] m. Mourning (douleur); *deuil national,* national mourning; *plonger dans le deuil,* to throw into mourning; ‖ Bereavement, loss (perte); *en raison de son deuil récent,* because of his recent bereavement. ‖ Mourning (vêtements, période); *grand deuil,* deep mourning; *deuil de veuve,* weeds, widow's weeds; *en deuil,* in mourning; *porter le deuil,* to wear mourning; *prendre le deuil de,* to go into mourning for. ‖ Funeral procession (cortège); *celui qui conduit le deuil,* the chief mourner. ‖ Fam. *En faire son deuil,* to do (ou) to get along without it; *les ongles en deuil,* with one's nails in mourning.

deus ex machina [deysɛksmaʃina] m. Deus ex machina.

deutérium [døterjɔm] m. Chim. Deuterium.

deutéronome [døterɔnɔm] m. Ecclés. Deuteronomy.

deux [dø, døz] adj. num. invar. Two; *à deux tranchants,* two- (ou) double-edged; *deux fois,* twice; *une chose ou deux,* a thing or two; *un jour sur deux, tous les deux jours,* every other day; *pour nous deux,* for us two. ‖ Second; *le deux mai,* the second of May, May the second; U. S. May second; *Henri II,* Henry the Second. ‖ Both; *les deux côtés,* both sides.
— m. Two; *à deux,* together; *deux à deux,* two and two, in pairs; *deux par deux,* in twos (ou) pairs; two by two; *deux et un,* deuce-ace (aux dés); *deux et un font trois,* two and one are three; *deux p,* double p; *le deux de carreaux,* the two of diamonds (aux cartes); *en deux,* in two. ‖ Second; *le deux,* on the second of the month (date). ‖ Both; *je veux les deux,* I want them both. ‖ Fam. *A deux pas,* close at hand, hard by; *Pierre et Paul, ça fait deux,* Peter and Paul are two different men; *entre les deux,* so-so, betwixt and between. ‖ **Deux-mâts,** m. Naut. Two-master. ‖ **Deux-pièces,** m. Two-piece costume (ou) suit; bare-midriff dress. ‖ **Deux points,** m. Gramm. Colon. ‖ **Deux-ponts,** m. Naut. Double-decker. ‖ **Deux-roues,** m. Two-wheeler. ‖ **Deux-temps,** m. Mus. Two-four time; Techn. Two-stroke engine.

deuxième [døsjɛm] adj. num. Second.
— m. Second (par le rang). ‖ Second floor, U. S. third floor (étage).
— f. Fifth form (classe en Angleterre); second form (en France).

deuxièmement [-mã] adv. Secondly, in the second place.

dévaler [devale] v. tr., intr. (1). To run down; to rush down; to tumble down.

dévaliser [devalize] v. tr. (1). To burgle, to rifle, to clean out (un local); to rob, to strip (qqn).

dévaliseur [zœ:r] s. Robber.

dévalorisation [devalɔrizasjɔ̃] f. Fin. Devalorization. ‖ Comm. Fall (ou) loss in value.

dévaloriser [-ze] v. tr. (1). Fin. To devalorize.

dévaluateur, trice [devalɥatœ:r, tris] adj. Fin. Devaluation (manœuvres).

dévaluation [-sjɔ̃] f. Fin. Devaluation.

dévaluer [devalɥe] v. tr. (1). Fin. To devaluate.

devancer [devãse] v. tr. (6). To leave behind, to go on ahead of, to outstrip, to outdistance (dépasser); *se laisser devancer,* to drop behind. ‖ To go before, to precede (précéder). ‖ To get before, to forestall, to anticipate (anticiper, prévenir). ‖ Milit. *Devancer l'appel,* to anticipate the call-up, to enlist before the usual age. ‖ To be ahead of, to surpass (surclasser); *devancer son époque,* to be in advance of one's time.

devancier [-sje] s. Precursor; predecessor. ‖ Pl. Forefathers.

devant [dəvã] prép. Before, in front of; *devant l'église*, before the church; *devant vous*, in front of you. ‖ In advance of, in front of (en avant de); *partir devant le groupe*, to go (ou) move off in advance of (ou) in front of the party. ‖ In the presence of, before (en présence de); *devant le danger*, in face of danger; *devant ces faits*, in view of these facts. ‖ In the eyes of (aux yeux de); towards, with respect to (vis-à-vis de); *son attitude devant ses détracteurs*, his attitude towards his detractors. ‖ Loc. *Avoir de l'argent, du temps, devant soi*, to have money in hand, time to spare; *n'hésiter devant rien*, to stick at nothing.
— adv. Before, in front; *marcher, s'asseoir devant*, to walk, to sit in front. ‖ Naut. Forward (sur le bateau); ahead (sur la mer). ‖ Loc. *Devant derrière*, wrong side foremost.
— loc. adv. **Par-devant**, before, in front; *attaquer par-devant*, to attack in front. ‖ Jur. *Par-devant notaire*, in presence of a notary.
— m. Fore part, front (d'un objet); *le devant de la mairie*, the front of the town-hall; *devant de chemise, de cheminée*, shirt-front, fire screen; *pièce, porte sur le devant*, front room, door; *prendre les devants*, to go on ahead. ‖ Ecclés. *Devant d'autel*, altar-frontal. ‖ Zool. *Pattes de devant*, fore-legs. ‖ Fig. *Prendre les devants*, to forestall (couper l'herbe sous le pied); to make the first move (faire le premier pas).
devanture [-ty:r] f. Shop-window, display-window (étalage); shop-front (façade); *à la devanture*, in the window.
dévastateur, trice [devastatœ:r, tris] adj. Devastating, ravaging.
— s. Devastator, ravager.
dévastation [-sjɔ̃] f. Devastation, havoc, ravages.
dévasté, ée [devaste] adj. Ruined; wasted.
dévaster v. tr. (1). To devastate, to lay waste.
déveinard, arde [devɛna:r, ard] adj. Fam. Unlucky.
— s. Fam. Unlucky person.
déveine [devɛn] f. Fam. Tough (ou) ill luck; *avoir la déveine*, to be out of luck.
développable [devlɔpabl] adj. Developable.
développante [-pã:t] f. Math. Evolute.
développé [-pe] m. Développé (en chorégraphie). ‖ Sports. Press (en haltérophilie).
développée [-pe] f. Math. Evolute.
développement [-pmã] m. Spreading out (des ailes); stretching out (des bras); unfolding (d'un objet plié); unrolling (d'un objet roulé); unwrapping (d'un paquet). ‖ Spread (des branchages); extent (du paysage, de la route). ‖ Development, growth (du corps); en voie de développement, emerging (peuple); *qui a atteint son plein développement*, full-grown. ‖ Math. Expansion (en algèbre); evolution (en géométrie). ‖ Milit. Deployment (des troupes). ‖ Techn. Gear (d'une bicyclette); development (en photo). ‖ Comm. Promotion, growth. ‖ Méd. Evolution (d'une maladie). ‖ Sports. Lunge (à l'escrime). ‖ Fig. Development (de l'esprit, d'une idée); unfolding (d'un projet); exposition (d'un sujet); *long développement*, expatiation.
développer [-pe] v. tr. (1). To spread out (ses ailes); to stretch out (ses bras); to unfold (un objet plié); to unroll (un objet roulé); to unwrap (un paquet). ‖ To develop (les muscles, le corps). ‖ Math. To develop. ‖ Techn. To develop (une photo); to increase, to put on (la vitesse). ‖ Comm. To promote (la vente). ‖ Fin. To enlarge (sa fortune). ‖ Agric. To develop, to step up (la production). ‖ Fig. To develop, to improve (les dons); to develop, to enlarge (l'esprit, l'intelligence); to unfold (une idée, un plan); to work out, to amplify (des projets); to enhance (sa réputation); to expose, to develop (un sujet); *déve-

lopper longuement*, to expatiate, to enlarge upon.
— v. pr. Se **développer**, to spread out (ailes); to stretch out (bras); to unfold (objet plié); to unroll (objet roulé); to become unwrapped (paquet); to extend (paysage, route). ‖ Méd. To grow (corps); to develop (muscles). ‖ Comm. To grow (affaire); to augment, to increase, to grow (vente). ‖ Fin. To increase (fortune). ‖ Milit. To deploy (troupes). ‖ Fig. To develop, to expand, to enlarge (esprit, intelligence); to increase (habitude).
devenir [dəvni:r] v. tr. (101). To become; *il est devenu mon mari*, he became my husband. ‖ To grow, to turn, to wax, to get (par changement, croissance); *devenir fou*, to go mad; *devenir un grand garçon*, to grow into a young man; to shoot up; *devenir gris*, to turn grey (cheveux); *devenir riche, vieux*, to grow rich, old; *devenir soldat*, to turn soldier; *le jeune lieutenant a fini par devenir colonel*, the young lieutenant rose to be a colonel. ‖ To become of (advenir de); *qu'est devenu votre frère?*, what has become of your brother? ‖ Fam. *Devenir à rien*, to grow as thin as a lath (ou) rail; *ne savoir que devenir*, not to know what is to become of oneself; to be at one's wits' end; *que devenez-vous?*, how goes the world with you?, how are you getting on?, how's life?
— m. Development; state of flux.
déverbatif, ive [devɛrbatif, i:v] adj. Gramm. Deverbative.
dévergondage [devɛrgɔ̃da:ʒ] m. Licentiousness, libertinism. ‖ Fam. Extravagance, wildness (de l'imagination).
dévergondé, ée [-de] adj. Licentious, debauched, libertine; shameless. ‖ Fig. Fanciful, wild, disorderly, extravagant (imagination).
— s. Profligate.
dévergonder (se) [sədevɛrgɔ̃de] v. pr. (1). To run wild, to fall into profligacy; to deviate from the paths of virtue. ‖ Fig. To become extravagant.
dévernir [devɛrni:r] v. tr. (2). To unvarnish.
déverrouillage [devɛruja:ʒ] m. Unbolting.
déverrouiller [devɛruje] v. tr. (1). To unbolt.
devers [dəvɛ:r] prép. *Par-devers qqn*, in the presence of (ou) before s.o.; *par-devers soi*, in one's heart of hearts (en son for intérieur); in one's own hands (en sa possession).
déversement [devɛrsəmã] m. Discharge, outflow (d'un liquide); tilting (d'un véhicule). ‖ Sloping, slope (pente).
déverser [-se] v. tr. (1). To pour, to shed (de l'eau); to discharge (un trop-plein). ‖ To dump, to shoot (un chargement, des ordures). ‖ To pour out (une foule). ‖ Fig. To pour out (des injures); *déverser ce qu'on a sur le cœur*, to get it off one's chest.
— v. pr. Se **déverser**, to discharge, to empty, to pour (dans, into).
déverser [-se] v. tr. (1). To cant up (ou) over.
déversoir [-swa:r] m. Outfall; waste-weir. ‖ Fig. Outlet (pour, for).
dévêtir [devɛti:r] v. tr. (104). To unclothe, to undress (qqn).
— v. pr. Se **dévêtir**, to undress, to take off one's clothes, to disrobe. ‖ Jur. To divest oneself (de, of).
déviance [devjã:s] f. Deviance, deviancy.
déviateur, trice [devjatœ:r, tris] adj. Deviative, deviatory.
— m. Aviat. *Déviateur de jet*, jet-deflector.
déviation [devjasjɔ̃] f. Deviation (de la route). ‖ Méd. Curvature (de la colonne vertébrale). ‖ Phys., Milit., Naut., Aviat. Deviation. ‖ Autom. Diversion. ‖ Ch. de f. Change of route. ‖ Techn. Deflection (d'un outil). ‖ Fig. Deviation (de, from).
déviationnisme [-sjɔnism] m. Deviationism.
déviationniste [-sjɔnist] s. Deviationist.

dévidage [devida:ʒ] m. Unwinding; winding off.

dévider [-de] v. tr. To unwind; to wind off. ‖ Fɪɢ. To reel off (des paroles).

dévideur [-dœ:r] s. Tᴇᴄʜɴ. Winder.

dévidoir [-dwa:r] m. Winder; reel; *dévidoir de machine à coudre*, shuttle-winder, U. S. bobbin. ‖ Eʟᴇᴄᴛʀ. Drum.

dévié, ée [devje] adj. Circuitous; *route déviée*, diversion, loop-way, U. S. detour.

dévier v. intr. (1). To deviate, to swerve, to turn aside (*de*, from); *faire dévier*, to deflect; to drive out of one's (ou) its course. ‖ Sᴘᴏʀᴛs. To break (balle). ‖ Fɪɢ. To deviate, to diverge, to swerve (*de*, from); *faire dévier*, to divert (la conversation).
— v. tr. To turn aside (un coup); to divert (une route). ‖ Eʟᴇᴄᴛʀ. To divert (le courant). ‖ Pʜʏs. To deflect (la lumière). ‖ Mᴇᴅ. *Dévier la colonne vertébrale*, to cause curvature of the spine.
— v. pr. Se dévier. Mᴇᴅ. To curve.

devin [dəvɛ̃] m. Sooth-sayer, fortune-teller. ‖ Fᴀᴍ. Wizard.

devinable [dəvinabl] adj. Foreseeable, guessable.

deviner [dəvine] v. tr. To guess (par l'imagination); to feel (par l'intuition); to foretell, to divine (par la prédiction); to find out (par la recherche); *ce n'est pas chose facile à deviner*, it is no easy guess; *je devine que je réussirai*, I have a feeling that I shall succeed.
— v. intr. To guess.
— v. pr. Se deviner, to be obvious (ou) manifest.

devineresse [-nrɛs] f. Fortune-teller.

devinette [-nɛt] f. Riddle, conundrum, puzzle.

devineur [-nœ:r] s. Guesser.

devis [dəvi] m. Estimate (état); tender, U. S. bid (soumission).

dévisager [devizaʒe] v. tr. (7). To stare at; *dévisager qqn avec insistance*, to scrutinize (ou) scan s.o.'s face, to peer (ou) stare into s.o.'s face, to give s.o. a hard look.
— v. récipr. Se dévisager, to stare at each other.

devise [dəvi:z] f. Motto (d'un livre); slogan (d'un parti, d'une société). ‖ Bʟᴀs. Device. ‖ Fɪɴ. Currency; *devises étrangères*, foreign bills.

deviser [-ze] v. intr. (1). To chat, to have a chat, to talk. (V. ᴄᴀᴜsᴇʀ.)

dévissage [devisa:ʒ] m. Unscrewing.

dévisser [-se] v. tr. (1). To unscrew.

de visu [devizy] adv. With one's own eyes; *constater de visu*, to witness.

dévitaliser [devitalize] v. tr. (1). To devitalize.

dévitrification [devitrifikasjɔ̃] f. Devitrification.

dévitrifier [-fje] v. tr. (1). To devitrify.

dévoiement [devwamɑ̃] m. Mᴇᴅ. Diarrhoea. ‖ Aʀᴄʜɪᴛ. Slope. ‖ Fɪɢ. Perversion, going astray.

dévoilement [devwalmɑ̃] m. Unveiling (d'une statue). ‖ Fɪɢ. Disclosure, revelation, discovery.

dévoiler [-le] v. tr. (1). To unveil (qqn, une statue). ‖ Fɪɢ. To lay bare (une fraude); to unmask (une imposture); to open (ses plans); to reveal, to disclose, to let out (un secret); *dévoiler son jeu*, to show one's hand; *dévoiler la vérité*, to bring truth to light.
— v. pr. Se dévoiler, to unveil (personne). ‖ Fɪɢ. To reveal oneself; to come out, to come to light.

devoir [dəvwa:r] v. aux. (39). Ought, should (obligation morale); *je crois devoir vous dire que*, I think I ought (ou) I think it my duty to tell you that; *les jeunes doivent respecter la vieillesse*, the young should respect old age. ‖ Must, to be compelled (ou) obliged, to have to (contrainte ou très forte obligation morale); *bientôt vous devrez le faire de force*, soon you will be compelled to do it; *bien qu'il n'aime pas protester, il a dû le faire*, though he does not like to protest,

he had to do so; *je dois absolument le voir*, I absolutely must see him. ‖ Must, to have to, to be obliged to (nécessité partielle); *j'ai dû parler au médecin*, I had to speak to the doctor; *je dois le mettre au courant*, I have to inform him; *vous auriez dû prendre un parapluie*, you ought to have taken an umbrella; *vous devez le faire, je le veux*, you shall do it. ‖ To be to (convention); *je devais le rencontrer à 5 heures*, I was to meet him at five; *le départ doit avoir lieu à cinq heures*, the departure is scheduled for five o'clock; *nous devons dîner ensemble*, we are to dine together. ‖ To be to, to be likely to (destinée, probabilité); *cela devait se produire*, that was likely to happen (appamement); that was bound (ou) meant to happen (obligatoirement); *il doit faire un discours*, he is expected to speak. ‖ Must, to have to (supposition); *ce doit être un étranger*, he must be a foreigner; *dussé-je être blâmé*, should I be blamed; were I to be blamed; *dût-il me couper le bras*, even if he had to cut off my arm; *elle devait être en colère*, she must have been angry; *si je dois le lire, il faut me le prêter*, if I am to read it, you must lend it to me. ‖ Cʜ. ᴅᴇ ꜰ. *Le train doit arriver à minuit*, the train is due at midnight. ‖ Loc. *Fais ce que dois, advienne que pourra*, do what you ought and come what may.
— v. tr. To owe, to be in debt (avoir une dette d'argent ou morale); *je lui dois deux mille francs*, I am indebted to him for (ou) I owe him two thousand francs; *elle doit partout*, she owes money all round; *il ne doit plus rien à personne*, he no longer owes anyone a penny, he is clear of debt; *la somme qui lui est due*, the sum owing (ou) due to him.
— v. pr. Se devoir, to owe oneself (*à*, to); to have to care (*à*, for). ‖ Loc. *Comme (il) se doit*, as it is necessary (ou) obligatory; *comme (il) se devait*, as it ought.
— m. Duty; *faire son devoir*, to fulfil (ou) to perform one's duty; *par devoir*, for duty's sake, from a sense of duty, as in duty bound; *se faire un devoir de*, to make it a point of duty to; *se mettre en devoir de faire*, to prepare to do, to set about doing. ‖ Exercise, task (d'écolier). ‖ Pl. Duties, regards (civilités); *présenter ses devoirs à*, to pay one's respects to. ‖ Pl. Honours (honneurs); *rendre les derniers devoirs à*, to pay the last honours to, to perform the last offices to.

dévolter [devɔlte] v. tr. (1). Eʟᴇᴄᴛʀ. To step down (le courant).

dévolu, ue [devɔly] adj. *Dévolu à*, vested in (la Couronne); escheated (ou) lapsing to (l'Etat); devolved (ou) devolving upon (qqn); *ce travail m'est dévolu*, it fell to my lot to do it. ‖ Fɪɢ. Appertaining (*à*, to).
— m. Fɪɢ. Choice; *jeter son dévolu sur*, to fix one's choice upon.

dévolution [devɔlysjɔ̃] f. Jᴜʀ. Devolution, disposal. ‖ Eᴄᴄʟᴇ́s. Lapsing.

dévorant, ante [devɔrɑ̃, ɑ̃:t] adj. Devouring (animal). ‖ Mᴇᴅ. Wasting (maladie); rodent (ulcère). ‖ Fɪɢ. Consuming, carking (chagrin); ravenous (faim); devouring (passion); consuming (soif); parching (vent).

dévorateur, trice [-ratœ:r, tris] adj. Devouring.
— s. Devourer.

dévorer [-re] v. tr. (1). To devour, to raven (une proie); to eat up, to gulp down, to wolf down (un repas). ‖ To destroy, to burn down (ou) out (feu); to eat away (vagues). ‖ Cʜɪᴍ. To eat away (acide). ‖ Fɪɢ. To eat up (ambition); to devour (angoisse). ‖ Fɪɢ. To devour, to eat out, to run through (une fortune); to swallow (une insulte); to swallow, to gulp back (ses larmes); to devour (une lettre, un livre); *dévorer l'espace* (ou) *la*

route, to eat up the miles; *dévorer des yeux,* to devour with one's eyes.
— v. intr. To gorge, to stuff oneself.
— v. récipr. Se **dévorer,** to devour each other (ou) one another.
dévoreur [-rœ:r] s. Devourer.
dévot, ote [devɔ] adj. Devout, pious (pieux); sanctimonious (tartufe). ‖ Fɪɢ. Attached, faithful (à, to).
— s. Devout person. ‖ Religious bigot, devotee; *un faux dévot,* a Tartufe; *une vieille dévote,* an old church hen (fam.). ‖ Fɪɢ. Devotee (*de,* of, to).
dévotement [-tmã] adv. Devoutly.
dévotion [-sjɔ̃] f. Devotion, devoutness, piety; *dévotion des lèvres,* lip-service; *donner dans la dévotion,* to take to religion; *faire ses dévotions,* to be at one's devotions (ou) at prayers. ‖ Eᴄᴄʟᴇ́s. Devotion, cult. ‖ Fɪɢ. Devotion, attachment (*à,* to); *avoir à sa dévotion,* to have at one's beck and call; *être à la dévotion de qqn,* to be at s.o.'s devotion (ou) disposal.
dévoué, ée [devwe] adj. Devoted; attached, faithful; *dévoué au bien public,* public-spirited; *votre dévoué,* yours faithfully (ou) truly. ‖ Cᴏᴍᴍ. *Dévoué à vos ordres,* at your service.
dévouement [devumã] m. Devotion, self-sacrifice, self-devotion (abnégation); devotedness, devotion (altruisme); *dévouement à la science,* dedication (ou) devotion to science.
dévouer [devwe] v. tr. (1). To devote, to dedicate (vouer) (*à,* to]. ‖ To devote, to give over (livrer) [à, to].
— v. pr. Se **dévouer,** to devote (ou) to dedicate (ou) to sacrifice oneself (*à,* to; *pour,* for). ‖ Fᴀᴍ. To volunteer.
dévoyé, ée [devwaje] adj. Having lost one's way (égaré). ‖ Fɪɢ. Perverted, warped (esprit); depraved, perverted (personne).
— s. Pervert; depraved person.
dévoyer v. tr. (9 *a*). To lead astray (pr. et fig.).
— v. pr. Se **dévoyer,** to go astray.
déwatté, ée [dewate] adj. Eʟᴇᴄᴛʀ. Wattless.
dextérité [dɛksterite] f. Dexterity, skill (habileté); *avec dextérité,* skilfully, dexterously.
dextre [dɛkstr] f. † Right hand.
— adj. Bʟᴀs. Dexter.
dextrine [dɛkstrin] f. Cʜɪᴍ. Dextrin.
dey [dɛ] m. Dey.
dia! [dja] interj. Ho!, heck!, haw!
diabète [djabɛt] m. Mᴇ́ᴅ. Diabetes.
diabétique [-betik] adj., s. Mᴇ́ᴅ. Diabetic.
diable [dja:bl] m. Devil, old Nick (fam.) [démon]. ‖ Tomboy (fillette); terror (garçon); *faire le diable,* to romp; *faire le diable à quatre,* to kick up a shindy. ‖ Fellow, wretch; *un bon, grand diable,* a good, big fellow; *un bon petit diable,* a good little chap; *un pauvre diable,* a poor wretch. ‖ Jack-in-the-box (jouet). ‖ Cʜ. ᴅᴇ ꜰ. Trolley, porter's barrow; U. S. porter's dolly (chariot). ‖ Lᴏᴄ. *A la diable,* hurriedly, perfunctorily, in a slovenly way; *allez au diable!* go to the devil (ou) to blazes (ou) to Jericho; to hell with you!; *au diable, au diable Vauvert,* miles away, at the back of beyond; *avoir le diable au corps,* to be possessed of a devil, to be full of devilment; *il a le diable au corps,* the devil is in him; *la beauté du diable,* the freshness of youth; *c'est le diable à confesser,* it's the very devil; *c'est le diable à réussir,* it's devilishly hard to bring it off; *ce sera bien le diable si,* it'll be bad luck if; *ce n'est pas le diable,* it's no great matter; *comment, où, pourquoi, quand diable,* how, where, why, when the devil (ou) the deuce (ou) the blazes; *un diable de courage,* terrific courage; *en diable,* awfully, dreadfully, terribly; *quand le diable y serait,* though the deuce were in it; *que le diable l'emporte!,* the devil take him!, confound him!,

bother him!; *que le diable m'emporte si,* I'll be hanged if; *tirer le diable par la queue,* to be hard up; *un vacarme du diable,* a devil of a row.
— adj. Rompish, boisterous.
— interj. Well!, I'm damned!; *diable non!,* no fear!; *que diable!,* by Jove!, hang it!
diablement [-bləmã] adv. Devilishly, fearfully, dreadfully, awfully; hellishly; *diablement chaud,* devilish hot; *c'est diablement embêtant,* it's a fearful nuisance.
diablerie [-bləri] f. Devilry, devilment, witchcraft (sorcellerie). ‖ Fiendishness, devilishness (nature diabolique). ‖ Devilry, U. S. deviltry; boisterousness, rompishness (turbulence).
diablesse [-blɛs] f. She-devil, devil's dam (démon). ‖ Shrew, virago, termagant (mégère). ‖ Fᴀᴍ. Tomboy (fillette).
diablotin [-blɔtɛ̃] m. Imp (démon). ‖ Little imp (enfant). ‖ Jack-in-the-box (jouet). ‖ Cᴜʟɪɴ. Cracker. ‖ Nᴀᴜᴛ. Mizzen-top staysail.
diabolique [-bɔlik] adj. Eᴄᴄʟᴇ́s. Diabolic, diabolical. ‖ Fᴀᴍ. Devilish, fiendish, demoniacal, infernal, hellish (pernicieux).
diaboliquement [-bɔlikmã] adv. Diabolically, fiendishly; devilishly.
diabolo [-bɔlo] m. Diabolo.
diachronie [djakroni] f. Gʀᴀᴍᴍ. Diachronism, diachrony.
diachronique [-nik] adj. Gʀᴀᴍᴍ. Diachronic.
diaconal [djakɔnal] adj. Eᴄᴄʟᴇ́s. Diaconal.
diaconat [-na] m. Eᴄᴄʟᴇ́s. Deaconship; diaconate.
diaconesse [-nɛs] f. Deaconess. ‖ Deacon's wife.
diacre [djakr] m. Eᴄᴄʟᴇ́s. Deacon.
diacritique [-itik] adj. Gʀᴀᴍᴍ. Diacritical; *signe diacritique,* diacritic.
diadème [djadɛm] m. Diadem.
diagnose [djagno:z] f. Bᴏᴛ. Diagnosis. ‖ Mᴇ́ᴅ. Diagnostics.
diagnostic [djagnɔstik] m. Mᴇ́ᴅ. Diagnosis.
diagnostique adj. Mᴇ́ᴅ. Characteristic, diagnostic.
diagnostiquer [-ke] v. tr. (1). Mᴇ́ᴅ. To diagnose.
diagonal, ale [djagɔnal] adj. Gᴇ́ᴏᴍ. Diagonal.
— f. Mᴀᴛʜ. Diagonal; *en diagonale,* diagonally. ‖ Cʜ. ᴅᴇ ꜰ. *Voie diagonale,* cross-over. ‖ Sᴘᴏʀᴛs. *En diagonale,* across the court (au tennis). ‖ Sᴘᴏʀᴛs. Pl. Ski-bindings.
diagonalement [-gɔnalmã] adv. Diagonally.
diagramme [-gram] m. Diagram; *sous forme de diagramme,* diagrammatically.
diagraphe [-gra:f] m. Diagraph.
dialectal, ale [djalɛktal] adj. Dialectal.
dialecte [-lɛkt] m. Dialect.
dialecticien, enne [-lɛktisjɛ̃, ɛn] s. Dialectician.
dialectique [-lɛktik] adj. Dialectic.
— f. Dialectics.
dialectiquement [-lɛktikmã] adv. Dialectically.
dialectologie [-lɛktɔlɔʒi] f. Dialectology.
dialogue [-lɔg] m. Dialogue.
dialoguer [-ge] v. tr., intr. To dialogue.
dialoguiste [-gist] m. Tʜᴇ́ᴀᴛʀ. Dialogue writer, dialogist.
dialyse [djali:z] f. Cʜɪᴍ. Dialysis.
dialyser [-ze] v. tr. (1). Cʜɪᴍ. To dialyse.
diamagnétisme [djamaɲetism] m. Pʜʏs. Diamagnetism.
diamant [djamã] m. Diamond; *diamant de vitrier,* glazier's diamond; *parer de diamants,* to diamond. ‖ Tᴇᴄʜɴ. Diamond (en typographie).
diamantaire [-tɛ:r] adj. Diamond-like.
— s. Diamond-cutter (tailleur); diamond-merchant (vendeur).
diamanté, ée [-te] adj. Set with diamonds. ‖ Tᴇᴄʜɴ. Frosted (fleurs); *étoffe diamantée,* diamanté.
diamanter [-te] v. tr. (1). To diamond, to set with diamonds. ‖ Fɪɢ. To make diamond-like (ou) sparkling.

diamantifère [-tifɛ:r] adj. Diamond-bearing (ou) -yielding; *champ diamantifère*, diamond-field.
diamantin, ine [-tɛ̃, in] adj. Adamantine; diamond-like.
diamétral, ale [djametral] adj. Diametral, diametrical. ‖ NAUT. Sheer (plan).
diamétralement [-mɑ̃] adv. Diametrally, diametrically; *diamétralement opposé*, antipodal, diametrically opposite.
diamètre [djamɛtr] m. MATH. Diameter.
diane [djan] f. Diana. ‖ MILIT. Reveille. ‖ NAUT. Morning-watch.
diantre [djɑ̃:tr] interj. Well !, by Jove ! (V. DIABLE.)
diantrement [djɑ̃trəmɑ̃] adv. Infernally; devilishly. (V. DIABLEMENT.)
diapason [djapazɔ̃] m. MUS. Tuning-fork, diapason (instrument); diapason, pitch (registre). ‖ FIG. Level; *se mettre au diapason de*, to fall in with the mood of. ‖ FAM. *Monter le diapason*, to shout at the top of one's voice.
diaphane [djafan] adj. Diaphanous, filmy.
diaphorèse [djafɔrɛ:z] f. MÉD. Diaphoresis.
diaphragmatique [djafragmatik] adj. Diaphragmatic.
diaphragme [-fragm] m. Sound box (du phonographe); diaphragm (en photo). ‖ MÉD. Diaphragm; midriff (fam.). ‖ BOT., TECHN. Diaphragm.
diaphragmer [-fragme] v. tr. (1). To diaphragm, to fit with a diaphragm (en photo).
— v. intr. To stop down (en photo).
diapositive [djapoziti:v], **diapo** [djapo] f. Slide, transparency.
diapré, ée [djapre] adj. Diapered, dappled, speckled, mottled, variegated. ‖ FIG. Besprinkled.
diaprer v. tr. (1). To diaper, to variegate. ‖ FIG. To adorn (ou) to sprinkle (ou) to set with.
diaprure [-pry:r] f. Diapering; variegation; variegated pattern.
diarrhée [djare] f. MÉD. Diarrhoea.
diarrhéique [-ik] adj. MÉD. Diarrhoeic, diarrhoeal.
— s. Diarrhoeic patient.
diascopie [djaskɔpi] f. PHYS. Diascopy.
diaspora [djaspɔra] f. Diaspora.
diastase [djastɑ:z] f. MÉD. Diastase.
diastole [djastɔl] f. MÉD. Diastole.
diathermie [djatɛrmi] f. MÉD. Diathermy; *traiter à la diathermie*, to diathermize.
diathèse [djatɛ:z] f. MÉD. Diathesis.
diatomée [djatɔme] f. CHIM. Diatom.
diatomique [-mik] adj. CHIM. Diatomic.
diatonique [djatɔnik] adj. MUS. Diatonic.
diatribe [djatrib] f. Diatribe.
dichotomie [dikɔtɔmi] f. ASTRON., BOT., PHILOS. Dichotomy. ‖ MÉD. Fee-splitting.
dichotomique [-mik] adj. ASTRON., BOT., PHILOS. Dichotomic, dichotomous. ‖ MÉD. Fee-splitting.
dichromatique [dikrɔmatik] adj. Dichromatic.
dico [dikɔ] m. FAM. Dictionary.
dicotylédone [dikɔtiledɔn] adj. BOT. Dicotyledonous.
— f. BOT. Dicotyledon (pl. dicotyledones).
dictame [diktam] m. BOT. Dittany. ‖ FIG. Balm, comfort, solace.
Dictaphone [diktafo:n] m. Dictaphone.
dictateur [diktatœ:r] m. Dictator.
dictatorial, ale [-tɔrjal] adj. Dictatorial.
dictature [-ty:r] f. Dictatorship.
dictée [dikte] f. Dictation (action et texte); *écrire sous la dictée de qqn*, to write at (ou) from s.o.'s dictation. ‖ FIG. Dictation, guidance.
dicter v. tr. (1). To dictate (un texte) [à, to]. ‖ FIG. To dictate, to lay down (des conditions).
diction [diksjɔ̃] f. Diction (style). ‖ Elocution, delivery; voice-production.

dictionnaire [diksjɔnɛ:r] m. Dictionary. ‖ FAM. *Dictionnaire ambulant*, walking dictionary.
dicton [diktɔ̃] m. By-word, saw, old tag.
didactique [didaktik] adj. Didactic.
— f. Didactics.
dièdre [diɛ:dr] adj. MATH. Dihedral.
— m. MATH. Dihedron.
diélectrique [dielɛktrik] adj., m. Dielectric.
diérèse [dierɛ:z] f. MÉD., GRAMM. Diaeresis.
dièse [djɛ:z] adj., m. MUS. Sharp; *double dièse*, double sharp.
diesel [dizɛl] m. TECHN. Diesel engine; *adoption de moteurs diesels*, dieselization; *équiper de moteurs diesels*, to dieselize.
diéser [djeze] v. tr. (5). MUS. To sharp(en).
diésis [djezis] m. Double dagger (en typo).
diète [djɛt] f. Diet (assemblée).
diète f. MÉD. Low diet (abstinence); diet (régime); *diète absolue*, starvation diet; *se mettre à la diète*, to put oneself on a low diet.
diététicien, enne [djetetisjɛ̃, ɛn] s. MÉD. Dietetician, U. S. dietician.
diététique [-tik] adj. MÉD. Dietetic.
— f. MÉD. Dietetics.
dieu [djø] (pl. **dieux**) m. God, deity (divinité païenne); *demi-dieu*, demi-god; *jurer ses grands dieux*, to swear by all that is sacred; *se faire un dieu de*, to make a god of.
Dieu m. God; the Deity; *le Bon Dieu*, God, the Heavenly Father. ‖ LOC. *A Dieu ne plaise* (ou) *Dieu m'en préserve*, God forbid; *à la grâce de Dieu*, come what may; *Dieu vous bénisse*, God bless you; *Dieu merci*, thank God; *la maison du Bon Dieu*, Liberty Hall; *pour l'amour de Dieu*, for God's (ou) goodness' sake; *s'il plaît à Dieu*, please God, God willing; *tous les jours que le Bon Dieu fait*, every blessed day.
— interj. *Bon Dieu !*, *nom de Dieu !*, damn !, hell !; *mon Dieu !*, dear !, dear me !, good gracious !, my !, my goodness !; *mon Dieu oui*, *non, peut-être !*, why yes !, well no !, well, indeed !
diffamant, ante [difamɑ̃, ɑ̃:t] adj. Defamatory, slanderous, libellous.
diffamateur, trice [-matœ:r, tris] s. Defamer, slanderer, libeller.
diffamation [-masjɔ̃] f. Defamation. ‖ JUR. *Diffamation écrite, orale*, libel, slander.
diffamatoire [-matwa:r] adj. Defamatory, slanderous, libellous; *écrit diffamatoire*, libel.
diffamer [-me] v. tr. (1). To defame, to slander, to libel, to traduce.
différé, ée [difere] adj. Delayed (action). ‖ FIN. Deferred (capital, paiement).
différé m. RADIO. *Emission en différé*, recorded (ou) pre-recorded programme.
différemment [diferamɑ̃] adv. Differently.
différence [diferɑ̃:s] f. Difference (dissemblance, divergence) [*avec*, from; *de*, in, of; *entre*, between]; *à la différence de*, unlike, contrary to. ‖ Difference, disparity, discrepancy (écart) [*de*, in]; *différence d'âge*, disparity in age; *différence entre deux récits*, discrepancy between two accounts. ‖ Difference, discrimination (distinction); *faire la différence avec*, to discriminate (ou) to distinguish between. ‖ MATH. Difference. ‖ FIN. Difference, margin. ‖ AVIAT. Variation (de surface).
différenciateur, trice [-rɑ̃sjatœ:r, tris] adj. Differentiating, distinguishing.
différenciation [-rɑ̃sjasjɔ̃] f. Differentiation. ‖ MÉD. Specialization.
différencier [-rɑ̃sje] v. tr. (1). To differentiate, to discriminate (ou) to distinguish between. ‖ MATH. To differentiate. ‖ MÉD. To specialize.
— v. pr. **Se différencier**, to differentiate. ‖ MÉD. To specialize.

différend [-rã] m. Difference, contention; *en cas de différend relatif à,* in case of dispute regarding.

différent, ente [rã, ã:t] adj. Different, unlike, dissimilar, distinct (dissemblable). ‖ Different, distinct (*de,* from). ‖ Pl. Different, various, sundry. (V. DIVERS.)

différentiel, elle [-rãsjεl] adj. MATH., TECHN., MÉD., FIN. Differential.
— m. TECHN. Differential.

différentielle [-rãsjεl] f. MATH. Differential.

différer [-re] v. tr. (5). To delay (une action, un départ); to postpone (un départ, un projet); *différer de faire,* to put off doing. ‖ JUR. To postpone (une affaire); to put off (un jugement). ‖ COMM., FIN. To defer (une affaire, un paiement); to put off (un paiement, une vente).
— v. intr. To put things off (retarder). ‖ To differ, to be different (ne pas se ressembler); *différer de,* to differ from, to be unlike. ‖ To disagree, to be at variance (être en désaccord) [*avec,* with].

difficile [difisil] adj. Difficult (chose, leçon, tâche, tour, problème) [*à,* to]; hard, trying (circonstances); hard (temps, texte); *il est difficile de se procurer des épices,* spices are hard to find; *il m'est difficile de croire,* I find it difficult to believe; I can't very well believe. ‖ Dainty, fastidious, overnice, finicky, finical, faddy (pour la nourriture); particular (pour les relations, le travail). ‖ FIG. Difficult, crotchety, prickly (caractère); wayward (enfant); cranky, crotchety, difficult, hard to please, hard to manage (personne); *difficile à manier,* hard to handle, choosy; *difficile à vivre,* difficult to get on with.
— m. Difficulty; hard thing. ‖ FAM. *Faire le difficile,* to pick and choose (chipoter).

difficilement [-silmã] adv. With difficulty.

difficulté [-kylte] f. Difficulty (sens général); hardness (des circonstances, de l'époque); toilsomeness (d'un travail); *d'exécution difficile,* hard to accomplish, difficult of accomplishment. ‖ Difficulty, obstacle. ‖ Difficulty, trouble, perplexity (ennui); *avoir des difficultés pour faire,* to have trouble in doing; *en difficultés,* in difficulties. ‖ Pl. Difficulties, objections; *faire des difficultés,* to make difficulties. ‖ Pl. Difficulties, differences (différend); *avoir des difficultés avec,* to be at variance with.

difficultueux [-kyltɥø] adj. Fussy (personnage). ‖ FAM. Difficult, toilsome (travail).

difforme [difɔrm] adj. Deformed, misshapen (mal formé); shapeless (sans forme).

difformité [-mite] f. Deformity, malformation.

diffracter [difrakte] v. tr. (1). PHYS. To diffract.

diffraction [-sjɔ̃] f. PHYS. Diffraction.

diffus, use [dify, y:z] adj. PHYS. Diffused (lumière). ‖ MÉD. Diffusc. ‖ FIG. Prolix, wordy, long-winded (personne); lengthy (récit); diffuse, loose (style).

diffusément [-zemã] adv. Diffusely.

diffuser [-ze] v. tr. (1). PHYS. To diffuse (la chaleur, la lumière). ‖ RADIO. To broadcast. ‖ FIG. To diffuse.
— v. pr. Se diffuser. PHYS., FIG. To diffuse.

diffuseur [-zœ:r] m. TECHN. Diffuser, spray-cone. ‖ RADIO. Cone loud-speaker (appareil); broadcaster (personne).

diffusif, ive [-zif, i:v] adj. Diffusive.

diffusion [-zjɔ̃] f. PHYS. Diffusion (de la chaleur, de la lumière). ‖ RADIO. Broadcasting (action); broadcast (programme). ‖ MÉD. Spread (d'une maladie). ‖ FIG. Diffusion (des idées, des nouvelles); diffuseness (des paroles, du style).

digérer [diʒere] v. tr. (5). MÉD. To mature (un abcès); to digest (la nourriture, une préparation). ‖ FIG. To digest (assimiler); to digest, to classify,

to summarize (ordonner, résumer); *mal digéré,* ill-digested. ‖ FAM. To digest, to stomach, to get over (encaisser); *il ne digère pas ça,* it sticks in his gizzard (ou) crop.
— y. intr. MÉD. To digest; *elle digère bien,* her digestion is good; *faire digérer,* to digest. ‖ FIG. *Dur à digérer,* unpalatable, hard to put up with.
— v. pr. Se digérer. MÉD. To digest (aliments).

digest [dajdʒεst] m. Digest. (V. ABRÉGÉ.)

digeste [diʒεst] adj. Digestible.

digestible [diʒεstibl] adj. MÉD. Digestible.

digestif, ive [-tif, i:v] adj. MÉD. Digestive.
— m. Digestive, after-dinner drink, liqueur.

digestion [-tjɔ̃] f. MÉD. Maturing (d'un abcès); digestion (de la nourriture). ‖ FIG. Digestion (des faits, du savoir).

digit [diʒit] m. INFORM. Digit; *digit binaire,* binary digit.

digital, ale [diʒital] adj. Digital; *empreinte digitale,* finger print. ‖ INFORM. Digital.

digitale [-ta:l] f. BOT. Digitalis, foxglove.

digitaline [-talin] f. MÉD. Digitalin.

digité, ée [-te] adj. BOT. Digitate.

digitigrade [-tigrad] adj., m. ZOOL. Digitigrade.

digne [diɲ] adj. Worthy (honorable); dignified (solennel). ‖ *Digne de,* worthy of, becoming of, appropriate to (approprié à); fit to (capable de); worthy of, deserving of (méritant); *digne d'attention,* worthy of notice; *digne d'éloges, d'envie, de remarque,* praiseworthy, enviable, noteworthy; *digne d'être mentionné,* worth mentioning; *digne d'une mère,* motherly.

dignement [diɲmã] adv. Fitly, properly, meetly (convenablement); worthily (honorablement); with dignity (solennellement).

dignitaire [diɲitε:r] s. Dignitary.

dignité [-te] f. Dignity (gravité); dignity, self-respect (respect de soi); seriousness (sérieux); *qui manque de dignité,* undignified. ‖ Dignity, high rank (ou) office (fonction). ‖ FAM. *C'est contraire à sa dignité,* it doesn't go with his dignity.

digon [digɔ̃] m. SPORTS. Fish-gig (à la pêche). ‖ NAUT. Flagstaff.

digramme [digram] m. GRAMM. Digraph.

digression [digrεsjɔ̃] f. Digression; *faire une digression,* to digress; *se lancer dans des digressions,* to ramble off into digressions.

digue [dig] f. Dam (en travers d'un cours d'eau); dyke, dam, sea-wall (de la mer); bank, enbankment (d'une rivière). ‖ FIG. Barrier (à, to); *élever une digue contre,* to stem, to curb, to throw up a barrier against.

diktat [diktat] m. Diktat, dictate.

dilapidateur, trice [dilapidatœ:r, tris] adj. Prodigal, lavish, wasteful.
— s. Squanderer, waster; *dilapidateur des deniers publics,* peculator.

dilapidation [-dasjɔ̃] f. Dilapidation, squandering, wasting; *dilapidation des deniers publics,* peculation of public funds.

dilapider [-de] v. tr. (1). To dilapidate, to squander, to waste. ‖ To peculate, to misappropriate (les deniers publics).

dilatabilité [dilatabilite] f. Dilatability.

dilatable [-bl] adj. Dilatable.

dilatant, ante [dilatã, ã:t] adj. Dilating.
— m. MÉD. Dilatant.

dilatateur, trice [dilatatœ:r, tris] adj. Dilating.
— m. MÉD. Dilator.

dilatation [-tasjɔ̃] f. MÉD. Dilatation, distension.

dilater [-te] v. tr. (1). To dilate. ‖ MÉD. To distend. ‖ FIG. To gladden (le cœur).
— v. pr. Se dilater, to dilate. ‖ MÉD. To distend (estomac); to become enlarged (pores); to dilate

(pupille). ‖ Fig. To rejoice (cœur). ‖ Fam. *Se dilater la rate,* to shake (ou) to split one's sides.
dilatoire [dilatwa:r] adj. Dilatory.
dilection [dilεksjɔ̃] f. Loving-kindness; dilection.
dilemme [dilεm] m. Philos. Dilemma; *enfermer dans un dilemme,* to fix on the horns of a dilemma; to corner (fam.). ‖ Fig. Quandary; *pris dans un dilemme,* in a quandary.
dilettante [dilεttã:t] s. Dilettante.
dilettantisme [-tãtism] m. Dilettantism.
diligemment [diliʒamã] adv. Diligently (avec diligence); quickly (avec promptitude).
diligence [-ʒã:s] f. Diligence, application, care (soin). ‖ Speed, haste (v. rapidité); *faire toute diligence,* to make all speed. ‖ Stage-coach (voiture); *aller en diligence à,* to go by coach to. ‖ Jur. *A la diligence de,* at the suit of; *faire ses diligences contre,* to sue.
diligent, ente [-ʒã, ã:t] adj. Diligent, busy, industrious, painstaking (travailleur). ‖ Quick, speedy (rapide).
diligenter [-ʒãte] v. tr. (1). To press on, to stimulate (qqn). ‖ Jur. To urge on.
diluant [dilɥã] m. Techn. Thinner, paint thinner.
diluer [dilɥe] v. tr. (1). To dilute (*de,* with).
— v. pr. **Se diluer,** to become diluted.
dilution [dilysjɔ̃] f. Dilution. ‖ Milit. Spacing out (de troupes).
diluvien, enne [dilyvjɛ̃, ɛn] adj. Diluvial. ‖ Fam. *Il tombe une pluie diluvienne,* it is raining cats and dogs.
dimanche [dimã:ʃ] m. Sunday; *les habits du dimanche,* Sunday (ou) party clothes, Sunday best; *le dimanche, tous les dimanches,* on Sundays; *venez dimanche,* come on Sunday.
dîme [di:m] f. Ecclés. Tithe. ‖ Fin. U. S. Dime.
dimension [dimãsjɔ̃] f. Dimension, size; *à trois dimensions,* three-dimensional; *de grandes dimensions,* large-sized; *prendre les dimensions de,* to measure out, to take the measurements of.
dîmer [dime] v. tr. (1). Ecclés. To tithe.
— v. intr. Ecclés. To levy tithe (*sur,* on).
diminué, ée [diminɥe] adj. Full-fashioned (bas); decreased (tricot). ‖ Mus. Diminished. ‖ Méd. Deficient; disabled; handicapped. ‖ Fig. Lowered (personne).
diminuer v. tr. (1). To diminish; to shorten; to narrow (en dimension). ‖ To diminish, to lower, to decrease, to reduce (réduire). ‖ To take in (au tricot). ‖ Fin. To cut down (les charges); to curtail (les dépenses); to reduce (les prix); to bring down (la valeur). ‖ Méd. To reduce, to assuage (la douleur); to impair (les forces). ‖ Fig. To lessen, to weaken (l'autorité); to lighten (le chagrin); to damp (l'enthousiasme); to lower (qqn).
— v. intr. To subside (crue); to relax (froid); to grow shorter (jour); to decline (lumière); to fall off (nombre); to slacken (vitesse). ‖ Comm. To run low (réserves). ‖ Fin. To fall off (bénéfices); to go down (prix); *faire diminuer,* to lower. ‖ Méd. To abate (fièvre); to decline (forces, santé); to fail (mémoire, vue). ‖ Fig. To decline (influence); to wane (renommée).
— v. pr. **Se diminuer,** to lower oneself.
diminutif, ive [diminytif, i:v] adj. Diminutive.
— m. Pet name, nickname (nom). ‖ Miniature (édifice). ‖ Gramm. Diminutive.
diminution [-sjɔ̃] f. Diminution, shortening (en dimension); decrement (en nombre); decrease (en quantité). ‖ Full-fashioning (des bas); taking-in (d'un tricot). ‖ Fin. Cutting down (des charges); curtailment (des dépenses); reduction, falling (des prix); depreciation (de la valeur). ‖ Techn. Slackening (de la vitesse). ‖ Méd. Assuagement (de la

douleur); abatement (de la fièvre); impairment (des forces, de la santé, de la vue). ‖ Fig. Lessening (de l'autorité, du prestige).
dimorphe [dimɔrf] adj. Chim., Bot. Dimorphous.
dimorphisme [-fism] m. Chim., Bot. Dimorphism. ‖ Méd. *Dimorphisme sexuel,* sexual dimorphism.
dinanderie [dinãdri] f. Braziery, dinanderie.
dinatoire [dinatwa:r] adj. Substantial (déjeuner).
dinde [dɛ̃:d] f. Zool. Turkey-hen, turkey. ‖ Culin. Turkey. ‖ Fam. *Petite dinde,* little goose; *vieille dinde,* old hen.
dindon [dɛ̃dɔ̃] m. Zool. Turkey-cock. ‖ Fam. Ninny; *dindon de la farce,* dupe, gull.
dindonneau [-dɔno] m. Zool. Young turkey.
dîner [dine] v. intr. (1). To dine (*de,* off, on); to take one's dinner; *dîner par cœur,* to go without eating, to dine with Duke Humphrey; *dîner en ville,* to dine out; *en train de dîner,* at dinner; *prier qqn à dîner,* to invite s.o. to dinner.
— m. Dinner; *donner un dîner,* to give a dinner party; *l'heure du dîner,* dinner-time; *faire son dîner de,* to dine off (ou) on.
dinette [-nɛt] f. Dolls' dinner-party (d'enfants); *faire la dînette,* to have a dolls' dinner-party. ‖ Snack meal (d'adultes); *faire la dînette,* to have a snack.
dineur [-nœ:r] m. Diner. ‖ Fam. Good trencherman.
dingo [dɛ̃go] adj. Fam. Loopy, crazy, U. S. nuts.
— s. Fam. Screwball, crackpot, goon, U. S. nut.
dingue [dɛ̃:g] adj. Pop. Crazy, loony, nuts (personne); *devenir dingue,* to go nuts (ou) bananas. ‖ Crazy, incredible (histoire).
— s. Pop. Nut, nutcase, loony.
dinguer [dɛ̃ge] v. intr. Pop. *Envoyer dinguer qqch., qqn,* to chuck sth. up; to turn s.o. out.
dinosaure [dinɔsɔ:r] m. Zool. Dinosaur.
diocésain, aine [djosezɛ̃, ɛn] adj., s. Ecclés. Diocesan.
diocèse [djosɛ:z] m. Ecclés. Diocese.
diode [djɔd] f. Electr. Diode.
dionysiaque [djɔnizjak] adj. Dionysiac, Dionysian.
dioptrie [djɔptri] f. Phys. Diopter, dioptre.
dioptrique [-trik] adj. Phys. Dioptric.
— f. Phys. Dioptrics.
diorama [djɔrama] m. Diorama.
dioxyde [diɔksid] m. Chim. Dioxide.
diphasé [difaze] adj. Electr. Two-phase, diphase.
diphtérie [difteri] f. Méd. Diphtheria.
diphtérique [-rik] adj. Méd. Diphtheric.
diphtongaison [diftɔ̃gɛzɔ̃] f. Gramm. Diphthongization.
diphtongue [-tɔ̃:g] f. Gramm. Diphthong.
diphtonguer [-tɔ̃ge] v. tr. To diphthongize.
diplodocus [diplɔdɔkys] m. Zool. Diplodocus.
diploïde [diplɔid] adj. Méd. Diploid.
diplomate [diplɔmat] m. Jur. Diplomat. ‖ Fig. Diplomat, diplomatist.
diplomatie [-si] f. Diplomacy.
diplomatique [-tik] adj. Diplomatic; *valise diplomatique,* dispatch-box; diplomatic bag (fam.), U. S. diplomatic pouch.
— f. Diplomatics.
diplomatiquement [-tikmã] adv. Diplomatically.
diplôme [diplo:m] m. Diploma; certificate; *il a pris ses diplômes à,* he graduated at; U. S. he got his degree at.
diplômé, ée [diplome] adj. Certificated; graduated.
diplômer v. tr. (1). To grant a diploma (ou) U. S. degree to.
diplopie [diplɔpi] f. Méd. Diplopia.
dipsomane [dipsɔman] s. Méd. Dipsomaniac.
dipsomanie [-ni] f. Méd. Dipsomania.
diptère [diptɛ:r] adj. Archit. Dipteral.

diptère adj. ZOOL. Dipterous, two-winged.
— m. ZOOL. Dipteran. ‖ Pl. Diptera.
diptyque [diptik] m. Diptych.
dire [diːr] v. tr. (40).

---

1. Affirmer, énoncer. — 2. Divulguer, ordonner, préciser. — 3. Assurer. — 4. Décider. — 5. Employer. — 6. Critiquer. — 7. Parler, raconter. — 8. Penser. — 9. Plaire. — 10. Rappeler. — 11. Ressembler, sembler. — 12. Réciter. — 13. Signifier. — 14. FAM. — 15. LOC. — 16. Entendre dire. — 17. Envoyer dire. — 18. Faire dire. — 19. Vouloir dire.

---

1. To say (affirmer, énoncer, indiquer) [à, to]; *à ce qu'on dit*, according to what they say; *cela va sans dire*, it goes without saying, it's a matter of course; *comme dit l'autre*, as they say; *comme dit le proverbe*, as the saying is; *comment dit-on roi en anglais?*, what's the English for « roi »?; *elle dit ne pas savoir*, she says she does not know; *il est dit dans le Coran*, it says in the Koran; *il y a beaucoup à dire sur*, much may be said on; *j'avais beau dire*, say what I would; *je ne saurais dire combien je suis heureux*, I can't tell you how happy I am; *on le dit riche*, he is said to be rich; *le moins qu'on puisse dire*, to say the least; *pour ainsi dire* (ou) *comme qui dirait*, so to say, so to speak, as it were, in a way; *quoi qu'on dise*, whatever may be said, say what they will; *sans mot dire*, without a word; *soit dit en passant*, be it said in passing; *vous disiez?*, you were saying? ‖ 2. To tell (divulguer, ordonner, préciser); *à qui le dites-vous?*, you are telling me! (fam.); *à vrai dire*, to tell the truth; *c'est moi qui vous le dis*, I can tell you; let me tell you; *c'est tout dire*, there is nothing to add; *cela en dit long*, that speaks volumes; *je lui ai dit de venir*, I told her to come; *je vous l'avais bien dit*, I told you so; *je ne vous dis que ça*, I can tell you so; *je vous dis que non*, I tell you it is not so; *on m'a dit de le faire*, I was told to do it; *qqch. me le dit*, sth. tells me so. ‖ 3. To confirm, to assure (assurer); *il n'est pas dit que*, it is by no means sure that; *qui me dit que?*, how can I be sure that? ‖ 4. To settle, to decide (décider); *c'est dit*, it's settled; *disons la semaine prochaine?*, shall we say next week? ‖ 5. To use (employer); *ne dites pas ce mot*, don't use this word. ‖ 6. To object, to oppose; to criticize (critiquer, objecter); *dire qqch. contre*, to bring sth. against; *trouver à dire contre*, to raise an objection against, to find fault with. ‖ 7. To speak, to talk (parler, raconter); *c'est facile à dire*, it's easy to talk; *dire ce qu'on pense*, to speak one's mind; *dire des sottises*, to talk nonsense, *elle sait ce qu'elle dit*, she knows what she is talking about; *j'ai dit*, I have spoken; *pour ainsi dire*, so to speak. ‖ 8. To say, to think (penser); *dire qu'il est parti!*, and to think he has gone away!; *que dites-vous de lui?*, what do you think of him?; *qu'en diront les gens?*, what will people say?; *qui l'eût dit!*, who would have thought it!; *se dire que*, to think that. ‖ 9. To please (plaire); *ça ne me dit rien*, that does not appeal to me; I don't like it; I am not in the humour for it; U. S. I don't go much for it; *ça ne me dit rien qui vaille*, it looks fishy to me; *si le cœur vous en dit*, if you feel like it, if you have a fancy for it. ‖ 10. To say, to recall, to put in mind (rappeler); *ça me dit qqch.*, that puts me in mind of sth.; *ça ne me dit rien*, that conveys nothing to me. ‖ 11. To look (ressembler, sembler); *on dirait que*, it looks as if; *on dirait que qqn marche*, it sounds as if s.o. were walking; *on dirait du velours*, it looks like velvet. ‖ 12. To recite (réciter); *dire*

un poème, to recite a poem. ‖ 13. To mean (signifier); *qu'est-ce à dire?*, what does it mean? ‖ 14. FAM. *Dis donc!*, look here!; I say!; *dites toujours*, go on, get on with it, fire away; *il n'y a pas à dire*, there's no doubt about it, there's no denying it; *il ne le lui a pas envoyé dire*, he told him to his face, he let him have it straight from the shoulder. ‖ 15. LOC. *C'est-à-dire*, that is to say, i.e., namely; *cela revient à dire*, that amounts to saying; *content?*, *que dis-je!*, *ravi!*, glad?, nay, delighted!; *d'après les on-dit*, as the story goes, by what people say; *je me suis laissé dire*, I heard that, it would seem that; *ou pour mieux dire*, or rather; *se le tenir pour dit*, to need no second warning; *soit dit sans vous offenser*, without offence to you; *vous l'avez dit!*, exactly!; U. S. you said it! ‖ 16. Entendre dire, to hear; *c'est ce que j'ai entendu dire*, it is what I heard; *j'ai entendu dire qu'il était malade*, I heard that he was ill. ‖ 17. Envoyer dire, faire dire, to send word, to announce (annoncer, faire savoir); *faire dire qqch. à qqn*, to let s.o. know sth.; to send word of sth. to s.o.; *faire dire qqch. à qqn*, to send s.o. word of sth. through s.o.; *il ne se l'est pas fait dire deux fois*, he didn't want (ou) need telling twice. ‖ 18. Faire dire, to make tell (obliger à dire); *je lui ai fait tout dire*, I made him tell everything; *je ne vous le fais pas dire!*, you say so yourself. ‖ 19. Vouloir dire, to mean (signifier); *savoir ce que parler veut dire*, to know what it means.

— v. pr. Se dire, to be used (mot); *cela ne se dit pas*, you shouldn't say that; *cela ne se dit plus*, that word is obsolete. ‖ To claim to be, to pass oneself off for (se prétendre); *il se dit mon parent*, he claims to be a relative of mine.
— v. récipr. Se dire, to say to (ou) to tell each other.
— m. Saying; statement; *au dire de mon voisin*, according to what my neighbour says; *au dire de tous*, by all accounts; *d'après ses dires*, from what he says. ‖ JUR. Allegation; *à dire d'experts*, at a valuation.

direct, ecte [dirɛkt] adj. Direct (action, cause, intérêt, riposte); flat (démenti); direct, straight (ligne); *partisan de l'action directe*, direct-actionist. ‖ FIN. Direct (impôt). ‖ JUR. Lineal (héritier); immediate, direct (preuves); private (traité); *descendre en ligne directe de*, to be a direct descendant of. ‖ CH. DE F. Through (billet, train). ‖ GRAMM. Direct (complément, discours).
— m. SPORTS. *Direct du gauche*, straight left. ‖ RADIO. *Emission en direct*, live broadcast; *monté en direct*, direct-coupled (antenne).

directement [-təmɑ̃] adv. Directly, straight (en ligne droite); directly, exactly (exactement); directly (sans intermédiaire); *répondre directement*, to give a straight answer. ‖ COMM. Direct (par expédition). ‖ CH. DE F. *Aller directement à*, to run straight through to.

directeur, trice [-tœːr, tris] adj. Directional, managing (comité). ‖ MATH. Director (cercle). ‖ TECHN. Controlling (force); driving, steering (roue). ‖ FIG. Leading, master (idée); directive (fonction); master (plan); guiding (principe).
— m. Director, manager (sens général); president (d'académie); headmaster (d'école); editor (de journal). ‖ THÉÂTR. Manager. ‖ JUR. Governor, warden (de prison); head (d'un service administratif). ‖ COMM. Head (d'une affaire); leader (d'une entreprise). ‖ ECCLÉS. *Directeur de conscience*, spiritual director (ou) adviser. ‖ V. DIRECTRICE.

direction [-sjɔ̃] f. Direction, way, course, quarter (orientation, sens); *dans la direction de Paris*, towards Paris; *elle a pris cette direction*, she went this way; *la direction du vent*, the quarter from which the wind is blowing. ‖ Direction, guidance, lead (conduite); *avoir la direction de*, to be at the head of. ‖ Board of directors; board; directorate; staff (conseil directeur). ‖ Manager's office (bureau directorial). ‖ Bureau, offices, department (services); *direction du contentieux*, legal department. ‖ Directorship (fonction); headship (d'une école); editorship (d'un journal); leadership (d'un parti). ‖ Jur. Government (des affaires publiques); committee (de créanciers). ‖ Comm. Management, control (d'une affaire); *se plaindre à la direction*, to make a complaint to the management. ‖ Milit. Conduct, direction (de la guerre). ‖ Naut. Course, route; *changer de direction*, to alter one's route (ou) course. ‖ Aviat., Naut., Autom. Steering (conduite); steering gear (mécanisme). ‖ Ch. de f. *En direction de*, for; running to. ‖ Pl. Directions, instructions. ‖ Fig. Direction, course (de l'opinion); walk (de vie); *donner une direction*, to impart a direction; *donner une mauvaise direction à*, to misdirect; *la bonne direction*, the right way.

directive [-ti:v] f. Instruction; directive.
directoire [-twa:r] m. † Directory.
directorat [-tɔra] m. Directorate. ‖ Directorship.
directorial, ale [-tɔrjal] adj. Directorial.
directrice [-tris] f. Directress, manageress (sens général). ‖ Head-mistress (d'école). ‖ Math. Directrix. ‖ V. directeur.
dirigé, ée [diriʒe] adj. Managed, run (fam.) [école]. ‖ Radio. Directional (antenne); beam (émission); *dirigée vers*, beamed to (émission). ‖ Jur. Planned (économie). ‖ Fin. Controlled (monnaie).
dirigeable [diriʒabl] m. Aviat. Dirigible; airship; *dirigeable éclaireur*, observation balloon; blimp (fam.).
dirigeant, ante [diriʒɑ̃, ɑ̃:t] adj Governing, ruling (classe); guiding, directing (principe).
— s. Leader, ruler.
diriger [-ʒe] v. tr. (7). To point (son doigt) [*vers*, at]; to bend (ses pas) [*vers*, towards]; to turn (ses regards) [*vers*, to]; to train (un projecteur) [*sur*, on]; to level, to point (un télescope) [*sur*, at]. ‖ To direct, to guide, to lead, to conduct (conduire); to control (la circulation); to manage (une école); to edit (un journal); to superintend (des travaux); *mal diriger*, to misdirect, to misguide, to misconduct, to mismanage. ‖ Naut. To sail, to steer, to navigate. ‖ Aviat. To steer. ‖ Autom. To drive (une voiture). ‖ Bot. To train (une plante). ‖ Milit. To aim (un fusil) [*sur*, at]; to train (un canon) [*sur*, on]. ‖ Ch. de f. To send (le train) [*sur*, towards]. ‖ Milit. To control (le tir). ‖ Comm. To manage, to run, to handle, to work (une entreprise). ‖ Jur. To administer (les affaires publiques); to institute (des poursuites); to conduct (un procès). ‖ Mus. To conduct (un orchestre). ‖ Théâtr. To manage. ‖ Fig. To aim (une accusation); to level (l'animosité); to turn (un argument, son attention, ses pensées); to address (une critique); to conduct (la discussion, les études, une expérience, les négociations); to direct (ses efforts, ses forces); to guide (le jugement); *diriger un élève vers la littérature*, to interest a pupil in literature; *se laisser diriger par ses passions*, to allow oneself to be governed by one's passions. ‖ Fam. *Diriger sa barque*, to paddle one's own canoe.
— v. pr. Se **diriger**, to head (*vers*, for); to turn (*vers*, towards); to go up (*vers*, to). ‖ To be managed (affaire). ‖ To be aimed (accusation, critique) [*vers*, at].
dirigisme [-ʒism] m. Planning; planned economy; controlled finance; dirigisme.
dirigiste [-ʒist] adj. In favour of State control

in economics, dirigiste (personne, Etat); dirigiste, dirigistic (mesure, politique).
— s. Partisan of State control in economics.
dirimant, ante [dirimɑ̃, ɑ̃:t] adj. Jur. Diriment.
dirimer [-me] v. tr. (1). Jur. To nullify.
discal, ale [diskal] adj. Méd. *Hernie discale*, slipped disc.
discernable [disɛrnabl] adj. Discernible, visible.
discernement [-nəmɑ̃] m. Discrimination (différenciation). ‖ Discernment, discretion (jugement); *avec discernement*, with discrimination.
discerner [-ne] v. tr. (1). To discern (qqch.); to discriminate (*entre*, between); to distinguish (*de*, from). ‖ To make out, to detect, to descry (percevoir).
disciple [disipl] m. Disciple; pupil, follower.
disciplinable [disiplinabl] adj. Disciplinable.
disciplinaire [-nɛ:r] adj. Disciplinary (mesure).
— m. Disciplinarian. ‖ Milit. Soldier of a disciplinary company.
disciplinairement [-nɛrmɑ̃] adv. Disciplinarily.
discipline [-plin] f. Discipline, branch of instruction (enseignement); discipline (règlements, soumission). ‖ Milit. Discipline; *compagnie de discipline*, disciplinary company. ‖ Aviat. *Discipline de piste*, ground discipline. ‖ Ecclés. Scourge; *se donner la discipline*, to scourge oneself.
discipliné, ée [-ne] adj. Disciplined.
discipliner v. tr. (1). To discipline, to bring under control (qqn). ‖ Fig. To discipline, to school, to regulate (ses émotions).
discobole [diskɔbɔl] m. † Discobolus, discus-thrower.
discoïde [diskɔid] adj. Disc-shaped.
discontinu, ue [diskɔ̃tiny] adj. Discontinuous.
— m. Philos. Discontinuity.
discontinuation [-nɥasjɔ̃] f. Discontinuance.
discontinuer [-nɥe] v. tr., intr. (1). To discontinue; *sans discontinuer*, without stopping, without a break, at a stretch.
discontinuité [-nɥite] f. Discontinuity.
disconvenance [diskɔ̃vnɑ̃:s] f. Disparity, disproportion; incompatibility, unsuitableness.
disconvenir [-vni:r] v. intr. (101). ‖ Not to agree (*de*, with); *je n'en disconviens pas*, I don't deny it (ou) gainsay it, I don't object to it.
discophile [diskɔfil] s. Discophile, record enthusiast.
discordance [diskɔrdɑ̃:s] f. Discordance, lack of harmony, clashing (des couleurs). ‖ Mus. Dissonance, discordance. ‖ Fig. Difference (des avis); disagreement, contradiction (des preuves); *en discordance avec*, at variance with.
discordant, ante [dɑ̃, ɑ̃:t] adj. Discordant; clashing, jarring (couleurs). ‖ Mus. Discordant, inharmonious, dissonant; out of tune. ‖ Fig. Conflicting; inconsistent.
discorde [diskɔrd] f. Discord, dissension.
discorder [-de] v. intr. (1). To clash (couleurs). ‖ Mus. To be discordant.
discothèque [diskɔtɛk] f. Record collection (collection). ‖ Disco, discothèque (dancing). ‖ Record library (d'emprunt).
discount [diskaunt] m. Comm. Discount.
discoureur [diskurœ:r] s. Fam. Speechifier; twaddler; U. S. spieler, soap-box orator.
discourir [-ri:r] v. intr. (32). To discourse (*sur*, on); to enlarge, to expatiate (*sur*, upon). ‖ Fam. To speechify, U. S. to go into a spiel.
discours [disku:r] m. Speech; address. ‖ Oration de Cicéron); dissertation, discourse (sur un sujet). ‖ Gramm. Speech; *partie du discours*, part of speech. ‖ Fam. Twaddle; hot air; *tenir des discours*, to hold forth, to launch out into explanations.
discourtois, oise [diskurtwa, waz] adj. Discourteous. (V. incivil.)

discourtoisement [-twazmɑ̃] adv. Discourteously.

discourtoisie [-twazi] f. Discourtesy.

discrédit [diskredi] m. Disrepute; discredit.

discréditer [-te] v. tr. (1). To discredit, to bring discredit on (qqch.). ‖ To discredit, to ruin the reputation of (qqn). [V. DÉCRIER.]
— v. pr. **Se discréditer**, to fall into discredit (auprès de, with).

discret, ète [diskrɛ, ɛ:t] adj. Unobtrusive, modest (effacé); sober (peu voyant); circumspect, cautious (prudent); discreet, reserved (réservé); secret, secretive, silent (secret); quiet (tranquille); demande discrète, modest request; être discret sur ses intentions, to keep one's own counsel; être discret au sujet de qqch., to keep sth. a secret; sous pli discret, under plain cover, in a plain wrapper. ‖ MATH. Discrete, discontinuous.

discrètement [-tmɑ̃] adv. Discreetly; moderately; unobtrusively; circumspectly; soberly.

discrétion [discresjɔ̃] f. Discretion (discernement). ‖ Discretion; moderation; circumspection; reservedness. ‖ Secrecy, discreetness; recommander la discrétion, to enjoin secrecy. ‖ Discretion (merci); à la discrétion de qqn, at s.o.'s mercy. ‖ Forfeit (au jeu). ‖ MILIT. Se rendre à discrétion, to surrender unconditionally. ‖ LOC. A discrétion, unlimitedly, without stint, ad libitum; lait à discrétion, unlimited supply of milk.

discrétionnaire [-sjɔnɛ:r] adj. Discretionary.

discriminant, ante [diskriminɑ̃, ɑ̃:t] adj., m. MATH. Discriminant.

discrimination [-nasjɔ̃] f. Discrimination.

discriminatoire [-natwa:r] adj. Discriminatory, discriminative.

discriminer [-ne] v. tr. (1). To discriminate.

disculpation [diskylpasjɔ̃] f. Disculpation, exculpation, exoneration.

disculper [-pe] v. tr. (1). To disculpate, to exculpate, to exonerate (de, from); to clear (de, of).
— v. pr. **Se disculper**, to exonerate oneself (de, from).

discursif, ive [diskyrsif, i:v] adj. Discursive.

discussion [diskysjɔ̃] f. Discussion, debate, argument (débat); avoir l'art de la discussion, to be a good debater; chaude discussion, heated argument; en discussion, in debate (débattu); under discussion, pending, at issue (non décidé). ‖ Difference, contest, dispute.

discutable [-tabl] adj. Debatable, disputable. ‖ Questionable, doubtful (douteux); non discutable, unquestionable, incontestable.

discutailler [-taje] v. tr. (1). FAM. To argiebargie; to argle-bargle; to argue the toss; to quibble; to argufy.

discuter [-te] v. tr. (1). To discuss, to debate, to dispute (débattre); discuter qqch. à fond, to thrash sth. out; discuter une question, to talk a question over; discuter la question de savoir si, to discuss whether. ‖ To question, to controvert, to challenge, to dispute (mettre en question); discuter un ordre, to dispute an order. ‖ FAM. Discuter le coup, to argie-bargie, U. S. to hash it over.
— v. intr. To talk things over; to argue (avec, with; de, about); ce n'est pas à discuter, it's not worth arguing about. ‖ To quarrel, to wrangle (disputer).
— v. pr. **Se discuter**, to be questionable (ou) doubtful (être contestable); to be debatable (ou) disputable (être discutable); to be under discussion (être en discussion); point qui se discute, moot point.

discuteur, euse [-tœ:r, ø:z] s. Arguer.

disert, erte [dizɛ:r, ɛrt] adj. Fluent. ‖ FAM. Talkative, speechifying, gabby.

disette [dizɛt] f. Famine, dearth (en vivres). ‖

Shortage, want (manque); jours de disette, lean days.

diseur [dizœ:r] m. Talker; U. S. spieler; diseur de fariboles, twaddler. ‖ THÉÂTR. Diseur.

diseuse [-zø:z] f. Talker; teller; diseuse de bonne aventure, fortune-teller. ‖ THÉÂTR. Diseuse.

disgrâce [disgrɑ:s] f. Disgrace, disfavour; tomber en disgrâce, to fall into disgrace. ‖ FAM. Ugliness, plainness, U. S. homeliness (laideur).

disgracié, ée [-grasje] adj. Disgraced, out of favour (en disgrâce). ‖ Plain-featured, ugly, U. S. homely (laid).

disgracier [-grasje] v. tr. (1). To disgrace. ‖ To dismiss from court (un courtisan).

disgracieusement [-grasjøzmɑ̃] adv. Ungraciously.

disgracieux, euse [grasjø, ø:z] adj. Ungracious, unpleasant (désagréable); ungraceful, ugly, U. S. homely (laid).

disjoindre [disʒwɛ̃:dr] v. tr. (59). To disjoin, to sunder. ‖ JUR. To sever, to dissociate, to separate.
— v. pr. **Se disjoindre**, to separate, to disunite, to come apart (ou) asunder.

disjoint, ointe [-ʒwɛ̃, ɛ̃:t] adj. Disjointed, disjoined. ‖ MUS. Disjunct.

disjoncteur [disʒɔ̃ktœ:r] m. ELECTR. Underload release, circuit-breaker.

disjonctif, ive [-tif, i:v] adj., f. Disjunctive.

disjonction [-sjɔ̃] f. Disjunction, sundering. ‖ JUR. Severance (de causes).

dislocation [dislɔkasjɔ̃] f. Separation, dislocation. ‖ Dismemberment (démembrement); breaking-up, dispersal (dispersion). ‖ MÉD. Dislocation.

disloqué, ée [-ke] s. THÉÂTR. Contortionist.

disloquement [-kmɑ̃] m. Dislocation.

disloquer [-ke] v. tr. (1). To dislocate, to separate (séparer). ‖ To dismember (démembrer); to break up, to scatter, to disperse, to disband (disperser); to rout (mettre en fuite). ‖ MÉD. To dislocate, to put out of joint.
— v. pr. **Se disloquer**, to break up. ‖ MÉD. To come out of joint.

dispache [dispaʃ] f. NAUT., COMM. Average adjustment.

dispacheur [-ʃœ:r] m. NAUT., COMM. Average adjuster.

disparaître [disparɛ:tr] v. intr. (74). To disappear, to vanish, to be lost to sight, to fade out of sight (à la vue); disparaître sous, to be hidden under (ou) covered with (ou); faire disparaître aux regards, to hide from sight. ‖ To disappear, to be missing (manquer). ‖ To disappear, to die, to pass away (mourir). ‖ To go out (partir, passer); qui tend à disparaître, dying out (usage); faire disparaître, to smooth out (un pli); to clear away, to make away with (qqch.); to take out, to wash out, to remove (une tache). ‖ FAM. To abscond, to make off, to take oneself off (filer); to withdraw (se retirer); faire disparaître, to sweep off, to pinch (rafler).

disparate [disparat] adj. Ill-matched, made up of odd pieces (désassorti); clashing, jarring (discordant); dissimilar, disparate (dissemblable).
— f. Disparity; incongruity. ‖ Clash (des couleurs).

disparité [-rite] f. Disparity.

disparition [-risjɔ̃] f. Disappearing, vanishing (action); disappearance (fait).

disparu, ue [-ry] adj. Dead, departed, deceased (personne); extinct (race). ‖ MILIT. Porté disparu, reported missing. ‖ JUR. Absconding.
— s. Deceased; dead person; notre cher disparu, our dear departed. ‖ MILIT. Missing soldier.

dispatcher [dispatʃœ:r] m. Dispatcher.

dispatching [-ʃiŋ] m. Dispatching.

dispendieusement [dispɑ̃djøzmɑ̃] adv. Expensively.

dispendieux, euse [-djø, ø:z] adj. Expensive.
dispensaire [dispãsɛ:r] m. Méd. Dispensary, welfare centre.
dispensateur, trice [-satœ:r, tris] s. Dispenser.
dispensation [-sasjɔ̃] f. Dispensation; distribution. ‖ Méd. Dispensing.
dispense [dispã:s] f. Exemption (de service). ‖ Ecclés. Dispensation. ‖ Jur. *Dispense d'âge*, waiving of age limit; *dispense de bans*, marriage licence.
dispenser [-se] v. tr. (1). To dispense, to distribute, to mete out (distribuer). ‖ To dispense, to excuse, to exempt (*de*, from); to relieve (*de*, of); *dispenser qqn d'une corvée*, to spare s.o. a chore; *dispenser qqn de tout travail*, to let s.o. off work. ‖ Ecclés. To administer (les sacrements); *dispenser de*, to dispense from. ‖ Fam. *Je vous dispense de vos observations*, I can do without your remarks.
— v. pr. **Se dispenser de,** to do without (d'un travail); to avoid, to get out of (d'une obligation); *je n'ai pas pu me dispenser de faire une remarque*, I couldn't help making a remark.
dispersement [dispɛrsəmã] m. Dispersing.
disperser [-se] v. tr. (1). Tα disperse, to scatter, to spread, to break up (une foule). ‖ Milit. To break up, to rout (une armée); *en ordre dispersé*, in extended order. ‖ Phys. To decompose, to scatter (la lumière). ‖ Fig. To dissipate, to fritter away (ses efforts).
— v. pr. **Se disperser,** to disperse, to break up (nuages); to break up, to scatter (foule); *se disperser par petits groupes*, to drift (ou) to straggle off. ‖ Fig. To have too many irons in the fire.
dispersion [-sjɔ̃] f. Dispersion, breaking up, scattering (d'une foule); blowing away (d'un obstacle). ‖ Phys. Leakage; straying (d'une force magnétique); scattering (de la lumière). ‖ Milit. Rout (d'une armée); *dispersion du tir*, fire dispersion. ‖ Fig. Dissipation (des efforts).
disponibilité [disponibilite] f. Availability (des biens, des objets). ‖ Fin. Pl. Liquid assets, available funds; cash on hand; *manquer de disponibilités*, to be short of available funds. ‖ Comm. Pl. Available stocks (en matériel). ‖ Jur. *En disponibilité*, temporarily unattached (ou) suspended. ‖ Milit. *En disponibilité*, unattached, unassigned; on the inactive list; on half-pay; *mise en disponibilité*, release.
disponible [-nibl] adj. Unoccupied, unengaged, disengaged, free (lieu); available (objet); disengaged, unengaged (personne); spare, free (temps). ‖ Fin. Available (capitaux); *avoir de l'argent disponible*, to have funds available. ‖ Jur. Unattached, detached (fonctionnaire); disposable (quotité). ‖ Milit. Unattached, unassigned.
— m. Fin. Disposable funds; cash in hand.
dispos, ose [dispo, oz] adj. Well, fit, fresh, in good form (personne); alert, brisk, fresh (esprit).
disposant [dispozã] adj. Jur. Alienator; settlor.
disposé, ée [-ze] adj. Disposed, arranged (arrangé); organized (organisé). ‖ Disposed, inclined, prepared, willing, in the humour (enclin) [à, to]; *n'être pas disposé à rire*, to be in no laughing mood; *peu disposé à*, indisposed (ou) unwilling to. ‖ Disposed (intentionné) [*envers*, towards]. ‖ Predisposed, liable (prédisposé) [à, to].
disposer [-ze] v. tr. To dispose. (V. ARRANGER, INCLINER, PRÉPARER.)
— v. intr. To dispose (décider). ‖ To prescribe, to enjoin, to decide, to determine (prescrire). ‖ To retire (s'en aller); *vous pouvez disposer*, you may go. ‖ *Disposer de*, to dispose of, to have at one's disposal (ou) at one's command (ou) in one's possession, to make use of (qqch., qqn); *disposer de sa vie*, to order one's own life; *les moyens dont on dispose*, available means. ‖ Fin.

Disposer d'argent, to have money in hand (ou) at one's command. ‖ Jur. *Disposer de ses biens*, to dispose of (ou) to alienate (ou) to convey one's property; *disposer par testament de sa fortune en faveur de*, to will one's fortune to.
— v. tr. To dispose, to arrange; to organize. ‖ To dispose; to predispose (incliner, prédisposer).
— v. pr. **Se disposer,** to prepare, to make ready, to compose oneself (se préparer) [à, to]; to be thinking (songer) [à, of].
dispositif [-zitif] m. Techn. Apparatus, device, contrivance, appliance. ‖ Milit. Disposition, formation; *dispositif d'attaque*, attack formation. ‖ Jur. Enacting terms, purview enactment. ‖ Comm. Public sale catalogue.
disposition [-zisjɔ̃] f. Disposition, ordering, disposal, arrangement; *disposition d'un livre en chapitres*, division of a book into chapters; *disposition du terrain*, lie of the land. ‖ Disposal, command; *à ma disposition*, at my disposal, in my possession; *avoir la libre disposition de*, to be free to dispose of; *libre disposition de soi-même*, self-determination. ‖ Disposition, bent, inclination; propensity, tendency (tendance); *disposition d'esprit*, bent (ou) frame of mind; *disposition au mensonge*, propensity for lying. ‖ Intention, purpose; humour; *être dans la disposition de*, to intend (ou) to mean to; *être dans de bonnes dispositions à l'égard de*, to be well inclined (ou) disposed towards. ‖ Liability, predisposition, proneness (à, to). ‖ Pl. Arrangements; *prendre des dispositions*, to make arrangements. ‖ Pl. Aptitude, disposition, talent; *avoir quelques dispositions pour*, to have a turn (ou) bent for. ‖ Jur. Provision, clause (d'un accord); *sauf disposition contraire*, except as otherwise provided. ‖ Jur. Pl. *Dispositions légales*, statutory provisions; *dispositions testamentaires*, dispositions of a will; *dispositions de trésorerie*, financial arrangements.
disproportion [disprɔpɔrsjɔ̃] f. Disproportion.
disproportionné [-sjɔne] adj. Disproportionate (à, to); out of proportion (à, with).
disputable [dispytabl] adj. Disputable.
disputailler [-tɑje] v. intr. (1). To wrangle.
disputailleur, euse [-tɑjœ:r, ø:z] s. Wrangler.
— adj. Disputacious.
dispute [dispyt] f. Debate, disputation (débat). ‖ Dispute, squabble, wrangle, quarrel, contest (v. QUERELLE); *avoir une dispute*, to quarrel.
disputer [-te] v. tr. (1). To dispute, to contest (à, with); *disputer qqch. à qqn*, to contend with s.o. for sth.; *disputer le terrain à*, to keep the ground against. ‖ To rival; *le disputer à*, to vie (ou) contend (ou) compete with. ‖ Sports. To play (un match); *chèrement disputé*, hard-won (victoire).
— v. intr. To dispute, to argue.
— v. pr. **Se disputer,** to be debated (ou) discussed (être débattu). ‖ To be contested, to be contended for (être disputé); *se disputer qqch.*, to fight over sth., to struggle (ou) to battle for sth. ‖ Sports. To be played (match).
— v. récipr. **Se disputer,** to quarrel, to wrangle, to have words (*pour*, about; *pour savoir*, as to).
disputeur, euse [-tœ:r, ø:z] adj. Quarrelsome.
— s. Wrangler, disputer (querelleur). ‖ Arguer (discuteur).
disquaire [diskɛ:r] m. Comm. Record-dealer.
disqualification [diskalifikasjɔ̃] f. Sports. Disqualification.
disqualifier [-fje] v. tr. (1). Sports. To disqualify.
— v. pr. **Se disqualifier,** to disqualify oneself.
disque [disk] m. Disc, disk (de la lune, du téléphone). ‖ Sports. Discus; *lancement du disque*, throwing the discus. ‖ Mus. Record, disc. ‖ Milit. Plate. ‖ Ch. de f. Disc-signal, target-

disc; *disque de fermeture*, block-signal. ‖ Autom.
Disc, plate; *disque d'embrayage*, clutch-disc. ‖
Electr. Plate-disc. ‖ Méd. Disc.
disrupteur [disryptœ:r] m. Electr. Spark-
breaker.
dissécable [disekabl] adj. Dissectible.
dissecteur [disɛktœ:r] m. Dissector.
dissection [-sjɔ̃] f. Dissection.
dissemblable [disɑ̃blabl] adj. Dissimilar (*de*, to);
different (*de*, from).
dissemblance [-blɑ̃:s] f. Dissimilarity; unlikeness.
dissémination [diseminasjɔ̃] f. Dissemination.
disséminer [-ne] v. tr. (1). To disseminate; to
scatter, to spread.
— v. pr. Se **disséminer**, to spread; *se disséminer
largement*, to become widespread.
dissension [disɑ̃sjɔ̃] f. Dissension.
dissentiment [-timɑ̃] m. Dissent, disagreement.
disséquer [diseke] v. tr. (5). To dissect.
disséqueur [-kœ:r] m. Dissector.
dissertation [disɛrtasjɔ̃] f. Dissertation (d'un
auteur); essay, U. S. term-paper (d'un élève). ‖
Fam. Expatiation.
disserter [-te] v. intr. (1). To dissert, to discourse,
to descant (*sur*, on). ‖ Fam. To expatiate.
dissidence [disidɑ̃:s] f. Dissidence. ‖ Ecclés.
Schism.
dissident, ente [-dɑ̃, ɑ̃:t] adj. Brcak-away (gouvernement); dissident (groupe, individu). ‖ Ecclés.
Etre dissident, to dissent.
— s. Dissident, dissentient. ‖ Ecclés. Dissenter;
non-conformist.
dissimilaire [dissimilɛ:r] adj. Dissimilar, unlike.
dissimilation [-lasjɔ̃] f. Gramm. Dissimilation.
dissimilitude [-lityd] f. Dissimilarity.
dissimulateur, trice [disimylatœ:r, tris] s. Dissimulator, deceiver.
dissimulation [-sjɔ̃] f. Dissimulation; concealment; *avec dissimulation*, deceitfully, dissem-
blingly. ‖ Jur. Concealment (de bénéfices).
dissimulé, ée [disimyle] adj. Dissembling, secretive. ‖ Hidden.
dissimuler v. tr. (1). To cover (sa confusion, un
objet); to dissimulate (un fait); to keep dark (ses
intentions); to disguise (une odeur, sa pensée);
to dissemble (ses sentiments); to conceal, to cover
up (la vérité); *dissimuler que*, to conceal the fact
that. ‖ Jur. To conceal (ses bénéfices).
— v. intr. To dissemble.
— v. pr. Se **dissimuler**, to conceal oneself, to
lurk, to skulk (se cacher). ‖ To be concealed (ou)
dissimulated (être caché). ‖ *Se dissimuler que*, to
dissemble (ou) to overlook the fact that; *il n'y a
pas à se dissimuler que*, there is no blinking (ou)
disguising the fact that.
dissipateur, trice [disipatœ:r, tris] adj. Prodigal, wasteful, lavish.
— s. Squanderer, spendthrift.
dissipation [-sjɔ̃] f. Dissipation, squandering,
wasting (de l'argent); dispersion (du brouillard,
des nuages); wasting (de l'énergie). ‖ Inattention,
misbehaviour, fooling (d'un enfant). ‖ Dissipation, profligacy (d'un viveur).
dissipé, ée [disipe] adj. Restless, unruly, inattentive (écolier); dissipated, dissolute (personne, vie).
dissiper v. tr. (1). To dissipate, to squander, to
make away with, to fritter away (l'argent, sa fortune). ‖ To dissipate, to scatter, to dispel (le
brouillard, les nuages). ‖ To dispel (les craintes,
les illusions); to clear away (les doutes); to waste
(l'énergie); to clear up (un malentendu); to run
out of (ses réserves); to allay (les soupçons);
dissiper en riant les craintes de qqn, to laugh
away s.o.'s fears. ‖ To distract the attention of;
to divert (qqn).
— v. pr. Se **dissiper**, to clear up, to dissipate

(brouillard, orage); to break (nuages). ‖ Fig. To
abate, to subside (colère); to vanish (doutes,
soupçons); to wear off (fatigue, timidité); to fail,
to flag (forces). ‖ To become inattentive and noisy
(enfant); to dissipate (personne).
dissociable [disɔsjabl] adj. Chim. Dissociable.
dissociation [-sjasjɔ̃] f. Dissociation.
dissocier [-sje] v. tr. (1). To dissociate.
dissolu, ue [disɔly] adj. Dissolute, profligate.
dissoluble [disɔlybl] adj. Jur. Dissolvable (union).
‖Chim. Soluble.
dissolutif, ive [-tif, i:v] adj. Dissolvent, solvent.
dissolution [-sjɔ̃] f. Chim. Dissolution; decomposition; solution (d'un corps). ‖ Jur. Dissolution
(d'une assemblée, d'un mariage); breaking-up,
winding-up (d'une association). ‖ Autom. Rubber
solution (pour pneu). ‖ Fig. Dissoluteness, profligacy (des mœurs).
dissolvant, ante [disɔlvɑ̃, ɑ̃:t] adj. Dissolvent,
solvent.
— m. Solvent; *dissolvant de vernis à ongles*, nail-
varnish (ou) U. S. nail-polish remover.
dissonance [disɔnɑ̃:s] f. Dissonance. ‖ Mus.
Discord.
dissonant, ante [-nɑ̃, ɑ̃:t] adj. Dissonant, discordant.
dissoudre [disudr] v. tr. (10). Chim. To dissolve;
faire dissoudre, to melt. ‖ Jur. To break up (une
assemblée); to annul (un mariage); to dissolve
(le parlement, une société).
— v. pr. Se **dissoudre**, to dissolve, to melt. ‖
Jur. To break up (assemblée); to be annulled
(mariage); to be wound up (ou) dissolved (société).
dissous, oute [disu, ut] adj. Dissolved, melted. ‖
Chim. *Corps dissous*, solute. ‖ Jur. Annulled
(mariage); dissolved (réunion, société).
dissuader [disɥade] v. tr. (1). To dissuade (*de*,
from); to talk, to argue (*de*, out of).
dissuasif, ive [-zif, i:v] adj. Dissuasive.
dissuasion [-zjɔ̃] f. Dissuasion.
dissyllabe [disillab] adj. Gramm. Dissyllabic.
— m. Dissyllable.
dissyllabique [-bik] adj. Gramm. Dissyllabic.
dissymétrie [disimetri] f. Dissymmetry.
dissymétrique [-trik] adj. Dissymmetrical.
distance [distɑ̃:s] f. Distance (espace); *à distance*, at (ou) from a distance; *à deux kilomètres
de distance*, at two kilometres' distance; *de distance en distance*, at intervals; *quelle distance
y a-t-il de X à Y?*, how far is it from X to Y? ‖
Distance, difference (temps); *à deux cents ans de
distance*, at a distance of two centuries. ‖ Phys.
Distance focale, focal length. ‖ Autom. *Distance
au sol*, ground-clearance. ‖ Milit. *Distance de tir*,
range. ‖ Electr. *Distance explosive*, spark gap. ‖
Fig. Distance; *garder les distances*, to keep one's
distance; *savoir garder les distances*, to know
one's place; *tenir à distance*, to hold off, to keep
at a distance (ou) at arm's length.
distancer [-tɑ̃se] v. tr. (6). To distance, to outdistance, to outrun; to outstrip; *se laisser distancer*, to fall behind, to be left behind ‖ Naut.
To outsail.
distanciation [-tɑ̃sjasjɔ̃] f. Théâtr. Alienation.
‖ Fig. Perspective.
distancier (se) [sədistɑ̃sje] v. pr. (1). To
detach oneself (*de*, from).
distant, ante [distɑ̃, ɑ̃:t] adj. Distant, remote,
far-off. ‖ Fig. Stand-offish, aloof, distant.
distendre [distɑ̃:dr] v. tr. (4). To distend. ‖ Méd.
To strain (un muscle); to distend (un organe); to
stretch (la peau).
— v. pr. Se **distendre**, to become distended; to
become overstretched (caoutchouc). ‖ Méd. To
swell out, to become distended.
distension [-sjɔ̃] f. Distension. ‖ Méd. Straining

(d'un muscle); distension (d'un organe); over-stretching (de la peau).

distillateur [distilatœ:r] m. CHIM. Distiller.

distillation [-lasjɔ̃] f. CHIM. Distillation.

distillatoire [-latwa:r] adj. Distillatory.

distiller [-le] v. tr. (1). CHIM. To distil. ‖ FIG. To distil, to exude, to secrete (du venin).

distillerie [-lri] f. Distillery (lieu).

distinct, incte [distɛ̃kt, ɛ̃:kt] adj. Distinct, separate (de, from). ‖ Clear-cut, distinct (contour); visible, perceptible (objet); distinct (souvenir); clear, distinct, audible (voix).

distinctement [-təmɑ̃] adv. Distinctly; clearly.

distinctif, ive [-tif, i:v] adj. Distinctive, distinguishing, characteristic.

distinction [-sjɔ̃] f. Distinction, discrimination; *établir une distinction entre,* to distinguish (ou) to discriminate between; *sans distinction de race,* without any racial discrimination. ‖ Distinction, honour, decoration. ‖ Distinction, refinement, distinguished manners (courtoisie); distinction, eminence (rang); *de grande distinction,* highly distinguished.

distinguable [distɛ̃gabl] adj. Distinguishable.

distingué, ée [distɛ̃ge] adj. Distinguished, noted, eminent. (V. REMARQUABLE.) ‖ Distinguished, refined, genteel, polished (manières); distingué, gentlemanly, ladylike (personne). ‖ *Sentiments distingués,* yours very faithfully (fin de lettre).

distinguer v. tr. (1). To mark out (délimiter); to distinguish, to differentiate (différencier) [*de,* from]. ‖ To distinguish, to detect, to make out, to perceive (entendre, voir); to know, to tell (reconnaître). ‖ To draw attention to, to bring into prominence (mettre en relief); to honour (honorer); to single out (remarquer).
— v. intr. To distinguish, to discriminate.
— v. pr. **Se distinguer,** to be distinguished (ou) distinguishable (ou) marked off; to differ (se différencier) [*de,* from]. ‖ To be audible (ou) noticeable (ou) remarkable (ou) conspicuous (ou) visible (être entendu, remarqué, vu). ‖ To distinguish oneself, to gain distinction (par son courage, son talent); to attract attention, to make oneself conspicuous (par son originalité); to push oneself forward, to show off (par vanité).

distinguo [-go] m. FAM. Distinction.

distique [distik] m. Distich; couplet.

distordre [distɔrdr] v. tr. (4). To distort. ‖ MÉD. To twist.

distorsion [-sjɔ̃] f. MÉD., PHYS. Distorsion.

distraction [distraksjɔ̃] f. Absent-mindedness, absence of mind (absence). ‖ Inattention, inadvertency, inadvertence, distraction; *avoir des distractions,* to be subject to fits of absent-mindedness, to be absent-minded; *donner des distractions à qqn,* to give s.o. sth. else to think about. ‖ Amusement, distraction, entertainment, diversion. (V. RÉCRÉATION.) ‖ JUR. Abstraction, separation, setting aside (prélèvement); *distraction de fonds,* peculation, embezzlement, misappropriation.

distraire [distrɛ:r] v. tr. (11). To distract (l'attention); *distraire qqn de sa douleur, de ses préoccupations,* to take s.o.'s mind off his sorrow, his cares (ou) worries; *distraire qqn de ses soucis,* to charm away s.o.'s cares; *distraire qqn de son travail,* to take s.o. away from his work. ‖ To divert, to amuse, to entertain. (V. AMUSER.) ‖ To abstract, to set aside, to divert (un objet, une somme); *distraire de,* to take out of (ou) from, to divert from. ‖ JUR. To misappropriate, to embezzle (des fonds).
— v. pr. **Se distraire,** to entertain (ou) to amuse oneself, to take relaxation (ou) recreation.

distrait, aite [distrɛ, ɛt] adj. Absent-minded; heedless; listless; inattentive; wool-gathering (personne); *écouter d'une oreille distraite,* to listen with half an ear; *regarder qqch. d'un air distrait,* to gaze vacantly (ou) to look abstractedly at sth.

distraitement [-tmɑ̃] adv. Absently, absent-mindedly, abstractedly, inattentively, vacantly.

distrayant, ante [distrɛjɑ̃, ɑ̃:t] adj. Diverting, amusing, entertaining.

distribuable [distribɥabl] adj. Distribuable.

distribuer [-bye] v. tr. (1). To distribute (sens général); to dispense (des aumônes); to give out (des bulletins); to deal (les cartes); to deliver (des colis, des lettres); to deal out (des coups); to serve (l'eau, le gaz); to portion out (des parts); to give away (des prix); to issue (des provisions); to allot, to assign (des rôles); *distribuer du lait aux enfants,* to issue children with milk; U. S. to issue milk to children; *distribuer à la ronde,* to circulate; *distribuer parcimonieusement,* to dole out. ‖ To arrange the rooms in (un appartement). ‖ To distribute, to classify (la population). ‖ FIN. To allot (des actions); to pay (des dividendes). ‖ THÉÂTR. Distribuer des rôles, to cast the parts.

distributeur, trice [-bytœ:r, tris] s. Distributor; *distributeur automatique,* slot-machine, penny-in-the-slot machine; *distributeur de timbres,* stamp machine. ‖ AUTOM. Distributor; *distributeur d'essence,* petrol-pump; U. S. fuel-pump. ‖ CH. DE F. Distributeur de billets, ticket-clerk.

distributif, ive [-bytif, i:v] adj., m. Distributive.

distribution [-bysjɔ̃] f. Distribution, allotment (d'argent); dispensation (d'aumônes); giving out (de bulletins, de prospectus); dealing (de cartes); delivery (de colis, de lettres); service, supply (de l'eau, du gaz); apportionment, sharing out (des parts); giving away (des prix); issuing (des provisions); assignment (des rôles); sharing out (du travail); *distribution parcimonieuse,* doling out; *distribution des prix,* prize-giving. ‖ Arrangement, disposition (d'un appartement). ‖ Classification, distribution, division (répartition). ‖ FIN. Allotment (des actions). ‖ THÉÂTR. Cast of characters (personnages); casting (des rôles). ‖ COMM. Handling.

distributivement [-bytivmɑ̃] adv. Distributively.

distributivité [-bytivite] f. MATH. Distributivity.

district [distrik] m. District. ‖ FAM. Province.

dit [di] adj. Appointed, indicated (heure, jour); *autrement dit,* in other words; *c'est dit,* it's settled. ‖ So-called, alias, surnamed, nicknamed; *Jean, dit Leclerc,* John, known as Leclerc; *ledit.* the said; *proprement dit,* properly, so-called.
— m. † Word; saying. ‖ Tale (en poésie). ‖ **Dit-on,** m. Saying.

dithyrambe [ditirɑ̃:b] m. Dithyramb. ‖ FAM. Rhapsody.

dithyrambique [-bik] adj. Dithyrambic. ‖ FAM. Eulogistic, laudatory, extravagant.

dito [dito] adv. Ditto, do.

diurèse [djyrɛ:z] f. MÉD. Diuresis.

diurétique [-retik] adj., m. MÉD. Diuretic.

diurnal, ale [djyrnal] adj., m. ECCLÉS. Diurnal.

diurne [djyrn] adj. Diurnal; *température diurne,* day temperature.

diva [diva] f. THÉÂTR. Diva.

divagant, ante [divagɑ̃, ɑ̃:t] adj. Wandering (errant). ‖ FIG. Rambling.

divagation [-gasjɔ̃] f. Wandering (errance). ‖ FIG. Divagation, rambling; incoherence. ‖ FAM. Desultoriness (décousu).

divaguer [-ge] v. intr. To wander (errer). ‖ FIG. To ramble, to rave. ‖ FAM. To talk wildly, to ramble.

divagueur [-gœ:r] s. Rambler.

divan [divɑ̃] m. Divan, couch (meuble). ‖ Divan (en Orient).

dive [di:v] adj. f. † Divine; *adorateur de la dive bouteille*, devotee to Bacchus.

divergence [divɛrʒɑ̃:s] f. Phys., Math. Divergence. ‖ Fig. Divergence, difference (d'opinions).

divergent, ente [-ʒɑ̃, ɑ̃:t] adj. Phys., Math. Divergent. ‖ Bot. Diverging. ‖ Fig. Divergent, different.

diverger [-ʒe] v. intr. (7). To diverge, to fork (routes). ‖ Phys., Math., Bot. To diverge. ‖ Fig. To diverge, to differ.

divers [divɛr] adj. † Changeful, varying (inconstant). ‖ Diverse, various, different. ‖ Several, some (quelques). ‖ Various (conversation); varied (opinions, style). ‖ Pl. Miscellaneous (extraits); sundry, various (occasions); various (raisons, types). ‖ Comm. *Articles divers*, sundries.

diversement [-səmɑ̃] adv. Diversely; variously.

diversification [-sifikasjɔ̃] f. Diversification.

diversifier [-sifje] v. tr. (1). To diversify, to vary (ses lectures). ‖ To variegate (les couleurs).
— v. pr. **Se diversifier**, to become different; to vary.

diversion [-sjɔ̃] f. Milit. Diversion. ‖ Méd. Drawing off. ‖ Fig. Diversion, distraction, change; *faire diversion*, to create a diversion; *faire diversion à la douleur de qqn*, to divert s.o. from his grief.

diversité [-site] f. Diversity; variety; difference.

divertir [divɛrti:r] v. tr. (2). To divert, to distract (détourner) [*de*, from]. ‖ To divert, to amuse, to entertain.
— v. pr. **Se divertir**, to amuse (ou) to entertain (ou) to enjoy oneself (se récréer). ‖ To make fun (ou) game (se moquer) [*de*, of].

divertissant, ante [-tisɑ̃, ɑ̃:t] adj. Diverting.

divertissement [-tismɑ̃] m. Amusement, recreation, relaxation. ‖ Game, pastime (jeu). ‖ Théâtr. Divertissement.

divette [divɛt] f. Théâtr. Star.

dividende [dividɑ̃:d] m. Math. Dividend. ‖ Fin. Dividend; *sans dividendes*, ex-dividend.

divin, ine [divɛ̃, in] adj. Ecclés. Divine; *le Divin Enfant*, the Holy Child. ‖ Fig. Heavenly, godlike (personnage). ‖ Fam. Divine, sublime, exquisite.

divinateur, trice [divinatœ:r, tris] adj. Divining.
— s. Diviner, soothsayer.

divination [-sjɔ̃] f. Divination.

divinatoire [-twa:r] adj. Divinatory (art); divining (baguette); perspicacious (esprit).

divinement [divinmɑ̃] adv. Divinely.

divinisation [-nizasjɔ̃] f. Divinization.

diviniser [-nize] v. tr. (1). To divinize, to deify. ‖ Fig. To exalt, to glorify.

divinité [-nite] f. Divinity, deity (du paganisme). ‖ Ecclés. God (Dieu); divinity, godhead (nature).

diviser [divize] v. tr. (1). To divide, to break up; to mark out (par des bornes); to cut up (en coupant); to carve up (en démembrant); to portion out, to parcel out, to split up (en partageant); *diviser d'avec*, to separate (ou) to divide from. ‖ Math. To divide (par, by); *machine à diviser*, graduator. ‖ Fig. To divide, to set at variance (désunir).
— v. pr. **Se diviser**, to divide, to break up (*en*, into). ‖ To part, to separate (se séparer). ‖ To be divided (se répartir) [*en*, into].

diviseur [-zœ:r] m. Math. Divisor; *plus grand commun diviseur*, highest common factor. ‖ Electr. Divider.
— adj. Divisor (fraction).

diviseuse [-zø:z] f. Techn. Graduator; dividing machine.

divisibilité [-zibilite] f. Divisibility.

divisible [-zibl] adj. Divisible.

division [-zjɔ̃] f. Division, partition (*en*, into); dividing; sharing out (des biens); splitting up (d'une question, d'un terrain); *division du travail*, division of labour. ‖ Branch, department (d'une administration); division, section (d'une école); part, chapter (d'un ouvrage). ‖ Milit. Division. ‖ Math. Division; *division à un chiffre*, simple division. ‖ Mus. Double bar. ‖ Fig. Division, disunion, discord.

divisionnaire [-zjɔnɛ:r] adj. Milit. Divisional.
— m. Milit. Major-general.

divorce [divɔrs] m. Jur. Divorce (*d'avec*, from); *demander, obtenir le divorce*, to sue for, to procure a divorce; *ordonnance de divorce*, bill of divorcement, decree absolute. ‖ Fig. Disagreement, severance; divorcement (*d'avec*, from).

divorcé, ée [-se] s. Divorcee.

divorcer [-se] v. intr. (6). Jur. To obtain a divorce, to be divorced; *avoir divorcé*, to have been divorced; *chercher à divorcer d'avec*, to seek a divorce from; *divorcer d'avec sa femme, son mari*, to divorce one's wife, one's husband. ‖ Fig. To withdraw (*de*, from); to break (*de*, with).

divulgateur, trice [divylgatœ:r, tris] s. One who divulges (ou) discloses, publicizer.

divulgation [divylgasjɔ̃] f. Divulgation, disclosure (*de*, of).

divulguer [-ge] v. tr. (1). To divulge.
— v. pr. **Se divulguer**, to come out, to emerge.

dix ([di] devant consonne; [diz] devant h muette ou voyelle; [dis] seul) adj. num. Ten; tenth; *dix œufs*, ten eggs; *dix septembre*, the tenth of September, September the tenth.
— m. Ten (chiffre); *le dix de carreau*, the ten of diamonds. ‖ **Dix-sept**, seventeen; seventeenth. ‖ **Dix-septième**, seventeenth. ‖ **Dix-huit**, eighteen; eighteenth. ‖ **Dix-huitième**, eighteenth. ‖ **Dix-neuf**, nineteen; nineteenth. ‖ **Dix-neuvième**, nineteenth.

dixième [dizjɛm] adj., m. Tenth.

dixièmement [dizjɛmmɑ̃] adv. Tenthly.

dizain [dizɛ̃] m. Packet of ten packs of cards. ‖ Ten-line stanza.

dizaine [dizɛn] f. Ten (nombre exact); half a score. ‖ About ten (nombre approximatif); *une dizaine d'œufs*, ten eggs or so.

djinn [dʒin] m. Djin, jinn.

do [do] m. Mus. Do, C.

docile [dɔsil] adj. Docile; submissive; tractable.

docilement [-lmɑ̃] adv. Docilely; submissively.

docilité [-lite] f. Docility; submissiveness; tractability; meekness.

docimologie [dɔsimɔlɔʒi] f. Study (ou) analysis of examination marks.

dock [dɔk] m. Naut. Dock (bassin); dock-warehouse, store (magasin).

docker [dɔkɛr] m. Naut. Docker.

docte [dɔkt] adj. Learned.

doctement [-təmɑ̃] adv. Learnedly. ‖ Fam. Priggishly, pedantically.

docteur [dɔktœ:r] m. Doctor; *docteur en droit, en médecine, ès lettres, ès sciences, en théologie*, Doctor of Laws (Ll. D.), of Medicine (M. D.), of Literature (D. Litt.), of Science (D. Sc.), of Divinity (D. D.). ‖ Méd. Doctor (appellation); *le docteur X*, Doctor X. ‖ Ecclés. Doctor (de l'Eglise).

doctoral, ale [-ral] adj. Doctoral. ‖ Pedantic.

doctoralement [-ralmɑ̃] adv. Pompously.

doctorat [-ra] m. Doctorate; *passer son doctorat*, to take one's doctorate (ou) doctor's degree.

doctoresse [-rɛs] f. Méd. Woman (ou) lady doctor, doctoress.

doctrinaire [dɔktrinɛ:r] adj., s. Doctrinaire, doctrinarian.

doctrinal, ale [-nal] adj. Doctrinal.

doctrine [dɔktrin] f. Doctrine; *c'est de doctrine courante*, it is a matter of doctrine.

document [dɔkymɑ̃] m. Document. ‖ Jur. Written evidence, document.

documentaire [-tɛ:r] adj. Documentary; eviden-

tial. ‖ Comm. *Traité documentaire,* draft with documents attached.
— m. Ciném. Documentary film.
documentaliste [-talist] s. Research assistant; information scientist (or) officer.
documentariste [-tarist] m. Ciném. Documentary director; producer of documentary films.
documentation [-tasjɔ̃] f. Documentation; documents. ‖ Comm. Literature.
documenté, ée [-te] adj. Documented (récit); supported (ou) proved by documents (œuvre); *bien documenté sur,* well-informed on.
documenter v. tr. (1). To document; to support by documents. ‖ To brief (qqn) [*sur, on*].
— v. pr. **Se documenter,** to collect documents (ou) material.
dodécaèdre [dɔdekaɛdr] m. Dodecahedron.
dodécagone [-gɔn] m. Math. Dodecagon.
dodécaphonique [dɔdekafɔnik] adj. Mus. Dodecaphonic, twelve-tone (ou) -note.
dodécaphonisme [-nism] m. Mus. Dodecaphonism, twelve-note (ou) -tone system.
dodelinement [dɔdlinmɑ̃] m. Rocking, swaying. ‖ Wagging (de la tête).
dodeliner [-ne] v. tr. (1). To rock (un enfant).
— v. intr. *Dodeliner de la tête,* to nod one's head, to wag one's head as one walks along.
— v. pr. **Se dodeliner,** to sway, to waddle.
dodo [dɔdo] m. Fam. Bed (lit); sleep (sommeil); *aller faire dodo,* to go to bye-bye, to go bye-bye.
— interj. Hushaby!
dodu, ue [dɔdy] adj. Plump, chubby, roly-poly.
dogaresse [dɔgarɛs] f. Dogaressa.
dogat [dɔga] m. Dogate, Doge-ship.
doge [dɔʒ] m. Doge.
dogmatique [dɔgmatik] adj. Ecclés., Philos. Dogmatic. ‖ Fam. Dogmatic, oracular; sententious.
— m. Philos. Dogmatist.
— f. Ecclés. Dogmatics; dogmatic theology.
dogmatiquement [-kmɑ̃] adv. Dogmatically. ‖ Fam. Peremptorily; sententiously.
dogmatiser [-ze] v. intr. (1). To dogmatize.
dogmatiseur [-zœ:r] m. Dogmatizer.
dogmatisme [dɔgmatism] m. Dogmatism.
dogmatiste [-tist] m. Dogmatist.
dogme [dɔgm] m. Ecclés. Dogma. ‖ Fam. Tenet, doctrine.
dogre [dɔgr] m. Naut. Dogger.
dogue [dɔg] m. Zool. Mastiff. ‖ Fam. Cerberus; *d'une humeur de dogue,* as cross as two sticks.
doguin [dɔgɛ̃] m. Zool. Pug.
doigt [dwa] m. Finger (de la main); toe (du pied); *au doigt,* on one's finger; *aux doigts agiles,* light-fingered; *doigt de gant,* glove-finger; *montrer du doigt,* to point at. ‖ Stick (de chocolat); thimbleful, finger (de liqueur). ‖ Digit, inch (mesure); *à deux doigts de,* within an ace (ou) an inch of, on the verge of. ‖ Méd., Zool. Digit. ‖ Loc. *Donner sur les doigts à qqn,* to take s.o. down a peg; *être comme les deux doigts de la main,* to be hand in glove; *gagner les doigts dans le nez,* to romp home; *mettre le doigt dessus* (ou) *sur la plaie,* to put one's finger on it, to hit the nail on the head, to hit it, to touch the spot; *mon petit doigt me l'a dit,* a little bird told me, I know it by the pricking of my thumbs; *ne pas bouger le petit doigt pour,* not to lift a finger for; *ne rien faire de ses dix doigts,* not to do a hand's turn; *obéir au doigt et à l'œil,* to be at s.o.'s beck and call; *recevoir sur les doigts,* to catch it; *se fourrer* (ou) *se mettre le doigt dans l'œil,* to take the wrong sow by the ear; *se lécher les doigts,* to lick one's lips; *se mettre les doigts dans le nez,* to pick one's nose; *se mordre les doigts,* to bite one's nails.

doigté [-te] m. Mus. Fingering. ‖ Fig. Tact; savoir-faire.
doigter v. tr. (1). To finger.
doigtier [-tje] m. Finger-stall, U. S. finger cot.
doit [dwa] m. Comm. Debtor side; *le doit et l'avoir,* debtor and creditor.
— indic. prés. V. devoir (39).
dol [dɔl] m. Jur. Fraud; wilful misrepresentation.
doléance [dɔleɑ̃:s] f. Complaint. (V. plainte.)
dolent, ente [dɔlɑ̃, ɑ̃:t] adj. Doleful; plaintive.
doler [dɔle] v. tr. (1). To shave (du bois); to skive (des peaux).
dolichocéphale [dɔlikɔsefal] adj. Dolichocephalic.
— m. Dolichocephalus.
dollar [dɔla:r] m. Dollar; U. S. buck (pop.).
dolman [dɔlmɑ̃] m. Dolman.
dolmen [dɔlmɛn] m. Dolmen.
doloire [dɔlwa:r] m. Techn. Adze, chip-axe.
dolomie [dɔlɔmi] f. Géol. Dolomite.
Dolomites [-mit] f. pl. Géogr. Dolomites.
dolomitique [-mitik] adj. Dolomitic.
dolorisme [dɔlɔrism] m. Philos. Algolagnia.
dom [dɔ̃] m. Ecclés. Dom.
D. O. M. [dɔm] m. Abrév. de *département d'outremer,* French department overseas.
domaine [dɔmɛn] m. Domain, demesne, estate, lands; *domaine de la Couronne,* Crown lands; *domaine de l'Etat, les Domaines,* public property, property of the State. ‖ Jur. *Tomber dans le domaine public,* to become public property (invention); to be out of copyright (ouvrage). ‖ Fig. Range (d'un art); field, province, sphere, scope, domain (d'une personne).
domanial, ale [dɔmanjal] adj. Domanial. ‖ Jur. Crown; State (forêts).
dôme [do:m] m. Archit. Dome, cupola. ‖ Ecclés. Cathedral (en Italie). ‖ Géogr. Puy, small volcanic cone. ‖ Ch. de f. Dome. ‖ Fig. Vault, canopy (des cieux, de verdure).
domestication [dɔmɛstikasjɔ̃] f. Domestication.
domesticité [-tisite] f. Domesticity, service, menial condition (état). ‖ Staff of servants, household (ensemble des domestiques). ‖ Domesticated state (d'un animal). ‖ Fig. Servility.
domestique [-tik] adj. Family (affaires); domestic (animal, économie, querelles); domestic, menial (service); *foyer domestique,* home. ‖ Milit. Domestic, internal, intestine (guerre).
— s. Servant; domestic.
domestiquer [-tike] v. tr. (1). To domesticate.
— v. pr. **Se domestiquer,** to become domesticated (animal). ‖ Fam. To become sociable (personne).
domicile [dɔmisil] m. Residence, abode, domicile, home (v. demeure); *domicile légal,* permanent residence; *sans domicile connu,* of no fixed abode; *élire domicile,* to take up one's abode, to elect domicile. ‖ Comm. *Livrable à domicile,* « to be delivered »; *livraison à domicile,* home delivery.
domiciliaire [-ljɛ:r] adj. Domiciliary.
domiciliataire [-ljatɛ:r] m. Comm. Paying agent.
domiciliation [-ljasjɔ̃] f. Comm. Domiciliation.
domicilié, ée [-lje] adj. Domiciled, resident.
domicilier v. tr. (1). To domicile (qqn). ‖ Comm. To domicile (un billet); to make payable (un chèque).
— v. pr. **Se domicilier,** to take up one's residence (à, at).
dominance [dɔminɑ̃:s] f. Dominance (d'un gène, d'un hémisphère cérébral).
dominant, ante [dɔminɑ̃, ɑ̃:t] adj. Dominant (hauteur). ‖ Dominant, dominating (caractère, caractéristique); prevailing (couleur, opinion, vent); governing, leading, master (idée); predominant (intérêt;) ruling (passion); dominant,

predominant, outstanding (trait). ‖ Mus. *Note dominante*, key-note, dominant.

dominante [-nɑ̃:t] f. Leading characteristic; governing idea. ‖ Mus. Dominant.

dominateur, trice [-natœ:r, tris] adj. Overbearing (attitude); domineering (caractère, personne, ton); dominating (nation); ruling, dominant (passion).

domination [-nasjɔ̃] f. Domination, dictation (de qqn); domination, dominion, mastery (d'un peuple); dominion (*sur*, over); *sous la domination de*, under entire submission to, dominated by; *sous la domination russe*, under Russian control.

dominer [-ne] v. tr. (1). To rise above (le bruit); to dominate, to command, to look down on (un lieu, la vallée); *dominer en hauteur*, to tower above. ‖ To dominate, to keep down (un peuple); to dominate, to have command over (qqn); to gain an ascendancy over (par l'autorité morale); to dominate (par la contrainte); to keep under one's thumb (par l'emprise); to lord it over (par l'orgueil); to tower above (par la taille, par la valeur); *dominer sa femme*, to crush one's wife; *dominer son mari*, to henpeck one's husband. ‖ Fig. To master, to keep down (ou) in (sa colère); to sway (l'opinion); to bridle, to command, to master, to control (ses passions); to master (son sujet); *dominé par ses passions*, a slave to one's passions.
— v. intr. To dominate, to rule; to rise to ascendancy (nation). ‖ To lord it (personne). ‖ To be outstanding (affaire, couleur, trait); to be dominant (caractère); to predominate (défaut, qualité); to govern (idée); to prevail (opinion, théorie).
— v. pr. **Se dominer**, to control oneself.

dominicain, aine [dɔminikɛ̃, ɛn] adj. Géogr. Dominican; *république Dominicaine*, Dominican Republic. ‖ Ecclés. Dominican (moine).
— m. Géogr., Ecclés. Dominican.

dominicaine [-kɛn] f. Ecclés. Dominican nun.

dominical, ale [-kal] adj. Dominical; *repos dominical*, Sunday rest; *oraison dominicale*, Lord's Prayer.

dominion [dɔminjɔ̃] m. Dominion.

domino [dɔmino] m. Domino (jeu, vêtement); *jouer aux dominos*, to play dominoes.

dommage [dɔma:ʒ] m. Damage (dégât). ‖ Prejudice, harm, injury, damage, hurt. (V. PRÉJUDICE.) ‖ Pity; *quel dommage!*, what a pity! ‖ Jur. *Dommage causé à un tiers*, third party damage; *dommages de guerre*, war damage compensation. ‖ **Dommages-intérêts**, m. pl. Damages; *réclamer des dommages-intérêts*, to sue for damages.

dommageable [dɔmaʒabl] adj. Damageable; prejudicial, detrimental. ‖ Jur. *Acte dommageable*, tort.

domptable [dɔ̃tabl] adj. Tamable. ‖ Fig. Subduable.

domptage [-ta:ʒ] m. Taming (d'un animal); breaking-in (d'un cheval).

dompter [-te] v. tr. (1). To tame (un animal); to break in (un cheval). ‖ To subdue, to master, to subjugate (qqn). ‖ Fig. To master, to govern, to control, to subdue (ses passions).

dompteur, euse [-tœ:r, ø:z] s. Tamer.

don [dɔ̃] m. Gift, present, bestowal (v. CADEAU); *faire don de*, to give. ‖ Jur. Donation, legacy; *faire don*, to bestow, to donate. ‖ Fig. Gift, talent (*de*, for); *avoir le don de*, to have a talent for (ou) the knack of. ‖ Fam. *Cela n'a pas le don de le satisfaire*, it does not happen to please him; *il a le don de me taper sur les nerfs*, he has a way (ou) knack of jarring on my nerves.

don [dɔ̃] m. Don (titre espagnol).

doña [dɔɲa] f. Donna.

donataire [dɔnatɛ:r] s. Jur. Donee, grantee.

donateur [-tœ:r] m. Jur. Donor, grantor.

donation [-sjɔ̃] f. Jur. Donation; *acte de donation*, deed of gift; *donation entre vifs*, disposition inter vivos.

donatrice [-tris] f. Jur. Donatrix.

donc [dɔk, dɔ̃] conj. Then (ainsi, alors); *or donc*, well then. ‖ Well, so, now (maintenant); *donc, comme je disais*, well, as I was saying. ‖ Therefore, consequently (par conséquent); *j'ai de la fièvre, donc je suis malade*, I have a temperature, therefore (ou) so I am ill. ‖ Loc. *Allons donc!* nonsense!, come, come!; you don't mean it! *c'est donc lui!*, so it was he!; *comment donc pouvait-il faire autrement?*, how on earth could he do anything else?; *écoutez donc!*, do listen!; *qui donc a pu vous voir?*, who ever can have seen you?; *quoi donc?*, what?, what's that?; *regardez donc ça*, just look at that.

dondon [dɔ̃dɔ̃] f. Fam. Whacker, whopper, dump.

donjon [dɔ̃ʒɔ̃] m. Archit. Keep, donjon. ‖ Turret.

don Juan [dɔ̃ʒɥɑ̃] m. Don Juan, philanderer, womanizer.

donjuanesque [dɔ̃ʒyanɛsk] adj. Donjuanesque.

donjuanisme [-nism] m. Philandering, womanizing, donjuanism.

donnant, ante [dɔnɑ̃, ɑ̃:t] adj. Generous. ‖ Loc. *Donnant donnant*, give and take; gift for gift.

donne [dɔn] f. Deal (aux cartes).

donné, ée [dɔne] adj. Given (condition, délai); *étant donné que*, considering (ou) seeing that; *étant donné le problème*, given the problem; *étant donné sa situation*, considering (ou) in view of his situation. ‖ Loc. *C'est donné!*, that's giving it away!

donnée f. Basic principle; admitted fact (de l'histoire); theme, subject, motif, donnée (d'une œuvre). ‖ Pl. Instructions; notions; data. ‖ Math. Datum, pl. data (d'un problème).

donner v. tr. (1).

---

1. Offrir. — 2. Aboutir. — 3. Accorder. — 4. Administrer. — 5. Assigner. — 6. Attribuer. — 7. Causer. — 8. Céder. — 9. Confier. — 10. Consacrer. — 11. Distribuer. — 12. Faire passer. — 13. Fournir. — 14. Prescrire. — 15. Poser. — 16. Souhaiter. — 17. Agric. — 18. Fin. — 19. Comm. — 20. Jur. — 21. Chim., Phys. — 22. Méd. — 23. Techn. — 24. Electr. — 25. Pop. — 26. Loc.

---

1. To give, to bestow, to present (v. OFFRIR); *donner qqch. à qqn*, to give s.o. sth., to give sth. to s.o.; *donner à manger à qqn*, to give s.o. sth. to eat; *donner le bras, la main à*, to give one's arm, hand to; *donner une fête, une interview*, to give a feast, an interview; *donner sa parole de*, to give one's word for; *je me le suis fait donner*, I had it given to me. **2.** To lead (aboutir); *ne pas donner ce qu'on escomptait*, not to turn out as anticipated; *ne rien donner*, to give no results. ‖ **3.** To give, to bestow, to yield (accorder); *donner libre cours à*, to give free vent to; *donner la permission de*, to grant leave to; *donner raison à*, to agree with, to say that s.o. is in the right. ‖ **4.** To give, to administer, to deal (administrer); *donner un coup à*, to strike a blow at. ‖ **5.** To assign, to fix (assigner); *donner rendez-vous à*, to fix (ou) make an appointment with. ‖ **6.** To give, to ascribe, to confer (attribuer); *donner du Monsieur à qqn*, to address s.o. as My Lord; *donner un titre*, to confer a title; *je lui donne cinquante ans*, I put him down as fifty; *on lui donne X pour père*, they say that X is his father; *on ne lui donnerait pas son âge*, he does not look his age. ‖ **7.** To give, to cause, to inspire (causer);

donner faim à qqn, to make s.o. hungry ; *donner de la peine,* to give trouble ; *donner du souci,* to cause worry. ‖ **8.** To give (céder) ; *donner sa place à,* to give up one's seat to. ‖ **9.** To commit, to entrust (confier) ; *donner à qqn la garde de,* to entrust s.o. with, to leave s.o. in charge of. ‖ **10.** To give up (consacrer) ; *donner sa vie au travail,* to give up one's life to work. ‖ **11.** To deal (distribuer) ; *donner les cartes,* to deal cards. ‖ **12.** To give up (faire passer) ; *donner qqn pour mort,* to give s.o. up for dead. ‖ **13.** To give (fournir) ; *donner des conseils,* to give advice ; *donner un exemple,* to give (ou) to set an example ; *donner une idée,* to convey an idea ; *donner une idée de,* to give an idea of ; *donner des signes de,* to evince, to show signs of. ‖ **14.** To give (prescrire) ; *donner des ordres,* to give orders. ‖ **15.** To set (poser) ; *donner un problème,* to set a problem. ‖ **16.** To wish (souhaiter) ; *donner le bonjour à qqn,* to wish s.o. good day. ‖ **17.** AGRIC. To bear (des fruits). ‖ **18.** FIN. *Donner des bénéfices,* to yield profits. ‖ **19.** COMM. *Donner une chambre à qqn,* to accommodate s.o. with a room ; to let s.o. have a room ; *donner un article à qqn pour un prix donné,* to let s.o. have an article at a given price ; *en donner deux mille francs,* to pay two thousand francs for it. ‖ **20.** JUR. *Donner en mariage,* to give in marriage ; *donner qqch. à qqn par testament,* to will sth. to s.o. ‖ **21.** CHIM., PHYS. To give off (de la chaleur) ; to give out (de la lumière). ‖ **22.** MÉD. *Donner des ampoules,* to raise blisters ; *donner la fièvre à,* to throw into a fever ; *donner la grippe à qqn,* to give s.o. the flu ; *donner des nausées à qqn,* to make s.o. sick (ou) seasick ; *elle lui donna deux fils,* she bore him two sons ; *donner du sang,* to give (ou) to donate blood. ‖ **23.** TECHN. *Donner de la vitesse,* to get up speed. ‖ **24.** ELECTR. *Donner à qqn la communication avec,* to put s.o. through to. ‖ **25.** POP. To give away, to rat on (un complice). ‖ **26.** LOC. *Je vous le donne en mille,* I give you a thousand guesses.

— v. intr. To give ; *donnez et vous recevrez,* give and it shall be given unto you. ‖ To deal (aux cartes). ‖ To give, to yield (corde). ‖ MILIT. To attack ; to be engaged ; *faire donner,* to send (ou) to bring into action. ‖ NAUT. *Donner à la côte,* to run aground. ‖ MÉD. To run (abcès). ‖ LOC. *Donner à croire,* to lead to believe ; *donner à entendre,* to give to understand ; *donner à réfléchir,* to give matter for reflection ; to give food for thought ; *donner contre* (ou) *donner de la tête contre,* to run (ou) to bump one's head against ; *donner dans,* to have a taste for, to lean to (une manie) ; to fall into (un piège) ; *donner dans le panneau,* to walk right into the trap ; *donner sur,* to abut on (aboutir) ; to overlook, to look out on, to look on to (avoir vue sur) ; to lead to (conduire).

— v. pr. **Se donner,** to give oneself up (s'adonner) ; to abandon oneself (se livrer) [à, to] ; *se donner du bon temps,* to give oneself a good time ; *se donner la mort,* to kill oneself ; *se donner un travail,* to set oneself a task ; *se donner de la peine,* to take trouble. ‖ To be given (être donné) ; *ça ne se donne pas,* that's not given away. ‖ *Se donner pour,* to give oneself out for, to pass oneself off for. ‖ LOC. *S'en donner à cœur joie,* to have one's fling, to indulge oneself to the full. — v. récipr. **Se donner,** to give one another ; *se donner le mot,* to pass the word round, U. S. to be in cahoots (fam.).

donneur, euse [dɔnœːr, øːz] adj., s. Giver. ‖ Dealer (aux cartes). ‖ MÉD. Donor (pour insémination artificielle) ; *donneur de sang,* blood donor. ‖ FAM. *Il n'est pas donneur,* he is close-fisted. ‖ POP. Informer (dénonciateur).

dont [dɔ̃] pron. relat. Of which, of whom, whose (duquel) ; *la chose, l'homme dont nous parlons,* the thing, the man we are speaking of ; *le professeur dont je connais la sœur,* the professor whose sister I know ; *la rose dont l'épine est blanche,* the rose the thorn of which is white. ‖ By which (ou) whom ; from which (ou) whom (par lequel) ; *le mur dont la ville est entourée,* the wall by which the city is surrounded ; *la personne dont vous tenez ces faits,* the person from whom you learned these facts. ‖ About which (ou) whom (au sujet duquel) ; *la pièce dont nous parlions,* the play we were talking about. ‖ At which, at whom (aux dépens duquel) ; *le sot dont ils se moquaient,* the nincompoop that they were laughing at. ‖ (Traduit selon la préposition gouvernée par le verbe anglais) ; *la chose dont il se sépare,* the thing he parts with ; *le résultat dont il s'assure,* the result he makes sure of ; *la victoire dont dépend notre sécurité,* the victory on which our security depends. ‖ (Sans préposition si le verbe anglais est transitif) ; *le chien dont j'ai peur,* the dog that I fear ; *l'individu dont je me méfie,* the fellow I distrust ; *le stylo dont je me sers,* the fountain pen which I use. ‖ Of which (ou) whom (au sens restrictif) ; *j'ai deux amis dont l'un est médecin,* I have two friends, one of whom is a doctor ; *des pommes dont plusieurs sont gâtées,* apples, several of which are rotten ; *voici dix crayons, dont deux rouges,* here are ten pencils, including two red ones.

donzelle [dɔ̃zɛl] f. † Damsel. ‖ FAM. Wench.

dopage [dɔpaːʒ] m. SPORTS. Doping, use of illicit stimulants.

dopant [dɔpɑ̃] adj. SPORTS. Stimulant.
— m. Drug, stimulant.

doper [dɔpe] v. tr. (1). SPORTS. To dope. ‖ FIG. To buck up (encourager).
— v. pr. **Se doper,** to dope oneself.

doping [dɔpiŋ] m. SPORTS. Doping (action) ; dope (excitant).

dorade [dɔrad] f. ZOOL. Sea-bream.

dorage [-raːʒ] m. TECHN. Gilding.

doré, ée [-re] adj. Golden (couleur d'or) ; *cheveux dorés,* golden hair. ‖ Gilt (couvert de dorure) ; *doré sur tranche,* gilt-edged. ‖ Gilded (riche) ; *jeunesse dorée,* gilded youth. ‖ CULIN. Glazed (gâteau) ; browned (poulet). ‖ FIG. *Légende dorée,* Golden Legend.
— m. Gilt.

dorée [-re] f. ZOOL. Dory.

dorénavant [dɔrenavɑ̃] adv. Henceforth, henceforward, from now on.

dorer [dɔre] v. tr. (1). To gild. ‖ CULIN. To coat with yolk of egg ; to egg (un gâteau) ; to brown (un poulet). ‖ FIG. *Dorer la pilule,* to sugar-coat (ou) to gild the pill.

doreur, euse [-rœːr, øːz] s. Gilder.

dorien, enne [dɔrjɛ̃, ɛn] adj., s. GÉOGR., MUS. Dorian. ‖ GRAMM. Doric (dialecte).

dorique [dɔrik] adj., m. ARCHIT. Doric.

doris [dɔris] m. NAUT. Dory.

dorlotement [dɔrlɔtmɑ̃] m. Coddling, pampering, mollycoddling.

dorloter [dɔrlɔte] v. tr. (1). To coddle ; to cosset ; to pamper.
— v. pr. **Se dorloter,** to coddle oneself.

dormant, ante [dɔrmɑ̃, ɑ̃ːt] adj. Stagnant, still (eau) ; sleeping (personne) ; dormant (volcan). ‖ TECHN. Fixed (châssis) ; dead (pène). ‖ FIN. Unproductive (capital) ; dormant (compte).
— m. Frame (d'une fenêtre, d'une porte).

dormeur, euse [-mœːr, øːz] s. Sleeper (qui dort). ‖ Sleepy-head, slug-a-bed (paresseux) ; slacker (peu dégourdi).
— adj. Sleeping (poupée).

dormeur m. ZOOL. Crab, edible crab.

dormeuse [-mø:z] f. Dormeuse (siège, voiture). ‖ Stud ear-ring (bijou). ‖ Clairvoyant (médium).

dormir [-mi:r] v. intr. (41). To sleep, to be asleep ; to repose ; *avoir envie de dormir*, to feel sleepy ; *dormir debout*, to be unable to keep one's eyes open ; *dormir comme un loir*, to sleep like a top ; *dormir un peu*, to get a little sleep ; *dormir du sommeil du juste*, to sleep the sleep of the just ; *dormir toute la nuit*, to sleep the night through ; *empêcher de dormir*, to keep awake ; *envie de dormir*, sleepiness ; *faire passer sa migraine en dormant*, to sleep off one's headache ; *il n'en dort plus*, he can't sleep for brooding over it ; *ne pas dormir de la nuit*, not to sleep a wink all night ; *passer son temps à dormir*, to sleep the hours away ; *parler en dormant*, to talk in one's sleep. ‖ To sleep (être mort). ‖ To be stagnant (eau). ‖ FIN. To lie idle, to be unproductive (capitaux). ‖ COMM. To lie dormant, to be shelved, to stand over (affaire). ‖ TECHN. Not to be working (machine). ‖ FIG. To lie dormant (passions). ‖ FAM. To do nothing (ne rien faire) ; *dormir sur son travail*, to sleep over one's work. ‖ LOC. *Dormir sur ses deux oreilles*, to rest easy ; *histoire à dormir debout*, incredible story ; *ne dormir que d'un œil*, to cat-nap.

dormitif, ive [-mitif, i:v] adj., m. MÉD. Dormitive, soporific.

dormition [-misjõ] f. ARTS., ECCLÉS. Dormition.

dorsal, ale [dɔrsal] adj. MÉD. Dorsal ; *épine dorsale*, backbone, spine.

dorsale f. GRAMM. Dorsal sound (ou) phoneme. ‖ GÉOL. Ridge. ‖ GÉOGR. *Dorsale barométrique*, ridge of high pressure.

dortoir [dɔrtwa:r] m. Dormitory.

dorure [dɔry:r] f. Gilding (action) ; gilt (or appliqué). ‖ CULIN. Egging (d'un gâteau) ; browning (d'un poulet).

doryphore [dɔri:ɔr] m. ZOOL. Colorado beetle ; potato bug. ‖ FAM. Jerry (soldat allemand).

dos [do] m. Back (des animaux, de l'homme) ; *au dos large, rond*, broad-backed, round-shouldered ; *aller à dos d'âne*, to ride on a donkey ; *faire le gros dos*, to set up one's back (chat) ; *tourner le dos à*, to stand with one's back to (qqch.) ; to turn one's back upon (qqn). ‖ Back (d'un livre, de la main, d'une maison, d'une page, d'un siège, d'un vêtement) ; back, rear (d'une maison) ; *voir au dos*, see overleaf. ‖ GÉOGR. Ridge (d'une montagne). ‖ SPORTS. *Sac au dos*, with one's rucksack (ou) kit-bag on one's back. ‖ JUR. *Renvoyer dos à dos*, to nonsuit both parties. ‖ TECHN. *Dos-d'âne*, hog-back ; *en dos d'âne*, hog-backed (pont) ; high-crowned (route). ‖ FIG. *Tendre le dos*, to hump one's back ; *tourner le dos à*, to run away from (l'ennemi) ; to turn one's back upon (qqn). ‖ FAM. *Avoir bon dos*, to have broad shoulders (ou) a broad back ; *être toujours sur le dos de*, to be always carping at (critiquer) ; to have one's eye on (surveiller) ; *en avoir plein le dos*, to be fed up with it ; *mettre qqch. sur le dos de qqn*, to saddle s.o. with sth., to let s.o. else shoulder sth. ; *n'avoir rien à se mettre sur le dos*, not to have a rag to one's back ; *se mettre qqn à dos*, to make an enemy of s.o. ; *tomber sur le dos de*, to come down heavily on (critique) ; to crack down on (surveillant) ; to drop in on (visiteur).

dosable [dozabl] adj. CHIM. Measurable.

dosage [-za:ʒ] m. CHIM. Proportioning ; measurement. ‖ MÉD. Dosage.

dose [do:z] f. CHIM. Proportion. ‖ MÉD. Dose. ‖ FIG. Admixture (d'un défaut) ; *avoir sa bonne dose de*, to have one's share of ; *par petites doses*, in small quantities.

doser [doze] v. tr. (1). CHIM. To titrate, to pro-portion. ‖ MÉD. To determine the dose of. ‖ FIG. To measure out, to apportion.

doseur [-zœ:r] m. Measure ; *bouchon doseur*, measuring cap.

dosimétrie [dozimetri] f. CHIM. Dosimetry.

dosologie [dozɔlɔʒi] f. MÉD. Dosology.

dossard [dɔsa:r] m. SPORTS. Number, number-card.

dosseret [dɔsrɛ] m. ARCHIT. Pier. ‖ TECHN. Back.

dossier [dɔsje] m. Head (d'un lit) ; back (d'un siège) ; *à haut dossier*, high-backed. ‖ NAUT. Backboard.

dossier m. Documents, file, papers (d'une affaire) ; dossier (d'une administration) ; record (d'un fonctionnaire). ‖ JUR. *Dossier de procédure*, counsel's brief ; *établir un dossier*, to brief a case. ‖ FIN. Portfolio (en banque) ; holding, investment (de valeurs). ‖ MÉD. Case-history (d'un malade).

dossière [dɔsjɛ:r] f. Backplate (de cuirasse) ; backstrap (harnais.)

dot [dɔt] f. Dowry, marriage portion (ou) settlement ; *épouser une dot*, to marry a fortune, to marry for money ; *sans dot*, portionless. ‖ ECCLÉS. Portion (de religieuse).

dotal, e [dɔtal] adj. JUR. Dotal (régime) ; *apport dotal*, dowry.

dotation [dɔtasjõ] f. Dotation, endowment ; *dotation des enfants*, education insurance. ‖ Jointure (douaire).

doter [dɔte] v. tr. (1). To portion, to endow (une fille) ; to endow (une fondation) [de, with]. ‖ FIG. To equip (de, with) ; to give (de, to) ; to bestow (de, upon).

douaire [dwɛ:r] m. JUR. Jointure (d'une épouse) ; dower (d'une veuve).

douairière [dwɛrjɛ:r] adj., f. Dowager. ‖ FAM. Old lady.

douane [dwan] f. Board of Customs, Customs, U. S. Bureau of Customs (administration) ; custom-house (bureau) ; custom-duties (droits) ; *en douane*, bonded (marchandises) ; *exempt de douane*, non-dutiable ; custom-free ; *passer en douane*, to clear, to pass through ; *soumis à la douane*, dutiable, customable.

douanier, ère [dwanje, ɛ:r] adj. Customs (tarif, union, visite).
— m. Custom-house officer. ‖ NAUT. Tide-waiter.

douar [dwa:r] m. Douar.

doublage [dubla:ʒ] m. Doubling (pliage). ‖ Lining (d'un vêtement). ‖ Doubling (d'un textile). ‖ NAUT. Copper bottom. ‖ CINÉM. Dubbing. ‖ AUTOM. Overtaking, passing.

double [dubl] adj. Double, twofold (dimension, quantité) ; *à double face*, reversible (étoffe) ; *à double fond*, double-bottomed (caisse) ; *double emploi*, duplication, overlapping ; *double porte*, folding door. ‖ Double (excellent) ; *bière double*, double ale. ‖ Duplicate (reproduit) ; *en double exemplaire*, in duplicate. ‖ ASTRON., BOT., CH. DE F., GÉOGR., MATH., MÉD., PHYS. Double. ‖ AUTOM. *A double étage*, double-decker (autobus) ; *double allumage*, dual ignition ; *faire un double débrayage*, to double-declutch ; U. S. to double-clutch. ‖ AVIAT. *Double commande*, dual control. ‖ SPORTS. *Faire coup double*, to kill two birds at one shot (à la chasse) ; *partie double*, foursome (au golf). ‖ CINÉM. Double-feature (programme). ‖ FIN. Double (imposition). ‖ FIG. *A double effet, face, usage, sens*, double-acting, -faced, -handed, meaning ; *jouer double jeu*, to play a double game ; *mener une vie double*, to lead a double life. ‖ **Double-blanc**, m. Double-blank. ‖ **Double-corde**, f. MUS. Double-stopping. ‖ **Double-crème**, f. CULIN. Cream-cheese. ‖ **Double-croche**, f. MUS. Semi-quaver, U. S. sixteenth note.
— adv. Double ; *voir double*, to see double.
— loc. adv. **Au double**, twofold.

— m. Double; *coûter le double*, to cost twice as much; *le double de la distance*, twice the distance; *plus grand du double*, twice as tall. ‖ Duplicate, counterpart, antigraph (d'un écrit); copy, replica (d'une œuvre); carbon-copy (à la machine à écrire); *en double*, in duplicate; in double original. ‖ Méd. Doppelganger, doubleganger, co-walker, double (en psychiatrie, spiritisme). ‖ Sports. Double (au tennis). ‖ Loc. *Avoir tout en double*, to have two of everything; *plier en double*, to fold in half.

doublé, ée [-ble] adj. Lined (habit). ‖ Techn. Plated; gold-plated. ‖ Fig. *Un héros doublé d'un modeste*, a hero and yet modest; *un soldat doublé d'un artiste*, a soldier crossed with an artist.
— m. Plated jewellery (ou) wares; *en doublé*, gold-filled. ‖ Sports. Cushion shot (au billard).

doubleau [-blo] m. Archit. Ceiling-beam.

doublement [-bləmɑ̃] adv. Doubly.
— m. Doubling, twofold increase.

doubler [-ble] v. tr. (1). To double (en dimension, poids, quantité). ‖ To line (un vêtement). ‖ To double, to fold in two (en pliant). ‖ Autom. To overtake, to pass (une voiture). ‖ Naut. To round, to double, to weather (un cap); to make head against (un courant); to overhaul (un navire). ‖ Sports. To pass (à la course). ‖ Théâtr. To understudy (un acteur, un rôle); to double, to dub (un film); to be the stand-in (ou) the stuntman of (une vedette de cinéma). ‖ Fig. *Doubler le cap*, to get out of a scrape; *avoir doublé le cap de la cinquantaine*, to be on the wrong side of fifty.
— v. intr. To double; to increase twofold.

doublet [-blɛ] m. Doublet.

doubleur [-blœ:ʳ] m. Techn. Lapping machine (machine); doubler (ouvrier).

doubleuse [-blø:z] f. Techn. Doubling frame.

doublon [-blɔ̃] m. Double (en typographie). ‖ Fin. Doubloon (monnaie).

doublure [dubly:ʳ] f. Lining (d'habit). ‖ Théâtr. Understudy (d'acteur); stunt man (de vedette de cinéma pour les exercices acrobatiques); stand-in (de vedette de cinéma pendant les mises au point). ‖ Naut. Coppering (de coque).

douce [du:s] adj. V. doux. ‖ **Douce-amère**, f. Bot. Bitter-sweet.

douceâtre [dusɑ:tr] adj. Sweetish (au goût). ‖ Fam. Wishy-washy (discours); honeyed (paroles); mealy-mouthed (personne).

doucement [-smɑ̃] adv. Kindly, softly, mildly, gently (aimablement); stealthily (furtivement); cautiously, discreetly (prudemment); softly, lightly, sweetly, quietly (sans bruit); slowly, easily (sans hâte); smoothly, easily (sans heurt); quietly, peacefully (tranquillement); *il va tout doucement*, he is so-so.
— interj. Steady!, easy!, not so fast!; *doucement sur le champagne!*, go easy on the champagne!

doucereusement [-srøzmɑ̃] adv. With a soapy voice; in a soft-spoken manner.

doucereux, euse [-srø, ø:z] adj. Sweetish (au goût). ‖ Honeyed (paroles); mealy-mouthed (personne); sugary (ton); *femme doucereuse*, mim.

doucet [-sɛ] adj. Meek, mild.

doucette [-sɛt] f. Bot. Corn-salad, lamb's lettuce.

doucettement [-sɛtmɑ̃] adv. Meekly; coyly.

douceur [-sœ:ʳ] f. Sweetness (au goût, à l'odorat); softness, sweetness (à l'oreille); softness, pleasantness (à la vue). ‖ Clemency (du climat); mildness (du temps). ‖ Smoothness (d'une machine en marche); softness (d'un mouvement). ‖ Gentleness (du caractère); mildness, meekness, kindness (d'une personne); sweetness (du sourire); charm, quietness (de la vie); *en douceur*, gently; calmly; tactfully; with indulgence; *employer la*

douceur, to use gentle methods; *traiter qqn avec douceur*, to deal gently with s.o. ‖ Pl. Pretty speech, compliments; *dire des douceurs à*, to say sweet nothings to. ‖ Pl. Sweets, comforts (de la vie). ‖ Culin. Sweets, U. S. candies; *aimer les douceurs*, to have a sweet tooth.

douche [duʃ] f. Shower; *douche écossaise*, hot and cold shower. ‖ Méd. Douche (injection). ‖ Fam. Sousing, dousing (averse); disappointment (déception); rebuke (réprimande); *recevoir une douche*, to be dashed (être décontenancé); to get a dousing (être trempé); *jeter une douche sur*, to throw a wet blanket over (ou) cold water on.

doucher [-ʃe] v. tr. (1). To give a shower to. ‖ Méd. To douche. ‖ Fam. To souse, to douse (par une averse); to cool off (l'enthousiasme).
— v. pr. Se doucher, to shower, to take a shower. ‖ Méd. To douche.

doué, ée [due] adj. Gifted, endowed (de, with); *bien doué*, talented; *être doué pour*, to have a turn (ou) gift for.

douelle [dwɛl] f. Stave (de tonneau). ‖ Archit. Soffit (de voussoir).

douer [dwe] v. tr. (1). To gift, to endow (de, with).

douille [du:j] f. Sconce (de bougeoir). ‖ Electr. Socket (d'ampoule). ‖ Techn. Bushing. ‖ Milit. Cartridge case.

douillet, ette [dujɛ, ɛt] adj. Downy (lit); cosy, snug (pièce); cosy (vêtement); easy (vie). ‖ Soft (personne).
— m. Molly-coddle; sissy.

douillette [dujɛt] f. Quilted wrap (d'enfant). ‖ Ecclés. Overcoat (de prêtre).

douillettement [-mɑ̃] adv. Cosily; snugly; softly.

douleur [dulœ:ʳ] f. Pain, ache (physique); *sans douleur*, painless. ‖ Grief, sorrow, woe (morale); *avoir la douleur de*, to experience the grief of; *douleur affreuse*, agony. ‖ Méd. Pl. Pains, throes, labour (de l'enfantement); *dans les douleurs*, in the throes. ‖ Fam. Pl. Rheumatism.

douloureuse [duluxø:z] f. Fam. Bill (note).

douloureusement [duluxøzmɑ̃] adv. Painfully. ‖ Sorrowfully, grievously.

douloureux, euse [-rø, ø:z] adj. Aching, painful (blessure); sore (endroit); *très douloureux*, excruciating. ‖ Dolorous (accents); mournful (air, voix); painful (effort, spectacle, sujet); distressing, woeful (nouvelle); grievous (perte); sorrowful (regard); heart-rending (soupir); aching (vide); *très douloureux*, agonizing, harrowing (cri).

doura [dura] m. Agric. Durra.

douro [duro] m. Fin. Douro.

doute [dut] m. Doubt (*au sujet de*, as to; *sur*, about); *dans le doute s'abstenir*, when in doubt abstain; *d'un air de doute*, dubiously; *en doute*, in question; *être dans la doute au sujet de*, to be doubtful of (ou) about (ou) as to; *hors de doute*, unquestionable, beyond all question; *mettre en doute que*, to question whether; *nul doute*, no doubt; *sans aucun doute*, undoubtedly, unquestionably; *sans doute*, no doubt, doubtless, probably; *son sort ne fait plus de doute*, there is no longer any doubt as to his fate. ‖ Doubt, misgiving; suspicion (soupçons) [*sur*, about].

douter [-te] v. intr. (1). *Douter de*, to doubt, to question, to have doubts about, to be doubtful of; *douter que* (ou) *si*, to doubt whether; *faire douter de la vertu de qqn*, to bring s.o.'s virtue into question; *ne pas douter que*, to have no doubt of, not to doubt but that, to be confident that. ‖ *Douter de*, to distrust, to mistrust (se méfier). ‖ Loc. *A n'en pas douter*, certainly, unquestionably; *il est jeune? j'en doute!*, is he young? I am afraid he is not; *il ne doute de rien*, he is over-confident (ou) far too self-confident.
— v. pr. Se douter de, to suspect, to have an

idea of; *se douter que,* to suspect that, to have an idea that; *je m'en doutais,* I thought as much; *il a oublié! je m'en doutais!,* he's forgotten! I thought he would!; *sans s'en douter,* unawares, unwittingly.

douteusement [-tøzmɑ̃] adv. Doubtfully.

douteux, euse [-tø, ø:z] adj. Doubtful, questionable (v. INCERTAIN); *cesser d'être douteux,* to be no longer a matter of doubt. ‖ Doubtful, indeterminate, imprecise, indefinite (vague); *lumière douteuse,* dubious light; *souvenir douteux,* shadowy remembrance. ‖ Doubtful, questionable, dubious (suspect); *linge douteux,* dubious linen.

douve [du:v] f. Stave (pour tonneau). ‖ Moat (de château). ‖ SPORTS. Water-jump (aux courses). ‖ BOT. Spearwort. ‖ MÉD. Fluke.

doux, ouce [du, us] adj. Fresh (eau); sweet (miel); mild (tabac); sweet, new (vin). ‖ Soft (brise); mild, genial (climat); mellow, sober, subdued (couleur); soft, subdued (lumière); sweet (musique, parfum); smooth (plume, velours). ‖ Loving, soft (paroles); soft, smooth (peau); gentle (regard); sweet (sourire, visage). ‖ Smooth (allure, mouvement); easy (escalier); easy, gentle (pente); smooth-running (voiture). ‖ Quiet (animal); gentle, meek, lenient, mild (personne). ‖ Pleasant (nouvelle, rêve, souvenir); mild, lenient (règlement); easy, quiet, calm, smooth (vie); *il m'est doux de,* it gives me pleasure to; *la douce sensation d'avoir accompli sa tâche,* a comfortable sense of achievement. ‖ COMM. Moderate (prix). ‖ MÉD. Mild (remède). ‖ CULIN. Sweet (plat); *à feu doux,* over a slow fire; *trop doux,* flavourless, insipid, wishy-washy. ‖ GRAMM. Soft (consonne). ‖ FAM. *Se la couler douce,* to lead a soft life.
— adv. *Filer doux,* to sing small; *tout doux!,* gently!, take it easy!
— loc. adv. *En douce,* on the quiet.
— m. Soft; *passer du fort au doux, du grave au doux,* to pass from loud to soft, from grave to gay.

douzain [duzɛ̃] m. Twelve-line stanza (ou) poem.

douzaine [duzɛn] f. Dozen (douze); *à la douzaine,* by the dozen; *deux douzaines d'huîtres,* two dozen oysters; *treize à la douzaine,* a baker's dozen. ‖ About twelve, ten or twelve (douze environ); *une douzaine d'invités,* about a dozen guests. ‖ FAM. *Il s'en trouve à la douzaine,* they swarm like bees; *on n'en trouve pas à la douzaine,* you don't come across them every day, they don't grow on trees.

douze [du:z] adj. Twelve; twelfth; *douze mois,* twelve months; *le douze septembre,* September the twelfth, the twelfth of September.
— m. Twelfth, twelfth part.

douzième [duzjɛm] adj., s. Twelfth.

douzièmement [-mɑ̃] adv. Twelfthly.

doxologie [dɔksɔlɔʒi] f. ECCLÉS. Doxology.

doyen [dwajɛ̃] s. Doyen (du corps diplomatique); dean (d'une faculté); senior, oldest member (d'une société); *le doyen des artistes,* the senior artist. ‖ ECCLÉS. Dean.

doyennat [dwajɛna] m. Deanship (de faculté).

doyenné [-ne] m. ECCLÉS. Deanery (circonscription, dignité); dean's residence (habitation).

doyenné f. AGRIC. Doyenné du Comice, Doyenné pear.

doyenneté [-nte] f. Seniority.

Dr [dɛɛr] abrév. de *docteur,* Dr.

drachme [drakm] f. Drachma (monnaie). ‖ MÉD. Drachm, dram.

draconien, enne [drakɔnjɛ̃, ɛn] adj. Draconian.

drag [drag] m. Drag (voiture).

dragage [draga:ʒ] m. Dredging (pour nettoyage); dragging (pour recherche).

dragée [draʒe] f. Sugared almond. ‖ MÉD. Dragee. ‖ SPORT. Small shot (à la chasse). ‖ MILIT.,

FAM. Bullet. ‖ FIG. *Une dragée amère,* a bitter pill; *tenir la dragée haute à,* to be high-handed with, to act high-handedly with.

drageifié, ée [-ʒeifje] adj. Sugared (médicament, confiserie).

drageoir [-ʒwa:r] m. Comfit-box.

drageon [draʒɔ̃] m. AGRIC. Sucker.

drageonner [-ʒɔne] v. tr. (1). AGRIC. To sucker.

dragon [dragɔ̃] m. Dragon (astre, démon, monstre). ‖ MILIT. Dragoon. ‖ BLAS. Wyvern. ‖ FAM. Dragon, virago (femme); Cerberus (gardien).

dragonnades [dragɔnad] f. pl. † Dragonnades, persecution of Protestants by Louis XIV's dragoons.

dragonne [dragɔn] f. Tassel (de parapluie.) ‖ MILIT. Sword knot.

dragonnier [-nje] m. BOT. Dragon-tree.

drague [drag] f. Dredger (machine). ‖ NAUT. Drag-net (filet).

draguer [drage] v. tr. (1). To dredge (pour curage); to drag (pour recherche). ‖ NAUT. To sweep for (des mines); *draguer le fond,* to drag. ‖ FAM. To chat up, to try and pick up.
— v. intr. To chase after girls (ou) men, to cruise.

dragueur [-gœ:r] m. Dredger (machine, ouvrier); dragman (pêcheur). ‖ NAUT. *Dragueur de mines,* mine-sweeper.
— adj. *Bateau dragueur,* dredger.

dragueur, euse [-gœ:r, ø:z] s. FAM. Man (ou) woman out for pick-ups, cruiser.

drain [drɛ̃] m. Drain-pipe. ‖ MÉD. Drain.

drainable [dɛnabl] adj. Drainable.

drainage [-na:ʒ] m. Drainage, draining.

drainer [-ne] v. tr. (1). To drain. ‖ FIG. To drain, to tap.

draineur [-nœ:r] m. Drainer.

draisienne [drɛzjɛn] f. CH. DE F. Handcar. ‖ † Hobby-horse.

draisine [drɛzin] f. CH. DE F. Rail maintenance car.

dramatique [dramatik] adj. Dramatic (art, littérature); *auteur dramatique,* dramatist, playwright ‖ FIG. Tragic, dramatic; striking, sensational.
— m. Drama. ‖ Dramatic element.

dramatique f. TV play.

dramatiquement [-tikmɑ̃] adv. Dramatically.

dramatisation [-tizasjɔ̃] f. Dramatization. ‖ FAM. Dramatization, piling on the agony.

dramatiser [-tize] v. tr. (1). To dramatize. ‖ FAM. To dramatize, to pile on the agony.

dramaturge [-tyrʒ] m. Dramatist, playwright.

dramaturgie [-tyrʒi] f. Dramaturgy (art). ‖ Treatise on dramaturgy (traité).

drame [dram] m. Drama. ‖ FIG. Tragedy, tragic occurrence.

drap [dra] m. Cloth (tissu); *drap mortuaire,* pall, hearse cloth; *du drap,* woollen (commerce). ‖ Sheet, bed-sheet, bedclothes (literie). ‖ MÉD. *Drap d'hôpital,* waterproof sheeting; *drap mouillé,* pack-sheet. ‖ FAM. *Dans de beaux draps,* in a fine pickle. ‖ **Drap-housse,** m. Fitted sheet.

drapage [-pa:ʒ] m. Draping.

drapé [-pe] m. Drapery.

drapeau [drapo] m. Colours; flag; standard; *drapeau blanc, rouge,* white, red flag; *le drapeau tricolore,* the tricolour. ‖ MILIT. *Etre sous les drapeaux,* to serve with the colours. ‖ AVIAT. *Hélice en drapeau,* feathered propeller; *mettre en drapeau,* to feather (une hélice). ‖ RADIO. Irregular synchronism (en télévision).

draper [drape] v. tr. (1). To drape (une étoffe, une fenêtre, une statue).
— v. pr. **Se draper,** to drape oneself (*dans,* in). ‖ FAM. *Se draper dans sa dignité,* to be standoffish, to drape oneself in one's dignity.

draperie [-pri] f. Drapery (drapé, étoffe, manufacture, métier).

drapier [-pje] s. Cloth-manufacturer (fabricant); draper, clothier (marchand).

drapière [-pjɛːr] f. Blanket-pin (épingle).

drastique [drastik] adj., m. MÉD. Drastic.

dravidien, enne [dravidjɛ̃, ɛn] adj. GÉOGR., GRAMM. Dravidian.

drawback [drobak] m. COMM. Drawback; *certificat de drawback*, debenture.

drayer [drɛje] v. tr. (9*b*). To flesh.

dreadnought [drɛdnoːt] m. NAUT. Dreadnought.

drêche [drɛʃ] f. Draff.

drège [drɛːʒ] f. Drag-net (filet). ‖ Hackle (peigne).

drelin [drəlɛ̃] m. Tinkle; ting-a-ling.

dressage [drɛsaːʒ] m. Setting up (d'un échafaudage); erection, erecting, raising (d'un monument); pitching (d'une tente). ‖ Training (d'un animal); dressage (en équitation). ‖ Trimming (d'une haie); dressing (d'une pierre). ‖ MILIT. Truing up (d'un canon); laying (d'une embuscade).

dressement [-smɑ̃] m. Making out (d'une liste); drawing up, preparation (d'un plan).

dresser [-se] v. tr. (1). To raise, to lift, to hold up (la tête); *dresser l'oreille,* to cock (ou) to prick up one's ears. ‖ To set up (une barrière, un échafaud, une statue); to pitch (un camp, une tente); to erect, to put up (un échafaudage); to put up (une échelle, un monument); to raise, to rear (une échelle, un mât); to erect, to step, to set up (un mât). ‖ To draw, to lay down (une carte); to lay, to set (le couvert); to draw up (une liste); to prepare (un plan). ‖ To train (un animal); to break, to break in (un cheval); *non dressé,* unbroken (cheval). ‖ To trim (une haie); to dress (une pierre). ‖ TECHN. To true up (une machine). ‖ MILIT. To establish (une batterie); to lay out (un camp); to drill (une recrue). ‖ JUR. To draw up (un acte); to prepare (l'accusation); to make up, to schedule (un inventaire). ‖ CULIN. To dish up (un plat). ‖ FAM. *Dresser qqn,* to make s.o. toe the line, to make s.o. watch his step, to put the screw on s.o.; *dresser contre,* to rouse (ou) work up (ou) stir up against; *à faire dresser les cheveux,* hair-raising; *faire dresser les cheveux sur la tête,* to make s.o.'s hair stand on end. — v. pr. Se **dresser,** to rear up, to rise on its hind legs (cheval); to stand on end (cheveux); to prick up, to cock up (oreilles). ‖ To stand (monument). ‖ To sit up (en s'asseyant); to rise (en se levant); to draw oneself up (de toute sa taille); *se dresser sur la pointe des pieds,* to stand on tiptoe. ‖ To stand (obstacle); *se dresser face à,* to make a stand against; *se dresser contre,* to rise up against.

dresseur [-sœːr] s. Trainer (d'animaux); breaker (de chevaux). ‖ TECHN. Dresser, trimmer.

dressoir [-swaːr] m. Sideboard.

dreyfusard, arde [drɛfyzaːr, ard] adj. † Dreyfusard, supporting Dreyfus. — s. Dreyfusard, supporter of Dreyfus.

dribble [dribl] m. SPORTS. Dribble.

dribbler [-ble] v. tr., intr. (1). SPORTS. To dribble.

drill [driːj] m. AGRIC., ZOOL. Drill.

drille m. FAM. Chap, fellow; *de joyeux drilles,* gay dogs.

drille f. TECHN. Hand-drill. ‖ Pl. Rags.

driller [-drije] v. tr. (1). To drill.

drink [drink] m. FAM. Drink.

drisse [dris] f. NAUT. Halyard.

drive [draiv] m. SPORTS. Drive (au tennis).

driver [-ve] v. intr. (1). SPORTS. To drive. — v. tr. To drive (un cheval).

drogman [drɔgmɑ̃] m. Dragoman.

drogue [drɔg] f. Drug (stupéfiant). ‖ MÉD. Drug. ‖ CHIM. Chemical.

drogué, ée [-ge] s. Drug taker, drug addict, junkie.

droguer [-ge] v. tr. (1). SPORTS. To dope, to hobble (un animal). ‖ MÉD. To physic (qqn). ‖ FAM. To doctor (le vin). — v. intr. FAM. To dance attendance; *faire droguer,* to keep waiting. — v. pr. Se **droguer,** MÉD. To physic oneself. ‖ FAM. To be a drug addict.

droguerie [-gri] f. Drysalter's shop, U. S. drugstore (boutique); drysaltery (drogues).

droguet [-gɛ] m. Drugget (tissu).

droguiste [-gist] m. Drysalter. ‖ MÉD. Drug-manufacturer; druggist.

droit [drwa] adj. Straight (ligne, route); plumb (mur); erect, upright (personne); true (planche); *couper droit fil,* to cut on the straight; *en droite ligne,* in a straight line; *marcher en ligne droite vers,* to make a bee-line for; *se tenir droit,* to stand upright (debout); *se tenir erect (dressé).* Stand-up, stiff (col); single-breasted (veston). ‖ Right (côté, main). ‖ GÉOM. Right (angle, ligne). ‖ SPORTS. *Coup droit,* straight thrust, lunge (à l'escrime); forehand drive (au tennis). ‖ FIG. Right (conduite); straightforward (esprit); straight, straightforward, upright (personne); *un coup droit,* a direct blow; *le droit chemin,* the right path; *bras droit,* right-hand man. — adv. Straight, directly; *droit au fait,* straight to the point, directly to the purpose; *droit dans le nez,* flush in the face; *tout droit,* straight on (ou) ahead.

droit m. Right (faculté, justification); *à bon droit,* rightly, legitimately, with good reason; *avoir droit à,* to have a right to, to be entitled to; *avoir le droit de faire,* to have a right to do; *de droit, de plein droit,* by right, as of right, lawfully; *quel droit entrez-vous?,* what right have you to enter?; *être dans son droit,* to be within one's right; *faire droit à,* to accede to, to acquiesce in, to admit; *n'avoir pas le droit de faire,* not to be justified (ou) warranted in doing. ‖ Power (pouvoir); *avoir des droits sur,* to have power over; *droit du plus fort,* jungle law; *droit de grâce,* right of reprieve; *droit de vie et de mort,* power of life and death; *s'adresser à qui de droit,* to apply to the proper authority. ‖ Right, title (titre); *droit d'association,* right to organize; *droit à la couronne,* title to the Crown; *donner des droits à,* to entitle to. ‖ Pl. Rights, claim; *droits acquis,* vested interests; *faire valoir ses droits,* to vindicate one's rights; *to put in a claim;* to put one's rights into effect. ‖ JUR. Law; *droit des gens,* law of nations; *étudiant en droit,* law student; *faire son droit,* to take a degree in law, to read for the bar; *par voies de droit,* by legal means. ‖ FIN. Dues, duty; tax; fee; *exempt de droits,* duty free; *soumis aux droits,* dutiable. ‖ FIN. *Sans droit aux actions, au dernier dividende, au tirage,* ex-new, ex-coupon, ex-drawing.

droite [drwat] f. Right, right hand, right-hand side (côté); *à droite,* on the right; *de droite à gauche,* from right to left. ‖ Right; *la droite,* the Right, the Conservatives (en politique). ‖ MATH. Straight line (ligne).

droitement [-tmɑ̃] adv. Rightly. ‖ Uprightly.

droitier [-tje] adj. Right-handed. — m. Right-handed person. ‖ FAM. Conservative, Rightist (en politique).

droiture [-tyːr] f. Right-mindedness (de l'esprit); uprightness, rectitude (des mœurs).

drolatique [drɔlatik] adj. Comical, funny, droll.

drôle [droːl] adj. Comical, funny, droll (amusant); *ce n'est pas drôle de vivre seul,* it is no joke living alone; *je ne trouve pas ça drôle,* I don't see the fun of it. ‖ Queer, funny, rum, odd (bizarre); *c'est drôle que,* it's funny (ou) strange that; *c'est vraiment drôle!,* that's rum!, that's really odd!; *se sentir tout drôle,* to feel queer.

— s. Rogue, rascal, scamp, knave (voyou). ‖ *Une drôle d'idée,* a funny (ou) queer idea; *un drôle de numéro,* a rum (ou) queer chap. ‖ MILIT. *La drôle de guerre,* the phoney war.

drôlement [drolmɑ̃] adv. Funnily, drolly, comically; queerly. ‖ FAM. Terribly; *drôlement contente,* jolly glad, really glad; *drôlement difficile,* devilish hard. (V. BIGREMENT.)

drôlerie [-ri] f. Drollness (cocasserie); drollery, fun, joke (plaisanterie).

drôlesse [-lɛs] f. Hussy, baggage.

drôlet, ette [-lɛ, ɛ:t] adj. Quaint, queer.

dromadaire [drɔmadɛ:r] m. ZOOL. Dromedary.

drop [drɔp], **drop-goal** [-gol] m. SPORTS. Drop goal.

drosera [drɔzɛra] m. BOT. Sundew.

drosse [drɔs] f. NAUT. Wheel-rope, rudder-chain (de gouvernail); *drosse de vergue,* truss.

drosser [-se] v. tr. (1). NAUT. To drive.

dru, ue [dry] adj. Scrubby (barbe); thick-set (broussailles); thick (coups); dense (herbe); close (pluie).

— adv. Hard (cogner); heavily, thick and fast (neiger, pleuvoir); thickly (pousser).

drugstore [drœgstɔ:r] m. Drugstore.

druide [drɥid] m. Druid.

druidique [-dik] adj. Druidic.

druidisme [-dism] m. Druidism.

drupe [dryp] f. BOT. Drupe.

dryade [drijad] f. Dryad.

du [dy] art. V. DE, LE.

dû, due adj. Due, owing (attribuable) [à, to]; *dû à la fatigue,* due to weariness. ‖ Due, proper, fitting (convenable) [à, to]. ‖ COMM. Owing [à, to]; *l'argent qui lui est dû,* the money owing to him; *en port dû,* carriage forward. ‖ JUR. Adequate; *en bonne et due forme,* in due form; *contrat en bonne et due forme,* formal contract.

— m. COMM. Due.

dualisme [dɥalism] m. PHILOS. Dualism.

dualiste [-list] adj., m. PHILOS. Dualist.

dualité [-lite] f. Duality.

dubitatif, ive [dybitatif, i:v] adj. Dubitative.

dubitativement [-tivmɑ̃] adv. Dubitatively.

duc [dyk] m. Duke (titre) [*de,* of]. ‖ ZOOL. Horned owl; *grand duc,* eagle-owl.

ducal, ale [-kal] adj. Ducal.

ducat [-ka] m. FIN. Ducat.

ducaton [-tɔ̃] m. FIN. Ducaton.

duché [dyʃe] m. Dukedom (terres et titre); duchy (territoire).

duchesse [-ʃɛs] f. Duchess. ‖ Duchesse satin. ‖ BOT. Duchess pear (poire).

ducroire [dykrwa:r] m. COMM. Del credere agent (ou) commission.

ductile [dyktil] adj. Ductile, tensile.

ductilité [-lite] f. Ductility.

duègne [dɥɛɲ] f. Duenna.

duel [dɥɛl] m. GRAMM. Dual.

duel m. Duel, encounter; *duel à l'épée,* duel with swords; *provoquer en duel,* to challenge to a duel; *se battre en duel,* to fight a duel. ‖ AVIAT. *Duel aérien,* dog-fight.

duelliste [dɥelist] m. Duellist.

duettiste [dɥetist] s. MUS. Duettist.

duffle-coat [dœfəlkot] m. Duffle- (ou) duffel-coat.

dulcifier [dylsifje] v. tr. (3). To dulcify.

dulcine [-sin] f. CHIM. Dulcin.

dulcinée [-sine] f. Dulcinea. ‖ FAM. Lady-love.

dulie [dyli] f. ECCLÉS. Dulia.

dum-dum [dumdum] m. MILIT. Dum-dum.

dûment [dymɑ̃] adv. Duly, properly, in due form.

dumping [dœmpiɲ] m. COMM. Dumping; *faire du dumping,* to dump.

dundee [dœndi] m. NAUT. Ketch.

dune [dyn] f. Dune. ‖ Pl. Downs (crayeuses); dunes (sableuses).

dunette [dynɛt] f. NAUT. Poop.

duo [dɥo] m. MUS. Duo; duet. ‖ FAM. *Duo d'injures,* duet of curses.

duodécimal, ale [dɥɔdesimal] adj. Duodecimal.

duodénal, ale [dɥɔdenal] adj. MÉD. Duodenal.

duodénite [-nit] f. MÉD. Duodenitis.

duodénum [-nɔm] m. MÉD. Duodenum.

duopole [dɥɔpɔl] m. Duopoly.

dupe [dyp] f. Dupe; gull, gudgeon, U. S. sucker (fam.); *être dupe de,* to be taken in by (ou) fooled by.

duper [-pe] v. tr. (1). To dupe, to fool, to take in, to gull.

duperie [-pri] f. Dupery, cheating, trickery.

dupeur [-pœ:r] s. Trickster; hoaxer.

duplex [duplɛks] m. ARCHIT. Duplex apartment. ‖ RADIO. Duplex operation (ou) transmission, duplexing.

duplexer [-se] v. tr. (1). RADIO. To duplex.

duplicata [dyplikata] m. Duplicate; replica.

duplicateur [-tœ:r] m. Duplicator, duplicating machine.

duplicatif, ive [-tif, i:v] adj. Duplicative, duplicating.

duplication [-sjɔ̃] f. Duplication.

duplicité [dyplisite] f. Duplicity, double-dealing.

duquel [dykɛl] pron. V. LEQUEL.

dur [dy:r] adj. Hard (bois, pierre, métal); stiff, hard (brosse). ‖ Harsh (couleur); grating (son). ‖ Hard, rigorous (climat, hiver); choppy (mer); stiff (montée). ‖ Stiff (examen); hard, difficult (question, travail); hard (temps, vie). ‖ Stony, hard (cœur); hard, unfeeling, severe (personne); stony, stern (regard); *dur pour qqn,* hard on s.o. ‖ MILIT. Stiff (bataille). ‖ AVIAT. Rough, bumpy (atterrissage). ‖ CULIN. Hard (eau); hard-boiled (œuf); stale (pain); tough (viande); harsh (vin). ‖ GRAMM. Hard (consonne). ‖ LOC. *A la tête dure,* thick-headed; *aux traits durs,* hard-featured; *avoir la peau dure,* to have a thick skin (ou) hide; *avoir la vie dure,* to have nine lives, to die hard; *dur à la douleur,* stoical; *dur à la main,* heavy on the hand (cheval); *dur d'oreille,* hard of hearing; *dur au travail,* hard-working; *mener la vie dure à qqn,* to lead s.o. a wretched life.

— adv. Hard; *travailler dur,* to work hard. ‖ FAM. *Croire dur comme fer à qqch.,* to pin one's faith to sth.

— m. ARCHIT. Concrete; *en dur,* in concrete, in stone. ‖ FAM. Tough customer, U. S. tough guy.

durabilité [dyrabilite] f. Durability.

durable [-bl] adj. Durable, lasting.

durablement [-bləmɑ̃] adv. Durably, lastingly.

Duralumin [dyralymɛ̃] m. Duralumin; U. S. duraluminum.

durant [dyrɑ̃] prép. During, for (v. PENDANT); *durant des jours,* for many days; *sa vie durant,* his whole life long; *vingt-quatre heures durant,* twenty-four hours by the clock (ou) on end.

duratif, ive [-ratif, i:v] adj. GRAMM. Durative.

durcir [dyrsi:r] v. tr. (2). To harden; to make hard. ‖ CULIN. To hardboil (un œuf).

— v. intr. To harden. ‖ To set (ciment); *durcir à la chaleur,* to bake.

— v. pr. Se durcir, to harden, to grow hard.

durcissement [-sismɑ̃] m. Hardening. ‖ Setting (du ciment); induration (de la glaise). ‖ AUTOM. Stiffening (de la suspension). ‖ FIG. Hardening (d'une position).

dure [dy:r] f. FAM. *A la dure,* painfully; *en avoir vu de dures,* to have seen service (être usé); *en voir de dures,* to have a hard time of it; *sur la dure,* on the cold hard ground.

durée [dyre] f. Term (d'un bail); duration (de

la guerre); continuance (d'un règne); period (de séjour); length (des vacances); *courte durée*, shortness, short duration. ‖ Lasting quality (résistance); *étoffe de bonne durée*, stuff that will stand hard wear. ‖ Techn. Life (d'une machine); *essai de durée*, endurance test. ‖ Electr. Life (d'une ampoule). ‖ Mus. *Disque longue-durée*, long-playing record. ‖ Jur. Currency (d'une police).

durement [-mɑ̃] adv. Hardly, with difficulty (difficilement); hard (fort); severely, harshly (sévèrement).

durer [-re] v. intr. (1). To last (en général); to hold (chance, réserves); to wear well, to last (étoffe); to endure (œuvre); to hold out, to last, to last out (personne); *ça dure depuis deux ans*, it has been going on for two years; *combien dure votre séjour?* how long is your stay?; *elle durera plus que lui*, she will outlast him; *le temps me dure*, I find life dull; *mangez du pain tant qu'il dure*, eat bread as long as there is any; *trop beau pour durer*, too good to last.

dureté [dyrte] f. Hardness (du bois, du métal, de la pierre). ‖ Hardness, difficulty (du travail). ‖ Harshness, severity (du châtiment); hardness (du cœur); austerity, hardships (de l'époque); hardheartedness, severity, unkindness (d'une personne); steeliness (du regard); harshness (de la voix). ‖ Culin. Hardness (de l'eau); toughness (de la viande). ‖ Pl. Harsh words (paroles).

durillon [dyrijɔ̃] m. Méd. Callosity (aux mains); corn (au pied).

durio(n) [dyrjɔn] f. Bot. Durian (fruit).

Durit [dyrit] f. (nom déposé). Autom. Radiatorhose.

dus, dut [dy]. V. devoir (39).

duumvirat [dyɔmvira] m. † Duumvirate.

duvet [dyvɛ] m. Down (plume, poil). ‖ Fluff (d'étoffe). ‖ Bot. Down (de chardon); bloom (de fruit); cotton-like flake (d'arbre). ‖ Fam. Featherbed (lit); down quilt (édredon).

duveté, ée [dyvte] adj. Downy.

duveter (se) [sədyvte] v. pr. (8 a). To become downy (ou) fluffy.

duveteux, euse [-tø, ø:z] adj. Downy. ‖ Fluffy; flaky.

duvetine [dyvtin] f. Duvetyn (tissu).

dynamique [dinamik] adj. Phys. Dynamic. ‖ Fam. Energetic; full or drive (ou) push; *être très dynamique*, to be a live wire, U. S. to be a go-getter (ou) hustler.
— f. Phys. Dynamics.

dynamiquement [-mikmɑ̃] adv. Phys. Dynamically. ‖ Dynamically, energetically.

dynamisme [-mism] m. Phys. Dynamism. ‖ Fam. Drive, push.

dynamitage [dinamita:ʒ] m. Dynamiting.

dynamite [dinamit] f. Dynamite.

dynamiter [-te] v. tr. (1). To dynamite, to blow up with dynamite.

dynamiteur, euse [-tœ:r, ø:z] s. Dynamiter.

dynamo [dinamo] f. Electr. Dynamo; U. S. generator. ‖ **Dynamo-électrique**, adj. Dynamo-electric. ‖ **Dynamo-quantité**, f. Low-tension dynamo. ‖ **Dynamo-tension**, f. High-tension dynamo.

dynamogène [dinamɔʒɛn] adj. Méd. Dynamogenic, dynamogenous.

dynamomètre [dinamɔmɛtr] m. Dynamometer.

dynamométrie [-tri] f. Electr. Dynamometry.

dynamométrique [-trik] adj. Electr. Dynamometric.

dynamoteur [-tœ:r] m. Electr. Dynamotor.

dynastie [dinasti] f. Dynasty.

dynastique [-tik] adj. Dynastic.

dyne [din] f. Phys. Dyne.

dysenterie [disɑ̃tri] f. Méd. Dysentery.

dysentérique [-terik] adj. Méd. Dysenteric.

dysfonctionnement [disfɔksjɔnmɑ̃] m. Dysfunction, malfunction.

dyslexie [dislɛksi] f. Dyslexia.

dyslexique [-sik] adj., s. Dyslectic, dyslexic.

dysménorrhée [dismenore] f. Méd. Dysmenorrhea.

dyspepsie [dispɛpsi] f. Méd. Dyspepsia.

dyspeptique [-tik] adj., s. Méd. Dyspeptic.

dyspnée [dispne] f. Méd. Dyspnoea.

dysprosium [disprɔzjɔm] m. Chim. Dysprosium.

dystrophie [distrɔfi] f. Méd. Dystrophy.

dytique [ditik] m. Dytiscus, diving beetle.

E

e [ə], **é** [e], **è** [ɛ] m. E, e.

E abrév. de *Est*, East, E.

eau [o] f. Water (en général); *eau de mer, de pluie, de roche, de source*, sea-, rain-, rock-, spring-water; *se passer les mains à l'eau*, to rinse one's hands. ‖ Water, rain (pluie). ‖ Water (éclat); *l'eau d'un diamant*, the water of a diamond. ‖ Water (salive); *faire venir l'eau à la bouche de qqn*, to make s.o's mouth water. ‖ Sweat (sueur); *être en eau*, to be in a sweat. ‖ Pl. Waters (d'une inondation); *les eaux baissent*, the waters are abating. ‖ Pl. Waterworks (fontaines; installation); *eaux de la ville*, main water; *grandes eaux, jeux d'eaux*, ornamental fountains. ‖ Pl. Waters; *eaux du port*, confines; *dans les eaux occidentales de la Manche*, in the western area of the Channel. ‖ Naut. Wake; *dans les eaux de*, in the wake of; *faire de l'eau*, to take in water; *faire eau*, to leak; *mettre à l'eau*, to lower (une barque); to set afloat, to launch (un navire). ‖ Méd. Water (urine, sérosité); *eau blanche*, Goulard water; *eau de Cologne, de rose*, eau de Cologne, rosewater; *eau de toilette*, lotion. ‖ Chim. *Eau lourde*, heavy water. ‖ Culin. *Eau de riz*, rice-water. ‖ Ecclés. *Eau bénite*, holy water. ‖ Loc. *De la plus belle eau*, of the first water; *mettre de l'eau dans son vin*, to draw in one's horns; *porter de l'eau à la rivière*, to carry coals to Newcastle; *revenir sur l'eau*, to be afloat again; *tomber à l'eau*, to fizzle out, to come to nothing. ‖ **Eau-de-vie** (pl. *eaux-de-vie*) f. Brandy; *eau-de-vie de cidre*, apple-jack, apple-brandy. ‖ **Eau-forte**, f. Arts. Etching; Chim. aqua-fortis.

ébahi, ie [ebai] adj. Dumbfounded, stupefied, gaping. (V. AHURI, ÉBERLUÉ.)

ébahir [-i:r] v. tr. (2). To amaze, to astound.
— v. pr. **S'ébahir**, to be dumbfounded (ou) amazed ; to stand gaping ; *s'ébahir de*, to wonder at, to be astounded at.

ébahissement [-ismã] m. Amazement.

ébarbage [ebarba:ʒ] m. TECHN. Trimming, burring (en métallurgie) ; trimming (en reliure). ‖ AGRIC. Clipping (ou) trimming of roots.

ébarber [-be] v. tr. (1). TECHN. To trim, to burr (en métallurgie) ; to trim (en reliure). ‖ AGRIC. To clip (ou) trim the roots of.

ébarbeuse [-bø:z] f. TECHN. Trimming-machine.

ébarboir [-bwa:r] m. TECHN. Chipping chisel.

ébarbure [-by:r] f. Shavings (de métal); trimmings (de papier).

ébats [eba] m. pl. Frolics, sports, gambols; *prendre ses ébats*, to frolic, to gambol.

ébattre (s') [sebatr] v. pr. (20). To frolic, to gambol, to frisk about, to disport oneself.

ébaubi, ie [ebobi] adj. Flabbergasted, staggered, tongue-tied.

ébaubir (s') [sebobi:r] v. pr. (2). To be flabbergasted ; to stand gaping.

ébauchage [eboʃa:ʒ] m. Roughing out (de qqch.); outlining (d'une œuvre littéraire). ‖ ARTS. Sketching out.

ébauche [ebo:ʃ] f. Rough shape (de qqch.); rough outline (d'une œuvre littéraire). ‖ ARTS. Rough sketch. ‖ FIG. Prefiguration, germ (de l'avenir); outline (d'un projet); ghost (d'un sourire).

ébaucher [eboʃe] v. tr. (1). To rough out (en général); to outline, to sketch (une œuvre littéraire). ‖ ARTS. To rough-hew (une sculpture); to outline, to rough (ou) to sketch out (un tableau). ‖ FIG. To begin (un geste); to rough (ou) to sketch out (un projet); to give the ghost of (un sourire).

ébauchoir [-ʃwa:r] m. Paring-chisel (de charpentier); roughing-chisel (de maçon). ‖ ARTS. Ebauchoir, boaster, roughing-chisel.

ébaudir (s') [sebodi:r] v. pr. (2). † To rejoice; to make merry (*de*, over, at).

ébène [ebɛn] f. Ebony; *noir d'ébène*, ebony.

ébénier [ebenje] m. BOT. Ebony-tree; *faux ébénier*, laburnum.

ébéniste [-nist] m. Cabinet-maker.

ébénisterie [-nistəri] f. Cabinet-making (art); cabinet-work (meubles).

éberlué, ée [ebɛrlɥe] adj. Flabbergasted, dumbfounded; in a daze. (V. ÉBAHI.)

éberluer v. tr. (1). To flabbergast, to astound.

éblouir [eblui:r] v. tr. (2). To dazzle. ‖ FIG. To fascinate.

éblouissant, ante [-sã, ã:t] adj. Dazzling.

éblouissement [-smã] m. Dazzling, dazzle (éclat); dazzling sight (spectacle). ‖ MÉD. Dizziness. ‖ FIG. Bewilderment.

ébonite [ebɔnit] f. Ebonite.

éborgner [ebɔrɲe] v. tr. (1). To blind in one eye; *éborgner qqn*, to put out s.o.'s eye. ‖ AGRIC. To disbud (un arbre).
— v. pr. **S'éborgner**, to lose an eye; to put out one of one's eyes.

ébouer [ebue] v. tr. (1). To scavenge (les rues).

éboueur [ebœ:r] m. Scavenger.

ébouillantage [ebujãta:ʒ] m. Scalding.

ébouillanter [ebujãte] v. tr. (1). To scald. ‖ CULIN. To dip in boiling water, to scald.

éboulement [ebulmã] m. Falling in; collapsing (action). ‖ Landslide (de terrain).

ébouler [-le] v. tr. (1). *Faire ébouler*, to cause to fall in, to bring down.
— v. pr. **S'ébouler**, to fall in, to crumble (mur); to slip (rocher); to cave in, to slide (terrain).

ébouleux, euse [-lø, ø:z] adj. Crumbling.

éboulis [-li] m. Debris. ‖ Scree (en montagne).

ébourgeonner [eburʒɔne] v. tr. (1). AGRIC. To disbud.

ébouriffant, ante [eburifã, ã:t] adj. FAM. Amazing, striking, startling. (V. MIROBOLANT.)

ébouriffer [-ife] v. tr. (1). To ruffle, to tousle (les cheveux); to dishevel, to ruffle (ou) to tousle the hair of (qqn). ‖ To ruffle, (les plumes, les poils). ‖ FAM. To stun, to ruffle.

ébourrer [ebure] v. tr. (1). To unhair (des peaux).

ébrancher [ebrãʃe] v. tr. (1). AGRIC. To lop off the branches from; to prune.

ébranchoir [-ʃwa:r] m. AGRIC. Lopping-bill.

ébranlement [ebrãlmã] m. Shaking (d'un objet). ‖ MÉD. *Ebranlement nerveux*, shock. ‖ FIG. Commotion, perturbation, disturbance.

ébranler [-le] v. tr. (1). To shake (en général); to set ringing (une cloche); to unsettle (un piédestal); to rattle (une vitre). ‖ MÉD. To loosen (une dent); to shake (les nerfs); to unhinge (la raison); to affect, to attack (la santé). ‖ PHYS. To disturb (l'atmosphère). ‖ FIG. To shake (le crédit, la confiance, la résolution); to disturb, to impress, to shock, to move (qqn); to weaken (la résistance); *se laisser ébranler par*, to let oneself be impressed by.
— v. pr. **S'ébranler**, to move off, to start (en général); to rumble off (carriole); to set out on a march, to march off (colonne); to totter (mur); to start (train). ‖ FIG. To be shaken (confiance); to be disturbed (ou) moved (personne); to totter (raison); to falter (résolution).

ébraser [ebrɑze] v. tr. (1). To splay (une fenêtre).

ébrasure [-zy:r] f. Splay.

ébrécher [ebreʃe] v. tr. (5). To chip (une assiette); to notch (une lame, un outil); *couteau ébréché*, jagged knife. ‖ FIG. To make a hole in, to break into (son capital, sa fortune).

ébréchure [-ʃy:r] f. Chip (d'assiette, de couteau, de verre); notch (de lame, d'outil).

ébriété [ebrijete] f. Ebriety (v. IVRESSE); *en état d'ébriété*, ebriated, inebriated, intoxicated.

ébrouement [ebrumã] m. Snorting, snort.

ébrouer [ebrue] v. tr. (1). To bran (la laine).

ébrouer (s') [sebrue] v. pr. (1). To snort (cheval); *s'ébrouer dans l'eau*, to splash about in the water; *s'ébrouer dans la poussière*, to take a dust-bath (oiseau). ‖ FAM. To shake oneself (personne).

ébruitement [ebrɥitmã] m. Noising abroad (d'une nouvelle); divulgation, disclosure (d'un secret).

ébruiter [-te] v. tr. (1). To noise abroad, to bruit abroad (ou) about (une nouvelle); to divulge, to disclose, to blab out (un secret).
— v. pr. **S'ébruiter**, to get noised abroad (ou) bruited about, to spread, to get round (nouvelle); to get out, to leak out (secret).

ébullition [ebylisjɔ̃] f. Ebullition; boiling; *point d'ébullition*, boiling point. ‖ FIG. Ebullience, effervescence, ferment, turmoil; *être en ébullition*, to be boiling over (ou) seething with excitement.

éburnéen, enne [ebyrneɛ̃, ɛn] adj. Eburnean, ivory-like.

écaillage [ekaja:ʒ] m. Shelling (des coquillages); scaling (des poissons). ‖ Flaking off (de la peinture); scaling off (du vernis).

écaille [ekaj] f. Scute (de crocodile); shell (d'huître, de tortue); scale (de poisson). ‖ Chip (de bois); scale, flake (de peinture, de vernis). ‖ FIG. Scale (des yeux).

écailler [ekaje] v. tr. (1). To shell (des huîtres); to scale (un poisson). ‖ To flake off (la peinture).
— v. pr. **S'écailler**, to flake (ou) scale (ou) peel off.

écailler m. Oyster-sheller; oyster-seller.

écaillère [-jɛːr] f. Oyster-knife (couteau).

écailleux, euse [-jø, øːz] adj. Scaly, squamous (animal). ‖ Fissile (ardoise); splintery (bois); flaky (peinture, vernis).

écaillure [-jyːr] f. Flake.

écale [ekal] f. Shuck (de châtaigne); husk (de noix); shell, pod (de pois).

écaler [-le] v. tr. (1). To shuck (des châtaignes); to husk, to hull (des noix); to shell (des pois). — v. pr. S'écaler, to burst the husk (châtaigne); to come out of the pod (pois).

écarlate [ekarlat] adj., f. Scarlet.

écarquiller [ekarkije] v. tr. (1). To open wide (les yeux); aux yeux écarquillés, wide-eyed; écarquiller les jambes, to straddle, to stand with legs wide apart; regarder en écarquillant les yeux, to goggle at, to gaze open-eyed (ou) round-eyed at.

écart [ekaːr] m. Divergence; difference (de chiffre, de température); disparity, gap (entre, between). ‖ Extension (en gymnastique); faire le grand écart, to do the splits. ‖ Step aside, side-step (mouvement de côté); swerve (du cheval); faire un écart, to shy (cheval); to step aside (personne). ‖ Remote spot (lieu). ‖ Discard (aux cartes). ‖ MÉD. Error (de régime). ‖ FIN. Margin (des prix); supprimer l'écart entre, to close the gap between. ‖ TECHN. Scarf. ‖ BLAS. Quarter. ‖ MILIT. Error; deviation. ‖ AVIAT. Range (de vitesse). ‖ FIG. Lapse, slip (de conduite); flight (d'imagination); error (de jeunesse); lapse, slip (de langage). — loc. adv. A l'écart, aside, apart; out of the way; se tenir à l'écart, to keep out of the way; tenir à l'écart, to keep out of the way. ‖ A l'écart de, off, away (ou) apart from (un lieu); aloof from (une préoccupation, un sujet); se tenir à l'écart de, to keep (ou) hold aloof from; tenir à l'écart de, to keep out of.

écarté, ée [ekarte] adj. Isolated, remote, out-of-the-way; secluded (lieu); chemin écarté, by-path. ‖ Apart, spread out, asunder (jambes); debout les jambes écartées, standing with one's legs apart, standing astride.

écarté m. Écarté (jeu de cartes).

écartelé, ée [ekartəle] adj. BLAS. Quartered.

écartèlement [-tɛlmɑ̃] m. Quartering.

écarteler [-təle] v. tr. (6). To quarter.

écartement [ekartəmɑ̃] m. Spacing (action). ‖ Space, distance, gap (de, between). ‖ CH. DE F. Gauge (de la voie). ‖ AUTOM. Wheelbase (empattement). ‖ AVIAT. Gap (des plans). ‖ MÉD. Gaping (d'une plaie).

écarter [-te] v. tr. (1). To scatter (des éléments rassemblés, une foule); to separate (des objets unis); to draw aside (une tenture). ‖ To open (les bras); to square (les coudes); to spread (les doigts, les jambes). ‖ To keep away (éloigner) [de, from]; écarter un coup, to ward off a blow. ‖ To keep off (tenir à distance); écarter d'un geste, to brush aside; écarter d'une poussée, to push aside; écarter qqn pour passer, to push (ou) to thrust past s.o. ‖ Fig. To set aside (un avis, une hypothèse, une opinion); to turn down (une candidature, une protestation); to dismiss (une idée); to brush aside (une objection); to divert (les soupçons). — v. intr. To discard (aux cartes). ‖ To scatter (fusil). — v. pr. S'écarter, to open (doigts, volets); to diverge (routes). ‖ To move (ou) to step (ou) to draw aside (se détourner). ‖ To move, to stand, to keep away (de, from). ‖ To make way (devant, for); to get out of the way (devant, of). ‖ To deviate (dévier) [de, from]; s'écarter de son chemin, to go out of one's way. ‖ Fig. S'écarter de, to swerve from (son devoir); to depart from (l'ori-

ginal); to deviate from (la règle); to deviate (ou) to wander from (son sujet).

écarteur [-tœːr] m. MÉD. Retractor.

ecchymose [ɛkimoːz] f. MÉD. Ecchymosis.

Ecclésiaste [ɛklezjast] m. ECCLÉS. Ecclesiastes (livre) ; Ecclesiast, the Preacher (personnage).

ecclésiastique [-tik] adj. ECCLÉS. Ecclesiastical (en général); clerical (costume); spiritual (tribunaux); état ecclésiastique, priesthood. — m. ECCLÉS. Ecclesiastic, clergyman. ‖ Pl. Clergy. ‖ Ecclesiasticus (livre).

écervelé, ée [esɛrvəle] adj. Hare-brained, scatter-brained (étourdi); giddy, flighty (léger). — s. Scatter-brain, madcap.

échafaud [eʃafo] m. Staging, stage, platform (pour spectateurs). ‖ Scaffold (instrument de supplice); gallows, gibbet (gibet); monter sur l'échafaud, to mount the scaffold.

échafaudage [-daːʒ] m. Scaffolding (de maçons). ‖ Heap, pile (d'objets entassés). ‖ FIG. Building up, amassing (d'une fortune); drawing up (d'un plan); elaboration (de théories) [action]; structure (d'un raisonnement, d'un système) [état].

échafauder [-de] v. intr. (1). To erect a scaffolding, to scaffold. — v. tr. To pile up (des objets en tas). ‖ FIG. To make up (une fortune, une histoire); to draw up (un plan); to build up (des théories).

échalas [eʃala] m. AGRIC. Pole (de jardin); échalas de vigne, vine-prop. ‖ FAM. Maypole, spindle-shanks.

échalasser [-se] v. tr. (1). To prop (une vigne).

échalier [eʃalje] m. Stile (échelle). ‖ Hurdle (clôture).

échalote [eʃalɔt] f. BOT. Shallot, scallion.

échancré, ée [eʃɑ̃kre] adj. Indented, ragged, jagged (côte). ‖ Open-necked, with a plunging neck-line (vêtement).

échancrer [eʃɑ̃kre] v. tr. (1). To indent, to notch (un objet). ‖ To open (au col); to ease (sous le bras).

échancrure [-kryːr] f. Indentation, notch (dans un objet). ‖ Décolleté, opening at the neck, neck-line (à une robe).

échange [eʃɑ̃ːʒ] m. Interchange (de lettres); exchange (d'objets, de promesses); comparison (de remarques); en échange de, in exchange for; faire l'échange de, to interchange; leur échange de coups, the blows that passed between them. ‖ COMM. Barter, truck (troc); valeur d'échange, exchange value.

échangeable [eʃɑ̃ʒabl] adj. Interchangeable, exchangeable.

échanger [-ʒe] v. tr. (7). To exchange (des compliments, des idées, des objets, des promesses, des vues); to interchange (des lettres, un mot); to bandy (des plaisanteries, des reproches); to compare (des remarques); échanger des baisers, to kiss; échanger des injures, to bandy words; ils échangèrent quelques coups, there was an exchange of blows between them; échanger des sourires, to smile at each other. ‖ To barter (troquer); to swap (fam.); échanger pour, to exchange for.

échangeur [-ʒœːr] m. AUTOM. Interchange. ‖ TECHN. Échangeur de chaleur, heat-exchanger. ‖ PHYS., CHIM. Échangeur d'ions, ion exchanger.

échangiste [-ist] m. COMM. Exchanger.

échanson [eʃɑ̃sɔ̃] m. † Cup-bearer. ‖ Butler.

échantillon [eʃɑ̃tijɔ̃] m. Sample (de denrées); sample, pattern (de tissu); carnet d'échantillons, pattern book; prélever un échantillon, to sample. ‖ TECHN. Standard dimension (ou) size (des briques, du bois); standard (des poids et mesures). ‖ NAUT. Scantling. ‖ FIG. Taste (avant-goût); example, instance (exemple); specimen, sample.

échantillonnage [-jɔnaːʒ] m. Sampling.

échantillonner [-jɔne] v. tr. (1). To sample, U.S. to spot-check (des marchandises); to gauge (des poids et mesures).

échappatoire [eʃapatwaːr] f. Loop-hole; elusion, evasion; *chercher des échappatoires,* to hedge.

échappé, ée [eʃape] adj. Runaway (cheval).
— s. Runaway (personne); *échappé de l'asile,* crackpot, bedlamite.

échappée f. Glimpse (vision rapide); vista (vue); *échappée sur la mer,* glimpse of the sea; *échappée de lumière,* touch (ou) passage of light. ‖ SPORTS. Break-away (à bicyclette); spurt (à la course).

échappement (-pmɑ̃] m. TECHN. Escapement (en horlogerie). ‖ ARCHIT. Head-room (d'un escalier). ‖ AUTOM. Exhaust; *échappement libre,* cut-out; *pot d'échappement,* silencer; U.S. muffler; *tuyau d'échappement,* exhaust-pipe.

échapper [-pe] v. intr. (1). To slip away, to pass out (autorité, puissance); to slip out (parole); to escape (personne); *l'échapper belle,* to have a narrow escape. ‖ *Echapper à,* to escape from, to break loose from (l'autorité, le contrôle); to shun (son destin); to escape (la mémoire, la mort, qqn); to get out of, to dodge (une obligation); to elude, to baffle (la poursuite, la recherche); to be an exception to (la règle); to elude (la remarque); *échapper à l'attention de qqn* (ou) *à qqn,* to escape s.o.'s notice; *échapper à l'œil,* to be invisible to the naked eye; *je ne peux y échapper,* there is no escape for me; *la patience m'a échappé,* my patience gave out; *son nom m'échappe,* his name slips (ou) has slipped my mind. ‖ *Laisser échapper,* to give vent to (donner libre cours à); to blunder (ou) blurt out, to let out, to let fly (lâcher, révéler); to let go (laisser

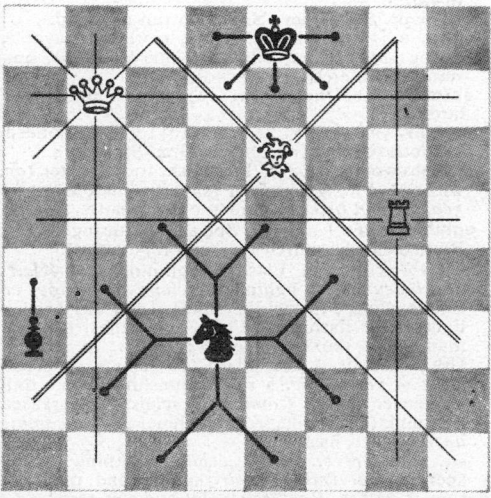

ÉCHECS (CHESS) : roi (king) — cheval (knight) — reine, dame (queen) — tour (rook, castle) — fou (bishop) — pion (pawn)

fuir); to let slip, to miss (laisser perdre, manquer); to drop (laisser tomber); to fail to hear (ne pas entendre); to overlook, to pass over, to be blind to (ne pas remarquer); *ne rien laisser échapper,* to miss nothing, to let nothing get past one.
— v. pr. **S'échapper,** to slip (objet) [de, from]. ‖ To escape, to break free (ou) loose; to run away; to get away (personne) [de, from]. ‖ To slip its collar (ou) its chain (chien); to fly away (oiseau). ‖ To leak out (eau, gaz); to burst out (feu); to gush out (jet d'eau); to flash, to burst (lumière). ‖ FIG. To slip out (chance, occasion); to burst (cri); to vanish (espoir).

écharde [eʃard] f. Splinter.

échardonner [eʃardɔne] v. tr. (1). To nap (un drap). ‖ AGRIC. To clear of thistles.

écharner [eʃarne] v. tr. (1). To flesh (une peau).

écharnoir [-nwaːʳ] m. Fleshing knife.

écharpe [eʃarp] f. Scarf, stole (de femme); sash (de maire); *en écharpe,* slantwise across the chest. ‖ AUTOM. *Prendre en écharpe,* to run obliquely into. ‖ MÉD. Sling; *en écharpe,* in a sling (membre). ‖ MILIT. *Prendre en écharpe,* to attack from an oblique angle.

écharper [-pe] v. tr. (1). To scribble (la laine). ‖ To slash, to hack, to gash (blesser). ‖ To rough-handle, to lynch, to mob (qqn); *se faire écharper,* to be torn to pieces. ‖ MILIT. To cut to pieces; to smash (fam.) [l'ennemi].

échasse [eʃas] f. Stilt (objet). ‖ ZOOL. Stilt. ‖ FAM. *Monter,* être *monté sur des échasses,* to be stilted.

échassier [-sje] m. Wader. ‖ FAM. Spindleshanks.

échaudé, ée [eʃode] adj. Scalded (personne). ‖ AGRIC. Shrivelled (blé). ‖ CULIN. Scalded. ‖ FAM. Fleeced.
— m. CULIN. Echaudé, light pastry.

échauder v. tr. (1). To scald (ébouillanter). ‖ FAM. To fleece, to cheat; U. S. to gyp, to rook; *se faire échauder dans,* to burn one's fingers over.

échauder v. tr. (1). To whitewash (à la chaux).

échaudoir [-dwaːr] m. Scalding-room (lieu); scalding-tub (vase).

échaudure [-dyːr] f. Scald.

échauffaison [eʃofɛzɔ̃] f. MÉD. Heat-rash.

échauffant, ante [-fɑ̃, ɑ̃ːt] adj. Heating (nourriture). ‖ MÉD. Binding (constipant). ‖ FIG. Exciting.

échauffé, ée [-fe] adj. Overheated (lieu, sang). ‖ Heated, fermented (grain, nourriture). ‖ FIG. Excited, heated; *les esprits sont échauffés,* feeling is running very high.
— m. Close smell (odeur).

échauffement [-fmɑ̃] m. TECHN. Heating. ‖ MÉD. Constipation; chafing (de la peau). ‖ FIG. Over-excitement.

échauffer [-fe] v. tr. (1). To heat (beaucoup); to warm (un peu). ‖ MÉD. To chafe (la peau); to bind, to constipate (qqn). ‖ FIG. To warm up; to inflame. ‖ FAM. *Echauffer les oreilles de qqn,* to make s.o.'s blood boil, to stir up s.o.'s bile, to get s.o.'s dander up.
— v. pr. **S'échauffer,** to get heated (chose, personne); to overheat oneself (personne). ‖ MÉD. To chafe (peau). ‖ FIG. To warm up (s'enthousiasmer); to chafe, to take fire, to flare up (s'irriter).

échauffourée [eʃofure] f. Scuffle, affray, brawl, U. S. ruckus (bagarre). ‖ MILIT. Skirmish.

échauguette [eʃogɛt] f. ARCHIT. Bartizan, watch-tower.

èche [ɛʃ] f. V. AICHE.

échéance [eʃeãːs] f. COMM. Date, maturity (de crédit); term (d'un effet); pay-day (jour d'échéance); *à deux mois d'échéance,* at two months' date; *à courte, longue échéance,* short-, long-dated (effet); *payable à l'échéance,* payable at maturity; *venir à échéance,* to fall due. ‖ JUR.

Expiration, expiry (d'occupation). ‖ FIG. *A longue échéance*, deferred, long-term, long to come.
échéancier [-ɑ̃sje] m. COMM. Bill-book.
échéant, ante [-ɑ̃, ɑ̃:t] adj. COMM. Falling due, payable. ‖ FIG. *Le cas échéant*, in case of need, should the occasion arise, should such be the case.
échec [eʃɛk] m. Check (au jeu); *échec et mat*, checkmate. ‖ Pl. Chess-board (échiquier); chess (jeu); chessmen (pièces); *faire une partie d'échecs*, to play a game of chess; *jouer aux échecs*, to play chess. ‖ MILIT. Check, reverse, defeat; *faire échec à*, to check; *subir un échec*, to suffer a defeat; *tenir en échec*, to keep at bay, to hold in check. ‖ FIG. Failure, ill-success (insuccès); failure (à un examen); miscarriage (d'un plan); *courir au-devant d'un échec*, to court failure.
échelle [eʃɛl] f. Ladder; *échelle à crochets, de corde, double, pliante*, hook-, rope-, step-, folding-ladder; *échelle à incendie* (ou) *de sauvetage*, fire-escape. ‖ NAUT. *Echelle de coupée, de dunette, de poupe*, gangway, quarter, stern ladder; *échelle de débarquement*, landing steps. ‖ TECHN. Scale (de mesure); *échelle d'étiage*, water-gauge; *à l'échelle*, to scale; *à grande échelle*, large-scale (carte). ‖ COMM. Scale (barème); *échelle mobile des salaires*, sliding scale of wages. ‖ FIG. Range (des coloris); ladder, U. S. run (dans un bas démaillé); scale (des prévisions); *échelle mobile, sociale*, sliding, social scale; *échelle des valeurs*, scale of values; *sur une grande échelle*, on a large scale. ‖ LOC. *Faire la courte échelle à qqn*, to give s.o. a leg up; *il n'y a plus qu'à tirer l'échelle*, that puts paid to it; U. S. that wraps it up; *monter à l'échelle*, to swallow it.
échelon [eʃlɔ̃] m. Round, rung (d'une échelle). ‖ MUS. Degree (de la gamme). ‖ MILIT. Echelon; *échelon d'attaque*, assault echelon. ‖ AVIAT. Echelon; *en échelon vers le bas, vers le haut*, stepped-down, stepped-up (formation). ‖ JUR. Grade (de l'administration); stage (de l'avancement); *à l'échelon ministériel*, at ministerial level. ‖ FIG. Step (vers la réussite).
échelonnement [eʃlɔnmɑ̃] m. Spacing out (des objets). ‖ FIN. Spreading out (des paiements). ‖ MILIT. Echelon formation. ‖ FIG. Staggering (des congés).
échelonner [-ne] v. tr.(1). To space out, to dispose (ou) to place at intervals (des objets). ‖ FIN. To spread out (les paiements); to shade (les prix). ‖ MILIT. To echelon, to draw up (ou) to place in echelon. ‖ FIG. To stagger (les congés); to grade (des exercices); to organize in stages (une opération).
— v. pr. **S'échelonner**, to be disposed (ou) placed at intervals. ‖ FIN. To be spread (sur, over). ‖ MILIT. To be echeloned. ‖ FIG. To be staggered (congés).
échenillage [eʃnija:ʒ] m. AGRIC. Clearing of caterpillars.
écheniller [-je] v. tr. (1). AGRIC. To clear of caterpillars.
échenilloir [-jwa:r] m. AGRIC. Averruncator.
écherra [eʃɛra]. V. ÉCHOIR (42).
écheveau [eʃvo] m. Skein. ‖ FIG. Maze.
échevelé, ée [eʃəvle] adj. Dishevelled. ‖ FIG. Wild (course).
écheveler v. tr. (8 a). To dishevel.
échevin [eʃvɛ̃] m. † Alderman.
échine [eʃin] f. Spine; back. ‖ CULIN. Chine; loin. ‖ FIG. *Avoir l'échine souple*, to be a lick-spittle; *courber l'échine devant*, to cringe to.
échine f. ARCHIT. Echinus.
échinée [eʃine] f. CULIN. Griskin.
échiner v. tr. (1). To break the back of (qqn). ‖ FAM. To wear out, to knock up (ou) U. S. out (accabler).

— v. pr. **S'échiner**, to tire oneself out; *s'échiner à faire qqch.*, to work oneself to death over sth.
échinoderme [ekinɔderm] m. ZOOL. Echinoderm.
échiquier [eʃikje] m. Chess-board; *en échiquier*, chequerwise, chequered. ‖ FIN. Exchequer.
écho [eko] m. Echo; *faire écho à;* to echo; *renvoyer un écho*, to send back an echo, to re-echo. ‖ News item; social gossip (dans un journal). ‖ FIG. Repetition; *se faire l'écho de qqch.*, to repeat (ou) to tell sth. again; *se faire l'écho de qqn*, to repeat s.o.'s words.
échographie [ekɔgrafi] f. MÉD. Ultrasonography.
échoir [eʃwa:r] v. intr. (42). To fall (à, to); to devolve (à, on); *échoir en partage à*, to fall to s.o.'s lot. ‖ FIN. To mature, to fall due (billet, traite); *à échoir*, accruing (intérêts).
échoppe [eʃɔp] f. Small workshop (de savetier). ‖ Booth, stall (dans la rue).
échoppe f. ARTS. Burin.
échotier [ekɔtje] m. Paragraphist; columnist; gossip-writer (ou) reporter.
échouage [eʃua:ʒ] m. NAUT. Stranding, grounding (accidentel); beaching (à sec); beaching-place (lieu).
échouer [eʃue] v. tr. (1). NAUT. To strand, to ground (accidentellement); to beach (à sec).
— v. intr. NAUT. To ground, to be stranded, to run aground. ‖ FIG. To strand (arriver) [à, in]; *échouer en prison*, to land in prison, to end up in prison. ‖ FIG. To fail (en général); to be ploughed, U. S. to flunk (à un examen); to miscarry (projet); *l'argument échoua*, the argument fell to the ground; *faire échouer*, to frustrate, to thwart.
— v. pr. **S'échouer**. NAUT. To run aground.
échu, e [eʃu] adj. FIN. Due, matured, payable, owing; *billet échu*, bill due; *intérêts échus*, outstanding interest. (V. ÉCHOIR.)
écimage [esima:ʒ] m. AGRIC. Topping, pollarding.
écimer [esime] v. tr. (1). To top, to pollard.
éclaboussement [eklabusmɑ̃] m. Splashing.
éclabousser v. tr. (1). To splash, to bespatter (de, with). ‖ FIG. To smirch (salir); *éclabousser les gens de son luxe*, to parade one's wealth.
éclaboussure [-sy:r] f. Splash, spattering. ‖ FIG. Blot, blemish, smirch (sur une réputation).
éclair [eklɛ:r] m. Flash of lightning; *des éclairs de chaleur*, heat lightning; *éclairs en nappe, en zigzag*, sheet-, forked-lightning; *il fait des éclairs*, lightning is flashing. ‖ Flash (des balles, des diamants, des yeux); *lancer des éclairs*, to flash. ‖ CULIN. Eclair. ‖ FIG. Flash (de génie); *un éclair dans sa vie morne*, a ray of sunshine in his dull existence. ‖ LOC. *Comme un éclair*, like greased lightning (ou) a bolt from the blue; *passer comme un éclair*, to flash by.
— adj. *Grève, vitesse éclair*, lightning strike, speed; *intervention éclair*, split-second intervention. ‖ MILIT. *Raid éclair*, hit-and-run raid.
éclairage [eklɛra:ʒ] m. Lighting; *éclairage par projecteurs*, floodlighting. ‖ Light (pour photo). ‖ MILIT. Scouting, reconnaissance. ‖ AUTOM. *Eclairage route*, full lights, U. S. high beams; *heure d'éclairage*, lighting-up time; *sans éclairage*, without lights.
éclairagiste [-raʒist] m. Electric lighting engineer.
éclairant, ante [-rɑ̃, ɑ̃:t] adj. Lighting (pouvoir). ‖ Illuminating.
éclaircie [eklɛrsi] f. Rift, break (dans le brouillard, les nuages); spell of sunny weather, fair period (après la pluie). ‖ Clearing, glade (dans une forêt). ‖ FIG. Bright period (dans la vie).
éclaircir [-si:r] v. tr. (2). To clear up (le brouil-

lard); to clear (le ciel, le teint, la voix); to clean (les carreaux). ‖ To thin (la chevelure, une forêt, les rangs); to thin out (une plate-bande). ‖ CULIN. To clarify (un liquide); to thin out (une sauce). ‖ FIG. To clear up (un doute); to clarify (une idée); to clear up, to elucidate (un mystère, une question); to make clear (la situation).
— v. pr. S'éclaircir, to clear up (ciel, temps); to get clearer (teint). ‖ To thin (cheveux); to thin out (rangs). ‖ FIG. To brighten up (front, visage); to grow clearer (idées); to clear up (mystère); to become clearer (situation).

éclaircissage [-sisa:ʒ] m. AGRIC. Thinning out. ‖ TECHN. Polishing; furbishing.

éclaircissement [-sismɑ̃] m. Clearing up (d'un mystère). ‖ Elucidation, explanation; *demander des éclaircissements sur,* to ask for enlightenment on.

éclairé, ée [eklɛre] adj. Light, lighted; *éclairé par la lune, les étoiles,* moonlit, starlit. ‖ FIG. Wise (conseil); enlightened (esprit, jugement); informed, experienced (personne); lit up (visage); *éclairé par un commentaire marginal,* side-lighted (ou) U. S. high-lighted by a commentary.

éclairement [-rmɑ̃] m. PHYS. Illumination.

éclairer [-re] v. tr. (1). To light (un lieu) [v. ILLUMINER]; *éclairer au néon,* to light by neon. ‖ To light the way for (qqn); *éclairer qqn qui descend l'escalier,* to light s.o. down the stairs. ‖ MILIT. To reconnoitre (la route). ‖ FIG. To illuminate, to throw a light on (une affaire, une question); to enlighten (l'esprit, qqn); to inform, to instruct (qqn); to light up, to brighten (le visage).
— v. intr. To give light; *éclairer peu,* to give a poor light. ‖ To shine (briller); to gleam, to glimmer (luire). ‖ MILIT. To scout, to reconnoitre.
— v. impers. To lighten (faire des éclairs)..
— v. pr. S'éclairer, to be lit up (pièce); *s'éclairer au gaz,* to have gas-lighting (personne, pièce); *s'éclairer sur la rue,* to be lighted from the street (pièce). ‖ FIG. To be enlightened (esprit); to become informed, to obtain enlightenment (ou) elucidation (personne); to clear up (question); to be lit up (visage).

éclaireur [-rœ:r] m. Boy Scout. ‖ MILIT. Scout. ‖ NAUT. Look-out ship. ‖ AVIAT. Blimp, observation balloon. ‖ AUTOM. *Éclaireur de tablier,* dashboard light.

éclaireuse [-ø:z] f. Girl Guide; U. S. Girl Scout.

éclampsie [eklɑ̃psi] f. MÉD. Eclampsia.

éclat [ekla] m. Chip, sliver, splinter (de bois); bort (de diamant); splinter (de pierre); chip (de verre); *voler en éclats,* to fly into pieces. ‖ Blaze-up (de colère); burst (de rire, de voix); peal (du tonnerre); blare (des trompettes); *des éclats de voix,* raised voices; *faire rire la tablée aux éclats,* to set the table roaring with laughter; *grand éclat de rire,* peal of laughter; *partir d'un furieux éclat de rire,* to burst into a roar of laughter; *rire aux éclats,* to roar with laughter. ‖ Brightness (de l'acier, d'une lampe, du soleil); glint (de l'aurore); glow (de la braise); vividness (des couleurs); sparkle (des étoiles); blaze (du jour, de la rampe); gleam (d'une lame); flash (de la lumière, des projecteurs); shimmer (de la lune, des pierreries); glare (des phares fixes); flare (d'un phare tournant); lustre, gloss (du satin, du vernis); glimmer (du ver luisant). ‖ Noise (bruit); scandal (esclandre); *faire un éclat,* to create a stir; *sans éclat,* without any scandal. ‖ Radiance (de la beauté); brightness (du regard); glint (du regard irrité); brilliancy, brightness (du teint); *dans tout son éclat,* in all its radiance (beauté). ‖ MILIT. *Éclat d'obus,* shell-splinter. ‖ MÉD. Splinter (d'os). ‖ FIG. Splendour, glamour, brilliancy (de la gloire); brightness (de l'intelligence); display, show, parade (des richesses

vaniteuses); *donner de l'éclat à,* to throw a glamour over, to give glamour to; *faux éclat,* cheapness, tawdriness, tinsel (du style).

éclatant, ante [-tɑ̃, ɑ̃:t] adj. Loud (bruit, rire, voix); ringing (son). ‖ Dazzling (blancheur); glowing (braise); vivid (couleur); blazing (feu, soleil); bright (lumière); glittering, shimmering (pierreries); glossy (satin, vernis); colourful (spectacle, paysage). ‖ Radiant (beauté); florid, dazzling (teint); *éclatant de santé,* bursting with health; *des yeux éclatants de convoitise,* gloating eyes. ‖ FIG. Striking (exemple); blazing, glaring (gaffe, sottise); obvious (preuve); signal (service, succès); brilliant (succès); terrible (vengeance).

éclatement [eklatmɑ̃] m. Burst; explosion. ‖ Splitting (du bois); shivering (du verre). ‖ MÉD. Rupture (d'une veine). ‖ MILIT. Burst; bursting (d'un obus). ‖ AUTOM. Bursting, burst, U. S. blowout (d'un pneu).

éclater [-te] v. intr. (1). To split, to splinter (bois); to burst, to explode (chaudière); to blow up (mine); to crack, to fly into pieces (verre); *faire éclater,* to splinter (le bois); to explode (une mine). ‖ To burst forth (bruit); to blare out (fanfare, trompettes); to crash (tonnerre). ‖ To shine, to glitter (lumière). ‖ To be lit, to burst out (incendie); to break out (orage). ‖ To break (ou) burst out (colère); to blaze out (joie, révolte); to come out (nouvelle, vérité); to flare up (personne irritée); to become obvious (preuve); *éclater en applaudissements,* to burst into applause; *éclater de rire,* to burst out laughing; *éclater en protestations contre,* to rise up in arms against; *éclater en sanglots,* to burst out crying (ou) sobbing; *faire éclater,* to raise (des difficultés); to rouse (l'indignation); to stir up (la révolte); *faire éclater de rire,* to set in a roar; *la surprise éclatait dans ses yeux,* his eyes were full of astonishment; *la vérité éclata à mes yeux,* the truth burst upon me. ‖ AUTOM. To burst, U. S. to blow out (pneu); *faire éclater un pneu,* to burst a tyre, U. S. to blow out a tire. ‖ MÉD. To burst (veine). ‖ MILIT. To burst, to explode (arme, obus); to go off (coup de fusil); to break out (guerre); *faire éclater la guerre,* to bring about war.
— v. tr. AGRIC. To divide (des pousses).

éclateur [-tœ:r] m. ELECTR. Spark-gap.

éclectique [eklɛktik] adj., s. Eclectic.

éclectisme [-tism] m. Eclecticism.

éclimètre [eklimɛtr] m. Eclimeter; clinometer.

éclipse [eklips] f. ASTRON. Eclipse. ‖ TECHN. Occultation (d'un phare). ‖ NAUT. *Feu à éclipses,* intermittent light. ‖ MILIT. *Cible à éclipses,* disappearing (ou) bobbing target. ‖ FIG. Eclipse; disappearance.

éclipser [-se] v. tr. (1). ASTRON. To eclipse. ‖ FIG. To eclipse, to outshine, to overshadow, to cast into the shade.
— v. pr. S'éclipser, to disappear. ‖ FAM. To slip away, to sneak off.

écliptique [-tik] m. ASTRON. Ecliptic; *obliquité de l'écliptique,* obliquity of the ecliptic.

éclisse [eklis] f. Wedge (coin). ‖ MUS. Rib (de violon). ‖ CULIN. Cheese-tray. ‖ MÉD. Splint. ‖ CH. DE F. Splice bar; fish plate.

éclisser [-se] v. tr. (1). MUS. To rib. ‖ MÉD. To splint. ‖ CH. DE F. To fish.

éclopé, ée [eklɔpe] adj. Lame, limping (v. BOITEUX); footsore.
— s. Lame person; cripple. ‖ MILIT. Crippled (ou) temporarily disabled soldier.

écloper v. tr. (1). To cripple.

éclore [eklɔ:r] v. intr. (43). To hatch (œuf, oiseau); *faire éclore,* to hatch. ‖ To burst (bourgeon); to bloom (fleur). ‖ FIG. To be born; to germinate; to dawn; *faire éclore,* to call up (une idée); to rouse, to kindle (une passion); to realize

(un projet); to bring about, to stir up (la révolte).
éclos [eklo]. V. ÉCLORE.
éclosion [eklozjɔ̃] f. Hatching (d'un œuf, d'un oiseau). ‖ Opening, blossoming (d'une fleur). ‖ FIG. Birth, dawn.
éclusage [eklyza:ʒ] m. Lockage.
écluse [ekly:z] f. Lock; lock-gate; sluice-gate; tide-gate; *écluse de moulin,* mill-dam. ‖ ECCLÉS. FIG. Flood-gate. ‖ FAM. *Lâcher les écluses,* to give vent to one's anger (se mettre en colère); to turn on the water-works (pleurer).
éclusée [eklyze] f. Lockage-water.
écluser v. tr., intr. (1). To lock.
éclusier, ère [-zje, ɛ:r] s. Lock-keeper.
écœurant, ante [ekœrɑ̃, ɑ̃:t] adj. Sickening. (V. NAUSÉEUX.) ‖ FIG. Loathsome, disgusting.
écœurement [-rmɑ̃] m. Nausea, disgust. ‖ FIG. Discouragement, disgust.
écœurer [ekœre] v. tr. (1). To nauseate, to sicken. ‖ FIG. To disgust; to dishearten.
écoinçon [ekwɛ̃sɔ̃] m. ARCHIT. Corner-stone.
école [ekɔl] f. School (en général). ‖ College, academy. ‖ MILIT. Drill, training, instruction; *école de guerre,* staff college, U. S. war college, staff school; *école militaire,* military academy; *école de pointage,* aiming drill; *école des tambours,* drum practice. ‖ SPORTS. *Haute école,* haute école, high-school riding, dressage. ‖ ARTS. School (d'un artiste, d'un écrivain). ‖ FIG. School (de l'adversité); *à l'école de,* schooled in; *à bonne école,* schooled, well trained; *faire école,* to gain adherents, to be imitated, to set a fashion; *la vieille école,* the old school.
écolier, ère [-lje, ɛ:r] adj. Schoolboy, schoolgirl (dispositions); foolscap (papier).
— m. Schoolboy. ‖ FAM. *Le chemin des écoliers,* the longest way round, U. S. the overland route.
écolière [-ljɛ:r] f. Schoolgirl.
écologie [ekɔlɔʒi] f. Ecology.
écologique [-ʒik] adj. Ecological.
écologiste [-ʒist] s. Ecologist.
éconduire [ekɔ̃dɥi:r] v. tr. (85). To reject, to send packing (un prétendant); to show out (un visiteur). [V. CONGÉDIER.]
économat [ekɔnɔma] m. Stewardship, bursarship (fonction). ‖ Bursar's (ou) steward's office (bureau). ‖ Truck-shop (magasin), U. S. vegetable market; tuck-shop (dans un pensionnat).
économe [-nɔm] adj. Economical, sparing, saving, thrifty. ‖ Sparing, chary (d'éloges).
— s. Bursar; steward; housekeeper.
économétrie [ekɔnɔmetri] f. Econometrics.
économétrique [-trik] adj. Econometric, econometrical.
économie [ekɔnɔmi] f. Economy (gestion); *économie domestique,* housekeeping. ‖ Economy, saving, sparing, sparingness, thrift, thriftiness (v. PARCIMONIE); *faire l'économie de,* to save; *par économie,* for economy's sake. ‖ Pl. Savings, sparings (v. ÉPARGNE); *économies ramassées sou à sou,* scrapings; *faire des économies de,* to economize on. ‖ JUR. *Economie politique,* economics. ‖ FIG. Saving; *économie de main-d'œuvre,* laboursaving.
économique [-mik] adj. Economic; *science économique,* economics. ‖ Economical (appareil, méthode); inexpensive, cheap (objet); *économique en gaz,* gas-saving. ‖ AUTOM. Economical (vitesse).
— f. Economics.
économiquement [-mikmɑ̃] adv. Economically, frugally, sparingly, thriftily, inexpensively.
économiser [-mise] v. tr. (1). To save, to put by (de l'argent) [*sur, on*]. ‖ FIG. To husband (ses forces); to be sparing of (ses paroles); to save (du temps).
— v. intr. To economize, to save up.

économiseur [-mizœ:r] m. Economizer, economizing device; *économiseur de gaz,* gas-saver.
économiste [-mist] m. Economist.
écoope [ekɔp] f. NAUT. Scoop, bailer.
écoper [-pe] v. tr. (1). NAUT. To bail out.
— v. intr. FAM. To cop it, to catch it; *écoper de,* to cop (qqch.).
écoperche [-pɛrʃ] f. ARCHIT. Upright pole; derrick.
écorçage [ekɔrsa:ʒ] m. Barking (d'un arbre); peeling (d'une orange).
écorce [ekɔrs] f. Bark (d'arbre); rind (d'une grenade); peel (d'une orange). ‖ GÉOGR. *Ecorce terrestre,* earth's crust. ‖ FIG. Exterior, aspect, appearance; *une rude écorce,* a rough diamond.
écorcer [-se] v. tr. (1). To bark (un arbre); to peel (une orange).
écorché [ekɔrʃe] m. ARTS. Ecorché.
écorcher v. tr. (1). To skin (un lapin); to flay (qqn). ‖ To scratch (par égratignure); to graze (par éraflure); to excoriate (par excoriation); to gall, to chafe (par frottement). ‖ FAM. To fleece, to strip (un client); to murder (une langue); to mispronounce (un mot); to rasp, to grate upon (les oreilles).
— v. pr. **S'écorcher,** to get scratched, to be chafed.
écorcheur, euse [-ʃœ:r, ø:z] s. Flayer, skinner. ‖ FAM. Fleecer.
écorchure [-ʃy:r] f. Scratch, graze. ‖ MÉD. Abrasion; excoriation; gall.
écorner [ekɔrne] v. tr. (1). To break the horns of, to poll (un animal). ‖ To chip (une assiette); to dog's-ear (un livre); to break a corner of (une table). ‖ FIG. To curtail (diminuer); to make a hole in (entamer).
écornifler [ekɔrnifle] v. tr. (1). To cadge, to scrounge; *écornifler un dîner à qqn,* to sponge on s.o. for a dinner, to scrounge a dinner out of s.o.; U.S. to bum a dinner off s.o.
écornifleur [-flœ:r] s. Cadger, sponger.
écossais, aise [ekɔse, ɛ:z] adj. GÉOGR. Scots, Scottish, Scotch. ‖ COMM. Tartan, check (tissu).
— m. Scotsman, Scot. ‖ Scots (langue). ‖ COMM. Tartan, plaid (tissu).
Écossaise [ekɔsɛ:z] f. Scotswoman.
Écosse [ekɔs] f. GÉOGR. Scotland; *la Nouvelle-Ecosse,* Nova Scotia.
écosser [-se] v. tr. (1). To shell, to hull.
écosystème [ekosistɛm] m. Ecosystem.
écot [eko] m. Share (v. QUOTE-PART); *payer son écot,* to pay one's share. ‖ Bill, score, U. S. check (au restaurant).
écoulé, ée [ekule] adj. Elapsed, past, gone. ‖ COMM. Of last month, ultimo, ult.
écoulement [-lmɑ̃] m. Flow, outflow; flowing (de l'eau). ‖ TECHN. *Ecoulement d'eau,* drainage; *tuyau d'écoulement,* drain, drain-pipe. ‖ MÉD. Discharge (de pus); gleet (de l'urètre); flux, issue, flow (de sang). ‖ ELECTR. Flow. ‖ COMM. Disposal, sale; *article d'écoulement facile,* quick-selling line, quick seller. ‖ FIG. Dispersal (d'une foule).
écouler [-le] v. tr. (1). To put into circulation, to pass (de la fausse monnaie); *faire écouler,* to move on (la foule); to pass (de faux billets). ‖ COMM. To dispose of (des marchandises).
— v. pr. **S'écouler,** to flow out (ou) away (liquide); to pour out (à flots); to leak out (par une fuite); to ooze out (en suintant); *faire écouler,* to drain off; *laisser écouler,* to allow to run out. ‖ COMM. To be disposed of, to sell (marchandises); to run low (provisions). ‖ FIG. To melt away (argent). ‖ FIG. To elapse, to pass (temps); to glide on (imperceptiblement); to wear on (péniblement); to slip away, to run on, to fly by (vite); *laisser s'écouler du temps,* to

let time slip by; *sa vie s'écoule heureuse*, he lives a happy life. ‖ Fig. To flow out, to pour out, to stream out (foule).

écoumène [ekumɛn] m. Géogr. Ecumene.

écourter [ekurte] v. tr. (1). To shorten, to curtail (en général); to clip (les oreilles); to dock, to bob (la queue). ‖ Fig. To curtail.

écoute [ekut] f. Naut. Sheet.

écoute f. Radio. Listening, listening-in; *être à l'écoute de*, to be listening to (ou) tuned in to; *heure de grande écoute*, peak listening hour (à la radio), peak viewing hour (à la télévision); *taux d'écoute*, rating. ‖ Milit. Listening; *poste d'écoute*, listening-post. ‖ Techn. *Ecoutes téléphoniques*, phone tapping; *brancher sur une table d'écoute*, to tap. ‖ Loc. *Etre aux écoutes*, to be eavesdropping (d'une conversation); to keep one's ears pricked, to have one's ears to the ground (de l'actualité). ‖ Pl. Zool. Ears (d'un sanglier).

écouter [-te] v. tr. (1). To listen to; *écouter jusqu'au bout*, to hear out; *écouter chanter qqn*, to listen to s. o. singing; *savoir écouter*, to be a good listener; *se faire écouter*, to obtain a hearing. ‖ To listen to, to obey (obéir à). ‖ To heed, to pay attention to (faire attention à); *ne l'écoutez pas!*, take no notice of what he says. ‖ Radio. To listen in to (la radio).
— v. intr. To listen; *écouter aux portes*, to eavesdrop. ‖ Radio. To listen in.
— v. pr. **S'écouter**, to coddle (ou) to indulge oneself. ‖ *S'écouter parler*, to talk with self-complacency; *aimer à s'écouter parler*, to love the sound of one's own voice.

écouteur [-tœ:r] m. Receiver, ear-piece (de téléphone); headphones, head-piece (de T. S. F.).
— s. Listener (personne); *écouteur aux portes*, eaves-dropper.

écoutille [ekuti:j] f. Naut. Hatchway.

écoutillon [-tijõ] m. Naut. Scuttle.

écouvillon [ekuvijõ] m. Mop (de boulanger); bottle-brush (à bouteilles). ‖ Milit. Sponge, cleaning brush.

écouvillonner [-jɔne] v. tr. To mop out; to brush out. ‖ Milit. To sponge out.

écrabouillage [ekrabuja:ʒ] m. Crushing.

écrabouiller [-je] v. tr. (1). Fam. To crush, to squash. (V. écraser.)

écran [ekrã] m. Screen; *écran de foyer*, fire-screen. ‖ Filter (en photo). ‖ Ciném. Screen; *porter à l'écran*, to put on the screen, to film. ‖ Milit. *Ecran de protection aérienne*, air umbrella. ‖ Phys. Ecran thermique, biological shield.

écrasant, ante [ekrazã, ã:t] adj. Crushing (poids). ‖ Stifling (chaleur); crushing (défaite, mépris); overwhelming (preuve, supériorité).

écrasement [-zmã] m. Crushing (en général); grinding (à la meule); pounding (au pilon). ‖ Autom. Running over. ‖ Aviat. Crash. ‖ Milit. Crushing. ‖ Fig. Oppression (d'un peuple); prostration, collapse (d'une personne).

écraser [-ze] v. tr. (1). To crush (en général); to flatten out (en aplatissant); to grind (à la meule); to mash (au moulin à légumes); to pound (au pilon); to crush, to squash (au pressoir); to squeeze (en serrant); to trample (sous les pieds); *écraser une mouche*, to swat a fly. ‖ Autom. To run over; *se faire écraser*, to get run over. ‖ Milit. To crush, to defeat. ‖ Sports. To kill. ‖ Fig. To oppress, to crush (la population); to overwhelm (d'impôts, de travail); to crush (par le mépris); to outshine (par le mérite); to dwarf (par la taille); *écrasé de douleur*, crushed with grief.
— v. intr. Fam. *En écraser*, to sleep like a log.
— v. pr. **S'écraser**, to get crushed; to be flattened out (ou) ground (ou) mashed (ou) pounded

(ou) squashed (ou) squeezed (ou) trampled. ‖ Autom. To crash (*contre*, into). ‖ Fig. To be crushed, to crush (foule, personnes); *on s'écrasait pour entrer*, there was a great crush to get in.

écraseur, euse [-zœ:r, ø:z] s. Crusher. ‖ Autom. Road-hog.

écrémage [ekrema:ʒ] m. Creaming, skimming.

écrémer [-me] v. tr. (5). To cream, to skim (le lait); *non écrémé*, full-cream, whole (lait). ‖ Techn. To skim, to dross. ‖ Fig. To cream.

écrémeuse [-mø:z] f. Cream-separator, creamer.

écrémoir [-mwa:r] m. Culin. Skimmer.

écrêter [ekrɛte] v. tr. (1). To cut off the comb of (un coq). ‖ Archit. To cut down, to lower the crest of. ‖ Agric. To cut off the tops of, to top.

écrevisse [ekrəvis] f. Zool. Crayfish, U. S. crawfish. ‖ Tech. Lever-tongs.

écrier (s') [sekrje] v. pr. (1). To cry out, to exclaim.

écrin [ekrɛ̃] m. Jewel-case (ou) -casket (ou) -box.

écrire [ekri:r] v. tr. (44). To write (en général); to pencil (au crayon); to pen (à l'encre); to type-write, to type (à la machine). ‖ To write down, to set down in black and white. (V. inscrire, noter.) ‖ To spell (orthographier) [un mot]. ‖ To write (composer). ‖ Loc. *C'était écrit*, it was written (ou) fated; *c'est écrit sur sa figure*, it is written (ou) stamped all over his face.
— v. intr. To write; *il écrit comme un chat*, he writes a dreadful scrawl.
— v. pr. **S'écrire**, to be written. ‖ To be spelt (ou) U. S. spelled (s'orthographier).
— v. récipr. **S'écrire**, to write to each other.

écrit, ite [ekri, it] adj. Written. ‖ Jur. *Droit écrit*, statute-law.
— m. Writing; *par écrit*, in writing. ‖ Written examination (examen). ‖ Pl. Writings, works.

écriteau [-to] m. Notice-board, U. S. bulletin-board. (V. pancarte.)

écritoire [-twa:r] f. Writing-desk.

écriture [-ty:r] f. Writing; *avoir une belle écriture*, to write a good hand; *écriture à la main*, handwriting; *écriture de chat*, scrawl. ‖ Script, writing (ensemble de signes). ‖ Writing, penmanship (art d'écrire). ‖ Ecclés. Scriptures; Holy Writ (ou) Scripture. ‖ Comm. Accounts, entries, books, records; *commis aux écritures*, book-keeper; *passer une écriture*, to post an item; *tenir les écritures*, to keep the accounts, to do the book-keeping.

écrivailler [-vɑje] v. intr. (1). To scribble.

écrivailleur, euse [-vɑjœ:r, ø:z] s., **écrivaillon** [-vɑjõ] m. Fam. Scribbler, hack.

écrivain [-vɛ̃] m. Writer, author (v. auteur); *écrivain à gages*, hack-writer; *écrivain public*, letter-writer; *femme écrivain*, woman writer, authoress.

écrivais [-vɛ]. V. écrire (44).

écrivasser [-vase] v. intr. To scribble.

écrivassier, ère [-vasje, ɛ:r] s. Scribbler.

écrou [ekru] m. Techn. Nut. ‖ Ecrou-raccord, m. Union-nut.

écrou m. Jur. Entry in prison register; *levée d'écrou*, discharge; *ordre d'écrou*, warrant of commitment; *registre d'écrou*, prison register.

écrouelles [ekruɛl] f. pl. Méd. Scrofula, king's evil. (V. scrofule.)

écrouelleux, euse [ekru-lø, ø:z] adj. Méd. Scrofulous.

écrouer [ekrue] v. tr. Jur. To lock up.

écrouir [ekrui:r] v. tr. (2). Techn. To cold-hammer.

écroulé [ekrule] adj. Tumble-down (mur).

écroulement [-lmã] m. Collapse, tumbling down, giving way (d'un bâtiment); fall (d'un rocher). ‖ Fin. Slump (des cours). ‖ Fig. Collapse (d'un empire); breakdown (d'une entreprise); downfall, ruin (des espérances); crumbling (de la fortune).

écrouler (s') [sekrule] v. pr. To collapse, to tumble down, to give way, to fall down (bâtiment); to fall (rocher); to crumble (terre) [v. CROULER]. ‖ FIN. To slump (cours). ‖ FIG. To collapse (empire, personne); to break down (entreprise); to be ruined (espérances); to crumble away (fortune, influence); *s'écrouler sur le divan*, to slump down (ou) to sink down on to the sofa.

écru, ue [ekry] adj. Ecru (couleur); raw (soie); unbleached, natural-coloured (toile); *toile écrue*, holland.

ectoplasme [ɛktɔplasm] m. MÉD. Ectoplasm. ‖ Ectoplasm (en parapsychologie).

écu [eky] m. Shield (bouclier). ‖ BLAS. Shield, escutcheon. ‖ ZOOL. Scutum. ‖ FIN. Crown. ‖ Pl. Plenty of money.

écubier [ekybje] m. NAUT. Hawse-hole, hawse-pipe.

écueil [ekœ:j] m. Reef, shelf, rock. ‖ FIG. Stumbling-block (achoppement); danger, risk (danger).

écuelle [ekɥɛl] f. Bowl, porringer (contenant); bowlful (contenu). ‖ NAUT. Saucer. ‖ TECHN. Pan.

écuellée [-le] f. Bowlful.

éculé, ée [ekyle] adj. Down-at-heel (soulier).

éculer v. tr. (1). *Eculer ses souliers*, to wear one's shoes down at the heel.
— v. pr. **S'éculer**, to wear down at heel (souliers).

écumage [ekyma:ʒ] m. Scumming, skimming.

écumant, ante [-mɑ̃, ɑ̃:t] adj. Foaming (bière, mer); frothing, frothy (boisson, bouche); in a foam (ou) lather (cheval). ‖ FIG. Foaming (de, with).

écume [eky:m] f. Froth (de la bière, du bouillon); foam, froth (à la bouche, du cheval en sueur, de la mer); scum (des confitures, du lait bouillant); dross, scum (d'un métal en fusion). ‖ FIG. Scum (de la société). ‖ LOC. *Pipe en écume de mer*, meerschaum pipe.

écumer [ekyme] v. intr. (1). To froth (bière, bouillon); to foam, to froth (bouche); to be in a foam (cheval); to scum (confitures, lait bouillant, métal en fusion); to foam (mer). ‖ FIG. To foam with rage.
— v. tr. To scum, to skim (le bouillon, les confitures). ‖ To dross (le métal en fusion). ‖ To scour (les mers). ‖ FIG. To pick up.

écumeur [-mœ:r] m. FIG. *Écumeur de mer*, sea-wolf. ‖ FAM. *Écumeur de marmite*, sponger.

écumeux, euse [-mø, ø:z] adj. Frothy; foamy.

écumoire [-mwa:r] f. Skimmer.

écureuil [ekyrœ:j] m. ZOOL. Squirrel.

écurie [ekyri] f. Stable (lieu); stabling (logement, place); *écurie de course*, racing stable; *mettre à l'écurie*, to stable. ‖ FIG. Pigsty (lieu sale). ‖ FAM. *Sentir l'écurie*, to be in a hurry to get home.

écusson [ekysɔ̃] m. BLAS. Escutcheon; *écusson mortuaire*, hatchment. ‖ TECHN. Scutcheon, sheave (de serrure). ‖ ZOOL. Scutum. ‖ AGRIC. Bud (de greffe). ‖ NAUT. Scutcheon. ‖ MILIT. Badge; tab.

écussonnage [-sɔna:ʒ] m. AGRIC. Budding.

écussonner [-sɔne] v. tr. (1). AGRIC. To bud.

écussonneur, euse [-sɔnœ:r, ø:z] s. AGRIC. Grafter.

écussonnoir [-sɔnwa:r] m. AGRIC. Budding-knife.

écuyer [ekɥije] m. † Esquire (gentilhomme, titre); squire, armour-bearer (serviteur); *écuyer tranchant*, carver. ‖ † Equerry; *grand écuyer*, Master of the Horse. ‖ Rider, horseman (cavalier); riding-master (professeur); *écuyer de cirque*, equestrian.

écuyère [-jɛ:r] f. Horsewoman; *bottes à l'écuyère*, riding-boots; *écuyère de cirque*, equestrienne.

eczéma [ɛgzema] m. MÉD. Eczema.

eczémateux, euse [-tø, ø:z] adj. MÉD. Eczematous.
— m. MÉD. Eczematous patient.

édaphique [edafik] adj. Edaphic.

edelweiss [edɛlwais] m. BOT. Edelweiss.

Éden [edɛn] m. Eden.

édénique [edenik] adj. Edenic.

édenté, ée [edɑ̃te] adj. Broken-toothed (aux dents manquantes); gap-toothed (brèche-dent); toothless (sans dents). ‖ ZOOL. Edentate.
— m. pl. ZOOL. Edentata.

édenter v. tr. (1). To break the teeth of (un peigne). ‖ To remove the teeth of (qqn); *il l'a édenté*, he knocked his teeth out.

E. D. F. [edeɛf] f. Abrév. de *Electricité de France*, French electricity board.

édicter [edikte] v. tr. (1). To decree, to enact, to promulgate (une loi); to inflict (une peine).

édicule [edikyl] m. Kiosk. ‖ FAM. Public convenience; street urinal.

édifiant, ante [edifjɑ̃, ɑ̃:t] adj. Edifying. ‖ Convincing (convaincant); improving (profitable).

édificateur [edifikatœ:r] m. ARCHIT. Builder.

édification [-sjɔ̃] f. ARCHIT. Building. ‖ FIG. Edification. ‖ FAM. Information, enlightenment.

édifice [edifis] m. ARCHIT. Building, edifice (V. BÂTIMENT.) ‖ FIG. Fabric, structure.

édifier [-fje] v. tr. (1). ARCHIT. To build, to erect, to set up. ‖ FIG. To edify (moralement). ‖ FIG. To build up (une fortune, une réputation); to build (un monde). ‖ FAM. To inform, to enlighten; *édifié sur le fait que*, satisfied that.

édile [edil] m. † Aedile. ‖ FAM. Town-councillor; local official.

Édimbourg [edɛ̃bu:r] m. GÉOGR. Edinburgh.

édit [edi] m. Edict, decree.

éditer [-te] v. tr. (1). To publish (publier); *se faire éditer chez*, to have one's books published by. ‖ To edit (un manuscrit, un texte).

éditeur, trice [-tœ:r, tris] s. Publisher. ‖ Editor (d'un texte critique).

édition [-sjɔ̃] f. Issue (d'un journal). ‖ Edition (publication, tirage); *atteindre sa vingtième édition*, to run into twenty editions. ‖ Publishing (action); publishing trade (commerce); *maison d'édition*, publishing house (ou) firm.

éditorial [-tɔrjal] adj. Editorial.
— m. Editorial, leader.

éditorialiste [-tɔrjalist] m. Leader-writer; U. S. editorial writer.

édredon [edrədɔ̃] m. Eiderdown, counterpane, U. S. comforter, puff (couvre-pied); *édredon piqué*, eiderdown quilt. ‖ Eiderdown (duvet).

éducabilité [edykabilite] f. Educability.

éducable [-kabl] adj. Educable.

éducateur, trice [-katœ:r, -tris] adj. Educative; educational.
— s. Educator.

éducatif, ive [-katif, i:v] adj. Educative (méthode); educational (ouvrage).

éducation [-kasjɔ̃] f. Training (des animaux); bringing up, upbringing (des enfants); training (des sens); *éducation physique*, physical training (ou) culture (ou) U. S. education; *établissement d'éducation*, school; *faire l'éducation de*, to educate. ‖ Breeding; *la bonne éducation*, good breeding, good manners; *sans éducation*, ill-bred. ‖ Education (courtoisie et instruction).

édulcoration [edylkɔrasjɔ̃] f. Edulcoration; sweetening. ‖ FIG. Extenuation, palliation.

édulcorer [-re] v. tr. (1). To edulcorate, to sweeten. ‖ FIG. To extenuate, to gloss over.

éduquer [edyke] v. tr. (1). To oring up, to educate (un enfant). ‖ To train (une faculté, un sens).

effaçable [ɛfasabl] adj. Erasable, removable (tache); effaceable, eradicable (impression, souvenir).

effaçage [ɛfasa:ʒ] m. Rubbing out; erasing; striking out.

effacé, ée [-se] adj. Fig. Retiring (genre); unobtrusive (personne, rôle); retired, secluded (vie).

effacement [-smɑ̃] m. Rubbing out, erasing (d'une tache); obliteration (d'un souvenir). ‖ *Tête d'effacement,* erasing head (d'un magnétophone). ‖ Sideways position (du corps); throwing-back (des épaules). ‖ Fig. Unobtrusiveness, self-effacement.

effacer [-se] v. tr. (6). To efface (en général); to blot out (à l'encre); to rub out, to erase (à la gomme); to erase (au grattoir); to sponge out (avec une éponge); to strike out (d'un trait); to wipe out (en essuyant); to wash out (en lavant); to obliterate (par oblitération); to wear away (ou) off (par le temps). ‖ To throw back (les épaules). ‖ Fig. To blot out, to wipe out (une impression) [*de,* of]; to smooth out (des rides). — v. pr. **S'effacer,** to become obliterated, to rub off; to fade away (en pâlissant); to wear away (en vieillissant). ‖ To draw back (ou) aside, to get out of the way (se détourner); *s'effacer devant,* to make way for (pour laisser passer). ‖ Sports. To stand sideways (à l'escrime). ‖ Fig. To efface oneself, to keep out of the way, to remain in the background (se tenir à l'écart); *s'effacer devant,* to yield precedence to (par déférence). ‖ Fig. To fade away, to die out, to grow dim (impression).

effarant, ante [ɛfarɑ̃, ɑ̃:t] adj. Bewildering.

effaré, ée [-re] adj. Aghast (terrifié). ‖ Alarmed, startled, shaken (ému).

effarement [-rmɑ̃] m. Bewilderment, fluster.

effarer [-re] v. tr. (1). To scare, to bewilder, to fluster, to flurry. — v. pr. **S'effarer,** to get bewildered (ou) flustered; to become scared (de, at).

effaroucher [ɛfaruʃe] v. tr. (1). To scare away. ‖ Fig. To alarm; to shock. — v. pr. **S'effaroucher,** to be scared (ou) frightened (de, at) [par crainte]; to be shocked, to blush (de, at) [par pudeur]; to shy (de, at) [par timidité].

effectif, ive [ɛfɛktif, i:v] adj. Effective; positive. ‖ Fin. Active (circulation); real (valeur). — m. Effective, manpower (potentiel humain); *effectif scolaire,* size of classes. ‖ Naut. Complement. ‖ Milit. Strength; *effectif de base,* basic establishment. ‖ Fig. Credit (actif).

effectivement [-vmɑ̃] adv. Effectively (efficacement); actually, really (réellement). ‖ Indeed; quite true, right enough (dans une réponse).

effectuer [ɛfɛktɥe] v. tr. (1). To work out (un calcul); to carry out (une expérience); to execute (une opération); to effect (un paiement); to bring about (une réconciliation); to hold (une vente publique); to accomplish (un voyage). — v. pr. **S'effectuer,** to be worked out (calcul); to be carried out (expérience); to be realized (projet); to be performed (trajet).

effémination [ɛfeminasjɔ̃] f. Effeminacy.

efféminé, ée [-ne] adj. Effeminate, womanish; sissy.

efféminer [-ne] v. tr. (1). To render effeminate, to unman. — v. pr. **S'efféminer,** to become effeminate.

efférent, ente [ɛferɑ̃, ɑ̃:t] adj. Méd. Efferent.

effervescence [ɛfɛrvɛsɑ̃:s] f. Effervescence; *être en effervescence,* to effervesce. ‖ Fig. Effervescence, over-excitement, turmoil.

effervescent, ente [-sɑ̃, ɑ̃:t] adj. Effervescent. ‖ Fig. Over-excited, in a turmoil.

effet [ɛfɛ] m. Effect, result, consequence; *à cet effet,* for that purpose, to that end (ou) effect; *avoir pour effet de,* to result (ou) to come (ou) to lead to. ‖ Action, effect; *faire de l'effet,* to be effective; *ne faire aucun effet,* to be ineffective (ou) of no avail; *produire un effet,* to have an effect; *sans effet,* ineffective. ‖ Operation, execution; *prendre effet,* to take effect, to become operative. ‖ Impression (émotion); *faire de l'effet,* to affect, to move, to give a shock; to make an impression; *faire un effet sur,* to impress, to strike, to make an impression on; *si c'est tout l'effet que ça te fait!,* if that's the way you feel about it! ‖ Impression, sensation; *faire l'effet de,* to seem like, to look like (ou) as if, to give the idea of; *faire bon effet,* to look (ou) to sound well; *ça me fait l'effet d'être vrai,* it sounds true to me. ‖ Show, parade, display; *à effet,* spot (éclairage); showy (objet); affected (personne); *couper ses effets à qqn,* to steal s.o.'s thunder; *faire de l'effet,* to make a show, to cut a dash; *faire beaucoup d'effet,* to make a splendid appearance; *faire des effets,* to flaunt oneself, to parade; *faire des effets de torse,* to throw out one's chest; *phrases à effet,* claptrap. ‖ Pl. Effects, belongings (biens); things, clothes (vêtements); *effets mobiliers,* movables. ‖ Milit. Pl. Kit. ‖ Techn. Efficiency; *à double, à simple effet,* double-, simple-effect. ‖ Milit. Effect, power. ‖ Théâtr. Gag. ‖ Electr., Méd., Arts. Effect. ‖ Sports. Break, twist (de balle); screw (de bille); spin (au billard). ‖ Fin. *Effets au porteur,* bearer stock; *effets publics,* public bonds. ‖ Comm. Bill; *effets à payer, à recevoir,* bills payable, receivable; *effet à vue,* draft at sight, U. S. sight draft. ‖ Loc. **En effet,** indeed, as a matter of fact, effectively (effectivement); true, quite so, sure enough (dans une réponse); *vous n'avez pas l'air de me croire. — En effet,* you don't seem to believe me. — I don't.

effeuillage [ɛfœja:ʒ] m. Thinning out of leaves; plucking off of petals. ‖ Théâtr. Fam. Strip-tease.

effeuillaison [-jɛzɔ̃] f. Fall of the leaves.

effeuiller [-je] v. tr. (1). To thin out the leaves of (un arbre); to pluck off the petals of (une fleur). — v. pr. **S'effeuiller,** to shed its leaves (arbre); to shed its petals (fleur).

effeuilleuse [-jø:z] f. Théâtr. Strip-teaser.

efficace [ɛfikas] adj. Efficacious, effective.

efficacement [-smɑ̃] adv. Efficaciously, effectively.

efficacité [-site] f. Efficaciousness, efficacy, effectiveness.

efficience [ɛfisjɑ̃:s] f. Efficiency.

efficient, ente [-jɑ̃, ɑ̃:t] adj. Efficient.

effigie [ɛfiʒi] f. Effigy; *à l'effigie de,* bearing the head (ou) effigy of.

effilé, ée [ɛfile] adj. Tapered, tapering (doigt); pointed (outil); slender (taille). ‖ Frayed (tissu). ‖ Naut. Rakish. ‖ Aviat. Tapered. ‖ Autom. Streamlined. — m. Fringe (garniture).

effiler v. tr. (1). To fray (un tissu). ‖ To thin out (les cheveux); to taper (un outil). — v. pr. **S'effiler,** to fray out (tissu). ‖ To taper off (colonne, flèche).

effilochage [ɛfilɔʃa:ʒ] m. Fraying.

effilocher [-ʃe] v. tr. (1). To fray, to unravel. — v. pr. **S'effilocher,** to fray, to become unravelled.

effilocheur [-ʃœ:r] m. Teaser, rag-tearer (ou) -picker.

effilocheuse [-ʃø:z] f. Tech. Devil.

effilochure [-ʃy:r] f. Ravelling.

effilure [ɛfily:r] f. Ravelling.

efflanqué, ée [ɛflãke] adj. Lean-flanked (animal); lanky, lank (personne).

efflanquer v. tr. (1). To make thin, to emaciate.

effleurement [ɛflœrmã] m. Grazing (en général); skimming (de l'eau). ‖ Light touch.

effleurer [-re] v. tr. (1). To graze (en général, en écorchant); to brush (avec douceur); to shave (en rasant); to skim (l'eau). ‖ Fig. To come into, to cross (l'esprit); to come into the mind of (qqn); to touch lightly on (un sujet).

effloraison [ɛflɔrɛzɔ̃] f. Bot. Flowering.

efflorescence [-sã:s] f. Chim., Bot. Efflorescence. ‖ Méd. Eruption.

effluent, ente [ɛflɥã, ã:t] adj. Effluent.
— m. Phys. *Effluent radioactif,* radio-active effluent. ‖ Géogr. *Effluent pluvial,* surface runoff, overland flow. ‖ Techn. *Effluent urbain,* sewage.

effluve [ɛfly:v] m. Effluvium (pl. effluvia).

effondré, ée [ɛfɔ̃dre] adj. Collapsed (bâtiment); caved in (plancher); rutted, cut up (route); boggy (terrain); fallen in (toit). ‖ Agric. Ploughed up. ‖ Fig. Prostrate.

effondrement [-dremã] m. Collapse, collapsing, crumbling (d'un bâtiment); caving in (du plancher); subsidence (d'un terrain). ‖ Fin. Slump (des cours); collapse (du marché). ‖ Méd. Breakdown (de la santé). ‖ Fig. Collapse (des espérances, d'un établissement, du moral); breakdown (d'un projet, d'un système).

effondrer [-dre] v. tr. (1). To break open (un coffre, une porte); to break down (un plancher). ‖ Agric. To trench.
— v. pr. **S'effondrer,** to subside, to crumble, to collapse (bâtiment); to collapse, to crumple up; to flop (fam.) [personne]; to cave in, to give way (plancher); to subside (sol); to fall in (toit). ‖ Fin. To slump (cours). ‖ Méd. To break down (raison, santé); to collapse, to break down (personne); to come to nothing (projet).

efforcer (s') [sefɔrse] v. pr. (6). To make efforts, to exert oneself (v. essayer); *s'efforcer à* (ou) *vers,* to aim at, to struggle for, to strain after, to strive after; *s'efforcer de,* to endeavour to, to struggle to, to strive to, to do one's best to.

effort [ɛfɔ:r] m. Effort, exertion, strain (au moral et au physique); attempt, endeavour (tentative); *faire effort, des efforts pour,* to strive, to strain to; *faire des efforts pour vomir,* to heave, to retch; *faire un effort pour,* to make an effort (ou) an endeavour to; *faire un effort sur soi-même pour,* to constrain oneself to; *faire tous ses efforts pour,* to use every endeavour to, to try one's utmost to; *loi du moindre effort,* line of least resistance; *obtenir qqch. grâce à ses efforts personnels,* to get sth. off one's own bat (ou) on one's own hook; *prodiguer ses efforts en vain,* to spend oneself in a vain endeavour; *sans effort,* effortless; *travail qui sent l'effort,* work that smells of the lamp. ‖ Techn. Stress; *effort de rupture,* breaking stress; *effort de tension,* torque. ‖ Méd. Strain, rick; rupture; *attraper un effort,* to strain one's back. ‖ Fin. *Effort financier,* financial outlay.

effraction [ɛfraksjɔ̃] f. Jur. Breaking open; *s'introduire chez qqn par effraction,* to break into s.o.'s house; *vol avec effraction,* house-breaking (de jour); burglary (de nuit).

effraie [ɛfrɛ] f. Zool. Screech-owl, barn-owl.

effrangement [ɛfrãʒmã] m. Fraying.

effranger [-ʒe] v. tr. (7). To fray.
— v. pr. **S'effranger,** to fray.

effrayant, ante [ɛfrɛjã, ã:t] adj. Frightful, fearful; awful, ghastly (pr. et fig.).

effrayé, ée [-je] adj. Afraid, frightened, full of fear, startled.

effrayer [-je] v. tr. (9 *b*). To frighten, to startle.
— v. pr. **S'effrayer,** to take fright (ou) alarm; *s'effrayer de,* to be frightened of (ou) at, to be afraid of.

effréné, ée [ɛfrene] adj. Unbridled, unrestrained. ‖ Ungovernable (désir); frantic (efforts); extravagant (luxe); unruly, unbridled (passion); rampant (vice).

effritement [ɛfritmã] m. Crumbling away; weathering.

effriter [-te] v. tr. (1). To desintegrate; to cause to crumble.
— v. pr. **S'effriter,** to crumble away; to weather.

effroi [ɛfrwa] m. Dread, fright, fear (v. peur); *jeter l'effroi,* to spread terror.

effronté, ée [ɛfrɔ̃te] adj. Jaunty, rakish (air); barefaced (mensonge); saucy, pert, cheeky, brazen-faced, U. S. fresh (personne).
— s. Brazen-face (en général); brazen hussy (femme); cheeky devil (homme).

effrontément [-temã] adv. Impudently, brazenly, shamelessly, barefacedly.

effronterie [tri] f. Barefacedness, effrontery; cheekiness, sauciness; front.

effroyable [ɛfrwajabl] adj. Dreadful, fearful, frightful (effrayant); terrifying (terrifiant); ghastly (pr. et fam.).

effroyablement [-bləmã] adv. Dreadfully, fearfully, frightfully; awfully.

effusion [ɛfyzjɔ̃] f. Effusion; *effusion de sang,* bloodshed. ‖ Ecclés. Effusion. ‖ Fig. Demonstration; effusiveness. (V. épanchement.)

égaiement [egɛmã] m. Cheering (ou) brightening up, enlivening.

égailler [egaje] v. tr. (1). To scatter.
— v. pr. **S'égailler,** to scatter, to disperse.

égal [egal] adj. Equal (en degré, mesure, valeur); *à armes égales,* on equal terms; *à poids égal,* weight for weight; *de force égale,* evenly matched; *toutes choses égales,* other things being equal. ‖ Even (chaleur); even, smooth (chemin); regular (mouvement); steady (vent). ‖ Fig. Equable, even (caractère). ‖ Fam. *Ça m'est égal,* it's all the same to me, it's all one to me (ça m'est indifférent); I don't care (je ne m'en soucie pas); I don't mind (je n'y vois pas d'inconvénient); *c'est égal!,* well!, indeed!
— s. Equal, peer (en rang); equal (en valeur); *à l'égal de,* as much as, no less than; *être l'égal de,* to be equal to; *traiter d'égal à égal,* to treat as an equal; *sans égal,* peerless, matchless, not to be equalled.

égalable [-labl] adj. That can be equalled.

également [-lmã] adv. Equally (avec égalité); alike (de même manière). ‖ Also, too, as well (aussi).

égaler [-le] v. tr. (1). To equal, to be equal to, to match (qqn); *chercher à égaler,* to emulate; *égaler à,* to compare with, to rank as equal to. ‖ Math. To equal.
— v. pr. **S'égaler,** to equal, to come up (à, to) [par son mérite]; to claim equality of rank (à, with) [par son orgueil].

égalisateur [egalizatœ:r] m. Techn. Leveller.

égalisation [-zasjɔ̃] f. Equalization. ‖ Levelling, smoothing (nivellement).

égaliser [-ze] v. tr. (1). To equalize, to make equal, to level out; *la mort égalise tout,* death is the great leveller. ‖ To trim (en coupant); to level (en nivelant). ‖ Sports. To equalize (la marque).
— v. pr. **S'égaliser,** to become equal (ou) level (ou) even.

égalitaire [-tɛ:r] adj., s. Equalitarian, egalitarian.

égalitarisme [-tarism] m. Egalitarianism.

égalité [-te] f. Equality (v. parité); *à égalité de prix,* at even prices; *égalité de salaires,* equal pay; *sur un pied d'égalité,* on an equal footing. ‖ Levelness, evenness, smoothness (nivellement). ‖ SPORTS. *A égalité,* equal on points; *égalité de points,* tie. ‖ FIG. Regularity, equability, evenness; *égalité d'âme,* equanimity.

égard [ega:r] m. Consideration; *avoir égard à,* to consider, to pay respect to; *eu égard à,* having regard to, considering, in consideration of. ‖ Attention, regard (v. DÉFÉRENCE); *avec beaucoup, avec peu d'égards,* considerately, slightingly; *avoir des égards pour,* to be attentive to (ou) considerate of; *manque d'égards,* slight; *par égard pour,* out of respect for; *sans égard pour,* regardless of. ‖ LOC. *A certains égards,* in some respects (ou) ways; *à cet égard,* on that account, in that respect; *à l'égard de,* as regards; towards; with respect to.

égaré, ée [egare] adj. Stray (animal); lonely (chemin); out-of-the-way (lieu); lost, misplaced (objet); lost, wandering (personne). ‖ Haggard, bewildered, wild (air, regard). ‖ MILIT. Stray (balle).

égarement [-rmã] m. Mislaying (d'un objet); wandering (de qqn). ‖ FIG. Bewilderment (de l'air, du regard); disorder, deviation, wildness (de la conduite); aberration (de l'esprit).

égarer [-re] v. tr. (1). To mislay (qqch.); to lead astray (qqn). ‖ FIG. To derange, to distract.
— v. pr. **S'égarer,** to be mislaid (objet); to go astray, to lose one's way (personne). ‖ FIG. To become unhinged (esprit); to lose one's bearings (personne). ‖ FAM. To digress, to wander from the point.

égayant, ante [egɛjɑ̃, ɑ̃:t] adj. Cheery, lively.
égayer [-je] v. tr. (9 *b*). To enliven (la conversation, le trajet); to lighten, to brighten up (un lieu); to cheer up, to enliven (qqn); to relieve (un vêtement).
— v. pr. **S'égayer,** to cheer up (personne); to brighten up (pièce); *s'égayer aux dépens de,* to make merry at, to make fun of.

Égée [eʒe] m. Aegeus.
— adj. GÉOGR. *La mer Egée,* the Aegean sea.
égéen, enne [eʒeɛ̃, ɛn] adj. GÉOGR. Aegean.
Égérie [eʒeri] f. Egerie (pr. et fig.).
égide [eʒid] f. Shield, protection, aegis (v. AUSPICES); *prendre sous son égide,* to take under one's wing; *sous l'égide de,* under the care of.
églantier [eglɑ̃tje] m. BOT. Eglantine, wild (ou) dog rose-bush.
églantine [-tin] f. BOT. Wild (ou) dog rose
églefin [egləfɛ̃] m. ZOOL. Haddock.
église [egli:z] f. ECCLÉS. Church (édifice, société).
églogue [eglɔg] f. Eclogue.
ego [egɔ] m. PHILOS. Self, ego.
égocentrique [-sɑ̃trik] adj. Egocentric, self-centred.
égocentrisme [-sɑ̃trism] m. Egocentricity, self-centredness.
égoïne [egɔin] f. TECHN. Compass saw.
égoïsme [egɔism] m. Egoism, selfishness; *sans égoïsme,* unselfish.
égoïste [egɔist] adj. Egoistic, selfish.
— s. Egoist; selfish person.
égoïstement [-təmɑ̃] adj. Selfishly.
égomanie [egɔmani] f. Egomania.
égorgement [egɔrʒmɑ̃] m. Throat-cutting. ‖ Murder.
égorger [-ʒe] v. tr. (6). To cut the throat of. ‖ To butcher, to slaughter. ‖ FAM. To fleece.
— v. pr. **S'égorger,** to cut one's throat.
— v. récip. **S'égorger,** to cut each other's throats.
égorgeur, euse [-œ:r, ø:z] s. Sticker (de porc). ‖ Cut-throat (assassin). ‖ FAM. Fleecer.
égosiller (s') [segɔzije] v. pr. (1). To sing

ÉGLISE - CHURCH

païen	pagan, heathen(ish)
brahmane, -isme	brahmin (-ism)
mahométan, musulman	Mohammedan, Moslem, Muslim
le christianisme	Christianity
la chrétienté	Christendom
Messie	Messiah
Rédempteur	Redeemer
auréole	aureole, halo
sainte Croix	Holy Rood, H. Cross
Saint-Esprit	Holy Ghost
Ecriture sainte	Holy Scripture
Evangile	Gospel
chemin de Croix	Stations of the Cross
théologien	theologian, divine
le dogme	dogma
fanatisme	fanaticism
libre pensée	free-thought
un laïque	a layman
le salut	salvation
un réprouvé	a reprobate
péché mortel	deadly sin
paroisse, paroissien	parish, parishioner
soutane	cassock
goupillon	aspergillum, sprinkler
évêque	bishop
évêché	bishopric
mitre, crosse	mitre, crosier
doyen	dean
diacre	deacon
chanoine	canon
sacristain	sexton
bedeau	verger
enfant de chœur	altar-boy
faire la quête	to take the collection
faire pénitence	to do penance
rendre grâces	to return thanks
un dissident	a dissenter
élu, bienheureux	elect, blessed

---

loudly (oiseau); to shout like mad, to shout one's head off, to strain one's voice (personne); *je m'égosille à vous le dire,* I've told you till I am sick of it.
égotisme [egɔtism] m. Egotism.
égotiste [-tist] s. Egotist.
égout [egu] m. Draining, dripping (action). ‖ Eaves (du toit). ‖ Sewer (de rue); *eaux d'égout,* sewage. ‖ **Tout-à-l'égout,** m. Modern sanitation. ‖ FIG. Sink, cesspool.
égoutier [-tje] m. Sewerman.
égouttage [-ta:ʒ] m. Draining; dripping.
égoutter [-te] v. tr. (1). To drain; *faire égoutter,* to drain off (l'eau); to strain (le fromage).
— v. pr. **S'égoutter,** to drain. to drip.
égouttoir [-twa:r] m. Draining-rack (à bouteilles); drainer (à fromage); dish-drainer, plate-rack (à vaisselle); draining board, U. S. drainboard (d'évier); drip-pan (de porte-parapluie).
égoutture [-ty:r] f. Drops, drippings.
égrainage [egrɛna:ʒ], **égrainer** [-ne] V. ÉGRENAGE, ÉGRENER.
égrappage [egrapa:ʒ] m. Stalking (des raisins).
égrapper [-pe] v. tr. (1). To stalk (des raisins).
égratigner [egratiɲe] v. tr. (1). To scratch (qqch., qqn). ‖ FIG. To nettle, to sting, to rub up the wrong way (qqn).
égratignure [-ɲy:r] f. Scratch (v. ÉCORCHURE); *sans une égratignure,* without a scratch, unhurt. ‖ FIG. Gibe.
égrenage [egrəna:ʒ] m. AGRIC. Shelling (des pois, des céréales); picking off (des raisins). ‖ Striking, chiming (des heures).
égrener [egrəne] v. tr. (5). To shell (des pois); to pick off (des raisins). ‖ To unstring (des perles);

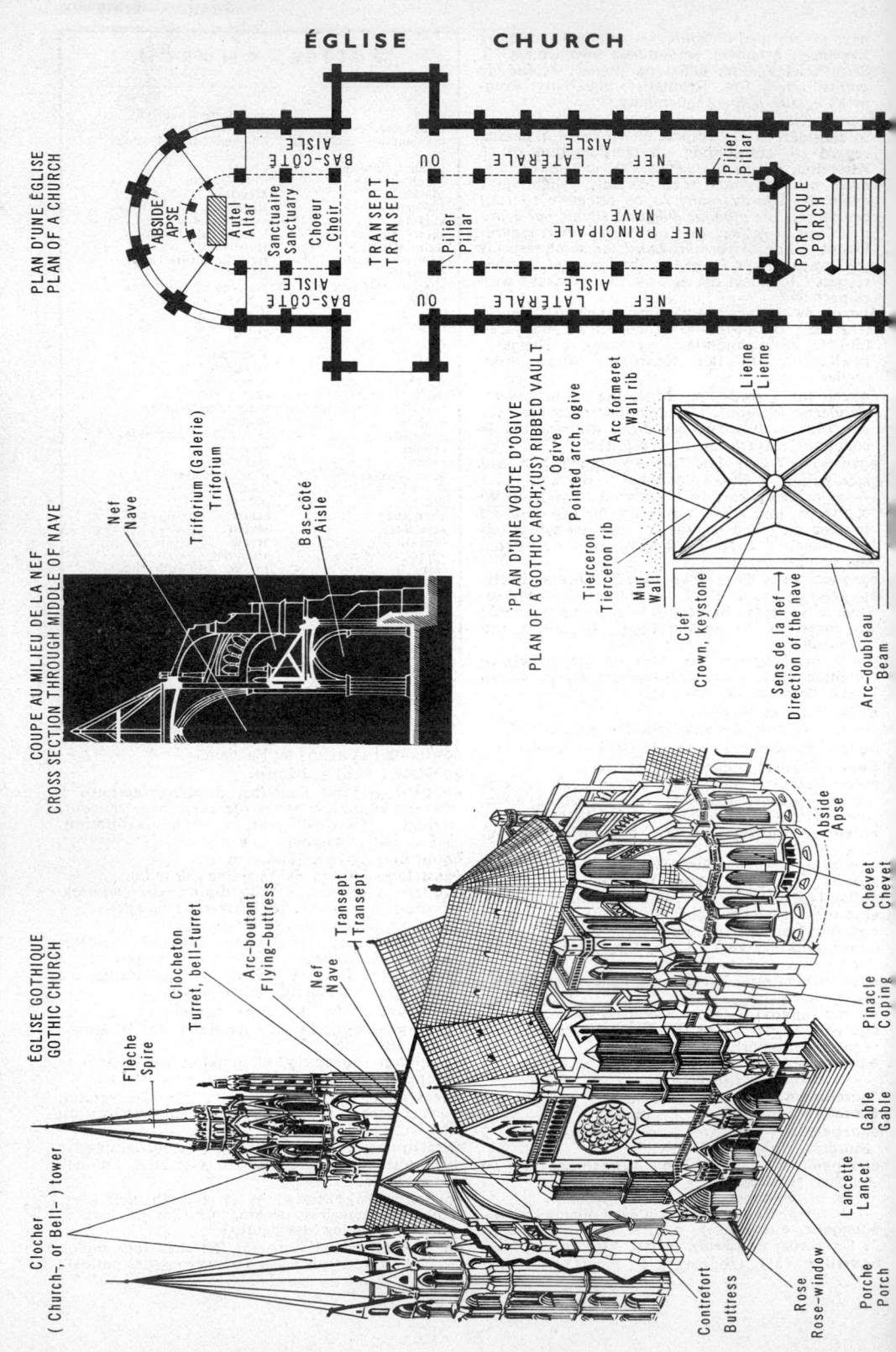

ÉGLISE   CHURCH

PLAN D'UNE ÉGLISE
PLAN OF A CHURCH

ABSIDE
APSE

Autel
Altar

Sanctuaire
Sanctuary

Chœur
Choir

BAS-CÔTÉ
AISLE

TRANSEPT
TRANSEPT

Pilier
Pillar

NEF
LATÉRALE
OU
AISLE

NEF PRINCIPALE
NAVE

Pilier
Pillar

PORTIQUE
PORCH

COUPE AU MILIEU DE LA NEF
CROSS SECTION THROUGH MIDDLE OF NAVE

Nef
Nave

Triforium (Galerie)
Triforium

Bas-côté
Aisle

PLAN D'UNE VOÛTE D'OGIVE
PLAN OF A GOTHIC ARCH;(US) RIBBED VAULT

Ogive
Pointed arch, ogive

Arc formeret
Wall rib

Lierne
Lierne

Tierceron
Tierceron rib

Mur
Wall

Clef
Crown, keystone

Sens de la nef
Direction of the nave

Arc-doubleau
Beam

ÉGLISE GOTHIQUE
GOTHIC CHURCH

Flèche
Spire

Clocheton
Turret, bell-turret

Arc-boutant
Flying-buttress

Nef
Nave

Transept
Transept

Abside
Apse

Clocher
(Church-, or Bell-) tower

Contrefort
Buttress

Rose
Rose-window

Porche
Porch

Lancette
Lancet

Gable
Gable

Pinacle
Coping

Chevet
Chevet

égrener son chapelet, to tell one's beads. ‖ To strike, to chime (des heures).
— v. pr. **S'égrener,** to drop, to drop away. ‖ Fig. To drop like pearls (chant); to ripple (rire); *s'égrener le long de la route,* to straggle along the street (retardataires).

égreneuse [-nø:z] f. Techn. Shelling machine.

égrillard, arde [egrija:r, ard] adj. Libidinous, lecherous, shameless (personne); spicy (propos); lewd (sourire). [V. grivois.]

égrisée [egrize] f. Diamond-dust.

égriser [egrize] v. tr. (1). To grind (des diamants).

égrotant, ante [egrɔtɑ̃, ɑ̃:t] adj. Sickly.

égrugeoir [egryʒwa:r] m. Culin. Small mortar; salt-mill.

égruger [egryʒe] v. tr. (7). Culin. To pound.

Égypte [eʒipt] f. Géogr. Egypt.

égyptien, enne [-jɛ̃, ɛn] adj., m., Egyptian.

égyptienne [-sjɛn] f. Géogr. Egyptian woman. ‖ Clarendon (en typogr.).

égyptologie [-tɔlɔʒi] f. Egyptology.

égyptologue [-tɔlɔg] s. Egyptologist.

eh [e] interj. Hey! Hi! Hallo there! V. bien.

éhonté, ée [eɔ̃te] adj. Shameless, brazen, barefaced, unblushing. (V. impudent.)

eider [edɛ:r] m. Zool. Eider.

eidétique [ɛjdetik] adj. Philos., Psych. Eidetic; *image eidétique,* eidetic image.

einsteinium [ajnʃtɛnjɔm] m. Chim. Einsteinium.

éjaculation [eʒakylasjɔ̃] f. Ejaculation.

éjaculatoire (-latwa:r] adj. Ejaculatory.

éjaculer [-le] v. tr. (1). To ejaculate.

éjectable [eʒɛktabl] adj. Aviat. Ejector (siège).

éjecter [-te] v. tr. (1). To eject.

éjecteur [-tœ:r] adj., m. Ejector.

éjection [-sjɔ̃] f. Ejection.

élaboration [elabɔrasjɔ̃] f. Elaboration.

élaborer [-re]v. tr. (1). To elaborate (pr. et fig.).
— v. pr. **S'élaborer,** to be elaborated, to form.

élagage [elaga:ʒ] m. Pruning (des arbres); lopping (des branches).

élaguer [-ge] v. tr. (1). To prune (un arbre); to lop off (des branches). ‖ Fig. To cut out (des détails); to curtail, to prune (un ouvrage).

élagueur [-gœ:r] m. Pruner.

élan [elɑ̃] m. Zool. Elk; eland.

élan m. Spring; *avec élan, sans élan,* running, standing (saut); *d'un élan,* at a (ou) one bound; *prendre son élan,* to take off, to take a run. ‖ Impetus, momentum; *emporté par son propre élan,* carried away by one's momentum (ou) impetus. ‖ Fig. Burst (d'éloquence, d'énergie); transport (d'enthousiasme); *plein d'élan,* full of dash. ‖ Pl. Fits of enthusiasm; impulses.

élancé, ée [-se] adj. Slim, slender.

élancement [-smɑ̃] m. Méd. Stabbing (ou) shooting pain. ‖ Fig. Yearning (vers, towards).

élancer [-se] v. intr. (1). Méd. To twinge, to stab, to give stabbing pains.
— v. pr. **S'élancer,** to shoot, to dart (comme un trait); to spring, to bound (d'un bond) [v. foncer]; *s'élancer sur,* to rush at, to hurl oneself at; *s'élancer vers,* to soar up to (cime, clocher); to dash at, to run towards (personne).

élargir [elarʒi:r] v. tr. (2). To let out (une robe); to widen (un passage); to stretch (des souliers); to enlarge (un trou). ‖ Jur. To release, to set free (un détenu). ‖ Fig. To extend (les connaissances); to broaden (les idées); to enlarge, to develop (l'intelligence).
— v. pr. **S'élargir,** to get wider, to widen (en général); to stretch (souliers). ‖ Fig. To enlarge, to develop, to widen.

élargissement [-ʒismɑ̃] m. Letting out (d'une robe); widening (d'un passage); enlarging (d'une propriété); stretching (des souliers). ‖ Jur. Release, discharge. ‖ Fig. Widening (des connaissances); broadening (des idées).

élasticité [elastisite] f. Elasticity (d'un corps); springiness, spring (de la marche). ‖ Fig. Buoyancy (du caractère); laxity (de la morale).

élastique [-tik] adj. Springy, resilient (fauteuil); elastic (gaz, tissu). ‖ Springy (démarche). ‖ Fig. Flexible (caractère); lax, elastic (conscience); lax (morale); elastic (règlement).
— m. India-rubber, rubber (caoutchouc, gomme); elastic, rubber band (ruban caoutchouté).

élastomère [-tɔmɛ:r] m. Chim. Elastomer.

Elbe [ɛlb] f. Géogr. Elbe (fleuve); Elba (île).

électeur [elɛktœ:r] m. † Elector. ‖ Elector, constituent, voter.

électif, ive [-tif, i:v] adj. Elective.

élection [-sjɔ̃] f. Election (v. choix); *terre d'élection,* land of dreams. ‖ Election; polling; *élections générales, législatives,* general, parliamentary election; *élections partielles,* by-election; *jour des élections,* polling day, U. S. election day. ‖ Ecclés. Election; *vase d'élection,* chosen vessel. ‖ Fig. Preference.

électoral, ale [-tɔral] adj. Election (affiche, comité); electoral (campagne, propagande); electioneering (agent); vote-catching (manœuvres); *faire une campagne électorale,* to canvass, to electioneer; *corps électoral,* electorate; *période électorale,* election-time.

électoralisme [-tɔralism] m. Vote-catching, electioneering.

électorat [-tɔra] m. Electorate (corps); franchise (droit).

électrice [-tris] f. Electress.

électricien [elɛktrisjɛ̃] m. Electr. Electrician.
— adj. Electrical (ingénieur).

électricité [-site] f. Electr. Electricity; *à l'électricité,* by electricity, electrically.

électrification [-fikasjɔ̃] f. Electr. Electrification.

électrifier [-fje] v. tr. (1). Electr. To electrify.

électrique [elɛktrik] adj. Electric (courant, lumière, véhicule); electrical (machine). ‖ Fam. Electric.

électriquement [-kmɑ̃] adv. Electr. Electrically.

électrisable [-zabl] adj. Electr. Electrifiable.

électrisant, ante [-zɑ̃, ɑ̃:t] adj. Electr. Electrifying. ‖ Fig. Galvanizing.

électrisation [-zasjɔ̃] f. Electr. Electrification.

électriser [-ze] v. tr. (1). Electr. To electrify. ‖ Fig. To electrify, to thrill. (V. galvaniser.)

électroacoustique [elɛktroakustik] adj. Electroacoustic, electroacoustical; *musique électroacoustique,* electronic music.
— f. Electroacoustics.

électro-aimant [elɛktroɛmɑ̃] m. Electr. Electromagnet.

électrocardiogramme [-kardjɔgram] m. Méd. Electrocardiogram.

électrocardiographe [-kardjɔgraf] f. Méd. Electrocardiograph.

électrocardiographie [-kardjɔgrafi] f. Méd. Electrocardiography.

électrochimie [-ʃimi] f. Chim. Electrochemistry.

électrochimique [-ʃimik] adj. Electrochemical.

électrochoc [-ʃɔk] m. Méd. Electroshock.

électrocuter [-kyte] v. tr. (1). To electrocute.

électrocution [-kysjɔ̃] f. Electrocution.

électrode [elɛktrɔd] f. Electr. Electrode.

électrodynamique [-dinamik] f. Electrodynamics.

électrodynamomètre [-dinamɔmɛtr] m. Electr. Electrodynamometer.

électrogalvanique [-galvanik] adj. Electr. Electrogalvanic.

électrogène [-gε:n] adj. Generating ; *groupe électrogène,* power plant.
électrolyse [-li:z] f. ELECTR. Electrolysis; *génératrice pour électrolyse,* electroplating generator.
électrolyser [-lize] v. tr. (1). To electrolyze.
électrolyseur [-lizœ:r] m. ELECTR. Electrolyzer.
électrolyte [-lit] adj. Electrolyte.
électrolytique [-litik] adj. Electrolytic.
électromagnétique [-maɲetik] adj. ELECTR. Electromagnetic.
électromagnétisme [-maɲetism] m. ELECTR. Electromagnetism.
électromécanique [-mekanik] adj. ELECTR. Electro-mechanical.
— f. Electromechanics.
électroménager [-menaʒe] adj. m. Domestic, household.
— m. Domestic (ou) household appliances (appareils) ; household (ou) household appliance industry (industrie).
électrométallurgie [-metalyrʒi] f. ELECTR. Electro-metallurgy.
électromètre [-mεtr] m. ELECTR. Electrometer.
électrométrie [-metri] f. ELECTR. Electrometry.
électromoteur, trice [-mɔtœ:r, tris] adj., f. Electromotive.
— m. Electromotor.
électron [elεktrɔ̃] m. Electron.
électronégatif, ive [elεktrɔnegatif, i:v] adj. Electro-negative.
électronicien, enne [-nisjε̃, εn] s. Electronics engineer (ou) specialist.
électronique [-nik] adj. Electronic (action) ; electron (faisceau, lentille, microscope, optique, tube).
— f. Electronics.
électronucléaire [-nykleε:r] adj. *Centrale électronucléaire,* nuclear power-station.
— m. Nuclear energy (ou) power.
électrophone [-fɔn] m. Record player.
électrophorèse [-fɔrε:z] f. CHIM. Electrophoresis.
électroponcture [-põkty:r] f. MÉD. Electro-puncture.
électropositif, ive [-pɔzitif, i:v] adj. Electro-positive.
électroscope [-skɔp] m. ELECTR. Electroscope.
électrostatique [-statik] adj. Electrostatic.
— f. Electrostatics.
électrotechnique [-tεknik] adj. TECHN. Electrotechnic, electrotechnical.
— f. Electrotechnics, electrotechnology.
électrothérapie [-terapi] f. MÉD. Electropathy, electrotherapeuthics, electrotherapy.
électrovalence [-valɑ̃:s] f. CHIM. Electrovalence, electrovalency.
électrum [elεktrɔm] m. Electrum.
électuaire [elεktɥε:r] m. MÉD. Electuary.
élégamment [elegamɑ̃] adv. Elegantly, smartly. ‖ FIG. Elegantly.
élégance [-gɑ̃:s] f. Elegance, smartness. ‖ FIG. Handsomeness (du comportement) ; refinement (du goût, des manières).
élégant, ante [-gɑ̃, ɑ̃:t] adj. Elegant; dressy, smart, stylish (habit) ; well-dressed, dressy (personne) ; fashionable (société). ‖ FIG. Handsome (comportement) ; polished, refined (manières) ; elegant (solution).
— m. Man of fashion, dandy, swell (fam.) ; U. S. dude (fam.).
élégante [-gɑ̃:t] f. Woman of fashion.
élégiaque [eleʒjak] adj. Elegiac.
élégie [-ʒi] f. Elegy.
élément [elemɑ̃] m. Element (corps, principe). ‖ Element, component, item, constituent (composant) ; unit (partie). ‖ Element (milieu; *dans son*

élément, in one's element, at home, on one's own ground. ‖ CHIM., PHYS., GRAMM. Element. ‖ ELECTR. Cell. ‖ MÉD. Ingredient. ‖ Pl. Elements, rudiments. ‖ MILIT. Element, unit. ‖ FIG. Constituent (du bonheur) ; element (d'incertitude) ; matter (d'un ouvrage) ; item (de preuve) ; datum (d'un problème) ; factor (du succès) ; *élément comique,* comical side ; *élément principal,* staple.
élémentaire [-mɑ̃tε:r] adj. Elemental, elementary (corps). ‖ Elementary, rudimentary, basic (connaissances, ouvrage) ; *professeur de classes élémentaires,* primary (ou) elementary teacher, U. S. grade-school teacher.
éléphant [elefɑ̃] m. ZOOL. Elephant; *éléphant femelle, mâle,* cow-, bull-elephant. ‖ FAM. Whacker (personne forte) ; *comme un éléphant dans un magasin de porcelaine,* like a bull in a china-shop.
éléphanteau [-to] m. ZOOL. Young elephant.
éléphantesque [-tεsk] adj. FAM. Elephantine; colossal, enormous.
éléphantiasis [-tjazis] f. MÉD. Elephantiasis.
éléphantin, ine [-tε̃, i:n] adj. Elephantine.
élevable [eləvabl] adj. Trainable (animal) ; educable (personne).
élevage [-va:ʒ] m. Culture (des abeilles) ; breeding, rearing (des bestiaux) ; *élevage des animaux à fourrure,* fur-farming ; *faire l'élevage de,* to breed. ‖ Stock-farm, U. S. ranch.
élévateur, trice [elevatœ:r, tris] adj. Lifting. ‖ MÉD. Elevator (muscle).
— m. Elevator, hoist, lift. ‖ MÉD. Elevator.
élévation [-sjɔ̃] f. Elevation, erection, raising (d'un édifice) ; raising (de la voix). ‖ Elevation, height (v. HAUTEUR) ; rise, swell (de terrain). ‖ Ascent; elevation, raising, promotion (avancement) [à, to]. ‖ ARCHIT., MILIT., ECCLÉS. Elevation. ‖ MATH. Involution. ‖ MÉD. Quickening (du pouls) ; raising, rise (de température). ‖ FIN. Raising, rise (des prix). ‖ FIG. Uplifting, lifting up (de l'âme) [vers, to] ; loftiness (de la pensée) ; nobility, grandeur (du style) ; *élévation d'esprit,* high-mindedness.
élévatoire [-twa:r] adj. Elevating, lifting, hoisting.
élévator [-tɔr] m. Escalator, moving staircase.
élevé, ée [elve] adj. High (montagne) ; lofty (tour) ; *peu élevé,* low. ‖ High (niveau) ; elevated (position) ; exalted, high (rang) ; *d'une situation élevée,* in a high position ; *occuper un rang élevé parmi,* to rank high among. ‖ MÉD. Frequent, rapid (pouls) ; high (température). ‖ COMM. High (prix). ‖ FIG. Exalted (conception) ; noble (esprit, style) ; high (motif, principe) ; elevated (pensée, style) ; *aux principes élevés,* high-principled. ‖ FIG. Bred ; brought-up ; *bien, mal élevé,* well-, ill-bred ; *élevé dans le luxe,* cradled in luxury ; *élevé à la diable,* dragged up.
élève [elε:v] m. Pupil (d'une école, d'un maître) ; student (d'une université) ; *être l'élève de,* to study under. ‖ MILIT., NAUT., AVIAT. Cadet ; *élève officier,* officer cadet.
— f. Pupil. ‖ AGRIC. Seedling.
élever [elve] v. tr. (5). To erect (un autel, un édifice, un monument) ; to raise (une barrière, un mur) ; to erect, to set up (une statue). [V. ÉRIGER.] ‖ To raise (l'eau) ; to lift up (un poids). ‖ To raise (le niveau, la température, la voix). ‖ To breed, to rear, to keep (un animal) ; to bring up, to nurse, to educate (un enfant). ‖ To exalt, to extol (par des louanges) ; to elevate, to raise, to promote (par une promotion). ‖ MATH. To erect (une perpendiculaire). ‖ FIN. To increase, to put up (les prix). ‖ ECCLÉS. To elevate (l'hostie). ‖ FIG. To improve (l'âme) ; to lift up (son âme) [vers, to] ; to elevate (l'esprit) ; to raise, to set up (une protestation).

— v. pr. **S'élever,** to soar, to rise (clocher).
‖ To ascend, to rise up (ballon); to lift (brume);
to rise (fumée); *s'élever en grimpant,* to climb up
(personne). ‖ To spring up (brise); to rise (tempête, vent). ‖ To be uttered (cris); to be raised
(protestations); *s'élever contre,* to protest against.
‖ To stand (édifice) [*sur,* on]. ‖ To rise, to swell
(terrain). ‖ To be bred (animal); to be brought up
(enfant). ‖ To exalt oneself (par vanité); to rise
(socialement); *s'élever au faîte de la gloire,* to
soar to the heights of fame; *s'élever au niveau
de,* to rise (ou) come up to the level of ‖ FIN. To
mount up (dépenses); to come, to amount, to run
up (facture, somme) [*à,* to]. ‖ NAUT. To beat off
the wind. ‖ FIG. To rise (âme); to arise (difficultés, doutes).

éleveur, euse [-vœ:r, ø:z] s. Farmer (d'abeilles,
d'animaux à fourrure); fancier (d'animaux **d'appartement**); breeder, stockbreeder (de bétail).

éleveuse [-vø:z] f. Incubator; brooder.

élevure [-vy:r] f. MÉD. Pimple.

elfe [ɛlf] m. Elf. (V. LUTIN.)

élider [elide] v. tr. (1). GRAMM. To elide.

Élie [eli] m. ECCLÉS. Elijah.

éligibilité [eliʒibilite] f. Eligibility.

éligible [-ʒibl] adj. Eligible.

élimé, ée [elime] adj. Threadbare, shiny. (V. USÉ.)

élimer v. tr. (1). To wear out.
— v. pr. **S'élimer,** to become threadbare.

élimination [eliminasjɔ̃] f. Elimination.

éliminatoire [-natwa:r] adj. Eliminatory (examen); disqualifying (note). ‖ SPORTS. Eliminating,
trial (épreuve).
— f. SPORTS. Eliminating heat.

éliminer [-ne] v. tr. (1). To exclude (un candidat);
to weed out (les importuns); to get rid of (qqn). ‖
MÉD., MATH. To eliminate.
— v. intr. MÉD. To eliminate.
— v. pr. **S'éliminer.** MATH. To cancel out. ‖
MÉD. To be eliminated.

élingue [elɛ̃:g] f. NAUT. Sling.

élinguer [-ge] v. tr. (1). NAUT. To sling.

élire [eli:r] v. tr. (60). To choose, to elect (V. CHOI-
SIR). ‖ To elect (un candidat, un président); to
elect, to return (un député); *être élu député,* to be
elected, to get in. ‖ JUR. To elect (domicile).

élisabéthain, aine [-tɛ̃, ɛn] adj. Elizabethan.

élision [elizjɔ̃] f. GRAMM. Elision.

élite [elit] f. Elite; *d'élite,* elite, picked.

élitisme [-tism] m. Elitism.

élitiste [-tist] adj., s. Elitist.

élixir [eliksi:r] m. MÉD. Elixir.

elle [ɛl] pron. pers. f. She (pour les personnes);
it (pour les choses); they (au pl.) [sujet]. ‖ Her
(pour les personnes); it (pour les choses); them
(au pl.) [complément]; *je suis plus grand qu'elle,*
I am taller than she; *je suis souffrant, mais elle
non,* I am unwell but she isn't; *elle a une maison
à elle,* she has a house of her own; *c'est à elle de
jouer,* it's her turn to play; *une amie à elle,* a
friend of hers. ‖ (Non traduit); *la fenêtre est-elle
fermée?,* is the window shut? ‖ **Elle-même,**
herself (pers.); itself (chose); themselves (au pl.).

ellébore [elebɔ:r] m. BOT. Hellebore.

ellipse [ɛlips] f. MATH. Ellipse. ‖ GRAMM. Ellipsis.

ellipsoïdal, ale [-sɔidal] adj. Ellipsoidal.

ellipsoïde [-sɔid] m. Ellipsoid.

elliptique [-tik] adj. MATH., GRAMM. Elliptical.

elliptiquement [-tikmã] adv. GRAMM. Elliptically.

élocution [elɔkysjɔ̃] f. Elocution, delivery, voice-
production; *difficulté d'élocution,* impediment in
one's speech, stammering articulation; *facilité
d'élocution,* fluency, flow of language.

éloge [elɔ:ʒ] m. Praise, laud, commendation,

encomium (v. LOUANGE); *adresser des éloges à,* to
praise; *être à l'éloge de qqn,* to speak well for
s.o., to be to s.o.'s credit; *faire l'éloge de,* to
praise, to speak highly of; *faire un éloge excessif
de,* to overpraise; *faire son propre éloge,* to blow
one's own trumpet. ‖ Eulogy (discours); *prononcer l'éloge de,* to eulogize.

élogieusement [elɔʒjøzmã] adv. Glowingly,
eulogistically, in high terms.

élogieux, euse [-ʒjø, ø:z] adj. Laudatory, commendatory, eulogistic; *en termes élogieux, très
élogieux,* in high, glowing terms.

éloigné, ée [elwaɲe] adj. Outlying, remote,
removed, distant, far-away, far-off (lieu); *être éloigné de deux kilomètres,* to be two kilometres away
(ou) distant; *se tenir éloigné de,* to keep away
from, to stand aloof from; *très éloigné de la gare,*
a long way from (ou) far distant from the station.
‖ Distant, remote, far-away, far-off (temps); *dans
un avenir peu éloigné,* in the near future. ‖ Far-
off, distant (parent). ‖ Remote (cause); removed,
far (sentiment) [*de,* from]; *rien n'est plus éloigné
de mes intentions,* nothing is farther from my
mind.

éloignement [-ɲmã] m. Withdrawal (action de
s'éloigner); removal (fait d'éloigner). ‖ Remoteness, distance (de, from). ‖ Separation, absence.
‖ FIG. Difference (entre, between). ‖ FIG. Aversion, dislike (pour, of, for); antipathy (pour, to,
for, against). ‖ FIG. Estrangement (de, from);
neglect (de, of).

éloigner [-ɲe] v. tr. (1). To remove, to take away
(ou) back (qqch.). ‖ To keep away, to keep off
(écarter); to send away, to dismiss (faire partir);
to drive away (repousser); to keep at a distance
(tenir à distance) [*de,* from]. ‖ To alienate, to
indispose, to estrange (aliéner); to divert, to turn
(détourner) [*de,* from]; to put off, to postpone
(remettre). ‖ To avert, to ward off (un danger);
to drive away, to banish (une idée); to avert, to
allay (les soupçons).
— v. pr. **S'éloigner,** to get (ou) to go away, to
withdraw, to move (ou) to make off; *s'éloigner
en courant,* to run away. ‖ To get farther away;
*la victoire semble s'éloigner chaque jour de plus
en plus,* victory seems to get farther and farther
away every day. ‖ To stand farther back (se
reculer); to keep aloof (se tenir à distance) [*de,*
from]. ‖ To grow fainter (bruit); to pass over
(danger, orage). ‖ FIG. *S'éloigner de,* to become
estranged from, to turn away from (ses amis);
to differ from (une conception); to swerve from
(son devoir); *s'éloigner du droit chemin, du sujet,*
to stray from the right path, from the point.

élongation [elɔ̃gasjɔ̃] f. Elongation.

élonger [-ʒe] v. tr. (7). NAUT. To run out (un
câble); to skirt (le littoral); to pass alongside
(un navire).

éloquemment [elɔkamã] adv. Eloquently.

éloquence [-kã:s] f. Eloquence, oratory.

éloquent, ente [-kã, ã:t] adj. Eloquent.

élu, ue [ely] adj. Elect.
— s. Chosen person. ‖ Elected member (au Parlement). ‖ ECCLÉS. *Les élus,* the elect.

élucidation [elysidasjɔ̃] f. Elucidation.

élucider [-de] v. tr. (1). To elucidate, to clear up.

élucubration [elykybrasjɔ̃] f. Lucubration.

élucubrer [-bre] v. tr. (1). FAM. To lucubrate.

éluder [elyde] v. tr. (1). To elude, to evade, to
dodge (une difficulté, un règlement); to evade
(une question); to shirk (un travail). [V. ÉVITER.]

Élysée [elize] m. † Elysium. ‖ Elysée (à Paris).
— adj. Elysian (champs). ‖ *Les Champs-Elysées,*
Champs Elysées (à Paris).

élyséen, enne [-ẽ, ɛn] adj. Elysian.

élytre [elitr] m. ZOOL. Elytron (pl. elytra).

elzévir [ɛlzevi:r] m. Elzevir (en typogr.).

émaciation [emasjasjɔ̃] f. Emaciation.

émacié, ée [-sje] adj. Emaciated. (V. DÉCHARNÉ.)

émacier (s') [semasje] v. pr. (1). To become emaciated.

émail [ema:j] (pl. **émaux** [emo]) m. Enamel; *en émail*, enamelled. ‖ ARTS. Enamel; glaze (de la céramique). ‖ MÉD. Enamel (des dents). ‖ BLAS. Tincture.

émaillage [-ja:ʒ] m. Enamelling. ‖ Glazing (de la céramique).

émailler [-je] v. tr. (1). To enamel (l'acier); to glaze (la céramique). ‖ FIG. To sprinkle, to dot, to speckle (*de*, with); *émaillé de*, dotted (ou) studded with (citations); dotted with (fleurs).

émaillerie [-jri] f. Enamelling.

émailleur, euse [-jœ:r, ø:z] s. Enameller.

émanation [emanasjɔ̃] f. Emanation; efflux (de gaz). ‖ CHIM. Radium emanation, radon. ‖ FIG. Emanation, exhalation.

émancipateur, trice [emɑ̃sipatœ:r, tris] adj. Emancipatory.
— s. Emancipator.

émancipation [-pasjɔ̃] f. Emancipation.

émancipé, ée [-pe] adj. Emancipated. ‖ FIG. Forward, fast.

émanciper [-pe] v. tr. (1). To emancipate.
— v. pr. S'émanciper, to get out of hand (ou) control; to throw off all restraint; *s'émanciper de*, to free oneself from.

émaner [emane] v. intr. (1). To emanate (*de*, from). [V. DÉCOULER.]

émargement [emarʒəmɑ̃] m. Cutting down of the margins. ‖ Marginal note. ‖ Signing, initialling (pour paiement); *feuille d'émargement*, pay-sheet.

émarger [-ʒe] v. tr. (7). To cut down the margins of. ‖ To write a marginal note in. ‖ To sign (pour paiement).
— v. intr. To draw one's salary, to be paid (v. TOUCHER); *émarger aux fonds secrets*, to be subsidized from secret funds.

émasculation [emaskylasjɔ̃] f. Emasculation.

émasculer [-le] v. tr. (1). To emasculate.

embâcle [ɑ̃bɑ:kl] m. Ice-jam, obstruction.

emballage [ɑ̃bala:ʒ] m. Packing, wrapping; *frais d'emballage*, package, packing charges. ‖ Package; *emballage compris*, ready packed; *emballage perdu*, packing free; *on ne reprend pas les emballages vides*, empties not returnable (ou) not taken back. ‖ SPORTS. Burst of speed.

emballement [-lmɑ̃] m. TECHN. Racing. ‖ FIN. *Emballement des cours*, boom in prices. ‖ FAM. Excitement; enthusiasm; passing fancy.

emballé, ée [-le] adj. FAM. Fiery (personne); carried away (*par*, by); keen (*pour*, on).

emballer [-le] v. tr. (1). To pack up, to wrap up. ‖ TECHN. To race (le moteur). ‖ FIG. To thrill (électriser); to transport; to carry away (entraîner). ‖ FAM. To run in (arrêter); to blow up (semoncer).
— v. intr. TECHN. To spurt.
— v. pr. S'emballer, to bolt, to run away (cheval). ‖ TECHN. To race. ‖ FAM. To get worked up; to fly into a temper (s'emporter); *s'emballer pour*, to take a fancy to (qqn); to become a fan of (une vedette).

emballeur, euse [-lœ:r, ø:z] s. Packer.

embarcadère [ɑ̃barkadɛ:r] m. NAUT. Wharf; landing-stage. ‖ CH. DE F. Platform.

embarcation [-sjɔ̃] f. NAUT. Boat, small boat.

embardée [ɑ̃barde] f. Lurch; *faire une embardée dans la rue*, to lurch across the road. ‖ AUTOM. Skid, swerve. ‖ NAUT. Yaw, lurch. ‖ FAM. Slip, lapse (écart).

embarder v. intr. (1). AUTOM. To skid, to swerve. ‖ NAUT., AVIAT. To yaw, to lurch.

embargo [ɑ̃bargo] m. NAUT. Embargo; *lever, mettre l'embargo sur*, to raise, to lay an embargo on. ‖ COMM. Embargo; *mettre l'embargo sur*, to forbid the sale of.

embarquement [ɑ̃barkəmɑ̃] m. NAUT. Shipping (de marins, d'un paquet de mer); embarking, embarcation, boarding (de passagers); shipment, loading (de marchandises). ‖ AVIAT., CH. DE F. Boarding (de passagers); loading (de marchandises).

embarquer [-ke] v. tr. (1). NAUT. To ship (des marins, un paquet de mer); to embark, to ship, to take on board (prendre à bord des passagers, des marchandises); to put on board, to load (charger des marchandises à bord). ‖ FAM. To walk off with (voler). ‖ FAM. To pull in, to run in (arrêter). ‖ FIG. To drag (entraîner) : *mal, bien embarqué*, off to a bad, good start.
— v. intr. NAUT. To go aboard, to board, to embark. ‖ AVIAT. To board, to embark, to emplane. ‖ CH. DE F. To board, to embark, to entrain. ‖ NAUT. *Le bateau embarque*, the boat is shipping water.
— v. pr. S'embarquer. NAUT. To go aboard, to board, to embark. ‖ FAM. To launch into.

embarras [ɑ̃bara] m. Encumbrance; *embarras de voitures*, traffic-block (ou) jam. ‖ Inconvenience, trouble (dérangement); *causer de l'embarras à*, to put to a lot of trouble. ‖ Embarrassment; difficulty, quandary (perplexité); *être, mettre dans l'embarras*, to be, to put at a loss (ou) in a fix; *se mettre dans l'embarras*, to get into a fix; *tirer qqn d'embarras*, to get s.o. out of a scrape. ‖ Embarrassment, confusion; awkwardness (v. TIMIDITÉ); *avec embarras*, confusedly. ‖ Pl. Difficulties; *embarras d'argent*, pecuniary (ou) money difficulties. ‖ MÉD. *Embarras gastrique*, weak digestion, upset stomach; *embarras de parole*, speech defect, impediment of speech. ‖ FAM. To-do; fuss; *faire des embarras*, to make a fuss.

embarrassant, ante [-sɑ̃, ɑ̃:t] adj. Cumbersome (encombrant). ‖ Perplexing; puzzling (problème); embarrassing, awkward (question, situation).

embarrassé, ée [-se] adj. Encumbered (encombré); blocked up, obstructed (obstrué). ‖ Hampered, entangled (empêtré); hindered (entravé); *embarrassé de sa personne*, awkward, gawky. ‖ At a loss, in a fix (en difficulté) [*pour*, for]; puzzled, perplexed (perplexe); *embarrassé pour trouver une réponse*, at a loss for an answer. ‖ Embarrassed, confused (confus); awkward (gauche); *avec un sourire embarrassé*, smiling diffidently. ‖ Embarrassed (gêné financièrement). ‖ MÉD. Heavy, upset (estomac); stammering (parole).

embarrasser [-se] v. tr. (1). To encumber (encombrer); to impede, to obstruct, to block up (obstruer). ‖ To hamper, to entangle, to hinder (empêtrer, entraver). ‖ To intrude on (importuner); *je ne l'embarrasse pas souvent*, I don't often darken his door. ‖ To embarrass, to puzzle, to perplex, to nonplus, to put at a loss. ‖ To confuse, to disconcert, to discompose, to abash (déconcerter). ‖ MÉD. To upset, to cloy (l'estomac); to impede (la parole).
— v. pr. S'embarrasser, to burden oneself (se charger) [*de*, with]; to cumber (ou) to hamper oneself (s'encombrer) [*de*, with]. ‖ To trouble oneself, to bother (se préoccuper) [*de*, about]. ‖ To feel awkward (être gauche); to be perplexed (ou) at a loss (être perplexe); to feel shy (être timide); *s'embarrasser dans ses explications*, to flounder in an explanation; *il ne s'embarrasse pas pour dire ce qu'il pense*, he is a plain speaker, he gives it you straight from the shoulder.

embastiller [ɑ̃bastije] v. tr. (1). To imprison.

embauche [ɑ̃bo:ʃ] m. Hiring (acte) [à la ferme];

engaging, taking on (à l'usine). ‖ Job (travail); *pas d'embauche!*, no hands wanted!

embaucher [ãboʃe] v. tr. (1). To hire (à la ferme); to engage, to take on (à l'usine).

embaucheur, euse [-ʃœːr, øːz] s. Hirer; taker-on, labour contractor.

embauchoir [ãboʃwaːr] m. Boot-tree, shoe-tree.

embaumé, ée [ãbome] adj. Balmy, fragrant.

embaumement [-mmã] m. Embalming.

embaumer [-me] v. tr. (1). To embalm (un mort). ‖ To be fragrant (ou) redolent of.
— v. intr. To give out a sweet smell, to be fragrant.

embaumeur, euse [-mœːr, øːz] s. Embalmer.

embecquer [ãbɛke] v. tr. (1). To feed (un oiseau).

embellie [ãbɛli] f. Fair period, spell of sunny weather.

embellir [-liːr] v. tr. (2). To embellish, to beautify, to improve the looks of (qqn). ‖ FAM. To doll up. (V. ORNER.)
— v. intr. To grow more beautiful (ou) handsome, to improve in looks.
— v. pr. **S'embellir**, to look better (chose); to grow more beautiful (ou) handsome (personne). ‖ FAM. To adorn oneself.

embellissement [-lismã] m. Embellishing (action); embellishment (résultat); *l'embellissement d'une ville*, the improvement of a town. ‖ Adornment (ornement).

emberlificoter [ãbɛrlifikɔte] v. tr. (1). FAM. To entangle, to ensnare.
— v. pr. **S'emberlificoter**. FAM. To get entangled (ou) U. S. snarled up (*dans*, in).

embêtant, ante [ãbɛtã, ãːt] adj. FAM. Tiresome, boring. [V. ENNUYEUX.]

embêté, ée [ãbɛte] adj. Bored, fed up (importuné) [*de*, with]; worried (tourmenté) [*de*, about].

embêtement [-tmã] m. Nuisance; bother, bore; *se préparer des embêtements*, to look for trouble.

embêter [-te] v. tr. (1). To annoy, to rile (agacer); to bore; to bother, to pester (importuner); to worry (tourmenter).
— v. pr. **S'embêter**, to be bored (à, with).

emblave [ãblaːv] f. AGRIC. Land sown with corn.

emblaver [ãblave] v. tr. (1). AGRIC. To sow (ou) crop with corn.

emblavure [-vyːr] f. AGRIC. Land sown with corn.

emblée (d') [dãble] loc. adv. Right away, straight away (ou) off, at the very first, at the first go.

emblématique [ãblematik] adj. Emblematic.

emblème [ãblɛːm] m. Emblem (attribut, symbole). ‖ Pl. Insignia. ‖ FIG. Symbol.

embobeliner [ãbɔbline], **embobiner** [-bine] v. tr. (1). FAM. To bamboozle, to blarney, to hoodwink, to get round.

emboîtage [ãbwataːʒ] m. Packing, boxing, casing. ‖ Casing; cover (en reliure). ‖ FAM. Hooting, U. S. razzing.

emboîtement [-tmã] m. Encasing (de boîtes); jointing, interlocking (de pièces). ‖ MÉD. Socket (d'un os).

emboîter [-te] v. tr. (1). To box. ‖ TECHN. To joint, to interlock. ‖ MILIT. *Emboîter le pas à*, to fall into step with. ‖ FAM. To jug (coffrer); to hoot, U. S. to razz (huer); *emboîter le pas à qqn*, to dog s.o.'s footsteps.
— v. pr. **S'emboîter**, to fit (*dans*, into).

emboîture [-tyːr] f. Fit; socket.

embolie [ãbɔli] f. MÉD. Embolism.

embonpoint [ãbɔ̃pwɛ̃] m. Stoutness; portliness; rotundity; *prendre de l'embonpoint*, to put on flesh.

emboquer [ãbɔke] v. tr. (1). To cram.

embosser [ãbɔse] v. tr. (1). NAUT. To moor fore and aft (ou) alongside.
— v. pr. **S'embosser**, to moor fore and aft.

embossure [ãbɔsyːr] f. NAUT. Spring.

embouche [ãbuʃ] f. AGRIC. Pasture land.

embouché, ée [ãbuʃe] adj. *Mal embouché*, foul-mouthed.

emboucher v. tr. (1). To blow. ‖ FAM. *Emboucher la trompette*, to trumpet the news.

embouchoir [-ʃwaːr] m. MUS. Mouthpiece. ‖ MILIT. Upper band, nose-cap.

embouchure [-ʃyːr] f. Mouth (d'un vase). ‖ MUS. Mouthpiece. ‖ GÉOGR. Mouth (d'un fleuve).

embouquer [ãbuke] v. tr. (1). NAUT. To enter the mouth of.

embourber [ãburbe] v. tr. (1). To bog, to mire.
— v. pr. **S'embourber**, to get bogged, to stick in the mud. ‖ FIG. To get entangled (*dans*, in).

embourgeoisement [ãburʒwazmã] m. Adoption of bourgeois ideas and habits.

embourgeoiser (s') [sãburʒwaze] v. pr. (1). To become « suburban »; to adopt the habits and the ideas of the middle-class.

embout [ãbu] m. Ferrule.

embouteillage [ãbutɛjaːʒ] m. Bottling (d'un liquide). ‖ AUTOM. Traffic-jam; bottleneck (dans un goulet). ‖ NAUT. Blocking-up (d'un port). ‖ COMM. Bottleneck (de la production).

embouteiller [-je] v. tr. (1). To bottle (un liquide). ‖ AUTOM. To jam. ‖ NAUT. To block up. ‖ COMM. To bottleneck.

embouter [ãbute] v. tr. (1). To ferrule; to tip.

emboutir [ãbutiːr] v. tr. (2). TECHN. To stamp; to emboss. ‖ AUTOM. To crash into, to bump into.
— v. pr. **S'emboutir**, AUTOM. To crash (*contre*, into); to collide (*contre*, with).

emboutissage [-tisaːʒ] m. TECHN. Stamping. ‖ AUTOM. Collision.

emboutissoir [-tiswaːr] m. TECHN. Stamper.

embranchement [ãbrãʃmã] m. Branching off (d'un arbre). ‖ Branching off (d'une rivière); junction, fork (de routes); junction (de tuyaux). ‖ Embranchment (rivière); branch-road (route); branch-pipe (tuyau). [V. RAMIFICATION.] ‖ Siding; *embranchement particulier*, own (ou) private siding. ‖ CH. DE F. Junction (de lignes); branch-line (ligne). ‖ ZOOL., BOT. Branch, phylum.

embrancher [-ʃe] v. tr. (1). To branch.
— v. pr. **S'embrancher**, to branch off (*sur*, from).

embrasement [ãbrazmã] m. Conflagration, blaze (par le feu). ‖ Illumination (par la lumière); glow (par le soleil). ‖ FIG. Conflagration.

embraser [-ze] v. tr. (1). To set aflame (ou) ablaze, to set fire to (par le feu). ‖ To illuminate (par la lumière); to set aglow (par le soleil). ‖ FIG. To inflame, to fire up (qqn).
— v. pr. **S'embraser**, to blaze up, to glow (feu); to take fire, to flare up, to blaze up (par le feu). ‖ To become illuminated (par la lumière); to glow (par le soleil). ‖ FIG. To become infatuated (par l'amour); to flare up (par la colère); to blaze up (par la guerre).

embrassade [ãbrasad] f. Kissing (baiser); embrace (enlacement).

embrasse [ãbras] f. Curtain-loop (pour rideau).

embrassement [-smã] m. Embracement; embrace.

embrasser [-se] v. tr. (1). To hug, to embrace, to clasp in one's arms (enlacer). ‖ To kiss (donner un baiser); *je vous embrasse affectueusement*, with my best love, all my love, love to you (par lettre). ‖ To cover, to span (couvrir); to embrace, to encircle, to encompass (englober); *embrasser par l'esprit*, to comprehend, to take in; *embrasser du regard*, to survey, to take in. ‖ FIG. To take up, to enter upon (une carrière); to espouse (une cause); to adopt, to embrace (une doctrine); to undertake (un travail); *embrasser le parti de,* to stand by, to side with.

embrasseur, euse [-sœːr, øːz] s. Person fond of kissing; gushing person; smoocher (fam.).

embrasure [ãbrazyːr] f. Embrasure. ‖ MILIT. Embrasure, crenel. ‖ NAUT. Gun-port.

embrayage [ãbrɛjaːʒ] m. TECHN. Putting (ou) throwing into gear; engaging of the clutch (action); clutch; connecting gear (appareil).

embrayer [-je] v. tr. (9 *b*). TECHN. To put (ou) to throw into gear. ‖ AUTOM. To engage (ou) let in the clutch. ‖ FAM. To start work.
— v. pr. **S'embrayer,** to come into gear.

embrayeur [-jœːr] m. TECHN. Clutch-fork.

embrigadement [ãbrigadmã] m. MILIT. Brigading. ‖ FIG. Enrolling (*dans,* into).

embrigader [-de] v. tr. (1). MILIT. To brigade. ‖ FIG. To enrol (*dans,* into).

embringuer [ãbrɛ̃ge] v. tr. (1). FAM. To involve (*dans,* in), to drag (*dans,* into).
— v. pr. **S'embringuer.** FAM. To get involved (ou) mixed up (*dans,* in).

embrocation [ãbrɔkasjɔ̃] f. MÉD. Embrocation.

embrochement [ãbrɔʃmã] m. CULIN. Spitting.

embrocher [-ʃe] v. tr. (1). CULIN. To spit, to skewer. ‖ FAM. To run through, to spit (qqn).

embrouillage [ãbrujaːʒ] m. V. EMBROUILLEMENT.

embrouillamini [ãbrujamini] m. FAM. Pretty kettle of fish, nice pickle.

embrouille [ãbruːj] f. POP. Skulduggery (tractation louche); muddle, mix-up (confusion); *sac d'embrouilles,* shady business.

embrouillé, ée [-je] adj. Tangled (écheveau, fil). ‖ FIG. Intricate (affaire, situation); involved (style); *aux idées embrouillées,* muddle-headed.

embrouillement [-jmã] m. Tangle, entanglement. ‖ FIG. Intricacy, embroilment.

embrouiller [-je] v. tr. (1). To tangle, to ravel (un écheveau); to mix up (des papiers). ‖ FIG. To embroil (une affaire); to confuse (une question, qqn).
— v. pr. **S'embrouiller,** to get tangled. ‖ FIG. To become complicated (ou) intricate (affaire, question); to grow confused, to lose count (personne).

embroussaillé, ée [ãbrusɑje] adj. Overgrown with brushwood (lieu). ‖ Tousled (cheveux); bushy (sourcils). ‖ FIG. Intricate (affaire).

embruiné, ée [ãbrɥine] adj. Misty. ‖ AGRIC. Spoiled by drizzle.

embrumé, ée [ãbryme] adj. Foggy, hazy; misty. ‖ FIG. Foggy (idée); clouded, gloomy (visage).

embrumer v. tr. (1). To haze, to cover with fog. ‖ FIG. To muddle (les idées); to cloud (le visage).
— v. pr. **S'embrumer,** to become foggy (ou) hazy. ‖ FIG. To become gloomy.

embrun [ãbrœ̃] m. Spray, spindrift.

embryogénie [ãbrijɔʒeni] f. MÉD. Embryogeny.

embryologie [ãbrijɔlɔʒi] f. MÉD. Embryology.

embryologique [-ʒik] adj. MÉD. Embryologic, embryological.

embryologiste [-ʒist] s. MÉD. Embryologist.

embryon [ãbrijɔ̃] m. Embryo. ‖ FIG. Embryo. (V. GERME.) ‖ FAM. Shrimp.

embryonnaire [-jɔnɛːr] adj. Embryonic. ‖ FIG. In embryo.

embu, ue [-ãby] adj. ARTS. Dull.
— m. ARTS. Dullness.

embûche [ãbyːʃ] f. Trap. (V. PIÈGE.)

embûcher (s') [sãbyʃe] v. pr. (1). To enter covert.

embué, ée [ãbye] adj. Misty.

embuer v. tr. (1). To mist.

embuscade [ãbyskad] f. Ambush, ambuscade; *attirer dans une embuscade,* to waylay.

embusqué [-ke] m. MILIT. Shirker, dodger, U. S. gold-bricker. ‖ SPORTS. *Les embusqués,* third-row forwards.

embusquer v. tr. (1). To station in ambush. ‖ To place under cover.
— v. pr. **S'embusquer,** to lie in ambush (ou) in wait. ‖ MILIT. To shirk, U. S. to gold-brick.

éméché, ée [emeʃe] adj. FAM. Fuddled, tight, squiffy, lit up; U. S. high. (V. GRIS.)

émécher v. tr. (5). To divide into locks (les cheveux). ‖ FAM. To fuddle (qqn).

émendation [emãdasjɔ̃] f. Emendation.

émender [-de] v. tr. (1). To emend. ‖ JUR. To amend.

émeraude [emroːd] f. Emerald.
— adj. Emerald green (couleur).

émergence [emɛrʒãːs] f. Emergence.

émerger [-ʒe] v. intr. (5). To emerge. ‖ FIG. To come out.

émeri [emri] m. Emery; *bouché à l'émeri,* stoppered; *papier émeri,* emery paper. ‖ FAM. *Bouché à l'émeri,* wood from the neck up.

émerillon [emrijɔ̃] m. ZOOL. Merlin. ‖ NAUT. Swivel.

émerillonné [-jɔne] adj. Bright, gleaming (œil); brisk, bright (personne).

émérite [emerit] adj. Emeritus (en retraite). ‖ FAM. Experienced, eminent, remarkable.

émersion [emɛrsjɔ̃] f. Emersion.

émerveillé, ée [emɛrvɛje] adj. Wonderstruck.

émerveillement [-jmã] m. Wonder, amazement.

émerveiller [-je] v. tr. (1). To amaze, to fill with wonder.
— v. pr. **S'émerveiller,** to marvel, to wonder (*de,* at). [V. ÉTONNER (s').]

émétique [emetik] adj., m. MÉD. Emetic.

émetteur, trice [emetœːr, tris] adj. RADIO. Transmitting; *poste émetteur,* transmitter. ‖ FIN. Issuing (établissement).
— m. RADIO. Transmitter; *émetteur-récepteur portatif,* walkie-talkie. ‖ FIN. Issuer.

émettre [emɛtr] v. tr. (64). To emit (de la chaleur, de la lumière); to give off (une odeur); to utter (un son). ‖ FIN. To issue (un chèque, un emprunt, des titres, un timbre); to put into circulation (de la monnaie); to utter (de la fausse monnaie). ‖ RADIO. To transmit. ‖ FIG. To express, to set forth (une opinion, un souhait); to put forward (des prétentions); to cast (un vote).
— v. intr. RADIO. To broadcast.

émeu [emø] m. ZOOL. Emu.

émeute [emøːt] f. Riot. (V. INSURRECTION.)

émeutier [emøtje] m. Rioter.

émiettement [emjɛtmã] m. Crumbling.

émietter [-te] v. pr. (1). To crumb (du pain). ‖ FIG. To crumble, to fritter away.
— v. pr. **S'émietter,** to crumble away (pr. et fig.).

émigrant, ante [emigrã, ãːt] adj., s. Emigrant.

émigration [-grasjɔ̃] f. Emigration.

émigré, ée [-gre] s. † Emigré (pendant une révolution). ‖ Emigrant.

émigrer [-gre] v. intr. (1). To emigrate. ‖ To migrate (oiseaux).

émincé [emɛ̃se] m. CULIN. Sliced meat.

émincer v. tr. (6). CULIN. To mince.

éminemment [eminamã] adv. Eminently, prominently.

éminence [-nãːs] f. Rise, eminence, hill (lieu). ‖ Eminence (titre). ‖ FIG. Eminence, prominence.

éminent, ente [-nã, ãːt] adj. Eminent, conspicuous, prominent.

éminentissime [-nãtisim] adj. Most eminent.

émir [emiːr] m. Emir.

émirat [emira] m. Emirate. ‖ **Émirats arabes unis,** m. pl. GÉOGR. United Arab Emirates.

émissaire [emisɛ:r] m. Emissary. (V. MESSAGER.)

émissif, ive [-sif, i:v] adj. Emissive.

émission [-sjɔ̃] f. Emission (de chaleur, lumière, parfum); utterance (d'un son); release (de vapeur). ‖ Sending out (de messages, de signaux). ‖ FIN. Coining (de monnaie); utterance (de fausse monnaie); issuing, issue (de chèques, de titres); *prix d'émission,* issue price. ‖ RADIO. Transmitting, broadcasting (action); broadcast, transmission (émission). ‖ GRAMM. *D'une seule émission de voix,* in one breath.

emmagasinage [ãmagazina:ʒ] m. Storage, warehousing; *droits d'emmagasinage,* storage charges. ‖ FIG. Accumulation, storing up.

emmagasiner [-ne] v. tr. (1). To store, to warehouse. ‖ FIG. To accumulate, to store up.

emmaillotement [ãmajɔtmã] m. Swaddling. ‖ FAM. Binding up (d'un membre).

emmailloter [-te] v. tr. (1). To swaddle (un enfant). ‖ FAM. To bind up (un membre).

emmanchement [ãmãʃmã] m. Fitting of a handle (d'un outil). ‖ Fitting (d'une pièce).

emmancher [ãmãʃe] v. tr. (1). To haft, to helve. ‖ To joint, to fit on (embouter). ‖ FAM. To start (une affaire); *bien emmanché,* well organized, well in hand.
— v. pr. **S'emmancher,** to fit (*dans,* into). ‖ FAM. To start, to set going.

emmanchure [-ʃy:r] f. Arm-hole, sleeve-hole.

emmêlement [ãmɛlmã] m. Tangle, entanglement.

emmêler [-le] v. tr. (1). To tangle, to entangle, to ravel. ‖ FIG. To mix up.
— v. pr. **S'emmêler,** to become entangled. ‖ FIG. To get muddled.

emménagement [ãmenaʒmã] m. Moving in; installation.

emménager [-ʒe] v. intr. (7). To move in; to move house.
— v. tr. To install, to move in (les meubles, qqn).

emmener [ãmne] v. tr. (5). To take (ou) to lead away (ou) out; *emmenez-le,* take him away (ou) with you; *emmenez-la faire une promenade,* take her out for a walk; *je l'ai emmené dîner,* I took him to dinner; *le train m'a emmené à Lyon,* the train took (ou) carried me to Lyons; *un agent l'a emmené,* a policeman took him away.

emment(h)al [emãtal] m. CULIN. Emmenthal.

emmerdant, ante [ãmɛrdã, ã:t] adj. ARG. Bloody boring (ennuyeux); bloody sickening (ou) irritating (agaçant); *c'est emmerdant,* it gets on one's wick (ou) tits, it's a bloody drag; *elle est emmerdante,* she's a pain in the arse.

emmerdement [ãmɛrdəmã] m. ARG. Bloody nuisance; *avoir des emmerdements,* to be in the shit.

emmerder [ãmɛrde] v. tr. (1). ARG. To muck, to crap on (conchier). ‖ FIG. To bother (qqn); *je l'emmerde!,* to hell with him!
— v. pr. **S'emmerder,** to be bored stiff.

emmerdeur [-dœ:r] s. ARG. Bloody (ou) damn nuisance.

emmieller [ãmjɛle] v. tr. (1). To sweeten with honey. ‖ POP. To bother.

emmitoufler [ãmitufle] v. tr. (13). To muffle up (*dans, de,* in).
— v. pr. **S'emmitoufler,** to muffle up.

emmouscailler [ãmuskaje] v. tr. (1). POP. To get on s.o.'s nerves, to be a pain in the neck.

emmurer [ãmyre] v. tr. (1). To wall in, to immure (qqn); to wall in (un terrain).

émoi [emwa] m. Emotion; flutter; *en émoi,* agitated, all of a flutter. ‖ Sensation, disturbance; *soulever l'émoi,* to spread alarm.

émollient, ente [emɔljã, ã:t] adj., m. MÉD. Emollient, counter-irritant.

émoluments [emɔlymã] m. pl. Emoluments.

émonctoire [emɔ̃ktwa:r] m. MÉD. Emunctory.

émondage [emɔ̃da:ʒ] m. AGRIC. Pruning, lopping. ‖ FIG. Cutting down.

émonder [-de] v. tr. (1). AGRIC. To prune, to lop. ‖ FIG. To cut down.

émondeur [-dœ:r] m. Pruner.

émondoir [-dwa:r] m. Pruning-hook.

émotif, ive [emɔtif, i:v] adj. Emotional (personne); emotive (trouble); *peu émotif,* unemotional, irresponsive, U. S. unresponsive.

émotion [-sjɔ̃] f. Emotion, feeling. (V. ÉMOI.) ‖ Shock, turn (choc). ‖ Sensation, disturbance, agitation.

émotionnable [emɔsjɔnabl] adj. Emotional.

émotionnant, ante [-nã, ã:t] adj. Moving. ‖ Stirring; thrilling.

émotionnel, elle [-nɛl] adj. Emotional (réaction, état).

émotionner [-ne] v. tr. (1). To move. (V. ÉMOUVOIR.) ‖ To stir; to thrill (effrayer).
— v. pr. **S'émotionner,** to be moved; to get excited.

émotivité [emɔtivite] f. Emotivity, emotiveness.

émotter [emɔte] v. tr. (1). AGRIC. To crush the clods of.

émoucher [emuʃe] v. tr. (1). To drive away the flies from.

émouchet [emuʃɛ] m. ZOOL. Kestrel.

émouchette [emuʃɛt] f. Fly-net (pour chevaux).

émouchoir [emuʃwa:r] m. Fly-whisk.

émoudre [emudr] v. tr. (65). To sharpen.

émoulu, ue [emuly] adj. FIG. *Frais émoulu de,* fresh from.

émoussé, ée [emuse] adj. Blunt (lame, tranchant). ‖ FIG. Blunted, dulled (sens, sentiments).

émousser v. tr. (1). To blunt (le tranchant). ‖ FIG. To take the edge off (l'appétit); to dull (l'esprit); to blunt (les sentiments).
— v. pr. **S'émousser,** to become blunt (tranchant). ‖ FIG. To lose its edge (appétit); to become dull (esprit); to become blunted (sentiments).

émoustillant, ante [emustijã, ã:t] adj. Titillating, exciting, arousing.

émoustillé, ée [emustije] adj. Excited, randy (pop.) [allumé]; frisky (folâtre); exhilarated (joyeux).

émoustiller v. tr. (1). To ginger up; to elate.
— v. pr. **S'émoustiller,** to get excited (ou) jolly (ou) elated.

émouvant, ante [emuvã, ã:t] adj. Moving, touching; *fort émouvant,* stirring, thrilling.

émouvoir [-wa:r] v. tr. (67). To move, to touch, to affect (toucher). ‖ To disturb, to alarm, to upset (bouleverser); to excite, to stir, to rouse (exciter); to thrill (impressionner).
— v. pr. **S'émouvoir,** to be moved (ou) touched (*de,* by). ‖ To get alarmed (*de,* at); to be disturbed (*de,* by). ‖ To get excited (*de,* at); to be stirred up (*de,* by); to be thrilled (*de,* at, by).

empaillage [ãpãja:ʒ] m. Stuffing (d'un animal); taxidermy (métier).

empailler [-je] v. tr. (1). To stuff (un animal). ‖ To rush-bottom (une chaise). ‖ To pack in straw (des objets); to cover with straw (des plantes).

empailleur [-jœ:r] m. Taxidermist.

empalement [ãpalmã] m. Impalement.

empaler [-le] v. tr. (1). To impale.

empan [ãpã] m. Span.

empanacher [ãpanaʃe] v. tr. (1). To plume.

empanner [ãpane] v. tr. (1). NAUT. To bring by the lee.

empaquetage [ãpakta:ʒ] m. Packing.

empaqueter [-te] v. tr. (8 a). To pack, to wrap up.

empaqueteur, euse [-tœ:r, ø:z] s. Packer.

emparer (s') [sãpare] v. pr. (1). To lay hands (*de,* on); to lay (ou) to catch (ou) to take (ou) to seize hold (*de,* of); to take possession (*de,* of);

s'emparer de la meilleure place, to secure the best seat. ‖ MILIT. *S'emparer par surprise de,* to take by surprise. ‖ FIG. *S'emparer de,* to come over, to fall upon, to grow upon, to lay hold on, to steal over, to possess (idée, sentiment); *s'emparer de la conversation,* to monopolize the conversation.

empâtement [ᾶpɑtmᾶ] m. Cramming d'une volaille). ‖ Putting on flesh (du corps). ‖ Furring (de la langue); huskiness (de la voix). ‖ Over-inking (en typogr.).

empâter [-te] v. tr. (1). To cram (une volaille). ‖ To make fleshy (le corps). ‖ To coat (la bouche); to make husky (la voix). ‖ To over-ink (en typogr.). — v. pr. **S'empâter,** to put on flesh (corps); to become coated (langue); to become husky (voix).

empathie [ᾶpati] f. Empathy.

empattement [ᾶpatmᾶ] m. ARCHIT. Foundation (de bâtiment); footing (de mur); basement (de pont). ‖ AUTOM. Wheelbase. ‖ AVIAT. Width.

empaumer [ᾶpome] v. tr. (1). To catch in (ou) to strike with the palm of the hand. ‖ FIG. To catch hold of (une affaire). ‖ FAM. To bamboozle (qqn) [v. ENTORTILLER]; *se laisser empaumer,* to allow oneself to be hoodwinked.

empaumure [-my:r] f. Palm piece (de gant). ‖ Palm (du cerf).

empêché, ée [ᾶpεʃe] adj. Prevented; *empêché d'aller à,* prevented from going to. ‖ Engaged, tied up (retenu). ‖ At a loss, puzzled (embarrassé); *bien empêché de trouver la réponse,* somewhat at a loss for an answer.

empêchement [ᾶpεʃmᾶ] m. Impediment, bar, hindrance (v. ENTRAVE, OBSTACLE); *mettre empêchement à,* to hinder, to oppose, to prevent. ‖ Prevention; *en cas d'empêchement,* in case of prevention; *j'ai eu un empêchement,* I was prevented from coming. ‖ JUR. Bar.

empêcher [-ʃe] v. tr. (1). To avert (détourner); to preclude, to exclude (exclure); to prevent, to hinder (mettre obstacle à); to obviate (obvier à); *empêcher qqn de faire,* to prevent (ou) hinder (ou) to keep s.o. from doing; *empêcher d'entrer,* to lock out (en enfermant); to keep out (en retenant); *je ne puis empêcher cela,* I cannot help it. — v. impers. *Il n'empêche que c'est un menteur,* that does not prevent him from being a liar; *n'empêche que c'est aimable de votre part,* it's nice of you all the same. — v. pr. **S'empêcher,** to refrain (de, from); *elle ne peut s'empêcher de se demander si,* she cannot help wondering whether; *je ne peux m'empêcher d'en douter,* I cannot but doubt it.

empêcheur [-ʃœ:r] m. Hinderer; *empêcheur de danser en rond,* spoil-sport, wet-blanket.

empeigne [ᾶpεɲ] f. Upper (de soulier). ‖ POP. *Gueule d'empeigne,* ugly mug, nasty puss.

empennage [ᾶpεna:ʒ] m. Feathering (de flèche). ‖ MILIT. Fin assembly (de bombe). ‖ AVIAT. Tail unit (ou) group (ou) surface.

empenner [ᾶpεne] v. tr. (1). To feather (une flèche). ‖ MILIT. To provide with fins (une bombe).

empereur [ᾶprœ:r] m. Emperor. (V. IMPÉRATRICE.)

emperlé, ée [ᾶpεrle] adj. FIG. Pearled, beaded (de, with).

emperler v. tr. (1). To ornament with pearls. ‖ FIG. To cover with pearls (ou) beads; *la sueur emperla son front,* his forehead was beaded with perspiration.

empesage [ᾶpəza:ʒ] m. Starching.

empesé, ée [-ze] adj. Boiled, U. S. stiff (chemise); starched, starchy (étoffe). ‖ FIG. Starchy, stiff.

empeser [-ze] v. tr. (1). To starch.

empesté, ée [ᾶpεste] adj. Pestilential, foul; stinking. ‖ FIG. Pestilent; depraved.

empester v. tr. (1). To infect. ‖ To stink (ou) reek of (une odeur); to stink out (une pièce). ‖ FIG. To deprave, to taint. — v. intr. To stink. (V. PUER.)

empêtré, ée [ᾶpεtre] adj. FAM. Entangled (dans, in); *empêtré dans une sale histoire,* mixed up in a nasty business. ‖ FAM. Gawky (gauche); *empêtré comme une poule qui a trouvé un couteau,* as flustered as an old hen with one chick.

empêtrer v. tr. (1). To hobble (un animal); to entangle (qqn). ‖ FIG. To puzzle (embarrasser); to involve, to mix up (engager) [dans, in]. — v. pr. **S'empêtrer,** to hamper (ou) encumber oneself (s'encombrer) [de, with]; to get entangled (s'entraver) [dans, in]. ‖ FIG. To get involved (ou) mixed up (dans, in).

emphase [ᾶfɑ:z] f. Bombast, grandiloquence.

emphatique [ᾶfatik] adj. Bombastic, grandiloquent (v. AMPOULÉ). ‖ GRAMM. Emphatic.

emphatiquement [-kmᾶ] adv. Bombastically; in a bombastic way.

emphysémateux, euse [ᾶfizematø, ø:z] adj. MÉD. Emphysematous. — s. MÉD. Emphysematous patient.

emphysème [-zε:m] m. MÉD. Emphysema.

empiècement [ᾶpjεsmᾶ] m. Yoke (de robe).

empierrement [ᾶpjεrmᾶ] m. TECHN. Metalling (action); metal (résultat). ‖ CH. DE F. Ballasting; ballast.

empierrer [-re] v. tr. (1). To metal (une route). ‖ CH. DE F. To ballast.

empiétement [ᾶpjetmᾶ] m. Encroachment (sur, on, upon); infringement (sur, of). ‖ Inroad (sur, into); intrusion (sur, on).

empiéter [ᾶpjete] v. tr. (1). To appropriate (un terrain) [sur, from]. — v. intr. To encroach (sur, on, upon); to infringe, to intrude (sur, upon). ‖ FAM. To trespass (sur, on) [les plates-bandes].

empiffrer (s') [sᾶpifre] v. pr. (1). FAM. To stuff oneself (de, with).

empilage [ᾶpila:ʒ], **empilement** [ᾶpilmᾶ] m. Stacking, piling up.

empiler [-le] v. tr. (1). To stack (du bois); to pile up (des draps). ‖ FIG. To crowd, to squeeze (des gens). ‖ FAM. To diddle, to rook, U. S. to gouge (filouter) [de, out of]. — v. pr. **S'empiler,** to crowd (ou) pack (dans, into).

empileur, euse [-lœ:r, ø:z] s. Stacker, piler. ‖ FAM. Trickster, swindler; U. S. gouger.

empire [ᾶpi:r] m. Empire (état, style); *le Bas Empire,* the Lower Empire; *l'empire colonial,* the Colonial Empire. ‖ Empire, power (puissance); dominion, sway (sur, over). ‖ Authority, hold, control (ascendant) [sur, over]; *empire sur soi,* self-command, self-control; *prendre de l'empire sur,* to acquire control over, to gain a hold over. ‖ Pressure, stress (pression); *sous l'empire du besoin,* under the pressure of necessity.

empirer [ᾶpire] v. tr. (1). To worsen, to make worse. — v. intr. To worsen, to grow worse; to deteriorate.

empirique [-rik] adj. Empiric, empirical. — s. Empiric, empiricist.

empiriquement [-rikmᾶ] adv. Empirically.

empirisme [-rism] m. Empiricism. ‖ FAM. Guesswork.

empiriste [-rist] s. Empiric, empiricist.

emplacement [ᾶplasmᾶ] m. Site (de, of, for). ‖ Place, location. ‖ MILIT. Emplacement (d'un canon); position (des troupes).

emplanture [ᾶplᾶty:r] f. NAUT. Step (de mât). ‖ AVIAT. Socket (d'aile).

emplâtre [ᾶplɑ:tr] m. MÉD. Plaster; *mettre un*

emplâtre sur, to plaster. ‖ AUTOM. Patch. ‖ FAM.
Boob, wet, U. S. poor fish.
emplâtrer [ɑ̃plɑtre] v. tr. (1). MÉD. To plaster. ‖
FAM. To lumber up, to clutter up, to encumber.
emplette [ɑ̃plɛt] f. Purchase (v. ACHAT); *aller
faire des emplettes,* to go shopping; *faire l'emplette de,* to purchase.
emplir [ɑ̃pli:r] v. tr. (2). To fill, to fill up *(de,*
with); *emplir de monde,* to crowd (ou) to throng
with people. ‖ FIG. To overwhelm; *emplir de joie,*
to overjoy.
— v. pr. **S'emplir,** to fill, to fill up *(de,* with). ‖
NAUT. To fill, to become swamped.
emploi [ɑ̃plwa] m. Employment, use; *double
emploi,* duplication, overlapping; *faire emploi de
la force,* to resort to force. ‖ Handling (maniement); use (usage); *emploi du temps,* daily routine
(quotidien); time-table (tableau); *faire un bon
emploi de,* to make good use of, to put to good
use. ‖ Employment (occupation); *demande, offre
d'emploi,* situation wanted, vacant; *sans emploi,*
out of work, jobless. ‖ Employment, place, post,
position, situation (fonction); *emploi public,*
public office, official situation. ‖ THÉÂTR. Line. ‖
FIN. Employment, appropriation (des crédits). ‖
GRAMM. Use (d'un mot).
employé [-je] m. Employee; *employé de bureau,
de magasin, de l'Etat,* clerk, salesman (ou) shop-
assistant, official. ‖ CH. DE F. Railway employee,
railwayman.
employée [-je] f. Employee; *employée de bureau,
de magasin,* lady-clerk, saleswoman (ou) salesgirl
(ou) shop-assistant.
employer [-je] v. tr. (9 a). To use, to employ, to
make use of, to put to use (utiliser). ‖ To take,
to require (nécessiter); *ce gâteau emploie beaucoup de farine,* this cake takes a lot of flour. ‖
To spend (son argent, son temps); *mal employer,*
to mis-spend. ‖ To use (un mot); *mal employer,*
to misuse. ‖ To employ (qqn) [à, to]; *être employé
par qqn,* to be in s.o.'s employ. ‖ To have
recourse to, to resort to (la force); to exert (son
intelligence; to make use of (les protections).
— v. pr. **S'employer,** to be used (ou) employed;
s'employer à, to occupy oneself with; to endeavour
to; to do one's best to; *s'employer en faveur* (ou)
pour, to exert oneself on behalf of.
employeur [-jœ:r] s. Employer.
emplumé, ée [ɑ̃plyme] adj. Feathered.
empocher [ɑ̃pɔʃe] v. tr. (1). To pocket.
empoignade [ɑ̃pwaɲad] f. FAM. Set-to.
empoignant, ante [ɲɑ̃, ɑ̃:t] adj. Thrilling, gripping, sensational.
empoigne [ɑ̃pwaɲ] f. Grabbing, grab.
empoigner [-ɲe] v. tr. (1). To grab, to grip, to
grasp (saisir). ‖ To collar, to catch (arrêter). ‖
FIG. To grip, to thrill (émouvoir).
— v. pr. **S'empoigner.** FAM. To have a set-to;
to fight.
empois [ɑ̃pwa] m. Starch.
empoisonnant, ante [ɑ̃pwazɔnɑ̃, ɑ̃:t] adj. FAM.
Irritating, vexing; *c'est empoisonnant,* it's a
confounded nuisance.
empoisonné, ée [-ne] adj. Poisoned (flèche, nourriture). ‖ FIG. Poisonous (doctrine); envenomed
(louanges). ‖ FAM. Bored (importuné); worried
(inquiet).
empoisonnement [-nmɑ̃] m. Poisoning (pr. et
fig.). ‖ FAM. Nuisance, bother. (V. EMBÊTEMENT.)
empoisonner [-ne] v. tr. (1). To poison. ‖ FIG.
To corrupt (les mœurs); to embitter, to poison (la
vie). ‖ FAM. To infect (l'air); *empoisonner le gaz,*
to reek of gas. ‖ FAM. V. EMBÊTER.
— v. intr. To reek. (V. PUER.)
— v. pr. **S'empoisonner,** to be poisoned (par
accident); to poison oneself (volontairement). ‖
FAM. To be bored.

empoisonneur, euse [-nœ:r, ø:z] s. Poisoner.
emporté, ée [ɑ̃pɔrte] adj. Fiery, warm (caractère); quick-tempered, touchy, peppery, huffy
(personne). ‖ Runaway (cheval).
emportement [-tmɑ̃] m. † Transport. ‖ Anger,
fury (colère); fieriness (fougue); *avec emportement,* angrily.
emporte-pièce [-təpjɛs] m. invar. Punch; *découper à l'emporte-pièce,* to punch (ou) stamp out. ‖
FIG. *A l'emporte-pièce,* cutting, incisive (remarque); trenchant (style).
emporter [-te] v. tr. (1). To take away (ou) off (en
général); *emporter qqn à la morgue,* to take s.o.
to the mortuary. ‖ To bear off; to carry off (à la
main); *emportez votre parapluie,* take your
umbrella with you. ‖ To carry off (ou) away (en
voiture). ‖ To tear away (en arrachant); to sweep
away (en balayant); to punch out (en découpant
net). ‖ To shoot off (balle, obus); to remove
(décapant); to wash away (eau, mer); to blow off
(explosion); to blow off (ou) away (vent); *emporté
par le courant,* carried away by the stream;
emporté de-ci de-là par le vent, blown about; *
un passager fut emporté par une lame,* a passenger was washed overboard. ‖ MILIT. To carry,
to take (une place forte); to win (la victoire). ‖
MÉD. To carry off (un malade). ‖ CULIN. *A emporter,* for off-consumption, U. S. to take home (ou)
to go (fam.); *emporter la bouche,* to be highly-
seasoned, to be as hot as pepper, to burn the
mouth. ‖ JUR. To imply, to involve (décision). ‖
FIG. To transport (enthousiasme); to carry away
(passion); *emporter une douce image de,* to bring
away pleasant memories of; *se laisser emporter
par la colère,* to give way to anger; *se laisser
emporter par l'enthousiasme,* to let oneself be
carried away by enthusiasm. ‖ FAM. *Le diable
m'emporte si,* I'll be hanged if; *le diable vous
emporte!,* the devil take you!, go to the devil! ‖
L'emporter sur, to outshine, to overshadow (par
l'éclat); to outnumber (en nombre); to outweigh
(en poids); to preponderate over, to prevail over,
to have the best of (par la prédomination); to outmanœuvre (par la tactique); to be worth more
than (en valeur); to overcome, to triumph over,
to get the better of, to get the upper hand of (par
la victoire).
— v. pr. **S'emporter,** to be taken away, to be
carried off (ou) away (objet). ‖ To bolt (cheval).
‖ FIG. To flare (ou) to blaze up; *s'emporter
contre,* to lose one's temper with; *s'emporter pour
un rien,* to get worked up about nothing (fam.).
empotage [ɑ̃pɔta:ʒ] m. Potting.
empoté, ée [ɑ̃pɔte] adj. FAM. Clumsy.
— s. Muff, gawk.
empoter v. tr. (1). AGRIC. To pot (une plante).
empourprer [ɑ̃purpre] v. tr. (1). To purple, to
crimson. ‖ To flush (le teint).
— v. pr. **S'empourprer,** to glow red, to turn
crimson (ciel); to purple (raisins); to flush, to
blush, to burn red (teint).
empoussiéré, ée [ɑ̃pusjere] adj. Dusty.
empoussiérer v. tr. (5). To cover with dust.
empreindre [ɑ̃prɛ̃:dr] v. tr. (59). To impress, to
imprint, to stamp, to mark.
empreint, einte [ɑ̃prɛ̃, ɛ̃:t] adj. Stamped *(de,*
with).
empreinte [ɑ̃prɛ̃:t] f. Imprint, impression, print
(en général); impress (d'un tampon); *empreintes
digitales,* thumb- (ou) finger-prints, dabs (fam.);
empreinte de doigts, de pas, de roue, finger-,
mark-, foot-print, wheel-trace (ou) -track; *prendre
l'empreinte de,* to take an impression of. ‖ TECHN.
Mould (en typo). ‖ FIG. Stamp; mark *(sur,* upon).
empressé, ée [ɑ̃prɛse] adj. Anxious, willing *(à,*
to); eager *(de,* for, to); keen *(de,* on); *peu*

empressé à faire, backward in doing. ‖ Bustling, busy (affairé). ‖ Attentive (*auprès de,* to); assiduous (*auprès de,* about); faire *un accueil empressé à qqn,* to receive s.o. effusively; *se montrer empressé à l'égard de,* to show marked attentions to.
— s. Busybody; *faire l'empressé,* to fuss about.

empressement [-smɑ̃] m. Willingness (bonne volonté); haste, promptitude (rapidité); eagerness, forwardness (zèle); *avec empressement,* readily; *défaut d'empressement,* backwardness. ‖ Attentions (*auprès de,* to).

empresser (s') [sɑ̃prɛse] v. pr. (1). To be eager (*à,* to); to be sedulous (*à,* in) [avoir du zèle]. ‖ To be prompt (*de,* in); to hasten (*de,* to) [se hâter]. ‖ To busy oneself (*auprès de,* about) [s'occuper de]. ‖ To be assiduous (*auprès de,* about); to be attentive, to pay attention (*auprès de,* to) [être prévenant]. ‖ To bustle, to fuss (*autour de,* around) [s'affairer].

emprise [ɑ̃priz] f. Ascendancy (*sur,* over) [v. INFLUENCE]; hold (*sur,* on). ‖ JUR. Expropriation; requisitioning.

emprisonnement [ɑ̃prizɔnmɑ̃] m. Imprisonment.

emprisonner [-ne] v. tr. (1). To imprison, to put in prison, to take into custody. (V. ÉCROUER, INCARCÉRER.) ‖ To lock up, to box up, to cage (enfermer). ‖ FIG. To confine.

emprunt [ɑ̃prœ̃] m. Borrowing (argent, mot); *d'emprunt,* assumed, false (nom). ‖ FIN. Loan.

emprunté, ée [-te] adj. Borrowed (idée, mot) [*à,* from]. ‖ Assumed, false (nom). ‖ Clumsy, awkward (personne). ‖ FIG. Artificial, fictitious (éclat).

emprunter v. tr. (1). To borrow (de l'argent, un objet) [*à,* from, of]. ‖ To borrow (une idée); to borrow, to take (un mot) [*à,* from]. ‖ To assume (une identité, un nom, un titre). ‖ CH. DE F. To make use of (une voie). ‖ FIG. To derive (*à,* from). ‖ FAM. To take (un chemin).

emprunteur, euse [tœ:r, ø:z] adj. Given to borrowing.
— s. Borrower; *emprunteur sur gage,* pawner.

empuantir [ɑ̃pɥɑ̃ti:r] v. tr. (2). To make stink; to infect.

Empyrée [ɑ̃pire] adj., m. Empyrean.

ému, ue [emy] adj. Affected, moved (personne) [*par,* by]; tender (souvenir); *parler d'une voix émue,* to speak feelingly. ‖ Upset, agitated, nervous (v. TROUBLÉ); *ému de,* alarmed by.

émulateur, trice [emylatœ:r, tris] adj. Emulative.

émulation [-sjɔ̃] f. Emulation; *rivaliser d'émulation avec,* to vie with.

émule [emyl] s. Emulator; *être l'émule de,* to emulate.

émulseur [emylsœ:r] m. Emulsifier.

émulsif, ive [-sif, i:v], **émulsifiant, ante** [-sifjɑ̃, ɑ̃:t] adj. Emulsifying.
— m. Emulsifier, emulsifying agent.

émulsion [-sjɔ̃] f. Emulsion.

émulsionner [-sjɔne] v. tr. (1). To emulsify, to emulsionize.

en [ɑ̃] ([ɑ̃n] before a vowel) prép.

---

1. Lieu sans mouvement. — 2. Lieu avec mouvement. — 3. Etat. — 4. Manière. — 5. A la manière de. — 6. Matière. — 7. Moyen. — 8. But. — 9. Changement. — 10. Objet. — 11. Profession. — 12. Rang. — 13. Temps. — 14. Chez. — 15. En tant que. — 16. Lorsque. — 17. Par le fait que. — 18. Non traduit.

---

1. In, at (lieu, sans mouvement); *en nourrice,* at nurse; *en ville,* in town, U. S. downtown. ‖ **2.** To, into (lieu, avec mouvement); *aller en ville,* to go to town; *entrer en ville,* to go into town. ‖ **3.** In, on, at, with (état); *en bonne santé,* in good health; *en chapeau,* with a hat on; *en défaut,* at fault; *en grève,* on strike; *en guerre avec,* at war with; *en prière,* in prayer; *en robe du soir,* in evening dress. ‖ **4.** In, into (manière); *déchirer en morceaux,* to tear into pieces; *en bloc,* in the lump; *en hâte,* in haste. ‖ **5.** Like (à la manière de); *agir en roi,* to act like a king. ‖ **6.** Of (matière); *un mur en pierre,* a wall of stone, a stone wall. ‖ **7.** In, by (moyen); *aller en taxi à,* to go in a taxi-cab to; *venir en avion,* to come by air. ‖ **8.** In (but); *en l'honneur de,* in honour of. ‖ **9.** To, into (changement); *réduire en cendres,* to reduce to ashes; *tomber en poussière,* to crumble to dust. ‖ **10.** In, at (objet); *fertile en blé,* fertile in wheat; *fort en math,* good at math. ‖ **11.** Of (profession); *docteur en médecine,* doctor of medicine. ‖ **12.** In, at (rang); *en premier,* in the first place; *en tête du,* at the head of. ‖ **13.** During, in, within (temps); *en deux heures,* in two hours; *en été,* in summer; *livraison en un mois,* delivery within a month. ‖ **14.** In, about (chez); *ce qui me déplaît en elle,* what I dislike about her; *il n'y a pas l'ombre de vanité en lui,* there is no vanity about him. ‖ **15.** As (en tant que); *en punition de,* as a punishment for; *traiter en ennemi,* to treat as an enemy. ‖ **16.** On, when (lorsque); *en entrant dans la pièce,* on entering the room; *en passant je suis entré dire bonjour,* I looked in on my way by. ‖ While, as (pendant que); *tout en écrivant il bavardait,* he chattered as he wrote. ‖ **17.** By (par le fait de); *en n'en prenant pas davantage,* by not taking more. ‖ **18.** (Non traduit); *conduire qqn en voiture à,* to drive s.o. to; *en longueur,* lengthwise; *en or,* gold, golden; *fenêtre en ogive,* ogive window; *il marchait en lisant son journal,* he was walking along reading his paper; *mettre en bouteille,* to bottle; *partir en courant,* to run away; *peintre en bâtiments,* house-painter.

en [ɑ̃] (ɑ̃n before a vowel) pron. [sens personnel = de cela, d'elle, d'elles, d'eux, de lui, avec préposition correspondant au sens]; *elle ne s'en soucie pas,* she doesn't worry about it; *il en était aimé,* he was loved by her; *il est né dans la maison et il en connaît tous les recoins,* he was born in the house and he knows every corner of it; *j'en ai besoin,* I need it. ‖ Some, any, not any, none (sens partitif); *en voulez-vous?,* will you have some?; *je n'en ai pas,* I haven't any; *je vous en donnerais si j'en avais,* I would give you some if I had any. ‖ From there (sens adverbial); *elle en vient, elle en est originaire,* she comes from there. ‖ (Non traduit); *combien en voulez-vous?,* how much (ou) many do you want?; *elle m'en a donné trente,* she gave me thirty; *j'en ai fini de tout cela,* I have done with all that; *s'en aller,* to go away.

E. N. A. [ena] f. Abrév. de *Ecole nationale d'Administration,* school of higher education for future State officials.

enamouré, ée [ɑ̃namure] adj. Amorous (regard); enamoured (personne) [*de,* of].

enamourer (s') [sɑ̃namure] v. pr. (1). To fall in love (*de,* with).

énarque [enark] s. Student (ou) former student of the Ecole nationale d'Administration.

en-avant [ɑ̃navɑ̃] m. inv. SPORTS. Forward pass (passe); knock-on (balle qui touche terre).

encablure [ɑ̃kably:r] f. NAUT. Cable's length.

encadré [ɑ̃kadre] m. TECHN. Box (texte à l'intérieur d'un autre); inset (photo à l'intérieur d'une autre).

encadrement [ɑ̃kadrəmɑ̃] m. Framing (d'un tableau). ‖ Frame (de fenêtre, de porte); *dans l'encadrement de la porte,* in the doorway. ‖ Border (de lettre). ‖ Ciném. Field (de l'image). ‖ Milit. Officering (des troupes).
encadrer [-dre] v. tr. (1). To frame (un tableau). ‖ To border (une lettre). ‖ Milit. To bracket (le but); to officer (les hommes); *encadrer de bombes,* to straddle with bombs. ‖ Fig. To guide (qqn); to frame (le visage).
encadreur [-drœːr] m. Framer.
encager [ɑ̃kaʒe] v. tr. (1). To encage.
encaissable [ɑ̃kɛsabl] adj. Fin. Encashable, cashable (chèque); collectable (effet).
encaisse [ɑ̃kɛs] f. Fin. Cash in hand; cash balance; *encaisse métallique,* gold and silver reserve; *pas d'encaisse,* no funds. ‖ Sports. Punishment (à la boxe).
encaissé, ée [-se] adj. Sunk, hollow (chemin); deeply embanked (rivière); deep (vallée); lying between hills (village).
encaissement [-smɑ̃] m. Boxing, encasing, crating (de marchandises); tubbing (de plantes). ‖ Embankment (d'un canal); embanking (d'une rivière). ‖ Fin. Encashment, collection (d'argent, de traites); *présenter à l'encaissement,* to pay in, to present for payment (un chèque).
encaisser [-se] v. tr. (1). To box, to encase (des marchandises); to tub (des plantes). ‖ Fin. To encash; to cash (un chèque); to collect (un effet). ‖ Sports. To take (un coup). ‖ Fam. To pocket, to swallow (un affront); to bear (des reproches); *elle encaisse sans broncher,* she grins and bears everything; *je n'encaisse pas ça,* I can't stand that. ‖ Fam. To stand (v. blairer); *je ne peux pas l'encaisser,* I can't stick (ou) stand him.
— v. intr. Sports. To take punishment. ‖ Fam. To take it.
— v. pr. S'encaisser, to be steeply embanked (rivière); to lie between hills (vallée, village).
encaisseur, euse [-sœːr, øːz] adj. Collecting.
— s. Cashier (à la caisse); collector (de chèques, d'effets, de factures).
encalminé, ée [ɑ̃kalmine] adj. Naut. Becalmed.
encan [ɑ̃kɑ̃] m. Auction; *mettre, vendre à l'encan,* to put up for, to sell by auction.
encanailler [ɑ̃kɑnɑje] v. tr. (1). To drag down, to debase.
— v. pr. S'encanailler, to keep low company; to lower oneself.
encaper [ɑ̃kape] v. tr. (1). Naut. To embay.
— v. intr. Naut. To get embayed.
encapuchonner [ɑ̃kapyʃɔne] v. tr. (1). To hood (qqch.); to put a hood on (qqn).
— v. pr. S'encapuchonner, to put on a hood (personne). ‖ To curve the neck (cheval).
encaquer [ɑ̃kake] v. tr. (1). To barrel.
encart [ɑ̃kar] m. Inset (en reliure).
encartage [-taːʒ] m. Insetting, inset (en reliure). ‖ Carding (des boutons). ‖ Card-indexing (mise sur fiches).
encarter [-te] v. tr. (1). To inset, to inlay (en reliure); to insert (en page volante). ‖ To card (des boutons). ‖ To card-index (des renseignements sur fiches). ‖ To register (une prostituée).
en-cas [ɑ̃kɑ] m. invar. Emergency-supply (ou) -stock. ‖ Short umbrella (ombrelle). ‖ Emergency snack (collation).
encaserner [ɑ̃kazɛrne] v. tr. (1). Milit. To quarter in barracks.
encastrement [ɑ̃kastrəmɑ̃] m. Techn. Embedding, housing (action) [*dans,* into]. ‖ Recess, housing (endroit).
encastrer [-tre] v. tr. (1). Techn. To embed; to house; to impact; to recess (*dans,* into).
— v. pr. S'encastrer, to be embedded (ou) housed (*dans,* in); to fit, to tail (*dans,* into).

encaustique [ɑ̃kostik] f. Furniture-polish (pour meubles); wax- (ou) floor-polish (à parquet). ‖ Arts. Encaustic.
encaustiquer [-ke] v. tr. (1). To polish (un meuble); to wax (le parquet).
encaver [ɑ̃kave] v. tr. (1). To cellar.
enceinte [ɑ̃sɛ̃ːt] f. Compass (entourage). ‖ Enclosure (murs). ‖ Precinct, enclosed space; *dans cette enceinte,* within these walls, in this room. ‖ Milit. Enceinte. ‖ Sports. Ring (à la boxe); paddock (aux courses). ‖ Techn. Speaker, speaker enclosure (haut-parleur).
enceinte adj. f. Méd. Pregnant, with child; in the family way; *enceinte de trois mois,* three months gone (ou) gone with child; *enceinte de* (ou) *des œuvres de,* in child by.
encens [ɑ̃sɑ̃] m. Incense, frankincense. ‖ Fig. Flattery; praise; incense.
encensement [-smɑ̃] m. Ecclés. Censing.
encenser [-se] v. tr. (1). To incense, to cense. ‖ Fig. To flatter.
— v. intr. To toss its head (cheval).
encenseur [-sœːr] s. Censer-bearer. ‖ Fig. Flatterer, adulator.
encensoir [-swaːr] m. Ecclés. Censer. ‖ Fam. Flattery; *manier l'encensoir,* to flatter.
encéphale [ɑ̃sefal] m. Méd. Encephalon.
encéphalique [-lik] adj. Méd. Encephalic.
encéphalite [-lit] f. Méd. Encephalitis.
encerclement [ɑ̃sɛrkləmɑ̃] m. Encircling.
encercler [-kle] v. tr. (1). To encircle; to gird; to shut (ou) hem in.
enchaîné [ɑ̃ʃɛne] m. Ciném. Lap dissolve.
enchaînement [-nmɑ̃] m. Chaining up. ‖ Théâtr. Lap dissolve (d'images); passage (de scènes). ‖ Fig. Chain, sequence (d'événements); chain, concatenation (d'idées).
enchaîner [-ne] v. tr. (1). To chain (un animal, une personne) [*à,* to]. ‖ To put in chains (ou) irons (ou) fetters, to chain down (qqn). ‖ Fig. To captivate, to rivet (l'attention); to captivate (les cœurs, qqn); to fetter (l'inspiration); to paralyse (les mouvements); to curb, to enchain (les passions). ‖ Fig. To carry on (la conversation); to link up (des idées); to connect up (des raisonnements).
— v. intr. To go on (en parlant). ‖ Théâtr. To take up one's cue quickly. ‖ Ciném. To fade in.
— v. pr. S'enchaîner, to be linked (idées); to be connected (raisonnements, preuves).
enchanté, ée [ɑ̃ʃɑ̃te] adj. Enchanted (chose); spellbound (personne) [ensorcelé]. ‖ Enchanted, charmed, delighted (de, at, with); *enchanté de vous voir,* delighted to see you. ‖ Delightful, charming (lieu, séjour).
enchantement [-tmɑ̃] m. Enchantment, charm, spell; *comme par enchantement,* as if by magic; *rompre l'enchantement,* to break the spell. ‖ Delight, rapture; *dans l'enchantement,* delighted. ‖ Fig. Enchantment (d'un paysage); magic (d'un poème); fascination (d'un regard).
enchanter [-te] v. tr. (1). To enchant, to bewitch. ‖ Fig. To charm, to delight. (V. charmer.) ‖ Fam. *Ça ne m'enchante pas,* it doesn't appeal to me.
enchanteresse [-trɛs] f. Enchantress.
enchanteur, teresse [-tœːr, trɛs] adj. Fascinating (beauté, regard); glamorous (nuit); charming, delightful (séjour); bewitching (sourire).
— m. Enchanter.
enchâssement [ɑ̃ʃɑsmɑ̃] m. Setting (d'une pierre). ‖ Ecclés. Enshrining.
enchâsser [-se] v. tr. (1). To set (une pierre). ‖ Ecclés. To enshrine. ‖ Fig. To insert.
enchatonner [ɑ̃ʃatɔne] v. tr. (1). To set.
enchausser [ɑ̃ʃose] v. tr. (1). Agric. To straw, to earth up.
enchemiser [ɑ̃ʃəmize] v. tr. (1). To jacket.

enchère [ᾶ∫ε:r] f. Bid, bidding; *faire une enchère de X francs,* to bid another X francs. ‖ Auction; *être mis aux enchères,* to come under the hammer; *mettre aux enchères,* to put up to (ou) for auction; *vente aux enchères,* auction sale.

enchérir [ᾶ∫eri:r] v. tr. (2). To bid for (à une vente). ‖ Comm. To raise the price of (une marchandise).
— v. intr. To bid; *enchérir sur,* to improve on (une offre); to outbid (qqn). ‖ Comm. To grow dearer (prix). ‖ Fig. To improve (*sur,* on).

enchérissement [-rismᾶ] m. Rise in price, increase in cost.

enchérisseur [-risœ:r] m. Bidder; *dernier enchérisseur,* highest bidder.

enchevêtré, ée [ᾶ∫vεtre] adj. Tangled (écheveau); intergrown (feuillage). [V. ENTORTILLÉ.] ‖ Fig. Confused (idées); involved (style).

enchevêtrement [-trəmᾶ] m. Tangle, ravel (d'un écheveau); criss-cross (de fils de fer, de sentiers); tangle, entanglement (de fils téléphoniques, de ronces). ‖ Fig. Confusion (des idées).

enchevêtrer [-tre] v. tr. (1). To halter up (un cheval). ‖ To tangle up, to entangle. ‖ Archit. To join, to trim in. ‖ Fig. To confuse; to make a muddle of (une affaire).
— v. pr. **S'enchevêtrer,** to become entangled (*dans,* in); to be hampered (*dans,* by). ‖ To get mixed up (ou) jumbled (ou) entangled. ‖ Fig. To become very complicated (affaire); to get confused (idées).

enchifrené, ée [ᾶ∫ifrəne] adj. Stuffed up (nez); snuffling, sniffling (personne); *être enchifrené,* to have the snuffles (ou) sniffles.

enchymose [ᾶkimo:z] f. Méd. Flush of blood.

enclave [ᾶkla:v] f. Enclave.

enclavé, ée [ᾶklave] adj. Hemmed in, enclosed.

enclavement [ᾶklavmᾶ] m. Surrounding, hemming in (action); hemmed in situation (état).

enclaver [ᾶklave] v. tr. (1). To enclave.

enclenche [ᾶklᾶ:∫] f. Techn. Gab.

enclenchement [ᾶklᾶ∫mᾶ] m. Interlocking (action); interlocking gear (appareil).

enclencher [-∫e] v. tr. (1). To interlock, to throw into gear (*avec,* with). ‖ Fig. To set going, to start.
— v. pr. **S'enclencher,** to interlock (*avec,* with).

enclin, ine [ᾶklɛ̃, in] adj. Inclined, disposed, prone (à, to). [V. PORTÉ.]

encliqueter [ᾶklikte] v. tr. (8a). Techn. To ratch, to cog (une roue).

enclitique [ᾶklitik] adj., f. Gramm. Enclitic.

enclore [ᾶklɔ:r] v. tr. (27). To enclose, to close in (en général); *enclore d'une grille, de haies, de murs, d'une palissade,* to rail in, to hedge in, to wall in, to fence in.

enclos [ᾶklo] m. Enclosure, close (en général). ‖ Pen (pour bestiaux); paddock (pour chevaux); sheep-fold (pour moutons).

enclouer [ᾶklue] v. tr. (1). To prick in shoeing (un cheval). ‖ Milit. To spike (un canon).

enclume [ᾶklym] f. Techn. Anvil. ‖ Méd. Incus, anvil (de l'oreille). ‖ Loc. *Entre le marteau et l'enclume,* between the devil and the deep blue sea.

encoche [ᾶkɔ∫] f. Notch; nick; slot. ‖ Techn. Gap.

encocher [-∫e] v. tr. (1). To notch, to nick; to slot.

encochure [-∫y:r] f. Naut. Notch.

encoignure [ᾶkɔɲy:r] f. Corner, angle. (V. COIN.) ‖ Corner-cabinet, corner-cupboard (meuble).

encollage [ᾶkɔla:ʒ] m. Gumming; sizing.

encoller [-le] v. tr. (1). To size (l'étoffe); to gum (le papier).

encolure [ᾶkɔly:r] f. Neck, withers (de cheval); neck (de personne). ‖ Neck, neck-opening (de robe); size of collar (pointure). ‖ Sports. *D'une encolure,* by a neck (aux courses).

encombrant, ante [ᾶkɔ̃brᾶ, ᾶ:t] adj. Cumbersome, lumbering (chose); clumsy, always in the way (personne).

encombre [ᾶkɔ̃:br] f. Cumbrance; *sans encombre,* without hindrance (ou) mishap.

encombrement [ᾶkɔ̃brəmᾶ] m. Congestion, crowding (de la rue); *encombrement de voitures,* traffic-block (ou) -jam. ‖ Cumbersomeness, bulkiness (d'un objet); room occupied, floor-space, space required (espace occupé). ‖ Autom. Measurements, length (d'une voiture). ‖ Naut. *Tonneau d'encombrement,* measurement ton. ‖ Comm. Overstocking; glut; congestion (du marché).

encombrer [-bre] v. tr. (1). To encumber, to cumber, to embarrass; to litter, to lumber up (*de,* with); *table encombrée de livres,* table littered with books. ‖ To overcrowd, to congest (la rue); *rue encombrée par la foule,* crowded street. ‖ To jam, to block, to block up (la chaussée, la circulation, le passage). ‖ To choke up, to block (un tuyau). ‖ Comm. To glut, to overstock (le marché). ‖ Fig. To cumber, to load (la mémoire). ‖ Fam. To be always in the way of (qqn); *encombré de six enfants,* saddled with six children; *les scrupules ne l'encombrent pas,* he is not overburdened with scruples.
— v. pr. **S'encombrer,** to cumber (ou) to hamper oneself (*de,* with). ‖ To be obstructed (route). ‖ Fig. To saddle (ou) burden oneself (*de,* with).

encontre [ᾶkɔ̃:tr] f. † Opposite direction.
— loc. adv. **A l'encontre de,** contrary to, in opposition to; *aller à l'encontre de,* to run counter to.

encorbellement [ᾶkɔrbɛlmᾶ] m. Archit. Cantilever; *en encorbellement,* corbelled, cantilever, overhanging; oriel (fenêtre). ‖ Milit., Aviat. Blister.

encorder [ᾶkɔrde] v. tr. (1). To rope, to put on the rope.
— v. pr. **S'encorder,** to rope each other together, to rope up.

encore [ᾶkɔ:r] adv. Still (toujours); *elle est encore là,* she is still there; *il n'est encore que lieutenant,* he is still only a lieutenant; *j'en suis encore à l'attendre,* I am still waiting for him. ‖ Yet (jusqu'à présent); *elle n'est pas encore arrivée,* she has not yet arrived; *je n'avais pas encore subi une telle déception,* I had never experienced such a disappointment before. ‖ More, still, yet, else, moreover (de plus, en outre); *apportez encore une chaise,* bring another chair; *encore une fois,* once again (ou) more; *encore un mot,* just one word more; *encore les circonstances sont-elles favorables,* moreover, circumstances are favourable; *encore quelques jours,* a few more days; *il y avait encore une autre raison,* there was yet another reason; *l'avenir vous réserve encore d'autres joies,* life has still other joys in store for you; *pour quelque temps encore,* for some time yet; *que vous rappelez-vous encore?,* what else do you remember? ‖ More (davantage); *donnez-m'en encore,* give me some more. ‖ As recently as (dernièrement encore); *il y a une semaine encore,* only a week ago. ‖ Again (de nouveau); *encore autant,* as much again; *prononcez encore ce mot,* pronounce this word again. ‖ Nevertheless, for all that (néanmoins); *c'est encore un brave homme,* he is a good fellow for all that; *encore aurait-il fallu me le dire,* for all that, you should have told me. ‖ At least, only (au moins); *si encore elle était belle!,* if at least (ou) if only she were beautiful! ‖ Still, yet (avec un comparatif); *une chose plus incroyable encore,* a still (ou) yet more incredible thing. ‖ Loc. *Il est encore bizarre,* *celui-là!*, he is a queer chap too!; *elle est jolie. Mais encore?*, she is pretty. Is that all? — interj. THÉÂTR. Encore! — loc. conj. **Encore que**, though, although.

encorné, ée [ɑ̃kɔrne] adj. Horned.

encorner v. tr. (1). To provide with horns (orner). ‖ To gore (blesser). ‖ FAM. To cuckold (cocufier).

encornet [ɑ̃kɔrnɛ] m. ZOOL. Squid.

encourageant [ɑ̃kuraʒɑ̃] adj. Hopeful (avenir); cheerful (nouvelle); comforting, cheering, encouraging (paroles).

encouragement [-ʒmɑ̃] m. Incitement, encouragement (*à*, to); support, encouragement (*de la part de*, from).

encourager [-ʒe] v. tr. (7). To encourage, to inspirit, to cheer up (remonter); to stimulate, to cheer on, to spur on (stimuler). ‖ To instigate; to incite (pousser) [*à*, to]. ‖ To promote, to patronize (les arts); to abet (le crime); to favour (une entreprise); to flatter (une passion); to promote (un projet); to encourage, to foster (un sentiment).

encourir [ɑ̃kuri:r] v. tr. (32). To incur.

encrage [ɑ̃kra:ʒ] m. Inking.

encrassement [ɑ̃krasmɑ̃] m. Furring (d'une chaudière); sooting (d'une cheminée); clogging (d'un poêle); choking (d'un tuyau). ‖ Dirtying, (d'un vêtement). ‖ MILIT. Fouling (d'une arme). ‖ AUTOM. Sooting-up, oiling-up (d'une bougie). ‖ TECHN. Gumming-up (d'une machine).

encrasser [-se] v. tr. (1). To fur (une chaudière); to soot (une cheminée); to clog (un poêle); to choke (un tuyau). ‖ To dirty, to soil (un vêtement). ‖ MILIT. To foul (une arme). ‖ AUTOM. To soot up (une bougie). ‖ TECHN. To gum up (une machine).

— v. pr. **S'encrasser**, to fur (chaudière); to soot up (cheminée); to clog (poêle); to get choked (tuyau). ‖ To become dirty (habit). ‖ MILIT. To foul (arme). ‖ AUTOM. To soot up (bougie). ‖ TECHN. To gum up (machine).

encre [ɑ̃:kr] f. Ink; *encre de Chine*, Indian ink; *encre d'imprimerie*, printing-ink; *encre à stylo*, fountain-pen ink; *écrire à l'encre*, to write in ink; *repasser à l'encre*, to ink over.

encrer [ɑ̃kre] v. tr. (1). To ink.

encreur, euse [ɑ̃krœ:r, ø:z] adj. Inking (ruban). — m. Inker, ink-roller.

encrier [ɑ̃krje] m. Inkstand, ink-pot (ordinaire); ink-well (de pupitre). ‖ Ink-trough (en imprimerie).

encroûtant, ante [ɑ̃krutɑ̃, ɑ̃:t] adj. Crusting, encrusting. ‖ FAM. Humdrum, destroying (vie).

encroûter [-te] v. tr. (1). To crust, to encrust. ‖ FIG. To encrust (l'esprit); to fossilize, to put into a rut (qqn).

— v. pr. **S'encroûter**, to crust. ‖ FIG. To fossilize, to get rusty.

encyclique [ɑ̃siklik] adj. ECCLÉS. Encyclical. — f. ECCLÉS. Encyclical letter.

encyclopédie [-klɔpedi] f. Encyclopædia, cyclopædia. ‖ FIG. *Encyclopédie vivante*, walking encyclopædia.

encyclopédique [-dik] adj. Encyclopædic.

encyclopédiste [-dist] m. Encyclopædist.

endémie [ɑ̃demi] f. MÉD. Endemic disease.

endémique [-mik] adj. MÉD. Endemic.

endenter [ɑ̃dɑ̃te] v. tr. (1). MÉD. To provide with teeth. ‖ TECHN. To indent (le bois); to cog, to tooth (une roue).

endetté, ée [ɑ̃dɛte] adj. In debt; indebted (*envers*, to).

endettement [ɑ̃dɛtmɑ̃] m. Getting into debt (action); indebtedness (état).

endetter v. tr. (1). To get into debt. — v. pr. **S'endetter**, to run (ou) get into debt.

endeuiller [ɑ̃dœje] v. tr. (1). To cast deep gloom

over; *le pays est endeuillé par la catastrophe*, the country is in mourning over the catastrophe.

endêver v. intr. (1). FAM. *Faire endêver qqn*, to drive s.o. mad (ou) wild.

endiablé, ée [ɑ̃djable] adj. † Possessed of the devil. ‖ FAM. Frantic, wild (entrain); rattling, boisterous, full of devilment (personne); *plein d'une verve endiablée*, bubbling over with high spirits.

endiamanté, ée [ɑ̃djamɑ̃te] adj. Bediamonded, bejewelled, covered with diamonds.

endiguement [ɑ̃digmɑ̃] m. Damming (par barrage); embanking, dyking (sur les rives).

endiguer [-ge] v. tr. (1). To dam up (par barrage); to dyke, to embank (sur les rives). ‖ MILIT. To localize. ‖ FIG. To check, to stop, to stem.

endimanché, ée [ɑ̃dimɑ̃ʃe] adj. In one's Sunday best, in Sunday attire.

endimancher v. tr. (1). To dress in one's best.

endive [ɑ̃di:v] f. BOT. Chicory, endive.

endoblaste [ɑ̃dɔblast] m. MÉD. Endoblast.

endocarde [ɑ̃dɔkard] m. MÉD. Endocardium.

endocardite [-dit] f. MÉD. Endocarditis.

endocarpe [ɑ̃dɔkarp] m. BOT. Endocarp.

endocrine [ɑ̃dɔkrin] adj. MÉD. Endocrine.

endocrinien, enne [-njɛ̃, ɛn] adj. MÉD. Endocrinal, endocrinic, endocrinous.

endocrinologie [-nɔlɔʒi] f. MÉD. Endocrinology.

endoctrinement [ɑ̃dɔktrinmɑ̃] m. Indoctrination.

endoctriner [-ne] v. tr. (1). To indoctrinate.

endoderme [ɑ̃dɔdɛrm] m. MÉD. Endoderm.

endogame [-gam] adj. Endogamous.

endogène [-ʒɛn] adj. BOT., MÉD. Endogenous. ‖ GÉOL. Endogenic, endogenous.

endolori, ie [ɑ̃dɔlɔri] adj. Sore, aching.

endolorir [-ri:r] v. tr. (2). To make sore, to make ache.

endolorissement [-rismɑ̃] m. Soreness.

endommagement [ɑ̃dɔmaʒmɑ̃] m. Damaging.

endommager [-ʒe] v. tr. (7). To damage, to injure, to hurt.

endormant, ante [ɑ̃dɔrmɑ̃, ɑ̃:t] adj. Soporific, soporiferous. ‖ Lulling (rythme). ‖ FAM. Dull, humdrum.

endormeur [-mœ:r] s. MÉD. Anæsthetist. ‖ FAM. Hypnotist. ‖ FAM. Opiate-monger, sweet-talker (bourreur de crâne); bore (raseur).

endormi, ie [-mi] adj. Asleep, sleeping, slumbering; *à moitié endormi*, drowsy, sleepy. ‖ Numb (jambe). ‖ FIG. Dormant (passion). ‖ FAM. Sleepy, sluggish, apathetic (personne). — s. FAM. Sleepy-head.

endormir [ɑ̃dɔrmi:r] v. tr. (41). To lull to sleep (musique, voix); to send to sleep, to make sleep (somnifère); *endormir en chantant*, to sing to sleep; *le sermon du curé m'a endormi*, the vicar's sermon sent me to sleep. ‖ To numb (un membre). To hypnotize (par magnétisme). ‖ MÉD. To anæsthetize, to chloroform. ‖ FIG. To lull (la crainte, les soupçons); to deaden (la douleur). ‖ FAM. To circumvent; to hoodwink.

— v. pr. **S'endormir**, to go to sleep; to fall asleep. ‖ FAM. To go to sleep (*sur*, over); to slack off (se relâcher).

endormissement [-mismɑ̃] m. Falling to sleep, going to sleep.

endos [ɑ̃dɔ] m. FIN. Endorsement.

endoscope [ɑ̃dɔskɔp] m. MÉD. Endoscope.

endoscopie [-skɔpi] f. MÉD. Endoscopy.

endosmose [ɑ̃dɔsmo:z] f. PHYS. Endosmosis.

endossataire [ɑ̃dɔsatɛ:r] m. FIN. Endorsee.

endosse [ɑ̃dɔ:s] f. Liability, responsibility, burden.

endossement [ɑ̃dosmɑ̃] m. V. ENDOS.

endosser [-se] v. tr. (1). To put on (un habit). ‖

FIN. To endorse. || TECHN. To back (en reliure). || FIG. To assume, to shoulder, to saddle oneself with.

endosseur [-sœ:r] m. Endorser.

endothermique [-tɛrmik] adj. CHIM. Endothermic.

endroit [ɑ̃drwa] m. Place, spot (lieu) ; *à quel endroit ?,* where ? ; in what place ? ; *en quelque autre endroit,* somewhere else ; *en quelque endroit que,* wherever ; *le petit endroit,* the lavatory, the lav ; *par endroits,* in places. || Side (côté) ; part, passage (d'un livre) ; point (point) ; *un endroit sensible,* a tender spot. || Right side, face (d'une étoffe) ; *une maille à l'envers, une maille à l'endroit,* knit one, purl one ; *sans endroit ni envers,* reversible.
— loc. prép. **A l'endroit de,** with regard (ou) respect to, as regards.

enduire [ɑ̃dɥi:r] v. tr. (85). *Enduire de,* to coat (ou) to plaster with (boue) ; to render with (ciment) ; to smear, to besmear with (crème) ; to coat with (goudron, jaune d'œuf, peinture) ; to anoint with (huile) ; to daub with (peinture, torchis). || AVIAT. To dope.

enduit [ɑ̃dɥi] m. Coating, coat ; plastering, plaster ; daub. || Glaze (de céramique). || AVIAT. Dope.

endurable [ɑ̃dyrabl] adj. Endurable, bearable.

endurance [-rɑ̃:s] f. Endurance, stamina, staying-power ; *course d'endurance,* reliability (ou) endurance test. || FIG. Grit, stamina.

endurant, ante [-rɑ̃, ɑ̃:t] adj. Patient, enduring ; *peu endurant,* hot-tempered. || Of great powers of endurance, tough (enduaci).

endurci, ie [ɑ̃dyrsi] adj. Confirmed (célibataire) ; callous, obdurate (cœur) ; hardened (criminel, pécheur) ; unfeeling, hard (personne). || Seasoned ; inured (à, to). [V. AGUERRI.]

endurcir [-si:r] v. tr. (2). To harden (le cœur, qqn) ; to sear (la conscience). || To season ; to inure (à, to).
— v. pr. **S'endurcir,** to harden (cœur, personne). || To become seasoned (ou) inured (à, to).

endurcissement [-sismɑ̃] m. Hardening, induration (de la chair). || Seasoning ; inurement (à, to) ; *endurcissement à la fatigue,* toughening. || FIG. Callousness (du cœur).

endurer [ɑ̃dyre] v. tr. (1). To endure, to undergo (souffrir). || To bear, to tolerate, to put up with, to brook (tolérer).

énergétique [enɛrʒetik] adj. Energy (ressources, politique). || Energy giving (aliment).

énergie [enɛrʒi] f. Energy ; *avec énergie,* energetically ; *faire appel à toute son énergie,* to rouse one's energies ; *sans énergie,* apathetically. || Expressiveness, vigour (d'un mot). || MÉD. Efficacy (d'un remède). || TECHN., PHYS. Energy. || ÉLECTR. Energy ; power.

énergique [-ʒik] adj. Energetic (caractère) ; strenuous (effort) ; forcible (mesures, paroles) ; energetic, spirited (personne) ; emphatic (refus) ; arduous (travailleur). || MÉD. Powerful, drastic (remède).

énergiquement [-ʒikmɑ̃] adv. Energetically.

énergisme [-ʒism] m. PHILOS. Energism.

énergumène [enɛrgymɛn] m. Energumen ; tub-thumper, loud-mouthed ranter (fam.).

énervant, ante [enɛrvɑ̃, ɑ̃:t] adj. Enervating (déprimant). || Irritating, provoking ; aggravating (fam.) [agaçant].

énervé, ée [-ve] adj. Nerveless (abattu). || Irritated, provoked (agacé) ; excitable, nervy, highly-strung, U. S. nervous (nerveux).

énervement [-vəmɑ̃] m. Exasperation (agacement) ; high-strung (ou) wound-up state (nervosité) ; excitement (surexcitation).

énerver [-ve] v. tr. (1). To unnerve (couper les nerfs). || To enervate (abattre). || To irritate, to provoke (agacer) ; *ça m'énerve,* it gets on my nerves.
— v. pr. **S'énerver,** to become enervated (s'affaiblir). || To become excited (ou) irritable ; to grow nervy (ou) U. S. nervous (s'agacer).

enfaîteau [ɑ̃fɛto] m. ARCHIT. Ridge-tile.

enfaîter [-te] v. tr. (1). ARCHIT. To ridge.

enfance [ɑ̃fɑ̃:s] f. Infancy, childhood (en général) ; girlhood (d'une fille) ; boyhood (d'un garçon) ; *dès ma plus tendre enfance,* from my earliest childhood, from babyhood. || Second childhood ; *retomber en enfance,* to be in one's dotage (ou) second childhood. || Children (sens collectif). || FIG. Infancy. || FAM. *L'enfance de l'art,* child's play.

enfant [ɑ̃fɑ̃] s. Child (en général) ; infant, baby (bébé) ; girl (fille) ; boy (garçon) ; *enfant trouvé,* foundling. || Child (progéniture) ; *sans enfant,* childless, without issue. || Native (originaire) ; *enfant de Paname,* native of Paris ; *une enfant du Limousin,* a daughter of Limousine. || Child ; *mon enfant,* my child, my boy, my girl. || MILIT. *Enfant de troupe,* barracks-bred child. || ECCLÉS. *Enfant de chœur,* altar-boy. || MÉD. *En mal d'enfant,* in labour. || FAM. Brain-child (idée, ouvrage qu'on a conçu). || LOC. *Faire l'enfant,* to behave childishly ; *il n'y a plus d'enfants !,* children know everything nowadays !
— adj. Childish (puéril) ; *femme-enfant,* child-wife. || Childlike (air, sourire) ; *bon enfant,* good-humoured ; good-natured.

enfantement [-tmɑ̃] m. MÉD. Parturition, childbirth. || FIG. Giving birth (de, to).

enfanter [-te] v. tr. (1). MÉD. To give birth to. || FIG. To beget, to produce (engendrer). || FAM. To father, to be the father of (une idée).

enfantillage [-tija:ʒ] m. Childishness. (V. PUÉRILITÉ.) || Enfantillage, childish action. || Pl. Childish pranks.

enfantin, ine [-tɛ̃, in] adj. Infantile ; *classe, école enfantine,* infant class, school ; *contes enfantins,* nursery tales. || Childish (attitude) ; childlike (candeur). || FAM. Just too easy ; *un travail enfantin,* child's play.

enfariné, ée [ɑ̃farine] adj. Floury. || FAM. Mealy (visage) ; *la gueule enfarinée,* as sleek as a cat, mealy-mouthed.

enfariner v. tr. (1). To flour, to cover with flour.

enfer [ɑ̃fɛ:r] m. Hades (de la mythologie). || Inferno (de la *Divine Comédie,* de Stalingrad). || ECCLÉS. Hell. || TECHN. Stoke-hole (de chaufferie). || FIG. Hell ; *ma vie est un enfer,* my life is hell. || LOC. *Aller un train d'enfer,* to go hell (ou) U. S. hell bent for leather ; *un bruit d'enfer,* an infernal noise ; *un feu d'enfer,* a roaring fire.

enfermer [ɑ̃fɛrme] v. tr. (1). To shut in, to shut up ; *enfermer à clef,* to lock up ; *tenir enfermé,* to keep in. || To confine, to keep in confinement (un coupable) ; to shut up in an asylum (un fou). || To surround, to hem, to hedge, to enclose (entourer). || FIG. To contain (un sens, une vérité).
— v. pr. **S'enfermer,** to shut oneself in ; *s'enfermer à clef,* to lock oneself in ; *s'enfermer dans son bureau avec qqn,* to be closeted with s.o. || To live shut up, to live indoors (ne pas sortir). || FIG. To bury (ou) to wrap oneself (dans, in) [se plonger].

enferrer [ɑ̃fɛre] v. tr. (1). To run through.
— v. pr. **S'enferrer,** to spit oneself (sur, on). || FAM. To be hoisted with one's own petard (ou) caught in one's own trap ; to flounder (dans, in).

enfièvrement [ɑ̃fjɛvrəmɑ̃] m. Feverishness.

enfiévrer [-vre] v. tr. (5). To fever. || FIG. To fever, to fire.
— v. pr. **S'enfiévrer,** to grow feverish. || FIG. To become excited (ou) nervy (ou) U. S. nervous.

enfilade [ɑ̃filad] f. Row (d'immeubles); suite (de pièces); series (de portes); *des pièces en enfilade,* a suite of rooms. ‖ String (de paroles). ‖ MILIT. Enfilade; *battre d'enfilade,* to enfilade.

enfile [ɑ̃fi:l]. V. ENFILER. ‖ **Enfile-aiguille,** m. Needle-threader.

enfiler [-le] v. tr. (1). To thread (une aiguille) [*de,* with]. ‖ To string (des oignons, des perles). ‖ To spit (qqn, d'un coup d'épée). ‖ To turn the corner of, to go along (une rue en marchant); to look down (ou) up (en regardant). ‖ To slip on (un vêtement). ‖ MILIT. To enfilade. ‖ FAM. To get outside (un repas); to down (un verre).

enfin [ɑ̃fɛ̃] adv. At last (à la fin); lastly, last of all (à la fin d'une énumération); *enfin et surtout,* last but not least. ‖ Finally, ultimately, in the end (finalement). ‖ In conclusion, in short, in a word (bref). ‖ After all; well; *mais enfin, s'il répondait!,* but still, if he did answer!; *enfin c'est ainsi,* well (ou) anyhow, that's how it is.

enflammé, ée [ɑ̃flame] adj. On fire, ablaze. ‖ Fiery (ciel); glowing (joues); fiery, blazing (regard). ‖ Passionate, fiery (cœur); fighting (discours); fiery, heated (paroles); burning (*de,* with). ‖ MÉD. Inflamed, angry.

enflammer v. tr. (1). To set on fire (en général); to strike (une allumette). ‖ FIG. To inflame, to heat (v. ÉCHAUFFER); to fire (*de,* with).
— v. pr. **S'enflammer,** to take fire; to ignite; to flare up, to blaze up. ‖ MÉD. To inflame. ‖ FIG. To catch fire, to warm (s'animer); to fire up, to flare up (s'emporter); *s'enflammer d'amour pour,* to lose one's heart to.

enflé, ée [ɑ̃fle] adj. MÉD. Swollen, tumid, bloated (figure, jambe); puffy (yeux). ‖ FIN. Inflated (prix). ‖ FIG. Bombastic, turgid (style). ‖ FAM. Swollenhead; puffed up (*de,* with) [orgueil].
— s. FAM. Puffed up person; *quel enflé!,* what a conceited ass!

enfléchure [ɑ̃fleʃy:r] f. NAUT. Ratline.

enfler [ɑ̃fle] v. tr. (1). To swell, to tumefy. ‖ To puff out (les joues); to raise (la voix). ‖ NAUT. To fill (les voiles). ‖ FIN. To inflate (les prix). ‖ FIG. To puff up (d'orgueil).
— v. intr. To swell, to swell up (membre).
— v. pr. **S'enfler,** to swell. ‖ To rise, to swell (rivière); to swell, to surge (vagues). ‖ To swell, to rise (voix). ‖ NAUT. To fill (voiles). ‖ FIN. To swell (prix). ‖ FIG. To be puffed up; *s'enfler d'orgueil,* to swell with importance.

enflure [ɑ̃fly:r] f. MÉD. Swelling. (V. TUMÉFACTION.) ‖ FIG. Turgidity (du style).

enfoncé, ée [ɑ̃fɔ̃se] adj. Low-lying (lieu); deep (recoin). ‖ Deep-set (yeux). ‖ MÉD. Broken (côtes). ‖ FAM. Bowled over (démonté); outstripped (dépassé); bested, done, U. S. taken (roulé).

enfoncement [-smɑ̃] m. Driving in (d'un clou); breaking open (d'une porte).

enfoncer [-se] v. tr. (6). To drive (un clou) [*dans,* into]. ‖ To hammer in (à coups de marteau); to plough in (en labourant); to stick in (en piquant); to push in (en poussant); *enfoncer les mains, un poignard dans,* to thrust one's hands, a dagger into; *on y enfonce jusqu'au genou, au menton,* it's knee-deep, chin-deep. ‖ To smash (un mur); to break open (une porte). ‖ MILIT. To break through (le front). ‖ FAM. To bowl over (démonter); to outstrip (dépasser); to best, U. S. to gyb (rouler).
— v. intr. To sink (pr. et fig.).
— v. pr. **S'enfoncer,** to penetrate (balle, clou, racine) [*dans,* into]; *s'enfoncer une écharde dans le doigt,* to run a splinter into one's finger. ‖ To form a recess (ou) a niche (mur). ‖ To subside, to give way (sol). ‖ *S'enfoncer dans,* to dive into (un chemin); to sink into (l'eau); to plunge into

(une forêt); to disappear into (l'ombre); *s'enfoncer vers le nord,* to thrust northwards. ‖ NAUT. To settle down, to sink. ‖ FIG. *S'enfoncer dans,* to sink deeper in (le crime); to bury oneself in (les livres, les recherches); to sink into (le rêve); to plunge into (le vice); *en train de s'enfoncer,* on the downgrade. ‖ FAM. To sink (endetté).

enfonceur [-sœ:r] m. FAM. *Enfonceur de portes ouvertes,* braggart.

enfouir [ɑ̃fwi:r] v. tr. (2). To bury (un cadavre, des graines, un trésor) [*dans,* in]. ‖ To enclose, to embower (une maison) [*dans,* in]. ‖ FIG. To bury, to conceal.
— v. pr. **S'enfouir,** to burrow (animal); to become buried (chose); to bury (ou) to hide oneself (personne).

enfouissement [ɑ̃fwismɑ̃] m. Burying; hiding.

enfouisseur [-sœ:r] m. Burier.

enfourcher [ɑ̃furʃe] v. tr. (1). To bestride, to mount (une bicyclette, un cheval). ‖ To pitchfork (à la fourche). ‖ FIG. To get on (son dada); to ride to death (une idée).

enfourchure [-ʃy:r] f. Fork (des branches).

enfournage [ɑ̃furna:ʒ] m. Placing in an oven (ou) kiln. ‖ TECHN. Charging.

enfourner [-ne] v. tr. (1). To place in an oven (le pain). ‖ ARTS. To place in a kiln (la céramique). ‖ TECHN. To charge (un fourneau). ‖ POP. To gobble (la nourriture).
— v. pr. **S'enfourner.** FAM. To crowd, to surge, to rush (*dans,* into).

enfourneur [-nœ:r] m. Oven-man; kiln-man. ‖ Charger.

enfreindre [ɑ̃frɛ̃:dr] v. tr. (59). To infringe, to transgress, to break, to offend against.

enfuir (s') [sɑ̃fɥi:r] v. pr. (56). To flee, to run away, to fly; to turn tail (v. FUIR); *s'enfuir de prison,* to escape from prison. ‖ FIG. To fly, to slip by, to be fleeting (temps).

enfumé, ée [ɑ̃fyme] adj. Smoke-blackened (mur); smoky (pièce).

enfumer v. tr. (1). To blacken with smoke (un mur); to fill with smoke (une pièce). ‖ To smoke out (un animal, qqn).

enfutailler [ɑ̃fytaje] v. tr. (1). To barrel.

engagé, ée [ɑ̃gaʒe] adj. In pawn, U. S. in hock (mis en gage). ‖ ARCHIT. Engaged. ‖ NAUT. Foul (cordage, hélice); waterlogged (navire). ‖ MILIT. Enlisted. ‖ FIG. Committed (littérature).
— m. MILIT. Volunteer.

engageant, ante [-ʒɑ̃, ɑ̃:t] adj. Tempting, inviting (aspect); prepossessing, attractive (dehors); attractive, engaging (sourire).

engagement [-ʒmɑ̃] m. Pawning, pledging (mise en gage). ‖ Engagement, indenture, obligation (contrat); *sans engagement,* without obligation. ‖ Pledge, agreement, engagement (promesse). ‖ Pl. Liabilities, commitments (d'argent); *faire face à ses engagements,* to meet one's liabilities. ‖ Engagement (d'un artiste, d'un travailleur); indenture (d'un apprenti). ‖ MILIT. Affair, skirmish (escarmouche); enlistment (recrutement). ‖ SPORTS. Entry (dans une course); engagement (à l'escrime).

engager [-ʒe] v. tr. (7). To pawn, to pledge, U. S. to hock (sa montre). ‖ To engage, to hire (un domestique); to take on (un ouvrier). [V. EMBAUCHER.] ‖ To plight, to pledge (sa parole); to be binding on (qqn); *ça ne vous engage pas,* it does not bind you. ‖ To engage, to book (qqn par invitation). ‖ To start upon, to enter into (des négociations); *engager la conversation avec,* to engage in conversation with. ‖ To engage, to incite, to induce (*à, to*); *engager vivement à,* to urge to. ‖ To insert, to fit (qqch.) [*dans,* into]; to engage, to involve, to implicate (qqn) [*dans,* in]. ‖ TECHN. To engage, to put into gear (un

mécanisme). ‖ MILIT. To enlist (des hommes); *engager le combat contre*, to engage. ‖ NAUT. To foul (l'ancre); to catch (l'aviron); to engage (des marins). ‖ FIN. To invest, to tie up (de l'argent); *les frais engagés*, expenses incurred. ‖ JUR. To institute (des poursuites). ‖ SPORTS. To enter (un cheval); to engage (le fer).
— v. intr. TECHN. To gear. ‖ NAUT. To be thrown on her beam-ends.
— v. pr. **S'engager**, to take (ou) to go into service (domestique) [*chez*, with]. ‖ To bind (ou) to commit oneself, to pledge one's word, to promise, to undertake (*à*, to); *je veux savoir à quoi je m'engage*, I want to know what I am letting myself in for; *ne s'engager à rien*, to be non-committal; *s'engager par contrat à*, to contract to. ‖ To begin (conversation, négociations). ‖ *S'engager dans*, to engage in, to get involved in (une affaire); to enter (un chemin); to join (un parti); *la clé s'engagea dans la serrure*, the key was fitted into the lock. ‖ TECHN. To gear (*dans*, with, on). ‖ MILIT. To begin (combat); to enlist, to sign on (homme). ‖ SPORTS. To enter (*dans*, for).

engainer [ãgɛne] v. tr. (1). To sheathe (un poignard). ‖ FIG. To ensheathe.

engeance [ãʒãːs] f. FAM. Brood.

engelure [ãʒlyːr] f. MÉD. Chilblain.

engendrement [ãʒãdrəmã] m. MÉD. Giving birth (*de*, to), begetting (d'un enfant); breeding (d'une maladie). ‖ MATH., GRAMM., Generation. ‖ FIG. Giving birth, creation, breeding.

engendrer [ãʒãdre] v. tr. (1). MÉD. To beget (un enfant); to breed (une maladie). ‖ ZOOL. To sire. ‖ MATH. To generate. ‖ ELECTR. To produce. ‖ PHYS. To generate, to develop. ‖ FIG. To engender, to breed, to create.

engin [ãʒɛ̃] m. Engine, appliance; *comment s'appelle cet engin?*, what do you call that gadget? ‖ MILIT. Weapon; *engins de guerre*, engines of war; *engin meurtrier*, deadly weapon. ‖ AVIAT. Aircraft. ‖ TECHN. Machine.

engineering [ɛndʒinəriŋ] m. Industrial (ou) management engineering.

englober [ãglɔbe] v. tr. (1). To include; to embrace. ‖ To take, to merge (*dans*, in). ‖ COMM. To absorb (une maison).

engloutir [ãglutiːr] v. tr. (2). To gobble, to down, to gulp down (un repas). [V. AVALER.] ‖ NAUT. To engulf, to swallow up, to submerge (un navire). ‖ FIG. To swallow up, to sink (sa fortune).
— v. pr. **S'engloutir**. NAUT. To sink, to be engulfed (naufragé, navire). ‖ FIG. To be swallowed up (fortune).

engloutissement [-tismã] m. Gobbling up, bolting (d'un repas). ‖ NAUT. Engulfment, sinking. ‖ FIG. Swallowing up (d'une fortune).

engluage [ãglyaːʒ] m. Liming.

engluer [ãglɥe] v. tr. (1). To catch with bird-lime (un moineau); to lime (un piège). ‖ FIG. To catch, to ensnare.
— v. pr. **S'engluer**, to get caught with bird-lime. ‖ FIG. To be caught in the toils.

engommer [ãgɔme] v. tr. (1). To gum.

engoncé, ée [-se] adj. Bundled up (*dans*, in).

engoncement [ãgõsmã] m. Squat (ou) neckless appearance.

engoncer v. tr. (6). To give a squat (ou) neckless appearance to.

engorgé, ée [ãgɔrʒe] adj. Foul (pompe); choked up (tuyau). ‖ MÉD. Congested (foie); swollen (ganglion). ‖ FIG. Congested, obstructed (issue).

engorgement [-ʒmã] m. Fouling (d'une pompe); choking (d'un tuyau). ‖ MÉD. Engorgement. ‖ COMM. Glutting (du marché). ‖ FIG. Congestion, obstruction (d'une issue).

engorger [-ʒe] v. tr. (7). To choke up (un tuyau). ‖ MÉD. To engorge, to congest. ‖ COMM. To glut (le marché). ‖ FIG. To congest, to obstruct (une issue).
— v. pr. **S'engorger**, to foul (pompe); to become choked (tuyau). ‖ MÉD. To become engorged (ou) congested. ‖ FIG. To become congested (ou) obstructed.

engouement [ãgumã] m. MÉD. Obstruction. ‖ FIG. Infatuation (*pour*, with).

engouer [ãgue] v. tr. (1). MÉD. To obstruct.
— v. pr. **S'engouer**, to become infatuated (*de*, with); to go crazy (*de*, over); to have a crush (*de*, on). [V. ENTICHER (S').]

engouffrer [ãgufre] v. tr. (1). To engulf. ‖ FAM. To gobble up (son repas).
— v. pr. **S'engouffrer**, to sink, to be swallowed up (navire). ‖ FAM. To dive, to crowd, to rush, to surge (foule) [*dans*, into]; *le vent s'engouffra dans la pièce*, the wind swept in; *le vent s'engouffra par la fenêtre*, the wind blew in at the window.

engoulevent [ãgulvã] m. ZOOL. Goatsucker.

engourdi, ie [ãɡurdi] adj. Numb, benumbed (*de*, *par*, with). ‖ FIG. Dull, torpid (esprit); sleepy, sluggish (personne).

engourdir [-diːr] v. tr. (2). To numb, to benumb. ‖ FIG. To dull (l'esprit).
— v. pr. **S'engourdir**, to grow numb. ‖ FIG. To become dull (ou) sluggish.

engourdissement [-dismã] m. Numbness. ‖ Torpor, torpidity. ‖ COMM. Slackness (du marché). ‖ FIG. Dullness (de l'esprit).

engrais [ãgrɛ] m. Fattening pasture (herbage); fattening food (pâture); *à l'engrais*, fattened up. ‖ Manure (fumier); *engrais chimique*, fertilizer.

engraissage [-saːʒ] m. Fattening (du bétail); cramming (des oies).

engraissement [-smã] m. Putting on flesh (d'une personne).

engraisser [-se] v. tr. (1). To fatten (le bétail, les porcs); to cram (les oies); *engraisser à l'étable*, to stall-feed. ‖ To manure, to fertilize (la terre). ‖ To make fat (qqn).
— v. intr. To fatten (animaux); to put on flesh, to grow fat, to plump out (personnes).
— v. pr. **S'engraisser**, to fatten (animaux); to grow fat (personnes); to grow fertile (terre). ‖ FIG. To batten (*de*, on).

engraisseur [-sœːr] m. Fattener (de bestiaux); crammer (de volailles).

engrangement [ãgrãʒmã] m. AGRIC. Garnering.

engranger [-ʒe] v. tr. (7). AGRIC. To garner, to get in.

engraver [ãgrave] v. tr. (1). To gravel (une route). ‖ NAUT. To strand (un bateau); to silt up (un port).
— v. pr. **S'engraver**, NAUT. To run aground, to ground.

engrenage [ãgrənaːʒ] m. TECHN. Gearing; gear; mesh. ‖ FIG. Mesh (des circonstances); *engrenage des travaux journaliers*, daily round of work.

engrener [-ne] v. tr. (5). To feed with corn (une batteuse). ‖ To feed on corn (la volaille). ‖ TECHN. To gear, to engage, to mesh (des roues dentées); to throw into gear, to connect. ‖ MÉD. *Fracture engrenée*, impacted fracture. ‖ FIG. To set going.
— v. intr. TECHN. To interlock, to connect, to be in mesh.
— v. pr. **S'engrener**, TECHN. To gear (*dans*, into); to mesh (*dans*, with).

engrosser [ãgrose] v. tr. (1). To put in the family way, to make pregnant; U. S. to knock up (pop.).

engrumeler (s') [sãgrymle] v. pr. (8 a). To clot.

engueulade [ãgølad] f. Pop. Telling-off, bawling out; *envoyer une lettre d'engueulade à qqn*, to send s.o. a rocket (ou) a blast.

engueuler [-le] v. tr. (1). Pop. To tell off, to blow up, to bawl out; *se faire engueuler*, to catch a rocket, to get a bawling-out.
— v. pr. **S'engueuler**, Pop. To have a row (*avec*, with).

enguirlander [ãgirlãde] v. tr. (1). To garland, to wreathe (*de*, with). ‖ Fam. To give a rocket to, to smack down (qqn).

enhardir [ãardi:r] v. tr. (2). To embolden (qqn); to encourage (*à*, to).
— v. pr. **S'enhardir**, to grow bold. ‖ To make bold (*à*, to).

enharmonie [ãnarmɔni] f. Mus. Enharmonic change.

enharmonique [-nik] adj. Mus. Enharmonic.

énième [enjɛm] adj., s. Fam. Umpteenth, nth; *pour la énième fois, enlève tes coudes de la table*, if I've told you once, I've told you a thousand times, take your elbows off the table.

énigmatique [enigmatik] adj. Enigmatic; *d'une manière énigmatique*, enigmatically.

énigme [enigm] f. Riddle, enigma, puzzle; *le mot de l'énigme*, the key to the enigma; *parler par énigmes*, to speak (ou) talk in riddles. ‖ Puzzle; *ce garçon est une énigme pour moi*, that boy is a puzzle to me.

enivrant, ante [ãnivrã, ã:t] adj. Intoxicating, heady (pr. et fig.).

enivrement [-vrəmã] m. Intoxication, inebriation. (V. IVRESSE.) ‖ Fig. Intoxication (du plaisir); elation (du succès).

enivrer [-vre] v. tr. (1). To intoxicate. (V. GRISER.) ‖ Fig. To intoxicate, to elate.
— v. pr. **S'enivrer**, to grow drunk, to become intoxicated (*de*, with). ‖ Fig. *S'enivrer de*, to grow wild with (colère); to be elated with (joie, succès); to revel in (paroles).

enjambée [ãʒãbe] f. Stride; *faire de grandes enjambées*, to stride along.

enjambement [-bmã] m. Enjambment (en prosodie). ‖ Fly-over (d'un pont).

enjamber [-be] v. tr. (1). To stride (ou) step over (qqch.). ‖ Fig. To span (une rivière).
— v. intr. To stride along. ‖ To run the line on (poète); to run on (vers).

enjeu [ãʒø] m. Stake; *être l'enjeu de*, to be at stake in.

enjoindre [ãʒwɛ̃:dr] v. tr. (59). *Enjoindre à*, to enjoin, to order (*de*, to); *enjoindre le secret à qqn*, to enjoin s.o. to secrecy.

enjôlement [ãʒolmã] m. Inveigling (action); inveiglement (résultat).

enjôler [-le] v. tr. (1). To inveigle; to wheedle, to blarney.

enjôleur, euse [-lœ:r, ø:z] adj. Coaxing (air); wheedling (parole); cajoling (personne).
— s. Cajoler, wheedler.

enjolivement [ãʒolivmã] m. Embellishment. ‖ Fig. Embroidery (d'un récit).

enjoliver [-ve] v. tr. (1). To embellish, to ornament. (V. ORNER.) ‖ Fig. To embroider (un récit).

enjoliveur [-vœ:r] m. Autom. Wheel-disc, hubcap.

enjolivure [-vy:r] f. Flourish, frill.

enjoué, ée [ãʒwe] adj. Sprightly (caractère); playful, lively, mirthful (personne) [v. GAI]; *d'un ton enjoué*, pleasantly.

enjouement [ãʒumã] m. Sprightliness; cheerfulness, liveliness.

enjuponné, ée [ãʒypɔne] adj. Tied to one's mother's apron-strings (enfant); henpecked, uxorious (mari).

enjuponner v. tr. (1). To put into petticoats.

enkysté, ée [ãkiste] adj. Méd. Encysted.

enkystement [-tmã] m. Méd. Encystment.

enkyster (s') [sãkiste] v. pr. (1). Méd. To become encysted.

enlaçage [ãlasa:ʒ] m. Interlacing (d'un cordon); enlacing (par un lacet).

enlacement [-smã] m. Embrace, clasp (étreinte). ‖ Sports. Trip, lock.

enlacer [-se] v. tr. (1). To interlace, to intertwine (un cordon); to enlace, to entwine (un tronc d'arbre). ‖ To embrace, to clasp, to hug (étreindre); *être enlacés*, to be folded (ou) clasped in each other's arms.
— v. pr. **S'enlacer**, to interlace, to intertwine; *s'enlacer autour de*, to twine round (liane); to coil round (serpent). ‖ To be folded (ou) clasped in each other's arms (personnes). ‖ Sports. To hold, to hug each other (lutteurs).

enlaidir [ãlɛdi:r] v. tr. (2). To make ugly (ou) plain (qqn); to disfigure, to deform (le visage).
— v. intr. To grow ugly (ou) plain.

enlaidissement [-dismã] m. Growing ugly; disfigurement.

enlevage [ãlva:ʒ] m. Sports. Spurt.

enlevant, ante [ãlvã, ã:t] adj. Fam. Rousing, stirring, swinging.

enlevé, ée [-ve] adj. Fam. Spirited (conversation); snappy (récit). ‖ Arts., Mus. Dashed off.

enlèvement [ãlɛvmã] m. Lifting up (d'un poids). ‖ Removing (d'un meuble); carrying off (d'un objet); clearing away (des ordures); *enlèvement par avion, bateau, camion, train*, U. S. enplaning, embarking, entrucking, entraining. ‖ Removal, washing out (d'une tache). ‖ Jur. *Enlèvement d'un enfant, d'une mineure, d'une personne*, baby-snatching, abduction, kidnapping; *enlèvement d'une jeune fille consentante*, elopement. (V. RAPT.) ‖ Méd. Ablation. ‖ Milit. Carrying (ou) sweeping away (d'une position). ‖ Ecclés. Translation. ‖ Comm. Snapping up, removal (des marchandises).

enlever [ãlve] v. tr. (5). To lift up, to raise (un poids). ‖ To remove (un meuble); to take (ou) to carry away (ou) off (un objet); to clear away (les ordures) [*de*, from]. ‖ To remove (une marque, une tache); *enlever en arrachant, en balayant, en brossant, en déchirant, en effaçant, en grattant, en lavant, en soufflant*, to snatch away, to sweep away, to brush away, to tear away, to rub away, to scrape off, to wash away, to blow away; *enlever l'écorce de*, to strip the bark from (un arbre); *enlever la peau de*, to peel off the skin of (une orange). ‖ To take up (une carpette); to take down (un lustre); to take off (un vêtement); *enlever sa jupe*, to slip off one's skirt. ‖ To lift (des animaux qu'on vole); to snatch (un enfant); to abduct (une mineure); to kidnap (qqn); *se faire enlever par*, to elope with. ‖ To pull off (une affaire); to snap up (une occasion); to bear off (un prix). ‖ To take (une somme) [*de*, from, out of]. ‖ *Enlever qqch. à qqn*, to deprive s.o. of sth., to take sth. away from s.o.; *enlever à qqn l'envie de*, to stop s.o. from wanting to. ‖ Ecclés. *Enlevé au ciel*, translated to heaven. ‖ Méd. To carry off. ‖ Milit. To carry (une position); to win (la victoire). ‖ Comm. To snap up, to remove (des marchandises); *enlever une affaire*, to secure an order. ‖ Mus., Arts. To dash off (un morceau, un portrait). ‖ Sports. To urge on, to spur (éperonner); to lift (faire sauter). ‖ Fam. To carry away (son auditoire).
— v. pr. **S'enlever**, to strip off (écorce); to tear off (morceau); to peel off (peau); to scale off (peinture); to come off, to wash off (tache). ‖ To be snapped up (marchandises). ‖ Sports, Aviat. To take off. ‖ Ecclés. To rise.

enliasser [ãljase] v. tr. (1). To tie up in bundles.

enlisement [ãlizmã] m. Sinking into quicksands. ‖ AUTOM. Bogging. ‖ FIG. Floundering; involvement (dans, in).

enliser [-ze] v. tr. (1). To suck in (sables). — v. pr. S'enliser, to sink in a quicksand. ‖ AUTOM. To get bogged. ‖ FIG. To flounder; to get involved (dans, in).

enluminé, ée [ãlymine] adj. FAM. Flushed, rubicund, fiery red.

enluminer v. tr. (1). To illuminate. ‖ To colour (colorier). ‖ FIG. To flush (le teint).

enlumineur [-nœ:r] m. Illuminator.

enluminure [-ny:r] f. ARTS. Illumination. ‖ Colouring. ‖ FAM. Rubicundity, ruddiness, redness (du teint).

enneigé, ée [ãnɛʒe] adj. Snow-covered (ou) -capped (montagne); snow-clad (pente).

enneigement [-ʒmã] m. Condition of the snow; bulletin d'enneigement, snow report.

ennemi [ɛnmi] m. Enemy; foe (†); se faire un ennemi de, to make an enemy of. ‖ MILIT. Enemy; occupé par l'ennemi, enemy-occupied. — adj. Hostile, inimical. ‖ Hostile, averse (de, to); être ennemi du bruit, to hate noise. ‖ MILIT., NAUT. Enemy (armée, flotte, nation).

ennoblir [ãnobli:r] v. tr. (2). To ennoble (qqn). — v. intr. To be ennobling (travail).

ennoblissement [-blismã] m. Ennoblement.

ennuager [ãnɥaʒe] v. tr. (7). To cloud over, to becloud. ‖ FIG. To cast a shadow over. — v. pr. S'ennuager, to cloud over.

ennui [ãnɥi] m. Ennui, tedium, boredom, weariness, dullness (lassitude morale); mourir d'ennui, to be bored to tears. ‖ Nuisance, annoyance, vexation (désagrément). ‖ Pl. Worries, vexations, troubles (tracas); avoir des ennuis à propos de, to worry over (ou) about; avoir des ennuis avec, to be in trouble with; créer des ennuis à, to make trouble for; se préparer des ennuis, to be looking for trouble.

ennuyant, ante [-jã, ã:t] adj. Annoying, vexing.

ennuyé, ée ι-je] adj. Annoyed, troubled, bothered, worried (inquiet); mopish (morose). ‖ Bored (assommé).

ennuyer [-je] v. tr. (9 a). To bore (v. ASSOMMER); ennuyer mortellement, to bore stiff (ou) to death. ‖ To pall on (rassasier); toujours jouer l'ennuie, playing all the time palls on him. ‖ To bother, to worry, to pester, to plague (importuner). ‖ To annoy, to worry, to vex (contrarier); cela vous ennuie-t-il de venir? do you mind coming? ‖ To trouble (v. DÉRANGER); je ne voudrais pas vous ennuyer, I don't want to put you to any trouble. ‖ To worry, to trouble (inquiéter). — v. pr. S'ennuyer, to be (ou) get bored, to mope; s'ennuyer à attendre, to get bored waiting; s'ennuyer avec, to feel dull with (qqn); s'ennuyer de, to be bored with (qqch.); to long for (qqn); je m'ennuie de vous, I miss you.

ennuyeusement [-jøzmã] adv. Tediously, boringly.

ennuyeux, euse [-jø, ø:z] adj. Boring, tedious, tiresome, wearisome (assommant); annoying, vexing (désagréable); bothering, troublesome (importun).

énoncé [enɔse] m. Wording (d'un acte); terms (d'un problème). ‖ Statement, expression, account (exposé). ‖ GRAMM. Utterance.

énoncer v. tr. (6). To word (un problème). ‖ To state (une condition); to word, to express (une idée); to enunciate (une opinion). — v. pr. S'énoncer, to be worded (ou) expressed (ou) stated.

énonciation [-sjasjɔ̃] f. Wording (des idées, d'un problème). ‖ Statement, enunciation (des faits).

enorgueillir [ãnɔrgøji:r] v. tr. (2). To make proud (qqn). — v. pr. S'enorgueillir, to be proud (de, of); to pride oneself (de, upon, on); to glory (de, in); to boast (de, of, about).

énorme [enɔrm] adj. Huge, monster (animal, bâtiment); oversized (volume). ‖ Heinous (crime); huge (différence); flagrant, thumping (mensonge); grievous (perte); tremendous (quantité); enormous, huge (succès).

énormément [-memã] adv. Hugely, tremendously; énormément de, lots of, a great deal of.

énormité [-mite] f. Hugeness (par la taille). ‖ Enormity, heinousness (d'un crime); grossness (d'une faute). ‖ FAM. Thumper, blunder, whopper, U. S. boner; dire des énormités, to make dreadful statements. ‖ FAM. Pl. Howlers, U. S. boners (dans un devoir).

enquérir (s') [sãkeri:r] v. pr. (13). To inquire, to make inquiries (de, about, after) [qqch.]; to ask (de, about); to inquire (de, after, for) [qqn].

enquête [ãkɛt] f. Inquiry, investigation; survey; après enquête, on inquiry; enquête par sondage, sample survey; faire une enquête, to hold an inquiry; ouvrir une enquête sur, to set up an inquiry regarding (ou) into; procéder à une enquête sur, to conduct an inquiry regarding (ou) into. ‖ JUR. Inquiry (en général); inquest (en cas de mort suspecte).

enquêter [-te] v. intr. (1). To hold (ou) conduct an inquiry (sur, about); to inquire (sur, into). ‖ To make investigations.

enquêteur [-tœ:r] m. Investigator, inquirer. ‖ JUR. Inquisitor; coroner (sur une mort suspecte).

enquiquinant, ante [ãkikinã, ã:t] adj. FAM. Boring (ennuyeux); irritating (agaçant); c'est enquiquinant, it's a pain in the neck, it gets on my nerves.

enquiquinement [-kinmã] m. FAM. Trouble, bother; chercher les enquiquinements, to look for trouble.

enquiquiner [ãkikine] v. tr. (1). FAM. To plague.

enraciné, ée [ãrasine] adj. AGRIC. Rooted. ‖ FIG. Deep-rooted.

enracinement [ãrasinmã] m. AGRIC. Rooting, taking root. ‖ FIG. Taking root, rootedness (de personnes, d'idées); entrenchment, ingrainedness (d'idées).

enraciner v. tr. (1). AGRIC. To root. ‖ FIG. To implant, to plant, to instil. — v. pr. S'enraciner. AGRIC. To root, to take root. ‖ FIG. To become rooted (ou) fixed (ou) ingrained.

enragé, ée [ãraʒe] adj. Mad, rabid (chien); devenir enragé, to go mad. ‖ FIG. Enthusiastic; rabid, confirmed (fanatique); mad, keen (de, on). ‖ FIG. Mad, wild (danse, jeu); enraged, mad, raging, fuming (personne); wild (contre, with). — s. Fanatic, fan, enthusiast; enragé de tennis, tennis enthusiast.

enrageant, ante [-ʒã, ã:t] adj. Maddening, irritating.

enrager [-ʒe] v. intr. (7). To be enraged, to be in a rage (v. RAGER); faire enrager, to enrage (rendre furieux); to tease (taquiner). ‖ To be itching (brûler) [to, de].

enrayage [ãrɛja:ʒ] m. Fitting of spokes (d'une roue). ‖ Jamming (d'un revolver).

enrayement [ãrɛjmã] m. Locking (d'une roue). ‖ TECHN. Jamming (d'une arme). ‖ MÉD. Stemming (d'une maladie), staunching (d'une hémorragie). ‖ FIG. Curbing, checking, stemming.

enrayer [-je] v. tr. (9 b). To skid, to lock (une roue). ‖ TECHN. To jam (une arme, une machine). ‖ MÉD. To stem, to check (une épidémie). ‖ FIG. To stem, to stop, to check (un progrès).

— v. pr. **S'enrayer**, to jam (arme, machine). ∥ MÉD. To abate, to be stemmed (maladie). ∥ FIG. To be stopped (ou) checked.

enrayer [-je] v. tr. (9 b). AGRIC. To ridge.

enrayure [-jy:r] f. TECHN. Skid-shoe; lock-chain.

enrégimenter [ãreʒimãte] v. tr. (1). MILIT. To enregiment. ∥ FIG. To incorporate.

enregistrable [ãreʒistrabl] adj. Registrable.

enregistrement [-trəmã] m. JUR. Registration, recording (d'un acte, d'un fait); registry-office (bureau); *droits d'enregistrement*, registration fees. ∥ CH. DE F. Registering, U. S. checking (des bagages); booking-office, U. S. checking-office (bureau). ∥ TECHN. Record (disque); recording (d'un disque, de la voix); *enregistrement sur magnétophone*, tape recording.

enregistrer [-tre] v. tr. (1). JUR. To register, to record (un acte, un fait). ∥ To record, to observe (des températures, des ·hausses); *enregistrer des chutes de neige*, to record snowfalls. ∥ AVIAT., CH. DE F. To register, to check in (des bagages). ∥ TECHN. To record (sur disque, sur bande), to tape (sur bande), to videotape (sur magnétoscope). ∥ FIG. To set down (noter par écrit), to take in (noter en mémoire); *question mal enregistrée, badly grasped point*.

enregistreur [-trœ:r] m. TECHN. Recorder; *enregistreur du son, de vitesse*, sound-, speed-recorder. — adj. Recording; *caisse enregistreuse*, cash register.

enrhumer [ãryme] v. tr. (1). To give a .cold to; *être enrhumé*, to have a cold. — v. pr. **S'enrhumer**, to catch a cold.

enrichi, ie [ãriʃi] adj. Enriched (de, with). ∥ New-rich. — s. Nouveau-riche, new-rich; parvenu; *un enrichi du marché noir*, a spiv, a black-marketeer.

enrichir [-ʃi:r] v. tr. (2). To enrich, to make rich (de, with). ∥ FIG. To enrich, to enlarge (l'intelligence); to embellish (un vêtement). — v. pr. **S'enrichir**, to grow rich, to come into a fortune. ∥ FIG. To grow richer (intelligence) [de, with; en, in]; to be rich (ou) resplendent (vêtement) [de, with].

enrichissement [-ʃismã] m. Enriching (action); enrichment (résultat).

enrobage [ãrɔba:ʒ], **enrobement** [-bmã] m. Coating, wrapping.

enrober [-be] v. tr. (1). To coat (de, with).

enrochement [ãrɔʃmã] m. Stone bed; riprap.

enrocher [-ʃe] v. tr. (1). ARCHIT. To riprap.

enrôlé [ãrole] m. MILIT. Recruit.

enrôlement [ãrolmã] m. Enrolment. ∥ MILIT. Enlistment. ∥ NAUT. *Enrôlement forcé*, impressment.

enrôler [-le] v. tr. (1). To enrol(l), to enlist (qqn). ∥ MILIT. To enlist. ∥ NAUT. *Enrôler de force*, to impress. — v. pr. **S'enrôler**, to enrol(l) [dans, in]. ∥ MILIT. To enlist.

enrôleur [-lœ:r] m. Recruiter. ∥ MILIT. Recruiting sergeant. ∥ NAUT. Shipping-master.

enroué, ée [ãrue] adj. Hoarse, husky (personne, voix); *d'une voix enrouée*, hoarsely, huskily.

enrouement [-mã] m. Hoarseness, huskiness.

enrouer [-e] v. tr. (1). To make hoarse (ou) husky. — v. pr. **S'enrouer**, to grow hoarse; *s'enrouer à force de chanter*, to sing oneself hoarse.

enrouillement [ãrujmã] m. Rusting.

enroulement [ãrulmã] m. Coiling up (en cercle), rolling up (en rouleau); winding (en pelote). ∥ BOT. Twisting, wreathing (d'une plante). ∥ ARCHIT. Volute.

enrouler [-le] v. tr. (1). To coil up (en cercle); to roll up (en rouleau); to wind (en pelote); to twist (en torsade). ∥ To wrap, to fold (qqn, un tissu) [autour, round; dans, in]. ∥ ARCHIT. To volute.

— v. pr. **S'enrouler**, to coil (en cercle); to roll up (en rouleau); to wind (en pelote); to twist, to twine (en torsade). ∥ To wrap (ou) to fold oneself (autour de, round); to wrap, to roll up (dans, in). ∥ ARCHIT. To form a volute.

enroutiné, ée [ãrutine] adj. Stick-in-the-mud, hidebound, routine-bound, routine-minded.

enrubanner [ãrybane] v. tr. (1). To trim with ribbons.

ensablement [ãsabləmã] m. Sanding up (d'un objet); silting up (d'un port). ∥ Sinking in the sand (enlisement). ∥ Sand-bank. ∥ NAUT. Stranding.

ensabler [-ble] v. tr. (1). To sand over (une allée); to blind (une route). ∥ To choke with sand (un égout); to silt up (un port). — v. pr. **S'ensabler**, to get choked with sand (égout); to silt up (port). ∥ To sink in sand (personne). ∥ NAUT. To strand, to run aground, to settle in the sand.

ensachage [ãsaʃa:ʒ] m. Sacking, bagging.

ensacher [-ʃe] v. tr. (1). To sack, to bag (du blé).

ensanglanté, ée [ãsãglãte] adj. Gory, bloody, blood-stained. (V. SANGLANT.)

ensanglanter v. tr. (1). To bloody, to cover (ou) stain with blood. ∥ FIG. To drench (ou) to steep in blood, to cover with blood.

enseignant, ante [ãsɛɲã, ã:t] adj. Teaching. — s. Teacher.

enseigne [ãsɛɲ] f. Sign, sign-board, style (d'un commerce); *enseigne lumineuse*, electric sign; *logés à la même enseigne*, all in the same boat. ∥ MILIT. Flag (drapeau). ∥ NAUT. Ensign (pavillon). ∥ JUR. *A telle enseigne que*, so much so that. — m. MILIT. Ensign. ∥ NAUT. Sub-lieutenant, U. S. ensign.

enseignement [ãsɛɲmã] m. Teaching (action); education (fait); *enseignement par correspondance*, postal tuition, U. S. correspondence school; *enseignement professionnel*, vocational training; *enseignement supérieur*, university education. ∥ FIG. Lesson.

enseigner [-ɲe] v. tr. (1). To teach, to profess (qqch.) [v. PROFESSER]; to teach, to instruct (qqn) [v. INSTRUIRE]; *enseigner qqch. à qqn*, to teach s.o. sth. ∥ To inform (faire savoir). ∥ FIG. To give a lesson in.

ensemble [ãsã:bl] adv. Together; *aller ensemble*, to go together (de conserve); to match (de pair). ∥ At the same time (à la fois). — m. Whole (totalité); *dans l'ensemble*, on the whole; *dans son ensemble*, as a whole; *d'ensemble*, general (impression); comprehensive (mesure). ∥ Concord, concert, harmony, unity; *avec ensemble*, simultaneously, like one man, unanimously. ∥ Ensemble (costume). ∥ Suite (de meubles); set (d'objets, d'outils). ∥ ARTS. *L'ensemble*, the nude; the altogether (fam.). ∥ MUS. *Musique d'ensemble*, concert music; *ensemble vocal*, vocal ensemble. ∥ MATH. Set; *théorie des ensembles*, set theory. ∥ ARCHIT. *Grand ensemble*, high-rise housing estate. ∥ FIG. Set, body (de doctrines).

ensemblier [ãsãblje] m. Decorative artist, decorator.

ensemencement [ãsəmãsmã] m. AGRIC. Sowing.

ensemencer [-se] v. tr. (6). AGRIC. To sow; *ensemencer en avoine*, to put under oats.

enserrer [ãsɛre] v. tr. (1). To enclose (enclore). ∥ To embrace, to hug, to clasp (embrasser).

enserrer v. tr. (1). AGRIC. To put in a hothouse.

ensevelir [ãsəvli:r] v. tr. (2). To shroud (un mort). ∥ To bury (un vivant) [sous, under]. ∥ FIG. To bury, to hide away (cacher); to sink (plonger) [dans, in].

ensevelissement [-lismɑ̃] m. Shrouding.
ensilage [ɑ̃sila:ʒ], **ensilotage** [-lɔta:ʒ] m. AGRIC. Ensilage.
ensiler [-le], **ensiloter** [-lɔte] v. tr. (1). AGRIC. To ensile, to silo, to silage.
ensoleillé, ée [ɑ̃sɔlɛje] adj. Sunny (endroit, maison); sun-kissed (paysage); *situation ensoleillée,* sunny exposure, sunniness. ‖ FIG. Sunny.
ensoleillement [-lɛjmɑ̃] m. Amount of (ou) exposure to sunshine, sunshine, sunniness.
ensoleiller v. tr. (1). To make sunny; to sun (un endroit). ‖ FIG. To brighten, to light up (la vie).
ensommeillé, ée [ɑ̃sɔmɛje] adj. Sleepy.
ensorcelant, ante [ɑ̃sɔrsəlɑ̃, ɑ̃:t] adj. Bewitching, fascinating, enchanting. (V. FASCINANT.)
ensorcelé, ée [-le] adj. Bewitched, spell-bound; enchanted. ‖ FIG. Bewitched, charmed, fascinated.
ensorceler [-le] v. tr. (8 a). To bewitch, to enchant. ‖ FIG. To bewitch, to fascinate, to charm.
ensorceleur, euse [-lœ:r, ø:z] adj. Bewitching. — m. Sorcerer, wizard. ‖ FIG. Charmer.
ensorceleuse [-lø:z] f. Sorceress, witch, enchantress. ‖ FIG. Witch, enchantress.
ensorcellement [ɑ̃sɔrsɛlmɑ̃] m. Bewitchment. ‖ FIG. Witchery, fascination, enchantment.
ensuite [ɑ̃sɥit] adv. Next; *que va-t-il faire ensuite?,* what will he do next? ‖ After; *passez devant, je viendrai ensuite,* go on ahead, I'll follow. ‖ Then (puis); *et ensuite?,* what then?
ensuivre (s') [sɑ̃sɥi:vr] v. pr. (45). To come after (suivre); *tout ce qui s'ensuit,* all the rest of it. ‖ To ensue, to follow, to spring (de, from) [v. RÉSULTER]; *les résultats qui s'ensuivent,* the results attendant upon it; *il s'ensuit que,* hence it follows that.
entablement [ɑ̃tabləmɑ̃] m. ARCHIT., TECHN. Entablature.
entabler [-ble] v. tr. (1). TECHN. To scarf, to half-joint.
entacher [ɑ̃taʃe] v. tr. (1). To blemish (la réputation); to taint (de, with). ‖ JUR. To vitiate; *entaché de nullité,* null and void, voidable.
entaillage [ɑ̃tɑja:ʒ] m. Notching (par encoche); slitting (par taillade).
entaille [ɑ̃tɑ:j] f. Notch, nick (encoche); slit (fente, taillade). ‖ Hack, gash, cut, slash (dans le corps). ‖ TECHN. Gap.
entailler [ɑ̃tɑje] v. tr. (1). To notch (en encoche); to slit (en taillade). ‖ To hack, to gash, to cut, to slash (la peau).
entame [ɑ̃tam] f. First slice (du pain).
entamer [-me] v. tr. (1). To take a gulp of (en buvant); to cut the first slice of (en coupant); to take a bite out of (en mordant). ‖ To give the first snip of the scissors to (en coupant); to open (en ouvrant). ‖ To cut (ou) to bite into, to break (la peau). ‖ JUR. To institute (des poursuites). ‖ FIG. To impair, to encroach on, to make a big dent in, to dip pretty deeply into, to make a hole in (son capital); to weaken (la confiance); to open (une discussion, des pourparlers, une querelle); to enter into (des négociations); to broach (une question); to start on (un travail).
— v. pr. **S'entamer,** to become abraded (ou) excoriated (peau).
entartrage [ɑ̃tartra:ʒ] m. Furring, scaling, coating, incrustation.
entartrer [ɑ̃tartre] v. tr. (1). To scale, to fur.
— v. pr. **S'entartrer,** to scale, to fur.
entassement [ɑ̃tasmɑ̃] m. Heaping (ou) piling up (action); heap, pile (résultat). ‖ Hoarding (d'argent); cramming (de gens). ‖ FIG. Accumulation, collection, pack.
entasser [-se] v. tr. (1). To heap (ou) pile up (des objets en tas); to huddle up (pêle-mêle). ‖ To

hoard up (de l'argent); to crowd, to cram, to pack, to huddle (des gens).
— v. pr. **S'entasser,** to crowd, to pack (dans, into).
ente [ɑ̃:t] f. AGRIC. Scion, graft. ‖ ARTS. Handle.
entendant, ante [ɑ̃tɑ̃dɑ̃, ɑ̃:t] adj. *Mal entendant,* hard of hearing.
— s. *Les mal entendants,* the hard of hearing.
entendement [ɑ̃tɑ̃dəmɑ̃] m. Understanding.
entendeur [-dœ:r] m. Quick-witted man; *à bon entendeur salut,* if the cap (ou) shoe fits, wear it.
entendre [ɑ̃tɑ̃:dr] v. tr. (4). To hear (un bruit); *entendre chanter,* to hear s.o. singing. ‖ To hear, to listen to (écouter); *à l'entendre,* according to him; *entendre jusqu'au bout,* to hear out; *ne rien vouloir entendre,* to turn a deaf ear to all advice. ‖ To understand (comprendre); *entendre la plaisanterie,* to know how to take a joke; *entendre raison,* to listen to reason. ‖ To know all about, to be clever at, to be versed in (être doué pour); *il n'y entend rien,* he doesn't know the first thing about it. ‖ To mean, to intend (vouloir dire); *entendre malice,* to mean mischief; *entendre par là que,* to mean by that that. ‖ To like (aimer); to wish, to want (souhaiter); *agir comme on l'entend,* to have one's own way; *comme vous l'entendez,* as you like (ou) please (ou) prefer (ou) choose. ‖ To hear, to attend (assister à); *entendre un cours,* to attend a lecture. ‖ To propose (envisager); *quelle suite entendez-vous donner à cette affaire?,* what do you propose to do in the matter? ‖ To intend, to demand (exiger); *entendre faire qqch.,* to intend to do (ou) doing sth.; *j'entends qu'on ne m'insulte pas,* I won't be insulted; *je n'entends pas être traité de la sorte,* I won't stand being treated in such a way. ‖ JUR. To hear (un témoin).
‖ **Entendre dire,** to hear it said, to hear (que, that); *entendre dire qqch. à qqn,* to hear sth. said to s.o.; *entendre qqn dire qqch.,* to hear s.o. say sth.; *je ne sais par ce qu'on entend dire,* I know it by hearsay; *on entend dire que,* it is rumoured that; *on entend dire du vilain sur son compte,* there are nasty reports afloat about him. ‖ **Entendre parler,** to hear (de, of); *il en a entendu parler,* he has heard of it; *il n'entend plus les gens parler de lui,* he no longer hears himself talked of; *on n'entend plus parler de lui,* he is no longer heard (ou) talked of; *elle ne veut pas en entendre parler,* she won't hear of it (de qqch.); she wants nothing to do with him, she won't hear his name mentioned (de qqn). ‖ **Faire entendre,** to utter (un mot); to express (une opinion); to raise (une revendication); *faire entendre raison à,* to bring to reason.
— v. intr. To hear; *entendre mal,* to be hard of hearing. ‖ To understand; *entendre à demi-mot,* to take the hint, to be quick on the uptake.
— v. pr. **S'entendre,** to be heard (bruit); to hear oneself (soi-même). ‖ To be understood, to be obvious (explication, raison); *je m'entends!,* I know what I mean! ‖ To understand, to be skilled (ou) versed (à, in); to be a good judge (à, of); *s'entendre aux autos,* to know all about cars.
— v. récipr. **S'entendre,** to hear each other (ou) one another; *on ne s'entend plus,* there is such a noise that people can't hear one another. ‖ To agree (se mettre d'accord) [avec, with; sur, about]. ‖ To understand each other, to get on, to be on good terms (s'accorder) [avec, with]; *elles ne s'entendent pas,* they don't hit it off; *s'entendre comme les deux doigts de la main,* to get along like turtle doves. ‖ To plot, to conspire (conspirer); to band together (contre, against).
entendu, ue [ɑ̃tɑ̃dy] adj. Stipulated, appointed; *c'est une affaire entendue,* that's settled (ou) agreed; right-o!; *étant entendu que,* it being understood that, on the understanding that. ‖ Capable, efficient, up to one's work; *être entendu*

à, to be well up (ou) versed in, to be a good judge of, to have a good grasp of. ‖ Jur. Understood; *intérêt bien entendu*, enlightened self-interest.
— interj. Right-o!, O. K.!; U. S. check! *bien entendu!*, of course!, naturally!, no wonder!, as a matter of course!

enténébrer [ãtenebⓇe] v. tr. (5). To darken.
— v. pr. **S'enténébrer**, to become gloomy.

entente [ãtã:t] f. Meaning; *expression à double entente*, expression with a double meaning, double entendre. ‖ Understanding, agreement (accord); *Entente cordiale*, Entente Cordiale; *bonne entente*, good feeling. ‖ Grasp (*de*, of) [compréhension]; skill (*de*, in) [habileté]. ‖ Comm. *Entente industrielle*, combine.

enter [ãte] v. tr. (1). Agric. To graft. ‖ Fig. To implant (*sur*, in).

entérinement [ãterinmã] m. Confirmation, ratification.

entériner [-ne] v. tr. (1). To confirm, to ratify.

entérite [ãterit] f. Méd. Enteritis.

entérocolite [-rɔkolit] f. Méd. Enterocolitis.

enterrement [ãtɛrmã] m. Burial (acte); burial-service (messe). ‖ Fam. *Une mine d'enterrement*, a funereal look.

enterrer [-re] v. tr. (1). To bury (un cadavre, un trésor). ‖ To attend the burial-service of (suivre le convoi de); to outlive (survivre à). ‖ To bury (un vivant) [*dans*, in]. ‖ Fig. To shelve, to bury and forget (une affaire); to scrap, to give up, to throw up (un projet). ‖ Fam. *Enterrer sa vie de garçon*, to give a bachelor's farewell party.
— v. pr. **S'enterrer**, to dig oneself in (volontairement); to sink in a quicksand (involontairement). ‖ Fig. To bury oneself (*à*, in).

entêtant, ante [ãtɛtã, ã:t] adj. Stifling (chaleur); heady (vin); head-achy (fam.).

en-tête [ãtɛ:t] (pl. **en-têtes**) m. Head, heading, U. S. caption (de chapitre); headline (de journal); printed address (de papier à lettres). ‖ Comm. Bill-head (de facture).

entêté [ãtɛte] adj. Wilful, perverse; obstinate, stubborn, heady, pig-headed, mulish, obdurate.

entêtement [-tmã] m. Wilfulness; pig-headedness, obstinacy, stubbornness.

entêter [-te] v. tr. (1). To go to s.o.'s head (alcool, vin). ‖ To give a headache to (atmosphère). ‖ Fig. To intoxicate.
— v. pr. **S'entêter**, to be stubborn (ou) mulish; *s'entêter à faire qqch.*, to persist in doing sth.; *s'entêter dans*, to persist in, to stick stubbornly to, to be steadfast in.

enthalpie [ãtalpi] f. Phys. Enthalpy.

enthousiasmant, ante [ãtuzjasmã, ã:t] adj. Exhilarating, exciting, thrilling.

enthousiasme [ãtuzjasm] m. Enthusiasm (*pour*, for, about) [v. Engouement]; *avec enthousiasme* (ou) *d'enthousiasme*, enthusiastically; *montrer de l'enthousiasme pour*, to enthuse over.

enthousiasmer [-zjasme] v. tr. (1). To make enthusiastic, to transport, to enrapture (qqn).
— v. pr. **S'enthousiasmer**, to be moved, to enthusiasm. ‖ To become enthusiastic, to enthuse (*pour*, over); to be carried away (*pour*, by).

enthousiaste [-zjast] adj. Enthusiastic.
— s. Enthusiast (*de*, for); *enthousiaste du ping-pong*, table-tennis enthusiast.

entiché, ée [ãtiʃe] adj. *Entiché de*, infatuated with, keen on, mad on, U. S. nuts about (fanatique); wedded to (obstiné); proud of (orgueilleux).

entichement [-ʃmã] m. Infatuation (*de*, for).

enticher [-ʃe] v. tr. (1). To infatuate (*de*, with)'.
— v. pr. **S'enticher**, to become infatuated (*de*, with); to go daft (ou) batty (*de*, over) [fam.].

entier, ère [ãtje, ɛr] adj. Whole, entire (complet); full, whole (total); *le monde entier*, the whole world; *paye entière*, full pay; *la population entière*, the entire population. ‖ Culin. Full-cream, U. S. whole (lait). ‖ Ch. de f. *Place entière*, full fare. ‖ Math. Whole; *nombre entier*, integer. ‖ Zool. Entire (animal); *cheval entier*, stallion. ‖ Fig. Entire (confiance). ‖ Fam. Absolute, unyielding (personne).
— m. Whole, entirety; *en entier*, in full, at full length (au long); fully, entirely, completely (complètement); *le travail doit être recommencé en entier*, the work must be done all over again. ‖ Math. Whole.

entièrement [ãtjɛrmã] adv. Wholly, entirely; fully, completely; *entièrement pourri*, rotten to the core. ‖ Unreservedly, entirely (sans réserve); *entièrement pour*, completely in favour of.

entièreté [-te] f. Entirety.

entité [ãtite] f. Philos. Entity.

entoilage [ãtwala:ʒ] m. Mounting on cloth (d'une carte). ‖ Stiffening (d'un revers d'habit). ‖ Aviat. Covering.

entoiler [-le] v. tr. (1). To mount on cloth (une carte). ‖ To stiffen (un revers). ‖ Aviat. To cover.

entoir [ãtwa:r] m. Agric. Grafting-knife.

entôlage [ãtola:ʒ] m. Pop. Diddling, swindling, fleecing.

entôler [-le] v. tr. (1). Pop. To diddle, to trick, to take in, to gyp; *se faire entôler*, to be done down, to be taken in (ou) rooked.

entomologie [ãtɔmɔlɔʒi] f. Zool. Entomology.

entomologique [-ʒik] adj. Zool. Entomological.

entomologiste [-ʒist] s. Zool. Entomologist.

entonner [ãtɔne] v. tr. (1). To break into (un air); to intone (un chant); to sound (une trompette). ‖ Fig. To sing, to sound (des louanges).

entonner v. tr. (1). To cask, to tun (enfutailler). ‖ To force down (un liquide) [*à*, to]. ‖ Fam. To drink, to toss off, to swill (du vin).
— v. tr. To drink like a fish.
— v. pr. **S'entonner**, to swill (du vin).

entonnoir [-nwa:r] m. Funnel; *en entonnoir*, funnelled, funnel-shaped. ‖ Milit. Shell-hole. ‖ Fam. Soak (ivrogne).

entorse [ãtɔrs] f. Méd. Sprain; *se donner une entorse*, to sprain (ou) to twist one's ankle. ‖ Fig. Infringement (au règlement); stretching (à la vérité).

entortillage [ãtɔrtija:ʒ], **entortillement** [-jmã] m. Winding; twisting; wrapping. ‖ Fig. Entanglement, intricacy.

entortiller [-je] v. tr. (1). To twist, to twine, to wind (autour de, round); to wrap up (dans, in). [V. Enchevêtrer.] ‖ Fig. To make intricate (ses idées, ses réponses). ‖ Fam. To wheedle, to bamboozle, to twist round one's little finger (qqn).
— v. pr. **S'entortiller**, to twist, to twine (autour de, round); to wrap oneself (dans, in); *le serpent s'entortilla autour de l'arbre*, the snake coiled itself round the tree. ‖ Fam. To get muddled.

entour [ãtur] m. A l'entour, à l'entour de, around, round about; *les maisons à l'entour*, the neighbouring houses.

entourage [-ra:ʒ] m. Frame (de tableau). ‖ Edging (bordure); fencing, hedging (clôture); *avec un entourage de petites maisons*, with little houses clustering around. ‖ Fig. Surroundings (milieu); entourage (personnes).

entourer [-re] v. tr. (1). To edge, to border (border); to fence, to hedge (clôturer); to surround, to encircle, to encompass (encercler); to sheathe (gainer); *entourer de murs*, to wall in (un terrain); *une église entourée de petites maisons*, a church hemmed in by cottages. ‖ To set (un bijou); *entouré de brillants*, set round with dia-

monds. ‖ MILIT. To hem in, to surround (l'ennemi). ‖ FIG. To surround (adversaires, périls); *entouré de dangers*, surrounded by (ou) with dangers. ‖ FIG. To surround; to press (ou) to hang round (qqn); *entourer d'attentions*, to lavish attentions on; *entourer de mystère*, to wrap in mystery, to make a mystery of; *entourer de respect*, to show great respect to, to have due consideration for; *entouré de ses partisans*, supported by his backers; *être très entouré*, to have a large following.
— v. pr. S'entourer, to surround oneself (*de*, with); *savoir s'entourer*, to know how to choose one's counsellors. ‖ To wrap oneself (*de*, in) [mystère]; *s'entourer de précautions contre*, to take every precaution against.

entourloupette [ɑ̃turlupɛt] f. FAM. Dirty trick; *faire une entourloupette à*, to play a dirty trick on.

entournure [ɑ̃turny:r] f. Arm-hole. ‖ FAM. *Gêné aux entournures*, ill at ease.

entozoaire [ɑ̃tɔzɔɛ:r] m. ZOOL. Entozoon (pl. entozoa).

entraccuser (s') [sɑ̃trakyze] v. récipr. (1). To accuse each other (ou) one another.

entracte [ɑ̃trakt] m. THÉÂTR. Interval; U. S. intermission; *pendant l'entracte*, during the interval, between the acts, U. S. during the intermission. ‖ Entr'acte (intermède). ‖ FIG. Interlude, pause.

entraide [ɑ̃trɛ:d] f. Mutual help.

entraider (s') [sɑ̃trɛde] v. récipr. (1). To help each other (ou) one another.

entrailles [ɑ̃trɑ:j] f. pl. Guts (d'un animal); entrails, bowels (d'une personne); bowels, womb (de la terre). ‖ ECCLÉS. *Le fruit de vos entrailles*, the fruit of thy womb. ‖ FIG. Pity; *sans entrailles*, heartless; merciless.

entr'aimer (s') [sɑ̃trɛme] v. récipr. (1). To love each other (ou) one another.

entrain [ɑ̃trɛ̃] m. Spirit, liveliness, cheerfulness (gaieté). ‖ Dash, go, fire, mettle, spunk (allant); *retrouver son entrain*, to recover one's spirits.

entraînant, ante [ɑ̃trɛnɑ̃, ɑ̃:t] adj. Stirring (action, musique, paroles); catchy (musique).

entraînement [-nmɑ̃] m. TECHN. Driving, drive. ‖ SPORTS. Training; *à l'entraînement*, in training; *d'entraînement*, practice. ‖ NAUT. Coaching. ‖ FIG. Urge, impulse (des passions); *céder à l'entraînement*, to yield to temptation.

entraîner [-ne] v. tr. (1). To sweep away (qqch.) [en balayant]; to carry along (ou) away (en emportant); to wash away (en lavant); to draw (ou) drag along (en tirant). ‖ To lead, to induce, to incite, to instigate, to occasion (v. INCITER) [à, to]; *se laisser entraîner trop loin*, to let oneself go too far, to give too free a rein to one's feelings. ‖ To involve, to inveigle (v. IMPLIQUER) [dans, into]. ‖ To carry away, to sweep along (son auditoire). ‖ To bring about (un accident, la ruine); to entail (des conséquences, des dépenses); to involve (des difficultés, des frais); to occasion (une révolte); *les malheurs qu'entraîne la guerre*, the evils that follow in the train of war. ‖ TECHN. To drive. ‖ SPORTS. To train (un sportif); to pace (dans une course). ‖ FAM. To train [à, for, to]; *entraîné à*, schooled in.
— v. pr. S'entraîner. SPORTS. To train, to be in training, to go into training (à, for).

entraîneur [-nœ:r] adj. TECHN. Driving.
— m. SPORTS. Coach (d'une équipe); trainer (d'un sportif); pace-maker (dans une course).

entraîneuse [-nø:z] f. FAM. Dance hostess, U. S. B-girl, shill.

entrait [ɑ̃trɛ] m. TECHN. Tie-beam; tie-rod.

entrant [ɑ̃trɑ̃] adj. Ingoing, incoming. ‖ JUR. Newly-appointed.
— s. Ingoer, incomer.

entr'apercevoir [ɑ̃trapɛrsəwa:r] v. tr. (3). To get a faint glimpse of.

entr'appeler (s') [sɑ̃trapəle] v. récipr. (8 a). To call each other (ou) one another.

entrave [ɑ̃tra:v] f. Clog (bois); shackle, hobble (lien). ‖ SPORTS. Trammel (pour dressage). ‖ FIG. Shackle, trammel, hindrance; *mettre une entrave à l'action de*, to hamper (ou) hinder (ou) balk (qqn).

entraver [ɑ̃trave] v. tr. (1). To fetter (avec des fers); to shackle, to hobble (avec des liens); to clog (avec un morceau de bois). ‖ To trammel, to shackle (qqn); *jupe entravée*, hobble-skirt. ‖ SPORTS. To trammel (un cheval au dressage). ‖ FIG. To clog (une entreprise); to check, to thwart (un projet); to hamper, to hinder, to impede, to balk (qqn) [dans, in]; *entraver la marche de mes affaires*, to hinder me in my business.
— v. pr. S'entraver, to be hampered (dans, by); to get entangled (dans, in).

entre [ɑ̃tr] prép. Between (au milieu); *entre la vie et la mort*, between life and death. ‖ Between (de l'un à l'autre); *entre quatre yeux*, in private; *nous réunir entre nous*, to meet by ourselves; *soit dit entre nous*, between ourselves, between you and me and the lamp-post (fam.). ‖ Between (sens réciproque); *ils se battent entre eux*, they fight between themselves; *ils se dévorent entre eux*, they devour one another; *il n'y a pas d'amitié entre eux*, there is no love lost between them. ‖ Between (environ); *entre 20 et 30*, between 20 and 30. ‖ Through (à travers); *passer entre les mailles*, to slip through the meshes. ‖ In (dans); *entre de bonnes mains*, in good hands. ‖ Out of (tiré de); *un jour entre mille*, a day in a thousand. ‖ Among (parmi); *entre tous mes amis*, among all my friends; *ma tante entre autres*, my aunt for one. ‖ D'entre, of, from, among, from among, out of; *celles d'entre mes amies qui*, those among my friends who; *ceux d'entre eux qui*, those of them who; *se différencier d'entre*, to differ from; *sortir d'entre la foule*, to come out from among the crowd; *un d'entre les cinq*, one out of the five. ‖ **Entre-déchirer (s')**, v. récipr. To tear each other (ou) one another. ‖ **Entre-détruire (s')**, v. récipr. To destroy each other (ou) one another. ‖ **Entre-deux**, m. Insertion (de lingerie); interval (dans le temps); *l'entre-deux-guerres*, the interwar years. ‖ **Entre-dévorer (s')**, v. récipr. To devour each other (ou) one another. ‖ **Entre-luire**, v. intr. (61). To glimmer. ‖ **Entre-nœud**, m. BOT. Internode. ‖ **Entre-pilastre**, m. ARCHIT. Interpilaster. ‖ **Entre-quereller (s')**, v. récipr. To quarrel with each other (ou) one another. ‖ **Entre-rail**, m. CH. DE F. Four-foot way; gauge. ‖ **Entre-regarder (s')**, v. récipr. To look at each other (ou) one another. ‖ **Entre-temps**, adv., m. Meanwhile. ‖ **Entre-tuer (s')**, v. récipr. To kill each other (ou) one another. ‖ **Entre-voie**, f. CH. DE F. Six-foot way, space between the tracks.

entrebâillé, ée [ɑ̃trəbɑje] adj. Half-open; ajar.

entrebâillement [ɑ̃trəbɑjmɑ̃] m. Narrow (ou) slight opening.

entrebâiller v. tr. (1). To half-open.

entrebâilleur [-jœ:r] m. Door-stop.

entrechat [ɑ̃trəʃa] m. ARTS. Entrechat (à la danse). ‖ FAM. Pl. Capers.

entrechoquement [ɑ̃trəʃɔkmɑ̃] m. Rattling, knocking together (d'objets); clash (d'armes, d'idées); clinking (de verres); chattering (des dents).

entrechoquer [ɑ̃trəʃɔke] v. tr. (1). To touch, to clink (les verres).
— v. récipr. S'entrechoquer, to clash (armes);

to chatter (dents); to knock against one another (objets). ‖ Fig. To clash (idées).

entrecolonne [ãtrəkɔlɔn] m. Archit. Intercolumniation.

entrecôte [ãtrəko:t] f. Culin. Entrecôte, ribsteak, rib of beef, sirloin steak.

entrecoupé, ée [ãtrəkupe] adj. Intersected (terrain) [de, with]. ‖ Broken (sommeil, voix) [de, with]; *d'une voix entrecoupée*, with a catch in one's voice, brokenly. ‖ Jerky, halting (style); *entrecoupé de digressions*, interspersed with digressions.

entrecouper v. tr. (1). To intersect (un terrain). ‖ Fig. To interrupt (un discours); to break (le sommeil, la voix); to intersperse, to sprinkle (de, with).
— v. récipr. S'entrecouper, to cut each other (ou) one another. ‖ To intersect.

entrecroisement [ãtrəkrwazmã] m. Interlacing (de fils); intersection (de routes).

entrecroisé, ée [-ze] adj. Intersected, interwoven. ‖ Géol. *Stratification entrecroisée*, cross-bedding.

entrecroiser [-ze] v. tr. (1). To interlace (des fils); to cross (des lignes); to intersect (des routes).
— v. récipr. S'entrecroiser, to interlace (fils); to cross one another (lignes); to intersect (routes).

entrée [ãtre] f. Entering, entry, incoming, coming in (action); *faire une entrée majestueuse*, to stride (ou) stalk in; *faire son entrée dans*, to make one's entrance into; *faire son entrée dans le monde*, to come out. ‖ Admittance, access (chez, to); *entrée interdite*, no admittance; *on lui refusa l'entrée*, he was denied admittance. ‖ Admission; *examen d'entrée*, entrance examination. ‖ Entrée, entrance fee (droits); *entrée de faveur*, free pass; *entrée gratuite*, free admission. ‖ Entrance-hall, hall, U. S. entry (de maison); street-door, frontdoor (porte); *entrée de service*, tradesmen's entrance. ‖ Edge (d'un bois); outskirts (d'une forêt); mouth (d'une grotte, d'un puits, d'un tunnel, d'un sac). ‖ Aviat. *Entrée d'air des réacteurs*, jet engine air intake. ‖ Naut. Arrival (d'un navire); mouth (d'un port). ‖ Jur. *Entrée en fonction*, taking over one's duties (d'un employé); accession to office (d'un ministre); *entrée en jouissance*, entry, taking possession. ‖ Comm. Entry (inscription); receipt (recette). ‖ Culin. Entrée. ‖ Sports. Receipts, gate-money, gate. ‖ Théâtr. Entrance. ‖ Inform. Input. ‖ Gramm. Entry (dans un dictionnaire). ‖ Fig. Beginning (de l'hiver); *entrée en matière*, opening. ‖ Loc. D'entrée, point-blank, outright; from the very first.

entrefaite [ãtrəfɛt] f. *Sur ces entrefaites*, in the meantime, at that time, in the midst of all this.

entrefer [ãtrəfɛ:r] m. Phys. Air gap (d'un aimant).

entrefilet [ãtrəfilɛ] m. Notice, paragraph.

entregent [ãtrəʒã] m. Social sense; aplomb; *avoir de l'entregent*, to be a good mixer.

entr'égorger (s') [sãtregɔrʒe] v. récipr. To cut each other's (ou) one another's throats.

entrejambe [ãtrəʒã:b] m. Length from fork to heel.

entrelacement [ãtrəlasmã] m. Interlacing, interweaving (action). ‖ Network. ‖ Radio. Interlacing, interlaced scanning (en T.V.).

entrelacer [-lase] v. tr. (6). To interlace (des fils). ‖ To link (des anneaux); to interweave, to weave, to wreathe (des branches, des fleurs); to wreathe (de, with).

entrelacs [-lɑ] m. Knot-work (en broderie). ‖ Tangle (d'épines).

entrelardé, ée [ãtrəlarde] adj. Streaky, streaked (viande).

entrelarder v. tr. (1). Culin. To lard. ‖ Fam. To interlard, to intersperse (de, with).

entremêlement [ãtrəmɛlmã] m. Intermixing, intermingling (action). ‖ Mixture, medley.

entremêler [-mɛle] v. tr. (1). To intermix, to intermingle, to mix, to mingle (de, with). ‖ Fig. To intersperse (de, with).
— v. pr. S'entremêler, to intermingle; to get entangled.

entremets [ãtrəmɛ] m. Culin. Sweet, U. S. dessert.

entremetteur [ãtrəmɛtœ:r] m. Procurer, pander, pimp (v. Maquereau); *jouer le rôle d'entremetteur auprès de*, to pander to. ‖ Comm. Middleman. ‖ Fam. Go-between.

entremetteuse [-tø:z] f. Procuress.

entremettre (s') [sãtrəmɛtr] v. pr. (64). To intervene. ‖ To mediate (entre, between); to intercede (pour, for).

entremise [ãtrəmi:z] f. Intervention; interposition; mediation; *par l'entremise de*, through the medium (ou) agency of (action); by the hand of (lettre).

entrepas [ãtrəpɑ] m. Sports. Amble.

entreplan [ãtrəplã] m. Aviat. Wing-gap.

entrepont [ãtrəpɔ̃] m. Naut. Between-decks, 'tween-decks.

entreposage [ãtrəpoza:ʒ] m. Warehousing. ‖ Jur. Bonding (en douane).

entreposer [-ze] v. tr. (1). To warehouse, to store. ‖ Jur. To bond (en douane).

entreposeur [-zœ:r] m. Warehouseman.

entrepositaire [-zitɛ:r] m. Comm. Owner (ou) keeper of warehoused goods. ‖ Jur. Bonder (des douanes).

entrepôt [ãtrəpo] m. Warehouse, storehouse. ‖ Jur. Bonded warehouse (des douanes); depot (de l'Etat). ‖ Milit. Depot. ‖ Fig. Emporium.

entreprenant, ante [ãtrəprənã, ã:t] adj. Enterprising; go-ahead, go-getting (actif); daring (audacieux); *esprit entreprenant*, enterprise. ‖ Enterprising, forward (osé).

entreprendre [-prã:dr] v. tr. (80). To undertake, to take in hand, to assume, to take up (qqch.); *entreprendre de faire*, to undertake to do. ‖ To undertake (qqn); to tackle (au sujet de, sur, about). ‖ Archit. To contract for (des travaux).

entrepreneur [-prənœ:r] m. Contractor; *entrepreneur de camionnage*, carter, haulier, U. S. trucker; *entrepreneur de construction*, masterbuilder, master-mason; *entrepreneur de pompes funèbres*, undertaker; funeral director, U. S. mortician; *entrepreneur de transports*, carrier. ‖ Jur. Entrepreneur (en économie politique).

entreprise [-pri:z] f. Undertaking; *manifester un grand esprit d'entreprise*, to show enterprise. ‖ Techn. Contract (de travaux); *comité d'entreprise*, joint production (ou) works committee. ‖ Comm. Concern, undertaking; *une grosse entreprise*, a large firm; *entreprise rémunératrice*, profitable concern; *entreprise de transport*, carriers.

entrer [ãtre] v. intr. (1). To enter; to go in; to come in; to get in (v. Pénétrer); *entrez!*, go in! (si l'on est à l'extérieur); come in! (si l'on est à l'intérieur); *entrer par la fenêtre*, to get in through the window; *entrer à pas de loup, en courant*, to steal in, to run in; *entrer et sortir*, to pass in and out; *entrer par une porte et sortir par l'autre*, to go in at one door and come out at the other; *faire entrer*, to call in (en appelant); to bring in (en conduisant); to show in (en introduisant); to push in (en poussant); *faire entrer de force*, to force in; *ne faire qu'entrer et sortir*, to drop in (visiteur). ‖ To ride in (cavalier); to walk in (piéton); to blow in (vent); to drive in (voiture). ‖ To go, to come, to get (dans, into);

entrer dans sa chambre, to enter one's room; *entrer dans une boutique,* to go into a shop; *entrer dans la cour,* to drive into the yard (voiture); *entrer à pas de loup dans,* to steal into; *faire entrer dans,* to call into (en appelant); to bring into (en conduisant); to show into (en introduisant); to push (ou) to cram into (en poussant); *faire entrer la clé dans la serrure,* to get the key into the lock. ‖ Comm. *Entrer dans,* to join in, to enter into (une affaire); *entrer en,* to enter into (concurrence). ‖ Jur. *Entrer au barreau,* to become a barrister, to be admitted to the Bar; *entrer au Parlement,* to enter Parliament; *entrer en jouissance,* to enter into the possession of; *entrer en ligne de compte,* to be relevant; *entrer en possession,* to come into possession; *entrer en vigueur,* to come into force; to become effective. ‖ Milit. *Entrer dans l'armée,* to enter the army. ‖ Ecclés. *Entrer en religion,* to become a monk (ou) a nun. ‖ Culin. *Entrer en ébullition,* to begin to boil. ‖ Méd. *Entrer en moiteur,* to break into perspiration. ‖ Loc. *Entrer dans un complot,* to take part in a plot; *entrer en conversation avec,* to engage in conversation with; *entrer dans les détails, les explications,* to go into details, explanations; *entrer dans une famille,* to marry into a family; *entrer en ménage,* to set up housekeeping; *entrer dans les plans de qqn de,* to be a part of s.o.'s plans to; *entrer pour qqch. dans,* to play a part in; *entrer dans la tête de qqn,* to enter s.o.'s head; *faire entrer qqch. dans la tête de qqn,* to get sth. into s.o.'s head; *entrer dans les vues de qqn,* to meet s.o.'s views. ‖ Fam. *Il n'entre pas là-dedans,* he has nothing to do with it.

entresol [ãtrəsɔl] m. Mezzanine, entresol.
entretaille [ãtrətɑ:j] f. Arts. Slight cut.
entre-temps [ãtrətã] adv., m. Meantime, meanwhile.
entretenir [ãtrətəni:r] v. tr. (101). To keep up (le feu, la maison, les vêtements). ‖ To keep, to maintain (une armée, une famille, une femme). ‖ To feed (la conversation); to keep up, to maintain (une correspondance, des rapports); to make conversation with, to speak (ou) converse with (qqn); to talk to (qqn) [*de,* about]; *entretenir des relations avec,* to keep in touch with, to have dealings with. ‖ To foster (une agitation, l'amitié); to cherish (des espérances); to nurse (des illusions); to entertain (des intentions, des sentiments); to keep alive (la mémoire, le souvenir); to maintain (qqn) [*dans,* in].
— v. pr. **S'entretenir,** to be kept in good condition (maison, objets). ‖ To keep one's hand in (conserver la main); to keep oneself fit (se maintenir en forme); to keep (ou) support oneself (subvenir à ses besoins). ‖ To have a talk, to make conversation (converser); to converse (*avec,* with); to talk (*avec,* to, with; *de,* about).
entretenu, ue [ãtrətəny] adj. Kept (femme, maison).
entretien [-tjɛ̃] m. Keeping in good condition; upkeep (d'un animal, d'une maison, d'un objet); upkeep (frais d'entretien); keep, maintenance (d'une personne); maintenance (d'un appareil). ‖ Talk, conversation; *entretien des plus importants,* vital discussion.
entretoile [ãtrətwal] f. Lace insertion.
entretoise [ãtrətwa:z] f. Techn. Strut, crosspiece. ‖ Milit. Transom. ‖ Aviat. Brace.
entretoiser [-twaze] v. tr. (1). To strut, to brace.
entrevoir [ãtrəvwa:r] v. tr. (106). To catch a glimpse of (un objet, qqn). ‖ To foresee (une difficulté); to glimpse (la mort); to have an idea of (une solution); to have a feeling of, to sense (la vérité); *laisser entrevoir,* to give to under-

stand; to foretell, to foreshadow (faire pressentir); to hint (suggérer).
entrevue [-vy] f. Interview.
entrisme [ãtrism] m. Entrism (dans un parti politique).
entropie [ãtrɔpi] f. Phys., Psych. Entropy.
entropion [ãtrɔpjɔ̃] m. Méd. Entropion.
entrouvert, erte [ãtruvɛr, ɛ:rt] adj. Half-open, ajar (porte). ‖ Parted (lèvres); half-open (yeux). ‖ Bot. Half-open (fleur). ‖ Fig. Gaping (abîme).
entrouvrir [-vrir] v. tr. (72). To half-open (la porte, les yeux); to draw slightly aside (les rideaux).
— v. pr. **S'entrouvrir,** to half-open (porte). ‖ Fig. To open up (abîme).
entuber [ãtybe] v. tr. (1). Pop. To do, to diddle, to con; *je me suis fait entuber,* I've been had.
enturbanné, ée [ãtyrbane] adj. Turbaned.
enture [ãty:r] f. Agric. Incision for grafting. ‖ Archit. Scarf.
énucléation [enykleasjɔ̃] f. Méd. Enucleation.
énucléer [-klee] v. tr. (1). Méd. To enucleate.
énumératif, ive [enymeratif, i:v] adj. Enumerative.
énumération [-rasjɔ̃] f. Enumeration.
énumérer [-re] v. tr. (5). To enumerate.
énurésie [enyrezi] f. Méd. Enuresis.
envahi, ie [ãvai] adj. Milit. Occupied, invaded (pays). ‖ *Envahi par,* overrun with (les mauvaises herbes, les souris); swarming with (la vermine, les visiteurs); *envahi par l'eau,* flooded. ‖ Fig. Overcome (*par,* by) [les regrets]; *envahi par la peur,* panic-stricken. ‖ Fam. Pestered (*par,* by) [des importuns].
envahir [ãva:ir] v. tr. (2). To overspread, to flood (eau); to rush (ou) to break into (foule); to overrun (herbes, rats); to swarm over (vermine, visiteurs). ‖ Milit. To invade; to occupy. ‖ Fig. To steal over (appréhension, émotion, sommeil); to seize (effroi, regrets). ‖ Fam. *Envahir qqn,* to invade s.o.'s privacy.
envahissant, ante [-isã, ã:t] adj. Milit. Invading. ‖ Fam. Invasive, invading (étrangers, voyageurs); encroaching (mal, vice).
envahissement [-ismã] m. Invading, overrunning.
envahisseur [-isœ:r] m. Milit. Invader.
envasement [ãvazmã] m. Naut. Sticking in the mud (d'un bateau); silting up (d'un port).
envaser [-ze] v. tr. (1). To run on the mud (un bateau); to silt up (un port).
— v. pr. **S'envaser.** Naut. To stick in the mud (bateau); to silt up (port).
enveloppant, ante [ãvlɔpã, ã:t] adj. Enveloping, wrapping. ‖ Milit. Encircling.
enveloppe [ãvlɔp] f. Envelope (de lettre); *sous enveloppe,* under cover. ‖ Wrapper, wrapping (emballage). ‖ Techn. Jacket; casing; lagging; lag. ‖ Autom. Cover, casing (de pneu). ‖ Aviat. Bag (de ballon). ‖ Phys. *Enveloppe de l'atome,* shell. ‖ Fig. Exterior, outside, appearance.
enveloppé, ée [-pe] adj. Enveloped, wrapped. ‖ Fig. Roundabout (critique); soft (lumière); *enveloppé de,* wrapped (ou) enshrouded in (mystère).
enveloppement [-pmã] m. Envelopment, wrapping up (action); wrappage (emballage). ‖ Méd. *Enveloppement humide,* wet pack; *enveloppement sinapisé,* mustard plaster (ou) poultice. ‖ Milit. Encirclement.
envelopper [-pe] v. tr. (1). To envelop, to wrap up, to tie up (qqch., qqn); *envelopper d'un couvre-livre, d'un enduit, d'un étui* (ou) *d'une housse* (ou) *d'un revêtement, d'un fourreau,* to jacket, to coat, to encase, to sheathe; *envelopper qqn d'un manteau,* to wrap a cloak round s.o. ‖ Méd. To

pack off. ‖ Milit. To encircle. ‖ Fig. *Envelopper de*, to bathe in (calme, lumière); to wrap (ou) to shroud in (mystère); *envelopper de caresses*, to pay flattering attentions to.

nvenimer [ãvnime] v. tr. (1). Méd. To inflame. Fig. To envenom, to embitter.
— v. pr. **S'envenimer.** Méd. To become inflamed, to fester. ‖ Fig. To become envenomed, to grow bitter.

nverguer [ãvɛrge] v. tr. (1). Naut. To bend.

nvergure [ãvɛrgy:r] f. Wing-spread, spread. ‖ Naut. Head (ou) spread of sail. ‖ Aviat. Wing-spread; airfoil span. ‖ Fig. Scale, scope (d'une entreprise); sweep, range (d'un esprit); range (des idées); *d'envergure*, large-scale (entreprise); of great ability (personne).

nverrai [ãvɛre]. V. envoyer (46).

nvers [ãvɛːr] prép. Towards, to.

nvers m. Verso, back (d'une page); reverse (d'une pièce); wrong side, back (d'un tissu); seamy side (d'un vêtement); *à l'envers*, inside out (du mauvais côté); wrong side up (retourné); upside down (sens dessus dessous); *maille à l'envers*, purl stitch. ‖ Fig. *A l'envers*, upside down, topsy-turvy; *l'envers du décor*, the seamy side of life; *l'envers de la médaille*, the other side of the picture, the reverse of the medal; *avoir la tête à l'envers*, to be in a whirl; *le monde à l'envers*, a state of topsy-turvy.

nvi [ãvi] m. A l'envi, emulously, vying with one another.

nviable [ãvjabl] adj. Enviable; *peu enviable*, not to be envied.

nvie [ãvi] f. Envy (jalousie); *avec envie*, enviously; *être un objet d'envie pour*, to be the envy of; *faire envie à qqn*, to excite (ou) to raise s.o.'s envy, to make s.o. envious, to be envied by s.o. ‖ Desire, longing (désir); *avoir envie de*, to have a fancy for (attirance); to long for (désir); to be in the mood for (disposition); *avoir bonne* (ou) *grande envie de*, *presque envie de*, to have a good (ou) great mind to; half a mind to; *chose qui lui fait envie*, thing he fancies; *faire envie à qqn*, to take s.o.'s fancy; *envie de rire*, laughing mood; *envie d'être admiré*, desire for admiration. ‖ Want (besoin); craving (besoin irrésistible); *envie de tabac*, craving for tobacco. ‖ Méd. Agnail, hangnail; cuticle (au doigt); birth-mark (nævus). ‖ Fam. *Avoir envie*, to want to wee-wee.

nvié, ée [ãvje] adj. Envied (jalousé). ‖ Longed-for (désiré).

nvier v. tr. (1). To envy (jalouser); *envier qqn*, to envy (ou) to be envious of s.o. ‖ To envy, to covet (convoiter); *envier la beauté de qqn*, to wish one had s.o.'s beauty; *faire envier qqch. à qqn*, to make s.o. envious of sth.

nvieusement [ãvjøzmã] adv. Enviously.

nvieux, euse [ãvjø, ø:z] adj. Envious, jealous (jaloux) [*de*, of]; *jeter un regard envieux sur qqch.*, to look at sth. with envious eyes, to look enviously at sth. ‖ Desirous (désireux) [*de*, of]; *envieux de succès*, wishful (ou) eager to succeed; *être envieux de louanges*, to have a craving for praise.
— s. Envious person; *faire des envieux*, to cause (ou) to excite envy.

nviron [ãvirõ] adv. About; or so; *environ vingt ans*, about twenty years.
— m. pl. Surroundings; environs (v. alentours); *aux environs*, in the environs (ou) neighbourhood (ou) vicinity. ‖ Fam. *Aux environs de la quarantaine*, about forty; *aux environs de Noël*, towards Christmas.

nvironnant, ante [-rɔnã, ã:t] adj. Circumambient (atmosphère); circumfluent (fluide). ‖ Surrounding, neighbouring (lieux).

nvironnement [-rɔnmã] m. Environment.

environner [-rɔne] v. tr. (1). To environ, to surround, to be around, to encircle, to encompass (un lieu). ‖ Fig. To wrap, to shroud (*de*, in) [mystère]; *environné de difficultés*, beset with difficulties; *se sentir environné d'ennemis*, to feel enemies everywhere about one.

envisager [ãvizaʒe] v. tr. (7). To face, to envisage (le danger, les difficultés, la mort). ‖ To look at, to envisage (une affaire); *envisager qqch. sous un mauvais jour*, to see sth. in a bad light. ‖ To intend, to plan (un dessein); *envisager de faire*, to think of doing.

envoi [ãwa] m. Sending (action); forwarding; consignment, dispatch (expédition); *envoi par bateau*, shipment; *envoi de fonds*, remittance of funds; *votre envoi de livres*, your consignment of books. ‖ Envoy (d'une ballade). ‖ Sports. *Coup d'envoi*, kick-off (au football).

envol [ãvɔl] m. Flight (d'un oiseau). ‖ Aviat. Taking off (action); take-off (résultat). ‖ Fig. Flight, soaring (de l'esprit).

envolée [-le] f. Flying off, taking wing (d'un oiseau). ‖ Fig. Flight (d'éloquence, d'imagination); *de haute envolée*, high-soaring.

envoler (s') [sãvɔle] v. pr. (1). To fly off, to take flight (ou) wing (oiseau). ‖ To fly away, to blow off (ou) away (chapeau). ‖ Aviat. To take off. ‖ Fig. To fly, to elapse (temps). ‖ Fam. To make off. (V. décamper.)

envoûtement [ãvutmã] m. Bewitchment. ‖ Fig. Spell.

envoûter [-te] v. tr. (1). To bewitch. ‖ Fig. To bewitch, to charm.

envoyé, ée [ãvwaje] adj. Fam. *Ça c'est envoyé!*, that's got him!
— s. Messenger; *envoyé spécial*, special correspondent. ‖ Jur. *Envoyé extraordinaire*, envoy extraordinary.

envoyer v. tr. (46). To send (qqn) [*à*, to]; *envoyer qqn chercher qqch.*, to send s.o. for sth.; *envoyer chercher qqn*, to send for s.o.; *envoyer qqn dire que*, to send s.o. to say that; *il m'a envoyé chercher son manteau*, he sent me to bring his coat back; *envoyer en mission*, to send on a mission. ‖ To remit (de l'argent); to send (une lettre, un colis; *envoyer un mot*, to drop a line. ‖ To deliver (un coup); to emit, to send forth (de la fumée); *envoyer un baiser*, to blow a kiss. ‖ Milit. To shoot (une balle); to fire (une décharge). ‖ Fam. *Ne pas l'envoyer dire*, to tell s.o. to his face.
— v. intr. To send. ‖ Naut. *Envoyez!*, ready about!
— v. pr. **S'envoyer.** Fam. To treat oneself to (un bon repas); to gulp down (un verre). ‖ Fam. To get through (le travail).

envoyeur [-jœːr] s. Sender.

enzyme [ãzim] m. Chim. Enzym(e).

éocène [eɔsɛːn] adj. Eocene.

Éole [eɔl] m. Aeolus.

éolien, enne [eɔljɛ̃] adj. Aeolian (harpe, mode).

éolienne [eɔljɛn] f. Techn. Windmill, wind pump, wind motor.

éolithe [eɔlit] m. Eolith.

éon [eɔ̃] m. Eon, aeon.

épacte [epakt] f. Epact.

épagneul [epaɲœl] m. Zool. Spaniel.

épais, aisse [epɛ, ɛːs] adj. Thick (objet); *barbe épaisse*, bushy beard; *aux lèvres épaisses*, thick-lipped; *épais de dix centimètres*, ten centimetres thick. ‖ Thick, dense (brouillard, foule); thick (cheveux); close, thick, closely set (herbe); thick-set, dense (taillis). ‖ Thick, turbid (liquide). ‖ Fig. Thick (esprit); thick-headed (personne).
— adv. Thick, thickly.

épaisseur [-sœːr] f. Thickness (d'un objet). ‖ Depth (d'une couche). ‖ Thickness, density (du brouillard) ; thickness (des cheveux, de l'herbe, d'un liquide, d'une soupe). ‖ Fig. Denseness, dullness (de l'esprit). ‖ Fam. *De l'épaisseur d'un cheveu,* by a hair's breadth.

épaissir [-si:r] v. tr. (2). To make deeper (une couche) ; to thicken, to make thicker (un objet). ‖ To coarsen (les traits) ; *cette toilette l'épaissit,* that dress makes her look stouter. ‖ To thicken (les ténèbres). ‖ Culin. To thicken (une sauce). ‖ Fig. To make dull (l'esprit).
— v. intr. To get deeper (couche, neige) ; to become denser (feuillage) ; to grow darker (ténèbres). ‖ To grow fatter (personne) ; to coarsen (traits). ‖ Culin. To thicken (sauce).
— v. pr. **S'épaissir.** [V. ÉPAISSIR (v. intr.).]

épaississement [-sismã] m. Thickening. ‖ Culin. Thickening (d'une sauce). ‖ Coarsening (des traits). ‖ Fig. Dullness (de l'esprit).

épanchement [epãʃmã] m. Discharge, effusion (d'un liquide). ‖ Méd. *Epanchement pleural, synovial,* pleural, synovial extravasation ; *épanchement sanguin,* effusion of blood. ‖ Fig. Effusion, out-pouring (du cœur, des sentiments).

épancher [epãʃe] v. tr. (1). To discharge (un liquide). ‖ Fig. To open (son cœur) ; *épancher sa bile,* to vent one's spleen.
— v. pr. **S'épancher,** to pour out (liquide). ‖ Méd. To extravasate. ‖ Fig. To unbosom oneself (*auprès de,* to) ; *s'épancher de qqch.,* to get sth. off one's chest.

épandage [epãda:ʒ] m. Agric. Manuring ; *champ d'épandage,* sewage farm.

épandeur [-dœ:r] s. Agric. Manure-spreader.

épandre [epã:dr] v. tr. (4). To spread (du fumier). ‖ To pour out (un liquide).
— v. pr. **S'épandre,** to spread. ‖ To flow out, to pour forth (ou) out (liquide).

épanoui, ie [epanui] adj. Bot. Full-blown, blooming, full-bloomed, in blossom, in full bloom. ‖ Fig. Whole-hearted (rire) ; jubilant, radiant (personne) ; beaming, glowing, wreathed in smiles (visage).

épanouir [-nwi:r] v. tr. (2). Bot. To cause to bloom. ‖ Fig. To brighten up, to light up (le visage).
— v. pr. **S'épanouir.** Bot. To bloom, to blossom, to be in bloom. ‖ Fig. To blossom out (beauté). [*en,* into] ; to spread (sourire) ; to brighten up, to light up (visage).

épanouissement [-nwismã] m. Bot. Blooming. ‖ Fig. Blooming, flowering, ripening (des charmes) ; heyday (de la jeunesse) ; brightening up (du visage).

éparcet [eparsɛ] m. Bot. Sainfoin.

épargnant, ante [eparɲã, ã:t] adj. Saving.
— s. Fin. Investor.

épargne [eparɲ] f. Saving. ‖ Fin. *Caisse d'épargne,* savings-bank ; *dépôts d'épargne,* savings ; *la petite épargne,* small investors.

épargner [-ɲe] v. tr. (1). To save, to put by (de l'argent) ; to spare, to economize (son avoir). [V. ÉCONOMISER.] ‖ To spare, to stint (la peine) ; *épargnez vos pas,* save your shoe-leather. ‖ To spare, to have mercy on (un adversaire, la vie).
— v. pr. **S'épargner,** to be saved (argent). ‖ To spare one's pains (personne).

éparpillement [eparpijmã] m. Scattering. ‖ Fig. Frittering away (des efforts) ; dissipation (d'une fortune).

éparpiller [-je] v. tr. (1). To scatter. ‖ Fig. To dissipate, to fritter away (ses efforts).
— v. pr. **S'éparpiller,** to scatter. ‖ Fig. To be frittered away (efforts).

épars, arse [epa:r, a:rs] adj. Scattered about (objets). ‖ Sparse (population) ; *fait d'être épars,* sparseness.

épart [epa:r] m. Cross-bar (de porte) ; shaft-ba (de véhicule).

éparvin [eparvɛ̃] m. Spavin.

épatamment [epatamã] adv. Fam. Marvellously stunningly, terrifically ; *ça marche épatammen* it's going first-rate.

épatant, ante [-tã, ã:t] adj. Fam. Stunnin (étonnant) ; marvellous, first-rate, terrific (exce lent) ; *tireur épatant,* crack shot ; *type épatan* stunner, jolly good chap, U. S. great guy ; *êtr épatant à,* to be hot at.

épate [epat] f. Fam. Swank, U. S. splurge ; *fair de l'épate,* to show off, to swank, to swagger U. S. to splurge.

épaté, ée [-te] adj. Flat (nez) ; *au nez épaté,* fla nosed. ‖ Fam. Amazed, flabbergasted. (V. ÉBAHI

épatement [-tmã] m. Flatness (du nez).

épater [epate] v. tr. (1). To flatten (une base). Fam. To flabbergast, to knock, to stun (qqn) *épater le bourgeois,* to shock the conventionally minded ; *ça m'épate,* that beats me !
— v. pr. **S'épater,** to flatten out. ‖ Fam. To b stunned ; *ça m'épate de vous,* you amaze me ; *ça t'épate ?,* that knocks you, doesn't it ? ; *il n'y pas de quoi s'épater,* it's nothing to be startled a

épateur [-tœ:r] s. Swanker, U. S. splurger ; ho rock (pop.).

épaule [epo:l] f. Shoulder ; *aux épaules large.* broad-shouldered ; *à cheval sur les épaules,* pick a-back ; *charger sur l'épaule, pousser de l'épaul* to shoulder. ‖ Shoulder (de mouton, de vêtement ‖ Naut. Loof. ‖ Fig. *Donner un coup d'épaule à* to give s.o. a leg-up.

épaulé-jeté [epoleʒəte] m. Sports. Clean and jerk (en haltérophilie).

épaulement [-lmã] m. Archit. Retaining-wall. Milit. Epaulement. ‖ Naut. Luff.

épauler [-le] v. tr. (1). To splay the shoulder c (un cheval). ‖ Milit. To raise to the shoulder (u: fusil) ; to rest the flank of (ses troupes) [*sur, on* ‖ Archit. To shoulder. ‖ Fig. To back up, t give a leg-up to, to lend a hand to (qqn).

épaulette [-lɛt] f. Shoulder-piece (de vêtement) ‖ Milit. Epaulette. ‖ Naut. Shoulder (de mât).

épave [epa:v] f. Naut. Derelict (navire aban donné) ; wreck (navire naufragé). ‖ Piece c wreckage ; flotsam (flottante) ; jetsam (rejetée). Fig. Wreck.

épeautre [epo:tr] m. Bot. Spelt.

épée [epe] f. Sword ; *l'épée nue,* with draw sword ; with swords bared ; *passer au fil de l'épée* to put to the sword ; *se battre à l'épée,* to figh with the sword. ‖ Swordsman (épéiste) ; *une bonn épée,* a good swordsman. ‖ Techn. Pricker (d bourrelier). ‖ Fig. *Un coup d'épée dans l'eau* beating the air ; *pousser l'épée dans les reins, t* press too hard, to prod on.

épéiste [-ist] m. Swordsman.

épeler [eple] v. tr. (8 a). To spell, to spell out.

épellation [epɛllasjõ] f. Spelling.

épépinage [epepina:ʒ] m. Seeding, stoning.

épépiner [-ne] v. tr. (1). To seed, to stone.

éperdu, ue [epɛrdy] adj. Distracted, frantic.

éperdument [-mã] adv. Madly ; desperately.

éperlan [epɛrlã] m. Zool. Smelt ; sparling.

éperon [eprõ] m. Spur (de cavalier, de coq, d fortification, de montagne). ‖ Archit. Buttres (de mur) ; cutwater (de pont). ‖ Naut. Stem, ram ‖ Fig. Spur (de la douleur, de la nécessité).

éperonner [eprɔne] v. tr. (1). To spur, to rowel to clap spurs to (un cheval). ‖ To spur (un coq) ‖ Naut., Aviat. To ram. ‖ Fig. To spur on (qqn)

épervier [epɛrvje] m. Zool. Sparrow-hawk. ‖ Cast-net (filet).

épeuré, ée [epøre] adj. Frightened.

éphèbe [efɛb] m. Ephebe.

éphélide [efelid] f. Méd. Freckle.

éphémère [efemε:r] adj. Ephemeral. || Fleeting, transient.
— m. Zool. Ephemera, may-fly.

éphéméride [efemerid] f. Ephemeris. || Pl. Ephemerides.

épi [epi] m. Bot. Ear (de céréale); spike (de fleur); cob (de maïs); à épi, spicate (plante); blé en épi, grain in the ear; épi de blé, ear of wheat, wheat-ear; monter en épi, to ear. || Cow-lick (de cheveux). || Cluster (en bijouterie). || Méd. Spica. || Archit. Spike. || Ch. de F. Spur-tracks.

épiaire [epjε:r] f. Bot. Woundwort.

épice [epis] f. Culin. Spice; pain d'épice, gingerbread; quatre épices, allspice, mixed spices. || Jur. Bribe.

épicé, ée [-se] adj. Culin. Spiced, seasoned; goût épicé, spiciness. || Fam. Spicy (propos).

épicéa [episea] m. Bot. Picea.

épicène [episε:n] adj. Gramm. Epicene.

épicentre [episᾶ:tr] m. Epicentre.

épicer [epise] v. tr. (6). Culin. To spice, to season. || Fig. To spice.

épicerie [-sri] f. Grocery (commerce); grocer's shop, U.S. grocery (magasin); groceries (produits); à l'épicerie, at the grocer's; être dans l'épicerie, to be in the grocery trade (ou) business.

épicier, ère [-sje, εr] s. Grocer.

épicrâne [epikrᾶ:n] m. Méd. Epicranium.
— adj. Epicranial.

épicurien, enne [epikyrjε̃, εn] adj. Philos. Epicurean. || Fam. Hedonistic, sensual, self-indulgent, pleasure-loving.
— s. Philos. Epicurean. || Fam. Epicurean, hedonist, sybarite.

épicurisme [-rism] m. Philos. Epicureanism. || Fam. Epicurism.

épicycle [episikl] m. Math. Epicycle.

épidémie [epidemi] f. Méd., Fig. Epidemic.

épidémiologie [-mjɔlɔʒi] f. Méd. Epidemiology.

épidémique [-mik] adj. Méd. Epidemic(al).

épiderme [epidεrm] m. Méd. Epidermis. || Bot. Cuticle. || Fig. Avoir l'épiderme sensible, to be ticklish (ou) thin-skinned.

épidermique [-mik] adj. Epidermic, epidermal.

épididyme [epididim] m. Méd. Epididymis.

épier [epje] v. int. (1). Bot. To ear.

épier v. tr. (1). To spy upon, to play the spy on. (V. espionner.) || To be on the look-out for, to look out for (une occasion); épier l'arrivée de qqn, to watch for s.o. to come.

épierrer [epjεre] v. tr. (1). To stone (un champ).

épieu [epjø] m. Pike. || Boar-spear.

épigastre [epigastr] m. Méd. Epigastrium.

épiglotte [epiglɔt] f. Méd. Epiglottis.

épigone [epigɔn] m. Epigone.

épigramme [epigram] f. Epigram.

épigraphe [-graf] f. Epigraph. || Motto. || Chapter-heading.

épigraphie [-grafi] f. Epigraphy.

épigraphique [-grafik] adj. Epigraphic.

épilation [epilasjɔ̃] f. Depilation.

épilatoire [-twa:r] adj., m. Depilatory.

épilé [epile] adj. Depilated. || Plucked (sourcils).

épilepsie [epilεpsi] f. Méd. Epilepsy.

épileptique [-tik] adj., s. Méd. Epileptic.

épiler [epile] v. tr. (1). To depilate (en général); to pluck (les sourcils).

épilogue [epilɔg] m. Epilogue.

épiloguer [-ge] v. intr. (1). To carp, to cavil (sur, at). || Fam. To speechify, to enlarge (sur, upon); to make a fuss, to waffle (sur, about).

épilogueur [-gœ:r] s. Caviller. || Fam. Speechifier.

épiloir [epilwa:r] m. Tweezers.

épinard [epina:r] m. Bot., Culin. Spinach.

épine [epin] f. Bot. Thorn; prickle; épine blanche, hawthorn; sans épines, thornless. || Méd. Epine dorsale, spine, backbone. || Fig. Sur des épines, on thorns. || Epine-vinette, f. Bot. Barberry.

épinette [-nεt] f. Agric. Hen-coop. || Mus. Spinet. || Thornhook. || Bot. Spruce.

épineux, euse [-nø, ø:z] adj. Thorny, prickly; thistly. || Fig. Thorny (question); ticklish, tricky (situation).

épinglage [epε̃gla:ʒ] m. Pinning.

épingle [epε̃:gl] f. Pin; épingle à cheveux, à friser, à linge, hairpin, curling-pin, clothes-peg (ou) U.S. -pin; épingle de cravate, tie-pin, scarf-pin, U.S. stick-pin; épingle de nourrice (ou) de sûreté, safety-pin. || Autom. Virage en épingle à cheveux, hairpin bend. || Fig. Discuter sur des pointes d'épingle, to split hairs, to argue upon the point of a needle; monter en épingle, to spotlight, to make a song and dance about; piqûre d'épingle, pin-prick; tiré à quatre épingles, dressed up to kill; U.S. dressed to the teeth; tirer son épingle du jeu, to turn circumstances to account.

épinglé [epε̃gle] m. Terry (étoffe).

épingler v. tr. (1). To pin; to pin on (à, to). || Fam. To pin down (qqn).

épinglerie [-glɚi] f. Pin-trade (commerce); pin-factory (fabrique).

épinière [epinjε:r] adj. f. Méd. Moelle épinière, spinal cord.

épinoche [epinɔʃ] f. Zool. Stickleback.

Épiphanie [epifani] f. Ecclés. Epiphany; Twelfth Night.

épiphénomène [epifenɔmεn] m. Philos. Epiphenomenon.

épiphyse [epifi:z] f. Méd. Epiphysis.

épique [epik] adj. Epic (combat, texte); poème épique, epic. || Fam. Spirited (discussion); agitated (séance); eventful (voyage).

épirogenèse [epirɔʒɔnε:z] f. Géol. Epeirogeny, epeirogenesis, epirogeny.

épiscopal, ale [episkɔpal] adj. Ecclés. Episcopal, bishop.

épiscopalien, enne [-paljε̃, εn] adj., s. Ecclés. Episcopalian.

épiscopat [-pa] m. Ecclés. Bishopric, episcopate (dignité); episcopacy (évêques).

épisode [epizɔd] m. Episode. || Ciném. A épisodes, serial (film).

épisodique [-dik] adj. Episodic. || Temporary, transitory, adventitious.

épisodiquement [-dikmᾶ] adv. Episodically.

épisser [epise] v. tr. (1). To splice.

épissure [-sy:r] f. Splice.

épistémologie [epistemɔlɔʒi] f. Epistemology.

épistolaire [epistɔlε:r] adj. Epistolary.

épistolier [-lje] s. Epistolarian.

épitaphe [epitaf] f. Epitaph.

épithalame [epitalam] m. Ephithalamium.

épithélial, ale [epiteljal] adj. Méd., Bot. Epithelial.

épithélium [epiteljɔm] m. Méd., Bot. Epithelium.

épithète [epitεt] f. Gramm. Epithet.

épitoge [epitɔ:ʒ] f. † Epitogium. || Graduate's hood.

épitomé [epitɔme] m. Epitome.

épitre [epi:tr] f. Epistle (lettre). || Ecclés. Epistle.

épizootie [epizɔɔti] f. Méd. Epizooty.

éploré, ée [eplɔre] adj. In tears, tearful (pleurant). || Distressed, grieved, afflicted (affligé). || Fig. Weeping (feuillage).

éployé, ée [eplwaje] adj. Blas. Spread.

épluchage [eplyʃa:ʒ] m. Peeling (des fruits, des pommes de terre); picking (de la laine, de la salade); husking (du maïs, des noix); shelling, hulling (des pois). || Agric. Pruning (d'un arbre); weeding (d'un terrain). || Fig. Sifting (des témoignages); pulling to pieces (d'un texte).

éplucher [-ʃe] v. tr. (1). To peel (des fruits, des pommes de terre); to pick (de la laine, de la salade); to husk (du maïs, des noix); to shell, to hull (des pois). ‖ Agric. To prune (un arbre); to thin out (des fruits); to weed (un terrain). ‖ Fig. To pick holes in (la conduite); to sift (des rapports); to pull to pieces (un texte).

éplucheur [-ʃœ:r] s. Peeler. ‖ Fam. Critic, fault-finder.

épluchoir [-ʃwa:r] m. Potato-peeler (ou) -knife.

épluchure [-ʃy:r] f. Peeling.

épointage [epwɛ̃ta:ʒ] m. Blunting (ou) breaking of a point.

épointer [-te] v. tr. (1). To blunt (ou) to break the point of (une aiguille).
— v. pr. S'épointer, to get blunt.

éponge [epɔ̃:ʒ] f. Sponge; donner un coup d'éponge à qqch., to give sth. a sponge-down; nettoyage à l'éponge, sponging. ‖ Culin. Eponge métallique, pan-scraper, metallic sponge. ‖ Zool. Sponge. ‖ Méd. Eponge chirurgicale, surgical sponge. ‖ Fig. Passer l'éponge sur, to pass the sponge over. ‖ Eponge-tampon, f. Culin. Saucepan-brush.

éponger [epɔ̃ʒe] v. tr. (7). To sponge up, to mop up (un liquide); to sponge, to mop (une table); to sponge off (ou) out (une tache). ‖ To mop (la transpiration); s'éponger le front, to mop one's brow; s'éponger les yeux, to dab one's eyes.

épontille [epɔ̃ti:j] f. Naut. Stanchion (de cale). ‖ Shore, prop (accore).

éponyme [epɔnim] adj. Eponymous.
— m. Eponym.

épopée [epɔpe] f. Epic, epic poem, epopee, epos. ‖ Fig. Epic.

époque [epɔk] f. Epoch, age (v. Ère); qui fait époque, epoch-making. ‖ Time, period; à l'époque des Romains, at the time of the Romans; l'époque des semailles, sowing season, seed-time. ‖ Astr. Periodic time. ‖ Méd. Pl. Periods.

épouillage [epuja:ʒ] m.

épouiller [-je] v. tr. (1). To delouse.

époumoné, ée [epumɔne] adj. Out of breath, panting, puffed, gasping.

époumoner v. tr. (1). To put out of breath.
— v. pr. S'époumoner, to shout oneself out of breath (crier); to pant for breath (panteler).

épousailles [epuzɑ:j] f. pl. Espousals, nuptials.

épouse [epu:z] f. Wife, spouse. ‖ Fam. Mon épouse, the wife.

épousé [epuze] m. Bridegroom.

épousée f. Bride.

épouser v. tr. (1). To marry; to wed (poét.). ‖ Fig. To assume (une forme); to espouse (une idée); to take up (une querelle).

époussetage [epusta:ʒ] m. Dusting.

épousseter [epuste] v. tr. (8 a). To dust.

époustouflant, ante [epustuflɑ̃, ɑ̃:t] adj. Fam. Staggering, terrific; c'est époustouflant, it knocks you sideways, it bowls you over.

épouti [eputi] m. Burl.

épouvantable [epuvɑ̃tabl] adj. Dreadful, terrifying, horrid, hideous, appalling. ‖ Fam. Awful.

épouvantablement [-tabləmɑ̃] adv. Dreadfully, frightfully, horribly. ‖ Fam. Awfully, frightfully.

épouvantail [-ta:j] m. Scarecrow (à moineaux). ‖ Fig. Bugbear (cauchemar); bogey (croquemitaine); hobgoblin (lutin). ‖ Fam. Fright (personne).

épouvante [epuvɑ̃:t] f. Dread, terror; fou d'épouvante, scared out of one's wits; frapper d'épouvante, to strike with terror.

épouvanté, ée [-vɑ̃te] adj. Scared. (V. Terrifié.)

épouvantement [-vɑ̃tmɑ̃] m. Deadly terror.

épouvanter [-vɑ̃te] v. tr. (1). To scare, to appal.
— v. pr. S'épouvanter, to be scared, to stand appalled.

époux [epu] m. Husband (mari). ‖ Pl. Husban[d] and wife, married couple; les époux Dupon[t], the man Dupont and his wife, the Dupont couple[.]

époxyde [epɔksid] m. Chim. Epoxide; résine époxyde, epoxy, epoxy resin.

épreinte [eprɛ̃:t] f. Méd. Tenesmus; gripes (fam.)[.] ‖ Pl. Spraints (de la loutre); U. S. otter's dung[.]

éprendre (s') [seprɑ̃:dr] v. pr. (47). To fall i[n] love, to become infatuated (de, with) [amour]; to take a fancy (de, to) [béguin].

épreuve [eprœ:v] f. Test, proof, trial; à l'épreuv[e] de, proof against; à l'épreuve du feu, fire-proof[.] à toute épreuve, unwearying (patience); mettre à l'épreuve, to put to the test (éprouver); to giv[e] the acid test to, to try (exercer); prendre à l'épreuve, to take on trial. ‖ † Epreuve du feu, ordeal by fire. ‖ Test (d'examen); épreuve écrite orale, examination-paper, oral examination (ou viva). ‖ Proof (d'imprimerie); épreuve en page en placard, revise (ou) U. S. page proof, galley proof; dernière épreuve, press-revise, U. S. fina[l] proof. ‖ Arts. Proof (de gravure); print (de photo). ‖ Sports. Event (de course). ‖ Fig. Trial hardship.

épris, ise [epri, i:z] adj. In love, infatuated smitten (de, with). ‖ Fig. Burning (de, for).

éprouvant, ante [epruvɑ̃, ɑ̃:t] adj. Trying (personne, travail); testing (climat, travail).

éprouvé, ée [epruve] adj. Tried (objet, valeur). ‖ Fig. Tried, afflicted (personne).

éprouver v. tr. (1). To test, to try, to prove (qqch.)[.] ‖ To give the acid test to, to put to the test (qqn) to try (la patience). ‖ To try (qqn); duremen[t] éprouvé, sorely afflicted. ‖ To meet with (un échec); to suffer (une perte); to feel (du respect de la sympathie) [pour, for]; éprouver des doutes, to feel doubtful; éprouver un ennui, to be in difficulty.

éprouvette [epruvɛt] f. Chim. Test-tube, test-glass. ‖ Techn. Test-bar, test-piece. ‖ Méd. Probe[.]

épucer [epyse] v. tr. (6). To clean of fleas.

épuisant, ante [epɥizɑ̃, ɑ̃:t] adj. Exhausting.

épuisé, ée [-ze] adj. Out of print (livre); exhausted (provision); dried up (source). ‖ Comm. Exhausted (stock). ‖ Electr. Dead, burned out (pile). ‖ Agric. Exhausted (terre). ‖ Fig. Exhausted, worn out (personne) [fam.]; complètement épuisé, in a state of complete exhaustion.

épuisement [-zmɑ̃] m. Drainage, pumping, empty-ing (d'un liquide). ‖ Comm. Consumption (d'un stock). ‖ Agric., Fig. Exhaustion.

épuiser [-ze] v. tr. (1). To pump out, to drain (un liquide). ‖ To fork, to work out (une mine). ‖ Comm. To consume, to exhaust (des provisions, un stock). ‖ Fig. To use up (ses forces); to use (les moyens); to exhaust, to tire out (qqn); épuiser sa veine d'écrivain, to write oneself out.
— v. pr. S'épuiser, to be drained (liquide); to run low (source). ‖ To be worked out (mine). ‖ To sell out (ouvrage). ‖ Comm. To get exhausted, to run low (provisions, stock). ‖ Fig. To tire (ou) wear (ou) fag oneself out, to overstrain oneself; s'épuiser à faire, to wear oneself out doing.

épuisette [epɥizɛt] f. Scoop, bailer (écope). ‖ Landing-net (de pêcheur).

épurateur [epyratœ:r] m. Purifier; filter. ‖ Fig. Purge-organizer (en politique).

épuration [-sjɔ̃] f. Purifying (action); puri-fication (état). ‖ Filtering (de l'air, de l'eau); refining (du pétrole). ‖ Jur. Purging (action); purge (fait) [en politique]. ‖ Fig. Purging (des mœurs).

épure [epy:r] f. Arts. Working drawing; dia-gram. ‖ Math. Diagrám.

épurement [epyrmɑ̃] m. Fig. Purging.

épurer [-re] v. tr. (1). To purify (en général); to filter (l'air); to refine (le pétrole). ‖ FIG. To refine (le goût, une langue); to purge (les mœurs, la société).

équarrir [ekari:r] v. tr. (2). To square (une pierre). ‖ To quarter the carcass of (un animal).

équarrissage [-risa:ʒ] m. Squaring (du bois, de la pierre). ‖ Quartering (d'animaux).

équarrisseur [-risœ:r] m. Squarer (de pierre, de bois). ‖ Knacker (d'animaux).

équateur [ekwatœ:r] m. GÉOGR. Equator (ligne); Ecuador (république).

équation [ekwasjɔ̃] f. MATH. Equation.

équatorial, ale [ekwatɔrjal] adj. Equatorial.

équerrage [ekɛra:ʒ] m. Bevelling (action); bevel, bevel-angle.

équerre [ekɛ:r] f. Square (de dessinateur); *équerre à coulisse,* sliding cal(l)ipers. ‖ TECHN. Cross-staff (d'arpenteur); *équerre d'angle,* angle-plate; *équerre en T,* T-iron, U. S. T square; *d'équerre,* square at right angles; *mettre d'équerre,* to square, to true.

équerrer [ekɛ:e] v. tr. (1). To bevel.

équestre [ekɛstr] adj. Equestrian.

équeuter [ekøte] v. tr. (1). To tail (un fruit).

équiangle [ekɥiɑ̃:gl] adj. MATH. Equiangular.

équidé [ekide, ekɥide] m. ZOOL. Equid.

équidistance [ekɥidistɑ̃:s] f. MATH. Equidistance. ‖ *A équidistance de,* half-way between.

équidistant, ante [-distɑ̃, ɑ̃:t] adj. MATH. Equidistant.

équilatéral, ale [-lateral] adj. MATH. Equilateral.

équilibrage [ekilibra:ʒ] m. Balancing.

équilibre [ekilibr] m. Equilibrium, balance; *faire perdre l'équilibre à qqn,* to throw s.o. off his balance; *se tenir en équilibre,* to keep one's balance; *tenir qqch. en équilibre sur,* to balance sth. on. ‖ Counterbalance, counterpoise (contre-poids); *faire équilibre à,* to counterbalance. ‖ Balance of power (en politique). ‖ FIN. *Assurer l'équilibre budgétaire,* to balance the budget. ‖ FIG. Balance (des couleurs, de l'esprit); stead-iness (d'un Etat).

équilibré, ée [-bre] adj. Balanced (choses). ‖ FIG. Balanced; sedate (esprit); *à l'esprit bien équili-bré,* level-headed; *non équilibré,* unbalanced (esprit, forces).

équilibrer [-bre] v. tr. (1). To balance (des objets). To equilibrate, to counterbalance (des forces). ‖ FIN. To balance (le budget). ‖ AVIAT. To trim. — v. pr. **S'équilibrer,** to balance (objets). ‖ To equilibrate (forces). ‖ FIG. To recover one's balance (esprit).

équilibriste [-brist] s. Equilibrist.

équille [eki:j] f. ZOOL. Lance-fish.

équimultiple [ekɥimyltipl] adj., m. MATH. Equi-multiple.

équin, ine [ekɛ̃, in] adj. ZOOL. Equine.

équinoxe [ekinɔks] m. Equinox; *d'équinoxe,* equinoctial (marée).

équinoxial, ale [-sjal] adj. Equinoctial.

équipage [ekipa:ʒ] m. Retinue, suite, equipage (du roi). ‖ Attire, state (de qqn); *en grand équi-page,* in state, in array. ‖ Turn-out, carriage and horses, U. S. horse and carriage (attelage); *équi-page à deux, quatre chevaux,* carriage and pair, and four. ‖ Pack of hounds (à la chasse). ‖ MILIT. Train; *équipage d'un char,* tank-crew. ‖ NAUT. Crew; ship's company. ‖ AVIAT. Air-crew. ‖ TECHN. Outfit (d'un appareil); train (d'une ma-chine); plant (d'une usine); *équipage de pompe,* pump gear.

équipe [ekip] f. Gang, shift, team (d'ouvriers); *équipe de jour,* day-shift. ‖ Party (de secouristes); *équipe de dépannage,* repair party (ou) U. S. crew;

équipe de secours, rescue squad. ‖ CH. DE F. *Homme d'équipe,* yardman. ‖ NAUT. Crew. ‖ SPORTS. Team (en général); crew (à la rame); *jeux d'équipe,* team games. ‖ NAUT. Crew. ‖ Equipe-écoute, f. RADIO. Interception-station team.

équipée [-pe] f. Prank, escapade. (V. FRASQUE.) ‖ Crazy enterprise.

équipement [-pmɑ̃] m. Equipment, outfit; gear; appurtenances. ‖ TECHN. Fitting-up (action); equipment (résultat) [d'une usine]. ‖ NAUT. Out-fit. ‖ MILIT. Equipment, accoutrement, outfit.

équiper [-pe] v. tr. (1). TECHN., MILIT. To equip, to fit out (un homme). ‖ NAUT. To man. ‖ FAM. To fit out, to rig out (qqn). — v. pr. **S'équiper,** to equip oneself, to fit oneself out (de, with).

équipier, ère [-pje, ɛ:r] s. Crew (ou) team member.

équipollence [ekipɔlɑ̃:s] f. Equipollence.

équipollent, ente [-lɑ̃, ɑ̃:t] adj. Equipollent (à, with).

équipotent [ekɥipɔtɑ̃] adj. m. MATH. Equipotent.

équitable [ekitabl] adj. Equitable; upright.

équitablement [-bləmɑ̃] adv. Equitably, justly; uprightly, impartially.

équitation [ekitasjɔ̃] f. Riding, horsemanship, equitation (art). ‖ Riding (action).

équité [ekite] f. Equity. (V. JUSTICE.)

équivalence [ekivalɑ̃:s] f. Equivalence, equi-valency.

équivalent, ente [-lɑ̃, ɑ̃:t] adj. Equivalent (à, to). — m. Equivalent. ‖ Offset (à, to); making up, compensation (à, for).

équivaloir [-lwa:r] v. intr. (81). To be equivalent (à, to). ‖ FIG. To amount (à, to).

équivoque [ekivɔk] adj. Equivocal (ambigu). ‖ Shady, suspicious, doubtful (louche). — f. Ambiguity (d'une expression). ‖ Misinter-pretation; *sans équivoque,* clearly, unquestion-ably. ‖ Equivocation, quibble (faux-fuyant); *user d'équivoques,* to equivocate.

équivoquer [-ke] v. intr. (1). To equivocate.

érable [erabl] m. BOT. Maple, maple-tree (arbre); maple-wood (bois).

érablière [-blijɛ:r] f. BOT. Maple plantation.

éradication [eradikasjɔ̃] f. AGRIC. Eradication.

éraflement [erafləmɑ̃] m. Scratching, grazing.

érafler [erafle] v. tr. (1). To graze (la peau). ‖ MILIT. To score. — v. pr. **S'érafler,** to peel off; *s'érafler la jambe,* to bark one's shin.

éraflure [-fly:r] f. Graze, scratch. ‖ MILIT. Score.

éraillé, ée [erɑje] adj. Unravelled (bas); frayed (tissu). ‖ Fretted (corde). ‖ Bloodshot (œil); husky (voix). ‖ Scratchy (son).

éraillement [-jmɑ̃] m. Unravelling (d'un bas); fraying (d'un tissu). ‖ Chafing (d'une corde). ‖ Huskiness (de la voix).

érailler [-je] v. tr. (1). To unravel (un bas); to fray (un tissu). ‖ To chafe, to fret (une corde). ‖ To scratch (une peinture). ‖ To make husky (la voix). — v. pr. **S'érailler,** to become unravelled (bas); to fray (étoffe). ‖ To become fretted (corde). ‖ To get scratched (peinture). ‖ To become husky (voix).

éraillure [-jy:r] f. Scratch.

erbium [ɛrbjɔm] m. CHIM. Erbium.

ère [ɛ:r] f. Era.

Érèbe [erɛb] m. Erebus.

érectile [erɛktil] adj. Erectile.

érection [-sjɔ̃] f. Erection, raising, setting up (d'un monument, d'une statue). ‖ MÉD. Erection. ‖ FIG. Setting up, establishment.

éreintage [erɛta:ʒ] m. V. ÉREINTEMENT.

éreintant, ante [erɛ̃tɑ̃, ɑ̃:t] adj. FAM. Backbreaking, killing. (V. EXTÉNUANT.)

éreinté, ée [-te] adj. FAM. Fagged, jaded, dead beat, all in, done up, worn out, U. S. bushed.

éreintement [-tmɑ̃] m. FAM. Exhaustion (fatigue). ‖ Slating, slashing, roasting (critique); un éreintement sous des fleurs, damning with faint praise.

éreinter [-te] v. tr. (1). To break the back of (casser les reins); to thrash (donner une raclée). ‖ FAM. To exhaust, to jade, to tire out, to work to death, to fatigue (fatiguer). ‖ FAM. To slash, to slate, to vilify (critiquer); to scalp (fam.). — v. pr. S'éreinter, to wear oneself out, to work oneself to death; je m'éreinte à vous le dire, I've told you till I'm sick of it!

éreinteur [-tœ:r] m. FAM. Destructive critic.

érémitique [eremitik] adj. Eremitical.

érésipèle [erezipɛl] m. V. ÉRYSIPÈLE.

éréthisme [eretism] m. MÉD. Erethism.

erg [ɛrg] m. PHYS. Erg, ergon.

erg m. GÉOGR. Erg.

ergonomie [ɛrgɔnɔmi] f. Ergonomics.

ergot [ɛrgo] m. ZOOL. Dew-claw (de chien); spur (de coq). ‖ BOT. Spur (d'arbre fruitier); ergot (du seigle). ‖ ELECTR. Pin. ‖ TECHN. Stop. ‖ FAM. Dressé sur ses ergots, with one's hackles up, mounting one's high horse.

ergotage [ɛrgɔta:ʒ] m. Cavilling, quibbling, wrangling, bandying of words (action); argumentativeness (disposition). ‖ Cavil, quibble, arglebargle, argy-bargy (fait).

ergoter [-te] v. intr. (1). To argufy, to argue the toss; to argle-bargle; ergoter sur, to cavil at, to quibble about.

ergoteur, euse [-tœ:r, ø:z] adj. Argumentative. — s. Quibbler, arguer, caviller.

ergothérapie [ɛrgɔterapi] f. PSYCH. Occupational therapy.

ériger [eriʒe] v. tr. (7). To erect, to raise, to set up (un monument, une statue). ‖ To establish, to found (une institution). ‖ FIG. To erect (en, into); ériger en principe, to set up (ou) to lay down as a principle. — v. pr. S'ériger. FIG. To set up; to pose (en, as).

Érinnyes [erinni] f. pl. Erinnyes.

ermitage [ɛrmita:ʒ] m. Hermitage.

ermite [ɛrmit] m. Hermit. ‖ FIG. Recluse; vivre en ermite, to live a secluded life.

éroder [erɔde] v. tr. (1). To erode.

érogène [erɔʒɛn] adj. Erogenous; zone érogène, erogenous zone.

érosif, ive [-zif, i:v] adj. Erosive.

érosion [-zjɔ̃] f. Erosion.

érotique [erɔtik] adj. Erotic.

érotisme [-tism] m. Eroticism.

érotomane [-tɔman] adj., s. MÉD. Erotomaniac.

érotomanie [-tɔmani] f. MÉD. Erotomania.

errance [ɛrɑ̃:s] f. Wandering, roaming; odyssey.

errant, ante [ɛrɑ̃, ɑ̃:t] adj. Stray (chien); wandering, rambling, roaming, roving (personne); vagrant (vagabond); chevalier errant, knighterrant; le Juif errant, the Wandering Jew. — s. Wanderer; vagrant, roamer, rover.

erratique [eratik] adj. Erratic.

erratum [ɛratɔm] (pl. errata) m. Erratum (pl. errata).

erre [ɛ:r] f. NAUT. Headway; sternway; courir sur son erre, to forge ahead; prendre de l'erre, to gather way. ‖ Pl. Track.

errements [ɛrmɑ̃] m. pl. Bad habits; lapses, mistakes; errors.

errer [ɛre] v. intr. (1). To wander, to ramble, to roam, to rove (vagabonder). ‖ To err, to make a mistake (ou) an error, to be wrong, to be mistaken (se tromper). ‖ FIG. To flit, to hover; un sourire erra sur son visage, a smile flitted across his face.

erreur [ɛrœ:r] f. Error (de, of, in); mistake erreur d'adresse, de calcul, de date, d'interprétation, de traduction, misdirection, miscount (ou miscalculation, misdating, misinterpretation, mistranslation; erreur d'étiquetage, mistake in labelling; erreur de transcription, clerical error; être dans l'erreur, to be (ou) to stand in error, to labour under a delusion; par erreur, by mistake in error; pas d'erreur!, no mistake!, no error! sauf erreur, errors excepted. ‖ JUR. Erreur judiciaire, miscarriage of justice. ‖ Pl. Lapse, erro (de jeunesse); revenir de ses erreurs, to see the errors of one's ways.

erroné, ée [ɛrɔne] adj. Erroneous.

ersatz [ɛrzats] m. invar. Substitute, ersatz.

erse [ɛrs] f. NAUT. Strap, strop.

erse adj., m. GRAMM. Erse.

erseau [ɛrso] m. NAUT. Grummet.

érubescent, ente [erybɛsɑ̃, ɑ̃:t] adj. Erubescent

éructation [eryktasjɔ̃] f. Eructation; belch (fam.

éructer [-te] v. intr. (1). To eructate. — v. tr. FAM. To give vent to (des injures).

érudit, ite [erydi, it] adj. Erudite; learned, scholarly (personne, ouvrage); érudit en, widely read in, well up in. — s. Scholar; les érudits, the erudite.

érudition [-sjɔ̃] f. Erudition, scholarship; avec érudition, learnedly, eruditely.

éruptif, ive [eryptif, i:v] adj. Eruptive.

éruption [-sjɔ̃] f. GÉOGR., MÉD. Eruption.

érysipèle [erizipɛl] m. MÉD. Erysipelas.

érythème [eritɛ:m] m. MÉD. Erythema.

érythrocyte [eritrɔsit] m. MÉD. Erythrocyte.

ès [ɛs] prép. Of; docteur ès sciences, doctor of science.

es, est [ɛ]. V. ÊTRE (48).

esbigner (s') [sɛsbiɲe] v. pr. (1). POP. To clear off, to split.

esbroufe [ɛsbruf] f. Swagger, bounce, swank faire de l'esbroufe, to swank, U. S. to splurge. ‖ JUR. A l'esbroufe, snatch-and-grab (vol).

esbroufeur [-fœ:r] s. FAM. Swaggerer, swank line-shooter. ‖ JUR. Snatch-and-grab thief (voleur).

escabeau [ɛskabo] m. Step-ladder, pair of steps (pour monter); stool (pour s'asseoir).

escabelle [ɛskabɛl] f. Stool.

escadre [ɛska:dr] f. NAUT. Squadron. ‖ AVIAT. Wing.

escadrille [-dri:j] f. AVIAT. Flight. ‖ NAUT. Flotilla.

escadron [-drɔ̃] m. MILIT., AVIAT. Squadron.

escalade [ɛskalad] f. Scaling (d'une échelle); climbing, climb (d'une montagne, d'un mur). ‖ Cat-burglary (pour voler). ‖ MILIT. Escalade.

escalader [-de] v. tr. (1). To scale, to climb. ‖ MILIT. To escalade.

escale [ɛskal] f. NAUT. Call (action); port of call (lieu); faire escale à, to call at, to put in at. ‖ AVIAT. Stop, intermediate landing; sans escale non-stop (vol).

escalier [ɛskalje] m. Flight of stairs (par étage); stairs, stairway, staircase (en totalité); escalier roulant, escalator; escalier de service, backstairs escalier de secours, fire-escape; escalier tournant, winding stairs. ‖ NAUT. Companion (ou) accommodation ladder (ou) way. ‖ FAM. L'esprit de l'escalier, belated repartee (ou) uptake, after-wit.

escalope [ɛskalɔp] f. CULIN. Escalope, collop.

escamotable [ɛskamɔtabl] adj. AVIAT. Retractable (train d'atterrissage).

escamotage [-ta:ʒ] m. Juggling, conjuring, legerdemain, sleight of hand (art). ‖ Smuggling away (action de faire disparaître); pinching (action de dérober). ‖ AVIAT. Retraction. ‖ CINÉM. Phase *l'escamotage*, cut-off period. ‖ Fig. Skipping d'une difficulté); hushing up (d'un scandale); lodging (d'une question); shirking, scamping d'un travail).

scamoter [-te] v. tr. (1). To juggle, to conjure away (prestidigitateur). ‖ To pinch, to filch (voleur). ‖ To smuggle away (personne habile). ‖ Aviat. To retract (le train). ‖ Fig. To skip (une difficulté); to slur (un mot); to dodge (une question); to hush up (un scandale); to shirk, to camp (un travail).

scamoteur [-tœ:r] s. Juggler, conjurer (prestidigitateur). ‖ Sharper (voleur).

scampette [ɛskɑ̃pɛt] f. *Prendre la poudre d'escampette*, to bolt, U. S. to take a powder.

scapade [ɛskapad] f. Escapade. ‖ Prank (fredaine).

scarbille [ɛskarbi:j] f. Cinder. ‖ Pl. Ashes, clinkers.

scarbot [ɛskarbo] m. Zool. Beetle.

scarboucle [-bukl] f. Carbuncle. ‖ Blas. Escarbuncle.

scarcelle [ɛskarsɛl] f. † Purse, wallet.

scargot [ɛskargo] m. Zool. Snail. ‖ Fam. *En escargot*, spiral, corkscrew (escalier).

scargotière [-tjɛ:r] f. Snailery. ‖ Culin. Pan for cooking snails.

scarmouche [ɛskarmuʃ] f. Milit. Skirmish.

scarmoucher [-ʃe] v. intr. (1). Milit. To skirmish.

scarole [ɛskarɔl] f. Bot. Endive, escarole.

scarpe [ɛskarp] f. Milit. Scarp.

scarpe m. Ruffian.

scarpé, ée [ɛskarpe] adj. Steep (chemin); craggy, cragged (montagne, rocher); sheer, abrupt (pente).

scarpement [-pəmɑ̃] m. Craggedness; steepness, abruptness. ‖ Crag (roc); steep slope (pente). ‖ Milit., Géol. Escarpment.

scarpin [ɛskarpɛ̃] m. Pump.

scarpolette [ɛskarpɔlɛt] f. Swing.

scarre [ɛska:r] f. Méd. Eschar, scab; bed-sore.

scarrifier [ɛskarifje] v. tr. (1). Méd. To form a scab (ou) scabs on.

scaut [ɛsko] m. Géogr. Scheldt (fleuve).

sche [ɛʃ] f. V. Aiche.

scient [ɛsjɑ̃] m. *A bon escient*, well knowing, wittingly; *à mon escient*, to my certain knowledge.

sclaffer (s') [sɛsklafe] v. pr. (1). Fam. To guffaw, to shake with laughter.

sclandre [ɛsklɑ̃:dr] m. Scandal; disturbance.

sclavage [ɛsklava:ʒ] m. Slavery, thraldom; *réduire en esclavage*, to enslave. ‖ Fig. Thraldom *(de*, to) [asservissement]; drudgery *(de*, of) [métier].

sclavagisme [-vaʒism] m. Slavery, slave system.

sclavagiste [-vaʒist] adj. Zool. Slave-holding, dulotic (fourmi). ‖ Slave (Etat); in favour of slavery (personne).
— s. Partisan of negro slavery.

sclave [ɛskla:v] s. Slave, thrall; *marchand d'esclaves*, slave-dealer (ou) -trader; *vente des esclaves*, slave-traffic; Slave, drudge; *mener une vie d'esclave*, to lead the life of a drudge, to drudge and slave; *travailler comme un esclave à*, to slave away at. ‖ Fig. Slave; *esclave de la mode*, slave of fashion; *être esclave du devoir, d'une habitude*, to be a slave to duty, to a habit.

sclavine [-in] f. Duffle-coat.

scoffier [ɛskɔfje] v. tr. (1). Pop. To murder, to do in, to bump off (qqn).

scogriffe [ɛskɔgrif] m. Fam. Gawk, lubber, great lump of a man.

scomptable [ɛskɔ̃tabl] adj. Comm., Fin. Discountable. ‖ Fam. To be expected (résultat).

scompte [ɛskɔ̃:t] m. Fin., Comm. Discount.

escompter [-te] v. tr. (1). Fin., Comm. To discount (un effet); *escompter à terme*, to call for delivery before the settlement (en Bourse). ‖ Fig. To bank on, to reckon upon, to hope for, to look for (un résultat, un succès).

escompteur [-tœ:r] s. Discounter.
— adj. Discounting.

escopette [ɛskɔpɛt] f. † Blunderbuss.

escorte [ɛskɔrt] f. Train, retinue (d'un prince). ‖ Milit. Escort. ‖ Naut. Convoy. ‖ Fig. Accompaniment.

escorter [-te] v. tr. (1). To escort, to accompany (qqn). ‖ Milit. To escort. ‖ Naut. To convoy.

escorteur [-tœ:r] m. Naut. Escort vessel. ‖ Fam. Follower.

escouade [ɛskwad] f. Milit. Section. ‖ Fam. Gang, squad.

escrime [ɛskrim] f. Sports. Fencing; swordplay, swordsmanship; *salle d'escrime*, fencing-school; *faire de l'escrime*, to fence, to go in for fencing.

escrimer [-me] v. intr. (1). Sports. To fence.
— v. pr. S'escrimer. Sports. To fence (*contre*, with). ‖ Fam. To strain (à, to); to peg away (à, sur, at); to work with might and main (à, at).

escrimeur [-mœ:r] m. Sports. Fencer, swordsman.

escroc [ɛskro] m. Swindler, sharper, U. S. racketeer. (V. Aigrefin.)

escroquer [-ke] v. tr. (1). To swindle; to cheat; *escroquer de l'argent à qqn*, to swindle s.o. out of money.

escroquerie [ɛskrokri] f. Swindling (action); swindle (résultat); rook, U. S. racket.

ésotérique [ezote:rik] adj. Esoteric.

ésotérisme [-terism] m. Esotericism.

espace [ɛspɑ:s] m. Space (indéfini). ‖ Space, area, surface, room (en surface); *manquer d'espace*, to be cramped for room. ‖ Space, interval (*entre*, between). ‖ Space, interval (de temps); *dans l'espace d'un an*, in the space of (ou) within a year. ‖ Techn. Clearance.
— f. Techn. Space (en typogr.).

espacé, ée [ɛspase] adj. Spaced, far apart (ou) between, spaced out (objets). ‖ Far apart, far distant (époques); occasional (visites).

espacement [-smɑ̃] m. Spacing (d'objets). ‖ *Barre d'espacement*, space-bar (d'une machine à écrire). ‖ Techn. Spacing (en typogr.).

espacer [-se] v. tr. (6). To space (des objets); to make less frequent (des périodes). ‖ Techn. To space, to space out (en typogr.).
— v. pr. S'espacer, to become less frequent; *s'espacer sur*, to spread over.

espadon [ɛspadɔ̃] m. Zool. Sword-fish.

espadrille [ɛspadri:j] f. Canvas shoe (with cord sole); U. S. espadrille.

Espagne [ɛspaɲ] f. Géogr. Spain.

espagnol, ole [-ɲɔl] adj. Géogr. Spanish.
— m. Spanish (langue).
— s. Géogr. Spaniard.

espagnolette [-ɲɔlɛt] f. Espagnolette.

espalier [ɛspalje] m. Espalier tree (arbre); espalier, fruit-wall (treillis); *en espalier*, espalier-trained.

espar [ɛspa:r] m. Naut. Spar.

espèce [ɛspɛs] f. Breed (race); kind, sort (sorte); *une espèce d'arbre*, a sort of tree; *l'espèce humaine*, the human species; *elle sait quelle espèce d'homme c'est*, she knows the sort of man he is. ‖ Sort; kind (genre, type); *des gens de son espèce*, people of his kind; *une espèce d'idiot*, a silly ass; *une sale espèce*, a rotter, a bounder, a cad. ‖ Bot., Zool., Philos. Species. ‖ Ecclés. Species, kind; *sous les deux espèces*, in both kinds. ‖ Jur. Case; *en l'espèce*, in this particular case. ‖ FIN. Pl. Specie; cash (fam.); *en espèces,* in hard cash.

espérance [ɛsperɑ̃:s] f. Hope (v. ESPOIR); *mettre son espérance en,* to found one's hopes on; *plein d'espérance,* hopeful. ‖ Expectation (attente); *tromper les espérances de qqn,* to fall short of s.o.'s expectations. ‖ Promise (promesse); *donner de belles espérances,* to promise well, to look promising. ‖ Pl. Prospects (avenir). ‖ JUR. Pl. Expectations (d'héritage).

espérantiste [-rɑ̃tist] adj., s. Esperantist.

espéranto [-to] m. GRAMM. Esperanto.

espérer [-re] v. tr. (5). To hope for (qqch.); to be in hopes (*que,* that); *espérer faire,* to hope to do; *espérer quand même,* to hope against hope. ‖ To expect, to look for, to reckon upon, to bank on (escompter); *j'espère bien qu'il le fera,* I'm banking on his doing it (fam.). ‖ COMM. *Bénéfice espéré,* estimated profits. ‖ FAM. *J'espère que voilà un gentil garçon,* what a nice boy you are! — v. intr. To hope, to trust (*en,* in).

espiègle [ɛspjɛgl] adj. Mischievous, full of mischief (enfant); arch, roguish (femme). ‖ Mischievous, arch (air, regard); *d'un air espiègle,* archly; *frimousse espiègle,* roguish little face.
— m. Imp, monkey.
— f. Minx, imp.

espièglerie [-gləri] f. Mischievousness (disposition); trick, monkey-trick (tour); *par pure espièglerie,* out of pure mischief.

espion, onne [ɛspjɔ̃, ɔn] s. Spy. ‖ MILIT. Spy. ‖ FAM. Concealed microphone (instrument); Paul Pry, snooper (personnage indiscret).

espionnage [ɛspjɔnaː3] m. Espionage, spying.

espionner [-ne] v. tr. (1). To spy upon (des agissements, qqn). ‖ FAM. To spy into (qqch.).

esplanade [ɛsplanad] f. Esplanade.

espoir [ɛspwaːr] m. Hope (v. ESPÉRANCE); *avoir bon* (ou) *ferme espoir,* to hope and trust; *avoir bon espoir de réussir,* to have good hopes of succeeding; *mettre son espoir dans,* to hope in, to set all one's hopes on; *sans espoir,* hopeless. ‖ Promise (promesse); *donner de grands espoirs,* to be (ou) to look promising. ‖ Hope (d'une famille, d'une nation).

esprit [ɛspri] m. Spirit (être immatériel); spirit, control (entité); ghost (fantôme). ‖ Spirit, soul (âme); *rendre l'esprit,* to give up the ghost. ‖ Mind; intellect (intelligence); *à l'esprit clair, ouvert,* clear-headed, open-minded. ‖ Thought (pensée); *avoir l'esprit ailleurs,* to be thinking of sth. else; *en esprit,* in spirit; *sortir de l'esprit de qqn,* to slip s.o's mind; *venir à l'esprit de qqn,* to enter (ou) to cross s.o.'s mind, to occur to s.o., to come home to s.o. ‖ Spirit, tendency, turn of mind, disposition; *avoir bon esprit,* to be well-meaning; *esprit d'aventure,* enterprise, adventurousness; *esprit de contradiction, de suite,* contrariness, consistence; *par esprit de,* in a spirit of. ‖ Spirit (sens); *esprit d'équipe,* team spirit. ‖ Sense; *avoir le bon esprit de,* to have the sense to. ‖ Genius (d'une langue); spirit (d'un règlement). ‖ Wit; *faire de l'esprit,* to try to be witty; *faire de l'esprit aux dépens de,* to sharpen one's wits on; *plein d'esprit,* witty. ‖ Spirit, mind (personne); *un esprit chagrin,* a peevish man; *un bel esprit,* a wit; *un grand esprit,* a great mind. ‖ Pl. *Esprits animaux,* animal spirits; *reprendre ses esprits,* to come to. ‖ ECCLÉS. *Les pauvres d'esprit,* the poor in spirit; *le Saint-Esprit,* the Holy Ghost. ‖ **Esprit-de-sel,** m. CHIM. Spirits of salt. ‖ **Esprit-de-vin,** m. CHIM. Spirit of wine.

esquif [ɛskif] m. NAUT. Skiff.

esquille [ɛskiːj] f. MÉD. Splinter.

esquilleux, euse [ɛskijø, øːz] adj. MÉD. Splintery, splintered; comminuted.

esquimau, aude [ɛskimo, oːd] adj., s. GÉOGR. Eskimo, Eskimau.
— m. ZOOL. Eskimo dog, husky. ‖ Siren sui (vêtement d'enfant); U. S. snow suit. ‖ CULIN Eskimo-pie, choc-ice, icebrick (glace).

esquintant, ante [ɛskɛ̃tɑ̃, ɑ̃:t] adj. FAM Tiring, exhausting, back-breaking.

esquinter [ɛskɛ̃te] v. tr. (1). FAM. To jade, t tire out, to fatigue (fatiguer). ‖ FAM. To slate, t slash, to run down (critiquer). ‖ FAM. To spoil to ruin, U. S. to mess up (abîmer).
— v. pr. **S'esquinter.** V. S'ÉREINTER.

esquisse [ɛskis] f. Sketch. ‖ FIG. Outline sketch.

esquisser [ɛskise] v. tr. (1). To sketch, to outline to frame (un dessin, un ouvrage). ‖ To start (un attaque, un geste); *esquisser une révérence, t* make a vague curtsey; *esquisser un sourire, t* put on the ghost of a smile.

esquive [ɛskiːv] f. SPORTS. Dodge, side-step. ‖ FIG. Dodge, dodging, evasion.

esquiver [ɛskive] v. tr. (1). To shirk, to dodg (une corvée); to elude, to skip, (une difficulté) to dodge, to side-step (une question); to scamp (un travail); U. S. to fluff (fam.).
— v. pr. **S'esquiver,** to dodge, to take avoidin action. ‖ To sneak away (partir).

essai [ɛsɛ] m. Trial, test (épreuve); *à l'essai, o* trial; *essai sur modèles,* model experiment; *fair l'essai de qqch.,* to try sth. out, to give sth. trial. ‖ Try; attempt (pour, to) [tentative]; *à titr d'essai,* tentatively; as a trial measure; *cou d'essai,* first try. ‖ Essay (composition littéraire). AUTOM. *Essai de vitesse,* speed trial. ‖ NAUT. CH. DE F. *Voyage d'essai,* trial trip. ‖ AVIAT Pilote *d'essai,* test pilot; *vol d'essai,* trial flight. MILIT. *Essais de tir,* gun trials. ‖ CHIM. Test assay (des métaux). ‖ SPORTS. Try (au rugby).

essaim [ɛsɛ̃] m. ZOOL. Swarm (d'abeilles); *essain posé,* cluster of bees. ‖ FIG. Swarm.

essaimage [ɛsɛmaː3] m. ZOOL. Swarming, hivin off (action); swarming time (époque).

essaimer [ɛsɛme] v. intr. (1). ZOOL. To swarm, t hive off (abeilles). ‖ FIG. To emigrate.

essanger [ɛsɑ̃3e] v. tr. (7). To soak (du linge).

essarder [ɛsarde] v. tr. (1). NAUT. To swab.

essarter [ɛsarte] v. tr. (1). AGRIC. To grub up.

essayage [ɛsɛjaː3] m. Trying (d'un objet). Trying-on, fitting (d'une robe). ‖ CHIM. Testing.

essayer [-je] v. tr. (9 *b*). To try, to test (un objet) ‖ To try on, to fit (un vêtement). ‖ To tr [v. TÂCHER, TENTER]; *essayez par vous-même* have a try yourself; *essayer de faire,* to try to do to have a try at doing; to try and do (fam.).
— v. pr. **S'essayer,** to have a try, to try one' skill (à, at).

essayeur, euse [-jœːr, øːz] s. Trier-on, fitter (e couture). ‖ TECHN. Trier, tester (de machines) assayer (de métaux).

essayiste [-jist] s. Essayist.

esse [ɛs] f. S-hook (crochet). ‖ MUS. Sound-hole

essence [ɛsɑ̃:s] f. Essence; essential . element *par essence,* essentially. ‖ Pith (d'une affaire); gis (d'une conversation, d'une question); essentia part (d'une doctrine); substance, marrow (d'u livre). ‖ Oil (de lavande, de térébenthine); atta (de roses); *essence de citron,* lemon-oil. ‖ AUTOM Petrol, U. S. gasoline, benzine, gas (fam.); *essenc* aviation, aviation grade petrol. ‖ BOT. Specie (d'arbres). ‖ PHILOS., ECCLÉS. Essence.

essentiel, elle [ɛsɑ̃sjɛl] adj. Essential (huile propriété). ‖ Essential (donnée); key (industrie) *être une condition essentielle de,* to be vital to.
— m. Essential point (ou) thing.

essentiellement [-mɑ̃] adv. Essentially.

esseulé, ée [ɛsøle] adj. Lonely. (V. ISOLÉ.)

essieu [ɛsjø] m. Axle-tree, axle, spindle.

essor [ɛsɔːr] m. Flight, launch (v. ENVOL); *prendre son essor*, to take flight. ‖ AVIAT. Taking off; *prendre son essor*, to take off. ‖ FIG. Progress, development (d'une affaire); *donner libre essor à*, to give vent to (sa colère); to give full scope to (son talent); *prendre un grand essor*, to develop rapidly, to make great strides (affaire).

essorage [ɛsɔraːʒ] m. Drying.

essorer [-re] v. tr. (1). To wring dry (du linge).

essoreuse [-røːz] f. Mangle, wringer (à linge). ‖ TECHN. Drainer (à mélasse).

essorillé, ée [ɛsɔrije] adj. Crop-eared (chien).

essoriller v. tr. (1). To crop the ears of (un chien).

essoucher [ɛsuʃe] v. tr. (1). AGRIC. To stub.

essoufflé, ée [ɛsufle] adj. Puffed, winded, blown, out of breath; *essoufflé par la course*, breathless with running. ‖ MÉD. Short-winded.

essoufflement [-fləmɑ̃] m. Panting, breathlessness. ‖ MÉD. Breathlessness, shortness of breath.

essouffler [-fle] v. tr. (1). To wind, to blow (qqn).
— v. pr. S'essouffler, to get winded (ou) out of breath. ‖ MÉD. To be short-winded.

essuie [ɛsɥi]. V. ESSUYER. ‖ **Essuie-glace, m.** AUTOM. Windscreen-wiper, U.S. windshield wiper. ‖ **Essuie-mains, m.** Hand-towel. ‖ **Essuie-plume, m.** Pen-wiper. ‖ **Essuie-verres, m.** Glass-cloth.

essuyage [-ja:ʒ] m. Dusting; wiping.

essuyer [-je] v. tr. (9 a). To dust (un objet poussiéreux). ‖ To wipe, to mop (un objet humide); *essuyer ses larmes*, to wipe away one's tears; *essuyer le tableau*, to wipe (ou) clean the blackboard; *s'essuyer le front*, to mop one's brow; *s'essuyer les yeux*, to wipe one's eyes. ‖ MILIT. To suffer (une défaite); to come under (le feu); *essuyer un coup de feu*, to be shot at. ‖ NAUT. To weather (une tempête). ‖ FIG. To suffer (un affront, une perte); to meet with (un échec, une perte, un refus). ‖ FAM. *Essuyer l'orage*, to bear the brunt of the storm.

est [ɛst] m. East; *à l'est*, in the east; *à l'est de*, east of, on (ou) to the east of; *d'est*, east (vent).
— adj. East (côte). ‖ **Est-allemand**, adj., s. East German.

estacade [ɛstakad] f. MILIT. Stockade. ‖ NAUT. Breakwater. ‖ CH. DE F. Coal-tip.

estafette [ɛstafɛt] f. MILIT. Dispatch-rider, U. S. messenger. ‖ † Estafette.

estafilade [ɛstafilad] f. Slash, gash.

estaminet [ɛstaminɛ] m. Tavern. (V. CABARET.)

estampage [ɛstɑ̃pa:ʒ] m. TECHN. Stamping, swaging. ‖ FAM. Fleecing.

estampe [ɛstɑ̃:p] f. ARTS. Print. ‖ TECHN. Stamp.

estamper [ɛstɑ̃pe] v. tr. (1). TECHN. To stamp, to swage. ‖ FAM. To fleece (écorcher); to gull, to swindle (escroquer).

estampeur [-pœ:r] m. TECHN. Stamper. ‖ FAM. Fleecer.

estampeuse [-pø:z] f. TECHN. Stamping-machine.

estampillage [-pija:ʒ] m. TECHN. Stamping.

estampille [-pi:j] f. TECHN. Stamp. ‖ FIG. Mark, stamp.

estampiller [-pije] v. tr. (1). TECHN. To stamp. ‖ FAM. To mark.

este [ɛst] adj., s. V. ESTONIEN.

ester [ɛstɛ:r] m. CHIM. Ester.

ester [ɛste] v. intr. (1). JUR. To bring an action, to go to law, to sue in a civil action.

esthète [ɛstɛ:t] m. Aesthete.

esthéticien, enne [ɛstetisjɛ̃, ɛn] s. Beauty specialist, U.S. beautician, cosmetologist.

esthétique [ɛstetik] f. Aesthetics.
— adj. Aesthetic. ‖ MÉD. Plastic (chirurgie).

esthétiquement [-kmɑ̃] adv. Aesthetically.

esthétisme [ɛstetism] m. Aestheticism.

estimable [ɛstimabl] adj. Estimable, respectable.

estimateur [-matœ:r] m. Valuer, estimator.

estimatif, ive [-matif, i:v] adj. Estimative; estimated (coût). ‖ Approximative.

estimation [-masjɔ̃] f. Estimation, estimating (des frais, d'un prix). ‖ Valuation, estimate (d'un objet).

estimatoire [-matwa:r] adj. Estimatory.

estime [ɛstim] f. Esteem, respect, regard; *jouir de l'estime de*, to be held in high esteem by; *tenir en haute, petite estime*, to hold in high, low esteem. ‖ Estimation; *baisser, monter dans l'estime de*, to fall, to rise in the estimation of; *succès d'estime*, succès d'estime. ‖ Estimate; *à l'estime*, at a rough estimate. ‖ NAUT. Dead reckoning; *à l'estime*, by reckoning.

estimée [ɛstime] f. COMM. Esteemed favour (lettre).

estimer v. tr. (1). To estimate (les frais, un prix); to value, to appraise (un objet). [V. ÉVALUER.] ‖ To prize, to appreciate (qqch.); to esteem, to appreciate (qqn); *être estimé de qqn*, to stand well with s.o., to stand high in s.o.'s estimation. ‖ To consider; *il estime de son devoir de*, he considers it his duty to; *estimer inutile de*, to see no point in; *le pays n'est pas si froid que vous l'estimez*, the country is not so cold as you make it out to be. ‖ NAUT. To reckon.
— v. pr. S'estimer, to esteem oneself; *s'estimer heureux que*, to esteem (ou) to consider oneself happy that.

estivage [ɛstiva:ʒ] m. AGRIC. Summering.

estivage m. NAUT. Stowing.

estival, ale [-val] adj. Aestival; estival. ‖ Summer (station, tenue).

estivant [-vɑ̃] s. Summer-resident, holiday-maker, U. S. vacationist.

estivation [-vasjɔ̃] f. ZOOL., BOT. Aestivation.

estiver [-ve] v. intr. (1). AGRIC. To summer.

estiver v. tr. (1). NAUT. To stow.

estoc [ɛstɔk] m. † Rapier; *frapper d'estoc et de taille*, to cut and thrust. ‖ SPORTS. *Coup d'estoc*, thrust (à l'escrime). ‖ AGRIC. Stock (d'arbre).

estocade [ɛstɔkad] f. Thrust. ‖ FIG. Onrush.

estomac [ɛstɔma] m. MÉD. Stomach; *avoir l'estomac creux*, to feel empty; *l'estomac garni, vide*, on a full, on an empty stomach; *mal d'estomac*, stomach-ache. ‖ TECHN. Web (d'enclume); breast-plate (outil). ‖ FAM. *Avoir de l'estomac*, to have guts; *estomac d'autruche*, ostrich-like stomach, U.S. cast-iron stomach.

estomaquer [-ke] v. tr. (1). FAM. To flabbergast; *cela m'a estomaqué*, it took my breath away.

estompage [ɛstɔ̃pa:ʒ], **estompement** [-pmɑ̃] m. ARTS. Shading off. ‖ FIG. Blurring (des contours); dimming (des souvenirs).

estompe [-tɔ̃:p] f. ARTS. Stump; stump drawing.

estomper [-tɔ̃pe] v. tr. (1). ARTS. To stump, to shade off. ‖ FIG. To blur (les contours); to tone down (une couleur, des détails); to dim (la lumière, la mémoire).
— v. pr. S'estomper, to grow blurred (contours); to dim (gloire, souvenir).

Estonie [ɛstɔni] f. GÉOGR. Estonia.

estonien, enne [-njɛ̃, ɛn] adj., s. Estonian.

estourbir [ɛsturbi:r] v. tr. (2). POP. To do in, to bump off (tuer); to knock out (ou) senseless (assommer).

estrade [ɛstrad] f. Platform, stand; *estrade d'honneur*, dais.

estragon [ɛstragɔ̃] m. BOT., CULIN. Tarragon.

estran [ɛstrɑ̃] m. GÉOGR. Foreshore.

estrapade [ɛstrapad] f. † Strappado.

estrope [ɛstrɔp] f. NAUT. Strop.

estropié, ée [ɛstrɔpje] adj. Lame (boiteux). ‖ Crippled, maimed (membre, personne). ‖ MILIT. Disabled.
— s. Cripple.

estropier v. tr. (1). To cripple, to maim, to lame (qqn). ‖ Milit. To disable. ‖ Fam. To mangle, to murder (une citation, un mot, un vers).

estuaire [ɛstɥɛːr] m. Géogr. Estuary.

estudiantin, ine [ɛstydjɑ̃tɛ̃, in] adj. Student.

esturgeon [ɛstyrʒɔ̃] m. Zool. Sturgeon.

et [e] conj. And ; *et Pierre et Paul,* both Peter and Paul.

étable [etabl] f. Byre, cow-shed (ou) -house (à bestiaux) ; rabbit-hutch (à lapins) ; sheep-fold (à moutons) ; sty (à porcs).

établi [etabli] m. Techn. Work-bench.

établi, ie adj. Established (fait) ; standing (habitude) ; determined (limite).

établir [-bliːr] v. tr. (2). To build (un barrage) ; to set up (une barrière) ; to pitch (un camp, une tente) ; to set up, to settle (sa demeure, qqn dans un lieu) ; to lay (des fondations). ‖ To settle (ses enfants en mariage). ‖ To make out (ou) up (un document, une liste, une mémoire) ; to institute (un ordre) ; to lay down (un plan, un programme) ; to establish (un système). ‖ To establish (son crédit, des faits, des relations) ; to settle, to lay down (des conditions) ; to draw (des conclusions) ; to lay down (un principe, une règle) ; to work out, to build up (une théorie) ; *établir sa domination sur,* to assume dominion over ; *établir son opinion sur,* to base one's opinion on. ‖ Jur. To establish (une accusation, le gouvernement) ; to lay, to place (des impôts) ; to institute, to lay down (une loi). ‖ Comm. To settle (ses affaires) ; to set up, to establish (un magasin) ; *établir qqn dans une affaire,* to set s.o. up in business. ‖ Fin. To quote (un bilan, un prix) ; to make out (un chèque, un compte, une facture) ; to work out (un prix). ‖ Sports. To set up (un record). ‖ Ch. de f. To lay down (une voie ferrée).
— v. pr. **S'établir,** to settle (dans un lieu ; dans le mariage) ; to settle down (se fixer). ‖ Comm. To set up (commerçant). ‖ Fin. To be worked out (prix). ‖ Milit. *S'établir sur des positions,* to take up positions.

établissement [-blismɑ̃] m. Laying ; setting up ; erection (d'une construction). ‖ Establishment (bâtiment) ; settlement (colonial) ; establishment, installation (commercial, industriel) ; establishment, institution (éducatif) ; foundation, institution (religieux). ‖ Establishment, creation, institution (d'une affaire). ‖ Setting up (dans les affaires) ; Settling, settlement (dans le mariage). ‖ Making out (ou) up (d'un document, d'une liste) ; establishment (d'un fait, d'un système) ; laying down (d'un principe, d'un programme).

étage [etaːʒ] m. Story (extérieur), floor (intérieur) ; *de trois étages,* three-storied (maison) ; *au troisième étage,* on the third (ou) U. S. fourth floor. ‖ Level (d'une mine). ‖ Techn. Stage (de fusée). ‖ Fig. Rank ; *de bas étage,* low-class.

étagé, ée [-ʒe] adj. Terraced (jardin) ; rising in tiers (plateau). ‖ Carried out in stages (opération).

étagement [-ʒmɑ̃] m. Tiering, terracing (des cultures) ; scaling (des prix).

étager [-ʒe] v. tr. (7). To tier up. ‖ Fig. To do (ou) to carry out in stages.
— v. pr. **S'étager,** to rise in tiers. ‖ Fig. To be done in stages.

étagère [-ʒɛːr] f. Set of shelves, what-not (meuble) ; shelf (rayon).

étai [etɛ] m. Prop, strut, shore. ‖ Naut. Stay.

étaiement [etɛmɑ̃] m. Propping (ou) shoring up (action d'étayer) ; shoring (ensemble d'étais).

étain [etɛ̃] m. Tin ; *étain oxydé, pyriteux,* cassiterite, stannite ; *étain de roche,* lode tin ; *mine d'étain,* stannary ; *papier d'étain,* tinfoil. ‖ Arts. Pewter.

étal [etal] m. Stall (de boucherie) ; stand (de marché).

étalage [etalaːʒ] m. Comm. Show, display (de marchandises, d'objets) ; shop- (ou) show- (ou) display-window (vitrine) ; *à l'étalage,* in the window ; *art de l'étalage,* window-dressing, window display. ‖ Stand (de marché) ; *droits d'étalage,* stallage. ‖ Fig. Show, display ; *faire étalage de,* to make a parade of, to show off.

étalager [-laʒe] v. tr. (7). Comm. To display in a window.

étalagiste [-laʒist] m. Window-dresser, display artist (de magasin) ; stall-keeper (de marché).

étale [etal] adj. Naut. Slack (mer).
— m. Naut. Slack water.

étalement [-lmɑ̃] m. Displaying (action) ; display (état). ‖ Fig. Staggering (des congés).

étaler [-le] v. tr. (1). To flatten (aplatir) ; to spread (étendre). ‖ To display, to lay out (déployer). ‖ Comm. To display, (en magasin) ; to patch (sur le marché). ‖ Naut. To weather (la rafale) ; to ride out (la tempête). ‖ Fig. To display, to parade, to show off (faire étalage de).
— v. intr. Naut. To hold water (sur les avirons).
— v. pr. **S'étaler,** to spread (beurre). ‖ To be displayed (ou) deployed. ‖ To stretch (paysage). ‖ To stretch oneself (en s'étendant) ; to sprawl (en se vautrant). ‖ To spread (période, temps) [*sur,* over]. ‖ Fam. To measure one's length, to go sprawling (tomber).

étalinguer [ɛtalɛ̃ge] v. tr. (1). Naut. To bend, to clinch (un câble).

étalingure [-gyːr] f. Naut. Bend, clinch.

étalon [etalɔ̃] m. Zool. Stallion, stud-horse.

étalon m. Fin. Standard ; *poids-étalon,* troy weight. ‖ **Etalon-or,** m. Fin. Gold-standard.

étalonnage [-lɔnaːʒ] m. Gauging (d'un appareil) ; standardization (des poids et mesures) ; calibration (des tubes). ‖ Stamp (estampille). ‖ Electr. Logging (des stations de radio).

étalonner [-lɔne] v. tr. (1). To gauge (un appareil) ; to standardize (les poids et mesures) ; to calibrate (des tubes). ‖ To stamp (estampiller). ‖ To grade (des photos).

étamage [etamaːʒ] m. Tinning (à l'étain). ‖ Silvering (au tain).

étambot [etɑ̃bo] m. Naut. Sternpost.

étambrai [etɑ̃brɛ] m. Naut. Mast-hole.

étamer [etame] v. tr. (1). To tin (une casserole). ‖ To silver (un miroir).

étameur [-mœːr] m. Tinsmith. ‖ Tinker (rétameur). ‖ Silverer (de miroir).

étamine [etamin] f. Bot. Stamen.

étamine f. Bunting (tissu épais). ‖ Butter-muslin, U. S. cheesecloth (tissu gaze). ‖ Bolting-cloth (pour tamiser).

étampe [etɑ̃ːp] f. Techn. Stamp ; swage ; punch.

étamper [etɑ̃pe] v. tr. (1). Techn. To stamp ; to swage ; to punch.

étamperche [etɑ̃pɛrʃ] f. Scaffolding-pole.

étamure [etamyːr] f. Tinning (action) ; tinning-metal (métal).

étanche [etɑ̃ːʃ] adj. Impervious, tight ; *étanche à l'air, à l'eau, au gaz,* air-, water-, gas-tight.

étanchéité [etɑ̃ʃeite] f. Imperviousness, watertightness.

étanchement [-ʃmɑ̃] m. Mopping-up, sponging-up (d'un liquide) ; stopping (d'une fuite). ‖ Quenching (de la soif). ‖ Méd. Stanching (du sang).

étancher [-ʃe] v. tr. (1). To mop up, to sponge up (un liquide). ‖ To stop (une fuite). ‖ To make tight (un compartiment). ‖ To quench, to assuage (la soif). ‖ Méd. To stanch (le sang).

étançon [etɑ̃sɔ̃] m. Naut. Stanchion.

étançonnement [-sɔnmɑ̃] m. Archit. Shoring ; underpinning.

étançonner [-ɔne] v. tr. (1). ARCHIT. To shore up ; to underpin.

étang [etã] m. Pond (artificiel) ; pool (naturel).

étant pr. prés. Being. (V. ÊTRE.)

étape [etap] f. Stopping-place (lieu) ; stage (marche) ; *à la dernière étape*, on the last lap ; *par petites étapes*, by easy stages. ‖ MILIT. Halting-place ; *fournir une étape*, to do a day's march. ‖ FIG. Step (*vers*, towards) ; stage (d'une carrière, d'une évolution, de la vie) ; *étape importante*, landmark (dans l'histoire d'un pays).

étarquer [etarke] v. tr. (1). NAUT. To swig, to swig up.

état [eta] m. State (v. CONDITION) ; *état des choses*, state of things ; *état d'esprit*, frame of mind ; *à l'état de neuf*, as good as new ; *dans son état actuel*, as it stands ; *dans un triste état*, in a sad way (ou) plight ; *dans tous ses états*, in a great state, all of a dither ; *en bon état*, well-conditioned (animal, terrain) ; in good repair (bâtiment) ; undamaged (colis) ; in good order (machine) ; in good condition (marchandises, personne) ; in good trim (ou) shape (sportif) ; *en mauvais état*, ill-conditioned ; in bad repair, out of order ; in bad condition ; *en état d'ivresse*, in a state of intoxication ; *être en état de faire*, to be in a fit state to do ; *être hors d'état* (ou) *n'être plus en état de*, to be unable (ou) no longer able to ; *n'être plus en état de travailler*, to be past one's work ; not to be up to doing one's work ; *laisser les choses en l'état*, to leave the things as they stand ; *réduit à l'état de*, reduced to ; *remettre en état*, to recondition. ‖ Condition, social station (condition sociale) ; trade, profession (métier) ; *de son état*, by profession (ou) trade. ‖ Account, schedule, statement, list, roll (document) ; *état de comptes*, statement of accounts ; *état de frais*, bill of costs ; *état des lieux*, inventory of fixtures ; *état mensuel*, monthly return ; *état nominatif*, roll, list of names. ‖ State (gouvernement, nation) ; *les Etats-Unis*, the United States ; *homme d'Etat*, statesman ; *raison d'Etat*, reason of State. ‖ Estate (corps) ; *Etats généraux*, States General ; *tiers état*, Third Estate. ‖ ECCLÉS. State (de grâce). ‖ MÉD. State (de santé). ‖ TECHN. *En état de marche*, in working order. ‖ MILIT. *Etats de service*, record of service ; *état de solde*, pay-bill. ‖ JUR. *Etat civil*, status, family-status ; vital statistics ; *bureau, officier de l'état civil*, register-office, registrar. ‖ LOC. *En tout état de cause*, in any case, under any circumstances ; *faire état de*, to take into a account ; *faire grand état de*, to think highly of. ‖ **Etat-major**, m. MILIT. Staff ; *officier d'état-major*, staff officer. ‖ **Etat-tampon**, m. Buffer-state.

étatique [-tik] adj. Under State control.

étatisation [-tizasjɔ̃] f. Nationalization, bringing under State control.

étatisé, ée [-tize] adj. State-controlled.

étatiser [-tize] v. tr. (1). To establish State control over.

étatisme [-tism] m. State control, etatism.

étatiste [-tist] s. Partisan of State control,

étau [eto] m. TECHN. Vice, U. S. vise ; *étau d'ébéniste, d'établi*, cramp, bench-vice. ‖ FIG. Stranglehold (des restrictions).

étaupiner [etopine] v. tr. (1). AGRIC. To clear of moles.

étayage [etɛja:ʒ] m. V. ÉTAIEMENT.

étayer [etɛje] v. tr. (9 b). ARCHIT. To prop up, to shore, to stay ; to underpin. ‖ NAUT. To stay. ‖ FIG. To bolster (ou) to back up (une théorie) [*de*, with].
— v. pr. **S'étayer**, to be supported (*sur*, by, on). ‖ FIG. To lean (*sur*, on) ; to be based (ou) grounded (ou) founded (*sur*, on, upon).

et cetera, etc. [etsetera] loc. adv. Et cetera, etc.

été [ete] m. Summer ; *été de la Saint-Martin*, Indian summer ; *été comme hiver*, summer and winter alike.

été p. p. V. ÊTRE (48).

éteigneur [etɛɲœ:r] m. Extinguisher (personne).

éteignoir [-ɲwa:r] m. Extinguisher ; snuffer. ‖ FAM. Wet blanket.

éteindre [etɛ̃:dr] v. tr. (59). To blow out, to put out (une chandelle) ; to extinguish, to put out (le feu, la lampe, la lumière) ; to switch off (l'électricité) ; to turn out (ou) off (le gaz). ‖ JUR. To extinguish (une dette, une famille, une servitude). ‖ CHIM. To slake (la chaux). ‖ FIG. To deaden (un bruit) ; to fade (une couleur) ; to quench (la soif) ; To cool down (la colère) ; to quench (l'enthousiasme) ; to extinguish (l'espérance, les passions) ; to dim (la gloire, le lustre).
— v. pr. **S'éteindre**, to go out ; to burn out (faute de charbon) ; to blow out (par courant d'air, souffle) ; To pass away, to die (personne) ; *il s'éteint*, his life is flickering out. ‖ JUR. To die out (coutume, famille, race, titre). ‖ FIG. To die away (bruit, couleur, voix) ; to fade (couleur, espoir, jour, lumière, sourire) ; to dim (éclat, gloire) ; to die down (passions).

éteint, einte [etɛ̃, ɛ̃:t] adj. Dead (combustible) ; out (feu, lumière) ; extinct (feu, volcan). ‖ Slaked (chaux). ‖ JUR. Paid off, extinguished (dette) ; extinct (famille, race). ‖ FIG. Dying (bruit, voix) ; faded (beauté, couleur, visage) ; washed out (personne) ; dim (regard) ; stifled (voix).

étendage [etãda:ʒ] m. Hanging out (du linge). ‖ Drying-yard (lieu).

étendard [etãdar] m. MILIT., BOT. Standard. ‖ FIG. Banner, standard.

étendoir [etãdwa:r] m. Drying-yard (lieu). ‖ Clothes-line. ‖ TECHN. Peel (en typogr.).

étendre [etã:dr] v. tr. (4). To spread (en déployant, en étalant) ; to stretch out (en étirant) ; to hammer out (en martelant) ; to hang out (en suspendant). ‖ To spread (de la colle, un tapis) [*sur*, on] ; to strew (des fleurs, de la paille) [*sur*, over] ; to hang out (du linge) ; to lay (une nappe). ‖ To spread out, to expand (les ailes) ; to stretch out (le bras, la main) ; to lay (qqn) [*sur*, on]. ‖ To extend (les dimensions) ; to expand, to extend (les limites). ‖ To extend (une appellation, ses connaissances, sa domination, la durée, son influence, ses ravages) ; to enlarge (sa fortune, sa propriété, ses relations) ; to extend (le sens d'un mot). ‖ To dilute ; *étendre d'eau*, to water down. ‖ COMM. To extend (un commerce). ‖ JUR. To extend (la validité). ‖ CULIN. To roll out (la pâte). ‖ FAM. To plough, U. S. to flunk (un candidat) ; to knock down, to stretch out, to flatten (qqn).
— v. pr. **S'étendre**, to lie (côtes) ; to spread (plaine) ; to extend, to stretch out (procession) ; to stretch, to lie (route). ‖ To extend (mur, propriété) [*jusqu'à*, to]. ‖ To stretch oneself out (personne) [par terre] ; to lie down (sur un lit). ‖ MÉD. To extend (blessure) ; to spread (cancer, épidémie). ‖ FIG. To expand (empire, intelligence) ; to reach (empire, regard) ; to spread (idées, odeur, renommée, rumeur) ; to stretch (moyens) ; *s'étendre sur*, to enlarge upon, to expatiate on, to dwell on (un sujet).

étendu, ue [etãdy] adj. Outspread (ailes) ; outstretched (bras). ‖ Lying, stretched (personne) ; supine (sur le dos). ‖ Diluted ; *étendu d'eau*, watered. ‖ Extensive, large (lac, plaine). ‖ FIG. Extensive (connaissances, mémoire) ; comprehensive (connaissances, programme, sens) ; wide (expérience, influence, savoir).

étendue f. Expanse (d'eau, de pays); spread (de pays); extent (de terrain). ‖ Dimensions, size (d'une parcelle, d'une pièce). ‖ Stretch (du bras). ‖ Compass (du temps); length (de la vie). ‖ Range (de la vue). ‖ Mus. Range (d'un instrument); compass, range (de la voix). ‖ Sports. Reach (à l'escrime). ‖ Fig. Scope (d'une action); scope, compass (de l'esprit, du savoir); extent (d'un dommage, d'une perte); coverage (d'information); range (des lectures, du sens).

éternel, elle [etɛrnɛl] adj. Ecclés. Eternal. ‖ Fig. Eternal, endless, everlasting.
— m. Ecclés. Eternal.

éternellement [-nɛlmɑ̃] adv. Eternally, endlessly, everlastingly, ceaselessly, perpetually.

éterniser [-nize] v. tr. (1). To eternalize, to perpetuate. ‖ Fam. To drag on (ou) out.
— v. pr. S'éterniser, to drag on, to last ceaselessly; s'éterniser chez qqn, to overstay an invitation, to wear out one's welcome.

éternité [-nite] f. Eternity; de toute éternité, from the beginning of time. ‖ Fam. Ages; eternity; il y a une éternité que, it is an age since, it has been ages since.

éternuement [etɛrnymɑ̃] m. Sneeze; sneezing (répété). ‖ Méd. Sternutation.

éternuer [-nɥe] v. intr. (1). To sneeze.

êtes [ɛt]. V. être (48).

étêtage [etɛta:ʒ], **étêtement** [-tmɑ̃] m. Agric. Pollarding, topping.

étêter [etɛte] v. tr. (1). To cut off the head of (une pointe). ‖ Agric. To poll, to pollard, to top (un arbre); to top, to head down (une plante).

éteule [etœ:l] f. Agric. Stubble.

éthane [etan] m. Chim. Ethane.

éther [etɛ:r] m. Ether (espace). ‖ Chim. Ether.

éthéré, ée [etere] adj. Ethereal. ‖ Skyey (voûte).

éthérifier [-rifje] v. tr. (1). Chim. To etherify.

éthériser [-rize] v. tr. (1). Méd. To etherize.

éthéromane [-roman] s. Ether addict.

éthéromanie [-romani] f. Méd. Addiction to ether.

Éthiopie [etjɔpi] f. Géogr. Ethiopia.

éthiopien, enne [-pjɛ̃, ɛn] adj., s. Géogr. Ethiopian.

éthique [etik] adj. Ethical.
— f. Philos. Ethics.

ethnie [ɛtni] f. Ethnic group.

ethnique [-nik] adj. Ethnic, ethnical.

ethnocentrisme [-nɔsɑ̃trism] m. Ethnocentrism.

ethnocide [-nɔsid] m. Genocide.

ethnographe [etnɔgraf] s. Ethnographer.

ethnographie [-fi] f. Ethnography.

ethnographique [-fik] adj. Ethnographic, ethnographical.

ethnologie [etnɔlɔʒi] f. Ethnology.

ethnologique [-lɔʒik] adj. Ethnologic, ethnological.

ethnologue [-lɔg] m. Ethnologist.

éthologie [etɔlɔʒi] f. Zool. Ethology.

éthyle [eti:l] m. Chim. Ethyl.

éthylène [etilɛ:n] m. Chim. Ethylene.

éthylique [etilik] adj. Chim. Ethyl, ethylic; alcool éthylique, ethyl alcohol. ‖ Alcoholic.
— s. Alcoholic (alcoolique).

éthylisme [-lism] m. Alcoholism.

étiage [etja:ʒ] m. Low-water mark. ‖ Fig. Level.

étincelant, ante [etɛ̃slɑ̃, ɑ̃:t] adj. Sparkling (bijou, étoile, regard); étincelant de colère, de convoitise, glaring, covetous (yeux). ‖ Fig. Sparkling, brilliant (conversation, esprit).

étinceler [-sle] v. intr. (5). To spark (feu). ‖ To glitter (argenterie); to glitter, to sparkle (bijou); to glow (ver luisant). ‖ To sparkle (regard joyeux); to flash, to glow (regard furieux); to

twinkle (regard malicieux) [de, with]. ‖ Fig. To sparkle (conversation, esprit).

étincelle [-sɛl] f. Spark (du feu); flake (à la forge) [v. flammèche]; faire des étincelles, to spark (feu). ‖ Sparkle, twinkle (des étoiles, du ver luisant); twinkle (du regard); sparkle (du vin mousseux). ‖ Electr. Spark. ‖ Autom. Étincelle d'allumage, ignition spark. ‖ Fig. Spark (d'esprit, de la vie); flash (de génie); faire des étincelles, to be sparkling with wit.

étincellement [-sɛlmɑ̃] m. Sparkling, glittering, twinkling (action); sparkle, glitter, twinkle (éclat).

étiolement [etjɔlmɑ̃] m. Méd., Bot., Fig. Etiolation, wilting.

étioler [-le] v. tr. (1). Bot. To etiolate. ‖ Méd. To weaken.
— v. pr. S'étioler. Bot. To wilt, to droop. ‖ Méd. To decline; to be weakening.

étiologie [-lɔʒi] f. Etiology.

étique [etik] adj. Raw-boned, skinny (animal); weakly, skinny, bony (personne).

étiquetage [etikta:ʒ] m. Labelling (d'un paquet). ‖ Comm. Ticketing.

étiqueter [-kte] v. tr. (8b). To label (une bouteille, un paquet); to ticket (avec le prix).

étiquette [-kɛt] f. Label, U. S. sticker (pour bouteilles, colis); tally (pour plantes); ticket (indiquant le prix). ‖ Label (en politique). ‖ Etiquette (protocole); il n'est pas conforme à l'étiquette de, it's not etiquette to.

étirable [etirabl] adj. Ductile (fil, métal); extensible (matière).

étirage [-ra:ʒ] m. Stretching out. ‖ Drawing out (d'un métal).

étiré, ée [-re] adj. Stretched, worn out (élastique); wire-drawn, drawn out (métal).

étirer [-re] v. tr. (1). To stretch (un élastique, ses membres). ‖ To wiredraw, to draw out (un métal).
— v. pr. S'étirer, to draw out (métal). ‖ To stretch, to string out (colonne, procession); to stretch away (route). ‖ To stretch, to stretch oneself (personne).

étireur [-rœ:r] s. Techn. Drawer (personne).

étireuse [-rø:z] f. Techn. Wire-drawer (machine).

étoffe [etɔf] f. Fabric, material (v. tissu); étoffe de laine, stuff, wool fabric, woollen. ‖ Fig. Stuff, matter (d'une œuvre); stuff, mettle (d'une personne); avoir l'étoffe de, to have the makings of, to be cut out for; il a de l'étoffe, there is good stuff in him.

étoffé, ée [etɔfe] adj. Ample (habit). ‖ Fig. Full of substance (discours). ‖ Fam. Plump (personne).

étoffer v. tr. (1). To give fullness to (un habit); to fill out (qqn). ‖ Fig. To fill out, to substantiate (un discours).

étoile [etwal] f. Astron. Star; à la belle étoile, under the stars; loger à la belle étoile, to sleep out in the open; sans étoile, starless. ‖ Star-shaped crack (brisure sur un verre). ‖ Star (décoration, insigne du grade). ‖ Asterisk (en typogr.). ‖ Théâtr. Star; avoir un rôle d'étoile, to star; danseuse étoile, prima ballerina; principal dancer; dancing star. ‖ Zool. Étoile de mer, starfish. ‖ Fig. Star (du destin); né sous une bonne étoile, born under a lucky star.

étoilé [-le] adj. Starry, star-studded (firmament); starlit (nuit). ‖ Star-spangled (bannière). ‖ Star-shaped (cassure); starred (glace, vitre). ‖ Bot. Starry; anis étoilé, star anise.

étoiler [-le] v. tr. (1). To star (casser). ‖ To stud with stars (orner).
— v. pr. S'étoiler, to become starry (ciel). ‖ To be starred (glace, vitre).

étole [etɔ:l] f. Ecclés. Stole.

eton [etɔn] m. Eton jacket (veste).

étonnamment [etɔnamɑ̃] m. Astonishingly.

étonnant, ante [-nɑ̃, ɑ̃:t] adj. Astonishing, wonderful, surprising; *pas* (ou) *rien d'étonnant*, no wonder !, small wonder !, that isn't to be wondered at ! ‖ Queer, peculiar, odd (bizarre).

étonnement [-nmɑ̃] m. Astonishment, wonder, amazement.

étonner [-ne] v. tr. (1). To astonish, to amaze, to surprise; *air étonné*, look of surprise; *être étonné de*, to wonder at.
— v. pr. S'étonner, to wonder, to marvel, to be astonished (*de*, at); *cela ne m'étonne pas*, I'm not surprised, I don't wonder at it.

étouffant, ante [etufɑ̃, ɑ̃:t] adj. Stuffy (atmosphère); stifling (chaleur); sultry (chaleur, temps); sweltering (local, lieu).

étouffe-chrétien [etufkretjɛ̃] m. inv. Stodgy dish, stodge.

étouffée [-fe] f. CULIN. *Cuire à l'étouffée*, to casserole.

étouffement [etufmɑ̃] m. Stifling (par la chaleur); suffocation (par la fumée); choking (par strangulation). ‖ Smothering (d'un feu). ‖ MÉD. Suffocation; suffocating fit. ‖ FIG. Shelving (d'une affaire); smothering (d'une enquête); hushing up (d'un scandale).

étouffer [-fe] v. tr. (1). To choke, to smother, to suffocate (qqn). ‖ To smother (un feu). ‖ FIG. To muffle, to deaden (un bruit); to stifle (un cri); to drown (la voix). ‖ FIG. To shelve (une affaire); to smother (une enquête); to strangle (le mal); to suppress (une nouvelle); to stamp out (une révolte); to hush up (un scandale). ‖ FIG. To oppress (qqn); to stifle (les sentiments).
— v. intr. To choke, to swelter, to suffocate. ‖ To be smothered to death (par entassement). ‖ To choke (*de*, with) [colère].
— v. pr. S'étouffer, to choke, to suffocate. ‖ FAM. *On s'étouffait pour entrer*, people crushed in.

étouffoir [-fwa:r] m. Extinguisher (de feu). ‖ MUS. Damper. ‖ FAM. Stuffy room, oven.

étoupe [etup] f. Tow; oakum.

étouper [-pe] v. tr. (1). To pack, to caulk.

étoupille [-pi:j] f. Fuse (de mines). ‖ MILIT. Tube, priming tube.

étoupiller [-pije] v. tr. (1). To fuse. ‖ MILIT. To insert the firing tube.

étourderie [eturdəri] f. Heedlessness, thoughtlessness, carelessness (inattention); *par étourderie*, in an unthinking moment. ‖ Giddiness, flightiness (légèreté). ‖ Oversight (inadvertance); *par étourderie*, through (ou) by an oversight.

étourdi, ie [eturdi] adj. Giddy, dizzy (pris de vertige). ‖ Heedless, thoughtless, light-headed, feather-brained, harum-scarum. (V. ÉTOURNEAU.)
— s. Scatter-brain, harum-scarum.

étourdie (à l') loc. adv. Giddily, thoughtlessly.

étourdiment [-dimɑ̃] adv. Heedlessly, thoughtlessly; giddily. ‖ Unintentionally.

étourdir [-di:r] v. tr. (2). To make giddy (ou) dizzy (qqn). ‖ To stupefy (boisson); to deafen (bruit); to stun, to daze, to make groggy (coup). ‖ FIG. To numb (ou) to soothe (la douleur); to stun, to daze, to stagger (qqn).
— v. pr. S'étourdir. FIG. To try to forget; to seek diversion.

étourdissant, ante [-disɑ̃, ɑ̃:t] adj. Deafening (bruit); stunning (coup, toilette); staggering, amazing (succès); giddy, vertiginous (vitesse).

étourdissement [-dismɑ̃] m. Giddiness, dizziness (vertige); *avoir un étourdissement*, to have a fit of giddiness, to feel faint (ou) dizzy. ‖ FIG. Diversion.

étourneau [eturno] m. ZOOL. Starling. ‖ FAM. Feather-brain. (V. ÉCERVELÉ.)

étrange [etrɑ̃:ʒ] adj. Strange, queer, odd (v. BIZARRE); *chose étrange*, strange to say; *le plus*

étrange, c'est qu'il soit venu, the oddest thing is that he came at all. ‖ Weird (inquiétant). ‖ Singular, odd, eccentric, queer, quaint (original et étonnant).

étrangement [etrɑ̃ʒmɑ̃] adv. Strangely, queerly, oddly; weirdly. ‖ Wonderfully, surprisingly (étonnamment).

étranger, ère [etrɑ̃ʒe, ɛ:r] adj. Foreign (nation, personne); alien (avec sens péjoratif); *de marque étrangère*, foreign-built (auto). ‖ Strange (lieu, maison, visage); *être étranger à*, to be a stranger in (un lieu). ‖ MÉD. Foreign (corps). ‖ FIG. Extraneous (considération, influence); *être étranger à*, to be extraneous to (ou) unconcerned in (ou) unacquainted with (une affaire); to be a stranger to (la peur); to be foreign to (une question).
— s. Foreigner; alien (d'une autre nationalité). ‖ Stranger (à un groupe, à un lieu). ‖ Foreign country (ou) part; *vivre à l'étranger*, to live abroad; *voyage à l'étranger*, trip abroad, foreign travel.

étrangeté [-ʒəte] f. Strangeness, oddness, queerness, quaintness (v. BIZARRERIE); weirdness. ‖ Pl. Oddities (travers).

étranglé, ée [etrɑ̃gle] adj. Strangled (personne). ‖ MÉD. Strangulated (hernie). ‖ FIG. Narrow (chemin); stifled, choking, strangled (voix).

étranglement [-gləmɑ̃] m. Strangling (action); strangulation. ‖ Garrotting (supplice). ‖ MÉD. Strangulation (d'une hernie). ‖ TECHN. Throttling. ‖ FIG. Narrowing, neck (d'un passage).

étrangler [-gle] v. tr. (1). To strangle, to throttle (qqn). ‖ To garrot (supplicier). ‖ To choke (étouffer) [*de*, with]; *la colère l'étranglait*, he was choking with anger. ‖ MÉD. To strangulate (une hernie). ‖ TECHN. To throttle down (le moteur). ‖ NAUT. To spill (une voile).
— v. intr. To choke (étouffer).
— v. pr. S'étrangler, to strangle oneself (par accident, suicide). ‖ To choke (s'étouffer) [*de*, with]. ‖ MÉD. To become strangulated (hernie). ‖ FIG. To narrow (passage); to become strangled (ou) stifled (voix).

étrangleur [-glœ:r] s. Strangler, garrotter.
— m. TECHN. Throttle.

étrangloir [-glwa:r] m. NAUT. Compressor; spilling line.

étrave [etra:v] f. NAUT. Stem; cutwater.

être [e:tr] v. intr. (48).

---

1. Exister. — 2. Se porter. — 3. Avoir lieu. — 4. Appartenir. — 5. Venir de. — 6. Echoir. — 7. Incomber. — 8. Se trouver. — 9. Etre avec attribut. — 10. Etre au sens passif et pronominal. — 11. FAM. Aller. — 12. En être. — 13. Y être.

---

1. To be, to exist (exister); *il n'est plus*, he is no more; *le meilleur homme qui soit*, the best man in the world; *si cela est*, if so. ‖ 2. To be (se porter); *comment êtes-vous?*, how are you?; *je ne suis guère bien*, I'm not too well. ‖ 3. To be (avoir lieu); *ça y est*, it is done; *c'était l'an passé*, it was last year. ‖ 4. To be, to belong (appartenir); *à qui est ce chapeau?*, whose hat is this?; *ce champ est à mon père*, this field belongs to my father; *je suis à vous*, I am at your service (à votre disposition). ‖ 5. To be (venir de); *il est de Rome*, he is from Rome; *le vent est au nord*, the wind is blowing north. ‖ 6. To be (échoir); *c'est à vous de parler*, it is your turn to speak; *pour ce qui est de*, as regards. ‖ 7. To belong to, to lie (ou) to rest with (incomber); *ce fut à Pierre de*, it was left to Peter to; *c'est à vous d'agir*, it rests with you (ou) it's up to you to act; *la faute est à Jean*, the fault lies with John. ‖ 8. To be,

to lie, to stand (se trouver); *être à l'ancre*, to lay at anchor; *être debout près de la porte*, to stand near the door; *où est-elle?*, where is she? ‖ **9.** To be (avec attribut); *c'est ça*, that's it; *c'est bien ·mon frère*, he is my brother; *c'est moi*, it is I; *c'est son père tout craché*, he is the very spit of his father; *c'était à qui des deux arriverait le premier*, they were both out to get there first; *être content, fatigué, lourd*, to be glad, tired, heavy; *imbécile que vous êtes!*, you fool!; *qui a mangé le gâteau? C'est moi*, who has eaten the cake? I have; *sotte que je suis!*, how silly of me!; *voilà ce que c'est que d'être vieux*, you see what it means to grow old. ‖ **10.** To be (sens passif); *être vu*, to be seen. ‖ To have; *elle est douée pour*, she has a gift for; *il est soutenu par*, he has the support of; *il y est autorisé*, he has leave to do it; *il s'est endetté*, he has got into debt; *il s'est repenti*, he has repented. ‖ **11.** FAM. To go (aller); *avoir été à Paris*, to have been to Paris; *où avez-vous été voir ce film?*, where did you go to see that film? ‖ **12. En être**; *l'affaire en est là*, so the matter rests; *elle en est à mendier son pain*, she is reduced to begging for her bread; *en êtes-vous?*, will you join us? (voulez-vous nous accompagner); do you belong to it? (en faites-vous partie?); *il en a été pour ses frais*, he got nothing out of it, all his trouble went for nothing; *il en est encore à chercher ça*, he is still looking for it; *il en est pour son idée*, he is set on his idea; *il ne sait plus où il en est*, he is all at sea; *j'en suis pour mon argent*, I am out of pocket because of it; *je n'en suis plus*, I give it up (j'abandonne); *où en êtes-vous?*, how far have you got with it? (lecture, travail); *où en sont-ils au point de vue argent?*, how do they stand in the matter of money?; *voir où j'en suis*, to see how I stand; *vous n'en êtes pas à votre coup d'essai*, you are no new hand at it. ‖ **13. Y être**; *ça y est*, it's finished (c'est fait); *elle n'y est pas*, she is not at home; *elle n'y est pour personne*, she is at home to nobody; *il n'y est pas*, he is all at sea (il s'y perd); he is not all there (il est détraqué); *je n'y suis pas*, I don't get you (fam.) [je ne comprends pas]; I don't follow (je ne suis pas); *le surmenage y est pour beaucoup*, overworking is largely responsible for it; *n'y être pour rien*, to have no part in it; *y être pour qqch.*, to have a hand (ou) a part in it, to have sth. to do with it; *y êtes-vous?*, are you ready? (êtes-vous prêt?); *vous y êtes!*, you've got (ou) hit it! (vous avez trouvé); *vous n'y êtes pas*, you have missed it; U. S. you're not with it (pop.).

— v. impers. **Il est**, it is; there is (il y a); *il est 4 heures*, it is four o'clock; *il était une fois*, once upon a time there was; *il est des gens qui*, there are people who; *il n'en.est rien*, it is not so; *il en est de lui comme des autres*, it is with him as with the others; *comme si de rien n'était*, as if nothing had happened; *savoir ce qu'il en est*, to know how things stand. ‖ **Est-ce que** (non traduit); *est-ce qu'elle est chez elle?*, is she at home?; *est-ce qu'il vient?*, is he coming? ‖ **N'est-ce pas**; *il est jeune, n'est-ce pas?*, he is young, is he not? (ou) isn't he?; *il n'est plus jeune, n'est-ce pas?*, he is no longer young, is he?; *il possède une maison, n'est-ce pas?* he owns a house, doesn't he?; *il ne possède pas de maison, n'est-ce pas?*, he doesn't own a house, does he?; *il viendra ce soir, n'est-ce pas?*, he will come this evening, won't he?; *n'est-ce pas que vous me comprenez?*, don't you understand me? ‖ **N'était**, but for, were it not for; *n'eût été*, had it not been for (qqch.); *n'était sa maladie*, but for his illness. ‖ **N'était que, si ce n'est que**, were it not that; *n'eût été que*, had it not been that; *ne*

fût-ce que pour l'aider, if only to help him. ‖ V. CE, ÉTANT, POUR, SOIT.

— m. Being, existence. ‖ Being, creature, soul; *être humain*, human being; *un drôle d'être*, a queer fellow; *un petit être*, a little creature; *pauvre être!*, poor soul! ‖ Being, body (corps); *dans tout son être*, in his whole being.

étreindre [etrɛ̃:dr] v. tr. (59). To embrace, to hug, to squeeze (embrasser). ‖ To grip, to grasp, to clutch, to clench (empoigner). ‖ To twist round (liane, lierre); to coil round (serpent). ‖ FIG. To grip (douleur, émotion); *la peur l'étreignit à la gorge*, fear took him by the throat.

étreinte [etrɛ̃:t] f. Embrace, hug, clasp (embrassement). ‖ Grip, grasp, clutch, clasp (empoignade). ‖ FIG. Grip, gripping (de la douleur, de la maladie, de la peur); pressure (de la misère).

étrenne [etrɛn] f. COMM. First sale. ‖ Pl. New Year's gift, Christmas box (ou) gift (ou) present. ‖ LOC. *Avoir l'étrenne de*, to be the first to use.

étrenner [-ne] v. tr. (1). To use (ou) to wear for the first time (qqch.). ‖ COMM. To be the first customer of.
— v. intr. COMM. To make the first sale of the day. ‖ FAM. To be told off, to catch it.

étrésillon [etrezijɔ̃] m. Strut, brace.

étrier [etrje] m. Stirrup; *à franc étrier*, full speed. ‖ Tread (d'échasse); climbing-iron (de grimpeur). ‖ Link (de balance); tool-post (de tour). ‖ MÉD. Stirrup-bone (de l'oreille); stirrup, leg-rest (de table opératoire). ‖ NAUT. Stirrup. ‖ AUTOM. Bridle (de ressort).

étrillage [etrija:ʒ] m. Currying (du cheval). ‖ FAM. Thrashing.

étrille [etri-j] f. Curry-comb. ‖ ZOOL. Swimming crab.

étriller [-je] v. tr. (1). To curry, to comb (un cheval). ‖ FAM. To thrash, to leather.

étripage [etripa:ʒ] m. Gutting (d'un poisson, d'une volaille). ‖ FIG., FAM. Butchery, blood-bath.

étriper [etripe] v. tr. (1). To gut (un animal); to disembowel (qqn). ‖ CULIN. To draw (une volaille).
— v. pr. **S'étriper.** NAUT. To become frayed (cordage).
— v. récipr. **S'étriper**, FIG., FAM. To fight, to battle.

étriqué, ée [etrike] adj. Skimpy, scrimpy, skimpily made (habit). ‖ FIG. Sketchy (exposé); narrow (esprit); cramped (position); skimpy (ressources).

étriquer v. tr. (1). To make skimpily (un vêtement). ‖ FIG. To curtail (un ouvrage).

étrivière [etrivjɛ:r] f. Stirrup-leather. ‖ Pl. Leathering, belting; *donner les étrivières à*, to leather, to belt.

étroit, oite [etrwa, wat] adj. Narrow (objet, passage); *assez étroit*, narrowish. ‖ Tight (vêtement). ‖ Narrow, limited (espace); *à l'étroit*, cramped for room. ‖ FIG. Narrow (conceptions, esprit, limites, sens, vue); strict (discipline, obligation, règlement, sens); close (liens, parenté, rapport, ressemblance, union); scanty (ressources); *à l'esprit étroit*, narrow-minded.

étroitement [-tmɑ̃] adv. Narrowly. ‖ Strictly (rigidement). ‖ Closely (intimement). ‖ Scantily (insuffisamment).

étroitesse [-tɛ:s] f. Narrowness. ‖ FIG. Closeness (des relations); *étroitesse d'esprit*, narrow-mindedness.

étron [etrɔ̃] m. POP. Turd.

étrusque [etrysk] adj., s. GÉOGR. Etruscan.

étude [ety:d] f. Study (d'une science); *faire ses études*, to go to school, to be educated; *homme d'étude*, scholar, student, erudite. ‖ Study, investigation (recherche); *à l'étude*, under consideration; *bureau d'études*, assay-office (pour recherches); *commission d'études*, working party;

comité d'études, committee of inquiry; *étude de marché,* marketing; *service d'études,* designing (ou) planning department. ‖ Essay (écrit) [*sur,* on, about]. ‖ Preparation; prep (fam.) [travail à l'école]; *fait en étude,* done in prep. ‖ Prep room, study (salle d'étude). ‖ Mus., Arts. Study. ‖ Jur. Office, chambers (d'avoué, de notaire). ‖ Fig. Study (préoccupation); *sans étude,* unstudied.

étudiant [etydjã] m. Student.

étudiante [-djɑ:t] f. Student, woman student, U. S. co-ed.

étudié, ée [-dje] adj. Fig. Studied (affecté); elaborate (minutieux). ‖ Comm. Cut (prix).

étudier [-dje] v. tr. (1). To learn (une leçon); to study (une matière; to make a study of (une période); to study (une science). ‖ To study (une affaire, qqn); to scrutinize (une proposition); to scan (un visage); to study, to go (ou) look into (une question). ‖ To calculate, to study (ses gestes); to elaborate (son style). ‖ Mus. To practise on (le piano).
— v. intr. To study.
— v. pr. S'étudier, to introspect (par introspection). ‖ To be affected (par affectation). ‖ To study, to try (chercher) [*à,* to]; *on s'était étudié à préparer qqch.,* much thought had gone to the preparation of sth.

étui [etᶩi] m. Case; *étui à cigarettes, à lunettes,* cigarette-, spectacle- (ou) glasses-case. ‖ Méd. Holder (de brosse à dents). ‖ Naut. Cover.

étuve [ety:v] f. Drying-room (pour séchage); sterilizer (pour stérilisation). ‖ Sweating-room (pour transpiration). ‖ Hot press (pour le linge). ‖ Fam. Oven.

étuvée [etyve] f. Culin. *Cuire à l'étuvée,* to steam.

étuver v. tr. (1). To stove (au four); to steam (à la vapeur). ‖ To dry (sécher); to sterilize (stériliser). ‖ Culin. To steam.

étymologie [etimɔlɔʒi] f. Etymology.

étymologique [-ʒik] adj. Etymological.

étymologiquement [-ʒikmã] adv. Etymologically.

étymologiste [-ʒist] s. Etymologist.

étymon [etimõ] m. Gramm. Etymon.

É.-U. [əy] abrév. de *Etats-Unis,* U. S.

eucalyptus [økaliptys] m. Bot. Eucalyptus, gum-tree (arbre). ‖ Méd. Eucalyptus, eucalyptus oil (essence).

eucharistie [økaristi] f. Ecclés. Eucharist.

eucharistique [-tik] adj. Eucharistic(al).

euclidien, enne [øklidjẽ, ɛn] adj. Euclidean; *géométrie euclidienne,* Euclidean geometry; *géométrie non euclidienne,* non-Euclidean geometry.

eudiomètre [ødjɔmɛtr] m. Eudiometer.

eugénique [øʒenik] adj. Eugenic.
— f. Eugenics. (V. eugénisme.)

eugénisme [øʒenism] m. Eugenism, eugenics.

euh [ø] interj. Hum!

eunuque [ønyk] m. Eunuch.

euphémique [øfemik] adj. Euphemistic.

euphémisme [-mism] m. Euphemism.

euphonie [øfɔni] f. Euphony.

euphonique [-nik] adj. Euphonic.

euphorbe [øfɔrb] f. Bot. Euphorbia.

euphorie [øfɔri] f. Euphory, euphoria, bliss.

euphorique [-rik] adj. Euphoric.

euphorisant, ante [-rizã, ã:t] adj. Euphoriant.
— m. Euphoriant; pep pill (fam.).

euphuisme [øfᶩism] m. Euphuism.

eurafricain, aine [ørafrikẽ, ɛn] adj. Géogr. Euro-african, Eurafrican.

eurasiatique [ørazjatik] adj. Géogr. Eurasian.

Eurasie [ørazi] f. Géogr. Eurasia.

eurasien, enne [-zjẽ, ɛn] adj., s. Eurasian.

Euratom [øratɔm] m. Euratom.

euristique [øristik] adj., f. V. heuristique.

eurodollar [ørɔdɔla:r] m. Eurodollar.

Europe [ørɔp] f. Géogr. Europe. ‖ † Europa (déesse).

européaniser [ørɔpeanize] v. tr. (1). To europeanize.

européanisme [ørɔpeanism] m. Europeanism.

européen, enne [ørɔpeẽ, ɛn] adj., s. Géogr. European.

eurythmie [øritmi] f. Eurhythmy.

eurythmique [øritmik] adj. Eurhythmic.

eus, eusse, eut. V. avoir (19).

Eustache [østa:ʃ] m. Eustace (prénom). ‖ Jack-knife, pig-sticker (couteau). ‖ Méd. *Trompe d'Eustache,* Eustachian tube.

euthanasie [øtanazi] f. Méd. Euthanasia.

eutrophisation [øtrɔfizasjõ] f. Eutrophication.

eux [ø] pron. pers. V. lui.

E.V. [əve], abrév. de *En ville,* by hand (sur une lettre).

évacuateur, trice [evakᶩatœ:r, tris] adj. Drainage, exhaust (conduit), evacuation (processus). ‖ Méd. Evacuative.
— m. Techn. *Evacuateur de crues,* overfall.

évacuation [-asjõ] f. Draining off, drainage (des eaux); exhaust (de la vapeur). ‖ Vacating, vacation (d'un domicile, d'une maison); clearing (d'une salle). ‖ Méd., Milit. Evacuation.

évacué, ée [-e] s. Evacuee.

évacuer [-e] v. tr. (1). To drain off (les eaux); to exhaust (la vapeur). ‖ To leave (une maison); to evacuate, to remove (qqn); *faire évacuer,* to clear (une salle). ‖ Méd., Milit. To evacuate.

évadé, ée [evade] adj. Escaped.
— s. Fugitive, escapee.

évader (s') [sevade] v. pr. (1). To escape. ‖ Fig. To slip away (se dérober).

évaluable [evalᶩabl] adj. Appraisable.

évaluation [-asjõ] f. Valuation, appraisement (d'un objet). ‖ Estimate, computation (d'un prix). ‖ Jur. Assessment.

évaluer [-e] v. tr. (1). To value, to appraise, to price (un objet). ‖ To evaluate, to compute (une distance, un prix). ‖ Jur., Fin. To assess (les dommages, les impôts).

évanescent, ente [evanɛssã, ã:t] adj. Evanescent.

évangélique [evãʒelik] adj. Ecclés. Evangelic. ‖ Evangelical (de la religion réformée).

évangéliquement [-kmã] adv. Evangelically.

évangélisateur, trice [-zatœ:r, tris] s. Evangelist.

évangélisation [-zasjõ] f. Evangelization.

évangéliser [-ze] v. tr. (1). To evangelize.

évangéliste [-list] m. Evangelist.

évangile [-ʒil] m. Ecclés. Gospel. ‖ Fam. *Parole d'évangile,* Gospel truth.

évanoui, ie [evanwi] adj. Unconscious, in a dead faint, in a swoon (personne). ‖ Fig. Vanished (espérance).

évanouir (s') [sevanwi:r] v. pr. (2). To faint, to swoon (personne). ‖ Radio. To fade. ‖ Fig. To disappear, to fade away (apparition); to vanish, to fade (espoir, projet, rêve).

évanouissement [evanwismã] m. Méd. Faint, swoon, fainting fit; *revenir de son évanouissement,* to come to. ‖ Radio. Fading. ‖ Fig. Vanishing, fading (d'un rêve).

évaporateur [evaporatœ:r] m. Evaporator.

évaporation [-sjõ] f. Evaporation.

évaporatoire [-twa:r] adj. Evaporating.

évaporé, ée [evapore] adj. Evaporated (liquide). ‖ Fig. Flighty, fluffy, skittish, giddy, dizzy.
— f. *Une blonde évaporée,* a dizzy blonde; *une jeune évaporée,* a skittish (ou) giddy young thing.

évaporer v. tr. (1). To evaporate (un liquide); *faire évaporer,* to evaporate. ‖ Fig. To vent, to give vent to (sa colère).
— v. pr. S'évaporer, to evaporate (liquide);

s'évaporer en bouillant, to boil away. ‖ Fɪɢ. To vanish (espoir, rêve). ‖ Fᴀᴍ. To evaporate (chose, personne) [disparaître].

évasé, ée [evɑze] adj. Splayed (ouverture); bell-mouthed (tuyau). ‖ Bell-shaped (jupe); flared (jupe, tuyau); cupped (objet).

évasement [-zmɑ̃] m. Flaring, flare (d'une jupe, d'un tuyau). ‖ Splaying, splay (d'une ouverture).

évaser [-ze] v. tr. (1). To flare (une cloche, une jupe, un tuyau); to splay (une ouverture).
— v. pr. **S'évaser,** to flare (jupe); to splay (ouverture); *qui s'évase,* broadening (chenal).

évasif, ive [-zif, i:v] adj. Evasive, shifty. ‖ Jᴜʀ. Escape (clause).

évasion [-zjɔ̃] f. Escape (de prison). ‖ Fɪɢ. Escapism; *d'évasion,* escapist (littérature).

évasivement [-zivmɑ̃] adv. Evasively.

évêché [eveʃe] m. Eᴄᴄʟᴇ́s. Bishopric (fonction); bishop's house (ou) palace (palais); see (siège); cathedral town (ville).

éveil [eve:j] m. Awakening. ‖ Fɪɢ. Alert; *donner l'éveil à qqn,* to arouse s.o.'s attention, to awaken s.o.'s suspicions. ‖ Fɪɢ. Dawning (de l'amour).

éveillé, ée [eveje] adj. Awake; *bien éveillé,* wide-awake. ‖ Fɪɢ. Wakeful, vigilant (en alerte). ‖ Fɪɢ. Brisk, sprightly (esprit). [V. ᴅᴇ́ɢᴏᴜʀᴅɪ.]

éveiller v. tr. (1). To wake up, to awake; *éveillez-moi à six heures demain,* call me at six tomorrow. ‖ Fɪɢ. To kindle (l'amour); to attract (l'attention); to awake (la curiosité, l'espoir, l'intelligence, une passion); to arouse (la jalousie, les soupçons); to stir up (qqn); *éveiller l'intérêt de,* to interest.
— v. pr. **S'éveiller,** to wake up, to awake. ‖ Fɪɢ. To awaken.

événement [evɛnmɑ̃] m. Event (à sensation); occurrence (fait).

événementiel, elle [-mɑ̃sjɛl] adj. *Histoire événementielle,* factual history.

évent [evɑ̃] m. Flatness (d'une boisson); staleness (de la nourriture). ‖ Open air (air libre); ventilation; vent-hole (trou d'aération). ‖ Zᴏᴏʟ. Spout, spout-hole (de baleine). ‖ Mɪʟɪᴛ. Windage.

éventail [evɑ̃ta:j] m. Fan; *se déployer en éventail,* to fan out. ‖ Fɪɴ. Range (des salaires).

éventaire [evɑ̃tɛ:r] m. Flower-basket (de bouquetière); stall, stand (de marché).

éventé, ée [evɑ̃te] adj. Flat (boisson); stale (nourriture); evaporated (odeur). ‖ Fɪɢ. Disclosed, out (nouvelle).

éventer v. tr. (1). To fan (avec un éventail). ‖ To air, to ventilate (aérer). ‖ To flatten (la boisson); to stale (la nourriture). ‖ Nᴀᴜᴛ. To fill (une voile). ‖ Fɪɢ. To discover (une piste); to disclose (un secret).
— v. pr. **S'éventer,** to fan oneself (personne). ‖ To go flat, to go off (boisson); to go stale, to go off (nourriture). ‖ Fɪɢ. To come out, to come to light (secret, vérité).

éventration [evɑ̃trasjɔ̃] f. Eventration.

éventrer [-tre] v. tr. (1). To disembowel (qqn). ‖ Fɪɢ. To break open (un coffre); to rip open (un paquet, un sac).

éventreur [-trœ:r] m. Ripper.

éventualité [evɑ̃tɥalite] f. Possibility (d'un fait); *dans l'éventualité de,* in the event of. ‖ Eventuality (fait); *prêt à toute éventualité,* ready for every emergency.

éventuel, elle [-ɛl] adj. Eventual, possible. ‖ Jᴜʀ. Conditional (clause); *à titre éventuel,* as a possibility.
— m. Eventuality. ‖ Jᴜʀ. Perquisiter; casual profit.

éventuellement [-ɛlmɑ̃] adv. Possibly, eventually; occasionally; on occasion.

évêque [evɛ:k] m. Eᴄᴄʟᴇ́s. Bishop (de, of).

évertuer (s') [sevɛrtɥe] v. pr. (1). Fᴀᴍ. To peg away (à, at); to exert oneself (à, to); U. S. to hump oneself.

éviction [eviksjɔ̃] f. Jᴜʀ. Eviction.

évidage [evida:ʒ] m. Hollowing out.

évidé, ée [-de] adj. Hollow (en creux); grooved (en long). ‖ Nᴀᴜᴛ. Clean.

évidement [evidmɑ̃] m. Hollow (creux); groove (rainure).

évidemment [evidamɑ̃] adv. Evidently, clearly, obviously (manifestement). ‖ Of course (naturellement).

évidence [-dɑ̃:s] f. Obviousness (d'un fait); matter of fact (fait); *il est de toute évidence,* it is obvious; *nier l'évidence,* to deny the obvious. ‖ Conspicuousness; *bien en évidence,* conspicuously; *mettre en évidence,* to place in a prominent position (qqch.); to put forward (qqn); *se mettre en évidence,* to push oneself forward, to cut a conspicuous figure.

évident, ente [-dɑ̃, ɑ̃:t] adj. Evident, obvious.

évider [evide] v. tr. (1). To hollow out (en creux); to groove (en long). ‖ To cut away (entailler).

évidoir [-dwa:r] m. Tᴇᴄʜɴ. Gouge.

évier [evje] m. Sink.

évincement [evɛ̃smɑ̃] m. Supplanting. ‖ Jᴜʀ. Evicting, ejecting.

évincer [-se] v. tr. (6). To supplant. ‖ Jᴜʀ. To evict, to dispossess.

éviscérer [evisere] v. tr. (5). To eviscerate, to disembowel (personne); to gut (animal).

évitable [evitabl] adj. Avoidable.

évitage [-ta:ʒ] m., **évitée** [-te] f. Nᴀᴜᴛ. Swinging (action); swinging-room (lieu).

évitement [-tmɑ̃] m. Cʜ. ᴅᴇ F. Shunting.

éviter [-te] v. tr. (1). To avoid (en général); to evade (un châtiment, un obstacle); to elude, to dodge, to avoid (un coup, une difficulté, une question); to shirk (une corvée, une responsabilité); to escape (un danger); to avoid (qqn); *les choses qu'on ne peut éviter,* things one cannot help; *éviter de faire,* to avoid doing; *éviter que qqn fasse qqch.,* to avoid s.o.'s doing sth.; *éviter d'être entendu,* to avoid being heard; *elle n'a pu éviter de le voir,* she could not help seeing him. ‖ To spare, to save (épargner); *éviter à qqn la peine de faire qqch.,* to spare s.o. the trouble of doing sth. ‖ Mᴇ́ᴅ. To abstain from (l'alcool).
— v. intr. Nᴀᴜᴛ. To swing.

évocable [evɔkabl] adj. Jᴜʀ. That may be removed to a higher court (cause).

évocateur, trice [-tœ:r, tris] adj. Evocative.
— s. Evocator.

évocation [-sjɔ̃] f. Evocation, raising (d'une entité). ‖ Jᴜʀ. Removal. ‖ Fɪɢ. Evocation, calling up, recalling.

évocatoire [-twa:r] adj. Evocatory, evocative.

évolué, ée [evɔlɥe] adj. Developed.

évoluer v. intr. (1). To progress (civilisation); to change (mœurs); to evolve (race). ‖ Tᴇᴄʜɴ. To revolve. ‖ Mɪʟɪᴛ. To manœuvre. ‖ Mᴇ́ᴅ. To run its course (maladie). ‖ Tʜᴇ́ᴀᴛʀ. To go through an act (sur la scène).

évolutif, ive [evɔlytif, i:v] adj. Evolutionary, evolutive. ‖ Mᴇ́ᴅ. Progressive.

évolution [evɔlysjɔ̃] f. Evolution (d'un acrobate); *faire des évolutions,* to perform evolutions. ‖ Mɪʟɪᴛ. Evolution, manœuvre. ‖ Fɪɢ. Evolution (d'une civilisation, d'un projet, d'une race); march (des événements); development (d'une question).

évolutionnisme [-sjɔnism] m. Evolutionism.

évolutionniste [-sjɔnist] s. Evolutionist.
— adj. Evolutionistic.

évoquer [evɔke] v. tr. (1). To evoke, to raise, to call up (une entité). ‖ Jᴜʀ. To remove (une affaire).

‖ Fɪɢ. To allude to (une information, une nouvelle); to evoke, to conjure up, to recall (le passé).

ex- [ɛks] préf. Ex-, late-; *ex-ambassadeur,* ex-ambassador, former ambassador.

ex abrupto [ɛksabrypto] loc. adv. All of a sudden, out of the blue.

exacerbation [ɛgzasɛrbasjɔ̃] f. Exacerbation.

exacerber [-bə] v. tr. (1). To exacerbate.

exact, acte [ɛgzakt] adj. Punctual; *exact à payer ses dettes,* punctual in paying his debts; *exact à ses rendez-vous,* punctual in keeping his appointments. ‖ Exact, true, right (juste); exact, precise, strict (précis); *au sens exact du mot,* in the strict sense of the word; *est-il exact que?,* is it true that?; *tout à fait exact,* true enough. ‖ Mᴀᴛʜ. Right, accurate (calcul); exact (science).

exactement [ɛgzaktəmɑ̃] adv. Exactly, punctually. ‖ Exactly, truly, rightly; precisely; *c'est exactement le portrait de son père,* he's the very picture of his father. ‖ Exactly, quite so, quite true (dans les réponses).

exacteur [ɛgzaktœːr] m. Exactor.

exaction [-sjɔ̃] f. Exaction. ‖ Extortion.

exactitude [ɛgzaktityːd] f. Exactitude. (V. ᴘᴏɴᴄᴛᴜᴀʟɪᴛᴇ́.) ‖ Exactness, exactitude. (V. ᴘʀᴇ́ᴄɪsɪᴏɴ.) ‖ Exactitude, accuracy (justesse); *d'une exactitude rigoureuse,* accurate to a hair's breadth.

ex æquo [egzekwo] loc. adv. Even; *classés ex aequo,* tying (ou) bracketed together for first place.

exagérateur, trice [egzaʒeratœːr, tris] adj. Exaggerator.

exagération [-rasjɔ̃] f. Exaggeration.

exagéré, ée [-re] adj. Exaggerated (outré); *complaisance, confiance exagérée,* over-complaisance, over-confidence. ‖ Cᴏᴍᴍ. Too high, exorbitant, outrageous (prix). ‖ Fᴀᴍ. Fond of exaggerating (person).

exagérément [-remɑ̃] adv. Exaggeratedly; *exagérément actif,* over-active.

exagérer [-re] v. tr. (1). To exaggerate (les éloges, un événement, une faute); to overcolour (un incident); to overrate (les qualités); to overdo (un rôle).
— v. intr. To exaggerate; *il exagère!,* he is going too far. ‖ Fᴀᴍ. To draw the long bow, to shoot a line (galéjer).

exaltant, ante [ɛgzaltɑ̃, ɑ̃ːt] adj. Elating.

exaltation [-tasjɔ̃] f. Exaltation (excitation). ‖ Elation, exultation. ‖ Exalting (action) [*de,* of]. ‖ Eᴄᴄʟᴇ́s. Exaltation.

exalté, ée [-te] adj. Exalted (imagination). ‖ Impassioned; excited; overstrung (personne).
— s. Hot-head; fire-eater.

exalter [-te] v. tr. (1). To exalt, to cry up (fam.) [glorifier]; to praise (louer). ‖ To exalt, to elevate, to spiritualize (élever). ‖ To excite, to animate, to fire (exciter).
— v. pr. **S'exalter,** to grow excited; to enthuse.

examen [ɛgzamɛ̃] m. Examination; investigation; *examen d'ensemble,* survey; *examen minutieux,* scrutinizing (action); scrutiny (résultat). ‖ Study (d'une question, d'un texte); *à l'examen,* under consideration (question). ‖ Examination; exam (fam.); U. S. quiz (petit examen) [à l'école]. ‖ Aᴜᴛᴏᴍ. *Examen pour le permis de conduire,* driving test, U. S. driver's test. ‖ Eᴄᴄʟᴇ́s. *Examen de conscience,* self-examination; *libre examen,* free enquiry. ‖ Jᴜʀ. Examination.

examinateur, trice [ɛgzaminatœːr, tris] s. Examiner.

examiner [-ne] v. tr. (1). To examine (en général); to survey (dans l'ensemble); to have a good look at (avec attention); to investigate (avec méthode); to scrutinize (avec minutie); to scan (en fouillant du regard); to observe (en observant); *examiner*

qqn d'un œil soupçonneux, to eye s.o. suspiciously. ‖ To study, to go into (une question). ‖ To examine (un candidat). ‖ Mᴇ́ᴅ. To examine; *examiner qqn sur toutes les coutures,* to put s.o. through a searching examination; *se faire examiner,* to get examined, to have oneself examined.
— v. pr. **S'examiner,** to examine oneself (au physique). ‖ To examine one's conscience (au moral).

exanthème [ɛgzɑ̃tɛm] m. Mᴇ́ᴅ. Exanthema.

exaspérant, ante [ɛgzasperɑ̃, ɑ̃ːt] adj. Exasperating, galling. ‖ Unbearable, insufferable (intolérable).

exaspération [-rasjɔ̃] f. Exasperation.

exaspérer [-re] v. tr. (5). To exasperate.
— v. pr. **S'exaspérer,** to become exasperated (ou) enraged (personne). ‖ Mᴇ́ᴅ. To become exasperated (ou) exacerbated (mal).

exaucement [-zosmɑ̃] m. Granting, fulfilment.

exaucer [ɛgzose] v. tr. (6). To grant, to fulfil (un souhait); *exaucer qqn,* to grant s.o.'s request. ‖ Eᴄᴄʟᴇ́s. To hear (une prière); *exaucer qqn,* to hear s.o.'s prayer.

ex cathedra [ɛkskatedra] loc. adv. Ex cathedra.

excavateur, trice [ɛkskavatœːr, tris] s. Tᴇᴄʜɴ. Excavator, digging-machine.

excavation [-vasjɔ̃] f. Excavating (action); excavation (résultat).

excaver [-ve] v. tr. (1). To excavate.

excédant, ante [ɛksedɑ̃, ɑ̃ːt] adj. Excess (poids). ‖ Fᴀᴍ. Exasperating.

excédent m. Excess, surplus; *excédent de poids,* excess weight, overweight; *avoir en excédent,* to have a surplus of. ‖ Fɪɴ. *Excédent budgétaire,* budget surplus; *excédents de caisse,* surplus in the cash, cash overs.

excédentaire [-dɑ̃tɛːr] adj. Excess (poids).

excéder [-de] v. tr. (5). To exceed (un chiffre, une quantité, une valeur). ‖ Fɪɢ. To overstep (les bornes, ses pouvoirs). ‖ Fᴀᴍ. To exasperate (exaspérer); to harass (harceler); *excédé de fatigue,* worn out.

excellemment [ɛksɛlamɑ̃] adv. Excellently.

excellence [-lɑ̃ːs] f. Excellence; *par excellence,* pre-eminently; particularly. ‖ Your Excellency (appellation); Excellency (titre).

excellent, ente [-lɑ̃, ɑ̃ːt] adj. Excellent. ‖ First-class, capital (fam.). ‖ Well-up (*en,* in) [une étude]. ‖ Tʜᴇ́ᴀᴛʀ. *Etre excellent dans un rôle,* to be a great success in a part.

exceller [-le] v. intr. (1). To excel (*en,* in); *exceller à faire,* to excel in doing.

excentré, ée [ɛksɑ̃tre] adj. Remote, outlying (région).

excentrer [-tre] v. tr. (1). Tᴇᴄʜɴ. To offset; to throw off centre.

excentricité [-trisite] f. Remoteness (d'un quartier). ‖ Mᴀᴛʜ., Fɪɢ. Eccentricity.

excentrique [-trik] adj. Remote, outlying (quartier). ‖ Mᴀᴛʜ. Eccentric. ‖ Fɪɢ. Eccentric, cranky, crotchety (personne).
— m. Mᴀᴛʜ. Eccentric.
— s. Fɪɢ. Eccentric, crank.

excentriquement [-trikmɑ̃] adv. Eccentrically.

excepté, ée [ɛksɛpte] adj. Excepted; *mon amie exceptée,* except my friend.
— prép. Except, save; *excepté mon amie,* except my friend; *excepté en ce qui me concerne,* except for me.
— loc. conj. *Excepté que,* except that.

excepter v. tr. (1). To except.

exception [-sjɔ̃] f. Exception; *à l'exception de,* except, with the exception of, barring; *à moins d'exception formelle,* unless expressly provided otherwise; *faire exception à,* to be an exception to; *faire une exception à,* to make an exception to; *sauf exception,* with certain exceptions. ‖ Jᴜʀ.

Bar, incidental plea; *soulever une exception contre*, to raise a protest against.

exceptionnel, elle [-sjɔnɛl] adj. Exceptional, outstanding. ‖ Unfrequent. (V. RARE.)

exceptionnellement [-sjɔnɛlmɑ̃] adv. Exceptionally; by way of exception, as an exception.

excès [ɛksɛ] m. Excess; *excès d'éclairage*, over-lighting; *excès de fatigue*, over-tiredness, over-fatigue; *à l'excès*, to excess, overmuch, excessively, U. S. overly; *pécher par excès de zèle*, to be over-zealous; *travailler avec excès*, to overwork. ‖ Pl. Intemperance; over-eating; *faire des excès de table*, to over-eat, to over-indulge in eating. ‖ JUR. Pl. Excesses; *se livrer à des excès contre*, to lay violent hands on.

excessif, ive [-sif, i:v] adj. Excessive, exaggerated (dépenses); too high, exorbitant, outrageous (prix); *rétribution excessive*, overpayment. ‖ Inordinate (orgueil); *c'est un travail excessif pour*, it's overmuch work for; *excessive confiance en soi*, overweening self-confidence.

excessivement [-sivmɑ̃] m. Excessively; over-much; inordinately (abusivement); exceedingly, extremely (extrêmement).

exciper [ɛksipe] v. intr. JUR. *Exciper de sa bonne foi*, to plead one's good faith; *exciper de sa qualité*, to allege one's quality.

excipient [-pjɑ̃] m. MÉD. Excipient.

excise [ɛksi:z] f. JUR. Excise.

exciser [-ze] v. tr. (1). MÉD. To excise.

excision [-zjɔ̃] f. MÉD. Excision.

excitabilité [ɛksitabilite] f. Excitability.

excitable [-tabl] adj. Excitable.

excitant, ante [-tɑ̃, ɑ̃:t] adj. Exciting (pr. et fig.). — m. Excitant.

excitateur, trice [-tatœ:r, tris] adj. Excitatory, excitative; provocative. ‖ ÉLECTR., MÉD. Exciting. — s. Instigator (*à*, of).

excitation [-tasjɔ̃] f. Excitement. ‖ Instigation, provocation (*à*, to). ‖ ÉLECTR., MÉD. Excitation.

excitatrice [-tatris] f. ÉLECTR. Exciter.

excité, ée [-te] adj. Excited, heated, fired (échauffé). ‖ Spurred on (stimulé).

exciter [-te] v. tr. (1). To excite, to work up, to fire (échauffer); to excite, to irritate (énerver). ‖ To egg on, to incite (encourager) [*à*, to]; to spur (ou) to urge on (stimuler) [*à*, to]; *exciter à agir*, to rouse to action; *exciter l'émulation de qqn*, to put s.o. on his mettle. ‖ To rouse, to work up, to stir up (dresser) [*contre*, against]. ‖ To call forth, to excite, to stir up (l'admiration); to kindle (l'amour); to excite (la curiosité, l'envie, l'intérêt, les passions); to stir up, to rouse (la curiosité, la haine); to sharpen (un désir, une passion). ‖ MÉD. To sharpen (l'appétit); to excite (qqn). ‖ ÉLECTR. To excite. — v. pr. S'exciter, to become excited, to get worked up, to work oneself up. ‖ FAM. To warm up. (V. ÉCHAUFFER [s'].)

exclamatif, ive [ɛksklamatif, i:v] adj. Exclamatory.

exclamation [-sjɔ̃] f. Exclamation. ‖ GRAMM. *Point d'exclamation*, exclamation mark.

exclamer (s') [sɛksklame] v. pr. (1). To exclaim (contre, at, against; devant, at).

exclu, ue [ɛkskly] adj. Excluded, not included (ou) counted (non compris). ‖ Excluded, left out (*de*, of); *il n'est pas exclu que*, it is not out of the question that. ‖ JUR. Debarred (*de*, from).

exclure [-kly:r] v. tr. (29). To exclude, to shut out (*de*, from); to leave out (*de*, of). ‖ To exclude, to prevent (empêcher). ‖ JUR. To debar (*de*, from). — v. pr. S'exclure, to be mutually exclusive, to be incompatible; *cela s'exclut de soi-même*, it is obviously out of the question.

exclusif, ive [ɛksklyzif, i:v] adj. COMM. Sole (agent); exclusive (vente). ‖ JUR. Exclusive (droit). ‖ FIG. Exclusive, jealous.

exclusion [-zjɔ̃] f. Exclusion; *à l'exclusion de*, to the exclusion of, excluding. ‖ Expulsion (d'un élève).

exclusive [-zi:v] f. JUR. Debarment; *prononcer l'exclusive contre*, to refuse to admit.

exclusivement [-zivmɑ̃] adv. Exclusively, exclusive; *un à dix exclusivement*, from one to ten exclusive. ‖ Exclusively, uniquely (seulement).

exclusivisme [-zivism] m. Exclusivism.

exclusivité [-zivite] f. Exclusiveness (caractère). ‖ THÉÂTR. Stage-rights (d'une pièce); *film en exclusivité*, exclusive film, U. S. first-run picture. ‖ COMM. Exclusive right.

excommunication [ɛkskɔmynikasjɔ̃] f. ECCLÉS. Excommunication.

excommunier [-nje] v. tr. (1). ECCLÉS. To excommunicate.

excorier [ɛkskɔrje] v. tr. (1). MÉD. To excoriate; to chafe; to gall (fam.). — v. pr. S'excorier. MÉD. To be excoriated; to peel off, to chafe (fam.).

excrément [ɛkskremɑ̃] m. Excrement.

excrémenteux, euse [-mɑ̃tø, ø:z], **excrémentiel, elle** [-mɑ̃sjɛl] adj. Excrementitious, excremental.

excréter [ɛkskrete] v. tr. (5). To excrete.

excrétion [-sjɔ̃] f. Excretion.

excroissance [ɛkskrwasɑ̃:s] f. Excrescence; protuberance.

excursion [ɛkskyrsjɔ̃] f. Excursion (en général); hiking, hike (en campant); walk, tramp (en se promenant); outing (randonnée, sortie); trip (petit voyage); *excursion accompagnée*, conducted tour. ‖ MILIT. Incursion, inroad.

excursionner [-sjɔne] v. tr. (1). To make an excursion.

excursionniste [-sjɔnist] s. Excursionist, tourist (en général); hiker (à pied).

excusable [ɛkskyzabl] adj. Excusable.

excuse [ɛksky:z] f. Excuse; *invoquer qqch. pour excuse*, to make sth. one's excuse; *ne pas avoir d'excuse*, to admit of no excuse (conduite); to have no excuse (personne). ‖ Excuse, pretext. ‖ Apology; *faire ses excuses à qqn pour*, to apologize to s.o. for.

excuser [-kyze] v. tr. (1). To excuse, to extenuate (une faute); to excuse, to pardon (une faute, qqn); *excuser qqn de faire qqch.*, to excuse s.o.'s doing sth., to excuse s.o. for (ou) from doing sth. ‖ To excuse (un absent) [*auprès de*, to]; *se faire excuser*, to ask to be excused. — v. pr. S'excuser, to apologize (*auprès de*, to; *de*, for); *s'excuser sur qqch.*, to make sth. one's excuse; *s'excuser sur qqn*, to shift the responsibility on to s.o.'s shoulders. ‖ To decline an invitation.

exécrable [ɛgsekrabl] adj. Execrable. (V. DÉTESTABLE.) ‖ Rotten, wretched (temps).

exécrablement [-bləmɑ̃] adv. Execrably.

exécration [-sjɔ̃] f. Execration. (V. HORREUR.)

exécrer [ɛgzekre] v. tr. (5). To execrate.

exécutable [ɛgzekytabl] adj. Feasible, workable, realizable (plan, projet). ‖ MUS. Playable.

exécutant, ante [-tɑ̃, ɑ̃:t] s. MUS. Executant; performer.

exécuter [-te] v. tr. (1). To execute (en général); to work (une broderie, un plan); to perform (un mouvement, un travail); to carry out (un ordre); to work out, to realize (un projet); to fulfil (une promesse). ‖ MUS. To perform, to execute (une danse, un morceau). ‖ COMM. To carry out (une commande). ‖ FIN. To sell out against (un acheteur). ‖ JUR. To distrain upon (un débiteur); to execute (un condamné). ‖ MÉD. To make up (une

ordonnance). ‖ Fam. To slash, to flay (éreinter).
— v. pr. S'exécuter, to be executed (ou) performed. ‖ Fam. To comply (agir); to shell out,
to put one's hand down (payer).

exécuteur [-tœ:r] m. Executor. ‖ Jur. Exécuteur
des hautes œuvres, public executioner, hangman,
headsman; exécuteur testamentaire, executor.

exécutrice [-tris] f. Executrix.

exécutif, ive [-tif, i:v] adj., m. Executive.

exécution [-sjɔ̃] f. Execution (en général); carrying
out (d'un ordre); working out (d'un projet); fulfilment (d'une promesse); accomplishment, performance (d'un travail); en exécution de, in pursuance of, conformably to, in conformance with;
mettre à exécution, to carry out; mise à exécution
de, enforcement (ou) operation of. ‖ Execution
travail); une belle exécution, show business; good
workmanship; finesse d'exécution, finish. ‖ Mus.
Performance, execution. ‖ Comm. Performance. ‖
Fin. Selling out. ‖ Jur. Distraint of property
(d'un débiteur); execution (d'un condamné). ‖
Fam. Slashing (éreintement).

exécutoire [-twa:r] adj. Jur. Enforceable (contrat);
executory (formule); mesure exécutoire, execution.
— m. Jur. Writ of execution.

exégèse [ɛgʒeʒɛ:z] f. Exegesis.

exégète [-ʒɛt] m. Exegete.

exemplaire [ɛgzɑ̃plɛ:r] adj. Condign (châtiment);
exemplary (punition, vie).
— m. Copy (d'un livre, d'un texte); en deux,
trois exemplaires, in duplicate, triplicate. ‖ Specimen, example (d'un travail).

exemplairement [-mɑ̃] adv. Exemplarily.

exemplarité [ɛgzɑ̃plarite] f. Exemplariness.

exemple [ɛgzɑ̃:pl] m. Example; à l'exemple de,
after the example of; donner l'exemple, to give
(ou) set the example; prendre exemple sur qqn,
to take s.o. as one's model. ‖ Example, warning;
faire un exemple, to make an example. ‖ Example,
precedent; sans exemple, unprecedented (fait). ‖
Example, instance; par exemple, for instance (ou)
example. ‖ Loc. Par exemple, on the other hand,
in compensation (en revanche); elle est laide,
mais par exemple elle est bonne, she is plain,
but, mind you, she is good-natured. ‖ Par
exemple !, well !, my word !, indeed !, to be sure !;
ah non, par exemple !, Good heavens, no !

exempt, empte [ɛgzɑ̃, ɑ̃:t] adj. Exempt (de,
from); exempt d'accidents, de soucis, accident-,
care-free. ‖ Milit. Excused (de, from).

exempt m. † Police officer.

exempté, ée [ɛgzɑ̃te] adj. Exempt, exempted.

exempter v. tr. (1). To exempt, to free (de, from).
[V. Exonérer.] ‖ Milit. To exempt. ‖ Méd. To
preserve (de, from).
— v. pr. S'exempter, to exempt oneself (de,
from). ‖ Milit. S'exempter de corvée, to shirk
fatigue.

exemption [ɛgzɑ̃psjɔ̃] f. Exemption (de, from).

exerçant, ante [ɛgzɛrsɑ̃, ɑ̃:t] adj. Méd. Practising.

exercé, ée [-se] adj. Experienced, practised,
trained (à, in). ‖ Milit. Trained.

exercer [-se] v. tr. (6). To exercise, to train (le
corps, qqn); to train (l'esprit); to give scope to
(son imagination, ses talents). ‖ To have (une
action); to exercise (un droit, une influence); to
exert (une emprise); to make (des représailles).
‖ To exercise, to carry on (un métier); to be
engaged in (une profession). ‖ Jur. To institute
(des poursuites). ‖ Méd. To practise (la médecine). ‖ Sports. To train (qqn). ‖ Milit. To
drill, to train.
— v. intr. Méd. To practise; il n'exerce plus, he
is no longer in practice.
— v. pr. S'exercer, to practise; s'exercer à sau-

ter, to practise jumping. ‖ To exert itself, to be
exerted (sur, on) [force, influence, talent].

exercice [-sis] m. Exercise (du corps); faire de
l'exercice, to do physical exercises. ‖ Training,
practice (entraînement). ‖ Exercise (d'un droit,
d'une faculté). ‖ Exercise (d'une fonction, d'un
métier); dans l'exercice de ses fonctions, in the
discharge of his duties; en exercice, practising,
in active employment. ‖ Sports. Practice, training.
‖ Milit. Drill; aller à l'exercice, to go on parade;
faire l'exercice, to drill; exercice à la cible, target
practice; exercices de pointage, aiming drill. ‖
Mus. Practice; faire des exercices, to practise. ‖
Méd. Practice (de la médecine). ‖ Fin. Fiscal (ou)
trading year; exercice budgétaire, financial (ou)
U. S. fiscal year. ‖ Ecclés. Exercise.

exérèse [ɛgzerɛ:z] f. Méd. Removal, excision,
resection.

exergue [ɛgzɛrg] m. Exergue.

exfoliation [ɛksfɔljasjɔ̃] f. Exfoliation.

exfolier (s') [sɛksfɔlje] v. pr. (1). To exfoliate.

exhalaison [ɛgzalɛzɔ̃] f. Exhalation. ‖ Pl. Fire-
damp (gaz); fumes (vapeurs). ‖ Smell (de la cuisine); bouquet (du vin).

exhaler [-le] v. tr. (1). To exhale (du gaz, une
odeur, des vapeurs); to emit (de la fumée, une
odeur). ‖ To give, to utter (un gémissement); to
exhale, to vent, to give free course to (sa rage);
to heave, to breathe (un soupir).
— v. pr. S'exhaler, to exhale (gaz, odeur, vapeur).
‖ To be uttered (gémissement); to find a vent
(colère); to be breathed (ou) heaved (soupir).

exhaussement [ɛgzosmɑ̃] m. Raising.

exhausser [-se] v. tr. (1). To raise.
— v. pr. S'exhausser, to rise.

exhaustif, ive [ɛgzostif, i:v] adj. Exhaustive.

exhaustivement [-tivmɑ̃] adv. Exhaustively,
thoroughly.

exhérédation [ɛgzeredasjɔ̃] f. Jur. Disinheritance.

exhéréder [-de] v. tr. (5). Jur. To disinherit.

exhiber [ɛgzibe] v. tr. (1). To exhibit; to display
(qqch.). ‖ Jur. To produce. ‖ Fam. To parade (ses
connaissances); to display, to flaunt, to make a
parade of (son érudition, son luxe); to show off
(sa force, ses talents); to sport, to show off, to
flaunt (ses toilettes).
— v. pr. S'exhiber, to show oneself, to make an
exhibition of oneself.

exhibition [-bisjɔ̃] f. Exhibition, display, parade.
‖ Jur. Producing, production. ‖ Théâtr. Exhibition.

exhibitionnisme [-bisjɔnism] m. Exhibitionism.

exhibitionniste [-bisjɔnist] s. Exhibitionist.

exhortation [ɛgzɔrtasjɔ̃] f. Exhortation.

exhorter [-te] v. tr. (1). To exhort. ‖ To appeal
to; exhorter qqn à, to urge s.o. to.

exhumation [ɛgzymasjɔ̃] f. Exhumation, disinterment. ‖ Fam. Unearthing, hunting out.

exhumer [-me] v. tr. (1). To exhume. (V. Déterrer.) ‖ Fig. To unearth, to bring to light.

exigeant, eante [ɛgziʒɑ̃, ɑ̃:t] adj. Exacting;
exigeant pour la nourriture, finicky, faddy, fastidious.

exigence [-ʒɑ̃:s] f. Exigency, exigence (nécessité);
les exigences de l'heure, the exigencies of the
hour. ‖ Exactingness (de qqn). ‖ Pl. Requirements,
unreasonable demands; céder aux exigences de,
to indulge the fancies of, to humour.

exiger [-ʒe] v. tr. (7). To demand (de, of, from);
exiger de savoir, to demand to know. ‖ To claim,
to require, to demand (nécessiter); exiger des
soins attentifs, to require (ou) demand great care.
‖ Jur. Exiger la mise aux voix, to insist on a
division.

exigibilité [-ʒibilite] f. Exigibility.

exigible [-ʒibl] adj. Exigible (*de,* from, against). ‖ FIN. Payable; *prêt exigible,* call loan.

exigu, uë [-gy] adj. Exiguous (lieu). ‖ FIN. Exiguous, scanty (revenu).

exiguïté [-gɥite] f. Exiguity (d'un lieu). ‖ FIN. Exiguousness, scantiness (des revenus).

exil [ɛgzil] m. Exile.

exilé, ée [-le] adj. Exiled. (V. BANNI.) — s. Exile.

exiler [-le] v. tr. (1). To exile [*de,* from]. — v. pr. **S'exiler,** to go into exile; to expatriate oneself.

existant, ante [ɛgzistɑ̃, ɑ̃:t] adj. Existing, being. ‖ Existent (actuel); extant, in existence (subsistant).

existence [-tɑ̃:s] f. Existence, being (être). ‖ Existence, life (vie).

existentialisme [-tɑ̃sjalism] m. PHILOS. Existentialism.

existentialiste [-tɑ̃sjalist] s. PHILOS. Existentialist.

existentiel, elle [-tɑ̃sjɛl] adj. Existential.

exister [-te] v. intr. (1). To exist, to be, to be in existence (être); *exister depuis cent ans,* to have been in existence for a hundred years. ‖ To be extant, to exist, to continue (subsister); *il en existe encore un,* there is still one.

ex-libris [ɛkslibris] m. invar. Book-plate, ex-libris; *collectionneur d'ex-libris,* ex-librist.

exode [ɛgzɔd] m. ECCLÉS. Exodus. ‖ FIG. Exodus. ‖ *Exode rural,* drift from the countryside. ‖ *Exode des cerveaux,* brain drain.

exogame [ɛgzɔgam] adj. Exogamous.

exonération [ɛgzɔnerasjɔ̃] f. Exoneration (*de,* from); remission (*de,* of).

exonérer [-re] v. tr. (5). To exonerate (*de,* from).

exophtalmie [ɛgzɔftalmi] f. MÉD. Exophthalmus.

exorbitant, ante [ɛgzɔrbitɑ̃, ɑ̃:t] adj. Exorbitant, unreasonable, extravagant (demande); exorbitant, outrageous (prix); *d'une façon exorbitante,* exorbitantly.

exorbité, ée [-te] adj. *Les yeux exorbités,* with one's eyes starting out of one's head.

exorcisation [ɛgzɔrsizasjɔ̃] f. Exorcizing.

exorciser [-size] v. tr. (1). ECCLÉS. To exorcize.

exorcisme [-sism] m. ECCLÉS. Exorcism.

exorciste [-sist] m. ECCLÉS. Exorcist.

exorde [ɛgzɔrd] m. Exordium. ‖ FAM. Beginning.

exosmose [ɛgzɔsmo:z] f. PHYS. Exosmosis.

exotérique [ɛgzɔterik] adj. Exoteric.

exothermique [ɛgzɔtɛrmik] adj. CHIM. Exothermic.

exotique [ɛgzɔtik] adj. Exotic.

exotisme [-tism] m. Exoticism.

expansé, ée [ɛkspɑ̃se] adj. Expanded; *polystyrène expansé,* expanded polystyrene.

expansibilité [ɛkspɑ̃sibilite] f. PHYS. Expansibility. ‖ FIG. Expansiveness.

expansible [-sibl] adj. PHYS. Expansible.

expansif, ive [-sif, i:v] adj. PHYS. Expansive (force, gaz). ‖ FIG. Expansive (v. COMMUNICATIF); *devenir expansif,* to expand.

expansion [-sjɔ̃] f. Expansion, spread (élargissement). ‖ PHYS. Expansion. ‖ FIG. Expansiveness.

expansionnisme [-sjɔnism] m. Expansionism.

expansionniste [-sjɔnist] adj., s. Expansionist.

expansivité [-sivite] f. Expansivity (d'un matériau). ‖ Expansiveness, openness (d'une personne).

expatriation [ɛkspatrjasjɔ̃] f. Expatriation.

expatrier [-trje] v. tr. (1). To banish, to expatriate. — v. pr. **S'expatrier,** to expatriate oneself.

expectant, ante [ɛkspɛktɑ̃, ɑ̃:t] adj. Expectant.

expectative [-tati:v] f. Expectancy; *en expectative,* in expectancy; *dans l'expectative,* expectantly; waiting (*de,* for).

expectorant [ɛkspɛktɔrɑ̃] adj., m. MÉD. Expectorant.

expectoration [-rasjɔ̃] f. MÉD. Expectoration (action); sputum (crachat).

expectorer [-re] v. tr. (1). MÉD. To expectorate.

expédient [ɛkspedjɑ̃] m. Expedient; *homme d'expédient,* man of resource; *vivre d'expédients,* to live by one's wits. — adj. Expedient (*de,* to); advisable.

expédier [-dje] v. tr. (1). To dispatch, to send, to forward (un colis, une dépêche, une lettre); *expédier par avion, par voiture,* to send by airmail, by car; *expédier par bateau, par la poste,* to ship, to post (ou) to mail. ‖ To send off (qqn) [dépêcher]; *expédiez-le chez moi,* send him along. ‖ To get rid of (qqn) [se débarrasser de]. ‖ To dispatch, to expedite (une affaire, un repas); *expédier un verre de vin,* to down (ou) toss off a glass of wine. ‖ JUR. To draw up a copy of (un acte). ‖ FAM. To finish off (un animal); to dispatch, to account for (qqn) [tuer].

expéditeur, trice [-ditœ:r, tris] s. Sender, forwarder, consigner (d'un colis); sender, addresser (d'une lettre). ‖ COMM. Forwarding agent (expéditionnaire). — adj. Forwarding (agence, gare).

expéditif, ive [-ditif, i:v] adj. Expeditious, speedy, quick.

expédition [-disjɔ̃] f. Sending, dispatch, forwarding (action); consignment, shipment (envoi); *service des expéditions,* dispatch service. ‖ Dispatch (d'une affaire). ‖ Copy (exemplaire); *en quatre expéditions,* in quadruplicate. ‖ MILIT. Expedition; *en expédition en,* on an expedition to.

expéditionnaire [-disjɔnɛ:r] m. COMM. Forwarding agent. ‖ JUR. Copying clerk, writer. — adj. MILIT. Expeditionary. ‖ JUR. Copying.

expéditivement [-ditivmɑ̃] adv. Expeditiously.

expérience [ɛksperjɑ̃:s] f. Experience; *avoir de l'expérience,* to be experienced; *avoir fait l'expérience de qqch.,* to know sth. from experience; *faire une expérience,* to have an experience; *l'expérience des affaires,* business experience; *l'expérience de la cuisine,* experience in cooking; *par expérience,* from experience. ‖ CHIM., PHYS. Experiment, test (épreuve); *faire une expérience,* to make (ou) do an experiment, to experiment (*sur,* on).

expérimental, ale [ɛksperimɑ̃tal] adj. Experimental.

expérimentalement [-talmɑ̃] adv. Experimentally.

expérimentateur, trice [-tatœ:r, tris] s. Experimentalist; experimenter.

expérimentation [-tasjɔ̃] f. Experimenting (action); experimentation (résultat).

expérimenté, ée [-te] adj. Experienced, practised, trained. ‖ Wise (vieillard).

expérimenter [-te] v. tr. (1). To test (qqch.). — v. intr. To experiment (*sur,* on, upon).

expert [ɛkspɛr] adj. Expert, skilled, skilful (*en,* in); *d'un œil expert,* with the eye of an expert. — s. Expert (*en, in, at*). ‖ Valuer, appraiser (estimateur); *expert juré,* official referee. ‖ MÉD. Medical expert. ‖ **Expert-comptable,** m. Chartered accountant.

expertise [-ti:z] f. Expert valuation (ou) appraisal (d'un objet). ‖ Expert advice (avis); expert evidence (document); survey (rapport). ‖ NAUT. Survey.

expertiser [-tize] v. tr. (1). To value, to appraise (un objet); *expertiser à dix mille francs,* to estimate (ou) to put down as worth ten thousand francs. ‖ NAUT. To survey.

expiable [ɛkspjabl] adj. Expiable.

expiation [-sjɔ̃] f. Expiation. ‖ ECCLÉS. Atonement (*de,* for).

expiatoire [-twa:r] adj. Expiatory.

expier [εkspje] v. tr. (1). To expiate. ‖ ECCLÉS. To atone for.

expirant, ante [εkspirᾶ, ᾶ:t] adj. Expiring (personne) ; dying (jour, regard, voix).

expiration [-rasjɔ̃] f. MÉD. Expiration. ‖ FIG. Expiration, expiry; *venir à expiration,* to expire.

expirer [-re] v. tr. (1). To expire, to breathe out. — v. intr. To expire, to breathe out. ‖ To expire, to pass away. (V. MOURIR.) ‖ JUR. To expire (bail, contrat). ‖ FIG. To expire (espoir); to die out (voix).

explétif, ive [εkspletif, i:v] adj., m. GRAMM. Expletive.

explicable [εksplikabl] adj. Explainable, explicable.

explicateur, trice [-tœ:r, tris] s. Explainer.

explicatif, ive [-tif, i:v] adj. Explicative, explanatory ; *mot explicatif,* explicative.

explication [-sjɔ̃] f. Explanation ; exposition. ‖ Explanation, reason ; *fournir des explications,* to enter into explanations ; *un fait qui demande une explication,* a fact which needs explaining. ‖ Explication ; *explication grammaticale,* grammatical remarks ; *explication de texte,* close analysis, textual commentary. ‖ Explanation (avec, with) ; *avoir une explication avec,* to come to an explanation with.

explicite [εksplisit] adj. Explicit ; *en termes explicites,* explicitly.

explicitement [-tmᾶ] adv. Explicitly.

expliciter [-te] v. tr. (1). To make clearer, to be more explicit in (ses affirmations). — v. pr. **S'expliciter,** to be explicit (*au sujet de,* about).

expliquer [εksplike] v. tr. (1). To explain (en général) ; to expound (des principes, une théorie) ; to explain, to comment upon (un texte). ‖ To unriddle (une énigme, un rêve) ; to explain, to unshroud (un mystère) ; to solve (un problème). ‖ To make known, to disclose (ses desseins). ‖ To account for (une circonstance, un échec) ; *explique cela qui pourra,* it is unaccountable. — v. pr. **S'expliquer,** to explain oneself ; *je m'explique,* this is what I mean. ‖ To explain one's intentions (ou) actions. ‖ To have it out (avec, with) ; *s'expliquer vivement avec qqn,* to have words with s.o. ‖ To be accounted for (circonstance, fait) ; *il ne se l'explique pas,* he can't account for it.

exploit [εksplwa] m. Exploit, feat, prowess. ‖ JUR. Writ (d'huissier); *dresser, signifier un exploit,* to draw up, to serve a writ.

exploitable [-tabl] adj. Exploitable, workable (mine, procédé). ‖ JUR. Distrainable (biens).

exploitant, ante [-tᾶ, ᾶ:t] s. Worker (d'une mine). ‖ AGRIC. Exploiter, farmer, cultivator. ‖ JUR. Writ-server. — adj. Operating. ‖ AGRIC. Working, farming. ‖ JUR. Writ-serving.

exploitation [-tasjɔ̃] f. Exploitation ; management, quarrying (d'une carrière) ; working (d'une forêt, d'une mine) ; *matériel d'exploitation,* working stock. ‖ Management (d'une affaire, d'une usine) ; *exploitation en régie,* State management. ‖ AGRIC. Farming (action) ; farm (propriété). ‖ COMM. Concern. ‖ FIG. Exploitation, exploiting (de qqn) ; sweating (des ouvriers).

exploiter [-te] v. tr. (1). To exploit ; to manage, to quarry (une carrière) ; to work (une forêt, une mine). ‖ To manage (une affaire, une usine). ‖ AGRIC. To farm (une propriété). ‖ COMM. To run (un fonds). ‖ FAM. To exploit (qqn, la sottise, le talent) ; to exploit, to take unfair advantage of (qqn) ; to sweat (des ouvriers).

exploiteur, euse [-tœ:r, ø:z] s. FAM. Exploiter ; sweater. — m. Operative (d'une mine). ‖ AGRIC. Farmer.

explorateur, trice [-tœ:r, tris] s. Explorer. — m. MÉD. Probe, trocar.

exploration [-rasjɔ̃] f. Exploration. ‖ ELECTR. Dissection, U. S. scanning (en T. V.).

explorer [-re] v. tr. (1). To explore (les lieux, le terrain). ‖ MÉD. To explore, to probe. ‖ RADIO. To scan (en T. V.). ‖ FIG. To explore, to examine (les archives).

exploser [εksploze] v. intr. (1). To explode, to blow up, to burst (appareil, ballon, bombe, mine, poudrière) ; *faire exploser,* to explode, to blow up, to touch off. ‖ FIG. To burst out (colère). ‖ FAM. To flare up (personne).

explosibilité [-zibilite] f. Explosiveness.

explosible [-zibl] adj. Explosive.

explosif, ive [-zif, i:v] adj., m. Explosive.

explosive f. GRAMM. Explosive, plosive.

explosion [-zjɔ̃] f. Blowing up, explosion (d'un appareil, d'une bombe, d'une mine, de la poudre) ; bursting (d'un ballon, d'une bombe) ; *faire explosion,* to explode. ‖ TECHN. A explosion, internal combustion (moteur). ‖ FIG. Burst, outburst (de colère) ; outburst, passion (de douleur).

exponentiel, elle [εkspɔnᾶsjἔl] adj. MATH. Exponential.

exportable [εkspɔrtabl] adj. Exportable.

exportateur, trice [-tatœ:r, tris] s. Exporter. — adj. Exporting.

exportation [-tasjɔ̃] f. COMM. Exportation ; export (*en provenance de,* from) ; *article d'exportation,* export item, export ; *d'exportation,* export (commerce). ‖ Pl. Exports (articles). ‖ FIN. *Exportation de capitaux,* export of money (ou) currency.

exporter [-te] v. tr. (1). COMM. To export (*de,* from).

exposant [εkspozᾶ] m. Exhibitor (dans une exposition. ‖ MATH. Exponent, index.

exposé, ée [-ze] adj. Exposed, exhibited, displayed (objets) ; hung (tableau) ; *demeurer exposé,* to be on display ; *être exposé,* to lie in state (mort). ‖ Facing (maison) ; *exposé au nord,* facing north. ‖ Exposed, dangerous (lieu dangereux) ; exposed, open (lieu découvert). ‖ Exposed, subject, liable (à, to) ; *exposé à la critique,* subject to criticism ; *exposé à l'erreur,* liable to error. ‖ JUR. Liable (à, to) [des poursuites]. — m. Exposé, account, statement ; *faire un exposé de,* to give an account of ; *faire un exposé sur Ruskin,* to read a paper on Ruskin. ‖ JUR. Recital (des faits) ; pleading (des moyens).

exposer [-ze] v. tr. (1). To expose, to display (en général). ‖ To show (des animaux) ; to exhibit (des collections). ‖ To lie in state (un défunt). ‖ To expose (un enfant). ‖ To build facing (sa maison) ; *être exposé à l'est,* to face (ou) to look east. ‖ To expose, to jeopardize, to endanger (sa vie) ; to expose, to subject (à, to). ‖ To expose, to state, to set forth (des faits, un grief, une réclamation). ‖ To expose, to disclose (ses idées, ses projets). ‖ PHYS. To expose (en photo). ‖ ECCLÉS. To expose (le Saint Sacrement). — v. pr. **S'exposer,** to risk one's life ; to take risks ; *s'exposer à,* to expose oneself to (la critique, la mort) ; to render oneself liable to (des ennuis, des poursuites). ‖ To risk ; *s'exposer à attendre,* to run the risk of waiting.

exposition [-zisjɔ̃] f. Exposition, exposure, display (d'objets). ‖ Show (d'animaux, de fleurs) ; exhibition (de collections, de manuscrits, de tableaux) ; *Exposition universelle,* Universal Exhibition, World Fair ; *salle d'exposition,* showroom. ‖ Lying in state (d'un défunt). ‖ Exposure (d'un enfant). ‖ Exposure (à, to) [l'air, la critique, le danger]. ‖ Lie (d'une côte) ; aspect (d'une maison). ‖ Exposition, disclosure (des idées) ; exposition, statement (des faits) ; exposition, commentary (d'une œuvre). ‖ Exposure, showing up (révélation). ‖ Introduction (dans un texte).

exprès, esse [εksprε, ε:s] adj. Express, absolute, formal. ‖ JUR. *Convention expresse,* stated agreement.
— m. Express messenger.

exprès adv. On purpose, purposely, intentionally (volontairement); *faire exprès,* to do on purpose (ou) deliberately; *vous m'avez fait mal!, Je l'ai fait exprès,* you hurt me!, I meant to! ‖ FAM. *Un fait exprès,* something done on purpose.

express [εksprεs] adj. COMM., CH. DE F. Express.
— m. CH. DE F. Express, express train.

expressément [-semɑ̃] adv. Expressly.

expressif, ive [-sif, i:v] adj. Expressive, significant (geste); expressive (mot, style).

expression [-sjɔ̃] f. Pressing, squeezing out, expression (du jus, du suc). ‖ Expression (de la pensée, des sentiments); *au-delà de toute expression,* beyond (ou) past expression, inexpressibly. ‖ Expression (du visage). ‖ Expression, idiom, phrase (locution); word, term (mot). ‖ MUS. Expression. ‖ MATH. Expression; *réduire à la plus simple expression,* to reduce to the simplest expression (ou) to the lowest terms. ‖ FAM. *Réduit à la plus simple expression,* in one's birthday-suit.

expressionnisme [-sjɔnism] m. ARTS. Expressionism.

expressionniste [-sjɔnist] adj. ARTS. Expressionist, expressionistic.
— s. ARTS. Expressionist.

expressivement [-sivmɑ̃] adv. Expressively.

expressivité [sivite] f. Expressiveness.

exprimable [εksprimabl] adj. Expressible.

exprimer [-me] v. tr. (1). To press, to squeeze; *exprimer en écrasant, en pressant, en tordant,* to crush out, to squeeze out, to wring out. ‖ To express, to word (une idée); to express, to manifest (un sentiment); *qu'on ne peut exprimer,* inexpressible, unspeakable, unutterable. ‖ To convey (communiquer); *exprimer ses conceptions, ses vœux,* to convey one's meaning, wishes.
— v. pr. **S'exprimer,** to be expressed (ou) conveyed (chose, idée, sentiment); to express oneself (personne); *si l'on peut s'exprimer ainsi,* if one may put it in that way.

expropriateur, trice [εksproprijatœ:r, tris] adj. Expropriator.

expropriation [εksproprijasjɔ̃] f. Expropriation.

exproprier [-je] v. tr. (1). To expropriate.

expulser [εkspylse] v. tr. (1). To evict, to eject, to turn out (un locataire, qqn). ‖ To expel (un élève); to send down, to expel (un étudiant). ‖ To deport (un étranger). ‖ MÉD. To evacuate (des gaz, des matières). ‖ TECHN. To discharge (de la vapeur). ‖ FAM. To oust (évincer) [*de,* from].

expulsif, ive [-sif, i:v] adj. Expulsive.

expulsion [-sjɔ̃] f. Expulsion, ejection, eviction, turning out (d'un locataire, de qqn). ‖ Expulsion (d'un élève); expulsion, rustication, sending down (d'un étudiant). ‖ Deportation (d'un étranger). ‖ MÉD. Evacuation (des matières). ‖ TECHN. Discharge (des vapeurs).

expurgation [εkspyrgasjɔ̃] f. Expurgation.

expurgatoire [-gatwa:r] adj. Expurgatory.

expurgé, ée [-ʒe] adj. Expurgated, bowdlerized.

expurger v. tr. (7). To expurgate, to bowdlerize.

exquis, ise [εski, iz] adj. Exquisite.

exquisément [-zemɑ̃] adv. Exquisitely.

exsangue [εksɑ̃:g] adj. Exsanguine (anémique); bloodless (dépourvu de sang).

exsudat [εksyda] m., **exsudation** [εksydasjɔ̃] f. MÉD. Exudation.

exsuder [-de] v. tr., intr. (1). MÉD. To exude.

extase [εkstɑ:z] f. ECCLÉS., MÉD. Ecstasy; *en extase,* in an ecstasy. ‖ FIG. Ecstasy, rapture (v. TRANSPORT); *être en extase devant,* to go into

extasies (ou) raptures over; *plonger qqn dans l'extase,* to send s.o. into ecstasies.

extasié, ée [-tɑzje] adj. Ecstatic, enraptured.

extasier (s') [sεkstazje] v. pr. (1). To go into ecstasies (ou) raptures (*devant,* over); *faire s'extasier qqn,* to throw s.o. into raptures.

extatique [εkstatik] adj. ECCLÉS., MÉD. Ecstatic. ‖ FIG. Ecstatic, rapturous, transported, entranced.

extemporané, ée [εkstɑ̃pɔrane] adj. MÉD. Extemporaneous; *pour administration extemporanée,* ready for use. ‖ JUR. Unpremeditated (délit).

extenseur [εkstɑ̃sœ:r] m. Developer (de gymnastique). ‖ MÉD. Extensor. ‖ AVIAT. Shock-absorber.

extensibilité [-sibilite] f. Extensibility.

extensible [-sibl] adj. Extensible, extensile.

extensif, ive [-sif, i:v] adj. TECHN. Tensile. ‖ AGRIC. Extensive. ‖ FIG. Wide (sens).

extension [-sjɔ̃] f. Extension (en général); stretching (d'une peau, d'un tissu). ‖ Prolongation (de la durée); extension (de la validité). ‖ Extension, enlargement (d'un territoire). ‖ Extent (étendue); *dans toute son extension,* in its full extent. ‖ MÉD. Extension (d'un membre, d'un muscle). ‖ CH. DE F. Extension (d'une ligne). ‖ COMM. Extension, development, growth (d'une affaire); widening (de la clientèle); spreading (d'une industrie); *prendre de l'extension,* to grow, to develop. ‖ JUR. Extension (d'un droit) [*à,* to]. ‖ PHILOS. Denotation. ‖ GRAMM. Widening (du sens); *par extension,* in a wider sense.

extenso (in) [inεkstɛ̃so] loc. adv. In extenso, in full.

extensomètre [εkstɑ̃sɔmɛtr] m. TECHN. Extensometer.

exténuant, ante [εkstenɥɑ̃, ɑ̃:t] adj. Exhausting. (V. ÉREINTANT.)

exténuation [-asjɔ̃] f. Exhaustion. ‖ GRAMM. Extenuation.

exténuer v. tr. (1). To exhaust, to tire out; to jade; to knock up (ou) U. S. out, to take it out of (fam.)
— v. pr. **S'exténuer,** to tire oneself out, to fag; *s'exténuer au travail,* to work oneself to death.

extérieur, eure [εksterjœ:r] adj. Exterior (*à,* to). ‖ External (apparence, monde, mur); outside (bord, façade, monde); outer (côté, mur). ‖ COMM. External, foreign. ‖ JUR. Foreign (dette); *Affaires extérieures,* external events. ‖ ECCLÉS. *Les ténèbres extérieures,* the outer darkness. ‖ FAM. Unreserved; *il est très extérieur,* he wears his heart on his sleeve.
— m. Exterior, outside; *à l'extérieur,* outside, outdoors, without; *de l'extérieur,* from outside. ‖ Exterior, appearance (v. DEHORS); *extérieur aimable,* pleasing appearance. ‖ Externals; *juger par l'extérieur,* to judge by externals. ‖ Foreign parts (ou) countries (étranger); *de l'extérieur,* from abroad. ‖ CINÉM. Exterior.

extérieurement [-rjœ:rmɑ̃] adv. Exteriorly, externally; outside, without. ‖ In appearance.

extériorisation [-rjorizasjɔ̃] f. Exteriorization.

extérioriser [-rjorize] v. tr. (1). To manifest, to express (ses sentiments). ‖ PHILOS. To exteriorize.
— v. pr. **S'extérioriser,** to be expressed (sentiments). ‖ To reveal oneself outwardly (personne); to unbosom oneself, to open one's heart (*auprès de,* to).

extériorité [-rjorite] f. Exteriority.

exterminateur, trice [εkstɛrminatœ:r, tris] adj. Exterminating. ‖ ECCLÉS. Destroying (ange).
— s. Exterminator, destroyer.

extermination [-nasjɔ̃] f. Extermination.

exterminer [-ne] v. tr. (1). To exterminate, to wipe out (qqn, une race). ‖ FIG. To root out, to annihilate.

externat [ɛkstɛrna] m. Day-school. ‖ Méd. Non-resident studentship; dressership (en chirurgie).
externe [-tɛrn] adj. External, outer. ‖ Math. External (angle). ‖ Méd. External (médicament); *usage externe,* external application (ou) use.
— s. Day-pupil, non-resident (élève). ‖ Méd. Non-resident assistant, dresser (en chirurgie); non-resident medical student, U. S. extern (en médecine). ‖ Sports. Mid-on (au cricket).
exterritorialité [ɛkstɛritɔrjalite] f. Extraterritoriality, extrality.
extincteur, trice [ɛkstɛ̃ktœ:r, tris] adj. Extinguishing; *liquide extincteur,* fire-extinguishing fluid.
— m. Fire-extinguisher; *extincteur à mousse,* foam sprayer (ou) extinguisher.
extinction [-sjɔ̃] f. Extinction, extinguishing (du feu, de la lumière); *extinction des lumières,* blackout. ‖ Chim. Slaking (de la chaux). ‖ Jur. Extinction (d'une dette). ‖ Milit. *Extinction des feux,* lights out, U. S. taps. ‖ Méd. Loss (de voix). ‖ Fig. Extirpation, rooting out (d'un abus, d'un vice); extinction (d'une famille, d'une race).
extirpable [ɛkstirpabl] adj. Eradicable.
extirpateur [-patœ:r] m. Extirpator. ‖ Agric. Cultivator, scarifier.
extirpation [-pasjɔ̃] f. Extirpation.
extirper [-pe] v. tr. (1). To extirpate, to eradicate, to root out (pr. et fig.).
extorquer [ɛkstɔrke] v. tr. (1). To extort, to squeeze de l'argent) [*à,* out, of]; to extort (des aveux, une promesse, une signature) [*à,* from]; to wring (une faveur, un secret) [*à,* out of]; *extorquer la confiance de,* to take advantage of.
extorqueur, euse [-kœ:r, ø:z] s. Extortioner, extortionist.
extorsion [-sjɔ̃] f. Extortion.
extorsionnaire [-sjɔnɛ:r] adj. Extortionate.
extra [ɛkstra] adj. invar. First-rate. ‖ Comm. Prime, superfine.
— m. Extra; extra charge (frais). ‖ Temporary servant, hired waiter (personne); temporary job (travail). ‖ Treat (repas); *faire un extra,* to give oneself a treat.
— adv. Extra, apart. ‖ **Extra-conjugal,** adj. Extra-conjugal. ‖ **Extra-courant,** m. Electr. Extra-current. ‖ **Extra-fin,** adj. Superfine. ‖ **Extra-fort,** m. Prussian binding, U. S. hem-binding. ‖ **Extra-muros,** adv. Outside the town (ou) the walls; adj. extramural. ‖ **Extra-utérin,** adj. Méd. Extra-uterine.
extracteur [ɛkstraktœ:r] m. Extractor.
extractif, ive [-tif, i:v] adj. Techn. Extractive.
extraction [-sjɔ̃] f. Extraction (d'un clou, d'un objet enfoncé). ‖ Extraction (du charbon); winning (de l'or); extraction, extracting (du pétrole); extraction, quarrying (de la pierre). ‖ Extraction, pressing out (du jus, de l'huile, du suc). ‖ Méd., Math. Extraction. ‖ Agric. *Extraction en motte,* lifting. ‖ Fig. Extraction, origin, parentage.
extrader [ɛkstrade] v. tr. (1). To extradite.
extradition [-disjɔ̃] f. Extradition.
extrados [ɛkstrado] m. Archit. Extrados.
extragalactique [ɛkstragalaktik] adj. Astron. Extragalactical.
extraire [ɛkstrɛ:r] v. tr. (11). To extract (un clou, un objet enfoncé, un passage de texte) [*de,* from]; to bring out (qqn) [*de,* of]. ‖ To extract, to raise (du charbon); to win (de l'or); to extract, to pump (du pétrole); to extract, to quarry (de la pierre). ‖ To extract (du jus, de l'huile); *extraire en écrasant, en pressant, en tordant,* to crush out, to press (ou) to squeeze out, to wring out. ‖ Méd. To extract (une balle, une dent). ‖ Math. To extract (une racine carrée).
extrait [ɛkstrɛ] m. Extract (de fleurs, de viande); *extrait de bœuf,* beef extract. ‖ Extract (d'un

ouvrage); *tirer des extraits de,* to make extracts from. ‖ Abstract (abrégé). ‖ Jur. Certificate (de mariage, de naissance); *extrait du casier judiciaire,* extract from police records. ‖ Ecclés. Certificate (de baptême).
extralégal, ale [ɛkstralegal] adj. Extra-legal, which is outside the law.
extraordinaire [ɛkstraɔrdinɛ:r] adj. Extraordinary, uncommon, rare (peu commun). ‖ Queer, odd, singular (bizarre); surprising, wonderful (étonnant). ‖ Jur. Special (assemblée); emergency (impôt); *ambassadeur extraordinaire,* ambassador extraordinary.
— m. Extraordinary. ‖ Milit. Extraordinaries.
— loc. adv. *Par extraordinaire,* for a wonder.
extraordinairement [-mɑ̃] adv. Extraordinarily; singularly, wonderfully.
extraparlementaire [ɛkstraparləmɑ̃tɛ:r] adj. Extraparliamentary.
extrapolation [ɛkstrapɔlasjɔ̃] f. Extrapolation.
extrapoler [-le] v. tr. (1). To extrapolate.
extrasensible [ɛkstrasɑ̃sibl] adj. Supersensible, supersensory.
extraterrestre [ɛkstraterɛstr] adj. Extra-terrestrial.
— s. Being from outer space (en science-fiction).
extraterritorialité [ɛkstratɛritɔrjalite] f. Extra-territoriality.
extravagance [ɛkstravagɑ̃:s] f. Extravagance (de la conduite, de qqn). ‖ Extravagant action, crank (action); extravagant talk (discours); piece of extravagance (dépense); *faire des extravagances,* to act foolishly.
extravagant, ante [-gɑ̃, ɑ̃:t] adj. Extravagant (goût); extravagant, absurd (idée, propos); preposterous (histoire, prétentions, questions, toilette); eccentric, unbalanced, fantastic, cranky (personne); extravagant, outrageous, exorbitant, prohibitive (prix); *histoire extravagante,* extravaganza.
— s. Eccentric, crank, oddity.
extravaguer [-ge] v. intr. (1). To extravagate, to maunder; to talk nonsense.
extravasation [ɛkstravazasjɔ̃] f. Extravasation.
extravaser [-ze] v. tr. (1). To extravasate.
— v. pr. S'extravaser, to extravasate.
extraversion [ɛkstravɛrsjɔ̃] f. Extroversion.
extraverti, e [-vɛrti] adj. Extrovert, extroverted.
— s. Extrovert.
extrême [ɛkstrɛ:m] adj. Extreme, farthest (très éloigné). ‖ Extreme, intense, deep (profond); *d'un intérêt extrême,* extremely interesting. ‖ Extreme (très grand); *extrême misère,* extreme poverty. ‖ Extreme, excessive; *d'opinions extrêmes,* extreme in one's views. ‖ Extreme, drastic (rigoureux); *mesures extrêmes,* drastic measures. ‖ **Extrême-Orient,** m. Géogr. Far East. ‖ **Extrême-oriental,** adj. Far-Eastern. ‖ **Extrême-onction,** f. Ecclés. Extreme unction.
— m. Extreme; *à l'extrême,* in the extreme; to a degree; *d'un extrême à l'autre,* from one extreme to the other; *pousser à l'extrême,* to carry to extremes.
extrêmement [-trɛmmɑ̃] adv. Extremely, highly, deeply; excessively; *d'un air extrêmement intéressé,* with a keenly interested look.
extrémisme [-tremism] m. Extremism.
extrémiste [-tremist] adj. Extremist; extreme.
— s. Extremist.
extrémité [-tremite] f. Extremity (d'un arbre, d'une corde, d'un village); end (d'un bâton, d'une rue); farther part (du monde). ‖ Pl. Extremities, drastic measures (mesures extrêmes); *pousser qqn à des extrémités,* to drive s.o. to extremities. ‖ Pl. Violence; *se livrer à des extrémités sur,* to commit an assault on. ‖ Méd. Extremity (du corps); tip

(des doigts); *à la dernière extrémité,* on the point of death, at one's last gap. ‖ Fig. Urgency (du besoin); extremity (du malheur); *réduit à la dernière extrémité,* reduced to the last extremity.

extrinsèque [εkstrēsεk] adj. Extrinsic.

extroverti, e [εkstrɔvεrti] adj., s. V. EXTRA-VERTI.

exubérance [εgzyberɑ̃:s] f. Exuberance (de l'esprit, des idées, d'une personne, des propos). ‖ Exuberance, luxuriance (de la végétation).

exubérant, ante [-rɑ̃, ɑ̃:t] adj. Exuberant (esprit, personne, vitalité); immoderate (joie); gushing (personne, propos); *exubérant de vie,* bubbling over with high spirits, overflowing with vitality.

exulcération [εgzylserasjɔ̃] f. Méd. Exulceration.

exulcérer [-re] v. tr. (5). Méd. To exulcerate.

exultant, ante [-tɑ̃, ɑ̃:t] adj. Exultant (cri, sentiment); exulting (personne).

exultation [εgzyltasjɔ̃] f. Exultation, exultancy; *avec exultation,* exultantly.

exulter [-te] v. intr. (1). To exult (de, at, in); to be exultant.

exutoire [εgzytwa:r] m. Méd. Exutory. ‖ Fig. Issue, outlet (de, for).

ex-voto [εksvɔto] m. invar. Ex-voto, ex-voto (ou) votive offering.

eye-liner [ajlajnœ:r] m. Eye-liner.

Ézéchiel [ezekjεl] m. Ezekiel.

F

f [εf] m. F, f (lettre).

F. Abrév. de *franc,* French franc, franc.

fa [fa] m. Mus. F.

fable [fabl] f. Fable (genre littéraire). ‖ Tale, fable (histoire); lie, falsehood (mensonge). ‖ Laughing-stock (objet de risée). ‖ Talk (objet de conversation); *la fable du pays,* the talk of the neighbourhood.

fabliau [-bljo] m. Fabliau.

fablier [-blje] m. Book of fables.

fabricant [fabrikɑ̃] m. Manufacturer; mill-owner; maker.

fabricateur, trice [-katœ:r, tris] s. Forger (de documents); coiner (de fausse monnaie); fabricator (de fausses nouvelles).

fabrication [-kasjɔ̃] f. Manufacture (industrielle); *de bonne fabrication,* well made, of good workmanship; *de fabrication anglaise,* made in England, of English make; *service de la fabrication,* manufacturing department. ‖ Forging (de documents); coining (de fausse monnaie); fabrication (de fausses nouvelles).

fabrique [fabrik] f. Factory, manufactory; works; (v. MANUFACTURE); *fabrique de papier,* paper-mill. ‖ Manufacture; *prix de fabrique,* cost price. ‖ Ecclés. Vestry.

fabriquer [-ke] v. tr. (1). To manufacture, to make, to produce (un objet). ‖ To forge (un document); to coin (de la fausse monnaie, un mot); to fabricate (une histoire, une nouvelle); to forge, to fake (un objet faux). ‖ Fam. To be up to (qqch.).

fabulateur, trice [fabylatœ:r, tris] adj. Pathologically lying (ou) mendacious.
— s. Pathological liar.

fabulation [fabylasjɔ̃] f. Development, working out (action); texture (trame). ‖ Psych. Pathological lying, fabrication.

fabuler [-le] v. intr. (1). To fabricate, to make up stories.

fabuleusement [-løzmɑ̃] adv. Fabulously.

fabuleux, euse [-lø, ø:z] adj. Fabulous, legendary. ‖ Fam. Fabulous (récit, prix, somme).

fabuliste [-list] m. Fabulist.

façade [fasad] f. Façade, front, frontage (d'une maison); *sa façade est sur la rue,* it faces the street. ‖ Fig. Façade. ‖ Fam. Window-dressing (parade); *tout de façade,* all façade, all on the surface.

face [fas] f. Face (de l'homme). [V. FIGURE.] ‖ Obverse (d'une médaille); head (d'une pièce). ‖ Face, surface (de l'eau, d'une feuille, de la terre). ‖ Face, side (d'un dé à jouer); *à double face,* double-sided (disque); reversible (tissu). ‖ Face; *à double face,* double-dealing (personne); *perdre la face,* to lose face; *sauver la face,* to save one's face. ‖ Face, angle, aspect; *la face des choses,* the face of things; *sous toutes ses faces,* from every aspect (ou) side. ‖ Ecclés. *La Sainte Face,* the Holy Face. ‖ Milit. Flat (de lame); *face à droite, à gauche,* face to the right, to the left. ‖ Math. Face (d'un cube). ‖ **A la face de,** before. ‖ **De face,** full-face (portrait); front (vue); *attaqué de face,* attacked in front (ou) from the front; *regarder une maison de face,* to look at the front of a house; *voir qqn de face,* to see s.o. full face. ‖ **En face;** *la dame d'en face,* the lady from across the street; *la maison d'en face,* the house opposite (ou) over the way; *dire qqch. à qqn en face,* to say sth. to s.o.'s face; *regarder en face,* to look straight in the face. ‖ **En face de,** in front of, facing opposite, over against, in the presence of; *en face de lui,* in front of him; *en face de l'église,* opposite the church; *en face l'un de l'autre,* opposite each other; *se trouver en face d'un problème,* to be confronted with a problem. ‖ **Face à,** facing; *face à face avec,* face to face with; *face à moi,* facing me; *face à l'ennemi,* face to the enemy. ‖ **Faire face à,** to defray (des dépenses); to face, to front (un lieu, un objet); to face, to face up to, to oppose (un ennemi); to meet, to face up to (une dépense, un engagement); to face, to face up to (une difficulté); to bear up against (une épreuve); to cope with, to face up to (la situation). ‖ **Face-à-face,** m. invar. TV Debate (ou) encounter. ‖ **Face-à-main** (pl. *faces-à-main*) m. Lorgnette.

facétie [fasesi] f. Joke. ‖ Pl. Facetiae; pranks.

facétieusement [-sjøzmɑ̃] adv. Facetiously.

facétieux, euse [-sjø, ø:z] adj. Facetious.
— m. Wag, joker.

facette [fasεt] f. Facet (de diamant); *à facette,* segmented (miroir); in facets, faceted (pierre). ‖ Zool. Facet (d'un œil d'insecte).

facetter [-te] v. tr. (1). To facet.

fâché, ée [fɑʃe] adj. Sorry (de, about) [contrarié]. ‖ Angry (en colère) [contre, with]; il a l'air fâché, he looks very cross. ‖ Not on speaking terms (brouillé); être fâché, to have fallen out (avec, with).

fâcher v. tr. (1). To grieve (ennuyer); to anger, to irritate, to annoy, to vex (irriter); to offend (offenser).
— v. pr. **Se fâcher**, to get angry (s'irriter) [contre, with; pour, over]; to take offence (s'offenser) [pour, at]; se fâcher tout rouge, to blaze up. ‖ To fall out (se brouiller) [avec, with].

fâcherie [-ʃri] f. Tiff, quarrel.

fâcheusement [-ʃøzmɑ̃] adv. Annoyingly; tiresomely; disagreeably.

fâcheux, euse [-ʃø, ø:z] adj. Sad (erreur, nouvelle); untoward, unfortunate, distressing (événement); awkward (position); c'est vraiment fâcheux, that's a nuisance; il est fâcheux que, it's a pity (ou) regrettable that.
— m. † Bore.

facial, ale [fasjal] adj. Facial (angle, muscle).

faciès [fasjɛs] m. Facies. ‖ FAM. Features.

facile [fasil] adj. Easy (ascension, travail, vie) [à, for; de, to]; d'un accès facile, easy of access, easily reached; c'est facile pour lui de donner des ordres, mais..., it's all very well for him to give orders, but... ‖ Easy (caractère); facile à satisfaire, easily satisfied; facile à vivre, easy-going, easy to live with; facile en affaires, accommodating. ‖ Of easy virtue (femme); easy (mœurs). ‖ Facile, fluent, smooth (style); avoir la parole facile, to be a fluent (ou) ready speaker. ‖ FAM. Ready; avoir la larme facile, to weep easily; il a le pourboire facile, he's always good for a tip.

facilement [-lmɑ̃] adv. Easily.

facilité [-lite] f. Facility, easiness (d'un travail). [V. AISANCE.] ‖ Facility, ease (absence d'effort); avec facilité, easily; avoir de la facilité pour apprendre, to learn easily. ‖ Fluency (du style); facilité de travail, capacity for work; facilité de parole, readiness of speech; s'exprimer avec facilité, to talk fluently. ‖ Facility, yieldingness, pliancy, accommodativeness (complaisance); solution de facilité, line of least resistance. ‖ Pl. Facilities, opportunities. ‖ COMM. Facilités de paiement, deferred payments, easy terms, instalment system, U. S. instalment plan.

faciliter [-lite] v. tr. (1). To make easy, to facilitate; faciliter qqch. à qqn, to make sth. easier for s.o.

façon [fasɔ̃] f. Making, fashioning; bonne façon, good workmanship; de ma façon, of my own making; la façon d'une robe, the making-up of a dress; tailleur à façon, jobbing (ou) bespoke tailor, U. S. custom tailor; travailler à façon, to make up the customer's own material. ‖ Aspect, appearance, look; avoir bonne façon, to look well (personne, robe). ‖ Imitation; façon loutre, imitation otter. ‖ Composition; façon japonaise, Japanese pattern; un procédé de sa façon, a process of his own invention. ‖ Fashion, way, manner (v. MANIÈRE); à la façon des Indiens, after the Indian fashion; à sa façon, in his own way, after his manner (ou) fashion; avoir une façon à soi de travailler, to have one's own way of working; de cette façon, je pourrai vous voir, that way I shall be able to see you; de façon à, so as to; de façon que (ou) de telle façon que, so that; de la belle façon, severely; d'une façon ou d'une autre, one way or another, by some means or other; d'une drôle de façon, oddly, queerly; de quelle façon?, how?; de toute façon, anyhow, in any case; en aucune façon, by no means, in no wise; en quelque façon, in a way,

in a sense; en toutes façons, in every respect; façon de parler, mode of speaking; simple façon de parler, mere talk; penser de la même façon, to think in the same way. ‖ Pl. Manners, ways, address; behaviour, demeanour; des façons plaisantes, a pleasant manner; de gracieuses petites façons, pretty (ou) taking ways. ‖ Pl. Ceremony, ado, fuss, frills; flummery (fam.) [v. CHICHI]; faire des façons, to stand on ceremony, to make a fuss, to put on frills; être sans façon, to be informal (ou) unceremonious (ou) rough and ready; faire qqch. sans façon, to do sth. unceremoniously, in an off-hand manner, informally; sans plus de façons, without further ado. ‖ AGRIC. Dressing. ‖ NAUT. Run.

faconde [fakɔ̃:d] f. Facundity, glibness; gift of the gab (fam.).

façonnage [fasɔna:ʒ], **façonnement** [fasɔnmɑ̃] m. Manufacturing, making, forming; fashioning, working (du bois, des métaux); fashioring, moulding (de la glaise); figuring (des tissus); hewing (des troncs d'arbre); façonnement au tour, turning. ‖ FIG. Shaping, moulding, forming (de l'esprit).

façonner [-ne] v. tr. (1). To work, to shape (du bois, du fer); to fashion, to mould (la glaise); to shape (des meubles); to figure (du tissu). ‖ AGRIC. To dress (la terre). ‖ FIG. To form, to mould (le caractère).
— v. pr. **Se façonner**, to acquire polish (personne).

façonnier, ère [-nje, ɛ:r] adj. Jobbing, bespoke (ouvrier). ‖ FAM. Fussy (personne).
— m. Home-worker, jobbing workman. ‖ FAM. Fussy person, fusspot. (V. CHICHITEUR.)

fac-similé [faksimile] (pl. **fac-similés**) m. Facsimile.

factage [fakta:ʒ] m. COMM. Cartage, porterage; entreprise de factage, parcels-delivery company.

facteur, trice [-tœ:r, tris] s. Maker (d'instruments de musique). ‖ Carman, carrier (de messageries); postman, U. S. mailman, letter carrier (des postes). ‖ CH. DE F. Porter. ‖ COMM. Factor, agent. ‖ JUR. Customs agent (ou) broker (aux douans). ‖ MATH. Factor. ‖ ELECTR., MÉD., FIG. Factor.

factice [faktis] adj. Artificial, imitation, false (objet). ‖ FIG. Factitious (beauté); sham (piété).

facticement [-tismɑ̃] adv. Falsely, feignedly.

factieux, euse [faksjø, ø:z] adj. Factious.
— s. Factious person, factionist, malcontent.

faction [-sjɔ̃] f. Faction (en politique); esprit de faction, factiousness. ‖ MILIT. Sentry-duty; de (ou) en faction, on sentry duty; mettre en faction, to post.

factionnaire [-sjɔnɛ:r] m. MILIT. Sentry, sentinel.

factitif, ive [faktitif, i:v] adj., m. GRAMM. Factitive, causative.

factorerie [faktɔreri] f. COMM. Factory, foreign trading-station; sub-office.

factorielle [faktɔrjɛl] adj. f. MATH. Analyse factorielle, factor analysis.
— f. MATH. Factorial; la factorielle de 5, 5 factorial.

factotum [faktɔtɔm] m. Factotum.

factuel, elle [faktɥɛl] adj. Factual.

factum [faktɔm] m. Controversial pamphlet (en politique). ‖ JUR. Brief, factum, memorial.

facturation [faktyrasjɔ̃] f. COMM. Invoicing, billing. ‖ Invoicing department (bureau).

facture [fakty:r] f. Structure, construction, treatment (d'un texte); d'une bonne facture, well-made, well-constructed. ‖ MUS. Manufacture (d'instruments de musique); treatment (d'un morceau). ‖ ARTS. Execution (d'un tableau). ‖ COMM. Make, workmanship (d'un article).

facture f. COMM. Invoice, bill; *compte de factures,* statement of account; *suivant facture,* as per invoice.

facturer [-tyre] v. tr. (1). COMM. To invoice.

facturier, ère [-tyrje, ɛ:r] s. COMM. Sales-book (livre); invoice-clerk (personne).

facule [faky:l] f. ASTRON. Facula.

facultatif, ive [fakyltatif, i:v] adj. Facultative, optional. ‖ JUR. Permissive (législation). ‖ AUTOM. *Arrêt facultatif,* request stop, U. S. flag stop.

facultativement [-tivmɑ̃] adv. Optionally.

faculté [fakylte] f. Faculty, capacity (de l'esprit). ‖ Faculty, power (possibilité); *avec faculté de,* with right of, with the option of. ‖ Property, capacity, power (propriété). ‖ Faculty, U. S. department, school (de droit). ‖ JUR. *Constituer une faculté,* to be permissive. ‖ FAM. *La Faculté,* the Faculty (of Medicine).

fada [fada] m. FAM. Ninny, simpleton.

fadaises [fadɛ:z] f. pl. Twaddle (v. BALIVERNE); *débiter des fadaises,* to reel off platitudes.

fadasse [fadas] adj. FAM. Mawkish, cloying (goût); washy (teinte).

fade [fad] adj. Flat (boisson); tasteless, insipid, flavourless (goût, mets); stale (odeur); washed-out (teinte). ‖ Mawkish, namby-pamby (histoire, style); milk-and-water, wishy-washy (personne); tame (plaisanterie).

fadement [-dmɑ̃] adv. Insipidly.

fadeur [-dœ:r] f. Tastelessness insipidity (du goût); sickliness (d'une odeur); washiness (d'une teinte). ‖ Tameness (d'une histoire); mawkishness (d'un sentiment). ‖ Pl. Insipid talk; platitudes.

fading [fediɲ] m. ELECTR. Fading.

fafiot [fafjo] m. FAM. Bradbury, flimsy; U. S. greenback. ‖ POP. *Sans un fafiot pour se le torcher,* without a penny to scratch one's arse.

fagot [fago] m. LOC. *De derrière les fagots,* from the hidden store; *ressembler à un fagot,* to look like a scarecrow; *sentir le fagot,* to smell of heresy.

fagotage [-ta:ʒ] m. Faggotting (du bois). ‖ FAM. Dowdy get-up (habillement).

fagoté, ée [-te] adj. Dowdy, frumpish (personne); *femme mal fagotée,* frump, mess.

fagoter [-te] v. tr. (1). To faggot (du bois). ‖ FAM. To tog up (qqn). [V. ACCOUTRER.]
— v. pr. **Se fagoter.** FAM. To dress like a guy, to get oneself up, to rig oneself out like a scarecrow.

fagoteur [-tœ:r] s. Faggot-maker (de bois).

fagotin [-tɛ̃] m. Bundle of firewood.

faiblard [fɛbla:r] adj. FAM. Weakish, rather feeble; *un homme faiblard,* a weakling.

faible [fɛbl] adj. Weak, feeble (corps); low, slight (gémissement); weak, feeble, faint (voix); weak, dim (yeux); *faible de la vue* (ou) *à la vue faible,* weak-sighted; *le sexe faible,* the weaker sex. ‖ Low (lueur); feeble, weak, dim (lumière); faint, slight (odeur); light, soft (vent). ‖ Slight (différence); bare (majorité); small (nombre, quantité). ‖ Slight (dommage, effet); slender (espoir); weak, small (mérite). ‖ Weak, feeble, unconvincing (argument); weak, feeble tame (style); *faible en,* weak in. ‖ Weak (chair, côté, point); weak, feeble (esprit); *faible d'esprit,* weak-minded. ‖ Weak (caractère, personne) [avec, with]; weak, fond (mère, parents). ‖ MÉD. Slight (amélioration); feeble, faint (pouls); weak, delicate (santé). ‖ CULIN. Weak (thé); weak, thin (vin). ‖ COMM. Slack (demande). ‖ FIN. Low (chiffre, prix); soft (devises); weak (marché); small, slight (ressources). ‖ AGRIC. Poor (récolte). ‖ TECHN. Low, slow (vitesse). ‖ MUS. Unaccented (temps). ‖ GRAMM. Weak (conjugaison, déclinaison).

— m. Weak person; *les faibles,* the weak. ‖ Foible, weak side (ou) point; *prendre qqn par son faible,* to get on s.o.'s weak side. ‖ Weakness, liking (pour, for) [qqch.]; partiality, liking, soft spot (pour, for) [qqn]. ‖ MÉD. *Les faibles d'esprit,* the mentally deficient. ‖ JUR. *Les économiquement faibles,* the lowest income-groups, U. S. the underprivileged.

faiblement [-bləmɑ̃] adv. Weakly, feebly, faintly, dimly, slightly.

faiblesse [-blɛs] f. Weakness, feebleness (du corps); weakness, feebleness, faintness (de la voix); weakness, dimness (de la vue). ‖ Dimness (de la lumière); lightness (du vent). ‖ Slightness (d'une différence); smallness (du nombre). ‖ Slightness (d'un dommage); smallness (des mérites). ‖ Weakness, lameness, feebleness (du style). ‖ Weakness (d'esprit); *faiblesse d'esprit,* weak-mindedness. ‖ Weakness (du caractère); partiality, over-indulgence (des parents). ‖ Pl. Shortcomings, failings; *il a ses petites faiblesses,* he has his little weaknesses, he is only human. ‖ FIN. Smallness, slightness (des ressources); lowness (d'une somme). ‖ MILIT. Weakness (d'une armée). ‖ MÉD. Weakness (de santé); fainting fit (malaise).

faiblir [-bli:r] v. intr. (2). To weaken, to grow weaker (forces); to lose strength (personne); to fail (vue); to abate, to slacken (vent). ‖ FIG. To flag (courage); to fail (espoir); to yield (personne); to grow weaker (résistance); to abate (résolution).

faïence [fajɑ̃:s] f. Faïence, earthenware, crockery. ‖ LOC. *Se regarder en chiens de faïence,* to stare at each other.

faïencerie [-jɑ̃sri] f. Earthenware works.

faïencier [-jɑ̃sje] s. Earthenware maker (fabricant) [ou] dealer (marchand).

faignant, ante [fɛɲɑ̃, ɑ̃:t] adj., s. V. FEIGNANT.

faille [fɑ:j] f. Fault (fente, imperfection).

faille f. Faille (tissu).

faille. V. FALLOIR (51).

failli, ie [faji] adj. Bankrupt. ‖ FAM. *Failli chien !,* scoundrel !, dirty dog !
— m. Bankrupt. (V. BANQUEROUTIER.)

faillibilité [-bilite] f. Fallibility.

faillible [fajibl] adj. Fallible.

faillir [faji:r] v. intr. (49). To fail (manquer); *faillir à,* to fail in (son devoir); to fail to keep (ses promesses). ‖ To slip, to make a slip (fauter). ‖ To go bankrupt (banqueroutier). ‖ To be on the point of, to come near, to be within an inch of; *cela a failli réussir,* it very nearly succeeded; *j'ai failli me faire écraser,* I narrowly escaped (ou) just missed being run over; *j'ai failli me perdre,* I almost lost my way.

faillite [fajit] f. Failure, bankruptcy; *déclarer* (ou) *mettre qqn en faillite,* to declare s.o. bankrupt; *faire faillite,* to fail, to go bankrupt; *faire une faillite de cent millions,* to fail for a hundred million. ‖ FIG. Failure.

faim [fɛ̃] f. Hunger; *avoir faim,* to be hungry; *avoir une faim de loup,* to be as hungry as a hunter (ou) U. S. as a bear; *manger à sa faim,* to eat one's fill; *mourir de faim,* to die of starvation (au pr.); to be starving (au fig.). ‖ FIG. Hunger, craving (de, for).

faine [fɛ:n] f. BOT. Beech-nut.

fainéant, ante [fɛneɑ̃, ɑ̃:t] adj. Idle, lazy (v. PARESSEUX); *roi fainéant,* sluggard king.
— s. Lazy-bones.

fainéanter [-te] v. intr. (1). To do nothing. (V. PARESSER.)

fainéantise [-ti:z] f. Laziness. (V. PARESSE.)

faire [fɛ:r] v. tr. (50).

1. Créer. — 2. Engendrer. — 3. Fabriquer. — 4. Former. — 5. Causer. — 6. Fournir. — 7. Agir, s'occuper. — 8. Accomplir. — 9. Effectuer. — 10. Exécuter. — 11. Réaliser. — 12. Etablir. — 13. Gagner. — 14. Adresser. — 15. Formuler. — 16. Décrire. — 17. Instituer. — 18. Transmettre. — 19. S'approvisionner. — 20. Parcourir. — 21. Arranger. — 22. Nettoyer. — 23. Contrefaire. — 24. Etre. — 25. Destiner. — 26. Devenir. — 27. Importer. — 28. Faire de. — 29. Faire que. — 30. Faire que (ou) en sorte que. — 31. Ne faire que. — 32. Faire, suivi d'un infinitif à sens actif. — 33. Faire, suivi d'un infinitif à sens passif. — 34. Faire faire. — 35. Ecclés. — 36. Culin. — 37. Arts. — 38. Mus. — 39. Théâtr. — 40. Autom. — 41. Sports. — 42. Milit. — 43. Méd. — 44. Math. — 45. Jur. — 46. Fin. — 47. Comm. — 48. Fam.

◼. To make, to create (créer); *Dieu fit l'homme à Son image,* God made man in His own image; *on l'a fait baron,* he has been made a baron (ou) created baron. ‖ 2. To beget, to have (engendrer, mettre au monde); *faire un enfant à,* to make pregnant; *faire des enfants,* to have children; *faire des petits chiens,* to have pups, to pup, to whelp. ‖ 3. To make (fabriquer); *faire du pain, des souliers,* to make bread, shoes; *faire un poème,* to make (ou) write (ou) compose a poem. ‖ 4. To make, to form (former); *faire un angle,* to form an angle; *faire une paire d'amis,* to make a pair of friends; *faire partie de,* to form part of. ‖ 5. To make (causer); *faire un affront à qqn,* to offer s.o. an affront; *faire du bien à qqn,* to do s.o. good; *faire du dégât,* to make a mess; *faire de la peine à qqn,* to hurt s.o.'s feelings; *ne faites pas à autrui ce que vous ne voudriez pas qu'on vous fît,* do as you would be done by; *on ne peut rien me faire,* they can't hurt me. ‖ 6. To give, to make (fournir); *faire un avantage à,* to give an advantage to; *faire les cartes,* to deal the cards; *faire la mise de fonds,* to supply the capital. ‖ 7. To do (agir, s'occuper); *avoir qqch. à faire,* to have sth. to do; *en faire trop,* to do too much, to overdo; *faire de la couture,* to do sewing; *faire du latin,* to do Latin; *il n'a rien à faire ici,* he has no business here; *ne rien faire,* to do nothing; *pourquoi faire?,* what for?, why?; *que fait-il?,* what is his profession (ou) business (ou) job?; *que fait-il là?,* what is he about (ou) up to?; *rester sans rien faire,* to remain idle. ‖ 8. To do (accomplir); *faire une bonne action, son travail,* to do a good deed, one's work; *il l'a fait par bonté,* he did it out of kindness. ‖ 9. To make (effectuer); *faire son apprentissage,* to serve one's apprenticeship; *faire une commission,* to do (ou) to run an errand; *faire un petit voyage,* to make a trip; *faire une visite,* to pay a visit. ‖ 10. To make (exécuter); *faire un bond,* to give a jump; *faire un mouvement,* to make a movement. ‖ 11. To make (réaliser); *faire fortune,* to make a fortune; *faire une importante opération,* to bring off an important transaction. ‖ 12. To make out (établir); *faire une carte,* to draw a map; *faire une liste,* to make out (ou) to draw up a list. ‖ 13. To make (gagner); *faire école,* to set a fashion; *faire des disciples,* to make disciples. ‖ 14. To give (adresser); *faire un discours,* to make a speech; *faire une politesse à,* to show s.o. civility; *faire un sourire à,* to smile at, to give a smile to. ‖ 15. To make (formuler); *faire une déclaration, une promesse,* to make a declaration, a promise; *faire des reproches à,* to reproach. ‖ 16. To make out, to give out (décrire); *vous me*

faites pire que je ne suis, you make me out worse than I am. ‖ 17. To make (instituer); *faire de qqn son héritier,* to make s.o. one's heir; *faire qqn juge,* to ask s.o. to umpire. ‖ 18. To give (transmettre); *faites-lui mes amitiés,* give him my kindest regards. ‖ 19. To take in (s'approvisionner); *faire de l'eau,* to take in water; *faire provision de,* to get in a supply of. ‖ 20. To do, to cover, to go, to travel (parcourir, visiter); *faire un long trajet,* to travel a long way; *faire six kilomètres à pied,* to walk six kilometres; *faire six kilomètres en une heure,* to cover six kilometres in an hour; *faire la vallée de la Loire,* to tour the Loire valley. ‖ 21. To make (arranger); *faire le lit,* to make the bed; *faire une malle,* to pack a trunk. ‖ 22. To do, to clean (nettoyer); *faire la chambre,* to clean the room; *faire ses chaussures,* to do (ou) to clean one's shoes; *faire la vaisselle,* to wash up, to wash the dishes. ‖ 23. To play, to feign (contrefaire); *faire le mort,* to sham dead (au propre); to play 'possum (fam.); *faire le singe,* to play the ape. ‖ 24. To be (être); *quel sot je fais!,* what a fool I am! ‖ 25. To make (destiner); *le ciel a voulu faire de lui un prêtre,* God meant him for a priest. ‖ 26. To make, to become (devenir); *faire un bon chirurgien,* to make a good surgeon. ‖ 27. To matter (importer); *ça ne fait rien,* it does not matter; it makes no difference; *cela ne vous fait rien que j'ouvre la fenêtre?,* would you mind my opening (ou) if I opened the window?; *do you mind if I open the window?; qu'est-ce que ça peut me faire!,* what is that to me! ‖ 28. Faire... de, to make... of; *faire une chambre d'un grenier,* to make a room of a garret, to turn an attic into a room; *faire de qqn son ami,* to make s.o. one's friend; *cela fait de lui un homme important,* that makes him an important man. ‖ 29. Faire que; *cela fait que,* the result is that, it follows that (s'ensuivre). ‖ 30. Faire que (ou) en sorte que; *faire en sorte que tout se passe sans accroc,* to take steps to ensure that everything goes off without a hitch. ‖ 31. Ne faire que; *ne faire que pleurer,* to do nothing but cry; to keep on crying; *il ne fait que de sortir,* he has only just gone out. ‖ 32. Faire (suivi d'un infinitif à sens actif); to make, to cause, to order, to bid, to have, to get; *faire arrêter la machine,* to cause the machine to stop; *faire croire qqch. à qqn,* to make s.o. believe sth.; *faire entrer qqn,* to show s.o. in; U. S. to have s.o. come in; *faire monter qqn,* to get s.o. to come up; *faire partir,* to order off; *faire reprendre le travail,* to get the work started again; *cela fait réfléchir,* that makes you think; *cela fait rire,* that makes one laugh; *ils m'ont fait poster leur lettre,* they got me to post (ou) U. S. to mail their letter; *il veut me faire croire que,* he tries to persuade me that; *on lui fit promettre que,* he was made to promise that. ‖ 33. Faire (suivi de l'infinitif à sens passif); *faire bâtir une maison,* to have a house built (faire qu'une maison soit bâtie); *faire oublier le passé,* to cause the past to be forgotten; *faire pendre qqn,* to get s.o. hanged. ‖ 34. Faire faire; *faire faire qqch.,* to have sth. done (ou) made; *faire faire qqch. à qqn,* to have (ou) to get sth. done by s.o.; to get (ou) cause s.o. to do sth.; *faire faire ses commissions à qqn,* to get s.o. to run one's errands; *un costume qu'il a fait faire,* a suit he has had made. ‖ 35. Ecclés. *Faire un miracle,* to work a miracle. ‖ 36. Culin. To make (une omelette); *faire la cuisine,* to cook. ‖ 37. Arts. *Faire de la peinture,* to paint. ‖ 38. Mus. *Faire de la musique,* to go in for music (étudier); to play some music, to make music (jouer). ‖ 39. Théâtr. *Faire le roi,* to act the king's part (rôle); *faire du théâtre,* to go in for dramatics (en amateur); to be on the

stage (en professionnel). ‖ **40.** AUTOM. *Faire de l'auto,* to be a motorist ; *faire du cent à l'heure,* to do sixty miles an hour. ‖ **41.** SPORTS. *Faire une partie de cricket,* to play (ou) to have a game of cricket ; *faire la planche,* to float (à la nage) ; *faire du ski,* to ski. ‖ **42.** MILIT. *Faire l'appel,* to call the roll ; *faire feu,* to fire ; *faire la paix,* to make peace. ‖ **43.** MÉD. To develop (une maladie) ; to carry out (une opération) ; to have, to run (une température) ; *faire ses besoins,* to relieve oneself (ou) nature. ‖ **44.** MATH. To perform (une addition) ; to work out (un problème) ; *ça fait cent francs,* it comes to a hundred francs (montant) ; *deux et deux font quatre,* two and two are (ou) make four. ‖ **45.** JUR. To bring (un procès). ‖ **46.** FIN. To make out (un chèque). ‖ **47.** COMM. *Faire un article à « x » francs,* to ask « x » francs for a commodity ; to let s.o. have a commodity for x francs ; *faire un bénéfice,* to make a profit ; *faire la banlieue,* to do the suburbs (voyageur de commerce) ; *faire du commerce,* to be in business (ou) trade. ‖ **48.** FAM. *Comment est-il fait?,* what does he look like? ; what sort of man is he? ; *faire les poches de qqn,* to go through s.o.'s pockets ; *on m'a fait mon portefeuille,* they have sneaked my wallet (ou) U. S. my bill-fold ; *on ne me la fait pas,* I'm not to be had ; *vous êtes fait!,* you've had it!
— v. intr.

---

1. Agir. — 2. Procéder. — 3. Faire de. — 4. Y faire. — 5. Avoir besoin. — 6. Obtenir. — 7. Paraître. — 8. Dire. — 9. Durer. — 10. Distribuer. — 11. MÉD.

---

1. To do, to act (agir) ; *avoir fort à faire,* to have much to do ; *avoir fort à faire pour,* to have difficulty in ; *avoir tôt fait de venir,* not to be long in coming ; *avoir vite fait,* to be quick about it ; *avoir vite fait de dîner,* to be quick over dinner ; *empêcher qqn de mal faire,* to keep s.o. right ; *faire à sa guise,* to have one's way, to do as one likes ; *faire au mieux de,* to act to the best of ; *faire bien d'écouter,* to do well (ou) right to listen ; *faire de son mieux,* to do one's best ; *faire mal,* to do wrong ; *faire mieux d'écouter,* to do better to listen, to have better listen ; *faire pour le mieux,* to act for the best ; *il a bien fait,* he did right ; *il n'y a pas moyen de faire autrement,* there is no help for it, there is nothing else that can be done ; *il n'y a rien à faire,* there is no remedy, it is quite hopeless ; there's nothing doing, it's no go (fam.); *je ne peux faire autrement que d'écouter,* I can but listen ; *je vais l'avertir. N'en faites rien,* I'll warn him. Don't ; *je n'en ferai rien,* I'll do nothing of the sort ; *la seule chose à faire c'est de,* there is nothing for it but to ; *laisser faire qqn,* to leave it to s.o. (laisser agir) ; to let s.o. alone (laisser tranquille). ‖ **2.** To do, to proceed (procéder) ; *comment faites-vous pour écrire?,* how do you set about writing? ; *comment fait-il pour réussir?,* how does he manage to succeed? ; *comment faire pour?,* what must one do to? ‖ **3. Faire de,** to make with ; *qu'avez-vous fait de mon parapluie?,* what have you done with my umbrella? ; *que faire de ces poires?,* what is to be done with these pears? ‖ **4. Y faire ;** *rien n'y fait,* it would not do ; *qu'y faire?,* what can be done about it? ; *que voulez-vous que j'y fasse?,* what can I do about it? ‖ **5.** To have need (avoir besoin) ; *n'avoir que faire de,* to have no need of, to have no use for ; *pour ce que j'en fais,* for all the use it is to me. ‖ **6.** To get, to obtain (obtenir) ; *on peut faire de lui ce qu'on veut,* you can get anything you like out of him. ‖ **7.** To look (paraître) ; *faire bien sur,* to

look well on (costume) ; *faire jeune,* to look young. ‖ **8.** To say (dire) ; *je le pense, fit-elle,* I think so, she said. ‖ **9.** To do, to last (durer) ; *cela fera encore quelque temps,* it will still last for some time. ‖ **10.** To deal (distribuer) ; *c'est à vous de faire,* it's your turn to deal (aux cartes). ‖ **11.** MÉD. To evacuate.
— v. (remplaçant un verbe déjà exprimé). To do ; *n'agissez pas comme font ces gens-là,* don't act as those people do ; *puis-je regarder votre livre? Faites,* may I have a look at your book? Please do.
— v. impers. To be ; *il fait à peine jour,* it is hardly light ; *il fait beau, froid, nuit,* it is fine, cold, dark ; *il fait bon flâner,* it is nice to stroll about. ‖ FAM. *Il fait soif,* I am beginning to feel thirsty.
— v. pr. Se faire, to be done (ou) made (sens passif) ; to be worked out (calcul) ; to be carried out (expérience) ; to be effected (paiement) ; to be performed (trajet) ; *cela ne se fait pas,* that is not done ; *se mêler de ce qui se fait chez les autres,* to meddle with (ou) in other people's business ; *savoir ce qui se fait,* to know what is going on (ou) being done ; *le vin se fait avec du raisin,* wine is made from grapes. ‖ To make oneself (sens réfléchi) ; *se faire belle,* to make oneself beautiful ; *se faire tout à tous,* to be made all things to all men. ‖ To grow, to become, to turn (devenir) ; *se faire avocat,* to become a barrister (ou) U. S. a lawyer ; *se faire plus aigu,* to grow sharper ; *se faire vieux,* to get (ou) to grow old. ‖ To grow better, to improve (s'améliorer) ; *il se fera avec le temps,* he will develop with time ; *ces souliers se feront,* those shoes will wear to the shape of your feet. ‖ To adapt oneself (s'habituer) ; *se faire à qqch.,* to get used to sth. ; *se faire à voir qqch.,* to get used (ou) accustomed to seeing sth. ‖ To happen (advenir) ; *comment se fait-il que?,* how does it happen that? ; *comment se fait-il que vous soyez ici?,* how do you come to be here? ‖ To be (être) ; *il se fait tard,* it is getting late ; *la nuit se fait,* night is falling, it is getting dark. ‖ Se faire (suivi d'un complément) ; *se faire une idée de,* to conceive an idea of ; *se faire un lit, une réputation,* to make oneself a bed, a reputation ; *se faire un mérite de,* to make a virtue of ; *se faire une opinion,* to form an opinion ; *se faire du souci* (ou) *s'en faire pour,* to worry about ; *ne vous en faites pas,* don't worry. ‖ Se faire (suivi d'un infinitif) ; *se faire comprendre,* to make oneself understood ; *se faire entendre,* to be heard (bruit) ; to make oneself heard (personne) ; *se faire friser,* to get (ou) to have one's hair curled ; *se faire plomber une dent,* to have a tooth filled ; *se faire respecter de tous,* to make oneself respected by all ; *se faire tuer,* to get killed ; *il se fait envoyer des livres,* he has some books sent him ; *il se fait offrir ses livres par un ami,* he has his books given to him by a friend, he gets a friend to give him his books. ‖ CULIN. To ripen (fromage, fruit).
— m. Doing, making (action). ‖ ARTS. Technique, manner. ‖ **Faire-part,** m. invar. Notice ; announcement ; *faire-part de décès,* notification of death ; *faire-part de mariage,* wedding card (ou) U. S. invitation ; *le présent avis tiendra lieu de faire-part,* will friends please accept this as the only notification. ‖ **Faire-valoir,** m. inv. Stooge, straight man, foil.

fair-play [fɛrplɛ] m. Fair play, sportsmanship.
— adj. inv. Sportsmanlike, sporting.

faisable [fəzabl] adj. Feasible, performable.

faisan [fəzɑ̃] m. ZOOL. Pheasant, cock-pheasant.

faisandé, ée [-de] adj. CULIN. High (gibier) ; gamy (viande). ‖ FIG. Spicy, corrupt (littérature).

faisandeau [-do] m. ZOOL. Young pheasant.
faisander [-de] v. tr. (1). To hang, U. S. to age.
— v. pr. **Se faisander**, to get high (gibier).
faisanderie [-dri] f. Pheasant-preserve.
faisandier [-dje] m. Pheasant breeder.
faisane [fəzan] f. ZOOL. Hen-pheasant.
faisceau [fɛso] m. Fasces (des licteurs). ‖ Fascio (des fascistes). ‖ Bundle (de piquets). ‖ MÉD. Fasciculus (nerveux). ‖ BOT. Head (de feuilles); fascicle (de fibres). ‖ MILIT. Pile (d'armes); sheaf (de tir, de trajectoires); *former, rompre les faisceaux*, to pile (ou) to stack, to unpile arms. ‖ ELECTR. Beam (de lumière); pencil (de rayons). ‖ CH. DE F. *Faisceau de voies*, grid-iron sidings.
faiseur [fəzœ:r] s. Maker; *bon faiseur*, first-rate tailor; *faiseur d'embarras*, fusspot; *faiseur de miracles*, miracle-worker; *faiseur de projets*, schemer. ‖ FAM. Bluffer; fraud.
faisons [fəzɔ̃]. V. FAIRE (50).

fait [fɛ] adj. Done (accompli); *ce qui est fait est fait*, what is done is done. ‖ Made (fabriqué); *fait à la main*, hand-made; *tout fait*, ready-made (expressions, vêtements). ‖ Made (bâti); *bien fait*, well made, well built, shapely (personne). ‖ Grown, full-grown (adulte); *un homme fait*, a grown man. ‖ Apt, formed, suited, cut out (propre) [*pour*, for]; *ce n'est pas fait pour nous encourager*, it's not calculated to encourage us; *il n'est pas fait pour ça*, he is not fitted (ou) cut out for that. ‖ Used, accustomed (habitué) [*à*, to]; *il n'y est pas fait*, he is new to it. ‖ FIG. *Bien fait*, well constituted (esprit). ‖ FAM. *Bien fait!*, *c'est bien fait pour vous*, it serves you right; *comme te voilà fait!*, what a sight you are!; *je suis fait*, I've had it; *son affaire est faite*, it's all up with him. ‖ LOC. *C'en est fait*, it is done; *c'en est fait de lui*, it is all over (ou) up with him; *c'en est fait de notre argent*, our money is all gone.
— m. [fɛ, fɛt]. Fact, matter of fact (réalité); *c'est un fait*, it is a fact; *de fait ou de nom*, in fact or in name; *le fait est que*, the fact is that; *le fait de savoir lire*, the fact of being able to read. ‖ Occurrence (événement); *fait journalier*, daily occurrence; *fait nouveau*, new development; *faits divers*, news items. ‖ Act, deed (action); *c'est de mon fait*, that's my doing; *faits et gestes*, doings; *hauts faits*, feats, exploits; *prendre sur le fait*, to catch red-handed (ou) in the very act. ‖ Line, strong point (affaire, fort); *ce n'est guère mon fait*, that's scarcely in my line. ‖ Way (manière); *ce n'est pas le fait d'un escroc de*, it is not like a swindler to. ‖ Point; *aller droit, en venir au fait*, to go straight, to come to the point. ‖ Information; *être au fait*, to know all about it; *être au fait de*, to be conversant (ou) acquainted with, to be well posted in (ou) fully aware of; *être sûr de son fait*, to be sure of what one says; *mettre qqn au fait*, to lay the facts before s.o., to acquaint s.o. with the situation; *mettre qqn au fait de*, to acquaint s.o. with. ‖ MILIT. Feat (d'armes); *fait de guerre*, war occurrence. ‖ JUR. *Le fait du prince*, restraint of princes; *gouvernement de fait*, de facto government; *situation de fait*, actual situation; *voies de fait*, violence, assault. ‖ LOC. *Dire son fait à qqn*, to give s.o. a piece of one's mind; *prendre fait et cause pour*, to take sides with, to stand up for.
— loc. adv. **Au fait**, by the way, after all; *au fait, où est-il?*, by the way, where is he? ‖ **De fait, en fait, par le fait**, in fact, in effect, in point of fact, in actual fact, as a matter of fact; actually; *de fait, c'est agréable*, it is really pleasant. ‖ **De ce fait**, for that reason, thereby, therefore; hence. ‖ **Du fait que**, because, for the reason that; owing to the fact that; *du seul fait que*, by the mere fact of, merely by.

— loc. prép. **En fait de**, as regards, in the matter of, by way of, as for.
faîtage [fɛta:ʒ] m. ARCHIT. Ridge-pole; roof-piece (ou) tree; ridge.
faîte [fɛ:t] m. Top (d'un arbre); ridge (d'une maison, d'une montagne). [V. SOMMET.] ‖ FIG. Height. (V. COMBLE.)
faîteau [fɛto] m. ARCHIT. Finial.
faites. V. FAIRE (50).
faîtière [fɛtjɛ:r] adj. Ridge (tuile).
— f. ARCHIT. Ridge-tile. ‖ Ridge-pole (de tente).
fait-tout, faitout [fɛtu] m. CULIN. Stew-pan, cooking pot.
faix [fɛ] m. Burden. (V. FARDEAU.) ‖ ARCHIT. Settling. ‖ MÉD. Foetus and placenta.
faix m. NAUT. Bolt-rope.
fakir [faki:r] m. Fakir.
fakirisme [-kirism] m. The art of fakirs.
falaise [falɛ:z] f. Cliff.
falbalas [falbala] m. pl. Furbelows.
falerne [falɛrn] m. Falernian wine.
fallacieusement [falasjøzmɑ̃] adv. Fallaciously.
fallacieux, euse [-sjø, ø:z] adj. Fallacious.
falloir [falwa:r] v. impers. (51).

---

1. Etre nécessaire. — 2. Etre obligatoire. — 3. Etre besoin. — 4. Etre convenable. — 5. Demander, prendre. — 6. Etre fatal. — 7. Etre possible. — 8. Valoir la peine.

---

1. To have to, must (être nécessaire); *des choses qu'il faut savoir*, things that must be known; *il faut obéir*, you must obey; *il faut que cela soit décidé*, that must be settled; *il faut que cette dent soit arrachée*, that tooth will have to come out; *il me fallut retourner chez moi*, I had to return home; *puisqu'il le faut, j'irai*, since I must go, I shall; *s'il le faut, j'irai*, I shall go if need be; *vous avez cédé?, il a bien fallu*, did you give in?, I had to. ‖ **2.** To be obliged to (être obligatoire); *il m'a fallu obéir*, I was obliged to obey; *il lui faut convenir que*, he is bound to admit that. ‖ **3.** To want, to need, to require (être besoin); *ce qu'il faut*, the very thing that is wanted; *il faut bien vivre*, one has to live; *il faudrait être peintre pour*, one would have to be a painter to; *il faudrait un peintre pour*, it would take a painter to; *il me faudrait un manteau neuf*, I want (ou) I ought to have a new coat (désir); I should have to have a new coat (nécessité); *j'ai tout ce qu'il me faut*, I have all that I want (ou) need; *l'homme qu'il faut*, the very man we want; *que vous faut-il de plus?*, what more do you want?; *tout ce qu'il faut pour écrire*, all that is necessary to write with; *vous avez de la volonté!, Il le faut*, you're strong-willed! I have to be. ‖ **4.** To be fitting to (être convenable); *agir comme il faut*, to act properly (ou) suitably (ou) correctly; *comme il faut*, respectable (femme); gentlemanly, well-bred (homme); *il ne faudrait pas croire que*, you should not believe that; *il fallait me le dire!*, why didn't you tell me?; *il ne faut pas se fier à elle*, she is not to be trusted; *il ne faut pas y songer*, it is not to be thought of; *juste ce qu'il ne faut pas dire!*, just what should not be said!; *pas plus qu'il ne faut*, not overmuch; *que faut-il que je dise si*, what am I to say if; *s'il faut partir de bonne heure, il faudra nous lever tôt*, if we are to start early, we'll have to get up in good time. ‖ **5.** To take, to require (demander, prendre); *combien de temps faut-il pour?*, how long will it take you to?; *il m'a fallu trois heures pour le faire*, I was three hours in doing it, it took me three hours to do it; *il aurait fallu trop d'argent*, it would have taken too much money; *il faudra seulement un effort pour*, it will need only an

effort to. ‖ **6.** To have to (être fatal); *il a fallu qu'elle apprenne cet accident!,* she had to hear of that accident! ‖ **7.** Must (être possible); *faut-il qu'il soit bête!,* how stupid he must be!; *il faut qu'elle ait perdu la tête,* she must have lost her head. ‖ **8.** To be worth (valoir la peine); *il fallait entendre ça!,* that was worth hearing!
— v. pr. **S'en falloir,** to be lacking (ou) wanting; *il s'en fallait d'une heure pour que se levât le soleil,* it wanted but an hour to sunrise; *il n'est pas attentif, il s'en faut de beaucoup,* he is far from being attentive; he is not attentive, far from it; *il s'en est fallu de peu qu'elle se fasse écraser,* she was within an ace (ou) a hair's breadth of being run over; she came near being run over; *peu s'en faut,* very nearly; *tant s'en faut,* far from it.

fallu, fallut. V. FALLOIR (51).
falot [falo] m. Big lantern.
falot, ote adj. Wan (lumière); tame (personnage).
falsifiable [falsifjabl] adj. Falsifiable.
falsificateur, trice [-fikatœːr, tris] s. Adulterator (de denrées); falsifier (de documents); debaser (de monnaie); forger (de signature).
falsification [-fikasjɔ̃] f. Falsification (en général); adulteration (de denrées); forgery (de documents, de signatures); debasement (de monnaie); tampering with (de registres, de textes).
falsifier [-fje] v. tr. (1). To adulterate (des denrées); to falsify, to forge (des documents); to twist (les faits); to debase (une monnaie); to fake, to tamper with (des registres, des textes).
falzar [falzaːr] m. ARG. Trousers, pants.
famé, ée [fame] adj. *Bien famé,* of good repute; *mal famé* (ou) *malfamé,* of evil repute, ill-famed.
famélique [famelik] adj. Starving, hungry (aspect); half-starved, famished-looking (personne).
— s. Starveling.
fameusement [famøzmɑ̃] adv. Famously. ‖ FAM. Jolly, awfully.
fameux, euse [famø, øːz] adj. Famous, famed. (V. ILLUSTRE.) ‖ CULIN. Excellent, first-rate, jolly good. ‖ FAM. Precious, regular (canaille, imbécile); mighty, big (erreur); capital, first-rate (idée); *ce n'est pas fameux,* it's not up to much; *il n'est pas fameux en histoire,* he is not too bright in history.
familial, ale [familjal] adj. Family (lien, maison, vie); *placement familial des enfants,* placing of children in foster-homes, foster care.
familiale [-ljaːl] f. AUTOM. Seven-seater saloon, U. S. seven-passenger sedan.
familiariser [-ljarize] v. tr. (1). To familiarise (avec, with); to accustom (avec, to).
— v. pr. **Se familiariser,** to accustom oneself (avec, to) [qqch.]; *se familiariser avec,* to master (un instrument, une langue). ‖ To grow familiar (avec, with) [qqn].
familiarité [-ljarite] f. Familiarity, intimacy (intimité); intimate terms (relations intimes). ‖ Familiarity (de l'attitude); undue familiarity (privauté); *se permettre des familiarités avec,* to take liberties with, to be over-free with.
familier, ère [-lje, ɛːr] adj. Familiar, domestic, household (du foyer). ‖ Familiar, intimate (intime); pet, pet animal. ‖ Familiar (attitude, personne); *trop familier avec,* over-familiar (ou) over-free with (qqn). ‖ Habitual (défaut, manière); *cette attitude lui est familière,* that is his habitual position. ‖ Familiar, well-known (sujet, visage); *familier avec,* conversant (ou) well-acquainted (ou) familiar with (un sujet). ‖ Colloquial (expression, langage); familiar (terme); *expression familière,* colloquialism.
— m. Close acquaintance, intimate (d'une personne); regular (d'un lieu).

familièrement [-ljɛrmɑ̃] adv. Familiarly. ‖ Colloquially.
famille [fami:j] f. Family, lineage (lignage); *de bonne famille,* well-connected, of a good family; *c'est de famille,* it runs in the blood (ou) the family, it is bred in the bone. ‖ Relatives, relations, kindred, next-of-kin (parenté); *la belle famille,* wife's (ou) husband's family, the in-laws. ‖ Family (ensemble familial); household (maisonnée); *sa petite famille,* her children. ‖ JUR. *Indemnité de charges de famille,* family allowance. ‖ ECCLÉS. *Sainte Famille,* Holy Family.
famine [famin] f. Famine (disette); starvation (inanition); *crier famine,* to cry hunger; to plead poverty (péj.); *réduire à la famine,* to starve; *salaire de famine,* starvation wages.
fan [fan] s. FAM. Fan.
fana [fana] adj. FAM. Crazy, wild (de, about).
— s. FAM. Fanatic; *c'est une fana de tennis,* she's a tennis freak, she's crazy about tennis.
fanage [fana:ʒ] m. AGRIC. Tedding, turning.
fanal [fanal] m. Lantern; lighthouse lamp, fanal; beacon light. ‖ CH. DE F. Headlight. ‖ NAUT. Signal light.
fanatique [fanatik] adj., s. Fanatic.
fanatiquement [-tikmɑ̃] adv. Fanatically.
fanatiser [-tize] v. tr. (1). To fanaticize.
fanatisme [-tism] m. Fanaticism; zealotry.
fanchon [fɑ̃ʃɔ̃] m. Kerchief.
fandango [fɑ̃dɑ̃go] m. Fandango.
fane [fan] f. AGRIC. Top (de carottes); haulm (de pommes de terre).
fané, ée [fane] adj. Faded (couleur, fleur); withered (peau, personne). [V. FLÉTRI.]
faner v. tr. (1). AGRIC. To ted, to turn (le foin).
— v. intr. AGRIC. To make hay.
— v. pr. **Se faner,** to fade (couleur, fleur).
faneur [-nœːr] s. AGRIC. Tedder, hay-maker.
faneuse [-nøːz] f. AGRIC. Tedder, tedding-machine.
fanfare [fɑ̃faːr] f. MUS. Fanfare (de cor de chasse); flourish (de trompettes); brass-band (musiciens); *fanfare du régiment,* bugle-band.
fanfaron, onne [fɑ̃farɔ̃, ɔn] adj. Bragging, blustering.
— s. Braggart, blusterer.
fanfaronnade [-rɔnad] f. Fanfaronade, brag, bluster.
fanfaronner [-rɔne] v. intr. (1). To brag, to bluster, to boast.
fanfreluche [fɑ̃frəlyʃ] f. Fal-lal; pl. frills.
fange [fɑ̃:ʒ] f. Mire. (V. BOUE.)
fangeux, euse [-ʒø, øːz] adj. Miry.
fanion [fanjɔ̃] m. Pennon, pennant.
fanon [fanɔ̃] m. Whalebone (de baleine); dewlap (de bœuf); fetlock (de cheval). ‖ NAUT. Hanging fold (de voile). ‖ ECCLÉS. Pendant (de bannière).
fantaisie [fɑ̃tɛzi] f. Fancy (imagination); *de fantaisie,* fanciful (récit). ‖ Fancy, fantasy, freak, whim (v. LUBIE); *prendre fantaisie de,* to take a fancy to; *satisfaire les fantaisies de qqn,* to humour s.o.'s fancy; *par fantaisie,* out of sheer caprice. ‖ Liking, manner (goût, guise); *à sa fantaisie,* as it pleases him, as he pleases. ‖ MUS. Fantasia. ‖ COMM. Fancy goods (articles); *de fantaisie,* fancy (pain).
fantaisiste [-zist] adj. Fanciful, fantastic.
— s. Fanciful person. ‖ Fanciful (ou) whimsical writer (écrivain).
fantasia [fɑ̃tazja] f. Fantasia.
fantasmagorie [fɑ̃tasmagɔri] f. Phantasmagoria.
fantasmagorique [-rik] adj. Phantasmagoric.
fantasmatique [fɑ̃tasmatik] adj. Phantasmal, phantasmic.
fantasme [-tasm] m. PSYCH. Fantasy. ‖ Phantasm (image hallucinatoire).
fantasmer [-tasme] v. intr. (1). To fantasize.

fantasque [fɑ̃task] adj. Fantastic (idée); whimsical, crotchety, changeable, flighty (personne).
fantassin [fɑ̃tasɛ̃] m. MILIT. Foot-soldier, infantryman.
fantastique [fɑ̃tastik] adj. Fantastic. ‖ FAM. Outrageous, extravagant.
— m. The fantastic; the literature of fantasy (ou) of the fantastic.
fantastiquement [-mɑ̃] adv. Fantastically.
fantoche [fɑ̃tɔʃ] adj., m. Puppet (pr. et fig.).
fantomatique [fɑ̃tɔmatik] adj. Ghostly, ghostlike.
fantôme [fɑ̃to:m] m. Ghost, phantom. ‖ NAUT., MUS. *Le vaisseau fantôme,* the Flying Dutchman. ‖ FIG. Shadow.
— adj. Shadow.
F.A.O. [ɛfao] abrév. de *Food and Agricultural Organization,* FAO.
faon [fɑ̃] m. ZOOL. Fawn.
faonner [fane] v. intr. (1). ZOOL. To fawn.
faquin [fakɛ̃] m. † Knave.
farad [farad] m. ELECTR. Farad.
faradique [-dik] adj. ELECTR. Farad(a)ic.
farandole [farɑ̃dɔl] f. Farandole.
faraud, aude [faro, od] adj. Swell, smart.
— s. FAM. Swanker; *faire le faraud,* to put on side. (V. FENDANT.)
farce [fars] f. Joke (plaisanterie); trick (tour); *faire une farce à,* to play a trick on. (V. ATTRAPE.) ‖ THÉÂTR. Farce. ‖ CULIN. Stuffing, forcemeat. ‖ FIG. *Faire ses farces,* to sow one's wild oats.
— adj. Farcical.
farceur, euse [-sœ:r, ø:z] adj. Waggish.
— s. Wag. ‖ FAM. Bluffer, joker. (V. BOUFFON.)
farcin [farsɛ̃] m. Farcy (des chevaux).
farcir [farsi:r] v. tr. (2). CULIN. To stuff. ‖ FIG. To cram (l'esprit).
— v. pr. **Se farcir,** CULIN. To be stuffed. ‖ FIG. *Se farcir la tête de,* to cram one's head with.
fard [fa:r] m. Paint. (V. MAQUILLAGE.) ‖ FIG. *Parler sans fard,* to speak candidly (ou) undisguisedly. ‖ FAM. *Piquer un fard,* to blush.
fard m. NAUT. Sails.
fardage [farda:ʒ] m. NAUT. Top-hamper (agrès); dunnage (arrimage). ‖ COMM. Camouflage (des cageots, des fruits).
fardeau [fardo] m. Burden, load. ‖ FIG. Weight (des ans); *c'est un fardeau qu'il traînera jusqu'à sa mort,* it will be a millstone round his neck all his life.
farder [farde] v. tr. (1). To paint (qqn). ‖ COMM. To camouflage. ‖ FIG. To disguise. (V. DÉGUISER.)
— v. pr. **Se farder,** to paint. (V. SE MAQUILLER.)
farder v. intr. (1). To weigh heavily. ‖ ARCHIT. To sink. ‖ NAUT. To fit.
fardier [fardje] m. Truck, dray; bar-wheels.
farfadet [farfadɛ] m. Brownie, sprite. (V. LUTIN.)
farfelu, ue [farfəly] s. Whipper-snapper.
— adj. Hare-brained (projet).
farfouiller [farfuje] v. intr. (1). FAM. To rummage (dans, in).
fargue [farg] f. NAUT. Washboard.
faribole [faribɔl] f. Piece of nonsense (ou) twaddle. (V. BALIVERNE.) ‖ Pl. Nonsense, twaddle.
farinacé, ée [farinase] adj. Farinaceous; mealy.
farine [farin] f. Flour, meal; *farine de froment,* wheaten (ou) U. S. whole-wheat flour; *farine de riz,* ground rice; *farine lactée,* malted milk; *farine de pâtisserie,* farina; pastry flour; *couvert de farine,* floury; *saupoudrer de farine,* to flour.
fariner [-ne] v. tr. (1). CULIN. To flour.
farineux, euse [-nø, ø:z] adj. Farinaceous, farinose (aliment); floury, mealy (goût).
— m. Farinaceous food.
farinier [-nje] m. COMM. Flour-merchant.
farinière [-njɛ:r] f. Flour bin.

farniente [farnjɛ̃nte] m. invar. Dolce farniente, blissful ease.
farouche [faruʃ] adj. Fierce, grim (cruel); unsociable (insociable); wild (sauvage); shy (timide).
farouchement [-ʃmɑ̃] adv. Fiercely.
farrago [farago] m. AGRIC. Mixed corn. ‖ FAM. Farrago; hodge-podge.
fart [fa:r] m. Wax used on skis.
fartage [farta:ʒ] m. SPORTS. Waxing (des skis).
farter [-tə] v. tr. (1). To wax (les skis).
fascicule [fasikyl] m. Instalment, part; *vente par fascicule,* instalment selling. ‖ MÉD. Fascile, fascicule, bunch. ‖ MILIT. *Fascicule de mobilisation,* mobilisation instructions (ou) card.
fascié, ée [fasje] adj. BOT. Fasciate.
fascinage [fasina:ʒ] m. MILIT. Fascine work.
fascinant, ante [fasinɑ̃, ɑ̃:t] adj. Fascinating.
fascinateur, trice [fasinatœ:r, tris] adj. Fascinating.
— s. Fascinating person; spell-binder (fam.).
fascination [-sjɔ̃] f. Fascination (pr. et fig.)
fascine [fasin] f. MILIT. Fascine.
fasciné, ée [fasine] adj. Fascinated, spellbound. ‖ U. S. Corduroy (route).
fasciner v. tr. (1). To fascinate. (V. ENSORCELER.)
fasciner v. tr. (1). MILIT. To fascine.
fascisant, ante [faʃizɑ̃, ɑ̃:t] adj. Fascistic.
fascisme [faʃism] m. Fascism.
fasciste [-ʃist] s. Fascist.
faséyer [fazeje] v. intr. (9 c). NAUT. To shiver.
faste [fast] m. State (apparat); display, show (étalage).
faste adj. Lucky, auspicious. (V. BÉNÉFIQUE.) ‖ JUR. *Jour faste,* legal court-day.
fastes m. pl. † Fasti. ‖ FAM. Annals, records.
fastidieusement [fastidjøzmɑ̃] adv. Tediously.
fastidieux, euse [-djø, ø:z] adj. Tedious. (V. LASSANT.)
fastueusement [fastɥøzmɑ̃] adv. Gorgeously (avec éclat); ostentatiously (avec ostentation).
fastueux, euse [-tɥø, ø:z] adj. Gorgeous. ‖ Gaudy, showy (de mauvais goût).
fat [fat] adj. m. Foppish. ‖ Conceited (vaniteux).
— m. Fop. ‖ Conceited young man.
fatal, ale [fatal] adj. Fatal (à, to); fatal (coup, erreur); inevitable (événement); fateful (jour); *femme fatale,* vamp.
fatalement [-lmɑ̃] adv. Fatally.
fatalisme [-lism] m. Fatalism.
fataliste [-list] s. Fatalist.
— adj. Fatalistic.
fatalité [-lite] f. Fatality (adversité, destin).
fatidique [fatidik] adj. Fatidical, fateful.
fatigant, ante [fatigɑ̃, ɑ̃:t] adj. Tiring, fatiguing (besogne); trying (enfant, lumière); tiresome (personne). [V. LASSANT.]
fatigue [fatig] f. Fatigue, tiredness, weariness; *à bout de fatigue,* over-tired. ‖ Pl. Fatigues, toils, hardships. ‖ MÉD. *Fatigue des yeux,* eye-strain. ‖ COMM. Wear and tear (d'un tissu); *de fatigue,* strong (souliers); working (vêtements). ‖ TECHN. Wear and tear (d'une machine); fatigue (du matériel). ‖ NAUT. Strain (d'un cordage).
fatigué, ée [-ge] adj. Tired, weary, fatigued; *fatigué de, de faire,* tired of, of doing. ‖ Worn, shabby (tissu, vêtements). ‖ MÉD. Strained (cœur, yeux); tired (visage, voix). ‖ FAM. *Fatigué d'entendre cette rengaine,* sick of hearing the same old story.
fatiguer [-ge] v. tr. (1). To tire, to weary (qqn); *fatiguer exagérément,* to overwork, to overstrain. ‖ To override (un cheval). ‖ To thumb (un livre); to make shabby (les vêtements). ‖ MÉD. To strain (le cœur, la vue); to make hoarse (la voix). ‖ TECHN. To overdrive, to overstrain, to overtax

(une machine, un moteur). ‖ CULIN. To mix (la salade). ‖ FAM. *Il me fatigue!*, he bores me! — v. intr. TECHN. To be overloaded (pont, poutre). ‖ NAUT., AUTOM. To labour. — v. pr. **Se fatiguer**, to tire (ou) to weary oneself; *se fatiguer à faire*, to tire oneself out doing. ‖ FAM. To get tired, to grow sick, to weary (*de*, *of*). ‖ FAM. *Il ne se fatigue pas les méninges*, he doesn't overtax his brain.

fatras [fatrα] m. Rubbish, farrago, hotch-potch.

fatuité [fatɥite] f. Self-conceit. ‖ Foppishness.

fauberder [fobɛrde] v. tr. (1). NAUT. To swab.

faubert [fobɛ:r] m. NAUT. Swab.

faubourg [fobu:r] m. Suburb (d'une ville); *faubourgs extérieurs*, outskirts. ‖ LOC. *Le faubourg Saint-Germain*, the aristocratic quarter (quartier); the aristocracy (personnes).

faubourien, enne [foburjɛ̃, ɛn] adj. Suburban; U. S. downtown (quartier). ‖ Common, vulgar, Cockney (accent). — s. Suburbanite; U. S. downtowner.

faucarder [fokarde] v. tr. (1). To clear of weeds.

fauchage [foʃa:ʒ] m. AGRIC. V. FAUCHAISON. ‖ FIG. Bringing down, running down (d'un piéton).

fauchaison [-ʃɛzɔ̃] f. AGRIC. Mowing, reaping (action); mowing (ou) reaping time (temps).

fauche [fo:ʃ] f. AGRIC. † V. FAUCHAISON. ‖ POP. Theft, ripping off, pilfering.

fauchage [foʃa:ʒ] m. AGRIC. V. FAUCHISON. ‖ FIG. Bringing down, running down (d'un piéton).

fauchaison [-ʃɛzɔ̃] f. AGRIC. Mowing, reaping (action); mowing (ou) reaping time (temps).

fauche [fo:ʃ] f. AGRIC. V. FAUCHAISON. ‖ POP. Theft, ripping off, pilfering.

fauché, ée [-ʃe] adj. FAM. Broke; *fauché comme les blés*, stony-broke, dead (ou) U.S. flat broke.

faucher [-ʃe] v. tr. (1). AGRIC. To mow (de l'herbe), to reap (des céréales); to scythe (avec une faux). ‖ FIG. To cut down (des cultures); to fell, to bring down (des arbres); to run down (un piéton); to chop (ou) bring down (un footballeur); to mow down (des troupes); to decimate, to wipe out (une famille, une population). ‖ FAM. To pinch, to rip off, to pilfer. (V. BARBOTER.)

faucheur, euse [-ʃœ:r, ø:z] s. AGRIC. Mower.

faucheuse [-ʃø:z] f. AGRIC. Mowing-machine.

faucheux [-ʃø] n. Daddy-long-legs.

faucille [fosi:j] f. AGRIC. Sickle.

faucillon [-sijɔ̃] f. Small sickle.

faucon [fokɔ̃] m. ZOOL. Falcon, hawk.

fauconneau [fokɔno] m. ZOOL. Young falcon. ‖ † Falconet.

fauconnerie [-nri] f. Falconry, hawking.

fauconnier [-nje] m. Falconer.

faudra, faudrait. V. FALLOIR (51).

faufil [fofil] m. Tacking (ou) basting thread.

faufilage [-la:ʒ] m. Tacking, basting.

faufiler [-le] v. tr. (1). To tack, to baste. — v. pr. **Se faufiler**, to thread (ou) to worm one's way, to creep, to edge (*dans*, into); *se faufiler au milieu des voitures*, to nip (ou) dodge in and out of the traffic. (V. GLISSER [SE].) ‖ To insinuate oneself. (V. INSINUER [s'].)

faufilure [-ly:r] f. Tacking, basting.

faune, esse [fo:n, ɛ:s] s. Faun.

faune f. ZOOL. Fauna. ‖ FIG. Set. (V. CLIQUE.)

faunesque [fonɛsk] adj. Faunlike.

faussaire [fosɛ:r] m. Forger (de documents). ‖ Falsifier (de faits).

fausse [fo:s]. V. FAUX.

faussement [fosmɑ̃] adv. Falsely, untruly. ‖ Wrongfully, erroneously (à tort).

fausser [fose] v. tr. (1). To bend, to buckle, to warp, to wrench (une clé, un objet); to force, to strain, to tamper with (une serrure). ‖ MUS. To strain (la voix). ‖ FIG. To warp (l'esprit, les idées, le jugement); to falsify, to alter, to pervert (les faits, la vérité); to wrest, to distort (le sens).

fausset [fosɛ] m. MUS. Falsetto.

fausset m. Spigot, U. S. faucet.

fausseté [foste] f. Falsehood, untruth (mensonge). ‖ Duplicity (duplicité). ‖ Falsity (de jugement). ‖ Falseness (d'une accusation, d'une prétention). ‖ Spuriousness (d'un document). ‖ MUS. *Fausseté de l'oreille*, lack of musical sense.

faut [fo:]. V. FALLOIR (51).

faute [fo:t] f. Lack, want, scarcity, dearth (manque); *faute de mieux, de parler*, for want of something better, of speaking; *faute de quoi*, failing which; *faire faute*, to be lacking (ou) missing; *cela pourrait vous faire faute*, you might miss (ou) need it; *il ne se fait pas faute de critiquer*, he is not backward in criticizing; *se faire faute de*, to fail to; *sans faute*, without fail. ‖ Fault, offence, misdeed (mauvaise action); lapse; indiscretion (mauvaise conduite); sin (péché). ‖ Fault, mistake, error (erreur); *faute de calcul, de jugement*, error of calculation, of judgment; *faute d'impression*, misprint; *faute d'orthographe*, misspelling, spelling mistake. ‖ Blunder (gaffe); *c'est plus qu'un crime, c'est une faute*, it is more than a crime, it is a blunder. ‖ Fault (responsabilité); *à qui la faute?*, whose fault is it?; *c'est ma faute*, the blame is mine, it is my fault; *ce n'est pas ma faute*, it is no fault of mine.

fauter [-te] v. intr. (1). To slip, to make a slip.

fauteuil [fotœ:j] m. Armchair, easy-chair; *fauteuil roulant, tournant*, bath- (ou) wheel-, swivel-chair. ‖ Seat (à l'Académie); chair (de président). ‖ THÉÂTR. *Fauteuil d'orchestre*, orchestra-stall (ou) -seat. ‖ FAM. *Arriver dans un fauteuil*, to win in a canter (ou) in a bath chair (ou) hands down.

fauteur, trice [fotœ:r, tris] s. Fomenter (de désordre); *fauteur de guerre*, warmonger; *fauteur de troubles*, agitator, ringleader.

fautif, ive [fotif, i:v] adj. Defective, faulty (chose); blamable, at fault, guilty (personne).

fautivement [-tivmɑ̃] adv. Faultily.

fauve [fo:v] adj. Wild (bête); fulvous, fallow (couleur); tawny (poil). — m. Fawn (couleur). ‖ ZOOL. Wild beast; *les fauves*, deer; *les grands fauves*, the larger wild beasts, big game. ‖ ARTS. *Les Fauves*, the « wild men », the Fauves.

fauvette [-vɛt] f. ZOOL. Warbler.

faux, fausse [fo, fo:s] adj. False, untrue (contraire à la vérité); *fausse nouvelle*, false report; *faux témoin*, false witness. ‖ False, wrong, mistaken, erroneous (erroné); *date fausse*, wrong date; *idée fausse*, false idea; *faux numéro*, wrong number; *faux sens*, misinterpretation. ‖ False, bad (mauvais); *faux jour*, wrong light (clarté); false light (interprétation); *vers faux*, faulty verse. ‖ False, counterfeit (contrefait); *faux billet*, false (or) forged note; *fausse boîte*, dummy box; *fausse clé*, skeleton key; *faux col*, detachable collar; *fausse fenêtre, porte*, blind window, door; *fausse interview*, fake interview; *faux nom*, assumed (ou) false name; *faux ourlet*, false hem; *bijou faux*, imitation jewel. ‖ False, deceptive (trompeur); *fausse bonhomie*, feigned (ou) assumed joviality. ‖ False, deceitful (peu franc); *il a l'air faux*, he has a shifty look. ‖ False (peu clair); *position fausse*, false position. ‖ Defective (défectueux); *balance fausse*, inaccurate balance. ‖ MUS. Wrong (note). ‖ MÉD. False, floating (côtes); *fausse position*, cramped position. ‖ THÉÂTR. *Fausse sortie*, sham exit, moves to the door. ‖ SPORTS. *Faux départ*, false start. ‖ FIN. *Faux frais*, incidental expenses, incidentals. — adv. Wrongly, not true. ‖ MUS. Out of tune. — loc. adv. **A faux**, wrongly; *accuser à faux*, to accuse wrongly; *porter à faux*, to be irrelevant (ou) inapposite (argument). ‖ Beside the mark;

frapper à faux, to miss one's mark; *poser le pied à faux*, to miss one's footing. ‖ Out of true; *être en porte à faux*, *porter à faux*, to be out of plumb. — m. False, untrue (chose fausse); *plaider le faux pour savoir le vrai*, to angle for the truth with a lie. ‖ JUR. Forgery; *faire un faux*, to commit forgery; *usage de faux*, use of a forged instrument; *s'inscrire en faux contre*, to deny. ‖ COMM. Sham article, imitation, fake. ‖ **Faux-bourdon**, m. MUS. Faux-bourdon. ‖ **Faux bras**, m. NAUT. Warp. ‖ **Faux filet**, m., CULIN. Sirloin. ‖ **Faux-fuyant**, m. Subterfuge, evasion; dodge; put-off (fam.); *user de faux-fuyants*, to hedge. ‖ **Faux jeton**, m. FAM. Shifty customer, double-dealer, double-crosser, U. S. two-timer. ‖ **Faux-monnayeur**, m. Coiner, counterfeiter. ‖ **Faux pont**, m. NAUT. Orlop deck. ‖ **Faux-semblant**, m. Sham, pretence. ‖ **Faux-sens**, m. inv. Mistranslation.

faux [fo] f. AGRIC. Scythe.

faveur [favœ:r] f. Favour (bienveillance); *accorder sa faveur à*, to favour; *en grande faveur auprès de*, high (ou) much in favour with; *perdre la faveur générale*, to fall out of favour. ‖ Favour (marque de bienveillance); *solliciter une faveur*, to ask for (ou) to seek a favour. ‖ Favour (marque de partialité); *de faveur*, free, complimentary (billet); preferential (prix, traitement); *tour de faveur*, preferential treatment. ‖ Pl. Favours (d'une femme); *menues faveurs*, small favours. ‖ Favour (ruban). — loc. prép. A la faveur de, under cover of. ‖ En faveur de, in favour of; *quête en faveur de*, collection in aid of.

favorable [favɔrabl] adj. Favourable, propitious (propice); *favorable à*, friendly (ou) favourable to, in favour of; *se rendre qqn favorable*, to propitiate s.o. ‖ Favourable, suitable (convenable); *moment* (ou) *occasion favorable*, favourable opportunity. ‖ Favourable, kind (bienveillant); *une oreille favorable*, a favourable ear.

favorablement [-rabləmɑ̃] adv. Favourably; *écouter favorablement*, to lend a sympathetic ear to.

favori, ite [-ri, it] adj. Pet (animal); favourite (chose, personne). — s. Favourite, darling; blue-eyed (ou) U. S. fair-haired boy (fam.). [V. PRÉFÉRÉ.] ‖ SPORTS. Favourite. ‖ Pl. Side-whiskers.

favoriser [-rize] v. tr. (1). To favour [*with*, de] (v. AVANTAGER); to favour, to foster, to promote, to patronize (encourager); *favoriser un dessein*, to further an object. ‖ To favour, to assist, to aid, to facilitate (faciliter); *favoriser la fuite de*, to assist the escape of.

favoritisme [-ritism] m. Favouritism.

fayard [faja:r] m. BOT. Beech.

fayot [fajo] m. CULIN., FAM. Kidney bean. ‖ POP. Toady, creep.

fayoter [-ɔte] v. intr. (1). To toady, to creep.

féal, ale [feal] adj. Feal.

fébrifuge [febrify:ʒ] adj. MÉD. Febrifugal, anti-febrile. — m. MÉD. Febrifuge.

fébrile [febril] adj. MÉD. Febrile. ‖ FIG. Feverish.

fébrilement [-lmɑ̃] adv. Feverishly.

fébrilité [-lite] f. MÉD. Febrility. ‖ FIG. Feverishness.

fécal, ale [fekal] adj. Fecal; *matières fécales*, faeces.

fèces [fɛ:s] f. pl. MÉD. Faeces. ‖ FAM. Dregs.

fécond, onde [fekɔ̃, ɔ̃:d] adj. Fecund, fertile (terre). ‖ Prolific (femme, race). ‖ Inventive, fertile (esprit); fruitful (sujet).

fécondant, ante [-dɑ̃, ɑ̃:t] adj. Fecundating.

fécondateur, trice [-datœ:r, tris] adj. Fertilizing. — s. Fertilizer.

fécondation [-dasjɔ̃] f. Fecundation. ‖ MÉD. Impregnation; *fécondation artificielle*, artificial insemination.

féconder [-de] v. tr. (1). To fecundate. ‖ AGRIC. To fertilize. ‖ MÉD. To impregnate.

fécondité [-dite] f. Fecundity. ‖ AGRIC. Fertility.

fécule [fekyl] f. Faecula, starch; *fécule de pommes de terre*, potato-starch (ou) -flour.

féculence [fekylɑ̃:s] f. Faeculence.

féculent, ente [-lɑ̃, ɑ̃:t] adj. Faeculent, starchy (aliment). ‖ CHIM. Turbid. — m. Starchy food.

fed(d)ayin [fedajin] m. inv. Fedayee (pl. fedayeen).

fédéral, ale [federal] adj. Federal.

fédéraliser [-lize] v. tr. (1). To federalize.

fédéralisme [-lism] m. Federalism.

fédéraliste [-list] adj., s. Federalist.

fédératif, ive [-tif, i:v] adj. Federative.

fédération [-sjɔ̃] f. Fédération; *fédération syndicale ouvrière*, trade union; amalgamated unions.

fédéré, ée [federe] adj., s. Federate.

fédérer v. tr. (1). To federate. — v. pr. Se fédérer, to federate.

fée [fe] f. Fairy; *pays des fées*, fairy-land. — adj. Fairy; *arbre fée*, fairy tree.

feed-back [fidbak] m. inv. ELECTR., MÉD. Feedback.

feeder [fi:dœ:r] m. ELECTR. Feeder.

féerie [feri] f. Fairyhood (art); fairy-land (pays des fées). ‖ THÉÂTR. Fairy-play; pantomime. ‖ FIG. Magic spectacle.

féerique [-rik] adj. Fairy, fairy-tale (château). ‖ THÉÂTR. Fairy (jeu). ‖ FIG. Fairy-like, fairy-tale, enchanting (spectacle).

féeriquement [-rikmɑ̃] adv. Magically.

feignant, ante [fɛɲɑ̃, ɑ̃:t] adj. POP. Idle, lazy, bone idle. — s. POP. Lazy-bones, loafer, layabout.

feindre [fɛ̃:dr] v. tr. (59). To feign, to simulate, to counterfeit, to sham, to play (simuler); *feindre la maladie*, to sham sickness, to malinger. ‖ To pretend (faire semblant) [*de*, to]. ‖ To dissemble (dissimuler). — v. intr. To limp slightly (cheval).

feint, einte [fɛ̃, ɛ̃:t] adj. Sham (attaque, maladie); assumed (bonhomie); feigned (chagrin); pretended (émotion, qualité); mock (modestie).

feinte [fɛ̃:t] f. Feint, pretence, fake, sham (faux-semblant); trick, dodge (ruse). ‖ SPORTS. Feint.

feinter [fɛ̃te] v. intr. (1). SPORTS. To feint.

feinteur [fɛ̃tœ:r] m. SPORTS. Feinter.

feld-maréchal [fɛldmareʃal] m. MILIT. Field-marshal.

feldspath [fɛldspat] m. Feldspar.

fêlé, ée [fɛle] adj. Cracked (vase, voix); *rendre un son fêlé*, to sound cracked. ‖ FAM. Cracked, crackpot, crack-brained. (V. CINGLÉ.)

fêler [fɛle] v. tr. (1). To crack. — v. pr. Se fêler, to crack.

félibre [felibr] m. Provençal poet.

félibrige [-bri:ʒ] m. Félibrige, Provençal literary society.

félicitation [felisitasjɔ̃] f. Congratulation; *envoyer ses félicitations*, to send a message of congratulation; *recevoir des félicitations*, to be congratulated; *lettre de félicitations*, congratulatory letter.

félicité [-te] f. Felicity, bliss. (V. BONHEUR.)

féliciter [-te] v. tr. (1). To congratulate (*de*, on); *féliciter qqn d'avoir achevé*, to congratulate s.o. on having completed. (V. COMPLIMENTER.) ‖ FAM. *Je vous félicite, c'est réussi!*, I wish you a joy of it, you have made a fine mess of things (ironiquement). — v. pr. Se féliciter, to congratulate oneself (*de*, on) [qqch.]; to pat oneself on the back (fam.);

je n'ai eu qu'à me féliciter de lui, I am highly satisfied with him.

félidé [felide] m. Zool. Felid.

félin, ine [felɛ̃, in] adj. Zool. Feline. ‖ Fig. Cat-like.

— s. Zool. Feline.

félir [feli:r] v. intr. (2). To spit (chat).

fellag(h)a [fɛlaga] m. Fellagha.

fellah [fɛlla] m. Fellah. ‖ Pl. Fellaheen.

félon, onne [felɔ̃, ɔn] adj., m. Felon.

félonie [feloni] f. Felony, disloyalty.

felouque [fəluk] f. Naut. Felucca.

fêlure [fely:r] f. Split (du bois); crack (du verre). ‖ Méd. Fracture.

femelle [fəmɛl] f. Zool. Female; cow (de l'éléphant); hen (des oiseaux); *c'est une femelle,* it's a she. ‖ Pop. Female (femme).

— adj. Female; cow- (éléphant); hen- (oiseau). ‖ Techn. Female.

féminin, ine [feminɛ̃, in] adj. Feminine (monde, sexe). ‖ Feminine (grâce, personne); womanly (personne, vertu, vêtements); womanish (voix). ‖ Gramm. Feminine.

— m. Gramm. Feminine.

féminisation [-nizasjɔ̃] f. Feminization (du mâle); increase in the number of women (d'une profession). ‖ Gramm. Making (ou) becoming feminine.

féminiser [-nize] v. tr. (1). To feminize. ‖ Gramm. To make feminine.

— v. pr. Se **féminiser,** to feminize.

féminisme [-nism] m. Feminism.

féministe [-nist] adj., s. Feminist.

féminité [-nite] f. Femineity, femininity, womanliness.

femme [fam] f. Woman; *les femmes,* women, womankind; *femme agent, soldat, police-, service-woman; femme de chambre,* chambermaid, house-maid, parlour maid; *femme de charge,* house-keeper; *femme docteur,* lady (ou) U. S. woman doctor; *femme écrivain,* authoress; *femme peintre,* woman painter; *femme d'intérieur,* housewife, home-maker; *elle est très femme,* she is very feminine. (V. bonne *femme.*) ‖ Wife (épouse); *sa future femme,* his bride-to-be; *sa femme le mène,* he is henpecked; *prendre femme,* to marry; *prendre pour femme,* to take to wife; *mes femmes,* my womenfolk. ‖ Jur. *Femme en puissance de mari, seule,* feme covert, sole.

femmelette [-lɛt] f. Little (ou) weak woman (femme); weakling, womanish man (homme).

fémoral, ale [femɔral] adj. Méd. Femoral.

fémur [-my:r] m. Méd. Femur.

fenaison [fənɛzɔ̃] f. Agric. Haymaking (action); hay-time (époque).

fendage [fɑ̃da:ʒ] m. Splitting.

fendant [fɑ̃dɑ̃] m. Comm. Fendant, white wine from Valais in Switzerland.

fendeur [-dœ:r] s. Splitter (de bois); cleaver (de diamants).

fendillé, ée [-dije] adj. Crackled, cracked.

fendillement [-dijmɑ̃] m. Crackle (en surface); cracking (de la peinture).

fendiller [-dije] v. tr. (1). To crack, to fissure (le bois, la peinture); to craze (le vernis).

— v. pr. Se **fendiller,** to crack; to craze.

fendoir [-dwa:r] m. Cleaver, chopper.

fendre [fɑ̃:dr] v. tr. (4). To split (du bois); to cleave (en long). ‖ To fissure, to crack (un mur); to crack (la peinture, le plafond); to slit (le tissu); to craze (le vernis). ‖ Fig. To cleave (l'air); to break (le cœur); to elbow one's way through (la foule); to cleave (la mer); *à fendre l'âme, les oreilles,* heart-rending, ear-splitting.

— v. pr. Se **fendre,** to crack, to cleave asunder (bois, peinture). ‖ Sports. To lunge (à l'escrime).

‖ Méd. *Se fendre la main,* to cut one's hand. ‖ Fam. *Se fendre de mille francs,* to stump (ou) cough up a thousand francs; *il s'est fendu,* he has put his hand down, U. S. he crashed through.

fendu, ue [fɑ̃dy] adj. Split (anneau); slit, slashed (jupe); *la bouche fendue jusqu'aux oreilles,* with his mouth stretching from ear to ear.

fenestrage [fənɛstra:ʒ], **fenêtrage** [fenɛtra:ʒ] m. Archit. Fenestration.

fenêtre [-nɛ:tr] f. Window; sash-window (à l'anglaise, à guillotine); casement (à battants); balance (ou) pivoted window (à bascule); French window (porte-fenêtre); *fenêtre treillissée,* lattice window; *regarder à, par la fenêtre,* to look in at, out of the window; *sans fenêtre,* windowless. ‖ Window (d'enveloppe); *enveloppe à fenêtre,* window-envelope. ‖ Ciném. *Fenêtre d'observation,* observation post. ‖ Naut. Aperture. ‖ Méd. Fenestra. ‖ Fam. *Jeter l'argent par les fenêtres,* to throw money down the drain.

fenêtrer [-nɛtre] v. tr. (1). To put windows in.

fénian [fenjɑ̃] m. Fenian.

fenil [fəni] m. Agric. Hay-loft.

fennec [fenɛk] m. Zool. Fennec.

fenouil [fənu:j] m. Bot. Fennel.

fenouillet [fənuje] m. Bot. Fennel-apple.

fente [fɑ̃:t] f. Crack, split (dans le bois); crack, chink, fissure (dans un mur); cleft (dans un roc). ‖ Slit (dans une jupe); slash (dans un vêtement). ‖ Slot (d'une boîte aux lettres, d'un distributeur, d'une tirelire, d'une vis); chink (d'un entrebâillement). ‖ Méd. Chap, crack (aux mains); slash (de la peau). ‖ Sports. Lunge.

fenugrec [fənygrɛk] m. Bot. Fenugreek.

féodal, ale [feɔdal] adj. Feudal.

— m. Feudal landlord.

féodalité [-lite] f. Feudality.

fer [fɛr] m. Iron (métal). ‖ Head (de flèche, de lance, de marteau); fluke (de gaffe); tag (de lacet); ferrule (de parapluie); shoe (de piolet); blade (de rabot); hobnail, metal tip (de semelle). ‖ Horseshoe (à cheval); *fer à glace,* calk; *perdre un fer,* to cast a shoe. ‖ Flat-iron, smoothing-iron (à repasser); *donner un coup de fer à,* to iron up, to press up. ‖ Curling-iron, crisper (à friser). ‖ Brand, red-hot iron (fer rouge); *marquer au fer rouge,* to brand. ‖ Steel, sword (épée). ‖ Pl. Irons; *les fers aux mains,* with his hands fettered. ‖ Naut. *Mettre aux fers,* to clap in irons. ‖ Méd. Pl. Forceps. ‖ Techn. *Fer à souder,* soldering-iron. ‖ Loc. *Discipline de fer,* iron discipline; *faire feu des quatre fers,* to be full of drive; *tomber les quatre fers en l'air,* to fall backwards. ‖ **Fer-blanc,** m. Tin; *boîte en fer blanc,* can.

ferblanterie [fɛrblɑ̃tri] f. Tin-shop (local); tin-ware (marchandise).

ferblantier [-tje] m. Tinsmith, tinman (fabricant); dealer in tinware (marchand).

férial, ale [ferjal] adj. Ecclés. Ferial.

férie [feri] f. Ecclés. Feria.

férié, ée [ferje] adj. *Jour férié,* official holiday, Bank Holiday.

férir [feri:r] v. tr. (52). † To strike; *sans coup férir,* without striking a blow.

ferlage [fɛrla:ʒ] m. Naut. Furling.

ferler [-le] v. tr. (1). Naut. To furl.

fermage [fɛrma:ʒ] m. Agric. Tenant farming (action); rent (loyer).

fermail [fɛrma:j] m. † Clasp.

fermant, ante [fɛrmɑ̃, ɑ̃:t] adj. Lock-up (bureau); closing (meuble).

ferme [fɛrm] adj. Solid (chair, sol); firm (terre). ‖ Firm (écriture, main, voix); steady (main, pas); *marcher d'un pas ferme,* to walk steadily. ‖ Culin. Firm (gelée); stiff (pâte); tough (viande). ‖ Fin. Firm (achat, vente); strong (marché); steady (prix). ‖ Fig. Confirmed, solid (conviction);

staunch (courage); firm (personne, proposition);
steadfast (politique); steady (résistance); resolute
(ton); unfaltering (volonté); *ferme devant le dan-*
ger, steadfast in danger; *attendre de pied ferme*,
to wait resolutely for.
— adv. Firmly, steadily; *frapper ferme*, to hit
hard; *tenir ferme*, to stand fast.
ferme f. AGRIC. Farming-lease (bail); farm-house
(bâtiment); farm (exploitation); *donner, prendre*
à ferme, to farm, to rent; *petite ferme*, small
holding, croft. ‖ FIN. Farm.
ferme f. ARCHIT. Truss, roof truss.
fermé, ée [-me] adj. Shut, closed (fenêtre, porte);
closed (voiture); *fermé au public*, closed to the
public. ‖ Exclusive (cercle, milieu). ‖ FIG. Impenetrable, irresponsive (expression, visage); *fermé*
à, blind to (une idée); impervious to, inaccessible
to (un sentiment).
fermement [-məmɑ̃] adv. Firmly; steadily.
ferment [fɛrmɑ̃] m. Ferment. ‖ ECCLÉS. Fer-
mentum. ‖ FIG. Ferment (de discorde).
fermentable [-tabl] adj. Fermentable.
fermentatif, ive [-tatif, i:v] adj. Fermentative.
fermentation [-tasjɔ̃] f. Fermentation; working
(fam.) [du vin]. ‖ MÉD. Flatulence. ‖ FIG. Ferment, effervescence; *en fermentation*, at work.
fermenter [-te] v. intr. (1). To ferment; to work
(fam.). ‖ FIG. To ferment.
ferme-porte [fɛrməpɔrt] m. invar. Door-spring.
fermer [fɛrme] v. tr. (1). To shut (la fenêtre, la
porte); to shut up (la maison) [v. CLORE]; *fermer*
à clef, au verrou, to lock, to bolt. ‖ To shut (une
boîte); to furl (un éventail, un parapluie); to
close (une lettre, un livre); to close, to shut (un
parapluie); to draw (les rideaux); to pull down
(un store); *fermer les yeux*, to shut (ou) to close
one's eyes. ‖ To enclose, to shut in (un terrain).
‖ To shut up (condamner). ‖ To stop up, to bar
(l'accès); to cut off (la route). ‖ To close (un cortège); *fermer la marche*, to bring up the rear. ‖
To turn off, to shut off (l'eau); to turn out (le
gaz) [au brûleur], to turn off (au compteur), to
cut off (en le coupant); to switch off, U. S. to turn
off (la lumière électrique). ‖ ELECTR. To close (un
circuit); to /switch off (le courant). ‖ COMM. To
shut down (une entreprise, une usine); *fermer*
boutique, to shut up shop. ‖ FIN. To close (un
compte). ‖ NAUT. To brace in (une vergue). ‖ FIG.
To close (une carrière, un débouché); *fermer*
l'oreille à, to shut one's ears to; *fermer les yeux*
sur, to shut one's eyes to, to wink at. ‖ POP.
Ferme ça, la ferme!, cut it out!, shut up!
— v. intr. To close, to shut (fenêtre, porte). ‖ To
close (magasin, musée); *l'heure de fermer*, closing
time; *on ferme!*, all out! ‖ To fasten up (une
ouverture dans un vêtement); *un manteau qui*
ferme bien, a coat that wraps well round. ‖ COMM.
To close down (maison).
— v. pr. Se fermer, to close, to shut. ‖ MÉD. To
heal. ‖ FIG. To freeze, to become inscrutable.
fermeté [fɛrməte] f. Firmness (des chairs); hardness (du sol). ‖ Firmness, steadiness (de l'écriture,
de la main); steadiness (du regard). ‖ FIN. Firmness (des cours). ‖ FIG. Firmness, resoluteness
(du caractère).
fermette [fɛrmɛt] f. Small farm, farmhouse.
fermeture [-ty:r] f. Shutting, closing (action);
closing-time (heure). ‖ Fastening (moyen); *ferme-*
ture de boutique, de porte, shutter, door-fastening.
‖ COMM. Closing down, lock-out (d'une maison,
d'une usine). ‖ TECHN. Cut-off (de l'arrivée). ‖
ELECTR. Closing (du circuit). ‖ SPORTS. *Ferme-*
ture de la chasse, end of the shooting season. ‖
Fermeture Eclair (nom déposé), **à glissière, à**
crémaillère, f. Zip, zip-fastener, zipper, slide-
fastener.

fermier, ère [fɛrmje, ɛ:r] adj. AGRIC. Farm-
house (beurre, produits); *poulet fermier*, free-
range chicken.
fermier [fɛrmje] m. AGRIC. Farmer; tenant-
farmer; crofter. ‖ *Fermier d'entreprise*, contractor. ‖ † *Fermier général*, farmer-general.
fermière [-mjɛ:r] f. AGRIC. Farmer's wife.
fermion [fɛrmjɔ̃] m. PHYS. Fermion.
fermoir [fɛrmwa:r] n. Snap (de collier, de livre,
de sac, de valise); clasp (de livre); fastener (de
vêtements).
féroce [ferɔs] adj. Wild (bête); fierce, ferocious
(personne). ‖ Ravenous (appétit); ferocious
(regard).
férocement [-smɑ̃] adv. Ferociously, fiercely.
férocité [-site] f. Ferocity, fierceness, ferociousness. (V. CRUAUTÉ.)
ferrage [fɛra:ʒ] m. Shoeing (d'un cheval, d'une
roue); *ferrage à glace*, calking. ‖ Tagging (de
lacet). ‖ SPORTS. Strike (à la pêche).
ferraillage [feraja:ʒ] m. TECHN. Steel reinforcement (pour le béton).
ferraille [fɛrɑ:j] f. Scrap-iron (débris); scrap-
heap (tas); *bruit de ferraille*, rattling noise.
ferrailler [fɛrɑje] v. intr. (1). FAM. To fight with
swords.
ferrailleur [-jœ:r] m. Dealer in scrap.
ferrailleur m. Swashbuckler. (V. BRETTEUR.) ‖
FAM. Wrangler.
ferrant [fɛrɑ̃] adj. m. *Maréchal-ferrant*, farrier,
shoeing-smith.
ferrate [fɛrrat] m. CHIM. Ferrate.
ferré, ée [fɛre] adj. Shod (cheval); tagged (lacet);
iron-shod (piolet); hobnailed (souliers). ‖ CH.
DE F. *Voie ferrée*, railway track. ‖ FAM. Well up,
posted up (sur, in). [V. CALÉ.]
ferrements [-mɑ̃] m. pl. Iron works.
ferrer [-re] v. tr. (1). To shoe (un cheval, un piolet); to tag (un lacet); to iron (un meuble, une
porte); to hobnail (un soulier); *ferrer à glace*,
to calk, to rough-shoe. ‖ SPORTS. To strike (un
poisson). ‖ TECHN. To metal (une route).
ferret m. Tag (de lacet). ‖ Ferret (de verrier). ‖
GÉOL. Hard core (de pierre).
ferreur [fɛrœ:r] m. Shoeing-smith, farrier (de chevaux); tagger (de lacets); iron-fitter (de meubles).
ferreux, euse [fɛrø, ø:z] adj. CHIM. Ferrous;
non ferreux, non-ferrous (métaux).
ferrifère [-rifɛ:r] adj. Ferriferous.
ferrique [-rik] adj. CHIM. Ferric.
ferrite [fɛrit] m. Ferrite.
ferro-alliage [fɛroalja:ʒ] m. TECHN. Ferroal-
loy, ferrous alloy.
ferrocérium [fɛroserjɔm] m. Ferrocerium.
ferrochrome [-kro:m] m. CHIM. Ferrochromium.
ferrocyanure [-sjany:r] m. CHIM. Ferrocyanide.
ferromagnétique [-maɲetik] adj. PHYS. Ferromagnetic.
ferronnerie [fɛrɔnri] f. Ironworks, iron-foundry
(fabrique); iron-work, ironmongery, hardware
(objets).
ferronnier [-nje] s. Ironmonger.
ferronnière [-njɛ:r] f. Ferroniere, frontlet.
ferrotypie [-tipi] f. Ferrotype.
ferroviaire [-vjɛ:r] adj. CH. DE F. Railway.
ferrugineux, euse [fɛryʒinø, ø:z] adj. Ferruginous.
ferrure [fɛry:r] f. Iron fitting (de meuble, de
porte). ‖ Shoeing (action); shoe (fer). ‖ Shoe (de
canne, de piolet); clout (de sabot).
ferry [fɛri], **ferry-boat** [fɛribot] m. NAUT.
Train (ou) car ferry.
fertile [fɛrtil] adj. Fertile, fruitful (en, in).
[V. FÉCOND.] ‖ FIG. Rich, fertile (imagination);
fertile en émotions, thrilling; *fertile en expé-*

dients, fruitful of expedients; *fertile en événements,* eventful.

fertilisable [-lizabl] adj. Fertilizable.

fertilisant, ante [-lizɑ̃, ɑ̃:t] adj. Fertilizing.
— m. Fertilizer.

fertilisation [-lizasjɔ̃] f. Fertilization.

fertiliser [-lize] v. tr. (1). To fertilize.
— v. pr. Se **fertiliser,** to become fertile.

fertilité [-lite] f. Fertility, fruitfulness.

féru, ue [fery] adj. Struck (ou) set *(de,* on) [une idée]; *féru d'amour pour,* smitten with, enamoured of.

férule [feryl] f. Cane; ferule †. ‖ Boт. Ferula. ‖ Fɪɢ. Sway; *sous la férule de qqn,* under s.o.'s thumb. (V. ᴅᴏᴍɪɴᴀᴛɪᴏɴ.)

fervent, ente [fɛrvɑ̃, ɑ̃:t] adj. Fervent.
— s. Devotee *(de,* of). ·

ferveur [-vœ:r] f. Fervour *(à,* in); *avec ferveur,* fervently. ‖ Earnestness (v. ᴀʀᴅᴇᴜʀ); *avec ferveur,* earnestly, zealously.

fesse [fɛs] f. Buttock. ‖ Pl. V. ᴅᴇʀʀɪ̀ᴇʀᴇ. ‖ **Fesse-mathieu** (pl. *fesse-mathieux*) m. Skinflint.

fessée [fɛse] f. Spanking; *donner une fessée à,* to spank.

fesser v. tr. (1). To spank, to whack; to skelp.

fessier [fɛsje] adj. Méᴅ. Gluteal (muscle); *le grand fessier,* gluteus maximus.
— m. Fᴀᴍ. Buttocks. ‖ V. ᴅᴇʀʀɪ̀ᴇʀᴇ.

fessu, ue [fɛsy] adj. Broad-buttocked.

festin [fɛstɛ̃] m. Feast, banquet; spread (fam.); *faire un festin à tout casser,* to have a tremendous spread.

festiner [-tine] v. intr. (1). To banquet.

festival [-tival] (pl. **festivals**) m. Mᴜs. Festival. ‖ Fête (réjouissance).

festivité [-tivite] f. Festivity.

festoiement [-twamɑ̃] m. Banqueting.

feston [fɛstɔ̃] m. Festoon (guirlande). ‖ Scallop (broderie); *point de feston,* button-hole stitch.

festonner [-tɔne] v. tr. (1). To scallop.
— v. intr. Fᴀᴍ. To zigzag along (ivrogne).

festoyer [fɛstwaje] v. intr. (9 *a*). To banquet (nourriture); to booze (fam.) [beuverie].

fêtard [fɛtɑ:r] m. Reveller, boozer; U. S. hellbender.

fête [fɛ:t] f. Feast, festival; *fête légale,* bank (ou) public holiday, U. S. statutory (ou) legal holiday; *jour de fête,* feast-day, high day, holiday. ‖ Name-day, fête-day (de qqn); *souhaiter une bonne fête à qqn,* to wish s.o. many happy returns. (V. ᴀɴɴɪᴠᴇʀsᴀɪʀᴇ.) ‖ Fête, entertainment, festive party; *donner une fête, une petite fête,* to give an entertainment, a party. ‖ Festivity, merry-making; *fête champêtre,* village fête; *être en fête,* to be holiday- (ou) merry-making. ‖ Rejoicing; *air de fête,* festal (ou) festive air; *se faire une fête de venir,* to look forward to coming. ‖ Spree (noce); *faire la fête,* to carouse. ‖ Welcome (accueil); *faire fête à,* to welcome warmly, to fête. ‖ Eᴄᴄʟᴇs. Feast. ‖ Aᴠɪᴀᴛ. *Fête de l'air,* air display (ou) pageant. ‖ **Fête-Dieu** (pl. *fêtes-Dieu*) f. Eᴄᴄʟᴇ́s. Corpus Christi.

fêter [fɛte] v. tr. (1). To keep (un anniversaire, une fête); to celebrate (un événement); to fête (qqn).

fétiche [fetiʃ] m. Fetish. ‖ Aᴜᴛᴏᴍ., Aᴠɪᴀᴛ., Nᴀᴜᴛ. Mascot.

fétichisme [-ʃism] m. Fetishism.

fétichiste [-ʃist] s. Fetishist.

fétide [fetid] adj. Fetid. (V. ᴘᴜᴀɴᴛ.)

fétidité [-dite] f. Fetidness.

fétu [fety] m. Straw (de paille).

feu [fø] (pl. **feux**) m.

FÊTES DE L'ANNÉE
FEAST-DAYS OF THE YEAR

Annonciation	Lady-Day, Annunciation
Ascension	Ascension Day
Assomption	Assumption Day
Avent	Advent
Carême	Lent
Cendres (mercredi des)	Ash Wednesday
Chandeleur (la)	Candlemas
Epiphanie	Epiphany, Twelfth Night
Fête-Dieu	Corpus Christi
jour des Morts	All Souls' Day
jour des Rois	Twelfth Day
mardi gras	Shrove Tuesday
Mi-Carême	Mid-Lent
Nativité de la Vierge	Nativity of the Virgin
Noël	Christmas (*abr.* Xmas)
Noël (fêtes de)	Christmas, Yule-Tide
Noël (le Père)	Father Christmas
Noël (la veille de)	Christmas Eve
Nouvel An	New Year, New Year's Day
octave de la Fête-Dieu	Octave of Corpus Christi
Pâques	Easter
Passion (semaine de la)	Passion Week
Pentecôte	Whitsuntide
Pentecôte (lundi de)	Whit Monday
Quadragésime	Quadragesima
Quasimodo	Low Sunday
Quatre-Temps	Ember-Days
Ramadan, Ramadhan	Ramadan
Rameaux (les)	Palm Sunday
Rogations (les)	Rogation Week
Sabbat	Sabbath-Day, the Sabbath
Sacré-Cœur (fête du)	Feast of the Sacred Heart
Saint-Jean (la)	Midsummer Day
Saint-Nicholas (la)	Santa Claus
semaine sainte	Holy Week
Toussaint	All Saints' Day
Trinité	Trinity Sunday
vendredi saint	Good Friday
Vigile des Quatre-Temps	Ember-eve

---

1. Chauffage. — 2. Incendie. — 3. Divertissement. — 4. Supplice. — 5. Foudre. — 6. Lumière. — 7. Foyer. — 8. Eclat. — 9. Amour. — 10. Congestion. — 11. Mɪʟɪᴛ. — 12. Aᴠɪᴀᴛ. — 13. Nᴀᴜᴛ. — 14. Aᴜᴛᴏᴍ. — 15. Tʜᴇ́âᴛʀ. — 16. Cᴜʟɪɴ. — 17. Fɪɢ. Ardeur. — 18. Loc.

1. Fire (de chauffage); *faire du feu,* to make a fire *(avec,* of); *feu de bois, de charbon,* wood, coal fire. ‖ 2. Fire (incendie); *crier au feu,* to shout «Fire!»; *en feu,* on fire, ablaze; *feu de cheminée,* chimney on fire; *le feu a pris au rideau,* the curtain caught fire; *mettre le feu à,* to set fire to; *prendre feu,* to take (ou) catch fire. ‖ 3. Fire (divertissement); *feu d'artifice,* fireworks; *feu de joie,* bonfire. ‖ 4. Stake (supplice); *condamner au feu,* to condemn to the stake. ‖ 5. Lightning (éclair); *feu du ciel,* thunderbolt. ‖ 6. Light (lumière); *feu fixe, tournant,* fixed, revolving light (de phare). ‖ 7. Hearth (foyer); *un hameau de dix feux,* a hamlet of ten houses; *sans feu ni lieu,* homeless. ‖ 8. Fire, sparkle (éclat); *feux du diamant,* sparkle (ou) lights (ou) dispersion of a diamond. ‖ 9. † Love (amour); *brûler d'un feu ardent,* to love ardently (ou) passionately. ‖ 10. Fire (congestion); *feu du rasoir,* barber's itch, razor-itch; *la figure en feu,* blushing hotly, with a flushed face; *mettre la bouche en feu,* to take the skin off s.o.'s tongue. ‖ 11. Mɪʟɪᴛ. *Aller au feu,* to go into action; *cesser le feu,* to cease firing; *faire feu,* to shoot, to fire; *feu!* fire!; *feu grégeois,* Greek fire; *par le fer et le feu,* by fire and sword. ‖ 12. Aᴠɪᴀᴛ. *Feux de bord* (ou) *de position,* navigation lights. ‖ 13. Nᴀᴜᴛ. *Feux de route,* navigation (ou) signal lights; *tous feux éteints,* without lights. ‖ 14. Aᴜᴛᴏᴍ. *Feu arrière,*

rear (ou) tail light; *feux de côté, de position,* side, parking lights; *feux rouges,* traffic lights; *feux de croisement,* dipped lights, U. S. low beams. ‖ **15.** THÉÂTR. *Feux de la rampe,* footlights. ‖ **16.** CULIN. *A feu doux, vif,* on a gentle, brisk fire; *à deux feux,* double- (ou) two-burner (réchaud); *à petit feu,* on a slow fire. ‖ **17.** FIG. Heat (de la colère); heat, glow, warmth (de la discussion); fire (de l'inspiration, de la jeunesse, du talent) [v. ARDEUR]; *avec feu,* with fire; *feu de paille,* flash in the pan; *plein de feu,* full of drive (personne); flashing (regard); *prendre feu,* to catch fire, to flare (ou) fire up. ‖ **18.** LOC. *Donner du feu à qqn,* to give s.o. a light; *faire long feu,* to fizzle out, to misfire; *feu vert!,* green light, U. S. go-ahead; *jouer avec le feu,* to play with fire; *la part du feu,* a necessary sacrifice; *n'y voir que du feu,* to be bamboozled; *se jeter au feu pour,* to go through fire and water for; *tuer à petits feux,* to kill by inches. ‖ **Feu pilote,** n. Pilot-light.
— adj. Flame, flame-coloured, tan (couleur).

feu, eue adj. Late, deceased.
feudataire [fødatɛ:r] m. † Feudatory.
feuillage [føja:ʒ] m. Foliage.
feuillaison [-jɛzɔ̃] f. Foliation.
feuillard [-ja:r] m. Hoop-wood; hoop-iron.
feuille [fø:j] f. BOT. Leaf (d'arbre, d'artichaut, de chou, de plante, de vigne); petal, rose-leaf (de rose); *mettre ses feuilles,* to come into leaf. ‖ TECHN. Leaf, foil (d'or); foil (de plomb); sheet (de tôle). ‖ Leaf (d'un paravent, d'un volet). ‖ Sheet (de papier); *feuille de garde,* fly-leaf; *les bonnes feuilles,* the advance sheets. ‖ Newspaper (journal); *feuille de chou,* rag. ‖ JUR. *Feuille d'audience,* cause list; *feuille d'impôt,* notice of assessment; *feuille de paie,* salary (ou) wage sheet, pay-roll; *feuille de présence,* time-sheet; *feuille de route,* way-bill. ‖ MILIT. *Feuille de route,* marching orders. ‖ AVIAT. *Descente en feuille morte,* falling-leaf roll. ‖ ARTS. *Feuille de vigne,* fig-leaf (sur une statue). ‖ **Feuille-morte,** adj. invar. Filemot, russet, dead leaf (couleur).
feuillée [føje] f. Foliage; leaves. ‖ MILIT. Pl. Straddle trench, camp latrine.
feuilleret [føjrɛ] m. TECHN. Grooving-plane.
feuillet [føjɛ] m. Leaf (de livre). ‖ Panel (de bois); layer (d'écorce); plate, sheet (de métal). ‖ ZOOL. Psalterium (des ruminants).
feuilletage [-jta:ʒ] m. CULIN. Puff-pastry.
feuilleté, ée [-jte] adj. CULIN. *Pâte feuilletée,* puff-paste. ‖ GÉOL. Foliated.
— m. CULIN. Flaky-pastry, puff-pastry.
feuilleter v. tr. (8a). To flip through (un livre); to finger (des papiers). ‖ CULIN. To make flaky (la pâte).
— v. pr. **Se feuilleter.** CULIN. To become flaky. ‖ GÉOL. To split into layers.
feuilleton [føjtɔ̃] m. Feuilleton; serial (roman); *publier en feuilleton,* to serialize.
feuilletoniste [-tɔnist] m. Feuilletonist.
feuillette [føjɛt] f. Leaflet.
feuillette f. Quarter-cask, half hogshead (fût).
feuillettement [-tmɑ̃] m. Flipping (ou) running through the pages (de, of).
feuillu, ue [føjy] adj. Leafy; *forêt d'arbres feuillus,* hardwood forest.
feuillure [-jy:r] f. Groove.
feuler [føle] v. intr. (1). To roar (tigre); to growl (chat).
feutrage [føtra:ʒ] m. Felting.
feutre [fø:tr] m. Felt hat (chapeau); felt (étoffe). ‖ Felt-tipped pen, felt-pen (stylo).
feutré, ée [føtre] adj. Felt, felty (étoffe). ‖ Padded (fenêtre, selle). ‖ FIG. Soft, stealthy (pas); *marcher à pas feutrés,* to pad along.

feutrer v. tr. (1). To felt. ‖ To pad (capitonner).
— v. pr. **Se feutrer,** to felt, to become matted.
feutrier [-trje] m. Felt-maker.
feutrine [-tri:n] f. Imitation felt.
fève [fɛ:v] f. BOT. Bean. ‖ CULIN. *Fève du gâteau des rois,* bean hidden in a Twelfth-Night cake.
féverole [fevrɔl] f. BOT. Horse-bean.
février [fevrije] m. February.
fez [fɛ:z] m. Fez.
fi [fi] interj. Fy!, Faugh! *fi de!,* a fig for!; *faire fi de,* to turn up one's nose at.
fiabilité [fjabilite] f. Reliability.
fiable [fjabl] adj. Reliable (appareil); trustworthy (personne).
fiacre [fjakr] m. Cab.
fiançailles [fjɑ̃sɑ:j] f. pl. Betrothal, engagement (avec, to); *bague de fiançailles,* engagement ring.
fiancé, ée [fjɑ̃se] s. Fiancé.
fiancer v. tr. (6). To betroth, to engage (qqn); *fiancé à* (ou) *avec,* engaged to.
— v. pr. **Se fiancer,** to get (ou) become engaged (à, avec, to).
fiasco [fjasko] m. FAM. Fiasco, wash-out, flop; *faire fiasco,* to be a fiasco, to fizzle out.
fiasque [fjask] f. Italian flask.
fibranne [fibran] f. Staple fibre.
fibre [fibr] f. BOT., MÉD. Fibre. ‖ TECHN. Staple (de tissu). ‖ FIG. *A la fibre sensible,* sensitive. ‖ **Fibre-cellule,** f. MÉD. Fibre-cell.
fibreux, euse [-brø, ø:z] adj. Fibrous.
fibrillaire [-brilɛ:r] adj. Fibrillary.
fibrillation [-brilasjɔ̃] f. MÉD. Fibrillation.
fibrille [-bri:j] f. Fibril.
fibrine [-brin] f. CHIM. Fibrine.
fibrinogène [-brinɔʒɛn] m. MÉD. Fibrinogen.
fibrociment [fibrɔsimɑ̃] m. Fibro-cement.
fibroïde [fibrɔid] adj. MÉD. Fibroid.
fibrome [fibro:m] m. MÉD. Fibroma, fibrous tumour; fibroid (fam.).
fic [fik] m. Wart.
ficaire [fikɛ:r] f. BOT. Pilewort.
ficelage [fisla:ʒ] m. Tying up.
ficeler [-sle] v. tr. (8 a). To tie up (un paquet). ‖ FAM. To tog up. (V. ACCOUTRER.)
ficelle [-sɛl] f. String, twine, pack-thread (à paquets). ‖ MILIT. Stripe. ‖ FIG. Wire; *tirer les ficelles,* to pull the strings. ‖ FAM. Tricks; *connaître les ficelles,* to know the ropes; *vieille ficelle,* old hand.
— adj. Putty-coloured (couleur). ‖ FAM. Knowing.
ficellerie [-sɛlri] f. String-factory.
fiche [fiʃ] f. Filing-card, index-card, slip; *fiche auteur, sujet,* author, subject entry; *fiche de police,* registration form; *fiche scolaire,* school record-card; *fiche de versement,* paying-in (ou) U. S. deposit slip; *mettre sur fiche,* to card-index; *mise en fiches,* card-indexing. ‖ TECHN. Peg, pin (de bois, de fer). ‖ ELECTR. Plug (de prise); key (de tableau).
fiche [fiʃ] v. tr. V. FICHER.
fiché, ée [fiʃe] adj. *Fiché sur place,* nailed to the spot; *rester fiché,* to stand frozen (ou) stock-still.
ficher v. tr. (1). To stick (un poignard) [dans, in]; to drive (une pointe) [dans, into]. ‖ To point (des joints de maçonnerie). ‖ To file (un renseignement); to have a file (ou) record on, to put on file (ou) record (une personne). ‖ FAM. *Allez vous faire fiche!,* go to hell!; *fichez le camp!,* scram!, beat it!, hop it!, clear off!; *ficher dehors,* to chuck out (expulser); to sack, to fire (renvoyer); *ficher la paix à qqn,* to let s.o. alone; *ficher dedans,* to have, to get, to do (tromper); *ne rien ficher,* not to do a stroke, to do damn all.
— v. pr. **Se ficher,** to stick (clou, poignard) [dans, in]. ‖ FAM. Not to care a rap (de, about) [qqch.]; *il s'en fiche,* he doesn't care a tinker's cuss; U. S. he doesn't give a darn. ‖ FAM. To

make fun (ou) game (*de*, of) [qqn]; *il se fiche de vous*, he is pulling your leg (se moquer); he has got you (tromper). ‖ Fam. *Se ficher une idée dans le crâne*, to get a bee into one's bonnet; *se ficher par terre*, to go sprawling, to take a spill.

fichier [fiʃje] m. Card-index, card-file, card catalogue, card record file. ‖ Card-index box.

fichtre [fiʃtr] interj. Fam. Phew!; Gosh!; *fichtre non!*, no fear!

fichtrement [-trəmɑ̃] adv. Fam. Terribly, awfully.

fichu, ue [fiʃy] adj. Fam. Awful (caractère); deuced (ennui); God-forsaken (pays); rotten (temps); *fichu idiot*, absolute fool; *fichue position*, dreadful position. ‖ Lost (perdu); *il est fichu*, he's done for, it's all up with him, he's had his chips; *mon chapeau est fichu*, my hat has had it (ou) is done for. ‖ Togged up (accoutré); *fichu comme l'as de pique*, dressed like a guy (ou) U. S. a slob. ‖ Shaped (tourné); *bien fichu*, good-looking, well-built; *mal fichu*, bad-looking (mal bâti); in poor shape, under the weather, off colour (souffrant). ‖ Able (capable); *elle n'est pas fichue de chanter*, she is not up to singing; *elle est fichue de se marier*, it's quite on the cards she will marry.

fichu m. Fichu, neckerchief, scarf.

fictif, ive [fiktif, iːv] adj. Fictitious (personnage). ‖ Comm. Impersonal, dead (compte); pro forma (facture); nominal (prix). ‖ Jur. Feigned (action); nominal (associé); unbonded (entrepôt).

fiction [-sjɔ̃] f. Fiction.

fictivement [-tivmɑ̃] adv. Fictitiously.

fidéicommis [fideikɔmi] m. Jur. Deposit, trust.

fidéicommissaire [-sɛ:r] m. Jur. Beneficiary, trustee.

fidéjusseur [fideʒysœːr] m. Jur. Guarantor.

fidéjussion [-ʒysjɔ̃] f. Jur. Suretyship, security.

fidèle [fidɛl] adj. Faithful (ami, époux) [à, to]; faithful, trusty (chien, serviteur) [v. LOYAL]; *rester fidèle à qqn*, to stick to s.o. ‖ Faithful, trustworthy (chroniqueur, récit); accurate, faithful (compte, traduction); regular (lecteur); faithful, retentive (mémoire); *être fidèle à*, to hold to (des idées, des opinions); to keep (sa parole). — s. Supporter. ‖ Ecclés. *Les fidèles*, the faithful.

fidèlement [-mɑ̃] adv. Faithfully.

fidélité [fidelite] f. Faithfulness, fidelity; *fidélité à ses engagements*, faith; *fidélité envers le roi*, loyalty to the king. ‖ Trustworthiness (d'un chroniqueur, d'un employé); accuracy, accurateness (d'un compte, d'une traduction).

fiduciaire [fidysjɛːr] adj. Fin. Fiduciary; *acte fiduciaire*, writ; *circulation fiduciaire*, paper currency.

fiducie [-si] f. Jur. Trust.

fief [fjɛf] m. Fief, feud, fee.

fieffé, ée [fjɛfe] adj. Fam. Arrant, absolute (coquin); precious, egregious (imbécile); consummate, confounded, arrant (menteur).

fiel [fjɛl] m. Gall (de l'animal); bile (de l'homme). ‖ Fig. Gall (amertume); venom (venin).

fielleux, euse [-lø, øːz] adj. Gall-like. ‖ Fig. Rancorous (caractère); bitter (remarque).

fiente [fjɑ̃ːt] f. Droppings (d'oiseau).

fienter [-te] v. intr. (1). To mute (oiseau); to dung (vache).

fier (se) [səfje] v. pr. (1). To rely (à, on) [qqch.]; to trust (à, to) [qqn]; *il ne faut pas se fier à lui*, he is not to be trusted; *on ne peut se fier à ses dires*, you can never depend on what he says; *on peut se fier à cet ouvrage*, it is a reliable work; *vous pouvez vous fier à moi sur ce point*, you may take my word for it.

fier, ière [fjɛːr] adj. Proud, dignified (digne); *au cœur fier*, proud-hearted; *trop fier pour demander*, too proud to ask. ‖ Proud (noble); *un fier coursier*, a proud steed. ‖ Proud (orgueilleux);

être fier de, to be proud of, to glory in; *il n'y a pas là de quoi être fier*, that is not much to boast of. ‖ Self-satisfied (content de soi); *il n'était pas fier*, he felt rather small, he cut a rather poor figure; *avoir fière allure*, to cut a fine figure. ‖ Fam. Famous, fine. (V. FIEFFÉ.) — s. *Faire le fier*, to put on airs, to swank (se pavaner); to stand on one's dignity (se piquer). ‖ Fier-à-bras, m. Bully. (V. BRAVACHE.)

fièrement [fjɛrmɑ̃] adv. Proudly. ‖ Fam. Famously.

fiérot [-ro] adj. Fam. Stuck-up, snobbish, uppish.

fierté [-te] f. Pride, dignity. ‖ Pride, vanity.

fiesta [fjɛsta] f. Fam. Party, shindig.

fieu [fjø] (pl. FIEUX) m. † Son.

fièvre [fjɛːvr] f. Méd. Fever; *avoir de la fièvre*, to have a temperature, to be feverish; *fièvre de croissance*, growing pains. ‖ Fig. Fever-heat, excitement, restlessness; *avec fièvre*, feverishly.

fiévreusement [fjevrøzmɑ̃] adv. Feverishly (pr. et fig.).

fiévreux, euse [-vrø, øːz] adj. Feverish (climat, personne, pouls); fevered (front). ‖ Fig. Feverish. — s. Méd. Fever patient.

fifre [fifr] m. Mus. Fife-player, fifer (artiste); fife (instrument).

fifrelin [fifrəlɛ̃] m. Fam. Farthing; U. S. red cent.

fig. Abrév. de *figure*, figure (schéma, dessin). ‖ Abrév. de *figuré*, figuratively.

figaro [figaro] m. Fam. Barber.

figé, ée [fiʒe] adj. Congealed (huile). ‖ Fig. Stiff (corps); starched (manières, personne); set (sourire); *figé sur place*, nailed to the spot.

figement [-ʒmɑ̃] m. Congealing (de l'huile); clotting (du sang).

figer [fiʒe] v. tr. (7). To congeal (l'huile); to curdle, to clot (le sang). ‖ Fam. To freeze (qqn). — v. pr. Se figer, to congeal (huile); to curdle, to clot (sang). ‖ Fam. To stiffen (personne); to freeze (sourire).

fignolage [fiɲɔlaːʒ] m. Finicking, fiddle-faddling.

fignoler [-le] v. intr. (1). To finick, to fiddle-faddle. — v. tr. To finick over (un travail).

figue [fig] f. Bot. Fig. ‖ Fam. *Mi-figue, mi-raisin*, wavering, half one thing and half another.

figuerie [figri] f. Fig-orchard.

figuier [figje] m. Bot. Fig-tree; *figuier de Barbarie*, prickly pear.

figurant [figyrɑ̃, ɑ̃:t] m. Théâtr. Super, supernumerary, walker-on; *rôle de figurant*, walk-on (ou) non-speaking part. ‖ Ciném. Extra, crowd artist.

figurante [-rɑ̃:t] f. Théâtr. Figurante.

figuratif, ive [-ratif, iːv] adj. Figurative. ‖ Arts. *Art figuratif*, figurative art. — m. Arts. Figurative artist.

figuration [-rasjɔ̃] f. Figuration. ‖ Ciném. Extras. ‖ Théâtr. Supers.

figurativement [-rativmɑ̃] adv. Figuratively.

figure [figy:r] f. Figure (forme); *figure de bronze*, bronze figure. ‖ Face (v. VISAGE); *à la figure ronde*, round-faced; *faire bonne figure à*, to give a warm welcome to. ‖ Look, air (apparence); *chevalier à la triste figure*, Knight of the Rueful Countenance; *faire figure, piètre figure*, to cut a figure, a sorry figure; *faire figure de*, to play the part of; *faire figure d'imbécile*, to look a fool. ‖ Figure (personnage); *une grande figure*, a great character. ‖ Court card (aux cartes). ‖ Math., Gramm., Arts. Figure. ‖ Naut. *Figure de proue*, figurehead.

figuré, ée [figyre] adj. Represented. ‖ Archit. Decorated. ‖ Math. Representative (plan). ‖ Gramm. Figurative. — m. Gramm. Figurative use (emploi); figurative sense (sens); *au figuré*, figuratively.

figurer v. tr. (1). To figure. (V. REPRÉSENTER.)

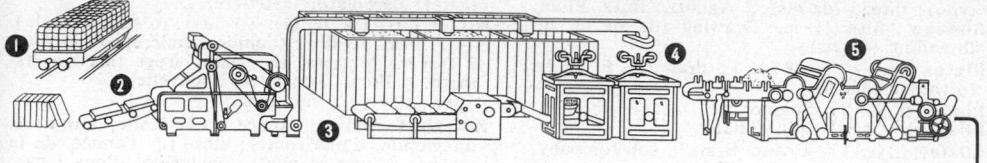

1. Balles de coton   Cotton bales
2. Chargeuse-mélangeuse   Scutcher
3. Stockage   Storage
4. Ouvreuse   Bale-opener, opener
5. Batteur   Bale-breaker, cleaner
6. Cardeuse   Carding machine, carder
7. Boîtes tournantes   Cans
8. Étireuse   Combing machine, comber
9, 10. Bancs à broches   Roving frames

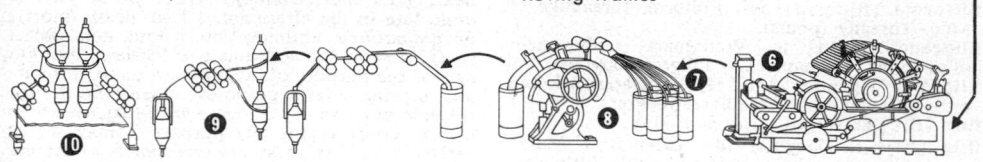

— v. intr. To figure (*dans*, in ; *sur*, on). ‖ THÉÂTR. To appear (comédien) ; to dance (danseuse).
— v. pr. **Se figurer,** to imagine, to fancy (imaginer) ; to think, to believe (penser).

figurine [-rin] f. Figurine.

fil [fil] m. Thread ; *fil à coudre*, sewing thread ; *fil à fil*, end-on-end. ‖ Linen (toile) ; *fil de lin*, yarn ; *bas de fil*, lisle stocking ; *pur fil*, all linen. ‖ Wire (de métal) ; *fil à beurre*, cheese-wire ; *fil de fer*, wire ; *fil d'or*, spun gold. ‖ String (de haricot) ; *plein de fils*, stringy. ‖ Grain (du bois) ; vein (du marbre) ; warp (du tissu) ; *droit fil*, with the grain (dans le bois) ; on the straight (dans le tissu). ‖ Thread (d'araignée) ; *fil de la Vierge*, gossamer. ‖ Edge (d'une lame) ; *passer au fil de l'épée*, to put to the sword. ‖ Current (de l'eau) ; *au fil de l'eau*, with the stream. ‖ TECHN. *Fil à plomb*, plumb-line. ‖ ELECTR. *Fil souple, torsadé*, flex, twin flex ; *fil de terre*, earth-wire ; *fil du téléphone*, telephone wire ; *au bout du fil*, on the phone (ou) line ; *un coup de fil*, a ring, a call ; *sans fil*, wireless. ‖ FIG. Thread (de la conversation, d'un discours, des idées, d'une intrigue) ; *ne tenir qu'à un fil*, to hang by a thread. ‖ FAM. *Avoir un fil à la patte*, not to be a free agent ; *cousu de fil blanc*, obvious ; *donner du fil à retordre à*, to give a lot of trouble to ; *il n'a pas inventé le fil à couper le beurre*, he won't set the Thames (ou) the world on fire ; *c'est un vrai fil*, she is a mere slip of a woman. ‖ **Fil-à-fil,** m. inv. Pepper-and-salt.

filage [fila:ʒ] m. Spinning ; yarn. ‖ Drawing (du métal).

filament [filamɑ̃] m. Filament, fibre. ‖ ELECTR. Filament.

filamenteux, euse [-tø, ø:z] adj. Filamentous. ‖ Stringy (viande).

filandière [filɑ̃djɛ:r] f. † Spinner. ‖ Pl. The Fates.

filandre [filɑ̃:dr] f. String (de la viande). ‖ Pl. Gossamer (fils de la Vierge).

filandreux, euse [-drø, ø:z] adj. Stringy (viande). ‖ FIG. Long-drawn-out (explication).

filant, ante [filɑ̃, ɑ̃:t] adj. Ropy (liquide). ‖ ASTRON. Shooting (étoile).

filasse [fila:s] f. BOT. Tow (de chanvre). ‖ FAM. Tow-coloured, flaxen.
— adj. inv. *Cheveux filasse*, tow-coloured (ou) flaxen hair.

filateur [filatœ:r] s. Spinner.

filature [-ty:r] f. Spinning (action). ‖ Spinning-mill (fabrique). ‖ FAM. Shadowing ; *prendre en filature*, to shadow.

fildefériste [fildəferist] s. Tightrope walker.

file [fi:l] File (d'objets) ; queue (de personnes) ; *à la file*, in file ; *faire la file*, to queue up. ‖ MILIT. File ; *par file à droite*, right wheel. ‖ LOC. *A la file*, at a stretch, without stopping, on end.

filé, ée [file] adj. Spun (chanvre, verre). ‖ NAUT. Flowing. ‖ MUS. Sustained (note) ; drawn-out (son). ‖ CULIN. Spun (sucre).

filer v. tr. (1). To spin (de la laine, une quenouille, une toile, du verre). ‖ NAUT. To ease off (une amarre, le foc) ; to pay out (une corde) ; to pour (de l'huile) ; to run (des nœuds). ‖ MUS. To sustain (une note) ; to draw out (un son). ‖ FIG. *Filer le parfait amour*, to live love's young dream. ‖ FAM. To shadow (qqn).
— v. intr. To spin (filandière). ‖ To smoke (lampe). ‖ NAUT. To run out (câble) ; *laisser filer*, to pay out (un câble). ‖ CULIN. To rope (liquide) ; to go stringy (macaroni). ‖ FIG. To fly (temps) ; to spin along (voiture). ‖ FAM. To buzz off, to scram, to scuttle off, to make tracks (v. DÉCAMPER) ; *il faut que je file*, I must away (or) be off. ‖ LOC. *Filer doux*, to sing small, to tread softly.

filerie [filri] f. Spinning-shed.

filet [filɛ] m. Net ; *filet à cheveux*, hair-net, filet ; *filet à papillons*, butterfly-net. ‖ Network (ouvrage) ; *faire du filet*, to net. ‖ SPORTS. *Filet de pêche, de tennis*, fishing-, tennis-net. ‖ CH. DE F. Rack (à bagages). ‖ CULIN. String (ou) net bag (à provisions). ‖ FIG. *Coup de filet*, haul ; *prendre dans ses filets*, to net.

filet m. Small thread (fil). ‖ Thin trickle (d'eau) ; thin streak (de lumière) ; *un filet de voix*, a thin voice. ‖ MÉD. String (sous la langue) ; *couper le filet*, to loosen the tongue ; *filet nerveux*, nervous filament. ‖ CULIN. Fillet (de bœuf, de sole, de veau); dash (de vinaigre). ‖ TECHN. Rule (en typo); thread (de vis). ‖ ARCHIT., BLAS. Fillet.

filetage [filta:ʒ] m. Drawing (de fil de fer); threading (de vis).

fileter [-te] v. tr. (8 b). To draw (du fil de fer); to thread (une vis).

fileur [filœ:r] s. Spinner.

filial, ale [filjal] adj. Filial.

filiale [filja:l] f. COMM. Branch, sub-company.

filialement [-lmɑ̃] adv. Filially.

filiation [-sjɔ̃] f. Filiation; *en filiation directe*, in direct line. ‖ FIG. Affiliation.

filière [filjɛ:r] f. Draw-plate (à fil de fer); screwing-plate (à vis). ‖ ZOOL. Spinneret (d'araignée). ‖ NAUT. Man-rope; guard rail. ‖ TECHN. Circular die. ‖ ARCHIT. Ledger (d'échafaudage). ‖ COMM. Circulating contract; transfer note (ou) warrant. ‖ FIG. Regular steps; *passer par* (ou) *suivre la filière*, to go through the usual channels (demande); to work one's way up (personne). ‖ FIG. Network (réseau de malfaiteurs).

filiforme [filifɔrm] adj. Filiform, threadlike. ‖ MÉD. Thready (pouls).

filigrane [-gran] m. Watermark, embossment (d'un billet, du papier). ‖ Filigree (ouvrage).

filigraner [-grane] v. tr. (1). To watermark (un billet, du papier). ‖ To filigree (ouvrer).

filin [filɛ̃] m. Rope; *vieux filin*, junk.

fille [fi:j] f. Daughter (des parents). ‖ Maid; *jeune fille*, young lady, girl; *petite fille*, little girl; *petite-fille*, grand-daughter; *fille-mère*, unmarried mother; *vieille fille*, spinster, old maid; *rester fille*, to remain single. ‖ Maid (servante); *fille de salle*, waitress; *fille de vaisselle*, washer-up, kitchen hand. ‖ † *Fille d'honneur*, maid of honour. ‖ FAM. Prostitute (v. PROSTITUÉE); *courir les filles*, to wench. ‖ LOC. *Jouer la fille de l'air*, to skedaddle, to give leg-bail.

fillette [fijɛt] f. Little girl, lassie. ‖ Half-bottle (bouteille).

filleul [fijœ:l] m. Godson.

filleule [fijœ:l] f. God-daughter.

film [film] m. CINÉM. Film; motion picture, U. S. movie (fam.); *film d'actualités*, newsreel; *film-annonce*, trailer, U. S. teaser; *film d'enseignement*, educational film, film-strip; *relatif aux films*, cinematic.

filmer [-me] v. tr. (1). To film.

filmique [-mik] adj. Film, cinematic, filmic.

filmographie [-mɔgrafi] f. Filmography.

filmologie [-mɔlɔʒi] f. Film (ou) cinema studies.

filmothèque [-mɔtɛk] f. Film library.

filon [filɔ̃] m. Sill (en géologie); lode, vein (en minéralogie); *filon guide*, leader, leader vein. ‖ FAM. Cushy (ou) soft job; U. S. bonanza; *trouver le filon*, to strike oil. ‖ Filon-couche, m. Bedvein.

filoselle [filɔzɛl] f. Filoselle, floss-silk.

filou [filu] m. Sharper, crook. (V. VOLEUR.)

filouter [-te] v. tr. (1). To take in, to cheat (qqn).

filouterie [-tri] f. Cheating, swindling.

fils [fis] m. Son; *X et son fils*, X and his son; *le fils X*, young X; *X et fils*, X and son; *M. X fils*, Mr X junior; *avec mes deux fils*, with my two boys. ‖ ECCLÉS. *Le Fils de Dieu*, the Son of God. ‖ LOC. *Fils de famille*, young man of good family; *fils à papa*, rich man's son, playboy, U.S. papa's boy; *fils de ses œuvres*, self-made man.

filtrage [filtra:ʒ] m. Filtering.

filtrant, ante [-trɑ̃, ɑ̃:t] adj. Filtering; *bout filtrant*, filter-tip (de cigarette). ‖ MÉD. Filterable.

filtrat [-tra] m. Filtrate.

filtration [-trasjɔ̃] f. Filtration.

filtre [filtr] m. Filter, strainer (cornet); filter-

paper (papier). ‖ CULIN. Demi-tasse, drip-coffee (café); percolator (cafetière).

filtrer [-tre] v. tr. (1). To filter, to strain (qqch.). — v. intr. To filter (liquide, lumière); *l'eau filtre à travers la terre*, the water seeps through the earth. ‖ FIG. To leak out (nouvelle).

filure [fily:r] f. Spinning.

fin [fɛ̃] f. End (de l'année, d'une étoffe, d'un livre, du monde, d'une route); close (de l'année, de la journée, d'une séance); conclusion (d'une lettre, d'un ouvrage) [v. BOUT]; *fin de semaine*, weekend; *fin de siècle*, advanced (idées); fin de siècle (personne); *en fin de*, at the end of; *jusqu'à la fin*, to the very end; *le troisième en commençant par la fin*, the third from the end, the last but two; *mener à bonne fin*, to bring to a successful conclusion (une affaire); to deal successfully with (une tâche); *mettre fin à*, to put an end to, to make an end of, to bring to an end; *prendre fin*, to come to an end; *sans fin*, endless; *tirer à sa fin*, to draw to a close (année, soirée); to be nearing its end (réunion); *vers la fin de l'après-midi*, late in the afternoon. ‖ End, death (mort); *fin prématurée*, untimely end. ‖ End, aim, object (but); *à cette fin*, with this end in view; *aux fins de*, for the purpose of, with a view to; *à plusieurs fins*, serving several purposes; *à seule fin de*, for the sole purpose of; *à toutes fins utiles*, to whom it may concern, for any purpose it may serve; *arriver à ses fins*, to secure one's ends, to accomplish one's object. ‖ COMM. *Fin courant*, at the end of the present month; *fin de mois*, monthly statement. ‖ JUR. Expiration (d'un bail, d'un terme); *fin de non-recevoir*, exception, demurrer; *renvoyer des fins de la poursuite*, to nonsuit. ‖ LOC. *Faire une fin*, to settle down, to marry; *fin de non-recevoir*, mere put-off.

— loc. adv. *A la fin*, at last, in the end; *à la fin des fins*, at long last; *à la fin c'est trop!*, that's really outrageous!

fin, ine [fɛ̃, in] adj. Fine (aiguille, cheveux, fleur, linge, pluie, poussière, sable, tissu, travail); small, fine (écriture); thin (papier, pluie, tranche); small-tooth (peigne); sharp (pointe). ‖ Fine (or); real (perle). ‖ Neat (attaches); slender (doigts, taille); delicate (traits). ‖ Fine, expert (dégustateur); nice (goût); sharp, keen (nez, odorat, ouïe). ‖ Expert; *fine lame*, fine swordsman; *fin tireur*, crack shot. ‖ NAUT. Fast (voilier). ‖ COMM. High-class (produits). ‖ CULIN. Exquisite (dîner); choice (vin). ‖ FIG. Subtle (allusion, ironie); fine, delicate (esprit); sharp, shrewd (personne); *fin comme l'ambre*, sharp as a needle. ‖ FIG. Shrewd, astute, clever, smart (rusé); *fine mouche*, knowing bird; shrewd customer; *on ne peut être plus fin que tous les autres*, you can't fool all the people all the time. ‖ LOC. *Au fin fond de*, in the depths of (la campagne); at the very bottom of (un tiroir); *savoir le fin mot de l'affaire*, to get to the bottom of it.

— m. Fine linen (linge). ‖ FIG. Clever (ou) smart person; *jouer au plus fin avec*, to try to outwit.

— adv. Fine, finely; *écrire fin*, to write small; *moulu fin*, finely ground; *fin prêt*, absolutely ready; *taillé fin*, sharp-pointed (crayon).

finage [fina:ʒ] m. Refining.

final, ale [final] (pl. **finals**) adj. Last (lettre, mot); final (résultat). ‖ PHILOS., ECCLÉS. Final.

finale [fina:l] m. MUS. Finale. — f. SPORTS. Final. ‖ MUS. Keynote. ‖ GRAMM. End syllable.

finalement [-lmɑ̃] adv. Finally; at last.

finalisme [-lism] m. PHILOS. Finalism.

finaliste [-list] s. SPORTS. Finalist.

finalité [-lite] f. PHILOS. Finality.

finance [finɑ.s] f. FIN. Financial circles (ou)

world (monde); finance (profession, science). ‖ Money, cash (argent); *moyennant finance,* for money, for a consideration. ‖ Pl. Finances (ressources); *mes finances sont en baisse,* my finances are in a low water (ou) in bad shape. ‖ Pl. Finances (trésor public); *le ministère des Finances,* the Exchequer, U. S. the Treasury Department.

financement [-smɑ̃] m. FIN. Financing.

financer [-se] v. tr. (6). To finance.
— v. intr. FAM. To shell out. [V. CASQUER.]

financiér, ère [-sje, ɛ:r] adj. FIN. Financial.
— m. Financier.

financière [-sjɛ:r] f. CULIN. Financière sauce.

financièrement [-sjɛrmɑ̃] adv. Financially.

finasser [finase] v. tr. (1). FAM. To finesse.

finasserie [-sri] f. FAM. Trickery, foxiness. ‖ Pl. Wiles. (V. RUSE.)

finasseur, euse [-sœ:r, ø:z], **finassier, ère** [-sje, sjɛ:r] s. FAM. Slyboots, trickster.

finaud, aude [fino, o:d] adj. Wily, foxy, cute.
— m. Sly fox.

finaude [fino:d] f. Sly minx, slyboots.

finauderie [-nodri] f. Craftiness, wiliness, slyness, foxiness.

fine [fi:n] f. Fine champagne, liqueur brandy.

fine-de-claire [-dəklɛ:r] f. ZOOL., CULIN. Green oyster raised in an oyster-farm.

finement [finmɑ̃] adv. Delicately (avec délicatesse); shrewdly (avec habileté); knowingly (d'un air entendu).

finesse [finɛs] f. Fineness (d'une aiguille, des cheveux, du linge, du travail); smallness (de l'écriture); thinness (de la pluie); sharpness (d'une pointe); sharpness, keenness (du tranchant). ‖ Neatness (des attaches); slenderness (de la taille); delicacy (des traits). ‖ Delicacy (du goût); sharpness (de l'odorat, de l'ouïe). ‖ FIG. Subtlety (d'une allusion, de l'esprit, de la pensée); shrewdness, cleverness (de qqn). ‖ Wile, trick, finesse (ruse). ‖ Pl. Niceties (de la langue); tricks (du métier, du style).

finette [finɛt] f. Flannelette.

fini, ie [fini] adj. Finished, ended (v. ACHEVÉ); *c'en est fini,* it's all over; *fini de s'amuser,* the fun is over; *le dîner est fini,* dinner is over; *tout est fini entre nous,* it's all over between us. ‖ Finished (parfait); *ouvrage fini,* finished work. ‖ PHILOS. Finite. ‖ FAM. Done for (usé); *il est fini,* he's done for. ‖ FAM. Consummate (fieffé); *un idiot fini,* a perfect idiot, an absolute fool.
— m. Finish (du travail). ‖ PHILOS. Finite.

finir [fini:r] v. tr. (2). To finish, to end (v. ACHEVER); *finir la soirée,* to finish the evening; *avoir fini sa sieste,* to have had one's nap. ‖ To finish, to put the finishing touch to. (V. FIGNOLER.) ‖ MILIT. *Il a fini son temps,* his time is up.
— v. intr. To finish (achever); *avez-vous bientôt fini?,* have you nearly finished? ‖ To end, to die (mourir). ‖ To come to an end (avoir une fin); *il finira mal,* he will come to a bad end. ‖ To finish, to end, to stop (cesser); *cela ne finit pas,* it is endless. ‖ Finir en, to finish (ou) end in; *finir en queue de poisson,* to end in smoke, to fizzle out. ‖ Finir de; *il n'a pas fini de s'habiller,* he has not finished (ou) done dressing; *on avait fini de danser,* the dancing was over. ‖ Finir par, to end by (en arriver à); *cela finit par me lasser,* in the long run it tires me; *il a fini par l'acheter,* in the end he bought it; *elle a fini par l'admirer,* she came to admire him. ‖ Finir par, to end in (s'achever par); *finir par une dispute,* to end in a quarrel. ‖ En finir, to finish, to stop; *ça n'en finit pas,* there is no end of it; *des excuses à n'en plus finir,* never-ending (ou) endless apologies; *en finir avec,* to have done with (qqch., qqn); *finissons-en,* let us get it over (ou) make an end of it; *il n'en*

finit pas, he never stops (il ne s'arrête pas); he dawdles, he is a slowcoach (il lambine); *on n'en finit pas de travailler,* there's no end to the work, it's nothing but work, work, work.

finish [finiʃ] m. SPORTS. Finishing power; *au finish,* at the last moment, at the very end.

finissage [finisa:ʒ] m. Finishing.

finissant, ante [-sɑ̃, ɑ̃:t] adj. Finishing, ending; *le jour finissant,* dusk, gloaming.

finisseur [-sœ:r] s. Finisher.

finition [-sjɔ̃] f. Finishing.

finlandais, aise [fɛ̃lɑ̃dɛ, ɛ:z] adj. Finnish.
— s. Finn, Finlander.

Finlande [fɛ̃lɑ̃:d] f. GÉOGR. Finland.

finnois, oise [finwa, wa:z] adj. GÉOGR. Finnish.
— s. GÉOGR. Finn.
— m. GRAMM. Finnish (langue).

finno-ougrien, enne [finougrijɛ̃, ɛn] adj., m. GRAMM. Finno-Ugric, Finno-Ugrian.

fiole [fjɔl] f. Phial, flask. ‖ POP. Mug; *se payer la fiole de qqn,* to chip s.o., to pull s.o.'s leg.

fion [fjɔ̃] m. FAM. Finish; *coup de fion,* finishing touch.

fiord [fjɔrd] m. GÉOGR. Fiord.

fioriture [fjɔrity:r] f. Flourish; frill. ‖ MUS. Grace-note.

firmament [firmamɑ̃] m. Firmament. (V. CIEL.)

firme [firm] f. COMM. Firm.

fisc [fisk] m. FIN. Inland Revenue; U. S. Internal Revenue; *agent du fisc,* Inland Revenue official, U. S. Collector of Internal Revenue.

fiscal, ale [fiskal] adj. Fiscal; *année fiscale,* taxable (ou) U. S. fiscal year; *fraude fiscale,* tax-evasion; *régime fiscal,* system of taxation; *ressources fiscales,* financial resources; *timbre fiscal,* revenue stamp.

fiscalisation [fiskalizasjɔ̃] f. FIN. Making subject to tax (imposition); funding through taxation (financement).

fiscaliser [-lize] v. tr. (1). FIN. To make subject to tax (imposer); to fund through taxation (financer).

fiscalité [-lite] f. Fiscal policy (politique); mode of taxation (système).

fissible [fisibl] adj., **fissile** [fisil] adj. Fissile. ‖ PHYS. Fissile, fissionable.

fission [-sjɔ̃] f. Fission. ‖ PHYS. Splitting (de l'atome); *fission nucléaire,* nuclear fission.

fissuration [fisyrasjɔ̃] f. TECHN. Fissuring, cracking.

fissure [fisy:r] f. Fissure, crack, slit, grike. ‖ MÉD. Fissure. ‖ FIG. Split, crack. (V. FENTE.)

fissurer [-syre] v. tr. (1). To fissure, to split.
— v. pr. Se fissurer, to fissure.

fiston [fistɔ̃] m. FAM. Sonny, sonny-boy.

fistulaire [fistylɛ:r] adj. MÉD. Fistular.

fistule [-ty:l] f. MÉD. Fistula.

fistuleux, euse [-tylø, ø:z] adj. MÉD. Fistulous.

fixage [fiksa:ʒ] m. Fixing.

fixateur [fiksatœ:r] m. Fixer. ‖ Fixing bath (en photo).

fixatif, ive [-tif, i:v] adj., m. Fixative.

fixation [-sjɔ̃] f. Fixing (de date); settling (de rendez-vous). ‖ FIN. Assessment (d'impôt); determination (d'indemnité). ‖ CHIM. Fixation. ‖ SPORTS. Binding (de ski). ‖ MÉD. *Abcès de fixation,* abscess of the anchorage.

fixe [fiks] adj. Fixed (demeure, point); permanent (emploi). ‖ Stationary (machine); fast (poulie). ‖ Intent (regard); set (yeux). ‖ Fixed, set (heures); regular (jour). ‖ COMM. Fixed (prix). ‖ FIN. Permanent (capital); fixed (revenu); regular (traitement). ‖ CHIM. Fixed (corps, couleur). ‖ FIG. Fixed (idée). ‖ LOC. *Beau fixe,* set fair. ‖ Fixe-chaussettes, m. Sock suspenders, U. S. garters.
— m. FIN. Fixed (ou) regular salary.
— interj. MILIT. *Fixe!,* eyes front!

fixé, ée [fikse] adj. Fixed (choix, décision, époque) ; fixed, appointed (date, jour, heure) ; *fixé à demain*, fixed for tomorrow. ‖ Fɪɢ. *Etre fixé*, to have definite plans (savoir ce qu'on veut) ; to know what to think (savoir que penser).

fixement [-səmɑ̃] adv. Fixedly ; *regarder fixement*, to stare at.

fixer [-se] v. tr. (1). To fix (une agrafe, son domicile) ; to fasten (des papiers, un volet). ‖ To fix (les yeux) [*sur*, on] ; to stare at (qqn). ‖ To settle (un choix) ; to fix, to settle, to appoint (une date) ; to make (un rendez-vous) [*à*, with]. ‖ To fix, to hold (l'attention) ; to stabilize (un esprit fuyant) ; *fixer qqch. dans la mémoire de qqn*, to fix sth. in s.o.'s memory. ‖ Jᴜʀ. To assess (des dommages) ; to determine (une indemnité). ‖ Fɪɴ. To assess (l'impôt). ‖ Mɪʟɪᴛ. To immobilize (l'ennemi). ‖ Fᴀᴍ. To let know (informer) ; *fixer qqn sur*, to give s.o. definite information as to.
— v. pr. Se fixer, to fix oneself, to fasten (s'attacher). ‖ To settle (résider) [*à*, in, at]. ‖ Fɪɢ. To fasten, to concentrate (attention) [*sur*, on].

fixité [-site] f. Fixity. ‖ Steadiness (du regard). ‖ Fixedness (des opinions).

fjord [fjɔrd] m. Fiord.

flac [flak] interj. Flop (dans l'eau) ; crack (d'un fouet).

flaccidité [flaksidite] f. Flaccidity. ‖ Looseness (des chairs).

flacon [flakɔ̃] m. Flagon, flask ; *flacon de parfum*, scent-bottle, perfume bottle.

flaconnet [flakɔnɛ] m. Small flask (ou) bottle.

flaconnier [-nje] m. Flask-maker.

fla-fla [flafla] m. Fᴀᴍ. Show ; *faire du fla-fla*, to show off. (V. CHICHI.)

flagada [flagada] adj. inv. Pᴏᴘ. On one's last legs ; *je me sens flagada*, I feel a wreck (ou) washed out (ou) run down.

flagellant [flaʒɛllɑ̃] m. Flagellant.

flagellateur, trice [-tœ:r, tris] s. Flagellator.

flagellation [-lasjɔ̃] f. Flagellation, scourging, whipping.

flagelle [flaʒɛl] m. Mᴇ́ᴅ., Zᴏᴏʟ. Flagellum.

flagellé, ée [flaʒɛlle] adj., m. Zᴏᴏʟ. Flagellate.

flageller [-le] v. tr. (1). To flagellate, to scourge, to whip. ‖ Fɪɢ. To stigmatize.

flageoler [flaʒɔle] v. intr. (1). To shake.

flageolet [flaʒɔlɛ] m. Mᴜs., Bᴏᴛ. Flageolet.

flagorner [flagɔrne] v. tr. (1). To toady to, to fawn on, to blarney. (V. FLATTER.)

flagornerie [-nri] f. Toadyism, flunkeyism.

flagorneur [-nœ:r] s. Flunkey, toady, yes-man.

flagrant, ante [flagrɑ̃, ɑ̃:t] adj. Flagrant ; glaring, rank (injustice) ; *pris en flagrant délit*, caught red-handed (ou) in the very act.

flair [flɛ:r] m. Scent, sense (du chien). ‖ Flair (d'une personne) ; *avoir du flair pour*, to have a flair for. (V. PERSPICACITÉ.)

flairer [flɛre] v. tr. (1). To scent, to nose out (le gibier) ; to smell, to sniff (qqch.). ‖ Fᴀᴍ. To smell, to nose (le danger).

flamand, ande [flamɑ̃, ɑ̃:d] adj. Gᴇ́ᴏɢʀ. Flemish.
— s. Gᴇ́ᴏɢʀ. Fleming.
— m. Flemish (langue).

flamant m. Zᴏᴏʟ. Flamingo.

flambage [flɑ̃ba:ʒ] m. Singeing (des cheveux). ‖ Tᴇᴄʜɴ. Buckling. ‖ Cᴜʟɪɴ. Singeing.

flambant, ante [-bɑ̃, ɑ̃:t] adj. Flaming. ‖ Fᴀᴍ. *Tout flambant*, dressed up to the nines (personne).
— adv. *Flambant neuf*, brand new.
— m. Coal.

flambard [-ba:r] adj. Fᴀᴍ. Smart, gorgeous (chic) ; blustering (fanfaron) ; (self-)conceited (vaniteux). ‖ Nᴀᴜᴛ. Fishing-smack.
— m. Swanker ; *faire le flambard*, to strut.

flambé, ée [flɑ̃be] adj. Fᴀᴍ. Down and out ; finished, done for. (V. CUIT.)

flambeau [flɑ̃bo] m. Torch ; *aux flambeaux*, by torchlight ; *course aux flambeaux*, torch-race. ‖ Candlestick ; electric table-standard (ou) lamp.

flambée [flɑ̃be] f. Blaze. ‖ Fɪɢ. Rocketing (des prix).

flambement [flɑ̃bmɑ̃] m. Tᴇᴄʜɴ. V. FLAMBAGE.

flamber [flɑ̃be] v. tr. (1). Cᴜʟɪɴ. To singe (une volaille). ‖ Mᴇ́ᴅ. To flame (une aiguille).
— v. intr. To burn (bois) ; to flame (ou) blaze up, to go up in a blaze (feu) ; to blaze (incendie) ; *flamber comme une allumette*, to burn like matchwood. ‖ Cᴜʟɪɴ. To be pungent (ou) highly seasoned (nourriture). ‖ Fɪɢ. To flame (passions).

flamberge [flɑ̃bɛrʒ] f. † Sword.

flambeur [flɑ̃bœ:r] m. Aʀɢ. Gambler.

flamboiement [flɑ̃bwamɑ̃] m. Flaming, blazing.

flamboyant, ante [-jɑ̃, ɑ̃:t] adj. Blazing, flaming (feu) ; flaring (lumière). ‖ Aʀᴄʜɪᴛ. Flamboyant. ‖ Fɪɢ. Flaming (couleur) ; flamboyant, florid (discours) ; fiery (regard) ; dazzling (toilette) ; *titres de journaux flamboyants*, banner (ou) screaming headlines.

flamboyer [-je] v. intr. (9a). To flame, to blaze. ‖ Fɪɢ. To glow, to flash (yeux).

flamine [flamin] m. † Flamen.

flamingant, ante [flamɛ̃gɑ̃, ɑ̃:t] adj. Flemish-speaking.
— s. Flemish speaker.

flamme [fla:m] f. Flame ; *en flammes*, in flames, on fire, ablaze. ‖ Flame ; *la flamme de ses yeux*, his flashing (ou) fiery eyes. ‖ † Love, passion (amour). ‖ Mɪʟɪᴛ., Nᴀᴜᴛ. Pennon, pennant. ‖ Fɪɢ. Fire (fougue) ; *plein de flamme*, full of dash. ‖ Fᴀᴍ. *Jeter feu et flamme contre*, to fume and rage at.

flammé, ée [flame] adj. Flambé, glazed (céramique). ‖ Flame-shaped.

flammèche [-mɛʃ] f. Flake (ou) burning particle of fire.

flan [flɑ̃] m. Cᴜʟɪɴ. Custard-tart. ‖ Tᴇᴄʜɴ. Flong (en typogr.). ‖ Pᴏᴘ. *A la flan*, botched (travail) ; *un discours à la flan*, all flummery.

flanc m. Flank (d'animal, de personne) ; *battre du flanc*, to pant. ‖ Slope (de montagne) ; *flanc de coteau*, hillside. ‖ Mɪʟɪᴛ. Flank ; *prendre de flanc*, to take (ou) catch in the flank ; *tirer au flanc*, to swing the lead, U. S. to goof off, to gold-brick. ‖ Nᴀᴜᴛ. Flank (de navire). ‖ Fɪɢ. *Prêter le flanc à*, to lay oneself open to. ‖ Fᴀᴍ. *Sur le flanc*, laid up (couché) ; done up (éreinté). ‖ **Flanc-garde,** m. Mɪʟɪᴛ. Flank-guard.

flancher [flɑ̃ʃe] v. intr. (1). Aᴜᴛᴏᴍ. To break down (auto) ; to give out (moteur). ‖ Fᴀᴍ. To flinch, to give in.

flanchet [flɑ̃ʃɛ] m. Cᴜʟɪɴ. Flank.

Flandre(s) [flɑ̃:dr] f. (ou) f. pl. Gᴇ́ᴏɢʀ. Flanders.

flandrin [flɑ̃drɛ̃] m. Fᴀᴍ. *Grand flandrin*, great lump.

flanelle [flanɛl] f. Flannel ; *flanelle de coton*, flannelette ; *de flanelle*, flannel (gilet). ‖ Sᴘᴏʀᴛs. Flannels, whites.

flâner [flɑne] v. intr. (1). To idle about ; to dawdle ; to loiter about.

flânerie [-nri] f. Idling (ou) dawdling about (lambinage). ‖ Stroll (promenade).

flâneur [-nœ:r] s. Idler, dawdler, loiterer, loafer.

flanquer [flɑ̃ke] v. tr. (1). Mɪʟɪᴛ. To flank. ‖ Fᴀᴍ. To escort (qqn) ; to flank (qqch.).

flanquer v. tr. (1). Fᴀᴍ. To fetch (appliquer) ; *flanquer une torgniole à qqn*, to give s.o. a clout. ‖ To chuck (jeter) ; *flanquer son argent en l'air*, to toss one's money about ; *flanquer dehors un ivrogne*, to throw (ou) chuck out a drunkard ; *flanquer qqn à la porte*, to sack (ou) fire s.o.

— v. pr. **Se flanquer.** FAM. To throw oneself ; *se flanquer par terre,* to come a cropper.
flanqueur [-kœ:r] m. MILIT. Flanker.
flapi, ie [flapi] adj. FAM. Fagged out, done up.
flaque [flak] f. Puddle, pool (d'eau). ‖ Pool (mare).
flash [flaʃ] m. Flashlight, flash (en photographie) ; news flash, flash (en radiodiffusion) ; flash (en cinéma). ‖ **Flash-back,** m. inv. CINÉM. Flash-back.
flasque [flask] adj. Flaccid (chair) ; flabby (main). [V. MOU.] ‖ FIG. Limp (style).
flasque m. MILIT. Flask, cheek. ‖ NAUT., TECHN. Cheek.
flatter [flate] v. tr. (1). To stroke, to pat (caresser). ‖ To flatter (qqn) ; *flatter bassement,* to fawn upon ; *être flatté de,* to feel flattered by. ‖ ARTS. To flatter (un portrait, qqn). ‖ FIG. To flatter (l'amour-propre) ; to charm (l'oreille) ; to tickle (l'oreille, le palais) ; to delight (le regard). ‖ FIG. To indulge, to humour, to gratify (un caprice, un défaut) ; to cater to, to pander to (un vice) ; *flatter qqn d'un vain espoir,* to delude s.o. with an idle hope.
— v. pr. **Se flatter,** to flatter oneself (imaginer) [*de,* with] ; to pretend, to claim (prétendre) ; *se flatter de tout savoir,* to profess to be omniscient. ‖ To boast (s'enorgueillir) [*de,* of] ; *se flatter de son succès,* to plume oneself on one's success. ‖ To delude oneself (se bercer) ; *se flatter d'un vain espoir,* to harbour a vain hope.
flatterie [-tri] f. Flattery, blandishment.
flatteur, euse [-tœ:r, ø:z] adj. Flattering (regard, remarque, portrait) ; high (termes).
— s. Flatterer ; *vil flatteur,* fawner, lickspittle, sycophant.
flatteusement [-tøzmã] adv. Flatteringly.
flatulence [-tylã:s] f. MÉD. Flatulence.
flatulent, ente [-tylã, ã:t] adj. MÉD. Flatulent.
flavescent, ente [flavɛssã, ã:t] adj. BOT. Flavescent.
fléau [fleo] m. Beam (d'une balance) ; bar (d'une porte). ‖ AGRIC. Flail. ‖ FIG. Plague, pest, calamity ; *le fléau de Dieu,* the Scourge of God.
fléchage [flɛʃa:ʒ] m. Arrowing, sign-posting.
flèche [flɛ:ʃ] f. Arrow (d'arbalète) ; shaft (d'arc) ; *les flèches de l'amour,* Cupid's shafts. ‖ Pointer (de balance) ; jib (de grue). ‖ Pole (de voiture) ; *atteler en flèche,* to drive tandem ; *cheval de flèche,* head horse. ‖ Arrow (de direction). ‖ ARCHIT. Spire (d'église) ; sag, dip (de soutien) ; rise (de voûte). ‖ AGRIC. Beam (de charrue). ‖ MILIT. Trail (d'affût) ; flèche (de fortifications) ; *flèche de la trajectoire,* maximum ordinate. ‖ NAUT. Pôle (d'un mât) ; *mât de flèche,* top-mast. ‖ AVIAT. Camber ; *en flèche,* swept-back (aile) ; *monter en flèche,* to zoom up. ‖ AUTOM. Trafficator, U. S. turn indicator. ‖ MATH. Versed sine. ‖ COMM. *Montée en flèche des prix et des salaires,* wage-price spiral ; *qui montent en flèche,* rocketing (prix). ‖ CULIN. Flitch (de lard). ‖ FIG. Shaft (de la critique). ‖ LOC. *Comme une flèche,* like a shot, like a bolt from the blue, like greased lightning ; *faire flèche de tout bois,* to use every possible means ; *partir comme une flèche,* to dart off.
flécher [fleʃe] v. tr. (5). To arrow.
fléchette [-ʃɛt] f. Dart.
fléchir [fleʃi:r] v. tr. (2). To bend, to flex (une articulation) ; to bow (le genou). ‖ FIG. To assuage (la colère). ‖ To move (qqn) ; *se laisser fléchir par,* to relent at, to be touched by.
— v. intr. To bend, to sag, to yield (ployer) ; to give way (membre) ; to sag (poutre) ; *fléchir sur ses jambes,* to stagger. ‖ FIN. To sag (cours) ; to fall off (recettes). ‖ FIG. To flag (attention) ; to fall off (popularité, talent, zèle).

fléchissement [-ʃismã] m. Bending (du genou). ‖ Sagging, yielding (d'un câble, d'une poutre). ‖ FIN. Sagging (des cours) ; falling off (des recettes). ‖ ELECTR. Weakening (du courant). ‖ MÉD. Deterioration (de la santé). ‖ FIG. Yielding, giving way, weakening (de la volonté).
fléchisseur [-ʃisœ:r] adj., m. MÉD. Flexor.
flegmatique [flɛgmatik] adj. Phlegmatic, stolid. ‖ MÉD. Lymphatic.
flegmatiquement [-mã] adv. Phlegmatically.
flegme [flɛgm] m. Phlegm, stolidness. ‖ MÉD. Phlegm.
flegmon [flɛgmɔ̃] m. MÉD. Phlegmon.
flemmard, arde [flɛma:r, ard] adj. FAM. Slack, supine.
— s. FAM. Lazybones, slacker, never-sweat.
flemmarder [-marde] v. intr. (1). FAM. To slack, to laze.
flemmardise [-mardi:z] f. FAM. Laziness, idleness.
flemme [flɛm] f. FAM. Slackness ; *j'ai la flemme d'y aller,* I can't be bothered to go ; *ça me donne la flemme,* I can't be bothered to do it ; *tirer sa flemme,* to laze about.
flet [flɛ] m. ZOOL. Flounder, fluke.
flétan [fletã] m. ZOOL. Halibut.
flétri, ie [fletri] adj. Withered, faded (fleur, peau).
flétri, ie adj. Tarnished (réputation).
flétrir [-tri:r] v. tr. (2). To wither up, to shrivel (les fleurs). ‖ To make fade (les couleurs). ‖ FIG. To wither, to fade (la peau, le visage).
— v. pr. **Se flétrir,** to wither, to wilt, to fade (fleurs). ‖ To fade (couleurs). ‖ FIG. To shrivel up (peau) ; to fall into the sear and yellow, to grow old and gray (personne).
flétrir [-tri:r] v. tr. (2). JUR. To brand (un condamné). ‖ FIG. To stigmatize, to denounce (un acte, la conduite, qqn) ; to stain, to sully, to tarnish (une réputation).
flétrissure [-trisy:r] f. Withering, fading (d'une fleur, de la peau).
flétrissure f. JUR. † Branding. ‖ FIG. Blemish, blight, stigma, brand.
flettner [flɛtnœ:r] m. AVIAT. Trimmer, trimming tab.
fleur [flœ:r] f. Flower ; *fleur d'oranger,* orange-blossom. ‖ Blossom, bloom (floraison) ; *arbre en fleur,* in blossom (arbre) ; in bloom (nature) ; in flower (rosier). ‖ Blossom (d'un arbre) ; bloom (d'un fruit). ‖ Flower (sur un tissu) ; *tissu à fleurs,* flowered material. ‖ Flowers (de soufre, du vin) ; *fleur de farine,* best wheaten flour. ‖ GRAMM. *Fleurs de rhétorique,* flowers of speech. ‖ BLAS. *Fleur de lis,* fleur-de-lis. ‖ FIG. Flower ; *fleur de l'âge,* prime of life ; *fleur de la jeunesse,* bloom of youth ; *fine fleur de la race,* flower of the nation ; *jeunes filles en fleur,* maidens in the bloom of youth. ‖ LOC. *Couvrir de fleurs,* to shower with congratulations ; *s'envoyer des fleurs,* to blow one's own trumpet.
— loc. prép. **A fleur de,** on the surface of ; *à fleur de terre,* on the surface of the ground. ‖ On a level with ; *à fleur d'eau,* at water level ; *à fleur de peau,* skin-deep (beauté, sensibilité) ; *à fleur de tête,* prominent, goggle ; U. S. bug (yeux). ‖ NAUT. *A fleur d'eau,* between wind and water ; awash (sous-marin).
fleurage [-ra:ʒ] m. Floral pattern.
fleurdelisé, ée [flœrdəlize] adj. Decorated with fleur-de-lis.
fleurer [flœre] v. intr. (1). To smell ; *fleurer la rose,* to smell of roses.
fleuret [flœrɛ] m. SPORTS. Foil. ‖ TECHN. Borer.
fleureter [flœrte] v. intr. (8 a). To flirt.
fleurette [flœrɛt] f. Floweret. ‖ FIG. *Conter fleurette à,* to flirt with.

fleurettiste [-tist] m. Sports. Foil-play expert.

fleuri, ie [flœri] adj. In blossom (arbre); in bloom, in flower (buisson, plante); flowery (chemin). || Fig. White (barbe); decorated (boutonnière); grog-blossomed (nez); florid (style, teint).

fleurir [-ri:r] v. intr. (53). To blossom (arbre); to flower, to bloom, to burst into bloom (buisson, plante); *faire fleurir*, to bring out. || Fig. To flourish (art, science). [V. FLORIR.]
— v. tr. To put a flower in (la boutonnière); to decorate with flowers (une pièce, la table); to put a flower in the buttonhole of (qqn); to lay flowers on (une tombe). || Fig. To make florid (le style).

fleuriste [-rist] s. Florist.

fleuron [-rɔ̃] m. Fleuron (de couronne). || Archit. Finial. || Techn. Finial (en typogr.). || Bot. Floret. || Fig. *Le fleuron de sa couronne*, the gem of his collection.

fleuve [flœ:v] m. River. || Fig. River (de sang).

flexibilité [flɛksibilite] f. Flexibility.

flexible [-sibl] adj. Flexible, pliant. (V. SOUPLE.) || Fig. Pliant.
— m. Electr. Flex.

flexion [-sjɔ̃] f. Flexion. || Techn. Deflexion. || Gramm. Flexion.

flexionnel, elle [-sjɔnɛl] adj. Gramm. Flexional.

flexueux, euse [flɛksɥø, ø:z] adj. Flexuous. || Bot. Flexuose.

flexuosité [-ozite] f. Flexuosity.

flexure [flɛksy:r] f. Géol. Monocline.

flibuste [flibyst] f. Buccaneering, freebooting, filibustering (piraterie); buccaneers, freebooters, filibusters (pirates).

flibustier [-tje] m. Buccaneer, freebooter, filibuster. || Fig. Sharper, crook.

flic [flik] m. Fam. Cop, bobby, slop, flattie; U. S. flat-foot.

flic. V. FLAC.

flingot [flɛ̃go] m. Milit. Rifle.

flingue [flɛ̃g] m. Arg. Heater, gat, rod, gun.

flinguer [-ge] v. tr. (1). Arg. To shoot.

flint [flint] m. Phys. Flint glass.

flipper [flipər] m. Pin-ball machine (appareil); pin-ball (jeu); flipper (levier).

flipper [flipe] v. intr. (1). Fam. To freak out.

flirt [flœrt] m. Flirting (action); flirtation (manège). || Boy-friend, girl-friend (personne); *un de mes anciens flirts*, an old flame of mine.

flirtage [-ta:ʒ] m. Flirting.

flirter [-te] v. intr. (1). To flirt.

flirteur [-tœ:r] m. Flirt, philanderer.

floc! [flɔk] interj. Flop!, plop!

floc m. Tassel.

floche [flɔʃ] adj. Flossy; floss (soie).

flocon [flɔkɔ̃] m. Flock (de laine); flake (de neige). || Culin. *Flocons d'avoine*, rolled oats. || Chim. Floccule.

floconner [-kɔne] v. intr. (1). To flake. || Chim. To form into floccules.

floconneux, euse [-kɔnø, ø:z] adj. Flaky (neige); fleecy (nuage); fluffy (tissu). || Chim. Flocculent.

floculation [flɔkylasjɔ̃] f. Chim., Méd. Flocculation.

flonflon [flɔ̃flɔ̃] m. Mus. Pom pom (des cuivres).

flopée [flɔpe] f. Fam. Heaps, piles, lots. (V. TAS.)

floraison [flɔrɛzɔ̃] f. Blooming, flowering, blossoming, florescence (épanouissement); flower-time (époque).

floral, ale [-ral] adj. Floral.

floralies [-rali] f. pl. Flower show.

flore [flɔ:r] f. Flora.

floréal [flɔreal] m. Floréal, eighth month in French Republican calendar (April-May).

Florence [flɔrɑ̃:s] f. Géogr. Florence.

florentin, ine [-rɑ̃tɛ̃, in] adj., s. Géogr. Florentine.

florès [flɔrɛ:s] m. *Faire florès*, to be a success, to catch on; *ne pas faire florès*, to be no great shakes, to be nothing to write home about.

floriculture [flɔrikylty:r] f. Floriculture.

florifère [flɔrifɛ:r] adj. Bot. Floriferous; *plante florifère*, flowerer.

florilège [-lɛ:ʒ] m. Florilegium. (V. ANTHOLOGIE.)

florin [flɔrɛ̃] m. Florin.

florir [flɔrir] v. intr. Fig. To flourish.

florissant, ante [flɔrisɑ̃, ɑ̃:t] adj. Flourishing (v. PROSPÈRE); *avoir une mine florissante*, to be bursting with health.

floss [flɔs] m. Floss.

flot [flo] m. Flood, wave, waters; *les flots de la mer*, the seas; *le flot montant*, the flow of the tide, the flood-tide. || Cascade (de dentelles); knot (de rubans). || Naut. *A flot*, afloat; *mise à flot*, floating; *remettre à flot*, to refloat, to float off. || Comm. *Remettre à flot*, to refloat (les finances, qqn). || Fig. Flood (d'idées, de larmes, de lumière, de paroles); stream (de gens, de sang); tide (de haine); *le flot des voitures*, the stream of traffic; *à flots*, in torrents; *couler à flots*, to gush forth; *entrer à flots*, to stream in (foule); *to flood* in (soleil); *se mettre à flot dans son travail*, to get up to date in one's work.

flottabilité [flɔtabilite] f. Buoyancy.

flottable [-tabl] adj. Floatable (bois, rivière).

flottage [-ta:ʒ] m. Floating (du bois); *bois de flottage*, raft-wood; *train de flottage*, timber-raft.

flottaison [-tɛzɔ̃] f. Naut. Floating; *ligne de flottaison*, water-line.

flottant, ante [-tɑ̃, ɑ̃:t] adj. Floating (corps, île, ligne). || Flowing (cheveux, vêtements); loose (manteau); baggy (pantalon). || Naut. Floating, drifting (mine). || Méd. Floating (rein). || Techn. Floating (moteur). || Fin. Floating (dette, police). || Fig. Floating, wavering, vacillating (esprit).

flotte [flɔt] f. Naut. Fleet. || Aviat. *Flotte aérienne*, air fleet. || Fam. Adam's ale.

flotte f. Float (de câble, de filet, de ligne).

flotté, ée [flɔte] adj. *Bois flotté*, driftwood, floating logs.

flottement [flɔtmɑ̃] m. Milit. Flapping (du drapeau); swaying (des troupes). || Fin. Floating (des monnaies). || Fig. Wavering, hesitation.

flotter [-te] v. intr. (1). To float (dans l'air, sur l'eau). || To stream, to flow (cheveux); to float, to wave (drapeau); to hang loose (rênes). || Milit. To waver (troupes). || Fin. To float (monnaies). || Fig. To fluctuate.
— v. tr. To float (du bois).
— v. impers. Pop. To rain.

flotteur [-tœr] m. Raftsman (de train de bois); Ball (de chasse d'eau); float (de filet, de ligne). || Autom. Float (de carburateur). || Aviat. Float; *hydravion à flotteurs*, float plane.

flottille [-ti:j] f. Naut. Flotilla; *flottilles fluviales*, rivercraft.

flou, oue [flu] adj. Fluffy (cheveux); loose-fitting (robe). || Blurred (contour); fuzzy (image, peinture). || Fig. Nebulous (caractère); muzzy, woolly (idées). [V. VAGUE, VAPOREUX.]
— m. Fuzziness, woolliness (d'une image); *éclairage de flou*, soft-lighting. || Dressmaking (en couture).
— adv. Arts. In a fuzzy manner.

flouer [flue] v. tr. (1). Fam. To do, U. S. to take.

fluctuant, ante [flyktɥɑ̃, ɑ̃:t] adj. Méd. Fluctuant. || Fig. Wavering.

fluctuation [-asjɔ̃] f. Fluctuation. (V. VARIATION.) || Techn. Variation (de charge). || Milit. Tide (de la bataille). || Fin. Fluctuation.

fluctuer [-e] v. intr. (1). To fluctuate.

fluer [flɥe] v. intr. Phys. To creep.

fluet, ette [flɥɛ, ɛ:t] adj. Slender (corps, personne); thin (voix).

flueurs [flyœːr] f. pl. MÉD. *Flueurs blanches,* leucorrhoea ; whites (fam.).

fluide [flyid] adj., m. Fluid.

fluidifier [-difje] v. tr. (1). To fluidify.

fluidité [-dite] f. Fluidity.

fluor [flyɔːr] m. CHIM. Fluorine.

fluorescéine [-ɔrɛsein] f. Fluorescein.

fluorescence [flyɔrɛssãːs] f. Fluorescence.

fluorescent, ente [-sã, ãːt] adj. Fluorescent.

fluorine [flyɔrin] f. Calcium fluoride, fluor-spar.

fluorure [flyɔryːr] m. CHIM. Fluoride.

flush [flœʃ] m. Flush ; *quinte flush,* straight flush (au poker).

flûte [flyːt] f. MUS. Flute ; *flûte de Pan,* syrinx, Pan-pipe ; *grande flûte,* concert flute ; *petite flûte,* piccolo. ‖ Long French loaf (de pain). ‖ Flute glass (à champagne). ‖ FAM. Pl. Legs ; *jouer (ou) se tirer des flûtes,* to leg it.

flûte! interj. Bother!, dash!, darn!, blow ! (V. ZUT.)

flûté, ée [flyte] adj. Flute-like, fluty, piping (voix). ‖ MUS. *Sons flûtés,* harmonics.

flûter v. intr. (1). MUS. To play the flute.

flûtiste [-tist] s. MUS. Flutist, flautist.

fluvial, ale [flyvjal] adj. Fluvial (eaux) ; river (bassin, brigade, navigation).

fluvio-glaciaire [-vjɔglasjɛːr] adj. GÉOGR. Fluvio-glacial.

flux [fly] m. Flood (d'eau) ; flow (de la marée) ; ebb (marée). ‖ MÉD. Flux. ‖ FIG. Flux (de lumière, d'opinion) ; flow (de paroles).

fluxion [flyksjõ] f. MÉD. Fluxion : *fluxion à la joue,* swollen cheek ; *fluxion de poitrine,* inflammation of the lungs. ‖ MATH. Fluxion.

FM [ɛfɛm] f. Abrév. de *frequency modulation,* FM.

fob [fɔb] adj. inv., adv. Abrév. de *free on board,* f.o.b.

foc [fɔk] m. NAUT. Jib ; *grand, petit foc,* outer, inner jib ; *les focs,* the head sails ; *foc d'artimon,* mizzen-topmast staysail.

focal, ale [fɔkal] adj. PHYS., MATH. Focal.

focaliser [-lize] v. tr. (1). TECHN., FIG. To focus.

foëne [fwɛn] f. Fishgig.

fœtal, ale [fetal] adj. MÉD. Fœtal.

fœtus [fetyːs] m. MÉD. Fœtus.

fofolle [fɔfɔːl] adj. f. FAM. Flighty.

foi [fwa] f. Faith, pledge (fidélité) ; *la foi jurée,* pledged word ; *sous la foi du serment,* upon oath ; *sur la foi des traités,* on the faith of treaties. ‖ Faith (sincérité) ; *de bonne, mauvaise foi,* in good, bad faith ; *bona, mala fide ; une personne de bonne, mauvaise foi,* a genuine, insincere person. ‖ Faith, word (parole) ; *foi de gentilhomme,* on the word of a gentleman ; *ma foi, non!,* upon my word, no ! ‖ Faith, trust (confiance) ; *digne de foi,* trustworthy. ‖ Faith, credence, credit (créance) ; *digne de foi,* credible, reliable. ‖ Faith, evidence (témoignage) ; *en foi de quoi,* in testimony whereof ; *faire foi de,* to be evidence of ; *faire foi que,* to attest that ; *qui fait foi,* authentic, conclusive. ‖ Opinion, conviction ; *profession de foi,* statement of policy (en politique). ‖ ECCLÉS. Faith, belief ; *la foi chrétienne,* the Christian faith ; *il est de foi que,* it is of faith (ou) an article of faith that.

foie [fwa] m. Liver ; *huile de foie de morue,* cod-liver oil. ‖ MÉD. *Maladie de foie,* liver-complaint. ‖ CULIN. *Mousse de foie gras,* liver paste ; *pâté de foie gras,* pâté de foie gras. ‖ POP. *Il a les foies,* he is white-livered, U. S. he's chicken.

foin [fwɛ̃] m. AGRIC. Hay ; *faire les foins,* to make hay. ‖ Choke (d'artichaut). ‖ MÉD. *Rhume des foins,* hay-fever. ‖ FAM. *Avoir du foin dans ses bottes,* to have feathered one's nest ; *faire du foin,* to kick up a row, to make a great song and dance.

foin! interj. Pooh! (v. FI) ; *foin de!,* a plague on !

foirage [fwaraːʒ] m. TECHN. Stripping. ‖ POP. Flop. (V. FIASCO.)

foirail [fwarɑːj] m. Fair-ground (champ de foire).

foire [fwaːr] f. Fair ; *foire aux chevaux,* horse-fair. ‖ FAM. Spree (bombe) ; crowd (foule) ; *foire d'empoigne,* game of grab.

foire f. POP. Squitters, U. S. trots.

foirer [fware] v. intr. (1). To hang fire (fusée) ; to strip (vis). ‖ FAM. To flop (rater). ‖ POP. To feel funky (ou) jittery (trembler).

foireux, euse [fwarø, øːz] adj. FAM. Funky, scared, jittery. ‖ POP. Diarrhoeic.
— s. POP. Funky (ou) diarrhoeic person.

fois [fwa] f. Time ; *une, deux fois,* once, twice ; *trois fois,* thrice, three times ; *quatre fois,* four times ; *une fois en passant,* once in a while ; *une fois pour toutes,* once and for all ; *une seule fois,* once only ; *autant de fois que,* as often as ; *bien des fois,* many a time ; *cette fois,* this time ; *combien de fois?,* how often? how many times? *encore une fois,* once more ; *maintes et maintes fois,* many a time ; *la première fois que je l'ai vu,* the first time I saw him, when I saw him first ; *neuf fois sur dix,* in nine cases out of ten ; *plusieurs fois,* several times ; *pour la première fois dans les annales,* for the first time in history ; *pour une fois,* for once ; *que de fois,* how often ; *y regarder à deux fois,* to think twice about it. ‖ MATH. Time ; *deux fois moins, plus d'avions,* half, twice as many planes ; *deux fois plus long que,* twice as long as ; *en trois fois moins de temps,* in a third of the time ; *trois fois deux font six,* three times two are six. ‖ JUR. *Une fois, deux fois, adjugé!,* going, going, gone !
— loc. **A la fois,** at once, both (ensemble) ; at the same time (en même temps) ; *à la fois la fortune et la gloire,* both fame and fortune ; *à la fois riant et pleurant,* laughing and crying at the same time ; *parler tous les deux à la fois,* to speak both together. ‖ **De fois à autre,** from time to time, at times. ‖ **Une fois que,** as soon as.

foison [fwazõ] f. Plenty. (V. PROFUSION.)
— loc. adv. **A foison,** plentifully, in abundance ; *des fruits à foison,* fruit galore.

foisonnement [-zɔnmã] m. Multiplication. ‖ Swelling, dilating, expansion. ‖ PHYS. Dilating, dilation.

foisonner [-zɔne] v. intr. (1). To abound (de, in, with) ; *foisonner en blé,* to abound in corn. ‖ To pullulate, to multiply (animal, plante) ; *foisonner de serpents,* to swarm with snakes. ‖ PHYS. To swell.

fol [fɔl]. V. FOU.

folâtre [-lɑːtr] adj. Frolicsome, frisky, sprightly, coltish. ‖ FAM. *Ce n'est vraiment pas folâtre,* it's no joke.

folâtrer [fɔlɑtre] v. intr. (1). To frolic, to frisk, to gambol, to sport ; *en folâtrant,* playfully.

folâtrerie [-latrɔri] f. Sportiveness, friskiness.

foliacé, ée [fɔljase] adj. Foliaceous, leaf-like.

foliation [fɔljasjõ] f. BOT. Foliation.

folichon, onne [fɔliʃõ, ɔn] adj. FAM. Frolicsome, playful, sportive (caractère, personne) ; funny (situation) ; *ce n'est pas folichon,* it's not really funny.

folichonner [-ʃɔne] v. intr. (1). FAM. To frolic.

folichonnerie [-ʃɔnri] f. FAM. Sportiveness.

folie [fɔli] f. MÉD. Dementia, madness, insanity, lunacy (v. DÉMENCE) ; *accès de folie,* fit of madness ; *folie des grandeurs,* megalomania. ‖ Madness, folly, extravagance ; *avoir la folie de,* to be so foolish as to ; *c'est une vraie folie que de,* it is sheer folly (ou) lunacy to. ‖ Act of folly (ou) extravagance ; *faire une folie,* to act foolishly, to play the fool ; *dire des folies,* to say foolish things ; *faire des folies,* to act extravagantly, to be over-generous (ou) too free with one's money, to spend money like water. ‖ Folly, passion ; *aimer à la folie,* to love to distraction ; *avoir la folie de,* to be mad on (ou) about. ‖ Pl. Follies (écarts) ; *folies de jeunesse,* the follies of youth. ‖ THÉÂTR. *Folies-Bergère,* the Follies.

folié, ée [fɔlje] adj. BOT. Foliate.

folio [fɔljo] m. Folio.

foliole [fɔljɔl] f. BOT. Leaflet, foliole.

foliotage [fɔljɔta:ʒ] m. Pagination.

folioter [-te] v. tr. (1). To paginate, to foliate.

folique [fɔlik] adj. MÉD. *Acide folique,* folic acid.

folklore [fɔlklɔr] m. Folklore. ‖ FIG. Picturesque stuff.

folklorique [-rik] adj. Folkloristic ; *danse (ou) chant folklorique,* folk-dance (ou) folk-song. ‖ FAM. Exotic, colourful.

folksong, folk [fɔlksɔg, fɔlk] m. Folk-music, folk.

folle [fɔ:l] adj. V. FOU.
— f. Madwoman. (V. FOU.)

follement [fɔlmɑ̃] adv. Madly. ‖ Desperately, distractedly, madly (éperdument) ; exceedingly ; highly (extrêmement) ; foolishly, stupidly (sottement) ; rashly, recklessly (témérairement) ; *c'est follement drôle,* it's a perfect scream.

follet [fɔlɛ] adj. *Esprit follet,* sprite ; *feu follet,* jack-o'-lantern, will-o-the-wisp ; *poil follet,* down.

folliculaire [fɔlikylɛ:r] m. FAM. Hack writer, penny-a-liner.

follicule [fɔlikyl] m. BOT., MÉD. Follicle.

folliculine [-lin] f. MÉD. Folliculin.

fomentateur, trice [fɔmɑ̃tatœ:r, tris] s. Fomenter.

fomentation [-tasjɔ̃] f. MÉD., FIG. Fomentation.

fomenter [-te] v. tr. (1). MÉD., FIG. To give rise to (un événement) ; to foment (la révolte).

fonçage [fɔ̃sa:ʒ] m. TECHN. Boring, sinking (d'un puits de mine).

foncé, ée [fɔ̃se] adj. Dark, mazarine (bleu) ; dark (couleur, objet).

foncer v. tr. (6). To darken (une couleur). ‖ To bore (un puits) ; to bottom (un tonneau).
— v. intr. To rush, to dash (*sur,* at) ; to make a run-up (*sur,* to). ‖ To speed up ; to go faster (augmenter la vitesse). ‖ FAM. To shell (ou) fork out. (V. CASQUER.)
— v. pr. Se foncer, to grow darker (couleur).

fonceur, euse [-sœ:r, ɸ:z] adj. FAM. Go-ahead, full of go, enterprising.
— s. FAM. Live wire, dynamo.

foncier [fɔ̃sje] adj. Landed (biens, impôt). ‖ FIG. Fundamental ; *honnêteté foncière,* innate (ou) natural honesty.
— m. FIN. Land-tax.

foncièrement [fɔ̃sjɛrmɑ̃] adv. Fundamentally, thoroughly (au fond) ; naturally (naturellement) ; *foncièrement égoïste,* selfish to the core.

fonction [fɔ̃ksjɔ̃] f. Function, duty, office (V. CHARGE, EMPLOI) ; *de par ses fonctions,* ex officio ; *entrer en fonctions,* to take up (ou) to enter upon one's duties ; *être en fonctions,* to be in (ou) to hold office ; *faire fonction de,* to serve (ou) act as ; *fonctions publiques,* public offices. ‖ MÉD., MATH. Function. ‖ GRAMM. *Faire fonction de,* to function as. ‖ FIG. *Etre fonction de,* to depend on, to be conditional upon, to be a function of.

fonctionnaire [-nɛ:r] m. Official, civil servant, U. S. office-holder ; *haut, moyen, petit fonctionnaire,* higher, senior, minor official.

fonctionnalisme [fɔ̃ksjɔnalism] m. Functionalism.

fonctionnariat [-narja] m. Civil service.

fonctionnarisation [-narizasjɔ̃] f. Turning into a public service (des institutions) ; assimilation into the civil service (des personnes).

fonctionnariser [-narize] v. tr. (1). To turn into a public service (les institutions) ; to assimilate into the civil service (les personnes).

fonctionnarisme [-narism] m. Officialdom, red tape, bureaucracy.

fonctionnel, elle [-nɛl] adj. Functional.

fonctionnellement [-nɛlmɑ̃] adv. Functionally.

fonctionnement [-nmɑ̃] m. MÉD. Functioning. ‖ TECHN. Working (d'une machine). ‖ FIG. Work ; *bon fonctionnement,* smoothness, smooth working.

fonctionner [-ne] v. tr. (1). To function (comité) ; *fonctionner parfaitement,* to be in excellent working order. ‖ TECHN. To work, to act, to operate, to function ; *faire fonctionner,* to run, to work (une machine). ‖ MÉD. To function (organe).

fond [fɔ̃] m. Bottom (d'une boîte, d'un placard, d'un trou) ; *au fin fond de,* at the very bottom of ; *de fond en comble,* from top to bottom ; *enfoncer qqch. au fond d'un panier,* to thrust sth. deep down into a basket. ‖ Back, bottom, far end (d'une cour) ; back, far end (d'une pièce) ; back (d'une voiture) ; *maison au fond de la cour,* house giving on to a central courtyard. ‖ Bosom, depth, heart (d'un bois). ‖ Foundation ; *un fond solide de construction,* a sound building site. ‖ Kick (d'une bouteille) ; crown (d'un chapeau) ; seat (d'une chaise, d'un pantalon) ; bottom (d'un tonneau) ; *à double fond,* double-bottomed, with a false bottom. ‖ Dregs (de bouteille) ; dregs, heeltap (de verre) ; *fond de café,* coffee grounds. ‖ Foundation, grounding (d'une tapisserie) ; ground (d'un tissu) ; *fond de teint,* make-up foundation ; *noir sur fond blanc,* black on a white ground. ‖ Background (arrière-plan) ; *dans le fond,* in the background ; *servir de fond à,* to serve as a background to. ‖ ARTS. Background (d'un tableau) ; *fond de toile,* foundation. ‖ THÉÂTR. Back-drop ; *bruit de fond,* ground noise ; *toile de fond,* backdrop (ou) -cloth. ‖ NAUT. Bottom (de la mer) ; depth (hauteur d'eau) ; *grands, hauts-fonds,* deeps, shoals ; *par dix brasses de fond,* in ten fathoms of water, at a depth of ten fathoms ; *s'envoyer par le fond,* to scuttle one's ship ; *trouver le fond au sondage,* to strike bottom ; *sans fond,* bottomless (abîme). ‖ SPORTS. Staying power (d'un cheval). ‖ MÉD. Back (de la gorge). ‖ CULIN. Bottom, heart (d'artichaut). ‖ JUR. Main issue (d'une cause) ; *juger au fond,* to decide the main issue ; *proposition de fond,* substantive motion. ‖ TECHN. Margin (en typogr.). ‖ FIG. Ground ; *faire fond sur,* to build upon, to rely on (qqch.) ; to rely (ou) to depend on (qqn). ‖ FIG. Bottom (de l'âme, du cœur) ; essential feature (du caractère) ; *au, du fond du cœur,* at, from the bottom of one's heart ; *au fond de soi,* in one's secret heart ; *le fond du caractère national,* the basis of the national character ; *manquer de fond,* to be shallow. ‖ FIG. Undercurrent (d'humour, de mécontentement) ; *un fond de vérité,* a substratum of truth. ‖ FIG. Root, bottom (d'une affaire) ; content, substance (d'un ouvrage) ; gist, substance (d'une question).
— loc. **A fond,** home ; thoroughly ; *aller à fond,* to go the limit (ou) the whole hog (tout risquer) ; *connaître à fond,* to know through and through, to have a thorough knowledge of ; *partir à fond,* to start all out ; *traiter à fond,* to treat exhaustively. ‖ **A fond de ; à fond de course,** at lower dead centre, at dead point (piston) ; on one's last legs (personne) ; *à fond de train,* at top speed. ‖ **Au fond, dans le fond,** at bottom (au fond de soi) ; after all, on the whole, all things considered (après tout) ; *au fond il est heureux,* deep down inside (ou) in his heart of hearts he is happy ; *au fond elle a raison,* after all she is right. ‖ **De fond,** fundamental ; *article de fond,* leader, editorial.

fondage [fɔ̃da:ʒ] m. TECHN. Melting.

fondamental, ale [fɔ̃damɑ̃tal] adj. Fundamental, basic; *le principe fondamental de l'ordre nouveau*, the essential quality of the New Order.

fondamentalement [-talmɑ̃] adv. Fundamentally, basically.

fondant, ante [fɔ̃dɑ̃, ɑ̃:t] adj. Melting (glace); luscious (poire). ‖ MÉD. Softening.
— m. Fondant (bonbon). ‖ ARTS. Base (d'émail).

fondateur [fɔ̃datœ:r] m. Founder. ‖ FIN. Promoter (de société); *part de fondateur*, founder's share.

fondation [-sjɔ̃] f. Foundation, founding (action); foundation, institution (établissement); donation, endowment (legs). ‖ ARCHIT. Foundation. ‖ FAM. *De fondation*, regular, customary; *une habitude de fondation*, the standing custom.

fondatrice [-tris] f. Foundress.

fondé, ée [fɔ̃de] adj. Founded, grounded (appuyé) [sur, on]. ‖ Grounded, founded; *bien, mal fondé*, well, ill founded; sound, unsound. (V. BIEN-FONDÉ.) ‖ Justified, authorized, entitled; *être fondé à, croire*, to be entitled to believe (ou) justified in believing, to have grounds for believing; *il n'y a rien de fondé dans*, there are no grounds for.
— m. JUR. *Fondé de pouvoir*, proxy. ‖ COMM. Managing (ou) signing clerk; authorized agent.

fondement [-dəmɑ̃] m. Foundation (d'un bâtiment). ‖ Foundation, basis, groundwork (d'un empire, du gouvernement). ‖ Foundation, ground (d'une accusation, d'un bruit); *dénué de tout fondement*, quite groundless, entirely without foundation; *sans fondement*, groundless, unfounded. ‖ MÉD. Fundament. ‖ FAM. Bottom, backside.

fonder [-de] v. tr. (1). To found (un bâtiment, un empire, une institution); to start (une famille, un journal). ‖ COMM. To start (un commerce). ‖ FIN. To fund (une dette); to float (une société). ‖ JUR. To base (un recours). ‖ FIG. To ground, to base, to build (un espoir, une théorie) [sur, on].
— v. pr. Se **fonder**, to base oneself; *se fonder sur*, to be grounded (ou) based (espoir, théorie); to rely on, to place reliance on, to take one's stand on, to build upon (personne).

fonderie [fɔ̃dri] f. TECHN. Founding (art); foundry (usine).

fondeur [-dœ:r] s. TECHN. Founder (en bronze); caster (en médailles).

fondeuse [-ø:z] f. TECHN. Melting-machine (à bougies); founding-machine (en typogr.).

fondre [fɔ̃:dr] v. tr. (4). To melt (la cire, un métal); to thaw, to melt (la glace); to smelt (un minerai); *faire fondre*, to dissolve, to melt (du sucre). ‖ To cast, to found (une cloche, une statue). ‖ CINÉM. To dissolve (une scène). ‖ COMM. To amalgamate, to combine, to fuse (des sociétés). ‖ FIG. To blend (des couleurs).
— v. intr. To melt (beurre, glace, fruit, métal, sucre). ‖ MÉD. To disperse (abcès). ‖ ELECTR. To blow out (fusible). ‖ FIG. *Fondre en larmes*, to burst into tears; *fondre sur*, to swoop on, to pounce on, to rush at; *fondre à l'improviste*, to attack unexpectedly. ‖ FAM. To melt away (argent); to lose flesh (personne); *il fond à vue d'œil*, he gets thinner every day.
— v. pr. Se **fondre**, to melt (glace, sucre). ‖ MÉD. To dissolve (abcès). ‖ FIG. To blend (couleurs); *se fondre dans*, to fade into.

fondrière [fɔ̃drjɛ:r] f. Pot-hole (sur route). ‖ Morass. (V. MARÉCAGE.)

fonds [fɔ̃] m. AGRIC. Estate, land (terre). ‖ COMM. Goodwill and stock-in-trade, business assets (capitaux); *fonds de commerce*, business house; *exploiter un fonds de commerce*, to carry on a business. ‖ FIN. Pl. Funds, cash, capital; stocks; *fonds d'Etat*, Government stocks; *fonds de roule-*

ment, trading (ou) floating capital; *à fonds perdus*, without security; *en fonds*, in funds; *rentrer dans ses fonds*, to recover one's outlay. ‖ FIG. Fund (d'érudition, d'humour, de probité); vein (d'imagination); *bon fonds*, good nature, fondamental qualities.

fondu, ue [fɔ̃dy] p. p. (V. FONDRE.) ‖ CULIN. Clarified, melted (beurre).
— m. ARTS. Blending (des couleurs); mellowness (d'un tableau). ‖ CINÉM. Dissolve; *fermeture, ouverture en fondu*, fade-out, fade-in.

fondue [fɔ̃dy] f. CULIN. Fondue, melted cheese.

fongible [fɔ̃ʒibl] adj. JUR. Fungible.

fongicide [fɔ̃ʒisid] adj. Fungicidal.
— m. Fungicide.

fongus [fɔ̃gys] m. MÉD. Fungus.

fontaine [fɔ̃tɛ:n] f. Fountain. ‖ Wash-basin (d'appartement). ‖ Spring (source).

fontanelle [fɔ̃tanɛl] f. MÉD. Fontanel.

fonte [fɔ̃:t] f. Thawing, melting (de la glace, des neiges); melting (du sucre); smelting (du minerai). ‖ Casting, founding (d'une cloche, d'une statue). ‖ Cast- (ou) pig-iron (alliage); *en fonte*, cast-iron. ‖ TECHN. Fount, U. S. font (en typogr.).

fonte f. Holster (pour pistolet).

fonts [fɔ̃] m. pl. ECCLÉS. *Fonts baptismaux*, font.

FOOTBALL — FOOTBALL (soccer)

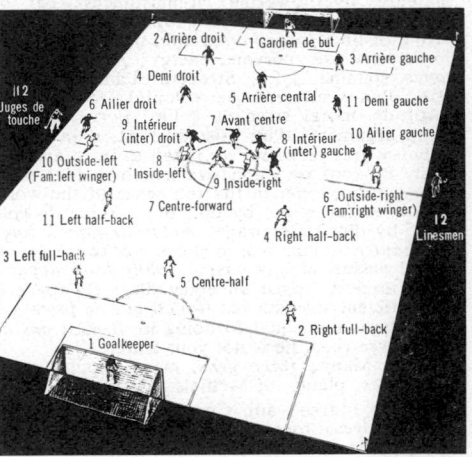

football [futbol], foot [fut] m. SPORTS. Football, soccer; *terrain de football*, football ground (ou) field.

footballeur [-lœ:r] m. SPORTS. Footballer.

footing [futiŋ] m. SPORTS. Walking (ou) jogging; *faire du footing*, to go jogging, to go for a walk.

for [fɔ:r] m. † Tribunal. ‖ FIG. *For intérieur*, conscience; *dans mon for intérieur*, in my secret heart, deep down inside.

forage [fɔra:ʒ] m. Boring (d'un conduit, d'un trou); sinking (d'un puits); drilling (d'un puits de pétrole).

forain [fɔrɛ̃] adj. Itinerant (v. NOMADE); *fête foraine*, fun (ou) street fair; *marchand forain*, itinerant vendor; booth- (ou) stall-keeper at a fair. ‖ THÉÂTR. Strolling (acteur); travelling (théâtre).
— s. Stall-keeper at a fair. ‖ Peddler (colporteur).

foramen [fɔramɛn] m. MÉD., BOT. Foramen.

forban [fɔrbɑ̃] m. Pirate. ‖ Bandit.

forçage [fɔrsa:ʒ] m. AGRIC. Forcing.

forçat [fɔrsa] m. Convict. ‖ FAM. *Mener une vie de forçat*, to slave, to drudge.

force [fɔrs] f. Strength, power, force; *à bout de forces*, worn out; *à la force du poignet*, by sheer strength; *de toutes ses forces*, with all one's might; *n'avoir pas la force de*, to have no strength left to; *prendre des forces*, to grow strong; *reprendre des forces*, to regain strength, to pick up. ‖ Strength (d'un câble, du papier, d'une étoffe). ‖ Strength (du thé, du vin); *force en alcool*, alcoholic strength. ‖ Compulsion, force (contrainte); *de force, par force*, by force, on compulsion, compulsorily; *de vive force*, by sheer (ou) main force, by open attack; *entrer de force*, to force one's way in; *faire avancer, descendre, sortir de force*, to force on, down, out; *force lui fut de*, he was compelled to; *recourir à la force*, to resort to force. ‖ Proficiency; skill (habileté); *de première force en*, highly proficient (ou) skilful in. ‖ PHYS. Force; *force vive*, kinetic energy, vis viva. ‖ ELECTR., TECHN. Power. ‖ AUTOM. *Force en chevaux*, horsepower. ‖ AVIAT. *Force aérodynamique*, drag, air resistance; *force ascensionnelle*, lift. ‖ NAUT. Strength (du courant); *faire force de rames*, to ply the oars; *faire force de voiles*, to cram on sail. ‖ MILIT. *Forces aériennes*, armées, air, armed forces; *en force*, in force; *faire appel à la force armée*, to call out the troops; *prendre de vive force*, to take by storm. ‖ JUR. *Force des choses*, force of circumstances; *force d'inertie*, inertia; *force majeure*, vis major, force majeure, overpowering circumstances; *cas de force majeure*, act of God. ‖ MÉD. *Force de l'âge*, prime of life; *force musculaire*, muscular power; *force nerveuse*, nervous energy; *force de résistance*, stamina. ‖ FIG. Strength (d'âme, de caractère, d'un sentiment, de volonté); *force d'âme*, fortitude, moral strength. ‖ FIG. Force, strength (d'un argument, d'un raisonnement, d'un texte); *appuyer avec force sur un point*, to insist emphatically on (ou) to emphasize a point; *dans toute la force du terme*, in the full sense of the word. ‖ LOC. **A force de**, by dint of; *à force de courage*, by dint of courage; *endormir qqn à force de chanter*, to sing s.o. to sleep. ‖ **A toute force**, by all means, at any cost; *vouloir faire qqch. à toute force*, to insist on doing sth. ‖ **De force à**, of sufficient strength to; *il n'est pas de force à le faire*, he is not equal to doing it; *il n'est pas de force avec vous*, he is not your match.
— adv. Many; *force gens*, many people; *force victuailles*, plenty of victuals.

forcé, ée [fɔrse] adj. Compulsory, forced (contraint); *aveux forcés*, forced confession; *forcé à*, compelled to; *la carte forcée*, Hobson's choice. ‖ Affected (amabilité); forced (rire, sourire). [V. AFFECTÉ.] ‖ Inevitable, ineluctable (conséquence, dénouement). [V. INÉVITABLE, FATAL.] ‖ COMM. Forced (vente). ‖ FIN. Compulsory (emprunt). ‖ AVIAT. Forced, emergency (atterissage). ‖ MILIT. Forced (marche).

forcement [-səmɑ̃] m. Forcing, breaking open (d'un coffre, d'une serrure, d'une porte); forcing, breaking through (d'un blocus, d'un barrage).

forcément [-mɑ̃] adv. Necessarily, of necessity; inevitably, perforce.

forcené, ée [fɔrsəne] adj. Wild, mad, frantic, frenzied (personne). ‖ Furious, desperate (attaque, lutte); frenzied (travail).
— s. Frantic person. (V. FOU.) ‖ FAM. *Travailler comme un forcené*, to work like a black (ou) U. S. dog.

forceps [fɔrseps] m. MÉD. Forceps.

forcer [fɔrse] v. tr. (6). To force (ouvrir); to break into (la caisse); to force, to break open (un coffre, une porte); to wrench open (un couvercle); to force (une serrure). ‖ To bend (v. FAUSSER); to buckle, to bend (une clé); to jam (un méca-

nisme); to tamper with (une serrure). ‖ To run (un blocus); to force (un passage); *forcer la consigne*, to enter in spite of orders; to gatecrash; *forcer la porte de qqn*, to force one's way into s.o.'s house. ‖ To violate, to abuse (une femme). ‖ To hunt (ou) to run down (un cerf); to override (un cheval). ‖ To exaggerate (les éloges); *forcer la note*, to force the note, to overdo it. ‖ To overstrain (un argument, la vérité); to wrench, to strain (un sens, son talent). ‖ To force (le pas); to strain (sa voix, sa vue). ‖ To compel, to win (l'admiration); to compel, to command (l'obéissance). ‖ To compel, to force, to constrain (v. CONTRAINDRE); *être forcé de*, to be obliged (ou) compelled to; *forcer la main à qqn*, to force s.o.'s hand. ‖ AGRIC. To force (une culture). ‖ MÉD. To increase (la dose). ‖ FAM. *Forcer la dose*, to go a bit too far.
— v. intr. To be jammed (ou) strained (mécanisme); *la porte force*, the door is sticking. ‖ To increase; *forcer sur l'apéritif*, to drink too much; *forcer sur le sucre*, to take too much sugar. ‖ *Forcer sur*, to overcall, to overbid (une annonce, une enchère). ‖ FAM. To overwork (se surmener).
— v. pr. **Se forcer**, to force (ou) to compel oneself (à, pour, to). ‖ To overwork (se surmener); *se forcer la voix*, to strain one's voice.

forcerie [-səri] f. AGRIC. Forcing house.

forcing [fɔrsiŋ] m. SPORTS. All-out attack, pressure; *faire le forcing*, to put the pressure on.

forcir [fɔrsi:r] v. intr. (2). FAM. To grow, to fill out (enfant); to put on weight (adulte).

forclore [fɔrklɔ:r] v. tr. (27). JUR. To foreclose, to preclude, to bar.

forclos [-klo] adj. JUR. Foreclosed.

forclusion [-klyzjɔ̃] f. JUR. Foreclosure.

forer [fɔre] v. tr. (1). To bore (une clé, un trou); to sink (un puits); to drill (un puits de pétrole).

forestier, ière [fɔrɛstje, jɛ:r] adj. Forest (arbre); *chemin forestier*, forest road; *garde forestier*, forester; *maison forestière*, forester's lodge.
— m. Forester.

foret [fɔrɛ] m. TECHN. Drill.

forêt f. BOT. Forest; *connaissance de la forêt*, woodcraft. ‖ JUR. *Service des Eaux et Forêts*, Forestry Commission. ‖ **Forêt-galerie**, f. Gallery-forest.

foreur [fɔrœ:r] m. Driller, borer.

foreuse [-rø:z] f. TECHN. Drill, machine-drill.

forfaire [fɔrfɛ:r] v. intr. (54). To fail (à, in); *forfaire à*, to fail in (ses engagements); to forfeit (l'honneur).

forfait [fɔrfɛ] m. Heinous crime.

forfait m. COMM. Contract; *à forfait*, outright (acheter); by contract, by the job (travailler).

forfait m. SPORTS. Forfeit; *déclarer forfait*, to scratch (un cheval). ‖ FIG. *Déclarer forfait*, to give it up, to throw one's hand in.

forfaitaire [-tɛ:r] adj. COMM., FIN. Contractual; outright (marché); presumptive (méthode); contract (prix); *paiement forfaitaire*, lump sum.

forfaiture [-ty:r] f. Forfeiture, breach of honour. ‖ FIG. Prevarication; maladministration.

forfanterie [fɔrfɑ̃tri] f. Bragging, boasting.

forge [fɔrʒ] f. Forge, smithy (atelier); forge (feu); *comité des Forges*, Association of Heavy Industries; *maître de forges*, iron-master, steel-manufacturer.

forgé, ée [-ʒe] adj. Wrought (fer).

forgeage [-ʒa:ʒ] m. Forging.

forger [-ʒe] v. tr. (7). To forge (le fer). ‖ FIG. To forge (un document); to fabricate, to invent, to get up, to make up, to trump up (une histoire); to coin, to mint (un mot).
— v. intr. To forge.

forgeron [-ʒerɔ̃] m. Blacksmith, ironsmith.

forgeur [-ʒœ:r] s. FAM. Forger, fabricator.
formage [fɔrma:ʒ] m. TECHN. Shaping, moulding, forming.
formaldéhyde [fɔrmaldeid] m. CHIM. Formaldehyde.
formalisation [fɔrmalizasjɔ̃] f. Formalization.
formaliser [-lize] v. tr. (1). To formalize.
— v. pr. Se **formaliser**, to take offence (de, at).
formalisme [-lism] m. Formalism; precisianism; conventionalism.
formaliste [-list] adj. Formalistic, formal.
— s. Formalist, precisian; conventionalist.
formalité [-lite] f. Formality, formal procedure; pure formalité, mere matter of form; accomplir des formalités, to comply with formalities.
formant [fɔrmɑ̃] m. GRAMM. Formant; formative (en grammaire générative).
format [fɔrma] m. Format, size; format de poche, pocket-size.
formateur, trice [fɔrmatœ:r, tris] adj. Formative.
— s. Teacher in adult education.
formatif, ive [fɔrmatif, i:v] adj. Formative.
formation [-sjɔ̃] f. Formation. || Education, training (instruction); ses années de formation, his formative years; formation professionnelle, vocational training; formation permanente, further education for adults.
forme [fɔrm] f. Form, shape (configuration); de forme étrange, queer-shaped; en forme de cœur, heart-shaped; sans forme, shapeless. || Form, shape (corps); de formes athlétiques, of athletic build; mouler les formes, to bring out the lines of the figure. || Shape (concrétisation); donner forme à, to embody, to shape; prendre forme, to materialize (corps); to take shape (idée). || Form, appearance (apparence). || Form, aspect; forme de l'énergie, de gouvernement, form of energy, of government; sous sa pire forme, in its worst form. || Form (expression); le fond et la forme, form and content; y mettre des formes, to behave tactfully (ou) considerately. || Shape (de chapeau de femme); crown (de chapeau d'homme); jupe en forme, gored (ou) flared skirt. || Block (de chapelier); shoe-tree (de cordonnier); mettre à la forme, to stretch (des chaussures). || Form (formalité); dans les formes, en bonne et due forme, in due form; de pure forme, purely formal; pour la forme, for form's sake, as a matter of form. || JUR. Cassé pour vice de forme, quashed on a technical point; les formes établies, the established procedure; sans autre forme de procès, without any form of trial; vice de forme, informality. || TECHN. Form (en typogr.). || SPORTS. Form; en forme, fit, in form, in fine fettle; très en forme, at the top of one's form. || FAM. Etre en forme, to be up to the mark (ou) to scratch.
formé, ée [-me] adj. Formed (caractère, style). || BOT. Set (fruit). || MÉD. Puberal, pubescent (fille); full-grown (garçon).
formel, elle [fɔrmɛl] adj. Formal, express (défense); categorical, flat (démenti); explicit (loi); distinct, positive (promesse); absolute (veto).
formellement [-mɑ̃] adv. Absolutely; affirmer formellement, to state emphatically.
former [fɔrme] v. tr. (1). To form (un corps, un chiffre, une lettre, des nuages); former croûte, to form a crust. || To form, to shape, to mould (une statue, un vase). || To form (un cabinet, une coalition, un complot, un cortège, un gouvernement, un projet, une société). || To train (un apprenti); to mould (le caractère); to school (un enfant); to turn out (un étudiant).
— v. pr. Se **former**, to take form (ou) shape (prendre forme); to form (se produire). || To form, to gather (s'assembler) [en, in]. || To be formed

(être organisé); il se forma une société, a company was formed. || To improve (goût); to be trained (travailleur).
formeret [fɔrmərɛ] m. ARCHIT. Wall-rib.
Formica [fɔrmika] m. (nom déposé). Formica.
formidable [fɔrmidabl] adj. Formidable. || FAM. Awful, stupendous, smashing; c'est formidable!, really!, did you ever!; il est formidable, he's a caution (ou) character (bizarre); he's a smasher, U. S. he's tops (ou) a neat guy (extraordinaire).
formidablement [-blǝmɑ̃] adv. Formidably.
formique [fɔrmik] adj. CHIM. Formic.
formol [-mɔl] m. CHIM. Formalin.
Formose [fɔrmo:ʒ] f. GÉOGR. Formosa.
formulable [fɔrmylabl] adj. Expressible.
formulaire [-lɛ:r] m. Form (imprimé). || JUR., MÉD. Formulary.
formulation [-lasjɔ̃] f. Formulation, way of stating (ou) formulating.
formule [-myl] f. Formula; formule toute faite, set form; formule épistolaire, form of words used in correspondence. || Form : formule de télégramme, telegraph form (ou) U. S. blank. || JUR., MÉD., CHIM., MATH. Formula.
formuler [-myle] v. tr. (1). To formulate (une doctrine); to state (des griefs, une opinion); to define (sa pensée); to put forward, to set forth (des prétentions); to make (une remarque); to express, to formulate (un vœu); formuler une demande, to make an application. || MATH., CHIM. To formulate. || JUR. To draw up (un acte); to lodge (une plainte).
fornicateur [fɔrnikatœ:r] m. Fornicator.
fornicatrice [-katris] f. Fornicatress.
fornication [-kasjɔ̃] f. Fornication.
forniquer [-ke] v. intr. (1). To fornicate.
fors [fɔr] prép. † Except, save. (V. EXCEPTÉ.)
forsythia [fɔrsitja] m. BOT. Forsythia.
fort, orte adj. Strong (résistant, vigoureux, violent); câble, tissu, vent fort, strong cable, fabric, wind. || Considérable; forte chaleur, différence, great heat, difference; forte pente, steep slope. || Loud (bruit, son, voix); heavy (choc, secousse); strong (lumière, odeur). || Strong (argument, motif, preuve); big (sensation); employer la manière forte, to use strong methods. || Able (capable); se faire fort de, to undertake to, to engage to, to take it upon oneself to; se porter fort pour, to answer for, to stand bail for. || Strong, good, well up, proficient (en, in); pas très fort en, not very bright in. (V. CALÉ.) || Clever (malin); c'est trop fort pour moi, it's too deep for me; trouver plus fort que soi, to meet one's master. || Jaunty (désinvolte); esprit fort, freethinker. || Stubborn (têtu); forte tête, pig-headed fellow. || Stout, lusty (corpulent); big, large (gros); c'est une forte femme, she is a stout woman. || COMM. Stiff (prix); prix fort, full price (du catalogue). || FIN. Hard (devise); large (somme). || MILIT. Strong (position); place forte, fortress. || MÉD. Large (dose); high (fièvre); strong (pouls). || CULIN. Strong (café, fromage, thé, vin). || GRAMM. Strong (verbe). || FAM. Ça c'est plus fort que tout, that takes the cake; c'est plus fort que lui, he can't help it; c'est plus fort que jouer au bouchon, it beats cock-fighting; c'est trop fort, that's too thick (ou) bad; celle-là est forte, that's a thumper; il est fort pour les bons vins, he has a partiality for good wines; fort en gueule, loud-mouthed.
— adv. Hard, heavily, strongly (violemment); pleuvoir très fort, to rain heavily; sentir trop fort, to have too strong a smell; serrer fort, to squeeze tight. || Loud (haut); parler plus fort, to speak more loudly. || Very, greatly (v. TRÈS); fort beau, very fine; fort remarqué, highly admired.

— m. Strong (ou) sturdy (ou) hefty man (costaud); *les forts de la Halle,* the market porters. ‖ Milit. Fort (fortification). ‖ Naut. *Fort maritime,* sea-coast work (ou) fort. ‖ Fig. Strong point, forte; *c'est mon fort,* it's my forte; *un fort en thème,* a swot, U. S. a grind. ‖ Loc. *Au plus fort de,* in the utmost heat of (la discussion); at the height of (l'été); in the heart (ou) depth of (l'hiver); in the thick of (la mêlée).

fortement [fɔrtəmɑ̃] adv. Hard (durement); strongly (énergiquement); tightly (étroitement); firmly (fermement); heavily (lourdement); very, very much (très).

forteresse [-rɛs] f. Milit. Fortress; stronghold; *la forteresse européenne,* Fortress Europe. ‖ Aviat. *Forteresse volante,* Flying Fortress. ‖ Fig. Stronghold.

fortiche [fɔrtiʃ] adj. Pop. Crafty, smart; burly.

fortifiable [fɔrtifjabl] adj. Fortifiable.

fortifiant, ante [-fjɑ̃, ɑ̃:t] adj. Fortifying, strengthening.

— m. Méd. Tonic, fortifier.

fortification [-fikasjɔ̃] f. Milit. Fortification (action et ouvrage).

fortifier [-fje] v. tr. (1). Milit. To fortify (une ville). ‖ Méd. To strengthen, to fortify. ‖ Fig. To strengthen (l'esprit, une position); to confirm (une opinion).

— v. pr. **Se fortifier.** Milit. To fortify oneself. ‖ Méd. To grow stronger (ou) more robust. ‖ Fig. To be strengthened (ou) confirmed.

fortin [fɔrtɛ̃] m. Milit. Fortlet.

fortiori (a) [afɔrsjɔri] loc. adv. A fortiori.

fortran [fɔrtrɑ̃] m. Inform. Fortran.

fortuit, ite [fɔrtɥi, it] adj. Fortuitous, casual, chance. (V. accidentel.) ‖ Jur. *Cas fortuit,* fortuitous event; act of God.

fortuitement [-tmɑ̃] adv. Fortuitously.

fortune [fɔrtyn] f. Fortune, Fate (sort). ‖ Fortune, wealth (richesse); *après fortune faite,* after making one's pile (fam.); *avoir de la fortune,* to have private means; *faire fortune,* to make a fortune. ‖ Fortune, chance, luck (chance); *dans la bonne et la mauvaise fortune,* come rain or come shine; *faire contre mauvaise fortune bon cœur,* to put a good face on a bad business; *tenter fortune,* to try one's luck. ‖ Chance, hazard (hasard); *de fortune,* chance (compagnon); rough and ready (installation); makeshift (moyens); emergency (réparations); of fortune (soldat); *manger à la fortune du pot,* to take pot-luck; *repas à la fortune du pot,* scratch (ou) U. S. potluck meal. ‖ Naut. *Fortunes de mer,* sea-going risks. ‖ Jur. *Impôt* (ou) *prélèvement sur la fortune,* general property tax. ‖ Pl. *Bonnes fortunes,* womanizing affairs; *un homme à bonnes fortunes,* a ladies' man, a lady killer; *en quête de bonnes fortunes,* on the prowl.

fortuné, ée [-ne] adj. Fortunate. (V. chanceux, heureux.) ‖ Wealthy. (V. riche.)

forum [fɔrɔm] m. † Forum. ‖ Fam. Politics; *les luttes du forum,* political strife.

fosse [fo:s] f. Pit, hole (trou). ‖ Deep (dans la mer). ‖ Pit; *fosse d'aisances,* cesspool; *fosse à purin,* cess-pit; *fosse septique,* septic tank. ‖ Den (antre); *fosse aux lions, aux ours,* lions', bears' den. ‖ Grave (tombe); *fosse commune,* common (ou) pauper's grave; potter's field. ‖ Autom. Inspection pit. ‖ Théâtr. Orchestra pit. ‖ Méd. Fossa; *fosses nasales,* nasal fossae.

fossé [fose] m. Ditch (de la route). ‖ Drain (de dessèchement); *fossé d'arrêt pour les feuilles,* trap-ditch for leaves. ‖ Milit. *Fossé antichar,* anti-tank ditch. ‖ Fig. Breach, gulf (*entre,* between).

fossette [fɔsɛt] f. Dimple (sur le visage). ‖ Géol. Socket.

fossile [fɔsil] adj., m. Fossil.

fossilifère [-lifɛ:r] adj. Fossiliferous.

fossilisation [-lizasjɔ̃] f. Fossilization.

fossiliser [-lize] v. tr. (1). To fossilize.

fossoyage [fɔswaja:ʒ] m. Ditching (des routes). ‖ Grave-digging (au cimetière).

fossoyer [-je] v. tr. (9 a). To ditch.

fossoyeur [-jœ:r] m. Grave-digger.

fou [fu] (m. **fol** [fɔl] before a vowel or a mute h; f. **folle** [fɔ:l]) adj. Méd. Mad, insane (v. aliéné, dément); *devenir fou,* to go mad; *fou furieux,* raving mad; *mourir fou,* to die insane; *rendre fou,* to distract, to drive mad (ou) out of one's head. ‖ Crazy (v. cinglé, toqué); *il n'est pas si fou qu'il en a l'air,* there is method in his madness; ‖ Mad, wild, frantic (surexcité); *fou de,* mad with (colère); wild with (joie); frantic with (peur); *d'une gaieté folle,* wild with mirth; *rage folle,* tearing rage. ‖ Passionately fond (passionné); *fou d'amour pour,* madly in love with; *être folle d'une nouvelle amie,* to be crazy about a new friend; *être fou de chocolat,* to be passionately fond of chocolate. ‖ Extravagant (dépenses); irresponsible (enchère); foolhardy (entreprise); foolish (espoir). ‖ Splitting (migraine); tremendous (succès); breakneck (vitesse); *gagner un argent fou,* to make pots of money; *un monde fou,* a fearful crowd. ‖ Rank (herbes); stray (mèches); *brise folle,* baffling wind. ‖ Unsteady (balance); loose (poulie); idle, free, loose (roue). ‖ **Fou-fou,** adj. Fam. Foolish.

— m. Méd. Maniac, lunatic; *un fou, une folle,* a madman, a madwoman; *maison de fous,* lunatic asylum, mental institution. ‖ Madcap (écervelé); *faire le fou,* to frolic, to act the fool, to play the giddy goat. ‖ Fool, jester (bouffon). ‖ Bishop (aux échecs). ‖ Zool. Gannet. [V. folle.]

fouace [fwas] f. Culin. Flat-cake, bannock.

fouailler [fwaje] v. tr. (1). To lash, to whip. ‖ Fig. To lather.

foucade [fukad] f. Fam. Craze, whim.

foudre [fudr] f. Lightning (du ciel); *frappé par la foudre,* struck by lightning; *la foudre est tombée à,* lightning struck at. ‖ Fig. Thunderbolt; *coup de foudre,* love at first sight; *frappé d'un coup de foudre réciproque,* smitten with each other; *tomber sur qqn comme la foudre,* to come upon s.o. like a thunderbolt. ‖ Fig. Pl. Thunder; ‖ Ecclés. Pl. Anathema; excommunication.

— m. *Foudre de guerre,* great captain. ‖ Electr. Danger sign.

foudre m. Tun (tonneau).

foudroiement [fudrwamɑ̃] m. Striking down by lightning (de qqn). ‖ Blasting (d'un arbre).

foudroyant, ante [-jɑ̃, ɑ̃t] adj. Thundering. ‖ Overwhelming, crushing (attaque); lightning (avance, progrès, vitesse); withering (regard); *nouvelle foudroyante,* bolt from the blue, thunderbolt. ‖ Méd. Fulminant (maladie).

foudroyer [-je] v. tr. (9 a). To blast (un arbre); to strike down (qqn). ‖ Electr. To kill by electric discharge (qqn). ‖ Méd. To strike down (qqn). ‖ Fig. To confound (confondre); to dumbfound (étonner); *foudroyer du regard,* to cast a withering glance at.

fouène [fwɛn] f. V. foëne.

fouet [fwɛ] m. Whip; *chasser à coup de fouet,* to whip out. ‖ Birch, rod (verge); *donner le fouet à,* to flog, to whip, to give a flogging to. ‖ Culin. Egg-whisk.

fouettard [-tar] adj. *Père Fouettard,* Bogy-man.

fouettée [-te] f. Flogging. (V. fessée.)

fouettement [-mɑ̃] m. Lashing (de la pluie); lashing, whipping (des verges). ‖ Naut. Flapping (des voiles).

fouetter [-te] v. tr. (1). To flog, to birch (un

enfant). [V. FESSER.] ‖ To whip, to lash (un cheval). ‖ CULIN. To whip (de la crème); to whisk (des œufs). ‖ FIG. To lash, to whip (pluie); to beat (vent); *fouetter l'air*, to switch the air; *fouetter le sang de qqn*, to send the blood rushing through s. o. ‖ FIG. To stimulate, to spur on (désir, émulation). ‖ LOC. *Avoir d'autres chats à fouetter*, to have other fish to fry; *il n'y a pas de quoi fouetter un chat*, there is nothing to make a fuss about.
— v. intr. To lash (pluie). ‖ NAUT. To flap (voile).

ougasse [fugas] f. V. FOUACE.

ougeraie [fuʒrɛ] f. Fernery.

ougère [fuʒɛːr] f. BOT. Fern.

ougue [fug] f. Fire (de la jeunesse); heat (des passions); *plein de fougue*, fiery (animal); full of dash (personne).

ougueusement [fugøzmɑ̃] adv. Impetuously.

ougueux, euse [-gø, øːz] adj. Fiery, mettlesome (animal); impetuous, full of dash (personne).

ouille [fuːj] f. Digging, excavating (action); excavation (résultat); *faire des fouilles dans*, to excavate. ‖ Searching, search (des poches, de qqn).

ouillé, ée [fuje] adj. Elaborate (style, travail).

ouiller v. tr. (1). To dig, to excavate, to turn up (le sol). ‖ To scour (un bois); to go through (les poches, qqn); to ransack (un tiroir). ‖ ARTS. To undercut (une sculpture). ‖ FIG. To go thoroughly into (un sujet); *fouiller du regard*, to scan (une pièce); to peer into (l'ombre).
— v. intr. To dig (creuser). ‖ To grub; *fouiller dans les plates-bandes*, to grub among the flowerbeds. ‖ To burrow (taupe). ‖ To rummage (pour chercher); *fouiller dans*, to rummage in, to ransack. (V. FOURGONNER.)
— v. pr. Se fouiller, to go through (ou) to search one's pockets. ‖ POP. *Tu peux te fouiller!*, nothing doing!

ouilleur, euse [-jœːr, øːz] s. Digger (pour creuser). ‖ Searcher (de poches).

ouilleuse [-jøːz] f. TECHN. Excavator; subsoil plough.

ouillis [fuji] m. Muddle, jumble, tangle.

ouinard, arde [fwinaːr, ard], **fouineur, euse** [-nœːr, øːz] adj. FAM. Inquisitive, ferrety.
— s. Nosy Parker.

ouine [fwin] f. ZOOL. Stone- (ou) beech-marten. ‖ FAM. *À figure de fouine*, weasel-faced; *des yeux de fouine*, ferrety eyes. (V. FOUINARD.)

ouine f. AGRIC. Pitchfork.

ouiner [-ne] v. intr. (1). FAM. To ferret (ou) to nose about; *fouiner dans les affaires des autres*, to poke one's nose into other people's business, to meddle.

ouineur, euse [-nœːr, øːz] adj., s. V. FOUINARD.

ouir [fwiːr] v. tr. (2). To burrow in, to grub, to dig (le sol).

ouisseur, euse [fwisœːr, øːz] adj. ZOOL. Burrowing, fossorial (animal).
— m. ZOOL. Burrower, fossorial.

oulage [fulaːʒ] m. Fulling (du drap). ‖ Pressing (du raisin). ‖ Impression (en typogr.).

oulant, ante [-lɑ̃, ɑ̃:t] adj. TECHN. *Pompe foulante*, force-pump. ‖ FAM. Back-breaking.

oulard [fulaːr] m. Foulard (étoffe); scarf (fichu).

oule [ful] f. Crowd, throng (de, of); *accourir en foule à*, to crowd in, to throng (ou) to flock to; *encombré par la foule*, crowded, thronged. (V. COHUE, PRESSE.) ‖ Mob, crowd, throng (peuple); *psychologie des foules*, mob (ou) mass psychology. ‖ Piles, lots, heaps (de choses); host, world, crowd (de gens, de serviteurs); host (d'idées, de questions); *venir en foule à l'esprit*, to crowd upon one.

oulé, ée [fule] adj. Fulled (drap). ‖ MÉD. Sprained, wrenched.

foulée f. Print, tread (d'un cheval); foil, slot, track (du gibier). ‖ Stride (enjambée); *marcher à longues foulées*, to stride along.

fouler v. tr. (1). To full (un drap). ‖ To crush (des raisins). ‖ To tread, to tread on (le sol). ‖ MÉD. To sprain, to wrench (un membre). ‖ FIG. *Fouler aux pieds*, to trample underfoot, to tread down.
— v. pr. Se fouler. FAM. To fag (ou) to knock oneself out; *il ne se foule par*, he doesn't kill himself.

fouleur [fulœːr] s. Fuller.

fouloir [-lwaːr] m. TECHN. Beater (de drap); rammer (de métal).

foulon [fulɔ̃] m. Fuller; *terre à foulon*, fuller's earth.

foulque [fulk] f. ZOOL. Coot.

foultitude [fultity:d] f. FAM. Heaps, lots, piles.

foulure [fuly:r] f. MÉD. Sprain, wrench.

four [fu:r] m. CULIN. Oven; *faire cuire au four*, to roast; *plat allant au four*, fireproof dish; U. S. ovenware platter; *petits fours*, petits fours, cup-cakes. ‖ Oven (de boulanger). ‖ TECHN. Kiln, furnace; *séché au four*, kiln dried. ‖ FAM. Flop, foozle, fiasco, frost, washout; U. S. turkey.

fourbe [furb] adj. Deceitful, sly. (V. SOURNOIS.)
— s. Cheat, double-dealer.

fourberie [-bəri] f. Deceit; cheating. ‖ Double-dealing. (V. DUPLICITÉ.)

fourbi [furbi] m. FAM. Whole caboodle (v. BAZAR); thingummy. (V. MACHIN.)

fourbir [furbi:r] v. tr. (2). To furbish, to polish (ou) shine up. (V. BRIQUER.)

fourbissage [-bisa:ʒ] m. Furbishing, shining up.

fourbu, ue [furby] adj. Foundered (cheval). ‖ FAM. Dog (ou) dead tired. (V. ÉREINTÉ.)

fourche [furʃ] f. Fork, pitchfork (outil). ‖ Fork (d'arbre); forking (de routes); *à fourche*, branching, Y-shaped, forked (route); *faire une fourche*, to fork (ou) to branch off.

fourchée [-ʃe] f. Forkful.

fourcher [-ʃe] v. intr. (1). To fork (arbre); to fork (ou) branch off (route). ‖ FIG. *La langue lui a fourché*, he made a slip of the tongue.

fourchetée [-ʃəte] f. (Table-)forkful.

fourchette [-ʃɛt] f. Fork; *à la fourchette*, knife-and-fork (repas). ‖ TECHN. Fork. ‖ MILIT. Bracket; *prise en fourchette*, bracketing. ‖ MÉD. *Déformation en fourchette*, dinner-fork deformity. ‖ FAM. *Une bonne fourchette*, a good trencherman; *jouer de la fourchette*, to ply a good knife and fork.

fourchon [-ʃɔ̃] m. Prong.

fourchu, ue [-ʃy] adj. Forked (arbre, langue, perche); branching, Y-shaped, furcate, bifurcated (route); *pied fourchu*, cloven hoof.

fourgon [furgɔ̃] m. CH. DE F. Luggage (ou) goods van; U. S. baggage car; *fourgon à bestiaux*, cattle-truck; U. S. cattle-car. ‖ MILIT. Waggon. ‖ AUTOM. Motor van, truck; *fourgon de déménagement*, furniture van.

fourgonner [-gɔne] v. intr. (1). To poke (ou) to rake (dans le feu). ‖ FAM. To rummage (ou) to poke about (*dans*, in.) [V. FOUILLER, FOURRAGER.]
— v. tr. To poke (le feu).

fourgonnette [-gɔnɛt] f. Delivery van (ou) U. S. truck.

fourguer [furge] v. tr. (1). ARG. To flog, to sell off.

fourmi [furmi] f. ZOOL. Ant; *fourmi rouge*, red ant. ‖ FAM. *J'ai des fourmis dans les jambes*, I have pins and needles (ou) a tingling in my legs. ‖ **Fourmi-lion**, m. ZOOL. Ant-lion.

fourmilier [-lje] m. ZOOL. Ant-eater (animal); ant-catcher (oiseau).

fourmilière [-ljɛ:r] f. Ant-hill, ants' nest. ‖ FIG. Hive, swarm.

fourmillement [-jmɑ̃] m. Swarming (des fourmis). ‖ Formication, tingling, pins and needles (des membres). ‖ Fig. Swarming (de la foule).

fourmiller [-je] v. intr. (1). To swarm (en général). ‖ To crawl, to swarm, to be alive (de, with) [vermine, vers]. ‖ To tingle (membre). ‖ Fig. To teem (de, with). [V. foisonner.]

fournaise [furnɛ:z] f. Furnace. ‖ Fam. Oven.

fourneau [-no] m. Culin. Cooker, kitchen- (ou) cooking range; fourneau à gaz, gas-range (ou) stove (ou) cooker. ‖ Techn. Furnace; fourneau de mine, mine chamber; haut fourneau, blast-furnace. ‖ Bowl (de pipe). ‖ Fam. Muff, U. S. dumbbell.

fournée [-ne] f. Ovenful, batch (de pain). ‖ Kiln (de briques); charge (de fourneau). ‖ Fig. Batch, bunch (de gens).

fourni, ie [furni] adj. Bushy (barbe); thick (chevelure, forêt). ‖ Comm. Supplied; bien fourni en, well-stocked in (ou) with.

fournil [furni] m. Bakehouse, bakery.

fourniment [furnimã] m. Milit. Kit.

fournir [-ni:r] v. tr. (2). To furnish, to yield, to afford (produire); fournir un bon approvisionnement de, to provide a good supply of. ‖ To furnish, to provide, to supply (approvisionner); fournir qqch. à qqn, to supply s. o. with sth. ‖ To furnish (un exemple); to afford (une occasion); to do (un travail); fournir un travail gratuit, to give one's labour gratuitously; fournir du travail à qqn, to give s. o. work. ‖ Sports. To run (une course). ‖ Jur. To give (caution); to produce (des documents); to adduce (des preuves).
— v. intr. To provide (à, for); fournir aux besoins de qqn, to supply s.o.'s wants (ou) needs. ‖ To follow suit (aux cartes).
— v. pr. Se fournir, to provide oneself (de, with); se fournir chez, to get one's supplies from.

fournissement [-nismã] m. Comm. Contribution. ‖ Fin. Repartition account.

fournisseur [-nisœ:r] s. Comm. Supplier, purveyor; dealer (de, in); fournisseur du gouvernement, contractor to the Government; fournisseur de la reine, by special appointment to the Queen; les fournisseurs, tradespeople, tradesmen. ‖ Milit. Contractor. ‖ Naut. Ship-chandler.

fourniture [-nity:r] f. Supplying, providing, purveying (action). ‖ Pl. Materials, supplies, requisites; fournitures de bureau, office stationery (ou) supplies.

fourrage [fura:ʒ] m. Agric. Fodder. ‖ Milit. Forage; envoyer au fourrage, to send out foraging.

fourrager [-ʒe] v. tr. (7). To forage. ‖ Fam. To forage. (V. fourgonner.)

fourragère [-ʒɛ:r] adj. f. Fodder (plante); farines fourragères, meal.
— f. Forage waggon, U. S. feed truck (voiture). ‖ Milit. Regimental lanyard, fourragère. ‖ Autom. Luggage carrier, U. S. baggage rack.

fourrageur [-ʒœ:r] m. Forager. ‖ Milit. En fourrageurs, in extended order (charge).

fourré, ée [fure] adj. Furred, fined (gants, manteau). ‖ Culin. Chocolats fourrés, chocolates, chocolate creams; dattes fourrées, stuffed dates. ‖ Sports. Coup fourré, double hit. ‖ Fam. Être toujours fourré chez qqn, to be never off s. o. 's doorstep.
— m. Thicket; cover.

fourreau [furo] m. Sheath, scabbard (d'épée); mettre au fourreau, to sheathe; tirer du fourreau, to unsheathe. ‖ Case, cover (de parapluie). ‖ Sheath, fourreau (robe collante).

fourrer [fure] v. tr. (1). To line (ou) to cover with fur (un vêtement). ‖ Culin. To stuff. ‖ Fam. To tuck, to shove, to stick (qqch.) [dans, into]; fourrer son nez partout, to poke one's nose into everything, to meddle; fourrer dedans, to put in quod (emprisonner); to bamboozle (tromper).

— v. pr. Se fourrer, to stick oneself (se placer) ne savoir où se fourrer, not to know where to hide oneself; se fourrer dans un trou de souris, to want to go through the floor.

fourre-tout [furtu] m. invar. Hold-all, catchall.

fourreur [furœ:r] s. Furrier.

fourrier [furje] m. Milit. Quatermaster-sergeant.

fourrière [-rjɛ:r] f. Pound; mettre en fourrière, to impound.

fourrure [fury:r] f. Comm., Blas. Fur. ‖ Autom. Techn. Lining.

fourvoiement [furvwamã] m. Leading astray. ‖ Fig. Error.

fourvoyer [-je] v. tr. (9a). To mislead.
— Se fourvoyer, to go astray. [V. s'égarer.] ‖ Fig. To go astray, to go off the rails.

foutaise [futɛ:z] f. Fam. Twaddle, rot, bunkum, poppycock.

foutoir [-twa:r] m. Pop. Damned mess (ou) shambles.

foutre [futr] v. tr. (4). Pop. V. ficher, fourrer.

foutrement [-trəmã] adv. Pop. Bloody (avec adjectif et adverbe); bloody well (avec verbe).

foutriquet [futrikɛ] m. Pop. Little squirt.

foutu, ue [futy] adj. Pop. V. fichu.

fox [fɔks], **fox-terrier** [-tɛrje] m. Zool. Fox-terrier. ‖ Fox-hound, m. Zool. Foxhound. ‖ Fox-trot, m. Foxtrot.

foxhound [fɔksaund] m. Zool. Foxhound.

foyer [fwaje] m. Hearth, fire-place (âtre); hearthstone (dalle); hearth-rug (tapis). ‖ Techn. Furnace (de chaudière). ‖ Ch. de f. Fire-box (de locomotive). ‖ Math., Phys. Focus. ‖ Méd. Seat, focus, centre. ‖ Théâtr. Green-room (des artistes); foyer (du public). ‖ Milit. Rentrer dans ses foyers, to return home. ‖ Fig. Home (demeure, maison d'accueil); foyer des étudiants, students' Union (club); students' hostel (hôtel); la vie au foyer, home life. ‖ Fig. Hotbed (de conspiration).

frac [frak] m. Dress-coat, tails.

fracas [fraka] m. Crash (d'objet brisé ou écroulé); roll, peal (du tonnerre); roar (des vagues). ‖ Fam. Faire du fracas, to kick up a shindy. (V. boucan.)

fracassant, ante [-sã, ã:t] adj. Deafening, ear-splitting (bruit); staggering, stunning (déclaration).

fracasser [-se] v. tr. (1). To crash, to smash to pieces. (V. briser.)

fraction [fraksjõ] f. Fraction, subdivision, portion, unit. ‖ Math. Fraction. ‖ Ecclés. Breaking, fraction (du pain). ‖ Fin. Instalment (paiement).

fractionnaire [-sjɔnɛ:r] adj. Math. Fractional; nombre fractionnaire, improper fraction.

fractionnel, elle [-sjɔnɛl] adj. Divisive.

fractionnement [-sjɔnmã] m. Fractionation; splitting up.

fractionner [-sjɔne] v. tr. (1). To divide into fractions. ‖ To split up (des parts).
— v. pr. Se fractionner, to split up.

fracture [frakty:r] f. Breaking open (d'une porte). ‖ Méd. Fracture. ‖ Gramm. Breaking.

fracturer [-tyre] v. tr. (1). To fracture, to break open (une porte). ‖ Méd., Gramm. To break.
— v. pr. Se fracturer, to fracture. ‖ Méd. Se fracturer un bras, to break (ou) fracture one's arm.

fragile [fraʒil] adj. Fragile; frangile, brittle (cassant). ‖ Comm. « Fragile », « with care ». ‖ Fig. Weak (argument, vertu); frail (bonheur, personne, vertu); precarious (santé). [V. frêle.]

fragilité [-lite] f. Fragility (en général); flimsiness (du papier); brittleness (du verre). ‖ Fig. Weakness; frailty.

fragment [fragmã] m. Fragment. (V. morceau.) ‖ Fig. Fragment (v. passage); fragment de chanson, snatch of a song.

fragmentaire [-tɛ:r] adj. Fragmentary.

fragmentairement [-tɛrmɑ̃] adv. Fragmentarily, sketchily.

fragmentation [-tasjɔ̃] f. Fragmentation.

fragmenter [-te] v. tr. (1). To break up.

frai [frɛ] m. Spawning-season (époque); spawning (ponte); spawn (œufs). ‖ Fry (fretin).

frai m. Abrasion, wear.

fraîche [frɛ:ʃ] adj. f. V. FRAIS.
— f. *A la fraîche*, in the cool of the evening.

fraîchement [frɛʃmɑ̃] adv. Coolly (au frais). ‖ FIG. Freshly, newly. (V. RÉCEMMENT.) ‖ FAM. Coldly, coolly (sans chaleur).

fraîcheur [-ʃœ:r] f. Coolness, freshness, cool (froid agréable); chilliness (froidure). ‖ CULIN. Freshness (des aliments.) ‖ FIG. Freshness, newness. (V. NOUVEAUTÉ.) ‖ FIG. Freshness (d'une couleur, du teint); *fraîcheur d'esprit*, freshness of approach. ‖ FAM. Chilliness (d'un accueil).

fraîchir [-ʃi:r] v. intr. (2). To freshen (temps).

frairie [frɛri] f. Village fête (ou) fair.

frais, aîche [frɛ, ɛ:ʃ] adj. Fresh (air, eau, vent); cool (cave, pièce); fresh, cool, chilly (temps); *il commence à faire frais*, it is getting cool. ‖ Cool (léger); new, new-looking (neuf) [vêtement]. ‖ Wet (encre, peinture). ‖ Fresh (odeur, teint, personne); *frais et dispos*, as fresh as a daisy. ‖ Fresh (chagrin, souvenir); recent (date, empreinte, nouvelle); *de fraîche date*, recent, newly formed. ‖ CULIN. Fresh (boisson, nourriture, poisson, viande); newlaid (œuf); new (pain). ‖ MÉD. Fresh, green (blessure). ‖ MILIT. Fresh (troupes). ‖ FAM. *Etre frais*, to be in a nice mess.
— adv. Freshly; *boire frais*, to have a cool drink. ‖ Newly; *frais arrivé*, just arrived; *fraîche cueillie*, freshly gathered; *frais éclos*, new-blown. ‖ NAUT. *Venter frais*, to blow freshly.
— m. Cool, fresh air; *prendre le frais*, to enjoy the cool air, to take a breath of fresh air. ‖ *Au frais*, in a cool place. ‖ **De frais**, newly, freshly.

frais [frɛ] m. pl. Expenses, charges, cost; *à grands frais*, at great expense; *à mes frais*, at my own expense (ou) charge; *à peu de frais*, at little cost; *aux frais de*, at the expense of; *aux frais de la princesse*, on the house, buckshee; *faire les frais de*, to bear the expense of; *se mettre en frais pour*, to go to expense for; *sans frais*, free of charge. ‖ COMM. *Couvrir ses frais*, to pay its way (entreprise); to cover one's expenses (personne); *frais de bureau*, office expenses (débours); office allowance (indemnité); *frais de déplacement*, travelling and hôtel expenses; *frais divers*, sundries; miscellaneous expenses; *frais d'emballage*, packing costs; *frais d'entretien*, cost of upkeep; *frais d'expédition*, forwarding (ou) shipping charges; *frais d'exploitation* (ou) *de marche*, working expenses, U. S. operating costs; *frais généraux*, overhead charges (ou) expenses; overheads (fam.); *frais d'installation*, initial outlay; *frais de magasinage*, warehousing (ou) storage charges; *frais de représentation*, entertainment allowance; *sans frais*, «no expenses». ‖ JUR. *Condamné aux frais*, ordered to pay costs; *frais d'instance*, costs; *frais de procédure*, Court fees. ‖ FIG. *En être pour ses frais*, to have lost one's time and money; *faire les frais de la conversation*, to keep the conversation going (l'alimenter); to be the topic of the conversation (en être le sujet); *se mettre en frais pour*, to lay (ou) put oneself out for.

fraisage [frɛza:ʒ] m. TECHN. Milling; countersinking. ‖ MÉD. Drilling (des dents).

fraise [frɛ:z] f. BOT. Strawberry. ‖ MÉD. Strawberry-mark (nævus).

fraise f. Fraise, ruff (collet). ‖ CULIN. Frill (de veau). ‖ ZOOL. Wattle (de dindon).

fraise f. TECHN. Milling cutter (à découper); fraise (à élargir). ‖ MÉD. Drill (du dentiste).

fraiser [frɛze] v. tr. (1). To frill (un col).

fraiser v. tr. (1). TECHN. To mill (découper); to countersink (élargir). ‖ MÉD. To drill.

fraiseur [-zœ:r] m. TECHN. Miller.

fraiseuse [-zø:z] f. TECHN. Milling-machine. ‖ MÉD. Drill.

fraisier [frɛzje] m. BOT. Strawberry-plant.

fraisure [frɛzy:r] f. Countersink, countersunk hole.

framboise [frɑ̃bwa:z] f. BOT. Raspberry.
— adj. Murrey, purple-red.

framboisé, ée [-ze] adj. Raspberry-flavoured.

framboisier [-zje] m. BOT. Raspberry-bush.

franc [frɑ̃] m. Franc (monnaie); *une pièce de dix francs*, a ten-franc piece; *pour vingt francs de*, twenty francs' worth of.

franc, anche [frɑ̃, ɑ̃:ʃ] adj. Frank (v. SINCÈRE); *il est très franc*, he is very sincere. ‖ Frank, open-hearted, outspoken, straightforward (carré, direct); *avoir son franc-parler*, to be outspoken; *un ami trop franc*, a candid friend; *franc du collier*, straightforward; *réponse franche*, straight answer. ‖ Clear, unequivocal, straightforward (clair); *jouer franc jeu*, to play the game; *net et franc*, open and above-board; *situation franche*, unequivocal position. ‖ Downright, regular, rank (vrai); *une franche fripouille*, an arrant scoundrel. ‖ Real, absolute (absolu); *joie franche*, unmixed joy. ‖ † Free (libre); *port franc*, free port. ‖ JUR. Free (exempt); *franc de tout droit*, duty-free; *franc de port*, carriage paid, U. S. postpaid (colis); postage free (colis postal). ‖ JUR. Whole, complete (entier); *huit jours francs*, eight clear days. ‖ SPORTS. *Coup franc*, free kick. ‖ MILIT. *Corps franc*, free corps, commando. ‖ LOC. *A franc étrier*, at full speed. ‖ **Franc-bord**, m. NAUT. Free-board. ‖ **Franc-bourgeois**, m. Freeman. ‖ **Franc-comtois**, adj. GÉOGR. Of (ou) from Franche-Comté; s. native (ou) inhabitant of Franche-Comté. ‖ **Franc-maçon**, m. Freemason. ‖ **Franc-maçonnerie**, f. Freemasonry. ‖ **Franc-parler**, m. Candour, plain-speaking, outspokenness. ‖ **Franc-tireur**, m. MILIT. Franc-tireur, sniper; FIG. free-lance.
— adv. Frankly, clearly, candidly.

franc, anque [frɑ̃, ɑ̃:k] adj. Frankish.
— s. Frank.

français, aise [frɑ̃sɛ, ɛ:z] adj. French.
— m. Frenchman; *les Français*, the French. ‖ French (langue).

française [-sɛ:z] f. Frenchwoman. ‖ LOC. *A la française*, in (ou) after the French manner.

France [frɑ̃:s] f. GÉOGR. France.

franchement [frɑ̃ʃmɑ̃] adv. Frankly, sincerely (en toute vérité). ‖ Absolutely, really (absolument). ‖ Straightforwardly, bluntly, plainly, candidly (catégoriquement); boldy (hardiment).

franchir [frɑ̃ʃi:r] v. tr. (2). To jump over (un fossé); to clear (un obstacle); to cross, to pass (une rivière). ‖ To pass through (une porte); to step over, to cross (le seuil). ‖ To cross, to cover (une distance). ‖ NAUT. To pump (une pompe). ‖ AVIAT. To break through (le mur du son). ‖ FIG. To go beyond, to overstep (les bornes); to get over (une difficulté).

franchise [frɑ̃ʃi:z] f. Frankness, candour, outspokenness (franc-parler); plain speaking, sincerity (v. SINCÉRITÉ, VÉRACITÉ); *en toute franchise*, quite frankly. ‖ Exemption; *en franchise*, duty-free (colis); frank (lettre); *franchise postale*, On Her Majesty's Service (O. H. M. S.), U. S. franking privilege. ‖ Immunity; *franchise diplomatique*, diplomatic immunity. ‖ † Freedom, franchise (d'une ville).

franchissable [frɑ̃ʃisabl] adj. Negotiable (montagne); passable (rivière).

franchissement [-sm$\tilde{a}$] m. Jumping (d'un fossé) ; negotiating (d'une montagne) ; crossing, passing (d'une rivière). ‖ MILIT. *Capacité de franchissement,* spanning ability.

francisation [fr$\tilde{a}$sizasj$\tilde{o}$] f. NAUT., GRAMM. Gallicizing.

franciscain, aine [fr$\tilde{a}$sisk$\tilde{\epsilon}$, ϵn] adj., m. ECCLÉS. Franciscan.

franciser [fr$\tilde{a}$size] v. tr. (1). GRAMM. To gallicize, to Frenchify. ‖ NAUT. To register as French.

francisque [-sisk] f. Frankish battle-axe, francisca.

francium [fr$\tilde{a}$sj$\Im$m] m. CHIM. Francium.

franco [fr$\tilde{a}$ko] adv. Carriage-free ; *franco de port,* carriage-paid ; U. S. postpaid ; *envoyé franco sur demande,* sent free on request.

franco- [fr$\tilde{a}$ko] préf. Franco-. ‖ **Franco-allemand,** adj. Franco-German ; *guerre franco-allemande,* Franco-Prussian war. ‖ **Franco-anglais,** adj. Anglo-French. ‖ **Franco-canadien,** adj. Franco-Canadian ; adj., s. GRAMM., GÉOGR. French Canadian.

francophile [fr$\tilde{a}$k$\Im$fil] adj., s. Francophile.

francophilie [-fili] f. Francophilia.

francophobe [-f$\Im$b] adj., s. Francophobe.

francophobie [-f$\Im$bi] f. Francophobia.

francophone [-f$\Im$n] adj. French-speaking, francophone.
— s. French speaker, francophone.

francophonie [-f$\Im$ni] f. Community of French-speaking peoples (collectivité).

frange [fr$\tilde{a}$:$\Im$] f. Fringe (de cheveux, de rideau). ‖ MILIT. Bullion (d'épaulettes).

franger [-$\Im$e] v. tr. (6). To fringe.

frangin [fr$\tilde{a}$$\Im\tilde{\epsilon}$] m. POP. Brother.

frangine [-$\Im$in] f. POP. Sister.

frangipane [fr$\tilde{a}$$\Im$ipan] f. CULIN. Frangipane.

franglais [fr$\tilde{a}$glϵ] m. Franglais, French corrupted by anglicisms.

franquette [fr$\tilde{a}$kϵt] f. *A la bonne franquette,* simply, without ceremony.

franquisme [fr$\tilde{a}$kism] m. Francoism.

franquiste [-kist] adj. Pro-Franco, Franquista.
— s. Supporter of Franco, Franquista.

frappage [frapa:$\Im$] m. Striking (des médailles, de la monnaie). ‖ Icing (du champagne).

frappant, ante [-p$\tilde{a}$, $\tilde{a}$:t] adj. Conspicuous (exemple) ; striking (ressemblance) ; *de façon frappante,* strikingly. ‖ FAM. *Argument frappant,* blow.

frappe [frap] f. Striking (d'une médaille) ; coinage, striking, mintage (d'une monnaie) ; type, stamp (empreinte). ‖ Set of matrices (en typogr.). ‖ Striking of the keys (en dactylogr.); *faute de frappe,* typing mistake, typist's error. ‖ MILIT. *Force de frappe,* striking-force, strike force.

frappé, ée [frape] adj. Struck (de, with) ; *frappé d'horreur,* horror-stricken. ‖ Embossed (velours). ‖ Iced (champagne). ‖ MÉD. Stricken (de, with) ; *frappé à mort,* mortally wounded. ‖ FIG. Struck, impressed. (V. IMPRESSIONNER.)

frappement [frapm$\tilde{a}$] m. Knock, bang, tap (bruit) ; knocking, banging, tapping (action) ; stamping (avec les pieds).

frapper v. tr. (1). To strike (un coup) ; to hit (qqn). ‖ To stamp (du cuir, du métal) ; to strike (une médaille) ; to strike, to coin (une monnaie) ; to emboss (du velours). ‖ To type (une lettre à la machine). ‖ To ice (du champagne). ‖ THÉÂTR. *Frapper les trois coups,* to give the three knocks. ‖ JUR. *Frapper d'une amende,* to impose a fine on ; *frapper d'un impôt,* to lay a tax on ; *frapper d'une peine de,* to sentence to ; *frapper de nullité,* to render void. ‖ FIG. To strike, to smite (l'oreille) ; *frapper le regard de qqn,* to meet s.o.'s eyes. ‖ FIG. To fall (ou) come upon, to overtake (malheur) ; to strike, to impress (impression).
— v. intr. To strike ; *frapper juste,* to strike

home ; *frapper du pied,* to stamp one's foot. To knock, to tap ; *frapper deux coups à la porte* to give a double knock (ou) rap at the door ; o *frappe,* s.o.'s knocking, there's a knock ; *entre sans frapper,* to walk straight in. ‖ To rap (tabl tournante).
— v. pr. Se frapper, to hit, to knock ; *se frappe la poitrine,* to beat one's breast. ‖ FIG. To becom panicky ; to get into a state (fam.).

frappeur, euse [-p∞:r, ø:z] adj. Rapping (esprit)
— m. TECHN. Hammer (outil) ; hammerma (ouvrier).

frasque [frask] f. Prank, escapade ; *faire se frasques,* to sow one's wild oats.

fraternel, elle [fratϵrnϵl] adj. Brotherly, fra ternal.

fraternellement [-nϵlm$\tilde{a}$] adv. Fraternally.

fraternisation [-nizasj$\Im$] f. Fraternizing (action) fraternization (fait).

fraterniser [-nize] v. intr. (1). To fraternize.

fraternité [-nite] f. Brotherhood, fraternity. MILIT. Comradeship.

fratricide [fratrisid] m. JUR. Fratricide (crime criminel).
— adj. Fratricidal.

fraude [fro:d] f. Fraud ; *par fraude,* fraudulently ‖ Smuggling ; *faire la fraude,* to smuggle ; *passe en fraude,* to smuggle in. ‖ JUR. *Fraude pénale* cheating.

frauder [-de] v. tr. (1). To defraud, to cheat (l douane).
— v. intr. To smuggle. ‖ To cheat (v. TRICHER) to crib (aux examens).

fraudeur, euse [-d∞:r, ø:z] adj. Defrauding (du fisc) ; smuggling (de la douane) ; cheating, cribbing (aux examens).
— s. Defrauder, tax evader ; smuggler ; cheat, cribber.

frauduleusement [-dyl∞zm$\tilde{a}$] adv. Fraudulently

frauduleux, euse [-dylø, ø:z] adj. Fraudulent.

frayer [frϵje] v. tr. (9b). To open up, to trace ou (un chemin). ‖ To fray (frotter). ‖ FIG. To clear to pave (la voie) [à, for].
— v. intr. To spawn (poisson). ‖ To consort, tc mix, to associate (avec, with).
— v. pr. Se frayer ; *se frayer un chemin à tra vers,* to break (ou) to force (ou) to elbow (ou to plough one's way through.

frayeur [frϵj∞:r] f. Fright, fear. (V. ÉPOUVANTE.)

fredaine [fr$\Im$dϵn] f. Prank. (V. ÉQUIPÉE, FRASQUE.)

fredonnement [fr$\Im$d$\Im$nm$\tilde{a}$] m. Humming.

fredonner [fr$\Im$d$\Im$ne] v. tr. (1). To hum.

freezer [friz∞:r] m. Freezing-compartment freezer.

frégate [fregat] f. NAUT. Frigate. ‖ ZOOL. Frigate-bird.

frein [fr$\tilde{\epsilon}$] m. Bit (de cheval). ‖ TECHN. Brake ; *frein à main, au pied,* hand-, foot-brake ; *frein à rétropédalage,* back-pedalling brake ; *bloquer le freins,* to jam on the brakes ; *donner un coup de frein,* to brake suddenly. ‖ FIG. *Mettre un frein à,* to curb to bridle ; *ronger son frein,* to champ the bit ; *sans frein,* unbridled.

freinage [frϵna:$\Im$] m. Braking (action).

freiner [-ne] v. tr. (1). To brake, to apply the brakes to. ‖ FIG. To check, to restrain.
— v. intr. To put on the brakes, to brake.

freinte [fr$\tilde{\epsilon}$:t] f. Wastage, waste ; *freinte de route* loss in transit.

frelatage [fr$\Im$lata:$\Im$] m. Adulteration.

frelater [-te] v. tr. (1). To adulterate.

frelateur [-t∞:r] m. Adulterator, sophisticator.

frêle [frϵ:l] adj. Fragile (tige). ‖ Slender, frail (membre), frail, weak (personne). ‖ FIG. Frail, precarious (bonheur). [V. FRAGILE.]

frelon [fr$\Im$l$\tilde{o}$] m. ZOOL. Hornet, U. S. yellow-jacket.

freluquet [frəlykɛ] m. Whipper-snapper, puppy.

frémir [fremi:r] v. intr. (2). To simmer (eau prête à bouillir); to rustle (feuilles); to sough (vent). ‖ Mus. To quiver (corde). ‖ To quiver, to tremble, to shudder; *frémir de*, to shake with (colère); to boil over with (impatience); to shake (ou) quiver with (peur); *faire frémir qqn*, to give s.o. the shivers; *une histoire à faire frémir*, a blood-curdling (ou) horror story, a thriller (fam.).

frémissant, ante [-misɑ̃, ɑ̃:t] adj. Simmering (eau); rustling (feuilles); sighing (vent). ‖ Quivering, shuddering (de, with); *frémissant de fièvre*, throbbing with fever.

frémissement [-mismɑ̃] m. Simmering (de l'eau); rustling (des feuilles). ‖ Quivering (des lèvres). ‖ Quivering (d'impatience, d'irritation); shuddering (de peur).

frênaie [frɛnɛ] f. Ash-plantation.

frêne [frɛ:n] m. Bot. Ash, ash-tree (arbre); ash, ash-timber (bois).

frénésie [frenezi] f. Frenzy; *avec frénésie*, frantically; furiously.

frénétique [-tik] adj. Frantic, frenzied.

frénétiquement [-tikmɑ̃] adv. Frantically.

Fréon [freɔ̃] m. Chim. Freon.

fréquemment [frekamɑ̃] adv. Frequently.

fréquence [-kɑ̃:s] f. Frequency. ‖ Techn. Frequency; *à basse, haute fréquence*, low-, high-frequency; *fréquence téléphonique*, audio-frequency; *modulation de fréquence*, frequency modulation.

fréquent, ente [-kɑ̃, ɑ̃:t] adj. Frequent; *il est fréquent que*, it often happens that. ‖ Méd. Quick, rapid (pouls).

fréquentable [-kɑ̃tabl] adj. Fit to associate with (personne); recommendable (endroit); *peu fréquentable*, disreputable.

fréquentatif, ive [-kɑ̃tatif, i:v] adj., m. Gramm. Frequentative.

fréquentation [-kɑ̃tasɔ̃] f. Frequenting (action); frequentation (fait); *mauvaises fréquentations*, bad company. (V. relations.) ‖ Ecclés. Frequent receiving (des sacrements).

fréquenté, ée [-kɑ̃te] adj. Frequented (lieu); *mal fréquenté*, ill-frequented.

fréquenter [-kɑ̃te] v. tr. (1). To frequent (un lieu); to frequent, to visit, to consort with (qqn); *fréquenter un milieu différent*, to keep different company. ‖ Ecclés. To frequent (l'église, les sacrements).
— v. intr. † To be a frequent caller (chez, at).
— v. récipr. Se fréquenter, to visit each other; to meet each other socially.

frère [frɛ:r] m. Brother; *frère de lait*, foster-brother; *frères siamois*, Siamese twins. ‖ Milit. *Frère d'armes*, brother in arms. ‖ Ecclés. Friar, brother (moine); *mes bien chers frères*, dearly beloved brethren (fidèles). ‖ Fam. *Frère Trois-Points*, Freemason; *faux frère*, traitor; *vieux frère*, old chap.
— adj. Brother, sister, fellow.

frérot [frero] m. Fam. Little brother.

fresque [frɛsk] f. Arts. Fresco.

fresquiste [-kist] s. Arts. Fresco painter.

fressure [frɛsy:r] f. Culin. Pluck.

fret [frɛ] m. Naut. Freight (cargaison, louage).

frètement [frɛtmɑ̃] m. Naut. Freighting, chartering.

fréter [frete] v. tr. (5). Naut. To freight, to charter, to equip. ‖ Autom. To hire.

fréteur [-tœ:r] m. Naut. Freighter, charterer.

rétillant, ante [fretijɑ̃, ɑ̃:t] adj. Frisky, lively (chien, personne); wagging (queue du chien); wriggling (poisson).

rétillement [-jmɑ̃] m. Frisking (d'un chien, d'une personne); wagging (de la queue); wriggling (d'un poisson).

frétiller [-je] v. intr. (1). To frisk (chien, personne); to wag (queue); to wriggle (poisson).

frétillon [-tijɔ̃] m. Fam. Fidget.

fretin [frətɛ̃] m. Fry. ‖ Fig. *Menu fretin*, small fry.

frette [frɛt] f. Band, hoop. ‖ Milit. Frette, hoop.

fretter [frɛte] v. tr. (1). To band, to hoop. ‖ Milit. To wire.

freudien [frødjɛ̃] adj., m. Philos. Freudian.

freudisme [-dism] m. Philos. Freudianism.

freux [frø] m. Zool. Rook.

friabilité [frijabilite] f. Friability, friableness.

friable [-jabl] adj. Friable, crumbly.

friand, ande [frijɑ̃, ɑ̃:d] adj. Dainty, tasty (mets); fond (personne) [de, of].
— m. Culin. Sausage-roll.

friandise [-di:z] f. Daintiness (gourmandise). ‖ Delicacy, dainty tit-bit (mets). ‖ Pl. Sweets, candies (sucreries).

fric [frik] m. Pop. Dough, oof; U. S. jack.

fricandeau [frikɑ̃do] m. Culin. Fricandeau, larded braised veal.

fricassé, ée [frikase] adj. Culin. Fricasseed.

fricassée f. Culin. Fricassee. ‖ Fam. *Fricassée de museaux*, smooching.

fricasser v. tr. (1). Culin. To fricassee.

fricative [frikati:v] adj. f. Gramm. Fricative.

fricfrac [frikfrak] m. Pop. Burglary, housebreaking.

friche [friʃ] f. Fallow; *être en friche*, to lie fallow. ‖ Fig. Undeveloped, unimproved.

frichti [friʃti], **fricot** [friko] m. Fam., Culin. Grub, U. S. chow (mangeaille); stew (ragoût).

fricoter [-te] v. intr. (1). Fam., Culin. To cook. ‖ Fam. To feather one's nest, to make one's pile.
— v. tr. Fam. Culin. To cook. ‖ Fam. To work underhand (manigancer).

fricoteur [-tœ:r] s. Fam. Embezzler.

friction [friksjɔ̃] f. Rubbing (des membres). ‖ Dry shampoo (pour cheveux). ‖ Sports. Rub-down. ‖ Techn. Friction.

frictionner [-sjɔne] v. tr. (1). To rub, to friction, to give a rub-down to (qqn).
— v. pr. Se frictionner, to rub oneself; *se frictionner le genou avec*, to rub one's knee with.

Fridolin [fridolɛ̃] m. Fam. Jerry, U. S. Kraut.

frigide [friʒid] adj. Méd. Frigid.

frigidité [-dite] f. Méd. Frigidity.

frigo [frigo] m. Fam. Fridge, U. S. ice-box (réfrigérateur); frozen meat (viande).

frigorifié [frigorifje] adj. Frozen (viande). ‖ Fam. Chilled to the bone (personne).

frigorifier v. tr. (1). To refrigerate (la viande). ‖ Fam. *Il me frigorifie*, he makes my blood run cold.

frigorifique [-fik] adj. Frigorific, refrigerating; *entrepôt frigorifique*, cold store, U. S. deepfreeze. ‖ Ch. de f. *Wagon frigorifique*, refrigerator van (ou) U. S. car.
— m. Refrigerator. (V. glacière.)

frileusement [frilœzmɑ̃] adv. Shiveringly; snugly.

frileux, euse [-lø, ø:z] adj. Chilly, shivery; *être frileux*, to feel the cold; to be a chilly mortal.

frimaire [frimɛ:r] m. Frimaire, third month in French Republican calendar (November-December).

frimas [frimɑ] m. Frost, rime, hoar. ‖ Pl. Winter.

frime [frim] f. Fam. Sham, make-believe, eyewash, U. S. hooey, malarkey.

frimer [frime] v. intr. (1). Fam. To show off, to sham.

frimousse [frimus] f. Fam. Little face.

fringale [frɛ̃gal] f. Fam. Ravenous hunger.

fringant, ante [frɛ̃gɑ̃, ɑ̃:t] adj. Frisky, brisk (animal); smart, dashing (personne).

fringuer [-ge] v. tr. (1). Fam. To rig out.

fringues [frɛ̃:g] f. pl. Fam. Togs.

fripé, ée [fripe] adj. Crumpled, creased (tissu). ‖ Fig. Wrinkled (visage).

friper v. tr. (1). To crumple, to crease (un tissu). ‖ Fig. To wrinkle (la peau).
— v. pr. **Se friper,** to get crumpled (tissu). ‖ Fig. To wrinkle (peau).

friperie [-pri] f. Second-hand trade (commerce); second-hand clothes shop (boutique); second-hand goods (marchandises). [V. brocante.]

fripes [frip] f. pl. Fam. Rags.

fripier [-pje] m. Old-clothes-dealer; U. S. junkman. (V. chiffonnier.)

fripon [fripɔ̃] adj. Roguish, knavish.
— m. Rogue, knave. ‖ Fam. Rascal. (V. coquin.)

friponne [-pɔn] f. Fam. Minx.

friponnerie [-pɔnri] f. Knavishness (état); piece of roguery, knavish trick (tour).

fripouille [fripu:j] f. Fam. Rogue, blackguard, rotter. (V. canaille.)

fripouillerie [-pu:jri] f. Fam. Roguery (malhonnêteté); dirty trick (sale tour).

frire [fri:r] v. tr. (55). Culin. To fry (le poisson); *faire frire,* to fry.
— v. intr. Culin. To fry.

frise [fri:z] f. Border (de papier peint). ‖ Théâtr. Pl. Sky-pieces. ‖ Archit. Frieze.

Frise f. Géogr. Friesland.

frisé, ée [frize] adj. Curly (bouclé); frizzy, crisp (crépu). ‖ Culin. Curly (chicorée); *chou frisé,* kale, savoy.

frisée f. Bot. Endive.

friselis [-zli] m. Rustle, rustling (des feuilles).

friser [-ize] v. tr. (1). To curl (les cheveux); to twirl (sa moustache) [v. boucler, onduler]; *frisé au fer,* tong-curled. ‖ Fig. To border on (l'indiscrétion); *friser la soixantaine,* to be close on to (ou) to be pushing sixty. ‖ Fig. To skim, to graze (v. raser); *friser le trottoir,* to graze the pavement. ‖ Fig. To be within a hair's breadth of; *friser la prison,* to scrape clear of prison.
— v. intr. To curl (cheveux).
— v. pr. **Se friser,** to curl one's hair.

frisette [-zɛt] f. Frisette, ringlet.

frisoir [-zwa:r] m. Curling-pin, curler (épingle); curling-iron (fer).

frison, onne [frizɔ̃, ɔn] adj. Géogr. Frisian. ‖ Agric. Friesian, U. S. Holstein (vache).
— s. Géogr. Frisian.

frison [frizɔ̃] m. Curl.

frisonne [frizɔn] f. Agric. Friesian, U. S. Holstein (vache).

frisotter [-zɔte] v. tr., intr. (1). To frizz.

frisquet [friskɛ] adj. Chilly; *il fait frisquet,* it is a bit chilly.

frisson [frisɔ̃] m. Shiver (de froid). ‖ Méd. Horror, rigor. ‖ Fig. Thrill, shudder (d'horreur); *à donner le frisson,* blood-curdling; *j'en ai le frisson,* it gives me the creeps.

frissonnant, ante [-sɔnɑ̃, ɑ̃:t] adj. Shivering; shuddering.

frissonnement [-sɔnmɑ̃] m. Shivering, shuddering. ‖ Rustling (des feuilles).

frissonner [-sɔne] v. intr. (1). To shiver (de froid); to shudder (de crainte, d'horreur). ‖ To rustle, to quiver (feuilles).

frisure [frizy:r] f. Curliness (état); curls, wave (ondulation).

frit [fri] adj. Culin. Fried. ‖ Fam. *Il est frit,* his number is up, he 's had it.

friterie [fritri] f. Chip shop (ou) stall.

frites [frit] f. pl. Culin. Chips, U. S. French-fries.

friteuse [fritø:z] f. Culin. Frying-basket, potato-chipper.

fritte [frit] f. Techn. Frit (en verrerie).

friture [frity:r] f. Culin. Frying (action); oil, grease (graisse); dish of fried fish (ou) food (plat). ‖ Fam. Crackling, mush, static (à la radio); sizzling, frying (au téléphone).

Fritz [frits] m. Fritz (en 1914); Jerry, U. S. Kraut (en 1939). [V. fridolin.]

frivole [frivɔl] adj. Frivolous, flighty (conduite, personne); light (propos). [V. futile, léger.]

frivolement [-lmɑ̃] adv. Frivolously.

frivolité [-lite] f. Frivolity, frivolousness (d'une personne); idleness (des propos). ‖ Tatting (dentelle); *en frivolité,* tatted; *faire de la frivolité,* to tat

froc [frɔk] m. Ecclés. Frock; *jeter le froc aux orties,* to cast one's frock on the dung-hill.

froid, oide [frwa, wad] adj. Cold (eau, lieu, membre, objet, temps); *à sang froid,* cold-blooded. ‖ Fig. Cold, frigid, cool (accueil); frigid, cold (personne, tempérament); lifeless (style); *laisser froid,* to leave cold.
— m. Cold; *froid glacial,* bitter cold; *les grands froids,* winter cold; *à froid,* cold, when cold; *il a froid aux mains,* his hands are cold; *il fait froid,* it is cold. ‖ Méd. *Prendre froid,* to catch a cold. ‖ Comm. *Conservation par le froid,* cold-storage; *industrie du froid,* refrigeration industry. ‖ Fig. Coldness, coolness; *être en froid,* not to be on the best of terms; *jeter un froid,* to cast a chill; *n'avoir pas froid aux yeux,* to be plucky.

froidement [-dmɑ̃] adv. Coldly, coolly (sans chaleur, sans passion); calmly (calmement).

froideur [-dœ:r] f. Coldness (d'un objet, du temps). ‖ Fig. Coldness, coolness (d'une personne, des sentiments); frigidity (des sens); *envisager les choses avec froideur,* to look at things calmly.

froidir [-dir]. V. refroidir.

froidure [-dy:r] f. Cold season, cold weather.

froissement [frwasmɑ̃] m. Crumpling (d'un papier, d'un tissu). ‖ Méd. Straining (d'un muscle). ‖ Fig. Clash, conflict (d'intérêts); *froissement d'amour-propre,* ruffling of susceptibilities.

froisser [frwase] v. tr. (1). To crumple (du papier); to crumple, to crease (du tissu). [V. chiffonner, friper.] ‖ Méd. To strain (un muscle). ‖ Fig. To offend (v. blesser); to hurt (les sentiments); *cela ne vous froisse pas que je l'aie invité?,* you don't mind my inviting him?
— v. pr. **Se froisser,** to take offence (ou) umbrage (de, at). [V. vexer (se).]

froissure [-sy:r] f. Crumple, crease.

frôlement [frolmɑ̃] m. Brush, brushing, grazing.

frôler [-le] v. tr. (1). To brush, to graze. (V. effleurer, raser.) ‖ Aviat. To buzz (un autre avion); to skim (la cime des arbres).

fromage [frɔma:ʒ] m. Cheese; *fromage à la crème, de chèvre, frais,* cream, goat's milk, green cheese. ‖ Culin. *Fromage de tête,* potted head, U. S. head-cheese. ‖ Fam. Soft job; cushy billet.

fromager [-maʒe] s. Cheese-maker (fabricant); cheese-monger (ou) -dealer (marchand).
— adj. Cheese (industrie).
— m. Bot. Ceiba tree, silk-cotton tree, kapok tree.

fromagerie [-maʒri] f. Cheesemonger's, U. S. cheese store (boutique); cheese-dairy (lieu de fabrication).

froment [frɔmɑ̃] m. Bot. Wheat.

fronce [frɔ̃:s] f. Gather (dans le tissu); *à fronces,* gathered, U. S. shirred.

froncement [frɔ̃smɑ̃] m. Gathering (du tissu). ‖ Knitting (du front); *froncement de sourcils,* frown.

froncer [-se] v. tr. (6). To gather (un tissu). ‖ To knit (le front); to purse (les lèvres); *froncer les sourcils,* to frown.

— v. pr. **Se froncer**, to gather (tissu). ‖ To knit, to pucker up (front, sourcils).

°roncis [-si] m. Gathering (en couture).

°rondaison [frɔ̃dɛzɔ̃] f. Foliage. ‖ Foliation, frondescence. ‖ Canopy (ensemble feuillu).

fronde [frɔ̃:d] f. Sling (arme). ‖ Catapult, slingshot (lance-pierre). ‖ Fronde (revolt).

fronder [frɔ̃de] v. tr. (1). † To sling. ‖ FIG. To criticize, to nag at.

frondeur [-dœ:r] m. † Slinger. ‖ FAM. Faultfinder (critique); rebel (indiscipliné).

front [frɔ̃] m. Forehead, brow (de l'homme). ‖ Front (d'un bâtiment); crest (d'une montagne). ‖ *Front commun, populaire*, United (ou) Common, Popular Front (en politique). ‖ MILIT. Front, front line; *de front*, frontal (attaque); *sur le front*, at the front. ‖ *Front de mer*, water-front. ‖ PHYS. *Front d'onde*, wave-surface. ‖ FIG. Countenance (attitude); *le front haut*, keeping one's head up; *le front serein*, with an unruffled look; *faire front*, to face it; *faire front à*, to face. ‖ FIG. Cheek, front (audace); *avoir le front de*, to have the face (ou) nerve to. [V. TOUPET.] ‖ LOC. **De front**, abreast (côte à côte); at the same time, together (ensemble); in front, front (par devant).

frontal [-tal] adj. MÉD. Frontal (os).
— m. Front, frontlet, forehead strap (harnais). ‖ MÉD. Frontal bone.

frontalier, ère [frɔ̃talje, ɛr] adj. Frontier (région).
— s. Borderer (en Angleterre); frontier-inhabitant, frontiersman.

fronteau [frɔ̃to] m. NAUT. *Fronteau de dunette, d'écoutille*, poop-break, headledge. ‖ ECCLÉS. Frontlet. ‖ ARCHIT. Frontal.

frontière [-tjɛ:r] adj., f. Frontier.

frontispice [-tispis] m. Frontispiece.

fronton [-tɔ̃] m. ARCHIT. Fronton, pediment. ‖ NAUT. Stern-rails.

frottage [frɔta:ʒ] m. Polishing.

frotté, ée [frɔte] adj. FAM. With a smattering (de, of) [connaissances livresques].

frottée f. FAM. Dusting, pasting, licking.

frottement [frɔtmɑ̃] m. Rubbing; *blesser, user par frottement*, to chafe, to abrade. ‖ Shuffling (des pieds). ‖ TECHN. Friction. ‖ MÉD. *Frottement pleural*, pleural rub. ‖ FIG. Rubbing shoulders (*avec*, with) [contact]. ‖ FIG. Pl. Friction (tiraillements).

frotter [-te] v. tr. (1). To rub (un membre); to polish (le parquet). ‖ To shuffle (les pieds en marchant). ‖ To strike (une allumette). ‖ FAM. *Frotter les oreilles à qqn*, to box s.o.'s ears.
— v. intr. To rub (*contre*, against).
— v. pr. **Se frotter**, to rub (*contre*, against); *se frotter les mains*, to rub one's hands. ‖ FIG. To rub shoulders (*à*, with) [contact amical]; to come up (*à*, against) [contact désagréable].

frotteur [-tœ:r] m. Floor-polisher. ‖ TECHN. Friction piece. ‖ ÉLECTR. Brush (de dynamo); shoe (de trolley).

frottis [-ti] m. ARTS. Scumble.

frottoir [-twa:r] m. Polisher (à parquets). ‖ Friction-strip (d'allumettes). ‖ ÉLECTR. Brush.

frou-frou [frufru] m. Rustle (des feuilles); froufrou, swish (de la soie).

froufrouter [-te] v. intr. (1). To rustle, to swish.

froussard, arde [frusa:r, ard] adj. FAM. Funky, yellow, U. S. jittery, chicken.
— s. FAM. Funk; yellow-belly (pop.).

frousse [fru:s] f. FAM. Funk, jitters (v. TROUILLE); *flanquer la frousse à qqn*, to give s. o. the jitters, to put the wind up s.o.

fructidor [fryktidɔ:r] m. Fructidor, twelfth month in French Republican calendar (August-September).

fructifère [fryktifɛ:r] adj. Fructiferous.

fructification [-fikasjɔ̃] f. Fructification.

fructifier [-fje] v. intr. (1). To fructify. ‖ FIN. To bear interest. ‖ FIG. To bear fruit.

fructueusement [fryktyøzmɑ̃] adv. Fruitfully.

fructueux, euse [-tɥø, ø:z] adj. Fruitful, fructuous. ‖ FIN. Lucrative.

frugal, ale [frygal] adj. Frugal (personne, vie).

frugalement [-mɑ̃] adv. Frugally.

frugalité [-lite] f. Frugality. (V. SOBRIÉTÉ.)

fruit [frɥi] m. ARCHIT. Batter.

fruit m. Fruit; *aimer les fruits*, to be fond of fruit. ‖ CULIN. *Fruits confits*, comfits, U. S. preserved fruit; *fruits au sirop*, tinned (ou) U. S. canned fruit. ‖ ZOOL. *Fruits de mer*, fish and shell-fish, U. S. sea-food. ‖ JUR. Profits, revenues; *fruits naturels*, emblements. ‖ ECCLÉS. *Fruit défendu*, forbidden fruit; *le fruit de ses entrailles*, the fruit of her womb. ‖ FIG. Fruit, profit : *avec fruit*, with profit; *porter fruit*, to bear fruit. ‖ FIG. Result, fruit; *le fruit de nos efforts*, the outcome of our labours; *sans fruit*, fruitlessly. ‖ FAM. *Fruit sec*, failure, dud, U. S. flop (personne).

fruité [-te] adj. Fruity.

fruiterie [-tri] f. Fruiterer's shop (boutique); fruit-trade (commerce).

fruitier [-tje] adj. Fruit (arbre, jardin).
— s. Fruiterer, greengrocer, U. S. vegetable man (marchand); fruit-room (pièce).

frusquer [fryske] v. tr. (1). FAM. To rig out.

frusques [frysk] f. pl. FAM. Duds, togs, clobber.

fruste [fryst] adj. Worn (médaille, pièce); rough (objet). ‖ FAM. Rough, unpolished (manières, personne, style).

frustration [frystrasjɔ̃] f. Frustrating (action); frustration (fait). ‖ JUR. Defrauding. ‖ FIG. Disappointing.

frustré, ée [frystre] adj. Frustrated.

frustrer [frystre] v. tr. (1). To frustrate, to defraud, to deprive (qqn) [*de*, of]. ‖ FIG. To disappoint (l'attente); *frustrer qqn dans ses espérances*, to frustrate s. o. in his hopes.

fuchsia [fyksja] m. BOT. Fuchsia.

fuchsine [fyksin] f. CHIM. Fuchsine.

fucus [fyky:s] m. BOT. Fucus.

fuel [fjul], **fuel-oil** [-ɔ:jl] m. Fuel-oil.

fugace [fygas] adj. Fugacious; transient.

fugacité [fygasite] f. Fugacity, transience.

fugitif, ive [fyʒitif, i:v] adj. Fugitive, flying, runaway (personne). ‖ FIG. Transient (beauté, bonheur); passing (désir, moment); fleeting (espoir, passion, ombre); evanescent (gloire, splendeur); short (mémoire).
— s. Fugitive.

fugitivement [-tivmɑ̃] adv. Fugitively.

fugue [fyg] f. Running away from home; *faire une fugue*, to run away from home. ‖ MUS. Fugue.

fugué, ée [-ge] adj. Mus. Fugued, fugal.

fugueur, euse [-gœ:r, ø:z] adj., s. Runaway.

fuir [fɥi:r] v. intr. (56). To flee, to run away, to fly (v. ENFUIR [s']); *faire fuir*, to put to flight. ‖ To elope (femme) [*avec*, with]. ‖ To whirl past (arbres, voiture); to vanish away, to slip (ou) glide away (heures, temps); to recede (front, horizon, paysage); to give way (sol). ‖ To escape (gaz); to leak out, to run out (liquide); to leak (robinet, tonneau).
— v. tr. To flee, to run away from (un endroit). ‖ To shun (le danger, les gens); to avoid (qqn).

fuite [fɥit] f. Flight; *devoir son salut à la fuite*, to save oneself by flight; *prendre la fuite*, to take to flight; *une voiture qui a pris la fuite*, a non-stop car. ‖ Escape (de gaz); leak, leakage (de liquide); leak (fissure). ‖ Shift. (V. FAUX-FUYANT.) ‖ JUR. Elopement (du domicile conjugal); absconding (d'un escroc); escape (prisonnier). ‖ TECHN. Outlet. ‖ FIG. Flight (du temps). ‖ FIG. Leak, leakage (des secrets).

fulgurant, ante [fylgyrᾶ, ᾶ:t] adj. Flashing (lumière). ‖ Mɛ́ɒ. Fulgurating (douleur). ‖ Fɪɢ. Withering (regard).
fulguration [-rasjɔ̃] f. Summer lightning, heat lightning.
fulgurer [-re] v. intr. (1). To flash, to fulgurate.
fuligineux, euse [fyliʒinø, ø:z] adj. Fuliginous.
fulmicoton [fylmikɔtɔ̃] m. Gun-cotton.
fulminant, ante [fylminᾶ, ᾶ:t] adj. Fulminant, fulminating (pr. et fig.).
fulminate [-nat] m. Cɦɪᴍ. Fulminate; *capsule de fulminate*, percussion cap.
fulmination [-nasjɔ̃] f. Fᴀᴍ. Storming, ranting and raving.
fulminer [-ne] v. tr., intr. Eccʟɛ́s. To fulminate, to thunder out. ‖ Fᴀᴍ. To fulminate, to thunder forth.
fulminique [-nik] adj. Cɦɪᴍ. Fulminic.
fumage [fyma:ʒ] m., **fumaison** [-mɛsɔ̃] f. Cᴜʟɪɴ. Smoking, smoke-curing (du jambon).
fumage m. Aɢʀɪc. Manuring (d'un champ).
fumant, ante [fymᾶ, ᾶ:t] adj. Smoking (cendres). ‖ Smoking (flancs, narines d'un cheval). ‖ Cᴜʟɪɴ. Steaming (liquide); piping-hot (plat). ‖ Fᴀᴍ. Fuming with anger (furieux).
fume [fym]. (V. ꜰᴜᴍᴇʀ.) ‖ **Fume-cigare** (pl. *fume-cigares*), m. Cigar-holder. ‖ **Fume-cigarette** (pl. *fume-cigarettes*), m. Cigarette-holder.
fumé, ée [fyme] adj. Cᴜʟɪɴ. Smoked, smoke-cured (jambon). ‖ Smoked; *verres fumés,* sunglasses, smoked glasses.
fumée f. Smoke; *rideau de fumée,* smoke screen; *sans fumée,* smokeless. ‖ Tobacco-smoke (du tabac); *la fumée vous gêne-t-elle?,* do you mind smoke? ‖ Cᴜʟɪɴ. Steam (de la nourriture); fumes (du vin). ‖ Fɪɢ. *Les fumées de l'orgueil,* the fumes of pride; *partir en fumée,* to end in smoke, to dissolve into thin air, to peter out.
— adj. *Gris fumée,* smoke-grey.
fumer v. intr. (1). To smoke (bois, cheminée). ‖ To smoke (personne). ‖ Cᴜʟɪɴ. To smoke, to steam. ‖ Fᴀᴍ. To fume.
— v. tr. To smoke (une cigarette). ‖ Cᴜʟɪɴ. To smoke, to smoke-cure (un jambon).
fumer v. tr. (1). Aɢʀɪc. To manure; to muck.
fumerie [-mri] f. Smoking-den, opium-den.
fumerolle [-mrɔl] f. Fumarole.
fumeron [-mrɔ̃] m. Smoky charcoal.
fumet [fymɛ] m. Scent (du gibier). ‖ Cᴜʟɪɴ. Smell (de la nourriture); bouquet (du vin).
fumeur, euse [-mœ:r, ø:z] s. Smoker.
fumeux, euse [-mø, ø:z] adj. Smoky, fumy. ‖ Fɪɢ. Hazy, nebulous.
fumier [fymje] m. Aɢʀɪc. Manure (engrais); manure-heap, dung-hill (tas). ‖ Fᴀᴍ. Muck.
fumigateur [fymigatœ:r] m. Fumigator.
fumigation [-sjɔ̃] f. Fumigation.
fumigatoire [-twa:r] adj. Fumigatory.
fumigène [fymiʒɛ:n] adj. Smoke-producing; *bombe fumigène,* smoke-bomb.
fumiste [fymist] m. Chimney-sweep (ramoneur). ‖ Fᴀᴍ. Joker, crackpot (plaisantin); *c'est un fumiste,* he is a fraud (monteur de coup).
fumisterie [-tri] f. Chimney-building (ou) sweeping. ‖ Fᴀᴍ. Hoax; *c'est de la fumisterie,* it's all bunkum (ou) eyewash (ou) U. S. hooey.
fumivore [fymivɔ:r] adj. Smoke-consuming.
— m. Smoke-consumer.
fumoir [-mwa:r] m. Smoking-room. ‖ Cᴜʟɪɴ. Curing-room.
fumure [-my:r] f. Aɢʀɪc. Manuring (action); manure (fumier).
funambule [fynᾶbyl] m. Funambulist, tight-rope walker.
funambulesque [-lɛsk] adj. Funambulic, funambulatory. ‖ Fᴀᴍ. Fantastic, incredible.

funèbre [fynɛbr] adj. Funeral (marche, oraison). ‖ Fɪɢ. Funereal, mournful.
funèbrement [-brəmᾶ] adv. Funereally, mournfully.
funérailles [fynerɑ:j] f. pl. Funeral, burial.
funéraire [-rɛ:r] adj. Funeral.
funeste [fynɛst] adj. Fatal, deadly (coup); disastrous (événement); baneful (influence); ill-fated (jour); *funeste à,* fatal to.
funestement [-təmᾶ] adv. Fatally; balefully.
funiculaire [fynikylɛ:r] adj. Cɦ. ᴅᴇ ꜰ. Funicular.
— m. Cɦ. ᴅᴇ ꜰ. Funicular (ou) cable railway.
fur [fy:r] m. *Au fur et à mesure,* simultaneously and proportionately; as one goes along; *au fur et à mesure que,* in proportion as.
furax [fyraks] adj. inv. Fᴀᴍ. Raging, fuming, mad, livid.
furet [fyrɛ] m. Zooʟ. Ferret. ‖ Hunt-the-slipper, who's got the button (jeu). ‖ Fᴀᴍ. Nosy Parker, Paul Pry.
furetage [fyrta:ʒ] m. Ferreting. ‖ Fɪɢ. Rummaging, nosing about.
fureter [-te] v. intr. (8 *b*). To ferret. ‖ Fɪɢ. To ferret (ou) to nose about.
fureteur, euse [-tœ:r, ø:z] s. Ferreter. ‖ Fɪɢ. Searcher, rummager. ‖ Fᴀᴍ. Nosy Parker, Paul Pry, busybody.
— adj. Ferrety, prying.
fureur [-rœ:r] f. Fury (colère); *en fureur,* in a rage; *entrer en fureur,* to fly into a rage. ‖ Fury, furor, passion (transport). ‖ Fury (violence); *la fureur de la tempête,* the fury of the storm. ‖ Furore (mode); *faire fureur,* to create a furore, to be all the rage (ou) all the go.
furfural [fyrfyral] m. Cɦɪᴍ. Furfural.
furibard [fyriba:r], **furibond, onde** [-bɔ̃, ɔ̃:d] adj. Furious (personne); withering (regard).
furie [fyri] f. Fury (divinité). ‖ Fury, termagant (femme). [V. ʜᴀʀᴘɪᴇ.] ‖ Fury, rage (colère); fury (violence); *avec furie,* furiously; *en furie,* furious, infuriated; *soulever une furie meurtrière,* to set off a murderous rampage. ‖ Fᴀᴍ. Craze (de, for).
furieusement [fyrjøzmᾶ] adv. Furiously. ‖ Fᴀᴍ. Awfully.
furieux, euse [fyrjø, ø:z] adj. Furious, in a rage (en colère); *furieux contre,* wild with; *rendre furieux,* to infuriate. ‖ Desperate, furious (combat); wild (galop); raging (orage); furious, wild (torrent, vent). ‖ Fᴀᴍ. Awful, tremendous.
furoncle [fyrɔ̃kl] m. Mɛ́ɒ. Furuncle; boil (fam.).
furonculose [-kylo:z] f. Mɛ́ɒ. Furunculosis.
furtif, ive [fyrtif, i:v] adj. Furtive, stealthy, sly. ‖ Gʀᴀᴍᴍ. *Voyelle furtive,* glide.
furtivement [-tivmᾶ] adv. Furtively, stealthily.
fusain [fyzɛ̃] m. Bᴏᴛ. Euonymus, spindle-tree. ‖ Aʀᴛs. Fusain, charcoal pencil (crayon); fusain, charcoal sketch (dessin).
fuseau [fyzo] m. Bobbin (de dentelière); spindle (de fileuse); *au fuseau,* bobbin (dentelle); *en forme de fuseau,* tapered. ‖ Tapering (ou) peg-top trousers (pantalon). ‖ Aᴠɪᴀᴛ. Gore (de ballon); *fuseau moteur,* engine nacelle. ‖ Tᴇcʜɴ. Link-pin (de chaîne). ‖ Mᴀᴛʜ. *Fuseau horaire,* time zone. ‖ Fᴀᴍ. Spindle-shank (jambe).
fusée [fyze] f. Rocket (d'artifice); flare, Verey light (éclairante); *fusée-parachute,* parachute flare; *lancer une fusée,* to send up a flare. ‖ Mɪʟɪᴛ. Fuse (d'obus). ‖ Pʜʏs. Rocket.
fuselage [fyzla:ʒ] m. Aᴠɪᴀᴛ. Fuselage.
fuselé, ée [fyzle] adj. Tapered, spindle-shaped; *doigts fuselés,* tapering fingers. ‖ Aᴜᴛᴏᴍ., Aᴠɪᴀᴛ. Streamlined.
fuseler v. tr. (8a). To taper. ‖ Aᴜᴛᴏᴍ., Aᴠɪᴀᴛ. To streamline.
fuser [fyze] v. intr. (1). To flash (éclairer); to

fuse (fondre). ‖ FIG. To burst out, to break out (chant, rire).

fusibilité [fyzibilite] f. Fusibility.

fusible [-zibl] adj. Fusible.
— m. ELECTR. Fuse.

fusiforme [fysifɔrm] adj. Spindle-shaped, fusiform.

fusil [fyzi] m. Steel (de briquet). ‖ Gun (arme); *fusil à air comprimé, mitrailleur*, air-, light-machine gun; *fusil de chasse*, shot-gun, fowling-piece; *fusil rayé*, rifle. ‖ Shot (personne); *un bon fusil*, a good shot. ‖ FAM. *Changer son fusil d'épaule*, to change one's opinion.

fusilier [-lje] m. MILIT. Fusilier; automatic rifle-man. ‖ **Fusilier-marin**, m. NAUT., MILIT. Marine.

fusillade [-jad] f. Fusillade, volley of shots.

fusiller [-je] v. tr. (1). To shoot (qqn). ‖ FAM. To smash.

fusion [fyzjɔ̃] f. Fusion, melting; *en fusion*, molten; *point de fusion*, melting point. ‖ Smelting (d'un minerai). ‖ CHIM. Dissolving. ‖ COMM. Amalgamation, merger; *opérer une fusion*, to amalgamate. ‖ FIG. Coalescing, blending (des idées).

fusionnement [fyzjɔnmɑ̃] m. Fusion, amalgamation, merging.

fusionner [-ne] v. tr., intr. (1). To combine (en politique). ‖ COMM. To amalgamate, to merge. ‖ FIG. To coalesce, to blend.

fustigation [fystigasjɔ̃] f. Fustigation.

fustiger [-ʒe] v. tr. (6). To fustigate.

fût [fy] m. Bole, trunk (d'un arbre); *à fût plein*, non-tapering (arbre). ‖ ARCHIT. Shaft (d'une colonne). ‖ Barrel, cask (tonneau); *tirer au fût*, to draw from the wood.

futaie [fytɛ] f. Forest; *arbre de haute futaie*, fully-grown tree.

futaille [fytɑ:j] f. Barrel. (V. FÛT.)

futaine [fytɛn] f. Fustian.

futé, ée [fyte] adj. Sharp, cunning (v. FINAUD); *petite futée*, sly little minx, slyboots.

futile [fytil] adj. Trifling (chose, incident); idle (désir, prétexte); frivolous, futile (personne).

futilement [-lmɑ̃] adv. Futilely.

futilité [-lite] f. Futility. ‖ Pl. Trifles; *s'occuper à des futilités*, to fool around, to footle about.

futur [fyty:r] adj. Future (à venir); *les temps futurs*, the ages (ou) the years to come. ‖ Chosen, elect, intended (choisi); *son futur gendre*, his future son-in-law. ‖ Intending (décidé); *futur client*, intending customer.
— m. PHILOS., GRAMM. Future, intended.
— s. FAM. Intended. [V. FIANCÉ, FIANCÉE.]

futurisme [fytyrism] m. ARTS. Futurism.

futuriste [-rist] adj. Futuristic, space-age. ‖ ARTS. Futurist.
— s. ARTS. Futurist.

futurologie [-rɔlɔʒi] f. Futurology.

fuyant, ante [fɥijɑ̃, ɑ̃:t] adj. Receding (front, menton); shifty, evasive, foxy (regard).
— m. ARTS. Perspective line.

fuyard [-ja:r] m. Fugitive, runaway.

G

g [ʒe] m. G, g.

gabardine [gabardin] f. Gabardine (tissu); twill raincoat (vêtement).

gabare [gabar] f. NAUT. Sailing-barge, lighter, smack (bateau); drag-net (filet).

gabarit [gabari] m. Gauge, pattern, former (format). ‖ NAUT. Model; mould. ‖ ARCHIT. Outline. ‖ CH. DE F. Gauge.

gabegie [gabʒi] f. † Fraudulent dealings. ‖ Disorder in administration or in finance. ‖ Trickery.

gabelle [gabɛl] † Salt-tax.

gabelou [gablu] m. † Salt-tax collector. ‖ FAM. Custom-house officer; exciseman; tax-collector.

gabier [gabje] m. NAUT. Topman.

gabion [gabjɔ̃] m. MILIT. Gabion.

gable [gɑ:bl] m. ARCHIT. Gable.

Gabon [gabɔ̃] m. GÉOGR. Gabon.

gaburon [gaburɔ̃] m. NAUT. Fish-front (mât).

gâchage [gɑʃa:ʒ] m. Slaking (de la chaux); mixing (du mortier). ‖ AGRIC. Harrowing. ‖ FIG. Spoiling, wasting, bungling.

gâche [gɑʃ] f. Spatula (de cuisinier); trowel (de maçon). ‖ Catch (pêne); staple (serrure).

gâcher [-ʃe] v. tr. (1). ARCHIT. To slake (de la chaux); to mix, to wet (du mortier). ‖ To undersell, to underprice; *gâcher le métier*, to spoil the trade. ‖ AGRIC. To harrow. ‖ FIG. To spoil, to waste (l'étoffe, le pain); to dissipate (ses forces); to squander (sa fortune); to ruin (sa vie).

gâchette [gɑʃɛt] f. Trigger (de fusil); spring-catch (de serrure). ‖ TECHN. Pawl.

gâcheur, euse [gɑʃœ:r, ø:z] adj. Spoiling, bungling. ‖ COMM. Underselling, cut-price.
— s. Mason's (ou) bricklayer's labourer. ‖ COMM. Underseller, cut-price dealer, spoil-trade. ‖ FAM. Botcher, bungler.

gâchis [gɑʃi] m. Wet mortar. ‖ Mud, slush (boue). ‖ FAM. Disorder, mess; *quel gâchis!*, what a hash (ou) mess!

gadget [gadʒɛt] m. Gadget.

gadoue [gadu] f. Night-soil (engrais). ‖ Dirt, filth; mud. (V. BOUE.)

gaélique [gaelik] adj., m. Gaelic.

gaffe [gaf] f. NAUT. Boat-hook; gaff (harpon). ‖ MILIT. FAM. Sentry-duty. ‖ FAM. Blunder, break. bloomer, gaffe, U.S. boner (v. BÉVUE); *faire une gaffe*, to drop a brick, U.S. to pull a boner.

gaffer [-fe] v. tr. (1). To hook; to gaff.
— v. i. FAM. To drop a brick, U. S. to pull a boner.

gaffeur, euse [-fœ:r, ø:z] m. FAM. Blunderer.

gag [gag] m. THÉÂTR. Gag; gag-line; wheeze.

gaga [gaga] adj. Doddering, dotty, gaga.
— s. Dotard, driveller. (V. GÂTEUX.)

gage [gɑ:ʒ] m. Pledge, pawn, security; pawned article. ‖ Forfeit (amende); *jouer aux gages*, to play at forfeits. ‖ Pl. Wages, hire (paie); *homme à gages*, hired man, paid servant. ‖ JUR. Pledged chattels; *prêteur sur gages,* pawnbroker. ‖ Fig. Token, sign.

gager [gaʒe] v. tr. (7). To wager, to bet, to lay, to stake (parier). ‖ To hire, to pay wages to (payer). ‖ Jur. To place under distraint; *meubles gagés,* furniture under distraint; *gager sur,* to secure on.

gagerie [-ʒri] f. Jur. Security of pledge.

gageur [-ʒœ:r] m. Bettor, wagerer.

gageure [-ʒy:r] f. Wager, bet; stake; *c'est une gageure,* it's a long (ou) risky shot.

gagiste [-ʒist] m. Wage-earner. ‖ Jur. Pledger, pawner; *créancier gagiste,* pledge-holder. ‖ Théâtr. Supernumerary actor, U. S. extra.

gagnable [gaɲabl] adj. Obtainable, procurable. ‖ Agric. Reclaimable.

gagnant, ante [gaɲã, ã:t] adj. Winning.
— s. Winner, victor.

gagne [gaɲ]. V. Gagner. ‖ Gagne-pain, m. invar. Livelihood, means of subsistence (moyens); breadwinner (personne). ‖ Gagne-petit, m. invar. Fam. Knife-grinder; cheap-jack.

gagner [gaɲe] v. tr. (1). To earn (un salaire); *gagner de l'argent,* to make money; *gagner sa vie,* to earn one's living. ‖ To reach (une destination). ‖ To gain (du poids, du temps, du terrain); to save (du temps). ‖ To win (un pari, un prix). ‖ Sports. To win (une course). ‖ Jur. To win (un procès). ‖ Milit. To win (la guerre). ‖ Naut. To reach (le port).
— v. intr. To spread (feu). ‖ *Gagner à,* to gain (ou) profit by; *gagner à être connu,* to improve upon acquaintance; *gagner au change,* to benefit by the change; *gagner sur,* to gain ground upon. ‖ Sports. To win. ‖ Méd. To spread (contagion).
— v. pr. Se gagner, to be earned; to be gained. ‖ Méd. To be catching (ou) contagious (maladie).

gagneur [-ɲœ:r] m. Winner; earner; gainer.

gai, aie [ge] adj. Gay, cheerful, merry, high-spirited (personne, visage); bright, vivid (couleur); spicy, ribald (histoire). ‖ Techn. Free (serrure). ‖ Fam. Jolly (pompette).

gaiement [gɛmã] adv. Gaily, cheerfully, merrily.

gaieté [gɛte] f. Gaiety, gayness, cheerfulness, high spirits; *de gaieté de cœur,* out of sheer wantonness.

gaillard, arde [gaja:r, ard] adj. Strong, vigorous, strapping (personne). ‖ Spicy, broad (propos). [V. Grivois.]
— m. Jolly chap, merry fellow; *grand gaillard,* strapping fellow, U. S. husky guy. ‖ Naut. Castle; *gaillard d'avant, d'arrière,* forecastle, quarter deck.

gaillarde [-ja:rd] f. Strapping wench, U.S. husky girl. ‖ Galliard (danse).

gaillardement [-jardəmã] adv. Vigorously (avec entrain); pluckily (crânement); spiritedly, cheerfully (jovialement).

gaillardise [-jardi:z] f. Broad speech, wanton language; spicy story. (V. Gauloiserie.)

gain [gɛ̃] m. Gain; profit; winnings (au jeu); earnings (par le travail); *avoir gain de cause,* to win one's case; to carry one's point; *donner gain de cause à,* to decide in favour of.

gaine [gɛn] f. Cover, case, wrapping (étui); sheath, scabbard (fourreau). ‖ Girdle (corset); roll-on (fam.). ‖ Archit. Terminal; shaft, passage (à aération). ‖ Naut. Tabling, edging (d'une voile).
‖ Gaine-culotte f. Pantie-belt (ou) -girdle.

gainer [-ne] v. tr. (1). To cover, to encase, to sheathe. ‖ To corset (vêtement). ‖ Naut. To hem, to table (une voile).

gainier [-nje] m. Sheath-maker, case-maker. ‖ Bot. Judas-tree.

gala [gala] m. Festivity, fête, gala; *habits de gala,* full dress; glad rags (fam.).

galactique [galaktik] adj. Astron. Galactic; *plan galactique,* galactic plane.

galactogène [-tɔʒɛn] adj., s. Galactogogue.

galactomètre [galaktomɛtr] m. Lactometer.

galactose [-to:z] m. Galactose.

galalithe [galalit] f. Galalith.

galamment [galamã] adv. † Gallantly. ‖ Politely, courteously.

galandage [-lãda:ʒ] m. Brick partition.

galant, ante [-lã, ã:t] adj. Courteous, gentleman-like; *galant homme,* gentleman, man of honour. ‖ Gallant, attentive to the ladies (homme). ‖ *Femme galante,* kept woman, courtesan. ‖ Complimentary, gallant (propos).
— s. Lover, gallant; *vert galant,* gay old spark.

galanterie [-lãtri] f. Courtesy, gentlemanliness (v. Courtoisie); gallantry (envers les femmes). ‖ Pl. Compliments; sweet nothings; *dire des galanteries,* to pay compliments.

galantin [-lãtɛ̃] m. Fop, dandy, coxcomb.

galantine [galãtin] f. Culin. Galantine.

galapiat [galapja] m. Fam. Good-for-nothing.

galaxie [galaksi] f. Astron. Galaxy.

galbe [galb] m. Archit. Entasis (d'une colonne); outline, sweep (d'un meuble). ‖ Autom. Lines (d'une voiture). ‖ Fig. Contours, curves, shapeliness (d'un corps).

galbé, ée [-be] adj. Shapely (partie du corps); curving outwards (ligne). ‖ Techn. Serpentine front (ou) shaped (meuble); *pied galbé,* cabriole, cabriole leg.

galber [-be] v. tr. (1). Archit. To curve, to contour, to round.

gale [gal] f. Méd. Scabies, mange, itch. ‖ Bot. Scurf, scale; worm-hole (du bois). ‖ Techn. Defect (du tissu). ‖ Fam. Scold, shrew (femme); nuisance, pest (homme).

galéjade [galeʒad] f. Tall story, far-fetched tale.

galéjer [-ʒe] v. tr. (1). To tell tall stories; to shoot a line (fam.).

galène [galɛn] f. Galena, sulphide of lead. ‖ Radio. *Poste à galène,* crystal set.

galère [galɛ:r] f. Naut. Galley, convict ship. ‖ Pl. Hulks; galleys. ‖ Fam. Drudgery, hard work. ‖ Loc. *Vogue la galère!,* come what may!, here goes!, sink or swim!

galerie [galri] f. Gallery, long room; corridor (d'appartement); arcade, covered walk (de rue). ‖ Cornice, moulding, beading (à un meuble). ‖ Comm. Department store (grand magasin). ‖ Arts. Picture gallery. ‖ Théâtr. Balcony. (V. Balcon.) ‖ Naut. Stern gallery. ‖ Autom. Luggage-rail, U. S. baggage-rack. ‖ Fam. On-lookers.

galérien [-lerjɛ̃] m. Galley-slave; convict. ‖ Fam. *Vie de galérien,* dog's life.

galet [galɛ] m. Pebble, shingle, gravel (caillou); cobble-stone (pour chaussée). · ‖ Techn. Roller; small pulley. ‖ Sports. Shuffle-board.

galetas [galtɑ] m. Garret. (V. Mansarde.)

galette [galɛt] f. Culin. Pancake, girdle-cake, griddle-cake. ‖ Naut. Ship's biscuit, hard-tack. ‖ Techn. Presscake; slab (projectiles). ‖ Fam. Hard, thin mattress (matelas); *plat comme une galette,* flat as a pancake. ‖ Pop. Brass, oof, dough. (V. Pèze.)

galeux, euse [galø, ø:z] adj. Méd. Mangy, scabby, itchy. ‖ Bot. Scurfy. ‖ Fig. *Brebis galeuse,* black sheep.

galhauban [galobã] m. Naut. Backstay.

galibot [galibo] m. Pit-boy (ou) -lad.

galiléen, enne [galileɛ̃, ɛn] adj., m. Géogr. Galilean.

galimatias [galimatjɑ] m. Balderdash, gibberish, rubbish, garble. (V. Baragouin, Charabia.)

galion [galjɔ̃] m. Naut. Galleon, treasure-ship.

galipette [galipɛt] f. Fam. Antic. (V. Cabriole.)

galipot [galipo] m. White resin. ‖ NAUT. Blacking.

galle [gal] f. BOT. Gall, oak-apple.

Galles (pays de) [peidəgal] m. GÉOGR. Wales.

gallican, ane [galikɑ̃, an] adj., s. ECCLÉS. Gallican.

gallicanisme [-kanism] m. ECCLÉS. Gallicanism.

gallicisme [-sism] m. GRAMM. Gallicism.

gallinacé, ée [galinase] adj. ZOOL. Gallinaceous, gallinacean.
— m. pl. ZOOL. Gallinaceae, gallinaceans.

gallique [galik] adj. Gallic, pertaining to Gaul. ‖ CHIM. Gallic (acide).

gallium [galjɔm] m. CHIM. Gallium.

gallois, oise [galwa, wa:z] adj. Welsh, pertaining to Wales.
— m. Welshman (habitant); Welsh (langue).

gallon [galɔ̃] m. Gallon (mesure).

gallo-romain, aine [galorɔmɛ̃, ɛn] adj. Gallo-Roman.

gallup [galœp] m. Gallup poll.

galoche [galɔʃ] f. Galosh, wooden-soled clog. ‖ NAUT. Snatch-block; chock; belaying-cleat. ‖ FAM. *Menton en galoche*, undershot jaw.

galon [galɔ̃] m. Galloon, gold braid, gold lace. ‖ MILIT. Pl. Stripes.

galonner [-lɔne] v. tr. (1). To trim with braid (ou) with lace. ‖ MILIT. To promote, to confer rank upon.

galop [galo] m. Gallop; *grand galop*, full gallop; *petit galop*, canter; *prendre le galop*, to break into a gallop. ‖ FAM. Scolding, wigging (semonce); *déjeuner au galop*, to rush through lunch.

galopade [-lɔpad] f. Galloping, gallop, canter (action); distance galloped (espace).

galopant, ante [-lɔpɑ̃, ɑ̃:t] adj. Galloping. ‖ MÉD. *Phtisie galopante*, galloping consumption.

galope [galɔp] f. Book-binder's tool.

galoper [-lɔpe] v. intr. (1). To gallop; *faire galoper*, to gallop. ‖ FAM. To run (personne).

galopin [galɔpɛ̃] m. Urchin (gamin); scamp (garnement). ‖ TECHN. Loose pulley, jockey wheel.

galuchat [galyʃa] m. Shark-skin, dogfish-skin.

galure [galy:r], **galurin** [galyrɛ̃] m. FAM. Topper, tile, lid.

galvanique [galvanik] adj. Galvanic; *plaqué galvanique*, electro-plate.

galvanisation [-zasjɔ̃] f. Galvanization, galvanizing.

galvaniser [-ze] v. tr. (1). To galvanize. ‖ FIG. To stimulate.

galvanisme [galvanism] m. Galvanism.

galvano [-no] m. TECHN. Electrotype plate.

galvanomètre [galvanɔmɛtr] m. ÉLECTR. Galvanometer.

galvanoplastie [-plasti] f. Galvanoplasty. ‖ TECHN. Electro-plating.

galvanoplastique [-plastik] adj. Galvanoplastic.

galvanoscope [-skɔp] m. Galvanoscope.

galvanotype [-tip] m. Electrotype.

galvanotypie [-tipi] f. Electrotyping.

galvauder [galvode] v. tr. (1). To botch (son travail). ‖ To sully, to lower (sa réputation).
— v. pr. Se galvauder, to debase (ou) to lower oneself.

galvaudeux [-dø] s. Tramp. (V. VAGABOND.) ‖ Loose liver (débauché).

gambade [gɑ̃bad] f. Leap, gambol. ‖ SPORTS. Gambade (à l'équitation).

gambader [-de] v. intr. To leap, to gambol.

gambe [gɑ̃:b] f. NAUT. Futtock-shrouds. ‖ MUS. *Viole de gambe*, viola da gamba.

gamberge [gɑ̃bɛrʒ] f. FAM. Imagination, fantasy.

gamberger [-ʒe] v. intr. FAM. To imagine all sorts of things, to fantasize.
— v. tr. FAM. To think up, to concoct.

gambette [gɑ̃bɛt] m. ZOOL. Red-shank.

gambette f. FAM. Leg.

Gambie [gɑ̃bi] f. GÉOGR. Gambia.

gambiller [gɑ̃bije] v. intr. (1). FAM. To skip about. (V. GAMBADER.)

gambit [gɑ̃bi] m. Gambit (aux échecs).

gamelle [gamɛl] f. Tin container. ‖ MILIT. Mess-tin.

gamète [gamɛt] m. MÉD. Gamete.

gamin [gamɛ̃] m. Urchin, gamin, kid; street-boy.

gamine [gamin] f. Girl; street-girl.

gaminerie [-ri] f. Adolescent pranks, tricks, mischievousness.

gamma [gama] m. Gamma; *rayons gamma*, gamma rays.

gamme [gam] f. MUS. Scale, gamut. ‖ FIN. Range (des prix). ‖ FIG. Gamut, range, series. ‖ FAM. *Changer de gamme*, to change one's tune.

gammé, ée [game] adj. *Croix gammée*, swastika.

ganache [ganaʃ] f. ZOOL. Lower jaw, jowl (de cheval). ‖ Upholstered chair. ‖ FAM. Blockhead.

Gand [gɑ̃] m. GÉOGR. Ghent.

gandin [gɑ̃dɛ̃] m. Dandy, dude, swell.

gang [gɑ̃g] m. Gang.

Gange [gɑ̃:ʒ] m. GÉOGR. Ganges.

gangliforme [gɑ̃gliform] adj. MÉD. Gangliform.

ganglion [gɑ̃glijɔ̃] m. MÉD. Ganglion; gland.

ganglionnaire [-glionɛ:r] adj. MÉD. Ganglionary, ganglionic.

gangrène [gɑ̃grɛ:n] f. MÉD. Gangrene. ‖ BOT. Canker. ‖ FIG. Gangrene, canker.

gangrené, ée [-grəne] adj. MÉD. Gangrened, gangrenous. ‖ FIG. Rotten, corrupt.

gangrener [-grəne] v. tr. (1). MÉD. To gangrene. ‖ BOT. To canker. ‖ FIG. To rot, to corrupt.

gangréneux, euse [-grenø, ø:z] adj. Gangrened, gangrenous. ‖ BOT. Cankerous.

gangster [gɑ̃gstɛ:r] m. Gangster, gang member; U. S. racketeer. (V. BANDIT.)

gangstérisme [-sterism] m. Gangsterism.

gangue [gɑ̃:g] f. Gangue, matrix.

ganse [gɑ̃s] f. Braid; edging, piping.

ganser [-se] v. tr. (1). To trim with braid; to pipe (une couture).

gant [gɑ̃] m. Glove; *gant de boxe*, boxing-glove; *gant de crin*, flesh-glove; *gant de toilette*, washing-glove, glove-sponge. ‖ LOC. *Aller comme un gant*, to fit like a glove, to suit to a T; *jeter, relever le gant*, to throw down, to pick up the gauntlet; *prendre des gants pour*, to put on kid gloves to.

gantelet [gɑ̃tlɛ] m. Gauntlet. ‖ MÉD. Glove-bandage.

ganter [-te] v. tr. To glove. ‖ FIG. To suit, to be convenient to.
— v. pr. Se ganter, to put on gloves; to buy gloves for oneself.

ganterie [-tri] f. Glove-making (fabrication); glove-factory (fabrique); glove-counter (rayon de magasin); glove-trade (vente).

gantier, ière [-tje, ɛ:r] adj. Pertaining to glove manufacture.
— s. COMM. Glover, glove-manufacturer.

garage [gara:ʒ] m. AUTOM. Garage; *garage en bord de route*, lay-by, U. S. roadside stop. ‖ Storage depot (remise). ‖ CH. DE F. Shunting, side-tracking; engine-shed; *voie de garage*, siding. ‖ NAUT. Docking; *garage pour canots*, boat-house.

garagiste [-raʒist] m. AUTOM. Garage-man, garage-proprietor.

garance [garɑ̃:s] f. BOT. Madder, madder-wort.
— adj. Madder (couleur).

garant, ante [garɑ̃, ɑ̃:t] adj. Guaranteeing.

— m. Jur. Security, warrant, voucher (garantie). ‖ Naut. Tackle-fall.

— s. Jur. Guarantor, warrantor, surety, bail (personne); *se porter garant de*, to guarantee, to vouch (ou) answer for. (V. caution, répondant.)

garanti, ie [garãti] adj. Guaranteed, warranted.

garantie f. Jur. Guarantee; pledge (de contrat); guaranty (de paiement). ‖ Comm. Warranty (de qualité); *contrat de garantie*, underwriting contract. ‖ Fig. Safeguard, insurance (*contre*, against).

garantir [-ti:r] v. tr. (2). To guarantee (en général). ‖ To guarantee, to certify (certifier). ‖ *Garantir contre*, to guarantee (ou) secure (ou) to defend against. ‖ Fin. To guarantee, to secure (une dette).

garce [gars] f. Pop. Wench, hussy (femme); strumpet, trollop (putain).

garcette [garsɛt] f. Naut. Rope-end, cat-o'-nine tails (fouet); gasket (raban).

garçon [garsõ] m. Boy, lad; young fellow. ‖ Bachelor (célibataire). ‖ *Garçon de bureau*, office-boy; *garçon de café*, waiter; *garçon coiffeur*, hairdresser's assistant; *garçon d'étage*, floor waiter; *garçon d'honneur*, best man. ‖ Fam. *Bon garçon*, good sort, decent chap; *mon garçon*, my son (fils).

garçonne [-sɔn] f. Tomboy, hoyden; *coiffure à la garçonne*, Eton crop, U. S. boyish bob.

garçonnet [-sɔnɛ] m. Small (ou) little boy.

garçonnier, ère [-sɔnje, ɛ:r] adj. Mannish, boyish.

garçonnière [-sɔnjɛ:r] f. Bachelor's quarters.

garde [gard] f. Care, guarding, watching; *monter la garde*, to keep watch; to mount guard. ‖ Guard, guards; *de garde*, on (guard) duty; *Garde républicaine*, Horse Guards. ‖ Guardianship, care, protection, custody; *garde d'enfants*, baby-sitting (fonction); baby-sitter (personne). ‖ Fly-leaf, end-paper (d'un livre). ‖ Ward (d'une serrure). ‖ Comm. *Longue garde*, keeping quality. ‖ Méd. Nurse. ‖ Naut. *Garde descendante, montante*, check-spring, ahead, astern. ‖ Sports. *En garde!*, on guard! (à l'escrime). ‖ Fig. *Prendre garde à*, to take care to; *prendre garde de*, to take care not to; to be careful not to; *prendre garde que*, to notice that; *prendre garde que ... ne*, to be careful lest.

garde m. Guardian, watchman; keeper, warden; *garde champêtre*, rural constable; *garde forestier*, forester, ranger; *Garde des sceaux*, Keeper of the Seals. ‖ Milit. Guardsman, U. S. military policeman. ‖ **Garde-à-vous**, m. Milit. Attention; *être au garde-à-vous*, to stand to attention. ‖ **Garde-barrière**, m. Ch. de f. Signalman, gate-keeper. ‖ **Garde-boue**, m. invar. Autom. Mudguard, U. S. fender. ‖ **Garde-canal**, m. Water-bailiff; fishing-warden. ‖ **Garde-chasse**, m. Gamekeeper, game-warden. ‖ **Garde-chiourme**, m. Warder (de forçats). ‖ **Garde-corps**, m. invar. Naut. Life-line, manrope. ‖ **Garde-côte**, m. Naut. Coastguard ship (bateau); coastguard (homme). ‖ **Garde-feu**, m. invar. Fire-screen, fender. ‖ **Garde-fou**, m. Hand-rail, railing; parapet (d'un pont). ‖ **Garde-frein**, m. Ch. de f. Brakesman. ‖ **Garde-magasin**, m. Comm. Warehouseman. ‖ **Garde-main**, m. Hand-shield. ‖ **Garde-malade**, m. Méd. Male nurse; f. nurse. ‖ **Garde-manche**, m. Oversleeve, cuff-protector. ‖ **Garde-manger**, m. invar. Culin. Meat-safe, larder, pantry. ‖ **Garde-meuble**, m. Furniture storehouse. ‖ **Garde-nappe**, m. invar. Table-mat; doily. ‖ **Garde-pêche**, m. invar. Fishery protection vessel (bateau); fishing-warden, water-bailiff, river-keeper (homme). ‖ **Garde-phare**, m. Lighthouse-keeper. ‖ **Garde-place**, m. Reserved seat voucher. ‖ **Garde-port**, m. Naut. Wharf-master, harbour-master. ‖ **Garde-rivière**,

m. River-policeman. ‖ **Garde-robe**, f. Wardrob (meuble, penderie, vêtements); toilet, waterclose (toilettes). ‖ **Garde-voie**, m. Ch. de f. Track-watch man. ‖ **Garde-vue**, m. invar. Eyeshade, visor.

gardénia [gardenja] m. Bot. Gardenia.

garden-party [gardɛnparti] (pl. **garden-parties**) f. Garden-party.

garder [garde] v. tr. (1). To keep, to preserve (v. conserver). ‖ To guard, to protect, to keep watch over, to watch over, to look after; *garder des enfants*, to baby-sit. ‖ To keep up (les apparences); to stay in (la chambre); to respect (sa parole); to observe (le silence); *gardez ça pour vous*, keep it under your hat, let it go no further; *gardez vos observations pour vous*, keep your remarks to yourself; *garder rancune*, to harbour resentment, to nurse a grudge (à, against).
— v. pr. **Se garder**, to protect oneself; *se garder de tomber*, to take care not to fall. ‖ To keep to preserve (aliments).

garderie [gardəri] f. Boarding-home (pour animaux); day nursery (pour enfants).

gardeur [-dœ:r] m. Keeper; preserver. ‖ Herder

gardian [gardjã] m. Herdsman in the Camargue.

gardien [-djɛ̃] m. Guardian; keeper (v. garde); attendant (d'un garage); caretaker (d'une propriété). ‖ Jur. Protector (des intérêts publics) warden, U. S. guard (de prison); *gardien de la paix*, policeman, police constable. ‖ Sports. *Gardien de but*, goalkeeper. ‖ Ecclés. Guardian angel (ange).

gardiennage [-djɛnaʒ] m. Guarding; caretaking; conservancy.

gardienne [-djɛ:n] f. Guardian; keeper; care-taker.

gardon [gardõ] m. Zool. Roach (poisson).

gare [gar] f. Ch. de f. Station; stop; terminus; *gare aérienne*, airport; *gare de manœuvre*, sidings; *gare de ravitaillement*, rail-head; *gare de triage*, marshalling yard; *gare de voyageurs*, passenger station. ‖ Naut. *Gare maritime*, harbour station. ‖ Fam. The railway people (employés).

gare! [gar] interj. Beware! (V. attention!)

garenne [garɛn] f. Warren (pour la chasse); fishing preserve (pour la pêche).

garer [gare] v. tr. (1). Autom. To park, to garage. ‖ Avion. To put into a hangar. ‖ Ch. de f. To shunt on to a siding. ‖ Naut. To dock, to moor. ‖ Agric. To garner, to gather in. ‖ Fam. To secure.
— v. pr. **Se garer**, to stand aside; to get out of the way (de, of); to take cover. ‖ Ch. de f. To shunt on to a siding.

Gargantua [gargãtɥa] m. Gargantua. ‖ Glutton, guzzler.

gargantuesque [-tɥɛsk] adj. Gargantuan. ‖ Gluttonous.

gargariser (se) [sə gargarize] v. pr. (1). To gargle.

gargarisme [gargarism] m. Gargle, mouth-wash, throat-wash.

gargote [gargɔt] f. Cook-shop, U. S. hash-house, beanery, greasy spoon.

gargoter [-te] v. intr. (1). To eat in cheap restaurants. ‖ To cook wretchedly.

gargotier [-tje] m. Cook-shop operator, bad cook, U. S. hasher.

gargouille [gargu:j] f. Archit. Gargoyle; roof water-spout; gutter spout.

gargouillement [-jmã] m. Gurgling, bubbling. ‖ Méd. Rumbling.

gargouiller [-je] v. intr. (1). To gurgle, to bubble; to dabble, to paddle (dans l'eau). ‖ Méd. To rumble.

gargouillis [-ji] m. Gurgling.

gargoulette [-lɛt] f. Water-jug, water-cooler.

garnement [garnmɑ̃] m. Good-for-nothing, scamp. (V. GALOPIN.)

garni, ie [garni] adj. Garnished (v. ORNÉ); trimmed (chapeau). ‖ Equipped (de, with). ‖ Well-lined, heavy (bourse). ‖ Furnished (chambre). — m. Furnished apartment, lodging house, U. S. rooming house. ‖ FAM. Digs.

garnir [-nir] v. tr. (2). To furnish, to stock. (V. EMPLIR.) ‖ To garnish, to trim [de with]. (V. ORNER.) ‖ To bait (un hameçon). ‖ MILIT. To garrison, to strengthen.
— v. pr. **Se garnir**, to fill, to fill up.

garnison [-nizɔ̃] f. MILIT. Garrison.

garnissage [-nisa:ʒ] m. Garnishing, furnishing. ‖Trimming, ornamenting. ‖ Facing (couture).

garnisseur [-nisœ:r] m. Garnisher, trimmer (couturier); fitter (maroquiniste); ‖ Filler (de lampes); napper, teazler (de tissus).

garniture [-nity:r] f. Garniture, furniture; fittings (accessoires); trimmings, ornaments (ornements); garniture de boutons, set of buttons; garniture de cheminée, set of mantelpiece ornaments. ‖ CULIN. Garnish, garnishing. ‖ NAUT. Rigging. ‖ AUTOM. Lining (de freins); upholstery (de sièges). ‖ TECHN. Lagging (de chaudière); packing-ring (de piston); gear (de pompe).

garou [garu] m. BOT Spurge-flax, mezereon.

garrigue [garig] f. Garrigue, oak plantation.

garrot [garo] m. MÉD. Garrot. ‖ TECHN. Tongue (d'une scie). ‖ † Garrotte, garrotting (supplice).

garrot m. ZOOL. Withers (du cheval).

garrotter [garɔte] v. tr. (1). † To garrotte, to strangle. ‖ To bind, to tie, to pinion (lier).

gars [gɑ] m. FAM. Lad, stripling.

Gascogne [gaskɔɲ] f. GÉOGR. Gascony.

gascon, onne [gaskɔ̃, ɔn] adj., s. Gascon.
— m. Gascon dialect (langage); Gascon (personne). ‖ FIG. Boaster. (V. FANFARON.)

gasconnade [-kɔnad] f. Bragging, gasconade.

gas-oil, gasoil [gazɔjl (ou) gazwal] m. Fuel oil, diesel oil; derv (fam.).

gaspacho [gaspatʃo] m. CULIN. Gazpacho.

gaspillage [gaspija:ʒ] m. Waste, wasting, squandering.

gaspiller [-ije] v. tr. (1). To waste, to squander (son argent); to fritter away (son temps); to dissipate (sa vie).

gaspilleur, euse [-jœ:r, ø:z] adj. Wasteful; spendthrift, extravagant, squandering (personne). — s. Waster, squanderer, spendthrift.

gastéropodes [gasterɔpɔd] m. pl. ZOOL. Gast(e)ropods.

gastralgie [gastralʒi] f. MÉD. Gastralgia.

gastralgique [-ʒik] adj. MÉD. Gastralgic, dyspeptic.

gastrique [gastrik] adj. MÉD. Gastric.

gastrite [-trit] f. MÉD. Gastritis.

gastro- [gastro] préf. Gastro-. ‖ **Gastro-entérite**, f. MÉD. Gastro-enteritis. ‖ **Gastro-entérologie**, f. MÉD. Gastro-enterology. ‖ **Gastro-entérologue**, s. MÉD. Gastro-enterologist. ‖ **Gastro-intestinal**, adj. Gastro-intestinal.

gastronome [gastrɔnɔm] m. Gastronome(r).

gastronomie [-mi] f. Gastronomy.

gastronomique [-mik] adj. Gastronomic.

gastropodes [gastrɔpɔd] m. pl. V. GASTÉ-ROPODES.

gâte [gɑt]. V. GÂTER. ‖ **Gâte-métier**, m. Scribbler. ‖ **Gâte-sauce**, m. Scullion, kitchen-boy.

gâté, ée [gɑte] adj. Spoiled, tainted, damaged, deteriorated (aliment). ‖ FIG. Spoiled, pampered, petted (enfant).

gâteau [gɑto] m. CULIN. Cake; gâteau; sweet pudding. ‖ Honeycomb (de miel); lump (de plomb). ‖ FAM. Profits, benefits; partager le gâteau, to go shares, to split the profits. ‖ FAM. Papa gâteau, over-indulgent father.

gâter [gɑte] v. tr. (1). To spoil, to taint, to damage (un aliment). [V. AVARIER.] ‖ FIG. To spoil, to indulge, to pamper (un enfant).
— v. pr. **Se gâter**, to spoil, to deteriorate (aliment). ‖ FIG. To indulge (ou) pamper oneself.

gâterie [-tri] f. Treat, goodie (fam.). ‖ FIG. Spoiling, pampering, over-indulgence.

gâteur [-tœ:r] m. Spoiler, waster (de matériel). ‖ FIG. Spoiler, pamperer, indulger (d'enfants).

gâteux, euse [gɑtø, ø:z] adj. Doddering, in a state of senile decay.
— s. Dotard, dodderer. (V. GAGA.)

gâtine [gɑtin] f. Marshland.

gâtisme [gɑtism] m. Dotage.

gatte [gat] f. NAUT. Manger.

gauche [goːʃ] adj. Left (côté). ‖ FIG. Awkward, bungling, clumsy, maladroit, gawky (geste, personne). [V. EMPOTÉ.] ‖ FAM. Mariage de la main gauche, left-handed marriage; se lever du pied gauche, to get out on the wrong side of the bed.
— m. SPORTS. Left (à la boxe).
— f. Left side, left-hand side; à gauche, on the left; tourner à gauche, turn to the left. ‖ FIG. Left-wing party; homme de gauche, leftist. ‖ AUTOM. Tenir sa gauche, to keep to the left. ‖ FAM. Jusqu'à la gauche, up to the hilt.

gauchement [goʃmɑ̃] adv. Awkwardly, clumsily.

gaucher, ère [-ʃe, ɛːr] adj. Left-handed.
— s. Left-handed person, U. S. southpaw (fam.).

gaucherie [-ʃri] f. Left-handedness. ‖ FIG. Awkwardness, clumsiness, gaucherie. (V. MALADRESSE.)

gauchir [goʃi:r] v. intr. (2). To swerve, to turn aside. ‖ To warp (bois); to buckle (métal).
— v. tr. To give camber to. ‖ AVIAT. To bank, to warp (l'aileron).

gauchisant, ante [-ʃizɑ̃, ɑ̃:t] adj. With left-wing tendencies.

gauchisme [-ʃism] m. Leftism, extreme leftism.

gauchissement [-ʃismɑ̃] m. Getting out of true; warping (du bois); buckling (du métal). ‖ AVIAT. Banking, warping (de l'aileron).

gaucho [goʃo] m. Gaucho.

gaudriole [godriɔl] f. Broad joke; coarse jest.

gaufrage [gofraʒ] m. Embossing, stamping (du cuir); goffering (du linge); crinkling, puckering (du papier, du tissu); blocking (d'une reliure); corrugating, chequering (de la tôle). ‖ Embossment (sur cuir); goffers (sur lingerie).

gaufre [gofr] f. CULIN. Wafer (biscuit); waffle (gâteau); moule à gaufres, waffle-iron. ‖ Honeycomb (de miel). ‖ POP. Mug (face).

gaufré, ée [-fre] adj. Embossed (cuir); goffered, wafer-stamped (linge); crinkled, puckered (papier, tissu); blocked (reliure); corrugated, chequered (tôle); tissu gaufré, seersucker.

gaufrer [-fre] v. tr. (1). To emboss, to stamp (du cuir); to goffer (du linge); to crinkle, to pucker (du papier, du tissu); to block (une reliure); to corrugate (de la tôle).

gaufrette [-frɛt] f. CULIN. Thin chequered wafer, sugar-wafer; wafer-biscuit.

gaufreur [-frœ:r] m. Gofferer, embosser, stamper.

gaufrier [-frije] m. CULIN. Waffle-iron.

gaufrure [-fryr] f. Embossing (du cuir); goffering (du linge); puckering, crinkling (du papier, du tissu).

gaulage [gola:ʒ] m. AGRIC. Beating (d'un arbre).

Gaule [gol] f. GÉOGR. Gaul.

gaule f. Long thin pole (ou) stick. ‖ SPORTS. Fishing-rod (à pêche). ‖ NAUT. Small flag-staff.

gaulée [-le] f. Fruit shaken down by beating.

gauleiter [golaitɛ:r] m. Gauleiter.

gauler [gole] v. tr. (1). AGRIC. To beat, to thrash.

gaullien, enne [goljɛ̃, ɛn] adj. Reminiscent of de Gaulle.

gaullisme [golism] m. Gaullism.

gaulliste [-list] s. Gaullist.
gaulois, oise [golwa, waz] adj. GÉOGR. Gallic. ‖ FAM. Spicy; *esprit gaulois,* broad Gallic humour. — s. Gallic (langue); Gaul (personne).
gauloise [golwaːz] f. FAM. Popular brand of French cigarettes.
gauloisement [-zmã] adv. Spicily, bawdily.
gauloiserie [-zri] f. Broad joke, racy story.
gaupe [gop] f. POP. Slut, drab, trollop.
gauss [goːs] m. PHYS. Gauss.
gausser (se) [səgose] v. pr. To scoff (*de,* at); *se gausser de,* to mock, to ridicule.
gavage [gavaːʒ] m. MÉD. Forcible feeding, U. S. gavage. ‖ FAM. Gorging, stuffing (d'une personne); cramming (d'une volaille).
gave [gaːv] m. Mountain torrent.
gaver [gave] v. tr. (1). MÉD. To force-feed, to feed by gavage. ‖ FAM. To gorge, to stuff, to glut (une personne); to cram (la volaille). — v. pr. **Se gaver,** to gorge, to stuff oneself.
gaveur [-vœːr] s. Crammer (appareil, personne).
gavotte [gavɔt] f. Gavotte.
gavroche [gavrɔʃ] m. FAM. Parisian street urchin.
gaz [gaz] m. Gas; *gaz d'éclairage,* illuminating gas; *usine à gaz,* gas works, gas plant. ‖ AUTOM. *Gaz d'échappement,* exhaust gas; *couper les gaz,* to throttle back; *ouvrir les gaz,* to open the throttle, U. S. to step on the gas. ‖ MÉD. Wind.
gaze [gɑːz] f. Gauze; butter muslin; veiling; *gaze métallique,* wire gauze. ‖ MÉD. Antiseptic (ou) sterilized gauze. ‖ FAM. Softening.
gazé, ée [gɑze] adj. MÉD. Gassed. — s. MÉD. Poison-gas victim (ou) casualty.
gazéification [gazeifikasjɔ̃] f. CHIM. Gasification; aeration, charging (d'une eau minérale).
gazéifier [-fje] v. tr. (1). CHIM. To gasify, to volatilize. ‖ To aerate, to charge, to carbonate (une eau minérale).
gazéiforme [-fɔrm] adj. CHIM. Gasiform.
gazelle [gazɛl] f. ZOOL. Gazelle.
gazer [gɑze] v. tr. (1). To gas (du tissu). — v. intr. To smoke. ‖ AUTOM. To roll (ou) whiz along. ‖ FAM. *Ça gaze?,* how goes it?, how're tricks?
gazer v. tr. (1). To cover with gauze. ‖ FIG. To soften, to tone down.
gazetier [gaztje] m. Gazetteer.
gazette [gazɛt] f. Gazette. (V. JOURNAL.) ‖ FAM. Gossip (personne).
gazeux, euse [gazø, øːz] adj. Aerated, charged, carbonated, sparkling, fizzy (boisson). ‖ CHIM. Gazeous (corps). ‖ FAM. Windy (flatulent).
gazier, ère [-zje, ɛːr] adj. Gas (industrie). — m. Gas employee, gasman.
gazoduc [-zɔdyk] m. Gas pipeline.
gazogène [gɑzɔʒɛːn] adj. Gas-producing; aerating. — m. Gas-generator, gas-producer; producer gas plant; gasogene, seltzogene. ‖ AUTOM. Gas-propelled car.
gazoline [gazɔlin] f. Gasoline, gasolene.
gazomètre [-mɛtr] m. Gasometer.
gazon [gazɔ̃] m. Grass (herbe); grass-plot, lawn, turf, green, greensward (pelouse).
gazonnement [gazɔnmã], **gazonnage** [-naːʒ] m. Turfing.
gazonner [-ne] v. tr. (1). To turf. — v. intr. To sward.
gazonneux, euse [-nø, øːz] adj. Grassy, swarded; turfy, turf-like.
gazouillant, ante [gazujã, ãːt] adj. Babbling, prattling (enfant); warbling, chirping, twittering (oiseau); murmuring, purling (ruisseau).
gazouillement [-jmã], **gazouillis** [-ji] m. Babbling, prattling (d'un enfant); warbling, chirping,

twittering (d'un oiseau); murmuring, purling, babbling (d'un ruisseau).
gazouiller [-je] v. intr. (1). To babble, to prattle (enfant); to warble, to chirp, to twitter (oiseau); to murmur, to purl, to babble (ruisseau).
gazouilleur, euse [-jœːr, øːz] adj. V. GAZOUILLANT. — s. Babbler, prattler (enfant).
G.D.F. [ʒedeɛf] abrév. de *Gaz de France,* French gas board.
geai [ʒɛ] m. ZOOL. Jay.
géant, ante [ʒeã, ãːt] adj. Giant, gigantic. — m. Giant.
géante [ʒeãt] f. Giantess.
gecko [ʒeko] m. ZOOL. Gecko.
géhenne [ʒeɛn] f. Gehenna, Hell.
geignant, ante [ʒɛɲã, ãːt] adj. Whining, whimpering, complaining, fretful.
geignard, arde [-ɲaːr, ard] adj. Whining, whimpering, querulous, fretful. — s. Whiner, sniveller.
geignement [ʒɛɲmã] m. Whine, whimper.
geindre [ʒɛ̃dr] v. intr. (59). To whine, to whimper.
geisha [gɛʃa] f. Geisha.
gel [ʒɛl] m. Frost; freezing.
gélatine [ʒelatin] f. Gelatin; *gélatine explosive,* gum (ou) U. S. gelatin dynamite.
gélatiné, ée [-ne] adj. Gelatinized.
gélatineux, euse [-nø, øːz] adj. Gelatinous.
gelée [ʒəle] f. Frost; *gelée blanche,* hoar-frost, rime. ‖ CULIN. Jelly; *à la gelée,* jellied.
geler v. tr. (8b). To freeze, to convert into ice. (V. CONGELER.) ‖ MÉD., AGRIC. To frostbite. — v. intr. To freeze, to become frozen; to jell, to solidify. — v. pr. **Se geler,** to freeze; *se geler à attendre qqn,* to get frozen waiting for s.o.
gélifier [ʒelifje] v. tr. To gelatinize, to jellify.
gelinotte [ʒəlinɔt] f. ZOOL. Hazel-grouse; fat pullet.
gelivure [ʒelivyr] f. Frost-crack, frost-cleft.
gélose [ʒeloːz] f. Agar, agar-agar.
gélule [ʒelyːl] f. MÉD. Capsule.
gelure [ʒəlyːr] f. MÉD. Frost-bite.
gémeaux [ʒemo] m. pl. ASTRON. Gemini, the Twins.
gémellaire [ʒemɛlɛːr] adj. MÉD. Gemellary, bigeminal.
gémination [ʒeminasjɔ̃] Gemination. ‖ GRAMM. Gemination (de phonèmes), reduplication (de syllabes).
géminé, ée [ʒemine] adj. Geminate, twin. ‖ Mixed, co-educational (école).
gémir [ʒemir] v. intr. (2). To groan, to moan, to wail (v. GEINDRE); *gémir de ses péchés,* to bewail one's sins; *gémir sur son sort,* to bemoan one's fate.
gémissant, ante [-misã, ãːt] adj. Moaning, groaning; wailing. ‖ Creaking (essieu).
gémissement [-mismã] m. Moaning, groaning, wailing (action); moan, groan, wail. (V. PLAINTE.) ‖ Creaking (d'un essieu).
gémisseur [-misœːr] m. Moaner, groaner; wailer.
gemmage [ʒɛmaːʒ] m. AGRIC. Tapping for resin (d'un pin).
gemme [ʒɛm] f. Gem, precious stone; *sel gemme,* rock salt. ‖ BOT. Leaf-bud; pine resin. ‖ ZOOL. Gemma.
gemmé, ée [-me] adj. Bejewelled, set with precious stones.
gemmer [-me] v. intr. (1). BOT. To bud, to gemmate. — v. tr. To tap for resin (un arbre).
gémonies [ʒemɔni] f. pl. The Gemonies, Gemonian stairs. ‖ FIG. Pillory; *vouer qqn aux gémonies,* to hold s.o. up to public obloquy (ou) scorn.

gênant, ante [ʒɛnɑ̃, ɑ̃:t] adj. Inconvenient, annoying (objet); bothersome, troublesome (personne); awkward, embarrassing (silence, situation).

gencive [ʒɑ̃siv] f. MÉD. Gum.

gendarme [ʒɑ̃darm] m. Gendarme, soldier of the police militia; constable. ‖ Rock pinnacle (pic). ‖ Flaw (dans une pierre gemme). ‖ FIG. Termagant, virago (femme). ‖ POP. Red herring.

gendarmer (se) [səʒɑ̃darme] v. pr. (1). To make violent protest, to be up in arms (contre, against).

gendarmerie [-məri] f. Gendarmerie, constabulary. ‖ Gendarmerie barracks (ou) headquarters (caserne).

gendre [ʒɑ̃dr] m. Son-in-law.

gêne [ʒɛn] f. Annoyance, bother, trouble, inconvenience (ennui). ‖ Constraint, discomfort, embarrassment (inconfort). ‖ Financial embarrassment (pénurie); dans la gêne, in straitened circumstances; gêne de trésorerie, shortness of cash. ‖ Loc. Sans gêne, unconstrained, free and easy, offhand.

gène m. MÉD. Gene.

gêné, ée [ʒɛne] adj. Annoyed, bothered, inconvenienced (ennuyé). ‖ Financially embarrassed, hard up (impécunieux). ‖ Constrained, embarrassed, ill-at-ease (mal à l'aise). ‖ Awkward, uneasy (embarrassé).

généalogie [ʒenealɔʒi] f. Genealogy; descent, lineage. ‖ Pedigree (d'un animal).

généalogique [-ʒik] adj. Genealogical.

généalogiste [-ʒist] m. Genealogist.

gêner [ʒɛne] v. tr. (1). To impede, to hinder, to interfere with (contrarier); to embarrass, to inconvenience (embarrasser); to annoy, to bother, to trouble (ennuyer); to intrude on, to disturb (déranger). ‖ To cramp, to constrict (vêtement).
— v. pr. Se gêner, to constrain oneself; to trouble (ou) inconvenience oneself; ne vous gênez pas, don't stand on ceremony; do make yourself at home (ironiquement).

général, ale [ʒeneral] adj. General, universal; consentement général, common consent; en général (ou) d'une façon générale, en règle générale, in general, generally, generally speaking. ‖ THÉÂTR. Répétition générale, dress rehearsal. ‖ JUR. Direction générale, head office.
— m. MILIT. General; général de brigade, de division, brigadier, major-general. ‖ AVIAT. Général d'aviation, air marshal.

généralat [-rala] m. MILIT., ECCLÉS. Generalship.

générale [-ra:l] f. General's wife. ‖ MILIT. Alarm call; battre la générale, to call to arms. ‖ THÉÂTR. Pre-view; dress rehearsal.

généralement [ʒeneralmɑ̃] adv. Generally; as a rule; généralement parlant, broadly speaking.

généralisable [-lizabl] adj. Generalizable.

généralisateur, trice [-lizatœ:r, tris] adj. Generalizing.
— s. Generalizer.

généralisation [-lizasjɔ̃] f. Generalization; generalizing.

généraliser [-lize] v. tr. (1). To generalize.
— v. pr. Se généraliser, to become generalized, to become widespread, to come into general use.

généralissime [-lisim] m. MILIT. Generalissimo, commander-in-chief.

généraliste [-list] s. MÉD. General practitioner, G.P.

généralité [-lite] f. Generality. ‖ Pl. Generalizations.

générateur, trice [ʒeneratœ:r, tris] adj. Primary (couleur). ‖ Generating (fonction, machine); productive (de, of). ‖ MÉD. Generative (force, organe). ‖ MUS. Son générateur, fundamental tone, generator. ‖ ELECTR. Station génératrice,

generating plant, power-house. ‖ TECHN. Chaudière génératrice, steam-boiler.
— m. TECHN. Boiler; générateur à gaz, gas-producer. ‖ ELECTR. Générateur de courant, current-generator.

génératif, ive [-tif, i:v] adj. Generative; grammaire générative, generative grammar.

génération [-sjɔ̃] f. Generation; generating.

génératrice [-tris] f. MATH. Generating line, generant.

généreusement [ʒenerøzmɑ̃] adv. Generously, bountifully, munificently. ‖ Nobly, bravely.

généreux, euse [-rø, ø:z] adj. Generous (pour, to); bountiful, munificent (personne); fertile (terre); generous (vin). ‖ FIG. Noble (âme).

générique [ʒenerik] adj. Generic.
— m. CINÉM. Production credits and cast.

génériquement [-mɑ̃] adv. Generically.

générosité [ʒenerozite] f. Generosity, bounteousness, munificence. (V. LIBÉRALITÉ.) ‖ Pl. Acts of generosity. ‖ Body, generousness (d'un vin). ‖ FIG. Nobility, magnanimity (d'âme).

Gênes [ʒɛ:n] n. GÉOGR. Genoa. ‖ CULIN. Pain de Gênes, Genoa cake.

genèse [ʒənɛ:z] f. Genesis.

génésique [ʒenezik] adj. Genetic; instinct génésique, reproductive instinct.

genêt [ʒənɛ] m. BOT. Genista, broom; genêt épineux, furze, gorse.

généticien, enne [ʒenetisjɛ̃, ɛn] s. MÉD. Geneticist.

génétique [ʒenetik] adj. MÉD. PHILOS. Genetic.
— f. Genetics.

génétiquement [ʒenetikmɑ̃] adv. MÉD. Genetically.

gêneur [ʒɛnœ:r] s. Intruder; nuisance; spoilsport.

Genève [ʒənɛ:v] n. GÉOGR. Geneva.

genevois, oise [ʒənvwa, a:z] adj., s. Genevan, Genevese.

genévrier [ʒənevrije] m. BOT. Juniper tree.

génial, ale [ʒenjal] adj. Ingenious, clever, inspired; idée géniale, brilliant idea; œuvre géniale, work of genius.

génialement [-mɑ̃] adv. Ingeniously, cleverly. ‖ FAM. In an inspired manner, brilliantly.

géniculation [ʒenikylasjɔ̃] f. Geniculation.

géniculé, ée [-le] adj. Geniculate; kneed. ‖ TECHN. Action géniculée, knee-action.

génie [ʒeni] m. Genius (v. TALENT); homme de génie, man of genius. ‖ Bent (penchant); suivre son génie, to follow one's bent. ‖ Spirit, nature, character (essence). ‖ Genie (démon); pl. genii. ‖ TECHN. Génie civil, civil engineers (personnel); civil engineering (science). ‖ MILIT. Corps du génie, engineers, U. S. engineer corps; soldat du génie, sapper. ‖ NAUT. Génie maritime, naval construction; corps of naval constructors. ‖ FIG. Mauvais génie, evil genius.

genièvre [ʒənjɛ:vr] m. BOT. Juniper-tree (arbre); juniper berry (baie). ‖ CULIN. Gin, Geneva (boisson).

génique [ʒenik] adj. MÉD. Genic.

génisse [ʒenis] f. ZOOL. Heifer.

génital, ale [ʒenital] adj. MÉD. Genital; organes génitaux, genitals, genitalia.

géniteur, trice [-tœ:r, tris] adj. Generating, engendering.
— m. Generator; sire.

génitif, ive [-tif, i:v] adj. Genitive.
— m. GRAMM. Genitive, genitive case.

génito-urinaire [ʒenitoyrinɛ:r] adj. MÉD. Genito-urinary.

génitrice [-tris] f. Genitrix.

génocide [ʒenɔsid] m. Genocide.

génois [ʒenwa] adj., s. GÉOGR. Genoese.

génoise [-nwa:z] f. CULIN. Génoise, Genoese cake.

génome [ʒenom], **génotype** [ʒenɔtip] m. MÉD. Genotype.

genou [ʒənu] (pl. **genoux**) m. Knee; *avoir les genoux en dedans*, to be knock-kneed; *à genoux!*, down on your knees!, kneel down!; *être à genoux*, to be on one's knees (ou) kneeling; *se mettre à genoux*, to kneel; *tenir un enfant sur les genoux*, to hold a child on one's lap. ‖ TECHN. Ball-and socket joint; knee piece. ‖ NAUT. Lower futtock (d'un navire); arm, loom (d'une rame). ‖ FAM. Bald head (crâne chauve).

genouillère [ʒənujɛ:r] f. Knee-pad, knee-guard; knee-piece (d'une armure); knee-cap (d'un cheval); *bottes à genouillère*, top-boots, jack-boots. ‖ TECHN. *Articulation à genouillère*, knuckle- (ou) ball-and-socket joint. ‖ MILIT. Firing-step.

genre [ʒɑ̃:r] m. Genus, family, race, kind (v. ESPÈCE); *le genre humain*, the human race, mankind. ‖ Kind, sort, type, species (v. SORTE); *tous les genres*, all kinds; *étui genre maroquin*, imitation leather case. ‖ Manners, fashion, taste; *avoir un petit genre*, to have quite a way of one's own; *se donner un petit genre*, to cultivate a gimmick; *se donner du genre*, to put on airs. ‖ GRAMM. Gender (d'un substantif). ‖ ARTS. Genre; *peinture de genre*, genre painting. ‖ COMM. Line (d'articles). ‖ PHILOS. Genus.

gens [ʒɛ̃s] f. Gens (dans l'Antiquité romaine).

gens [ʒɑ̃] m. et f. pl. People, persons, folk; men and women; *gens de bien*, respectable people, honest folk; *jeunes gens*, young men, youths; *gens de lettres*, writers, literary people; *gens du monde*, fashionable society, socialites (fam.); *gens ordinaires*, ordinary people; *gens en place*, jobholders; *petites gens*, little people, small fry; *vieilles gens*, old folks. ‖ Servants, domestics; *gens de maison*, household retainers, domestic servants. ‖ MILIT. *Gens d'épée*, soldiers. ‖ NAUT. *Gens de mers*, sailors, seafarers. ‖ THÉÂTR. *Gens de théâtre*, stage folk. ‖ JUR. *Gens de robe*, lawyers.

gent f. invar. Race, tribe, brood; *gent ailée*, feathered tribe.

gentiane [ʒɑ̃sjan] f. BOT. Gentian. ‖ COMM. Gentian-bitters.

gentil, ille [ʒɑ̃ti, i:j] adj. Noble (cavalier); gentle (dame); nice, pretty, pleasing (enfant); kind, amiable, nice, obliging (personne); *gentil avec qqn*, kind to s.o.; *c'est gentil à vous*, it's kind of you.

gentil m. ECCLÉS. Gentile.

gentilhomme [ʒɑ̃tijom] (pl. **gentilshommes** [ʒɑ̃tizɔm]) m. Nobleman, man of gentle birth. ‖ Gentleman.

gentilhommière [-jomjɛ:r] f. Country seat, manor house.

gentillesse [ʒɑ̃tijɛs] f. Niceness, kindness, obligingness (amabilité); prettiness, graciousness, engaging manner (gracieuseté).

gentillet [-jɛ] adj. Rather nice, sweet, engaging.

gentiment [-mɑ̃] adv. Nicely, kindly; sweetly.

gentleman [ʒɑ̃tlman] m. Gentleman, man of breeding.

génuflexion [ʒenyflɛksjɔ̃] f. Genuflexion, kneeling; *faire une génuflexion*, to genuflect, to bend the knee.

géocentrique [-ʒeosɑ̃trik] adj. Geocentric.

géochimie [ʒeoʃimi] f. Geochemistry.

géodésie [ʒeodezi] f. Geodesy.

géodésien [-dezjɛ̃] m. Geodesist.

géodésique [-dezik] adj. Geodetic, geodesic; *point géodésique*, triangulation point.
— f. Geodetic line.

géodynamique [-dinamik] f. Geodynamics.
— adj. Geodynamic.

géographe [-graf] m. GÉOGR. Geographer.

géographie [-grafi] f. GÉOGR. Geography (science); geography book (livre); *géographie économique*, statistical (ou) economic geography; *géographie humaine*, anthropogeography.

géographique [-grafik] adj. GÉOGR. Geographic, geographical; *carte géographique*, map; *dictionnaire géographique*, gazetteer.

géoïde [ʒeoid] m. ASTRON. Geoid.

geôle [ʒo:l] f. Gaol, jail, prison. ‖ Jailer's quarters.

geôlier [-lje] m. Gaoler, jailer, turnkey; warder.

geôlière [-ljɛ:r] f. Female jailer, wardress. ‖ Jailer's wife.

géologie [ʒeolɔʒi] f. Geology; *faire de la géologie*, to geologize.

géologique [-lɔʒik] adj. Geologic, geological.

géologue [-lɔg] m. Geologist.

géomagnétique [-maɲetik] adj. Geomagnetic.

géomagnétisme [-maɲetism] m. Geomagnetism.

géomancie [-mɑ̃si] f. Geomancy.

géomètre [-mɛtr] m. MATH. Geometer, geometrician; *arpenteur géomètre*, land-surveyor. ‖ ZOOL. Geometer, geometrid moth.

géométrie [-metri] f. MATH. Geometry; *géométrie dans l'espace, plane, à trois dimensions*, solid, plane, three-dimensional geometry.

géométrique [-metrik] adj. MATH. Geometric, geometrical.

géométriquement [-metrikmɑ̃] adv. Geometrically.

géomorphologie [-mɔrfɔlɔʒi] f. Geomorphology.

géophysique [-fizik] f. Geophysics.

géopolitique [-pɔlitik] adj. Geopolitical.
— f. Geopolitics.

géorama [-rama] m. Georama.

georgette [ʒɔrʒɛt] m. COMM. Georgette (crèpe).

géorgien, enne [ʒeorʒjɛ̃, ɛn] adj., s. GÉOGR. Georgian.

géorgique [-ʒik] adj. Georgic.
— f. pl. The Georgics (de Virgile).

géostationnaire [ʒeostasjɔnɛ:r] adj. ASTRONAUT. Geostationary.

géostatique [ʒeostatik] f. Geostatics.

géosynclinal [-sɛ̃klinal] m. GÉOL. Geosyncline.

géothermie [-tɛrmi] f. Geothermics.

géothermique [-tɛrmik] adj. Geothermal; *gradient géothermique*, geothermal gradient; *énergie géothermique*, geothermal energy.

géotropisme [-trɔpism] m. Geotropism.

gérance [ʒerɑ̃s] f. Managership, administratorship; management, direction (d'un commerce); editorship (d'un journal).

géranium [ʒeranjom] m. BOT. Geranium; pelargonium.

gérant [ʒerɑ̃] m. Manager, director; managing director (d'une société); *rédacteur-gérant*, managing editor.

gérante [-rɑ̃:t] f. Manageress, directress; managing directress.

gerbage [ʒɛrba:ʒ] m. AGRIC. Binding, sheaving.

gerbe [ʒɛrb] f. AGRIC. Sheaf (de blé); spray (de fleurs). ‖ Spray, column (d'eau); shower (d'étincelles). ‖ MILIT. Cone of fire. ‖ BLAS. Garb.

gerber [-be] v. tr. (1). AGRIC. To bind, to sheave (le blé). ‖ TECHN. To stack, to pile (des tonneaux). ‖ MILIT. To bombard (un fort).
— v. intr. AGRIC. To tiller, to stool. ‖ To spray (étincelles).

gerbier [-bje] m. Stack (de blé); barn (grenier).

gerboise [ʒɛrbwa:z] f. ZOOL. Jerboa.

gercement [ʒɛrsmɑ̃] m. Cracking (du bois, du sol). ‖ MÉD. Chapping (de la peau).

gercer [-se] v. tr., intr. (6). To crack (le bois, le sol). ‖ MÉD. To chap (la peau).
— v. pr. Se gercer, to crack (bois). ‖ MÉD. To chap (peau).

gerçure [-sy:r] f. Crack, cleft, chink, fissure,

flaw (du bois) ; hair-crack, hair-line (du métal). ‖ MÉD. Chap (de la peau).

gérer [ʒere] v. tr. (5). To conduct (un commerce) ; to direct, to manage, to run (un hôtel, un journal) ; to administer (une tutelle) ; *mal gérer,* to mismanage.

gerfaut [ʒɛrfo] m. ZOOL. Gerfalcon, U. S. gyrfalcon.

gériatrie [ʒerjatri] f. MÉD. Geriatrics.

gériatrique [-trik] adj. MÉD. Geriatric.

germain, aine [ʒɛrmɛ̃, ɛn] adj. Germanic, Teutonic.
— s. German, Teuton.

germain adj. German, first (cousin) ; *cousin issu de germain,* second cousin, cousin once removed.

germanique [ʒɛrmanik] adj. GÉOGR. Germanic, Teutonic ; German (empire).
— m. GRAMM. Germanic (langue).

germanisant, ante [-nizɑ̃, ɑ̃:t] adj. Germanizing.
— s. Student of Germanic languages.

germanisation [-nizasjɔ̃] f. Germanization, Germanizing ; Teutonization.

germaniser [-nize] v. tr. (1). To Germanize ; to Teutonize.

germanisme [-nism] m. Germanism ; Teutonism. ‖ GRAMM. German phrase or idiom.

germaniste [-nist] s. Germanist, German scholar.

germanium [-njɔm] m. CHIM. Germanium.

germanophile [-nɔfil] adj., s. Germanophile.

germanophilie [-nɔfili] f. Germanophilia.

germanophobe [-nɔfɔb] adj. Germanophobic.
— s. Germanophobe.

germanophobie [-nɔfɔbi] f. Germanophobia.

germe [ʒɛrm] m. MÉD. Germ. ‖ BOT. Eye (d'une pomme de terre). ‖ ZOOL. Tread (d'un œuf). ‖ FIG. Principle, source, origin ; seed (de la corruption) ; germ (d'une idée) ; *étouffer dans le germe,* to nip in the bud.

germer [-me] v. intr. (1). AGRIC. To germinate ; to sprout, to shoot, to spring up. ‖ FIG. To germinate, to spring up (idée).

germicide [-misid] m. Germicide.

germinal, ale [-minal] adj. Germinal ; *feuille germinale,* seed-leaf.
— m. Germinal, seventh month in French Republican calendar (March-April).

germinateur, trice [-minatœ:r, tris] adj. Germinative.

germinatif, ive [-minatif, i:v] adj. Germinative, germinal.

germination [-minasjɔ̃] f. Germination.

germoir [-mwa:r] m. BOT. Hot-bed, seed-bed. ‖ Malt-house, malt-floor (malterie).

gérondif [ʒerɔ̃dif] m. GRAMM. Gerund, gerundial infinitive ; *au gérondif,* in the gerundive.

gérontocratie [ʒerɔ̃tɔkrasi] f. Gerontocracy.

gérontologie [ʒerɔ̃tɔlɔʒi] f. Gerontology, geriatrics.

gésier [ʒezje] m. ZOOL. Gizzard. ‖ FAM. Breadbasket. (V. GILET.)

gésir [ʒezi:r] v. intr (57). To lie, to be lying ; *ci-gît,* here lies.

gestaltisme [gɛstaltism] m. PHILOS. Gestalt psychology.

Gestapo [gɛstapo] m. Gestapo.

gestation [ʒɛstasjɔ̃] f. MÉD. Gestation ; cyesis.

geste [ʒɛst] m. Gesture, action, motion, movement (v. MIMIQUE) ; wave (de la main) ; shrug (de résignation) ; *écarter qqn d'un geste,* to motion (ou) to wave s.o. away ; *faire un geste,* to gesticulate, to gesture ; *joindre le geste à la parole,* to suit the action to the word. ‖ FIG. Act, gesture ; *faire un beau geste,* to do the handsome thing (fam.).

geste f. Heroic achievement, deed (exploit) ; *faits et gestes,* doings, deeds (actions) ; behaviour (conduite).

gesticulaire [-tikylɛ:r] adj. Gesticulatory ; of gesture.

gesticulant, ante [-tikylɑ̃, ɑ̃:t] adj. Gesticulating, making gestures.

gesticulation [-tikylasjɔ̃] f. Gesticulation, gesticulating.

gesticuler [-tikyle] v. intr. (1). To gesticulate, to gesture.

gestion [ʒɛstjɔ̃] f. Administration, conduct, management (d'un commerce) ; administration, care (des deniers publics) ; *mauvaise gestion,* mismanagement, maladministration. ‖ Administratorship, stewardship (fonctions).

gestionnaire [-tjɔnɛ:r] adj. JUR. *Administration gestionnaire,* administration by agent.
— m. Manager, administrator ; official in charge (d'un service gouvernemental).
— f. Manageress, administratrix.

gestuel, elle [ʒɛstɥɛl] adj. Gestural. ‖ ARTS. *Peinture gestuelle,* action painting.

geyser [ʒezɛ:r] m. Geyser.

Ghana [gana] m. GÉOGR. Ghana.

ghanéen, enne [-neɛ̃, ɛn] adj., s. GÉOGR. Ghanaian.

ghetto [gɛto] m. Ghetto.

ghilde [gild] f. V. GILDE.

gibbeux, euse [ʒibbø, ø:z] adj. Gibbous, gibbose, convex, protuberant. ‖ MÉD. Humped, hunchbacked (bossu).

gibbon [ʒibbɔ̃] m. ZOOL. Gibbon, gibbon-ape.

gibbosité [ʒibbozite] f. Gibbosity, swelling, protuberance. ‖ MÉD. Hump. ‖ ASTRON. Gibbosity.

gibecière [ʒibsjɛ:r] f. Game-bag. (V. CARNASSIÈRE.) ‖ Satchel. (V. SACOCHE.) ‖ Conjuror's pocket, bag (d'escamoteur).

gibelin, ine [ʒiblɛ̃, in] adj., s. † Ghibelline.

gibelotte [ʒiblɔt] f. CULIN. Rabbit-stew, fricassee of hare.

giberne [ʒibɛrn] f. MILIT. Cartridge-pouch.

gibet [ʒibɛ] m. Gibbet, gallows. ‖ ECCLÉS. Tree, cross (croix). ‖ TECHN. Shear-legs (de puisatier).

gibier [ʒibje] m. Game ; *gibier à plume,* winged game ; *gibier à poil,* ground-game, venison ; *gros, menu gibier,* big, small game. ‖ FIG. *Gibier de potence,* gallows-bird, jailbird.

giboulée [ʒibule] f. Sudden shower (ou) downpour ; *giboulées de Mars,* April showers. ‖ FAM. Drubbing, shower (de coups). [V. GRÊLE.]

giboyer [ʒibwaje] v. intr. (9 a). To shoot, to hunt small game.

giboyeux, euse [-jø, ø:z] adj. Abounding in game, well-stocked with game ; *pays giboyeux,* good game country.

gibus [ʒibys] m. Crush- (ou) opera-hat, folding hat, gibus.

giclée [ʒikle] f. Squirt, spurt.

giclement [ʒikləmɑ̃] m. Splashing up, squelching (de la boue) ; gushing, squirting, spouting, spurting (en jet).

gicler [ʒikle] v. intr. (1). To splash up, to squelch (boue) ; to gush, to squirt, to spurt, to spout (en jet).

gicleur [ʒiklœ:r] m. Spray nozzle ; atomizer. ‖ AUTOM. Nozzle, jet.

gifle [ʒifl] f. Smack, slap in the face.

gifler [ʒifle] v. tr. (1). *Gifler qqn,* to smack (ou) to slap s.o.'s face ; to box s.o.'s ears.

gigantesque [ʒigɑ̃tɛsk] adj. Gigantic, giant.

gigantisme [-tism] m. MÉD. Gigantism, giantism.

gigogne [ʒigɔɲ] f. Gigogne (marionnette) ; *mère Gigogne,* Old Woman who lived in a shoe. ‖ COMM. *Table gigogne,* nest of tables. ‖ NAUT. *Bateau gigogne,* landing-craft carrier ; *vaisseau gigogne,* mother ship.

gigolo [ʒigɔlo] m. Pop. Gigolo, fancy man.

gigot [ʒigo] m. CULIN. Leg of mutton. ‖ *Manches gigot,* leg of-mutton sleeves.

gigoter [ʒigɔte] v. intr. (1). To kick, to fling about (jambes) ; to jig, to dance, to shake a leg (personne) ; to fidget (s'agiter).

gigue [ʒig] f. ZOOL. Hind leg ; haunch (d'un chevreuil, d'un sanglier). ‖ MUS. Jig. ‖ FAM. Pl. Pins.

gilde [gild] f. Guild, gild.

gilet [ʒilɛ] m. Waistcoat, vest ; *gilet de corps,* singlet ; *gilet fermé, ouvert,* high-cut, low-cut waistcoat. ‖ NAUT. *Gilet de sauvetage,* life-jacket. ‖ SPORTS. *Gilet d'armes,* fencing-jacket. ‖ FAM. Bread-basket ; *se remplir le gilet,* to stuff oneself.

giletier [-ltje] m. Waistcoat-maker.

giletière [-ltjɛ:r] f. Albert watch-chain (ou) watch-guard ; albert.

gin [dʒin] m. Gin.

gindre [ʒɛ̃dr] m. Baker's man, journeyman-baker.

gingembre [ʒɛ̃ʒɑ̃:br] m. BOT., CULIN. Ginger.

gingival, ale [ʒɛ̃ʒival] adj. MÉD. Gingival.

gingivite [-vit] f. MÉD. Gingivitis.

gipsy [ʒipsi] m. Gipsy.

girafe [ʒiraf] f. ZOOL. Giraffe. ‖ THÉÂTR. Traveller (du micro).

girandole [ʒirɑ̃dɔl] f. Girandole, chandelier. ‖ Cluster (de fleurs). ‖ BOT. *Girandole d'eau,* water horse-tail.

girasol [ʒirasɔl] m. Girasole.

giration [-sjɔ̃] f. Gyration. ‖ NAUT. Turning.

giratoire [-twa:r] adj. Gyratory ; rotary (carrefour) ; *sens giratoire,* roundabout.

giravion [ʒiravjɔ̃] m. AVIAT. Gyroplane.

girl [gœ:rl] f. THÉÂTR. Chorus-girl.

girofle [ʒirɔfl] m. BOT. Clove.

giroflée [ʒirɔfle] f. BOT. Stock, gillyflower (des jardins) ; wallflower (des murailles). ‖ FAM. *Giroflée à cinq feuilles,* slap in the face.

giroflier [-flje] m. BOT. Clove-tree.

girolle [ʒirɔl] f. BOT., CULIN. Mushroom, chanterelle.

giron [ʒirɔ̃] m. Lap. (V. SEIN.) ‖ Tread, treadboard (de marche d'escalier). ‖ NAUT. Loom (d'une rame). ‖ BLAS. Gyron. ‖ FIG. Bosom (de l'Eglise).

girondin [ʒirɔ̃dɛ̃] m. Girondist.

girouette [ʒirwɛt] f. Weathercock, vane. ‖ FAM. Weathercock (personne).

gisant, ante [ʒizɑ̃, ɑ̃:t] adj. Felled, fallen (bois) ; lying, recumbent (corps). ‖ NAUT. Stranded (vaisseau).
— m. ARTS. Recumbent effigy.

gisement [ʒizmɑ̃] m. Layer, bed, deposit, stratum ; lode, seam (de minerai) ; *gisement de charbon, de pétrole,* coal-, oil-field ; *gisement houiller,* coal-seam. ‖ NAUT. Trend (d'une côte) ; position, lie (d'une île) ; bearing (d'un vaisseau).

gît [ʒi]. V. GÉSIR.

gitan, ane [ʒitɑ̃, an] adj., s. Gipsy.

gitane [ʒitan] f. Gitane, popular brand of French cigarettes.

gîte [ʒit] m. Lodging, home ; *sans gîte,* homeless. ‖ Halting-place, accommodation (de voyageur). ‖ Shelter, refuge (abri) ; lie, cover, couch (d'animal) ; form (de lièvre). ‖ TECHN. Bed, stratum, deposit (de minerai). ‖ ARCHIT. Joist, sleeper (de plancher). ‖ Nether millstone (de moulin). ‖ CULIN. *Gîte à la noix,* silverside, U. S. top round. ‖ **Gîte-gîte,** m. CULIN. Gravy-beef.
— f. NAUT. Bed (d'un navire échoué) ; heel, list, tilt (d'un navire en perdition).

gîter [-te] v. intr. (1). To lie, to couch, to lair (animal) ; to perch (oiseau). ‖ NAUT. To list, to heel, to lie over. ‖ FAM. To lodge, to put up.

givrage [ʒivra:ʒ] m. Frosting. ‖ AVIAT. Icing.

givre [ʒi:vr] m. Rime, hoar-frost. ‖ Flaw (des pierres précieuses).

givré, ée [ʒivre] adj. Frosted, rimy, rimed.

givrer v. tr. (1). To frost, to ice, to cover with rime.

givreux, euse [-vrø, ø:z] adj. Flawy (pierre).

glabre [gla:br] adj. Glabrous. (V. IMBERBE.) ‖ Beardless, clean-shaven (visage).

glaçage [glasa:ʒ] m. Glazing, glossing ; surfacing (du papier). ‖ CULIN. Icing, frosting.

glaçant, ante [-sɑ̃, ɑ̃:t] adj. Chilly, glacial, icy (accueil, vent).

glace [glas] f. Ice ; *glace flottante,* drift ice ; *pris dans les glaces,* icebound. ‖ Freezing-point (au thermomètre). ‖ Glass, plate-glass (verre) ; *une glace,* sheet of plate-glass ; *glace Securit,* safety-glass. ‖ Looking-glass, mirror (miroir) ; *glace de cheminée,* chimney glass ; *gallerie des glaces,* Hall of Mirrors. ‖ CULIN. Ice, ice cream (à la crème) ; icing (glaçage). ‖ AUTOM. Window (de portière). ‖ TECHN. Flaw (défaut). ‖ FIG. *Rompre la glace,* to break the ice.

glacé, ée [-se] adj. Frozen, freezing (eau) ; ice-cold, cold as ice (main) ; chill, biting, icy (vent) ; *glacé jusqu'aux os,* chilled to the bone. ‖ Smooth, polished, glacé (cuir) ; glazed (fil, papier) ; glossy (photographie) ; watered (soie). ‖ CULIN. Iced (café) ; candied, crystallized, glacé (fruits) ; iced, covered with sugar-icing (gâteau) ; polished (riz) ; glazed (viande). ‖ FIG. Frigid, chilly (accueil) ; stony (regard).
— m. Gloss (d'une étoffe) ; glaze (du papier).

glacer [-se] v. tr. (5). To freeze, to chill. ‖ To surface, to glaze (du papier) ; to gloss (une photographie) ; to water (de la soie). ‖ CULIN. To ice (une boisson) ; to crystallize, to candy (des fruits) ; to glaze (une galantine) ; to ice, to frost (un gâteau) ; to polish (du riz). ‖ FIG. To chill, to dispirit, to freeze, to dampen (l'enthousiasme) ; *glacer le sang à qqn,* to chill s.o.'s blood.

glacerie [-sri] f. TECHN. Glass-making ; glass factory. ‖ Ice-making. ‖ CULIN. Ice-cream trade.

glaceur [-sœ:r] m. TECHN. Glazing-machine. ‖ Glazer (personne).

glaciaire [-sjɛ:r] adj. Glacial ; *boue glaciaire,* glacier mud ; *époque glaciaire,* ice age.

glacial, ale [-sjal] (pl. **glacials**) adj. Glacial, icy (température) ; frosty, frigid, chilling, bitter (vent) ; frigid (zone). ‖ FIG. Icy, chilly, frigid (accueil).

glacialement [-sjalmɑ̃] adv. Glacially, icily.

glaciation [-sjasjɔ̃] f. Freezing, turning to ice. ‖ GÉOL. Glaciation, glacial period, ice age.

glacier [-sje] m. Glacier, ice-field. ‖ Maker of plate-glass and mirrors. ‖ Ice-man (vendeur de glace en vrac). ‖ CULIN. Ice-cream dealer. ‖ **Glacier-confiseur,** m. CULIN. Confectioner and ice-cream vendor.

glacière [-sjɛ:r] f. Ice-house, ice-pit (dépôt) ; ice-box, ice-chest, refrigerator (réfrigérateur) ; freezer (sorbetière). ‖ CH. DE F. Refrigerator van (ou) U. S. car.

glaciologie [-sjolɔʒi] f. Glaciology.

glacis [-si] m. Slope, bank (d'un jardin). ‖ MILIT. Glacis. ‖ ARTS. Glaze, scumble (d'un tableau).

glaçon [-sɔ̃] m. Block (ou) cake of ice (en général) ; ice-floe (flottant) ; icicle (au bord d'un toit). ‖ Pl. Drift-ice. ‖ FIG. Icicle, iceberg (personne).

glaçure [-sy:r] f. ARTS. Glaze ; glazing.

gladiateur [gladjatœ:r] m. † Gladiator.

glaïeul [glajœl] m. BOT. Gladiolus.

glaire [glɛ:r] f. MÉD. Mucus, phlegm, glair. ‖ CULIN. Glair, white of egg. ‖ TECHN. Flaw (dans un diamant) ; glair (de reliure).

glairer [glɛre] v. tr. (1). To glair (une reliure).

glaireux, euse [-rø, ø:z] adj. Glaireous, glairy.

glaise [glɛ:z] f. Clay, loam (terre). ‖ Pug, pugging (à briques). ‖ Puddle (pour enduit).

glaiser [glɛze] v. tr. (1). To clay, to improve with clay (une terre). ‖ TECHN. To pug, to puddle (les berges d'un canal).

glaiseux, euse [glɛzø, ø:z] adj. Clayey, loamy.

glaisière [-zjɛ:r] f. TECHN. Clay-pit.

glaive [glɛ:v] m. Glaive, sword. ‖ ZOOL. Swordfish. ‖ FIG. Sword.

glanage [glana:ʒ] m. AGRIC. Gleaning.

gland [glɑ̃] m. Tassel (de bonnet, de dragonne); *à gland*, tasselled. ‖ BOT. Acorn (de chêne). ‖ Pl. Mast (nourriture de porcs). ‖ MÉD. Glans. ‖ ZOOL. *Gland de mer*, acorn-shell, U. S. acorn barnacle.

glande [glɑ̃d] f. BOT. Gland, kernel. ‖ MÉD. Gland. ‖ ZOOL. *Glande venimeuse*, poison-gland.

glander [glɑ̃de] v. intr. (1). POP. To mooch (ou) lounge (ou) loaf around.

glandeur, euse [-dœ:r, ø:z] s. POP. Moocher, loafer, layabout.

glandouiller [-duje] v. intr. (1). V. GLANDER.

glandulaire [-dylɛ:r] adj. MÉD. Glandular.

glane [glan] f. Gleaning (action); handful, small sheaf (de blé); string (d'oignons); cluster, bunch (de poires). ‖ FAM. Pl. Gleanings, pickings.

glaner [-ne] v. tr. (1). To glean, to gather. ‖ FAM. To pick and steal, to pilfer.

glaneur [-nœ:r] s. AGRIC. Gleaner.

glanure [-ny:r] f. AGRIC. Gleanings.

glapir [glapi:r] v. intr. (2). To yap, to yelp (chien); to bark (renard). ‖ FAM. To yelp (personne).

glapissant, ante [-pisɑ̃, ɑ̃:t] adj. Yelping, yapping (chien); barking (renard). ‖ FAM. Yelping (voix).

glapissement [-pismɑ̃] m. Yapping, yelping.

glas [gla] m. Knell, passing-bell, tolling; *pour qui sonne le glas*, for whom the bell tolls.

glass [glas] m. FAM. Glassful (contenu); glass (verre).

glatir [glati:r] v. intr. (2). To scream (aigle).

glaucome [gloko:m] m. MÉD. Glaucoma.

glauque [glok] adj. Glaucous, sea-green.

glaviot [glavjo] m. POP. Gob.

glèbe [glɛb] f. Clod, sod, glebe; *attaché à la glèbe*, bound to the soil.

glène f. NAUT. Coil.

gléner [glene] v. tr. (5). NAUT. To coil.

glinglin [glɛ̃glɛ̃] m. FAM. *Jusqu'à la Saint-Glinglin*, till hell freezes over.

glissade [glisad] f. Slip, slipping; slide, sliding. ‖ Landslide (de terrain). ‖ Glide, glissade (de danse). ‖ SPORTS. Glissade; *faire des glissades*, to glissade. ‖ MUS. Glissando, slide. ‖ AVIAT. *Glissade sur l'aile*, side-slip; *glissade sur la queue*, tail-dive. ‖ AUTOM. Skid.

glissant, ante [-sɑ̃, ɑ̃:t] adj. Slippery (route, terrain). ‖ Sliding (porte); *joint glissant*, slip-joint. ‖ FIG. Slippery, treacherous (affaire).

glissé [-se] m. Glide (en dansant).

glissement [-smɑ̃] m. Slip, slipping; slide, sliding; *glissement de terrain*, landslide. ‖ Gliding, glide (pas). ‖ TECHN. Creeping (d'une bande transporteuse). ‖ FIN. *Glissement en Bourse*, falling away, sagging of the Stock market. ‖ FIG. Falling off, deterioration (des mœurs).

glisser [-se] v. intr. (1). To glide (sur l'eau); to slide, to slip (sur la glace). ‖ To skid (déraper). ‖ To be slippery (plancher, rue). ‖ To glance off, to graze (coup d'épée). ‖ AVIAT. To side-slip (sur l'aile); to tail-dive (sur la queue). ‖ TECHN. To creep (bande transporteuse). ‖ SPORTS. *Se laisser glisser*, to glissade down (sur la neige). ‖ FIG. To make no impression (*sur*, on) [qqn]. ‖ FAM. *Se laisser glisser*, to slip one's cable (mourir).
— v. tr. To slide; to slip (qqch.). ‖ To drop, to whisper (un mot); *impossible de glisser un mot*, I couldn't get a word in edgeways.
— v. pr. **Se glisser**, to glide, to steal (se faufiler); to worm one's way (s'insinuer). ‖ FIG. To creep (erreur).

glisseur [-sœ:r] m. Slider. ‖ AVIAT. Glider. ‖

NAUT. Hydroplane, speed-boat. ‖ TECHN. Slide-block.

glissière [-sjɛ:r] f. Slide, groove; *porte à glissières*, sliding-door. ‖ Chute. (V. GLISSOIR.) ‖ TECHN. Slipper, guide, slide-bar; recoil (d'un fusil). ‖ Pl. Shears (d'un tour mécanique). ‖ NAUT. *Banc à glissières*, sliding seat. ‖ AVIAT. Cable-guide. ‖ AUTOM. Window-guide.

glissoir [-swa:r] m. Slide, chute (conduit incliné); flume (canal). ‖ TECHN. Slide, sliding-block.

glissoire [-swa:r] f. Slide (sur la glace).

global, ale [global] adj. Total (capital, montant); entire, aggregate, gross (déplacement, poids); global (méthode); lump (paiement, somme); *total global*, sum (ou) grand total.

globalement [-mɑ̃] adv. In the mass (ou) lump.

globe [glɔb] m. Globe (v. SPHÈRE); orb (du soleil); *faire le tour du globe*, to circle the earth; *globe terrestre*, globe. ‖ Light bulb (de lampe); glass cover (de pendule); *sous globe*, under glass. ‖ Ball (boule); *globe de feu*, fire-ball. ‖ MÉD. Eye-ball (de l'œil). ‖ BLAS. Mound. ‖ **Globe-trotter**, m. Globe-trotter, world traveller.

globulaire [-bylɛ:r] adj. Globular.
— f. BOT. Globe-daisy, globularia.

globule [-byl] m. Globule (d'air); drop (d'eau). ‖ Globule, capsule, pill (pilule). ‖ MÉD. Globule, cell, corpuscle (du sang); *globules blancs*, leucocytes, white blood cells.

globuleux, euse [-bylø, ø:z] adj. Globular; globulous, globulose.

globuline [-bylin] f. MÉD. Globulin.

gloire [glwa:r] f. Glory; fame (v. RÉPUTATION); *rendre gloire à*, to glorify. ‖ Boast, pride; vain-glory (orgueil); *se faire gloire de*, to glory in, to pride oneself on. ‖ Splendour, glory (splendeur). ‖ ARTS. Gloriole, glory. (V. AURÉOLE.) ‖ FAM. *Pour la gloire*, for love, for nothing.

glorieusement [glɔrjøzmɑ̃] adv. Gloriously. ‖ Proudly, vaingloriously (orgueilleusement)ː

glorieux, euse [-rjø, ø:z] adj. Glorious; illustrious (illustre). ‖ Glorious, bright, splendid (beau). ‖ Proud, vainglorious, conceited. (V. VANITEUX.) ‖ ECCLÉS. Glorious (corps).
— m. Boaster, braggart; conceited person; *faire le glorieux*, to swagger.

glorificateur, trice [glɔrifikatœ:r, tris] s. Praiser, glorifier, panegyrist.

glorification [-kasjɔ̃] f. Glorification, glorifying.

glorifier [-fje] v. tr. (1). To glorify, to praise; to apotheosize, to deify.
— v. pr. **Se glorifier**, to glory (de, in); to boast (de, of); to brag.

gloriole [glɔrjɔl] f. Vainglory, petty vanity; *par pure gloriole*, out of sheer conceit.

glose [glo:z] f. Gloss, explanatory note (v. COMMENTAIRE); *glose marginale*, marginal note. ‖ Comment, remark, criticism. (V. CRITIQUE.)

gloser [gloze] v. tr. (1). To censure (un auteur); to gloss, to expound, to comment upon (un texte).
— v. intr. To criticize, to find fault (*sur*, with), to carp (*sur*, at).

glossaire [glɔsɛ:r] m. Glossary.

glossateur [-satœ:r] m. Glossator, glossarist.

glossine [-sin] f. ZOOL. Glossina, tsetse fly.

glottal, ale [glɔtal] adj. Glottal.

glotte [glɔt] f. MÉD. Glottis; *coup de glotte*, glottal stop.

glottique [-tik] adj. MÉD. Glottal.

glouglou [gluglu] m. FAM. Glug-glug, gurgle (d'une bouteille); gobble, gobbling (d'un dindon).

glouglouter [-te] v. intr. (1). To gurgle (bouteille); to gobble (dindon).

gloussant, ante [glusɑ̃, ɑ̃:t] adj. Chuckling (personne); clucking (poule).

gloussement [-smɑ̃] m. Gobble, gobbling (du dindon); cluck, clucking (de la poule). ‖ FAM. Chuckle, chuckling (d'une personne).

glousser [-se] v. intr. To gobble (dindon); to cluck (poule). ‖ FAM. To chuckle (personne).

glouton, onne [glutɔ̃, ɔn] adj. Gluttonous, greedy.
— m. Glutton, gormandizer. ‖ ZOOL. Glutton.

gloutonnement [-tɔnmɑ̃] adv. Gluttonously, greedily.

gloutonnerie [-tɔnri] f. Gluttony, greediness.

gloxinia [gloksinja] m. BOT. Gloxinia.

glu [gly] f. Bird-lime; *prendre à la glu*, to lime, to take with bird-lime. ‖ FIG. Trap, snare.

gluant, ante [glyɑ̃, ɑ̃ːt] adj. Sticky, gluey, gummy; glutinous. (V. POISSEUX.)

gluau [glyo] m. Lime-twig, bird-snare.

glucide [glysid] m. MÉD. Carbohydrate.

glucine [glysin] f. CHIM. Glucinium oxide, beryllia.

glucinium [-njɔm] m. CHIM. Glucinium.

glucose [glykoːz] m. CHIM. Glucose.

gluer [glɥe] v. tr. (1). To lime (des gluaux). ‖ To make gluey (ou) sticky (les mains).

glutamate [glytamat] m. Glutamate.

gluten [glytɛn] m. Gluten.

glycémie [glisemi] f. MÉD. Glycaemia; blood-sugar.

glycérine [gliserin] f., **glycérol** [-rol] m. Glycerine, glycerol.

glycine [glisin] f. BOT. Wistaria, wisteria. ‖ CHIM. Glycine.

glycogène [glikɔʒɛn] m. CHIM. Glycogen.

glycogénique [-ʒenik] adj. MÉD. Glycogenic.

glycol [glikɔl] m. CHIM. Glycol.

glyptique [gliptik] f. ARTS. Glyptography.

G.M.T. [ʒeɛmte] Abrév. de *Greenwich Mean Time*, GMT.

gnaf [ɲaf] m. POP. Cobbler.

gnangnan [ɲɑ̃ɲɑ̃] adj. FAM. Namby-pamby, mawkish (livre); lackadaisical (personne).
— m. FAM. Dawdler, slow-coach.

gnaule [ɲol] f. V. GNOLE.

gneiss [gnɛs] m. GÉOL. Gneiss.

gnocchi [ɲɔki] m. CULIN. Gnocchi.

gnognote [ɲɔɲɔt] f. FAM. Trash, rubbish, junk.

gnole [ɲɔl] f. POP. Booze, hooch, U. S. hard liquor.

gnome [gnoːm] m. Gnome.

gnomique [gnɔmik] adj. Gnomic.

gnon [ɲɔ̃] m. POP. Biff, U. S. bop. (V. BEIGNE.)

gnose [gnoːz] f. PHILOS. Gnosis. ‖ ECCLÉS. Gnosticism.

gnosticisme [gnɔstisism] m. PHILOS. Gnosticism.

gnostique [-tik] adj., m. PHILOS. Gnostic.

gnou [gnu] m. ZOOL. Gnu.

go [go] adv. *Tout de go*, right off, straight off, straightway.

goal [gol] m. SPORTS. Goal (but); goalkeeper (gardien).

gobelet [gɔblɛ] m. Mug, cup, goblet (v. TIMBALE); screw-cap top (d'une thermos); *gobelet gradué*, measuring cup; *verre gobelet*, tumbler. ‖ † Buttery. ‖ BOT. Acorn cup. ‖ TECHN. Rocket-case.

gobeleterie [-tri] f. Making (ou) selling of hollow-glass-ware (fabrication ou vente); hollow-glass-ware (marchandise).

gobeletier [-tje] m. Maker of hollow-glass-ware (fabricant); dealer in hollow-glass-ware (marchand).

gobe-mouches [gɔbmuʃ] m. ZOOL. Fly-catcher; king-bird. ‖ BOT. Fly-trap, sundew. ‖ FAM. Gull, U. S. sucker (personne crédule).

gober [gɔbe] v. tr. (1). To suck (un œuf). ‖ FAM. To be gullible; to swallow, U. S. to be a sucker for (qqch.); to have a strong liking for, to be taken with (qqn); *gober le morceau*, to swallow the bait, hook, line and sinker.

— v. pr. **Se gober**, FAM. To be swollen-headed (ou) U. S. swellheaded; to fancy oneself.

goberger (se) [sɔgɔbɛrʒe] v. pr. (7). To guzzle.

gobeur [gɔbœːr] m. Swallower, gulper. ‖ FIG. Gullible person, gull, U. S. sucker.

godage [gɔdaːʒ] m. Cockling (du papier); bagging (d'un pantalon); wrinkling, puckering (d'un tissu).

godaille [gɔdaːj] f. POP. Drinking, tippling, swilling, guzzling (boisson); feast, revel, guzzle (nourriture).

godailler [gɔdaje] v. intr. (1). FAM. To guzzle, to tipple, to swill (boire); to feast, to gormandize, to guzzle (manger).

godailler v. intr. V. GODER.

godailleur [-jœːr] m. FAM. Guzzler, swiller, tippler (buveur); guzzler (mangeur).

godasse [gɔdas] f. POP. Beetle-crusher, U. S. gunboat, clodhopper, puddlejumper.

godelureau [gɔdlyro] m. FAM. Coxcomb, popinjay. (V. GALANTIN.)

goder [gɔde] v. intr. (1). To bag (pantalon); to cockle (papier); to pucker, to wrinkle, to ruck up (tissu).

godet [gɔdɛ] m. Drinking-bowl, small mug, cup, noggin (à boire); saucer (à couleurs); bowl (d'une pipe). ‖ Pucker, wrinkle (faux pli). ‖ Flare, gore (d'une jupe en forme); *jupe à godets*, flared (ou) gored skirt. ‖ TECHN. *Godet graisseur*, lubricating cup; *godet à huile*, waste-oil cup. ‖ BOT. Calyx (d'une fleur); cup (d'un gland).

godiche [gɔdiʃ] adj. Simple, U. S. dumb (benêt); awkward, clumsy, gawky (maladroit).
— s. Simpleton, fool, booby, U. S. dumbbell (benêt); gawk, lout, clumsy fool (maladroit).

godille [gɔdiːj] f. NAUT. Stern-oar.

godiller [gɔdije] v. tr. (1). NAUT. To single-scull.

godillot [gɔdijo] m. MILIT. Army boot; hob-nailed boot. ‖ POP. Beetle-crusher, U. S. gunboat.

godron [gɔdrɔ̃] m. ARCHIT. Gadroon. ‖ TECHN. Goffering-iron (fer à gaufrer).

goéland [gɔelɑ̃] m. ZOOL. Sea-gull.

goélette [gɔelɛt] f. NAUT. Schooner (bateau); *barque goélette*, barquantine. ‖ NAUT. Trysail, spencer (voile). ‖ ZOOL. Sea-swallow.

goémon [gɔemɔ̃] m. BOT. Seaweed.

gogo [gogo] m. POP. Gull, U. S. sucker.

gogo (à) [agogo] loc. adv. FAM. Galore, in abundance; *argent à gogo*, money to burn.

goguenard, arde [gɔgnaːr, ard] adj. Jeering, bantering, scoffing, mocking.
— m. Jeerer, scoffer, mocker, banterer.

goguenarder [gɔgnarde] v. intr. (1). To jeer, to banter, to scoff.

goguenardise [-diz] f. Banter, bantering, jeering.

goguenots [gɔgno], **gogues** [gɔg] m. pl. POP. Jakes, U.S. john.

goguette [gɔgɛt] f. FAM. Lively frolic (festin); merry jest (propos); *en goguette*, on the spree, U.S. on a bender.

goï [gɔj] m. (pl. *goïm*). V. GOY.

goinfre [gwɛ̃ːfr] m. Gormandizer, gobbler, guzzler; greedy-guts (pop.). [V. GLOUTON.]

goinfrer [gwɛ̃fre] v. intr. (1). FAM. To gormandize, to guzzle, to gorge. (V. BAFRER.)
— v. pr. **Se goinfrer**, to stuff oneself, to guzzle.

goinfrerie [-frəri] f. Gluttony, guzzling.

goitre [gwaːtr] m. MÉD. Goitre.

goitreux, euse [-trø, øːz] adj. MÉD. Goitrous.
— s. MÉD. Goitrous person.

golden [gɔldɛn] f. BOT. Golden delicious.

golf [gɔlf] m. SPORTS. Golf (jeu); golf-course, golf-links (terrain); *joueur de golf*, golfer.

golfe m. GÉOGR. Gulf, bay; *golfe de Gascogne*, Bay of Biscay. ‖ MÉD. Sinus; bulb.

golfeur, euse [gɔlfœːr, øːz] s. SPORTS. Golfer.

Gomina [gɔmina] f. Solid brilliantine, hair dressing.

gominé, ée [-ne] adj. Plastered down (chevelure).
gommage [gɔma:ʒ] m. Gumming. || Erasing, rubbing-out (effaçage). || TECHN. Sticking, gumming (d'un piston, d'une soupape).
gomme [gɔm] f. Gum. || Eraser, rubber (à effacer); *gomme à encre*, ink-eraser. || *Gomme explosive*, explosive gelatine; *gomme laque*, shellac. || MÉD. Gumma. || BOT. Gum. || CULIN. *Boule de gomme*, gumdrop; gum (bonbon). || FAM. *Transactions à la gomme*, bogus transactions, U.S. phony dealings. || **Gomme-gutte,** f. Gamboge. || **Gomme-laque,** f. Lac, shellac. || **Gomme-résine,** f. Gum resin.
gommé, ée [gɔme] adj. Gummed, adhesive, sticking; *enveloppe gommée*, gummed envelope; *taffetas gommé*, sticking plaster, adhesive tape; *toile gommée*, oil-cloth. || TECHN. Gummed (piston). || CULIN. With syrup.
gommer v. tr. (1). To gum. || To erase, to rub out (effacer). || CULIN. To mix with gum.
— v. intr. To stick, to jam, to gum.
gommeux, euse [-mø, ø:z] adj. Gummy; sticky. || BOT. Gum-yielding. || MÉD. Gummatous.
— m. FAM. Swell, toff, dandy, U.S. high-hat.
gommier [-mje] m. BOT. Gum-tree, gum.
gonade [gɔnad] f. MÉD. Gonad.
gond [gɔ̃] m. Hinge; *hors de ses gonds*, off its hinges. || NAUT. Pin, pintle (d'un gouvernail). || FAM. *Hors de ses gonds*, beside oneself with rage; *sortir de ses gonds*, to fly off the handle.
gondolage [gɔ̃dɔla:ʒ] m. Warping (du bois); lifting (d'une chaussée, d'un plancher); cockling, wrinkling (du papier); blistering (d'une peinture); buckling, crumpling (d'une tôle).
gondolant, ante [-lɑ̃, ɑ̃:t] adj. FAM. Killing.
gondole [gɔ̃dɔl] f. NAUT. Gondola. || AVIAT. Nacelle, gondola (d'un dirigeable). || MÉD. Eye-bath, eye-cup.
gondolement [-lmɑ̃] m. V. GONDOLAGE.
gondoler [-le] v. intr. (1). To warp (bois); to lift (chaussée, plancher); to cockle, to wrinkle (papier); to blister (peinture); to buckle, to crumple (tôle).
— v. pr. Se **gondoler,** to warp (bois); to lift (chaussée, plancher); to cockle, to wrinkle (papier); to blister (peinture); to buckle, to crumple (tôle). || POP. To split one's sides, to rock with laughter.
gondolier [-lje] m. NAUT. Gondolier.
gonfalon [gɔ̃falɔ̃], **gonfanon** [gɔ̃fanɔ̃] m. Gonfalon.
gonfalonier [-lɔnje], **gonfanonier** [-nɔnje] m. Gonfalonier.
gonflage [gɔ̃fla:ʒ] m. AUTOM. Inflating, blowing-up (d'un pneu); *gonflage excessif*, over-inflation.
gonflé, ée [gɔ̃fle] adj. Swollen; inflated, blown up (ballon, pneu); full, heavy (cœur); distended (estomac); bulging (poche); bloated (visage); bellying out (voile); puffy (yeux). || CULIN. Puffed (riz). || FIG. *Gonflé d'orgueil*, puffed up (ou) swelling with pride; *gonflé à bloc*, U.S. hopped-up.
gonflement [-flɑ̃mɑ̃] m. Swelling, bulging. || Inflation (des stocks, des chiffres). || MÉD. Swelling.
gonfler v. tr. (1). To blow up, to inflate (un ballon, un pneu). || To puff out, to blow out (les joues). || To swell (un torrent). || NAUT. To fill, to swell (les voiles). || CULIN. To puff (du riz). || FAM. U.S. To high-pressure.
— v. intr. To swell; to become inflated. || CULIN. To rise (pâte).
— v. pr. Se **gonfler,** to swell (cœur); to become distended (estomac); to belly (voile); to become swollen (ou) puffy (yeux). || FIG. To swell with (d'orgueil).
gonfleur [-flœ:r] m. AUTOM. Inflator, air- (ou) tyre-pump, U.S. tire-pump.

gong [gɔ̃g] m. Gong.
gonio [gɔnjo] m. NAUT., AVIAT. Radiogoniometer, direction-finder.
goniomètre [-mɛtr] m. Goniometer, angle gauge. || MILIT. Dial-sight.
goniométrie [-metri] f. Goniometry.
gonne [gɔn] f. Drum; tar-barrel (à goudron).
gonocoque [gɔnɔkɔk] m. MÉD. Gonococcus.
gonzesse [gɔ̃zɛs] f. ARG. Bird, broad, chick (femme); woman (homme lâche).
gordien [gɔrdjɛ̃] adj. m. Gordian; *trancher le nœud gordien*, to cut the Gordian knot.
goret [gɔrɛ] m. ZOOL. Piglet, porker, little pig. || NAUT. Hog (balai). || FAM. Dirty pig, swine, U.S. slob (personne).
gorge [gɔrʒ] f. Throat, neck (cou); *tenir à la gorge*, to have a stranglehold on. || Bosom, breast (de femme). || Throat, gullet (gosier); *avoir mal à la gorge*, to have a sore throat; *crier à pleine gorge*, to shout loudly; *rire à gorge déployée*, to laugh heartily, to roar with laughter; *serrement de gorge*, lump in one's throat. || ARCHIT. Quirk, gorge; throat (de cheminée). || GÉOGR. Gorge, pass, gill, glen. || TECHN. Groove (de cannelure); notch, score (de poulie); tumbler (de serrure). || FIG. *Faire des gorges chaudes de*, to gloat over; to scoff at; *faire rentrer à qqn les mots dans la gorge*, to make s.o. eat his words; *rendre gorge*, to make restitution; to stump up. || **Gorge-de-pigeon,** adj. invar. Dove-colour.
gorgée [-ʒe] f. Mouthful; gulp; *petite gorgée*, sip; *d'une seule gorgée*, at one gulp (ou) draught.
gorger [-ʒe] v. tr. (7). To stuff, to gorge (une personne); to cram (une poule). [V. GAVER.] || FIG. To glut (combler).
— v. pr. Se **gorger,** to stuff oneself, to gorge, to glut oneself.
gorgerette [-ʒərɛt] f. Gorget, small collar. || ZOOL. Black-cap.
gorget [-ʒɛ] m. TECHN. Moulding-plane.
gorgonzola [gɔrgɔ̃zɔla] m. CULIN. Gorgonzola.
gorille [gɔri:j] m. ZOOL. Gorilla.
gosier [gozje] m. Throat; gullet (gorge). || MÉD. Fauces. || FAM. Wind-pipe, weasand; *avoir le gosier pavé*, to have a cast-iron throat; *s'humecter le gosier*, to wet one's whistle; *à plein gosier*, loudly, lustily.
gosse [gɔs] m. FAM. Youngster, kid, kiddy (v. GAMIN); brat (péj.).
— f. *Une gosse*, a mere chit of a girl.
gotha [gota] m. AVIAT. Gotha.
gothique [gɔtik] adj. Gothic, black-letter (caractères). || FIG. Barbarous, rude, uncouth (barbare); old-fashioned (démodé).
— m. ART., ARCHIT. Gothic art (ou) architecture.
— f. Black letter, old English (caractères).
gotique adj., m. Gothic (langue).
goton [gɔtɔ̃] f. † Country lass (ou) wench. || POP. Trollop, drab.
gouache [gwaʃ] f. ARTS. Gouache, body-colour.
gouaille [gwɑ:j] f. FAM. Bantering, jeering.
gouailler [-je] v. intr., v. tr. (1). FAM. To banter, to jeer, to chaff. (V. GOGUENARDER.)
gouaillerie [-jri] f. FAM. Raillery, chaff, banter.
gouailleur, euse [-jœr, ø:z] adj. Waggish (humeur); jeering, bantering (personne).
gouape [gwap] f. POP. Blackguard, hooligan.
goudron [gudrɔ̃] m. Tar; *goudron de houille*, coal-tar.
goudronnage [gudrɔna:ʒ] m. Tarring.
goudronné, ée [-ne] adj. Tarred; *carton goudronné*, tarred felt, roofing felt; *toile goudronnée*, tarpaulin.
goudronner [-ne] v. tr. (1). To tar. || NAUT. To pay (une couture).
goudronnerie [-nri] f. Tar-works; tar-shed (dépôt).
goudronneur [-nœ:r] m. Tar-worker (ouvrier).

goudronneuse [-nøz] f. Tar-sprayer, tar-spreader.

goudronneux, euse [-nø, ø:z] adj. Tarry; gummy.

gouffre [gufr] m. Gulf, abyss, pit, chasm. ‖ Whirlpool, vortex (tournoiement d'eau). ‖ Fig. *Au bord du gouffre,* on the verge of ruin.

gouge [gu:ʒ] f. Techn. Gouge, hollow chisel. ‖ Méd. Gouge.

gougnafier [guɲafje] m. Pop. Botcher, bungler.

gouine [gwin] f. Pop. Dike, dyke, lesbian.

goujat [guʒa] m. Techn. Apprentice; hodman (de maçon). ‖ Fam. Boor, churl, cad, ill-bred fellow.

goujaterie [guʒatri] f. Caddishness, boorishness, scurrilousness.

goujon [guʒɔ̃] m. Zool. Gudgeon.

goujon m. Archit. Gudgeon. ‖ Techn. Stud, studbolt; gudgeon (d'arbre); link-pin (de chaîne de bicyclette); pin, pintle (de charnière).

goujonner [-ʒɔne] v. tr. (1). To pin, to stud, to bolt (des pièces); to joggle (des pierres, des poutres); to dowel (des planches); to key (des plaques).

goulache, goulasch [gulaːʃ] m. Culin. Goulash.

goulée [gule] f. Techn. Channel. ‖ Fam. Big mouthful, gulp.

goulet [gulɛ] m. Géogr. Narrow passage, gully, defile. ‖ Naut. Sound, strait, narrows; neck. ‖ Archit. Neck-gutter (de toit). ‖ Sports. *Homme de goulet,* gully (au cricket).

goulot [gulo] m. Neck (d'une bouteille); spout (d'un broc). ‖ Pop. Mouth, gullet.

goulu, ue [guly] adj. Greedy. (V. glouton.)
— s. Glutton.

goulûment [gulymɑ̃] adv. Greedily, gluttonously, voraciously.

goupille [gupi:j] f. Pin, peg, keeper-pin; gudgeon; cotter.

goupiller [gupije] v. tr. (1). Techn. To pin, to key; to cotter (un écrou). ‖ Fam. To manage, to arrange.
— v. pr. Se goupiller, Fam. To work, to work out, to shape up.

goupillon [-jɔ̃] m. Ecclés. Aspergillum, sprinkler; *le sabre et le goupillon,* the army and the clergy. ‖ Techn. Bottle-brush, cylinder brush.

goupillonner [-jɔne] v. tr. (1). To clean, to brush.

gourance [gurɑ̃:s], **gourante** [-rɑ̃:t] f. Pop. Bloomer, botch-up.

gourbi [gurbi] m. Gourbi, Arab hut; shack. ‖ Milit. Wattle-hut. ‖ Fam. Funk-hole.

gourd, ourde [gur, urd] adj. Numb, benumbed, stiff (de froid).

gourde [gurd] adj. Fam. Dumb.
— f. Water-bottle, water-vessel, flask. ‖ Bot. Gourd, calabash. ‖ Fam. Dolt, U. S. dumbbell.

gourdin [gurdɛ̃] m. Club, bludgeon, cudgel, cosh; *frapper avec un gourdin,* to bludgeon, to cudgel, to cosh. (V. matraquer.)

gourer (se) [səgure] v. pr. (1). Fam. To be mistaken, to blunder, to make a bloomer.

gourgandine [gurgɑ̃din] f. Harlot, trollop, strumpet. (V. grue.) ‖ Low-necked bodice (vêtement).

gourmand, ande [gurmɑ̃, ɑ̃:d] adj. Gourmand, greedy, gluttonous.
— s. Gourmand, gormandizer. (V. gourmet.)

gourmander [-de] v. tr. (1). To scold, to rebuke, to rebuff, to reprimand, to chide, to snub. (V. gronder.) ‖ To saw (la bouche d'un cheval).

gourmandise [-diz] f. Greediness, gluttony (péché capital); love of good food (péché mignon); *faire un péché de gourmandise,* to indulge oneself in good food. ‖ Pl. Delicacies, dainties, titbits, sweetmeats. (V. friandise.)

gourme [gurm] f. Strangles (du cheval). ‖ Méd. Impetigo. ‖ Fig. *Jeter sa gourme,* to sow one's wild oats.

gourmé, ée [gurme] adj. Stiff, formal, aloof, starched, stuck-up (manière); stand-offish, distant, aloof (personne). [V. guindé.]

gourmet [gurmɛ] m. Gourmet, epicure.

gourmette [gurmɛt] f. Curb, curb-chain (de harnais). ‖ Curb-bracelet, U. S. link bracelet (bracelet); curb watch-chain (chaîne). ‖ Techn. Polishing chain.

gourou [guru] m. Guru.

gousse [gus] f. Bot. Clove (d'ail); pod, hull, shell (de haricot, de pois); bean (de vanille). ‖ Sinker (de plomb).

gousset [gusɛ] m. Fob, watch-pocket, waistcoat-pocket (poche); *avoir le gousset bien garni,* to have a well-lined purse. ‖ Archit. Bracket, stay-plate, gusset.

goût [gu] m. Taste (sens); *goût fin,* fine palate. ‖ Taste, flavour, savour, relish (saveur); bouquet (du vin); *avoir un goût de,* to taste of, to taste like, to smack of. ‖ Taste, liking, inclination, fancy (penchant); *à son goût,* to one's liking; *chacun son goût,* tastes differ, there's no accounting for tastes; *par goût,* from inclination; *prendre goût à,* to take to, to acquire a taste for, to take a fancy to. ‖ Taste, judgment (v. discernement); *avec goût,* tastefully; *faute de goût,* lapse in taste; *de mauvais goût,* in bad taste. ‖ Fam. Manner, taste, style (manière); *dans le goût de,* in the style of, after the manner of.

goûter [gute] v. tr. (1). To taste, to try, to sample (un mets); *goûter à,* to take a little of, to sample; *goûter de,* to taste for the first time. ‖ To taste, to perceive (ou) to catch the flavour of. (V. déguster.) ‖ Fig. To relish, to appreciate, to enjoy, to like (aimer); to approve of (approuver).
— v. intr. To have a snack, to eat something, to have a bite; *goûter sur l'herbe,* to picnic.
— m. Snack, light collation, refreshments.

goutte [gut] f. Drop (de liquide); blob (de liquide épais); bead (de sueur); *tomber goutte à goutte,* to drip. ‖ Drop, dash, nip, sip (d'alcool); *une petite goutte?,* will you have one?, will you indulge? ‖ Spot, splash (de couleur). ‖ Archit. Gutta. ‖ Méd. Gout (maladie); minim, drop (médicament). ‖ Fig. *Une goutte d'eau dans la mer,* a mere drop in the ocean; *se ressembler comme deux gouttes d'eau,* to be as like as two peas. ‖ **Goutte-à-goutte,** m. invar. Méd. Drip, dripfeed.
— loc. adv. *Ne... goutte, pas... goutte,* not at all, not in the least; *n'y comprendre goutte,* not to understand at all.

gouttelette [-lɛt] f. Droplet, tiny drop, globule.

goutter [gute] v. intr. (1). To drip; to leak.

goutteux, euse [gutø, ø:z] adj. Méd. Gouty, goutish.
— s. Méd. Sufferer from gout, gouty person.

gouttière [gutjɛ:r] f. Gutter, guttering (de toit); shoot, spout, rain-pipe (tuyau). ‖ Pl. Eaves (de toit). ‖ Méd. Cradle-splint. ‖ Naut. *Gouttière de pont,* waterway. ‖ Fig. Roof.

gouvernable [guvɛrnabl] adj. Manageable, governable, controlable; *peu gouvernable,* unmanageable. ‖ Naut. Steerable.

gouvernail [-na:j] m. Naut. Rudder; helm, wheel (v. barre); *gouvernail de fortune,* jury rudder; *gouvernail de plongée,* horizontal rudder; *prendre le gouvernail,* to take the helm; *roue du gouvernail,* steering-wheel; *tenir le gouvernail,* to be at the helm, to steer. ‖ Aviat. *Gouvernail de profondeur,* elevator; *gouvernail de direction,* vertical rudder.
‖ Fig. Managing, governing; *tenir le gouvernail de l'Etat,* to steer the Ship of State.

gouvernant, ante [-nɑ̃, ɑ̃:t] adj. Governing, ruling. ‖ In power (parti politique).

— m. Pl. Those who govern; *gouvernants et gouvernés*, governors and governed.

gouvernante [-nɑ̃t] f. Governess (d'enfants). ‖ Housekeeper (d'intérieur).

gouverne [guvɛrn] f. Guidance, guide, guiding principle, rule of conduct; *pour votre gouverne*, for your future guidance. ‖ Aviat. Pl. Control surfaces, rudders and ailerons; *gouverne de profondeur*, tail flap. ‖ Naut. Steering.

gouvernement [guvɛrnəmɑ̃] m. Government, management, direction, governance, U. S. administration. ‖ Governorship (fonction). ‖ Government, cabinet (en politique). ‖ Government House, U. S. Executive Mansion (hôtel du gouverneur).

gouvernemental, ale [-tal] adj. Governmental; *le parti gouvernemental*, the Government Party.

gouvernementalisme [-talism] m. Governmentalism.

gouverner [guvɛrne] v. tr. (1). To direct, to manage, to run (une maison); to govern (un pays). ‖ To rein up (un cheval). ‖ To educate, to bring up (un enfant). ‖ Gramm. To govern. ‖ Naut. To steer; to handle; *gouverner sur un port*, to head for a port. ‖ Aviat. To navigate, to pilot. ‖ Fig.

GOUVERNEMENT
Parlement et Administration

GOVERNMENT
Parliament and Civil Service

être au pouvoir	to be in power
loi	law, act
projet de loi	bill
arrêté	decree
décret-loi	Order in Council
Parlement	Parliament
convoquer	to summon
vacance (parlemᵗ)	recess
voter une loi	to pass a law
abroger	to repeal
droit de vote	franchise; (fam.) vote
tour de scrutin	ballot
urne	ballot box
scrutin	poll
agent électoral	canvasser
circonscription	constituency
programme	platform, programme
être élu	to be returned, elected
être blackboulé	to be blackballed
amendement	amendment
vote de confiance	vote of confidence
commission	committee
commission du budget	Committee of Ways & Means
budget	budget
budget de la guerre	Army Estimates
un impôt	a tax
les impôts	taxation, taxes
la tendance (pol.)	the trend
le salut (bien) public	public welfare
l'Administration	Civil Service
fonctionnaire	Civil Servant, official
attributions	province
traitement	salary
avancement	promotion, preferment
nomination	appointment
renvoyer	to dismiss, to remove
donner sa démission	to resign
prendre sa retraite	to retire
mettre à la retraite	to pension off
retraite (payée)	retiring pension
un retraité	a pensioner
bureaucratie	red tape
diplomate	diplomat, diplomatist
Ambassade de France	French Embassy
non-intervention	non-interference
— — (en guerre)	non-intervention
lettres de créance	credentials
lettres de rappel	letters of recall
valise diplomatique	Embassy dispatch-bag

To rule, to command, to control (une passion). — v. intr. Naut. To steer; to answer the helm. — v. pr. **Se gouverner**, to control oneself; to behave oneself.

gouvernés m. pl. Subjects.

gouverneur [-nœːr] m. Governor (de banque, de province); *gouverneur général*, governor-general. ‖ Governor, U. S. warden (de prison). ‖ Tutor (de prince). ‖ Naut. Steersman. ‖ Milit. Commanding officer (de place forte).

gouvernorat [-nɔra] m. Governorship; rank of governor.

goy [gɔi] m. Goy. ‖ Pl. Goyim.

goyave [gɔja:v] f. Bot. Guava. ‖ Culin. *Confiture de goyave*, guava jelly.

goyavier [-vje] m. Bot. Guava-tree.

Graal [graal] m. Grail.

grabat [graba] m. Pallet; wretched bed, litter of rags. ‖ Fig. Poverty; *mourir sur un grabat*, to die in a garret.

grabataire [-tɛːr] adj. Bed-ridden. — s. Bed-ridden person.

grabuge [graby:ʒ] m. Fam. Row, ructions, rumpus; *il y aura du grabuge*, there'll be a row.

grâce [grɑːs] f. Grace, gracefulness, charm, attractiveness (charme); prettiness, comeliness (joliesse); *avec grâce*, gracefully; *faire des grâces*, to put on airs and graces. ‖ Grace, graciousness (bonne volonté); *de bonne grâce*, willingly; readily; *de mauvaise grâce*, ungraciously, unwillingly, reluctantly, grudgingly. ‖ Grace (divinité); *les Trois Grâces*, The Three Graces. ‖ Favour, grace, boon (faveur); *demander en grâce*, to beseech; *gagner les bonnes grâces de*, to get into the good graces of; *rechercher les bonnes grâces de*, to curry favour with; *trouver grâce devant*, to find favour with (ou) in the eyes of. ‖ Act of grace, mercy, clemency, pity (miséricorde); *crier grâce*, to cry for mercy; *de grâce*, for mercy's sake, for pity's sake. ‖ Remission (d'une dette); pardon, forgiveness (pardon); *droit de grâce*, right of pardon; *faire grâce à qqn de qqch.*, to spare s.o. sth., to let s.o. off sth. ‖ Thanks, gratitude (remerciement); *action de grâces*, thanksgiving; *grâce à*, thanks to; *rendre grâces à qqn de*, to give thanks to s.o. for. ‖ Jur. Free pardon, reprieve. ‖ Ecclés. Grace (de Dieu); grace (avant un repas); *état de grâce*, state of grace. ‖ Loc. *Sa Grâce*, His Grace.

graciable [grasjabl] adj. Pardonable.

gracier [grasje] v. tr. To reprieve, to pardon.

gracieusement [-sjøzmɑ̃] adv. Gracefully, with grace, becomingly (avec grâce). ‖ Graciously, kindly (avec bienveillance). ‖ Gratuitously, free, without payment (gratuitement).

gracieuseté [-sjøzte] f. Graciousness, affability, kindness (amabilité). ‖ Gratuitousness (gratuité).

gracieux, euse [-sjø, øːz] adj. Graceful, pleasing, attractive, charming (charmant). ‖ Affable (aimable); *gracieux sourire*, winning smile. ‖ Gratuitous, complimentary, free (gratuit); *à titre gracieux*, gratis, as a gift, free; *exemplaire à titre gracieux*, presentation copy. ‖ Gracious (indulgent, miséricordieux); *notre gracieuse reine*, our gracious queen.

gracile [grasil] adj. Gracile, slim, slender (personne, tige); thin (voix).

gracilité [-lite] f. Gracility, slimness, slenderness.

gradation [gradasjɔ̃] f. Gradation, gradual process; *avec une gradation lente*, by slow degrees; *par gradation*, gradually. ‖ Gramm. *Gradation ascendante, inverse*, climax, anti-climax.

grade [grad] m. Rank, grade, rating, degree, dignity; *détenir un grade*, to hold a rank (ou) rating; *monter en grade*, to be promoted. ‖ Degree (diplôme); *prendre ses grades*, to take one's degree, to graduate. ‖ MILIT. Rank; *être élevé au grade d'officier*, to be commissioned, to obtain a commission. ‖ NAUT. Rating. ‖ MATH. Grade.

gradé [-de] m. MILIT. Non-commissioned officer, N. C. O.; *gradés et soldats*, « Other Ranks ». ‖ NAUT. Petty officer.

gradient [gradjã] m. Gradient.

gradin [gradɛ̃] m. Step (marche). ‖ Tier, stepped row of seats (banc). ‖ Gradin (d'un amphithéâtre); *disposé en gradins*, stepped, tiered. ‖ MILIT. *Gradin de tir*, fire-step. ‖ TECHN. *Assemblage à gradins*, joggle-joining.

graduation [gradu̜asjõ] f. Graduating, graduation (d'un instrument). ‖ Scale (échelle).

gradué, ée [gradu̜e] adj. Graduated (échelle). ‖ Progressive (exercices); graded (couleurs). ‖ CHIM. *Verre gradué*, graduate.

graduel [-ɛl] adj., m. Gradual.

graduellement [-ɛlmã] adv. Gradually, progressively, by degrees.

graduer [gradu̜e] v. tr. (1). To graduate, to proportion; to grade (des études); to calibrate (un instrument). ‖ To confer a degree upon (qqn).

graffiti [grafiti] m. pl. Graffiti.

grailler [grɑje] v. intr. (1). To caw, to croak (d'une corneille); to croak (parler d'une voix enrouée).

grailler v. tr. (1). ARG. To nosh, to eat.

graillon [grajõ] m. CULIN. Broken meat, scraps; *odeur de graillon*, smell of burnt fat. ‖ MÉD. FAM. Hawked-up phlegm.

graillonner [grajɔne] v. intr. (1). CULIN. To smell (ou) taste of burnt fat. ‖ MÉD. To bring up phlegm; to hawk (fam.).

grain [grɛ̃] m. BOT. Grain (d'avoine, de blé); bean (de café); berry (de groseille); seed (de moutarde); grape (de raisin). ‖ Corn, grain; *marchand de grains*, corn-chandler, U. S. grain merchant. ‖ Bead (de chapelet, de collier). ‖ Grain, atom (particule); grain (de poudre, de sable, de sel); speck (de poussière); *réduire en grains*, to granulate, to grind. ‖ Grain, texture (du bois); rough side (du cuir); *grain dense* (ou) *fin* (ou) *serré*, close grain; *gros grain*, grogram, gross-grain (étoffe, ruban); *à gros grains*, coarse-grained. ‖ NAUT. Heavy shower (averse); squall (vent). [V. BOURRASQUE.] ‖ MÉD. Pellet, minute pill (pilule); *grain de beauté*, mole, beauty-spot. ‖ TECHN. Cam-roller (de machine); bushing, lining (de roulement à billes); chisel (de tailleur de pierres). ‖ CULIN. *Poulet de grain*, corn-fed pullet. ‖ † Grain (poids). ‖ FIG. Grain, dash; touch (de coquetterie, de folie); touch, spice (de méchanceté). ‖ FAM. *Avoir un grain*, to be slightly cracked (ou) weak in the upper storey; *veiller au grain*, to watch out for danger. ‖ Grain-d'orge, m. MÉD. Stye; TECHN. Diamond-point chisel.

graine [grɛn] f. BOT. Seed; *graine de lin*, linseed; *monter en graine*, to seed. ‖ ZOOL. Graine, silkworm eggs. ‖ MILIT., FAM. *Graine d'épinards*, bullion, U. S. scrambled eggs. ‖ FAM. Breed, strain; *mauvaise graine*, bad lot; *monter en graine*, to grow into an old maid, to go on the shelf (femme); *prendre de la graine de*, to profit by (ou) from (un exemple).

grainer [grɛne] v. intr. (1). V. GRENER.

graineterie [grɛntri] f. COMM. Seed-trade (commerce); seed-shop (magasin).

grainetier [-tje] m. COMM. Seed-merchant. ‖ BOT. Collection of seeds. ‖ **Grainetier-fleuriste**, m. Seedsman.

graissage [grɛsaʒ] m. Greasing (à la graisse); oiling, lubrication (à l'huile); *circuit de graissage*, circulating, lubrication system; *huile de graissage*, lubricating oil. ‖ AUTOM. *Graissage central*,

one-shot lubrication. ‖ FAM. *Graissage de patte*, palm-greasing.

graisse [grɛs] f. CULIN. Fat (de viande); grease (fondue); *graisse alimentaire, de ménage*, edible, cooking fat; *graisse minérale*, mineral jelly, U. S. petrolatum; *graisse de porc*, lard; *graisse de rôti*, dripping. ‖ Fat, fatness (d'une personne); *prendre de la graisse*, to put on fat, to get fat, to put on weight. ‖ Oiliness ropiness (du vin). ‖ AUTOM. Lubricant, oil, grease; *boîte à graisse*, grease-box; *graisse pour essieux*, axle-grease. ‖ MILIT. *Graisse d'armes*, rifle-oil. ‖ FAM. *Boniments à la graisse d'oie*, blarney, bunkum, U. S. hooey, baloney. ‖ POP. Oof, dough. (V. FRIC.)

graisser [grɛse] v. tr. (1). To grease (à la graisse); to oil, to lubricate (à l'huile). ‖ To make greasy, to soil with grease (salir). ‖ FAM. *Graisser ses bottes*, to prepare for kingdom come; *graisser la patte à qqn*, to grease s.o.'s palm.

— v. intr. To become ropy (bière, vin).

graisseur, euse [-sœ:r, ø:z] adj. TECHN. Self-oiling, self-lubricating; *robinet graisseur*, grease-cock.

— m. Greaser, oiler (ouvrier). ‖ TECHN. Lubricator, oil-cup, grease-cup. ‖ AVIAT. *Graisseur centrifuge*, banjo-oiler.

graisseux, euse [grɛsø, ø:z] adj. Greasy, oily, unctuous. ‖ Soiled with grease (sali). ‖ Ropy (vin). ‖ MÉD. Fatty (dégénérescence); adipose (tissu).

gram [gram] m. CHIM. Gram; *liqueur de Gram*, Gram's solution.

graminacée [graminase], **graminée** [-ne] f. BOT. Graminaceous (ou) gramineous plant. ‖ Pl. Graminaceae.

grammaire [grammɛ:r] f. Grammar; *grammaire raisonnée*, analytical grammar. ‖ Grammar book (livre).

grammairien, enne [-mɛrjɛ̃, ɛn] s. Grammarian.

grammatical, ale [-matikal] adj. Grammatical.

grammaticalement [-matikalmã] adv. Grammatically.

grammaticalité [-matikalite] f. Grammaticality.

gramme [gram] m. Gramme, gram.

gramophone [gramɔfɔn] m. Gramophone.

grand, ande [grã, ã:d] adj.

---

1. Sens général. — 2. Considérable. — 3. Nombreux. — 4. Élevé. — 5. Fort. — 6. Noble. — 7. Pompeux. — 8. Notable. — 9. Principal. — 10. Adulte. — 11. Plein. — 12. Complet. — 13. Titre. — 14. TECHN. — 15. ASTRON. — 16. RADIO. — 17. CH. DE F. — 18. ZOOL. — 19. MATH. — 20. BOT. — 21. MÉD. — 22. MILIT. — 23. NAUT.

---

1. Big, large, great (sens général); tall, high, lofty (en hauteur); long (en longueur); tall (en taille); wide (en surface); *grande barbe*, long beard; *grand bras*, big (ou) long arm; *grands fauves*, big game; *grande maison*, large (ou) big house; *à grands pas*, with great (ou) long strides; *grande ville*, big city, large town; *grand voyage*, long journey; *homme grand*, tall man; *ouvrir de grands yeux*, to open one's eyes wide; *sur une grande échelle*, on a large scale; *trop grand pour son âge*, overgrown. ‖ 2. Great, considerable (considérable); *grande multitude*, great multitude; *grande nation*, great (ou) mighty nation; *en grande partie*, to a large extent; *grand public*, general public; *grand soin*, good (ou) great care; *prendre grand intérêt à*, to take great interest in. ‖ 3. Great, large, big, numerous (nombreux); *grande famille*, numerous (ou) large family; *un grand nombre de*, a great number of, a great

many; *pas grand monde*, not many people. ‖
4. Great (élevé); *au grand cœur*, great-hearted;
grand homme, great man; *les grands et les petits
poètes*, the major and the minor poets. ‖
5. Great (fort); loud (bruit); intense (chaleur);
great (découverte); wide (différence); severe
(froid); extreme (jeunesse); heavy (pluie); high,
strong (vent); high (vitesse); *à cause de son grand
âge*, because of his extreme age. ‖ **6.** Great, high,
lofty (noble); noble (art, pensée, sentiment);
grande manière, grand manner; *grandes pensées*,
noble thoughts; *se montrer grand*, to show oneself magnanimous. ‖ **7.** Big, extravagant (pompeux); *de grands mots*, big words; *faire de grandes
phrases*, to talk big, to be bombastic; *prendre de
grands airs*, to give oneself airs, to act big. ‖
8. Great (notable); *grands amis*, great friends; *les
grands blessés*, the seriously wounded, the serious
cases; *grand buveur*, hard (ou) heavy drinker;
grands crus, high-class wines, great vintages;
grande misère, dire poverty, severe distress; *couleur grand teint*, fast-colour dye. ‖ **9.** Great, principal, main (principal); *grand chemin*, main road,
high road, highway; *grand escalier*, grand staircase; *grandes marées*, spring-tides; *grandes
vacances*, summer holidays. ‖ **10.** Grown, grown-
up, adult (personne); *son grand frère*, his big
brother; *grandes personnes*, grown-ups (fam.). ‖
11. High, full (plein); *grand air*, open air; *grand
galop*, full gallop; *grand jour*, broad daylight;
grand temps, high time; *grande tenue* (ou) *toilette*, full dress. ‖ **12.** Quite, full, good; *une
grande heure*, a full (ou) good hour. ‖ **13.** Grand,
great, high (appellations); *Grande Armée*, Grand
Army; *grand prêtre*, high priest; *grand maître*,
Grand Master; *grand seigneur*, great nobleman;
le Grand Turc, the Grand Turk; *Pierre le Grand*,
Peter the Great. ‖ **14.** TECHN. *Explosif à grande
puissance*, high explosive; *grand ressort*, mainspring. ‖ **15.** ASTRON. *Grande Ourse*, Great Bear.
‖ **16.** RADIO. Long (onde). ‖ **17.** CH. DE F. *Grande
ligne*, main line, trunk line, trunk. ‖ **18.** ZOOL.
Grand duc, Eagle-owl, great horned owl, grand
duke. ‖ **19.** MATH. *Grand axe*, major axis (d'une
ellipse). ‖ **20.** BOT. Full-grown (plante). ‖
21. MÉD. *Les grands malades*, the seriously ill.
‖ **22.** MILIT. *Grand uniforme*, full regimentals,
U.S. dress uniform. ‖ **23.** NAUT. *Grand mât*, mainmast. ‖ **Grand-angle, grand-angulaire,** m.
TECHN. Wide-angle lens. ‖ **Grand-chose,** m. Much;
ne pas valoir grand-chose, not to amount to much. ‖
Grand-croix, f. Grand Cross (décoration); m.
Knight Grand Cross (personne). ‖ **Grand-duc,** m.
Grand duke (personne). ‖ **Grand-ducal,** adj.
Grand ducal. ‖ **Grand-duché,** m. Grand duchy. ‖
Grande-Bretagne, f. GÉOGR. Great Britain. ‖
Grande-duchesse, f. Grand duchess. ‖ **Grand-
Guignol,** m. *C'est du Grand-Guignol*, it's all
blood and thunder. ‖ **Grand-guignolesque,** adj.
Gory, bloody, blood curdling. ‖ **Grand-livre,** m.
Ledger (dans le commerce). ‖ **Grand-maman,** f.
FAM. Grand-mamma, grandma, granny, gran. ‖
Grand-mère, f. Grandmother. ‖ **Grand-messe,** f.
ECCLÉS. High mass. ‖ **Grand-oncle,** m. Great-
uncle, grand-uncle. ‖ **Grand-papa,** m. Grand-
papa, grandpa, grandad. ‖ **grand-peine (A),** loc.
adv. With great difficulty, with much trouble. ‖
 Grand-père, m. Grand-father, grand-sire. ‖
Grand-route, f. Highway, high road, main road.
‖ **Grands-parents,** m. pl. Grandparents. ‖ **Grand-
tante,** f. Great-aunt, grand-aunt. ‖ **Grand-voile,**
f. NAUT. Mainsail. ‖

— adv. On a large scale; *faire grand*, to do on a
large scale; *en grand*, on a large scale; large-
scale; full-size; *grand ouvert*, wide open; *voir
grand*, to have large views, to see (ou) to plan
on a large scale, to have big ideas. ‖ ARTS. *En
grand*, life-size (portrait, statue); *reproduction en

grand, enlarged copy. ‖ NAUT. *Amenez en grand*,
lower amain; *arriver en grand*, to bear around.
— m. *Le grand*, the great. ‖ Senior (élève). ‖
Grandee (d'Espagne). ‖ Pl. The great; *les grands
de la terre*, the great ones of the earth. ‖ Pl.
Grown-ups, grown people (adultes); *grands et
petits*, old and young; *les Trois Grands*, the Big
Three.

grandelet [grãdlɛ] adj. Biggish, tallish.

grandement [-dmã] adv. Grandly, handsomely
(généreusement); *faire grandement les choses*, to
do things lavishly. ‖ Greatly, amply, largely (largement); *avoir grandement le temps*, to have
plenty of (ou) ample time; *avoir grandement de
quoi vivre*, to have more than sufficient to live on.
‖ Widely, greatly (de beaucoup); *avoir grandement raison*, to be altogether right; *se tromper
grandement*, to be greatly mistaken.

grandet [-dɛ] adj. Biggish, largish; tallish.

grandeur [-dœːr] f. Size (dimension); extent
(étendue); height (hauteur); wideness (largeur);
length (longueur); bigness, bulk (masse); spaciousness (place); *étoile, gaffe de première grandeur*, star, blunder of the first magnitude; *grandeur naturelle*, full-size, life-size. ‖ Greatness (en
son espèce, en son genre); loudness (du bruit);
scale (d'une entreprise); length (d'un voyage). ‖
Greatness, loftiness, nobility (de l'âme, de la pensée, du sentiment); grandeur, sublimity (d'une
œuvre, d'un spectacle). ‖ Greatness, grandeur,
splendour (majesté, puissance); *au faîte de la
grandeur humaine*, at the summit of human grandeur. ‖ Extent, greatness, importance, magnitude;
grandeur d'un crime, enormity of a crime; *grandeur d'une perte*, extent of a loss. ‖ Pride, proud-
ness, disdain (dédain, orgueil); *regarder qqn du
haut de sa grandeur*, to look down upon s.o. ‖
ECCLÉS. *Sa Grandeur*, his Grace (archevêque);
his Lordship (évêque).

grandiloquence [grãdilɔkãs] f. Grandiloquence,
magniloquence, bombast.

grandiloquent, ente [-kã, ãːt] adj. Grandiloquent, magniloquent (personne); bombastic,
turgid, pompous (style).

grandiose [grãdjoːz] adj. Grandiose, grand,
imposing, majestic; *spectacle grandiose*, awe-
inspiring spectacle.
— m. Grandiosity, grandeur, majesty.

grandiosement [-mã] adv. Grandiosely, imposingly, majestically.

grandir [grãdiːr] v. intr. To grow up (personne);
to grow taller (ou) bigger (personne, plante). ‖
FIG. To increase; *grandir en sagesse*, to grow in
wisdom.
— v. tr. To make taller (ou) larger; to add to the
size (ou) height of (qqn, qqch.). ‖ FIG. To increase,
to magnify; to exaggerate. (V. GROSSIR.)

grandissant, ante [-disã, ãːt] adj. Growing (personne, plante); increasing (puissance, sagesse);
rising (tempête).

grandissement [-dismã] m. Growth, growing (de
personne, de plante). ‖ PHYS. Magnification. ‖
FIG. Increase (de puissance).

grange [grãːʒ] f. AGRIC. Barn, grange; *mettre
le blé en grange*, to garner the wheat.

granit(e) [granit] m. GÉOL. Granite. ‖ FIG. *Cœur
de granit*, heart of stone.

granité [-te] adj. Grained; granulated; granular.
— m. Pebble-weave (étoffe).

graniter [-te] v. tr. (1). ARTS. To grain.

graniteux, euse [-tø, øːz] adj. Granitoid, granitic.

granitique [-tik] adj. Granitic.

granivore [granivɔːr] adj. ZOOL. Granivorous.
— s. ZOOL. Granivore.

granulaire [granylɛːr] adj. Granular.

granulation [granylasjõ] f. Granulation, graining

(de la poudre). ‖ Méd. Pl. Granulations, granular formations.

granule [-nyl] m. Granule.

granulé, ée [-nyle] adj. Granulated, granular. — m. Méd. Pharmaceutical preparation in granular form.

granuler [-nyle] v. tr. (1). To granulate. ‖ Techn. To grain (de la poudre). ‖ Arts. To stipple (une gravure).

granuleux, euse [-nylø, ø:z] adj. Granular, granulous. ‖ Méd. Cellule granuleuse, granule-cell.

grapefruit [grɛpfrut] m. Bot. Grapefruit.

graphe [graf] m. Math. Graph.

graphie [grafi] f. Writing; written form.

graphique [-fik] adj. Graphic; arts graphiques, graphic arts; dessin graphique, diagram. — m. Graph (courbe); diagram (dessin).

graphiquement [-fikmɑ̃] adv. Graphically, diagrammatically.

graphisme [-fism] m. Writing.

graphiste [-fist] s. Graphic designer.

graphite [-fit] m. Graphite, plumbago, black-lead.

graphiteux, euse [-fitø, ø:z], **graphitique** [-fitik] adj. Graphitic, plumbaginous.

graphologie [-fɔlɔʒi] f. Graphology.

graphologique [-fɔlɔʒik] adj. Graphological.

graphologue [-fɔlɔg] m. Graphologist.

grappe [grap] f. Cluster (de fruits); bunch (de raisins); croître en grappe, to cluster. ‖ Bot. Raceme. ‖ Milit. Grapeshot (mitraille).

grappillage [grapija:ʒ] m. Gleaning (de raisins). ‖ Fam. Pilfering, scrounging; pickings.

grappiller [-je] v. intr. (1). To glean (des raisins). ‖ Fig. To pilfer. — v. tr. To pick from a bunch (des raisins). ‖ To pick at (la nourriture). ‖ Fig. To pilfer.

grappilleur, euse [-jœ:r, ø:z] adj. Gleaning (des raisins). ‖ Fig. Pilfering, cadging, scrounging. — s. Gleaner (de raisins). ‖ Fig. Pilferer, cadger.

grappillon [-pijɔ̃] m. Small cluster (ou) bunch.

grappin [grapɛ̃] m. Naut. Grapnel, grappling-hook, grappling-anchor. ‖ Techn. Cant-hook, gripper (de bûcheron); anchor-tie; iron-anchor (de construction); climbing-irons (de grimpeur). ‖ Electr. Grab-dredger, grab. ‖ Fam. Mettre le grappin sur, to get one's hooks on to.

gras, asse [grɑ̃, as] adj. Fat, fattened, fatted (animal); fleshy, fat, stout, corpulent (personne); fat (viande); bœuf gras, fat ox; poulet bien gras, plump pullet; veau gras, fatted calf. ‖ Culin. Meaty, rich (aliment, nourriture); cream (fromage); meat (potage); corps gras, fat; matière grasse, fat, fat content. ‖ Greasy, smeary, oily (graisseux); cheveux gras, oily hair; eaux grasses, swill, swilling. ‖ Thick; greasy, thick (boue); slippery (pavé); thick, oily (peinture). ‖ Fat (argile); soft, fat, bituminous (charbon); soft (crayon, pierre); thick (poutre); rich, fat (prairie); heavy, clayey (terre). ‖ Rolling, thick (voix); rire gras, fat chuckle. ‖ Chim. Acide gras, fatty acid. ‖ Bot. Plante grasse, thick leaf, succulent plant. ‖ Méd. Phlegmy, loose (toux). ‖ Théâtr. Crayon de gras, grease-paint stick (pour maquillage). ‖ Techn. Caractères gras, thick (ou) heavy (ou) bold-faced type; toile grasse, tarred canvas. ‖ Arts. Soft (silhouette); contours gras, softened (ou) woolly outlines. ‖ Naut. Temps gras, thick (ou) foggy weather. ‖ Ecclés. Mardi gras, Shrove Tuesday; faire gras, to eat meat; jour gras, meat-eating day; semaine grasse, Shrovetide. ‖ Fam. Faire la grasse matinée, to have a lie-in, to sleep late (à l'occasion); to be a slug-a-bed (habituellement). ‖ Pop. Coarse, smutty (plaisanterie); parler gras, to talk smut; rire gras, to gurgle with laughter.

— adv. Tousser gras, to have a phlegmy cough; parler gras, to speak gutturally; manger gras, to eat fatty food; rire gras, to laugh dirtily. ‖ Fam. Il n'y a pas gras à manger, it's not much of a feast. — m. Thick part; fleshy part (du dos); calf (de la jambe). ‖ Culin. Fat (de viande). ‖ Zool. Speck, blubber (de baleine). ‖ Archit. Superfluous thickness (de pilier, de poutre). ‖ **Gras-double**, m. Culin. Tripe.

grassement [grɑsmɑ̃] adv. Comfortably, handsomely; vivre grassement, to live comfortably (ou) on the fat of the land. ‖ Liberally, plentifully; grassement rétribué, handsomely paid.

grasseyement [grasɛjmɑ̃] m. Burr.

grasseyer [-je] v. intr. (9c). To burr, to speak with a strong uvular (ou) guttural r.

grasseyeur [-jœ:r] m. Person who speaks with a burr.

grassouillet [grasujɛ] adj. Chubby, plump, podgy.

gratifiant, ante [gratifjɑ̃, ɑ̃:t] adj. Gratifying, rewarding.

gratification [gratifikasjɔ̃] f. Gratification, gratuity, perquisite, reward, tip (pourboire). ‖ Bonus, bounty (libéralité). ‖ Milit., Naut. Gratuity.

gratifier [-fje] v. tr. (1). To gratify (de, with); to present (de, with); to confer, to award, to bestow (de, upon). ‖ Fig. To favour (de, with) [accorder]; to ascribe, to attribute (de, to) [attribuer].

gratin [gratɛ̃] m. Culin. Browned part (d'un plat); gratin, seasoned breadcrumbs (plat); au gratin, au gratin. ‖ Fig. Smart set (de la société).

gratiné, ée [-tine] adj. Culin. Cooked au gratin. ‖ Fam. Fine; spicy, juicy (plaisanterie, scandale); une interro gratinée, a real bastard of a test; c'est gratiné, it's really something.

gratinée [-tine] f. Culin. Onion soup au gratin.

gratiner [-tine] v. tr. (1). Culin. To cook au gratin. — v. intr. Culin. To brown; to crisp; to stick to the side of the pan.

gratis [gratis] adv. Fam. Gratis, free of charge; buckshee (pop.); entrée gratis, admission free.

gratitude [gratityd] f. Gratitude, gratefulness, thankfulness. (V. reconnaissance.)

grattage [grata:ʒ] m. Scraping, scratching (d'une surface). ‖ Erasure, scratching out (effacement). ‖ Techn. Napping, teaseling.

gratte [grat] f. Techn. Chisel (de calfat); scraper (de maçon). ‖ Fig. Pickings, graft, rake-off, side-profits. ‖ Fam. Itch (gale). ‖ **Gratte-ciel**, m. skyscraper. ‖ **Gratte-cul**, m. Bot. Hip. ‖ **Gratte-dos**, m. Back-scratcher. ‖ **Gratte-papier**, m. Copy-clerk (copiste); scribbler, quilldriver, pen-pusher (écrivaillon). ‖ **Gratte-pieds**, m. Door-(ou) shoe-scraper.

grattement [-tmɑ̃] m. Scratch, scratching.

gratter [-te] v. tr. (1). To scratch (avec les ongles); to scrape (avec un outil); to rake (avec une ratissoire). ‖ To erase (effacer); to scrape off (une tache). ‖ Techn. To raise, to nap (du drap); to brush up (de la laine). ‖ Naut. To grave (une coque). ‖ Fam. To out distance, to get the better of (un concurrent); to overtake, to pass (un coureur, une voiture). ‖ Fam. To graft (faire des petits profits illégitimes); gratter du papier, to drive a quill, to push a pen. — v. intr. To scratch, to scrape. ‖ To knock gently, to tap (à une porte). ‖ To have a bite (vin). ‖ Fam. To itch (démanger); to be prickly (barbe); to be rough (laine).

gratteur [-tœ:r] m. Scraper, scratcher. ‖ Techn. Napper (du drap). ‖ Fam. Gratteur de papier, copyist, quill-driver, pen-pusher.

grattoir [-twa:r] m. Eraser; grattoir de bureau,

erasing-knife, scraper-eraser. ‖ TECHN. Slice (en typogr.); *grattoir à peinture*, paint-scrubber.

gratture [-ty:r] f. Scraping.

gratuit, uite [gratɥi, ɥit] adj. Gratuitous, free of charge; *école gratuite*, free school; *entrée gratuite*, admission free; *à titre gratuit*, gratis, free of charge. ‖ Gratuitous, unwarranted (sans fondement); gratuitous, unmotivated (acte); gratuitous, unprovoked (insulte); unfounded (supposition). ‖ FIN. *Action gratuite*, bonus share.

gratuité [-te] f. Gratuitousness.

gratuitement [-tmɑ̃] adv. Gratuitously, gratis, for nothing, free of charge (gratis). ‖ Without cause, wantonly, without provocation (sans fondement).

gravats [grava] m. pl. Screenings (de plâtre). ‖ Rubble, debris.

grave [gra:v] adj. Grave, sedate, solemn, staid (air); grave, sober (visage). ‖ Important, weighty (affaire); grave, grievous, serious (erreur). ‖ MÉD. Severe, serious, dangerous (maladie). ‖ PHYS. Heavy. ‖ MUS. Low-pitched, deep, full-toned (note, voix). ‖ GRAMM. Grave (accent).
— m. Grave; *passer du grave au doux*, to pass from grave to gay. ‖ PHYS. Pl. Heavy bodies. ‖ MUS. Deep notes, low notes.

gravé, ée [grave] adj. Graven (image); pitted (métal); engraved (pierre).

gravelage [grava:ʒ] m. Gravelling (d'une route). ‖ Gravel (gravier).

graveler [gravle] v. tr. (8 a). To gravel.

graveleux, euse [-lø, ø:z] adj. Gritty (craie); gravelly (terrain). ‖ MÉD. Gravelly. ‖ BOT. Gritty (fruit). ‖ FIG. Smutty, bawdy, obscene (propos).

gravelle [-vɛl] f. MÉD. Gravel.

gravelure [gravly:r] f. Lewdness (caractère licencieux); dirty talk (propos).

gravement [gravmɑ̃] adv. Gravely, solemnly, soberly, sedately (d'un air grave). ‖ Heavily (endetté); grievously (offensé). ‖ MÉD. Seriously, severely, gravely.

graver v. tr. (1). ARTS. To engrave, to cut, to carve (un dessin); to engrave (une médaille); *graver sur bois*, to engrave on wood; *graver en relief*, to emboss. ‖ TECHN. To sink (un creux, une matrice). ‖ FIG. *Graver dans*, to imprint on, to impress on (l'esprit, la mémoire).

graveur [-vœ:r] m. ARTS. Engraver; carver (sur marbre); *graveur sur bois*, wood-engraver. ‖ TECHN. *Graveur de matrices*, die-sinker.

gravide [gravid] adj. Gravid.

gravier [-vje] m. Gravel (petits cailloux); grit (sable dans une machine). ‖ MÉD. Pl. Gravel.

gravillon [-vijɔ̃] m. Fine gravel.

gravillonner [-vijɔne] v. tr. To gravel.

gravimétrie [gravimetri] f. PHYS., CHIM. Gravimetry.

gravir [gravi:r] v. tr. (2). To climb, to mount (une échelle); to climb, to ascend (une montagne).

gravitation [gravitasjɔ̃] f. Gravitation; gravitational pull.

gravité [-te] f. Gravity, solemnity, sobriety, staidness (du maintien). ‖ Grievousness, seriousness (d'une erreur); importance, significance (d'une situation). ‖ MÉD. Gravity, severity, seriousness (d'une maladie). ‖ PHYS. Gravity, weight (pesanteur); *centre de gravité*, centre of gravity.

graviter [-te] v. intr. (1). PHYS. To gravitate (vers, towards). ‖ FAM. To revolve, to turn (autour de, around).

gravois [gravwa] m. pl. † Syn. de GRAVATS.

gravure [gravy:r] f. ARTS. Engraving; carving (sur pierre); *gravure sur acier, sur bois*, steel-, wood-engraving; *gravure en creux*, intaglio engraving, incised work; *gravure à l'eau-forte*, etching; *gravure au pointillé*, stipple-engraving; *gravure*

en relief, line-work, half-tone work; *gravure en taille douce*, copper-plate engraving; *gravure au trait*, line engraving. ‖ Engraving, print, picture, etching (image); *gravure sur bois*, wood-cut; *gravure en couleurs*, colour-print; *marchand de gravures*, print-dealer. ‖ TECHN. *Gravure en creux*, die-sinking.

gré [gre] m. Will, pleasure (caprice, volonté); *à votre gré*, as you please, as you will; *au gré des flots*, at the mercy of the waves; *bon gré mal gré*, willy-nilly, whether one likes it or not; *contre mon gré*, against my will; *de bon gré*, willingly; *de gré ou de force*, willy-nilly; *de gré à gré*, by mutual consent (ou) agreement; by private contract; *de mauvais gré*, reluctantly, grudgingly; *de son plein gré*, of his own free will. ‖ Liking, taste, mind (goût); *à mon gré*, to my liking, to my taste. ‖ Gratitude; *savoir gré à qqn de*, to be grateful to s.o. for; *savoir mauvais gré à qqn de*, to be annoyed with s.o. about sth.

gréage [grea:ʒ] m. NAUT. Rigging.

grèbe [grɛb] m. ZOOL. Grebe.

grec, ecque [grɛk] adj. GÉOGR. Greek; Grecian (arts, coiffure, profil).
— m. Greek (langue, personne).

Grèce [grɛs] f. GÉOGR. Greece.

gréco-latin, ine [grɛkɔlatɛ̃, in] adj. Græco-Latin.

gréco-romain, aine [grɛkɔrɔmɛ̃, ɛn] adj. Græco-Roman.

grecque [grɛk] f. ARCHIT., ARTS. Greek key-pattern, Greek border. ‖ TECHN. Saw (de relieur).

gredin [grədɛ̃] m. Scoundrel, rascal, rogue.

gredinerie [-dinri] f. Rascally trick, piece of roguery (action); rascality, roguery, villainy (état).

gréement [gremɑ̃] m. NAUT. Rigging, rig (d'un bateau); gear (d'un canot).

gréer [gree] v. tr. (1). NAUT., AVIAT. To rig; to sling (un hamac); to fit (une vergue).

gréeur [-œ:r] m. NAUT. Rigger.

greffage [grɛfa:ʒ] m. MÉD., BOT. Grafting.

greffe [grɛf] m. JUR. Office of clerk of a court. ‖ COMM. Registry (d'une société).

greffe f. MÉD. Grafting, graft. ‖ BOT. Graft, scion, slip (ente); grafting (greffage); *greffe en couronne, en écusson*, crown-, shield-grafting; *greffe par œil détaché*, budding.

greffer [-fe] v. tr. (1). MÉD. To graft. ‖ BOT. To graft; *greffer en écusson*, to bud. ‖ FIG. *Greffer sur*, to add to, to engraft upon.

greffeur [-fœ:r] m. MÉD., BOT. Grafter.

greffier [grɛfje] m. JUR. Town-clerk, recorder, registrar (municipal); clerk (de tribunal).

greffoir [grɛfwa:r] m. Grafting-knife.

greffon [-fɔ̃] m. BOT. Graft, scion, slip.

grégaire [grege:r] adj. Gregarious.

grégarisme [-garism] m. Gregariousness.

grège [grɛ:ʒ] adj. Raw (soie).
— f. Raw silk, grege.

grégeois [greʒwa] adj., m. *Feu grégeois*, Greek fire.

grégorien, enne [gregɔrjɛ̃, ɛn] adj. ECCLÉS. Gregorian.

grêle [grɛ:l] adj. Slender, thin, slim, lank (bras, tige); spindle (jambes); thin, acute, high-pitched, shrill (voix). ‖ MÉD. *Intestin grêle*, small intestine.
— m. MÉD. Small intestine.

grêle f. Hail; *averse de grêle*, hail-storm. ‖ FIG. Hail, shower (de balles, de coups). ‖ FAM. *Méchant comme la grêle*, wicked as the devil.

grêlé, ée [grɛle] adj. BOT. Hail-damaged (plante). ‖ MÉD. Pock-marked (visage).

grêler v. intr. (1). To hail. ‖ FIG. To hail, to rain down thick.
— v. tr. To damage (ou) ruin crops by hail. ‖ MÉD. To pock-mark (le visage).

grelin [grəlɛ̃] m. NAUT. Cablet, hawser, warp; *grelin de remorque*, tow-rope.

grêlon [grɛlɔ̃] m. Hail-stone.
grelot [grəlo] m. Small round bell (clochette); sleigh-bell (de traîneau). ‖ FAM. *Attacher le grelot,* to bell the cat. ‖ Pl. FAM. Funk, jitters.
grelottant, ante [-tɑ̃, ɑ̃:t] adj. Jingling (grelot). ‖ Shivering, shaking, trembling (personne).
grelottement [-tmɑ̃] m. Jingling (d'un grelot); shiver, shivering (d'une personne).
grelotter [-te] v. intr. (1). To jingle (grelot). ‖ To shiver, to shake, to tremble (personne).
grenade [grənad] f. BOT. Pomegranate. ‖ MILIT. Grenade, bomb; *grenade adhérente,* sticky bomb; *grenade éclairante,* flare; *grenade à main,* hand-grenade. ‖ NAUT. *Grenade sous-marine,* depth-charge.
grenader [-de] v. tr. (1). MILIT. To attack with grenades; to bomb. ‖ NAUT. To launch depth-charges at.
grenadier [-dje] m. BOT. Pomegranate-tree.
grenadier m. MILIT. Grenadier.
grenadine [grənadin] f. CULIN. Grenadine.
grenaille [grənɑ:j] f. Grains (de métal); pellets, shot (de plomb); *en grenaille,* granulated. ‖ AGRIC. Refuse grain.
grenaison [grənɛzɔ̃] f. AGRIC. Seeding, corning.
grenat [grəna] adj. invar. Garnet-red.
— m. Garnet.
grené, ée [grəne] adj. Seeded, corned (céréales). ‖ Shredded (cire); granulated, corned (poudre); grained (sel). ‖ ARTS. Stippled (gravure).
— m. ARTS. Stipple.
greneler [grənle] v. tr. (8 a). To grain.
grener [grəne] v. tr. (5). To shred (de la cire); to granulate (de la poudre); to grain (du sel). ‖ ARTS. To stipple (une gravure).
— v. intr. AGRIC. To seed (céréales).
grenier [grənje] m. Loft (à fourrage); granary, garner (à grain); store-house (réserve); *grenier à foin,* hay-loft. ‖ Lumber-room (débarras); attic, garret (mansarde); *de la cave au grenier,* high and low, all over the house. ‖ NAUT. Dunnage. ‖ FIG. Granary (région fertile).
grenouillage [grənuja:ʒ] m. FAM. Skulduggery, monkey business, shady dealings.
grenouille [grənu:j] f. ZOOL. Frog; *grenouille mugissante* (ou) *taureau,* bullfrog. ‖ NAUT. *Homme-grenouille,* frogman. ‖ FAM. Kitty (caisse); *manger la grenouille,* to make off with the kitty. ‖ FAM. *Grenouille de bénitier,* church hen.
grenouillette [-jɛt] f. BOT. Water-crowfoot. ‖ MÉD. Ranula.
grenu, ue [grəny] adj. Grained (cuir, peau); clotted (huile); rough-grained, granular (surface); coarse-grained (toile). ‖ MÉD. Granular (fracture). ‖ AGRIC. Grainy (épi).
— m. Granularity (du marbre).
grenure [-ny:r] f. ARTS. Stippling, stipple. ‖ Graining (du cuir).
grès [grɛ] m. Sandstone, gritstone; *grès dur,* grit. ‖ Stone ware (grès cérame); *cruche de grès,* stone jug; *grès flammé,* glazed earthenware.
gréseux, euse [grezø, ø:z] adj. Gritty, sandy.
grésil [grezil] m. Small hard hail (grêle menue); frozen snow pellets (neige dure). ‖ TECHN. Cullet, pounded glass (verre).
grésillement [grezijmɑ̃] m. Crackling, sputtering (de flamme); sizzling (de friture). ‖ Chirping (de grillon). ‖ Whirring (au téléphone).
grésiller [-je] v. intr., impers. (1). To patter (grésil).
— v. intr. To crackle, to sputter (flamme); to sizzle (friture); *mourir en grésillant,* to sputter out (flamme). ‖ To chirp (grillon). ‖ To whirr (téléphone).
— v. tr. To scorch (brûler); to shrivel up (rétrécir).
gressin [grɛsɛ̃] m. CULIN. Grissino.

grève [grɛv] f. Beach, shore, strand (plage); bank, strand (rive). ‖ FIG. Strike, walk-out; *grève de la faim,* hunger-strike; *grève perlée,* go-slow (ou) U. S. slow-down strike; *grève sur le tas,* sit-down (ou) stay-in strike; *grève du zèle,* work-to-rule action; *faire grève,* to strike, to be on strike; *se mettre en grève,* to strike, to go on strike.
grever [grəve] v. tr. (5). FIN. To burden, to encumber (d'une hypothèque); to saddle (d'un impôt). ‖ JUR. To entail (un héritage); to rate, to lay a rate on (un immeuble); to mortgage (une propriété).
gréviste [grevist] s. Striker.
gribouillage [gribuja:ʒ], **gribouillis** [-ji] m. FAM. Scrawl, scribble (écriture); daub (peinture).
gribouille [gribu:j] m. Simpleton, booby.
gribouiller [-je] v. tr., intr. (1). FAM. To scrawl, to scribble (en écrivant); to daub (en peignant).
gribouilleur [-jœ:r] s. FAM. Scrawler, scribbler (qui écrit mal); dauber, daubster (qui peint mal).
grief [grijɛf] m. Wrong, injury, grievance (dommage); grievance, complaint, ground for complaint (plainte); *faire grief à qqn de qqch.,* to hold sth. against s.o., to reproach s.o. with sth.
grièvement [-jɛvmɑ̃] adv. MÉD. Grievously, badly, sorely, gravely, seriously, dangerously. ‖ FIG. Deeply.
grièveté [-jɛvte]. V. GRAVITÉ.
griffe [grif] f. Claw, talon (d'un faucon); claw, nail (d'un quadrupède); *faire ses griffes,* to sharpen its claws (chat). ‖ COMM. Signature stamp, facsimile stamp, label (d'un couturier). ‖ TECHN. Claw (d'établi); hook-wrench (de forgeron); glass-holder, globe-holder (de galerie de lampe); grip, clamp, clip (de serrage); *griffe à papiers,* paper-clip (ou) -fastener. ‖ BOT. Root (d'asperge); tendril (de vigne); blaze, notch (encoche sur un arbre). ‖ FIG. Jaws (de la mort). ‖ FAM. Malicious (ou) sarcastic remark, dig (fam.); *sortir les griffes,* to show one's claws; *tomber sous la griffe de qqn,* to fall into s.o.'s clutches.
griffer [-fe] v. tr. (1). To scratch, to claw (égratigner); to seize in one's claws (saisir). ‖ To stamp with a signature (signer). ‖ To clamp, to clip (fixer). ‖ To mark, to blaze, to notch (un arbre).
griffeur [-fœ:r] m. Scratcher, clawer.
griffon [-fɔ̃] m. ZOOL. Griffon (chien); tawny vulture (vautour). ‖ SPORTS. Large hook (hameçon). ‖ BLAS. Griffin, gryphon.
griffonnage [-fɔna:ʒ] m. Rough sketch (brouillon, dessin); scrawl, scribble (écriture).
griffonnement [-fɔnmɑ̃] m. ARTS. Sketch.
griffonner [-fɔne] v. tr. (1) To sketch roughly, to block in (un dessin); to scrawl, to scribble (un texte); to doodle.
griffonneur [-fɔnœ:r] s. Scrawler, scribbler.
griffu, ue [grify] adj. Equipped with claws.
griffure [-fy:r] f. Scratch. (V. ÉGRATIGNURE).
grigner [griɲe] v. intr. To puckle (tissu).
grignon [griɲɔ̃] m. Crust.
grignotage [-ɲɔta:ʒ] m. Attrition (tactique); gradual erosion (destruction).
grignotement [-ɲɔtmɑ̃] m. Nibbling, nibble.
grignoter [-te] v. tr. (1). To peck at, to pick at (mangeoter); to nibble, to nibble at (ronger). ‖ FIG. To encroach (empiéter) [*sur,* on].
grignoteur [-tœ:r] s. Nibbler.
grignotis [-ti] m. ARTS. Dotting.
grigou [grigu] m. FAM. Skinflint, U.S. tightwad.
gri-gri [grigri] m. FAM. Greegree, U. S. grigri.
gril [gri] m. Grill (instrument de torture). ‖ CULIN. Gridiron, grid, grill. ‖ TECHN. Grating, grid. ‖ FIG. *Sur le gril,* on the rack, on tenterhooks, on pins and needles.
grillade [-jad] f. CULIN. Toasting (du pain); grill-

ing, broiling (de la viande); piece of toast (pain); grill, grilled meat (viande).

grillage [grija:ʒ] m. CULIN. Roasting (du café); toasting (du pain); grilling, broiling (de la viande). ‖ TECHN. Singeing (d'une étoffe); calcining, roasting (d'un minerai). ‖ ELECTR. Burning-out (d'une lampe).

grillage m. Lattice, lattice-work (en bois); grating, wire-netting (en fil de fer). ‖ TECHN. Grate, grid (de chaudière). ‖ ELECTR. Grid, frame.

grillager [-jaʒe] v. tr. (7). To lattice, to grate, to equip with lattice-work (griller). ‖ To surround with grating (ou) wire-netting (entourer de grillages).

grille [gri:j] f. Grating, railing (de clôture); iron bars (de prison); *entourer d'une grille,* to rail in; *séparer par une grille,* to rail off. ‖ Gate, iron gate (d'entrée). ‖ ECCLÉS. Grille, grill (de couvent). ‖ TECHN. Grating (d'égout, d'évier); grate (de foyer); rack (de turbine). ‖ Cross-word puzzle form (ou) pattern (de mots croisés). ‖ ELECTR. Grid. ‖ CHIM. *Grille à analyse,* combustion furnace. ‖ AUTOM. Grille (de radiateur). ‖ MILIT. Cipher-grid, cipher-stencil (d'un code). ‖ **Grille-écran,** f. RADIO. *Lampe à grille-écran,* screen grid valve.

grille-pain [gri:jpɛ̃] m. invar. CULIN. Toaster, bread-toaster.

griller [grije] v. tr. (1). CULIN. To roast (du café); to toast (du pain); to broil, to grill (de la viande). ‖ AGRIC. To frost, to nip (gelée); to burn, to parch, to scorch (soleil). ‖ TECHN. To singe (une étoffe); to calcine, to roast (du minerai). ‖ ELECTR. To burn out (une lampe). ‖ AUTOM. To jam, to seize, to burn out, U. S. to fry (fam.) [un moteur]. ‖ FAM. To burn, to scorch (qqch.); to spot, to detect (qqn); *griller une cigarette,* to smoke a cigarette.
— v. intr. CULIN. To toast (pain); to grill, to broil (viande). ‖ ELECTR. To burn out (lampe). ‖ AVIAT. To burn up (ou) out (avion). ‖ FIG. *Griller d'envie* (ou) *d'impatience de,* to be burning to, to be itching to.

griller v. tr. (1). To grate, to bar (une fenêtre); to rail in, to rail off (un monument).

grilloir [-jwa:r] m. CULIN. Griller, broiler. ‖ TECHN. *Grilloir de minerai,* ore-roaster.

grillon [grijɔ̃] m. ZOOL. Cricket; *grillon des champs,* field-cricket.

grill-room [grilrum] m. Grill-room, restaurant.

grimaçant, ante [grimasɑ̃, ɑ̃:t] adj. Grimacing, grinning; *sourire grimaçant,* grin, twisted smile. ‖ FAM. Full of creases, wrinkled (vêtement).

grimace [grimas] f. Grimace, wry face (moue, rictus); *faire des grimaces,* to make (ou) to pull a face; *faire la grimace,* to make a long face (de déception); to make a wry face (de dégoût); *faire une grimace de douleur,* to wince; *faire la grimace à une proposition,* to give a proposal an unfavourable reception. ‖ FIG. Sham, humbug, feigning (feinte). ‖ Pl. Grimaces, affectation (simagrées); *faire des grimaces,* to simper, to mince, to smirk, to put on airs. ‖ FAM. Crease, pucker, wrinkle (mauvais pli); *faire des grimaces,* to be full of creases, to be wrinkled (vêtement).

grimacer [-se] v. intr. (1). To grimace, to make a wry face; *grimacer de douleur,* to wince. ‖ FIG. To simper, to smirk, to mince (minauder). ‖ FAM. To pucker, to crease, to wrinkle (faire des plis).
— v. tr. *Grimacer un sourire,* to grin.

grimacerie [-sri] f. Grimacing, grinning. ‖ FIG. Affectation, smirking, mincing.

grimacier, ère [-sje, ɛ:r] adj. Given to grimacing (ou) to grinning. ‖ FIG. Affected, hypocritical.
— s. Person given to grimacing, grimacer. ‖ FIG. Affected person, humbug.

grimage [grima:ʒ] m. THÉÂTR. Making-up.

grimer [-me] v. tr. (1). THÉÂTR. To make up (un acteur) [en, as].
— v. pr. **Se grimer,** to make up, to put on greasepaint. (V. SE MAQUILLER.)

grimoire [grimwa:r] m. Magician's book (livre de magie). ‖ FIG. Unintelligible book (livre obscur). ‖ FAM. Scrawl, scribble (gribouillis).

grimpant, ante [grɛ̃pɑ̃, ɑ̃:t] adj. Climbing (animal); climbing, trailing, creeping (plante); *plante grimpante,* creeper.
— m. POP. Slacks, bags (pantalon).

grimpée [-pe] f. FAM. Climb.

grimper [-pe] v. intr. (1). To climb (en général); to swarm up (en s'aidant des genoux ou des jambes); to clamber up, to scramble up (en s'aidant des pieds et des mains); *grimper à l'échelle,* to go up the ladder. ‖ BOT. To creep, to climb, to trail (plante).
— v. tr. To climb, to ascend; to clamber up; *grimper une côte,* to climb a slope.

grimpette [pɛt] f. Steep climb. (V. CÔTE.)

grimpeur, euse [-pœ:r, ø:z] adj. Climbing. ‖ ZOOL. Scansorial, climbing (oiseau). ‖ TECHN. *Appareil grimpeur,* set of climbing irons.
— s. Climber. ‖ ZOOL. Pl. Climbers (oiseaux).

grinçant, ante [grɛ̃sɑ̃, ɑ̃:t] adj. Creaking, grating (bruit). ‖ FIG. Biting, caustic, scathing (humour, remarque, satire); grating (rire).

grincement [grɛ̃smɑ̃] m. Grinding, gritting, gnashing (de dents); grinding, creaking, grating (d'un gond); scratching (d'une plume).

grincer [-se] v. intr. (6). To grind, to grit, to gnash (dents); to grind, to creak, to grate (gond); to scratch (plume).

grincheux, euse [-ʃø, ø:z] adj. Grumpy, cranky, crabby, sour, cross, peevish. (V. ACARIÂTRE.)
— s. Grumbler, crab, cross-patch.

gringalet [grɛ̃galɛ] m. Weak (ou) puny person; weedy person, stripling; shrimp, poor fish (fam.).

griot [grijo] m. Griot, African story-teller.

griotte [grijɔt] f. BOT. Morello, morello cherry.

grippage [gripaʒ] m. TECHN. Seizing (d'un piston); scoring (d'un roulement); rubbing, friction (d'une surface).

grippal, ale [gripal] adj. MÉD. Influenzal.

grippe [grip] f. MÉD. Grippe, influenza; flu (fam.); *grippe intestinale,* intestinal flu, gastric influenza. ‖ FIG. Dislike, aversion, antipathy; *prendre en grippe,* to take a dislike to.

grippé, ée [-pe] adj. MÉD. Suffering from influenza; down with the flu (fam.); *être grippé,* to have influenza; to have the flu (fam.).

grippement [gripmɑ̃] m. V. GRIPPAGE.

gripper [gripe] v. tr. (1). To pounce upon, to snatch (agripper); to grip, to clutch (saisir). ‖ FIG. To steal (dérober).
— v. intr. TECHN. To seize up, to bind, to jam (piston); to get hot, to become abraded (ou) scored (roulement); to adhere, to stick (surface). ‖ To crinkle, to wrinkle, to pucker (étoffe).

grippe-sou [gripsu] m. FAM. Money-grubber, skinflint, screw, U.S. tightwad. (V. GRIGOU.)

gris, ise [gri, iz] adj. Grey, gray (en général); grey, grizzled (cheveux, barbe); cloudy, overcast (ciel); dull, gloomy (temps); pale red, pinkish (vin); *gris bleu,* blue-grey; *gris clair, foncé,* light, dark grey; *gris fer,* iron-grey; *gris perle,* pearl-grey. ‖ ZOOL. Grizzly (ours). ‖ COMM. *Petit-gris,* grey squirrel (fourrure). ‖ FAM. Tipsy, fuddled, tight, U. S. high (v. ÉMÉCHÉ, PAF); *en voir de grises,* to have a bad time of it; *en faire voir de grises à qqn,* to give s.o. a rough time; *faire grise mine à,* to cold-shoulder.
— m. Grey (couleur). ‖ Ordinary tobacco.

grisaille [grizɑ:j] f. ARTS. Grisaille, monochrome painting; pencil-sketch on grey paper (dessin);

tint-graving (gravure); first sketch with shadows laid in (peinture). ‖ Grey colour, dullness, gloom (du ciel, du temps).

grisailler [-zɑje] v. tr. (1). To grey, to paint in grisaille.
— v. intr. To grey, to grow (ou) to become (ou) to turn grey.

grisant, ante [grizɑ̃, ɑ̃:t] adj. Exhilarating, intoxicating, heady.

grisâtre [-zɑ:tr] adj. Greyish.

grisbi [grisbi] m. ARGOT. Oof, dough, brass, U.S. jack, green stuff. (V. FRIC.)

grisé, ée [grize] adj. ARTS. Tinted grey, painted grey. ‖ FIG. Inebriated, intoxicated (de, with).
— m. ARTS. Grey tint (ou) wash.

griser v. tr. (1). ARTS. To paint (ou) tint with grey. ‖ FIG. To inebriate, to intoxicate (de, with). ‖ FAM. To fuddle, to make tipsy. (V. ENIVRER.)
— v. pr. **Se griser**, to become inebriated, to get tipsy (ou) tight (s'enivrer). ‖ FIG. *Se griser de*, to revel in, to luxuriate in (espoir); to be intoxicated by, to have one's head turned by (succès).

griserie [-zri] f. Inebriation, intoxication, tipsiness. (V. IVRESSE.) ‖ FIG. Intoxication, exhilaration, rapture.

grisette [grizɛt] f. Grisette (étoffe, ouvrière). ‖ ZOOL. Whitethroat.

grison, onne [grizɔ̃, ɔn] adj. Grey, grizzled, grey-haired.
— m. † Greybeard (vieillard). ‖ ZOOL. FAM. Donkey.

grisonnant, ante [-zɔnɑ̃, ɑ̃:t] adj. Greying, turning grey, touched with grey (cheveux).

grisonnement [-zɔnmɑ̃] m. Greying, turning grey.

grisonner [-zɔne] v. intr. (1). To turn grey, to grow grey.
— v. tr. To paint (ou) to stain grey.

grisotte [grizɔt] f. Clock (sur les bas).

grisou [grizu] m. Fire-damp, pit-gas; *coup de grisou*, fire-damp explosion.

grive [griv] f. ZOOL. Thrush; *grive chanteuse*, throstle, song thrush. ‖ LOC. *Faute de grives, on mange des merles*, half a loaf is better than none; beggars can't be choosers.

griveler [grivle] v. tr. (8 a). To graft, to scrounge (de l'argent); to cadge, U.S. to chisel (un repas).
— v. intr. To graft, to scrounge; to sponge, U.S. to chisel. ‖ *Grivelé*, speckled (plumage).

grivèlerie [-vɛlri] f. Graft (gain illicite); scrounging, sponging, U.S. chiseling (repas).

griveton [grivtɔ̃] m. POP. Soldier, squaddy.

grivois, oise [grivwa, a:z] adj. Spicy, racy, licentious, broad, bawdy.
— s. Libertin, rake.

grivoiserie [-zri] f. Licentiousness, raciness. ‖ Broad joke, smutty story.

grizzli [grizli] m. ZOOL. Grizzly bear, grizzly.

grœnendael [grɔnɛndal] m. ZOOL. Grœnendael, Belgian sheepdog.

groenlandais, aise [grɔɛnlɑ̃dɛ, ɛ:z] adj. GÉOG. Greenlandic, of Greenland.
— s. Greenlander (habitant); Greenlandic (langue).

grog [grɔg] m. CULIN. Grog, toddy.

groggy [grɔgi] adj. Groggy.

grognard, arde [grɔɲa:r, a:rd] adj. Grumbling, grousing, U.S. griping.
— m. Grumbler, grouser, grunter, U.S. griper. ‖ MILIT. Veteran of Napoleon's armies.

grogne [grɔɲ] f. FAM. Grousing, grumbling, moaning.

grognement [-mɑ̃] m. Growl, snarl (de chien); grunt, grunting (de porc, de personne). ‖ Snort (d'incrédulité); growl, grunt, grumble (de mécontentement).

grogner [grɔɲe] v. intr. (1). To growl, to snarl (chien); to grunt (porc, personne). ‖ To snort (d'incrédulité); to growl, to grunt (de mécontentement).
— v. tr. To growl, to snarl (des injures).

grogneur, euse [-ɲœ:r, ø:z] adj. Grumbling, grousing, peevish, U. S. griping. (V. BOUGON.)
— m. Grumbler, grouser, U. S. griper.

grognon [-ɲɔ̃] adj. Grumbling, peevish, cross, grouchy. (V. RONCHON.)
— m. Grumbler, cross-patch.

groin [grwɛ̃] m. Snout (de porc). ‖ POP. Ugly mug (figure).

grol(l)e [grɔl] f. POP. Shoe.

grommeler [grɔmle] v. intr. (8 a). To grumble, to growl (grogner); to mutter (marmonner).
— v. tr. To mutter (un juron).

grommellement [-mɛlmɑ̃] m. Grumbling, muttering (grognement).

grondement [grɔ̃dmɑ̃] m. Rumble, rumbling (de bruit sourd, de tonnerre); roar, roaring, boom, booming (de canon, d'orage, de vagues); growl, snarl (de chien); snort (de colère, d'incrédulité); muttering (d'un orage en préparation).

gronder [grɔ̃de] v. intr. (1). To rumble (bruit sourd, tonnerre); to roar, to boom (canon, orage, vagues); to growl, to snarl (chien); to mutter (orage qui débute).
— v. tr. To scold, to reproach, to chide, to rate (v. RÉPRIMANDER); *gronder sans cesse*, to nag.

gronderie [-dri] f. Scolding, chiding, rating.

grondeur, euse [-dœ:r, ø:z] adj. Scolding, grumbling, nagging.
— m. Scolder, scold.

grondeuse [-døz] f. Scold, shrew (mégère).

grondin [-dɛ̃] m. ZOOL. Gurnet, gurnard.

groom [grum] m. Groom (d'écurie); page-boy, buttons, U. S. bell-hop, bell-boy (d'hôtel).

gros, osse [gro, o:s] adj.

---

1. Sens général. — 2. Solide. — 3. Gras. — 4. Important. — 5. Long. — 6. Sonore. — 7. NAUT. — 8. ARCHIT. — 9. MILIT. — 10. MÉD. — 11. TECHN. — 12. ZOOL. — 13. CULIN. — 14. COMM. — 15. FIG. — 16. FAM. — 17. LOC.

---

1. Big, large (en général); bulky (paquet); fat (portefeuille); *gros caractères*, big letters, large print; *gros morceau*, large piece, lump; *gros orteil*, big toe. ‖ 2. Strong (solide); strong, stout, thick (corde); heavy (tôle); *gros bout*, thick end; *gros fil*, heavy thread; *gros souliers*, stout shoes, heavy boots; *grosse toile*, coarse linen. ‖ 3. Fat, stout (gros); *gros et gras*, fleshy, portly; *grosses lèvres*, thick lips. ‖ 4. Large, big, considerable, substantial (important); *gros bourgeois*, solid citizen, wealthy burgher; *jouer gros jeu*, to play for high stakes; *gros travail*, heavy work. ‖ 5. Good, full (long); *il y a une grosse heure*, a good hour ago. ‖ 6. Loud (sonore); guffaw, loud (rire); heavy, deep (soupir); deep, booming (voix). ‖ 7. NAUT. Rough, high, heavy (mer, vent); heavy, hard (pluie); swollen (rivière); bad, heavy, foul (temps); *grosse chaleur*, hot weather. ‖ 8. ARCHIT. *Gros murs*, main walls; *grosse poutre*, thick (ou) stout beam. ‖ 9. MILIT. Heavy (artillerie, cavalerie); big (bataillon). ‖ 10. MÉD. Swollen (enflé); pregnant (femme enceinte); high, raging (fièvre); bad, heavy (rhume); *yeux gros de larmes*, eyes swollen with tears. ‖ 11. TECHN. High-powered, heavy (moteur); *grosse pièce de forge*, heavy forging; *gros tour*, heavy lathe. ‖ 12. ZOOL. *Gros bétail*, cattle; *gros gibier*, big game. ‖ 13. CULIN. Coarse, cooking (sel); heavy, full-

bodied (vin). ‖ **14.** Comm. *Grosse affaire*, big concern, large business. ‖ Fin. Substantial (bénéfice) ; high (intérêt) ; large (somme). ‖ **15.** Fig. Important ; great, big, serious (difficulté) ; bad, serious, gross (erreur) ; *gros buveur,* heavy drinker ; *gros mangeur,* big eater. ‖ Fig. Coarse, vulgar, broad (mot, plaisanterie) ; *gros bon sens,* plain (ou) broad common sense ; *grosse indélicatesse,* gross impropriety ; *gros mensonge,* big lie, whacker, whopper ; *gros mots,* swear-words. ‖ Fig. *Gros de,* big (ou) fraught (ou) pregnant with ; *tentative grosse de risques,* attempt fraught with risks. ‖ **16.** Fam. *Gros bonnet, grosse légume,* bigwig, big shot, U. S. big wheel, big-time operator. ‖ **17.** Loc. *Avoir le cœur gros,* to have a heavy heart ; *faire le gros dos,* to arch its back (chat) ; *faire la grosse voix,* to speak gruffly ; *faire les gros yeux à,* to glare at.
— m. Fat man (homme) ; big one (objet). ‖ Bulk, mass, chief (ou) major part (en général) ; worst part (d'un orage) ; *le gros de la besogne,* the bulk of the heavy (ou) rough work ; *le plus gros est fait,* the hardest part is done. ‖ Body, party, strong force (d'un groupe) ; mass (du peuple). ‖ Méd. *Gros de l'avant-bras,* swell of the forearm. ‖ Bot. Thickest part (d'un arbre). ‖ Milit. Naut. Main part, bulk (d'une armée, d'une flotte). ‖ Comm. Best part (d'une affaire) ; wholesale trade, wholesale dealing (commerce) ; *boucher en gros,* carcass-butcher ; *commerce de gros,* wholesale trade ; *gros et détail,* wholesale and retail ; *marchand en gros,* wholesaler, wholesale dealer. ‖ *Gros de l'eau,* high water of springtide. ‖ *Gros de Naples,* silk cloth (soie). ‖ Fig. Essential part (d'une doctrine) ; *gros de l'été,* height of summer ; *gros de l'hiver,* depth of winter.
— adv. Much ; *coûter gros,* to cost a lot ; *écrire gros,* to write in large characters ; *gagner gros,* to earn a lot, to make a lot of money ; *il y a gros à parier,* it's a safe bet. ‖ Comm. *En gros,* wholesale, in bulk. ‖ Fig. *En gros,* approximately, roughly (environ) ; on the whole, in the main (en somme) ; *évaluation en gros,* rough estimate. ‖ **Gros-bec,** m. Zool. Hawfinch. ‖ **Gros-grain,** m. Grogram, gros grain, petersham. ‖ **Gros-porteur,** m. Aviat. Jumbo jet.

groseille [grozɛːj] f. Bot. White (ou) red currant ; *groseille à maquereau,* gooseberry. ‖ Culin. *Gelée de groseille,* red-currant jelly.

groseillier [-je] m. Bot. Currant-bush ; *groseillier à maquereau,* gooseberry-bush.

grosse [gros] f. Fat (ou) stout woman (femme). ‖ Text-hand, round-hand (écriture) ; *plume de grosse,* round-nibbed pen. ‖ Comm. Gross, twelve dozen. ‖ Jur. Engrossed copy, engrossed document, engrossment (d'un acte).

grosserie [-ri] f. Comm. Wholesale dealing.

grossesse [-sɛs] f. Méd. Pregnancy.

grosseur [-sœːr] f. Bulk, size, volume. ‖ Bulkir.ess, thickness (épaisseur). ‖ Coarseness (d'un fil, du grain, d'une pierre, d'un tissu). ‖ Méd. Stoutness, heaviness (du corps) ; thickness (des lèvres) ; swelling (enflure) ; tumour (tumeur).

grossier, ère [-sje, ɛr] adj. Coarse, rough (drap, vêtement). ‖ Culin. Common, coarse, gross (nourriture). ‖ Fig. Unrefined, coarse (sans délicatesse) ; unpolished, boorish, loutish (incivil) ; *air grossier,* uncouth appearance ; *gens grossiers,* low company ; *grossier personnage,* unmannerly fellow ; *réponse grossière,* offensive answer ; *traits grossiers,* coarse features. ‖ Fig. Coarse, crude, artless (sans art) ; *image grossière,* crude image ; *travail grossier,* unpolished work. ‖ Fig. Gross, flagrant, glaring (erreur, mensonge) ; crass, rank (ignorance). ‖ Fig. Coarse, vulgar, ribald, foul (plaisanterie) ; abusive (propos).
— m. Boor (v. butor). ‖ Fig. Coarseness.

grossièrement [-sjɛrmɑ̃] adv. Grossly (nourri) ; coarsely (vêtu). ‖ Flagrantly, glaringly (mentir) ; grossly (se tromper). ‖ Coarsely, boorishly, rudely (sans politesse). ‖ Coarsely, rudely, crudely, clumsily (sans art). ‖ Roughly, broadly (grosso modo). ‖ Coarsely, offensively, indecently (d'une manière choquante).

grossièreté [-sjɛrte] f. Coarseness, roughness (d'une étoffe). ‖ Rudeness, churlishness, unmannerliness (manque d'éducation). ‖ Coarseness, crudeness, rudeness, clumsiness (d'un travail). ‖ Grossness, glaring nature (d'une erreur) ; flagrancy (d'un mensonge). ‖ Coarseness, boorishness, rudeness (des manières) ; broadness, coarseness, foulness (d'une plaisanterie, d'un propos) ; *dire des grossièretés,* to be offensive, to make rude remarks.

grossir [grosiːr] v. tr. (2). To enlarge, to make bigger, to swell, to magnify ; *cette robe la grossit,* that dress makes her look stouter. ‖ To swell (une rivière). ‖ Phys. To magnify (loupe, microscope). ‖ Fin. To increase (des frais). ‖ Fig. To exaggerate, to magnify (un défaut, un incident).
— v. intr. To increase, to swell (foule) ; to grow fatter (ou) stouter (personne). ‖ To get up, to rise (mer, vent) ; to swell (rivière). ‖ Fin. To increase (dépenses). ‖ Bot. To grow bigger (fruit). ‖ Fig. To increase, to swell (émotion).

grossissant, ante [-sisɑ̃, ɑ̃ːt] adj. Growing bigger (ou) more numerous ; increasing, swelling. ‖ Phys. Amplifying, enlarging, magnifying (verre).

grossissement [-sismɑ̃] m. Swelling out, increase in bulk (ou) in number. ‖ Phys. Enlargement, magnifying (par une loupe) ; power, magnifying power, magnification (d'une loupe) ; *à fort grossissement,* high-power (jumelles).

grossiste [-sist] s. Comm. Wholesaler, wholesale dealer.

grosso modo [grosomɔdo] loc. adv. Roughly, at a rough guess.

grotesque [grotɛsk] adj. Arts., Archit. Grotesque. ‖ Grotesque, ludicrous. (V. ridicule.)
— m. Grotesque personage ; freak.

grotte [grot] f. Grotto (artificielle) ; cave (naturelle).

grouillant, ante [grujɑ̃, ɑ̃ːt] adj. Teeming, swarming, seething (foule) ; crawling, wriggling (vers) ; *grouillant de,* crawling (ou) swarming (ou) teeming (ou) alive with.

grouillement [-jmɑ̃] m. Crawling, swarming, wriggling (bruit, mouvement) ; swarming mass (masse). ‖ Méd. Rumbling (des intestins). ‖ Ciném. Swarming.

grouiller [-je] v. intr. (1). To teem, to swarm ; *grouiller de,* to be alive (ou) crawling with. ‖ Méd. To rumble (intestins). ‖ Fam. To move, to budge. ‖ Pop. To hustle.
— v. pr. **Se grouiller,** Fam. to get a move on, to stir one's stumps.

grouillot [grujo] m. Fam. Errand-boy.

group [grup] m. Comm. Sealed bag of cash.

groupage [-paːʒ] m. Comm. Collecting, bulking.

groupe [grup] m. Group (d'amis, d'objets) ; clump (d'arbres) ; knot, party (de promeneurs) ; *par groupes de deux ou trois,* in twos and threes, U. S. in twos or threes. ‖ Méd. *Groupe sanguin,* blood group. ‖ Astron. Cluster (d'étoiles). ‖ Electr. *Groupe électrogène,* generator set ; *groupe motopropulseur,* motor drive. ‖ Milit. Section. ‖ Aviat. Group. ‖ Zool. Division.

groupement [-pmɑ̃] m. Grouping (v. assemblage) ; group (groupe). ‖ Electr. Connection, connecting up, arrangement (de piles). ‖ Comm. *Groupement des sociétés industrielles,* grouping, trustification ; trust, pool.

grouper [-pe] v. tr. (1). To group, to arrange in groups (des articles, des personnes). ‖ Comm.

To collect (des colis). ‖ ELECTR. To connect up, to join up, to couple, to group (des piles). ‖ FIG. To concentrate (ses efforts).
— v. pr. **Se grouper**, to gather (se rassembler); to unite, to rally, to join forces (s'unir).
groupuscule [-pyskyl] m. FAM. Small political group, clique.
grouse [-gruz] f. ZOOL. Grouse.
gruau [gryo] m. BOT. Hulled grain, groats. ‖ CULIN. Gruel (tisane de gruau); *gruau d'avoine*, oatmeal; grits, groats; *farine de gruau*, finest wheat flour; *pain de gruau*, fine wheaten bread.
grue [gry] f. ZOOL. Crane. ‖ TECHN. Crane; *grue d'applique* (ou) *à potence*, wall-crane; *grue à bras* (ou) *à flèche*, jib-crane; *grue de chargement*, loading hoist; *grue à pivot*, revolving-crane; *grue roulante* (ou) *transportable*, travelling (ou) loco crane. ‖ CH. DE F. *Grue d'alimentation*, water-pillar, water-crane. ‖ FAM. Whore, streetwalker. (V. CATIN.) ‖ FAM. *Faire le pied de grue*, to be kept waiting, to cool one's heels.
gruger [gryʒe] v. tr. (7). To fleece, to plunder, to sponge on. (V. ESTAMPER.)
grume [grym] f. Bark; *bois en grume*, rough (ou) undressed timber. ‖ Log (bûche).
grumeau [grymo] m. Clot; lump (de farine); curd (de lait caillé).
grumeler (se) [səgrymle] v. pr. (8 a). To clot; to curdle (lait).
grumeleux, euse [-lø, ø:z] adj. Clotted, lumpy; curdled (lait); gritty (poire); granular (surface).
grumelure [-ly:r] f. TECHN. Cavity.
gruppetto [grupɛto] m. MUS. Turn, gruppetto.
grutier [grytje] m. Crane-driver, crane operator.
gruyère [gryjɛ:r] m. CULIN. Gruyère, U. S. Swiss cheese.
Guadeloupe [gwadlup] f. GÉOGR. Guadeloupe.
guadeloupéen, enne [-peɛ̃, ɛn] adj. GÉOGR. Of (ou) from Guadeloupe.
— s. Native (ou) inhabitant of Guadeloupe.
guano [gwano] m. Guano.
Guatemala [gwatemala] m. GÉOGR. Guatemala.
guatémaltèque [gwatemaltɛk] adj., s. GÉOGR. Guatemalan.
gué [ge] m. Ford; *passer à gué*, to ford.
guéable [geabl] adj. Fordable.
guelfe [gɛlf] adj. † Guelphic.
— m. † Guelph.
guelte [gɛlt] f. COMM. Bonus, percentage. (V. BONI.)
guenille [gəni:j] f. Rag (chiffon); tattered garment (vêtement). ‖ Pl. Rags and tatters. (V. HAILLON.) ‖ FIG. Body (corps).
guenilleux, euse [gənijø, ø:z] adj. Ragged.
guenon [gənɔ̃] f. ZOOL. Long-tailed monkey (espèce); she-monkey (femelle). ‖ FAM. Hag, fright, ugly old bag.
guenuche [gənyʃ] f. ZOOL. Young she-ape.
guépard [gepa:r] m. ZOOL. Cheetah, guepard.
guêpe [gɛ:p] ZOOL. Wasp; ‖ FIG. *Taille de guêpe*, wasp-waist. ‖ **Guêpe-frelon**, f. ZOOL. Hornet.
guêpier [-pje] m. Wasp's nest (nid); wasp-trap (piège). ‖ ZOOL. Bee-eater. ‖ FAM. Tricky situation; *tomber dans un guêpier*, to stir up a hornets' nest.
guêpière [-pjɛ:r] f. Wasp-waisted corset, U. S. waist-cincher.
guère [gɛ:r] adv. *Ne... guère*, hardly, scarcely, barely (rarement); not much, little (quantité); few, not many (nombre); *n'aimer guère*, not to like very much; *n'avoir guère d'amis*, to have very few friends; *n'avoir guère d'argent*, to have hardly any money; *je ne le vois guère*, I scarcely ever see him.
guéret [gerɛ] m. Unsown ploughed land; fallow. ‖ Pl. Fields.
guéridon [geridɔ̃] m. Pedestal (ou) occasional table, stand. ‖ NAUT. Bailing scoop.

guérilla [gerija] f. MILIT. Guerilla warfare (guerre); pl. guerilla troops (troupes).
guérillero [gerijerɔ] m. MILIT. Guerilla (personne).
guérir [geri:r] v. tr. (2). MÉD. To heal (une blessure, une plaie); to cure (qqn) [*de*, of]. ‖ FIG. To remedy, to redress (un abus); to relieve (un chagrin); *guérir de*, to cure, to break off (une habitude).
— v. intr. MÉD. To heal, to mend (blessure, plaie); to recover, to be restored to health, to get well again (personne).
guérison [-zɔ̃] f. Healing (d'une blessure); cure (d'une maladie); recovery (d'une personne).
guérissable [-sabl] adj. MÉD. Curable (malade); medicable (maladie).
guérisseur, euse [-sœːr, ø:z] adj. Healing.
— m. Healer; faith healer. ‖ Quack (charlatan); medicine-man (sorcier).
guérite [gerit] f. Cabin, shelter (d'un gardien). ‖ MILIT. Sentry-box. ‖ ARCHIT. Look-out turret. ‖ TECHN. Cab, house (de grue). ‖ CH. DE F. *Guérite d'aiguillage, à signaux*, signal-box (ou) -cabin; *guérite de serre-frein*, brakesman's cabin. ‖ NAUT. Cowl.
guerre [gɛ:r] f. MILIT. War, warfare; *guerre d'embuscade*, bush-fighting; *guerre de mouvement*, open (ou) field warfare, war of movement; *guerre-éclair*, blitzkrieg; *guerre froide*, cold war; *guerre sur mer*, naval warfare; *guerre des nerfs*, war of nerves; *guerre à outrance*, war to the knife, all-out war; *guerre sainte*, holy war; *guerre totale*, total warfare; *guerre des tranchées*, trench warfare; *guerre d'usure*, war of attrition; *drôle de guerre*, phoney war; *être en guerre avec*, to be at war with; *faire la guerre à*, to war against, to wage war against; *la Grande Guerre*, the Great War, World War I; *ministère de la Guerre*, War Office, U. S. Department of Defense, the Pentagon; *ministre de la Guerre*, Secretary of State for War, U. S. Secretary of Defense. ‖ FIG. Strife, quarrel (conflit, discorde, dispute); feud (entre familles, tribus). ‖ FIG. *De guerre lasse*, for the sake of peace and quietness; *être de bonne guerre*, to be fair, to be cricket; *nom de guerre*, pseudonym; *partir en guerre*, to go on the warpath; *partir en guerre contre, pour*, to enter the lists against, to take up the cudgels on behalf of.
guerrier, ère [gɛrje, ɛ:r] adj. MILIT. War (danse); warlike (humeur, peuple).
— m. MILIT. Warrior.
guerrière [gɛrjɛ:r] f. Amazon; female warrior.
guerroyant, ante [gɛrwajɑ̃, ɑ̃:t] adj. Warlike; bellicose.
guerroyer [-je] v. intr. (9 a). MILIT. To war, to fight; *guerroyer contre*, to wage war against.
guerroyeur, euse [-jœːr, ø:z] adj. Fighting.
— m. Fighter, knight-errant.
guet [gɛ] m. Watch, watching, look-out (aguets); *avoir l'œil au guet*, to keep a sharp look-out; *avoir l'œil et l'oreille au guet*, to keep one's eyes and ears open; *faire le guet*, to be on the watch. ‖ Watch, night patrol (patrouille). ‖ **Guet-apens**, m. invar. Ambush, ambuscade (embuscade); trap, snare (piège); *tomber dans un guet-apens*, to be waylaid; FIG. Treacherous scheme, snare, trap (piège); foul play (attentat); *tomber dans un guet-apens*, to meet with foul play, to fall into a trap.
guêtre [gɛ:tr] f. Legging (en cuir); gaiter (en étoffe); demi-guêtres, spats. ‖ FAM. *Traîner ses guêtres*, to loaf about, to lounge around.
guetter [gɛte] v. tr. To watch (surveiller). ‖ To watch for, to be on the look-out for; *guetter l'occasion*, to watch for the opportunity. ‖ To lie in wait for, to waylay (dans une intention hostile).
guetteur [-tœːr] m. Watchman, watcher (de bef-

froi). ‖ Milit., Naut. Look-out man; signalman (à un poste); *guetteur sémaphorique*, coast signalman; *poste de guetteurs*, lookout post.

gueulante [gœlã:t] f. Pop. Howl, yell; *pousser une gueulante*, to let out a yell (ou) howl; to holler.

gueulard, arde [gœla:r, ard] adj. Pop. Loudvoiced (ou) -mouthed, noisy. ‖ Mus. Noisy, loud. — m. Naut. Megaphone, speaking-trumpet. ‖ Techn. Mouth, throat (de haut-fourneau); *gueulard de mine*, pit-head. ‖ Milit. Muzzle (d'un canon). ‖ Pop. Bawler, bellower, loud-mouth (braillard).

gueule [gœl] f. Firehole (d'un four); mouth (d'un animal, d'un sac). ‖ Milit. Muzzle (d'un canon); *gueules cassées*, soldiers wounded in the face. ‖ Pop. Mouth, U. S. yap (bouche); phiz, mug, map, pan (visage); *avoir de la gueule*, to have an air; to have sth. about one; *avoir la gueule de bois*, to have a hangover; *être fort en gueule*, to be a bawler (ou) bellower; *fine gueule*, gourmet, epicure; *sale gueule*, ugly mug; *ta gueule!* shut up!, shut your trap!, none of your lip! ‖ **Gueulede-loup** (pl. *gueules-de-loup*) f. Bot. Antirrhinum, snapdragon; Archit. Cowl, turn-cap (de cheminée).

gueuler [-le] v. intr. (1). Pop. To bawl, to bellow. — v. tr. Pop. To bawl out, to shout out (une chanson).

gueules [gœl] m. Blas. Gules.

gueuleton [-ltɔ̃] m. Pop. Slap-up meal, spread, beanfeast.

gueuletonner [-ltɔne] v. intr. (1). Pop. To tuck in, to guzzle, to junket.

gueusaille [gøza:j] f. Fam. Rabble, riff-raff, scum.

gueusard [gøza:r] m. Rascal, scoundrel (coquin); beggar, ragamuffin (mendiant).

gueuse [gø:z] f. Techn. Pig-iron (fonte); pigmould (moule); *gueuse de fonte*, pig.

gueuse f. Trollop, harlot; *courir la gueuse*, to wench, to go wenching.

gueux, euse [gø, ø:z] adj. Beggarly, poor, destitute (personne); shabby (vêtements). — m. Beggar, cadger (mendiant); ragamuffin, tatterdemalion, tramp (vagabond); *vie de gueux*, beggarly existence.

gui [gi] m. Bot. Mistletoe.

gui m. Naut. Guy (cordage); boom (vergue).

guibolle [gibɔl] f. Fam. Shank, pin, U. S. gam.

guibre [gi:br] f. Naut. Cutwater.

guiche [giʃ] f. Buckler strap (courroie). ‖ Pl. Small curls, side-curls, kiss-curls (mèches).

guichet [giʃɛ] m. Wicket, wicket-door, wicketgate (d'une grande porte). ‖ Gateway, archway (du Louvre). ‖ Grating (grille); peep-hole, spyhole (judas). ‖ Turnstile, entrance gate (de l'octroi). ‖ Counter, position, window (d'un bureau de poste). ‖ Slit, mouth (d'une boîte à lettres). ‖ Ch. de F. Booking-office (ou) U. S. ticket window. ‖ Théâtr. Box-office. ‖ Fin. Cashier's window, counter (d'une banque). ‖ Sports. Wicket (au cricket).

guichetier [giʃtje] m. Turnkey (de prison).

guidage [gida:ʒ] m. Techn. Guiding; guidance.

guide [gid] m. Guide, cicerone (dans un musée). ‖ Guide-book, guide, handbook (catalogue). ‖ Sports. Guide (en montagne). ‖ Techn. *Guide de clapet, de courroie*, valve-, belt-guide. ‖ Fig. Leader, guide. ‖ **Guide-âne**, m. Manual, handbook (pour débutants); sheet of lined paper, line guide (transparent).

guide f. Rein (v. Rêne). ‖ Girl guide; U. S. girl scout; *guide de France*, Catholic girl guide. ‖ Fig. *Mener la vie à grandes guides*, to live in style, to live high.

guider [gide] v. tr. (1). To steer (un bateau); to drive (un cheval); to guide, to conduct, to direct,

to lead (une personne). ‖ Autom. To drive (une voiture). ‖ Fig. To govern (les actions).

guiderope [gidro:p] m. Aviat. Guide-rope, trailrope, drag.

guidon [gidɔ̃] m. Handlebars (d'une bicyclette). ‖ *Guidon de renvoi*, reference mark (d'un livre). ‖ Milit. Field-colours, camp-colours, guidon (drapeau); foresight, bead (d'un fusil). ‖ Naut. Pennant (de commandement); burgee (de signaux, de yacht).

guignard, arde [giɲa:r, ard] adj. Fam. Unlucky. — s. Fam. Unlucky person, U. S. jinx. ‖ Zool. Dotterel.

guigne [giɲ] f. Bot. Mazard, sweet cherry, heartcherry. ‖ Fam. Bad (ou) ill luck, hoodoo, U. S. jinx, hex; *porter la guigne*, to bring bad luck. U. S. to jinx.

guigner [giɲe] v. intr. (1). Fam. To peer, to peep, to gaze. — v. tr. Fam. To steal a glance at, to look stealthily at, to peep at (regarder à la dérobée); to leer at, to ogle (lorgner). ‖ Fig. To covet (convoiter).

guignol [giɲɔl] m. Théâtr. Punch (personnage); Punch-and-Judy show (spectacle). ‖ Aviat. Kingpost; elevator lever.

guignolet [giɲɔlɛ] m. Cherry liqueur.

guignon [giɲɔ̃] m. Fam. Run of bad luck, unluckiness, hoodoo; U. S. jinx. (V. Guigne.)

guilde [gild] f. V. Gilde.

Guillaume [gijo:m] m. William (nom).

guillaume m. Techn. Rabbet.

guilledou [gijdu] m. Fam. *Courir le guilledou*, to lead a gay life, to gad about, to gallivant.

guillemet [gijmɛ] m. Quotation mark, inverted comma; *mettre entre guillemets*, to enclose in quotation marks (ou) in quotes (fam.).

guilleret [gijrɛ] adj. Brisk, lively, sprightly (personne); racy, spicy, broad (plaisanterie, propos).

guillochage [gijɔʃa:ʒ] m. Arts. Guilloche, chequered pattern. ‖ Techn. Rose-engine turning.

guillocher [-ʃe] v. tr. (1). Techn. To engine-turn; to chequer.

guillochis [-ʃi] m., **guillochure** [-ʃy:r] f. Techn. Guilloche.

guillotine [gijɔtin] f. Guillotine; *fenêtre à guillotine*, sash-window; *obturation à guillotine*, drop shutter.

guillotiner [-ne] v. tr. (1). To guillotine.

guillotineur [-nœ:r] m. Guillotiner.

guimauve [gimo:v] f. Bot., Culin. Marshmallow.

guimbarde [gɛ̃bard] f. Mus. Jew's harp. ‖ Techn. Plough, grooving-plane (rabot). ‖ Fam. Old crock, ramshackle vehicle, U. S. jalopy, flivver.

guimpe [gɛ̃p] f. Ecclés. Wimple (de religieuse). ‖ Guimpe, tucker, chemisette (de robe).

guincher [gɛ̃ʃe] v. intr. (1). Pop. To shake a leg, to dance.

guindage [gɛ̃da:ʒ] m. Techn. Hoisting (action); hoisting-tackle, hoist (appareil).

guindant [-dã] m. Naut. Hounding (de mât); hoist, drop (de pavillon); hoist (de voile).

guindé, ée [-de] adj. Stiff, formal, starched, starchy, tight-laced (attitude, personne); stilted, affected (manière); stiff, stilted (style).

guindeau [gɛ̃do] m. Naut. Windlass.

guinder [gɛ̃de] v. tr. (1). Techn. To hoist, to raise; to windlass. ‖ Naut. To send up, to sway up (un mât). ‖ Fig. To strain, to force (affecter). — v. pr. **Se guinder**, to behave in a stiff (ou) affected manner.

Guinée [gine] f. Géogr. Guinea; *Nouvelle-Guinée*, New Guinea. ‖ Comm. *Toile de Guinée*, Guinea cloth (ou) cotton. ‖ **Guinée-Bissau**, f. Géogr. Guinea-Bissau. ‖ **Guinée Equatoriale**, f. Géogr. Equatorial Guinea.

guinée f. Fin. Guinea (monnaie).

guinéen, enne [gineɛ̃, ɛn] adj., s. GÉOGR. Guinean.

guingois [gɛ̃gwa] m. Crookedness, twist, skew; *de guingois,* awry, askew; lop-sided; *marcher de guingois,* to walk lop-sidedly.

guinguette [gɛ̃gɛt] f. Suburban tavern, roadside inn, U. S. road house, highway stand.

guipure [gipy:r] f. Guipure, point-lace, pillow-lace. ‖ ELECTR. Wrapping.

guirlande [girlɑ̃:d] f. Garland, festoon, wreath (de fleurs); rope (de perles); string (de pierreries); coronal (pour la tête). ‖ NAUT. Breast-hook. ‖ FIG. *Tresser des guirlandes à qqn,* to praise s.o. to the skies.

guirlander [-de] v. tr. (1). To garland, to festoon.

guise [gi:z] f. Manner, way (v. FAÇON); *en guise de,* in place of, for (au lieu de); by way of (comme); *faire à sa guise,* to have one's way, to do as one pleases.

guitare [gita:r] f. MUS. Guitar.

guitariste [-rist] s. MUS. Guitarist.

guitoune [gitun] f. MILIT., FAM. Shelter, dug-out, funk-hole, fox-hole.

guivre [gi:vr] f. BLAS. Wyvern.

guru [guru] m. Guru.

gustatif, ive [gystatif, i:v] adj. Gustative. ‖ MÉD. Gustatory (nerf).

gustation [-sjɔ̃] f. Gustation, tasting.

gutta-percha [gytapɛrka] f. Gutta-percha.

gutte [gyt] f. BOT. Gamboge.

guttural, ale [gytyral] adj. Guttural (son, voix); throaty (voix). ‖ MÉD. Guttural.
— f. GRAMM. Guttural.

Guyana [gɥijana] m. GÉOGR. Guyana.
Guyane [gɥijan] f. GÉOGR. Guiana.
gymkhana [ʒimkana] m. SPORTS. Obstacle race (d'autos, de motos).
gymnase [ʒimna:z] m. Gymnasium.
gymnaste [-nast] s. Gymnast.
gymnastique [-nastik] adj. Gymnastic; *au pas gymnastique,* at the double.
— f. Gymnastics; *gymnastique respiratoire,* breathing exercises; *gymnastique rythmique,* eurhythmics. ‖ FIG. Gymnastic (de l'esprit).
gymnique [-nik] adj. Gymnastic.
gymnique f. Gymnastics.
gynécée [ʒinese] m. Gynaeceum.
gynécologie [ʒinekɔlɔʒi] f. MÉD. Gynaecology.
gynécologique [-lɔʒik] adj. MÉD. Gynaecological.
gynécologue [-lɔg] s. MÉD. Gynaecologist.
gypaète [ʒipaɛt] m. ZOOL. Lammergeyer, bearded vulture.
gypse [ʒips] m. Gypsum, plaster-stone. ‖ COMM. Plaster of Paris.
gypseux, euse [-sø, ø:z] adj. Gypseous.
gyrocompas [ʒirokɔ̃pa] m. AVIAT., NAUT. Gyro-compass.
gyroscope [ʒirɔskɔp] m. Gyroscope.
gyroscopique [-pik] adj. Gyroscopic. ‖ NAUT., AVIAT. *Compas gyroscopique,* gyro-compass. ‖ AVIAT. *Appareil gyroscopique de pilotage,* gyro-pilot; George (fam.).
gyrostabilisateur [-stabilizatœ:r] m. AVIAT. Gyrostabilizer.

h [aʃ] m., f. H, h. ‖ MILIT. Zero, H (heure).
H [aʃ] m. CHIM. Hydrogen; *bombe H.,* hydrogen bomb, H-bomb.
ha [*a] interj. Ha! Haw! (rire); ah! (surprise).
habanera [*abanera] f. MUS. Habanera.
habile [abil] adj. Clever, skilful, able, capable (adroit); cunning, smart, artful, crafty (intrigant). ‖ JUR. Apt, fit; *habile à succéder,* capacitated (ou) qualified (ou) competent to inherit.
habilement [-mɑ̃] adv. Cleverly, skilfully, ably, capably.
habileté [-te] f. Cleverness, skilfulness, ability, capability (adresse); cleverness, smartness (en affaires); *habileté technique,* ingenuity; U. S. know-how (fam.). ‖ JUR. Qualification.
habilitation [abilitasjɔ̃] f. JUR. Qualifying, capacitation.
habilité [-te] f. JUR. Capacity, legal competency, title; *avoir habilité à,* to be entitled to.
habiliter [-te] v. tr. (1). JUR. To capacitate, to qualify; to entitle, to empower (qqn).
habillage [abija:ʒ] m. Preparation. ‖ BOT. Pruning, trimming (d'un arbre). ‖ COMM. Boxing, packaging, packing, get-up (d'une marchandise). ‖ CULIN. Cleaning (du poisson); dressing (de la viande); drawing and dressing (d'une volaille). ‖ TECHN. Setting (d'un texte typographique).
habillé, ée [-je] adj. Dressed, attired, clad (personne). ‖ Dressy, dress-up; stylish (robe).

habillement [-jmɑ̃] m. Clothing, dressing (action); clothes, garments, dress, apparel (vêtement). ‖ MILIT. Clothing, kit. ‖ NAUT. Slops.
habiller [-je] v. tr. (1). To dress, to clothe (des enfants). ‖ To suit (aller bien à). ‖ To cover, to wrap, to envelop (couvrir, envelopper). ‖ BOT. To prepare for planting (une racine). ‖ CULIN. To clean (un poisson); to dress, to trim (un rôti); to draw, to dress, to truss (une volaille). ‖ TECHN. To prepare for tanning (le cuir); to place type around (une illustration). ‖ COMM. To dress, to clothe, to make clothes for (des clients); to package, to pack, to box, to get up (une marchandise). ‖ FIG. To pull to pieces (qqn).
— v. pr. **S'habiller,** to dress, to get dressed, to dress oneself (habituellement); to dress up (en grande tenue); *s'habiller de bleu,* to dress in blue. ‖ To buy one's clothes (chez, at, from).
habilleur [-jœ:r] m. THÉÂTR. Dresser.
habilleuse [-jø:z] f. THÉÂTR. Wardrobe mistress, dresser.
habit [abi] m. Dress, costume, outfit; pl. clothes, attire; *marchand d'habits,* old-clothes man, second-hand-clothes dealer. ‖ Coat; *en habit,* in evening dress, in tails; *habit vert,* green coat (des académiciens). ‖ ECCLÉS. Frock (de moine); cloth (de prêtre); habit (de religieuse); *prendre l'habit,* to take the veil.
habitabilité [abitabilite] f. Habitability, habi-

tableness (conditions de vie); spaciousness, capacity (espace).

habitable [abitabl] adj. Habitable, inhabitable, fit for habitation.

habitacle [-takl] m. † Habitacle, dwelling-place. ‖ NAUT. Binnacle. ‖ AVIAT. Cockpit.

habitant [-tɑ̃] m. Inhabitant; dweller, occupant, occupier, resident, inmate (d'une maison); inhabitant, citizen (d'une ville). ‖ Settler, planter (dans les colonies). ‖ Habitant (au Canada, en Louisiane). ‖ Denizen (des bois).

habitat [-ta] m. Habitat; *amélioration de l'habitat*, improvement of the living conditions.

habitation [-tasjɔ̃] f. Habitation, inhabiting, dwelling, occupancy. ‖ Habitation, residence, dwelling-place, abode. ‖ Habitat (d'une plante). ‖ JUR. House, domicile, tenement.

habiter [-te] v. intr. (1). To live, to dwell, to reside.
— v. tr. To inhabit, to live (ou) to dwell in.

habituation [abitɥasjɔ̃] f. PSYCH. Habituation.

habitude [abityd] f. Habit, custom, practice, use (v. COUTUME, USAGE); *avoir l'habitude de*, to be in the habit of, to be accustomed to, to be used to, to make a practice of; *comme d'habitude*, as usual; *d'habitude*, generally, usually, ordinarily; *par habitude*, from force of habit, out of habit; *plus que d'habitude*, more than usual; *prendre l'habitude de*, to get into the habit of. ‖ FIG. *Avoir ses habitudes chez qqn*, to be a constant caller at s.o.'s house.

habitué, ée [-tɥe] adj. Accustomed, used (à, to); familiar (à, with). ‖ ECCLÉS. Non-beneficed, unbeneficed (prêtre).
— m. Frequenter, haunter, regular visitor, habitué; regular customer (client); *habitué du cinéma*, patron of the cinema, regular cinemagoer, U. S. movie-fan (ou) -goer.

habituel, elle [-tɥɛl] adj. Habitual, wonted, regular. ‖ ECCLÉS. *Péché habituel*, besetting sin.

habituellement [-tɥɛlmɑ̃] adv. Habitually, usually, regularly, customarily, ordinarily.

habituer [-tɥe] v. tr. (1). To habituate, to accustom, to make used (à, to); to familiarize (à, with); *habituer à faire*, to get into the habit of doing. ‖ To inure (aguerrir) [à, to]; *habituer à la fatigue*, to inure to fatigue.
— v. pr. S'habituer, to get used (ou) accustomed (ou) inured (à, to).

hâblerie [*ɑblǝri] f. Bragging, boasting, braggadocio (attitude); boast, brag; big talk (parole).

hâbleur [*ɑblœ:r] m. Boaster, braggart.

hachage [*aʃa:ʒ] m. Chopping, cutting fine; grinding, hashing (de la viande).

hache [*aʃ] f. Axe (grande); hatchet (petite); *hache d'abordage, d'armes, de bûcheron*, boarding- (ou) pole-, battle-, felling-axe. ‖ FIG. *Enterrer la hache de guerre*, to bury the hatchet. ‖ Hache-légumes, m. invar. CULIN. Vegetable chopper. ‖ Hache-paille, m. invar. AGRIC. Chaff-cutter, chaff-cutting machine. ‖ Hache-viande m. invar. Meat cutter, meat-grinder.

haché, ée [*aʃe] adj. CULIN. Chopped; *haché menu*, minced. ‖ ARTS. Hatched, cross-hatched (dessin). ‖ FIG. Staccato, jerky (style).
— m. CULIN. Mince; minced meat.

hachement [*aʃmɑ̃] m. V. HACHAGE.

hacher v. tr. (1). To mangle, to hack (déchiqueter). ‖ CULIN. To chop, to hash; *hacher menu*, to mince. ‖ AGRIC. To chop, to cut (de la paille) ; to destroy, to cut to pieces (des récoltes par la grêle). ‖ ARTS. To cross-hatch, to hachure (un dessin). ‖ FIG. To jerk out, to chop (ses mots).

hachereau [*aʃro] m. Hatchet.

hachette [*aʃɛt] f. Hatchet; *hachette à marteau*, hammer-head hatchet.

hachis [*aʃi] m. CULIN. Force-meat; mince, hash ‖ FIG. Hash, mess.

hachisch [*aʃiʃ] m. Hashish, hasheesh; bhang.

hachoir [*aʃwa:r] m. CULIN. Chopping-knife, chopper (couperet); mincing-machine, grinder (machine); chopping-board, butcher's block (table).

hachure [*aʃy:r] f. ARTS. Hatching, hatch, hachure; *en hachures*, hachured; *hachures croisées, parallèles*, ruled, crossed tint.

hachuré, ée [*aʃyre] adj. Streaked.

hachurer v. tr. (1). ARTS. To hatch, to hachure.

haddock [*adɔk] m. ZOOL. Haddock.

hagard, arde [*aga:r, ard] adj. Haggard (air, personne); gaunt, haggard, drawn (visage); wild, staring (yeux).

hagiographe [aʒjɔgraf] adj. Hagiographal, hagiographic, hagiographical.
— m. Hagiographer.

hagiographie [-fi] f. Hagiography.

hagiographique [-fik] adj. Hagiographic.

haie [*ɛ] f. BOT. Hedge, hedgerow; *haie vive*, quickset hedge. ‖ AGRIC. Beam (d'une charrue). ‖ MILIT. Fence (clôture); *haie barbelée*, barbed-wire entanglement. ‖ SPORTS. Hurdle; *course de haies*, hurdle race. ‖ FIG. Line, row (de personnes); *faire la haie*, to line the streets.

haillon [*ajɔ̃] m. Rag (v. LOQUE); *en haillons*, in rags and tatters.

haillonneux, euse [*ajɔnø, ø:z] adj. Ragged, tattered (vêtement); in rags (personne).

haine [*ɛ:n] f. Hate, hatred, detestation; *par haine de*, out of hatred of; *prendre en haine*, to take a strong aversion to.

haineusement [*ɛnøzmɑ̃] adv. Malignantly.

haineux, euse [*ɛnø, ø:z] adj. Hateful, malignant (caractère); full of hatred (paroles).

haïr [*ai:r] v. tr. (58). To hate, to detest, to abhor; *haïr qqn comme la peste*, to hate s.o. like poison, to loathe s.o.

haire [*ɛ:r] f. Hair-cloth (tissu); hair-shirt (vêtement).

haïssable [*aisabl] adj. Hateful, detestable.

Haïti [aiti] f. GÉOGR. Haiti.

haïtien, enne [aisjɛ̃, ɛn] adj., s. GÉOGR. Haitian.

halage [*ala:ʒ] m. NAUT. Warping, hauling, haulage (remorquage); towing (par chemin); *corde de halage*, tow-line.

hâle [*a:l] m. Burning, browning, tanning (action); sunburn, suntan, coat of tan (effet).

hâlé, ée [*ale] adj. Sunburnt, suntanned, tanned, weather-beaten. (V. BRONZÉ.)

haleine [alɛ:n] f. Breath; wind; *avoir l'haleine courte, longue*, to be short-winded, long-winded; *hors d'haleine*, out of breath, breathless, winded; *perdre haleine*, to get out of breath, to get winded; *reprendre haleine*, to take a breath, to get one's second wind. ‖ MÉD. *Haleine forte*, halitosis, strong (ou) bad breath. ‖ FIG. *De longue haleine*, long-term (travail); long and exacting (travail); *tenir qqn en haleine*, to hold s.o. breathless; *tout d'une haleine*, all in one breath, all at one go.

haler [*ale] v. tr. (1). NAUT. To pull in, to heave (une corde); to haul; to tow (une péniche); to track (une péniche).
— v. intr. NAUT. To haul (vent); *haler sur une manœuvre*, to haul (ou) pull on a rope.

hâler [*ɑle] v. tr. (1). To sunburn, to tan, to brown. (V. BRONZER.)

haletant, ante [*altɑ̃, ɑ̃:t] adj. Breathless, out of breath, winded, panting, gasping; heaving (poitrine); *tout haletant*, panting, puffing and blowing.

halètement [*alɛtmɑ̃] m. Panting, gasping; puffing and blowing.

haleter [*alte] v. intr. (8b). To pant, to gasp, to puff and blow.

haleur [*alœ:r] m. NAUT. Hauler (directement); tower (sur chemin).

hall [*ol] m. Hall, entrance hall (d'entrée); house, shop (de fonderie); hall (de gare); lounge, lobby (d'hôtel).

hallali [alali] m. Death; mort; *assister à l'hallali*, to be in at the death; *sonner l'hallali*, to blow the mort.

halle [*al] f. Market hall, covered market; *halle au blé*, Corn Exchange; *halles centrales*, central market.

hallebarde [*albard] f. † Halberd, halbert, poleaxe; bill. ‖ FIG. *Tomber des hallebardes*, to rain cats and dogs.

hallebardier [-dje] m. † Halberdier.

hallier [*alje] m. BOT. Copse, thicket, brake; pl. brushwood.

hallucinant, ante [alysinɑ̃, ɑ̃:t] adj. Hallucinating, haunting.

hallucination [-nasjɔ̃] f. Hallucination.

hallucinatoire [-natwa:r] adj. Hallucinatory.

halluciné, ée [-ne] adj. Hallucinated; moonstruck. — m. Hallucinated (ou) moonstruck person.

halluciner [-ne] v. tr. (1). To hallucinate.

hallucinogène [-nɔʒɛn] adj. Hallucinogenic. — m. Hallucinogen.

halo [*alo] m. ASTRON. Halo, ring (de la lune); corona (du soleil). ‖ PHYS. Blurring (optométrique). ‖ TECHN. Halation (photographique).

halogène [alɔʒɛn] adj. CHIM. Halogenous. — m. CHIM. Halogen.

haloïde [alɔid] adj., m. CHIM. Haloid.

halte [*alt] f. Stopping-place, halting-place (lieu); stop, halt (v. PAUSE); *faire halte à*, to halt at, to stop at. ‖ MILIT. *Faire halte*, to halt; *halte-là!* halt! ‖ CH. DE F. Halt, wayside station; *faire halte*, to stop, to call (train). ‖ FIG. Pause, respite, interruption, recess; *halte-là!*, listen to me!; just a minute!

haltère [altɛ:r] m. SPORTS. Dumb-bell, weight. ‖ Pl. ZOOL. Halters, poisers.

haltérophile [-terɔfil] m. SPORTS. Weight-lifter.

haltérophilie [-terɔfili] f. SPORTS Weight-lifting.

hamac [*amak] m. Hammock; *hamac à l'anglaise* (ou) *à cadre*, cot.

hamadryade [amadrijad] f. Hamadryad.

hamamélis [amamelis] BOT., MÉD. Witch-hazel.

hamburger [*ãburgœ:r] m. CULIN. Hamburger.

hameau [*amo] m. Hamlet.

hameçon [amsɔ̃] m. Fish-hook; *prendre à l'hameçon*, to hook. ‖ FIG. *Mordre à l'hameçon*, to swallow the bait, to bite.

hammam [*amam] m. Hammam.

hammerless [amɛrlɛs] m. Hammerless gun.

hampe [*ɑ̃p] f. Staff, pole (de drapeau); shaft, staff, stave (de hallebarde, de lance); shank (de hameçon); handle (de pinceau). ‖ Down-stroke (jambage). ‖ BOT. Scape, stem.

hampe [*ɑ̃p] f. CULIN. Flank (du bœuf); breast (du cerf).

hamster [*amstɛ:r] m. ZOOL. Hamster.

han [*ɑ̃] interj. Hah!, huh!; *pousser un han*, to give a grunt, to grunt.

hanap [*anap] m. Hanap, goblet, tankard.

hanche [*ɑ̃:ʃ] f. MÉD. Hip; haunch; huckle; *les poings sur les hanches*, arms akimbo, with hands on hips. ‖ ZOOL. Hook (du bœuf); haunch (du cheval). ‖ NAUT. Quarter.

handball [*ɑ̃dbal] m. SPORTS. Handball.

handicap [*ɑ̃dikap] m. SPORTS. Handicap. ‖ FIG. Handicap, disadvantage.

handicapé, ée [-pe] adj. Handicapped, disabled. — s. Handicapped (ou) disabled person; *les handicapés*, the handicapped; *les handicapés mentaux*, the mentally handicapped.

handicaper [-pe] v. tr. (1). To handicap

handicapeur [-pœ:r] m. SPORTS. Handicapper.

hangar [*ɑ̃ga:r] m. Shed, lean-to, penthouse, NAUT. Boat-house. ‖ AVIAT. Hangar.

hanneton [*antɔ̃] m. ZOOL. May-beetle, may-bug cockchafer, U. S. June bug. ‖ FIG. Harum-scarum

hanovrien, enne [*anɔvrijɛ̃, ɛn] adj., s. Hanoverian.

hanse [*ɑ̃:s] f. † Hanse (guilde); *la Hanse*, the Hanse, the Hanseatic League (en Allemagne).

hanséatique [*ɑ̃seatik] adj. † Hanseatic.

hanter [*ɑ̃te] v. tr. (1). To frequent, to haun (un lieu, une maison); to frequent (qqn). ‖ FIG To haunt, to obsess (par la pensée, le souvenir)

hantise [*ɑ̃ti:z] f. Haunting memory, obsession ‖ MÉD. Perseveration (psychologique); *vivre dan la hantise de*, to be obsessed by.

happeau [*apo] m. Snare (pour les oiseaux).

happement [*apmɑ̃] m. Snapping up, snatchin up, seizing.

happening [*apəniŋ] m. ARTS., THÉÂTR. Happening.

happer [*ape] v. tr. (1). To snap up, to snatch up to seize. ‖ To catch (un voleur). ‖ FIG. T waylay (qqn au passage). — v. intr. To adhere, to cling, to stick.

happy end [*apiɛnd] m., f. Happy ending.

haquenée [*akne] f. ZOOL. † Palfrey; hackney ambling horse.

haquet [*akɛ] m. Dray; *haquet à main*, hand cart, push-cart.

harakiri [*arakiri] m. Hara-kiri.

harangue [*arɑ̃:g] f. Harangue.

haranguer [*arɑ̃ge] v. tr. (1). To harangue, t address; to hold forth to, to spout to (fam.).

harangueur [-rɑ̃gœ:r] m. Orator, speaker (ora teur); speechifier, spouter, tub-thumper, soap-bo orator (phraseur).

haras [*arɑ] m. Stud-farm, haras.

harassant, ante [*arasɑ̃, ɑ̃:t] adj. Exhausting, gruelling.

harasse [*aras] f. Crate.

harassement [*arasmɑ̃] m. Harassing, harass ment, worrying (action); exhaustion, weariness fatigue (état).

harasser [-se] v. tr. (1). To exhaust, to wear out

harcelant, ante [*arslɑ̃, ɑ̃:t] adj. Harassing harrying, tormenting, worrying; pestering, badg ering, plaguing.

harcèlement [-sɛlmɑ̃] m. Harassment, worrying badgering, plaguing, pestering.

harceler [-səle] v. tr. (8b). To bait, to worry (un animal); to worry, to pester, to badger, to heckle (qqn); *harceler qqn de querelles, de ques tions*, to nag at, to heckle s. o.; *être harcelé par ses créanciers*, to be dunned by one's creditors ‖ MILIT. To harass (l'ennemi).

harceleur, euse [-səlœ:r, ø:z] adj. Harassing worrying. — s. Tormentor, harasser, worrier (fatigant) heckler (questionneur); nagger (querelleur).

harde [*ard] f. ZOOL. Herd (de bêtes fauves).

harde [*ard] f. Leash (lien); set of hounds (chiens).

hardes f. pl. Togs. (V. FRUSQUES.)

hardi, ie [*ardi] adj. Bold, daring, fearless plucky, hardy (courageux); brazen, forward impudent (effronté). ‖ FIG. Rash, risky, venture some (projet); bold, audacious (style).

hardiesse [-djɛs] f. Boldness, daring, hardihood pluck (courage); audacity, brazenness, forward ness (effronterie). ‖ Bold act, daring act. ‖ FIG Boldness, audacity (d'une image, d'un style).

hardiment [-dimɑ̃] adv. Boldly, hardily, fear lessly (courageusement); boldly, audaciously impudently (effrontément). ‖ FIG. Boldly, auda ciously.

hardware [*ardwɛ:r] m. INFORM. Hardware.

harem [*arɛm] m. Harem.

hareng [*rɑ̃] m. ZOOL. CULIN. Herring; *hareng bouffi*, bloater; *hareng fumé*, kipper, kippered herring; *hareng saur*, red herring.

harengère [-ʒɛ:r] f. Fishwife. (V. POISSARDE.)

hargne [*arɲ] f. Ill-temper, churlishness.

hargneusement [-ɲøzmɑ̃] adv. Cantankerously, peevishly, ill-temperedly (réagir); nastily (regarder, aboyer).

hargneux, euse [-ɲø, ø:z] adj. Ill-tempered, vicious (cheval); snarling (chien); nagging (femme); surly, churlish (humeur); peevish, cross, cantankerous (personne); harsh, cross (ton).

haricot [*ariko] m. BOT. Bean; *haricot beurre*, butter (ou) U. S. wax bean; *haricot blanc*, haricot (ou) kidney bean, U. S. Navy bean; *haricot vert*, French bean, U. S. string bean. ‖ CULIN. Stew, haricot; *haricot de mouton*, haricot mutton, U. S. lamb stew. ‖ POP. *C'est la fin des haricots*, that's torn it; that takes the cake, that's the limit.

haridelle [*aridɛl] f. ZOOL. FAM. Nag, jade, hack.

harmonica [armɔnika] m. MUS. Harmonica, mouth-organ.

harmonie [-ni] f. MUS. Harmony; consonance (des sons); brass and reed band. ‖ FIG. Harmony, harmoniousness, concordance, congruence (entre les choses); harmony, concord, agreement (entre les personnes); *en harmonie avec*, in keeping with, consistent with; in line with; *vivre en harmonie*, to live harmoniously.

harmonieusement [-njøzmɑ̃] adv. MUS. Harmoniously, musically, melodiously. ‖ FIG. Harmoniously, consistently, fittingly (en accord); peaceably (en paix).

harmonieux, euse [-njø, ø:z] adj. MUS. Harmonious, tuneful. (V. MÉLODIEUX.) ‖ Harmonious, blending (couleurs); harmonious, symmetrical (formes); harmonious, friendly (rapports).

harmonique [-nik] adj. MUS., MATH. Harmonic.
— m. MUS. Harmonic; *harmoniques supérieurs*, overtones.

harmoniquement [-nikmɑ̃] adv. MUS., MATH. Harmonically.

harmonisation [-nizasjɔ̃] f. Harmonization, bringing into harmony, harmonizing.

harmoniser [-nize] v. tr. (1). MUS. To harmonize. ‖ To match, to blend (des couleurs); to harmonize, to attune (des idées).
— v. pr. **S'harmoniser**, to harmonize; to be in keeping, to agree; to match, to tone in (couleurs); to be attuned (idées).

harmoniste [-nist] m. MUS. Harmonist (musicien); voicer (d'orgue).

harmonium [-njɔm] m. MUS. Harmonium.

harnachement [*arnaʃmɑ̃] m. Harnessing (action). ‖ Harness, trappings, saddlery; gear (d'un cheval). ‖ FAM. Accoutrement.

harnacher [-ʃe] v. tr. (1). To harness; to gear (un cheval de trait). ‖ FAM. To rig out, to attire.

harnacheur [-ʃœ:r] m. Harness-maker; saddler (fabricant). ‖ Groom (d'écurie).

harnais [*arnɛ] m. Harness; saddlery; trappings (en général); gear (de cheval de trait); *harnais d'attelage*, draught (ou) U. S. draft-harness. ‖ TECHN. *Harnais d'engrenages*, train of gear wheels; gearing.

harnois [*arnwa] m. FIG. *Blanchi sous le harnois*, grown grey in the service.

haro [*aro] m. Harrow, haro; *crier haro*, to cry shame (ou) haro, to raise a hue and cry; *crier haro sur*, to denounce.

harpagon [arpagɔ̃] m. Shylock, Scrooge.

harpe [*arp] f. MUS. Harp; *harpe éolienne*, Aeolian (ou) wind-harp; *jouer, pincer de la harpe*, to play, to touch the harp.

harpie [*arpi] f. Harpy. ‖ ZOOL. Harpy-eagle;

harpy-bat. ‖ FIG. Harpy, shrew, old hag, hell-cat, battle-axe. (V. MÉGÈRE.)

harpin [*arpɛ̃] m. NAUT. Boat-hook.

harpiste [*arpist] s. MUS. Harpist, harp-player.

harpon [*arpɔ̃] m. NAUT. Harpoon. ‖ TECHN. Angle-iron (de construction); cross-cut saw (de menuisier).

harponnage [*arpɔna:ʒ], **harponnement** [-nmɑ̃] m. Harpooning.

harponner [-ne] v. tr. (1). NAUT. To harpoon. ‖ FIG. To waylay, to buttonhole (qqn).

harponneur [-nœ:r] m. NAUT. Harpooner.

hart [*ar] f. Withe; band, binder (lien). ‖ † Halter, noose, rope (corde).

hasard [*aza:r] m. Risk, danger, hazard; *courir le hasard*, to run the risk. ‖ Chance, luck, accident; *à tout hasard*, at all hazards, on the off chance; *au hasard*, haphazardly, at random, blindly (au petit bonheur); aimlessly (sans but); *comme par hasard*, casually; *par hasard*, by chance, by accident; *remarque faite par hasard*, chance remark; *rencontre de hasard*, chance meeting; *trouver par hasard*, to happen to find, to stumble upon. ‖ MILIT. Hazard (de la guerre).

hasardé, ée [-de] adj. Hazardous, risky, rash, dangerous (action); indiscreet, risky (chanson, mot); ventured lightly (proposition).

hasarder [-de] v. tr. To hazard (v. AVENTURER, RISQUER); *hasarder une opinion*, to venture an opinion.
— v. intr. To run the risk (de, of).
— v. pr. Se hasarder, to take risks; to run risks; *se hasarder à*, to venture to.

hasardeusement [-døzmɑ̃] adv. Hazardously.

hasardeux, euse [-dø, ø:z] adj. Hazardous, risky (entreprise); rash, venturesome, foolhardy (person).

haschich [*aʃiʃ], **hasch** [*aʃ] m. Hashish; hash (fam.).

haschisch [*aʃiʃ]. V. HACHISCH.

hase [*ɑ:z] f. ZOOL. Doe-hare, doe-rabbit.

hassidisme [*asidism] m. Hassidism, hasidism.

hasté, ée [*aste] adj. BOT. Hastate.

hâte [*ɑ:t] f. Longing, looking forward eagerly (de, to) [désir impatient]. ‖ Haste, hurry, quickness (rapidité); *à la hâte*, in a hurry, hurriedly; *en hâte*, in haste, hastily; *en toute hâte*, with all possible dispatch.

hâter [*ɑte] v. tr. (1). To hurry on, to hasten, to speed up, to push forward (v. ACCÉLÉRER); *hâter le pas*, to quicken one's pace. ‖ To expedite (la besogne). ‖ JUR. To accelerate (la procédure).
— v. pr. Se hâter, to hasten, to haste, to make haste, to hurry, to hie.

hâtif, ive [*ɑtif, i:v] adj. Hasty, hurried. (V. RAPIDE.) ‖ Cursory, hasty (examen); ill-considered, ill-regulated (mesure, précaution). ‖ Precocious (esprit); early, forward (fruit, saison); premature (vieillesse).

hâtivement [-tivmɑ̃] adv. Hastily, hurriedly, rapidly. ‖ Prematurely.

hauban [*obɑ̃] m. NAUT. Shroud; guy, stay.

haubanner [*obane] v. tr. (1). NAUT. To guy, to stay.

haubert [*obɛ:r] m. Hauberk, coat of mail.

hausse [*os] f. Rise, rising, increase (de prix, de température); *à la hausse*, on the rise; *en hausse*, advancing, going up; *hausse rapide*, boom. ‖ TECHN. Underlay (en typogr.). ‖ Wedge, underlay block (d'un meuble); heel-tap, lift (de talon). ‖ MILIT. Sight, backsight, rear-sight (de fusil). ‖ FIN. Rise; *jouer à la hausse*, to speculate on a rise, to bull the market; *spéculateur à la hausse*, bull.

haussement [*osmɑ̃] m. Shrug, shrugging

(d'épaules) ; lifting, raising (d'un mur, d'une voix) ; banking (du niveau d'une rivière).

hausser [*ose] v. tr. (1) To raise, to heighten, to make higher (une maison, un mur) ; to shrug (les épaules). ‖ COMM. To raise (les prix). ‖ FIG. To raise (la voix).
— v. pr. Se **hausser**, to raise oneself ; to rise ; *se hausser sur la pointe des pieds*, to stand on tiptoe ; *se hausser pour voir*, to crane one's neck.

haussier [*osje] m. FIN. Bull, speculator.

haussière [*osjɛ:r] f. NAUT. Hawser.

haut, haute [*o, *o:t] adj. High (front, siège) ; high, tall (herbe) ; high, lofty, towering (montagne) ; *de haute taille*, tall ; *haut de six pieds*, six feet high (ou) tall ; *hautes terres*, highlands. ‖ High (marée, rivière) ; *haute mer*, open sea, high seas ; *mer haute*, high tide. ‖ High, aristocratic, noble (naissance). ‖ High, exalted, eminent (grade, rang) ; *haute couture*, haute couture, high-style dressmaking ; *haute cuisine*, high-class cooking ; *haut fonctionnaire*, high-ranking official ; *de haut rang*, high-ranking. ‖ Lofty, noble ; honourable ; *avoir l'âme haute*, to be high-minded ; *de haute mine*, of noble presence. ‖ High (pression, température). ‖ High, high-pitched, loud (voix) ; *lire à haute voix*, to read aloud. ‖ Upper, higher (opposé à bas) ; *hautes classes*, upper classes (de la société) ; *le plus haut étage*, the topmost floor ; *haut Rhin*, Upper Rhine. ‖ GRAMM. High (en linguistique) ; *haut allemand*, High German. ‖ COMM. High, dear (prix). ‖ GÉOGR. High (latitude). ‖ ÉLECTR. High (fréquence). ‖ MATH. Higher (mathématiques). ‖ NAUT. Upper (voiles). ‖ MÉD. *Haut mal*, epilepsy, falling sickness. ‖ ECCLÉS. High (église). ‖ JUR. *Haute trahison*, high treason.
— adv. High ; high up (par rapport au niveau) ; *de haut en bas*, from top to bottom ; *du haut de*, from, down from ; *chercher du haut en bas*, to hunt high and low ; *en haut*, upstairs ; above ; *en haut de la page*, at the top of the page ; *haut les mains !*, hands up ! ‖ High (moralement ou socialement) ; *arriver haut*, to reach a high station in life ; *haut placé*, in a high position. ‖ Loud, loudly ; aloud ; *lire tout haut*, to read out loud ; *parler haut*, to speak loudly ; *plus haut*, louder, more loudly. ‖ Back (dans le temps, dans un texte) ; *paragraphe plus haut*, paragraph above ; *plus haut*, above, further back. ‖ COMM. *Haut*, this side up (sur un colis). ‖ MUS. High. ‖ FIG. *Gagner haut la main*, to win hands down ; *porter haut la tête*, to carry one's head high ; *viser haut*, to aim high.
— m. Height ; *six pieds de haut*, six feet in height (ou) high (ou) tall. ‖ Head (d'un escalier, d'une table) ; top, upper part (d'une page) ; *haut du bras*, upper arm ; *sur le haut des collines*, on the hill-tops. ‖ NAUT. *En haut tout le monde*, all hands on deck ; *haut du mât*, mast-head. ‖ NAUT. Pl. Superstructure, topsides, upper works (d'un navire). ‖ TECHN. *Haut de course*, top of stroke, upper dead-centre (d'un piston) ; *haut de casse*, upper case (en typogr.). ‖ FIG. *Les hauts et les bas*, the ups and downs ; *tomber de son haut*, to be taken aback, to be dumbfounded. ‖ **Haut-commissaire**, m. High Commissioner (diplomate) ; commissioner (haut fonctionnaire). ‖ **Haut-commissariat**, m. High Commissionership. ‖ **Haut-de-chausses**, m. Trunk-hose, breeches. ‖ **Haut-de-forme**, m. Top hat, silk hat, opera hat ; topper, plug hat (fam.). ‖ **Haute-contre**, f. MUS. Alto, counter-tenor. ‖ **Haute-fidélité**, f. TECHN. High-fidelity, hi-fi. ‖ **Haute-Volta**, f. GÉOGR. Upper Volta. ‖ **Haut-fond**, m. Shallow, shoal. ‖ **Haut-le-cœur**, m. inv. MÉD. Heave, qualm, retching. ‖ **Haut-le-corps**, m. inv. Sudden start, jump. ‖ **Haut le pied**, adj. CH. DE F. Running, light (locomotive) ; empty (train, voiture) ; MILIT.

Spare, in reserve. ‖ **Haut-parleur**, m. Amplifier, loud-speaker. ‖ **Haut-relief**, m. ARTS. High relief, alto-relievo.

hautain, aine [*otɛ̃, ɛn] adj. Proud, haughty, lordly, lofty. (V. ALTIER.)

hautainement [-tɛnmɑ̃] adv. Haughtily.

hautbois [*obwa] m. MUS. Hautboy, oboe (instrument) ; oboist, oboe-player (soliste).

hautboïste [*oboist] m. MUS. Oboist.

haute [*ot] f. FAM. Smart set, upper ten, upper crust. (V. GRATIN.)

hautement [*otmɑ̃] adv. Openly, boldly (nettement). ‖ Loudly ; clearly, distinctly (d'une voix forte). ‖ Nobly, loftily (fièrement).

hautesse [*otɛs] f. Highness (titre).

hauteur [*otœ:r] f. Height, elevation. ‖ Height, rising ground, eminence. ‖ Level (niveau) ; *à la hauteur de*, on a level with ; opposite, abreast of. ‖ Head (d'une chute d'eau) ; drop (d'une chute libre) ; head-room (de passage sous une voûte) ; depth (profondeur) ; *hauteur du dos*, length of back (d'une robe). ‖ AUTOM. Ground-clearance (du châssis). ‖ AVIAT. *Prendre de la hauteur*, to gain height, to climb. ‖ ASTRON. Altitude (d'un astre). ‖ MATH. Altitude (d'un triangle). ‖ COMM. Highness (des cours, des tarifs). ‖ MUS. Pitch (d'une note). ‖ FIG. Arrogance, haughtiness (arrogance) ; elevation, loftiness, grandeur, dignity (supériorité) ; *être à la hauteur de*, to be equal to, to be up to. ‖ FAM. *A la hauteur*, thoroughly efficient ; *tomber de sa hauteur*, to be taken aback, to be dumbfounded.

havage [*ava:ʒ] m. TECHN. Cutting.

havanais, aise [*avanɛ, ɛ:z] adj., s. GÉOGR. Havanese.

havane [*avan] m. Havana cigar ; Havana tobacco.
— adj. inv. Brown, tobacco-coloured.

Havane (La) [laavan] f. GÉOGR. Havana.

hâve [*ɑ:v] adj. Sunken, emaciated (joues) ; pale, wan, gaunt, haggard (visage). [V. BLÊME.]

haveneau [*avno], **havenet** [*avnɛ] m. Purse-net.

haver [*ave] v. tr. (1). TECHN. To cut.

haveuse [-vø:z] f. TECHN. Cutting machine.

havrais, aise [avrɛ, ɛ:z] adj. GÉOGR. Of (ou) from Le Havre.
— s. Native (ou) inhabitant of Le Havre.

havre [*ɑ:vr] m. Harbour, haven. (V. PORT.) ‖ GÉOGR. *Le Havre*, Havre (ville et port maritime).

havresac [*avrəsak] m. Haversack (de campeur) ; tool bag (d'ouvrier). ‖ MILIT. Knapsack, pack.

Hawaii (îles) [*awai] f. pl. GÉOGR. Hawaii.

hawaiien, enne [*awajɛ̃, ɛn] adj., s. GÉOGR. Hawaiian.

Haye (La) [laɛ] f. GÉOGR. The Hague.

hayon [ɛjɔ̃] m. AUTOM. Tail-board, tail-gate.

hé ! [*e] interj. Hullo ! hallo ! hi ! I say ! oy ! (pour attirer l'attention) ; what ! hey ! eh ? (pour marquer la surprise).

heaume [*o:m] m. Helmet, helm.

hebdomadaire [ɛbdɔmadɛ:r] adj. Weekly, hebdomadal.
— m. Weekly publication.

hebdomadairement [-mɑ̃] adv. Weekly.

hébergement [ebɛrʒmɑ̃] m. Lodging, housing, accommodation (action) ; shelter, lodging, accommodation (abri). ‖ Overnight charge (frais).

héberger [-ʒe] v. tr. (7). To lodge, to house, to accommodate, to take in, to shelter ; to entertain. ‖ FIG. To harbour, to entertain.

hébétant, ante [ebetɑ̃, ɑ̃:t] adj. Dulling, stupefying, besotting.

hébété, ée [-te] adj. Dazed, stupefied, hebetated (air) ; dull, stupid, obtuse (personne).

hébétement [-tmɑ̃] m. Daze, numbness, stupor.

hébéter [-te] v. tr. (5). To hebetate, to stupefy; to besot; to daze.
hébétude [-tyd] f. Daze, dazed condition. ‖ MÉD. Hebetude.
hébraïque [ebraik] adj. Hebraic, Hebrew.
hébraïsant, ante [-zɑ̃, ɑ̃:t], **hébraïste** [-st] adj. Hebraistic, Hebraistical.
— s. Hebraist.
hébraïsme [-ism] m. GRAMM. Hebraism.
hébreu [ebrø] adj. m. (au fém., on dit *hébraïque*). Hebrew.
— m. GRAMM. Hebrew (langue). ‖ FAM. *Pour moi, c'est de l'hébreu,* it's all Greek to me.
hécatombe [ekatɔ̃:b] f. Hecatomb. (V. MASSACRE.)
hectare [ɛkta:r] m. Hectare (2.47 acres).
hectique [ɛktik] adj. MÉD. Hectic.
hecto [ɛkto] m. Hectogram(me); hectolitre.
hectogramme [-gram] m. Hectogram(me).
hectolitre [-litr] m. Hectolitre (2.75 bushels).
hectomètre [-mɛtr] m. Hectometre.
hectowatt [-wat] m. ELECTR. Hectowatt.
hédonisme [edɔnism] m. PHILOS. Hedonism.
hédoniste [-nist] adj. PHILOS. Hedonist, hedonistic.
— s. PHILOS. Hedonist.
hégélianisme [egeljanism] m. PHILOS. Hegelianism.
hégélien, enne [egeljɛ̃, ɛn] adj., s. PHILOS. Hegelian.
hégémonie [eʒemɔni] f. Hegemony.
hégire [eʒi:r] f. Hegira.
hein? [*ɛ̃] interj. FAM. Eh? What?
hélas [elɑ:s] interj. Alas.
héler [*ele] v. tr. (5). To hail. (V. APPELER.) ‖ NAUT. To speak (un navire).
hélianthe [eljɑ̃:t] m. BOT. Helianthus.
hélianthine [eljɑ̃tin] f. CHIM. Helianthine, methyl orange.
hélice [elis] f. Screw, propeller. ‖ NAUT. *Navire à deux hélices,* twin-screw steamer. ‖ AVIAT. *Hélice propulsive,* propeller. ‖ MATH. Helix, spiral line. ‖ TECHN. Archimedean screw. ‖ MÉD. Helix (de l'oreille). ‖ ZOOL. Helix (mollusque); spinner (poisson).
hélicoïdal, ale [elikɔidal] adj. MATH. Helicoidal, helical.
hélicoïde [elikɔid] adj., m. MATH. Helicoid.
hélicon [elikɔ̃] m. MUS. Helicon.
hélicoptère [elikɔptɛ:r] m. AVIAT. Helicopter.
héliocentrique [eljɔsɑ̃trik] adj. Heliocentric.
héliochromie [eljɔkrɔmi] f. Heliochrome, colour photography.
héliographe [-graf] m. Heliograph.
héliographie [-grafi] f. TECHN., ASTRON. Heliography.
héliogravure [-gravy:r] f. Heliogravure, photogravure.
héliomarin, ine [-marɛ̃, in] adj. Sunshine and sea water (cure); *centre héliomarin,* health farm specializing in treatment through sea water and sunshine.
hélion [eljɔ̃] m. Helium nucleus.
hélioscope [eljɔskɔp] m. ASTRON. Helioscope.
héliostat [-sta] m. ASTR. Heliostat. ‖ MILIT. Heliograph.
héliothérapie [-terapi] f. MÉD. Heliotherapy, sunlight treatment.
héliotrope [eljɔtrɔp] m. BOT. Heliotrope.
héliotypie [-tipi] f. Heliotypy.
héliport [elipɔ:r] m. AVIAT. Heliport, helicopter landing site (ou) ground.
héliporté [elipɔrte] adj. AVIAT. Helicopter-borne.
hélium [eljɔm] m. CHIM. Helium.
hélix [eliks] MÉD., ZOOL. Helix.
hellène [ɛllɛn] adj. Hellenic, Greek.
— s. Hellene.

hellénique [ɛllenik] adj. GÉOGR. Hellenic, Greek.
hellénisant, ante [-nizɑ̃, ɑ̃:t] s. Hellenist.
hellénisation [-nizasjɔ̃] f. Hellenization.
helléniser [-nize] v. tr., v. intr. (1). To Hellenize.
hellénisme [-nism] m. Hellenism.
helléniste [-nist] m. Hellenist.
helminthe [ɛlmɛ̃:t] m. MÉD., ZOOL. Helminth.
Helvète [ɛlvɛt] s. GÉOGR. Helvetian.
helvétien, enne [-vesjɛ̃, ɛn] adj. GÉOGR. Helvetian, Swiss.
helvétique [-vetik] adj. GÉOGR. Helvetic, Swiss; *Confédération helvétique,* Helvetic confederacy, Switzerland.
helvétisme [-vetism] m. GRAMM. Word (ou) idiom peculiar to Swiss French.
hem! [*ɛm] interj. Hem! ahem!
hématie [emati (ou) emasi] f. MÉD. Red blood corpuscle, erythrocyte.
hématite [ematit] f. Hæmatite.
hématologie [ematɔlɔʒi] f. MÉD. Hæmatology.
hématome [ematɔm] m. MÉD. Hematoma.
hématurie [ematyri] f. MÉD. Hæmaturia.
hémicycle [emisikl] m. ARCHIT. Hemicycle.
hémiplégie [emipleʒi] f. MÉD. Hemiplegia.
hémiplégique [-ʒik] adj. MÉD. Hemiplegic.
hémiptère [emiptɛ:r] adj. ZOOL. Hemipterous.
— m. Hemipter.
hémisphère [emisfɛ:r] m. Hemisphere.
hémisphérique [-sferik] adj. Hemispheric.
hémistiche [emistiʃ] m. Hemistich.
hémoglobine [emɔglɔbin] f. MÉD. Hæmoglobin.
hémolyse [-liz] f. MÉD. Hæmolysis.
hémophile [-fil] s. MÉD. Hæmophiliac.
hémophilie [-fili] f. MÉD. Hæmophilia, hæmorrhagic diathesis.
hémoptysie [-ptizi] f. MÉD. Hæmoptysis.
hémorragie [-raʒi] f. MÉD. Hæmorrhage.
hémorragique [-raʒik] adj. MÉD. Hæmorrhagic.
hémorroïdaire [-rɔidɛ:r] adj. MÉD. Affected with hæmorrhoids (ou) piles.
— s. MÉD. Hæmorrhoid (ou) piles sufferer.
hémorroïdal, ale [-rɔidal] adj. MÉD. Hæmorrhoidal.
hémorroïdes [-rɔid] f. pl. MÉD. Hæmorrhoids; piles (fam.).
hémostatique [-statik] adj. MÉD. Hæmostatic.
— m. MÉD. Hæmostat.
hendécagone [ɛ̃dekagɔn] adj. MATH. Hendecagonal.
— m. MATH. Hendecagon.
hendécasyllabe [ɑ̃dekasilab] adj. Hendecasyllabic.
— m. Hendecasyllable.
henné [*ɛnne] m. Henna; *teindre au henné,* to henna.
hennin [*ɛnɛ̃] m. † Hennin.
hennir [*ɛni:r] v. intr. (2). To neigh, to whinny.
hennissement [*ɛnismɑ̃] m. Whinny, whinnying, neigh, neighing.
henry [ɑ̃ri] m. ELECTR. Henry (pl. *henrys*).
hep [*ɛp] interj. Hey! hey there!
héparine [eparin] f. MÉD. Heparin.
hépatique [epatik] adj. MÉD. Hepatic; *colique hépatique,* biliary colic.
— s. MÉD. Hepatic.
— f. BOT. Hepatica, liverwort.
hépatisme [-tism] m. MÉD. Hepatism.
hépatite [-tit] f. MÉD. Hepatitis. ‖ Hepatite (minerai).
heptaèdre [ɛptaɛdr] m. MATH. Heptahedron.
heptagonal, ale [ɛptagɔnal] adj. MATH. Heptagonal.
heptagone [-gɔn] m. MATH. Heptagon.
heptarchie [ɛptarʃi] f. Heptarchy.
heptateuque [ɛptatøk] m. ECCLÉS. Heptateuch.

héraldique [eraldik] adj. Blas. Heraldic.
— f. Blas. Heraldry.
héraldiste [-dist] m. Blas. Heraldist.
héraut [*ero] m. Herald ; harbinger.
herbacé, ée [ɛrbase] adj. Bot. Herbaceous.
herbage [-ba:ʒ] m. Grass, herbage (herbe) ; grass-land, meadow-land. (V. pâturage.) ‖ Culin. Green vegetables ; greens (fam.).
herbager, ère [-baʒe, ɛ:r] s. Agric. Grazier.
herbe [ɛrb] f. Grass ; *en herbe*, in the blade, green, unripe. ‖ Bot. Weed (herbe folle, mauvaise herbe) ; *herbe aux chats*, catmint, U. S. catnip ; *herbes marines*, seaweed. ‖ Culin. Herb ; *fines herbes*, fines herbes, savoury herbs, herbs for seasoning ; *omelette aux fines herbes*, savoury omelette ; *herbes potagères*, pot-herbs. ‖ Méd. *Herbes médicinales*, medicinal herbs, simples. ‖ Fig. *En herbe*, budding, in embryo ; *couper l'herbe sous le pied à qqn*, to cut the ground out from under s.o.'s feet ; to steal a march on s.o.
herbette [-bɛt] f. Bot. Lawn grass ; greensward.
herbeux, euse [-bø, ø:z] adj. Bot. Grassy. (V. herbu.) ‖ Herbous, herby (végétation).
herbicide [-bisid] m. Weed-killer, herbicide.
herbier [-bje] m. Agric. Grass-shed (hangar). ‖ Bot. Herbarium (collection).
herbivore [-bivɔ:r] adj. Herbivorous, grass-eating.
— m. Herbivore. (V. végétarien.)
herborisation [ɛrbɔrizasjɔ̃] f. Bot. Herborizing, botanizing, herborization.
herboriser [-ze] v. intr. (1). Bot. To herborize, to botanize.
herboriseur [-zœ:r] m. Bot. Herborizer, botanizer, plant-collector.
herboriste [-rist] m. Bot. Herborist, herbalist.
herboristerie [-tri] f. Comm. Herborist's shop (boutique) ; herb trade (commerce).
herbu, ue [ɛrby] adj. Grassy, herby, grass-grown.
hercule [ɛrkyl] m. Hercules. ‖ Strong man (de foire).
herculéen, enne [-leɛ̃, ɛn] adj. Herculean.
hercynien, enne [ɛrsinjɛ̃, ɛn] adj. Géol. Hercynian ; *plissement hercynien*, Hercynian orogeny.
herd-book [*œrdbuk] m. Herd-book.
hère [*ɛ:r] m. Wretch, down-and-outer ; *pauvre hère*, poor devil, U. S. poor guy.
hère m. Zool. Young stag.
héréditaire [ereditɛ:r] adj. Hereditary.
héréditairement [-tɛrmɑ̃] adv. Hereditarily.
héréditarisme [-tarism] m. Méd. Hereditism.
hérédité [-te] f. Méd. Heredity. ‖ Jur. Inheritance, heritage (héritage) ; heredity, heirship (succession).
hérédosyphilitique [eredɔsifilitik] adj. Méd. Heredosyphilitic.
hérésiarque [erezjark] m. Heresiarch.
hérésie [-zi] f. Heresy.
hérétique [-tik] adj. Heretical.
— s. Heretic.
hérissé, ée [*erise] adj. Erect, bristling, spiky, on end (cheveux, poil). [V. hirsute.] ‖ Bristly, shaggy, untrimmed (barbe, moustache) ; *hérissé de*, bristling with (piquants). ‖ Bot. Prickly (fruit, tige). ‖ Zool. Rough-coated (cheval). ‖ Fig. *Hérissé de*, bristling (ou) beset (ou) fraught (ou) teeming with.
hérisser v. tr. (1). To erect, to bristle up, to ruffle (plumes, poil). ‖ To spike, to stick (de, with) [pointes]. ‖ Archit. To rough-cast (un mur). ‖ Fig. To enliven, to interlard (de, with).
— v. pr. **Se hérisser**, to stand on end (cheveux) ; to bristle up (plumes, poil). ‖ Fig. To bristle up, to bridle up, to get one's back up, to get one's dander up.
hérisson [*erisɔ̃] m. Zool. Hedgehog ; *hérisson de mer*, sea-urchin (oursin) ; porcupine-fish (poisson). ‖ Bot. Hedgehog-mushroom. ‖ Milit. Che-

vaux de frise (engin) ; strong point (lieu). ‖ Techn. Urchin (de cardeuse) ; sprocket-wheel ; crown-wheel (en mécanique) ; flue-brush (de ramoneur). ‖ Agric. Spiked roller, toothed cylinder. ‖ Archit. Row of spikes (sur un mur).
héritage [erita:ʒ] m. Heritage, inheritance, legacy (v. hoirie, succession) ; *faire un héritage*, to come into an inheritance ; *recueillir son héritage*, to come into one's property. ‖ Fig. Legacy.
hériter [-te] v. intr. (1). To inherit ; *hériter d'une fortune*, to come into a fortune, to inherit a fortune ; *hériter de qqn*, to become s.o.'s heir, to inherit s.o.'s property. ‖ Fam. To get (attraper).
— v. tr. *Hériter qqch. de qqn*, to inherit sth. from s.o.
héritier [-tje] m. Heir, inheritor ; *héritier légitime*, rightful heir ; *héritier naturel*, heir-at-law ; *héritier présomptif*, heir presumptive (ou) apparent.
héritière [-tjɛ:r] f. Heiress, inheritress.
hermaphrodisme [ɛrmafrɔdism] m. Méd. Hermaphrodism, hermaphroditism.
hermaphrodite [-dit] adj. Méd. Hermaphroditic, hermaphrodite.
— s. Hermaphrodite. (V. androgyne.)
herméneutique [ɛrmenøtik] adj. Hermeneutic, hermeneutical.
— f. Hermeneutics.
hermétique [ɛrmetik] adj. Hermetic, hermetically sealed (ou) closed ; air-tight, water-tight. ‖ Abstruse (style).
hermétiquement [-mɑ̃] adv. Hermetically ; tightly.
hermétisme [ɛrmetism] m. Abstruseness.
hermine [ɛrmin] f. Zool. Stoat, ermine. ‖ Comm. Ermine (fourrure).
herminette [-nɛt] f. Techn. Adze (de charpentier) ; howel (de tonnelier).
herniaire [ɛrnjɛ:r] adj. Méd. Hernial ; *bandage herniaire*, truss.
hernie [ɛrni] f. Méd. Hernia, rupture ; *hernie discale*, slipped disc ; *hernie étranglée*, strangulated hernia ; *hernie inguinale*, inguinal hernia. ‖ Fam. Autom. Bulge (d'un pneu).
hernié, ée [-nje] adj. Méd. Herniated ; protruding (intestin).
hernieux, euse [-njø, ø:z] adj. Méd. Ruptured, hernial, suffering from hernia.
héroï-comique [erɔikɔmik] adj. Heroi-comic, mock-heroic, serio-comic.
héroïne [erɔin] f. Heroine (personnage).
héroïne f. Chim. Heroin (stupéfiant).
héroïque [-ik] adj. Heroic, heroical. ‖ Méd. Heroic, kill-or-cure (remède).
héroïquement [-ikmɑ̃] adv. Heroically.
héroïsme [-ism] m. Heroism.
héron [*erɔ̃] m. Zool. Heron, hern.
héros [*ero] m. Hero.
herpe [*ɛrp] f. Naut. Head-board (de guibre) ; head-rail (de poulaine).
herpès [ɛrpɛs] m. Méd. Herpes.
herpétique [ɛrpetik] adj. Méd. Herpetic.
hersage [*ɛrsa:ʒ] m. Agric. Harrowing.
herse [*ɛrs] f. Agric. Harrow. ‖ Archit. Portcullis, herse. ‖ Ecclés. Hearse (pour cierges). Pl. Théâtr. Stage lights, battens.
herser [*ɛrse] v. tr. (1). Agric. To harrow.
hertz [ɛrts] m. Electr. Hertz.
hertzien, enne [ɛrtsjɛ̃, ɛn] adj. Electr. Hertzian.
hésitant, ante [ezitɑ̃, ɑ̃:t] adj. Hesitating, undecided, wavering (caractère) ; halting, shilly-shallying (politique) ; faltering (voix).
hésitation [-tasjɔ̃] f. Hesitation, hesitancy, wavering (v. indécision) ; *avec une certaine hésitation*, hesitatingly, tentatively ; *sans hésitation*, unhesitatingly ; unfalteringly.
hésiter [-te] v. tr. (1). To hesitate, to waver (v. balancer) ; *hésiter à*, to hesitate to ; to be

reluctant to, to scruple to ; *hésiter sur,* to hesitate over ; *sans hésiter,* unhesitatingly, unfalteringly. ‖ To hesitate, to falter (en parlant).

hétaïre [etai:r] f. Hetaera, hetaira.

hétéroclite [eterɔklit] adj. Irregular, unusual, strange ; incoherent. ‖ Nondescript (bâtiment) ; eccentric (conduite) ; incongruous (mélange). ‖ Gramm. Heteroclite.

hétérodoxe [eterɔdɔks] adj. Heterodox, unorthodox.

hétérodoxie [-dɔksi] f. Heterodoxy.

hétérodyne [-din] adj., m. Radio. Heterodyne.

hétérogamie [-gami] f. Bot. Heterogamy.

hétérogène [-ʒɛn] adj. Heterogeneous, dissimilar. (V. différent.) ‖ Fig. Incongruous (collection) ; uncongenial, mixed (société).

hétérogénéité [-ʒeneite] f. Heterogeneousness, heterogeneity.

hétéromorphe [-mɔrf] adj. Bot., Chim. Heteromorphous, heteromorphic.

hétéroplastie [-plasti] f. Méd. Heteroplasty.

hétérosexualité [-sɛksɥalite] f. Heterosexuality.

hétérosexuel, elle [-sɛksɥɛl] adj., s. Heterosexual.

hêtraie [*ɛtrɛ] f. Bot. Beech-grove.

hêtre [*ɛtr] m. Bot. Beech (arbre, bois).

heu! [*ø] interj. Ah! well! Hum! h'm! (exprimant le doute) ; pooh, h'mph (exprimant le mépris).

heur [œ:r] m. † Luck, chance ; good luck.

heure f. Hour (soixante minutes) ; *une grande heure,* a good (ou) full hour ; *une petite heure,* just under an hour ; *d'heure en heure,* hour by hour, every hour, hourly. ‖ Time, hour (à la pendule) ; *avancer, retarder l'heure,* to put the clock forward, back ; *avant l'heure,* ahead of time ; *heure d'été,* summer time, U. S. daylight-saving time ; *heure de Greenwich,* Greenwich mean time, standard time ; *heure légale,* civil time ; *trois heures du matin, de l'après-midi,* three o'clock in the morning, afternoon, three a.m., p.m. ; *trois heures et quart,* three-fifteen (ou) a quarter past three ; *trois heures et demie,* three-thirty (ou) half-past three ; *à l'heure qu'il est,* by this time, by now ; *c'est* (ou) *il est l'heure,* the time has come, time is up ; *quelle heure est-il ?* what time is it? ‖ Time, day, period, hour ; *attendre son heure,* to bide one's time ; *chacun a son heure,* every dog has its day (de célébrité). ‖ Comm. *Heures supplémentaires,* overtime ; *payé cent francs l'heure,* paid one hundred francs an hour ; *semaine de quarante heures,* forty-hour week ; *travailler à l'heure,* to work by the hour (ou) on an hourly basis. ‖ Milit. *Heure H,* H-hour. ‖ Ecclés. *Livre d'heures,* Book of Hours, prayer-book. ‖ Loc. *A la bonne heure !* Well done!, capital!, grand!, good!, fine! ; *à ses heures,* when he liked (ou) felt like it ; *à l'heure,* at the right time, at the appointed time ; *être à l'heure,* to be on time, to be punctual ; *de bonne heure,* early ; *dernière heure,* latest news, news flash, stop-press news (dans un journal, à la radio) ; *de meilleure heure,* earlier ; *à l'heure militaire,* prompt to the minute ; *mauvais quart d'heure,* bad (ou) nasty quarter of an hour ; *pour l'heure,* for the present, for the time being ; *sur l'heure,* at once, immediately ; *tout à l'heure,* just now, a little while ago (dans le passé) ; soon, in a little while, presently (dans un proche avenir) ; *à tout à l'heure,* I'll see you in a few moments (ou) in a little while ; see you later (fam.).

heureusement [œrøzmɑ̃] adv. Happily, successfully ; auspiciously, prosperously (d'une manière heureuse). ‖ Felicitously, happily, aptly (avantageusement). ‖ *Heureusement que,* luckily, fortunately, happily (par bonheur).

heureux, euse [œrø, ø:z] adj. Happy, glad, delighted. (V. content, joyeux.) ‖ Lucky, fortunate (chanceux) ; lucky, successful (prospère). ‖ Happy, favourable, auspicious, propitious (favorable). ‖ Happy, felicitous, seasonable (opportun) ; *réponse heureuse,* apt reply, neat rejoinder. — s. Happy (ou) fortunate person.

heuristique [øristik] adj. Philos. Heuristic. — f. Philos. Heuristics.

heurt [*œ:r] m. Shock, bump, knock (choc) ; blow (coup) ; *heurt des armes,* clash of arms.

heurté, ée [-te] adj. In violent contrast, clashing, hard (couleurs) ; harsh, abrupt (style).

heurtement [-tmɑ̃] m. Clash, collision, clashing.

heurter [-te] v. tr. (1). To knock against, to strike, to hit. (V. cogner.) ‖ To jostle, to collide with, to bump into (qqch., qqn) ; *heurter du pied,* to stumble, to stub one's toe (*contre,* against). ‖ Fig. To come into collision with, to encounter, to shock. (V. choquer.)
— v. intr. To knock (*à,* at) ; to strike (*contre,* against).
— v. pr. Se heurter, to collide, to run into each other ; *se heurter à, contre qqch.,* to bang against sth. ; *venir se heurter contre qqn,* to barge into s.o. (fam.). ‖ Autom. To collide, to be in collision. ‖ Fig. To clash (idées, intérêts).

heurtoir [*-twa:r] m. Door-knocker. ‖ Ch. de f. Buffer. (V. butoir.)

hévéa [evea] m. Bot. Hevea.

hexaèdre [ɛgzaɛdr] adj. Math. Hexahedral. — m. Hexahedron.

hexagonal, ale [-gɔnal] adj. Math. Hexagonal.

hexagone [-gɔn] m. Math. Hexagon. ‖ Fig., Géogr. France.

hexamètre [-mɛtr] m. Hexameter. — adj. Hexametric.

hiatus [jatys] m. Hiatus.

hibernal, ale [ibɛrnal] adj. Hibernal.

hibernant, ante [-nɑ̃, ɑ̃:t] adj. Hibernating. — s. Hibernant, U. S. hibernator.

hibernation [-nasjɔ̃] f. Hibernation.

hiberner [-ne] v. intr. (1). To hibernate.

hibiscus [ibisky:s] m. Bot. Hibiscus.

hibou [*ibu] (pl. **hiboux**) m. Owl ; *jeune hibou,* owlet.

hic [*ik] m. Fam. Snag, hitch, catch ; *voilà le hic,* there's the rub.

hickory [ikɔri] m. Bot. Hickory.

hidalgo [idalgo] m. Hidalgo.

hideur [*idœ:r] f. Hideousness. (V. laideur.)

hideusement [*idøzmɑ̃] adv. Hideously.

hideux, euse [*idø, ø:z] adj. Hideous.

hie [*i] f. Techn. Beetle ; pile-driver.

hier [*jɛr] adv. Yesterday ; *hier matin,* yesterday morning ; *hier soir,* last night ; *il y a eu hier huit jours,* yesterday week ; *pendant toute la journée d'hier,* all day yesterday. ‖ Fam. *Né d'hier,* green.

hiérarchie [*jerarʃi] f. Hierarchy.

hiérarchique [-ʃik] adj. Hierarchical ; *par la voie hiérarchique,* through the official (ou) usual channels.

hiérarchiquement [-ʃikmɑ̃] adv. Hierarchically.

hiérarchisation [-ʃizasjɔ̃] f. Grading (action) ; hierarchical organization.

hiérarchiser [-ʃize] v. tr. (1). To grade.

hiératique [jeratik] adj. Hieratic.

hiéroglyphe [jerɔglif] m. Hieroglyph. ‖ Pl. Hieroglyphics. ‖ Fig. Unintelligible scribble, scrawl.

hiéroglyphique [-flik] adj. Hieroglyphic.

hi-fi [*ifi] f. Hi-fi, high-fidelity.

hi-han! [*iɑ̃] interj. Hee-haw.

hilarant, ante [ilarɑ̃, ɑ̃:t] adj. Laughable. (V. désopilant.) ‖ Chim. Laughing (gaz).

hilare [ila:r] adj. Hilarious.

hilarité [ilarite] f. Hilarity; *soulever l'hilarité générale*, to raise a general laugh.

hile [*i:l] m. Bot. Hilus, hilum. ‖ Méd. Hilus; *porta* (du foie).

hilote [ilɔt] m. V. ilote.

Himalaya [imalaja] m. Géogr. The Himalayas, the Himalaya Mountains.

himalayen, enne [-jɛ̃, ɛn] adj. Géogr. Himalayan.

hindi [indi] m. Gramm. Hindi (langue).

hindou, oue [ɛ̃du] adj., s. Géogr. Indian (habitant de l'Inde). ‖ Ecclés. Hindu (fidèle).

hindouisme [-ism] m. Ecclés. Hinduism.

hinterland [intɛrlɑ̃d] m. Géogr. Hinterland.

hippie, hippy [*ipi] adj., s. Hippie, hippy.

hippique [ipik] adj. Hippic, equine; *concours hippique*, horse-show.

hippisme [ipism] m. Sports. Horse-racing.

hippocampe [ipɔkɑ̃:p] m. Zool. Hippocampus, sea-horse.

hippodrome [-dro:m] m. † Hippodrome. ‖ Sports. Race-course, race-track.

hippogriffe [-grif] m. Hippogriff, hippogryph.

hippologie [-lɔʒi] f. Hippology.

hippomobile [-mɔbil] adj. Horse-drawn.

hippophage [-fa:ʒ] adj. Hippophagous.

hippophagique [-faʒik] adj. *Boucherie hippophagique*, horse butcher's.

hippopotame [-pɔtam] m. Zool. Hippopotamus.

hippotechnie [-tɛkni] f. Horse-training.

hirondelle [irɔ̃dɛl] f. Zool. Swallow.

hirsute [irsyt] adj. Hirsute. (V. hérissé.)

hispanique [ispanik] adj. Hispanic.

hispanisant, ante [-nizɑ̃, ɑ̃:t], **hispaniste** [-nist] adj., s. Hispanist.

hispanisme [-nism] m. Gramm. Hispanicism.

hispanisant [-nizɑ̃] s. Hispanist.

hispano-américain, aine [-noamerikɛ̃, ɛn] adj., s. Géogr. Spanish-American.

hispano-moresque [-nomorɛsk] adj. Hispano-Moresque.

hisser [*ise] v. tr. (1). To hoist; to pull up; *oh! hisse!*, hoist away!, yo heave ho! ‖ Fam. *Hisser qqn sur*, to hoist s.o. on to.
— v. pr. **Se hisser**, to hoist (ou) pull oneself up; *se hisser sur un mur*, to climb up a wall; *se hisser sur la pointe des pieds*, to rise oneself on tiptoe.

histamine [istamin] f. Méd., Chim. Histamine.

histoire [istwa:r] f. History (science); *l'histoire d'Angleterre*, English history; *histoire naturelle, sainte*, natural, Bible (ou) Biblical history. ‖ History, history-book (livre). ‖ Story (v. conte, récit); *histoire de fou*, a shaggy dog story; *raconter de longues histoires*, to spin long yarns. ‖ Trouble (ennui); *avoir une histoire avec*, to have a difference with; *faire des histoires*, to raise difficulties; *sale histoire*, nasty business. ‖ Pl. Story, fib (v. baliverne); *conter des histoires*, to draw the long bow; *raconter des histoires sur*, to tell stories about. ‖ Fam. Pl. Fuss (embarras); *faire un tas d'histoires pour*, to make an awful fuss about; *pas d'histoires*, no fuss. ‖ Loc. *C'est une autre histoire*, that's another story; *le plus beau de l'histoire*, the best of it; *histoire de rire*, just for fun, for the fun of it; *histoire de s'informer*, out of curiosity.

histologie [istɔlɔʒi] f. Méd. Histology.

histologique [-lɔʒik] adj. Histological.

historicité [-risite] f. Historicity.

historié, ée [-rje] adj. Historiated (lettre). ‖ Archit. Storiated, storied.

historien [-rjɛ̃] s. Historian.

historier [-rje] v. tr. (1). To ornament.

historiette [-rjɛt] f. Short story, storiette.

historiographe [-rjɔgraf] m. Historiographer.

historiographie [-rjɔgrafi] f. Historiography.

historique [-rik] adj. Historic (château); historical (fait, roman). ‖ Théâtr. *Pièce historique*, historical (ou) costume play. ‖ Arts. *Eglises et monuments historiques*, religious and historical monuments.
— m. Historical account (relation).

historiquement [-rikmɑ̃] adv. Historically.

histrion [istrijɔ̃] m. Théâtr. Histrion. (V. bouffon.) ‖ Fam. Mountebank (de la politique).

hitlérien, enne [itlerjɛ̃, ɛn] adj. Hitlerite.

hitlérisme [-rism] m. Hitlerism.

hit-parade [*itparad] m. Mus. Hit parade; *premier au hit-parade*, top of the pops.

hittite [*itit] adj., s. Géogr. Hittite.

hiver [ivɛ:r] m. Winter; *d'hiver*, winter (jardin, journée, sports, vêtements); wintry (pluie, temps); *passer l'hiver à*, to winter in. ‖ Fig. Winter.

hivernage [ivɛrna:ʒ] m. Rainy season (saison des pluies). ‖ Polar exploration. ‖ Naut. Winter harbour. ‖ Agric. Winter ploughing (labour); wintering (du bétail).

hivernal, ale [-nal] adj. Hibernal; winter; wintry.

hivernant [-nɑ̃] s. Winterer, winter resident.

hiverner [-ne] v. intr. (1). To winter. ‖ Zool. To hibernate. ‖ Milit. To go into winter quarters.

H. L. M. [aʃɛlɛm] m. ou f. Abrév. de *habitation à loyer modéré*, council flat, block of council flats.

ho [*o] interj. Hey! (appel); oh! (surprise).

hobereau [*ɔbʰ:o] m. Squire, country gentleman. ‖ Zool. Hobby.

hochement [*ɔʃmɑ̃] m. Shaking, shake, toss (de tête).

hochepot [*ɔʃpo] m. Culin. Hotchpotch.

hochequeue [*ɔʃkø] m. Zool. Wagtail.

hocher [*ɔʃe] v. tr. (1). To shake, to toss (la tête); to nod.

hochet [*ɔʃɛ] m. Rattle. ‖ Fig. Toy.

hockey [*ɔkɛ] m. Sports. Hockey.

hockeyeur [*ɔkɛjœ:r] m. Sports. Hockey-player.

hoirie [wari] f. Jur. Inheritance, heirdom (v. héritage); *avance d'hoirie*, advance on a legacy.

holà [*ɔla] interj. Hallo!, hullo! (appel). ‖ Stop!, hold on! (pour arrêter).
— m. Stop; *mettre le holà à*, to put a stopper on, to put a stop to.

hold up [*ɔldœp] m. Hold-up; stick-up (pop.).

holding [*ɔldiɲ] m. Fin. Holding company.

hollandais, aise [*ɔlɑ̃dɛ, ɛ:z] adj. Géogr. Dutch.
— m. Géogr. Dutchman (habitant); Dutch (langue); *les Hollandais*, the Dutch.

Hollandaise [*ɔlɑ̃dɛ:z] f. Dutchwoman.

Hollande [*ɔlɑ̃:d] f. Géogr. Holland. ‖ Holland (toile).
— m. Culin. Dutch cheese (fromage).

holocauste [ɔlɔkost] m. Holocaust.

hologramme [ɔlɔgram] m. Techn. Hologram.

holographie [-grafi] f. Techn. Holography.

homard [*ɔma:r] m. Zool. Lobster.

homélie [ɔmeli] f. Ecclés. Homily. ‖ Fam. Lecture.

homéopathe [ɔmeɔpat] adj. Méd. Homœopathic.
— s. Méd. Homœopath.

homéopathie [-ti] f. Méd. Homœopathy.

homéopathique [-tik] adj. Homœopathic.

homéostasie [-stazi] f. Homœostasis.

homéostatique [-statik] adj. Homœostatic.

homéotherme [-tɛrm] adj. Med., Zool. Homoiothermic, warm-blooded.
— m. Méd., Zool. Homoiotherm, homoiothermic animal.

homérique [ɔmerik] adj. Homeric (récit, rire).

homicide [ɔmisid] adj. Homicidal. ‖ Fig. Murderous.
— s. Homicide. (V. meurtrier.)

— m. Jur. Homicide (acte); *homicide par imprudence*, manslaughter.

homilétique [ɔmiletik] adj. Ecclés. Homiletic.

hommage [ɔma:ʒ] m. † Homage (du vassal). ‖ Homage; *rendre hommage à*, to pay homage (ou) a tribute to. ‖ Complimentary copy (livre); *hommage de l'auteur*, with the author's compliments. ‖ Token (témoignage); *faire hommage de qqch.*, to offer sth. as a token of esteem (ou) gratitude. ‖ Pl. Respects; *présenter ses hommages à*, to pay one's respects to.

hommasse [ɔmas] adj. Mannish, masculine.

homme [ɔm] m. Man, mankind (espèce humaine); *l'homme est mortel*, man is mortal; *de mémoire d'homme*, within living memory. ‖ Man (être humain); *homme des bois*, wild man; *l'abominable homme des neiges*, the abominable snowman; *les grands hommes*, great men. ‖ Man (être masculin); *l'homme et la femme*, man and woman. ‖ Man (adulte); *homme fait*, grown man. ‖ Hand (ouvrier); *homme à tout faire*, Jack-of-all-trades, handyman; *homme de peine*, labourer. ‖ Upholder (partisan); *homme de droite, de gauche*, rightist, leftist; *voilà mon homme*, he's the man for me. ‖ Milit. Man (soldat); *homme d'armes*, man-at-arms; *homme de troupe*, private; *vingt mille hommes*, twenty thousand men. ‖ Jur. *Homme de loi* (ou) *de robe*, lawyer. ‖ Comm. *Homme de paille*, man of straw, cat's-paw, dummy, stooge. ‖ Ecclés. *Homme d'Eglise*, clergyman; *le vieil homme*, the Old Adam. ‖ Fam. Man, husband (mari). ‖ Loc. *Comme un seul homme*, like one man; *d'homme à homme*, between man and man; *être homme à*, to be the sort of man to. ‖ **Homme-Dieu**, m. Ecclés. God made man. ‖ **Homme-grenouille**, m. Frogman. ‖ **Homme-orchestre**, m. Mus. One-man band. ‖ **Homme-sandwich**, m. Sandwich-man. ‖ **Homme-serpent**, m. Contortionist.

homocentrique [ɔmosɑ̃trik] adj. Math., Phys. Homocentric.

homogène [ɔmoʒɛn] adj. Homogeneous.

homogénéisation [-ʒeneizasjɔ̃] f. Homogenization.

homogénéisé, ée [-ʒeneize] adj. Homogenized; *lait homogénéisé*, homogenized milk.

homogénéiser v. tr. (1). To homogenize.

homogénéité [-ʒeneite] f. Homogeneity, homogeneousness.

homographe [ɔmɔgraf] m. Gramm. Homograph.

homogreffe [ɔmɔgrɛf] f. Méd. Homograft, homotransplant.

homologation [ɔmɔlɔgasjɔ̃] f. Jur. Confirmation.

homologie [-lɔʒi] f. Homology.

homologue [-lɔg] adj. Homologous.
— m. Counterpart.

homologué, ée [-lɔge] adj. Recognized; *plusieurs avions abattus, trois homologués*, several planes brought down, three confirmed.

homologuer [-lɔge] v. tr. (1). Jur. To confirm, to homologate (un acte); to ratify (une décision); to prove (un testament). ‖ Sports. To recognize (un record).

homoncule [ɔmɔ̃kyl] m. V. homuncule.

homonyme [ɔmɔnim] adj. Homonymous.
— m. Gramm. Homonym. ‖ Namesake (personne).

homonymie [-mi] f. Homonymy.

homonymique [-mik] adj. Homonymic.

homophone [ɔmɔfɔn] adj. Gramm. Homophonous. ‖ Mus. Homophonous, homophonic.
— m. Gramm. Homophone.

homophonie [-ni] f. Mus., Gramm. Homophony.

homosexualité [ɔmɔsɛksɥalite] f. Homosexuality.

homosexuel, elle [ɔmɔsɛksɥɛl] adj., s. Homosexual.

homuncule [ɔmɔ̃kyl] m. Homuncule, homunculus; manikin.

Honduras [ɔ̃dyras] m. Géogr. Honduras.

hondurien, enne [*ɔ̃dyrjɛ̃, ɛn] adj., s. Géogr. Honduran.

hongre [*ɔ̃:gr] adj. Gelded (cheval).
— m. Gelding.

hongrer [*ɔ̃gre] v. tr. To geld.

hongreur [*ɔ̃grœ:r] m. Gelder.

Hongrie [*ɔ̃gri] f. Géogr. Hungary.

hongrois, oise [*ɔ̃grwa, waz] adj., s. Hungarian.
— m. Gramm. Hungarian (langue).

honnête [ɔnɛ:t] adj. Honest, good, virtuous (femme); honest, upright (homme); honest, respectable, decent (personnes). (V. intègre, probe). ‖ Decent, seemly (attitude); square, fair (procédé). ‖ Reasonable, moderate (prix); *une honnête aisance*, a decent competency. ‖ Polite.

honnêtement [ɔnɛtmɑ̃] adv. Honestly, uprightly, respectably. ‖ Decently; fairly. ‖ Politely.

honnêteté [-te] f. Honesty, uprightness. (V. intégrité, probité.) ‖ Modesty; *l'honnêteté des femmes*, virtue in women. ‖ Fairness, fair dealing (loyauté). ‖ † Politeness. ‖ † Decency; *braver l'honnêteté*, to offend against propriety.

honneur [ɔnœ:r] m. Hono(u)r (probité, réputation); *donner sa parole d'honneur*, to give one's word of honour; *engagé d'honneur*, bound in honour; *faire honneur à*, to meet (ses obligations); to honour (sa signature); *homme d'honneur*, man of honour; *perdre qqn d'honneur*, to ruin s.o.'s honour. ‖ Honour (distinction); *avoir l'honneur de parler à*, to have the honour of speaking to; *j'ai l'honneur de demander*, I beg to ask; *en l'honneur de*, in honour of; *être à l'honneur*, to be held in honour (chose); to hold a place of honour (personne); *faire honneur à*, *l'honneur de*, to do honour to, the honour of. ‖ Honour; *place d'honneur*, seat of honour; *président d'honneur*, honorary president. ‖ Honour, credit; *c'est à votre honneur*, it's to your credit, it speaks well for you; *faire à qqn l'honneur de qqch.*, to credit s.o. with sth. ‖ Honour, pride (fierté); *être l'honneur de*, to be the pride of; *faire honneur à*, to be an honour to; to do credit to; *se piquer d'honneur pour*, to make it a point of honour to. ‖ Pl. Honours; *derniers honneurs*, last (ou) funeral honours; *faire les honneurs de*, to do the honours of (la maison). ‖ Pl. Honours (aux cartes). ‖ Milit. *Champ d'honneur*, battlefield; *honneurs de la guerre*, honours of war; *rendre les honneurs*, to render honours, to present arms. ‖ Archit. *D'honneur*, great, main (cour); grand (escalier). ‖ Fam. *En quel honneur êtes-vous venu?*, to what do we owe your visit?, what's the occasion of your coming?; *faire honneur au repas*, to do justice to the meal. ‖ Loc. *En tout bien tout honneur*, nothing untoward taking place, with no nonsense; *pour l'honneur*, for love.

honnir [*ɔnni:r] v. tr. (2). To shame, to spurn.

honorabilité [ɔnɔrabilite] f. Honourableness.

honorable [-rabl] adj. Honourable (conduite, personne, profession). [V. respectable.] ‖ Creditable (action, travail). ‖ Blas. *Pièce honorable*, honourable ordinary.

honorablement [-rabləmɑ̃] adv. Honourably. ‖ Creditably.

honoraire [-rɛ:r] adj. Honorary (président); emeritus (professeur, recteur).
— m. pl. Fees (d'homme de loi, de médecin, de professeur).

honorariat [-rarja] m. Honorary membership.

honoré, ée [-re] adj. Respected (confrère); *très honoré de faire votre connaissance*, greatly honoured to make your acquaintance.

honorée [-re] f. COMM. Favour.
honorer [-re] v. tr. (1). To honour (qqn); to respect (une qualité). ‖ To do credit to (qqn); *votre attitude vous fait honneur*, your attitude does you honour (ou) credit. ‖ To be an honour to (qqn); *honorer de sa présence*, to grace with one's presence; *honorer qqn de*, to honour (ou) favour s.o. with; *votre amitié m'honore*, I am honoured by your friendship. ‖ To fee, U. S. to pay (un avocat, un médecin). ‖ COMM. To honour (un effet).
— v. pr. **S'honorer**, to consider oneself honoured; *s'honorer de*, to pride oneself on, to be proud of.
honorifique [-rifik] adj. Honorary.
honoris causa [ɔnɔriskoza] loc. adj. Honoris causa.
honte [*ɔ̃:t] f. Shame, disgrace (déshonneur); *couvrir de honte*, to shame; *être la honte de*, to be a shame (ou) disgrace to. ‖ Shame (confusion); *avoir honte de*, to be ashamed of; *faire honte à qqn*, to put s.o. to shame; *faire honte à qqn de*, to make s.o. ashamed of; *fausse honte*, shamefacedness; *sans honte*, shamelessly. ‖ Shame, scandal; *c'est une honte !*, it's scandalous !
honteusement [*ɔ̃tøzmɑ̃] adv. Shamefully. ‖ In a shamefaced manner.
honteux, euse [*ɔ̃tø, ø:z] adj. Shameful, disgraceful (déshonorant); *c'est honteux*, it's a shame. ‖ Ashamed (confus) [*de*, of]. ‖ Shamefaced, shy, sheepish (timide). ‖ MÉD. Secret (maladie); privy, private (parties).
hop [*ɔp] interj. Hop it !, off with you !
hôpital [ɔpital] m. MÉD. Hospital. ‖ MILIT. *Hôpital de campagne*, military, field, station hospital. ‖ NAUT. *Navire-hôpital*, hospital ship. ‖ Workhouse. (V. HOSPICE.)
hoquet [*ɔkɛ] m. MÉD. Hiccough, hiccup; *avoir le hoquet*, to have the hiccups. ‖ Gasp (d'étouffement); retch (de nausée).
hoqueter [*ɔkte] v. intr. (8a). To hiccough, to hiccup.
horaire [ɔrɛ:r] adj. Horary (cercle). ‖ TECHN. Per hour.
— m. Time-table; teaching duties (d'un professeur). ‖ CH. DE F. Time-table. ‖ SPORTS. Programme.
horde [*ɔrd] f. Horde. ‖ FAM. Host. (V. BANDE.)
horion [*ɔrjɔ̃] m. Punch, clout. (V. COUP.)
horizon [ɔrizɔ̃] m. Horizon, sky-line. ‖ ARTS. *Ligne d'horizon*, vanishing line. ‖ FIG. Scope (champ); outlook (perspective).
horizontal, ale [-tal] adj., f. Horizontal.
horizontalement [-talmɑ̃] adv. Horizontally.
horizontalité [-talite] f. Horizontality.
horloge [ɔrlɔ:ʒ] f. Clock (v. PENDULE); *horloge normande*, grandfather clock; *l'horloge parlante*, the speaking clock, « Tim »; *durant deux heures d'horloge*, for two hours by the clock.
horloger [ɔrlɔʒe] adj. Horological.
— s. Clock-maker.
horlogerie [-ʒri] f. Clock-making (fabrication); watchmaker's (magasin); clocks and watches (marchandise); *d'horlogerie*, clockwork (mouvement).
hormis [ɔrmi] prép. Except, but, save (v. EXCEPTÉ); *hormis que*, except that.
hormonal, ale [ɔrmɔnal] adj. MÉD. Hormonal, hormonic.
hormone [-mɔn] f. MÉD. Hormone.
hornblende [*ɔrnblɑ̃:d] f. Hornblende.
horodateur [ɔrɔdatœ:r] m. TECHN. Time and date stamping machine.
horographie [ɔrografi] f. Horography.
horométrie [-metri] f. Horometry.
horoscope [-skɔp] m. Horoscope; *faire* (ou) *tirer un horoscope*, to cast an horoscope.

horreur [ɔrrœ:r] f. Horror (v. ÉPOUVANTE); *saisi d'horreur*, horror-stricken. ‖ Horror, abhorrence, loathing (v. RÉPUGNANCE); *avoir horreur de*, to loathe, to abhor, to hate; *faire horreur à*, to horrify; *inspirer à qqn de l'horreur pour*, to inspire s.o. with an abhorrence for. ‖ Horror, horribleness (v. HIDEUR); *l'horreur d'un spectacle*, the horror of a sight. ‖ Pl. Horrors (atrocités); horrid things (propos). ‖ FAM. *Une horreur*, an horrible thing (chose); a fright (personne); *quelle horreur !*, how dreadful ! how shocking !; *quelle horreur d'enfant !*, what a horrid child !; *quelle horreur ce sac !*, what an awful handbag !
horrible [ɔrribl] adj. Horrible; horrid. (V. AFFREUX.) ‖ Hideous. (V. HIDEUX.) ‖ Gruesome, ghastly. (V. TERRIFIANT.) ‖ FAM. Shocking.
horriblement [-blømɑ̃] adv. Horribly, horridly; hideously. ‖ FAM. Awfully.
horrifiant, ante [-ɔrrifjɑ̃, ɑ̃:t] adj. Horrifying, appalling, shocking.
horrifier [-ifje] v. tr. (1). To horrify.
horrifique [-fik] adj. Horrific.
horripilant, ante [-pilɑ̃, ɑ̃:t] adj. Horripilant. ‖ FAM. Exasperating.
horripilation [-pilasyɔ̃] f. Horripilation. ‖ FAM. Exasperation.
horripiler [-pile] v. tr. (1). To cause horripilation. ‖ FAM. To exasperate. (V. EXASPÉRER.)
hors [*ɔ:r] adv. Out, outside. (V. DEHORS.)
— prép. Save, except. (V. EXCEPTÉ.) ‖ Outside; *hors les murs*, outside the walls. ‖ *Hors de*, outside, out of; *hors d'atteinte, de danger, de vue*, out of reach, danger, sight; *hors d'affaire*, out of the wood; *hors de combat*, disabled, knocked down; *hors de doute*, beyond doubt; *hors de soi*, beside oneself; *les poires sont hors de prix*, the price of pears is prohibitive. ‖ LOC. *Hors cadre, hors concours, hors concours*; *hors ligne*, matchless; *hors programme*, outside the syllabus; *mettre hors la loi*, to outlaw. ‖ **Hors-bord**, m. invar. NAUT. Speed-boat. ‖ **Hors-cote**, adj. inv. FIN. Curb, curbstone (marché, argent), unlisted (action); m. inv. FIN. Curb (ou) curbstone market. ‖ **Hors-d'œuvre**, m. inv. CULIN. Hors-d'œuvre. ‖ **Hors-jeu**, adj. inv. Out of play; m. Offside. ‖ **Hors-la-loi**, m. inv. Outlaw. ‖ **Hors-taxes**, adj. inv. Before tax, duty-free; adv. duty-free. ‖ **Hors-texte**, m. inv. TECHN. Plate.
horsain [ɔrsɛ̃] m. Foreigner, outsider.
hortensia [ɔrtɑ̃sja] m. BOT. Hydrangea.
horticole [ɔrtikɔl] adj. Horticultural.
horticulteur [-kyltœ:r] m. Horticulturist.
horticultural, ale [-kyltyral] adj. Horticultural.
horticulture [-kylty:r] f. Horticulture.
hosanna [ɔzanna] interj. m. ECCLÉS. Hosanna.
hospice [ɔspis] m. Hospice, home, poor-house, workhouse, almshouse; *hospice des enfants assistés*, foundling hospital; *hospice des vieillards*, home for the aged. ‖ ECCLÉS. Hospice.
hospitalier, ère [ɔspitalje, ɛr] adj. Charitable (établissement); hospitable (personne). ‖ ECCLÉS. Hospitalier.
— s. Hospitaller.
hospitalièrement [-ljɛrmɑ̃] adv. Hospitably.
hospitalisation [-lizasjɔ̃] f. MÉD. Hospitalization; *frais d'hospitalisation*, hospital charges.
hospitalisé [-lize] s. MÉD. In-patient.
hospitaliser [-lize] v. tr. (1). MÉD. To hospitalize.
hospitalité [-lite] f. Hospitality.
hospitalo-universitaire [ɔspitaloynivɛrsitɛ:r] adj. *Centre hospitalo-universitaire*, teaching hospital.
hostellerie [ɔstɛlri] f. Country inn.
hostie [ɔsti] f. † Victim, offering. ‖ ECCLÉS. Host.
hostile [ɔsti:l] adj. Hostile; *être hostile à*, to be against, to be opposed to.

387

hostilement [-lmɑ̃] adv. Hostilely.
hostilité [-lite] f. Hostility (*contre*, against). ‖ Opposition (*à* to). ‖ Milit. Pl. Hostilities.
hôte [o:t] m. Host (amphitryon); guest (invité). ‖ Landlord (hôtelier); *table d'hôte*, table d'hôte. ‖ Pl. Denizens (habitants).
hôtel [otɛl] m. Hotel; hostelry; *descendre à l'hôtel*, to put up at a (ou) an hotel. ‖ Mansion, town-house (maison particulière). ‖ Public building; *Hôtel des ventes*, general auction-rooms; *hôtel de ville*, town hall.
hôtelier, ère [otəlje, ɛ:r] adj. Hotel; *école hôtelière*, catering (ou) hotel management school. — s. Hotel-keeper, hotelier.
hôtellerie [-ri] f. Hostelry. ‖ Hotel trade. ‖ Ecclés. Guest-house.
hôtesse [o:tɛs] f. Hostess (maîtresse de maison). ‖ Landlady (hôtelière). ‖ Aviat. *Hôtesse de l'air*, air hostess.
hotte [*ɔt] f. Basket (à dos). ‖ Hod (de maçon). ‖ Archit. Hood (de cheminée).
hottée [*ɔte] f. Basketful. ‖ Hodful.
hou! [*u] interj. Fie! (pour désapprouver); boo! (pour faire peur).
houblon [*ublɔ̃] m. Bot. Hop, hops.
houblonner [*ublɔne] v. tr. (1). To hop.
houblonnière [-njɛr] f. Agric. Hop-field.
houe [*u] f. Hoe.
houer [*ue] v. tr. (1). Agric. To hoe.
houille [*u:j] f. Coal (charbon); *houille blanche*, white coal.
houiller, ère [*uje, ɛ:r] adj. Coal (bassin, industrie); coal-bearing, carboniferous (terrain); *production houillère*, output of coal.
houillère [*ujɛ:r] f. Coal-mine, colliery.
houilleux, euse [*ujø, ø:z] adj. Coal-bearing.
houle [*u:l] f. Swell.
houlette [*ulɛt] f. Crook (de berger).
houleux, euse [*ulø, ø:z] adj. Swelling (mer). ‖ Fig. Tumultuous (assemblée, foule); stormy (débats, réunion).
houp [*up] interj. Hoop!; *houp là!*, upsadaisy!
houppe [*up] f. Tuft (de cheveux, de plumes); crest (de feuillage); tassel (de soie); *houppe à poudre*, powder-puff.
houppelande [*uplɑ:d] f. Greatcoat.
houppette [*upɛt] f. Small tuft (de cheveux, de plumes). ‖ Powder-puff (à poudrer).
hourder [*urde] v. tr. (1). Archit. To rough-cast.
hourdis [-di] m. Archit. Pugging.
houri [*uri] f. Houri (femme).
hourque [*urk] f. Naut. Hooker.
hourra [*ura] interj. m. Hurrah!; *pousser des hourras*, to cheer.
hourvari [*urvari] m. Fam. Uproar.
houseau [*uzo] m. Legging.
houspiller [*uspije] v. tr. (1). Fam. To hustle (v. malmener); to rate, to tell (ou) tick off. (V. réprimander.)
housse [*us] f. Garment-bag (à habits); dust-sheet, slip-cover (à meubles). ‖ Horse-cloth (de cheval).
houssine [*usin] f. Switch (fouet).
houx [*u] m. Bot. Holly.
hovercraft [ɔvœrkraft] m. Hovercraft.
hoyau [*ɔjo] m. Agric. Grubber, grubbing-hoe.
H.T. [aʃte] Abrév. de *haute-tension*, high tension, H.T.
hublot [*yblɔ] m. Naut. Side-scuttle, port-hole; *hublot d'aération*, air scuttle (ou) port.
huche [*yʃ] f. Bin (à farine, à pain). ‖ Trough (à pétrir); hopper (de moulin).
huchet [*yʃɛ] m. Blas. Hunting-horn.
hue! [*y] interj. Gee! ‖ Loc. *Tirer à hue et à dia*, to pull in opposite directions.
huée [*ɥe] f. Hoot, howl; *chasser qqn sous les*

huées, to hoot s.o. out. ‖ Sports. Halloo (à la chasse).
huer v. tr. (1). To hoot, to boo. — v. intr. To hoot (chouette).
huguenot [*ygno] adj., s. Huguenot.
huilage [ɥila:ʒ] m. Oiling; lubrication.
huile [ɥil] f. Oil; *huile de table*, salad oil; *cuisine à l'huile*, oil cooking. ‖ Oil; *huile de graissage, de machine*, lubricating, engine oil. ‖ Arts. *Peinture à l'huile*, oil-painting. ‖ Ecclés. *Saintes huiles*, holy oil, chrism. ‖ Fam. *Huile de coude*, elbow-grease; *jeter de l'huile sur le feu*, to pour oil on the flames, to add fuel to the fire; *faire tache d'huile*, to spread; *une huile*, a bigwig, a big pot; *mer d'huile*, calm glassy sea.
huilé, ée [-le] adj. *Manteau de pluie en toile huilée*, oilskin rain-coat; *papier huilé*, oil-paper.
huiler [-le] v. tr. (1). To oil. (V. lubrifier.)
huilerie [-lri] f. Oil-mill (fabrique); oil-store (magasin).
huileux, euse [-lø, ø:z] adj. Oily.
huilier [-lje] m. Oil-cruet; cruet-stand (burette). ‖ Oilman (fabricant).
huis [ɥi] m. † Door. ‖ Jur. [*ɥi] *A huis clos*, behind closed doors, in camera; *ordonner le huis clos*, to clear the court. ‖ Fam. *A huis clos*, in private.
huisserie [ɥisri] f. Techn. Door- (ou) window-frame.
huissier [ɥisje] m. Usher (gardien). ‖ Jur. Process-server.
huit [*ɥit] ([*ɥi] before a consonant) adj. num. Eight; *huit pages*, eight pages; *d'aujourd'hui en huit*, a week to day, today week. ‖ Eighth; *Henri VIII*, Henry the Eighth; *le huit avril*, the eighth of April, April the eighth. ‖ Loc. *Donner ses huit jours*, to give notice. — m. Eight; *faire des huit*, to sprinkle water in figure eights; *plier en huit*, to fold in eights. ‖ **Huit-reflets**, m. invar. Fam. Silk hat.
huitain [-tɛ̃] m. Octet.
huitaine [-tɛn] f. About eight, eight or so (environ huit); a week or so (une semaine environ).
huitième [-tjɛm] adj. num. s. Eighth. — f. Eighth class (in French schools); first or second form.
huitièmement [-tjɛmmɑ̃] adv. Eighthly.
huître [ɥi:tr] f. Oyster. ‖ Fam. Ninny.
huîtrier [ɥitrje] adj. Oyster-, pertaining to oysters.
huîtrière [-trjɛ:r] f. Oyster-bed.
hulotte [ylɔt] f. Zool. Brown owl, screech-owl, howlet.
hululer [ylyle] v. intr. (1). To ululate.
hum! [œm] interj. Hem! hm!
humage [yma:ʒ] m. Inhaling.
humain, aine [ymɛ̃, ɛn] adj. Human (corps, être, nature); *genre humain*, mankind. ‖ Humane. (V. compatissant.) ‖ Personal (facteur). — m. Human being.
humainement [ymɛnmɑ̃] adv. Humanly. ‖ Humanely (avec humanité).
humanisation [ymanizasjɔ̃] f. Humanization.
humaniser [ymanize] v. tr. (1). To humanize. — v. pr. S'humaniser, to grow (ou) to become more humane. ‖ To grow more sociable.
humanisme [-nism] m. Humanism.
humaniste [-nist] m. Humanist.
humanitaire [-nitɛ:r] adj., s. Humanitarian.
humanitarisme [-nitarism] m. Humanitarianism.
humanité [-nite] f. Humanity, human nature (nature). ‖ Humanity, mankind (genre humain). ‖ Humaneness, human feeling (sentiments humains). ‖ Pl. Humanities; classics.
humanoïde [-nɔid] adj., s. Humanoid.

humble [œ̃:bl] adj. Humble (modeste); humble, obscure (obscur); humble, meek (soumis).
— s. Humble person; *les humbles*, the humble.
humblement [-bləmɑ̃] adv. Humbly.
humectage [ymɛkta:ʒ] m. Moistening, wetting.
humectation [-tasjɔ̃] f. Humectation.
humecter [-te] v. tr. (1). To moisten, to damp, to wet. (V. HUMIDIFIER.)
— v. pr. **S'humecter,** to become moist (ou) damp. ‖ FAM. *S'humecter le gosier,* to wet one's whistle.
humer [*yme] v. tr. (1). To breathe in (l'air); to inhale (une odeur). ‖ To sip (un liquide); to suck up (un œuf).
— v. intr. To sniff.
huméral, ale [ymeral] adj. MÉD. Humeral.
humérus [-rys] m. MÉD. Humerus.
humeur [ymœ:r] f. Humour, spirits, temper; *avec bonne, mauvaise humeur,* good-humouredly, testily; *de bonne humeur,* in a good humour, in good spirits; *d'excellente humeur,* in high feather; *de mauvaise humeur,* in a bad humour, out of trim, out of temper; *d'une humeur massacrante,* in a filthy mood. ‖ Bad temper, ill humour (v. IRRITATION); *accès d'humeur,* fit of temper; *passer son humeur sur,* to vent one's spleen on. ‖ Mood (disposition); *humeur belliqueuse,* bellicose mood, fighting spirit; *être d'humeur à,* to be in a mood to (ou) in the vein to. ‖ Temper (caractère); *d'humeur égale, sombre,* even-minded, gloomy; *incompatibilité d'humeur,* incompatibility of temperament. ‖ MÉD. Humour; *humeurs froides,* scrofula.
humide [ymid] adj. Wet, damp, humid. (V. MOITE.) ‖ Damp, dank (maison, mur). ‖ Damp (temps); *humide et chaud,* muggy; *humide et froid,* raw; *chaleur humide,* U. S. sticky heat. ‖ Watery (œil, terrain).
humidificateur [ymidifikatœ:r] m. Humidor.
humidification [-sjɔ̃] f. Damping, moistening.
humidifier [ymidifje] v. tr. (1). To humidify. (V. HUMECTER.)
humidité [-te] f. Humidity, moisture, dampness, damp, wetness, wet; *chargé d'humidité,* heavy with moisture.
humiliant, ante [ymiljɑ̃, ɑ̃:t] adj. Humiliating.
humiliation [-ljasjɔ̃] f. Humiliation (action). ‖ Humiliation. (V. AFFRONT, MORTIFICATION.)
humilier [-lje] v. tr. (1). To humble (l'orgueil); to humiliate; to humble (qqn).
— v. pr. **S'humilier,** to humble oneself (*jusqu'à,* to); *s'humilier devant,* to cringe to, to eat humble pie before.
humilité [-lite] f. Humility, humbleness. ‖ Lowliness (de la condition).
humoral, ale [ymɔral] adj. MÉD. Humoral.
humoriste [ymɔrist] adj. Humoristic.
— s. Humorist. ‖ MÉD. Humoralist.
humoristique [-tik] adj. Humoristic, humorous.
humour [ymu:r] m. Humour; U. S. humor; *humour noir,* macabre (ou) graveyard humour.
humus [ymys] m. Humus.
hune [*yn] f. NAUT. Top; *hune d'artimon, de misaine,* mizzentop, foretop.
hunier [*ynje] m. NAUT. Topsail.
huppe [*yp] f. Tuft, crest (d'oiseau). ‖ Tuft. (V. HOUPPE.) ‖ ZOOL. Hoopoe.
huppé, ée [*ype] adj. ZOOL. Tufted, crested. ‖ FAM. Smart, swell; *les gens huppés,* the toffs, the swells.
hure [*y:r] f. ZOOL. Head (de sanglier); jowl (de saumon). ‖ CULIN. Brawn, potted head, U. S. head-cheese. ‖ FAM. Tousled head.
hurlement [*yrləmɑ̃] m. Howl, howling (du chien, du loup); *pousser un hurlement,* to howl, to give a howl. ‖ Howling (de la tempête, du vent). ‖

Roar (de colère); howl, yell (de douleur); *pousser des hurlements de rage,* to roar with rage.
hurler [-le] v. intr. (1). To howl (chien, loup). ‖ To howl (tempête, vent). ‖ To roar (de colère); to howl, to yell (de douleur). ‖ To bawl. (V. BRAILLER.)
— v. tr. To howl out, to bawl out (des ordres).
hurleur, euse [-lœ:r, ø:z] adj. Howling.
— s. Howler.
— m. ZOOL. Howler. ‖ RADIO. Extra-loud, loud speaker.
hurluberlu [yrlybɛrly] adj. Scatter-brained.
— s. Harum-scarum, flibbertigibbet.
huron [*yrɔ̃] m. GÉOGR. Huron. ‖ FAM. Boor.
hurrah [*ura] interj., m. V. HOURRA.
hussard [*ysa:r] m. MILIT. Hussar.
hussarde [*ysard] f. Hussarde (danse). ‖ FAM. *A la hussarde,* cavalierly.
hutte [*yt] f. Hut. (V. CABANE.)
hyacinthe [jasɛ̃:t] f. BOT. Hyacinth.
— adj. Hyacinthine (couleur).
hyalin [jalɛ̃] adj. Hyaline.
hyaloïde [jalɔid] adj. MÉD. Hyaloid.
hyalurgie [jalyrʒi] f. Hyalurgy, glass-making.
hybridation [ibridasjɔ̃] f. Hybridization.
hybride [ibrid] adj., m. Hybrid.
hybrider [-de] v. tr. (1). To hybridize.
hybridité [-dite] f., **hybridisme** [-dism] m. Hybridity, hybridism.
hydracide [idrasid] m. CHIM. Hydracid.
hydratant, ante [idratɑ̃, ɑ̃:t] adj. Moisturizing; *crème hydratante, lait hydratant,* moisturizer.
hydratation [-tasjɔ̃] f. CHIM. Hydration.
hydrate [idrat] m. CHIM. Hydrate; *hydrates de carbone,* carbohydrates.
hydraté, ée [idrate] adj. Hydrated.
hydrater [-te] v. tr. (1). To hydrate.
— v. pr. **S'hydrater.** To hydrate.
hydraulicien, enne [idrolisjɛ̃, ɛn] s. Hydraulic engineer.
hydraulique [idrolik] adj. Hydraulic; *roue hydraulique,* water-wheel.
— f. Hydraulics.
hydravion [idravjɔ̃] m. AVIAT. Sea-plane; *hydravion à coque,* flying boat.
hydrazine [idrazin] f. CHIM. Hydrazine.
hydre [i:dr] f. Hydra.
hydrique [idrik] adj. Hydrous; pertaining to water. ‖ MÉD. Water (diète).
hydro-aérien [idroaerjɛ̃] adj. AVIAT. Sea-plane.
hydrocarbure [-karby:r] m. CHIM. Hydrocarbon.
hydrocèle [-sɛl] f. MÉD. Hydrocele.
hydrocéphale [-sefal] adj. MÉD. Hydrocephalic, hydrocephalous.
— s. MÉD. Hydrocephalic person.
hydrocéphalie [-sefali] f. MÉD. Hydrocephalus, hydrocephaly.
hydrocortisone [-kɔrtizɔn] f. MÉD. Hydrocortisone.
hydrocution [-kysjɔ̃] f. MÉD. Loss of consciousness (ou) death through sudden immersion in cold water.
hydrodynamique [-dinamik] adj. Hydrodynamic.
— f. Hydrodynamics.
hydroélectricité [-elɛktrisite] f. Hydroelectricity.
hydroélectrique [-elɛktrik] adj. Hydroelectric.
hydrogénation [-ʒenasjɔ̃] f. CHIM. Hydrogenation; *hydrogénation du charbon,* coal hydrogenation.
hydrogène [-ʒɛn] m. CHIM. Hydrogen; *à hydrogène,* hydrogen (bombe).
hydrogéner [-ʒene] v. tr. CHIM. To hydrogenate.
hydroglisseur [-glisœ:r] m. AVIAT. Hydroplane.
hydrographe [-graf] m. Hydrographer.

hydrographie [-grafi] f. Hydrography.
hydrographique [-grafik] adj. Hydrographical.
hydrologie [-lɔʒi] f. Hydrology.
hydrologique [-lɔʒik] adj. Hydrologic, hydrological.
hydrologiste [-lɔʒist], **hydrologue** [-lɔg] s. Hydrologist.
hydrolyse [-li:z] f. CHIM. Hydrolysis.
hydrolyser [-lize] v. tr. (1). CHIM. To hydrolyze.
hydromel [-mɛl] m. Hydromel, mead.
hydromécanique [-mekanik] f. Hydromechanics.
hydromètre [-mɛtr] m. Hydrometer.
hydrométrie [-metri] f. Hydrometry.
hydrométrique [-metrik] adj. Hydrometric.
hydrophile [-fi:l] adj. Absorbent (coton).
hydrophobe [-fɔb] adj. Hydrophobic.
— s. MÉD. Hydrophobic patient.
hydrophobie [-fɔbi] f. MÉD. Hydrophobia, rabies.
hydropique [-pik] adj. Dropsical.
— s. MÉD. Dropsical patient.
hydropisie [-pizi] f. MÉD. Dropsy, hydropsy.
hydropneumatique [-pnømatik] adj. Hydropneumatic.
hydroptère [-ptɛ:r] m. NAUT. Hydrofoil.
hydrosol [-sɔl] m. CHIM. Hydrosol.
hydrosoluble [-sɔlybl] adj. Water-soluble.
hydrosphère [-sfɛ:r] f. GÉOGR. Hydrosphere.
hydrostat [-sta] m. AVIAT. Hydrostat.
hydrostatique [-statik] adj. Hydrostatic.
— f. Hydrostatics.
hydrosulfite [-sylfit] m. CHIM. Hydrosulphite.
hydrothérapie [-terapi] f. MÉD. Hydrotherapy, hydrotherapeutics, water cure.
hydrothérapique [-terapik] adj. Hydrotherapeutic; *établissement hydrothérapique*, hydropathic establishment.
hydrothermal, ale [-tɛrmal] adj. Hydrothermal.
hydroxyde [-ksid] m. CHIM. Hydroxide.
hydroxyle [-ksil] m. CHIM. Hydroxyl.
hydrure [idry:r] m. CHIM. Hydride.
hyène [jɛn] f. ZOOL. Hyena.
hygiène [iʒjɛn] f. Hygiene, sanitation (propreté); hygienics (science); *mauvaise hygiène alimentaire*, malnutrition.
hygiénique [iʒjenik] adj. Hygienic. ‖ Sanitary (serviette); *papier hygiénique*, toilet paper.
hygiéniquement [-nikmɑ̃] adv. Hygienically.
hygiéniste [-nist] m. Hygienist, sanitarian.
hygrologie [igrɔlɔʒi] f. Hygrology.
hygromètre [-mɛtr] m. Hygrometer.
hygrométrie [-metri] f. Hygrometry.
hygrométrique [-metrik] adj. Hygrometric.
hygroscope [-skɔp] m. Hygroscope.
hygroscopique [-skɔpik] adj. Hygroscopic.
hymen [imɛn] m. Marriage. ‖ MÉD. Hymen.
hyménée [imɛne] m. Marriage. (V. MARIAGE.)
hyménoptère [imenɔptɛ:r] m. ZOOL. Hymenopter (pl. hymenoptera).
hymnaire [imnɛ:r] m. ECCLÉS. Hymnary, hymnbook.
hymne [imn] m. Anthem (national); hymn.
— f. ECCLÉS. Hymn.
hymnique [imnik] adj. Hymnic, hymnal.
hyoïde [iɔid] adj., m. MÉD. Hyoid.
hypallage [ipala:ʒ] m. GRAMM. Hypallage.
hyperacide [ipɛrasid] adj. CHIM. Hyperacid.
hyperbole [-bɔl] f. GRAMM. Hyperbole. ‖ MATH. Hyperbola.
hyperbolique [-bɔlik] adj. Hyperbolic.
hypercorrect, e [-kɔrɛkt] adj. GRAMM. Hypercorrect.
hyperémotivité [-emɔtivite] f. Hyperemotionality.
hyperesthésie [-ɛstezi] f. MÉD. Hyperaesthesia.

hyperglycémie [-glisemi] f. MÉD. Hyperglycaemia.
hypermarché [-marʃe] m. Hypermarket.
hypermétrope [-metrop] adj. MÉD. Hypermetropic.
— s. MÉD. Hypermetrope, long- (ou) far-sighted.
hypermétropie [-metrɔpi] f. MÉD. Hypermetropia.
hypernerveux, euse [-nɛrvø, ø:z] adj. Over-excitable.
— s. Over-excitable person.
hypersensibilité [-sɑ̃sibilite] f. Hypersensitiveness, hypersensitivity.
hypersensible [-sɑ̃sibl] adj. Hypersensitive.
hypersonique [-sɔnik] adj. AVIAT. Hypersonic.
hypertendu, ue [-tɑ̃dy] adj., m. MÉD. Hypertensive.
hypertension [-tɑ̃sjɔ̃] f. MÉD. Hypertension, high blood-pressure.
hyperthermie [-tɛrmi] f. MÉD. Hyperthermia.
hypertrophie [-trɔfi] f. MÉD. Hypertrophy.
hypertrophier [-trɔfje] v. tr. (1). MÉD. To hypertrophy.
hypertrophique [-trɔfik] adj. MÉD. Hypertrophic.
hypnogène [ipnɔgɛn] adj. MÉD. Hypnogenetic.
hypnologie [-lɔʒi] f. MÉD. Hypnology.
hypnose [ipnɔ:z] f. MÉD. Hypnosis; *hypnose provoquée*, induced hypnosis.
hypnotique [ipnɔtik] adj. Hypnotic.
hypnotiser [-tize] v. tr. (1). To hypnotize.
— v. pr. **S'hypnotiser**, FIG. To fasten (sur, onto), to be mesmerized (sur, by).
hypnotiseur [-tizœ:r] s. Hypnotizer, hypnotist.
hypnotisme [-tism] m. Hypnotism.
hypocondre [-kɔ̃:dr] m. MÉD. Hypochondrium.
hypocondriaque [-kɔ̃drijak] adj. Hypochondriac; splenetic. (V. BILIEUX.)
— s. Hypochondriac.
hypocondrie [-kɔ̃dri] f. MÉD. Hypocondria.
hypocrisie [-krizi] f. Hypocrisy. (V. FOURBERIE.)
hypocrite [-krit] adj. Hypocritical. (V. FOURBE, SOURNOIS.)
— s. Hypocrite. (V. TARTUFE.)
hypocritement [-kritmɑ̃] adv. Hypocritically.
hypocycloïde [-siklɔid] f. MATH. Hypocycloid.
hypodermique [-dɛrmik] adj. MÉD. Hypodermic.
hypogastre [-gastr] m. MÉD. Hypogastrium.
hypogastrique [-gastrik] adj. MÉD. Hypogastric.
hypogée [ipɔʒe] m. Hypogeum (pl. hypogea).
hypoglosse [ipɔglɔs] adj. MÉD. Hypoglossal.
hypoglycémie [-glisemi] f. MÉD. Hypoglycaemia.
hypophosphite [-fɔsfit] m. CHIM. Hypophosphite.
hypophyse [ipɔfiz] f. MÉD. Pituitary gland, hypophysis.
hypostase [ipɔsta:z] f. ECCLÉS. Hypostasis.
hyposulfite [ipɔsylfit] m. CHIM. Hyposulphite.
hypotension [-tɑ̃sjɔ̃] f. MÉD. Low blood-pressure.
hypoténuse [-teny:z] f. MATH. Hypotenuse.
hypothalamus [-talamys] m. MÉD. Hypothalamus.
hypothécable [ipɔtekabl] adj. JUR. Mortgageable.
hypothécaire [-tekɛ:r] adj. JUR. Hypothecary; *créance hypothécaire*, mortgage claim; *créancier, débiteur hypothécaire*, mortgagee, mortgager; *prêt hypothécaire*, mortgage loan.
hypothèque [-tɛk] f. JUR. Mortgage; *bureau des hypothèques*, mortgage registry; *grevé d'hypothèques*, mortgaged; *prendre, purger une hypothèque*, to raise, to pay off a mortgage.
hypothéquer [-teke] v. tr. (1). JUR. To hypothecate, to mortgage (un bien); to secure by mortgage (une créance).
hypothermie [-tɛrmi] f. MÉD. Hypothermia.
hypothèse [ipɔtɛ:z] f. Hypothesis (v. SUPPOSITION); *se livrer à des hypothèses*, to speculate; *en toute hypothèse*, in all eventualities.

hypothétique [-tetik] adj. Hypothetic.
hypothétiquement [-tetikmɑ̃] adv. Hypothetically.
hypothyroïdie [-tirɔidi] f. MÉD. Hypothyroidism.
hypsographie [ipsɔgrafi] f. Hypsography.

hypsométrie [-metri] f. Hypsometry.
hysope [izɔp] f. BOT. Hyssop.
hystérectomie [-tɔmi] f. MÉD. Hysterectomy.
hystérie [isteri] f. MÉD. Hysteria.
hystérique [-rik] adj. MÉD. Hysteric, hysterical.

I [i] m. I, i; *i grec*, y. ‖ FIG. *Mettre les points sur les i*, to speak plainly, not to mince one's words.
ïambe [iɑ̃:b] m. ARTS. Iambus, iamb (en vers anciens ou anglais); iambic (poème).
ïambique [iɑ̃bik] adj., m. ARTS. Iambic.
ibère [ibɛ:r] adj., s. GÉOGR. Iberian.
ibérique [iberik] adj. GÉOGR. Iberian.
ibidem [ibidɛm] adv. Ibidem, ibid., ib.
ibis [ibis] m. ZOOL. Ibis.
icarien, enne [ikarjɛ̃, ɛn] adj. GÉOGR. Icarian (mer). ‖ SPORTS. *Jeux icariens*, trapeze acrobatics.
iceberg [isbɛrg] m. Iceberg.
ichneumon [iknømɔ̃] m. ZOOL. Ichneumon.
ichtyol [iktjɔl] m. CHIM. Ichthyol.
ichtyologie [-lɔʒi] f. ZOOL. Ichthyology.
ichtyologique [-lɔʒik] adj. ZOOL. Ichthyological.
ichtyologiste [-lɔʒist] s. Ichthyologist.
ichtyosaure [iktjosɔ:r] m. ZOOL. Ichthyosaurus.
ici [isi] adv. Here (lieu); *hors d'ici!*, begone!, go away!; get out; clear off (ou) out (fam.); *il y a un mille d'ici à la ville*, the town's a mile from here; *je ne suis pas d'ici*, I'm a stranger here; *jusqu'ici*, up to here, as far as this; *près d'ici*, nearby, hereabouts; *venez ici*, come here. ‖ Now (temps); *d'ici là*, between now and then; *d'ici peu*, shortly, before long; *d'ici samedi*, before next Saturday; *jusqu'ici*, so far, up till now. ‖ RADIO. *Ici Londres*, London calling. ‖ **Ici-bas**, loc. Here below, on earth.
icône [iko:n] f. ECCLÉS. Icon, ikon, eikon.
iconoclasme [ikɔnɔklasm] m. Iconoclasm.
iconoclaste [ikɔnɔklast] adj. Iconoclastic.
— s. Iconoclast, image-breaker.
iconogène [-ʒɛn] m. Eikonogen.
iconographe [-graf] s. Iconographer.
iconographie [-grafi] f. Iconography.
iconographique [-grafik] adj. Iconographic, iconographical.
iconologie [-lɔʒi] f. Iconology.
iconoscope [-skɔp] m. View-finder (en photographie). ‖ RADIO. Iconoscope.
icosaèdre [ikɔzaɛ:dr] m. MATH. Icosahedron.
— adj. MATH. Icosahedral.
ictère [iktɛ:r] m. MÉD. Jaundice. (V. JAUNISSE.)
ictérique [ikterik] adj. MÉD. Icteric (maladie); jaundiced (personne).
— s. MÉD. Sufferer from jaundice.
ictus [ikty:s] m. MÉD. Stroke, fit, ictus.
idéal, ale [ideal] (pl. **idéals, idéaux**) adj. Ideal.
— m. Ideal.
idéalement [-lmɑ̃] adv. Ideally.
idéalisation [-lizasjɔ̃] f. Idealization.
idéaliser [-lize] v. tr. (1). To idealize.
idéalisme [-lism] m. Idealism.

idéaliste [-list] adj. Idealistic.
— s. Idealist.
idée [ide] f. Idea, notion; *avoir soudain l'idée de*, to hit upon the idea of; *idée du beau*, idea of beauty; *idée fixe*, obsession, idée fixe; *idée lumineuse*, brainwave; *idées noires*, the blues; *je n'ai pas la moindre idée*, I haven't the slightest idea; I haven't the foggiest (fam.); *quelle idée!*, what an idea!, the very idea! ‖ Fancy; *ce ne sont que des idées*, that's just idle fancy; *se faire des idées*, to imagine things. ‖ Mind (esprit); *cela m'est sorti de l'idée*, it's gone clean out of my mind; *cela ne m'est pas venu à l'idée*, the thought never crossed my mind; *en idée*, in the mind's eye; *il me vient à l'idée que*, it occurs to me that. ‖ Opinion, view; *à son idée*, as one thinks fit, according to one's lights; *changer d'idée*, to change one's mind, to alter one's opinion; *dans cet ordre d'idées*, on this connection. ‖ FAM. Very little, touch, suspicion. (V. BRIN, SOUPÇON.) ‖ **Idée-force**, f. Key idea, keystone.
idem [idɛm] adv. Idem, id.; ditto, do.
identifiable [idɑ̃tifjabl] adj. Identifiable.
identification [idɑ̃tifikasjɔ̃] f. Identification. ‖ AVIAT. *Feu d'identification*, identification light.
identifier [-fje] v. tr. (1). To identify, to consider to be identical (deux genres). ‖ To identify, to establish the identity of (qqch.).
— v. pr. **S'identifier**, to identify oneself (*à, avec*, with).
identique [idɑ̃tik] adj. Identical (*à*, with); the same (*à*, as). [V. SEMBLABLE.]
identiquement [-mɑ̃] adv. Identically.
identité [idɑ̃tite] f. Identity; sameness. ‖ MILIT. *Plaque d'identité*, identity disc. ‖ JUR. *Carte d'identité*, identity card; *pièces d'identité*, identification papers. ‖ MATH. Identity.
idéogramme [ideogram] m. Ideogram, ideograph.
idéographie [-grafi] f. Ideography.
idéographique [-grafik] adj. Ideographic, ideographical.
idéologie [-lɔʒi] f. PHILOS. Ideology. ‖ FIG. Speculation, abstract theorizing.
idéologique [-lɔʒik] adj. Ideologic, ideological.
idéologue [-lɔg] m. PHILOS. Ideologist. ‖ FIG. Visionary, theorist.
ides [id] f. pl. Ides.
idiolecte [idjɔlɛkt] m. GRAMM. Idiolect.
idiomatique [idjɔmatik] adj. Idiomatic.
idiome [idjo:m] m. Idiom. (V. LANGAGE.)
idiosyncrasie [-sɛ̃krazi] f. MÉD. Idiosyncrasy.
idiot, ote [idjo, ɔt] adj. Idiotic, absurd (v. STUPIDE); *c'est idiot!*, it's crazy! what nonsense! ‖ MÉD. Idiot, imbecile.
— s. Idiot, ass, fool, loon. ‖ MÉD. Idiot, imbecile.
idiotement [idjɔtmɑ̃] adv. Idiotically, foolishly, stupidly.

idiotie [idjɔsi] f. Idiocy, crass stupidity. ‖ Stupid action, piece of nonsense. ‖ MÉD. Idiocy, imbecility.

idiotisme [idjɔtism] m. GRAMM. Idiom, idiomatic expression; *idiotisme écossais,* scotticism.

idoine [idwan] adj. Adequate (approprié). ‖ Fit, able (capable). ‖ Competent, suitable (qualifié).

idolâtre [idolɑ:tr] adj. Idolatrous (culte, personne). ‖ Inordinately fond (*de,* of) [qqch., qqn]. — s. Idolater (f. idolatress).

idolâtrer [-lɑtre] v. intr. (1). To worship idols, to practise idolatry.
— v. tr. To idolize, to worship, to be inordinately fond of (qqch., qqn). [V. ADORER.]

idolâtrie [-lɑtri] f. Idolatry.

idole [idɔl] f. Idol, image; *culte des idoles,* idol worship. ‖ FIG. Idol.

idylle [idil] f. ARTS. Idyll. ‖ FIG. Idyll, romance.

idyllique [-lik] adj. ARTS. Idyllic.

idylliste [-list] m. ARTS. Idyllist.

if [if] m. BOT. Yew, yew-tree. ‖ ECCLÉS. Triangular stand (pour cierges). ‖ TECHN. Rack (pour bouteilles).

igloo [iglu] m. Igloo.

igname [iɲam] f. BOT. Yam.

ignare [iɲa:r] adj. Ignorant, uneducated.
— s. Ignoramus.

igné, ée [iɲe] adj. Igneous.

ignifugation [ignifygasjɔ̃] f. Fireproofing.

ignifuge [-fy:ʒ] adv. Fireproof, non-inflammable.
— m. Fireproofing material.

ignifuger [-fyʒe] v. tr. (7). To fireproof.

ignition [-sjɔ̃] f. Ignition (état).

ignoble [iɲɔbl] adj. Ignoble, disgraceful, unspeakable (action); ignoble, base, vile (personne).

ignoblement [-bləmɑ̃] adv. Ignobly, unspeakably, basely.

ignominie [iɲɔmini] f. Ignominy, disgrace.

ignominieusement [-njøzmɑ̃] adv. Ignominiously.

ignominieux, euse [-njø, ø:z] adj. Ignominious, disgraceful.

ignorance [iɲɔrɑ̃:s] f. Ignorance; *dans l'ignorance,* in ignorance; *par ignorance,* out of ignorance.

ignorant, ante [-rɑ̃, ɑ̃:t] adj. Ignorant, uneducated. (V. IGNARE.) ‖ Ignorant (*de,* of); uninformed (*de,* about); unacquainted (*de,* with).
— s. Ignoramus.

ignoré, ée [-re] adj. Unknown.

ignorer [-re] v. tr. (1). To be ignorant (ou) unaware of (qqch.); to know nothing of (ou) about (qqch.); not to know (qqch.); *ne pas ignorer,* to be fully aware of (qqch.). ‖ To ignore, to snub (qqn); *ignorer complètement,* to be totally oblivious of.

iguane [igwan] m. ZOOL. Iguana.

il [il] (pl. **ils**) pron. pers. sujet, m. It (chose); she (navire); he (personne). ‖ Pl. They.
— pron. impers. It; *il est 3 heures,* it is three o'clock. ‖ There; *il était une fois,* once upon a time there was (ou) were; *il y a,* there is, there are.

île [i:l] f. Island, isle.

iléon [ileɔ̃] m. MÉD. Ileum.

îlet [ilɛ] m., **îlette** [ilɛt] f. Islet, small island.

ilex [ilɛks] m. BOT. Ilex.

Iliade [iljad] f. ARTS. Iliad.

iliaque [iljak] adj. MÉD. Iliac.

ilien, enne [iljɛ̃, ɛn] s. Islander, native of the Breton islands.

illégal, ale [illegal] adj. JUR. Illegal, unlawful.

illégalement [-lmɑ̃] adv. JUR. Illegally, unlawfully.

illégalité [-lite] f. JUR. Illegality; illegal (ou) unlawful act.

illégitime [illeʒitim] adj. JUR. Unlawful (action);

illegitimate; natural (enfant). ‖ FIG. Unwarranted (prétention).

illégitimement [-timmɑ̃] adv. JUR. Illegitimately.

illégitimité [-timite] f. JUR. Illegitimacy.

illettré, ée [illɛtre] adj. Uneducated; illiterate.
— s. Illiterate (ou) uneducated person.

illicite [illisit] adj. JUR. Illicit.

illicitement [-mɑ̃] adv. JUR. Illicitly.

illico [iliko] adv. FAM. At once, straight away.

illimitable [illimitabl] adj. Illimitable.

illimité, ée [-te] adj. Unlimited, boundless, unbounded.

illisibilité [illisibilite] f. Illegibility.

illisible [-zibl] adj. Illegible (écriture) [v. INDÉCHIFFRABLE]; unreadable (livre).

illisiblement [-zibləmɑ̃] adv. Illegibly.

illogique [illoʒik] adj. Illogical, irrational.

illogiquement [-ʒikmɑ̃] adv. Illogically.

illogisme [-ʒism] m. Illogicality, illogicalness. ‖ Piece of illogicality, non sequitur, inconsistency.

illuminable [illyminabl] adj. Illuminable.

illuminant, ante [-nɑ̃, ɑ̃:t] adj. Illuminant.

illuminateur, trice [-natœ:r, tris] s. Illuminator.

illumination [-nasjɔ̃] f. Illumination; *illumination par projecteurs,* floodlighting. ‖ FIG. Enlightenment, inspiration, inner light.

illuminé, ée [-ne] adj. Illuminated. ‖ ECCLÉS. Visionary.
— s. ECCLÉS. Visionary. ‖ Pl. Illuminati.

illuminer [-ne] v. tr. (1). To illuminate, to light up (v. ÉCLAIRER); *illuminer par projecteurs,* to floodlight. ‖ FIG. To enlighten, to illumine (qqn); to light up, to brighten (le visage).
— v. intr. To illuminate, to light up.
— v. pr. S'illuminer, to light up (visage).

illusion [illyzjɔ̃] f. Illusion (de la vue). ‖ Delusion; *chérir une illusion,* to cherish a delusion; *faire illusion à,* to deceive; *se faire illusion,* to deceive oneself, to labour under a delusion.

illusionner [-zjone] v. tr. (1). To delude, to deceive.
— v. pr. S'illusionner, to deceive (ou) delude oneself.

illusionnisme [-zjonism] m. Illusion.

illusionniste [-zjonist] m. Illusionist, conjurer.

illusoire [-zwa:r] adj. Illusory, illusive, deceptive.

illusoirement [-zwarmɑ̃] adv. Illusorily, illusively.

illustrateur, trice [illystratœ:r, tris] s. ARTS. Illustrator.

illustration [-sjɔ̃] f. Illustriousness; making illustrious. ‖ Illustrious person; celebrity. ‖ ARTS. Illustration, picture.

illustre [illystr] adj. Illustrious, famous, well-known.

illustré, ée [-tre] adj. ARTS. Illustrated.
— m. Illustrated (ou) picture paper.

illustrer v. tr. (1). To make illustrious (ou) famous. ‖ ARTS. To illustrate; to do the pictures for (un livre); to elucidate, to explain (un texte).
— v. pr. S'illustrer, to become famous; to find fame.

illustrissime [-trisim] adj. Most illustrious.

I.L.M. [iɛlɛm] m. Abrév. de *Immeuble à loyer moyen,* block of council flats.

îlot [ilo] m. Islet, small island. (V. ÎLE.) ‖ Block (de maisons). ‖ MILIT. *Chef d'îlot,* air-raid warden. ‖ AUTOM. Island.

ilote [ilɔt] m. Helot.

ilotier [-tje] m. Policeman whose beat covers a certain block.

ilotisme [-tism] m. Helotism, helotry.

image [ima:ʒ] f. Image, picture (représentation); *livre d'images,* picture-book; *sage comme une image,* as good as gold. ‖ Image, likeness (ressemblance). ‖ Image, mental picture (impression); *tournure qui fait image,* picturesque way of putting it. ‖ RADIO. Picture. ‖ PHYS., ECCLÉS. Image.

imagé, ée [imaʒe] adj. Vivid, picturesque.
imager v. tr. (7). To make vivid (ou) picturesque ; to colour (son style).
imagerie [-ʒri] f. Coloured print ; coloured print trade.
imagier [-ʒje] s. Designer of coloured prints. ‖ † Painter ; sculptor.
imaginable [imaʒinabl] adj. Imaginable, thinkable, conceivable.
imaginaire [-nɛ:r] adj. Imaginary, fictitious, fancied, make-believe. ‖ MÉD. *Malade imaginaire,* hypochondriac ; *maladie imaginaire,* imagined (ou) imaginary illness. ‖ MATH. Imaginary.
imaginatif, ive [-natif, i:v] adj. Imaginative.
imagination [-nasjɔ̃] f. Imagination (faculté). ‖ FIG. Fancy, invention ; *c'est pure imagination,* it's idle fancy ; *événement qui dépasse l'imagination,* undreamt-of happening.
imaginer [-ne] v. tr. (1). To imagine, to fancy, to picture, to conceive ; *le plus beau climat qu'on puisse imaginer,* the finest climate imaginable. ‖ To contrive (un dispositif) ; to devise, to invent, to think out (une méthode, un plan).
— v. pr. **S'imaginer,** to be imagined. ‖ To imagine, to think, to suppose, to fancy (v. SE FIGURER) ; *n'allez pas vous imaginer que,* don't run away with the idea that ; *ne vous imaginez pas être parfait,* don't think you are perfect.
iman [imɑ̃] m. ECCLÉS. Iman, imaum.
imbattable [ɛ̃batabl] adj. Unbeatable, invincible.
imbattu, ue [-ty] adj. Unbeaten.
imbécile [ɛ̃besil] adj. Imbecile, half-witted, idiotic.
— s. Imbecile, idiot, half-wit (v. SOT) ; *faire l'imbécile,* to play the fool, to act the goat ; *le premier imbécile venu,* any fool.
imbécilement [-lmɑ̃] adv. FAM. Stupidly, foolishly.
imbécillité [-lite] f. Imbecility, stupidness (état). ‖ Foolish act (action) ; *dire des imbécillités,* to talk nonsense ; to talk through one's hat (fam.).
imberbe [ɛ̃bɛrb] adj. Beardless, smooth-faced. (V. GLABRE.) ‖ FIG. Callow, raw.
imbiber [ɛ̃bibe] v. tr. (1). To soak, to make wet, to saturate, to steep (qqch.). ‖ To soak, to drench, to permeate (liquide).
— v. pr. **S'imbiber,** to absorb, to become saturated (de, with). ‖ To be absorbed, to sink in (liquide).
imbrication [ɛ̃brikasjɔ̃] f. Imbrication.
imbriqué, ée [-ke] adv. Overlapping, imbricated.
imbriquer [-ke] v. tr. (1). To overlap (des tuiles).
imbrisable [ɛ̃brizabl] adj. Unbreakable.
imbroglio [ɛ̃brɔljoˈm. Imbroglio.
imbrûlable [ɛ̃brylabl] adj. Fireproof.
imbrûlé, ée [ɛ̃bryle] adj. Unburnt.
imbu, ue [ɛ̃by] adj. Imbued (de, with) ; possessed (de, of) ; steeped (de, in).
imbuvable [ɛ̃byvabl] adj. Undrinkable. ‖ FAM. Insufferable (personne).
imitable [imitabl] adj. Imitable.
imitateur, trice [-tœ:r, tris] s. Imitator.
— adj. Imitative.
imitatif, ive [-tif, i:v] adj. Imitative.
imitation [-sjɔ̃] f. Imitation ; imitating, copying ; counterfeiting (de la monnaie) ; forging (d'une signature) ; *à l'imitation de,* in imitation of. ‖ Imitation, copy, forgery ; *bijoux imitation,* imitation jewellery. ‖ ECCLÉS. Imitation (de Jésus-Christ).
imiter [imite] v. tr. (1). To imitate, to copy, to model oneself on. (V. COPIER.) ‖ To mimic, to imitate, to take off. (V. SINGER.) ‖ To counterfeit (la monnaie) ; to forge (une signature). [V. CONTREFAIRE.]
immaculé, ée [immakyle] adj. Immaculate, stainless, spotless. ‖ ECCLÉS. Immaculate (Concep-

tion). ‖ FIG. Unsullied, spotless, unstained (caractère).
immanence [immanɑ̃:s] f. Immanence, immanency.
immanent, ente [-nɑ̃, ɑ̃:t] adj. Immanent.
immangeable [ɛ̃mɑ̃ʒabl] adj. Uneatable.
immanquable [ɛ̃mɑ̃kabl] adj. Impossible to miss (but). ‖ Inevitable, sure (événement).
immanquablement [-blɑ̃mɑ̃] adv. Inevitably, without fail, surely.
immatérialité [-lite] f. Immateriality.
immatériel, elle [immaterjɛl] adj. Immaterial.
immatériellement [-mɑ̃] adv. Immaterially.
immatriculation [immatrikylasjɔ̃] f. Registering, registration. ‖ MILIT. Enrolling, taking on the strength. ‖ AUTOM. *Numéro d'immatriculation,* registration number ; *plaque d'immatriculation,* numberplate, U. S. license plate.
immatriculer [-kyle] v. tr. (1). To register, to enter in (ou) on a register (qqch., qqn). ‖ MILIT. To enroll. ‖ AUTOM. To register.
immature [immaty:r] adj. Immature.
immaturité [-tyrite] f. Immaturity.
immédiat, ate [immedja, at] adj. Immediate, near (avenir) ; urgent (besoin) ; immediate (cause), close (contact) ; instant (soulagement) ; *à action immédiate,* quick-acting. ‖ CHIM. Proximate.
— m. *Dans l'immédiat,* for the moment (ou) present.
immédiatement [-tmɑ̃] adv. Immediately, at once, without delay.
immédiateté [-tate] f. Immediacy.
immédité, ée [immedite] adj. Unpremeditated.
immémorable [immemɔrabl] adj. Immemorable.
immémoré, ée [-re] adj. Unremembered.
immémorial, ale [-rjal] adj. Immemorial ; *de temps immémorial,* from (ou) since time immemorial, time out of mind.
immense [immɑ̃:s] adj. Immense, huge, vast, immeasurable.
immensément [-semɑ̃] adv. Immensely, hugely.
immensité [-site] f. Immensity, hugeness, vastness, boundlessness.
immensurable [-syrabl] adj. Immeasurable.
immerger [immɛrʒe] v. tr. (7). To immerse, to plunge, to sink, to dip. ‖ ASTRON. To immerge. ‖ TECHN. To lay under the sea (un câble).
immérité, ée [immerite] adj. Undeserved, unmerited.
immersion [immɛrsjɔ̃] f. Immersion, plunging, dipping (dans un liquide). ‖ NAUT. Submerging, submersion (d'un sous-marin). ‖ ASTRON. Immersion. ‖ TECHN. Laying under the sea (d'un câble).
immesurable [immɜzyrabl] adj. Immeasurable.
immettable [ɛ̃mɛtabl] adj. Unwearable.
immeuble [immœbl] adj. JUR. Real, unmovable, fixed (bien).
— m. ARCHIT. House, building. ‖ JUR. Real estate ; *immeuble par destination,* landlord's fixtures.
immigrant, ante [immigrɑ̃, ɑ̃:t], **immigré, ée** [gre] adj., s. Immigrant.
immigration [-grasjɔ̃] f. Immigration.
immigrer [-gre] v. intr. (1). To immigrate.
imminence [imminɑ̃:s] f. Imminence.
imminent, ente [-nɑ̃, ɑ̃:t] adj. Imminent, impending.
immiscer [immise] v. tr. (1). To mix, to involve (qqn) [dans, in].
— v. pr. **S'immiscer,** to interfere (dans, with) ; to involve oneself, to get involved (dans, in).
immiscible [immisibl] adj. Immiscible ; unmixable.
immixtion [immiksjɔ̃] f. JUR. Interference, meddling.
immobile [immɔbil] adj. Immobile, motionless, still. ‖ FIG. Firm, unshakable.

immobilier, ère [-lje, ɛr] adj. JUR. Real; *agence immobilière*, estate agency; U. S. real estate agency; *agent immobilier*, estate agent; U. S. real estate broker, realtor; *biens immobiliers*, real estate, immovables; *société immobilière*, building society; *vente immobilière*, house-sale, sale of property.
— m. Real estate, property.

immobilisation [-lizasjɔ̃] f. Immobilization, immobilizing. ‖ JUR. Conversion into real estate (de valeurs immobilières). ‖ FIN. Locking (ou) tying up (de capitaux); pl. Fixed assets (capitaux).

immobiliser [-lize] v. tr. (1). To immobilize; to bring to a stop (ou) standstill; to fix. ‖ MÉD. To immobilize (un membre). ‖ JUR. To convert into real estate (des valeurs). ‖ FIN. To lock (ou) tie up (des capitaux); *capital immobilisé*, fixed assets. ‖ COMM. To lock up (le stock).
— v. pr. S'**immobiliser,** to come to a stop (ou) standstill; to rest.

immobilisme [-lism] m. Systematic opposition to progress.

immobiliste [-list] s. Die-hard, U. S. standpatter (fam.).

immobilité [-lite] f. Immobility, motionlessness.

immodéré, ée [immɔdere] adj. Immoderate, inordinate, intemperate. (V. EXCESSIF.)

immodérément [-mɑ̃] adv. Immoderately.

immodeste [immɔdɛst] adj. Immodest, indecent, shameless. (V. IMPUDIQUE.)

immodestie [-ti] f. Immodesty, shamelessness (qualité). ‖ Immodest (ou) shameless act (action).

immolateur, trice [immɔlatœ:r, tris] m. Immolater, sacrificer.

immolation [-lasjɔ̃] f. Immolation.

immoler [-le] v. tr. (1). To immolate.

immonde [immɔ̃:d] adj. Filthy, unclean (animal). ‖ ECCLÉS. Unclean (esprit). ‖ FIG. Foul.

immondices [-dis] f. pl. Dirt, filth, refuse.

immoral, ale [immɔral] adj. Immoral.

immoralement [-lmɑ̃] adv. Immorally.

immoralisme [-lism] m. Immoralism.

immoraliste [-list] s. Immoralist.

immoralité [-lite] f. Immorality.

immortaliser [immɔrtalize] v. tr. (1). To immortalize, to make immortal.
— v. pr. S'**immortaliser,** to make oneself immortal; to win immortality.

immortalité [-talite] f. Immortality. ‖ PHILOS. Athanasy.

immortel, elle [-tɛl] adj. ECCLÉS. Immortal (âme). ‖ FIG. Everlasting, undying, imperishable (gloire).
— m. pl. Immortals; members of the French Academy.

immortelle [-tɛ:l] f. BOT. Immortelle, everlasting; straw flower.

immortellement [-tɛlmɑ̃] adv. Immortally.

immotivé, ée [immɔtive] adj. Unmotived, groundless.

immuabilité [immɥabilite] f. Immutability.

immuable [-abl] adj. Immutable, unalterable, fixed, immovable.

immuablement [-ablǝmɑ̃] adv. Immutably, unalterably, immovably.

immunisant, ante [immynizɑ̃, ɑ̃:t] adj. MÉD. Immunizing.

immunisation [-zasjɔ̃] f. MÉD. Immunization.

immuniser [-ze] v. tr. (1). MÉD. To immunize.

immunitaire [-tɛ:r] adj. MÉD. Immune.

immunité [-te] f. MÉD. Immunity. ‖ JUR. Privilege; *immunité diplomatique,* diplomatic immunity; *immunité parlementaire,* M.P.'s immunity from arrest. ‖ FIN. Exemption from taxation.

immunologie [immynɔlɔʒi] f. MÉD. Immunology.

immutabilité [immytabilite] f. Immutability.

impact [ɛ̃pakt] m. Impact. ‖ MILIT. *Point d'impact,* point of impact.

impair, aire [ɛ̃pɛ:r] adj. Odd, uneven; *jours impairs,* odd dates. ‖ CH. DE F. *Voie impaire* down line. ‖ MÉD. Unpaired (organe); single (os).
— m. FAM. Blunder (v. GAFFE); *commettre un impair,* to make a bloomer (ou) U. S. a boner.

impalpabilité [ɛ̃palpabilite] f. Impalpability.

impalpable [-pabl] adj. Impalpable.

imparable [ɛ̃parabl] adj. SPORTS. Unstoppable.

impardonnable [ɛ̃pardɔnabl] adj. Unpardonable, unforgivable.

imparfait, aite [ɛ̃parfɛ, ɛt] adj. Imperfect, defective, faulty (ouvrage); unfinished, uncompleted (tâche). ‖ GRAMM. Imperfect.
— m. GRAMM. Imperfect.

imparfaitement [-fɛtmɑ̃] adv. Imperfectly.

imparité [ɛ̃parite] f. Inequality, disparity; unevenness, oddness.

impartageable [ɛ̃partaʒabl] adj. Indivisible; unable to be shared.

impartial, ale [ɛ̃parsjal] adj. Impartial, equitable (jugement); even-handed (justice); candid (opinion); impartial, unbiassed, unprejudiced (personne).

impartialement [-lmɑ̃] adv. Impartially.

impartialité [-lite] f. Impartiality, fair-mindedness, disinterestedness.

impartir [ɛ̃parti:r] v. tr. (2). JUR. To grant, to allow; to bestow (une faveur); to invest (un pouvoir).

impassable [ɛ̃pɑsabl] adj. Impassable.

impasse [ɛ̃pɑ:s] f. Blind-alley, cul-de-sac, dead-end. ‖ *Faire une impasse,* to finesse (aux cartes). ‖ FIG. Impasse, deadlock; *dans une impasse,* in a quandary.

impassibilité [ɛ̃pasibilite] f. Impassibility, impassiveness.

impassible [-sibl] adj. Impassive; unmoved, unperturbed. ‖ Unimpressionable. (V. FLEGMATIQUE, IMPERTURBABLE.)

impassiblement [-siblǝmɑ̃] adv. Impassively.

impatiemment [ɛ̃pasjamɑ̃] adv. Impatiently.

impatience [-sjɑ̃:s] f. Impatience (irritation); *montrer de l'impatience contre,* to chafe under (ou) against. ‖ Impatience, lack of patience; *avec impatience,* impatiently. ‖ Eagerness, hastiness (vivacité). ‖ Pl. Fidgets.

impatient, ente [-sjɑ̃, ɑ̃:t] adj. Impatient, intolerant. ‖ Impatient, lacking in patience. ‖ Eager (pressé); *impatient de faire qqch.,* eager (ou) in a hurry (ou) anxious to do sth.

impatientant, ante [-sjɑ̃tɑ̃, ɑ̃:t] adj. Annoying, vexing, provoking, irritating.

impatiente [-sjɛ̃:t], **impatiens** [-sjɑ̃:s] f. BOT. Impatiens, balsam, busy Lizzie.

impatienter [-sjɑ̃te] v. tr. (1). To make impatient, to provoke, to irritate, to put out of patience; *vous m'impatientez,* I'm losing patience with you.
— v. pr. S'**impatienter,** to lose patience, to become impatient.

impatroniser [ɛ̃patrɔnize] v. tr. (1). To assert the authority of.
— v. pr. S'**impatroniser,** to assert one's authority, to set oneself up as master; to take charge.

impavide [ɛ̃pavid] adj. Impavid, fearless.

impayable [ɛ̃pɛjabl] adj. Invaluable, priceless, of inestimable value. ‖ FAM. Killing, screamingly funny. (V. CREVANT.)

impayé, ée [-je] adj. Unpaid, unsettled, outstanding (dette); dishonoured (facture, note).
— m. Unpaid debt; unpaid instalment.

impeccabilité [ɛ̃pɛkabilite] f. Impeccability, faultlessness.

impeccable [-kabl] adj. Impeccable; faultless. ‖ ECCLÉS. Impeccable, sinless, without sin.

impeccablement [-kabləmɑ̃] adv. Impeccably; faultlessly.
impécunieux, euse [ɛ̃pekynjø. ø:z] adj. Impecunious.
impécuniosité [-njozite] f. Impecuniosity.
impédance [ɛ̃pedɑ̃:s] f. ELECTR. Impedance.
impedimenta [ɛ̃pedimɑ̃ta] m. pl. Impedimenta.
impénétrabilité [ɛ̃penetrabilite] f. Impenetrability, imperviousness. ‖ FIG. Inscrutability.
impénétrable [-trabl] adj. Impenetrable, impervious (à, to). ‖ FIG. Inscrutable (figure); unfathomable (mystère).
impénétrablement [-trabləmɑ̃] adv. Impenetrably, inscrutably.
impénitence [ɛ̃penitɑ̃:s] f. Impenitence, unrepentance. ‖ ECCLÉS. Impenitence. ‖ FAM. Obduracy.
impénitent, ente [-tɑ̃, ɑ̃:t] adj. Impenitent, unrepentant. ‖ FAM. Obdurate.
impensable [ɛ̃pɑ̃sabl] adj. FAM. Unthinkable.
imper [ɛ̃pɛr] m. FAM. Mac, U. S. slicker.
impératif, ive [ɛ̃peratif, i:v] adj. Imperious (air); imperative (ordre); peremptory (ton). ‖ GRAMM. Imperative.
— m. PHILOS., GRAMM. Imperative.
impérativement [-vmɑ̃] adv. Imperatively.
impératrice [ɛ̃peratris] f. Empress.
imperceptibilité [ɛ̃pɛrsɛptibilite] f. Imperceptibility.
imperceptible [-tibl] adj. Imperceptible.
imperceptiblement [-tibləmɑ̃] adv. Imperceptibly.
imperdable [ɛ̃pɛrdabl] adj. Unlosable.
imperfectible [ɛ̃pɛrfɛktibl] adj. Imperfectible.
imperfectif, ive [-tif, i:v] adj., m. GRAMM. Imperfective.
imperfection [-sjɔ̃] f. Imperfection, incompleteness, defectiveness, faultiness (état). ‖ Imperfection, fault, defect (défaut).
imperforé, ée [ɛ̃pɛrfore] adj. MÉD. Imperforate.
impérial, ale [ɛ̃perjal] adj. Imperial; *couronne impériale,* Crown Imperial.
— m. pl. MILIT. *Impériaux,* imperial troops.
impériale [-rja:l] f. Imperial (barbiche). ‖ AUTOM. Top-deck, outside (d'un autobus); *monter à l'impériale,* to go upstairs (ou) on top. ‖ SPORTS. Four cards of one suit (aux cartes).
impérialement [-jalmɑ̃] adv. Imperially.
impérialisme [-jalism] m. Imperialism.
impérialiste [-jalist] adj. Imperialist(ic).
— s. Imperialist.
impérieusement [ɛ̃perjøzmɑ̃] adv. Imperiously; imperatively.
impérieux, euse [-rjø, ø:z] adj. Imperious, haughty, commanding, overbearing (ton). ‖ FIG. Urgent, pressing, imperative (besoin, nécessité).
impérissable [ɛ̃perisabl] adj. Imperishable, undying, deathless; unperishing (souvenir); *caractère impérissable,* imperishableness.
impéritie [ɛ̃perisi] f. Incapacity, inefficiency.
imperméabilisation [ɛ̃pɛrmeabilizasjɔ̃] f. Waterproofing, proofing.
imperméabiliser [-ze] v. tr. (1). To waterproof, to proof.
imperméabilité [-te] f. Impermeability, imperviousness.
imperméable [ɛ̃pɛrmeabl] adj. Impermeable; impervious (à, to); waterproof (à l'eau). ‖ NAUT. Watertight (cloison). ‖ ARCHIT. Damp-proof (couche).
— m. Waterproof, mackintosh, raincoat. ‖ Raincape (cape transparente).
impersonnalité [ɛ̃pɛrsɔnalite] f. Impersonality.
impersonnel, elle [-nɛl] adj. Impersonal.
impersonnellement [-nɛlmɑ̃] adv. Impersonally.
impertinemment [ɛ̃pɛrtinamɑ̃] adv. Impertinently. ‖ JUR. Irrelevantly.

impertinence [-nɑ̃:s] f. Impertinence, rudeness (qualité). ‖ Impertinence, rude word (ou) deed (acte); *dire des impertinences,* to utter impertinences. ‖ JUR. Irrelevance.
impertinent, ente [-nɑ̃, ɑ̃:t] adj. Impertinent, rude. (V. INSOLENT.) ‖ JUR. Irrelevant.
imperturbabilité [ɛ̃pɛrtyrbabilite] f. Imperturbability, imperturbableness.
imperturbable [ɛ̃pɛrtyrbabl] adj. Imperturbable.
imperturbablement [-bləmɑ̃] adv. Imperturbably.
impétigo [ɛ̃petigo] MÉD. Impetigo.
impétrant, ante [ɛ̃petrɑ̃, ɑ̃:t] s. JUR. Grantee.
impétrer [-tre] v. tr. (5). To impetrate.
impétueusement [ɛ̃petɥøzmɑ̃] adv. Impetuously.
impétueux, euse [-tɥø, ø:z] adj. Headlong, rushing (torrent); violent (vent). ‖ FIG. Impetuous; hot-headed (exalté); impulsive (impulsif); passionate (passionné).
impétuosité [-tɥozite] f. Rush (d'un torrent); violence (du vent). ‖ FIG. Impetuosity, impulsiveness. (V. FOUGUE.)
impie [ɛ̃pi] adj. Blasphemous, profane (ouvráge, paroles); godless, irreligious, impious (personne).
impiété [ɛ̃pjete] f. Impious deed (action); impiety, ungodliness (qualité). ‖ Disrespect, undutifulness (d'un fils ingrat).
impitoyable [ɛ̃pitwajabl] adj. Pitiless, merciless, unmerciful, ruthless.
impitoyablement [-bləmɑ̃] adv. Pitilessly, mercilessly, unmercifully.
implacabilité [ɛ̃plakabilite] f. Implacability, ruthlessness.
implacable [-kabl] adj. Implacable, relentless, unrelenting, ruthless.
implacablement [-kabləmɑ̃] adv. Implacably, relentlessly, unrelentingly, ruthlessly.
implant [ɛ̃plɑ̃] m. MÉD. Implant.
implantation [-tasjɔ̃] f. AGRIC. Implantation, planting. ‖ MILIT. Introduction. ‖ MÉD. Implantation.
implanter [-te] v. tr. (1). AGRIC. To implant, to plant. ‖ MILIT. To introduce. ‖ MÉD., FIG. To implant.
— v. pr. **S'implanter.** AGRIC., FIG. To take root; *s'implanter chez,* to foist oneself on.
implication [ɛ̃plikasjɔ̃] f. PHILOS. Contradictory implication. ‖ JUR. Implication.
implicite [ɛ̃plisit] adj. Implicit, implied (condition): absolute (foi).
implicitement [-tmɑ̃] adv. Implicitly.
impliquer [ɛ̃plike] v. tr. (1). To implicate, to involve; to include; *impliqué dans une affaire,* mixed up in an affair; *impliquer dans une accusation,* to include in an accusation. ‖ PHILOS. To implicate, to imply; *impliquer contradiction,* to imply a contradiction.
implorable [ɛ̃plorabl] adj. Able to be entreated, open to entreaty.
implorant, ante [-rɑ̃, ɑ̃:t] adj. Imploring, entreating.
implorateur, trice [-ratœ:r, tris] s. Implorer.
imploration [-rasjɔ̃] f. Imploration, entreaty; imploring, beseeching.
implorer [-re] v. tr. (1). To beg for, to crave, to implore (une faveur); to implore, to beseech, to entreat (qqn).
imploser [ɛ̃ploze] v. intr. (1). TECHN. To implode.
implosion [-zjɔ̃] f. TECHN. Implosion.
impoli, ie [ɛ̃pɔli] adj. Impolite, rude.
impoliment [-mɑ̃] adj. Impolitely.
impolitesse [-tɛs] f. Discourteous (ou) rude act (action); impoliteness, discourtesy (qualité).
impolitique [ɛ̃pɔlitik] adj. Impolitic, ill-advised.
impolitiquement [-kmɑ̃] adv. Ill-advisedly.

impondérabilité [ɛ̃pɔ̃derabilite] f. Imponderability.

impondérable [-rabl] adj., m. Imponderable.

impopulaire [ɛ̃pɔpylɛ:r] adj. Unpopular.

impopularité [-larite] f. Unpopularity.

importable [ɛ̃pɔrtabl] adj. Comm. Importable.

importable adj. Unwearable (vêtement).

importance [ɛ̃pɔrtɑ̃:s] f. Importance, consequence, gravity (en général); extent (des dégâts); magnitude (d'un désastre); *avoir de l'importance*, to be important; *d'importance*, momentous (décision); *de la première importance*, of the first importance; *de peu d'importance*, of little importance, unimportant; *d'une certaine importance*, sizable (groupement); *sans importance*, of no importance, inconsequential. ‖ Importance, authority, social standing; *homme d'importance*, *sans importance*, man of consequence, of no account; *prendre de l'importance*, to come into prominence; *se donner de l'importance*, to put on a show of importance; to put on side (fam.).
— loc. adv. **D'importance**, thoroughly; *rosser qqn d'importance*, to give s.o. a good thrashing.

important, ante [-ɑ̃, ɑ̃:t] adj. Important, weighty, grave (affaire); material (changement); considerable (chiffre, somme); important, momentous, outstanding (événement); *peu important*, unimportant, immaterial, of little account. ‖ Important, consequential (personne); *personnage important*, important figure, V.I.P. (Very Important Person).
— m. Important thing, main (ou) essential point.
— s. Fam. *Faire l'important*, to give oneself airs, to put on side.

Importateur, trice [ɛ̃pɔrtatœ:r, tris] s. Comm. Importer.
— adj. Comm. Importing.

importation [-tasjɔ̃] f. Comm. Importing, importation (action); imports (marchandise).

importer [-te] v. tr. (1). Comm. To import (des denrées). ‖ Fig. To import, to introduce (une mode).

importer [-te] v. intr. (1). To import, to matter, to be of importance (ou) significance (ou) consequence; *il importe que*, it is important (ou) essential that; *n'importe*, it doesn't matter, no matter, never mind; *n'importe comment, où, quand, qui, quoi*, no matter how, where, when, who, what; *n'importe lequel*, no matter which (chose) [ou] any one (personne); *n'importe quel jour*, any day; *peu importe que*, no matter if; *peu m'importe*, it doesn't matter to me; *qu'importe?*, what does it matter?

import-export [ɛ̃pɔ:rɛkspɔ:r] m. Comm. Import-export business.

importun, une [ɛ̃pɔrtœ̃, yn] adj. Importunate, intrusive, obtrusive, tiresome (personne); inopportune, untimely (visite).
— s. Importunate (ou) tiresome person; pest, bore (fam.).

importunément [-tynemɑ̃] adv. Importunately.

importuner [-tyne] v. tr. (1). To bother, to pester (de, with); to importune (harceler). ‖ To inconvenience, to intrude upon (déranger); *je crains de vous importuner*, I don't want to bother you.

importunité [-tynite] f. Importunity; *assaillir qqn de ses importunités*, to badger s.o.

imposable [ɛ̃pozabl] adj. Fin. Ratable, assessable (propriété); taxable (revenu).

imposant, ante [-zɑ̃, ɑ̃:t] adj. Imposing, impressive, dignified (cérémonie); stately (édifice); commanding, noble (figure).

imposé, ée [-ze] adj. Comm. Fixed (prix). ‖ Fin. Taxed (revenu).
— s. Tax-payer.

imposer [-ze] v. tr. (1). Ecclés. To lay on (les mains). ‖ Comm. To fix (un prix). ‖ Fin. To tax

(un produit); to assess (une propriété). ‖ Techn. To impose (une feuille). ‖ Fig. To give, to assign, to attribute (en général); to impose (des conditions); to enforce (l'obéissance); to lay down (une règle); to compel (le respect); to enjoin (le silence); to prescribe, to set (une tâche).
— v. intr. To impress, to command respect; *en imposer à*, to impress, to make an impression on; *sa fermeté m'en (ou) m'impose*, I'm impressed by his firmness.
— v. pr. **S'imposer**, to assert oneself (personne); to gain credence (vérité). ‖ To be necessary (ou) indispensable (ou) essential (patience). ‖ *S'imposer à*, to intrude on; *s'imposer chez*, to thrust (ou) foist oneself on.

imposition [-zisjɔ̃] f. Ecclés. Laying on (des mains). ‖ Comm. Fixing (d'un prix). ‖ Fin. Imposition, buying (d'un impôt); assessment (d'une propriété). ‖ Techn. Imposition (en typogr.) ‖ Fig. Imposing (d'une condition); giving, assigning (d'un nom); laying down (d'une règle); prescribing, setting (d'une tâche).

impossibilité [ɛpɔsibilite] f. Impossibility (état); *être dans l'impossibilité de*, to find it impossible to, to be unable to. ‖ Impossible thing; impossibility (chose).

impossible [-sibl] adj. Impossible; *c'est impossible!* it's impossible!, it's out of the question!, it can't be done!; *impossible à réaliser*, unrealizable, unfeasible; *il m'est impossible de faire cela*, I can't do that, that's beyond me. ‖ Impossible, extravagant, absurd (idée).
— m. Impossibility; *faire l'impossible pour*, to do one's utmost to; *tenter l'impossible*, to attempt the impossible. ‖ Loc. *Par impossible*, against all possibility.

imposte [ɛ̃pɔst] f. Archit. Impost; fan-light; transom; transom-window.

imposteur [ɛ̃pɔstœ:r] m. Impostor; humbug; sham (fam.).

imposture [-ty:r] f. Imposture, imposition, deception.

impôt [ɛ̃po] m. Fin. Tax : *frapper d'un impôt*, to tax, to levy (ou) put (ou) lay a tax on; *impôt sur le revenu*, income tax.

impotence [ɛ̃pɔtɑ̃:s] f. Impotence, helplessness.

impotent, ente [-tɑ̃, ɑ̃:t] adj. Impotent, helpless, infirm; *rendu impotent*, disabled.
— s. Cripple, invalid.

impraticabilité [ɛ̃pratikabilite] f. Impracticability.

impraticable [-kabl] adj. Impracticable; unfeasible, unworkable (projet); impassable (route). ‖ Sports. Unplayable (court).

imprécation [ɛ̃prekasjɔ̃] f. Imprecation, curse.

imprécatoire [-twa:r] adj. Imprecatory.

imprécis, ise [ɛ̃presi, iz] adj. Unprecise.

imprécision [-zjɔ̃] f. Vagueness, looseness (d'une expression); lack of precision, haziness (de la pensée); *rester volontairement dans l'imprécision*, to be deliberately vague.

imprégnation [ɛ̃preɲasjɔ̃] f. Impregnation.

imprégné, ée [-ɲe] adj. Impregnated; saturated; *imprégné de préjugés*, steeped in prejudice.

imprégner v. tr. (1). To impregnate (de, with). ‖ Fig. To imbue (de, with).
— v. pr. **S'imprégner**, to become saturated (de, with). ‖ Fig. To become imbued (de, with).

imprenable [ɛ̃prənabl] adj. Impregnable.

impréparation [ɛ̃preparasjɔ̃] f. Lack of preparation.

imprésario [ɛ̃prezarjo] m. Théâtr. Impresario.

imprescriptibilité [ɛ̃prɛskriptibilite] f. Jur. Imprescriptibility, indefeasibility.

imprescriptible [ɛ̃prɛskriptibl] adj. Jur. Imprescriptible, indefeasible.

impression [ɛ̃prɛsjɔ̃] f. Impression, impress, mark, imprint (marque). ‖ Printing, impression (d'un livre); stamping (de pièces); printing (d'un tissu); *à l'impression*, in the press; *envoyer à l'impression*, to send to press. ‖ FIG. Impression, sensation, feeling; *avoir l'impression que*, to have an idea that, to be under the impression that; *donner l'impression de*, to create an impression of; *faire impression*, to create an impression; *faire une impression sur*, to make an impression on (ou) upon; *faire une très grosse impression*, to cause a sensation (ou) a stir.

impressionnabilité [-sjɔnabilite] f. Impressionability.

impressionnable [-sjɔnabl] adj. Impressionable.

impressionnant, ante [-sjɔnɑ̃, ɑ̃:t] adj. Impressive; moving.

impressionner [-sjɔne] v. tr. (1). To act on, to affect. (V. ÉMOUVOIR.) ‖ FIG. To impress, to strike, to make an impression on; *se laisser impressionner*, to be overawed.
— v. pr. **S'impressionner**, to be impressed.

impressionnisme [-sjɔnism] m. ARTS. Impressionism.

impressionniste [-sjɔnist] adj. ARTS. Impressionistic.
— s. Impressionist.

imprévisibilité [ɛ̃previsibilite] f. Unpredictability.

imprévisible [-vizibl] adj. Unpredictable, unforeseeable.

imprévision [-vizjɔ̃] f. Lack of foresight.

imprévoyance [-vwajɑ̃:s] f. Lack of foresight, improvidence.

imprévoyant, ante [-vwajɑ̃, ɑ̃:t] adj. Improvident, unforeseeing.

imprévu, ue [-vy] adj. Unforeseen, unexpected.
— m. Unexpected (ou) unforeseen event; *à moins d'imprévu, sauf imprévu*, unless sth. unforeseen happens, barring accidents; *en cas d'imprévu*, in case of emergency.

imprimable [ɛ̃primabl] adj. Printable.

imprimante [-mɑ̃:t] f. INFORM. Printer.

imprimatur [-maty:r] m. Imprimatur.

imprimé, ée [-me] adj. Printed; *se voir imprimé*, to find oneself in print.
— m. Printed paper (ou) work. ‖ Printed form (formule). ‖ Pl. Printed matter. ‖ COMM. Print, cotton print, U. S. calico.

imprimer v. tr. (1). To mark, to impress, to print, to imprint, to stamp; *imprimer ses pas dans la neige*, to leave one's footprints in the snow. ‖ To print (une étoffe, un livre). ‖ FIG. To communicate (un mouvement).

imprimerie [-mri] f. Printing-house (maison); printing-plant, printing-press (presse).

imprimeur [-mœ:r] m. Printer, master-printer. ‖ Imprimeur-éditeur (ou) -libraire, m. Printer and publisher.
— adj. *Ouvrier imprimeur*, working printer.

improbabilité [ɛ̃prɔbabilite] f. Improbability, unlikelihood (qualité). ‖ Unlikely (ou) improbable event (fait).

improbable [-babl] adj. Improbable, unlikely.

improbablement [-bablǝmɑ̃] adv. Improbably.

improbant, ante [ɛ̃prɔbɑ̃, ɑ̃:t] adj. Unconvincing.

improbité [ɛ̃prɔbite] f. Dishonesty, improbity (défaut). ‖ Dishonest act (acte).

improductif, ive [ɛ̃prɔdyktif, i:v] adj. AGRIC. Unproductive (terre). ‖ FIN. Idle (argent).

improductivement [-tivmɑ̃] adv. Unproductively.

improductivité [-tivite] f. Unproductiveness.

impromptu [ɛ̃prɔ̃pty] adv. Impromptu, extempore; on the spur of the moment; *parler impromptu*, to speak off the cuff.
— adj. Impromptu, extempore. (V. IMPROVISÉ.)
— m. MUS. Impromptu.

imprononçable [ɛ̃prɔnɔ̃sabl] adj. Unpronounceable.

impropre [ɛ̃prɔpr] adj. Improper, inappropriate, misplaced (expression). ‖ Unsuitable, unfit (objet) [à, for].

improprement [-prǝmɑ̃] adj. Improperly, wrongly.

impropriété [-priete] f. Impropriety.

improuvable [ɛ̃pruvabl] adj. Unprovable.

improvisateur, trice [ɛ̃prɔvizatœ:r, tris] s. Improviser.

improvisation [-zasjɔ̃] f. Improvising, extemporaneous speaking (ou) playing (action); improvisation (résultat). ‖ MUS. Impromptu.

improvisé, ée [-vize] adj. Improvised, unprepared, impromptu, extemporized (discours); makeshift (moyen). ‖ SPORTS. Scratch (équipe).

improviser v. tr. (1). To improvise, to make up on the spur of the moment (un discours); to ad-lib (fam.). ‖ To arrange at short notice, to get up (un bal).
— v. intr. MUS. To improvise, to extemporize.

improviste (à l') [alɛ̃prɔvist] loc. adv. Unexpectedly; without warning, out of the blue (sans prévenir); by surprise, unawares (contre toute attente).

improvoqué, ée [ɛ̃prɔvɔke] adj. Unprovoked.

imprudemment [ɛ̃prydamɑ̃] adv. Imprudently.

imprudence [-dɑ̃:s] f. Imprudence, rashness, lack of caution. ‖ Imprudent, rash (ou) ill-advised act; *commettre des imprudences*, to take risks.

imprudent, ente [-dɑ̃, ɑ̃:t] adj. Imprudent, ill-advised (acte); imprudent, incautious, rash, foolhardy, venturesome (personne).

impubère [ɛ̃pybɛ:r] adj. JUR. Under the age of puberty.

impubliable [ɛ̃pybliabl] adj. Unpublishable.

impudemment [ɛ̃pydamɑ̃] adv. Impudently, shamelessly, brazenly.

impudence [-dɑ̃:s] f. Impudence, effrontery. ‖ Impudent (ou) impertinent act (ou) remark; piece of impudence.

impudent, ente [-dɑ̃, ɑ̃:t] adj. Impudent (personne); pert (visage).
— s. Impudent (ou) rude person.

impudeur [-dœ:r] f. Immodesty, shamelessness.

impudicité [-disite] f. Impudicity, lewdness. ‖ Lewd (ou) indecent act.

impudique [-dik] adj. Immodest, lewd.

impudiquement [-dikmɑ̃] adv. Immodestly, lewdly.

impuissance [ɛ̃pɥisɑ̃:s] f. Impotence, powerlessness, helplessness; *réduire à l'impuissance*, to overpower; to render powerless. ‖ MÉD. Impotence.

impuissant, ante [-sɑ̃, ɑ̃:t] adj. Unavailing, idle, futile (acte); impotent, powerless, helpless (personne); *impuissant à*, powerless to. ‖ MÉD. Impotent.
— m. MÉD. Impotent man.

impulsif, ive [ɛ̃pylsif, i:v] adj. Impulsive.

impulsion [-sjɔ̃] f. TECHN. Impulse; *d'impulsion*, impulsive (force). ‖ ELECTR. Impulse. ‖ RADIO. *A impulsion*, impact (transmetteur). ‖ FIG. Stimulus, impulsion; boost; shot in the arm (fam.) [élan]. ‖ FIG. Impulse, instigation, prompting; *sous l'impulsion du moment*, on the spur of the moment.

impulsivité [-sivite] f. Impulsiveness, rashness.

impunément [ɛ̃pynemɑ̃] adv. With impunity.

impuni, ie [-ni] adj. Unpunished.

impunité [-nite] f. Impunity.

impur, ure [ɛ̃py:r] adj. Impure, polluted, tainted (air, eau); adulterated (produit). ‖ ECCLÉS. Unclean. ‖ FIG. Impure, unchaste, lewd.

impureté [ɛ̃pyrte] f. Impurity, pollution, foulness. ‖ Pl. Impurities, foreign matter. ‖ ECCLÉS. Uncleanness. ‖ FIG. Impurity, unchastity.

imputabilité [ɛ̃pytabilite] f. Imputability.
imputable [-tabl] adj. Imputable, ascribable (à, to). ‖ FIN. Chargeable (frais). ‖ ECCLÉS. Imputable.
imputation [-tasjɔ̃] f. JUR. Imputation, accusation, charge. ‖ FIN. Charge, charging up. ‖ ECCLÉS. Imputation.
imputer [-te] v. tr. (1). To impute, to ascribe (v. ATTRIBUER); *imputer un crime à qqn,* to charge s.o. with a crime; *imputer la faute à qqn,* to lay the blame on s.o.'s shoulders; *imputer qqch. à l'ignorance,* to put sth. down to ignorance. ‖ FIN. To charge (une dépense); to assign, to appropriate (une somme). ‖ ECCLÉS. To impute.
imputrescibilité [ɛ̃pytrɛsibilite] f. Imputrescibility, rot-resisting properties.
imputrescible [ɛ̃pytrɛsibl] adj. Imputrescible; rot-proof.
in [in] adj. inv. FAM. In, trendy (à la mode).
inabordable [inabɔrdabl] adj. Inaccessible (lieu). ‖ FIN. Prohibitive (prix). ‖ FIG. Unapproachable (personne).
inabrité, ée [inabrite] adj. Unsheltered.
inabrogé, ée [inabrɔʒe] adj. JUR. Unabrogated.
inabrogeable [-ʒabl] adj. JUR. Unrepealable.
inaccentué, ée [inaksɑ̃tɥe] adj. GRAMM. Unstressed (syllabe); unaccented (voyelle).
inacceptable [inaksɛptabl] adj. Unacceptable.
inaccepté, ée [-te] adj. Unaccepted.
inaccessibilité [inaksɛsibilite] f. Inaccessibility.
inaccessible [-sibl] adj. Inaccessible; unreachable; un-get-at-able (fam.) [lieu]. ‖ FIG. Inaccessible, impervious (à, to); proof (à, against). ‖ FIG. Unapproachable (person).
inaccompli, ie [inakɔ̃pli] adj. Unaccomplished.
inaccomplissement [-smɑ̃] m. Non-accomplishment, non-fulfilment.
inaccordable [inakɔrdabl] adj. Ungrantable (faveur). ‖ Incompatible (caractères).
inaccostable [inakɔstabl] adj. Unapproachable.
inaccoutumé, ée [inakutyme] adj. Unaccustomed, unused (à, to).
inachevé, ée [inaʃve] adj. Unfinished.
inachèvement [-ʃɛvmɑ̃] m. Incompletion, incompleteness.
inacquitté, ée [inakite] adj. JUR. Undischarged (criminel). ‖ FIN. Undischarged (dette); unpaid (facture).
inactif, ive [inaktif, i:v] adj. Inactive, idle; indolent, sluggish. ‖ FIN. Idle, unproductive (capitaux). ‖ COMM. Dull (marché). ‖ CHIM. Inert (matière).
— s. Unproductive person.
inaction [-sjɔ̃] f. Inaction. ‖ Idleness (oisiveté).
inactivité [-tivite] f. Inactivity. ‖ Unemployment (d'un fonctionnaire). ‖ COMM. Dullness (d'un marché). ‖ CHIM. Inertness (d'une matière).
inactuel, elle [inaktɥɛl] adj. Out-of-date; out-of-season.
inadaptation [inadaptasjɔ̃] f. Maladjustment.
inadapté, ée [-te] s. Misfit; square peg (fam.).
— adj. Maladjusted (enfant).
inadéquat, ate [inadekwa, at] adj. Inadequate, unbalanced, discrepant.
inadéquation [-kwasjɔ̃] f. Imbalance, discrepancy, inadequacy.
inadmissibilité [inadmisibilite] f. Inadmissibility.
inadmissible [-sibl] adj. Inadmissible (prétention); *c'est inadmissible!,* it's out of the question!
inadmission [-sjɔ̃] f. Non-admittance.
inadvertance [inadvɛrtɑ̃:s] f. Inadvertence, inadvertency; *par inadvertance,* inadvertently, by an oversight.
inaliénabilité [inaljenabilite] f. JUR. Inalienability.
inaliénable [-nabl] adj. JUR. Inalienable.
inaliéné, ée [-ne] adj. JUR. Unalienated.
inalliable [inaljabl] adj. Non-alloyable (métal). ‖ FIG. Incompatible (idées).

inaltérabilité [inalterabilite] f. Inalterability, unchangeableness.
inaltérable [-rabl] adj. Not subject to deterioration (substance). ‖ MÉD. Sound (santé). ‖ FIG. Unfailing (bonne humeur).
inaltéré, ée [-re] adj. Unimpaired, unspoilt.
inamical, ale [inamikal] adj. Unfriendly, inimical.
inamovibilité [inamɔvibilite] f. JUR. Irremovability.
inamovible [-vibl] adj. JUR. Irremovable, permanent (fonctionnaire); permanent, held for life (poste); *agencements inamovibles,* fixtures, permanent fittings.
inanimé, ée [inanime] adj. Inanimate, lifeless (corps); dull, lifeless (regard); insensible, unconscious (personne). ‖ FIN. Dull (marché).
inanité [inanite] f. Inanity, futility, emptiness. ‖ Inane remark, inanity.
inanition [-sjɔ̃] f. Inanition, starvation; *mourir d'inanition,* to starve to death.
inapaisable [inapɛzabl] adj. Unable to be soothed (ou) assuaged (douleur); unappeasable (faim); unquenchable (soif).
inapaisé, ée [-ze] adj. Unassuaged (douleur); unappeased (faim); unquenched (soif).
inaperçu, ue [inapɛrsy] adj. Unperceived, unnoticed; *passer inaperçu,* to escape notice.
inapparent [inaparɑ̃] adj. Unapparent.
inappétence [inapetɑ̃:s] f. MÉD. Inappetence.
inapplicable [inaplikabl] adj. Inapplicable.
inapplication [-kasjɔ̃] f. Inapplication.
inappliqué, ée [-ke] adj. Lacking in application (écolier); unapplied (méthode). ‖ In abeyance (loi).
inappréciable [inapresjabl] adj. Inappreciable; imperceptible (quantité). ‖ FIG. Inestimable, invaluable (service).
inapprécié, ée [-sje] adj. Unappreciated.
inapprêté, ée [inaprɛte] adj. CULIN. Unprepared (aliment). ‖ FIG. Unrehearsed (discours); unstudied (style).
inappris, ise [inapri, i:z] adj. Unlearnt.
inapprivoisable [inaprivwazabl] adj. Untamable.
inapprivoisé, ée [-vwaze] adj. Untamed.
inapprochable [inaprɔʃabl] adj. Unapproachable.
inapte [inapt] adj. Inapt, unapt; unfit (à, for).
— m. pl. Unfit; throw-outs, washouts, duds (fam.).
inaptitude [-tityd] f. Inaptitude, inaptness, unfitness. (V. INCAPACITÉ.)
inarrangeable [inarɑ̃ʒabl] adj. Which cannot be settled (ou) arranged.
inarticulé, ée [inartikyle] adj. Inarticulate (cri). ‖ ZOOL. Inarticulate.
inasservi, ie [inasɛrvi] adj. Unenslaved.
inassimilable [inasimilabl] adj. Inassimilable.
inassouvi, ie [inasuvi] adj. Unappeased, unsatisfied (faim); unslaked, unquenched (soif). ‖ FIG. Unsatisfied, unsated, unquenched (désir).
inassouvissable [-sabl] adj. Insatiable, unappeasable.
inassouvissement [-smɑ̃] m. Insatiability.
inattaquable [inatakabl] adj. MILIT. Unassailable (position). ‖ CHIM. Inattaquable par les acides, acid-resisting. ‖ FIG. Unchallengeable, unquestionable (théorie).
inattendu, ée [inatɑ̃dy] adj. Unexpected, unforeseen. (V. IMPRÉVU.)
inattentif, ive [inatɑ̃tif, i:v] adj. Inattentive. ‖ Heedless, unmindful, careless (à, of).
inattention [-sjɔ̃] f. Inattention; absent-mindedness (distraction). ‖ Heedlessness, carelessness. (V. ÉTOURDERIE.)
inaudible [inodibl] adj. Inaudible.
inaugural, ale [inogyral] adj. Inaugural.
inaugurateur, trice [-ratœ:r, tris] s. Inaugurator.
inauguration [-rasjɔ̃] f. Inauguration (d'un monu-

ment) ; unveiling (d'une statue). ‖ Fig. Beginning, opening.
inaugurer [-re] v. tr. (1). To inaugurate (un monument) ; to open (un pont) ; to unveil (une statue). ‖ Fig. To open, to initiate ; to mark the beginning of.
inauthenticité [inotãtisite] f. Inauthenticity.
inauthentique [inotãtik] adj. Unauthentic.
inautorisé, ée [inotɔrize] adj. Unauthorized.
inaverti, ie [inavɛrti] adj. Unwarned.
inavouable [inavwabl] adj. Unavowable. ‖ Low, shameful, base (mœurs).
inavoué, ée [inavwe] adj. Unavowed, unacknowledged.
Inca [ɛ̃ka] m. Inca.
incalculable [ɛ̃kalkylabl] adj. Math. Incalculable, beyond calculation. ‖ Fig. Incalculable.
incalculablement [-bləmã] adv. Incalculably.
incalescence [ɛ̃kalɛssã:s] f. Incalescence.
incandescence [ɛ̃kãdɛssã:s] f. Incandescence, glow. ‖ Electr. A incandescence, glow (lampe).
incandescent, ente [ɛ̃kãdɛssã, ã:t] adj. Incandescent, glowing.
incantation [ɛ̃kãtasjɔ̃] f. Incantation.
incantatoire [ɛ̃kãtatwa:r] adj. Incantatory, spellbinding ; spell-like.
incapable [ɛ̃kapabl] adj. Incapable, unfit, incompetent, inefficient ; *incapable d'une telle action,* incapable of (ou) above such an action ; *incapable de faire,* incapable of doing, unable to do. ‖ Jur. Incapable, incompetent, disqualified.
— s. Incompetent (ou) incapable person.
incapacité [-site] f. Incapacity, inefficiency, incompetence, unfitness (v. inaptitude) ; *incapacité de faire,* inability to do, incapacity (ou) unfitness for doing. ‖ Jur. Incapacity, disability.
incarcération [ɛ̃karseɾasjɔ] f. Jur. Incarceration.
incarcérer [-re] v. tr. (5). Jur. To incarcerate ; *faire incarcérer,* to send to prison.
incarnat [ɛ̃karna] adj. invar. Flesh-coloured, rosy.
— m. Flesh-colour, rosiness ; bloom, carnation.
incarnation [ɛ̃karnasjɔ̃] f. Ecclés. Incarnation.
incarné, ée [-ne] adj. Incarnate. ‖ Méd. Ingrowing, U. S. ingrown (ongle).
incarner v. tr. (1). To incarnate, to embody. ‖ Théâtr. To play the part of.
— v. pr. **S'incarner.** Ecclés. To become incarnate. ‖ Méd. To grow in, to become ingrowing.
incartade [ɛ̃kartad] f. Insult, sudden outburst. (V. algarade.) ‖ Prank, indiscretion, folly (frasque). ‖ Swerve, shy (écart).
incassable [ɛ̃kɑsabl] adj. Unbreakable.
incendiaire [ɛ̃sãdjɛ:r] adj. Incendiary (bombe). ‖ Fig. Incendiary, inflammatory (discours).
— s. Incendiary. ‖ Fig. Fire-brand.
incendie [-di] m. Fire, conflagration (en général) ; burning (d'une ville) ; *incendie volontaire,* arson, fire-raising. ‖ Fig. Conflagration.
incendié, ée [-dje] adj. Burnt down (édifice).
— s. Person whose house has been burnt down.
incendier v. tr. (1). To set fire to, to set on fire, to burn down (un édifice).
incertain, aine [ɛ̃sɛrtɛ̃, ɛn] adj. Indistinct, blurred (contours) ; indistinct, fitful, vague (lumière) ; uncertain, dubious (personne) ; unreliable, doubtful, dubious (renseignement) ; doubtful (résultat) ; unsettled (temps) ; *incertain de,* uncertain of, dubious about.
incertitude [-tityd] f. Indecision (d'esprit) ; unreliability (d'un renseignement) ; dubiousness (d'un résultat) ; unsettled state (du temps) ; *dans l'incertitude,* in doubt, in a state of uncertainty.
incessamment [ɛ̃sɛsamã] adv. Incessantly, unceasingly, ceaselessly (sans cesse). ‖ At once, without delay, immediately (aussitôt).

incessant, ante [-sã, ã:t] adj. Incessant, ceaseless, unceasing (bruit) ; unremitting, uninterrupted (soins).
incessibilité [ɛ̃sɛsibilite] f. Jur. Inalienability.
incessible [-sibl] adj. Jur. Inalienable.
inceste [ɛ̃sɛst] m. Incest.
— s. Incestuous person.
incestueux, euse [ɛ̃sɛstɥø, ø:z] adj. Incestuous.
— s. Incestuous person.
inchangé, ée [ɛ̃ʃãʒe] adj. Unchanged, unaltered.
inchangeable [-ʒabl] adj. Unchangeable.
inchantable [ɛ̃ʃãtabl] adj. Unsingable.
inchauffable [ɛ̃ʃofabl] adj. Impossible to heat, unheatable.
inchavirable [ɛ̃ʃavirabl] adj. Naut. Uncapsizable.
inchoatif, ive [ɛ̃kɔatif, i:v] adj., m. Gramm. Inceptive, inchoative.
incidemment [ɛ̃sidamã] adv. Incidentally.
incidence [-dã:s] f. Phys. Incidence.
incident, ente [-dã, ã:t] adj. Incidental. ‖ Gramm. Relative, subordinate. ‖ Phys. Incident.
— m. Incident, occurrence, happening, event. ‖ Difficulty, hitch ; *faire naître des incidents,* to raise difficulties. ‖ Jur. Point of law. ‖ Radio. *Incident technique,* break in transmission, technical hitch.
incidente [-dã:t] f. Gramm. Subordinate (ou) relative clause.
incidentel, elle [-dɑ̃tɛl] adj. Incidental.
incinérateur [ɛ̃sineratœ:r] m. Incinerator.
incinération [-rasjɔ̃] f. Incineration ; cremation.
incinérer [-re] v. tr. (5). To incinerate ; to cremate.
incise [ɛ̃si:z] f. Gramm. Incidental clause.
inciser [ɛ̃size] v. tr. (1). To incise, to make an incision in. ‖ Méd. To lance (un abcès). ‖ Bot. To tap (un pin).
incisif, ive [-zif, i:v] adj. Méd. Incisive. ‖ Fig. Incisive (critique) ; cutting (paroles) ; trenchant (ton). [V. mordant.]
— f. Méd. Incisor.
incision [-zjɔ̃] f. Incision, cut. ‖ Méd. Lancing. ‖ Bot. Tapping.
incisivement [-zivmã] adv. Incisively.
incitateur, trice [ɛ̃sitatœ:r, tris] adj. Inciting.
incitation [-sjɔ̃] f. Incitement, inciting (à, to).
inciter [ɛ̃site] v. tr. (1). To incite (à, to) ; to instigate, to spur, to urge. (v. encourager.)
incivil, ile [ɛ̃sivil] adj. Uncivil, rude. (V. impoli.)
incivilité [-lite] f. Incivility, rudeness. (V. impolitesse.) ‖ Incivility ; impolite act (ou) remark.
incivisme [ɛ̃sivism] m. Incivism.
inclassable [ɛ̃klasabl] adj. Which cannot be classified (ou) categorized, unclassifiable.
inclémence [ɛ̃klemã:s] f. Inclemency.
inclément, ente [-mã, ã:t] adj. Inclement, severe (climat). ‖ Fig. Harsh, pitiless (personne).
inclinaison [ɛ̃klinɛzɔ̃] f. Incline, gradient, slope. ‖ Naut. Rake (d'un mât) ; list (d'un navire). ‖ Archit. Batter (d'un mur) ; pitch (d'un toit). ‖ Astron. Inclination. ‖ Electr. *Inclinaison magnétique,* magnetic dip. ‖ Fig. Inclination.
inclination [-nasjɔ̃] f. Bow, bowing (du corps) ; nod (de la tête). ‖ Fig. Inclination, propensity, bent, bias. (V. penchant.) ‖ Fig. Affection, liking ; *mariage d'inclination,* love-match.
incliné, ée [-ne] adj. Inclined, tilting, tilted ; *plan incliné,* inclined plane. ‖ Bent (corps) ; bowed (tête). ‖ Fig. Disposed, inclined (à, vers, to).
incliner v. tr. (1). To incline, to slope, to cant, to tilt (un objet). ‖ To bend (le corps) ; to bow, to nod (la tête) [v. pencher]. ‖ Fig. To incline, to dispose ; *incliner qqn à faire qqch.,* to influence s.o. in favour of doing sth.
— v. intr. To slope, to lean (mur). ‖ Naut. To list (navire). ‖ Fig. To incline, to be inclined (ou) disposed (à, to).

— v. pr. **S'incliner**, to slope, to lean, to slant. ‖ To bow, to bend (*sur*, over; *devant*, before). ‖ FIG. To give in; to yield (*devant*, to).

inclure [ɛ̃kly:r] v. tr. (4). To enclose, to include. ‖ JUR. To insert (une clause).

inclus, use [ɛ̃kly, y:z] adj. Included; *ci-inclus la copie de*, herewith copy of; *la lettre ci-incluse*, enclosed letter; *de lundi à vendredi inclus*, from Monday to Friday inclusive; *jusqu'à la page 20 incluse*, up to and including page 20.

inclusif, ive [-zif, i:v] adj. Inclusive.

inclusion [-zjɔ̃] f. Inclusion.

inclusivement [-zivmɑ̃] adv. Inclusively; *jusqu'à samedi inclusivement*, up to and including Saturday.

incoagulable [ɛ̃kɔagylabl] adj. Incoagulable.

incoercible [ɛ̃kɔɛrsibl] adj. Incoercible.

incognito [ɛ̃kɔɲito] adv. Incognito; incog (fam.). — m. Incognito; *garder l'incognito*, to preserve one's incognito, to keep one's identity secret.

incognoscible [ɛ̃kɔɲɔssibl] adj. Incognizable.

incohérence [ɛ̃kɔerɑ̃:s] f. PHYS., FIG. Incoherence.

incohérent, ente [-rɑ̃, ɑ̃:t] adj. PHYS. Incoherent. ‖ FIG. Incoherent, disjointed (idées).

incollable [ɛ̃kɔlabl] adj. Which does not stick. ‖ FAM. Who cannot be caught out.

incolore [ɛ̃kɔlɔ:r] adj. Colourless. ‖ FIG. Colourless, flat, insipid (style).

incomber [ɛ̃kɔ̃be] v. intr. (1). To be incumbent (*à*, on); to rest (*à*, with); to devolve (*à*, upon); to fall (*à*, on, to).

incombustibilité [ɛ̃kɔ̃bystibilite] f. Incombustibility.

incombustible [-tibl] adj. Incombustible; fireproof.

incommensurabilité [ɛ̃kɔmmɑ̃syrabilite] f. Incommensurability.

incommensurable [-rabl] MATH. Incommensurable. ‖ FAM. Immeasurable, outsize.

incommodant, ante [ɛ̃kɔmɔdɑ̃, ɑ̃:t] adj. Annoying, troublesome, offensive. ‖ Uncomfortable, stifling (chaleur).

incommode [ɛ̃kɔmɔd] adj. Incommodious, inconvenient (chambre); untimely, inconvenient (heure); unwieldy (objet); awkward, clumsy (outil).

incommodé, ée [-de] adj. MÉD. Not well, off colour. (V. INDISPOSÉ.) ‖ FIG. Upset, disturbed.

incommodément [-demɑ̃] adv. Inconveniently, uncomfortably.

incommoder [-de] v. tr. (1). To make unwell, to disagree with (indisposer). ‖ To bother (gêner). ‖ To disturb, to annoy, to inconvenience (déranger).

incommodité [-dite] f. Inconvenience, discomfort.

incommunicabilité [ɛ̃kɔmynikabilite] f. Incommunicability.

incommunicable [-kabl] adj. Incommunicable.

incommutabilité [ɛ̃kɔmytabilite] f. JUR. Incommutability.

incommutable [-tabl] adj. JUR. Absolute (propriétaire); incommutable (propriété, peine).

incomparable [ɛ̃kɔ̃parabl] adj. Incomparable, peerless, matchless; beyond compare; unrivalled.

incomparablement [-blamɑ̃] adv. Incomparably.

incompatibilité [ɛ̃kɔ̃patibilite] f. Incompatibility.

incompatible [-tibl] adj. Incompatible, inconsistent (*avec*, with); inappropriate (*avec*, to).

incompatiblement [-blamɑ̃] adv. Incompatibly.

incompétence [ɛ̃kɔ̃petɑ̃:s] f. Incompetence, inefficiency. ‖ JUR. Incompetence.

incompétent, ente [-tɑ̃, ɑ̃:t] adj. Incompetent, inefficient. ‖ JUR. Incompetent.

incomplet, ète [ɛ̃kɔ̃plɛ, ɛt] adj. Incomplete, unfinished (v. INACHEVÉ); defective.

incomplètement [-tmɑ̃] adv. Incompletely.

incomplétude [-tyd] f. Incompleteness (en logique). ‖ PSYCH. Deficiency, inadequacy.

incompréhensibilité [ɛ̃kɔ̃preɑ̃sibilite] f. Incomprehensibility.

incompréhensible [-sibl] adj. Incomprehensible.

incompréhensiblement [-siblamɑ̃] adv. Incomprehensibly.

incompréhensif, ive [-sif, i:v] adj. Uncomprehending.

incompréhension [-sjɔ̃] f. Incomprehension.

incompressibilité [ɛ̃kɔ̃prɛsibilite] f. Incompressibility.

incompressible [-sibl] adj. Incompressible.

incompris, ise [ɛ̃kɔ̃pri, iz] adj. Misunderstood. — s. Misunderstood person.

inconcevable [ɛ̃kɔ̃səvabl] adj. Inconceivable.

inconcevablement [-blamɑ̃] adv. Inconceivably.

inconciliabilité [ɛ̃kɔ̃siljabilite] f. Irreconcilability.

inconciliable [-ljabl] adj. Irreconcilable.

inconciliablement [-ljablamɑ̃] adv. Irreconcilably.

inconciliant, ante [-ljɑ̃, ɑ̃:t] adj. Unconciliatory.

inconditionné, ée [ɛ̃kɔ̃disjɔne] adj. Unconditioned.

inconditionnel, elle [-nɛl] adj. Unconditional. — s. Unconditional supporter (d'une politique); enthusiast devotee (d'une activité).

inconditionnellement [-nɛlmɑ̃] adv. Unconditionally, absolutely.

inconduite [ɛ̃kɔ̃dɥit] f. Loose living; immoral conduct. ‖ JUR. Misconduct.

inconfort [ɛ̃kɔ̃fɔ:r] m. Lack of comfort, discomfort.

inconfortable [-fɔrtabl] adj. Uncomfortable.

inconfortablement [-fɔrtablamɑ̃] adv. Uncomfortably.

incongelable [ɛ̃kɔ̃ʒəlabl] adj. Uncongealable.

incongru, ue [ɛ̃kɔ̃gry] adj. Incongruous, unbecoming, improper.

incongruité [-grɥite] f. Incongruity, incongruousness. ‖ Improper (ou) unbecoming act (ou) remark.

incongrûment [-grymɑ̃] adv. Incongruously.

inconnaissable [ɛ̃kɔnɛsabl] adj. Incognizable, unknowable.

inconnu, ue [ɛ̃kɔny] adj. Unknown (*à*, de, to) [artiste]; unexplored, unknown (pays). — s. Unknown person, stranger. — m. PHILOS. Unknown.

inconnue f. MATH. Unknown quantity.

inconquérable [ɛ̃kɔ̃kerabl] adj. Unconquerable.

inconquis, ise [-ki, iz] adj. Unconquered.

inconsciemment [ɛ̃kɔ̃sjamɑ̃] adv. Unconsciously.

inconscience [-sjɑ̃:s] f. Unconsciousness; ignorance (*de*, of); *inconscience de qqch.*, inability to realize sth.

inconscient, ente [-sjɑ̃, ɑ̃:t] adj. Unconscious (acte); unconscious, insensible, oblivious (personne). ‖ FIG. Unconscious of the nature of one's actions, unaware. — s. Unconscious (ou) insensible person. — m. PHILOS. Unconscious.

inconséquemment [ɛ̃kɔ̃sekamɑ̃] adv. Inconsequently, inconsistently.

inconséquence [-kɑ̃:s] f. Inconsequence; lack of consistence. ‖ Inconsistent act; non-sequitur remark; indiscretion.

inconséquent, ente [-kɑ̃, ɑ̃:t] adj. Inconsequent, irresponsible, thoughtless (conduite); rambling, disjointed (discours); unstable, inconsistent, harebrained (personne).

inconservable [ɛ̃kɔ̃sɛrvabl] adj. Unpreservable.

inconsidéré, ée [ɛ̃kɔ̃sidere] adj. Ill-considered, thoughtless (acte); inconsiderate, thoughtless, imprudent (personne).

inconsidérément [-mɑ̃] adv. Inconsiderately.

inconsistance [ɛ̃kɔ̃sistɑ̃:s] f. Lack of consistence (ou) consistency (d'une substance). ‖ FIG. Flabbiness (de caractère); inconsistency (d'une personne).

inconsistant, ante [-tɑ̃, ɑ̃:t] adj. Lacking in consistency (ou) firmness, yielding (substance). ‖ FIG. Flabby (caractère); inconsistent (personne).
inconsolable [ɛ̃kɔ̃sɔlabl] adj. Inconsolable; disconsolate.
inconsolablement [-bləmɑ̃] adv. Inconsolably, disconsolately.
inconsolé, ée [ɛ̃kɔ̃sɔle] adj. Grief-stricken, disconsolate.
inconsommable [ɛ̃kɔ̃sɔmabl] adj. JUR. Unable to be consummated (mariage). ‖ CULIN. Unconsumable (nourriture).
inconsommé, ée [-me] adj. JUR. Unconsummated (mariage). ‖ CULIN. Uneaten, unconsumed (nourriture). ‖ MILIT. Unexpended (vivres).
inconstance [ɛ̃kɔ̃stɑ̃:s] f. Inconstancy, fickleness (d'une personne); changeableness (du temps).
inconstant, ante [-stɑ̃, ɑ̃:t] adj. Inconstant, fickle (personne); changeable, variable (temps).
inconstatable [ɛ̃kɔ̃statabl] adj. Which cannot be checked (ou) proved, unverifiable.
inconstitutionnalité [ɛ̃kɔ̃stitysjɔnalite] f. Unconstitutionality.
inconstitutionnel, elle [ɛ̃kɔ̃stitysjɔnɛl] adj. Unconstitutional.
inconstitutionnellement [-nɛlmɑ̃] adv. Unconstitutionally.
incontestabilité [ɛ̃kɔ̃tɛstabilite] f. Incontestability.
incontestable [-tabl] adj. Incontestable, unquestionable, indisputable, incontrovertible; *c'est incontestable*, it's beyond all question.
incontestablement [-tabləmɑ̃] adv. Incontestably, indubitably, unquestionably.
incontesté, ée [-te] adj. Undisputed, unquestioned.
incontinence [ɛ̃kɔ̃tinɑ̃:s] f. Incontinence, lack of restraint; *incontinence de langage,* incontinence of speech. ‖ † Unchastity. ‖ MÉD. Incontinence; *incontinence d'urine,* bed-wetting.
incontinent, ente [-nɑ̃, ɑ̃:t] adj. Incontinent. ‖ Unchaste. ‖ MÉD. Bed-wetting.
incontinent [-nɑ̃] adv. Incontinently, forthwith, straightway, at once. (V. IMMÉDIATEMENT.)
incontrôlable [ɛ̃kɔ̃trolabl] adj. Unverifiable, uncheckable.
incontrôlé, ée [-le] adj. Uncontrolled, unrestrained (rire, tremblement); unruly (élément). ‖ Unchecked (rumeur).
inconvenance [ɛ̃kɔ̃vnɑ̃:s] f. Unseemliness, indecency, impropriety, indelicacy, indecorousness. ‖ Unseemly (ou) indecent (ou) improper act (ou) remark (V. INCORRECTION): *commettre une inconvenance,* to be guilty of a breach of good behaviour.
inconvenant, ante [-nɑ̃, ɑ̃:t] adj. Unseemly, indecent, improper, indelicate.
inconvénient [ɛ̃kɔ̃venjɑ̃] m. Disadvantage, inconvenience, drawback; *sans inconvénient,* without inconvenience, conveniently; *voir un inconvénient à,* to have an objection to.
inconvertible [-tibl] adj. Inconvertible.
incoordination [ɛ̃kɔɔrdinasjɔ̃] f. Lack of coordination.
incorporable [ɛ̃kɔrpɔrabl] adj. Which can be mixed, mixable (produit); incorporable. ‖ MILIT. Liable for military service.
incorporation [ɛ̃kɔrpɔrasjɔ̃] f. Incorporation. ‖ MILIT. Enrolment, embodiment.
incorporéité [-reite] f. Incorporeality, incorporeity.
incorporel, elle [-rɛl] adj. Incorporeal. ‖ JUR. *Biens incorporels,* intangible property.
incorporer [-re] v. tr. (1). To incorporate, to blend, to mix (à, with); to merge, to incorporate (*dans,* in). ‖ MILIT. To enrol, to embody (des conscrits). ‖ COMM. To incorporate (un agent).

— v. pr. **S'incorporer,** to incorporate, to blend.
incorrect, ecte [ɛ̃kɔrɛkt] adj. Incorrect, wrong, inaccurate (renseignement); improper, indecorous (tenue).
incorrectement [-təmɑ̃] adv. Incorrectly, inaccurately. ‖ GRAMM. Ungrammatically.
incorrection [-sjɔ̃] f. Incorrectness, inaccuracy (inexactitude). ‖ Incorrect (ou) improper act. (V. INCONVENANCE.) ‖ GRAMM. Faultiness, incorrectness. ‖ FIG. Incorrectness, impropriety, indecorousness (de la tenue).
incorrigible [ɛ̃kɔriʒibl] adj. Incorrigible (enfant); irremediable (erreur).
incorrigiblement [-bləmɑ̃] adv. Incorrigibly.
incorruptibilité [ɛ̃kɔryptibilite] f. Incorruptibility.
incorruptible [-tibl] adj. Proof against decay. ‖ FIG. Incorruptible (personne).
incrédibilité [ɛ̃kredibilite] f. Incredibility.
incrédule [-dyl] adj. Incredulous. ‖ ECCLÉS. Unbelieving.
— s. ECCLÉS. Unbeliever.
incrédulité [-dylite] f. Incredulity. ‖ ECCLÉS. Unbelief.
incréé, ée [ɛ̃kree] adj. Uncreated. ‖ ECCLÉS. Increate.
incrément [ɛ̃kremɑ̃] m. FIN. Increment.
increvable [ɛ̃krəvabl] adj. AUTOM. Unpuncturable, puncture proof. ‖ POP. Tireless (personne); which will never break down (ou) wear out (appareil).
incriminable [ɛ̃kriminabl] adj. JUR. Indictable (délit); chargeable (personne).
incrimination [-nasjɔ̃] f. JUR. Crimination, incriminating, arraignment. ‖ Indictment, charge.
incriminer [-ne] v. tr. (1). JUR. To incriminate, to charge, to impeach. ‖ FIG. To condemn, to reprove. ‖ FAM. To lay the blame on.
incrochetable [ɛ̃krɔʃtabl] adj. Burglar-proof (coffre-fort); unpickable (serrure).
incroyable [ɛ̃krwajabl] adj. Unbelievable, incredible.
incroyablement [-bləmɑ̃] adv. Unbelievably, incredibly.
incroyance [-jɑ̃:s] f. Unbelief.
incroyant, ante [-jɑ̃, ɑ̃:t] adj. Unbelieving.
— s. ECCLÉS. Unbeliever.
incrustation [ɛ̃krystasjɔ̃] f. Incrustation. ‖ TECHN. Fur, furring (d'une chaudière); inlay, inlaid work (en ébénisterie).
incruster [-te] v. tr. (1). To incrust. ‖ TECHN. To fur (une chaudière); to inlay (un meuble).
— v. pr. **S'incruster,** to become incrusted. ‖ TECHN. To fur up (chaudière). ‖ FIG. To become ingrained (préjugé). ‖ FAM. To dig oneself in, to take root, to outstay one's welcome (personne).
incubateur, trice [ɛ̃kybatœ:r, tris] adj. Incubating.
— m. Incubator. (V. COUVEUSE.)
incubation [-sjɔ̃] f. Incubating, incubation (des œufs). ‖ MÉD. Incubation (d'une maladie); *d'incubation,* incubation (période).
incube [ɛ̃kyb] m. Incubus.
incuber [-be] v. tr. (1). MÉD. To incubate.
inculcation [ɛ̃kylkasjɔ̃] f. Inculcation.
inculpable [ɛ̃kylpabl] adj. JUR. Chargeable, indictable, liable to prosecution.
inculpation [-pasjɔ̃] f. JUR. Inculpation, charge, indictment; *sur l'inculpation de,* on a charge of.
inculpé, ée [-pe] adj. JUR. Charged.
— s. Accused.
inculper [-pe] v. tr. (1). JUR. To inculpate, to charge, to indict. (V. ACCUSER.)
inculquer [ɛ̃kylke] v. tr. To inculcate.
inculte [ɛ̃kylt] adj. AGRIC. Uncultivated (jardin);

waste (terre). ‖ Fig. Straggly (barbe); unkempt (cheveux); rough, unpolished (nature, personne).

incultivable [-tivabl] adj. Agric. Unfit for cultivation.

incultivé, ée [ɛ̃kyltive] adj. Agric. Uncultivated, untilled. ‖ Fig. Uncultured (esprit, personne).

inculture [-ty:r] f. Ignorance, lack of education.

incunable [ɛ̃kynabl] adj. Incunabular.
— m. Incunabulum, incunable.

incurabilité [ɛ̃kyrabilite] f. Méd. Incurability.

incurable [-rabl] adj., s. Méd. Incurable.

incurablement [-bləmɑ̃] adv. Incurably.

incurie [ɛ̃kyri] f. Negligence, carelessness.

incursion [ɛ̃kyrsjɔ̃] f. Incursion, inroad. ‖ Milit. Raid, foray. ‖ Fig. Excursion (dans, into).

incurvation [ɛ̃kyrvasjɔ̃] f. Incurvation.

incurver [-ve] v. tr. (1). To incurve, to incurvate.
— v. pr. **S'incurver,** to curve, to bend.

indatable [ɛ̃databl] adj. Undatable.

Inde [ɛ̃:d] f. Géogr. India; *les Indes,* the Indies.

indébrouillable [ɛ̃debrujabl] adj. Unable to be disentangled, inextricable.

indécachetable [ɛ̃dekaʃtabl] adj. That cannot be opened (lettre).

indécemment [ɛ̃desamɑ̃] adv. Indecently.

indécence [-sɑ̃:s] f. Indecency, immodesty. ‖ Indecent (ou) immodest act.

indécent, ente [-sɑ̃, ɑ̃:t] adj. Indecent, immodest.

indéchiffrable [ɛ̃deʃifrabl] adj. Undecipherable, illegible. (V. illisible.) ‖ Fig. Incomprehensible.

indéchirable [ɛ̃deʃirabl] adj. Untearable, tear-proof.

indécis, ise [ɛ̃desi, iz] adj. Undefined, indistinct, blurred (forme); dim, uncertain (lumière); hesitant, irresolute, wavering, undecided (personne); unsettled, open (question); indecisive, drawn, doubtful (victoire).
— s. Waverer, undecided person; don't know.

indécision [-sizjɔ̃] f. Indecision, indecisiveness.

indéclinable [ɛ̃deklinabl] adj. Impossible to decline (invitation). ‖ Gramm. Indeclinable.

indécollable [ɛ̃dekɔlabl] adj. That cannot be unglued (ou) unstuck.

indécomposable [ɛ̃dekɔpozabl] adj. Indecomposable.

indécouvrable [ɛ̃dekuvrabl] adj. Undiscoverable.

indécrottable [ɛ̃dekrɔtabl] adj. Uncleanable (chaussures). ‖ Fam. Hopeless (cancre); loutish, boorish (lourdaud); incorrigible (paresseux).

indéfectibilité [ɛ̃defɛktibilite] f. Indefectibility.

indéfectible [-tibl] adj. Indefectible.

indéfendable [ɛ̃defɑ̃dabl] adj. Indefensible.

indéfini, ie [ɛ̃defini] adj. Indefinite, undetermined. ‖ Gramm. Indefinite.

indéfiniment [-mɑ̃] adv. Indefinitely.

indéfinissable [-sabl] adj. Indefinable, nondescript (couleur). ‖ Fig. Undefinable, difficult to describe (sentiment, trouble).

indéformable [ɛ̃defɔrmabl] adj. That keeps its shape.

indéfrichable [ɛ̃defriʃabl] adj. Agric. Unable to be cleared.

indéfrisable [ɛ̃defrizabl] adj. That cannot be uncurled (cheveux).
— f. Permanent wave.

indélébile [ɛ̃delebil] adj. Indelible (encre); kiss-proof (rouge à lèvres). [V. ineffaçable.] ‖ Fig. Undying, everlasting.

indélébilité [-bilite] f. Indelibility.

indélicat, ate [ɛ̃delika, at] adj. Indelicate, coarse, tactless (sans tact). ‖ Dishonest (employé); unscrupulous (procédé).

indélicatement [-tmɑ̃] adv. Indelicately. ‖ Dishonestly, unscrupulously.

indélicatesse [-tes] f. Indelicacy, lack of tact. ‖

Dishonesty, unscrupulousness (manque de scrupule). ‖ Indelicate (ou) unscrupulous act (action).

indémaillable [ɛ̃demɑjabl] adj. Ladder-proof, U. S. non-run, runproof.

indemne [ɛ̃dɛmn] adj. Unharmed, uninjured, unhurt (v. sauf); *sortir indemne,* to be unhurt, to get off scot-free, to come out unscathed (personne). ‖ Undamaged, intact (chose).

indemnisable [ɛ̃dɛmnizabl] adj. Jur. Entitled to indemnification (ou) compensation.

indemnisation [-zasjɔ̃] f. Jur. Indemnification, compensation.

indemniser [-ze] v. tr. (1). Jur. To indemnify, to compensate.

indemnité [-te] f. Fin. Indemnity, indemnification, compensation. ‖ Allowance, grant; *indemnité de chômage,* unemployment benefit; *indemnité de logement, de séjour,* living-out (ou) U. S. housing, subsistence allowance; *indemnité de vie chère,* cost-of-living bonus. ‖ Jur. *Indemnité parlementaire,* M.P.'s emoluments.

indémontable [ɛ̃demɔ̃tabl] adj. That cannot be taken to pieces (ou) dismantled (machine, meuble); not detachable (pièce).

indémontrable [ɛ̃demɔ̃trabl] adj. Undemonstrable.

indéniable [ɛ̃denjabl] adj. Undeniable.

indéniablement [-njabləmɑ̃] adv. Undeniably.

indénouable [ɛ̃denuabl] adj. That cannot be untied (ou) unravelled.

indentation [ɛ̃dɑ̃tasjɔ̃] f. Indentation.

indépassable [ɛ̃depasabl] adj. That cannot be exceeded (limite); who cannot be overtaken (coureur); unbreakable (record).

indépendamment [ɛ̃depɑ̃damɑ̃] adv. Independently (de, of).

indépendance [-dɑ̃:s] f. Independence. (V. liberté.) ‖ Independence (de l'Irlande); self-government (autonomie). ‖ Independence (d'esprit); self-reliance.

indépendant, ante [-dɑ̃, ɑ̃:t] adj. Independent, free, sovereign (pays). ‖ Independent (de, of); unconnected (de, with) [aspect, question]. ‖ Self-contained (appartement).

indépendantisme [-dɑ̃tism] m. Separatism (au Québec).

indéracinable [ɛ̃derasinabl] adj. Agric. Unable to be uprooted. ‖ Fig. Ineradicable.

indéréglable [ɛ̃dereglabl] adj. Fool-proof; that cannot get out of order; never-failing.

indescriptible [ɛ̃dɛskriptibl] adj. Indescribable.

indescriptiblement [-bləmɑ̃] adv. Indescribably.

indésirable [ɛ̃dezirabl] adj., s. Undesirable.

indestructibilité [ɛ̃dɛstryktibilite] f. Indestructibility.

indestructible [-tibl] adj. Indestructible.

indestructiblement [-tibləmɑ̃] adv. Indestructibly.

indéterminable [ɛ̃detɛrminabl] adj. Indeterminable.

indétermination [-nasjɔ̃] f. Indetermination, indefiniteness. ‖ Irresolution. (V. indécision.)

indéterminé, ée [-ne] adj. Undetermined, indeterminate. (V. indéfini.) ‖ Math. Indeterminate.

indétraquable [ɛ̃detrakabl] adj. Fool-proof.

index [ɛ̃deks] m. Forefinger, index-finger (doigt). ‖ Index (d'un livre). ‖ Techn. Hand, pointer (aiguille). ‖ Ecclés. Index; *mettre à l'Index,* to put on the Index. ‖ Fam. *A l'index,* tabooed, black-listed, banned.

indexation [-sasjɔ̃] f. Pegging (des prix) [sur, to].

indexer [ɛ̃dɛkse] v. tr. (1). To index (livre). ‖ Techn. To index. ‖ Fin. To peg (sur, to); *indexé,* index-linked.

indianiste [ɛ̃djanist] s. Indianist.

indic [ɛ̃dik] m. Fam. Nark, grass, stool-pigeon.

indicateur, trice [ε̃dikatœːr, tris] adj. Indicatory ; *plaque indicatrice,* street-sign ; *poteu indicateur,* finger-post, sign-post. ‖ Electr. Tell-tale.
— m. Techn. Indicator, pointer ; *indicateur de pression,* pressure-gauge. ‖ Ch. de F. Time-table.
‖ Autom. *Indicateur du niveau d'essence,* petrol-(ou) U. S. gasoline-gauge ; *indicateur de vitesse,* speedometer. ‖ Fam. Informer, police spy ; nark (fam.).
indicatif, ive [-tif, iːv] adj. Indicative (*de,* of).
‖ Gramm. Indicative (mode).
— m. Radio. Station-signal (du poste) ; signature-tune (musical). ‖ Gramm. Indicative. ‖ Aviat. Call-sign.
indication [-sjɔ̃] f. Indication, indicating, pointing out. ‖ Information, instruction ; *à titre d'indication,* for guidance ; *fausse indication,* wrong direction ; *sauf indication contraire,* unless otherwise stated ; *sur l'indication de,* at the suggestion of.
indice [ε̃dis] m. Indication sign, mark, clue. ‖ Math. Index. ‖ Chim. *Indice d'octane,* octane number. ‖ Phys. Index (de réfraction). ‖ Naut. Landmark. ‖ Comm. *Indice des prix de gros,* wholesale price index. ‖ Fin. *Indice du prix de la vie,* cost of living index, consumer's price index.
indicible [ε̃disibl] adj. Inexpressible.
indiciblement [-bləmɑ̃] adv. Unspeakably.
indiction [ε̃diksjɔ̃] f. Indiction. ‖ Ecclés. Convocation (d'un concile) ; proclamation (d'un jeûne).
indien [ε̃djε̃] adj., s. Géogr. Indian. (V. hindou.)
indienne [ε̃djεn] f. Comm. Chintz ; printed cotton.
indifféremment [ε̃diferamɑ̃] adv. Indifferently, without interest, coolly (froidement). ‖ Impartially, indiscriminately ; *manger de tout indifféremment,* to eat everything without discrimination ; *tourner indifféremment à droite ou à gauche,* to turn either way or left.
indifférence [-rɑ̃ːs] f. Indifference, coolness, unconcern. ‖ Phys., Chim. Inertness, indifference.
indifférenciation [-rɑ̃sjasjɔ̃] f. Uniformity. ‖ Méd., Bot. Absence of differenciation.
indifférencié, ée [-rɑ̃sje] adj. Uniform, unvaried. ‖ Méd., Bot. Undifferentiated.
indifférent, ente [-rɑ̃, ɑ̃ːt] adj. Indifferent, unconcerned ; *indifférent à son sort,* indifferent to one's fate. ‖ Indifferent, of no consequence, immaterial ; *cela m'est indifférent,* it doesn't matter to me, it makes no difference to me ; *parler de choses indifférentes,* to talk about trifling matters, to engage in small talk. ‖ Phys., Chim. Inert, indifferent (corps).
indifférentisme [-rɑ̃tism] m. indifferentism.
indifférer [-re] v. tr. (5). To be all the same to ; *cela m'indiffère,* I don't give a fig.
indigénat [ε̃diʒena] m. Indigenousness. ‖ Jur. Right of citizenship.
indigence [ε̃diʒɑ̃ːs] f. Indigence. (V. besoin, pauvreté.) ‖ Fig. Lack, want ; *indigence d'idées,* poverty (ou) dearth of ideas.
indigène [ε̃diʒεn] adj. Indigenous, native.
— s. Native. (V. autochtone, naturel.)
indigent, ente [ε̃diʒɑ̃, ɑ̃ːt] adj. Indigent, poor, poverty-stricken, destitute.
— s. Pauper ; *les indigents,* the poor.
indigeste [ε̃diʒεst] adj. Méd. Indigestible (aliment). ‖ Fig. Undigested, heavy, confused (livre).
indigestibilité [-tibilite] f. Méd. Indigestibility.
indigestion [-tjɔ̃] f. Méd. Indigestion. ‖ Fam. Surfeit ; *avoir une indigestion de,* to be fed up with.
indignation [ε̃diɲasjɔ̃] f. Indignation ; *avec indignation,* indignantly.
indigne [ε̃diɲ] adj. Unworthy, undeserving (*de,* of) ; *indigne d'un frère,* unbrotherly ; *indigne d'un Anglais,* un-English ; *indigne de vivre,* unfit to live. ‖ Unbecoming, unworthy, shameful (conduite) ; worthless, evil, odious (personne).

indigné, ée [-ɲe] adj. Indignant. (V. outré.)
indignement [-ɲmɑ̃] adv. Unworthily, shamefully.
indigner [-ɲe] v. tr. (1). To make indignant, to rouse to indignation (qqn).
— v. pr. **S'indigner,** to be indignant (*contre, de,* with, at).
indignité [-ɲite] f. Unworthiness, baseness, worthlessness (bassesse). ‖ Indignity, slight (affront).
indigo [ε̃digo] m. Indigo.
indigotier [-gɔtje] m. Bot. Indigo-plant. ‖ Techn. Manufacturer of indigo.
indiquer [ε̃dike] v. tr. (1). To point out, to show (v. montrer) ; *indiquer le chemin à qqn,* to tell (ou) show s.o. the way ; *indiquer du doigt,* to point out. ‖ To mark, to read, to show. (V. marquer.) ‖ To fix, to specify (v. fixer) ; *à l'heure indiquée,* at the scheduled time ; *indiquer le jour,* to name the day. ‖ To recommend, to tell of (v. signaler) ; *indiquer un bon dentiste,* to recommend a good dentist. ‖ Milit. *Indiquer l'emplacement exact,* to pin-point. ‖ Fig. To indicate, to denote, to show, to betoken (v. dénoter) ; *ce n'est pas très indiqué,* it is not very advisable ; *être tout indiqué pour,* to be the very man for.
indirect, ecte [ε̃dirεkt] adj. Indirect (chemin). ‖ Gramm., Milit., Fin. Indirect. ‖ Jur. Circumstancial (preuve). ‖ Fig. Oblique (allusion) ; indirect (critique).
indirectement [-təmɑ̃] adv. Indirectly.
indiscernable [ε̃disεrnabl] adj. Indistinguishable (*de,* from).
indisciplinable [ε̃disiplinabl] adj. Unruly ; unmanageable ; unamenable to discipline.
indiscipline [-plin] f. Indiscipline, lack of discipline.
indiscipliné, ée [-pline] adj. Undisciplined, unruly. (V. indocile.)
indiscret, ète [ε̃diskrε, εːt] adj. Indiscreet, tactless (personne) ; indiscreet (question) ; prying (regard).
— s. Tactless person.
indiscrètement [-tmɑ̃] adv. Indiscreetly.
indiscrétion [-sjɔ̃] f. Indiscretion, indiscreetness, tactlessness. ‖ Indiscreet (ou) tactless remark.
indiscutable [ε̃diskytabl] adj. Unquestionable, indisputable.
indiscutablement [-tabləmɑ̃] adv. Unquestionably, indisputably.
indiscuté, ée [-te] adj. Unquestioned ; beyond question.
indispensable [ε̃dispɑ̃sabl] adj. indispensable, essential ; *homme indispensable,* key-man.
— m. The necessary ; what is essential.
indispensablement [-bləmɑ̃] adv. Indispensably.
indisponibilité [ε̃dispɔnibilite] f. Unavailability (d'une personne). ‖ Fin. Unavailability (d'un capital). ‖ Jur. Inalienability (d'une propriété).
indisponible [-nibl] adj. Unavailable (personne). ‖ Fin. Unavailable. ‖ Jur. Inalienable.
indisposé, ée [ε̃dispoze] adj. Méd. Indisposed, unwell. ‖ Fig. Ill-disposed (*contre,* towards).
indisposer v. tr. (1). Méd. To indispose, to make unwell ; *mon dîner m'a indisposé,* my dinner did not agree with me. ‖ Fig. To antagonize, to make hostile (qqn) ; to set (*contre,* against).
indisposition [-zisjɔ̃] f. Méd. Indisposition, upset.
indissociable [ε̃disɔsjabl] adj. That cannot be dissociated, inseparable, indissociable.
indissolubilité [ε̃disɔlybilite] f. Chim. Insolubility. ‖ Ecclés., Fig. Indissolubility.
indissoluble [-lybl] adj. Chim. Insoluble (métal). ‖ Ecclés., Fig. Indissoluble.
indissolublement [-lybləmɑ̃] adv. Indissolubly.
indistinct, incte [ε̃distε̃, εːkt] adj. Hazy, faint,

blurred (contour); dim (lumière); confused (son); indistinct (voix).
indistinctement [-təmɑ̃] adv. Indistinctly, faintly (vaguement). ‖ Indiscriminately, without distinction (sans discrimination).
indistinguible [ɛ̃distɛ̃gibl] adj. Indistinguishable.
individu [ɛ̃dividy] m. Individual, human being. ‖ FAM. Person, fellow, chap, bloke; *drôle d'individu,* odd character, queer fish.
individualisation [-alizasjɔ̃] f. Individualization.
individualiser [-alize] v. tr. (1). To individualize, to particularize.
— v. pr. **S'individualiser,** to become individualized, to assume individual characteristics.
individualisme [-alism] m. Individualism.
individualiste [-alist] adj. Individualistic.
— s. Individualist.
individualité [-alite] f. Individuality.
individuel, elle [-ɛl] adj. Separate (article); personal (liberté); individual (qualité).
individuellement [-ɛlmɑ̃] adv. Individually.
indivis, ise [ɛ̃divi, iz] adj. JUR. Joint (héritiers).
— loc. adv. *Par indivis,* jointly.
indivisibilité [-zibilite] f. Indivisibility.
indivisible [-zibl] adj. Indivisible.
indivisiblement [-zibləmɑ̃] adv. Indivisibly.
indivision [-zjɔ̃] JUR. Joint possession.
indo-aryen, enne [ɛ̃doarjɛ̃, ɛn] adj. GRAMM. Indo-Aryan, Indic (langues).
Indochine [ɛ̃doʃin] f. GÉOGR. Indo-China.
indochinois, oise [ɛ̃doʃinwa, waz] adj., s. GÉOGR. Indo-Chinese.
indocile [ɛ̃dɔsil] adj. Indocile, unmanageable, intractable, unruly.
indocilité [-lite] f. Indocility, disobedience, unmanageableness, intractability.
indo-européen, enne [ɛ̃doørɔpeɛ̃, ɛn] adj., s. Indo-European.
indo-germanique [ɛ̃doʒɛrmanik] adj. Indo-Germanic.
indolemment [ɛ̃dɔlamɑ̃] adv. Indolently, idly, slothfully.
indolence [-lɑ̃:s] f. Indolence. ‖ Idleness, sloth (paresse). ‖ MÉD. Painlessness.
indolent, ente [-lɑ̃, ɑ̃:t] adj. Indolent, idle, sluggish, slothful. ‖ MÉD. Painless.
— s. Idler, sluggard. (V. PARESSEUX.)
indolore [ɛ̃dɔlɔ:r] adj. MÉD. Painless.
indomptable [ɛ̃dɔ̃tabl] adj. Untamable (animal); unmanageable (enfant); unconquerable (nation). ‖ FIG. Indomitable (orgueil); ungovernable, uncontrollable (passion).
indomptablement [-bləmɑ̃] adv. Unconquerably, indomitably.
indompté, ée [ɛ̃dɔ̃te] adj. Untamed (animal); unbroken (cheval); unconquered (nation). ‖ FIG. Uncontrolled, ungoverned (passion).
Indonésie [ɛ̃dɔnezi] f. GÉOGR. Indonesia.
indonésien, enne [-zjɛ̃, ɛn] adj., s. GÉOGR. Indonesian.
— m. GRAMM. Indonesian.
in-douze [indu:z] adj., m. invar. Duodecimo, twelvemo; 12 mo.
indu, ue [ɛ̃dy] adj. Undue (hâte); unseasonable, unseemly (heure); unwarranted (remarque); *à des heures indues,* at all hours. ‖ FIN. Not owed, not due (argent).
indubitable [ɛ̃dybitabl] adj. Indubitable, unquestionable, beyond all possible doubt.
indubitablement [-bləmɑ̃] adv. Indubitably, unquestionably, without doubt, doubtless.
inductance [ɛ̃dyktɑ̃:s] f. ELECTR. Inductance; inductance coil.
inducteur [-tœ:r] adj., m. ELECTR. Inducing (courant); inductive (pouvoir).
— m. ELECTR. Inductor.
inductif, ive [-tif, i:v] adj. Inductive.

inductile [-til] adj. Inductile.
induction [-sjɔ̃] f. PHILOS. Induction; *par induction,* inductively, by induction. ‖ ELECTR. Induction; *bobine d'induction,* induction coil. ‖ JUR. Inference, conclusion.
induire [ɛ̃dɥi:r] v. tr. (85). To induce; to lead, to beguile (*à,* into); to lead (*en,* into). ‖ ELECTR. To induce. ‖ *Induire en tentation,* to mislead.
induit [ɛ̃dɥi] adj., m. ELECTR. Induced (courant).
— m. ELECTR. Induced circuit.
indulgemment [ɛ̃dylʒamɑ̃] adv. Indulgently.
indulgence [-ʒɑ̃:s] f. Indulgence, leniency, forbearance. ‖ ECCLÉS. Indulgence.
indulgencier [-ʒɑ̃sje] v. tr. (1). ECCLÉS. To attach an indulgence to (un chapelet).
indulgent, ente [-ʒɑ̃, ɑ̃:t] adj. Lenient (*pour,* with); indulgent (*pour,* to) [clément]. ‖ Longsuffering, forbearing (tolérant).
indult [ɛ̃dylt] m. ECCLÉS. Indult.
indûment [ɛ̃dymɑ̃] adv. Unduly.
induration [ɛ̃dyrasjɔ̃] f. MÉD. Induration; hardened tissue.
indurer [-re] v. tr. (1). MÉD. To indurate.
— v. pr. **S'indurer,** to indurate.
industrialisation [ɛ̃dystrializasjɔ̃] f. Industrialization.
industrialiser [-trialize] v. tr. (1). To industrialize.
— v. pr. **S'industrialiser,** to become industrialized.
industrie [-tri] f. † Industry, dexterity. ‖ COMM. Industry, manufacture; *industrie chimique,* chemical engineering. ‖ FIG. Trickery; *vivre d'industrie,* to live by one's wits. ‖ **Industrie-clef,** f. Key-industry.
industriel, elle [-triɛl] adj. Industrial (en général); business (bénéfices).
— m. Manufacturer.
industriellement [-triɛlmɑ̃] adv. Industrially.
industrieusement [-trijøzmɑ̃] adv. Industriously.
industrieux, euse [-trijø, ø:z] adj. Industrious.
inébranlable [inebrɑ̃labl] adj. Unshakeable, immovable, solid (édifice). ‖ FIG. Resolute, steadfast, unshakeable, staunch (personne).
inébranlablement [-bləmɑ̃] adv. Unshakeably, immovably, steadfastly, inflexibly.
inéchangeable [ineʃɑ̃ʒabl] adv. Unexchangeable.
inécoutable [inekutabl] adj. Unbearable.
inécouté, ée [-te] adj. Ignored, unheeded, disregarded.
inédit, ite [inedi, it] adj. Unpublished (livre, poème). ‖ FAM. Unprecedented (événement); new, novel, original (spectacle).
— m. Unpublished material; original matter.
inéducable [inedykabl] adj. Ineducable, unteachable.
ineffabilité [inɛfabilite] f. Ineffability.
ineffable [-fabl] adj. Ineffable. (V. INEXPRIMABLE.)
ineffablement [-fabləmɑ̃] adv. Ineffably.
ineffaçable [inɛfasabl] adj. Indelible (tache). ‖ FIG. Ineffaceable (impression).
ineffaçablement [-bləmɑ̃] adv. Indelibly. ‖ FIG. Ineffaceably.
inefficace [inɛfikas] adj. Ineffective, ineffectual (moyen). ‖ MÉD. Inefficacious (remède).
inefficacement [-smɑ̃] adv. Ineffectually.
inefficacité [-site] f. Ineffectiveness, inefficacy.
inégal, ale [inegal] adj. Unequal (lignes); irregular (mouvement); rough, uneven (terrain). ‖ FIG. Changeable (humeur); uneven (style).
inégalable [-labl] adj. Matchless, incomparable, unparalleled.
inégalé, ée [-le] adj. Unequalled.
inégalement [-lmɑ̃] adv. Unequally; unevenly.
inégalitaire [-litɛ:r] adj. Inegalitarian.
inégalité [-lite] f. Inequality, roughness, bumpiness (du terrain). ‖ MATH., ASTRON. Inequality.

|| FIG. Inequality, disparity (d'aptitude); changeableness, capriciousness (d'humeur); unevenness (de style).

inélégamment [inelegamɑ̃] adv. Inelegantly.
inélégance [-gɑ̃:s] f. Inelegance, inelegancy.
inélégant, ante [-gɑ̃, ɑ̃:t] adj. Inelegant.
inéligibilité [ineliʒibilite] f. Ineligibility.
inéligible [-ʒibl] adj. Ineligible.
inéluctabilité [inelyktabilite] f. Ineluctability.
inéluctable [inelyktabl] adj. Ineluctable.
inéluctablement [-bləmɑ̃] adv. Ineluctably.
inemployable [inɑ̃plwajabl] adj. Unemployable.
inemployé, ée [-je] adj. Unemployed, unused; not made use of.
inénarrable [inenarabl] adj. Indescribable. || FAM. Screamingly funny.
inepte [inɛpt] adj. Inept, unfit (personne); foolish, absurd, stupid, silly, inept (remarque).
ineptie [-si] f. Ineptitude, ineptness, incapacity (état). || Inept (ou) foolish remark; *dire des inepties,* to talk nonsense (ou) bunkum (ou) bosh.
inépuisable [inepɥizabl] adj. Inexhaustible; *tampon inépuisable,* self-inking pad. || FIG. Never-failing, unfailing (bonté).
inépuisablement [-zabləmɑ̃] adv. Inexhaustibly.
inépuisé, ée [-ze] adj. Unexhausted.
inéquation [inekwasjɔ̃] f. MATH. Inequality.
inéquitable [inekitabl] adj. Inequitable, unfair.
inerte [inert] adj. MÉD. Inert, motionless, still (cadavre). || CHIM. Inert, neutral (matière). || FIG. Dull, sluggish (esprit); inactive (personne).
inertie [inɛrsi] f. TECHN., PHYS. Inertia; *force d'inertie,* force of inertia, vis inertiae. || FIG. Inertia, apathy, sluggishness (indolence); *force d'inertie,* passive resistance.
inescomptable [inɛscɔ̃tabl] adj. FIN. Not subject to discount. || FIG. Unexpected, unpredictable.
inespéré, ée [inɛspere] adj. Unhoped-for.
inesthétique [inɛstetik] adj. Unaesthetic.
inestimable [inɛstimabl] adj. Inestimable, invaluable, without price.
inévitable [inevitabl] adj. Inevitable, unavoidable.
inévitablement [-bləmɑ̃] adv. Inevitably, unavoidably.
inexact, acte [inɛgzakt] adj. Inexact, incorrect, inaccurate (calcul); inaccurate, unreliable (nouvelle); loose, inexact (traduction). || Unpunctual (employé).
inexactement [-təmɑ̃] adv. Inexactly, inaccurately (sans justesse); unpunctually (sans ponctualité).
inexactitude [-tityd] f. Inexactitude, inaccuracy, inexactness (manque de justesse). || Unpunctuality, mistake, inaccuracy (erreur). || Unpunctuality (manque de ponctualité).
inexaucé, ée [inɛgzose] adj. ECCLÉS. Unanswered (prière). || FIG. Unfulfilled (vœu).
inexcitable [inɛksitabl] adj. MÉD. Inert.
inexcusable [inɛkskyzabl] adj. Inexcusable, unforgivable, unpardonable, unwarranted (acte); inexcusable (personne). [V. IMPARDONNABLE.]
inexcusablement [-bləmɑ̃] adv. Inexcusably.
inexécutable [inɛgzekytabl] adj. Inexecutable (ordre); impracticable, unfeasible, unworkable (projet).
inexécuté, ée [-te] adj. Unexecuted, unperformed (projet); unfulfilled (vœu).
inexécution [-sjɔ̃] f. Non-execution, non-performance, inexecution (d'un projet); non-fulfilment (d'un vœu).
inexercé, ée [inɛgzɛrse] adj. Unexercised, unpractised, unskilled. || MILIT. Untrained (soldat).
inexhaustible [inɛgzostibl] adj. Inexhaustible.
inexigibilité [inɛgziʒibilite] f. Non-exigibility.

inexigible [-ʒibl] adj. Inexigible. || FIN. Not due.
inexistant, ante [inɛgzistɑ̃, ɑ̃:t] adj. Non-existent.
inexistence [-tɑ̃:s] f. Non-existence.
inexorabilité [inɛgzɔrabilite] f. Inexorability.
inexorable [-rabl] adj. Inexorable, unrelenting (personne). || FIG. Harsh, inexorable (destin, loi).
inexorablement [-bləmɑ̃] adv. Inexorably.
inexpérience [inɛksperjɑ̃:s] f. Inexperience.
inexpérimenté, ée [inɛksperimɑ̃te] adj. Inexperienced, unskilled, unpractised, inexpert (ouvrier); untried, untested, unproved (procédé).
inexpert, erte [inɛkspɛ:r, ɛrt] adj. Inexpert.
inexpiable [inɛkspjabl] adj. Inexpiable.
inexpié, ée [-pje] adj. Unexpiated.
inexplicable [inɛksplikabl] adj. Inexplicable, unaccountable (énigme); weird, unaccountable (personne).
inexplicablement [-bləmɑ̃] adv. Inexplicably, unaccountably.
inexpliqué, ée [inɛksplike] adj. Unexplained, unaccounted for.
inexploitable [inɛksplwatabl] adj. TECHN. Unworkable (mine). || AGRIC. Uncultivable (terre).
inexploité, ée [-te] adj. Unexploited.
inexplorable [inɛksplɔrabl] adj. Inexplorable.
inexploré, ée [-re] adj. Unexplored.
inexplosible [inɛksplozibl] adj. CHIM. Inexplosive.
inexpressif, ive [inɛksprɛsif, i:v] adj. Inexpressive (mot); expressionless; deadpan (fam.) [physionomie].
inexprimable [inɛksprimabl] adj. Inexpressible. — m. *L'inexprimable,* the inexpressible.
inexprimablement [-mabləmɑ̃] adv. Inexpressibly, unutterably.
inexprimé, ée [-me] adj. Unexpressed.
inexpugnable [inɛkspyɲabl] adj. MILIT. Impregnable, inexpugnable (forteresse). || FIG. Unassailable, steadfast (vertu).
inextensibilité [inɛkstɑ̃sibilite] f. Inextensibility.
inextensible [-sibl] adj. Inextensible.
in extenso [inɛkstɛ̃so] loc. adv. In extenso, in full.
in extremis [inɛkstremis] loc. adv. By the skin of one's teeth, at the last minute.
inextinguible [inɛkstɛ̃gibl] adj. Inextinguishable (feu). || FIG. Uncontrollable, irrepressible (rire); unquenchable (soif).
inextirpable [inɛkstirpabl] adj. Inextirpable, ineradicable.
inextricable [inɛkstrikabl] adj. Inextricable.
inextricablement [-bləmɑ̃] adv. Inextricably.
infaillibilité [ɛ̃fajibilite] f. Infallibility.
infaillible [-jibl] adj. Infallible (personne). || MÉD. Certain, sure, infallible (remède).
infailliblement [-jibləmɑ̃] adv. Infallibly, unfailingly, without fail.
infaisable [ɛ̃fɛzabl] adj. Unfeasible, impracticable.
infamant, ante [ɛ̃famɑ̃, ɑ̃:t] adj. Infamatory, defamatory; degrading. || JUR. Involving loss of civil rights (peine).
infâme [ɛ̃fɑ:m] adj. Infamous, disgraceful, dishonourable (acte); infamous, disreputable (personne); vile, filthy, squalid (taudis).
infamie [ɛ̃fami] f. Infamy, disgrace, opprobrium. || Infamous (ou) disgraceful deed (ou) expression; *dire des infamies sur qqn,* to blacken s.o.'s character.
infant [ɛ̃fɑ̃] m. Infante.
infante [ɛ̃fɑ̃:t] f. Infanta.
infanterie [ɛ̃fɑ̃tri] f. MILIT. Infantry; *soldat d'infanterie,* foot soldier.
infanticide [ɛ̃fɑ̃tisid] adj. Infanticidal.

— s. Infanticide, child-murderer (meurtrier).
— m. JUR. Infanticide, child-murder (crime).
infantile [-til] adj. MÉD. Infantile. ‖ FIG. Childish.
infantiliser [-tilize] v. tr. (1). To make infantile.
infantilisme [-tilism] m. Infantilism.
infarctus [ɛ̃farktys] n. MÉD. Infarct.
infatigable [ɛ̃fatigabl] adj. Indefatigable, tireless.
infatigablement [-bləmɑ̃] adv. Indefatigably, tirelessly.
infatuation [ɛ̃fatyasjɔ̃] f. Self-conceit.
infatué, ée [-tɥe] adj. Conceited, self-important.
infécond, onde [ɛ̃fekɔ̃, ɔ̃d] adj. Barren, sterile, unproductive. (V. STÉRILE.)
infécondité [-dite] f. Barrenness, sterility, unproductiveness.
infect, ecte [ɛ̃fɛkt] adj. Foul (haleine, odeur); noisome, stinking (marais). ‖ FIG. Vile, beastly (livre); abject (personne).
infecter [-te] v. tr. (1). To infect, to taint, to pollute (l'air). ‖ FIG. To corrupt (les mœurs).
— v. pr. **S'infecter**, to go septic, to become infected.
infectieux, euse [-sjø, ø:z] adj. MÉD. Infectious, catching (maladie).
infection [-sjɔ̃] f. MÉD. Infection. ‖ FIG. Corruption, contamination. ‖ FAM. Stink, stench.
inféodation [ɛ̃feɔdasjɔ̃] f. † Enfeoffment, infeudation. ‖ FIG. Subservience.
inféoder [-de] v. tr. (1). † To enfeoff. ‖ FIG. To make dependent, to vassalize.
— v. pr. **S'inféoder**, to give one's allegiance (à, to).
inférence [ɛ̃ferɑ̃:s] f. Inference.
inférer [-re] v. tr. (5). To infer, to conclude, to gather [de, from].
inférieur, eure [ɛ̃ferjœ:r] adj. MÉD. Lower, nether (lèvre, membres). ‖ GÉOGR. *Cours inférieur*, lower reaches (d'un fleuve); *inférieur au niveau de la mer*, below sea level. ‖ FIG. Inferior, poorer (qualité); inferior, lower (race, rang); *inférieur à soi-même*, below one's usual standard.
— s. Inferior. (V. SUBALTERNE, SUBORDONNÉ.)
inférieurement [-mɑ̃] adv. In a lower position (plus bas). ‖ FIG. In an inferior way; not as well (moins bien).
infériorité [ɛ̃ferjorite] f. Inferiority.
infernal, ale [ɛ̃fɛrnal] adj. ECCLÉS. Infernal. (V. DIABOLIQUE.) ‖ FIG. Infernal (machine); diabolical, devilish (ruse). ‖ FAM. Infernal (tapage).
infernalement [-lmɑ̃] adv. Infernally.
infertile [ɛ̃fɛrtil] adj. Unfertile.
infertilité [-lite] f. Infertility, barrenness.
infestation [ɛ̃fɛstasjɔ̃] f. MÉD. Infestation.
infester [ɛ̃fɛste] v. tr. (1). To infest, to overrun.
infidèle [ɛ̃fidɛl] adj. Faithless, unfaithful, untrue (déloyal); false, inaccurate (inexact); dishonest (malhonnête). ‖ ECCLÉS. Infidel.
— s. ECCLÉS. Infidel.
infidèlement [-dɛlmɑ̃] adv. Unfaithfully (déloyalement); inaccurately (inexactement).
infidélité [-delite] f. Infidelity, unfaithfulness. ‖ Unfaithful (ou) faithless act. ‖ ECCLÉS. Unbelief.
infiltration [ɛ̃filtrasjɔ̃] f. Infiltration, percolation. ‖ MÉD., MILIT. Infiltration.
infiltrer (s') [sɛ̃filtʳe] v. pr. (1). To infiltrate, to seep, to percolate, to filter (eau) [dans, into]. ‖ MÉD., MILIT. To infiltrate. ‖ FIG. To infiltrate (dans, into); to creep (dans, in).
infime [ɛ̃fim] adj. Low, mean, lowly (condition, rang). ‖ Tiny (morceau); minute, very small, infinitesimal (parcelle).
infini, ie [ɛ̃fini] adj. Infinite, boundless, immeasurable (espace); unlimited (patience); eternal, never-ending (supplice).
— m. Infinite.

— loc. adv. À *l'infini*, infinitely, ad infinitum, without limit.
infiniment [-ɑ̃] adv. Infinitely. ‖ MATH. *Infiniment petits*, infinitely small quantities. ‖ FAM. Awfully, terribly (énormément).
infinité [-te] f. Infinity. ‖ FAM. A great number; *infinité de maux*, host of evils.
infinitésimal, ale [-tezimal] adj. MATH., FIG. Infinitesimal.
infinitif, ive [ɛ̃finitif, i:v] adj., m. GRAMM. Infinitive.
infinitude [-tyd] f. Infinitude.
infirmable [ɛ̃firmabl] adj. JUR. Able to be quashed (ou) invalidated.
infirmatif, ive [-tif, i:v] adj. JUR. Invalidating.
infirmation [-sjɔ̃] f. JUR. Invalidation, quashing.
infirme [ɛ̃firm] adj. Infirm, weak, feeble (vieillard). ‖ MÉD. Disabled; crippled (de, in).
— s. Invalid; cripple.
infirmer [-me] v. tr. (1). JUR. To quash (un jugement); to invalidate (un témoignage). ‖ FIG. To weaken (un argument).
infirmerie [-məri] f. MÉD. Infirmary, hospital, sick-room, sick-bay (dans une école). ‖ MILIT. Hospital, sick-ward. ‖ NAUT. Sick-bay, sick-berth.
infirmier [-mje] m. MÉD. Male nurse. ‖ MILIT. Medical orderly. ‖ NAUT. Sick-berth attendant, U. S. aid man, hospital corpsman.
infirmière [-mjɛ:r] f. MÉD. Nurse. ‖ **Infirmière-major**, f. MÉD. Sister, head nurse.
infirmité [-mite] f. MÉD. Infirmity, illness, disability. ‖ FIG. Frailty.
infixe [ɛ̃fiks] m. GRAMM. Infix.
inflammabilité [ɛ̃flamabilite] f. Inflammability.
inflammable [-mabl] adj. Inflammable, combustible (matière). ‖ FIG. Excitable, easily roused (personne).
inflammation [-masjɔ̃] f. Inflammation, ignition. ‖ MÉD. Inflammation.
inflammatoire [-matwa:r] adj. MÉD. Inflammatory.
inflation [ɛ̃flɑsjɔ̃] f. FIN. Inflation; *d'inflation*, inflationary (politique).
inflationniste [-sjɔnist] adj. FIN. Inflationary.
— m. FIN. Inflationist.
infléchi, e [ɛ̃fleʃi] adj. Curved, bent. ‖ GRAMM. Modified, mutated (voyelle).
infléchir [ɛ̃fleʃi:r] v. tr. (2). To bend, to inflect, to curve.
— v. pr. **S'infléchir**, to bend, to curve.
infléchissement [-ʃismɑ̃] m. Slight deviation (ou) modification (d'une politique, d'une courbe); slackening off (d'une tendance).
inflexibilité [ɛ̃flɛksibilite] f. Inflexibility, rigidity. ‖ FIG. Inflexibility, rigidity, inexorability.
inflexible [-sibl] adj. Inflexible. (V. INEXORABLE.)
inflexiblement [-sibləmɑ̃] adv. Inflexibly.
inflexion [ɛ̃flɛɛksjɔ̃] f. Bending, bow (du corps); inflexion, modulation (de la voix). ‖ PHYS., MATH. Inflexion. ‖ GRAMM. Mutation, modification.
infliction [ɛ̃fliksjɔ̃] f. JUR. Infliction.
infliger [ɛ̃fliʒe] v. tr. (7). To inflict (une blessure); to impose (un châtiment).
inflorescence [ɛ̃flɔrɛsɑ̃:s] f. BOT. Inflorescence.
influençable [ɛ̃flɥɑ̃sabl] adj. Easily influenced, susceptible to influence.
influence [-ɑ̃:s] f. Influence (des astres). ‖ FIG. Influence (sur, with); control, authority.
influencer [-ɑ̃se] v. tr. (6). To influence, to have an influence on (qqch.); to have influence with, to carry weight with (qqn).
influent, ente [-ɑ̃, ɑ̃:t] adj. Influential.
influenza [ɛ̃flɥɑ̃za] f. MÉD. Influenza.

influer [ɛ̃flɥe] v. intr. (1). To have an influence (*sur*, on); *influer sur*, to influence, to affect.

influx [ɛ̃fly] m. MÉD. *Influx nerveux*, nerve impulse.

in-folio [infɔljo] adj. m. invar. Folio.

informateur, trice [ɛ̃fɔrmatœ:r, tris] s. Informant, informer.

informaticien, enne [-tisjɛ̃, ɛn] s. INFORM. Computer scientist.

informatif, ive [-tif, i:v] adj. Informative, informatory.

information [-sjɔ̃] f. JUR. Investigation. ‖ Pl. Information; *prendre des informations sur*, to make enquiries about. ‖ Pl. *Agence d'informations*, news agency; *les informations*, news items; U. S. news coverage (dans la presse). ‖ MILIT. *Service d'informations*, Intelligence. ‖ RADIO. Pl. News bulletin, news.

informatique [-tik] f. INFORM. Data processing, computer science.

— adj. INFORM. Computer (techniques, science).

informatisation [-tizasjɔ̃] f. INFORM. Computerization.

informatiser [-tize] v. tr. (1). INFORM. To computerize.

informe [ɛ̃fɔrm] adj. Shapeless, formless (bloc). ‖ JUR. Irregular, informal, not in order (acte). ‖ FIG. Crude, unpolished (ouvrage).

informé [ɛ̃fɔrme] m. *Jusqu'à plus ample informé*, until further inquiries have been made, until further information is available.

informel, elle [-mɛl] adj. Informal.

informer v. tr. (1). To inform, to tell, to advise. ‖ To acquaint (*de*, with); to apprise (*de*, of).

— v. intr. JUR. To investigate (enquêter); to inform, to lodge information (*contre*, against).

— v. pr. S'**informer**, to make enquiries, to enquire (*de*, about). [V. S'ENQUÉRIR.]

informulé, ée [ɛ̃fɔrmule] adj. Unformulated.

infortune [ɛ̃fɔrtyn] f. Misfortune, mischance, trouble. ‖ Pl. Woes, troubles.

infortuné, ée [-ne] adj. Unfortunate, hapless, ill-fated, unlucky, luckless.

— s. Unfortunate (ou) hapless person.

infra [ɛ̃fra] adv. Infra, below.

infraction [ɛ̃fraksjɔ̃] f. JUR. Infraction, infringement, offense (délit); breach (*à*, of).

infraliminaire [ɛ̃fraliminɛ:r] adj. Subliminal.

infranchissable [ɛ̃frɑ̃ʃisabl] adj. Impassable (abîme). ‖ FIG. Unsurmountable (difficulté).

infrangible [ɛ̃frɑ̃ʒibl] adj. Infrangible.

infrarouge [ɛ̃fraru:ʒ] adj., m. PHYS. Infrared.

infrason [-sɔ̃] m. PHYS. Infrasound.

infrasonore [-sɔnɔ:r] adj. PHYS. Infrasonic.

infrastructure [-strykty:r] f. Infrastructure (en économie, en sociologie); *infrastructure routière*, road system. ‖ AVIAT. Ground structure. ‖ MILIT. Infrastructure. ‖ TECHN. Substructure (d'une construction).

infréquentable [ɛ̃frekɑ̃tabl] adj. Unfit to associate with, disreputable (personne); disreputable (endroit).

infroissable [ɛ̃frwasabl] adj. Uncreasable, crease-resisting, wrinkle-proof.

infructueusement [ɛ̃fryktɥøzmɑ̃] adv. Fruitlessly, without profit.

infructueux, euse [-tɥø, ø:z] adj. Unfruitful, barren (champ). ‖ FIG. Fruitless (effort).

infumable [ɛ̃fymabl] adj. Unsmokable.

infus, use [ɛ̃fy, y:z] adj. Inborn, innate (science). ‖ FAM. Natural; *il a la science infuse*, he's a born genius.

infuser [ɛ̃fyse] v. tr. (1). CULIN. To infuse, to steep; *faire infuser dans*, to infuse in. ‖ FIG. To infuse, to instil.

— v. intr. CULIN. To infuse, to draw, to mast.

— v. pr. S'**infuser**, to infuse, to draw (thé).

infusible [-zibl] adj. Infusible.

infusion [-zjɔ̃] f. CULIN. Infusion, steeping. ‖ ECCLÉS. Affusion.

infusoire [-zwa:r] m. ZOOL. Infusorian. ‖ Pl. Infusoria.

ingambe [ɛ̃gɑ̃:b] adj. FAM. Nimble, alert; *vieillard ingambe*, spry old chap.

ingénier (s') [sɛ̃ʒenje] v. pr. (1). To rack one's brains; *s'ingénier à faire*, to strive hard to do.

ingénierie [ɛ̃ʒeniri] f. Industrial (ou) management engineering.

ingénieur [ɛ̃ʒenjœ:r] m. Engineer; *ingénieur des mines, du son*, mining, sound engineer. ‖ **Ingénieur-radio** (pl. *ingénieurs-radio*), m. Radio engineer.

ingénieusement [-njøzmɑ̃] adv. Ingeniously.

ingénieux, euse [-njø, ø:z] adj. Ingenious (machine); ingenious, clever, skilful (personne).

ingéniosité [-njozite] f. Ingenuity, skilfulness, ingeniousness.

ingénu, ue [ɛ̃ʒeny] adj. Ingenuous, artless, innocent, unsophisticated. (V. NAÏF.)

— f. THÉÂTR. Ingenue.

ingénuité [-ite] f. Ingenuousness.

ingénument [-mɑ̃] adv. Ingenuously.

ingérence [ɛ̃ʒrɑ̃:s] f. Interference, ingerence.

ingérer [-re] v. tr. (5). MÉD. To ingest.

— v. pr. S'**ingérer**, to interfere, to meddle, to intrude (v. S'INSINUER); *s'ingérer dans*, to poke one's nose into (les affaires d'autrui).

ingestion [ɛ̃ʒɛstjɔ̃] f. MÉD. Ingestion.

ingouvernable [ɛ̃guvɛrnabl] adj. Ungovernable, unruly. (V. INDISCIPLINÉ.)

ingrat, ate [ɛ̃gra, at] adj. Awkward (âge); disagreeable, displeasing, unpleasant, unattractive (figure). ‖ FIG. Ungrateful (personne); sterile, barren (sol); unprofitable, unrewarding (sujet); thankless (tâche).

— s. Ungrateful person.

ingratitude [-tityd] f. Ingratitude. ‖ FIG. Sterility, barrenness (du sol); unprofitableness (d'un sujet); thanklessness (d'une tâche).

ingrédient [ɛ̃gredjɑ̃] m. Ingredient.

inguéable [ɛ̃geabl] adj. Unfordable.

inguérissable [ɛ̃gerisabl] adj. MÉD. Incurable. ‖ FIG. Inconsolable (chagrin).

inguinal, ale [ɛ̃gɥinal] adj. MÉD. Inguinal.

ingurgitation [ɛ̃gyrʒitasjɔ̃] f. MÉD. Ingurgitation.

ingurgiter [ɛ̃gyrʒite] v. tr. (1). MÉD. To ingurgitate. ‖ FAM. To swallow, to take down (boisson); to wolf (nourriture).

inhabile [inabil] adj. Unpractised (main); unskilled (ouvrier). ‖ Inapt, unfitted (*à*, to). ‖ JUR. Incompetent.

inhabilement [inabilmɑ̃] adv. Unskilfully.

inhabileté [-lɔte] f. Lack of skill. (V. MALADRESSE.) ‖ Clumsiness. (V. GAUCHERIE.)

inhabilité, ée [-lite] f. JUR. Incompetency, incapacity.

inhabitable [inabitabl] adj. Uninhabitable.

inhabité, ée [-te] adj. Uninhabited.

inhabitué, ée [inabitɥe] adj. Unaccustomed, unused (*à*, to).

inhabituel, elle [-tɥɛl] adj. Unusual.

inhalateur, trice [inalatœ:r, tris] adj. MÉD. Inhaling, inhalant.

— m. MÉD. Inhaler (appareil).

inhalation [-sjɔ̃] f. MÉD. Inhalant, inhalation. ‖ BOT. Inhalation.

inhaler [inale] v. tr. (1). MÉD. To inhale.

inharmonie [inarmoni] f. MUS. Discordance.

inharmonieux, euse [-mɔnjø, ø:z] adj. MUS. Inharmonious (accord); unmusical (voix).

inhérence [inerɑ̃:s] f. Inherence.

inhérent, ente [-rɑ̃, ɑ̃:t] adj. Inherent; adherent (*à*, to).

inhiber [inibe] v. tr. (1). To inhibit.

nhibiteur, trice [-bitœ:r, tris] adj. Inhibitory, inhibitive.

nhibition [-bisjɔ̃] f. Inhibition.

nhospitalier, ère [inɔspitalje, ɛr] adj. Inhospitable.

nhospitalièrement [-ljɛrmɑ̃] adv. Inhospitably.

nhospitalité [-lite] f. Inhospitality.

nhumain, aine [inymɛ̃, ɛn] adj. Inhuman.

nhumainement [-mɛnmɑ̃] adv. Inhumanly.

nhumanité [-manite] f. Inhumanity, cruelty.

nhumation [inymasjɔ̃] f. Inhumation, burial.

nhumer [-me] v. tr. (1). To inhume, to bury.

nimaginable [inimaʒinabl] adj. Unimaginable, inconceivable. ‖ Unthought-of; undreamt-of.

nimitable [inimitabl] adj. Inimitable.

nimitablement [-bləmɑ̃] adv. Inimitably.

nimitié [inimitje] f. Enmity.

ninflammabilité [inɛ̃flamabilite] f. Uninflammability, non-inflammability.

ninflammable [-mabl] adj. Uninflammable, non-inflammable.

nintelligemment [inɛ̃tɛliʒamɑ̃] adv. Unintelligently.

nintelligence [-ʒɑ̃:s] f. Lack of intelligence.

nintelligent, ente [-ʒɑ̃, ɑ̃:t] adj. Unintelligent.

nintelligibilité [-ʒibilite] f. Unintelligibility.

nintelligible [-ʒibl] adj. Unintelligible. (V. INCOMPRÉHENSIBLE.)

nintelligiblement [-ʒibləmɑ̃] adv. Unintelligibly.

nintéressant, ante [inɛ̃terɛsɑ̃, ɑ̃:t] adj. Uninteresting, without interest.

ninterrompu, ue [inɛ̃tɛrɔ̃py] adj. Uninterrupted, continuous. (V. INCESSANT.)

nique [inik] adj. Iniquitous. (V. INJUSTE.)

niquement [-kmɑ̃] adv. Iniquitously.

niquité [-kite] f. Iniquity, iniquitousness, unfairness. ‖ Iniquitous (ou) unfair action.

nitial, ale [inisjal] adj. Initial. ‖ MILIT. *Vitesse initiale,* muzzle velocity.

nitiale [-sja:l] f. Initial.

nitialement [-sjalmɑ̃] adv. Initially, in the first place.

nitiateur, trice [inisjatœ:r, tris] adj. Initiatory.
— s. Initiator, originator.

nitiation [-sjɔ̃] f. Initiation.

nitiatique [-tik] adj. Initiatory; *rite, cérémonie initiatique,* initiation rite, ceremony.

nitiative [-ti:v] f. Initiative; *de sa propre initiative,* on one's own initiative; *initiative privée,* private enterprise; *syndicat d'initiative,* tourist office, information bureau.

nitié, ée [inisje] adj., s. Initiate.

nitier v. tr. (1). To initiate (à, into) [un art]. ‖ To admit (à, into) [une société]. ‖ FIG. To acquaint (à, with); *initier qqn à un secret,* to let s.o. into a secret.
— v. pr. **S'initier,** to initiate oneself (à, to), to get acquainted (à, with).

njectable [ɛ̃ʒɛktabl] adj. MÉD. Injectable.

njecté, ée [ɛ̃ʒɛkte] adj. MÉD. Injected, congested (visage); bloodshot (yeux).

njecter v. tr. (1). To impregnate (le bois). ‖ MÉD. To inject (un liquide).
— v. pr. **S'injecter.** MÉD. To become injected (visage); to become bloodshot (yeux).

njecteur, trice [-tœ:r, tris] adj. Injecting.
— m. Injector.

njection [-sjɔ̃] f. MÉD. Injection, injecting (action); injection (liquide). ‖ GÉOGR. Intrusion. ‖ TECHN. Injection.

njonction [ɛ̃ʒɔ̃ksjɔ̃] f. JUR. Injunction; order.

njouable [ɛ̃ʒwabl] adj. Unplayable.

njure [ɛ̃ʒy:r] f. Insult. ‖ JUR. Tort. ‖ FIG. *L'injure des ans,* the ravages of time.

injurier [ɛ̃ʒyrje] v. tr. (1). To insult, to abuse.

injurieusement [-rjøzmɑ̃] adv. Injuriously, insultingly, abusively.

injurieux, euse [-rjø, ø:z] adj. Insulting, abusive (parole); derisive (rire); *injurieux pour,* insulting towards.

injuste [ɛ̃ʒyst] adj. Unjust, unfair (*envers,* to) [personne]; ill-founded (soupçon). [V. INIQUE.]
— m. Wrong.

injustement [təmɑ̃] adv. Unjustly, unfairly.

injustice [-tis] f. Injustice, unfairness. ‖ Unjust (ou) unfair action.

injustifiable [-tifjabl] adj. Unjustifiable.

injustifié, ée [-tifje] adj. Unjustified. ‖ JUR. Frivolous (plainte).

inlassable [ɛ̃lɑsabl] adj. Untiring (efforts); tireless, indefatigable (personne).

inlassablement [-bləmɑ̃] adv. Untiringly, tirelessly, indefatigably.

inné, ée [inne] adj. Innate, inborn, natural.

innervation [innɛrvasjɔ̃] f. MÉD. Innervation.

innerver [-ve] v. tr. (1). MÉD. To innervate.

innocemment [inɔsamɑ̃] adv. Innocently; guilelessly.

innocence [-sɑ̃:s] f. Innocence, guiltlessness (non-culpabilité). ‖ Guilelessness, artlessness (candeur).

innocent, ente [-sɑ̃, ɑ̃:t] adj. Innocent, guiltless (non coupable). ‖ Guileless, artless, simple (naïf); *air innocent,* an innocent expression. ‖ MÉD. Harmless, inoffensive (remède).
— s. Innocent (ou) guiltless person (non coupable). ‖ Guileless (ou) simple person; simpleton (benêt); *faire l'innocent,* to play the idiot boy, to play dumb. ‖ ECCLÉS. Pl. Innocents. ‖ FAM. *Aux innocents les mains pleines,* beginners' luck.

innocenter [-sɑ̃te] v. tr. (1). To prove innocent, to clear (un accusé).

innocuité [innɔkɥite] f. Innocuity, innocuousness.

innombrable [innɔ̃brabl] adj. Innumerable, countless, without number.

innombrablement [-bləmɑ̃] adv. Innumerably.

innomé, ée [innɔme] adj. Unnamed, nameless. ‖ JUR. Innominate.

innommable [-mabl] adj. Unnameable.

innovateur, trice [innɔvatœ:r, tris] adj. Innovating.
— s. Innovator.

innovation [-vasjɔ̃] f. Innovation.

innover [-ve] v. tr. (1). To make changes (ou) innovations in.
— v. intr. To innovate.

inobservable [inɔpsɛrvabl] adj. Inobservable (phénomène). ‖ FIG. That cannot be observed (ou) complied with (recommandation).

inobservance [-vɑ̃:s] f. Inobservance.

inobservation [-vasjɔ̃] f. Failure to keep (d'une promesse); non-compliance (de, with); disregard (de, of) [une règle].

inobservé, ée [-ve] adj. Unobserved, unnoticed (phénomène); uncomplied with, unobserved (règle).

inoccupation [inɔkypasjɔ̃] f. Inoccupation, unemployment, idleness.

inoccupé, ée [-pe] adj. Vacant, unoccupied (logement). ‖ Unoccupied, unemployed, idle (personne).

in-octavo [inɔktavo] adj. invar., m. Octavo.

inoculable [inɔkylabl] adj. MÉD. Inoculable.

inoculateur, trice [-latœ:r, tris] adj. MÉD. Inoculating.
— s. MÉD. Inoculator.

inoculation [-lasjɔ̃] f. MÉD. Inoculation.

inoculer [-le] v. tr. (1). MÉD. To inoculate (*contre,* against) [qqch., qqn]. ‖ FIG. To inoculate; to instil (à, into).

inodore [inɔdɔ:r] adj. Inodorous, odourless.

inoffensif, ive [inɔfɑ̃sif, iːv] adj. Inoffensive, innocuous, harmless.

inondable [inɔ̃dabl] adj. That can be flooded; *aisément inondable,* easily (ou) readily flooded.

inondation [-dasjɔ̃] f. Flood, inundation. ‖ Fɪɢ. Flood, deluge.

inondé, ée [-de] adj. Flooded (champ). ‖ Fɪɢ. Flooded (*de,* with); overrun (*de,* by); *inondé de larmes, de lumière,* bathed in tears, in light.
— s. Flood victim.

inonder [-de] v. tr. (1). To flood, to inundate. ‖ Fɪɢ. To overrun, to flood (envahir). ‖ Fᴀᴍ. To drench, to soak. (V. TREMPER.)

inopérable [inɔperabl] adj. Mᴇᴅ. Inoperable.

inopérant, ante [-rɑ̃, ɑ̃:t] adj. Jᴜʀ. Inoperative.

inopiné, ée [inɔpine] adj. Unexpected, unlooked-for, unforeseen. (V. IMPRÉVU.)

inopinément [-mɑ̃] adv. Unexpectedly, suddenly; out of the blue (fam.).

inopportun, une [inɔpɔrtœ̃, yːn] adj. Inopportune, inconvenient, ill-timed.

inopportunément [-tynemɑ̃] adv. Inopportunely, inconveniently.

inopportunité [-tynite] f. Untimeliness, inopportuneness.

inorganique [inɔrganik] adj. Inorganic.

inorganisé, ée [-nize] adj. Unorganized; non-party (ou) -union.
— s. Non-party (ou) -union member.

inoubliable [inublabl] adj. Unforgettable, never-to-be-forgotten.

inouï, ïe [inwi] adj. Unheard-of, unprecedented, unparalleled (phénomène). ‖ Fɪɢ. Outrageous, shocking (cruauté).

inoxydable [inɔksidabl] adj. Inoxidizable, rust-proof, stainless.

in petto [inpetɔ] loc. adv. To oneself, inwardly. ‖ Eᴄᴄʟés. In petto.

inqualifiable [ɛ̃kalifjabl] adj. Unjustifiable (agression); infamous, unspeakable, scandalous (conduite).

in-quarto [inkwarto] m., adj. invar. Quarto.

inquiet, ète [ɛ̃kjɛ, ɛt] adj. Restless, broken (sommeil); restless, unsettled (vie). ‖ Uneasy, anxious, worried, apprehensive, concerned (personne).

inquiétant, ante [ɛ̃kjetɑ̃, ɑ̃:t] adj. Mᴇᴅ. Grave, alarming (symptôme). ‖ Fɪɢ. Disquieting, disturbing (nouvelle).

inquiéter [-te] v. tr. (1). To disquiet, to worry, to harass. (V. TOURMENTER.) ‖ Jᴜʀ. To challenge.
— v. pr. **S'inquiéter,** to worry, to trouble oneself. (V. SOUCIER [SE].)

inquiétude [-tyd] f. Restlessness, inquietude (agitation); ‖ Disquiet, anxiety, uneasiness (anxiété); *éprouver des inquiétudes,* to have qualms (ou) misgivings.

inquisiteur, trice [ɛ̃kizitœːr, tris] m. Eᴄᴄʟés. Inquisitor. ‖ Fᴀᴍ. Snooper, Paul Pry.
— adj. Inquisitorial, searching, scrutinizing.

inquisition [-sjɔ̃] f. Inquisition, enquiry. ‖ Eᴄᴄʟés. *L'Inquisition,* the Inquisition.

inquisitorial, ale [-tɔrjal] adj. Inquisitorial.

inracontable [ɛ̃rakɔ̃tabl] adj. Unexpressible, indescribable (sentiment); which cannot be told (histoire).

insaisissable [ɛ̃sɛzisabl] adj. Unseizable (chose); elusive, slippery (personne). ‖ Jᴜʀ. Not distrainable, unattachable. ‖ Fɪɢ. Imperceptible, intangible, elusive (nuance).

insalissable [ɛ̃salisabl] adj. Unsoilable.

insalubre [ɛ̃salybr] adj. Unhealthy, insalubrious.

insalubrité [-brite] f. Unhealthiness, insalubrity.

insanité [ɛ̃sanite] f. Insanity, madness, lunacy. ‖ Insane (ou) mad action (ou) statement.

insapide [ɛ̃sapid] adj. Tasteless. (V. INSIPIDE.)

insatiabilité [ɛ̃sasjabilite] f. Insatiability; covetousness.

insatiable [-sjabl] adj. Insatiable (appétit); unquenchable (soif). ‖ Fɪɢ. Insatiable.

insatiablement [-sjabləmɑ̃] adv. Insatiably.

insatisfaction [ɛ̃satisfaksjɔ̃] f. Unsatisfiedness,

insatisfait, aite [-fɛ, ɛt] adj. Unsatisfied.

inscriptible [ɛ̃skriptibl] adj. Mᴀᴛʜ. Inscribable

inscription [-sjɔ̃] f. Inscription, writing down (détails); entry (d'un acte de mariage); inscriptio (sur un tombeau). ‖ Registration (à l'école); *droit d'inscription,* registration fee; *prendre ses inscrip tions,* to keep terms (ou) to register at the Uni versity. ‖ Fɪɴ. *Inscription sur le grand-livre* inscribed stock. ‖ Jᴜʀ. *Inscription de faux,* ple of forgery; *inscription hypothécaire,* registratio of mortgage. ‖ Nᴀᴜᴛ. *Inscription maritime,* sea board conscription.

inscrire [ɛ̃skriːr] v. tr. (44). To inscribe, to write down, to note, to register; to schedule; *se fair inscrire à,* to put one's name down for, to ente one's name for. ‖ Mᴀᴛʜ. To inscribe.
— v. pr. **S'inscrire,** to put one's name down. ‖ Tᴏ register (à l'école); *s'inscrire pour,* to enter fo to go in for (un concours). ‖ Jᴜʀ. *S'inscrire e. faux contre.* to dispute the validity of. ‖ Cᴏᴍᴍ To register (*chez,* with) [un commerçant].

inscrit, ite [-kri, it] adj. Registered, enrolled (à l'école). ‖ Mᴀᴛʜ. Inscribed. ‖ Jᴜʀ. Scheduled (*pour,* to).
— m. Registered student. ‖ Nᴀᴜᴛ. *Inscrit mari time,* naval conscript. ‖ Sᴘᴏʀᴛs. Entry.

insécable [ɛ̃sekabl] adj. Indivisible.

insecte [ɛ̃sɛkt] m. Zᴏᴏʟ. Insect.

insecticide [-tisid] adj. Insecticide; *poudre insec ticide,* insect-powder.
— m. Insecticide, insect-killer.

insectivore [-tivɔːr] adj. Zᴏᴏʟ. Insectivorous.
— s. Zᴏᴏʟ. Insectivore.

insécurité [ɛ̃sekyrite] f. Insecurity.

in-seize [insɛ:z] m., adj. invar. Sixteenmo.

insémination [ɛ̃seminasjɔ̃] f. Mᴇᴅ. Insemination

inséminer [-ne] v. tr. (1). To inseminate artifi cially.

insensé, ée [ɛ̃sɑ̃se] adj. Senseless, mad, absurd *idée insensée,* crazy notion.
— m. Madman. (V. FOU.)

insensée f. Madwoman. (V. FOLLE.)

insensibilisateur, trice [ɛ̃sɑ̃sibilizatœːr, tris adj. Mᴇᴅ. Anaesthetizing.
— m. Mᴇᴅ. Anaesthetic (anesthésique); anaesthe tizing apparatus (appareil).

insensibilisation [-zasjɔ̃] f. Mᴇᴅ. Anaesthetiza tion.

insensibiliser [-ze] v. tr. (1). Mᴇᴅ. To anaesthe tize.

insensibilité [-te] f. Insensibility, unconscious ness. ‖ Fɪɢ. Insensibility, insensitiveness, callous ness. (V. INDIFFÉRENCE.)

insensible [ɛ̃sɑ̃sibl] adj. Insensate, insentien (matière); ‖ Numb (membre); insensible (per sonne). ‖ Fɪɢ. Imperceptible (mouvement); insen sitive, callous, indifferent (*à,* to) [personne].

insensiblement [-bləmɑ̃] adv. Insensibly, imper ceptibly.

inséparable [ɛ̃separabl] adj. Inseparable.
— s. Inseparable companion. ‖ Zᴏᴏʟ. Love-bird

inséparablement [-bləmɑ̃] adv. Inseparably.

insérable [ɛ̃serabl] adj. Insertable.

insérer [-re] v. tr. (5). To insert (*dans,* into) *prière d'insérer,* for favour of publication in you columns, please publish, for release.
— v. pr. **S'insérer,** to settle in, to become integrated (personne); to be (ou) form part o (événement, projet); to fit in (personne, chose).

insermenté, ée [ɛ̃sɛrmɑ̃te] adj. Eᴄᴄʟés. Non juring.

insertion [ɛ̃sɛrsjɔ̃] f. Mᴇᴅ., Bᴏᴛ., Fɪɢ. Insertion

insidieusement [ɛ̃sidjøzmɑ̃] adv. Insidiously.

insidieux, euse [-djø, ø:z] adj. MÉD. Insidious (maladie). ‖ FIG. Insidious, sly (personne).

insigne [ɛsiɲ] adj. Noteworthy, distinguished (personne); signal (service); conspicuous, remarkable (vertu). ‖ Notorious (malfaiteur); arrant (mensonge); glaring (sottise).

insigne m. Sign, badge, mark. ‖ Pl. Insignia.

insignifiance [ɛsiɲifjɑ̃:s] f. Insignificance, unimportance.

insignifiant, ante [-fjɑ̃, ɑ̃:t] adj. Trivial, trifling (affaire); unimportant, insignificant (personne) [v. FALOT]; vacuous (visage).

insinuant, ante [ɛsinɥɑ̃, ɑ̃:t] adj. Insinuating (fluide). ‖ FIG. Smooth (langage); winning, ingratiating (manières).

insinuation [-asjɔ̃] f. Insinuation, insertion. ‖ FIG. Insinuation, innuendo.

insinuer [-e] v. tr. (1). To insinuate, to introduce, to insert (dans, into). ‖ FIG. To insinuate, to imply, to hint at (qqch.).
— v. pr. **S'insinuer**, to insinuate oneself. ‖ FIG. To work (ou) worm oneself (dans, into); to thread one's way (entre, through).

insipide [ɛsipid] adj. Insipid, tasteless, without flavour. (V. FADE.) ‖ FIG. Tame, dull, uninteresting (conte); flat, insipid (style).

insipidement [-ɪdmɑ̃] adv. Insipidly.

insipidité [-dite] f. CULIN. Tastelessness, lack of flavour. ‖ FIG. Tameness, flatness, insipidity.

insistance [-tɑ̃:s] f. Insistence, insistency. ‖ Emphasis.

insistant, ante [-tɑ̃, ɑ̃:t] adj. Persistent, insistent. ‖ Stubborn (entêté).

insister [-te] v. intr. (1). To insist, to lay stress (sur, on, upon); insister sur l'affaire, to rub it in; insister sur un point, to press (ou) stress a point; n'insistez pas!, don't keep on!

in situ [insity] loc. adv. In situ.

insociabilité [ɛsɔsjabilite] f. Unsociability, unsociableness.

insociable [-sjabl] adj. Unsociable.

insolation [ɛsɔlasjɔ̃] f. PHYS. Solar heat. ‖ MÉD. Sunstroke. ‖ Daylight printing (en photographie).

insolemment [ɛsɔlamɑ̃] adv. Insolently, impertinently.

insolence [-lɑ̃:s] f. Insolence, impudence, lack of respect. (V. IMPERTINENCE.) ‖ Insolent (ou) impertinent remark; piece of insolence.

insolent, ente [-ɑ̃, ɑ̃:t] adj. Haughty, overbearing (arrogant); insolent, impudent (impertinent). ‖ Unwonted, unexpected, extraordinary (insolite).
— s. Insolent (ou) impertinent person.

insolite [-lit] adj. Unwonted, unaccustomed, unusual. (V. INUSITÉ.)

insolubiliser [ɛsɔlybilize] v. tr. (1). CHIM. To render insoluble.

insolubilité [-te] f. CHIM. Insolubility. ‖ FIG. Insolubleness.

insoluble [ɛsɔlybl] adj. CHIM. Insoluble. ‖ FIG. Unsolvable, insoluble.

insolvabilité [ɛsɔlvabilite] f. FIN. Insolvency.

insolvable [-vabl] adj. FIN. Insolvent.

insomniaque [ɛsɔmnjak], **insomnieux, euse** [-njø, ø:z] adj., s. Insomniac.

insomnie [ɛsɔmni] f. MÉD. Insomnia, sleeplessness.

insondable [ɛsɔ̃dabl] adj. Bottomless (abîme); unfathomable, unsoundable (océan). ‖ FIG. Impenetrable, unfathomable (mystère).

insonore [ɛsɔnɔ:r] adj. Insonorous, sound-proof.

insonorisation [-nɔrizasjɔ̃] f. Sound-proofing, sound-damping.

insonoriser [-nɔrize] v. tr. (1). To soundproof; insonorisé, soundproof.

insouciamment [ɛsusjamɑ̃] adv. Carelessly, heedlessly.

insouciance [-sjɑ̃:s] f. Carelessness, heedlessness, jauntiness, unconcern.

insouciant, ante [-sjɑ̃, ɑ̃:t] adj. Care-free, heedless, jaunty.

insoucieux, euse [-sjɔ̃, ø:z] adj. Careless, unmindful, heedless (de, of).

insoumis, ise [ɛsumi, iz] adj. Unsubmissive, unruly, disobedient (enfant); unconquered, unsubjugated (peuple). ‖ MILIT. Defaulting, absent (soldat).
— m. MILIT. Defaulter, absentee.

insoumission [-misjɔ̃] f. Unsubmissiveness, insubordination. ‖ MILIT. Defaulting, going absent.

insoupçonnable [ɛsupsɔnabl] adj. Beyond (ou) above suspicion.

insoupçonné, ée [-ne] adj. Unsuspected.

insoutenable [ɛsutnabl] adj. MÉD. Unbearable (douleur). ‖ FIG. Untenable (théorie).

inspecter [ɛspɛkte] v. tr. (1). To inspect (une école); to survey (un terrain).

inspecteur [-tœ:r] m. Inspector; inspecteur dans un magasin, shop-walker; U. S. floorwalker; inspecteur des mines, surveyor of mines; inspecteur sanitaire, public health officer; inspecteur du travail, factory inspector. ‖ JUR. Detective inspector.

inspection [-sjɔ̃] f. Inspection, examination, survey (action); inspectorship, inspectorate (fonction). ‖ MILIT. Inspection, muster parade; passer l'inspection de, to inspect.

inspectorat [-tɔra] m. Inspectorate.

inspectrice [-tris] f. Inspectress.

inspirant, ante [ɛspirɑ̃, ɑ̃:t] adj. Inspiring.

inspirateur, trice [-ratœ:r, tris] adj. Inspiring. ‖ MÉD. Inspiratory.
— s. Inspirer, source of inspiration.

inspiration [-rasjɔ̃] f. Inspiration, impulse (impulsion); sous l'inspiration du moment, on the spur of the moment. ‖ Inspiration (enthousiasme créateur). ‖ MÉD. Inspiration, inhaling.

inspiré, ée [-re] adj. Inspired.

inspirer [-re] v. tr. (1). MÉD. To inspire, to breathe in (de l'air). ‖ FIG. To inspire, to prompt (qqn, un sentiment); inspirer à qqn de, to inspire (ou) prompt s.o. to; inspirer qqch. à qqn, to inspire s.o. with sth.
— v. pr. **S'inspirer de**, to take as a pattern (imiter); to draw one's inspiration from (tirer son inspiration).

instabilité [ɛstabilite] f. Instability, unsteadiness (d'un meuble). ‖ NAUT. Crankiness. ‖ CHIM. Instability. ‖ FIG Instability, flightiness.

instable [ɛstabl] adj. Unstable, shaky, unsteady (meuble). ‖ NAUT. Cranky (navire). ‖ CHIM. Unstable (substance). ‖ FIG. Unstable, capricious, flighty (caractère, personne).

instablement [-bləmɑ̃] adv. Unsteadily.

installateur [ɛstalatœ:r] m. ECCLÉS. Inductor. ‖ TECHN., ELECTR. Fitter.

installation [-lasjɔ̃] f. ECCLÉS. Induction (d'un curé). ‖ TECHN. Installation, fitting up (acte); plant, equipment, fittings (pièces) [d'un atelier, d'une usine]. ‖ ELECTR. Putting in (de l'électricité). ‖ ARCHIT. Appointing, furnishing (acte); fixtures, appointments, fittings (agencements) [d'une maison].

installer [-le] v. tr. (1). To set. ‖ ECCLÉS. To induct (un curé). ‖ TECHN. To equip, to fit out (un atelier, une usine). ‖ ELECTR. To put in (l'électricité). ‖ ARCHIT. To furnish (une maison). ‖ LOC. Vous êtes très bien installés ici, you are very comfortable here; installé dans un fauteuil, seated (or) settled in an armchair.
— v. pr. **S'installer**, to install oneself, to settle oneself, to settle; s'installer chez, to foist oneself on (de façon importune).

instamment [ɛstamɑ̃] adv. Insistently, urgently.

instance [-tɑ̃:s] f. Instancy, solicitation; *avec instance*, earnestly; *en instance de départ*, about to leave, on the point of departure. ‖ Pl. Entreaties. ‖ JUR. Instance, suit; *affaire en instance*, pending matter; *en seconde instance*, on appeal; *introduire une instance*, to start proceedings; *tribunal de première instance*, court of first instance.

instant, ante [ɛ̃stɑ̃, ɑ̃:t] adj. Instant.

instant m. Instant, moment; *à chaque instant*, at every moment, constantly; *attendez un instant!* wait a minute!; half a sec! (fam.); *dans un instant*, in a minute; in a jiffy (fam.); *de tous les instants*. ceaseless, unremitting; *en un instant*, in no time; *par instants*, off and on.
— loc. adv. **À l'instant**, just now; at once; *faites-le à l'instant*, do it straight away; *il est arrivé à l'instant*, he's just arrived this minute.
— loc. conj. **Dès l'instant que**, seeing that, since. (V. PUISQUE.)

instantané, ée [-tane] adj. Instantaneous.
— m. Snapshot; snap (fam.).

instantanéité [-ite] f. Instantaneousness.

instantanément [-mɑ̃] adv. Instantaneously; immediately, at once.

instar [ɛ̃sta:r] m. Imitation; *à l'instar de*, like, after the fashion of, in imitation of, in the manner of.

instaurateur, trice [ɛ̃stɔratœ:r, tris] s. Founder.

instauration [-rasjɔ̃] f. Founding, establishing. ‖ JUR. Setting up (d'un conseil).

instaurer [-re] v. tr. (1). To found, to establish.

instigateur, trice [ɛ̃stigatœ:r, tris] s. Instigator.

instigation [-sjɔ̃] f. Instigation; *à l'instigation de*, at the instigation of, prompted by.

instillation [ɛ̃stilasjɔ̃] f. MÉD. Instillation.

instiller [-le] v. tr. (1). MÉD., FIG. To instil.

instinct [ɛ̃stɛ̃] m. Instinct.

instinctif, ive [-tif, i:v] adj. Instinctive.

instinctivement [-tivmɑ̃] adv. Instinctively.

instinctuel, elle [-tɥɛl] adj. PSYCH. Instinctual.

instituer [ɛ̃stitɥe] v. tr. (1). To found, to establish, to set up (une institution). ‖ JUR. To appoint (un héritier); to institute (des poursuites).

institut [-ty] m. Institute, institution; *institut de beauté*, beauty parlour. ‖ ECCLÉS. Monastic order.

instituteur [-tytœ:r] s. Founder, institutor (d'un hôpital, d'un ordre). ‖ School-teacher, schoolmaster.

institution [-tysjɔ̃] f. Institution, establishment, founding (établissement). ‖ Academy, private school, establishment (école). ‖ JUR. Appointing (d'un héritier); pl. institutions (d'un pays).

institutionnalisation [-tysjɔnalizasjɔ̃] f. Institutionalization.

institutionnaliser [-tysjɔnalize] v. tr. (1). To institutionalize.

institutionnel, elle [-tysjɔnɛl] adj. Institutional.

institutrice [-tytris] f. Governess (dans une famille). ‖ Schoolmistress (dans une école).

instructeur [ɛ̃stryktœ:r] m. MILIT. Instructor.
— adj. m. MILIT. *Sergent instructeur*, drill sergeant. ‖ JUR. *Juge instructeur*, examining magistrate.

instructif, ive [-tif, i:v] adj. Instructive.

instruction [-sjɔ̃] f. Instruction, guidance (renseignement). ‖ Education, teaching (enseignement); *avoir de l'instruction*, to be educated, to have had a good education; *instruction publique*, State education; *sans instruction*, uneducated. ‖ Pl. Directions, instructions (directives); *instructions permanentes*, standing orders. ‖ JUR. Preliminary examination.

instruire [ɛ̃strɥi:r] v. tr. (85). To inform (de, of); to tell (renseigner). ‖ To instruct, to teach (enseigner). ‖ JUR. To prepare (un procès). ‖ MILIT. To train, to drill (les soldats).

— v. pr. **S'instruire**, to educate oneself, t improve one's mind.

instruit, ite [-trɥi, it] adj. Educated, well-read *fort instruit*, well-educated.

instrument [ɛ̃strymɑ̃] m. TECHN. Instrument tool (outil). ‖ MUS. Musical instrument. ‖ JUR Instrument, deed. ‖ AVIAT. Instrument; *voler au instruments*, to fly by dead reckoning. ‖ FIG Tool; *servir d'instrument*, to be used as a tool

instrumentaire [-tɛ:r] adj. JUR. *Témoin instru mentaire*, witness to a deed.

instrumental, ale [-tal] adj. MUS., GRAMM. Ins trumental.
— m. GRAMM. Instrumental.

instrumentation [-tasjɔ̃] f. MUS. Instrumenta tion, orchestration.

instrumenter [-te] v. tr. (1). MUS. To instrument to score.
— v. intr. JUR. To draw up a deed, to implemen (rédiger); to take legal proceedings (*contre* against).

instrumentiste [-tist] m. MUS. Instrumentalist.

insu [ɛ̃sy] m. Ignorance; *à l'insu de*, unknow to, without the knowledge of.

insubmersible [ɛ̃sybmɛrsibl] adj. Insubmersible

insubordination [ɛ̃sybɔrdinasjɔ̃] f. Insubordina tion.

insubordonné, ée [-ne] adj. Insubordinate.

insubstantiel, elle [ɛ̃sybstɑ̃sjɛl] adj. Insubstan tial, unsubstantial.

insuccès [ɛ̃syksɛ] m. Lack of success. ‖ Failur (d'une entreprise); breakdown (d'un projet).

insuffisamment [ɛ̃syfizamɑ̃] adv. Insufficiently

insuffisance [-zɑ̃:s] f. Insufficiency, inadequacy shortage (manque); *insuffisance de main-d'œuvre* labour shortage. ‖ MÉD. Insufficiency (valvulaire) *insuffisance mitrale*, mitral regurgitation. ‖ FIG Unsatisfactoriness.

insuffisant, ante [-zɑ̃, ɑ̃:t] adj. Insufficien inadequate (quantité). ‖ FIG. Inefficient, incompeten (personne).

insufflateur [ɛ̃syflatœ:r] m. MÉD. Insufflator throat-spray, nose-spray.

insufflation [-flasjɔ̃] f. MÉD. Insufflation.

insuffler [-fle] v. tr. (1). MÉD. To insufflate.

insulaire [ɛ̃sylɛ:r] adj. Insular.
— s. Islander.

insularité [-larite] f. Insularity.

insuline [ɛ̃sylin] f. MÉD. Insulin.

insultant, ante [ɛ̃syltɑ̃, ɑ̃:t] adj. Insulting, abu sive.

insulte [ɛ̃sylt] f. Insult (v. INJURE, OFFENSE) *faire insulte à*, to insult.

insulter [-te] v. tr. (1). To insult, to affront, t offend (qqn).
— v. intr. *Insulter à*, to jeer at (malheur); t insult, to give insult to, to outrage (qqn).

insupportable [ɛ̃sypɔrtabl] adj. Intolerable (con duite); unbearable, unendurable (douleur); insuf ferable (personne).

insupportablement [-bləmɑ̃] adv. Unbearably insufferably.

insurgé, ée [ɛ̃syrʒe] adj., s. Insurgent, rebel.

insurger (s') [sɛ̃syrʒe] v. pr. (7). To rise, to revolt, to rebel (*contre*, against).

insurmontable [ɛ̃syrmɔ̃tabl] adj. Insurmountable insuperable.

insurmontablement [-bləmɑ̃] adv. Insurmount ably, insuperably.

insurpassable [ɛ̃syrpasabl] adj. Unsurpassable

insurrection [ɛ̃syrɛksjɔ̃] f. Insurrection.

insurrectionnel, elle [-sjɔnɛl] adj. Insurrectional insurrectionary.

intact, acte [ɛ̃takt] adj. Intact, undamaged, whol (objet). FIN. Complete (somme). ‖ FIG. Unsul lied, unblemished (réputation).

intaille [ɛ̃tɑ:j] f. ARTS. Intaglio; intaglio work

ntangibilité [ɛ̃tɑ̃ʒibilite] f. Intangibility.

ntangible [-ʒibl] adj. Intangible.

ntarissable [ɛ̃tarisabl] adj. Inexhaustible, perennial (source). [V. INÉPUISABLE.] ‖ FIG. Unfailing (imagination).

ntarissablement [-bləmɑ̃] adv. Inexhaustibly, unfailingly.

ntégrable [ɛ̃tegrabl] adj. MATH. Integrable.

ntégral, ale [ɛ̃tegral] adj. Integral, full, complete. ‖ MATH. Integral.

ntégrale [ɛ̃tegra:l] f. MATH. Integral.

ntégralement [-gralmɑ̃] adv. Integrally, wholly, completely ; in full.

ntégralité [-gralite] f. Integrality, completeness, wholeness ; *dans son intégralité*, in its entirety, in toto.

ntégrant, ante [-grɑ̃, ɑ̃:t] adj. *Partie intégrante*, integral part ; *faire partie intégrante de*, to be part and parcel of.

ntégration [-grasjɔ̃] f. Integration, fusion. ‖ MATH. Integration.

ntègre [ɛ̃tɛgr] adj. Honest, righteous, upright.

ntégré, ée [ɛ̃tegre] adj. ELECTR. *Circuit intégré*, integrated circuit.

ntègrement [-grəmɑ̃] adv. Honestly.

ntégrer [ɛ̃tegre] v. tr. (5). To integrate (*dans*, into). ‖ MATH. To integrate (*une fonction*).
— v. intr. FAM. To be admitted (à une grande école).
— v. pr. **S'intégrer**, to join, to combine (*dans*, with) ; to form an integral part (*dans*, of).

ntégrisme [-grism] m. ECCLÉS. Integrism, religious traditionalism.

ntégrité [-grite] f. Completeness, wholeness, entirety (d'un tout). ‖ FIG. Integrity, honesty (d'une personne).

ntellect [ɛ̃tɛlɛkt] m. Intellect.

ntellectualisation [-tɥalizasjɔ̃] f. Intellectualization.

ntellectualiser [-tɥalize] v. tr. (1). To intellectualize.

ntellectualisme [-tɥalism] m. Intellectualism.

ntellectualiste [-tɥalist] adj., s. Intellectualist.

ntellectualité [-tɥalite] f. Intellectuality.

ntellectuel, elle [-tɥɛl] adj. Intellectual, mental.
— s. Intellectual ; highbrow, U. S. egg-head (fam.). ‖ Pl. The intelligentsia.

ntellectuellement [-tɥɛlmɑ̃] adv. Intellectually.

ntelligemment [ɛ̃tɛliʒamɑ̃] adv. Intelligently.

ntelligence [-ʒɑ̃:s] f. Intelligence, intellect (faculté) ; *à l'intelligence vive*, bright (enfant) ; quick-witted (personne). ‖ Understanding (compréhension) ; *avoir l'intelligence des affaires*, to have a good grasp of business matters. ‖ Intelligence, mind (personne) ; *une des grandes intelligences de l'époque*, one of the great minds of the day. ‖ Intercourse, understanding (entente) ; *en bonne, mauvaise intelligence avec*, on good, bad terms with. ‖ Conspiring (complicité) [*avec*, with]. ‖ Pl. Communications ; *avoir des intelligences avec*, to have dealings with.

ntelligent, ente [-ʒɑ̃, ɑ̃:t] adj. Intelligent, smart, brainy, clever.

ntelligentsia [-ʒɛntsja] f. Intelligentsia.

ntelligibilité [-ʒibilite] f. Intelligibility.

ntelligible [-ʒibl] adj. Intelligible, clear, understandable (propos) ; audible, distinct (vo:x) ; *à haute et intelligible voix*, in a clear and audible voice.

ntelligiblement [-ʒibləmɑ̃] adv. Intelligibly, clearly ; audibly, distinctly.

ntempérance [ɛ̃tɑ̃perɑ̃:s] f. Intemperance, insobriety (de vie). ‖ FIG. Intemperance, immoderation, excess, lack of restraint (de langage).

ntempérant, ante [-rɑ̃, ɑ̃:t] adj. Intemperate.

intempérie [ɛ̃tɑ̃peri] f. Inclemency (du temps). ‖ Pl. Bad weather.

intempestif, ive [ɛ̃tɑ̃pɛstif, i:v] adj. Untimely, unseasonable. (V. INOPPORTUN.)

intempestivement [-tivmɑ̃] adv. Unseasonably, inopportunely.

intemporalité [ɛ̃tɑ̃pɔralite] f. Timelessness ; immateriality.

intemporel, elle [-rɛl] adj. Timeless (hors du temps) ; immaterial (immatériel).

intenable [ɛ̃tnabl] adj. Untenable, unmaintainable.

intendance [ɛ̃tɑ̃dɑ̃:s] f. Administration, management. ‖ MILIT. Commissariat ; supply services. ‖ NAUT. Naval paymaster's department.

intendant [-dɑ̃] m. Intendant, superintendent, manager. ‖ Bursar (à l'école). ‖ MILIT. *Intendant militaire*, commissary, senior officer of Quartermaster General's Staff.

intendante [-dɑ̃:t] f. Intendant's (ou) manager's wife. ‖ ECCLÉS. Mother Superior.

intense [ɛ̃tɑ̃:s] adj. Intense, excessive (chaleur) ; deep (couleur) ; keen, intense (froid) ; intense, strong (lumière). ‖ MÉD. High (fièvre). ‖ MILIT. Concentrated (bombardement). ‖ FIG. Violent (effort) ; strong (émotion).

intensément [ɛ̃tɑ̃semɑ̃] adv. Intensely.

intensif, ive [-sif, i:v] adj. Intensive.

intensification [-sifikasjɔ̃] f. Intensification.

intensifier [-sifje] v. tr. (1). To intensify.
— v. pr. **S'intensifier**, to intensify.

intensité [-site] f. Intensity (de chaleur), depth (de couleur) ; keenness (du froid) ; intensity, strength (de la lumière). ‖ MÉD. Height (de la fièvre). ‖ ELECTR. Intensity (d'un courant). ‖ FIG. Violence, strength (d'effort, d'émotion).

intensivement [-sivmɑ̃] adv. Intensively.

intenter [ɛ̃tɑ̃te] v. tr. (1). JUR. To bring, to enter.

intention [ɛ̃tɑ̃sjɔ̃] f. Intention, purpose (dessein) ; *avoir l'intention de*, to intend to ; *dans une bonne intention*, with good intent ; *fait dans l'intention de*, meant to ; *intention arrêtée de*, determination to ; *sans intention*, unintentionally. ‖ Will, wish, desire, intention (désir). ‖ MÉD. Intention.
— loc. prép. **À l'intention de**, for the sake (ou) benefit of ; *j'ai dit cela à son intention*, I said that for his benefit ; that was aimed at him.

intentionné, ée [-sjɔne] adj. *Bien (ou) mal intentionné*, well- (ou) ill-disposed, well- (ou) ill-meaning.

intentionnel, elle [-sjɔnɛl] adj. Intentional, deliberate.

intentionnellement [-nɛlmɑ̃] adv. Intentionally, deliberately ; on purpose.

inter [ɛ̃tɛ:r] m. Trunk, U. S. long distance (au téléphone). ‖ SPORTS. Inside-forward (au football). ‖ **Inter-droit**, m. SPORTS. Inside-right.

interaction [ɛ̃tɛraksjɔ̃] f. Interaction.

interallié, ée [-alje] adj. Interallicd.

interarmes [-arm] adj. inv. MILIT. Inter-service.

intercalaire [-kalɛ:r] adj. Intercalated, inserted (en général) ; interpolated (feuille) ; intercalary (jour).
— m. Guide-card (dans un fichier).

intercalation [-kalasjɔ̃] f. Intercalation.

intercaler [-kale] v. tr. (1). To interpolate, to insert, to slip in (une feuille) ; to intercalate (un jour). ‖ CH. DE F. To put on (un wagon).

intercéder [-sede] v. intr. (5). To intercede, to plead (*auprès de*, with ; *pour*, for, on behalf of).

intercellulaire [-selylɛ:r] adj. MÉD. Intercellular.

intercepter [-sɛpte] v. tr. (1). To tap (une communication) ; to cut off, to shut out (la lumière) ; to intercept (un message).

intercepteur [-sɛptœ:r] m. AVIAT. Fighter.

interception [-sɛpsjɔ̃] f. Interception. ‖ AVIAT. *Raid d'interception*, intruder raid.
intercesseur [-sɛsœːr] m. Intercessor.
intercession [-sɛsjɔ̃] f. Intercession.
interchangeabilité [-ʃãʒabilite] f. Interchangeability, interchangeableness.
interchangeable [-ʃãʒabl] adj. Interchangeable.
interclasse [-klɑːs] m. Gap between two classes; *pendant l'interclasse*, between the lessons.
intercommunal, ale [-kɔmynal] adj. Common to several municipalities.
interconnecter [-kɔnɛkte] v. tr. (1). To interconnect.
interconnexion [-kɔnɛksjɔ̃] f. Interconnection.
intercontinental, ale [-kɔ̃tinãtal] adj. Intercontinental.
intercostal, ale [-kɔstal] adj. MÉD. Intercostal.
intercurrent, ente [-kyrã, ãːt] adj. MÉD. Intercurrent.
interdépartemental, ale [-departəmãtal] adj. Interdepartmental.
interdépendance [-depãdãːs] f. Interdependence.
interdépendant, ante [-depãdã, ãːt] adj. Interdependent.
interdiction [-diksjɔ̃] f. Interdiction, prohibition, ban. (V. DÉFENSE.) ‖ JUR. Prohibition, injunction; *interdiction légale*, loss of civil rights; *interdiction de séjour*, prohibition from entering a specified area. ‖ MILIT. *Tir d'interdiction*, denying fire. ‖ ECCLÉS. Interdict.
interdigital, ale [-diʒital] adj. Interdigital.
interdire [ɛ̃tɛrdiːr] v. tr. (63). To forbid, to prohibit (défendre); *interdire qqch. à qqn*, to forbid s.o. sth.; *interdire à qqn de faire qqch.*, to forbid s.o. to do sth., to prohibit s.o. from doing sth. ‖ To amaze, to confound, to bewilder, to disconcert (étonner). ‖ JUR. To interdict, to prohibit, to veto; *faire interdire qqn*, to have s.o. placed under restraint. ‖ ECCLÉS. To interdict.
interdisciplinaire [ɛ̃tɛrdisiplinɛːr] adj. Interdisciplinary.
interdit, ite [-di, it] adj. Forbidden, prohibited. (V. DÉFENDU.) ‖ Confounded, amazed, bewildered (déconcerté); *demeurer interdit*, to be taken aback. ‖ JUR. Under restraint. ‖ ECCLÉS. Laid under an interdict.
— m. Prohibition, taboo. ‖ ECCLÉS. Interdict; *mettre en interdit*, to lay under an interdict.
intéressant, ante [ɛ̃tɛrɛsã, ãːt] adj. Attractive (avantageux); satisfactory (satisfaisant); *ce n'est pas intéressant pour nous*, it is not worth our while. ‖ Interesting (divertissant). ‖ FAM. *Avoir l'air intéressant*, to be rather fetching; *dans un état intéressant*, in the family way; *un type peu intéressant*, a shady character.
intéressé, ée [-se] adj. Interested (par, in); *être intéressé dans*, to have (ou) take an interest in. ‖ Closely concerned; *la gare intéressée*, the station involved; *les parties intéressées*, the interested parties. ‖ Interested, self-seeking (motif); self-interested, calculating (personne); *amour intéressé*, cupboard love.
— s. Person (ou) party concerned (ou) involved.
intéressement [-smã] m. FIN. Profit-sharing.
intéresser [-se] v. tr. (1). To interest, to concern, to affect (concerner); *cela m'intéresse*, that concerns me. ‖ To interest, to gain (ou) win the interest of [inspirer de l'intérêt]. ‖ To appeal to, to be interesting to (captiver). ‖ COMM., FIN. To give a share (ou) a financial interest to (qqn). ‖ MÉD. To affect (un organe). ‖ SPORTS. To fix a stake for (la partie) [aux cartes].
— v. pr. **S'intéresser**, to be interested, to have an interest (à, in); to concern oneself (à, with).
intérêt [ɛ̃tɛrɛ] m. Interest, advantage, profit

(avantage); *avoir un intérêt personnel en vue*, to have an axe to grind; *c'est l'intérêt qui le guide*, he is guided by self-interest; *il est de votre intérêt de, vous avez intérêt à*, it is in your interest to, it would pay you to; *il y a intérêt à*, it is desirable to; *intérêt bien entendu*, enlightened self-interest; *intérêt personnel*, self-interest; *savoir où est son intérêt*, to know on which side one's bread is buttered. ‖ FIN. Interest (bénéfice); interest, share, part (dans, in); *à intérêts*, interest-bearing (valeurs). ‖ CH. DE F. *D'intérêt local*, local branch (ligne). ‖ FIG. Interest (curiosité); attraction, charm (séduction); *plein d'intérêt*, most diverting; *sans intérêt*, uninteresting, dull. ‖ FIG. Interest, concern (sollicitude); *ressentir un vif intérêt pour qqn*, to take a keen interest in s.o.
interface [ɛ̃tɛrfas] f. Interface.
interférence [ɛ̃tɛrferãːs] f. PHYS., RADIO. Interference.
interférent, ente [-rã, ãːt] adj. PHYS., RADIO. Interfering.
interférer [-re] v. tr. (5). PHYS., RADIO. To interfere.
interféromètre [-rɔmɛtr] m. PHYS. Interferometer.
interféron [-rɔ̃] m. MÉD. Interferon.
interfluve [ɛ̃tɛrflyːv] m. GÉOGR. Interfluve.
intergouvernemental, ale [-guvɛrnəmãtal] adj. Intergovernmental.
intérieur, eure [ɛ̃terjœːr] adj. Inner, inside, interior (chambre, cour). ‖ JUR. Interior; *ministère de l'Intérieur*, Home Office, U. S. Department of the Interior. ‖ COMM., FIN. Domestic, home (marché). ‖ NAUT. Inland (eaux). ‖ FIG. Inward (sentiment); spiritual (vie).
— m. Inside, interior (d'une maison); interior (d'un pays); *à l'intérieur*, inside, on the inside, indoors. ‖ Household affairs (travail ménager); *d'intérieur*, indoor (vêtement); *chaussures d'intérieur*, house-shoes; *femme d'intérieur*, domesticated (ou) houseproud woman; U. S. homemaker; *robe d'intérieur*, house coat.
intérieurement [-mã] adv. Internally. ‖ FIG. Inwardly.
intérim [ɛ̃terim] m. Interim; *dans l'intérim*, in the interim, in the meantime, meanwhile; *par intérim*, acting (gérant).
intérimaire [-mɛːr] adj. Temporary, interim. ‖ Acting (directeur). ‖ U. S. Caretaker (gouvernement).
— s. Substitute, deputy; locum tenens. ‖ Temporary worker, temp. (travailleur).
interindividuel, elle [ɛ̃tɛrɛ̃dividɥɛl] adj. Interpersonal, interindividual.
intériorisation [ɛ̃terjɔrizasjɔ̃] f. Interiorization, internalization.
intérioriser [-rize] v. tr. (1). To interiorize, to internalize.
intériorité [-rite] f. Interiority.
interjectif, ive [ɛ̃tɛrʒɛktif, iːv] adj. GRAMM. Interjectional.
interjection [ɛ̃tɛrʒɛksjɔ̃] f. GRAMM. Interjection. ‖ JUR. Lodging (d'appel).
interjeter [-te] v. tr. (1). GRAMM. To interject. ‖ JUR. To lodge (un appel).
interlignage [ɛ̃tɛrliɲaːʒ] m. Leading out.
interligne [-liɲ] m. Space between the lines; *double interligne*, double space.
— f. Lead.
interligner [-liɲe] v. tr. (1). To interline (un document). ‖ To lead out (en typographie).
interlinéaire [-lineɛːr] adj. Interlinear.
interlinéation [-lineasjɔ̃] f. Interlineation.
interlocuteur [ɛ̃tɛrlɔkytœːr] m. Interlocutor.
interlocution [-sjɔ̃] f. Interlocution.
interlocutoire [-twaːr] adj. JUR. Interlocutory.
— m. JUR. Interlocutory judgment.
interlocutrice [-tris] f. Interlocutress.

interlope [ɛ̃tɛrlɔp] adj. COMM., NAUT. Unauthorized, irregular, illegal. ‖ FIG. Suspect, shady.
— m. NAUT. Interloper, blockade-runner.
interloquer [-lɔke] v. tr. (1). JUR. To award an interlocutory decree against (qqn). ‖ FIG. To disconcert, to nonplus, to take aback. (V. ÉBAHIR.)
interlude [-lyd] m. MUS.. THÉÂTR. Interlude.
intermède [-mɛd] m. THÉÂTR. Interlude.
intermédiaire [-medjɛ:r] adj. Intermediate, intermediary. ‖ TECHN. *Arbre intermédiaire,* countershaft.
— m. Intermediary, medium, go-between; *par l'intermédiaire de,* through the medium of. ‖ Adapter (en photo). ‖ COMM. Middleman.
intermezzo [-mɛdzo] m. MUS. Intermezzo.
interminable [ɛ̃tɛrminabl] adj. Interminable, endless, never-ending.
interminablement [-bləmɑ̃] adv. Interminably.
interministériel, elle [ɛ̃tɛrministɛrjɛl] adj. Interministerial.
intermission [ɛ̃tɛrmisjɔ̃] f. Intermission.
intermittence [-mitɑ̃:s] f. Intermittence; *par intermittence,* intermittently, now and again, off and on. ‖ MÉD. Irregularity (du pouls).
intermittent, ente [-mitɑ̃, ɑ̃:t] adj. Intermittent; occasional. ‖ MÉD. Intermittent (fièvre); irregular (pouls).
intermoléculaire [-mɔlekylɛ:r] adj. PHYS. Intermolecular.
internat [ɛ̃tɛrna] m. Boarding-school (école); boarders; boarding, living-in (régime). ‖ MÉD. Resident medical studentship, U. S. internship.
international, ale [ɛ̃tɛrnasjɔnal] adj., m. GÉOGR., SPORTS. International.
internationale [-na:l] f. International Workers' Association. ‖ « Internationale » (hymne).
internationalisation [-nalizasjɔ̃] f. Internationalization.
internationaliser [-nalize] v. tr. (1). To internationalize.
internationalisme [-nalism] m. Internationalism.
internationalité [-nalite] f. Internationality.
interne [ɛ̃tɛrn] adj. Inner (face). ‖ MATH. Interior. ‖ MÉD. Internal.
— m. Boarder (dans un lycée). ‖ MÉD. Resident medical student, U. S. intern. ‖ SPORTS. Mid-on.
internement [-nəmɑ̃] m. MÉD. Confinement (d'un aliéné). ‖ JUR. Internment (d'un prisonnier); *camp d'internement,* detention camp.
interné, ée [-ne] adj. Interned (prisonnier); confined, certified (aliéné).
— s. Internee (prisonnier); mental hospital inmate.
interner [-ne] v. tr. (1). MÉD. To confine (un aliéné). ‖ JUR. To intern (un prisonnier).
interocéanique [ɛ̃tɛrɔseanik] adj. GÉOGR. Interoceanic.
interosseux, euse [-ɔsø, ø:z] adj. MÉD. Interosseal.
interparlementaire [-parləmɑ̃tɛ:r] adj. JUR. *Commission interparlementaire,* joint committee.
interpellateur, trice [-pɛlatœ:r, tris] s. JUR. Interpellant, questioner.
interpellation [-pɛlasjɔ̃] f. Interpellation; peremptory questioning. ‖ JUR. Question (au Parlement); interpellation, summons (au Parquet).
interpeller [-pɛle] v. tr. (1). To call on, to speak peremptorily to. (V. APOSTROPHER.) ‖ JUR. To question (au Parlement); to summon, to interpellate (au Parquet).
interpénétration [-penetrasjɔ̃] f. Interpenetration.
interpénétrer (s') [-penetre] v. pr. (5). To interpenetrate.
interphone [-fɔn] n. Interphone.

interplanétaire [-planetɛ:r] adj. Interplanetary; outer (espace). ‖ Space (voyage).
interpolateur, trice [-pɔlatœ:r, tris] s. Interpolator.
interpolation [-pɔlasjɔ̃] f. Interpolation.
interpoler [-pɔle] v. tr. (1). To interpolate.
interposer [-poze] v. tr. (1). To interpose (entre, between). ‖ JUR. *Personne interposée,* intermediary. ‖ FIG. To interpose, to bring into play.
— v. pr. S'interposer, to interpose (ou) place oneself (entre, between).
interposition [-pozisjɔ̃] f. Interposition. ‖ JUR. Substitution (de personnes). ‖ FIG. Intervention.
interprétable [-pretabl] adj. Interpretable.
interprétariat [-pretarja] m. Interpretation.
interprétation [-pretasjɔ̃] f. Interpretation, explanation. ‖ MUS., THÉÂTR. Interpretation, rendering.
interprète [-prɛt] s. Interpreter (homme); interpretress (femme). ‖ Expounder, interpreter (d'un texte). ‖ THÉÂTR. Exponent, interpreter.
interpréter [-prete] v. tr. (5). To interpret (traduire). ‖ To explain, to expound, to elucidate (expliquer). ‖ FIG. To interpret, to understand (comprendre); *mal interpréter,* to misunderstand, to misinterpret, to misconstrue, to take amiss.
— v. pr. S'interpréter, to be interpreted.
interprofessionnel, elle [-prɔfɛsjɔnɛl] adj. Interprofessional; *salaire minimum interprofessionnel de croissance,* minimum legal wage.
interrègne [-rɛɲ] m. Interregnum.
interrogateur, trice [ɛ̃tɛrɔgatœ:r, tris] adj. Inquiring, questioning, interrogative.
— s. Interrogator.
interrogatif, ive [-tif, i:v] adj., m. GRAMM. Interrogative.
interrogation [-sjɔ̃] f. Interrogation, questioning. ‖ GRAMM. *Point d'interrogation,* question-mark.
interrogativement [-tivmɑ̃] adv. Interrogatively.
interrogatoire [-twa:r] m. JUR. Interrogatory, examination, questioning.
interroger [ɛ̃tɛrɔʒe] v. tr. (7). To interrogate, to examine, to question. ‖ FIG. To consult.
interrompre [ɛ̃tɛrɔ̃:pr] v. tr. (90). To interrupt, to break in on (une conversation); to interrupt (qqn); to break off, to suspend (des travaux); to interrupt, to break (un voyage). ‖ ELECTR. To break, to cut off, to switch off (un courant).
— v. pr. S'interrompre, to break off, to stop speaking.
interrompu, ue [-rɔ̃py] adj. Interrupted, broken.
interrupteur, trice [-ryptœ:r, tris] adj. Interrupting.
— s. Interruptor.
— m. ELECTR. Contact-breaker, switch.
interruption [-rypsjɔ̃] f. Interruption (d'une conversation, de qqn); suspension, interruption (des travaux); termination (d'un contrat). ‖ ELECTR. Breaking, switching (ou) cutting off. ‖ MÉD. Termination (d'une grossesse).
intersecté, ée [ɛ̃tɛrsɛkte] adj. ARCHIT. Interlacing, intersected. ‖ MATH. Intersected.
intersecter v. tr. (1). To intersect.
— v. pr. S'intersecter, to intersect.
intersection [-sjɔ̃] f. Intersection, crossing (de routes); U. S. intersection. ‖ MATH. Intersection.
intersession [ɛ̃tɛrsesjɔ̃] f. Recess (parlementaire).
intersidéral, ale [ɛ̃tɛrsideral] adj. ASTRON. Intersidereal, interstellar.
intersigne [ɛ̃tɛrsiɲ] m. Portent.
interstellaire [-stɛlɛ:r] adj. ASTRON. Interstellar.
interstice [-stis] m. Interstice, chink, crack.
interstitiel, elle [-stisjɛl] adj. MÉD. Interstitial.
intersyndical, ale [-sɛ̃dikal] adj. Inter-union.
intersyndicale f. Inter-union committee.
intertropical, ale [-trɔpikal] adj. GÉOGR. Intertropical.
interurbain, aine [-yrbɛ̃, ɛn] adj. Interurban. ‖

ELECTR. *Ligne interurbaine,* trunk line, U. S. long distance.
— m. ELECTR. Long distance phone.

intervalle [ɛ̃tɛrval] m. Interval, gap, space, distance (entre deux objets). ‖ Interval, lapse, period (de temps); *dans l'intervalle,* in the meantime; *par intervalles,* intermittently, off and on, now and then. ‖ MUS. Interval.

intervenant, ante [ɛ̃tɛrvənɑ̃, ɑ̃:t] adj. JUR. Intervening.
— s. Intervener.

intervenir [-vəni:r] v. intr. (101). To intervene, to interfere, to step in (personne); *faire intervenir,* to call in. ‖ To happen, to take place, to intervene (événement); to arise (situation). ‖ JUR. To intervene.
— v. impers. *Il intervint un accord,* an arrangement has been made.

intervention [-vɑ̃sjɔ̃] f. Intervention, intervening, interference. ‖ MÉD. Operation, surgical intervention. ‖ JUR. *Intervention parlementaire,* sponsoring of claims.

interventionnisme [-vɑ̃sjɔnism] m. Interventionism.

interventionniste [-vɑ̃sjɔnist]s.Interventionist.

interversion[-vɛrsjɔ̃]f. Inversion, transposition.

intervertébral, ale [-vɛrtebral] adj. MÉD. Intervertebral.

intervertir [-vɛrti:r] v. tr. (2). To invert, to transpose.

interview [ɛ̃tɛrvju] f. Interview.

interviewer [-vjuve] v. tr. (1). To interview.

interviewer [-vjuvœ:r] m. Interviewer.

intervocalique [ɛ̃tɛrvɔkalik] adj. Intervocalic.

intestat [ɛ̃tɛsta] adj. invar. JUR. Intestate.
— loc. prép. *Ab intestat,* intestate (succession); *hériter ab intestat,* to succeed to the estate of one who has died intestate.

intestin, ine [ɛ̃tɛstɛ̃, in] adj. Intestine.
— m. MÉD. Intestine, bowel.

intestinal, ale [-tinal] adj. MÉD. Intestinal.

intimation [ɛ̃timasjɔ̃] f. JUR. Intimation.

intime [ɛ̃tim] adj. Intimate, close (ami); cosy (lieu, pièce); homely, U. S. homelike (soirée). ‖ Inward, deep-seated; rooted (conviction); innermost (nature).
— s. Intimate; close friend.

intimé [ɛ̃time] s. JUR. Respondent.

intimement [ɛ̃timmɑ̃] adv. Intimately.

intimer [ɛ̃time] v. tr. (1). To intimate (v. NOTIFIER); *intimer qqch. à qqn,* to notify s.o. of sth. ‖ JUR. To summons.

intimidable [ɛ̃timidabl] adj. Easily intimidated.

intimidant, ante [ɛ̃timidɑ̃, ɑ̃:t] adj. Intimidating.

intimidateur, trice [-datœ:r, tris] adj. Intimidating.
— s. Intimidator.

intimidation [-dasjɔ̃] f. Intimidation.

intimider [-de] v. tr. (1). To intimidate, to threaten, to frighten, to overawe; to make self-conscious (ou) shy.
— v. pr. **S'intimider,** to get (ou) become nervous; to turn shy.

intimisme [ɛ̃timism] m. Intimism.

intimiste [-mist] adj., s. Intimist.

intimité [ɛ̃timite] f. Intimity, intimacy, familiarity; *dans l'intimité,* in private.

intitulé [ɛ̃tityle] m. Heading (d'un chapitre); title (d'un livre). ‖ JUR. Premises (d'un acte).

intituler v. tr. (1). To entitle, to give a title to.
— **S'intituler,** to call (ou) style oneself, to pass oneself off as.

intolérable [ɛ̃tɔlerabl] adj. Intolerable. (V. INSUPPORTABLE.)

intolérance [-rɑ̃:s] f. Intolerance. ‖ MÉD. *Intolérance à,* inability to assimilate.

intolérant, ante [-rɑ̃] adj. Intolerant.

intolérantisme [-rɑ̃tism] m. ECCLÉS. Intolerance.

intonation [ɛ̃tɔnasjɔ̃] f. Intonation. ‖ MUS. Modulation, pitch.

intouchable [ɛ̃tuʃabl] adj. Untouchable (paria). [V. INTANGIBLE.] ‖ FIN. Uncashable (chèque).
— s. Untouchable.

intoxicant, ante [ɛ̃tɔksikɑ̃, ɑ̃:t] adj. MÉD. Toxic, poisonous.

intoxication [-kasjɔ̃] f. MÉD. Poisoning; *intoxication alimentaire,* food-poisoning.

intoxiquer [-ke] v. tr. (1). MÉD. To poison.

intracellulaire [ɛ̃traselylɛ:r] adj. MÉD. Intracellular.

intradermique [ɛ̃tradɛrmik] adj. MÉD. Intracutaneous, intradermal.

intradermo-réaction [-moreaksjɔ̃] f. MÉD. Intracutaneous (ou) intradermal test.

intrados [ɛ̃trado] m. ARCHIT. Intrados.

intraduisible [ɛ̃tradɥizibl] adj. Untranslatable.

intraitable [ɛ̃trɛtabl] adj. MÉD. Untreatable (maladie). ‖ FIG. Intractable, uncompromising, obstinate (caractère, personne).

intra-muros [ɛ̃tramyro:s] adv. Within the walls.
— adj. invar. Intramural.

intramusculaire [-myskylɛ:r] adj. MÉD. Intramuscular.

intransférable [ɛ̃trɑ̃sferabl] adj. Untransferable.

intransigeance [ɛ̃trɑ̃siʒɑ̃:s] f. Intransigence.

intransigeant, ante [-siʒɑ̃, ɑ̃:t] adj. Intransigent, uncompromising.
— s. Intransigent; die-hard.

intransitif, ive [-zitif, i:v] adj. GRAMM. Intransitive.

intransitivement [-zitivmɑ̃] adv. GRAMM. Intransitively.

intransitivité [-zitivite] f. GRAMM. Intransitivity.

intransmissibilité [ɛ̃trɑ̃smisibilite] f. Intransmissibility.

intransmissible [ɛ̃trɑ̃smisibl] adj. Intransmissible.

intransportable [-pɔrtabl] adj. Untransportable (objet). ‖ MÉD. Unfit to be moved (malade).

intra-utérin, ine [ɛ̃trayterɛ̃, in] adj. MÉD. Intra-uterine.

intraveineux, euse [-vɛnø, ø:z] adj. MÉD. Intravenous.
— f. MÉD. Intravenous injection.

intrépide [ɛ̃trepid] adj. Intrepid, bold, fearless (héros); brazen (menteur).

intrépidement [-dmɑ̃] adv. Intrepidly, boldly.

intrépidité [dite] f. Intrepidity, boldness, fearlessness.

intrigant, ante [-gɑ̃, ɑ̃:t] adj. Intriguing, scheming.
— m. Intriguer, schemer.

intrigue [ɛ̃trig] f. Love-affair (amourette). ‖ Intrigue, machination, plot (complot). ‖ Lobbyism (en politique). ‖ Underhand manœuvres; wire-pulling (brigue). ‖ Plot (en littérature).

intrigué, ée [-ge] adj. Intrigued, puzzled, curious.

intriguer v. tr. (1). To intrigue, to puzzle, to make curious (qqn).
— v. intr. To intrigue, to scheme, to plot.

intrinsèque [ɛ̃trɛ̃sɛk] adj. Intrinsic.

intrinsèquement [-mɑ̃] adv. Intrinsically.

intriqué, ée [ɛ̃trike] adj. Intricate.

introducteur, trice [ɛ̃trɔdyktœ:r, tris] s. Introducer.

introductif, ive [-dyktif, i:v] adj. Introductory.

introduction [-dyksjɔ̃] f. Introduction, insertion (action). ‖ Introduction, bringing in (d'un article); introduction, showing in (de qqn). ‖ Introduction, preface, foreword (avant-propos). ‖ JUR. *Introduc-*

tion d'instance, writ of summons, institution of formal proceedings.

Introduire [-dɥiːr] v. tr. (85). To introduce; to insert (*dans,* in). [V. INSÉRER.] ‖ To introduce, to usher (ou) show in (faire entrer). ‖ JUR. To institute (une instance). ‖ FIG. To introduce, to bring in (une mode).
— v. pr. **S'introduire,** to get in, to find one's way in.

introït [ɛ̃trɔit] m. ECCLÉS. Introit.

introjection [ɛ̃trɔʒɛksjɔ̃] f. PSYCH. Introjection.

intromission [ɛ̃trɔmisjɔ̃] f. BOT., PHYS. Intromission.

intronisation [-nizasjɔ̃] f. Enthronement.

introniser [-nize] v. tr. (1). To enthrone. ‖ FIG. To establish, to set up, to implant (une mode); *introniser parmi,* to foist upon.
— v. pr. **S'introniser,** to become established (mode); to establish oneself.

introspectif, ive [ɛ̃trɔspɛktif, iːv] adj. Introspective.

introspection [-spɛksjɔ̃] f. Introspection.

introuvable [ɛ̃truvabl] adj. Undiscoverable.

introversion [ɛ̃trɔvɛrsjɔ̃] f. Introversion.

introverti, e [-vɛrti] adj. Introvert, introverted.
— s. Introvert.

intrus, use [ɛ̃try, yːz] adj. Intruding.
— s. Intruder, trespasser.

intrusion [-zjɔ̃] f. Intrusion.

intubation [ɛ̃tybaɔjɔ̃] f. MÉD. Intubation.

intuitif, ive [ɛ̃tɥitif, iːv] adj. Intuitive.

intuition [-sjɔ̃] f. Intuition.

intuitivement [-tivmɑ̃] adv. Intuitively.

intumescence [ɛ̃tymɛssɑ̃ːs] f. Intumescence.

intumescent, ente [-sɑ̃, ɑ̃ːt] adj. Intumescent.

inuline [inylin] f. CHIM. Inulin.

inusable [inyzabl] adj. Proof against wear; everlasting. ‖ Long-wearing, giving endless wear (vêtement).

inusité [inyzite] adj. Unusual, uncommon, unwonted (bienveillance); not in use (mot).

inusuel, elle [-zɥɛl] adj. Unusual. (V. RARE.)

inutile [inytil] adj. Useless, fruitless, unavailing (infructueux). ‖ Unnecessary, needless, superfluous (superflu); *estimer inutile de,* to see no point in; *inutile de vous dire,* I need hardly tell you, needless to say. ‖ Hopeless (vain).

inutilement [-lmɑ̃] adv. Uselessly, fruitlessly. ‖ Unnecessarily, needlessly.

inutilisable [-lizabl] adj. Unusable.

inutilisé, ée [-lize] adj. Unused.

inutilité [-lite] f. Inutility, uselessness. ‖ Useless thing.

invagination [ɛ̃vaʒinasjɔ̃] f. MÉD. Invagination.

invaincu, ue [ɛ̃vɛ̃ky] adj. Unconquered, unvanquished.

invalidant, ante [ɛ̃validɑ̃, ɑ̃ːt] adj. *Maladie invalidante,* disabling illness.

invalidation [ɛ̃validasjɔ̃] f. Invalidation.

invalide [ɛ̃valid] adj. MÉD. Invalid, infirm, disabled. ‖ JUR. Invalid.
— s. MÉD. Invalid; infirm (ou) disabled person. ‖ MILIT. Pensioner.

invalider [-de] v. tr. (1). JUR. To unseat (un député); to invalidate (un testament); to quash (une élection).

invalidité [-dite] f. MÉD. Infirmity (d'une personne). ‖ JUR. Invalidity, nullity (d'un contrat).

invariabilité [ɛ̃varjabilite] f. Invariability.

invariable [-rjabl] adj. Invariable, unchanging. ‖ GRAMM. Invariable. ‖ MATH. Constant.

invariablement [-rjabləmɑ̃] adv. Invariably.

invariant, ante [-rjɑ̃, ɑ̃ːt] adj., m. MATH. Invariant.

invasion [ɛ̃vasjɔ̃] f. MILIT. Invasion, inroad. ‖ MÉD. Invasion. ‖ FIG. Invasion, spread.

invective [ɛ̃vɛktiv] f. Invective. ‖ Pl. Abuse.

invectiver [-ve] v. intr. (1). To rail (*contre,* at); to inveigh (*contre,* against).
— v. tr. To rail at, to abuse, to hurl abuse at.

invendable [ɛ̃vɑ̃dabl] adj. COMM. Unsaleable, unmarketable.

invendu, ue [-dy] adj. COMM. Unsold; left over.
— m. COMM. Unsold article, left over (article). ‖ Pl. Returns (journaux).

inventaire [ɛ̃vɑ̃tɛːr] m. COMM. Inventory, stocktaking; *faire son inventaire,* to take stock. ‖ JUR. Inventory.

inventer [-te] v. tr. (1). To invent, to contrive (une machine). [V. DÉCOUVRIR.] ‖ FIG. To manufacture (une excuse); to make up, to invent, to contrive (un mensonge); to coin (un mot). [V. FORGER.]

inventeur, trice [-tœːr, tris] adj. Inventive.
— m. Inventor, discoverer. ‖ JUR. Finder (de trésors). [V. INVENTRICE.]

inventif, ive [-tif, iːv] adj. Inventive; *génie inventif,* inventiveness.

invention [-sjɔ̃] f. Invention, discovery, contrivance (découverte). ‖ Invention, fabrication, fiction, lie (fiction); *tout cela est pure invention,* that's all my eye. ‖ ECCLÉS. *L'invention de la Sainte Croix,* Invention of the Cross.

inventorier [ɛ̃vɑ̃tɔrje] v. tr. (1). COMM. To enter on an inventory (ou) stock-list (un article); to take stock of (des denrées).

inventrice [ɛ̃vɑ̃tris] f. Inventress.

invérifiable [ɛ̃verifjabl] adj. Unverifiable.

inversable [ɛ̃versabl] adj. Uncapsizable.

inverse [ɛ̃vɛrs] adj. Inverse, inverted, opposite. ‖ MATH. *En raison inverse,* in inverse ratio.
— m. Inverse, contrary, opposite; *à l'inverse de,* contrary to; *faire l'inverse,* to do the opposite.

inversement [-səmɑ̃] adv. Inversely.

inverser [-se] v. tr. (1). To reverse, to invert. ‖ ELECTR. To reverse (le courant).
— v. intr. ELECTR. To reverse (courant).

inverseur [-sœːr] m. ELECTR. Throw-over (ou) change-over switch. ‖ TECHN. Reversing device. ‖ AUTOM. *Inverseur des phares,* dip-switch, dimmer.

inversible [-sibl] adj. THÉÂTR. Reversible (film).

inversion [-sjɔ̃] f. ELECTR. Reversal (du courant). ‖ GRAMM., MÉD., MATH., Inversion.

invertébré, ée [ɛ̃vɛrtebre] adj., m. ZOOL. Invertebrate.

inverti, ie [ɛ̃vɛrti] adj. CHIM. Invert.
— s. MÉD. Invert; sexual pervert.

invertir [-tiːr] v. tr. (2). To invert, to reverse (un objet, une image). ‖ ELECTR. To reverse (un courant).

investigateur, trice [ɛ̃vɛstigatœr, tris] adj. Investigating, inquiring, searching.
— s. Investigator.

investigation [-sjɔ̃] f. Investigation, enquiry.

investir [ɛ̃vɛstiːr] v. tr. (2). To invest (*de,* with); to bestow (*de,* on). ‖ FIN. To invest (des fonds). ‖ MILIT. To invest, to beleaguer, to lay siege to (une forteresse). ‖ FIG. *Investir qqn de qqch.,* to bestow sth. on s.o.; *investi de l'autorité,* vested with power; *investir qqn de sa confiance,* to give s.o. one's trust, to place one's trust in s.o.

investissement [-tismɑ̃] m. FIN. Investment. ‖ MILIT. Investment, beleaguering.

investiture [-tityːr] f. Investiture. ‖ ECCLÉS. Induction.

invétéré, ée [ɛ̃vetere] adj. Inveterate, deep-rooted (habitude, mal); confirmed (ivrogne, scélérat).

invétérer (s') [sɛ̃vetere] v. pr. To become inveterate.

invincibilité [ɛ̃vɛ̃sibilite] f. Invincibility.

invincible [-sibl] adj. Invincible (armée). ‖ FIG. Irrefutable (argument); invincible, unshakeable (courage); insuperable (difficulté).

invinciblement [-sibləmɑ̃] adv. Invincibly.

inviolabilité [ɛ̃vjɔlabilite] f. Inviolability.

inviolable [-labl] adj. Inviolable.
inviolablement [-labləmɑ̃] adv. Inviolably.
inviolé, ée [ɛ̃vjɔle] adj. Inviolate.
invisibilité [ɛ̃vizibilite] f. Invisibility.
invisible [-zibl] adj. Invisible.
invisiblement [-zibləmɑ̃] adv. Invisibly.
invitation [ɛ̃vitasjɔ̃] f. Invitation ; *sans invitation,* uninvited ; *sur l'invitation de,* at the invitation (ou) call (ou) request of.
invite [ɛ̃vit] f. Lead, call (aux cartes). ‖ FIG. Incitement, inducement.
invité [-te] s. Guest.
inviter v. tr. (1). To invite, to ask (v. CONVIER) ; *inviter qqn à dîner,* to invite s.o. to dine. ‖ To call for (aux cartes). ‖ FIG. To invite, to court.
invocation [ɛ̃vɔkasjɔ̃] f. Invocation.
invocatoire [-twa:r] adj. Invocatory.
involontaire [ɛ̃vɔlɔ̃tɛ:r] adj. Involuntary, unintentional.
involontairement [-mɑ̃] adv. Involuntarily, unintentionally.
involuté, ée [ɛ̃vɔlyte] adj. BOT. Involute.
involution [-sjɔ̃] f. BOT., MÉD. Involution.
invoquer [ɛ̃vɔke] v. tr. (1). To invoke, to call upon (les saints). ‖ To refer to (une clause). ‖ FIG. To invoke, to put forward ; *invoquer le témoignage de qqn,* to call s.o. to witness ; *invoquer que,* to plead that.
invraisemblable [ɛ̃vrɛsɑ̃blabl] adj. Improbable, unlikely, hard to believe.
invraisemblablement [-blabləmɑ̃] adv. Improbably.
invraisemblance [-blɑ̃:s] f. Improbability, unlikelihood.
invulnérabilité [ɛ̃vylnerabilite] f. Invulnerability.
invulnérable [-rabl] adj. Invulnerable.
iode [jɔd] m. CHIM. Iodine ; *teinture d'iode,* tincture of iodine ; iodine (fam.).
ioder [-de] v. tr. (1). To iodize.
iodique [-dik] adj. CHIM. Iodic.
iodisme [-dism] m. MÉD. Iodism.
iodoforme [-dɔfɔrm] m. MÉD. Iodoform.
iodure [-dy:r] m. CHIM. Iodide.
ion [jɔ̃] m. ELECTR., CHIM., PHYS. Ion.
ionien, enne [jɔnjɛ̃, ɛn] adj., s. GÉOGR. Ionian.
ionique [jɔnik] adj. ARCHIT. Ionic.
ionisation [jɔnizasjɔ̃] f. ELECTR., CHIM., PHYS. Ionization ; *chambre d'ionisation,* cloud chamber.
ioniser [-ze] v. tr. (1). To ionize.
iota [jɔta] m. Iota. ‖ FAM. Jot, whit, iota, tittle.
ipécacuana [ipekakɥana] m. MÉD. Ipecacuanha ; ipecac (fam.).
ira [ira]. V. ALLER (15).
Iran [irɑ̃] m. GÉOGR. Iran.
iranien, enne [iranjɛ̃, ɛn] adj., s. GÉOGR. Iranian.
irascibilité [irassibilite] f. Irascibility, temper ; rattiness (fam.).
irascible [-sibl] adj. Irascible, short-tempered.
ire [i:r] f. † Ire.
iridescence [iridɛssɑ̃:s] f. Iridescence.
iridescent, ente [-sɑ̃, ɑ̃:t] adj. Iridescent.
iridium [iridjɔm] m. CHIM. Iridium.
iris [iris] m. † Iris. ‖ MÉD. Iris (de l'œil). ‖ BOT. Iris, flag.
irisation [-zasjɔ̃] f. Irisation, iridescence.
irisé, ée [-ze] adj. Iridescent.
iriser v. tr. (1). To make iridescent.
irlandais, aise [irlɑ̃dɛ, ɛz] adj. GÉOGR. Irish.
— m. Irishman.
Irlandaise [-dɛ:z] f. Irishwoman.
Irlande [irlɑ̃:d] f. GÉOGR. Ireland.
ironie [irɔni] f. Irony.
ironique [-nik] f. Ironic, ironical.
ironiquement [-nikmɑ̃] adv. Ironically.
ironiser [-nize] v. intr. (1). To speak ironically.
ironiste [-nist] s. Ironist.

irons, iront [irɔ̃]. V. ALLER (15).
irraccommodable [irrakɔmɔdabl] adj. Unmendable.
irrachetable [irraʃtabl] adj. Unredeemable.
irradiation [irradjasjɔ̃] f. Irradiation.
irradier [-dje] v. intr. (1). To radiate, to irradiate.
— v. tr. To irradiate.
irraisonnable [irrɛzɔnabl] adj. Irrational.
irraisonné, ée [-ne] adj. Unreasoned, unreasoning.
irrationnel, elle [irrasjɔnɛl] adj. Irrational.
irrationnellement [-mɑ̃] adv. Irrationally.
irréalisable [irrealizabl] adj. Unrealizable.
irréalisé, ée [-ze] adj. Unrealized.
irréalité [-te] f. Unreality.
irrecevable [irrəsəvabl] adj. Inadmissible (témoignage) ; inacceptable (théorie).
irréconciliabilité [irrekɔ̃siljabilite] f. Irreconcilability.
irréconciliable [-ljabl] adj. Irreconcilable.
irrécouvrable [irrekuvrabl] adj. Irrecoverable, unrecoverable. ‖ FIN. *Créance irrécouvrable,* bad debt.
irrécusable [irrekyzabl] adj. Irrecusable, unimpeachable.
irréductibilité [irredyktibilite] f. Irreductibility.
irréductible [-tibl] adj. MÉD., MATH. Irreductible. FIG. Indomitable, unyielding. (V. INTRAITABLE.)
irréel, elle [irreɛl] adj. Unreal.
irréfléchi, ie [irrefleʃi] adj. Rash, hasty, precipitate (action) ; thoughtless, hare-brained, unthinking (personne).
irréflexion [-flɛksjɔ̃] f. Thoughtlessness.
irréformable [irrefɔrmabl] adj. Unalterable.
irréfragable [-fragabl] adj. Irrefragable.
irréfrangible [-frɑ̃ʒibl] adj. PHYS. Irrefrangible.
irréfutable [irrefytabl] adj. Irrefutable.
irréfutablement [-bləmɑ̃] adv. Irrefutably.
irréfuté, ée [irrefyte] adj. Unrefuted, which has not been refuted (ou) disproved.
irrégularité [irregylarite] f. Irregularity, looseness (de conduite) ; unpunctuality (d'un employé). ‖ Irregularity, unevenness (d'une surface). ‖ GRAMM. Irregularity (d'un verbe). ‖ MÉD. Irregularity, unevenness (du pouls).
irrégulier, ère [-lje, ɛ:r] adj. Unpunctual (employé). ‖ Irregular, uneven (surface). ‖ GRAMM. Irregular (verbe). ‖ MÉD. Irregular, uneven (pouls) ; broken (sommeil). ‖ MILIT. Irregular (troupes). ‖ NAUT. *Navire irrégulier,* tramp steamer. ‖ FIG. Irregular, disorderly (conduite).
— m. pl. MILIT. Irregulars.
irrégulièrement [-ljɛrmɑ̃] adv. Irregularly.
irreligieusement [irreliʒjøzmɑ̃] adv. Irreligiously.
irréligieux, euse [-ʒjø, ø:z] adj. Irreligious.
irréligion [-ʒjɔ̃] f. Irreligion.
irrémédiable [irremedjabl] adj. Irremediable (mal) ; irreparable, irretrievable (désastre).
irrémédiablement [-bləmɑ̃] adv. Irreparably ; irremediably.
irrémissible [irremisibl] adj. Irremissible.
irrémissiblement [-siblmɑ̃] adv. Irremissibly.
irremplaçable [irrɑ̃plasabl] adj. Irreplaceable.
irréparable [irreparabl] adj. Irreparable, irretrievable.
irrépréhensible [irrepreɑ̃sibl] adj. Irreprehensible.
irrépressible [irreprɛsibl] adj. Irrepressible.
irréprochable [irreprɔʃabl] adj. Irreproachable, blameless.
irréprochablement [-bləmɑ̃] adv. Irreproachably.
irrésistible [irrezistibl] adj. Irresistible.
irrésistiblement [-bləmɑ̃] adv. Irresistibly.
irrésolu, ue [irrezɔly] adj. Irresolute, hesitant (personne) ; unsolved (problème).

irrésolument [-lymɑ̃] adv. Irresolutely.

irrésolution [-lysjɔ̃] f. Irresolution.

irrespect [irrɛspɛ] m. Disrespect, disregard.

irrespectueusement [-pɛktɥøzmɑ̃] adv. Disrespectfully.

irrespectueux, euse [-pɛktɥø, ø:z] adj. Disrespectful.

irrespirable [irrɛspirabl] adj. Irrespirable, unbreathable.

irresponsabilité [irrɛspɔ̃sabilite] f. Irresponsibility.

irresponsable [-sabl] adj. Irresponsible.

irrétrécissable [irretresisabl] adj. Unshrinkable.

irrévérence [irreverɑ̃:s] f. Irreverence.

irrévérencieusement [-rɑ̃sjøzmɑ̃] adv. Irreverently, disrespectfully.

irrévérencieux, euse [-rɑ̃sjø, ø:z] adj. Irreverent, disrespectful.

irréversibilité [irrevɛrsibilite] f. Irreversibility, irreversibleness.

irréversible [irrevɛrsibl] adj. Irreversible.

irrévocabilité [irrevɔkabilite] f. Irrevocability.

irrévocable [-kabl] adj. Irrevocable.

irrévocablement [-kabləmɑ̃] adv. Irrevocably.

irrigable [irigabl] adj. Irrigable.

irrigateur [-gatœ:r] m. AGRIC. Hose. ‖ MÉD. Irrigator (pour blessures); enema, douche (pour injections, lavements).

irrigation [-gaɛjɔ̃] f. AGRIC., MÉD. Irrigation.

irriguer [-ge] v. tr. (1). AGRIC., MÉD. To irrigate.

irritabilité [iritabilite] f. Irritability.

irritable [-tabl] adj. Irritable.

irritant, ante [-tɑ̃, ɑ̃:t] adj. Irritating.
— m. Irritant.

irritation [-tasjɔ̃] f. MÉD. Irritation, inflammation. ‖ FIG. Irritation, annoyance.

irrité, ée [-te] adj. MÉD. Inflamed (peau). ‖ FIG. Irritated, angry (personne).

irriter [-te] v. tr. (1). MÉD. To irritate, to inflame (la peau). ‖ FIG. To irritate, to make angry, to vex (qqn).
— v. pr. S'**irriter**. MÉD. To become inflamed. ‖ FIG. To become annoyed (ou) angry (personne).

irruption [irrypsjɔ̃] f. Irruption, invasion (des barbares); *faire irruption dans,* to burst into. ‖ Overflowing (d'une rivière).

Isabelle [izabɛl] adj. invar. Biscuit-coloured.
— m. Biscuit-colour. ‖ ZOOL. Light bay horse.

isard [iza:r] m. ZOOL. Izard.

isba [isba] f. Isba, izba.

islam [islam] m. Islam.

islamique [-mik] adj. Islamic.

islamisation [-mizasjɔ̃] f. Islamization.

islamiser [-mize] v. tr. (1). To Islamize.

islamisme [-mism] m. Islamism.

islandais, aise [islɑ̃dɛ, ɛ:z] adj. GÉOGR. Icelandic.
— s. GÉOGR. Icelander.

Islande [islɑ̃:d] f. GÉOGR. Iceland.

isobare [izɔba:r] adj. Isobaric.
— f. Isobar.

isocèle [izɔsɛl] adj. MATH. Isosceles.

isochromatique [izɔkrɔmatik] adj. Isochromatic.

isochrone [izɔkrɔn], **isochronique** [-nik] adj. Isochronous.

isocline [izɔklin] adj. PHYS. Isoclinal.
— f. PHYS. Isoclinal line.

isogone [izɔgɔn] adj. MATH. Isogonic.

isolable [izɔlabl] adj. Isolable. ‖ ELECTR. Insulatable.

isolant, ante [-lɑ̃, ɑ̃:t] adj. Isolating. ‖ *Bouteille isolante,* vacuum (ou) Thermos flask. ‖ ELECTR. Insulating. ‖ ARCHIT. *Couche isolante, imperméable,* damp-proof course.
— m. ELECTR. Insulator.

isolateur, trice [-latœ:r, tris] adj. ELECTR. Insulating.
— m. ELECTR. Insulator.

isolation [-lasjɔ̃] f. TECHN., ELECTR. Insulation. ‖ PSYCH. Isolation.

isolationnisme [-lasjɔnism] m. Isolationism.

isolationniste [-lasjɔnist] adj., s. Isolationist.

isolé, ée [-le] adj. Isolated (cas); detached, lonely (maison); single (son). ‖ ELECTR. Insulated. ‖ MILIT. Sporadic (attaque).

isolement [-lmɑ̃] m. Isolation, loneliness, seclusion. ‖ ELECTR. Insulation.

isolément [-lemɑ̃] adv. Individually, singly, separately.

isoler [-le] v. tr. (1). To isolate, to detach (des objets). ‖ CHIM. To isolate. ‖ ELECTR. To insulate.
— v. pr. S'**isoler,** to become isolated, to cut oneself off.

isoloir [-lwa:r] m. Polling-booth. ‖ ELECTR. Insulator.

isomère [izɔmɛ:r] adj. CHIM. Isomeric.
— m. CHIM. Isomer.

isométrique [izɔmetrik] adj. GÉOL., MATH., MÉD. Isometric.

isomorphe [izɔmɔrf] adj. Isomorphous, isomorphic.

isomorphisme [-fism] m. Isomorphism.

isotherme [izɔtɛrm] adj. GÉOGR. Isothermal. ‖ AUTOM. *Camion isotherme,* insulated truck.
— f. GÉOGR. Isotherm, isothermal line.

isotope [izɔtɔp] adj. PHYS. Isotopic.
— m. PHYS. Isotope.

isotrope [-trɔp] adj. CHIM., PHYS. Isotropic.

Israël [israɛl] m. GÉOGR. Israel.

israélien, enne [-ɛljɛ̃, ɛn] adj., s. GÉOGR. Israeli.

israélite [-elit] adj. Israelite, Israeli, Jewish.
— s. Israelite, Israeli, Jew.

issu, ue [isy] adj. Born (de, of); sprung (de, from); descended (de, from).
— m. By-product.

issue f. Outlet, exit, way out (sortie). ‖ AGRIC. Pl. Middlings, sharps (de blé). ‖ FIG. Outcome, end, upshot, issue, result; *à l'issue de,* at the end (ou) close of; *situation sans issue,* deadlock, impasse; dead end (fam.).

isthme [ism] m. GÉOGR. Isthmus.

isthmique [-mik] adj. GÉOGR. Isthmian.

italianisant, ante [italjanizɑ̃, ɑ̃:t] s. Italianist. ‖ ARTS. Italianizer.

italianiser [italjanize] v. tr. (1). To Italianize.

italianisme [-nism] m. Italianism.

Italie [itali] f. GÉOGR. Italy.

italien, enne [-ljɛ̃, ɛn] adj., s. GÉOGR. Italian.
— m. GRAMM. Italian (langue).

italique [-lik] adj., m. Italic.

item [itɛm] adv., m. invar. Item, ditto.

itératif, ive [iteratif, i:v] adj. JUR. Reiterated (sommation). ‖ GRAMM. Iterative.

itinéraire [itinerɛ:r] adj. Itinerary.
— m. Itinerary; route; guide-book.

itinérant, ante [-rɑ̃, ɑ̃:t] adj. Itinerant.

itou [itu] adv. POP. Also, likewise, too.

I.U.T. [iyte] m. Abrév. de *Institut universitaire de technologie,* polytechnic.

ivoire [ivwa:r] m. Ivory. ‖ MÉD. Dentine.

ivoirerie [-rəri] f. Ivory trade.

ivoirien, enne [-rjɛ̃, ɛn] adj. GÉOGR. Of (ou) from the Ivory Coast.
— s. GÉOGR. Native (ou) inhabitant of the Ivory Coast.

ivoirin [-rɛ̃] adj. Ivory.

ivraie [ivrɛ] f. BOT. Darnel, tare. ‖ FIG. *Le bon grain et l'ivraie,* the wheat and the tares.

ivre [i:vr] adj. Drunk, intoxicated; *ivre mort,* dead drunk. ‖ FIG. Drunk (de joie, d'orgueil).

ivresse [ivrɛs] f. Drunkenness, intoxication. (V. ÉBRIÉTÉ.) ‖ FIG. Transport, ecstasy, rapture.

ivrogne, esse [ivrɔɲ, ɛs] s. Drunkard, tippler; boozer, soak, pub-crawler (fam.).

— (f. IVROGNE) adj. Drunken.
ivrognerie [-ri] f. Drunkenness.

J

J [ʒi] m. J, j.
jabiru [ʒabiry] m. ZOOL. Jabiru.
jable [ʒabl] m. CHIM. Croze (de tonneau).
jabler [-ble] v. tr. (1). To croze.
jaborandi [ʒabɔrɑ̃di] m. BOT., MÉD. Jaborandi.
jabot [ʒabo] m. Frill; jabot (parure). ‖ Crop (d'oiseau). ‖ FAM. Bread-basket; enfler le jabot, to put on airs; se remplir le jabot, to have a good tuck-in; to eat a bellyful (pop.).
jabotage [ʒabɔta:ʒ] m. FAM. Jabbering, chattering; gossiping.
jaboter [-te] v. intr. (1). FAM. To jabber.
jaboteur [-tœ:r] f. Jabberer, chatterer; gossiper.
jacasse [ʒakas] f. ZOOL. Magpie. ‖ FAM. Chatterbox (femme).
jacasser [-se] v. intr. (1). To chatter (pie). ‖ FAM. To jabber, to chatter, to gossip; U. S. to yak, to chin (pop.).
jacasserie [-sri] f. Chatter, gossip.
jacasseur, euse [-sœ:r, ø:z] s. FAM. Chatterbox, gasbag, gossip.
jachère [ʒaʃɛ:r] f. AGRIC. Fallow; fallow ground; laisser une parcelle en jachère, to let a plot lie fallow.
jachérer [ʒaʃere] v. tr. (5). AGRIC. To plough up; U. S. to plow; to fallow.
jacinthe [ʒasɛ̃:t] f. BOT. Hyacinth; bluebell (des bois).
Jack [ʒak] m. Jack (du téléphone).
jacobin [ʒakɔbɛ̃] m. Jacobin.
jacobinisme [-binism] m. Jacobinism.
jacobite [ʒakɔbit] adj. Jacobite, Jacobitical.
— s. Jacobite.
jacquard [ʒaka:r] m. Jacquard loom (métier); Jacquard weave (tricot).
jacquerie [ʒakri] f. Peasant revolt, jacquerie.
Jacques [ʒa:k] m. James. ‖ FAM. Faire le jacques, to play the fool; Maître Jacques, Jack-of-all-trades.
jacquet [ʒakɛ] m. Backgammon (jeu); backgammon board (table, trictrac).
Jacquot [ʒako] m. Polly, Poll (perroquet). ‖ Jimmy, Jim (personne).
jactance [ʒaktɑ̃s] f. Bragging; boasting; swank.
jacter [-te] v. tr., intr. POP. To jaw.
jaculatoire [ʒakylatwa:r] adj. ECCLÉS. Ejaculatory (oraison).
jade [ʒad] m. Jade.
jadis [ʒadis] adv. Once upon a time; in days of old, in days gone by; formerly; du temps jadis, of long ago. (V. ANCIENNEMENT.)
jaguar [ʒagwa:r] m. ZOOL. Jaguar.
jaillir [ʒaji:r] v. intr. (2). To gush out, to rush out, to burst forth (eau); to spout (geyser); to shoot (flamme); to flash (lumière); to spurt (sang) [v. GICLER]; faire jaillir des étincelles, to strike sparks. ‖ FIG. To burst forth (cri); to rise (colonne); faire jaillir la vérité, to force the truth out.
jaillissant, ante [-jisɑ̃, ɑ̃:t] adj. Gushing, spout-

ing; flashing; une source jaillissante, gusher (de pétrole).
jaillissement [-jismɑ̃] m. Gush, spurt; spouting, gushing out; flashing; springing out. ‖ ELECTR. Sparking, flash.
jais [ʒɛ] m. Jet; noir comme du jais, jet-black.
jalon [ʒalɔ̃] m. Levelling-rod; surveyor's staff; pole. ‖ FIG. Plan, foundation, path; poser des jalons pour, to broach (une transaction); to prepare the ground for (un travail).
jalonnement [-lɔnmɑ̃] m. Staking out; marking.
jalonner [-lɔne] v. tr. (1). To stake out, to mark out; jalonner une route, to blaze a trail (à, for). ‖ FIG. To mark out.
jalonneur [-lɔnœ:r] m. Leader, staffman. ‖ MILIT. Marker.
jalousement [ʒaluzmɑ̃] adv. Jealously.
jalouser [-ze] v. tr. (1). To be jealous of; to envy.
jalousie [-zi] f. Jealousy; envy. ‖ ARCHIT. Awning, Venetian blind. ‖ BOT. Sweet-William.
jaloux, ouse [ʒalu, u:z] adj. Watchful, careful (œil); jealous, envious (de, of) [envieux]. ‖ FIG. Jaloux de, eager for, anxious to (anxieux).
— s. Jealous person; faire des jaloux, to make people jealous, to arouse jealousy.
jamaïquain, aine [ʒamaikɛ̃, ɛn] adj., s. GÉOGR. Jamaican.
Jamaïque [-maik] f. GÉOGR. Jamaica.
jamais [ʒamɛ] adv. Never (sens négatif); ever (sens positif); ne... jamais, never; jamais de la vie!, never!, no fear!, out of the question!, not on your life!; pour jamais, for ever, U. S. forever; jamais plus, never again, nevermore.
jambage [ʒɑ̃ba:ʒ] m. Down-stroke, pot-hook (de lettre). ‖ ARCHIT. Jamb; foundation-wall.
jambe [ʒɑ̃:b] f. Leg; jambe de bois, wooden leg; il a couru à toutes jambes, he ran as fast as his legs could take him. ‖ ARCHIT. Prop, strut, brace, stay. ‖ FAM. Ça vous fera une belle jambe, that won't get you very far; par-dessous la jambe, careless, perfunctory (travail); prendre ses jambes à son cou, to take to one's heels; tirer dans les jambes de, to play a low trick on.
jambé, ée [ʒɑ̃be] adj. Bien jambé, with well-shaped legs; with a neat ankle, U. S. with a nice pair of gams (fam.).
jambette [-bɛt] f. Small leg. ‖ ARCHIT. Stanchion, purlin-post, prop.
jambier [-bje] m. MÉD. Tibialis.
jambière [-bjɛ:r] f. † Greave. ‖ MILIT. Legging. ‖ MÉD. Stocking. ‖ SPORT. Shin-guard, pad.
jambon [-bɔ̃] m. CULIN. Ham; jambon blanc, pale ham; œufs au jambon, ham and eggs.
jambonneau [-bɔno] m. CULIN. Knuckle of ham.
jamboree [ʒɑ̃bɔri] m. Jamboree.
janissaire [ʒanisɛ:r] m. Janissary.
jansénisme [ʒɑ̃senism] m. Jansenism.
janséniste [-nist] adj. s. Jansenist.
jante [ʒɑ̃:t] f. Rim.
jantille [ʒɑ̃ti:j] f. Paddle.

janvier [ʒɑ̃vje] m. January; *le premier janvier,* January the first, the first of January, U. S. January first.
Japon [ʒapɔ̃] m. GÉOGR. Japan. ‖ ARTS. Japanese porcelain.
Japonais, aise [ʒapɔnɛ, ɛːz] adj., s. GÉOGR. Japanese.
— m. GRAMM. Japanese (langue).
japonaiserie [-nɛzri] f. ARTS. Japanese curio.
japonisant [-nizɑ̃] m. Student of Japanese.
japoniste [-nist] m. ARTS. Japonist.
jappement [ʒapəmɑ̃] m. Yelping, yelp, yapping, yap.
japper [-pe] v. intr. (1). To yelp, to yap.
jappeur, euse [-pœːr, øːz] adj. Yelping, yapping.
— s. Yelping (ou) yapping dog.
jaquette [ʒakɛt] f. Jacket, coat (de femme); morning-coat; U. S. cut away (d'homme).
jarde [ʒard] f. Bog-spavin (du cheval).
jardin [ʒardɛ̃] m. Garden; *jardin d'acclimatation,* Zoo; *jardin potager,* market-garden, vegetable garden; *jardin anglais,* landscape (ou) informal garden. ‖ *Jardin d'enfants,* kindergarten. ‖ THÉÂTR. *Côté jardin,* prompt-side, « P. S. ».
jardinage [ʒardina:ʒ] m. Gardening (action); garden-produce (produit). [V. HORTICULTURE.] ‖ Flaw (du diamant).
jardiner [-ne] v. intr. (1). To garden.
jardinet [-nɛ] m. Small garden.
jardineux, euse [-nø, øːz] adj. Cloudy, spotty.
jardinier [-nje] s. Gardener; *jardinier paysagiste,* landscape gardener (ou) U. S. architect.
— adj. *Culture jardinière,* horticulture.
jardinière [-njɛːr] f. Flower-stand. ‖ Two-wheeled hand-cart (voiture). ‖ CULIN. Mixed vegetables (plat); vegetable soup (potage); *bœuf jardinière,* beef jardinière. ‖ ZOOL. Ortolan.
jardon [ʒardɔ̃] m. V. JARDE.
jargon [ʒargɔ̃] m. Jargon, cant; *jargon administratif,* officialese. ‖ Gibberish (d'animal, d'idiot). ‖ FAM. Lingo.
jargonner [-gɔne] v. intr. (1). To talk jargon.
jarre [ʒaːr] f. Jar. ‖ ELECTR. *Jarre électrique,* Leyden jar.
jarret [ʒarɛ] m. Hock (de cheval); back of the knee (d'homme); *couper le jarret à,* to hamstring. ‖ CULIN. *Jarret de bœuf, de veau,* shin of beef, knuckle of veal. ‖ ARCHIT. Bulge. ‖ FAM. *Avoir du jarret,* to be strong in the leg.
jarreté, ée [ʒarte] adj. ZOOL. Close-hocked (cheval). ‖ ARCHIT. Bulging.
jarretelle [ʒartɛl] f. Suspender, U. S. garter.
jarretière [ʒartjɛːr] f. Garter. ‖ NAUT. Gasket.
jarrettes [ʒarɛt] f. pl. Socks, half-hose.
jars [ʒaːr] m. ZOOL. Gander.
jas [ʒɑ] m. NAUT. Stock (d'une ancre).
jaser [ʒaze] v. intr. (1). To chatter, to gossip, to prate, to gab, to jabber; to talk, to twaddle; U. S. to yak (v. BAVARDER); *cela a fait jaser,* that caused a lot of gossip. ‖ To twitter (oiseau); to cackle (poule); to babble (ruisseau). ‖ FAM. To blab, to blow the gaff (avec indiscrétion).
jaseur, euse [-zœːr, øːz] adj. Talkative; gossiping, U. S. tattletale.
— s. Jabberer, gossip (bavard); blabber, U. S. tattler, tattletale (indiscret). ‖ ZOOL. Waxwing.
jasmin [ʒasmɛ̃] m. BOT. Jasmine.
jaspage [ʒaspa:ʒ] m. Mottling, marbling.
jaspe [ʒasp] m. Jasper; *jaspe sanguin,* bloodstone. ‖ Marbling (en reliure).
jasper [ʒaspe] v. tr. (1). To marble, to dot, to vein, to mottle.
jaspiner [ʒaspine] v. intr. (1). POP. To jaw, to chatter (bavarder); to tattle, to let the cat out of the bag (vendre la mèche).
jaspure [ʒaspyːr] f. Marbling.

jatte [ʒat] f. Flat bowl; basin.
jattée [-te] f. Bowlful; basinful.
jauge [ʒoːʒ] f. Gauge. ‖ AUTOM. Dipstick, petrol-gauge. ‖ NAUT. Tonnage. ‖ AGRIC. Trench. ‖ TECHN. Gauge, gauging-rod.
jaugeage [ʒoʒa:ʒ] m. Gauging, measurement.
jauger [-ʒe] v. tr. (1). To gauge, to measure. ‖ FIG. To size up (un homme).
jaugeur [-ʒœːr] m. Gauger.
jaunâtre [ʒonɑːtr] adj. Yellowish; sallow (teint).
jaune [ʒoːn] adj. Yellow (couleur, race); tan (cuir); brown (souliers); sallow (teint); *au teint jaune,* sallow-looking; bilious-looking. ‖ MÉD. Yellow (fièvre). ‖ GÉOGR. *La mer Jaune,* the Yellow Sea.
— m. Yellow (couleur); man of yellow race (homme). ‖ *Jaune d'œuf,* yolk. ‖ FAM. Blackleg, scab (gréviste).
— adv. *Rire jaune,* to give a forced laugh, to give a sickly smile.
jaunet, ette [ʒonɛ, ɛːt] adj. Yellowish.
— m. BOT. Yellow water-lily. ‖ FAM. Gold coin.
jaunir [-niːr] v. tr. (2). To yellow, to colour yellow.
— v. intr. To turn yellow; to fade.
jaunissant, ante [-nisɑ̃, ɑ̃ːt] adj. Turning yellow (en général); ripening (moissons).
jaunisse [ʒonis] f. MÉD. Jaundice. ‖ FAM. *En faire une jaunisse,* to be green with envy.
jaunissement [-nismɑ̃] m. Yellowing.
Java [ʒava] f. GÉOGR. Java.
java f. MUS. Java, popular waltz. ‖ FIG., POP. *Faire la java,* to go on a binge, to paint the town red.
javanais, aise [-nɛ, ɛːz] adj., s. GÉOGR. Javanese.
— m. GRAMM. Javanese. ‖ FAM. Slang in which *ave* is inserted into syllables.
javel [ʒavɛl] f. *Eau de Javel,* bleaching water, bleach, U. S. Javelle water.
javelage [ʒavla:ʒ] m. AGRIC. Laying in loose sheaves (ou) swaths.
javeler [-le] v. tr. (5). AGRIC. To lay ready for sheafing.
javeleur [-lœːr] s. AGRIC. Reaper, harvester.
javeline [ʒavlin] f. † Javelin (arme).
javeline f. AGRIC. Loose sheaf.
javelle [ʒavɛl] f. AGRIC. Swath, loose sheaf (de blé); bunch of vine-twigs (de vigne).
javellisation [ʒavɛlizasjɔ̃] f. Chlorination, sterilization (de l'eau).
javelliser [-ze] v. tr. (1). To chlorinate.
javelot [ʒavlo] m. Javelin. ‖ SPORTS. *Lancement du javelot,* throwing the javelin.
jazz [dja:z] m. MUS. Jazz (musique); jazz band (orchestre).
J.-C. Abrév. de *Jésus-Christ* (v. JÉSUS).
je [ʒə] pron. pers. I. ‖ **Je-m'en-fichisme, je-m'en-foutisme,** m. POP. Couldn't-care-less attitude, U. S. don't-give-a-damn attitude. ‖ **Je-m'en-fichiste, je-m'en-foutiste,** adj. POP. Casual, cynical; s. casual (ou) cynical sort of person. ‖ **Je-ne-sais-quoi,** m. inv. Indefinable something (ou) touch. ‖ **Je-sais-tout,** m. Know-all.
Jean [ʒɑ̃] m. John (diminutif : Jack, Jackie, Johnny). ‖ **Jean-foutre,** m. inv. POP. Slob, bastard, good-for-nothing.
jean [dʒin], **jeans** [dʒins] m. Jeans (pantalon). ‖ Denim (tissu); *jupe en jean,* denim skirt.
Jeanne [ʒan] f. Jean, Jane, Joan; *Jeanne d'Arc,* Joan of Arc; *à la Jeanne d'Arc,* bobbed (cheveux).
Jeannette [ʒanɛt] f. Janet, Jenny (nom). ‖ Gold cross (ornement). ‖ Sleeve-board (à repasser). ‖ Brownie (girl-guide).
Jeep [dʒip] f. (nom déposé). MILIT. Jeep.
Jéhovah [ʒeova] m. Jehovah, Yahveh.
jejunum [ʒeʒynɔm] m. MÉD. Jejunum.
jenny [ʒɛni] f. TECHN. Spinning jenny.

jérémiade [ʒeremja:d] f. FAM. Jeremiad.
jeroboam [ʒerɔbɔam] m. Jeroboam, double magnum.
jerrycan [djɛrikan] m. Petrol-can, jerrycan.
Jersey [ʒɛrzɛ] f. GÉOGR. Jersey.
jersey m. Jersey (chandail, tissu); *point de jersey*, stocking-stitch.
jersiais, aise [-zjɛ, ɛ:z] adj. GÉOGR. Of (ou) from Jersey. ‖ AGRIC. Jersey (vache).
— s. GÉOGR. Native (ou) inhabitant of Jersey.
jésuite [ʒesɥit] m. ECCLÉS. Jesuit, Jesuit priest. ‖ FIG. Hypocrite, Jesuit.
— adj. FAM. Jesuitical, Jesuit-like; hypocritical.
jésuitique [-tik] adj. Jesuitical, Jesuit-like; plausible.
jésuitisme [-tism] m. Jesuitism.
Jésus [ʒezy] m. ECCLÉS. Jesus Christ, Jesus; *av. J.-C.*, B. C. (Before Christ); *apr. J.-C.*, A. D. (Anno Domini).
— adj. Imperial (papier).
jet [ʒɛ] m. Throwing, casting (action); throw (résultat). ‖ Jet, stream (d'eau, de gaz); burst (de flammes); flash (de lumière); spurt (de sang); jet, blast (de vapeur); *jet d'eau*, fountain, jet of water. ‖ AGRIC. Shoot (pousse). ‖ SPORTS. Pitching (au baseball); ball, bowling (au cricket); cast (à la pêche). ‖ MILIT. *Arme de jet*, missile. ‖ TECHN. Casting (du métal). ‖ NAUT. Jetsam. ‖ LOC. *A jet continu*, continuously; *à un jet de pierre*, at a stone's throw; *d'un seul jet*, at one go; *du premier jet*, at the first attempt; *un premier jet*, a first (ou) rough sketch.
jet [dʒɛt] m. AVIAT. Jet.
jeté [ʒəte] m. Step (à la danse). ‖ Over (au tricot).
jetée f. Pier, jetty; breakwater.
jeter v. tr. (8 a). To throw, to cast, to throw away. (V. LANCER.) ‖ To toss (négligemment); to shed (en versant); to dart, to fling, to hurl, to dash (violemment); *jeter à bas*, to throw down, to pull down; *jeter une cigarette*, to throw away a cigarette; *jeter une pierre à*, to throw a stone at. ‖ To let out, to utter (un cri); to emit (des étincelles); to throw out (des flammes); to jot down (des notes); to cast (une ombre, un sort); *jeter qqch. au nez de qqn*, to fling sth. in s.o.'s face; *jeter qqn à la porte*, to turn s.o. out; *jeter un regard sur*, to cast a glance at. ‖ ARCHIT. To lay (des fondements); *jeter un pont par-dessus une brèche*, to bridge a gap. ‖ NAUT. *Jeter à la mer*, to jettison. ‖ MÉD. *Jeter du pus*, to discharge pus. ‖ LOC. *Jeter son argent par les fenêtres*, to squander one's money; *jeter son bonnet par-dessus les moulins*, to throw propriety to the winds, to throw one's cap over the wind-mill; *jeter le discrédit sur*, to throw discredit upon. ‖ FAM. *N'en jetez plus!*, dry up!, that's enough!
— v. intr. BOT. To shoot (plante). ‖ MÉD. To run, to discharge (abcès). ‖ ZOOL. To swarm (abeilles).
— v. pron. Se jeter, to throw oneself, to rush; *se jeter sur* (ou) *contre un arbre*, to crash into a tree (auto); *se jeter au cou de qqn*, to fall on s.o.'s neck; *se jeter sur*, to pounce on (aigle); to rush at (personne); *se jeter tête baissée sur*, to run headlong at; *elle s'est jetée à sa tête*, she threw herself at him. ‖ To flow (cours d'eau) [*dans*, into].
jeteur [-tœ:r] s. Thrower (aux dés); *jeteuse de sort*, witch, sorceress.
jeton [-tɔ̃] m. Counter; *jeton de téléphone*, telephone token, U. S. slug. ‖ JUR. *Jetons de présence*, director's fees. ‖ FIG. *Faux comme un jeton*, false to the core.
jeu [ʒø] (pl. **jeux**) m. Play, game, sport (v. AMUSEMENT); *jeu d'adresse*, sleight of hand, game of skill; *jeu de cartes*, pack (ou) U. S. deck of cards; *jeu de croquet*, croquet set; *jeu de dames*, draughts, U. S. checkers; *jeu de patience*, puzzle;

jeux de plein air, outdoor games; *jeu de quilles*, skittles (jeu); skittle-alley (lieu); *jeu de société*, parlour game; *avoir un beau jeu*, to have a good hand; *étaler son jeu*, to reveal one's hand, to lay one's cards on the table. ‖ Gambling, gaming (jeu d'argent); stake (enjeu); *jeu de hasard*, game of chance; *jouer gros jeu*, to play for high stakes; *maison de jeu*, gambling house; *perdre une fortune au jeu*, to gamble away a fortune. ‖ Set, assortment (assortiment). ‖ FIG. Speculation (à la Bourse); *intérêts en jeu*, interests at stake. ‖ COMM. *Jeu d'écritures*, trick of accounting. ‖ SPORTS. *Jeu serré*, close game; *en jeu*, in play; *hors jeu*, out, out of play, off-side. ‖ THÉÂTR. Acting; *jeu de lumière*, play of light; *jeu de scène*, stage business; *jeu muet*, dumb-show. ‖ ARTS. Playing (musique); style, stop (d'orgue). ‖ TECHN. Looseness, slack; *avoir du jeu*, to be loose, to be slack. ‖ FIG. Action; *y aller franc jeu*, to go right ahead; *dévoiler son jeu*, to show one's hand; *entrer en jeu*, to come into play (ou) action; *être en jeu*, to be at stake; *faire le jeu de qqn*, to play into s.o.'s hand; *double jeu*, U. S. double cross; *jouer franc jeu*, to play fair; *mettre tout en jeu*, to stake everything, to use all one's resources. ‖ FIG. *Jeu de mots*, play upon words, pun; *jeu d'esprit*, witticism; *jeu de physionomie*, expression of the face; *vieux jeu*, old-fashioned.
jeudi [ʒødi] m. Thursday; *jeudi saint*, Maundy Thursday; *la semaine des quatre jeudis*, a month of Sundays.
jeun (à) [aʒœ̃] adv. Fasting; before breakfast, on an empty stomach. ‖ Sober.
jeune [ʒœn] adj. Young (d'âge); youthful (d'esprit); junior (plus jeune); *jeune âge*, youth; *jeune garçon*, lad, youth, youngster; *jeune fille*, girl, young lady, lass; *il est plus jeune que moi de deux ans*, he is my junior by two years; *Pline le Jeune*, Pliny the Younger. ‖ Juvenile (aspect). ‖ FAM. Green, immature, callow, adolescent-minded (inexpérimenté).
— adv. Youthfully.
— s. Young one; youth; young man (garçon); young girl (fille); *les jeunes*, the young; the younger ones. ‖ Pl. Young (d'un animal). ‖ THÉÂTR. *Jeune premier*, juvenile (ou) U. S. romantic lead; *jeune première*, leading lady.
jeûne [ʒø:n] m. Fast; fasting; *jour de jeûne*, fast-day; *rompre le jeûne*, to break one's fast.
jeûner [-ne] v. intr. (1). To fast, to abstain from food.
jeunesse [ʒønɛs] f. Youth; boyhood; girlhood; *il faut que jeunesse se passe*, boys will be boys, youth will have its fling; *ne pas être de la première jeunesse*, to be no longer in the first flush of youth. ‖ Young people; *la jeunesse d'aujourd'hui*, the youth of to-day, modern youth; *livres pour la jeunesse*, children's books. ‖ FAM. Girl.
jeunet, ette [-nɛ, ɛt] adj. Youngish, rather young.
jeûneur [ʒønœ:r] s. One who fasts.
jeunot, otte [ʒøno, ɔt] adj. FAM. Young and raw.
— m. FAM. Raw youth.
jiu-jitsu [dʒy-dʒitsy] m. SPORTS. Jiu-jitsu.
J.O. [ʒio] m. Abrév. de *Journal officiel*, official French government publication.
— m. pl. Abrév. de *jeux Olympiques*, Olympic Games.
joaillerie [ʒɔɑjri] f. Jewellery, U. S. jewelry (bijoux); jeweller's trade (commerce).
joaillier [-je] s. Jeweller, U. S. jeweler.
job [ʒɔb] m. FAM. Job, position, employment.
jobard [ʒɔba:r] s. FAM. Dupe, simpleton, U. S. sucker. (V. GOBEUR.)
jobarder [-de] v. tr. (1). To take in, to fool, to dupe, to make an ass of, to suck in.

jobardise [-diːz] f. Gullibility. ‖ Spoof; mug's game (tromperie).

jockey [ʒɔke] m. Sports. Jockey.

jocrisse [ʒɔkris] m. Clown. ‖ Fam. Mug, dolt.

jodler [ʒɔdle] v. intr. (1). To yodel.

jogging [dʒɔgiŋ] m. Sports. Jogging.

joie [ʒwa] f. Joy, mirth, gladness (en général); glee, delight, merriment (grande joie); *avec joie,* gladly, joyfully; *à cœur joie,* to one's heart's content; *être fou de joie,* to be beside oneself with joy; *je me ferai une joie de vous aider,* I shall be delighted to help you; *je me fais une joie de le revoir,* I'm eagerly looking forward to seeing him again. ‖ Pleasure, enjoyment, delight; *être plein de la joie de vivre,* to be full of joie de vivre, to enjoy life to the full; *les joies du monde,* the good things of life, the world's delights. ‖ Loc. *Feu de joie,* bonfire; *fille de joie,* tart.

joignant, ante [ʒwaɲɑ̃, ɑ̃ːt] adj. Adjoining, next (à, to).
— prép. Next to, adjoining.

joindre [ʒwɛ̃ːdr] v. tr. (59). To join (en général); to add (additionner); to unite, to combine, to associate (associer); to be next to (ou) adjacent to (être proche de); *joindre les mains,* to clasp one's hands; *joindre l'utile à l'agréable,* to combine utility with beauty (ou) business with pleasure. ‖ To meet, to come up with, to get hold of (entrer en contact). ‖ To enclose (inclure); *joindre un timbre,* to enclose a stamp. ‖ Techn. To weld, to join. ‖ Fam. *Joindre les deux bouts,* to make ends meet.
— v. pron. **Se joindre,** to join, to unite. ‖ To be adjacent to, to be contiguous, to be next to each other (domaines, contrées). ‖ *Se joindre à,* to join; to join in.

joint, ointe [ʒwɛ̃, wɛ̃ːt] adj. Joined (v. UNI); *joint à,* added to, combined with; *les mains jointes,* with clasped (ou) folded hands; *sauter à pieds joints,* to take a standing jump. ‖ Comm. *Ci-joint,* attached, enclosed, herewith; *pièces jointes,* enclosures. ‖ Fig. *Sauter à pieds joints sur,* to snatch (ou) jump at (une proposition).
— m. Joint; join. ‖ Techn. Joint (en général); seam (d'une chaudière). ‖ Archit. Jointing (d'un mur). ‖ Fam. Solution; *trouver le joint,* to find the clue (ou) a way round it. ‖ Arg. Joint (drogue).

jointif, ive [-tif, iːv] adj. Joined; butt-jointed (planches).

jointoyer [-twaje] v. tr. (9a). Archit. To point.

jointure [-tyːr] f. Joint (v. articulation); *les jointures des doigts,* the knuckles.

jojo [ʒɔʒo] m. Pop. *Affreux jojo,* pest, holy terror, little devil (ou) menace.

joker [ʒɔkœːr] m. Joker.

joli, ie [ʒɔli] adj. Pretty, nice; good-looking, fine. (V. BEAU.) ‖ Fam. Pretty, comfortable, tidy; *un joli revenu,* a tidy (ou) sizeable income.
— m. Fam. *Le joli de l'affaire,* the best of it; *vous avez fait du joli!,* nice work!, you have made a fine mess of it!; *c'est du joli!,* it's disgraceful!

joliesse [-ljɛs] f. Prettiness. (V. BEAUTÉ.)

joliet, ette [-ljɛ; ɛ] adj. Rather pretty, dainty.

joliment [-limɑ̃] adj. Prettily, nicely. ‖ Fam. Extremely, terribly, awfully, jolly; *il s'est joliment trompé,* he has made a nice mistake; *elle est joliment contente,* she is awfully (ou) terribly pleased; *vous avez joliment raison,* how right you are, U. S. you are so right.

jonc [ʒɔ̃] m. Bot. Rush; bulrush (des chaisiers); calamus (odorant); *jonc marin,* furze. ‖ Malacca cane, rattan walking-stick (canne). ‖ Guard ring (bijou).

jonchaie [ʒɔ̃ʃɛ] f. Bot. Rush-bed.

jonchée f. Strewing (de fleurs, de joncs). ‖ Culin. Cream-cheese, U. S. cottage cheese.

joncher v. tr. (1). To strew. ‖ To cover, to litter, to be scattered about on. (V. recouvrir.)

joncheraie [-ʃrɛ], **jonchère** [-ʃɛːr] f. Rush-bed.

jonchet [ʒɔ̃ʃɛ] m. Spillikin; *jouer aux jonchets,* to play pick-up sticks (ou) spillikins.

jonction [ʒɔ̃ksjɔ̃] f. Junction; joining; meeting. (V. connection, union.) ‖ Ch. de f. Junction. ‖ Jur. Joinder. ‖ Milit. *Opérer une jonction,* to join hands. ‖ Electr. Connector.

jongler [ʒɔ̃gle] v. intr. (1). To juggle (pr. et fig.).

jonglerie [-gləri] f. Jugglery, juggling. ‖ Fig. Trickery, fraud.

jongleur [-glœːr] m. Juggler (moderne). ‖ Jongleur, minstrel; tumbler (au Moyen Age). ‖ Fig. Trickster, charlatan.

jonque [ʒɔ̃k] f. Naut. Junk.

jonquille [ʒɔ̃kij] f. Bot. Jonquil.
— adj. Pale yellow (couleur).

Jordanie [ʒɔrdani] f. Géogr. Jordan.

jordanien, enne [-njɛ̃, ɛn] adj., s. Géogr. Jordanian.

jouable [ʒwabl] adj. Playable. ‖ Usable (cartes).

joual [ʒwal] m. Gramm. Joual, French Canadian dialect.

joubarbe [ʒubarb] Bot. Houseleek, stonecrop, sempervivum.

joue [ʒu] f. Cheek; *joue contre joue,* cheek to cheek (amoureux), cheek by jowl (complices). ‖ Milit. *En joue,* Present!; *coucher (ou) mettre en joue,* to level a gun at, to take aim at. ‖ Techn. Cheek (de poulie); flange (de treuil). ‖ Archit. Cheek (mortaise). ‖ Ch. de f. Guard-rail. ‖ Pop. *Se caler les joues,* to have a good blow-out, to stuff oneself to the gills.

jouée [ʒwe] f. Archit. Reveal (de fenêtre); side (de lucarne); thickness (de mur).

jouer v. intr. (1). To play (v. s'amuser); *jouer au billard, aux cartes, au football,* to play billiards, cards, football; *jouer à la marchande, à la poupée, aux soldats,* to play shops, dolls, at soldiers; *bien, mal jouer,* to play a good, a bad game; *c'est à vous de jouer,* it is your turn to play (aux cartes); it is your move (aux dames, aux échecs). ‖ To gamble (pour de l'argent). ‖ Fin. To speculate, to gamble on the Stock Exchange, U.S. to play the market (à la Bourse); *jouer à la hausse,* to bull, to speculate on a rise. ‖ Mus. To play; *jouer de la flûte, du piano,* to play the flute, the piano. ‖ Théâtr. To play, to act; *jouer la comédie,* to act a play. ‖ Techn. To work, to go (agir); to be loose, to have too much play (avoir du jeu); to shrink, to warp (bois); *faire jouer,* to set going; to start; to set off. ‖ Jur. To operate, to take effect (clause). ‖ Fig. *Jouer avec,* to play (ou) to toy (ou) to trifle with (le danger, une idée); *jouer la comédie,* to act a part; *jouer de la fourchette,* to tuck in; *jouer des jambes,* to take to one's heels; *jouer de malheur,* to have a run of bad luck; *jouer de la prunelle,* to ogle; *jouer sur les mots,* to play with words; to quibble; *le soleil joue sur le toit,* the sun is dancing on the roof.
— v. tr. To play; to gamble (de l'argent); to back (un cheval); *jouer le jeu,* to play the game; *jouer petit jeu,* to play for small stakes. ‖ Mus. To play, to perform (une sonate). ‖ Théâtr. To play (un rôle); *on a joué longtemps sa pièce,* his play has had a long run. ‖ To look like; to copy, to imitate, to mimic; to pretend to be; to affect, to feign; *cette étoffe joue la soie,* this material looks like silk. ‖ Fig. To venture; to risk (sa vie). ‖ Fam. To deceive, to fool, to take in, to humbug, to bamboozle (qqn); *jouer un tour à,* to play a trick on.
— v. pron. **Se jouer,** to play, to gambol, to frisk; *il a écrit ce sonnet en se jouant,* writing this sonnet was child's play to him. ‖ *Se jouer de,* to make sport of, to deride (se moquer); to make nothing of, to make light of (surmonter); to deceive, to baffle (tromper).

jouet [ʒwɛ] m. Plaything, toy. ‖ Fɪɢ. Victim; sport; toy; laughing-stock; *être le jouet des vents*, to be the sport of the wind.

joueur, euse [ʒwœːr, øːz] adj. Sᴘᴏʀᴛs. Fond of games (au jeu); fond of gambling (aux jeux d'argent).
— s. Player; *mauvais joueur*, bad loser. ‖ Fɪɴ. Speculator (à la Bourse); gambler (aux jeux d'argent); *jouer à la hausse, à la baisse*, bull, bear. ‖ Tʜᴇ́ᴀ̂ᴛʀ. Actor, player. ‖ Mᴜsɪᴄ. Player, performer.

jouffiu, ue [ʒufly] adj. Chubby, chubby-cheeked.

joug [ʒu] m. Yoke (des bœufs). ‖ Tᴇᴄʜɴ. Beam (de balance). ‖ Fɪɢ. Yoke, power, influence; *secouer le joug*, to throw off the yoke; *sous le joug*, under the yoke.

jouir [ʒwiːr] v. intr. (2). To enjoy; *jouir de*, to enjoy, to be possessed of, to own, to have (droits, fortune); to enjoy (santé, vacances). ‖ Mᴇ́ᴅ. To have an orgasm, to come (fam.).

jouissance [ʒwisɑ̃ːs] f. Enjoyment, delight, pleasure (joie). ‖ Jᴜʀ. Possession, enjoyment, use. ‖ Fɪɴ. *Jouissance fin mai*, dividend payable during last week of May. ‖ Mᴇ́ᴅ. Orgasm, sexual climax.

jouisseur, euse [sœːr, øːz] adj. Self-indulgent, sensual.
— s. Pleasure seeker, hedonist, sensualist; good-time Charley.

jouissif, ive [-sif, iːv] adj. Pᴏᴘ. Orgasmic. ‖ Fɪɢ., Pᴏᴘ. Exhilarating, mind-blowing.

joujou [ʒuʒu] (pl. **joujoux**) m. Fᴀᴍ. Plaything, toy. (V. ᴊᴏᴜᴇᴛ.)

joule [ʒul] m. Pʜʏs. Joule.

jour [ʒuːr] m. Day (journée); *un jour de retard*, one day's delay; *jour de pluie*, rainy day; *combien de fois par jour?*, how many times a day?; *de jour en jour*, from day to day; *de deux jours en avance*, two days in advance; *de tous les jours*, everyday (habits); *tous les jours*, daily, every day; *tous les deux jours*, every other day; *tous les trois jours*, every third day; *tous les jours que le Bon Dieu fait*, every day that God sends; day in, day out. ‖ Day (date); *au premier jour*, as soon as possible; *Jour de l'An*, New Year's Day; *jour des anciens élèves*, old boys' day, U.S. class day; *jour de Noël, de Pâques, de la Pentecôte, des Rois, de la Saint-Sylvestre*, Christmas Day, Easter Sunday, Whitsunday, Twelfth Night, New Year's Eve; *jour de réception*, at-home day; *jour des prix*, prize (ou) speech day, U. S. commencement day; *un jour*, one day (passé); some day (à venir); *un jour exceptionnel*, a red-letter day; *à un de ces jours*, so long!: *dans huit, quinze jours*, in a week, in a fortnight; *dès le premier jour*, from the first (ou) outset; *du jour au lendemain*, soon; at a moment's notice; *le journal du jour*, today's paper; *prendre jour avec*, to fix a day with. ‖ Day, time (époque); *au jour d'aujourd'hui*, nowadays; *aux jours d'autrefois*, in former times, formerly; *de nos jours*, these days; in our time nowadays; *les beaux jours du règne*, the heyday of the reign; *les jours de Noël*, Christmas-time, Yuletide. ‖ Days, life (vie); *attenter aux jours de*, to attempt to murder; *donner le jour à*, to give birth to; *jour de naissance*, birthday; *un de ses mauvais jours*, one of his off-days; *mes beaux jours sont finis*, my dancing days are over; *sur mes vieux jours*, in my old age; *vivre au jour le jour*, to live from hand to mouth; *voir le jour*, to be born, to see the light. ‖ Day, daylight, light (lumière); *demi-jour*, dim light; half-light; twilight (crépuscule); *au grand jour*, in broad daylight; *au lever du jour*, at daybreak; *au petit jour*, at dawn; *le jour se lève*, the sun is rising; *se lever avant le jour*, to get up before dawn. ‖ Opening; aperture, gap (ouverture); *jour dans le mur*, opening (ou) crack in the wall; *jour à*

fils tirés, drawn-work, open-work; *jour échelle*, hemstitch bar; *ourlet à jours*, hemstitch; *prendre jour sur*, to open into (ou) on. ‖ Way (passage); *se faire jour*, to emerge, to come out. ‖ Aspect, appearance, light (aspect); *se présenter sous un beau jour*, to show oneself to good advantage; *sous un faux, nouveau, vrai jour*, in a wrong, new, proper light. ‖ Cᴏᴍᴍ. Information, preparation; *mettre, tenir à jour*, to bring, to keep up to date. ‖ Cᴜʟɪɴ. *Plat du jour*, today's special dish. ‖ Fɪɴ. *Au cours du jour*, at the current market rate. ‖ Lᴏᴄ. *Au grand jour*, publicly; *clair comme le jour*, clear as daylight; *dès le premier jour*, from the beginning; *mettre au jour*, to bring to light; *percer qqn à jour*, to see through s.o.'s intentions; *se faire jour*, to come out, to come to the surface (vérité).

journal [ʒurnal] m. Paper, newspaper (v. ɢᴀ-ᴢᴇᴛᴛᴇ); *journal parlé*, news; *crieur de journaux*, newsboy; *marchand de journaux*, newsagent; *vendeur de journaux*, newsvendor, paper-seller, U.S. news dealer. ‖ Diary, journal (particulier). ‖ Cᴏᴍᴍ. Journal; register. ‖ Nᴀᴜᴛ. Logbook.

journalier, ère [-lje, ɛːr] adj. Daily, everyday. ‖ Changing, uncertain, unsettled, variable (caractère).
— s. Journeyman, day-labourer.

journalisme [-lism] m. Journalism; *faire du journalisme*, to go in for journalism, to write for the papers; *style de journalisme*, journalese.

journaliste [-list] m. Journalist; reporter; correspondent; *journaliste indépendant*, free-lance.

journalistique [-listik] adj. Journalistic.

journée [ʒurne] f. Day, day-time. ‖ Day's work (travail); *femme de journée*, daily help, charwoman. ‖ Day's wages (paye); *à la journée*, by the day. ‖ Stage (étape); *à grandes journées*, by forced marches; *à petites journées*, by short stages.

journellement [-nɛlmɑ̃] adv. Daily, every day.

joute [ʒut] f. Joust, tilt. (V. ᴛᴏᴜʀɴᴏɪ.) ‖ Contest (oratoire). ‖ Sᴘᴏʀᴛs. Tournament.

jouter [-te] v. intr. (1). † To joust, to tilt. ‖ Fɪɢ. To fight, to dispute, to duel.

jouteur [-tœːr] m. Tilter, jouster. ‖ Fɪɢ. Fighter.

jouvence [ʒuvɑ̃ːs] f. Youth.

jouvenceau [-vɑ̃so] m. Young boy, young girl; stripling, youngster. (V. ᴀᴅᴏʟᴇsᴄᴇɴᴛ.)

jouvencelle [-vɑ̃sɛl] f. Lass, maiden.

jouxter [ʒukste] v. tr. (1). To be next to (ou) adjacent to.

jovial, ale [ʒɔvjal] (pl. **jovials**) adj. Jovial, good-humoured, jolly. (V. ɢᴀɪ.)

jovialement [-lmɑ̃] adv. Jovially, merrily.

jovialité [-lite] f. Joviality, jollity, good humour.

joyau [ʒwajo] m. Jewel, precious stone, gem.

joyeusement [ʒwajøzmɑ̃] adv. Joyfully, gladly; joyously.

joyeuseté [-jøzte] f. Mirth (joie); pleasantry, jest, joke, drollery, fun (plaisanterie).

joyeux, euse [-jø, øːz] adj. Merry, joyful, cheerful, gay (v. ɢᴀɪ); blithe (poétique); *le cœur joyeux*, with a light heart.

jubé [ʒybe] m. Eᴄᴄʟᴇ́s. Rood-screen, rood-loft.

jubilaire [ʒybilɛːr] adj. Jubilee (année).

jubilant, ante [-lɑ̃, ɑ̃:t] adj. Jubilant, in high glee (ou) feather.

jubilation [-lasjɔ̃] f. Jubilation, exultation, elation, high glee.

jubilé [-le] m. Jubilee, golden wedding.

jubiler [-le] v. intr. (1). To jubilate, to glory; to feel in high spirits (v. ᴇxᴜʟᴛᴇʀ); to gloat (fam.).

juché, ée [ʒyʃe] adj. Gone to roost, roosting, perched (oiseaux).

juchée f. Perch.

jucher v. intr. (1). To perch, to roost (oiseau). ‖ Fᴀᴍ. To perch (personne).
— v. tr. To place (ou) to hang high up.

— v. pron. **Se jucher,** to go to roost (oiseau). [V. PERCHER (SE).] ‖ FAM. To perch oneself.
juchoir [-ʃwaːr] m. Roosting-place (endroit); perch (objet).
Judaïque- [ʒydaik] adj. Judaic; Jewish.
Judaïsme [-ism] m. Judaism.
Judas [ʒyda] m. ECCLÉS. Judas. ‖ Betrayer, traitor (traître). ‖ Spy- (ou) peep-hole, judas (ouverture).
judéo- [ʒydeo] préf. Judaeo-. ‖ **Judéo-allemand,** adj., m. GRAMM. Judaeo-German, Yiddish (langue). ‖ **Judéo-chrétien,** adj. Judaeo-Christian. ‖ **Judéo-christianisme,** m. ECCLÉS. Judaeo-Christianism, Early Christianity. ‖ **Judéo-espagnol,** m. GRAMM. Judaeo-Spanish, Ladino (langue).
Judicature [ʒydikatyːr] f. JUR. Judicature; judgeship.
judiciaire [-sjɛːr] adj. Judicial, judiciary; legal. JUR. *Eloquence judiciaire,* forensic eloquence; *erreur judiciaire,* miscarriage of justice; *poursuites judiciaires,* legal proceedings. ‖ † *Combat judiciaire,* ordeal, trial by combat.
judiciairement [-sjɛrmɑ̃] adv. Judicially, legally.
judicieusement [-sjøzmɑ̃] adv. Judiciously, sensibly; discreetly.
judicieux, euse [-sjø, øːz] adj. Judicious, sensible, wise, sound; discreet, prudent. (V. AVISÉ.)
judo [ʒydo] m. SPORTS. Judo.
judoka [-dɔka] s. SPORTS. Judoka.
juge [ʒyːʒ] m. JUR. Judge, justice, magistrate (v. MAGISTRAT); *juge d'instruction,* examining magistrate; *juge de paix,* Justice of the Peace, J. P., magistrate. ‖ SPORTS. *Juge de touche,* linesman (au football). ‖ FIG. Judge, umpire; *prendre pour juge,* to appeal to.
jugé, ée [ʒyʒe] adj. *Chose jugée,* a matter already settled, closed case.
— m. *Au jugé,* at a guess, by guesswork; *tirer au jugé,* to fire without taking aim, to fire blind (ou) blindly.
jugeable [-ʒabl] adj. Subject to a legal decision.
jugement [-ʒmɑ̃] m. JUR. Judgment, trial (épreuve); decision, award, judgment (sentence); *mettre en jugement,* to bring to trial; *passer en jugement,* to be tried; *prononcer le jugement,* to pass sentence. ‖ † *Jugement de Dieu,* ordeal. ‖ ECCLÉS. *Le Jugement dernier,* the Last Judgment, doomsday. ‖ FIG. Opinion, estimation, discrimination, judgment; *de bon jugement,* of sound judgment, of good sense.
jugeote [-ʒɔt] f. FAM. Gumption, common sense.
juger [-ʒe] v. tr. (7). JUR. To judge; to try; to decide (v. STATUER); *juger un différend,* to decide a dispute; *juger pour vol,* to try for theft. ‖ FIG. To deem, to estimate, to appreciate (estimer); *juger sur la mine,* to judge from (ou) by appearances; *juger le cas, la situation,* to weigh (up) the case, the situation; *juger la solution absurde,* to find the solution absurd; *je le juge le plus intelligent des deux,* I consider him to be the more intelligent; *le médecin le juge perdu,* the doctor has given him up; *mal juger,* to misjudge (qqn). ‖ FIG. To consider, to fancy, to think, to imagine (penser); *juger bon de,* to think it right (ou) wise to; *juger à propos de,* to think it advisable to; *que jugez-vous qu'il faille faire?,* what do you think ought to be done?; *vous pouvez juger quelle fut ma réaction,* you can imagine what my reaction was.
— v. intr. *Juger de,* to judge of; *jugez de ma surprise,* you can imagine my surprise; *juger d'après,* to judge from; *juger par,* to judge by; *à en juger par ses paroles,* judging from his talk; *autant que j'en puis juger,* as far as I can judge.
— v. pr. **Se juger,** to consider (ou) deem oneself.
jugulaire [ʒygylɛːr] adj. MÉD. Jugular.
— f. MÉD. Jugular vein. ‖ MILIT. Chin-strap.

juguler [-le] v. tr. (1). To strangle, to throttle, to choke. ‖ MÉD. To jugulate.
juif, ive [ʒɥif, iːv] adj. Jewish.
— m. Jew; *le Juif errant,* the Wandering Jew; *petit juif,* funny-bone, U. S. crazy bone.
juillet [ʒɥijɛ] m. July.
juin [ʒɥɛ̃] m. June.
Juive [ʒɥiːv] f. Jewess.
juiverie [-vri] f. Jewry; the Jews. ‖ Ghetto, Jewish quarter (quartier). ‖ FIG. Usury.
jujube [ʒyʒyb] m. BOT. Jujube.
jujubier [-bje] m. BOT. Jujube-tree.
juke-box [dʒukbɔks] m. Juke-box.
julep [ʒylɛp] m. MÉD. Julep.
Jules [ʒyl] m. JUR. Julius. ‖ POP. Chamber-pot, jerry. ‖ FAM. Feller, bloke, boy-friend (mari, amant). ‖ POP. Pimp (souteneur).
julien, enne [ʒyljɛ̃, ɛn] adj. ASTRON. Julian (calendrier, année).
julienne [ʒyljɛn] f. CULIN. Vegetable soup, julienne.
jumeau, elle [ʒymo, ɛːl] adj. Twin (frères, lits); semi-detached (maison). ‖ NAUT. *Hélices jumelles,* twin screws; *navires jumeaux,* sister ships. ‖ AGRIC. Double (fruits).
— m. Twin; twin brother.
jumelage [ʒymlaːʒ] m. Coupling, arrangement in pairs.
jumelé, ée [-le] adj. Coupled, twin. ‖ NAUT. Twin-turret (canon).
jumeler [-le] v. tr. (5). To couple, to arrange in pairs. ‖ To reinforce.
Jumelle [ʒymɛl] f. Twin sister. ‖ Pl. Opera-glasses, field-glasses, binoculars. (V. LUNETTES.) ‖ Cuff-links (de chemise). ‖ TECHN. Cheeks, side-pieces, guide-poles, slide-bars. ‖ NAUT. Fishes (du mât). ‖ BLAS. Gemels.
jument [ʒymɑ̃] f. ZOOL. Mare. (V. CAVALE.)
jumper [ʒœpɛːr] m. Sweater, jumper.
jumping [dʒœmpiŋ] m. SPORT. Jumping.
jungle [ʒɔ̃gl] f. Jungle.
junior [ʒynjɔr] adj., m. Junior; *Martin junior,* Martin Junior. ‖ SPORTS. Junior.
Junon [ʒynɔ̃] f. Juno.
junte [ʒɔ̃t] f. Junta. ‖ FAM. Clique.
jupe [ʒyp] f. Skirt. ‖ FAM. *Toujours fourré dans ses jupes,* always hanging about her; *pendu aux jupes de sa mère,* tied to his mother's apron-strings. ‖ **Jupe-culotte,** f. Trouser-skirt, culottes.
jupette [-pɛt] f. Skirt, short skirt.
Jupiter [ʒypitɛr] m. Jupiter, Jove (dieu). ‖ ASTRON. Jupiter.
jupon [ʒypɔ̃] m. Petticoat; slip; kilt (écossais). ‖ FIG. Girl, woman; *courir le jupon,* to be a skirt-hunter (ou) -chaser.
Jura [ʒyra] m. GÉOGR. Jura.
jurassien, enne [-sjɛ̃, ɛn] adj. GÉOGR. Of (ou) from Jura.
— s. Native (ou) inhabitant of Jura.
jurassique [ʒyrasik] adj. GÉOL. Jurassic.
juratoire [ʒyratwaːr] adj. JUR. Juratory; sworn.
juré, ée [-re] adj. Sworn; *ennemi, expert juré,* sworn enemy, expert.
— m. JUR. Juryman, juror. ‖ Pl. Jury; *liste des jurés,* jury-panel.
jurement [-rmɑ̃] m. Oath; swearing.
jurer [-re] v. tr. (1). To swear; to take an oath; *jurer de dire la vérité,* to swear to tell the truth. ‖ To swear, to vow (v. PROMETTRE); *jurer fidélité,* to swear faithfulness; *il a juré de ne plus boire d'alcool,* he has sworn off drinking, he has signed the pledge, he has gone on the wagon.
— v. intr. To swear; *je n'en jurerais pas,* I would not swear to it; *il ne faut jurer de rien,* you never can tell; *ne jurer que par,* to swear by (qqn). ‖ To clash, to jar (v. CONTRASTER); *ces deux couleurs jurent,* these two colours clash. ‖ FAM. *Jurer*

ses. grands dieux, to swear by all one's gods.
— v. pr. **Se jurer,** to swear (ou) vow to oneself
(réfléchi); to swear (ou) vow (ou) pledge each
other (réciproque).

juridiction [ȝyridiksjɔ̃] f. Jurisdiction; *tombant
sous la juridiction de,* within the jurisdiction of.
‖ FAM. Province; authority.

juridique [-dik] adj. JUR. Juridical, legal; *conseiller, texte juridique,* legal adviser, instrument.

juridiquement [-dikmɑ̃] adv. JUR. Juridically,
according to the law, legally.

jurisconsulte [ȝyriskɔ̃sylt] m. JUR. Jurisconsult;
legal expert. (V. JURISTE.)

jurisprudence [-prydɑ̃:s] f. JUR. Jurisprudence;
cas faisant jurisprudence, test case.

juriste [ȝyrist] m. JUR. Jurist, legal writer.

juron [ȝyrɔ̃] m. Oath, swear-word, curse.

jury [ȝyri] m. Examining board (d'examen);
board of admission, selection committee (d'exposition); jury, judges (au concours d'élégance). ‖
JUR. Jury, jurors, jurymen.

jus [ȝy] m. Juice; *le jus de la treille,* wine; *plein
de jus,* juicy. ‖ CULIN. Gravy. ‖ FAM. Dishwater,
dirty water, U. S. joe (café); juice (électricité);
petrol, U. S. gas (essence); *donner du jus,* to open
out the throttle, U. S. to step on the gas.

jusant [ȝyzɑ̃] m. Ebb, ebb-tide. (V. REFLUX.)

jusque [ȝysk] prép. Down to, to; as far as (lieu);
up to; as much (ou) many as (quantité); till,
until, up to (temps); *aller jusqu'à dire,* to go so
far as to say; *depuis le Moyen Age jusqu'à notre
époque,* from the Middle Ages down to our time;
jusqu'alors, till (ou) until then; *jusqu'à quand?,*
how long?; *jusqu'au bout,* to the end, to the
bitter end; *jusqu'au dernier,* to the last man. ‖
Even; *avaler les prunes jusqu'aux noyaux,* to
swallow the plums, stones and all. ‖ † *Jusques
à quand?,* how long?; *jusques et y compris,* up
to and including. ‖ **Jusqu'à ce que,** till, until.
‖ **Jusqu'auboutisme,** m. Die-hard attitude. ‖
Jusqu'auboutiste, s. Die-hard, U. S. bitter-ender.

jusquiame [ȝyskjam] f. BOT. Henbane.

justaucorps [ȝystokɔr] m. † Jerkin.

juste [ȝyst] adj. Righteous, upright, just (droit).
‖ Just, fair, legitimate (v. ÉQUITABLE); deserved,
condign (châtiment); legitimate (colère); fair
(traitement); *obligé pour être juste de,* bound in
justice to; *le juste et l'injuste,* right and wrong.
‖ Right (calcul, heure); right, accurate, exact
(mot); sound (raisonnement); pertinent (réflexion);
avoir l'esprit juste, to see things in their true light;
juste milieu, middle course; happy medium. ‖
Tight (souliers, vêtement). ‖ MUS. Perfect
(octave); good (oreille); in tune (piano); true
(voix). ‖ COMM. *Au plus juste prix,* at rock-bottom
price, at the lowest price. ‖ CULIN. Barely sufficient (nourriture). ‖ LOC. *Au juste,* exactly, precisely.
— m. Just (équité). ‖ ECCLÉS. Righteous, just.
— adv. Rightly, justly, soundly, correctly; *comme
de juste,* of course, naturally; *deviner juste,* to
guess right, to hit it; *frapper juste,* to strike home,

to hit the nail on the head; *voir juste,* to have
a sound view of things. ‖ Exactly; *juste à ce
moment,* just at this very moment; *à six heures
juste,* at six o'clock sharp; *tout juste,* barely, narrowly. ‖ FAM. *Ça a été juste!,* it was a near thing!;
it was a close shave!

justement [-təmɑ̃] adv. Justly, rightly (v. ÉQUI-
TABLEMENT). ‖ Exactly, just (v. PRÉCISÉMENT); *justement il disait que,* as a matter of fact (ou) as it
happened, he was saying that.

justesse [-tɛs] f. Soundness; justness; correctness, accuracy (v. EXACTITUDE, PRÉCISION); *de justesse,* barely; *il s'en est tiré de justesse,* he just
scraped out of it.

justice [-tis] f. Justice, fairness, right; *rendre justice à,* to do justice to. ‖ JUR. Justice, legal proceedings, law; *aller en justice,* to go to law;
demander justice, to seek redress; *rendre la justice,* to administer justice. ‖ LOC. *Se faire justice,*
to take the law into one's own hands, to revenge
oneself (se venger); to commit suicide (se tuer).

justiciable [-tisjabl] adj. Amenable, subject (de,
to); justiciable (de, of); *il est justiciable des tribunaux français,* he can be brought before the
French courts.
— s. Justiciable; *parmi nos justiciables,* among
those coming under our jurisdiction.

justicier, ère [-tisje, ɛ:r] adj., s. Justiciary.

justifiable [-tifjabl] adj. Justifiable (crime). ‖
FIG. Defensible (action).

justifiant, ante [-tifjɑ̃, ɑ̃:t] adj. Justifying.

justificateur, trice [ȝystifikatœ:r, tris] adj. Justificatory, vindicating.
— s. Justifier.

justificatif, ive [-tif, i:v] adj. Justificative;
numéro justificatif, reference number; *pièce justificative,* voucher, document in proof, relevant
(ou) supporting document.
— m. FIN. Voucher.

justification [-sjɔ̃] f. Justification, vindication,
warrant, proof. ‖ Type area, justification (en
typographie).

justifié, ée [ȝystifje] adj. Justified; *peu justifié,*
unwarranted.

justifier v. tr. (1). To justify, to vindicate (sa
conduite); *justifier qqn de,* to clear s.o. of. ‖ To
prove (prouver). ‖ To justify, to adjust (en typo).
— v. intr. JUR. *Justifier de,* to account for (son
action); to prove (son identité, une origine).
— v. pr. **Se justifier,** to justify oneself, to vindicate one's character, to clear oneself (de, of).

jute [ȝyt] m. Jute.

juter [ȝyte] v. intr. (1). To be juicy, to run with
juice.

juteux, euse [-tø, ø:z] adj. Juicy.
— m. POP., MILIT. Sergeant-major.

juvénile [ȝyvenil] adj. Juvenile, youthful.

juvénilité [-lite] f. Youthfulness, juvenility.

juxtalinéaire [ȝykstalineɛ:r] adj. Juxtalinear,
line for line.

juxtaposer [-poze] v. tr. (1). To juxtapose, to
place side by side.

juxtaposition [-pozisjɔ̃] f. Juxtaposition.

K

k [ka] m. K, k.

kabyle [kabil] adj., s. Kabyle.

kacha [kaʃa] m. CULIN. Kasha.

kafkaïen, enne [kafkajɛ̃, ɛn] adj. Kafkaesque.

kaiser [kaizɛr] m. Kaiser, German emperor.

kakatoès [kakatɔɛs] m. ZOOL. Cockatoo.

kaki [kaki] adj., m. Khaki.

kaléidoscope [kaleidɔskɔp] m. Kaleidoscope.

kaléidoscopique [-pik] adj. Kaleidoscopic.
kamikaze [kamikaze] m. Kamikaze.
Kampuchéa [kãputʃea] m. GÉOGR. Kampuchea.
kangourou [kanguru] m. ZOOL. Kangaroo.
kantien [kãtjɛ̃] adj. PHILOS. Kantian.
kantisme [kãtism] m. PHILOS. Kantism.
kaolin [kaɔlɛ̃] m. Kaolin, China clay.
kapok [kapɔk] m. BOT. Kapok.
karakul [karakyl] m. ZOOL., COMM. Karakul.
karaté [karate] m. SPORTS. Karate.
karma [karma] m. PHILOS. Karma.
karstique [karstik] adj. GÉOGR. Karstic, karst.
kart [kart] m. Kart, go-kart.
karting [-tiŋ] m. SPORTS. Karting.
kasbah [kasba] f. Kasba. ‖ POP. Hut.
kasher [kaʃɛ:r] adj. inv. Kosher.
kayak [kajak] m. NAUT. Kayak.
keepsake [ki:pseik] m. Keepsake, souvenir.
kelvin [kɛlvin] m. PHYS. Kelvin.
Kenya [kenja] m. GÉOGR. Kenya.
kenyan, anne [-jã, an] adj., s. GÉOGR. Kenyan.
képi [kepi] m. MILIT. Képi.
kératine [keratin] f. ZOOL. Keratin.
kératite [kɛratit] f. MÉD. Keratitis.
kermès [kɛrmɛs] m. Kermesite (minéral). ‖ BOT. Kermes oak.
kermesse f. Kermesse; village fair; charity fête.
kérosène [kerɔsɛn] m. CHIM. Paraffin-oil, kerosene.
ketch [kɛtʃ] m. NAUT. Ketch.
ketchup [ketʃœp] m. CULIN. Ketchup, catsup.
kg abrév. de *kilogramme*, kg, kilogram.
khâgne [kaŋ] f. FAM. Preparatory class for the entrance exam to the École normale supérieure.
khâgneux, euse [-ŋø, øz] s. FAM. Student in a khâgne.
khalife [kalif] m. V. CALIFE.
khan [kã] m. Khan.
khédive [kedi:v] m. Khedive.
khmer, khmère [kmɛ:r] adj., s. GÉOGR. Khmer. — m. GRAMM. Khmer (langue).
khôl [kol] m. Kohl.
kibboutz [kibuts] m. Kibbutz.
kidnapper [kidnape] v. tr. (1). To kidnap; to snatch (pop.).
kidnappeur [-pœ:r] s. Kidnapper.
kidnapping [-piŋ] m. Baby-snatching.
kieselguhr [kieselgy:r] m. Kieselguhr, diatomite.
kif [kif] m. Kif (marijuhana).
kif-kif [kifkif] adj. inv. FAM. All one, all the same; *c'est kif-kif*, it comes to the same thing.
kiki [kiki] m. FAM. *Serrer le kiki à qqn*, to throttle s.o., to wring s.o.'s neck.
kil [kil] m. POP. *Un kil de rouge*, a bottle of plonk.
kilo [kilo], **kilogramme** [kilɔgram] m. Kilogram, kilogramme.
kilocalorie [-kalɔri] f. PHYS. Kilocalorie.
kilocycle [-sikl] m. ELECTR. Kilocycle.
kilolitre [-litr] m. Kilolitre.
kilométrage [-metra:ʒ] m. Mileage (d'une voiture); marking with kilometre-stones (d'une route).
kilomètre [-mɛtr] m. Kilometre.
kilométrer [-metre] v. tr. (1). To measure in kilometres.
kilométrique [-metrik] adj. Kilometrical.
kilotonne [-tɔn] f. PHYS. Kiloton.

kilowatt [-wat] m. ELECTR. Kilowatt. ‖ **Kilowattheure**, m. ELECTR. Kilowatt-hour.
kilt [kilt] m. Kilt.
kimono [kimɔno] m. Kimono.
kinase [kina:z] f. MÉD. Kinase.
kinésithérapeute [kineziterapø:t] s. MÉD. Physiotherapist.
kinesthésie [kinɛstezi] f. Kinesthesia.
kiosque [kjɔsk] m. Summer-house (de jardin). ‖ Kiosk, stall, stand (de vendeurs). ‖ MUS. Bandstand. ‖ NAUT. Conning-tower (de sous-marin); *kiosque de navigation*, chart-house.
Kippour [kipu:r] m. V. YOM KIPPOUR.
kir [ki:r] m. Black currant liqueur with dry white wine, kir.
kirsch [kirʃ] m. Kirsch.
kitchenette [kitʃənɛt] f. CULIN. Kitchenette.
kitsch [kitʃ] adj. inv. Kitsch, kitschy. — m. Kitsch.
kiwi [kiwi] m. ZOOL. Kiwi. ‖ BOT. Kiwi, kiwi fruit, Chinese gooseberry.
klaxon [klaksɔ̃] m. AUTOM. Motor-horn, hooter, horn, klaxon.
klaxonner [-sɔne] v. intr. (1). AUTOM. To hoot, to blow (ou) toot one's horn, to honk.
kleptomane [klɛptɔman] s. MÉD. Kleptomaniac.
kleptomanie [-mani] f. MÉD. Kleptomania.
klystron [klistrɔ̃] m. PHYS. Klystron.
km abrév. de *kilomètre*, km, kilometre.
knout [knut] m. Knout.
K.O. [kao], **knock-out** [nɔkawt] m. inv. SPORTS. Knock-out, K. O. — adj. FIG., FAM. *Être K. O.*, to be shattered, wrecked. ‖ SPORTS. *Mettre K. O.*, to knock out.
koala [kɔala] m. ZOOL. Koala, koala bear.
kohol [kɔɔl] m. Kohl.
kola [kɔla] f. Kola, cola.
kolinski [kɔlinski] m. ZOOL. Kolinski. ‖ COMM. Kolinski fur (fourrure).
kolkhoze [kolkoz] m. Kolkhoz.
komintern [kɔmintɛrn] m. Comintern.
kommandanture [kɔmãdãtyr] f. MILIT. Kommandanture.
kopeck [kɔpɛk] m. Kopeck, copeck. ‖ FAM. Penny, cent, dime.
Koweit [kɔwɛjt] m. GÉOGR. Kuwait.
koweïtien, enne [-tjɛ̃, ɛn] adj., s. GÉOGR. Kuwaiti.
krach [krak] m. FIN. Financial crash, smash, collapse.
kraft [kraft] m. Kraft (ou) brown paper.
Kremlin [kremlɛ̃] m. Kremlin.
krypton [kriptɔ̃] m. CHIM. Krypton.
Ku-Klux-Klan [kyklyksklã] m. Ku Klux Klan; *membre du Ku-Klux-Klan*, Ku Klux Klanner, Klansman.
kummel [kymɛl] m. Kümmel.
kung-fu [kungfu] m. SPORTS. Kung fu.
kurde [kyrd] s. GÉOGR. Kurd (peuple). — m. GRAMM. Kurdish (langue). — adj. GÉOGR. Kurdish.
Kurdistan [kyrdistã] m. GÉOGR. Kurdistan.
kwashiorkor [kwaʃjɔrkɔr] m. MÉD. Kwashiorkor.
kymrique [kimrik] adj., m. Cymric, kymric.
kyrielle [kirjɛl] f. FAM. Long rigmarole; string (*de*, of).
kyste [kist] m. MÉD. Cyst.
kystique [-tik] adj. MÉD. Cystic.

L

l [ɛl] m. L, l (lettre).
l. Abrév. de litre, l.
la [la] art. pr. V. LE.
la [la] m. Mus. A; donner le la, to give the pitch.
là [la] adj. There (lieu); à quelques pas de là, a few paces (ou) steps away; là en bas, down there; là où, where; votre père est-il là?, is your father at home?; par-ci par-là, here and there. ‖ Then (temps); à quelque temps de là, some time after; d'ici là, till then. ‖ That (cela); de là, whence; en passer par là, to go through that; par-là, thereby; thereabout. ‖ Loc. Il n'en est pas encore là, he has not come to that yet; il est un peu là, he is all there; il s'ensuit de là que, it follows that; sortir de là, to get out of it. ‖ Là-bas, over there, yonder. ‖ Là-dedans, in there, inside. ‖ Là-dessous, underneath. ‖ Là-dessus, thereupon; on that. ‖ Là-haut, up there; upstairs (à l'étage supérieur); in heaven above (au ciel).
— interj. Là, là!, there now!, gently!, oh là là!, oh dear me!, you don't mean that!
labarum [labarɔm] m. Labarum.
label [labɛl] m. COMM. Stamp, seal (d'origine); hallmark (de qualité).
labeur [labœːr] m. Work, toil.
labial, ale [labjal] adj. Labial.
labiale f. GRAMM. Labial.
labialisation [-lizasjɔ̃] f. GRAMM. Labialization.
labialiser [-lize] v. tr. (1). GRAMM. To labialize.
labié, ée [labje] adj., BOT. Labiate.
labile [labil] adj. CHIM., PSYCH. Labile.
labiodentale [labjodɑ̃tal] adj. f., f. GRAMM. Labiodental.
laborantin, ine [labɔrɑ̃tɛ̃, in] s. Laboratory (ou) lab assistant.
laboratoire [-ratwaːr] m. Laboratory; laboratoire d'essai, testing plant.
laborieusement [-rjøzmɑ̃] adv. Laboriously, painstakingly, industriously.
laborieux, euse [-rjø, øːz] adj. Laborious, painstaking, industrious (v. TRAVAILLEUR); classes laborieuses, working classes. ‖ Heavy, laboured, plodding, halting (style); difficult, hard, wearisome (tâche).
labour [labuːr] m. AGRIC. Ploughing, tillage, tilling, U. S. plowing; bœuf de labour, plough-ox. ‖ Pl. Ploughed fields (ou) land.
labourable [laburabl] adj. AGRIC. Arable (terre).
labourage [-raːʒ] m. AGRIC. Ploughing, tilling, U. S. plowing.
labourer [-re] v. tr. (1). AGRIC. To plough, U. S. to plow. ‖ NAUT. To graze, to drag. ‖ FIG. Labouré de rides, furrowed (front).
laboureur [-rœːr] m. AGRIC. Ploughman, U. S. plowman.
Labrador [labradɔːr] m. GÉOGR. Labrador. ‖ GÉOL. Labradorite, Labrador spar. ‖ ZOOL. Labrador, Labrador retriever.
labyrinthe [labirɛ̃ːt] m. Maze, labyrinth.
labyrinthique [-rɛ̃tik] adj. Maze-like, labyrinthine.
lac [lak] m. GÉOGR. Lake; loch (en Écosse); tarn (de montagne). ‖ FAM. Dans le lac, in the soup; c'est dans le lac, U. S. the jig is up.
laçage [lasaːʒ], lacement [-smɑ̃] m. Lacing up.
lacédémonien, enne [lasedemɔnjɛ̃, ɛn] adj., s. GÉOGR. Lacedaemonian.
lacer [-se] v. tr. (6). To lace. ‖ NAUT. To belay.

— v. pr. Se lacer, to lace (corset); to lace oneself in (femme).
lacération [laserasjɔ̃] f. Laceration, tearing. ‖ Defacing (d'une affiche). ‖ Mauling (par un fauve).
lacéré, ée [-re] adj. BOT. Lacerate (feuille).
lacérer [-re] v. tr. (5). To lacerate; to maul.
laceret [lasre] m. TECHN. Gimlet, auger.
lacet [lase] m. Lace; lacets de souliers, shoelaces, U. S. shoestrings. ‖ Hairpin bend (d'un chemin); en lacets, twisting, winding (route). ‖ Noose, snare (pour lapins). ‖ Bowstring (pour étrangler). ‖ NAUT. Lacing (de voile).
lâchage [lɑʃaːʒ] m. Releasing, letting go. ‖ FAM. Dropping.
lâche [lɑːʃ] adj. Slack, lax (corde); loose (nœud). ‖ Lax (style); careless, perfunctory (travail). ‖ FIG. Cowardly, dastardly, faint-hearted, craven (personne).
— m. Coward, dastard, craven. (V. COUARD.)
lâchement [-ʃmɑ̃] adv. In a cowardly manner.
lâcher [-ʃe] v. tr. (1). To loosen, to slacken (en général); to unleash (un chien); to let out (son corset); lâcher pied, to give ground; lâcher prise, to let go. ‖ AUTOM. To release (le frein). ‖ TECHN. Lâcher la vapeur, to blow off steam. ‖ AVIAT. To drop, to release (une bombe); to drop (un parachutiste). ‖ FAM. To blurt out (un mot); to jilt, to drop (qqn); to chuck (un travail); to let off, to break (un vent); lâcher une bordée d'insultes, to let fly a volley of abuse.
— v. intr. FAM. To turn tail, to give up (abandonner); to loosen (se desserrer).
— m. Release (de pigeons).
lâcheté [-ʃte] f. Cowardice, dastardliness. ‖ Cowardly act. ‖ Baseness, villainy.
lâcheur [-ʃœːr] s. FAM. Funk, quitter.
lacis [lasi] m. Network.
laconique [lakɔnik] adj. Laconic; of few words.
laconiquement [-nikmɑ̃] adv. Laconically, tersely.
laconisme [-nism] m. Laconicism. (V. BRIÈVETÉ.)
lacrymal, ale [lakrimal] adj. MÉD. Lachrymal; conduit lacrymal, tear-duct.
lacrymatoire [-matwaːr] adj., m. Lachrymatory.
lacrymogène [-mɔʒɛːn] adj. Lachrymatory, tear-producing; gaz lacrymogène, tear-gas.
lacs [lɑ] m. Noose, springs, snare. ‖ FIG. Toils.
lactaire [laktɛːr] adj. Lactary, lacteous.
— m. BOT. Lacteous mushroom.
lactalbumine [-talbymin] f. MÉD. Lactalbumine.
lactarium [-tarjɔm] m. MÉD. Milk-bank.
lactase [-taz] f. MÉD. Lactase.
lactation [-tasjɔ̃] f. MÉD. Lactation.
lacté, ée [-te] adj. Lacteous, milky. ‖ ASTRON. Voie lactée, Milky Way. ‖ MÉD. Lacteal (vaisseau).
lactique [-tik] adj. CHIM. Lactic.
lactose [-toːz] m. CHIM. Lactose, milk sugar.
lacunaire [lakynɛːr] adj. Incomplete, deficient, with gaps.
lacune [-kyn] f. Gap, deficiency, lacuna.
lacuneux, euse [-kynø, øːz] adj. Incomplete, deficient, with gaps. ‖ BOT. Lacunal, lacunary.
lacustre [lakystr] adj. Lacustral; cité lacustre, lake-village.
lad [lad] m. Stable-boy.
ladite [ladit] adj. JUR. The aforesaid.
ladre [laːdr] adj. MÉD. Leprous (personne);

measly (porc). || Fig. Stingy, niggardly, tight-fisted. (V. pingre.)
— m. Méd. Leper. || Fig. Miser; tightwad (fam.).
ladrerie [ladrəri] f. Measles (du porc). || Lazar-house (léproserie). || Fam. Avarice, miserliness.
lagon [lagɔ̃] m. Lagoon (au centre d'un atoll); salt-water pool (étang).
lagunaire [lagynɛ:r] adj. Géogr. Lagoon, lagoonal.
lagune [lagyn] f. Géogr. Lagoon.
lai [lɛ] adj. Ecclés. Lay (brother).
lai [lɛ] m. Lay (poème).
laïc [laik]. V. laïque.
laîche [lɛʃ]. Bot. Sedge.
laïcisation [laisizasjɔ̃] f. Laicisation, seculari-sation.
laïciser [-ze] v. tr. (1). To secularize.
laïcisme [laisism] m. Secularism.
laïcité [-te] f. Secularity, undenominationalism.
laid, e [lɛ, ɛ:d] adj. Ugly, mean, vile, base, unseemly, repulsive (chose); ugly, plain, mis-shapen, ill-shaped (ou) -favoured, U. S. homely (personne).
laidement [-dmɑ̃] adv. In an ugly way, meanly.
laideron [-drɔ̃] m. Ugly person. || Fam. Fright; *petit laideron*, ugly duckling; *laideronne*, plain Jane.
laideur [-dœ:r] f. Meanness, unsightliness (des choses); ugliness, plainness, U. S. homeliness (des personnes).
laie [lɛ] f. Zool. Wild sow.
laie f. Forest-path; ride, rack.
laie f. Techn. Stone-cutter's hammer.
lainage [lɛna:ʒ] m. Woollen (tissu); teaseling, napping (travail).
laine [lɛn] f. Wool; *laine filée, peignée*, yarn, worsted; *laine à tricoter*, knitting wool. || Woolly hair (chevelure). || Fam. *Se laisser tondre la laine sur le dos*, to let oneself be fleeced.
lainer [-ne] v. tr. (1). Techn. To teasel.
laineux, euse [-nø, ø:z] adj. Woolly.
lainier, ère [-nje, ɛ:r] adj. Wool (industry).
— s. Manufacturer of woollens (fabricant); wool-merchant (marchand).
laïque [laik] adj. Lay, secular (en général); undenominational (école)
— s. Layman, laywoman; *les laïques*, the laity.
lais [lɛ] m. Staddle (baliveau). || Alluvium, warp, silt (alluvion).
laisse [lɛs] f. Leash, lead. || Fam. *Tenir en laisse*, to keep in leading-strings.
laisse f. Naut. Foreshore, high (ou) low water-mark (en mer). || Laisse (strophe).
laissées [lɛse] f. pl. Droppings (des grosses bêtes).
laissé-pour-compte [lɛsepu:rkɔ̃t] m. Comm. Returned article, reject. || Fam. Reject, cast-off.
laisser v. tr. (1). To leave (sens général); *cela me laisse froid*, it leaves me cold; *laisser sa voiture à la gare*, to leave one's car at the station. || To leave, to quit, to go away from (quitter); *allons, je vous laisse*, well, I'm going; *je les ai laissés avant qu'ils aient fini*, I left them before they finished. || To leave, to reserve (remettre); *laissez cela pour l'an prochain*, save (ou) leave that for next year. || To leave out, to omit (omettre); *laissez cela de côté*, leave that out. || To let, to allow (permettre); *laisser entrer*, to let in, to give admittance to; *laissez-les dire*, let them talk; *laissez-moi voir*, let me see; *ne pas laisser voir qqn*, not to show to s.o., not to let s.o. see; *on ne le laisse pas sortir seul*, he is not allowed to go out alone; *on ne le laissa pas s'approcher de*, he was denied access to. || To let have (prêter); *je vous laisse mes outils pendant mon absence*, I will let you have (ou) leave you my tools while I am away. || To give (donner); *laisser la place à*, to give way to. || Comm. To let have, to leave (vendre); *il le laissera pour trois cents francs*,

he will let it go at three hundred francs; *laissé pour compte*, left unpaid (ou) on hand. || Fin. *Laisser un bénéfice*, to yield a profit. || Loc. *Laisser aller*, to let go; to let things go their way; *laisser faire*, not to interfere; *laisser tout aller*, to let things slide; *laisser tranquille*, to let (ou) to leave alone; *elle y laissa la vie*, it cost her her life.
— v. intr. *Laisser à penser*, to leave ample food for thought; *ne pas laisser de*, not to fail to; *cela ne laisse pas de m'inquiéter*, it worries me all the same, I can't help feeling worried.
— v. pr. *Se laisser*, to let oneself; *se laisser aller*, to let oneself go; to slip; *se laisser aller à*, to give way to (un regret); *se laisser boire*, to be very drinkable (vin); *se laisser lire*, to be easy to read; *je me suis laissé dire que*, I have been told that. ||
Laisser-aller, m. invar. Abandon, lack of res-traint (en général); slovenliness (de l'allure). || **Laisser-faire**, m. Non-interference, laissez-faire. || **Laissez-passer**, m. invar. Permit, pass. (V. coupe-file, sauf-conduit.)
lait [lɛ] m. Milk; *lait concentré, écrémé*, con-densed (ou) evaporated, skim milk. || Culin. *Lait de poule*, egg-nog. || Techn. *Lait de chaux*, white-wash, limewash. || Méd. *Lait d'amandes*, almond-milk. || Fam. *Boire du lait*, to lap it up.
laitage [-ta:ʒ] m. Dairy produce.
laitance [-tɑ̃s], **laite** [lɛt] f. Culin. Soft roe.
laiterie [-tri] f. Dairy; dairy-work; dairy farm. || Milk-shop, U. S. creamery.
laiteux, euse [-tø, ø:z] adj. Milky, milk-like, lacteous. || Méd. Lacteal.
laitier, ère [-tje, ɛ:r] adj. Milk (industrie); *vache laitière*, milch-cow.
— m. Milkman, dairyman. || Techn. Dross, slag.
laitière [lɛtjɛ:r] f. Dairymaid (femme). || Milk-cart (voiture). || Zool. Milch-cow.
laiton [lɛtɔ̃] m. Brass; *fil de laiton*, brass-wire.
laitonner [-tɔne] v. tr. (1). To cover with brass.
laitue [lɛty] f. Bot. Lettuce.
laïus [lajys] m. Fam. Speech; lecture.
laïusser [-se] v. intr. (1). Fam. To jaw, to speechify.
laïusseur [-sœ:r] m. Fam. Speechifier, tub-thumper, soap-box orator.
laize [lɛ:z] f. Width (d'une étoffe).
lakiste [lakist] adj., m. Lake-poet.
lama [lama] m. Lama.
lama m. Zool. Llama.
lamaneur [lamanœ:r] m. Naut. Branch-pilot; river-pilot.
lamantin [lamɑ̃tɛ̃] m. Zool. Manatee, sea-cow.
lamaserie [lamazri] f. Lamasery, lama monastery.
lambda [lɑ̃bda] m. Lambda.
— adj. Fam. Average.
lambeau [lɑ̃bo] m. Rag, scrap, shred; *mettre en lambeaux*, to tear to tatters; *tomber en lambeaux*, to fall to pieces. || Méd. Flap.
lambin [lɑ̃bɛ̃] adj. Slothful, sluggish. (V. lent.)
— s. Dawdle, laggard, loafer, idler.
lambiner [-bine] v. intr. (1). Fam. To dawdle, to loaf, to loiter.
lambourde [lɑ̃burd] f. Archit. Sleeper, bridging-joist; beam-bearing. || Agric. Fruit-branch.
lambrequin [lɑ̃brəkɛ̃] m. Techn. Valance, pelmet.
lambris [lɑ̃bri] m. Wainscoting, panelling (en bois); lining (en marbre). || Ceiling (plafond).
lambrissage [-sa:ʒ] m. Wainscoting, panelling; lining.
lambrisser [-se] v. tr. (1). To wainscot, to panel; to line.
lambswool [lɑ̃bswul] m. Lamb's-wool.
lame [lam] f. Lamina, chin plate (de métal); floor-board (de parquet); slide (de verre). || Blade (de couteau, de rasoir); knife (de faucheuse). || Wave, billow (vague); *lame de fond*, ground

swell. ‖ ELECTR. Plate. ‖ SPORTS. *Une fine lame,* a skilful swordsman. ‖ FIG. *Une fine lame,* a sly baggage (femme); a very clever fellow (homme); U. S. a shrewd guy; *visage en lame de couteau,* hatchet face.

lamé, ée [-me] adj. Spangled.
— m. Lamé (tissu); *lamé argent,* silver lamé; *lamé or,* samite; *brocart lamé,* brocade.

lamelle [-mɛl] f. Thin plate; lamella, lamina.

lamellibranche [-mɛllibrɑ̃:ʃ] m. ZOOL. Lamellibranch. bivalve.

lamentable [lamɑ̃tabl] adj. Mournful, dismal, sad (aspect, voix); lamentable, deplorable, grievous (événement); contemptible, pitiable, wretched (personne). ‖ FAM. Rotten.

lamentablement [-tabləmɑ̃] adv. Lamentably.

lamentation [-tasjɔ̃] f. Lamentation, wailing. ‖ Complaint. (V. PLAINTE.)

lamenter (se) [səlamɑ̃te] v. pr. (1). To lament, to moan, to complain (sur, about, for, over); *se lamenter de,* to deplore.

lamento [lamɛnto] m. MUS. Lament.

lamifié, ée [lamifje] adj. TECHN. Laminated.
— m. TECHN. Laminate.

laminage [lamina:ʒ] m. TECHN. Laminating, rolling (du métal); calendering (du papier); throttling (de la vapeur).

laminaire [-nɛ:r] adj. PHYS., GÉOL. Laminar.
— f. BOT. Laminaria, oar-weed, kelp.

laminer [-ne] v. tr. (1). To laminate; to roll (un métal); to calender (le papier); *verre laminé,* plate-glass.

lamineur [-nœ:r] m. TECHN. Roller (métallurgiste); calender (papetier).
— adj. m. TECHN. Rolling; *cylindre lamineur,* roller.

laminoir [-nwa:r] m. TECHN. Rolling mill (à métal); rolling press (à papier).

lampadaire [lɑ̃padɛ:r] m. Candelabrum, sconce (lustre). ‖ Lamp-stand (support).

lampant, ante [-pɑ̃, ɑ̃:t] adj. Refined (huile).

lamparo [lɑ̃paro] m. NAUT. Lamp; *pêche au lamparo,* fishing by lamplight.

lampe [lɑ̃:p] f. Lamp; *lampe à arc,* arc-light; *lampe à incandescence,* glow lamp, fluorescent (ou) strip lighting; *lampe de poche,* flash-lamp, torch, flashlight; *lampe de travail,* reading-lamp. ‖ TECHN. *Lampe à souder,* blow lamp, U. S. blow torch. ‖ RADIO. *Poste à cinq lampes,* five-valve (ou) -tube set. ‖ AUTOM. *Lampe de bord,* dashboard light. ‖ **Lampe témoin,** f. Pilot-lamp.

lampée [lɑ̃pe] f. Draught; *d'une seule lampée,* at one gulp.

lamper v. tr. (1). To gulp down, to toss off.

lamperon [lɑ̃prɔ̃] m. Wick-holder.

lampion [-pjɔ̃] m. Chinese lantern. ‖ Fairy light (pour illumination).

lampiste [-pist] m. Lamp-maker (ou) -lighter (ou) -trimmer. ‖ FAM. Underling, scapegoat; U. S. fall guy.

lampisterie [-pistri] f. COMM. Lamp-trade (ou) making. ‖ CH. DE F. Lamp-room.

lamproie [lɑ̃prwa] f. ZOOL. Lamprey.

lançage [lɑ̃sa:ʒ] m. V. LANCEMENT.

lance [lɑ̃:s] f. Spear, lance (arme). ‖ *Lance d'arrosage,* water-hose nozzle. ‖ TECHN. Slice-bar (de chaufferie). ‖ FIG. *Rompre une lance avec,* to break a lance with, to cross swords with, to enter into contest with. ‖ **Lance-bombes,** m. MILIT. Trench mortar. ‖ **Lance-flammes,** m. MILIT. Flame-thrower. ‖ **Lance-fusées,** m. MILIT. Rocket-launcher. ‖ **Lance-grenades,** m. MILIT. Grenade thrower. ‖ **Lance-mines,** m. Mine-layer. ‖ **Lance-missiles,** m. MILIT. Missile launcher. ‖ **Lance-pierres,** m. Catapult. ‖ **Lance-roquettes,** m. MILIT. Rocket launcher. ‖ **Lance-torpilles,** m. MILIT. Torpedo-tube.

lancé, ée [lɑ̃se] adj. Started; going; *lancé à fond de train,* at full speed. ‖ SPORTS. *Départ lancé,* flying start. ‖ FIG. *Une fois lancé, il ne s'arrête plus,* once he gets going, there is no stopping him; *acteur lancé,* actor in the limelight. ‖ FAM. Dashing; *être lancé dans le monde,* to cut a figure in society.

lancée f. Impetus. ‖ Pl. MÉD. Shooting pains.

lancement [-smɑ̃] m. Throwing, casting, flinging, tossing, hurling. ‖ NAUT. Launching (de navire). ‖ SPORTS. Pitch (au baseball); *lancement du disque,* throwing (ou) tossing the discus; *lancement du poids,* putting the weight. ‖ COMM. Starting, floating, launching (d'une affaire).

lancéolé, ée [-seɔle] adj. BOT. ARCHIT. Lanceolate.

lancer [-se] v. tr. (6). To throw; to cast; to fling; to toss (en l'air); to harl (avec violence). ‖ To hit, to strike (un coup); to puff out (de la fumée); to loose (une flèche); to throw (une pierre). ‖ MILIT. To hurl (une armée); to launch (une attaque); to drop (une bombe); to send up (une fusée). ‖ AVIAT., AUTOM. To swing (l'hélice, la manivelle). ‖ NAUT. To launch (un navire). ‖ SPORTS. To pitch (au baseball); to throw, to toss (le disque); to put (le poids). ‖ SPORTS. To start (le cerf à la chasse); to throw, to cast (une ligne à la pêche). ‖ COMM. To float, to launch, to start (une affaire); to bring out (des marchandises). ‖ FIN. To float (un emprunt). ‖ JUR. To level (une accusation); to move (un projet de loi). ‖ THÉÂTR. To bring into the limelight (un acteur). ‖ TECHN. To start (une machine, un moteur). ‖ FIG. To crack (une plaisanterie); to give a start to (qqn); to fire (une remarque); to advance, to put forth, to set up (une théorie).
— v. pr. **Se lancer,** to rush, to dash, to throw oneself (contre, at, on, against, through); *se lancer à la poursuite de,* to rush in pursuit of. ‖ FIG. *Se lancer dans,* to embark on (une affaire); to tackle (un sujet).
— m. Release (de pigeons). ‖ SPORTS. Starting (à la chasse); casting (à la pêche).

lancette [-sɛt] f. MÉD. Lancet.

lanceur, euse [-sœ:r, ø:z] s. SPORTS. Thrower (de javelot, de poids). ‖ COMM. *Lanceur d'affaires,* business promoter.
— m. ASTRONAUT. Launcher.

lancier [-sje] m. MILIT. Lancer. ‖ Pl. Lancers (danse).

lancinant, ante [lɑ̃sinɑ̃, ɑ̃:t] adj. Haunting, nagging (souvenir). ‖ MÉD. Lancinating, shooting (douleur).

lanciner [-ne] v. tr. (1). To rack, to haunt, to nag away at.
— v. intr. MÉD. To shoot, to stab, to throb.

landais, aise [lɑ̃dɛ, ɛ:z] adj. GÉOGR. Of (ou) from the Landes.
— s. Native (ou) inhabitant of the Landes.

landau [lɑ̃do] (pl. **landaus**), m. Landau (voiture attelée). ‖ Pram, U. S. baby carriage (voiture d'enfant).

landaulet [-lɛ] m. Landaulet, landaulette.

lande [lɑ̃:d] f. Moor, heath.

landgrave [lɑ̃dgra:v] s. Landgrave.

landgravine [-vin] f. Landgravine.

landier [lɑ̃dje] m. Tall kitchen andiron.

laneret [lanərɛ] m. ZOOL. Lanneret, lanner.

langage [lɑ̃ga:ʒ] m. Language; speech; *langage ordinaire,* common parlance. ‖ LOC. *En voilà un langage!,* that's no way to talk! ; *ayez recours au langage des fleurs,* say it with flowers.

lange [lɑ̃:ʒ] m. Baby's napkin, U. S. diaper. ‖ Pl. Swaddling clothes.

langer [lɑ̃ʒe] v. tr. (7). To swaddle.

langoureusement [lɑ̃gurøzmɑ̃] adv. Languidly, languorously.

langoureux, euse [-rø, ø:z] adj. Languid, languorous; lackadaisical.

langouste [lãgust] f. Zool. Spiny lobster; crayfish (fam.).

langoustine [-tin] f. Zool. Norway lobster, Dublin prawn, scamp, U. S. prawn.

langue [lã:g] f. Tongue; *tirer la langue*, to put out (ou) to stick out one's tongue. ‖ Tongue, language; *don des langues*, gift of tongues; *langue maternelle*, mother-tongue; *de langue anglaise*, English-speaking; *langue verte*, slang; *langues vivantes*, modern languages. ‖ Language, style; *écrire une belle langue*, to write beautiful English (ou) French, to have an elegant style. ‖ Géogr. Neck (de terre). ‖ Naut. Gore (de voile). ‖ Fig. *Avoir la langue bien pendue*, to have a glib tongue; *l'avoir sur le bout de la langue*, to have it on the tip of one's tongue; *délier la langue à qqn*, to loosen s.o.'s tongue; *donner sa langue aux chats*, to give it up; *ne pas avoir sa langue dans sa poche*, to have a quick (ou) ready tongue; U. S. to be quick on the come back; *prendre langue*, to establish contact; to open up a conversation. ‖ **Langue-de-chat** (pl. *langues-de-chat*), f. Culin. Finger-biscuit, U. S. ladyfinger.

languedocien, enne [lãgədɔsjɛ̃, ɛn] adj. Géogr. Of (ou) from the Languedoc.
— s. Native (ou) inhabitant of the Languedoc.

languette [lãgɛt] f. Small tongue (de métal); tongue (de soulier). ‖ Pointer (de balance); tongue (de plancher). ‖ Techn. Spline, feather. ‖ Mus. Languet.

langueur [lãgœ:r] f. Languor, languidness. ‖ Méd. *Maladie de langueur*, decline.

languir [-gi:r] v. intr. (2). To languish, to pine; *languir d'amour*, to be love-sick. ‖ Méd. To decline. ‖ Fig. To flag, to drag (action, conversation, intérêt); *les affaires languissent*, business is slack. ‖ Fig. To burn (*après*, for); to languish (*après*, after); *ne me faites pas languir*, don't keep me on thorns (ou) tenterhooks.

languissamment [-gisamɑ̃] adv. Languidly.

languissant, ante [-gisɑ̃, ɑ̃:t] adj. Languishing (au moral); languid, languorous (au physique). ‖ Fig. Slack (affaires); lagging, dragging (conversation).

lanière [lanjɛ:r] f. Thong, thin strap (courroie); lash (fouet). ‖ Blas. Bend.

lanifère [lanifɛ:r] adj. Laniferous, wool-bearing.

lanoline [lanɔlin] f. Lanolin, wool-fat.

lansquenet [lãskənɛ] m. Lansquenet.

lanterne [lãtɛrn] f. Lantern; *lanterne arrière*, tail lamp; *lanterne magique*, magic lantern, epidiascope; *lanterne sourde*, bull's eye lantern; *lanterne tempête*, hurricane lamp; *lanterne vénitienne*, Chinese lantern. ‖ Loc. *A la lanterne!*, string him up! ‖ Pl. Autom. Sidelights.

lanterneau [-no] m. Sky-light.

lanterner [-ne] v. intr. (1). Fam. To linger, to loiter, to dawdle, to lag, to hang about, to dilly-dally, to shilly-shally. (V. lambiner, remettre.)
— v. tr. Fam. *Lanterner qqn*, to waste s.o.'s time; to put s.o. off.

lanthane [lãtan] m. Chim. Lanthanum.

Laos [laɔs] m. Géogr. Laos.

laotien, enne [laɔsjɛ̃, ɛn] adj., s. Géogr. Laotian.

lapalissade [lapalisad] f. Truism.

laparotomie [laparɔtɔmi] f. Méd. Laparotomy.

lapement [lapmɑ̃] m. Lapping, lapping up.

laper [-pe] v. tr. (1). To lap, to lap up.

lapereau [lapro] m. Zool. Young rabbit.

lapidaire [lapidɛ:r] adj., m. Lapidary.

lapidation [-dasjɔ̃] f. Stoning, lapidation.

lapider [-de] v. tr. (1). To stone, to lapidate. ‖ Fig. To vilify.

lapin [lapɛ̃] m. Zool. Rabbit; *lapin de garenne*,

wild rabbit. ‖ Fam. *C'est un chaud lapin*, he's a bit of a lad; *coup du lapin*, rabbit punch (coup), whiplash (voiture); *poser un lapin à qqn*, to let s.o. down, U. S. to stand s.o. up; *se sauver comme un lapin*, to turn tail and run.

lapine [-pin] f. Zool. Female rabbit, doe.

lapiner [lapine] v. intr. (1). To litter.

lapinière [-njɛ:r] f. Rabbit-hutch (clapier); rabbit-warren (garenne).

lapis-lazuli [lapislazyli] m. Lapis lazuli (pierre). ‖ Bright blue (couleur).

lapon, onne [lapɔ̃, ɔn] adj. Lapp; Lappish.
— s. Géogr. Laplander.
— m. Lapp, Lappish (langue).

Laponie [laponi] f. Géogr. Lapland.

laps [laps] m. *Laps de temps*, lapse, space of time.

lapsus [lapsys] m. Slip (de la langue, de la plume).

laquage [laka:ʒ] m. Lacquering.

laquais [lakɛ] m. Lackey, footman (serviteur). ‖ Flunkey. (V. larbin.)

laque [lak] f. Lacquer (vernis); lacquer, hair spray (pour les cheveux). ‖ Bot. Lac, gum lac (résine).
— m. Arts. Lacquer ware, japan.

laquelle [lakɛl] v. lequel.

laquer [lake] v. tr. (1). To lacquer, to japan.

laqueur [-kœ:r] m. Lacquerer, japanner.

larbin [larbɛ̃] m. Flunkey.

larcin [larsɛ̃] m. Larceny, pilfering. (V. vol.)

lard [la:r] m. Fat (de porc). ‖ Culin. Bacon. ‖ Fam. *Faire du lard*, to get fat; *gras à lard*, as fat as a pig.

lardage [larda:ʒ] m. Culin. Larding.

lardé, ée [-de] adj. Culin. Larded. ‖ Géol. Interbedded.

larder [-de] v. tr. (1). Culin. To lard. ‖ Fig. To stab at, to thrust at (accabler, cribler); *larder de coups*, to shower with blows; *larder de brocards*, to sneer at, to carp at. ‖ Fig. To interlard, to lard (parsemer); *éloges lardés d'insinuations*, praise interlarded with innuendoes; *larder sa prose d'allusions classiques*, to sprinkle one's prose with classical allusions.

lardoire [-dwa:r] f. Culin. Larding-needle. ‖ Techn. Shoe.

lardon [-dɔ̃] m. Culin. Lardon; lardoon; piece of larding bacon. ‖ Fig. Taunt, sarcasm, gibe. ‖ Fam. Kid, brat (gosse).

lardonner [-dɔne] v. tr. (1). Culin. To cut into lardoons. ‖ Fig. To taunt. (V. brocarder.)

lare [la:r] m. Lar; *dieux lares*, Lares, household gods.

largable [largabl] adj. Aviat. Releasable.

largage [-ga:ʒ] m. Naut. Letting go (d'une amarre); unfurling (d'une voile). ‖ Aviat. *Largage des réservoirs*, tank-slipping.

large [larʒ] adj. Wide, broad (étendu); *à larges bords*, broad-brimmed; *au front large*, broad-browed; *geste large*, sweeping gesture; *large ouvert*, wide-open; *mot employé dans un sens large*, word used in a broad sense. ‖ Loose, full (ample); *jupe large*, full skirt; *pardessus large*, loose overcoat. ‖ Fig. Liberal, broad; *avoir l'esprit large*, to be broad-minded; *avoir la conscience large*, to have an elastic (ou) adaptible conscience; *avoir la main large*, to be liberal with one's money; *pratiquer une large tolérance*, to be broad-minded. ‖ Free (libre); *mener la vie large*, to spend freely. ‖ Bold, free (hardi); *peinture large*, bold painting; *style large*, free style. ‖ Large (vaste, important); *on lui a donné une large marge*, he was given plenty of scope; *une large part*, a large share; *de larges pouvoirs*, extensive powers.
— adv. Loosely; *s'habiller large*, to wear loose

garments. ‖ Boldly; *peindre large,* to paint boldly.
— m. Breadth, width (étendue); *dix mètres de large,* ten metres in width; *ce terrain a plus de long que de large,* this plot is wider than it is long. ‖ NAUT. Open sea, offing; *au large du port,* off the harbour; *au grand large,* in the open sea, on the high sea; *le cuirassé est resté au large,* the battle-ship remained in the offing; *passer au large des brisants,* to take a course wide of the breakers, to give the breakers a wide berth; *prendre le large,* to put out to sea. ‖ Loc. *De long en large,* to and fro; *au large!,* away, hold off!; *donnez-lui du large,* give him elbow-room.

largement [-ʒəmɑ̃] adv. Broadly, widely (en étendue); *une idée largement répandue,* a widely accepted idea. ‖ FIG. Freely (généreusement); boldly (hardiment). ‖ Fully, well (tout à fait); *avoir largement dépassé la quarantaine,* to be well past forty; *il a en largement assez,* he has had his fill; *nous avons largement le temps,* we have plenty of time.

largesse [-ʒɛs] f. Liberality, bounty, largesse; *avec largesse,* generously, bountifully. ‖ Pl. Gifts; *faire des largesses,* to make generous gifts.

largeur [-ʒœ:r] f. Width, breadth; *distance en largeur,* distance across; *dans la largeur,* in the width; *étoffe grande largeur,* double-width (ou) extra-wide cloth. ‖ NAUT. Beam. ‖ FIG. Breadth (intelligence); *largeur d'esprit,* broadness of mind; *largeur de vues,* breadth of outlook. ‖ FAM. *Dans les grandes largeurs,* in a big way, unstintedly, with a vengeance.

largue [larg] adj. NAUT. Loose (cordage); free (vent); *aller vent largue,* to sail free.
— m. NAUT. Broad sweep; *avoir du largue,* to sail free.

larguer [-ge] v. tr. (1). NAUT. To let go, to loose (une amarre); to release (un ballon); to slip (un corps mort); to shake out (un ris); to let out (une voile). ‖ AVIAT. To drop.

larme [larm] f. Tear (v. PLEUR); *avec des larmes dans la voix,* in a tearful voice; *yeux baignés de larmes,* eyes brimming over with tears; *pleurer à chaudes larmes,* to weep bitterly; *il a ri aux larmes,* he laughed till he cried; *les larmes me vinrent aux yeux,* tears welled up in my eyes; *verser des larmes de joie,* to shed tears of joy. ‖ BOT. Tear (de résine, de sève). ‖ FAM. *Y aller de sa larme,* to shed a tear; *la faire aux larmes,* to play the comedy of tears. ‖ FAM. Drop (goutte); *une larme de cognac,* just a drop of brandy.

larmier [-mje] m. MÉD. Corner of the eye near the nose. ‖ ARCHIT. Dripstone; coping (de pont). ‖ ZOOL. Tear-bag (du cerf).

larmoiement [-mwamɑ̃] m. Weeping. ‖ MÉD. Watering of the eyes.

larmoyant, ante [-mwajɑ̃, ɑ̃:t] adj. Whimpering (enfant); tearful, plaintive, lachrymose (personne); watering (yeux). ‖ FIG. Sentimental (comédie); doleful, maudlin, lachrymose (récit).

larmoyer [-mwaje] v. intr. (9 *a*). To water (yeux). ‖ To whimper, to snivel, to blubber (enfant).

larron, onnesse [larɔ̃, ɔnɛs] m. Robber, pilferer. (V. VOLEUR.) ‖ TECHN. Uncut dog's-ear (dans un livre); crease (dans le papier). ‖ Loc. *S'entendre comme larrons en foire,* to be as thick as thieves.

larronner [-rɔne] v. intr. (1). To pilfer, to filch.

larvaire [larvɛ:r] adj. ZOOL. Larval. ‖ FIG. Immature (œuvre).

larve [larv] f. ZOOL. Larva, grub. ‖ † Larva, ghost.

larvé, ée [-ve] adj. MÉD. Larval, larvated (fièvre). ‖ FIG. Masked, disguised; latent.

laryngien, enne [larɛ̃ʒjɛ̃, ɛn] adj. MÉD. Laryn-geal.

laryngite [-ʒit] f. MÉD. Laryngitis.

laryngologie [-gɔlɔʒi] f. MÉD. Laryngology.

laryngologiste [-gɔlɔʒist], **laryngologue** [-gɔlɔg] s. MÉD. Laryngologist, throat specialist.

laryngoscope [-gɔskɔp] m. MÉD. Laryngoscope.

laryngoscopie [-gɔskɔpi] f. MÉD. Laryngoscopy.

laryngotomie [-gɔtɔmi] f. MÉD. Laryngotomy.

larynx [larɛ̃:ks] m. MÉD. Larynx.

las [la] interj. † Alas! (V. HÉLAS.)

las, asse [lɑ, ɑs] adj. Tired, weary. (V. FATIGUÉ.)

lasagne [lazaɲ] f. pl. CULIN. Lasagne, lasagna.

lascar [laska:r] m. NAUT. Lascar, tar. ‖ FAM. Smart fellow; tough guy. (V. LURON.)

lascif, ive [lasif, i:v] adj. Lascivious, lewd, wanton.

lascivement [-sivmɑ̃] adv. Lasciviously, lewdly.

lasciveté [-sivte] f. Lewdness, lust, lasciviousness.

laser [lazɛ:r] m. PHYS. Laser.

lassant, ante [lasɑ̃, ɑ̃:t] adj. Tiring, wearying, wearisome, tedious.

lasser [-se] v. tr. (1). To tire, to weary (au moral et au physique); *tout passe, tout casse, tout lasse,* all is vanity; everything comes to an end.
— v. pr. Se lasser, to grow weary, to tire (de, of); *se lasser à faire,* to tire oneself out doing; *se lasser de faire,* to tire of doing.

lassitude [-sityd] f. Weariness, lassitude.

lasso [laso] m. Lasso, lariat; *prendre au lasso,* to lasso.

latence [latɑ̃:s] f. Latency; *temps de latence,* latent period, time-lag (temps de réaction). ‖ PSYCH. *Période de latence,* latency period.

latent, ente [latɑ̃, ɑ̃:t] adj. Latent, dormant, hidden; *état latent,* latency, latence.

latéral, ale [lateral] adj. Lateral side; *canal latéral,* side-canal; *chapelle latérale,* side-chapel; *sortie latérale,* side-exit.

latéralement [-mɑ̃] adv. Laterally, sideways, sidewise.

latérite [laterit] f. GÉOL. Laterite.

latéritique [-tik] adj. GÉOL. Lateritic.

latex [latɛks] m. BOT. Latex.

latifundium [latifɔdjɔm] m. Latifundium.

latin, ine [latɛ̃, in] adj. Latin; *le Quartier latin,* the Latin Quarter; *thème latin,* translation into Latin. ‖ NAUT. Lateen (voile).
— m. Latin (personne); *les Latins,* the Latin peoples. ‖ Latin (langue); *latin de cuisine,* dog-Latin, U. S. pig Latin. ‖ FAM. *Perdre son latin,* to be all at sea, not to make head or tail of it.

latiniser [latinize] v. tr. (1). To latinize.

latinisme [-nism] m. Latinism.

latiniste [-nist] m. Latinist, Latin scholar.

latinité [-nite] f. Latinity.

latino-américain, aine [-noamerikɛ̃, ɛn] adj., s. GÉOGR. Latin-American.

latitude [latityd] f. Latitude; *par 25° de latitude Nord,* in latitude 25° North. ‖ Pl. Latitudes, regions. ‖ Breadth (espace). ‖ FIG. Scope, range (champ d'action); freedom (liberté); *avoir toute latitude,* to have full discretion; *ne pas laisser trop de latitude à qqn,* not to give s.o. too much scope (ou) rope (fam.).

latitudinaire [-dinɛ:r] adj. Latitudinarian.

Latran [latrɑ̃] m. ECCLÉS. Lateran; *de Latran,* Lateran (Conciles).

latrie [latri] f. ECCLÉS. Latria.

latrines [latrin] f. pl. Latrines; U. S. privies. ‖ MILIT. Bogs, jakes, rears. ‖ NAUT. Head.

lattage [lata:ʒ] m. TECHN. Lathing (action); lath-work, lathing (surface).

latte [lat] f. Lathe, slat. ‖ NAUT. Futtock-plate. ‖ MILIT. Straight cavalry sword.

latter [-te] v. tr. (1). To lath. ‖ TECHN. To lag.

lattis [-ti] m. Lathing. ‖ TECHN. Lagging.

laudanisé, ée [lodanize] adj. MÉD. Containing laudanum.

laudanum [-nɔm] m. MÉD. Laudanum.

laudateur, trice [lodatœ:r, tris] s. Praiser, eulogizer.

laudatif, ive [lodatif, i:v] adj. Laudatory, lauding.
lauré, ée [lɔre] adj. Laureate.
lauréat, ate [lɔrea, at] adj. Laureate ; *poète lauréat*, poet laureate.
— s. Laureate. ‖ Prize-winner (concours).
laurelle [lɔrɛl] f. Bot. Oleander.
laurier [lɔrje] m. Bot. Laurel. ‖ Fig. Laurels ; *cueillir des lauriers*, to reap laurels, to win glory ; *se reposer sur ses lauriers*, to rest on one's laurels (ou) oars. ‖ **Laurier-cerise**, m. Bot. Cherry-laurel. ‖ **Laurier-rose**, m. Bot. Oleander.
lavable [lavabl] adj. Washable ; *papier lavable*, washable wall-paper.
lavabo [-bo] m. Wash-stand, wash-bowl (cuvette). ‖ Lavatory (d'école) ; pit-head bath (de mines) ; washroom (d'usine). ‖ Ecclés. Lavabo.
lavage [lava:ʒ] m. Washing. ‖ Fin. *Lavage des titres*, fraudulent conversion of stocks, faking of shares. ‖ Pop. Popping, U. S. hocking.
lavallière [lavaljɛ:r] f. Windsor tie.
lavande [lavɑ̃:d] f. Lavender ; *eau de lavande*, lavender water.
lavandière [lavɑ̃djɛ:r] f. † Washerwoman.
lavasse [lavas] f. Watery soup, tasteless sauce, skilly (sauce). ‖ Fam. Slops, dish-water ; wish-wash, wishy-washy stuff, hog-wash (écrit).
lavatory [lavatɔri] m. Public convenience, U. S. comfort station.
lave [lav] f. Lava.
lave [lav] V. Laver. ‖ **Lave-glace**, m. Autom. Windscreen (ou U. S.) windshield washer. ‖ **Lave-mains**, m. inv. Hand-basin. ‖ **Lave-vaisselle**, m. inv. Dishwasher.
lavé, ée [lave] adj. Washed, cleaned ; *les mal lavés*, the great unwashed. ‖ Washy, washed out (couleur). ‖ Arts. *Dessin lavé*, wash-drawing.
lavement [-vmɑ̃] m. Ecclés. Washing. ‖ Méd. Rectal injection ; enema.
laver [-ve] v. tr. (1). To wash (sens général) ; to swill (à grande eau) ; to scrub (à la brosse) ; to wash up (la vaisselle) ; *cuvette pour se laver les mains*, basin to wash one's hands in. ‖ To clean, to wash out, to cleanse (nettoyer) ; *produit pour laver les taches*, stain remover. ‖ To lave (le rivage). ‖ Méd. To bathe (une plaie). ‖ Arts. To wash (un dessin). ‖ Fig. To clear (disculper) ; *laver d'une accusation*, to clear of a charge ; *s'en laver les mains*, to wash one's hands of it. ‖ Fin. To obliterate the writing on (un chèque). ‖ Fam. *Laver la tête à*, to rebuke, to call down. ‖ Pop. To sell off (vendre).
— v. pr. **Se laver**, to wash (linge) ; to wash oneself, to bathe (personne) ; *se laver le bout du nez*, to give oneself a cat-lick (ou) a lick and a promise ; *se laver les mains*, to wash one's hands.
laverie [-vri] f. Washery ; scullery.
lavette [-vɛt] f. Dish-mop.
laveur [-vœ:r] s. Washer.
laveuse [-vø:z] f. Washerwoman (v. blanchisseuse) ; *laveuse de vaisselle*, scullery-maid. ‖ Techn. *Laveuse mécanique*, washing machine.
lavis [-vi] m. Washing, tinting. ‖ Arts. Wash-drawing.
lavoir [-vwa:r] m. Wash-house ; *lavoir de cuisine*, scullery. ‖ Techn. Washing-plant (pour charbon).
lavure [-vy:r] f. Dish-water. ‖ Fam. Thin (ou) tasteless soup. ‖ Techn. Pl. Scourings, sweepings.
lawrencium [lɔrɑ̃sjɔm] m. Chim. Lawrencium.
laxatif, ive [laksatif, i:v] adj. Méd. Laxative, aperient.
— m. Méd. Laxative, aperient.
laxisme [-sism] m. Laxity, laxness.
laxiste [-sist] adj. Lax.
— s. Lax person.
laxité [-site] f. Techn., Méd. Laxity.
laye [lɛ] f. Techn. Stone-cutter's hammer.
layer [lɛ:je] v. tr. (1). To cut a path through (un

bois) ; to mark out (une coupe). ‖ Techn. To tool (une pierre).
layette [lɛ:jɛt] f. Baby-linen, layette. ‖ Packing-case.
layon [lɑjɔ̃] m. Narrow path, rack, ride.
lazaret [lazarɛ] m. Naut. Lazaret, lazaretto, quarantine station.
lazariste [-rist] m. Ecclés. Lazarist.
lazulite [lazylit] f. Lazuli.
lazzi [lazi] m. pl. Jests, jokes, gibes. ‖ Théâtr. Comic pantomime.
le [lə] (f. **la** [la], pl. **les** [lɛ]) art. déf.

---

1. Devant les noms déterminés. — **2.** Devant les parties du corps. — **3.** Devant les éléments d'une région ou les parties de l'univers. — **4.** Devant les moments de la journée. — **5.** Devant les noms au singulier désignant un groupe entier. — **6.** Devant un nom au singulier symbolisant une fonction. — **7.** Devant les noms collectifs généraux. — **8.** Devant les noms de mers, rivières, au singulier ; d'îles et de montagnes, au pluriel. — **9.** Devant les noms de maladies courantes. — **10.** Devant les noms de mesure. — **11.** Devant certains noms de temps. — **12.** Devant les points cardinaux. — **13.** Devant les noms de phénomènes atmosphériques. — **14.** Devant les adjectifs pris substantivement. — **15.** Devant les noms de durée, mesure, etc., précédés d'un nom de nombre. — **16.** Devant les noms de parties du corps précédés d'un adjectif. — **17.** Devant les parties du corps ou facultés de l'âme appartenant au sujet. — **18.** Non traduit devant les noms de collectivités réduites. — **19.** Non traduit devant les noms d'espèce au pluriel. — **20.** Non traduit devant les noms abstraits indéterminés. — **21.** Non traduit devant les noms d'art, de jeux, de langue, de matière, de science. — **22.** Non traduit devant les noms propres précédés d'une désignation ou d'un titre. — **23.** Non traduit devant les noms de lieux familiers ; les noms de montagnes et de pays au pluriel. — **24.** Non traduit devant les noms de jours de fêtes et jours de la semaine. — **25.** Non traduit devant les noms de repas. — **26.** Non traduit devant les noms savants de maladies.

---

1. The (devant les noms déterminés) ; *l'eau de notre puits*, the water from our well ; *la prudence qu'il a montrée*, the prudence which he showed. ‖ **2.** The (devant les parties du corps en général) ; *le cerveau, le cœur*, the brain, the heart. ‖ **3.** The (devant les éléments d'une région familière ou les parties de l'univers) ; *les passants*, the passers-by ; *le ciel, la côte, la lune, la mer, les vagues*, the sky, the shore, the moon, the sea, the waves. ‖ **4.** The (devant les moments de la journée) ; *l'après-midi, le matin, le soir*, the afternoon, the morning, the evening. ‖ **5.** The (devant un nom au sing. désignant un groupe entier) ; *le chien est fidèle*, the dog is a faithful animal ; *la charrue est supplantée par le tracteur*, the horse-plough is replaced by the tractor. ‖ **6.** The (devant un nom au sing. symbolisant une fonction) ; *le barreau, la pourpre, la soutane*, the Bar, the purple, the cloth. ‖ **7.** The (devant les noms collectifs généraux) ; *l'armée, la canaille, la foule*, the army, the riff-raff, the crowd ; *les Anglais, les masses*, the English, the masses. ‖ **8.** The (devant les noms de mers et de rivières au sing. ; devant les noms d'îles et de montagnes au plur.) ; *le Pacifique, la Tamise*, the Pacific, the Thames ; *les Alpes, les Sorlingues*, the Alps, the Scilly Isles. ‖ **9.** The (devant les noms de maladies courantes) ; *la grippe, les oreillons, la rougeole*, the flu (fam.), the mumps, the measles. ‖ 10. The (devant les noms de mesure); *la livre, le mètre, la tonne,* the pound, the metre, the ton. ‖ 11. The (devant certains noms de temps); *l'avenir, le passé, le présent,* the future, the past, the present. ‖ 12. The (devant les points cardinaux); *le nord, le sud,* the north, the south. ‖ 13. The (devant les noms de phénomènes atmosphériques); *le temps,* the weather. ‖ 14. The (devant les adj. pris substantivement); *le beau, le vrai,* the beautiful, the true; *les grands, les riches,* the great, the rich. ‖ 15. A, an (devant les noms de durée, de mesure, de poids, précédés d'un nom de nombre); *vingt francs la livre,* twenty francs a pound (ou) per pound; *soixante kilomètres à l'heure,* sixty kilometres an hour (ou) per hour. ‖ 16. A (devant les noms de parties du corps précédées d'un adj.); *avoir le bras cassé,* to have a broken arm; *avoir mal à la gorge,* to have a sore throat. ‖ 17. His, her, its (devant les parties du corps ou les facultés de l'âme appartenant au sujet); *je me suis cassé la jambe,* I broke my leg; *elle a perdu la raison,* she has lost her reason. ‖ 18. (Non traduit devant les noms de collectivités réduites); *les Françaises sont jolies,* Frenchwomen are pretty. ‖ 19. (Non traduit devant les noms d'espèce au pluriel); *les artistes sont imprévoyants,* artists are improvident; *les hommes de lettres,* men of letters. ‖ 20. (Non traduit devant les noms abstraits indéterminés); *la chrétienté,* Christendom; *la danse, la vitesse,* dancing, speed; *la grandeur d'âme, le respect de soi,* greatness of soul, self-respect; *la vieillesse,* old age. ‖ 21. (Non traduit devant les noms d'art, de jeux, de langue, de matière, de sciences); *la littérature, la musique,* literature, music; *les billes, le football,* marbles, football; *l'allemand, le français,* German, French; *l'acier, l'eau douce,* steel, fresh water; *la chimie, la physique,* chemistry, physics. ‖ 22. (Non traduit devant les noms propres précédés d'un titre ou d'une désignation); *le Cardinal Newman,* Cardinal Newman; *le jeune Nickleby,* young Nickleby; *le lac Ontario,* Lake Ontario; *le prince Philippe,* Prince Philip. ‖ 23. (Non traduit devant les noms de lieux familiers; devant les noms de montagnes et de pays au sing.); *aller à l'école, à l'église,* to go to school, to church; *l'Etna, la France,* Etna, France. ‖ 24. (Non traduit devant les noms des jours de fêtes et des jours de la semaine); *la fête du travail,* U. S. Labour Day; *la Toussaint,* All Saints' Day; *le lundi est mon jour de congé,* Monday is my free day (ou) my day off. ‖ 25. (Non traduit devant les noms de repas); *le petit déjeuner, le thé,* breakfast, tea. ‖ 26. (Non traduit devant les noms savants de maladies); *l'asthme, la diphtérie, la tuberculose,* asthma, diphtheria, tuberculosis.

le [lə] (f. **la** [la], pl. **les** [lɛ]) pron. pers. compl. Him, her, it, them; *je le* (ou) *la* (ou) *les connais,* I know him (ou) her (ou) them.
— pron. neutre. So; *une chose n'est impossible que lorsqu'on croit qu'elle l'est,* a thing is impossible only when one thinks it so; *je le crois,* I believe (ou) think so; *il l'espère,* he hopes so. ‖ One (pour remplacer un substantif); *mon frère est médecin, j'espère le devenir aussi,* my brother is a doctor, I hope to become one too. ‖ It (pour remplacer une proposition); *j'espère aller en France, mais je ne l'ai pas encore dit à mon père,* I hope to go to France, but I haven't mentioned it yet to my father. ‖ That (par emphase); *et pourquoi le ferai-je?,* why should I do that? ‖ (Non traduit); *êtes-vous prêt? je le suis,* are you ready? I am; *il ne croit pas qu'il y ait la guerre, je ne le crois pas non plus,* he does not think there will be a war, nor do I.

lé [le] m. Breadth, width (d'étoffe); *à quatre lés,* four-gored. ‖ Tow-path (d'une rivière).

leader [li:dœ:r] m. Leader (article, chef).
leadership [-ʃip] m. Leadership.
leasing [liziŋ] m. FIN. Leasing.
lebel [ləbɛl] m. MILIT. Lebel rifle.
léchage [leʃa:ʒ] m. Licking.
lèche [lɛʃ] f. FAM. Thin slice (de pain, de viande). ‖ POP. *Faire de la lèche à qqn,* to suck up to s.o., to lick s.o.'s boots. ‖ **Lèche-cul,** m. invar. POP. Arse-crawler (ou) -creeper, U. S. ass-licker, brown nose. ‖ **Lèche-vitrine,** m. invar. FAM. Window-shopping.
léché, ée [leʃe] adj. Overwrought, finical (peinture, style). ‖ Licked (ourson).
lèchefrite [leʃfrit] f. Dripping (ou) drip pan.
lécher [leʃe] v. tr. (5). To lick. ‖ FIG. To lick (les murs). ‖ FAM. To lick (les bottes).
— v. pr. **Se lécher,** to lick oneself.
lécheur [-ʃœ:r] s. Gormandiser. ‖ FAM. Lick-spittle, toady, U. S. apple-polisher; *lécheur de bottes,* boot-licker. ‖ POP. Creeper, toady.
leçon [ləsɔ̃] f. Lesson; *leçon de choses,* object lesson; *donner des leçons particulières,* to tutor, to coach, to give private lessons; *prendre des leçons particulières,* to take private lessons; U. S. to be coached (ou) tutored. ‖ Lecture (à l'université). ‖ Reading (dans un manuscrit). ‖ FIG. Warning, lesson; *faire la leçon à,* to lecture; *que cela lui serve de leçon,* let that be a lesson to him. ‖ Advice; *on lui a fait la leçon,* he was prompted as to what to say, he was primed in advance.
lecteur, trice [lɛktœ:r, tris] s. Reader; *avis au lecteur,* foreword. ‖ Proof-reader (d'épreuves). ‖ Assistant (à l'université).
— m. ELECTR. Head; *lecteur de cassettes,* cassette player. ‖ INFORM. Read head.
lecture [-ty:r] f. Reading; *être d'une lecture agréable,* to make pleasant reading. ‖ Reading, perusal (fait de parcourir). ‖ Reading, book; *abonnement de lectures,* circulating library; *lectures pour la jeunesse,* juvenile reading, children's stories. ‖ CINÉM. *Lecture au son,* sound reproduction. ‖ FIG. Culture.
ledit [lədi] adj. JUR. The aforesaid.
légal, ale [legal] adj. Legal, lawful; *adresse légale,* registered address.
légalement [-lmɑ̃] adv. Legally, lawfully.
légalisation [-lizɑsjɔ̃] f. Legalization, authentication, certification (d'une signature).
légaliser [-lize] v. tr. (1). To legalize, to authenticate, to certify; *déclaration légalisée,* duly attested declaration.
légalisme [-lism] m. Legalism.
légaliste [-list] adj. Legalistic.
— s. Legalist.
légalité [legalite] f. JUR. Legality, lawfulness; *rester dans la légalité,* to keep within the law.
légat [lega] m. ECCLÉS. Legate. (V. NONCE.)
légataire [-tɛ:r] m. JUR. Legatee (v. HÉRITIER); *légataire universel,* sole legatee.
légation [-sjɔ̃] f. Legation (fonction, hôtel, personnel). ‖ ECCLÉS. Legateship.
légendaire [leʒɑ̃dɛ:r] adj. Legendary.
légende [-ʒɑ̃:d] f. Legend, fable. ‖ Key (de carte); legend (de dessin); caption (d'illustration); inscription, legend (de médaille).
léger, ère [leʒe, ɛ:r] adj. Light (poids). ‖ Mild (bière); weak (thé); light (vin). ‖ MILIT. Light (artillerie). ‖ FIG. Slight (amélioration); light (démarche); light, frivolous, fast (femme); trivial (perte); *au pied léger,* fleet-footed; *propos légers,* frivolous (ou) risqué talk. ‖ Loc. *A la légère,* lightly, rashly, thoughtlessly (étourdiment); unthinkingly, impulsively (impulsivement); *traiter qqn à la légère,* to trifle with s.o.
légèrement [leʒɛrmɑ̃] adv. Lightly (en poids); *vêtu légèrement,* scantily clad. ‖ Slightly, rather

(un peu); *légèrement dissolu,* slightly intemperate; *légèrement susceptible,* rather thin-skinned. ‖ Unthinkingly, impulsively; inconsiderately; flippantly (à la légère).

légèreté [-te] f. Lightness (d'un poids). ‖ Buoyancy (de la démarche); nimbleness (des doigts); lightness (du toucher). ‖ Mildness (du tabac); weakness (du thé); lightness (du vin). ‖ Levity, flightiness, indulgence (de la conduite); slightness (d'une faute).

leggings [legiŋs] f. pl. Leggings.

légiférer [leʒifere] v. tr. (5). To legislate.

légion [leʒjɔ̃] f. MILIT. Legion; *Légion étrangère,* Foreign Legion. ‖ FIG. *Ils sont légion,* there are crowds of them.

légionnaire [-ʒjɔnɛ:r] m. Legionary (à Rome). ‖ MILIT. Légionnaire.

législateur [leʒislatœ:r] m. Legislator, law-giver.

législatif, ive [-tif, i:v] adj. Legislative; *élection législative,* Parliamentary (ou) U. S. Congressional election.

législation [-sjɔ̃] f. JUR. Legislation, law-making (action); law, set of laws (lois).

législature [-ty:r] f. Legislature; session (d'une assemblée élue).

légiste [leʒist] m. JUR. Legist. (V. JURISTE.) ‖ MÉD. *Médecin légiste,* medical expert.

légitimation [leʒitimasjɔ̃] f. Legitimation.

légitime [-tim] adj. Legitimate, lawful. ‖ Just, justifiable; *en état de légitime défense,* acting in self-defence.
— f. POP. *Ma légitime,* my better half, the missus, my trouble and strife.

légitimement [-timmã] adv. Legitimately, lawfully, justly.

légitimer [-time] v. tr. (1). To legitimate (une action); to legitimize (un enfant); to recognize (un titre).

légitimisme [-timism] m. Legitimism.

légitimiste [-timist] s. Legitimist.

légitimité [-timite] f. Lawfulness (d'une action); justness (d'une cause); legitimacy (d'un enfant).

legs [lɛg] m. Legacy, bequest; *faire un legs,* to leave a legacy; *hériter d'un legs,* to come into a legacy.

léguer [lege] v. tr. (5). To bequeath, to leave, to hand over.

légume [legym] m. Vegetable; *légumes secs,* dried vegetables; *légumes verts,* greens, green vegetables.
— f. FAM. *Grosses légumes,* bigwigs, big bugs, U. S. big wheels. (V. BONNET.)

légumier, ère [-mje, ɛ:r] adj. AGRIC. Vegetable (cultures).
— m. Vegetable dish.

légumineuse [-minø:z] f. BOT. Leguminous plant.

légumineux, euse [-minø, ø:z] adj. Leguminous.

leitmotiv [lɛtmɔtif] (pl. **leitmotive**) m. Leitmotiv; theme-song.

lémurien [lemyrjɛ̃] m. ZOOL. Lemur.

lendemain [lɑ̃dmɛ̃] m. Morrow, day after, next day; *du jour au lendemain,* overnight; *le lendemain matin,* the next morning; *succès sans lendemain,* short-lived success.

lénifiant, ante [lenifjɑ̃, ɑ̃:t] adj. Soothing (apaisant); enervating (amollissant).

lénifier [lenifje] v. tr. (1). To attenuate, to soften. (V. ADOUCIR.) ‖ MÉD. To assuage, to soothe.

léninisme [leninism] m. Leninism.

léniniste [-nist] adj., s. Leninist.

lénitif, ive [-tif, i:v] adj., m. Lenitive.

lent, ente [lɑ̃, ɑ̃:t] adj. Slow; *à l'esprit lent,* dull-minded; *à la parole lente,* slow in speech. ‖ NAUT. *Lent à virer,* slow in tacking, slack in stays. ‖ MÉD. Low (fièvre); lingering (mort).

lente [lɑ̃:t] f. ZOOL. Nit, egg (de pou).

lentement [lɑ̃tmɑ̃] adv. Slowly, sluggishly. ‖ Deliberately. ‖ NAUT. *Avant lentement,* slow ahead.

lenteur [lɑ̃tœ:r] f. Sluggishness (du comportement); backwardness (de la croissance); dullness (de l'intelligence); slowness (du mouvement, du temps). ‖ Pl. Delays, slackness, dilatoriness.

lenticulaire [lɑ̃tikylɛ:r] adj. MÉD. Lenticular.

lentille [lɑ̃ti:j] f. BOT., CULIN. Lentil. ‖ TECHN. Bob (de pendule). ‖ PHYS. Lens. ‖ NAUT. Deck-light, side-light. ‖ ELECTR. *Lentille électronique,* electronic lens.

lentisque [lɑ̃tisk] m. BOT. Lentisk, lentiscus.

léonin, ine [leonɛ̃, in] adj. Leonine, lion-like.

léopard [leopa:r] m. ZOOL. Leopard.

léopardé, ée [leoparde] adj. Spotted. ‖ BLAS. Lion passant gardant.

lépidoptère [lepidɔptɛ:r] m. ZOOL. Lepidopteran; pl. lepidoptera.

léporide [lepɔrid] m. ZOOL. Leporide.

lèpre [lɛpr] f. MÉD. Leprosy.

lépreux, euse [leprø, ø:z] adj. MÉD. Leprous.
— s. MÉD. Leper.

léproserie [-prozri] f. Lazar-house, leper-hospital, leprosery, leprosarium.

lequel [ləkɛl] (f. **laquelle** [lakɛl]; pl. **lesquels** [lɛkɛl], **lesquelles** [lɛkɛ:l]). [Contracted with *a* : **auquel, auxquels** [okɛl], **auxquelles** [okɛ:l]; contracted with *de* : **duquel** [dykɛl], **desquels** [dekɛl], **desquelles** [dɛkɛ:l] (v. DONT) pr. rel. Who, whom (pour les personnes); *la lutte fut plus longue pour savoir lequel serait roi,* there was a longer struggle as to who should be king; *le professeur auquel vous avez écrit,* the professor to whom you wrote; *le professeur à la maison duquel je suis allée,* the professor to whose house I have been. ‖ Which (pour les choses); *l'affaire à laquelle il se consacre,* the business to which he devotes himself.
— adj. Which; *prenez ce livre, lequel livre vous me rendrez dans une semaine,* take this book, which book you will return to me in a week.
— pron. inter. Which; *laquelle de ces deux roses est la plus jolie?,* which of these two roses is the prettier?

lès, lez [le] prép. GÉOGR. Near; *Plessy-lès-Tours,* Plessy near Tours.

lesbien, enne [lɛsbjɛ̃, ɛn] adj., s. Lesbian.

lèse [lɛz] adj. f. Outraged. ‖ **Lèse-humanité,** f. Outrage against humanity. ‖ **Lèse-majesté,** f. High treason.

léser [leze] v. tr. (5). To injure, to wrong (qqn). ‖ JUR. To encroach upon (les droits); to endanger (les intérêts); *la partie lésée,* the injured party. ‖ MÉD. To injure (un organe).

lésiner [lezine] v. intr. (1). To strike hard bargains; U. S. to dicker. (V. LIARDER.) ‖ To haggle (*sur,* over).

lésinerie [-inri] f. Stinginess, niggardliness (défaut). ‖ Stingy, miserly act (action).

lésineur, euse [-nœ:r, ø:z] adj. Stingy, close fisted, niggardly. (V. CHICHE.)
— s. Stingy person, skin-flint. (V. AVARE.)

lésion [lezjɔ̃] f. MÉD. Lesion, injury. ‖ JUR. Injury, damage.

Lesotho [lezoto] m. GÉOGR. Lesotho.

lessivage [lɛsiva:ʒ] m. Washing; cleaning. ‖ CHIM. Leaching. ‖ FAM. Selling off. ‖ FAM. *Lessivage de crâne,* brain-washing.

lessive [-si:v] f. Household washing, wash (lavage); washed linen (linge); lye, soda (produit); *faire la lessive,* to do the washing (ou) laundry; *jour de lessive,* washing-day, U. S. wash-day.

lessivé, ée [-sive] adj. POP. Washed out; cleaned out.

lessiver v. tr. (1). To wash (du linge); to scrub

LETTRES ET ARTS — LETTERS AND ARTS

littérature, lettres	literature, letters	argile	clay
avoir des lettres	to be well-read	modèle	sitter, model
écrivain	writer	poser pour	to sit for
auteur	author	maquette	clay model
auteur classique	classical writer	taille directe	rough dressing
	standard author	mobile	mobile
poète	poet	ébauchoir	roughing chisel
vers	line	moulage (action)	moulding
couplet, strophe	verse	moulage (objet)	cast
rime	rhyme, rime	moule	mould
métrique	metrics	sculpter	to carve
scander (un vers)	to scan (a line)	en buste	half-length
accent	stress	en pied	full-length
lyrisme	lyricism	gravure sur bois	wood-engraving
auteur dramatique	playwright	eau-forte	etching
intrigue	plot	dessinateur	drawer, draughtsman
personnages	characters	ressemblance	likeness
vraisemblance	verisimilitude	calquer	to trace, to calk
romancier	novelist	pochoir	stencil
roman	novel	esquisse, croquis	sketch, draft
histoire merveilleuse	romance	pochade	rough sketch
conte	tale	peindre, peintre	to paint, painter
nouvelle	short story	peinture	painting, picture
feuilleton	serial	toile	canvas
écrivain besogneux	hack-writer	aquarelle	water-colour
plagiaire	plagiarist	fresque	fresco
plagier	to plagiarize	paysage	landscape
cliché, poncif	« cliché »	marine	sea-scape
rebattu	hackneyed	nature morte	still life
banal	commonplace, trite	nu	nude
lieu commun	commonplace truism	chevalet	easel
obscur, abscons	abstruse, obscure	vernis, médium	varnish, medium
prolixe	diffuse, wordy	cadre	frame
paradoxal	paradoxical	clair-obscur	chiaroscuro
emphatique	bombastic	teinte	tint, hue
absurde	absurd, preposterous	nuance, ombre	shade
féerique	fairy-like	dégrader	to shade off
pittoresque	picturesque	grandeur nature	life-size
styliser	to stylize	(non) figuratif	(non) representational
licencieux	profane	empâtement	impasting
ennuyeux	tedious, boring	glacis	glazing
banal	banal, trite	musique, -icien	music, -ician
maniéré	over-nice, finical	compositeur	composer
recherché	studied, far-fetched	exécutant, -tion	performer, -ance
saisissant, frappant	striking	virtuose	virtuoso
émouvant	stirring, moving	diapason	tuning-fork
distrayant	entertaining	donner le *la*	to tune up
passionnant	thrilling, exciting	battre la mesure	to beat time
évocateur	evocative	accorder	to tune
animé, vif	lively, vivid	accordeur	tuner
ingénieux	ingenious	désaccordé	out of tune
ingénu	ingenuous	faux	wrong, out of tune
joyeux, jovial	genial	juste, accordé	in tune
homme de génie, génial	man of genius	en mesure	in time
homme de talent	talented man	pupitre	music-desk
l'éditeur	the publisher	violon, violoniste	violin, violinist
le rédacteur en chef	the editor	violoncelle, violoncelliste	'cello, 'cellist
les collaborateurs (journal)	the contributors	archet	bow
		flûte, hautbois	flute, oboe
les abonnés	the subscribers	basson, cor	bassoon, horn
reportage	report	cornemuse	bagpipe
article de tête	leader, editorial	trombone à coulisse	slide trombone
pamphlet	pamphlet, lampoon	embouchure	mouth-piece
manchette	heading, headline	tambour, timbale	drum, kettle-drum
épreuve	proof	accordéon	accordeon
placard	galley (-proof)	harmonica	harmonica
épuisé	out of print		mouth-organ
feuille mobile	loose leaf	jeu d'orgue	organ stop
broché	paper-bound	orgue de barbarie	barrel-organ
relié	bound	carillon	chime
d'occasion	second-hand	les cuivres	the brass (instruments)
art (beaux-arts)	art (fine arts)	les bois	the wood-winds
connaisseur, amateur	connoisseur	les cordes	the strings
profane	layman	chef d'orchestre	conductor
architecte, -ture	architect, -ture	soliste	soloist
plan	plan, design	clavecin	harpsichord
devis	estimate	pianoter	to strum
édifice	edifice, fabric	clavier	keyboard
sculpture, -teur	sculpture, -tor	piano à queue	grand piano
atelier	studio	faire des gammes	to practise scales
ciseau	chisel	déchiffrer	to play at sight
mannequin	lay-figure	improviser	to extemporize

(le plancher). ‖ Chim. To lixiviate, to leach. ‖ Fam. To sell off. (V. laver.) ‖ To blue, U. S. to blow (son argent).

lessiveuse [-sivø:z] f. Washing-machine, washer. ‖ Washerwoman (personne).

lest [lɛst] m. Ballast. ‖ Naut. *Jeter du lest,* to throw out ballast ; *sur lest,* on ballast. ‖ Fig. *Jeter du lest,* to make a serious sacrifice ; to cut one's losses.

lestage [-ta:ʒ] m. Naut. Ballasting.

leste [lɛst] adj. Light, nimble (v. agile) ; *qui a la main leste,* free with one's hands. ‖ Unscrupulous (conduite) ; loose, broad (propos).

lestement [-təmɑ̃] adv. Quickly, briskly, smartly, nimbly (agir) ; freely, broadly (plaisanter) ; flippantly, cavalierly, freely (répondre).

lester [-te] v. tr. (1). Naut. To ballast (un navire). ‖ Fig. To fill ; *se lester l'estomac,* to cram one's stomach.

letchi [lɛtʃi] m. V. litchi.

léthargie [letarʒi] f. Lethargy.

léthargique [-ʒik] adj. Lethargic. ‖ Fam. Sluggish. (V. endormi.)

Léthé [lete] m. Lethe ; *les eaux du Léthé,* the Lethean waters.

letton, onne [lɛtɔ̃, ɔn] adj., s. Géogr. Lett, Lettish, Latvian.
— m. Gramm. Lett, Lettish, Latvian (langue).

Lettonie [-tɔni] f. Géogr. Latvia.

lettre [lɛtr] f. Letter, character (caractère) ; *en toutes lettres,* in full, in clear and complete terms, written out. ‖ Letter (v. missive, pli) ; *lettre collective,* official circular ; *lettre chargée,* registered letter ; *lettre de convocation,* notice of meeting ; *lettre d'introduction, de recommandation,* letter of introduction, of recommendation ; *lettre missive,* private letter. ‖ Fin. Letter (de crédit). ‖ Jur. *Lettre d'introduction,* credentials ; *lettre de naturalisation,* naturalization papers ; *lettres patentes,* letters patent ; *lettre de voiture,* way-bill, consignment note. ‖ Naut. *Lettre de mer,* sea-letter (ou) -brief. ‖ Pl. Letters, literature ; *avoir des lettres,* to be well-read ; *homme de lettres,* man of letters. ‖ Fam. *Passer comme une lettre à la poste,* to go down (ou) through without any difficulty. ‖ Loc. *Avant la lettre,* in advance, premature ; *à la lettre, au pied de la lettre,* literally, to the letter ; *lettre morte,* dead letter ; *rester lettre morte pour,* to be Greek to.

lettré, ée [lɛtre] adj. Lettered, literate, well-read.
— m. Well-read person ; scholar. (V. savant.)

lettrine [-trin] f. Head letter, ornamental capital (lettre ornée) ; reference letter (petite lettre).

leu [lø] m. *A la queue leu leu,* in Indian file.

leucémie [løsemi] f. Méd. Leucocythaemia, leukemia, Hodgkin's disease ; lymphadenoma.

leucémique [-mik] adj., s. Méd. Leukemic.

leucocyte [løkɔsit] m. Méd. Leucocyte.

leucoderme [løkɔdɛrm] adj. Leucoderm, leucodermic ; white-skinned.

leucorrhée [-re] f. Méd. Leucorrhoea ; whites.

leude [lø:d] m. † Feudatory, vassal.

leur [lœ:r] pr. pers. invar. pl. To them. (V. lui.)
— adj. poss. Their.
— pron. poss. Theirs, their own ; *des étrangers pour les leurs,* strangers to their own people ; *plus petit que le leur,* smaller than theirs.

leurre [lœ:r] m. Lure, decoy. ‖ Fig. Allurement, enticement ; *ce n'est qu'un leurre,* it's only a catch.

leurrer [lœre] v. tr. (1). To lure. ‖ Fig. To deceive, to inveigle, to delude. (V. tromper.)
— v. pr. Se leurrer, to delude oneself.

levage [ləva:ʒ] m. Lifting, raising.

levain [ləvɛ̃] m. Culin. Leaven ; *sans levain,* unleavened (pain). ‖ Fig. Leaven (de révolte).

levant [ləvɑ̃] adj. Rising.
— m. East. (V. orient.)

levantin, ine [ləvɑ̃tɛ̃, in] adj. Géogr. Levantine.
— m. Géogr. Levantine. ‖ Naut. Levanter (vent).

levé, ée [ləve] adj. Up (debout) ; *personne tôt levée,* early riser. ‖ Raised (main). ‖ Culin. Raised (pâte). ‖ Jur. *Voter à main levée,* to vote by show of hands. ‖ Arts. *A main levée,* free-hand (dessin). ‖ Fig. *Au pied levé,* unprepared, on the spur of the moment, impromptu.
— m. Survey ; *faire le levé d'un terrain,* to survey a site (ou) a piece of ground.

levée f. Raising, lifting ; *la levée du corps aura lieu à,* the funeral will leave at. ‖ Clearance (de la boîte aux lettres) ; collection, U. S. pickup (des lettres) ; *la levée est faite,* the letter-box (ou) U. S. mailbox has been cleared. ‖ Trick (aux cartes). ‖ Embankment, dyke, levee (d'un fleuve). ‖ Jur. Breaking, levying (des impôts) ; breaking (des scellés) ; closing (d'une séance). ‖ Fin. Taking up (des titres) ; *levée d'une prime,* exercise of an option. ‖ Milit. Raising (d'un siège) ; levy (des troupes). ‖ Agric. Germination (du blé). ‖ Fig. Cancellation (des punitions).

lever v. tr. (1). To raise, to lift (sens général). ‖ To shrug (les épaules) ; to pull up (la glace, un store) ; to raise (la main) ; to heave, to hoist, U. S. to heft (un objet lourd). ‖ To clear, U. S. to pick up (le courrier d'une boîte aux lettres). ‖ To survey (des plans). ‖ Sports. To start (un lièvre) ; to spring (un oiseau). ‖ Théâtr. *Levez le rideau !,* curtain up ! ‖ Milit. To raise (le siège) ; to levy (des troupes) ; *lever le camp,* to break (ou) strike camp. ‖ Jur. To exercise (une option) ; to lift (une saisie) ; to break (les scellés) ; to adjourn, to close (une séance). ‖ Méd. *Lever un malade,* to get a sick person out of bed. ‖ Fig. To remove (une difficulté) ; to satisfy (les doutes) ; to take off (le masque) ; to cancel (des punitions). ‖ Fam. *Lever une fille,* to pick up a tart ; *lever le pied,* to hop it, U. S. to fly the coop.
— v. intr. To rise, to get up (mettre debout) ; *faire lever,* to rouse, to wake, to get out of bed. ‖ Culin. To rise (pâte) ; *faire lever,* to raise (la pâte). ‖ Bot. To shoot, to sprout (plante).
— v. pr. **Se lever,** to get up (du lit) ; to stand up (quand on est assis) ; *se lever brusquement,* to start up ; *se lever de table,* to rise from table. ‖ To break (jour) ; to come on (orage) ; to rise (soleil) ; to clear (temps) ; to spring up (vent).
— m. Levee (du roi) ; *le lever du soleil,* sunrise. ‖ Théâtr. Rise (du rideau) ; *un lever de rideau,* a curtain-raiser (pièce).

levier [ləvje] m. Techn. Lever ; crow-bar ; *levier de commande,* control lever. ‖ Fig. *Levier de commande,* reins of power ; *s'emparer des leviers de commande d'un parti,* to get control of the party machine.

lévitation [levitasjɔ̃] f. Levitation.

lévite [levit] m. Levite.
— f. Long frock-coat, dressing-gown (vêtement).

lévitique [levitik] adj. Levitical.
— m. Ecclés. Leviticus.

levraut [ləvro] m. Zool. Leveret.

lèvre [lɛ:vr] f. Lip ; *lèvre inférieure, supérieure,* lower, upper lip. ‖ Loc. *Parler des lèvres et non de cœur,* to pay lip-service ; *rire du bout des lèvres,* to force a laugh ; *se mordre les lèvres d'avoir parlé,* to regret having spoken ; *sourire du bout des lèvres,* to give a faint smile.

levrette [ləvrɛt] f. Zool. Greyhound bitch.

lévrier [levrje] m. Zool. Greyhound.

lévulose [levylo:z] f. Chim. Levulose, fructose.

levure [ləvy:r] f. Yeast ; *levure artificielle,* baking-powder ; *levure de bière,* barm.

lexème [lɛksɛm] m. Gramm. Lexeme.

lexical, ale [-sikal] adj. GRAMM. Lexical.
lexicalisation [-sikalizasjɔ̃] f. GRAMM. Lexicalization.
lexicaliser [-sikalize] v. tr. (1). GRAMM. To lexicalize.
lexicographe [lɛksikɔgraf] m. Lexicographer.
lexicographie [-fi] f. Lexicography.
lexicologie [leksikɔlɔʒi] f. Lexicology.
lexicologique [-lɔʒik] adj. Lexicological.
lexicologue [-lɔg] s. Lexicologist.
lexie [lɛksi] f. GRAMM. Lexical unit.
lexique [lɛksik] m. Lexicon.
lez [lɛ] prép. GÉOGR. Near.
lézard [lezaːr] m. ZOOL. Lizard. ‖ FAM. *Faire le lézard,* to bask in the sun.
lézarde [lezard] f. Crack, cranny, chink, split.
lézardé, ée [lezarde] adj. Cracked, crannied, split.
lézarder v. tr. (1). To crack, to split.
— v. intr. FAM. To bask in the sun.
— v. pr. **Se lézarder,** to crack, to split.
liage [lja:ʒ] m. Binding, tying, fastening.
liaison [ljɛzɔ̃] f. Blinding, linking, joining, connection ; junction ; *en liaison avec,* in connection with. ‖ MILIT. *Officier de liaison,* liaison officer ; *effectuer la liaison avec,* to liaise with. ‖ COMM. *Liaison d'affaires,* business connection. ‖ AVIAT. *Pilote de liaison,* liaison pilot. ‖ ARCHIT. Mortar, cement. ‖ CULIN. Thickening (d'une sauce). ‖ GRAMM. *Faire la liaison,* to link two words together. ‖ MUS. *Liaison des notes,* slurring, gliding. ‖ FIG. Connection, relationship (relations) ; *liaison amoureuse,* love-affair, liaison.
liane [ljan] f. BOT. Liana, creeper.
liant, ante [ljɑ̃, ɑ̃:t] adj. Sociable, responsive ; good-natured (v. AFFABLE) ; *peu liant,* stand-offish. ‖ TECHN. Flexible, pliant (métal).
— m. Amiability, winning manner ; *avoir du liant,* to be a good mixer. ‖ Binder (substance). ‖ TECHN. Binder (en peinture) ; flexibility, elasticity (en métallurgie).
liard [ljaːr] m. Farthing, U. S. cent.
liarder [ljarde] v. intr. (1). To pinch and scrape, to scrimp. (V. LÉSINER.)
liasse [ljas] f. File (de documents) ; bundle (de lettres). ‖ FIN. Sheaf, roll, U. S. wad (fam.) [de billets de banque].
Liban [libɑ̃] m. GÉOGR. Lebanon.
libanais, aise [libanɛ, ɛ:z] adj., s. GÉOGR. Lebanese.
libation [libasjɔ̃] f. Libation, potation ; drink-offering. ‖ Pl. Libations, drinking session.
libelle [libɛl] m. Lampoon. (V. SATIRE.) ‖ JUR. Libel.
libellé [-le] m. Wording ; lettering. ‖ COMM. Trade description.
libeller v. tr. (1). To draw up, to word.
libelliste [-list] m. Lampoonist, satirist.
libellule [libɛllyl] f. ZOOL. Dragonfly, adderfly.
liber [libɛ:r] m. BOT. Inner bark.
libérable [liberabl] adj. MILIT. *Congé libérable,* full discharge.
libéral, ale [-ral] adj. Liberal, generous, open-handed. (V. LARGE, MUNIFICENT.) ‖ Liberal, broad-minded, tolerant.
— m. Liberal. ‖ Lib-Lab (union des Libéraux et du Labour Party).
libéralement [-ralmɑ̃] adv. Liberally, bountifully.
libéralisation [-ralizasjɔ̃] f. Liberalization.
libéraliser [-ralize] v. tr. (1). To liberalize.
libéralisme [-ralism] m. Liberalism.
libéralité [-ralite] f. Liberality, openhandedness.
libérateur, trice [-ratœ:r, tris] adj. Liberating, rescuing.
— s. Liberator, deliverer, rescuer.
libération [-rasjɔ̃] f. Liberation, delivery. (V. DÉLIVRANCE.) ‖ Discharging (d'une dette). ‖ Release (d'un prisonnier) ; discharge (d'un soldat).

libératoire [-ratwa:r] adj. Liberating.
libéré, ée [-re] adj. FIN. Paid-up (action, police).
— m. MILIT. Discharged soldier. ‖ JUR. Discharged prisoner.
libérer v. tr. (5). To liberate, to free, to set free (de, from). ‖ FIN. To pay up (une action). ‖ JUR. To release (un prisonnier) ; *forçat libéré,* returned (ou) ex-convict. ‖ MILIT. To discharge (un soldat).
— v. pr. **Se libérer,** to free oneself (de, from) [un joug] ; to shake oneself free (de, from) [un préjugé] ; *je me suis libéré pour aujourd'hui,* I have taken the day off. ‖ FIN. *Se libérer de,* to pay, to redeem (une dette).
Liberia [liberja] m. GÉOGR. Liberia.
libérien, enne [-rjɛ̃, ɛn] adj., s. GÉOGR. Liberian.
libertaire [libɛrtɛ:r] adj. Libertarian.
liberté [-te] f. Liberty, freedom ; *j'ai un jour de liberté par semaine,* I have one day off every week. ‖ JUR. *Liberté provisoire* (ou) *sous caution,* release on bail ; *le coupable est encore en liberté,* the culprit is still at large. ‖ ARTS. *Liberté de pinceau,* boldness of touch. ‖ FIG. *En toute liberté,* with perfect freedom ; *je prends la liberté de dire,* I take the liberty to say, I make so bold as to say ; *libertés d'allure,* unconventionality ; *prendre des libertés de langage,* to be too free of speech ; *prendre des libertés avec qqn, avec un texte,* to take liberties with s.o., with a text. ‖ Pl. JUR. Rights.
libertin, ine [-tɛ̃, in] adj. Libertine, dissolute.
— s. Libertine, rake. (V. DÉBAUCHÉ.)
libertinage [-tina:ʒ] m. Libertinage, profligacy, looseness. (V. DÉBAUCHE.) ‖ † Free-thinking.
libidinal, ale [libidinal] adj. PSYCH. Libidinal.
libidineux, euse [libidinø, ø:z] adj. Libidinous, lewd, salacious, lecherous.
libido [libido] f. PHILOS., MÉD. Libido.
libraire [librɛ:r] s. Bookseller. ‖ **Libraire-éditeur,** m. Publisher and bookseller.
librairie [librɛri] f. Bookshop, U. S. bookstore (magasin). ‖ Bookselling, book-trade (commerce) ; *en librairie,* published.
libre [libr] adj. Free (sans entraves) ; *libre arbitre, parole, pensée,* free will, speech, thinking ; *libre à vous de croire,* you are welcome to believe ; *libre de ses mouvements,* free to do what one pleases ; *à l'air libre,* in the open air ; *école libre,* denominational (ou) U. S. private school ; *champ libre,* open field ; *France libre,* Free France ; *union libre,* companionate marriage. ‖ Free, disengaged, unoccupied (sans occupation) ; *je serai libre demain,* I shall be free tomorrow ; *je suis libre de mon temps,* my time is my own. ‖ Unoccupied (chambre, place) ; *pas libre,* line engaged (ou) U. S. busy (au téléphone) ; *taxi libre,* taxi for hire. ‖ TECHN. Free, unimpeded (chute) ; free (roue). ‖ FIN. Clear of (de dettes) ; *libre de droits,* duty-free. ‖ COMM. Unlicensed (courtier). ‖ FIG. Loose, unguarded, exceptionable (conduite, propos) ; *libre de,* free from (préjugés). ‖ FAM. *Le champ est libre,* the coast is clear. ‖ **Libre-échange,** n. Free-trade. ‖ **Libre-échangiste,** n. Free-trader. ‖ **Libre-service,** adj. COMM. Self-service ; *magasin libre-service,* self-service store.
librement [-brəmɑ̃] adv. Freely, unrestrainedly.
librettiste [librɛttist] m. MUS. Librettist.
libretto [librɛtto] m. MUS. Libretto.
Libye [libi] f. GÉOGR. Libya.
libyen, enne [-bjɛ̃, ɛn] adj., s. GÉOGR. Libyan.
lice [lis] f. † Lists, tilt-yard. ‖ LOC. *Entrer en lice contre,* to enter the lists against.
lice f. ZOOL. Bitch, hound.
lice f. NAUT., TECHN. V. LISSE.
licence [lisɑ̃:s] f. Licence (permission). ‖ Licence (en poésie). ‖ *Licence en droit, ès lettres, ès sciences,* bachelor's degree in law (ou) Ll. B., in

arts (ou) B. A., in science (ou) B. Sc.; U. S. Master's degree. ‖ JUR. Licence (de débit de boissons); *licence d'importation*, import licence. ‖ FIG. Licentiousness (dérèglement des mœurs); licence (excès de liberté); *prendre des licences*, to take liberties.

licencié, ée [-sje] adj. Dismissed, sacked. ‖ MILIT. Disbanded, demobilized.
— s. *Licencié ès lettres, ès sciences*, Bachelor of Arts, of Sciences; U. S. Master of Arts, of Sciences.

licenciement [-simɑ̃] m. Redundancy, dismissal, sacking. ‖ MILIT. Disbanding, demobilization.

licencier [-sje] v. tr. (1). To make redundant, to dismiss, to sack (un travailleur). ‖ MILIT. To disband, to demobilize, to demob (des troupes).

licencieux, euse [-sjø, ø:z] adj. Licentious, loose.

lichen [likɛn] m. BOT. Lichen.

licher [liʃe] v. tr. (1). POP. To lick, to lap (lécher). ‖ FAM. To tipple, to booze.

lichette [-ʃɛt] f. FAM. Wee bit (nourriture); wee drop (boisson).

licitation [lisitasjɔ̃] f. JUR. Sale by (ou) at auction, auction-sale.

licite [lisit] adj. Licit, legal, lawful.

licitement [-sitmɑ̃] adv. Licitly, legally, lawfully.

licol [likɔl], **licou** [liku] m. Halter.

licorne [likɔrn] f. Unicorn.

licteur [liktœ:r] m. † Lictor.

lie [li] adj. † *Faire chère lie*, to carouse, to feast.

lie f. Lees, dregs; *boire la coupe jusqu'à la lie*, to drain the cup to the dregs. ‖ FIG. *La lie du peuple*, the scum of the population, the rabble, the riff-raff. ‖ **Lie-de-vin**, adj. Wine-coloured.

lié, ée [lje] adj. Tied, bound (objets). ‖ Intimate, intimately acquainted (amis). ‖ Linked, related (questions, sujets).

Liechtenstein [liʃtɛnʃtajn] m. GÉOGR. Liechtenstein.

lied [li:d] m. MUS. Lied.

liège [ljɛ:ʒ] m. Cork.

liégeois, oise [ljeʒwa, a:z] adj. GÉOGR. Of (ou) from Liège. ‖ CULIN. *Café, chocolat liégeois*, coffee, chocolate ice-cream with whipped cream.
— s. GÉOGR. Native (ou) inhabitant of Liège.

lien [ljɛ̃] m. Bond (de gerbes); withe (d'osier). ‖ JUR. Bond, tie; *les liens de l'amitié*, friendly ties; *le lien du mariage*, the marriage tie. ‖ FIG. Link (relation) [*entre*, between].

lier [lje] v. tr. (1). To tie, to bend, to fasten (V. ATTACHER); *lier en gerbe*, to bind in a sheaf. ‖ CULIN. To thicken. ‖ GRAMM. To link. ‖ FIG. To link (unir) [*par*, by]; *lier amitié avec*, to strike up a friendship with; *lier conversation avec*, to enter into conversation with, to strike up a conversation with.
— v. pr. Se lier, to make friends (*avec*, with). ‖ To bind oneself (par contrat, serment). ‖ FIG. To agree with one another (idées).

lierre [ljɛ:r] m. BOT. Ivy.

liesse [ljɛ:s] f. Gaicty, jollity.

lieu [ljø] m. ZOOL. Pollack (lieu jaune); coal-fish, coley, saithe (lieu noir).

lieu [ljø] m. Place, spot, locality, site (endroit); *en lieu sûr*, in a safe place; *en quelque lieu que*, wherever; *en tous lieux*, everywhere; *les lieux du crime*, the scene of the crime; *lieux d'aisance*, privy, toilet; *sur les lieux*, on the spot (ou) premises; *vider les lieux*, to move out. ‖ Occasion, reason (raison); *avoir lieu de croire*, to have good grounds for believing, to have reason to believe; *il y aurait lieu de croire*, there is reason to believe; *donner lieu à*, to give rise to, to be the occasion for; *s'il y a lieu*, if need be. ‖ MATH. Locus. ‖ GRAMM. *Lieux communs*, commonplaces. ‖ ECCLÉS. *Lieux saints*, Holy places. ‖ LOC. *Au*

lieu de, instead of; *au lieu que*, whereas; *avoir lieu*, to take place, to happen (arriver); *en dernier lieu*, lastly, finally; *en premier lieu*, firstly, in the first place (ou) instance; *en temps et lieu*, in due course; *tenir lieu de tout*, to take the place of everything. ‖ **Lieu-dit**, m. Place. locality.

lieue [ljø] f. League; *bottes de sept lieues*, seven league boots. ‖ FIG. *Etre à cent lieues de penser que*, not to dream that.

lieur [ljœ:r] m. AGRIC. Binder (ouvrier).

lieuse [ljø:z] f. AGRIC. Binder (ouvrière, machine).

lieutenant [ljøtnɑ̃] m. MILIT. Lieutenant. ‖ NAUT. Lieutenant; *lieutenant de vaisseau*, lieutenant-commander. ‖ AVIAT. Flying officer. ‖ **Lieutenant-colonel**, m. MILIT. Lieutenant-colonel; AVIAT. Wing-commander.

lièvre [ljɛ:vr] m. ZOOL. Hare. ‖ FIG. *Courir deux lièvres à la fois*, to try to do two things at once; *lever un lièvre*, to start it; *prendre le lièvre au gîte*, to catch s.o. napping.

liftier [liftje] m. Liftman, lift boy; U. S. elevator boy (ou) operator.

lifting [liftiŋ] m. MÉD. Face-lift.

ligament [ligamɑ̃] m. MÉD. Ligament.

ligamenteux, euse [-tø, ø:z] adj. MÉD. Ligamentous. ‖ FAM. Fibrous, stringy.

ligature [ligaty:r] f. Ligature, binding. ‖ ELECTR. Splice. ‖ MUS. Tie.

ligaturer [-tyre] v. tr. (1). To bind. (V. LIER.) ‖ MÉD. To ligature, to ligate.

lige [li:ʒ] adj. † Liege; *homme lige*, liegeman.

lignage [liɲa:ʒ] m. Lineage; *de haut lignage*, of high degree.

lignard [liɲa:r] m. FAM., MILIT. Foot-slogger.

ligne [liɲ] f. Line (trait); *ligne de la main*, line of the hand. ‖ Line, row (rang); *assis en ligne*, sitting in a row. ‖ Line, part (partie); *les grandes lignes de son discours*, the main topics (ou) lines of his speech. ‖ Line (de journal, de livre); *à la ligne*, next line; indent; *aller à la ligne*, to begin a fresh paragraph, to indent; *tirer à la ligne*, to swell one's pages with trash. ‖ GÉOGR. Line (de l'équateur). ‖ MILIT. *Infanterie de ligne*, line infantry; *ligne Maginot*, Maginot Line; *ligne de mire*, line of sight. ‖ NAUT. *Ligne de flottaison*, water-line; *bâtiment de ligne*, capital ship. ‖ AVIAT. *Pilote de ligne*, airline pilot. ‖ CH. DE F. Railway line; *grande ligne*, main line; *ligne secondaire*, branch line, U. S. spur line. ‖ AUTOM. *Ligne d'autobus*, bus service; *ligne élégante d'une voiture*, good outline (ou) sleek lines of a car. ‖ SPORTS. Crease (du batteur au cricket); *ligne de touche*, touch line (au football, au rugby). ‖ FIG. Descent (descendance); *descendre en ligne droite de*, to be a lineal descendant of. ‖ FIG. *Hors ligne*, unrivalled, outstanding; *rester fidèle à sa ligne de conduite*, to be consistent in one's behaviour; *suivre la ligne du devoir*, to follow the path of duty; *venir en première ligne*, to be of primary importance. ‖ LOC. *Elle a de la ligne*, she has a good figure (ou) build; *garder la ligne*, to preserve one's figure.

lignée [-ɲe] f. Line, issue, stock. (V. RACE.)

ligneux, euse [liɲø, ø:z] adj. Ligneous, woody.

lignifier [-ɲifje] v. tr. (1). To lignify; to turn into wood.
— v. pr. Se lignifier, to lignify, to turn into wood, to become woody.

lignite [-ɲit] m. Lignite, brown coal.

lignosité [-ɲozite] f. Woodiness.

ligot [ligo] m. Bundle of firewood.

ligotage [ligota:ʒ] m. Binding, tying.

ligoter [-te] v. tr. (1). To bind hand and foot; U. S. to hog-tie. ‖ To lash together (les choses); to tie up (les personnes).

ligue [lig] f. League. (V. COALITION.)
liguer [lige] v. tr. (1). To league, to bend together.
— v. pr. **Se liguer**, to league, to form a league.
ligueur [-gœ:r] s. Leaguer.
lilas [lilα] m. BOT. Lilac.
— adj. Lilac coloured.
lilial, ale [liljal] adj. Lily-like.
lilliputien, enne [lilipysjɛ̃, ɛ:n] adj. Lilliputian.
lillois, oise [lilwa, a:z] adj. GÉOGR. Of (ou) from Lille.
— s. Native (ou) inhabitant of Lille.
limace [limas] f. ZOOL. Slug. ‖ TECHN. Archimedean screw.
limaçon [-sɔ̃] m. ZOOL. Snail. ‖ MÉD. Cochlea.
limage [lima:ʒ] m. Filing.
limaille [lima:j] f. Filings.
limande [limɑ̃d] f. ZOOL. Limanda; dab. ‖ TECHN. Sheeting (d'une mine).
limbes [lɛ̃:b] m. pl. Limbo.
lime [lim] f. File; *lime à ongles*, nail-file; *lime émeri*, emery board; *donner un coup de lime*, to give a touch up with a file; *enlever à la lime*, to file off.
limer [-me] v. tr. (1). To file. ‖ FIG. To polish.
limeur [-mœ:r] s. Filer.
limicole [limikɔl] adj. ZOOL. Limicolous.
limier [limje] m. ZOOL. Bloodhound. ‖ FAM. Sleuth, dick (détective).
liminaire [liminɛ:r] adj. Preliminary; *épître liminaire*, prefatory letter, foreword.
limitable [limitabl] adj. Limitable.
limitatif, ive [-tif, i:v] adj. Limiting.
limitation [-sjɔ̃] f. Limitation (v. RESTRICTION); *limitation des naissances*, birth-control. ‖ AUTOM. *Sans limitation de vitesse*, unrestricted (route).
limite [limit] f. Limit, boundary (d'un pays). [V. FRONTIÈRE.] ‖ Limit; bound; margin; *dans les limites de vos possibilités*, within the limits of your capacities; as far as your means will allow; *date limite*, latest date, U. S. deadline; *son orgueil n'a pas de limites*, his pride knows no bounds; *sans limite*, limitless, boundless. ‖ TECHN. *Limite critique de résistance*, breaking point; *limite de rupture*, ultimate stress; *charge limite*, limit load; *vitesse limite*, maximum speed.
limité, ee [-te] adj. Limited.
limiter [-te] v. tr. (1). To bound, to limit (v. BORNER); to restrict. (V. RESTREINDRE.)
— v. pr. **Se limiter**, to be limited (*à*, to) [avoir pour limites]; to limit (ou) restrict oneself (*à*, to) [s'imposer des limites].
limitrophe [limitrɔf] adj. Limitrophe, adjoining, bordering (v. ADJACENT); *limitrophe de*, bordering on, adjacent to; *pays limitrophe*, borderland.
limnologie [limnɔlɔʒi] f. Limnology.
limogeage [-ʒa:ʒ] m. Superseding. ‖ MILIT., FAM. Bowler-hatting, U. S. shelving.
limoger [-ʒe] v. tr. (7). MILIT. To supersede. ‖ FAM. To bowler-hat, to sack, U. S. to shelve.
Limoges [limɔʒ] f. GÉOGR. Limoges. ‖ ARTS. Limoges ware (ou) porcelain.
limon [limɔ̃] m. Mud, clay, loam.
limon m. BOT. Sour lime.
limon m. TECHN. Shaft (d'une voiture); string, stair-horse (d'un escalier).
limonade [limɔnad] f. Lemonade, U. S. limeade.
limonadier, ère [-dje, ɛ:r] s. Café- (ou) bar-owner (cafetier); lemonade manufacturer (fabricant).
limoneux, euse [-nø, ø:z] adj. Muddy. ‖ GÉOL. Alluvial.
limonier [limɔnje] m. ZOOL. Shaft horse.
limousin, ine [limuzɛ̃, in] adj. GÉOGR. Of (ou) from the Limousin. ‖ AGRIC. Limousin (bovin).
limousine [limuzin] f. Long woollen cloak. ‖ AUTOM. Limousine.
limpide [lɛ̃pid] adj. Limpid, clear.

limpidité [-dite] f. Limpidity, limpidness, clarity.
lin [lɛ̃] m. BOT. Flax; *bleu de lin*, flax-blue; *huile de lin*, linseed oil. ‖ TECHN. Linen (tissu).
linceul [lɛ̃sœl] m. Shroud, winding-sheet. ‖ FIG. *Le linceul de pourpre où dorment les dieux morts*, the dust of creeds outworn.
linéaire [lineɛ:r] adj. Linear; *dessin linéaire*, geometrical drawing.
linéament [lineamɑ̃] m. Lineament, feature (trait du visage). ‖ FIG. Outline (d'un ouvrage); prefiguration, germ (d'un événement).
linge [lɛ̃:ʒ] m. Linen; *linge de corps*, underlinen, underwear; *linge de maison*, de table, house, table linen; *linge de toilette*, towelling. ‖ LOC. *Lavez votre linge sale en famille*, do not wash your dirty linen in public.
lingère [lɛ̃ʒɛ:r] f. Seamstress. ‖ Wardrobe-keeper (dans une école).
lingerie [lɛ̃ʒri] f. Linen-drapery, U. S. white goods (commerce); linen, underwear (linge); linen-room (pièce).
lingot [lɛ̃go] m. Ingot.
lingotière [-tjɛ:r] f. TECHN. Ingot-mould.
lingual, ale [lɛ̃gwal] adj. Lingual.
linguiste [lɛ̃gɥist] s. Linguist.
linguistique [-tik] adj. Linguistic.
— f. Linguistics.
linguistiquement [-tikmɑ̃] adv. Linguistically.
linier, ère [linje, ɛ:r] adj. Flax, linen (industrie).
liniment [linimɑ̃] m. MÉD. Liniment.
linoléum [linoleɔm], **lino** [lino] m. Linoleum; lino (fam.).
linon [linɔ̃] m. Lawn (tissu).
linotte [linɔt] f. ZOOL. Linnet. ‖ FAM. *Avoir une tête de linotte*, to be feather-brained (ou) hare-brained.
linotype [linɔtip] f. TECHN. Linotype.
linotypiste [-pist] m. Linotyper, linotypist.
linteau [lɛ̃to] m. Lintel.
lion [ljɔ̃] m. ZOOL. Lion. ‖ ASTRON. Leo. ‖ FIG. *On en a fait le lion du jour*, he was lionized; *Richard Cœur de Lion*, Richard the Lion-heart.
lionceau [ljɔ̃so] m. ZOOL. Lion-cub.
lionne [ljɔn] f. ZOOL. Lioness.
lipide [lipid] m. MÉD. Lipid, lipide.
lippe [lip] f. Thick lower lip; blubber lip; *faire la lippe*, to pout. (V. MOUE.)
lippée [lipe] f. FAM. Mouthful; *franche lippée*, full meal, blow-out.
lippu, ue [lipy] adj. Thick-lipped, blubber-lipped.
liquéfaction [likefaksjɔ̃] f. Liquefaction.
liquéfiable [-fjabl] adj. Liquefiable.
liquéfiant, ante [-fjɑ̃, ɑ̃:t] adj. Liquefying. ‖ FAM. Gruelling (chaleur).
liquéfier [-fje] v. tr. (1). To liquefy.
— v. pr. **Se liquéfier**, to liquefy. ‖ FAM. To go to pieces, to fall apart.
liquette [likɛt] f. FAM. Shirt. (V. CHEMISE.)
liqueur [likœ:r] f. Liquor; alcoholic drink, liqueur; *liqueurs fortes*, strong drink, hard liquor. ‖ CHIM. Liquid solution.
liquidateur [likidatœ:r] m. Liquidator.
liquidation [-sjɔ̃] f. Liquidation; winding up. ‖ COMM. Clearance sale. ‖ FIN. Settlement; *entrer en liquidation*, to go into liquidation; *liquidation d'actif*, administration of assets.
liquide [likid] adj. Liquid, fluid. ‖ FIN. *Argent liquide*, ready money; available cash.
— m. Liquid. ‖ Liquid drink (boisson). ‖ GRAMM. Liquid.
liquider [-de] v. tr. (1). To liquidate; to pay up (l'arriéré); to settle (des comptes); to realize (sa fortune). ‖ COMM. To wind up (un commerce); to sell off, to realize (des marchandises); to pay (une note); to clear (un stock). ‖ FAM. To liquidate, to get rid of (qqn); to settle (une question).

— v. pr. **Se liquider**, to clear oneself of debt (personne); to be settled (question).

liquidité [-dite] f. Liquidity.

liquoreux, euse [likɔrø, ø:z] adj. Liqueur-like.

liquoriste [-rist] m. Wine and spirit merchant; U. S. liquor dealer.

lire [li:r] v. tr. (60). To read (sur, about); *ce livre se laisse lire*, this book is quite interesting; *c'est un livre à lire*, it's a book well worth reading; *une personne qui a beaucoup lu*, a well-read person. ‖ Mus. *Lire à première vue*, to read at sight. ‖ Comm. *A vous lire, dans l'attente de vous lire*, looking forward to hearing from you. — v. intr. To read; *lire tout bas, tout haut*, to read to oneself, aloud. — v. pr. **Se lire**, to be read; *cela se lit avec plaisir*, it makes enjoyable reading, it reads well. ‖ Fig. *Cela se lisait sur son visage*, it showed in his face; *la joie se lisait dans ses yeux*, his eyes sparkled with joy.

lis [lis] m. Bot. Lily; *lis d'eau*, water-lily; *lis de la vallée*, lily of the valley; *blanc comme un lis*, lily-white; *fleur de lis*, fleur de lis.

liséré [lizere] m. Border, edge.

lisérer v. tr. (5). To border, to edge.

liseron [lizrɔ̃] m. Bot. Bind-weed, convolvulus.

liseur [lizœ:r] s. Reading person, great reader. ‖ Fig. *Liseur d'âmes*, thought (ou) mind reader.

liseuse [-zø:z] f. Reading lamp (lampe). ‖ Book-wrapper (de livre). ‖ Bed jacket (vêtement).

lisibilité [lizibilite] f. Legibility.

lisible [-zibl] adj. Readable; legible.

lisiblement [-ziblǝmɑ̃] adv. Legibly.

lisière [lizjɛ:r] f. List, selvage, selvedge (d'étoffe). ‖ Leading-strings (pour bébé). ‖ Edge, border (d'un bois); skirt (d'une forêt). ‖ Fig. *En lisières*, in leading-strings.

lissage [lisa:ʒ] m. Smoothing, polishing, glazing.

lisse [lis] adj. Smooth, polished, glossy, sleek.

lisse f. Techn. Warp, heddle (de métier).

lisse f. Naut. Hand-rail of the bulwark.

lisser [-se] v. tr. (1). To smooth, to polish, to gloss (pierre); to glaze (papier); to sleek (les cheveux, les poils); to preen (ses plumes). — v. pr. **Se lisser**, to become smooth. ‖ *Se lisser les plumes*, to preen its feathers (oiseau).

lisseur [-sœ:r] s. Techn. Smoother, polisher.

lisseuse [-sø:z] f. Techn. Smoothing-machine.

lissoir [-swa:r] m. Techn. Smoothing-tool.

listage [lista:ʒ] m. Listing; list.

listing [listiŋ] m. Inform. Listing, print-out.

liste [list] f. List, register, roll (v. nomenclature); *liste civile*, civil list; *scrutin de liste*, vote for a list; *venir en tête de liste*, to top the poll. ‖ Milit. *Liste des hommes de service*, roster.

lit [li] m. Bed; *à deux lits, à un lit*, double-bedded (ou) double, single (chambre); *lit de camp*, camp-bed; *lit à colonnes*, four-poster; *lit de douleur, de mort*, sick-, death-bed; *lit d'enfant*, cot, U. S. crib. ‖ Bed, marriage; *enfant du second lit*, child of the second marriage. ‖ Layer (de cailloux); bed (d'une rivière). ‖ Harbour (de ccrf); form (de lièvre). ‖ **Lit-cage**, m. Collapsible metal bed.

litanie [litani] f. Litany. ‖ Fig. Long list.

litchi [litʃi] m. Bot. Lychee, litchi.

litée [lite] f. Litter.

literie [litri] f. Bedding; bed linen.

lithlase [litja:z] f. Méd. Lithiasis.

lithique [-tik] adj. Lithic.

lithium [-tjɔm] m. Chim., Méd. Lithium.

lithographie [litɔgrafi], **litho** [lito] f. Arts. Lithography; poster (fam.). ‖ Techn. Lithography.

lithographier [-grafje] v. tr. (1). To lithograph.

lithographique [-grafik] adj. Lithographic.

lithopone [litɔpɔn] f. Chim. Lithopone.

litière [litjɛ:r] f. Litter, palanquin. ‖ Litter

(d'écurie). ‖ Fig. *Faire litière de ses scrupules*, to stifle one's scruples.

litigant, ante [litigɑ̃, ɑ̃:t] adj. Jur. Litigant.

litige [-ti:ʒ] m. Jur. Litigation, contest; *cas en litige*, case under dispute; *être en litige*, to be at issue, in question.

litigieux, euse [-tiʒjø, ø:z] adj. Litigious; disputable (question).

litote [litɔt] f. Gramm. Litotes; understatement.

litre [litr] m. Litre.

litron [-trɔ̃] m. Fam. Litre (ou) bottle of plonk.

littéraire [literɛ:r] adj. Literary. — s. Person gifted for the arts; arts teacher (professeur); arts student (étudiant).

littérairement [-rɛrmɑ̃] adv. Literarily.

littéral, ale [-ral] adj. Literal. ‖ Jur. *Preuve littérale*, documentary evidence.

littéralement [-lmɑ̃] adv. Literally.

littéralisme [-lism] m. Literalism.

littéralité [-lite] f. Literalness, literality.

littérateur [-tœ:r] m. Man of letters, literary man, littérateur. (V. auteur, écrivain.)

littérature [-ty:r] f. Literature; *littérature alimentaire*, hackwork, pot-boilers.

littoral, ale [litɔral] adj. Littoral, coastal. — m. Littoral, coast-line, seaboard, shore; *du littoral*, coastal.

lituanien, enne [litɥanjɛ̃, ɛn] adj., s. Géogr. Lithuanian. — m. Gramm. Lithuanian (langue).

liturgie [lityrʒi] f. Ecclés. Liturgy.

liturgique [-ʒik] adj. Ecclés. Liturgical.

liturgiste [-ʒist] m. Ecclés. Liturgist.

livide [livid] adj. Livid, ghastly. (V. blême.)

lividité [-dite] f. Lividness, ghastliness. (V. pâleur.)

living-room [liviŋrum], **living** [liviŋ] m. Living-room.

livrable [livrabl] adj. Comm. Deliverable, ready for delivery.

livraison [livrɛzɔ̃] f. Comm. Delivery. ‖ Instalment (d'un livre).

livre [livr] f. Pound; *vingt francs la livre*, twenty francs a pound; *vendu à la livre*, sold by the pound. ‖ Pound, pound sterling (monnaie). ‖ Fam. *Vingt mille livres de rentes*, an income of twenty thousand francs.

livre m. Book (v. volume); *livre de classe, du maître*, school, answer book; *livre relié, non relié*, bound, paper-covered book; *livre à succès*, best-seller; *traduire à livre ouvert*, to translate at sight. ‖ Book; *en cinq livres*, in five books. ‖ Fin. *Grand livre*, ledger; *livre de caisse*, cash book; *livre de comptabilité*, account book; *livre de la dette publique*, Register of the National Debt. ‖ Ecclés. *Livre de messe*, prayer-book. ‖ Naut. *Livre de bord*, log-book. ‖ Culin. *Livre de cuisine*, cookery book, U. S. cook book. ‖ Sports. *Faire un livre*, to make book (hippisme). ‖ Loc. *Livre jaune*, White Paper.

livrée [livre] f. Livery; *porter la livrée de qqn*, to be in s.o.'s service.

livrer v. tr. (1). To deliver, to give up, to surrender, to yield. (V. céder.) ‖ To commit (abandonner) [à, to]. ‖ Comm. To deliver. ‖ Milit. *Livrer bataille*, to give battle. ‖ Jur. To hand over (à la justice). ‖ Fig. To betray; to give up (révéler) [à, to]; *livré à lui-même*, left to himself; *livré à la risée publique*, made a laughing-stock. — v. pr. **Se livrer**, to surrender oneself (à, to) [qqn]. ‖ Fig. *Se livrer à la boisson*, to indulge in drink, to take to the bottle; *se livrer au désespoir*, to give way to despair; *se livrer à l'étude*, to devote oneself to study. (V. s'adonner.)

livresque [-vrɛsk] adj. Got (ou) U. S. gotten from books, bookish (savoir); *connaissances livresques*, book-knowledge; *imagination livresque*, bookish imagination.

livret [-vrɛ] m. Booklet. ‖ *Livret de l'étudiant,* scholastic record-book. ‖ Fin. *Livret de caisse d'épargne,* savings-bank book. ‖ Milit. *Livret militaire,* military record. ‖ Mus. Libretto (d'opéra).

livreur [livrœːʳ] m. Comm. Delivery-man.

livreuse [-vrøːz] f. Comm. Delivery-girl (personne); delivery-van (ou) U. S. -truck (voiture).

Lloyd [lɔjd] m. Comm. Lloyd's.

lob [lɔb] m. Sports. Lob (au tennis).

lobby [lɔbi] m. Lobby (groupe de pression).

lobe [lɔb] m. Méd. Lobe (du foie, de l'oreille); flap (de l'oreille). ‖ Archit. Foil (d'une fenêtre).

lobé, ée [lɔbe] adj. Bot. Lobate.

lober v. intr. (1). Sports. To lob (au tennis).

lobotomie [lɔbɔtɔmi] f. Méd. Lobotomy.

lobulaire [lɔbylɛːr], **lobulé, ée** [-le] adj. Lobular.

lobule [lɔbyl] m. Méd., Bot. Lobule.

local, ale [-lɔkal] adj. Local (couleur, intérêt, heure).

— m. Premises, building, site; *locaux professionnels,* business premises.

localement [-lmɑ̃] adv. Locally.

localisable [-lizabl] adj. Locatable (que l'on peut situer); localizable (que l'on peut circonscrire).

localisation [-lizasjɔ̃] f. Localisation.

localiser [-lize] v. tr. (1). To locate (qqch., qqn). ‖ To localize (un incendie). [V. Circonscrire.]
— v. pr. **Se localiser,** to fix one's abode. ‖ To become localized (incendie).

localité [-lite] f. Locality; inhabited place, settlement; *de la localité,* local.

locataire [-tɛːr] m. Tenant; lessee (ou) leaseholder (avec bail); lodger, U. S. roomer (pour une chambre); *locataire de bonne foi,* conventionary.

locatif, ive [lɔkatif, iːv] adj. Referring to letting (ou) leasing (ou) renting; *réparations locatives,* tenantable repairs; *risques locatifs,* tenant's risks; *valeur locative,* rental value.
— m. Gramm. Locative.

location [lɔkasjɔ̃] f. Hiring, letting out on hire, U. S. renting; *agent de location,* house-agent, U. S. renting agent; *en location,* on hire, rented, for rent; *prix de location,* rent, rental. ‖ Théâtr. Releasing (d'un film); booking, reserving (d'une place); *bureau de location,* box-office. ‖ **Location-vente,** f. Hire-purchase system.

loch [lɔk] m. Naut. Ship's log.

loche [lɔʃ] f. Zool. Grey slug (limace); loach (poisson).

lock-out [lɔkaut] m. invar. Lock-out. (V. Grève.)

lock-outer [-aute] v. tr. (1). To lock out.

locomobile [lɔkɔmɔbil] adj. Locomotive; transportable (en général); travelling (grue).
— f. Agric. Transportable steam-engine.

locomoteur, trice [lɔkɔmɔtœːr, tris] adj. Techn., Méd. Locomotor.

locomotion [-sjɔ̃] f. Locomotion.

locomotive [-tiv] f. Ch. de f. Locomotive, engine.

locomotrice [-tris] f. Ch. de f. Electric engine.

locuste [lɔkyst] f. Zool. Locust.

locuteur, trice [lɔkytœːr, tris] s. Gramm. Speaker; *locuteur natif,* native speaker.

locution [lɔkysjɔ̃] f. Phrase, idiom.

loden [lɔdɛn] m. Loden (tissu); loden coat (manteau).

lœss [løs] m. Géol. Loess.

lof [lɔf] m. Naut. Windward side (d'un navire); *aller au lof,* to sail into the wind.

lofer [-fe] v. intr. (1). Naut. To luff.

logarithme [lɔgaritm] m. Math. Logarithm; *échelle des logarithmes,* logarithmic scale.

logarithmique [-ritmik] adj. Math. Logarithmic.

loge [lɔːʒ] f. Hut, cabin. ‖ Lodge (de concierge,

de franc-maçon). ‖ Théâtr. Box; *loges des artistes,* artists' dressing-rooms; *loge d'avant-scène,* stage-box. ‖ Arts. Separate studio; *entrer en loge,* to start working for the « Prix de Rome ». ‖ Fig. *Être aux premières loges,* to have a front seat, to be in an excellent position.

logeable [lɔʒabl] adj. Habitable, inhabitable, fit for occupation.

logement [-ʒmɑ̃] m. Lodging, housing; *logement et nourriture,* board and lodging. ‖ Accommodation, room (place). ‖ Lodging, apartment, dwelling. (V. Appartement.) ‖ Comm. Container (des liquides); packing (des marchandises). ‖ Milit. Quarters (quartier); billeting (des troupes); *effectuer un logement,* to gain a foot-hold (sur l'ennemi). ‖ Naut. Berth; berthing. ‖ Aviat. *Logement du moteur,* engine nacelle. ‖ Techn. Seating; housing; recess, socket.

loger [lɔʒe] v. intr. (7). To live, to lodge (v. Habiter); *loger à l'hôtel,* to stay at a hotel; *loger en garni,* to live in lodgings (ou) in furnished rooms. ‖ To find room (v. Tenir); *pouvons-nous tous loger dans ce compartiment?,* can we all get into this compartment? ‖ Milit. *Loger chez l'habitant,* to go into billets. ‖ Fam. *Où logez-vous?,* where do you stay (ou) live?
— v. tr. To lodge, to house, to put up; *cet hôtel vous logera bien,* this hotel will give you good accommodation; *je ne sais où loger cette armoire,* I don't know where to put this wardrobe; *logez les manteaux à l'arrière de la voiture,* put the coats in the back of the car. ‖ Comm. To cask (liquide); *vin logé,* wine in the wood.
— v. pr. **Se loger,** to lodge (choses, projectile); to take lodgings, to put up, to room (personne); *il se loge selon ses moyens,* he puts up with such accommodation as he can afford; *où ces chauves-souris se logent-elles le jour?,* where do these bats lurk in the daytime? ‖ Milit. To get a lodgment (ou) a footing.

logette [-ʒɛt] f. Small lodge (ou) cell.

logeur [-ʒœːr] m. Lodging-house keeper, landlord.

logeuse [-ʒøːz] f. Landlady.

loggia [lɔdʒja] f. Archit. Loggia.

logiciel [lɔʒisjɛl] m. Inform. Software.

logicien [-ʒisjɛ̃] m. Philos. Logician.

logique [lɔʒik] adj. Logical (en général); consistent (raisonnement). ‖ Culin. Reasoned (menu).
— f. Philos. Logic.

logiquement [-mɑ̃] adv. Logically, consistently.

logis [lɔʒi] m. Dwelling, lodging, abode (v. Habitation); *corps de logis,* main part of a building; *rentrer au logis,* to go home. ‖ Fig. *La folle du logis,* the imagination.

logistique [lɔʒistik] adj. Logistic; *soutien logistique,* logistic support.
— f. Logistics.

logogriphe [lɔgɔgrif] m. Logogriph, word-puzzle.

logomachie [-maʃi] f. Logomachy.

logorrhée [-re] f. Psych. Logorrhoea. ‖ Fig. Rambling, verbal diarrhoea.

loi [lwa] f. Jur. Law; *avoir force de loi,* to have the force of law; *conformément à la loi,* as required by law, in pursuance of law; *force est restée à la loi,* the law prevailed; *loi Bérenger,* First Offender's Act; *sa parole fait loi,* his word is law. ‖ Law, rule, point (règle); *faire la loi,* to lay down the law; *se faire une loi de,* to make a point of. ‖ **Loi-cadre,** f. Jur. Law outlining general principles of a reform. ‖ **Loi-programme,** f. Jur. Law authorizing long-term government spending.

loin [lwɛ̃] adv. Far (espace); *il y a loin de Paris à Rome,* it's a long way from Paris to Rome; *moins loin,* less far; *plus loin,* farther (ou) farther on; *la nouvelle se répandit au loin*, the news spread abroad; *dans un pays très loin*, in a far distant country. ‖ Far (temps); *loin dans le passé*, far back in the past; *avec lui, cet héritage n'ira pas loin*, that legacy of his won't last long (ou) will not take him far; *le jour est encore loin où*, the day is still far off when; *de loin en loin*, every now and then; *du plus loin que je me souvienne*, as far back as I can remember. ‖ FIG. *Il est allé trop loin*, he overdid it, he overreached himself, he went too far; *il ira loin*, he will go a long way; *il y a loin de la coupe aux lèvres*, there's many a slip 'twixt the cup and the lip; *il revient de loin*, he was at death's door; *loin du but*, wide of the mark; *loin de là*, far from it; *loin de moi la pensée de*, far be it from me to; *loin que cela lui soit utile*, far from being useful to him; *loin des yeux, loin du cœur*, out of sight, out of mind.

lointain, aine [lwɛ̃tɛ̃, ɛ:n] adj. Distant, far, far off (lieu, période). [V. ÉLOIGNÉ.] ‖ Remote (causes); vague (souvenir).
— m. Distance; *dans le lointain*, in the far distance; *les lointains*, the background. ‖ ARTS. Pl. Distances.

loir [lwa:r] m. ZOOL. Dormouse.

loisible [lwazibl] adj. Permissible; optional; *il vous est loisible de*, you are free to, you are at liberty to.

loisir [-zi:r] m. Leisure, spare time; leisure hours; *à loisir*, at leisure, leisurely; *organisation des loisirs*, organizing of spare time activities.

lokoum [lɔkum] m. V. LOUKOUM.

lombago [lɔ̃bago] m. MÉD. Lumbago.

lombaire [lɔ̃bɛ:r] adj. MÉD. Lumbar.

lombard, arde [lɔ̃ba:r, a:rd] adj., s. GÉOGR. Lombard.

lombes [lɔ̃:b] m. pl. MÉD. Loins; lumbar region.

lombo-sacré, ée [lɔ̃bosakre] adj. MÉD. Lumbosacral.

lombric [lɔ̃brik] m. ZOOL. Earthworm.

londonien, enne [lɔ̃dɔnjɛ̃, ɛn] adj. Pertaining to London; *la vie londonienne*, London life.
— s. Londoner.

Londres [lɔ̃dr] m. London; *le Grand Londres*, Greater London.

londrès [lɔ̃drɛs] m. Havana cigar.

long, ongue [-lɔ̃, ɔ̃:g] adj. Long; *longue barbe*, flowing beard; *long de deux pieds*, two feet long; *long de vingt-huit jours*, twenty-eight days long; *il a eu une longue vie*, he was long-lived. ‖ JUR. *A longue échéance*, long (bail). ‖ CULIN. Thin (sauce). ‖ LOC. *Avoir les dents longues*, to be ambitious (ambitieux); to be greedy (avide); *avoir la langue trop longue*, to be unable to hold one's tongue; *de longue date*, of long standing; *être long à venir*, to be long in coming.
— adv. *Cela en dit long sur*, that speaks volumes for; *en savoir long sur*, to know quite a lot about; *il n'en sait pas plus long*, this is all he knows; *un mot, un regard qui en dit long*, a tell-tale word, an eloquent look.
— m. Length; *deux pieds de long*, two feet long (ou) in length; *de long en large*, to and fro, up and down, backward and forward; *en long*, lengthwise; *être étendu de tout son long sur le dos* (ou) *sur le ventre*, to lie flat on one's back (ou) prone. ‖ LOC. *Le long de*, along; *le long l'un de l'autre*, alongside each other; *le long de la pente*, down the slope; *tout au long*, at full length; *tout le long du jour*, all day long. ‖ **Long-courrier**, adj. AVIAT. Long-distance; NAUT. ocean-going.

longanimité [-mite] f. Forbearance, long-suffering, longanimity.

longe [lɔ̃:ʒ] f. Tether, lunge, longe; *faire trotter un cheval à la longe*, to lunge a horse. ‖ Thong (d'un fouet). ‖ CULIN. Loin (de veau).

longer [lɔ̃ʒe] v. tr. (7). To run along. ‖ To skirt (le bois).

longeron [lɔ̃ʒrɔ̃] m. TECHN. Longitudinal girder. ‖ CH. DE F. Side-frame. ‖ AUTOM. Side-member, sill. ‖ AVIAT. Front spar; wing spar; longeron.

longévité [lɔ̃ʒevite] f. Longevity.

longiligne [lɔ̃ʒiliɲ] adj. Rangy, long-limbed, tall and thin.

longitude [lɔ̃ʒityd] f. Longitude; *par 20⁰ longitude Ouest*, in the longitude of 20⁰ West.

longitudinal, ale [-dinal] adj. Longitudinal. ‖ NAUT. Fore and aft.

longitudinalement [-dinalmɑ̃] adv. Longitudinally. ‖ NAUT. Fore and aft.

longtemps [lɔ̃tɑ̃] adv. Long, a long time; *il n'en a pas pour longtemps*, it won't take him long (durée); he's nearing the end (vie); *il y a longtemps que je l'ai appris*, I learned it long ago; *il y a longtemps que nous avons rompu*, it's a long time since we broke off; *j'ai été longtemps avant de m'en apercevoir*, it was a long time before I realized it; *j'ai mis longtemps à la connaître*, it took me a long time to get to know her; *vous ne verrez pas de longtemps un si beau film*, you won't see such a fine film (ou) picture for a long time.

longue [lɔ̃:g] f. GRAMM. Long syllable. ‖ *A la longue*, at length, after a time; in the long run. ‖ **Longue-vue**, f. Telescope, field-glass.

longuement [lɔ̃gmɑ̃] adv. Long, for a long time. ‖ Slowly, deliberately. ‖ Lengthily, at great length.

longuet [-gɛ] adj. FAM. Rather long, longish.

longueur [-gœ:r] f. Length; *deux mètres de longueur*, two metres long; *en longueur, dans la longueur*, lengthwise. ‖ SPORTS. *D'une longueur*, by a length. ‖ RADIO. *Longueur d'onde*, wavelength. ‖ Pl. Delays, dilatoriness (délais); slowness (lenteurs); dull parts, tedious passages (textes); *traîner en longueur*, to drag on.

looping [lupiŋ] m. AVIAT. Loop; *faire un looping*, to loop the loop; *looping à l'envers*, bunt.

lopin [lɔpɛ̃] m. Bit, piece, plot, strip (de terre).

loquace [lɔkwas] adj. Loquacious, talkative (personne); garrulous (vieillard). [V. BAVARD.]

loquacité [lɔkwasite] f. Loquacity, loquaciousness, talkativeness; garrulity (d'un vieillard).

loque [lɔk] f. Rag (v. GUENILLE); *en loques*, falling to pieces, in tatters. ‖ FIG. *Comme une loque*, as limp as a rag.

loquet [lɔkɛ] m. Latch; *fermer au loquet*, to latch.

loqueteau [lɔkto] m. Small latch.

loqueteux, euse [lɔktø, ø:z] adj. Ragged, tattered, in tatters. (V. DÉGUENILLÉ.)
— s. Tatterdemalion; ragged fellow, ragamuffin.

lord [lɔ:r] m. Lord. ‖ **Lord-maire**, m. Lord Mayor.

lordose [lɔrdo:z] f. MÉD. Lordosis.

lorette [lɔrɛt] f. † Tart.

lorgner [lɔrɲe] v. tr. (1). To cast sidelong glances, to ogle, to leer, U. S. to lamp; *en train de lorgner qqn*, looking at s.o. out of the corner of one's eye. ‖ To look through opera-glasses (à la jumelle). ‖ FIG. To have one's eyes on, to covet.

lorgnette [lɔrɲɛt] f. Opera glasses.

lorgnon [lɔrɲɔ̃] m. Pince-nez, eye-glasses.

loriot [lɔrjo] m. ZOOL. Oriole.

lorrain, aine [lɔrɛ̃, ɛn] adj. Pertaining to Lorraine.
— s. GÉOGR. Lorrainer; native of Lorraine.
— m. GRAMM. Dialect spoken in Lorraine.

lors [lɔ:r] adv. † Then. ‖ *Dès lors*, from that time; *dès lors que*, since; *lors de*, at the time of; *lors même que*, though, even though; *pour lors*, then; in that case.

lorsque [lɔrsk] conj. When (v. QUAND); *lorsqu'il sera arrivé*, when he has come.

losange [lɔzɑ̃:ʒ] m. Lozenge, diamond; *en losange*, diamond-shaped.

losanger [-ʒe] v. tr. (7). To divide into lozenges.

lot [lo] m. Share, portion. (V. PART.) ǁ Fate, lot, fortune (sort). ǁ Prize (de loterie); *gros lot*, first prize; jackpot (fam.). ǁ COMM. Lot, parcel (de marchandises).

loterie [lɔtri] f. Lottery; *mettre en loterie*, to raffle.

loti [lɔti] adj. FAM. *Bien loti*, well provided for; *mal loti*, poorly (ou) badly off.

lotion [lɔsjɔ̃] f. Washing, bathing; *lotion pour les cheveux*, hair-lotion.

lotionner [-sjɔne] v. tr. (1). To wash, to bathe, to sponge.

lotir [lɔti:r] v. tr. (2). To divide into lots (v. MORCELER); *lotir un domaine*, to parcel out an estate. ǁ To sort (trier).

lotissement [-tismɑ̃] m. Dividing into lots, parcelling out (morcelage). ǁ Allotment; building plot (terrain). ǁ Development of building land.

loto [lɔto] m. Lotto; lotto-set. ǁ FAM. *Yeux en boule de loto*, goggle-eyes.

lotte [lɔt] f. ZOOL. Eel-pout, burbot; *lotte de mer*, angler-fish.

lotus [lɔty:s] m. BOT. Lotus.

louable [luabl] adj. Laudable, commendable, praiseworthy (digne de louange).

louable adj. Rentable.

louablement [-bləmɑ̃] adv. Laudably, commendably.

louage [lwa:ʒ] m. Hiring out; renting; *voiture de louage*, hackney-carriage, cab, U. S. rented car. ǁ Hiring, engaging (de domestiques).

louange [luɑ̃:ʒ] f. Praise, encomium (v. ÉLOGE); *chanter les louanges de qqn*, to sing the praises of s.o.; *chanter ses propres louanges*, to blow one's own trumpet (ou) U. S. horn; *c'est à sa louange*, it is to his credit.

louanger [luɑ̃ʒe] v. tr. (7). To praise, to commend, to eulogize. (V. LOUER.) ǁ To cry up, to extol, to sing the praises of. (V. EXALTER.)

louangeur, euse [-ʒœ:r, ø:z] adj. Laudative, laudatory (laudatif). ǁ Flattering (flatteur).

— s. Praiser, laudator. ǁ Flatterer.

loubard [luba:r] m. V. LOULOU.

louche [luʃ] adj. MÉD. Squint- (ou) cross-eyed. ǁ FIG. Doubtful, shady (choses); cloudy (liquide); suspicious, shifty (personne); *ça c'est louche!*, it's all rather fishy.

— m. Fishiness, shadiness.

louche f. CULIN. Soup-ladle. ǁ TECHN. Reamer.

loucher [-ʃe] v. intr. (1). To squint; to have a cast in one eye. ǁ FAM. To cast longing eyes (*vers*, at). [V. LORGNER.]

loucherie [-ʃri] f. MÉD. Squinting.

louer [lwe] v. tr. (1). To hire out, to let, to let out, U. S. to rent (*à*, to) [par le propriétaire]; *louer à bail*, to lease; *maison à louer*, house to let (ou) U. S. for rent. ǁ To take (une chambre, une maison); to rent (une maison); to hire, U. S. to rent (une voiture). ǁ THÉÂTR. To book; to reserve; *place louée*, reserved seat.

— v. pr. **Se louer**, AGRIC. To engage oneself.

louer v. tr. (1). To praise, to commend.

— v. pr. **Se louer**, to be satisfied (*de*, with); to congratulate oneself (*de*, on).

loueur [lwœ:r] s. Hirer out; *loueur de chevaux*, livery-stable keeper; *loueur d'habits*, clothes agency, U. S. clothes rental store. ǁ Praiser, flatterer.

loufiat [lufja] m. POP. Waiter.

loufoque [lufɔk] adj. FAM. Crazy, cracked, daft; U. S. nutty, screwy.

— s. Crank, crack-pot, U. S. screwball.

loufoquerie [-kri] f. Craziness, eccentricity, daftness.

louftingue [luftɛ̃:g] s. V. LOUFOQUE.

lougre [lugr] m. NAUT. Lugger.

Louis [lwi] m. Lewis (prénom). ǁ Louis, twenty-franc piece (monnaie).

louise-bonne [lwizbɔn] f. BOT. Louise-bonne pear.

lo(u)koum [lukum] m. Turkish delight.

loulou [lulu] m. ZOOL. *Grand loulou*, spitz; *loulou de Poméranie*, Pomeranian.

loulou [lulu], **loubard** [luba:r] m. POP. Yob, yobbo, hooligan.

loup [lu] m. ZOOL. Wolf. ǁ Black velvet half mask (masque). ǁ Flaw, fault (défaut). ǁ NAUT. *Loup de mer*, tar, old salt. ǁ FIG. *A pas de loup*, stealthily; *connu comme le loup blanc*, known to everybody; *de loup*, ravenous (faim); bitter (froid); *elle a vu le loup*, she has lost her innocence; *enfermer le loup dans la bergerie*, to set the fox to keep the geese; *se jeter dans la gueule du loup*, to rush into the lion's mouth; *les loups ne se mangent pas entre eux*, dog doesn't eat dog; *quand on parle du loup, on en voit la queue*, talk of the devil and he will pop up. ǁ FAM. *Mon petit loup*, my sweet, U. S. honey. ǁ **Loup-cervier**, m. ZOOL. Lynx. ǁ **Loup-garou**, m. Werewolf; FAM. bogeyman.

loupe [lup] f. MÉD. Wen. ǁ PHYS. Lens, magnifying glass. ǁ TECHN. Burr (du bois); lump (du métal).

loupé [lupe] m. Slip-up.

louper [lupe] v. tr. (1). FAM. To miss (son train); to botch, to bungle (son travail). ǁ TECHN. *Loupé*, defective (pièce).

loupiot, otte [lupjo, ɔt] s. POP. Kid, nipper.

loupiote [lupjɔt] f. POP. Small lamp (lampe).

lourd, ourde [lu:r, u:rd] adj. Heavy, weighty; ponderous (en poids). ǁ Too rich, hard to digest (aliment); heavy (sommeil); sultry (temps). ǁ Burdensome (charge); ungainly, clumsy (démarche); gross (erreur); dull (esprit); dull-witted (personne); severe (perte); grievous, grave, heavy (tâche); *lourd de*, big (ou) fraught with (conséquences); heavy with (sommeil); *l'affaire est lourde pour lui*, the business is rather too much for him. ǁ AUTOM. *Poids lourd*, heavy lorry (ou) U. S. truck. ǁ MILIT. Heavy (artillerie). ǁ LOC. *Avoir la main lourde*, to be heavy-handed.

— adv. Heavy; *il n'en reste pas lourd*, there's not much left; *cela pèse lourd sur sa conscience*, it weighs heavy on his conscience.

lourdaud, aude [lurdo, o:d] adj. Heavy, clumsy, awkward. ǁ FIG. Dull (esprit).

— s. Lout, bumpkin, gawk. (V. BALOURD.) ǁ FIG. Dullard, blockhead.

lourde [lu:rd] f. POP. Door; *boucle la lourde*, put wood in hole.

lourdement [-dəmɑ̃] adv. Heavily. ǁ FIG. Heavily, clumsily, awkwardly (avec gaucherie); *se tromper lourdement*, to make a gross mistake.

lourder [lurde] v. tr. (1). POP. To chuck (ou) kick out, to bounce.

lourderie [-dəri] f. Loutishness, doltishness. ǁ Gross blunder.

lourdeur [-dœ:r] f. Heaviness (du poids); sultriness, closeness (du temps). ǁ Clumsiness, awkwardness (du comportement); dullness (de l'esprit); ponderousness (du style). ǁ Severity (d'une perte); weight (d'une responsabilité).

loustic [lustik] m. Wag, joker, jester. (V. LASCAR.)

loutre [lutr] f. ZOOL. Otter. ǁ COMM. Sealskin.

louve [lu:v] f. ZOOL. She-wolf. ǁ TECHN. Lewis, lewisson. ǁ NAUT. Rudder-case.

louver [luve] v. tr. (1). TECHN. To lewis.

louveteau [-vto] m. ZOOL. Wolf-cub. ǁ FAM. Wolf-cub (scout).

louveterie [-vtri] f. Wolf-hunting; wolf-hunting organization.

louvetier [-vtje] m. SPORTS. Master of the wolf-hunt.
louvoiement [luvwɑmɑ̃], **louvoyage** [luwaja:ʒ] m. NAUT. Tacking. ‖ FIG. Shuffling.
louvoyer [-vwɑje] v. intr. (9a). NAUT. To tack, ot tack about. ‖ FIG. To be evasive.
lover [lɔve] v. intr. (1). NAUT. To coil (une corde). ‖ ZOOL. Serpent lové, coiled snake.
— v. pr. **Se lover**, to coil up (serpent).
loyal, ale [lwajal] adj. Frank, honest, faithful, dependable, fair (personne). ‖ Sincere, staunch, frank (comportement). ‖ COMM. Loyal et marchand, sound, fair quality.
loyalement [-lmɑ̃] adv. Frankly, faithfully, sincerely, honestly; agir loyalement, to behave honourably; to play the game (fam.).
loyalisme [-lism] m. Loyalty; loyalism.
loyaliste [-list] adj., s. Loyalist.
loyauté [lwajote] f. Honesty, straightforwardness. (V. DROITURE.) ‖ Fairness (franc jeu). ‖ Loyalty (envers, to).
loyer [lwaje] m. Rent; rental; prendre à loyer, to rent. ‖ FIN. Price (de l'argent).
L.S.D. [ɛlɛsde] m. MÉD. L.S.D.
lu [ly]. V. LIRE (60).
lubie [lybi] f. Whim, crotchet, freak, fad; qui a des lubies, crotchety.
lubricité [lybrisite] f. Lewdness, lust, lubricity, lechery.
lubrifiant, ante [lybrifjɑ̃, ɑ̃:t] adj. Lubricating. — m. Lubricant.
lubrification [-fikasjɔ̃] f. Lubrication.
lubrifier [-fje] v. tr. (1). To lubricate.
lubrique [lybrik] adj. Libidinous, lewd, lustful.
lubriquement [-brikmɑ̃] adv. Lewdly, lustfully, lecherously.
lucarne [lykarn] f. Attic- (ou) dormer-window (v. TABATIÈRE); lucarne faîtière, skylight.
lucide [lysid] adj. Lucid, clear (esprit); clear-headed (personne).
lucidement [-dmɑ̃] adv. Lucidly, clearly.
lucidité [-dite] f. Lucidity. (V. CLAIRVOYANCE.) ‖ MÉD. Intervalle de lucidité, lucid interval.
luciole [lysjɔl] f. ZOOL. Luciola, firefly.
lucratif, ive [lykratif, i:v] adj. Lucrative, paying.
lucre [lykr] m. Lucre. (V. GAIN.)
ludion [lydjɔ̃] m. Cartesian diver.
ludique [lydik] adj. Ludic, play.
luette [lyɛt] f. MÉD. Uvula.
lueur [lyœ:r] m. Gleam, glimmer; flash; à la lueur des étoiles, by the faint light of the stars; jeter une lueur, to gleam; lueur d'un coup de feu, flash of a shot. ‖ Ray (rayon); premières lueurs de l'aube, first rays of dawn.
luge [ly:ʒ] f. SPORTS. Luge, toboggan.
luger [lyʒe] v. intr. (7). SPORTS. To sleigh, to toboggan.
lugeur, euse [-ʒœ:r, ø:z] s. SPORTS. Sleigher, tobogganer.
lugubre [lygybr] adj. Lugubrious, dismal, mournful, gloomy (aspect); sad, distressing, dreary (récit, spectacle); sorrowful, doleful (ton).
lugubrement [-brəmɑ̃] adv. Lugubriously.
lui [lɥi] (pl. **eux** [ø] sujet; **leur** [lœ:r] compl.) pr. pers. **He** (sujet); c'est lui, it's he; elle est plus obligeante que lui, she is more obliging than he; il n'aurait pas dit cela, lui! he would not have said that! ; son frère et lui, he and his brother. ‖ **Him**, her, it; to him, to her, to it (complément); c'est à lui, it's his; de lui c'est étonnant, from him it is surprising; dites-le-lui, tell him; donnez-le-lui, give it to him; elle ne viendra pas, je le lui ai défendu, she will not come, I have forbidden her to; je ne lui ai jamais dit cela, I never said that to him (ou) to her; j'ai fait un grand feu, venez vous sécher près de lui, I have made a big

fire, come and dry yourselves around it; je les connais bien, son frère et lui, I know him and his brother well. ‖ **Lui-même**, pr. réfl. Himself; il viendra de lui-même, he will come himself.
luire [lɥi:r] v. intr. (61). To shine (soleil); to gleam, to glimmer, to glint. (V. BRILLER.) ‖ To be shining (nez). ‖ FIG. To dawn (espoir).
luisant, ante [lɥizɑ̃, ɑ̃:t] adj. Shining (v. BRILLANT); shiny (nez, surface); glossy (satin); gleaming (yeux); luisant de sueur, glistening with perspiration. ‖ ZOOL. Ver luisant, glow-worm.
— part. prés. V. LUIRE (61).
— m. Gloss, shine; sheen.
lumbago [lɔ̃bago] m. Lumbago.
lumière [lymjɛ:r] f. Light; à la lumière de la lampe, by lamplight; la lumière de la lune, du soleil, moonlight, sunlight. ‖ ELECTR. Light; donner de la lumière, to turn the light on; éteindre la lumière, to turn the light out. ‖ TECHN. Mouth (d'un rabot); oil-hole (d'un engrenage); slot (d'un piston). ‖ FIG. Light, enlightenment; à la lumière de la science, in the light of science; avoir recours aux lumières de qqn, to have recourse to s.o.'s learning; mettre en lumière, to bring out; une de nos lumières, one of our luminaries; le siècle de lumière, the age of enlightenment; la ville-lumière, the City of Light (Paris).
lumignon [lymiɲɔ̃] m. Candle-end, bit of candle.
luminaire [-nɛ:r] m. Luminary.
luminescence [-nɛssɑ̃:s] f. ELECTR. Luminescence; éclairage par luminescence, fluorescent (ou) strip lighting; tension de luminescence, blue-glow voltage.
lumineusement [-nøzmɑ̃] adv. Luminously.
lumineux, euse [-nø, ø:z] adj. Luminous; bande, onde lumineuse, light strip, wave. ‖ FIG. Brilliant (idée); idée lumineuse, magnificent idea, brain-wave.
luminosité [-nozite] f. Luminosity, sheen.
lumpenprolétariat [lumpənproletarja] m. Lumpenproletariat.
lunaire [lynɛ:r] adj. Lunar.
lunaire f. BOT. Honesty, moonwort, satin-pod.
lunaison [lynɛzɔ̃] f. ASTRON. Lunar (ou) synodic month, lunation.
lunatique [lynatik] adj. Whimsical, unsteady. (V. CAPRICIEUX.) ‖ Moon-eyed (cheval).
lunch [lœʃ] (pl. **lunches**) m. Lunch, luncheon (en Angleterre). ‖ Buffet-lunch (en France); lunch debout, stand-up lunch.
lundi [lœdi] m. Monday; le lundi de Pâques, de la Pentecôte, Easter Monday, Whit-Monday.
lune [lyn] f. ASTRON. Moon; lune rousse, April moon. ‖ FIG. Lune de miel, honeymoon. ‖ FAM. Whim, mood (disposition); moonface (visage); dans une bonne lune, in a good humour; demander, promettre la lune, to ask for, to promise the moon and stars; être dans la lune, to be absent-minded (ou) wool-gathering (ou) miles away; faire un trou dans la lune, to shoot the moon; faire voir la lune en plein midi à, to gull, to take in. ‖ POP. Bum, U. S. ass.
luné [-ne] adj. FAM. Bien luné, in good humour; mal luné, in a bad mood.
lunetier [-ntje] m. Spectacle- (ou) glasses-maker.
lunette [-nɛt] f. Telescope, spy-glass. (V. LONGUE-VUE, LORGNETTE.) ‖ Pl. Spectacles; lunettes d'automobiliste, goggles; lunettes fumées, smoked glasses, U. S. cheaters (fam.); lunettes noires, dark glasses; lunettes de soleil, sun-glasses; lunettes à verres obliques, harlequin glasses. ‖ CH. DE F. Cab-window (de locomotive). ‖ TECHN. Back-rest (d'un tour); die (outil à fileter). ‖ ARCHIT. Lunette. ‖ AUTOM. Rear-window.
lunetterie [-nɛtri] f. Spectacle- (ou) glass-making. ‖ Spectacle- (ou) eye-glass trade.

lunule [lynyl] f. Math. Lunula. ‖ Méd. Lunula, half-moon.

lupanar [lypana:r] m. Brothel ; U. S. whorehouse, cat-house. (V. bordel.)

lupin [lupɛ̃] m. Bot. Lupin, lupine.

lupus [lypys] m. Méd. Lupus.

lurette [lyrɛt] f. *Il y a belle lurette,* that was long ago.

luron [lyrɔ̃] m. Strapping (ou) U. S. husky fellow. (V. costaud.) ‖ Gay dog. (V. drille.)

luronne [lyrɔn] f. Strapping lass ; tomboy. ‖ Gay hussy.

lusitanien, enne [lyzitanjɛ̃, ɛn], **lusitain, aine** [-tɛ̃, ɛn] adj., s. Géogr. Lusitanian.

lustrage [lystra:ʒ] m. Glazing, glossing. ‖ Shininess (par l'usage).

lustral, ale [lystral] adj. Lustral.

lustre [lystr] m. Lustrum (période).

lustre m. Lustre, glaze, sheen, gloss. (V. brillant.) ‖ Chandelier (candélabre) ; corona (d'église). ‖ Fig. Lustre, radiance.

lustré, ée [-tre] adj. Lustrous, glossy ; *lustré par l'usage,* shiny with age.

lustrer [-tre] v. tr. (1). To lustre, to glaze, to gloss.

lustrine [-trin] f. Lustrine, lutestring ; *manches en lustrine,* oversleeves.

luth [lyt] m. Mus. Lute.

luthéranisme [lyteranism] m. Ecclés. Lutheranism.

lutherie [lytri] f. Stringed-instrument making (ou) trade.

luthérien, enne [lyterjɛ̃, ɛn] adj., s. Ecclés. Lutheran.

luthier [lytje] m. Mus. Stringed-instrument maker (fabricant) [ou] seller (marchand).

luthiste [-tist] s. Mus. Lutanist, lutenist.

lutin, ine [lytɛ̃, in] adj. Mischievous, roguish. — m. Elf, goblin, sprite. ‖ Imp (enfant). ‖ Aviat. *Lutins malfaisants,* gremlins (fam.).

lutiner [lytine] v. tr. (1). To tease, to bother ; *lutiner les filles,* to fondle the girls.

lutrin [lytrɛ̃] m. Ecclés. Lectern ; *chanter au lutrin,* to sing in the choir.

lutte [lyt] f. Struggle, strife (effort) ; *au fort de la lutte,* in the thick of the fight ; *la lutte pour la vie,* the struggle for life ; *la lutte des classes,* the class struggle. ‖ Conflict, contest (opposition) ; *entrer en lutte avec,* to clash with ; *luttes parlementaires,* parliamentary clashes. ‖ Sports. Wrestling (corps à corps) ; *lutte à la corde de traction,* tug-of-war. ‖ Loc. *De haute lutte,* by force ; *de bonne lutte,* by fair means ; *soutenir une lutte inégale,* to fight against odds.

lutter [-te] v. intr. (1). To fight (se battre) ; *lutter des pieds et des mains,* to fight tooth and nail. ‖ Sports. To wrestle (*avec,* with) [corps à corps] ; *lutter de vitesse avec,* to race. ‖ To offer resistance (*contre,* to) ; *lutter contre le sommeil,* to strive to keep awake. ‖ Fig. To struggle, to fight, to contend (*contre,* with, against) [v. batailler] ; *lutter contre l'adversité,* to struggle against adversity ; *lutter*

contre la calomnie, to fight against slander ; *lutter contre l'incendie,* to battle with the fire.

lutteur [-tœ:r] m. Wrestler (de foire). ‖ Fighter (opposant). ‖ Fam. U. S. Grunter.

luxation [lyksasjɔ̃] f. Méd. Luxation, dislocation.

luxe [lyks] m. Luxury (faste, splendeur) ; *de luxe,* luxury, de luxe. ‖ Wealth, abundance (richesse) ; *vivre dans le luxe,* to live in luxury (ou) in the lap of ease. ‖ Fig. Profusion (d'explications). ‖ Fam. *Je vais me donner le luxe de dormir demain matin,* I shall treat myself to a « lie-in » (ou) U. S. late sleep tomorrow morning.

Luxembourg [lyksɑ̃bu:r] m. Géogr. Luxembourg.

luxembourgeois, oise [-burʒwa, a:z] adj. Géogr. Of (ou) from Luxembourg, Luxembourgeois. — s. Géogr. Native (ou) inhabitant of Luxembourg, Luxembourger.

luxer [lykse] v. tr. (1). Méd. To luxate, to dislocate, to put out of joint. — v. pr. Méd. *Se luxer l'épaule,* to dislocate one's shoulder, to put one's shoulder out of joint.

luxueusement [lyksyøzmɑ̃] adv. Luxuriously.

luxueux, euse [-ø, ø:z] adj. Luxurious, showy, sumptuous. (V. fastueux.)

luxure [lyksy:r] f. Lechery, lust, lewdness.

luxuriance [lyksyrjɑ̃:s] f. Luxuriance ; opulence.

luxuriant, ante [-rjɑ̃, ɑ̃:t] adj. Luxuriant ; *une chevelure luxuriante,* a magnificent head of hair.

luxurieux, euse [-rjø, ø:z] adj. Lecherous, lustful, lewd.

luzerne [lyzɛrn] f. Bot. Lucerne ; U. S. alfalfa.

lycanthropie [likɑ̃trɔpi] f. Méd. Lycanthropy.

lycée [lise] m. † Lyceum. ‖ State grammar (ou) secondary school (en France).

lycéen, enne [liseɛ̃, ɛn] adj. Pertaining to a lycee. — s. Pupil (dans un lycée).

lycopode [likɔpɔd] m. Bot. Lycopode.

lymphangite [lɛ̃fɑ̃ʒit] f. Méd. Lymphangitis.

lymphatique [-fatik] adj. Méd. Lymphatic.

lymphe [lɛ̃:f] f. Méd. Lymph.

lymphocyte [lɛ̃fɔsit] m. Méd. Lymphocyte.

lynchage [lɛ̃ʃa:ʒ] m. Lynching.

lyncher [-ʃe] v. tr. (1). To lynch.

lynx [lɛ̃ks] m. Zool. Lynx ; *aux yeux de lynx,* lynx-eyed.

Lyon [liɔ̃] m. Géogr. Lyons.

lyonnais, aise [liɔnɛ, ɛ:z] adj. Géogr. Of (ou) from Lyons. — s. Native (ou) inhabitant of Lyons.

lyophilisation [ljɔfilizasjɔ̃] f. Techn. Freeze-drying, lyophilization.

lyre [li:r] f. Mus. Lyre. ‖ Zool. *Oiseau-lyre,* lyre-bird. ‖ Fam. *Toute la lyre,* the whole range.

lyrique [lirik] adj. Lyric ; lyrical ; *théâtre lyrique,* opera-house. — m. Lyric poet.

lyrisme [lirism] m. Lyricism. ‖ Fam. Excessive enthusiasm ; gush.

lys [lis] m. V. lis.

lysergique [lizɛrʒik] adj. Chim. *Acide lysergique,* lysergic acid.

M

M [ɛm] m. M, m (lettre).

M. Abrév. de *Monsieur,* Mr.

ma [ma] adj. poss. f. V. mon.

maboul, oule [mabul] adj. Fam. Cracked, crazy, U. S. nuts. (V. cinglé.) — s. Fam. Crazy person, loony, U. S. nut.

maboulisme [mabulism] m. Fam. Craziness.
macabre [makaːbr] adj. Macabre, gruesome; ghastly. ‖ Loc. *La danse macabre,* the dance of Death.
macache [makaʃ] adv. interj. Pop. Not likely!, nothing doing!
macadam [makadam] m. Macadam (v. bitume); macadamized road (rue).
macadamiser [-mize] v. tr. (1). To macadamize.
macaque [makak] m. Zool. Macaque.
macareux [makarø] m. Zool. Puffin.
macaron [makarɔ̃] m. Culin. Macaroon. ‖ Fam. Tight coils (coiffure).
macaroni [makarɔni] m. Culin. Macaroni. ‖ Fam. Wop (Italien).
macaronique [makarɔnik] adj. Macaronic; *latin macaronique,* dog-Latin; U. S. pig Latin.
macassar [makassar] m. *Huile de macassar,* macassar oil.
macchabée [makabe] m. Ecclés. Macchabeus. ‖ Fam. Stiff'un, stiffy, U. S. stiff.
Macédoine [masedwan] f. Géogr. Macedonia.
macédoine f. Culin. Diced vegetables; fruit salad, U. S. cut-up fruit. ‖ Fig. Hotch-potch, farrago.
macédonien, enne [-dɔnjɛ̃, ɛn] adj., s. Géogr. Macedonian.
macération [maserasjɔ̃] f. Maceration; steeping; soaking. ‖ Fig. Mortifying of the flesh.
macérer [-re] v. tr. (5). To macerate; *faire macérer,* to steep, to soak. ‖ Fig. To mortify (la chair).
macfarlane [macfarlan] m. Inverness cape, ulster.
Mach [mak] m. Phys., Aviat. *Nombre de Mach,* Mach number; *voler à Mach 2,* to fly at Mach 2.
mâche [mɑːʃ] f. Bot. Lamb's lettuce, corn salad.
mâchefer [mɑʃfɛr] m. Clinker, slag, scoria.
mâcher [mɑʃe] v. tr. (1). To masticate, to chew. (V. mâchonner, mastiquer.) ‖ To champ (cheval). ‖ To tear (outil). ‖ Fig. *Il n'a pas mâché ses mots,* he didn't mince matters; *on lui a mâché la besogne,* the work was half done for him.
machette [maʃɛt] f. Machete.
machiavélique [makjavelik] adj. Machiavellian.
machiavélisme [-lism] m. Machiavellism.
mâchicoulis [mɑʃikuli] m. Machicolation; *à mâchicoulis,* machicolated.
machin [maʃɛ̃] m. Fam. What's-it, thingumijig, thingumbob (chose); what's-his-name (personne); *Madame Machin,* Mrs. What's-her-name. (V. truc.)
machinal, ale [maʃinal] adj. Mechanical (v. automatique); unconscious. (V. involontaire.)
machinalement [-mɑ̃] adv. Mechanically; unconsciously.
machinateur [maʃinatœːr] m. Plotter, schemer, machinator.
machination [-sjɔ̃] f. Machination, plot, scheme. ‖ Pl. Scheming, plotting. (V. agissements.)
machine [maʃin] f. Machine; *machine à affranchir,* franking machine; *machine à calculer,* calculating (ou) adding machine, calculator, arithmometer, comptometer; *machine à composer, à coudre, à laver, à sous,* typesetting, sewing, washing, slot machine; *machine à écrire,* typewriter. ‖ Ch. de f. Engine (locomotive); *machine à vapeur, de manœuvre, routière,* steam, shunting, traction engine. ‖ Fig. Machinery; *la machine de l'Etat,* the machinery of Government. ‖ Fam. Contraption; gadget. (V. engin.) ‖ **Machine comptable,** f. Fin. Accounting machine. ‖ **Machine-outil,** f. Techn. Machine-tool.
machiner [-ne] v. tr. (1). To scheme, to plot, to contrive (v. ourdir); *machiné à l'avance,* put-up (affaire). ‖ Théâtr. To devise stage effects.
machinerie [-nri] f. Machine construction. ‖ Techn. Machine-group, machine shops. ‖ Naut. Engine-room.

machinisme [-nism] m. Mechanization. ‖ Philos. Machinism.
machiniste [-nist] m. Machinist. (V. mécanicien.) ‖ Théâtr. Scene-shifter, stage-hand. ‖ Loc. *Faire signe au machiniste,* to signal the driver to stop.
machisme [maʃism] m. Machism.
macho [matʃo] m. Macho.
mâchoire [mɑʃwaːr] f. Méd. Jaw; jaw-bone. (V. maxillaire.) ‖ Techn. Jaws, chaps, chops (d'étau); flange (de poulie). ‖ Autom. Brake-shoes. ‖ Milit. *Mâchoire d'un mouvement en tenailles,* arm of a pincer movement.
mâchonnement [mɑʃɔnmɑ̃] m. Chewing.
mâchonner [mɑʃɔne] v. tr. (1). To chew, to munch. (V. mâcher.) ‖ Fig. To mutter (des injures); to mumble (des paroles vagues).
mâchouiller [mɑʃuje] v. tr. (1). Fam. To chew, to munch. (V. mâchonner.)
mâchure [mɑʃyːr] f. Flaw (du velours). ‖ Bruise (sur un fruit).
mâchurer [mɑʃyre] v. tr. (1). To bruise, to crush (une pièce métallique). ‖ To smudge (du papier).
mackintosh [makintɔʃ] m. Mackintosh.
macle [makl] f. Macle. ‖ Blas. Mascle.
macler [makle] v. intr. (1). To twin (cristal).
— v. pr. **Se macler,** to twin.
mâcon [makɔ̃] m. Comm. Mâcon (vin).
maçon [masɔ̃] m. Archit. Mason, bricklayer. ‖ Fam. Freemason.
— adj. Zool. *Abeille maçonne,* mason-bee.
maçonnage [-naːʒ] m. Archit. Bricklaying, mason's work.
maçonner [-ne] v. tr. (1). Archit. To build, to mason (un mur); to face (une paroi); to wall-up (une porte).
maçonnerie [-nri] f. Archit. Masonry; stone-work, brick-work. ‖ Fam. Freemasonry.
maçonnique [-nik] adj. Masonic (loge).
macramé [makrame] m. Macramé, knotted-bar work.
macreuse [makrøːz] f. Zool. Scoter.
macreuse f. Culin. Shoulder of beef.
macrobiotique [makrɔbjɔtik] adj. Macrobiotic.
— f. Macrobiotics.
macrocéphale [makrɔsefal] adj. Méd. Macrocephalic.
macrocosme [-kɔsm] m. Philos. Macrocosm.
macro-économie [-ekɔnɔmi] f. Macro-economics.
macromolécule [-mɔlekyl] f. Chim. Macromolecule.
macrophage [-faːʒ] adj. Méd. Macrophagic.
— m. Méd. Macrophage.
macrophotographie [-fɔtɔgrafi] f. Macrophotography.
macroscopique [-skɔpik] adj. Macroscopic.
maculage [makylaːʒ] m. Maculation. ‖ Blurring.
maculature [makylatyːr] f. Mackle, spoilt sheet.
macule [makyl] f. Spot, stain. (V. tache.) ‖ Astron. Macula.
maculer [makyle] v. tr. (1). To maculate. (V. salir.) ‖ To mackle, to blur (mâchurer),
— v. intr. To mackle, to blur (papier).
Madagascar [madagaskaːr] f. Géogr. Madagascar.
madame [madam] (pl. **mesdames** [mɛdam]) f. Mrs. (devant un nom propre); *Mme Durand,* Mrs. Durand, the Mrs. Durand; *Mmes Durand et Joly,* Mrs. Durand and Mrs. Joly; *Mme Vve Crillon,* Mrs. Crillon, widow of the late Mr. Crillon. ‖ *Madame est sortie,* Mrs. X (ou) her Ladyship (dans le cas d'une personne titrée) is not at home; *Madame est servie,* dinner is served; *Madame veut-elle me dire son nom?,* will you please tell me your name? ‖ Madam (ou) your ladyship (dans la conversation); ladies (au

MACHINES (ÉLÉMENTS DE) — MACHINE ELEMENTS

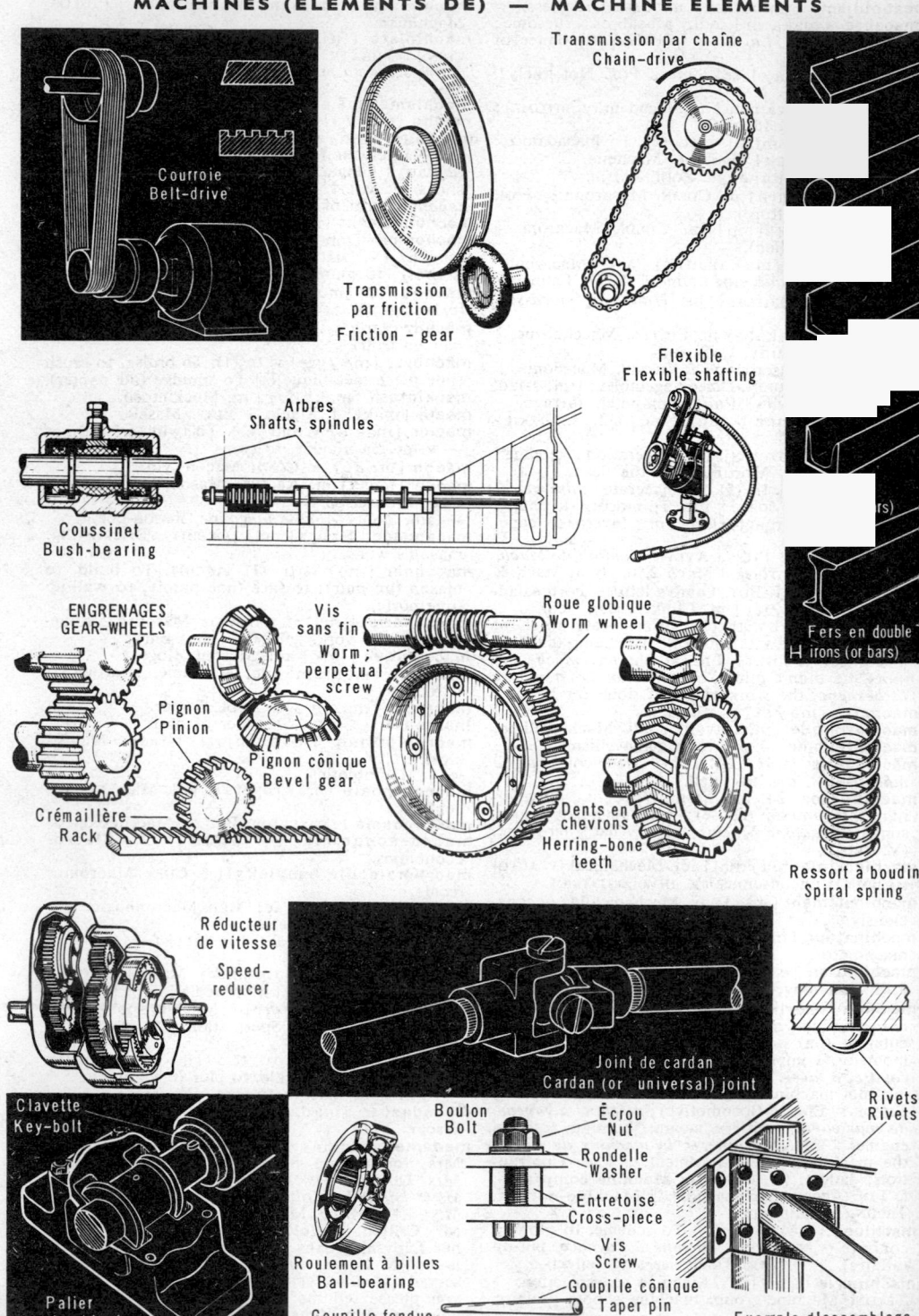

Courroie
Belt-drive

Transmission par friction
Friction – gear

Transmission par chaîne
Chain-drive

Flexible
Flexible shafting

Arbres
Shafts, spindles

Coussinet
Bush-bearing

Fers en double
H irons (or bars)

ENGRENAGES
GEAR-WHEELS

Vis sans fin
Worm; perpetual screw

Roue globique
Worm wheel

Pignon
Pinion

Pignon cônique
Bevel gear

Crémaillère
Rack

Dents en chevrons
Herring-bone teeth

Ressort à boudin
Spiral spring

Réducteur de vitesse
Speed-reducer

Joint de cardan
Cardan (or universal) joint

Rivets
Rivets

Clavette
Key-bolt

Boulon
Bolt

Écrou
Nut

Rondelle
Washer

Entretoise
Cross-piece

Vis
Screw

Roulement à billes
Ball-bearing

Palier
Bearing block

Goupille fendue
Split pin

Goupille cônique
Taper pin

Exemple d'assemblage
Example of assembling

début d'un discours); Dear Madam, Dear Mrs. X (au début d'une lettre). ‖ (Non traduit devant un titre ou devant un nom commun); *Mme la Marquise de S.*, the Marchioness of S.; *rappelez-moi au souvenir de Mme votre mère*, please remember me to your mother. ‖ † Madame (titre).

Madeleine [madlɛn] f. Magdalen, Madeleine. ‖ CULIN. Sponge-cake, madeleine (gâteau); Magdalen pear (poire). ‖ FAM. Reformed prostitute.

Madelon [madlɔ̃] f. Maud.

mademoiselle [madmwazɛl] (pl. **mesdemoiselles** [mɛdmwazɛl]) f. Miss (toujours suivi du nom ou du prénom de la personne); *Mlle Durand*, Miss Durand; *Mlles Boivin*, the Misses Boivin; *Mlles Durand et Boivin*, the Misses Durand and Boivin; *mademoiselle est sortie*, Miss X is out; *pardon, mademoiselle*, pardon (ou) excuse me, Miss X; excuse me, please (quand on ignore le nom de la personne). ‖ (Non traduit devant un nom commun); *rappelez-moi au souvenir de mademoiselle votre sœur*, please remember me to your sister. ‖ Dear Miss X (en commençant une lettre). ‖ † Mademoiselle (titre).

Madère [madɛ:r] m. Madeira wine. ‖ GÉOGR. Madeira.

Madone [madɔn] f. Madonna.

madras [madras] m. Madras (étoffe); Madras kerchief (foulard).

madré, ée [madre] adj. Spotted, veined (bois). ‖ FIG. Sly, wily, artful, U. S. cagey. (V. FINAUD.) — s. Sly one.

madrépore [madrepɔ:r] m. Madrepore.

madrier [madrije] m. Beam.

madrigal [madrigal] m. Madrigal.

madrilène [madrilɛn] adj. GÉOGR. Madrilenian.

maelström [malstrø:m] m. Maelstrom, whirlpool (pr., fig.).

maestria [maɛstrija] f. Masterly skill.

maestro [-tro] m. MUS. Maestro.

maf(f)ia [mafja] f. Mafia (société secrète). ‖ Gang, mob (bande).

maf(f)ioso [-fjozo] m. Mafioso.

mafflu, ue [mafly] adj. Fat-cheeked, chubby-faced. — s. Fat-chops.

magasin [magazɛ̃] m. Shop, U. S. store (v. BOUTIQUE); *grand magasin*, department store; *marchandises en magasin*, stock in hand; *magasin à succursales multiples*, chain stores; *magasins généraux*, public bonded warehouse; *magasin universel*, U. S. general store. ‖ Warehouse, storeroom (dépôt); *avoir en magasin*, to have in stock. ‖ MILIT. Armoury (d'armes); magazine (d'équipement, de munitions).

magasinage [-zina:ʒ] m. Storing, warehousing.

magasinier [-zinje] m. Warehouse man. ‖ MILIT. Storeman.

magazine [-zin] m. Magazine, mag (fam.).

magdalénien, enne [magdalenjɛ̃, ɛn] adj. GÉOL. Magdalenian.

mage [ma:ʒ] m. Magus (pl. Magi); seer; *les Rois Mages*, the Three Wise Men.

Maghreb [magrɛb] m. GÉOGR. Maghreb, Maghrib.

maghrébin, ine [-rebɛ̃, in] adj. GÉOGR. Maghrebi, Maghribi.

magicien [maʒisjɛ̃] m. Wizard; magician.

magicienne [-sjɛ:n] f. Woman magician.

magie [maʒi] f. Magic. (V. SORCELLERIE.) ‖ FIG. Witchery.

magique [maʒik] adj. Magic, magical.

magiquement [-mɑ̃] adv. Magically.

magisme [maʒism] m. Magianism.

magister [maʒistɛr] m. † Schoolmaster, dominie.

magistère [-tɛ:r] m. Ministry, agency.

magistral, ale [-tral] adj. Masterly, skilful (action); magisterial, masterful (air, ton). ‖ MÉD.

Magistral. ‖ FAM. First-rate, signal; *correction magistrale*, sound thrashing.

magistralement [-tralmɑ̃] adv. In a masterly manner. ‖ Magisterially.

magistrat [-tra] m. JUR. Magistrate. (V. JUGE.)

magistrature [-traty:r] f. Magistrature. ‖ Magistracy (fonction). ‖ The Bench, the judges (magistrature assise); the body of public prosecutors (magistrature debout).

magma [magma] m. Magma. (V. MÉLANGE.)

magnanime [maɲanim] adj. Magnanimous.

magnanimement [-mmɑ̃] adv. Magnanimously.

magnanimité [-mite] f. Magnanimity.

magnat [maɲa] m. Magnate; *magnat de la finance*, financial magnate, tycoon.

magner (se) [səmaɲe] v. pr. (1). POP. To get a move on, to shift.

magnésie [maɲezi] f. CHIM., MÉD. Magnesia; *sulfate de magnésie*, Epsom salts.

magnésium [maɲezjɔm] m. CHIM. Magnesium; *éclair de magnésium*, magnesium flash; *lampe au magnésium*, flash-lamp.

magnétique [maɲetik] adj. Magnetic (attraction, champ, ruban).

magnétisable [-tizabl] adj. Magnetizable.

magnétisation [-tizasjɔ̃] f. Magnetization.

magnétiser [-tize] v. tr. (1). To magnetize; to mesmerize.

magnétiseur [-tizœ:r] m. Magnetizer; mesmerizer.

magnétisme [-tism] m. Magnetism.

magnétite [-tit] f. Magnetite, lodestone.

magnéto [-to] f. Magneto. ‖ **Magnéto-électrique,** adj. PHYS. Magneto-electric.

magnétophone [-tofo:n] m. Tape recorder.

magnétoscope [-tɔskɔp] m. TECHN. Video tape recorder.

magnétron [-trɔ̃] m. ELECTR. Magnetron.

magnificat [magnifikat] m. ECCLÉS., MUS. Magnificat.

magnificence [maɲifisɑ̃:s] f. Magnificence.

magnifier [-fje] v. tr. (1). To magnify.

magnifique [-fik] adj. Sumptuous (repas, vêtement); magnificent, splendid, grand (spectacle); glorious (temps). ‖ Pompous, high-sounding (paroles). ‖ † Liberal, generous. — m. Magnifico (à Venise).

magnifiquement [-fikmɑ̃] adv. Magnificently.

magnitude [-tyd] f. ASTRON. Magnitude.

magnolia [magnɔlja] m. BOT. Magnolia.

magnolier [-lje] m. BOT. Magnolia-tree.

magnum [magnɔm] m. Magnum.

magot [mago] m. Treasure, hoard, pile (argent).

magot m. ZOOL. Barbary ape. ‖ COMM. Chinese porcelain figure. ‖ FAM. Paunchy fellow.

magouillage [maguja:ʒ] m. FAM. Shady dealing, skulduggery; gerrymandering (en matière électorale).

magouille [magu:j] f. FAM. Shady deal (ou) business, sharp practice; gerrymandering (en matière électorale).

magouiller [maguje] v. tr. (1). FAM. To intrigue, to plot.

magyar, e [magjar] adj., s. GÉOGR. Magyar.

maharajah [maaraʒa] m. Maharajah.

maharani [-rani] f. Maharanee.

mahatma [-tma] m. Mahatma.

mah-jong [maʒɔ̃(g)] m. Mah-jong.

Mahomet [maɔmɛ] m. Mohammed, Mahomet.

mahométan, ane [maɔmɛtɑ̃, an] adj. Mohammedan, Moslem, Muslim.

mai [mɛ] m. May (mois); *le premier mai*, May-day (fête). ‖ May-pole (mât).

maie [mɛ] f. Kneading-trough. ‖ Flour- (ou) bread-bin.

maïeutique [majøtik] f., pl. Maieutics.

maigre [mɛ:gr] adj. Lean, thin, skinny. ‖ CULIN.

Skim-milk (fromage); vegetable (potage); lean (viande); *maigre repas,* meagre (ou) scanty meal. ‖ AGRIC. Poor, scanty, meagre (récolte); poor, barren (sol); scanty, sparse (végétation). ‖ ARTS. Meagre (pinceau); meagre, bald (style). ‖ ECCLÉS. Meatless (jour); *faire maigre,* to abstain from meat; *repas maigre,* meatless meal. ‖ FIG. Scant (assistance); sparse (chevelure); poor (résultat). — m. CULIN. Lean, lean meat. ‖ ECCLÉS. Abstinence.

maigrelet, ette [mɛgrəlɛ, ɛt] adj. Rather thin (ou) lean (personne).

maigrement [-grəmã] adv. Meagrely.

maigreur [-grœ:r] f. Thinness, leanness, lankiness (des personnes). ‖ Spareness, scantiness, poorness, meagreness (des choses). ‖ FIG. Baldness (du style).

maigrichon, onne [-griʃɔ̃, ɔn], **maigriot, otte** [-grio, ɔt] adj. Rather thin (ou) lean, skinny.

maigrir [-gri:r] v. intr. (2). To get lean (ou) thin; to lose flesh. (V. MINCIR.)

— v. tr. To make s.o. thinner (maladie); to make s.o. look thinner (vêtement); *faites-vous maigrir,* trim down your waistline; *se faire maigrir,* to slim, to diet. ‖ TECHN. To thin down (le bois).

mail [ma:j] m. Maul, sledge-hammer (maillet). Mallet, mall (allée, jeu). ‖ Avenue, promenade.

maille [ma:j] f. Link (de chaîne); mesh (de filet); stitch (de tricot); *cotte de mailles,* coat of mail, mail. ‖ Silver grain (du bois). ‖ MÉD. Spot (sur l'œil). ‖ ZOOL. Speckle (sur le plumage).

maille f. † Penny. ‖ LOC. *Avoir maille à partir avec,* to have a bone to pick with; *n'avoir ni sou ni maille,* to be hard up.

maillé, ée [maje] adj. † Mail-clad, mailed. ‖ ZOOL. Speckled (oiseau); netted (poisson).

maillechort [majʃɔ:r] m. Nickel-silver.

mailler [maje] v. tr. (¹) To net. ‖ NAUT. To shackle (deux chaînes); to lace (deux voiles).

maillet [majɛ] m. Maul, mallet. ‖ Mallet (jeu).

mailloche [majɔʃ] f. Large maul (ou) mallet. ‖ MUS. Bass drumstick.

maillon [majɔ̃] m. Link.

maillot [majo] m. Swaddling-band (pour bébé). ‖ FIG. *Encore au maillot,* still in swaddling-clothes.

maillot m. SPORTS. Vest (pour la course); jersey (pour le football); *maillot de bain,* bathing costume (ou) U. S. suit. ‖ THÉÂTR. Tights.

main [mɛ̃] f.

---

1. Partie du corps. — 2. Dessin, écriture. — 3. Aide. — 4. Attaque. — 5. Commodité. — 6. Direction, maîtrise. — 7. Travail. — 8. Générosité. — 9. Connaissances. — 10. Etude. — 11. Au jeu. — 12. COMM. — 13. MUS. — 14. TECHN. — 15. AUTOM. — 16. LOC.

---

1. Hand (partie du corps); *donnez-moi la main,* give me your hand; *la main dans la main,* hand in hand; *serrer la main de qqn,* to shake hands with s.o., to give s.o. a hand-shake; *soins des mains,* manicuring; *tendre la main à,* to hold out one's hand to. ‖ **2.** Hand (dessin, écriture); *à main levée,* freehand; *ce n'est pas de sa main,* it's not in his hand; *une belle main,* a fine hand. ‖ **3.** Hand (aide); *appuyer qqn des deux mains,* to give s.o. one's full support; *homme de main,* thug, bully; *prêter la main à qqch.,* to help s.o. to do sth.; *prêter main forte à,* to help; *remettre qqch. entre les mains de qqn,* to put sth. into s.o.'s hands; *se donner la main,* to join forces. ‖ **4.** Hand (attaque); *attaque à main armée,* armed attack; *avoir la main leste,* to be free with one's hand; *en venir aux mains,* to come to blows; *lever la main sur,* to raise a threatening hand to; *mettre*

l'épée à la main, to draw one's sword; *porter la main sur,* to lay a hand on. ‖ **5.** Hand (commodité); *avoir tout sous la main,* to have everything near at hand; *faire main basse sur,* to lay hands on, to grab, to make a clean sweep of; *mettre la main sur ce qu'on cherchait,* to manage to find what one was looking for; *tomber sous la main,* to come to hand. ‖ **6.** Hand (direction, maîtrise); *avoir la haute main sur,* to rule, to control; *avoir bien en main,* to have well in hand; *changer de mains,* to change hands; *lâcher la main à qqn,* to give s.o. the rein; *tenir la main à ce que,* to make it a point that; *tenir à qqn la main haute,* to keep s.o. under control. ‖ **7.** Hand (travail); *s'entretenir, se faire la main,* to keep, to get one's hand in. ‖ **8.** Hand (générosité); *avoir la main large,* to be open-handed; *acquiescer des deux mains,* to agree whole-heartedly; *donner à pleines mains,* to give unstintingly; *puiser à pleines mains,* to dig deep into, to dip one's hand into. ‖ **9.** Hand (connaissances); *de première main,* at first hand; *savoir de longue main,* to have known for a long time; *tenir de bonnes mains,* to have from a reliable source. ‖ **10.** Hand (étude); *en mains,* in s.o.'s hands (livre); *passer son examen haut la main,* to pass one's exam with flying colours. ‖ **11.** Deal (au jeu); *avoir, passer la main,* to have, to pass the deal; *jouer à la main chaude,* to play at hot cockles. ‖ **12.** COMM. *Main courante,* cash- (ou) waste-book; *main de papier,* quire; *payer de la main à la main,* to pay without a deed (ou) without anyone knowing; *une petite main,* a dressmaker's apprentice; *main-d'œuvre,* labour; manpower; *rareté de la main-d'œuvre,* labour shortage. ‖ **13.** MUS. *Jouer du piano à quatre mains,* to play a piano duet. ‖ **14.** TECHN. *Main courante,* handrail (d'escalier); side-rail (de locomotive). ‖ **15.** AUTOM. *Main de ressort,* dumb spring-rest. ‖ **16.** LOC. *A main droite,* on (ou) to the right-hand side; *bas, haut les mains!,* hands off, up!; *demander la main de qqn,* to ask for s.o.'s hand; *faire qqch. en sous main,* to do sth. in an underhand way; *j'en mettrai ma main au feu,* I would swear to it; *passer la main dans le dos,* to coax, to soft-soap, to butter up, U. S. to apple-polish; *se passer la main dans le dos,* to pat oneself on the back; *ne pas y aller de main morte,* to make no bones about it.

mainate [mɛnat] m. ZOOL. Mina, myna.

mainlevée [-ləve] f. JUR. Restoration of goods, withdrawal of opposition.

mainmise [-mi:z] f. Seizure, grasp. ‖ FIG. Influence.

mainmorte [-mɔrt] f. † Mortmain.

maint [mɛ̃] adj. Many a; *à maintes reprises,* over and over again; *maintes fois,* many a time.

maintenance [mɛ̃tnã:s] f. TECHN., INFORM., MILIT. Maintenance (entretien).

maintenant [mɛ̃tnã] adv. Now; *dès maintenant,* already now, now, from now on, henceforth. — loc. conj. *Maintenant que,* now that.

maintenir [mɛ̃tni:r] v. tr. (101). To hold up (v. SOUTENIR); *maintenir un pont,* to hold up a bridge. ‖ To keep up (une allure, une vitesse). ‖ To maintain, to hold (conserver); *maintenir en fonction,* to maintain in office; *maintenir sa position,* to hold one's own; *ne pas maintenir son opinion,* to give up one's opinion. ‖ To maintain (v. AFFIRMER); *je maintiens qu'il a tort,* I maintain (ou) I positively affirm that he is wrong.

— v. pr. **Se maintenir,** to keep on, to continue; *son enthousiasme se maintient,* his enthusiasm does not flag. ‖ To remain fine (temps). ‖ MÉD. To hold out (malade). ‖ FIN. To remain firm (actions); to keep up (prix). ‖ MILIT. To keep one's position (à, at).

maintien [mɛ̃tjɛ̃] m. Keeping (de l'ordre). ‖ Upholding (d'une opinion). ‖ Carriage, bearing (attitude, port); *noble maintien,* commanding demeanour; *se donner un maintien,* to keep oneself in countenance.

maire [mɛːr] m. Mayor; *Lord Maire,* Lord Mayor.

mairesse [mɛrɛs] f. Mayoress.

mairie [-ri] f. Town-hall (bâtiment); mayoralty (fonction).

mais [mɛ] conj. But; *intelligent, mais trop hardi,* clever, but cheeky; *non seulement... mais encore,* not only... but. — adv. Indeed, well, why; *mais non!,* oh no!, decidedly not!; *il était vieux, mais vieux, archi-vieux,* he was old, very old indeed; *mais c'est votre anniversaire aujourd'hui!,* well, it's your birthday today!; *mais, qu'est-ce qui le prend?,* why, what's biting him? ‖ More; *il n'en pouvait mais,* he could do nothing more. — m. Difficulty, rub (v. HIC); *il y a un mais,* there is an objection.

maïs [mais] m. BOT. Maize, Indian corn; U. S. corn.

maison [mɛzɔ̃] f. House (v. HABITATION); *maison de campagne,* country-house; *maison d'éducation,* educational establishment; *maison d'habitation,* dwelling-house; *maison de jeu,* gambling house; *maison de maître,* gentleman's residence; *maison de plaisance,* week-end house; *maison de rapport,* apartment house, tenement. ‖ Home (foyer); *fait à la maison,* home-made; *je vous invite à la maison,* do come to my house; *rester à la maison,* to stay at home; *revenir à la maison,* to return home. ‖ House, household (famille, personnel, vie de famille); *de bonne maison,* of a good family (personne), well-trained (serviteur); *entrer en maison,* to go into service; *être de la maison,* to be one of the family; *la maison de Hanovre,* the house of Hanover; *mener bien sa maison,* to manage one's household well. ‖ COMM. *Maison de commerce,* firm, business; *avoir une très grosse maison,* to have a very large business; *faire maison nette,* to dismiss all the employees. ‖ JUR. *Maison d'arrêt,* prison; *maison close,* brothel, U.S. whorehouse; *maison de correction,* approved school, Borstal institution; U. S. reform school. ‖ MÉD. *Maison de fous,* lunatic asylum; *maison de repos, de santé,* rest, mental home. ‖ ECCLÉS. *Maison religieuse,* convent. ‖ CULIN. Home-made (tarte).

maisonnée [-zɔne] f. Household; *toute la mai-sonnée,* every member of the household.

maisonnette [-zɔnɛt] f. Little house, cottage.

maistrance [mɛstrɑ̃ːs] f. NAUT. Petty officers.

maître [mɛːtr] m. Master (qui commande); *les Russes sont maîtres d'une moitié de l'Asie,* the Russians are masters of half Asia. ‖ Master (qui est libre); *maître chez soi,* master in one's own house; *être entièrement son maître,* to be entirely independent, to be one's own master; *être maître de faire ce qu'on veut,* to be free to do what one likes. ‖ Master (qui domine); *maître de soi,* self-controlled; *être parfaitement maître de ses mou-vements,* to have all one's movements under per-fect control; *être passé maître en,* to be a past master of (ou) in; *n'être plus maître de son auto,* to have lost control of one's car; *l'œil du maître,* the master's eye; *se rendre maître de,* to get the upper hand of; *voiture de maître,* chauffeur-driven car. ‖ Master, teacher (qui enseigne); *mon maître d'anglais,* my English teacher; *maître de confé-rences,* lecturer; *maître à danser,* dancing master; *maître d'école,* school-master, U. S. school-teacher; *maître d'étude,* usher, U. S. study hall assistant. ‖ Master (personne éminente); *les maîtres de la peinture,* the masters of painting; *le grand maître de l'Université,* the Minister of Education. ‖ Master (chef); *maître d'équipage,*

boatswain; *maître d'hôtel,* maître d'hôtel, head-waiter; butler; *maître mécanicien,* chief engineer; *maître mineur,* colliery (ou) mine foreman. ‖ CULIN. *Maître queux,* cook. ‖ FAM. *Maître chan-teur,* blackmailer; *maître Jacques,* man-of-all-work, Jack-of-all-trades. ‖ **Maître-assistant,** s. Lecturer. ‖ **Maître-autel,** m. ECCLÉS., ARCHIT. High altar.

maîtresse [mɛtrɛs] f. Mistress; *maîtresse d'école,* school-mistress; *maîtresse de maison,* house-keeper, housewife. ‖ Mistress, paramour (amante); sweetheart, lady-love (bien-aimée). — adj. *Maîtresse femme,* managing (ou) capable woman; *maîtresse poutre,* main beam, girder; *branche maîtresse d'un cours d'eau,* main stream of a river; *idée maîtresse,* basic idea, governing principle; *position maîtresse,* key position.

maîtrisable [mɛtrizabl] adj. Manageable; con-trollable.

maîtrise [-triːz] f. Mastership; *maîtrise de confé-rences,* lectureship. ‖ Mastery (domination); *avoir la maîtrise de ses passions,* to be in control of one's passions; *maîtrise de soi,* self-control. ‖ ARTS. Mastery. ‖ ECCLÉS. Choir.

maîtriser [-trize] v. tr. (1). To master (un cheval). ‖ FIG. To deal with (une difficulté); to subdue (une émeute); to curb, to bridle (l'orgueil); to control (ses passions). — v. pr. Se maîtriser, to control oneself.

majesté [maʒɛste] f. Majesty; *la majesté divine,* divine majesty; *Sa Majesté,* Her Majesty (la reine), His Majesty (le roi). ‖ Stateliness, gran-deur; *air de majesté,* stately bearing.

majestueusement [-tɥœzmɑ̃] adv. Majestically.

majestueux, euse [-tɥø, øːz] adj. Majestic (imposant); *démarche majestueuse,* stately tread.

majeur [maʒœːr] adj. Major; *en majeure partie,* for the major part. ‖ *Devenir majeur,* to reach one's majority. ‖ Important; *affaire majeure,* very important transaction; *cas de force majeure,* act of God, case of absolute necessity; *pour des raisons majeures,* for imperative reasons. ‖ PHILOS. *Terme majeur,* major term. ‖ MUS. Major (tierce). ‖ ECCLÉS. Major (ordres). ‖ GÉOGR. Lac Majeur, Lake Maggiore. — m. MÉD. Second (ou) long finger (doigt).

majeure [maʒœːr] f. PHILOS. Major premise.

majolique [maʒɔlik] f. Majolica.

major [maʒɔːr] m. MILIT. Regimental adjudant; *major général,* chief of staff. ‖ NAUT. *Major géné-ral,* Admiral Maritime Superintendent. ‖ MILIT., NAUT. Medical officer. ‖ Head of the list (d'une grande école).

majoration [maʒɔrasjɔ̃] f. Over-estimation (dans un apport). ‖ Increase; raising (des prix, des salaires). ‖ COMM. Additional item (sur facture).

majordome [maʒɔrdɔm] m. Majordomo, chief steward.

majorer [maʒɔre] v. tr. (1). To overestimate, to overvalue. ‖ To swell (une note); to increase (un prix). [V. AUGMENTER, REHAUSSER.]

majorette [-rɛt] f. Majorette.

majoritaire [-ritɛːr] adj. Pertaining to the majority. — s. FIN. Person holding a majority of shares.

majorité [-rite] f. Majority, greater part; *la majo-rité des participants,* the greater part (ou) the majority of the participants; *la majorité des personnes présentes,* most of the people present; *élu à une majorité de,* elected by a majority of; *être en majorité,* to be in the majority. ‖ JUR. Coming of age, majority. ‖ MILIT. Function of adjutant, adjutancy.

Majorque [maʒɔrk] f. GÉOGR. Majorca.

majorquin, ine [-kɛ̃, in] adj., s. GÉOGR. Ma-jorcan.

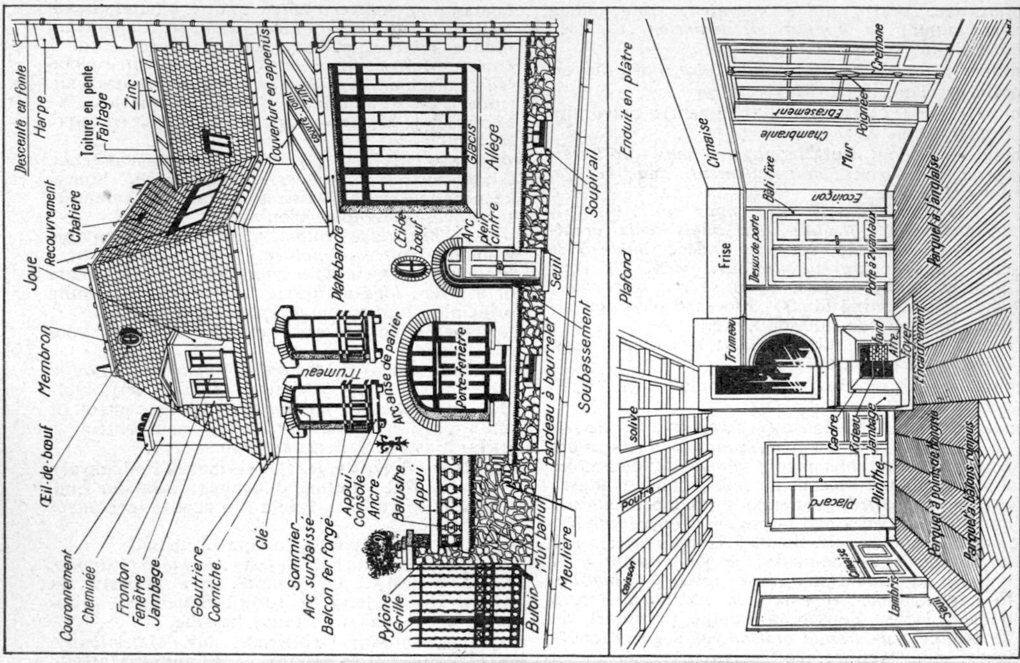

MAISON ▶

▲ HOUSE

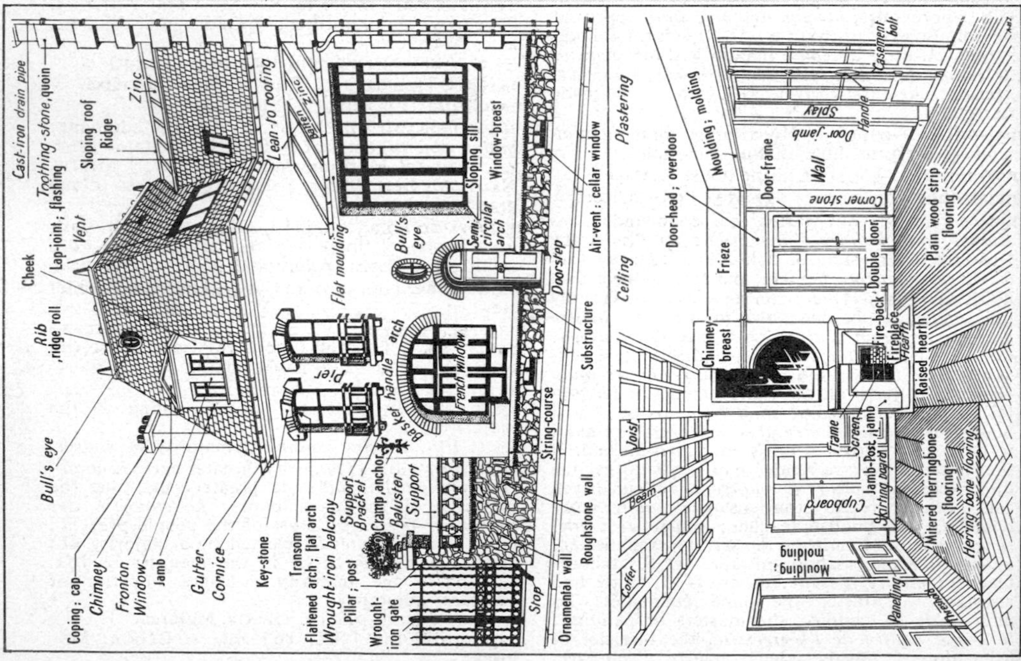

majuscule [maʒyskyl] adj. Capital.
— f. Capital letter.
maki [maki] m. Zool. Lemur; Madagascar cat.
mal m. Méd. Ailment, disease, illness (maladie);
mal de cœur, nausea; *mal de dents*, toothache;
mal de gorge, sore throat; *mal de mer*, sea-sickness; *mal des montagnes*, mountain sickness; *mal
de reins*, lumbago; *mal de tête*, headache; *mal
des transports*, car-sickness; *mal blanc*, whitlow;
mal du pays, homesickness; *avoir mal au pied*,
to have a pain in the foot; *attraper du mal*, to
catch an infection; *supporter ses maux*, to bear
one's ailments. ‖ Pain (douleur); *j'ai mal au dos*,
le dos me fait mal, my back hurts, I have a pain
in the back; *vous me faites mal*, you're hurting
me. ‖ Fig. Sorrow, affliction, trouble (souffrances).
‖ Harm, hurt, evil, ill, damage, mischief (tort);
faire du mal, to do harm; *il n'y aurait pas de
mal à le lui dire*, there would be no harm in
telling him so; *prendre qqch. en mal*, to take
offense at sth. ‖ Evil, wrong, wrongdoing; *le bien
et le mal*, good and evil; *dire du mal de*, to
speak ill of, to run down; *faire le mal*, to commit
evil; *je ne pensais pas à mal quand j'ai dit cela*,
I said that with the best intentions. ‖ Trouble,
difficulty, pains; *avoir du mal à suivre*, to have
much difficulty in following; *j'ai eu tout le mal
possible à ne pas lui dire son fait*, I was hard
put to it not to say what I think of him; *ne vous
donnez pas de mal pour ce garçon*, don't give
yourself any trouble over that boy; *se donner du
mal*, to take pains (ou) trouble.
mal adv. Badly, ill (contrairement à la morale);
biens mal acquis, ill-gotten goods; *c'est mal à
lui de*, it is shameful (ou) unkind (ou) wicked
(ou) wrong of him to. ‖ Ill, in bad health;
au plus mal, at death's door; *se porter mal*,
to be in bad health; *se trouver mal*, to feel
faint, to faint; *très mal*, dangerously ill. ‖ Ill,
wrongly, badly (sans habileté); *mal choisir*, to
choose wrongly; *mal conseiller*, to misadvise;
mal informé, ill-informed; *mal juger*, to misjudge;
mal léché, unlicked; raw (fam.); *mal mener une
affaire*, to make a mess of a transaction; *s'y
prendre mal*, to tackle the matter badly, to go
at it the wrong way, to mismanage the whole
thing; *travail mal fait*, botched work. ‖ On bad
terms; *être mal avec*, to be at loggerheads with;
être au plus mal avec, to be at daggers drawn
with; *se mettre mal avec*, to fall out with;
prendre mal qqch., to take offence at sth., to
take sth. the wrong way; *vous ne trouverez pas
mal que je me retire*, you will not mind my
withdrawing. ‖ Uncomfortable (sans confort); *on
est mal chez lui*, one is uncomfortable (ou)
there is no comfort in his house; *nous ne sommes
pas mal ici*, we are not badly off here. ‖ Ugly,
plain, U. S. homely (d'aspect); *elle n'est pas mal*,
she is quite good-looking; *ce tableau n'est pas
mal*, this picture is not at all bad. ‖ Fam. *Pas
mal de*, a great deal of, quite a lot of, a good
many; *pas mal de gens*, a lot of people, a good
many people; *il y a pas mal de temps que je
ne l'ai vu*, it is a long time since I saw him;
il n'a pas mal fait d'en discuter avec elle, it was
a rather good idea to discuss it with her; *vous
ne feriez pas mal de venir*, it would be a good
thing if you came; *s'en tirer tant bien que mal*,
to get out of it somehow. ‖ **Mal-en-point**, adj.
Out of sorts; in poor shape (souffrant); in a
bad way (en mauvaise posture). ‖ **Mal-jugé**, m.
Jur. Miscarriage of justice. ‖ **Mal-logé**, s. Person
living in inadequate housing conditions.
mal adj. See Mauvais. ‖ Loc. *Bon an, mal an*, year
in, year out; *bon gré mal gré*, willy-nilly.
malabar [malaba:r] adj. Pop. Hefty, beefy,
brawny.
— m. Tough guy, muscle man.

Malabar m. Géogr. Malabar; *côte de Malabar*,
Malabar Coast.
malachite [malakit] f. Malachite.
malade [malad] adj. Méd. Ill; poorly, sick,
unwell; *avoir l'air malade*, to look unwell (ou)
ill (ou) sick; *il en est malade*, he is quite upset
about it; *être malade d'une bronchite*, to be ill
with bronchitis; *être malade du foie*, tó have
liver-trouble; *être malade du cœur*, to suffer
from heart trouble; *être malade de la poitrine*,
to be tubercular (ou) consumptive (ou) chesty.
‖ Bad, injured, sore; *ma jambe malade*, my bad
leg; *ses yeux malades*, his sore eyes. ‖ Fam.
Ce livre est bien malade, this book is in very
bad condition (ou) in a wretched state; *vous êtes
malade!*, you must be mad!, you're not well!
— s. Méd. Sick person, invalid; *rester constamment malade*, to remain a permanent invalid; *les
malades*, sick people, the sick, the ill; *faire le
malade*, to malinger. ‖ Méd. Patient. ‖ Naut.
Poste des malades, sick bay.
maladie [-di] f. Méd. Illness (affection); sickness
(indisposition); disease, complaint, malady; *maladie des chiens*, distemper; *maladie de foie*, liver
complaint; *maladie de peau*, skin disease; *maladie
légère*, ailment; *mourir de maladie*, to die of
disease. ‖ Bot. *Maladie de la vigne*, vine disease.
‖ Fig. Malady.
maladif, ive [-dif, i:v] adj. Méd. Sickly, weakly,
unhealthy. ‖ Fig. Morbid (curiosité).
maladivement [-divmɑ̃] adv. Morbidly.
maladrerie [drəri] f. † Leper hospital, lazar
house.
maladresse [maladrɛs] f. Clumsiness, awkwardness (d'expression, de gestes). ‖ Inexpediency
(d'une démarche). ‖ Blunder (bévue); maladroitness (gaucherie).
maladroit, oite [-drwa, at] adj. Heavy, lubberly
(d'allure); clumsy, awkward, maladroit (de
gestes). ‖ Blundering (gaffeur). ‖ Impolitic,
inopportune (démarches).
— s. Clumsy (ou) awkward person; clumsy clot
(fam.). ‖ Fig. Bungler, fumbler, blunderer.
maladroitement [-drwatmɑ̃] adv. Clumsily, awkwardly. ‖ Fig. Blunderingly.
malaga [malaga] m. Géogr., Comm. Malaga.
malais, aise [malɛ, ɛ:z] adj., s. Géogr. Malay.
— m. Gramm. Malay (langue).
malaise [malɛ:z] m. Indisposition, discomfort,
malaise; *avoir un malaise*, to feel faint. ‖ Fig.
Unrest.
malaisé, ée [malɛze] adj. Uneasy. (V. difficile.)
‖ Toilsome (chemin).
malaisément [-mɑ̃] adv. Uneasily.
Malaisie [malɛzi] f. Géogr. Malaysia, Malaya;
Malay Archipelago.
malandrin [malɑ̃drɛ̃] m. Burglar, highwayman,
marauder. (V. bandit.) ‖ † Freebooter.
malappris [malapri] adj. Rude, boorish; ill-bred.
— s. Ill-bred person, lout, boor, U. S. slob (fam.).
malard [mala:r] m. Zool. Mallard.
malaria [malarja] f. Méd. Malaria; *de la malaria*, malarial.
malavisé, ée [malavize] adj. Ill-advised, unwise
(personne). ‖ Blundering (acte); inexpedient,
impolitic (démarche).
Malawi [malawi] m. Géogr. Malawi.
malaxage [malaksa:ʒ] m. Mixing (du ciment);
kneading (de la pâte). ‖ Méd. Massage.
malaxer [-se] v. tr. (1). To work (du beurre);
to mix (du ciment); to knead (de la pâte). ‖
Méd. To massage (le corps).
malaxeur [-sœ:r] m. Kneading-machine, mixing
machine; mixer; cement-mixer; butter-worker.
Malaysia [malɛzja] f. Géogr. Malaysia.

malbâti, ie [malbati] adj. Misshapen, ill made, ill-favoured.

malchance [malʃɑ̃:s] f. Bad (ou) ill luck; *avoir de la malchance*, to be unlucky; *par malchance*, as ill luck would have it, because of bad luck.

malchanceux, euse [malʃɑ̃sø, ø:z] adj. Unlucky, luckless. — s. Unlucky person.

malcommode [malkɔmɔd] adj. FAM. Inconvenient.

maldonne [maldɔn] f. Misdeal (aux cartes). ‖ FAM. Error, mistake.

mâle [mɑ:l] adj. Male; bull (éléphant); buck (lapin); cock (oiseau); *enfant mâle*, man (ou) male child. ‖ ARTS. Bold, virile (facture). ‖ TECHN. Male (vis). ‖ FIG. Masculine, virile, manly (qualités); vigorous, strong, virile (style). — m. Male; *un beau mâle*, a fine looking fellow, a he-man (fam.).

malédiction [malediksjɔ̃] f. Curse, malediction; *appeler la malédiction sur*, to curse. — interj. Curse it!

maléfice [malefis] m. Malefice, evil spell.

maléfique [-fik] adj. Maleficent; baleful (influence).

malemort [malmɔr] f. † Violent death.

malencontre [malɑ̃kɔ̃:tr] f. † Mishap.

malencontreusement [-kɔ̃trøzmɑ̃] adv. Unfortunately, unluckily.

malencontreux, euse [-kɔ̃trø, ø:z] adj. Unlucky, unfortunate, untoward (événement). ‖ Unhappy (malheureux); ill met (malvenu).

malentendant, ante [malɑ̃tɑ̃dɑ̃, ɑ̃:t] adj. Hard of hearing. — s. Person who is hard of hearing; *les malentendants*, the hard of hearing.

malentendu [-tɑ̃dy] m. Misunderstanding, misapprehension (différence d'appréciation). ‖ Dispute, quarrel (différend).

malfaçon [malfasɔ̃] f. Defect, bad workmanship (mauvais travail). ‖ Cheating (profit illicite).

malfaisance [malfɛzɑ̃:s] f. Maleficence, mischievousness.

malfaisant, ante [-zɑ̃, ɑ̃:t] adj. Maleficent, mischievous; harmful. (V. NUISIBLE.)

malfaiteur, trice [malfɛtœ:r, tris] s. Crook, criminal, law-breaker.

malfamé, ée [malfame] adj. Of ill fame, in bad repute, disreputable.

malformation [malfɔrmasjɔ̃] f. MÉD. Malformation, malconformation.

malfrat [malfra] m. ARG. Crook.

malgache [malgaʃ] adj., s. GÉOGR. Madagascan, Malagasy.

malgracieux, euse [malgrasjø, ø:z] adj. Churlish, discourteous. ‖ Surly; frowning. (V. RENFROGNÉ.)

malgré [malgre] prép. In spite of, notwithstanding; *malgré moi*, in spite of myself, against my will; *malgré tout*, yet, still; *malgré tous mes efforts*, in spite of all my efforts; *malgré toute ma fortune*, for all my wealth. — loc. conj. *Malgré que*, FAM. though, although; *malgré que j'en aie*, for all I can do.

malhabile [malabil] adj. Unskilful (v. MALADROIT); *malhabile dans l'art de*, untutored in the art of.

malheur [malœ:r] m. Bad luck (v. MALCHANCE); *jouer de malheur*, to be out of luck; *malheur à vous!*, woe unto you!; *par malheur*, as ill luck would have it; *porter malheur*, to bring bad luck. ‖ Misfortune; *avoir le malheur de*, to be unfortunate enough to; *lui est-il arrivé malheur?*, has any misfortune befallen him?; *faire le malheur de*, to be the ruin of; *faire le malheur de sa famille*, to be the curse of one's family; *quel malheur!*, what a terrible thing! ‖ FAM. *Faire un malheur*, to run amok, to do sth. irrepa-

rable; *le beau malheur!*, what harm is there in it!; *pour comble de malheur*, as the crowning misfortune; to crown it (fam.).

malheureusement [malœrøzmɑ̃] adv. Unhappily; unfortunately; unluckily.

malheureux, euse [malœrø, ø:z] adj. Unlucky, luckless; ill-fated (malchanceux); *avoir la main malheureuse aux cartes*, to be unlucky at cards. ‖ Unfortunate, unhappy, miserable (infortuné); *le malheureux!*, the poor man!; *malheureux comme les pierres*, utterly wretched, in great straits. ‖ Ill-starred (entreprise); unfortunate, unlucky, disastrous (événements, situations); *avoir la main malheureuse pour les choses fragiles*, to play havoc with anything fragile, to be a bull in a china-shop; *c'est malheureux que vous ne puissiez venir*, it's a pity you can't come. ‖ FAM. Paltry, wretched, trivial; *s'emporter pour une malheureuse remarque*, to lose one's temper over a trivial remark; *pour un malheureux billet de mille*, for a paltry thousand francs; *vous voici, ce n'est pas malheureux*, here you are, and about time too! — s. Unfortunate (ou) unlucky person; *une malheureuse de plus!*, one more unfortunate!; *secourir les malheureux*, to help the destitute.

malhonnête [malɔnɛ:t] adj. Dishonest (personne); dishonest, fishy, sharp (transaction). ‖ Impolite, ill-bred. (V. IMPOLI.)

malhonnêtement [-nɛtmɑ̃] adv. Dishonestly. ‖ Impolitely.

malhonnêteté [-nɛtəte] f. Dishonesty, improbity. ‖ Dishonest act, fishy transaction, sharp practice. ‖ Impoliteness. ‖ Rude remark, coarse expression.

Mali [mali] m. GÉOGR. Mali.

malice [malis] f. Malice, malevolence (méchanceté); *ne pas voir malice à*, not to see any harm in. ‖ Mischievousness, mischief, archness (taquinerie); *des yeux pleins de malice*, eyes full of mischief. ‖ Arch (ou) roguish remark; sly trick; *dire des malices à*, to say sly things to; *faire des malices à*, to play practical jokes on.

malicieusement [-sjøzmɑ̃] adv. Maliciously. ‖ Mischievously. ‖ Archly, slyly, impishly.

malicieux, euse [-sjø, ø:z] adj. Malicious (méchant). ‖ Mischievous, arch, impish (coquin).

malien, enne [maljɛ̃, ɛn] adj., s. GÉOGR. Malian.

malignement [maliɲmɑ̃] adv. Maliciously, malignly, malignantly (avec malignité); mischievously (avec taquinerie).

malignité [maliɲite] f. Malignity. ‖ Mischievousness (taquinerie). ‖ MÉD. Malignancy.

malin, igne [malɛ̃, i:ɲ] adj. Malignant, malign; *le Malin*, the Evil One. ‖ Mischievous (malicieux); *malin comme un singe*, mischievous as a box of monkeys. ‖ ARCH. Roguish, sly (rusé). ‖ Cunning, clever, sharp, smart, U. S. cagey (fam.) [à l'esprit délié]. ‖ MÉD. Malignant. ‖ FAM. Difficult; *ce n'est pas malin*, it's easy. — s. Smart (ou) sharp (ou) knowing one; *c'est un malin*, he has all his wits about him; *ne fais pas le malin*, don't try to be clever; *petite maligne*, little slyboots; *vieux malin*, old fox.

Malines [malin] f. GÉOGR. Malines, Mechlin. ‖ COMM. Mechlin lace (dentelle).

malingre [malɛ̃gr] adj. Puny, weakly, stunted.

malintentionné, ée [malɛ̃tɑ̃sjɔne] adj. Ill-intentioned.

malle [mal] f. Trunk; *malle de cabine*, cabin (ou) U. S. steamer trunk; *malle en osier*, basket trunk; *faire ses malles*, to pack one's things; *défaire ses malles*, to unpack one's trunks. ‖ Pack (de colporteur). ‖ † *La malle des Indes*, the Indian mail. ‖ **Malle-poste**, f. Mail-coach.

malléabilité [maleabilite] f. Malleability. ‖ FIG. Pliability.

malléable [-abl] adj. Malleable. ‖ FIG. Pliant.

malletier [maltje] m. Trunk-maker.

mallette [malɛt] f. Small trunk (ou) box; suit-case, attaché-case; U. S. fitted suitcase; *mallette garnie*, dressing case. ‖ Bot. Shepherd's purse.

malmener [malmənə] v. tr. (1). To handle roughly, to maul; to harry; to knock about (fam.). [V. MALTRAITER, MOLESTER.] ‖ To browbeat, to bully. (V. HOUSPILLER.)

malnutrition [malnytrisjɔ̃] f. Malnutrition.

malodorant, ante [malɔdɔrã, ã:t] adj. Ill-smelling, malodorous.

malotru, ue [malɔtry] adj. Coarse, caddish.
— m. Cad, boor, churl.

malouin, ine [malwɛ̃, in] adj. GÉOGR. Of (ou) from Saint-Malo.
— s. Native (ou) inhabitant of Saint-Malo.

malpoli, e [malpɔli] adj. Ill-behaved, bad-mannered, impolite.
— s. Ill-behaved child (ou) person.

malpropre [malprɔpr] adj. Unclean, filthy, untidy, dirty. (V. SALE.) ‖ Nasty (conduite); smutty, dirty (histoire).
— s. Dirty person; swine (fam.); *partir comme un malpropre*, to run away with one's tail between one's legs.

malproprement [-prəmã] adv. Dirtily. ‖ Nastily.

malpropreté [-prəte] f. Dirtiness, filthiness, foulness. (V. SALETÉ.) ‖ Slovenliness, slatternliness (habituelle). ‖ Dirt (impureté, résidu). ‖ FIG. Smuttiness; nastiness; *raconter des malpropretés*, to talk smut, to tell dirty stories.

malsain, aine [malsɛ̃, ɛn] adj. Unhealthy, unsound, unhygienic, insalubrious (air); unwholesome (nourriture); unhealthy, sickly (personne). ‖ FIG. Unsound (doctrine, littérature).

malséance [malseã:s] f. Impropriety, indecorousness, unseemliness.

malséant, ante [-ã, ã:t] adj. Improper, indecorous, unseemly. ‖ Unbecoming.

malsonnant, ante [malsɔnã, ã:t] adj. FAM. Objectionable, offensive, shocking.

malt [malt] m. Malt.

maltage [-ta:ʒ] m. Malting.

maltais, e [maltɛ] adj., s. GÉOGR. Maltese.

Malte [malt] f. GÉOGR. Malta.

malter [malte] v. tr. (1). To malt.

malterie [-təri] f. Malt-house.

malteur [-tœ:r] m. Malster.

malthusianisme [maltyzjanism] m. Malthusianism; birth control (fam.).

malthusien, enne [-zjɛ̃, ɛn] adj. Malthusian.

maltose [malto:z] f. CHIM. Maltose.

maltraiter [maltrɛte] v. tr. (1). To maltreat, to ill-treat, to ill-use.

malus [maly:s] m. FIN. Loss of no-claims bonus.

malveillance [malvɛjã:s] f. Malevolence, ill-will, spite; *avec malveillance*, malevolently. ‖ Evil intent, foul play; *dû à la malveillance*, due to some criminal machination.

malveillant, ante [-jã, ã:t] adj. Malevolent, malignant, ill-willed (personne); spiteful (remarque). ‖ Carping (censeur).

malvenu, ue [malvəny] adj. Ill-advised; *vous seriez malvenu à vous plaindre*, you have no right to complain.

malversation [malvɛrsasjɔ̃] f. Malversation.

malvoisie [malvwazi] m. Malmsey (vin).

maman [mamã] f. Mamma; *bonne maman*, grandma. ‖ FAM. Mother; *maman Dupont*, old mother Dupont.

mamellaire [mamɛllɛ:r] adj. MÉD. Mammary.

mamelle [mamɛl] f. Udder, teat (d'un animal); breast (d'une femme).

mamelon [mamlɔ̃] m. MÉD. Dug (d'un animal); nipple (d'une femme). ‖ GÉOGR. Hillock, knoll.

mamelonné, ée [-lɔne] adj. MÉD. Mamillate. ‖ Hilly (terrain).

mameluk [mamlyk] m. Mameluke.

mamillaire [mamillɛ:r] adj. Mamillary.

mammaire [mammɛ:r] adj. MÉD. Mammary.

mammalien, enne [mammaljɛ̃, ɛn] adj. ZOOL. Mammalian.

mammectomie [mammɛktɔmi] f. MÉD. Mastectomy.

mammifère [mamifɛ:r] m. ZOOL. Mammal.

mammite [mammit] f. MÉD. Mammitis.

mammouth [mamut] m. ZOOL. Mammoth.

mamours [mamur] m. pl. Billing and cooing; *faire des mamours à*, to coax.

Man [man] f. *Ile de Man*, Isle of Man.

mana [mana] m. Mana (dans les croyances animistes).

manade [manad] f. Herd of bulls or horses in Camargue.

management [manaʒmã] m. Management (gestion).

manager [manaʒɛr] m. Manager.

manant [manã] m. † Villein. ‖ FIG. Churl, boor, yokel.

manceau, elle [mãso, ɛl] adj. GÉOGR. Of (ou) from Le Mans.
— s. Native (ou) inhabitant of Le Mans.

manche [mã:ʃ] f. Sleeve; *en manches de chemise*, in one's shirt-sleeves. ‖ SPORTS. Games (aux cartes); set (au tennis); *gagner la première manche*, to win the first game (ou) set. ‖ NAUT. *Manche à air (ou) à vent*, wind scoop (ou) sail; *manche à charbon*, coal-chute. ‖ AVIAT. *Manche à air*, wind sock. ‖ GÉOGR. *La Manche*, the Channel. ‖ LOC. *Avoir qqn dans sa manche*, to have s.o. in one's pocket; *mettre qqn dans sa manche*, to put s.o. up one's sleeve; *c'est une autre paire de manches*, that is quite a different kettle of fish; *faire la manche*, to pass the hat round, U.S. to panhandle.

manche m. Handle (de couteau); crop (de cravache); stock (de fouet); helve (de hache); neck (d'outil); handle, stick (de parapluie); *manche à balai*, broomstick. ‖ CULIN. *Manche à gigot*, leg-of-mutton (ou) U. S. lamb holder. ‖ MUS. Neck (de violon). ‖ AVIAT. *Manche à balai*, control column. ‖ LOC. *Ne jetez pas le manche après la cognée*, never say die; *se mettre du côté du manche*, to side with the strongest.

mancheron [mãʃrɔ̃] m. Plough-stock, plough-tail (de charrue); handle (d'objet).

manchette [-ʃɛt] f. Cuff, wrist-band (de chemise); *manchette mousquetaire*, double cuff. ‖ Oversleeves, false cuffs (garde-manches). ‖ Headline (de journal); *mettre en manchette*, to splash. ‖ NAUT. Lizard. ‖ POP. Pl. Handcuffs (menottes).

manchon [-ʃɔ̃] m. Muff (de dame). ‖ Flange (en bourrelet). ‖ NAUT. *Manchon d'écubier*, hawse-pipe; *manchon de gouvernail*, rudder-casing. ‖ TECHN. *Manchon de bec de gaz*, mantle; *manchon de chaîne*, chain-pipe; *manchon intérieur*, cylinder-liner; *manchon de refroidissement*, cooling-jacket. ‖ TECHN. Sleeve; *manchon taraudé*, sleeve-nut; *manchon à vis*, screw-coupling. ‖ AUTOM. *Manchon d'embrayage*, clutch.

manchot, ote [mãʃo, ɔt] adj. One-armed. ‖ FIG. Clumsy (v. MALADROIT); *il n'est pas manchot*, he is skilful with his hands; he is no fool.
— s. One-armed person.

manchot m. ZOOL. Penguin.

mandant [mãdã] m. JUR. Mandator; principal. ‖ COMM. Agent. ‖ Constituent (d'un député).

mandarin, ine [mãdarɛ̃, in] adj. ZOOL. Mandarin (canard). ‖ *La langue mandarine*, Mandarin.
— m. Mandarin (en Chine). ‖ GRAMM. Mandarin (langue). ‖ FAM. Big whig, high priest (à l'université).

mandarinat [-rina] m. Mandarinate (en Chine). ‖ FAM. Academic authoritarianism (à l'université).

mandarine [mãdarin] f. Tangerine, mandarine.

mandarinier [mãdarinje] m. BOT. Tangerine-orange tree.

mandat [mãda] m. Mandate; *sous mandat*, mandated (territoire). ‖ Mandate (de député). ‖ JUR. Power of attorney, proxy. ‖ JUR. Warrant, writ; *mandat d'arrêt*, writ of arrest, capias; *mandat de dépôt*, warrant of commitment; *mandat de perquisition*, search-warrant. ‖ FIN. Money-order (postal); *mandat international*, international money-order; *mandat télégraphique*, telegraphic money-order; *mandat du Trésor*, Treasury warrant. ‖ **Mandat-carte**, m. Postcard money-order. ‖ **Mandat-lettre**, m. Letter money-order. ‖ **Mandat-poste**, m. Postal money-order.

mandataire [-tɛ:r] m. Mandatory. (V. ENVOYÉ.) ‖ Inside broker (aux Halles). ‖ JUR. Proxy; representative, agent.

mandatement [-tmã] m. Commissioning.

mandater [-te] v. tr. (1). To commission, to give a mandate to (qqn). ‖ To write a money-order for (une somme).

mandchou [mãdʃu] adj., s. GÉOGR. Manchu.

Mandchourie [mãdʃuri] f. GÉOGR. Manchuria.

mandement [mãdmã] m. Mandate, instructions. ‖ ECCLÉS. Pastoral letter.

mander [-de] v. tr. (1). † To say by letter; to announce. ‖ FAM. To call, to summon.

mandibule [mãdibyl] f. MÉD. Mandible.

mandoline [mãdɔlin] f. MUS. Mandoline.

mandoliniste [-nist] m. MUS. Mandolinist.

mandore [mãdɔ:r] f. MUS. Mandola.

mandragore [mãdragɔ:r] f. BOT. Mandragora; mandrake (fam.).

mandrill [mãdril] m. ZOOL. Mandrill.

mandrin [mãdrɛ̃] m. TECHN. Drift (à élargir); punch (à percer); hammer (d'abattage); mandrel, mandril, chuck (de tour).

manducation [mãdykasjɔ̃] f. Chewing, mastication. ‖ ECCLÉS. Manducation.

manécanterie [manekãtri] f. Choir school.

manège [manɛ:ʒ] m. Riding school, manege, ring (d'équitation). ‖ Roundabout, merry-go-round, U. S. carousel (de chevaux de bois). ‖ FIG. Trick, stratagem; pl. wiles.

mânes [mɑ:n] m. pl. Manes.

maneton [mantɔ̃] m. TECHN. Handle (de manivelle); pin (de vilebrequin).

manette [manɛt] f. TECHN. Hand-lever. ‖ AUTOM. *Manette des gaz*, throttle-lever. ‖ ELECTR. Key (d'interrupteur). ‖ NAUT. Spoke (de gouvernail).

manganate [mãganat] m. CHIM. Manganate.

manganèse [mãganɛ:z] m. CHIM. Manganese.

mangeable [mãʒa:bl] adj. Edible, eatable; fit to eat. (V. COMESTIBLE.)

mangeaille [mãʒa:j] f. Victuals; grub (fam.); U. S. chow (fam.). ‖ Feed (des volailles).

mangeoire [mãʒwa:r] f. Manger.

manger [mãʒe] v. tr. (7). To eat (dans, off, from [une assiette]; in [un lieu]); *manger la soupe*, to drink one's soup, to sup one's broth. ‖ To eat (attaquer); *mangé des vers*, worm-eaten; *route mangée d'herbe*, road overgrown with weeds. ‖ To fray, to scratch (effriter); *le rivage est mangé par la mer*, the shore is eaten away by the waves. ‖ To use up, to consume (consommer). ‖ FIG. To spend, to run through, to squander (dilapider); *manger de l'argent*, to run through money; *manger jusqu'à son dernier sou*, to spend one's last penny. ‖ FIG. To ignore (négliger); *manger la consigne*, to disregard orders. ‖ FAM. To clip, to drop (avaler); *manger ses mots en parlant*, to swallow one's words. ‖ FAM. To devour (dévorer); *manger qqn des yeux*, to devour s.o. with one's eyes; *il ne vous mangera pas!*, he won't swallow you whole (ou) eat you up!; *manger le morceau*, to squeal; *il y a à boire*

et à manger là-dedans, this business has its advantages and its drawbacks.

— v. intr. To eat; *manger au-dehors*, to have a meal out; *manger comme quatre*, to eat like a horse; *ne pas manger à sa faim*, not to have enough to eat; *on mange bien chez eux*, they keep a good table, one eats well at their house.

— m. Food; *apporter son manger*, to bring one's own food; *perdre le boire et le manger*, to lose one's appetite; *à prendre après manger*, to be taken after meals.

mange-tout [mãʒtu] m. invar. Spendthrift. ‖ CULIN. Pl. Large French beans, string bean.

mangeur [mãʒœ:r] s. Eater; *gros mangeur*, great (ou) big eater.

mangouste [mãgust] f. ZOOL. Mongoose. ‖ BOT. Mangosteen.

mangue [mã:g] f. BOT. Mango.

manguier [-gje] m. BOT. Mango-tree.

maniabilité [manjabilite] f. Handiness (d'un outil). ‖ AVIAT., AUTOM. Manœuvrability.

maniable [-njabl] adj. Supple (corde); workable (glaise); easy to handle (objet); handy (outil); *peu maniable*, unhandy, awkward (outil). ‖ NAUT. Manageable (navire); moderate (vent). ‖ FIG. Tractable, pliable (caractère).

maniaco-dépressif, ive [manjakodeprɛsif, i:v] adj., s. PSYCH. Manic-depressive.

maniaque [manjak] adj. Crotchety, whimsical (bizarre); faddy (à marotte); fussy (exigeant); finical, finicky (méticuleux).

— s. Crank, faddist. ‖ MÉD. Maniac. (V. ALIÉNÉ.)

maniaquerie [-kri] f. Crankiness, fussiness, fastidiousness, finicalness.

manichéen, enne [manikeɛ̃, ɛn] adj., s. PHILOS. Manich(a)ean.

manichéisme [-keism] m. PHILOS. Manich(a)eism.

manie [mani] f. Crotchet, mania, fad; *elle ne peut pas se faire à ses manies*, she cannot get accustomed to his eccentricities. ‖ Craze, fad (v. DADA, MAROTTE); *la manie des vieilles monnaies*, a craze for old coins. ‖ Trick; *la manie de corner les livres*, the habit of dog-earing books. ‖ Idiosyncrasy (trait personnel). ‖ MÉD. Mental derangement.

maniement [manimã] m. Handling (des gens, d'un outil); use (de la langue). ‖ Handling, management (des affaires).

manier [manje] v. tr. (1). To handle (de l'argent). ‖ To ply (l'aiguille); to ply, to pull (l'aviron); to deal (les cartes); to wield (l'épée). ‖ FIG. To manage (les hommes); to employ (l'ironie).

— m. Feel, touch.

manière [manjɛ:r] f. Way, manner (v. FAÇON). *manière d'agir*, line of conduct, manner of proceeding; *manière d'être*, usual behaviour; *manière de faire*, one's own way; *manière de voir*, outlook, point of view; *à la manière de*, after the manner of; *à ma manière*, in my own way; *de la bonne manière*, in the right way; *d'une autre manière*, otherwise; *d'une manière ou d'une autre*, somehow or other; *en aucune manière*, in no wise; *en quelque manière*, in a way; *manière de donner vaut mieux que ce qu'on donne*, it's not the gift that matters, it's the sentiment. ‖ Way, wise (guise); *en manière de compliment*, by way of compliment. ‖ Sort, kind (espèce); *manière de potentat*, sort of potentate. ‖ Pl. Way, manners; *faire des manières*, to put on airs, to swank (v. CHICHI); *je n'aime pas ses manières*, I don't like his attitude. ‖ ARTS. Manner; *un Turner dernière manière*, a late Turner, a Turner in his last manner.

— loc. conj. De manière à, so as to. ‖ De manière que, so that.

maniéré, ée [manjere] adj. Affected, simpering, finical (femme); finicky, pretentious (homme). ‖ Finical, over-wrought mannered (style).

maniérisme [-rism] m. Mannerism.

manieur [manjœ:r] m. Handler, user; *grand manieur d'argent*, big financier; tycoon (fam.).

manifestant [manifɛstã] s. Demonstrator; one of the crowd.

manifestation [-fɛstɑsjɔ̃] f. Public demonstration; political meeting.

manifeste [-fɛst] adj. Manifest, obvious (v. ÉVIDENT, NOTOIRE); *une erreur manifeste*, an unmistakable error.

manifeste m. Manifesto, broadside. ‖ NAUT. Manifest.

manifestement [-fɛstəmã] adv. Manifestly.

manifester [-fɛste] v. tr. (1). To manifest, to show, to evince (des sentiments).
— v. intr. To demonstrate, to take part in a public demonstration.
— v. pr. **Se manifester**, to appear, to come out.

manigance [manigã:s] f. Wangling. ‖ Pl. Wiles, intrigue.

manigancer [-gãse] v. tr. (6). FAM. To wangle; to engineer, U. S. to finagle (v. OURDIR); *qu'est-ce qu'ils manigancent?*, what trick are they up to? ‖ To gerrymander (une élection).

Manille [mani:j] f. GÉOGR. Manila; *chanvre de Manille*, Manila hemp.
— m. Manila cigar (ou) cheroot (cigare). ‖ Manila straw hat (chapeau).

manille f. Manille (jeu de cartes).

manille f. TECHN. Shackle.

manioc [manjɔk] m. BOT. Manioc.

manipulateur [manipylatœ:r] m. Manipulator, handler. ‖ TECHN. Transmitter, tapper; sending key (au télégramme).

manipulation [-pylasjɔ̃] f. Manipulation, handling.

manipule [-pyl] m. ECCLÉS. Maniple.

manipuler [-pyle] v. tr. (1). To manipulate. (V. MANIER.) ‖ To operate (au télégraphe). ‖ FAM. To wangle; to gerrymander (une élection).

manique [mani:k] f. Pot-holder.

manitou [manitu] m. Manitou. ‖ FAM. Bigwig.

manivelle [manivɛl] f. TECHN. Crank, handle. ‖ AUTOM. Starting handle, U. S. crank.

manne [ma:n] f. ECCLÉS. Manna.

manne f. Basket, hamper. ‖ Corf (à charbon); creel (à poisson).

mannequin [mankɛ̃] m. Mannequin, fashion model (de couturière); dummy (de tailleur). ‖ ARTS. Lay figure.

manœuvrabilité [manœvrabilite] f. Manœuvrability.

manœuvrable [-vrabl] adj. Manœuvrable.

manœuvre [manø:vr] f. Manœuvring, handling, managing. ‖ TECHN. Driving (d'une machine). ‖ NAUT. Working, manœuvring, rigging. ‖ MILIT. Tactical movement; drill, manœuvre; *grandes manœuvres*, army manœuvres. ‖ CH. DE F. Shunting. ‖ FIG. Move (mouvement); *fausse manœuvre*, wrong move. ‖ FIG. Pl. Manœuvre; intrigue (v. AGISSEMENTS); *manœuvre électorale*, vote-catching manœuvre; *manœuvres frauduleuses*, swindling; *manœuvres d'obstruction*, obstructive tactics, U. S. filibustering (en politique).
— m. Labourer; *travail de manœuvre*, unskilled labour. ‖ FIG. Hack-writer (écrivain); *travail de manœuvre*, hack-work.

manœuvrer [-vre] v. tr. (1). TECHN. To work, to drive (une machine). ‖ NAUT. To manage, to handle, to sail (un navire). ‖ CH. DE F. To shunt. ‖ FIG. To manœuvre, to drive (une personne); *on le manœuvre comme on veut*, you can do what you like with him; *se laisser manœuvrer*, to let oneself be outmanœuvred.
— v. intr. MILIT., NAUT. *Faire manœuvrer*, to manœuvre.

manœuvrier, ère [-vrije, ɛ:r] adj. MILIT. Skilful (ou) successful in manœuvring.
— m. MILIT. Tactician. ‖ NAUT. First-class seaman. ‖ FAM. Filibuster, U. S. filibusterer.

manoir [manwa:r] m. † Manor, manor-house. ‖ Country seat (ou) residence.

manomètre [manɔmɛtr] m. Manometer. ‖ CH. DE F. Steam gauge.

manouvrier [manuvrije] m. Day-labourer.

manquant, ante [mãkã, ã:t] adj. Missing, wanting. ‖ Absent; *porté manquant*, missing, reported missing. ‖ COMM. Out of stock (article).
— m. Absentee; *les manquants*, the missing. ‖ COMM. Shortage.

manque [mã:k] m. Want, lack (v. DÉFAUT); *manque de sommeil*, want of sleep, insufficient sleep; *par manque de*, for lack of. ‖ Insufficiency (insuffisance); *le manque d'écoles*, insufficiency of schools. ‖ Breach (manquement); *manque de parole*, breach of faith. ‖ Slip, stumble (du cheval). ‖ Defect, error (en typographie). ‖ COMM. Shortage (d'une marchandise); *manque à gagner*, lost opportunity. ‖ FIG. Deficiency; *manque de cœur*, heartlessness. ‖ LOC. *Être en état de manque*, to suffer from withdrawal symptoms (méd., fig.).
— f. FAM. *A la manque*, poor, lousy, dud (à la noix).

manqué, ée [-ke] adj. Missed, unsuccessful; *coup manqué*, abortive attempt, failure; *mariage manqué*, broken engagement; marriage that didn't come off; *ouvrage manqué*, botched work. ‖ FIG. *C'est un danseur manqué*, he ought to have been a dancer, U. S. he's a disappointed dancer; *un garçon manqué*, a tomboy; *un héros manqué*, a caricature of (ou) a failure as a hero.

manquement [-kmã] m. Breach, lapse; *manquement au devoir*, lapse from duty; *manquement à l'étiquette*, breach of etiquette. ‖ Pl. Shortcomings.

manquer [-ke] v. intr. (1). To be missing, to run short, to give out (faire défaut); *il me manque dix francs*, I am ten francs short; *le pain manque*, there is no bread to be had; *les vivres commencèrent à manquer*, supplies began to give out; *n'allez pas me manquer au dernier moment*, don't let me down at the last moment; *une page du livre manque*, a page of the book is missing; *si je viens à manquer*, if I happen to die (mourir); *vous me manquez*, I miss you. ‖ **Manquer à,** to fail, to lack (faire défaut); *cela me manque*, I feel the lack of it; *le cœur lui a manqué*, his heart failed him; *le courage lui a manqué pour*, he lacked the necessary courage to; *les mots me manquent pour*, I cannot find words to; *le pied m'a manqué*, my foot slipped; *le sol a manqué*, the ground gave way. ‖ **Manquer de,** to lack, to want, to be out of (être à court de); *manquer d'argent*, to be short of money; *manquer d'esprit*, to be deficient in wit, to lack wit; *manquer de charbon*, to run short of coal; *manquer de sucre*, to be out of sugar; *avoir toujours peur de manquer*, to be always afraid of being penniless; *ne manquer de rien*, not to want for anything. ‖ To fail (faillir); *manquer à l'amitié*, to commit a breach of friendship; *manquer à la consigne*, to disobey an order; *manquer au devoir*, to fail to do one's duty; *manquer à sa parole, à sa promesse*, to break one's word, one's promise; *manquer à la règle*, to fail to observe the rule; *manquer au respect dû à l'âge*, to be disrespectful towards old age; *ne pas manquer de*, not to fail to; *ne pas manquer de venir*, to come without fail. ‖ To miss, to miscarry (avor-

ter); *faire manquer un coup*, to cause an undertaking to fail (ou) to fall flat. ‖ To miss (rater); *cela n'a pas manqué!*, it happened just as I thought!; *cela ne pouvait manquer d'arriver*, that was bound to happen; *le fusil a manqué*, the gun missed fire; *plusieurs de nos coups ont manqué de peu*, we scored several near misses. ‖ To come near (*de*, to) [être à deux doigts]; *manquer de faire qqch.*, to be nearly to do sth.; *il a manqué de se noyer*, he was nearly drowned, he almost drowned.
— v. tr. To miss (l'avion, le train). ‖ SPORTS. To miss (le but). ‖ COMM. To slip (une affaire); to miss (la vente). ‖ FIG. To miss, to lose, to let go (une occasion); *manquer sa vie*, to make a mess of one's life; *manquer sa vocation*, to miss one's true vocation. ‖ FAM. To botch (un travail).
— v. impers. *Il lui manque de l'assurance*, he lacks assurance; *il lui manque un œil*, he has lost one eye; *il ne manquerait plus que ça*, that would be the last straw. ‖ *Il s'en manque que*, it is far from; *il s'en manque que les préparatifs soient achevés*, the preparations are far from being completed.
— v. pr. **Se manquer**, to fail; *il a voulu se tuer, mais il s'est manqué*, he attempted suicide, but failed.
— v. récipr. **Se manquer**, to miss each other (ou) one another.

mansarde [mᾶsard] f. Garret, attic (pièce). ‖ Dormer-window (fenêtre).

mansardé, ée [-de] adj. Mansard-roofed; *chambre mansardée*, attic; *étage mansardé*, attic storey.

mansuétude [mᾶsyetyd] f. Mansuetude, gentleness, clemency.

mante [mᾶ:t] f. Woman's sleeveless mantle.

mante f. ZOOL. *Mante religieuse*, praying mantis.

manteau [mᾶto] m. Cloak, coat, overcoat, U. S. top coat (en général). ‖ MILIT. Great coat. ‖ FIG. Mantle, cloak, veil; *manteau de lierre*, cloak of ivy; *sous le manteau de la poésie*, under the cloak (ou) veil of poetry; *sous le manteau*, sub rosa, confidentially; on the quiet, on the Q. T. (fam.).

mantelet [-tlɛ] m. Mantlet, short mantle. ‖ MILIT. Mantlet. ‖ NAUT. Port-lid.

mantille [-ti:j] f. Mantilla.

manucure [manyky:r] m. Manicure.

manucuré [-kure] adj. Manicured.

manuel, elle [manɥɛl] adj. Manual.
— s. Manual worker.
— m. Manual, text-book; handbook.

manuellement [-mᾶ] adv. Manually.

manufacture [manyfakty:r] f. † Making by hand. ‖ Factory, plant; mill. (V. FABRIQUE.)

manufacturer [-tyre] v. tr. (1). To manufacture.

manufacturier [-tyrje] adj. Manufacturing (région, ville).
— m. Manufacturer, mill-owner.

manu militari [manymilitari] loc. adv. Forcibly.

manuscrit, ite [manyskri, it] adj. Manuscript, written by hand, hand-written.
— m. Manuscript.

manutention [manytᾶsjɔ̃] f. Handling. ‖ Working up (du pain). ‖ MILIT. Bakery; storehouse.

manutentionnaire [-sjɔnɛ:r] s. Warehouse man, porter.

manutentionner [-sjɔne] v. tr. (1). To handle. ‖ To work up (du pain). ‖ MILIT. To bake (le pain); to store (les provisions).

maoïsme [maɔism] m. Maoism.

maoïste [-ist] adj., s. Maoist.

maous, ousse [mau:s] adj. POP. Whopping, whacking, dirty great.

mappemonde [mapmɔ̃:d] f. GÉOGR. Map of the world.

maquereau [makro] m. ZOOL. Mackerel. ‖ POP. Procurer; pimp, ponce, pander, prostitute's bully.

maquerelle [-rɛl] f. POP. Procuress, Madame.

maquette [makɛt] f. Dummy, lay-out, mock-up (d'un livre). ‖ TECHN., ARCHIT., THÉÂTR. Model, mock-up. ‖ ARTS. Maquette (d'un sculpteur).

maquettiste [-tist] s. Lay-out artist (dans l'édition). ‖ TECHN., ARCHIT., THÉÂTR. Model maker.

maquignon [makiɲɔ̃] m. Horse-dealer. ‖ FAM. Spiv; jobber.

maquignonnage [-ɲɔna:ʒ] m. Horse-dealing. ‖ FAM. Jobbery, spivvery.

maquignonner [-ɲɔne] v. tr. (1). To practise crooked horse dealing. ‖ FAM. To practise jobbery; to jockey.

maquillage [makija:ʒ] m. Make-up; making-up. ‖ FIG. Faking.

maquiller [-je] v. tr. (1). To make up. (V. FARDER.) ‖ FIG. To fake, to tamper with; *maquiller les faits*, to distort the facts; *auto maquillée*, disguised car. (V. FALSIFIER.)
— v. pr. **Se maquiller**, to make up; to paint; *se maquiller exagérément*, to make up heavily.

maquilleur [-jœ:r] m. CINÉM., THÉÂTR. Make-up man.

maquilleuse [-jø:z] f. CINÉM., THÉÂTR. Make-up girl.

maquis [maki] m. Bush (en Corse); *prendre le maquis*, to take to the bush. ‖ Maquis (pendant la guerre 39-45); *prendre le maquis*, to take to the maquis, to go underground. ‖ FIG. Maze; *le maquis de la procédure*, the intricacies of legal procedure.

maquisard [-zar] m. Member of the maquis; underground (ou) resistance fighter; partisan.

marabout [marabu] m. Marabout (prêtre). ‖ Marabou-feather (plume); marabou silk (soie). ‖ ZOOL. Marabou (oiseau).

maraîcher [marɛʃe] m. Market-gardener; U. S. truck-gardener (ou) -farmer.
— adj. Market- (ou) U. S. truck-gardening.

marais [marɛ] m. Marsh (v. MARÉCAGE); *gaz des marais*, marsh gas; *marais salant*, salt marsh, saltern. ‖ GÉOGR. *Le Marais*, an old quarter of Paris; part of Poitou.

marasme [marasm] m. Despondency; depression; the dumps. ‖ Stagnation; *les affaires sont dans le marasme*, business is in the doldrums.

marasquin [maraskɛ̃] m. Maraschino.

marathon [maratɔ̃] m. SPORTS. Marathon.

marâtre [marɑtr] f. † Stepmother. ‖ Harsh stepmother; unnatural mother.

maraud [maro] m. † Knave, rogue, rascal.

maraudage [maroda:ʒ] m. Pilfering.

maraude [-ro:d] f. Thieving, robbing (par des galopins). ‖ MILIT. Marauding. ‖ FIG. *Un taxi en maraude*, a fare-hunting (ou) crawling (ou) cruising taxi.

marauder [-rode] v. intr. (1). To pilfer, to steal. ‖ MILIT. To maraud. ‖ FIG. To crawl, to cruise (taxi).

maraudeur [-rodœ:r] m. Marauder; pilferer, petty thief. ‖ FIG. Fare-hunting (ou) crawling taxi.

maravédis [maravedi] m. FIN. Maravedi. ‖ FAM. Penny.

marbre [marbr] m. Marble (matière, objet). ‖ Marble top (de commode). ‖ Marbling (de tranche de livre). ‖ Bed; *livre sur marbre*, book at press, (ou) U. S. on the press. ‖ Slab (à couleurs).

marbrer [-bre] v. tr. (1). To marble, U. S. to vein (un livre). ‖ MÉD. *Peau marbrée*, mottled skin. ‖ FIG. To mottle.

marbrerie [-brəri] f. Marbre-cutter's workshop (atelier); marble-working (industrie); marble-work (ouvrage).

marbrier, ère [-brije, ɛr] adj. Marble (industrie).
— m. Marble-cutter. ‖ Grainer (en peinture).

marbrière [-brijɛːr] f. Marble-quarry.
marbrure [-bryːr] f. Marbling (sur un livre). ‖ Mottling (sur la peau).
marc [mark] m. Mark (monnaie).
marc [maːr] m. Marc (de raisin); *eau-de-vie de marc*, marc-brandy. ‖ Grounds; *marc de café*, coffee grounds.
marcassin [markasɛ̃] m. ZOOL., CULIN. Young wild boar.
marcassite [markasit] f. Marcasite.
marchand, ande [marʃɑ̃, ɑ̃ːd] adj. COMM. Good value (bon); marketable, saleable (vendable); *prix marchand*, market price; *valeur marchande*, sale value. ‖ NAUT. Commercial, mercantile, merchant; *navire marchand*, merchant ship, cargo-boat; *port marchand*, naval port.
— m. Dealer, tradesman, merchant (gros marchand); shopkeeper, U. S. storekeeper (petit marchand); *marchand au détail*, retail dealer; *marchand en gros*, wholesale merchant; *marchand de chevaux*, horse-dealer; *marchand de poisson*, fishmonger; *marchand des quatre-saisons*, costermonger, barrow boy, U. S. push-cart man, huckster; *marchand de vins en gros*, wine-merchant.
marchandage [-ʃɑ̃daːʒ] f. Bargaining, haggling.
marchande [-ʃɑ̃ːd] f. Tradeswoman; *marchande de beurre*, butter-seller.
marchander [-ʃɑ̃de] v. tr. (1). To bargain for, to haggle over; U. S. to dicker over; *marchander qqn*, to haggle with s.o. ‖ FIG. To grudge, to skimp; *ne pas marchander sa peine*, not to spare oneself; *marchander les éloges*, to grudge one's praise.
— v. intr. To bargain, to haggle, U. S. to dicker.
marchandeur [-ʃɑ̃dœːr] s. Bargainer, haggler.
marchandise [-ʃɑ̃diːz] f. COMM. Merchandise, goods, wares (v. DENRÉE); *marchandises en magasin*, stock in hand; *une marchandise*, a commodity. ‖ FIG. *Étaler sa marchandise*, to parade, to push oneself.
marchant, ante [marʃɑ̃, ɑ̃ːt] adj. Marching. ‖ MILIT. *Aile marchante*, wheeling flank.
marche [marʃ] f. March, border. (V. FRONTIÈRE.)
marche f. Walking, walk (acte); gait (démarche); pace (vitesse); *continuer sa marche*, to walk on; *faire une heure de marche*, to go for an hour's walk, to take an hour's constitutional; *faire de grandes marches dans la campagne*, to hike in the country; *marche lourde*, awkward gait; *ralentir sa marche*, to slacken one's pace. ‖ MILIT. *En marche*, on the march, in motion. ‖ Moving, progress (aux échecs). ‖ AUTOM. *Changement de marche*, reverse gear; *mettre en marche*, to switch on, to put into gear. ‖ CH. DE F. Running (des trains); *mettre un train en marche*, to start a train; *ne montez pas dans un train en marche*, don't get into a moving train. ‖ TECHN. *En état de marche*, in working order; *mettre une machine en marche*, to set a machine going. ‖ ARCHIT. Step, stair; *les marches sont raides*, the stairs are steep. ‖ MUS. *Marche funèbre, nuptiale*, dead (ou) funeral, wedding march. ‖ MÉD. Progress (de la maladie). ‖ CINÉM. Action (de la caméra); motion (d'un film). ‖ COMM. *Entreprise en marche*, going concern; *l'affaire est en pleine marche*, the business is in full swing. ‖ FIG. Progress, march, course (en général); development (d'une action romanesque); run (de la phrase); *la marche des années*, the march of time, the flight of years; *né sur les marches du trône*, born on the steps of the throne.
marché [marʃe] m. Market (v. FOIRE, HALLE); *marché couvert, aux fleurs, en plein air, au poisson, à la volaille*, covered, flower, open-air, fish, poultry market; *marché aux puces*, rag fair, junk (ou) flea market; *aller au marché*, to go to market; *place du marché*, market square; *vendeuse au*

marché, market woman. ‖ Market; *marché gris, noir*, grey, black market; *vendeur au marché noir*, black marketeer. ‖ Marketing, mart; *faire son marché*, to do the shopping; *connaître les grands marchés*, to know the great trade marts. ‖ COMM. Market, transaction, bargain, contract; *à bon marché*, cheap, cheaply; *au marché le plus bas*, in the cheapest market; *article qui n'a pas de marché*, article for which there is no market; *le bon marché ruine l'acheteur*, the bargain ruins the buyer; *être en marché avec*, to be negotiating with; *faire marché de tout*, to haggle over everything; *faire marché avec*, to contract (ou) to sign a contract with; *faire un marché avantageux*, to make a good bargain; *lancer un article sur le marché*, to put an article on the market; to market an article; *mettre le marché en main à qqn*, to force s.o. to make up his mind one way or another; *marché conclu!*, that's settled!, U. S. it's a deal; *on ne revient pas sur un marché conclu*, a bargain is a bargain; *rompre un marché*, to break a contract. ‖ Market; *le marché du travail*, the labour market. ‖ FIN. Market, transaction; *le marché a haussé*, the market has risen; *le marché se tient bien*, the market is steady (ou) strong; *marché des valeurs*, stock market. ‖ FIG. *En être quitte à bon marché*, to get off cheaply; *faire bon marché de sa vie*, to hold one's life cheap; *faire bon marché de ses pertes*, to make little of one's losses; *par-dessus le marché*, into the bargain, on top of that.
marchepied [marʃəpje] m. Footboard (de voiture). ‖ Step-ladder, pair of steps (escabeau). ‖ AUTOM. Running board (d'auto); tail-board (de camion). ‖ NAUT. Foot-rope (de beaupré); stretcher (de canot). ‖ AVIAT. Foot-rest (d'hélicoptère). ‖ FIG. *Se faire un marchepied de qqch. pour arriver*, to use sth. as a stepping-stone in order to get on.
marcher [marʃe] v. intr. (1).

---

1. Sens général. — 2. Piétiner. — 3. Aller. — 4. MILIT. — 5. CH. DE F. — 6. NAUT. — 7. TECHN. — 8. ELECTR. — 9. COMM. — 10. FAM.

---

1. To go, to walk, to march (sens général); *marcher à grandes enjambées*, to stride; *marcher dans l'eau*, to wade through water; *marcher de biais*, to sidle; *marcher dans la direction du nord*, to head north; *marcher de-ci, de-là*, to gad about; *marcher loin dans la campagne*, to go for a long walk in the country; *marcher lourdement*, to walk awkwardly, to clump about, to slouch along; *marcher péniblement à travers champs*, to plod (ou) plough one's way through the fields; *marcher en père peinard*, to stroll, to saunter along; *marcher en prenant des airs*, to strut about; *marcher à quatre pattes*, to walk on all fours; *marcher sur qqn*, to walk quickly towards s.o.; *le bébé ne marche pas encore*, the baby is not walking yet; *façon de marcher*, walk; *prenez la voiture, moi je marcherai*, get into the car, I will walk (ou) take Shanks's pony. ‖ **2.** To tread (piétiner); *défense de marcher sur le gazon*, keep off the grass; *marcher sur les pas de qqn*, to follow in s.o.'s footsteps; *marcher sur les pieds de qqn*, to tread on s.o.'s feet. ‖ **3.** To go (aller); *des choses qui marchent toujours ensemble*, things that always go together; *marcher à sa ruine*, to head for ruin; *faire marcher la maison*, to run the house. ‖ **4.** MILIT. *En avant, marche!*, forward, march!; *marcher à l'ennemi*, to advance against the enemy; *marcher au pas*, to keep step; *marcher en queue*, to

bring up the rear; *marcher en tête*, to lead. ‖
5. Сн. DE F. To go, to work (machine); to run
(train); to head (se diriger vers); *faire marcher
une machine*, to work a machine; *marcher à vide,
à toute vitesse*, to run idle, at full speed; *qui
marche à la vapeur*, steam-driven (machine). ‖
6. NAUT. To steam; *le navire marche vers les
Indes occidentales*, the ship is heading for the
West Indies. ‖ **7.** TECHN. To go, to run (montre);
ma montre ne marche plus, my watch is out of
order (ou) has stopped (ou) is broken. ‖ **8.** ELECTR.
Marcher sur tous courants, to work on all volt-
ages. ‖ **9.** COMM. To go, to go off; *cela fera
marcher les affaires*, that will be good for business; *faire marcher une affaire*, to run (ou) to
manage a business; *les affaires marchent, ne
marchent pas*, business is brisk, slack; *une affaire
qui marche bien*, a thriving business; *tout marche
à souhait pour moi*, all is going swimmingly for
me. ‖ **10.** FAM. *Cela fera marcher les langues*,
that will start tongues wagging; *ça n'a pas marché*, it did not work; *je marche avec vous*, I agree
with you; *je ne marche pas*, nothing doing, don't
count on me; *je ne marcherai pas pour vos beaux
yeux*, I won't do it just to please you; *il ne faut
pas lui marcher sur les pieds*, he won't let anyone
trample on him; *quoi qu'on lui raconte, il marche
toujours*, whatever you tell him, he swallows it
all; *on vous a fait marcher*, you have been had;
they fooled you; *sa femme le fera marcher droit*,
his wife will make him toe the mark (ou) walk
the straight and narrow path.
— m. Walking, gait. (V. DÉMARCHE). ‖ Ground
(terrain); *très rude au marcher*, very heavy going.
marcheur [-ʃœ:r] s. Walker; *bon marcheur,*
good walker. ‖ FIG. *Un vieux marcheur*, an old
roué (ou) profligate.
— adj. NAUT. *Bon marcheur*, fast sailer.
marcottage [markɔta:ʒ] m. AGRIC. Layering.
marcotte [markɔt] f. AGRIC. Layer.
marcotter [-te] v. tr. (1). AGRIC. To layer.
mardi [mardi] m. Tuesday; *mardi gras*, Shrove
Tuesday.
mare [ma:r] f. Pond (étang); pool (flaque). ‖ FIG.
Pool (de sang).
marécage [mareka:ʒ] m. Swamp; morass;
marsh; bog; quagmire. (V. MARAIS).
marécageux, euse [-ʒø, ø:z] adj. Marshy, boggy,
swampy.
maréchal [mareʃal] m. Blacksmith, farrier. ‖
MILIT. Marshal; *maréchal des logis*, cavalry (ou)
artillery sergeant.
maréchalat [-ʃala] m. Marshalship.
maréchale [-ʃal] f. Marshal's wife.
maréchalerie [-ʃalri] f. Horse-shoeing. ‖ Smithy,
smith's forge.
maréchaussée [-ʃose] f. Mounted constabulary.
marée [mare] f. Tide; *marée descendante*, ebb-
tide; *marée montante*, rising tide, flood-tide; *la
marée descend, monte*, the tide is going out, is
coming in; *grande marée*, spring tide; *marée
noire*, oil slick. ‖ COMM. Fresh fish; *train de
marée*, fish-train. ‖ FIG. *Marée humaine*, flood
(ou) surge of people. ‖ LOC. *Contre vents et
marées*, against wind and tide.
marégraphe [-gra:f] m. Self-registering tide-
gauge.
marelle [marɛl] f. Hopscotch (jeu).
marémotrice adj. f. *Usine marémotrice*, tide-
powes plant.
marengo [marɛgo] m. CULIN. *Poulet à la
Marengo*, chicken Marengo. ‖ Reddish-brown
(couleur).
marennes [marɛn] f. ZOOL., CULIN. Marennes
oyster.
mareyeur [marɛjœ:r] m. Fishmonger.

margarine [margarin] f. CULIN. Margarine.
marge [marʒ] f. Margin (d'un cahier, d'un livre);
edge, border (d'une route). ‖ Tympan-sheet (en
typogr.). ‖ Margin; *une marge de quelques francs,*
a margin of a few francs; *laisser de la marge
pour l'imprévu*, to make an allowance for
unexpected items (ou) occurrences. ‖ COMM. *Marge
bénéficiaire*, margin of profit. ‖ FIG. *En marge
de l'histoire*, a footnote to history; *en marge de
la société*, on the fringe of society.
margelle [marʒɛl] f. Curb (d'un puits).
marger [marʒe] v. tr. (7). To feed (en imprimerie); to set the margin of (sur une machine à
écrire).
margeur [-ʒœ:r] m. Feeder (sur une presse);
margin stop (sur une machine à écrire).
marginal, ale [marʒinal] adj. Marginal.
— s. Drop-out.
marginaliser [-nalize] v. tr. (1). To set aside of
conventional society.
— v. pr. **Se marginaliser**, to drop out.
margis [marʒi] m. ARG., MILIT. Sarge.
margotin [margɔtɛ̃] m. Bundle of firewood;
U. S. kindling.
margouillet [margujɛ] m. NAUT. Bull's-eye.
margoulette [margulɛt] f. FAM. Mug.
margoulin [margulɛ̃] m. Small tradesman. ‖ FAM.
Black marketeer.
margrave [margra:v] m. Margrave.
Marguerite [margərit] f. Margaret; Maggie,
Peggy (nom). ‖ BOT. Marguerite (à grande fleur);
daisy (à petite fleur). ‖ NAUT. Deck-tackle. ‖
FAM. *Effeuiller la marguerite*, to play « she loves
me, she loves me not ».
marguillier [margije] m. ECCLÉS. Churchwarden.
mari [mari] m. Husband.
mariable [marjabl] adj. Marriageable.
mariage [-rja:ʒ] m. Marriage, match (union);
mariage de convenance (ou) de raison, marriage
of convenience; *mariage de la main gauche*,
companionate marriage; *apporter une fortune en
mariage à qqn*, to bring s.o. a fortune as a dowry;
donner en mariage, to give away; *promesse de
mariage*, engagement, betrothal. ‖ Wedding, nuptials (noce); *mariage en grande pompe*, grand
wedding; *jour du mariage*, wedding-day. ‖ Wedlock; *né en dehors du mariage*, born out of
wedlock.
marial, ale [marjal] adj. ECCLÉS. Marian.
Marianne [marjan] f. Marian, Marianne. ‖
GÉOGR. *Iles Mariannes*, Marianas.
Marie [mari] f. Mary. ‖**Marie-salope**, f. Slut;
TECHN. mud-barge; MILIT. field-kitchen.
marié, ée [marje] adj. Married; *non marié,*
unmarried, single.
— s. Married person; *le jeune marié*, the bridegroom; *la jeune mariée*, the bride; *nouveaux
mariés*, newly married couple, honeymooners;
robe de mariée, wedding dress, bridal gown. ‖
FAM. *Faire la mariée plus belle qu'elle n'est*, to
gild the lily; *la mariée est trop belle*, it's too
much of a good thing; *se plaindre que la mariée
est trop belle*, to complain without reason.
marier v. tr. (1). To marry, to unite in marriage,
to join in wedlock (par le prêtre). ‖ To marry
(à, avec, to); to marry off, to give in marriage
(par les parents); *fille à marier*, daughter of
marriageable age, eligible daughter. ‖ NAUT. To
marry (des cordages). ‖ FIG. To unite, to join,
to wed, to match; *marier des couleurs*, to match
(ou) to blend colours.
— v. pr. **Se marier**, to marry, to get married;
se marier avec, to marry, to wed. ‖ FIG. To go
together, to blend, to harmonize (à, avec, with).
marieur, euse [-rjœ:r, rjø:z] s. Matchmaker.
marigot [marigo] m. GÉOGR. Marigot, divergent
river channel.

marihuana [marirwana], **marijuana** [-ʒɥana] f. Marihuana, marijuana.

marin, ine [marɛ̃, in] adj. NAUT. Marine (plante); *carte marine*, sea-chart; *costume marin*, sailor suit; *mille marin*, nautical mile; *avoir le pied marin*, to be a good sailor, to be free of sea-sickness. ‖ AGRIC. *Chou marin*, cole.
— m. Sailor (v. MATELOT); mariner; *marin d'eau douce*, land-lubber.

marina [marina] f. Marina.

marinade [marinad] f. CULIN. Marinade; *marinade de chevreuil*, soused (ou) U. S. marinated venison.

marine [marin] f. NAUT. Marine, Navy; *marine de guerre*, Navy; *marine marchande*, merchant marine, mercantile navy; *le ministère de la Marine*, the Admiralty; *ministre de la Marine*, First Lord of the Admiralty, U. S. Secretary of the Navy; *officier de marine*, naval officer. ‖ ARTS. Seascape, sea-piece.
— adj. Navy-blue, navy.

marine m. MILIT. Marine (fusilier marin).

mariner [-ne] v. tr. (1). CULIN. To souse, to marinade, U. S. to marinate; to pickle.
— v. intr. To be in pickle.

marinier, ère [-nje, ɛr] adj. NAUT. Marine, naval; *officier marinier*, petty officer. ‖ ARCHIT. *Arche marinière*, navigation arch.
— m. NAUT. Waterman, bargee.

marinière [-njɛ:r] f. Tee-shirt, over-blouse, jersey (blouse). ‖ CULIN. *Sauce marinière*, thin sauce with onions. ‖ SPORTS. Side-stroke (nage).

mariole [marjɔl] adj. FAM. Knowing, cute.
— m. FAM. *Faire le mariole*, to show off, to try to be clever. (V. MALIN.)

mariolâtrie [marjɔlɑtri] f. ECCLÉS. Mariolatry.

marionnette [marjɔnɛt] f. Puppet; *théâtre de marionnettes*, marionette (ou) puppet-show.

marionnettiste [-tist] s. Puppeteer.

Mariotte [mariɔt] m. PHYS. *Loi de Mariotte*, Boyle's law.

mariste [marist] m. ECCLÉS. Marist.

marital, ale [marital] adj. Marital; *autorisation maritale*, husband's authorisation.

maritalement [-mɑ̃] adv. Maritally; *vivre maritalement*, to live together as husband and wife.

maritime [maritim] adj. NAUT. Shipping, sea-borne (commerce); harbour (gare); maritime (législation, province, puissance); coastal, seaside (ville); *courtier maritime*, ship-broker.

maritorne [maritɔrn] f. Slut, slattern.

marivaudage [marivoda:ʒ] m. Witty and sophisticated conversation. ‖ Playful flirting (badinage).

marivauder [-de] v. intr. (1). To say witty and sophisticated nothings. ‖ To flirt verbally.

marjolaine [marʒɔlɛn] f. BOT. Marjoram.

mark [mark] m. Mark (monnaie).

marketing [markɛtiŋ] m. Marketing.

marlou [marlu] m. POP. Pimp, ponce. V. MAQUEREAU.

marmaille [marma:j] f. FAM. Kids, brats.

marmelade [marmǝlad] f. CULIN. Compote (de fruits); marmalade (d'oranges); apple sauce (de pommes). ‖ FIG. *En marmelade*, pounded to a jelly; smashed up. (V. CAPILOTADE.)

marmitage [marmita:ʒ] m. FAM. Heavy bombardment.

marmite [-mit] f. CULIN. Pot, pan; *marmite norvégienne*, pressure-cooker. ‖ MILIT. Dixie (gamelle); heavy shell (obus). ‖ GÉOL. Pot-hole. ‖ FAM. *Faire bouillir la marmite*, to keep the pot boiling; *nez en pied de marmite*, bulbous nose.

marmiter [-mite] v. tr. (1). MILIT. To shell.

marmiton [-mitɔ̃] m. † Scullion. ‖ CULIN. Kitchen-hand, cook's helper.

marmonnement [marmɔnmɑ̃] m. Mumbling.

marmonner [marmɔne] v. tr., intr. (1). To mumble. (V. BOUGONNER.)

marmoréen, enne [marmɔreɛ̃, ɛn] adj. Marmorean, marble-like. ‖ Marble (blancheur).

marmot [marmo] m. Brat, urchin, kid.

marmottage [-mɔta:ʒ] m. Mumbling, muttering (action); mumble, mutter (résultat).

marmotte [marmɔt] f. ZOOL. Marmot, U. S. woodchuck. ‖ COMM. Kerchief (fichu). ‖ LOC. *Dormir comme une marmotte*, to sleep like a log.

marmottement [marmɔtmɑ̃] m. V. MARMOTTAGE.

marmotter [marmɔte] v. tr., intr. (1). To mutter.

marmouset [marmuzɛ] m. FAM. Urchin, kid.

marnage [marna:ʒ] m. AGRIC. Marling.

marnage m. NAUT. Tidal range.

marne [marn] f. AGRIC. Marl.

marner [-ne] v. tr. (1). AGRIC. To marl.
— v. intr. NAUT. To flow; to rise (marée). ‖ POP. To slog away. (V. TRIMER.)

marneux, euse [-nø, ø:z] adj. Marly.

marnière [-njɛ:r] f. Marl-pit.

Maroc [marɔk] m. GÉOGR. Morocco.

marocain, aine [marɔkɛ̃, ɛn] adj. GÉOGR. Moroccan.
— s. GÉOGR. Moroccan. ‖ COMM. Marocain (tissu).

maronite [marɔnit] adj., s. ECCLÉS. Maronite.

maronner [marɔne] v. intr. (1). To grumble, to growl. (V. BOUGONNER.)

maroquin [marɔkɛ̃] m. Morocco leather (cuir). ‖ FIG. Minister's portfolio; *ambitionner le maroquin*, to covet an appointment.

maroquin m. NAUT. Spring stay.

maroquinerie [-kinri] f. Morocco-dressing, Morocco-leather tanning. ‖ COMM. Morocco- (ou) fancy-leather goods (ou) trade.

maroquinier [-kinje] m. Morocco-leather tanner. ‖ COMM. Seller of fancy-leather goods.

marotte [marɔt] f. † Court-jester's cap and bells. ‖ Dummy head (de coiffeuse, de modiste). ‖ FIG. Fad (v. DADA, MANIE); *un homme à marotte*, a faddist; *flatter la marotte de qqn*, to humour s.o.'s whim.

maroufle [marufl] m. † Rascal. (V. COQUIN.)
— f. ARTS. Paste.

maroufler [marufle] v. tr. (1). ARTS. To remount, to back. ‖ AVIAT. To tape.

marquage [marka:ʒ] m. Marking.

marquant, ante [-kɑ̃, ɑ̃:t] adj. Outstanding, remarkable, striking, conspicuous (événement); prominent, eminent, of note (personnage).

marque [mark] f. Mark, stamp (d'identification); *marque à la craie, au crayon, à la plume, au pochoir*, chalk-, pencil-, pen-, stencil-mark; *marque d'un corps sur le gazon*, imprint of a body on the grass; *marques distinctives du métier*, earmarks of the trade; *marque de pas*, footprint, track; *porter la marque infamante*, to be branded. ‖ ZOOL. Star, blaze (sur le pelage d'un cheval). ‖ TECHN. Marking tool; branding iron, marker (instrument). ‖ MÉD. Trace; *marque d'un coup de fouet*, weal; *marque de la petite vérole*, mark, pit; *laisser une marque*, to leave a mark. ‖ SPORTS. Score (au jeu); *tenir la marque*, to keep the score. ‖ COMM. Mark, brand; *marque déposée (ou) de fabrique*, registered trade-mark; *la meilleure marque*, the best make (de bicyclettes); the best brand (de cigarettes, de cognac); *liqueur de marque*, choice liqueur; *marque d'origine*, maker's name. ‖ AUTOM. Make (de voiture). ‖ FIG. Token (d'affection, de respect); imprint (de l'éducation); stamp (du génie). ‖ FIG. Notability; *personnages de marque*, persons of note (ou) distinction.

marqué, ée [-ke] adj. Marked (linge). ‖ Appointed (date, jour). ‖ COMM. *Au prix marqué*, at the labelled (ou) marked price; *prix marqué,* catalogue price, price on the label. ‖ Méd. Strongly marked, clear-cut (traits); *marqué de la petite vérole,* pock-marked. ‖ Fig. Marked, pronounced, distinct, distinctive (accusé, net); marked (taré); *sympathie marquée pour,* strong liking for.

marquer [-ke] v. tr. (1). To mark, to blaze (les arbres); to brand (le bétail); to stencil (une caisse); to mark (un endroit, sa place); *marquer une page,* to put a book-mark at a certain page, to dog-ear a page; *faire marquer son linge à ses initiales,* to have one's linen marked with one's initials; *faire marquer son papier à lettres à son adresse,* to have one's note-paper stamped with one's address. ‖ To point to (l'heure); to record (la température). ‖ To show off, to bring out (la silhouette, la taille). ‖ To make a note of (une adresse); to write down (une date). ‖ Comm. To mark, to label (un article). ‖ Sports. To score (un point); *marquer un adversaire de trois points,* to be three up; *marquer un but,* to score; *marquer un coup,* to register a hit (à l'escrime). ‖ Milit. *Marquer le pas,* to mark time. ‖ Mus. *Marquer la mesure,* to beat time. ‖ Fig. To stress (un danger); to single out (une époque); to mark, to show (une réaction, un sentiment).
— v. intr. To mark; *ce crayon ne marque pas bien,* this pencil does not write well; *ses doigts ont marqué sur les pages,* his fingers have left marks on the pages. ‖ Naut. *Faire marquer un drapeau,* to dip a flag. ‖ Fig. To make a mark (personnalité); *les faits qui marquent,* outstanding events. ‖ Fig. To look (paraître); *marquer plus que son âge,* to look older than one is.

marqueter [markəte] v. tr. (8 a). To inlay (un meuble). ‖ To speckle (une fourrure).

marqueterie [-tri] f. Inlaid-work, marquetry. ‖ Fig. Patchwork.

marqueteur [-tœ:r] m. Marquetry worker.

marqueur [markœ:r] m. Marker. ‖ Brander (de bétail); stenciller (de caisses). ‖ Sports. Scorer (de but). ‖ Aviat. Marker-bomb, target indicator bomb. ‖ Comm. Marker pen (crayon-feutre).

marquis [marki] m. Marquess, marquis. ‖ Fop (au XVIIᵉ siècle).

marquisat [-kiza] m. Marquisate.

marquise [-ki:z] f. Marchioness (titre). ‖ Carriage awning (d'hôtel); glass-roof (verrière); glass porch (au-dessus d'un perron). ‖ Marquise (bague). ‖ Agric. Marquise pear. ‖ Naut. Awning (de bateau).

Marquises [-ki:z] f. pl. Géogr. Marquesas.

marquoir [markwa:r] m. Sampler (de brodeuse); marker (de tailleur).

marraine [marɛn] f. Godmother (d'un enfant); sponsor (d'un candidat à une société); *marraine de guerre,* pen-friend, soldier's correspondent.

marrant, ante [marã, ã:t] adj. Pop. Splitting; side-splitting; *c'est marrant,* it's a riot.

marre [ma:r] f. Pop. *J'en ai marre,* I'm cheesed off (ou) fed up; *j'en ai marre des maths,* maths bore (ou) U. S. math bores me stiff.

marrer (se) [səmare] v. pr. (1). Pop. To split one's sides with laughing.

marri, ie [mari] adj. † Sorry, grieved.

marron [marɔ̃] m. Chestnut; *marrons glacés,* iced chestnuts, marrons glacés; *marrons d'Inde,* horse-chestnuts; *marchand de marrons,* chestnut-man. ‖ Maroon (pétards). ‖ Maroon, chestnut (couleur). ‖ Fig. *Tirer les marrons du feu,* to pull the chestnuts out of the fire. ‖ Fam. Blow; *un marron sur le nez,* one on the snout.
— adj. invar. Maroon, chestnut (couleur).

marron adj. *Nègre marron,* runaway slave, maroon. ‖ Comm. *Courtier marron,* unlicensed broker. ‖ Méd. *Médecin marron,* shady doctor.
— m. Pirated book. ‖ Stencil plate.

marronnier [marɔnje] m. Bot. Chestnut-tree; *marronnier d'Inde,* horse-chestnut-tree.

Mars [mars] m. Mars. ‖ *Champ de Mars,* parade ground (à Paris); Campus Martius (à Rome). ‖ Fig. *Le métier de Mars,* the profession of arms.

mars m. March; *fin mars,* at the end of March; *le 20 mars,* March the twentieth. ‖ Zool. *Grand mars,* purple emperor.

marseillais, aise [marsɛjɛ, ɛ:z] adj. Géogr. Marseillais; *la Marseillaise,* the Marseillaise (chant).

Marseille [marsɛ:j] f. Géogr. Marseilles.

marsouin [marswɛ̃] m. Zool. Porpoise; sea-hog. ‖ Naut. Forecastle awning; *marsouin avant, arrière,* stemson, sternson. ‖ Naut., Fam. Marine.

marsupial, ale [marsypjal] adj., m. Zool. Marsupial.

marte [mart] f. V. MARTRE.

marteau [marto] m. Hammer; *marteau à deux mains, à panne fendue,* sledge-, claw-hammer; *marteau de porte,* knocker; *marteau pneumatique,* pneumatic tool (ou) drill. ‖ Méd. Malleus, hammer (de l'oreille). ‖ Zool. Hammer-head. ‖ Comm. Hammer (de commissaire-priseur); *passer sous le marteau,* to be sold by (ou) U. S. at auction. ‖ Fam. *Avoir un coup de marteau, être complètement marteau,* to be cracked (ou) absolutely barmy. ‖ **Marteau-pilon,** m. Power-hammer.

martel [martɛl] m. † Hammer. ‖ Fam. *Se mettre martel en tête,* to worry.

martelage [martəla:ʒ] m. Hammering. ‖ Agric. Marking (ou) blazing of trees.

martelé, ée [-le] adj. Hammered, wrought. ‖ Fig. Plodding, laboured (vers).

martèlement [martɛlmã] m. Hammering, pounding (bruit de coups frappés); tramp (bruit de pas).

marteler [-le] v. tr. (8b). To hammer; to hammer out, to beat out (du métal). ‖ Agric. To mark, to blaze (des arbres). ‖ Milit. To pound away at (une position). ‖ Fig. To hammer out (ses mots, des vers); *marteler le cerveau à qqn,* to batter s.o.'s brains out.

marteleur [-lœ:r] m. Hammersmith, hammerman.

martelures [-ly:r] f. Hammer-scales.

martensite [martɛsit] f. Techn. Martensite.

martial, ale [marsjal] adj. Soldierly (allure); martial, warlike (humeur); *cour martiale,* court-martial (pl. courts martial).

martialement [-mã] adv. Martially.

martien [marsjɛ̃] s. Astron. Martian.

Martin [martɛ̃] m. Martin. ‖ Neddy (âne); Teddy Bear, Bruin (ours). ‖ **Martin-bâton,** m. Stick, cudgel. ‖ **Martin-pêcheur,** m. Zool. Kingfisher.

martinet [martinɛ] m. Whip, scourge (pour corriger); whisk (pour épousseter). ‖ Flat candlestick. ‖ Naut. Peak-halyard. ‖ Techn. Tilt-hammer, trip-hammer.

martinet m. Zool. Swift, martlet, martin.

martingale [martɛ̃gal] f. Martingale (harnais). ‖ Half-belt (ceinture). ‖ Martingale (au jeu). ‖ Naut. Martingale.

martiniquais, aise [-kɛ, ɛ:z] adj., s. Géogr. Martinican.

Martinique [martinik] f. Géogr. Martinique.

martre [martr] m. Zool. Marten.

martyr [marti:r] s. Ecclés. Martyr (supplicié). ‖ Loc. *Poser au martyr,* to play the martyr.
— adj. Martyred.

martyre m. Ecclés., Fig. Martyrdom (supplice).

martyriser [-tirize] v. tr. (1). Ecclés. To martyr. ‖ Fam. To martyrize, to torment.

martyrologe [-tirɔlɔ:ʒ] m. Ecclés. Martyrology.

marxien, enne [marksjɛ̃, ɛn] adj. Marxian.

marxisme [-sism] m. Marxism. ‖ **Marxisme-léninisme,** m. Marxism-Leninism.

marxiste [-sist] adj., s. Marxist.

maryland [marilɑ̃] m. Maryland tobacco.
mas [mas] m. Farm- (ou) country-house.
mascara [maskara] m. Mascara.
mascarade [maskarad] f. Masquerade.
mascaret [maskarɛ] m. Tidal wave, bore.
mascaron [maskarɔ̃] m. Grotesque mask.
mascotte [maskɔt] f. Mascot ; lucky charm.
masculin, ine [maskylɛ̃, in] adj. Masculine (genre, rime). ‖ Male (sexe). ‖ Mannish (femme). — m. GRAMM. Masculine, masculine gender.
masculiniser [-linize] v. tr. (1). To make mannish.
masculinité [-linite] f. Masculinity.
maser [mazɛ:r] m. PHYS. Maser.
masochisme [mazɔʃism] m. Masochism.
masochiste [-ʃist] s. Masochist.
masque [mask] m. Mask ; *le Masque de fer*, the Man in the Iron Mask ; *masque mortuaire*, death-mask. ‖ Face, features (expression) ; *masque mobile*, expressive (ou) mobile features. ‖ Masque, masker, mummer (personne masquée). ‖ SPORTS. Fencing-mask (à l'escrime). ‖ MILIT. *Masque à gaz*, gas-mask, respirator. ‖ ARCHIT. Grotesque mask. ‖ THÉÂTR. Opera mask. ‖ MUS. *Placer la voix dans le masque*, to pitch the voice forward. ‖ NAUT. Screen ; *masque à fumée*, smoke sail. ‖ FIG. Mask, cloak, screen ; *lever le masque*, to throw off the mask ; *sous le masque de la sympathie*, under the cloak of sympathy.
masque f. FAM. Hussy, hag (femme, fille) ; *petite masque*, little minx.
masqué, ée [-ke] adj. Masked (bal, personne).
masquer [-ke] v. tr. (1). To disguise (le goût, l'odeur). ‖ To mask, to hide, to conceal ; *masquer la lumière*, to shade the light ; *masquer la vue*, to hide the view. ‖ MILIT. To conceal (une batterie). ‖ NAUT. To cover (les feux) ; to back (les voiles) ; *tous feux masqués*, with all lights obscured. ‖ FIG. *Masquer ses batteries*, to conceal one's intentions. — v. pr. **Se masquer**, to mask oneself, to put on a mask. ‖ To masquerade (*en*, as).
massacrante [masakrɑ̃:t] adj. *D'une humeur massacrante*, in a vile temper.
massacre [-sakr] m. Massacre, slaughter. (V. CARNAGE.) ‖ *Jeu de massacre*, Aunt Sally ; U. S. Hit-the-Baby ; *avoir une tête à massacre*, to have the sort of face you'd like to punch. ‖ ZOOL. Stag's antlers. ‖ SPORTS. *Faire un massacre de perdrix*, to kill partridges wholesale.
massacrer [-sakre] v. tr. (1). To slaughter, to butcher, to massacre, to murder. ‖ CULIN. To hack to pieces (une pièce mal découpée). ‖ FIG. To murder (une langue) ; to botch (un ouvrage).
massacreur [-sakrœ:r] s. Slayer, butcher, massacrer, murderer (d'une langue, de la musique) ; bungler, botcher (d'un ouvrage).
massage [masa:ʒ] m. MÉD. Massage.
masse [mas] f. Mass, heap, bulk (tas) ; body (d'eau) ; bank (de nuages) ; mass (de terre) ; *la masse de platine dans le monde*, the volume of platinum in the world ; *production en masse*, mass production ; *tomber comme une masse*, to fall like a log, to slump down ; *vendre des pommes en masse*, to sell apples in bulk. ‖ Mass, body (de personnes) ; *en masse*, in a body ; *ils sont venus en masse*, a whole crowd of them came. ‖ Mass, mob, crowd, multitude (peuple) ; *le gouvernement des masses*, government by the masses. ‖ Mass (quantité) ; *exécutions en masse*, mass (ou) wholesale executions. ‖ MILIT. Main striking force. ‖ FIN. Fund, stock ; *masse active, passive*, assets, liabilities. ‖ ÉLECTR. Mass, earth ; U. S. ground ; *mettre à la masse*, to earth (ou) U. S. to ground the current. ‖ PHYS. Mass. ‖ FAM. *Il n'y en a pas des masses*, there isn't such a lot of it ; *une masse de livres*, heaps of books.
masse f. Sledge-hammer, maul ; beetle (en bois).

‖ Mace (d'huissier). ‖ Butt (d'une queue de billard). ‖ † *Masse d'armes*, mace.
masselotte [maslɔt] f. TECHN. Deadhead, runner ; counterweight.
massepain [maspɛ̃] m. CULIN. Marzipan, marchpane.
masser [mase] v. tr. (1). To mass. — v. pr. **Se masser**, to mass, to crowd together.
masser v. tr. (1). MÉD. To massage.
massette [masɛt] f. TECHN. Stone-mason's hammer. ‖ BOT. Bulrush, cat's-tail.
masseur [masœ:r] MÉD. Masseur.
masseuse [-sø:z] f. MÉD. Masseuse.
massicot [masiko] m. CHIM. Yellow lead, massicot.
massicot m. Guillotine, trimmer (d'imprimeur).
massicoter [-kɔte] v. tr. (1). To trim, to cut with a guillotine.
massier [masje] m. † Mace-bearer. ‖ ARTS. Treasurer.
massif, ive [masif, i:v] adj. Solid (argent, or) ; massive, bulky (choses) ; large, heavy (dose) ; heavy, dull (personne). ‖ COMM. *Licenciements massifs*, mass dismissals. ‖ MILIT. Massed (attaque) ; *action massive*, mass attack ; *lancer une attaque massive*, to attack in force. — m. Clump (d'arbustes) ; bed (de rosiers). [V. BOSQUET.] ‖ GÉOGR. Mountain mass, group. ‖ ARCHIT. Solid mass. ‖ NAUT. Dead-wood.
massique [masik] adj. PHYS. Of (ou) relating to mass.
massivement [-vmɑ̃] adv. Massively.
massiveté [-vəte] f. Massiveness.
mass media [masmedja] m. pl. Mass media, medias.
massue [masy] f. Club, bludgeon. ‖ FIG. *En coup de massue*, sledge-hammer (arguments) ; *recevoir un coup de massue*, to be knocked silly.
mastectomie [mastɛktɔmi] f. MÉD. Mastectomy.
mastic [mastik] m. Mastic (résine). ‖ Cement, filling (de menuiserie) ; putty (de vitrier). ‖ MÉD. Filling, stopping (de dentiste). ‖ AUTOM. Tyrestopping, U. S. tire cement (pour chambre à air). ‖ FIG. Muddle, mess, mix-up. — adj. invar. Putty-coloured.
masticage [-ka:ʒ] m. Filling, puttying, stopping.
masticateur, trice [mastikatœ:r, tris] adj. MÉD. Masticatory. — m. MÉD. Masticator.
mastication [-kasjɔ̃] f. MÉD. Mastication, masticating, chewing.
masticatoire [-katwa:r] adj., s. MÉD. Masticatory (substance. pâte).
mastiquer [-ke] v. tr. (1). TECHN. To fill, to stop (une fissure) ; to putty (une vitre).
mastiquer [-ke] v. tr. (1). MÉD. To masticate.
mastoc [mastɔk] adj. invar. FAM. Heavy, loutish.
mastodonte [mastɔdɔ̃t] m. ZOOL. Mastodon. ‖ MILIT. Mammoth tank.
mastoïde [mastɔid] adj. MÉD. Mastoid.
mastoïdite [-dit] f. MÉD. Mastoiditis.
mastroquet [mastrɔkɛ] m. FAM. Publican ; barkeeper, U. S. bar-keep.
masturbation [mastyrbasjɔ̃] f. Masturbation.
masturber [-be] v. tr. (1). To masturbate.
m'as-tu-vu [matyvy] m. FAM. Smart Aleck ; U. S. show-off.
masure [mazy:r] f. Hovel, tumbledown cottage.
mat, e [mat] adj. Dull, flat, lustreless (couleur) ; dead (or) ; mat (papier, teint). ‖ Dull, dead (bruit) ; *bruit mat*, thud.
mat [mat] adj. Checkmated. — m. Checkmate.
mât [mɑ] m. NAUT. Mast ; *grand mât*, main mast ; *à trois mâts*, three-masted ; *navire à trois mâts*, three-master. ‖ SPORTS. Pole (de gymnastique) ; *mât de cocagne*, greasy pole ; *mât de tente*, tent-

pole. ‖ Ch. de f. *Mât de signaux*, signal-post. ‖ Aviat. Strut.

matador [matadɔr] m. Matador.

matage [mata:ʒ] m. Matting (du métal).

matamore [matamɔr] m. Swashbuckler.

match [matʃ] (pl. **matches**) m. Sports. Match; *match d'aviron*, boat race; *match de boxe*, boxing contest; *match de boxe amicale*, sparring demonstration; *match de championnat*, league match; *match international de cricket*, test-match.

matcher [-ʃe] v. tr. (1). To match.
— v. intr. To play a match (*contre*, against).

maté [mate] m. Culin. Maté; Paraguayan tea.

matelas [matla] m. Mattress; *matelas de crin*, hair mattress; *retourner le matelas*, to turn the bed. ‖ Cushion; *matelas d'air*, air-cushion.

matelassé [-lase] m. Matelassé.

matelasser v. tr. (1). To pad (une fenêtre); to cushion (une porte, une voiture).

matelassier [-lasje] s. Mattress-maker.

matelot [matlo] m. Naut. Sailor, seaman (en général); blue-jacket (de la marine d'Etat); shipmate (camarade marin); *matelot de première, de deuxième, de troisième classe*, leading, able (ou) able-bodied, ordinary seaman; *servir comme simple matelot*, to serve before the mast. ‖ Naut. Ship (navire); *matelot d'avant, d'arrière*, next ship ahead, astern. ‖ Comm. Sailor suit (costume).

matelote [matlɔt] f. Culin. Matelote.

mater [mate] v. tr. (1). To mat, to dull (le métal). ‖ To caulk, to hammer (une chaudière). ‖ Culin. To work (de la pâte).

mater v. tr. (1). To checkmate (aux échecs). ‖ Fig. To humble (l'orgueil); to break in (qqn).

mater v. tr. (1). Arg. To have a butcher's (ou) dekko at.

mâter [mɑte] v. tr. (1). Naut. To toss up (les avirons); to up-end (un canot); to mast (un navire); *machine à mâter*, masting shears.

mâtereau [matro] m. Naut. Small mast, boom-spar.

matérialisation [materjalizasjɔ̃] f. Materialization.

matérialiser [-lize] v. tr. (1). To materialize.
— v. pr. **Se matérialiser**, to materialize.

matérialisme [-lism] m. Materialism.

matérialiste [-list] adj. Materialistic.
— s. Materialist.

matérialité [-lite] f. Materiality.

matériau [materjo] m. Archit. Material.

matériaux m. pl. Archit., Fig. Materials.

matériel, elle [materjɛl] adj. Material, physical. ‖ Bodily (besoins); materialistic, fleshly (goûts); real, material (impression, sensation). ‖ Jur. *Dommages matériels*, damage to property; *erreur matérielle*, clerical error.
— m. Furniture (d'une école). ‖ Agric. Implements (d'une ferme). ‖ Techn. Working stock (d'une usine). ‖ Milit. Stores (de l'armée); equipment (des hommes); *matériel de guerre*, war material; *service du matériel*, ordnance. ‖ Naut. Stores (de la marine). ‖ Ch. de f. Rolling stock. ‖ Sports. *Matériel de campement*, camping equipment.

matériellement [-mɑ̃] adv. Materially. ‖ Physically; utterly; *matériellement impossible*, physically impossible.

maternel, elle [matɛrnɛl] adj. Maternal, motherly; *l'amour maternel*, maternal affection, motherly love; *école maternelle*, infant (ou) U. S. nursery school, kindergarten; *langue maternelle*, native (ou) mother tongue; *grand-père maternel*, maternal grand-father.

maternelle [-nɛ:l] f. Nursery school.

maternellement [-nɛlmɑ̃] adv. Maternally.

materner [-ne] v. tr. (1). To mother, to baby, to nanny.

maternité [-nite] f. Maternity, motherhood. ‖ Méd. Maternity (ou) lying-in hospital.

math, maths [mat] f. pl. Fam. Maths.

mathématicien [matematisjɛ̃] s. Math. Mathematician.

mathématique [-tik] adj. Math. Mathematical.
— f. pl. Math. Mathematics; maths (fam.); mathematics class (classe).

mathématiquement [-tikmɑ̃] adv. Mathematically.

matheux, euse [matø, ø:z] s. Fam. Mathematician.

Mathurin [matyrɛ̃] m. Fam. Jack Tar (marin).

matière [matjɛ:r] f. Material, substance (matériau); *matière plastique*, plastic; *matières premières*, raw material. ‖ Material (base); *matière à conversation*, material for conversation; *matière à discussion, à procès*, ground for discussion, for litigation. ‖ Matter, subject, topic (v. sujet); *en matière de conseils*, as regards advice; *en matière de discipline*, in the matter of discipline; *il n'y a pas matière à rire*, it's no laughing matter; *table des matières*, table of contents; *versé en une matière*, well up in a subject. ‖ Philos. Matter. ‖ Méd. Pl. Faecal matter, faeces.

matin [matɛ̃] m. Morning; *demain matin*, tomorrow morning; *le lendemain matin*, next morning; *de bonne heure le matin*, early in the morning; *deux heures du matin*, two o'clock in the morning (ou) two a. m.; *tous les matins*, every morning; *le vendredi 3 au matin*, on the morning of Friday the third; *il travaille du matin au soir*, he works from morning till night; *rentrer au petit matin*, to come home in the early hours (ou) with the milkman (fam.).
— adv. Early; *je me lève matin*, I get up early.

mâtin [mɑtɛ̃] m. Zool. Mastiff, watch-dog.
— interj. Fam. Indeed!, my word!

matinal, ale [matinal] adj. Morning, matutinal. ‖ Early; *comme vous êtes matinal!*, what an early riser you are!

matinalement [-mɑ̃] adv. Early in the morning.

mâtine [mɑtin] f. Minx. ‖ Fam. *Ma mâtine de mémoire*, my confounded memory.

mâtiné, ée [mɑtine] adj. Cross-bred; crossed (*de*, with).

matinée [matine] f. Morning, forenoon; *dans la matinée*, in the forenoon; *faire la grasse matinée*, to have a lie-in, to sleep late. ‖ Morning wrapper (vêtement). ‖ Théâtr. Matinée, morning (ou) afternoon performance.

mâtiner v. tr. (1). To cross.

matines [-tin] f. pl. Ecclés. Matins.

matir [matir] v. tr. (2). To mat (le métal).

matité [matite] f. Deadness (ou) dullness of sound. ‖ Méd. Dullness.

matoir [matwa:r] m. Techn. Matting tool; riveting-hammer; caulking-tool.

matois, oise [matwa, waz] adj. Sly, cunning, crafty. (V. finaud.)
— m. Slyboots; *fin matois*, wily dog, slippery (ou) U. S. slick customer (fam.).

maton, onne [matɔ̃, ɔn] s. Pop. Screw (gardien de prison).

matou [matu] m. Zool. Tom-cat.

matraquage [matraka:ʒ] m. Coshing (par un cambrioleur); hitting with a truncheon, beating up (par la police). ‖ Stinging, soaking, clipping (des clients). ‖ Plugging (publicitaire).

matraquer [-ke] v. tr. (1). To cosh (avec une matraque de cambrioleur), to hit (ou) beat up with a truncheon (avec une matraque de policier). ‖ To sting, to soak, to clip (les clients). ‖ To assault, to shower, to bombard (le public avec des slogans).

matras [matra] m. Chim. Matrass.

matriarcal, ale [matriarkal] adj. Matriarchal.
matriarcat [-ka] m. Matriarchy.
matrice [matris] f. MÉD. Uterus. ‖ TECHN. Die, matrix; mother (ou) U. S. master record (de disque). ‖ Standard (des poids). ‖ FIN. Original (des contributions).
— adj. Primary (couleur).
matricide [-sid] adj. Matricidal.
— s. Matricide (crime, criminel).
matriciel, elle [-sjɛl] adj. FIN. Pertaining to the assessment of taxes; *loyer matriciel*, rent assessed.
matriculaire [matrikylɛ:r] adj. Pertaining to registration (ou) enrolment. ‖ MILIT. *Feuille matriculaire*, history sheet.
matricule [-kyl] f. Roll, register, list. ‖ Entry on the roll; enrolment. ‖ Registration certificate.
— m. Official (ou) reference number. ‖ MILIT. Serial (ou) army number.
— adj. MILIT. Army (ou) serial (numéro).
matriculer [-kyle] v. tr. (1). To register.
matrilinéaire [matrilinɛ:r] adj. Matrilineal.
matrilocal, ale [-lɔkal] adj. Matrilocal.
matrimonial, ale [-mɔnjal] adj. Matrimonial.
matrone [matrɔn] f. Matron; *faire matrone*, to look matronly.
maturation [matyrasjɔ̃] f. Maturation (acte).
mâture [mɑty:r] f. NAUT. Masting (action); masts and spars; masthouse (mâts); *dans la mâture*, in the rigging, aloft. ‖ Sheers (grue).
maturité [matyrite] f. Maturity, ripeness (d'un fruit). ‖ MÉD. Maturity (d'un abcès). ‖ FIG. Maturity, ripeness (des idées); maturity, full growth (d'une personne); *amener à maturité*, to bring to maturity, to put the finishing touch to (un projet); *manquer de maturité*, to be immature.
matutinal, ale [matytinal] adj. Matutinal.
maudire [modir] v. tr. (62). To curse.
maudit, ite [modi, it] adj. Cursed, accursed; damnable, damned; *maudit soit-il!*, a curse on him!, confound the fellow! ‖ FAM. *Cette maudite lettre*, this confounded letter!; *quel maudit temps*, what wretched weather!; *ce maudit rhumatisme*, this beastly rheumatism.
— m. ECCLÉS. *Le maudit*, the Evil One; *les maudits*, the damned.
maugréer [mogree] v. intr. (1). To grumble, to growl. ‖ FAM. To grouse, U. S. to gripe (*contre*, at).
maure [mo:r] adj. Moorish.
— m. Moor.
mauresque [morɛsk] adj. Moorish (chose).
— f. Moorish woman, Moresque. ‖ ARCHIT. Moresque.
Maurice [moris] m. Maurice (nom). ‖ GÉOGR. Mauritius (île).
mauricien, enne [morisjɛ̃, ɛn] adj., s. GÉOGR. Mauritian.
Mauritanie [moritani] f. GÉOGR. Mauritania.
mauritanien, enne [-njɛ̃, ɛn] adj., s. GÉOGR. Mauritanian.
mauser [mozɛr] m. MILIT. Mauser.
mausolée [mozole] f. Mausoleum.
maussade [mosad] adj. Sullen, cranky, glum, moody, surly; grumpy, crusty, disgruntled (personne); *avoir l'air maussade*, to have a hang-dog look. ‖ Dull, cloudy, depressing (temps).
maussadement [-mɑ̃] adv. Sullenly, sulkily, peevishly, moodily.
maussaderie [-ri] f. Sullenness, sulkiness, glumness, moodiness, crankiness, spleen.
mauvais, aise [movɛ, ɛ:z] adj. Bad, ill, evil, wrong (choses); *avoir de mauvaises intentions*, to have bad intentions, to be ill-intentioned; *faire mauvais usage de son argent*, to put one's money to bad use; *prendre tout du mauvais côté*, to take exception to everything. ‖ Bad, unkind

(personne); *avoir mauvais cœur*, to be hard hearted; *être de mauvaise humeur*, to be in a bad temper; *faire mauvaise mine à qqn*, to give s.o. a cool shoulder; *un mauvais garçon*, a hooligan, U. S. hoodlum; *voir d'un mauvais œil*, to bear a grudge against. ‖ Bad (défectueux); *de mauvaise construction*, jerry-built (maison); *mauvais siège*, uncomfortable chair; *de mauvais vers*, sorry (ou) third-rate verses. ‖ Bad, nasty, poor, rotten, sorry (déplaisant, déplorable); *mauvaise affaire*, nasty business; rotten case (fam.); *mauvaise année*, bad (ou) unlucky year; *mauvaise éducation*, faulty upbringing, ill-breeding; *mauvaise excuse*, poor (ou) lame excuse; *mauvais goût*, bad (ou) unpleasant taste; *mauvaise influence, nouvelles*, bad influence, news; *mauvaise odeur*, bad (ou) offensive smell; *mauvaise saison pour les commerçants*, bad season for tradespeople; *mauvais signe*, bad (ou) ominous sign; *il fait de mauvaises affaires*, his business is doing badly (ou) in a bad way; *prendre qqch. en mauvaise part*, to put a wrong construction on sth.; *trouver mauvais qu'on fasse qqch.*, to object to s.o. doing sth. ‖ Bad, nasty, dangerous (funeste, pénible); *mauvaise grippe*, severe attack of flu; *mauvaise plaisanterie*, untimely practical joke; *mauvais tour*, dirty trick. ‖ Wrong (erroné); *arriver au mauvais moment*, to arrive at an awkward moment; *prendre le mauvais chemin*, to take the wrong way (ou) road; *prendre qqn par le mauvais bout*, to rub s.o. the wrong way. ‖ MÉD. Bad (coup); dangerous (blessure); *mauvaise grippe*, severe attack of flu; *mauvaise vue*, defective vision, deficient eyesight.
— adv. *Qu'il fait mauvais aujourd'hui!*, what wretched weather to-day!; *il fait mauvais lui répondre*, it is unsafe to answer him back; *sentir mauvais*, to smell bad, to stink.
— m. Evil, ill (v. MAL); *distinguer le bon du mauvais*, to distinguish good from evil; *ne voir que le mauvais*, to see only the bad side of things; *les mauvais*, the wicked.
mauvaisement [-zmɑ̃] adv. Evilly, badly, wickedly.
mauve [mov] adj., m. Mauve, light purple.
— f. BOT. Mallow. ‖ ZOOL. Sea-gull.
mauviette [movjɛt] f. ZOOL. Skylark. ‖ FAM. Milk toast.
maxillaire [maksilɛ:r] adj. Maxillary.
— m. MÉD. Jaw-bone; *maxillaire supérieur*, maxilla.
maxima [maksima] adj. V. MAXIMUM.
maximal, ale [-mal] adj. Maximal.
maxime [maksim] f. Maxim, saying.
maximum [maksimɔm] adj. Greatest, maximum.
— m. Maximum; *maximum de rendement*, highest (ou) maximum efficiency; *condamné au maximum de la peine*, sentenced to the severest penalty; *deux cents au maximum*, two hundred at most; *donner son maximum*, to exert oneself to the utmost; *thermomètre à maxima*, maximum thermometer.
mayonnaise [majɔnɛ:z] f. CULIN. Mayonnaise.
mazagran [mazagrɑ̃] m. Beaker for coffee.
mazdéisme [mazdeism] m. Mazdeism.
mazer [maze] v. tr. (1). TECHN. To refine.
mazette [mazɛt] f. SPORTS. Duffer (au jeu); rabbit (au tennis).
— interj. My!, Gosh!
mazout [mazut] m. Fuel oil; oil; mazout, mazut. ‖ MILIT. *Bombe à mazout*, oil bomb.
mazurka [mazyrka] f. MUS. Mazurka.
me [mə] pron. pers. Me (compl. direct); me, to me (compl. ind.); *il me voit*, he sees me; *il me parle*, he speaks to me; *me voici*, here I am;

on me l'a dit, I was told so; *donne-m'en,* give me some.
— pron. réfléchi. Myself; *je m'examine,* I examine myself; *je me suis dit que,* I said to myself that. ‖ (Non traduit avec les verbes pronominaux); *je me demande,* I wonder; *je m'éloignai,* I went off.

mea-culpa [meakylpa] m. invar. One's own fault; *faire son mea-culpa,* to beat one's breast.

méandre [meã:dr] m. Meander, winding (v. SINUO-SITÉ); *faire des méandres,* to wind along (rivière); *les méandres du ruisseau,* the ins and outs of the brook.

méat [mea] m. MÉD. Meatus.

mec [mɛk] m. POP. Bloke, cove, U. S. guy.

mécanicien [mekanisjɛ̃] m. TECHN. Mechanic (v. MACHINISTE); *ingénieur mécanicien,* mechanical engineer. ‖ MÉD. *Mécanicien dentiste,* dental mechanic. ‖ NAUT. *Ouvrier mécanicien,* engine-room artificer. ‖ CH. DE F. Engine driver; U. S. engineer.

mécanicienne [-sjɛ:n] f. Machinist; sewing-machine operator.

mécanique [mekanik] adj. TECHN. Mechanical (art, geste, moyen); machine made (broderie, dentelle); clock-work (jouets); *métier mécanique,* power-loom. ‖ MÉD. Mechanical (mouvement).
— f. TECHN. Mechanism (rouages); mechanics (science). ‖ MUS. Technique. ‖ FAM. Gadget.

mécaniquement [-nikmã] adv. Mechanically.

mécanisation [-nizasjɔ̃] f. Mechanization.

mécaniser [-nize] v. tr. (1). To mechanize.

mécanisme [-nism] m. TECHN. Mechanism; works (de, of). ‖ PHILOS. Mechanism. ‖ MUS. Technique.

mécaniste [-nist] adj. PHILOS. Mechanistic.
— s. PHILOS. Mechanist.

mécano [mɜkano] m. TECHN., FAM. Mechanic.

mécanographe [-nɔgraf] m. Multicopier.

mécanographie [-nɔgrafi] f. Multicopying (acte); multicopying business (industrie).

mécanothérapie [-nɔterapi] f. MÉD. Mechano-therapy.

mécénat [mesena] m. Patronage.

mécène [mesɛ:n] m. Maecenas; patron.

méchage [meʃa:ʒ] m. Fumigation.

méchamment [meʃamã] adv. Wickedly, naughtily, malignantly, spitefully.

méchanceté [meʃɑ̃ste] f. Wickedness (état coupable). ‖ Nastiness, maliciousness (aigreur); spite, spitefulness (besoin de nuire); malice (cruauté); mischievousness (malice); *par pure méchanceté,* out of sheer spite. ‖ Naughtiness (d'un enfant). ‖ Spiteful (ou) malicious deed (ou) word (acte, parole).

méchant, ante [meʃɑ̃, ɑ̃:t] adj. Mischievous, naughty (enfant); wicked, bad, ill-natured (personne); *ce n'est pas un méchant homme,* he is not so bad as all that. ‖ Spiteful, malicious, malevolent (regard); spiteful, nasty, cutting (remarque); *de méchante humeur,* in a bad temper; *lettre méchante,* unkind letter; *roman méchant,* bitingly satirical novel. ‖ Paltry, mean, unimportant (médiocre); *un méchant manteau de fourrure,* a skimpy fur-coat; *un méchant roman,* a third-rate novel; *un méchant billet de dix francs,* a miserable ten francs.
— s. Ill-natured person; *les méchants,* the wicked. ‖ Naughty child (enfant).

mèche [mɛ:ʃ] f. Wick (de bougie); match fuse (de mine). ‖ Lash (de fouet). ‖ Lock (de cheveux); forelock (tombant sur le front). ‖ Bit (de vilebrequin); *mèche à cuiller,* spoon-bit. ‖ Auger-bit (de charpentier). ‖ FAM. *Etre de mèche avec,* to be hand in glove (ou) U. S. in cahoots with; *il n'y a pas mèche,* there is not the ghost of a chance,

nothing doing; *vendre la mèche,* to let the cat out of the bag; to blow the gaff (fam.).

mécher [meʃe] v. tr. (5). To fumigate.

méchoui [meʃwi] m. Barbecue.

mécompte [mekɔ̃:t] m. Miscalculation, error. ‖ FIG. Disappointment, unpleasant surprise; *avoir un grave mécompte,* to be badly let down.

méconnaissable [mekɔnɛsabl] adj. Unrecognizable.

méconnaissance [-nɛsɑ̃:s] f. Misappreciation, non-recognition. ‖ Repudiation (de ses devoirs).

méconnaître [-nɛ:tr] v. tr. (74). To refuse to recognize, to ignore, to cut (un ami pauvre). ‖ To neglect; to disregard (ses intérêts). ‖ To misunderstand, to misinterpret (des faits); to disown, to disclaim (une obligation); to misappreciate, to slight, to underrate (qqn).
— v. pr. **Se méconnaître,** to undervalue (ou) underrate oneself. ‖ To forget what one owes to others.

méconnu, ue [-ny] adj. Misunderstood (personne); unrecognized (talent).

mécontent, ente [mekɔ̃tɑ̃, ɑ̃:t] adj. Displeased, discontented, dissatisfied (de, with); *être mécontent que,* to be annoyed that.
— s. Grumbler. ‖ Malcontent (en politique).

mécontentement [-tmã] m. Discontent, dissatisfaction. ‖ Displeasure (v. DÉPLAISIR); *des sujets de mécontentement,* grounds for complaint.

mécontenter [-te] v. tr. (1). To displease, to annoy (ennuyer); to irritate (irriter).

Mecque (La) [lamɛk] f. GÉOGR. Mecca.

mécréant, ante [mekreɑ̃, ɑ̃:t] adj. Misbelieving, unbelieving.
— m. Misbeliever, unbeliever, miscreant. ‖ FAM. Wretch.

médaille [medɑ:j] f. Medal (pièce). ‖ Badge (insigne). ‖ ARCHIT. Medallion.

médaillé, ée [medaje] adj. MILIT. Holding a medal, decorated (soldat). ‖ Licensed (commissionnaire).
— s. MILIT. Holder of a medal. ‖ Medallist, prize winner (d'un concours).

médailler v. tr. (1). MILIT. To award a medal to. ‖ To issue a badge to (un commissionnaire).

médailliste [-jist] m. ARTS Medallist.

médaillon [-jɔ̃] m. Medallion. ‖ Locket. ‖ Inset (dans un journal). ‖ CULIN. Pat (de beurre).

médecin [medsɛ̃] m. MÉD. Doctor; physician; *femme médecin,* lady doctor. ‖ NAUT. *Le médecin du bord,* the ship's doctor. ‖ FIG. *Le temps est un grand médecin,* time is a great healer.

médecine [-sin] f. MÉD. Medicine (art); dose, drug, medicine (médicament); *étudiant en médecine,* medical student; *médecine de cheval,* horse drench (ou) draught.

média [medja] m. Medium (pl. *media*).

médial, ale [medjal] adj. Medial.

médian, ane [medjɑ̃, an] adj. Median. ‖ Centre (raie). ‖ SPORTS. Half-way (ligne).

médiane [-djan] f. MATH., MÉD. Median.

médiante [-djɑ̃:t] f. MUS. Mediant.

médiastin [med astɛ̃] m. MÉD. Mediastinum.

médiat, ate [-dja, at] adj. Mediate.

médiateur, trice [medjatœ:r, tris] adj. Mediatory.
— m. Mediator. ‖ CHIM. *Médiateur chimique,* transmitter. ‖ JUR. Ombudsman.

médiation [-sjɔ̃] f. Mediation. (V. ENTREMISE.)

médiatisation [-tizasjɔ̃] f. Mediatization.

médiatiser [-tize] v. tr. (1). To mediatize.

médiator [-tɔr] m. MUS. Plectrum.

médiatrice [-tris] f. Mediator. ‖ ECCLÉS. Mediatrix. ‖ MATH. Perpendicular bisector.

médical, ale [medikal] adj. MÉD. Medical.

médicalement [-kalmã] adv. MÉD. Medically.

médicament [-kamã] m. MÉD. Medicine, medicament.

médicamenter [-kamãte] v. tr. (1). MÉD. To doctor, to dose.
— v. pr. Se médicamenter, to doctor (ou) to dose oneself. (V. DROGUER [SE].)

médicamenteux, euse [-kamãtø, ø:z] adj. MÉD. Medicinal (eau); medicated (vin).

médicastre [-kastr] m. MÉD. Medicaster.

médication [-kasjõ] f. MÉD. Medication.

médicinal, ale [-sinal] adj. MÉD. Medicinal.

medicine ball [mɛdsinbol] m. SPORTS. Medicine ball.

médico- [mediko] préf. Medico-. ‖ **Médico-légal**, adj. Medico-legal; expertise médico-légale, forensic evidence. ‖ **Médico-social**, adj. Medico-social.

médiéval, ale [medjeval] adj. Mediaeval.

médiéviste [-vist] m. Mediaevalist.

médiocre [medjokr] adj. Medium, middling (taille). ‖ Average (intelligence); indifferent, mediocre, poor (qualité); de médiocre apparence, shoddy (chose); unimpressive, shabby-looking (personne).
— s. Poor performer; nonentity, mediocrity (personne). ‖ Ordinary; au-dessous du médiocre, worse than mediocre.

médiocrement [-krəmã] adv. Indifferently, poorly.

médiocrité [-krite] f. Mediocrity; poorness (de l'esprit); slenderness (des ressources). ‖ Dull-brained person, nonentity, mediocrity (individu).

médire [medi:r] v. intr. (63). To speak ill (de, of); to cast aspersions (de, on); médire de, to backbite, to vilify, to abuse, to run down.

médisance [-zã:s] f. Slander, scandal, backbiting; l'école de la médisance, the school for scandal; dire des médisances, to talk scandal.

médisant, ante [-zã, ã:t] adj. Scandalmongering; carping, slanderous, backbiting.
— s. Slanderer, backbiter, scandalmonger.

méditatif, ive [meditatif, i:v] adj. Meditative, meditating; d'un air méditatif, musingly, meditatively.

méditation [-tasjõ] f. Meditation. ‖ Cogitation, rumination, musing.

méditer [-te] v. intr. (1). To meditate (sur, on); to cogitate (sur, over); méditer longuement sur, to brood (ou) to ponder over.
— v. tr. To think over, to meditate on, to ponder over (qqch.); méditer de faire, to think of (ou) to contemplate doing. ‖ To prepare, to plan, to contemplate (une entreprise, une œuvre).

Méditerranée [meditɛrane] f. GÉOGR. Mediterranean.

méditerranéen, enne [-neɛ̃, ɛn] adj., s. Mediterranean.

médium [medjom] (pl. médiums) m. Medium (spirite). ‖ Mus. Middle register.

médiumnique [-nik] adj. Mediumistic.

médius [medjys] m. MÉD. Middle finger.

médoc [medɔk] m. COMM. Médoc (vin).

médullaire [medylɛ:r] adj. MÉD. Medullary. ‖ BOT. Medullary; rayon médullaire, pith ray.

médullo-surrénale [-losyrrenal] f. MÉD. Adrenal medulla.

Méduse [medy:z] f. † Medusa. ‖ ZOOL. Jelly-fish.

méduser [-dyze] v. tr. (1). FAM. To petrify, to gorgonize. (V. INTERLOQUER.)

meeting [mitiŋ] m. Meeting. ‖ AVIAT. Air-show.

méfait [mefɛ] m. Misdeed, misdemeanour, wrongdoing. ‖ Pl. Damage (ravages).

méfiance [mefjã:s] f. Mistrust, distrust; avec méfiance, distrustfully.

méfiant, ante [-fjã, ã:t] adj. Distrustful.

méfier (se) [səmefje] v. pr. (1). To be on one's guard; se méfier de, to mistrust, to distrust; to beware of; to watch out for; to guard against; il y a longtemps que je m'en méfie, I have suspected it for some time; méfiez-vous, keep your eyes open, be on the look-out, watch out.

mégalithe [megalit] m. Megalith.

mégalithique [-tik] adj. Megalithic.

mégalomane [megaloman] m. Megalomaniac.

mégalomanie [-ni] f. Megalomania.

mégaphone [megafɔn] m. SPORTS. Megaphone.

mégarde [megard] f. Par mégarde, inadvertently, through carelessness, by an oversight.

mégatonne [megatɔn] f. Megaton.

mégère [meʒɛ:r] f. Shrew, termagant, scold.

mégir [meʒi:r] v. tr. (2). To taw.

mégisserie [-ʒisri] f. Tawing, dressing (action); tawery (lieu).

mégissier [-ʒisje] m. Tawer, leather-dresser.

mégot [mego] m. FAM. Fag-end, cigarette-end, butt.

mégoter [-gɔte] v. intr. (1). POP. To be stingy cheese-paring (sur, with).

méhari [meari] (pl. méharis; méhara [-ra]) m. ZOOL. Fast dromedary.

méhariste [-rist] m. MILIT. Mehariste; member of desert-raiding camel corps.

meilleur, eure [mejœ:r] adj. Better (comparatif); devenir meilleur, to grow better, to improve; de meilleur cœur, more willingly; de meilleure heure, earlier; être sur un meilleur terrain, to stand on more solid ground; prendre meilleure tournure, to take a better turn. ‖ The best (superlatif); le meilleur moyen de se mettre à l'abri, the best thing is to take shelter.
— adv. Better; il fait meilleur aujourd'hui, the weather is better to-day; où fait-il meilleur vivre?, where is it more pleasant to live?
— s. The better (des deux); the best (de plusieurs); du meilleur de mon cœur, with all my heart.

méiose [mejo:z] f. MÉD. Meiosis.

méiotique [-ɔtik] adj. MÉD. Meiotic.

méjuger [meʒyʒe] v. tr. (7). To misjudge.
— v. pr. Se méjuger, to underestimate oneself.

mélancolie [melãkɔli] f. Melancholy, despondency, gloom; blues, dumps (fam.); il n'engendre pas la mélancolie, he is as gay as a lark.

mélancolique [-lik] adj. Melancholy, despondent, gloomy, glum; avoir l'air mélancolique, to look downcast (ou) in the dumps (ou) mopish.

mélancoliquement [-likmã] adv. Melancholically, dejectedly, gloomily.

mélange [melã:ʒ] m. Mixing, blending (action). ‖ Mixture, blend; sans mélange, unalloyed, pure. ‖ Miscellany (en littérature). ‖ AUTOM. Mixture.

mélangé, ée [-ʒe] adj. Mixed; aux couleurs mélangées, motley.

mélanger [-ʒe] v. tr. (7). To mix, to blend, to mingle; mélanger à, to mix with.
— v. pr. Se mélanger, to mix, to get mixed. ‖ To blend (thés). ‖ To mingle, to intermingle (races).

mélangeur [-ʒœ:r] m. Mixing machine.

mélanine [melanin] f. MÉD. Melanin.

mélanoderme [-nɔdɛrm] adj. Melanoderm, black-skinned (races).

mélasse [melas] f. Treacle; U. S. molasses. ‖ POP. Dans la mélasse, in the soup.

melba [mɛlba] adj. inv. CULIN. Pêche melba, peach (ou) pêche Melba.

mêlé, ée [mɛle] adj. Mixed (société); sang mêlé, half-breed. ‖ Tangled (cheveux, écheveau).

mêlée f. Fray, jostle, scuffle. ‖ SPORTS. Scrimmage.

mêler v. tr. (1). To mix, to mix together. (V. MÉLANGER.) ‖ To shuffle (les cartes). ‖ To tangle (les

cheveux). ‖ To spoil (une serrure). ‖ To mix, to mingle (ajouter) [*à*, with]. ‖ Fig. To mingle [*à*, with] ; *joie mêlée de tristesse*, joy mingled with sadness. ‖ Fig. To involve (impliquer) [*à*, in] ; *être mêlé à une querelle*, to be dragged into a quarrel ; *être mêlé à tout*, to have a finger in every pie.
— v. pr. **Se mêler**, to mix (se mélanger). ‖ To mingle (*à*, with) ; *se mêler à un groupe*, to mingle with (ou) to join a group ; *se mêler à la conversation*, to join in the conversation. ‖ To interfere ; to meddle (*de*, with) ; to take a hand (*de*, in) ; *mêlez-vous de vos affaires*, mind your own business ; *le diable s'en mêle*, the devil is taking a hand in it ; *ne vous en mêlez pas*, let it alone ; *ne vous mêlez pas de controverses*, keep out of controversy ; *se mêler de politique*, to dabble in politics.

mélèze [melɛ:z] m. Bot. Larch.

méli-mélo [melimelo] m. Fam. Jumble ; hotch-potch, U. S. hodgepodge.

méliioratif, ive [meljɔratif, i:v] adj. Melio-rative.

mélisse [melis] f. Méd. Melissa, lemon balm ; *eau de mélisse*, melissa cordial (or) water.

mellification [melifikasjɔ̃] f. Honey-making.

mélo [melo] m. Fam. Tear-jerker.
— adj. Fam. Tear-jerking.

mélodie [melɔdi] f. Melody, tune. ‖ Melodious-ness (v. harmonie).

mélodieusement [-djøzmɑ̃] adv. Melodiously.

mélodieux, euse [-djø, ø:z] adj. Melodious, tune-ful. (V. harmonieux.)

mélodique [-dik] adj. Mus. Melodic.

mélodiste [-dist] m. Mus. Melodist.

mélodramatique [-dramatik] adj. Melodramatic.

mélodramatiser [-dramatize] v. tr. (1). To melo-dramatize.

mélodrame [-dram] m. Théâtr. Melodrama.

mélomane [-man] m. Melomaniac ; *être mélo-mane*, to be music-mad.

mélomanie [-mani] f. Melomania.

melon [məlɔ̃] m. Bot. Melon. ‖ Comm. Bowler, billycock, U. S. derby hat (chapeau).

mélopée [melɔpe] f. † Melopoeia. ‖ Chant, sing-song. ‖ Recitative.

membrane [mɑ̃bran] f. Membrane, film. ‖ Web (de palmipède).

membraneux, euse [-nø, ø:z] adj. Membranous.

membre [mɑ̃:br] m. Méd. Limb, member. ‖ Naut. Rib, timber (de navire). ‖ Math. Side (d'une équation). ‖ Fig. Member (d'une société).

membré, ée [mɑ̃bre] adj. Limbed.

membru, ue [-bry] adj. Strong-limbed, big-limbed.

membrure [-bry:r] f. Méd. Limbs. ‖ Aviat., Naut. Frame, framework.

même [mɛ:m] adj. Same (placé avant le nom) ; *le même jour*, on the same day ; *en un même lieu*, in one spot ; *en même temps*, at the same time ; *une seule et même chose*, one and the same thing ; *de la même manière*, in the same way. ‖ Very, self (placé après le nom) ; *le jour même*, the very day ; *le livre même*, the actual book ; *les animaux mêmes l'aiment*, the very animals (ou) the animals themselves like him ; *elle est la bonté même*, she is kindness itself ; *c'est cela même*, that's just it. ‖ Self (pl. selves) [après un pronom personnel] ; *lui-même se récuse*, he himself balks at it ; *ils se sont trahis eux-mêmes*, they betrayed themselves ; *je fais mes cigarettes moi-même*, I make (ou) roll my own cigarettes ; *faire qqch. de soi-même*, to do sth. of one's own accord.
— s. Same ; *il est toujours le même*, he is still the same ; *ces deux idées sont les mêmes*, the two concepts are identical ; *donnez-moi les mêmes*

qu'hier, give me the same ones as yesterday ; *un autre moi-même*, my other self, my alter ego ; *revenir au même*, to come (ou) to amount to the same thing.
— adv. Even ; *il ne m'a même pas fait un signe de tête*, he did not even nod to me. ‖ Loc. *A même la bouteille*, straight out of the bottle ; *à même la peau*, next to the skin ; *à même de répondre*, able to answer ; *de même que..., de même*, as..., so ; *faire de même*, to do likewise, to follow suit ; *faites de même que moi*, do as I do ; *tout de même*, all the same, for all that.

mémé [meme] f. Fam. Grandma, granny (grand-mère). ‖ Old bag (femme d'un certain âge). ‖ Bird, chick (bonne femme).

mêmement [mɛmmɑ̃] adv. Likewise.

mémento [memɛ̃to] m. Memorandum. ‖ Memento, reminder. ‖ Note-book (carnet). ‖ Ecclés. Memento.

mémère [memɛ:r] f. V. mémé.

mémoire [memwa:r] f. Memory (faculté) ; *ma mémoire baisse*, my memory is failing ; *si j'ai bonne mémoire*, if I remember rightly. ‖ Memory, recollection, remembrance, mind (souvenir) ; *garder la mémoire de qqch.*, to keep sth. in mind ; *rappeler qqch. à la mémoire de qqn*, to call (ou) to recall sth. to s.o.'s mind, to give s.o. a reminder of sth. ; *réciter de mémoire*, to recite from mem-ory ; *remettre en mémoire*, to bring back to memory, to refresh s.o.'s memory about. ‖ Mem-ory, remembrance ; *en mémoire de*, in memory of ; *de glorieuse mémoire*, of illustrious memory. ‖ Inform. Memory, storing device, store.

mémoire m. Memorial ; report. ‖ Dissertation, memoir (pour une université). ‖ Jur. Abstract, statement. ‖ Comm. Bill (de fournisseur). ‖ Pl. Memoirs. (V. autobiographie.)

mémorable [memɔrabl] adj. Memorable, note-worthy (événement) ; eventful (journée) ; historical (séance).

mémorablement [-rabləmɑ̃] adv. Memorably.

mémorandum [-rɑ̃dɔm] m. Memorandum. ‖ Note-book (carnet). ‖ Naut. *Mémorandum de combat*, battle orders.

mémorial [-rjal] m. Memorial.

mémorialiste [-rjalist] s. Memorialist.

mémorisation [-rizasjɔ̃] f. Memorization. ‖ Inform. Storage.

mémoriser [-rize] v. tr. (1). To memorize. ‖ Inform. To store.

menaçant, ante [mənasɑ̃, ɑ̃:t] adj. Threatening, menacing, forbidding (regard). ‖ Lowering, threat-ening (ciel).

menace [-nas] f. Threat, menace ; *des menaces en l'air*, idle threats ; *obliger qqn sous la menace à faire qqch.*, to bully s.o. into doing sth.

menacer [-nase] v. tr. (6). To threaten, to menace (*de*, with) ; *nous sommes menacés d'un orage*, a storm is brewing ; *la tuberculose le menace*, tuberculosis is hanging over him.

ménade [menad] f. Maenad (prop., fig.).

ménage [mena:ʒ] m. Housekeeping (soins du ménage) ; *tenir le ménage de*, to keep house for. ‖ Household, family (famille) ; *ménage de six personnes*, household of six. ‖ Household goods (appareils ménagers) ; *un ménage complet*, a full set of furniture ; *liqueur de ménage*, home-made liqueur. ‖ Housework (nettoyage) ; *faire le ménage*, to do housework ; *femme de ménage*, charwoman, daily help, U. S. cleaning woman ; *le ménage à fond*, general house-cleaning. ‖ Couple, married pair (époux) ; *ménage à trois*, domestic triangle ; *engager un ménage*, to hire a couple ; *faux ménage*, unmarried couple living together ; *jeune ménage*, newly married couple ; *faire bon, mauvais ménage*, to be happy, unhappy in wedlock; *mon chien et mon chat font bon mé-nage*, my dog and my cat get along well together.

ménagement [menaʒmɑ̃] m. Prudence, discretion, care; *avec ménagement*, carefully; *user de ménagement pour*, to take precautions to; *sans ménagement*, roughly, bluntly.

ménager [-ʒe] v. tr. (7). To husband, to save, to be sparing of (épargner); *ménager ses forces*, to husband one's strength; *un homme qui ménage ses paroles*, a man of few words; *ménager ses vêtements*, to save one's clothes; *ne rien ménager*, to go the whole hog. ‖ To treat considerately, to handle gingerly, to spare (prendre des précautions); to approach gently, to humour, to indulge (ne pas heurter); *obtenir beaucoup de qqn en le ménageant*, to get a great deal out of s.o. by humouring him; *ménager la fierté d'un pauvre*, to take a poor man's self-respect into consideration; *on vous a ménagé*, you have been treated considerately. ‖ To arrange, to plan (organiser); *ménager une entente entre*, to bring about an understanding between; *ménager une rencontre*, to arrange a meeting; *ménager une surprise à*, to prepare a surprise for; *ménager de la place pour*, to allow room for; *transition ménagée de, à*, gradual transition from, to.
— v. pr. **Se ménager**, to spare oneself; to take care of oneself.

ménager, ère [-ʒe, ɛːr] adj. Household (du ménage). ‖ Sparing (économe) [de, of].

ménagère [-ʒɛːr] f. Housewife, housekeeper. ‖ Cruet-stand (burette). ‖ FAM. Wife.

ménagerie [menaʒri] f. Menagerie. ‖ FAM. *Une vraie ménagerie*, a perfect zoo.

mendelevium [mɛ̃delevjɔm] m. CHIM. Mendelevium.

mendélisme [mɑ̃delism] m. Mendelism.

mendiant, ante [mɑ̃djɑ̃, ɑ̃ːt] adj. Begging. ‖ ECCLÉS. Mendicant (ordre).
— s. Beggar. ‖ CULIN. Dessert of nuts, almonds, figs and raisins.

mendicité [-disite] f. Mendicity, mendicancy, begging (acte); beggary (état); beggars (gens).

mendier [-dje] v. intr. (1). To beg.
— v. tr. To beg for.

mendigot [-digo] s. FAM. Beggar, U. S. panhandler.

mendigoter [-digote] v. intr. (1). FAM. To beg, U. S. to panhandle.

meneau [mǝno] m. ARCHIT. Mullion; transom; *à meneaux*, mullioned.

menée [mǝne] f. Sly manœuvre, intrigue (v. AGISSEMENT); *déjouer les menées de qqn*, to thwart (ou) to outmanœuvre s.o.

mener v. tr. (1). To lead, to take, to conduct (conduire); *mener un chien en laisse*, to lead a dog on the leash; *menez-moi voir ce film*, take me to see this film. ‖ To rule; to boss (fam.) [diriger]; *mener la bande, la danse*, to lead the band, the dance; *mener tout le bazar*, to rule the roost; *mener tout le monde*, to boss everybody (fam.); *mener le mouvement*, to be the backbone of the movement; *mener par le bout du nez*, to lead by the nose. ‖ To carry (porter); *mener le lait de sa ferme à la ville*, to carry the milk from one's farm to town. ‖ To manage (organiser); *bien mener sa barque*, to manage one's affairs well; *mener qqch. à bien*, to carry sth. through successfully; *mener plusieurs choses de front*, to have several irons in the fire. ‖ To lead (suivre); *mener la vie à grandes guides*, to go the pace; *mener une vie de patachon*, to lead a fast life. ‖ To take (amener); *cet héritage le mènera jusqu'à la fin de ses études*, this inheritance will see him through his course of studies. ‖ To carry (entraîner); *cela peut le mener loin*, that may take him a long way; *mené par ses passions*,

swayed by one's passions. ‖ AUTOM. To drive. ‖ MATH. To draw (une ligne). ‖ JUR. To carry out (une enquête). ‖ MILIT. To concentrate (une attaque); *rapidement mené*, concentrated.
— v. intr. To lead (aboutir) [à, to]. ‖ SPORTS. To lead (par, by). ‖ LOC. *Ne mener à rien*, to fall flat, to peter out; *ne pas en mener large*, to be in a tight corner, to feel small.

ménestrel [menɛstrɛl] m. Minstrel.

ménétrier [menetrije] m. † Fiddler.

meneur [mǝnœːr] m. Leader; ring-leader (dans une révolte). ‖ AGRIC. *Meneur de bœufs*, cattle-driver. ‖ THÉÂTR. *Meneur de jeu*, narrator. ‖ FIG. *Meneur de jeu*, moving spirit.

menhir [mɛniːr] m. Menhir, standing stone.

méninge [menɛ̃ːʒ] f. MÉD. Meninx (pl. meninges). ‖ FAM. *Se torturer les méninges*, to rack one's brains.

méningé, ée [-ʒe] adj. MÉD. Meningeal.

méningite [-ʒit] f. MÉD. Meningitis.

ménisque [menisk] m. PHYS. Meniscus. ‖ MÉD. Meniscus; *se faire opérer du ménisque*, to have a cartilage operation.

ménopause [menɔpoːz] f. MÉD. Menopause.

ménorragie [-raʒi] f. MÉD. Menorrhagia.

ménorrhée [-re] f. MÉD. Menorrhoea.

menotte [mǝnɔt] f. Tiny hand. ‖ Pl. Handcuffs, manacles; *mettre les menottes à*, to handcuff; *menottes aux poignets*, handcuffed.

mensonge [mɑ̃sɔ̃ːʒ] m. Lie, untruth, falsehood (v. CONTREVÉRITÉ); *faire un mensonge*, to tell a lie; *faire un petit mensonge*, to fib; *gros mensonge*, big (ou) whopping lie; *petit mensonge*, fib, white lie. ‖ Fallacy; delusion (de l'imagination).

mensonger, ère [-ʒe, ɛr] adj. Lying, false, mendacious, untrue (faux); illusory, fallacious, delusive (illusoire).

mensongèrement [-ʒɛrmɑ̃] adv. Falsely, untruthfully, mendaciously.

menstruation [mɑ̃stryasjɔ̃] f. MÉD. Menstruation.

menstruel, elle [-stryɛl] adj. MÉD. Menstrual.

menstrues [-stry] f. pl. MÉD. Menses.

mensualisation [mɑ̃syalizasjɔ̃] f. Payment by the month (d'un salarié); monthly payment (d'un salaire). ‖ FIN. Payment by the month (de l'impôt sur le revenu).

mensualiser [-lize] v. tr. (1). To pay by the month (un salarié); to pay monthly (un salaire).

mensualité [mɑ̃syalite] f. Monthly nature (du paiement). ‖ Monthly instalment (ou) allowance.

mensuel, elle [-ɛl] adj. Monthly.

mensuellement [-ɛlmɑ̃] adv. Monthly; every (ou) per month.

mensurabilité [mɑ̃syrabilite] f. Mensurability.

mensurable [-rabl] adj. Mensurable, measurable.

mensuration [-rasjɔ̃] f. Mensuration.

mental, ale [mɑ̃tal] adj. Mental. ‖ MÉD. Mental (maladie); *spécialiste de maladies mentales*, mental specialist, psychiater, U. S. psychiatrist. ‖ MATH. *Calcul mental*, mental arithmetic.

mentalement [-lmɑ̃] adv. Mentally.

mentalité [-lite] f. Mentality; turn of mind.

menterie [mɑ̃tri] f. FAM. Fib. (V. MENSONGE.)

menteur, euse [-tœːr, øːz] adj. Lying, false, mendacious, given to lying (faux); false, deceptive, illusory (illusoire).
— s. Liar; fibber (fam.).

menthe [mɑ̃ːt] f. Mint; *pastille de menthe*, peppermint lozenge (ou) drop. ‖ CULIN. *Sauce à la menthe*, mint-sauce.

menthol [mɛ̃tɔl] m. CHIM. Menthol.

mentholé, ée [-le] adj. Mentholated.

mention [mɑ̃sjɔ̃] f. Mention; *faire mention de*, to mention (ou) refer to; *faire mention expresse*, to stipulate. ‖ Honours (à un examen); *avec mention*, with honours; *être reçu sans mention*, to receive a pass, to just pass. ‖ JUR. Endorsement; *portant la mention « inconnu »*, endorsed « not known ». ‖ MILIT. Pl. Particulars (au livret).

mentionner [-sjɔne] v. tr. (1). To mention (v. CITER); *ci-dessus, ci-dessous mentionné*, aforesaid (ou) above-mentioned, undermentioned. ‖ To specify (préciser).

mentir [mɑ̃tiːr] v. intr. (93). To lie; to fib, to tell stories (fam.); *sans mentir*, to tell the truth, truth to tell; honour bright (fam.); *faire mentir le proverbe*, to belie the proverb.

menton [mɑ̃tɔ̃] m. Chin; *prendre qqn par le menton*, to chuck s.o. under the chin.

mentonnet [-tɔnɛ] m. TECHN. Lug; tappet. ‖ MILIT. Lug (de bombe); cocking piece (de revolver). ‖ CH. DE F. Flange (de roue).

mentonnier [-tɔnje] adj. MÉD. Mental.

mentonnière [-tɔnjɛːr] f. MILIT. Chin-strap. ‖ MÉD. Chin-bandage. ‖ MUS. Chin-rest (de violon). ‖ TECHN. Muffle-plate.

mentor [mɑ̃tɔːr] m. Mentor.

menu, ue [məny] adj. Slim, slender (mince); small, tiny (petit); *menue monnaie*, small change; *menu plomb*, small shot. ‖ Small, trifling (insignifiant); *menus détails*, minute details; *menus frais*, petty expenses.
— adv. Fine, small; *écrire menu*, to write small; *hacher menu*, to mince; *trotter menu*, to trip along, to mince along.
— m. *Raconter par le menu*, to tell in detail, U. S. to spell out.

menu m. CULIN. Bill-of-fare, menu; *menu à prix fixe*, table d'hôte.

menuet [mənɥɛ] m. Minuet.

menuiser [mənɥize] v. tr. (1). To cut down, to whittle (du bois).
— v. intr. To do joiner's work (ou) woodwork.

menuiserie [-zri] f. Joiner's (ou) carpenter's shop (atelier); piece of joinery (ouvrage); joiner's work, joinery, woodwork, carpentry (travail).

menuisier [-zje] m. Joiner, U. S. carpenter.
— adj. *Ouvrier menuisier*, joiner, carpenter.

méphistophélique [mefistɔfelik] adj. Mephistophelean.

méphitique [mefitik] adj. Mephitic.

méphitisme [-tism] m. Mephitis.

méplat, ate [mepla, at] adj. Flat, flat-laid.
— Flat part (d'un visage).

méprendre (se) [səmeprɑ̃ːdr] v. pr. (80). To be mistaken (*au sujet de, sur*, about); *il n'est pas possible de s'y méprendre*, there is no mistaking it, there is no possible mistake about it; *imiter qqch. à s'y méprendre*, to imitate sth. so well that you could be easily taken in.

mépris [mepri] m. Contempt, scorn; *au mépris de*, in contempt of, in defiance of; *on n'a que du mépris pour lui*, he is despised by all; *regarder avec mépris*, to look down upon.

méprisable [-zabl] adj. Contemptible, despicable (individu); piddling (offre).

méprisant, ante [-zɑ̃, ɑ̃ːt] adj. Contemptuous, scornful.

méprise [mepriːz] f. Mistake, misapprehension.

mépriser [-prize] v. tr. (1). To despise (qqch., qqn). ‖ To spurn, to scorn (des avances, une offre). [V. DÉDAIGNER.]

mer [mɛr] f. Sea; *mer d'huile*, sea as smooth as a mill-pond; *capable de prendre la mer*, seaworthy (navire); *de haute mer*, sea-going (navire); *en pleine mer*, out at sea, in the open sea; *gens de mer*, seamen; *mettre à la mer*, to lower (un canot); to launch (un navire); *prendre la mer*, to put out to sea; *voyage par mer*, sea-voyage. ‖ Tide (marée); *à haute mer*, at high tide; *la mer descend, monte*, the tide is going down (ou) out, is coming up (ou) in. ‖ FAM. *Porter de l'eau à la mer*, to carry coals to Newcastle.

mercanti [mɛrkɑ̃ti] m. FAM. Profiteer, shark.

mercantile [-til] adj. COMM. Mercantile, commercial. ‖ FIG. Grabbing, mercenary, covetous; *esprit mercantile*, money-grubbing mentality.

mercantilisme [-tilism] m. COMM. Mercantilism. ‖ FIG. Mercenary spirit.

mercenaire [mɛrsənɛːr] adj. Mercenary; money-minded. ‖ MILIT. Mercenary, hired (troupes).
— m. Hireling. ‖ MILIT. Mercenary.

mercerie [mɛrsri] f. Haberdashery (commerce); haberdasher's shop, dressmaker's supplies shop, U. S. notions shop (magasin); U. S. notions (marchandises).

mercerisé, ée [-sərize] adj. Mercerized.

merceriser [-sərize] v. tr. (1). To mercerize.

merci [mɛrsi] f. † Favour (v. MISÉRICORDE); *Dieu merci*, by the grace of God, thank God. ‖ Mercy; *accorder merci à qqn*, to grant s.o. quarter; *être à la merci de*, to be at the mercy of; *implorer merci*, to beg for mercy; *se mettre à la merci de qqn*, to put oneself in s.o.'s power; *se rendre à merci*, to surrender unconditionally; *sans merci*, merciless, mercilessly. ‖ ECCLÉS. *Notre-Dame de la Merci*, our Lady of Ransom.
— adv. Thank you, thanks (*de*, for) [assentiment]; *merci mille fois*, very many thanks; thanks very much. ‖ No, thank you (refus).
— m. Thanks; *adresser un merci sincère à*, to give sincere thanks to.

mercier [mɛrsje] m. Haberdasher; dealer in dressmaker's supplies.

mercredi [mɛrkrədi] m. Wednesday.

mercure [mɛrkyːr] m. CHIM. Mercury, quicksilver. ‖ † Mercury (dieu).

mercuriale [mɛrkyrjal] f. Remonstrance. (V. RÉPRIMANDER.) ‖ COMM. Market price-list.

mercuriel, elle [-rjɛl] adj. CHIM. Mercurial.

mercurochrome [-rɔkrom] m. MÉD., CHIM. Mercurochrome.

merde [mɛrd] f. ARGOT. Shit.
— interj. Oh hell!

merdeux, euse [-dø, ø:z] adj. POP. Shitty. ‖ POP. Uppish (prétentieux).
— s. POP. Shit; *faire le merdeux*, to look big.

merdier [-dje] m. POP. Bloody mess (ou) fix; balls-up (arg.).

merdique [-dik] adj. POP. Crappy, shitty.

mère [mɛːr] f. Mother, parent; *mère de famille*, mother of a family; *Madame votre mère*, your mother; *reine mère*, Queen Mother; *sans mère*, motherless. ‖ CULIN. Mother (de vinaigre). ‖ ECCLÉS. *Mère abbesse*, abbess; *Révérende Mère X.*, Reverend Mother X.; *maison mère*, parent monastery. ‖ COMM. *Maison mère*, head office. ‖ FIG. Mother, root; source (origine); *langue mère*, mother tongue; *mère de tous les maux*, root of all evils. ‖ FAM. *La mère Michel*, old Mrs. Michel. ‖ **Mère-grand,** f. FAM. † Grandma. ‖ **Mère patrie,** f. Mother country.

méridien, enne [meridjɛ̃, ɛ:n] adj. Meridian; *lunette méridienne*, transit instrument.
— m. Meridian; *passer le méridien*, to south.

méridienne [-djɛ:n] f. Meridian line (ligne). ‖ Midday siesta, nap (sieste). ‖ Sofa (lit).

méridional, ale [-djɔnal] adj. South, southern, meridional.
— s. Southerner.

meringue [mərɛ̃:g] f. CULIN. Meringue.

meringuer [-rɛ̃ge] v. tr. (1). CULIN. To coat (ou) top with meringue.

mérinos [merinos] m. ZOOL., COMM. Merino.

merise [məri:z] f. BOT. Wild cherry, merry.

merisier [mərizje] m. BOT. Wild cherry tree.

méritant, ante [meritɑ̃, ɑ̃:t] adj. Deserving, meritorious, worthy.

mérite [merit] m. Merit, desert, worth, worthiness (v. VALEUR); *avoir le mérite d'être bon* *marché,* to have the merit of being cheap; *homme de mérite,* a man of sterling qualities; *revendiquer le mérite de,* to claim credit for; *traiter qqn selon son mérite,* to deal with s.o. according to his deserts; *sans mérite,* undeserving. ‖ *Mérite agricole,* French decoration awarded to prominent farmers.

mériter [-te] v. tr. (1). To merit, to deserve; *mériter d'être lu, vu,* to be worth reading, seeing; *mériter examen,* to deserve looking into; *n'avoir que ce qu'on mérite,* to get what one deserves, to get one's just deserts. ‖ To entitle, to win, to earn, to secure (valoir); *mériter à qqn une promotion,* to win to s.o. a promotion. ‖ To require (demander); *mériter confirmation,* to need confirmation.
— *v.* intr. To merit, to deserve; *il a bien mérité de la patrie,* he has served his country well.

méritoire [-twa:r] adj. Meritorious, deserving, commendable.

merlan [mɛrlɑ̃] m. ZOOL. Whiting. ‖ FAM. *Tourner des yeux de merlan frit,* to turn up one's eyes like a duck in thunder; to stare blankly. ‖ POP. Hairdresser.

merle [mɛrl] m. ZOOL. Blackbird; *merle bleu,* blue rock thrush; *merle à collier,* ring-ouzel. ‖ FIG. *Merle blanc,* white crow, rara avis, blue dahlia. ‖ FAM. *Vilain merle,* nasty fellow.

merlette [-lɛt] f. ZOOL. Hen blackbird. ‖ BLAS. Martlet.

merlin [mɛrlɛ̃] m. Heavy (ou) cleaving axe. ‖ ‖ NAUT. Marline.

merluche [mɛrly:ʃ] f. ZOOL. Hake. ‖ CULIN. Dried cod.

mérou [meru] m. ZOOL. Grouper.

mérovingien, enne [merɔvɛ̃ʒjɛ̃, ɛn] adj., s. Merovingian.

merrain [mɛrɛ̃] m. Cask- (ou) stave-wood.

merveille [mɛrvɛ:j] f. Marvel, wonder (v. PRODIGE); *dire des merveilles de,* to speak in glowing terms of; *faire merveille,* to work wonders (ou) miracles; *les sept merveilles du monde,* the seven wonders of the world. ‖ BOT. *Merveille-du-Pérou,* Marvel of Peru.
— loc. adv. **A merveille,** wonderfully, admirably; *il l'a fait à merveille,* he made a wonderful job of it (fam.); *se porter à merveille,* to be in the pink of condition; *votre robe vous va à merveille,* your dress is most becoming; *tout marche à merveille,* everything is going beautifully (ou) swimmingly (ou) first rate; *poli à merveille,* ever so polite (ironique).

merveilleusement [-jøzmɑ̃] adv. Marvellously, wonderfully.

merveilleux, euse [-jø, ø:z] adj. Marvellous, wonderful (v. MAGNIFIQUE); *elle est merveilleuse,* she is wonderful. ‖ FAM. *Vous êtes merveilleuse!,* you are a wonder (extraordinaire).
— m. The marvellous; the supernatural element. ‖ † Fop, dandy.

mes [mɛ]. V. MON.

mésalliance [mɛsaljɑ̃:s] f. Misalliance.

mésallier [-lje] v. tr. (1). To misally.
— *v.* pr. **Se mésallier,** to marry beneath one's station.

mésange [mezɑ̃:ʒ] f. ZOOL. Titmouse, tomtit.

mésaventure [mezavɑ̃ty:r] f. Misadventure, misfortune, mishap (infortune); mischance (malchance).

mescaline [meskalin] f. CHIM. Mescaline.

mesdames, mesdemoiselles [mɛdam, mɛdmwazɛl] f. pl. V. MADAME, MADEMOISELLE.

mésentente [mesɑ̃tɑ̃:t] f. Misunderstanding, disagreement.

mésentère [mezɑ̃tɛ:r] m. MÉD. Mesentery.

mésestimation [mezɛstimasjɔ̃] f. Underestimation, underrating, undervaluing.

mésestime [mezɛstim] f. Disesteem, low esteem; poor opinion.

mésestimer [-me] v. tr. (1). To underestimate, to underrate; to have a poor opinion of.

mésintelligence [mezɛ̃tɛliʒɑ̃:s] f. Misunderstanding, disagreement (v. BROUILLE); *en mésintelligence avec,* at loggerheads with.

mesmérisme [mɛsmɛrism] m. Mesmerism.

mesmériste [-rist] m. Mesmerist.

mésomorphe [mezɔmɔrf] adj. GÉOL. Mesomorphous, mesomorphic.

méson [mezɔ̃] m. PHYS. Meson.

Mésopotamie [mezɔpɔtami] f. GÉOGR. Mesopotamia.

mésopotamien, enne [-mjɛ̃, ɛn] adj., s. GÉOGR. Mesopotamian.

mésozoïque [mezɔzɔik] adj., m. GÉOL. Mesozoic.

mesquin [mɛskɛ̃] adj. Mean, stingy, niggard, niggardly (personne). ‖ Paltry, shabby, beggarly (cadeau); shabby, mean (demeure); petty, narrow, small (esprit); poor, scanty (repas); *à l'esprit mesquin,* small-minded; *c'est bien mesquin de sa part de,* it is very petty of him to.

mesquinement [mɛskinmɑ̃] adv. Shabbily, meanly, niggardly, poorly. ‖ Scantily, pettily.

mesquinerie [-ri] f. Stinginess, meanness, niggardliness (de qqn). ‖ Scantiness, shabbiness, pettiness, paltriness, poorness (de qqch.). ‖ Shabby, mean action, meanness (action).

mess [mɛs] m. MILIT. Mess.

message [mɛsa:ʒ] m. Message; *message chiffré, téléphoné,* code, telephone message. ‖ NAUT., AVIAT. *Message de détresse, d'urgence,* distress, emergency message; *message de position,* position report. ‖ FIG. Message (d'un philosophe, poète).

messager [mɛsaʒe] m. Messenger; *messager de malheur,* bearer of bad news; *messager de printemps,* harbinger of spring. ‖ Public carrier (de messagerie).

messagerie [-ʒri] f. Carrying trade; conveyance by a common carrier; express transport service. ‖ CH. DE F. *Bureau des messageries,* parcels office. ‖ NAUT. *Messagerie maritime,* shipping company, sea-transport. ‖ AVIAT. *Messageries aériennes,* air-mail service.

messe [mɛs] f. ECCLÉS., MUS. Mass.

messeigneurs [mɛsɛɲœ:r]. V. MONSEIGNEUR.

messianique [mɛsjanik] adj. ECCLÉS. Messianic.

messianisme [-nism] m. ECCLÉS. Messianism.

messidor [mɛsidɔ:r] m. Messidor, tenth month in French Republican calendar (June-July).

messie [mɛsi] m. ECCLÉS. Messiah.

messin, ine [mɛsɛ̃, in] adj. GÉOGR. Of (ou) from Metz.
— s. GÉOGR. Native (ou) inhabitant of Metz.

messire [mɛsi:r] m. † My Lord; Master.

mesurable [məzyrabl] adj. Measurable; mensurable.

mesurage [-ra:ʒ] m. Measuring, measurement.

mesure [məzy:r] f. Measurement (mensuration); *prendre les mesures d'une pièce,* to take the measurements of a room. ‖ Measure; *mesure de longueur,* measure of length; *mesure de capacité, de superficie, de volume,* liquid (ou) dry, square, cubic measure; *une mesure de vin,* a measure of wine; *faire bonne mesure,* to give good measure; *poids et mesures,* weights and measures. ‖ Extent, proportion, measure degree (limite); *dans une certaine, une large mesure,* to some (ou) a certain, a large extent; *dans la mesure de mes moyens,* in so far as it lies within my power; *dans la mesure où,* in so far as; in proportion to; *dépasser la mesure,* to overstep the bounds; *garder la mesure,* to keep within

bounds; *ne garder aucune mesure,* to fling aside all restraint, to know (ou) keep no bounds; *outre mesure,* beyond measure; *sans mesure,* unbounded (ambition). || Moderation; *en toute chose il y a une mesure,* there is a limit to everything. || Measure, step (disposition); *mesure disciplinaire,* disciplinary measure (ou) action; *une habile mesure de sa part,* a clever move on his part; *prendre toutes les mesures nécessaires,* to take all necessary steps; *prendre des mesures sévères contre,* to take strong measures against. || Position, ability (possibilité); *être en mesure de,* to be in a position to, to have the power to. || Measure (dans les vêtements); *costume fait sur mesure,* suit made to measure, suit to order, U. S. custom-made suit; *prendre les mesures de qqn,* to take s.o.'s measurements. || Mus. Measure; bar; *battre la mesure,* to beat time; *jouer quelques mesures,* to play a few bars; *mesure composée,* compound time. || Milit. Pl. Measures; *mesures de défense,* defence measures. || Fig. Measure; *donner sa mesure,* to show what one is capable of (ou) what one is made of; *prendre la mesure de qqn,* to size s.o. up.
— loc. conj. A **mesure que,** as, in proportion as.
mesuré, ée [məzyre] adj. Temperate, moderate, restrained, guarded (expression, parole); measured, regular (marche, pas).
mesurer v. tr. (1). To measure (en général); to measure up (du bois); to measure off (du drap); to measure out (un terrain). || To measure (avoir une dimension); *mesurer six pieds,* to stand six feet high (taille); *mesurer dix pieds sur vingt,* to measure ten feet by twenty. || To calculate, to proportion, to measure (apprécier); *mesurer au pas,* to pace off; *mesurer à la vue,* to judge by the eye. || To measure, to gauge, to estimate (jauger); *mesurer la force de qqn,* to judge of s.o.'s strength; *mesurer qqn du regard,* to look s.o. up and down. || To measure out, to mete out, to stint (départir); *mesurer ses désirs à ses moyens,* to cut one's coat according to one's cloth; *mesurer ses efforts,* to stint one's efforts; *mesurer les fonds à,* to grudge funds to; *mesurez vos paroles,* weigh your words, be careful what you say, curb your tongue.
— v. pr. **Se mesurer,** to tackle, to cope (*avec, contre,* with); to pit oneself (*avec,* against); *être de taille à se mesurer avec un géant,* to be a match for a giant.
mesureur [-rœːr] m. Measurer.
mésuser [mezyze] v. intr. (1). *Mésuser de,* to abuse (son pouvoir); to misuse (ses richesses).
métabolisme [metabɔlism] m. Méd. Metabolism.
métacarpe [metakarp] m. Méd. Metacarpus.
métacarpien, enne [-pjɛ̃, ɛn] adj. Méd. Metacarpal.
métairie [metɛri] f. Agric. Métairie, small farm.
métal [metal] m. Metal.
métalangage [metalɑ̃gaːʒ] m. Inform., Philos., Math. Metalanguage.
métalangue [-lɑ̃ːg] f. Philos., Math. Metalanguage.
métallifère [metalifɛːr] adj. Metalliferous. || Géogr. *Monts Métallifères,* Ore Mountains, Erzgebirge.
métallique [-lik] adj. Metallic. || Fin. *Encaisse métallique,* gold reserve. || Archit. All-metal.
métallisation [-lizasjɔ̃] f. Metallization.
métalliser [-lize] v. tr. (1). To metallize, to plate.
métallo [-lo] m. Fam. Metallurgist.
métallographie [-lɔgrafi] f. Metallography.
métallographique [-lɔgrafik] adj. Metallographic.
métalloïde [-lɔid] m. Metalloid.
métallurgie [-lyrʒi] f. Metallurgy.
métallurgique [-lyrʒik] adj. Metallurgic.

métallurgiste [-lyrʒist] m. Metallurgist.
métamorphique [metamɔrfik] adj. Géol. Metamorphic.
métamorphiser [metamɔrfize] v. tr. (1). Géol. To metamorphose.
métamorphisme [metamɔrfism] m. Metamorphism.
métamorphosable [metamɔrfozabl] adj. Capable of undergoing metamorphosis (ou) metamorphism.
métamorphose [-foːz] f. Metamorphosis.
métamorphoser [-foze] v. tr. (1). To metamorphose.
— v. pr. **Se métamorphoser,** to change, to be metamorphosed.
métaphonie [metafɔni] f. Gramm. Mutation.
métaphore [metafɔːr] f. Metaphor.
métaphorique [-fɔrik] adj. Metaphorical.
métaphoriquement [-fɔrikmɑ̃] adv. Metaphorically.
métaphysicien [metafizisjɛ̃] m. Philos. Metaphysician.
métaphysique [-zik] adj. Metaphysical.
— f. Philos. Metaphysics.
métapsychique [metapsiʃik] adj. Metapsychical.
— f. Metapsychics.
métargon [metargɔ̃] m. Chim. Metargon.
métastase [metastaːz] f. Méd. Metastasis.
métatarse [metatars] m. Méd. Metatarsus.
métatarsien, enne [-sjɛ̃, ɛn] adj. Méd. Metatarsal.
métathèse [metatɛːz] f. Metathesis.
métayage [metɛjaːʒ] m. Agric. Metayage system.
métayer [-je] m. Agric. Metayer, tenant farmer; U. S. share cropper (terme régional).
métazoaire [metazɔɛːr] m. Zool. Metazoan.
méteil [metɛj] m. Agric. Wheat and rye grown together.
métempsycose [metɑ̃psikoːz] f. Metempsychosis.
météo [meteɔ] f. Weather report (bulletin); meteorological office, U. S. weather bureau (office).
— m. Meteorologist.
météogramme [-gram] m. Symbol weather report.
météore [meteɔːr] m. Astr. Meteor. (V. bolide.)
météorique [-rik] adj. Meteoric.
météorisation [-rizasjɔ̃] f., **météorisme** [-rism] m. Méd. Hoove, meteorism.
météorite [-rit] f. Meteorite.
météorologie [-rɔlɔʒi] f. Meteorology.
météorologique [-rɔlɔʒik] adj. Meteorological; *Office national météorologique,* Central Meteorological Office; *station météorologique,* weather station.
météorologiste [-rɔlɔʒist], **météorologue** [-rɔlɔg] s. Meteorologist, weatherman.
métèque [metɛk] m. Alien. || Fam. Dago.
méthadone [metadɔn] f. Méd. Methadone.
méthane [metan] m. Chim. Methane, marsh-gas.
méthanier [-nje] m. Naut. Gas tanker.
méthanol [-nɔl] m. Chim. Methanol.
méthode [metɔd] f. Method, system, way (v. procédé); *il a sa méthode à lui,* he has his own way of doing things; *lecture sans méthode,* desultory reading; *livre écrit sans méthode,* disconnected book. || Manual school-book (livre).
méthodique [-dik] adj. Methodical. (V. réglé.)
méthodiquement [-dikmɑ̃] adv. Methodically.
méthodisme [metɔdism] m. Methodism.
méthodiste [-dist] s. Ecclés. Methodist.
méthodologie [-dɔlɔʒi] f. Methodology.
méthyle [metil] m. Chim. Methyl.
méthylène [-lɛn] m. Chim. Methylene. || Méd. *Bleu de méthylène,* methylene blue.
méthylique [-lik] adj. Chim. Methylic.
méticuleusement [metikyløzmɑ̃] adv. Meticulously, over-scrupulously, painstakingly.

5

méticuleux, euse [-lø, ø:z] adj. Meticulous, over-scrupulous, punctilious, finical ; *soin méticuleux,* thoroughness.

méticulosité [-lozite] f. Meticulosity, over-carefulness, over-scrupulousness.

métier [metje] m. Trade, craft, business (v. PROFESSION) ; *corps de métier,* trade association, craft corporation ; *être du métier,* to belong to the trade ; *homme de métier,* professional. ‖ Professional skill, experience, talent (art) ; *manquer de métier,* to lack experience ; *parler métier,* to talk shop ; *un peintre qui a du métier,* a painter of sound technique ; *posséder son métier sur le bout du doigt,* to know the tricks of the trade. ‖ TECHN. Loom ; *métier à filer,* spinning jenny ; *métier mécanique,* power-loom ; *métier à tapisserie,* tapestry frame ; *métier à tisser,* weaving loom ; ‖ MILIT. *Armée de métier,* professional army ; *le métier des armes,* the profession of arms. ‖ FIG. Occupation, work, business (travail) ; *ne pas avoir le cœur au métier,* to have no heart for one's work ; *vilain métier,* nasty piece of work ; *ce n'est pas mon métier,* that's not in my line.

métis [metis] adj. Half-bred, cross-bred (animal). — s. Cross-breed (animal) ; half-breed ; mestizo, metif, metis (personne).

métissage [-sa:ʒ] m. Cross-breeding.

métisser [-se] v. tr. (1). To cross (des espèces).

métonymie [metɔnimi] f. Metonymy.

métonymique [-mik] adj. Metonymical.

métope [metɔp] f. ARCHIT. Metope.

métrage [metra:ʒ] m. Measurement, measuring. ‖ Length ; *quel métrage désirez-vous?,* how many yards do you want? ‖ CINÉM. Footage ; *un film de court métrage,* a short ; *long métrage,* full-length film.

mètre [mɛtr] m. Metre, U. S. meter ; *mètre articulé,* pliant joint folding rule ; *mètre en bois,* yard-stick ; *mètre droit,* straight ruler ; *mètre à ruban,* tape-measure, measuring tape.

mètre m. Metre (du vers).

métré [metre] m. Measurement (mesure) ; estimate (devis).

métrer [metre] v. tr. (5). To survey (de grandes étendues) ; to measure (de petites longueurs).

métreur [-trœ:r] m. Quantity surveyor.

métrique [-trik] adj. MATH. Metric.

métrique f. GRAMM. Metrics.

métrite [metrit] f. MÉD. Metritis.

métro [metro] m. FAM. Underground railway, tube ; U. S. subway ; *métro aérien,* elevated railway.

métrologie [metrɔlɔʒi] f. Metrology.

métrologique [-lɔʒik] adj. Metrological.

métrologiste [-lɔʒist] s. Metrologist.

métronome [metronɔm] m. MUS. Metronome.

métropole [metropɔl] f. Metropolis ; capital (ville). ‖ Mother country (pays).

métropolitain, aine [-litɛ̃, ɛn] adj. Metropolitan. — m. Metropolitan railway. (V. MÉTRO.) ‖ ECCLÉS. Metropolitan.

mets [mɛ] m. CULIN. Article of food, food (nourriture) ; dish (plat).

mettable [mɛtabl] adj. Wearable.

metteur [metœ:r] s. Placer. ‖ THÉÂTR. *Metteur en scène,* director (d'un film) ; producer, stage-manager (d'une pièce). ‖ TECHN. *Metteur en pages,* type-setter.

mettre [metr] v. tr. (64).

---

1. Sens général. — 2. Disposer. — 3. Placer. — 4. Poser. — 5. Organiser. — 6. Vêtir. — 7. Suivi d'un infinitif. — 8. Employer. — 9. Admettre. — 10. Traduire. — 11. THÉÂTR. — 12. COMM. — 13. FIN. — 14. ZOOL. — 15. MILIT. — 16. FAM.

---

1. To put (en général) ; *mettre une couverture à,* to put a cover on ; *mettre une pièce dans la main de qqn,* to put a coin in s.o.'s hand ; *mis en congé,* sent on leave. ‖ 2. To set (disposer) ; *mettre la lampe droite,* to set the lamp straight. ‖ 3. To place, to set, to put (placer) ; *mettre un crayon dans le trou de la serrure,* to stick a pencil in the key-hole ; *mettre l'opinion de qqn au-dessus de tout,* to place s.o.'s opinion above everything else. ‖ 4. To lay (poser) ; *mettre le pain sur la table,* to lay the bread on the table. ‖ 5. To put, to set (dans un état défini) ; *mettre qqn à l'aise,* to put s.o. at his ease ; *mettre qqn en colère,* to make s.o. angry ; *mettre qqn à contribution,* to lay s.o. under contribution ; *mettre qqn dans de mauvais draps,* to get s.o. into a scrape ; *mettre qqn en garde,* to put s.o. on his guard ; *mettre qqn à mort,* to put s.o. to death ; *mettre à nu,* to lay bare ; *mettre qqch. en tête à qqn,* to put sth. into s.o.'s head ; *mettre le feu à,* to set fire to. ‖ 6. To put on (enfiler) ; to wear (porter) [un habit]. ‖ 7. To put, to set (suivi d'un infinitif) ; *mettre chauffer la soupe,* to put the soup on to heat ; *mettre refroidir la crème,* to set the custard to cool ; *mettre sécher du linge,* to put washing out to dry. ‖ 8. To take (employer) ; *mettre tout son soin à,* to take great care to ; *y mettre le temps voulu,* to take all due time. ‖ 9. To grant, to suppose (admettre) ; *mettons qu'il soit honnête,* let us suppose he is honest ; *mettons qu'il joue franc jeu,* let us assume that he plays the game. ‖ 10. To turn into (traduire) ; *mettre un discours en français,* to turn (ou) put a speech into French ; *mettre des vers en musique,* to set verse to music. ‖ 11. THÉÂTR. *Mettre en scène,* to stage. ‖ 12. COMM. *Mettre à exécution,* to implement (un contrat) ; *mettre une maison en vente,* to put a house up for sale. ‖ 13. FIN. To put, to invest [dans, in] (de l'argent) ; *mettre trop d'argent à,* to pay too much for ; *mettre de l'argent à la caisse d'épargne,* to put money in the savings-bank ; *mettre de l'argent sur un cheval,* to put money on (ou) to bet on a horse ; *mettre aux enchères,* to put up for auction. ‖ 14. ZOOL. *Mettre bas,* to lamb (brebis) ; to whelp (chienne, lionne) ; to litter (chienne) ; to foal (jument) ; to throw its young (lapine) ; to pig, to farrow (truie) ; to calve (vache). ‖ 15. MILIT. *Mettre bas les armes,* to lay down one's arms. ‖ 16. FAM. *Alors on les met?,* well, are we off? ; *en mettre un coup,* to put some vim into it.

— v. pr. **Se mettre,** to place oneself (se placer) ; *se mettre au lit,* to go to bed ; *se mettre devant qqn,* to stand in front of (ou) before s.o. ; *se mettre dans la politique,* to go in for (ou) to go into politics ; *se mettre en rangs,* to draw in (ou) to form ranks ; *se mettre du rouge aux lèvres,* to put on some lipstick ; *il se met bien,* he's doing himself well ; *le feu s'est mis chez nous,* our house caught fire, we have had a fire ; *mettez-vous là,* take this seat ; stand there : *ne savoir où se mettre,* not to know where to stand (ou) to hide. ‖ **Se mettre à,** to begin, to start, to take to, to set to ; *se mettre à boire,* to take to drink ; *se mettre à écrire,* to start writing ; *se mettre à la diète,* to put oneself on a diet ; *se mettre ensemble,* to live together (en concubinage) ; *se mettre à hurler,* to set up a howl ; *se mettre à manger,* to begin eating ; *se mettre à l'œuvre, à une tâche,* to set to work, to address oneself to a task ; *se mettre à pleurer,* to start to cry, to burst into tears ; *se mettre à pleuvoir,* to begin to rain ; *se mettre sur les rangs,* to run as a candidate ; *se mettre à rire,* to start laughing ; *s'y mettre,* to set about it, to take a hand in it ; *il est temps de s'y mettre,* it is time to get (ou) to buckle down to it ; *il va enfin se mettre* à faire beau, the weather is going to clear up at last; mettons-nous-y à deux, let us tackle the difficulty together. ‖ **Se mettre en,** to dress (s'habiller); to fall (ou) to get into (se livrer à); se mettre en colère, to get angry; se mettre en fureur, to fall into a passion; se mettre en grande toilette, to dress for the occasion; se mettre en route, to start off; se mettre en smoking, to put on a dinner-jacket (ou) U. S. tuxedo.

meublant, ante [mœblɑ̃, ɑ̃:t] adj. Decorative; être très meublant, to fill out the room nicely.

meuble [mœbl] adj. Uncemented (pierre); light (sol); loose (terre). ‖ JUR. Biens meubles, movables, personal estate.
— m. Piece of furniture. ‖ Pl. Furnishings, furniture. ‖ Set of furniture; meuble de coin, cornerpiece (or) cabinet; meuble de famille, heirloom; meubles de salon, drawing room suite.

meublé, ée [-ble] adj. Furnished; loué meublé, let out (ou) rented as furnished; non meublé, unfurnished; maison meublée, service flats, U. S. apartment house. ‖ FIG. Mémoire bien meublée de faits, memory well stocked with facts.
— m. Furnished apartment; vivre en meublé, to live in furnished rooms.

meubler [-ble] v. tr. (1). To furnish (un appartement). ‖ AGRIC. To stock (une ferme). ‖ FIG. To store (son esprit).
— v. intr. To be decorative.
— v. pr. **Se meubler,** to furnish one's home.

meuglement [mœgləmɑ̃] m. Lowing; mooing.

meugler [-gle] v. intr. (1). To low; to moo.

meule [mœl] f. Millstone (de moulin); grindstone (de rémouleur). ‖ CULIN. Meule de fromage, round cheese. ‖ AGRIC. Hayrick, haycock, haystack (de foin); mettre le foin en meules, to stack the hay.

meuler [-le] v. tr. (1). To hone (une lame); to grind (un outil); to grind down (du métal).

meulerie [-lri] f. Grindstone factory.

meulière [mœljɛ:r] f. Millstone-quarry (carrière); coarse-grained limestone (pierre).

meunerie [mœnri] f. Milling (action); milling-trade (commerce).

meunier [-nje] m. Miller.

meunière [-njɛ:r] f. Miller's wife; proprietress of a flour-mill.

meurs, meurt [mœ:r]. V. MOURIR (66).

meurt-de-faim [mœrdəfɛ̃] m. Starveling; salaire de meurt-de-faim, starvation wages.

meurtre [mœrtr] m. JUR. Murder (avec préméditation); manslaughter (sans préméditation). ‖ FIG. Crime, crying shame, discreditable act.

meurtri, ie [mœrtri] adj. Bruised, sore (personne). ‖ Damaged (fruit). ‖ FIG. Distressed.

meurtrier, ère [mœrtrije, ɛr] adj. Murderous, deadly (arme); deadly (fusillade).
— s. Murderer.

meurtrière [-trijɛ:r] f. Murderess (femme). ‖ ARCHIT. Loophole.

meurtrir [mœrtri:r] v. tr. (2). To bruise.

meurtrissure [-trisy:r] f. Bruise.

meute [mø:t] f. Pack of hounds. ‖ FIG. Crowd, pack.

meuvent [mœ:v]. V. MOUVOIR (67).

mévente [mevɑ̃:t] f. COMM. Sale at a loss; lack of sale, slump.

mexicain, aine [mɛksikɛ̃, ɛn] adj., s. GÉOGR. Mexican.

Mexico [mɛksiko] m. GÉOGR. Mexico City.

Mexique [mɛksik] m. GÉOGR. Mexico.

mezcal [mɛzkal] m. Mescal (boisson). ‖ BOT. Mescal buttons.

mezzanine [medzanin] f. ARCHIT. Mezzanine.

mezzo-soprano [mɛdzosɔprano] m. MUS. Mezzo-soprano.

mezzo-tinto [-tinto] m. ARTS. Mezzotint.

M⁹ʳ abrév. de Monseigneur, Mgr.

mi [mi] adj. invar. Half. ‖ **Mi-août,** f. Mid-August. ‖ **Mi-bas,** m. Half-hose. ‖ **Mi-carême,** f. Mid-Lent; dimanche de la mi-carême, Simnel (ou) U. S. Refreshment Sunday. ‖ **Mi-chemin (à),** adv. Half-way, midway. ‖ **Mi-clos,** adj. Half-closed. ‖ **Mi-corps (à),** adv. To the waist; saisi à mi-corps, caught round the waist; nu jusqu'à mi-corps, naked to the waist. ‖ **Mi-côte (à),** adv. Half-way up the hill. ‖ **Mi-jambes (à),** adv. Half-way up the leg; être dans l'eau jusqu'à mi-jambes, to wade up to the knees. ‖ **Mi-lourd,** adj., m. SPORTS. Light heavyweight. ‖ **Mi-moyen,** adj., m. SPORTS. Welterweight. ‖ **Mi-nu,** adj. Half-naked. ‖ **Mi-parti,** adj. Motley; half one colour, half another. ‖ **Mi-temps,** f. SPORTS. Half (période), half-time (pause); loc. adv. A mi-temps, part-time; m. inv. Part-time work. ‖ **Mi-terme (à),** adv. Half-way through the period, on half-quarter-day. ‖ **Mi-vitesse (à),** adv. At half-speed. ‖ **Mi-voix (à),** adv. In a subdued voice, in an under-tone, under one's breath.

mi m. MUS. E, mi.

miaou [mjau] m. Miaow, mew; faire miaou, to mew, to miaou.

miasmatique [mjasmatik] adj. Miasmatic, miasmal.

miasme [mjasm] m. MÉD. Miasma.

miaulement [mjolmɑ̃] m. Mewing, miaowing, caterwauling. ‖ FAM. Catcall (de personnes).

miauler [-le] v. intr. (1). To miaow, to mew, to miaul; to caterwaul.
— v. tr. FAM. To screech out (une chanson).

miauleur [-lœ:r] adj. Miaowing, mewing.

mica [mika] m. Mica.

micaschiste [-ʃist] m. Mica-schist.

miche [miʃ] f. CULIN. Large round loaf (de pain).

Michel [miʃɛl] m. Michael; la Saint-Michel, Michaelmas.

micheline [miʃlin] f. CH. DE F. Rail-car.

micheton [miʃtɔ̃] m. ARG. Prostitute's customer.

micmac [mikmak] m. FAM. Contrivance, trick, manœuvre, jobbery; fiddle, fiddling; U. S. finagling. (V. MANIGANCE.)

micocoulier [mikɔkulje] m. BOT. Nettle tree.

micro [mikro] m. FAM. Mike; parler au micro, to speak (ou) talk over the radio; peur du micro, mike nerves.

micro-ampère [mikrɔɑ̃pɛ:r] m. Microampere.

microanalyse [-analiz] f. CHIM. Microanalysis.

microbalance [-balɑ̃:s] f. Microbalance.

microbe [mikrɔb] m. MÉD. Microbe. ‖ FAM. Little brat.

microbicide [-bisid] m. MÉD. Microbicide.

microbien, enne [-bjɛ̃, ɛn] adj. MÉD. Microbial, microbic, microbian. ‖ MILIT. Biological (guerre).

microbiologie [mikrɔbiɔlɔʒi] f. MÉD. Microbiology.

microcéphale [-sefal] adj. MÉD. Microcephalous, microcephalic.

microcircuit [-sirkɥi] m. ÉLECTR. Microcircuit; chip.

microclimat [-klima] m. GÉOGR. Microclimate.

microcoque [-kɔk] m. MÉD. Micrococcus.

microcosme [-kɔsm] m. Microcosm.

micro-électronique [-elɛktrɔnik] f. ÉLECTR. Microelectronics.

microfiche [-fiʃ] f. Microfiche, fiche.

microfilm [-film] m. Microfilm.

microfilmer [-filme] v. tr. To microfilm.

micrographie [-grafi] f. Micrography.

microhm [mikro:m] m. ÉLECTR. Microhm.

micro-imprimé [-ɛ̃prime] m. Microprint.

micromètre [mikrɔmɛtr] m. Micrometer.

micromillimètre [-millimɛtr] m. Micromillimeter.

micron [mikrɔ̃] m. PHYS. Micron.

micro-organisme [-ɔrganism] m. Micro-organism.

microphone [mikrɔfɔn] m. Microphone; *microphone à perche*, boom microphone.
— adj. Microphonic.
microphotographie [mikrɔfɔtɔgrafi] f. Microphotograph.
microphotographique [-fik] adj. Microphotografic.
microprocesseur [-prɔsɛsœːr] m. ÉLECTR. Microprocessor.
microscope [mikrɔskɔp] m. PHYS. Microscope.
microscopie [-pi] f. PHYS. Microscopy.
microscopique [-pic] adj. Microscopic.
microsillon [mikrɔsiljɔ̃] m. MUS. Long-playing record. ‖ Microgroove, minigroove.
microtome [mikrɔtom] m. Microtome.
miction [miksjɔ̃] f. MÉD. Urination, micturition.
midi [midi] m. Midday, twelve o'clock (heure); *midi et demi*, half-past twelve; *midi moins le quart*, a quarter to twelve; *en plein midi*, in broad daylight. ‖ South (sud); *exposé au midi*, with a southern exposure (ou) facing south. ‖ GÉOGR. *Le Midi*, the South of France. ‖ FIG. Heyday (point culminant); noontide (de la vie). ‖ FAM. *Chercher midi à quatorze heures*, to be over-subtle; *ne pas voir clair en plein midi*, to be blind to the obvious.
midinette [midinɛt] f. Dressmaker's assistant; midinette. (V. COUSETTE.)
midship [midʃip] m. NAUT. Midshipman, middy.
mie f. † Sweetheart; lady-love.
mie [mi] f. CULIN. Crumb, soft bread.
miel [mjɛl] m. CULIN. Honey. ‖ ZOOL. *Mouche à miel*, honey bee. ‖ FIG. *Lune de miel*, honeymoon.
miellé, ée [mjɛle] adj. Honeyed. ‖ Honey-sweet.
miellée [mjɛle], **miellure** [-lyːr] f. BOT. Honeydew (exsudation); nectar (nectar).
mielleusement [-løzmɑ̃] adv. With sugared (ou) honeyed words (en parlant); blandly, silkily (en souriant).
mielleux, euse [-lø, øːz] adj. Honey-like, honeyish (goût). ‖ FIG. Honeyed, sugary (paroles); mealy-mouthed, soft-spoken, oily, greasy, unctuous (personne); bland (sourire).
mien, ienne [mjɛ̃, jɛn] adj. poss. † Of mine; *un mien ami*, a friend of mine.
— pron. poss. Mine; *voici sa maison, à côté de la mienne*, here is his house, next to mine.
— m. Mine, my own, my property; *faites la différence entre le mien et le vôtre*, discriminate between mine and yours; *je n'y mets pas du mien*, I am not adding anything of my own. ‖ Pl. *Les miens*, my people (ou) family.
miette [mjɛt] f. Crumb (de pain). ‖ FIG. Bit, morsel, scrap (brin); piece (morceau); *réduit en miettes*, smashed to smithereens.
mieux [mjø] adv. compar. Better (avantage); *mieux vaut tard que jamais*, better late than never; *vous auriez mieux fait de ne rien dire*, you would have done better to say nothing; *vous feriez mieux de m'écouter*, you had better listen to me. ‖ Better, rather (choix); *j'aimerais mieux ne pas avoir à dire non*, I would rather not say no; *je ne demande pas mieux que de le rencontrer*, I should be very pleased to meet him; *plus tôt ce sera fait, mieux cela vaudra*, the sooner it is done, the better. ‖ More comfortable (aise); *mettez-vous là, vous serez mieux*, sit down here, you will be more comfortable. ‖ Better (qualité); *c'est le portrait de sa mère, mais en mieux*, she is the very likeness of her mother, but a shade prettier; *c'est on ne peut mieux*, it could not be better: *de mieux en mieux*, better and better; *espérer mieux*, to hope for sth. better; *faute de mieux*, for lack of sth. better; *il est mieux que son frère*, he has more about him than his brother; *on ne saurait mieux dire*, that's putting it in a nutshell; *pour mieux dire*, to be more exact; *pour ne pas dire mieux*, to say the least; *pouvez-vous faire mieux que ça?*, can you beat that?; *qui mieux est*, better still; *à qui mieux mieux*, one trying to do better than (ou) to outdo the other; emulously; in eager emulation; vying with one another. ‖ Better (satisfaction); *rien de mieux*, nothing better; *il n'y a rien de mieux*, it's the best there is; *tant mieux!*, so much the better. ‖ Better (supériorité); *ce qu'il y a de mieux dans l'homme, c'est le chien*, the best thing about man is his dog; *décider mieux que personne*, to decide better than anybody. ‖ MÉD. *Aller mieux*, to feel better, to be better.
— adv. superl. **Le mieux**, the best (aspect); *c'est elle la mieux des trois*, she is the best-looking of the three; *deviner le mieux*, to make the best guess; *la femme la mieux habillée de Paris*, the best-dressed woman in Paris; *tout est pour le mieux dans le meilleur des mondes*, all is for the best in the best of all possible worlds. ‖ Best (choix); *ce que j'aime le mieux au monde*, what I like best in the world; *ce que nous avons de mieux à faire*, the best thing we can do. ‖ Best (degré); *agir au mieux des intérêts de qqn*, to act in s.o.'s best interests; *c'est lui qui peut le mieux vous aider*, he is the best person to help you; *en mettant les choses au mieux*, at best; *il s'en est tiré le mieux du monde*, no one could have managed it better; *toujours à mieux*, always the best quality. ‖ Best, utmost (soin); *faire pour le mieux*, to do one's very best, to do what is best; *j'ai fait de mon mieux pour vous*, I did my best for you. ‖ Best (relations); *être le mieux du monde avec*, to be on the best terms with. ‖ **Mieux-être**, m. invar. Greater comfort, improved condition.
— m. The best (le meilleur parti). ‖ Improvement (amélioration). ‖ MÉD. *Un léger mieux*, a slight improvement.
mièvre [mjɛvr] adj. Delicate (enfant); effete (personne). ‖ Finical, affected (style).
mièvrerie [-vrəri] f. Daintiness, affected refinement (d'une personne); false elegance, finicality (du style).
mignard, arde [miɲaːr, aːrd] adj. Dainty, delicate. (V. DÉLICAT.) ‖ Affected, mincing, simpering, finicking (affecté). ‖ Affected, finical (gestes).
mignarder [miɲarde] v. tr. (1). To fondle (un enfant). ‖ To prettify (son style).
— v. intr. To simper. (V. MINAUDER.)
mignardise [-diːz] f. Affected winsomeness, finicality (des manières); delicacy, daintiness (des traits); Affected (ou) finicking act (ou) word. ‖ BOT. Pink.
mignon, onne [miɲɔ̃, on] adj. Dainty, delicate, gracefully pretty. ‖ FIG. Darling; *péché mignon*, besetting sin, particular weakness.
— s. Dear, darling (enfant); sweet (femme).
— m. Favourite; minion (†).
mignonnement [miɲɔnəmɑ̃] adv. Delicately.
mignonnet, ette [-nɛ, ɛt] adj. Dainty, tiny, delicately made.
mignonnette [-nɛt] f. Mignonette lace (dentelle). ‖ Fine gravel (pour allées). ‖ BOT. Mignonette.
mignoter [miɲɔte] v. tr. (1). To caress, to pet.
migraine [migrɛn] f. MÉD. Sick headache, migraine.
migrant, ante [migrɑ̃, ɑ̃:t] adj., s. Migrant.
migrateur, trice [migratœːr, tris] adj. Migrant (peuple). ‖ ZOOL. Migratory (oiseau).
— m. ZOOL. Migratory bird.
migration [-sjɔ̃] f. ZOOL. Migration.
migratoire [-twaːr] adj. Migratory (mouvement).
migrer [migre] v. intr. (1). To migrate.
mijaurée [miʒɔre] f. Conceited, affected person;

stuck-up woman ; *faire la mijaurée,* to be all affectation.

mijoter [miʒɔte] v. tr. (1). CULIN. To stew slowly, to let simmer. ‖ FAM. To plot, to concoct (un dessein) ; to plan (une mystification) ; to nurse (une revanche).
— v. intr. CULIN., FAM. To simmer.
— v. pr. **Se mijoter.** FAM. To be in preparation, to mature ; *il se mijote qqch.,* something is brewing, there is sth. in the wind.

mikado [mikado] m. Mikado.

mil [mil] m. SPORTS. Indian club.

mil adj. Thousand ; *l'an mil huit cent trois,* the year one thousand eight hundred and three (ou) eighteen hundred and three.

mil m. V. MILLET.

milady [miladi] f. My lady. ‖ Lady.

milan [milɑ̃] m. ZOOL. Kite.

milanais, aise [milanɛ, ɛ:z] adj., s. GÉOGR. Milanese. ‖ CULIN. *Escalope milanaise (ou) à la milanaise,* Wiener schnitzel.

mildiou [mildju] m. AGRIC. Mildew.

miliaire [miljɛ:r] adj. MÉD. Miliary.

milice [milis] f. MILIT. Militia. ‖ FIG. Host.

milicien [-sjɛ̃] m. MILIT. Militia man.

milicienne [-sjɛn] f. Militia woman.

milieu [miljø] m. Middle, midst (centre) ; *au milieu de sa carrière,* in mid-career ; *au milieu de l'été,* in the height of summer ; *au milieu de l'hiver,* in mid-winter ; *au milieu de la montée,* half-way up the hill ; *au milieu de nous,* in our midst ; *au milieu de tous ces inconvénients,* in the midst of all these drawbacks ; *le milieu du jour,* midday, noon. ‖ Middle course, mean (position moyenne) ; *le juste milieu,* the happy medium ; *il n'y a pas de milieu,* there is no middle course. ‖ Class, set, circle (classe sociale) ; medium, environment, surroundings (entourage) ; *milieu humide,* damp atmosphere (ou) climate ; *influence du milieu,* influence of the milieu (ou) environment ; *les milieux autorisés,* responsible quarters. ‖ POP. *Le milieu,* the underworld, gangsterdom.

militaire [militɛ:r] adj. MILIT. Soldier-like, soldierly (allure) ; military (classe, exercices, questions) ; warlike (peuple) ; *main-d'œuvre militaire,* Service labour. ‖ FAM. Exact ; *à cinq heures, heure militaire,* at five o'clock sharp.
— m. MILIT. Military man, Serviceman, soldier ; *familles de militaires,* Service families, dependents.

militairement [-tɛrmɑ̃] adv. In a soldierly manner, like a soldier ; militarily. ‖ Punctually (à heure fixe).

militant, ante [-tɑ̃, ɑ̃:t] adj. Militant. ‖ ECCLÉS. *Eglise militante,* Church Militant.
— s. Militant. (V. PARTISAN.)

militantisme [-tɑ̃tism] m. Militancy.

militarisation [-tarizasjɔ̃] f. MILIT. Militarization.

militariser [-tarize] v. tr. (1). MILIT. To militarize.

militarisme [-tarism] m. MILIT. Militarism.

militariste [-tarist] s. MILIT. Militarist.

militer [-te] v. intr. (1). To militate (*en faveur de* [ou] *pour, contre,* for, against). ‖ FIG. *Cela milite en sa faveur,* that speaks in his favour (ou) well for him.

mille [mil] adj. invar. Thousand, one thousand ; *mille dollars,* a (ou) one thousand dollars ; *trois cent mille,* three hundred thousand ; *mille cinq,* one thousand and five ; *mille fois,* a thousand times ; *les Mille et Une Nuits,* the Arabian (ou) Thousand and One Nights ; *c'est mille fois trop,* it's far too much ; *merci mille fois,* thanks a million. ‖ **Mille-feuille,** f. BOT. Milfoil, yarrow ; m. CULIN. Mille-feuille pastry, U. S. napoleon. ‖ **Mille-pattes,** m. inv. ZOOL. Centipede, millepede. ‖ **Mille-pertuis, millepertuis,** m. inv. BOT. St. John's wort.

— m. Thousand. ‖ FIG. *Mettre dans le mille,* to hit the nail on the head, to score a direct hit.

mille m. Mile ; *à trois milles de là,* three miles off. ‖ NAUT. Nautical mile.

millénaire [milenɛ:r] adj. Millenial, millenary.
— m. Thousand years ; millenary ; millenium.

millésime [-zim] m. Date (sur une pièce) ; vintage (d'un vin).

millésimé, ée [-zime] adj. Vintage (vin).

millet [milɛ] m. Millet ; *grains de millet,* birdseed.

milliaire [miljɛ:r] adj. Milliary ; *borne milliaire,* milestone.

milliampère [miljɑ̃pɛr] m. ELECTR. Milliampere.

milliard [milja:r] m. Thousand million, milliard ; U. S. billion.

milliardaire [-dɛ:r] adj., s. Multi-millionaire.

milliardième [-djɛm] adj., s. Thousand millionth ; U. S. billionth.

millibar [milibar] m. Millibar.

millième [miljɛ:m] adj. Thousandth.

millier [milje] m. Thousand ; a thousand or so.

milligramme [miligram] m. Milligram(me).

millilitre [-litr] m. Millilitre.

millimètre [-mɛtr] m. Millimetre.

millimétrique [-metrik], **millimétré, ée** [-metre] adj. Millimetric ; *papier millimétrique,* graph paper.

million [miljɔ̃] m. Million ; *un million d'hommes,* one (ou) a million men ; *riche à millions,* worth millions, millionaire.

millionième [miljɔniɛm] adj., m. Millionth.

millionnaire [-nɛ:r] s. Millionaire.

milord [milɔ:r] m. My lord (appellation) ; lord (noble). ‖ FAM. Very rich man.

miltonien, enne [miltɔnjɛ̃, ɛn] adj. Miltonian.

mime [mim] m. THÉÂTR. Mime, pantomime ; mummery (jeu) ; mimic ; mummer (personne).

mimer [mime] v. tr. (1). THÉÂTR. To mime, to act in dumb show, U. S. to pantomime. ‖ FIG. To mimic. (V. IMITER.)

mimétique [mimetik] adj. Mimetic.

mimétisme [-tism] m. Mimicry.

mimique [mimik] f. Dumb show, sign language.

mimodrame [mimɔdram] m. Mime-drama.

mimosa [mimoza] m. BOT. Mimosa.

min abrév. de *minute,* min.

minable [minabl] adj. TECHN. Minable. ‖ FIG. Shabby, dingy, pitiable (aspect) ; down at heel, seedy, shabby (personne). [V. MITEUX.]

minaret [minarɛ] m. ARCHIT. Minaret.

minauder [minode] v. intr. (1). To simper, to smirk ; *parler en minaudant,* to mince.

minauderie [-dri] f. Simpering, smirking (action). ‖ Pl. Mincing ways. (V. SIMAGRÉES.)

minaudier [-dje] adj. Simpering, smirking.
— s. Simperer.

mince [mɛ̃:s] adj. Thin, slim, slight, spare. ‖ FIG. Slender, slight (de peu de valeur) ; *mince personnage,* unimportant person.
— interj. *Mince alors!,* Gosh! ; *mince de rigolade!,* what a lark!

minceur [mɛ̃sœ:r] f. Thinness, slimness. ‖ FIG. Slightness, scantiness.

mincir [-si:r] v. intr. (2). To get lean (or) thin.

mine [min] f. Mine ; *mine de houille,* colliery, coal-mine ; *mine d'or, de sel,* gold-, salt-mine. ‖ Graphite, black-lead (de plomb). ‖ Lead (de crayon). ‖ MILIT., NAUT. Mine ; *mine terrestre,* landmine ; *faire sauter une mine,* to spring (ou) to blow up a mine. ‖ FIG. Fund (de bons mots). ‖ **Mine-piège,** f. MILIT. Booby-trap.

mine f. Look, mien, face (apparence) ; *avoir belle mine,* to be good-looking (ou) of attractive appearance (être beau) ; *de bonne mine,* well-favoured ; *avoir mauvaise mine,* to be ill-looking, to have

MILITAIRE (vocabulaire) — MILITARY TERMS

être dans l'armée	to be in the army	sous-marin	submarine
le grade	rank	porte-avions	aircraft-carrier
la troupe	the rank and file	dragueur de mines	mine-sweeper
soldat de 2e classe	private	flotte aérienne	airfleet
bon pour le service	fit for service	base aérienne	air base
monter en grade	to be promoted	avion de combat	fighter
ancienneté	seniority	chasseur, avion de chasse	fighter, chaser
caporal ; sergent	corporal ; sergeant	lâcher une bombe	to release a bomb
adjudant	warrant-officer	bombardier	bomber
sous-officier	non-commissioned officer	bombe incendiaire	incendiary bomb
lieutenant	lieutenant	avion de reconnaissance	reconnoissance plane
capitaine	captain	D. C. A.	A. A., « ack-ack »
commandant	major	avion-estafette	courier-plane
colonel	colonel	faire une reconnaissance	to reconnoitre, to scout
officiers supérieurs	field (ou) senior officers	maîtrise de l'air	command of the air
général de brigade	brigadier	ravitaillement en vol	aerial refuelling
général de division	major-general	propulsion par réaction	jet propulsion
général de corps d'armée	lieutenant-general	turboréacteur	turbo-jet engine
général d'armée	general	avion à réaction	jet (propelled) plane
maréchal	marshal (field-)	avion-fusée	rocket-plane
généralissime	commander-in-chief	fusée éclairante	star-shell
être au garde-à-vous	to stand to attention	engin téléguidé	guided missile
Garde à vous !	Attention !	guerre aérienne	air warfare
En avant... marche !	Forward... march !	guerre mondiale	world war
sorti du rang	risen from the ranks	guerre de mouvement	war of movement
officier sorti du rang	ranker	guerre de tranchée	trench warfare
officier de l'état-major	staff officer	guerre de position	static warfare
état-major général	general Staff	guerre d'usure	war of attrition
fantassin	foot soldier, infantry man	tactique, tacticien	tactics, tactician
fusil	rifle	stratégie, stratège	strategy, strategist
recul	recoil	carte d'état-major	Ordnance map
à l'épreuve des balles	bullet-proof	repérer	to detect, to spot
mitrailleuse	machine-gun	repérage	spotting, detecting
mitrailleur	machine-gunner	repérage par le son	sound-ranging
artillerie	artillery	radar	radar
artilleur	artilleryman	station de radar	radar station
pièce (d'artillerie)	piece of ordnance	antenne de radar	radar scanner
canon	gun, cannon	reconnaissance	reconnoissance
canon à tir rapide	quick-firer	éclaireur	scout
bouche à feu	muzzle	agent de transmission	runner
lance-flammes	flame-thrower	officier de liaison	liaison officer
tirer à blanc	to fire blank	cantonnement	cantonment
affût	carriage	billet de logement	billeting order
rectifier le tir	to correct the fire	réquisition	requisitioning (de bâtiments)
mettre en batterie	to bring into action		
mortier (de tranchée)	(trench) mortar	réquisition	commandeering (de voitures)
coup au but	hit		
coup manqué	miss	campagne	campaign
bon tireur	crack shot, marksman	l'agresseur	the aggressor
munitions	munitions, ammunition	contre-attaquer	to counter-attack
projectile	projectile ; missile	escarmouche	skirmish
balle perdue	spent bullet	tirailleur	skirmisher
mitraille	grape-shot	dresser une embuscade	to lay an ambush
salve	volley ; salvo	se tenir en embuscade	to lie in ambush
à portée de fusil	within rifle-shot	harceler	to harass
mine ; contre-mine	mine, countermine	faire une sortie	to break out
auto blindée	armoured car	percée	break-through
division blindée	armoured division	prendre l'assaut	to carry by storm
chenille	caterpillar	groupe d'assaut	assault force
canon de tourelle	turret gun	coup de main	raid
parachutiste	paratrooper	renforts	reinforcements
troupes aéroportées	airborne troops	mouvement enveloppant	encircling movement
soldat du génie	engineer	débâcle	downfall, collapse
pionnier, pontonnier	pioneer	retraite ; déroute	retreat ; rout
sapeur	sapper	mettre en déroute	to rout
la Marine ; la Flotte	Navy ; the Fleet	corps-à-corps	hand-to-hand fight
fusiliers marins	Marines	débandade	stampede
officier de marine	naval officer	déborder	to outflank
navire de guerre	man of war, warship	mêlée	mêlée
cuirassé	battleship	repousser	to push back
croiseur	cruiser	hôpital de campagne	clearing hospital
torpilleur	torpedo-boat	pertes	casualties, losses
contre-torpilleur	destroyer	cessez-le-feu	cease-fire

an unprepossessing appearance ; *avoir la mine longue*, to pull a long face ; *faire piteuse mine*, to hang one's lip ; *homme à la mine hautaine*, man of lofty mien ; *il ne faut pas juger les gens sur la mine*, one must not judge people by their looks ; *il ne paie pas de mine*, his looks are not much in his favour, he is not much to look at. ‖ Reception (accueil) ; *faire bonne mine à qqn*, to welcome s.o., to show courtesy to s.o., to treat s.o. well ; *faire mauvaise mine à qqn*, to frown at s.o., to give the cold shoulder to s.o., to treat s.o. coldly. ‖ Show (indication) ; *faire mine d'être fâché*, to make a show of being angry ; *faire mine de frapper qqn*, to make as though to strike s.o. ‖ Pl. Airs, simperings. (V. SIMAGRÉES.) ‖ MÉD. *Avoir bonne, mauvaise mine*, to look well, poorly ; *avoir meilleure mine*, to look better.

miner [mine] v. tr. (1). To mine, to undermine. (V. SAPER.) ‖ FIG. *Miné par l'inquiétude*, undermined by anxiety.
— v. pr. **Se miner**, to pine (*dans l'attente de, pour*, for).

minerai [minrɛ] m. Ore.

minéral, ale [mineral] adj. Mineral. ‖ CHIM. Inorganic.
— m. Mineral.

minéralier [-lje] m. NAUT. Ore carrier.

minéralisation [-lizasjɔ̃] f. Mineralization.

minéraliser [-lize] v. tr. (1). To mineralize.

minéralogie [-lɔʒi] f. Mineralogy.

minéralogique [-lɔʒik] adj. Mineralogical.

minéralogiste [-lɔʒist] m. Mineralogist.

Minerve [minɛrv] f. Minerva.

minerve f. MÉD. Surgical collar.

minestrone [minɛstrɔn] m. CULIN. Minestrone.

minet, ette [minɛ, ɛt] s. ZOOL., FAM. Pussy, kitty-cat. ‖ FAM. Darling. ‖ FAM. Teeny bopper (jeune fille), young trendy (jeune homme).

minette [minɛt] f. TECHN. Minette, iron ore. ‖ BOT. Black medick, nonesuch, nonsuch.

mineur [minœr] m. Miner, collier (ouvrier) ; *mineur de fond*, underground worker.

mineur, eure adj. Minor, lesser. ‖ GÉOGR. *L'Asie Mineure*, Asia Minor. ‖ ECCLÉS. *Frère mineur*, Franciscan Friar, Friar Minor. ‖ MUS. Minor. ‖ JUR. Minor, under age.
— s. JUR. Minor.

mineure [minœːr] f. PHILOS. Minor premise.

miniature [minjatyːr] f. ARTS. Miniature.
— adj. Miniature, model (locomotive).

miniaturisation [-tyrizasjɔ̃] f. Miniaturization.

miniaturiser [-tyrize] v. tr. (1). To miniaturize.

miniaturiste [-tyrist] m. ARTS. Miniaturist.

minibus [minibys], **minicar** [-kaːr] m. AUTOM. Minibus.

minicassette [-kasɛt] m. TECHN. Cassette-player.

minier, ère [minje, ɛːr] adj. Mining (district).

minière [-njɛːr] f. Ore-bearing earth. ‖ Opencast mine.

minijupe [miniʒyp] f. Miniskirt, mini.

minimal, ale [minimal] adj. Minimal.

minime [minim] adj. Tiny. (V. MODIQUE.)
— s. SPORTS. Under fifteen. ‖ ECCLÉS. Minim.

minimiser [-mize] v. tr. (1). To minimize.

minimum [-mɔm] m. Minimum ; *au minimum*, at least ; *avec le minimum d'efforts*, with the least effort possible ; *minimum vital*, minimum living wage.
— adj. Minimum ; *la valeur minimum* (ou) *minima*, the minimum value.

ministère [ministɛːr] m. Help, service (aide) ; *prêter son ministère à qqn*, to lend s.o. a hand. ‖ Ministry, cabinet, government (en politique) ; *entrer au ministère*, to take office. ‖ Ministry, U.S. department ; *ministère du Commerce*, Board of Trade, U.S. Department of Commerce ; *ministère*

du Travail, Ministry of Labour, U.S. Department of Labor. ‖ JUR. *Le ministère public*, the Public Prosecutor.

ministériel, elle [-terjɛl] adj. Ministerial (circulaire, déclaration) ; departmental (comité) ; cabinet (crise). ‖ JUR. *Officier ministériel*, law official.

ministériellement [-terjɛlmɑ̃] adv. Ministerially.

ministrable [-trabl] adj. Likely to become a Minister of State.

ministre [ministr] m. Minister, agent. ‖ Minister, Secretary of State; U.S. Government (ou) Cabinet Secretary ; *ministre des Finances*, Chancellor of the Exchequer, U.S. Secretary of the Treasury ; *ministre de l'Intérieur*, Home Secretary, U.S. Secretary of the Interior ; *ministre de la Marine*, First Lord of the Admiralty, U.S. Secretary of the Navy ; *ministre plénipotentiaire*, minister plenipotentiary. ‖ ECCLÉS. Minister, clergyman, parson.

ministresse [-trɛs] f. FAM. Wife of a Minister of State.

minium [minjɔm] m. CHIM. Minium ; red lead.

minois [minwa] m. Face, countenance, visage.

minoration [minɔrasjɔ̃] f. Undervaluing, underestimation.

minorer [-re] v. tr. (1). To play down (minimiser) ; to undervalue, to underestimate (sous-estimer).

minoritaire [minɔritɛːr] adj. Minority.
— s. Member of the minority.

minorité [minɔrite] f. Minority (en politique) ; *être en minorité*, to be outvoted (ou) defeated ; *mettre en minorité*, to defeat. ‖ Minority, nonage (jeune âge). ‖ JUR. Legal infancy.

Minorque [minɔrk] f. GÉOGR. Minorca.

minorquin, ine [-kɛ̃, in] adj., s. GÉOGR. Minorcan.

minotaure [minɔtoːr] m. Minotaur.

minoterie [minɔtri] f. Flour-milling (action, métier) ; flour-mill (lieu).

minotier [-tje] m. Miller.

minuit [minɥi] m. Midnight, twelve o'clock at night ; *vers minuit*, about midnight ; *messe de minuit*, midnight mass.

minus [minys] m. FAM. Nitwit, chump, nincompoop ; *c'est un minus (ou) minus habens*, he is loose in the head.

minuscule [minyskyl] adj. Minute, tiny. (V. MINIME.) ‖ Small (lettre).

minutage [minyta:ʒ] m. Timing.

minute [minyt] f. Minute ; *attendez une minute*, wait a minute ; *être toujours à la minute*, to be always punctual to the minute (ou) there on the tick ; *réparations à la minute*, repairs while you wait ; *prêt à la minute*, ready in a jiffy. ‖ JUR. Draft, minute (brouillon) ; minutes (compte rendu) ; record, minute (copie d'un acte) ; *déposer la minute au greffe*, to enter upon the rolls ; *faire la minute d'un acte*, to draft a deed.
— interj. Hold on !, just a minute !

minuter [-te] v. tr. (1). To minute (rédiger). ‖ To time (chronométrer).

minuterie [-tri] f. Set of wheels (d'une montre). ‖ ELECTR. Time-switch.

minutie [minysi] f. Minute detail, trifle. ‖ Pl. Minutiae. ‖ FIG. Scrupulousness, minuteness ; *avec minutie*, in minute detail, minutely.

minutieusement [-sjøzmɑ̃] adv. Minutely, scrupulously ; closely.

minutieux, euse [-sjø, øːz] adj. Minute, searching, detailed, thorough (examen) ; scrupulous, particular, punctilious, fastidious (personne).

miocène [miɔsɛn] m. GÉOL. Miocene.

mioche [mjɔʃ] s. FAM. Kid, youngster, mite, tot.

mirabelle [mirabɛl] f. Mirabelle plum.

mirabellier [-belje] m. BOT. Mirabelle, mirabelle tree.

miracle [mira:kl] m. Ecclés. Miracle. ‖ Théâtr. Miracle-play. ‖ Fig. Wonder, miracle, prodigy (v. merveille); *c'est miracle qu'il ait échappé*, he had a narrow escape.

miraculé, ée [-kyle] adj. Ecclés. Miraculously healed.

miraculeusement [-kyløzmɑ̃] adv. Miraculously.

miraculeux, euse [-kylø, ø:z] adj. Miraculous.

mirador [mirador] m. Mirador, belvedere (pavillon). ‖ Platform (d'agent de police). ‖ Milit. Observation post (ou) look-out.

mirage [mira:ʒ] m. Mirage (dans le désert). ‖ Fig. Illusion.

mire [mi:r] f. Sighting, aiming. ‖ Milit. Sight, bead (d'un fusil); *angle de mire*, angle of elevation; *point de mire*, aim, point aimed at. ‖ Techn. Levelling staff (ou) rod, surveyor's pole (d'arpenteur). ‖ Techn. Test pattern (en télévision). ‖ Fig. Point de mire, cynosure.

mirer [mire] v. tr. (1). To take a sight on (arpenteur). ‖ To scrutinize; *mirer du drap*, to look at a piece of cloth against the light; *mirer un œuf*, to candle an egg.
— v. pr. **Se mirer**, to look at oneself (*dans*, in). ‖ To be reflected. ‖ Fig. To look at oneself complacently.

mirettes [-rɛt] f. pl. Pop. Peepers, daylights.

mirifique [mirifik] adj. Fam. Mirific.

mirifiquement [-mɑ̃] adv. Fam. Mirifically.

mirliton [mirlitɔ̃] m. Mus. Toy flute. ‖ Culin. Cream puff. ‖ Loc. *Vers de mirliton*, doggerel verse.

mirobolant, ante [mirɔbɔlɑ̃, ɑ̃:t] adj. Fam. Tremendous, terrific, staggering.

miroir [mirwa:r] m. Mirror. (V. glace.) ‖ Sports. *Miroir à alouettes*, lark-mirror, twirl. ‖ Culin. *Œufs au miroir*, fried eggs. ‖ Zool. Speculum; ocellus.

miroitant, ante [mirwatɑ̃, ɑ̃:t] adj. Dazzling (brillant); glistening (clignotant); sparkling (étincelant).

miroitement [-tmɑ̃] m. Glistening.

miroiter [-te] v. intr. (1). To gleam (briller); to flash, to glisten, to shimmer (clignoter); to sparkle (étinceler). ‖ Fig. *Faire miroiter*, to show to advantage, to show off, to flaunt (un avantage).

miroiterie [-tri] f. Manufacture of mirrors (arts); mirror-trade (commerce).

miroitier [-tje] m. Mirror seller (marchand); mirror maker (fabricant).

mironton mirontaine [mirɔ̃tɔ̃-mirɔ̃tɛn] loc. With a link a down and a day; refrain used in folk songs.

miroton [mirɔtɔ̃] m. Beef-stew with onions.

mis, ise [mi, iz] adj. Placed, put. (V. mettre.) ‖ Dressed (habillé); *bien mis*, well dressed.

misaine [mizɛn] f. Naut. Foresail; *mât de misaine*, foremast; *hune de misaine*, foretop.

misanthrope [mizɑ̃trɔp] adj. Misanthropic.
— m. Misanthrope, misanthropist.

misanthropie [-pi] f. Misanthropy.

misanthropique [-pik] adj. Misanthropic.

miscellanées [misɛlane] f. pl. Miscellany.

miscible [missibl] adj. Chim. Miscible.

mise [miz] f. Placing, putting, setting (en un lieu); *mise en bouteilles*, bottling; *mise en place*, placing, putting, setting; *mise à la poste*, posting, mailing; *mise à terre*, landing. ‖ Putting, setting (en un état); *mise à exécution*, implementing (d'un contrat); *mise en circulation*, putting into circulation; *mise en demeure*, formal demand; *mise en jeu*, bringing into play; *mise en liberté*, setting free, freeing, setting loose, liberation, release, letting out; *mise en ligne*, alignment; *mise au net*, recopying, writing a fair copy of (d'une rédaction); *mise en pages*, make-up, making up, lay-out

(en typogr.); *mise en position*, set-up, setting-up; *mise en pratique*, putting into action, putting to use, utilizing, utilization; *mise ' aux voix*, vote, division. ‖ Dress, garb, attire (vêtement); *mise irréprochable, négligée*, faultless, slovenly (ou) sloppy (ou) careless dress; *mise recherchée*, elaborate attire; *mise simple*, plain (ou) simple dress. ‖ Stake (enjeu); *doubler sa mise*, to double one's stake; *sauver sa mise*, to get back one's outlay. ‖ Comm. *Mise à prix*, upset price. ‖ Fin. Outlay; *mise d'un associé*, partner's holding; *mise de fonds*, putting up of money, outlay; *principale mise de fonds*, chief share of (ou) in the capital. ‖ Théâtr. *Mise en scène*, staging, production. ‖ Milit. *Mise en ligne*, bringing up (de renforts); *mise en marche*, moving on (d'une troupe). ‖ Naut. *Mise à l'eau*, launching. ‖ Autom. *Mise en marche* (ou) *en route*, starting; *mise en marche automatique*, self-starter; *mise au point*, tuning (d'un moteur). ‖ Phys. *Mise à feu*, blast-off (de fusée). ‖ Méd. *Mise à nu*, laying bare, baring (d'un membre malade). ‖ Fig. *Etre de mise*, to be suitable (ou) appropriate; *ne plus être de mise*, to be old-fashioned (ou) out of fashion. ‖ Fam. *Mise à pied*, sacking, firing. ‖ **Mise-bas**, f. Zool. Dropping (d'un animal); Techn. downing of tools, strike (grève).

miser [mize] v. intr. (1). To stake, to bet, to wager (parier); to bid (aux enchères). ‖ Fam. To bank, to count (*sur*, on); *miser sur le mauvais cheval*, to back the wrong horse; *miser sur les deux tableaux*, to try to have it both ways.
— v. tr. To stake, to bid (une somme).

misérabilisme [mizerabilism] m. Arts. Concentration on life's wretchedness.

misérabiliste [-list] adj. Arts. Concentrating on life's wretchedness.
— s. Arts. Writer (ou) artist who concentrates on life's wretchedness.

misérable [mizerabl] adj. Miserable, wretched, unfortunate. (V. malheureux.) ‖ Miserable, wretched, sorry (minable); *d'aspect misérable*, of mean appearance. ‖ Despicable, mean (piètre); *une misérable petite baraque*, a poky little place; *pour une misérable somme d'argent*, for a paltry sum of money.
— s. Wretch (malheureux). ‖ Wretch, scoundrel, rascal (coquin).

misérablement [-blɑ̃] adv. Miserably, wretchedly.

misère [mizɛ:r] f. Poverty, destitution, distress, need, want, wretchedness (v. pauvreté); *être dans la misère*, to be badly off, to be down and out; *la misère des temps*, hard times such as these; *parer à la misère*, to keep the wolf from the door; *secourir la misère*, to relieve the destitute (ou) the wretched. ‖ Misfortune, misery, woe (douleur); *crier misère*, to lament, to bewail; *reprendre le collier de misère*, to go back to drudgery (ou) to one's daily toil; *vêtements qui crient misère*, shabby (ou) threadbare clothes. ‖ Pl. Trouble, bother, worries; *faire des misères à qqn*, to give s.o. a bad time. ‖ Bot. Wandering Jew, tradescantia, spiderwort. ‖ Fam. *Une misère!*, a mere trifle.

miserere [mizerere] m. invar. Ecclés. Miserere. ‖ Méd. *Colique de miserere*, iliac passion, severe intestinal colic.

miséreux, euse [-rø, ø:z] adj. Wretched, destitute, poverty-stricken.
— s. Needy person.

miséricorde [mizerikɔrd] f. Mercy, mercifulness; *à tout péché miséricorde*, no sin but should find mercy; *crier miséricorde*, to cry for mercy. ‖ Misericord (poignard). ‖ Ecclés. Misericord, miserere.
— interj. Mercy on me!, mercy!

miséricordieusement [-djøzmɑ̃] adv. Mercifully.

miséricordieux, euse [-djø, ø:z] adj. Merciful.
misogyne [misɔʒin] adj. Misogynous.
— m. Misogynist, woman-hater.
misogynie [-ni] f. Misogyny.
miss [mis] f. Beauty queen; *miss Monde,* Miss World.
missel [misɛl] m. Missal, mass-book; prayer-book.
missile [misi:l] adj., m. Missile (arme).
missilier [-lje] n. Missileman.
mission [misjɔ̃] f. Mission; *lettre de mission,* detached-service warrant; *en mission spéciale,* on a special mission; *mission désagréable,* unpleasant errand; *recevoir mission de faire qqch.,* to be commissioned to do sth. ‖ Assignment (tâche). ‖ Mission; envoys (diplomates). ‖ ECCLÉS. Mission (acte); mission station (local).
missionnaire [-sjɔnɛr] m. ECCLÉS. Missionary; mission priest.
— adj. Mission (sacerdoce).
missive [misi:v] f. Missive.
mistelle [mistɛl] f. Alcoholized must (moût); mistelle wine (vin).
mistenflûte [mistɑ̃fly:t] m. FAM. What's-his-name; thingummy.
mistigri [mistigri] m. FAM. Puss; grimalkin.
mistral [mistral] m. Mistral, north wind.
mit [mi]. V. METTRE (64).
mitaine [mitɛn] f. Mitten. ‖ FAM. Boxing glove.
mitan [mitɑ̃] m. Middle, centre.
mitard [mita:r] m. POP. Cooler (prison).
mite [mit] f. ZOOL. Moth; *mangé aux mites,* moth-eaten. ‖ CULIN. Mite (dans le fromage).
mité, ée [mite] adj. Moth-eaten.
miter (se) [səmite] v. pr. (1). To get moth-eaten.
miteux, euse [mitø, ø:z] adj. FAM. Shabby, shabbily-dressed, seedy-looking. (V. MINABLE.)
mithridatiser [mitridatize] v. tr. (1). To immunize against poison.
mitigation [mitigɑsjɔ̃] f. Mitigation.
mitigé [-ʒe] adj. Mitigated, softened (châtiment, rebuffade). ‖ Loose, lax (morale).
mitochondrie [mitɔkɔ̃dri] f. MÉD. Mitochondrion.
mitonner [-tɔne] v. tr. CULIN. To let simmer. ‖ FAM. To concoct.
— v. intr. CULIN. To simmer.
mitose [mito:z] f. MÉD. Mitosis.
mitoyen, enne [mitwajɛ̃, ɛn] adj. Party (mur); common (puits).
mitoyenneté [-jɛnte] f. Joint ownership (de possession); joint use (d'usage).
mitraillade [mitrajad] f. Burst of fire, volley of shots.
mitraillage [mitraja:ʒ] m. MILIT. Machine-gunning.
mitraille [mitra:j] f. TECHN. Scraps (de métaux). ‖ MILIT. Grapeshot; canister-shot; machine-gun fire. ‖ NAUT. Langrage; *boîte à mitraille,* canister. ‖ FAM. Coppers, U. S. chink (petite monnaie).
mitrailler [mitraje] v. tr. (1). MILIT. To machine-gun; to mow down (ou) to rake (ou) to pepper with machine-gun fire.
mitraillette [-jɛt] f. MILIT. Tommy-gun, sub-machine-gun.
mitrailleur, euse [-jœ:r, ø:z] adj. MILIT. *Fusil mitrailleur,* Bren-gun.
— m. MILIT. Machine-gunner; *mitrailleur arrière,* rear-gunner.
mitrailleuse [-jø:z] f. MILIT. Machine-gun.
mitral, ale [mitral] adj. MÉD. Mitral.
mitre [mitr] m. ECCLÉS. Mitre. ‖ ARCHIT. Cowl (de cheminée).
mitré, ée [-tre] adj. ECCLÉS. Mitred.
mitron [-mitrɔ̃] m. Baker's apprentice, pastry-cook's boy. ‖ Baker's cap (bonnet). ‖ ARCHIT. Chimney pot.

mixage [miksa:ʒ] m. Mixing.
mixer [-se] v. tr. (1). RADIO., CINÉM. To mix.
mixer, mixeur [-sœ:r] m. CULIN. Mixer, liquidizer, blender.
mixité [-site] f. Mixedness, mixed character (en général); coeducation (à l'école).
mixte [mikst] adj. Joint (commission); mixed (école, ligne, mariage, race); U. S. co-educational (école); *assurance mixte,* life and endowment insurance. ‖ SPORTS. *Mixte double,* mixed doubles.
mixtion [mikstjɔ̃] f. MÉD. Mixing.
mixture [miksty:r] f. Mixture. (V. MÉLANGE.)
M.J.C. [ɛmʒise] f. Abrév. de *Maison des jeunes et de la culture,* leisure centre.
Mlle abrév. de *Mademoiselle,* Miss.
MM. Abrév. de *Messieurs,* Messrs.
Mme abrév. de *Madame,* Mrs.
mnémonique [mnemɔnik] adj. Mnemonic.
mnémotechnie [-tɛkni] f. Mnemonics.
mnémotechnique [-tɛknik] adj. Mnemonic.
— f. Mnemonics.
mobile [mɔbil] adj. Movable (fête, objet). ‖ AUTOM. Detachable (carrosserie). ‖ MILIT. Mobile (colonne); *garde mobile,* mobile guard, mounted police. ‖ MÉD. Floating (rein). ‖ JUR. *Echelle mobile,* sliding scale. ‖ FIG. Mobile, changeable; *esprit mobile,* unstable mind (instable); quick, nimble mind (vif); *physionomie mobile,* mobile features; *regard mobile,* roving look.
— m. ASTRON. *Premier mobile,* primum mobile. ‖ PHILOS. *Premier mobile,* originator, prime mover. ‖ FIG. Spring, motive power; motive (d'un crime); *quel mobile l'a poussé?,* what drove him to act in this way?
mobilier [mobilje] adj. Movable, personal; *biens mobiliers,* personal estate; *valeurs mobilières,* stocks and shares; U. S. stocks and bonds; *vente mobilière,* sale of furniture, furniture sale.
— m. Furniture; *mobilier de salon,* suite of drawing-room (ou) living-room furniture.
mobilisable [mɔbilizabl] adj. MILIT. Mobilizable (troupes); *effectifs mobilisables,* potential strength. ‖ FIN. Mobilizable, readily available (ou) disposable (capitaux).
mobilisateur, trice [-zatœ:r, tris] adj. Motivating, activating, rallying.
mobilisation [-zasjɔ̃] f. MILIT. Mobilization. ‖ FIN. Mobilization (de biens); liquidation (de capitaux); conversion (en valeurs négociables). ‖ FIG. Motivation, activation, rallying (de personnes en faveur d'une cause).
mobilisé [-ze] m. MILIT. Serviceman.
mobiliser [-ze] v. tr. (1). MILIT. To mobilize, to call up. ‖ FIN. To mobilize (des biens immobiliers); to make available (des capitaux); to convert (en valeurs négociables). ‖ FIG. To motivate, to activate, to rally (des personnes en faveur d'une cause).
— v. pr. **Se mobiliser,** to rally, to rally round, to mobilize.
mobilité [mɔbilite] f. Mobility. ‖ FIG. Fickleness; instability (du caractère).
Mobylette [mɔbilɛt] f. Motor-bicycle, power-assisted bicycle; motor-bike; moped.
mocassin [mɔkasɛ̃] m. Moccasin.
moche [mɔʃ] adj. FAM. Ugly, misshapen (aspect); rotten, lousy (conduite); dowdy (femme); rotten, dud (spectacle); lousy (tableau); poor, shoddy (travail); gawky, unfashionable (vêtement).
mocheté [mɔʃte] f. FAM. Ugly mug, gargoyle (personne); eyesore, hideous thing (chose).
modal, ale [mɔdal] adj. JUR., PHILOS., MUS. Modal.
modalité [-ite] f. PHILOS. Modality. ‖ MUS. Form of scale. ‖ FIN. *Modalités de paiement,* methods of payment; scheme of payments, U.S. instalment plan. ‖ Pl. Modalities, methods, details; *régler*

les modalités d'un accord, to settle the ways and means of an agreement.

mode [mɔd] m. Mode, form, method; *mode d'emploi,* directions for use; *mode de propulsion,* method of propulsion. ‖ Mus. Mode; mood. ‖ Philos. Mode. ‖ Gramm. Mood.

mode f. Fashion, manner, way (manière); *à ma mode,* as I wish, the way I want to, according to my idea; *à la mode russe,* in the Russian way, as the Russians do. ‖ Fashion (v. vogue); *à l'ancienne mode,* old-fashioned; *à la dernière mode,* in the latest (ou) newest fashion (ou) style; in the height of fashion; *à la mode,* in fashion, fashionable, stylish; *coloris mode,* leading shades; *gravure de mode,* fashion-plate; *passé de mode,* outmoded, out of fashion; *passer de mode,* to go out of fashion. ‖ Pl. Millinery; *magasin de modes,* milliner's shop. ‖ Culin. *A la mode,* à la mode (bœuf).

modelage [mɔdla:ʒ] m. Arts. Modelling (action); *boîte de modelage,* plasticine set.

modèle [mɔdɛl] m. Model, pattern (forme); *sur le même modèle,* on the same pattern; *sur le modèle de Wagner,* modelled on Wagner. ‖ Pattern (patron); *le modèle d'une robe,* the style of a dress; *modèle de Dior,* Dior's model; *nouveaux modèles de chapeaux,* new hat-styles; *présenter des modèles de,* to model. ‖ Comm. *Grand modèle,* large size. ‖ Techn. Template; pattern (prototype); *modèle déposé,* registered pattern; *modèle réduit,* small-scale model. ‖ Arts. Model (de peintre). ‖ Jur. Form (de contrat). ‖ Fig. Model (exemple); *le modèle des amis,* a model friend, the best of friends; *un modèle de vertu,* a model of all virtues; *prendre qqn pour modèle,* to take s.o. as (ou) for one's model, to model oneself on s.o.
— adj. Model; *appartement modèle,* show-flat, U. S. model apartment.

modelé [mɔdle] m. Arts. Relief; richness of form.

modeler v. tr. (8 b). Arts. To model, to mould, to shape (la cire); to bring out (les formes). ‖ Fig. To mould (*sur,* on).
— v. pr. **Se modeler,** to mould oneself (*sur,* upon); *se modeler sur,* to take as one's pattern.

modeleur [-lœ:r] m. Arts. Modeller; statuette-maker. ‖ Techn. Model-maker (pour l'industrie).

modéliste [modelist] m. Pattern-maker, dress-designer. ‖ Théâtr. Model-maker.

modérantisme [mɔderãtism] m. Moderatism (en politique).

modérantiste [-rãtist] adj., s. Moderate (en politique).

modérateur, trice [-ratœ:r, tris] adj. Moderating.
— s. Moderator, restrainer, regulator. ‖ Électr. *Modérateur de son,* volume-control.

modération [-rasjɔ̃] f. Moderation, restraint, forbearance. (V. retenue.) ‖ Temperance (v. sobriété); *avec modération,* temperately.

modéré, ée [-re] adj. Moderate, temperate, sober, sparing, frugal (comportement). ‖ Moderate, temperate, mild, gentle (chaleur); gentle (vent); moderate, safe (vitesse). ‖ Moderate, centre (parti). ‖ Comm. Conservative (estimation); moderate, reasonable, just, fair (prix).
— s. Moderate (ou) temperate person. ‖ Moderate (en politique).

modérément [-remã] adv. Moderately.

modérer [-re] v. tr. (5). To moderate, to reduce, to lessen, to regulate (la chaleur, la vitesse). ‖ To soften, to subdue (la voix). ‖ To moderate, to soothe, to sober, to keep within bounds (qqn). ‖ To moderate, to temper, to repress, to control, to subdue, to govern (les sentiments).
— v. pr. **Se modérer,** to moderate (ou) to control

oneself, to keep oneself in check (ou) in hand (personne). ‖ To abate, to subside (vent).

moderne [mɔdɛrn] adj. Modern, up-to-date (maison); modern (style, temps); *l'enseignement moderne,* modern education; *vivre à la moderne,* to live in the modern style.
— m. Modern; *les Anciens et les Modernes,* the Ancients and the Moderns. ‖ Modern style.

modernisation [-nizasjɔ̃] f. Modernization.

moderniser [-nize] v. tr. (1). To modernize, to bring up-to-date.
— v. pr. **Se moderniser,** to modernize.

modernisme [-nism] m. Modernism.

moderniste [-nist] adj., s. Modernist.

modernité [-nite] f. Modernity.

modern style [mɔdɛrnstil] adj., m. inv. Arts. Art nouveau.

modeste [mɔdɛst] adj. Modest, unassuming, unobtrusive, retiring, unostentatious; *trop modeste,* over-modest. ‖ Quiet, simple, unpretentious (vêtements); *condition modeste,* modest background; *des gens modestes,* people of modest resources. ‖ Modest (ambition, requête). ‖ Comm. Moderate (prix). ‖ † Decent, virtuous.
— s. Modest person.

modestement [-təmã] adv. Modestly, moderately, quietly, simply.

modestie [-ti] f. Modesty, unpretentiousness, bashfulness (caractère); *fausse modestie,* false modesty, decency, propriety (conduite). ‖ Quietness, modesty, unpretentiousness (train de vie).

modicité [mɔdisite] f. Moderateness (des demandes); paucity, scantiness (des ressources).

modifiable [mɔdifjabl] adj. Modifiable.

modifiant, ante [-fjã, ã:t] adj. Modifying.

modificateur, trice [-fikatœ:r, tris] adj. Modificatory.

modificatif, ive [-fikatif, i:v] adj., m. Modificative.

modification [-fikasjɔ̃] f. Modification.

modifier [-fje] v. tr. (1). To modify, to qualify (une affirmation); to modify, to alter, to change (une loi, un plan). ‖ Gramm. To modify.
— v. pr. **Se modifier,** to change, to alter.

modique [mɔdik] adj. Small, slender (fortune, moyens); moderate, limited, reasonable (prix).

modiquement [-mã] adv. Poorly, modestly (rétribuer); simply, modestly (vivre).

modiste [mɔdist] f. Milliner, modiste.

modulaire [mɔdylɛ:r] adj. Modular.

modulateur [mɔdylatœ:r] m. Électr. Modulator.

modulation [-sjɔ̃] f. Modulation (d'un son); inflexion (d'une voix); adjustment (d'un prix). ‖ Phys., Radio. Modulation; *modulation de fréquence,* frequency modulation.

module [mɔdyl] m. Archit., Astronaut., Techn. Module. ‖ Math. Modulus.

modulé, ée [mɔdyle] adj. Modulated (son); *puissance modulée,* modulated output of power.

moduler v. tr. (1). To modulate.

modus vivendi [mɔdysvivɛ̃di] m. inv. Modus vivendi.

moelle [mwal] f. Marrow. ‖ Méd. Medulla; *moelle épinière,* spinal cord. ‖ Bot. Pith. ‖ Fig. Pith, marrow, core (v. quintessence); *jusqu'à la moelle,* thoroughly, to the bone (ou) core (ou) marrow. ‖ Fam. *Sucer qqn jusqu'à la moelle,* to suck s.o. dry (intellectuellement); to bleed s.o. white (pécuniairement).

moelleusement [-løzmã] adv. Softly, luxuriously.

moelleux, euse [-lø, ø:z] adj. Soft, downy (lit). ‖ Soft, mellow (voix). ‖ Bot. Juicy, sappy (fruit). ‖ Arts. Soft, rounded.
— m. Softness, mellowness (de la couleur, de la voix); juiciness, sappiness, velvety feeling (du velours); mellowness (du vin).

moellon [mwalɔ̃] m. ARCHIT. Quarry-stone; *moellon de roche*, rock rubble.

mœurs [mœːrs] f. pl. Manners, morals (moralité); *avoir de bonnes mœurs*, to be of good moral character; *femme de mauvaises mœurs*, loose woman. ‖ Customs (coutumes); *autres temps, autres mœurs*, other times, other ways; *c'est entré dans les mœurs*, it has become a custom.

mofette [mɔfɛt] f. Choke-damp; gas-spring.

mohair [mɔɛr] m. Mohair.

moi [mwa] pr. pers. I (sujet); *moi je ne l'ai pas dit*, I didn't say so; *moi qui suis son oncle*, I who am his uncle; *c'est moi*, it is I; *il n'est pas riche, ni moi non plus*, he is not rich, nor am I; *je l'ai vu moi*, I did see it; *vous et moi nous nous cotiserons*, you and I will club together; *vous êtes moins susceptible que moi*, you are less touchy than I; *vous vous êtes insurgé et moi aussi*, you rebelled and so did I. ‖ Me (compl. direct); *il va recevoir ma femme et moi*, he is going to entertain my wife and me; *il ne me reconnaît pas, moi qu'il a vu plusieurs fois*, he does not recognize me whom he has seen several times. ‖ Me (compl. indirect); *c'est une idée à moi*, it's an idea of mine; *cette lettre n'est pas de moi*, this letter is not one that I wrote; *c'est un parent à moi*, he is one of my relatives; *de vous à moi*, between you and me; *faites-le pour moi*, do it for my sake (ou) for me; *revenez avec moi*, come back with me. ‖ (Explétif, non traduit); *faites-moi partir ces gens-là*, send these people away; *envoyez-moi cet importun au diable!*, send this bore about his business! ‖ Loc. *A moi!*, help!
— m. Ego; self; *le culte du moi*, egotism, the cult of the self. ‖ **Moi-même**, pron. réfl. Myself; *je le ferai moi-même*, I will do it myself; *c'est un autre moi-même*, he is my other self (ou) alter ego.

moignon [mwaɲɔ̃] m. MÉD. Stump.

moindre [mwɛ̃ːdr] adj. compar. Less, lesser, smaller (*que*, than); *de moindre importance*, of lesser (ou) less importance; *entre deux maux choisissez le moindre*, of two evils choose the lesser (ou) the less.
— superl. The least, the smallest; *dans les moindres détails*, in the smallest (ou) minutest details; *il n'y a pas le moindre espoir*, there is not the faintest shadow of a hope; *il n'a pas dit le moindre mot*, he never said a word; *le dernier, mais non le moindre*, last but not least; *le moindre bruit le gêne*, the slightest noise troubles him.

moindrement [-drəmɑ̃] adv. *Pas le moindrement*, not in the least.

moine [mwan] m. Bed-warmer, hot-water bottle (bouillotte). ‖ ECCLÉS. Monk, friar. ‖ ZOOL. Monk-seal. ‖ TECHN. Blister, flaw (défaut). ‖ ARCHIT. Pin maul. ‖ NAUT. Long-burning light. ‖ Loc. *Gras comme un moine*, as fat as Friar Tuck.

moineau [mwano] m. ZOOL. Sparrow. ‖ COMM. *Tête de moineau*, nuts (charbon). ‖ FAM. *Vilain moineau*, dirty dog.

moinerie [mwanri] f. FAM. Monkery.

moinillon [-nijɔ̃] m. FAM. Young monk.

moins [mwɛ̃] adv. comp. Less (*que*, than) [en degré]; *moins bon*, less good; *moins coûteux*, less costly; *il est obligeant, mais sa sœur l'est moins*, he is obliging but his sister is less so. ‖ Less (en valeur); *cela a coûté moins que je ne croyais*, it cost less than I thought; *cela ne coûtera pas moins de cent francs*, that will cost no less than a hundred francs; *il faut dépenser moins*, you must spend less; *je l'ai payé cinq francs de moins que vous*, I paid five francs less for it than you. ‖ Fewer (en nombre); *il y a eu moins de monde aux courses aujourd'hui qu'hier*, there were fewer people at the races today than yesterday. ‖ **Moins-value**, f. Decrease in value, depreciation.
— superl. Least; *son moins grand effort*, his slightest effort; *la moins longue de ses interventions*, the least extensive of his interventions; *le moins de temps possible*, the least time possible.
— prép. Less, minus; *cinq moins trois égale deux*, five less (ou) minus three is two; *c'est sa mère moins les rides*, she is her mother over again, without (ou) but for (ou) except for the wrinkles; *quatre heures moins le quart*, a quarter to four. ‖ FAM. *C'était moins cinq!*, it was a hair-breadth escape, it was a close shave!
— m. MATH. Minus, minus sign.
— loc. adv. **A moins de**; *à moins d'indication contraire*, barring any indication to the contrary; *à moins d'être fou*, unless he were mad; *à moins d'un mille*, within a mile; *à moins de mille francs*, for less than a thousand francs. ‖ **Au moins, pour le moins, tout au moins**, at least; *quatre navires au moins*, at least four ships; *vous pourriez au moins me remercier*, you might at least thank me; *vous le paierez au moins deux cents francs*, you will pay at least two hundred francs for it. ‖ **De moins**, less, the less, the fewer; *ce sera autant de copies de moins à corriger*, that will be all the fewer (ou) just so many fewer papers to correct; *ce sera autant de moins à consommer*, there will be so much the less to consume; *ici vous paierez cela dix francs de moins*, here you will pay ten francs less for that; *il a un bras de moins*, he has lost one arm. ‖ **De moins en moins**, less and less; *il est de moins en moins violent*, he is less and less hot-headed; *nous le voyons de moins en moins*, we see less and less of him. ‖ **Du moins**, at least; *du moins vous n'aurez rien à payer*, at least you will have nothing to pay. ‖ **En moins**, less, missing; *en moins de*, in less than; *il y a deux paires en moins*, two pairs are missing; *en moins de rien*, in less than no time, before you could say Jack Robinson. ‖ **Le moins**, least, the least; *celui qui mange le moins se porte le mieux*, he who eats least enjoys the best health (parmi plusieurs); he who eats less enjoys the better health (de deux); *pas le moins du monde*, not in the least. ‖ **Moins... moins**, the less... the less; *moins on parle, moins on se trompe*, the less you speak, the fewer mistakes you make; *moins on est soucieux, plus on rit*, the less careworn you are, the more you laugh. ‖ **Pas moins**, all the same; just the same; *il n'en est pas moins ruiné*, he is ruined all the same. ‖ **Pas moins de**, no less than; *il n'a pas perdu moins de cent mille francs*, he has lost no less than one hundred thousand francs. ‖ **Plus... moins, the more... the less**; *plus on souffre, moins on est gai*, the more pain you endure, the less gay you are. ‖ **Ni plus ni moins**, neither more nor less; *il a cinquante ans ni plus ni moins*, he is fifty years old, neither more nor less.
— loc. conj. **A moins que**, unless; *à moins qu'il ne proteste*, unless he protests. ‖ **Pas moins que**, no less than; *elle n'a pas gagné moins que je vous le dis*, she has not won less than I say; *il n'en est pas moins vrai que*, it is none the less true that. ‖ **Rien moins que**, anything but, not at all; *il n'est rien moins qu'agréable*, he is anything but pleasant, he is not at all pleasant.

moirage [mwaraːʒ] m. TECHN. Watering.

moire, ée [mwaːr, e] f. TECHN. Watered silk, moire. ‖ Watering.

moiré [mware] adj. TECHN. Watered, moiré (étoffe); moiré (métal).
— m. Watered (ou) clouded effect (effet); moiré (étoffe). ‖ Moiré tin (ou) zinc (métal).

moirer v. tr. (1). TECHN. To water, to cloud (une étoffe) ; to cloud, to moiré (un métal).

moirure [-ry:r] f. TECHN. Watered effect.

mois [mwa] m. Month ; *un bébé de trois mois,* a three-month-old baby. ‖ Month's pay (ou) wage (ou) salary ; *mille francs par mois,* a thousand francs a month ; *salaire au mois,* salary by the month ; *toucher son mois,* to draw one's pay for the month. ‖ COMM. *Le vingt de ce mois, du mois dernier, du mois prochain,* the twentieth instant (ou) inst., ultimo (ou) ult., proximo (ou) prox.

Moïse [mɔi:z] m. Moses (prénom). ‖ Moses basket ; basket cot ; bassinet. (V. BERCEAU.)

moiser [mwaze] v. tr. (1). TECHN. To brace.

moisi, ie [mwazi] adj. Mouldy, musty, mildewed (objet) ; musty, fusty, stale (odeur).
— m. Mould, must, mildew ; *goût de moisi,* musty (ou) stale taste ; *sentir le moisi,* to smell musty (ou) fusty.

moisir [-zi:r] v. intr. (2). To mildew, to become mouldy. ‖ FIG. To rot.
— v. tr. To mildew, to make mouldy.
— v. pr. **Se moisir,** to become mouldy.

moisissure [-zisy:r] f. Mould, mildew ; mouldiness.

moisson [mwasɔ̃] f. AGRIC. Harvest, crop ; *faire la moisson,* to harvest. ‖ FIG. Harvest.

moissonner [-sɔne] v. tr. (1). AGRIC. To reap, to harvest, to gather in. ‖ FIG. To reap (des lauriers) ; *vie trop tôt moissonnée,* life cut off too soon.

moissonneur [-sɔnœ:r] s. AGRIC. Harvester, reaper. ‖ ZOOL. Rook.

moissonneuse [-sɔnøːz] f. AGRIC. Harvester, reaping-machine. ‖ **Moissonneuse-batteuse,** f. AGRIC. Combine-harvester. ‖ **Moissonneuse-lieuse,** f. AGRIC. Self-binder, sheaf-binding harvester.

moite [mwat] adj. Moist, damp, humid (front, main) ; sweaty, clammy (main). [V. HUMIDE.]

moiteur [-tœ:r] f. Moistness, dampness, clamminess. ‖ MÉD. Perspiration.

moitié [mwatje] f. Half ; *à moitié prix,* at half-price ; *à moitié ivre,* half drunk ; *couper par moitié,* to cut in half ; *faire qqch. à moitié,* to half-do sth. ; *la moitié du temps,* half the time ; *partager par moitié,* to go shares (ou) half-and-half ; *réduit de moitié,* reduced by half ; *s'arrêter à moitié chemin,* to stop half-way ; *se mettre de moitié avec qqn,* to go halves (ou) fifty-fifty with s.o. ‖ FAM. Helpmate (épouse) ; *ma chère moitié,* my better half.
— adv. Half ; *moitié laine, moitié coton,* half wool, half cotton ; *moitié moins cher, moitié plus cher,* half as dear (ou) expensive, half as dear again (ou) again as expensive ; *moitié plus,* half as much again.

moitir [mwati:r] v. tr. (2). To make damp (ou) moist ; to dampen, to moisten.

moka [mɔka] m. CULIN. Mocha coffee (café) ; mocha cake (gâteau).

mol [mɔl]. V. MOU.

molaire [mɔlɛ:r] adj., f. MÉD. Molar.

molaire adj. PHYS. Molar.

moldave [mɔldav] adj., s. GÉOGR. Moldavian.

Moldavie [mɔldavi] f. GÉOGR. Moldavia.

mole [mɔl] f. PHYS. Mole.

môle [mo:l] m. Mole (jetée).

môle f. MÉD. Mole.

moléculaire [mɔlekylɛ:r] adj. CHIM. Molecular.

molécule [-kyl] f. CHIM. Molecule. ‖ **Molécule-gramme,** f. PHYS., CHIM. Gram molecule.

molène [mɔlɛn] f. BOT. Mullein.

moleskine [mɔleskin] f. Imitation leather.

molestation [mɔlɛstasjɔ̃] f. Molestation.

molester [-te] v. tr. (1). To molest. (V. MALMENER.)

moleter [mɔlte] v. tr. (8 a). TECHN. To mill.

molette [-lɛt] f. Rowel (d'éperon). ‖ TECHN. Knurling tool ; *appareil à molette,* cutting-wheel ; *clef à molette,* adjustable spanner. ‖ Winding pulley (de mine). ‖ Pestle (à broyer).

moliéresque [mɔljerɛsk] adj. Relating to Molière, reminiscent of Molière.

mollah [mɔla] m. Mullah.

mollasse [mɔlas] adj. FAM. Soft, lacking in body (chose) ; slow, lazy (enfant) ; soft, flabby (personne). [V. FLASQUE.]

mollasse f. GÉOL. Molasse, sandy (ou) clayey limestone.

mollasserie [-sri] f. FAM. Softness, flabbiness, gutlessness.

mollasson [-sɔ̃] s. FAM. Molly-coddle.

mollement [mɔlmɑ̃] adv. Softly, flabbily (attitude) ; slackly, lazily (travail).

mollesse [-lɛs] f. Flabbiness (des chairs) ; softness (d'un tapis). ‖ ARTS. Softness (des contours). ‖ FIG. Flabbiness, spinelessness ; listlessness (du caractère) ; laxity, slackness, tameness (du comportement) ; slackness, indolence (de la vie).

mollet [mɔlɛ] adj. Soft, softish. ‖ CULIN. Soft-boiled (œuf).

mollet m. MÉD. Calf (de la jambe).

molletière [mɔltjɛ:r] adj. *Bande molletière,* puttee.

molleton [mɔltɔ̃] m. Soft flannel (ou) cotton ; duffel ; swansdown.

molletonné, ée [-tɔne] adj. With raised nap (étoffe) ; lined with swansdown (habit).

moletonner [-tɔne] v. tr. (1). To raise the nap of (une étoffe) ; to line with swansdown (un habit).

mollir [mɔli:r] v. intr. (2). To become soft, to soften (sens général). ‖ NAUT. To ease away (sur une manœuvre) ; to shorten the stroke (en ramant) ; to abate, to slacken, to die (ou) go down (vent). ‖ MILIT. To slacken, to drop off, to abate (énergie) ; to flag, to fail, to sag (force) ; to give way (jambes) ; to go off, to deteriorate (personne).
— v. tr. NAUT. To ease (la barre) ; to slack off (une corde) ; to ease, to slacken, to slack off (une manœuvre).

mollo [mɔlo] adv. POP. Easy !, easy does it !

mollusque [mɔlysk] m. Mollusc. ‖ FAM. Slow-coach (lambin) ; molly-coddle (mollasson).

molosse [mɔlɔs] m. ZOOL. Mastiff.

molybdène [mɔlibdɛn] m. CHIM. Molybdenum.

môme [mo:m] s. POP. Kid, brat, youngster.

moment [mɔmɑ̃] m. Moment, while, instant, second (court espace de temps) ; *dans un moment,* in a second (ou) a trice ; *d'un moment à l'autre,* at any time ; *en un moment,* in a flash, in the twinkling of an eye ; *n'avoir pas un moment à soi,* not to have a moment to oneself (ou) to spare ; *pour le moment,* at present, for the time being ; *pour un moment,* for a while ; *sur le moment,* for a moment, on the spur of the moment ; *un moment !,* hold on !, wait a minute ! ‖ Moment (point précis du temps) ; *à un moment donné,* at one time ; *au moment de parler,* just as he was about to speak, at the moment when he was about to speak ; *au moment de partir,* as I was getting ready to start ; *au moment où,* just when ; *au moment voulu,* in due course ; *à tout moment,* constantly, at every turn ; *dès ce moment,* from that moment ; *en ce moment,* at this moment, at the present time ; *jusqu'au moment où,* till, until ; *le moment venu,* in good time ; *par moments,* at times, now and then ; *les préoccupations du moment,* the preoccupations of the hour. ‖ Moment (de la vie) ; *à ses derniers moments,* in his last moments ; *à ses moments perdus,* in his spare time ; *arriver au bon, au mauvais moment,* to arrive in the nick of time, at an awkward moment ; *avoir ses bons moments,* to have one's good days ; *le bon moment pour,* the time to ;

passer un bon moment ensemble, to have a good time together; *profiter du moment,* to take advantage of the opportunity. ‖ Stage (d'un développement).

— loc. conj. **Du moment où** (ou) **que,** seeing that, since. (V. PUISQUE.)

momentané, ée [mɔmɑ̃tane] adj. Momentary (absence, présence); temporary (difficulté).

momentanéité [-ite] f. Momentaneity, momentariness.

momentanément [-mɑ̃] adv. Momentarily, temporarily, for a while.

momerie [mɔmri] f. Mummery.

momie [mɔmi] f. Mummy. ‖ ARTS. Mummy. ‖ FAM. Sleepy-head (endormi); fossil (vieillard).

momification [-fikasjɔ̃] f. Mummification.

momifier [-fje] v. tr. (1). To mummify.

— v. pr. **Se momifier,** to become mummified. ‖ To shrivel (ou) dry up (se ratatiner). ‖ FAM. To grow sluggish (ou) inert.

mon [mɔ̃] (f. **ma** [ma], pl. **mes** [mɛ]) adj. poss. My; *mon corps,* my body; *mon existence, ma vie,* my life; *mes jours,* my days; *un de mes cousins,* one of my cousins, a cousin of mine; *oui, mon oncle,* yes, uncle.

monacal, ale [mɔnakal] adj. ECCLÉS. Monachal, monastic.

monachisme [-ʃism] m. ECCLÉS. Monachism, monasticism.

Monaco [mɔnako] f. GÉOGR. Monaco.

monade [mɔnad] f. PHILOS. Monad.

monarchie [mɔnarʃi] f. Monarchy.

monarchique [-ʃik] adj. Monarchic.

monarchiser [-ʃize] v. tr. (1). To monarchize.

monarchisme [-ʃism] m. Monarchism.

monarchiste [-ʃist] adj., s. Monarchist.

monarque [mɔnark] m. Monarch. (V. ROI.)

monastère [mɔnastɛ:r] m. ECCLÉS. Monastery.

monastique [-tik] adj. ECCLÉS. Monastic.

monastiquement [-tikmɑ̃] adv. ECCLÉS. Monastically.

monaural, ale [mɔnoral] adj. ÉLECTR. Monaural, monophonic. ‖ MÉD. Monaural.

monceau [mɔso] m. Heap (v. AMAS); ton (de chiffons); mountain (de ferrailles); stack (de journaux).

mondain, aine [mɔ̃dɛ̃, ɛn] adj. Worldly, mundane, earthly (pensées, plaisirs); *elle est très mondaine,* she leads a very active social life, she's a socialite; *événements de la vie mondaine,* social events; *réunions mondaines,* social (ou) society functions.

— s. Worldly-minded (ou) worldly person; wor dling; man of fashion; man-about-town.

mondanité [-danite] f. Worldliness, mundanity. ‖ Love of fashionable gatherings (ou) social functions (goût). ‖ Pl. Society news (rubrique).

monde [mɔ̃:d] m. World, universe, earth (v. UNIVERS); *l'Ancien, le Nouveau Monde,* the Old, the New World; *au bout du monde,* at the back of beyond; *courir le monde,* to travel far and wide; *dans le monde entier,* all over the world, throughout the whole world; *jusqu'au bout du monde,* to the edges of the earth. ‖ World, life (vie); *depuis que je suis au monde,* since I was born; *être encore de ce monde,* to be still living (ou) in the land of the living; *mettre au monde,* to give birth to, to bring forth; *ne plus être de ce monde,* to be no more; *passer dans un monde meilleur,* to go to a better world; *venir au monde,* to be brought into the world, to come into the world, to be born. ‖ World, people (gens); *c'est se moquer du monde,* that's making fools of us all, you must think people are mad; *comme tout le monde,* like everyone else, like other people; *il y avait beaucoup de monde à la soirée,* there were a lot of people at the party; *il connaît*

son monde, he knows the people he deals with; *je n'ai pas encore tout mon monde,* my guests haven't all arrived yet; *prendre le monde comme il est,* to take the world as it is, to take things as they come; *renvoyer tout son monde,* to dismiss all one's servants (ses domestiques); *tout le monde en parle,* everyone is speaking of it; *le petit monde,* the little ones (ou) children. ‖ World, society, set (société); *aller dans le monde,* to go out, to lead an active social life; *dans le monde cela ne se fait pas,* it is not done in good society; *être du même monde que qqn,* to belong to s.o.'s set; *le grand monde,* high life (ou) society, the best circles; *le monde lancé,* the fast set; *un homme du monde,* a gentleman, a man of good breeding; *une femme du monde,* a lady, a woman of good breeding. ‖ ASTRON. Pl. Planets, stars, spheres. ‖ FIG. World; *en ce monde,* in this world; *dans l'autre monde,* in the next world, in the hereafter; *depuis que le monde est monde,* since the beginning of things (ou) time; *être seul au monde,* to be alone in the world; *expédier qqn dans l'autre monde,* to send s.o. to kingdom come; *le monde renversé,* the world turned upside down; *s'entendre le mieux du monde,* to be on the best of terms, to get on famously; *vieux comme le monde,* as old as the hills.

mondé, ée [mɔ̃de] adj. Hulled (orge).

mondial, ale [-djal] adj. World-wide, worldly, universal; *guerre mondiale,* world war.

mondialement [-djalmɑ̃] adv. Universally, all over the world.

mondialisation [-djalizasjɔ̃] f. World-wide expansion, spreading to a world scale.

mondovision [mɔ̃dovizjɔ̃] f. World-wide television relayed by satellites.

monégasque [mɔnegask] adj., s. GÉOGR. Of Monaco; Monégasque.

monétaire [mɔnetɛ:r] adj. FIN. Money (marché); monetary (réforme); *système monétaire,* coinage.

monétisation [-tizasjɔ̃] f. FIN. Monetization.

monétiser [-tize] v. tr. (1). FIN. To monetize, to mint.

mongol, ole [mɔ̃gol] adj., s. GÉOGR. Mongol, Mongolian.

— m. GRAMM. Mongol, Mongolian (langue).

Mongolie [mɔ̃gɔli] f. GÉOGR. Mongolia.

mongolien, enne [-ljɛ̃, ɛn] adj. MÉD. Mongolian.

— s. MÉD. Mongol.

mongolique [-lik] adj. GÉOGR. Mongolian.

mongolisme [-lism] m. MÉD. Mongolism.

moniale [mɔnjal] f. ECCLÉS. Nun of a contemplative order.

monisme [mɔnism] m. PHILOS. Monism.

moniste [-nist] adj. PHILOS. Monistic, monist.

— s. PHILOS. Monist.

moniteur [mɔnitœ:r] m. Monitor, coach.

monition [-sjɔ̃] f. Monition.

monitoire [-twa:r] adj., f. ECCLÉS. Monitory.

monitrice [-tris] f. Monitress.

monnaie [mɔnɛ] f. Money, currency; *la monnaie française,* French currency; *monnaie forte,* hard currency; *papier monnaie,* paper money. ‖ Change; *la monnaie de mille francs,* change for a thousand francs. ‖ Mint; *l'Hôtel de la Monnaie,* the Mint. ‖ FIG. Change, coin; *la monnaie courante de la diplomatie,* the small change of diplomacy; *rendre à qqn la monnaie de sa pièce,* to pay s.o. back in his own coin. ‖ FAM. *Payer en monnaie de singe,* to bilk. ‖ **Monnaie-du-pape,** f. BOT. Honesty, moonwort, satinpod.

monnayable [-jabl] adj. Coinable (métal); saleable, negotiable (marchandise).

monnayage [-ja:ʒ] m. Minting, coining; mintage.

monnayer [-je] v. tr. (9b). To coin, to mint; to

monetize. ‖ FIG. *Monnayer son talent*, to cash in on one's talent.

monnayeur [-jœ:r] m. Coiner, minter; *faux-monnayeur*, counterfeiter.

mono [mɔnɔ] adj. inv., f. TECHN. Mono (monophonie).
— m. SPORTS. Mono-ski (objet); mono-skiing (activité).

monoacide [mɔnɔasid] adj. CHIM. Monoacid, monacid, monoacidic, monacidic.

monoatomique [mɔnɔatɔmik] adj. PHYS. Monoatomic, monatomic.

monobloc [-blɔk] adj. Made all in one piece.

monocamérisme [-kamerism] m. Unicameralism.

monochromatique [-krɔmatik] adj. PHYS. Monochromatic.

monochrome [-krɔ:m] adj., s. Monochrome.

monocle [mɔnɔkl] m. Monocle, eye-glass.

monocoque [mɔnɔkɔk] f. AVIAT. Monocoque.

monocorde [-kɔrd] m. MUS. Single-string instrument. ‖ PHYS. Monochord.
— adj. FIG. Monotonous.

monocotylédone [-kɔtiledɔn] adj. BOT. Monocotyledon.

monoculture [mɔnɔkylty:r] f. AGRIC. Monoculture.

monocylindrique [-cylɛ̃drik] adj. AUTOM. Single-cylinder (moteur).

monocyte [-sit] m. MÉD. Monocyte.

monodactyle [-daktil] adj. ZOOL. Monodactylous.

monodie [-di] f. MUS. Monody.

monogame [-gam] adj. Monogamous.
— s. Monogamist.

monogamie [-gami] f. Monogamy.

monogamique [-gamik] adj. Monogamous.

monogramme [-gram] m. Monogram; initials.

monographe [-graf] m. Monographer.
— adj. Monographic.

monographie [-grafi] f. Monograph.

monokini [-kini] m. Monokini, topless swimsuit.

monolingue [-lɛ̃g] adj., s. GRAMM. Monolingual.

monolinguisme [-lɛ̃gɥism] m. GRAMM. Monolingualism.

monolithe [-lit] m. Monolith.
— adj. Monolithic.

monolithique [-litik] adj. Monolithic (doctrine, organisation).

monolithisme [-litism] m. Monolithism (d'une doctrine, d'une organisation).

monologue [-lɔg] m. Monologue.

monologuer [-lɔge] v. intr. (1). To soliloquize.

monologueur [-lɔgœ:r] m. Monologist, soliloquist.

monomane [-man] adj., s. MÉD. Monomaniac.

monomanie [-mani] f. MÉD. Monomania.

monôme [mɔno:m] m. MATH. Monomial. ‖ Students' rag (ou) parade (défilé d'étudiants).

monomère [mɔnɔmɛ:r] adj. CHIM. Monomeric.
— m. CHIM. Monomer.

monométallisme [mɔnɔmetallism] m. FIN. Monometallism.

monomoteur [-mɔtœ:r] adj. AVIAT. Single-engined.
— m. AVIAT. Single-engined aircraft.

mononucléaire [-nyklεɛ:r] adj. MÉD. Mononuclear.
— m. MÉD. Mononuclear, mononucleate.

mononucléose [-nykleo:z] f. MÉD. Mononucleosis.

monophasé, ée [-faze] adj. ÉLECTR. Monophase, monophasic, single-phase.

monophonie [-fɔni] f. TECHN. Monophony.

monophonique [-fɔnik] adj. TECHN. Monophonic.

monoplace [-plas] adj., m. AVIAT., AUTOM. Single-seater.

monoplan [-plɑ̃] m. AVIAT. Monoplane.

monopode [-pɔd] adj. ZOOL. Monopodous, one-footed.
— m. Monopode.

monopole [mɔnɔpɔl] m. Monopoly; *monopole de fait*, de facto monopoly.

monopolisateur [-lizatœ:r] m. Monopolizer.

monopolisation [-lizasjɔ̃] f. Monopolization.

monopoliser [-lize] v. tr. (1). To monopolize.

monopolistique [-listik] adj. Monopolistic; *contrôle monopolistique*, monopoly control.

monoprix [mɔnɔpri] m. One-price shop.

monorail [-ra:j] adj., m. CH. DE F. Monorail.

monoski [-ski] m. SPORTS. Mono-ski (objet); mono-skiing (activité).

monosyllabe [-sillab] m. Monosyllable.

monosyllabique [-sillabik] adj. Monosyllabic.

monosyllabisme [-sillabism] m. GRAMM. Monosyllabism.

monothéisme [-teism] m. Monotheism.

monothéiste [-teist] s. Monotheist.
— adj. Monotheistic.

monotone [-mɔnɔtɔn] adj. Monotonous. (V. UNIFORME.) ‖ FIG. Unvaried (occupation); drab, humdrum (vie).

monotonie [-tɔni] f. Monotony, sameness, dullness.

monotype [mɔnɔtip] adj. BOT. Monotypical.
— f. Monotype (en typogr.) [nom déposé].
— m. ARTS. Monotype. ‖ NAUT. One-design craft.

monovalence [-valɑ̃:s] f. CHIM. Monovalence.

monovalent, ente [-valɑ̃, ɑ̃:t] adj. CHIM. Monovalent.

monozygote [-zigɔt] adj. MÉD. Monozygotic, one-egg.

Monseigneur [mɔ̃sɛɲœ:r] (pl. **messeigneurs** [mɛsɛɲœ:r]) m. Your Grace (à un archevêque, un duc); Your Eminence (à un cardinal); my Lord, your Lordship (à un évêque); Your Royal Highness (à un prince); *donner du monseigneur à*, to give the title of Monseigneur to.

Monsieur [məsjø] (pl. **messieurs** [mɛsjø]) m. Mr. (devant un nom propre); Master (pour un enfant); *M. Smith*, Mr. Smith; *Monsieur Jean*, Master John. ‖ (Non traduit devant un titre); *M. le duc de*, the Duke of; *M. le Ministre*, the Minister; *Monsieur l'abbé O'Leary*, Father O'Leary. ‖ Pl. Messieurs; *Messieurs Steerforth Frères et Cⁱᵉ*, Messrs. Steerforth Brothers & Co. ‖ Dear Mr. X (en tête d'une lettre amicale); Dear Sir (dans une lettre d'affaires). ‖ (En s'adressant à une personne) *Monsieur le comte*, your Lordship; *Monsieur le duc*, Your Grace; *Monsieur le juge*, your Lordship, your Worship; *Monsieur le maire*, Mr. Mayor; *Monsieur le président*, Mr. President; *Mesdames et Messieurs*, Ladies and Gentlemen. ‖ Gentleman (personne de bonne compagnie); *un jeune monsieur*, a youngster, a youth; *un monsieur d'un certain âge*, an elderly gentleman; *reconduisez ces messieurs à la porte*, please show these gentlemen to the door. ‖ Sir (de la part d'un domestique); *Monsieur a-t-il sonné?*, did you ring, Sir?; *Monsieur veut-il me dire où je pourrai lui téléphoner?*, may I ask, Sir, where I can call you?; *Monsieur est sorti*, the master (ou) Mr. Smith is out; *que prendront ces messieurs?*, what will you have, gentlemen? ‖ FAM. *Un joli monsieur*, a bad lot.

monstre [mɔ̃str] m. Monster (animal mythique). ‖ Monster, freak (v. PHÉNOMÈNE); *un mouton à cinq pattes est un monstre*, a five-legged sheep is a freak of nature; *les monstres marins*, the monsters of the deep. ‖ FIG. Monster (personne); *un monstre de cruauté*, a monster of cruelty. ‖ FAM. *Petit monstre!*, little imp!; *quel monstre de*

femme !, what a fright she is !; *se faire un monstre de tout,* to make mountains out of molehills.
— adj. FAM. Huge, enormous, prodigious ; *un culot monstre,* the cheek of the devil ; *un navet monstre,* a monster (ou) whacking turnip.

monstrueusement [-trɥozmɑ̃] adv. Monstrously.

monstrueux, euse [-trɥo, ø:z] adj. Monstrous, prodigious (anormal). ‖ Monstrous, huge (colossal). ‖ Monstrous, shocking, outrageous (odieux).

monstruosité [-trɥozite] f. Monstrosity, abomination (horreur). ‖ Monstrousness, heinousness, outrageousness (chose choquante).

mont [mɔ̃] m. Mount, mountain ; *le mont Blanc,* Mont Blanc ; *passer les monts,* to cross the Alps. ‖ FIG. *Etre toujours par monts et par vaux,* to be always on the move ; *promettre monts et merveilles,* to promise s.o. wonders (ou) the moon and the stars. ‖ **Mont-blanc,** m. CULIN. Chestnut cake (ou) purée with whipped cream. ‖ **Mont-de-piété,** m. Pawn-shop ; *mettre au mont-de-piété,* to pawn ; to pop (fam.) ; U. S. to hock ; *retirer du mont-de-piété,* to take out of pawn.

montage [mɔ̃ta:ʒ] m. Taking up, carrying up ; lifting, raising ; hoisting. ‖ CULIN. Boiling up (du lait). ‖ TECHN. Fitting out (d'un atelier) ; setting (d'un bijou) ; setting up, assembling (d'une machine) ; putting together, assembling, mounting (d'une montre) ; *atelier, bande de montage,* assembly shop, line. ‖ THÉÂTR. Montage ; cutting, editing (d'un film) ; staging (d'une pièce) ; *montage sonore, visuel,* sound-, picture-cutting. ‖ RADIO. Lay-out, building (d'un poste).

montagnard, arde [mɔ̃taɲa:r, a:rd] adj. Mountain, highland.
— s. Mountaineer, highlander. ‖ Pl. Mountain folk, hillfolk, U. S. hillbillies (fam.) [au Sud].
— m. † Montagnard.

montagne [mɔ̃taɲ] f. GÉOGR. Mountain ; *aussi haut qu'une montagne,* mountain-high ; *les montagnes d'Ecosse,* the Highlands ; *les montagnes Rocheuses,* the Rocky Mountains, the Rockies ; *passer l'été à la montagne,* to spend the summer in the mountains (ou) hills. ‖ *Montagnes russes,* scenic railway, switchback, U. S. roller-coaster. ‖ FIG. Mountain (v. AMAS) ; *montagne de glace,* iceberg. ‖ FAM. *Se faire une montagne de rien,* to make a mountain out of a mole-hill.

montagneux, euse [-taɲø, ø:z] adj. Mountainous, hilly.

montant, ante [mɔ̃tɑ̃, ɑ̃:t] adj. Uphill, rising (chemin). ‖ High, stand-up (col) ; high-necked (robe) ; *chaussures montantes,* boots, U. S. high shoes. ‖ MUS. *Gamme montante,* ascending scale. ‖ CH. DE F. *Voie montante,* up line. ‖ TECHN. Vertical (joint) ; uptake, raising (tuyau) ; *course montante,* up-stroke (du piston). ‖ MILIT. *Garde montante,* new (ou) relief guard.
— m. Flood, inflow (flot) ; rising tide (marée). ‖ Post, pole, upright ; *montant d'échelle, d'escalier, de fenêtre, de lambris, de machine, de portail, de porte, de tréteau, de trépied, de réverbère,* upright, riser, cheek, stile, column (ou) pillar (ou) vertical standard, gate-post, jamb, leg, stand, lamp-post. ‖ AVIAT. *Montant de cellules,* interplane strut. ‖ SPORTS. *Montants du but,* goal-posts (au football). ‖ NAUT. *Montant de tente,* awning stanchion. ‖ FIN. Amount, total amount, sum total ; *montant d'une facture,* value of an invoice. ‖ CULIN. High flavour, strong aroma, tastiness ; *une boisson qui a du montant,* a drink with a kick in it (fam.). ‖ FIG. Allure, enticement. ‖ POP. *Les montants,* a pair of trousers.

monte [mɔ̃:t] f. Covering (accouplement) ; *monte d'une chienne, d'une jument,* lining, covering. ‖ SPORTS. Mounting, horsemanship ; *partants et montes probables,* probable starters and jockeys. ‖ **Monte-charge,** m. Hoist, goods-lift, U. S.

freight (ou) service elevator. ‖ **Monte-en-l'air,** m. POP. Cat-burglar, U. S. porch-climber. ‖ **Monteplats,** m. Kitchen-lift, U. S. dumb-waiter.

monté, ée [mɔ̃te] adj. Mounted (cavalier, police). ‖ Organized, set up, got up (organisé). ‖ Provided (fourni) ; *cave, boutique bien montée,* well-stocked cellar, shop ; *garde-robe bien montée,* extensive wardrobe ; *le libraire le mieux monté de la ville,* the best-stocked bookshop (ou) U. S. bookstore in town. ‖ MUS. Tuned. ‖ TECHN. Set (sur, in) [diamant]. ‖ THÉÂTR. *Bien montée,* well-staged (pièce). ‖ FAM. *Coup monté,* put-up job, U. S. frame-up ; *être très monté contre,* to have a bitter grudge against, to be down on.

montée f. Going up, ascending (action) ; *la montée est dure,* it is a hard climb. ‖ Slope, gradient (v. CÔTE) ; *en montée,* going up-hill, on the up-grade ; *en haut de la montée,* at the top of the hill. ‖ ARCHIT. Height (d'une voûte). ‖ TECHN. Inflow (des eaux dans un bac) ; up-stroke (d'un piston) ; *tuyau de montée,* uptake pipe, riser. ‖ MÉD. *La montée du lait,* milk-fever. ‖ AVIAT., CH. DE F. *Essai de montée,* climbing test ; *vitesse en montée,* climbing speed. ‖ BOT. Rising.

monter v. intr. (1). To go up, to climb up, to ascend (v. GRAVIR, GRIMPER) ; *monter dans un arbre,* to climb up a tree ; *monter jusqu'au bout de la colline d'un pas tranquille,* (ou) *en courant* (ou) *en soufflant* (ou) *en traînant la jambe,* to walk slowly (ou) to run (ou) to pant (ou) to limp up to the top of the hill ; *monter à une échelle,* to go up (ou) to climb a ladder ; *monter sur les épaules de qqn,* to climb on s.o.'s shoulders ; *monter en toute hâte,* to run up ; *monter en flèche,* to soar, U. S. to skyrocket (fam.) ; *monter se coucher,* to go upstairs to bed ; *faire monter le visiteur,* to ask the caller upstairs. ‖ To mount, to ride ; *monter à bicyclette,* to ride a bicycle ; *monter à cheval,* to ride horseback (chevaucher) ; to mount one's horse (enfourcher) ; *elle monte bien,* she is a good rider. ‖ To slope up (terrain). ‖ To rise (marée, rivière, soleil). ‖ AVIAT. *Monter en avion,* to get into an aeroplane. ‖ ECCLÉS. *Monter en chaire,* to ascend the pulpit. ‖ NAUT. *Monter en bateau,* to get into a boat ; *monter sur un navire,* to go aboard a ship. ‖ AUTOM. *Monter dans* (ou) *en voiture,* to get into a carriage (ou) a car ; *voulez-vous monter dans ma voiture ?,* shall I give you a lift ? ‖ CH. DE F. *Monter dans le train,* to get into the train. ‖ FIN. To amount (à, to) [dépense] ; to rise, U. S. to skyrocket, to zoom (prix) ; *faire monter les prix,* to send up prices. ‖ CULIN. *Le lait monte,* the milk is just on the boil. ‖ MÉD. *Faire monter le sang aux joues de qqn,* to cause s.o. to blush ; *le sang lui monta au visage,* the blood rushed to his face. ‖ FIG. To come to a head (colère). ‖ FIG. To be promoted (personne) ; *[au grade de,* to the rank of]. ‖ FAM. *Faire monter qqn,* to take (ou) U. S. to get a rise out of s.o.
— v. tr. To go up, to climb, to ascend (grimper) ; *monter un escalier,* to climb the stairs ; *monter une pente,* to ascend a slope. ‖ To carry up, to bring up ; *montez-moi mon courrier,* bring my mail up ; *montez cet enfant au lit,* carry this child up to bed ; *se faire monter son dîner,* to have one's dinner brought up to one's room. ‖ To mount, to ride (un cheval) ; to mount (un escadron). ‖ To line, to serve (une chienne) ; to cover, to serve (une jument). ‖ To make (une robe). ‖ To turn up (une mèche de lampe). ‖ To wind up (un mécanisme, une montre, une pendule). ‖ To fit out (organiser) ; *monter une fabrique,* to set up a factory ; *monter un magasin,* to stock (ou) to furnish a shop ; *monter son ménage,* to set up house ; *monter qqn en meubles,* to provide s.o. with furniture. ‖ TECHN. To mount (un bijou,

n hameçon, une photo); to assemble (ou) to put
ogether (ou) to set up (une machine); to hang
une porte). ‖ AUTOM. To fit on (des pneus). ‖
ÉLECTR. To connect up (des piles). ‖ Mus. *Mon-
er de deux tons,* to tune two tones higher. ‖
ARTS. To tone up (la couleur). ‖ COMM. To found,
» build up, to promote (une société). ‖ THÉÂTR.
'o set, to mount (un décor); to stage (une pièce).
FAM. To excite, to urge (qqn); *on lui a monté
à tête contre moi,* they've set him against me;
n vous a monté contre nous, you have been set
ou) egged on against us. ‖ FAM. *Monter le coup
qqn,* to take s.o. in, U. S. to frame s.o.
– v. pr. **Se monter,** to fit oneself out (de, with);
e monter en meubles, to furnish one's house. ‖
'IN. To amount (à, to). ‖ FAM. To get excited;
» raise Cain; *ne vous montez pas pour des riens,*
on't get worked up (ou) go into hysterics over
trifle; *se monter la tête,* to get worked up.

onteur [-tœːr] m. TECHN. Setter (joaillier);
tter (mécanicien); mounter (photographe);
uvrier monteur, erector. ‖ THÉÂTR. Stager, pro-
ucer; film-editor (ou) -cutter. ‖ COMM. Promoter.

ontgolfière [mõgɔlfjɛːr] f. AVIAT. Montgolfier
alloon.

onticule [mõtikyl] m. Hillock, monticule, knoll,
10und, hummock. (V. BUTTE.)

ontmartrois, oise [mõmartrwa, aːz] adj.
iÉOGR. Of (ou) from Montmartre.
– s. GÉOGR. Native (ou) inhabitant of Mont-
1artre.

ontmorency [mõmɔrãsi] f. BOT. Sour (ou)
Iontmorency cherry.

ontoir [mõtwaːr] m. Horse-block.

ontrable [mõtrabl] adj. Fit to be shown.

ontre [mõtr] f. Show, display (apparat); *faire
1ontre de sa richesse,* to show off one's wealth.
OMM. Shop-window (étalage); *mettre en montre,*
» put in the shop-window; to display in a show-
ase. ‖ Watch (chronomètre); *montre à double
oîtier,* hunter; *montre à répétition,* repeater; *dix
eures et demie à ma montre,* half past ten by my
atch; *une heure, montre en main,* an hour by
1e clock. ‖ Mus. Front (d'un orgue). ‖ NAUT.
fficier des montres, navigator. ‖ SPORTS. *Course
ontre la montre,* time race. ‖ FIG. *Faire montre
e,* to display. ‖ **Montre-bracelet,** f. Wrist-watch.

ontréal [mõreal] f. GÉOGR. Montreal.

ontréalais, aise [-lɛ, ɛːz] adj. GÉOGR. Of (ou)
om Montréal.
– s. GÉOGR. Montrealer.

ontrer [-tre] v. tr. (1). To show, to display, to
xhibit (faire voir). ‖ To show, to indicate (indi-
uer); *montrer le chemin à qqn,* to show s.o. the
ay. ‖ To show, to manifest, to evince (mani-
ester); *montrer du courage,* to show courage;
1ontrez-lui ce que vous valez,* show him your
nettle. ‖ To teach (enseigner); *montrer la manière
e faire,* to teach how to do it. ‖ FAM. *Se faire
1ontrer la porte,* to be turned out.
– v. pr. **Se montrer,** to show oneself, to make
n appearance; to appear (apparaître); *le pape
e montra à sa fenêtre,* the Pope appeared at his
'indow. ‖ To show oneself, to prove, to turn
ut (se révéler); *se montrer accommodant,* to
rove accommodating; *se montrer lamentable,*
» cut a sorry figure.

ontreur [-trœːr] m. Showman; *montreur d'ours,*
ear-leader.

ontueux, euse [mõtɥø, øːz] adj. Hilly.

onture [mõtyːr] f. Mount (animal). ‖ Mount-
1g, fitting up, assembling (ajustage). ‖ Tackle
pour la pêche). ‖ Setting (d'une bague); stock
l'un fusil); frame (de lunettes, de parapluie);
1ounting (d'une photo, d'un tableau); *à monture
'écaille,* shell-rimmed; *sans monture,* rimless
unettes).

monument [mɔnymã] m. Monument, memorial.
‖ Monument, building (bâtiment); *monuments
historiques,* ancient monuments; *les monuments
publics,* public buildings, the sights.

monumental, ale [mɔnymãtal] adj. Monumental.
‖ FAM. Colossal.

moque [mɔk] f. NAUT. Bull's-eye.

moquer [mɔke] v. tr. (1). † To mock.
– v. pr. **Se moquer,** to mock (ou) to scoff, to
laugh (de, at); to make fun (de, of) [v. RAILLER];
se faire moquer de soi, to get laughed at, to
become a laughing-stock. ‖ FAM. *Je m'en moque
comme de ma première chemise,* I don't care a
tinker's cuss; U. S. I don't give a tinker's damn;
vous vous moquez, je suppose!, you are joking!;
se moquer du monde, to have a confounded cheek
(ou) U. S. nerve.

moquerie [mɔkri] f. Mockery, scoffing, ridicule
(v. RAILLERIE); *par moquerie,* mockingly.

moquette [mɔkɛt] f. Decoy bird (oiseau).

moquette f. Moquette, carpeting.

moqueur, euse [mɔkœːr, øːz] adj. Mocking;
jeering (remarque); derisive (rire). ‖ Sarcastic,
waggish, ironical (personne).
– s. Mocker, derider, scoffer. ‖ ZOOL. Mocking-
bird.

moqueusement [-køzmã] adv. Mockingly.

moraine [mɔrɛn] f. GÉOGR. Moraine.

morainique [-nik] adj. GÉOGR. Morainal,
morainic.

moral, ale [mɔral] adj. Moral (loi, sens). ‖ Moral
(certitude, courage); mental (facultés). ‖ Moral
(écrit, influence). ‖ COMM. *Rapport moral,* secretary's report.
– m. Mind, moral faculties (moralité). ‖ Morale,
spirits (confiance en soi); *bon moral,* good
morale; *son moral est bas,* his spirits are low.

morale [mɔraːl] f. Morals (v. ÉTHIQUE); *acte
que la morale réprouve,* act condemned by the
moral law (ou) contrary to good morals. ‖ Advice,
lecture (conseils); *faire de la morale à,* to lecture.
‖ Moral (d'une fable, d'un récit).

moralement [mɔralmã] adv. Morally, honestly.
‖ Morally, virtually, practically (intuitivement).

moralisant, ante [-lizã, ãːt] adj. Moralizing.

moralisateur, trice [-lizatœːr, tris] adj. Moralizing (personne); elevating (principe).
– s. Moralizer.

moralisation [-lizasjõ] f. Moralization.

moraliser [-lize] v. tr. (1). To moralize.
– v. pr. **Se moraliser,** to rise to a higher moral
level.

moraliste [-list] m. Moralist.
– adj. Moralist, moralistic.

moralité [-lite] f. Morality (d'un acte). ‖ Morality,
morals (d'une personne); *d'une moralité impeccable,* of unimpeachable character; *que pensez-
vous de sa moralité?,* what do you think of his
honesty?; *sans moralité,* devoid of morals.

morasse [mɔras] f. Brush-proof; U. S. galley-proof.

moratoire [mɔratwaːr] adj. JUR. Moratory, post-
poned; *intérêts moratoires,* interest on overdue
payments.
– m. Moratorium.

morave [mɔraːv] adj., s. GÉOGR., ECCLÉS.
Moravian.

Moravie [mɔravi] f. GÉOGR. Moravia.

morbide [mɔrbid] adj. Morbid (maladif);
unhealthy (malsain).

morbidesse [-dɛs] f. Languor, languid grace. ‖
ARTS. Morbidezza, delicacy in flesh-tints.

morbidité [-dite] f. Morbidity, morbidness.

morbleu [mɔrblø] interj. † Zounds!, Ye gods!

morceau [mɔrso] m. Bit, piece (d'étoffe); piece
(de bois). ‖ Piece (d'un objet brisé); *se casser
en morceaux,* to fall to pieces; *mettre qqch. en
morceaux,* to break sth. into pieces. ‖ *Morceaux*

choisis de, selections from. ‖ CULIN. Helping (de gâteau) ; morsel, bit, piece, chunk (de pain) ; cut (de rôti) ; lump (de sucre) ; *c'est un morceau de roi,* it's a dainty tit-bit (ou) U. S. tid-bit, it's fit for a king ; *manger un morceau,* to have a snack ; *sucre en morceaux,* lump sugar. ‖ MUS. Piece of music ; *jouez-nous un morceau,* play sth. for us ; *morceau à deux voix,* two-part song. ‖ FAM. *Avoir qqch. pour un morceau de pain,* to get sth. for a song ; *gober le morceau,* to swallow the bait, to fall for it ; *manger le morceau,* to blow the gaff ; U. S. to spill the beans ; *n'en faire qu'un morceau,* to swallow it all at one gulp.

morceler [mɔrsəle] v. tr. (5). To break up, to parcel out (une propriété). ‖ To carve up (un pays vaincu).

morcellement [-sɛlmɑ̃] m. Cutting up, parcelling out.

mordache [mɔrdaʃ] f. TECHN. Clamp, claw.

mordacité [mɔrdasite] f. CHIM. Corrosiveness, mordacity. ‖ FIG. Mordancy, causticity.

mordant, ante [-dɑ̃, ɑ̃:t] adj. CHIM. Corrosive (acide). ‖ TECHN. Sharp (lime, scie). ‖ FIG. Biting, sharp, caustic, pungent (paroles) ; trenchant, pointed, keen (sarcasme) ; scathing, stinging (trait). — m. Tartness (d'un goût) ; pungency (d'une odeur). ‖ Mordant (teinture, vernis). ‖ CHIM. Corrosiveness (d'un acide). ‖ MILIT. Dash, keenness, vigour (d'une troupe). ‖ SPORTS. Fighting spirit, aggressiveness. ‖ MUS. Mordent. ‖ FIG. Sharpness, pointedness, trenchancy, sting.

mordeur, euse [-dœ:r, ø:z] adj. Biting. — s. Biter.

mordicus [mɔrdikys] adv. FAM. Stubbornly, doggedly, tenaciously ; *soutenir une opinion mordicus,* to stick to one's guns.

mordienne [mɔrdjɛn], **mordieu** [-djø] interj. † Zounds !

mordillage [mɔrdija:ʒ], **mordillement** [-dijmɑ̃] m. Nibbling.

mordiller [mɔrdije] v. tr. (1). To pretend to bite, to bite playfully (jeune chien). ‖ To nibble (grignoter).

mordoré, ée [mɔrdɔre] adj. Golden-brown, bronze-coloured ; *poterie mordorée,* lustre ware.

mordorer v. tr. (1). To bronze.

mordorure [mɔrdɔry:r] f. Bronze finish.

mordre [mɔrdr] v. tr. (4). To bite (animal) ; *essayer de mordre,* to snap at ; *mordre qqn à la main,* to bite s.o.'s hand. ‖ To nip (froid). ‖ CHIM. To eat into (acide). ‖ TECHN. To bite into (lime, scie, vis). ‖‖ FIG. To bite, to sting, to burn (colère, parole, remarque) ; *mordu par la fureur,* stung to fury ; *mordre la poussière,* to bite the dust ; *s'en mordre les doigts,* to kick oneself about it ; *se mordre les lèvres,* to bite one's lips. — v. intr. To bite (*dans,* into). ‖ NAUT. To bite ; *l'ancre a mordu,* the anchor has gripped (ou) held. ‖ SPORTS. To bite (poisson) ; *ça a mordu,* I've got a bite. ‖ ARCHIT. To overlap (tuiles). ‖ COMM. To encroach (*sur,* on) [transactions]. ‖ TECHN. To catch (engrenage). ‖ ARTS. To etch (acide des graveurs). ‖ FAM. To take (à, to) ; *ne pas mordre au grec,* to find Greek very hard going.

mordu, ue [-dy] adj. FAM. Mad (*de,* on, about). — s. FAM. Fan.

more [mɔ:r] adj., s. V. MAURE.

morelle [mɔrɛl] f. BOT. Morel.

moresque [mɔrɛsk] adj., s. V. MAURESQUE.

morfil [mɔrfil] m. TECHN. Wire-edge.

morfiler [-file] v. tr. (1). TECHN. To remove the wire-edge from.

morfondre [mɔrfɔ̃dr] v. tr. (4). To freeze, to chill to the bone. — v. pr. **Se morfondre,** to feel dejected (ou) melancholy. ‖ To kick one's heels (en attendant).

morganatique [mɔrganatik] adj. Morganatic.

morgue [mɔrg] f. Arrogance, haughtiness, stan offishness ; *la morgue littéraire,* the pomposi of literary men.

morgue f. Mortuary ; U. S. morgue.

moribond, onde [mɔribɔ̃, ɔ̃:d] adj. Moribun dying, at death's door. — s. Dying person. (V. AGONISANT, MOURANT.)

moricaud, aude [mɔriko, o:d] adj. Dark-skinne dusky. — s. Blackamoor ; darky (fam.).

morigéner [mɔriʒene] v. tr. (5). To lecture, take to task, to rate, to give a good talking (o ticking-off to. (V. RÉPRIMANDER.)

morille [mɔri:j] f. BOT. Morel.

morillon [mɔrijɔ̃] m. Rough emerald (pierre). BOT. Morillon. ‖ ZOOL. Mussel-duck.

mormon, one [mɔrmɔ̃, ɔn] adj. Mormon. — s. Mormon ; Latter-day-Saint.

mormonisme [-mɔnism] m. ECCLÉS. Mo monism.

morne [mɔrn] adj. Dismal, cheerless (avenir dejected, doleful, despondent (personne) ; ble (plaine) ; gloomy (silence).

morne m. Hillock, knoll. (V. BUTTE.)

mornifle [mɔrnifl] f. FAM. Bump.

morose [mɔrɔ:z] adj. Gloomy, forbidding (aspe visage) ; morose, sullen, surly (personne).

morosité [-zite] f. Moroseness.

Morphée [mɔrfe] m. Morpheus.

morphème [mɔrfɛm] m. GRAMM. Morpheme.

morphine [mɔrfin] f. MÉD. Morphine, morphi

morphinomane [-nɔman] m. MÉD. Morphinom niac, morphia (ou) morphine addict.

morphinomanie [-nɔmani] f MÉD. Morphir addiction, morphinism.

morphisme [mɔrfism] m. MATH. Morphism.

morphologie [mɔrfɔlɔʒi] f. Morphology.

morphologique [-ʒik] adj. Morphological.

morpion [mɔrpjɔ̃] m. MÉD. Crab-louse, crab. POP. Brat.

mors [mɔ:r] m. Bit ; *prendre le mors aux den* to bolt (cheval). ‖ TECHN. Jaw (d'un étau). ‖ FA *Prendre le mors aux dents,* to take the bit in on teeth (personne).

morse [mɔrs] m. ZOOL. Walrus, sea-cow, mor

morse m. Morse (télégraphie).

morsure [mɔrsy:r] f. Bite (avec les dents). CHIM. Biting (d'un acide). ‖ TECHN. Biting (d' étau). ‖ FIG. Stings (de la calomnie) ; gnawin (de la faim) ; nip (du froid).

mort, orte [mɔ:r, ɔ:rt] p. p. Died. (V. MOURI — adj. Dead (sans vie) ; *morte la bête, mort venin,* dead dogs don't bite ; *être plus mort q vif,* to be more dead than alive ; *il y a une semai qu'elle est morte,* she has been dead a week, s died a week ago ; *tomber raide mort,* to fall sto dead. ‖ Dead (sans vigueur) ; *arriver au poi mort,* to come to a standstill (ou) to a deadloc *doigts morts,* numb (ou) dead fingers. ‖ AGR Bois mort, dead wood. ‖ COMM. *Marché mo* dead market. ‖ ARTS. *Nature morte,* still lif *feuille-morte,* dead-leaf (couleur). ‖ AUTOM. *point mort,* into neutral ; *point mort,* neutral ge ‖ AVIAT. *Descente en feuille morte,* falling-le roll. ‖ MILIT. *Balle morte,* spent bullet. ‖ NAU Still. stagnant (eau) ; upper (œuvres). ‖ SPORT *Ballon mort,* dead (ou) out-of-play ball. ‖ TECH *Poids mort,* dead load (ou) weight ; *point mo* bottom dead centre. ‖ GÉOGR. *La mer Morte,* t Dead Sea. ‖ FIG. *Devenir lettre morte,* to becom a dead letter ; *langues mortes,* dead language *mort de fatigue,* dog-tired ; dead-beat, U. bushed ; *un trou à moitié mort,* a dull dum (localité). — s. Dead person ; *faire le mort,* to sham dea to play possum (fam.) ; *pâle comme un mort,* white as a sheet. ‖ Dummy (aux cartes) ; *faire*

mort, to be dummy. ‖ ECCLÉS. *Jour des morts,* All Souls Day ; *l'office des morts,* the service for the dead ; *ressuscité d'entre les morts,* risen from the dead. ‖ MILIT. *Morts et blessés,* dead and wounded, casualties. ‖ CULIN. *Tête de mort,* Dutch cheese (fromage). ‖ FIG. *Faire le mort,* to lie low, to play possum.
— f. Death ; *à mort les traîtres!,* death to the traitors! ; *attraper la mort,* to catch one's death, to run the risk of death ; *être à l'article de la mort,* to be at the point of death (ou) at death's door (ou) on the verge of death ; *fidèle jusqu'à la mort,* faithful unto death ; *mourir de mort accidentelle,* to die accidentally (ou) an accidental death ; *mourir de sa belle mort,* to die a natural death (ou) in one's bed ; *semblable à la mort,* death-like ; *silence de mort,* dead (ou) deathly silence. ‖ JUR. *Arrêt de mort,* death sentence ; *condamner à mort,* to sentence (ou) to condemn to death. ‖ MILIT. *Blessé à mort,* mortally wounded ; *combat à mort,* fight to the death ; *il n'y a pas eu mort d'hommes,* no one was killed ; there were no casualties. ‖ ECCLÉS. *Faire une bonne mort,* to die a Christian death. ‖ FIG. *Avoir la mort dans l'âme,* to be sick at heart ; *ennemis à mort,* deadly (ou) mortal enemies ; *germes de mort,* germs of decay ; *il a la mort dans l'âme,* the iron has entered into his soul. ‖ **Mort-aux-rats,** f. invar. Ratsbane, rat-poison. ‖ **Morte-eau,** f. Neap-tide. ‖ **Morte-saison,** f. Dead season. ‖ **Mort-né** (pl. *mort-nés*), adj. Still-born (enfant) ; foredoomed to miscarry, U. S. stillborn (projet).

mortadelle [mɔrtadɛl] f. CULIN. Bologna sausage.
mortaisage [mɔrtɛza:ʒ] m. Mortising.
mortaise [-tɛ:z] f. Mortise. ‖ NAUT. Key-hole.
mortaiser [-tɛze] v. tr. (1). To mortise.
mortalité [mɔrtalite] f. Mortality, mortal nature. ‖ Mortality ; *mortalité infantile,* infant mortality. ‖ Mortality, number of deaths (fréquence des morts) ; *tables de mortalité,* mortality tables ; *taux de mortalité,* death-rate.
mortel, elle [mɔrtɛl] adj. Mortal (sujet à la mort) ; *dépouille mortelle,* mortal remains. ‖ Mortal, deadly (causant la mort) ; *accident mortel,* fatal accident ; *blessure mortelle,* mortal wound. ‖ Mortal, deadly (cruel) ; deathly (de mort) ; *douleur mortelle,* mortal pain ; *d'une pâleur mortelle,* deathly pale. ‖ Mortal, deadly (haineux) ; *ennemi mortel,* mortal enemy ; *haine mortelle,* deadly hatred. ‖ PHYS. *Rayon mortel,* death ray. ‖ FAM. Weary, wearying, deadly (ennuyeux) ; *attente mortelle,* trying delay ; *pendant cinq heures mortelles,* for five mortal hours.
— s. Mortal ; *un heureux mortel,* a fortunate mortal ; *les mortels,* mortals, mortal beings.
mortellement [-tɛlmɑ̃] adv. Mortally, fatally. ‖ FAM. *S'ennuyer mortellement,* to be bored to death.
morticole [-tikɔl] m. FAM. Saw-bones.
mortier [mɔrtje] m. ARCHIT. Mortar ; *mortier liquide,* grout. ‖ MÉD. Mortar. ‖ ECCLÉS. Cap. ‖ MILIT. Mortar.
mortifiant, ante [mɔrtifjɑ̃, ɑ̃:t] adj. Mortifying.
mortification [-fikasjɔ̃] f. MÉD. Mortification, necrosis. ‖ ECCLÉS. Mortification. ‖ CULIN. Hanging (du gibier) ; keeping (de la viande). ‖ FIG. Mortification. (V. HUMILIATION.)
mortifié, ée [-fje] adj. Mortified.
mortifier [-fje] v. tr. (1). MÉD. To gangrene. ‖ CULIN. To keep, to hang (la viande). ‖ ECCLÉS. To mortify. ‖ FIG. To mortify. (V. HUMILIER.)
— v. pr. **Se mortifier.** MÉD. To mortify. ‖ ECCLÉS., FIG. To mortify oneself.
mortinatalité [mɔrtinatalite] f. Rate of still births.
mortuaire [mɔrtɥɛ:r] adj. Mortuary ; *avis mor-*

tuaire, announcement of death, death notice ; *chambre mortuaire,* death-chamber ; *drap mortuaire,* pall ; *maison mortuaire,* house of the deceased ; *service mortuaire,* burial service.
morue [mɔry] f. ZOOL. Cod ; *huile de foie de morue,* cod-liver oil. ‖ POP. Tart, U. S. slut (femme).
morutier, ère [-tje, ɛ:r] adj. Cod-fishing.
— m. Cod-fishing boat (bateau) ; cod-fisherman (marin).
morve [mɔrv] f. Nasal mucus ; snot (fam.) [de l'homme]. ‖ Glanders (du cheval). ‖ BOT. Rot (de la laitue).
morveux, euse [-vø, ø:z] adj. Snotty ; *être morveux,* to snivel.
— s. FAM. Whipper-snapper (freluquet).
mosaïque [mɔzaik] f. ARTS. Mosaic. ‖ RADIO. Test-card.
mosaïque adj. Mosaic (loi).
mosaïste [-zaist] m. ARTS. Mosaic-maker.
Moscou [mɔsku] f. GÉOGR. Moscow.
moscovite [-kɔvit] adj., s. GÉOGR. Muscovite.
mosquée [mɔske] f. Mosque.
mot [mo] m. Word (parole) ; *à ces mots,* thereupon ; *en d'autres mots,* in other words ; *en un mot,* in a word, briefly ; *gros mots,* bad (ou) coarse language ; *mot historique,* historical (ou) memorable saying ; *mot-à-mot,* word-for-word (traduction) ; *ne plus dire un mot,* to cease to speak ; to shut up (fam.) ; *sans mot dire,* without a word. ‖ Word (élément de la connaissance) ; *ne pas savoir le premier mot de la physique,* not to have the least smattering of physics ; *ne pas savoir un traître mot d'anglais,* not to know a single word of English. ‖ Word (explication) ; *j'aurais un mot à vous dire,* I'd like a word with you ; *je vais lui en dire un mot,* I will speak to him about it, I'll give him a piece of my mind ; *parler à mots couverts,* to hint about, to allude to. ‖ Word, key (révélation) ; *avoir le fin mot,* to be in the know, to see through the whole thing ; *le fin mot de l'affaire,* the first and last of it ; *c'est le mot de l'énigme,* it is the key to the mystery (ou) riddle ; *vous avez dit le mot,* you have thrown light on the matter. ‖ Word, war of words (discussion) ; *avoir le dernier mot,* to have the last word, to have the best of it ; *avoir des mots avec qqn,* to have words with s.o. ; to fall out with s.o. ; *échanger des mots vifs avec qqn,* to exchange words with s.o. ; *n'avoir pas un mot entre soi,* not to have a cross word. ‖ Word, aid (soutien) ; *dire un mot pour qqn,* to say something in s.o.'s favour ; to back s.o. up, to lend countenance to s.o. ‖ Word, note, letter (billet) ; *envoyer un mot à,* to send a note to, to drop a line to ; *recevoir un mot de,* to have a few lines from. ‖ Witticism, joke (plaisanterie) ; *il a le mot pour rire,* he has a good sense of humour, he always has sth. funny to say ; *bon mot,* witticism, witty remark, smart saying, U. S. wisecrack (fam.) ; *faire des mots,* to be witty, to crack jokes, to play the wag ; *jouer sur les mots,* to play on words. ‖ Instructions ; *aller prendre le mot chez qqn,* to go to s.o. for instructions ; *donner le mot à,* to give the word to ; *mot d'ordre,* key-word, key-note ; watch-word, slogan ; shibboleth (d'un parti) ; *se donner le mot,* to pass the word on. ‖ *Mots croisés,* cross-word puzzle. ‖ MILIT. Watch-word, pass-word (consigne). ‖ COMM. Word, estimate, figure (estimation) ; *au bas mot,* at the lowest estimate ; *est-ce votre dernier mot?,* is that your final offer? ‖ CULIN. *Dire deux mots au rôti,* to tuck into the joint, to cut into the roast. ‖ FIG. *Comprendre à demi-mot,* to take the hint, to be quick on the uptake (fam.) ; *prendre qqn au mot,* to take s.o. at his word. ‖ LOC. *C'est le mot,* that's just it ; *tranchons le mot,* let us have it out, let us put it plainly ; *voilà le*

abstracted	distrait, inattentif
abuse	injurier, dénigrer
acceptation	acception (d'un mot)
accost	racoler
achieve	accomplir, réaliser
actual	véritable, effectif
actually	en réalité, en fait
adept	expert (en)
advertisement	annonce, réclame
affluent	opulent, riche
agenda	ordre du jour
agreeable (to be)	consentant, d'accord (être)
alien	étranger
alienation	brouille, éloignement
anxious	impatient, désireux
apologetic	qui contient des excuses
apparel	vêtements, habillements
appointment	nomination, rendez-vous
appreciation	évaluation, augmentation
assumption	affectation ; hypothèse
attend	accompagner, assister à
auditor	vérificateur de comptes
balance	équilibre ; restant
beldame	vieille femme
billion	trillion (en Angleterre)
billion	milliard (aux Etats-Unis)
blemish	abîmer, gâter, défigurer
bless	bénir, rendre heureux
blouse	corsage, chemisier
brigadier	général (de brigade)
brutalize	abrutir, dégrader
candid	franc, sincère, impartial
canteen	bidon de soldat
cargo	chargement, cargaison
castor-oil	huile de ricin
chandelier	lustre
chemist	pharmacien ; chimiste
chord	accord
combine	trust, cartel
commodious	spacieux, vaste
comprehensive	complet
confections	confiseries
confident	confiant, convaincu
crapulous	ivre, adonné à l'ivrognerie
cynical	sceptique, sarcastique, caustique
deception	tromperie, fraude
deliberately	lentement ; avec réflexion
deride	railler, se moquer de
destitution	misère
dilapidated	dépenaillé, délabré
draper	marchand de nouveautés
editor	rédacteur en chef
educated (well)	instruit, cultivé
endive	chicorée (frisée)
enervated	affaibli, sans vigueur
engineer	1º ingénieur ; 2º soldat du génie
engross	absorber, accaparer
epicure	gourmet
extenuate	diminuer, atténuer
fastidious	exigeant, difficile
female	femme ; féminin (non péjor.)
figure	ensemble du corps ; silhouette, ligne
fresh water	eau douce, eau non salée
furniture	meubles
genial	jovial, cordial, sympathique
grange	château, manoir
indifferently	avec indifférence ; médiocrement
indulge	céder à ; s'abandonner à
ingenuity	habileté, ingéniosité
ingenuousness	ingénuité, sincérité
injure	blesser, détériorer
invalid	1º souffrant ; 2º invalide
journey	voyage (voir VOYAGE)
large	grand, gros (jamais large)
lastly	finalement
library	bibliothèque
location	emplacement, position
lubricity	onctuosité ; inconstance ; lubricité
luxurious, luxury	luxueux, luxe
malicious	malveillant, méchant
mercer	marchand de nouveautés
miscreant	misérable, gredin
moral	la morale (d'une histoire)
morale	le moral (des troupes)
morals	les mœurs
mystify	embarrasser ; troubler
neat	pur ; élégant, joli
novel	roman
officer	fonctionnaire ; officier
oil	pétrole ; huile
ostensible ; ostensibly	feint ; prétendument
pair of stairs (a)	étage (un)
pamphlet	brochure, opuscule
panel	panneau ; liste des jurés, jury
parents	le père et la mère
pass (exam)	être reçu (examen)
passion	douleur ; colère
patron	client habituel ; saint patron
pedestrian (adj.)	pédestre ; vulgaire
perverse	entêté ; revêche, acariâtre
petrol	essence
petulant	irritable, susceptible
phrase	locution ; membre de phrase
physic	médecine ; drogue
physician	médecin
plain	simple, clair ; sans charme
plume	panache
poignant	piquant (propre et fig.)
portmanteau	valise
prejudice	préjugé ; préjudice
presently	bientôt (jamais à présent)
pretend	feindre, prétendre
prevarication	équivoque, faux-fuyant
privy (adj.)	secret, caché, clandestin
procurer	entremetteur
profane	grossier, mal embouché
propriety	convenance, bienséance
provoking	agaçant, impatientant
prune	pruneau sec
publisher	éditeur (v. EDITOR)
raisins	raisins secs
refuse	ordures, détritus
relations	parents ; rapports.
resume	reprendre, recommencer
route	itinéraire, ordre de marche
saucer	soucoupe
savour	odeur, parfum, arôme
scabrous	rugueux ; raboteux
sequestration	séparation, isolement
sot	ivrogne invétéré
sporting (adj.)	d'esprit sportif
sportsman (sens pr.)	amateur de chevaux, de chasse, de pêche
stable	écurie
surname	nom de famille
sympathetic	compatissant, compréhensif
talon	serres ; griffes (de fauve)
terrace	rangée de maisons identiques
traduce	calomnier, dénigrer
trivial	insignifiant ; sans intérêt
truculent	féroce, brutal
umbrella	parapluie
uncompromising	intraitable, intransigeant
unmoved	immobile, inexorable
variance	discorde, différend
versatile	souple ; très varié
vest	gilet ; tricot, maillot de corps
viand	mets, aliments
vicar	curé, pasteur (dans l'Eglise anglicane)
vicious	méchant, haineux ; rigoureux
villain	scélérat, coquin
vindication	défense, apologie
virtually	effectivement, en fait
voyage	voyage en bateau
wag(g)on	chariot, charrette
zest	1º saveur, plaisir ; 2º zeste

grand mot lâché, the cat is out of the bag. ‖ **Mot-souche**, n. Head-word, catchword.

motard [mɔta:r] m. FAM. Motorcyclist (motocycliste); courtesy cop, U. S. motorcycle cop (policier).

motel [mɔtɛl] m. Motel.

motet [mɔtɛ] m. Mus. Motet.

moteur, trice [mɔtœ:r, tris] adj. Motive, driving (arbre, force, roue); *appareil moteur*, driving machinery; *force motrice*, driving power; *unité motrice*, power unit. ‖ MÉD. Motor, motory. — m. PHILOS. Mover. (V. MOBILE.) ‖ TECHN. Motor, engine; *moteur à deux ou quatre temps, à essence, à explosion, à gaz, à pétrole, à réaction*, two- (ou) four-stroke, petrol (ou) U. S. gasoline, internal combustion, gas, oil, jet engine; *moteur électrique, fixe, rotatif, sans soupapes*, electric, stationary, rotary, sleeve-valve engine. ‖ FIG. Instigator.

motif [mɔtif] m. Motive (V. CAUSE, MOBILE); *avoir un motif pour faire qqch.*, to have a motive for doing sth.; *motif d'espérance*, reason to hope; *pour le bon motif*, for an honest purpose; *sans motif*, gratuitously, without good reason. ‖ Pattern, design (de broderie); ornament, trimming (en couture). ‖ JUR. Charge; *motifs d'un jugement*, grounds for a judgment. ‖ ARTS. Motif; *motifs de bijouterie*, jewellery motifs. ‖ Mus. Theme, motif; U. S. motive.

motilité [mɔtilite] f. Motility.

motion [mɔsjɔ̃] f. Motion (proposition); *motion de censure*, motion of censure; *présenter une motion pour que*, to move that.

motivant, ante [mɔtivã, ã:t] adj. Motivating, stimulating, incentive.

motivation [-vasjɔ̃] f. Justification (d'un acte). ‖ PSYCH. Motivation. ‖ FIN. *Etude de motivation*, motivational research.

motivé, ée [mɔtive] adj. Justified, considered (opinion); *avis motivé*, counsel's advice; *non motivé*, unjustified, unwarranted. ‖ JUR. Based on specific reasons; *motivé par*, owing to.

motiver v. tr. (1). To justify, to warrant (justifier); to cause, to bring about (causer); to motivate, to stimulate (stimuler). ‖ JUR. To state the reasons for (un arrêt, une décision).

moto [mɔto] f. FAM. Motor-bike; *à moto*, on a motor-bike.

motocross [-krɔs] m. SPORTS. Motocross.

motoculteur [-kyltœ:r] m. AGRIC. Cultivator.

motoculture [-kylty:r] f. AGRIC. Mechanized farming.

motocycle [-sikl] m. Motor bicycle.

motocyclette [-siklɛt] f. Motor-bicycle; *à motocyclette*, on a motor-cycle.

motocyclisme [-siklism] m. Motorcycling; motorcycle racing.

motocycliste [-siklist] s. Motor-cyclist.

motoglisseur [-glisœ:r] m. NAUT. Speed-boat.

motogodille [-gɔdi:j] m. NAUT. Motor-driven scull.

motonautique [-notik] adj. NAUT. Motor-boat.

motonautisme [-notism] m. NAUT. Motorboating; motorboat racing.

motopompe [-pɔ̃:p] f. Motor-pump.

motorisation [-risasjɔ̃] f. Motorization.

motorisé, ée [-rize] adj. MILIT. Motorized. ‖ FAM. *Etre motorisé*, to have transport.

motoriser [-rize] v. tr. (1). To motorize.

motrice [mɔtris] f. CH. DE F. Motor-carriage.

motricité [-site] f. MÉD. Motor functions.

motte [mɔt] f. Pat, block (de beurre). ‖ Turf (de gazon); clod, lump (de terre).

motter [mɔte] v. tr. (1). To throw clods at. — v. pr. Se motter, to hide behind a clod, to clod.

motus [mɔtys] interj. Mum's the word!

mou [mu] (f. **molle** [mɔl]) adj. Soft (en général). ‖ Soft (col, chemise). ‖ Muggy (temps); squashy,

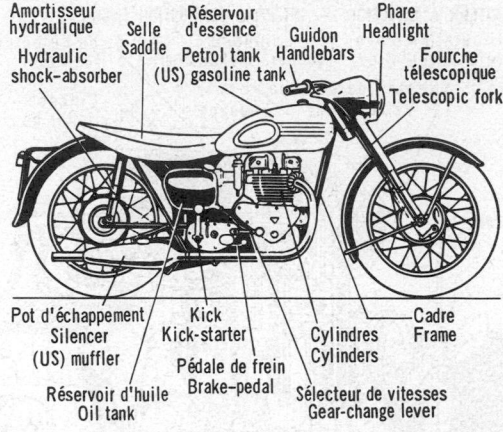

Amortisseur hydraulique — Hydraulic shock-absorber

Selle — Saddle

Réservoir d'essence — Petrol tank (US) gasoline tank

Guidon — Handlebars

Phare — Headlight

Fourche télescopique — Telescopic fork

Pot d'échappement Silencer (US) muffler

Kick — Kick-starter

Pédale de frein — Brake-pedal

Réservoir d'huile — Oil tank

Cylindres — Cylinders

Cadre — Frame

Sélecteur de vitesses — Gear-change lever

soggy, muddy (terrain). ‖ Flabby, flaccid, limp (chairs). ‖ PHYS. Soft (rayons). ‖ MÉD. Soft (chancre). ‖ NAUT. Light (brise); slack (cordage); smooth (mer). ‖ ARTS. Woolly, flabby (dessin); flat (pinceau). ‖ FIG. Feeble, relaxed, languid (effort); lax, flabby, indolent, spineless, slothful, listless (personne); lax, soft (vie); lax, languid, half-hearted (zèle). — m. NAUT. Slack; *donner, prendre du mou*, to slacken.

mou m. Lights, lungs (de veau).

mouchard [muʃa:r] m. FAM. Sneak, tell-tale, tattle-tale (à l'école). ‖ FAM. Police-spy, informer, U. S. stool-pigeon, canary (indicateur). ‖ TECHN. Black box (d'un camion, d'un avion).

mouchardage [muʃarda:ʒ] m. FAM. Squealing, grassing.

moucharder [-de] v. tr. (1). FAM. To spy on (espionner); to blab, to squeal on (rapporter).

mouche [muʃ] f. ZOOL. Fly; *mouche commune*, house-fly; *mouche à miel*, bee; *mouche à viande* (ou) *à vers*, blow-fly; *taché par les mouches*, fly-blown, fly-specked. ‖ Patch (sur la joue d'une femme); tuft of hair (sur le menton d'un homme). ‖ NAUT. Advice-boat (d'escadre); *bateau-mouche*, river-steamer. ‖ SPORTS. Button-cover (de fleuret); fly (à la pêche); bull's-eye (au tir); *pêche à la mouche noyée, sèche*, wet-fly, dry-fly fishing; *faire mouche au tir*, to hit the bull's eye, to score a hit; *poids mouche*, fly-weight (à la boxe). ‖ MÉD. *Mouches volantes*, muscae volitantes, floating specks, spots before the eyes. ‖ LOC. *Faire d'une mouche un éléphant*, to make a mountain out of a mole-hill; *fine mouche*, sly minx (femme); *slick customer* (homme); *la mouche du coche*, a busybody; *on aurait entendu voler une mouche*, you could have heard a pin drop; *on prend plus de mouches avec du miel qu'avec du vinaigre*, honey catches more flies than vinegar; *prendre la mouche*, to fly into a temper, to take offence, to get huffy; *quelle mouche vous pique?*, what's biting you?

moucher [muʃe] v. tr. (1). To wipe, to blow (son nez); to wipe (ou) to blow the nose of (un enfant); *moucher du sang*, to bring blood in blowing one's nose. ‖ To snuff, to trim (une chandelle). ‖ NAUT. To cut off the frayed end of (un cordage). ‖ TECHN. To square up the end of (une pièce de bois). ‖ FAM. *Moucher qqn*, to put s.o. in his place; *il a été mouché de la belle*

MOTEURS — MOTORS

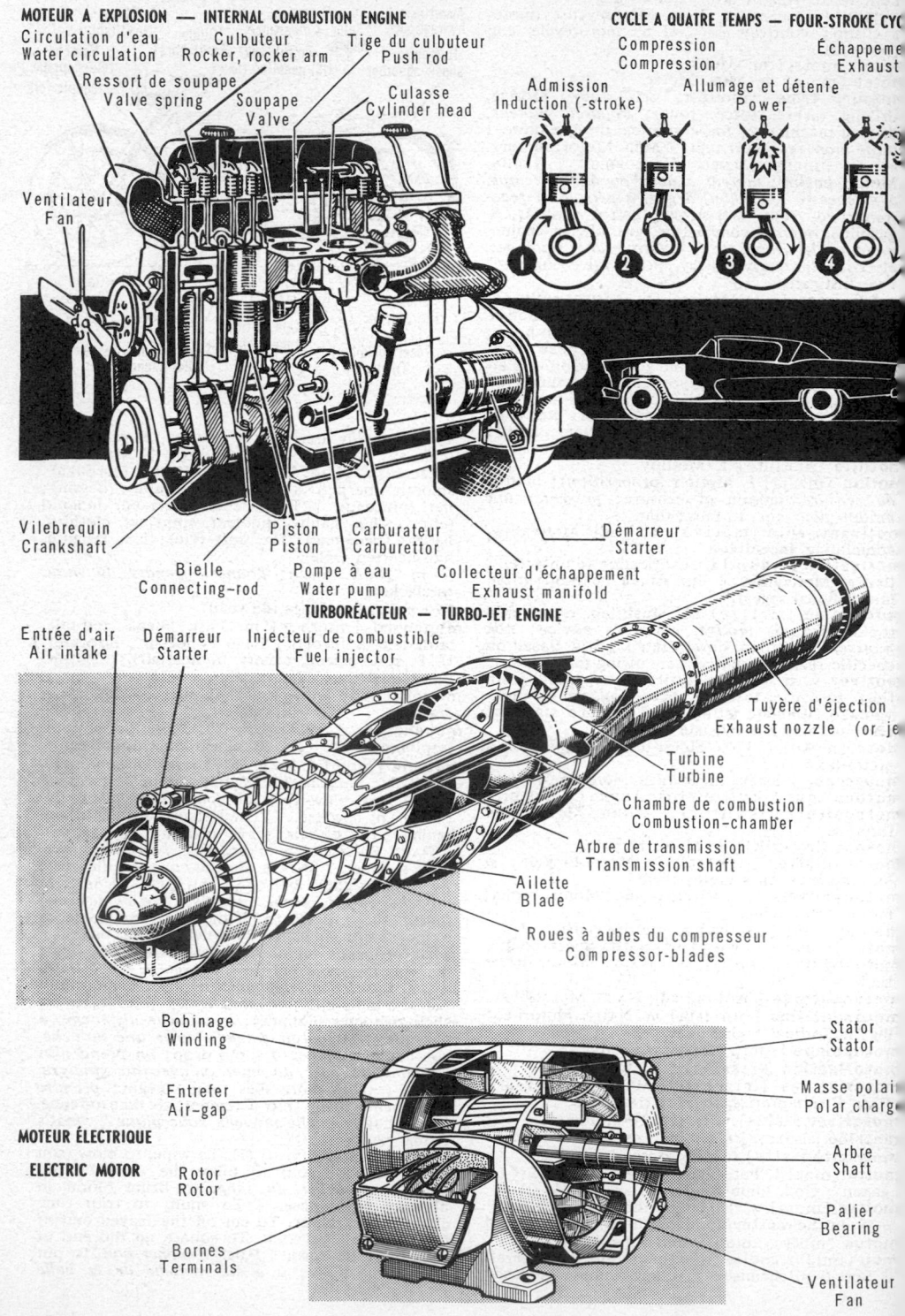

MOTEUR A EXPLOSION — INTERNAL COMBUSTION ENGINE

Circulation d'eau
Water circulation

Culbuteur
Rocker, rocker arm

Tige du culbuteur
Push rod

Ressort de soupape
Valve spring

Soupape
Valve

Culasse
Cylinder head

Ventilateur
Fan

Vilebrequin
Crankshaft

Piston
Piston

Carburateur
Carburettor

Démarreur
Starter

Bielle
Connecting-rod

Pompe à eau
Water pump

Collecteur d'échappement
Exhaust manifold

CYCLE A QUATRE TEMPS — FOUR-STROKE CYC

Compression
Compression

Échappeme
Exhaust

Admission
Induction (-stroke)

Allumage et détente
Power

TURBORÉACTEUR — TURBO-JET ENGINE

Entrée d'air
Air intake

Démarreur
Starter

Injecteur de combustible
Fuel injector

Tuyère d'éjection
Exhaust nozzle (or je

Turbine
Turbine

Chambre de combustion
Combustion–chamber

Arbre de transmission
Transmission shaft

Ailette
Blade

Roues à aubes du compresseur
Compressor-blades

MOTEUR ÉLECTRIQUE

ELECTRIC MOTOR

Bobinage
Winding

Entrefer
Air-gap

Rotor
Rotor

Bornes
Terminals

Stator
Stator

Masse polai
Polar charg

Arbre
Shaft

Palier
Bearing

Ventilateur
Fan

façon, he was made to sing small; *mouche ton nez,* mind your own business.
— v. intr. To blow one's nose.
— v. pr. **Se moucher,** to wipe (ou) to blow one's nose. ‖ FIG. *Il ne se mouche pas du coude* (ou) *du pied,* he does things in great style.

moucherolle [-rɔl] f. ZOOL. Fly-catcher.

moucheron [-rɔ̃] m. ZOOL. Gnat, midge. ‖ FAM. Kid, nipper.

moucheron m. Snuff (de chandelle).

moucheronner [-rɔne] v. intr. (1). SPORTS. To rise (à la pêche).

mouchet [muʃɛ] m. ZOOL. Hedge-sparrow.

moucheté, ée [muʃte] adj. Dappled, flecked, spotty, speckled. ‖ AGRIC. Smutty (blé).

moucheter v. tr. (8a). To fleck, to speckle, to spot (une étoffe). ‖ SPORTS. To button (un fleuret). ‖ NAUT. To mouse (un croc).

mouchetis [-ʃti] m. TECHN. Rough-cast.

mouchette [-ʃɛt] f. Snuffers, wick-scissors (pour chandelle). ‖ Nose-ring (pour un porc). ‖ ARCHIT. Fillet of drip-moulding. ‖ TECHN. Moulding plane.

moucheture [-ʃəty:r] f. Speckle, spot, fleck.

moucheur [-ʃœ:r] m. THÉÂTR. † Candle-snuffer.

mouchoir [-ʃwa:r] m. Handkerchief; *mouchoir de tête,* kerchief. ‖ NAUT. Knee-plate. ‖ TECHN. Facing (de maçonnerie).

mouchure [-ʃy:r] f. Mucus (du nez). ‖ Snuff (de chandelle). ‖ NAUT. Frayed end (of cordage).

moudre [mudr] v. tr. (65). To grind (en général); to grind, to mill (du blé). ‖ FAM. To grind out (un air).

moue [mu] f. Pout; *faire la moue,* to pout.

mouette [mwɛt] f. ZOOL. Gull, sea-mew.

moufette [mufɛt] f. ZOOL. Skunk.

moufle [mufl] f. Mitten, mitt; mufflers (gants). ‖ TECHN. Tackle-block, pulley-block; tie-bar.

moufler [mufle] v. tr. (1). TECHN. To tie (un mur); to set in a tackle (une poulie).

mouflet, ette [muflɛ, ɛt] s. FAM. Kid, nipper.

mouflon [muflɔ̃] m. ZOOL. Moufflon.

moufter [mufte] v. intr. (1). POP. To object, to say something; *sans moufter,* without turning a hair.

mougeotte [muʒɔt] f. Private posting box.

mouillage [muja:ʒ] m. Watering, adulterating (du lait, du vin). ‖ AGRIC. Damping, wetting (du tabac). ‖ NAUT. Anchoring, mooring; anchorage (lieu); anchoring berth (poste); *droit de mouillage,* harbour dues; *être au mouillage,* to ride at anchor. ‖ MILIT., NAUT. Laying (d'une mine).

mouillé, ée [-je] adj. Wet (joues, lèvres); watery (yeux). ‖ Damp, wet, sodden, spongy, soggy (sol). ‖ NAUT. Lying at anchor, anchored, moored; *mouillé au large,* at her moorings, moored in the open sea. ‖ GRAMM. Palatalized (consonne); liquid (l). ‖ LOC. *Mouillé comme un rat,* like a drowned rat; *mouillé jusqu'aux os,* wet to the skin, soaked through; *mouillé à tordre,* dripping (ou) soaking (ou) wringing wet.

mouiller [-je] v. tr. (1). To wet, to damp, to moisten; *mouiller son linge,* to dampen (ou) sprinkle one's laundry; *vous allez vous faire mouiller,* you are going to get wet. ‖ To water, to adulterate (le lait, le vin). ‖ NAUT. To cast, to drop (l'ancre); to stream (une bouée); to lay, to sink (une mine); to moor, to bring to anchor (un navire).
— v. intr. NAUT. To come to.
— v. pr. **Se mouiller,** to water (yeux); *ses yeux commencèrent à se mouiller,* her eyes turned misty with tears, tears came to her eyes. ‖ To get wet (personne).

mouillette [-jɛt] f. Sprinkling brush (pour la lessive). ‖ CULIN. Sippet. ‖ ELECTR. Tongue.

mouilleur [-jœ:r] m. Damper (pour timbres). ‖ NAUT. Tumbler (d'ancre); *mouilleur de mines,* mine-layer.

mouilleux, euse [-jø, ø:z] adj. Damp, wet, sodden (sol).

mouilloir [-jwa:r] m. Dampener (pour le linge). ‖ TECHN. Damper, water-can.

mouillure [-jy:r] f. Wetting, damping; wetness, dampness. ‖ Damp-mark.

mouise [mwi:z] f. FAM. Poverty; *dans la mouise,* hard up, up against it.

moujik [muʒik] m. Moujik.

moulage [mula:ʒ] m. Moulding, casting (action); cast (résultat).

moule [mul] m. Mould; *mettre au moule,* to cast (ou) to pour (ou) to run in a mould. ‖ CULIN. *Moule à beurre,* butterprint; *moule à fromages,* cheese-tub; *moule à gâteaux,* cake-tin. ‖ ARTS. Matrix, form. ‖ MILIT. *Moule à balles,* bullet-mould. ‖ FIG. *Coulés dans le même moule,* cast in the same mould; *fille faite au moule,* shapely (ou) exquisitely shaped girl; *le moule en est brisé,* we shan't see his like again.

moule f. ZOOL. Mussel. ‖ FAM. Simpleton (benêt); molly-coddle (mollasson).

moulé, ée [mule] adj. Moulded, cast (acier). ‖ Copperplate (écriture); block (lettre). ‖ Exquisitely shaped; with a fine figure (personne).

mouler v. tr. (1). To mould (une matière plastique); to cast (un métal); to press (le verre). ‖ To show off (les formes); *robe qui moule,* form-fitting dress.

mouleur [-lœ:r] m. TECHN. Caster, moulder.

moulier [mulje] adj. Mussel (industrie).

moulière [-ljɛr] f. Marshy ground (marais). ‖ Mussel-bed (parc).

moulin [mulɛ̃] m. Mill; *roue de moulin,* mill-wheel; *moulin à eau,* water-, wind-mill. ‖ Wheel; *moulin à prières,* prayer-wheel. ‖ CULIN. Mill; *moulin à café,* coffee-mill. ‖ TECHN. *Moulin à minerai,* ore-crusher. ‖ MILIT., FAM. *Moulin à café,* machine-gun. ‖ FAM. *Moulin à paroles,* chatterbox; *on entre chez eux comme dans un moulin,* they keep open house; *porter de l'eau au moulin,* to bring grist to the mill.

mouliner [-ne] v. tr. (1). TECHN. To polish (du marbre); to paddle (des peaux); to throw (de la soie).

moulinet [mulinɛ] m. Reel (de canne à pêche). ‖ Flourish, twirl; *faire un moulinet avec sa canne,* to twirl (ou) whirl one's stick. ‖ *Moulinet à musique,* toy musical box. ‖ AVIAT. Windmilling.

Moulinette [-nɛt] f. (nom déposé). CULIN. Food-mill; Moulinette.

moulineur [-nœ:r] m. Thrower (de soie). ‖ Putter (dans une mine).

moult [mult] adv. † Much; very.

moulu, ue [muly] adj. Ground, powdered. ‖ FAM. Aching all over (courbatu); beaten, done up (éreinté).

moulure [muly:r] f. ARCHIT. Moulding.

moulurer [mulyre] v. tr. (1). ARCHIT. To decorate with mouldings.

moumoute [mumut] m. FAM. Wig (perruque); sheepskin jacket (veste).

mourant, ante [murɑ̃, ɑ̃:t] adj. Dying. ‖ FIG. Faint, dying, languid (voix); *d'une voix mourante,* faintly, weakly; like a dying duck (fam.). ‖ FAM. Screamingly funny, killing. (V. CREVANT.)
— s. Dying person; *les mourants,* the dying.

mourir [-ri:r] v. intr. (66). To die (perdre la vie); *au moment de mourir,* in the hour of death; *mourir avant l'âge,* to come to an untimely end; *mourir à la peine,* to die in harness; *faire mourir,* to put to death. ‖ AGRIC. To fade, to droop (fleur). ‖ FIG. To die out (ou) away (s'affaiblir); to die out (feu); to die away (voix). ‖ FIG. To vanish (disparaître); to wither, to come to nothing (ambition); to die, to fall (espoir). ‖ FIG. To be dejected (être accablé); *aimer qqn à en mourir*, to be desperately in love with s.o.; *mourir d'ennui*, to be bored to tears; *mourir d'inquiétude, de peur*, to be worried, frightened to death; *mourir de rire*, to die of laughing, to be tickled to death; *c'est à mourir de rire*, it's absolutely killing; *vous me ferez mourir de rire*, you're killing me. ‖ FIG. To be dying (ou) bursting to; *mourir d'impatience de*, to be dying (ou) longing to.

— v. pr. **Se mourir**, to die, to die away, to die out; *se mourir d'envie de*, to be dying to.

mouron [murɔ̃] m. BOT. Chickweed.

mourrai, mourrais. V. MOURIR (66).

mousmé [musme] f. Mousmee. ‖ FAM. Broad, woman.

mousquet [muskɛ] m. MILIT. Musket.

mousquetaire [muskətɛ:r] m. MILIT. Musketeer. ‖ COMM. *Gants à la mousquetaire*, gauntlet gloves.

mousqueterie [muskɛtri] f. Musketry.

mousqueton [muskətɔ̃] m. † Musketoon. ‖ MILIT. Cavalry magazine rifle. ‖ Snap-hook (de chaîne).

moussaillon [musajɔ̃] m. NAUT. Ship's boy.

moussaka [musaka] f. CULIN. Moussaka, mousaka.

moussant, ante [musɑ̃, ɑ̃:t] adj. Foamy, foaming, frothy, frothing.

mousse [mus] f. Moss; *couvert de mousse*, mossy, moss-grown; *lit de mousse*, mossy bed. ‖ Froth, foam (de bière, de champagne, d'eau); lather (de savon). ‖ *Caoutchouc mousse*, foam-rubber. ‖ *Mousse de platine*, platinum sponge. ‖ CULIN. *Mousse à la Chantilly*, whipped cream; *mousse au chocolat*, chocolate mousse. ‖ LOC. *Pierre qui roule n'amasse pas mousse*, a rolling stone gathers no moss.

mousse m. NAUT. Ship's boy; deck-boy.

mousse adj. Blunt (pointe).

mousseline [muslin] f. Muslin; *mousseline de soie*, chiffon; *verre mousseline*, muslin glass, mousseline. ‖ CULIN. *Gâteau mousseline*, spongecake; *pommes mousseline*, purée, mashed potatoes.

mousser [muse] v. intr. (1). To froth, to foam (bière, champagne, eau); to sparkle, to effervesce; to fizz (fam.) [limonade]; to lather (savon). ‖ CULIN. *Faire mousser de la crème*, to whip (ou) to whisk cream. ‖ FIG. *Faire mousser qqn*, to make s.o. foam at the mouth (irriter); to crack s.o. up (vanter); *se faire mousser*, to advertize oneself.

mousseron [musrɔ̃] m. BOT. Edible mushroom.

mousseux, euse [musø, ø:z] adj. Mossy (banc, pierre). ‖ Foaming, frothy (bière); sparkling (vin). ‖ BOT. *Rose mousseuse*, moss-rose.

— m. Sparkling wine, mousseux.

mousson [musɔ̃] f. Monsoon.

moussu, ue [musy] adj. Mossy, moss-grown.

moustache [mustaʃ] f. Whiskers (de chat); moustache, U. S. mustache (d'homme). ‖ NAUT. Gobline.

moustachu, ue [-ʃu] adj. Moustached, moustachio-ed, U. S. mustached.

moustiquaire [mustikɛ:r] f. Mosquito curtain (ou) U. S. net.

moustique [mustik] m. ZOOL. Mosquito; gnat.

moût [mu] m. Must (du raisin).

moutard [muta:r] m. FAM. Kid. (V. GOSSE.)

moutarde [mutard] f. CULIN. Mustard. ‖ MILIT. *Gaz moutarde*, mustard-gas. ‖ FIG. *La moutarde lui est montée au nez*, he flared up, he flew off the handle.

— adj. Mustard-coloured, mustard.

moutardier [-dje] m. Mustard-maker (fabricant);

mustard-pot (pot). ‖ LOC. *Se prendre pour le pr[emier] mier moutardier du pape*, to think no small be[er] of oneself, to think oneself somebody.

moutier [mutje] m. † Monastery.

mouton [mutɔ̃] m. ZOOL. Sheep; *peau de mouto[n]* sheepskin (reliure, vêtement). ‖ Fluff (de pou[s-] sière). ‖ CULIN. Mutton (viande). ‖ NAUT. P[...] White horses, whitecaps. ‖ TECHN. Monkey (ma[-] chine); ram, beetle (pilon). ‖ LOC. *C'est un vr[ai] mouton*, he is as mild as a lamb; *ce sont des mo[u-] tons de Panurge*, they follow blindly; *revenons [à] nos moutons*, let us get back to our subject. ‖ POP. Spy (en prison).

— adj. Sheep-like.

moutonnant, ante [mutɔnɑ̃, ɑ̃:t] adj. Covere[d] with white horses (ou) whitecaps (mer); whi[te] (vagues).

moutonné, ée [-ne] adj. *Ciel moutonné*, macke[-] rel sky; *roche moutonnée*, sheep-back, roch[e] moutonnée.

moutonnement [-nmɑ̃] m. Covering with whi[te] horses (ou) whitecaps (de la mer); breaking int[o] foam (des vagues).

moutonner [-ne] v. intr. (1). To curl (cheveux). To break into white horses (ou) whitecaps, t[o] froth (mer); *ciel moutonné*, mackerel sky.

— v. tr. To curl, to frizz (la chevelure).

— v. pr. **Se moutonner**, to become covered wit[h] fleecy clouds (ciel); to become covered with whi[te] horses (ou) whitecaps (mer).

moutonneux, euse [-nø, ø:z] adj. Fleecy (ciel[)]; covered with white horses (ou) whitecaps (mer[)].

moutonnier, ère [-nje, ɛr] adj. ZOOL. Pertainin[g] to sheep, ovine (race). ‖ FIG. Sheep-like, easi[-] led (personne).

mouture [muty:r] f. Grinding, milling (action[)]. ‖ Multure, milling dues (droits).

mouvance [muvɑ̃:s] f. † Tenure. ‖ Sphere o[f] influence.

mouvant, ante [muvɑ̃, ɑ̃:t] adj. Moving; *sable[s] mouvants*, quicksands, shifting (ou) moving sand[s]. ‖ MILIT. Fluid (front).

mouvement [muvmɑ̃] m. Motion, movement[;] *aimer le mouvement*, to be fond of change; êtr[e] *toujours en mouvement*, to be always on th[e] move; *mettre en mouvement*, to start off; *mou[-] vement brusque*, jerk; *mouvement brusque e[n] avant, de côté*, lunge, dodge (ou) sidestep; *mou[-] vement des épaules, des paupières, de la têt[e]*, shrug, wink, nod; *mouvement de recul*, sta[rt] back. ‖ Traffic (circulation); *être en mouvemen[t] de bonne heure*, to be early astir; *petite ville sans mouvement*, lifeless (ou) sleepy (ou) du[ll] little place; *ville au mouvement intense*, bus[y] town. ‖ MÉD. *Faire un faux mouvement*, to strai[n] oneself (ou) a muscle. ‖ ARTS. Fall, hang (d'u[n] rideau); line (d'une robe). ‖ FIN. Fluctuatio[n] (du marché); trend (des prix); *mettre en mo[u-] vement une affaire*, to launch a business; *l[e] mouvement a été nul en Bourse*, the Stoc[k] Exchange was extremely quiet. ‖ GÉOGR. Ris[e,] swell (de terrain); *mouvements de terrain*, hill[s] and valleys, mounds and dells. ‖ JUR. Trend (d[e] la natalité); change, appointment (du personnel[)]; *un mouvement au ministère des Finances*, ne[w] appointments at the Exchequer. ‖ MILIT. Move[-] ment, manœuvre, move; *mouvements de troupe[s]*, troop movements. ‖ NAUT. *Mouvement d[e] navires*, shipping entries and clearances. ‖ Mus[.] Movement; time. ‖ PHYS. *Mouvement acqui[s,]* impressed motion, impetus; *mouvement d'osci[l-] lation*, swing; *mouvement de va-et-vient*, to an[d] fro movement; *quantité de mouvement d'u[n] corps*, momentum of a body. ‖ TECHN. Work[s,] movement (d'une montre, d'une pendule). ‖ FI[G.] Movement, stir, change, evolution (des esprit[s,] des idées); *être dans le mouvement*, to be i[n] the swim (ou) abreast of the time (ou) up to date ; *le mouvement d'Oxford*, the Oxford Movement ; *mouvement populaire*, popular uprising ; *mouvement révolutionnaire*, revolutionary agitation ; *suivre le mouvement*, to go with the stream ; *toute la ville est en mouvement*, the whole city is seething (ou) agog (ou) astir (ou) in a state of excitement. ‖ Fig. Motion, impulse, burst, outburst (accès, impulsion) ; *avoir un bon mouvement*, to act on a kindly impulse ; *de son propre mouvement*, of one's own accord ; *mouvement de colère, d'humeur*, fit of anger, of temper ; *mouvement de répulsion*, recoil ; *mouvement de surprise*, start of surprise ; *premier mouvement*, first impulse.

mouvementé, ée [-te] adj. Lively, spirited (discussion); lively, agitated (entrevue, séance); eventful, stirring (époque, vie) ; exciting (jeu, partie) ; lively (style) ; thrilling, eventful (voyage). ‖ Géogr. Undulating, uneven (terrain).

mouvementer [-te] v. tr. (1). To enliven, to give life to (une description) ; to enliven, to animate (une discussion).

mouver [muve] v. tr. (1). To turn over (la terre). ‖ To stir (un liquide).

mouvette [muvɛt] f. Stirrer. (V. MIXEUR.)

mouvoir [muvwa:r] v. tr. (67). To move, to stir, to set in motion ; *mouvoir la roue du moulin*, to set the mill-wheel moving. ‖ Techn. *Mû à la vapeur*, steam-propelled. ‖ Fig. To move, to urge, to prompt (inciter) ; *mû par l'intérêt*, actuated by self-interest.
— v. pr. Se **mouvoir**, to move, to stir ; *lent à se mouvoir*, slow to stir ; *se mouvoir autour du soleil*, to move round the sun.

moyen, enne [mwajɛ̃, ɛn] adj. Middle (position); medium (qualité) ; *d'âge moyen*, middle-aged ; *classe moyenne*, middle class ; *de taille moyenne*, middle-sized ; *Moyen Age*, Middle Ages ; *moyen terme*, middle course. ‖ Average, mean ; *l'homme moyen*, the average man, the man in the street ; *température moyenne*, mean temperature. ‖ Ordinary, imperfect, mediocre, middling, moderate (médiocre) ; *capacité moyenne*, middling capacity ; *très moyen*, middling only, nothing to boast of. ‖ Intermediate course in literature. ‖ Gramm. Middle (voix). ‖ Philos. Middle (terme). ‖ Géogr. *Moyen-Orient*, Middle East. ‖ Comm. Moderate (prix). ‖ Fin. *Cours moyen*, middle price. ‖ Autom. *Voiture de puissance moyenne*, medium-powered car. ‖ Radio. Medium (onde). ‖ **Moyen-courrier**, adj. Aviat. Medium-distance (ou) -haul. m. Medium distance (ou) haul aircraft.
— m. Math. Mean ; *le moyen arithmétique*, the arithmetical mean.

moyen m. Means, way (manière) ; *le moyen de ne pas aboutir*, the straight way to failure ; *le moyen de réussir*, the way to success. ‖ Means, way (possibilité) ; *s'arranger pour trouver moyen de*, to contrive to, to make shift to ; *il n'y a aucun moyen de se tirer d'embarras*, there is no getting out of the scrape, there is no way out ; *le moyen de faire autrement!*, what else can one do! ; *pas moyen*, it can't be done, nothing doing. ‖ Contrivance (invention) ; *trouver un moyen de fabriquer*, to find a way of manufacturing. ‖ Means (intervention) ; *au moyen de*, by means of ; *les grands moyens*, exceptional measures ; *par le moyen de*, through the, by the instrumentality of, with the co-operation of ; *tous les moyens lui sont bons*, he will stick at nothing, he will resort to any means. ‖ Means, powers (capacité) ; *avoir les moyens qu'il faut*, to have the necessary ability ; *dans la mesure de mes moyens*, as far as it lies in my capacity ; *dans la pleine mesure de mes moyens*, to the best of my ability ; *enlever ses moyens à qqn*, to upset (ou) to disconcert s.o. ;

faire appel à tous ses moyens, to put forth all one's powers, to do all that lies in one's power, to put one's best foot forward (fam.). ‖ Means (ressources) ; *il en a, il n'en a pas les moyens*, he can, he cannot afford it ; *faire qqch. par ses propres moyens*, to draw upon one's own resources, to do sth. off one's own bat (fam.) ; *il a largement les moyens de payer*, he has ample means to pay for this ; *ils y sont allés par leurs propres moyens*, they have gone there under their own steam (fam.). ‖ Means (instrument) ; *moyen de transport*, means of conveyance (ou) U. S. transportation. ‖ Jur. *Voies et moyens*, ways and means.

moyenâgeux, euse [mwajɛnaʒø, ø:z] adj. Mediaeval, medieval (du Moyen Age) ; sham mediaeval (de genre médiéval).

moyennant [-nã] prép. At the cost of, thanks to ; *moyennant votre approbation*, subject to your approval ; *moyennant beaucoup de peine*, with great difficulty ; *moyennant quoi*, in consideration of which.
— loc. prép. † *Moyennant que*, on condition that, provided that.

moyenne [mwajɛn] f. Average ; *en moyenne*, on an average ; *taille au-dessous, au-dessus de la moyenne*, below, above average height. ‖ Half-marks, pass-marks, U. S. passing mark (note) ; *avoir la moyenne*, to get the pass-mark, U. S. to get a passing mark. ‖ Comm. *Faire la moyenne des recettes journalières*, to calculate the average daily receipts. ‖ Math. Mean.

moyennement [-nmã] adv. Moderately, fairly ; middling, so-so (fam.). ‖ On an average.

moyenner [-ne] v. tr. (1). Pop. To obtain a result ; *pas moyen de moyenner*, it's no good.

moyette [mwajɛt] f. Agric. Shock (de blé).

moyeu [mwajø] m. Techn. Nave (de roue de charrette) ; hub (de roue de bicyclette). ‖ Aviat. Boss (d'hélice).

Mozambique [mɔzãbik] m. Géogr. Mozambique.

mû [my]. V. MOUVOIR (67).

muable [myabl] adj. Mutable. (V. CHANGEABLE.)

muance [myɑ̃:s] f. Mus. Mutation. ‖ Méd. Breaking (de la voix).

mucilage [mysilaʒ] m. Méd. Mucilage.

mucilagineux, euse [-ʒinø, ø:z] adj. Méd. Mucilaginous.

mucosité [mykɔzite] m. Mucosity.

mucus [-kys] m. Mucus.

mue [my] f. Moult, moulting (d'un oiseau) ; shedding of the coat (ou) of the hair (ou) of the antlers (d'un cerf, d'un mammifère) ; sloughing (d'un reptile). ‖ Mew (de faucon) ; coop (de poule). ‖ Méd. Breaking (de la voix).

muer [mye] v. intr. (1). To cast its antlers (cerf) ; to moult (oiseau) ; to slough (serpent). ‖ Méd. To break (voix).
— v. pr. Se **muer**, to change (en, into).

muet, ette [myɛ, ɛ:t] adj. Dumb (privé de l'usage de la parole) ; *muet de naissance*, dumb from birth, born dumb. ‖ Dumb, mute, speechless (sans parole) ; *muet de colère*, speechless with rage. ‖ Silent (silencieux) ; *rester muet devant le juge*, to remain silent before the magistrate. ‖ Théâtr. Dumb (jeu, scène) ; *film muet*, silent film ; *personnage muet*, non-speaking (or) mute character. ‖ Géogr. Blank, skeleton (carte). ‖ Gramm. Mute, silent (consonne). ‖ Fig. Mute, silent (douleur, mécontentement) ; *accablement muet*, silent despondency ; *muet désespoir*, mute despair.
— s. Dumb, mute person ; *sourd-muet*, deaf-mute ; *sourde-muette*, deaf-and-dumb woman.

muette [myɛt] f. Sports. Hunting-box (à la chasse). ‖ Gramm. Mute (ou) unsounded letter. ‖

Loc. *A la muette,* without speaking, with gestures.
muezzin [myezɛ̃] m. Muezzin.
mufle [myfl]m. Muffle (de bœuf); muzzle (de bison, de chien); nose (de lion). || Fam. Face, mug, pan (visage). || Fam. Cad, skunk, bounder, rotter (v. GROSSIER; *quel mufle!,* what a twirp!
muflerie [myflǝri] f. Caddishness (défaut); rotten trick (tour).
muflier [myflije] m. Bot. Snap-dragon.
mufti [myfti] m. Mufti (musulman).
muge [my:ʒ] m. Zool. Mullet.
mugir [myʒi:r] v. intr. (2). To low, to moo, to bellow (taureau, vache). || To roar, to boom (mer); to howl (vent). || Autom. To hoot, to honk (klaxon).
mugissant, ante [-ʒisɑ̃, ɑ̃:t] adj. Bellowing (taureau); lowing (vache). || Roaring, booming (flots); howling (vent).
mugissement [-ʒismɑ̃] m. Bellowing, bellow (taureau); lowing (vache). || Roaring, roar, booming, boom (mer, vent); howling, wailing (vent). || Hooting, hoot, blowing (corne, sirène).
muguet [mygɛ] m. invar. Bot. Lily of the valley. || Méd. Thrush.
muid [myi] m. Hogshead, large barrel (tonneau).
mulatier, ère [mylatje, ɛ:r] adj. Connected with mule-breeding.
— s. Mule-breeder.
mulâtre [mylɑ:tr] adj. Mulatto.
— m. Mulatto.
mulâtresse [-trɛs] f. Mulatto, mulattress; U. S. griffin.
mule [myl] f. Mule, she-mule. || Fam. *Têtu comme une mule,* mulish, stubborn as a mule.
mule f. Slipper, mule (chaussure); *baiser la mule du pape,* to kiss the Pope's toe. || Méd. Chilblain. || **Mule-jenny,** f. Techn. Mule-jenny.
mulet [mylɛ] m. Zool. Mule, he-mule (quadrupède); mullet (poisson).
muletier, ère [-ltje, ɛr] adj. Mule; *sentier muletier,* pack-trail, bridle-path.
— m. Mule-driver, muleteer.
mulot [mylo] m. Zool. Field-mouse.
mulsion [mylsjɔ̃] f. Milking.
multicellulaire [myltiselylɛ:r] adj. Multicellular.
multicolore [myltikɔlɔ:r] adj. Multi-coloured, many-coloured, pied, variegated, polychromatic, U.S. parti-colored.
multiforme [-fɔrm] adj. Multiform (objet). || Fig. Many-sided (explication).
multilatéral, ale [-lateral] adj. Multilateral.
multimilliardaire [-miljardɛ:r] adj., s. Multi-billionaire.
multimillionnaire [-miljɔnɛ:r] adj., s. Multi-millionaire.
multinational, ale [-nasjɔnal] adj., f. Multinational.
multipare [-pa:r] adj. Méd., Zool. Multiparous.
— f. Méd. Multipara. || Zool. Multiparous animal.
multiphasé, ée [-faze] adj. Electr. Multiphase.
multiplace [-plas] adj. Multi-seat.
multiplan [-plɑ̃] adj., m. Aviat. Multiplane.
multiple [myltipl] adj. Multiple, manifold (nombreux); multifarious (varié).
— m. Multiple.
multiplex [mytipleks] adj. Electr. Multiplex.
multipliable [-pliabl] adj. Math. Multipliable, multiplicable.
multipliant, ante [-pliɑ̃, ɑ̃:t] adj. Math. Multiplying.
multiplicande [-plikɑ̃:d] m. Math. Multiplicand.
multiplicateur [-plikatœ:r] adj. Math. Multiplying.
— m. Multiplier.
multiplicatif, ive [-plikatif, i:v] adj. Math. Multiplicative.

multiplication [-plikasjɔ̃] f. Math. Multiplication. || Techn. *Grande, petite multiplication,* high, low gear. || Fig. Increase.
multiplicité [-plisite] f. Multiplicity.
multiplier [-plije] v. tr. (1). Techn. To gear up. || Math. To multiply. || Fig. To multiply; to propagate (descendants, espèces).
— v. intr. To multiply; to increase.
— v. pr. Se multiplier, to be multiplied, to multiply; to increase, to grow in numbers. || Fig. To exert oneself to the utmost, to be everywhere; to bustle about (se dépenser); *plus il se multiplie, moins il obtient de résultats,* the more he fusses, the less he achieves; more haste, less speed.
multipolaire [myltipɔlɛ:r] adj. Electr., Méd. Multipolar.
multirisque [-risk] adj. Fin. *Assurance multirisque,* comprehensive insurance.
multitude [-ityd] f. Multitude, crowd, the many; *l'élite et la multitude,* the few and the many. || Fig. Multiplicity, heap, hosts, scores, shoals (v. FOULE); *une multitude d'occupations,* lots of things to do.
munichois, oise [mynikwa, a:z] adj. Géogr. Of (ou) from Munich.
— s. Géogr. Native (ou) inhabitant of Munich. || † Municheer, Munichite.
municipal, ale [mynisipal] adj. Municipal; *la Garde municipale,* the Paris Municipal Guard.
— m. Member of the Paris Municipal Guard.
municipaliser [-lize] v. tr. (1). To municipalize.
municipalité [-lite] f. Municipality. || Incorporated borough (ville). || Municipal corporation; town council (conseil).
munificence [mynifisɑ̃:s] f. Munificence, bounty; *avec munificence,* bounteously, bountifully.
munificent, ente [-sɑ̃, ɑ̃:t] adj. Munificent, bounteous.
munir [myni:r] v. tr. (2). To provide, to supply (de, with); *muni d'argent,* supplied with money; *muni du nerf de la guerre,* provided with the sinews of war; *non muni de,* lacking, short of. || Ecclés. *Muni des sacrements de l'Eglise,* fortified with the rites of the Church. || Milit. To supply, to provision, to furnish (de, with) [vivres, munitions]; to garrison (de, with) [troupes].
— v. pr. Se munir, to provide (ou) to supply (ou) to furnish oneself (de, with).
munition [mynisjɔ̃] f. † Equipping; *pain de munition,* ration bread. || Milit. Pl. Ammunition; *à court de munitions,* short of ammunition. || Fig. *Munitions de bouche,* provisions, provender.
munitionnaire [-sjɔnɛ:r] m. Milit. Supply officer.
munitionner [-sjɔne] v. tr. (1). Milit. To provide with munitions.
munster [mœstɛ:r] m. Culin. Munster, Munster cheese.
muphti [mufti] m. V. MUFTI.
muqueuse [mykø:z] f. Méd. Mucous membrane.
muqueux, euse [mykø, ø:z] adj. Mucous. || Méd. *Fièvre muqueuse,* mild typhoïd fever.
mur [my:r] m. Wall; *mur d'appui, de clôture, d'enceinte,* breast-high, enclosing, surrounding wall; *entourer un jardin de murs,* to wall a garden in; *maison aux murs de briques,* brick-walled house. || Aviat. *Mur du son,* sonic (ou) sound barrier; *franchir le mur du son,* to break through the sound barrier. || Sports. *Parer au mur,* to stonewall; *tirer au mur,* to practise shadow-fencing (à l'escrime). || Fig. *Chassé de nos murs,* banished, outlawed, sent to Coventry; *l'ennemi est dans nos murs,* the enemy is within our walls; *mettre qqn au pied du mur,* to drive s.o. into a corner, to demand a « yes » or a « no » from s.o.; *les murs ont des oreilles!,* walls have ears!; *poussé au pied du mur,* with his back to

the wall. ‖ FAM. *Coller qqn au mur*, to put s.o. up against a wall and shoot him; *faire le mur*, to climb over the wall.

mûr [my:r] adj. Ripe (fruit); *pas mûr*, unripe, green; *poire bien mûre*, mellow pear; *mûr seulement en hiver*, winter-ripe. ‖ MILIT. Seasoned (soldat). ‖ FIG. Mature, ripe, middle (âge); *femme assez mûre*, woman well on in years; *femme plus que mûre*, more than middle-aged woman. ‖ MÉD. Ripe (abcès). ‖ FIG. Ready (prêt); *il est mûr pour encaisser toutes leurs balivernes*, he is about ready to believe all their stories. ‖ FIG. Mature (qualités); *jugement mûr*, well-balanced judgment (réfléchi); reliable judgment (sûr). ‖ FAM. Mellow, half-seas over; U. S. high, tight (éméché); mellow (influençable); *en faire avaler des vertes et des pas mûres à qqn*, to make s.o. swallow one's tallest stories.

murage [myra:z] m. Walling in (ou) up (clôture). ‖ Masonry, walling (maçonnerie).

muraille [-ra:j] f. High (ou) thick wall (v. MUR); *muraille de clôture*, enclosing wall. ‖ NAUT. Side, wall. ‖ FIG. Wall.

mural, ale [myral] adj. Mural; *carte murale*, wall-map; *peinture murale*, mural painting, U.S. mural.

mûre [my:r] f. BOT. Mulberry; blackberry; brambleberry.

mûrement [myrmɑ̃] adj. Maturely; *après avoir mûrement réfléchi*, after mature reflection.

murène [myrɛn] f. ZOOL. Muraena.

murer [m̥yre] v. tr. (1). To wall up (une porte); to wall in (une propriété); *murer avec des briques*, to brick up. ‖ ·FIG. To shut up (enfermer); *se murer dans son obstination*, to take refuge in sheer obstinacy.

murette [-rɛt] f. Low wall.

murex [myrɛks] m. ZOOL. Murex.

muriate [myrjat] m. CHIM. Muriate; chloride.

muriatique [-tik] adj. CHIM. Muriatic.

mûrier [myrje] m. BOT. Mulberry-tree.

mûri, ie [myri] adj. *Mûri au soleil*, sun-ripened. ‖ FIG. Carefully studied, long-considered (projet); *mûri par les combats*, tempered in battle; *mûri par les siècles*, age-old.

mûrir [-ri:r] v. tr. (2). BOT. To ripen, to mature. ‖ MÉD. To mature; *faire mûrir un abcès*, to bring an abscess to a head. ‖ FIG. To work out; to strengthen; *mûrir le goût de qqn*, to develop s.o.'s taste.
— v. intr. AGRIC. To ripen, to mellow. ‖ MÉD. To be brought to a head (abcès). ‖ FIG. To mature (projet).

mûrissant, ante [-risɑ̃, ɑ̃:t] adj. Ripening, mellowing, maturing.

murmurant, ante [myrmyrɑ̃, ɑ̃:t] adj. Murmuring (arbres); brawling (cascade); babbling (enfant); murmuring, muttering (personne); chirping (oiseau); purling, babbling (ruisseau); hissing (scierie); sighing, soughing (vent).

murmure [myrmy:r] m. Murmuring, murmur, muttering, whispering (de personnes); *un murmure d'approbation*, a buzz of approval; *un murmure hostile*, a hostile muttering. ‖ FIG. Soughing (des arbres); brawling (d'une cascade); babble, babbling (d'un enfant); whisper, whispering (de la parole); chirp, chirping (des oiseaux); purl, purling, babbling (d'un ruisseau); hiss, hissing (d'une scierie); sighing, soughing (du vent).

murmurer [-myre] v. intr. (1). To murmur, to whisper (parler bas). ‖ To complain, to growl, to hoot. (V. BOUGONNER.) ‖ FIG. To sough (arbres); to brawl (cascade); to babble (enfant); to chirp (oiseaux); to purl, to babble (ruisseau); to hiss (scierie); to sigh, to sough (vent).
— v. tr. To whisper, to breathe (un secret).

musaraigne [myzarɛɲ] f. ZOOL. Shrew-mouse.

musard, arde [myza:r, a:rd] adj. Dawdling.
— m. Dawdler.

musarder [-zarde] v. intr. (1). To dawdle, to fribble away one's time, to dilly-dally.

musardise [-zardi:z] f. Dawdling, dilly-dallying.

musc [mysk] m. Musk. ‖ ZOOL. Musk-deer; *couleur de musc*, musk-coloured.

muscade [myskad] f. BOT. Nutmeg. ‖ Thimble-rigger's pea; *passez muscade!*, hey presto!

muscadet [myskadɛ] m. Muscatel wine.

muscadier [myskadje] m. BOT. Nutmeg-tree.

muscadin [myskadɛ̃] m. Beau, blade.

muscat [myska] adj. Muscat (raisin, vin).
— m. Musk-pear (poire); muscat grape, muscadine (raisin); muscat wine, muscatel (vin).

muscle [myskl] m. MÉD. Muscle; *tendre tous ses muscles*, to strain every nerve.

musclé, ée [myskle] adj. Brawny, athletic, muscular; beefy (fam.).

muscler v. tr. (1). To develop the muscles of.

musculaire [-kylɛ:r] adj. MÉD. Muscular (action).

musculation [-kylasjɔ̃] f. Muscle- (ou) body-building.

musculature [-kylaty:r] f. MÉD. Musculature.

musculeux, euse [-kylø, ø:z] adj. Sinewy (viande).

musculosité [-kylozite] f. Muscularity.

muse [my:z] f. Muse.

museau [myzo] m. Nose, snout, muzzle (d'un animal). ‖ FAM. Nose.

musée [myze] m. ARTS. Museum.

museler [myzle] v. tr. (1). To muzzle (un chien). ‖ FAM. To silence; *être vite muselé*, to be soon made to shut up.

muselière [-zəljɛ:r] f. Muzzle; *mettre une muselière à*, to muzzle.

musellement [-zɛlmɑ̃] m. Muzzling (pr. et fig.).

muser [myze] v. intr. (1). To dawdle, to dilly-dally, to fritter away one's time. (V. FLÂNER.)

muserolle [myzərɔl] f. Nose-band, musrole.

musette [myzɛt] f. Nose-bag (pour cheval). ‖ MUS. Musette, country bag-pipe; *bal musette*, popular dance-hall. ‖ MILIT. Haversack, U. S. musette-bag.

muséum [myzeɔm] m. Natural history museum.

museur [myzœ:r] m. Dawdler. (V. FLÂNEUR.)

musical, ale [myzikal] adj. MUS. Musical; *avoir l'oreille musicale*, to have an ear for music (ou) a musical ear. ‖ AUTOM. *Avertisseur à tonalité musicale*, musical horn.

musicalement [-kalmɑ̃] adv. MUS. Musically.

musicalité [-kalite] f. MUS. Musicality; musicalness.

music-hall [-kol] (pl. **music-halls**) m. THÉÂTR. Music-hall, variety theatre; U. S. vaudeville theater. ‖ Show business (métier).

musicien, enne [-sjɛ̃, ɛn] adj. MUS. Musical; *être musicien*, to be fond of music, to be musical.
— s. MUS. Musician. ‖ MILIT. Bandsman.

musicographe [-kɔgraf] m. MUS. Musicographer.

musicographie [-kɔgrafi] f. MUS. Writing on music.

musicologie [-kɔlɔʒi] f. MUS. Musicology.

musicologue [-kɔlɔg] m. MUS. Musicologist.

musique [myzik] f. MUS. Music; *musique de chambre, de danse, d'orchestre*, chamber, dance, orchestral music; *faire de la musique*, to make (ou) study music; *mettre des vers en musique*, to set verses to music; *voulez-vous nous faire un peu de musique?*, won't you play (ou) sing for us? ‖ MUS. Band (orchestre). ‖ THÉÂTR. Incidental music (pour une pièce). ‖ ECCLÉS. *Musique d'église*, sacred music. ‖ FAM. *Faire une musique du diable*, to make an awful row; *musique de chats*, caterwauling.

musiquer [-ke] v. intr. (1). FAM. To make music.

musiquette [-kɛt] f. FAM. Cheap music.

musoir [myzwa:r] m. Pier, jetty-head.
musqué, ée [myske] adj. Musky, musk; *rat musqué*, musk-rat; musquash; *rose musquée*. musk-rose. ‖ FIG. Affected.
musquer v. tr. (1). To musk.
mussif, ive [mysif, iv] adj. Mosaic (or).
musulman, ane [myzylmɑ̃, an] adj., s. Moslem, Mussulman, Mohammedan, Muslim; *le parti musulman,* the Moslem party.
mutabilité [mytabilite] f. Mutability.
mutable [-tabl] adj. Mutable.
mutage [-ta:ʒ] m. Mutage (du vin).
mutant, ante [-tɑ̃, ɑ̃:t] adj., m. Mutant (bot., zool., science-fiction).
mutation [-tasjɔ̃] f. Change, alteration. ‖ Transfer (dans un personnel). ‖ JUR. *Impôt sur les mutations,* tax on transfer of property; *mutation par décès,* transfer by death; *mutation entre vifs,* transfer (ou) conveyance inter vivos. ‖ MUS. Shifting; *jeux de mutation,* mutation stops (orgue). ‖ ZOOL. Mutation (des espèces).
mutatis mutandis [-tatismytɑ̃dis] loc. Mutatis mutandis.
muter [-te] v. tr. (1). To transfer, to change (un fonctionnaire). ‖ To mute (du vin).
— v. intr. BOT., ZOOL. To mutate.
mutilant, ante [mytilɑ̃, ɑ̃:t] adj. MÉD. Mutilative.
mutilateur, trice [mytilatœ:r, tris] s. Mutilator, maimer. ‖ Defacer.
mutilation [-lasjɔ̃] f. MÉD. Mutilation, maiming, mayhem (d'une personne). ‖ FIG. Defacement (d'une statue); mutilation (d'un texte).
mutilé, ée [-le] adj. MÉD. Mutilated, maimed. ‖ MILIT. Disabled, maimed (du corps); disfigured (de la face).
— m. MILIT. Disabled soldier; *grand mutilé,* badly-disabled ex-Service man, U. S. disabled veteran.
mutiler [-le] v. tr. (1). To deface (un monument, une statue); to mangle (un objet); to mutilate, to mangle, to maim (une personne). ‖ FIG. To garble, to mangle (une citation); to mutilate (un texte).
mutin, ine [mytɛ̃, in] adj. Rebellious, unruly. ‖ MILIT., NAUT. Mutinous. ‖ FAM. Saucy, pert (personne); *frimousse mutine,* pert little face. (V. ESPIÈGLE.)
— m. Mutineer. ‖ MILIT., NAUT. Mutineer.
mutiné, ée [-tine] adj. Mutinous.
— s. MILIT., NAUT. Mutineer.
mutiner (se) [səmytine] v. pr. (1). To revolt. ‖ MILIT., NAUT. To mutiny.
mutinerie [mytinri] f. Unruliness, disobedience (d'enfant). ‖ Unruliness, insubordination, refractoriness (du peuple). ‖ MILIT., NAUT. Mutiny.
mutisme [mytism] m. Mutism, muteness; dumbness; stolid silence.
mutité [-tite] f. MÉD. Muteness, dumbness.
mutualisme [mytɥalism] m. Mutualism.
mutualiste [-list] m. Mutualist.
mutualité [-lite] f. Mutuality, reciprocity. ‖ JUR. Mutual insurance (assurance).
mutuel, elle [mytɥɛl] adj. Mutual (aide, assurance, consentement). ‖ JUR. *Société de secours*

mutuels, friendly society. ‖ SPORTS. *Pari mutuel,* pari mutuel, totalizator betting.
mutuelle [-tɥɛl] f. JUR. Mutual insurance company.
mutuellement [-tɥɛlmɑ̃] adv. Mutually.
mycélium [miseljɔm] m. BOT. Mycelium.
mycénien, enne [misenjɛ̃, ɛn] adj., s. Mycenaean.
mycologie [mikɔlɔʒi] f. Micology.
micologique [-lɔʒik] adj. Mycologic, mycological.
mycologue [-lɔg] s. Mycologist.
mycose [miko:z] f. MÉD. Mycosis.
myéline [mjelin] f. MÉD. Myelin.
myélite [mjɛlit] f. MÉD. Myelitis.
myélome [mjelo:m] m. MÉD. Myeloma.
mygale [migal] f. ZOOL. Mygale, bird spider.
myocarde [mjɔkard] m. MÉD. Myocardium.
myocardite [mjɔkardit] f. MÉD. Myocarditis.
myope [mjɔp] adj. MÉD. Short- (ou) near-sighted; myopic (œil).
— s. MÉD. Short- (ou) near-sighted person.
myopie [mjɔpi] f. MÉD. Near- (ou) short-sightedness; myopia.
myosotis [mjɔzɔtis] m. BOT. Myosotis, forget-me-not.
myriade [mirjad] f. Myriad.
myriapode [mirjapɔd] m. ZOOL. Myriapod.
myrmidon [mirmidɔ̃] m. Myrmidon. ‖ Dwarf.
myrobolan [mirɔbɔlɑ̃] m. BOT. Myrobalan.
myrrhe [mi:r] f. Myrrh.
myrte [mirt] m. BOT. Myrtle.
myrtille [mirti:l] f. BOT. Whortleberry, bilberry.
mystère [mistɛ:r] m. Secrecy (attitude); mysteriousness (caractère); mystery, secret (secret); *pourquoi faire tant de mystère?,* why act in such secrecy? ‖ THÉÂTR., ECCLÉS. Mystery.
mystérieusement [-terjøzmɑ̃] adv. Mysteriously.
mystérieux, euse [-terjø, ø:z] adj. Mysterious.
mysticisme [mistisism] m. Mysticism.
mysticité [-site] f. Mysticity.
mystificateur, trice [mistifikatœ:r, tris] adj. Mystifying.
— s. Mystifier. ‖ FAM. Hoaxer, humbug.
mystification [-fikasjɔ̃] f. Mystification. ‖ FAM. Hoaxing, hoax, humbug, hocus-pocus.
mystifier [-fje] v. tr. (1). To mystify. ‖ FAM. To hoax, to fool, to humbug, to hocus-pocus, to bamboozle.
mystique [mistik] adj. Mystical, mystic.
— s. Mystic.
— f. Mystical doctrine.
mystiquement [-mɑ̃] adv. Mystically.
mythe [mit] m. Myth (fiction, légende); *faire un mythe de,* to mythicize, to mythologize.
mythifier [-tifje] v. tr. (1). To mythicize.
mythique [-tik] adj. Mythical.
mythologie [mitɔlɔʒi] f. Mythology.
mythologique [-lɔʒik] adj. Mythological.
mythologiquement [-lɔʒikmɑ̃] adv. Mythologically.
mythologue [-lɔg] m. Mythologist, mythologer.
mythomane [-man] s. MÉD. Mythomaniac.
mythomanie [-mani] f. MÉD. Mythomania.
mytiliculture [mitilikylty:r] f. Mussel-breeding.
myxomatose [miksɔmatoz] f. MÉD. Myxomatosis.

N

n [ɛn] m. N (lettre). ‖ MATH. *A la n^{ième} puis-sance,* to the nth power.

N abrév. de *nord,* N, north.

n' v. NE.

na [na] interj. There; *je ne répondrai pas, na!,* I won't answer, there!

nabab [nabab] m. Nabob.

nabot [nabo] adj. Dwarfish, tiny.
— s. Dwarf, midget.

Nabuchodonosor [nabykɔdɔnɔzɔ:r] m. Nebuchadnezzar.

nacelle [nasɛl] f. Skiff, wherry, dinghy (barque). ‖ AVIAT. Cockpit, nacelle (d'avion); basket, nacelle (de ballon).

nacre [nakr] f. Mother-of-pearl, nacre.

nacré, ée [nakre] adj. Pearly, nacreous.

nacrer v. tr. (1). To give a pearly glow to.

nadir [nadi:r] m. ASTRON. Nadir.

nævus [nevy:s] m. MÉD. Birth-mark, naevus.

nage [na:ʒ] f. NAUT. Rowing, sculling; *donner la nage,* to set the stroke. ‖ SPORTS. Swimming; *cent mètres nage libre,* hundred metres free style; *se sauver à la nage,* to swim to safety; *traverser une rivière à la nage,* to swim across a river. ‖ LOC. *Être en nage,* to be bathed in perspiration.

nagée [naʒe] f. SPORTS. Stroke's length.

nageoire [-ʒwa:r] f. ZOOL. Flipper (de baleine); fin (de poisson). ‖ SPORTS. Float, water-wings. ‖ POP. Fin, flipper (bras).

nager [-ʒe] v. intr. (7). To swim; *nager contre le courant,* to swim against the stream; *nager le crawl,* to swim the crawl; *nager entre deux eaux,* to swim under water. ‖ To be plunged in (être plongé dans); *légumes nageant dans le beurre,* vegetables swimming in butter; *nager dans le sang,* to welter in blood. ‖ To float (surnager); *une plume nage sur l'eau,* a feather floats on the water. ‖ NAUT. To row, to scull, to pull; *nagez partout!,* all pull away! ‖ FIG. *Nager contre le courant,* to struggle against ill luck; *nager entre deux eaux,* to run with the hare and hunt with the hounds; *nager dans la joie,* to float on air; *nager dans l'opulence,* to wallow in wealth, to have one's bread buttered on both sides. ‖ FAM. To be perplexed; *savoir nager,* to be a clever schemer, to be a master of the indirect approach; to play both sides against the middle.

nageret [-ʒrɛ] m. Duck-shooting punt.

nageur [-ʒœ:r] m. Swimmer. ‖ NAUT. Oarsman, rower.
— adj. Swimming (oiseau).

naguère [nagɛ:r] adv. Recently, lately, of late, a short time ago, not long ago.

naïade [najad] f. Naiad, water-nymph.

naïf, ive [naif, i:v] adj. Ingenuous, naive, unsophisticated, artless; *avoir l'air naïf,* to look innocent (ou) guileless. ‖ Simple-minded, simple; *plus naïf que bon,* more simple-minded than kind-hearted. ‖ FAM. Silly, green.
— m. Simpleton; green'un (fam.). [V. BENÊT.] ‖ ARTS. Simplicity; *le naïf,* unsophisticated style.

nain, aine [nɛ̃, ɛn] s. Dwarf, midget, pigmy. ‖ *Nain jaune,* Pope Joan (jeu).
— adj. Dwarfish, dwarf, undersized.

nais, naissais. V. NAÎTRE (68).

naissain [nɛsɛ̃] m. ZOOL. Oyster (ou) mussel larvae.

naissance [nɛsɑ̃:s] f. Birth; *donner naissance à,*

to give birth to; *Français de naissance,* French-born, of French birth; *de haute naissance,* high-born. ‖ Origin; *naissance du jour,* dawn; *naissance du printemps,* birth of spring; *donner naissance à,* to give rise to; *prendre naissance,* to arise, to spring, to come to being, to originate. ‖ Beginning (commencement); *naissance du monde,* beginning of the world; *à la naissance des cheveux,* where the hair begins, at the hair-line. ‖ MÉD. Root (de la langue, d'un muscle, d'un ongle). ‖ ARCHIT. Spring (d'un pilier).

naissant, ante [-sɑ̃, ɑ̃:t] adj. Just growing (barbe); newly-born (enfant). ‖ BOT. Newly-formed, new (bourgeon). ‖ MÉD. Incipient, nascent (maladie). ‖ FIG. Budding (amitié). [V. NAÎTRE.]

naître [nɛ:tr] v. intr. (68). To be born (v. NÉ); *encore à naître,* unborn; *il est né le,* he was born on the; *qui vient de naître,* new-born; *un fils lui était né de sa première femme,* his first wife had borne him a son; *la ville qui l'a vu naître,* the town where he was born. ‖ To come up, to rise, to spring up (fleur); to dawn (jour). ‖ FIG. To begin (amitié). ‖ FAM. *Je l'ai vu naître,* I have known him since he was a child; *n'être pas né d'hier,* not to be born yesterday. ‖ LOC. *Faire naître,* to cause; *faire naître l'admiration,* to breed admiration; *faire naître en qqn le désir de,* to inspire s.o. with the desire to.

naïvement [naivmɑ̃] adv. Naively, simply, ingenuously, artlessly.

naïveté [-te] f. Naivety, ingenuousness, guilelessness; simplicity. ‖ Artless (ou) childish (ou) innocent remark. ‖ FAM. Greenness; *avoir la naïveté de croire que,* to be so simple as to believe that.

naja [naʒa] m. ZOOL. Naja.

Namibie [namibi] f. GÉOGR. Namibia.

nana [nana] f. POP. Chick, bird (jeune fille); dame (femme).

nanan [nanɑ̃] m. Dainty. ‖ FAM. Lovely grub; U. S. tasty stuff; *c'est du nanan!,* yum-yum!

nanisme [nanism] m. MÉD. Dwarfism, nanism.

nankin [nɑ̃kɛ̃] m. Nankeen (tissu). ‖ GÉOGR. Nanking.

nantais, aise [nɑ̃tɛ, ɛ:z] adj. GÉOGR. Of (ou) from Nantes.
— s. Native (ou) inhabitant of Nantes.

nanti, e [nɑ̃ti] adj., s. pl. Wealthy, well-to-do.

nantir [nɑ̃ti:r] v. tr. (2). To provide (de, with); *maintenant me voilà nanti,* now I am provided for against a rainy day. ‖ JUR. To secure, to give security to.
— v. pr. Se nantir, to provide oneself (de, with); to equip oneself.

nantissement [nɑ̃tismɑ̃] m. JUR. Security, pledge; *donner en nantissement,* to give as security.

napalm [napalm] m. CHIM., MILIT. Napalm.

naphtaline [naftalin] f. CHIM. Naphthaline, naphthalene. ‖ COMM. Moth-balls (en boules).

naphte [naft] m. CHIM. Naphtha.

naphtol [-tɔl] m. CHIM. Naphthol.

napoléon [napɔleɔ̃] m. FIN. † Napoléon; twenty-franc piece.

napoléonien, enne [-leɔnjɛ̃, ɛn] adj. Napoleonic.

napolitain, aine [napolitɛ̃, ɛn] adj., s. Neapolitan.

nappe [nap] f. Table-cloth, cloth. ‖ ECCLÉS. *Nappe d'autel,* altar-cloth. ‖ FIG. Sheet (d'eau); layer (de brouillard).

napper [-pe] v. tr. (1). CULIN. To coat (de, with).

napperon [-prɔ̃] m. Tea-cloth; tray-cloth; *napperon individuel*, individual table-mat; *petit napperon*, doily.

naquis [naki]. V. NAÎTRE (68).

narcisse [narsis] m. BOT. Narcissus.

narcissique [-sisik] adj. Narcissistic.

narcissisme [-sisism] m. Narcissism.

narcose [narko:z] f. MÉD. Narcosis.

narcotique [-kɔtik] m. Opiate; drug; narcotic.
— adj. Narcotic. (V. SOPORIFIQUE.)

nard [na:r] m. MÉD., BOT. Nard, spikenard.

narghilé [nargile] m. V. NARGUILÉ.

narguer [-ge] v. tr. (1). To flout, to taunt, to snap one's fingers at (se moquer de). ‖ To set at defiance (défier).

narguilé [nargile] m. Narghile, hookah.

narine [narin] f. MÉD. Nostril.

narquois, oise [narkwa, waz] adj. Mocking, sneering, derisive.

narquoisement [-zmɑ̃] adv. Sneeringly, mockingly, derisively.

narrateur, trice [naratœ:r, tris] s. Narrator, teller, relater; story-teller.

narratif, ive [-tif, i:v] adj. Narrative.

narration [-sjɔ̃] f. Narration, narrative, account. (V. RÉCIT.) ‖ Composition, theme. (V. DISSERTATION.) ‖ GRAMM. *De narration,* historic (infinitif).

narrer [nare] v. tr. (1). To narrate. (V. RACONTER.)

narthex [nartɛks] m. ARCHIT. Narthex, lich-gate.

narval [narval] m. ZOOL. Narwhal.

nasal, ale [nazal] adj. Nasal. ‖ MÉD. *Gouttes nasales,* nose-drops.

nasale [-za:l] f. GRAMM. Nasal.

nasalisation [-lizasjɔ̃] f. GRAMM. Nasalization.

nasaliser [-lize] v. tr. (1). GRAMM. To nasalize.

nasalité [-lite] f. Nasality.

nasarde [nazard] f. Fillip (ou) rap on the nose (chiquenaude). ‖ FIG. Rebuff, snub.

naseau [nazo] m. Nostril (d'animal).

nasillard, arde [nazija:r, ard] adj. Nasal.

nasillement [-jmɑ̃] m. Nasal pronunciation (ou) twang, snuffle.

nasiller [-je] v. intr. (1). To talk through one's nose, to snuffle; to twang.
— v. tr. To snuffle out, to say through one's nose.

nasilleur [-jœ:r] m. Snuffler, one who speaks through his nose (ou) with a nasal twang.

nasse [nas] f. SPORTS. Basket, wicker-trap, U. S. fyke (pour la pêche).

natal, ale [natal] (pl. **natals**) adj. Native; *ville natale,* birth-place. ‖ Natal; *jour natal,* birthday.

nataliste [-list] adj. Encouraging an increase in the birth-rate.

natalité [-lite] f. Natality. ‖ Birth-rate.

natation [natasjɔ̃] f. SPORTS. Swimming, natation; *ceinture de natation,* swimming-belt.

natatoire [-twa:r] adj. ZOOL. Natatory, natatorial; *vessie natatoire,* swimming- (ou) air-bladder.

natif, ive [natif, i:v] adj. Native, born (né); *natif de Brive,* Brive-born. ‖ Native, natural (inné); *or natif,* free gold; *bon sens natif,* native wit.
— s. Native.

nation [nasjɔ̃] f. Nation; *Nations Unies,* United Nations.

national, ale [nasjɔnal] adj. National (hymne, histoire, industrie); nationwide (importance, échelle); *Assemblée nationale,* National Assembly, French Parliament. ‖ AUTOM. Main (route). ‖ FAM. Very own, this our great (iron.). ‖ **National-socialisme,** m. National Socialism. ‖ **National-socialiste** (pl. *nationaux-socialistes*), adj., s. National Socialist.
— f. AUTOM. Main road, A road.
— m. pl. *Les nationaux,* the nationals (d'un pays).

nationalisation [-lizasjɔ̃] f. Nationalization.

nationaliser [-lize] v. tr. (1). To nationalize.

nationalisme [-lism] m. Nationalism.

nationaliste [-list] m. Nationalist.
— adj. Nationalistic.

nationalité [-lite] f. Nationality.

nativisme [nativism] m. PSYCH. Nativism.

nativiste [-vist] adj. PSYCH. Nativistic.

nativité [nativite] f. ECCLÉS. Nativity.

natron [natrɔ̃] m. CHIM. Natron.

natte [nat] f. Mat, matting (de joncs). ‖ Plait, braid (de cheveux); pigtail (de Chinois, de petite fille). [V. TRESSE.]

natter [nate] v. tr. (1). To weave (des joncs). ‖ To cover with mats (une pièce). ‖ To plait, to braid (des cheveux).

naturalisation [natyralizasjɔ̃] f. Naturalization (d'une personne). ‖ Naturalizing, acclimatizing (d'un animal, d'une plante). ‖ Taxidermy, stuffing, mounting (empaillage).

naturalisé, ée [natyralize] adj. Naturalized (personne).
— s. Naturalized person, citizen by naturalization.

naturaliser [-lize] v. tr. (1). To naturalize, to nationalize (qqn). ‖ To naturalize, to acclimatize (un animal, une plante). ‖ TECHN. To stuff, to mount (empailler).
— v. pr. Se naturaliser, to become naturalized.

naturalisme [-lism] m. Naturalism.

naturaliste [-list] m. PHILOS., ARTS. Naturalist. ‖ TECHN. Taxidermist.
— adj. Naturalistic.

naturalité [-lite] f. Naturalness.

nature [naty:r] f. Nature (cours des choses); *contre nature,* unnatural; *ne pas forcer la nature,* not to constrain (ou) force nature; *laisser agir la nature,* to let nature follow her course; *lois de la nature,* laws of nature. ‖ Nature (v. CONSTITUTION); *bon par nature,* kind by nature, naturally kind; *être musicien de nature,* to have a natural bent for music. ‖ Nature (contexture); *de la même nature,* of the same kind; *film de nature à effrayer des enfants,* film likely to frighten children; *proposition de nature à,* proposal of such a nature as to; *tenir à la nature du climat,* to depend on the nature of the climate. ‖ Nature (monde physique); *aimer la nature,* to be fond of nature; *retour à la nature,* return to nature. ‖ Kind (produits matériels); *payer en nature,* to pay in kind. ‖ Nature (v. TEMPÉRAMENT); *une bonne nature,* a good (ou) genial disposition; *c'est une petite nature,* he is a weakly sort of person (ou) a weakling; *d'une nature exubérante,* of buoyant disposition; *nature accueillante,* receptive nature; *quelle nature insouciante!,* what a carefree fellow!; *quelle nature insupportable!,* what an unbearable fellow! ‖ ARTS. *D'après nature,* from nature; *plus grand que nature,* larger than life (portrait). ‖ FIG. Order, sort, kind (v. ESPÈCE); *n'accepter aucun service de quelque nature qu'il soit,* to accept no service of any kind; *des défauts d'une autre nature,* defects of another order; *de même nature,* similar, of the same sort.
— adj. invar. Neat, pure (pur); *à l'état nature,* in a state of nature. ‖ CULIN. Black (café); plain (omelette); boiled (pommes). ‖ ARTS. *Grandeur nature,* life-size. ‖ FAM. Unaffected (personne).

naturel, elle [-rɛl] adj. Natural (inné); innate (dons); instinctive (horreur); spontaneous (obligeance); natural, inevitable (réaction); native (vivacité); *mort naturelle,* death from natural causes. ‖ Natural (sans artifice); unaffected (attitude); unlaboured (effort); unstudied (langage); plain, sober (style); genuine (vin). ‖ Natural (normal) [à, to]. ‖ BOT., ZOOL. *Histoire naturelle,* natural history. ‖ JUR. Natural (droit).

— m. Native (habitant). ‖ Nature, disposition (caractère); *avoir un bon naturel*, to be kind-hearted. ‖ Naturalness (simplicité); *le naturel dans la littérature*, naturalness in literature. ‖ CULIN. *Au naturel*, unseasoned; boiled. ‖ LOC. *Au naturel*, as things are, realistically.

aturellement [-rɛlmɑ̃] adv. Naturally (simplement); *répondre naturellement*, to answer in plain language. ‖ Of course (bien entendu); *naturellement, il vous paiera!*, of course, he will pay you! ‖ Naturally (par nature); *naturellement scrupuleux*, naturally scrupulous.

aturisme [-rism] m. Naturism.

aturiste [-rist] m. Naturist.
— adj. Naturistic.

aufrage [nofra:ʒ] m. NAUT. Wreck, shipwreck; *faire naufrage*, to be wrecked; *périr dans un naufrage*, to be lost at sea. ‖ FIG. Ruin; shipwreck.

aufragé, ée [nofraʒe] adj. NAUT. Shipwrecked; castaway.
— s. NAUT. Shipwrecked person; castaway; marooned person (sur une île déserte).

aufrager v. tr. (7). NAUT. To wreck.

aufrageur [-ʒœ:r] m. Wrecker.

auséabond, onde [nozeabɔ̃, ɔ̃d] adj. Ill-smelling, nauseous, nauseating, reeking; stinking.

ausée [noze] f. MÉD. Nausea; sea-sickness (en mer); *avoir la nausée*, to feel sick (ou) sick to one's stomach; *sujet aux nausées*, squeamish. ‖ PHILOS. «Nausée» (existentialisme). ‖ FIG. Nausea.

auséeux, euse [-ø, ø:z] adj. Nauseous, nauseating, sickening. ‖ FIG. Loathsome.

autile [notil] m. ZOOL. Pearly nautilus, nautilus.

autique [notik] adj. Nautical; *sports nautiques*, water sports; *salon nautique*, boat show.

autisme [-tism] m. Water sports, yachting.

autonier [notɔnje] m. NAUT. Ferryman, pilot.

aval, ale [naval] (pl. **navals**) adj. Naval (en général); *constructions navales*, ship-building; *forces navales*, sea-forces, navy.

avarin [navarɛ̃] m. CULIN. Haricot-mutton, lamb stew with turnips.

avarrais, aise [navarɛ, ɛ:z] adj. GÉOGR. Of (ou) from Navarre.
— s. Native (ou) inhabitant of Navarre.

avet [navɛ] m. BOT. Turnip. ‖ ARTS., FAM. Daub, dud. ‖ FAM. Ass (personne); *avoir du sang de navet*, to be a twerp, to be without guts.

avette [navɛt] f. TECHN. Shuttle. ‖ NAUT. *Faire la navette*, to ply. ‖ CH. DE F. Shuttle-train. ‖ FIG. *Faire la navette*, to go to and fro (personne).

avette f. BOT. Rape; *de navette*, rape-seed (huile).

avicert [navisɛrt] m. NAUT. Navicert, navigation certificate.

aviculaire [-kylɛ:r] adj. MÉD. Navicular.

avigabilité [-gabilite] f. NAUT. Navigability (d'un fleuve); seaworthiness (d'un navire).

avigable [-gabl] adj. NAUT. Navigable (fleuve); seaworthy (navire).

avigant, ante [-gɑ̃, ɑ̃:t] adj. NAUT. Sailing. ‖ AVIAT. Flying.
— s. AVIAT. Member of flying staff.

avigateur, trice [-gatœ:r, tris] s. NAUT. Navigator, sailor. ‖ AVIAT. Navigator.
— adj. Seafaring (peuple).

avigation [-gasjɔ̃] f. Navigation, sailing; *navigation de plaisance*, yachting; *compagnie, routes de navigation*, shipping company, routes; *terme de navigation*, nautical term. ‖ AVIAT. *Navigation aérienne*, aeronautical navigation.

aviguer [-ge] v. intr. (1). NAUT. To sail, to navigate; *naviguer au cabotage*, to be in the coasting trade; *naviguer près de la terre*, to hug the land (ou) the coast.
— v. tr. NAUT. To navigate, to sail (un navire).

navire [navi:r] m. NAUT. Ship, boat, vessel (v. BATEAU); *navire de commerce*, merchantman, cargo-boat, trader; *navire de guerre*, warship, man-of-war; *navire de ligne*, capital ship; *navire à vapeur*, steamship, steamer; *navire à voiles*, sailing-ship. ‖ AVIAT. *Navire volant*, flying boat. ‖ **Navire-citerne**, m. NAUT. Tank-vessel, tanker. ‖ **Navire-école**, m. NAUT. Training ship. ‖ **Navire-hôpital**, m. NAUT. Hospital-ship.

navrant, ante [navrɑ̃, ɑ̃:t] adj. Heart-breaking, distressing, dreadful, heart-rending.

navré, ée [-vre] adj. Heart-broken, deeply grieved, broken-hearted; *avoir l'air navré*, to look downcast. ‖ FAM. Terribly sorry (de, for).

navrer [-vre] v. tr. (1). To hurt, to grieve, to cut to the heart (ou) to the quick. (V. ATTRISTER.)

nazaréen, éenne [nazareɛ̃, ɛɛn] adj. Nazarene.
— s. GÉOGR. Nazarene, Nazarite.

nazi [nazi] s. Nazi.

nazifier [-zifje] v. tr. (1). To nazify.

nazisme [-zism] m. Nazism.

n. b. [ɛnbe] abrév. de *nota bene*, N. B.

ne [nə] (n' devant voyelle ou h muette) adv.

---

1. Employé avec *cesser, importer, pouvoir, oser, savoir*. — 2. Employé après *autre... que*. — 3. Employé seul après *que, quel, qui*. — 4. Employé après *il y a... que, depuis que*. — 5. Employé après *si*. — 6. Employé avec une locution de temps. — 7. Explétif après *craindre, empêcher, éviter, pouvoir, prendre garde, à moins que, avant que, de crainte, peu s'en faut que*. — 8. Explétif après *douter, nier*. — 9. Explétif après le comparatif. — 10. Explétif après *autre, autrement*.

---

1. (Employé seul avec les verbes *cesser, importer, pouvoir, oser, savoir*); *ne cesser d'interrompre qqn*, to keep interrupting s.o.; *n'importe!*, never mind!; *je ne puis vous dire combien*, I cannot tell you how much; *n'oser contredire qqn*, not to dare contradict s.o.; *je ne sais*, I don't know. ‖ 2. (Employé seul après *autre... que*); *n'avoir d'autre soin que de s'enrichir*, to have no other aim than to get rich. ‖ 3. (Employé seul, après *que, quel, qui* interrogatifs ou exclamatifs); *que ne me l'avez-vous dit plus tôt!*, why didn't you tell me earlier!; *que ne diriez-vous si je le faisais?*, what wouldn't you say if I did it?; *quelle femme ne serait scandalisée!*, what woman would not be shocked! ‖ 4. (Employé seul, facultativement, après *il y a... [ou] depuis que*); *depuis que vous (ne) m'avez quitté*, since you have left me. ‖ 5. (Employé seul, facultativement, après *si*, exprimé ou sous-entendu); *il se serait noyé, n'eût été sa fille*, he would have been drowned, had it not been for his daughter; *s'il n'arrive dans cinq minutes, je partirai*, if he does not come within five minutes, I shall go; *si je ne me trompe*, if I am not mistaken. ‖ 6. (Employé seul dans une proposition principale contenant une locution de temps); *je ne lui parlerai de longtemps après cela*, it will be a long time before I speak to him again after that. ‖ 7. (Explétif, après les verbes : *avoir peur, craindre, empêcher, éviter, prendre garde*; après les locutions : *à moins que, avant que, de crainte que, peu s'en faut que*); *j'ai peur qu'il ne s'en repente*, I am afraid he will regret it; *évitez qu'on ne vous envie*, take care not to arouse envy; *prendre garde que les valeurs ne baissent tout d'un coup*, to take care that stocks do not fall suddenly; *à moins que vous ne preniez beaucoup de précautions*, unless you take many precautions; *avant que vous n'ayez fini*, before you have finished;

de crainte qu'on ne soit attaqué, for fear one may be attacked ; *peu s'en est fallu que la foudre ne soit tombée sur notre toit,* our roof barely escaped being struck by lightning. ‖ **8.** (Explétif après les verbes *douter, nier* employés négativement avec notion d'incertitude) ; *je ne doute pas qu'il n'ait des raisons de se défier,* I do not doubt that he has reasons to be distrustful ; *nous ne nions pas qu'il ne l'ait dit,* we do not deny that he has said it. ‖ **9.** (Explétif après un comparatif) ; *ce sera moins facile qu'il ne le dit,* it will be less easy than he says ; *ce sera plus long que vous ne pensez,* it will be longer than you think. ‖ **10.** (Explétif avec *autre, autrement*) ; *le problème se présente autrement que vous ne croyez,* the problem presents itself differently from what you believe. (V. PAS.)

né, ée [ne] adj. Born (v. NAÎTRE); *bien né,* of good family, well connected, gently (ou) high-born ; *né chanceux,* born lucky ; *né sous une bonne étoile,* born under a lucky star, well-starred ; *née Brown,* née Brown. ‖ FIG. Born ; *poète-né,* a born poet, a poet born ; *ruines nées de la guerre,* ruins caused by the war.
— s. Born ; *premier-né,* first-born.

néanmoins [neɑ̃mwɛ̃] adv. Nevertheless, notwithstanding, however, yet, still ; all the same, for all that. (V. CEPENDANT.)

néant [neɑ̃] m. Nothingness, nothing, naught, nought ; *néant des promesses,* emptiness (ou) worthlessness of promises ; *réduire à néant,* to reduce to nothing (ou) nought. ‖ Nil ; *actif, enfants : néant,* assets, children : nil.

nébuleuse [nebylø:z] f. ASTR. Nebula.

nébuleusement [-løzmɑ̃] adv. Nebulously.

nébuleux, euse [-lø, ø:z] adj. Nebulous ; cloudy, overcast, hazy, misty, foggy (ciel, horizon). [V. NUAGEUX.] ‖ Turbid, muddy, cloudy (cristal, liquide). ‖ Gloomy, clouded, sombre, frowning (front). ‖ FAM. Nebulous, recondite (écrit, écrivain); obscure, vague, hazy (idée).

nébuliseur [-lizœ:r] m. Spray, atomizer.

nébulosité [-lozite] f. Nebulosity, nebulousness, cloudiness (état) ; light cloud, patch of mist (nuage). ‖ FAM. Obscurity, haziness.

nécessaire [nesɛsɛ:r] adj. Necessary, needful, requisite, indispensable ; *nécessaire à,* necessary (ou) required for ; *il est nécessaire que vous teniez compte de ces choses,* you cannot afford to ignore these things ; *peu nécessaire,* unnecessary, needless.
— m. *Le nécessaire,* the necessary, the needful ; *faire le nécessaire,* to do the indispensable (ou) what is required. ‖ The necessities of life ; *manquer du nécessaire,* to lack the necessities of life. ‖ Outfit, kit ; *nécessaire à ouvrage,* sewing-outfit, sewing-kit, housewife ; *nécessaire à outils,* repair outfit ; tool-box ; *nécessaire de toilette,* dressing-case, toilet-set.

nécessairement [-mɑ̃] adv. Necessarily, of necessity (absolument) ; inevitably, of course (inévitablement). ‖ Willy-nilly (bon gré, mal gré).

nécessité [nesɛsite] f. Necessity, need (v. BESOIN). *être de toute nécessité de,* to be absolutely necessary to ; *nécessité absolue,* absolute necessity (ou) U. S. must. ‖ Necessity, inevitableness (caractère inévitable). ‖ Necessity, compulsion (obligation) ; *céder à la nécessité,* to yield under stress of necessity ; *se trouver dans la nécessité de partir,* to be under the necessity of going away. ‖ Indigence, poverty ; straitened circumstances (pauvreté) ; *état d'extrême nécessité,* state of extreme need. ‖ COMM. *Objet de première nécessité,* staple commodity.

nécessiter v. tr. (1). To necessitate, to require, to make necessary, to entail ; *nécessiter d'assez grandes dépenses,* to entail considerable expense.

nécessiteux, euse [-tø, ø:z] adj. Needy, necessitous, in want, deprived.
— s. Needy person ; *les nécessiteux,* the destitute the needy.

nec plus ultra [nɛkplyzyltra] m. Ne plu ultra, height, apex, dernier cri.

nécrologe [nekrɔlɔ:ʒ] m. ECCLÉS. Obituary lis death-roll.

nécrologie [-lɔʒi] f. Necrology, obituary.

nécrologique [-lɔʒik] adj. Necrological, obituary *notice nécrologique,* obituary notice.

nécromancie [-mɑ̃si] f. Necromancy.

nécromancien [-mɑ̃sjɛ̃] s. Necromancer.

nécrophilie [-fili] f. Necrophyly.

nécropole [-pɔl] f. Necropolis.

nécrose [nekro:z] f. MÉD. Necrosis. ‖ BOT Canker.

nécroser [-krɔze] v. tr. (1). MÉD. To cause necro sis in (un os). ‖ BOT. To canker (un arbre).
— v. pr. **Se nécroser.** MÉD. To necrotize. ‖ BOT To canker.

nectar [nɛkta:r] m. Nectar.

nectarine [-rin] f. AGRIC. Nectarine.

néerlandais, aise [neɛrlɑ̃dɛ, ɛ:z] adj. Dutch Netherlandish ; *les Indes néerlandaises,* the Dutch East Indies.
— m. GÉOGR. Netherlander, Dutchman. GRAMM. Dutch (langue).

Néerlandaise [-dɛ:z] f. GÉOGR. Dutchwoman.

nef [nɛf] f. † NAUT. Vessel. ‖ *Nef latérale,* aisle. ECCLÉS., ARCHIT. Nave.

néfaste [nefast] adj. Bringing ill luck, attende by evil circumstances ; ill-fated, ill-omened unlucky, ill-starred (événement, jour, signe). Harmful, mischievous (personne). ‖ Baneful pernicious, injurious, hurtful (action, influence)

nèfle [nɛfl] f. BOT. Medlar. ‖ POP. *Avoir qqch pour des nèfles,* to get sth. dirt-cheap ; *des nèfles .* nothing doing! ; U. S. nuts!

néflier [neflije] m. BOT. Medlar-tree.

négateur, trice [negatœ:r, tris] adj. Given t denying.
— s. Denier ; one who denies.

négatif, ive [-tif, -i:v] adj. Negative (position réponse). ‖ MATH. Minus (quantité). ‖ ARTS *Epreuve négative,* negative (photo).
— m. Negative (en photo).

négation [-sjɔ̃] f. Negation, denial (d'une asser tion, d'un fait). ‖ GRAMM. Negative.

négative [-tiv] f. Negative ; *se tenir sur la néga tive,* to maintain a negative attitude ; *soutenir l négative,* to oppose the motion, to uphold th negative.

négativement [-tivmɑ̃] adv. Negatively ; *répondr négativement,* to return a negative answer, t reply in the negative.

négativisme [-tivism] m. Negativism.

négativité [-tivite] f. Negativity.

négligé, ée [negliʒe] adj. Careless of one's perso (personne) ; untidy, slovenly, careless, loose (vête ment). ‖ Neglected, left out in the cold (ami) neglected, unheeded (obligation) ; neglected, over looked, missed (occasion) ; loose, careless, slip shod (style).
— m. Negligee, morning wrap, wrapper (d femme) ; dressing-gown (d'homme) ; *en néglig é* in informal attire, in undress.

négligeable [-ʒabl] adj. Negligible, unimportan insignificant, trifling, immaterial (acte, parole quantité).

négligemment [-ʒamɑ̃] adv. Negligently, care lessly (sans soin). ‖ Casually (indolemment).

négligence [-ʒɑ̃:s] f. Neglect, negligence, care lessness, remissness (manque de soin). ‖ Heedless ness, thoughtlessness (manque d'attention). Negligence, slovenliness, oversight (de style).

Negligence, looseness, carelessness, slovenliness (du vêtement).

négligent, ente [-ʒɑ̃, ɑ̃:t] adj. Negligent, neglectful, careless, remiss (sans soin). ‖ Heedless, thoughtless, careless, slack (sans attention).

négliger [-ʒe] v. tr. (7). To neglect, to be remiss about; *ne rien négliger pour aboutir,* to leave no stone unturned. ‖ To neglect (un ami); to slight, to ignore (un avis, qqn); to neglect, to leave out (un élément utile); to neglect, to disregard, to let go by (une occasion). ‖ To neglect, to be careless about (sa mise). ‖ To neglect, to omit, to fail (*de,* to); to overlook (omettre).
— v. pr. **Se négliger,** to neglect oneself; to become careless about (au sujet de sa santé, de sa tenue). ‖ To become slovenly (ou) slipshod (au sujet de son style).

négoce [negɔs] m. COMM. Trade, business; *entreprendre le négoce du pétrole,* to go into oil.

négociabilité [-sjabilite] f. Negotiability.

négociable [-sjabl] adj. FIN. Negotiable (effet); transferable (valeurs).

négociant, ante [sjɑ̃, ɑ̃:t] s. COMM. Wholesale dealer (ou) merchant; wholesaler.

négociateur, trice [-sjatœr, tris] m. Negotiator (d'un consortium, d'un traité). ‖ Transactor (d'une affaire).

négociation [-sjasjɔ̃] f. Negotiation, negotiating (d'un traité). ‖ COMM. Negotiating (d'un billet, d'une transaction). ‖ FIN. Transaction (de valeurs). ‖ MILIT. Parley, negotiation.

négocier [-sje] v. tr. (1). To negotiate (une association, un mariage, un traité). ‖ FIN. To place (un emprunt); to negotiate (des valeurs).
— v. intr. To negotiate; to deal (*avec,* with).

nègre [nɛ:gr] m. Negro, black; coloured man. ‖ Ghost, devil, U. S. stooge (rédacteur à gages); *faire le nègre,* to ghost, to devil, U. S. to stooge; *faire rédiger ses articles par des nègres,* to have one's articles written by ghost-writers. ‖ FAM. *Parler petit-nègre,* to talk broken French (ou) pidgin-English; *travailler comme un nègre,* to work like a nigger, to drudge.
— adj. Negro, black, coloured; *la race nègre,* the Negro race.

négresse [negrɛs] f. Negress, coloured woman.

négrier [negrije] m. NAUT. Slave-ship (bateau); captain of a slave-ship (commandant); slave-trader (trafiquant); *bateau négrier,* slave-ship.

négrillon [-jɔ̃] m. FAM. Nigger-boy, pickaninny.

négrillonne [-jɔn] f. FAM. Nigger-girl.

négritude [-tyd] f. Negritude.

négro [negro] m. FAM. Nigger.

négroïde [-grɔid] adj. Negroid.

négus [negy:s] m. Negus.

neige [nɛ:ʒ] f. Snow; *neiges éternelles,* perpetual snow; *neige fondue,* slush (à terre); sleet (tombant). ‖ CH. DE F. *Train de neige,* winter sports (ou) U. S. ski train. ‖ CULIN. *Œufs à la neige,* whipped eggs with cream, U. S. floating island; *œufs battus en neige,* whites of eggs beaten stiff. ‖ CHIM. *Neige carbonique,* dry ice. ‖ FIG. *De neige,* snowy (cheveux).

neiger [nɛʒe] v. imp. (7). To snow; *il neige dru,* it is snowing hard.

neigeux, euse [-ʒø, ø:z] adj. Snowy, snow-covered. ‖ Snow-white (blanc).

nemrod [nɛmrɔd] m. Nimrod.

néné [nene] m. POP. Tit, bub. (V. NICHON.)

nenni [nani] adv. † Nay, not I!

nénuphar [nenyfa:r] m. BOT. Water-lily, nenuphar.

néo- [neo] préf. Neo-. ‖ **Néo-calédonien,** adj., s. GÉOGR. New Caledonian. ‖ **Néo-hébridais,** adj., s. GÉOGR. New Hebridean. ‖ **Néo-zélandais,** adj. GÉOGR. New Zealand; s. New Zealander.

néocapitalisme [neokapitalism] m. Neo-capitalism.

néoclassicisme [-klasisism] m. Neo-classicism.

néocolonialisme [-kɔlɔnjalism] m. Neo-colonialism.

néodyme [-dim] m. CHIM. Neodymium.

néogothique [-gɔtik] adj., m. ARCHIT., ARTS. Neo-Gothic.

néolibéralisme [-liberalism] m. Neo-liberalism.

néolithique [-litik] adj., m. Neolithic.

néologique [-lɔʒik] adj. GRAMM. Neological.

néologisme [-lɔʒism] m. GRAMM. Neologism.

néon [neɔ̃] m. ELECTR. Neon; *éclairage au néon,* neon lighting.

néonatal, ale [neonatal] adj. MÉD. Neonatal.

néophyte [-fit] s. ECCLÉS. Neophyte. ‖ FIG. Neophyte, tyro (fam.).

néoplasme [-plasm] m. MÉD. Neoplasm.

Néoprène [-prɛn] m. (nom déposé). Neoprene.

néoréalisme [-realism] m. CINÉM. Neo-realism.

Népal [nepal] m. GÉOGR. Nepal.

népalais, aise [-lɛ, ɛ:z] adj., s. GÉOGR. Nepali, Nepalese.
— m. GRAMM. Nepali, Nepalese (langue).

néphrétique [nefretik] adj. MÉD. Nephritic; renal (colique).

néphrite [-frit] f. MÉD. Nephritis. ‖ Nephrite, jade (pierre).

néphrologie [-frɔlɔʒi] f. MÉD. Nephrology.

népotisme [nepɔtism] m. Nepotism.

neptunien, enne [nɛptynjɛ̃, ɛn] adj. Neptunian.

neptunium [-njɔm] m. CHIM. Neptunium.

Nérée [nere] m. Nereus.

néréide [-id] f. Nereid (divinité). ‖ ZOOL. Nereid, nereis, ragworm.

nerf [nɛr] m. MÉD. Nerve (filet nerveux); sinew (tendon); *attaque de nerfs,* hysterics; *avoir les nerfs malades,* to have a nervous complaint; *des jambes qui ont du nerf,* sinewy (ou) muscular legs. ‖ TECHN. Band (en reliure). ‖ ARCHIT. Rib (de voûte). ‖ MILIT. Sinews, nerves; *le nerf de la guerre,* the sinews of war. ‖ FIG. Nerve, sensitiveness, sensitivity, susceptibility (impressionnabilité); *avoir les nerfs à fleur de peau,* to be thin-skinned (ou) highly strung (ou) on edge; *avoir ses nerfs,* to be on edge; *avoir les nerfs à vif,* to be jumpy (fam.); *mettre les nerfs de qqn à vif,* to fray s.o.'s nerves; *paquet de nerfs,* bundle of nerves, fidget; *porter (ou) taper sur les nerfs à qqn,* to get on s.o.'s nerves (ou) U. S. in s.o.'s hair (fam.). ‖ FIG. Nerve; sinews, thews; energy, vigour, mettle, pep, vim (énergie, force); *avoir des nerfs d'acier,* to have nerves of steel; *du nerf, bon sang!,* wake up, man!; *elle voudrait lui voir plus de nerf,* she wishes he had more backbone; *manquer de nerf,* to be flabby (ou) lackadaisical; *sans nerf,* nerveless, weak (personne); slipshod, sloppy (style). ‖ **Nerf-de-bœuf,** m. Bull's pizzle.

néroli [nerɔli] m. Neroli; neroli oil; *essence de néroli,* orange-flower water.

Néron [nerɔ̃] m. Nero.

néronien, enne [-rɔnjɛ̃, ɛn] adj. Neronian.

nerprun [nɛrprœ̃] m. BOT. Buckthorn.

nervé, ée [nɛrve] adj. BOT. Nervate.

nerver v. tr. (1). To reinforce. ‖ To put hands on (en reliure). ‖ To strengthen (un panneau).

nerveusement [-vøzmɑ̃] adj. Nervously. ‖ Vigorously.

nerveux, euse [-vø, ø:z] adj. MÉD. Nerve (cellule, centre); sinewy, wiry (corps, membre); nervous (maladie, système). ‖ AUTOM. Responsive, lively (moteur). ‖ BOT. Nervate (feuille). ‖ FIG. Fidgety, nervy, jittery (impatient); excitable, highly-strung (impressionnable); *rendu nerveux par l'attente,* made jittery by long waiting; *rire nerveux,* hyster-

ical laughter. ‖ Fig. Vigorous, forceful, snappy (style).
— s. Excitable (ou) highly-strung (ou) oversensitive person.
nervi [nɛrvi] m. Pop. Hooligan, tough.
nervosisme [nɛrvozism] m. Méd. Nervous diathesis.
nervosité [-zite] f. Excitability (v. agitation); irritability; *en état de nervosité,* in a highly-strung condition; *nervy,* on edge (fam.).
nervure [nɛrvy:r] f. Piping. ‖ Techn. Rib, flange. ‖ Bot. Nervure, rib, vein (de feuille). ‖ Archit. Fillet (de colonne); rib (de voûte).
nervuré, ée [-vyre] adj. Veined, ribbed.
n'est-ce pas [nɛspɑ] adv. V. être, *v. impers.*
net, ette [nɛt] adj. Clean, spotless, stainless (propre); *faire plat net,* to leave a clean plate. ‖ Neat, tidy, spruce (aspect, costume); fair (copie); clear, distinct (écriture); clear-cut (lignes); sharp (image, photo). ‖ Fin. Net; *bénéfice net,* net return; *net de,* free from; *revenu net d'impôts,* tax-free income. ‖ Comm. *Faire maison nette,* to dismiss all one's employees. ‖ Fig. Unexceptionable, above-board (conduite); clear (conscience); clear, distinct, definite (idées); flat, downright, unmistakable (refus); clear, plain, candid (réponse); *un esprit net,* a clear-headed person. ‖ Fam. *En avoir le cœur net,* to get sth. clear, to know where one stands.
— m. *Mettre qqch. au net,* to write a fair copy of sth. ‖ Fin. *Net légal,* net proceeds.
— adv. Clearly, plainly, flatly; *refuser net,* to refuse point-blank. ‖ Short: *s'arrêter net,* to stop short. ‖ Bluntly; *parler net à,* to speak plainly to. ‖ Comm. Clear; *mille francs net,* thousand francs clear, a clear thousand francs.
nettement [-tmɑ̃] adv. Cleanly (proprement). ‖ Clearly, distinctly (clairement); plainly, sharply (sans détours). ‖ Definitely, obviously, decidedly (sans ambiguïté); *prendre nettement parti,* to take sides unmistakably.
netteté [-təte] f. Cleanness, neatness (propreté). ‖ Neatness (du costume, de la tenue). ‖ Sharpness (d'une cassure); sharpness, clearness (des lignes). ‖ Clearness (de l'écriture, d'un texte); distinctness, clearness (d'une illustration, d'une impression); distinctness, terseness, incisiveness (du style). ‖ Fig. Decidedness (d'une attitude mentale).
nettoiement [nɛtwamɑ̃] m. Clearing (d'une prairie). ‖ Cleaning (des rues); *service du nettoiement,* refuse collection, U. S. garbage service.
nettoie-pipe [nɛtwapi:p] m. Pipe-cleaning combination, pipe-cleaner.
nettoyage [nɛtwaja:ʒ] m. Cleaning (d'une maison); *nettoyage à sec,* dry cleaning; *grand nettoyage,* spring cleaning. ‖ Milit. Mopping up.
nettoyer [-je] v. tr. (9a). To clean, U. S. to cleanse (en général); to wash out (une bouteille); to scour (une casserole); to wash up (la vaisselle); *nettoyer à grande eau,* to swill out, to mop; *nettoyer à sec,* to dry-clean. ‖ Méd. To cleanse (une plaie). ‖ Agric. To screen (du blé); to clean (la terre). ‖ Techn. To pickle (du métal). ‖ Naut. To scour, to swab (le pont). ‖ Milit. To mop up (une tranchée). ‖ Fam. To clean out; *nettoyer les poches de qqn,* to rifle s.o.'s pockets; *nettoyer qqn à la roulette,* to clean s.o. out at roulette.
— v. pr. Se nettoyer, to clean oneself; to wash (personne). ‖ To clean (étoffe); *se nettoyer bien,* to clean easily.
nettoyeur, euse [-jœ:r, ø:z] adj. Cleaning.
— m. Cleaner; dry-cleaner (teinturier); street-cleaner (de rues); *nettoyeur de fenêtres,* window-cleaner, U. S. window-washer. ‖ Techn. *Nettoyeur de chaudières,* scurfer.
nettoyeuse [-jø:z] f. Techn. Cleaning machine.
neuf [nœf] adj. num. Nine; *Charles IX,* Charles

the Ninth; *les neuf dixièmes,* nine-tenths; *à neuf heures,* at nine o'clock; *le neuf octobre,* October the ninth, the ninth of October, U. S. October ninth.
— m. invar. *Le neuf de trèfle,* the nine of clubs. ‖ Math. *Faire la preuve par neuf,* to cast out the nines.
neuf, euve [nœf, nœv] adj. New (non usé); *auto neuve,* new car; *livre neuf,* new book; *presque neuf,* almost new, as good as new, « as new ». ‖ Fig. New, fresh, young, inexperienced, raw (inexpérimenté); *esprit neuf,* fresh mind; *neuf en affaires,* a novice in business; *regarder avec des yeux neufs,* to take a new (ou) fresh view of things. ‖ Fam. Yet unknown (non connu); new, unhackneyed (non rebattu).
— m. New; *à l'état de neuf,* practically new; *habillé de neuf,* dressed in new clothes. ‖ Fam. New (nouveau); *il y a du neuf,* there is something new; *quoi de neuf?,* what news?; is there anything new? ‖ Loc. A neuf, like new; anew; *reconstruire à neuf,* to build anew; *refaire à neuf,* to recondition, to renovate, to modernize; *remettre à neuf,* to renovate; to do up like new (fam.).
neume [nøm] m. Mus. Neume.
neural [nøral] adj. Méd. Nerval, neural.
neurasthénie [nørasteni] f. Méd. Neurasthenia.
neurasthénique [-nik] adj. Méd. Neurasthenic.
neurochirurgie [nørʃiryrʒi] f. Méd. Neurosurgery.
neuroleptique [nørɔlɛptik] adj., m. Méd. Neuroleptic.
neurologie [nørɔlɔʒi] f. Méd. Neurology.
neurologue [-lɔg] m. Méd. Neurologist.
neurone [nørɔn] m. Méd. Neuron.
neuropathologie [nørɔpatolɔʒi] f. Méd. Neuropathology.
neuropsychiatrie [nørɔpsikjatri] f. Méd. Neuropsychiatry.
neurovégétatif, ive [nørɔveʒetatif, i:v] adj. Méd. Autonomic nervous (système).
neutralisant, ante [-lizɑ̃, ɑ̃:t] adj. Chim. Neutralizing.
— m. Neutralizing agent.
neutralisation [-lizasjɔ̃] f. Neutralization.
neutraliser [-lize] v. tr. (1). To neutralize.
— v. pr. Se neutraliser, to neutralize each other, to cancel out.
neutralisme [-lism] m. Neutralism.
neutraliste [-list] m. Neutralist.
neutralité [-lite] f. Jur. Neutrality; *revendiquer la neutralité,* to declare oneself neutral; *sortir de la neutralité,* to take sides. ‖ Chim. Neutral state; neutrality, adiaphoria.
neutre [nø:tr] adj. Gramm., Zool. Neuter. ‖ Jur., Electr., Chim., Milit. Neutral. ‖ Bot. Sexless.
— s. Jur. Neutral. ‖ Gramm. Neuter.
neutrino [nøtrino] m. Phys. Neutrino.
neutron [nøtrɔ̃] m. Phys. Neutron.
neuvaine [nøvɛn] f. Ecclés. Novena.
neuvième [nøvjɛm] adj. Ninth.
— s. Ninth, ninth part.
— f. Ninth class (à l'école). ‖ Mus. Ninth.
neuvièmement [-mɑ̃] adv. Ninthly.
névé [neve] m. Géogr. Névé.
neveu [nəvø] m. Nephew. ‖ Pl. Descendants.
névralgie [nevralʒi] f. Méd. Neuralgia.
névralgique [-ʒik] adj. Méd. Neuralgic. ‖ Fig. *Point névralgique,* nerve-centre.
névrite [nevrit] f. Méd. Neuritis.
névritique [-tik] adj. Méd. Neuritic.
névropathe [-pat] m. Méd. Neuropath.
névrose [nevro:z] f. Méd. Neurosis.
névrosé, ée [nevroze] adj., s. Méd. Neurotic.
névrotique [-tik] adj. Méd. Neurotic.
newton [njutɔn] m. Phys. Newton (unité).
newtonien, enne [-tɔnjɛ̃, ɛn] adj. Newtonian.

new-yorkais, aise [njujɔrkɛ, ɛːz] adj. Of (ou) from New York.
— s. New Yorker.

nez [ne] m. Nose; *parler du nez,* to speak through one's nose, to snuffle. ‖ Scent (odorat); *avoir du nez,* to have a good nose; *chercher du nez,* to nose about. ‖ AVIAT. Nose (d'avion); nose end (d'hélicoptère); *piquer du nez,* to nose-dive. ‖ MILIT. Nose (de balle, d'obus). ‖ NAUT. Nose; *vaisseau sur le nez,* ship down at the bows. ‖ TECHN. Nosing (d'une marche d'escalier); nose (d'un outil). ‖ FIG. Nose, face; *avoir du nez* ou *bon nez,* to smell (ou) to scent trouble coming; *avoir le nez creux,* to have a flair for a bargain; *clair comme le nez au milieu de la figure,* as clear as the sun at noonday, as plain as the nose on one's face; *faire qqch. au nez de qqn,* to do sth. under s.o.'s nose; *fourrer son nez dans,* to stick one's nose into; *mettre le nez à la fenêtre,* to look out at the window; *rire au nez de qqn,* to laugh in s.o.'s face; *se trouver nez à nez avec,* to find oneself face to face with. ‖ FAM. *A vue de nez,* at a rough estimate; *avoir qqn dans le nez,* to bear s.o. a grudge; *cela lui pend au nez,* he's due for it; *filer sous le nez de qqn,* to slip through s.o.'s fingers; *mener par le bout du nez,* to twist round one's little finger; *se casser le nez,* to be balked, to find the door closed; *se manger le nez,* to be always quarrelling; *tirer les vers du nez à,* to worm a secret out of, to pump; *voir plus loin que le bout de son nez,* to see farther than one's nose; *voyez le nez qu'il fait!,* see what a face he is putting on!

ni [ni] conj. *Ni...ni,* neither...nor; *je ne vous demande ni de me secourir ni de me défendre,* I ask you neither to help nor to defend me; *ni vous ni moi ne l'estimons,* neither you nor I think well of him (ou) esteem him. ‖ *Ni...ni,* either...or (après : *jamais, personne*); *jamais je ne l'ai vu ni entendu,* I never either saw or heard him; *personne ne l'a jamais ni conseillé ni dirigé,* no one has ever either advised or directed him. ‖ *Ni,* nor (servant à lier deux propositions négatives); *je ne l'inviterai plus, ni n'irai le voir,* I will not invite him again, nor will I call on him.

niable [njabl] adj. Deniable, contestable; *il n'est pas niable que,* it is not to be denied that.

niais, aise [njɛ, ɛːz] adj. Silly, simple, foolish, soft, addle-pated.
— s. Simpleton, fool, nincompoop, U.S. sap (fam.).

niaisement [-zmɑ̃] adv. Foolishly.

niaiser [-ze] v. intr. (1). To play the fool. ‖ To fool away one's time, to dilly-dally (muser).

niaiserie [-zri] f. Silliness, simplicity, foolishness (état). ‖ foolish talk, twaddle, tomfoolery, nonsense (remarque).

niaule [ɲol] f. V. GNOLE.

Nicaragua [nikaragwa] m. GÉOGR. Nicaragua.

nicaraguayen, enne [-gwajɛ̃, ɛn] adj., s. GÉOGR. Nicaraguan.

niche [niʃ] f. Practical joke, trick; *faire des niches à,* to play tricks upon, to poke fun at.

niche f. Kennel (à chien). ‖ ARCHIT. Niche, nook.

nichée [niʃe] f. ZOOL. Brood (de chiots, de souris); nestful, nest (d'oiseaux). ‖ FIG. Swarm (d'enfants).

nicher v. tr. (1). To put in a nest (ou) a nook; to nich, to perch.
— v. intr. ZOOL. To nest, to build a nest (oiseau). ‖ FAM. *Où nichez-vous?* where do you hang out?, U.S. where do you hang your hat?
— v. pr. **Se nicher,** to nest, to build its nest (oiseau). ‖ FIG. To settle, to ensconce oneself.

nichet [niʃɛ] m. Nest-egg.

nichon [niʃɔ̃] m. POP. Tit, bub (de femme).

nickel [nikɛl] m. Nickel.

nickelage [nikla:ʒ] m. Nickel-plating.

nickeler [-le] v. tr. (8a). To nickel-plate.

niçois, oise [niswa, waːz] adj. GÉOGR. Of (ou) from Nice. ‖ CULIN. *Salade niçoise,* mixed salad with eggs, olives, anchovies, etc.
— s. Native (ou) inhabitant of Nice.

nicotine [nikɔtin] f. Nicotine.

nid [ni] m. Nest (de fourmis, d'oiseaux, de souris). ‖ MILIT. *Nid de mitrailleuses,* machine-gun nest. ‖ NAUT. *Nid-de-pie,* crow's-nest; *nid de sous-marins,* submarine base (ou) pen. ‖ COMM., ARCHIT. *Nid d'abeilles,* honeycomb. ‖ AUTOM. *Nid-de-poule,* pot-hole (sur route). ‖ FIG. *Nid douillet,* cosy little house. ‖ LOC. *Ecraser une rébellion au nid,* to crush a rebellion from the outset, to nip a revolution in the bud; *trouver la pie au nid,* to catch a runaway in his lair (ou) in his hide-out. ‖ **Nid-trappe,** m. Trap-nest.

nidifier [-difje] v. intr. (1). To nidificate.

nièce [njɛs] f. Niece.

nielle [njɛl] f. BOT. Corn-cockle, smut.

nielle m. TECHN. Niello, inlaid enamel-work.

niellé, ée [njele] adj. BOT. Blighted, smutty (blé).

nieller v. tr. (1). AGRIC. To smut, to blight.
— v. pr. **Se nieller.** BOT., AGRIC. To smut.

nieller v. tr. (1). TECHN. To niello.

nielleur [-lœ:r] m. TECHN. Niellist, niello-worker.

niellure [-ly:r] f. AGRIC. Blighting, smutting.

niellure f. TECHN. Niello-work (orfèvrerie).

nier [nje] v. tr. (1). To deny; *nier être impliqué dans une affaire,* to deny being involved in an affair. ‖ JUR. To deny (ou) to traverse (un fait); to repudiate (une dette).

nietzschéen, enne [nitʃeɛ̃, ɛn] adj. Nietzschean.

nigaud [nigo] s. Booby, fool, simpleton, nincompoop, noodle, fat-head, U. S. sap, dope (fam.).
— adj. Silly, foolish, soft.

nigauderie [-dri] f. Simplicity, silliness, softness (état). ‖ Tomfoolery, act of folly (action).

Niger [niʒɛ:r] m. GÉOGR. Niger (Etat, fleuve).

Nigeria [niʒerja] m. GÉOGR. Nigeria.

nigérian, ane [-jɑ̃, jan] adj., s. GÉOGR. Nigerian.

nigérien, enne [-jɛ̃, jɛn] adj. GÉOGR. Of (ou) from Niger.
— s. Native (ou) inhabitant of Niger.

night-club [najtklœb] m. Night-club.

nihilisme [niilism] m. Nihilism.

nihiliste [-list] m. Nihilist.
— adj. Nihilistic.

Nil [nil] m. GÉOGR. Nile.

nilotique [-lɔtik] adj. GÉOGR., GRAMM. Nilotic.

nimbe [nɛ̃:b] m. ECCLÉS. Nimbus, halo.

nimbé, ée [-be] adj. ECCLÉS. Nimbed, nimbused.

nimbus [-by:s] m. Nimbus, rain-cloud.

ninas [ninas] m. Cigarillo.

niobium [njɔbjɔm] m. CHIM. Niobium.

nipper [nipe] v. tr. (1). FAM. To rig out; to tog out. (V. ACCOUTRER.)
— v. pr. **Se nipper,** FAM. to rig oneself out.

nippes [nip] f. pl. FAM. Togs.

nippon [nipɔ̃] adj., s. GÉOGR. Nipponese.

nique [nik] f. *Faire la nique à,* to snap one's fingers at (qqch.); to turn up one's nose at (qqn).

nirvāna [nirvana] m. Nirvana.

nitouche [nituʃ] f. Demure (ou) coy girl; *faire la sainte nitouche,* to look as if butter would not melt in one's mouth.

nitrate [nitrat] m. CHIM. Nitrate.

nitraté, ée [-te] adj. CHIM. Nitrated.

nitre [nitr] m. CHIM. Nitre, saltpetre.

nitreux, euse [-trø, ø:z] adj. CHIM. Nitrous.

nitrière [nitrijɛ:r] f. Nitre-bed; nitre-works.

nitrification [-fikasjɔ̃] f. CHIM. Nitrification.

nitrifier [-fje] v. tr. (1). CHIM. To nitrify.

nitrique [nitrik] adj. CHIM. Nitric (acide).

nitrite [-trit] m. CHIM. Nitrite.

nitrobenzène [nitrobẽzɛn] m. CHIM. Nitrobenzene.
nitrocellulose [-sɛlylo:z] f. CHIM. Nitrocellulose.
nitrogène [-ʒɛn] m. CHIM. Nitrogen.
nitroglycérine [-gliserin] f. CHIM. Nitroglycerine.
nival [nival] adj. Nival.
niveau [nivo] m. Level (degré d'élévation); *au niveau de, de niveau avec,* on a level with; *au niveau de la mer,* at sea-level; *de niveau,* level, on a level; *élever au niveau de,* to level up to; *mettre à niveau,* to level. ‖ Level (instrument); *niveau à bulle d'air,* spirit-level; *niveau d'eau,* water-level; *niveau à lunettes,* surveyor's level; *niveau de maçon,* plumb-level. ‖ Level (étage dans les mines); *voie de niveau,* level. ‖ Level, standard (degré); *niveau des études, d'un examen,* standard of education, of an examination; *niveau intellectuel,* intellectual level; *niveau de vie,* standard of living. ‖ ELECTR. *Mettre un accumulateur à niveau,* to top up a battery. ‖ TECHN. Gauge (limite, marque). ‖ AUTOM. *Niveau d'essence, d'huile,* petrol-, oil-gauge. ‖ CH. DE F. *Passage à niveau,* level (ou) U. S. grade crossing. ‖ AVIAT. *Niveau de l'air respirable,* breathing level, ceiling for normal breathing. ‖ FIG. Level (de qqn); *au niveau de,* on a par with.
nivelage [nivla:ʒ] m. Levelling (v. NIVELLEMENT).
niveler [nivle] v. tr. (8 a). To survey, to bone (une route, une rue); to level (un terrain); *porte nivelée avec les murs,* door flush with the walls. ‖ FIG. To level, to even up (les conditions, les fortunes); *niveler par le bas,* to level down.
— v. pr. **Se niveler,** to become level, to settle down (terrain). ‖ FIG. To become equal, to level out (conditions, fortunes).
nivelette [-lɛt] f. Boning- (ou) U. S. leveling-rod.
niveleur, euse [-lœ:r, ø:z] adj. Levelling.
— s. Leveller.
nivellement [nivɛlmã] m. Surveying; *borne de nivellement,* bench-mark. ‖ Levelling (d'un terrain). ‖ FIG. Levelling (des conditions).
nivéole [niveɔl] f. BOT. Snow-flake.
nivôse [nivo:z] m. Nivôse, fourth month in French Republican calendar (december-january).
nobélium [nɔbeljɔm] m. CHIM. Nobelium.
nobiliaire [nɔbiljɛ:r] adj. Nobiliary.
— m. Peerage-list.
noble [nɔbl] adj. Noble; *de famille noble,* of aristocratic extraction. ‖ THÉÂTR. *Père noble,* heavy father. ‖ FIG. Noble, generous (sentiments); lofty (style).
— m. Noble, nobleman; *les nobles,* the nobility. ‖ FIG. Noble; *le noble,* the august, the memorable, the weighty.
— f. Noblewoman.
noblement [-bləmã] adv. Nobly. ‖ FIG. Nobly, generously; loftily.
noblesse [-blɛs] f. Nobility; *la haute et la petite noblesse,* the nobility and the gentry. ‖ FIG. Nobleness (des sentiments).
nobliau [-blijo] m. FAM. Minor noble.
noce [nɔs] f. Wedding, wedding festivities (fête); *être de noce,* to be a member of the wedding party (ou) one of the wedding-guests; *repas de noce,* wedding breakfast (ou) banquet. ‖ Pl. Marriage; *elle l'épousa en secondes noces,* he was her second husband; *voyage de noces,* honeymoon trip. ‖ FAM. Spree, high jinks (v. BOMBE); *faire la noce,* to go on the spree (ou) on a binge (ou) U. S. on a bender. ‖ FAM. Rapture; *ne pas être à la noce,* to be far from ecstatically happy.
nocer [-se] v. intr. (6). To go on the spree, to binge, to live fast; U. S. to live it up. ‖ To feast.
noceur [-sœ:r] s. Fast liver, debauchee, gay dog (fam.). ‖ Reveller, roisterer. (V. BAMBOCHEUR.)

nocher [nɔʃe] m. Ferryman (en mythologie); boatman, pilot (en poésie).
nocif, ive [nɔsif, i:v] adj. Noxious, nocuous, harmful, hurtful, injurious. (V. NUISIBLE.)
nocivité [-vite] f. Noxiousness, harmfulness.
noctambule [nɔktãbyl] adj. Noctambulant.
— s. Noctambulist. (V. SOMNAMBULE.) ‖ FAM. Fly-by-night; night-prowler; night hawk (ou) owl.
noctambulisme [-lism] m. Noctambulism.
nocturne [nɔktyrn] adj. Nocturnal, nightly; *silence nocturne,* silence of the night; *tapage nocturne,* disturbance in the night.
— s. ZOOL. Pl. Nocturnals. ‖ MUS. Nocturne. ‖ ECCLÉS. Nocturn.
nocuité [nɔkɥite] f. Noxiousness.
nodal, ale [nɔdal] adj. PHYS. Nodal.
nodosité [nɔdozite] f. Nodosity; knottiness (état); node, nodule; knot (nœud).
nodulaire [nɔdylɛ:r] adj. MÉD., GÉOL. Nodular.
nodule [nɔdyl] m. MÉD., GÉOL. Nodule.
noduleux, euse [-lø, ø:z] adj. GÉOL. Nodulous.
Noé [nɔe] m. Noah; *l'arche de Noé,* Noah's Ark.
Noël [nɔɛl] m. Christmas; *arbre de Noël,* Christmas-tree; *époque de Noël,* Christmas time; *le père Noël,* Father Christmas, Santa Claus; *veille de Noël,* Christmas Eve. ‖ Nowel; U. S. Noel; *chanter Noël,* to sing Nowel. ‖ Christmas-box (ou) -present (cadeau). ‖ MUS. Carol, Christmas carol.

nœud [nø] m. Knot; *défaire un nœud,* to untie a knot; *faire un nœud à son mouchoir,* to tie a knot in one's handkerchief; *nœud de tisserand,* weaver's knot; *nœud de vache,* carrick bend. ‖ Bow (de cravate, de ruban); favour (cocarde, faveur); *faire son nœud de cravate,* to knot one's tie, to tie one's bow. ‖ BOT. Knot, knar (dans le bois). ‖ ZOOL. Pl. Coils (d'un serpent). ‖ CH. DE F. Junction. ‖ ELECTR. *Nœud de potentiel,* potential node. ‖ PHYS. Node (d'une oscillation). ‖ TECHN. Bur, burl (dans une étoffe); *nœud d'empattement, de jonction,* T joint, T-joint. ‖ MATH. Node (d'une courbe). ‖ MÉD. *Nœud vital,* vital centre. ‖ NAUT. Knot; *filer quinze nœuds,* to make fifteen knots. ‖ COMM., JUR. Crux (d'une affaire, d'une question). ‖ THÉÂTR. Knot, crux (d'une pièce). ‖ FIG. Bond, tie, knot; *nœuds de l'amitié, de la parenté,* bonds of friendship, of kinship.

noir, oire [nwa:r] adj. Black, dark; *cheveux noirs,* dark (ou) black hair; *noir comme l'encre, le jais,* ink-, jet-black; *race noire,* Negro race; *tableau noir,* blackboard; *yeux noirs,* dark eyes. ‖ Dark (obscur); *faire noir,* to be dark; *noir comme dans un four,* pitch-dark. ‖ Dirty (sale); *figure noire,* grimy face; *ongle noir,* dirty nail. ‖ Dark, gloomy, cloudy; *ciel noir,* lowering sky. ‖ CULIN. *Beurre noir,* brown butter sauce; *café noir,* black coffee; *viande noire,* brown meat. ‖ GÉOGR. *La Forêt-Noire,* the Black Forest. ‖ AGRIC. *Blé noir,* buckwheat. ‖ MÉD. *Peste noire,* bubonic plague. ‖ FIG. Dark, gloomy; ominous (avenir); gnawing (chagrin); black (messe); utter (pauvreté); *bête noire,* bête noire, pet aversion; *donner son avis noir sur blanc,* to give one's opinion in black and white; *four noir,* dreadful failure, flop; *humour noir,* macabre humour; *idées noires,* the blues. ‖ FAM. Plastered (ivre); *œil au beurre noir,* black eye.
— m. Black man, black, Negro. (V. NÈGRE, NÉGRESSE, NOIRE.)
— m. Black (couleur); *noir de fumée,* lamp-black; *tourner au noir,* to turn dark. ‖ Black, mourning (vêtement); *prendre le noir,* to wear (ou) to go into mourning. ‖ MÉD. Bruise (meurtrissure). ‖ MILIT., SPORTS. Bull's eye (de cible); *mettre dans le noir,* to hit the mark. ‖ ARTS. Pl.

Shadows. ‖ Bot. Smut (nielle). ‖ Loc. *Broyer du noir*, to be in the dumps (ou) in the doldrums; *voir tout en noir*, to be down in the mouth; to look on the black side of things.

noirâtre [nwara:tr] adj. Blackish.

noiraud, aude [-ro, od] adj. Swarthy.
— s. Dark-skinned (ou) -complexioned person.

noirceur [-rsœ:r] f. Blackness (d'une teinte, d'un ton). ‖ Darkness, gloominess (du ciel, du temps). ‖ Méd. Black spot (sur le visage). ‖ Fig. Foulness (d'un acte); heinousness (d'un crime); Gloominess, dejection, despondency (de la disposition). ‖ Fam. Calumny.

noircir [-sir] v. tr. (2). To blacken, to darken; *noirci par la fumée*, smoky. ‖ To grime. ‖ To scribble on (du papier). ‖ Fig. To slander (calomnier); to darken (exagérer); *noircir qqn*, to make s.o. out to be worse than he is. ‖ Fig. To make sad (ou) gloomy (attrister). ‖ Fam. To fuddle (enivrer).
— v. intr. To grow (ou) to turn dark (ou) black, to darken.
— v. pr. **Se noircir**, to grow black. ‖ To grow cloudy (ciel, temps).

noircissement [-sismɑ̃] m. Blackening, darkening. ‖ Techn. Blackwashing.

noircisseur [-sisœ:r] m. Techn. Dyer in black. ‖ Fig. *Noircisseur de papier*, scribbler.

noircissure [-sisy:r] f. Black spot, smudge.

noire [nwa:r] f. Black woman, Negress (femme). ‖ Black (à la roulette). ‖ Mus. Crotchet; U. S. quarter note.

noise [nwa:z] f. Quarrel; *chercher noise à qqn*, to try to pick a quarrel with.

noisetier [nwaztje] m. Bot. Hazel-tree.

noisette [-zɛt] f. Bot. Hazel-nut; *aller aux noisettes*, to go nutting.
— adj. invar. Nut-brown, hazel (couleur).

noix [nwa] f. Bot. Walnut; *coquille de noix*, walnut shell; *huile de noix*, walnut oil. ‖ Nut; *noix de coco*, cocoa-nut; *noix de terre*, peanut. ‖ Culin. *Noix de gigot*, pope's eye; *noix de veau*, cushion. ‖ Techn. Drum-head (de cabestan); half round groove (en menuiserie). ‖ Pop. *A la noix*, lousy; *ce que tu es noix!* what an ass you are!

nolage [nɔla:ʒ] m. Comm. Freight, freighting.

nolisement [nɔlizmɑ̃] m. Comm. Freighting.

noliser [-ze] v. tr. (1). Comm. To freight.

nom [nɔ̃] m. Name (v. Appellation); *nom de famille*, surname; *nom de guerre*, assumed name, pseudonym; *nom de jeune fille*, maiden name; *nom de plume*, pen-name; *nom de théâtre*, stage-name; *au nom de*, in the name of; *avoir nom Alex*, to be named Alex; *connaître de nom*, to know by name; *décliner ses nom et prénoms*, to give one's full name; *du nom de Smith*, named Smith, Smith by name; *erreur de nom*, misnomer; *parler au nom de sa mère*, *en son nom*, to speak on one's mother's behalf, for oneself; *petit nom*, Christian name; *porter le nom de qqn*, to be called after s.o.; *sous le nom de*, by (ou) under the name of. ‖ Name, fame, reputation; *se faire un nom*, to achieve a name, to win fame, to become famous, to make a name for oneself. ‖ Comm. *Nom déposé*, registered trade name. ‖ Gramm. Noun. ‖ Loc. *Appeler les choses par leur nom*, to call a spade a spade, not to mince matters (ou) words; *nom de Dieu!*, by God!, damn!; *nom d'un bonhomme* (ou) *d'un chien* (ou) *de nom* (ou) *d'une pipe!*, *tonnerre de nom!*, by Jove!, good heavens!, heavens above!

nomade [nɔmad] adj. Migratory (animal); roving (instinct); wandering (tribu); nomadic (vie).
— s. Nomad, wanderer. ‖ Pl. Nomadic (ou) wandering tribes.

nomadisme [-dism] m. Nomadism.

no man's land [nomanzland] m. No man's land.

nombrable [nɔ̃brabl] adj. Numerable.

nombre [nɔ̃br] m. Number (chiffre). ‖ Numbers (groupement); *à nombre égal*, numbers being equal; *en grand nombre*, in large numbers; *submergé par le nombre*, overrun by numbers. ‖ Number (collection); *au nombre de 2 000*, to the number of 2000; *un bon nombre de*, *un certain nombre*, *nombre de*, a fairly large number of, a good many, a number of; *être au nombre des lauréats*, to be among the prize-winners; *mettre au nombre de*, to count among; *pour faire nombre*, to help to make a crowd; *sans nombre*, numberless, innumerable; *ennuis sans nombre*, no end of trouble; *tout fait nombre*, every little bit helps. ‖ Harmony (des vers). ‖ Gramm., Math. Number. ‖ Jur. *Nombre requis*, quorum. ‖ Aviat. *Nombre de Mach*, Mach number.

nombrer [-bre] v. tr. (1). To number, to count; to take stock of.

nombreux, euse [-brø, ø:z] adj. Numerous, large, many; *famille nombreuse*, large family; *moins nombreux que*, fewer than; *de nombreuses familles pauvres*, many poor families; *peu nombreux*, infrequent. ‖ Full-toned, harmonious (vers).

nombril [nɔ̃bri] m. Méd. Navel; belly-button (fam.). ‖ Bot. Eye (de fruit).

nomenclature [nɔmɑ̃klaty:r] f. Nomenclature; list of words; list of names.

nominal, ale [nɔminal] adj. Nominal; *appel nominal*, roll-call, call-over; *faire l'appel nominal*, to call over, to call the roll. ‖ Fin. Nominal; *valeur nominale*, face-value.

nominalement [-lmɑ̃] adv. Nominally; *appeler nominalement*, to call by name. ‖ Fin. *Nominalement sa fortune se monte à*, on the face of things, his fortune amounts to.

nominalisme [-lism] m. Philos. Nominalism.

nominatif, ive [-tif, i:v] adj. Nominal; *état nominatif*, list of names. ‖ Fin. *Titres nominatifs*, registered securities. ‖ Gramm. Nominative (cas).
— m. Gramm. Nominative; *au nominatif*, in the nominative.

nomination [-sjɔ̃] f. Appointment; *recevoir sa nomination*, to be appointed. ‖ Choice; *ce poste est à la nomination du ministre*, the Minister has the choice of a nominee for this post. ‖ Mention (au palmarès); *avoir deux nominations*, to be mentioned twice on the prize-list.

nominativement [-tivmɑ̃] adv. By name.

nommé, ée [nɔme] adj. Named (personne). ‖ Appointed (à un poste). ‖ Loc. *A point nommé*, in the nick of time.
— s. Jur. *Le nommé X*, the man named X.

nommément [-mɑ̃] adv. By name. ‖ Namely.

nommer [nɔme] v. tr. (1). To name, to give a name to. (V. Appeler.) ‖ To name, to mention by name; *un voyou que je ne nommerai pas*, a scoundrel who shall remain nameless; *nommer qqch. une négligence*, to call sth. an oversight. ‖ To appoint; *être nommé gérant*, to be appointed manager; *nommer qqn son exécuteur testamentaire*, to appoint s.o. one's executor. ‖ Milit. To appoint, to promote.
— v. pr. **Se nommer**, to be named (ou) called. (V. S'appeler.) ‖ To name oneself; to call oneself (se traiter). ‖ To give one's name; *se nommer en entrant*, to give one's name when one goes in.

nomogramme [nɔmɔgram] m. Nomogram.

non [nɔ̃] adv. No (réponse négative); *mais non!*, oh, no!; *que non!*, not a bit!; certainly not!; *non pas!*, not at all! ‖ Not (négation); *je crains que non*, I am afraid not; *je pense que non*, I think not; *voulez-vous me le dire, oui ou non?*, will you tell me, or not? ‖ Not (devant un adverbe, une conjonction, un participe, une pré-

position) ; *corsage non repassé,* unironed blouse ; *personnage non estimé,* person not highly thought of ; *non loin d'ici,* not far from here ; *non que ce soit facile,* not that it is easy ; *non sans difficulté,* not without difficulty. ‖ *Non pas,* v. PAS. ‖ FAM. *C'est formidable, non ?,* it's marvellous, isn't it ? ‖ **Non-acceptation,** f. Non-acceptance. ‖ **Non-activité,** f. Non-activity ; *mise en non-activité,* suspension. ‖ **Non-agression,** f. Non-aggression. ‖ **Non alcoolisé,** adj. Non-alcoholic ; *boissons non alcoolisées,* soft drinks. ‖ **Non-aligné,** adj. Non-aligned ; s. non-aligned state. ‖ **Non-assistance,** f. *Non-assistance à personne en danger,* not coming to the aid of a person in danger. ‖ **Non-belligérance,** f. MILIT. Non-belligerency. ‖ **Non-combattant,** adj., s. MILIT. Non-combatant. ‖ **Non conducteur,** adj. PHYS. Non-conducting ; m. non-conductor. ‖ **Non-conformisme,** m. Nonconformism (gén., ecclés.). ‖ **Non-conformiste,** s. Non-conformist (gén., ecclés.), dissenter (ecclés.). ‖ **Non-conformité,** f. Nonconformity. ‖ **Non-croyant,** adj. Non-believing ; s. non-believer. ‖ **Non-directif,** adj. PSYCH. Non-directive. ‖ **Non-engagé,** adj. Non-committed (ou) -aligned ; s. non-committed (ou) -aligned state. ‖ **Non-être,** m. PHILOS. Non-existence. ‖ **Non-exécution,** f. Non-fulfilment ; non-completion. ‖ **Non existant,** adj. Non-existent. ‖ **Non ferreux,** adj. Non ferrous. ‖ **Non-figuratif,** adj. ARTS. Non-figurative, non-representational. ‖ **Non-fumeur,** s. Non-smoker. ‖ **Non-ingérence,** f. Non-interference (ou) non-intervention. ‖ **Non-initié,** adj. Uninitiated ; s. layman. ‖ **Non-inscrit,** adj., s. Independent (au Parlement). ‖ **Non-intervention,** f. Non-intervention. ‖ **Non-interventionniste,** adj., s. Non-interventionist. ‖ **Non-jouissance,** f. JUR. Non-enjoyment. ‖ **Non-lieu,** m. JUR. No true bill ; *obtenir un non-lieu,* to be discharged ; *ordonnance de non-lieu,* nonsuit. ‖ **Non-livraison,** f. COMM. Non-delivery. ‖ **Non-métal,** m. CHIM. Non-metal. ‖ **Non-moi,** m. PHILOS. Non-ego. ‖ **Non-paiement,** m. COMM. Non-payment. ‖ **Non-présentation,** f. JUR. Concealment (d'enfant). ‖ **Non-prolifération,** f. Non-proliferation. ‖ **Non-recevoir,** m. *Opposer à qqn une fin de non-recevoir,* to turn s. o. down. ‖ **Non-retour,** m. *Point de non-retour,* point of no return. ‖ **Non-réussite,** f. Failure ; miscarriage (d'un projet). ‖ **Non-sens,** m. Meaningless word or phrase (dans un texte) ; piece of nonsense (idée). ‖ **Non-spécialiste,** adj., s. Non-specialist. ‖ **Non-stop,** adj. Non-stop (vol, émission). ‖ **Non syndiqué,** adj. Non-union (ouvrier) ; s. non-union worker. ‖ **Non-tissé,** m. TECHN. Non-woven. ‖ **Non-valeur,** f. valueless person or thing ; incompetent employee ; write-off, passenger (fam.). ‖ **Non-violence,** f. Non-violence. ‖ **Non-violent,** adj. Non-violent ; s. advocate of non-violence.
— m. invar. No ; *les non l'emportent,* the noes have it ; *se fâcher pour un oui, pour un non,* to lose one's temper over the merest trifle.

nonagénaire [nɔnaʒenɛ:r] adj., s. Nonagenarian.

nonante [nɔnɑ̃t] adj. † Ninety.

nonce [nɔ̃:s] m. ECCLÉS. Nuncio.

nonchalamment [nɔ̃ʃalamɑ̃] adv. Nonchalantly, languidly, listlessly, idly ; *s'avancer nonchalamment,* to loiter along, to saunter.

nonchalance [-lɑ̃:s] f. Nonchalance (indifférence). ‖ Languidness, languor (langueur). ‖ Laziness, sloth (paresse).

nonchalant, ante [-lɑ̃, ɑ̃:t] adj. Nonchalant. ‖ Languid. ‖ Slothful, sluggish, supine.

nonchaloir [-lwa:r] m. Nonchalance ; apathy.

nonciature [nɔ̃sjaty:r] f. ECCLÉS. Nunciature ; nuncio's residence.

nonnain [nɔnɛ̃] f. † Nun.

nonne [nɔn] f. ECCLÉS. Nun.

nonobstant [nɔnɔbstɑ̃] prép. Notwithstanding.
— adv. Nevertheless, for all that.
— loc. conj. Nonobstant que, although.

nonpareil, eille [nɔ̃parɛ:j] adj. † Peerless, matchless, unrivalled, unique, nonpareil.
— m. ZOOL. Nonpareil.

nonpareille f. Nonpareil, six-point type (en typo). ‖ BOT. Nonesuch (pomme). ‖ CULIN. Nonpareil.

nord [nɔ:r] m. North ; *au nord,* in the north ; *au nord de,* to the north of ; *du nord,* northern ; *du côté du nord,* on the north side ; *en plein nord,* due north ; *être au nord,* to face (ou) to look north (une chambre, une maison) ; *vent du nord,* north wind ; *vers le nord,* northward. ‖ GÉOGR. *La mer du Nord,* the North Sea. ‖ FIG. *Perdre le nord,* to lose one's bearings. ‖ FAM. *Du nord au midi,* from John o' Groat's to Land's End, U. S. all over the map.
— adj. GÉOGR. *Le cap Nord,* the North Cape ; *le pôle Nord,* the North Pole. ‖ **Nord-africain,** adj., s. GÉOGR. North African. ‖ **Nord-américain,** adj., s. GÉOGR. North American. ‖ **Nord-coréen,** adj., s. GÉOGR. North Korean. ‖ **Nord-est,** adj., m. North-east. ‖ **Nord-ouest,** adj., m. North-west.

nordique [-dik] adj. Nordic.

nordir [-di:r] v. intr. (2). To veer to the North.

nordiste [-dist] adj., s. Northerner.

noria [nɔrja] f. TECHN. Chain-pump, bucket-elevator, noria.

normal, ale [nɔrmal] adj. Normal, ordinary, usual (habituel). ‖ Normal, regular ; standard (dimensions, taille). ‖ *Ecole normale,* training college, U. S. normal school, teachers' college.

normale f. Normal ; *inférieur, supérieur à la normale,* below, above normal.

normalement [-lmɑ̃] adv. Normally ; ordinarily ; in the normal course of events.

normalien, enne [-ljɛ̃, ɛn] s. Student at an Ecole Normale.

normalisation [-lizasjɔ̃] f. Normalization, standardization.

normaliser [-lize] v. tr. (1). To normalize, to standardize.
— v. pr. Se normaliser, to normalize (relations).

normalité [-lite] f. Normality, normalcy.

normand, ande [nɔrmɑ̃, ɑ̃:d] adj. GÉOGR. Norman (conquête, race) ; *les Iles normandes,* the Channel Islands.
— s. Norman ; *faire une réponse de Normand,* to equivocate.

Normandie [-di] f. GÉOGR. Normandy.
— m. NAUT. Normandie (bateau).

normatif, ive [nɔrmatif, i:v] adj. Normative.

norme [nɔrm] f. Norm, standard ; *hors de la norme,* abnormal.

norois [nɔrwa] m. NAUT. North-west ; *vent de norois,* nor'wester.

norois, oise [nɔrwa, waz] adj., m. GÉOGR. Norse.

Norvège [nɔrvɛ:ʒ] f. GÉOGR. Norway.

norvégien, enne [-veʒjɛ̃, ɛn] adj., s. GÉOGR. Norwegian.
— m. GRAMM. Norwegian (langue).

nos [no]. V. NOTRE.

nostalgie [nɔstalʒi] f. MÉD. Nostalgia. ‖ FAM. Yearning, longing (aspiration) ; homesickness (mal du pays) ; *avoir la nostalgie de,* to yearn for.

nostalgique [-ʒik] adj. MÉD. Nostalgic. ‖ FAM. Home-sick.

nota bene [nɔtabene] m. inv. Nota bene.

notabilité [nɔtabilite] f. Notability, notableness (caractère). ‖ Notability, prominent person (personnage) ; V. I. P. (fam.).

notable [-tabl] adj. Notable, signal, noteworthy, noticeable. (V. REMARQUABLE.) ‖ Appreciable,

palpable, perceptible, sensible (choses); eminent, prominent (personnes); great (progrès).
— m. Notable.
notablement [-tabləmᾶ] adv. Notably.
notaire [nɔtɛ:r] m. JUR. Commissioner for oaths (en Angleterre); notary (en Ecosse, en France); notary public (aux Etats-Unis).
notamment [nɔtamᾶ] adv. Notably, especially, particularly. ‖ Namely; including.
notarial, ale [nɔtarjal] adj. JUR. Notarial.
notariat [-rja] m. JUR. Body of notaries (corps); profession of a notary (profession).
notarié [-rje] adj. JUR. Drawn up by a notary, notarial (acte).
notation [nɔtasjɔ̃] f. Notation.
note [nɔt] f. Note (observation); *prendre bonne note de,* to take due note of, duly to note; *prendre note de,* to make note of, to note, to keep track (ou) record of, to keep in mind. ‖ Note (remarque); *carnet de notes,* note-book; *prendre des notes,* to take (ou) to jot down notes. ‖ Note (renvoi); *notes en bas de page, en fin de volume,* foot-, end-notes. ‖ Mark (quotation); *avoir des notes élevées,* to score high marks, U. S. to win high grades; *bonne, mauvaise note,* good, bad mark (ou) U. S. grade. ‖ Note (billet, instructions); *note diplomatique,* diplomatic note. ‖ Note, mark (marque, ton); *note gaie,* cheerful note (ou) tone; *donner la note,* to give the key-note. ‖ Note (mesure); *forcer la note,* to force the note, to exaggerate. ‖ COMM. Bill, account (facture); *mettez-le sur la note,* charge it on the bill. ‖ MUS. Note; *donner la note,* to give the key-note.
noté, ée [nɔte] adj. FIG. Regarded, looked upon (considéré); *bien noté,* in good repute, in good esteem; *être bien noté au bureau,* to have a good record at the office; *mal noté,* in ill repute, of bad reputation.
noter v. tr. (1). To note; to remark, to take notice of (remarquer); *notez bien,* mind you. ‖ To note (ou) to jot down; to make (ou) to take note of, to record (prendre note de); *noter un nom dans la liste,* to enter a name on the list. ‖ To mark (marquer); *noter qqch. sur le calendrier,* to mark sth. on the calendar; *noter qqn d'infamie,* to brand s.o. with infamy. ‖ MUS. To write out, to take down (un air).
notice [nɔtis] f. Notice; account, review (compte rendu). ‖ Directions (mode d'emploi).
notificatif, ive [nɔtifikatif, i:v] adj. Of notification.
notification [-sjɔ̃] f. Notification, advice, information; *recevoir notification de,* to be notified of.
notifier [nɔtifje] v. tr. (1). To notify. (V. SIGNIFIER.) ‖ JUR. *Notifier une citation à,* to serve a summons to.
notion [nɔsjɔ̃] f. Notion, idea; *premières notions d'algèbre,* elementary algebra (livre); *quelques notions d'électronique,* a smattering of electronics.
notionnel, elle [-sjɔnɛl] adj. GRAMM. Notional.
notoire [nɔtwa:r] adj. Acknowledged (difficulté); notorious (ignorance); arrant (menteur).
notoirement [nɔtwarmᾶ] adv. Notoriously; plainly, evidently. [V. MANIFESTEMENT.]
notoriété [nɔtɔrjete] f. Notoriety, notoriousness; *de notoriété publique,* cf. common knowledge. ‖ Reputation, fame; *atteindre à la notoriété,* to make a name for oneself. ‖ JUR. *Acte de notoriété,* identity certificate.
notre [nɔtr] (pl. **nos** [no]) adj. poss. Our; *c'est de notre récolte,* it's from our own crop; *nos amis et connaissances,* our friends and acquaintances. ‖ **Notre-Dame,** f. ECCLÉS. Our Lady; ARCHIT. Church of Notre-Dame.
nôtre [no:tr] adj., pron. poss. Ours.

— m. Our efforts; *y mettre du nôtre,* to put our best foot forward. ‖ Pl. *Les nôtres,* our people; *vous serez des nôtres, n'est-ce pas?,* you will join us, won't you?
nouage [nwa:ʒ] m. Knotting, tying.
nouba [nuba] f. FAM. Spree; binge (v. BOMBE); *faire la nouba,* to paint the town red.
noue [nu] f. AGRIC. Water-meadow. ‖ ARCHIT. Valley channel; gutter-tile.
noué, ée [nue] adj. MÉD. Knotty (articulation); stiffened (membre). ‖ BOT. Set (fruit). ‖ BLAS. Nowed, knotted. ‖ FIG. Stunted (esprit). ‖ LOC. *Point noué,* lockstitch.
nouer v. tr. (1). To fasten, to braid (ses cheveux); to knot, to tie (un cordon, une cravate, une ficelle); *nouer les bras autour de la taille de qqn,* to clasp s.o. round the waist. ‖ MÉD. To stiffen (les membres). ‖ FIG. To seal (une alliance); to strike up (une amitié); to work up (un complot); to enter into (une conversation); to knit (une intrigue); to establish (des relations).
— v. intr. BOT. To set (fruit).
— v. pr. **Se nouer,** to become (ou) to get knotted, to knit (ficelle). ‖ BOT. To set (fruit). ‖ MÉD. To become knotted (ou) knotty (articulations). ‖ FIG. To knit (intrigue).
noueux, euse [-ø, ø:z] adj. BOT. Gnarled (arbre, branche); knotty (bois). ‖ MÉD. Knotted, knotty, gnarled (articulation); arthritic (rhumatisme).
nougat [nuga] m. CULIN. Nougat.
nouille [nu:j] f. CULIN. Noodle. ‖ FAM. Nincompoop.
nouillerie [nujəri] f. FAM. Wishy-washy story (histoire); stupidity (sottise).
nouillette [nujɛt] f. CULIN. Small noodle.
noumène [numɛn] m. PHILOS. Noumenon.
nounou [nunu] f. FAM. Nurse; Nanny.
nourri, ie [nuri] adj. Fed; *bien, mal nourri,* well, ill-fed; *logé et nourri,* with board and lodging; *nourri au biberon,* bottle-fed. ‖ CULIN. Well seasoned. ‖ TECHN. Thick, heavy (en typogr.). ‖ MILIT. Steady, well-sustained, intensive (canonnade, feu). ‖ FIG. Warm, rich, vigorous (applaudissements); well-furnished (récit); *nourri de faits,* packed with facts; meaty (fam.); *nourri de hautes pensées,* nurtured with noble thoughts; *nourri dans le respect de la règle,* brought up in observance of the rules.
nourrice [nuris] f. Nurse; wet nurse; *enfant en nourrice,* child at nurse; *enfant changé en nourrice,* changeling; *mettre un enfant en nourrice,* to put a child out to nurse; *nourrice sèche,* dry nurse. ‖ AUTOM., AVIAT. Feed-tank; jerrycan (bidon). ‖ TECHN. Service tank.
nourricier, ère [-sje, ɛr] adj. Nutritious, nutrient, nutritive (suc). ‖ Foster; *mère nourricière,* foster-mother; *père nourricier,* foster-father.
nourrir [nuri:r] v. tr. (2). To nourish, to nurture, to feed (alimenter). ‖ To nurse, to feed, to suckle (allaiter). ‖ To nourish, to feed (fournir le repas); *nourrir les ouvriers,* to feed workmen. ‖ To support, to maintain, to keep (entretenir); *assez pour nourrir une famille,* enough to maintain a family; *un métier qui ne nourrit pas son homme,* a trade that does not provide a decent living. ‖ To nourish, to train, to bring up (dans, in) [élever]. ‖ ARTS. To deepen (la couleur); *nourrir un trait,* to give breadth to a line. ‖ FIG. To hatch (un complot); to strengthen, to fortify (la conscience); to enrich (la conversation, l'esprit); to entertain (un doute, des intentions); to cherish (un espoir); to foster (un projet); to harbour (un sentiment); to indulge (un rêve).
— v. intr. To be nourishing (ou) nutritious.
— v. pr. **Se nourrir,** to feed, to eat, to live (de, on); *se bien nourrir,* to fare well. ‖ To keep oneself; *son travail lui fournit juste de quoi se*

nourrir, his work provides him with a bare subsistence (ou) just enough to keep body and soul together. ‖ FIG. *Se nourrir d'illusions*, to live on illusions.

nourrissant, ante [nurisɑ̃, ɑ̃:t] adj. Nourishing.

nourrisseur [-sœ:r] m. Feeder, keeper (de bestiaux); dairyman (de vaches laitières).

nourrisson [-sɔ̃] m. Infant, babe in arms, baby at the breast. ‖ FAM. Nursling, suckling (des Muses).

nourriture [-ty:r] f. Nourishment, nurture, nutriment (valeur nutritive). ‖ Food, fare, sustenance (aliment); *la nourriture et le logement*, board and lodging; *ne pas avoir une nourriture suffisante*, to be short of food. ‖ Feeding, suckling (d'un enfant); eating (d'une personne); *excès de nourriture*, over-eating. ‖ Feeding, rearing (du bétail). ‖ Keep, living (entretien); *gagner tout juste sa nourriture*, to earn just enough for one's keep. ‖ FIG. Pabulum, food, sustenance.

nous [nu] pron. pers. We (sujet); *vous vous en tirez mieux que nous*, you manage better than we do. ‖ Us (complément); *il nous prend à témoins*, he calls us to witness; *on nous l'a volé*, it was stolen from us. ‖ We, us (style officiel); *nous, préfet du Gard*, we, prefect of the Gard Department. ‖ Ourselves (sens réfléchi); *nous nous chauffons à votre feu*, we warm ourselves at your fire. ‖ Each other, one another (sens réciproque); *mon frère et moi nous nous aidons toujours*, my brother and I always help each other. ‖ (Non traduit); *nous nous en allons*, we are going; *nous nous en souvenons*, we remember it. ‖ FAM. *Nous en avons de belles étrennes, Jean!*, that's a fine Christmas-box for you, John! ‖ LOC. **A nous**; *ce jardin est à nous*, this garden is ours; *c'est à nous de*, it is our duty to (c'est notre devoir de); it is our turn to (c'est à notre tour de); *ce n'est pas à nous de*, it is not for us to (il ne nous appartient pas de). ‖ **Chez nous**, at our house; *rentrons chez nous*, let's go home; *venez chez nous*, come to our house; *il n'y a chez nous aucune répugnance*, there is no reluctance on our part. ‖ **De nous**; *ce que c'est que de nous!*, how precarious life is! ‖ **Entre nous**, between ourselves, between you and me. ‖ **Nous-mêmes**, ourselves; *nous le ferons nous-mêmes*, we shall do it ourselves; *c'est à nous-mêmes de prendre l'initiative*, it is up to us to take the initiative.

nouveau [nuvo], **nouvel, elle** [nuvɛl] adj. New (neuf); *habit nouveau*, suit of a new cut; *livre nouveau*, new book; *modèle le plus nouveau*, latest model; *nouvelle façon, mode*, new way, fashion; *plaisir toujours nouveau*, pleasure that never grows stale; *quelque chose de nouveau*, something new; *quoi de nouveau?*, what's new? what's the news? ‖ Another (autre); *faire une nouvelle tentative*, to make another attempt. ‖ New, fresh (renouvelé); *nos nouveaux ministres*, our new ministers; *nouvelle preuve de mauvaise volonté*, fresh proof of ill-will. ‖ New (sans précédents); *des sentiers nouveaux*, untrodden paths. ‖ New (inexpérimenté); *il est nouveau en politique*, he is a novice in politics. ‖ Newly (récent); *nouveaux pauvres*, new poor, recently impoverished; *nouveaux riches*, new rich, wealthy parvenus; *nouveau venu*, newcomer. ‖ CULIN. Yet untasted (goût). ‖ TECHN. Yet untried (procédé). ‖ **Nouveau-né**, adj. New-born. — m. New, news; *c'est du nouveau pour moi*, it's news to me. ‖ New pupil (à l'école). ‖ LOC. **A nouveau**, again, over again, anew, afresh. ‖ **De nouveau**, again, once more.

nouveauté [-te] f. Novelty, newness, freshness. ‖ Novelty, change (changement). ‖ Novelty, new invention (invention); latest book out (livre). ‖ COMM. Pl. Fancy goods, linen drapery; U. S. dry goods; *magasin de nouveautés*, fancy goods store.

nouvel [nuvɛl]. V. NOUVEAU.

nouvelle [nuvɛl] f. News, piece of news; *les dernières nouvelles*, the latest news; *triste nouvelle*, sad piece of news, sad news. ‖ News, information; *aller prendre des nouvelles de*, to go and enquire about; *demander des nouvelles de qqn*, to ask after s.o.; *donnez-moi de vos nouvelles*, let me hear from you. ‖ Short story (récit). ‖ FAM. *Vous aurez de mes nouvelles!*, you shall hear from me!; *goûtez ça, vous m'en direz des nouvelles*; taste that, I am sure you'll find it first rate. — adj. V. NOUVEAU. ‖ **Nouvelle-Angleterre**, f. GÉOGR. New England. ‖ **Nouvelle-Calédonie**, f. GÉOGR. New Caledonia. ‖ **Nouvelle-Écosse**, f. GÉOGR. Nova Scotia. ‖ **Nouvelle-Galles du Sud**, f. GÉOGR. New South Wales. ‖ **Nouvelle-Guinée**, f. GÉOGR. New Guinea. ‖ **Nouvelle-Orléans** (*La*), f. GÉOGR. New Orleans. ‖ **Nouvelles-Hébrides**, f. pl. GÉOGR. New Hebrides. ‖ **Nouvelle-Zélande**, f. New Zealand.

nouvellement [nuvɛlmɑ̃] adv. Newly, recently, lately; *nouvellement découvert*, newly-discovered.

nouvelliste [-list] m. Short-story writer; nouvelliste.

novateur, trice [nɔvatœ:r, tris] s. Innovator. — adj. Innovating.

novation [-sjɔ̃] f. JUR. Novation.

novembre [nɔvɑ̃:br] m. November.

nover [nɔve] v. tr. (1). JUR. To substitute.

novice [nɔvis] s. ECCLÉS. Novice. ‖ FAM. Novice, beginner; apprentice. — adj. Inexperienced, green; new (en, into).

noviciat [-sja] m. ECCLÉS. Noviciate. ‖ FAM. Apprenticeship.

novocaïne [nɔvɔkain] f. MÉD. Novocaine.

noyade [nwayad] f. Drowning.

noyau [nwajo] m. Stone, kernel, U. S. pit (de fruit); *enlever les noyaux de*, to stone, U. S. to pit; *fruit à noyau*, stone-fruit. ‖ Newel (d'escalier); hub (de roue). ‖ ELECTR. Core (d'électro-aimant). ‖ PHYS. Nucleus (de l'atome, de la cellule). ‖ FIG. Knot, group; cell; *noyau communiste*, communist cell; *un petit noyau de joueurs de cartes*, a little bunch of card-players.

noyautage [-ta:ʒ] m. TECHN. Coring. ‖ FIG. Infiltration (de, into).

noyauter [-te] v. intr. (1). TECHN. To core. ‖ FIG. To set up a cell, to create a nucleus.

noyauteur [-tœ:r] m. TECHN. Core-maker.

noyé, ée [nwaje] adj. Drowned (personne). ‖ AUTOM. Flooded (carburateur). ‖ TECHN. Countersunk (vis). ‖ FIG. *Noyé dans*, submerged in (les détails); sunk into (la nuit). — s. Drowned (ou) drowning person.

noyer v. tr. (9a). To drown (un animal, une personne). ‖ AUTOM. To flood (le carburateur). ‖ TECHN. To flood (une mine); to countersink (une vis). ‖ ARTS. To blur (les contours). ‖ FIG. To drown (son chagrin); to dilute (son vin). ‖ FAM. *Noyer le poisson*, to pigeon-hole, to blather, to set up a verbal smoke-screen. — v. pr. **Se noyer**, to drown, to be drowned (accidentellement); to drown oneself (volontairement); *un homme qui se noie*, a drowning man. ‖ FAM. To flounder (patauger); *se noyer dans un verre d'eau*, to drown in a puddle.

noyer m. BOT. Walnut-tree; *noyer d'Amérique*, hickory.

noyure [-jy:r] f. TECHN. Countersink.

nu, ue [ny] adj. Naked, nude, unclothed (sans vêtements). ‖ Bare (non couvert); *pieds nus*, barefooted; *tête nue*, bareheaded. ‖ Naked (épée); bare (mur); uncarpeted (plancher); *vin nu*, wine without the cask. ‖ AUTOM. Stripped (châssis). ‖ LOC. *Nu comme la main,* bare as the back of your hand; *se voir à l'œil nu,* to be visible to the naked eye. ‖ LOC. **A nu,** naked, bare; *mettre une plaie à nu,* to lay a wound open. ‖ **Nu-jambes,** adj. Bare-legged. ‖ **Nu-pieds,** adj. Barefooted; m. inv. Sandal, flip-flop. ‖ **Nu-proprié-taire,** s. JUR. Bare owner. ‖ **Nue-propriété,** f. JUR. Bare ownership. ‖ **Nu-tête,** adj. Bare-headed. — m. ARTS. Nude.

nuage [nɥa:ʒ] m. Cloud; *couvert de nuages,* overcast; *sans nuages,* cloudless. ‖ FIG. Trace, drop (de lait); cloud (de poussière); *bonheur sans nuage,* unalloyed happiness, perfect bliss; *pulvériser en nuage,* to spray, to atomize. ‖ FAM. *Se perdre, vivre dans les nuages,* to get lost, to live in the clouds.

nuageusement [nɥaʒøzmɑ̃] adv. Cloudily.

nuageux, euse [-ʒø, ø:z] adj. Overcast, clouded over (ciel); cloudy (temps). ‖ Muddy (pierre précieuse). ‖ FIG. Nebulous, misty, dim (idée).

nuance [nɥɑ̃:s] f. Shade, hue, tone (couleur). ‖ MUS. Nuance. ‖ ARTS. Lights and shades. ‖ FIG. Shading, nicety; shade of meaning; nuance; *ils ne diffèrent que par de légères nuances,* they diverge only on minute points. ‖ FAM. Touch (ombre).

nuancé, ée [nɥɑ̃se] adj. Delicately shaded (gravure); delicately expressive (style).

nuancement [-smɑ̃] m. Shading, blending (de tons). .

nuancer [-se] v. tr. (6). To shade (une peinture); to colour (un récit); to blend (des tons); *nuancer un discours,* to express delicate shades of thought in a speech.

nuancier [-sje] m. Colour card.

nubile [nybil] adj. Nubile, marriageable.

nubilité [-lite] f. Marriageable age; nubility.

nucléaire [nykleɛ:r] adj. PHYS. Nuclear.
— m. Nuclear energy.

nucléé, ée [-e] adj. MÉD. Nucleated, nucleate.

nucléique [-ik] adj. MÉD. *Acides nucléiques,* nucleic acids.

nucléole [-ɔl] m. MÉD. Nucleolus.

nucléon [-ɔ̃] m. PHYS. Nucleon.

nucléonique [-ɔnik] f. PHYS. Nucleonics.

nudisme [nydism] m. Nudism.

nudiste [-dist] s. Nudist.

nudité [-dite] f. Bareness (des membres); nudity, nakedness (d'une personne). ‖ Baldness, bareness (des pics). ‖ FIG. Bareness; *sa cupidité s'étala dans toute sa nudité,* his greed showed up shamelessly.

nue [ny] f. Cloud. ‖ Pl. Sky, high heavens, clouds. ‖ FIG. Skies, clouds; *porter aux nues,* to praise to the skies; *tomber des nues,* to be taken aback; to be struck all of a heap (fam.).

nuée [nɥe] f. Thick cloud, storm-cloud (au ciel). ‖ FIG. Cloud. (V. MULTITUDE.)

nuire [nɥi:r] v. intr. (69). To be hurtful (ou) harmful (ou) injurious; to do harm (à, to); *cela nuira à votre réputation,* that will do harm to your reputation; *nuire au bonheur de qqn,* to cloud s.o.'s happiness; *nuire aux intérêts de qqn,* to prejudice s.o.'s interests; *ne penser qu'à nuire,* to be always planning to do harm; *son caractère revêche lui a beaucoup nui,* his surly disposition has been prejudicial to him.

nuisance [nɥizɑ̃:s] f. Nuisance.

nuisibilité [-zibilite] f. Harmfulness, injuriousness.

nuisible [-zibl] adj. Harmful, hurtful; injurious, noxious; prejudicial; *bête nuisible,* vermin.

nuit [nɥi] f. Night-time; *cette nuit,* tonight (à venir); *cette nuit, la nuit dernière,* last night (passée); *de nuit,* by night; *passer la nuit en bombe,* to make a night of it; *passer la nuit chez des amis,* to stay overnight with friends; *il ne*

passera pas la nuit, he won't live through the night; *train de nuit,* night train; *vêtements de nuit,* night-wear, sleeping-garments. ‖ Night, dark; *à la tombée de la nuit,* at nightfall; *après la tombée de la nuit,* after dark. ‖ ARTS. *Effets de nuit,* night-piece. ‖ FIG. Darkness (du tombeau); *la nuit des temps,* the mists of time. ‖ FAM. *C'est le jour et la nuit,* they are as different as day and night (ou) chalk and cheese.

nuitamment [-tamɑ̃] adv. By night, nightly.

nuitée [-te] f. Hotel bed occupied (dans les statistiques sur le tourisme).

nul, ulle [nyl] adj. indéf. No (v. AUCUN); *nul homme,* no man.
— pron. indéf. No one, none, no man; *nul n'est prophète en son pays,* a prophet has no honour in his own country; *nul ne vous en veut,* no one has anything against you.
— adj. Worthless, of no value; *nul en maths,* a dud at mathematics. ‖ Not worth mentioning (influence); non-existent (moyens). ‖ JUR. Worthless (bulletin); invalid (mariage); *nul et non avenu,* null and void. ‖ SPORTS. *Course nulle,* no race; *faire match nul,* to tie (ou) to draw a game; *partie nulle,* drawn (ou) tied game, draw.

nullard, arde [nyla:r, ard] adj. FAM. Useless, good-for-nothing; *nullard en maths,* useless (ou) a dud at maths.
— s. FAM. Thickhead, dud, good-for-nothing.

nulle [ny:l] f. Null, dummy letter.

nullement [nylmɑ̃] adv. Not at all, in no way, no wise, by no means.

nullifier [nyllifje] v. tr. (1). To nullify.

nullité [-te] f. Non-existence, lack (manque). ‖ Nullity, inability, incapacity (d'une personne). ‖ Nonentity (personne). ‖ JUR. Nullity, invalidity (d'un acte).

nûment [nymɑ̃] adv. Bluntly, point blank.

numéraire [nymerɛ:r] adj. Numerary, coined; *valeur numéraire,* legal tender value.
— m. Currency, cash, specie; *en numéraire,* in cash.

numéral, ale [-ral] adj., m. Numeral.

numérateur [-ratœr] m. MATH. Numerator.

numération [-rasjɔ̃] f. Numeration.

numérique [-rik] adj. Numerical.

numériquement [-rikmɑ̃] adv. Numerically.

numéro [-ro] m. Number; *chambre n° 19,* room number 19. ‖ Number, copy, issue (de journal, de revue); *dernier numéro,* current issue; *vente au numéro,* single copies sold (journaux); *vieux numéro,* back number. ‖ Number (de téléphone); *faire un numéro,* to dial. ‖ MILIT. Number, regimental number. ‖ NAUT. Official number. ‖ COMM. *Numéro d'ordre,* serial number; *prière de rappeler le numéro de référence,* please quote in your reply. ‖ AUTOM. Registered number. ‖ THÉÂTR. Act (de cirque); number on the programme (spectacle); *numéro de vestiaire,* cloakroom ticket. ‖ FAM. *Mon complet numéro un,* my best suit; *un dîner numéro un,* an A-1 (ou) a slap-up dinner; *un drôle de numéro,* a queer card (ou) fish; *quel numéro!,* what a character!

numérotage [-rɔta:ʒ], **numérotation** [nymerɔtasjɔ̃] m. Numbering (de maisons, de tickets); paging (des pages).

numéroté, ée [-rɔte] adj. Paginated (livre); with registered number (voiture).

numéroter [-rɔte] v. tr. (1). To number (des maisons, des tickets); to page, to paginate (des pages).

numéroteur [-rɔtœ:r] m. Numbering machine (ou) stamp.

numerus clausus [nymeryskɔzys] m. Numerus clausus, restriction on number of admittances.

numismate [nymismat] m. Numismatist.

numismatique [-tik] adj. Numismatic.
— f. Numismatics.

nuncupatif, ive [nɔ̃kypatif, i:v] adj. JUR. Nuncupative.

nuptial, ale [nypsjal] adj. Wedding (anneau, cérémonie, marche); marriage (bénédiction); bridal (chambre, cortège, voile).

nuptialité [-sjalite] f. Marriage rate.

nuque [nyk] f. MÉD. Nape, nape of the neck.

nurse [nœ:rs] f. Nanny, nursemaid.

nutriment [nytrimɑ̃] m. MÉD. Nutrient, nutriment.

nutritif, ive [nytritif, i:v] adj. Nutritive, nutrient,

nourishing, nutritious; *valeur nutritive,* food value.

nutrition [-sjɔ̃] f. Nutrition.

nutritionnel, elle [-sjɔnɛl] adj. Nutritional.

nyctalope [niktalɔp] adj. MÉD. Hemeralopic.

nyctalopie [-pi] f. MÉD. Hemeralopia.

Nylon [nilɔ̃] m. (nom déposé). Nylon.

nymphe [nɛ̃:f] f. Nymph (déesse). ‖ ZOOL. Nymph.

nymphéa [nɛ̃fea] m. BOT. Nymphea, water-lily.

nymphette [nɛ̃fɛt] f. Nymphet.

nymphomane [-fɔman] adj., s. Nymphomaniac.

nymphomanie [-fɔmani] f. Nymphomania.

O

o [o] m. O (lettre).

O [o] abrév. de *ouest,* W, west.

ô [ɔ] interj. Oh! O!

oasis [oazis] f. Oasis.

obédience [ɔbedjɑ̃:s] f. ECCLÉS. Obedience. ‖ FAM. Submission (à, to).

obéir [ɔbeir] v. intr. (2). *Obéir à,* to obey, to yield to (une impulsion); to submit to (la force); to obey, to fulfil (un ordre); to obey (qqn) [v. OBTEMPÉRER]; *se faire obéir de,* to obtain (ou) to enforce obedience from. ‖ NAUT. To obey, to yield to (navire). ‖ AUTOM. To obey, to answer to.

obéissance [-isɑ̃:s] f. Obedience, submission; *devoir obéissance à qqn,* to owe s.o. obedience; *devoir obéissance au roi,* to owe allegiance to the king; *rentrer dans l'obéissance,* to submit to authority; to toe the line (fam.).

obéissant, ante [-isɑ̃, ɑ̃:t] adj. Obedient, dutiful (à, to) [enfant]; compliant (personne); submissive (sujet). ‖ NAUT., AUTOM. Responsive.

obéliscal, ale [ɔbeliskal] adj. Obeliscal.

obélisque [-lisk] m. Obelisk.

obérer [ɔbere] v. tr. (5). To encumber with debt (qqch.); to burden with debt (qqn); *obérer les finances,* to weigh heavily on the finances.
— v. pr. S'obérer, to run into debt.

obèse [ɔbɛ:z] adj. Obese, stout, corpulent, portly.

obésité [ɔbezite] f. Obesity, stoutness, corpulence, portliness, fatness.

obier [ɔbje] m. BOT. Guelder-rose, snow-ball tree.

obit [ɔbit] m. ECCLÉS. Obit, anniversary mass.

obituaire [-tɥɛ:r] adj. ECCLÉS. Obituary.
— m. ECCLÉS. Obit book, obituary list.

objecter [ɔbjɛkte] v. tr. (1). To object, to raise an objection (à, to); *objecter qqch. à qqn,* to allege sth. against s.o.; *on lui objecta son attitude passée,* his former attitude was held against him.

objecteur [-tœ:r] m. *Objecteur de conscience,* conscientious objector; conchie, U. S. c.o. (fam.).

objectif, ive [-tif, i:v] adj. Objective; unbiassed. ‖ PHILOS. Objective.
— m. MILIT. Objective, aim. ‖ PHYS. Object-glass (ou) lens. ‖ FIG. Target.

objection [-sjɔ̃] f. Objection (à, to); *faire des objections,* to argue; *objection de conscience,* conscientious objection.

objectivement [-tivmɑ̃] adj. Objectively.

objectiver [-tive] v. tr. (1). PHILOS. To objectify.

objectivisme [-tivism] m. Objectivism.

objectivité [-tivite] f. Objectivity, objectiveness.

objet [ɔbjɛ] m. Object (chose visible). ‖ Object, thing (chose utilisable); *objet d'art,* «objet d'art»; U. S. art object; *objet de luxe,* article of luxury, U. S. luxury article; *objets trouvés,* lost property, lost and found; *faites-lui cadeau d'un objet utile,* give him something useful as a present. ‖ Object, subject (sujet); *objet de la conversation,* subject of the conversation; *objet de risée,* object of ridicule, laughing-stock. ‖ Object, aim (but); *quel est son objet?,* what's the use of that? what is it (ou) that for? (chose); what is he aiming at? (personne); *remplir son objet,* to reach one's goal; *sans objet,* aimless, purposeless. ‖ Object, purpose, objective (dessein); *atteindre son objet,* to realize (ou) achieve one's purpose. ‖ COMM. Article, items; *ayant pour objet, re...* ‖ JUR. *Objets immobiliers,* realty. ‖ PHILOS. Object, non-ego. ‖ GRAMM. Object, complement.

objurgation [ɔbʒyrgasjɔ̃] f. Objurgation, plea.

objurgatoire [-twa:r] adj. Objurgatory.

oblat [ɔbla] m. ECCLÉS. Oblate.

oblation [-sjɔ̃] f. ECCLÉS. Oblation.

obligataire [ɔbligatɛ:r] f. FIN. Bondholder. JUR. Obligee.

obligation [-sjɔ̃] f. Obligation, duty, moral necessity; *être dans l'obligation de,* to be bound (ou) obliged to; *être d'obligation pour,* to be obligatory for, to be required of; *mettre, se trouver dans l'obligation de,* to place, to be under the necessity of; *se soustraire à l'obligation de,* to get out of, to avoid. ‖ Gratefulness; *avoir beaucoup d'obligation à qqn,* to be much obliged to s.o. ‖ JUR. Bond; *obligation contractuelle,* privity in deed. ‖ FIN. Bond, debenture; *obligation du chemin de fer,* railway debenture; *obligation au porteur,* bearer bond.

obligatoire [-twa:r] adj. Obligatory; compulsory. ‖ JUR. Binding (clause).

obligatoirement [-twarmɑ̃] adv. Obligatorily.

obligé, ée [ɔbliʒe] adj. Obliged, bound, compelled (de, to) [contraint]. ‖ Unavoidable, inevitable; *dans la tragédie un dénouement malheureux est obligé,* in a tragedy an unhappy ending is the rule. ‖ Obligatory, indispensable; *invitation obligée,* invitation required by etiquette. ‖ Obliged,

grateful; *je vous suis très obligé,* I am much obliged to you.
— s. Person under obligation; *je demeure votre obligé,* I remain under an obligation to you.
obligeamment [-ʒamɑ̃] adv. Obligingly.
obligeance [-ʒɑ̃:s] f. Obligingness, kindness; *ayez l'obligeance de,* be so kind as to; *d'une grande obligeance,* very obliging.
obligeant, ante [-ʒɑ̃, ɑ̃:t] adj. Obliging, kind, considerate (v. COMPLAISANT); *se montrer obligeant envers,* to show kindness to; *termes très obligeants,* glowing terms.
obliger [-ʒe] v. tr. (7). To oblige, to compel, to bind (à, to); *ma position m'y oblige,* I am bound to do it in my position; *rien ne vous oblige à,* you are under no obligation to. ‖ To oblige, to do a service; *vous m'obligeriez en allant le voir,* you would oblige me by calling on him. ‖ JUR. To oblige, to bind.
— v. pr. S'obliger, to bind (ou) constrain oneself; *s'obliger à faire la sieste,* to make a point of taking a nap every afternoon.
oblique [ɔblik] adj. Oblique (direction, ligne); slanting, aslant (rayon); sidelong (regard). ‖ FIG. Underhand (manœuvre); crooked (moyen).
— m. Oblique movement. ‖ MÉD. Oblique muscle. ‖ MILIT. *Oblique à droite,* right incline (ou) U. S. oblique.
— f. Oblique line.
obliquement [-kmɑ̃] adv. Obliquely, aslant; *pluie qui tombe obliquement,* slanting rain. ‖ ‖ FIG. Slyly, in an underhand way.
obliquer [-ke] v. intr. (1). To oblique, to advance obliquely. ‖ NAUT. To slant, to tack. ‖ MILIT. To incline; U. S. to oblique.
obliquité [-kɥite] f. Obliquity, obliqueness. ‖ FIG. Crookedness.
oblitérateur, trice [ɔbliteratœ:r, tris] adj. Obliterating.
— m. Cancel (de timbres).
oblitération [-rasjɔ̃] f. Obliteration. ‖ Cancelling (d'un timbre). ‖ MÉD. Obliteration (d'une artère).
oblitérer [-re] v. tr. (5). To obliterate, to efface, to erase (une inscription); to cancel (un timbre). ‖ MÉD. To obliterate (une artère).
oblong, ongue [ɔblɔ̃, ɔ̃g] adj. Oblong.
obnubilation [ɔbnybilasjɔ̃] f. Obnubilation.
obnubilé, ée [-le] adj. Overcast (ciel). ‖ Cloudy, dimmed (esprit).
obnubiler [-le] v. tr. (1). To obnubilate, to dim.
obole [ɔbɔl] f. Obol, obole, obolus. (V. AUMÔNE.) ‖ FAM. Farthing, mite; *donner son obole à,* to contribute one's mite to.
obscène [ɔbsɛ:n] adj. Obscene (en général); smutty (chanson); obscene, indecent (geste); lewd, filthy, dirty (parole).
obscénité [-senite] f. Obscenity (en général); lewdness, filthiness, looseness (d'une conversation); obscenity, indecency (des gestes).
obscur, ure [ɔbsky:r] adj. Dark (chambre, forêt, grotte); overcast (ciel); gloomy (temps); *il fait obscur,* it's dark. ‖ FIG. Obscure (parole, style, texte); abstruse, recondite (sujet). ‖ FIG. Obscure, unknown (écrivain); unassuming, humble (personne).
obscurantisme [ɔbskyrɑ̃tism] m. Obscurantism.
obscurantiste [-rɑ̃tist] s. Obscurantist.
obscuration [-rasjɔ̃] f. ASTRON. Obscuration.
obscurcir [ɔbskyrsi:r] v. tr. (2). To obscure, to darken, to overcast (le ciel); to darken (la lumière); to dim (la vue). ‖ FIG. To overshadow, to obfuscate (l'esprit); to darken, to obnubilate (les idées); to becloud, to bedim (l'intelligence); to obscure, to conceal (la vérité); to dim, to cloud (le visage); *la renommée de Racine obscurcit celle de Corneille,* Racine's fame outshines Corneille's.
— v. pr. S'obscurcir, to grow dark (ciel, temps);

to grow dim (vue). ‖ FIG. To grow dim (ou) obfuscated (idées, intelligence); to wane, to pale (renommée); to become obscure (style).
obscurcissement [-sismɑ̃] m. Obscuring, darkening (du ciel, de la lumière); dimming (de la vue). ‖ Black-out (des lumières). ‖ FIG. Obfuscation (de l'esprit); obscuration (du style).
obscurément [ɔbskyremɑ̃] adv. Obscurely, darkly, dimly. ‖ FIG. Obscurely, in retirement.
obscurité [-rite] f. Obscurity, darkness, gloom (d'un lieu, de la nuit). ‖ Obscurity, humbleness (de la naissance); obscurity, retirement, seclusion (de la vie). ‖ FIG. Confusion, vagueness, reconditeness, dimness (des idées); abstruseness (du style); obscurity, obscureness (d'un texte).
obsédant, ante [ɔbsedɑ̃, ɑ̃:t] adj. Obsessing, obsessive, haunting (pensée, souvenir); pressing, urgent, instant (sollicitation).
obsédé, ée [-de] adj. Obsessed (par, with); fanatic, maniac (de, about).
— s. Sex maniac; *c'est un obsédé,* he is oversexed.
obséder [-de] v. tr. (5). To obsess, to haunt (pensée); to press, to importune, to worry, to plague (solliciteur).
obsèques [ɔbsɛk] f. pl. Obsequies, funeral.
obséquieusement [ɔbsekjøzmɑ̃] adv. Obsequiously.
obséquieux, euse [-kjø, ø:z] adj. Obsequious.
obséquiosité [-kjɔzite] f. Obsequiousness (attitude); oily pleading (paroles).
observable [ɔbsɛrvabl] adj. Observable.
observance [-vɑ̃:s] f. Observance, observing, keeping (d'une règle). ‖ ECCLÉS. Observance (règle).
observateur, trice [-vatœ:r, tris] adj. Observant, observing; *il est très observateur,* he has a keen eye (ou) an observant mind.
— s. Observer, keeper (des règlements). ‖ Observer, watcher, student (savant). ‖ Observer, onlooker (spectateur); observer (surveillant). ‖ AVIAT. Observer, spotter.
observation [-vasjɔ̃] f. Observation, observance (d'une loi); fulfilment (d'un ordre). ‖ Observation, remark, comment; *faire une observation,* to make an observation, to put in a remark. ‖ Reprimand, reproof (reproche); *faire une observation à,* to reproach with. ‖ Observation (examen); *en observation,* under observation (chose); on the lookout (personne). ‖ ASTRON. Observation. ‖ MÉD. *En observation,* under observation. ‖ MILIT. *D'observation,* reconnoitring (corps).
observatoire [-vatwa:r] m. ASTRON. Observatory. ‖ MILIT. Observation post.
observer [-ve] v. tr. (1). To observe, to keep (la loi); to fulfil (un ordre); *faire observer,* to enforce (la loi). ‖ To observe, to watch, to note, to take note of (noter); *faire observer qqch. à qqn,* to draw s.o.'s attention to sth.; *observez comment il s'y prend,* watch how he proceeds. ‖ To observe, to remark, to offer a remark (remarquer); *faire observer,* to point out.
— v. pr. S'observer, to be careful (ou) wary (ou) cautious (ou) on one's guard (être circonspect). ‖ To watch (ou) to keep watch on one's words (ou) behaviour (se surveiller). ‖ To be observed, to occur (arriver).
— v. récipr. S'observer, to observe one another.
obsessif, ive [ɔbsɛsif, i:v] adj. Obsessive.
obsession [-sjɔ̃] f. Obsession, haunting thought.
obsessionnel, elle [-sjɔnɛl] adj. Obsessional. ‖ PSYCH. *Névrose obsessionnelle,* obsessive-compulsive neurosis.
— s. Obsessional neurotic, obsessive-compulsive.
obsidienne [ɔbsidjɛ:n] f. Obsidian.
obsolescent, ente [ɔbsɔlɛsɑ̃, ɑ̃:t] adj. Obsolescent (machine, technique).
obstacle [ɔbstakl] m. Obstacle. ‖ SPORTS. *Course*

d'obstacles, obstacle race. ‖ Fig. Obstacle; impediment, hindrance; *dresser des obstacles devant qqn,* to place (ou) to put obstacles in s.o.'s way; *faire obstacle à,* to bar the way to, to stand in the way of, to thwart, to oppose.

obstétrical, ale [ɔbstetrikal] adj. Méd. Obstetrical.

obstétrique [-trik] adj. Méd. Obstetrical.
— f. Méd. Obstetrics.

obstination [ɔbstinasjɔ̃] f. Obstinacy, stubbornness, headstrongness, pertinacity, pigheadedness (entêtement); waywardness, wilfulness (avec caprice); perversity (avec malice).

obstiné, ée [-ne] adj. Obstinate, stubborn, wayward (enfant); wilful, headstrong, self-willed, mulish, pigheaded (personne). [V. tÊtu.] ‖ Méd. Stubborn, persistent (fièvre, rhume). ‖ Fig. Stubborn, dogged (résistance); persevering, dogged (travail).

obstinément [-nemɑ̃] adv. Obstinately, subbornly, tenaciously.

obstiner [-ne] v. tr. (1). To make obstinate (qqn).
— v. pr. **S'obstiner,** to grow obstinate (ou) obdurate (v. s'entÊter); *s'obstiner à,* to persist in, to persevere in, to cling to, to stick to; *s'obstiner dans son opinion,* to dig one's heels in, to stick to one's guns.

obstructif, ive [ɔbstryktif, i:v] adj. Obstructive.

obstruction [-sjɔ̃] f. Blocking up, stopping up (d'un conduit). ‖ Jam (de la circulation routière). ‖ Obstruction, U. S. filibuster (en politique). ‖ Méd. Stoppage, obstruction.

obstructionnisme [-sjɔnism] m. Obstructionism, U. S. filibustering.

obstructionniste [-sjɔnist] m. Obstructionist, U. S. filibuster.

obstruer [ɔbstrye] v. tr. (1). To jam (la circulation, une entrée); to obstruct, to block (un conduit, un passage); to choke (un tuyau); to close up (la vue). [V. boucher.] ‖ Méd. To occlude.
— v. pr. **S'obstruer,** to become jammed (ou) blocked (ou) choked up.

obtempérer [ɔbtɑ̃pere] v. intr. (1). *Obtempérer à,* to obey (un ordre); to accede to, to yield to (une prière); to comply with, to fall in with (une requête). [V. se soumettre.]

obtenir [ɔbtəni:r] v. tr. (101). To obtain, to get, to come by (de l'argent, une subvention); to obtain, to achieve, to get, to secure, to gain (un avantage, un résultat); to procure (un livre, un objet); to secure (une place); to win (un prix); to achieve (un succès); *obtenir de faire,* to obtain permission to do; *obtenir de qqn qu'il fasse qqch.,* to persuade (ou) to induce (ou) to prevail upon s.o. to do sth.; *obtenir de qqn qqch. de force,* to wring sth. out of s.o.; *j'obtiendrai que cette omission soit passée sous silence,* I will see to it that this oversight is not mentioned.
— v. pr. **S'obtenir,** to be obtained (ou) got *(de,* from); to be procured *(chez,* from). ‖ To be effected *(à,* at) [être effectué].

obtention [ɔbtɑ̃sjɔ̃] f. Obtaining, obtainment, getting, procurement.

obturant, ante [ɔbtyrɑ̃, ɑ̃:t] adj. Obturating. ‖ Méd. Occluding.

obturateur, trice [-ratœ:r, tris] adj. Obturating.
— m. Stopper (en général). ‖ Méd. Obturator. ‖ Shutter (en photo). ‖ Techn. Stop-valve, plug. ‖ Milit. Obturator, breech-plug.

obturation [-rasjɔ̃] f. Obturation; *obturation des lumières,* black-out. ‖ Méd. Filling (d'une dent).

obturer [-re] v. tr. (1). To obturate, to block up (un conduit, une ouverture); to black out (les lumières). [V. boucher.] ‖ To close (un trou). ‖ Méd. To stop, to fill (une dent).

obtus, use [ɔbty, yz] adj. Blunted (pointe). ‖ Math. Obtuse (angle). ‖ Bot. Rounded (feuille).

‖ Fig. Dull, obtuse (esprit); slow, dull-witted, obtuse (personne).

obtusangle [-zɑ̃:gl] adj. Math. Obtuse-angled.

obus [ɔby] m. Milit. Shell; *obus à balles,* shrapnel; *obus non éclaté,* unexploded shell; dud (fam.).

obusier [-zje] m. Milit. Howitzer; *obusier à projectile ultra-rapide,* high-velocity howitzer.

obvenir [ɔbvəni:r] v. intr. (2). Jur. To escheat *(à,* to).

obvier [ɔbvje] v. intr. (1). *Obvier à,* to provide against, to obviate, to prevent, to preclude, to forestall.

oc [ɔk] adv. Yes; *langue d'oc,* langue d'oc, early Provençal.

ocarina [ɔkarina] m. Mus. Ocarina.

occase [ɔka:z] f. Pop. Bargain, good deal, giveaway.

occasion [ɔkazjɔ̃] f. Occasion (conjoncture); *l'occasion,* on occasion; *dans les grandes occasions,* on special (ou) great occasions; *en cette occasion,* in this case, at this juncture; *pour l'occasion,* for once, for the nonce. ‖ Chance (hasard); *par occasion,* by chance, now and then occasionally. ‖ Occasion (cas); *en toute occasion,* on all occasions; *suivant l'occasion,* as occasion requires (ou) demands. ‖ Opportunity, chance (opportunité); *avoir l'occasion de faire,* to happen to do, to have occasion to do; *si l'occasion s'en présente,* if we get an opportunity, if the opportunity comes our way. ‖ Occasion, circumstance (circonstances); *à l'occasion,* at times, as occasion offers; *en pareille occasion,* in a similar case; *cela dépend des occasions,* it depends on circumstances; *un musicien d'occasion,* a mere amateur musician. ‖ Occasion, motive, cause; *être l'occasion de,* to be the cause of, to be the reason for to entail. ‖ Comm. Bargain; *trouver une occasion,* to come across a bargain; *une voiture d'occasion,* a used (ou) second-hand car.

occasionnel, elle [ɔkazjɔnɛl] adj. Occasional; *rencontre occasionnelle,* chance meeting. ‖ Determining (cause).

occasionnellement [-nɛlmɑ̃] adv. Occasionally, from time to time, every so often, now and then.

occasionner [-ne] v. tr. (1). To occasion, to cause, to produce; to give rise to, to bring about, to start, to lead to.

Occident [ɔksidɑ̃] m. West, Occident.

occidental, ale [-tal] adj. Occidental, western.
— s. Occidental, Westerner.

occidentaliser [-talize] v. tr. (1). To westernize, to occidentalize.

occipital, ale [ɔksipital] adj. Méd. Occipital.
— m. Méd. Occipital bone.

occiput [-pyt] m. Méd. Occiput.

occire [ɔksi:r] v. tr. (4). † To kill, to slay.

occitan, ane [ɔksitɑ̃, an] adj. Gramm. Occitan, relating to the group of dialects spoken in Southern France.
— m. Gramm. Occitan, group of dialects spoken in Southern France.

occlure [ɔkly:r] v. tr. (29). To occlude.

occlusif, ive [ɔklyzif, i:v] adj. Occlusive.

occlusion [ɔklyzjɔ̃] f. Méd. Occlusion; *occlusion intestinale,* obstruction (ou) stoppage of the bowels. ‖ Techn. Closure (d'une soupape).

occlusive [-zi:v] f. Gramm. Plosive, stop.

occultation [ɔkyltasjɔ̃] f. Astron. Occultation.

occulte [ɔkylt] adj. Occult. (V. caché, secret.)

occulter [-te] v. tr. (1). To occult.

occultisme [-tism] m. Occultism.

occultiste [-tist] m. Occultist.

occupant, ante [ɔkypɑ̃, ɑ̃:t] adj. Occupying (troupes). ‖ Engrossing (travail).
— m. Occupant, occupier. ‖ Milit. Member of the occupying forces.

occupation [-pasjɔ̃] f. Occupation, occupancy; tenure; possession. ‖ Occupation, business, employment, work (travail). ‖ JUR. *Occupation de bonne foi*, precarious tenure (appartement). ‖ MILIT. Occupation; *forces d'occupation*, occupying forces.

occupé, ée [-pe] adj. Occupied (pays, appartement, usine); taken (siège); held (poste); engaged, U. S. busy (ligne téléphonique, toilettes); busy (personne), taken up with (esprit, temps).

occuper [-pe] v. tr. (1). To occupy, to hold (tenir); *occuper trop de place*, to take up too much room. ‖ To employ, to occupy (employer); *occuper deux cents ouvriers*, to have a force of two hundred workmen. ‖ To occupy, to fill in (remplir); *occuper ses loisirs*, to occupy (ou) to use one's leisure time. ‖ To occupy, to retain, to engage (retenir); *occuper l'attention de qqn*, to engross (ou) to hold s.o.'s attention; *occuper qqn*, to keep s.o. busy; *être occupé à écrire*, to be busy writing; *la ligne est occupée*, the number is engaged, U. S. the line is busy. ‖ MILIT. To hold (une hauteur); to occupy (une ville).
— v. intr. JUR. To be in charge of the case (*pour*, for).
— v. pr. **S'occuper**, to keep oneself busy, to occupy (ou) to employ oneself; *en peine de s'occuper*, looking for an occupation; *s'occuper à*, to busy oneself with, to employ oneself in, to be engaged in. ‖ To see, to look after, to look to (prendre soin de); *s'occuper d'une affaire*, to see to a case, to go into the matter; *s'occuper d'enfants*, to look after (ou) to mind children. ‖ To be interested (*de*, in); to give one's attention, to give oneself up (*de*, to); *je m'occupe surtout d'histoire romaine*, my speciality is Roman history; *je m'occupe d'œuvres sociales*, I go in for social work; *s'occuper d'un problème*, to turn one's attention to a problem. ‖ COMM. *S'occupe-t-on de vous?*, are you being served (ou) attended to (ou) waited on?; *s'occuper de la vente de*, to handle, to deal in. ‖ FAM. *Occupez-vous de vos affaires*, mind your own business.

occurrence [ɔkyrɑ̃:s] f. Occurrence, emergency, juncture, occasion; *en l'occurrence*, under the circumstances, on this occasion, in the present case. ‖ ECCLÉS. Occurrence.

occurrent, ente [-rɑ̃, ɑ̃:t] adj. Occurring, occurrent.

O.C.D.E. [osedeə] abrév. de *Organisation de coopération et de développement économiques*, OECD, Organization for Economic Cooperation and Development.

océan [ɔseɑ̃] m. Ocean. ‖ FIG. Sea, ocean.

océane [-a:n] adj. f. Ocean.

océanide [ɔseanid] f. Oceanid; sea-nymph.

Océanie [-ni] f. GÉOGR. Oceania.

océanien, enne [-njɛ̃, ɛn] adj. s. Oceanian.

océanique [-nik] adj. Oceanic.

océanographe [-nɔgraf] m. Oceanographer.

océanographie [-nɔgrafi] f. Oceanography.

ocelle [ɔsɛl] m. ZOOL. Ocellus.

ocellé, ée [ɔsɛlle] adj. Ocellate.

ocelot [ɔslɔ] m. ZOOL. Ocelot.

ocre [ɔkr] adj. Ochrous, ochry.
— m. Ochre (couleur); *ocre rouge*, red ochre, raddle.

ocrer [ɔkre] v. tr. (1). To ochre.

ocreux, euse [ɔkrø, ø:z] adj. Ochrous, ochry.

octaèdre [ɔktaɛ:dr] adj. MATH. Octahedral.
— m. MATH. Octahedron.

octaédrique [-edrik] adj. MATH. Octahedral.

octane [ɔktan] m. CHIM. Octane; *indice d'octane*, octane number (ou) rating.

octante [ɔktɑ̃:t] adj. † Eighty, fourscore.

octave [ɔkta:v] f. MUS. Octave.

octet [ɔktɛ] m. INFORM. Eight bit byte. ‖ PHYS. Octet.

octobre [ɔktɔbr] m. October.

octogénaire [ɔktɔʒenɛ:r] adj., s. Octogenarian.

octogonal, ale [-gɔnal] adj. Octagonal.

octogone [-gɔn] m. MATH. Octagon.

octopode [-pɔd] adj. Eight-footed, octopod.
— m. ZOOL. Octopod.

octosyllabe [-sillab] m. GRAMM. Octosyllabic.

octosyllabique [-sillabik] adj. GRAMM. Octosyllabic.

octroi [ɔktrwa] m. Grant, granting (d'un avantage). ‖ JUR. Toll-office, octroi (bureau); town-dues, city-toll (droits).

octroyer [-je] v. tr. (9a). To grant (*à*, to); to bestow (*à*, on). [V. CONCÉDER.]
— v. pr. **S'octroyer**, to indulge in, to treat oneself to.

octuor [ɔktyɔr] m. MUS. Octuor, octet (composition); octet (formation d'instrumentistes).

octuple [ɔktypl] adj. Octuple.

oculaire [ɔkylɛ:r] adj. Ocular; *témoin oculaire*, eye-witness.
— m. PHYS. Ocular, eye-piece.

oculiste [-list] m. MÉD. Oculist.

odalisque [ɔdalisk] f. Odalisk.

ode [ɔd] f. Ode.

odelette [ɔdlɛt] f. Short ode.

odéon [ɔdeɔ̃] m. † Odeum. ‖ THÉÂTR. Odeon.

odeur [ɔdœ:r] f. Smell, odour, scent; U. S. odor; *à l'odeur agréable*, sweet smelling. ‖ Perfume, scent (v. PARFUM); *se mettre des odeurs*, to scent oneself. ‖ ECCLÉS. *Mourir en odeur de sainteté*, to die in the odour of sanctity. ‖ FAM. *Etre en odeur de sainteté auprès de qqn*, to be in s.o.'s good graces.

odieusement [ɔdjøzmɑ̃] adv. Odiously.

odieux, euse [ɔdjø, ø:z] adj. Shocking (conduite); heinous (crime); detestable (mesure); odious, hateful (personne); invidious (tâche); *rendre odieux*, to cast odium on; *se rendre odieux*, to attract odium to oneself.
— m. Odium, odiousness, hatefulness.

odographe [ɔdɔgra:f] adj. MILIT. Odograph.

odontalgie [ɔdɔ̃talʒi] f. MÉD. Odontalgia.

odontologie [ɔdɔ̃tɔlɔʒi] f. MÉD. Odontology.

odorant, ante [ɔdɔrɑ̃, ɑ̃:t] adj. Odorous, fragrant, sweet-smelling (de bonne odeur); smelly, ill-smelling (de mauvaise odeur). ‖ Perfumed, scented (parfumé).

odorat [-ra] m. Smell; *avoir l'odorat fin*, to have a keen sense of smell. ‖ FAM. Nose.

odoriférant, ante [-riferɑ̃, ɑ̃:t] adj. Odoriferous, fragrant.

Odyssée [ɔdise] f. † Odyssey. ‖ FAM. Odyssey, wanderings; eventful journey.

œcuménique [ekymenik] adj. ECCLÉS. Ecumenical, oecumenical.

œcuménisme [-nism] m. ECCLÉS. Ecumenicalism, oecumenicalism, ecumenism.

œcuméniste [-nist] adj. ECCLÉS. Ecumenical, oecumenical, ecumenist.
— s. Ecumenicist, oecumenist, ecumenist.

œdémateux, euse [edematø, ø:z] adj. MÉD. Oedematous, U. S. edematous.

œdème [-dɛm] m. MÉD. Oedema, U. S. edema.

Œdipe [edip] m. Oedipus. ‖ PHILOS. *Complexe d'Œdipe*, Oedipus complex.

œil [œ:j] (pl. **yeux** [jø]) m.

---

1. Sens général. — 2. Regard, vue. — 3. Avis. — 4. Attention. — 5. Observation. — 6. CULIN. — 7. TECHN. — 8. COMM. — 9. ELECTR. — 10. LOC. — 11. FAM.

---

1. Eye (sens général); *avoir les larmes aux yeux*, to have tears in one's eyes; *avoir mal aux yeux*, to have sore eyes; *avoir un œil poché* (ou) *au beurre noir*, to have a black eye; *baisser, lever les yeux*, to look down, up; *faire de l'œil à qqn*, to give s.o. the (glad) eye; *faire les petits yeux*, to screw up one's eyes; *faire les doux yeux à*, to make goo-goo eyes at; *regarder du coin de l'œil*, to cast a sidelong glance (ou) look at; *regarder avec de grands yeux*, to gape (ou) stare at; *s'user les yeux à pleurer*, to cry one's eyes out; *virer de l'œil comme une chèvre mourante*, to turn up one's eyes like a duck in thunder. ‖ 2. Sight, eye (regard, vue); *avoir sous les yeux*, to have before one's eyes; *caché aux yeux*, out of sight; *ça crève les yeux*, it stands out a mile; *jeter les yeux sur*, to have a look at, to run one's eyes over; *mettre sous les yeux de qqn*, to set before s.o.; *perdre* (ou) *quitter des yeux*, to lose sight of; *sauter aux yeux*, to be glaringly obvious; *sous mes yeux*, under my eyes, before my face; *suivre des yeux*, to watch. ‖ 3. Eye, opinion, advice (avis); *à mes yeux*, in my eyes, in my opinion; *aux yeux de mes amis*, in my friends' eyes; *envisager l'affaire d'un autre œil*, to look upon the matter with a different eye; *ne pas voir les choses du même œil que qqn*, not to see eye to eye with s.o.; *voir d'un bon, d'un mauvais œil*, to look favourably, unfavourably upon; *à vue d'œil*, with the naked eye, visibly. ‖ 4. Eye, notice, attention; *accepter une assurance de qqn les yeux fermés*, to take s.o.'s word about sth.; *avoir l'œil sur*, to keep an eye upon; *avoir l'œil à tout*, to keep an eye on everything; *être tout yeux*, to be all eyes; *ouvrir l'œil*, to keep a sharp look-out, to keep one's eyes open, to have one's eyes about one; *ouvrir les yeux de qqn*, to open s.o.'s eyes; *signer les yeux fermés*, to sign on the dotted line; *tenir qqn à l'œil*, to keep s.o. in sight. ‖ 5. Eye, observation; *avoir un coup d'œil pour*, to have a good eye for. ‖ 6. CULIN. Eye; speck of fat (sur le bouillon); hole (de gruyère); eye (de pain). ‖ 7. TECHN. Eye (d'aiguille); face (en typogr.). ‖ 8. COMM. *Donner de l'œil à un article*, to give an article a better appearance. ‖ 9. ELECTR. *Œil électrique*, electric eye. ‖ 10. LOC. *Avoir le mauvais œil*, to have the evil eye; *avoir les yeux plus gros que le ventre*, to bite off more than one can chew; *coûter les yeux de la tête*, to cost the earth; *faire les gros yeux à*, to look sternly at; *œil pour œil*, an eye for an eye; *ne pas fermer l'œil*, not to have a wink of sleep; *tourner de l'œil*, to faint, to pass out. ‖ 11. FAM. *A l'œil*, free, on the house (v. GRATIS); *je m'en bats l'œil*, I don't care a rap; *mon œil!*, my foot! U. S. nuts!; *taper dans l'œil de qqn*, to catch s.o.'s fancy, to dazzle s.o. ‖ **Œil-de-bœuf**, m. Bull's-eye window. ‖ **Œil-de-chat**, m. Cat's eye. ‖ **Œil-de-perdrix**, m. Soft corn. ‖ **Œil-de-pie**, m. NAUT. Eyelet. ‖ **Œil-de-tigre**, m. V. ŒIL-DE-CHAT.

œillade [œjad] f. Glance, ogle; *lancer une œillade*, to ogle, to make sheep's eyes at.

œillère [œjɛ:r] f. Blinker, eye-flap, U. S. blinder. ‖ MÉD. Eye-bath; eye-cup. ‖ FIG. *Avoir des œillères*, to have narrow views, to wear blinkers.

œillet [œjɛ] m. BOT. Carnation, pink; *œillet d'Inde*, French marigold.

œillet m. Eyelet, eyelet-hole. ‖ NAUT. Grommet.

œilleton [œjtɔ̃] m. Eyepiece shade (de télescope). ‖ Sight (en photo). ‖ BOT. Eye, seed-bud; sucker.

œillette [œjɛt] f. BOT. Oil-poppy; opium-poppy; *huile d'œillette*, poppy-oil, U. S. poppy-seed oil.

œnologie [enɔlɔʒi] f. Oenology.

œnologue [-lɔg] s. Oenologist.

œsophage [ezɔfa:ʒ] m. MÉD. Oesophagus, U. S. esophagus.

œsophagien, enne [-ʒjɛ̃, ɛn] adj. MÉD. Oesophageal; U. S. esophageal.

œstral [ɛstral] adj. MÉD. Oestrous, U. S. estrous (cycle).

œstrogène [ɛstrɔʒɛn] adj. MÉD. Oestrogenic, U. S. estrogenic.
— m. MÉD. Oestrogen, U. S. estrogen.

œuf [œf] (pl. **œufs** [ø]) m. Egg; *œuf de cane de poule*, duck's, hen's egg. ‖ Egg (de mouche de serpent); spawn, hard roe (de poisson). ‖ CULIN. *Œufs au lait*, custard; *œuf sur le plat* fried egg; *faire cuire un œuf à la coque, sur le plat*, to boil, to fry an egg. ‖ FIG. *Œuf à repriser*, darning egg; *œuf à thé*, tea-infuser. ‖ LOC. *Dans l'œuf*, in the bud; *marcher sur des œufs*, to walk on very thin ice; *mettre tous ses œufs dans le même panier*, to keep (ou) to put all one's eggs in one basket; *plein comme un œuf*, cram- (ou) chock-full; *tondre un œuf*, to skin a flint, to be a skinflint.

œuvé, ée [œve] adj. ZOOL. Hard-roed.

œuvre [œ:vr] f. Work, action (action); *faire œuvre utile*, to do useful work; *faire œuvre d'ami dévoué*, to act as a devoted friend; *fils de ses œuvres*, self-made man; *mettre en œuvre*, to bring into play; *mettre en œuvre un traité*, to implement a treaty; *mettre tout en œuvre pour*, to do everything possible to, to resort to all possible means to; *mise en œuvre d'une décision*, implementing of a decision; *mise en œuvre d'un plan*, carrying out of a project; *la mort avait fait son œuvre*, death had done its work. ‖ Work, product, achievement (produit); *l'œuvre de trois siècles*, the work of three centuries. ‖ Work, occupation; *mettre qqn à l'œuvre*, to set s.o. to work; *se mettre à l'œuvre*, to set to work, to settle down to work. ‖ Effect, activity; *enceinte des œuvres de*, with child by; *s'il a réussi, c'est bien mon œuvre*, if he has succeeded, it is thanks to me. ‖ Work, production (ouvrage); *œuvre d'art*, work of art; *œuvre maîtresse*, master-work; magnum opus (livre). ‖ Work, works; society; *faire de bonnes œuvres*, to do good works; *œuvre de bienfaisance*, charitable society, charity (fam.). ‖ ECCLÉS. *Renoncer au démon, à ses pompes et à ses œuvres*, to renounce the devil and all his works; *salle des œuvres*, parish hall. ‖ NAUT. *Œuvres mortes*, upper (ou) dead works, topsides; *œuvres vives*, vitals.
— m. Work, production. ‖ MUS. Opus. ‖ ARCHIT. Main work; *gros œuvre*, carcassing. ‖ LOC. *Le grand œuvre*, the philosopher's stone.

œuvrer [œvre] v. intr. (1). To work.

off [ɔf] adj. inv. CINÉM. Off, from off-stage.

offensant, ante [-ɔfɑ̃sɑ̃, ɑ̃:t] adj. Offensive, insulting.

offense [ɔfɑ̃:s] f. Offence, insult, contumely; U. S. offense; *faire offense à qqn*, to treat s.o. with contumely, to offend. ‖ ECCLÉS. Trespass, sin. ‖ JUR. Contempt.

offensé [ɔfɑ̃se] adj. Offended (par, at [qqch.]; by [qqn]).
— m. JUR. Offended party.

offenser v. tr. (1). To offend; to hurt the feelings of; to treat with contumely (qqn). ‖ To offend, to injure (la réputation) ‖ To offend, to shock, to be an offence to (la vue). ‖ ECCLÉS. To trespass against.
— v. pr. **S'offenser**, to take offence (de, at).

offenseur [ɔfɑ̃sœ:r] m. Offender.

offensif, ive [-sif, i:v] adj. Offensive. ‖ Unexpected, sudden (brusque). ‖ MILIT. Offensive.

offensive [ɔfɑ̃si:v] f. MILIT. Offensive; *passer à l'offensive*, to switch over to the offensive.

offertoire [ɔfɛrtwa:r] m. ECCLÉS. Offertory.

office [ɔfis] m. Office, function, duty (emploi); *faire office de*, to be used as (chose); to act as (personne); *remplir l'office de*, to fill the office of; *remplir son office*, to do one's job. ‖ Office,

service ; *rendre de bons offices à*, to be helpful towards. ‖ Office, bureau ; *Office du blé*, National Wheat Board ; *Office de la main-d'œuvre*, Labour Exchange, U. S. Labor Relations Board ; *Office des relations internationales*, International Relations Bureau ; *Office du tourisme*, Tourist Information Centre, Travel and Holiday Centre, Travel Centre. ‖ CULIN. Servants (domestiques). ‖ ECCLÉS. Service. ‖ LOC. **D'office**, ex officio, according to regulations, without any special order, automatically ; *entraîner le renvoi d'office*, to imply dismissal as a matter of course ; *reculer les mises à la retraite d'office*, to postpone the age-limit for retirement.
— f. CULIN. Pantry, servant's hall (lieu) ; *dîner à l'office*, to have one's meals with the servants.

official [ɔfisjal] m. ECCLÉS. Official.

officialisation [-lizasjɔ̃] f. Officialization, officializing, making official.

officialiser [-lize] v. tr. (1). To officialize, to make official.

officialité [-lite] f. ECCLÉS. Officiality.

officiant, ante [ɔfisjɑ̃, ɑ̃:t] adj. Officiating.
— m. ECCLÉS. Officiant, celebrant.

officiel, elle [ɔfisjɛl] adj. Official ; *rendre officiel*, to make public.
— m. Official (personnalité). ‖ Gazette (journal) ; *être à l'Officiel*, to be gazetted.

officiellement [-mɑ̃] adv. Officially.

officier [ɔfisje] v. intr. (1). ECCLÉS., FIG. To officiate.

officier [ɔfisje] m. MILIT. Officer ; *officier de réserve*, reserve officer ; *officier supérieur*, senior (ou) field officer, U. S. top brass (fam.). ‖ NAUT. *Officier de marine, de manœuvre, de pont, de tir*, naval, navigating, deck, gunnery officer. ‖ JUR. Officer ; *officier de l'état civil*, municipal magistrate ; *officier ministériel*, member of the legal profession ; *officier de paix*, municipal police officer. ‖ Officer (d'un ordre) ; *officier de la Légion d'honneur*, Officer of the Legion of Honour. ‖ MÉD. *Officier de santé*, health officer, authorized practitioner.

officieusement [-sjøzmɑ̃] adv. Officiously. Informally, unofficially

officieux, euse [-sjø, ø:z] adj. Informal, semi-official (renseignement) ; unofficial (source). ‖ Over-obliging, officious (personne).
— m. Officious person, busybody.

officinal, ale [ɔfisinal] adj. MÉD. Officinal ; medicinal.

officine [-sin] f. MÉD. Chemist's shop, U. S. drugstore. ‖ FIG. Den of thieves (repaire) ; hot-bed (d'intrigue).

offrande [ɔfrɑ̃:d] f. Gift, offering. (V. DON). ‖ ECCLÉS. Offering, offertory.

offrant [ɔfrɑ̃] s. *Au plus offrant*, to the highest bidder.

offre [ɔfr] f. Offer, proposal ; *offres de compromis*, overtures for a compromise ; *offres de service*, services tendered, begging for employment ; *faire offre de*, to offer. ‖ COMM. *L'offre et la demande*, supply and demand.

offrir [ɔfri:r] v. tr. (72). To offer, to proffer ; *offrir le choix, ses services*, to offer the choice, one's services ; *offrir son bras à qqn*, to offer s.o. one's arm ; *offrir sa démission*, to tender one's resignation. ‖ To offer, to present, to give (donner) ; *offrir qqch. à qqn*, to present s.o. with sth., to give sth. to s.o. ; *offrir un dîner à qqn*, to give a dinner for s.o. ; *offrir un whisky à qqn*, to stand s.o. a whisky. ‖ To offer, to furnish, to give (fournir) ; *offrir une chance, un exemple, une porte de sortie*, to offer a chance, an example, a way out ; *offrir une explication*, to furnish an explanation ; *offrir une solution*, to admit a solution. ‖ To offer, to bid ; *combien en offrez-vous ?*, how much do you offer for it ? ‖ To offer (ses souffrances) ; to offer, to sacrifice (une victime). ‖ To offer, to propose (*de*, to) [proposer] ; *offrir le mariage à*, to propose to.
— v. pr. **S'offrir**, to offer, to offer oneself ; to volunteer (*à*, to) ; *s'offrir en sacrifice*, to offer oneself up. ‖ FIG. To offer itself, to turn up (chance) ; *un magnifique paysage s'offrait à leurs yeux*, a magnificent scene met their eyes ; *la solution qui s'offrait*, the solution that presented itself ; *s'offrir la satisfaction de*, to give oneself the satisfaction of.

offset [ɔfsɛt] m. TECHN. Offset.

offshore [ɔfʃɔ:r] adj. TECHN. Offshore (prospection, forage).
— m. TECHN. Offshore prospection (ou) drilling (ou) technics.

offusquer [ɔfyske] v. tr. (1). To obscure, to obfuscate, to darken (la vue) ; to dazzle, to blind (les yeux). ‖ To veil, to mask, to blurr (le paysage, le soleil). ‖ FAM. To offend, to upset, to shock (qqn).
— v. pr. **S'offusquer**, to take offence (*de*, at) ; to take exception (*de*, to) [v. SE SCANDALISER] ; *s'offusquer facilement*, to be very touchy, to be easily put out.

ogival, ale [ɔʒival] adj. ARCHIT. Pointed, ogival.

ogive [ɔʒi:v] f. ARCHIT. Gothic (ou) pointed arch ; ogive ; rib ; *d'ogives*, ribbed (voûte). ‖ MILIT. Ogival point.

ogre [ɔgr] m. Ogre.

ogresse [ɔgrɛs] f. Ogress.

oh! [o] interj. Oh ! [V. ô.]

ohé [oe] interj. Hi !, halloo, hullo ! ‖ NAUT. *Ohé du navire*, ship ahoy !

ohm [om] m. ELECTR. Ohm. ‖ **Ohm-mètre**, m. ELECTR. Ohmmeter.

oïdium [ɔidjɔm] m. BOT. Oidium.

oie [wa] f. ZOOL., CULIN. Goose. ‖ MILIT. *Pas de l'oie*, goose-step. ‖ LOC. *Bête comme une oie*, as stupid as a goose ; *jeu de l'oie*, snakes and ladders ; *oie blanche*, simple little goose.

oignon [ɔɲɔ̃] m. BOT. Onion (légume) ; bulb (de tulipe). ‖ CULIN. *Aux petits oignons*, stewed with spring onions. ‖ FAM. *Ce n'est pas mes oignons*, it's no business of mine, it is not my cup of tea ; *en rang d'oignons*, in a row. ‖ FAM. Turnip (montre).

oïl [ɔil] adv. † Yes ; *la langue d'oïl*, Old French (as spoken in the North of the Loire).

oindre [wɛ̃:dr] v. tr. (70). To anoint with oil.

oint, e [wɛ̃, :t] adj. m. Anointed.

oiseau [wazo] m. ZOOL. Bird ; *oiseau d'appartement*, cage-bird ; *oiseaux de basse-cour*, poultry ; *oiseau de proie*, bird of prey. ‖ LOC. *Etre comme l'oiseau sur la branche*, to be here today and gone tomorrow ; *oiseau rare*, rara avis, rare bird, black swan. ‖ FAM. *Un drôle d'oiseau*, a queer bird. ‖ **Oiseau moqueur**, m. ZOOL. Mocking-bird. ‖ **Oiseau-mouche**, m. ZOOL. Humming-bird.

oiseau m. TECHN. Bricklayer's hod.

oiseleur [wazlœ:r] m. Fowler, bird-catcher.

oiselier [wazəlje] m. Bird-seller ; bird fancier.

oiselle [wazɛl] f. ZOOL. Hen-bird. ‖ FAM. Damsel.

oisellerie [-ri] f. Bird-catching ; bird-breeding (élevage) ; bird-fancier's shop, bird-shop (magasin).

oiseux, euse [wazø, ø:z] adj. Idle, useless, trifling, trivial (chose) ; useless (développement) ; otiose (épithète) ; idle (personne) ; *affirmation oiseuse*, irrelevant statement.

oisif, ive [wazif, i:v] adj. Idle, unoccupied (personne) ; idle (vie) ; *vie oisive*, life of idleness.
— s. Unemployed person. ‖ Idler.

oisillon [wazijɔ̃] m. ZOOL. Fledgling.

oisivement [wazivmɑ̃] adv. Idly.

oisiveté [-vte] f. Idleness, sloth, inaction.

oison [wazɔ̃] m. Zool. Gosling.

O.I.T. [oite] f. Abrév. de *Organisation internationale du travail*, ILO, International Labour Organization.

O.K.! [ɔke] interj. O.K., okay, all right.

okapi [ɔkapi] m. Zool. Okapi.

okoumé [ɔkume] m. Gaboon (bois).

olé [ɔle] interj. Ole! ‖ **Olé olé**, adj. invar. Fam. Swinging (soirée); *une fille olé olé*, a swinger.

oléacée [ɔlease] f. Bot. Oleaceous plant.

oléagineux, euse [ɔleaʒinø, ø:z] adj. Oleaginous.
— m. Oil-seed.

oléfine [ɔlefin] f. Chim. Olefin.

oléiculteur, trice [ɔleikyltœ:r, tris] s. Agric. Olive grower.

oléiculture [-kylty:r] f. Agric. Olive growing.

oléifère [-fɛ:r] adj. Bot. Oleiferous.

oléine [ɔlein] f. Chim. Olein.

oléoduc [ɔleɔdyk] m. Oil pipeline.

olé olé [ɔleɔle] adj. V. olé.

oléum [ɔleɔm] m. Chim. Oleum.

olfactif, ive [ɔlfaktif, i:v] adj. Olfactive, olfactory.

olfaction [-sjɔ̃] f. Olfaction.

olibrius [ɔlibriy:s] m. Fam. Braggart.

olifant [ɔlifɑ̃] m. Mus. Oliphant, horn.

oligarchie [ɔligarʃi] f. Oligarchy.

oligarchique [-ʃik] adj. Oligarchic.

oligo–élément [ɔligɔelemɑ̃] m. Méd. Oligo-element.

oligopole [-pɔl] m. Oligopoly.

olivacé, ée [ɔlivase] adj. Olivaceous; olive-green.

olivaie [ɔlivɛ] f. V. oliveraie.

olivâtre [-va:tr] adj. Olive-hued; olive-coloured. ‖ Sallow (teint).

olive [ɔliv] f. Bot. Olive; *huile d'olive*, olive-oil. ‖ Comm. Olive-button (bouton). ‖ Méd. Olivary body. ‖ Archit. Olive-moulding.
— adj. invar. Olive-coloured.

oliveraie [-vrɛ] f. Agric. Olive-grove.

oliverie [-vri] f. Olive-oil factory.

olivier [-vje] m. Bot. Olive-tree. ‖ Ecclés. *Le Jardin des Oliviers*, the Garden of Gethsemani; *le Mont des Oliviers*, the Mount of Olives; *le rameau d'olivier*, the olive-branch.

olographe [ɔlɔgraf] adj. Jur. Holograph.

olympe [ɔlɛ̃:p] m. Olympus.

olympiade [ɔlɛ̃pjad] f. Olympiad.

olympien, enne [-jɛ̃, ɛn] adj., s. Olympian.

olympique [-pik] adj. Olympic.

Oman [oman] m. Géogr. Oman.

ombelle [ɔ̃bɛl] f. Bot. Umbel; *en ombelle*, umbellate.

ombellifère [-lifɛ:r] adj. Bot. Umbelliferous.
— f. Bot. Umbellifer.

ombilic [ɔ̃bilik] m. Méd. Umbilicus, navel. (V. nombril.) ‖ Bot. Hilum. ‖ Math. Umbilicus.

ombilical, ale [-kal] adj. Méd. Umbilical (cordon).

omble [ɔ̃:bl] m. Zool. Char.

ombrage [ɔ̃bra:ʒ] m. Shade (d'un arbre); shady place (lieu ombragé). ‖ Fig. Umbrage; *porter ombrage à*, to give umbrage to; *prendre ombrage de*, to shy at (cheval); to take umbrage at (personne).

ombragé, ée [ɔ̃braʒe] adj. Shaded, shady, umbrageous.

ombrager v. tr. (7). To shade, to give shade.

ombrageusement [-ʒøzmɑ̃] adv. Skittishly (cheval). ‖ Touchily, sensitively (personne).

ombrageux, euse [-ʒø, ø:z] adj. Shy, skittish (cheval); touchy, over-sensitive, umbrageous (personne). [V. ombragé.]

ombre [ɔ̃:br] f. Shade (d'un arbre); *trente-cinq degrés à l'ombre*, thirty-five degrees centigrade in the shade. ‖ Shadow (d'un objet, d'une personne); *à l'ombre du palais*, in the shadow of the palace; *ombres chinoises*, shadow-show. ‖ Shadow, shade, darkness (ténèbres); *à l'ombre de la nuit*, under the cloak of night; *les ombres de la nuit*, the shades of night. ‖ Shadow, shade, darkness (obscurité); *dans l'ombre de l'anonymat*, under the cloak of anonymity; *rejeter dans l'ombre*, to throw into the shade; *rester dans l'ombre*, to stay in the background. ‖ Shadow, protection; *à l'ombre du grand homme*, in the shadow of the great man. ‖ Shadow, illusion; *avoir peur de son ombre*, to be afraid of one's own shadow; *courir après une ombre*, to catch at shadows; *lâcher la proie pour l'ombre*, to let go the substance for the shadow; *vivre dans l'ombre de la peur*, to live under the shadow of fear. ‖ Shade, ghost (fantôme); *évoquer une ombre*, to raise a ghost; *il n'est plus que l'ombre de lui-même*, he is but the shadow of his former self; *le royaume des ombres*, shadow-land, the land of shades. ‖ Shade, shadow, bit (brin); *ombre de bon sens*, grain of common sense; *ombre d'espoir*, ray of hope; *ombre de lassitude*, note of despondency; *l'ombre d'un sourire*, the ghost of a smile; *ombre de tristesse*, shade of sadness; *ombre de vérité*, particle of truth. ‖ Sadness, veil; *jeter une ombre sur*, to cast a gloom (ou) shadow over; *une ombre au tableau*, a fly in the ointment. ‖ Arts. Shade. ‖ Fam. *A l'ombre*, in quod (ou) clink.

ombre f. *Terre d'ombre*, umber.

ombre m. Zool. Grayling, umber.

ombré, ée [ɔ̃bre] adj. Arts. Shaded (dessin).

ombrelle [ɔ̃brɛl] f. Sunshade, parasol. ‖ Aviat. Aerial umbrella.

ombrer [ɔ̃bre] v. tr. (1). Arts. To shade (au crayon); to hatch (avec des hachures). ‖ To darken (les paupières).

ombreux, euse [ɔ̃brø, ø:z] adj. Shady, umbrageous.

oméga [ɔmega] m. Omega.

omelette [ɔmlɛt] f. Culin. Omelette, omelet. ‖ Fig. *Faire une omelette sans œufs*, to make bricks without straw.

omettre [ɔmɛtr] v. tr. (64). To omit; to leave (ou) to miss out (une lettre, un mot); to pass over, to jump (un passage); *omettre de faire*, to omit (ou) to fail (ou) to neglect to do.

omission [ɔmisjɔ̃] f. Omission. ‖ Ecclés. *Action et omission*, commission and omission.

omnibus [ɔmniby:s] m. Ch. de F., Autom. Omnibus, bus.
— adj. Ch. de F. Slow, stopping, local, U.S. milk (train). ‖ Fam. Omnibus.

omnidirectionnel, elle [-dirɛksjɔnɛl] adj. All-direction, omnidirectional.

omnipotence [-pɔtɑ̃:s] f. Omnipotence.

omnipotent, ente [-pɔtɑ̃, ɑ̃:t] adj. Omnipotent.

omnipraticien, enne [-pratisjɛ̃, ɛn] adj. *Médecine omnipraticienne*, general practice.
— s. General practitioner, GP.

omniprésence [-prezɑ̃:s] f. Omnipresence.

omniprésent, ente [-prezɑ̃, ɑ̃:t] adj. Omnipresent.

omniscience [-sjɑ̃:s] f. Omniscience.

omniscient, ente [-sjɑ̃, ɑ̃:t] adj. Omniscient; all-knowing.

omnisports [-spɔ:r] adj. inv. Sports; *centre omnisports*, sports complex, leisure centre.

omnium [ɔmniɔm] m. Comm. General trading company; general store. ‖ Sport. Open race.

omnivore [ɔmnivɔ:r] adj. Omnivorous.
— m. Omnivore.

omoplate [ɔmɔplat] f. Méd. Shoulder-blade, scapula, omoplate.

O.M.S. [oɛmɛs] f. Abrév. de *Organisation mon-*

diale de la santé, WHO, World Health Organization.

on [ɔ̃] pron. indéf. Somebody, someone, one, a man (qqn); people (des gens); *on frappe à la porte,* someone is knocking at the door; *on n'en sait rien,* no one knows anything about it; *on n'est pas toujours de bonne humeur,* one is not always in a good mood; *on n'y peut rien,* one can do nothing; nothing can be done about it; *il faut bien qu'on mange,* a fellow must eat; *que faire quand on est à sec?,* what can a man do when he is hard up?; *que voulez-vous qu'on y fasse?,* what can one do?; *on n'a pas idée d'une pareille insolence,* who would have believed he could have so much cheek? ‖ I (je); *on n'est pas né d'hier,* I was not born yesterday; *on y va,* coming! I'm coming! ‖ He, she (lui, elle); *on s'est donné du bon temps,* he used to have a very good time; *on croyait que ça durerait toujours,* she thought it would last for ever. ‖ We (nous); *on ferme!,* closing!; time please!; *eh, on se retrouve!,* so we meet again!; *on n'est pas des millionnaires,* we're not millionaires; *on est tous partis à la montagne,* we all went to the mountains; *ici on refait les vieux souliers à neuf,* old shoes turned into new. ‖ You (vous); *alors on s'est payé un beau manteau,* so you have treated yourself to a nice coat; *on ne me fera pas avaler pareille baliverne,* you won't make me swallow such nonsense. ‖ They (ils, elles); *à Lilliput, on avait une manière originale de choisir les ministres,* in Lilliput they had a queer way of choosing their ministers; *on vous enverra promener si vous insistez,* they'll send you about your own business if you insist. ‖ (Sens neutre); *on dirait qu'il n'a pas de cœur,* it looks as if he had no heart; *on est bien ici,* it's quite cosy here; *on pourrait croire que,* it might be thought that. ‖ (Sens passif); *on a brisé une vitre,* a pane was (ou) has been broken; *on demande un bon traducteur,* a good translator is wanted; *on fait savoir de Lyon que,* it is reported from Lyons that. ‖ **On-dit,** m. invar. Rumour, gossip, hearsay.

onagre [ɔna:gr] m. Zool., Milit. Onager.

onanisme [ɔnanism] m. Méd. Onanism.

once [ɔ̃:s] f. Ounce (poids). ‖ Fig. Ounce, particle, bit; *il ne fait pas une once de travail,* he won't do a stroke (ou) U. S. a lick of work.

once f. Zool. Ounce, snow-leopard.

oncial, ale [ɔ̃sjal] adj. Uncial (lettre).

oncle [ɔ̃:kl] m. Uncle. ‖ Fam. Uncle, old man.

oncques [ɔ̃:k] adv. † Never.

onction [ɔ̃ksjɔ̃] f. Oiling (d'un athlète). ‖ Unction, anointing (d'un roi). ‖ Ecclés. *Extrême-onction,* extreme unction. ‖ Fig. Unction, unctuousness.

onctueusement [ɔ̃ktɥøzmɑ̃] adv. Unctuously.

onctueux, euse [-tɥø, ø:z] adj. Oily, greasy (graisseux). ‖ Arts. Mellow (couleur). ‖ Fig. Unctuous (éloquence); oily (ton).

onctuosité [-tɥozite] f. Oiliness, greasiness (d'un liquide). ‖ Fig. Unctuousness, oiliness.

onde [ɔ̃:d] f. Water (eau). ‖ Wave, billow (de la mer); *l'onde amère,* the briny ocean; *les ondes,* the watery realm, the deep. ‖ Wave, wavy line (mouvement onduleux); watering (de la soie); *ses cheveux tombaient en onde,* her hair streamed down. ‖ Phys. Wave; *onde à champ électrique horizontal,* sky-wave. ‖ Radio. *Mettre une pièce en ondes,* to put a play on the air, to adapt a play for broadcasting; *par ordre d'entrée en ondes,* in order of speaking. ‖ Aviat. *Onde de choc,* shock wave.

ondé, ée [ɔ̃de] adj. Waved, wavy (cheveux); waved, wavy, undulating (ligne); watered (soie).

ondée [ɔ̃de] f. Shower. (V. averse.)

ondin [ɔ̃dɛ̃] m. Water-sprite.

ondine [ɔ̃din] f. Undine.

ondoiement [ɔ̃dwamɑ̃] m. Undulation, wavy motion (du blé, de l'eau). ‖ Ecclés. Emergency (ou) private baptism.

ondoyant, ante [-jɑ̃, ɑ̃:t] adj. Undulating, waving (blé); waving, rippling (eau); flowing, sinuous (surface). ‖ Fig. Fluctuating, unstable (changeant).

ondoyer [-je] v. intr. (9 *a*). To undulate, to wave (cheveux, eau, foule, surface). ‖ Fig. To waver (personne).
— v. tr. Ecclés. To baptize privately (un enfant).

ondulant, ante [ɔ̃dylɑ̃, ɑ̃:t] adj. Waving (blé); wavy (cheveux); flowing (draperie); undulating (eau).

ondulation [-lasjɔ̃] f. Waving (du blé); flowing (d'une draperie); undulation, flow; *les ondulations du terrain,* the undulating nature of the ground, the folds in the ground. ‖ Wave (des cheveux); *se faire faire une ondulation,* to have one's hair waved.

ondulatoire [-latwa:r] adj. Undulatory. ‖ Techn. Wave (mécanique).

ondulé, ée [-le] adj. Wavy, waved (cheveux); undulating (terrain); corrrugated (tôle).

onduler [-le] v. tr. (1). To wave (les cheveux); *se faire onduler,* to have one's hair waved. ‖ To corrugate (la tôle).
— v. intr. To wave, to undulate, to feather (blé); to wave (cheveux); to flow (draperie).

onduleusement [-løzmɑ̃] adv. Sinuously.

onduleux, euse [-lø, ø:z] adj. Sinuous.

onéreusement [ɔnerøzmɑ̃] adv. Onerously.

onéreux, euse [-rø, ø:z] adj. Onerous, costly, burdensome, heavy; *à titre onéreux,* for a valuable consideration; *trop onéreux,* too costly.

one-step [wanstɛp] m. One-step (danse).

ongle [ɔ̃:gl] m. Nail, finger-nail; *se faire, se ronger les ongles,* to trim, to bite one's nails. ‖ Claw (d'un animal); talon (d'un oiseau de proie). ‖ Zool. Onyx (à l'œil). ‖ Loc. *Jusqu'au bout des ongles,* to the finger-tips, to the tips of one's fingers.

onglé, ée [ɔ̃gle] adj. With claws (animal); with talons (oiseaux).

onglée [ɔ̃gle] f. Méd. Numbness of the finger-tip.

onglet [ɔ̃glɛ]m. Thimble (de brodeuse). ‖ Nailhole, groove (de lame de couteau). ‖ Binding-strip (de carte); thumb-index (de livre). ‖ Techn. Mitre; *assemblage à onglet,* mitre-joint. ‖ Math. Ungula. ‖ Arts. Lozenge-shaped graver. ‖ Bot. Unguis. ‖ Méd. Nictitating membrane. ‖ Naut. Wedge.

onglier [ɔ̃glije] m. Manicure-set.

onguent [ɔ̃gɑ̃] m. Ointment, unguent, liniment.

onguiforme [ɔ̃gɥifɔrm] adj. Zool. Unguiform, claw-shaped.

ongulé, ée [ɔ̃gyle] adj., s. Zool. Ungulate.

onirique [ɔnirik] adj. Dreamlike, oneiric.

onirisme [-rism] m. Dreamlike quality.

onomastique [ɔnɔmastik] adj. Onomastic.

onomatopée [ɔnɔmatɔpe] f. Onomatopoeia.

onomatopéique [-peik] adj. Onomatopoeic.

ontogenèse [ɔ̃tɔʒənɛ:z] f. Méd. Ontogenesis.

ontologie [-lɔʒi] f. Philos. Ontology.

ontologique [-lɔʒik] adj. Philos. Ontological; *preuve ontologique,* ontological argument (ou) proof.

O.N.U. [ɔny] f. Abrév. de *Organisation des Nations unies,* UNO, United Nations Organization.

onusien, enne [ɔnyzjɛ̃, ɛn] adj. United Nations, UN.

onyx [ɔniks] m. Onyx.

onze [ɔ̃:z] adj. num. Eleven; *le onze juin,* the eleventh of June, June the eleventh; *Louis XI,* Louis the Eleventh; *le train de 11 heures,* the

eleven o'clock train. ‖ Fam. *Prendre le train onze,* to go on Shanks's poney.
— m. Eleven. ‖ Sports. Eleven (au cricket); team (au football).
onzième [ɔ̃zjɛm] adj., m. Eleventh.
onzièmement [-mɑ̃] adv. Eleventhly.
oolithe [ɔɔlit] m. Phys. Oolite.
oolithique [-tik] adj. Oolitic.
O. P. [ope] abrév. de *Ordre des prêcheurs,* OP, Dominican.
O. P. A. [opea] f. Fin. Abrév. de *offre publique d'achat,* take-over bid.
opacifier [ɔpasifje] v. tr. (1). To make opaque. ‖ Fig. To cloud.
opacité [ɔpasite] f. Opacity. ‖ Fig. Obtuseness.
opale [ɔpa:l] f. Opal.
opalescence [ɔpalɛssɑ̃:s] f. Opalescence.
opalescent, ente [-sɑ̃, ɑ̃:t] adj. Opalescent.
opalin, ine [ɔpalɛ̃, in] adj. Opaline.
opaline [-lin] f. Opaline.
opaque [ɔpak] adj. Opaque.
op art [ɔpart] m. Arts. Op art.
open [ɔpɛn] adj. Sports. Open, pro-am (tournoi). ‖ Aviat. Open (billet).
— m. Sports. Open competition, open tournament.
O. P. E. P. [ɔpɛp] abrév. de *Organisation des pays exportateurs de pétrole,* OPEC, Organization of Petroleum Exporting Countries.
opéra [ɔpera] m. Théâtr., Mus. Opera; *opéra bouffe,* comic opera; *grand opéra,* grand opera. ‖ Opera-house (bâtiment). ‖ **Opéra-comique,** m. Théâtr., Mus. Light opera.
opérable [ɔperabl] adj. Méd. Operable.
opérant, ante [-rɑ̃, ɑ̃:t] adj. Jur. Operative (décret). ‖ Ecclés. Operating (grâce).
opérateur, trice [-ratœ:r, tris] s. Operator. ‖ Fin. *Opérateur à la baisse, à la hausse,* bear, bull. ‖ Ciném. Camera-man; *opérateur du son,* mixer.
opération [-rasjɔ̃] f. Ecclés. Operation, working. ‖ Philos. Operation; process (de l'esprit). ‖ Comm. Operation, transaction, bargain; *cadre d'opérations,* line of business (d'une maison). ‖ Milit. Operation, move; *opération commune,* joint action. ‖ Aviat. *Centre d'opérations,* operational centre (ou) station. ‖ Méd. Operation; *opération à chaud, à froid,* emergency, interval operation; *salle d'opération,* operating theatre, U. S. operating room; *subir une opération,* to undergo an operation. ‖ Math. Operation.
opérationnel, elle [-rasjɔnɛl] adj. Operational (gén., milit.). ‖ Comm., Fin. *Recherche opérationnelle,* operational research, operations research.
opératoire [-ratwa:r] adj. Méd. Operative; *médecine opératoire,* surgery.
operculaire [ɔpɛrkylɛ:r] adj. Opercular.
opercule [-ky:l] m. Zool. Lid (de cellules d'abeilles); gill-cover (de poisson). ‖ Naut. Deadlight (de hublot).
operculé, ée [-kyle] adj. Bot. Operculate.
opéré [ɔpere] s. Méd. Patient who has been operated on. ‖ Fin. Execution, deal.
opérer v. tr. (5). To effect (une arrestation, un changement); to bring about (une conversion); to achieve (un effet); to work (un miracle). ‖ Milit. To operate; to effect (une jonction); to undertake (une retraite). ‖ Math. To operate, to perform (une multiplication). ‖ Chim. To produce, to make (un mélange). ‖ Méd. To operate on (un abcès, un malade) [*de,* for]; *opérer une appendicite à chaud,* to operate for acute appendicitis; *se faire opérer de,* to be operated on for, to undergo an operation for.
— v. intr. To operate, to work (agir). ‖ Milit. To carry on operations; to be in action; *opérer en liaison avec,* to act jointly with. ‖ Fin. To operate. ‖ Méd. To operate, to perform an opera-

tion (chirurgien); to have a good effect (remède). ‖ Fam. To manage; to manoeuvre.
— v. pr. **S'opérer,** to take place (changement); to be brought about (conversion); to be effected (déménagement).
opérette [ɔperɛt] f. Mus., Théâtr. Operetta; musical comedy.
ophidien, enne [ɔfidjɛ̃, ɛn] adj., m. Zool. Ophidian.
ophite [ɔfi:t] m. Ophite.
ophtalmie [ɔftalmi] f. Méd. Ophthalmia.
ophtalmique [-mik] adj. Méd. Ophthalmic.
ophtalmologie [-mɔlɔʒi] f. Méd. Ophthalmology.
ophtalmologique [-mɔlɔʒik] adj. Ophthalmologic.
ophtalmologiste [-mɔlɔʒist] m. Méd. Ophthalmologist.
ophtalmoscope [-mɔskɔp] m. Méd. Ophthalmoscope.
ophtalmoscopie [-mɔskɔpi] f. Méd. Ophthalmoscopy.
opiacé, ée [ɔpjase] adj. Opiated (médicament).
opiacer [ɔpjase] v. tr. (6). To opiate.
opiat [ɔpja] m. Opiate.
opimes [ɔpi:m] adj. f. pl. *Dépouilles opimes,* spolia opima. ‖ Fig. Profits, spoils.
opiner [ɔpine] v. intr. (1). To opine (*que,* that); to incline (*pour,* to); *opiner du bonnet,* to nod assent; *tous opinèrent,* all heads nodded in approval.
opiniâtre [ɔpinjɑ:tr] adj. Stubborn, self-opinionated, headstrong (personne). ‖ Dogged, unyielding, unremitting, unflagging (effort, résistance, travail); hide-bound (idée). ‖ Méd. Persistent, tenacious (maladie).
opiniâtrement [-trəmɑ̃] adv. Stubbornly, obstinately, obdurately, doggedly; tenaciously.
opiniâtreté [-trəte] f. Obstinacy, stubbornness (des vues). ‖ Méd. Tenaciousness (d'une maladie).
opinion [ɔpinjɔ̃] f. Opinion, notion, point of view, judgment, belief (conception); *changer d'opinion,* to change one's views; *être d'opinions contraires,* to hold different points of view; *poursuivi pour délit d'opinion,* prosecuted for one's opinions; *se faire une opinion sur,* to form an opinion about; *se soucier trop de l'opinion,* to pay too much attention to public opinion; *suivant mon opinion,* in my opinion, to my mind; *voilà mon opinion,* that is what I think. ‖ Opinion, esteem (estime); *avoir bonne, mauvaise opinion de,* to think highly, poorly of; *avoir trop bonne opinion de soi,* to be self-conceited; *donner bonne opinion de soi,* to dispose people favourably toward oneself; *piètre opinion de,* dim view of.
opiomane [ɔpjɔman] s. Opiomaniac; opium-fiend.
— adj. Addicted to opium.
opiomanie [-mani] f. Opium addiction, opium habitism.
opium [ɔpjɔm] m. Opium; *fumeur d'opium,* opium-smoker.
opossum [ɔpɔsɔm] m. Zool. Opossum; 'possum.
opothérapie [ɔpɔterapi] f. Méd. Opotherapy.
opportun, une [ɔpɔrtœ̃, yn] adj. Opportune, timely, seasonable, convenient; *être opportun de,* to be advisable to; *en temps opportun,* at the right time, seasonably.
opportunément [-tynemɑ̃] adv. Opportunely, seasonably, in time.
opportunisme [-tynism] m. Opportunism; time-serving.
opportuniste [-tynist] s. Opportunist, time-server.
— adj. Opportunist, time-serving.
opportunité [-tynite] f. Expediency, advisability, fitness, suitableness (d'une décision); timeliness, opportuneness, seasonableness (d'une mesure).
opposable [ɔpɔzabl] adj. Opposable.

opposant, ante [-zɑ̃, ɑ̃:t] adj. Opposing, adverse. — s. Opponent, antagonist, adverse party.

opposé, ée [-ze] adj. Opposite (en face de); *opposé à,* facing. ‖ Opposed (en antagonisme); conflicting (intérêts); contrary (opinions, solutions); *diamétralement opposé,* antipodal; diametrically opposed; *être d'un avis opposé,* to think differently. ‖ Opposed, hostile (*à,* to). ‖ BOT., MATH. Opposite.
— m. Opposite, contrary (*de,* of); *à l'opposé du bon sens,* contrary to common sense; *à l'opposé de tout le monde,* different from (ou) unlike everybody.

opposer [-ze] v. tr. (1). To oppose, to place opposite, to set over against; *opposer la peinture à la sculpture,* to set painting over against sculpture; *opposer le piano à la commode,* to place the piano opposite the chest of drawers. ‖ To object, to oppose, to set (ou) bring against; *opposer une défense à,* to offer a defence to; *opposer une dénégation,* to return a denial; *opposer une équipe à,* to match a team against; *opposer une résistance acharnée,* to offer dogged resistance; *opposer son véto,* to interpose one's veto.
— v. pr. **S'opposer,** to be conflicting (ou) in conflict; *s'opposer à,* to oppose, to be opposed to, to stand in opposition to, to strive (ou) to be against; *s'opposer à une motion,* to bar a motion.

opposite [-zit] m. **A l'opposite de,** contrary to, opposite, against; *être à l'opposite de,* to be just the opposite of.

opposition [-zisjɔ̃] f. Opposition, contradistinction (contraste); *mettre en opposition l'imagination et la fantaisie,* to define the imagination in contradistinction to the fancy; *par opposition à,* in contradistinction to. ‖ Opposition, resistance (hostilité); *faire opposition à,* to offer opposition to; *rencontrer l'opposition des braillards,* to meet with opposition from the hecklers. ‖ Opposition, clash (d'intérêts); *être en opposition avec,* to clash with. ‖ Opposition (au Parlement); *du côté de l'opposition,* in opposition. ‖ JUR. *Faire opposition à,* to appeal against; *mettre opposition sur,* to issue a writ of attachment against. ‖ FIN. *Opposition à la cote,* objection to mark. ‖ ASTRON. Opposition.

oppositionnel, elle [-zisjɔnɛl] adj. Oppositional.

oppressant, ante [ɔprɛsɑ̃, ɑ̃:t] adj. Oppresive.

oppressé, ée [ɔprɛse] adj. MÉD. Oppressed; *être oppressé,* to have difficulty in breathing.

oppresser v. tr. (1). † To oppress (un peuple). ‖ MÉD. To oppress, to lie heavy on. ‖ FIG. To squeeze, to crush, to cramp.

oppresseur [-soe:r] m. Oppressor.
— adj. Oppressive, oppressing.

oppressif, ive [-si, i:v] adj. Oppressive.

oppression [-sjɔ̃] f. MÉD. Weight on the chest, oppression. ‖ FIG. Oppression, tyranny.

opprimant, ante [ɔprimɑ̃, ɑ̃:t] adj. MÉD. Weighing heavily on the chest. ‖ FIG. Oppressing, oppressive; tyrannical.

opprimé, ée [-me] adj. Oppressed, down-trodden. — s. Oppressed (ou) persecuted person.

opprimer [-me] v. tr. (1). MÉD. To weigh heavily on (la poitrine). ‖ FIG. To oppress, to trample, to maul, to tread underfoot (les faibles).

opprobre [ɔprɔbr] m. Opprobrium, disgrace, contumely; *couvrir d'opprobre,* to cover with opprobrium, to load with insults.

optant, ante [ɔptɑ̃, ɑ̃:t] adj. Optant.
— m. FIN. Taker of an option.

optatif [ɔptatif] adj. m. GRAMM. Optative.

opter [ɔpte] v. intr. (1). To opt, to make a choice (ou) an option (v. CHOISIR); *opter entre,* to choose between; *opter pour,* to opt for, to declare for.

opticien [ɔptisjɛ̃] m. Optician. (V. OCULISTE.)

optimal, ale [ɔptimal] adj. Optimum, optimal.

optimiser [ɔptimize] v. tr. (1). To optimize (gén., inform.).

optimisme [ɔptimism] m. Optimism, sanguineness.

optimiste [-mist] adj. Optimist, optimistic, buoyant, sanguine.
— s. Optimist.

optimum [-mɔm] adj., m. Optimum.

option [ɔpsjɔ̃] f. Option (v. CHOIX); *à option,* optional, U. S. elective (matière). ‖ FIN. Option (*sur,* on); *option d'achat, de vente,* call, put.

optionnaire [-sjɔnɛ:r] s. FIN. Giver of an option.

optique [ɔptik] adj. Optic, optical.
— f. Optics; *illusion d'optique,* optical illusion. ‖ FIG. Perspective; *l'optique du théâtre,* stage perspective.

opulence [ɔpylɑ̃:s] f. Opulence, wealth (v. RICHESSE); *nager dans l'opulence,* to be rolling in money (ou) wallowing in wealth. ‖ FIG. Opulence; *l'opulence de ses formes,* her opulent charms (ou) figure.

opulent, ente [-lɑ̃, ɑ̃:t] adj. Opulent, wealthy, well-off (personne). ‖ Affluent (condition); *beauté opulente,* buxomness, opulent charms.

opuscule [ɔpysky:l] m. Opuscule; pamphlet.

or [ɔr] conj. Now; well.

or m. Gold; *en lettres d'or,* gilt-lettered; *la ruée vers l'or,* the gold rush; *vaisselle d'or,* gold plate; *veau d'or,* golden calf. ‖ GÉOGR. *La Côte-de-l'Or* (auj. Ghana), the Gold Coast. ‖ BLAS. Or. ‖ COMM. *Affaire d'or,* excellent bargain; *à prix d'or,* at a huge price; *ça vaut de l'or,* it's worth its weight in gold. ‖ LOC. *Âge d'or,* Golden Age; *cœur d'or,* heart of gold; *de l'or en barre,* as safe as the Bank of England, as good as ready money; *parler d'or,* to speak words of wisdom; *rouler sur l'or,* to be rolling in money.
— adj. Gold (couleur); *filet d'or,* gold fillet.

oracle [ɔra:kl] m. Oracle; *d'oracle,* oracular (paroles); *parler comme un oracle,* to speak sententiously.

orage [ɔra:ʒ] m. Storm, thunder-storm, tempest; *orages locaux,* local thunder. ‖ FIG. Turmoil (du cœur); *orages populaires,* popular disturbances.

orageusement [ɔraʒøzmɑ̃] adv. Stormily

orageux, euse [-ʒø, ø:z] adj. Stormy, tempestuous (mer, temps). ‖ Thundery, sultry, lowering (ciel, temps). ‖ FIG. Stormy, passionate, violent (discussion); stormy, troublous, troubled (époque); stormy, agitated (vie).

oraison [ɔrɛzɔ̃] f. Orison (v. PRIÈRE); *faire oraison,* to pray. ‖ Oration (discours); *oraison funèbre,* funeral oration.

oral, ale [ɔral] adj. Oral. (V. VERBAL.) ‖ MÉD. Oral.
— m. Oral examination, viva-voce; viva (fam.); *être collé à l'oral,* to be ploughed in the viva, U.S. to flunk the oral.

oralement [-mɑ̃] adv. Orally.

orange [ɔrɑ̃:ʒ] f. BOT. Orange; *écorce d'orange,* orange peel.
— m. Orange (couleur).
— adj. invar. Orange.

Orange f. GÉOGR. Orange.

orangé, ée [ɔrɑ̃ʒe] adj. Orange-coloured, orangy.
— m. Orange (couleur).

orangeade [-ʒad] f. Orangeade.

oranger [-ʒe] m. BOT. Orange-tree; *eau de fleur d'oranger,* orange-flower water; *fleur d'oranger,* orange-blossom. ‖ COMM. Orange-seller.

orangeraie [-ʒrɛ] f. Orange-grove (ou) -plantation.

orangerie [-ʒri] f. Orangery, orange-house (local); orange-grove (ou) plantation.

orangiste [-ʒist] m. Orangeman.

orang-outan [ɔrɑ̃utɑ̃] m. ZOOL. Orang-outang.

orant, ante [ɔrɑ̃, ɑ̃:t] s. ARTS. Kneeling (ou) praying figure.

orateur [ɔratœ:r] m. Orator, speaker; *orateur de carrefour,* tub-thumper, stump-speaker; mob-orator; soap-box orator (fam.). ‖ Spokesman (d'un parti). ‖ ECCLÉS. Preacher.

oratoire [-twa:r] adj. Oratorical (mouvement, période, talent); *art oratoire,* oratory.
— m. Chapel. ‖ ECCLÉS. Oratory (ordre).

oratorien [-tɔrjɛ̃] m. ECCLÉS. Oratorian.

oratorio [-tɔrjo] m. MUS. Oratorio.

oratrice [-tris] f. Woman orator, oratress.

orbe [ɔrb] m. Orb, globe, sphere.

orbiculaire [ɔrbikylɛ:r] adj. Orbicular (image). ‖ MÉD. Orbicular (muscle). ‖ ASTRON. Circular.

orbital, ale [ɔrbital] adj. ASTRON. Orbital; *véhicule orbital,* orbiter; *station orbitale,* space station, manned orbital laboratory.

orbite [ɔrbit] f. ASTRON. Orbit; *se placer sur son orbite,* to go (or) swing into orbit, to settle in one's orbit. ‖ MÉD. Socket (de l'œil). ‖ FIG. Orbit (d'une nation).

Orcades [ɔrkad] f. pl. GÉOGR. Orkneys.

orchestral, ale [ɔrkɛstral] adj. Orchestral.

orchestration [-trasjɔ̃] f. MUS. Orchestration, scoring. ‖ FIG. Orchestration.

orchestre [ɔrkɛstr] m. MUS. Band (de bal); orchestra (de théâtre); *chef d'orchestre,* conductor; *grand orchestre,* full orchestra. ‖ THÉÂTR. Orchestra.

orchestrer [-tre] v. tr. (1). MUS. To orchestrate, to score. ‖ FIG. To harmonize (deux opinions); to orchestrate (une protestation).

orchidée [ɔrkide] f. BOT. Orchid.

orchite [ɔrkit] f. MÉD. Orchitis.

orcine [ɔrsi:n] f. CHIM. Orcin.

ordalie [ɔrdali] f. † Ordeal.

ordinaire [ɔrdinɛ:r] adj. Ordinary, customary, usual, regular (v. HABITUEL); *à l'heure ordinaire,* at the regular hour; *de taille ordinaire,* of average size; *peu ordinaire,* unusual. ‖ Ordinary, common, normal (v. COURANT); *ration ordinaire,* normal ration; *vêtements ordinaires,* everyday clothes. ‖ Ordinary, common, mean (v. VULGAIRE); *expression ordinaire,* trite phrase; *femme très ordinaire,* plain woman; *homme peu ordinaire,* unusual man. ‖ In ordinary; *coiffeur ordinaire de la reine,* hairdresser in ordinary to the Queen. ‖ FIN. Ordinary (actions).
— m. Custom, usual practice, wont; *au-delà de l'ordinaire,* extraordinary; *contre l'ordinaire,* contrary to the rule; *d'ordinaire,* usually; *moins ennuyeux que d'ordinaire,* less tiresome than usual; *sortir de l'ordinaire,* to be off the beaten path, to be out of the ordinary. ‖ CULIN. Fare, meals, cooking. ‖ MILIT. Mess. ‖ ECCLÉS. Ordinary.

ordinairement [-mɑ̃] adv. Ordinarily, usually, as a rule.

ordinal, ale [ɔrdinal] adj., m. Ordinal.

ordinand [ɔrdinɑ̃] m. ECCLÉS. Ordinand.

ordinant m. ECCLÉS. Ordinant, ordainer.

ordinateur [ɔrdinatœ:r] m. INFORM. Computer, data processor.

ordination [-nasjɔ̃] f. ECCLÉS. Ordination.

ordo [ɔrdo] m. ECCLÉS. Ordo.

ordonnance [ɔrdɔnɑ̃:s] f. Order, ordonnance, arrangement; *l'ordonnance des personnages,* the grouping of the figures. ‖ Order, ordinance, edict, enactment (édit); *ordonnance de payement,* order to pay; *ordonnance de police,* police regulation; *ordonnance royale,* Order in Council. ‖ JUR. Order, writ (d'un juge). ‖ MÉD. Prescription. ‖ MILIT. Orderly, batman (soldat); *chaussures, revolver d'ordonnance,* regulation boots, revolver; *officier d'ordonnance,* aide-de-camp.

ordonnancement [-nɑ̃smɑ̃] m. Order to pay.

ordonnancer [-nɑ̃se] v. tr. (6). To order, to pass for, to certify (un paiement).

ordonnateur, trice [-natœ:r, tris] s. Director, organizer (d'une cérémonie). ‖ FIN. Person entitled to make a payment.

ordonné, ée [-ne] adj. Orderly, trim, well-ordered, well-regulated (chose); orderly, tidy (personne). ‖ ECCLÉS. Ordained.

ordonnée [-ne] f. MATH. Ordinate.

ordonner [-ne] v. tr. (1). To arrange; to organize (une cérémonie). ‖ To put in order, to order (une pièce). [V. RANGER.] ‖ To regulate (son travail). ‖ To order, to command, to direct, to enjoin (v. COMMANDER); *ordonner une grève,* to call a strike; *ordonner la vaccination,* to order vaccination; *ordonner à qqn de rentrer de bonne heure,* to order s.o. to come back early; *on a ordonné aux enfants de se taire,* the children were told to be silent. ‖ MATH. To arrange in regular order. ‖ MÉD. To prescribe. ‖ ECCLÉS. To ordain.
— v. intr. To dispose (de, of); to arrange (de, for); *ordonner du sort de qqn,* to decide s.o.'s fate.

ordre [ɔrdr] m. Order; course (de la nature); *selon l'ordre des choses,* in the nature of things. ‖ Order, succession, sequence; *numéro d'ordre,* serial number; *par ordre alphabétique,* in alphabetical order; *par ordre de date,* in rotation. ‖ Order, method; *avec ordre,* methodically; *en bon ordre,* in due array, ship-shape; *mettre de l'ordre dans ses affaires,* to set one's affairs in order (ou) to rights; *tout est maintenant rentré dans l'ordre,* all is now in order. ‖ Order, orderliness, tidiness (soin); *manquer d'ordre,* to be unmethodical; *sans ordre,* messy, higgledy-piggledy (chose); slovenly, slatternly, untidy (personne). ‖ Order, quiet, peace (paix); *ordre public,* law and order; *délit contre l'ordre public,* breach of peace; *rétablir l'ordre,* to restore order; *troubler l'ordre,* to disturb the peace; *service d'ordre,* police force on duty. ‖ Order, estate (classe sociale). ‖ Order, class, sort (rang); *de premier ordre,* first-class, of the first order (ou) rank, outstanding (en général); out-of-the-top-drawer (écrivain); *dans cet ordre d'idées,* in this connection; on these lines; *de l'ordre d'un million,* in the region of (ou) running to one milion; *d'un autre ordre,* of another category. ‖ Order (de chevalerie). ‖ Order, command, directions, instructions; *aux ordres de,* at the beck and call of; *jusqu'à nouvel ordre,* until further orders; *par ordre de,* by order of; *recevoir l'ordre de,* to be ordered to; *sous les ordres de qqn,* under s.o.'s command. ‖ JUR. *L'ordre des avocats,* the Bar; *ordres de succession,* canons of inheritance; *ordre du jour,* order (ou) business of the day; agenda of the meeting; *le conseil de l'ordre,* the Bar Council; *être à l'ordre du jour,* to be the main question of the day; *passer à l'ordre du jour,* to proceed with the business of the day. ‖ COMM. Order; *billet à ordre,* promissory note; *d'ordre et pour compte de,* by order and in the account of; *toujours à vos ordres,* yours obediently, assuring you of our devoted attention. ‖ FIN. *Ordre d'achat,* buying order; *chèque à mon ordre,* cheque to order. ‖ MILIT. Order; *ordre d'appel,* call-up papers; *porté à l'ordre du jour,* mentioned in dispatches. ‖ NAUT. *Ordres de marche,* sailing orders. ‖ TECHN. *Ordre de marche,* working order. ‖ ECCLÉS. Order (religieux, sacerdotal); *entrer dans les ordres,* to take orders. ‖ LOC. *Questions à l'ordre du jour,* questions of the day (ou) of the moment.

ordure [ɔrdy:r] f. Excrement, dung, ordure (immondices). ‖ Pl. Refuse, dirt, filth (détritus); *ordures ménagères,* household refuse, garbage; *service de l'enlèvement des ordures,* refuse disposal department, U.S. garbage disposal service. ‖ FIG. Nastiness, dirt (en littérature); dirt, smut (en paroles).

ordurier, ère [-dyrje, ɛːr] adj. Filthy, lewd, obscene (chanson, livre); lewd, ribald, indecent (écrivain); smutty, scurrilous (propos).

orée [ɔre] f. Skirt, edge, border.

oreillard [ɔrɛjaːr] adj. Zool. Lop-eared.
— m. Zool. Long-eared bat.

oreille [ɔrɛːj] f. Ear; *aux longues oreilles,* long-eared; *porter son chapeau sur l'oreille,* to cock one's hat; *sur l'oreille,* at an angle, cocked over one ear (chapeau); *tirer les oreilles à qqn,* to pull s.o.'s ears. ‖ Méd. Ear, hearing (ouïe); *avoir l'oreille fine,* to have sharp ears. ‖ Mus. *Avoir de l'oreille,* to have an ear for music; *avoir l'oreille juste,* to have a good ear for music. ‖ Techn. Handle, ear (anse). ‖ Naut. Palm (d'ancre); *oreille de lièvre,* leg-of-mutton sail. ‖ Agric. Mouldboard (d'une charrue). ‖ Fig. Attention, heed; *écouter d'une oreille distraite,* to listen absent-mindedly (ou) with half an ear; *entrer par une oreille et sortir par l'autre,* to go in at one ear and out at the other; *être tout oreilles,* to be all ears. ‖ Loc. *Avoir l'oreille de,* to have the ear of, to have influence over; *laisser passer le bout de l'oreille,* to show the cloven hoof (ou) one's true colours; *ne pas l'entendre de cette oreille,* not to see things in that light; *l'oreille basse,* crest-fallen, chap-fallen, with a flea in one's ear; *se faire tirer l'oreille,* to appear reluctant, to need a lot of persuading (pour, to).

oreiller [ɔrɛje] m. Pillow.

oreillette [-jɛt] f. Ear-flap (de casquette). ‖ Méd. Auricle, U. S. atrium (du cœur).

oreillon [-jɔ̃] m. Agric. Mould-board. ‖ Pl. Méd. Mumps.

ores [ɔːr] adv. Now; *d'ores et déjà,* from now on.

orfèvre [ɔrfɛːvr] m. Goldsmith.

orfèvrerie [-vrəri] f. Goldsmith's trade (métier). ‖ Gold plate.

orfraie [ɔrfrɛ] f. Zool. Osprey, sea-hawk. ‖ Fam. *Pousser des cris d'orfraie,* to shriek at the top of one's voice.

orfroi [ɔrfrwa] m. Orphrey (tissu).

organdi [ɔrgɑ̃di] m. Organdie, U. S. organdy.

organe [ɔrgan] m. Méd. Organ. ‖ Mus. Voice. ‖ Techn. *Organes de sécurité,* safety devices; *organes de transmission,* transmission gear. ‖ Fig. Agent, instrument; *par l'organe de,* through the agency of, by means of, through. ‖ Fig. Organ (journal); spokesman, mouthpiece (d'un parti).

organeau [-no] m. Naut. Anchor-ring.

organelle [ɔrganɛl] f. Méd. Organelle.

organigramme [ɔrganigram] m. Organization chart (d'une entreprise, d'un organisme). ‖ Inform. Flow chart.

organique [-nik] adj. Organic (chimie).

organiquement [-nikmɑ̃] adv. Organically.

organisateur, trice [-nizatœːr, tris] adj. Organizing.
— s. Organizer.

organisation [-nizasjɔ̃] f. Organization, set-up (fam.). ‖ Organization, staff (personnel).

organisationnel, elle [-nizasjɔnɛl] adj. Organizational.

organisé, ée [-nize] adj. Organized (décoration, fête); arranged (exposition). ‖ Méd., Bot. Organized. ‖ Fig. Well-ordered (esprit); well-organized (parti).

organiser [-nize] v. tr. (1). To organize, to arrange, to get up (une cérémonie, une société); to organize, to set up (la résistance). ‖ To organize, to constitute.
— v. pr. S'organiser, to get organized, to take shape, to get into working order (choses); to get settled, to settle down, to get going (personnes).

organisme [-nism] m. Organism. ‖ Body (en politique). ‖ Méd. Human frame; *organisme*

solide, tough (ou) stout constitution. ‖ Comm. Corporation.

organiste [-nist] s. Mus. Organist.

organite [ɔrganit] m. Méd. Organelle.

orgasme [ɔrgasm] m. Méd. Orgasm.

orge [ɔrʒ] f. Barley.

orgeat [ɔrʒa] m. Culin. Orgeat.

orgelet [ɔrʒəlɛ] m. Méd. Stye.

orgiaque [ɔrʒjak] adj. Orgiastic, orgiac.

orgie [ɔrʒi] f. Orgy, drunken (ou) bacchanalian revel. ‖ Fig. Profusion, luxuriance; riot (de couleurs).

orgue [ɔrg] m. Mus. Organ; *orgue d'accompagnement, de Barbarie, de cinéma,* choir-, barrel-, cinema-organ; *joueur d'orgue de Barbarie,* organ-grinder; *tenir l'orgue,* to play the organ. ‖ Géogr. Basalt-colonnade.
— f. pl. Mus. Organ; *les grandes orgues,* the grand organ.

orgueil [ɔrgœːj] m. Pride, conceit (défaut); *crever d'orgueil,* to be bursting with pride. ‖ Dignity (qualité); *avoir l'orgueil de ne pas se plaindre,* to make it a point of pride not to complain.

orgueilleusement [ɔrgœjøzmɑ̃] adv. Proudly.

orgueilleux, euse [-jø, øːz] adj. Proud, conceited, bumptious (v. Vaniteux); *orgueilleux de son argent,* purse-proud.
— s. Proud person; prig.

Orient [ɔrjɑ̃] m. East, Orient; *tapis d'Orient,* Turkish carpet, U. S. Oriental rug. ‖ Orient (d'une perle). ‖ Orient, lodge (des francs-maçons).

orientable [-tabl] adj. Swivelling. ‖ Aviat. Revolving (hangar).

oriental, ale [-tal] adj. Eastern, oriental; *les Indes orientales,* the East Indies.
— s. Oriental.

orientaliser [-talize] v. tr. (1). To orientalize.

orientalisme [-taiism] m. Orientalism.

orientaliste [-talist] s. Orientalist.

orientation [-tasjɔ̃] f. Orientation; *table d'orientation,* landmark indicator, panoramic table. ‖ Siting; aspect, exposure (d'une maison); lay, lie (d'un terrain). ‖ Naut. Training (d'un canon); trimming (des voiles). ‖ Fig. Trend (de la politique); *orientation professionnelle,* vocational guidance.

orienté, ée [-te] adj. Facing (vers le nord, le sud). ‖ Math. Directed (vecteur, ligne). ‖ Fig. Biased, slanted (de parti pris).

orienter [-te] v. tr. (1). To orient, to orientate (une construction). ‖ To set, to direct (une antenne, un cadre de réception). ‖ To orient, to orientate, to set (une carte, un plan). ‖ Naut. To train (un canon); to trim (les voiles). ‖ Fig. To turn (la conversation, les débats); to lead, to steer (qqn) [vers, towards]; to guide, to direct (les recherches).
— v. pr. S'orienter, to take one's bearings; to make out the lie of the land; to look about one. ‖ Fig. S'orienter vers, to show a trend towards.

orienteur [-tœːr] m. Orientator; *orienteur professionnel,* vocational guide.

orifice [ɔrifis] m. Orifice, opening; mouth. ‖ Autom., Aviat., Techn. *Orifice d'admission, d'échappement,* intake, exhaust port.

oriflamme [ɔriflam] f. Oriflamme.

origan [ɔrigɑ̃] m. Bot. Origan.

originaire [ɔriʒinɛːr] adj. Native (de, of); coming (de, from); *il est originaire de,* he comes from, he is a native of. ‖ Innate, inborn (défaut, qualité). ‖ Original, primary, primitive (condition).

originairement [-nɛːrmɑ̃] adv. Originally, in the beginning.

original, ale [-nal] adj. Original (texte, version). ‖ Original, odd, queer, singular (caractère, con-

duite, personne); original, inventive, creative (esprit, imagination); original, novel, fresh (imagination, pensée). [V. EXCENTRIQUE.]
— m. Original (d'une œuvre); top copy (d'un texte). ‖ ARTS. Model, pattern, prototype.
— s. Eccentric character, queer card, oddity, queer customer (personne).
originalement [-nalmã] adv. Originally.
originalité [-nalite] f. Originality. ‖ Eccentricity.
origine [ɔriʒin] f. Origin (d'une coutume, d'un peuple); *l'origine de cette institution remonte très haut,* this institution dates from the distant past. ‖ Birth, extraction, descent (d'une personne); *d'origine orientale,* of Oriental extraction, an Oriental by birth. ‖ Origin, source, starting-point, cause (d'un fait); *tirer son origine de,* to derive (ou) to originate from. ‖ Origin; beginning, outset (début); *à l'origine,* in the beginning; *dès l'origine,* from the outset. ‖ Origin; *bureau postal d'origine,* postal office of dispatch, U. S. post office of origin; *d'origine,* certified (marchandises); vintage (vins).
originel, elle [-nɛl] adj. Original, innate (inné). ‖ Fondamental, essential. ‖ ECCLÉS. Original (péché).
originellement [-nɛlmã] adv. Originally, from the beginning.
orillon [ɔrijɔ̃] m. Handle (d'écuelle). ‖ ARCHIT., MILIT. Orillion.
orin [ɔrɛ̃] m. NAUT. Buoy-rope. ‖ Weighing-line.
oripeaux [ɔripo] m. pl. Tinsel, tawdry, finery, flashy dress. ‖ FIG. Flourishes, fustian; purple patches (du style). ‖ FAM. Rags.
O.R.L. [ɔɛrɛl] f. Abrév. de *oto-rhino-laryngologie,* ENT diseases and therapy.
— s. Abrév. de *oto-rhino-laryngologiste,* ENT specialist.
orle [ɔrl] m. BLAS. Orle. ‖ GÉOGR. Funnel (d'un volcan). ‖ NAUT. Hem (de voile).
Orlon [ɔrlɔ̃] m. (nom déposé). Orlon.
ormaie [ɔrmɛ] f. Elm-grove.
orme [ɔrm] m. BOT. Elm.
ormeau [-mo] m. BOT. Young elm. ‖ ZOOL. Ormer, abalone.
orné, ée [-ne] adj. Adorned, decorated. ‖ Ornate (lettre); *orné de brandebourgs,* frogged; *orné d'une plume,* decked with a feather (chapeau). ‖ FIG. Cultivated (esprit); ornate, florid (style); *orné de métaphores,* glittering with metaphors (style).
ornemaniste [ɔrnəmanist] m. ARCHIT., ARTS. Ornamentalist.
ornement [ɔrnəmã] m. Ornament, adornment, embellishment; *dessin d'ornement,* decorative drawing. ‖ ECCLÉS. Vestments. ‖ MUS. Gracenote. ‖ FIG. Ornament (d'une époque); *ornements du langage,* flowers of speech; *sans ornements,* plain, unpolished (style).
ornemental, ale [-tal] adj. Ornamental, decorative.
ornementation [-tasjɔ̃] f. Ornamentation.
ornementer [-te] v. tr. (1). To ornament.
orner [ɔrne] v. tr. (1). To adorn, to embellish, to decorate, to trim (qqch.); to doll up (qqn); *sa maison était ornée de drapeaux,* his house displayed flags. ‖ FIG. To enrich, to enhance (une description, l'esprit).
ornière [ɔrnjɛːr] f. Rut (du chemin). ‖ TECHN. Groove. ‖ FIG. Rut.
ornithologie [ɔrnitɔlɔʒi] f. ZOOL. Ornithology.
ornithologique [-ʒik] adj. Ornithological.
ornithologiste [-ʒist] s. ZOOL. Ornithologist.
ornithorynque [ɔrnitɔrɛ̃ːk] m. ZOOL. Ornithorynchus, duck-billed platypus.
orogenèse [ɔrɔʒənɛːz] f. GÉOL. Orogenesis, orogeny.
orogénique [-ʒenik] adj. Orogenetic, orogenic.
orographie [ɔrɔgrafi] f. Orography.

oronge [ɔrɔ̃ːʒ] f. BOT. Orange-milk agaric.
orpaillage [ɔrpajaːʒ] m. Gold-washing.
orpailleur [-jœːr] m. Gold-washer.
Orphée [ɔrfe] m. Orpheus.
orphelin [ɔrfəlɛ̃] m. Orphan; *orphelin de guerre,* war orphan.
— adj. Orphan, orphaned; *orphelin de père et de mère,* fatherless and motherless.
orphelinage [-lina:ʒ] f. Orphanhood.
orphelinat [-lina] m. Orphanage.
orpheline [-liːn] f. Orphan-girl.
orphéon [ɔrfeɔ̃] m. MUS. Male-voice choir.
orphie [ɔrfi] f. ZOOL. Garfish.
orphique [ɔrfik] adj. ARTS. Orphic.
orpiment [ɔrpimã] m. Orpiment.
orpin [ɔrpɛ̃] m. Orpiment. ‖ BOT. Orpine.
Orsay [ɔrsɛ] m. *Le Quai d'Orsay,* the French Foreign Office, the Quai d'Orsay.
ORSEC (plan) [ɔrsɛk] m. Emergency measures taken whenever disasters occur in France.
orseille [ɔrsɛːj] f. BOT. Archil, orchil.
orteil [ɔrtɛːj] m. MÉD. Toe.
orthicon [ɔrtikɔ̃] m. RADIO. Orthicon.
orthocentre [ɔrtɔsãːtr] m. MATH. Orthocentre.
orthodontie [-dɔ̃ti] f. MÉD. Orthodontia, orthodontics.
orthodontiste [-dɔ̃tist] s. MÉD. Orthodontist.
orthodoxe [-dɔks] adj. ECCLÉS. Orthodox (doctrine, église). ‖ FIG. Orthodox, conventional, correct; *peu orthodoxe,* unorthodox, unconventional.
orthodoxie [-dɔksi] f. ECCLÉS. Orthodoxy. ‖ FIG. Soundness, reliableness (d'opinion); sound knowledge (de qqn).
orthogenèse [-ʒənɛːz] f. Orthogenesis.
orthogonal, ale [-gɔnal] adj. MATH. Orthogonal; *projection orthogonale,* orthogonal projection.
orthographe [-graːf] f. Spelling; orthography; *orthographe d'accord, d'usage,* grammatical, dictionary spelling; *concours d'orthographe,* spelling-bee.
orthographie [-grafi] f. Orthography. ‖ MATH. Orthogonal projection.
orthographier [-grafje] v. tr. (1). To spell correctly.
orthographique [-grafik] adj. Orthographical. ‖ MATH. Orthographic, orthogonal.
orthonormé, ée [-nɔrme] adj. MATH. Orthonormal.
orthopédie [-pedi] f. MÉD. Orthopaedy, orthopedics.
orthopédique [-pedik] adj. MÉD. Orthopaedic; *appareils orthopédiques,* surgical appliances.
orthopédiste [-pedist] m. MÉD. Orthopaedist.
orthophonie [-fɔni] f. MÉD. Speech therapy.
orthophoniste [-fɔnist] s. MÉD. Speech therapist.
orthoptère [-ptɛːr] adj. ZOOL. Orthopterous.
— m. pl. ZOOL. Orthoptera.
ortie [ɔrti] f. BOT. Nettle. ‖ ZOOL. Sea-anemone. ‖ MÉD. Seton.
ortier [ɔrtje] v. tr. (1). MÉD. To urticate.
ortolan [ɔrtɔlã] m. ZOOL. Ortolan.
orvet [ɔrvɛ] m. ZOOL. Blind-worm.
orviétan [ɔrvjetã] m. Nostrum, quack medicine.
oryx [ɔriks] m. ZOOL. Oryx.
O.S. [ɔɛs] m. Abrév. de *ouvrier spécialisé,* unskilled (ou) semi-skilled worker.
os [ɔs] (pl. **os** [o]) m. Bone; *os à moelle,* marrowbone; *os de seiche,* cuttle-bone; *jetons en os,* bone-counters. ‖ LOC. *Jeter un os à Cerbère,* to give a sop to Cerberus; *ne pas faire de vieux os,* not to make old bones, not to live long; *y laisser les os,* to work oneself to death; *trempé jusqu'aux os,* drenched to the skin.

O. S. B. [oɛsbe] abrév. de *Ordre de saint Benoît,* OSB, order of Saint Benedict.

Oscar [ɔskar] m. Oscar. ‖ CINÉM. Oscar.

oscillant, ante [ɔsillɑ̃, ɑ̃ːt] adj. Rocking (fauteuil); oscillating (machine, pendule). ‖ CINÉM. *Miroir oscillant,* mirror oscillator. ‖ ELECTR. Oscillatory (circuit). ‖ COMM. Fluctuating (prix).

oscillateur, trice [-latœːr, tris] adj. Oscillating. — s. Oscillator. ‖ RADIO. Oscillating coil.

oscillation [-lasjɔ̃] f. Oscillation, swing (d'un pendule). ‖ Rocking (d'un bateau, d'un siège). ‖ FIN. Fluctuation (des prix). ‖ FIG. Wavering.

oscillatoire [-latwaːr] adj. Oscillatory.

osciller [-le] v. intr. (1). To rock (bateau, siège); to oscillate, to sway, to swing (pendule); *faire osciller,* to swing (un pendule). ‖ FIN. To fluctuate (prix). ‖ FIG. To waver (personne).

oscillographe [-lɔgraːf] m. Oscillograph.

oscilloscope [-lɔskɔp] m. Oscilloscope.

osculaire [ɔskylɛːr] adj. MÉD. Oscular.

osculateur [-latœːr] adj. MATH. Osculating.

osculation [-lasjɔ̃] f. MATH. Osculation.

osé, ée [oze] adj. Bold, daring, audacious (entreprise); bold, daring, plain-spoken (personne); broad, spicy, risqué (propos); indecorous (sujet).

oseille [ɔzɛːj] f. BOT. Sorrel. ‖ POP. Oof, dough, U. S. jack. (V. GALETTE.)

oser v. tr.(1). To dare, to dare to; *oser répondre,* to dare answer, to venture (ou) to be bold enough to answer; *si j'ose dire,* if I may (ou) dare say so. — v. intr. To dare; *je n'oserai jamais,* I shall never dare.

oseraie [ozərɛ] f. Osiery, osier-holt; osier-bed.

oseur [ozœːr] adj. Daring, bold, venturesome.

osier [ozje] m. Osier, wicker; *branche d'osier,* withe, withy; *panier d'osier,* wicker-basket.

osmose [ɔsmoːz] f. PHYS. Osmosis, osmose.

osmotique [-mɔtik] adj. PHYS. Osmotic (pression).

ossature [ɔsatyːr] f. MÉD. Ossature, skeleton, frame. ‖ FIG. Structure; skeleton.

osselet [ɔslɛ] m. Knuckle-bone (jouet). ‖ MÉD. Ossicle.

ossement [ɔsmɑ̃] m. Bone.

osseux, euse [ɔsø, øːz] adj. Bony, osseous (éléments, partie); bony (personne).

Ossian [ɔsjɑ̃] m. Ossian.

ossianique [ɔsjanik] adj. Ossianic.

ossicule [ɔsikyl] m. MÉD. Ossicle.

ossification [ɔsifikasjɔ̃] f. MÉD. Ossification.

ossifier [-fje] v. tr. (1). To ossify. — v. pr. **S'ossifier,** to become ossified.

ossuaire [ɔsɥɛːr] m. Ossuary. (V. CHARNIER.)

ostéite [ɔsteit] f. MÉD. Osteitis.

ostensible [ɔstɑ̃sibl] adj. Conspicuous, ostensive, patent, obvious. (V. ÉVIDENT, VISIBLE.)

ostensiblement [-blømɑ̃] adv. Conspicuously, visibly, patently, obviously, evidently.

ostensoir [ɔstɑ̃swaːr] m. ECCLÉS. Monstrance, ostensory.

ostentation [ɔstɑ̃tasjɔ̃] f. Ostentation, display, show, parade; *faire ostentation de,* to display, to parade; *sans ostentation,* unostentatiously.

ostéologie [ɔsteɔlɔ3i] f. MÉD. Osteology.

ostéologue [-lɔg] m. MÉD. Osteologist.

ostéomyélite [-mjelit] f. MÉD. Osteomyelitis.

ostéopathe [ɔsteɔpat] m. MÉD. Osteopath.

ostracisme [ɔstrasism] m. Ostracism.

ostréicole [ɔstreikɔl] adj. Oyster (production), oyster-farming (méthodes).

ostréiculteur, trice [-kyltœːr, tris] s. Oyster-farmer, U.S. oysterman.

ostréiculture [-kylty:r] f. Oyster-breeding (ou) farming.

ostrogoth [ɔstrɔgo] adj. Ostrogothic. — s. Ostrogoth. ‖ FAM. Barbarian.

otage [ɔtaːʒ] m. Hostage (*de,* for). ‖ FIG. Security.

otalgie [ɔtalʒi] f. MÉD. Otalgia, ear-ache.

O. T. A. N. [ɔtɑ̃] f. Abrév. de *Organisation du traité de l'Atlantique Nord,* NATO, North Atlantic Treaty Organization.

otarie [ɔtari] f. ZOOL. Otary, sea-lion.

ôté [ote] prép. FAM. Except, barring.

ôter v. tr. (1). To take away (ou) out, to remove (v. ENLEVER, RETIRER); *ôter en effaçant, en tirant,* to rub out, to pull out; *ôter le couvert,* to clear the table; *ôter à qqn les morceaux de la bouche,* to take the bread out of s.o.'s mouth; *ôter qqch. à qqn,* to deprive s.o. of sth. ‖ To take off (ses vêtements). ‖ MATH. *Ôter deux de huit,* to take two from eight. ‖ FIG. To destroy (une illusion); *ôter le goût du travail à qqn,* to destroy s.o.'s inclination to work.
— v. pr. **S'ôter,** to get away. ‖ FAM. *Ôte-toi de là,* out of the way; *s'ôter qqch. de l'idée,* to get sth. out of one's head.

otite [ɔtit] f. MÉD. Otitis.

otologie [ɔtɔlɔʒi] f. MÉD. Otology.

otologiste [-ʒist] m. MÉD. Otologist, aurist.

oto-rhino-laryngologie [-rinolarɛ̃gɔlɔʒi] f. MÉD. Oto(rhino)laryngology; science of ear, nose and throat diseases.

oto-rhino-laryngologiste [-ist] s. MÉD. Oto(rhino)laryngologist; ear, nose and throat specialist.

otoscope [ɔtɔskɔp] m. MÉD. Otoscope.

ottoman [ɔtɔmɑ̃] adj., s. Ottoman. — m. Grogram (tissu).

ottomane [-man] f. Divan, ottoman.

ou [u] conj. Or (alternative); *ce soir ou demain,* this evening or to-morrow. ‖ Or (sinon); *ou bien,* or else; *ou plutôt,* or rather. ‖ Or (en d'autres termes); *Agathe, ou la vertu récompensée,* Agatha, or Virtue Rewarded. ‖ Or (approximation); *cinq ou six fois millionnaire,* a millionaire five or six times over. ‖ Either... or (choix); *c'est lui ou moi qui partons,* it is either he or I who will go. ‖ **Que... ou,** whether... or; *que ce soit vrai ou non,* whether it is true or not. ‖ **Si... ou,** if (ou) whether... or; *dites-moi si vous aimez ce plat ou non,* tell me if (ou) whether you like this dish or not.

où [u] adv. Where (lieu); *où allez-vous?,* where are you going? ‖ Where, to what (à quoi); *où ces vantardises veulent-elles le conduire?,* where will his boasting lead him?; *où voulez-vous en venir?,* what are you driving at?
— pron. relat. Where (lieu); *le quartier où a eu lieu l'incendie,* the district where the fire occurred. ‖ When, on which (temps); *le jour où vous aurez compris,* on the day when you finally understand. ‖ FIG. At (ou) to (ou) in which; *la situation délicate où vous vous trouvez,* the predicament in which you find yourself; *la solution où il tend,* the solution he is aiming at; *les rêveries où il se complaît,* the day-dreams in which he indulges. ‖ LOC. **D'où,** whence, where... from; from which; *on ne sait d'où cela vient,* no one knows where that comes from; *d'où je conclus que vous vous trompez,* from which I conclude that you are mistaken. ‖ **D'où que,** from wherever; *d'où que cela vienne,* wherever it comes from. ‖ **Jusqu'où,** how far; up to which; *jusqu'où vous pourrez aller,* how far you may go; *voici le point jusqu'où vous n'avez rien à craindre,* here is the point up to which you may safely go. ‖ **N'importe où,** anywhere; *qu'il vienne de n'importe où, je ne considère que ses qualités,* let him come from no matter where, the only thing that I take into consideration is his worth. ‖ **Où que,** wherever; *où que vous vous trouviez,* wherever you happen to be. ‖ **Par où,** which way; by which,

through which; *la fenêtre par où il est entré,* the window through which he got in; *par où sortirai-je?,* which is the way out? ‖ **Partout où,** wherever; *partout où vous vous établirez,* wherever you settle.

O. U. A. [ɔya] f. Abrév. de *Organisation de l'unité africaine,* OAU, Organization of African Unity.

ouailles [wa:j] f. pl. ECCLÉS. Flock.

ouais [wɛ] interj. Well!, 'pon my word! ‖ FAM. Yeah (oui).

ouate [wat] f. Wadding, quilting, padding; *doublé d'ouate,* padded. ‖ Cotton-wool; *ouate hydrophile,* absorbent cotton-wool (ou) U. S. cotton.

ouaté, ée [-te] adj. Padded, quilted, wadded (habit). ‖ FIG. Softened, deadened (bruit); blurred (contour); cushy, snugy, soft, easy (vie).

ouater v. tr. (1). To pad, to wad, to quilt (un vêtement). ‖ FIG. To soften, to deaden (un bruit); to blur (les contours).

ouateux, euse [-tø, ø:z] adj. Fleecy, soft.

ouatine [-ti:n] f. Quilting.

ouatiner [-tine] v. tr. (1). To quilt.

oubli [ubli] m. Omission, oversight; *par oubli,* through an oversight; *réparer un oubli,* to make up for an omission. ‖ Forgetting (des différends, des injures); *l'oubli de soi,* self-forgetfulness. ‖ Oblivion; *tirer de, tomber dans l'oubli,* to rescue from, to fall into oblivion.

oubliable [-abl] adj. Forgettable.

oublie [ubli] f. CULIN. Conical wafer.

oublier [ublje] v. tr. (1). To forget (ne plus se rappeler); *n'allez pas oublier ce que je viens de vous dire,* don't forget what I have just told you; *n'oubliez pas,* remember. ‖ To forget, to omit, to neglect (omettre); *oublier de prendre son carnet d'adresses,* to forget (ou) to neglect to take one's address-book; *oublier une personne importante dans ses invitations,* to omit an important person from one's invitations; *oublier une virgule,* to leave out a comma. ‖ To forget (pardonner); *oublier la rudesse de qqn,* to overlook (ou) condone s.o.'s discourtesy; *faire oublier un méfait passé,* to live down a past misdemeanour. ‖ To let go by, to miss (laisser passer); *oublier les limites de la patience de qqn,* to overstep the boundaries of s.o.'s patience; *oublier une occasion,* to miss an occasion, to let an occasion slip by; *on n'oublia rien pour le persuader de se tenir tranquille,* they left no stone unturned to persuade him to keep quiet. ‖ To forget (ne pas faire état de); *il sait oublier sa richesse,* he does not flaunt his wealth; *le malheur lui a fait oublier son arrogance,* misfortune has cured him of his arrogance.
— v. pr. **S'oublier,** to forget (ou) to lower oneself; to stoop to (s'abaisser à). ‖ To be unmindful of oneself, to forget one's own interests (ne pas songer à soi). ‖ To indulge in (se plaire à); *s'oublier à rêver,* to indulge in day-dreams.

oubliette [-jɛt] f. Oubliette.

oublieur [-jœ:r] s. FAM. Forgetful person.

oublieux, euse [-jø, ø:z] adj. Forgetful; *oublieux de,* unmindful of.

oued [uɛd] (pl. **oueds; ouadi** [wadi]) m. Wadi.

ouest [wɛst] m. West; *à l'ouest,* in the west; *à l'ouest de,* to the west of; *de l'ouest,* western; *vent d'ouest,* west wind; *vers l'ouest,* westward. ‖ **Ouest-nord-ouest,** adj., m. West-north-west. ‖ **Ouest-quart-nord-ouest,** adj., m. West by north. ‖ **Ouest-quart-sud-ouest,** adj., m. West by south. ‖ **Ouest-sud-ouest,** adj., m. West-south-west.
— adj. West, western, westerly. ‖ **Ouest-allemand,** adj., s. West German.

ouf [uf] interj. What a relief!, whew!; *avant de pouvoir dire ouf,* before you could say knife.

Ouganda [ugãda] m. GÉOGR. Uganda.

oui [wi] adv. Yes; yea; ay (†); *oui-da!,* yes, indeed!; *oui, oui!,* uh-huh!; *est-il bien portant?, oui,* is he in good health? yes he is; *je crois que oui,* I think so; *il m'assure que oui,* he assures me that it is so; *nous connaît-il?, oui,* does he know us?, he does.
— m. invar. Yes, ay; *les oui l'ont emporté,* the ayes carried the vote; *pour un oui, pour un non,* for a mere trifle.

ouï, ïe [ui] adj. Heard. ‖ **Ouï-dire,** m. Hearsay.
— prép. JUR. *Ouï les témoins,* after hearing the witnesses.

ouiche [wiʃ] interj. Pooh!, oh no!, bah!

ouïe [ui] f. Hearing; *avoir l'ouïe fine,* to be sharp of hearing; *être tout ouïe,* to be all ears. ‖ MUS. Sound-holes (de violon). ‖ Pl. ZOOL. Gills. (V. BRANCHIES.)

ouïe!, ouille [u:j] interj. Ouch, ooyah (expression de douleur).

ouïr [ui:r] v. tr. (71). To hear.

ouistiti [wistiti] m. ZOOL. Wistiti, marmoset.

oukase [uka:z] m. Ukase.

ouléma [ulema] m. V. ULÉMA.

ouragan [uragã] m. Hurricane. ‖ FAM. *Entrer en ouragan,* to burst in.

Oural [ural] m. GÉOGR. Ural (rivière); *les monts Oural,* the Ural Mountains, the Urals.

ouralo-altaïque [uraloaltaik] adj. GRAMM. Ural-Altaic (langues).

ourdir [urdi:r] v. tr. (2). To warp (une corde, de la toile). ‖ To plait (de la paille). ‖ FIG. To hatch (un complot); to weave (une intrigue).

ourdissage [urdisa:ʒ] m. Warping.

ourdisseur [-sœ:r] s. Warper. ‖ FIG. Plotter.

ourdissoir [-swa:r] m. Warp-beam.

ourdou [urdu] m. Urdu, Hindustani (langue).

ourler [urle] v. tr. (1). To hem.
— v. pr. **S'ourler,** to comb (vague). ‖ FIG. To become edged (de, with).

ourlet [urlɛ] m. Hem; *ourlet à jour,* openwork (ou) oversewn hem. ‖ Rim (de l'oreille). ‖ Lip (d'un cratère).

ours [urs] m. ZOOL. Bear; *ours des cavernes,* cave-bear; *ours en peluche,* teddy bear (jouet). ‖ FAM. Bear; *ours mal léché,* unmannerly fellow; *quel ours!,* what a boor! ‖ LOC. *Vendre la peau de l'ours,* to count one's chickens before they are hatched.

ourse f. ZOOL. She-bear. ‖ ASTRON. *La Grande Ourse,* Ursa Major, the Great Bear (ou) Dipper; *la Petite Ourse,* Ursa Minor, the Little Bear.

oursin [-sɛ̃] m. ZOOL. Sea-urchin, sea-hedgehog.

ourson [-sɔ̃] m. ZOOL. Bear's cub; *ourson mal léché,* unlicked cub.

ouste [ust] interj. Oust!, get out!, out of it!

outarde [utard] f. ZOOL. Bustard.

outardeau [-do] m. ZOOL. Young bustard.

outil [uti] m. TECHN. Tool, implement.

outillage [-ja:ʒ] m. TECHN. Set of tools (d'un ouvrier); plant, equipment, fixtures (d'une usine); *outillage ménager,* domestic equipment.

outillé, ée [-je] adj. Provided with tools (ouvrier); equipped, fitted out (usine). ‖ FIG. *Bien outillé en, pour,* well equipped with, for.

outiller [-je] v. tr. (1). To provide with tools (un ouvrier); to equip, to fit out (une usine). ‖ FIG. To supply with adequate means.
— v. pr. **S'outiller,** to provide oneself with tools. ‖ FIG. To provide oneself with adequate means.

outilleur [-jœ:r] m. Tool-maker; dealer in tools.

outrage [utra:ʒ] m. Outrage, insult (v. OFFENSE); *faire subir un outrage à,* to outrage (une femme); to commit an outrage against (qqn). ‖ JUR. Insulting behaviour; *outrage à magistrat,* contempt of court. ‖ FIG. Outrage, offence, impairment;

OUTILLAGE — TOOLS

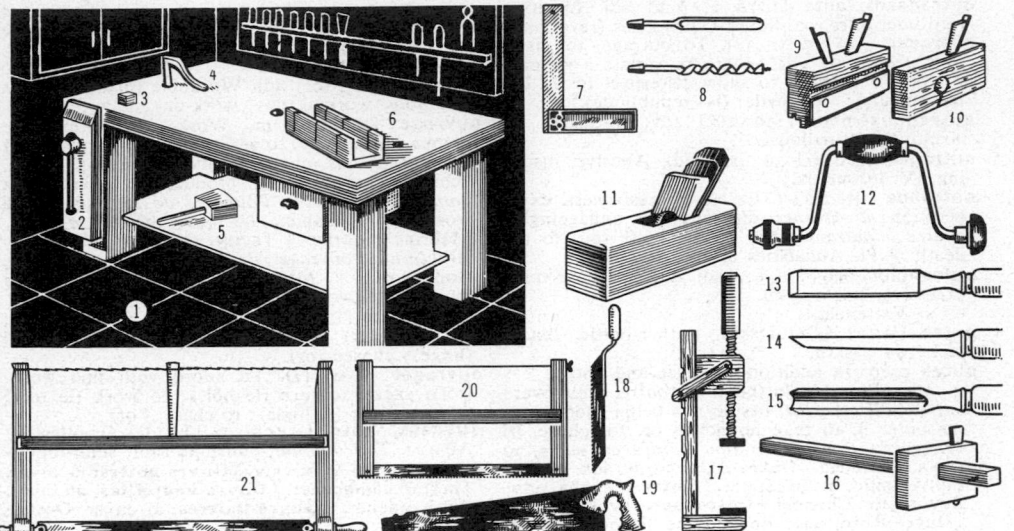

1. *Etabli*; Bench. — 2. *Presse*; Wood-vice. — 3. *Griffe*; Bench-stop. — 4. *Valet*; Clamp. — 5. *Maillet*; Mallet. — 6. *Boîte à onglet*; Mitre-box. — 7. *Equerre*; Square. — 8. *Mèche*; Bit. — 9. *Bouvet*; Tonguing-plane. — 10. *Guillaume*; Rabbet-plane. — 11. *Rabot*; Jack-plane, plane. — 12. *Vilebrequin*; Brace. — 13. *Ciseau à bois*; Chisel, wood chisel. — 14. *Bédane*; Mortise-chisel. — 15. *Gouge*; Gouge. — 16. *Trusquin*; Marking-gauge. — 17. *Serre-joint*; Clamp, cramp. — 18. *Scie à araser*; Tenon-saw, planing-saw. — 19. *Scie égoïne*; Hand-saw. — 20. *Scie à tenon*; Tenon-saw. — 21. *Scie à refendre*: Bow-saw.

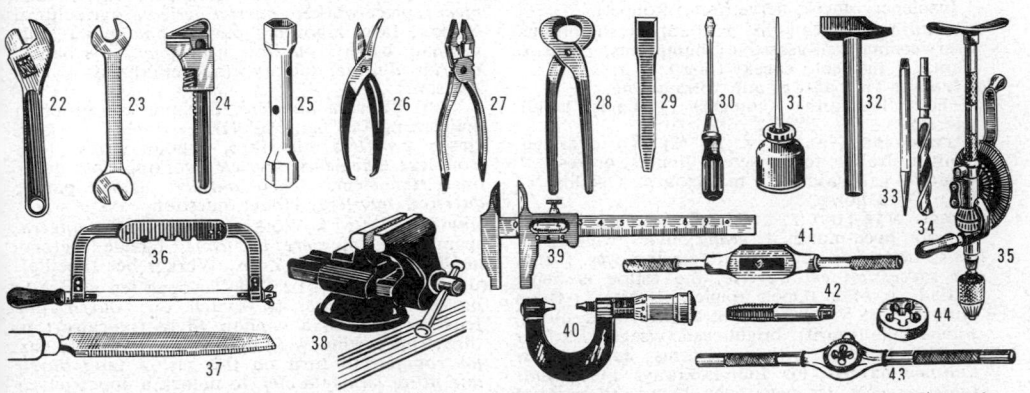

22. *Clef anglaise*; Crescent (-type) wrench. — 23. *Clef plate*; (Double-ended) spanner; (U. S.) open-end wrench. — 24. *Clef à molette*; Adjustable wrench; (U. S.) monkey wrench. — 25. *Clef à tube*; Box-spanner; (U. S.) socket wrench. — 26. *Cisailles*; Shears. — 27. *Pince universelle*; Universal pliers. — 28. *Tenailles*; Pincers. — 29. *Burin*; Cold chisel. — 30. *Tournevis*; Screwdriver. — 31. *Burette à huile*; Oil-can. — 32. *Marteau*; Hammer. — 33. *Pointeau*; Punch. — 34. *Foret*; Drill. — 35. *Chignole*; Breast-drill. — 36. *Scie à métaux*; Hack-saw. — 37. *Lime*; File. — 38. *Etau*; Engineer's vice. — 39. *Pied à coulisse*; Calipers. — 40. *Palmer*; Micrometer. — 41. *Tourne-à-gauche*; Wrench. — 42. *Taraud*: Screw-tap. — 43. *Porte-filière*; Circular die-stock. — 44. *Filière*; Circular die.

45. *Niveau*; Spirit level. — 46. *Truelle à plâtre*; Plaster trowel. — 47. *Truelle triangulaire*; Triangular trowel; (U. S.) brick trowel. — 48. *Taloche*; Hawk. — 49. *Pelle*; Shovel. — 50. *Coin à pierre*; Stone-wedge; plug. — 51. *Auge à plâtre*; Mortar-trough. — 52. *Fil à plomb*; Plumb-line. — 53. *Brosse à blanchir*; Whitening brush. — 54. *Tamis à sable*; Sieve. — 55. *Ciseau à pierre*; Stone-chisel.

outrage des ans, ravages of time; *outrage au bon sens*, insult to common sense.

outrageant, ante [utraʒɑ̃, ɑ̃:t] adj. Insulting (attitude, offre, parole). ‖ Outrageous (révoltant).

outrager [-ʒe] v. tr. (7). To outrage, to insult (qqn); *outrager une femme*, to violate a woman. ‖ Jur. To outrage, to show disrespect to (la loi, les mœurs); to revile (la république).

outrageusement [-ʒøzmɑ̃] adv. Outrageously, insultingly, scurrilously.

outrageux, euse [-ʒø, ø:z] adj. Abusive, insulting. [V. INJURIEUX.]

outrance [utrɑ̃:s] f. Excess, excessiveness, exaggeration; *à outrance*, unremittingly, unflaggingly; *guerre à outrance*, war to the knife (ou) to the death. ‖ Pl. Audacities (d'un écrivain).

outrancier, ère [-sje, ɛ:r] adj. Extreme; extremist, excessive, extravagant.
— s. Extremist.

outre [u:tr] f. Goatskin, leather-bottle, blackjack; water-skin.

outre prép. In addition to; over and above.
— adv. Beyond, further; *en outre*, moreover; *outre qu'il est petit*, besides his being short; *passer outre à*, to take no notice of, to ignore, to disregard; *transpercer qqn d'outre en outre*, to run s.o. through. ‖ **Outre-Atlantique**, adv. Across the Atlantic, in the States. ‖ **Outre-Manche**, adv. Beyond the Channel. ‖ **Outre-mer**, adv. Overseas. ‖ **Outre-Rhin**, adv. Beyond the Rhine. ‖ **Outre-tombe**, adv. Beyond the grave; *d'outre-tombe*, posthumous.

outré, ée [utre] adj. Exaggerated, extravagant, overdone, overstated (choses). ‖ Indignant, furious (personne); *outré de*, exasperated by.

outrecuidance [utrəkɥidɑ̃:s] f. Presumption, self-conceit; cocksureness, bumptiousness (fam.). ‖ Insolence; cheek, nerve (fam.) [toupet].

outrecuidant, ante [-dɑ̃, ɑ̃:t] adj. Presumptuous, overweening, self-assertive; bumptious, cocksure (fam.). ‖ Insolent; cheeky (fam.).

outremer [utrəmɛr] adj. Ultramarine.
— m. Ultramarine (couleur). ‖ Lapis lazuli (pierre).

outrepasser [-pase] v. tr. (1). To overstep (limites, droits); to transgress (limites, ordres).

outsider [autsaidœ:r] m. Sports. Outsider. ‖ Fam. Dark horse.

ouvert, erte [uvɛ:r, ɛ:rt] adj. Open; *la bouche ouverte*, open-mouthed; *grand ouvert*, wide open; *les yeux grands ouverts*, with staring eyes. ‖ Jur. *La succession est ouverte*, the estate is being settled. ‖ Méd. Open (plaie). ‖ Milit. Open (guerre, port, ville). ‖ Fig. Straightforward, quick, wide-awake (esprit); bright-eyed (visage); *les bras ouverts*, heartily, with open arms; *sa porte est toujours ouverte*, his door is always open; *tenir table ouverte*, to keep open house, to practise unstinted (ou) open-handed hospitality.

ouvertement [uvɛrtəmɑ̃] adv. Openly, overtly, frankly, undisguisedly.

ouverture [-ty:r] f. Opening, aperture, orifice (d'un lieu, d'un trou); gap, breach (dans une haie, un mur); *ouvertures d'une maison*, doors and windows of a house. ‖ Mouth (d'une grotte, d'un puits); cleft, fissure (entre deux rochers); *ouverture d'un nouveau continent*, opening-up of a new continent. ‖ Archit. Width, span (d'une arche). ‖ Phys. Aperture (en photo). ‖ Aviat. Drop (de parachute). ‖ Milit. Outbreak (des hostilités); overture (de paix). ‖ Naut. *Ouverture de la chauffe*, stoke-hole. ‖ Techn. Ports (d'une machine). ‖ Math. Aperture (d'un angle); spread (d'un compas). ‖ Mus. Overture. ‖ Comm. *Heures d'ouverture*, business hours. ‖ Sports. *Ouverture de la chasse*, first (ou) opening day of the shooting season. ‖ Fig. Beginning (d'une

réunion, d'une session); *séance d'ouverture*, inaugural meeting. ‖ Fig. Overture, proposal, offer; *faire des ouvertures*, to make overtures (ou) a tentative offer (à, to). ‖ Fig. *Ouverture de cœur*, open-heartedness; *ouverture d'esprit*, broad-mindedness.

ouvrable [uvrabl] adj. Workable (matière); *jour ouvrable*, working day, work-day.

ouvrage [uvra:ʒ] m. Work, occupation; *se mettre à l'ouvrage*, to set to work. ‖ Employment (emploi); *sans ouvrage*, unemployed. ‖ Work, achievement; product, production; *ouvrage de dames*, fancy-work; *l'ouvrage de ses mains*, the work of his hands; *les ouvrages de Mauriac*, Mauriac's works. ‖ Techn. *Ouvrages d'art*, constructions; *ouvrage de maçonnerie*, masonry, stone-work. ‖ Milit. Fortifications; *ouvrages avancés*, outworks.

ouvragé, ée [uvraʒe] adj. Carved, turned (bois); wrought (fer); patterned, diapered; embroidered (linge); chased (or).

ouvrager v. tr. (7). To adorn with fine work. ‖ To carve, to turn (le bois); to work (le fer); to embroider (le linge); to chase (l'or).

ouvrant, ante [uvrɑ̃, ɑ̃:t] adj. Opening. ‖ Autom. *Toit ouvrant*, sunshine roof, sun-roof.

ouvre [uvr]. V. OUVRIR. ‖ **Ouvre-boîtes**, m. invar. Tin (ou) can-opener. ‖ **Ouvre-bouteilles**, m. invar. Bottle-opener. ‖ **Ouvre-huîtres**, m. invar. Oyster-knife.

ouvré, ée [uvre] adj. Wrought.

ouvrer v. tr. (1). V. OUVRAGER.

ouvreur [uvrœ:r] m. Opener.

ouvreuse [uvrø:z] f. Théâtr. Usherette.

ouvrier [uvrije] m. Workman, worker, U. S. operator; *ouvrier à façons*, jobber; *ouvrier à la journée*, journeyman, day-labourer; *ouvrier aux pièces*, piece-worker; *ouvrier agricole*, agricultural worker, farm labourer; *ouvrier boulanger*, journeyman baker; *ouvrier mécanicien*, mechanic; *ouvrier d'usine*, factory- (ou) mill-hand. ‖ Fig. Artisan.
— adj. *Cheville ouvrière*, linchpin (au propre); mainspring (au figuré); *classe ouvrière*, working class; *conflits ouvriers*, labour unrest (ou) troubles; *logements ouvriers*, working-class dwellings, tenements;. *parti ouvrier*, labour party; *question ouvrière*, labour question.

ouvrière [-jɛ:r] f. Workwoman; *ouvrière lingère*, seamstress; *ouvrière en usine*, female factory-hand, factory-girl. ‖ Zool. Worker bee (abeille).

ouvrir [uvri:r] v. tr. (72). To open (en général); *ouvrir l'électricité*, to switch on; *ouvrir une fenêtre*, to open a window (à la française); to throw up a window (à guillotine); *ouvrir le gaz, un robinet*, to turn on the gas, a tap; *ouvrir une porte fermée à clef*, to unlock a door; *ouvrir de force, violemment une porte*, to force, to fling a door open; *ouvrir les rideaux*, to draw back the curtains. ‖ To open (pratiquer); *ouvrir un chemin dans*, to cut (ou) to blast a way through. ‖ To open (mettre en train); *ouvrir une galerie de peintures*, to open a picture-gallery; *ouvrir une école*, to start a school; *ouvrir un magasin*, to set up a shop; *ouvrir la marche*, to walk in front, to take the lead. ‖ To open (commencer); *ouvrir une enquête*, to open an enquiry; *ouvrir le bal, des négociations, la séance*, to open the ball, negotiations, the meeting. ‖ Méd. To lance (un abcès); to cut open (un membre); to open (une veine). ‖ Milit. To open (le feu, une tranchée); to begin, to start (les hostilités). ‖ Naut. To open (un port); to brace up (une vergue). ‖ Fin. To open (un crédit, un compte). ‖ Electr. To break (le circuit). ‖ Gramm. To open (une parenthèse). ‖ Fig. To open (un champ de recherches); *ouvrir l'appétit à qqn*, to sharpen

s.o.'s appetite; *ouvrir les idées à qqn*, to broaden s.o.'s mind; *ouvrir une parenthèse*, to digress for a moment; *ouvrir les portes à*, to open the doors to.
— v. intr. To let in; *ma sœur vous ouvrira*, my sister will let you in; *veuillez ouvrir*, please open the door. || To look out (fenêtre, porte) [*sur*, on]. || COMM. To open (magasin); *nous ouvrons de une à sept heures*, we are open from one to seven.
— v. pr. S'ouvrir, to open; to come open; *s'ouvrir violemment*, to fly open. || *S'ouvrir un passage dans*, to work one's way through. || FIG. To open (ère, époque, perspectives); to open one's heart (personne); *s'ouvrir à*, to confide in, to tell one's private thoughts to; *commencer à s'ouvrir*, to become more communicative.

ouvroir [uvrwa:r] m. Workroom, sewing-room.
ovaire [ɔvɛ:r] m. MÉD. Ovary.
ovale [ɔval] adj. Oval, oval-shaped.
— m. Oval.
ovalisation [-lizasjɔ̃] f. Ovalization.
ovaliser [-lize] v. tr. (1). To ovalize.
ovariectomie [ɔvarjɛktɔmi] f. MÉD. Ovariectomy.
ovarien, enne [ɔvarjɛ̃, ɛn] adj. MÉD. Ovarian.
ovariotomie [-rjɔtɔmi] f. MÉD. Ovariotomy.
ovarite [-ri:t] f. MÉD. Ovaritis.
ovation [ɔvasjɔ̃] f. Ovation; *faire une ovation à qqn*, to give s.o. an ovation.
ovationner [ɔvasjɔne] v. tr. FAM. To acclaim.
ove [ɔ:v] m. ARCHIT. Ovolo, ovum.
ové, ée [ɔve] adj. Ovate, egg-shaped.
ovidés [ɔvide] m. pl. ZOOL. Ovidæ.
oviducte [ɔvidykt] m. MÉD. Oviduct.
ovin, ine [ɔvɛ̃, in] adj. ZOOL. Ovine.
— m. pl. ZOOL. Sheep.
ovipare [ɔvipa:r] adj. ZOOL. Oviparous.
ovni [ɔvni] m. Abrév. de *objet volant non identifié*, UFO, unidentified flying object.

ovogenèse [ɔvoʒənɛ:z] f. MÉD. Oogenesis.
ovoïde [ɔvɔid] adj. Ovoid, oviform.
ovulaire [ɔvylɛ:r] adj. MÉD. Ovular; *ponte ovulaire*, egg release.
ovulation [ɔvylasjɔ̃] f. MÉD. Ovulation.
ovule [ɔvy:l] m. MÉD. Ovule.
oxacide [ɔksasid] m. CHIM. Oxyacid.
oxalate [ɔksalat] m. CHIM. Oxalate.
oxalique [-lik] adj. CHIM. Oxalic.
oxhydrile [ɔksidril] m. CHIM. Hydroxyl.
oxhydrique [ɔksidrik] adj. CHIM. Oxy-calcium, oxyhydrogen.
oxyacétylénique [ɔksiasetilenik] adj. Oxyacetylene.
oxydable [-dabl] adj. Oxidizable, oxidable.
oxydant, ante [-dɑ̃, ɑ̃:t] adj. Oxidizing.
— m. Oxidizer, oxidant.
oxydation [-dasjɔ̃] f. Oxidization, oxidation.
oxyde [ɔksid] m. CHIM. Oxide; *oxyde de carbone*, carbon monoxide.
oxyder [-de] v. tr. (1). To oxidize.
— v. pr. S'oxyder, to oxidize.
oxydoréduction [-doredyksjɔ̃] f. CHIM. Redox.
oxygénable [-ʒenabl] adj. CHIM. Oxygenizable.
oxygénation [-ʒenasjɔ̃] f. Oxygenation.
oxygène [-ʒɛn] m. CHIM. Oxygen. || MÉD. *Masque à oxygène*, oxygen mask.
oxygéné, ée [-ʒene] adj. Peroxided, bleached (cheveux); *eau oxygénée*, peroxide of hydrogen, U. S. hydrogen peroxide.
oxygéner [-ʒene] v. tr. (5). To oxygenate, to oxidize. || To bleach (les cheveux).
— v. pr. S'oxygéner, FAM. To get some fresh air; *aller s'oxygéner à la campagne*, to go to the country to get the city air out of one's lungs.
oxyton [ɔksitɔ̃] adj. GRAMM. Oxytone.
oyez [ɔje] interj. † Harken, hear ye (v. OUÏR [71]).
ozone [ɔzɔ:n] m. CHIM. Ozone.
ozoniser [ɔzɔnize] v. tr. (1). To ozonize.
ozonomètre [-nɔmɛtr] m. Ozonometer.

P

p [pe] m. P, p.
pacage [paka:ʒ] m. Pasture, pasture-land, pasturage. || JUR. *Droits de pacage*, grazing rights.
pacager [-ʒe] v. tr. (7). To graze, to pasture (une prairie).
— v. intr. To graze (bétail).
pacemaker [pɛsmɛkœ:r] m. MÉD. Pace-maker (instrument).
pacha [paʃa] m. Pasha, pacha.
pachyderme [paʃidɛrm] adj. Pachydermatous.
— m. ZOOL. Pachyderm. || Pl. Pachydermata.
pacificateur, trice [pasifikatœ:r, tris] adj. Pacifying, peace-making, pacificatory.
— s. Pacifier; peacemaker.
pacification [-fikasjɔ̃] f. Pacification.
pacifier [-fje] v. tr. (1). To pacify (un pays). || To pacify, to appease, to calm (l'esprit, qqn).
pacifique [-fik] adj. Pacific, calm, quiet (époque); pacific, peaceable, conciliatory (idées, mesures); peaceful, pacific (personne). || GÉOGR. Pacific (océan). || JUR. Undisputed (possesseur).

— s. Peaceable person; peacemaker.
— m. GEOGR. The Pacific.
pacifiquement [-fikmɑ̃] adv. Peacefully, peaceably.
pacifisme [-fism] m. Pacifism.
pacifiste [-fist] adj. Pacifist, pacifistic.
— s. Pacifist.
pacotille [pakɔti:j] f. Shoddy (ou) U. S. crummy goods (marchandises); job-lot (ramassis); *de pacotille*, gimcrack (bijoux); jerry-built (maison); poor-quality (vaisselle).
pacson [paksɔ̃] m. ARG. Parcel (colis); packet, bundle (somme d'argent).
pacte [pakt] m. Pact, agreement, contract, compact, covenant (v. TRAITÉ); *faire un pacte avec*, to make (ou) enter into an agreement with.
pactiser [-tize] v. intr. (1). To enter into an agreement (ou) a compact, to come to terms (avec, with); *pactiser avec sa conscience*, to compromise with one's conscience. || MILIT. *Pactiser avec l'ennemi*, to treat with the enemy.
Pactole [paktɔl] m. GÉOGR. Pactolus. || FIG. Gold mine.

paddock [padɔk] m. Paddock (pour les chevaux). ‖ Pop. Bed ; *aller au paddock,* to hit the sack (ou) the hay, to turn in.
Padoue [padu] f. Géogr. Padua.
paf! [paf] interj. Bang!, wallop!, whang!, slap! — adj. Fam. Tipsy, tight, blotto, shot, plastered.
pagaie [pagɛ] f. Naut. Paddle.
pagaïe, pagaille [paga:j] f. Fam. Muddle, jumble, clutter, mess (v. fatras, fouillis) ; *en pagaïe,* in disorder, at sixes and sevens, higgledy-piggledy.
paganiser [paganize] v. tr. (1). To paganize, to heathenize.
paganisme [-nism] m. Paganism, heathenism.
pagayer [pagɛje] v. tr., intr. (9 b). To paddle.
pagayeur [-jœ:r] m. Naut. Paddler.
page [pa:ʒ] f. Page ; leaf ; *un livre de huit cents pages,* an eight-hundred-page book. ‖ Page (d'histoire) ; *une page de Shakespeare,* a page from (ou) out of Shakespeare. ‖ Techn. *Mettre en pages,* to make up. ‖ Loc. *A la page,* in the picture, in the know (avisé) ; up-to-date (moderne) ; *ne plus être à la page,* to be behind the times ; *se tenir à la page,* to keep abreast of the times (ou) up to date.
page m. Page (à la cour, au mariage).
pageot [paʒo] m. Pop. Bed ; *se mettre au pageot,* to hit the sack (ou) the hay, to crash out.
pagination [paʒinasjɔ̃] f. Pagination ; paging.
paginer [-ne] v. tr. (1). To page, to paginate.
pagne [paɲ] f. Pagne, loin-cloth.
pagode [pagɔd] f. Pagoda (bâtiment, monnaie). — adj. Pagoda (manche).
paie [pɛ] f. V. paye.
paiement [pɛmɑ̃] m. Payment.
païen, enne [pajɛ̃, ɛn] adj., s. Pagan, heathen.
paillard, arde [paja:r, ard] adj. Pop. Ribald, profligate, lewd, lecherous. — m. Rake, libertine.
paillarde [pajard] f. Pop. Wanton.
paillardise [-di:z] f. Pop. Profligacy, lewdness.
paillasse [pajas] f. Straw mattress, paillasse. ‖ Draining-board, U. S. drainboard, deserter (d'évier). ‖ Pop. Belly ; *crever la paillasse à qqn,* to knife s.o. in the guts.
paillasse m. Clown, buffoon. ‖ Turncoat, Vicar of Bray (en politique).
paillasson [-sɔ̃] m. Mat, door-mat, matting ; *paillasson à grille,* wire-mat. ‖ Fam. *Mettre la clef sous le paillasson,* to flit, to abscond.
paillassonner [-sɔne] v. tr. (1). Agric. To mat.
paille [pa:j] f. Straw ; *chaise de paille,* straw-bottomed chair ; *paille d'Italie,* leghorn ; *paille de fer,* iron shavings. ‖ Crack, cleft (dans un métal) ; feather, flaw (dans une pierre précieuse) ; flaw (dans la porcelaine, le verre). ‖ Naut. Bitt pin. ‖ Loc. *Coucher sur la paille,* to live rough ; *mettre sur la paille,* to reduce to poverty ; *tirer à la courte paille,* to draw lots ; *voir la paille dans l'œil du prochain,* to see a mote in another's eye. — adj. invar. Straw-coloured.
paillé [pɑje] m. Agric. Stable-litter. — adj. Flawed (métal, pierre). ‖ Mulched (arbre).
pailler v. tr. To straw-bottom (une chaise). ‖ Agric. To mulch (un arbre). — m. Agric. Barn-yard ; straw-loft.
paillet adj. Pale red (vin).
pailleté, ée [pajte] adj. Spangled, sequined, sewn with paillettes.
pailleter [pɑjte] v. tr. (8a). To spangle.
pailleteur [-tœ:r] m. Gold-washer.
paillette [pɑjɛt] f. Spangle, paillette (ornement). ‖ Speck (d'or). ‖ Crystal (de mica) ; *savon en paillettes,* soap flakes. ‖ Flaw (dans une gemme).
pailleur [-jœ:r] m. Straw-merchant. ‖ Chair-bottomer.
paillis [-ji] m. Agric. Mulch ; matting.

paillon [-jɔ̃] m. Bread-basket (de boulanger) ; straw-case (de bouteille). ‖ Foil (en bijouterie).
paillote [-jɔt] f. Straw-hut. (V. case.)
pain [pɛ̃] m. Bread ; *pain de froment, de seigle,* wheat-, rye-bread ; *pain de maïs,* U. S. corn-bread ; *pain de ménage,* household bread ; *pain grillé,* toast ; *pain trempé,* sop. ‖ Loaf (miche) ; *pain de mie,* sandwich loaf ; *pain de 4 livres,* quartern loaf ; *petit pain,* roll. ‖ Loaf ; *pain à cacheter,* wafer ; *pain de savon,* cake (ou) brick of soap ; *pain de beurre,* butter pat ; *pain de sucre,* sugar loaf ; *sucre en pain,* loaf sugar. ‖ Culin. *Pain d'épice,* gingerbread ; *pain de Gênes,* Genoa cake. ‖ Milit. *Pain de munition,* ration bread. ‖ Bot. *Arbre à pain,* bread-tree. ‖ Loc. *Acheter pour une bouchée de pain,* to buy for a mere song ; *avoir du pain sur la planche,* to have plenty of work to do ; *bon comme du bon pain,* good-hearted ; *gagner son pain,* to make one's living, to earn one's bread ; *long comme un jour sans pain,* as long as a month of Sundays ; *manger son pain blanc le premier,* to begin with the dessert ; *ne pas manger de ce pain-là,* to have no stomach for it ; *ôter le goût du pain à qqn,* to bump off s.o. ; *rompre le pain,* to break bread ; *se vendre comme des petits pains,* to sell like hot cakes. ‖ Pop. Blow ; *je lui ai flanqué un pain,* I let him have one, I dotted him one.
pair, aire [pɛ:r] adj. Even (nombre).
pair m. Peer ; *Chambre des Pairs,* House of Lords ; *les pairs du royaume,* the Peers of the realm. ‖ Equal ; *de pair avec,* on a par with, on an equal footing with ; *aller de pair avec,* to be on all fours with ; *hors de pair,* unrivalled, unequalled, peerless ; *marcher de pair avec,* to be up to (qqch.) ; to keep pace with (qqn) ; *nos pairs,* our equals. ‖ Fin. Par ; *au-dessous, au-dessus du pair,* below, above par ; *au pair,* at par ; *valeur au pair,* par value. ‖ Loc. *Situation au pair,* « au pair » job.
pairage [pɛra:ʒ] m. Electr. Pairing (en T.V.).
paire [pɛ:r] f. Pair (d'amis, de bas) ; yoke (de bœufs) ; brace (de pistolets). ‖ Loc. *Une autre paire de manches,* quite another matter, a horse of another colour, another pair of shoes ; *faire la paire,* to pair off together.
pairesse [pɛrɛs] f. Peeress.
pairie [-ri] f. Peerage.
pairle [perl] m. Blas. Pall.
paisible [pɛzibl] adj. Peaceful, peaceable, calm, quiet, pacific (caractère, personne) ; peaceful, untroubled, uneventful, calm, quiet (situation, vie).
paisiblement [-bləmɑ̃] adv. Peacefully, peaceably, quietly, calmly.
paisseau [pɛso] m. Agric. Vine-prop.
paître [pɛ:tr] v. tr. (73). To graze, to put to grass (un troupeau). ‖ To graze on, to feed on, to browse (l'herbe). — v. intr. To graze, to feed (troupeau) ; *faire paître,* to graze, to take the grass. ‖ Fam. *Envoyer paître qqn,* to send s.o. to Jericho.
paix [pɛ] f. Peace, quiet (tranquillité) ; *en paix,* peacefully ; *la paix du tombeau,* the stillness (ou) silence of the grave. ‖ Milit. Peace ; *demander la paix,* to sue for peace. ‖ Fig. Reconciliation ; *faire la paix avec,* to be reconciled with. ‖ Fam. *Ficher la paix à qqn,* to leave s.o. alone, to let s.o. be. — interj. Peace! ; be quiet! ; *paix à ses cendres,* peace to his ashes!
Pakistan [pakistɑ̃] m. Géogr. Pakistan.
pakistanais, aise [-tanɛ, ɛ:z] adj., s. Géogr. Pakistani.
pal [pal] (pl. **pals**) m. Pale ; *supplice du pal,* impalement. ‖ Blas. Pale.
palabre [palabr] m. ou f. Useless discussion, palaver.

palabrer [-bre] v. intr. (1). To palaver.
palace [palas] m. Palace (cinéma, hôtel).
paladin [paladɛ̃] m. † Paladin.
palais [palɛ] m. ARCHIT. Palace. || JUR. Law-court (bâtiment, tribunal); lawyers, judges and barristers (gens de robe).
palais m. MÉD. Palate; *voile du palais,* soft palate. || FIG. Taste, delicacy of taste (goût).
palan [palɑ̃] m. Hoist. || NAUT. Tackle, pulley-block.
palançon [-sɔ̃] m. ARCHIT. Lath.
palanque [palɑ̃:k] f. MILIT. Stockade.
palanquin [palɑ̃kɛ̃] m. Palanquin.
palatal, ale [palatal] adj. MÉD. Palatal, palatine. || GRAMM. Palatal, front (consonne, voyelle).
palatale [palatal] f. GRAMM. Palatal; front consonant (ou) vowel.
palatalisation [-lizasjɔ̃] f. GRAMM. Palatalization.
palatalisé, ée [-lize] adj. GRAMM. Palatalized.
Palatin, ine [palatɛ̃, in] adj. Palatine; *la princesse Palatine,* the Princess Palatine. || GÉOGR. *Le mont Palatin,* the Palatine.
palatin, ine [palatɛ̃, in] adj. MÉD. Palatine.
palatinat [-tina] m. † Palatinate.
palatine [-tin] f. Palatine, fur tippet.
pale [pal] f. Pale, stake (de palissade). || Blade (de rame, d'hélice); sluice-gate (de réservoir); paddle (de roue).
pale f. ECCLÉS. Pall.
pâle [pɑ:l] adj. Colourless, pale (lèvres); pale (personne); pale, wan (visage). || Light, pale (couleur); faint (lumière); pale, wan (lune). || MÉD. Pallid. || FIG. Sickly (sourire); colourless (style). || FAM. *Se faire porter pâle,* to swing the lead, to malinger, U. S. to put on the sick act.
palé [pale] adj. BLAS. Paly.
palefrenier [palfrənje] m. Stableman, groom, ostler.
palefroi [-frwa] m. † Palfrey. (V. COURSIER.)
paléochrétien, enne [paleokretjɛ̃, ɛn] adj. ARTS. Early Christian.
paléographe [-graf] m. Palaeographer.
paléographie [-fi] f. Palaeography.
paléolithique [-litik] adj. Palaeolithic.
paléontologie [paleɔ̃tɔlɔʒi] f. Palaeontology.
paléontologique [-lɔʒik] adj. Palaeontologic, palaeontological.
paléontologiste [-lɔʒist], **paléontologue** [-lɔg] s. Palaeontologist.
— adj. *Savant paléontologiste,* palaeontologist, specialist in palaeontology.
paléozoïque [paleɔzɔik] adj., s. GÉOL. Palaeozoic.
paleron [palrɔ̃] m. Shoulder-blade (du cheval). || CULIN. Chuck (de bœuf).
Palestine [palɛsti:n] f. GÉOGR. Palestine.
palestinien, enne [palɛstinjɛ̃, ɛn] adj., s. Palestinian.
palestre [palɛstr] f. † Palaestra.
palet [palɛ] m. Quoit.
paletot [palto] m. Coat (de femme); overcoat, top-coat (d'homme).
palette [palɛt] f. Dasher (de baratte); pallet (de montre); blade (de rame); blade, paddle (de roue); *roue à palettes,* paddle-wheel. || Bat, U. S. paddle (de ping-pong). || ARTS. Palette (de peintre); pallet (de potier). || FIG. Scale of colours, palette.
palétuvier [paletyvje] m. BOT. Mangrove.
pâleur [pɑlœ:r] f. Paleness, pallidness (d'une personne); paleness, pallor (du teint); *d'une pâleur mortelle,* deathly pale. || Wanness (de la lune).
pali [pali] m. Pali (langue).
pâlichon, onne [pɑliʃɔ̃, ɔn] adj. FAM. Palish.
palier [palje] m. Landing (d'escalier); *être voisins de palier,* to live on the same floor; *sur le même palier,* on the same floor. || AUTOM.,

CH. DE F., AVIAT. Level; *en palier,* on the level; *voler en palier,* to fly level. || TECHN. Bearing. || FIG. Gradation; *par paliers,* by gradations, in graduated steps.
palière [-ljɛ:r] adj., f. Top (marche).
palimpseste [palɛ̃psɛst] adj., m. Palimpsest.
palinodie [palinɔdi] f. Palinode. || FAM. Recantation.
pâlir [pɑli:r] v. intr. (2). To pale, to grow pale; to blanch (de, with); *faire pâlir qqn,* to cause s.o. to turn pale. || To fade, to grow pale (couleur); to wane (jour); to grow dim (lumière); *faire pâlir une couleur,* to bleach a colour. || FIG. To be on the wane (étoile); *faire pâlir,* to outshine.
— v. tr. To bleach (une couleur); to make pale (le teint).
palis [pali] m. Palings, paling-fence (clôture); pale, stake (piquet).
palissade [-sad] f. Palissade, fence, paling. || Boarding (dans une rue). || MILIT. Stockade.
palissader [-sade] v. tr. (1). To palissade, to fence in.
palissage [palisa:ʒ] m. AGRIC. Training.
palissandre [palisɑ̃:dr] m. Rosewood (bois).
pâlissant, ante [pɑlisɑ̃, ɑ̃:t] adj. Blanching (couleur); waning (lumière); growing pale (personne).
palissé, ée [palise] adj. BLAS. Palissé.
palisser v. tr. (1). AGRIC. To train (une vigne).
palladium [paladjɔm] m. Palladium.
palliatif [paljatif] adj., m. Palliative.
pallier [palje] v. tr. (1). To palliate, to extenuate (un inconvénient, une faute). || MÉD. To palliate (une maladie).
— v. intr. FAM. To make up (à, for).
pallium [paljɔm] m. † ECCLÉS. Pallium, pall.
palmaire [palmɛ:r] adj. MÉD. Palmar.
palmarès [palmarɛs] m. Prize-list.
palme [palm] f. BOT. Palm-branch; *huile de palme,* palm-oil. || SPORTS. Flipper (d'un homme-grenouille). || ZOOL. Web (d'un palmipède). || FIG. Crown (du martyre); *les palmes académiques,* academic decoration; *remporter la palme,* to bear the palm, to win the victory.
palmé, ée [-me] adj. ZOOL. Web-footed (animal); webbed (patte). || BOT. Palmate (feuille).
palmer v. tr. (1). TECHN. To flatten the head of (une aiguille). || NAUT. To trim.
palmer [-mœ:r] m. TECHN. Micrometer caliper.
palmeraie [-mrɛ] f. Palm-grove, palm-plantation.
palmette [-mɛt] f. AGRIC. Fan-shaped espalier. || ARCHIT. Palm-leaf, palmette.
palmier [-mje] m. BOT. Palm-tree; *palmier nain,* palmetto. || **Palmier-éventail,** m. BOT. Fan-palm.
palmipède [-mipɛd] adj. ZOOL. Palmipede, web-footed.
— m. ZOOL. Palmipede.
palmiste [-mist] m. BOT. Areca.
— adj. ZOOL. *Rat, ver palmiste,* palm-squirrel, -worm.
palmite [-mit] m. Palm-marrow.
palmure [-my:r] f. ZOOL. Web (des palmipèdes).
palois, oise [palwa, wa:z] adj. GÉOGR. Of (ou) from Pau.
— s. Native (ou) inhabitant of Pau.
palombe [palɔ̃:b] f. ZOOL. Wood-pigeon, ring-dove.
palonnier [palɔnje] m. Swingle-tree. || AUTOM. Compensator. || AVIAT. Rudder-bar.
pâlot, otte [palo, ɔt] adj. Palish.
palourde [palurd] f. ZOOL. Clam, hard clam.
palpabilité [palpabilite] f. Palpability, tangibility. || FIG. Obviousness, evidence.
palpable [-pabl] adj. Palpable, tangible. || FIG. Obvious, evident.
palpation [-pasjɔ̃] f. MÉD. Palpation.

palpe [palp] f. Zool. Palpus, feeler (d'insecte); barbel (de poisson).

palper [-pe] v. tr. (1). To finger, to feel (un objet). ‖ Méd. To palpate. ‖ Fam. To pocket (de l'argent).
— v. intr. Fam. To pocket (ou) handle money.

palpitant, ante [palpitᾰ, ᾱ:t] adj. Méd. Palpitating. ‖ Fig. Thrilling, exciting. (V. passionnant.)

palpitation [-tasjɔ̃] f. Palpitation, throbbing, throb (du cœur); flickering, flicker (des paupières); heaving (du sein). ‖ Méd. *Avoir des palpitations,* to suffer from palpitation.

palpiter [-te] v. intr. (1). To palpitate, to throb (cœur); to flicker (paupières); to heave, to rise and fall (sein).

palsambleu [palsᾱblø] interj. Zounds!

paltoquet [paltokɛ] m. Nonentity.

paluche [paly:ʃ] f. Pop. Paw (main).

paludéen, enne [palydeɛ̃, ɛn] adj. Bot. Marsh (plante). ‖ Méd. Paludal, marsh, malarial (fièvre).

paludier [-dje] m. Worker in salt marsh.

paludisme [-dism] m. Méd. Impaludism, paludism, marsh fever; malaria.

palustre [palystr] adj. Marsh, paludous (plante); marshy, swampy (terrain).

palynologie [palinɔlɔʒi] f. Bot. Palynology.

pâmé, ée [pɑme] adj. In a swoon, swooning (personne). ‖ Gasping (poisson).

pâmer v. intr. (1). † To swoon.
— v. pr. **Se pâmer,** to swoon,.to faint. ‖ Fig. *Se pâmer de,* to gape with (admiration); to be convulsed with (rire).

pâmoison [pamwazɔ̃] f. Swoon, faint; *tomber en pâmoison,* to fall into a swoon.

pampa [pɑ̃pa] f. Pampas.

pamphlet [pɑ̃flɛ] m. Lampoon, hostile pamphlet.

pamphlétaire [-fletɛ:r] m. Lampoonist, pamphleteer.

pampille [pɑ̃pi:j] f. Tassel, bobble.

pamplemousse [pɑ̃pləmus] m. Bot. Grape-fruit.

pampre [pɑ̃:pr] m. Bot. Vine-branch.

pan [pɑ̃] m. Tail (de chemise); coat-tail, flap (d'habit). ‖ Side, face (de construction, de meuble, de prisme); section, piece (de mur). ‖ Autom. Flat (de carrosserie). ‖ Fig. Patch (de ciel).

Pan m. Pan (dieu).

pan! interj. Bang! slap! ‖ Fam. *Faire pan-pan à,* to smack (un enfant).

panacée [panase] f. Panacea, cure-all.

panachage [panaʃa:ʒ] m. Mixing (de couleurs, d'objets). ‖ Splitting one's vote (en politique).

panache [panaʃ] m. Plume, panache (au chapeau); wreath (de fumée). ‖ Archit. Triangular pendentive. ‖ Fig. Swagger, panache, show; *aimer le panache,* to be fond of show, to like to cut a dash.

panaché, ée [-ʃe] adj. Variegated, parti-coloured (fleur, étoffe); *panaché de,* dotted (ou) pied with. ‖ Sports. Scratch (équipe). ‖ Culin. Shandy (boisson); mixed (glace, salade). ‖ Fam. Mixed, motley (assemblée); variegated (style).
— m. Shandy, shandy-gaff, mixed drink.

panacher v. tr. (1). To variegate, to stripe (des plantes). ‖ To split (un vote).
— v. intr. To become variegated (plante).
— v. pr. **Se panacher,** to become variegated.

panachure [-ʃy:r] f. Streak, stripe.

panade [panad] f. Culin. Bread soup, boiled bread-and-butter panada. ‖ Fam. *Dans la panade,* in the soup.

panafricain, aine [panafrikɛ̃, ɛn] adj. Pan-African.

panafricanisme [-kanism] m. Pan-Africanism.

panais [panɛ] m. Bot. Parsnip.

panama [panama] m. Panama hat (chapeau). ‖ Géogr. Panama.

panaméricain, aine [panamerikɛ̃, ɛn] adj. Pan-American.

panaméricanisme [-kanism] m. Pan-Americanism.

panamien, enne [panamjɛ̃, ɛn], **panaméen, enne** [-meɛ̃, meɛn] adj. Panamanian.

panarabisme [panarabism] m. Pan-Arabism.

panard [panar] adj. Splay-footed, knock-kneed (cheval).

panard m. Pop. Foot, hoof.

panaris [panari] m. Méd. Whitlow, felon.

pancarte [pɑ̃kart] f. Placard, bill, poster. ‖ Show-card (pour réclame).

panchromatique [pɑ̃krɔmatik] adj. Techn. Panchromatic.

pancréas [pɑ̃kreas] m. Méd. Pancreas.

pancréatique [-atik] adj. Méd. Pancreatic.

panda [pɑ̃da] m. Zool. Panda.

pandectes [pɑ̃dɛkt] f. pl. Jur. † Pandects.

pandémique [pɑ̃demik] adj. Pandemic.

pandémonium [pɑ̃demɔnjɔm] m. Pandemonium; den of disorder.

pandit [pɑ̃di] m. Pundit.

pandore [pɑ̃dɔ:r] f. Pandora.
— m. Fam. Mounted policeman.

pané, ée [pane] adj. Culin. Breaded.

panégyrique [paneʒirik] m. Panegyric; encomium; *faire le panégyrique de,* to panegyrize.

panégyriste [-rist] m. Panegyrist.

panel [panɛl] m. Panel (enquête sociologique, échantillon étudié). ‖ Panel (débat).

paner [pane] v. tr. (1). Culin. To cover with bread-crumbs.

panerée [panəre] f. Basketful.

paneterie [pantəri] f. Pantry. ‖ Bread-store.

panetier [pantje] m. Bread-store keeper.

panetière [-tjɛ:r] f. Sideboard, dresser.

pangermanique [pɑ̃ʒɛrmanik] adj. Pan-Germanic.

pangermanisme [-nism] m. Pan-Germanism.

panier [panje] m. Basket; *panier à ouvrage, à papiers, à provisions,* work-, waste-paper-, shopping-basket; *panier à salade,* salad washer. ‖ Basketful (plein panier); *un panier de figues,* a basketful of figs. ‖ Bee-hive (ruche). ‖ † Pannier (de jupe). ‖ Archit. Pannier, corbel. ‖ Fam. *Le dessus du panier,* the cream of the crop, the pick of the bunch; *à mettre dans le même panier,* tarred with the same brush; *panier percé,* spendthrift; *panier à salade,* Black Maria, prison van, U. S. paddy-wagon. ‖ **Panier-repas,** m. Packed lunch.

panière [-jɛ:r] f. Large basket.

panifiable [panifjabl] adj. *Farine panifiable,* bread flour.

panification [-fikasjɔ̃] f. Panification.

panifier [-fje] v. tr. (1). To turn into bread.

paniquard [panikar] s. Fam. Alarmist, jitterbug.

panique [panik] adj. Panic (peur).
— f. Panic, scare; *pris de panique,* panic-stricken.

panislamisme [panislamism] m. Panislamism.

panne [pan] f. Techn. Breakdown; *panne d'électricité, de métro,* breakdown on the electric circuit, on the underground (ou) U. S. subway. ‖ Autom. Breakdown; *panne sèche* (ou) *d'essence,* engine failure through shortage of petrol; *avoir une panne d'essence,* to peter out, to run dry (ou) out of petrol (ou) U. S. gas; *avoir une panne de moteur,* to have engine-trouble. ‖ Naut. Boom (de port); *être en panne,* to be hove to; *mettre en panne,* to bring to. ‖ Théâtr. Poor part. ‖ Arts. Daub. ‖ Panne, plush (textile). ‖ Loc. *Laisser qqn en panne,* to let s.o. down; *rester en panne,* to be stuck; to be brought to a standstill.

panne f. Culin. Lard (de porc).

panne f. Claw (de marteau). ‖ Naut. Boom. ‖ Archit. Purlin, pantile.

panneau [pano] m. Panel (de porte, de robe); *à panneaux,* panelled (porte). ‖ Panel, board; *pan-*

neau d'affiches, boarding. ‖ Naut. Hatch. ‖ Aviat. Ground-signal. ‖ Fam. Trap, snarl.

panner [pane] v. tr. (1). To hammer out, to pane.

panneton [pantɔ̃] m. Web (de clef); catch (de fenêtre).

panonceau [panɔ̃so] m. Sign (enseigne).

panoplie [panɔpli] f. Panoply; suit of armour; soldier's equipment. ‖ Set of tools (jouet). ‖ Trophy (sur un mur).

panorama [panɔrama] m. Panorama; view-point.

panoramique [-mik] adj. Panoramic (vue); *wagon panoramique,* U. S. observation car.

— m. Ciném. Panoramic (ou) pan shot, pan.

pansage [pɑ̃sa:ʒ] m. Grooming (d'un cheval). ‖ Milit. *Au pansage,* stables (sonnerie).

panse [pɑ̃:s] f. Paunch, belly, pot-belly, corporation (d'une personne). ‖ Sound-bow (d'une cloche); belly (d'une cruche, d'un vase).

pansement [pɑ̃smɑ̃] m. Méd. Bandaging, dressing (action); bandage, dressing (objet); *faire un pansement à,* to dress, to bandage; *paquet de pansement,* first-aid kit (ou) outfit.

panser [pɑ̃se] v. tr. (1). To groom, to rub down (un cheval). ‖ Méd. To bandage (un blessé); to dress, to bandage (une plaie). ‖ Fig. To soothe, to soften, to mitigate (une douleur).

panslavisme [pɑ̃slavism] m. Pan-Slavism.

pansu, ue [pɑ̃sy] adj. Pot-bellied.

pantagruélique [pɑ̃tagrɥelik] adj. Pantagruelian.

pantagruélisme [-lism] m. Pantagruelism.

pantalon [pɑ̃talɔ̃] m. Trousers; pants (fam.). ‖ Slacks (long, pour femmes); knickers, panties (culotte de femme). ‖ Théâtr. Pantaloon.

pantalonnade [-lɔnad] f. Théâtr. Pantaloonery, farce. ‖ Fam. Humbugging, shamming.

pantelant, ante [pɑ̃tlɑ̃, ɑ̃:t] adj. Out of breath, panting (personne). ‖ Quivering (membre).

panteler [-le] v. intr. (8 *a*). To pant (personne). ‖ To throb (cœur); to quiver (poitrine).

pantenne [pɑ̃tɛn] f. Agric. Wicker-tray. ‖ Naut. *En pantenne,* apeak.

panthéisme [pɑ̃teism] m. Pantheism.

panthéiste [-ist] s. Pantheist.

— adj. Pantheistic.

Panthéon [pɑ̃teɔ̃] m. Pantheon.

panthère [pɑ̃tɛ:r] f. Zool. Panther.

pantin [pɑ̃tɛ̃] m. Jumping-jack (jouet). ‖ Fig. Puppet.

pantographe [pɑ̃tɔgraf] m. Pantograph.

pantois [pɑ̃twa] adj. Stupefied, flabbergasted, aghast; *rester pantois,* to be left all of a heap.

pantomime [pɑ̃tɔmim] f. Théâtr. Pantomime, dumb show (spectacle).

— m. Théâtr. Mime, mimic (acteur).

— adj. Théâtr. Dumb-show, U. S. pantomime.

pantouflard [pɑ̃tufla:r] m. Fam. Lie-a-bed, stay-at-home type.

pantoufle [-tufl] f. Slipper. ‖ Fam. Lucrative job in the private sector.

pantoufler [-tufle] v. intr. (1). Fam. To resign from government service in order to make more money in the private sector.

panure [pany:r] f. Culin. Bread-crumbs.

paon [pɑ̃] m. Zool. Peacock (oiseau); peacock moth (papillon).

— adj. Peacock-blue (couleur).

paonne [pan] f. Zool. Pea-hen.

paonneau [pano] m. Zool. Pea-chick.

papa [papa] m. Fam. Dad, daddy, papa, pa; *bon papa,* grand-dad; ‖ Fam. *Bon gros papa,* nice stout old party; *papa Tom,* old Tom.

papal, ale [papal] adj. Ecclés. Papal.

papauté [papote] f. Ecclés. Papacy; *de la papauté,* papal.

papavéracé, ée [papaverase] adj., n. f. Bot. Papaveraceous.

papavéracées f. pl. Bot. Papaveraceae.

papaye [papa:j] f. Bot. Papaw, pawpaw, papaya (fruit).

papayer [-je] m. Bot. Papaw, pawpaw (arbre).

pape [pap] m. Ecclés. Pope.

papegai [papəgɛ] m. Zool. Popinjay.

papelard [papəla:r] m. Fam. Paper.

papelard, arde [ard] adj. Fam. Sanctimonious, hypocritical.

— m. Fam. Canting (ou) mealy-mouthed humbug.

papelarder [-larde] v. intr. (1). Fam. To cant.

papelardise [-lardi:z] f. Fam. Sanctimoniousness.

paperasse [papəras] f. Fam. Old paper (papier).

paperasserie [-sri] f. Fam. Red-tape.

paperassier [-sje] adj. Fam. Fond of scribbling; fond of red tape.

— m. Fam. Scribbler (écrivailleur); bureaucrat (rond-de-cuir).

papesse [papɛs] f. She-Pope; *la papesse Jeanne,* Pope Joan.

papeterie [paptri] f. Paper-making (fabrication); paper-factory (fabrique). ‖ Stationer's shop (boutique); paper-trade (commerce); stationery (papier).

papetier [paptje] m. Paper-maker (fabricant); paper-merchant, stationer (marchand).

— adj. *Industrie papetière,* paper-making industry.

papier [papje] m. Paper; *papier d'emballage,* packing (ou) wrapping paper; *papier de journal,* newsprint; *papier à lettres,* writing- (ou) note-paper; *papier à machine,* typewriting (ou) typing paper; *papier peint,* wall-paper; *papier de verre,* glass- (ou) sand-paper. ‖ Story, write-up, flimsy (article); writing, document; *jeter des notes sur le papier,* to jot down notes; *sur le papier,* on paper; *tarif « papier d'affaires »,* printed paper rate. ‖ Papers (documents); *mettre de l'ordre dans ses papiers,* to set one's papers in order. ‖ Arts. *Papier à calquer, à musique,* tracing, music paper. ‖ Comm. Bills; *papier négociable,* bona-fide paper. ‖ Fin. *Papier timbré,* stamped paper; *payer en papier,* to pay in paper-money. ‖ Fam. *Être dans les petits papiers de,* to be in s.o.'s good books; *figure de papier mâché,* wan face; *réglé comme du papier à musique,* regular as clockwork. ‖ **Papier-calque,** m. Tracing paper. ‖ **Papier-émeri,** m. Emery-paper. ‖ **Papier-filtre,** m. Filter-paper. ‖ **Papier-monnaie,** m. Fin. Paper-money.

papilionacé, ée [papiljɔnase] adj. Bot. Papilionaceous.

— f. pl. Bot. Papilioneceae.

papillaire [papillɛ:r] adj. Bot., Méd. Papillary.

papille [papi:j] f. Méd., Bot. Papilla.

papillon [papijɔ̃] m. Zool. Butterfly; *papillon de nuit,* moth. ‖ Bat's wing gas-burner (de bec de gaz). ‖ Bow-tie (cravate); butterfly bow (nœud). ‖ Rider (ajouté); inset map (carte); inset (feuille encartée). ‖ Techn. Butterfly-valve (ou) throttle; butterfly-nut. ‖ Fam. Giddy-head (personne); *papillons noirs,* blues.

papillonnage [-jɔna:ʒ]. **papillonnement** [-jɔnmɑ̃] m. Fluttering (ou) flitting about.

papillonnant, ante [-jɔnɑ̃, ɑ̃:t] adj. Fluttering, flitting.

papillonner [-jɔne] v. intr. (1). To flutter, to flit about. ‖ Fam. To behave in a feather-brained manner; to flit from subject to subject; *papillonner auprès des dames,* to hover around the ladies.

papillotage [papijɔta:ʒ] m. Curling (des cheveux). ‖ Dazzling, dazzle (des lumières); blinking (des yeux). ‖ Mackling (en typogr.).

papillotant, ante [-jɔtɑ̃, ɑ̃:t] adj. Twinkling (étoile); flickering (lumière); blinking (yeux). ‖ Fam. Changeable (personne).

papillote [-jɔt] f. Curl-paper (à cheveux). ‖ Culin. Frill (à gigot); buttered paper (à rôti).

papillotement [-jɔtmɑ̃] m. Dazzling, dazzlement (des lumières). ‖ Electr. Flicker (en T. V.).

papilloter [-jɔte] v. intr. (1). To dazzle; to flicker (lumière). [V. VACILLER.] ‖ To blink (yeux).
papisme [papism] m. Papism.
papiste [-pist] s. Papist.
papotage [papɔta:ʒ] m. Tittle-tattle, chatter, chit-chat.
papoter [-te] v. intr. (1). To tittle-tattle, to chatter.
papou, e [papu] adj., s. GÉOGR. Papuan.
paprika [paprika] m. CULIN. Paprika.
papule [papy:l] f. MÉD., BOT. Papula.
papyrus [papiry:s] m. Papyrus.
pâque [pɑ:k] f. Passover (fête juive). ‖ Pl. ECCLÉS. *Pâques fleuries*, Palm Sunday.
— m. pl. ECCLÉS. Easter; *faire ses pâques*, to do one's Easter duties; *œufs de Pâques*, Easter-eggs.
paquebot [pakbo] m. NAUT. Packet-boat, steamer, liner.
pâquerette [pɑkrɛt] f. BOT. Daisy.
paquet [pakɛ] m. Packet, bundle (de, of); *faire un paquet de*, to pack up. ‖ Parcel (colis); *paquet postal*, parcel post; *faire un paquet de qqch.*, to tie sth. up in a parcel. ‖ NAUT. *Paquet de mer*, heavy sea; *embarquer un paquet de mer*, to ship a sea; *en paquet*, bundled (voile). ‖ FIN. Block, packet (d'actions). ‖ FAM. *Paquet de nerfs*, bundle of nerves; *faire ses paquets*, to pack up; *recevoir son paquet*, to get a dressing-down.
paquetage [pakta:ʒ] m. Making up into parcels, parcelling. ‖ MILIT. Pack.
paqueter [-te] v. tr. (8 a). To make up into a parcel; to parcel.
par [par] prép. By, through, at, out of (lieu); *arriver par la place*, to arrive via the square; *entrer par la fenêtre*, to come in through the window; *jeter par la fenêtre*, to throw out of the window; *par ici, par là*, this way, that way; *par mer et par terre*, by land and sea; *par monts et par vaux*, over hill and dale; *par tout le pays*, throughout the country; *par toute la ville*, all over the town; *par où êtes-vous venu?*, which way did you come?; *passer par Vierzon*, to go via Vierzon; *regarder par la fenêtre*, to look out of the window. ‖ On, in (temps); *par une froide journée d'hiver*, on a cold winter day; *par quatre fois*, four times; *par ce temps étouffant*, in this sultry weather; *sortir par tous les temps*, to go out in all sorts of weather. ‖ By, through (moyen); *conduire par la bride*, to lead by the bridle; *ne voir que par qqn*, to see only through s.o.'s eyes; *prendre par son faible*, to take advantage of s.o.'s special weakness; *réussir par un intermédiaire*, to succeed through the agency of a go-between; *tenir par le bras*, to hold by the arm; *venir d'Amérique par bateau*, to sail from America; *venir par air à Paris*, to fly to Paris; *venir par chemin de fer*, to come by rail. ‖ By, from, out of (agent); *écrit par mon père*, written by my father; *fait par un spécialiste*, made by a highly skilled craftsman; *se faire renseigner par*, to get information from. ‖ Out of, through (cause); *agir par complaisance*, to act out of kindness; *de par son âge*, by reason of his age; *par pitié*, for pity's sake; *remarquable par sa patience*, remarkable for his patience; *se ruiner par sa prodigalité*, to ruin oneself by one's extravagance. ‖ By, in (manière); *par hasard*, by chance; *par ordre numérique*, in numerical order. ‖ In, per, by (sens distributif); *défiler par trois*, to march past in threes; *douze fois par an*, twelve times a year; *une fois par dix années*, once in ten years; *se faire jour par jour*, to be done day by day; *venir par centaines*, to come in hundreds. ‖ By (au nom de); *par Dieu!*, by Jove!, my goodness! ‖ LOC. *Finir par ennuyer*, to get tiresome in the long run; *se montrer par trop insolent*, to prove far too insolent. ‖ *Par-ci, par-là*, here and there (lieu); now and then (temps). ‖ **Par-des-**

sous, beneath, under, underneath. ‖ **Par-dessus**, over (qqch.); *par-dessus bord*, overboard; *par-dessus le marché*, into the bargain; *par-dessus la tête*, over head and ears; *par-dessus tout*, above all; *en avoir par-dessus la tête*, to be absolutely fed up with it. ‖ **Par-devant**, JUR. Before, in presence of.
para [para] m. FAM. Para, paratrooper.
parabole [parabɔl] f. Parable. ‖ MATH. Parabola.
parabolique [parabɔlik] adj. Parabolic; *radiateur parabolique*, bowl-type electric fire (ou) U. S. heater.
paracentèse [parasɛtɛ:z] f. MÉD. Paracentesis.
parachèvement [paraʃɛvmɑ̃] m. Completion; completing; perfecting.
parachever [-ʃve] v. tr. (5). To complete, to perfect, to finish. (V. PARFAIRE.)
parachutage [paraʃyta:ʒ] m. AVIAT. Parachute drop; parachute landing.
parachute [-ʃyt] m. AVIAT. Parachute, 'chute (fam.); *parachute dorsal, ventral*, back-type, lap-pack parachute; *sauter en parachute*, to bale out ‖ TECHN. Safety-catch (dans les mines).
parachuter [-ʃute] v. tr. (1). AVIAT. To parachute, to drop by parachute.
parachutisme [-ytism] m. SPORTS. Parachute jumping, sky-diving.
parachutiste [-ʃytist] s. AVIAT. Parachutist; paratrooper; skyman (fam.); U. S. chutist; *parachutiste saboteur*, skieur, parasaboteur, paraskier.
Paraclet [paraklɛ] m. ECCLÉS. Paraclete.
parade [parad] f. Outside show (de cirque). ‖ MILIT. Parade, review. ‖ SPORT. Parry (à l'escrime); sudden stop, pulling up (au manège). ‖ FIG. Parade, display; U. S. come-on (fam.) [v. ÉTALAGE]; *érudition de parade*, surface display of learning; *faire parade de*, to parade, to show off; *lit de parade*, lying-in-state bed.
parader [-de] v. intr. (1). MILIT. To parade. ‖ SPORT. *Faire parader un cheval*, to put a horse through its paces. ‖ FIG. To show off.
paradigmatique [paradigmatik] adj. Paradigmatic.
paradigme [paradigm] m. Paradigm.
paradis [paradi] m. ECCLÉS. Paradise; *paradis terrestre*, Earthly Paradise, Eden. ‖ THÉÂTR. Gallery; the gods (fam.); U. S. peanut gallery. ‖ FIG. Paradise. ‖ FAM. *Tu ne l'emporteras pas en paradis!*, you won't get away with it!
paradisiaque [-zjak] adj. Paradisaic.
paradisier [-zje] m. ZOOL. Bird of paradise.
paradoxal, ale [paradɔksal] adj. Paradoxical.
paradoxalement [-mɑ̃] adv. Paradoxically.
paradoxe [paradɔks] m. Paradox.
parafe [paraf]. V. PARAPHE.
paraffinage [parafina:ʒ] m. Paraffining.
paraffine [parafin] f. Paraffin; *paraffine solide*, paraffin wax; *huile de paraffine*, mineral oil.
paraffiner [-ne] v. tr. (1). To paraffin.
parafoudre [parafudr] m. ÉLECTR. Lightning arrester.
parage [para:ʒ] m. † Lineage. (V. LIGNAGE.)
parages m. pl. Quarters, parts, regions; *dans ces parages*, in this part of the world, hereabouts. ‖ NAUT. Latitudes.
paraglace [paraglas] m. NAUT. Ice-fender.
paragraphe [paragraf] m. Paragraph.
paragrêle [paragrɛ:l] adj. Anti-hail (canon).
Paraguay [paragwɛ] m. GÉOGR. Paraguay.
paraguayen, enne [-jɛ̃, ɛn] adj., s. GÉOGR. Paraguayan.
paraître [parɛ:tr] v. intr. (74). To appear (en général); to dawn (poindre); to loom (se distinguer); to come up (se montrer); *un éclair parut*, there was a flash of lightning; *le jour paraît*, day is just dawning; *paraître à l'horizon*, to come up to the horizon; *des soucoupes volantes*

paraissent dans le ciel, flying saucers appear in the sky. ‖ To appear (être présent); *je ne désire pas que mon nom paraisse,* I don't wish my name to be mentioned. ‖ To be published, to come out (livre); to be issued, U. S. to appear (revue); *prêt à paraitre,* just off the press; *vient de paraître,* just out. ‖ To appear, to be visible; *la cicatrice ne paraît plus,* the scar no longer shows; *faire paraître,* to evince, to betray, to reveal. (V. MONTRER, RÉVÉLER, TRAHIR.) ‖ To show off, to make a display. (V. PARADER.) ‖ To look, to seem (v. SEMBLER); *cette étoffe paraît solide,* this stuff seems strong; *elle a cinquante ans et les paraît,* she is fifty and looks it. ‖ THÉÂTR. To make one's appearance, to come on (acteur).
— v. impers. *A ce qu'il me paraît,* as I see it, in my opinion (ou) view; *à ce qu'il paraît,* from all appearances, apparently; *il paraît que non, que oui,* it appears not, so; *il paraît qu'il est ruiné,* it seems he is ruined; *il paraît qu'il ment,* he is suspected of lying; *sans qu'il y paraisse,* without its being seen.
paralittérature [paraliteraty:r] f. Alternative literature.
parallactique [paralaktik] adj. ASTRON., PHYS. Parallactic.
parallaxe [-laks] f. ASTRON., PHYS. Parallax.
parallèle [parallɛl] adj. Parallel.
— f. MATH., MILIT. Parallel.
— m. Parallel (v. COMPARAISON); *mettre en parallèle,* to compare. ‖ Parallel, match. (V. ÉGAL.) GÉOGR. Parallel (de latitude). ‖ ELECTR. *Montage en parallèle,* parallel connection.
parallèlement [-lɛlmɑ̃] adv. Parallel, in a parallel direction (à, to).
parallélépipède [-lelepipɛd] m. MATH. Parallelepiped.
parallélisme [-lelism] m. Parallelism.
parallélogramme [-lelɔgram] m. MATH. Parallelogram. ‖ ELECTR. *Parallélogramme de Wheatstone,* Wheatstone bridge.
paralysant, ante [paralizɑ̃, ɑ̃:t] adj. Paralyzing.
paralysé, ée [-ze] adj. Paralyzed.
— s. MÉD. Paralytic.
paralyser [-ze] v. tr. (1). MÉD. To paralyze. ‖ FIG. To paralyze, to numb, to incapacitate (l'intelligence); to paralyze, to cripple (les moyens d'action); to nonplus, to inhibit (qqn).
paralysie [-zi] f. MÉD. Paralysis, palsy. ‖ FIG. Paralysis.
paralytique [-tik] adj., s. MÉD. Paralytic.
paramagnétique [paramaɲetik] adj. PHYS. Paramagnetic.
paramagnétisme [-tism] m. PHYS. Paramagnetism.
paramécie [paramesi] f. ZOOL. Paramoecium.
paramédical, ale [paramedikal] adj. Paramedical.
paramètre [paramɛtr] m. MATH., FIG. Parameter.
paramilitaire [paramilitɛ:r] adj. Paramilitary; semi-military.
parangon [parɑ̃gɔ̃] m. Paragon, unspotted precious stone (pierre). ‖ Paragon (v. MODÈLE); *parangon de vertu,* man of unparalleled virtue. ‖ TECHN. *Gros parangon,* double pica (en typogr.).
parangonnage [parɑ̃gɔna:ʒ] m. TECHN. Justification of different types.
parangonner [parɑ̃gɔne] v. intr. (1). TECHN. To justify different types.
paranoïa [paranɔja] f. MÉD. Paranoia.
paranoïaque [-nɔjak] adj., s. MÉD. Paranoiac.
paranoïde [-nɔid] adj. MÉD. *Délire paranoïde,* paranoid delusion.
paranormal, ale [paranɔrmal] adj. Paranormal (phénomène).

parapet [parapɛ] m. Parapet. ‖ MILIT. Breastwork, parapet.
paraphe [paraf] m. Flourish, paraph (fioritures). ‖ Initials (signature); *mettre son paraphe sur,* to initial.
parapher [-fe] v. tr. (1). To initial.
paraphrase [parafra:z] f. Paraphrase.
paraphraser [-ze] v. tr. (1). To paraphrase.
paraphrastique [-frastik] adj. Paraphrastic.
paraplégie [parapleʒi] f. MÉD. Paraplegia.
parapluie [paraplɥi] m. Umbrella. ‖ TECHN. Splashboard.
parapsychologie [parapsikɔlɔʒi] f. PHILOS. Parapsychology.
parascolaire [paraskɔlɛ:r] adj. Out of school (activité).
parasitaire [parazitɛ:r] adj. MÉD. Parasitical. ‖ RADIO. Interfering.
parasite [-zit] m. MÉD. Parasite. ‖ RADIO. Pl. Atmospherics; U. S. bugs (fam.). ‖ FIG. Parasite, hanger-on, blood-sucker.
— adj. MÉD. Parasitic. ‖ ELECTR. Extraneous, spurious.
parasiter [-zite] v. tr. (1). ZOOL., MÉD. To parasitize. ‖ RADIO. To interfer with. ‖ FIG. To live off, to sponge on.
parasitisme [-zitism] m. Parasitism.
parasitologie [-zitɔlɔʒi] f. MÉD. Parasitology.
parasol [parasɔl] m. Parasol, sunshade; beach-umbrella (sur la plage). ‖ AUTOM. Sun-shield, visor. ‖ AVIAT. Parasol.
parasympathique [parasɛ̃patik] adj. MÉD. Parasympathetic.
— s. MÉD. Parasympathetic nervous system, parasympathetic.
parathyroïde [paratirɔid] f. MÉD. Parathyroid.
paratonnerre [-tɔnɛ:r] m. Lightning-conductor (ou) rod.
parâtre [parɑ:tr] m. † Step-father.
paratyphique [paratifik] adj. MÉD. *Bacille paratyphique,* paratyphoid bacillus.
— s. Paratyphoid sufferer.
paratyphoïde [paratifɔid] f. MÉD. Paratyphoid fever.
paravent [paravɑ̃] m. Folding screen. ‖ FIG. *Se servir de qqn comme d'un paravent,* to hide behind s.o.
parbleu! [parblø] interj. Rather!, to be sure!, you bet!
parc [park] m. Park (de château, de ville); grounds (de maison). ‖ Play-pen, nursery pen (pour enfants). ‖ AGRIC. Pen, U. S. corral (à bestiaux); paddock (à chevaux); oyster-bed (ou) farm (à huîtres); sheep-fold (à moutons). ‖ AUTOM. *Parc de stationnement,* car park, parking place, U. S. parking lot. ‖ MILIT. *Parc à munitions,* ammunition-depot. ‖ NAUT. *Parc à charbon,* coalbin. ‖ AVIAT. *Parc à réparations,* maintenance unit. ‖ CH. DE F. Rolling-stock depot. ‖ GÉOGR. *Parc national,* national park, nature reserve. ‖ FIN. *Parc automobile, informatique,* total number of cars, of computers in use.
parcage [parka:ʒ] m. Bedding (d'huîtres). ‖ AGRIC. Penning, U. S. corralling (de bétail); folding (de moutons). ‖ AUTOM. Parking; *parcage interdit,* no parking.
parcellaire [parselɛ:r] adj. Piecemeal, bitty, fragmentary, compartmentalized (découpage, vision, tâche). ‖ AGRIC. Plot by plot (remembrement).
parcellarisation [-larizasjɔ̃] f. Fragmentation, compartmentalization.
parcelle [parsɛl] f. Parcel, fragment, particle (d'un corps). ‖ AGRIC. Compartment (de forêt); plot, parcel (de terrain). ‖ FIG. Bit, grain, ounce.
parceller [-səle] v. tr. (1). AGRIC. To parcel out.
parce que [parskə] conj. Because.

— m. *Les pourquoi et les parce que*, the whys and the wherefores.

parchemin [parʃəmɛ̃] m. Parchment (pour écrire); vellum (pour relier); *papier parchemin*, parchment-paper. ‖ FAM. Sheepskin (diplôme); deed (papier d'affaires).

parcheminé, ée [-mine] adj. Grease-proof (papier); parchment-like, shrivelled, wizened (peau).

parcheminer [-mine] v. tr. (1). To give a parchment finish to.

— v. pr. **Se parcheminer**, to become parchment-like; to shrivel up.

parchemineux, euse [-minø, ø:z] adj. Parchment-like.

parcimonie [parsimɔni] f. Parsimony, stinginess.

parcimonieusement [-njøzmɑ̃] adv. Parsimoniously, sparingly.

parcimonieux, euse [-njø, ø:z] adj. Parsimonious, sparing. (V. CHICHE.)

parcmètre [parkmɛtr] m. AUTOM. Parking-meter, meter.

parcourir [parkuri:r] v. tr. (32). To go (ou) to pass (ou) to proceed through (ou) over; *parcourir le pays*, to scour the country (en chercheur); *parcourir la France*, to tour France, to travel through France (en visiteur); to wander about (ou) through France (sans but précis). ‖ To travel, to cover (une distance); *un météore a parcouru le ciel*, a meteor flashed through the sky; *un frisson le parcourut*, a shiver ran over him. ‖ To look through, to skim, to go over (rapidement); *parcourir des yeux*, to glance at (ou) over. ‖ ÉLECTR. To traverse.

parcours [-ku:r] m. Distance covered; *du village à la ville, il y a trois kilomètres de parcours*, the distance from the village to the town is three kilometres; *parcours plus court*, shorter route. ‖ Trip, run, journey. (V. TRAJET.) ‖ CH. DE F. *Parcours d'essai*, trial run; *parcours à vide*, journey empty. ‖ TECHN. Path, stroke (d'un piston). ‖ AVIAT. *Parcours aérien*, air transit; *parcours à l'atterrissage*, landing run. ‖ NAUT. *Parcours maritime*, sea voyage (ou) transit. ‖ AUTOM. Drive.

pardessus [pardəsy] m. Overcoat, topcoat, great-coat.

pardi! [pardi], **pardieu!** [pardjø] interj. V. PARBLEU.

pardon [pardɔ̃] m. Forgiveness, pardon; *demander pardon de*, to beg pardon for; *pardon de vous interrompre*, sorry to have to interrupt you. ‖ ECCLÉS. Pardon.

— ¯interj. I beg your pardon!; excuse me.

pardonnable [-dɔnabl] adj. Forgivable, pardonable. (V. EXCUSABLE.)

pardonner [-dɔne] v. tr. (1). To forgive, to pardon (qqch.); *pardonnez la liberté que je prends de vous interrompre*, pardon my interrupting.

— v. intr. *Pardonner à qqn*, to forgive (ou) to pardon s.o. (de, for). ‖ MÉD. *Cela ne pardonne pas*, it is incurable. ‖ FIG. To spare (épargner). ‖ LOC. *Vous êtes tout pardonné*, don't mention it.

pare [pa:r]. V. PARER. ‖ **Pare-balles**, m. MILIT. Bullet-shield. ‖ **Pare-boue**, m. AUTOM. Mudguard. ‖ **Pare-brise**, m. AUTOM. Wind-screen; U. S. windshield. ‖ **Pare-chocs**, m. AUTOM. Bumper-bar, bumper. ‖ **Pare-éclats**, m. MILIT. Splinter-proof shield; NAUT. splinter-deck. ‖ **Pare-étincelles**, m. Fire-screen. ‖ **Pare-feu**, m. Hearth-screen, U. S. fire guard (de cheminée); fire-belt (en forêt). ‖ **Pare-flammes**, m. Flame-arrester (ou) trap. ‖ **Pare-fumée**, m. Smoke-shield. ‖ **Pare-lumière**, m. AUTOM. Anti-dazzle shield; RADIO. Lens screen, U. S. gobo (T. V.). ‖ **Pare-mines**, m. NAUT. Paravane. ‖ **Pare-oreilles** m. Ear-shields, U. S. ear muff. ‖ **Pare-soleil**, m.

AUTOM. Sun-glare shield. ‖ **Pare-torpilles**, m. MILIT. Torpedo-net. ‖ **Pare-vol**, m. Anti-theft device.

paré, ée [pare] adj. Adorned, dressed, decked out (personne). ‖ NAUT. Ready (à, for).

parégorique [paregɔrik] adj. Paregoric (elixir).

pareil, eille [parɛ:j] adj. Like, similar (semblable); *sans pareil*, unparalleled, peerless, unmatched; *tout pareil au vôtre*, just like yours. ‖ Such, of that kind (tel); *rien de pareil*, nothing like it; *on n'a jamais vu pareille générosité*, such generosity has never been seen.

— s. Equal, like, match (v. ÉGAL); *avoir le pareil*, to have the exact match; *lui et ses pareils*, he and his like; *n'avoir pas son pareil*, not to have one's equal. ‖ LOC. *Rendre la pareille à qqn*, to pay s.o. back in his own coin.

pareillement [parɛjmɑ̃] adv. In like manner (identiquement). ‖ Likewise (aussi).

parélie [pareli] f. V. PARHÉLIE.

parement [parəmɑ̃] m. Adorning, adornment. ‖ Cuff (de manche); facing (de revers). ‖ ARCHIT. Facing (d'un mur). ‖ CULIN. Dressing, trimming.

parenchyme [parɑ̃ʃim] m. MÉD. Parenchyma.

parent [parɑ̃] m. Pl. Parents, father and mother; *sans parents*, parentless. ‖ Relative, relation; *parents par alliance*, related by marriage; *proches parents*, closely related; *tous ses parents*, all his kinsmen, his kith and kin.

parental, ale [-rɑ̃tal] adj. Parental.

parente [-rɑ̃:t] f. Kinswoman.

parenté [-rɑ̃te] f. Kinship, relationship (liens de parenté). ‖ Kindred, relations (parents). ‖ FIG. Affinity.

parentéral, ale [parɑ̃teral] adj. MÉD. Parenteral.

parenthèse [parɑ̃tɛ:z] f. Parenthesis (phrase);

PARENTÉ (degrés de) **DEGREES OF RELATIONSHIP**	
arbre généalogique	genealogical table; family tree
parenté (avec qqn)	family relationship (with s.o.)
proche parent	next-of-kin
aïeux, ancêtres	ancestors, forefathers
descendance	descent
origine	offspring, issue
progéniture	progeny
lignage	lineage
le père et la mère	the parents
les autres parents	the relatives, the relations
grands-parents	grandparents
arrière-grand-père	great-grand father
petits-neveux	grand-nephews
cousin	cousin, male cousin
cousine	cousin, girl cousin
cousin germain	first cousin, cousin german
issu de germain	second cousin
beau-père	father-in-law
beaux-parents	wife's or husband's parents; « in-laws » (fam.).
parent par alliance	relative by marriage
chef de famille	head of the family
beau-père (2e père)	step-father
fils d'un 2e lit, beau-fils	step-son
tuteur	guardian
parrain, filleul	godfather, godson
enfant trouvé	foundling
orphelin	orphan
pupille	ward
père nourricier	foster-father
frère de lait	foster-brother
aîné	eldest; (de 2) elder
aînesse	primogeniture
puîné	younger brother
cadette (branche)	younger (branch)
paternel (le côté)	paternal
paternel (un ton)	fatherly

brackets (signe). ‖ Digression; *soit dit par paren-thèse*, incidentally; be it said parenthetically.

paréo [pareo] m. Sarong.

parer [pare] v. tr. (1). To ornament, to adorn, to deck. (V. ORNER.) ‖ COMM. To set off (la marchandise). ‖ CULIN. To dress, to trim (un plat). ‖ NAUT. To get ready (l'ancre). ‖ FIG. To adorn, to embellish (son style).
— v. pr. **Se parer**, to adorn (ou) to bedeck oneself. ‖ FIG. To show off (faire parade); *se parer des plumes du paon*, to bedeck oneself with peacock feathers; *se parer de qualités factices*, to parade false qualities.

parer v. tr. (1). To parry, to ward off (un coup). ‖ NAUT. To clear (un bas-fond); to steer away from, to clear of (un grain). ‖ FIG. To shield, to protect (qqn) [*contre*, against].
— v. intr. To provide (*à*, against, for); to guard (*à*, against); *parer à l'imprévu, au plus pressé*, to provide against the unforeseen, for the most immediate needs. ‖ NAUT. *Parer au grain*, to reduce sail for a squall; *parer à virer*, to stand ready to put (ou) go about.

paresse [parɛs] f. Laziness (en général); idleness (inactivité); sloth (indolence). ‖ MÉD. Sluggishness (d'intestin). ‖ FIG. Slowness (*à*, in).

paresser [-se] v. intr. (1). To laze, to idle. ‖ To loaf. (V. FLÂNER.)

paresseusement [-søzmɑ̃] adv. Lazily, idly.

paresseux, euse [-sø, ø:z] adj. Lazy, idle, sluggard. ‖ MÉD. Sluggish (organe). ‖ FIG. Slow (esprit); *prendre une solution paresseuse*, to take the line of least resistance.
— s. Lazy person; lazybones (fam.). ‖ ZOOL. Sloth.

paresthésie [parɛstezi] f. Paresthesis.

parfaire [parfɛ:r] v. tr. (50). To perfect. (V. FINIR.) ‖ To make up (une somme).

parfait, aite [parfɛ, ɛt] adj. Perfect; faultless (irréprochable); flawless (sans défaut); unblemished (sans tâche). ‖ Perfect, complete (achevé); *courtoisie parfaite*, exquisite courtesy; *d'une élégance parfaite*, well-groomed; *en parfait accord avec*, in perfect agreement with. ‖ Perfect; capital (fam.); *bonheur parfait*, unalloyed bliss; *c'est parfait*, that's fine!, splendid!; *en parfait état*, in excellent condition. ‖ Perfect (v. ACCOMPLI); *parfait gentilhomme*, real (ou) perfect gentleman. ‖ Perfect, arrant (fieffé); *parfait coquin*, utter scoundrel; *parfait crétin*, absolute idiot.
— m. CULIN. Ice-cream, parfait. ‖ GRAMM. Perfect.
— interj. Fine!, splendid!, capital!

parfaitement [-tmɑ̃] adj. Perfectly; *aller à qqn parfaitement*, to suit s.o. to a T. ‖ Perfectly (v. ABSOLUMENT); *être parfaitement d'accord*, to agree perfectly, to acquiesce unreservedly. ‖ Perfectly, thoroughly; *il a été parfaitement roulé*, he was well and truly (ou) U. S. thoroughly cheated. ‖ Of course!, quite so! (dans les réponses).

parfois [parfwa] adv. Sometimes; every so often, every now and then. (V. QUELQUEFOIS.)

parfum [parfœ̃] m. Perfume, scent (de toilette). ‖ Perfume, fragrance, scent, aroma (odeur). ‖ CULIN. Flavour (d'une glace). ‖ FIG. Flavour, odour.

parfumé, ée [parfyme] adj. Fragrant, perfumed, scented. (V. ODORANT.)

parfumer v. tr. (1). To scent, to perfume. ‖ CULIN. To flavour.
— v. pr. **Se parfumer**, to use scent, to perfume oneself.

parfumerie [-mri] f. Perfumery (magasin, métier); scent, perfume (marchandise).

parfumeur [-mœ:r] s. Perfumer.

parhélie [pareli] f. ASTRON. Parhelion, mocksun.

pari [pari] m. Bet, wager; *faire tenir un pari*, to hold s.o. to a bet; *les paris*, betting, bets. ‖ Bet, wager (somme pariée). ‖ SPORTS. Betting; *pari mutuel*, pari mutuel, totalizator system; tote (fam.).

paria [parja] m. Pariah (aux Indes). ‖ FIG. Outcast, pariah.

parier [parje] v. tr. (1). To bet (*avec*, with); to wager, to lay; *parier pour un cheval*, to back a horse; *parier deux mille francs*, to stake two thousand francs; *parier sur*, to bet on, to put money on. ‖ To bet (v. GAGER); *je vous parie qu'elle viendra*, I bet you she will come; *parier de faire qqch.*, to bet that one will do sth. ‖ LOC. *Il y a gros à parier que*, the odds are that.
— v. intr. To bet.

pariétal, ale [parjetal] adj. MÉD., BOT. Parietal. ‖ ARTS. Parietal, cave (art).
— m. MÉD. Parietal bone.

parieur [parjœ:r] s. Better, punter; backer (aux courses).

Parigot, ote [parigo] s. FAM. Parisian.

Paris [pari] m. GÉOGR. Paris. ‖ COMM. *Articles de Paris*, fancy goods.

parisianisme [-zjanism] m. Parisian habit; Parisian way of speaking; Paris centered ideology.

parisien, enne [-zjɛ̃, ɛn] adj. Parisian. ‖ NAUT. *Vergue parisienne*, monkey spar.
— s. Parisian.

paritaire [paritɛ:r] adj. Composed of equal numbers; *réunion paritaire*, round-table conference.

parité [parite] f. Parity. (V. ÉGALITÉ.) ‖ MATH. Evenness. ‖ FIN. Parity.

parjure [parʒy:r] m. Perjury (action); perjurer (personne).
— adj. Perjured, forsworn.

parjurer (se) [səparʒyre] v. pr. (1). To perjure (ou) forswear oneself; to commit perjury.

parka [parka] m. Parka.

Parkérisation [parkerizasjɔ̃] f. (nom déposé) TECHN. Parkerization.

parking [parkiŋ] m. AUTOM. Car-park, park; U. S. parking-lot.

parlant, ante [parlɑ̃, ɑ̃:t] adj. Speaking, talking. ‖ THÉÂTR. *Film parlant*, talking film (ou) U. S. movie; talkie (fam.). ‖ BLAS. Canting (armes). ‖ FIG. Speaking, life-like (dessin); eloquent (geste); expressive (physionomie).
— m. CINÉM. Talkies, sound films.

parlé, ée [-le] adj. Spoken.
— m. THÉÂTR. Spoken part.

parlement [parləmɑ̃] m. Parliament, U. S. Congress.

parlementaire [-tɛ:r] adj. Parliamentary.
— m. Parliamentarian; Member of Parliament; U. S. Congressman.

parlementaire m. White flag bearer.
— adj. *Drapeau parlementaire*, flag of truce.

parlementairement [-tɛrmɑ̃] adv. Parliamentarily.

parlementarisme [-tarism] m. Parliamentary government.

parlementer [-te] v. intr. (1). To parley, to discuss terms (*avec*, with). ‖ FIG. To palaver.

parler [parle] v. intr. (1).

---

1. S'exprimer. — 2. Converser. — 3. Etre en relations. — 4. S'entretenir. — 5. Déclarer. — 6. Exprimer une intention. — 7. Prononcer. — 8. Admonester. — 9. Faire un discours. — 10. Bavarder. — 11. FAM.

---

1. To speak, to talk (s'exprimer); *commencer à parler*, to begin to talk (enfant); *parler avec emphase, violemment*, to rant, to rail; *parler avec*

solennité, avec volubilité, to hold forth, to chatter; *parler d'abondance*, to have a glib tongue; *parler ferme*, to speak one's mind plainly; *parler franc*, not to mince words; *parler grossièrement, net, par signes*, to speak offensively, plainly, in signs; *parler pour ne rien dire*, to talk for the sake of talking; *parler sans ambages, sans réticences, sérieusement*, to speak to the point, out, in earnest; *faire parler les faits*, to bring the facts to the fore; *faire parler qqn*, to loosen s.o.'s tongue; *les faits parlent*, the facts speak for themselves. ‖ **2.** To speak (*à*, to); to confer, to converse (*à*, with); *il faudra que je vous parle*, I must have a talk with you; *parlez-lui de moi à l'occasion*, put in a word for me when the occasion present itself. ‖ **3.** To be on speaking terms (*à*, with) [être en relations]. ‖ **4.** To speak (*de*, of, about); to talk, to tell (*de*, about); *en parler*, to bring up the subject; *faire parler*, to set people talking; *il fait parler de lui*, he is much talked about; *n'en parlons plus*, let us drop the subject; *ne m'en parlez pas!*, don't mention the subject; *n'en parlez à personne*, keep your own counsel; *on m'a parlé de*, I was told of; *on parle d'une dévaluation*, it is rumoured that the franc will be devalued; *une façon de parler*, a manner of speaking; *un sujet dont on parle beaucoup*, a much talked-of matter; *parler abondamment de ses affaires*, to talk a great deal about one's business; *parler de tout avec assurance*, to be positive about everything; *parler bien, mal de qqn*, to speak well, ill of s.o.; *parlez-moi de vos parents*, tell me about your people; *sans parler de*, without mentioning. ‖ **5.** To speak out, to decide (déclarer); *à vous de parler*, it's for you to speak; *plus d'atermoiements, parlez*, no more shilly-shallying, speak out! ‖ **6.** To speak (ou) talk (*de*, about) [exprimer une intention]; *parler d'apprendre à conduire*, to talk about learning to drive. ‖ **7.** To speak (prononcer); *parler bas*, to speak softly; *parler distinctement*, to articulate distinctly; *parler du nez*, to speak through one's nose (ou) with a twang; *parler entre ses dents*, to mutter, to mumble; *parler fort*, to speak loudly; *parler haut*, to raise one's voice. ‖ **8.** To speak, to admonish (admonester); *depuis que je lui ai parlé, il se tient*, since I admonished him, he behaves. ‖ **9.** To lecture (faire une conférence); *de quoi le professeur a-t-il parlé?*, what did the professor lecture on? ‖ **10.** To talk (bavarder); *parler à tort et à travers*, to talk at random; *ne parlez pas tant, agissez!*, don't talk so much, do something! ‖ **11.** FAM. *Tu parles!*, not half!; you bet!, you said it!; *tu parles d'une surprise!*, talk about a surprise!; *parlez-moi d'un bon gâteau!*, give me a good cake!
— v. tr. To speak (une langue). ‖ To talk; *parler affaires, raison*, to talk business, sense; *parler mode*, to chat about fashions.
— v. pr. **Se parler**, to be spoken (langue). ‖ To speak to oneself; *se parler à mi-voix*, to mutter to oneself.
— v. récipr. **Se parler**, to speak to each other (ou) to one another.
— m. Speech, way of speaking; *parler distingué*, elegant speech; *parler nasillard*, twang.
parleur [-lœːr] s. Talker, speaker. ‖ Transmitter (au téléphone).
parloir [-lwaːr] m. Parlour, visiting room.
parlote [-lɔt] f. FAM. Empty chatter.
parmentier [parmɑ̃tje] adj. CULIN. Parmentier, potato.
parmesan [parməzɑ̃] adj. GÉOGR. Parmesan.
— m. CULIN. Parmesan cheese.
parmi [parmi] prép. Among, amongst, amid, amidst.

Parnasse [parnaːs] m. GÉOGR. Parnassus. ‖ FIG. Poetry, Parnassian school of poetry.
parnassien, enne [-nasjɛ̃, ɛːn] adj. Parnassian.
parodie [parɔdi] f. Parody; travesty.
parodier [-dje] v. tr. (1). To parody, to burlesque.
parodique [-dik] adj. Parodic.
parodiste [-dist] s. Parodist.
paroi [parwa] f. Wainscot (boiserie); partition (cloison); side (côté). ‖ Wall (de rocher). ‖ MÉD., BOT. Wall. ‖ THÉÂTR. Flat (d'une scène).
paroisse [parwas] f. ECCLÉS. Parish church (église); parish (lieu); parishioners (paroissiens).
paroissial, ale [-sjal] adj. Parochial; *école paroissiale*, parish (ou) U. S. parochial school.
paroissien, enne [-sjɛ̃, ɛn] s. Parishioner. ‖ FAM. *Un drôle de paroissien*, a queer fish.
— m. ECCLÉS. Prayer-book (livre).
parole [parɔl] f. Word (mot); *homme sobre de paroles*, man of few words. ‖ Speech (faculté); *avoir le don de la parole*, to be a brilliant speaker; *perdre la parole*, to lose one's tongue; *rester sans paroles*, to be left speechless; *retrouver la parole*, to find one's tongue again. ‖ Word, saying (expression); *parole d'Evangile*, Gospel truth; *la parole d'un sage*, a sage's saying; *parole souvent citée*, oft-quoted maxim; *selon la parole du Christ*, according to Christ's words. ‖ Chance (ou) occasion to speak; *donner la parole à*, to call upon; *prendre la parole*, to speak, to say a few words; *retirer la parole à qqn*, to cut s.o. short; *vous avez la parole*, you may speak, it's your turn to speak. ‖ Word (promesse); *croire qqn sur parole*, to take s.o.'s word for it; *donner sa parole*, to give one's word; *être de parole*, to be as good as one's word; *il n'a qu'une parole*, his word is as good as his bond; *parole d'honneur!*, honour bright!, upon my word! ‖ Eloquence; *talent de parole*, oratorical powers. ‖ MILIT. *Prisonnier sur parole*, prisoner on parole. ‖ THÉÂTR. *Sans paroles*, without words (pièce). ‖ LOC. *Passer parole*, to pass (aux cartes).
— interj. Pass!, no bid! (aux cartes).
parolier, ère [-rɔlje, ɛːr] s. Lyricist, lyric writer.
paronyme [parɔnim] m. Paronym.
paronymie [-mi] f. Paronymy.
Paros [parɔs] m. GÉOGR. Paros; *de Paros*, Parian.
parotide [parɔtid] adj., f. MÉD. Parotid.
paroxysmal, ale [-mal] adj. Paroxysmal.
paroxysme [parɔksism] m. MÉD. Paroxysm; *atteindre son paroxysme*, to reach its highest point. ‖ FIG. Paroxysm, climax.
parpaillot [parpajo] m. FAM. Protestant.
parpaing [parpɛ̃] m. Breeze-block (en béton); parpen, through-stone (en pierre).
Parque [park] f. One of the three Fates.
parquer [parke] v. tr. (1). AGRIC. To pen (du bétail); to fold (des moutons). ‖ AUTOM. To park (des voitures). ‖ FAM. To coop up (des gens).
— v. intr. AGRIC. To be penned (bétail).
— v. pr. **Se parquer**, AUTOM., MILIT. To park.
parquet [parkɛ] m. Floor; *lame de parquet*, floor-plank. ‖ FIN. Ring (à la Bourse). ‖ JUR. Public Prosecutor's Office; *déposer une plainte au parquet*, to lodge a plaint with the Public Prosecutor. ‖ NAUT. Dunnage (de chargement); floor-plates (de chauffe); engine-room platform (de machine).
parquetage [parkətaːʒ] m. Making of floors (fabrication); laying of floors (pose).
parqueter [-te] v. tr. (8a). To floor.
parqueteur [-tœːr] s. Floor-maker (fabricant); floor-layer (ouvrier).
parrain [parɛ̃] m. ECCLÉS. Godfather; *être parrain de*, to stand godfather to. ‖ FIG. Sponsor (dans un club).
parrainage [parɛnaːʒ] m. Sponsorship.

parrainer [-ne] v. tr. (1). To sponsor.
parricide [parisid] m. Parricide (meurtre et meurtrier).
— adj. Parricidal.
parsec [parsεk] m. ASTRON. Parsec.
parsemer [parsəme] v. tr. (5). To spangle, to sprinkle, to strew (de, with). ‖ To besprinkle, to bestrew.
parsi [parsi] adj., s. Parsee.
part [pa:r] f. Share (portion); la meilleure part, the best of the bargain; la part du lion, the lion's share. ‖ Part (partie); sa fortune, pour la plus grande part, est en terres, the greater part of his fortune is in land. ‖ Concern (participation); avoir part à, to have a concern (ou) a hand in; avoir part au gâteau, to have a finger in the pie; prendre part à, to attend (une cérémonie); to join in (une conversation); to participate in (une joie); to become a party to (une querelle); pour ma part, as for me, as far as I am concerned. ‖ Announcement (communication); faire part de qqch. à qqn, to announce sth. to s.o., to let s.o. know of sth., to acquaint s.o. with sth., to inform s.o. of sth. ‖ Allowance (considération); faire la part de, to make allowance for; prendre en bonne, mauvaise part, to take in good, bad part. ‖ Behalf, part (intervention); de la part de, on behalf of, on the part of; c'est aimable de votre part, it's kind on your part (ou) of you; c'est étonnant de sa part, it's astounding coming from him. ‖ CULIN. Slice (de gâteau); helping (de nourriture). ‖ JUR. Portion (d'héritage). ‖ FIN. Share (de fondateur). ‖ LOC. A part, aside (de côté); separately (séparément); à part cela, except for that; autre part, elsewhere, somewhere else; d'autre part, moreover; de bonne part, from a good source; des deux parts, on both sides; d'une part... d'autre part, on the one hand... on the other hand; de toutes parts, from all sides, on all hands; de part et d'autre, on both sides, here and there; de part en part, through and through; nulle part, nowhere, not anywhere; quelque part, somewhere, anywhere.
partage [-ta:ʒ] m. Sharing, partition (répartition); distribution (d'un domaine); faire le partage de, to divide, to share out; il y a partage des voix, the votes are divided; ligne de partage des eaux, watershed, U. S. divide. ‖ Portion, share (part); échoir à qqn en partage, to fall to s.o's share; il m'a échu en partage de, it behoves me to, it has fallen to me to.
partagé, ée [-taʒe] adj. Requited (amour). ‖ Endowed, gifted, treated (personne); le plus mal partagé, the worst of the bargain. ‖ Divided; partagé entre la colère et l'émotion, half angry, half moved.
partageable [-taʒabl] adj. Dividable.
partageant, ante [-taʒɑ̃, ɑ̃:t] s. JUR. Sharer.
partager [-taʒe] v. tr. (7). To share out, to parcel out (des provisions); to share (un repas). ‖ To share (un blâme, un chagrin, un danger, un point de vue); partager les travaux de qqn, to have a share in s.o.'s work. ‖ To divide (diviser); ce problème a partagé les avis, opinions were divided on this problem.
— v. intr. To divide, to share; partager équitablement, to divide evenly.
— v. pron. Se partager, to come in two, to divide, to split (se diviser); to differ (différer); les avis se partageaient, opinions were divided. ‖ To fork (route).
partageur, euse [-taʒœ:r, ø:z] s. Sharer; one claiming a share; one ready to share.
partance [partɑ̃:s] f. NAUT. Departure; en partance pour, sailing for. ‖ CH. DE F. En partance pour Londres, London-bound.
partant, ante [-tɑ̃, ɑ̃:t] adj. Être partant pour,

to be all for (sth.), to be in favor of (sth.).
— m. Person departing. ‖ SPORTS. Starter.
partant [-tɑ̃] adv. Consequently.
partenaire [partənɛ:r] s. Partner.
parterre [partɛ:r] m. Flower-bed, parterre (de jardin). ‖ THÉÂTR. Pit.
Parthe [part] m. Parthian; flèche du Parthe, Parthian shot (ou) shaft.
parthénogenèse [partenɔʒənɛ:z] f. MÉD. Parthenogenesis.
parti [parti] m. Party (groupe); être du parti de, to stand by, to support. ‖ Gang (bande); un parti de brigands, a gang of robbers. ‖ Choice (choix); resolution (décision); parti pris, obstinate opinion; settled prejudice; de parti pris, deliberately, obstinately (v. PRÉJUGÉ); prendre parti, to come to a decision; prendre parti pour, to side with; prendre son parti de, to resign oneself to. ‖ Advantage (profit); tirer parti de, to make use of, to turn to account. ‖ Match, suit, catch, parti (pour mariage); un beau parti, a desirable match. ‖ Treatment; faire un mauvais parti à, to ill-treat.
parti adj. BLAS. Party.
parti, ie adj. Bien parti, well under way; mal parti, bungled at the outset, muddled from the start (affaire). ‖ FAM. Tipsy, far gone, U. S. high (paf).
partial, ale [parsjal] adj. Partial (envers, to); prejudiced, biased, one-sided.
partialement [-lmɑ̃] adv. Partially.
partialité [-lite] f. Partiality, bias, one-sidedness.
participant, ante [partisipɑ̃, ɑ̃:t] adj. Participating, participant.
— s. Participant, participator, partaker.
participation [-pasjɔ̃] f. Participation; avec ma participation, with my help; sans ma participation, without my having any hand in it. ‖ FIN. Participation aux bénéfices, profit-sharing.
participe [partisip] m. GRAMM. Participle.
participer [-pe] v. intr. (1). To participate, to have a hand (ou) a share (à, in); to be a party (à, to) [prendre part]. ‖ To partake (de, of) [tenir de]; le singe participe de la race humaine, the ape resembles man. ‖ FIN. Participer aux bénéfices, to share the profits.
participial, ale [-pjal] adj. GRAMM. Participial.
particularisation [partikylarizasjɔ̃] f. Particularization.
particulariser [-rize] v. tr. (1). To particularize (individualiser). ‖ To specify. (V. PRÉCISER.)
— v. pron. Se particulariser, to make oneself conspicuous, to distinguish oneself from others.
particularisme [-rism] m. Particularism.
particulariste [-rist] adj. Particularist.
particularité [-rite] f. Particularity. ‖ Peculiarity, characteristic.
particule [partiky:l] f. PHYS., GRAMM. Particle. ‖ FAM. Avoir la particule, to have a handle to one's name (fam.).
particulier, ère [partikylje, ε:r] adj. Particular, peculiar (spécial); cas particulier, special case; qqch. de particulier à signaler, sth. special to point out; particulier à, peculiar to; signes particuliers, unusual signs. ‖ Particular, peculiar (singulier); don particulier pour, marked gift for; nasillement particulier, peculiar twang. ‖ Peculiar, queer (étrange); il a toujours été particulier, he has always been peculiar. ‖ Private (privé); à titre particulier, in one's private capacity; cabinet particulier, private room; entrée particulière, private entrance; intérêt général et particulier, public and private interest.
— s. Private individual (ou) person; simple particulier, ordinary member of the public. ‖ FAM. Fellow : drôle de particulier, queer fish.
— m. Particular, detail (aspect). ‖ Private life (vie privée). ‖ LOC. En particulier, privately (d'homme à homme); particularly (spécialement).

particulièrement [-ljɛrmɑ̃] adv. Particularly. (V. SPÉCIALEMENT.) ‖ In detail, in full (en détail). ‖ Intimately (intimement).

partie [parti] f. Part (élément) ; *dans les autres parties de la France*, elsewhere in France ; *en grande partie*, largely ; *en partie*, in part ; *faire partie de*, to be a part of (une attribution) ; to be one of (une famille) ; to belong to (un groupe) ; to pertain to (un sujet) ; *faire partie intégrante de*, to be an integral part of, to be part and parcel of ; *la plus grande partie de*, most of, the bulk of ; *une partie de*, part of ; *tout ou partie*, wholly or partly ; *vendre un domaine par parties*, to sell an estate by lots. ‖ SPORTS. Game (au jeu) ; *partie de cartes, de football*, game of cards, of football ; *partie de chasse*, shooting party ; *partie de plaisir*, outing, picnic, trip. ‖ JUR. Party ; *les parties*, parties, litigants ; *hautes parties contractantes*, high contracting parties. ‖ COMM. Line of business, trade. ‖ FIN. Entry ; *comptabilité en partie double*, book-keeping by double entry, U. S. double-entry bookkeeping. ‖ MUS. Part ; *à trois parties*, three-part (chant). ‖ GRAMM. Part (du discours). ‖ LOC. *Avoir affaire à forte partie*, to have a strong opponent against one ; *avoir la partie belle*, to hold all the cards ; U. S. to have it made (fam.) ; *lier partie avec*, to join hands with, to enter into partnership with ; *prendre qqn à partie*, to join (ou) take issue with s.o.

partiel, elle [parsjɛl] adj. Partial. ‖ JUR. *Élection partielle*, by-election.
— m. Periodic class examination. ‖ MUS., PHYS. Partial tone, partial.

partiellement [-mɑ̃] adv. Partly, partially, in part.

partir [parti:r] v. tr. (2). † To divide ; *avoir maille à partir avec*, to have a bone to pick with.

partir v. intr. (93). To start (de, from ; pour, for) ; to set off, to go away, to depart, to leave (personne) ; *partir à bicyclette, à cheval, au galop, en auto, en avion, en bateau, en courant, en voiture*, to cycle away (ou) off, to ride away (ou) off, to gallop away (ou) off, to motor away (ou) off, to fly away (ou) off, to sail away (ou) off, to run away (ou) off, to drive away (ou) off ; *partir de chez soi pour*, to leave one's home for ; *partir en excursion, en voyage*, to go on a trip, on a journey ; *partir en promenade*, to go out for a walk ; *vous feriez bien de partir*, you ought to be off. ‖ To start, to leave (chose) ; *partir du centre du village*, to start from the centre of the village. ‖ To come off (se détacher) ; *le bouton est parti*, the button has come off. ‖ CULIN. To boil over (lait) ; to strike (allumettes). ‖ AGRIC. To come out (plante). ‖ CH. DE F. To start (train) ; *le train qui part pour Londres*, the London-bound train ; *voici le train qui part*, the train is moving off. ‖ FIG. *Partir d'un bon naturel*, to be good natured ; *partir pour une période prospère*, to be in for a period of prosperity ; *partir de zéro*, to start from scratch ; *le mot est parti malgré lui*, the word escaped him. ‖ **A partir de**, from ; *à partir d'aujourd'hui*, from today on (ou) onwards. ‖ **Faire partir**, to let off, to fire (un fusil) ; to fire, to set off (une mine) ; to start (un moteur) ; to turn away (qqn).

partisan [partizɑ̃] m. Partisan, follower, supporter (de, for). ‖ MILIT. *Guerre de partisans*, guerilla warfare. ‖ FIG. *Etre partisan de*, to be in favour of.
— adj. Party (querelle).

partitif, ive [partitif, i:v] adj. GRAMM. Partitive.

partition [-sjɔ̃] f. Partition. ‖ MUS. Score.

partout [partu] adv. Everywhere ; *partout ailleurs*, everywhere else ; *partout où*, wherever ; *de partout*, from all sides, from everywhere ; *un peu partout*, all over the place.

· **partouze** [partu:z] f. POP. Wild party, orgy, binge.

parturiente [partyrjɑ̃:t] f. MÉD. Parturient woman.

parturition [-risjɔ̃] f. MÉD. Parturition.

paru, parut [pary]. V. PARAÎTRE (74).

parure [pary:r] f. Adornment. (V. ATOUR, ORNEMENT.) ‖ Set (de diamants) ; string (de perles). ‖ Trimmings (en boucherie).

parution [parysjɔ̃] f. Publication.

parvenir [parvəni:r] v. intr. (101). To reach, to attain, to come to (atteindre) ; *parvenir aux oreilles de qqn*, to reach s.o.'s ears ; *parvenir au sommet*, to reach the summit. ‖ To succeed (à, in) ; *parvenir à ses fins*, to attain one's ends ; *sans y parvenir*, without succeeding. ‖ To reach (ou) to achieve success ; *l'art de parvenir*, the art of getting on.

parvenu [-ny] m. Upstart, parvenu ; *orgueilleux parvenu*, beggar on horseback.

parvis [parvi] m. ECCLÉS. Parvis (devant une église) ; court (devant un temple) ; *célestes parvis*, courts of heaven.

pas [pa] m. Step, pace ; *à deux pas de*, within two paces of ; *à deux pas d'ici*, a few steps (ou) paces from here ; *à deux pas devant soi*, two steps ahead ; *avancer, reculer d'un pas*, to take a step forward, backward. ‖ Step, walk, gait (démarche) ; *aller au pas*, to go at a walking pace ; *à pas de géant*, with gigantic strides, in seven-league boots ; *à pas comptés*, with measured steps ; *à pas légers*, lightly, quietly ; *à pas de loup*, stealthily, with stealthy tread ; *à petits pas*, with short steps ; *diriger ses pas vers*, to wend one's way (ou) to bend one's ·steps toward ; *d'un pas mal assuré*, with unsteady gait ; *faire un faux pas*, to stumble ; *faux pas*, trip, stumble ; *marcher à grands pas*, *pas de promenade*, to stride along, to stroll ; *pas à pas*, step by step. ‖ Step (marche d'escalier) ; *le pas de la porte*, the doorstep ; *sur le pas de la porte*, in the doorway. ‖ Step (de danse). ‖ GÉOGR. Pass, strait ; *le pas de Calais*, the Straits of Dover. ‖ COMM. *Pas de porte*, premium, key money. ‖ CINÉM. Gauge (de l'image). ‖ TECHN. *Pas de vis*, thread of screw. ‖ AVIAT. Twist (d'hélice). ‖ AUTOM. *Aller au pas*, to go dead slow, to crawl along. ‖ FIG. Step, move ; *arriver à grands pas*, to come on apace (vieillesse) ; *faire un faux pas*, to blunder ; *faire le premier pas*, to make the first move ; *faux pas*, false step ; *prendre le pas sur*, to take precedence over ; *sauter le pas*, to take the plunge. ‖ FAM. *Ça ne se trouve pas dans le pas d'une mule*, they don't grow on every tree ; *être dans un mauvais pas*, to be in a tight corner ; *mettre qqn au pas*, to make s.o. toe the line ; *tirer qqn d'un mauvais pas*, to get s.o. out of fix (ou) jam.

pas adv. Not ; *ce n'est pas le cas*, it's not the case ; *ce n'est pas que je l'aime*, not that I love him ; *ne pas le faire*, not to do it. ‖ Not, not any, no ; *pas belle*, plain ; *pas encore*, not yet ; *pas du tout* not at all ; *pas de sitôt*, not so soon as all that ; *peu ou pas*, little or not at all ; *pourquoi pas?*, why not ? ‖ Not ; *l'hiver, non pas l'été*, winter not summer ; *non pas !*, not so.

pascal, ale [paskal] (pl. **pascals ; pascaux** [pasko]) adj. Paschal ; *communion pascale* Easter communion.

pascalien, enne [paskaljɛ̃, ɛn] adj. Of (ou) relating to Blaise Pascal.

pasquinade [paskinad] f. Pasquinade.

passable [pɑsabl] adj. Passable, acceptable, middling, not so bad, so-so (fam.) ; *mention passable*, pass, U. S. passing mark (à un examen).

passablement [-bləmɑ̃] adv. Passably, fairly rather well, middling (fam.).

passade [pɑsad] f. FAM. Brief (ou) fleeting love affair. ‖ Whim (caprice). ‖ SPORTS. Passade.

passage [pasa:ʒ] m. Passage, way (action) ; *de passage*, travelling, migratory (oiseau) ; *passing* (visiteur) ; casual (voyageur) ; *droit de passage,* right of way (privilège) ; toll (taxe) ; *livrer passage à,* to make way for ; *se frayer un passage dans,* to elbow one's way through (la foule) ; to thrust one's way through (un fourré) ; *sur mon passage,* as I went by. ‖ Passing (époque) ; *lors de mon passage à,* on my passing through. ‖ Way, passage, path ; U. S. walkway (lieu) ; U. S. areaway (entre divers corps de bâtiments) ; arcade, archway (dans une rue) ; *passage clouté,* pedestrian (ou) zebra crossing, U. S. crosswalk ; *passage souterrain,* subway, U. S. underpass. ‖ Passage (prix) ; *le passage est moins cher par Calais,* the passage is cheaper by Calais. ‖ Passage, change (changement) [*à,* to ; *de,* from]. ‖ Passage, excerpt (fragment) ; *un passage d'une lettre,* a few lines of a letter. ‖ Mus. Piece (de musique). ‖ Naut. Crossing, passage (traversée) ; *passage de la ligne,* crossing the line ; *passage sur l'eau,* ferry (à travers un détroit, une rivière). ‖ Ch. de f. *Passage à niveau,* level (ou) U. S. grade crossing ; *passage au-dessus de la voie,* railway bridge ; U. S. overpass ; *passage au-dessous de la voie,* railway arch ; U. S. underpass. ‖ Comm. Call, visit (d'un commis voyageur).

passager, ère [-ʒe, ɛːr] adj. Passing (hôte). ‖ Passing, momentary, transient. ‖ Zool. Migratory (oiseau).
— s. Aviat., Ch. de f., Naut. Passenger.

passagèrement [-ʒɛrmɑ̃] adv. Momentarily, transiently, for a short time.

passant, ante [pɑsɑ̃, -ɑ̃ːt] adj. Busy, well-trodden, well-frequented (rue). ‖ Blas. Passant.
— s. Passer-by.

passation [pɑsasjɔ̃] f. Jur. Drawing up and signing (d'un acte). ‖ Fin. *Passation d'écriture,* making an entry.

passavant [pɑsavɑ̃] m. Naut. Waist.

passe [pɑːs] f. Period, spell ; *une passe de froid,* a spell of cold. ‖ Pass (d'escamoteur, de magnétiseur). ‖ Techn. Overplus ; U. S. surplus ; *exemplaires de passe,* overs (en typogr.). ‖ Sports. Thrust (à l'escrime) ; pass (au football) ; *passe d'armes,* passage of arms. ‖ Milit. *Mot de passe,* password. ‖ Naut. Pass ; *passe étroite,* narrows. ‖ Comm. *Passe de caisse,* allowance left to a cashier. ‖ Loc. *En passe de,* in a fair way to ; *en passe de disparaître,* threatened by extinction (race) ; *en mauvaise passe,* in a tight corner ; *maison de passe,* bawdy house, brothel, U. S. cat house (pop.). ‖ **Passe-bouillon,** m. invar. Culin. Soup-strainer. ‖ **Passe-déversoir,** m. Spill-way. ‖ **Passe-droit,** m. Undue favour, injustice. ‖ **Passe-lacet,** m. Blunt, bodkin. ‖ **Passe-lait,** m. invar. Culin. Milk-strainer. ‖ **Passe-montagne,** m. Balaclava helmet. ‖ **Passe-partout,** m. invar. Latch- (ou) master-key (clé) ; Théâtr. Film of universal appeal. ‖ **Passe-passe,** m. invar. Sleight-of-hand, legerdemain ; *tour de passe-passe,* conjuring trick (prestidigitation) ; fraud (ruse). ‖ **Passe-plats,** m. invar. Service hatch. ‖ **Passe-purée,** m. invar. Culin. Potato-masher. ‖ **Passe-temps,** m. invar. Pastime. (V. récréation.) ‖ **Passe-thé,** m. invar. Culin. Tea-strainer.
— m. Passkey, skeleton key, master-key, latch-key.

passé, ée [pɑse] adj. Past (écoulé) ; *dans les années passées,* in years gone by ; *six heures passées,* past six. ‖ Faded (fleur). ‖ Over, finished, gone (achevé) ; *le pire était passé,* the worst was over.
— m. Past ; *comme par le passé,* as in past times. ‖ Jur. *Passé chargé,* bad record. ‖ Gramm. Past, past tense. ‖ Loc. *Broderie au passé,* satin-stitch embroidery.
— prép. invar. After ; *passé midi,* after twelve. ‖ Beyond ; *passé les ponts,* beyond the bridges.

passée f. Sports. Slot (du cerf).

passéisme [paseism] m. Attachment to the past, backwardness.

passéiste [-ist] adj. Attached to the past, old-fashioned, backward.
— s. One attached to the past.

passement [pasmɑ̃] m. Braid, trimming.

passementer [-mɑ̃te] v. tr. (1). To trim.

passementerie [-mɑ̃tri] f. Passementerie ; braid, trimmings.

passementier, ère [-mɑ̃tje, mɑ̃tjɛːr] s. Dealer in passementerie.

passepoil [-pwal] m. Piping.

passepoilé, ée [-pwale] adj. Piped, trimmed with piping.

passeport [paspɔr] m. Passport.

passer [pɑse] v. intr. (1).

---

1. Sens général. — 2. Changer de local. — 3. Se rendre. — 4. Visiter. — 5. Dépasser. — 6. Filtrer. — 7. Déteindre. — 8. Etre transmis. — 9. Disparaître. — 10. Fuir. — 11. Continuer. — 12. Omettre. — 13. Devenir. — 14. Aviat. — 15. Ch. de f. — 16. Autom. — 17. Jur. — 18. Milit. — 19. Méd. — 20. Passer par. — 21. Passer pour. — 22. Passer sur. — 23. En passant. — 24. Loc.

---

1. To pass (en général) ; *passer devant chez qqn,* to pass s.o.'s house ; *passer dans sa chambre,* to get into one's room ; *passer par la porte de derrière,* to go through the back door ; *passer en trombe,* to flash by ; *faire passer qqch. à,* to pass sth. on to ; *faire passer qqn par un endroit,* to take s.o. through a place ; *faire passer un pont sur la vallée,* to build a bridge over the valley ; *laisser passer,* to miss (une occasion) ; *laisser passer qqn,* to let s.o. pass ; *l'odeur a passé dans toute la maison,* the smell spread throughout the house ; *la route passe par le col,* the road goes over the mountain-pass. ‖ 2. To pass, to adjourn (changer de local) ; *passer au salon,* to adjourn to the drawing-room ; *passer au tableau,* to be sent to the blackboard ; *passer dans la classe au-dessus,* to be moved up. ‖ 3. To pass, to go (se rendre) ; *passer au guichet,* to go to the ticket-window. ‖ 4. To call (visiter) ; *passer voir qqn,* to call on s.o. ; *ne faire que passer,* just to drop in ; *le facteur passe à neuf heures,* the postman comes at nine. ‖ 5. To stick out (dépasser) ; *la queue du canard lui passe par la poche,* the tail of the duck is sticking out of his pocket. ‖ 6. To go through (filtrer) ; *passer par le tamis,* to go through the strainer. ‖ 7. To fade (déteindre) ; *le bleu passe vite,* blue fades quickly. ‖ 8. To be transmitted (être transmis) ; *la responsabilité passa au fils,* the responsibility was transferred to the son. ‖ 9. To disappear (disparaître) ; *tout chagrin passe,* all griefs abate in time ; *tout succès passe,* all success wears off. ‖ 10. To elapse (fuir) ; *faire passer le temps,* to while away the time ; *laisser passer le temps,* to let time go by ; *un siècle a passé,* a century has gone (ou) elapsed. ‖ 11. To pass on (continuer) ; *passer à la postérité,* to have one's name handed down to posterity. ‖ 12. To omit (omettre) ; *j'en passe,* I am skipping over many items. ‖ To pass (aux cartes). ‖ 13. To become (devenir) ; *cela a passé en proverbe,* it has become proverbial ; *passé maître en,* past master in ; *passé lieutenant,* promoted lieutenant. ‖ 14. Aviat. To fly (sur, over). ‖ 15. Ch. de f. *Passer près de la rivière,* to run along the river (train). ‖ 16. Autom. *Passer en seconde,* to change into second gear. ‖ 17. Jur. To go through the customs (à la douane) ; *la question passa à la chambre,* the question was brought up in the House. ‖ 18. Milit. To switch over to (à l'offensive). ‖ 19.

MÉD. To go down (nourriture); to pass away, to breathe one's last, to die (personne); *faire passer*, to get rid of, to cure (une maladie). ‖ **20. Passer par**, to go through; *j'ai passé par là*, I have been (ou) gone through it. ‖ **21. Passer pour**, to seem, to be looked upon as; *passer pour hanté*, to be supposed to be haunted; *passer pour vrai*, to be held to be true; *se faire passer pour*, to give oneself out for. ‖ **22. Passer sur**, to overlook, to let go by. ‖ **23. En passant**, by the way; once in a while; casually, in passing, incidentally. ‖ **24.** Loc. *Passons!* Let us not mention it any more; *passé au bleu*, cancelled; *faire passer le goût du pain à*, to do away with; *tout le monde y passe*, it's the common lot.
— v. tr. (1).

---

1. Traverser. — 2. Dépasser. — 3. Transmettre. — 4. Introduire. — 5. Glisser. — 6. Revêtir. — 7. Colorier. — 8. Omettre. — 9. Laisser écouler. — 10. Ne pas tenir compte. — 11. Déverser. — 12. Jur. — 13. Culin. — 14. Comm. — 15. Ciném. — 16. Méd. — 17. Milit. — 18. Fig.

---

1. To pass, to cross, to traverse (une place, une rue); to cross, to go over (un pont); *passer un cours d'eau en bac*, to be ferried across a stream; *passer une rivière à la nage*, to swim across a river; *passer un précipice en téléphérique*, to cross a ravine by aerial cable; *passer un ravin en ski*, to ski across a gully. ‖ 2. To go past (dépasser); *passer le poteau*, to go past the post; *passer les bornes*, to pass the limit. ‖ 3. To hand (transmettre); *passer son affaire à*, to hand over one's affairs to; *passer les fruits à qqn*, to hand the fruit to s.o. ‖ 4. To pass (introduire); *passer des cigarettes en fraude*, to smuggle in cigarettes; *passer un dollar faux*, to pass a counterfeit dollar. ‖ 5. To pass (glisser); *passer un lacet dans un œillet*, to slip a lace through an eyelet; *passer la tête à la fenêtre*, to stick one's head out of the window. ‖ 6. To put on (revêtir); *passer son pardessus*, to put on one's overcoat. ‖ 7. To stain (colorier); *passer au brun*, to stain brown. ‖ 8. To leave out, to skip (omettre); *passer sous silence*, to leave unmentioned. ‖ 9. To spend (laisser écouler); *passer l'été à la montagne*, to spend the summer in the mountains; *passer son temps à ne rien faire*, to idle one's time away. ‖ 10. To overlook, to ignore (ne pas tenir compte de); *passer une fantaisie à qqn*, to indulge s.o.'s fancy; *passer une faute à qqn*, to ignore s.o.'s misdeed; *son père ne lui passe rien*, his father doesn't let him get by with anything. ‖ To take, to sit for, to go up for (un examen); *passer avec succès*, to pass. ‖ 11. To vent (déverser); *passer sa mauvaise humeur sur*, to vent one's ill humour on. ‖ 12. Jur. To draw up (un acte). ‖ 13. Culin. To strain (filtrer) [v. TAMISER]; *passer au four*, to bake. ‖ 14. Comm. To place (une commande); *passer à profits et pertes*, to post to the profit and loss account. ‖ 15. Ciném. To show (un film). ‖ 16. Méd. *Passer la nuit auprès d'un malade*, to stay up all night with a sick man; *il ne passera pas la nuit*, he will not live out the night (malade). ‖ 17. Milit. *Passer à l'ennemi*, to go over to the enemy. ‖ 18. Fig. *Passer au crible*, to sift.
— v. pr. Se **passer**, to pass, to be spent (temps). ‖ To happen (arriver); *que se passe-t-il?*, what is going on?, what's up?; *que s'est-il passé à la conférence?*, what happened at the conference? ; *tout s'est bien passé*, all went off smoothly. ‖ To take place (avoir lieu); *où la noce s'est-elle passée?*, where did the wedding take place? ‖ To pass away, to cease (cesser); *cela ne se passera pas ainsi*, things will not rest at that. ‖ To

subside, to abate (s'apaiser); *sa colère se passera*, his anger will subside. ‖ **Se passer de**, to do without; to dispense with; *se passer de l'appui de qqn*, to dispense with s.o.'s help; *se passer de fumer*, to do without smoking.

passereau [pasro] m. Zool. Sparrow.
passerelle [pasrɛl] f. Foot-bridge; overpass. ‖ Naut. Bridge (de commandement); gangway (d'embarquement); compass-platform (de navigation); *passerelle volante*, flying bridge. ‖ Jur. Cross-channel (communication administrative).
passeur [pasœ:r] m. Naut. Ferryman.
passibilité [pasibilite] f. Liability (de, to).
passible [pasi:bl] adj. Liable, subject (de, to).
passif, ive [pasif, i:v] adj. Passive. ‖ Milit. *Défense passive*, air-raid precautions, civil defence; *poste de défense passive*, warden's post. ‖ Gramm. Passive. ‖ Fin. *Dettes passives*, liabilities.
— m. Gramm. Passive voice. ‖ Fin. Liabilities.
passiflore [pasiflɔ:r] f. Bot. Passiflora, passion-flower.
passion [pasjɔ̃] f. Passion; *aimer à la passion*, to be passionately in love; *passion du jeu*, passion for gambling. ‖ Love (amour). ‖ Ecclés. Passion; *la semaine de la Passion*, Holy Week, Passiontide.
passionnant, ante [pasjɔnɑ̃, ɑ̃:t] adj. Thrilling, exciting (livre, spectacle); absorbing, fascinating (travail).
passionné, ée [-ne] adj. Passionate, impassioned (pour, for); enthusiastic (de, about); *passionné de théâtre*, stage-struck. ‖ Passionate, impassioned, fiery (sentiment).
— s. Enthusiast; fan (fam.).
passionnel, elle [-nɛl] adj. Pertaining to the passions; *crime passionnel*, crime of jealousy, love tragedy.
passionnément [-nemɑ̃] adv. Passionately.
passionner [-ne] v. tr. (1). To impassion, to rouse the passions of, to excite (ou) work up to a fervour (enflammer). ‖ To captivate; to intrigue.
— v. pr. Se **passionner**, to get enthusiastic (pour, over); to get passionately fond (pour, of).
passivement [pasivmɑ̃] adv. Passively.
passivité [-vite] f. Passivity.
passoire [paswa:r] f. Strainer; colander.
pastel [pastɛl] m. Arts. Pastel, crayon; *bleu pastel*, pastel blue. ‖ Bot. Woad, dyer's woad.
pastelliste [-list] s. Arts. Pastellist.
pastèque [pastɛk] f. Bot. Water-melon.
pasteur [pastœ:r] m. Shepherd. ‖ Ecclés. Pastor; Protestant minister.
— adj. Pastoral.
pasteurisation [pastœrizasjɔ̃] f. Pasteurization.
pasteuriser [-rize] v. tr. (1). To pasteurize.
pastiche [pɑstiʃ] m. Pastiche. (V. IMITATION.)
pasticher [-ʃe] v. tr. (1). To imitate.
pasticheur, euse [-ʃœ:r, ø:z] s. Imitator, parodist.
pastille [pasti:j] f. Lozenge, jujube; *pastille de menthe*, peppermint. ‖ Méd. Pastille, pellet.
pastis [pastis] m. Pastis, aniseed aperitif. ‖ Fam. Muddle, mess.
pastoral, ale [pastɔral] adj. Pastoral.
pastorale [-ra:l] f. Pastoral play (ou) poem.
pastorat [-ra] m. Pastorate.
pastoureau [pasturo] m. Shepherd-boy.
pastourelle [-rel] f. Shepherd-girl. ‖ Dance-figure.
pat [pat] adj. Stalemated (aux échecs).
— m. Stalemate; *faire pat*, to stalemate.
patache [pataʃ] f. Naut. Water-police boat; revenue cutter (de la douane). ‖ Carrier's cart. ‖ Fam. Rickety cart, ramshackle conveyance.
patachon [-ʃɔ̃] m. Fam. *Mener une vie de patachon*, to lead a wild life.
pataphysique [patafizik] f. Pataphysics (word coined by Alfred Jarry), science of imaginary solutions.

patapouf [patapuf] s. Fattie, dump, humpty-dumpty (personne). ‖ Cropper (chute); *faire patapouf*, to fall down flop.
pataquès [patakɛːs] m. Mistake in pronunciation.
patata [patata] interj. *Et patati et patata!*, and so on, and all the rest of it.
patate [patat] f. Bot. Sweet potato. ‖ Fam. Spud.
patatras! [patatra] interj. Crash; *et patatras!*; down it came!
pataud [pato] m. Broad-pawed dog (chien); clumsy clot (personne).
— adj. Clumsy. (V. GAUCHE, LOURDAUD.)
pataugeage [patoʒaːʒ] m. Floundering, wallowing (dans l'eau). ‖ Fig. Floundering, muddling.
patauger [-ʒe] v. intr. (7). To flounder, to wallow (dans l'eau). ‖ Fig. To flounder, to stumble.
pataugeur, euse [-ʒœːr, øːz] s. Flounderer.
patchouli [patʃuli] m. Patchouli.
patchwork [patʃwœrk] m. Patchwork; *couverture en patchwork*, quilt.
pâte [pɑːt] f. Pulp (à papier). ‖ CULIN. Paste; *pâte d'anchois*, anchovy paste; *pâte à gâteaux, à pain*, pastry, dough; *pâte à frire*, batter; *pâtes alimentaires*, fancy pastes, macaroni, noodles, spaghetti. ‖ ARTS. *En pleine pâte*, with a full brush. ‖ Loc. *Une bonne pâte*, a good soul; *mettre la main à la pâte*, to lend a hand.
pâté [pɑte] m. Blot (d'encre). ‖ Block (de maisons). ‖ Sand-pie (de sable). ‖ CULIN. Pie, U.S. pâté. ‖ NAUT. Reef.
pâtée f. Dog food (du chien). ‖ Chicken feed, mash (des volailles).
patelin [patlɛ̃] adj. Fawning (manières, ton); soft-spoken, wheedling (personne).
— m. Wheedler.
patelin m. FAM. Native town (or) village. ‖ Small town (or) village.
pateliner [patline] v. intr. (1). To wheedle; to blarney.
— v. tr. To cajole, to wheedle.
patelle [patɛl] f. ZOOL. Limpet.
patène [patɛn] f. ECCLÉS. Paten.
patenôtre [patnoːtr] f. Paternoster. ‖ ARCHIT. Bead moulding.
patent, ente [patɑ̃, ɑ̃ːt] adj. Patent.
patentable [patɑ̃tabl] adj. Requiring a licence.
patente [patɑ̃ːt] f. COMM. Licence (document); licence tax (frais). ‖ NAUT. Bill (de santé).
patenté, ée [patɑ̃te] adj. Licensed.
— s. Licensee.
patenter v. tr. (1). To license.
Pater [patɛːr] m. ECCLÉS. Lord's Prayer.
patère [patɛːr] f. Hat-peg.
paternalisme [patɛrnalism] m. Paternalism.
paternaliste [-list] adj. Paternalistic.
— s. Paternalist.
paterne [patɛrn] adj. Placidly benevolent.
paternel, elle [-nɛl] adj. Paternal; *du côté paternel*, on the father's side. ‖ Fatherly, kindly.
— m. FAM. *Le paternel*, the governor, the pater, the old man.
paternellement [-nɛlmɑ̃] adv. Paternally.
paternité [-nite] f. Paternity, fatherhood; *recherche de la paternité*, research into paternity, action for affiliation. ‖Fig. *Attribuer la paternité d'un livre à*, to father a book on.
pâteux, euse [pɑtø, øːz] adj. Pasty. ‖ ARTS. Woolly (peinture). ‖ MÉD. Coated (langue). ‖ FIG. Thick (voix).
pathétique [patetik] adj. Pathetic, moving, touching. ‖ ANAT. Pathetic (muscle).
— m. Pathos.
pathétiquement [-mɑ̃] adv. Pathetically.
pathogène [patoʒɛn] adj. MÉD. Pathogenic.
pathogénie [-ʒeni] f. MÉD. Pathogeny.
pathologie [-loʒi] f. MÉD. Pathology.
pathologique [-loʒik] adj. MÉD. Pathological.

pathologiquement [-loʒikmɑ̃] adv. MÉD. Pathologically.
pathologiste [-loʒist] s. MÉD. Pathologist.
pathos [patos] m. Bathos, confused style.
patibulaire [patibylɛːr] adj. Gallows (mine).
patiemment [pasjamɑ̃] adv. Patiently.
patience [pasjɑ̃ːs] f. Patience (endurance); *prendre son mal en patience*, to bear one's grief patiently. ‖ Patience, forbearance, composure; *souffrir avec patience*, to bear and forbear. ‖ Constancy (persévérance). ‖ Jig-saw puzzle (jeu); patience (aux cartes). ‖ MILIT. Button-stick.
patience f. BOT. Patience (ou) spinach-dock.
patient, ente [-sjɑ̃, ɑ̃ːt] adj. Patient, enduring, long-suffering (endurant). ‖ Patient, forbearing, composed (calme).
— s. † Tortured criminal. ‖ MÉD. Patient.
patienter [-sjɑ̃te] v. intr. (1). To take (ou) have patience; to wait patiently.
patin [patɛ̃] m. Skate; *patins à roulettes*, roller-skates. ‖ Runner (de traîneau). ‖ TECHN. Shoe, brake-block (de frein). ‖ AVIAT. Skid. ‖ CH. DE F. Foot, flange (de rail).
patinage [patinaːʒ] m. SPORTS. Skating; *patinage à la voile*, ice sailing. ‖ Skidding, slipping (glissement).
patinage m. Patination (d'un meuble, d'un tableau).
patine [patin] f. Patina. ‖ FIG. *La patine du temps*, weathering.
patiné, ée [patine] adj. Weathered (meuble).
patiner v. tr. (1). To patine, to give a patina to.
patiner v. intr. (1). To skate. ‖ To skid, to slip (roue); to slip (courroie).
patinette [-nɛt] f. Scooter (jouet).
patineur, euse [-tinœːr, øːz] s. Skater.
patinoire [-nwaːr] f. Skating-rink.
patio [patjo] m. Patio.
pâtir [pɑtiːr] v. intr. (2). To suffer (de, from). ‖ To be impaired, to sustain loss; *vous en pâtirez*, you will rue it.
pâtisser [pɑtise] v. tr. (1). CULIN. To knead.
— v. intr. CULIN. To make pastry
pâtisserie [-sri] f. CULIN. Pastry. ‖ Cakes (gâteaux). ‖ Pastry-making (action); pastry-shop (magasin); pastry-cook's business (métier).
pâtissier, ère [-sje, ɛːr] s. Pastry-cook; owner of a pastry-shop.
patois [patwa] m. Dialect. ‖ Jargon, lingo.
patoisant, ante [-zɑ̃, ɑ̃ːt] adj. Dialect speaking (personne); full of dialectal expressions (style).
— s. Dialect speaker.
patoiser [-ze] v. intr. (1). To speak in dialect.
patouiller [patuje] v. intr. (1). FAM. To splash, to flounder.
patraque [patrak] adj. FAM. Worn out (machine); unwell, sickly, shaky (personne).
pâtre [pɑːtr] m. Shepherd. (V. BERGER.)
patriarcal, ale [patriarkal] adj. Patriarchal.
patriarcat [-ka] m. Patriarchate.
patriarche [patriarʃ] m. Patriarch.
patricien, enne [-sjɛ̃, ɛn] s. Patrician.
patrie [patri] f. Country, native land (ou) country, fatherland, home country; birth-place.
patrilinéaire [patrilineɛːr] adj. Patrilineal.
patrilocal, ale [-lokal] adj. Patrilocal.
patrimoine [patrimwan] m. Patrimony.
patrimonial, ale [-monjal] adj. Patrimonial.
patriotard, arde [patrijota:r, ard] adj. Chauvinistic, jingoist, jingoistic.
— s. Chauvinist, jingoist.
patriote [patriot] adj. Patriotic.
— s. Patriot.
patriotique [-tik] adj. Patriotic.
patriotiquement [-tikmɑ̃] adv. Patriotically.
patriotisme [-tism] m. Patriotism.
patristique [patristik] adj. ECCLÉS. Patristic.
— s. Patristics.

patron [patrɔ̃] m. Pattern; *patron de robe,* model-pattern. ‖ Template (en mécanique).
patron s. Patron. (V. PROTECTEUR.) ‖ Employer; boss (fam.) [d'une entreprise]. ‖ Proprietor, landlord (d'un hôtel). ‖ NAUT. Skipper, master; coxswain. ‖ ECCLÉS. Patron saint.
patronage [patrɔna:ʒ] m. Patronage, support. ‖ ECCLÉS. Young men's club.
patronal, ale [-nal] adj. Patronal; *fête patronale,* patronal feast, patron saint's day; *syndicat patronal,* employers' union.
patronat [-na] m. † Patronate. ‖ Body of employers; *le patronat et le salariat,* employers and employed.
patronne [patrɔn] f. Patroness (protectrice). ‖ Proprietress, landlady (d'un hôtel).
patronner [-ne] v. tr. (1). To patronize (une œuvre); to sponsor (une personne). [V. SOUTENIR.]
patronnesse [-nɛs] adj. f. Patroness; *dame patronnesse,* patroness.
patronyme [patrɔnim] m. Patronymic, surname.
patronymique [-mik] adj. Patronymic.
patrouille [patru:j] f. MILIT. Patrol; *activités de patrouille,* patrol activities. ‖ AVIAT. Section.
patrouiller [patruje] v. intr. (1). MILIT. To patrol; *patrouiller sur la ligne,* to patrol the line.
patrouilleur [-jœ:r] m. MILIT. Soldier on patrol. ‖ NAUT. Patrol vessel.

patte [pat] f. Paw (de chien, de félin); leg, foot (d'insecte, d'oiseau, de quadrupède); *pattes de derrière, de devant,* hindlegs, forelegs; *à quatre pattes,* four-footed (animal). ‖ Strap (d'épaulette); flap (de vêtement). ‖ *Pattes de mouches,* scrawl (écriture). ‖ FAM. Leg (de personnes); *marcher à quatre pattes,* to walk on all fours; *s'il me tombe sous la patte!,* if I catch him!, if I come across him!; *y aller à pattes,* to foot it, to leg it. ‖ **Patte-d'oie,** f. Crow's foot (d'antenne, de visage); crossroads (de route).
pattemouille [patmu:j] f. Damp cloth for ironing.
pattern [patərn] m. Pattern (schème).
pattu, ue [paty] adj. Large-pawed (chien); feather-legged (pigeon).
pâturage [patyra:ʒ] m. Pasture, grazing-ground (v. PACAGE). ‖ Grazing, pasturage (droit).
pâture [pɑty:r] f. Pasture, fodder (v. HERBAGE); food (v. NOURRITURE). ‖ Pasturage (droit); *droit de vaine pâture,* right of common pasturage. ‖ FIG. Pabulum, nourishment (de l'esprit).
pâturer [-re] v. intr., tr. (1). To pasture, to graze.
paturon [patyrɔ̃] m. ZOOL. Pastern.
paume [po:m] f. Palm (de la main). ‖ Hand (mesure). ‖ SPORTS. Tennis (jeu).
paumé, ée [pome] adj. FAM. Mixed up (perplexe), lost, at sea (perdu); *être paumé,* to be out of it (être désemparé); *un coin paumé,* a godforsaken place; *un type paumé,* a misfit.
— s. Misfit.
paumelle [pomɛl] f. Palm (de cordier, de sellier); grainer (de corroyeur). ‖ Hinge (penture).
paumer v. tr. (1). POP. To lose.
— v. pr. **Se paumer,** FAM. To get lost, to go the wrong way.
paupérisation [poperizasjɔ̃] f. Pauperization.
paupériser [-ze] v. tr. (1). To pauperize.
— v. pr. **Se paupériser,** to become pauperized.
paupérisme [poperism] m. Pauperism.
paupière [popjɛ:r] f. Eyelid, lid.
paupiette [popjɛt] f. CULIN. Olive, U. S. bird.
pause [po:z] f. Pause, stop; *faire une pause,* to stop. ‖ MUS. Pause, rest. ‖ SPORTS. Half-time (au football). ‖ **Pause café,** f. U. S. Coffee-break.
pauser [poze] v. intr. (1). MUS. To pause. ‖ FAM. To wait (attendre).
pauvre [po:vr] adj. Poor, poverty-stricken, hardup (v. BESOGNEUX, INDIGENT); *les classes pauvres,* the poorer classes. ‖ Poor (v. PIÈTRE); *pauvres chances de succès,* poor (ou) slight chance of success; *pauvre chère,* meagre fare; *pauvre mobilier,* rickety furniture; *pauvre raison,* paltry reason; *pauvre type,* failure; *gaz pauvre,* producer-gas; *matière pauvre,* meagre matter; *style pauvre,* bald style. ‖ Unfortunate, poor (malheureux); *le pauvre homme!,* unfortunate (ou) poor man! ‖ Regretted, poor (défunt); *mon pauvre ami,* my regretted (ou) poor friend. ‖ LOC. *Pauvre de moi!,* poor me!
— m. Poor person (indigent). ‖ Pauper (assisté). ‖ Beggar (mendiant).
pauvrement [-vrəmɑ̃] adv. Poorly. ‖ Feebly (éclairé); barely (meublé); meanly (nourri); scantily (payé); shabbily (vêtu).
pauvresse [-vrɛ:s] f. Poor woman.
pauvret [-vrɛ] s. Poor little thing.
pauvreté [-vrəte] f. Poverty, destitution. (V. BESOIN, INDIGENCE.) ‖ Beggary (mendicité). ‖ Humbleness (d'une maison); shabbiness (du mobilier, des vêtements). ‖ FIG. Poorness, banality (d'un argument, d'une raison); barrenness (du langage); poverty (du style).
pavage [pava:ʒ] m. Paving (action); pavement (ouvrage).
pavane [pavan] f. Pavane (danse).
pavaner (se) [səpavane] v. pr. (1). To strut, to peacock it, to peacock.
pavé [pave] m. Paving-stone (pierre). ‖ Pavement (empierrement); *pavé de bois,* wood pavement. ‖ The streets (rues); *battre le pavé,* to pound the pavement (en quête de travail); *jeter sur le pavé,* to throw out on to the streets. ‖ CULIN. Slab of pain d'épice). ‖ FIG. *Le pavé de l'ours,* ill-timed support; *tenir le haut du pavé,* to travel in the best company; U. S. to be one of the upper crust.
pavement [-vmɑ̃] m. Ornate pavement.
paver [-ve] v. tr. (1). To pave. ‖ FIG. *Pavé de bonnes intentions,* paved with good intentions.
paveur [-œ:r] m. Paviour.
pavillon [pavijɔ̃] m. Villa, lodge; pavilion; *pavillon de chasse,* shooting-box; *pavillon de jardin,* summer-house. ‖ Canopy (de lit). ‖ MÉD. Quarters (d'hôpital); external ear (oreille). ‖ MUS. Horn (de phonographe); bell (de trompette). ‖ TECHN. Mouth-piece (de téléphone); *pavillon d'écouteur,* ear-piece. ‖ NAUT. Flag; *pavillon de beaupré,* jack. ‖ BLAS. Pavilion. ‖ LOC. *Baisser pavillon devant,* to knuckle under to; *le pavillon couvre la marchandise,* the flag covers the goods.
pavillonnaire [-jɔnɛ:r] adj. *Banlieue pavillonnaire,* suburb characterized by private housing, suburbia; *hôtel pavillonnaire,* hotel with chalets.
pavlovien, enne [pavlɔvjɛ̃, ɛn] adj. Pavlovian.
pavois [pavwa] m. Shield. ‖ NAUT. Bulwark; flags. ‖ FIG. *Elever sur le pavois,* to extol.
pavoisement [-zmɑ̃] m. Decking with flags (d'un monument). ‖ NAUT. Dressing ship.
pavoiser [-ze] v. tr. (1). To deck with flags (un monument); *rue pavoisée,* beflagged street. ‖ NAUT. To dress (le vaisseau).
— v. intr. To dress the house (ou) monument with flags. ‖ NAUT. To dress ship.
pavot [pavo] m. BOT. Poppy.
payable [pɛjabl] adj. Payable.
payant, ante [-jɑ̃, ɑ̃:t] adj. Paying; *élève payant,* paying pupil; *travail payant,* work that pays.
paye [pɛ:j] f. Wages (d'ouvrier); *faire la paye,* to pay out the wages; *jour de paye,* pay-day. ‖ MILIT., NAUT. Pay.
payement, paiement [pɛmɑ̃] m. Payment.
payer [pɛje] v. tr. (9 b). To pay (qqn) [de, for]; *payer qqn de ses services,* to reward s.o. for his services; *trop payé,* overpaid; *trop peu payé,* underpaid. ‖ To pay (qqn) [de, with]; *payer qqn*

de la même monnaie, to pay s.o. back in his own coin. ‖ To pay (qqch.) ; *payer l'arriéré*, to pay up the arrears ; *payer une dette, une note*, to settle a debt, a bill ; *réponse payée*, answer prepaid. ‖ To pay (une somme) [*pour, for*] ; *payer qqch. cent francs*, to pay a hundred francs for sth. ; *voiture pas entièrement payée*, car not yet fully paid for ; *c'est payé cher*, it's high-priced. ‖ **Faire payer**, to charge ; *faire payer les riches*, to soak the rich ; *faire payer trop cher*, to charge too much for ; *se faire payer à dîner par*, to get a dinner out of ; U. S. to bum a dinner off (fam.). ‖ FIG. *Victoire chèrement payée*, dearly bought victory. ‖ FAM. *C'était à payer sa place*, it was worth paying a good price for it ; *vous me le paierez!*, you shall pay for it !

— v. intr. To pay ; *avoir de quoi payer*, to have the wherewithal to pay. ‖ FIG. *Payer pour les autres*, to pay for the misdeeds of others ; *payer de sa personne*, to incur risks, not to spare oneself ; *l'honnêteté ne paie pas*, honesty doesn't pay. ‖ FAM. *Payer pour savoir qqch.*, to learn sth. at a cost.

— v. pr. **Se payer**, to be paid (somme) ; *cela ne peut se payer en argent*, that cannot be paid for with money. ‖ To pay oneself (*sur*, out of) [se rembourser]. ‖ FIG. *Se payer de mots*, to dazzle people with words. ‖ FAM. *Se payer la tête de qqn*, to pull s.o.'s leg, to take (ou) U. S. to get a rise out of s.o. ; *s'en payer*, to have a good time.

payeur [-jœ:r] m. Payer. ‖ MILIT., NAUT. Paymaster.
— adj. Disbursing.

pays [pei] m. Land, country ; *pays chauds*, hot countries. ‖ Country, nation ; *pays de l'union postale universelle*, country in the Universal Postal Union. ‖ Country, native land (patrie) ; *avoir le mal du pays*, to be homesick ; *retourner dans son pays*, to go back home. ‖ Region ; *produits du pays*, home-grown produce. ‖ LOC. *Etre de son pays*, to come straight from one's village ; *être en pays de connaissance*, to be among friends, to feel at home. ‖ **Pays-Bas**, m. pl. GÉOGR. Netherlands, Low Countries.

pays [pei] m. FAM. Fellow-countryman.

paysage [peiza:ʒ] m. Landscape, scenery. ‖ FAM. Landscape painting.

paysagiste [-ʒist] s. AGRIC. *Jardinier paysagiste*, landscape gardener. ‖ ARTS. Landscape painter.

paysan, anne [peizɑ̃, an] adj. Peasant, country, rural (vie, mœurs) ; rustic (air, manières).
— m. Peasant, countryman.

paysannat [-zana] m. Peasantry.

paysanne [-zan] f. Peasant woman, countrywoman.

paysannerie [-zanri] f. Peasantry. ‖ Rustic manners.

payse [peiz] f. FAM. Fellow-countrywoman.

P. C. [pese] m. Abrév. de *parti communiste*, CP, communist party. ‖ MILIT. Abrév. de *poste de commandement*, command post.

P. C. C. [pesese] abrév. de *pour copie conforme*, certified accurate.

P. C. V. [peseve] m. Abrév. de *à Per Ce Voir*, reverse-charge (ou U. S.) collect call ; *téléphoner en P. C. V.*, to make a reverse-charge call, U. S. to call collect.

P.-D. G. [pedeʒe] m. inv. Abrév. de *président-directeur général*, chairman and managing director.

péage [pea:ʒ] m. Toll. ‖ NAUT. Wharfage.

peau [po] f. Skin (d'homme) ; *n'avoir que la peau et les os*, to be nothing but skin and bones ; *par la peau du cou*, by the scruff of the neck. ‖ Skin (d'animal) ; hide (de cheval, de vache) ; *peau brute*, undressed skin ; *peau de chamois*, chamois-leather. ‖ Fur. (V. FOURRURE.) ‖ COMM. *Peau*

d'ange, angel skin (tissu). ‖ BOT. Peel, skin (d'orange, de pommes). ‖ MUS. Head (de tambour). ‖ MÉD. *Maladie de peau*, skin disease. (V. MEMBRANE, TAIE.) ‖ CULIN. Skin, film, coating (sur le lait, un liquide). ‖ THÉÂTR. *Entrer dans la peau d'un personnage*, to get right inside a part. ‖ FAM. *J'aurai sa peau*, I'll get him ; *risquer sa peau*, to risk one's life ; *sauver sa peau*, to save one's skin (ou) bacon ; *tenir à sa peau*, to value one's skin. ‖ POP. Tart, bag (femme). ‖ FAM. *Il l'a dans la peau*, he's got her under his skin (ou) in his blood ; *peau de balle*, nothing doing ! ‖ **Peau-Rouge**, s. Redskin.

peaufiner [pofine] v. tr. (1). To polish with chamois-leather, to chamois. ‖ FIG. To hone, to go over (sth.) with a toothcomb, to put the final touch (to sth.).

peausserie [-sri] f. Skin-dressing (action) ; dressed skins (résultat).

peaussier [-sje] m. Skin-dresser.

pécaïre! [pekai:r] interj. Alas !

pécari [pekari] m. ZOOL. Peccary.

peccable [pekabl] adj. Peccant, liable to sin.

peccadille [-kadi:j] f. Peccadillo, slip.

pêchable [pɛʃabl] adj. Fishing (rivière).

pechblende [pɛʃblɑ̃:d] f. TECHN. Pitchblende.

pêche [pɛ:ʃ] f. BOT. Peach.

pêche f. SPORTS. Fishing (action) ; catch, take (prise) ; *pêche de la baleine, de la crevette*, whaling, shrimping ; *pêche au filet, au lancer, à la ligne*, netting, casting, angling ; *faire une bonne pêche*, to get a good catch.

péché [peʃe] m. Sin ; *à tout péché miséricorde*, there is forgiveness for every sin. ‖ ECCLÉS. Sin, transgression, offence ; *mourir dans le péché*, to die unrepentant.

pécher v. intr. (5). ECCLÉS. To sin, to trespass. ‖ FIG. To act contrary to the rules (personne) ; to be at fault (raisonnement) ; *pécher par défaut*, to fall short of the mark ; *pécher par excès*, to overrun the goal ; *par où pèche-t-il?*, what is his weak point ?

pêcher [pɛʃe] m. BOT. Peach-tree.

pêcher v. tr. (1). SPORTS. To fish for, to catch (du poisson). ‖ FAM. To get (une idée) ; to pull out (un soulier).
— v. intr. To fish, to angle (à la ligne) ; to cast (au lancer) ; to fly-fish (à la mouche). ‖ FIG. *Pêcher en eau trouble*, to fish in troubled waters.

pechère! [pøʃɛ:r] interj. By God, 'sblood, 'strewth.

pêcherie [pɛʃri] f. Fishery.

pêcheur, eresse [peʃœ:r, rɛ:s] ECCLÉS. Sinner, transgressor, offender.
— adj. Sinning ; sinful (âme).

pêcheur [pɛʃœ:r] (f. **pêcheuse** [pɛʃø:z]) m. SPORTS. Fisherman ; *pêcheur au chalut, à la ligne*, trawlerman (ou) trawler, angler ; *pêcheur de perles*, pearl-diver. ‖ ECCLÉS. *Pêcheur d'hommes*, fisher of men.
— adj. Fishing. ‖ NAUT. *Bateau pêcheur*, fishing smack.

pécore [pekɔ:r] f. FAM. Goose.

pectoral, e [pɛktɔral] adj. MÉD. Pectoral (muscle, sirop) ; *pastille de pâte pectorale*, cough-lozenge, cough-drop.
— m. MÉD. Pectoral.

péculat [pekyla] m. Peculation.

péculateur [-tœ:r] m. Peculator.

pécule [peky:l] m. Savings (économies). ‖ † Peculium. ‖ MILIT. Gratuity.

pécuniaire [pekynjɛ:r] adj. Pecuniary ; *perte pécuniaire*, financial loss.

pécuniairement [-njɛrmɑ̃] adv. Pecuniarily.

pédagogie [pedagɔʒi] f. Pedagogy.

pédagogique [-gɔʒik] adj. Pedagogical.

pédagogue [-gɔg] m. Pedagogue. (V. PROFESSEUR.)

pédale [pedal] f. Pedal (de bicyclette); treadle (de machine à coudre). ‖ Mus. Pedal (d'orgue, de piano). ‖ Autom. *Pédale d'embrayage, de frein,* clutch-, brake-pedal.
pédaler [-le] v. intr. (1). To pedal; to cycle, to bike (fam.).
pédaleur [-lœːr] s. Fam. Cyclist; U. S. pedalist.
pédalier [-lje] m. Crank-gear (de bicyclette). ‖ Mus. Pedalier, pedal-board.
pédalo [-lo] m. Fam. Pedal-craft, pedal-boat.
pédant [pedã] s. Pedant, prig.
— adj. Pedantic, priggish.
pédanterie [-tri] f. Pedantry, priggishness.
pédantesque [-tɛsk] adj. Pedantic.
pédantisme [-tism] m. Pedantry.
pédéraste [pederast] m. Pederast (v. homosexuel); pansy, U. S. fairy (fam.).
pédérastie [-ti] f. Pederasty.
pédestre [pedɛstr] adj. Pedestrian.
pédestrement [-trəmã] adv. On foot.
pédiatre [pedjaːtr] m. Méd. Pediatrician, pediatrist.
pédiatrie [-tri] f. Méd. Pediatrics.
pédicule [pedikyl] m. Bot., Méd. Pedicel, pedicle.
pédicure [pedikyːr] m. Chiropodist.
pedigree [pedigri] m. Pedigree.
pédologie [pedɔlɔʒi] f. Pedology, soil science.
pédologue [-lɔg] s. Pedologist.
pédoncule [pedɔ̃kyːl] m. Bot. Peduncle.
peeling [piliŋ] m. Facial.
Pégase [pegaːz] m. Pegasus.
pègre [pɛgr] f. Crooks; underworld.
peignage [pɛɲaːʒ] m. Hackling (du chanvre); combing, carding (de la laine).
peigne [pɛɲ] m. Comb, hair-comb (démêloir); *peigne de chignon,* back-comb; *se donner un coup de peigne,* to run the comb through one's hair. ‖ Toothed plate (de rasoir). ‖ Comb, card (de cardeur); hackle (à chanvre); reed (de tisserand). ‖ Zool. Scallop, pecten.
peigné, ée [pɛɲe] adj. Combed; *mal peigné,* unkempt, tousled (cheveux); untidy, dishevelled, slovenly (personne). ‖ Fam. Trim (jardin); affected (style); finical (travail).
— m. Worsted (étoffe).
peignée f. Cardful (de laine). ‖ Fam. Thrashing.
peigner v. tr. (1). To comb (les cheveux); *peigner qqn,* to comb s.o.'s hair. ‖ To hackle (le chanvre); to card, to comb (la laine). ‖ Fam. To polish (son style); to smooth out (son travail).
peigneur, euse [-ɲœːr, øːz] s. Wool-comber.
peigneuse [-ɲøːz] f. Hackling-machine (à chanvre); wool-combing machine (à laine).
peignoir [-ɲwaːr] m. Peignoir, négligé, housecoat, dressing-gown, morning-wrapper; U. S. negligee; *peignoir de bain,* bath-wrap, U. S. bath-robe.
peignure [-ɲyːr] f. pl. Combings (de cheveux). ‖ Naut. Combing (de cordages).
peinard [pɛnaːr] m. † Toiler. ‖ Fam. Slacker.
— adj. Fam. Quiet, sly; *en père peinard,* lazily; *rester peinard,* to take things easy.
peindre [pɛ̃ːdr] v. tr. (59). To paint, to coat with paint (un mur, un objet); *peint en blanc,* painted white. ‖ Arts. To paint (un tableau); *peindre à l'huile,* to paint in oils; *se faire peindre,* to have one's portrait painted. ‖ Fig. To paint, to portray, to describe (décrire). ‖ Fam. *Etre à peindre,* to be worth painting.
— v. intr. To paint.
— v. pr. Se peindre, to appear, to become visible, to show (sur, on) [apparaître]. ‖ Fam. To make up (se maquiller).
peine [pɛn] f. Pain, penalty, punishment (châtiment); *sous peine de mort,* under pain of death. ‖ Pain, suffering, anguish (souci); *avoir de la peine,* to be in sorrow, to grieve; *faire de la peine à,* to

grieve; *il fait peine à voir,* it grieves (ou) hurts one to see him. ‖ Labour, U. S. labor (travail); *peine perdue,* labour lost; *homme de peine,* day-labourer. ‖ Pain, trouble (effort); *avec un peu de peine,* by taking a little trouble; *donner de la peine à,* to give trouble to; *en valoir la peine,* to be worth while (ou) worth the trouble; *être fort en peine de,* to be at a loss to; *j'ai peine à croire que,* I can hardly believe that; *je perds ma peine à discuter,* this argument is a waste of breath; *n'avoir pas de peine à faire,* not to have any trouble in doing; *ne pas prendre la peine de,* not to bother to; *prendre toute la peine du monde pour,* to take tremendous trouble to; *prendre de la peine pour,* to take pains to.
— Loc. adv. A peine, hardly, barely, scarcely; *réponse à peine polie,* barely polite answer; *votre père était à peine arrivé que,* your father had scarcely come when. ‖ *A grand-peine,* with great difficulty; *avec peine,* with difficulty; *sans peine,* easily, without difficulty.
peiné, ée [pɛne] adj. Pained, distressed; *avoir l'air peiné,* to look grieved (ou) hurt.
peiner v. tr. (1). To pain, to afflict, to grieve, to distress. (V. attrister.)
— v. intr. To take pains, to labour, to toil (travailler). ‖ Archit. To bear a great weight (poutre, voûte). ‖ Autom. To labour (moteur).
peintre [pɛ̃ːtr] m. Painter; *peintre en bâtiments,* house-painter. ‖ Arts. Painter; *artiste peintre,* artist; *femme peintre,* woman artist. ‖ Fig. Painter.
peinture [pɛ̃tyːr] f. Paint, colour (couleur); *prenez garde à la peinture,* wet paint; *les peintures,* paint work (d'un bâtiment). ‖ Painting (action); *peinture au pistolet,* spray-painting. ‖ Arts. Painting (action); picture (tableau); *peinture à l'huile,* oil-painting. ‖ Fig. Portrayal; picture; painting (description); *peinture de mœurs,* portrayal of manners. ‖ Fam. *Je ne peux pas le voir en peinture,* I can't bear the sight of him.
peinturlurer [-tyrlyre] v. tr. (1). To daub, to bedaub. [V. peindre.]
péjoratif, ive [peʒɔratif, iːv] adj. Pejorative, derogatory, derogative, depreciatory (v. défavorable); *au sens péjoratif,* in a disparaging sense.
péjorativement [-tivmã] adj. Pejoratively, derogatorily, derogatively.
pékin [pekɛ̃] m. Fam. Civilian; *en pékin,* in mufti, in civvies.
pékiné, ée [pekine] adj. Candy-striped (étoffe).
pékinois, oise [pekinwa, waːz] adj. Géogr., Gramm., Zool. Pekinese.
— s. Géogr. Pekinese (habitant de Pékin).
— m. Gramm. Pekinese (langue). ‖ Zool. Pekinese, peke (chien).
pelade [pəlad] f. Méd. Alopecia, pelade.
pelage [pəlaːʒ] m. Hair, coat, pelage, fur, pelt.
pelage m. Taking off the hair (action). ‖ Techn. Unhairing.
pélagien, enne [pelaʒjɛ̃, ɛn] adj. Ecclés. Pelagian.
pélagique [pelaʒik] adj. Pelagian, pelagic (de haute mer).
pelard [pəlaːr] adj. Barked (bois).
pélargonium [pelargɔnjɔm] m. Bot. Pelargonium.
pelé, ée [pəle] adj. Bald, hairless (animal). ‖ Peeled (fruit, légume). ‖ Bald, bare, naked (terrain). ‖ Fam. Bald (chauve); fleeced (dépouillé).
— m. Bald person. ‖ Fam. *Quatre pelés et un tondu,* the rag-tag and bobtail, a few odds and sods.
pêle-mêle [pɛlmɛl] adv. Pell-mell, helter-skelter, in disorder, in confusion; indiscriminately, promiscuously.
peler [pəle] v. tr. (8b). To take the hair off (un ani-

mal); to bark (un arbre); to peel (un fruit). ‖
FAM. To fleece (dépouiller).
— v. intr. ZOOL. To slough (serpent). ‖ MÉD. To
peel, to peel off (peau); to desquamate, to peel
(personne).
— v. pr. **Se peler.** MÉD. To peel, to scale (peau).
‖ BOT. To scale, to scale off (arbre).
●èlerin [pɛlrɛ̃] s. ECCLÉS. Pilgrim. ‖ ZOOL. Peregrine falcon.
●èlerinage [-rina:ʒ] m. Pilgrimage (action); place
of pilgrimage (lieu).
●èlerine [-rin] f. Pelerine, tippet.
●élican [pelikɑ̃] m. ZOOL. Pelican. ‖ TECHN.
Holdfast.
●elisse [pəlis] f. Pelisse (d'enfant); fur-lined coat
(de personne). ‖ MILIT. Pelisse.
●ellagre [pɛla:gr] f. MÉD. Pellagra.
●elle [pɛl] f. Shovel, scoop (à charbon); dust-pan
(à poussière); spade (d'enfant); *ramasser à la
pelle,* to shovel up. ‖ AGRIC. Shovel, spade. ‖
TECHN. Steam-shovel. ‖ NAUT. Blade (d'aviron). ‖
FAM. *Ramasser une pelle,* to come a cropper;
U. S. to take a spill; *remuer l'argent à la pelle,*
to have tons of money. ‖ **Pelle-bêche** f. MILIT.
Short-handled shovel.
●elleron [-rɔ̃] m. Baker's peel.
●elletage [-ta:ʒ] m. Shovelling.
●elletée [-te] f. Shovelful, spadeful.
●elleter [-te] v. tr. (8a). To shovel.
●elleterie [pɛltri] f. Peltry, pelts (peaux). ‖ Fur-
trade (commerce); fur-making (fabrication).
●elleteuse [pɛltø:z] f. TECHN. Mechanical
shovel.
●elletier [-tje] m. Furrier. (V. FOURREUR.)
●ellicule [pɛliky:l] f. Pellicule (peau); dandruff,
scurf (de la tête). ‖ Film (au cinéma, en photo). ‖
CULIN. Film, mantle (sur le lait); cuticle (du riz).
●elliculeux, euse [-kylø, ø:z] adj. Scurfy.
●elotage [pəlɔta:ʒ] m. Winding into balls (de la
ficelle, de la laine). ‖ Knocking the balls about
(au billard). ‖ FAM. Cuddling, petting, pawing
(caresses); fawning upon (flatterie).
●elotari [-tari] m. SPORTS. Pelota player.
●elote [pəlɔt] f. Ball (de ficelle, de laine); *pelote
à épingles,* pin-cushion. ‖ SPORTS. Pelota. ‖ FAM.
Les nerfs en pelote, with one's nerves on edge;
faire sa pelote, to feather one's nest.
●eloter [-te] v. tr. (1). To wind into a ball (la
ficelle, la laine). ‖ FAM. To cuddle, to pet, to paw
(une femme); to toady, to fawn (un supérieur).
— v. intr. To knock the balls about (au billard).
●eloteur [-tœ:r] s. Ball-winder (de laine). ‖
FAM. Cuddler, pawer (de femme); toady (flatteur).
●eloton [-tɔ̃] m. Little ball (de laine). ‖ SPORTS.
Clump, cluster, group; U. S. pack. ‖ MILIT. Platoon, squad; *peloton d'exécution,* firing squad;
peloton de pièce, gun detachment.
●elotonner [-tɔne] v. tr. (1). To wind into a ball.
— v. pr. **Se pelotonner,** to coil oneself up; to
snuggle. (V. SE BLOTTIR.) ‖ ZOOL. To roll up into
a ball.
●elouse [pəlu:z] f. Lawn, green, greensward,
grass plot. ‖ SPORTS. Green.
●eluche [pəlyʃ] f. Plush, shag (étoffe). ‖ Fluff,
nap (duvet).
●eluché, ée [-ʃe] adj. Fluffy, shaggy. ‖ BOT.
Hairy.
●elucher [-ʃe] v. intr. (1). To get fluffy; to fluff.
●elucheux, euse [-ʃø, ø:z] adj. Fluffy, shaggy,
plushy, nappy.
●elure [pəly:r] f. Skin, peel (de fruit). ‖ Paring
(épluchure). ‖ FAM. Gossamer (étoffe très mince);
coat (vêtement). ‖ LOC. *Papier pelure,* copying
(ou) onionskin (ou) tissue paper; *pelure d'oignon,*
onion-peel coloured (vin).
●elvien, enne [pɛlvjɛ̃, ɛn] adj. MÉD. Pelvic.
●elvis [-vis] m. MÉD. Pelvis.

pénal, ale [penal] adj. Penal.
pénalisation [-lizasjɔ̃] f. Penalization.
pénaliser [-lize] v. tr. (1). To penalize.
pénalité [-lite] f. JUR., SPORTS. Penalty.
penalty [penalti] m. SPORTS. Penalty (au
football).
pénates [penat] m. pl. † Penates.
penaud, aude [pəno, o:d] adj. Shamefaced, crest-
fallen, chapfallen, sheepish. (V. DÉCONCERTÉ.)
penchant, ante [pɑ̃ʃɑ̃, ɑ̃:t] adj. Leaning; sloping.
— m. Slope, declivity (v. PENTE). ‖ FIG. Propensity
(à, to, for); bias (à, toward) [v. INCLINATION];
penchant naturel, natural bent; *penchant pour la
boisson,* fondness for drink; *penchant pour la
peinture,* passion for painting.
penché, ée [-ʃe] adj. Leaning (construction);
sloping (lettres); *penché en avant,* bending forward; *penché sur ses livres,* poring over his
books. ‖ FAM. *Air penché,* languid look.
pencher [-ʃe] v. tr. (1). To lean, to bend (v. INCLI-
NER); *pencher son assiette,* to tilt one's plate.
— v. intr. To lean (balance); to slope (colline);
to sag (mur); *faire pencher la balance,* to weigh
down the scale. ‖ NAUT. To list (navire). ‖ FIG.
To be inclined (vers, to); to tend (vers, toward)
[v. TENDRE]; *la balance penche de son côté,* the
turn of the balance is with him; *pencher vers le
point de vue de qqn,* to incline to s.o.'s point of
view.
— v. pr. **Se pencher,** to lean, to bend, to stoop.
‖ FIG. *Se pencher sur,* to take a sympathetic interest in (une infortune); to brood over (un problème).
pendable [pɑ̃dabl] adj. JUR. Liable to the death
penalty (crime); deserving hanging (criminel). ‖
FIG. Nasty, outrageous (action); bad (cas).
pendaison [-dɛsɔ̃] f. Hanging.
pendant, ante [pɑ̃dɑ̃, ɑ̃:t] adj. Hanging (en
général); drooping (branches); sagging, baggy
(joues); *aux oreilles pendantes,* floppy- (ou) flap-
eared. ‖ FIG. Pending, pendent, outstanding, undecided (affaire, question).
— m. Pendant; *pendant d'oreille,* drop ear-ring,
ear-drop, U. S. pendant earring. ‖ MILIT. Frog
(de ceinturon). ‖ FIG. Match, counterpart; *faire
pendant à,* to make a pair with, to go with, to
match.
— prép. During, for (v. DURANT); *pendant dix
ans,* for ten years.
— adv. *Après et pendant,* during and after.
— loc. conj. **Pendant que,** while, whilst. (V. TAN-
DIS QUE.)
pendard, arde [pɑ̃da:r, ard] s. Rascal. (V. COQUIN.)
pendeloque [pɑ̃dlɔk] f. Pendant.
pendentif [-dɑ̃tif] m. Pendant (collier). ‖ ARCHIT.
Pendentive.
penderie [-dri] f. Wardrobe.
pendiller [-dije] v. intr. (1). To dangle, to flap,
to bob.
pendillon [-dijɔ̃] m. Drop (de lustre).
pendoir [-dwa:r] m. Meat-hook.
pendouiller [-duje] v. intr. (1). FAM. To droop,
to hang losely (ou) flaccidly.
pendre [pɑ̃:dr] v. tr. (4). To hang (qqch.) [à,
from, on]. ‖ To hang (qqn); *pendre haut et
court,* to string up; *bon à pendre,* deserving
hanging. ‖ LOC. *Dire pis que pendre de,* to disparage; *il ne vaut pas la corde pour le pendre,* he's
not worth wasting powder and shot on (ou) U. S.
not worth the rope to hang him.
— v. intr. To hang; *pendre aux branches,* to hang
from the branches. ‖ To sag (corde, joue). ‖ To
hang down (cheveux, robes).
— v. pr. **Se pendre,** to hang oneself. ‖ To hang
on (à, to). ‖ FAM. *Se pendre aux jupes de,* to run
after; *se pendre à la sonnette de qqn,* to be
always knocking at s.o.'s door.

pendu, ue [pãdy] adj. Hanging (à, from, on) [choses]. ‖ Hanged (personne). — s. Person who has been hanged.
pendulaire [pãdylɛ:r] adj. Pendular.
pendule [pãdyl] m. Pendulum (balancier). — f. Clock, timepiece. (V. HORLOGE.)
pendulette [-lɛt] f. Little clock; *pendulette de voyage,* travelling clock.
pêne [pɛ:n] f. Bolt, latch.
Pénélope [penelɔp] f. Penelope; *toile (ou) travail de Pénélope,* never-ending task.
pénéplaine [peneplɛn] f. GÉOGR. Peneplain.
pénétrabilité [penetrabilite] f. Penetrability.
pénétrable [-trabl] adj. Penetrable.
pénétrant, ante [-trã, ã:t] adj. Penetrating (force); piercing, biting, penetrating (froid); piercing, sharp (objet); subtle, penetrating (odeur); pervasive (parfum); drenching (pluie). ‖ MÉD. Perforating (plaie). ‖ FIG. Keen, sharp (esprit); discerning, acute (personne); intent, searching (regard); sharp, acute (remarque).
pénétration [-trasjɔ̃] f. Penetration; *force de pénétration,* penetrating power. ‖ Pervasion (d'un parfum); *puissance de pénétration,* pervasiveness. ‖ MÉD. *Pénétration médicale,* availability of medical attention. ‖ FIG. Penetration, insight (perspicacité); keenness, acuteness, acumen (de l'esprit); *pénétration par sympathie,* empathy.
pénétré, ée [-tre] adj. Penetrated; imbued (*de,* with); convinced (*de,* of). [V. IMBU.] ‖ Convinced, earnest (ton).
pénétrer [-tre] v. intr. (5). To penetrate, to enter (*dans,* into); *l'eau a pénétré partout,* water seeped in everywhere; *pénétrer dans un groupe,* to gain admittance into a group; *pénétrer de force dans,* to break (ou) to burst into. ‖ FIG. To penetrate, to fill (l'âme).
— v. tr. To penetrate (en général) [v. ENTRER]; to pierce, to bite (froid); to invade (odeur); to pierce (pointe); to bite (vent); *la chaleur pénètre toute la maison,* the heat spreads throughout the house. ‖To penetrate (la conscience). ‖ To penetrate, to see into (discerner); *pénétrer les projets de qqn,* to fathom s.o.'s plans. ‖ To impress (*de,* with) [persuader]; *pénétrer qqn d'une idée,* to convince s.o. of an idea. ‖ To permeate, to imbue (*de,* with) [remplir]; *pénétrer qqn d'effroi,* to fill s.o. with dread.
— v. pr. **Se pénétrer,** to become filled with; *se pénétrer de notions fausses,* to let oneself be invaded by false notions.
— v. récipr. **Se pénétrer,** to interpenetrate (gaz, substances). ‖ To agree (intelligence); to understand each other (ou) one another (personnes).
pénible [penibl] adj. Hard, toilsome, irksome, tiresome (fatigant). ‖ Rough, arduous, difficult (chemin); toilsome (travail). ‖ Hard, trying, severe (coup); painful (décision); wearisome (effort); distressing, sad (événement); unpalatable (nouvelle) ; heart-rending (séparation); unpleasant, sorry (spectacle); unwelcome (surprise). ‖ Heavy, laboured, stiff (style). ‖ MÉD. Heavy, laboured (respiration).
péniblement [-bləmã] adv. Painfully, arduously, with difficulty.
péniche [peniʃ] f. NAUT. Barge, canal-boat; *péniche de débarquement,* landing-craft, invasion barge. ‖ Cutter (de la douane).
pénicillé, ée [penisile] adj. Penicillate.
pénicilline [-lin] f. MÉD. Penicillin.
péninsulaire [penɛ̃sylɛ:r] adj. Peninsular.
péninsule [-syl] f. GÉOGR. Peninsula.
pénis [penis] m. MÉD. Penis.
pénitence [penitã:s] f. Penitence; *en pénitence,* in the corner, U. S. in disgrace (enfant). ‖ ECCLÉS. Penance; *faire pénitence de,* to do penance for; *sacrement de pénitence,* sacrament of penance.

pénitencerie [-sri] f. ECCLÉS. Penitentiary.
pénitencier [-sje] m. JUR. Penitentiary. (V. PR SON.) ‖ NAUT. Reformatory ship.
pénitent, ente [penitã, ã:t] adj., s. Penitent.
pénitentiaire [-sjɛ:r] adj. Penitentiary.
pénitentiel [-sjɛl] adj., m. ECCLÉS. Penitential.
pennage [pɛnna:ʒ] m. Plumage.
penne [pɛn] f. Quill-feather (plume). ‖ Feath (de flèche). ‖ Warp end (de textile). ‖ NAUT. Pea
penné, ée [pɛnne] adj. BOT. Pinnate.
pennon [pɛnɔ̃] m. Pennon.
Pennsylvanie [pɛnsilvani] f. GÉOGR. Pennsy vania.
pénologie [penɔlɔʒi] f. JUR. Penology.
pénombre [penɔ̃br] f. Penumbra. ‖ Semi-obscu rity, half (ou) shadowy light (demi-jour).
pénon [penɔ̃] m. NAUT. Dog-vane.
pensable [pãsabl] adj. Conceivable; *pas per sable,* unthinkable, inconceivable.
pensant, ante [pãsã, ã:t] adj. Thinking. ECCLÉS. *Bien pensant,* right-thinking, orthodox.
pense-bête [pãsbɛt] m. FAM. Memory jogger.
pensée [pãse] f. BOT. Pansy, heart's-ease.
pensée f. Thought, thinking (fait de penser); *ag ter un sujet dans sa pensée,* to turn a subject ove in one's mind; *venir à la pensée de qqn,* to occu to s.o.'s mind. ‖ Thought (méditation); *s'absorbe dans ses pensées,* to become lost in thought. Thought, purpose, design (intention); *avoir la pen sée de,* to mean (ou) to intend to; *lire dans l pensée de qqn,* to read s.o.'s thoughts; *pénétrer l pensée de qqn,* to guess what s.o. thinks. Thought, idea (v. IDÉE); *suivre la pensée de qqr* to follow s.o.'s train of thought. ‖ Thought, vie of life (manière de voir); *ma pensée intime, m* inmost thoughts. ‖ Thought, opinion (v. AVIS); *révéler le fond de sa pensée,* to reveal exactl what one is thinking. ‖ Thought, memory (souve nir); *la pensée de son fils mort,* the memory c his dead son. ‖ LOC. *Libre pensée,* free though
penser v. intr. (1). To think (en général); *faço de penser,* way of thinking; *je pense que non, qu oui,* I think not, so; *penser par soi-même,* t think for oneself. ‖ To think, to have an op nion; *je n'en pense pas moins,* I have my ow opinion just the same. ‖ To think (à, of); *je n pense plus qu'à cela,* it's my constant and onl thought; *maintenant que j'y pense,* now that think of it; *rien que d'y penser,* at the very (ou bare idea of it; *sans y penser,* thoughtlessly. ‖ T remember (se rappeler); *faire penser qqn à qqch* to remind s.o. of sth., to put s.o. in mind of sth to suggest sth to s. o.; *on ne pense pas toujours tout,* one does not always take everything int consideration; *pensez à me montrer votre broui lon,* don't forget to show me your rough copy. To think (à, of, about) [v. RÉFLÉCHIR]; *penser au conséquences,* to think of the consequences. To think, to intend, to mean (avoir l'intention) *penser à se retirer des affaires,* to think of retirin from business. ‖ To expect, to hope (espérer); *j pensais bien que vous viendriez,* I really expectec you to come. ‖ To gather (v. DÉDUIRE); *d'après le journaux je pense que,* I gather from the paper that. ‖ FAM. To fear (craindre); *j'ai pensé ne pa pouvoir y arriver,* I feared it was beyond m strength.
— v. tr. To think (concevoir); *tout ce qu'o pense n'est pas bon à dire,* it's not expedient t say all that one thinks. ‖ To think, to suppose, t believe (croire); *pensez ce que vous voudrez,* thin that what you like. ‖ To think (de, of, about); *c qu'il pense de moi,* what he thinks about me; *j n'en pense pas grand-chose,* I don't think much o it; *penser le plus grand bien de,* to have th highest opinion of. ‖ To mean (vouloir dire); *vou ne le pensez pas au fond,* you don't really mea

it. ‖ PHILOS. To conceive of, to envisage. ‖ FAM. *Penser argent*, to be money-minded.
— m. † Thought.
penseur [-sœ:r] m. Thinker ; *libre penseur*, free thinker.
pensif, ive [-sif, i:v] adj. Pensive, thoughtful, contemplative. (V. RÊVEUR.)
pension [-sjɔ̃] f. Pension ; *pension alimentaire*, maintenance allowance, alimony ; *pension de retraite*, retiring (ou) U.S. retirement pension ; *attribuer* (ou) *servir une pension à*, to pension. ‖ Board and lodging (v. HÔTEL) ; charge for board and lodging (prix) ; *prendre pension chez*, to board at. ‖ Boarding-school (pensionnat) ; *mettre en pension*, to send to a boarding-school.
pensionnaire [pɑ̃sjɔnɛ:r] s. Boarder, resident (d'une école) ; lodger (dans une famille). ‖ MÉD. Inmate (d'un hôpital psychiatrique). ‖ THÉÂTR. Actor (ou) actress at the Comedie-Française.
pensionnat [-na] m. Private boarding school (école) ; boarders (élèves).
pensionné, ée [-ne] adj. Pensioned off.
— s. Pensioner.
pensionner [-ne] v. tr. (1). To pension off.
pensivement [pɑ̃sivmɑ̃] adv. Thoughtfully, pensively, wistfully.
pensum [pɛ̃sɔm] m. Imposition, U. S. extra work.
pentaèdre [pɛ̃taɛdr] m. MATH. Pentahedron.
pentagonal, ale [-gɔnal] adj. MATH. Pentagonal.
pentagone [-gɔn] m. MATH. Pentagon.
pentagramme [-gram] m. Pentagram.
pentamètre [-mɛtr] m. Pentameter.
pentane [pɛ̃tan] m. CHIM. Pentane.
Pentateuque [-tø:k] m. ECCLÉS. Pentateuch.
pentathlon [-tlɔ̃] m. SPORTS. Pentathlon.
pentavalent, ente [-valɑ̃, ɑ̃:t] adj. CHIM. Pentavalent.
pente [pɑ̃:t] f. Slope, declivity (d'une colline) ; gradient (d'une route) ; *pente rapide*, steep hill (ou) slope ; *descendre la pente*, to go downhill ; *en pente*, sloping, shelving ; *être en pente raide*, to slope up sharply. ‖ Side-band (d'encadrement). ‖ RADIO, MATH. Slope. ‖ CH. DE F. Gradient (de la voie). ‖ FIG. Bent (inclination) ; *avoir une pente naturelle pour*, to have a natural bent for ; *la pente du vice*, the downward path. ‖ FAM. *Avoir le gosier en pente*, to be a thirsty soul, to drink like a fish ; *sur l'autre côté de la pente*, on the downward slope. ‖ In the sear and yellow leaf.
Pentecôte [pɑ̃tko:t] f. ECCLÉS. Whitsuntide, Pentecost ; *lundi de la Pentecôte*, Whit-Monday.
pent(h)ode [pɛ̃tɔd] f. ELECTR. Pentode.
pentothal [pɑ̃tɔtal] m. MÉD. Pentothal.
pentu, e [pɑ̃ty] adj. Steep.
penture [pɑ̃ty:r] f. Strap-hinge (de porte). ‖ NAUT. Rudder-bands.
pénultième [penyltjɛm] adj. GRAMM. Penultimate, last but one.
— f. GRAMM. Last syllable but one.
pénurie [penyri] f. Penury, shortage, scarcity (v. DISETTE). ‖ Poverty (pauvreté).
pépé [pepe] m. FAM. Grandpa, U. S. gramps.
pépée [pepe] f. POP. Bird, chick, bit of fluff.
pépère [pepɛ:r] adj. FAM. Snug, comfortable (travail).
— m. FAM. Grandpa, U. S. gramps (v. PÉPÉ). ‖ Old man, quiet old buffer.
pépettes [pepɛt] f. pl. POP. Cash, lolly (argent).
pépie [pepi] f. Pip (des oiseaux). ‖ FAM. *Avoir la pépie*, to be thirsty.
pépiement [-mɑ̃] m. Cheeping, chirping.
pépier [pepje] v. intr. (1). To cheep, to chirp.
pépin [pepɛ̃] m. Pip, seed (de pomme) ; stone (de raisin). ‖ FAM. Hitch (ennui) ; *avoir un pépin*, to strike a snag. ‖ FAM. Gamp, brolly (parapluie).
pépinière [pepinjɛ:r] f. AGRIC. Nursery. ‖ FIG.

Nursery (de bons élèves) ; hotbed (de mauvais sujets).
pépiniériste [-njerist] m. Nurseryman, nursery-gardener.
pépite [pepit] f. Nugget.
péplum [peplɔm] m. Peplum, peplos.
peppermint [pepɛrmint] m. Peppermint.
pepsine [pɛpsin] f. MÉD. Pepsin.
peptique [-tik] adj. MÉD. Peptic.
peptone [-tɔn] f. MÉD. Peptone.
péquenot [pekno] m. POP. Bumpkin, yokel.
péquin [pekɛ̃] m. V. PÉKIN.
perçage [pɛrsa:ʒ] m. Piercing, boring, drilling, punching. ‖ Broaching, tapping (d'un fût).
percale [pɛrkal] f. Cambric muslin, percale.
percaline [-lin] f. Percaline.
perçant, ante [pɛrsɑ̃, ɑ̃:t] adj. Searching, penetrating (regard) ; sharp, shrill, high-pitched (voix) ; piercing, penetrating, keen (yeux) ; *cri perçant*, scream, shriek.
perce [pɛrs] f. Drill, borer, punch (outil). ‖ *En perce*, abroach, on tap (tonneau) ; *mettre en perce*, to broach. ‖ **Perce-bois**, m. invar. ZOOL. Woodborer. ‖ **Perce-neige**, f. invar. BOT. Snowdrop. ‖ **Perce-oreille** (pl. *perce-oreilles*) m. ZOOL. Earwig.
percé, ée [pɛrse] adj. Pierced, bored, holed (v. TROUÉ) ; *percé aux coudes*, out at elbows.
percée f. Clearing, cutting, glade (dans un bois) ; opening (dans un mur) ; *faire une percée*, to make a clearing. ‖ MILIT. Break-through. ‖ SPORTS. Run-through (au rugby).
percement [-səmɑ̃] m. Drilling, boring (d'un trou). ‖ Cutting (d'un canal) ; tunnelling (d'une montagne) ; sinking (d'un puits) ; opening (d'une rue). ‖ Driving (d'une galerie de mine).
percepteur, trice [pɛrsɛptœ:r, tris] adj. Perceiving.
— m. Tax collector.
perceptibilité [-tibilite] f. Perceptibility. ‖ JUR. Possibility of being collected.
perceptible [-tibl] adj. Perceptible, perceivable (v. AUDIBLE, VISIBLE) ; *à peine perceptible*, faint (bruit).
perceptiblement [-tibləmɑ̃] adv. Perceptibly.
perceptif, ive [-tif, i:v] adj. Apprehensive (faculté) ; perceptive (personne).
perception [sjɔ̃] f. Perception, perceiving (action) ; perception, feeling (sensation). ‖ JUR. Collection (action) ; tax collector's office (bureau) ; tax collectorship (fonction).
percer [pɛrse] v. tr. (6). To pierce, to drill, to bore. (V. FORER). ‖ To punch (à l'emporte-pièce). ‖ To pierce, to stab (au couteau, à l'épée). ‖ To broach (une barrique) ; to cut (un canal) ; to tunnel (une montagne) ; to break through (une palissade) ; to drive, to cut (une route). ‖ To make a hole in (une étoffe). ‖ To elbow one's way through (la foule) ; to break through (les nuages). ‖ To soak through (eau, pluie) ; to pierce, to penetrate, to go through (lumière, regard) ; *percer qqn du regard*, to give s.o. a sharp look. ‖ MÉD. To lance (un abcès) ; *percer ses dents*, to cut one's teeth, to teethe. ‖ FIG. To foresee (l'avenir) ; to stab (le cœur) ; to penetrate (un mystère, un secret). ‖ FAM. *Percer les oreilles à*, to deafen.
— v. intr. To come out (ou) through (ou) up. (V. APPARAÎTRE.) ‖ MÉD. To burst (abcès) ; to come through (dent). ‖ FIG. To win recognition (mérite) ; to come to the fore (personne) ; to become evident (vérité).
— v. pr. **Se percer**, to bore (bois). ‖ To wear into holes (vêtements). ‖ To perforate ; *se percer le nez*, to perforate one's nose.
perceur [-sœ:r] m. Driller, borer ; *perceur de coffres-forts*, safe-breaker (ou) U. S. -cracker.
perceuse [-sø:z] f. Borer, drilling-machine.

percevable [pɛrsəvabl] adj. Perceivable. ‖ Fin. Leviable, collectable (impôts).

percevoir [-wa:r] v. tr. (3). To perceive (v. discerner, saisir); to catch (un bruit). ‖ To sense, to be aware of (ou) sensitive to (une différence). ‖ Fin. To collect (les impôts); to charge (des frais).

perche [pɛrʃ] f. Pole (v. gaule); *perche d'étendoir*, clothes-prop (ou) U. S. pole. ‖ Sports. Jumping pole. ‖ Techn. Trolley-pole (de tramway). ‖ Naut. Pole; *conduire à la perche*, to punt. ‖ Fig. *Tendre la perche à qqn*, to give s.o. a helping hand. ‖ Fam. Maypole, U. S. beanpole (personne).

perche f. Zool. Perch.

perché, ée [-ʃe] adj. Perched (oiseau); roosting (volailles). ‖ Fam. Perched (personne).

percher [-ʃe] v. intr. (1). To perch (oiseau); to roost (volaille). ‖ Fam. To hang out (personne). — v. tr. To set in a high place (qqch.). — v. pr. Se percher, to perch (oiseau). ‖ Fam. To stick up (objet). [V. se jucher.]

percheron, onne [pɛrʃərɔ̃, ɔn] adj. Géogr. Of (ou) from Perche. — s. Native (ou) inhabitant of Perche. — m. Zool. Percheron.

percheur [pɛrʃœ:r] adj. Perching. — s. Zool. Percher.

perchiste [pɛrʃist] m. Sports. Pole-vaulter (sauteur à la perche); skilift operator (employé de téléski). ‖ Radio, Ciném. Boom operator.

perchlorate [pɛrklɔrat] m. Chim. Perchlorate.

perchlorure [-ry:r] m. Chim. Perchloride.

perchoir [pɛrʃwa:r] m. Perch.

perclus, use [pɛrkly, y:z] adj. Stiff (membre); crippled, stiff (personne).

perçoir [pɛrswa:r] m. Drill, borer, piercer (foret); gimlet (vrille). ‖ Punch (emporte-pièce).

percolateur [pɛrkɔlatoe:r] m. Percolator. ‖ Culin. Coffee-percolator.

percussion [pɛrkysjɔ̃] f. Percussion. (V. choc.) ‖ Méd. Percussion, sounding. ‖ Mus. Percussion; *de (ou) à percussion*, percussion (instrument).

percussionniste [-sjɔnist] s. Mus. Percussionist.

percutant, ante [-tɑ̃, ɑ̃:t] adj. Percussive. ‖ Milit. Percussion-fuse (obus).

percuter [-te] v. tr. (1). To strike, to tap. ‖ Aviat. To crash into, to crack up (un obstacle). ‖ Méd. To percuss, to sound. — v. intr. Aviat. *Percuter au sol*, to crash to the ground.

percuteur [-tœ:r] m. Milit. Hammer (de fusil); firing-pin (de mitrailleuse).

perdable [pɛrdabl] adj. Losable.

perdant, ante [-dɑ̃, a:t] adj. Losing; *billet perdant*, blank ticket (à la loterie). — s. Loser.

perdition [-disjɔ̃] f. Perdition. ‖ Naut. *En perdition*, in distress. ‖ Ecclés. Perdition, damnation.

perdre [pɛrdr] v. tr. (4). To lose (v. égarer); *perdre son porte-monnaie*, to lose one's purse. ‖ To lose, to miss, to wander from (s'égarer hors de); *perdre son chemin, la piste*, to lose one's way, the track. ‖ To lose (ne plus voir); *perdre qqn dans la nuit*, to lose s.o. in the dark. ‖ To lose, to waste, to fritter away (gaspiller); *perdre sa peine, son temps*, to waste one's pains, one's time; *il n'y a pas de temps à perdre*, there's no time to lose (ou) to be lost. ‖ To lose, to miss, to let slip (laisser échapper); *perdre une chance*, to lose a chance; *perdre une occasion*, to miss an opportunity. ‖ To get rid of (se débarrasser de); *perdre une habitude*, to get rid of a habit. ‖ To lose (au jeu); *perdre de l'argent, un pari*, to lose money, a bet. ‖ To spoil (gâter); *perdre un tableau*, to spoil a picture. ‖ To be deprived of (être privé de); *perdre pied*, to lose one's footing. ‖ To lose (voir mourir); *perdre son père*, to lose one's

father. ‖ To lose (ne plus conserver); *perdre l'esprit*, to go out of one's mind. ‖ To lose, to be the ruin of (faire le malheur de); *son insouciance l'a perdu*, recklessness was the ruin of him. ‖ To injure, to harm, to ruin (nuire à); *perdre qqn auprès de qqn*, to ruin s.o. in s.o.'s estimation; *perdre qqn de réputation*, to compromise s.o.'s reputation. ‖ Jur. *Perdre un procès*, to lose a case, to fail in a suit. ‖ Milit. To lose (une bataille). ‖ Loc. *N'avoir rien à perdre*, to stand to lose nothing; *perdre pied*, to lose one's grip on the situation. — v. intr. To lose; *y perdre*, to lose over (ou) by it. ‖ To leak. (V. fuir, suinter.) ‖ To retrograde (élève). ‖ Fin. To lose its value (monnaie). — v. pr. Se perdre, to lose oneself. (V. s'égarer.) ‖ To harm oneself (se nuire). ‖ To be lost (ne plus s'entendre); *sa voix se perd dans le bruit*, his voice is smothered by the noise. ‖ To disappear, to die out, to go out of fashion (se démoder); *cette pratique se perd*, this practice is falling into disuse. ‖ To be wasted (se gaspiller); *ces fruits trop mûrs se perdent*, these over-ripe fruit are going to waste. ‖ To be absorbed, to be wrapped (dans, in) [ses pensées]. ‖ To get confused (dans, in) [ses explications]; *je m'y perds*, I can't make head or tail of it. ‖ Naut. To sink, to be wrecked (navire).

perdreau [pɛrdro] m. Zool. Young partridge.

perdrix [-dri] f. Zool. Partridge.

perdu, ue [pɛrdy] adj. Lost (objet). ‖ Isolated (lieu); *un endroit perdu*, an out-of-the-way place. ‖ Lost (coutume, espèce, race). ‖ Odd (moments); wasted (peine, temps). ‖ Lost, ruined (récolte). ‖ Loose, depraved (femme); *fille perdue*, bad girl. ‖ Wrapped up, lost, absorbed (dans, in) [ses pensées]. ‖ Méd. Hopelessly ill (malade); *les médecins le déclarent perdu*, the doctors have given him up. ‖ Comm. Non-returnable, U. S. disposable (emballage). ‖ Milit. *Balle perdue*, stray bullet. ‖ Loc. *Crier comme un perdu*, to shout like mad; *perdu de dettes*, head over heels in debt.

perdurer [pɛrdyre] v. intr. (1). To persist, to linger on.

père [pɛ:r] m. Father; *père de famille*, father of family. ‖ Senior; *Durand père*, Durand senior. ‖ Ecclés. Father; *révérend père X*, Reverend Father X. ‖ Fam. *Le père Durand*, Old Durand, U. S. old man Durand; *de père de famille*, gilt-edged (placement).

pérégrination [peregrinasjɔ̃] f. Peregrination.

péremption [perɑ̃psjɔ̃] f. Jur. Lapse. ‖ Méd. *Date de péremption d'un médicament*, date beyond which a medicine is not to be used.

péremptoire [perɑ̃ptwa:r] adj. Peremptory.

péremptoirement [-mɑ̃] adv. Peremptorily.

pérenne [perɛn] adj. Perennial (rivière, source).

pérenniser [perɛnize] v. tr. (1). To perpetuate. ‖ Jur. To confirm in one's appointment (un fonctionnaire).

pérennité [perɛnite] f. Perennity.

péréquation [perekwasjɔ̃] f. Equalizing.

perfectibilité [perfɛktibilite] f. Perfectibility.

perfectible [-tibl] adj. Perfectible.

perfectif, ive [-tif, i:v] adj. Gramm. Perfective.

perfection [-sjɔ̃] f. Perfection; *à (ou) dans la perfection*, to perfection, perfectly.

perfectionnement [-sjɔnmɑ̃] m. Perfecting, improving. (V. amélioration.) ‖ Further training (études).

perfectionner [-sjɔne] v. tr. (1). To make better, to improve. (V. améliorer.) ‖ To perfect, to bring to perfection. — v. pr. Se perfectionner, to make oneself more skilful; to improve one's knowledge (en, of).

perfectionnisme [-sjɔnism] m. Perfectionism.

perfectionniste [-sjɔnist] s. Perfectionist.

perfide [pɛrfid] adj. Perfidious. (V. DÉLOYAL.)
perfidement [-dmɑ̃] adv. Perfidiously.
perfidie [-di] f. Perfidy, perfidiousness. (V. TRAÎ-TRISE.) ‖ Falseness. (V. FAUSSETÉ.)
perfolié, ée [pɛrfɔlje] adj. BOT. Perfoliate.
perforage [pɛrfɔra:ʒ] m. Perforating, drilling, boring. ‖ Punching.
perforant, ante [pɛrfɔrɑ̃, ɑ̃:t] adj. Perforating. ‖ MILIT. Penetrating (balle).
perforateur, trice [-ratœ:r, tris] adj. Perforating, perforative.
perforation [-rasjɔ̃] f. Perforation (trou); perforating, drilling, boring (action). ‖ INFORM. Punch, punching.
perforatrice [-ratris] f. TECHN. Drill. ‖ INFORM. Card punch.
perforer [-re] v. tr. (1). To perforate (v. PERCER); *cartes perforées*, IBM (ou) punched cards.
performance [pɛrfɔrmɑ̃:s] f. SPORTS. Performance. ‖ Pl. AUTOM. Performance, specifications.
performant, ante [-mɑ̃, ɑ̃:t] adj. TECHN. High performance (ou) output.
perfusion [pɛrfyzjɔ̃] f. MÉD. Perfusion.
pergola [pɛrgɔla] f. Pergola.
périanthe [perjɑ̃:t] m. BOT. Perianth.
péricarde [perikard] m. MÉD. Pericardium.
péricardique [-dik] adj. MÉD. Pericardial.
péricardite [-dit] f. MÉD. Pericarditis.
péricarpe [perikarp] m. BOT. Pericarp.
périclitant, ante [periklitɑ̃, ɑ̃:t] adj. Unsound, shaky (affaire).
péricliter [-te] v. intr. (1). To be shaky, to run to seed (affaire); to be tottering (empire).
péridot [perido] m. GÉOL. Peridot.
périgée [periʒe] m. ASTRON. Perigee.
périglaciaire [periglasjɛ:r] adj. GÉOL. Periglacial.
périgourdin, ine [perigurdɛ̃, in] adj. Of (ou) from Périgord (ou) Périgueux.
— s. Native (ou) inhabitant of Périgord (ou) Périgueux.
périhélie [perieli] m. ASTRON. Perihelion.
péril [peril] m. Peril, jeopardy (v. DANGER); *mettre en péril*, to imperil, to jeopardize.
périlleusement [perijœzmɑ̃] adv. Perilously.
périlleux, euse [-jø, ø:z] adj. Perilous.
périmé, ée [perime] adj. No longer available (billet). ‖ Lapsed, annulled (instance); out of date, outdated, outworn, superseded (méthode).
périmer v. intr. (1). To become unavailable (ou) invalid (billet). ‖ JUR. To lapse (instance); *laisser périmer un droit*, to forfeit a right.
périmètre [perimɛtr] m. MATH. Perimeter. (V. CIRCONFÉRENCE.) ‖ MÉD. *Périmètre thoracique*, chest measurement. ‖ FIG. Area, sphere (d'influence).
périnée [-ne] m. MÉD. Perineum.
période [perjɔd] f. Era, time, period (époque). ‖ ASTRON., MÉD. Period. ‖ MATH. Period, repetend. ‖ MILIT. *Période de repos*, spell of rest in billets; *période militaire*, course of training, U. S. hitch of duty (fam.). ‖ Period (de style).
— m. Period. (V. PHASE.) ‖ Climax. (V. APOGÉE.)
périodicité [-disite] f. Periodicity.
périodique [-dik] adj. Periodic, periodical. ‖ Periodic (style). ‖ MÉD. Recurrent (fièvre). ‖ NAUT. Regular (départs).
— m. Periodical publication.
périodiquement [-dikmɑ̃] adv. Periodically.
périoste [perjɔst] m. MÉD. Periosteum.
péripatéticien, enne [peripatetisjɛ̃, ɛn] adj., m. PHILOS. Peripatetic.
péripatéticienne [-tisjɛn] f. FAM. Street-walker.
péripatétisme [-tism] m. PHILOS. Peripateticism.
péripétie [peripesi] f. Peripeteia; episode. ‖ Pl. Vicissitudes, ups and downs.
périphérie [periferi] f. Outskirts (d'une ville). ‖ MATH. Periphery.
périphérique [-rik] adj. Outlying (quartier). ‖

MATH., MÉD., INFORM. Peripheral. ‖ AUTOM. *Boulevard périphérique*, ring road. ‖ RADIO. *Poste périphérique*, French radio station transmitting from abroad.
— m. INFORM. Peripheral. ‖ AUTOM. Ring road.
périphrase [perifra:z] f. Periphrasis, periphrase.
périphrastique [-tik] adj. Periphrastic.
périple [peripl] m. Periplus; long and complicated journey.
périr [peri:r] v. intr. (2). To perish (v. MOURIR); *faire périr*, to cause to die, to kill; *périr de froid*, to be frozen to death. ‖ To be destroyed, to decay (empire); to decay (entreprise). ‖ NAUT. To be wrecked, to sink (navire). ‖ FIG. *Ne jamais périr*, to live for ever (souvenir); *périr d'ennui*, to be bored to death.
périscope [periskɔp] m. NAUT. Periscope.
périscopique [-pik] adj. TECHN. Periscopic (objectif).
périssable [perisabl] adj. Perishable.
périssoire [periswa:r] f. NAUT. Canoe; *faire de la périssoire*, to canoe.
péristaltique [peristaltik] adj. MÉD. Peristaltic.
péristyle [peristil] m. ARCHIT. Peristyle.
péritoine [peritwan] m. MÉD. Peritoneum.
péritonite [-tɔnit] f. MÉD. Peritonitis.
perlaire [pɛrlɛ:r] adj. Pearly.
perle [pɛrl] f. Pearl ‖ Bead (de verre). ‖ FIG. Gem, jewel; *la perle des femmes*, a jewel of a wife. ‖ FAM. Gem, howler (bourde).
— adj. Pearl grey (couleur).
perlé, ée [-le] adj. Pearly (dents). ‖ Beaded, pearled (broderie); *coton perlé*, crochet (ou) corded cotton. ‖ BOT. *Orge perlé*, pearl-barley. ‖ MUS. Exquisitely done (chant). ‖ FIG. Rippling, rippled (rire); brilliantly done (travail).
perler [-le] v. tr. (1). To pearl (l'orge). ‖ To set with pearls (une broderie). ‖ FAM. To finish up.
— v. intr. To stand out in beads (larmes, sueur).
perlière [-ljɛ:r] adj. *Huître perlière*, pearl-oyster.
perlimpinpin [pɛrlɛ̃pɛ̃pɛ̃] m. *Poudre de perlimpinpin*, magic powder.
perm [pɛrm] f. FAM., MILIT. Leave (permission).
permafrost [pɛrmafrɔst] m. GÉOGR. Permafrost.
permanence [pɛrmanɑ̃:s] f. Permanence (v. PERSISTANCE); *en permanence*, permanently. ‖ Committee room (pièce); permanent (ou) all-day service, on-duty hours (service). ‖ MÉD. *Permanence de nuit*, all-night service.
permanent, ente [-nɑ̃, ɑ̃:t] adj. Permanent. (V. CONTINUEL, DURABLE.) ‖ MILIT. Standing (armée). ‖ CINÉM. *Spectacle permanent*, continuous (ou) non-stop performance (ou) show.
— m. Full-time official (d'un parti, d'un syndicat).
permanente [-nɑ̃:t] f. Permanent wave; perm.
permanganate [pɛrmɑ̃ganat] m. CHIM. Permanganate.
perméabilité [permeabilite] f. Permeability.
perméable [-abl] adj. Permeable. ‖ MILIT. Vulnerable. ‖ FIG. Pervious.
permettre [pɛrmɛtr] v. tr. (64). To permit, to allow, to let (v. AUTORISER); *permettre à qqn de faire qqch.*, to allow s.o. to do sth. ‖ To tolerate, to put up with. (V. SUPPORTER.) ‖ To allow, to grant leave to, to authorize (rendre possible); *cela m'a permis de prendre des vacances*, that enabled me to take a holiday; *mes moyens ne me permettent pas de voyager*, I can't afford to travel. ‖ To allow, to permit (autoriser); *vous permettez?*, may I?; *permettez!* excuse me!; *s'il est permis que je vous revoie*, if I may be allowed to see you again; *s'il m'est permis de placer un mot*, if I may put in a word; *si le temps le permet*, weather permitting. ‖ FAM. *Est-il permis d'être aussi ignorant!*, is it possible to be so ignorant!

— v. pr. Se **permettre**, to allow oneself (s'autoriser); *se permettre de faire la grasse matinée*, to indulge in a lie-in (ou) U. S. late sleep; to sleep in (ou) U. S. late; *se permettre une insolence envers qqn*, to allow oneself to be insolent toward s.o. ‖ To take upon oneself (s'aventurer); *se permettre de*, to make bold to, to take leave to, to be so bold as to, to venture to; *je me permets de vous écrire*, I am taking the liberty of writing to you.

permis, ise [-mi, iz] adj. Allowed, permitted. (V. ADMIS, AUTORISÉ.) ‖ Allowable, permissible. (V. LICITE.) ‖ Legitimate, lawful. (V. LÉGAL.)
— m. Permit, leave. (V. AUTORISATION.) ‖ SPORTS. *Permis de chasse*, hunting licence. ‖ CH. DE F. Free pass. ‖ JUR. *Permis d'inhumer*, permission to dispose of a body; U. S. burial permit; *permis de séjour*, certificate of registration. ‖ AUTOM. *Permis de conduire*, driving licence, U. S. driver's license. ‖ ARCHIT. *Permis de construire*, building licence (ou) U. S. permit.

permissif, ive [-misif, i:v] adj. Permissive.

permission [-misjɔ̃] f. Permission, leave (v. AUTORISATION); *avec votre permission*, with (ou) by your leave. ‖ MILIT. Leave, furlough; *en permission*, on leave.

permissionnaire [-misjɔnɛ:r] m. Holder of a permit. ‖ MILIT. Soldier on leave. ‖ NAUT. Liberty man.

permissivité [-misivite] f. Permissiveness.

permutabilité [pɛrmytabilite] f. Permutability.

permutable [-tabl] adj. Permutable.

permutant [-tɑ̃] s. Exchanger.

permutation [-tasjɔ̃] f. Permutation, exchange of posts.

permuter [-te] v. tr. (1). To exchange, to switch (un emploi).
— v. intr. To exchange posts (*avec*, with) (qqn).

pernicieusement [pɛrnisjøzmɑ̃] adv. Perniciously.

pernicieux, euse [-sjø, ø:z] adj. Pernicious (action); noxious (effet); baneful (influence). (V. NUISIBLE.) ‖ MÉD. Malignant (fièvre); *anémie pernicieuse*, Addison's (ou) pernicious anaemia.

Pernod [pɛrno] m. Pernod.

péroné [perɔne] m. MÉD. Fibula.

péronisme [perɔnism] m. Peronism.

péronnelle [perɔnɛl] f. Saucy (ou) pert woman.

péroraison [perɔrɛzɔ̃] f. Peroration.

pérorer [-re] v. intr. (1). To perorate, to speechify.

péroreur [-rœ:r] s. Speechifier, spouter.

Pérou [peru] m. GÉOGR. Peru. ‖ FAM. *Ce n'est pas le Pérou*, it's no great catch, it's nothing to write home about.

peroxyde [pɛrɔksid] m. CHIM. Peroxide.

peroxyder [-side] v. tr. (1). CHIM. To peroxidize.

perpendiculaire [pɛrpɑ̃dikylɛ:r] adj. MATH. Perpendicular. ‖ Upright (v. VERTICAL); sheer (falaise).
— f. MATH. Perpendicular.

perpendiculairement [-lɛrmɑ̃] adv. MATH. Perpendicularly. ‖ Sheer (verticalement).

perpendicularité [-larite] f. MATH. Perpendicularity.

perpétration [pɛrpetrasjɔ̃] f. Perpetration.

perpétrer [-tre] v. tr. (5). To perpetrate.

perpette (à) [apɛrpɛt] loc. adv. POP. For ever and ever, till doomsday; *être condamné à perpette*, to get life.

perpétuation [pɛrpetɥasjɔ̃] f. Perpetuation.

perpétuel, elle [-tɥɛl] adj. Perpetual, everlasting.

perpétuellement [-tɥɛlmɑ̃] adv. Perpetually, everlastingly. (V. ÉTERNELLEMENT.)

perpétuer [-tɥe] v. tr. (1). To perpetuate.
— v. pr. Se **perpétuer**, to last, to become permanent. (V. DURER.)

perpétuité [-tɥite] f. Perpetuity; *à perpétuité*, in perpetuity; for ever. ‖ JUR. *A perpétuité*, for life.

perplexe [pɛrplɛks] adj. Perplexed, puzzled (v. EMBARRASSÉ); *rendre perplexe*, to perplex, to puzzle.

perplexité [-site] f. Perplexity, puzzlement.

perquisiteur [pɛrkizitœ:r] m. JUR. Searcher.

perquisition [-sjɔ̃] f. JUR. House search; *faire une perquisition chez qqn*, to search s.o.'s premises; *mandat de perquisition*, search-warrant.

perquisitionner [-sjɔne] v. intr. (1). JUR. To make a search; *perquisitionner dans*, to search.

perron [pɛrɔ̃] m. Perron, flight of steps, U. S. stoop.

perroquet [pɛrɔkɛ] m. ZOOL. Parrot. ‖ NAUT. Topgallant.

perruche [pɛryʃ] f. ZOOL. Parakeet. ‖ NAUT. Mizzen topgallant sail.

perruque [pɛryk] f. Wig; periwig.

perruquier [-kje] m. Wig-maker (fabricant). ‖ Barber (coiffeur).

pers [pɛ:r] adj. Bluish-green, sea-green (yeux).

persan, ane [pɛrsɑ̃, an] adj., s. GÉOGR., ZOOL. Persian.

perse [pɛrs] adj., s. GÉOGR. Persian.
— m. GRAMM. Persian (langue).

Perse [pɛrs] f. GÉOGR. Persia. ‖ COMM. Chintz (étoffe); *de Perse*, Persian (tapis).

persécuté, ée [pɛrsekyte] adj. Persecuted.
— s. Persecuted person. ‖ MÉD. Sufferer from persecution.

persécuter v. tr. (1). To persecute. ‖ FAM. To worry, to beset. (V. IMPORTUNER.)

persécuteur, trice [-tœ:r, tris] adj. Persecuting.
— s. Persecutor.

persécution [-sjɔ̃] f. Persecution.

persévérance [pɛrseverɑ̃:s] f. Perseverance.

persévérant, ante [-rɑ̃, ɑ̃:t] adj. Persevering.

persévérer [-re] v. intr. (5). To persevere, to carry on (v. PERSISTER); to peg away (fam.); *persévérer dans la bienveillance*, to be persistently benevolent; *persévérer dans la résistance*, to be stubborn in resistance.

persienne [pɛrsjɛn] f. Blind, persienne, slatted shutter.

persiflage [pɛrsifla:ʒ] m. Persiflage, banter.

persifler [-fle] v. tr. (1). To banter. (V. RAILLER.)

persifleur, euse [-flœ:r, ø:z] adj. Bantering, jeering. (V. RAILLEUR.)
— s. Banterer.

persil [pɛrsi] m. BOT. Parsley.

persillade [-jad] f. CULIN. Beef salad with parsley sauce, cold sliced beef with chopped parsley.

persillé, ée [-je] adj. CULIN. Blue-moulded, mouldy (fromage); marbled (viande).

persique [pɛrsik] adj. ARCHIT. Persic. ‖ GÉOGR. Persian (golfe).

persistance [pɛrsistɑ̃:s] f. Persistence, persistency. (V. PERSÉVÉRANCE.) ‖ Doggedness. (V. OBSTINATION.) ‖ Continuance, continuation. ‖ MÉD. *Persistance rétinienne*, after-image.

persistant, ante [-tɑ̃, ɑ̃:t] adj. Persistent. (V. PERSÉVÉRANT.) ‖ Dogged (obstiné). ‖ Lasting, steady (continu). ‖ FIN. Steady (hausse).

persister [-te] v. intr. (1). To persist (*dans*, in) [v. PERSÉVÉRER]; to stick to it; to carry on (fam.); *persister à répondre*, to persist in answering back; *ne pas persister*, to give it up. ‖ To persist, to continue on one's course (v. DURER); *la pluie persiste*, it keeps raining.

persona grata [pɛrsɔnagrata] loc. adj. Persona grata.

personnage [pɛrsɔna:ʒ] m. Personage, person of rank. (V. PERSONNALITÉ.) ‖ Fellow (individu); *triste personnage*, contemptible individual. ‖ ARTS. Figure (d'un tableau). ‖ THÉÂTR. Character (d'une pièce); *les personnages*, the dramatis personae; *jouer le personnage de Macbeth*, to play Macbeth.

personnalisation [-nalizasjɔ̃] f. Personalization, impersonation.

personnaliser [-nalize] v. tr. (1). To personalize, to impersonate. (V. PERSONNIFIER.) ‖ COMM. *Simca personnalisée,* Simca designed to the customer's taste; U. S. custom-built Simca.

personnalité [-nalite] f. Personality, personal identity (identité). ‖ Personality, individuality; *avoir de la personnalité,* to have personality (ou) individuality. ‖ Person of mark, important person (v. PERSONNAGE, SOMMITÉ); *c'est une personnalité,* he is somebody. ‖ JUR. *Personnalité civile,* legal status. ‖ LOC. *Faire des personnalités,* to make personal remarks.

personne [pɛrsɔn] f. Person (être); *les grandes personnes,* the grown-ups; *plusieurs personnes,* several people; *une tierce personne,* a third party; *veuillez dire à toute personne qui viendra que,* please tell anybody who may come that. ‖ Person, individual (individu); *en personne,* in person, personally; *honorer l'armée en la personne de son chef,* to honour the Army in the person of the Commander-in-Chief; *s'appliquer à tout le monde sans acception de personne,* to apply to everybody whoever he may be. ‖ Person, body (corps); *payer de sa personne,* not to spare oneself. ‖ Person, personality, personal characteristics (individualité). ‖ Person, self (ego); *la bonté en personne,* kindness personified (ou) itself, the very soul of kindness; *ma petite personne,* little me; *prendre soin de sa petite personne,* to take care of Number One. ‖ Person, woman (femme); *belle, bonne personne,* fine-looking, kind-hearted woman; *jeune personne,* young lady; *personne mal fagotée,* dowdy creature. ‖ JUR. Person, body; *personne morale,* corporate body, legal entity; *erreur sur la personne,* mistaken identity; *s'assurer de la personne de,* to arrest. ‖ COMM. *Par personne,* per head. ‖ GRAMM. Person; *parler à la troisième personne,* to speak in the third person.
— pr. indéf. m. Anybody, anyone (qqn dans une phrase dubitative, interro-négative, ou négative); *est-il possible que personne soit entré?,* is it possible that anybody should have come in?; *il nie que personne soit parti avant lui,* he denies that anyone left before him. ‖ Anyone, anybody (qui que ce soit); *chanter mieux que personne,* to sing better than anyone; *porter l'uniforme mieux que personne,* to wear uniform to better advantage than anybody; *sans avoir pu remercier personne,* without having been able to thank anybody. ‖ No one, nobody, not... anybody (aucune personne); *il n'y a plus personne,* there is no one left; *ne se fier à personne d'autre,* to trust no one (ou) nobody else; *je ne le dirai à personne,* I shall tell it to no one; *qui attendez-vous? personne,* whom are you expecting? nobody; *personne de nous,* none of us.

personnel, elle [pɛrsɔnɛl] adj. Personal (affaire, lettre, question); private (fortune); *ce point de vue lui est personnel,* this point of view is his own. ‖ Selfish (égoïste); opinionated (imbu de ses opinions). ‖ JUR. *Contribution personnelle,* poll tax. ‖ GRAMM. Personal (pronom). ‖ CH. DE F. Non-transferable (billet).
— m. Staff, employees; *aimé de son personnel,* liked by one's employees; *manquer de personnel,* to be understaffed, to need hands; *service, chef du personnel,* personnel department, manager. ‖ MILIT., AVIAT. Personnel; *personnel à terre (ou) rampant,* ground staff (ou) crew.

personnellement [-nɛlmɑ̃] adv. Personally, in person.

personnification [-nifikasjɔ̃] f. Personification.

personnifier [-nifje] v. tr. (1). To personify (des abstractions). ‖ To impersonate, to embody, to personify (des vertus).

perspectif, ive [pɛrspɛktif, i:v] adj. Perspective.

perspective [-ti:v] f. Vista, view (vue). ‖ ARTS. Perspective. ‖ FIG. Prospect, perspective; *perspectives d'avenir,* future prospects; *en perspective,* in view, in prospect; *la seule perspective qui me reste,* the only future that remains open to me.

perspicace [pɛrspikas] adj. Perspicacious, acute, keen (esprit); sharp-witted, shrewd, discerning (personne).

perspicacité [-site] f. Perspicacity, acuteness, shrewdness; penetrating insight.

persuadant, ante [pɛrsɥadɑ̃, ɑ̃:t] adj. Impressive (convaincant); persuasive (persuasif).

persuadé, ée [-de] adj. Persuaded (de, of).

persuader [-de] v. tr. (1). To persuade (qqn) [v. CONVAINCRE]; *persuader qqch. à qqn (ou) qqn de qqch.,* to persuade s.o. of sth.; *persuader qqn à force de paroles,* to talk s.o. round.
— v. intr. To persuade; *persuader à qqn de faire qqch.,* to induce s.o. to do sth.; *persuader à qqn que,* to persuade s.o. that; *se laisser persuader,* to allow oneself to be persuaded (ou) prevailed upon; *persuadé que,* convinced that.
— v. pr. Se persuader, to be persuaded (v. SE CONVAINCRE) [de, of]; *il se persuade de son bon droit,* he persuades himself he is in the right; *il se persuade qu'il n'a pas d'ennemis,* he has got it into his head that he has no enemies.

persuasif, ive [-zif, i:v] adj. Persuasive (paroles, personne). [V. CONVAINCANT.] ‖ Smooth-tongued, insinuating. (V. INSINUANT.)

persuasion [-zjɔ̃] f. Persuasion, suasion. ‖ Firm belief (v. CONVICTION); *avoir l'intime persuasion que,* to be firmly convinced that.

persuasivement [-zivmɑ̃] adv. Persuasively.

perte [pɛrt] f. Waste (d'effort, de temps); loss (de temps); *c'est en pure perte,* it is sheer waste of time; *dépense en pure perte,* wasteful expenditure. ‖ Loss (d'argent); *perte sèche,* dead loss; *être en perte de mille francs,* to be one thousand francs to the bad. ‖ Leakage (de liquide). [V. FUITE.] ‖ Loss (de chaleur) [v. DÉPERDITION]; loss (d'une personne). [V. DEUIL.] ‖ Ruin, destruction (dommage); *courir à sa perte,* to head for ruin; *cette erreur a causé sa perte,* this error has brought about his failure. ‖ FIN. Discount (sur les valeurs); *vendre avec cent francs de perte,* to sell at one hundred francs' discount. ‖ MILIT. Loss (d'une bataille); *infliger de grosses pertes à l'ennemi,* to take heavy toll of the enemy. ‖ AVIAT. *Se mettre en perte de vitesse,* to stall. ‖ ELECTR. Leakage (de courant); loss (d'énergie). ‖ JUR. Loss (d'un procès). ‖ COMM. *Profits et pertes,* profit and loss; *passer aux profits et pertes,* to write off; *vendre à perte,* to sell at loss. ‖ MÉD. Flooding, uterine discharge; *pertes blanches,* leucorrhoea; whites (fam.). ‖ LOC. *A perte de vue,* as far as the eye can see; *discuter à perte de vue,* to argue endlessly.

pertinemment [pɛrtinamɑ̃] adv. Pertinently, to the point (ou) purpose, with knowledge, competently (avec compétence); ‖ Positively, with certainty (avec certitude); *savoir pertinemment que,* to be positive that.

pertinence [-nɑ̃:s] f. Pertinence, pertinency.

pertinent, ente [-nɑ̃, ɑ̃:t] adj. Pertinent, relevant.

pertuis [pɛrtɥi] m. † Hole (trou). ‖ GÉOGR. Pass; strait. ‖ TECHN. Tap hole.

pertuisane [pɛrtɥizan] f. † Partisan, halberd.

perturbateur, trice [pɛrtyrbatœ:r, tris] adj. Disturbing.
— s. Disturber, trouble-maker.

perturbation [-basjɔ̃] f. Perturbation (en général). ‖ Breakdown (dans l'administration); upheaval (dans le pays). ‖ MÉD. Disorder (de l'organisme). ‖ RADIO. *Perturbation atmosphérique,* atmospherics. ‖ FIG. Discomposure (de l'esprit).

perturber [-be] v. tr. (1). To perturb, to disturb.
péruvien, enne [pɛryvjɛ̃, ɛn] adj. GÉOGR. Peruvian.
pervenche [pɛrvɑ̃ːʃ] f. BOT. Periwinkle.
— adj. Periwinkle (couleur).
pervers [pɛrvɛːr] adj. Evil (dispositions); perverse (personne); vicious (tendances). [V. VICIEUX.]
— s. Evil-doer. ‖ MÉD. Pervert.
perversement [pɛrvɛrsəmɑ̃] adv. Perversely.
perversion [-sjɔ̃] f. Distortion, twist (de l'esprit); perversion (du goût, des mœurs).
perversité [-site] f. Perverseness, perversity.
pervertir [-tiːr] v. tr. (2). To distort (l'esprit); to pervert (qqn). [V. CORROMPRE.]
— v. pr. **Se pervertir**, to become perverted.
pervertissement [-tismɑ̃] m. Perverting.
pervertisseur [-tisœːr] adj. Perverting.
— s. Perverter.
pesage [pəza:ʒ] m. Weighing (action); *bureau de pesage*, weigh-house. ‖ SPORTS. Weighing in (du jockey); paddock, enclosure (enceinte).
pesamment [-zamɑ̃] adv. Heavily; weightily. (V. LOURDEMENT.) ‖ FIG. Clumsily, ponderously (v. MALADROITEMENT); *marcher pesamment*, to lumber along.
pesant, ante [-zɑ̃, ɑ̃:t] adj. Heavy, weighty, ponderous. (V. LOURD.) ‖ Heavy, lumbering (marche); *entrer à pas pesants*, to lumber in. ‖ PHYS. Ponderable (gaz). ‖ FIG. Sluggish (esprit); heavy, oppressive, grievous (joug); heavy, ponderous, clumsy (style).
— m. Weight (v. POIDS); *valoir son pesant d'or*, to be worth one's weight in gold.
pesanteur [-zɑ̃tœ:r] f. Weight. (V. POIDS.) ‖ Heaviness, unwieldiness, lumpishness (de la démarche, des mouvements). ‖ PHYS. Gravity; gravitation; *loi de la pesanteur*, law of gravitation. ‖ MÉD. Heaviness, dullness. ‖ FIG. Heaviness, dullness (de l'esprit, du style).
pèse [pɛz]. V. PESER. ‖ **Pèse-acide**, m. CHIM. Acidimeter. ‖ **Pèse-alcool**, m. invar. PHYS. Alcoholometer. ‖ **Pèse-bébé**, m. MÉD. Baby-weighing scale. ‖ **Pèse-lait**, m. invar. Lactometer, milk-tester. ‖ **Pèse-lettre**, m. Letter-balance (ou) U. S. scales. ‖ **Pèse-personne**, m. Scales. ‖ **Pèse-vin**, m. PHYS. Oenometer.
pesée [pəze] f. Weighing (action); quantity weighed (quantité). ‖ Leverage (poussée); *exercer une pesée sur une porte*, to try to force a door open; *pesée du poignet*, wrench.
peser v. tr. (5). To weigh (qqch.). [V. SOUPESER.] ‖ FIG. To ponder (un avis); to think out (une décision); to brood over (une idée); to weigh (ses mots); *j'ai tout pesé*, I have taken everything into consideration.
— v. intr. To weigh (un certain poids); *peser lourd*, to be heavy; *peser trois livres*, to weigh three pounds. ‖ To weigh (être pesant); *peser trop lourd sur le dos du cheval*, to weigh too heavily on the horse's back. ‖ MÉD. To lie heavy (nourriture) [sur, on]. ‖ TECHN. To bear, to press hard (sur, on) [exercer une pesée]. ‖ FIG. To weigh, to carry weight (argument); to lie heavy (crime) [sur, on]; to hang (ou) weigh heavily (responsabilité) [à, on]; to hang (silence) [sur, over]; *peser sur les bras de*, to be a burden to; *cette décision commence à me peser*, this decision is beginning to worry me; *ne pas peser lourd dans*, not to count for much in; *le temps me pèse*, time hangs heavy on my hands.
— v. pr. **Se peser**, to weigh in.
peseta [pezɛta] f. Peseta (monnaie).
pesette [pəzɛt] f. Assayer's scales.
peseur [-zœːr] s. Weigher.
peson [-zɔ̃] m. Balance.
pessaire [pesɛːr] m. Pessary.
pessimisme [pɛsimism] m. Pessimism.

pessimiste [-mist] s. Pessimist.
— adj. Pessimistic.
peste [pɛst] f. MÉD. Plague, pestilence; *peste noire*, bubonic plague. ‖ FAM. Nuisance (chose); pest, plague (personne); *fuir qqn comme la peste*, to shun s.o. like the plague.
— interj. Gosh!, Bless my soul!
pester [-te] v. intr. (1). To rail, to swear, to rave (contre, at).
pesticide [-tisid] adj. AGRIC. Pesticidal; *produit pesticide*, pesticide product.
— m. AGRIC. Pesticide.
pestiféré, ée [-tifere] adj. MÉD. Plague-stricken.
— s. MÉD. Plague-stricken patient. ‖ FIG. *Traiter qqn comme un pestiféré*, to keep s.o. at arm's length.
pestilence [-tilɑ̃:s] f. Pestilence.
pestilentiel, elle [-tilɑ̃sjɛl] adj. MÉD. Pestilential. ‖ FAM. Stinking, foetid; *odeur pestilentielle*, stench.
pet [pɛ] m. POP. Fart; *ça ne vaut pas un pet de lapin*, it's not worth a bean. ‖ **Pet-de-nonne**, m. (pl. *pets-de-nonne*). CULIN. Batter fritter. ‖ **Pet-en-l'air**, m. invar. POP. Bum-freezer; U. S ass-freezer.
pétainiste [petɛnist] s. Petainist.
pétale [petal] m. BOT. Petal.
pétanque [petɑ̃k] f. SPORTS. French bowls.
pétant, ante [petɑ̃, ɑ̃:t] adj. POP. Sharp, on the dot of; *à deux heures pétantes (ou) pétant*, at 2 o'clock sharp, on the dot of 2.
pétarade [petarad] f. Series of farts (du cheval). ‖ Crackling (du feu d'artifice). ‖ MILIT. Popping (d'un fusil). ‖ AUTOM. Popping back, backfire.
pétarader [-de] v. intr. (1). To let off a series of farts (cheval). ‖ To crackle (feu d'artifice). ‖ MILIT. To pop (armes). ‖ AUTOM. To pop back, to back-fire.
pétard [peta:r] m. Cracker, fire-cracker (d'enfant); *faire partir un pétard*, to fire a cracker. ‖ TECHN. Shot, blast (de mines). ‖ MILIT. Petard. ‖ CH. DE F. Fog-signal, U. S. torpedo. ‖ FAM. Row, din (v. BOUCAN, POTIN); *faire du pétard*, to kick up a row. ‖ POP. Bum, U. S. ass (derrière); gun (fusil); six-shooter, rod, U. S. heater (revolver).
Pétaud [peto] m. Prince of Misrule.
pétaudière [-djɛ:r] f. Ill-kept house, regular bear-garden.
péter [pete] v. intr. (5). POP. To fart, to break wind (personne). ‖ FAM. To burst (ballon); to pop (bouchon, fusée); to crackle (feu); to go bang (fusil). ‖ POP. To fizzle out (affaire); *envoyer péter*, to send to the devil.
— v. tr. FAM. *Péter du feu*, to be a live wire.
pète-sec [pɛtsɛk] m. invar. FAM. Martinet.
péteur [petœ:r] s. POP. Farter.
péteux [-tø] m. POP. Crestfallen person.
pétillant, ante [petijɑ̃, ɑ̃:t] adj. Crackling (bois, feu); semi-sparkling (vin). ‖ FIG. Coruscating, sprightly (esprit); sparkling (yeux) [de, with].
pétillement [-jmɑ̃] m. Crackling (du feu). [V. CRÉPITEMENT.] ‖ Sparkling, fizzing, fizzle (du vin). ‖ FIG. Sparkling (de l'esprit).
pétiller [-je] v. intr. (1). To crackle (feu). [V. CRÉPITER.] ‖ To sparkle, to fizz (vin). ‖ FIG. To sparkle (esprit, yeux); *pétiller d'esprit*, to sparkle with wit.
pétiole [pesjɔl] m. BOT. Petiole, leaf-stem.
petiot, ote [pətjo, ɔt] adj. Tiny, wee.
— s. Little one, tiny tot.
petit, ite [pəti, it] adj. Small, little (en dimension, taille); *petite maison, ville*, little house, town; *petit pied*, small foot; *tout petit*, tiny; teeny-weeny (fam.). ‖ Small, little (en nombre); *petit groupe*, small group. ‖ Little, small, young (en

âge); *petit chat, chien, ours,* kitten, pup (ou) puppy, bear-cub; *un petit Anglais,* an English boy; *une petite Italienne,* an Italian girl; *les petits Dupont,* the Dupont children; *le petit monde,* the youngsters; *la petite enfance,* infancy. ‖ Tight (étroit); *trop petit,* too tight (chaussure). ‖ Short (court); *à petites étapes,* by easy stages; *petite distance, durée,* short distance, duration; *un petit conte,* a short story; *un petit mot,* a few lines. ‖ Small, slight (léger); *petit choc,* slight shock; *petit coup,* tap; *petit ennui,* paltry vexation; *petit malheur,* slight misfortune. ‖ Little, small, petty (peu important); *petite affaire,* small matter; *petit commerçant,* small tradesman; *petites gens,* inconsiderable people; *petite noblesse,* minor nobility; *se faire petit,* to make oneself inconspicuous. ‖ Little, small, poor, delicate (piètre); *avoir une petite santé,* to be always ailing, to have poor health; *petit vin,* light wine. ‖ Small, little, mean (bas); *petit caractère,* small mind; *c'est bien petit de sa part,* it's mean of him; *petite querelle,* pitiable quarrel. ‖ Lower, minor (inférieur); *petites classes,* lower classes; *petite industrie,* smaller industries; *petit sujet,* minor subject. ‖ Humble; *quel petit garçon!,* how insignificant he is! ‖ RADIO. Short (onde). ‖ MILIT. *Petite tenue,* undress uniform. ‖ ECCLÉS. Minor (prophète); little (sœur); *Petit Jésus,* Infant Jesus. ‖ CULIN. *Petit four,* petit four. ‖ GRAMM. *Petit nègre,* pidgin-English. ‖ FAM. *Avoir ses petites entrées chez qqn,* to have the freedom of s.o.'s house; *j'étais dans mes petits souliers,* I was shaking in my shoes; *ma petite santé,* my precious health. ‖ LOC. *En petit,* in miniature, on a smaller scale; *petit à petit,* little by little, gradually; *un petit peu,* a little, a little bit. ‖ **Petit-beurre,** m. CULIN. Butter-biscuit. ‖ **Petit-bourgeois** (fém. *petite-bourgeoise),* adj., s. Petit (ou) petty bourgeois. ‖ **Petit-cousin,** m. Second cousin. ‖ **Petit-fils,** m. Grandson. ‖ **Petit-gris,** m. ZOOL. Siberian grey squirrel; COMM. Calabar (fourrure). ‖ **Petit-lait,** m. Whey. ‖ **Petit-maître,** m. Fop. ‖ **Petit-nègre,** m. FAM. Pidgin (charabia); gibberish, gobbledegook (discours incompréhensible). ‖ **Petit-neveu,** m. Grandnephew. ‖ **Petit-suisse,** m. CULIN. Small cream cheese. ‖ **Petite-cousine,** f. Second cousin. ‖ **Petite-fille,** f. Granddaughter. ‖ **Petite-nièce,** f. Grandniece. ‖ **Petits-enfants,** m. pl. Grandchildren.
— s. Child (enfant); kid (gosse); *grands et petits,* great and small; *la petite,* our little girl; *les petits,* the youngsters, the young ones; the juniors (en classe); *les tout petits,* the tiny tots; *un pauvre petit,* a poor little chap (ou) thing. ‖ ZOOL. Young, little one (d'un animal); *faire des petits,* to have young ones (en général); to kitten (chatte); to pup (chienne); to whelp (lionne, louve, ourse, tigresse); to farrow (truie). ‖ Small thing; *les infiniment petits,* the infinitesimals. ‖ FAM. *Faire des petits,* to multiply, to produce young.

petitement [-tmɑ̃] adv. Moderately (avec modération); meanly (chichement); basely (vilement); *logé petitement,* in mean (ou) poky lodgings.

petitesse [-tɛs] f. Smallness, littleness, tininess (de la personne, de la taille). ‖ Narrow dimensions (d'un local). ‖ FIG. Mean action (acte); narrow-mindedness (caractère). [V. MESQUINERIE.] ‖ FIG. Smallness, meanness, pettiness (d'esprit).

pétition [petisjɔ̃] f. Petition (de, from) [v. REQUÊTE]; *faire une pétition auprès de,* to petition. ‖ PHILOS. *Pétition de principe,* petitio principii; *faire une pétition de principe,* to beg the question.

pétitionnaire [-sjɔnɛːr] s. Petitioner.

pétitionner [-sjɔne] v. tr. (1). To petition.

pétoche [petɔʃ] f. POP. Fear, funk; *avoir la pétoche,* to have the wind up; *flanquer la pétoche à qqn,* to put the wind up s.o. (V. TROUILLE.)

pétoire [petwaːr] f. FAM. Pop-gun.

peton [pətɔ̃] f. FAM. Trotter, tootsy.

pétoncle [petɔ̃kl] m. ZOOL., Scallop, scollop.

pétrarquisme [petrarkism] m. Petrarchianism, petrarchism.

pétrel [petrɛl] ZOOL. Petrel.

pétri, ie [petri] adj. CULIN. Kneaded (pain). ‖ FIG. *Pétri de bonnes intentions,* full of good intentions; *pétri d'orgueil,* eaten up with pride.

pétrifiant, ante [petrifjɑ̃, ɑ̃ːt] adj. Petrifying. ‖ FAM. Dumbfounding.

pétrification [-fikasjɔ̃] f. Petrification, petrifaction.

pétrifié, ée [-fje] adj. Petrified. ‖ FAM. Dumbfounded. (V. INTERLOQUÉ.)

pétrifier [-fje] v. tr. (1). To petrify. ‖ To render callous (d'un). ‖ FAM. To dumbfound.
— v. pr. Se **pétrifier,** to petrify, to turn into stone.

pétrin [petrɛ̃] m. CULIN. Kneading-trough; *pétrin mécanique,* kneading machine. ‖ FAM. Mess; *être dans le pétrin,* to be in a nasty mess (ou) in the soup; *se tirer du pétrin,* to get out of a jam.

pétrir [petriːr] v. tr. (2). CULIN. To knead (de la pâte). ‖ ARTS. To mould (de l'argile). ‖ MÉD. To knead (les muscles). ‖ FIG. To mould (esprit).

pétrissage [petrisaːʒ] m. CULIN., MÉD. Kneading. ‖ ARTS. Moulding. ‖ FIG. Moulding, shaping.

pétrisseur [-sœːr] m. Kneader.
— adj. Kneading.

pétrisseuse [-søːz] f. Kneading-machine.

pétrochimie [petroʃimi] f. Petrochemistry.

pétrochimique [-mik] adj. Petrochemical; *produits pétrochimiques,* petrochemicals.

pétrochimiste [-mist] s. Petrochemical scientist.

pétrodollar [petrodɔlar] m. FIN. Petrodollar.

pétrographie [petrɔgrafi] f. Petrography.

pétrole [petrɔl] m. Petroleum, oil (sens générique); paraffin oil, U. S. kerosene (sens spécifique); *trouver du pétrole,* to strike oil.

pétrolette [-lɛt] f. FAM. Moped.

pétroleur [-lœːr] s. Incendiary using paraffin.

pétrolier, ère [-lje, ɛːr] adj. Petrol, mineral-oil (industrie); *établissements pétroliers,* oil installations.
— m. Oil magnate (industriel). ‖ NAUT. Tanker (navire).

pétrolifère [-lifɛːr] adj. Petroliferous; *gisement (ou) terrain pétrolifère,* oilfield; *région pétrolifère,* oil-bearing region.

pétrologie [-lɔʒi] f. Petrology.

pétulance [petylɑ̃ːs] f. Liveliness, sprightliness. (V. VIVACITÉ.) ‖ Friskiness (d'un cheval).

pétulant, ante [-lɑ̃, ɑ̃ːt] adj. Lively, sprightly, frolicsome. (V. VIF.) ‖ Frisky (cheval).

pétun [petœ̃] n. FAM. Baccy.

pétuner [-tyne] v. intr. (1). FAM. To smoke.

pétunia [petynja] m. BOT. Petunia.

peu [pø] adv. Little (en quantité ou en valeur) [v. GUERRE]; *c'est peu,* it's not much; *c'est peu de le louer,* he deserves more than mere praise; *ce n'est pas peu dire,* it means a lot, that's saying a good deal; *peu ou point,* little or none; *peu ou prou,* little if any, more or less. ‖ Few (en nombre); *il y en a peu qui viendront,* few will come; *il y en a peu qui vous connaissent,* few people know you. ‖ Not very, not much, non-, un- (sens négatif); *peu intelligent,* rather dull; *peu poétique,* unpoetical; *peu poli,* impolite; *peu utile,* not very useful. ‖ *Peu après, peu avant,* shortly after, shortly before. ‖ **Peu de,** little (au sg.); few (au pl.); a few (quelques); *peu ou point d'argent,* little if any money, little or no money; *peu de bonheur,* little happiness; *peu de choses,* nothing much; *peu d'élus,* few chosen; *peu d'entre vous,* few among you; *peu de gens,* few people; *à peu de*

chose près, little short of it ; *bien peu de confort*, very little comfort ; *en peu de mots*, in a few words ; *très* (ou) *trop peu d'exceptions*, very (ou) too few exceptions ; *y être pour peu de chose*, to have little to do with it. ‖ **Peu à peu**, little by little, by degrees. (V. PETIT À PETIT.) ‖ **Avant peu, sous peu**, before long. ‖ **A peu près**, nearly, almost, scarcely, hardly (v. ENVIRON, PRESQUE) ; *à peu près parfait*, verging on perfection ; *à peu près tout le monde*, practically everybody ; *à peu près rien*, hardly anything, next to nothing. ‖ **Depuis peu**, lately, of late, for a short time. ‖ **D'ici peu**, a short time hence. ‖ **Peu s'en faut**, very nearly ; *peu s'en faut qu'il ne soit tombé*, he almost fell. ‖ **Pour peu que**, if only, if ever. ‖ **Pour si peu**, for so small a matter. ‖ **Quelque peu**, slightly, to a slight extent ; *quelque peu inquiet*, somewhat anxious ; *quelque peu de fièvre*, a slight fever. ‖ **Si peu**, however little ; *si peu que vous m'en donniez*, however little you give me ; *si peu que rien*, the least little bit, next to nothing. ‖ **Tant soit peu**, ever so little, the least bit. ‖ **Un peu**, a little, somewhat, rather, a bit, slightly ; *un peu artiste*, something of an artist ; *un peu gros*, rather big ; *c'est un peu fort*, it's a bit thick ! ; *un petit peu troublé*, slightly disturbed.
— m. Bit, little ; *le peu de connaissances que j'ai*, the little learning I have ; *le peu d'ennemis qu'il a*, the few enemies he has ; *mon peu d'aide*, my little help ; *son peu d'éducation*, his lack of education ; *son peu de mémoire*, his shortness of memory. ‖ **De peu**, by a little bit ; *être plus grand de peu*, to be a shade taller ; *manquer de peu*, to miss by very little ; *il s'en est fallu de peu*, it was a near thing ; *il s'en est fallu de peu que je sois écrasé*, I was within an ace of being run over ; *un homme de peu*, low-born (ou) worthless fellow. ‖ **Un peu de**, a bit of ; *un peu de viande*, a little meat ; *un peu d'effronterie*, a bit of cheek ; *un tout petit peu*, a tiny bit ; *un tout petit peu de vin*, just a drop of wine ; *écoutez un peu !*, just listen !, listen a moment ! ; *je vous demande un peu !*, I ask you ! ; *viens un peu !*, come here ! ‖ **Pour un peu**, for a little, for two pins ; *pour un peu je serais parti*, I was within an ace of leaving. ‖ **Un tant soit peu de**, a modicum of ; *avec un tant soit peu de jalousie*, with a touch of jealousy. ‖ FAM. *Un peu beaucoup*, far too much.

peuchère ! [pøʃɛ:r] interj. V. PÉCHÈRE.
peuh ! [pø] interj. Pooh !
peuplade [pœplad] f. Small tribe. (V. TRIBU.)
peuple [pœpl] m. People (v. NATION) ; *tous les peuples d'Europe*, all the peoples of Europe. ‖ People, the masses ; *le bas peuple*, the lower classes, the riff-raff (v. POPULACE) ; *gens du peuple*, common people.
— adj. Plebeian (langage, mentalité) ; common, vulgar, rough-hewn, plebeian (personne) ; *être très peuple*, to be very plebeian (or) common.
peuplé, ée [-ple] adj. Populated (pays) ; *peuplé par une foule de gens*, thronged (ou) crowded with people. ‖ FIG. Peopled, filled (*de*, with).
peuplement [-pləmᾶ] m. Peopling (d'un pays). ‖ Stocking (d'une chasse, d'un étang). ‖ Planting (d'un terrain).
peupler [-ple] v. tr. (1). To people (une région). ‖ To stock (une chasse, un étang) ; to plant (un terrain). ‖ FIG. To people, to stock, to fill (sa mémoire) ; *les personnages qui peuplent ses livres*, the characters that are to be found in his books.
— v. intr. To multiply, to breed.
— v. pr. **Se peupler**, to become peopled ; *se peupler lentement*, to be gradually filled with people.
peuplier [pœplje] m. BOT. Poplar ; *peuplier d'Italie*, Lombardy poplar.
peur [pœ:r] f. Fear, fright, dread (v. CRAINTE, EFFROI) ; *avoir peur de qqch., qqn, de faire qqch.*,

to be afraid of sth., s.o., of doing sth. ; *avoir peur pour qqn*, to be anxious on s.o.'s account ; *avoir plus de peur que de mal*, to be more frightened than hurt ; *en être quitte pour la peur*, to get off with a bad fright ; *faire peur à qqn*, to frighten s.o., to give s.o. a fright ; *prendre peur*, to take fright ; *sans peur*, fearless ; *vilain à faire peur*, dreadfully ugly. ‖ Fear (crainte légère ou polie) ; *avoir peur que quelqu'un ne vienne*, to be anxious lest s.o. should come, to fear that s.o. may come (redouter la venue) ; to fear that s.o. may not come (redouter la non-venue) ; *j'en ai bien peur*, I am afraid it is so. ‖ MÉD. Phobia. ‖ FAM. *En voilà un qui n'a pas peur !*, he has got a nerve !, he has his nerve !
— loc. prép. **De peur de**, for fear of (qqch.) ; *de peur de faire qqch.*, for fear of doing sth. ; *de peur de me tromper*, for fear I may make a mistake.
— loc. conj. **De peur que**, lest, for fear that ; *de peur qu'il ne se fâche*, for fear he may get angry ; *de peur qu'on n'en abuse*, lest people should misuse it.
peureusement [pørøzmᾶ] adv. Fearfully, timorously. (V. CRAINTIVEMENT.)
peureux, euse [pørø, ø:z] adj. Fearful, timorous, timid (personne). [V. CRAINTIF.] ‖ Coward. (V. POLTRON.) ‖ Shy, timid, shrinking (caractère, nature) ; fearful (regard). ‖ Shy, skittish (cheval) ; gun-shy (chien de chasse).
— s. Timid (ou) fearful (ou) timorous person. ‖ Chicken-hearted person. (V. FROUSSARD.)
peut, peux [pø:]. V. POUVOIR (79).
peut-être [pøtɛ:tr] adv. Perhaps, maybe ; perchance ; *peut-être est-elle sortie*, she may be out ; *peut-être bien*, that may be so ; *peut-être que oui, peut-être que non*, perhaps so, perhaps not ; *je l'ai peut-être*, perhaps I have it. ‖ FAM. *J'en sais autant que vous, peut-être !*, I know as much as you, I suppose !
peuvent [pø:v]. V. POUVOIR (79).
peyotl [pejɔtl] m. BOT. Peyote.
pèze [pɛ:z] m. POP. Dough ; U. S. jack.
P. G. C. D. [peʒesede] m. MATH. Abrév. de *plus grand commun diviseur*, HCF, highest common factor (ou) GCD, greatest common divisor.
pH [peaʃ] m. CHIM. Abrév. de *potentiel hydrogène*, pH.
phacochère [fakɔʃɛ:r] m. ZOOL. Warthog.
phaéton [faetɔ̃] m. Phaeton.
phagocyte [fagɔsit] m. MÉD. Phagocyte.
phagocyter [-te] v. tr. (1). MÉD. To phagocitize. ‖ FIG. To smother.
phagocytose [-to:z] f. MÉD. Phagocytosis.
phalange [falᾶ:ʒ] f. † Phalanx (en Grèce). ‖ MILIT. Army, host. ‖ MÉD. Phalanx (des doigts). ‖ Falange (en Espagne).
phalangette [falᾶʒɛt] f. MÉD. Ungual phalanx.
phalangien, enne [-ʒjɛ̃, :ɛn] adj. MÉD. Phalangeal.
phalangiste [-ʒist] s. Falangist.
phalanstère [falᾶstɛ:r] m. Phalanstery.
phalène [falɛ:n] f. ZOOL. Phalaena, moth.
phallique [falik] adj. Phallic.
phallocrate [falɔkrat] adj. Male chauvinist.
— m. Male chauvinist, male chauvinist pig (fam.).
phallocratie [-krasi] f. Male chauvinism.
phalloïde [falɔid] adj. BOT. *Amanite phalloïde*, death cap.
phallus [falys] m. Phallus.
phanérogame [fanerɔgam] adj. BOT. Phanerogamic, phanerogamous.
— f. BOT. Phanerogam.
phantasme [fᾶtasm] m. MÉD., PHILOS. Phantasm.
pharamineux, euse [faraminø, ø:z] adj. FAM. Phenomenal, prodigious. (V. STUPÉFIANT.)
pharaon [faraɔ̃] m. Pharaoh. ‖ Faro (aux cartes).
phare [fa:r] m. Lighthouse ; *phare à éclipses*,

tournant, occulting-light, revolving-light lighthouse. ‖ AUTOM. Headlight; *phare dans l'aile,* built-in headlight. ‖ NAUT. Beacon. ‖ AVIAT. Beacon; *phare à éclats,* blinker; *phare d'atterrissage,* landing light. ‖ CH. DE F. Headlight. ‖ **Phare-balise,** m. NAUT., AVIAT. Beacon. ‖ **Phare-code,** m. AUTOM. Non-dazzle (ou) regulation headlight.

pharisaïque [farizaik] adj. Pharisaical.

pharisaïsme [-zaism] m. Pharisaism. ‖ FIG. Self-righteousness.

pharisien, enne [-zjɛ̃, ɛn] s. Pharisee. ‖ FIG. Pharisee, self-righteous person.

pharmaceutique [farmasøtik] adj. MÉD. Pharmaceutical; *spécialités pharmaceutiques,* patent medicines, proprietary medical articles.
— f. MÉD. Pharmaceutics.

pharmacie [-si] f. MÉD. Pharmacy, pharmaceutics (pharmaceutique). ‖ Chemist's (ou) druggist's shop, U. S. drugstore (magasin). ‖ Medicine-chest (armoire); *pharmacie de poche,* pocket medicine case, first-aid kit.

pharmacien, enne [-sjɛ̃, ɛn] s. MÉD. Chemist, druggist.

pharmacologie [-kɔlɔʒi] f. MÉD. Pharmacology.

pharmacopée [-kɔpe] f. MÉD. Pharmacopoeia.

pharyngien, enne [farɛ̃ʒjɛ̃, ɛn] adj. MÉD. Pharyngeal.

pharyngite [-ʒit] f. MÉD. Pharyngitis.

pharynx [farɛ̃:ks] m. MÉD. Pharynx.

phase [fa:z] f. ASTRON. Phase (de la lune). ‖ ELECTR. Phase; *à trois phases,* three-phase (moteur). ‖ MÉD. Phase (d'une maladie). ‖ FIG. Phase, stage (d'un cycle); angle, aspect.

Phébus [feby:s] m. Phoebus.

Phénicie [fenisi] f. GÉOGR. Phoenicia.

phénicien, enne [-sjɛ̃, ɛn] adj., s. Phoenician.

phénix [feniks] m. Phœnix (pr. et fig.).

phénobarbital [fenobarbital] m. MÉD. Phenobarbital, phenobarbitone.

phénol [fenɔl] m. CHIM. Phenol.

phénoménal, ale [fenomenal] adj. Phenomenal.

phénomène [-mɛn] m. Phenomenon (pl. phenomena). ‖ Freak (monstre); *montreur de phénomènes,* freak showman. ‖ FIG. Prodigy. (V. PRODIGE.) ‖ FAM. Caution, character, queer card (ou fish); *c'est un phénomène,* he's a character.

phénoménologie [-menɔlɔʒi] f. Phenomenology.

phénotype [fenɔtip] m. BOT., ZOOL., MÉD. Phenotype.

phényle [fenil] m. CHIM. Phenyl.

phéromone [feromɔn] f. ZOOL., MÉD. Pheromone.

philanthrope [filɑ̃trɔp] s. Philanthropist.

philanthropie [-trɔpi] f. Philanthropy.

philanthropique [-trɔpik] adj. Philanthropic.

philatélie [filateli] f. Philately, stamp collecting.

philatéliste [-list] s. Philatelist, stamp-collector.

philharmonie [filarmɔni] f. MUS. Philharmonic (orchestre).

philharmonique [filarmɔnik] adj. MUS. Philharmonic.

Philippe [filip] m. Philip.

philippin, ine [filipɛ̃, in] adj. GÉOGR. Philippine, Filipino.
— s. GÉOGR. Filipino.

philippine [filipin] f. Philippine (amande); Philippina (prénom). ‖ GÉOGR. Pl. Philippines.

philippique [filipik] f. Philippic.

Philistin [filistɛ̃] m. Philistine. ‖ FIG. Philistine; lowbrow (fam.).

philodendron [filɔdɛ̃drɔ̃] m. BOT. Philodendron.

philologie [filɔlɔʒi] f. Philology.

philologique [-ʒik] adj. Philological.

philologiquement [-ʒikmɑ̃] adv. Philologically.

philologue [filɔlɔg] s. Philologist.

Philomèle [filɔmɛl] f. Philomela.

philosophale [filozofal] adj. f. *Pierre philosophale,* philosopher's stone.

philosophe [-zɔf] s. PHILOS. Philosopher.
— adj. FAM. Philosophical.

philosopher [-zofe] v. intr. (1). PHILOS. To philosophize.

philosophie [-zofi] f. Philosophy. ‖ FAM. Philosophical attitude.

philosophique [-zofik] adj. PHILOS. Philosophical.

philosophiquement [-zofikmɑ̃] adv. Philosophically.

philosophisme [-zofism] m. Philosophism.

philtre [filtre] m. Philtre.

phlébite [flebit] f. MÉD. Phlebitis.

phlegmon [flegmɔ̃] m. MÉD. Phlegmon.

phlegmoneux, euse [-mɔnø, ø:z] adj. MÉD. Phlegmonous, phlegmonic.

phlogistique [flɔʒistik] m. Phlogiston.
— adj. Phlogistic.

phlox [flɔ:ks] m. BOT. Phlox.

phobie [fɔbi] f. Phobia.

phobique [fɔbik] adj., s. Phobic.

phocéen, enne [fɔseɛ̃, ɛn] adj. † Phocaean. ‖ GÉOGR. Of (ou) from Marseilles.
— s. † Phocaean. ‖ GÉOGR. Native (ou) inhabitant of Marseilles.

phonateur, trice [fɔnatœ:r, tris] **phonatoire** [-twa:r] adj. Phonatory; *organes phonateurs,* speech organs.

phonation [-sjɔ̃] f. Phonation.

phone [fɔn] m. PHYS., TECHN. Phon.

phonématique [fɔnematik] f. GRAMM. Phonemics.

phonème [fɔnɛm] m. GRAMM. Phone, phoneme.

phonémique [fɔnemik] adj. GRAMM. Phonemic.

phonéticien, enne [fɔnetisjɛ̃] s. Phonetician.

phonétique [-tik] adj. Phonetic.
— f. Phonetics; *phonétique historique,* phonology.

phonétiquement [-tikmɑ̃] adv. Phonetically.

phoniatrie [fɔnjatri] f. MÉD. Phoniatrics.

phonie [fɔni] f. MILIT. Radiotelephony, RT; *parler en phonie,* to communicate by RT.

phonique [fɔnik] adj. Phonic.

phono [fɔno], **phonographe** [-graf] m. Phonograph; gramophone.

phonogénique [-ʒenik] adj. Suitable for sound-recording.

phonographie [-grafi] f. Phonography. ‖ Phonetic spelling. ‖ Gramophone recording.

phonographique [-grafic] adj. Phonographic.

phonologie [-lɔʒi] f. GRAMM. Phonology.

phonologique [-lɔʒik] adj. GRAMM. Phonological.

phonologue [-lɔg] s. GRAMM. Phonologist.

phonométrie [-metri] f. TECHN. Phonometry.

phonothèque [-tɛk] f. Sound archives.

phoque [fɔk] m. ZOOL. Seal. ‖ COMM. Sealskin leather.

phosgène [fɔsʒɛn] m. CHIM. Phosgene (gaz).

phosphatage [fɔsfata:ʒ] m. AGRIC. Treating with phosphates.

phosphate [-fat] m. CHIM. Phosphate.

phosphaté, ée [-fate] adj. Phosphated.

phosphater [-fate] v. tr. (1). AGRIC. To treat with phosphates, to phosphatize.

phosphatique [-fatik] adj. CHIM. Phosphatic.

phosphène [fɔsfɛn] m. MÉD. Phosphene.

phosphine [fɔsfin] f. CHIM. Phosphine.

phosphore [fɔsfɔ:r] m. CHIM. Phosphorus.

phosphoré, ée [-fɔre] adj. Phosphorated.

phosphorer [-fɔre] v. intr. (1). FAM. To burn the midnight oil, to work one's brain.

phosphorescence [-fɔrɛsɑ̃:s] f. Phosphorescence.

phosphorescent, ente [-fɔrɛsɑ̃, ɑ̃:t] adj. Phosphorescent; *être phosphorescent,* to phosphoresce.

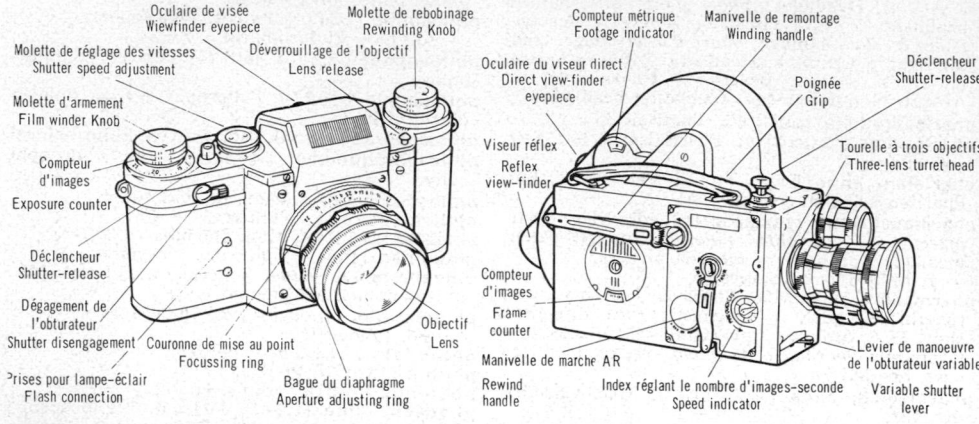

Oculaire de visée
Wiewfinder eyepiece

Molette de rebobinage
Rewinding Knob

Molette de réglage des vitesses
Shutter speed adjustment

Déverrouillage de l'objectif
Lens release

Molette d'armement
Film winder Knob

Compteur
d'images
Exposure counter

Déclencheur
Shutter-release

Dégagement de
l'obturateur
Shutter disengagement

Couronne de mise au point
Focussing ring

Prises pour lampe-éclair
Flash connection

Bague du diaphragme
Aperture adjusting ring

Objectif
Lens

Compteur métrique
Footage indicator

Manivelle de remontage
Winding handle

Oculaire du viseur direct
Direct view-finder
eyepiece

Poignée
Grip

Déclencheur
Shutter-release

Viseur réflex
Reflex
view-finder

Tourelle à trois objectifs
Three-lens turret head

Compteur
d'images
Frame
counter

Manivelle de marche AR
Rewind
handle

Index réglant le nombre d'images-seconde
Speed indicator

Levier de manoeuvre
de l'obturateur variable

Variable shutter
lever

---

phosphoreux, euse [-fɔrø, ø:z] adj. CHIM. Phos-phorous.
phosphorique [-fɔrik] adj. CHIM. Phosphoric.
phosphure [-fy:r] m. CHIM. Phosphide.
phosphuré, ée [-fyre] adj. CHIM. Phosphuretted.
photo [fɔto] f. V. PHOTOGRAPHIE. ‖ **Photo-finish,** m. SPORTS. Photograph showing (ou) camera filming a photofinish. ‖ **Photo-robot,** f. Identikit, identikit picture. ‖ **Photo-stoppeur,** m. Street-photographer.
photochimie [-ʃimi] f. CHIM. Photochemistry.
photocomposition [-kɔ̃pozisjɔ̃] f. TECHN. Photocomposition, photosetting, filmsetting (en imprimerie).
photocopie [-kɔpi] f. Photocopy; photostat.
photocopier [-kɔpje] v. tr. (1). To photocopy; to photostat; U.S. to xerox.
photocopieur [-kɔpjœ:r] m. Photocopier; photostat; xerox.
photocopieuse [-kɔpjø:z] f. V. PHOTOCOPIEUR.
photoélectrique [-elɛktrik] adj. Photo-electric; cellule photoélectrique, photocell.
photoémetteur, trice [-emɛtœ:r, tris] adj. Photo-emittent (cellule).
photogénique [-ʒenik] adj. Photogenic; être photogénique, to come out well on photographs.
photographe [-graf] s. Photographer.
photographie [-graphi] f. Photography; faire de la photo, to go in for photography; to take photographs; photographie en couleur, colour photography. ‖ Photograph, U.S. picture; se faire faire une photo, to have one's photograph taken.
photographier [-grafje] v. tr. (1). To photograph; photographier qqn, to take s.o.'s picture; se faire photographier, to be photographed, to have one's photograph taken.
photographique [-grafik] adj. Photographic; appareil photographique, camera. ‖ AVIAT. Reconnaissance photographique, photo-reconnaissance.
photographiquement [-grafikmɑ̃] adv. Photographically.
photograveur [-gravœ:r] m. Photoengraver.
photogravure [-gravy:r] f. Photogravure; photoengraving.
photomètre [-mɛtr] m. Photometer.
photométrie [-metri] f. Photometry.
photométrique [-metrik] adj. Photometric.
photomontage [-mɔ̃ta:ʒ] m. Photomontage.
photon [fɔtɔ̃] m. PHYS. Photon.
photophobie [fɔtofɔbi] f. MÉD. Photophobia.
photosensible [-sɑ̃sibl] adj. TECHN. Photosensitive.

photosphère [fɔtɔsfɛ:r] f. ASTRON. Photosphere.
photostat [fɔtɔsta] m. Photostat.
photosynthèse [-sɛ̃tɛ:z] f. BOT. Photosynthesis.
photothèque [-tɛk] f. Photographic library.
photothérapie [-terapi] f. MÉD. Phototherapy; light-cure.
phototype [-tip] m. Phototype.
phototypie [-tipi] f. Collotype.
photovoltaïque [-vɔltaik] adj. ELECTR. Photovoltaic (cellule).
phrase [frɑ:z] f. GRAMM. Sentence; membre de phrase, phrase; phrase toute faite, stock phrase. ‖ MUS., SPORTS. Phrase. ‖ FIG. Phrase; faire des phrases, to speechify, to use high-sounding words; sans phrases, without mincing matters.
phrasé [fraze] m. MUS. Phrasing.
phraséologie [frazeɔlɔʒi] f. Phraseology.
phraser [-ze] v. intr. (1). MUS. To phrase. ‖ FAM. To use flowery language; to speechify.
— v. tr. MUS. To phrase.
phraseur [-zœ:r] s. FAM. Phrase-monger, windbag, tub-thumper.
phratrie [fratri] f. Phratry.
phréatique [freatik] adj. Nappe phréatique, phreatic water, groundwater.
phrénologie [frenɔlɔʒi] f. Phrenology.
phrénologique [-ʒik] adj. Phrenological.
phrénologiste [-ʒist] m. Phrenologist.
Phrygie [friʒi] f. GÉOGR. Phrygia.
phrygien, enne [-ʒjɛ̃, ɛn] adj. Phrygian.
phtaléine [ftalein] f. CHIM. Phtalein.
phtisie [ftizi] f. MÉD. Phthisis, consumption.
phtisiologie [-zjɔlɔʒi] f. MÉD. Phthisiology, study of tuberculosis.
phtisiologue [-zjɔlɔg] s. MÉD. Specialist in tuberculosis.
phtisique [-zik] adj., s. MÉD. Consumptive.
phylactère [filaktɛ:r] m. † Phylactery, frontlet.
phylétique [filetik] adj. BOT., ZOOL. Phyletic.
phylloxéra [filɔksera] m. ZOOL. Phylloxera.
phylogenèse [filoʒənɛ:z] f. BOT., ZOOL. Phylogenesis.
phylum [filɔm] m. BOT., ZOOL. Phylum.
physalie [fizali] f. ZOOL. Physalia, portuguese man-of-war.
physicien, enne [fizisjɛ̃, ɛn] s. PHYS. Physicist.
physico-chimie, [fizikɔʃimi] f. PHYS., CHIM. Physical chemistry.
physico-chimique [-ʃimik] adj. Physico-chemical.

physiocrate [fizjɔkrat] adj. Physiocratic.
— s. Physiocrat.
physiocratie [-krasi] f. Physiocracy.
physiognomonie [fizjɔgnɔmɔni] f. Study of physiognomy.
physiographie [-grafi] f. GÉOGR. Physiography, physical geography.
physiologie [-lɔʒi] f. MÉD. Physiology.
physiologique [-lɔʒik] adj. Physiological; *sérum physiologique*, normal saline (ou) physiological salt solution.
physiologiste [-lɔʒist] s. Physiologist.
physionomie [-nɔmi] f. Physiognomy; countenance (aspect); set of features (traits); *physionomie fermée*, inscrutable coutenance. ‖ FIG. Aspect, appearance (des lieux); character (des événements); *physionomie littéraire*, literary profile (ou) character (ou) personality.
physionomiste [-nɔmist] s. Physionomist. ‖ FAM. *Ne pas être physionomiste*, to have no memory for faces.
physiothérapie [-terapi] f. MÉD. Physiotherapy.
physique [fizik] adj. Material (bien-être); physical (culture); bodily (douleur). ‖ PHYS. Physical (chimie, géographie, science).
— f. PHYS. Physics; *appareil de physique*, physical apparatus; *physique de la terre*, geophysics. ‖ Text-book on physics (livre).
— m. Physique (aspect); *au physique agréable*, good-looking. ‖ Body, physical constitution; *au physique et au moral*, in body and mind. ‖ THÉÂTR. *Avoir le physique de l'emploi*, to look the part, to be built for the part.
physiquement [-mɑ̃] adv. Physically. ‖ FAM. In appearance.
phytoplancton [fitoplɑ̃ktɔ̃] m. BOT. Phytoplankton.
phytozoaire [fitozɔɛːr] m. ZOOL. Phytozoon (pl. phytozoa).
pi [pi] m. MATH. Pi.
piaf [pjaf] m. POP. Sparrow.
piaffement [pjafmɑ̃] m. Pawing, stamping (du cheval). ‖ FIG. *Piaffement d'impatience*, prancing with impatience, fidgeting.
piaffer [-fe] v. intr. (1). To paw the ground, to stamp, to prance (cheval). ‖ FAM. To fidget (s'impatienter); to swagger (se pavaner).
piaffeur, euse [-fœːr, øːz] adj. Pawing, high-stepping (cheval). ‖ FAM. Fidgety (impatient); swaggering (vaniteux).
piaillement [pjajmɑ̃] m. Chirping, cheeping (d'oiseau); squeaking (de souris).
piailler [pjɑje] v. intr. (1). To chirp, to cheep (oiseau). ‖ To squeal, to squall (enfant).
— v. tr. FAM. To squeak out.
piaillerie [-jri] f. Chirping, cheeping (d'oiseau); squeaking (de souris). ‖ Squealing, squalling (d'enfants).
piailleur, euse [-jœːr, øːz] adj. Chirping (oiseau). ‖ Squalling (enfant).
— m. Chirper (oiseau). ‖ Squaller (enfant).
pianissimo [pjanisimo] adv. MUS. Pianissimo.
pianiste [-nist] s. MUS. Pianist, piano-player.
piano [-no] adv. MUS. Piano. ‖ FAM. Slowly, gently, quietly; *piano-piano*, very softly (ou) slowly.
— m. MUS. Piano, pianoforte (instrument); piano (mouvement); *piano automatique*, player piano, pianola; *piano à queue, crapaud* (ou) *demi-queue, droit*, grand, baby-grand, upright piano; *jouer du piano*, to play the piano; *tenir le piano*, to be at the piano.
Pianola [-nɔla] m. MUS. Pianola.
pianotage [-nɔtaːʒ] m. MUS. Strumming on (ou) plunking away at the piano. ‖ Drumming (des doigts sur la table).
pianoter [-nɔte] v. intr. (1). MUS. To strum on the piano. ‖ FIG. To rattle away (sur une machine

à écrire); to thrum, to drum, to play a tattoo (sur la table).
pianoteur [-nɔtoeːr] s. MUS. Strummer.
piastre [pjastr] f. FIN. Piastre.
piaule [pjo:l] f. POP. Digs, diggings, U. S. place.
piaulement [pjolmɑ̃] m. Peeping (d'oiseau). ‖ Squalling; whining, puling (d'enfant).
piauler [-le] v. intr. (1). To peep (poussin). ‖ To squall; to whine, to pule (enfant).
pic [pik] m. Pick, pickaxe; *pic pneumatique*, pneumatic drill. ‖ Pique (carte). ‖ GÉOGR. Peak (montagne). ‖ NAUT. Peak (de voile).
— loc. adv. **A pic**, perpendicularly, precipitously; *descendre à pic*, to go sheer down, to fall sheer; *descente à pic*, sheer drop. ‖ FAM. In the nick of time; *tomber à pic*, to come just in time.
pic [pik] m. ZOOL. Woodpecker.
picaillons [pikajɔ̃] m. pl. FAM. Ooze, U.S. dough.
picard, arde [pikaːr, ard] adj. GÉOGR. Of (ou) from Picardie.
— s. GÉOGR. Native of Picardie.
— m. GRAMM. Dialect of Picardie.
picaresque [pikarɛsk] adj. Picaresque.
piccolo [pikɔlo] m. MUS. Piccolo.
pichenette [piʃnɛt] f. Fillip, flick, flip (v. CHIQUENAUDE); *chasser d'une pichenette*, to flick off.
pichet [piʃɛ] m. Pitcher, jug.
pickpocket [pikpɔkɛt] m. Pickpocket.
pick-up [pikœp] m. Pick-up, record-player.
picoler [pikɔle] v. intr. (1). FAM. To lift the elbow.
picorer [pikɔre] v. tr., intr. (1). To peck, to pick up. ‖ FIG. To pilfer.
picot [piko] m. Picot (de dentelle). ‖ Splinter (de bois). ‖ TECHN. Pointed hammer (de carrier); wedge (de mineur).
picotement [-tmɑ̃] m. Tingling, prickling.
picoter [-te] v. tr. (1). To prick holes in (une feuille). ‖ To peck at (un arbre). ‖ To cause to tingle, to prickle (la peau); *picoter les mains*, to make s.o.'s hands smart. ‖ To work a picot on (une dentelle). ‖ To pit (le métal). ‖ TECHN. To wedge. ‖ FAM. To tease (qqn). [V. TAQUINER.]
picoterie [-tri] f. FAM. Pin-pricking.
picotin [-tɛ̃] m. Peck (mesure); feed (d'avoine).
picoture [-tyːr] f. Spot, mark (sur un fruit). ‖ Pinhole (dans le cuir).
picrate [pikrat] m. CHIM. Picrate.
picrique [pikrik] adj. CHIM. Picric.
pictographe [piktɔgraf] s. Pictograph.
pictographie [-fi] f. Pictography.
pictural, ale [piktyral] adj. ARTS. Pictorial.
pidgin [pidʒin] m. GRAMM. Pidgin.
pie [pi] f. ZOOL. Magpie. ‖ CULIN. *Fromage à la pie*, green cheese. ‖ FIG. Magpie, chatterbox (bavarde); *trouver la pie au nid*, to make a find. ‖ **Pie-grièche**, ZOOL. Shrike; FAM. Shrew.
— adj. invar. Piebald (cheval); *voiture pie*, police car, U. S. squad car.
pie adj. Pious; *œuvre pie*, good work.
pièce [pjɛs] f. Piece (étendue); *pièce d'eau*, sheet of water, ornamental water; *pièce de velours*, roll of velvet. ‖ Whole (tout); *d'une seule pièce*, one-piece; *inventé de toutes pièces*, entirely fabricated (ou) made up; *tout d'une pièce*, all of one piece, in one piece; *tomber tout d'une pièce*, to fall headlong. ‖ Piece, bit (fragment); *mettre en pièces*, to tear to pieces (un tissu); *pièce à pièce*, bit by bit. ‖ Patch (pour raccommoder); *mettre une pièce à, to patch; ouvrage fait de pièces et de morceaux*, patchwork. ‖ Pawn, man (aux échecs). ‖ Cask, barrel (de vin). ‖ Room (d'un appartement); *appartement de six pièces*, six-roomed flat (ou) U. S. apartment. ‖ AGRIC. Plot, field (champ). ‖ SPORTS. Head (à la chasse); *combien de pièces abattues?*, how many head brought down? ‖ ARTS. Piece (objet rare); *pièce de musée*, museum piece, show-piece. ‖ THÉÂTR. Play. ‖ MILIT. Gun.

‖ FIN. Coin (monnaie); gratuity (pourboire); *donner la pièce à qqn*, to give s.o. a tip, to tip s.o. ‖ JUR. Document, paper; *pièce jointe*, enclosure. ‖ NAUT. Coil of rope. ‖ MÉD. *Pièce anatomique*, anatomical specimen. ‖ CULIN. *Pièce montée*, set piece; *pièce de résistance*, pièce de résistance. ‖ COMM. Piece; *combien la pièce?*, how much apiece?; *se vendre à la pièce*, to be sold separately; *travail à la pièce*, piece-work; *travailler à la pièce*, to do piece-work, to work by the job. ‖ TECHN. Parts (de machine); *pièces de rechange*, spare parts. ‖ ARCHIT. Member (de charpente). ‖ BLAS. Ordinary; *pièce honorable*, honourable ordinary. ‖ FAM. *Faire pièce à qqn*, to play a trick on s.o.

piécette [pjesɛt] f. FIN. Small coin. ‖ THÉÂTR. Curtain-raiser, playlet.

pied [pje] m.

---

1. Membre. — 2. Organe de la marche. — 3. Assise. — 4. Pied d'objet. — 5. Mesure. — 6. TECHN. — 7. GRAMM. — 8. AGRIC. — 9. ARCHIT. — 10. ARTS. — 11. SPORTS. — 12. CULIN. — 13. MATH. — 14. MÉD. — 15. FIN. — 16. MILIT. — 17. LOC. — 18. POP.

---

1. Foot (de l'animal, de l'homme); *pieds de derrière, de devant*, hindfeet, forefeet; *pieds nus*, barefooted; *donner un coup de pied*, to kick; *fouler aux pieds*, to trample; *ne pouvoir mettre un pied devant l'autre*, to be unable to set one foot before the other; *sur la pointe des pieds*, on tiptoe; *sur ses pieds*, on one's feet (ou) toes. ‖ **2.** Foot (organe de la marche); *à pied*, on foot; *aller à pied*, to walk; *au pied léger*, swift-footed; *une heure de trajet à pied*, an hour's walk. ‖ **3.** Foothold (assise); *avoir pied*, to be within one's depth; to feel the ground under one's feet; *ne pas avoir pied*, to be out of one's depth; *le pied sûr*, sure of foot; *mettre pied à terre*, to dismount (de cheval); to alight (de voiture); *perdre pied*, to lose one's foothold; *prendre pied*, to gain a foothold. ‖ **4.** Foot (d'un arbre, d'une colline, d'une échelle, du lit, du mur, d'un verre); stand (d'un appareil photographique, d'un télescope); leg (de chaise, de table); base, foot (de colonne). ‖ Foot (d'un bas); sham (d'un col). ‖ **5.** Foot (mesure); *deux pieds de haut*, two feet high. ‖ **6.** TECHN. Size-stick (de cordonnier). ‖ **7.** GRAMM. Foot (du vers); *de douze pieds*, twelve-feet (vers). ‖ **8.** AGRIC. Head (de céleri, salade); stock (de vigne); *sur pied*, on the hoof (bétail); standing (récolte). ‖ **9.** ARCHIT. *A pied d'œuvre*, on the site. ‖ **10.** ARTS. *En pied*, full-length (portrait). ‖ **11.** SPORTS. Track (d'un animal, du gibier). ‖ **12.** CULIN. Trotter (de mouton, de porc); foot (de veau). ‖ **13.** MATH. Foot (d'une perpendiculaire). ‖ **14.** MÉD. *Remettre qqn sur pied*, to pull s.o. through, to set s.o. on his feet again. ‖ **15.** FIN. *Lever le pied*, to bolt; *lever le pied en emportant la caisse*, to abscond with the cash. ‖ **16.** MILIT. *A pied d'œuvre*, ready for action; *lâcher pied*, to give ground; *l'arme au pied*, with arms at order; *prendre pied dans*, to effect a lodgment in; *sur le pied de guerre*, on a war footing. ‖ **17.** LOC. *A pied d'œuvre*, in readiness; *au pied levé*, unprepared, at a moment's notice; *au petit pied*, third-rate, small-scale; *bon pied, bon œil*, lusty, hale and hearty; *cela lui fait les pieds*, it serves him right; *faire des pieds et des mains*, to move heaven and earth, to exert oneself to the utmost; *faire un pied de nez à*, to cock a snook at, to make a long nose at, to thumb one's nose at; *faire le pied de grue*, to kick one's heels, to stand and wait; *mettre à pied*, to sack, to suspend; *mettre au pied du mur*, to call

on for a straightforward answer; *mettre les pieds dans le plat*, to put one's foot in it, to drop a brick; *mettre sous les pieds*, to trample on; *mettre qqch. sur pied*, to work sth. out; *n'y avoir jamais mis les pieds*, never to have set foot there; *ne pas mettre les pieds chez qqn*, not to darken s.o.'s door; *nez en pied de marmite*, snub nose; *partir du bon pied*, to make a good start; *prendre pied*, to catch on; *sur le même pied que*, on the same footing as, on an equal footing with; *sur quel pied êtes-vous avec lui?*, how do you stand with him?; *sur quel pied vit-il?*, what is his style of living?; *tenir pied à*, to stand up to; *toujours le pied levé*, always on the hop; *un pied dans la tombe*, with one foot in the grave; *vivre sur le pied de cinquante mille francs par mois*, to live on an income of fifty thousand francs a month. ‖ **18.** POP. Duffer (imbécile); *comme un pied*, stupidly. ‖ **Pied-à-terre**, m. invar. Small occasional lodging, pied-à-terre. ‖ **Pied-bot**, m. MÉD. Club-footed person. ‖ **Pied-d'alouette**, m. BOT. Larkspur. ‖ **Pied-de-biche**, m. TECHN. Presser-foot (de machine à coudre); claw (de menuisier). ‖ **Pied-de-poule**, m. Broken-check; U. S. hound's-tooth check (dessin, tissu). ‖ **Pied-noir**, s. FAM. French colonial in North Africa. ‖ **Pied-plat**, m. Toady.

piédestal [pjedɛstal] m. Pedestal.

piège [pjeʒ:] m. Pit (fosse); snare (lacs); noose (nœud coulant); trap (trappe); *piège-à-loup*, mantrap; *prendre au piège*, to trap, to snare; *tendre un piège à*, to set a trap for. ‖ FIG. Trap (v. TRAQUENARD); *se laisser prendre à son propre piège*, to be hoist with one's own petard.

piégeage [pjeʒa:ʒ] m. Snaring, trapping.

piéger [-ʒe] v. tr. (5; 7). To snare, to trap. ‖ To booby-trap (mettre une charge explosive); *lettre piégée*, letter bomb.

pie-mère [pimɛ:r] f. MÉD. Pia mater.

Piémont [pjemɔ̃] m. GÉOGR. Piedmont.

piémontais, aise [pjemɔ̃tɛ, ɛ:z] adj., s. GÉOGR. Piedmontese.

piéride [pjerid] f. ZOOL. Pieridine butterfly, cabbage white.

pierraille [pjera:j] f. Rubble.

pierre [pjɛ:r] f. Stone (v. CAILLOU); *pierre calcaire*, limestone; *pierre de gué*, stepping stone; *pierre de taille*, freestone, hewn stone, ashlar; *pierre tombale*, tombstone; *poser la première pierre*, to lay the foundation stone. ‖ Stone; *pierre à aiguiser*, whetstone; *pierre à briquet*, flint; *pierre à fusil*, gun flint; *pierre à rasoir*, hone; *pierre fine*, semi-precious stone; *pierre précieuse*, precious stone; *pierre de touche*, touchstone. ‖ BOT. Grit (dans un fruit). ‖ MÉD. Stone. (V. CALCUL.) ‖ FIG. *Cœur de pierre*, heart of stone; *faire d'une pierre deux coups*, to kill two birds with one stone; *jeter une pierre dans le jardin de qqn*, to throw a stone in s.o.'s backyard; *une pierre dans votre jardin*, a fling at you; *ne pas laisser pierre sur pierre*, not to leave a stone standing; *lancer une pierre dans la mare aux grenouilles*, to cause a flutter in the dovecotes; *pierre d'achoppement*, stumbling-block.

pierreries [pjɛrri] f. pl. Jewels, precious stones.

pierrette [-rɛt] f. Small stone.

pierreuse [-rø:z] f. FAM. Street-walker.

pierreux, euse [-rø, ø:z] adj. Stony (chemin, lieu). ‖ BOT. Gritty (fruit). ‖ MÉD. Calculous (formation).

pierrot [-ro] m. Peter, young Peter (prénom). ‖ THÉÂTR. Pierrot. ‖ ZOOL. Sparrow. ‖ FAM. *Un drôle de pierrot*, a queer fish.

piétaille [pjeta:j] f. MILIT. Foot-soldiers, infantry. ‖ FIG. Lower ranks (subalternes).

piété [pjete] f. Piety; devotion (dévouement); *piété filiale*, dutifulness of children, filial devotion. ‖ ECCLÉS. Piety, godliness. ‖ COMM. *Articles de piété*, devotional articles.

759

piétement [pjetmɑ̃] m. ARTS., TECHN. Legs (d'un meuble).

piéter v. intr. (5). To run (gibier à plumes). ‖ SPORTS. To toe the line (joueur).
— v. tr. To cut close (le gazon). ‖ NAUT. To mark the draught.
— v. pr. **Se piéter**, to stand firm.

piétinement [-tinmɑ̃] m. Stamping, trampling.

piétiner [-tine] v. tr. (1). To stamp on, to trample on (qqch.). ‖ FIG. *Piétiner toute opposition*, to ride rough-shod over all opposition.
— v. intr. To stamp; *piétiner de colère*, to dance with rage. (V. TRÉPIGNER.) ‖ FIG. To mark time (ne pas avancer).

piétisme [pjetism] m. Pietism.

piétiste [-tist] s. Pietist.

piéton [pjetɔ̃] m. Pedestrian.

piéton, onne [-tɔ̃, ɔn], **piétonnier, ère** [-tɔnje, ɛːr] adj. Pedestrian; *zone piétonne*, pedestrian precinct.

piètre [pjɛtr] adj. Poor (animal); poor, lame (excuse); shabby, poor (individu); wretched (repas); *de piètre apparence*, poor-looking. ‖ FIG. Cold (consolation); poor, lame, paltry (excuse).

piètrement [-trəmɑ̃] adv. Poorly, wretchedly.

pieu [pjø] m. Post, stake. (V. PIQUET.) ‖ ARCHIT. Pale (de clôture); pile (de construction). ‖ NAUT. Bollard, pale (d'amarrage). ‖ POP. Doss, U. S. hay, sack (lit).

pieusement [pjøzmɑ̃] adv. Piously.

pieuter (se) [səpjøte] v. pr. (1). POP. To turn in, U. S. to hit the hay. (V. SE COUCHER.)

pieuvre [pjøːvr] f. ZOOL. Octopus, devil-fish.

pieux, euse [pjø, øːz] adj. Dutiful (enfant); devoted (soin). ‖ Godly (acte, lecture); pious, godly (personne). [V. DÉVOT.]

piézo-électricité [pjezoelɛktrisite] f. ELECTR. Piezo-electricity.

pif [pif] m. FAM. Conk, beak, U. S. schnozzle (nez). ‖ LOC. *Au pif*, v. PIFOMÈTRE.

pifomètre [pifɔmɛtr] m. FAM. *Au pifomètre*, by rule of thumb, at a rough guess.

pige [piːʒ] f. Measuring rod. ‖ Fee (d'un journaliste). ‖ TECHN. Take (en typogr.). ‖ FAM. *Faire la pige à*, to go one better than; to outdo.

pigeon [piʒɔ̃] m. ZOOL. Pigeon (v. RAMIER); *pigeon voyageur*, carrier pigeon, homing pigeon, homer; *couleur gorge-de-pigeon*, dove-coloured; *tir aux pigeons*, pigeon-shooting. ‖ ARCHIT. Builder's plaster. ‖ FAM. Gull (dupe). ‖ **Pigeon-ramier**, m. ZOOL. Wood-pigeon, ring dove.

pigeonne [piʒɔn] f. ZOOL. Hen-pigeon.

pigeonneau [-nɔ] m. ZOOL. Young pigeon (jeune); squab (naissant).

pigeonner [-ne] v. tr. (1). FAM. To gull, to con, to do.

pigeonnier [-nje] m. Dovecot, pigeon-house. ‖ FAM. High-perched house.
— adj. Pigeon (industrie).

piger [piʒe] v. tr. (7). To measure. ‖ FAM. To pinch, to collar (attraper); to twig (comprendre).
— v. intr. To be remunerated (journaliste). ‖ FAM. To get it (comprendre).

pigiste [piʒist] s. Freelance, freelancer; stringer (pour un journal).

pigment [pigmɑ̃] m. Pigment.

pigmentaire [-tɛːr] adj. Pigmentary.

pigmentation [-tasjɔ̃] f. Pigmentation.

pigmenté, ée [-te] adj. Pigmented.

pigne [piɲ] f. BOT. Pine- (ou) fir-cone.

pignocher [piɲɔʃe] v. intr. To pick and choose.

pignon [piɲɔ̃] m. ARCHIT. Gable; *à pignon*, gabled. ‖ TECHN. Pinion; *pignon de bicyclette*, chain-wheel. ‖ LOC. *Avoir pignon sur rue*, to own one's own house.

pignon m. BOT. Piñon, nut pine (pin parasol); pine nut (fruit).

pignouf [piɲuf] m. FAM. Skinflint, U. S. tightwad.

pilaf [pilaf] m. Pilau, pilaw.

pilage [pilaːʒ] m. Pounding, crushing, grinding.

pilaire [pilɛːr] adj. Pilary, pilar.

pilastre [pilastr] m. ARCHIT. Pilaster.

pile [piːl] f. Pile, stack (de bois); heap (d'objets). [V. AMAS.] ‖ Pier (de pont). ‖ ELECTR. Battery; *pile de rechange*, refill for a torch, U. S. flashlight battery.

pile f. POP. Thrashing. (V. RÂCLÉE.)
— adv. FAM. Short; *s'arrêter pile*, to stop short (ou) dead.

pile f. Reverse (v. AVERS); *pile ou face*, heads or tails; *jouer à pile ou face*, to toss up.

piler [pile] v. tr. (1). To pound, to crush, to grind, to pestle (v. ÉCRASER); *verre pilé*, ground glass.
— v. intr. FAM., AUTOM. To slam on the brakes.

pileux, euse [pilø, øːz] adj. Pilous, pilose, hairy.

pilier [pilje] m. ARCHIT. Pillar, shaft. (V. COLONNE.) ‖ MÉD. Pillar (du palais). ‖ FIG. Pillar, supporter.

pillage [pijaːʒ] m. Pillaging, looting, plundering; *mettre au pillage*, to plunder, to loot, to sack.

pillard, arde [-jaːr, ard] adj. Pillaging, plundering, looting; pilfering.
— m. Pillager, plunderer, looter; pilferer.

piller [-je] v. tr. (1). To rifle, to strip, to plunder (un jardin, une maison); to pillage, to plunder, to loot (une ville). ‖ FAM. To filch, to pirate (plagier).

pilleur, euse [-jœːr, øːz] adj., s. V. PILLARD. ‖ *Pilleur d'épaves*, wrecker.

pilon [pilɔ̃] m. TECHN. Rammer (de terrassier); *pilon de marteau*, hammer head; *pilon à vapeur*, steam hammer; *mettre au pilon*, to pulp (un livre). ‖ MÉD. Pestle (de pharmacien); wooden leg (d'unijambiste). ‖ CULIN. Drumstick (de poulet).

pilonnage [pilɔnaːʒ] m. Pounding, pestling. (V. PILAGE.) ‖ MILIT. Hammering, pounding. ‖ AVIAT. *Pilonnage aérien*, area bombing.

pilonner [-ne] v. tr. (1). To pound; to pestle. (V. PILER.) ‖ To ram, to beat (le sol). ‖ MILIT., AVIAT. To shell, to bomb. ‖ AVIAT. To prang.

pilori [pilɔri] m. Pillory; *mettre au pilori*, to pillory. ‖ FIG. *Clouer qqn au pilori*, to hold s.o. up to obloquy.

pilosité [pilɔzite] f. Pilosity.

pilot [pilo] m. Pile. (V. PIQUET.)

pilotage [pilɔtaːʒ] m. Pile-driving (action); pile-work (résultat).

pilotage m. NAUT. Piloting; *droits de pilotage*, pilotage. ‖ AVIAT. Piloting; *école de pilotage*, flying-school; *poste de pilotage*, cockpit.

pilote [pilɔt] m. NAUT. Pilot (v. TIMONIER); *bateau pilote*, pilot-boat. ‖ AVIAT. Pilot; *pilote automatique*, automatic pilot; George (fam.); *pilote de convoyage, d'essai, de ligne, de nuit*, ferry, test, air-line, night-fighter pilot; *sans pilote*, pilotless (avion). ‖ ZOOL. *Poisson pilote*, pilot-fish.

piloter [-te] v. tr. (1). NAUT. To pilot. ‖ AVIAT. To pilot, to fly. ‖ FAM. To guide, to lead, to show the way to.

piloter v. tr. (1). To drive piles into.

pilotis [piloti] m. Piling; piles; *sur pilotis*, on piles.

pilou [pilu] m. Flannelette (tissu).

pilulaire [pilylɛːr] adj. Pilular.

pilule [-lyːl] f. MÉD., FIG. Pill.

pimbêche [pɛ̃bɛʃ] f. FAM. Old cat, battle-axe.

piment [pimɑ̃] m. BOT. Pimento. ‖ CULIN. Red pepper. ‖ FIG. Spice (d'une aventure); relish (de la nouveauté).

pimenté, ée [-te] adj. CULIN. Highly spiced. ‖ FIG. Spicy. (V. SALÉ.)

pimenter [-te] v. tr. (1). CULIN. To spice, to season with red pepper. ‖ FIG. To give spice to.

pimpant, ante [pɛ̃pɑ̃, ɑ̃:t] adj. Smart, spruce (allure); trim, natty, spick and span (costume).

pimprenelle [pɛ̃prənɛl] f. BOT. Pimpernel.

pin [pɛ̃] m. Bot. Pine-tree; *pin maritime, de Norvège, sylvestre,* sea-, Norway, Scotch fir.

pinacle [pinakl] m. Pinnacle. (V. COMBLE.) ‖ FIG. *Porter au pinacle,* to praise to the skies, to extol.

pinacothèque [pinakɔtɛk] f. Picture gallery.

pinailler [pinaje] v. intr. (1). FAM. To quibble, to wrangle, to cavil, to niggle.

pinailleur, euse [-jœ:r, ø:z] adj. Quibbling, wrangling, cavilling.
— s. Quibbler, wrangler, caviller.

pinard [pina:r] m. FAM. Wine.

pinasse [pinas] f. NAUT. Pinnace.

pince [pɛ̃:s] f. Pliers, nippers (outil); *pince à cravates, à papier,* clip; *pince à épiler,* tweezers; *pince à linge,* clothes-pin (ou) -peg; *pinces à sucre,* sugar-tongs. ‖ Pleat, crease. (V. PLI.) ‖ ZOOL. Claw, nipper (de crabe). ‖ POP. Paw (main). ‖ **Pince-guiches,** m. invar. Hair grip; U. S. hair clip. ‖ **Pince-monseigneur,** f. Crowbar, jemmy. ‖ **Pince-nez,** m. invar. Pince-nez. ‖ **Pince-pantalon,** m. invar. Trouser-clip. ‖ **Pince-sans-rire,** m. invar. Straight-faced wag.

pincé, ée [pɛ̃se] adj. Stiff (air); pressed, tight, thin (lèvres); tight-lipped (sourire); sharp (ton); glum (visage maussade); prim (visage offusqué).

pinceau [pɛ̃so] m. Brush, paint-brush. ‖ PHYS. *Pinceau lumineux,* pencil of light. ‖ FIG. Touch.

pincée [pɛ̃se] f. Pinch, sprinkle.

pincement [-smɑ̃] m. Pinching, nipping. ‖ MUS. Plucking (des cordes).

pincer [-se] v. tr. (6). To pinch, to nip. ‖ To grip (dans un étau). ‖ To fit closely (la taille); to pleat (un tissu). ‖ AGRIC. To nip off (les bourgeons). ‖ MUS. To pluck (les cordes). ‖ FAM. To catch (qqch., qqn) [v. ATTRAPER]; *se faire pincer,* to get caught (ou) pinched (ou) copped (ou) nabbed.
— v. intr. To nip, to bite (froid). ‖ MUS. To touch; *pincer du banjo,* to strum on the banjo (fam.). ‖ FAM. *En pincer pour,* to be gone on, to have a crush on.
— v. pr. **Se pincer,** to nip one's skin; to pinch oneself; *se pincer les doigts,* to nip (ou) to squeeze one's fingers. ‖ FIG. *Se pincer les lèvres,* to purse one's lips (faire la moue); to keep a straight face (ne pas rire).

pincette [-sɛt] f. Light pinch, nip (pinçon). ‖ Pl. Tongs (à feu); pincers (petites pinces). ‖ FAM. *Il n'est pas à prendre avec des pincettes,* he is unapproachable (ou) like a bear with a sore head (en colère); I wouldn't touch him with a barge-pole (ou) U. S. ten-foot pole (sale).

pinçon [-sɔ̃] m. Pinch-mark (marque); nip, light pinch (pincette).

pinçure [-sy:r] f. Pinching; pinch. ‖ Crease (sur un tissu).

pindarique [pɛ̃darik] adj. Pindaric.

pinéal, ale [pineal] adj. MÉD. Pineal.

pinède [pinɛd] f. Pine-wood.

pineraie [pinərɛ] f. Pine-grove.

pingouin [pɛ̃gwɛ̃] m. ZOOL. Razorbill; auk.

Ping-Pong [piŋpɔ̃g] m. (nom déposé). SPORTS. Ping-pong, table tennis.

pingre [pɛ̃:gr] adj. Stingy. (V. CHICHE, LADRE.)
— s. Skinflint, U. S. tightwad. (V. RAPIAT.)

pingrerie [-grəri] f. Stinginess. (V. AVARICE.)

pinson [pɛ̃sɔ̃] m. ZOOL. Finch, chaffinch. ‖ LOC. *Gai comme un pinson,* as blithe (ou) gay as a lark.

pintade [pɛ̃tad] f. ZOOL. Guinea-hen (ou) -fowl.

pintadeau [-do] m. ZOOL. Guinea-poult.

pinte [pɛ̃:t] f. Pint, quart. ‖ CANADA, quart. ‖ FAM. *Une pinte de bon sang,* a loud laugh.

pinter [pɛ̃te] v. intr. (1). To booze, to tipple.
— v. tr. To make drunk (qqn).
— v. pr. **Se pinter,** to get drunk.

pin-up [pinœp] f. Pin-up girl.

pinyin [pinjin] m. GRAMM. Pinyin (écriture).

piochage [pjɔʃa:ʒ] m. AGRIC. Digging. ‖ FAM. Grinding, swotting (d'un sujet).

pioche [pjɔʃ] f. AGRIC. Pick, pickaxe. ‖ FIG. *Donner le premier coup de pioche,* to break up the ground. ‖ **Pioche-hache,** f. AGRIC. Mattock.

piocher [-ʃe] v. tr. (1). AGRIC. To dig up. ‖ FAM. To grind at, to swot at. (V. BÛCHER.)
— v. intr. AGRIC. To dig. ‖ SPORTS. To draw from the stock (aux dominos). ‖ FAM. To grind, to swot to dig; to peg (ou) U. S. to slug away at it.

piocheur, euse [-ʃœ:r, ø:z] adj. Digging. ‖ FAM. Hard-working.
— s. Digger. ‖ FAM. Swot, hard-worker.

piolet [pjɔlɛ] m. SPORTS. Ice-axe.

pion [pjɔ̃] m. Man (aux dames); pawn (aux échecs). ‖ Usher, assistant, under-master, U. S. proctor (à l'école).

pioncer [pjɔ̃se] v. intr. (6). POP. To snooze; to doss.

pionnier [pjɔnje] m. Pioneer, trail-blazer; *faire œuvre de pionnier,* to blaze a trail; *œuvre de pionnier,* pioneer work.

pioupiou [pjupju] m. FAM. Tommy, private of the line, foot-slogger.

pipe [pip] f. Pipe (pour fumer); *pipe de bruyère, de terre, hollandaise,* briar, clay, churchwarden pipe; *fumer la pipe,* to smoke a pipe, to be a pipe-smoker. ‖ Pipe (tuyau). ‖ Pipe (de vin). ‖ FAM. *Casser sa pipe,* to kick the bucket; *tant par tête de pipe,* so much per head. ‖ **Pipe-line,** m. Pipe-line.

pipé, ée [pipe] adj. Loaded (dé).

pipeau [pipo] m. Bird-call (d'oiseleur). ‖ Lime-twig (gluau). ‖ MUS. Pipe.

pipée f. Bird-catching.

pipée f. Pipe-full (de tabac).

pipelet [piplɛ] s. FAM. Door-keeper, concierge.

piper [pipe] v. intr. (1). To imitate the call of a bird. ‖ FAM. To speak; *ne pas piper,* to keep mum.
— v. tr. To decoy (des oiseaux.) To mark (les cartes); to load (les dés).

pipette [-pɛt] f. CHIM. Pipette.

pipeur [-pœ:r] m. Bird-snarer. ‖ FIG. Trickster.

pipi [pipi] m. FAM. Pee; wee-wee; *faire pipi,* to pee, to wee-wee.

pipistrelle [pipistrɛl] f. ZOOL. Pipistrelle.

pipit [pipit] m. ZOOL. Pipit, titlark.

piquage [pika:ʒ] m. Stitching (à la machine). ‖ Pitting (du métal); dressing (de la pierre). ‖ Staining (sur le linge); foxing, mildewing (sur le papier). ‖ Tapping (d'un fût).

piquant, ante [pikɑ̃, ɑ̃:t] adj. Rough, scraggy (barbe); sharp (épingle). ‖ CULIN. Hot, sharp (goût); sour, tart (vin). ‖ BOT. Prickly, thorny (plante). ‖ FIG. Stinging, biting, sharp (paroles); piquant, lively (physionomie); racy, lively (récit); sharp, biting (repartie).
— m. ZOOL. Quill, spine (du hérisson). ‖ BOT. Prickle, thorn (des plantes). ‖ FIG. Pungency, tang (d'une plaisanterie); gusto (d'un récit); zest (d'une repartie); liveliness, raciness, pointedness (du style).

pique [pik] f. Pike, spear, pointed staff. ‖ Spade (aux cartes). ‖ FAM. Pique, tiff (querelle). ‖ **Pique-assiette,** s. invar. Parasite, sponge, sponger. ‖ **Pique-bœufs,** m. invar. Bullock-driver; ox-pricker. ‖ **Pique-feu,** m. invar. Poker. ‖ **Pique-fleurs,** m. invar. Glass flower-block (ou) U. S. holder; pin-frog. ‖ **Pique-nique,** m. invar. Picnic; U. S. basket lunch. ‖ **Pique-niquer,** v. intr. (1). To picnic, to go on a picnic. ‖ **Pique-niqueur** (pl. *pique-niqueurs*), s. Picnicker. ‖ **Pique-notes,** m. invar. Bill-file.

piqué, ée [pike] adj. Outside-stitched (couture); sewn, stitched (linge); quilted (vêtement). ‖ Worm-eaten (bois); stained (linge); pitted, rust-eaten (métal); mildewed (papier); *piqué de mouches,* fly-blown. ‖ CULIN. Larded (viande); sour (vin). ‖ MUS. Staccato, detached (notes). ‖

FAM. Cracked (v. CINGLÉ); *ce n'est pas piqué des hannetons*, it's not so dusty (ou) not half bad. — m. Piqué, quilting (en couture). ‖ AVIAT. Dive; *attaque en piqué*, dive-attack; *attaquer en piqué*, to dive-bomb; *descente en piqué*, nose-dive.
piquer [-ke] v. tr. (1). To goad (avec un aiguillon); to spur (avec des éperons). ‖ To prickle (avec la barbe); to prick (avec une épingle). ‖ To irritate, to cause to smart (fumée). ‖ To stick (enfoncer); *piquer une fleur dans ses cheveux*, to stick a flower in one's hair. ‖ To stain, to mildew (humidité). ‖ BOT. To prickle (épine); to nettle (ortie). ‖ ZOOL. To sting (guêpe); to bite (puce); to sting, to bite (serpent); to eat into (vers). ‖ TECHN. To quilt (un couvre-pied); to stitch (du cuir); to prick (un dessin sur une étoffe); to sew, to prick (un ourlet); *piquer à la machine*, to machine, U. S. to machine-stitch. ‖ CULIN. To lard (un rôti). ‖ MÉD. To give an injection to (qqn); *piquer un chien*, to give a dog a lethal shot (fam.). ‖ SPORTS. To strike (un poisson); *piquer une tête*, to take a header, to dive (à la nage). ‖ FIG. To arouse (la curiosité, la jalousie); *piquer qqn au jeu*, to put s.o. on his mettle; *piquer au vif*, to cut to the quick. ‖ FAM. To filch (chiper); *piquer un fard*, to blush; *piquer un somme*, to snatch forty winks. — v. intr. To prick (aiguille, épingle). ‖ BOT. To sting (plante). ‖ MÉD. To smart (eau oxygénée). ‖ CULIN. To burn, to be hot (poivre); to have a sour taste (vin). ‖ NAUT. To head (*sur*, for). ‖ AVIAT. To dive down (*sur*, on, at); *piquer de l'aile*, to drop a wing; *piquer du nez*, to go into a nose-dive; *piquer à pleins gaz*, to power-dive. ‖ FIG. To bite (froid); to cut (vent). — v. pr. Se piquer, to prick oneself (avec une épingle); to sting oneself (avec une ortie). ‖ To get worm-eaten (bois); to spot, to stain (linge); to get rust-eaten (métal). ‖ CULIN. To turn sour (vin). ‖ MÉD. To give oneself an injection; *il se pique*, he is a drug-addict. ‖ FIG. To pride oneself (*de*, upon) [s'enorgueillir]; *se piquer au jeu*, to be on one's mettle. ‖ FIG. To get offended, to flare up (s'offusquer). ‖ FAM. *Se piquer le nez*, to hit the bottle, U. S. to liquor up.
piquet [pikɛ] m. Post, stake (v. PIEU); *entourer de piquets*, to stake (un champ). ‖ Corner (à l'école); *être au piquet*, to stand in the corner. ‖ Picket (d'ouvriers); *piquet de grève*, strike picket. ‖ MILIT. Picket; *piquet en armes*, inlying picket. ‖ SPORTS. *Piquet de coin*, corner-flag. ‖ FAM. *Raide comme un piquet*, as stiff as a poker.
piquet m. Piquet (aux cartes).
piquetage [pikta:ʒ] m. Staking out.
piqueter [-te] v. tr. (8a). To stake out, to mark out.
piquette [pikɛt] f. Light wine.
piqueur [pikœ:r] m. SPORTS. Whip, whipper-in (à la chasse). ‖ CH. DE F. Plate-layer. ‖ TECHN. Hewer (aux mines).
piqueuse [-kø:z] f. Stitcher (en couture).
piquier [-kje] m. MILIT. † Pikeman.
piqûre [piky:r] f. Prick (d'épingle). ‖ Stitching; quilting (en couture). ‖ Worm-hole (dans le bois); pit (dans le métal); foxing (sur le papier); stain (dans le tissu); *piqûre de mouche*, speck, flyblow. ‖ ZOOL. Sting (de guêpe); bite (de moustique, de serpent). ‖ MÉD. Injection; shot (fam.); *faire une piqûre à qqn*, to inject s.o.; to give s.o. an injection (ou) a shot (fam.).
piranha [piraɲa] m. ZOOL. Piranha, piraya, perai.
pirate [pirat] m. Pirate. ‖ AVIAT. *Pirate de l'air*, hijacker, skyjacker. — adj. Piratic, pirate; *radio, édition pirate*, pirate radio station, edition.
pirater [-te] v. intr., tr. (6). To pirate (pr. et fig.).
piraterie [-tri] f. Piracy. ‖ AVIAT. *Piraterie aérienne*, air piracy; hijacking, skyjacking (action); hijack (acte de piraterie).

piraya [piraja] m. V. PIRANHA.
pire [pi:r] adj. compar. Worse; *qqch. de pire*, sth. worse. ‖ Worst (v. PIS); *elle a fait pire*, she has done worse. — adj. superl. Worst. — m. *Le pire*, the worst; *au pire*, if the worst comes to the worst.
piriforme [pirifɔrm] adj. Pear-shaped.
pirogue [pirɔg] f. NAUT. Canoe.
piroguier [-gje] m. NAUT. Boatsman, native boatsman.
pirouette [pirwɛt] f. Pirouette (v. CABRIOLE); *faire une pirouette*, to pirouette. ‖ FIG. Sudden aboutface.
pirouetter [-te] v. intr. (1). To pirouette.
pis [pi] m. Udder, dug (de chèvre, de vache).
pis adv. compar. Worse; *de mal en pis*, from bad to worse. — adv. superl. Worst; *au pis aller*, if the worst comes; *à mettre les choses au pis*, if we look at things at their worst. — m. Worst; *le pis est que*, the worst is that. ‖ **Pis-aller**, m. Makeshift, last resource, pis aller; *au pis-aller*, at the worst; *c'est un pis-aller*, it's better than nothing.
pisciculteur [pisikyltœ:r] m. Pisciculturist.
pisciculture [-ty:r] f. Pisciculture.
pisciforme [-fɔrm] adj. Pisciform, fish-shaped.
piscine [pissin] f. Swimming-pool.
piscivore [pissivɔ:r] adj. Piscivorous.
Pise [pi:z] f. GÉOGR. Pisa.
pisé [pize] m. Pisé, mud bricks, rammed clay.
pissat [pisa] m. Urine (d'animal).
pisse [pi:s] f. POP. Piss. ‖ **Pisse-froid,** m. inv. POP. Killjoy, wet blanket.
pissement [pismɑ̃] m. POP. Pissing.
pissenlit [pisɑ̃li] m. BOT. Dandelion. ‖ FAM. *Manger les pissenlits par la racine*, to push up the daisies.
pisser [pise] v. intr. (1). POP. To piss, to make water, to pump ship. — v. tr. POP. *Pisser du sang*, to pass blood with the urine.
pisseux, euse [-sø, ø:z] adj. POP. Urine-coloured; stained with urine.
pissoir [-swa:r] m. POP. Urinal, piss-house.
pissoter [-sɔte] v. intr. (1). To dribble.
pissotière [-sɔtjɛ:r] f. POP. Urinal; piss-house.
pistache [pistaʃ] f. POP. Pistachio-nut. — adj. invar. Pistachio-green.
pistachier [-ʃje] m. BOT. Pistachio-tree.
pistage [pista:ʒ] m. Tracking. ‖ COMM. Touting (des clients).
pistard [pista:r] m. SPORTS. Track cyclist.
piste [pist] f. Ring (de cirque). ‖ AUTOM. Track (de course). ‖ AVIAT. *Piste d'atterrissage*, landing strip; *piste d'envol*, runway; *piste balisée*, flarepath. ‖ SPORTS. Rink (de patinage); *piste individuelle*, lane. ‖ SPORTS. Trail, track, scent (à la chasse). ‖ JUR. Track; trail; *fausse piste*, false trail; *sur la piste de*, on the track of.
pister [-te] v. tr. (1). SPORTS. To track (le gibier). ‖ JUR. To shadow (qqn); *faire pister qqn*, to have s.o. watched. (V. FILER.) ‖ COMM. To tout for.
pisteur [-tœ:r] m. Tracker. ‖ JUR. Police spy. ‖ COMM. Tout.
pistil [pistil] m. BOT. Pistil.
pistole [pistɔl] f. † Pistole.
pistolet [pistɔlɛ] m. Pistol (revolver). ‖ Gun, airgun (jouet). ‖ TECHN. Sprayer, spraying-gun, U. S. spray-gun (de peintre). ‖ ARTS. Curve (de dessinateur). ‖ NAUT. Davit. ‖ FAM. *Drôle de pistolet*, queer fish (ou) card. ‖ **Pistolet-mitrailleur**, m. MILIT. Automatic-pistol.
piston [pistɔ̃] m. Piston; *piston à clapet*, sucker (de pompe); pump-bucket. ‖ MUS. *Cornet à pistons*, cornet. ‖ FAM. Pull; influence; wire-pulling; *il est arrivé par le piston*, he got on through pull.

pistonner [-tɔne] v. tr. (1). To push, to back, to help to get on; *se faire pistonner*, to get s.o. to pull the strings (ou) wires for one.
pitance [pitɑ̃:s] f. Food.
pitch-pin [pitʃpɛ̃] m. Bot. Pitch-pine.
piteusement [pitøzmɑ̃] adv. Piteously.
piteux, euse [pitø, ø:z] adj. Piteous, pitiable, pitiful, woeful (v. PITOYABLE) ; *faire piteuse figure*, to cut a sorry figure.
pithécanthrope [pitekɑ̃trɔp] m. Pithecanthrope.
pitié [pitje] f. Pity (v. COMPASSION) ; *prendre pitié de qqn*, to take pity on s.o., to be merciful to s.o. ; *sans pitié*, merciless. ‖ Pity ; *c'est pitié de le voir*, he is a sorry sight, it is pitiful to see him ; *quelle pitié !*, what a shame (ou) pity !
piton [pitɔ̃] m. TECHN. Eyebolt, ringbolt ; *piton à vis*, screw eye ; *piton à crochet*, hook. ‖ GÉOGR. Piton, peak. ‖ FAM. Conk. (V. PIF.)
pitoyable [pitwajabl] adj. Pitiful, piteous, pitiable, lamentable. (V. PITEUX.) ‖ Compassionate, sympathetic. (V. COMPATISSANT.)
pitoyablement [-bləmɑ̃] adv. Pitifully, wretchedly. (V. LAMENTABLEMENT.) ‖ Compassionately (avec compassion).
pitre [pitr] m. Clown (de cirque). ‖ FAM. Fool, buffoon.
pitrerie [pitrəri] f. Clownery, clowning.
pittoresque [pitɔrɛsk] adj. Picturesque (paysage). ‖ Colourful (style).
— m. Picturesqueness (d'un site). ‖ Colour, vividness, brilliancy (du style).
pittoresquement [-mɑ̃] adv. Picturesquely.
pituitaire [pitɥitɛ:r] adj. MÉD. Pituitary.
pituite [-tɥit] f. MÉD. Water-brash (aigreurs) ; nasal mucus (morve) ; abnormal flow of saliva (salivation).
pituiteux, euse [-tɥitø, øz] adj. Pituitous.
pivert [pivɛ:r] m. ZOOL. Green woodpecker.
pivoine [pivwan] f. Bot. Paeony, peony.
pivot [pivo] m. Pivot, pin, swivel-pin. (V. AXE.) ‖ FIG. Central piece, hinge, hub. ‖ FAM. Pl. Pins (jambes).
pivotant, ante [pivɔtɑ̃, ɑ̃:t] adj. Pivoting, swivelling, turning. ‖ MILIT. Wheeling (mouvement). ‖ Bot. *Racine pivotante*, tap-root.
pivoter [-te] v. intr. (1). To pivot, to swivel, to swing round ; *faire pivoter*, to slew, to spin round. ‖ MILIT. To wheel, to swing round. ‖ FIG. *Faire pivoter qqn*, to keep s.o. on the go.
pizza [pidza] f. CULIN. Pizza.
pizzeria [-zerja] f. Pizzeria.
P.J. [peʒi] f. Abrév. de *Police judiciaire*, French Criminal Investigation Department, CID.
placage [plaka:ʒ] m. Veneer, veneering (de bois). ‖ Plating (de métal). ‖ MUS. Patchwork. ‖ SPORTS. Tackle (au rugby).
placard [plaka:r] m. Cupboard, closet, wall-press. ‖ Poster, bill. (V. AFFICHE.) ‖ Galley-proof, slip-proof (en typogr.).
placarder [-karde] v. tr. (1). To post, to stick up (une affiche) ; to stick bills on (un mur). ‖ To print in slips (un texte).
place [plas] f. Place (position) ; *changer les choses de place*, to change the place of things ; *chaque chose à sa place*, everything in its place. ‖ Room, space (espace) ; *nombre de places en voiture*, passenger capacity ; *tenir beaucoup de place*, to take up a lot of room. ‖ Place (endroit) ; *par places*, in places, here and there. ‖ Place, rank (rang) ; *avoir de bonnes places*, to have a good record (élève) ; *ne pas être à sa place*, not to have the position one deserves. ‖ Place, post, office (situation) ; job (fam.) ; *en place*, in service ; *sans place*, unemployed, without a job, out of work. ‖ Square (dans une ville) ; *place du marché*, market square. ‖ AUTOM., CH. DE F., THÉÂTR. Place, seat ; *cette place est-elle libre ?*, is this seat unoccupied ? ; *combien de places*

libres ?, how many seats are available ? ; *payer demi-place*, to pay half-fare ; *place assise*, sitting accommodation ; *places debout*, standing room ; *voiture à quatre places*, four-seater. ‖ AUTOM. *Voiture de place*, taxi. ‖ MILIT. Fortified town, stronghold (forteresse) ; drill-ground (place d'armes). ‖ COMM. Place, town, market ; *faire la place*, to canvass orders ; *sur place*, on the spot. ‖ FIN. *Chèque sur place*, town cheque. ‖ LOC. *A votre place*, in your place, if I were you ; *céder la place à*, to give up competing with ; *ne pas pouvoir tenir en place*, to be fidgety ; *place aux jeunes !*, give youth a chance ! ; *remettre qqn à sa place*, to put s.o. in his place ; to tell s.o. where to get off (fam.) ; *répondre à la place de qqn*, to answer on s.o.'s behalf ; *venir à la place de qqn*, to come instead of s.o.
placé, ée [-se] adj. Situated (maison). ‖ SPORTS. Placed (cheval) ; *non placé*, unplaced, « that also ran ». ‖ FIG. *Des gens bien placés*, people of good position ; *bien placé pour*, in a good position to.
placebo [plasebo] m. MÉD. Placebo.
placement ⌊plasmɑ̃] m. Placing (en général) ; *bureau de placement*, employment agency. ‖ FIN. Investment ; *placement de père de famille* (ou) *de tout repos*, gilt-edged investment ; *faire un placement d'argent*, to invest money.
placenta [plasɛ̃ta] m. MÉD. Placenta.
placentaire [-tɛ:r] adj. MÉD. Placentary.
placer [plase] v. tr. (5). To place, to put, to set (*sur*, on) [mettre] ; *placer la couchette dans la chambre d'ami*, to place the bedstead in the spare room ; *placer les choses où il faut*, to set (ou) put things where they ought to be. ‖ To seat (à table) ; *placer les enfants pour le déjeuner*, to seat the children for lunch. ‖ To lay (*sur*, on) [poser] : *placez votre serviette sur une chaise*, lay your briefcase on a chair ; *sa maison est placée en haut de la colline*, his house stands at the top of the hill. ‖ To place, to find a situation for (qqn) ; *placer sa fille comme secrétaire*, to place one's daughter as a secretary. ‖ To put, to place, to set (qqn) ; *se trouver placé dans une grande difficulté*, to find oneself in a quandary ; *il se plaint de la condition dans laquelle le sort l'a placé*, he complains of the situation in which Fate has placed him. ‖ To locate, to place (situer) ; *où placer Jean sans Terre dans la série des rois de France ?*, where should we place John Lackland in the succession of French kings ? ‖ To marry ; to settle. (V. CASER.) ‖ COMM. To sell, to dispose of (des billets, des marchandises). ‖ FIN. To invest, to put in (de l'argent) ; to negotiate (des valeurs). ‖ FIG. To repose, to place (*dans*, in) [sa confiance] ; *mal placé*, misplaced (espoir). ‖ FAM. To insert ; *je n'ai pu placer un mot*, I couldn't get (ou) put a word in.
— v. intr. To place (candidat). ‖ To place, to settle, to marry ; *difficile à placer*, difficult to settle. ‖ To slip in (excuse).
— v. pr. Se placer, to place oneself, to seat oneself, to find a seat (s'asseoir). ‖ To place oneself, to rank (prendre rang) ; *où êtes-vous placé à l'examen ?*, where did you rank (ou) come in the examination ? ‖ To get a job, to go into service (s'engager) ; *se placer chez un médecin*, to take service at a doctor's. ‖ To take place (se situer) ; *la conquête normande se place en 1066*, the Norman Conquest took place in 1066. ‖ COMM. To sell (article) ; *difficile à placer*, hard to dispose of ; *se placer facilement*, to sell readily.
placet [plasɛ] m. Petition. (V. REQUÊTE.)
placeur [plasœ:r] s. Employment agent (pour domestiques). ‖ COMM. Placer, seller. ‖ THÉÂTR. Seat-attendant, usher. (V. OUVREUSE.)
placide [plasid] adj. Placid, even-tempered.
placidement [-dmɑ̃] adv. Placidly.

placidité [-dite] f. Placidity. (V. CALME, SÉRÉNITÉ.)

placier [plasje] m. COMM. Canvasser.

plafond [plafɔ̃] m. Ceiling; *au plafond haut*, high-ceilinged. ‖ Contract bridge (aux cartes); *au plafond*, above the line. ‖ NAUT. Floor (de bassin, de cale). ‖ FIN. Ceiling (du budget, des prix); maximum (d'émission). ‖ AVIAT. Ceiling. ‖ AUTOM. Maximum speed. ‖ FIG. Maximum limit (des connaissances).

plafonnage [-fɔna:ʒ] m. ARCHIT. Ceiling work.

plafonnement [-fɔnmɑ̃] m. FIN. Maximum reached, levelling off (de la production, des prix).

plafonner [-fɔne] v. tr. (1). ARCHIT. To ceil.
— v. intr. To reach a ceiling (à, of), to level off (ou) out (à, at); to peak. ‖ *Salaire plafonné*, part of salary on which National Health contributions are paid.

plafonneur [-fɔnœ:r] m. Ceiling maker.

plafonnier [-fɔnje] m. Ceiling lamp.

plage [pla:ʒ] f. Beach, sea-shore (grève). ‖ Seaside resort (pour bains de mer). ‖ NAUT. Freeboard, deck (d'un cuirassé); *plage arrière, avant*, quarter-deck, forecastle. ‖ MUS. Band (de disque).

plagiaire [plaʒjɛ:r] s. Plagiarist.

plagiat [-ʒja] m. Plagiarism, literary piracy.

plagier [-ʒje] v. tr. (1). To plagiarize, to pirate.

plagiste [plaʒist] s. Beach attendant.

plaid [plɛ] m. Plaid, travelling-rug.

plaid m. † JUR. Plea, pleading.

plaidable [plɛdabl] adj. Pleadable.

plaidant, ante [-dɑ̃, ɑ̃:t] adj. JUR. Pleading (avocat); litigating (partie).

plaider [-de] v. intr. (1). JUR. To go to law, to litigate (intenter une action). ‖ To plead, to argue (*contre*, against; *pour*, for); *plaider coupable*, to plead guilty.
— v. tr. JUR. To plead (une cause); to allege, to maintain (une excuse); *plaider la jeunesse de l'accusé*, to plead the youth of the accused.
— v. pr. **Se plaider**, JUR. To come up, to come before the court (affaire).

plaideur [-dœ:r] s. JUR. Litigant, suitor. ‖ FAM. Litigious person.

plaidoirie [-dwari] f. JUR. Pleading (action); counsel's speech (discours).

plaidoyer [-dwaje] m. JUR. Counsel's speech. ‖ FIG. Plea (*en faveur de*, for).

plaie [plɛ] f. MÉD. Wound, sore. ‖ FIG. Plague, evil (calamité); sore (douleur); *mettre le doigt sur la plaie*, to put one's finger on the sore; *rouvrir la plaie*, to open an old sore. ‖ FAM. Plague (personne insupportable); *ne rêver que plaies et bosses*, to be bent on quarelling.

plaignant, ante [plɛɲɑ̃, ɑ̃:t] adj. JUR. Litigious; *partie plaignante*, plaintiff.
— s. JUR. Plaintiff, complainant.

plain, aine [plɛ̃, ɛn] adj. Level. ‖ **Plain-chant**, m. MUS. Plain-song (ou) -chant. ‖ **Plain-pied (de)**, loc. Easily, quickly (sans peine); *de plain-pied avec*, on a level with, flush with (qqch.); on an equal footing (ou) on a par with s.o.

plaindre [plɛ̃:dr] v. tr. (59). To pity, to feel sorry for (v. S'APITOYER); *aimer à être plaint*, to like to be an object of pity; *je vous plains de travailler avec lui*, I pity you for having to work with him; *ne pas être à plaindre*, to have nothing to complain about. ‖ To grudge (regretter); *plaindre la nourriture*, to stint on the food; *plaindre sa peine*, to spare one's pains, to grudge one's efforts.
— v. pr. **Se plaindre**, to moan, to groan (gémir); to complain (se lamenter); *qui toujours se plaint n'est jamais plaint*, he who always complains is never pitied. ‖ To grumble (ronchonner); *une bonne raison de se plaindre*, a good reason to grouse; *des gens qui ont à se plaindre*, people with a grievance. ‖ To complain [*de*, of] (être

insatisfait); *se plaindre de sa condition*, to be dissatisfied with one's lot; *se plaindre de qqn*, to complain of (ou) about s.o., to find fault with s.o. ‖ JUR. To lodge a complaint (*auprès de*, with); to complain (*à*, to).

plaine [plɛn] f. Plain, flat country.

plainte [plɛ̃:t] f. Moan, groan (gémissement). ‖ Protest (protestation). ‖ Complaint (mécontentement); *les plaintes du peuple*, the people's discontent; *un sujet de plainte*, sth. to complain about. ‖ JUR. Complaint, charge, accusation; *déposer une plainte contre, porter plainte contre*, to lay a charge against; *retirer sa plainte*, to withdraw one's charge.

plaintif, ive [plɛ̃tif, i:v] adj. Sorrowful (personne); plaintive, doleful (ton).

plaintivement [-tivmɑ̃] adv. Plaintively; dolefully; mournfully.

plaire [plɛ:r] v. intr. (75). To be pleasing (ou) pleasant. ‖ *Plaire à*, to please, to be agreeable to, to take s.o.'s fancy (chose); *ça ne me plaît guère*, I don't feel attracted by that, that scarcely appeals to me; *cela m'a beaucoup plu*, I was delighted; *la musique me plait*, I enjoy music; *quand cela vous plaira*, when you choose (ou) like. ‖ *Plaire à*, to please (personne); *ne rien faire pour plaire aux gens*, to do nothing to make oneself pleasant to people; *savoir plaire*, to have charm of manner. ‖ LOC. *A Dieu ne plaise*, God forbid; *plaise à Dieu que*, God grant that.
— v. impers. *Il me plaît de*, I choose to; *interprétez-le comme il vous plaira*, interpret it as you like (ou) please; *plaît-il?*, I beg your pardon?; *s'il vous plaît*, if you please; *vous plaît-il de sortir?*, would you like to go out?
— v. pr. **Se plaire**, to like, to take pleasure in (aimer); *se plaire à taquiner qqn*, to enjoy teasing s.o. ‖ To feel content, to prosper (personne); to thrive, to grow well (plante) [s'acclimater]; *se plaire dans le Midi*, to enjoy being in the South (personne).
— v. récipr. **Se plaire**, to please each other (ou) one another.

plaisais, plaisait [-zɛ]. V. PLAIRE (75).

plaisamment [plɛzamɑ̃] adv. Pleasantly. (V. AGRÉABLEMENT.) ‖ Amusingly, laughably (avec humour).

plaisance [-zɑ̃:s] f. Pleasure; *jardin de plaisance*, pleasure-ground; *maison de plaisance*, country-house. ‖ NAUT. Yachting; *bateau de plaisance*, pleasure boat; *port de plaisance*, marina; *salon de la plaisance*, boat show.

plaisancier [-zɑ̃sje] m. NAUT. Yachtsman, boating enthusiast, pleasure boater.

plaisancière [-zɑ̃sjɛ:r] f. NAUT. Yachtswoman.

plaisant, ante [-zɑ̃, ɑ̃:t] adj. Pleasant, pleasing, agreeable (agréable); *accueil plaisant*, kindly welcome; *visage plaisant*, gracious face. ‖ Amusing, funny, laughable (v. AMUSANT); *remarques plaisantes sur*, humorous remarks about. ‖ Ridiculous, ludicrous (v. RIDICULE); *plaisante situation*, ridiculous position.
— m. Jester, joker, wag (v. PLAISANTIN); *faire le plaisant*, to act the clown; *mauvais plaisant*, practical (ou) malicious joker. ‖ Amusing side (aspect drôle); *le plaisant de l'affaire*, the comical (ou) funny part of it.

plaisanter [-zɑ̃te] v. intr. (1). To jest, to joke (faire des plaisanteries). ‖ To joke, not to be in earnest (v. BADINER); *je ne plaisanterai pas sur cette question*, I will stand no fooling in the matter; *plaisanter sur tout*, to make a joke of everything; *plaisanter avec qqn*, to trifle (ou) to joke with s.o.; *pour plaisanter*, in jest, for a joke, for fun, by way of a joke.
— v. tr. To chaff (qqn) [*sur*, about]; *nous l'avons plaisanté tout le long du chemin*, we poked fun at him all along the way.

plaisanterie [-zɑ̃tri] f. Joke, jest, joking; *comprendre la plaisanterie*, to know how to take a joke; *dire des plaisanteries*, to crack jokes; *faire des plaisanteries à*, to play pranks on; *mauvaise plaisanterie*, silly (ou) malicious joke; *ne pas comprendre la plaisanterie*, to be impervious to joking. ‖ Trifle (bagatelle).

plaisantin [-zɑ̃tɛ̃] m. Jester, practical joker, wag, scoffer.

plaisir [-zi:r] m. Pleasure, delight, gladness (v. AGRÉMENT, JOIE); *apprendre avec plaisir que*, to be glad to hear that; *avec plaisir*, with pleasure, with great satisfaction; *avoir le plaisir d'annoncer*, to have pleasure in announcing; *ce sera un plaisir pour moi*, it will be a pleasure for me; *cela lui fera plaisir*, he will like (ou) enjoy it, it will give him great pleasure; *cela fait plaisir à voir*, it is pleasant to see; *faire plaisir à qqn*, to please s.o.; *le plaisir des yeux*, the delight of the eyes; *par plaisir*, for the pleasure (ou) the love of it; *prendre plaisir à*, to take pleasure in. ‖ Favour (faveur); *faire à qqn un petit plaisir*, to do s.o. a little favour; *faire à qqn le plaisir de lui écrire*, to favour s.o. with a letter, to do s.o. the favour of a letter; *Mᵐᵉ X vous prie de lui faire le plaisir de venir dîner chez elle*, Mrs X requests the pleasure of your company at dinner. ‖ Amusement, enjoyment (divertissement); *lieux de plaisir*, places of entertainment. ‖ Sensual delight (volupté); *ami des plaisirs*, pleasure-lover; *les plaisirs de la table*, the enjoyment of good food, the pleasures of the palate; *les plaisirs des sens*, sensual pleasures; *menus plaisirs*, minor (or) little luxuries. ‖ Pleasure, wish, will (volonté); *à plaisir*, wantonly, without cause; *mentir à plaisir*, to lie for the sake of lying; *le régime du bon plaisir*, the reign of despotism; *tel est notre bon plaisir*, such is our wish. ‖ CH. DE F. *Train de plaisir*, excursion train.

plan, ane [plɑ̃, an] adj. Flat, level, even. (V. ÉGAL, PLAT.) ‖ MATH. Plane.
— m. MATH., PHYS. Plane. ‖ ARCHIT. *Plan incliné*, chute. ‖ AVIAT. *Plan débordant, inférieur, supérieur*, overhanging, lower, upper plane. ‖ CINÉM. Shot; *gros plan*, close-up; *plan moyen*, medium shot. ‖ MILIT. *Plan de tir*, line of fire. ‖ ARTS. *Arrière-plan, premier plan*, background, foreground; *second plan*, middle distance. ‖ FIG. Ground (position); *être au premier plan*, to be in the limelight; *écrivain de premier plan*, writer of the first rank; *se placer au premier plan*, to come to the fore; *reléguer qqn à l'arrière-plan*, to push s.o. into the shade; *sur le plan politique*, from the political point of view. ‖ **Plan-concave**, adj. PHYS. Plano-concave. ‖ **Plan-convexe**, adj. PHYS. Plano-convex.

plan m. Skeleton, framework, scheme (d'un ouvrage); *plan détaillé d'une rédaction*, skeleton essay; *plan d'études*, course of study, curriculum; *faire le plan de*, to draw up the plan (ou) skeleton of, to plan. ‖ ARCHIT. Plan, draught, U. S. draft (de construction); *plans d'une maison*, plans of a house; *tirer des plans pour bâtir*, to plan a building. ‖ GÉOGR. Map (d'une ville); *plan en relief*, relief map; *lever le plan du terrain*, to survey a piece of ground. ‖ THÉÂTR. Plot (d'une pièce). ‖ NAUT. Plan. ‖ FIG. Plan (d'action, de vie); *auteurs de plans*, planners; *établissement d'un plan directeur*, overall planning; *sans plan arrêté*, following no preconceived plan. ‖ FAM. *Laisser qqn en plan*, to leave s.o. in the lurch; *laisser son travail en plan*, to stop working.

planchage [plɑ̃ʃa:ʒ] m. Boarding.

planche [plɑ̃:ʃ] f. Plank (épaisse); board (mince); *planche à laver, à repasser*, wash-, ironing board. ‖ ARCHIT. Batten (de parquet). ‖ CULIN. *Planche à pâtisserie*, pastry-board. ‖ ARTS. Plate (gra-

vure); *planche à dessin*, drawing-board; *planche de graveur*, woodcut. ‖ AGRIC. Bed (de légumes). ‖ NAUT. *Planche de débarquement*, gang-plank; *jour de planches*, lay-day. ‖ SPORTS. *Faire la planche*, to float on one's back (à la nage). ‖ THÉÂTR. *Monter sur les planches*, to go on the stage. ‖ FIG. *Planche de salut*, sheet anchor, last hope; *se fier à une planche pourrie*, to trust to a broken reed. ‖ FAM. *Planche à pain*, bony person, person as thin as a lath (ou) U. S. rail; *avoir du pain sur la planche*, to have plenty of work to do; *être entre quatre planches*, to get a wooden suit.

planchéiage [plɑ̃ʃeja:ʒ] m. Boarding, planking.
planchéier [-je] v. tr. (1). To floor, to batten (un parquet); to board, to plank (une pièce).
plancher [plɑ̃ʃe] v. intr. (1). FAM. To be sent to the blackboard.
plancher m. Floor. (V. PARQUET.) ‖ NAUT. Deck (du bateau). ‖ FAM. *Le plancher des vaches*, the cold, hard ground; *débarrasser le plancher*, to cut and run, to clear out.
planchette [-ʃɛt] f. Small plank. ‖ Planchette (de spirite). ‖ Plane-table (d'arpenteur).
plançon [plɑ̃sɔ̃] m. AGRIC. Sapling; slip.
plancton [plɑ̃ktɔ̃] m. Plankton.
plane [pla:n] f. TECHN. Drawing-knife (à bois); planisher (à métal).
plané, ée [plane] adj. AVIAT. Gliding; *descendre en vol plané*, to glide down; *faire du vol plané*, to glide; *vol plané*, glide, volplane.
planéité [-neite] f. Flatness, levelness, evenness. ‖ MATH. Planeness.
planer [-ne] v. intr. (1). To sail (ballon, fumée, nuage); to soar (oiseau); *planer sur*, to hang over. ‖ AVIAT. To glide, to volplane. ‖ FIG. To hang [*sur*, over] (danger, silence). ‖ FAM. To look down upon (dédaigner); to be superior to (s'élever au-dessus); *planer au-dessus du menu fretin*, to look down upon the common herd; *planer au-dessus des petits ennuis*, to rise above small annoyances.
planer v. tr. (1). TECHN. To plane, to trim (du bois); to planish, to flatten (du métal).
planétaire [planetɛ:r] adj. ASTRON., TECHN. Planetary. ‖ FIG. World, world-wide (conflit, guerre).
— m. ASTRON. Planetarium, orrery. ‖ TECHN., AUTOM. Planetary.
planétarium [-tarjɔm] m. ASTRON. Planetarium.
planète [-nɛt] f. ASTRON. Planet.
planeur [planœ:r] m. AVIAT. Glider.
planificateur, trice [planifikatœ:r, tri:s] adj. Planning.
— s. Economic planner.
planification [planifikasjɔ̃] f. Planning.
planifier [-fje] v. tr. (1). To plan, to blueprint.
planisme [-nism] m. Planning.
planisphère [-nisfɛ:r] m. Planisphere.
planning [planiŋ] m. COMM. Schedule, plan (programme de travail); planning department (service). ‖ *Planning familial*, family planning.
planque [plɑ̃:k] f. FAM. Hideout, U. S. plant (cachette); cushy job (situation).
planqué, ée [plɑ̃ke] adj. FAM. Hidden (argent); cushy (travail); shirking, dodging (soldat).
— s. FAM. Shirker, dodger.
planquer [plɑ̃ke] v. tr. (1). FAM. To hide, to throw aside, U. S. to plant.
— v. pr. **Se planquer.** FAM. To hide (ou) park oneself; to lie flat. ‖ To get a cushy job.
plant [plɑ̃] m. AGRIC. Plantation (d'arbres); bed (de légumes). ‖ Sapling, seedling, slip (plançon).
plantage [plɑ̃ta:ʒ] m. AGRIC. Planting.
plantain [-tɛ̃] m. BOT. Plantain, rib-grass.
plantaire [-tɛ:r] adj. MÉD. Plantar.
plantation [-tasjɔ̃] f. Planting (action); plantation (résultat).
plante [plɑ̃:t] f. BOT. Plant; *plante d'apparte-*

ment, indoor potted plant; *plante grimpante,* creeper; *plantes vertes,* evergreens.

plante f. Méd. Sole (du pied).

planté, ée [plɑ̃te] adj. Set, situated (édifice); *cheveux bien plantés,* well-set hair. ‖ Fig. *Gaillard bien planté,* well-set-up lad; *planté sur ses jambes,* firmly fixed on one's legs. ‖ Fam. *Ne restez pas planté là,* don't stand there gaping.

planter [-te] v. tr. (1). Agric. To plant, to set (des fleurs, des légumes); to plant, to lay out (un jardin). ‖ Fig. To stick [*dans,* in] (un couteau); to set up (un drapeau, une échelle); to drive in, to stick in (un pieu); to set up (une tente). ‖ Fam. *Planter là,* to desert (sa femme); to leave in the lurch, to jilt (qqn); to throw down (ses outils); to throw up (son travail); *tout planter là,* to cut oneself off from everything.
— v. pr. **Se planter,** to stand, to take one's stand; *se planter devant,* to take a close view of (qqch.); to stand before, to plant oneself before (qqn). ‖ Fam. To crap out.

planteur [-tœ:r] m. Agric. Planter, grower. ‖ Planter, plantation-owner (aux colonies).

planteuse [-tø:z] f. Agric. Planting-machine.

plantigrade [plɑ̃tigrad] adj., m. Zool. Plantigrade.

plantoir [plɑ̃twa:r] m. Agric. Dibble.

planton [plɑ̃tɔ̃] m. Milit. Orderly, sentry.

plantureusement [plɑ̃tyrøzmɑ̃] adv. Plentifully.

plantureux, euse [-rø, ø:z] adj. Abundant, plentiful (repas); fertile (pays). ‖ Fig. Buxom (femme).

plaquage [plaka:ʒ] m. Techn. Veneering (en menuiserie). ‖ Sports. Tackle, bringing down, grassing (au rugby). ‖ Fam. Throwing over, jilting (de qqn).

plaque [plak] f. Plank (de bois); patch (de boue); slat (de marbre); plate (de métal); *plaque d'ébéniste,* sheet of veneer; *plaque commémorative,* votive tablet; *plaque mortuaire,* church brass; U. S. memorial tablet; *plaque de porte,* doorplate, name-plate; *plaque de rue,* street plate; *avoir sa plaque dans une rue,* to have one's name up in a street. ‖ Number-plate (d'agent de police); badge (de commissionnaire); *plaque d'identité,* identification plate (d'un particulier); identity disc (d'un soldat). ‖ Plaque (décoration). ‖ Plate (de photographie). ‖ Electr. Plate (d'accu). ‖ Radio. Plate, anode. ‖ Naut. *Plaque de blindage,* armourplate. ‖ Ch. de f. *Plaque tournante,* turn-table, hinge. ‖ Méd. Patch, blotch. ‖ Culin. *Plaque chauffante,* hot plate. ‖ Autom. Number-plate, U. S. license-plate.

plaqué, ée [-ke] adj. Techn. Veneered (bois); plated (métal).
— m. Veneer, veneering. ‖ Plating (en métal).

plaquer v. tr. (1). To veneer (du bois); to plate (du métal); to flash (du verre). ‖ To daub (de la boue, des couleurs, du plâtre). ‖ Mus. To strike (un accord). ‖ Sports. To bring down, to grass (au rugby); *plaquer qqn contre,* to stand s.o. up against. ‖ Fam. To chuck, to get rid of (sa femme); *il nous a plaqués,* he left us in the lurch; *plaquer les affaires,* to give up business; *avoir envie de tout plaquer,* to feel like throwing everything up (ou) chucking it all.
— v. intr. To lie flat; *ses cheveux plaquent sur son front,* his hair lies flat on his forehead.
— v. pr. **Se plaquer,** to flatten oneself (s'aplatir); to lie flat (se coucher); *se plaquer les cheveux,* to plaster down one's hair. ‖ Aviat. To pancake.

plaquette [-kɛt] f. Small plate; plaquette (de bois, de métal); small slab (de marbre). ‖ Booklet, brochure, pamphlet (opuscule).

plaqueur [-kœ:r] s. Techn. Veneerer (de bois); plater (de métal). ‖ Sports. Tackler.

plasma [plasma] m. Méd. Plasma.

plaste [pla:st] m. Bot. Plast.

plastic [plastik] m. Plastic explosive.

plasticage [-ka:ʒ] m. V. PLASTIQUAGE.

plasticité [-site] f. Plasticity.

plastifiant [-fjɑ̃] m. Plasticizer.

plastifier [-fje] v. tr. (1). To plasticize.

plastiquage [plastika:ʒ] m. Bombing, blowing-up (attentat).

plastique [plastik] adj. Plastic (art); *aux formes plastiques,* having a well-moulded figure. ‖ Comm. *Matières plastiques,* plastic goods, plastics.
— f. Plastic art. ‖ Physique (d'une personne).
— m. Comm. Plastic goods; *manufacture de plastique,* plastic factory.

plastiquement [-mɑ̃] adv. Plastically.

plastiqueur [plastikœ:r] m. Bomber (auteur d'un attentat).

plastron [plastrɔ̃] m. Front (de corsage); *plastron de chemise,* shirt-front; *faux plastron,* detachable front, dickie (fam.). ‖ Breast-plate, plastron (d'armure). ‖ Sports. Body-shield (au baseball); fencing-jacket, plastron (à l'escrime). ‖ Fig. Butt, target (cible).

plastronner [-trɔne] v. tr. (1). To put a plastron on (s.o.).
— v. intr. Sports. To fence. ‖ Fam. To stick one's chest out, to attitudinize, to put on side.

plastronneur [-trɔnœ:r] m. Swaggerer.

plat, ate [pla, at] adj. Flat (assiette, surface); short-haired (fourrure); smooth (mer); low-heeled (souliers); flat, level, even (terrain); *à fond plat,* flat-bottomed. ‖ Lank, straight (cheveux); featureless (physionomie); *à la poitrine plate,* flat-chested. ‖ Naut. Dead (calme). ‖ Culin. Flat, tasteless (boisson, vin). ‖ Arts. Flat (couleur). ‖ Fig. Light, empty (bourse); flat, colourless, tame (style). ‖ Fam. Low (obséquiosité); cringing, servile (personne); *se montrer plat,* to eat humble pie.
— m. Flat (d'un couteau, de la main). ‖ Pl. Boards (d'une reliure). ‖ Dish, platter (vaisselle); *plat creux,* hollow dish. ‖ Culin. Dish (mets); course (service); *plat de côtes,* top ribs; *plat relevé,* savoury; *plat sucré,* pudding, dessert; *dîner à trois plats,* three-course dinner; *faire de bons petits plats,* to be a good cook; *mettre les petits plats dans les grands,* to give a big dinner. ‖ Naut. Blade (d'un aviron); *avirons à plat!,* feather your oars! ‖ Sports. *Se faire battre sur le plat,* to get beaten on the level stretch. ‖ Autom. *A plat,* run down (accu); deflated, down (pneu). ‖ Théâtr. *Tomber à plat,* to fall flat, to be a failure (ou) a flop. ‖ Fam. *En faire tout un plat,* to pile on the agony; to make a song and dance about it; *ne pas faire un plat de,* to make no bones about; *un plat de sa façon,* one of his nastiest tricks. ‖ **A plat,** flat, flatwise (objet); down and out (personne); *être complètement à plat,* to be completely run down, to feel washed out; *mettre qqn à plat,* te take it out of s.o.; *poser un livre à plat,* to lay a book down flat. ‖ **Plat-bord,** m. Naut. Gunwale. ‖ **Plate-bande,** f. Agric. Flower-bed; Fam. Private ground, preserves; *marcher sur les plates-bandes de qqn,* to encroach on s.o.'s preserves. ‖ **Plate-forme,** f. Autom. Platform (d'autobus); Naut. Half-deck; Ch. de f. Truck; Fig. Platform. ‖ **Plat-fond,** m. Naut. Well.

Plata [plata] f. Géogr. *Rio de la Plata,* River Plate, U. S. River Plata.

platane [platan] m. Bot. Plane-tree.

plateau [plato] m. Scale (de balance). ‖ Culin. Tray, salver (à servir); shelf (de four); *plateau à thé,* tea-tray. ‖ Géogr. Plateau, tableland, high plain. ‖ Naut. *Plateau d'ancre,* anchor-buoy. ‖ Milit. *Plateau chargeur,* loading platform. ‖ Techn. Table (de machine-outil). ‖ Théâtr. Stage.

‖ MÉD. Stationary condition. ‖ Mus. Turntable (de radiophono).

platée [plate] f. FAM. Dishful (d'aliments); dish.

platée f. ARCHIT. Foundation.

platement [platmã] adv. Flatly. (V. HUMBLEMENT.) ‖ Dully. (V. PROSAÏQUEMENT.)

platinage [platina:ʒ] m. Platting with platinum.

platine [-tin] f. Lock (de fusil); stage (de microscope); plate (de montre, de serrure); platen (de presse); deck (d'électrophone).

platine m. Platinum.

platiné, ée [-tine] adj. Platinum-plated; *iridium platiné*, platino-iridium. ‖ *Blonde platinée*, platinum blonde.

platineux, euse [-tinø, ø:z] adj. Platinous.

platinotypie [-tinɔtipi] f. Platinotype.

platitude [platityd] f. Baseness, obsequiousness, cringing attitude; *faire des platitudes à*, to fawn on. ‖ Flatness, banality, dullness (du comportement). ‖ Platitude, commonplace remark (dans la conversation, les écrits); flatness, vapidity (du style). ‖ Insipidity (du vin).

platonicien, enne [platɔnisjɛ̃, ɛn] adj. PHILOS. Platonic.

— m. PHILOS. Platonist.

platonique [-nik] adj. Platonic (amour). ‖ FAM. Futile, useless.

platonisme [-nism] m. Platonism.

platoniser [-nize] v. intr. (1). To platonize.

plâtrage [plɑtra:ʒ] m. ARCHIT. Plastering (action); plaster-work (résultat). ‖ Plastering (du vin). ‖ AGRIC. Liming (d'un champ). ‖ FIG. Rubbishy stuff (style).

plâtras [-trɑ] m. Rubbish, rubble.

plâtre [plɑ:tr] m. Plaster (produit); *plâtre à mouler*, plaster of Paris. ‖ Plaster-work (travail); *essuyer les plâtres*, to be the first occupant of a new house. ‖ ARTS. Plaster cast. ‖ MÉD. Medicinal plaster (produit); plaster-cast (appareil); *mettre dans le plâtre*, to put into plaster.

plâtré, ée [plɑtre] adj. Plastered (mur, vin). ‖ FIG. Patched-up (entente). ‖ FAM. Painted (femme).

plâtrer v. tr. (1). ARCHIT. To plaster (un mur). ‖ AGRIC. To lime (un champ); to plaster (du vin). ‖ MÉD. To put into plaster (un membre). ‖ FIG. To patch up (une amitié branlante). ‖ FAM. To paint (la figure).

plâtrerie [-trɛri] f. Plastering (action); plaster-work (résultat).

plâtreux, euse [-trø, ø:z] adj. Chalky (eau); limy (terrain).

plâtrier [-trije] m. Plasterer; plaster-maker.

plâtrière [-trijɛ:r] f. Gypsum quarry (carrière); gypsum kiln (four).

plausibilité [plozibilite] f. Plausibility.

plausible [-zibl] adj. Plausible. (V. VRAISEMBLABLE.)

plausiblement [-ziblǝmã] adv. Plausibly.

play-back [plɛbak] m. inv. RADIO. Pre-recording; *chanter en play-back*, to mime a song.

play-boy [plɛbɔj] m. Playboy.

plèbe [plɛb] f. Common people, plebeians; plebs (fam.).

plébéien, enne [plebejɛ̃, ɛn] adj., s. Plebeian.

plébiscitaire [plebissitɛ:r] adj. Plebiscitary.

plébiscite [-sit] m. Plebiscite.

plébisciter [-site] v. tr. (1). To vote by plebiscite; *plébisciter qqn*, to measure s.o.'s popularity.

plectre [plɛktr] m. Mus. Plectrum.

pléiade [plejad] f. Pleiad.

plein, eine [plɛ̃, ɛn] adj. Full [*de*, of] (v. REMPLI); *pleine cruche de vin*, jugful of wine; *pleine voiture*, cartful. ‖ Replete, crammed (bondé); *plein comme un œuf*, chock-full; *plein de fautes*, full of mistakes; *plein de monde*, swarming with people. ‖ Full, complete (entier); *pleine satis-*

faction, full (ou) entire satisfaction. ‖ Covered (couvert); *les doigts pleins d'encre*, with inky fingers. ‖ Full, round (rond); *joues pleines*, plump cheeks. ‖ ZOOL. With lamb (brebis); with kittens (chatte); in pup (chienne); in (ou) with foal (jument); in (ou) with calf (vache). ‖ ASTRON. Full (lune). ‖ ARTS. *Trait plein*, continuous line. ‖ ARCHIT. Solid (barre, brique). ‖ ELECTR. Solid (fil). ‖ AGRIC. *En pleine terre*, on open ground. ‖ NAUT. *Pleine mer*, high tide; *en pleine mer*, in the open sea. ‖ MILIT. Solid (boulet). ‖ MÉD. *Respirer à pleins poumons*, to breathe in deep. ‖ Mus. Full (voix); *chant à plein gosier*, full-throated song. ‖ JUR. *Plein pouvoir*, full power. ‖ FIG. *Plein de danger*, fraught with danger; *plein de bonne volonté*, full of good will; *plein de soi-même*, self-conceited, self-engrossed; *plein de soucis*, burdened with cares, full of trouble. ‖ LOC. *De plein gré*, of one's own free will, willingly; *en plein air*, outdoors; *en pleine chambre des Lords*, in the House of Lords itself; *en plein cœur*, right in the heart; *en pleine saison*, at the height of the season; *en plein travail*, in the middle of one's work; *en plein vent*, in the open; *mordre à pleine bouche*, to take a big bite. ‖ FAM. Drunk, top heavy (ivre); *plein comme une outre*, absolutely plastered. ‖ **Plein-emploi**, m. Full employment. ‖ **Plein-temps**, adj. inv. Full time; m. full-time job.

— adv. Full; *apporter des livres plein les bras*, to bring armfuls of books; *avoir de l'argent plein les poches*, to be rolling in money; *en plein dans l'œil*, straight (ou) right in the eye; *le vent en plein dans le nez*, the wind dead against one (ou) in one's face. ‖ FAM. *Tout plein*, very much, a lot; *tout plein gentil*, awfully nice, as nice as can be.

— s. Downstroke (de l'écriture). ‖ ASTRON. Full (de la lune). ‖ SPORTS. Bull's eye, middle; *mettre dans le plein*, to hit the bull. ‖ ARCHIT. Solid (d'un bâtiment). ‖ NAUT. Full load (charge); high water (mer); *avoir son plein*, to be fully laden; *faire le plein de*, to fill up with. ‖ AUTOM. *Faire le plein d'essence*, to refuel, to fill up with petrol (ou) U. S. gas.

pleinement [plɛnmã] adv. Fully, wholly. (V. ENTIÈREMENT, TOTALEMENT.)

pléistocène [pleistɔsɛn] m., adj. GÉOL. Pleistocene.

plénier, ère [plenje, ɛr] adj. Full, complete (liberté); plenary (séance). ‖ ECCLÉS. Plenary (indulgence).

plénipotentiaire [plenipotãsjɛ:r] adj., s. Plenipotentiary.

plénitude [plenity:d] f. Fullness (des facultés, des forces, du temps). ‖ Overabundance. (V. PLÉTHORE.)

pléonasme [pleonasm] m. GRAMM. Pleonasm.

plésiosaure [plezjozɔ:r] m. ZOOL. Plesiosaurus.

pléthore [pletɔ:r] f. MÉD. Plethora. ‖ FIG. Overabundance, repletion, superabundance. (V. PROFUSION, SURABONDANCE.)

pléthorique [-tɔrik] adj. MÉD. Plethoric. ‖ FIG. Overabundant (récolte); overcrowded (salle).

pleur [plœ:r] m. Tear. (V. LARME). ‖ ECCLÉS. Pl. *Pleurs et grincements de dents*, weeping and wailing and gnashing of teeth. ‖ BOT. Bleeding.

pleural, ale [plœral] adj. MÉD. Pleural.

pleurard, arde [plœra:r, ard] adj. Whining, whimpering (personne); tearful, plaintive, whining (ton). [V. PLEURNICHARD.]

— s. Whiner. (V. PLEURNICHEUR.)

pleurer [-re] v. intr. (1). To weep; to cry (de for); sur, over); *pleurer comme un veau*, to blubber; *pleurer bruyamment*, to bawl; *pleurer sur ses malheurs*, to lament one's misfortunes; *pleurer sur ses pertes d'argent*, to bewail one's money

losses; *pleurer tout son saoul,* to have a good cry. ‖ To water, to run (yeux); *faire pleurer les yeux,* to make s.o.'s eyes water. ‖ FAM. *Je veux ça ou je pleure,* give it me or I'll scream.
— v. tr. To weep, to lament, to mourn for; to regret (v. REGRETTER); *pleurer ses belles années,* to mourn the loss of one's happy days; *pleurer les morts,* to bemoan the dead, to weep for the dead; *pleurer toutes les larmes de son corps,* to cry one's eyes out. ‖ LOC. *Pleurer misère,* to cry poverty.

◾**leurésie** [-rezi] f. MÉD. Pleurisy, wet pleurisy.

◾**leurétique** [-retik] adj. MÉD. Pleuretic.

◾**leureur, euse** [-rœːr, øːz] adj. Whining (personne). ‖ BOT. Weeping (saule).
— s. Whiner. (V. PLEURNICHARD.)

◾**leureuse** [-røːz] f. † Mourner.

◾**leurite** [-rit] f. MÉD. Dry pleurisy.

◾**leurnichard, arde** [plœrniʃaːr, aːrd] adj. Whining, whimpering, puling, snivelling (personne). ‖ THÉÂTR. *Pièce pleurnicharde,* sloppy play, U. S. soap-opera (à la radio).

◾**leurnicher** [-ʃe] v. intr. (1). To whine, to snivel, to pule, to whimper. (V. LARMOYER.)

◾**leurnicherie** [-ʃri] f. Whining, snivelling, puling, whimpering.

◾**leurnicheur, euse** [-ʃœːr, øːz] adj. Whining. (V. PLEURNICHARD.)
— s. Whiner, whimperer, sniveller; cry-baby.

leut [pløː]. V. PLEUVOIR (76).

◾**leutre** [pløːtr] m. Cad; coward. (V. LÂCHE.)

◾**leutrerie** [pløːtrəri] f. Caddishness; cowardice.

leuvasser [pløvase], **pleuviner** [-vine] v. impers. (1). V. PLEUVOTER.

◾**leuvoir** [pløvwaːr] v. impers. (76). To rain; *il pleut à seaux,* it is raining in bucketfuls; *les jours où il pleut,* rainy days. ‖ FIG. To rain.
— v. intr. FIG. To rain, to hail, to shower (sur, on); *les applaudissements pleuvaient,* applause thundered forth; *les coups pleuvaient sur mon dos,* blows were raining on my back; *les félicitations pleuvaient sur lui,* congratulations were showered on him; *faire pleuvoir des coups, des malédictions sur,* to rain down blows, curses on.

◾**leuvoter** [pløvote] v. impers. (1). To drizzle. (V. BRUINER.)

◾**lèvre** [plɛːvr] f. MÉD. Pleura.

◾**lexiglas** [plɛksiglas] m. Plexiglas (trade mark).

◾**lexus** [plɛksyːs] m. MÉD. Plexus.

◾**li** [pli] m. Fold, pleat (garniture); crease (repliement); *pli du pantalon,* crease down the front of trousers; *pli du revers,* crease-edge; *faire des plis,* to fall into folds (rideaux); *faire des plis à,* to pleat; *gros pli,* large fold; *petit pli,* small tuck; *qui a un bon pli,* well-creased (pantalon). ‖ Crease, crinkle (du papier foncé); *faire un pli à une page de livre,* to turn down a page, to dog-ear a book. ‖ Crease (faux pli); *enlever les faux plis de,* to remove the creases from; *faire des faux plis a,* to crease. ‖ Wrinkle, pucker (boursouflure); *faire des plis,* to wrinkle, to pucker; *tomber sans un pli,* to hang well without a wrinkle. ‖ Form (forme); *se mettre au pli du corps,* to take the form of the body (vêtement). ‖ Waving, wave (de la coiffure); *mettre en plis,* to set the hair; *mise en pli,* setting, hair-setting. ‖ Trick (aux cartes); *faire un pli,* to take a trick. ‖ Envelope, cover (d'une lettre); *sous ce pli,* enclosed, herewith; *sous pli séparé,* under separate cover. ‖ Letter (missive); *pli cacheté,* sealed note (ou) letter. ‖ MÉD. Bend (du bras); line, wrinkle (du front); hollow (du genou); curl (de la lèvre). ‖ GÉOGR. Undulation, fold (du terrain). ‖ NAUT. *Plis cachetés,* sealed orders; *plis consulaires,* consular packages. ‖ FIG. Habit (habitude); *quand le pli est pris,* when

a habit has been acquired. ‖ FAM. *Ne pas faire un pli,* to be all plain sailing.

pliable [plijabl] adj. Folding (objet); foldable (tissu); flexible (verge). [V. PLIANT.]

pliage [plia:ʒ] m. Folding; creasing.

pliant, ante [plijɑ̃, ɑ̃:t] adj. Folding, foldable; *chaise, table pliante,* folding chair, table; *lit pliant,* folding bed. ‖ AUTOM. *Capote pliante,* collapsible hood; U. S. folding top. ‖ NAUT. *Canot pliant,* folding canoe, collapsible boat. ‖ FIG. Pliant, flexible, tractable, docile, pliable.
— m. Camp-stool, folding-stool.

plie [pli] f. ZOOL. Plaice.

plier [plije] v. tr. (1). To fold (une étoffe, un éventail, des vêtements); to roll up (son parapluie); to strike (sa tente). ‖ To bend (le bras, le genou); *plié en deux,* bent double (corps). ‖ FIG. To bend (qqn) [à, to]; *plier qqn à la discipline,* to bring s.o. under discipline; *plié à la volonté de qqn,* broken in; *qui ne veut pas plier,* unyielding.
— v. intr. To bend (sous, under) [arbre, moisson, personne, roseau]; to sag (poutre). ‖ MILIT. To give way (devant, before). ‖ FIG. To yield, to submit (v. CÉDER); *plier devant,* to bow to (ou) before; *plier le dos,* to knuckle down, to knock under; *tout plie devant lui,* he lords it over everybody.
— v. pr. Se plier, to fold up (objet). ‖ FIG. *Se plier à,* to bow to (ou) to submit to, to comply with, to humour; *se plier aux nécessités,* to yield to necessity.

plieur [-jœːr] s. Folder.

plieuse [-jø:z] f. TECHN. Folding-machine.

plinthe [plɛ̃:t] f. Plinth (de colonne, de mur); skirting-board (en bois).

pliocène [pliɔsɛn] m. GÉOL. Pliocene.

plioir [plijwa:r] m. Folder. ‖ SPORTS. Winder (à la pêche).

plissage [plisa:ʒ] m. Pleating (de l'étoffe); kilting (à plis verticaux). [V. GAUFRAGE, TUYAUTAGE.] ‖ Crinkling, creasing (du papier).

plissé, ée [-se] adj. Pleated, folded (étoffe); *plissé accordéon,* accordion pleated; *plissé en long,* kilted. ‖ Crinkled, creased (papier). ‖ Wrinkled (front); puckered, pursed (lèvre). ‖ **Plissé-tuyauté,** adj. Fluted.
— m. Pleating, pleat; kilting.

plissement [-smɑ̃] m. Wrinkling (du front); pursing (des lèvres). ‖ GÉOL. Fold, folding, plication.

plisser [-se] v. tr. (1). To pleat, to fold (une étoffe); *plisser en long,* to kilt; *plisser à la main,* to tuck. ‖ To crinkle, to crease (du papier). ‖ To crease. (V. CHIFFONNER.) ‖ To corrugate (du métal). ‖ To wrinkle (le front, le visage); to pucker, to purse (les lèvres); to screw up (les yeux); *plissé de douleur,* wincing, screwed up with pain.
— v. intr. To take pleats, to kilt (étoffe). ‖ To crease, to crumple (papier, tissu).
— v. pr. Se plisser, to pleat (étoffe). ‖ To wrinkle (front, visage); to pucker up, to purse (lèvres); to be screwed up (yeux).

plisseur [-sœːr] s. Folder, pleater.

plisseuse [-sø:z] f. TECHN. Pleating-machine.

plissure [-sy:r] f. Pleating, kilting.

pliure [plijy:r] f. Folding (action); folding-room (lieu).

ploiement [plwamɑ̃] m. Bending.

plomb [plɔ̃] m. Lead (métal); *sous plomb,* lead-covered. ‖ Plumb (pour alourdir). ‖ Seal (à sceller). ‖ Type (en typo.). ‖ ARCHIT. Leads (de toiture); sink (tuyauterie). ‖ SPORTS. Shot (pour la chasse); sinker (pour la pêche); *gros, petit plomb,* buck-shot, small shot. ‖ ÉLECTR. Fuse; *faire sauter les plombs,* to blow the fuses. ‖ NAUT. Sounding-lead, plummet (à sondage); *plombs de sécurité,* emergency ballast. ‖ Loc. *Avoir du plomb dans l'aile,* to be in a bad way (personne); *ciel, sommeil de plomb,* leaden sky, sleep; *n'avoir pas de plomb dans la tête,* to be feather-brained; *du plomb sur l'estomac,* a load on the stomach.

plombage [-ba:ʒ] m. Leading, plumbing. ‖ Sealing (d'un colis). ‖ Méd. Filling, stopping (d'une dent).

plombagine [-baʒin] f. Black-lead, graphite, plumbago.

plombé, ée [-be] adj. Leaded (canne). ‖ Sealed (colis). ‖ Archit. Lead-covered (toit). ‖ Sports. Shotted (ligne). ‖ Méd. Filled, stopped (dent); leaden-hued (teint).

plomber [-be] v. tr. (1). To weight (une canne). ‖ To seal (un colis). ‖ Archit. To lead (un toit). ‖ Sports. To weight (la ligne). ‖ Méd. To fill, to stop (une dent); to dull, to make leaden-hued (le teint).

plomberie [-bri] f. Plumbery, plumbing (action); lead industry (industrie); plumber's shop (magasin); lead-works (objets).

plombier [-bje] m. Plumber.

plombières [plɔ̃bjɛ:r] f. Culin. Ice-cream containing preserved fruit; U. S. tutti-fruti, Nesselrode pudding.

plombifère [plɔ̃bifɛ:r] adj. Plumbiferous.

plombique [-bik] adj. Plumbic.

plombure [-by:r] f. Leads, cames (de vitraux).

plonge [plɔ̃:ʒ] f. Fam. Dish-washing (dans un restaurant).

plongé, ée [plɔ̃ʒe] adj. Fig. Deep, buried, plunged, lost (dans, in).

plongeant, ante [plɔ̃ʒɑ̃, ɑ̃:t] adj. From above (vue); plunging (tir); plunge (ou) plunging (décolleté).

plongée f. Sports. Plunging, diving (à la nage). ‖ Naut. Diving, submersion (d'un sous-marin); *plongée raide,* crash-dive. ‖ Milit. Slope (de parapet). ‖ Géol. Incline, slope (de terrain).

plongement [-ʒmɑ̃] m. Plunging, dipping (dans un liquide). ‖ Fig. Immersion (dans un travail).

plongeon [-ʒɔ̃] m. Sports. Plunge, dive; *faire un plongeon,* to take a header, to dive. ‖ Zool. Diver, loon. ‖ Fig. Plunge; *faire le plongeon,* to take the plunge.

plonger [-ʒe] v. intr. (7). Sports. To dive, to plunge. ‖ Zool. To sound (baleine); to duck (canard). ‖ Naut. To send (bateau); to dive, to submerge, to go under (sous-marin). ‖ Géol. To dip, to go down, to slope (route, terrain). ‖ Fig. To plunge (v. s'enfoncer); *plonger dans le désespoir,* to plunge into despair; *notre regard plonge dans,* we look down into.
— v. tr. To plunge, to dip (qqch., qqn) [dans, into]; *plonger la main dans son sac,* to dive into one's handbag; *plonger le regard dans,* to look down into. ‖ Fig. To plunge, to throw (qqn) [dans, into].
— v. pr. Se plonger, to plunge (ou) to immerse oneself (dans, in) [l'eau]. ‖ Fig. To plunge (dans, into); to give oneself up (dans, to) [l'étude]; to be buried (dans, in) [la rêverie]; to be immersed (dans, in) [les soucis]; to be steeped (dans, in) [le vice].

plongeur, euse [-ʒœ:r, ø:z] adj. Zool. Diving (oiseau). ‖ Techn. Plunger (piston).
— m. Zool. Diver. ‖ Techn. Plunger.
— s. Sports. Diver. ‖ Fam. Dish-washer, washer-up (de restaurant).

plot [plo] m. Electr. Contact-stud; *à huit plots,* eight-point (distributeur).

plouc [pluk] adj. Fam. Boorish.
— m. Fam. Peasant, boor, clodhopper, U. S. hick.

plouf! [pluf] interj. Splash, plop.

ploutocrate [plutɔkrat] m. Plutocrat.

ploutocratie [-si] f. Plutocracy.

ploutocratique [-tik] adj. Plutocratic.

ployable [plwajabl] adj. Pliable. (V. flexible.)

ployer [-je] v. tr. (8 a). To bend (une branche, les genoux). ‖ Fig. To tame, to force to yield.
— v. intr. To bow, to yield, to give way (v. céder, plier); *faire ployer,* to bend down; *ses genoux ployèrent,* her knees gave way under her.

plu, plusse, plût. V. plaire (75).

pluches [ply:ʃ] f. pl. Milit. Corvée de pluches, cook-house fatigue; spud-bashing (fam.); U. S. kitchen-police, K. P.

pluie [plɥi] f. Rain (v. averse, ondée); *pluie fine,* drizzle; *se mettre à la pluie,* to be setting in for rain; *petite pluie,* sprinkle (v. crachin); *temps de pluie,* rainy weather. ‖ Fig. Rain (de félicitations); shower (d'or); shower, hail (de projectiles). ‖ Loc. *Faire la pluie et le beau temps,* to lay down the law; to boss the show (fam.); *il n'est pas tombé de la dernière pluie,* there are no flies on him, he wasn't born yesterday.

plumage [plyma:ʒ] m. Plumage, feathers.

plumard [-ma:r] m. Fam. Doss; U. S. hay, sack.

plumassier [-masje] s. Feather-dealer.

plume [plym] f. Feather (d'oiseau); *à plume* feathered (gibier); *lit de plume,* feather-bed; *sans plumes,* unfledged (oiseau). ‖ Feather, plume (de garniture); *à plumes,* plumed (chapeau). ‖ Pen (à écrire); *plume d'acier,* steel pen; *plume d'oie,* quill-pen; *plume en or,* gold nib (de stylo). ‖ Sports. Poids plume, feather-weight. ‖ Fig. *Avoir la plume facile,* to have a ready pen; *au courant de la plume,* as the pen runs on; *vivre de sa plume,* to make a living by one's pen; *y laisser des plumes,* not to come off unscathed.

plumeau [plymo] m. Feather-duster.

plumer [-me] v. tr. (1). To pluck (un oiseau). ‖ Fam. To fleece (qqn).
— v. intr. Naut. To feather.

plumet [-mɛ] m. Plume.

plumeté, ée [-məte] adj. Blas. Plumetty.

plumetis [-məti] m. Raised satin stitch, feather stitch (broderie); dotted swiss (tissu).

plumeux, euse [-mø, ø:z] adj. Featherlike, feathery.

plumier [-mje] m. Pen-tray; pen-box, pencil-box.

plumitif [-mitif] m. Fam. Scribbler, pen-pusher.

plum-pudding [plumpudiŋ] m. Culin. Plum-pudding.

plupart (la) [laplypa:r] f. Most, the most, the greater (ou) greatest part; *dans la plupart des cas,* in most cases; *la plupart des gens,* most people; *la plupart du temps,* most of the time; *pour la plupart,* mostly, for the most part.

plural [plyral] adj. Plural (vote).

pluraliser [-lize] v. tr. (1). To pluralize.

pluralisme [plyralism] m. Pluralism.

pluraliste [-list] adj. Pluralistic.
— s. Pluralist.

pluralité [-lite] f. Plurality.

pluricellulaire [plyriselylɛ:r] adj. Bot., Zool. Multicellular.

pluridisciplinaire [-disiplinɛ:r] adj. Multidisciplinary, interdepartmental.

pluridisciplinarité [-disiplinarite] f. Multidisciplinary (ou) interdepartmental approach.

pluriel, elle [plyrjɛl] adj., m. Plural.

plus ([ply] devant consonne et dans les locutions négatives; [ply:s] en calculant et en fin de phrase; [ply:z] devant voyelle) adv. Mor (devant les mots de plusieurs syllabes); -er (suffixe comparatif des mots d'une syllabe); *plu court,* shorter; *plus difficile,* more difficult; *plu près de chez moi que de chez vous,* nearer m place than yours; *de deux mois plus jeune qu moi,* two months younger than I. ‖ More (davan tage); *il y a plus,* there is something more; *il a plus de talent qu'elle,* he has more talent tha

she ; *il a plus de dix chevaux,* he has more than ten horses ; *plus d'une fois,* more than once ; *plus haut !,* speak up ! (ou) U. S. louder ! ; *dix ans et plus,* ten years and over. ‖ -est, most (superlatif) ; *la plus belle des promesses,* the fairest of promises ; *le plus malheureux des hommes,* the most unhappy of men ; *le plus de monde possible,* as many people as possible ; *celui que j'aime le plus,* the one I like best ; *ce qu'il aime le plus,* what he likes most. ‖ No more (négatif) ; *plus de soucis !,* no more worries ! ; *plus rien à faire,* nothing more to do ; *il n'y a plus le temps pour écrire,* there is not enough time left to write ; *sans plus tarder,* without further delay. ‖ Plus (en outre) ; *des dépenses plus les ennuis,* expenses plus bother ; *deux plus trois font cinq,* two and (ou) plus three are five ; *plus le pourboire,* plus tip, exclusive of gratuities. ‖ **Au plus, tout au plus,** at the most (ou) utmost, at the outside ; *dix ans au plus,* ten years at the utmost ; *c'est tout au plus s'il ne s'est pas trouvé mal,* he was on the verge of fainting. ‖ **Bien plus, plus encore,** moreover, besides, still more, what is more. ‖ **De plus,** more (en plus) ; *pas un mot de plus,* not one word more ; *quelque chose de plus,* something more ; *un jour de plus,* one day more ; *y a-t-il rien de plus à faire ?,* is there anything more to do ? ‖ **De plus,** moreover, further, furthermore (en outre) ; *de plus, il est méchant,* moreover he is wicked. ‖ **De plus en plus,** more and more ; *de plus en plus fort,* stronger and stronger ; *de plus en plus terrible,* more and more awful, increasingly awful. ‖ **En plus,** in addition, besides, extra (en surplus) ; *le chauffage en plus,* heating extra ; *en plus un encrier,* an inkstand as well ; *en plus de,* over and above. ‖ **Ne ... plus,** no more (quantité) ; not again, no longer (temps) ; *je ne peux plus rester,* I can't stay any longer ; *je n'en veux plus,* I want no more of it ; *nous ne vous en donnerons plus,* we shall not give you any more ; *votre grande amie n'est plus,* your great friend is no more (ou) is dead. ‖ **Ni plus ni moins,** neither more nor less ; *je ne ferai ni plus ni moins que je n'ai dit,* I will do neither more nor less than I said. ‖ **Non plus,** not either, nor, neither ; *moi non plus,* nor I either, nor do I ; *vous ne le pensez pas non plus,* nor do you think so, you don't think so either. ‖ **Plus ... moins** (ou) **plus,** the more ... the less (ou) ... the more ; *plus je le vois, moins je l'apprécie,* the more I see him, the less I think of him ; *plus il grandit, plus il s'assagit,* the older he gets, the more sensible he becomes. ‖ **Qui plus est,** what is more. ‖ **Tant et plus,** heaps of it ; *il en a tant et plus,* he has lots of it. ‖ **Tout au plus,** at most ; *c'est tout au plus s'il peut se tenir debout,* it's all be can do to stand up. ‖ **Tout... de plus,** the most ; *tout ce qu'il y a de plus difficile,* the most difficult thing in the world. ‖ **Plus-que-parfait,** m. GRAMM. Pluperfect. ‖ **Plus-value,** f. JUR. Gain in value, increase in yield.
— pron. More ; *plus d'un l'a vu,* more than one has seen him.
— m. *Le plus,* the most, the best ; *le plus qu'on puisse dire,* the most that can be said.

plusieurs [plyzjœːr] adj., pron. indéf. pl. Several ; *plusieurs personnes,* several people ; *j'ai eu plusieurs avis,* I have had more than one piece of advice.

plutonique [plytɔnik] adj. GÉOL. Plutonic (roches).

plutonium [plytɔnjɔm] m. CHIM. Plutonium.

plutôt [plyto] adv. More (davantage) ; *il est plutôt ennemi qu'ami,* he is more of an enemy than of a friend. ‖ Rather, sooner (de préférence) ; *tout plutôt que cela,* all rather than that. ‖ Instead (à la place) ; *n'écrivez pas, venez plutôt,* don't write, come instead. ‖ Somewhat, rather (quelque peu) ; *ce livre est plutôt ennuyeux,* this book is rather dull.

pluvial, ale [plyvjal] adj. Pluvial, of rain. ‖ Rain (eau) ; rainy (saison).

pluvier [pluvje] m. ZOOL. Plover.

pluvieux, euse [plyvjø, øːz] adj. Rainy, showery (journée) ; wet (temps).

pluviomètre [-vjɔmɛtr] m. Pluviometer, rain-gauge.

pluviométrie [-vjɔmetri] f. Pluviometry.

pluviométrique [-vjɔmetrik] adj. Pluviometric, pluviometrical.

pluviôse [-vjoːz] m. Pluviôse, fifth month in French Republican calendar (January-February).

pluviosité [-vjosite] f. Rainfall ; raininess.

P. M. E. [peɛmə] f. pl. COMM. Abrév. de *petites et moyennes entreprises,* small businesses.

P. M. U. [peɛmy] m. SPORTS. Abrév. de *pari mutuel urbain,* official organization taking bets on horses ; betting-shop.

P. N. B. [peɛnbe] m. FIN. Abrév. de *produit national brut,* GNP, gross national product.

pneu [pnø] m. FAM. V. PNEUMATIQUE.

pneumatique [pnømatik] adj. Pneumatic. ‖ NAUT. *Canot pneumatique,* rubber dinghy.
— m. AUTOM. Tyre, U. S. tire. ‖ Letter sent by pneumatic tube (lettre).

pneumocoque [pnømɔkɔk] m. MÉD. Pneumococcus.

pneumogastrique [-gastrik] adj. MÉD. Pneumogastric.

pneumologie [-lɔʒi] f. MÉD. Pneumology, study of the lungs and of lung diseases.

pneumologue [-lɔg] s. MÉD. Lung specialist.

pneumonie [-ni] f. MÉD. Pneumonia.

pneumonique [-nik] adj. MÉD. Pneumonic.
— s. MÉD. Pneumonic sufferer.

pneumothorax [-tɔraks] m. Pneumothorax.

pochade [pɔʃad] f. ARTS. Hasty sketch.

pochard, arde [-ʃaːr, ard] s. FAM. Drunkard, boozer.

pocharder (se) [səpɔʃarde] v. pr. FAM. To booze. (V. S'ENIVRER.)

poche [pɔʃ] f. Pocket (de vêtement) ; *poche intérieure, de pantalon, de revolver,* breast-, trouser-, hip-pocket ; *avoir de l'argent en poche,* to have money on one ; *argent de poche,* pocket-money. ‖ Bag, pucker (boursouflure) ; *faire des poches aux genoux,* to be (ou) get baggy at the knees. ‖ GÉOL. Pocket ; *poche d'eau,* water-pocket. ‖ MÉD. Bag, pouch, pocket (sous les yeux) ; *poche des eaux,* bag of waters. ‖ ZOOL. Honey-bag (de l'abeille) ; poison-bag (du serpent). ‖ CULIN. Ladle (à soupe). ‖ TECHN. Ladle (de fonderie). ‖ SPORTS. Bag-net (de chasseur) ; pocket (de pêcheur). ‖ FAM. *Connaître qqch. comme sa poche,* to know sth. like the palm of one's hand ; *en être de sa poche,* to be out of pocket by it ; *mettre ça dans sa poche avec son mouchoir dessus,* to put that in one's pipe and smoke it ; *mettre qqn dans sa poche,* to put s.o. up in a bag ; to be more than a match for s.o. ; *ne pas avoir sa langue dans sa poche,* to have a quick tongue ; *se remplir les poches,* to feather one's nest, to fill one's pockets.
— m. Paperback.

poché, ée [pɔʃe] adj. Black (œil).

pochée f. Pocketful.

pocher [-ʃe] v. tr. (1). CULIN. To poach (des œufs). ‖ FIG. To black, to bung up (les yeux).

pocher v. tr. (1). ARTS. To dash off.

pochet [pɔʃɛ] m. Nose-bag (de cheval).

pochetée [pɔʃte] f. Pocketful. ‖ POP. Duffer.

pocheter [-te] v. tr. (8a). To keep in one's pocket.

pochette [pɔʃɛt] f. Envelope, pocket-case (enveloppe) ; *pochette d'allumettes,* match-book ; *pochette à ouvrage,* lady's companion. ‖ Handbag (sac). ‖ Fancy handkerchief; pochette (de garniture). ‖ MATH. Flat case (à compas).

pocheuse [pɔʃøːz] f. CULIN. Egg-poacher.

pochoir [pɔʃwaːr] m. ARTS. Stencil; *peinture au pochoir*, stencilling.

podagre [pɔdaːgr] f. MÉD. Gout (in the foot).
— adj. MÉD. Gouty.
— s. MÉD. Gouty person.

podestat [pɔdɛsta] m. Podesta.

podium [pɔdjɔm] m. Podium.

podomètre [pɔdɔmɛtr] m. Pedometer.

poêle [pwɑl] m. ECCLÉS. Pall (drap mortuaire); *porteur de cordons du poêle*, pall-bearer.

poêle m. Stove (pour chauffage).

poêle [pwɑl] f. CULIN. Frying-pan, fryer. ‖ FAM. *Tenir la queue de la poêle*, to boss the show, to rule the roost.

poêlée [-le] f. Panful.

poêler [-le] v. intr. (1). To cook in a frying pan.

poêlier [-lje] m. Stove-manufacturer (fabricant); stove-dealer (marchand).

poêlon [-lɔ̃] m. CULIN. Pan, pipkin.

poème [pɔɛːm] m. Poem. ‖ FAM. *Ça c'est un poème*, that's a beauty!

poésie [poezi] f. Poetry (art); poem (morceau).

poétaillon [poɛtajɔ̃] m. FAM. Poetaster.

poète [pɔɛt] m. Poet.

poétesse [pɔɛtɛs] f. Poetess.

poétique [-tik] adj. Poetic, poetical; romantic.
— f. Poetics (art).

poétiquement [-tikmɑ̃] adv. Poetically.

poétisation [-tizasjɔ̃] f. Poetization, poeticization.

poétiser [-tize] v. tr., intr. (1). To poetize, to poeticize.

pogne [pɔɲ] f. FAM. Hand, grip.

pognon [pɔɲɔ̃] m. POP. Dough, oof, U. S. jack.

pogrom [pɔgrɔm] m. Pogrom.

poids [pwa] m. Weight (à peser); *poids et mesures*, Weights and Measures Department; *un poids d'un kilo*, a kilogram-weight. ‖ Weight, heaviness (pesanteur); *poids brut, mort, net*, gross, dead, net weight; *à poids égal*, weight for weight; *un complément pour faire le poids*, a make-weight; *faire bon poids*, to give good weight; *il n'y a pas le poids*, it's short weight; *tromper sur le poids*, to give short weight; *vendre au poids*, to sell by the weight. ‖ Weight (qu'on pèse); *perdre du poids*, to lose flesh (ou) weight; *peser de tout son poids sur*, to throw one's full weight on; *reprendre du poids*, to put on flesh again. ‖ TECHN. Weight (d'une horloge). ‖ SPORTS. Sinker (d'une ligne à pêcher); *poids coq, lourd, mi-lourd, mouche, moyen, plume, bantam-, heavy-, light heavy-, fly-, middle-, feather-weight* (à la boxe); *faire des poids*, to practise weight-lifting; *lancer le poids*, to put the weight (ou) U. S. shot. ‖ CHIM. *Poids spécifique*, specific gravity. ‖ AVIAT. *Poids utile*, payload. ‖ AUTOM. *Poids lourd*, heavy lorry (ou) U. S. truck. ‖ FIG. Load, burden (charge); weight, moment, import (importance); *poids des ans, des soucis*, burden of the years, of care; *acheter qqch. au poids de l'or*, to buy sth. for its weight of gold; *argument de poids*, weighty argument; *homme de poids*, man of weight; *ôter un poids à qqn*, to take a load off s.o.'s shoulders; *soutenir le poids du choc*, to bear the brunt of the onslaught.

poignant, ante [pwaɲɑ̃, ɑ̃ːt] adj. Agonizing, bitter (angoissant); harrowing, heart-rending (déchirant); poignant (pénible); sharp, keen (troublant).

poignard [pwaɲaːr] m. Dagger; *poignard écossais*, dirk.

poignarder [-ɲarde] v. tr. (1). To stab.

poigne [pwaɲ] f. FAM. Grip, grasp; *avoir de la poigne*, to show some grip; *homme à poigne*, strong man; *manquer de poigne*, to lack grip.

poignée [pwaɲe] f. Handful; *à poignées*, in handfuls. ‖ *Poignée de main*, handshake, handgrip; *donner une poignée de main à*, to shake hands with. ‖ AGRIC. Wisp (de paille). ‖ TECHN. Handle (de porte); haft, handle (d'outil); *avec poignée* ansate. ‖ CULIN. Handle (de casserole); haft (de couteau). ‖ MILIT. Hilt (d'épée); grip, butt (de pistolet); handle (de sabre). ‖ NAUT. Handle, grasp (d'aviron). ‖ AUTOM. *Poignée de portière*, door handle. ‖ FIG. Handful (d'hommes).

poignet [pwaɲɛ] m. Wrist; *à la force du poignet*, by sheer strength. ‖ Wristband; cuff (de vêtement). ‖ FIG. *A la force du poignet*, by sheer perseverance.

poil [pwal] m. Hair (d'animal, d'homme); *à poil dur, long*, rough-coated, long-haired (chien); *à rebrousse-poil*, the wrong way; *monter à cru*, to ride bareback (cavalier); *poil follet*, down; *sans poil au menton*, beardless, with a hairless face. ‖ Colour (pelage); *de tous poils*, all colours (animaux). ‖ Pile, nap (de tissu); *à trois poils*, three-pile (velours). ‖ Bristle (de brosse). ‖ SPORTS. *Le poil et la plume*, fur and feather (à la chasse). ‖ BOT. Bristle, down (de plante). ‖ FAM. *A poil*, naked; *au poil*, wizard!, bang on!; U. S. on the button!; *avoir un poil dans la main*, to be careful not to dirty one's hands; *c'est au poil!*, it fits me like a glove; *de tout poil*, of every shade and hue, of all sorts and conditions; *être de bon, de mauvais poil*, to be in a good, bad mood; *poil de carotte*, carroty (chevelure); carrots, ginger (personne); *reprendre du poil de la bête*, to be one's own self again; *se mettre à poil*, to strip to the skin; *tomber sur le poil à*, to go for.

poilant, ante [-lɑ̃, ɑ̃ːt] adj. POP. Killing.

poiler (se) [səpwale] v. pr. (1). POP. To laugh, to have a good laugh, to crease up.

poilu, ue [-ly] adj. Hairy, shaggy. (V. VELU.) ‖ BOT. Pilosc, pilous. (V. PUBESCENT, VILLEUX.)
— m. MILIT. Poilu, French soldier.

poinçon [pwɛ̃sɔ̃] m. Pricker, piercer (de brodeuse); awl (de cordonnier); stabber (de relieur). ‖ Punch, stamp, die (de fabricant); hall-mark (de garantie des bijoux). ‖ ARTS. Style, point (de graveur). ‖ CH. DE F. Punch. ‖ ARCHIT. King-post (de comble); scaffolding-pole (d'échafaudage).

poinçonnage [-sɔnaːʒ] m. Pricking (de brodeuse); awling (de cordonnier). ‖ Punching, stamping (de fabricant); hall-marking (de garantie). ‖ CH. DE F. Punching.

poinçonner [-sɔne] v. tr. (1). To prick (une broderie). ‖ To stamp (une marchandise); to hall-mark (des bijoux). ‖ CH. DE F. To punch (les billets).

poinçonneur [-sɔnœːr] s. Puncher.

poinçonneuse [-sɔnøːz] f. TECHN. Stamping-machine. ‖ CH. DE F. Ticket-punch.

poindre [pwɛ̃ːdr] v. tr. (77). † To sting.
— v. intr. To dawn, to break (jour). ‖ BOT. To peep, to sprout, to spring. ‖ FIG. To come up, to appear, to dawn.

poing [pwɛ̃] m. Fist; *menacer du poing*, to shake one's fist at; *pieds et poings liés*, bound hand and foot. ‖ LOC. *Dormir à poings fermés*, to sleep like a log; *on ne voyait pas le poing dans l'air*, you couldn't see your hand in front of you.

point [pwɛ̃] m. Stitch (en couture); *point arrière*, backstitch; *point de chausson*, faggoting; *point d'épine*, feather-stitch; *point devant*, running stitch; *point d'ourlet, de piqûre*, hem-, lock-stitch; *point de reprise*, darning stitch; *faire un point à*, to put a stitch in. ‖ Lace, needlework (de dentelle); *point d'Alençon*, French lace; *point de Venise*, Venice point. ‖ Mark (à l'école); *avoir de mauvais points*, to have a bad record. ‖ Point (au jeu); *marquer un point*, to score; *rendre des* *points à*, to give points to. ‖ Point, place (lieu); *point d'arrivée*, point of arrival; *point d'eau*, water-supply point. ‖ Moment, point; *arriver à point*, to arrive in the nick of time; *être sur le point de*, to be on the verge of, to be within an inch (ou) ace of, to be about to. ‖ Point, stage, state, situation; *en être au même point*, to have got no farther forward (être immobilisé); *to be level (ou) abreast* (être ex-æquo); *en être au point critique*, to have reached a critical juncture. ‖ Aspect; *le grand point, le point noir de l'affaire*, the best thing, the worst thing about the whole business. ‖ Point, reason, argument; *céder sur tous les points*, to yield on all points; *point d'honneur*, point of honour; *sur ce point*, on that head. ‖ Degree (degré); *à ce point que*, to such an extent that; *à tel point que*, so much so that; *au dernier point*, to the highest degree; *au plus haut point de son succès*, in the heyday of his success; *jusqu'à quel point*, to what extent. ‖ Point, position; *point de commande*, key-point; *point de vue*, viewpoint, standpoint, philosophical position; *point faible*, weak point, shortcoming, chink in the armour, joint in the harness; *point de mire de tous*, cynosure of every eye. ‖ Point, part (d'un discours, d'une question); *de point en point*, in every particular; *en tous points*, on all points; *un discours en trois points*, a formal speech; *point par point*, point by point, in order, bit by bit, in every particular. ‖ GRAMM. Period, full stop (en fin de phrase); *point d'exclamation*, exclamation mark (ou) U. S. point; *point d'interrogation*, question mark; *points de suspension*, points of suspension, pause-dots; U. S. ellipsis (typogr.); *mettre les points sur les i*, to dot the i's. ‖ GÉOGR. *Points cardinaux*, cardinal points; *point de repère*, landmark; *point de vue*, vista, landscape. ‖ MÉD. Point, condition; *point de côté*, stitch in one's side; *point de suture*, stitch; *bien mal en point*, in very poor shape. ‖ TECHN. *Point d'appui*, fulcrum, purchase. ‖ NAUT. *Point d'appui*, outlying station; *faire le point*, to take an observation (ou) the ship's position. ‖ MUS. *Point d'orgue*, pause. ‖ PHYS. Focus; *mettre au point*, to bring into focus; *pas au point*, out of focus. ‖ AUTOM. *Point mort*, neutral gear. ‖ ELECTR. *Points et traits*, dots and dashes (Morse). ‖ COMM. *Points textiles*, clothing coupons. ‖ FIN. *Point de vente*, point of sale. ‖ **A point**, just right, as was expected (comme attendu); in the nick of time (à temps); CULIN. medium (viande). ‖ **Au point**, in perfect running order (machine); *mettre un ouvrage au point*, to put the finishing touch to a work; *l'enquête n'est pas au point*, the enquiry is not yet completed; *la question n'est pas au point*, the question is not thoroughly worked out. ‖ **En tout point**, wholly, in all points (ou) respects. ‖ LOC. *Pour un point Martin perdit son âne*, for want of a nail the shoe was lost. ‖ **Point-virgule**, m. Semicolon.

point adv. Not, not at all, by no means. (V. PAS.) ‖ LOC. *Peu ou point*, little or not at all.

pointage [-ta:ʒ] m. Checking, ticking off (d'une liste). ‖ Timekeeping (des ouvriers à l'usine). ‖ Pointing (d'un télescope). ‖ MILIT. Aiming, laying (d'un canon). ‖ NAUT. Training (d'un canon).

pointe [pwɛ̃:t] f. Point (d'aiguille, d'épingle, de clou); head (de flèche); barb (de hameçon); nib (d'outil); *en pointe*, tapering (arbre); pointed (barbe); *se terminer en pointe*, to taper to a point. ‖ Tiptoe (du pied); *entrer sur la pointe des pieds*, to tiptoe into the room; *sur la pointe des pieds*, on tiptoe. ‖ Wire nail, spike, sprig. (V. CLOU.) ‖ Gore (en couture); *décolleté en pointe*, V-neck. ‖ Triangular fichu (fichu); diaper, triangular napkin (maillot). ‖ Quibble, conceit (mot d'esprit).

‖ Touch, soupçon, spice (v. BRIN); *pointe d'envie*, touch of envy. ‖ Dawn; *à la pointe du jour*, at daybreak. ‖ ARCHIT. Spire. ‖ CULIN. *Pointe d'asperge*, asparagus tip; *une pointe d'ail*, a touch of garlic. ‖ ARTS. *Pointe sèche*, dry-point engraving (gravure); point etching-needle (instrument); *pointes*, toe-dancing; *faire des pointes*, to dance on points (ou) on the tips of the toes (danseur). ‖ MILIT. Point (d'avant-garde); *à la pointe de l'épée*, at the point of the sword; *pousser une pointe*, to drive a wedge; *se trouver en pointe*, to be ahead. ‖ GÉOGR. Headland, foreland, tongue (de terre). ‖ MÉD. *Pointes de feu*, ignipuncture. ‖ ELECTR. Peak (d'une charge); *heures de pointe*, peak hours. ‖ SPORTS. Short trip (promenade); *pointe de vitesse*, spurt; *pousser une pointe jusqu'à*, to push on to. ‖ FIG. Touch; *une pointe d'acrimonie*, a touch of bitterness.

pointeau [pwɛto] m. TECHN. Centre punch. ‖ AUTOM. Needle.

pointer [pwɛte] v. tr. (1). To tick off (des chiffres); to check (des noms). ‖ To check, to tally, to prick off (les arrivages). ‖ MILIT. To aim, to lay (un canon). ‖ GÉOGR., NAUT. To prick (une carte); *pointer sur la carte*, to plot (ou) to pinpoint on the map. ‖ MUS. To dot (une note). ‖ GRAMM. To dot (un i).
— v. intr. TECHN. To clock in (à l'arrivée au travail); to clock out (au départ).
— v. pr. **Se pointer**, FAM. To show (ou) turn up.

pointer v. tr. (1). To prick up (les oreilles).
— v. intr. BOT. To sprout. ‖ NAUT. To stand up (récif). ‖ ARCHIT. To soar skywards (flèche). ‖ MÉD. To stick out (os).

pointeur [-tœ:r] m. Checker, tally clerk (des arrivages); time-keeper (des arrivées). ‖ MILIT. Gunlayer.

pointeuse [-tø:z] f. Time clock, clock.

pointillage [-tija:ʒ] m. Stippling, pointillage.

pointillé, ée [-tije] adj. Dotted (ligne). ‖ ARTS. Dotted, stippled (dessin). ‖ BOT. Spotted (fleur).
— m. Stippled drawing (dessin); dotted line (ligne).

pointiller [-tije] v. tr. (1). To stipple, to dot.
— v. intr. To make dots, to stipple.

pointilleusement [-tijøzmɑ̃] adv. Punctiliously, precisely (avec exigence); touchily (avec susceptibilité).

pointilleux, euse [-tijø, ø:z] adj. Punctilious (précis). ‖ Particular, fastidious (sur, as to, about). ‖ Touchy (susceptible).

pointillisme [-tijism] m. Punctiliousness, fussiness. ‖ ARTS. Pointillism.

pointilliste [-tijist] adj. Punctilious, fussy. ‖ ARTS. Pointillist.
— s. ARTS. Pointillist.

pointu, ue [-ty] adj. Pointed (en général); sharp-pointed (lame). ‖ Pointed (menton); pointed, sharp (nez); shrill (voix); *oreilles pointues*, prick-ears. ‖ NAUT. Scant, shy (vent). ‖ FIG. Angular, touchy (caractère).
— adv. *Parler pointu*, to talk posh (ou) like a Parisian.

pointure [pwɛty:r] f. Size. ‖ TECHN. Tympan point (en typogr.).

poire [pwa:r] f. BOT. Pear. ‖ MÉD. Bulb. ‖ ELECTR. Pear-shaped switch, bell-push. ‖ FAM. Mug, pan (v. BINETTE); *se payer la poire de qqn*, to pull s.o.'s leg; *tête en poire*, pear-shaped head. ‖ FAM. Gull, sucker, mug, juggins (v. GOBEUR); *une jolie poire*, a gullible fellow. ‖ LOC. *Couper la poire en deux*, to split the difference; *entre la poire et le fromage*, at a favourable moment; *garder une poire pour la soif*, to put sth. by for a rainy day.

poiré [pware] m. Perry; pear cider.

poireau [pwaro] m. BOT. Leek. ‖ FAM. French farmer's decoration. ‖ FAM. *Faire le poireau*, to dance attendance.

poireauter [-rɔte] v. intr. (1). Fam. To dance attendance; *faire poireauter qqn,* keep s.o. hanging about (ou) U. S. around.

poirier [pwarje] m. Bot. Pear tree (arbre); peartree wood (bois).

pois [pwa] m. Spot, polka dot (sur une étoffe); *à pois,* spotted, dotted. ‖ Bot. *Pois de senteur,* sweet p̣ea. ‖ Culin. Pea; *pois cassés, secs,* split, dried peas; *pois chiche,* chick-pea.

poison [pwazɔ̃] m. Poison. ‖ Fam. Plague.

poissant, ante [pwasɑ̃, ɑ̃:t] adj. Sticky. ‖ Fam. Bringing bad luck.

poissard, arde [pwasa:r, ard] adj. Fam. Billingsgate, bawdy (langage); vulgar, low (manières).

poissarde [-sard] f. Fam. Fish-wife (ou) -fag. ‖ Bawd.

poisse [pwas] f. Fam. Bad (ou) tough luck; jinx. (V. guigne.) ‖ Leech. (V. crampon.)

poisser [-se] v. tr. (1). To pitch (une corde); to wax (du fil). ‖ To make sticky (les mains). ‖ Fam. To bore.
— v. intr. To be sticky. (V. coller.) ‖ Fam. To stick like a leech.

poisseux, euse [-sø, ø:z] adj. Sticky. (V. gluant.) Covered with pitch. (V. englué.)

poisson [pwasɔ̃] m. Zool. Fish; *poisson d'eau douce, de mer,* fresh-water, salt-water fish; *poisson rouge, volant,* gold, flying fish. ‖ Astron. *Les Poissons,* the Fishes, Pisces. ‖ *Poisson d'avril,* April fool joke. ‖ **Poisson-chat,** m. Zool. Catfish. ‖ **Poisson-épée,** m. Zool. Swordfish. ‖ **Poisson-lune,** m. Zool. Sunfish, moonfish. ‖ **Poisson-scie,** m. Zool. Sawfish.

poissonnerie [pwasɔnri] f. Fish-shop (magasin); fish-market (marché).

poissonneux, euse [-nø. ø:z] adj. Full of fish.

poissonnier [-nje] m. Comm. Fishmonger.

poissonnière [-njɛ:r] f. Comm. Fishwife. ‖ Culin. Fish-kettle.

poitevin, ine [pwatvɛ̃, in] adj. Géogr. Of (ou) from Poitou (ou) Poitiers.
— s. Géogr. Native (ou) inhabitant of Poitou (ou) Poitiers.

poitrail [pwatra:j] m. Zool. Breast (cheval). ‖ Archit. Breastsummer.

poitrinaire [pwatrinɛ:r] adj., s. Méd. Consumptive. [V. tuberculeux.]

poitrine [-trin] f. Bosom (de femme); breast, chest (thorax); *qui n'a pas de poitrine,* flatchested. ‖ Mus. *Chanter de poitrine,* to sing from the chest. ‖ Méd. Chest; *malade de la poitrine,* consumptive. ‖ Culin. Brisket (de bœuf); breast (de veau).

poivrade [pwavrad] f. Culin. Poivrade, peppersauce.

poivre [pwa:vr] m. Culin. Pepper; *poivre de Cayenne,* Cayenne pepper. ‖ Fig. Spice, pep. (V. sel.) ‖ Fam. *Poivre et sel,* iron-grey (cheveux); grey-haired (personne).

poivré, ée [pwavre] adj. Culin. Peppery, peppered. ‖ Fig. Pungent (odeur); spicy (propos).

poivrer v. tr. (1). Culin. To season with pepper, to pepper. ‖ Fig. To spice, to pep up.
— v. pr. **Se poivrer,** Pop. To get pissed.

poivrier [-vrije] m. Bot. Pepper-plant. ‖ Culin. Pepper-box (ou) -pot.

poivrière [-vrijɛ:r] f. Culin. Pepper-box, U. S. pepper-shaker. ‖ Milit. Turret, pepper-box (fam.).

poivron [-vrɔ̃] m. Bot. Pimento, Jamaica pepper.

poivrot [pwavro] m. Fam. Boozer. (V. ivrogne.)

poix ⌊pwa⌋ f. Pitch. ‖ Wax (à cordonnerie).

poker [pɔkɛ:r] m. Poker (cartes, jeu).

polaire [pɔlɛ:r] adj. Géogr. Polar; *étoile polaire,* pole-star, lodestar. ‖ Math., Electr. Polar.

polar [pola:r] m. Arg. Detective novel, crime story, thriller.

polard, arde [pola:r, ard] adj. One-track-minded; *il est devenu complètement polard,* he has turned into a perfect swot.

polarimètre [pɔlarimɛtr] m. Phys. Polarimeter.

polarisateur, trice [-zatœ:r, tris] adj. Polarizing.
— m. Phys. Polarizer.

polarisation [-zasjɔ̃] f. Phys. Polarization.

polariser [-ze] v. tr. (1). Phys. To polarize.

polariseur [-zœ:r] m. Phys. Polarizer.

polarité [-te] f. Phys. Polarity.

Polaroïd [pɔlarɔid] m. (nom déposé). Techn. Polaroid (feuille, appareil photographique).

polder [pɔldɛ:r] m. Géogr. Polder.

pôle [po:l] m. Géogr., Phys., Math., Electr. Pole.

polémique [pɔlemik] adj., f. Polemic.

polémiquer [-mike] v. intr. (1). To polemize.

polémiste [-mist] m. Polemist.

polémologie [-mɔlɔʒi] f. Conflict study, scientific study of war.

poli, ie [pɔli] adj. Techn. Burnished (acier); polished (bois, métal, pierre); smooth (surface). ‖ Fig. Polite, courtly, civil (manières); polite, courteous, well-bred (personne). [V. courtois.] ‖ Fig. Cultured, refined (peuple); polished, elegant (style). [V. raffiné.]
— m. Polish, gloss.

police [pɔlis] f. Police (maintien de l'ordre); *faire la police,* to keep order; *police du roulage, de la route,* traffic, road regulations. ‖ Police, police force, constabulary (agents de l'ordre); *police judiciaire, P. J.,* Criminal Investigations Department, C. I. D.; *appeler police-secours,* to dial 999; U. S. to call emergency; *remettre qqn entre les mains de la police,* to give s.o. in charge, to turn s.o. over to the police. ‖ Jur. *Fiche de police,* registration form (à l'hôtel); *tribunal de simple police,* police-court. ‖ Milit. *Bonnet de police,* forage cap; *salle de police,* guard room.

police f. Policy; *police d'assurance contre l'incendie, sur la vie,* fire-, life-insurance policy; *police tout risque,* comprehensive policy. ‖ Comm. Bill (de chargement). ‖ Electr. *Police mixte,* electricity all-in agreement. ‖ Techn. Bill of type (en typogr.).

policer [-se] v. tr. (6). To police. (V. contrôler.) ‖ To civilize, to refine (v. civiliser); *mal policé,* unlicked, unmannerly.

polichinelle [pɔliʃinɛl] m. Punch (jouet). ‖ Théâtr. Punch; Punchinello; *théâtre de Polichinelle,* Punch and Judy show. ‖ Fig. Buffoon; jumping-jack, puppet (v. pantin); *secret de polichinelle,* everybody's (ou) open secret.

policier, ère [pɔlisje, ɛ:r] adj. Police (chien); detective (roman).
— m. Policeman, detective, police-officer, U. S. sleuth (limier). ‖ Police-dog (chien).

poliment ⌊pɔlimɑ̃⌋ adv. Politely.

polio [pɔljo] f. Fam. Polio (poliomyélite).
— s. Fam. Polio sufferer (poliomyélitique).

poliomyélite [pɔljɔmjelit] f. Méd. Poliomyelitis, infantile paralysis; polio (fam.).

poliomyélitique [-tik] adj. Méd. Poliomyelitic; *virus poliomyélitique,* poliovirus.
— s. Polio sufferer.

polir [pɔli:r] v. tr. (2). To polish (du bois); to burnish (du métal). ‖ To buff (faire reluire). ‖ Fig. To polish (les mœurs); to civilize (qqn); to give the finishing touch to (un texte).
— v. pr. **Se polir,** to become polished (ou) refined.

polissage ⌊pɔlisa:ʒ⌋ m. Techn. Polishing, smoothing (du bois); burnishing (du métal). ‖ Buffing (astiquage).

polisseur [-sœ:r] s. Polisher.

polissoir [-swa:r] m. Techn. Polisher, burnisher; polishing (ou) burnishing machine. ‖ Nail-polisher.

polisson [pɔlisɔ̃] s. Young scamp, rascal (gredin);

naughty child, imp (enfant). ‖ Dissolute person (débauché).
— adj. Dirty, smutty, loose (écrit); lascivious (personne); *regard polisson*, leer.
polissonner [-sɔne] v. intr. (1). To roam about (vagabond); to roam the street (enfant). ‖ To be lewd (ou) bawdy (ou) dissolute (débauché).
polissonnerie [-sɔnri] f. Naughty trick (d'enfant). ‖ Lewd act (débauche); smutty remark (propos).
polissure [pɔlisy:r] f. Polishing.
politesse [pɔlitɛs] f. Politeness, good manners (ou) breeding. (V. CIVILITÉ, COURTOISIE.) ‖ Pl. Polite (ou) courteous acts; civilities; *faire assaut de politesse avec*, to vie in civility with. ‖ LOC. *Brûler la politesse à qqn*, to jilt s.o.
politicaillerie [politikajri] f. Politician's trick, political jobbery.
politicard, arde [-tika:r, ard] adj. Politicking.
— s. Politico.
politicien, enne [-tisjɛ̃, ɛn] adj. Merely political, politicking; *faire de la politique politicienne*, to politick.
— s. Politician, politico.
politique [-tik] adj. JUR. Political (parti). ‖ FIG. Prudent, politic, wary (circonspect); guarded (discours).
— m. Politician, statesman.
— f. Policy (manière d'agir); *habile politique*, skilful policy; *politique extérieure*, foreign policy. ‖ Politics (action, débats). ‖ FIG. Cunning, shrewdness (astuce).
politiquement [-tikmɑ̃] adv. Politically.
politisation [-tizasjɔ̃] f. Politicization.
politiser [-tize] v. tr. (1). To politicize.
polka [pɔlka] f. ARTS. Polka (danse). ‖ TECHN. Heavy hammer.
pollen [pɔlɛn] m. BOT. Pollen.
pollinisation [pɔlinizasjɔ̃] f. BOT. Pollinization.
polluant, ante [pɔllɥɑ̃, ɑ̃:t] adj. Polluting, pollutant, pollutive.
— m. Pollutant, pollutive agent.
polluer [pɔllɥe] v. tr. (1). To pollute, to defile.
pollueur, euse [-lɥœ:r, ø:z] adj. Polluting.
— s. Polluter.
pollution [-lysjɔ̃] f. Pollution.
polo [polo] m. Polo (jeu). ‖ Toque (coiffure). ‖ Polo shirt (vêtement).
polochon [pɔlɔʃɔ̃] m. FAM. Bolster.
Pologne [pɔlɔɲ] f. GÉOGR. Poland.
polonais, aise [pɔlɔnɛ, ɛ:z] adj. GÉOGR. Polish.
— s. GÉOGR. Pole. ‖ GRAMM. Polish (langue).
polonaise [nɛz] f. Polonaise (danse). ‖ CULIN. Meringue pastry, Polish cake.
poltron, onne [pɔltrɔ̃, ɔn] adj. Cowardly, fearful, craven- (ou) faint-hearted; yellow, funky (fam.). [V. CAPON, PEUREUX.]
— m. Coward, poltroon. (V. FROUSSARD.)
poltronnerie [-trɔnri] f. Cowardliness, cowardice, poltroonery.
polyacide [pɔliasid] adj., m. CHIM. Polyacid.
polyamide [-amid] m. CHIM. Polyamid.
polyandre [pɔliɑ̃:dr] adj. Polyandrous.
polyandrie [pɔliɑ̃dri] f. Polyandry.
polybutadiène [pɔlibytadjɛn] m. CHIM. Polybutadiene, butadiene rubber.
polychrome [pɔlikro:m] adj. Polychromatic.
polychromie [-krɔmi] f. Polychromy.
polyclinique [-klinik] f. Polyclinic.
polyoopie [-kɔpi] f. Duplicating, stencilling, manifolding, mimeographing.
polycopié [-kɔpje] m. Roneoed course notes (à l'université).
polycopier [-kɔpje] v. tr. (1). To duplicate, to stencil, to manifold, to mimeograph.
polyculture [-kylty:r] f. AGRIC. General (ou) mixed farming.
polyèdre [pɔliɛdr] adj. Polyhedral.
— m. MATH. Polyhedron.

polyédrique [-edrik] adj. MATH. Polyhedral, polyhedric.
polyester [pɔliɛstɛ:r] m. CHIM., TECHN. Polyester.
polyéthylène [-etilɛn] m. CHIM., TECHN. Polythene, U. S. polyethylene.
polygame [pɔligam] adj. Polygamous.
— s. Polygamist.
polygamie [-gami] f. Polygamy.
polyglotte [-glɔt] adj. Polyglot.
polygonal, ale [-gɔnal] adj. MATH. Polygonal.
polygone [-gɔ:n] adj. Polygonal.
— m. MILIT. Polygon, range; proving-grounds.
polygraphe [-graf] m. Polygraph.
polymère [-mɛ:r] adj. CHIM., TECHN. Polymeric.
— m. CHIM., TECHN. Polymer.
polymérisation [-merizasjɔ̃] f. CHIM., TECHN. Polymerization.
polymériser [-merize] v. tr. (1). CHIM., TECHN. To polymerize.
polymorphe [-mɔrf] adj. Polymorphous, polymorphic.
polymorphisme [-mɔrfism] m. Polymorphism.
Polynésie [pɔlinezi] f. GÉOGR. Polynesia.
polynésien, enne [-nezjɛ̃, ɛn] adj., s. GÉOGR. Polynesian.
— m. GRAMM. Polynesian (langue).
polynôme [-no:m] m. MATH. Polynomial, multinominal.
polynucléaire [-nyklɛɛ:r] adj. MÉD. Polymorphonuclear (leucocyte).
polype [pɔlip] m. ZOOL. Polype. ‖ MÉD. Polypus.
polyphasé, ée [-faze] adj. ELECTR. Polyphase.
polyphonie [-fɔni] f. MUS. Polyphony.
polyphonique [-fɔnik] adj. MUS. Polyphonic, polyphonous.
polypode [pɔlipɔde] m. BOT. Polypod.
polypropylène [pɔliprɔpilɛn] m. CHIM., TECHN. Polypropelene.
polysémie [-semi] f. GRAMM. Polysemy.
polysémique [-semik] adj. GRAMM. Polysemic, polysemous.
polysoc [-sɔk] adj. Multiple, gang (charrue).
polystyrène [-stirɛn] m. CHIM., TECHN. Polystyrene.
polysyllabe [-sillab] adj. Polysyllabic.
— m. Polysyllable.
polytechnicien, enne [-tɛkniʃjɛ̃, ɛn] s. Student (ou) former student at the École polytechnique.
polytechnique [-tɛknik] adj. Polytechnic; *École polytechnique*, school of higher education in engineering.
polythéisme [-teism] m. Polytheism.
polythéiste [-teist] adj. Polytheistic.
— s. Polytheist.
polyuréthanne [-yretan] m. CHIM., TECHN. Polyurethane.
polyurie [-yri] f. MÉD. Polyuria.
polyvalence [-valɑ̃:s] f. Polyvalency.
polyvalent, ente [-lɑ̃, ɑ̃:t] adj. Polyvalent.
polyvinyle [-vinil] adj. CHIM., TECHN. *Chlorure de polyvinyle*, polyvinyl chloride, PVC.
pommade [pɔmad] f. MÉD. Pomade, pomatum; *pommade Rosat*, lip-salve. ‖ FAM. Soft soap; U.S. apple-polishing; *passer de la pommade à*, to curry favour with, to soft-soap, U. S. to apple-polish.
pommader [-de] v. tr. (1). To pomade.
pomme [pɔm] f. Apple; *pomme à cidre, à couteau, sauvage*, cider, eating, crab apple. ‖ Head (de chou, de laitue); *pomme de pin*, fir-cone. ‖ Knob (de canne); *pomme d'appareil à douche*, shower-bath rose; *pomme d'arrosoir*, sprinkling-rose. ‖ MÉD. *Pomme d'Adam*, Adam's apple. ‖ CULIN. *Pomme de terre*, potato; *pommes de terre à l'anglaise*, boiled potatoes; *pommes chips*, potato crisps (ou) chips. ‖ FIG. *Pomme de discorde*, bone of contention. ‖ FAM. Phiz, mug (tête); *tomber dans les pommes*, to pass out.

pommé, ée [-me] adj. BOT. Rounded; headed (chou, laitue); *chou pommé*, white-heart cabbage; *laitue pommée*, cabbage-lettuce. ‖ FAM. Terrific. — m. Cider.

pommeau [pɔmo] m. Pommel.

pommelé, ée [pɔmle] adj. Dappled.

pommeler (se) [səpɔmle] v. pr. (8*a*). To become dappled (ciel).

pommelle [pɔmɛl] f. Filter (d'un évier).

pommer [pɔme] v. intr. (1). BOT. To form a head.

pommeraie [-mrɛ] f. AGRIC. Apple-orchard.

pommette [-mɛt] f. MÉD. Cheek-bone. ‖ BOT. Small apple.

pommier [-mje] m. Apple-tree.

pompage [pɔpa:ʒ] m. TECHN., PHYS. Pumping.

pompe [pɔ:p] f. Pomp, display, state, array (v. APPARAT); *entrepreneur de pompes funèbres*, undertaker, funeral director, U.S. mortician.

pompe f. TECHN. Pump; *pompe aspirante et foulante*, lift and force pump; *pompe à incendie*, fire-engine. ‖ AUTOM. Tyre (ou) U. S. tire pump; *pompe à essence*, petrol pump, U. S. gas pump, gasoline pump (distributeur). ‖ NAUT. Pump. ‖ FAM. *Château-la-pompe*, Adam's ale. ‖ SPORTS., POP. Press-ups, U. S. push-ups. ‖ Pl. POP. Shoes; *marcher à côté de ses pompes*, to be out of it.

pompé, ée [pɔpe] adj. FAM. Washed (ou) pumped out (lessivé); done in (vanné).

pompéien, enne [pɔpejɛ̃, ɛn] adj., s. Pompeian.

pomper v. tr. (1). TECHN. To pump. ‖ FIG. To suck up (l'humidité). ‖ FAM. To pump (qqn).

pompette [pɔpɛt] adj. FAM. Squiffy, tipsy.

pompeusement [pɔpøzmɑ̃] adv. Pompously.

pompeux, euse [-pø, ø:z] adj. Pompous, stately (majestueux). ‖ Pompous. (V. FASTUEUX.) ‖ Stilted, high-sounding (ou) -flown, turgid (ampoulé).

pompier [pɔpje] m. Fireman. ‖ FAM. Pompous person.
— adj. FAM. High-falutin', pretentious, turgid, bombastic (style).

pompiste [pɔpist] m. AUTOM. Pump assistant, filling-station mechanic.

pompon [pɔpɔ̃] m. Tassel. (V. GLAND.) ‖ MILIT. Pompon. ‖ FAM. *A lui le pompon!*, he's taking the lead!; *avoir son pompon*, to be half seas over, U. S. to be high.

pomponner [-pɔne] v. tr. (1). To trick out, to deck out (qqn). ‖ FIG. To dress up.
— v. pr. **Se pomponner**, to smarten oneself up, to titivate.

ponant [pɔnɑ̃] m. † West, Occident. ‖ West wind.

ponçage [pɔsa:ʒ] m. Sandpapering, pumicing.

ponce [pɔ:s] f. Pumice-stone (pierre). ‖ Thick black ink, U. S. India ink (encre).

ponceau [pɔso] adj. invar. Poppy-coloured, flaming-red.

ponceau m. CH. DE F. Culvert.

poncer [pɔse] v. tr. (6). To pumice, to sandpaper. (V. POLIR.) ‖ To stone, to scour (du cuir). ‖ ARTS. To pounce (un dessin).

ponceuse [-sø:z] f. TECHN. Sander.

ponceux, euse [-sø, ø:z] adj. Pumiceous.

poncho [pɔʃo, pɔ̃ntʃo] m. Poncho (manteau).

poncif [pɔsif] m. Commonplace, cliché. ‖ ARTS. Pounced drawing.

ponction [pɔksjɔ̃] f. MÉD. Puncture. ‖ FIN. Levy.

ponctionner [-sjɔne] v. tr. (1). MÉD. To puncture. ‖ FIN. To levy.

ponctualité [pɔ̃ktɥalite] f. Punctuality.

ponctuation [-tɥasjɔ̃] f. Punctuation.

ponctué, ée [-tɥe] adj. Dotted (ligne); punctuated (texte). ‖ BOT. Punctulate, punctate.

ponctuel, elle [-tɥɛl] adj. Punctual (action). ‖ Punctual, prompt (personne).

ponctuellement [-tɥɛlmɑ̃] adv. Punctually.

ponctuer [-tɥe] v. tr. (1). To punctuate (un texte). ‖ MUS. To stop. ‖ FIG. To emphasize, to accentuate.

pondérateur, trice [pɔ̃deratœ:r, tris] adj. Moderating, stabilizing, counterbalancing.

pondération [-rasjɔ̃] f. Moderation, levelheadedness (du caractère, des jugements); counterbalancing (des forces, des pouvoirs). ‖ MATH. Weight, weighting (en statistique).

pondéré, ée [-re] adj. Level-headed (personne); well-balanced (esprit). ‖ MATH. Weighted (indice).

pondérer [-re] v. tr. (5). To balance, to counterbalance (forces, influences, pouvoirs). ‖ MATH. To weight (en statistique).

pondéreux, euse [-rø, ø:z] adj. COMM. Heavy. — m. pl. COMM. Heavy goods.

pondeuse [pɔ̃dœ:z] adj. Egg-laying (poule).
— f. Layer; *une bonne pondeuse*, a good layer.

pondre [pɔ̃:dr] v. tr. (4). To lay (un œuf). ‖ FAM. To produce, to turn out (un écrit).
— v. intr. To lay (poule).

poney [pɔnɛ] m. ZOOL. Poney.

pongé [pɔ̃ʒe] m. Pongee (tissu).

pongiste [pɔ̃ʒist] s. SPORTS. Ping-pong (ou) table tennis player.

pont [pɔ̃] m. Bridge; *pont à bascule, à consoles*, weigh, cantilever bridge; *pont de bateaux*, pontoon bridge; *pont pour piétons*, footbridge. ‖ *Ponts et chaussées*, Civil Department of Bridges and Highways (en France); *jeter un pont sur*, to bridge. ‖ Flap (de pantalon). ‖ NAUT. Deck; *pont abri*, awning deck; *pont d'envol, de manœuvre, de promenade*, flight, hurricane, promenade deck; *navire à deux, trois ponts*, two-, three-decker. ‖ CH. DE F. Pont roulant, traverser (ou) travelling crane. ‖ AVIAT. *Pont aérien*, airlift. ‖ AUTOM. *Pont arrière*, rear (ou) back axle. ‖ COMM. *Sur pont*, free on board. ‖ FIG. Bridge; *faire un pont d'or à qqn*, to pour money into s.o.'s hands. ‖ FAM. *Faire le pont*, to take off the days between two holidays. ‖ **Pont-l'évêque**, invar. CULIN. Pont-l'Evêque cheese. ‖ **Pontlevis**, m. Drawbridge. ‖ **Pont-Neuf**, m. New Bridge; FAM. *se porter comme le Pont-Neuf*, to be hale and hearty.

Pont m. GÉOGR. Pontus; *le Pont-Euxin*, the Euxine (ou) Black Sea.

ponte [pɔ̃:t] f. Laying (action); egg-laying season (époque).

ponte m. FAM. Magnifico, pontiff; U. S. kingpin. ‖ Punter, punt (joueur au baccara, à la roulette).

ponté, ée [-pɔte] adj. NAUT. Decked; *non ponté*, open (bateau). ‖ AUTOM. Launched.

pontée f. NAUT. Deck load.

ponter v. tr. (1) NAUT. To deck, to lay a deck on (un bateau). ‖ MILIT. To build pontoon-bridge over (une rivière).

ponter v. intr. (1). To punt (à la roulette, au baccara).

pontife [pɔ̃tif] m. Pontiff. ‖ ECCLÉS. *Le souverain pontife*, the Pope, the Sovereign Pontiff. ‖ FAM. Pontiff; *les grands pontifes*, the bigwigs.

pontifiant, ante [-fjɑ̃, ɑ̃:t] adj. Pontificating.

pontifical, ale [-fikal] adj. ECCLÉS. Pontifical.

pontificat [-fika] m. ECCLÉS. Pontificate.

pontifier [-fje] v. intr. (1). ECCLÉS. To officiate as a pontiff. ‖ FAM. To pontificate.

ponton [pɔ̃tɔ̃] m. NAUT. Pontoon (bac) [d'un pont de bateau]. ‖ Hulk, prison-ship (bateau-prison); floating platform (plate-forme). ‖ **Ponton-grue**, m. Floating-crane.

pontonnier [-tɔnje] m. MILIT. Pontonier.

pool [pu:l] m. COMM., FIN. Pool.

pop [pɔp] adj. inv. Pop (musique, groupe, art).
— m. ou f. MUS. Pop music.

pop art [pɔpart] m. ARTS. Pop art.

pope [pɔ:p] m. Pope.

popeline [pɔplin] f. Poplin.

popote [pɔpɔt] f. FAM. MILIT. Mess. ‖ FAM. CULIN. Canteen (cantine); cooking (cuisine).
— adj. FAM. Stay-at-home (personne).

populace [pɔpylas] f. Rabble, riff-raff, populace.
populacier, ère [-sje, ɛr] adj. FAM. Vulgar, low, coarse (goût, langage).
populaire [pɔpylɛ:r] adj. Folk (étymologie); popular, familiar (expressions); vulgar, common (goûts); popular (personne) [*auprès de*, with]; *mouvement populaire*, mass uprising.
— m. Populace, common herd.
populairement [-lɛrmɑ̃] adv. Popularly.
popularisation [-larizasjɔ̃] f. Popularization.
populariser [-larize] v. tr. (1). To popularize.
popularité [-larite] f. Popularity.
population [-lasjɔ̃] f. Population.
populeux, euse [-lø, ø:z] adj. Populous.
populisme [-lism] m. Populism.
populiste [-list] adj., s. Populist.
populo [-lo] m. FAM. Riff-raff, rabble.
porc [pɔ:r] m. ZOOL. Pig, hog, porker (v. COCHON); *troupeau de porcs*, herd of swine. ‖ CULIN. Pork; *côte de porc*, spare-rib. ‖ FAM. Dirty pig. ‖ **Porc-épic**, m. ZOOL. Porcupine, hedgehog.
porcelaine [pɔrsəlɛn] f. Porcelain; china; *porcelaine de Limoges*, Limoges ware. ‖ Chinaware (vaisselle).
porcelainier [-lɛnje] adj. Pertaining to porcelain.
— m. Porcelain-maker (ou) ¬manufacturer.
porcelet [pɔrsəle] m. ZOOL. Piglet, suckling-pig.
porche [pɔrʃ] m. Porch, portal.
porcher [-ʃe] m. Swineherd, swine-keeper.
porcherie [-ʃri] f. Piggery, pigsty, U. S. pigpen. ‖ FIG. Pig-sty.
porcin, ine [-sɛ̃, in] adj. Porcine. ‖ AGRIC., ZOOL. Pig.
— m. AGRIC., ZOOL. Swine, pig.
pore [pɔ:r] m. MÉD. Pore.
poreux, euse [pɔrø, ø:z] adj. Porous.
porion [pɔrjɔ̃] m. TECHN. Foreman.
porno [pɔrno] adj. FAM. Porno (pornographique); *film porno*, porno film, skinflick, blue movie.
— m. FAM. Porn, porno (pornographie).
pornographe [pɔrnograf] m. Pornographer, salacious writer.
pornographie [-grafi] f. Pornography.
pornographique [-grafik] adj. Pornographic; bawdy.
porosité [porozite] f. Porosity, porousness.
porphyre [pɔrfi:r] m. Porphyry.
porphyrique [-rik] adj. GÉOL. Porphyritic; *cuivre porphyrique*, porphyry copper.
porque [pɔ:rk] f. NAUT. Rider; web-frame.
port [pɔ:r] m. NAUT. Harbour (bassin); *de port*, harbour (capitaine, droits). ‖ GÉOGR. Port (ville); *port d'attache*, port of registry; *port de mer, de rivière*, sea-port, river-port. ‖ FIG. Home, land; *arriver à bon port*, to arrive safely; *échouer en vue du port*, to fail in sight of land; *mener à bon port*, to bring to a happy issue.
port m. Carrying (transport) [d'un objet]. ‖ Wearing (d'un numéro, d'un vêtement). ‖ NAUT. Burden (charge); *port réel*, load. ‖ MUS. *Port de voix*, portamento. ‖ FIN. Carriage (frais); *port dû*, *payé*, carriage forward, paid; postage due, paid; *port de lettres*, postage, postal charge. ‖ FIG. Carriage, bearing; *port de reine*, queenly bearing; *port de tête*, carriage of the head.
port m. GÉOGR. Pass, col.
portable [pɔrtabl] adj. Portable (faix, objet). ‖ Wearable (habit).
portage [-ta:ʒ] m. Portage, carrying (action). ‖ NAUT. Nip (d'un câble); portage (d'un canot). ‖ ELECTR. Bearing (des balais).
portail [-ta:j] m. Portal; doorway.
portance [-tɑ̃:s] f. AVIAT. Lifting capacity.
portant, ante [-tɑ̃, ɑ̃:t] adj. TECHN. Bearing, carrying (roue). ‖ AVIAT. Lifting (surface). ‖ NAUT. Fair, leading (vent). ‖ MÉD. *Bien, mal portant*, in good, bad health.

— m. Handle (de valise). ‖ ARCHIT. Stay. ‖ MILIT. Lengthening strap (de ceinturon). ‖ ELECTR. Armature (d'aimant). ‖ THÉÂTR. Upright, framework (de décor).
portatif, ive [-tatif, i:v] adj. Portable (objet); *dictionnaire portatif*, pocket dictionary. ‖ RADIO. *Poste portatif*, portable radio.
porte [pɔrt] f. Door; *porte de service*, tradesmen's entrance; *fausse porte*, blind door. ‖ Doorway (entrée); *passer par la porte*, to pass through the doorway. ‖ ARCHIT. Gate (de ville); arch (en arc); *Porte Saint-Martin*, St. Martin's Gate. ‖ TECHN. Door (de coffre-fort, de haut fourneau, de meuble). ‖ NAUT. Gate; *porte d'écluse*, lock gate. ‖ ECCLÉS. Gate (de l'enfer); *la porte étroite*, the narrow (ou) strait gate. ‖ GÉOGR. *La Sublime Porte*, the Sublime Porte. ‖ LOC. *Habiter porte à porte*, to be next-door neighbours. ‖ FIG. Outside (dehors); *à la porte!*, throw him out!; *mettre à la porte*, to turn out, to sack, to fire. ‖ FIG. Door (de la fortune); *la porte est ouverte à tous les abus*, the door is open to all abuses; *c'est la porte ouverte aux récriminations*, it affords a loop-hole for recriminations; *frapper à la bonne porte*, to apply to the right man; *parler à qqn entre deux portes*, to speak to s.o. for a brief instant. ‖ **Porte-à-porte**, m. COMM. Door-to-door transport; house-to-house canvassing. ‖ **Porte-fenêtre**, f. French window.
porte. V. PORTER. ‖ **Porte-adresse** (ou) **étiquette**, m. invar. Luggage-label (ou) U. S. baggage-tag hodler. ‖ **Porte-à-faux**, m. Overhang; *en porte à faux*, overhanging. ‖ **Porte-aiguille**, m. invar. Needle-case. ‖ **Porte-assiette**, m. invar. Tablemat. ‖ **Porte-avions**, m. invar. NAUT. Aircraft-carrier. ‖ **Porte-bagages**, m. invar. CH. DE F. Luggage rack; AUTOM. luggage-carrier, U. S. trunk-rack. ‖ **Porte-bébé**, m. invar. Baby-carrier. ‖ **Porte-billets**, m. invar. Note-case, U. S. billfold. ‖ **Porte-bombes**, m. invar. MILIT. Bomb-rack. ‖ **Porte-bonheur**, m. invar. Amulet, mascot, lucky charm. ‖ **Porte-bougie**, m. Candlestick. ‖ **Porte-bouquet**, m. Flower-vase. ‖ **Porte-bouteilles**, m. invar. Bottle-stand (ou) rack. ‖ **Porte-brancard**, m. invar. Lug. ‖ **Porte-bras**, m. invar. Arm-rest. ‖ **Porte-cartes**, m. invar. Card case. ‖ **Porte-chapeaux**, m. Hat-peg, hat-stand. ‖ **Porte-charbon**, m. ELECTR. Carbon-holder. ‖ **Porte-chars**, m. MILIT. Tank-transporter. ‖ **Porte-cigare**, m. Cigar holder. ‖ **Porte-cigarette**, m. invar. Cigarette-holder. ‖ **Porte-cigarettes**, m. invar. Cigarette-case (étui). ‖ **Porte-clefs**, m. invar. Key-ring (anneau); turnkey (geolier); key-board (tableau). ‖ **Porte-conteneurs**, m. invar. NAUT. Containership. ‖ **Porte-couteau**, m. Knife-rest. ‖ **Porte-crayon**, m. invar. Pencil-case. ‖ **Porte-croix**, m. invar. ECCLÉS. Cross-bearer. ‖ **Porte-documents**, m. Brief-case. ‖ **Porte-drapeau**, m. invar. MILIT. Standard (ou) banner (ou) colour bearer. ‖ **Porte-épée**, m. invar. Frog. ‖ **Porte-éperon**, m. invar. Stirrup-strap. ‖ **Porte-éponges**, m. invar. Sponge basket. ‖ **Porte-étendard**, m. invar. MILIT. Standard-bearer. ‖ **Porte-fanion**, n. invar. MILIT. Pennon-bearer. ‖ **Porte-fouet**, m. invar. Whip-socket. ‖ **Porte-greffe(s)**, m. BOT. Stock. ‖ **Porte-hauban**, m. invar. NAUT. Chanewale, channels. ‖ **Porte-hélicoptères**, m. invar. Helicopter carrier. ‖ **Porte-jarretelles**, m. invar. Suspender belt. ‖ **Porte-lanterne**, m. invar. AUTOM. Lamp-bracket. ‖ **Porte-lettres**, m. invar. Letter-case. ‖ **Porte-malheur**, m. invar. Bringer of ill-luck. ‖ **Porte-mine**, m. invar. Propelling pencil. ‖ **Porte-monnaie**, m. invar. Purse. ‖ **Porte-montre**, m. invar. Watch-stand (ou) -pocket. ‖ **Porte-musique**, m. invar. MUS. Music-case. ‖ **Porte-outil**, m. invar. TECHN. Tool-holder. ‖ **Porte-parapluies**, m. invar. Umbrella-stand. ‖ **Porte-parole**, m. invar. Spokesman, mouthpiece.

‖ **Porte-pincettes**, m. invar. Fire-iron stand. ‖ **Porte-pipes**, m. invar. Pipe-rack. ‖ **Porte-plat**, m. invar. CULIN. Table-mat, dish-stand. ‖ **Porte-plume**, m. invar. Pen-holder. ‖ **Porte-respect**, m. invar. Defensive weapon (arme) ; chaperon (personne). ‖ **Porte-savon**, m. invar. Soap-dish. ‖ **Porte-serviettes**, m. invar. Towel-rail, U. S. towel-rack. ‖ **Porte-voix**, m. invar. Megaphone ; speaking tube (ou) -trumpet ; *les mains en porte-voix*, with one's hands cupped around one's mouth.

porté, ée [-te] adj. Carried (transporté). ‖ MILIT. Portée (artillerie) ; mechanized (unité). ‖ MATH. Projected (ombre). ‖ FIG. Inclined, prone (*à*, to) ; *porté à la colère*, apt to get angry, irascible. ‖ FAM. *Bien porté*, fashionable.
— m. Wear (d'un vêtement).

portée [-te] f. ZOOL. Gestation (acte) ; brood, litter (animaux). ‖ ARCHIT. Span (d'une arche, d'une voûte) ; projection (d'un encorbellement) ; bearing (d'une poutre). ‖ MILIT. Range (de canon, de fusil). ‖ NAUT. Burden. ‖ MUS. Stave, staff (pour les notes) ; compass (de la voix). ‖ FIG. Import (des paroles) ; scope (d'un traité) ; *à portée*, within reach ; *hors de portée*, beyond (ou) out of s.o.'s reach, out of range ; *à portée de la main*, within reach ; *de grande portée*, of vital importance, of far-reaching consequence ; *mettre à la portée de qqn*, to bring within s.o.'s comprehension ; *rester à la portée de son auditoire*, not to speak over the heads of one's audience ; *se mettre à la portée de*, to adapt oneself to ; *vues à longue portée*, far-reaching views, far-sighted policy.

portefaix [pɔrtəfɛ] m. Porter.

portefeuille [-fœːj] m. Wallet, note-case ; U. S. billfold (pour argent) ; letter-case (pour lettres). ‖ Portfolio (de ministre) ; *le portefeuille de la Guerre*, the War Office. ‖ Connection (d'agent d'assurances). ‖ FIN. Investments, holdings ; *titres en portefeuille*, securities ; *vérifier son portefeuille*, to check one's stocks and shares (ou) U. S. bonds. ‖ FAM. *Lit en portefeuille*, apple-pie bed.

portemanteau [-mɑ̃to] m. Coat-stand, U. S. clothes-tree, clothes-stand. ‖ NAUT. Davits.

portement [-mɑ̃] m. ECCLÉS. Bearing (de croix).

porter [pɔrte] v. tr. (1).

---

1. Transporter. — 2. Supporter. — 3. Tenir.
— 4. Présenter. — 5. Lever. — 6. Revêtir. —
7. FIN. — 8. AGRIC. — 9. COMM. — 10. MILIT.
— 11. FIG. Supporter. — 12. Répandre. —
13. Montrer. — 14. Elever. — 15. Incliner. —
16. Enoncer. — 17. Nourrir. — 18. Nommer.
19. Renfermer.

---

1. To bear, to carry (transporter) ; *porter un fardeau*, to bear a burden ; *porter qqn à l'hôpital*, to remove s.o. to the hospital. ‖ 2. To support, to hold up, to sustain (supporter) ; *porter tout le poids*, to carry the whole weight (ou) to support the whole weight. ‖ 3. To carry (tenir) ; *porter haut la tête*, to carry one's head high. ‖ 4. To carry, to bear, to have (présenter) ; *porter les marques de l'incendie*, to carry (ou) bear the marks of the fire. ‖ 5. To carry, to raise (lever) ; *porter la main à son front*, to put one's hand to one's forehead ; *porter la main sur qqn*, to raise one's hand against s.o., to lay hands on s.o. ‖ 6. To wear (revêtir) ; *bien porter la toilette*, to wear one's clothes well ; *porter les cheveux ras*, to wear one's hair close-cropped ; *porter de la laine été comme hiver*, to wear woollen garments in summer as well as in winter. ‖ 7. FIN. To enter, to put down (*à*, *sur*, on) [une dépense] ; to bring in, to produce (un intérêt). ‖ 8. AGRIC. To bear (des fruits) ; to yield (des moissons). ‖ 9. COMM. To deliver (livrer) ; *porter les marchandises à domicile*, to deliver goods at customers' homes. ‖ 10. MILIT. To register ; *porté manquant*, reported missing ; *se faire porter absent*, to have oneself reported absent. ‖ 11. FIG. To bear (supporter) ; *porter des responsabilités*, to bear responsibilities ; *porter le vin allègrement*, to carry one's wine well. ‖ 12. FIG. To carry, to convey, to spread (répandre) ; *porter la nouvelle*, to carry the news ; *porter partout la terreur*, to spread terror everywhere ; *porter qqch. à la connaissance de qqn*, to bring sth. to s.o.'s knowledge. ‖ 13. FIG. To show (montrer) ; *porter son âge*, to look one's age ; *il porte la bonté sur son visage*, his face beams with (ou) conveys kindness. ‖ FIG. To carry, to turn (tourner) ; *porter ses regards sur*, to cast eyes on ; *partout où je porte mes pas*, wherever I go. ‖ 14. FIG. To bring, to raise (élever) ; *porter son ambition trop haut*, to aim too high ; *porter une fortune à plusieurs millions*, to bring a fortune to several millions. ‖ 15. FIG. To incline, to induce (incliner) ; *porter au mal*, to corrupt ; *cela me porte à croire que*, that leads me to believe that. ‖ 16. FIG. To state (énoncer) ; *le document porte que*, the document states that. ‖ 17. FIG. To feel (nourrir) ; *porter qqn dans son cœur*, to have a partiality for s.o. ; *porter amitié à*, to have kind feelings for, to be friendly towards. ‖ 18. FIG. To propose, to put forward (nommer) ; *être porté au décanat*, to be nominated for the deanship. ‖ 19. FIG. To carry (renfermer) ; *crime qui porte en soi son châtiment*, a crime carrying its own punishment.
— v. intr. To bear, to rest (reposer) ; *porter sur l'arrière*, to rest on the rear. ‖ To go to (monter) ; *porter à la tête*, to go to the head. ‖ MUS. To carry ; *voix qui porte bien*, voice that carries a long way. ‖ MILIT. To hit the target, to aim true (coup) ; to have a range (fusil) ; *porter à deux cents mètres* (fusil), to have a range of two hundred metres ; *porter sur la ville*, to hit the town (bombardement). ‖ NAUT. *Laisser porter*, to bear away. ‖ MÉD. To be pregnant, to be with child (femme) ; to carry its young (femelle). ‖ CINÉM. *Porter à l'écran*, to screen, to film, U. S. to make a movie of. ‖ FIG. To be effective ; *qui porte*, telling (argument). ‖ FIG. To bear (*sur*, upon) [critique] ; to be aimed (*sur*, at) [effort] ; *faire porter sa décision sur*, to bring one's decision to bear on. ‖ LOC. *Porter beau*, to have a noble bearing.
— v. pr. **Se porter**, to repair, to proceed (se diriger) ; *se porter vers le lieu d'où partent les cris*, to rush to the place from which the cries come. ‖ To indulge (se laisser aller) ; *se porter à des violences contre*, to commit physical violence against. ‖ To come forward, to stand (se présenter) ; *se porter candidat*, to stand (ou) run as candidate, *se porter fort pour* (ou) *garant de*, to answer for, to sponsor. ‖ To be worn (vêtement) ; *la fourrure se porte beaucoup*, furs are fashionable. ‖ MÉD. To be (aller) ; *comment vous portez-vous ?*, how are you ? *Je ne m'en suis pas plus mal porté*, I was none the worse for it ; *se porter comme un charme*, to be hale and hearty.

porteur, euse [-tœːr, øːz] s. Bearer, carrier, porter ; *porteur d'eau*, water-carrier. ‖ MÉD. *Porteur de germes*, germ-carrier. ‖ FIN. *Porteur d'actions, d'obligations*, stockholder, bondholder ; *porteur*, payable to bearer (chèque).
— adj. Bearing (essieu) ; carrying (roue). ‖ RADIO. Carrier (onde). ‖ TECHN. Carrier (fusée).

portier, ère [pɔrtje, ɛːr] s. Door-keeper.

portière [-tjɛːr] f. Door-curtain (rideau). ‖ CH. DE F. Door. ‖ NAUT. Raft.

portillon [-tijɔ̃] m. Wicket, side-gate, small gate. ‖ CH. DE F. Barrier.

portion [pɔrsjɔ̃] f. Part, share, portion (partie). ‖ CULIN. Helping. ‖ FAM. *Portion congrue,* bare subsistance.

portionner [-sjɔne] v. tr. (1). To divide, to portion out. (V. PARTAGER.)

portique [pɔrtik] m. ARCHIT. Porch, portico. ‖ SPORTS. Cross-beam. ‖ CH. DE F. Awning.

portland [pɔrtlɑ̃:d] m. TECHN. Portland cement.

porto [pɔrto] m. Port-wine, port (vin). ‖ GÉOGR. Porto.

portoricain, aine [pɔrtɔrikɛ̃, ɛn] adj., s. GÉOGR. Puerto-Rican.

Porto Rico [-ko] f. (ou) m. GÉOGR. Puerto Rico.

portrait [pɔrtrɛ] m. Portrait, likeness, picture; *être le portrait de,* to be the very image of. ‖ ARTS. Portrait, face; *portrait en pied,* full portrait. ‖ Pl. Character-sketches; profiles (en littérature). ‖ **Portrait-robot,** m. Identikit, identikit picture.

portraitiste [-tist] s. ARTS. Portrait-painter.

portraiturer [-tyre] v. tr. (1). FAM. To draw (ou) paint the portrait of; *se faire portraiturer,* to have one's portrait painted.

portuaire [pɔrtɥɛ:r] adj. NAUT. *Installation portuaire,* harbour works.

portugais, aise [pɔrtygɛ, ɛ:z] adj., s. GÉOGR. Portuguese.
— m. GRAMM. Portuguese (langue).

portugaise [-gɛ:z] f. ZOOL. Portuguese oyster.

Portugal [-gal] m. GÉOGR. Portugal.

posage [poza:ʒ] m. Placing, laying.

pose [po:z] f. TECHN. Placing, laying (d'un tuyau); putting in (d'une vitre). ‖ Time-exposure (en photo). ‖ MUS. Training (de la voix). ‖ FIG. Posture, attitude, pose; *le faire à la pose,* to attitudinize; to put it on, U. S. to put on the dog.

posé, ée [poze] adj. Composed, staid, solemn (attitude); careful (écriture); sober, steady, sedate (personne). ‖ MUS. Trained (voix).
— m. SPORTS. *Tirer un faisan au posé,* to shoot a sitting pheasant.

posément [-zemɑ̃] adv. Soberly, quietly, sedately, staidly, calmly, deliberately, composedly (agir); carefully, clearly, slowly (parler).

posemètre [pozmɛtr] m. TECHN. Light meter, exposure meter.

poser [-ze] v. tr. (1). To lay, to put, to place, to set (mettre). ‖ To take off (son chapeau, son manteau). ‖ To hang (un rideau); to lay down, to unroll (un tapis). ‖ TECHN. To put in (une vitre). ‖ ELECTR. To put in (l'électricité). ‖ ARCHIT. To lay (des fondations). ‖ CH. DE F. To lay (des rails). ‖ AVIAT. To land (un avion). ‖ MUS. To train (la voix). ‖ JUR. *Poser une candidature à,* to stand (ou) to run for; *poser la question de confiance,* to lay down a motion of confidence. ‖ FIG. To lay down (un principe); to ask, to put (une question). ‖ FAM. To give credit (ou) standing to (qqn).
— v. intr. To rest, to lie (reposer). ‖ ARTS. To pose (modèle); *poser pour son portrait,* to sit for one's portrait. ‖ FIG. To attitudinize, to pose, to swank; *poser pour,* to pass oneself off for. ‖ FAM. To cool one's heels; *faire poser qqn,* to keep s.o. waiting.
— v. pr. **Se poser,** to come up, to rise (s'élever). ‖ To rise socially, to achieve a certain standing (s'établir favorablement). ‖ *Se poser comme,* to pass oneself off as (se faire passer pour); to set up to be (se présenter comme). ‖ ZOOL. To alight, to perch (oiseau). ‖ AVIAT. To land (avion).

poseur [-zœ:r] m. TECHN. Layer (de tuyaux); *poseur d'affiches,* bill-sticker. ‖ NAUT. *Poseur de mines,* mine-layer. ‖ CH. DE F. *Poseur de rails,* plate-layer. ‖ FAM. Attitudinizer, poseur; U. S. fake (personne).
— adj. Affected. (V. MANIÉRÉ.) ‖ Supercilious. (V. HAUTAIN.)

positif, ive [pozitif, i:v] adj. Real, actual, positive (en général); undeniable (fait); unmistakable (preuve); definite (renseignement). ‖ Matter-of-fact (esprit). ‖ Positive (épreuve photographique). ‖ PHILOS., MATH., ELECTR. Positive.
— m. Solid reality; actual advantage; *s'en tenir au positif,* to have an eye to the main chance. ‖ Positive print (en photo). ‖ GRAMM. Positive; *au positif,* in the positive. ‖ FIN. Cash.

position [-sjɔ̃] f. Position, place. ‖ Position, attitude, posture. ‖ Position, job (emploi). ‖ Position, argument, point of view (point de vue); *s'en tenir à sa position initiale,* to maintain one's stand; *prendre position,* to take one's stand. ‖ Position, advantage; *position dominante,* ruling position. ‖ Position, situation; *être en position de,* to be in a position to. ‖ SPORTS. Lie (d'une balle de golf). ‖ AVIAT. Altitude (d'un avion); *feux de position,* navigation lights. ‖ NAUT. *Feux de position,* riding lights. ‖ AUTOM. *Feux de position,* parking lights (à l'arrêt); riding lights (en marche). ‖ **Position-clé,** f. Key-position.

positionner [-sjɔne] v. tr. (1). MILIT., NAUT. To locate, to get the bearings of. ‖ TECHN. To position (une pièce à usiner).

positivement [-tivmɑ̃] adv. Positively.

positivisme [-tivism] m. Matter-of-factness. ‖ PHILOS. Positivism.

positiviste [-tivist] s. PHILOS. Positivist.
— adj. Positivistic.

positivité [-tivite] f. Positivity.

posologie [pozɔlɔʒi] f. MÉD. Dosage.

possédant, ante [pɔsedɑ̃, ɑ̃:t] adj. Possessing.
— s. *Les possédants,* propertied classes.

possédé, ée [-de] adj. Possessed. ‖ ECCLÉS. Possessed by the devil. ‖ FIG. Possessed (par, with) [une idée].
— s. ECCLÉS. Person possessed. ‖ FAM. *Crier comme un possédé,* to shout like the very devil.

posséder [-de] v. tr. (5). To possess, to own, to be possessed (ou) owner of (une fortune). ‖ To have (avoir); *posséder qqch. peu de temps,* to have sth. for a short time. ‖ To engross (l'esprit); to haunt (qqn) [idée]. ‖ To possess (qqn) [mauvaise influence]. ‖ To be master of (une langue); to know perfectly (un sujet). ‖ ECCLÉS. To possess (qqn) [démon]. ‖ FAM. To take in, to impose on (qqn) [duper]; *il s'est fait posséder,* he has been taken in.
— v. pr. **Se posséder,** to master one's feelings, to have oneself under control (se maîtriser); *ne plus se posséder,* to be beside oneself.

possesseur [pɔsɛsœ:r] m. Possessor, owner; *devenir possesseur de,* to come by, to come into possession of.

possessif, ive [-sif, i:v] adj. GRAMM. Possessive. ‖ FIG. Grasping (avare); possessive (exclusif).

possession [-sjɔ̃] f. Possession, ownership; *entrer en possession de,* to enter into possession of (une propriété); *être mis en possession de,* to be furnished with; *être en possession d'une lettre,* to be in receipt of a letter; *prise de possession,* taking over. ‖ Having; *entrer en possession d'une fonction,* to take over a post. ‖ Pl. Possessions (d'un Etat). ‖ Command (d'une langue); perfect knowledge (d'un sujet). ‖ Engrossment (par, with) [de l'esprit]. ‖ ECCLÉS. Possession (par, by).

possibilité [pɔsibilite] f. Possibility (d'un fait); feasibility (d'un projet); *en voyez-vous la possibilité ?,* do you see any way of doing it ? ‖ Facilities; *possibilité de cuisiner,* cooking facilities.

possible [pɔsi:bl] adj. Possible (v. FAISABLE, RÉALISABLE); *aussitôt que possible,* as soon as possible; *est-il possible de ?,* is it possible to ?; *il est possible qu'il vienne,* he may come, it's possible that he will come; *le meilleur marché possible,* the cheapest possible; *le mieux possible,* the best possible; *si possible*, if possible; *tous les moyens possibles*, every possible means. ‖ Fam. Acceptable (mari); *possible!*, may be! it's quite possible!; *pas possible!*, you don't say so!, well I never! — m. Possible; *déroutant au possible*, as puzzling as can be; *dans la mesure du possible, dans toute la mesure possible*, as far as possible; *faire tout son possible*, to do one's best (ou) all one can.

possiblement [pɔsibləmɑ̃] adv. Possibly, may be.

postal, ale [pɔstal] adj. Postal; *carte postale*, postcard; *sac postal*, mail-bag; *code postal*, postcode, U. S. zip code.

postcure [pɔstky:r] f. After-care.

postdater [pɔstdate] v. tr. (1). To postdate.

poste [pɔst] f. † Post; *courir la poste*, to go posthaste; *maître de poste*, post-master. ‖ Post; *envoyer par la poste*, to send by post (ou) U. S. mail; *mettre à la poste*, to post, U. S. to mail. ‖ Post-office (bâtiment); branch post-office (bureau); *grande poste*, head (ou) U. S. main post-office.

poste m. Post (employé); *poste administratif*, administrative post, U. S. executive position; *rejoindre son poste*, to take up one's duties. (V. FONCTION.) ‖ Station (de police); *conduire qqn au poste*, to take s.o. to the police-station; *poste d'incendie*, fire-post, station. ‖ Set (de téléphone); *poste principal*, main set; *poste 22*, extension 22 (au téléphone). ‖ RADIO. Wireless set; *poste portatif*, portable radio. ‖ MÉD. *Poste de la Croix-rouge*, Red Cross station; *poste de secours*, first-aid post. ‖ CH. DE F. *Poste d'aiguillage*, signal post. ‖ AVIAT. *Poste de contrôle*, control-tower. ‖ NAUT. Station; *poste des malades*, sick-bay; *mettre au poste de combat*, to order to action stations, to station. ‖ FIN. Item (en comptabilité).

posté, ée [pɔste] adj. *Travail posté*, shift work.

poster [pɔste] v. tr. To post, U. S. to mail (une lettre). ‖ SPORTS. To set (un chasseur). ‖ MILIT. To post (une sentinelle).
— v. pr. **Se poster**, to take up one's position, to take post.

poster [pɔstɛr] m. Poster.

postérieur, eure [pɔsterjœ:r] adj. Later, posterior, subsequent. (V. ULTÉRIEUR.) ‖ Hinder, back (de derrière); *face postérieure*, rear side.
— m. FAM. Posterior, behind.

postérieurement [-rjœrmɑ̃] adv. Later, subsequently.

postériorité [-rjɔrite] f. Posteriority.

postérité [pɔsterite] f. Posterity; *la postérité*, later generations. ‖ Issue (descendance); *mourir sans postérité*, to die without issue.

postface [pɔstfas] f. Postface, afterword.

postglaciaire [-glasjɛ:r] adj. GÉOL. Post-glacial.

posthume [pɔstym] adj. Posthumous.

postiche [pɔstiʃ] adj. False (barbe, cheveux).
— m. Postiche; wig. ‖ Hair-pad, U. S. rat.

postier, ère [pɔstje, ɛ:r] s. Post-office employee, U. S. postal clerk.

postillon [pɔstijɔ̃] m. Postillion (cocher). ‖ FAM. Spluttering; *envoyer des postillons*, to splutter when speaking.

postillonner [-jɔne] v. intr. (1). To splutter.

postnatal, ale [pɔstnatal] adj. Post-natal.

postopératoire [-ɔperatwa:r] adj. MÉD. Post-operative.

post-partum [-partɔm] m. inv. MÉD. Post-partum.

postposer [pɔstpoze] v. tr. (1). GRAMM. To place after; *adjectif postposé*, postpositive adjective.

postposition [pɔstpozisjɔ̃] f. GRAMM. Postposition.

postscolaire [-skɔlɛ:r] adj. After-school; continuation (classe).

post-scriptum [-skriptɔm] m. Postscript.

postsynchronisation [-sɛ̃krɔnizasjɔ̃] f. CINÉM. Post-synchronization.

postsynchroniser [-sɛ̃krɔnize] v. tr. (1). CINÉM. To post-synchronize.

postulant, ante [pɔstylɑ̃, ɑ̃:t] adj., s. Applicant. ‖ ECCLÉS. Postulant.

postulat [-la] m. PHILOS. Postulate; *émettre un postulat*, to beg the question. ‖ ECCLÉS. Postulancy.

postuler [-le] v. tr. (1). To ask for, to apply for.

posture [pɔsty:r] f. Posture. ‖ Position, situation, state; *en bonne posture pour*, well situated to.

pot [po] m. Pot; *pot à colle*, glue-pot; *pot de colle*, pot of glue. ‖ Jug; U. S. pitcher; *pot à lait*, milk-jug; U. S. milk-pitcher. ‖ AGRIC. Pot (de plante); *mettre en pot*, to pot. ‖ CULIN. Cooking pot; *manger à la fortune du pot*, to take pot-luck. ‖ FIG. *Le pot de fer contre le pot de terre*, a giant against a pigmy; *découvrir le pot aux roses*, to smell out the mystery, U. S. to blow the lid off; *payer les pots cassés*, to pay for the damage, to pay the piper. ‖ POP. *Manque de pot!*, hard luck! ‖ **Pot-au-feu**, m. invar. CULIN. Boiled beef (mets); cooking-pot (ustensile); adj. FIG. Stay-at-home (personne); matter-of-fact (vie). ‖ **Pot-de-vin**, m. FAM. Gratuity, graft, palm oil. ‖ **Pot-pourri**, m. MUS. Medley.

potabilité [pɔtabilite] f. Potability, potableness.

potable [-tabl] adj. Drinkable; *eau potable*, drinking-water. ‖ FAM. Acceptable, decent, fairly good.

potache [pɔtaʃ] m. FAM. Schoolboy.

potage [pɔta:ʒ] m. CULIN. Soup. ‖ FAM. *Pour tout potage*, all told.

potager [pɔtaʒe] m. AGRIC. Kitchen-garden.
— adj. BOT. Vegetable.

potard [pɔta:r] m. FAM. Chemist.

potasse [pɔtas] f. CHIM. Potash.

potasser [-se] v. tr. FAM. To grind at, to swot up, U. S. to bone up on. (V. BURINER.)

potassique [-sik] adj. CHIM. Potassic.

potassium [-jɔm] m. CHIM. Potassium.

pote [pɔt] m. POP. Chum, pal; U. S. buddy.

poteau [pɔto] m. Post, pole (piquet); *poteau télégraphique*, telegraph-post (ou) pole. ‖ SPORTS. *Poteau d'arrivée, de but, de départ*, winning-, goal-, starting-post. ‖ MILIT. Place of execution; *coller au poteau*, to put against the wall. ‖ FAM. Fat leg (jambe).

potée [pɔte] f. Jugful. ‖ CULIN. Boiled vegetables with bacon. ‖ TECHN. Founder's clay.

potelé, ée [pɔtle] adj. Chubby (enfants); plump, roly-poly (personne).

potence [pɔtɑ̃:s] f. Gallows; *mériter la potence*, to deserve hanging. ‖ Saddle-pillar (de bicyclette). ‖ Bracket (d'enseigne). ‖ ARCHIT. Strut, bracket. ‖ NAUT. *Potence de chalut*, trawl-gallows.

potentat [pɔtɑ̃ta] m. Potentate. (V. PRINCE, ROI.)

potentialité [pɔtɑ̃sjalite] f. Potentiality.

potentiel, elle [pɔtɑ̃sjɛl] adj. Potentiality.
— m. Potentiality; *potentiel humain*, manpower. ‖ GRAMM. Potential mood. ‖ PHYS. Potential.

potentiellement [-mɑ̃] adv. Potentially.

potentiomètre [-sjɔmɛtr] m. ELECTR. Potentiometer.

poterie [pɔtri] f. Potter's workshop (atelier); earthenware (objets); pottery (travail).

poterne [pɔtern] f. Postern.

potiche [pɔtiʃ] f. Porcelain vase.

potier [pɔtje] m. Potter.

potin [pɔtɛ̃] m. FAM. Din, row, noise; U. S. ruckus; *faire du potin*, to make (ou) to kick up a row. ‖ Scandal, piece of gossip (médisance).

potinage [pɔtina:ʒ] m. Gossiping, scandal-mongering.

potiner [-ne] v. intr. FAM. To gossip, to talk scandal.

potinier, ière [-nje, njɛr] s. FAM. Scandal-monger, gossip.

— f. FAM. Gossip-shop; school for scandal.

potion [pɔsjɔ̃] f. MÉD. Potion.

potiron [pɔtirɔ̃] m. BOT. Pumpkin.

potron-jaquet [pɔtrɔ̃ʒakε], **potron-minet** [-minε] m. *Dès potron-jaquet (ou) -minet,* at cock-crow.

pou [pu] m. ZOOL. Louse; *pou de mer,* sea-louse. ‖ AVIAT. *Pou du ciel,* flying flea. ‖ FAM. *Laid comme un pou,* as ugly as sin.

pouah! [pwa] interj. Pooh!, ugh!

poubelle [pubεl] f. Dust-bin, U. S. garbage-can. ‖ LOC. *Chercher sa vie dans les poubelles,* to pick for a living in the gutter.

pouce [pu:s] m. Thumb (doigt). ‖ Inch (mesure). ‖ LOC. *Donner un coup de pouce,* to lend a hand (aider); to alter the course of things (détourner les événements); to finish off (fignoler); *manger un morceau sur le pouce,* to eat a snack in haste, to grab a bite on the run; *mettre les pouces,* to give in, to knuckle under; *pouce!,* pax!, U.S. truce!

Poucet [pusε] m. Tom Thumb.

poucettes [pusεt] f. pl. Thumb-fetters.

pouding [pudiŋ] m. CULIN. Pudding.

poudingue [pudε̃g] m. TECHN. Pudding-stone.

poudrage [pudra:ʒ] m. Powdering.

poudre [pu:dr] f. Dust (poussière). ‖ Powder; *poudre dentifrice,* tooth-powder; *poudre de riz,* face-powder. ‖ CULIN. *Café en poudre,* ground (ou) instant coffee; *chocolat en poudre,* powdered chocolate; *œufs en poudre,* dried (ou) dehydrated eggs. ‖ MILIT. Powder, gunpowder. ‖ LOC. *Jeter de la poudre aux yeux de qqn,* to throw dust in s.o.'s eyes; to bluff s.o.; *il n'a pas inventé la poudre,* he didn't invent gunpowder; *mettre le feu aux poudres,* to cause an uproar.

poudrer [pudre] v. tr. (1). To powder.

— v. pr. **Se poudrer,** to powder oneself.

poudrerie [-drəri] f. MILIT. Gunpowder factory.

poudreux, euse [-drø, ø:z] adj. Powdery, dusty.

poudreuse f. Powder snow. ‖ AGRIC. Duster (machine agricole).

poudrier [-drije] m. Powder-case (ou) -box, compact.

poudrière [-drijε:r] f. MILIT. Powder-magazine, powder-horn. ‖ FIG. Powder keg.

poudroiement [-drwamɑ̃] m. Dust-haze; dust hanging in the air.

poudroyer [-drwaje] v. intr. (9a). To form clouds of dust.

pouf [puf] m. Pouf, hassock, tuffet.

pouf! interj. Plump!, plop!

pouffant, ante [pufɑ̃, ɑ̃:t] adj. FAM. Rollicking.

pouffer [-fe] v. intr. (1). To burst out laughing.

pouffiasse [pufja:s] f. POP. Wench, U. S. floozey.

pouillerie [pujri] f. FAM. Beggarliness, squalor.

pouilles [pu:j] f. pl. Quarrel (v. NOISE); *chercher pouilles à,* to harrass.

pouilleux, euse [pujø, ø:z] adj. Lousy.

— s. FAM. Lousy person; down-and-out; U. S. crum.

poujadisme [puʒadism] m. † Poujadism, political trend in France in the 1950s characterized by antiparliamentarism, nationalism and reactionary demagogy.

poulailler [pulaje] m. Hen-house, hen-roost. ‖ THÉATR. Gods, U. S. peanut-gallery.

poulain [pulε̃] m. ZOOL. Colt, foal. ‖ COMM. Pony-skin (fourrure). ‖ SPORTS. Colt, trainee, promising youngster.

poulaine [pulεn] f. † Poulaine, crackowes (pl.), long pointed shoe.

poularde [pulard] f. CULIN. Fatted young fowl.

poulbot [pulbo] m. Street urchin.

poule [pu:l] f. ZOOL. Hen; *poule d'Inde,* turkey-hen. ‖ CULIN. Chicken. ‖ SPORTS. Sweepstake. ‖ FAM. *Poule mouillée,* milksop, mollycoddle; milk-toast; *poule aux œufs d'or,* goose with the golden eggs; *habiter au-delà des poules,* to live

at the back of beyond; *quand les poules auront des dents,* when pigs fly. ‖ FAM. Bird, U.S. pick-up (v. GRUE); *sa poule,* his mistress.

poulet [pulε] m. ZOOL., CULIN. Chicken. ‖ FAM. Ducky (enfant); love-letter (lettre).

poulette [-lεt] f. ZOOL. Pullet, young hen. ‖ FAM. Lassie; *ma poulette,* darling.

pouliche [puliʃ] f. ZOOL. Filly.

poulie [puli] f. TECHN. Pulley; block.

pouliner [puline] v. intr. (1). To foal (jument).

poulinière [-njε:r] adj. Brood (jument).

— f. ZOOL. Breeder, brood mare.

poulpe [pulp] m. ZOOL. Octopus; devil-fish.

pouls [pu] m. MÉD. Pulse; *prendre le pouls,* to take the pulse. ‖ FIG. *Se tâter le pouls,* to hesitate; *tâter le pouls à qqn,* to sound out s.o.'s intentions.

poumon [pumɔ̃] m. MÉD. Lung; *poumon d'acier,* iron lung; *respirer à pleins poumons,* to take a deep breath.

poupard [pupa:r] m. Baby in arms (enfant); baby doll (jouet). ‖ FAM. Chubby person.

— adj. Chubby. (V. POUPIN.)

poupe [pup] f. NAUT. Stern. ‖ FIG. *Avoir le vent en poupe,* to be in luck.

poupée [pupe] f. Doll; *poupée en chiffon,* rag-doll; *maison de poupée,* doll's house. ‖ LOC. *Poupées russes,* Chinese boxes. ‖ FAM. Bandaged finger. (V. NONNETTE.)

poupin, ine [-pε̃, in] adj. Baby-like (mine); chubby (visage).

poupon [-pɔ̃] m. Baby, infant.

pouponner [-pɔne] v. tr.(1). To mother, to coddle.

— v. intr. FAM. To nurse.

pouponnière [-pɔnjε:r] f. Public nursery, creche, U. S. day nursery.

pour [pu:r] prép.

---

1. Destiné à. — 2. A la place de. — 3. Dans l'opinion de. — 4. A l'avantage de. — 5. En faveur de. — 6. En considération de. — 7. Au prix de. — 8. Envers. — 9. Comme. — 10. Dans l'intention de. — 11. Par comparaison avec. — 12. A cause de. — 13. En ce qui concerne. — 14. A l'usage de. — 15. Parce que. — 16. A la date de. — 17. Pendant. — 18. En direction de. — 19. Afin de. — 20. De nature à. — 21. Par le fait de. — 22. Quoique. — 23. Considérant que. — 24. Sur le point de. — 25. Pour que. — 26. Pour ... que. — 27. Pour peu que. — 28. Loc.

---

1. For (destiné à); *pour vous,* for you. ‖ 2. For, instead of (à la place de); *signer pour qqn,* to sign instead of s.o. ‖ 3. For (dans l'opinion de); *pour moi il est honnête,* in my opinion he is honest. ‖ 4. For (à l'avantage de); *avoir peur pour qqn,* to fear for s.o. (ou) on s.o.'s account; *chacun pour soi,* every man for himself; *économiser pour sa famille,* to practise thrift for one's family. ‖ 5. For (en faveur de); *déposer pour qqn,* to give evidence on s.o.'s behalf; to testify for s.o.; *les personnes qui sont pour,* those in favour; *je n'ai rien à dire ni pour ni contre,* I have nothing to say one way or the other. ‖ 6. For, as for, with regard to (en considération de); *aimer qqn pour lui-même,* to love s.o. for his own sake; *pour l'amour de Dieu,* for heaven's sake; *l'art pour l'art,* art for art's sake; *faites-le pour moi,* do it for me; *pour son âge,* for (ou) considering his age. ‖ 7. For (au prix de); *j'en ai pour mon argent,* I've got my money's worth; *je l'ai cru pour mon malheur,* I believed it to my misfortune; *j'en suis pour mes frais,* I've gone to all that trouble for nothing; *pour deux sous de bonbons,* a pennyworth of sweets (ou)

U. S. candy; *travailler pour un maigre salaire,* to work for a meagre wage. ‖ **8.** For, toward (envers); *la bienveillance qu'on a montrée pour nous,* the kindness shown us. ‖ **9.** For, as (comme); *passer pour savant,* to be looked upon as learned; *prendre qqn pour secrétaire,* to engage s.o. as secretary; *se faire passer pour,* to pass oneself off as. ‖ **10.** For (dans l'intention de); *venir pour une affaire,* to come on business. ‖ **11.** For, per (par comparaison avec); *dix pour cent,* ten per cent. ‖ **12.** For (à cause de); *beaucoup de bruit pour rien,* much ado about nothing; *renvoyé pour négligence grave,* dismissed for grave negligence. ‖ **13.** For, as for (en ce qui concerne); *pour ma part,* as for me; *pour du toupet, c'est du toupet,* he's got the cheek of the devil. ‖ **14.** For (à l'usage de); *tailleur pour dames,* ladies' tailor; *vêtements pour hommes,* men's wear. ‖ **15.** Because (parce que); *compatir au mal de qqn pour y avoir passé,* to sympathize with s.o.'s complaint, having gone through it; *reconnaître qqn pour l'avoir déjà rencontré,* to recognize s.o. from having met him before. ‖ **16.** For (à la date de); *ce sera pour le mois prochain,* let us make it next month; *pour quand?* when? for when? ‖ **17.** For, during (pendant); *pour le peu de temps qu'il y est resté, il a fait beaucoup de choses,* during his short stay here, he has done many things; *pour toujours,* for ever. ‖ **18.** For (en direction de); *partir pour les colonies,* to set out for the colonies. ‖ **19.** To, for, in order to (afin de); *assez grand pour comprendre,* old enough to understand; *pour servir à l'application des règles,* for the enforcement of the rules; *trop malin pour ne pas se méfier,* too knowing not to be distrustful. ‖ **20.** Likely to, such as to (de nature à); *cela n'est pas pour me rajeunir,* that's not likely to make me look younger; *cela n'est pas pour me surprendre,* that doesn't come as a surprise to me. ‖ **21.** For, by (par le fait de); *ne rien perdre pour attendre,* to lose nothing by waiting; *usé pour avoir beaucoup servi,* worn out for having been much used. ‖ **22.** Though (quoique); *pour grand-père que je sois,* though I am a grand-father. ‖ **23.** For all (considérant que); *pour avoir tant étudié, il manque singulièrement de bon sens,* for all he has studied, he is singularly lacking in common sense. ‖ **24.** About to (sur le point de); *j'étais pour sortir quand la pluie a commencé,* I was about to go out when the rain began. ‖ **25. Pour que,** for; that, in order that (afin que); *il n'a pas assez de temps pour qu'il nous consacre une soirée,* he has not enough spare time for him to be able to spend an evening with us. ‖ **26. Pour... que,** however; *pour intelligent qu'il soit,* however intelligent he may be. ‖ **27. Pour peu que,** if ever, however little; *pour peu qu'il fasse froid, je m'enrhume,* at the least touch of cold, I catch a cold. ‖ **28.** Loc. *Pour ainsi dire,* so to speak; *pour de bon,* seriously, in earnest; *pour le moins,* at least; *partir pour partir, que ce soit tout de suite,* since we must go, let it be at once.

— m. *Le pour et le contre,* the pros and cons. ‖ Fig. *Tenir compte du pour et du contre,* to weigh both sides.

pourboire [purbwa:r] m. Tip, gratuity.

pourceau [purso] m. Zool. Pig, porker.

pourcentage [pursɑ̃ta:ʒ] m. Percentage.

pourchasser [purʃase] v. tr. (1). To pursue, to drive, to follow hard on the track of (qqn); *pourchassé par ses créanciers,* hounded by one's creditors.

pourfendeur [purfɑ̃dœ:r] m. Fam. Swashbuckler.

pourfendre [-fɑ̃:dr] v. tr. (4). To cleave in twain (fendre). ‖ To lunge at, to strike hard at (frapper).

pourlèchement [purlɛʃmɑ̃] m. Licking.

pourlécher (se) [səpurleʃe] v. pr. (1). To lick; *se pourlécher les babines,* to lick one's lips (ou) chops.

pourparlers [purparle] m. pl. Parley; diplomatic conversation, discussion. ‖ Pl. Negotiations.

pourpier [purpje] m. Bot. Purslane.

pourpoint [purpwɛ̃] m. Doublet.

pourpre [purpr] adj. Purple, crimson.

— f. Purple. ‖ Ecclés. *Porter la pourpre,* to wear purple.

— m. Purple (couleur); blush (rougeur). ‖ Méd. *Pourpre rétinien,* red pigment, visual purple.

pourpré, ée [-pre] adj. Purplish, purple, crimson.

pourquoi [purkwa] conj. adv. Why; *pourquoi faire?,* what for?; *c'est pourquoi,* that's why, that's the reason why; *dire pourquoi,* to say why.

— m. The reason why; the reason (de, for); *les pourquoi et les comment,* the whys and wherefores. ‖ Question (des enfants).

pourrai, pourrais. V. POUVOIR (79).

pourri, ie [puri] adj. Rotten, decayed (bois). ‖ Culin. Rotten (fruit, légumes); addled (œuf); spoilt (viande). ‖ Fig. Full of; *pourri d'orgueil,* puffed up with pride. ‖ Fam. Spoilt (enfant); dank, muggy (temps).

— m. Rotten part (d'un fruit).

pourrir [puri:r] v. intr. (2). Culin. To rot, to become rotten (fruit, légume); to addle (œuf).

— v. tr. To rot (le bois).

— v. pr. **Se pourrir,** to rot, to decay (bois). ‖ Culin. To rot (fruit, légume); to addle (œuf). ‖ Fig. To be spoilt (mentalité).

pourrissement [-smɑ̃] m. Deterioration, decaying.

pourriture [-ty:r] f. Rottenness, decay (action); rotten part (partie); *pourriture sèche,* dry rot. ‖ Rot (du bois). ‖ Fig. Corruption, rottenness.

poursuite [pursɥit] f. Pursuit (d'un fuyard); *à la poursuite de,* in pursuit of. ‖ Milit. Chase (de l'ennemi). ‖ Sports. Hunting (d'un cerf); chase (d'un lièvre); pursuit (en cyclisme). ‖ Jur. Pl. Proceedings, action, prosecution. ‖ Fig. Pursuit (de la gloire).

poursuiteur [-sɥitœ:r] m. Sports. Pursuit racer (en cyclisme).

poursuivant [-sɥivɑ̃] s. Pursuer. ‖ Jur. Prosecutor, plaintiff, ‖ Fam. Suitor (d'une femme).

— adj. Prosecuting.

poursuivre [-sɥi:vr] v. tr. (98). To pursue (un fuyard); to dog, to hound (qqn). ‖ Sports. To hunt, to chase. ‖ Milit. To pursue (l'ennemi). ‖ Jur. To prosecute, to sue, to take action against (qqn). ‖ Fig. To haunt, to worry, to importune (une femme, qqn). ‖ Fig. To follow up (son avantage); to go on (son chemin); to carry on (ses études); to prosecute, to work towards an end (un projet).

— v. intr. To continue, to go on.

— v. pr. **Se poursuivre.** Jur. To be proceeded with. ‖ Fig. To go on, to be carried on.

— v. récipr. **Se poursuivre,** to pursue one another.

pourtant [purtɑ̃] adv. Yet, however, nevertheless.

pourtour [purtu:r] m. Circumference, periphery; *dix mètres de pourtour,* ten metres round. ‖ Precincts (enceinte). ‖ Théâtr. Gangway, promenade.

pourvoi [purvwa] m. Jur. Appeal; petition.

pourvoir [purvwa:r] v. intr. (78). To provide (à, for) [des besoins]; to see (à, to) [un travail]; *pourvoir à un besoin,* to supply a want; *pourvoir aux besoins de,* to cater for, to support, to provide for; *pourvoir à ses propres besoins,* to keep oneself; *vous y pourvoirez,* you will see to it. ‖ ‖ Jur. *Pourvoir à une vacance,* to fill a vacancy.

— v. tr. To furnish, to provide, to supply (de,

with) [une maison]. ‖ Fɪɢ. To favour (*de*, with) [qqn].
— v. pr. **Se pourvoir**, to provide, to furnish, to supply oneself (*de*, with). ‖ Jᴜʀ. To appeal, to take action; to apply (*auprès de*, to); *se pourvoir en grâce*, to petition for mercy.

pourvoyeur, euse [-vwajœ:r, ø:z] a. Parveyor, provider, caterer.
— m. Mɪʟɪᴛ. Gunner, member of artillery-crew.

pourvoyons [-vwajɔ̃]. V. ᴘᴏᴜʀᴠᴏɪʀ (78).

pourvu, ue [purvy] adj. Provided (*de*, with); *bien pourvu d'argent*, flush with money.

pourvu conj. Provided, on condition (*que*, that); so long (*que*, as); *pourvu qu'il ne parle pas!* provided he doesn't talk!

poussah [pusa] m. Tumbler (jouet). ‖ Fᴀᴍ. Potbellied (ou) paunchy man, dump (personne).

pousse [pus] f. Bᴏᴛ. Growing, growth (action); sprout, young shoot (résultat).

pousse. V. ᴘᴏᴜssᴇʀ. ‖ **Pousse-café**, m. Liqueur, chaser. ‖ **Pousse-cailloux**, m. Mɪʟɪᴛ. Foot-slogger. ‖ **Pousse-pousse**, m. invar. Rickshaw, riksha (en Orient); pedicab (bicyclette).

poussé, ée [puse] adj. Tᴇᴄʜɴ. High-efficiency. ‖ Aʀᴛs. Elaborate (dessin); *trop poussé*, overelaborate, finicky. ‖ Fɪɢ. Deep (étude); exhaustive (recherche); highly finished, elaborate (travail).

poussée [puse] f. Push, thrust (de qqch., de qqn). ‖ Push, shove (secousse); *écarter qqn d'une poussée*, to push s.o. aside. ‖ Mɪʟɪᴛ. *Poussée de l'ennemi*, enemy thrust. ‖ Fɪɴ. *Poussée économique*, economic upsurge; *forte poussée en hausse*, strong upward tendency. ‖ Mᴇ́ᴅ. Rise (de fièvre); attack (de rhumatisme). ‖ Fɪɢ. *Poussée vitale*, vital impetus.

pousser v. tr. (1). To push, to shove, to thrust (qqch., qqn); *pousser la porte*, to push the door to; *pousser le verrou*, to shove the bolt across. ‖ To push, to hustle, to jostle (bousculer). ‖ To stir up (attiser); *pousser le feu*, to stir up the fire. ‖ To push, to urge (inciter); to urge on, to actuate, to stimulate (stimuler); *pousser qqn à faire qqch.*, to egg s.o. on to do sth.; *pousser un bon élève*, to push on a good pupil; *poussé par le besoin*, under stress of poverty. ‖ To carry forward, to extend (avancer); *pousser une conquête jusqu'à*, to carry a conquest so far as. ‖ To exaggerate (outrer); *ne poussez pas la plaisanterie plus loin*, don't carry the joke further. ‖ Mɪʟɪᴛ. To press hard (l'ennemi); *pousser une attaque à fond*, to strike home. ‖ Aᴜᴛᴏᴍ. *Pousser l'allure*, to drive hard, to push on. ‖ Fɪɴ. To run up (les enchères). ‖ Nᴀᴜᴛ. *Pousser l'allure*, to raise steam; *le vent pousse le navire à la côte*, the wind is blowing the ship ashore. ‖ Aʀᴛs. To elaborate, to finish (un dessin, un tableau). ‖ Mᴇ́ᴅ. To utter (un gémissement); to heave (un soupir). ‖ Tᴇᴄʜɴ. To push on, to press on (les travaux). ‖ Fᴀᴍ. *Aller à la va-comme-je-te-pousse*, to float along with the stream; *pousser qqn à bout*, to drive s.o. into a corner (acculer); to drive s.o. mad (irriter).
— v. intr. To push, to shove; *ne poussez pas!*, don't shove! ‖ Bᴏᴛ. To spring up, to grow (plante). ‖ Nᴀᴜᴛ. *Pousser au large*, to push off. ‖ Mɪʟɪᴛ. *Pousser droit sur*, to drive straight at. ‖ Fᴀᴍ. To grow (enfant); *pousser à la consommation*, to urge s.o. into expense; *pousser à la roue*, to put one's shoulder to the wheel; *pousser jusque chez qqn*, to push on as far as s.o.'s house; *demander à qqn d'en pousser une*, to knock s.o. down for a song, to ask s.o. to knock off a tune.
— v. pr. **Se pousser**, to get on, to push oneself to the fore.
— v. récipr. **Se pousser**, to push one another.

poussette [pusɛt] f. Push-chair, go-cart; U. S. stroller.

poussier [pusje] m. Coal-dust (charbon). ‖ Screenings (criblure).

poussière [-sjɛ:r] f. Dust; *enlever la poussière de*, to dust; *faire de la poussière*, to raise dust; *une poussière*, a speck of dust. ‖ *Poussière d'eau*, fine spray. ‖ Fɪɢ. Remains (cendres des morts). ‖Lᴏᴄ. *Mordre la poussière*, to bite the dust.

poussiéreux, euse [-sjerø, ø:z] adj. Dusty, covered with dust.

poussif, ive [pusif, i:v] adj. Broken-winded (cheval); short-winded, wheezy (personne).

poussin [pusɛ̃] m. Zᴏᴏʟ. Chicken, chick.

poussinière [-sinjɛ:r] f. Chicken-coop.

poussivement [pusivmɑ̃] adv. Wheezily.

poussoir [puswa:r] m. Push-button, pressbutton.

poutrage [putra:ʒ] m. Framework of beams.

poutre [pu:tr] f. Aʀᴄʜɪᴛ. Beam (en bois); girder (en fer); *poutre maîtresse*, main-beam; *aux poutres apparentes*, half-timbered. ‖ Aᴠɪᴀᴛ. *Poutre de liaison*, boom.

poutrelle [putrɛl] f. Aʀᴄʜɪᴛ. Small beam (ou) girder; joist.

pouvoir [puvwa:r] v. tr. (79). To be able; can, could (avoir la force, le pouvoir de); *cela ne peut se faire*, it cannot be done; *il a fait tout ce qu'il a pu*, he has done all he could; *il dit ne pouvoir le faire*, he says he cannot do it; *il aurait pu le faire*, he could have done it; *je n'aurais jamais pu le lire*, I could never have read it; *je ne puis le faire*, I am unable to do it; *je voudrais pouvoir vous dire oui*, I wish I could say yes; *nous ne voulons pas qu'on puisse dire que*, we don't want anyone to say that. ‖ Can (dénégation); *nous ne pouvons pas ne pas penser qu'il était au courant*, we cannot help thinking that he was perfectly aware of it; *vous ne pouvez dire que vous le connaissez bien*, you cannot say you know him well. ‖ May (possibilité); *cela a pu se passer comme vous le dites*, that may have happened as you say it has; *elle a pu sonner sans que je l'aie entendue*, she may have rung the bell without my hearing it; *il aurait pu m'attendre longtemps*, he might have waited for me a long time; *il peut venir à tout instant*, he may come at any moment; *sa femme, seule, sait ce qu'il peut bien penser*, his wife alone knows what he really thinks; *si faire se peut*, if it is possible; *si l'on peut dire*, if one may say so. ‖ May (suggestion); *elle pourrait répondre d'une façon péremptoire*, she might give a peremptory answer; *il aurait pu se montrer moins accommodant*, he might have proved less accommodating. ‖ May (souhait); *puissiez-vous dire vrai!*, may what you say be true! ‖ May (doute); *quelle a bien pu être sa vraie intention?*, what may his real intention have been?; *vous vous demandez qui a bien pu lui dire cela*, you are wondering who may have said that to him. ‖ Lᴏᴄ. *Il s'est conduit on ne peut mieux dans ces circonstances*, he behaved as well as one could expect under the circumstances; *il a été on ne peut plus content de cette nouvelle*, he was as delighted as could be with the news; *il faut, autant qu'on le peut, répondre poliment*, you must, as far as you can, answer politely; *nous sommes on ne peut plus heureux de vous voir guéri*, no one can be happier than we to see you well again; *son hospitalité est on ne peut plus large*, his hospitality is as liberal as may be. ‖ Fᴀᴍ. *N'en pouvoir plus*, to be at the end of one's resources; to be dispirited (être découragé); to be done in (ou) worn out (être éreinté); *palabrer à n'en plus pouvoir*, to talk oneself into a state of exhaustion.
— v. impers. May; *il peut arriver bien de l'imprévu*, many unforeseen things may happen; *il pourra se faire que*, it may happen that; *il aurait*

pu y avoir des conséquences graves à cette décision, the decision might have entailed serious consequences ; *il pourrait se faire qu'il ne se souvienne plus de moi,* he might very well not remember me.
— v. pr. impers. **Se pouvoir** ; *cela se peut,* that may be ; *il se peut qu'il n'ait pas reçu ma lettre,* he may not have received my letter.
— m. Power, ability (capacité, puissance) ; *de tout son pouvoir,* to the utmost of his ability ; *le pouvoir d'agir,* the power to act ; *le sauver dépasse mon pouvoir,* to rescue him is beyond my power. ‖ Power, rule, authority, domination ; *abus de pouvoir,* abuse of power ; *prendre le pouvoir,* to come into office (ministre) ; to ascend the throne (roi). ‖ Power, sway, ascendency ; influence ; *avoir du pouvoir sur soi-même,* to have self-control ; *avoir du pouvoir sur qqn,* to exert an influence over s.o. ‖ Jur. Power, authorization ; *avoir pouvoir de,* to have power to. ‖ Pl. Powers, authorities ; *les pouvoirs constitués,* the powers that be ; *obtenir les pleins pouvoirs,* to obtain full powers. ‖ Techn. *Pouvoir absorbant,* absorptive capacity.
P.P.C.M. [pepeseɛm] abrév. de *plus petit commun multiple,* Math. LCD, least (ou) lowest common denominator.
praesidium [prezidjɔm] m. Praesidium, presidium.
pragmatique [pragmatik] adj. Pragmatic.
pragmatisme [-tism] m. Philos. Pragmatism.
pragmatiste [-tist] s. Philos. Pragmatist.
praire [prɛːr] f. Zool., Culin. Clam.
prairial [prɛrjal] m. Prairial, ninth month in French Republican calendar (May-June).
prairie [prɛri] f. Agric. Meadow (pré) ; mead (en poésie). ‖ Grassland, U. S. prairie (région).
praline [prɑlin] f. Culin. Praline.
praliner [-line] v. tr. (1). Culin. To coat with almond-flavoured sugar.
praséodyme [prazeɔdim] m. Chim. Praseodymium.
praticabilité [pratikabilite] f. Practicability, feasibility.
praticable [-kabl] adj. Practicable, feasible (plan, projet) ; passable (route). ‖ Sociable (personne).
— m. Théâtr. Practicable, movable stage prop.
praticien [pratisjɛ̃] s. Méd. Practician, practitioner. ‖ Arts. Sculptor's assistant.
— adj. Practising.
pratiquant, ante [pratikɑ̃, ɑ̃ːt] adj. Ecclés. Practising.
— s. Ecclés. Church-goer.
pratique [-tik] adj. Practical, handy (chose) ; useful, convenient (mesure, moyen) ; practical (personne) ; *travaux pratiques,* field work, practical exercises.
— f. Practice ; *mettre en pratique,* to put into practice. ‖ Practice, use, experience ; *avoir la pratique des affaires,* to have business experience ; *avoir la pratique des enfants,* to know how to manage children ; *perdre la pratique,* to get out of practice. ‖ Proceeding ; *pratiques malhonnêtes,* dishonest proceedings. ‖ Comm. Customer (client) ; custom (clientèle). ‖ Jur. Legal procedure. ‖ Ecclés. *Libre pratique,* freedom of worship. ‖ Naut. *Libre pratique,* pratique.
pratiquement [-tikmɑ̃] adv. Practically ; in practice ; from a practical point of view.
pratiquer [-tike] v. tr. (1). To practise (un art) ; to practise, to pursue (une profession). ‖ To cut (une ouverture, un tunnel). ‖ Fin. To make, to do ; *cours pratiqués à la Bourse,* prices prevailing on the Exchange. ‖ Fig. To put into practice (des conseils) ; to practise (l'indulgence).
— v. intr. Méd. To practise ; *ne plus pratiquer,* to have retired ; to be no longer in practice. ‖

Ecclés. To be a church-goer, to go to church.
— v. pr. **Se pratiquer,** to be practised (ou) done. ‖ Fin. To be current (sur, on) [prix].
praxis [praksis] f. Philos. Praxis.
pré [pre] m. Agric. Meadow. ‖ † *Aller sur le pré,* to fight a duel. ‖ **Pré-salé,** m. Agric. Salt-meadow ; Zool. salt-meadow sheep ; Culin. salt-meadow mutton (ou) lamb.
préalable [prealabl] adj. Previous (question) ; preliminary.
— m. Preliminary ; *au préalable,* preliminarily, beforehand.
préalablement [-bləmɑ̃] adv. Previously, preliminarily. (V. auparavant.)
préambule [preɑ̃byl] m. Preamble.
préau [preo] m. Covered playground (d'école).
préavis [preavi] m. Previous warning (ou) notice ; advance notice.
prébende [prebɑ̃ːd] f. Ecclés. Prebend. ‖ Fam. Pay.
prébendé [-de] adj. m. Ecclés. Prebendal.
— m. Ecclés. Prebendary.
prébendier [-dje] s. Ecclés. Prebendary.
précaire [prekɛːr] adj. Precarious (possession) ; precarious, delicate (santé) ; precarious, uncertain, risky, unsafe (situation).
— m. Jur. Precarium.
précairement [-kɛrmɑ̃] adv. Precariously.
précambrien, enne [prekɑ̃brijɛ̃, ɛn] adj. Géol. Pré-Cambrian.
— m. Géol. Pre-Cambrian (ère).
précarité [-karite] f. Precariousness.
précaution [prekosjɔ̃] f. Precaution (mesure) ; *par précaution,* as a precaution (ou) a safety measure. ‖ Precaution, foresight (prudence) ; *avec précaution,* delicately, warily. ‖ Pl. *Précautions oratoires,* forestalling of objections, advance precautions.
précautionner [-sjɔne] v. tr. (1). To warn (qqn).
— v. pr. **Se précautionner,** to be on one's guard ; to take precautions (contre, against).
précautionneusement [-sjɔnøzmɑ̃] adv. Cautiously, warily.
précautionneux, euse [-sjɔnø, øːz] adj. Cautious, wary, prudent.
précédemment [presedamɑ̃] adv. Previously, beforehand. (V. avant.)
précédent, ente [-dɑ̃, ɑ̃ːt] adj. Preceding ; previous ; earlier ; *le jour précédent,* the day before.
— m. Precedent ; *sans précédent,* unprecedented.
précéder [-de] v. tr. (5). To precede, to antecede ; to go (ou) come before ; to take precedence over.
précepte [presɛpt] m. Precept.
précepteur, trice [-tœr- tris] s. Private tutor.
préceptoral, ale [-tɔral] adj. Tutorial.
préceptorat [-tɔra] m. Tutorship.
précession [presesjɔ̃] m. Astron. Precession.
prêche [prɛːʃ] m. Ecclés. Sermon.
prêcher [prɛʃe] v. tr. (1). Ecclés. To preach to (qqn). ‖ Fig. To preach, to preachify, to hold forth about.
— v. intr. Ecclés. To preach. ‖ Fig. *Prêcher d'exemple,* to set the example. ‖ Fam. *Prêcher pour son saint,* to have an axe to grind.
prêcheur [prɛʃœːr] m. Preacher, sermonizer.
prêchi-prêcha [prɛʃipreʃa] m. invar. Fam. Sermonizing.
précieusement [presjøzmɑ̃] adv. Preciously ; carefully. ‖ Affectedly (avec affectation).
précieux, euse [-sjø, øːz] adj. Precious (objet). ‖ Invaluable, precious, of great import (aide, avis) ; valuable, serviceable (person). ‖ Precious, affected, mincing. (V. maniéré.)
— s. Affected person. ‖ Preciosity.
précieuse f. † Précieuse, woman affecting excessive delicacy of language and taste.

préciosité [-sjɔzite] f. Preciosity.
précipice [presipis] m. Precipice. (V. GOUFFRE.)
précipitamment [presipitamã] adv. Precipitately.
précipitation [-tasjɔ̃] f. Hurry, rush, precipitation. ‖ CHIM., GÉOGR. Precipitation.
précipité, ée [-te] adj. Rash (action) : hasty (décision); hurried (départ); headlong (fuite). ‖ MÉD. Racing (pouls).
— m. CHIM. Precipitate.
précipiter [-te] v. tr. (1). To hurl, to throw (qqch., qqn); to push headlong, to rush (qqn). ‖ To hasten, to quicken, to accelerate, to hurry on. (V. HÂTER, PRESSER.) ‖ CHIM. To precipitate.
— v. pr. Se précipiter, to rush, to throw oneself (se jeter). ‖ To hasten, to hurry, to dash headlong. (V. S'ÉLANCER, SE RUER.) ‖ FIG. To rush forward (événements).
préciput [presipy] m. JUR. Portion; preference legacy.
précis, ise [presi, i:z] adj. Accurate, exact, distinct (idée); precise, definite (ordre). ‖ Precise (moment); *à cinq heures précises,* at five o'clock exactly, at five sharp. ‖ Careful (description); neat, clear (style); explicit (termes). ‖ MILIT. Accurate (tir).
— m. Primer (livre). ‖ Precis, abstract. (V. ABRÉGÉ.)
précisément [-zemã] adv. Precisely, exactly; *celui précisément qui,* the very man who.
préciser [-ze] v. tr. (1). To specify, to state precisely, to go into details regarding (qqch.).
— v. intr. To be precise (ou) explicit; to go into details.
— v. pr. Se préciser, to become clear (or) definite (idée). ‖ To take shape (danger).
précision [-zjɔ̃] f. Precision, preciseness, accuracy; *avec précision,* accurately; *de précision,* precision (instruments). ‖ Pl. Detailed information, particulars.
précité [presite] adj. Above-mentioned, aforesaid, already quoted. (V. SUSDIT.)
précoce [prekɔs] adj. Precocious. ‖ AGRIC. Early (fruit). ‖ FIG. Precocious, forward (enfant).
précocement [-smã] adv. Precociously.
précocité [-site] f. Precocity; precociousness. ‖ ‖ FIG. Precociousness, forwardness.
précolombien, enne [prekɔlɔ̃bjɛ̃, ɛn] adj. Pre-Columbian.
précombustion [-kɔ̃bystjɔ̃] f. Precombustion.
précompte [prekɔ̃:t] m. COMM. Previous deduction.
précompter [-kɔ̃te] v. tr. (1). To deduct beforehand.
préconception [-kɔ̃sɛpsjɔ̃] f. Preconception, anticipation.
préconcevoir [-kɔ̃səvwa:r] v. tr. (3). To preconceive, to anticipate.
préconçu, ue [-kɔ̃sy] adj. Preconceived; *idée préconçue,* preconception.
préconiser [prekɔnize] v. tr. (1). To advocate, to recommend, to vaunt (qqch.); to laud, to praise, to commend (qqn). ‖ ECCLÉS. To preconize.
préconnaissance [prekɔnɛsã:s] f. Foreknowledge, precognition.
préconstruction [-kɔ̃stryksjɔ̃] f. ARCHIT. Prefabrication, preconstruction.
précontraint, ainte [-kɔ̃trɛ̃, ɛ̃:t] adj. TECHN. Prestressed (béton, ciment).
précordial, ale [-kɔrdjal] adj. MÉD. Precordial.
précuit, uite [-kɥi, ɥit] adj. CULIN., AGRIC. Precooked.
précurseur [-kyrsœ:r] m. Precursor, forerunner.
— adj. Precursory, premonitory (signe).
prédateur, trice [predatœ:r, tris] adj. Predatory (animal); predacious (animal, instincts).

— m. Predator.
prédécesseur [predesesœ:r] m. Predecessor.
prédestination [predɛstinasjɔ̃] f. Predestination.
prédestiné, ée [-ne] adj. Predestined, foredoomed. ‖ Fated (*à,* to).
prédestiner [-ne] v. tr. (1). To predestine, to predestinate; to foredoom.
prédéterminer [predetermine] v. tr. (1). To predetermine.
prédicant [predikã] m. ECCLÉS. † Preacher among early French Protestants.
prédicat [predika] m. PHILOS., GRAMM. Predicate.
prédicateur [predikatœ:r] s. ECCLÉS. Preacher.
prédicatif, ive [-tif, i:v] adj. PHILOS., GRAMM. Predicative.
prédication [-sjɔ̃] f. ECCLÉS. Preaching.
prédiction [prediksjɔ̃] f. Prediction.
prédilection [predilɛksjɔ̃] f. Predilection, partiality; *de prédilection,* favourite.
prédire [predi:r] v. tr. (63). To predict, to foretell.
prédisposé, ée [predispoze] adj. Predisposed, prone, liable (*à,* to). ‖ Prejudiced (*contre,* against); predisposed (*en faveur de,* in favour of).
prédisposition [-zisjɔ̃] f. Predisposition, liability (*à,* to). ‖ Prejudice (*contre,* against); prepossession (*pour,* in favour of).
prédominance [predɔminã:s] f. Predominance.
prédominant, ante [-nã, ã:t] adj. Predominating, predominant.
prédominer [-ne] v. intr. (1). To predominate, to prevail, to have the upper hand (*sur,* over). [V. PRÉVALOIR.] ‖ To be uppermost.
— v. tr. To predominate over.
préélectoral, ale [preelɛktɔral] adj. Pre-election.
préemballé, ée [preãbale] adj. Prepacked.
prééminence [preeminã:s] f. Pre-eminence.
prééminent, ente [-nã, ã:t] adj. Pre-eminent.
préempter [preãpte] v. tr. (1). Jur. To pre-empt.
préemptif, ive [-tif, i:v] adj. JUR. Pre-emptive.
préemption [-sjɔ̃] f. JUR. Pre-emption.
préencollé, ée [preãkɔle] adj. Ready-pasted.
préétabli, ie [preetabli] adj. Pre-established.
préexistant, ante [preegzistã, ã:t] adj. Pre-existing, pre-existent.
préexistence [-tã:s] f. Pre-existence.
préexister [-te] v. intr. (1). To pre-exist.
préfabrication [prefabrikasjɔ̃] f. Prefabrication.
préfabriquer [-ke] v. tr. (1). To prefabricate; *maison préfabriquée,* prefabricated house; prefab (fam.).
préface [prefas] f. Preface, foreword. ‖ ECCLÉS. Preface.
préfacer [-se] v. tr. (1). To preface, to write a preface for.
préfacier [-sje] m. Prefacer.
préfectoral, ale [prefɛktɔral] adj. Prefectorial.
préfecture [-ty:r] f. Prefecture.
préférable [preferabl] adj. Preferable (*à,* to).
préférablement [-bləmã] adv. Preferably.
préféré, ée [prefere] adj. Preferred, favourite.
— s. Favourite. (V. FAVORI.)
préférence [-rã:s] f. Preference, special liking (v. PRÉDILECTION); *de préférence à, sur,* in preference to, over.
préférentiel, elle [-rãsjɛl] adj. Preferential.
préférer [-re] v. tr. (5). To prefer, to like better; *nous préférerions autre chose,* we should prefer (ou) we would rather have something else.
préfet [prefɛ] m. Prefect (civil); chief (de police).
préfète [-fɛt] f. Prefect's wife.
préfiguration [prefigyrasjɔ̃] f. Prefiguration.
préfigurer [prefigyre] v. tr. (1). To prefigure.
préfixal, ale [prefiksal] adj. GRAMM. Prefixal.
préfixe [prefiks] m. GRAMM. Prefix.

préfixer [-se] v. tr. Gramm. To prefix.
préformation [preformasjɔ̃] f. Preformation.
prégénital, ale [preʒenital] adj. Psych. Prege-
nital.
préhenseur [preɑ̃sœːr] adj. m. Prehensile.
préhensile [preɑ̃sil] adj. Prehensile.
préhension [-sjɔ̃] f. Prehension.
préhistoire [preistwaːr] f. Prehistory.
préhistorique [-tɔrik] adj. Prehistoric.
préindustriel, elle [preɛ̃dystriɛl] adj. Pre-
industrial.
préjudice [preʒydis] m. Injury, harm, detriment
(v. TORT); porter préjudice à qqn, to injure s.o.,
to do harm to s.o. ‖ Jur. Prejudice; sans préjudice de, without prejudice to.
préjudiciable [-disjabl] adj. Prejudicial, detrimental.
préjudiciel, elle [-disjɛl] adj. Prejudicial.
préjudicier [-disje] v. intr. To be prejudicial (ou)
detrimental (à, to).
préjugé [preʒyʒe] m. Prejudice, prepossession,
preconceived notion (v. PRÉVENTION); gens à préjugés, sans préjugés, prejudiced, unprejudiced
people; nourrir des préjugés à l'égard de, to
entertain prejudices toward; se garder des préjugés, to keep an open mind. ‖ Presupposition,
presumption; préjugé favorable, favorable assumption. ‖ Jur. Precedent.
préjuger v. intr., tr. (7). To prejudge.
prélart [prelar] m. Comm. Tarpaulin.
prélasser (se) [səprelɑse] v. pr. (1). To loll, to
sprawl, to take it easy.
prélat [prela] m. Prelate.
prélature [-tyːr] f. Prelacy.
prélavage [prelavaːʒ] m. Prewash.
prêle [prɛːl] m. Bot. Horsetail.
prélèvement [prelɛvmɑ̃] f. Appropriation. ‖
Drawing (action de soutirer). ‖ Méd. Sample;
quantity set aside. ‖ Fin. Levy.
prélever [prelve] v. tr. (5). To appropriate. ‖ To
take, to draw (un échantillon). ‖ Méd. To take.
‖ Fin. To levy; to charge (une commission).
préliminaire [preliminɛːr] adj. Preliminary; vue
préliminaire, preview.
— m. pl. Preliminaries (actes, documents); preliminary talks (entretiens).
prélude [prelyd] m. Mus. Prelude. ‖ Fig. Preliminary, precursory step.
préluder [-de] v. intr. Mus. To prelude. ‖ Fig.
To lead up (à, to); to pave the way (à, for).
prématuré, ée [prematyre] adj. Premature, untimely; avoir une fin prématurée, to come to an
early grave (ou) untimely end, to die prematurely.
— s. Méd. Premature baby, U.S. preemie (fam.).
prématurément [-mɑ̃] adv. Prematurely.
préméditation [premeditasjɔ̃] f. Premeditation;
avec préméditation, wilfully. ‖ Jur. Avec préméditation, with•malice aforethought.
préméditer [-te] v. tr. (1). To premeditate.
prémices [premis] f. pl. First-fruits.
premier, ère [prəmje, ɛːr] adj. First (en tête); le
premier arrivé (ou) venu, the first comer; les premiers jours du mois, the first days of the month.
‖ First (d'une série); Charles Iᵉʳ, Charles Iˢᵗ,
Charles the First. ‖ First, prime, head (titre);
premier clerc, head clerk; Premier ministre, Prime
Minister, Premier. ‖ First (du début); les premiers habitants du pays, the earliest inhabitants
of the country; the early settlers; premier livre
de littérature, literature primer. ‖ First (en avant);
tomber la tête la première, to fall head first. ‖
First, leading, best (meilleur); le premier chirurgien du pays, the best surgeon in the country. ‖
First, basic, essential (fondamental); premier
besoin, first (ou) basic need. ‖ First, exceptional;
de première importance, of paramount impor-

tance; de tout premier mérite, of sterling worth.
‖ Former, early (ancien); retrouver sa première
gaieté, to recover one's youthful sprightliness. ‖
Sports. First. ‖ Arts. Au premier plan, in the
foreground. ‖ Comm. Matières premières, raw
material. ‖ Math. Nombre premier, prime number.
‖ Fin. Premier cours, opening prices; premier
intéressé, preferential creditor. ‖ Milit. Premier
échelon, leading echelon; première ligne, front
line. ‖ Autom. Première vitesse, first (ou) low
gear. ‖ Loc. Au premier signal, at a moment's
notice. ‖ Premier-né, m. Firstborn.
— m. First; le premier de l'an, New Year's
day; le premier du mois, the first of the month.
‖ First floor, U. S. second floor (étage); au premier, on the first. ‖ Jur. Le premier, the Prime
Minister, the Premier, the French Premier. ‖
Naut. Lieutenant en premier, senior lieutenant.
‖ Loc. En premier, in the first place.
— s. First, first person; au premier de ces messieurs, next gentleman please; suis-je la première?, am I the first-comer? ‖ Théâtr. Jeune
premier, leading man.
première [-mjɛːr] f. Sixth form (classe); première
supérieure, class preparing for entrance to the
Ecole Normale Supérieure. ‖ Comm. Dressmaker's
forewoman (couturière); head saleswoman (vendeuse). ‖ Théâtr. First night, premiere; habitué
des premières, first-nighter. ‖ Ch. de f. First-
class ticket (billet) ou carriage (wagon); voyager
en première, to travel first class. ‖ Autom. First
(ou) low gear.
premièrement [-mjɛrmɑ̃] adv. First, firstly.
prémisse [premis] f. Premise, premiss.
prémolaire [premolɛr] adj. Méd. Premolar.
prémonition [-sjɔ̃] f. Premonition.
prémonitoire [-twaːr] adj. Premonitory.
prémunir [premyniːr] v. tr. (2). To protect (protéger). ‖ To caution, to warn (avertir).
— v. pr. Se prémunir, to protect (ou) secure
oneself; to take precautions (contre, against).
prenable [prənabl] adj. Pregnable; liable to be
taken.
prenant, ante [-nɑ̃, ɑ̃ːt] adj. Zool. Prehensile
(queue). ‖ Jur. Partie prenante, payee, creditor. ‖
Fig. Engaging, fascinating (manières, voix).
prénatal, ale [prenatal] (pl. prénatals) adj.
Prenatal, antenatal.
prendre [prɑ̃ːdr] v. tr. (80).

---

1. Saisir. — 2. Piéger. — 3. Voler. — 4. Aller
chercher. — 5. Retenir. — 6. Obtenir. —
7. Noter. — 8. Laisser pénétrer. — 9. Emprunter. — 10. Demander. — 11. Accepter. —
12. Saisir. — 13. Ressentir. — 14. Assumer.
— 15. Se donner. — 16. Occuper. — 17. S'octroyer. — 18. Recevoir. — 19. Capter. —
20. Manier. — 21. Reprendre. — 22. Reconnaître. — 23. Milit. — 24. Naut. — 25. Autom.
— 26. Ch. de f. — 27. Méd. — 28. Comm.
— 29. Fin. — 30. Fam. — 31. Loc.

---

1. To take, to take (ou) lay hold of, to grasp
(saisir); prendre le bout d'un bâton, to grasp
the tip of a stick; prendre un lapin par les
oreilles, to take a rabbit by the ears. ‖ 2. To
take, to catch, to trap, to snare (attraper au
piège); prendre une souris, to trap a mouse. ‖
3. To take, to wrench, to wrest, to steal (voler);
on m'a pris ma montre, I was robbed of my
watch. ‖ 4. To pick up (aller chercher); prendre
qqn chez lui, to pick s.o. up at his house; prenez-
moi dans votre voiture, give me a lift. ‖ 5. To
take (retenir); prendre une bonne, to engage a
maid; prendre une chambre, to rent a room;

prendre des places, to book (ou) reserve seats; *prendre un rendez-vous avec,* to make an appointment with. ‖ **6.** To have (obtenir); *prendre son B. A. à Trinity College,* to graduate as B. A. from (ou) to take one's B. A. at Trinity College. ‖ **7.** To take (noter); *prenez-en note,* jot it down, make a note of it. ‖ **8.** To let in (laisser pénétrer); *prendre l'eau,* to let in water, to leak. ‖ **9.** To follow (emprunter); *prendre la route d'en haut,* to take the high road. ‖ **10.** To ask (demander); *prendre conseil de qqn,* to ask, s.o.'s advice. ‖ **11.** To accept (accepter); *prendre un engagement,* to enter into an engagement; *prendre les choses comme elles viennent,* to take things as they come; to be easy-going; *prendre qqn pour ce qu'il est,* to accept s.o. for what he is; *prendre qqn en amitié,* to take to s.o.; *prendre qqn en grippe,* to take a dislike to s.o. ‖ **12.** To seize (saisir); *un frisson m'a pris,* I was seized by a shivering fit; *le froid vous prend,* the cold bites you. ‖ **13.** To feel (ressentir); *prendre grand plaisir à qqch.,* to enjoy sth. very much; *prendre pitié de,* to take pity on. ‖ **14.** To take (assumer); *prendre la défense de qqn,* to assume s.o.'s defence; *prendre qqch. sur soi,* to take sth. upon oneself. ‖ **15.** To assume (se donner); *prendre des airs,* to put on airs. ‖ **16.** To take up (occuper); *cela prendra plus d'une journée,* that will take up more than a day. ‖ **17.** To take (s'octroyer); *prendre une demi-heure de repos,* to take half-an-hour's rest. ‖ **18.** To take in (recevoir); *prendre une communication,* to take a call; *prendre des pensionnaires,* to take in boarders. ‖ **19.** To deceive (capter, tromper); *prendre qqn par des paroles douce-reuses,* to win s.o. over with honeyed words; *se laisser prendre,* to let oneself be taken in. ‖ **20.** To handle, to treat (manier); *on ne sait par quel bout le prendre,* one never knows how to deal with him; *prenez-le comme il faut,* handle him the right way. ‖ **21.** To catch (reprendre); *que je ne vous y prenne plus!* don't let me catch you at it again! ‖ **22.** To know (reconnaître); *prendre qqn pour,* to take s.o. for. ‖ **23.** MILIT. To attack (attaquer); to take, to conquer (conquérir); *être pris,* to be made prisoner; *prendre l'ennemi de front,* to make a frontal attack against the enemy; *prendre la fuite,* to take (to) flight. ‖ **24.** NAUT. To take on (des passagers); *prendre de l'eau,* to fill up with fresh water : *prendre la mer,* to put out to sea. ‖ **25.** AUTOM. *Prendre un tournant trop court,* to cut a corner too close. ‖ **26.** CH. DE F. To take, to catch (le train). ‖ **27.** MÉD. To drink, to eat (absorber); to get (attraper); *prendre une boisson forte,* to drink a stimulant; *prendre de l'âge,* to be getting old; *prendre des forces,* to get stronger; *prendre la grippe,* to catch the flu; *prendre du sang,* to draw off blood; *prendre du ventre,* to round out. ‖ **28.** COMM. To buy (acheter); to take, to choose (choisir); to charge (faire payer); *prendre un prix à qqn pour,* to charge s.o. a price for. ‖ **29.** FIN. To draw out, to withdraw (retirer); *prendre une option,* to acquire an option; *prendre une somme sur la caisse noire,* to draw (ou) take a sum out of the reserve fund. ‖ **30.** FAM. *Qu'est-ce qui lui prend?,* what's the matter with him?; *qu'est-ce qu'il a pris!,* he really caught it!, he didn't half catch it! ‖ **31.** LOC. *A tout prendre,* on the whole; *bien lui en a pris,* it was lucky for him he did it; *c'est à prendre ou à laisser,* take it or leave it; *j'en prends et j'en laisse,* I do as much as I feel inclined to (je ne me fatigue pas); I take it with a pinch of salt (je ne crois pas tout); *prendre l'air,* to go out for a breath of air; *prendre son vol,* to take flight; *prendre une solution,* to arrive at a solution.
— v. intr. To strike (allumette); to flame (charbon); *le charbon ne veut pas prendre,* the coal refuses to burn. ‖ To break out (feu, incendie); *le feu a pris à la meule de foin,* the hay-stack caught fire. ‖ To take (goût); *l'envie lui a pris de voyager,* a fancy has taken him to travel. ‖ To take (se diriger); *prendre par le plus court,* to take the shortest way. ‖ To get on, to succeed (réussir); *son livre a pris,* his book has made a hit; *sa ruse a pris,* his cunning trick worked well. ‖ To freeze, to congeal (se geler). ‖ TECHN. To thicken, to set (plâtre). ‖ CULIN. To thicken (crème). ‖ COMM. *Combien prenez-vous pour?,* How much do you charge for? ‖ BOT. To take root (plante). ‖ FAM. *Ça ne prend pas,* that cock won't (ou) wouldn't fight; *ça ne prend pas avec moi,* that won't work with me; *en prendre pour son grade,* to catch it hot, U. S. to get bawled out.
— v. pr. **Se prendre,** to be caught (dans un piège). ‖ To tackle (s'attaquer); *se prendre à un travail,* to undertake a task. ‖ To get (concevoir); *se prendre d'amitié pour,* to strike up a friendship with. ‖ To quarrel (s'attaquer). ‖ To become (ou) get cloudy (se couvrir); *le temps se prend,* the weather is getting cloudy. ‖ To be interpreted (se comprendre); *cette réponse peut se prendre dans les deux sens,* this answer could have two meanings. ‖ To turn (se laisser aller); *se prendre à pleurer,* to begin to weep. ‖ MÉD. To be affected; *son cerveau se prend,* he is threatened with insanity. ‖ **S'en prendre,** to find fault (à, with); *ne s'en prendre qu'à soi de,* to blame only oneself for; *qu'il s'en prenne à lui-même!,* let him realize his own responsibility! ‖ **S'y prendre,** to set about it; *s'y prendre à deux fois,* to make two attempts; *s'y prendre à temps,* to start doing it in time; *s'y prendre mal,* to tackle the difficulty the wrong way; *comment s'y prendre?* how can one go about it?; *savoir comment s'y prendre avec qqn,* to know how to deal with s.o.

preneur, euse [prənœ:r, ø:z] s. Taker, capturer. ‖ COMM., FIN. Taker, purchaser. ‖ JUR. Lessee; payee.
— adj. Buying, purchasing.

prénom [prenɔ̃] m. Christian (ou) first name.

prénommé, ée [-nɔme] adj. Called, whose Christian (ou) first name is. ‖ JUR. Above-named (susnommé).
— s. Person whose Christian (ou) first name is. ‖ JUR. Above-named.

prénommer [-nɔme] v. tr. (1). To give a Christian name to.
— v. pr. **Se prénommer,** to be called.

prenons [prənɔ̃]. V. PRENDRE (80).

prénuptial, ale [prenypsjal] adj. Prenuptial, antenuptial.

préoccupant, ante [preɔkypɑ̃, ɑ̃:t] adj. Preoccupying, engrossing, worrying.

préoccupation [preɔkypasjɔ̃] f. Preoccupation, absorption (absorbement). ‖ Preoccupation, anxiety, concern, care (souci).

préoccuper [-pe] v. tr. (1). To occupy beforehand (occuper avant). ‖ To preoccupy, to engross (absorber); to worry (inquiéter); *préoccupé de sa petite personne,* self-centred; *préoccuper qqn,* to make s.o. anxious; *avoir l'air préoccupé,* to look preoccupied.
— v. pr. **Se préoccuper,** to be engrossed (de, by). ‖ *Se préoccuper de,* to attend to, to take heed of, to keep in sight (veiller à); *il ne se préoccupe pas assez des problèmes financiers,* he treats financial problems too lightly, he takes financial problems too much in his stride. ‖ To get worried (de, about) [s'inquiéter].

préopératoire [preɔperatwa:r] adj. MÉD. Preoperative.

prépalatal, ale [prepalatal] adj. GRAMM. Ante-palatal.

préparateur, trice [preparatœ:r, trice] s. Planner, organizer (organisateur). ‖ MÉD. Assistant.

préparatifs [-tif] m. pl. Preparations. (V. APPRÊTS.)
préparation [-sjɔ̃] f. Preparation, preparing; *ouvrage en préparation*, work in preparation (chez l'auteur); work to appear shortly (en librairie); *sans préparation*, extemporaneous (discours). ‖ MÉD. Making up (en pharmacie). ‖ CULIN. Cooking. ‖ TECHN. Dressing (des peaux).

préparatoire [-twa:r] adj. Preparatory.

préparer [prepare] v. tr. (1). To prepare, to get ready. (V. APPRÊTER, DISPOSER.) ‖ To plan, to draw up (élaborer); *préparer un discours*, to prepare (ou) to draw up a speech. ‖ To train (instruire); *préparer des élèves*, to prepare (ou) to coach pupils; *préparer un examen*, to prepare (ou) to study for an exam. ‖ To prepare, to fit (disposer) [for, à]; *être préparé à tout*, to be prepared for whatever may happen. ‖ To lead up to (conduire à); *préparer le terrain*, to pave the way; *préparer l'union*, to pave the way for union. ‖ TECHN. To dress (des peaux). ‖ MÉD. To lay out (les instruments).
— v. pr. **Se préparer**, to prepare oneself (à, for); *se préparer à un examen*, to read (or) work for an exam. ‖ To be on the way (ou) in the wind (événements); to loom (malheur); to ferment (révolte); to brew (orage).

prépondérance [prepɔ̃derɑ̃:s] f. Preponderance.

prépondérant, ante [-rɑ̃, ɑ̃:t] adj. Preponderating, preponderant. ‖ JUR. *Voix prépondérante*, casting vote.

préposé [prepoze] s. Employee (en général); keeper (au vestiaire). ‖ JUR. Officer (aux douanes); collector (à l'octroi).

préposer v. tr. (1). To appoint (à, to); *être préposé à*, to be in charge of.

prépositif, ive [-zitif, i:v] adj. GRAMM. Prepositive; prepositional (locution).

préposition [-zisjɔ̃] f. GRAMM. Preposition.

prépositionnel, elle [-zisjɔnɛl] adj. GRAMM. Prepositional.

prépuce [prepy:s] m. MÉD. Prepuce; foreskin.

préraphaélisme [prerafaelism] m. ARTS. Pre-Raphaelitism, Pre-Raphaelism.

préraphaélite [-lit] adj., s. ARTS. Pre-Raphaelite.

préretraite [preratrɛt] f. Premature retirement; premature retirement benefit.

prérogative [prerogativ] f. Prerogative.

préromantique [preromɑ̃tik] adj., s. Preromantic.

préromantisme [-tism] m. Preromanticism.

près [prɛ] prép. Near; *près de Paris*, near (ou) close to Paris.
— adv. Near, close, close by, hard by, close at hand (v. PROCHE); *tenez-vous là tout près*, stand close by.
— loc. adv. **A ... près**; *à beaucoup près*, far from it; *à la beauté près*, beauty apart; *à cela près*, except for that, with that exception; *à peu de choses près*, almost, nearly; *dire l'âge de qqn à un an près*, to tell s.o.'s age to a year; *être d'accord à vingt francs près*, to agree to within twenty francs; *ne pas en être à cela près*, not to have come down to that. ‖ **A peu près**, nearly, almost; approximately; *à peu près pareil*, very much the same; *un à-peu-près*, an approximation. ‖ **De près**, when near, at a close distance (à côté); closely, carefully (avec soin); *tenir qqn de près*, to keep a close watch on s.o.; *voir qqn de près*, to see s.o. at close quarters; *voir qqch. de près*, to have a close look at sth.
— loc. prép. **Près de**, near, close to (à côté de); *près de l'Eglise*, close to the church; *habiter près de chez elle*, to live near her. ‖ Nearly, close upon (proche de); *près de sa fin*, nearing his end, about to die; *près de la perfection*, near perfection. ‖ About to (sur le point de); *je ne suis pas prêt de le revoir*, it will be long before I see him again; *il n'est pas prêt de recommencer*, he won't do it again in a hurry. ‖ Almost, nearly (presque); *près de cent francs*, almost a hundred francs; *il y a près de deux heures que vous êtes là*, you have been here for close on two hours. ‖ In comparison with, beside (à côté de); *près de lui*, beside him. ‖ LOC. *Près de ses intérêts*, close-fisted.

présage [preza:ʒ] m. Presage, omen, portent.

présager [-zaʒe] v. tr. (7). To presage, to foreshadow, to portend. ‖ To foresee, to predict.

présalaire [presalɛ:r] m. Salary paid to students.

presbyte [prɛsbit] adj. MÉD. Long-sighted, far-sighted, presbyopic.

presbytère [prɛsbitɛ:r] m. ECCLÉS. Parsonage, vicarage, rectory (de l'Eglise anglicane); presbytery, U. S. rectory (de l'Eglise catholique); manse (des presbytériens).

presbytérianisme [-terjanism] m. ECCLÉS. Presbyterianism.

presbytérien, enne [-terjɛ̃, ɛn] adj., s. ECCLÉS. Presbyterian.

presbytie [prɛsbisi] f. MÉD. Long-sightedness, far-sightedness, presbyopia.

prescient [presjɑ̃] adj. Prescient, foreseeing.

prescience [-sjɑ̃:s] f. Prescience, foresight, foreknowledge.

préscolaire [preskɔlɛ:r] adj. Pre-school.

prescriptible [prɛskriptibl] adj. Prescriptible.

prescription [-kripsjɔ̃] f. MÉD., JUR., FIG. Prescription.

prescrire [prɛskri:r] v. tr. (44). To prescribe, to ordain, to recommend (ordonner). ‖ To specify, to stipulate (les conditions, l'heure). ‖ JUR. To bar, to render invalid; *dans les délais prescrits*, within the stipulated time. ‖ MÉD. To prescribe. ‖ FIN. *Chèque prescrit*, stale (ou) U. S. lapsed cheque.
— v. pr. **Se prescrire**, MÉD., JUR. To be prescribed.

préséance [preseɑ̃:s] f. Precedence.

présélection [preselɛksjɔ̃] f. Preselection (en général), short-listing (des postulants à un emploi). ‖ RADIO. *Touche de présélection*, preset button.

présélectionner [-sjɔne] v. tr. (1). To preselect (en général), to short-list (les postulants à un emploi). ‖ RADIO. To preset.

présence [prezɑ̃:s] f. Présence (à, at); *feuille de présence*, attendance sheet. ‖ MÉD. Presence, trace (de, of). ‖ ECCLÉS. *Présence réelle*, real presence. ‖ MILIT. *Forces en présence*, opposing forces. ‖ FIG. *Présence d'esprit*, presence of mind. ‖ LOC. *En présence*, facing each other; *en présence de*, in presence (ou) front (ou) view of, face to face with; *faire acte de présence*, to put in an appearance.

présent, ente [prezɑ̃, ɑ̃:t] adj. Present, at hand (assistant); *les personnes présentes*, all those present. ‖ Present, current (actuel); *le mois présent*, the current month. ‖ GRAMM. Present. ‖ FIG. Present; *n'être pas présent à la conversation*, to be absent-minded, not to be aware of what is said. ‖ LOC. *A présent*, now, at present; in our time; *à présent que*, now, now that; *dès à présent*, even now; from now on; *jusqu'à présent*, until now, so far; *quant à présent*, as for now.
— m. Person present, bystander; *les présents*, those present. ‖ Present, time being (époque actuelle). ‖ GRAMM. Present, present tense.

présent m. Present, gift. (V. DON.)

présentable [prezɑ̃tabl] adj. Presentable, acceptable. (V. MONTRABLE.)

présentateur, trice [-tatœ:r, tris] s. Presenter.

présentation [-tasjɔ̃] f. Presentation; *faire les présentations*, to introduce people to one another. ‖ COMM. Get-up (d'une marchandise); *présenta-*

tion de collections, fashion parade, style show. ‖ Fin. Clearance (d'un chèque). ‖ Milit. *Présentation du drapeau*, trooping the colours. ‖ Théâtr. Trade-show, preview (d'un film). ‖ Ecclés. Presentation.

présente [prezɑ̃:t] f. Present letter (lettre). ‖ Jur. Pl. Presents.

présentement [prezɑ̃tmɑ̃] adv. Just now, at present; for the time being. (V. actuellement.)

présenter [-te] v. tr. (1). To present, to offer (offrir); *présenter son bras à qqn*, to offer s.o. one's arm; *présenter ses respects*, to pay one's respects. ‖ To present, to show (montrer); *présenter une lettre de recommandation*, to present a letter of introduction. ‖ To present, to hold out, to put forth (faire voir); *présenter les mains*, to hold out one's hands. ‖ To offer, to take (une matière d'examen). ‖ To present, to afford (fournir); *présenter des avantages, des difficultés*, to present advantages, difficulties; *présenter des ressources abondantes*, to afford abundant resources. ‖ To marshal (des faits); to present, to set forth (une idée). ‖ To present, to nominate, to propose (pour, for) [un candidat]. ‖ To introduce, to present (qqn) [à, to]; *je vous présente ma femme*, may I introduce my wife? ‖ Tech. To try (une serrure). ‖ Théâtr. To present (un acteur, une pièce). ‖ Milit. To parade (des troupes). ‖ Jur. To put (à, to) [une motion]; to submit (ses papiers d'identité); to produce (son passeport); to present (un rapport); to introduce (un projet de loi). ‖ Fin. To submit (ses comptes). ‖ Comm. To present (un modèle); to put up (*dans*, in) [un produit].
— v. pr. Se **présenter**, to present oneself (*devant*, before); to turn up (visiteur); *se présenter chez qqn*, to call on s.o. ‖ To introduce oneself (se faire connaître); *permettez-moi de me présenter*, allow me to introduce myself; *elle se présente bien, mal*, she makes a good, bad impression. ‖ To stand, U. S. to run (à, at) [une élection]; to sit (à, for) [un examen]; to apply (à, for) [un poste]. ‖ Fig. To come up, to occur, to arise (difficulté, solution); to come up (idée); to turn up (occasion favorable). ‖ To appear (affaire); *l'affaire se présente bien*, the affair looks well.

présentoir [-twa:r] m. Display stand.

préservateur, trice [prezɛrvatœ:r, tris] adj. Preservative, preserving.

préservatif, ive [-tif, i:v] adj. Preservative.
— m. Méd. Contraceptive sheath, condom.

préservation [-sjɔ̃] f. Preserving (action); preservation (résultat).

préserver [prezɛrve] v. tr. (1). To protect, to preserve, to save (de, from); *le ciel m'en préserve !*, Heaven forbid !

présidence [prezidɑ̃:s] f. Presidency (d'une nation); chairmanship (d'une réunion). ‖ President's residence (palais).

président, ente [-dɑ̃, ɑ̃:t] s. Speaker (de la Chambre des communes); Premier (du Conseil); president (de la République). ‖ Chairman (d'un comité, d'une réunion, d'une société); *Madame la Présidente*, Madam Chairman. ‖ Jur. *Président de Chambre*, presiding judge.

présidentialisme [-dɑ̃sjalism] m. Presidential government.

présidentiel, elle [-dɑ̃sjɛl] adj. Presidential.

présidentielles f. pl. Presidential election.

présider [-de] v. intr. (1). To preside (à, at, over); to be president (ou) chairman (à, of); to be in the chair (à, at) [une réunion]. ‖ To watch (à, over) [veiller sur]; *présider aux destinées de*, to be responsible for (ou) to preside over the destinies of; *présider à l'évolution de*, to regulate the evolution of.
— v. tr. To preside over, to be president of, to be in the chair at.

présidium [-zidjɔm] m. Presidium, praesidium.

présomptif, ive [prezɔ̃ptif, i:v] adj. Presumptive. ‖ Jur. *Héritier présomptif*, heir apparent (d'un trône).

présomption [-sjɔ̃] f. Presumption, supposition; *les présomptions jouent pour*, the presumptions are in favour of. ‖ Presumption, assurance (vanité). ‖ Jur. Presumption.

présomptueux, euse [-tɥø, ø:z] adj. Presumptuous.

presque [prɛsk] adv. Almost, nearly, well-nigh; *presque grandiose*, verging on grandeur; *presque mort*, all but dead; *presque ruinée*, little short of ruin; *presque toute la ville*, practically the whole town. ‖ Hardly, scarcely (sens négatif); *presque jamais*, almost never, hardly ever; *presque plus de ressources*, scarcely any resources left; *presque rien*, hardly anything.

presqu'île [prɛski:l] f. Géogr. Peninsula.

pressage [prɛsa:ʒ] m. Pressing.

pressant, ante [prɛsɑ̃, ɑ̃:t] adj. Cogent (argument); pressing, urgent, imperative (besoin); pressing, importunate (personne); *en un cas pressant*, in an emergency.

presse [prɛ:s] f. Press, crowd, throng (foule); *heures de presse*, rush hours. ‖ Haste (hâte); *moment de presse*, rush period, period of work at high pressure; *nous ne connaissons pas de presse*, we are never rushed. ‖ Techn. Press, pressing machine; squeezer; *presse à copier, à découper, à emballer, à forger*, copying-, punching-, baling-, forging-press; *presse à emboutir*, stamper. ‖ *Presse d'imprimerie*, printing press; *exemplaire du service de presse*, press (ou) review copy; *livre sous presse*, book in press; *prêt à mettre sous presse*, ready for press; *service de presse*, press copies. ‖ Press (journalistes); *tribune de la presse*, press-gallery. ‖ Newspapers (journaux); *avoir bonne, mauvaise presse*, to have a good, bad press. ‖ Naut. Impressment (action); press gang (recruteurs). ‖ **Presse-bouton**, adj. invar. Push-button. ‖ **Presse-citron**, m. invar. Lemon-squeezer. ‖ **Presse-étoupe**, m. invar. Stuffing box. ‖ **Presse-fruits**, m. invar. Fruit squeezer. ‖ **Presse-pantalon**, m. invar. Trouser-press (ou) -stretcher. ‖ **Presse-papiers**, m. invar. Paper-weight. ‖ **Presse-purée**, m. invar. Culin. Potato-masher. ‖ **Presse-raquette**, m. invar. Racket-press.

pressé, ée [prɛse] adj. Pressed, crowded, close together. (V. entassé.) ‖ In a hurry, pressed (plein de hâte). ‖ Hard pressed, beset (assailli); *pressé par le besoin*, under pressure of need. ‖ Urgent, pressing (urgent). ‖ Quick (rapide). ‖ Culin. Squeezed, pressed (citron).
— m. *Le plus pressé*, the most urgent business (chose); the one in the greatest hurry (personne).

pressentiment [prɛsɑ̃timɑ̃] m. Presentiment, foreboding; hunch. (V. prémonition.)

pressentir [-ti:r] v. tr. (93). To have a presentiment (ou) a foreboding (ou) an inkling of (prévoir); *faire pressentir*, to foreshadow. ‖ To have an intimation of (soupçon). ‖ To sound out (qqn) [au sujet de, sur, about, as to, on]; *président pressenti*, prospective Prime Minister.

presser [prɛse] v. tr. (1). To press, to squeeze (une éponge); to press (un pantalon); *presser qqn sur son cœur*, to clasp s.o. to one's breast. ‖ To hasten, to quicken (v. accélérer); *presser un enfant*, to hurry a child; *il n'y a rien qui vous presse*, there is no cause for you to hurry; *il ne presse jamais le pas*, he never hurries, he always walks at a deliberate pace. ‖ To urge, to bring pressure on (pousser); *pressé par la nécessité*, hard put to it by want; *on le pressera de se décider*, they will urge him to make a decision. ‖ To assail (accabler); *presser qqn d'arguments*, to assail s.o. with arguments; *presser qqn de ques-*

tions, to bombard s.o. with questions. ‖ MILIT. To pursue, to harry (l'ennemi). ‖ CULIN. To squeeze, to press (un citron).
— v. intr. To be urgent (question, travail); *cela ne presse pas,* there is no need to hurry; *le temps presse,* time is getting short.
— v. pr. Se presser, to crowd, to throng, to press (s'entasser). ‖ To heap up (s'amonceler [*sur,* on]. ‖ To hasten, to hurry (se dépêcher). ‖ To move swiftly (événements).

pressing [prɛsiŋ] m. Dry-cleaning (procédé); dry-cleaner's (boutique). ‖ SPORTS. Pressure; *faire du pressing,* to put the pressure on.

pression [-sjɔ̃] f. Pressure (acte, résultat). ‖ TECHN. Pressure; *machine sous pression,* engine under steam; *pression inverse,* reverse pressure. ‖ COMM. *Bière à la pression,* beer on draught; draught beer; *bouton-pression,* press-button, snap-fastener. ‖ MÉD. Blood-pressure (artérielle). ‖ FIG. *Etre sous pression,* to be under pressure; *faire pression sur,* to exert pressure on.

pressoir [-swa:r] m. Wine-press (appareil); press-house (local); *pressoir à huile,* oil-press.

pressurage [-syra:ʒ] m. Pressing. ‖ FIG. Extortion.

pressurer [-syre] v. tr. (1). To press (le raisin). ‖ FIG. To wring money out of, to bleed white.

pressurisation [-syrizasjɔ̃] f. Pressurization.

pressuriser [-syrize] v. tr. (1). To pressurize.

prestance [prɛstɑ̃:s] f. Presence, demeanour.

prestataire [prɛstatɛ:r] s. Recipient of an allowance, allocatee. ‖ *Prestataire de services,* company providing services.

prestation [prɛstasjɔ̃] f. JUR. *Prestation de serment,* taking of an oath (par l'assermenté); administration of an oath (par l'assermenteur). ‖ FIN. Tax-money (impôt); required service (travail); *prestations en espèces, en nature,* allowances in money, in kind; *prestations sociales,* social welfare provisions; *prestations familiales,* family allowance. ‖ Offering, gift (échange de dons). ‖ SPORTS., THÉÂTR. Performance; showing.

preste [prɛst] adj. Alert, lively, quick, agile, nimble. (V. AGILE.)

prestement [-təmɑ̃] adv. Nimbly, quickly, deftly.

prestesse [-tɛs] f. Agility, deftness, quickness.

prestidigitateur, trice [prɛstidiʒitatœ:r, tris] s. Conjuror, juggler; prestidigitator.

prestidigitation [-sjɔ̃] f. Conjuring, juggling, legerdemain, sleight-of-hand; prestidigitation.

prestige [prɛsti:ʒ] m. Prestige, glamour (éclat). ‖ Prestige, influence, reputation.

prestigieux, euse [-tiʒjø, ø:z] adj. Dazzling, glamorous, brilliant, splendid, marvellous.

presto [prɛsto] adv. MUS. Presto. ‖ FAM. Double quick.

présumable [prezymabl] adj. Presumable.

présumer [-me] v. tr. (1). To presume, to suppose, to guess; *le coupable présumé,* the supposed culprit; *il est à présumer que,* it is to be supposed (ou) inferred that; *trop présumer de ses forces,* to overestimate one's strength.

présupposé [presypoze] m. Presupposition, assumption.

présupposer v. tr. (1). To presuppose, to assume.

présupposition [-sjɔ̃] f. Presupposition.

présure [prezy:r] f. Rennet.

prêt, ête [prɛ, ɛt] adj. Ready, prepared (à, for); *prêt à fonctionner,* ready to work. ‖ Ready (disposé); *être tout prêt à,* to be willing and ready to. ‖ About, ready (à, to) [sur les limites de]; *être prêt à la révolte,* to be on the verge of revolt. ‖ CULIN. Ready (repas). ‖ FAM. *Fin prêt,* all tuned up, at concert pitch, all set. ‖ Prêt-à-porter, adj. Ready-made, ready-to-wear.

prêt [prɛ] m. Loan (d'un objet). ‖ Lending department (dans une bibliothèque); *exclu du prêt,* not

to be taken away (livre). ‖ FIN. Loan; *prêt à court terme,* short-term loan; *prêt sur salaire, sur titres,* advance on salary, on stocks. ‖ MILIT. Pay. ‖ Prêt-bail, m. Lease-lend.

prêtable [prɛtabl] adj. Lendable, loanable.

prétantaine [pretɑ̃tɛn] f. V. PRÉTENTAINE.

prêté [-te] m. Loan. ‖ FAM. *Un prêté pour un rendu,* tit for tat.

prétendant [pretɑ̃dɑ̃] s. Candidate (à, for) [un poste]. ‖ JUR. Claimant (à, to) [un héritage]; prétender (à, to) [un trône]. ‖ FAM. Suitor (à, for) [la main d'une femme].

prétendre [-tɑ̃:dr] v. tr. (4). To require, to mean (entendre); *il prétend que vous obéissiez,* he means you to obey. ‖ To maintain, to declare (affirmer); *je prétends être dans mon droit,* I maintain I have right on my side. ‖ To pretend, to affect, to claim (assurer prétentieusement); *il prétend savoir le français,* he claims (ou) pretends to know French. ‖ To insinuate (laisser entendre); *on prétend que,* it is rumoured that.
— v. intr. To pretend, to aspire (à, to); *prétendre à la pairie,* to aspire to the peerage. ‖ To lay claim (à, to); *il prétend à la science universelle,* he lays claim to universal knowledge; he thinks he knows everything.
— v. pr. Se prétendre, to say that one is, to profess to be (déclarer être); to claim to be, to pass oneself off for (se faire passer pour).

prétendu, ue [-tɑ̃dy] adj. So-called, would-be, alleged; *ces prétendus spécialistes,* these self-styled specialists; *prétendues preuves,* alleged proofs.
— m. FAM. Future husband (amoureux).

prétendue [-tɑ̃dy] f. FAM. Future wife (fiancée).

prétendument [-tɑ̃dymɑ̃] adv. Allegedly.

prête-nom [prɛtnɔ̃] m. Figurehead, lay-figure. ‖ FIN. Dummy, man of straw.

prétentaine [pretɑ̃tɛn] f. Free living; *courir la pretentaine,* to gad about; to run wild.

prétentieusement [pretɑ̃sjøzmɑ̃] adv. Pretentiously.

prétentieux, euse [-sjø, ø:z] adj. Pretentious, affected, ostentatious. (V. VANITEUX.)
— m. Coxcomb; fop.

prétention [-sjɔ̃] f. Pretention, ambition; *sans prétentions,* unassuming, unpretentious. ‖ Pretention, claim (revendication); *prétentions exorbitantes,* fantastic claims; *avoir des prétentions à,* to lay claim to; *émettre des prétentions,* to claim; *qui a des prétentions artistiques,* arty. ‖ Request (requête).

prêter [prɛte] v. tr. (1). To lend (à, to) [de l'argent]. ‖ To lend, to give, to grant (accorder); *prêter attention à,* to pay attention to; *prêter la main à,* to lend a hand to; *prêter l'oreille à,* to give ear to; *prêter secours,* to lend a helping hand; *prêter secours à qqn,* to go to s.o.'s help. ‖ To attribute (attribuer); *prêter une qualité à qqn,* to credit s.o. with a quality. ‖ To impart, to confer (conférer); *prêter du lustre à,* to add lustre to.
— v. intr. To lend; *prêter à intérêt,* to lend at interest. ‖ To afford matter (à, for); *prêter à discussion,* to be liable to be discussed; *prêter à la plaisanterie,* to invite ridicule. ‖ To give, to stretch (cuir, tissu).
— v. pr. Se prêter, to stretch (cuir). ‖ To lend itself (à, to) [chose]; *se prêter à plusieurs interprétations,* to be open to several constructions. ‖ To be favourable (à, to) [lieu]. ‖ To lend oneself (à, to) [personne]; *se prêter à toutes les expériences,* to be willing to try anything once. ‖ To fall in (à, with); *se prêter à une farce,* to join in a practical joke; *se prêter au rêve,* to give oneself up to one's dreams.

prétérit [preterit] m. GRAMM. Preterite.

prétérition [-risjɔ̃] f. GRAMM., JUR. Preterition.

préteur [pretœ:r] m. † Praetor (à Rome).
prêteur [prɛtœ:r] s. Lender; *prêteur sur gages,* pawnbroker.
— adj. Willing to lend.
prétexte [pretɛkst] m. Pretext (v. EXCUSE); *prendre prétexte que,* to allege (ou) put forward as a pretext that; *sous prétexte que,* under the pretext that, on the pretence that.
prétexte adj. Praetexta (robe).
prétexter [-tɛkste] v. tr. (1). To allege (ou) put forward as a pretext, to pretext.
— v. intr. *Prétexter de,* to give as a pretext.
prétoire [pretwa:r] m. † Praetorium. ‖ JUR. Tribunal; *de prétoire,* forensic (éloquence).
prétorien, enne [-tɔrjɛ̃, ɛn] adj., s. Praetorian.
prêtre [prɛ:tr] m. Priest; *grand prêtre,* high priest. ‖ ECCLÉS. Priest. ‖ **Prêtre-ouvrier,** m. Worker priest.
prêtresse [prɛtrɛs] f. Priestess.
prêtrise [-tri:z] f. ECCLÉS. Priesthood.
preuve [prœ:v] f. Proof, token (marque); *donner des preuves de son dévouement,* to give proof of one's devotion. ‖ Proof, evidence; *preuve absolue,* proof positive; *comme preuve,* by way of proof; *fournir la preuve de,* to produce proof of; *non appuyé de preuves,* non-substantiated. ‖ JUR. Evidence; *preuves extrinsèques, intrinsèques,* external, internal evidence; *commencement de preuves,* prima facie case; *pas de preuves contre,* no case against. ‖ MATH. *Faire la preuve de,* to prove the accuracy of (un calcul); *faire la preuve par neuf,* to cast out the nines. ‖ FIG. Proof; *faire preuve de,* to give proof of, to evince, to manifest; *faire ses preuves,* to prove oneself; to show one's ability (personne); to hold good (solution).
preux [prø] adj., m. invar. Valiant, doughty.
— m. Brave knight.
prévaloir [prevalwa:r] v. intr. (81). To prevail (sur, against); to get the advantage (sur, of); to have the upper hand (sur, over) [v. PRÉDOMINER]; *faire prévaloir son point de vue,* to gain acceptance for one's point of view. ‖ ECCLÉS. To prevail (contre, against).
— v. pr. **Se prévaloir,** to avail oneself (de, of); *se prévaloir de son titre,* to make capital out of one's title. ‖ To pride oneself (de, on) [s'enorgueillir].
prévaricateur, trice [prevarikatœ:r, tris] adj. Dishonest, unjust.
— s. Unjust judge; betrayer of one's trust.
prévarication [-kasjɔ̃] f. Embezzlement.
prévariquer [-ke] v. intr. (1). To violate one's trust.
prévenance [prevnɑ̃:s] f. Considerateness, kindness, obligingness; attention.
prévenant, ante [-nɑ̃, ɑ̃:t] adj. Prepossessing (manières); kind, obliging, considerate, thoughtful (personne). ‖ ECCLÉS. Prevenient (grâce).
prévenir [-ni:r] v. tr. (101). To anticipate, to forestall (une action, un adversaire, une objection); to anticipate (un désir). ‖ To ward off (un danger); to forestall, to prevent, to avert (un malheur); *mieux vaut prévenir que guérir,* prevention is better than cure. ‖ To bias, to prepossess (favorablement); to prejudice (défavorablement); *être prévenu en faveur de,* to have a partiality for; *être prévenu contre,* to have a prejudice against; *son abord prévient en sa faveur,* he has a prepossessing manner. ‖ To warn (v. AVERTIR); to tell (v. AVISER); *prévenez-moi quand vous serez arrivé,* let me know when you have arrived.
— v. pr. **Se prévenir,** to become prejudiced (contre, against); to become prepossessed (pour, in favour of).

— v. récipr. **Se prévenir,** to warn (ou) caution each other (ou) one another.
préventif, ive [prevɑ̃tif, i:v] adj. Preventive; forestalling; *campagne préventive contre les accidents,* accident prevention campaign; *état d'alerte préventive,* state of preparedness; *intervention préventive,* deterrent action. ‖ JUR. *Prison préventive,* remand in custody, imprisonment awaiting trial.
— m. Deterrent. ‖ MÉD. Preventive.
prévention [-sjɔ̃] f. Prevention (empêchement). ‖ Bias (inclination); prepossession (favorable); prejudice (défavorable); *un esprit libre de toute prévention,* an entirely candid (ou) an unbiased mind. ‖ JUR. Confinement pending trial; *faire plusieurs mois de prévention,* to be held for several months awaiting trial.
préventionnaire [-sjɔnɛ:r]. JUR. Person remanded in custody; prisoner awaiting trial.
préventivement [-tivmɑ̃] adv. Preventively. ‖ JUR. Awaiting trial; *détenu préventivement,* committed for trial.
préventorium [-tɔrjɔm] m. MÉD. Preventorium, observation sanatorium.
prévenu, ue [prevny] adj. Prepossessed, predisposed (en faveur de, in favour of); prejudiced (contre, against). ‖ Forewarned (de, of) [averti]. ‖ JUR. Accused (de, of); charged (de, with).
— s. JUR. Indicted (ou) accused person.
préverbe [prevɛrb] m. GRAMM. Verbal prefix.
prévisible [previzibl] adj. Foreseeable.
prévision [-zjɔ̃] f. Prevision, forecast (annonce); foresight, prevision, anticipation (idée); *contrairement à toute prévision,* contrary to all expectations; *en prévision des mauvais jours,* for a rainy day; *en prévision de,* in anticipation of. ‖ FIN. *Prévisions budgétaires,* budgetary estimates.
prévisionnel, elle [-zjɔnɛl] adj. Anticipatory, prospective (analyse); estimated, forecast, previsional (calcul, budget).
prévoir [prevwa:r] v. tr. (82). To foresee (anticiper); *prévoir le temps,* to forecast the weather; *rien ne le faisait prévoir,* we had no warning of it. ‖ JUR. To make provision for; to deal with; *prévoir un cas,* to make provision for a case; *ce cas n'est pas prévu par la loi,* this case does not fall within the scope (ou) purview of the law.
prévôt [prevo] m. † Provost (de, of); *prévôt des marchands,* Dean of the Guild. ‖ MILIT. Assistant Provost Marshal. ‖ SPORTS. *Prévôt de salle,* assistant fencing master.
prévôté [prevote] f. Provostship. ‖ MILIT. Military police.
prévoyance [prevwajɑ̃:s] f. Foresight, forethought (prescience). ‖ Precaution (prudence); *fonds de prévoyance,* reserve fund; *sans prévoyance,* improvident (personne); *société de prévoyance,* provident society.
prévoyant, ante [-jɑ̃, ɑ̃:t] adj. Provident, foreseeing, far-sighted, thoughtful; *peu prévoyant,* improvident, imprudent.
prévu, ue [prevy] adj. Foreseen (avenir); *comme prévu,* as anticipated. ‖ Provided, allowed, earmarked (pour, for); *prévu par les statuts,* provided by the articles of association.
prie-Dieu [pridjø] m. invar. ECCLÉS. Kneeling-chair, prie-Dieu, prayer-stool.
prier [prije] v. tr. (1). To pray to (Dieu, une divinité). ‖ To pray, to ask, to beg (demander); *écoutez-moi, je vous prie,* do listen to me, please; *je vous prie d'accepter mes sincères condoléances,* please accept my sincere sympathy. ‖ To ask, to supplicate, to entreat (implorer); *je vous prie de me pardonner,* I entreat you to forgive me. ‖ To request, to invite (inviter); *on vous prie de ne pas fumer,* you are requested not to smoke. ‖ To press, to urge (pousser); *elle veut se faire*

prier, she is making a show of reluctance; *sans se faire prier*, without any pressing, willingly. ‖ To pray (formule de politesse); *je vous prie*, please; *puis-je fermer la porte?* — *je vous en prie*, may I shut the door? — please do; *pardon!* — *je vous en prie*, I beg your pardon! — not at all!, granted!; *voulez-vous· me passer le sel, je vous prie?*, may I trouble you for the salt? ‖ To invite (inviter); *prier qqn à dîner*, to invite s.o. to dinner.
— v. intr. To pray (*pour*, for).

prière [-jɛ:r] f. ECCLÉS. Prayer (v. ORAISON); *prière en commun*, family prayers; *en prière*, at prayers; *livre de prières*, prayer-book. ‖ Prayer, request, entreaty (sollicitation); *céder aux prières de qqn*, to give way to s.o.'s entreaties. ‖ LOC. *Prière de ne pas fumer*, you are requested not to smoke; no smoking; *prière de fermer la porte*, please shut the door.

prieur [prijœ:r] m. ECCLÉS. Prior.

prieure [-jø:r] f. ECCLÉS. Prioress.

prieuré [-jœre] m. ECCLÉS. Priorship (fonction); priory (lieu).

primaire [primɛ:r] adj. Primary, elementary (école); primary (couleur, industries, élection). ‖ ELECTR. Primary (circuit). ‖ GÉOL. Primary, palaeozoic (ère). ‖ JUR. *Délinquant primaire*, first offender. ‖ FAM. Half-educated, narrow-minded.
— m. Primary school, primary education. ‖ Primary industries. ‖ ELECTR. Primary coil, primary. ‖ GÉOL. Primary, Palaeozoic.

primaire f. Primary (élection).

primarité [-marite] f. Primariness.

primat [prima] m. ECCLÉS. Primate. ‖ FIG. Primacy (d'une fonction).

primate [primat] m. ZOOL. Primate.

primauté [primote] f. ECCLÉS. Primacy. ‖ FIG. Primacy, pre-eminence. (V. SUPÉRIORITÉ.)

prime [prim] adj. First (fleur); early (jeunesse). ‖ LOC. *De prime abord*, at first sight; from the outset; *dans sa prime fleur*, in one's prime.

prime f. Bonus, bounty, subsidy (gratification); *prime de rendement*, output bonus; *prime journalière*, daily allowance. ‖ COMM. Premium; bounty; *prime d'importation*, bounty on imports; *prime de remboursement*, redemption premium. ‖ MILIT. *Prime de démobilisation*, gratuity on demobilization; U. S. mustering-out pay; *prime de rengagement*, bounty on re-enlistment. ‖ FIN. Premium (bénéfice, plus-value); *prime d'assurance*, insurance premium; *faire prime*, to be at a premium. ‖ FIN. Option money (en Bourse); *marché à prime*, option market. ‖ FIG. Encouragement (à, to); *faire prime*, to be highly appreciated.

primer [-me] v. tr. (1). To surpass, to outdo, to excel; *le droit doit primer la force*, right must take precedence over might. ‖ To take the lead of; *primer tous les concurrents*, to be ahead of all competitors. ‖ FIN. To premium. ‖ JUR. To have priority over; *primer qqn en hypothèque*, to rank before s.o. in claim of mortgaged property.
— v. intr. To take the lead (ou) the first place, to rank first, to come uppermost; *c'est la force qui prime*, force gets the upper hand.

primer [-me] v. tr. (1). To award a prize to; *roman primé*, prize-winning novel. ‖ AGRIC. *Bœuf primé*, prize ox.

primerose [primro:z] f. BOT. Hollyhock, rosemallow.

primesautier [primsotje] adj. Quick, ready, versatile (esprit); quick-witted, impulsive (personne). [V. SPONTANÉ.]

primeur [primœ:r] f. Newness (nouveauté). ‖ AGRIC. Early season (époque); early vegetables (produits); *asperges en primeur*, early asparagus. ‖ THÉÂTR. *Pièce dans sa primeur*, play when it

is first performed. ‖ FIG. Newness; *primeur d'une nouvelle sensationnelle*, scoop (fam.).

primevère [primvɛ:r] f. BOT. Primrose, primula.

primipare [primipa:r] adj. MÉD. Primiparous.
— f. MÉD. Primipara.

primitif, ive [-tif, i:v] adj. Original, primeval, pristine, earliest (état); primitive (être); unpolished, rude, crude, rough (mœurs). ‖ GRAMM. Early (langue); primitive (syllabe, temps). ‖ GÉOL. Primitive (roche). ‖ ECCLÉS. Early, ancient (église). ‖ ARTS. Primitive (art).
— m. ARTS. Primitive.

primitivement [-tivmã] adv. Primitively, originally.

primo [primo] adv. Primo, first, in the first place.

primogéniture [-ʒenity:r] f. Primogeniture.

primo-infection [-ɛ̃fɛksjɔ̃] f. MÉD. Primary infection.

primordial, ale [primɔrdjal] adj. Primordial, primeval, original (originel). ‖ Fundamental, essential, primordial (essentiel). ‖ FAM. Most important.

primordialement [-mã] adv. Primordially.

prince [prɛ̃:s] m. Prince; *prince consort*, prince consort. ‖ ECCLÉS. Prince (de l'Eglise). ‖ FAM. *Bon prince*, easy-going; *comme un prince*, sumptuously. ‖ **Prince-de-Galles**, m. Chequered cloth in different shades of the same colour.

princeps [prɛ̃sɛps] adj. First, original (édition).

princesse [-sɛs] f. Princess. ‖ *Dentelle princesse*, appliqué lace. ‖ FAM. *Aux frais de la princesse*, paid by the Government, at State expense.

princier, ère [-sje, ɛr] adj. Princely.

principal, ale [prɛ̃sipal] adj. Principal, chief, leading, main; *principaux personnages*, leading characters; *principal secteur*, key sector; *porte principale*, front door; *recherche principale*, main research. ‖ JUR. *Associé principal*, senior partner; *clerc* (ou) *commis principal*, head (ou) U. S. chief clerk; *principal créancier*, chief creditor; *principal locataire*, head lessee, immediate tenant. ‖ GRAMM. *Proposition principale*, principal (ou) main clause. ‖ MATH. Principal. ‖ ELECTR. Main.
— m. Headmaster (d'un collège); principal (d'une école normale). ‖ Main (ou) chief (ou) principal thing (ou) point (chose principale). ‖ FIN. Principal, capital sum. (V. CAPITAL.)

principalement [-mã] adv. Principally, chiefly, mainly, in the main.

principat [prɛ̃sipa] m. Principate.

principauté [-pote] f. Principality, princedom.

principe [prɛ̃sip] m. Principle, natural law (loi); *le principe de toutes ces expériences est le même*, the principle of all these experiments is the same. ‖ Principle, beginning, root (commencement); *dès le principe*, from the outset. ‖ Principle, premise, basic argument (donnée); *partir du même principe*, to start from the same initial datum; *poser en principe que*, to make it a matter of principle that; *poser un principe contestable*, to make a debatable assumption. ‖ Principle, settled rule (règle); *principes directeurs*, policy; *avoir pour principe de*, to make a point of; *en, par principe*, in, on principle, theoretically; *nous avons pour principe de*, our policy is to. ‖ MATH. Principle, original element (ou) law; *principe d'Archimède*, Archimedean principle; *les principes de l'algèbre*, the basic elements of algebra. ‖ CHIM. Principle, constituent. ‖ FIG. Pl. Principles, rules of conduct; *sans principes*, unprincipled (personne).

printanier, ère [prɛ̃tanje, ɛ:r] adj. Spring; spring-like. ‖ FIG. Youthful.

printemps [-tã] m. Spring; *au printemps*, in the spring; *au début du printemps*, in early spring; *de printemps*, vernal (équinoxe). ‖ FIG. Springtime, heyday (de la vie).

printing [printiɲ] m. Fam. Teleprinter, tape-machine.

priorat [priɔra] m. Ecclés. Priorship.

prioritaire [-ritɛːr] adj. Priority-holder, priority ; *être prioritaire*, to have a prior right. ‖ Fin. Pre-emptive (achat) ; preference (action). — s. Priority-holder.

priorité [-rite] f. Priority (*sur*, over). ‖ Priority, right to pass first (dans une file d'attente). ‖ Autom. Right to take the road, right of way ; *route de priorité*, major road ; *vous avez la priorité*, it's your road (fam.). ‖ Jur. Priority, prece-dence, ranking. ‖ Fin. *Action de priorité*, priority (ou) preference share.

pris, ise [pri, iz] adj. Taken, caught (objet). ‖ Occupied (place) ; taken up (temps) ; *il est très pris*, he is very busy. ‖ Shaped (taille) ; *elle a la taille bien prise*, she has a good figure. ‖ Under the influence of ; *pris de vin*, intoxicated, the worse for drink. ‖ Méd. *Avoir la gorge prise*, to have a sore throat ; *avoir la voix prise*, to be hoarse. ‖ Culin. Congealed (gelée). — p. p. V. PRENDRE (80).

prise [priːz] f. Grasp, hold (possibilité de saisir) ; *lâcher prise*, to lose one's hold ; *n'avoir pas de prise*, to offer no hold (objet) ; to have no pur-chase (personne). ‖ Take, catch (objet saisi) ; *une bonne prise*, a good catch ; *prise de tabac*, pinch of snuff. ‖ Catching, taking (action de saisir). ‖ Pl. Grips, dispute, fighting (querelle) ; *aux prises avec*, at grips with ; *en venir aux prises*, to get to grips ; *mettre aux prises*, to set by the ears ; *prise de bec*, bickering, row. ‖ Milit. Taking, capture (de prisonniers, d'une ville) ; storming (d'une position) ; taking up (d'un poste) ; *prise d'armes*, ceremonial parade. ‖ Naut. Prize ; *cour des prises*, prize-court ; *équipage de prise*, prize crew ; *être de bonne prise*, to be lawful prize ; *part de prise*, prize-money. ‖ Aviat. *Prise d'air*, air-scoop. ‖ Autom. *Etre en prise*, to be engaged ; *mettre en prise*, to engage ; *monter une côte en prise*, to climb a hill in top gear. ‖ Techn. Setting (du ciment, du plâtre) ; *faire prise*, to set ; *prise d'air*, air-inlet ; *prise d'eau*, hydrant ; main ; water-crane ; offtake. ‖ Méd. Dose (d'un médi-cament) ; *faire une prise de sang*, to take a blood specimen ; *prise de sang*, blood-taking. ‖ Electr. *Prise de courant*, intake of current (action) ; wall-plug (instrument) ; *prise de terre*, earth- (ou) U. S. ground connection. ‖ Jur. *Prise de posses-sion*, entering (ou) entry upon possession. ‖ Radio. *Prise de vue directe*, live broadcast (en télévision). ‖ Ciném. *Prise de son*, recording ; *prises de vues*, taking of pictures, shooting of the film. ‖ Fig. Catching ; *aux prises avec les diffi-cultés*, fighting against difficulties ; *donner prise à*, to expose oneself to, to lay oneself open to ; *on n'a pas de prise sur lui*, there is no catching him.

priser [prize] v. tr. (1). To appraise, to value (évaluer). ‖ To prize, to value (apprécier) ; to set store by (un objet précieux) ; to rate highly, to hold in high esteem (qqn).

priser v. tr. (1). To snuff up (du camphre) ; *priser du tabac*, to take snuff. — v. intr. To take snuff.

priseur [-zœːr] m. Jur. Appraiser, valuer ; *com-missaire-priseur*, auctioneer, official valuer.

priseur, euse s. Snuff-taker.

prismatique [prismatik] adj. Prismatic.

prisme [prism] m. Prism.

prison [prizɔ̃] f. Jur. Prison, gaol, jail (lieu) ; *aller en prison*, to go to jail ; *s'évader de prison*, to escape from prison. ‖ Jur. Imprisonment, confinement (détention) ; *prison perpétuelle*, life sentence, imprisonment for life ; *faire de la pri-son*, to be in prison, to do time. ‖ Milit. Prison

militaire, detention centre ; glass-house (fam.) ; *faire deux jours de prison*, to do two days in the cells.

prisonnier [-zɔnje] s. Prisoner. ‖ Jur. Prisoner, captive ; *se constituer prisonnier*, to give oneself up. ‖ Milit. *Prisonnier de guerre*, prisoner of war ; *camp de prisonniers*, prison camp ; *faire qqn prisonnier*, to take s.o. prisoner. — adj. Jur. Imprisoned. ‖ Milit. Captive.

privatif, ive [privatif, iːv] adj. Gramm. Priva-tive. — m. Gramm. Privative prefix.

privation [-sjɔ̃] f. Deprivation, privation (v. absence, perte) ; *privation de sortie*, gating (fam.). ‖ Privation (insuffisance) ; want (manque) ; *s'imposer des privations*, to deprive oneself. ‖ Méd. Loss (de la vue). ‖ Jur. Forfeiture (des droits civils).

privatisation [-tizasjɔ̃] f. Jur. Denationali-zation.

privatiser [-tize] v. tr. (1). Jur. To denatio-nalize.

privautés [privote] f. pl. Undue familiarity, liberties.

privé, ée [prive] adj. Private (entreprise, intérêt, réunion, vie) ; *mur de la vie privée*, privacy. — m. Private life.

priver v. tr. (1). To deprive (*de*, of) ; to debar (*de*, from) ; *cela vous prive-t-il ?*, do you miss it ? ; *privé de*, bereft of, without. — v. pr. **Se priver**, to deny oneself ; *se priver de*, to deprive oneself of, to do without, to abstain from.

privilège [privilɛːʒ] m. Privilege (prérogative) ; *avoir le privilège de*, to be entitled to. ‖ Privilege (droit exclusif) ; *avoir le privilège de*, to be privileged to. ‖ Jur. Lien, preference, charge ; *privilège de créancier*, creditor's preferential claim ; *privilège d'hypothèque*, mortgage charge. ‖ Fin. *Privilège de banque*, bank charter ; *action sans privilège*, ex all share.

privilégié, ée [-leʒje] adj. Privileged ; favoured. ‖ Fin. Preferred, preference (action). — s. Privileged person.

privilégier v. tr. (1). To privilege, to grant a privilege to.

prix [pri] m. Price, cost (coût) ; *au prix d'une fortune*, at enormous cost. ‖ Price (tarif) ; *à bas prix*, at a low price ; *dans mes prix*, within my means ; *hors de prix*, at an exorbitant price ; *faire un prix*, to give special terms ; *mettre le prix*, to pay the price ; *magasin à prix unique*, one-price store ; *repas à prix fixe*, table-d'hôte meal ; *restaurant à prix fixe*, restaurant with fixed charges. ‖ Comm. Price ; *prix d'achat, de vente*, purchase, selling price ; *prix coûtant* (ou) *de revient*, cost price ; *prix de détail, de gros*, retail, wholesale price ; *prix imposé*, agreed fair price ; *prix fort*, full price ; *prix minimum*, reserve price ; *prix net*, net (ou) trade price ; *faire connaître ses conditions de prix à qqn pour*, to quote s.o. a price for. ‖ Fin. Rate (en Bourse) ; *prix du change*, premium ; *prix d'émission*, issue price ; *prix des reports*, contango (ou) continuation rate. ‖ Jur. *Mise à prix*, upset price (d'un domaine) ; reserve price (aux enchères) ; *mettre la tête d'un homme à prix*, to set a price on a man's head. ‖ Price, charge (débours) ; *prix d'un billet* (ou) *d'une course*, fare ; *prix d'un colis postal*, charge by parcel post. ‖ Prize (distinction) ; *prix Nobel*, Nobel Prize. ‖ Reward ; prize (récompense) ; *le prix du dévouement*, the reward of devotion. ‖ Sports. Stakes (paris) ; *le grand prix*, the cham-pionship race. ‖ Fig. Value (valeur) ; *attacher un grand prix à*, to value highly, to set a high price on ; *n'avoir pas de prix*, to be invaluable. ‖ **Prix**

courant, m. COMM. Price-list. ‖ **Prix fixe,** m. Fixed-price restaurant.

pro [pro] m. SPORTS., FAM. Pro.

probabilisme [probabilism] m. PHILOS. Probabilism.

probabilité [-lite] f. Probability; *selon toute probabilité,* in all likelihood.

probable [probabl] adj. Probable, likely; *ce n'est guère probable,* it's hardly likely; *il est peu probable qu'il vienne,* he is not likely to come.

probablement [-bləmã] adv. Probably, in all likelihood; *il répondra très probablement,* he is very likely to answer.

probant, ante [probã, ã:t] adj. Convincing; *peu probant,* unconvincing.

probation [basjõ] f. JUR., ECCLÉS. Probation.

probatoire [-batwa:r] adj. Probationary, preliminary (examen, test). ‖ JUR. Probative (fait, force).

probe [prob] adj. Upright. (V. HONNÊTE.)

probité [-bite] f. Uprightness, honesty, probity; *être la probité même,* to be the soul of honesty.

problématique [problematik] adj. Problematical (issue); questionable, doubtful (sens).

problématique f. Field of enquiry, problems set.

problème [problɛm] m. Problem, enigma, puzzle, riddle (énigme). ‖ MATH. Sum (d'enfant); problem (d'algèbre, de géométrie). ‖ FIG. *Problème du logement,* housing problem.

procédé [prosede] m. Process, method (de fabrication). ‖ SPORTS. Tip (de queue de billard). ‖ FIG. Proceeding, dealing, action; *bons procédés,* civilities, fair dealings; *procédé honnête,* straightforward proceeding; *procédé de style,* trick of style, stylistic device; *vilains procédés,* unsavoury manœuvres, crooked methods.

procéder v. intr. (5). To proceed, to rise, to originate, to come, to flow (*de,* from). ‖ To proceed, to pass on (*à,* to); *procéder à une enquête, une expérience,* to conduct an inquiry, an experiment. ‖ To behave, to act, to demean oneself (agir); *façon de procéder,* behaviour, way of dealing (*avec,* with). ‖ JUR. To proceed (*contre,* against).

procédure [-dy:r] f. JUR. Procedure; *procédure civile,* civil proceedings; *procédure judiciaire,* judicial settlement.

procédurier [-dyrje] adj. JUR. Skilled in procedure. ‖ FAM. Pettifogging.

— s. JUR. Skilful practitioner. ‖ FAM. Pettifogger.

procès [prosɛ] m. MÉD. Process, method (processus). ‖ JUR. Case; *procès civil,* civil action, lawsuit; *procès criminel,* trial, criminal proceedings; *hors de procès,* nonsuited. ‖ FAM. *Sans autre forme de procès,* without more ado. ‖ **Procès-verbal,** m. Minutes, record (de séance); police officer's report, official statement (pour pénalité); *procès-verbal de carence,* memorandum of nulla bona; *dresser procès-verbal,* to draw up a report, to take down s.o.'s name and address, to make a report on s.o.

processif, ive [-sif, i:v] adj. Litigious, pettifogging. ‖ JUR. Of legal procedure (formes).

procession [prosɛsjõ] f. Procession. ‖ ECCLÉS. Procession; *suivant la procession,* walking in procession.

processionnaire [-sjonɛ:r] adj. Processionary. — f. ZOOL. Processionary caterpillar.

processionnel, elle [-sjonɛl] adj. Processional.

processionnellement [-sjonɛlmã] adv. Processionally.

processionner [-sjone] v. intr. (1). To process, to procession.

processus [prosɛsys] m. Process, method. ‖ Progress, march (d'une évolution). ‖ MÉD. Progress; evolution.

prochain, aine [proʃɛ̃, ɛn] adj. Nearest (très proche); next (suivant); neighbouring (voisin); *la prochaine fois,* next time; *la ville prochaine,* the neighbouring town. ‖ Near (dans le temps); *arrivée prochaine,* impending arrival; *fin prochaine,* coming (ou) proximate end; *prochain départ,* approaching departure. ‖ Direct, immediate; *cause prochaine,* proximate (ou) direct (ou) immediate cause. ‖ COMM. Next (livraison).

— m. Neighbour, fellow-creature (ou) -being (ou) -man.

prochainement [-ʃɛnmã] adv. In a short time, at an early date, before long, by and by, in a while, presently. (V. BIENTÔT.)

proche [proʃ] adj. Near, close (lieu); *la boulangerie la plus proche,* the nearest baker's shop (ou) U. S. bakery; *proche de la ville,* close to the town, near the town, adjoining the town. ‖ Near, close (temps); *l'heure est proche où,* the hour is near (ou) at hand when. ‖ Near (par le sang); *proches parents,* near kindred (ou) relatives; close family; *mes plus proches parents,* my next of kin. ‖ GÉOGR. *Proche Orient,* Near East. ‖ LOC. *De proche en proche,* by degrees.

— adv. FAM. Near; *tout proche,* hard by, close at hand. (V. PRÈS.)

— m. pl. Relations, relatives, next of kin.

proclamateur, trice [proklamatœ:r, tris] s. Proclaimer.

proclamation [-masjõ] f. Proclamation; *faire une proclamation,* to issue a proclamation.

proclamer [-me] v. tr. (1). To proclaim, to bruit about, to blazon forth, to spread about (répandre); *proclamer sur tous les toits,* to proclaim from the house-tops. ‖ To proclaim, to declare, to announce (annoncer); *proclamer les résultats du scrutin,* to declare the poll, to announce the results of the election. ‖ JUR. To publish (un édit).

proclitique [proklitik] adj., m. GRAMM. Proclitic.

proclivité [proklivite] f. Inclination, slope.

proconsul [prokõsyl] m. † Proconsul.

proconsulat [-la] m. † Proconsulship (fonction); proconsulate.

procréateur, trice [prokreatœ:r, tris] adj. Procreative.

— s. Procreator, parent.

— m. Sire, begetter.

procréation [-kreasjõ] f. Procreation, begetting.

procréer [-kree] v. tr. (1). To procreate.

procurable [prokyrabl] adj. Procurable.

procurateur [-ratœ:r] m. Procurator.

procuration [-rasjõ] f. ECCLÉS. Procuration. ‖ JUR. Procuration, letters procuratory, power of attorney; *procuration pour voter,* proxy; *donner procuration à,* to confer powers of attorney on, to empower; *par procuration,* by (ou) per procuration; by proxy.

procuratrice [-ratris] f. ECCLÉS. Procuratrix.

procurer [-re] v. tr. (1). To procure, to get, to furnish, to obtain.

— v. pr. **Se procurer,** to procure, to find; *où peut-on se procurer un petit chien?,* where can I get a puppy?

procureur [-rœ:r] m. Procurer (procurateur). ‖ JUR. Attorney at law; *procureur de la République,* Public Prosecutor (en Angleterre); Procurator fiscal (en Ecosse); U. S. district attorney; *procureur général,* Attorney-General (en Amérique, en Angleterre); Lord Advocate (en Ecosse). ‖ ECCLÉS. Bursar.

procureuse [-rø:z] f. FAM. Procuress (proxénète).

prodigalement [prodigalmã] adv. Prodigally.

prodigalité [-lite] f. Prodigality; extravagance, lavishness, wastefulness; squandermania (fam.).

prodige [prodi:ʒ] m. Prodigy, wonder (v. MERVEILLE); *faire des prodiges,* to work wonders.

— adj. Prodigy; *enfant prodige,* child prodigy; U. S. boy wonder.

prodigieusement [-diʒøzmã] adv. Prodigiously.
prodigieux, euse [-diʒjø, ø:z] adj. Prodigious, wonderful. ‖ FAM. Fabulous, enormous, amazing.
prodigiosité [-diʒjozite] f. Prodigiousness.
prodigue [prɔdig] adj. Prodigal; extravagant (*de*, with); wasteful (*de*, of); *prodigue de son argent*, free with one's money. ‖ Prodigal, lavish, unsparing (*de*, of); *prodigue de louanges*, lavish of praise. ‖ *L'enfant prodigue*, the Prodigal Son.
— s. Prodigal, spendthrift, waster, wastrel.
prodiguer [-ge] v. tr. (1). To waste, to squander, to throw away (de l'argent). ‖ To lavish, to give unstintingly (son affection); *il ne prodigue pas ses paroles*, he is a man of few words.
— v. pr. **Se prodiguer**, to lay oneself out (*auprès de*, for); to make oneself cheap (avec excès); *se prodiguer en compliments*, to pour out honeyed phrases.
pro domo [prodomo] adj. inv. In defence of one's own cause.
prodrome [prɔdro:m] m. Prodrome, preface. ‖ MÉD. Prodrome, premonitory symptom.
producteur, trice [prɔdyktœ:r, tris] adj. AGRIC. Producing (région); *producteur de*, productive of, bearing, yielding. ‖ FIN. *Producteur d'intérêts*, bearing interest.
— s. AGRIC. Grower; *producteur de fruits*, fruit-grower, orchardist. ‖ CINÉM. Producer.
productible [-tibl] adj. Producible.
productif, ive [-tif, i:v] adj. Producive.
production [-sjɔ̃] f. AGRIC. Production, growing (de blé); production, producing (de légumes); produce (produits). ‖ TECHN. Extraction (du charbon); generation (du gaz). ‖ TECHN. Production, producing (action); production, yield, output (rendement) [d'une usine]. ‖ JUR. Bringing forward (d'arguments, de témoins); production, exhibition (de pièces); adduction (de preuves). ‖ THÉÂTR. Production; *directeur de production*, producer. ‖ MUS. *Production de la voix*, voice production.
productivité [-tivite] f. Productivity; productiveness; yield-capacity.
produire [prɔdɥi:r] v. tr. (85). To produce, to bring forth, to give birth to (engendrer). ‖ To produce, to bring forth (une œuvre littéraire); to bring forth, to give birth to (un talent). ‖ To produce, to cause, to work (un effet), to bring about (une modification). ‖ To produce, to show, to bring out (qqn). ‖ AGRIC. To yield (une récolte); to yield, to bear (un rejeton). ‖ TECHN. To produce (du charbon); to manufacture, to make (des objets fabriqués); to generate (de la vapeur). ‖ JUR. To produce (des pièces); to adduce (des preuves); to bring forward (des témoins); to exhibit (ses titres). ‖ FIN. To bring in, to yield (des intérêts). ‖ CINÉM. To produce (un film).
— v. pr. **Se produire**, to be brought about (changement); to take place, to happen, to occur (événement); to arise (révolution). ‖ To show oneself (en société). ‖ THÉÂTR. To appear (sur la scène).
produit [-dɥi] m. Product (en général). ‖ Offspring (d'un animal). ‖ AGRIC. Pl. Produce. ‖ TECHN. Manufactured article (dans l'industrie); *produit accessoire* (ou) *secondaire*, by-product. ‖ CHIM. *Produits de beauté*, beauty preparations, cosmetics; *produits chimiques*, chemicals. ‖ COMM. Goods (denrées). ‖ FIN. Profit, proceeds (bénéfices, revenus); takings, receipts (recettes); *produit d'un capital*, yield of (ou) interest on (ou) income from a capital. ‖ MATH. Product.
proème [prɔɛm] m. Proem.
proéminence [prɔeminã:s] f. Protuberance, projection, bulge. ‖ FIG. Prominence, prominency.
proéminent, ente [-nã, ã:t] adj. Projecting, prominent, bulging, jutting out (saillant). ‖ FIG. Prominent (supérieur).

prof [prɔf] s. FAM. Teacher.
profanateur, trice [prɔfanatœ:r, tris] s. Profaner.
profanation [-sjɔ̃] f. ECCLÉS. Profanation, desecration. ‖ FAM. Misuse, defilement.
profane [prɔfan] adj. Sacrilegious (acte); impious, unholy (conduite). ‖ Profane, secular, worldly (art, littérature). ‖ Lay (personne).
— s. Uninitiated person, layman (non initié). ‖ FAM. Ignoramus, outsider.
profaner [-ne] v. tr. (1). ECCLÉS. To profane, to desecrate (un lieu saint). ‖ JUR. To violate (une tombe). ‖ FIG. To defile, to pollute (l'innocence); to abuse, to misuse (son talent).
proférer [prɔfere] v. tr. (5). To pour forth (des insultes); to utter (des paroles).
professer [prɔfɛse] v. tr. To declare, to put forth (une opinion); *professer être*, to set up to be, to boast of being. ‖ To exercise, to follow (un métier). ‖ To profess, to teach (une science). ‖ ECCLÉS. To profess (une religion).
— v. intr. To profess, to teach; *professer à l'Ecole de guerre*, to be an instructor at the Staff College.
professeur [-sœ:r] m. Teacher, master (de collège); professor, lecturer (d'université); *professeur adjoint*, assistant master (au lycée); *mon professeur de chant*, my singing master. ‖ *Femme professeur*, mistress, teacher (de collège); lady professor, lecturer (d'université); *mon professeur de dessin*, my drawing mistress. ‖ Professor (d'une opinion).
profession [-sjɔ̃] f. Occupation, calling, trade (métier); *profession libérale*, liberal profession; *appartenant à une profession libérale*, professional; *les membres des professions libérales*, the professional classes; *sans profession*, housewife (femme); independent, of private means (homme). ‖ Profession, declaration; *profession de foi*, declaration of political tenets (en politique); *faire profession de libéralisme*, to set up as a liberal, to proclaim oneself a liberal, to boast of being a liberal. ‖ ECCLÉS. Profession (de foi).
professionnalisme [-sjonalism] m. Professionalism.
professionnel, elle [-sjonɛl] adj. Professional, vocational; *école professionnelle*, technical school; *formation professionnelle*, training; *orientation professionnelle*, vocational guidance; *syndicat professionnel*, Trade Union; *test professionnel*, vocational test. ‖ MÉD. Occupational (maladie).
— s. Professional.
professionnellement [-sjonɛlmã] adv. Professionally.
professoral, ale [-sɔral] adj. Professorial.
professorat [-sɔra] m. Mastership, mistress-ship (de collège); professorship (d'université). ‖ Teacher's calling, teaching profession; *faire cinq ans de professorat*, to spend five years as a teacher.
profil [prɔfil] m. Profile, side-face; *de profil*, in profile. ‖ AUTOM. *Profil aérodynamique*, aerofoil section. ‖ AVIAT. Section. ‖ FIG. *Profil de l'horizon*, skyline; *profil littéraire*, profile; *profil du terrain*, contour.
profilé, ée [-le] adj. TECHN. Shaped (pièce). ‖ AUTOM., AVIAT. Streamlined.
— m. TECHN. Section.
profilée [-le] f. Row, range. (V. FILE, RANGÉE.)
profiler [-le] v. tr. (1). To profile, to draw in profile (une silhouette, un visage). ‖ ARCHIT. To profile, to give a sectional view of (une corniche). ‖ TECHN. To cut, to shape (une pièce); *profiler au tour*, to cut on a lathe.
— v. pr. **Se profiler**, to be outlined; *se profiler sur les nuages*, to stand out against the clouds.
profit [prɔfi] m. Advantage, profit (avantage); *au profit de*, in favour (ou) aid of, for the benefit of, to the advantage of; *à mon profit*, to my own

advantage; *mettre à profit*, to profit by, to turn to account; *tirer profit de*, to benefit by; *tout lui est profit*, everything is grist that comes to his mill; *y trouver son profit*, to get sth. out of it. ‖ Comm. Profit, benefit; *profit illicite*, illicit profit; *sans profit*, without returns, unprofitable (vente). ‖ Fig. Profit, benefit, improvement (v. bénéfice); *ce livre ne vous sera d'aucun profit*, that book will not improve your knowledge, you will reap no benefit from that book.

profitable [-tabl] adj. Profitable, advantageous. ‖ Comm. Paying, lucrative, gainful.

profitablement [-tabləmã] adv. Profitably, advantageously.

profiter [-te] v. intr. To grow, to put on weight (grossir); *ce bébé profite bien*, the baby is thriving, the baby is filling out apace. ‖ To be profitable (*à*, to); *profiter à*, to profit, to benefit (qqn). ‖ To avail oneself (*de*, of); *profiter de l'occasion*, to turn the occasion to account. ‖ To bring in a profit; *profiter des bons conseils*, to profit by good advice; *le voyage vous profitera*, the journey will be profitable to you; *il faut profiter de votre séjour en France*, you must make the most of your stay in France. ‖ Comm. To profit, to benefit (*de*, by); to draw profit (*de*, from).

profiterole [prɔfitrɔl] f. Culin. Profiterole.

profiteur, euse [-tœ:r, ø:z] s. Comm. Beneficiary, profit-taker. ‖ Fig. Profiteer; *profiteur de guerre*, war-profiteer.

profond, onde [prɔfɔ̃, ɔ̃:d] adj. Deep (en général); *profond de deux mètres*, two metres deep; *ruisseau peu profond*, shallow brook. ‖ Profound, thick (obscurité); deep, sound (sommeil). ‖ Deep, low (salut). ‖ Fig. Deep (cause, intérêt, mystère); profound, wide (différence); utter (ignorance); deep, heartfelt (respect); deep, profound, great, strong (sentiment).
— m. Bottom. (V. fond.) ‖ Depth. (V. profondeur.) ‖ Fig. *Au plus profond de mon âme*, in the bottom of my heart; *au plus profond du désespoir*, in the depths of despair; *au profond de la nuit*, at dead of night, in the dead of night.
— adv. Deep.

profonde [-fɔ̃:d] f. Pop. Pocket.

profondément [-fɔ̃demã] adv. Deeply, soundly (dormir); deeply (éprouver); intensely (mépriser); deep (pénétrer); intently (réfléchir); low (saluer).

profondeur [-fɔ̃dœ:r] f. Depth; *manque de profondeur*, shallowness; *trois cents pieds de profondeur*, three hundred feet in depth. ‖ Pl. Depths. ‖ Fig. Profundity (de l'esprit); profoundness, deepness (d'un mystère); profundity, depth, extent (du savoir); *manquer de profondeur*, to be superficial.

pro forma [prɔfɔrma] adj. inv. Comm. Pro forma (facture).

profusion [-zjɔ̃] f. Profusion, plenty (v. abondance); *à profusion*, plentifully, in plenty. ‖ Profusion, extravagance, lavishness (v. prodigalité); *à profusion*, unstintingly, lavishly.

progéniture [prɔʒenity:r] f. Progeniture, progeny, offspring.

progestérone [prɔʒɛsterɔn] f. Méd. Progesterone.

prognathe [prɔgnat] adj. Méd. Underhung (mâchoire); prognathous, prognathic (personne).
— s. Méd. Person with undershot jaw.

programmateur, trice [prɔgramatœ:r, tris] s. Radio. Programme planner (ou) manager.
— m. Cybern., Inform. Programmer (appareil). ‖ Techn. Timer (d'une cuisinière).

programmation [-sjɔ̃] f. Radio. Programming. ‖ Inform. Programming; *langage de programmation*, programming language.

programme [prɔgram] m. Programme, syllabus, curriculum, U. S. program (scolaire); *ayant au*

programme, featuring. ‖ Programme, platform (en politique). ‖ Programme (d'une réunion). ‖ Radio., Mus., Théâtr. Programme; *programme des auditeurs*, request programme. ‖ Inform. Program.

programmé, ée [-me] adj. Programmed, scheduled; *enseignement programmé*, programmed learning.

programmer v. tr. (1). To programme, to schedule. ‖ Inform. To program.

programmeur, euse [-mœ:r, ø:z] s. Inform. Programmer (personne).

progrès [prɔgrɛ] m. Improvement (d'un élève); *en progrès*, improving; *faire des progrès*, to improve, to come on. ‖ Progress, advancement (d'une affaire, de la science); *partisan du progrès*, progressive; *suivre les progrès de*, to keep track of (une affaire); to keep abreast of (science).

progresser [-se] v. intr. (1). To progress, to advance, to make progress (ou) headway (avancer). ‖ To come on, to improve (s'améliorer).

progressif, ive [-sif, i:v] adj. Progressive, graduated, gradual; *avec numérotage progressif*, numbered in succession. ‖ Fin. *Barème progressif*, progressive scale; *surtaxe progressive*, graduated surtax.

progression [-sjɔ̃] f. Progression, progress, advance (avance). ‖ Math. Progression.

progressiste [-sist] adj. Progressive (parti).
— s. Progressist, progressive.

progressivement [-sivmã] adv. Progressively.

progressivité [-sivite] f. Progressiveness.

prohibé, ée [prɔibe] adj. Sports. *Temps prohibé*, close (ou) U. S. closed season (pour la chasse). ‖ Jur. Prohibited (degré); *port d'armes prohibé*, illegal carrying of weapons.

prohiber v. tr. (1). To prohibit, to forbid.

prohibitif, ive [-bitif, iv] adj. Jur. Prohibitive, prohibitory (loi). ‖ Comm. Prohibitive (prix).

prohibition [-bisjɔ̃] f. Prohibition. (V. interdiction.) ‖ Prohibition (de l'alcool); *loi de prohibition*, prohibition law, U. S. Volstead Act. ‖ Comm. *Frapper de prohibition d'entrée*, to prohibit the import of.

prohibitionnisme [-bisjɔnism] m. Prohibitionism.

prohibitionniste [-bisjɔnist] s. Prohibitionist.

proie [prwa] f. Prey (butin); *devenir la proie de*, to be a prey to; *oiseau de proie*, bird of prey. ‖ Fig. Victim; *la proie des calomniateurs*, a victim of slanderers. ‖ Fig. Prey; *être en proie aux cauchemars*, to be a prey to nightmares; *être en proie au désespoir*, to be devoured with despair, to be eating one's heart out with despair; *en proie à un violent émoi*, under the stress of violent emotion. ‖ Loc. *Lâcher la proie pour l'ombre*, to lose the substance for the shadow.

projecteur [prɔʒɛktœ:r] m. Lecture-lantern, projector (de conférencier). ‖ Floodlight projector (de monuments); *éclairer par projecteur*, to floodlight. ‖ Milit. Searchlight; *repérage par projecteur*, searchlight location. ‖ Ciném. Picture-projector, projector.

projectif, ive [-tif, i:v] adj. Math., Psych. Projective (géométrie, test).

projectile [-til] m. Projectile, missile.

projection [-sjɔ̃] f. Projection (jet). ‖ Projection; *conférence avec projections*, lantern lecture. ‖ Math., Arts., Géogr. Projection. ‖ Naut. Plan, projection.

projectionniste [-sjɔnist] m. Ciném. Projectionist, operator (au cinéma).

projet [prɔʒɛ] m. Project, plan (v. dessein); *projets ambitieux*, ambitious schemes; *avoir des projets matrimoniaux sur*, to have designs on; *faire un projet*, to devise a plan; *homme à projets*, planner, schemer. ‖ Blue-print, plan (sur le papier); *à l'état de projet*, in the planning (ou) blue-print stage. ‖ Draft; *projet d'accord*, draft agreement; *établir un projet de contrat*, to draft a contract. ‖ JUR. *Projet de loi*, bill; *déposer un projet de loi*, to introduce a bill.

projeter [prɔʒte] v. tr. (8 *a*). To plan, to design, to be thinking of, to contemplate (nourrir le projet de). ‖ To throw, to hurl, to dash (jeter); *être projeté hors de*, to be hurled out of. ‖ To project, to cast (une ombre); to project (une silhouette). ‖ MATH., PHYS., CINÉM. To project.
— v. pr. Se projeter, to be planned (affaire, voyage). ‖ To be projected (ou) cast (ou) thrown (objet); to be projected, to fall (ombre). ‖ CINÉM. To be projected (film). ‖ ARCHIT. To jut out (encorbellement).

projeteur [-tœːr] m. Planner, schemer.

prolapsus [prɔlapsys] m. MÉD. Prolapse, prolapsus.

prolégomènes [prɔlegɔmɛn] m. pl. PHILOS. Prolegomena.

prolétaire [prɔletɛːr] adj., s. Proletarian.

prolétariat [-tarja] m. Proletariat (classe); proletarianism (condition).

prolétarien, enne [-tarjɛ̃, ɛn] adj. Proletarian.

prolétariser [-tarize] v. tr. (1). To proletarianize.

prolifération [prɔliferasjɔ̃] f. Proliferation.

prolifère [-fɛːr] adj. BOT., ZOOL. Proliferous.

proliférer [-fere] v. intr. (5). To proliferate.

prolifique [-fik] adj. Prolific.

prolixe [prɔliks] adj. Prolix, wordy, lengthy, diffuse, long-winded. (V. VERBEUX.)

prolixité [-site] f. Prolixity. (V. VERBOSITÉ.)

prolo [prɔlo] s. FAM. Prole.

prologue [prɔlɔg] m. Foreword (v. PRÉFACE); prologue (*de*, to).

prolongation [prɔlɔ̃gasjɔ̃] f. Protraction (d'attente); prolongation (de durée); extension, lengthening (de validité). ‖ COMM. Renewal (d'un effet); *clause de prolongation*, continuation clause. ‖ MUS. Holding (d'une note).

prolonge [-lɔ̃ːʒ] f. MILIT. Prolonge, trail-rope. ‖ MILIT. Ammunition waggon; *prolonge d'artillerie*, gun-carriage.

prolongé, ée [-lɔ̃ʒe] adj. Continued, prolonged (rue). ‖ Prolonged, protracted, lengthened (séjour). ‖ FIG. Sustained (effort).

prolongement [-lɔ̃ʒmɑ̃] m. Prolongation, extension (d'une rue); *sur le prolongement de*, in prolongation of. ‖ Pl. FIG. Sequel, repercussion, after-effect.

prolonger [-lɔ̃ʒe] v. tr. (7). To prolong, to extend (une rue). ‖ To extend (*de*, by) [un billet, une permission, la validité]. ‖ To lengthen, to protract (un séjour). ‖ MÉD. To protract (la maladie). ‖ COMM. To renew (un effet). ‖ MATH. To produce (une ligne). ‖ MUS. To prolong, to hold on to (une note). ‖ NAUT. To sail along (une côte).
— v. pr. Se prolonger, to be extended (rue). ‖ To be carried on (effort, lutte); to continue, to go on (séjour, vie). ‖ To live on (personne). ‖ MÉD. To be protracted (maladie, souffrance).

promenade [prɔmnad] f. Walking (action). ‖ Drive (en auto, en voiture); sail, row (en bateau); ride (à bicyclette, à cheval); walk (à pied); *petite promenade*, stroll; *faire faire une promenade à*, to take s.o. out for a walk; *partir en promenade*, to go out for a walk, to go for an outing. ‖ Promenade, public walk, avenue. ‖ MILIT. Route march (marche); walk-over (victoire rapide).

promener [-ne] v. tr. (1). To take out for a drive (en auto, en voiture); to take out for a sail (en bateau); to take out for a ride (en bicyclette, à cheval); to take out for a walk (à pied); *mes occupations me promenèrent par tout Paris*, my occupations took me all over Paris. ‖ To keep on the move (déplacer); *promener qqn du nord au sud*, to keep s.o. trotting from north to south. ‖ To move, to run (agiter); *promener ses doigts sur*, to run one's fingers over; *promener ses regards sur*, to run one's eyes over. ‖ FIG. To carry (sa mélancolie); *promener son attention sur*, to let one's thoughts dwell on. ‖ FAM. To keep dancing (faire attendre, leurrer).
— v. pr. Se promener, to take a drive (ou) a sail (ou) a ride (ou) a walk; *se promener de long en large*, to walk up and down. ‖ To run; *les punaises se promenaient partout*, bugs were running all over the place; *sa plume semblait se promener sur le papier*, his pen seemed to wander over the paper. ‖ FIG. To wander (pensée). ‖ FAM. *Envoyer promener qqn*, to send s.o. about his business, to turn s.o. out; *envoyer promener ses soucis*, to cast off all one's cares.

promeneur, euse [-nœːr, øːz] s. Walker, stroller (en général); tripper, hiker (excursionniste); loiterer (flâneur); *promeneuse d'enfants*, mother's help, baby-sitter. ‖ Guide (de touristes).

promenoir [-nwaːr] m. Covered gallery (ou) walk. ‖ THÉÂTR. Strolling gallery. (V. DÉAMBULATOIRE.)

promesse [prɔmɛs] f. Promise, assurance, pledge; *faire, manquer, tenir sa promesse*, to make, to break, to keep one's promise. ‖ JUR. *Rupture de promesse de mariage*, breach of promise. ‖ COMM. Promissory note. ‖ FIG. *Plein de promesses*, promising.

prometteur, euse [-mɛtœːr, øːz] adj. Promising, full of promise.
— s. Promiser; person ready to promise.

promettre [-mɛːtr] v. tr. (64). To promise (qqch.); *promettre monts et merveilles*, to make golden promises, to promise the moon. ‖ To announce, to give hope for (prédire); *promettre un bel avenir*, to foretell a happy future. ‖ To bid fair to; *il promet de devenir virtuose*, he bids fair to become a virtuoso. ‖ To promise, to assure (certifier); *je vous promets que je lui dirai*, I swear to tell him; *il ne promet pas que tout s'arrangera*, he cannot vouch for it that everything will go right. ‖ FAM. *Il faisait froid, je vous le promets!*, it was cold, I'll tell you!
— v. intr. To promise; *promettre facilement*, to promise readily. ‖ To promise, to look promising; *ça promet!*, it looks promising!; *c'est un garçon qui promet*, he is a promising boy, he has possibilities.
— v. pr. Se promettre, to promise oneself, to look forward to; *je me promets de belles vacances*, I am confident of having fine holidays.

promis, ise [-mi, iz] adj. Promised (objet, terre). ‖ Engaged (fiancé).
— s. FAM. Intended (v. FUTUR); *mon promis*, my intended.

promiscuité [prɔmiskɥite] f. Promiscuity; promiscuousness.

promontoire [prɔmɔ̃twaːr] m. GÉOGR. Promontory, headland.

promoteur, trice [prɔmɔtœːr, tris] s. Developer (immobilier). ‖ Promoter (d'une entreprise), mover (d'une réforme).
— m. CHIM. Promoter (d'un catalyseur).

promotion [-sjɔ̃] f. Promotion; move, raise (fam.); *promotion à l'ancienneté, au choix*, promotion by seniority, by selection; *il était de la même promotion universitaire que mon frère*, he took his degree in the same year as my brother, U. S. he was in the same class as my brother. ‖ Group of promoted persons (ensemble des promus); promotion list, list of preferments (liste).

promotionnel, elle [-sjɔnɛl] adj. COMM. Promotional.

promouvoir [prɔmuvwaːr] v. tr. (83). To promote.

prompt, ompte [prɔ̃, ɔ̃:t] adj. Quick, swift. (V. RAPIDE.) ‖ Agile, nimble (agile). ‖ Early, rapid (décision, retour); speedy (justice, revanche, vengeance); à l'esprit prompt, quick-witted; d'humeur prompte, hasty- (ou) quick-tempered; avoir la main prompte, to have a quick hand. ‖ Prompt (spontané); prompt à la riposte, prompt in repartee. ‖ MÉD. Rapid (guérison); quick (remède).
promptement [-tmɑ̃] adv. Quickly, promptly.
promptitude [-tity:d] f. Promptness, promptitude.
promu, ue [prɔmy] adj. Promoted, raised (à, to).
promulgateur, trice [prɔmylgatœ:r, tris] s. Promulgator.
promulgation [-gasjɔ̃] f. JUR. Promulgation, enactment.
promulguer [-ge] v. tr. (1). JUR. To issue, to publish (un décret); to promulgate, to enact (une loi).
prône [pro:n] m. ECCLÉS. Sermon, prone.
prôner [prone] v. tr. (1). To advocate, to favour, to recommend, to extol. (V. VANTER.)
prôneur [-nœ:r] m. FAM. Extoller; booster; prôneur d'un régime alimentaire, food faddist.
pronom [prɔnɔ̃] m. GRAMM. Pronoun.
pronominal, ale [prɔnɔminal] adj. GRAMM. Pronominal.
pronominalement [-mɑ̃] adv. GRAMM. Pronominally.
prononçable [prɔnɔ̃sabl] adj. Pronounceable.
prononcé, ée [-se] adj. Broad (accent); pronounced, marked (caractère, goût, trait); prominent (nez).
— m. JUR. Pronouncing, pronouncement (action); decision (résultat); prononcé d'un jugement, delivering of a judgment.
prononcer [-se] v. tr. (6). To pronounce, to utter (un mot, une phrase); prononcer distinctement, to articulate. ‖ To deliver (un discours). ‖ To utter (une parole). ‖ ARTS. To bring out, to stress (les traits). ‖ JUR. To deliver, to pass (une sentence); prononcer la peine de mort, to decree the death penalty; le jugement sera prononcé demain, the verdict will be given tomorrow.
— v. intr. To pronounce. (V. ARTICULER, PROFÉRER.) ‖ JUR. Prononcer sur une question, to adjudicate upon a question.
— v. pr. Se prononcer, to be pronounced (langage, mot). ‖ To come out (traits). [V. S'ACCUSER.] ‖ To declare, to decide (contre, against; pour, in favour of); se prononcer sur, to give one's opinion (ou) to come to a conclusion on.
prononciation [-sjasjɔ̃] f. Pronunciation. (V. ACCENT.) ‖ Delivery (d'un discours). ‖ JUR. Passing (d'un jugement).
pronostic [prɔnɔstik] m. Prediction (d'un événement); prognostic, forecast (du temps). ‖ Omen, pre-indication (présage). ‖ MÉD Prognosis.
pronostiquer [-ke] v. tr. (1). To prognosticate, to foretell (un événement); to forecast (le temps). ‖ MÉD. To prognose, to give the prognostic of.
pronostiqueur, euse [-kœ:r, ø:z] s. SPORTS. Forecaster, tipster.
pronunciamiento [prɔnunsjamjɛnto] m. Military coup, putsch.
propagande [prɔpagɑ̃:d] f. Propaganda; faire de la propagande, to carry on propaganda. ‖ COMM. Advertisement; faire de la propagande pour, to advertise, to boost.
propagandisme [-gɑ̃dism] m. Propagandism.
propagandiste [-gɑ̃dist] s. Propagandist.
propagateur, trice [-gatœ:r, tris] adj. Propagative.
— s. Propagator; propagateur de fausses nouvelles, spreader of false news. ‖ MÉD. Spreader.
propagation [-gasjɔ̃] f. Propagation, spreading.
propager [-ʒe] v. tr. (7). To propagate, to multiply

(une espèce). ‖ To extend (une influence); to spread abroad, to diffuse (des informations, des nouvelles); to promulgate (une théorie). ‖ PHYS. To propagate, to convey (la lumière, le son). ‖ MÉD. To spread (une épidémie).
— v. pr. Se propager, to multiply, to increase (espèce). ‖ To extend (influence); to · propagate, to spread (nouvelles); to be promulgated (théorie). ‖ PHYS. To be conveyed. ‖ MÉD. To spread.
propane [prɔpan] m. CHIM. Propane.
propédeutique [prɔpedøtik] adj. Propaedeutic.
— f. Propaedeutics.
propène [prɔpɛn] m. CHIM. Propene.
propension [prɔpɑ̃sjɔ̃] f. Propensity, leaning. ‖ FIG. Proneness, bias, appetency. (V. INCLINATION.)
propergol [prɔpergɔl] m. Fuel; propellant.
prophète [prɔfɛt] m. Prophet. ‖ FAM. Prophète de malheur, prophesier of calamity, Jeremiah; bon prophète, true prophet.
prophétesse [-tɛs] f. Prophetess.
prophétie [-si] f. Prophesying (action); prophetic utterance (paroles prophétiques); prophecy (prédiction).
prophétique [-tik] adj. Prophetic.
prophétiquement [-tikmɑ̃] adv. Prophetically.
prophétiser [-tize] v. tr. (1). To prophesy.
prophylactique [prɔfilaktik] adj. MÉD. Prophylactic.
prophylaxie [-laksi] f. MÉD. Prophylaxis.
propice [prɔpis] adj. Propicious, favourable, kind (divinité). ‖ Auspicious, favourable, opportune (occasion); étoile propice, lucky star; si le sort nous est propice, if Fate is kind to us.
propitiation [-sjasjɔ̃] f. Propitiation, atonement.
propitiatoire [-sjatwa:r] adj., m. Propitiatory; don propitiatoire, sop to Cerberus.
proportion [prɔpɔrsjɔ̃] f. Proportion, portion, part (en quantité). ‖ Proportion (mesure); à proportion que, in proportion as; toute proportion gardée, due allowance being made. ‖ Proportion, relation (entre, with) [rapport]; en proportion, proportionally; hors de proportion avec, out of proportion with, disproportionate with. ‖ Proportion, extent, scale (échelle); dans de vastes proportions, on a wide scale. ‖ Pl. Dimensions, size. ‖ ARCHIT., ARTS., MATH. Proportion.
proportionnalité [-sjɔnalite] f. Proportionality.
proportionné, ée [-sjɔne] adj. Proportioned (membre, taille). ‖ Proportionate (à, to); in proportion (à, with). ‖ Adequate (à, to).
proportionnel, elle [-sjɔnɛl] adj. Proportional (à, to); directement (ou) inversement proportionnel à, in direct (ou) inverse ratio to. ‖ MATH. Moyenne proportionnelle, geometrical mean. ‖ FIN. Droit proportionnel, ad valorem duty. ‖ JUR. Sliding (échelle); proportional (représentation).
proportionnelle [-nɛ:l] f. MATH. Proportional. ‖ JUR. Proportional representation (en politique).
proportionnellement [-sjɔnɛlmɑ̃] adv. Proportionately; in proportion (à, to, with).
proportionner [-sjɔne] v. tr. (1). To proportion, to make proportionate, to adapt, to adjust (à, to). ‖ JUR. Proportionner la peine au délit, to make the punishment fit the crime.
propos [prɔpo] m. Purpose, resolution; de propos délibéré, on purpose, of set purpose, deliberately. ‖ Matter, subject; à ce propos, in this connection; à propos de, about, concerning, à propos of, in connection with, with regard to; in reference to; à tout propos, at every turn; changer de propos, to change the subject. ‖ Convenience; à propos, opportunely, at the right time, just in time, by the way (sens adverbial); opportune, advisable, opposite, fitting, seasonable, appropriate (sens adjectival); hors de propos, irrelevant; juger à propos de, to think fit to; intervenir à propos, to talk to the point. ‖ Pl. Talk, conversation,

remarks; *tenir des propos malveillants sur,* to make malicious remarks about; *tenir des propos sans importance,* to be engaged in small talk.

proposable [prɔpɔzabl] adj. Proposable, fit to be proposed.

proposer [-ze] v. tr. (1). To propose (en général); to offer (de l'argent); to bring up (une difficulté); to suggest (une échappatoire); to bring forward (une explication); to propound (une idée); to propose (un mode d'action, un sujet); to bring up (un problème); to offer (une solution). ‖ To put forward (une invention, un objet). ‖ To recommend (une candidature, un candidat); to point to (un modèle). ‖ Jur. To move (une motion).
— v. intr. To propose.
— v. pr. **Se proposer,** to propose (ou) to offer oneself, to push oneself forward (s'offrir); *se proposer pour faire qqch.,* to offer to do sth. ‖ To mean, to intend, to purpose (*de, to*) [avoir l'intention]; *se proposer de faire qqch.,* to contemplate doing sth.

proposeur [-zœːr] m. Proposer (d'un mode d'action); propounder (d'une théorie). ‖ Jur. Mover (d'une motion).

proposition [-zisjɔ̃] f. Proposition, suggestion. ‖ Proposal, offer (offre); *faire une proposition,* to make an offer. ‖ Statement, assertion (déclaration). ‖ Recommendation (*pour,* for) [un poste]. ‖ Jur. Motion; *proposition de loi,* bill. ‖ Gramm. Clause. ‖ Math., Mus. Proposition. ‖ Milit. *Propositions de paix,* peace proposals. ‖ Philos. Proposition; *propositions d'un dilemme,* horns of a dilemma. ‖ Comm. Offer.

propre [prɔpr] adj. Clean, neat, spotless, unstained (objet); clean, cleanly (personne); *propre comme un sou neuf,* as clean as a new pin; *un petit vieux bien propre,* a well-groomed old man. ‖ Fig. Decent, fair (conduite, vie); *avoir les mains propres,* to be unimpeachable (ou) above reproach, to have clean hands. ‖ Fam. *Nous voilà propres!,* we are in a fine mess!
— m. Fam. *C'est du propre!* disgusting!, that's a fine mess!

propre adj. Own (à soi); *sa propre fille,* her own daughter. ‖ Proper, particular, peculiar (particulier); *propre à son âge,* natural for his age; *être propre à,* to be peculiar to (ou) characteristic of. ‖ Fit, appropriate, able (capable); *propre à,* appropriate to, well adapted to (paroles); able to, well fitted to (travailleur); *propre à rien,* good for nothing; *propre à tout,* versatile. ‖ Plain (net); *en propres termes,* in so many words, plainly. ‖ Personal; *à remettre en mains propres,* to be delivered to the addressee in person.
— m. Quality, attribute, characteristic, peculiarity; *le propre de Polichinelle, c'est sa bosse,* Punch's distinctive feature is his hump. ‖ Ecclés. Proper. ‖ Gramm. Proper meaning; *employé au propre,* used literally. ‖ Loc. *Un propre à rien,* a good-for-nothing, a ne'er-do-well; a dead loss, a rotter (fam.).

proprement [-prəmɑ̃] adv. Cleanly (avec propreté). ‖ Fairly, decently; *c'est proprement fait,* it's neatly done. ‖ Fig. Decently, honourably, cleanly. ‖ Fam. Fairly well; *passer un examen proprement,* to do fairly well at an exam.

proprement [-prəmɑ̃] adv. Properly, exactly; *à proprement parler,* strictly speaking; *proprement dit,* properly so called. ‖ Absolutely; simply; in fact. (V. RÉELLEMENT.)

propret, ette [-prɛ, ɛt] adj. Neat, tidy.

propreté [-prɛte] f. Cleanliness, cleanness, tidiness, neatness. ‖ Fig. Honesty, decency, virtue.

propriétaire [prɔprietɛːr] m. Owner, possessor, proprietor; *propriétaire foncier* (ou) *terrien,* landowner; *propriétaire indivis,* joint-owner; *être pro-* priétaire, to be a man of property; *être propriétaire de,* to own; *tour du propriétaire,* walk around the place. ‖ Landlord (d'une chambre, d'une maison). ‖ Comm. Grower (producteur).
— f. Proprietress. ‖ Landlady.

propriété [-te] f. Ownership, proprietorship, possession (droit et fait de posséder); *propriété industrielle,* patent rights; *propriété indivise,* parcenary; *propriété littéraire,* copyright; *nue-propriété,* bare ownership; *posséder en toute propriété,* to hold in fee simple. ‖ Estate, property (bien possédé); *propriétés bâties,* buildings; *propriété immobilière,* real estate; *petite propriété,* small holding. ‖ Landowners (les propriétaires); *la grande propriété,* the great landowners. ‖ Property, quality, attribute (caractéristique). ‖ Chim., Phys. Property. ‖ Gramm. Propriety (d'un mot).

proprio [prɔprjo] m. Fam. Landlord.

propulser [prɔpylse] v. tr. (1). To propel.
— v. pr. **Se propulser,** Fam. To make one's way.

propulseur [-sœːr] adj. Propelling, propulsive.
— m. Propeller.

propulsif, ive [-sif, iːv] adj. Propulsive.

propulsion [-sjɔ̃] f. Propulsion; *à propulsion mécanique,* mechanically propelled.

propyle [prɔpil] m. Chim. Propyl.

propylique [-lik] adj. Chim. Propyl.

prorata [prɔrata] m. invar. Share, proportional part (part). ‖ Proportion; *au prorata de,* in proportion to.

prorogatif, ive [prɔrɔgatif, iːv] adj. Proroguing.

prorogation [-gasjɔ̃] f. Extension (d'une durée); protraction (d'une mesure, d'un traité). ‖ Postponement, adjournment (remise). ‖ Jur. Prorogation (d'un Parlement).

proroger [-ʒe] v. tr. (7). To extend (un contrat, un délai); to postpone, to adjourn (un travail). ‖ Jur. To prorogue, to prorogate (le Parlement); *proroger une caution,* to extend bail.

prosaïque [prozaik] adj. Prosaic, prosaical, commonplace (objet, point de vue); pedestrian (style).

prosaïquement [-zaikmɑ̃] adv. Prosaically.

prosaïsme [-zaism] m. Prosaism; matter-of-factness (d'une personne); dullness, flatness, prosaicness (de la vie). ‖ Prosaic, pedestrian word (ou) phrase (expression).

prosateur [-zatœːr] m. Prose-writer.

proscenium [prɔsenjɔm] m. Théâtr. Proscenium.

proscripteur [prɔskriptœːr] m. Proscriber.

proscription [-sjɔ̃] f. Proscription, outlawry, exiling (bannissement). ‖ Abolition, rejection, exclusion (d'un usage). ‖ Comm. Prohibited articles.

proscrire [prɔskriːr] v. tr. (44). To proscribe, to outlaw, to exile (bannir). ‖ To abolish, to ban, to taboo (une coutume); to proscribe, to exclude, to reject, to interdict (qqch.); to forbid (l'usage d'une chose).

proscrit, ite [-kri, it] adj. Proscribed, outlawed (personne). ‖ Banned, forbidden (usage).
— s. Proscript, outlaw, exile.

prose [proːz] f. Prose. ‖ Ecclés. Prose, sequence. ‖ Fam. Letter (lettre); flat writing (texte plat).

prosecteur [prɔsɛktœːr] m. Prosector.

prosélyte [prozelit] s. Proselyte.

prosélytisme [-tism] m. Proselytism.

prosodie [prozodi] f. Prosody.

prosodique [-dik] adj. Prosodic.

prosodiste [-dist] s. Prosodist.

prosopopée [prozɔpɔpe] f. Prosopopoeia.

prospecter [prɔspɛkte] v. tr. (1). To prospect.

prospecteur [-tœːr] m. Prospector.

prospectif, ive [-tif, iːv] adj. Prospective.

prospection [-sjɔ̃] f. Prospecting (action); prospection (résultat). ‖ Comm. Canvassing.

prospective [-ti:v] f. Futurology, trend analysis.
prospectus [-ty:s] m. Prospectus, hand-bill, throw-away sheet.
prospère [prɔspɛ:r] adj. Prosperous, flourishing (affaires). ‖ Prosperous, flourishing, well-to-do, well-off (personne).
prospérer [-pere] v. intr. (5). To prosper, to flourish, to do well (affaires); to thrive (pays); to prosper, to be successful (personne).
prospérité [-perite] f. Prosperousness; prosperity; *vague de prospérité*, wave of prosperity, boom.
prostate [prɔstat] f. MÉD. Prostate.
prostatique [-tatik] adj. MÉD. Prostatic, prostate.
— s. MÉD. Prostate sufferer.
prostatite [-tatit] adj. MÉD. Prostatitis.
prosternation [prɔstɛrnasjɔ̃] f. Prostration, obeisance.
prosternement [-nəmɑ̃] m. Prostration.
prosterner (se) [səprɔstɛrne] v. pr. To prostrate oneself. ‖ To bow down to the ground; to grovel (*devant*, before).
prostituée [prɔstitɥe] f. Prostitute, harlot, whore.
prostituer [-tɥe] v. tr. (1). To prostitute (une femme). ‖ FIG. To prostitute, to misuse (son talent).
— v. pr. **Se prostituer**, to prostitute oneself (pr. et fig.).
prostitution [-tysjɔ̃] f. Prostitution; *maison de prostitution*, brothel. ‖ FIG. Prostitution, desecration, profanation.
prostration [prɔstrasjɔ̃] f. Prostration (prosternement). ‖ MÉD. Exhaustion, prostration.
prostré, ée [-tre] adj. Prostrate, prone (prosterné). ‖ MÉD. Prostrate, depressed.
protactinium [prɔtaktinjɔm] m. CHIM. Protactinium.
protagonisme [prɔtagonism] m. Protagonism.
protagoniste [-nist] s. THÉÂTR. Protagonist. ‖ FIG. Protagonist, promoter, instigator, leading spirit.
prote [prɔt] m. Foreman, overseer (d'imprimerie).
protecteur, trice [prɔtɛktœ:r, tris] adj. Protecting, protective; *société protectrice des animaux*, Society for the Prevention of Cruelty to Animals. ‖ JUR. Protective (droit, système, tarif). ‖ TECHN. Protective (appareil). ‖ FIG. Patronizing (attitude).
— m. Protector (d'une personne). ‖ ARTS. Patron. ‖ TECHN. Guard, shield. ‖ FAM. Man who keeps a mistress (amant); *son protecteur*, her lover.
protection [-sjɔ̃] f. Protection; *protection de l'enfance*, child welfare; *prendre sous sa protection*, to take under one's wing (fam.). ‖ Influence; wire-pulling, pull (aide politique). ‖ Support, influence (aide). ‖ JUR. Protection. ‖ ARTS. Patronage. ‖ TECHN. *Système de protection*, protective (ou) safety system. ‖ FAM. *Airs de protection*, patronizing airs.
protectionnisme [-sjɔnism] m. Protectionism.
protectionniste [-sjɔnist] adj. s. Protectionist.
protectorat [-tɔra] m. Protectorate.
protectrice [-tris] f. Protectress. ‖ Patroness.
Protée [prɔte] m. Proteus.
protège [prɔtɛ:ʒ] V. PROTÉGER. ‖ **Protège-cahier**, m. Exercise-book (ou) notebook cover. ‖ **Protège-dents**, m. inv. Gum-shield, mouthpiece (de boxeur). ‖ **Protège-jambes**, m. inv. Legshield. ‖ **Protège-pointe**, m. Pencil cap, point protector.
protégé, ée [-teʒe] adj. Protected. ‖ TECHN. Guarded. ‖ FAM. *Très protégé*, having a big pull, having many friends at court.
— m. Protégé, favourite.
protégée f. Protégée.
protéger [-teʒe] v. tr. (5,7). To protect (*de*, from); to guard, to shelter, to shield (*against*, de, contre).

(V. GARDER.) ‖ To protect, to champion (une cause, qqn). ‖ MILIT. To cover. ‖ JUR. To protect (l'industrie). ‖ ARTS. To patronize.
protéiforme [prɔteifɔrm] adj. Protean.
protéine [prɔtein] f. CHIM. Protein.
protestant, ante [prɔtɛstɑ̃, ɑ̃:t] adj. s. ECCLÉS. Protestant.
protestantisme [-tɑ̃tism] m. Protestantism.
protestataire [-tatɛ:r] s. Protester, objector.
protestation [-tasjɔ̃] f. Profession (d'amitié); protestation (d'innocence); declaration, asseveration (de fidélité). ‖ Protest; *élever une protestation*, to raise a protest; *réunion de protestation*, indignation meeting.
protester [-te] v. tr. (1). To protest, to affirm, to asseverate (*que*, that). ‖ COMM. To protest (un effet).
— v. intr. *Protester de*, to protest; *protester sa non-ingérence*, to protest one's non-interference. ‖ To rise in opposition; *protester contre*, to protest against, to challenge.
protêt [prɔtɛ] m. FIN. Protest; *lever un protêt*, to make a protest, to protest; *signifier un protêt*, to give notice of a protest.
prothèse [prɔtɛ:z] f. MÉD. Prothesis; *appareil de prothèse*, artificial teeth (dentier); artificial limb (membre artificiel).
prothrombine [prɔtrɔ̃bin] f. MÉD. Prothrombin.
protide [prɔtid] m. MÉD. Protein.
protiste [prɔtist] m. ZOOL., BOT. Protist.
protocolaire [prɔtɔkɔlɛ:r] adj. Official; formal.
protocole [-kɔl] m. Protocol; State etiquette; *chef du protocole*, Head of the Department of Etiquette and Ceremonial, U.S. Chief of Protocol. ‖ FAM. Etiquette, formalities.
protohistoire [prɔtɔistwa:r] f. Protohistory.
protomartyr [prɔtɔmartir] m. ECCLÉS. Protomartyr.
proton [prɔtɔ̃] m. PHYS. Proton.
protonotaire [prɔtɔnɔtɛ:r] m. ECCLÉS. Protonotary, prothonotary.
protoplasme [-plasm] m. MÉD. Protoplasm.
protoplasmique [-plasmik] adj. MÉD. Protoplasmal, protoplasmatic, protoplasmic.
prototype [-tip] m. Prototype, first model.
protoxyde [prɔtɔksid] m. CHIM. Protoxide.
protozoaire [prɔtɔzɔɛ:r] adj. ZOOL. Protozoan.
— m. ZOOL. Protozoon. ‖ Pl. Protozoa.
protracteur [prɔtraktœ:r] adj. MÉD. Protractor.
protrusion [prɔtryzjɔ̃] f. Protrusion.
protubérance [prɔtyberɑ̃:s] f. Protuberance. ‖ MÉD. Bump.
protubérant, ante [-rɑ̃, ɑ̃:t] adj. Protuberant.
prou [pru] adv. † Much, many; *peu ou prou*, more or less.
proue f. NAUT. Prow.
prouesse [pruɛs] f. Prowess. ‖ Pl. Exploits.
prouvable [pruvabl] adj. Provable.
prouver [-ve] v. tr. (1). To prove; *prouver par A plus B*, to prove mathematically; *ce n'est pas prouvé*, that remains to be proved. ‖ To prove, to give proof (ou) evidence of, to bear witness to; *ses manières prouvent l'excellence de son éducation*, his manner argues an excellent upbringing. ‖ JUR. *Prouver le bien-fondé de*, to substantiate.
provenance [prɔvənɑ̃:s] f. Origin, source, provenance; *en provenance de*, from; *de provenance française*, of French origin (ou) production. ‖ COMM. Produce (produit); *de provenance directe*, direct from the grower. ‖ NAUT. *En provenance de*, hailing from.
provenant, ante [-nɑ̃, ɑ̃:t] adj. Coming, originating (*de*, from). ‖ JUR. Derived, accruing (argent, biens); issuing (*de*, from) [enfants]; issuing (*de*, out of) [revenu].

provençal, ale [prɔvɑ̃sal] adj., s. GÉOGR. Provençal.
— m. GRAMM. Provençal (langue).
provende [prɔvɑ̃:d] f. Provender, food. ‖ AGRIC. Fodder.
provenir [prɔvni:r] v. intr. (101). To come, to derive, to issue, to originate, to proceed (de, from). ‖ To arise (difficultés); provenant de, due to, as a result of. ‖ COMM. Provenant d'Allemagne, manufactured in Germany.
proverbe [prɔvɛrb] m. Proverb; passé en proverbe, become proverbial. ‖ THÉÂTR. Proverb.
proverbial, ale [-bjal] adj. Proverbial.
proverbialement [-bjalmɑ̃] adv. Proverbially.
providence [prɔvidɑ̃:s] f. ECCLÉS. Providence. ‖ FAM. Etat Providence, Welfare State.
providentiel, elle [-dɑ̃sjɛl] adj. Providential.
providentiellement [-dɑ̃sjɛlmɑ̃] adv. Providentially.
provigner [-ɲe] v. tr. (1). AGRIC. To layer.
provin [prɔvɛ̃] m. AGRIC. Layer.
province [prɔvɛ̃:s] f. Province (d'un territoire). ‖ Province; country; la province, the provinces; aller en province, to leave town; to leave for the provinces; de province, provincial. ‖ FAM. Sentant sa province, countrified.
provincial, ale [prɔvɛ̃sjal] adj., s. Provincial.
provincialisme [-lism] m. Provincialism.
provincialité [-lite] f. Provinciality.
proviseur [prɔvizœ:r] m. Headmaster (d'un lycée).
provision [-zjɔ̃] f. Provision, store, supply, stock. ‖ Pl. Supplies, provisions, victuals; provisions de bouche, eatables, food; aller aux provisions, to go shopping; faire provision de, to get in a supply of. ‖ FIN. Cover, deposit, funds (en banque); défaut de provision, no funds (pour chèque); sans provision, without cover (ou) a deposit (chèque). ‖ FIN. Temporary allowance (indemnité professionnelle). ‖ JUR. Retainer, retaining fee (à un avocat, à un avoué); verser une provision, to pay a retaining fee. ‖ COMM. Instalment (v. ACOMPTE); verser une provision, to pay a commission (à un agent).
provisionnel, elle [-zjɔnɛl] adj. JUR. Provisional. ‖ FIN. Acompte provisionnel, instalment on account.
provisionner [-zjɔne] v. tr. FIN. (1). To give consideration for.
provisoire [prɔvizwa:r] adj. Provisional, temporary (v. TEMPORAIRE, TRANSITOIRE); conclusion provisoire, tentative conclusion; gérant provisoire, acting manager; gouvernement provisoire, interim government; habitation provisoire, emergency dwelling. ‖ JUR. Ad referendum (contrat); interim (dividende); provisional (sentence).
— m. Provisional state (état); temporary measure (mesure). ‖ FAM. Makeshift.
provisoirement [-zwarmɑ̃] adv. Provisionally, temporarily, in the meantime.
provisorat [-zɔra] m. Headmastership.
provocant, ante [prɔvɔkɑ̃, ɑ̃:t] adj. Provoking, provocative (agressif). ‖ Alluring, seductive, provocative, tempting (alléchant).
provocateur, trice [-katœ:r, tris] adj. Provoking (attitude, parole); agent provocateur, agent provocateur, professional agitator.
— s. Provoker; aggressor.
provocatif, ive [-katif, i:v] adj. Provocative.
provocation [-kasjɔ̃] f. Provocation, incitement, instigation; provocation au crime, incitement to crime. ‖ Challenge; provocation en duel, challenge to a duel. ‖ Affront, insult.
provoquer [-ke] v. tr. (1). To provoke, to incite, to egg on (pousser); provoquer à, to incite to. ‖ To provoke, to irritate (exciter). ‖ To provoke,

to challenge (défier). ‖ To tempt, to provoke, to allure, to make advances to; to vamp (fam.) (un homme). ‖ To cause, to bring about (un accident, une perte d'argent); to provoke (la colère); to create (une émeute); to rouse, to call forth (le mépris, la révolte); to draw (un rassemblement); to entail (un résultat). ‖ MÉD. To induce (un affaiblissement, l'hypnose, le sommeil).
proxénète [prɔksenɛt] m. Procurer, pander, pimp.
— f. Procuress, bawd.
proxénétisme [-netism] m. Procuring, pandering; white-slave trade.
proximité [prɔksimite] f. Proximity, vicinity, nearness, closeness, propinquity; à proximité, near; à proximité de, close to, near. ‖ JUR. Proximité de parenté, close kinship.
prude [pryd] adj. Prudish.
— f. Prude. (V. BÉGUEULE.)
prudemment [prydamɑ̃] adv. Prudently.
prudence [-dɑ̃:s] f. Prudence, caution, discretion; avec prudence, cautiously, prudently; faire preuve de prudence, to show wisdom (ou) discretion; relatif à la prudence, prudential.
prudent, ente [-dɑ̃, ɑ̃:t] adj. Prudent, cautious, wary. (V. AVISÉ, CIRCONSPECT.) ‖ Discreet, wise (sage); il serait prudent de, it would be advisable to; il faut être très prudent en, the greatest care must be taken in. ‖ Foreseeing, provident (précautionneux, prévoyant).
pruderie [prydri] f. Prudery, prudishness.
prud'homie [prydɔmi] f. Probity (intégrité); wisdom (sagesse).
prud'homme [-dɔm] m. Man of experience and integrity. ‖ JUR. Conseil des prud'hommes, Conciliation Board in labour disputes.
prudhommesque [-dɔmɛsk] adj. Banal, pompous, sententious.
prune [pryn] f. BOT. Plum; prune reine-claude, greengage. ‖ FAM. Pour des prunes, for nothing; des prunes!, nix!, U. S. nuts!
— adj. Plum-coloured.
pruneau [pryno] m. BOT. Prune. ‖ FAM. Bullet.
prunelle [-nɛl] f. BOT. Sloe. ‖ COMM. Sloe-gin (liqueur). ‖ MÉD. Apple of the eye, pupil. ‖ FAM. Jouer de la prunelle, to ogle. ‖ LOC. Tenir à qqch. comme à la prunelle de ses yeux, to prize sth. like the apple of one's eye.
prunellier [-nɛlje] m. BOT. Sloe-tree, blackthorn.
prunier [-nje] m. BOT. Plum-tree.
prurigineux, euse [pryriʒinø, ø:z] adj. MÉD. Pruriginous.
prurigo [pryrigo] m. MÉD. Prurigo.
prurit [-ri] m. MÉD. Pruritus. (V. DÉMANGEAISON.)
Prusse [prys] f. GÉOGR. Prussia; de Prusse, Prussian.
prussianiser [-sjanize] v. tr. (1). To Prussianize.
prussianisme [-sjanism] m. Prussianism.
prussiate [-sjat] m. CHIM. Prussiate, cyanide.
prussien, enne [-sjɛ̃, ɛn] adj., s. GÉOGR. Prussian.
prussique [-sik] adj. CHIM. Prussic (acide).
prytanée [pritane] m. † ARCHIT. Prytaneum. ‖ In France, military secondary school for sons of officers and public servants.
P.-S. [peɛs] m. Abrév. de post-scriptum, PS, postscript.
psallette [psalɛt] f. MUS. Choir.
psalmiste [psalmist] m. ECCLÉS. Psalmist.
psalmodie [-mɔdi] f. ECCLÉS. Psalmody; intoned psalm. ‖ FAM. Singsong, monotonous drone.
psalmodier [-mɔdje] v. intr., tr. (1). To psalmodize.
psalmodique [-mɔdik] adj. Psalmodic.
psaltérion [-terjɔ̃] m. ECCLÉS. Psaltery.
psaume [pso:m] m. Psalm.
psautier [psotje] m. ECCLÉS. Psalter.
pseudo [psødo] préf. Pseudo. ‖ **Pseudo-rubis**, m.

Rose quartz, Bohemian ruby. ‖ **Pseudo-saphir,** m. Blue quartz.
pseudonyme [-dɔnim] m. Pseudonym; *sous le pseudonyme de X,* signing himself X. ‖ Penname, nom de plume (d'écrivain).
— adj. Pseudonymous.
psitt [psit], **pst** [pst] interj. Psst.
psittacisme [psitasism] m. MÉD. Psittacism, parrotry.
psittacose [-kɔz] f. MÉD. Psittacosis.
psoriasis [psɔrjazis] m. MÉD. Psoriasis.
psychanalyse [psikanali:z] f. PSYCH. Psychoanalysis, analysis.
psychanalyser [-lize] v. tr. (1). PSYCH. To psycho-analyse, to analyse; to psych (fam.).
psychanalyste [-list] s. PSYCH. Psycho-analyst, analyst; shrink (fam.).
psychanalytique [-litik] adj. PSYCH. Psychoanalytic, psycho-analytical.
psychasthénie [psikasteni] f. PSYCH. Psychasthenia.
psyché [psiʃe] f. Psyche (nom). ‖ Cheval-glass, swing-mirror (miroir).
psychédélique [psikedelik] adj. Psychedelic.
psychédélisme [-lism] m. Psychedelic state.
psychiatre [psikja:tr] m. PSYCH. Psychiatrist.
psychiatrie [-kjatri] f. PSYCH. Psychiatry.
psychiatrique [-kjatrik] adj. PSYCH. Psychiatric, psychiatrical; *hôpital psychiatrique,* psychiatric (ou) mental hospital.
psychique [psiʃik] adj. Psychic, psychical.
psychisme [-ʃism] m. Psychism.
psychodrame [psikɔdram] m. Psychodrama.
psycholinguistique [-lɛ̃gɥistik] adj. PSYCH., GRAMM. Psycholinguistic.
— f. PSYCH., GRAMM. Psycholinguistics.
psychologie [psikɔlɔʒi] f. Psychology.
psychologique [-lɔʒik] adj. Psychological.
psychologiquement [-lɔʒikmɑ̃] adv. Psychologically.
psychologue [-lɔg] s. Psychologist.
psychomoteur, trice [-mɔtœ:r, tris] adj. Psychomotor.
psychopathe [-pat] m. PSYCH. Psychopath.
psychopathie [-pati] f. Psychopathy, mental illness.
psychopathologie [-patɔlɔʒi] f. Psychopathology.
psychopédagogie [-pedagɔʒi] f. Psychopedagogy, educational practice supported by psychological theory.
psychophysiologie [-fizjɔlɔʒi] f. Psychophysiology.
psychophysiologique [-fizjɔlɔʒik] adj. Psychophysiological.
psychose [psiko:z] f. PSYCH. Psychosis.
psychosensoriel, elle [psikɔsɑ̃sɔrjɛl] adj. Psychosensory.
psychosomatique [-sɔmatik] adj. Psychosomatic.
psychotechnicien, enne [-tɛknisjɛ̃, ɛn] s. Psychotechnician, psychotechnologist.
psychotechnie [-tɛknik] f. Psychotechnology, psychotechnics.
psychothérapeute [-terapø:t] s. Psychotherapist.
psychothérapie [-terapi] f. Psychotherapy.
psychothérapique [-terapik], **psychothérapeutique** [-terapøtik] adj. Psychotherapeutic.
psychotique [psikɔtik] adj., s. Psychotic.
psychotrope [psikɔtrɔp] adj. Psychotropic, psycho-active.
— m. Psychotropic (ou) psycho-active drug.
ptérodactyle [pterodaktil] m. ZOOL. Pterodactyl.
ptôse [pto:z] f. MÉD. Ptosis.
P.T.T. [petete] f. pl. Abrév. de *Postes et télécommunications,* French Post Office.
pu [py]. V. POUVOIR (79).

puant, ante [pɥɑ̃, ɑ̃:t] adj. Stinking, malodorous, noisome, fœtid; ill-smelling. ‖ FAM. Conceited, swollen-headed, U. S. swelled-headed.
puanteur [-tœ:r] f. Stink, stench, foul (ou) rank (ou) noisome smell; fœtidity, noisomeness.
pub [pœb] m. Pub.
pub [pyb] f. FAM. Advertising (publicité); *il travaille dans la pub,* he is an adman. ‖ Ad, advert (message, annonce publicitaire).
pubère [pybɛ:r] adj. Pubescent, puberal.
puberté [-bɛrte] f. MÉD. Puberty.
pubien, enne [-bjɛ̃, ɛn] adj. MÉD. Pubic.
pubis [-bis] m. MÉD. Pubis.
publiable [pybliabl] adj. Publishable, fit to be published.
public, ique [pyblik] adj. Public (national); *la chose publique,* the State, the Common weal; *la dette publique,* the National Debt; *la vie publique,* public life, politics. ‖ Public, open; *cours public,* course of public lectures; *fille publique,* prostitute, street-walker; *service public,* public utility service.
— m. Public; *le public est prié de,* the public are (ou) is requested to; *parler en public,* to speak in public. ‖ Public, audience; *avoir un public fidèle,* to have a faithful audience; *destiné au grand public,* intended for the general reader (livre); *le grand public,* the general public. ‖ **Public-relations,** f. pl. FAM. Public relations.
publicain [pyblikɛ̃] m. JUR. Tax-gatherer. ‖ ECCLÉS. Publican.
publication [pyblikasjɔ̃] f. Publication, publishing; bringing out (d'un livre); *en cours de publication,* printing. ‖ Publication, book, review.
publiciste [-sist] s. Publicist.
publicitaire [-sitɛ:r] adj. Advertising.
— s. Publicist, adman.
publicité [-site] f. Publicity; advertising; *agence de publicité,* advertising agency; *chef de la publicité,* advertising manager. ‖ JUR. Publicness.
publier [pyblje] v. tr. (1). To publish, to announce (faire connaître); *publier la nouvelle que,* to release the news that. ‖ To publish, to issue, to bring out (un livre); *être publié sur huit pages,* to run into eight pages. ‖ To edit (des documents, une édition critique). ‖ MÉD. To issue (un bulletin de santé).
publiquement [publikmɑ̃] adv. Publicly.
puce [pys] f. ZOOL. Flea. ‖ ZOOL. Puce de mer, sand-hopper, sand-flea. ‖ FAM. Marché aux puces, Flea market; *mettre la puce à l'oreille de qqn,* to awaken s.o.'s suspicions; *secouer les puces à qqn,* to give s.o. a good hiding.
— adj. invar. Puce-coloured.
puceau [pyso] adj., m. Virgin.
pucelage [-sla:ʒ] m. Maidenhead, maidenhood, virginity.
pucelle [-sɛl] adj. Virgin.
— f. Virgin, maid, maiden; *la Pucelle d'Orléans,* the Maid of Orleans.
puceron [pysrɔ̃] m. ZOOL. Plant-louse.
pucier [pusje] m. POP. Bed, kip.
pudding [pudiŋ] m. CULIN. Plum pudding.
puddlage [pydla:ʒ] m. TECHN. Puddling.
puddler [-le] v. tr. (1). TECHN. To puddle.
pudeur [pydœ:r] f. Modesty, sexual modesty; maidenly modesty; *attentat à la pudeur,* indecent assault. ‖ Modesty, moderation, decency; *sans pudeur,* shameless, wanton (adj.); shamelessly, wantonly (adv.).
pudibond, onde [pydibɔ̃, ɔ̃:d] adj. Prudish, modest, chaste. ‖ Easily shocked. (V. PRUDE.)
pudibonderie [-bɔ̃dri] f. Prudishness, excessive modesty.
pudicité [-site] f. Modesty, pudency; chastity.
pudique [pydik] adj. Modest; chaste.
pudiquement [-mɑ̃] adv. Modestly, chastely; blushingly.

puer [pɥe] v. intr. (1). To stink.
— v. tr. To stink (ou) reek of (l'alcool).
puéricultrice [pyerikyltris] f. Nurse trained in child care.
puériculture [pyerikylty:r] f. Rearing of children; child care.
puéril, ile [-ril] adj. Puerile, childish.
puérilité [-rilite] f. Puerility, childishness (état). ‖ Childish act (ou) expression.
puerpéral, ale [pyɛrperal] adj. MÉD. Puerperal.
pugilat [pyʒila] m. Pugilism. ‖ FAM. Set-to.
pugiliste [-list] m. SPORTS. Pugilist, boxer.
pugilistique [-listik] adj. SPORTS. Pugilistic.
pugnace [pygnas] adj. Pugnacious, full of fight.
pugnacité [-site] f. Pugnacity, pugnaciousness.
puiné, ée [pɥine] adj. Younger (brother or sister).
puis [pɥi] adv. Then; afterwards; next; *et puis,* moreover (ou) besides; *et puis après?,* well, what of it?; *puis donc,* since therefore.
puis. V. POUVOIR (79).
puisage [pɥiza:ʒ] m. Drawing, pumping up.
puisard [pɥiza:r] m. Draining well; sink, cesspool. ‖ TECHN. Sump.
puisatier [-zatje] m. Well-digger.
puiser [-ze] v. tr. (1). To draw (de l'eau). ‖ To draw, to borrow (emprunter); *Keats puisait dans Lemprière,* Keats drew material from Lemprière.
— v. intr. To draw (*dans,* on, upon).
puisque [pɥisk] conj. Since, as; considering (ou) seeing that; *puisque je vous l'ai dit!,* but I told you so!
puissamment [pɥisamɑ̃] adv. Powerfully, strongly. ‖ Exceedingly, excessively; *puissamment muni,* extremely well provided.
puissance [-sɑ̃:s] f. Power, force, strength (d'une personne); *la puissance de son bras,* the strength of his arm. ‖ Power, influence (d'une idée); power (d'imagination); power, faculty (d'organisation); power, efficacy (de raisonnement); power, force (de suggestion); *sa puissance de travail,* his capacity for work. ‖ Power, domination, sway, rule (emprise). ‖ Power (nation); *les Grandes Puissances,* the Great Powers. ‖ Potential; *en puissance,* potentially, in posse. ‖ JUR. Power, authority; *puissance paternelle,* parental control (ou) authority; *femme en puissance de mari,* feme covert. ‖ ECCLÉS. *Les puissances célestes,* the Powers above; *les puissances des ténèbres,* the Powers of Darkness. ‖ MATH. Power; *la n^{ième} puissance,* the nth power. ‖ MILIT. *Puissance offensive,* fighting efficiency; *puissance de feu,* firepower. ‖ TECHN. Power, strength, force (d'une machine); *puissance horaire,* output per hour; *calcul de la puissance motrice,* engine-rating; *moteur de grande puissance,* heavy-duty engine.
puissant, ante [-sɑ̃, ɑ̃:t] adj. Powerful, strong, mighty (homme, maître, volonté); *être assez puissant pour,* to be powerful enough to. ‖ Weighty (argument); powerful, efficacious (pression); adequate (résistance). ‖ COMM. Leading (firme). ‖ FAM. Stout (corpulent).
— m. pl. *Les puissants,* the mighty ones.
puisse, puissions, puissiez. V. POUVOIR (79).
puits [pɥi] m. Well. ‖ TECHN. Shaft (d'aération. d'extraction); pit (de mine); *puits de pétrole* oil-well. ‖ FIG. Well (de science).
pull [pyl], **pull-over** [-ɔvœr] m. Pullover, jumper, sweater.
pullman [pulman] m. CH. DE F. Pullman car. ‖ AUTOM. Pullman coach, pullman.
pullulation [pylylasjɔ̃] f., **pullulement** [-lmɑ̃] m. Pullulation, swarming.
pulluler [-le] v. intr. (1). To pullulate, to swarm.
pulmonaire [pylmɔnɛ:r] adj. MÉD. Pulmonary; *congestion pulmonaire,* congestion of the lungs.
— f. BOT. Pulmonaria.
pulpe [pylp] f. Pulp; *réduire en pulpe,* to crush, to pulp.

pulpeux, euse [-pø, ø:z] adj. Pulpous, pulpy.
pulsar [pylsa:r] m. ASTRON. Pulsar.
pulsation [pylsasjɔ̃] f. MÉD. Pulsation, throbbing (action); throb, heartbeat (battement).
pulser [pylse] v. tr. (1). TECHN. To force (air); *chauffage à air pulsé,* forced-air heating.
pulsion [pylsjɔ̃] f. PSYCH. Instinct, drive; *pulsion partielle,* component (ou) partial instinct.
pultacé, ée [pyltase] adj. Pultaceous, pulpy.
pulvérisable [pylverizabl] adj. Pulverizable.
pulvérisateur [-zatœ:r] m. Pulverizer, sprayer; atomizer, vaporizer.
pulvérisation [-zasjɔ̃] f. Pulverization, pulverizing, atomization, atomizing, spraying.
pulvériser [-ze] v. tr. (1). To pulverize, to grind, to crush (écraser). ‖ To spray, to atomize (vaporiser). ‖ FAM. To pulverize, to smash (les records).
pulvériseur [-zœ:r] m. AGRIC. Disk harrow.
pulvérulence [pylverylɑ̃:s] f. Pulverulence
pulvérulent, ente [-lɑ̃, ɑ̃:t] adj. Pulverulent, powdery.
puma [pyma] m. ZOOL. Puma, cougar.
punais, aise [pynɛ, ɛz] adj. Ill-smelling.
punaise [pynɛ:z] f. ZOOL. Bed-bug, bug. ‖ TECHN. Drawing-pin, U. S. thumbtack, pushpin (clou).
punaiser [-nɛze] v. tr. (1). To tack, to fix with drawing-pins (ou U.S.) thumbtacks.
punch [pɔ̃:ʃ] m. Punch; *bol à punch,* punch-bowl.
punch [pœ:nʃ] m. SPORTS. Punch (à la boxe). ‖ FIG. Punch (énergie, efficacité), drive (dynamisme).
puncheur [pœnʃœ:r] SPORTS. Hard hitter; *c'est un puncheur,* he packs quite a punch.
punching-ball [pœnʃiŋbol] m. Punch-ball, U.S. punching-bag.
punique [pynik] adj. Punic.
punir [pyni:r] v. tr. (2). To punish; *punir de prison,* to punish with imprisonment; *être puni pour avoir péché,* to pay for one's sins; *être puni par où on a péché,* to reap what one has sown.
punissable [-nisabl] adj. Punishable; liable to punishment.
punisseur, euse [-nisœ:r, ø:z] adj. Punishing.
— s. Punisher.
punitif, ive [-nitif, i:v] adj. Punitive.
punition [-nisjɔ̃] f. Punishment (v. CHÂTIMENT); *échapper à la punition,* to go unpunished. ‖ MILIT. *Registre des punitions,* defaulters' book.
punk [pœk] adj., s. Punk.
pupillaire [pypillɛ:r] adj. JUR., MÉD. Pupillar.
pupillarité [-larite] f. JUR. Pupillarity, pupillage.
pupille [pypil] s. JUR. Ward; *pupille de l'Assistance,* orphan, foundling; *pupille de la Nation,* Ward of the Nation, war orphan (in France).
— f. MÉD. Pupil.
pupitre [pypitr] m. Desk (pour écrire). ‖ MUS. Music stand. ‖ ECCLÉS. Lectern.
pur, ure [pyr] adj. Pure, unalloyed (sans mélange); *or pur,* pure gold; *vin pur,* unmixed (ou) neat wine. ‖ Pure, spotless, unspotted, unsullied (sans tache); *la blancheur la plus pure,* unsullied whiteness. ‖ Pure, innocent; *une jeune fille pure,* a chaste (ou) good girl; *pur de toute indélicatesse,* innocent of all rudeness; *pur de toute tache,* free from all taint. ‖ Perfect (parfait); *anglais pur,* pure English. ‖ Pure, simple, mere, sheer (absolu); *absurdité pure,* sheer absurdity; *folie pure,* utter folly; *pur hasard,* mere chance; *méchanceté pure,* unqualified wickedness; *par pure méchanceté,* out of sheer malice; *pur idiot,* unmitigated fool; *pur sectaire,* out-and-out sectarian; *vérité pure,* naked truth. ‖ ZOOL. *Pur sang,* thoroughbred. ‖ LOC. *En pure perte,* for nothing, to no purpose, uselessly; *pur et simple,* pure and simple; *c'est pur et simple!,* that's

clear ! || **Pur-sang,** m. Zool. Thoroughbred horse.
— s. Ecclés. *Les purs,* the pure in heart. || Fam.
Un pur, a diehard.

purée [pyre] f. Culin. Mash, puree ; *purée de
pommes de terre,* mashed potatoes ; *purée de
tomates,* tomato puree. || Fam. *Etre dans la purée,*
to be hard up.

purement [pyrmᾶ] adv. Purely (sans défaut,
sans tache). || Purely, merely ; *purement et sim-
plement,* purely and simply.

pureté [-te] f. Purity, pureness. || Chastity, inno-
cence.

purgatif, ive [pyrgatif, i:v] adj., m. Purgative.

purgation [-sjɔ̃] f. Méd. Purgation ; purge.

purgatoire [-twa:r] m. Ecclés. Purgatory. || Fam.
Bad time.

purge [pyrʒ] f. Méd. Purge, purgative, dose of
medicine. || Jur. Purge (en politique) ; redemption,
paying off (d'hypothèque). || Techn. Drain.

purger [-ʒe] v. tr. (7). Techn. To purge, to refine,
to purify (un métal) ; to drain (un radiateur). ||
Méd. To purge. || Jur. To redeem (une hypo-
thèque) ; *purger sa peine,* to serve one's sentence.
|| Fig. To purge, to rid, to clear (*de,* of).
— v. tr. **Se purger.** Méd. To take medicine. || Fig.
Se purger d'une accusation, to clear oneself of an
accusation.

purgeur [-ʒœ:r] m. Techn. Drain-cock.

purifiant, ante [pyrifjᾶ, ᾶ:t] adj. Purifying. ||
Méd. Cleansing.

purificateur, trice [pyrifikatœ:r, tris] adj.
Purifying.
— s. Purifier.

purification [-sjɔ̃] f. Purification. || Méd. Cleans-
ing (du sang).

purificatoire [-twa:r] adj. Purificatory.

purifier [pyrifje] v. tr. (1). To purify (en général).
|| To sweeten, to clear, to disinfect (l'air, l'eau).
[V. assainir.] || Techn. To refine (un métal). ||
Méd. To cleanse (le sang). || Ecclés. To cleanse,
to purge (l'âme).

purin [pyrɛ̃] m. Liquid manure.

purisme [pyrism] m. Purism.

puriste [-rist] s. Purist.
— adj. Puristical.

puritain, aine [pyritɛ̃, ɛn] adj. Puritan, puritanical.
— s. Puritan. || Fam. U.S. Blue nose. (V. bégueule.)

puritanisme [-tanism] m. Puritanism.

purotin [pyrɔtɛ̃] m. Fam. Hard-up (ou) penniless
person.

purpura [pyrpyra] m. Méd. Purpura.

purpurin, ine [-rɛ̃, in] adj. Purplish.

purulence [pyrylᾶ:s] f. Méd. Purulence.

purulent [-lᾶ] adj. Méd. Purulent.

pus [py] m. Méd. Pus, matter.

pus. V. pouvoir (79).

pusillanime [pyzillanim] adj. Pusillanimous ;
faint-hearted, chicken-hearted, lily-livered (fam.).

pusillanimité [-mite] f. Pusillanimity.

pustule [pystyl] f. Méd. Pustula.

pustuleux, euse [-lø, ø:z] adj. Méd. Pustular.

pût. V. pouvoir (79).

putain [pytɛ̃] f. Pop. Whore.

putatif, ive [pytatif, i:v] adj. Jur. Putative, supposed, presumed.

pute [pyt] f. V. putain.

putois [putwa] m. Zool. Polecat.

putréfaction [pytrefaksjɔ̃] f. Putrefaction ; rotting, decaying.

putréfiable [-fjabl] adj. Putrefiable.

putréfier [-fje] v. tr. (1). To putrefy ; to rot.
— v. pr. **Se putréfier,** to putrefy, to become
decomposed, to become putrid ; to go bad (fam.).

putrescence [pytrɛssᾶ:s] f. Putrescence. || Méd.
Sepsis.

putrescent, ente [-sᾶ, ᾶ:t] adj. Putrescent.

putrescible [-sibl] adj. Putrescible.

putride [pytrid] adj. Putrid.

putridité [-dite] f. Putridity, putridness.

putsch [putʃ] m. Putsch, military coup.

puy [pчi] m. Géogr. Peak.

puzzle [pœzl] m. Jigsaw-puzzle, jigsaw (propre,
fig.).

P.V. [peve] m. Abrév. de *procès-verbal,* Autom.
Ticket (contravention).

pygmée [pigme] m. Pygmy.

pygméen, enne [-meɛ̃, ɛn] adj. Pygmean, pygmy.

pyjama [piʒama] m. Pyjamas, U. S. pajamas.

pylône [pilo:n] m. Archit. Pylon, pilar. || Aviat.
Pylône de radar, radar tower.

pylore [pilɔ:r] m. Méd. Pylorus.

pyorrhée [piɔre] f. Méd. Pyorrhoea.

pyramidal, ale [piramidal] adj. Pyramidal.

pyramide [-mid] f. Pyramid.

pyrénéen, enne [pireneɛ̃, ɛn] adj. Pyrenean.

Pyrénées [pirene] f. pl. Géogr. Pyrenees.

pyrèthre [pirɛtr] m. Bot. Pyrethrum ; feverfew.

Pyrex [pirɛks] m. (nom déposé) Pyrex.

pyridine [piridin] f. Chim. Pyridine.

pyrite [pirit] m. Pyrites.

pyrogène [pirɔʒɛn] adj. Géol. Pyrogene.

pyrogravure [-gravy:r] f. Pyrogravure, poker-
work.

pyrolyse [-li:z] f. Pyrolysis.

pyromane [-man] s. Pyromaniac, fire bug (fam.).
|| Jur. Arsonist.

pyromètre [-mɛ:tr] m. Pyrometer.

pyrotechnie [-tɛkni] f. Pyrotechny.

pyrotechnique [-tɛknik] adj. Pyrotechnic,
pyrotechnical ; *compositions pyrotechniques,*
pyrotechnic (ou) firework compositions.

pyrrhique [pirik] adj., m. Pyrrhic.

pyrrhonien, enne [pirɔnjɛ̃, ɛn] adj. Pyrrhonian.
— s. Pyrrhonist.

pyrrhonisme [pirɔnism] m. Pyrrhonism.

Pyrrhus [pirys] n. Pyrrhus. || Fig. *Victoire à la
Pyrrhus,* Pyrrhic (ou) Cadmean victory.

Pythagore [pitagɔ:r] m. Pythagoras.

pythagoricien, enne [-gɔrisjɛ̃, ɛn] s. Philos.
Pythagorean.

pythagorisme [-gɔrism] m. Philos. Pytha-
gorism.

pythie [piti] f. Pythoness, Pythia.

pythique [pitik] adj. Pythian.

python [pitɔ̃] m. Zool. Python.

pythonisse [pitɔnis] f. Pythoness.

pyxide [piksid] f. Bot. Pyxidium. || Ecclés.
Pyx.

Q

q [ky] m. Q, q.

Qatar [kata:r] m. Géogr. Qatar.

Q.G. [kyʒe] m. Milit. Abrév. de *quartier général*, GHQ, General headquarters.

Q.I. [kyi] m. Psych. Abrév. de *quotient intellectuel*, IQ, intelligence quotient.

quadragénaire [kwadraʒenɛ:r] adj., s. Quadragenarian.

quadragésimal, ale [-zimal] adj. Quadragesimal.

quadragésime [-zim] f. Ecclés. Quadragesima.

quadrangulaire [kwadrãgylɛ:r] adj. Quadrangular; four-angled.

quadrant [kadrã] m. Math. Quadrant.

quadrat, ate [kwadra, at] adj. Astron. Quartile.

quadratique [-tik] adj. Math. Quadratic.

quadrature [-ty:r] f. Math. Quadrature. ‖ Fam. *Chercher la quadrature du cercle*, to try to square the circle.

quadriceps [kwadrisɛps] m. Méd. Quadriceps.

quadrichromie [-kromi] f. Techn. Four-colour printing.

quadriennal, ale [kwadriɛnal] adj. Quadrennial. ‖ Agric. Four-course (assolement).

quadrige [kwadri:ʒ] m. † Quadriga.

quadrijumeaux [kwadriʒymo] adj. m. pl. Méd. *Tubercules quadrijumeaux*, corpora quadrigemina, quadrigeminal body.

quadrilatéral, ale [kwadrilateral] adj. Math. Quadrilateral.

quadrilatère [-tɛ:r] m. Math., Milit. Quadrilateral.

quadrillage [kadrija:ʒ] m. Squaring (du papier); chequering, checkering (du tissu) [action]; chequer-work, checks (dessin).

quadrille [kadri:j] m. Quadrille, troop (de cavaliers). ‖ Arts. Quadrille (danse); *quadrille des lanciers*, lancers.

quadrillé, ée [kadrije] adj. Squared, graph (papier); checked, chequered, quadrilled (tissu); *carte quadrillée*, grid map.

quadriller v. tr. (1). To chequer, to checker, to cross-rule.

quadrimoteur [kwadrimɔtœ:r] adj. Aviat. Four-engined.
— m. Aviat. Four-engined plane.

quadripartite [-partit] adj. Quadripartite; *conférence quadripartite*, four-power conference (entre nations), four-party conference (entre partis).

quadriphonie [-fɔni] f. Techn. Quadraphonics, quadrophonics, four-channel sound.

quadriréacteur [-reaktœ:r] m. Aviat. Four-engined jet plane.

quadrisyllabe [-sillab] m. Gramm. Quadrisyllable.

quadrisyllabique [-sillabik] adj. Gramm. Quadrisyllabic.

quadrivalent [-valã] f. Chim. Quadrivalent, tetravalent.

quadrumane [kwadryman] adj. Quadrumanous, four-handed.
— m. Zool. Quadrumane (pl. quadrumana).

quadrupède [-pɛd] adj. Quadrupedal, four-footed.
— m. Zool. Quadruped.

quadruple [kwadrypl] adj., m. Quadruple, fourfold; *au quadruple*, fourfold. ‖ Mus. *Quadruple croche*, hemidemisemiquaver, U. S. sixty-fourth note.

quadrupler [-ple] v. tr., (1). To quadruple.

quadruplés [-ple] s. pl. Quadruplets; quads (fam.).

quai [kɛ] m. Embankment (avenue); *sur les quais*, on the embankment. ‖ Naut. Quay, wharf, pier; *amener à quai*, to berth; *à quai*, alongside the quay; *droits de quai*, wharfage, quayage (ou) pier dues; *vendre à quai*, to sell ex-wharf. ‖ Ch. de f. Platform; *à quai*, in. ‖ Fig. *Le Quai d'Orsay*, the French Foreign Office.

quaker, eresse [kwekœ:r, krɛs] n. Quaker.

qualifiable [kalifjabl] adj. Describable; that may be characterized (de, as).

qualificatif, ive [-fikatif, i:v] adj. Gramm. Qualifying; *adjectif, terme qualificatif*, qualifier. ‖ Sports. Qualifying.
— m. Epithet (propre, fig.).

qualification [-fikasjõ] f. Qualification; appellation. (V. désignation.) ‖ Jur. Appreciation. ‖ Fin. Qualifying. ‖ Sports. Qualification.

qualifié, ée [-fje] adj. Qualified, fit (pour, for) [v. compétent]; *ouvrier qualifié, non qualifié*, skilled, unskilled worker; *personne qualifiée*, qualified person. ‖ Qualified (de, as). [V. traité.] ‖ Jur. Aggravated (crime).

qualifier [-fje] v. tr. (1). To qualify, to style, to term (v. caractériser); *qualifier qqn de voleur*, to call s.o. a thief. ‖ Gramm. To qualify.
— v. pr. **Se qualifier**, to call (ou) to style oneself (se désigner). ‖ To qualify (pour, for) [prendre rang].

qualitatif, ive [kalitatif, i:v] adj. Qualitative.

qualitativement [-tativmã] adv. Qualitatively.

qualité [-te] f. Quality (v. attribut, propriété); *qualité soporifique*, soporific (ou) soporiferous property. ‖ Quality (valeur); *de première qualité*, first rate, prime, choice. ‖ Good quality (vertu); *avoir beaucoup de qualités*, to have many good qualities (ou) points. ‖ Quality (v. rang); *personne de qualité*, person of quality. ‖ Qualification (v. condition); *décliner ses nom et qualités*, to state one's name and status (ou) qualifications; *en qualité de*, as; *en sa qualité de*, in his capacity; *qualité officielle*, official status. ‖ Jur. Capacity (habilitation); *avoir qualité pour faire qqch.*, to be qualified (ou) entitled to do sth.; *avoir les qualités voulues pour remplir une fonction*, to have the necessary qualifications for a post. ‖ Mus. Tone quality.

quand [kã] conj. When (lorsque); *parlez-lui-en quand il viendra*, mention it to him when he comes; *quand il était enfant, il avait l'esprit vif*, he was quick-minded as (ou) when a boy. ‖ When (alors que); *je criais : « Arrêtez ! »*, *quand il fouetta son cheval et fila au galop*, I cried out « Stop ! », when he whipped up his horse and galloped away. ‖ As (comme); *il sortait quand vous entriez*, he went out as you were coming in. ‖ Even if (ou) though, although (bien que); *quand (ou) quand même (ou) quand bien même je le verrais, je n'y croirais pas*, even if I saw it, I should not believe it. ‖ Loc. *Quand même*, all the same, for all that, just the same (malgré tout); *c'est quand même un bon type*, he's a decent chap for all that; *il répond quand même*, he answers all the same. ‖ Fam. *Quand je vous le disais !*, didn't I tell you so !; *quand vous serez prêt !*, when you are ready !

— adv. When (à quel moment) ; *quand lui avez-vous écrit ?*, when did you write to him ? ; *à quand ce festin ?*, when will the celebration be ? ; *de quand est ce mariage ?*, what is the date of the wedding ? ; *depuis quand est-il là ?*, how long has he been there ? ; *jusqu'à quand resterez-vous ?*, how long (ou) till when shall you stay ? ; *n'importe quand*, no matter when ; *pour quand est-ce fixé ?*, when is it ?

quant [kɑ̃] adv. *Quant à*, as to, as for, as far as ; *quant à cela*, for that matter, as far as that is concerned ; *quant à vous*, as for you ; *quant à votre oncle*, as regards your uncle ; *exact quant à ses termes*, accurate as far as it goes ; *jeune quant au reste de l'assistance*, young compared with the rest of the company. ‖ **Quant-à-soi**, m. invar. Stand-offishness, reserve ; *se tenir sur son quant-à-soi*, to stand on one's dignity, to remain aloof.

quanta [kwɑ̃ta] m. pl. V. QUANTUM.

quantième [kɑ̃tjɛm] m. Day ; *quantième du mois*, day of the month. (V. COMBIEN.)

quantifiable [kɑ̃tifjabl] adj. Quantifiable.

quantification [-fikasjɔ̃] f. Quantification.

quantifier [-fje] v. tr. (1). To quantify. ‖ PHYS. To quantize.

quantique [kwɑ̃tik] adj. PHYS. Quantum (nombre, mécanique).

quantitatif, ive [kɑ̃titatif, i:v] adj. CHIM. Quantitative. ‖ GRAMM. Of quantity.

quantitativement [-tativmɑ̃] adv. Quantitatively.

quantité [-te] f. Quantity, amount (nombre) ; *en grande quantité*, in large quantities ; *en quantité*, in bulk ; *par petites quantités*, in small quantities (ou) amounts ; *quantité insuffisante*, insufficiency ; *des quantités de gens*, *quantité de gens*, lots of people. (V. FOULE, TAS.) ‖ Extent (étendue) ; *la quantité des champs*, the extent of the fields. ‖ MATH. Quantity. ‖ ELECTR. Quantity (du courant). ‖ GRAMM. Quantity (du vers, d'une voyelle). ‖ COMM. *Quantité de marchandises entreposées*, stock. ‖ FIG. Quantity ; *quantité négligeable*, negligible quantity.

quantum [kwɑ̃tɔm] m. Quorum (d'une société). ‖ Amount (des indemnités). ‖ CHIM., MATH. Quantum ; *théorie des quanta*, quantum theory.

quarantaine [karɑ̃tɛn] f. About forty, forty or so ; *une quarantaine de pommes*, about forty apples. ‖ Forty (âge) ; *approcher de la quarantaine*, to be verging on forty ; to be forty-ish (fam.). ‖ NAUT. Quarantine ; *mettre en quarantaine*, to quarantine. ‖ FIG. *Mettre en quarantaine*, to send to Coventry ; U. S. to give the silent treatment to.

quarante [karɑ̃:t] adj. num. Forty ; *quarante pommes*, forty apples ; *page quarante*, page forty. ‖ FAM. *S'en moquer comme de l'an quarante*, not to care a bean, not to give a hang.
— m. invar. Forty ; *habiter au quarante*, to live at number forty ; *les Quarante*, the Forty.

quarantenaire [karɑ̃tnɛ:r] adj. Forty-year. NAUT. Quarantine.

quarantième [-tjɛm] adj., m. Fortieth.

quark [kwark] m. PHYS. Quark.

quart [ka:r] m. Quarter (poids, portion) ; *une livre et quart*, a pound and a quarter ; *trois quarts*, three quarters. ‖ Quarter (heure) ; *quart d'heure*, a quarter of an hour ; *il est le quart*, it's a quarter past ; *trois heures et quart*, a quarter past three ; *trois heures moins le quart*, a quarter to three, two forty-five ; *trois heures trois quarts*, a quarter to four. ‖ MATH. Quadrant (de cercle). ‖ ARCHIT. *Quart-de-rond*, quarter round. ‖ MUS. *Quart de soupir*, semiquaver rest, U. S. sixteenth-note rest. ‖ MILIT. Tin mug (gobelet). ‖ NAUT. Point (aire de vent) ; watch (veille) ; *de quart*, of (ou) on the watch ; *prendre le quart*, to take charge of the

watch ; *relever le quart*, to change watch. ‖ LOC. *Aux trois quarts mort*, more than half dead ; *les trois quarts du temps*, most of the time ; *un petit quart d'heure*, a quarter of an hour or so ; *passer un mauvais quart d'heure*, to have a bad time of it ; *photo de trois quarts*, three-quarter face photography ; *pour le quart d'heure*, for the moment ; *vivre le quart d'heure de Rabelais*, to be at the hour of reckoning.

quarte [ka:rt] adj. f. MÉD. Quartan (fièvre).
— f. SPORTS. Quarte (à l'escrime). ‖ MUS. Fourth.

quarté [karte] m. SPORTS. Four-horse combination bet.

quarteron [kartərɔ̃] m. Handful, small bunch (petit groupe).

quarteron, onne [kartərɔ̃, ɔn] s. Quadroon (métis).

quartette [kwartɛt] m. MUS. Quartet, quartette.

quartier [kartje] m. Quarter, fourth part (morceau) ; *couper en quartiers*, to quarter ; *mettre en quartiers*, to tear to pieces. ‖ Quarter, district, ward (d'une ville) ; *quartier chic*, residential quarter ; fashionable neighbourhood ; *Quartier latin*, Latin Quarter ; *quartier populaire*, working-class district ; *quartier réservé*, red-light (ou) -lamp district ; *quartier des théâtres*, theatre-land ; *médecin de quartier*, local practitioner ; *poste de quartier*, branch post-office. ‖ Division (d'une école) ; *quartier des grands*, upper school. ‖ ASTRON. Quarter (de la lune) ; *au dernier, premier quartier*, in the last, first quarter. ‖ CULIN. Quarter (de bœuf) ; portion, piece (de gâteau) ; gammon (de lard) ; *quartier de chevreuil*, haunch of venison. ‖ BLAS. Quarter, quartering (de noblesse). ‖ JUR. Ward (de prison). ‖ MILIT. Quarters, barracks ; *quartier général*, headquarters ; *grand quartier général, G. Q. G.*, General Headquarters, G.H.Q. ; *quartiers d'hiver*, winter quarters ; *quartier libre*, off duty ; *consigné au quartier*, confined to barracks. ‖ FIG. Quarter, mercy ; *faire quartier à*, to grant quarter to ; *pas de quartier*, no quarter. ‖ **Quartier-maître**, MILIT. † Quartermaster ; NAUT. leading seaman.

quarto [kwarto] adv. Fourthly.

quartz [kwarts] m. Quartz, rock-crystal.

quartzite [-tsit] m. Quartzite.

quasar [kwaza:r, kaza:r] m. ASTRON. Quasar, quasi-stellar object, QSO.

quasi [kazi] m. CULIN. Chump-end, U.S. butt-end.

quasi, quasiment [-mɑ̃] adv. Quasi, almost, nearly (v. PRESQUE) ; *quasi certain*, practically certain ; *quasi mort*, almost dead.

Quasimodo [kazimodo] f. ECCLÉS. Low Sunday ; *lundi de Quasimodo*, Low Monday.
— m. Quasimodo (personnage).

quaternaire [kwatɛrnɛ:r] adj. CHIM., MATH., GÉOL. Quaternary.
— m. GÉOL. Quaternary.

quatorze [katɔrz] adj. num. Fourteen ; *page quatorze*, page fourteen. ‖ Fourteenth ; *Louis quatorze*, Louis the Fourteenth ; *le quatorze avril*, the fourteenth of April, April fourteenth.
— m. Fourteen.

quatorzième [-zjɛm] adj., m. Fourteenth.

quatorzièmement [-zjɛmmɑ̃] adv. Fourteenthly, in the fourteenth place.

quatrain [katrɛ̃] m. Quatrain.

quatre [katr] adj. num. Four ; *quatre pommes*, four apples ; *avoir quatre ans*, to be four. ‖ Fourth ; *Henri quatre*, Henry the Fourth ; *le quatre avril*, April the fourth. ‖ MUS. *Morceau à quatre mains*, duet. ‖ MILIT. *Colonne par quatre*, column of fours. ‖ BOT. *A quatre feuilles*, four-leaved. ‖ LOC. *A quatre pattes*, on all fours ; *à quatre pas d'ici*, close by ; just a step away ; *aux quatre vents*, to the four winds (of heaven) ; *aux quatre coins du monde*, to the four

corners of the earth; *de quatre sous*, twopenny-halfpenny; *comme quatre*, ravenously (manger); *entre quatre yeux*, between you and me; *les Quatre Grands*, the Big Four; *mes quatre sous*, my small savings; *monter quatre à quatre*, to go up four steps at a time; *se mettre en quatre*, to go out of one's way; *se tenir à quatre*, to keep one's temper, to control oneself in. ‖ **Quatre-épices**, f. pl. BOT. Allspice tree; CULIN. Allspice. ‖ **Quatre-feuilles**, m. invar. ARCHIT. Quaterfoil, quatrefoil. ‖ **Quatre-fleurs**, f. invar. MÉD. Tisane of dried flowers. ‖ **Quatre-huit**, m. inv. MUS. Four-eight time. ‖ **Quatre-mâts**, m. inv. NAUT. Four-master. ‖ **Quatre-quarts**, m. inv. CULIN. Pound cake, rich sponge cake. ‖ **Quatre-saisons**, f. plur. *Marchand des quatre-saisons*, street-trader, costermonger, barrow-boy. ‖ **Quatre-temps**, m. pl. ECCLÉS. Ember days. ‖ **Quatre-vingt-dix**, adj., m. Ninety. ‖ **Quatre-vingt-dixième**, adj., m. Ninetieth. ‖ **Quatre-vingtième**, adj., m. Eightieth. ‖ **Quatre-vingt-neuf**, m. Eighty-nine. ‖ **Quatre-vingts**, adj., m. Eighty; *quatre-vingt-un*, eighty-one. ‖ **Quatre-vingt-treize**, m. Ninety-three (année).
— m. Four (chiffre); number four (numéro).

quatrième [katrjɛm] adj. Fourth.
— m. Fourth; fourth part, quarter (partie); fourth (personne). ‖ Fourth floor (étage).
— f. Third form (classe). ‖ Quart (aux cartes).

quatrièmement [-mã] adv. Fourthly.

quatrillon [katriljɔ̃] m. MATH. Quadrillon, U.S. septillon.

quatuor [kwatɥɔr] m. MUS. Quartet, quatuor.

quayage [kɛja:ʒ] m. Quayage, wharfage.

que [kə], **qu'** [k] pron. relat. What (de qui, ce que); *advienne que pourra*, come what may; *coûte que coûte*, at all costs, cost what it may. ‖ Whom, that (pour les personnes); *l'enfant le plus turbulent que j'aie jamais vu*, the most unruly boy that I have ever seen; *la femme que vous voyez*, the woman whom you see. ‖ Which, that (pour les choses); *le livre que vous connaissez*, the book that you know, the book you know; *le tableau que j'ai trouvé*, the picture which I found. ‖ That, when (avec idée de temps); *la journée que j'ai passée*, the day that I spent; *pendant les années qu'il vécut*, during the years he lived; *un jour que je travaillais*, one day when I was working. ‖ (Emplois divers); *c'est un beau garçon que Paul*, he's a handsome boy, Paul; *c'est une erreur que de le penser*, it is a mistake to think so; *couvert de sang qu'il était*, covered with blood as he was; *d'ami qu'il était, il devint mon ennemi*, from being my friend, he became my enemy; *en ami qu'il était*, like the friend he was.
— pron. interrog. What (quoi); *que dit-il?*, what does he say?; what is he saying?; *n'avoir que faire de*, to have nothing to do with; *ne savoir que faire*, not to know what to do. ‖ What (à quoi); *que lui sert de courir?*, what is the good of his running? ‖ **Qu'est-ce?**, what is it?; *qu'est-ce qu'il y a?*, what's going on?; what's the matter?; *qu'est-ce que la grammaire?*, what is grammar?; *qu'est-ce que c'est que cela?*, what's that?; *qu'est-ce que vous pensez?*, what do you think?

que [kə] conj.

1. That (pouvant être non traduit); *je crois que vous êtes bon*, I think that you are good, I think you are good. ‖ That, so that (afin que); when (alors que, lorsque); before (avant que); since (depuis que, puisque); without (sans que); as long as, as far as (tant que); *allumez la bougie, que je lise ma lettre*, light the candle, so that I may read my letter; *à peine ma ligne était-elle à l'eau que le bouchon plongea*, hardly was my line in the water when the float dipped; *attendez que la voie soit libre*, wait till the way is clear; *ce n'est pas que je vous aime moins*, it is not that I love you less; *il y a un mois que nous avons eu la première gelée*, it is a month since we had the first frost; *il y a un mois que nous habitons ici*, we have been living here for a month; *il n'est que de travailler pour réussir*, there is nothing like working to succeed; *le travail n'avait pas duré six mois qu'ils étaient devenus amis*, before the work had lasted six months, they had become friends. ‖ 2. Let (impératif); *que la lumière soit!*, let there be light! ‖ 3. May (optatif); *que Dieu vous bénisse!*, God bless you! ‖ 4. Whether, but (dubitatif); *je doute qu'il réponde à votre lettre*, I doubt whether he will answer your letter; *je ne doute pas qu'il ne réponde*, I do not doubt but that he will answer. ‖ 5. Whether (alternatif); *qu'il soit d'accord ou non, j'agirai*, whether he agrees or not, I'll act. ‖ 6. That, lest (crainte); *j'ai peur que cette annonce ne crée un tumulte*, I fear lest this announcement should create a disturbance; *j'ai peur que nos hôtes ne soient déçus*, I am afraid that our guests will be disappointed. ‖ 7. That (intensité); *un tel bruit que*, such a noise that. ‖ 8. But (sauf); *elle ne veut être soignée que par sa mère*, she will be cared for by no one but her mother. ‖ 9. Only, but (seulement); *cela ne dura qu'un instant*, it lasted but a moment; *il n'y a pas qu'elle qui soit jolie*, she is not the only one who is pretty; *il n'y a pas que le bonheur*, happiness is not everything; *on n'a qu'une vie*, one has only one life; *que ça!*, that's all; *sans autre ami que moi*, having no other friend than me. ‖ 10. As (après *aussi, même, tel*); *aussi grand que mon frère*, as tall as my brother; *j'emploie la même grammaire que vous*, I use the same grammar as you; *tel que je l'ai connu*, such as I have ever known him. ‖ 11. Because, as (après *d'autant moins* [ou] *plus*); *d'autant moins* (ou) *plus puissant que*, the less (ou) the more powerful as (ou) because. ‖ 12. Than (après le comparatif); *plus âgé que*, older than. ‖ 13. Than, besides (après : *autre*); *il est autre chose qu'un homme*, he is more than a man; *il y en a d'autres que vous*, there are others besides you. ‖ 14. (Non traduit, après un verbe de volonté); *il ordonne que les élèves restent sous le préau*, he orders the pupils to stand under the playground shelter; *il tient à ce que les élèves se taisent*, he insists upon the pupils keeping quiet. ‖ 15. (Non traduit en cas de répétition); *lorsque les piquets eurent été plantés, que la tente fut montée et qu'on eut hissé le drapeau*, when the poles had been erected, the tent pitched and the flag hoisted. ‖ 16. LOC. *J'espère que oui*, I hope so; *que je sache*, as (ou) so far as I know; *que non, que si!*, surely not!, surely yes!; *qu'il aille au diable!*, he can go to hell! ‖ 17. POP. *Qu'il dit*, says he (dit-il); *qu'il dit!*, so he says! (d'après ce qu'il dit).
— adv. Why (pourquoi); *que n'êtes-vous venu?*, why didn't you come? ‖ How (comme); *que c'est joli!*, how fine it is!; *que cet homme est intelligent!*, how intelligent that man is!, what an intelligent man he is! ‖ How many (combien); *que de peine!*, what a lot of trouble!

---

1. Subordination. — 2. Impératif. — 3. Optatif. — 4. Dubitatif. — 5. Alternatif. — 6. Crainte. — 7. Intensité. — 8. Sauf. — 9. Seulement. — 10. Après *aussi, même, tel*. — 11. Après *d'autant moins* (ou) *plus*. — 12. Après le comparatif. — 13. Après *autre*. — 14. Non traduit après un verbe de volonté. — 15. Non traduit en cas de répétition. — 16. LOC. — 17. POP.

Québec [kebɛk] m. GÉOGR. Quebec.

québécois, oise [-bekwa, wa:z] adj. Of (ou) from Quebec.
— s. Quebecer, quebecois.

quel, elle [kεl, ε:l] adj. interrog. What; *quels poètes pouvez-vous nommer?* what poets can you name?; *quelle sorte d'homme est-ce?* what kind of man is he?; *dites-moi quel jour vous désirez que je vienne*, tell me on what day you wish me to come. ‖ Which (discriminatif); *quel poète préférez-vous?*, which poet do you prefer?; *quelle université a-t-il choisie?*, which university did he choose? ‖ Who, which, what (attribut); *quel est le meilleur moment?*, what is the best time?; *je ne sais quel est le plus savant des deux*, I don't know which is the more learned of the two; *on ne sait quel sera le premier*, there is no knowing who will be the first.
— adj. exclam. What; *quelle confusion!*, what confusion!; *quelle étrange idée!*, what a queer idea!
— adj. indéf. Whoever, whichever, whatever; *quels que soient les obstacles*, whatever obstacles may rise; *quel que soit le parti qui vienne au pouvoir*, whichever party comes to power.

quelconque [kεlkɔ̃:k] adj. indéf. Any, whatever (n'importe lequel); *dans le courant d'une journée quelconque*, in the course of any one day; *donnez-m'en un quelconque*, give me any one; *donnez-moi un livre quelconque à cinq shillings*, give me any book at five shillings. ‖ Some (quelque); *sous un quelconque prétexte*, on some pretence or other. ‖ Ordinary, commonplace (ordinaire); *il est très quelconque*, he is very ordinary; *c'est très quelconque*, it isn't up to much.

quelque [kεlk] adj. Some, any (certain); *elle a quelques notions d'anglais*, she has a smattering of English; *avoir quelque inquiétude*, to feel some uneasiness; *il a quelque moyen d'action*, he has some way of acting; *quelque autre étudiant*, some other student. ‖ Some, any; a little, a few (un certain nombre de); *avoir quelques melons de reste*, to have a few melons left; *il y a quelques jours*, a few days ago; *payer quelques francs de plus*, to pay a few francs more; *pendant quelques instants*, for a little while; *quelques autres*, some others. ‖ **Quelque ... qui (ou)... que**, whatever; whichever; *nous vous transmettrons quelque information qui nous parviendra*, we shall pass on to you any information that reaches us; *quelque chemin que vous preniez*, whichever way you go.
— adv. Some, about (environ); *pendant quelque six mois*, for some six months; *quelque deux ans auparavant*, some two years before; *quelque dix mille francs*, about ten thousand francs. ‖ **Quelque peu**, some, something, somewhat; *quelque peu alarmé*, somewhat alarmed, in some alarm; *quelque peu avant l'époque*, something before the time; *quelque peu voyageur*, something of a traveller; *ressembler quelque peu à*, to look something like. ‖ **Quelque ... que** (si ... que), however; *quelque pressants que lui paraissent ses besoins*, however pressing his needs may seem to him; *quelque bon qu'il soit*, however good he may be; *quelque méchant qu'il fût, il s'y refusa*, wicked as he was, he refused to do it.

quelque chose [kεlkəʃo:z] pron. indéf. invar. Something, anything; *dites-lui quelque chose*, tell him something; *être pour quelque chose dans*, to have something to do with; *il y a quelque chose d'un peu ridicule dans*, there is something a little ludicrous in; *quelque chose de drôle*, something funny; *quelque chose de semblable*, something similar (ou) of the same kind; *s'il y a quelque chose à lire*, if there is anything to read. ‖ Loc. *Ça me dit quelque chose*, that strikes my fancy, that sounds familiar to me; *ça me fait quelque chose*, that gives me a turn; *il y a sûrement*

quelque chose, there is something wrong indeed; *prendre quelque chose*, to have a drink (ou) a snack (boire, manger); *prendre quelque chose pour son grade*, to take a beating.

quelquefois [kεlkəfwa] adv. Sometimes, now and then. (V. PARFOIS.)

quelque part [kεlkəpa:r] loc. adv. Somewhere, anywhere; *j'ai trouvé quelque part, je ne sais où*, I found somewhere or other; *pouvez-vous le poser quelque part?*, can you put it down anywhere?

quelqu'un, une [kεlkœ̃, kyn]; pl. **quelques-uns, unes** [kεlkəzʌn, -zyn] pron. indéf. One, any one; some, any (certain); *pouvez-vous m'en prêter quelques-uns?*, can you lend me any?; *vous pouvez m'en prêter quelques-uns*, you can lend me some; *quelques-uns de mes amis*, some of my friends; *quelqu'un de ces ouvriers*, one of these workmen; *quelques-uns parmi nous*, a certain number of us; *si quelqu'un de vous*, if any of you. ‖ Someone, anyone; somebody, anybody (une personne); *quelqu'un est venu vous voir*, somebody has come to see you; *quelqu'un est-il venu me voir?*, has anybody come to see me?; *il y avait quelqu'un de trop*, there was one person too many; *si quelqu'un vient me voir*, if anyone calls. ‖ Loc. *C'est quelqu'un*, he is somebody; *se prendre pour quelqu'un*, to think no small beer of oneself.

quémander [kemɑ̃de] v. tr. (1). To beg for.
— v. intr. To beg.

quémandeur, euse [-dœ:r, ø:z] s. Beggar. (V. SOLLICITEUR.)

qu'en-dira-t-on [kɑ̃diratɔ̃] m. invar. What people say; public opinion; *se moquer du qu'en-dira-t-on*, not to care about what people say.

quenelle [kənεl] f. CULIN. Quenelle.

quenotte [kənɔt] f. FAM. Tooth.

quenouille [kənu:j] f. Distaff. ‖ AGRIC. Quenouille-trained fruit-tree. ‖ FIG. *Tomber en quenouille*, to fall to the distaff side.

querelle [kərεl] f. Quarrel (v. DISPUTE); *querelle d'Allemand*, forced quarrel; *querelle d'amoureux*, lovers' tiff; *querelles de ménage*, conjugal squabbles, domestic troubles (ou) strife; *chercher querelle à*, to try to pick a quarrel with; *chercher querelle à tout le monde*, to have a chip on one's shoulder; *épouser la querelle de qqn*, to take on (ou) up s.o.'s quarrel, to take up the cudgels on behalf of s.o.

quereller [kərεle] v. tr. (1). To quarrel with.
— v. pr. **Se quereller**, to quarrel; to fall out (fam.); *se quereller avec*, to quarrel with; to wrangle with.

querelleur, euse [kərεlœ:r, ø:z] adj. Quarrelsome.
— s. Quareller, quarrelsome person.

quérir [keri:r] v. tr. (84). † To look for.

questeur [kεstœ:r] m. Quaestor, questor.

question [kεstjɔ̃] f. Question (v. DEMANDE); *poser une question*, to ask a question. ‖ Question, point, matter (sujet); *questions d'actualité*, current affairs, topics of the day; *question en cours d'examen*, matter in hand; *question de vie ou de mort*, matter of life or death; *à côté de la question*, beside the point; *ce n'est pas la question*, that's not the point (ou) question; *de quoi est-il question?* what's the matter?; what's it all about?; *hors de question*, out of the question; *il est question de*, they are talking about; *il n'est pas question qu'il vienne*, there is no question of his coming; *il ne saurait en être question*, I could not think of it; *mettre en question*, to call in question; *ne pas faire question*, to be unquestionable; *ne plus en être question*, to talk no more about it; *remettre en question*, to bring the question up again; *tout remettre en question*, to put everything back into the melting pot. ‖ † Torture, question ; *soumettre à la question*, to put to the torture, to torture. ‖ FAM. *Question affaires*, with regard to business.

questionnaire [-tjɔnɛːr] m. Questionnaire, questionary. ‖ † Torturer.

questionner [-tjɔne] v. tr. (1). To question.

questionneur, euse [-tjɔnœːr, øːz] adj. Inquisitive.
— s. Inquisitive person ; person asking questions.

questure [kɛstyːr] f. Office of quaestor (en France). ‖ † Quaestorship.

quête [kɛːt] f. Quest (v. RECHERCHE) ; *en quête de*, in search of, on the look-out for. ‖ Collection (v. COLLECTE) ; *faire la quête*, to make a collection ; to pass the hat round (fam.). ‖ ECCLÉS. Collection ; *faire la quête*, to take the collection. ‖ SPORTS. Tracking (du chien de chasse). ‖ FIG. *En quête de compliments*, fishing for compliments ; *en quête de renseignements*, looking for information.

quêter [kɛte] v. tr. (1). To collect (de l'argent). ‖ SPORTS. To scent, to search for (le gibier). ‖ FIG. To angle (des compliments).
— v. intr. ECCLÉS. To take the collection. ‖ SPORTS. To quarter (chien).

quêteur, euse [-tœːr, øːz] s. Alms-collector. ‖ ECCLÉS. Sidesman, collection-taker. ‖ SPORTS. Quarterer.

quetsche [kwɛtʃ] f. AGRIC., CULIN. Quetsche.

queue [kø] f. Tail (d'animal) ; *queue écourtée*, bob-tail ; *queue de renard*, brush. ‖ Handle (de casserole) ; shank, handle (d'outil). ‖ Pig-tail (de cheveux) ; *queue de cheval*, pony-tail hair-do. ‖ Tail (d'habit) ; train (de robe) ; *queue de pie*, swallow-tail coat. ‖ Tail (de lettre). ‖ Bottom, tail (d'une classe, d'une liste, d'un cortège) ; *en queue*, at the tail-end ; *être en queue de*, to tail. ‖ Queue (v. FILE) ; *faire queue* (ou) *la queue*, to queue up, to form a queue ; U. S. to stand in line, to form a line, to line up ; *se mettre à la queue*, to fall in at the end of the queue. ‖ ASTRON. Tail (de comète). ‖ BOT. Stem, stalk (de fleur). ‖ MUS. Tail (de note) ; tail-piece (de violon) ; *piano à queue*, grand piano. ‖ AVIAT. Tail (d'avion). ‖ NAUT. Tail (de torpille). ‖ AUTOM. *Faire un tête-à-queue*, to swing tail-end first ; *queue-de-poisson*, tail-wobble. ‖ SPORTS. Cue (de billard) ; *arriver en queue*, to come in at the tail-end. ‖ AVIAT. Tail-end (d'hélicoptère). ‖ FIG. Tail-end (d'orage). ‖ FAM. *Finir en queue de poisson*, to fizzle out ; *histoire sans queue ni tête*, shaggy dog story ; *ni queue ni tête*, neither head nor tail ; *pas la queue d'un!*, not the tail-end of one ! ‖ **Queue-d'aronde,** f. TECHN. Dovetail. ‖ **Queue-de-cheval,** f. Pony-tail (coiffure) ; MÉD. filum terminale. ‖ **Queue-de-morue,** f. TECHN. Flat brush ; FAM. swallow-tail coat ; tails. ‖ **Queue-de-pie,** f. FAM. Tailcoat, tails. ‖ **Queue-de-rat,** f. TECHN. Rat-tail file ; NAUT. pointed rope end.

queuter [køte] v. intr. (1). SPORTS. To push the ball (au billard) ; to spoon (au croquet).

queux [kø] m. *Maître queux*, master cook.

qui [ki] pron. relat. Who, that (sujet, pour les personnes) ; *l'homme qui parle*, the man who is speaking ; *le maître qui vous apprend l'anglais*, the master who is teaching you English ; *un des plus grands hommes qui aient jamais vécu*, one of the greatest men who (ou) that ever lived. ‖ That, which (sujet, pour les choses) ; *le livre qui est dans le vestibule*, the book which (ou) that is in the hall ; *les livres qui doivent être reliés*, the books that are to be bound. ‖ Whom, that (ou non traduit) [complément, pour les personnes] ; *le commerçant à qui vous faites allusion*, the tradesman whom you are alluding to ; *le garçon à qui vous étiez si attaché*, the boy you were

so attached to. ‖ Who (celui qui) ; *crier à qui veut l'entendre*, to cry to all who will listen ; *qui vole mon temps vole mon argent*, time is money. ‖ Which, what (ce qui) ; *qui pis est*, what is worse. ‖ If one (si l'on) ; *comme qui dirait*, so to speak, as who should say, as you might say ; *tout vient à point à qui sait attendre*, all things come to him who waits. ‖ Qui... qui, one... the other ; some... the others ; *ils cherchent qui un appartement, qui une villa*, some are looking for a flat (ou) U. S. an apartment, others for a house. ‖ Qui... que, whoever, whomsoever ; *qui que vous soyez*, whoever you may be ; *qui que vous trouviez*, whomsoever you meet ; *à qui que ce soit*, to anybody ; *qui que ce soit qui*, whoever ; *donnez le sac à qui il appartient, qui que ce puisse être*, give the bag to whomsoever it belongs.
— pron. interrog. Who (sujet) ; whose ; whom (complément) ; *qui était en guerre aux Indes?* who was at war in India? ; *qui ce peut-il bien être?*, who in the world can it be? ; *qui ça?*, *qui donc?*, whom do you mean? ; *à qui est ce couteau?*, whose knife is this? ; *à qui appartient ce calepin?*, whom does this note-book belong to? ; *de qui avez-vous reçu cet argent?*, whom did you receive this money from? ‖ Which (sujet, sens discriminatif) ; *qui des deux* (ou) *de vous a perdu cette bourse?*, which of the two (ou) of you has lost this purse? ‖ **Qui est-ce qui?**, who? ; **qui est-ce que?**, whom ; *qui est-ce qui veut venir avec moi?*, who wishes to come with me? ; *qui est-ce que vous connaissez?*, whom are you acquainted with? ‖ **Qui-vive,** m. MILIT. Sentry's challenge ; *qui vive?*, who goes there? ; FIG. *sur le qui-vive*, on the alert.

quia (à) [akwja] loc. adv. Nonplussed, in a quandary ; *réduire à quia*, to nonplus, to stump.

quiche [kiʃ] f. CULIN. Quiche.

quiconque [kikɔ̃k] pron. indéf. Whoever, whosoever ; *quiconque le voit l'aime*, whoever sees him loves him. ‖ Anyone (n'importe qui) ; *il l'aime plus que quiconque*, he loves her more than anyone else.

quidam [qɥidam] m. Someone ; fellow, U. S. guy.

quiet, ète [kjɛ, ɛt] adj. Quiet, peaceful.

quiétisme [kɥietism] m. ECCLÉS. Quietism.

quiétiste [-tist] adj., s. ECCLÉS. Quietist.

quiétude [kietyd] f. Quietude. (V. TRANQUILLITÉ.)

quignon [kiɲɔ̃] m. Chunk, hunk (de pain).

quille [kiːj] f. Ninepin, skittle. (V. JEU.) ‖ Glove-stretcher (à gants). ‖ TECHN. Plug ; wedge. ‖ FAM. Pin (jambe).

quille f. NAUT. Keel.

quiller [kije] v. intr. (1). To set up the skittles (ou) pins. ‖ To throw for first play.

quillon [-jɔ̃] m. Cross-guard (d'épée) ; piling-pin (de fusil).

quinaud, aude [kino, oːd] adj. Confused, abashed. (V. EMBARRASSÉ.)

quincaillerie [kɛ̃kɑjri] f. Ironmongery, hardware (objets). ‖ Hardware shop, ironmonger's, U. S. hardware store (boutique).

quincaillier [-je] m. Ironmonger, hardware dealer.

quinconce [kɛ̃kɔ̃s] m. Quincunx ; *en quinconce*, in alternate rows, in fives.

quinine [kinin] f. MÉD. Quinine.

quinquagénaire [kɥɛ̃kwaʒenɛːr] adj. Quinquagenarian.
— s. Quinquagenarian, fifty-year-old.

quinquagésime [-ʒezim] f. ECCLÉS. Quinquagesima, Shrove Sunday.

quinquennal, ale [kɥɛ̃kɥənal] adj. Quinquennial ; five-year (plan).

quinquennat [-na] m. Quinquennium, five-year period.

quinquet [kɛ̃kɛ] m. † Oil burner. ‖ POP. Peepers

(yeux) ; *allumer ses quinquets,* to keep one's eyes skinned.

quinquina [kɛ̃kina] m. MÉD. Cinchona, quinquina. ‖ Quinquina (apéritif).

quinquinisme [-nism] m. MÉD. Cinchonism.

quint, inte [kɛ̃, ɛ̃:t] adj. Fifth (v. CINQUIÈME); *Charles Quint,* Charles the Fifth. ‖ MÉD. Quintan.

quintal [kɛ̃tal] m. Quintal.

quinte [kɛ̃:t] f. Quint (aux cartes). ‖ MÉD. Fit (de toux). ‖ MUS. Fifth. ‖ SPORTS. Quinte.

quintefeuille [kɛ̃tfø:j] f. BOT., ARCHIT. Cinquefoil.

quintessence [kɛ̃tɛssɑ̃:s] f. Quintessence.

quintette [kɛ̃tɛt] f. MUS. Quintet, quintette.

quinteux, euse [kɛ̃tø, ø:z] adj. Jibbing (cheval). ‖ MÉD. Fitful (toux). ‖ FIG. Crotchety.

quintillion [kwɛtiljɔ̃] m. MATH. Quintillion (10^{30}); U. S. trillion (10^{18}).

quintuple [kɛ̃typl] adj., m. Quintuple, fivefold.

quintuplé, ée [-ple] s. Quintuplet.
— adj. Quintuplicate.

quintupler [-ple] v. tr., intr. (1). To quintuple.

quinzaine [kɛ̃zɛn] f. Fifteen or so ; about fifteen (en nombre) ; *une quinzaine de pommes,* fifteen apples or so. ‖ Fortnight, U. S. two weeks (quinze jours). ‖ Fortnight's wages (paye).

quinze [kɛ̃:z] adj. num. Fifteen ; *avoir quinze ans,* to be fifteen ; *quinze jours,* a fortnight, U. S. two weeks. ‖ Fifteenth ; *le quinze avril,* the fifteenth of April, April fifteenth ; *Louis quinze,* Louis the Fifteenth.
— m. Fifteen ; *habiter au quinze,* to live at number fifteen. ‖ SPORTS. Fifteen (au football). ‖ **Quinze-vingts,** m. MÉD. Quinze-vingts Hospital.

quinzième [kɛ̃zjɛm] adj., s. Fifteenth.

quinzièmement [-zjɛmmɑ̃] adv. Fifteenthly, in the fifteenth place.

quiproquo [kiprɔko] m. Misunderstanding (malentendu) ; misapprehension, mistake (méprise). ‖ THÉÂTR. Mistaken identity.

quittance [kitɑ̃:s] f. COMM. Acquittance, receipt, discharge.

quittancer [-se] v. tr. (6). COMM. To receipt.

quitte [kit] adj. Clear (*de,* of) ; discharged (*de,* from) [dettes] ; *quitte envers qqn,* no longer in s.o.'s debt ; quits with s.o. ; *quitte ou double,* double or quits (ou) or nothing ; *tenir qqn quitte de,* to release s.o. from. ‖ Free, quit, rid (*de,* of) [qqch.] ; *en être quitte pour la peur,* to get off with a fright ; *en être quitte à bon compte,* to get off cheaply. ‖ **Quitte à,** even if ; at the risk of ; *je m'arrête quitte à recommencer,* I'm stopping even if I have to begin again (ou) if only to begin again ; *se marier quitte à le regretter,* to marry and be sorry for it.

quitter [kite] v. tr. (1). To leave (v. ABANDONNER) ; *quitter la place,* to give way ; *quitter son emploi,* to leave one's job. ‖ To leave (qqch., qqn) ; *quitter son mari,* to desert one's husband ; *je l'ai quitté hier en bonne santé,* I left him yesterday in good health ; *quitter la vie,* to depart this life. ‖ To take off, to lay aside (v. ÔTER) ; *quitter le deuil,* to go out of mourning ; *quitter son manteau,* to take off one's coat. ‖ LOC. *Ne quittez pas,* hold the line (au téléphone).
— v. récipr. Se **quitter,** to part, to separate.

quitus [kitys] m. invar. COMM., JUR. Discharge in full, acquittal.

quoi [kwa] pron. rel. What, which ; *ce à quoi je prétends,* what I am laying claim to ; *c'est en quoi elle a raison,* that is where she is right ; *c'est à peine de quoi vivre,* it's scarcely enough to live on ; *de quoi manger,* something to eat ; *il lui répondit non, sur quoi elle se mit en colère,* he answered her no, upon which she flew into a passion ; *il n'y a pas de quoi rire,* it is no laughing matter ; *il n'y a pas de quoi,* not at all, don't mention it ; *il n'y a pas de quoi s'étonner,* there is nothing surprising in that ; *il faut courir, sans quoi il nous rattrapera,* we must run, if not he will catch up with us ; *je ne sais quoi,* I don't know what, something or other ; *un je ne sais quoi de mélancolique,* a vague hint of melancholy ; *un homme qui a de quoi,* a man of substance ; *voilà comme quoi on se trompe,* that is how we make mistakes. ‖ **Quoi que,** whatever ; *quoi que ce soit,* anything, whatever ; *quoi que ce soit qu'il ait dit,* whatever he said ; *quoi qu'il arrive,* whatever may happen ; *quoi qu'il dise,* whatever he says, say what he will ; *quoi qu'il en soit,* however that may be ; *en quoi que ce soit,* in anything ; *je n'ai pas vu quoi que ce soit,* I saw nothing whatever.
— pron. interrog. What ; *quoi?, quoi donc?,* what?, what are you saying? ; *quoi de neuf?* what's the news? ; *quoi de plus bête que son attitude?,* what could be more stupid than his attitude? ; *à quoi bon?,* what's the good (ou) the use? ; *à quoi ça sert?,* what's the good of that? ; *alors, quoi?,* well, what about it ? ; *de quoi parlez-vous?,* what are you talking about? ; *en quoi est-ce?* what's it made of? ; *en quoi peut-elle vous aider?,* how can she help you? ; *le quoi?,* the what? ; *savez-vous de quoi il s'occupe?,* do you know what he does? (métier) [ou] what he is busy with? (travail).
— exclam. What! ; *eh quoi!,* well then!, what's that! ‖ FAM. *Enfin quoi, c'est ainsi,* well, such is life ; *il est mort, quoi!,* he is dead, and that's that!

quoique [kwak] conj. Though, although (v. BIEN QUE) ; *quoiqu'elle soit pauvre,* though she is poor ; *quoique presque mort,* although almost dead ; *quoique son chapeau fût bien laid,* in spite of her hat being terribly ugly ; *quoique son sourire fût aimable,* amiable as her smile was.

quolibet [kɔlibɛ] m. Gibe, dig, jeer (v. LAZZI) ; *couvrir de quolibets,* to jeer at.

quorum [kɔrɔm] m. Quorum ; *le quorum fut atteint,* there was a quorum.

quota [kɔta, kwɔta] m. Quota.

quote-part [kɔtpa:r] f. Quota, share.

quotidien, enne [kɔtidjɛ̃, ɛn] adj. Daily. (V. JOURNALIER.) ‖ Everyday (monotone). ‖ MÉD. Quotidian (fièvre). ‖ FAM. Everyday (monotone) ; *ah! que la vie est quotidienne!* life is just one damned thing after another.
— m. Daily, daily paper (journal). ‖ Everyday occurrence, everyday life.

quotidiennement [-djɛnmɑ̃] adv. Daily, every day. (V. JOURNELLEMENT.)

quotient [kɔsjɑ̃] m. MATH. Quotient.

quotité [kɔtite] f. JUR. Quota ; *quotité disponible,* disposable portion of estate ; *quotité imposable,* taxable quota.

R

r [ɛr] m. R, r.

rab(e) [rab] m. V. RABIOT.

rabâchage [rabɑʃa:ʒ] m. Tiresome repetition (d'idées, de mots) ; harping on the same string.

rabâcher [-ʃe] v. tr. (1). To be forever repeating the same old thing, to be always harping on the same string.

rabâcheur, euse [-ʃœ:r, ø:z] s. Person who is forever repeating the same old thing.

rabais [rabɛ] m. COMM. Allowance, reduction ; rebate (abattement) ; *acheté au rabais*, bought at a reduced price (ou) on the cheap ; *faire un rabais*, to make an allowance (ou) reduction ; *vendre au rabais*, to sell at a discount. ‖ FIN. Depreciation (de la monnaie). ‖ NAUT. Abatement, lowering (des eaux).

rabaissement [rabɛsmɑ̃] m. Lowering (d'un rideau). ‖ COMM. Lowering (des prix). ‖ FIN. Depreciation (de la monnaie). ‖ FIG. Running down, disparagement (dénigrement) ; humiliating, humbling (humiliation).

rabaisser [-se] v. tr. (1). To lower (un rideau). ‖ COMM. To lower (les prix). ‖ FIN. To depreciate (la monnaie). ‖ FIG. To run down, to disparage (dénigrer) ; to humble (humilier).

— v. pr. **Se rabaisser**, to abase oneself.

raban [rabɑ̃] m. NAUT. Swifter (de cabestan) ; head-earing (d'empointure) ; furling-line, gasket (de ferlage) ; reef-earing (de ris) ; roband (de têtière). ‖ Lashing (d'un hamac).

rabane [raban] f. Grass mat.

rabaner [rabane] v. tr. (1). NAUT. To fit rope bands into, to pass a gasket round (une voile).

rabat [raba] m. Top (de cage) ; band (d'habit) ; flap (de sac à main) ; *rabat gommé d'enveloppe*, flap. ‖ **Rabat-joie**, m. Kill-Joy, spoilsport ; wet-blanket (fam.) ; *faire le rabat-joie*, to spoil the fun.

rabattage [-ta:ʒ] m. COMM. Touting (des clients) ; lowering (des prix). ‖ SPORTS. Beating (du gibier).

rabattement [-tmɑ̃] m. Flattening (d'un pli) ; folding-back (d'un tissu) ; *charrette à rabattement*, tip-up cart, dump-cart. ‖ MATH. Rabatment. ‖ MILIT. Wheeling (ou) pivoting movement (d'une armée). ‖ NAUT. *Cheminée à rabattement*, hinged funnel.

rabatteur [-tœ:r] m. Decoy (de victimes). ‖ COMM. Tout, hotel tout. ‖ SPORTS. Beater (de gibier). ‖ FAM. Pimp, procurer ; ponce (pop.).

rabattre [rabatr] v. tr. (20). To turn down (un bord, son col) ; to press down, to flatten (une couture) ; to shut down (un couvercle) ; to tilt back (un siège) ; to pull down (un strapontin) ; to pull down (son voile) ; *rabattre les mailles*, to cast off (au tricot) ; *col rabattu*, turn-down collar ; *couture rabattue*, French seam ; *le vent rabat la fumée*, the wind is beating the smoke down. ‖ To tone down (une couleur). ‖ AGRIC. To cut back (un arbre). ‖ COMM. *Rabattre tant du prix*, to reduce the price by so much ; *combien en voulez-vous rabattre?*, what reduction will you make on it ? ; *je n'en rabattrai pas un sou*, I won't take (ou) knock a halfpenny off. ‖ MATH. To rabatte, to rotate (un plan). ‖ NAUT. To turn in (une poulie). ‖ SPORTS. To beat down (une épée) ; to beat up (le gibier) ; to head back (à courre). ‖ TECHN. To cut (une ardoise) ; to burr (un clou) ; to rough-polish (le marbre) ; *rabattre*

le bord d'une tôle, to flange a plate. ‖ FIG. To bring down (l'orgueil) ; *rabattre l'orgueil de qqn*, to make s.o. climb down (ou) take in sail. ‖ FAM. *Il faut rabattre la moitié de ce qu'il dit*, you must discount half of what he says.

— v. intr. To turn. ‖ COMM. *Rabattre de son prix*, to lower one's price. ‖ SPORTS. To beat up game. ‖ FIG. *En rabattre*, to climb down, to draw in one's horns ; *c'est ce qu'il dit mais il faut en rabattre*, so he says, but you have to take it with a pinch of salt ; *rabattre de son orgueil, de ses prétentions*, to put one's pride in one's pocket, to climb down.

— v. pr. **Se rabattre**, to drop down (col, couvercle) ; to fold (table) ; to drop, to fall down (strapontin). ‖ MILIT. To fall back on ; to swing round on ; to drop back (vers, towards). ‖ FAM. To fall back (sur, on) ; *faute de beurre, se rabattre sur la margarine*, to eke out the butter with margarine, to fall back on margarine when the butter runs out.

rabbin [rabɛ̃] m. Rabbi ; *grand rabbin*, Chief Rabbi.

rabbinat [rabina] m. Rabbinate.

rabbinique [rabinik] adj. Rabbinical.

rabbinisme [-nism] m. † Rabbinism.

rabelaisien, enne [rablɛzjɛ̃, ɛn] adj. Rabelaisian ; broad (esprit) ; earthy (humour).

rabibocher [rabibɔʃe] v. tr. (1). FAM. To tinker up ; to patch up (un objet). ‖ FAM. To reconcile, to make it up between (deux adversaires) ; to make up, to patch up (une querelle).

rabiot [rabjo] m. FAM. Bit more, extra, second helping (d'un plat) ; extra service (au service militaire) ; overtime (heures supplémentaires) ; *en rab, de rab*, spare.

rabique [rabik] adj. MÉD. Rabic.

râble [rɑ:bl] m. Back (de lapin, de lièvre). ‖ CULIN. *Râble de lièvre*, saddle of hare. ‖ FAM. Back (d'une personne).

râble m. Fire-rake. ‖ TECHN. Rabble.

râblé, ée [rɑble] adj. Broad- (ou) strong-backed (animal) ; plump-backed (lapin, lièvre). ‖ FAM. Broad- (ou) strong-backed (personne).

râblure [rɑbly:r] f. NAUT. Rabbet.

rabot [rabo] m. Plane ; *rabot à languette, à moulures, à rainures*, tongue-plane, moulding-plane, grooving-plane ; *rabot en caoutchouc*, squeegee ; *rabot coupe-cors*, corn-plane.

rabotage [rabɔta:ʒ] m. Planing.

raboter [-te] v. tr. (1). To plane (le bois) ; to file down (un sabot de cheval). ‖ FIG. To polish.

raboteur [-tœ:r] m. Planer.

raboteuse [-tø:z] f. Planing-machine.

raboteux, euse [-tø, ø:z] adj. Rough, rugged, uneven (chemin, pays) ; rough, unpolished (planche). ‖ FIG. Harsh, jarring, rough, unpolished (style, vers).

rabougri, ie [rabugri] adj. Dwarfish, stunted, undergrown (personne, plante) ; scraggy (végétation).

rabougrir [-gri:r] v. tr. (2). To dwarf, to stunt the growth of (qqch.).

— v. pr. **Se rabougrir**, to become stunted (ou) dwarfish.

rabougrissement [-grismɑ̃] m. Stuntedness, dwarfishness.

rabouter [rabute] v. tr. (1). To join up, to tack

(ou) sew together (des étoffes) ; to butt together (des longueurs) ; to join (ou) set end to end (des pièces).

rabrouer [rabrue] v. tr. (1). To snub ; to tick off.

racage [raka:ʒ] m. NAUT. Parrel, parral.

racaille [rakɑ:j] f. Trash, rubbish (choses) ; rabble, riff-raff (gens) ; dregs, scum (de la population).

raccommodable [rakɔmɔdabl] adj. Mendable, repairable.

raccommodage [-da:ʒ] m. Mending, repairing (action) ; darning (des bas) ; cobbling (des souliers). ‖ Mend, repair, darn.

raccommodement [-dmɑ̃] m. Reconciliation.

raccommoder [-de] v. tr. (1). To mend, to repair ; to darn (les bas) ; to cobble (les souliers). ‖ FIG. To retrieve, to restore (sa fortune). ‖ FAM. To reconcile, to bring together, to make it up between (deux adversaires). — v. pr. **Se raccommoder**, FAM. to make it up again (avec, with).

raccommodeur, euse [-dœr, ø:z] s. Mender, repairer.

raccompagner [rakɔ̃paɲe] v. tr. To accompany, to see home.

raccord [rakɔ:r] m. Connection, link, join, joining ; faire des raccords dans un roman, to join up parts of a novel ; faire un raccord de peinture, to paint over. ‖ CH. DE F. Raccord de rail, junction-rail. ‖ TECHN. Linking-up (au téléphone) ; connection, coupling, joint, junction, union (de tuyaux) ; raccord de câble, coupler.

raccordement [rakɔrdəmɑ̃] m. Coupling, linking-up, joining (action). ‖ CH. DE F. Voie de raccordement, junction- (ou) loop-line (sur rail) ; side-line (vers une usine). ‖ TECHN. Boîte de raccordement, connecting-box ; pièces de raccordement, making-up (ou) U. S. make-up lengths.

raccorder [-de] v. tr. (1). To connect, to link up, to join (v. ABOUTER) ; to bring into line, to make flush (les parties).

raccourci, ie [rakursi] adj. Bobbed (cheveux) ; shortened (jupe, manche). ‖ Abridged, concise, succinct (compte rendu, plan). ‖ Short, squat, dumpy (taille). ‖ FAM. A bras raccourcis, with might and main, with tooth and nail. — m. Abridgment, epitome, summary, abstract ; description en raccourci, thumbnail sketch ; histoire en raccourci, story in a nutshell. ‖ Short-cut, U. S. cutoff (chemin). ‖ ARTS. Foreshortening ; en raccourci, foreshortened.

raccourcir [-si:r] v. tr. (2). To shorten (un discours, une jupe) ; to abridge (un plan) ; to curtail (un séjour) ; raccourcir son chemin, to take a short-cut (ou) U. S. cutoff ; raccourcir ses cornes, to draw in its horns (escargot) ; raccourcir le pas, to shorten step (ou) one's stride. ‖ ARTS. To foreshorten. ‖ FAM. To behead (qqn). — v. intr. To shorten, to grow shorter. ‖ To shrink (au lavage). ‖ To grow shorter, to draw in, to close in (jours).

raccourcissement [-sismɑ̃] m. Shrinking (au lavage). ‖ Shortening (d'une jupe) ; abridgment (d'un livre) ; curtailment (d'un séjour). ‖ Shortening, drawing (ou) closing in (des jours).

raccoutumer (se) [sərakutyme] v. pr. (1). To reaccustom oneself (à, to).

raccroc [rakro] m. SPORTS., FIG. Fluke ; fluky (ou) lucky stroke (ou) shot ; par raccroc, by a fluke.

raccrochage [rakrɔʃa:ʒ] m. Accosting.

raccrocher [-ʃe] v. tr. (1). To hang (ou) hook up again ; raccrocher l'appareil, to hang up, to ring off ; raccrocher le récepteur, to hang up the receiver. ‖ FAM. To manage to get hold of (une place, un poste) ; again ; to get hold of (qqch.) again ; j'essaie de raccrocher l'affaire, I'm trying to get the deal going again. ‖ FAM. To buttonhole (un

ami) ; to accost, to solicit (un homme dans la rue). — v. intr. To ring off, to hang up (au téléphone). ‖ SPORTS. To make flukes. — v. pr. **Se raccrocher**, to clutch (à, at) ; to cling, to hold on (à, to). ‖ FIG. To cling (à, to) [un espoir] ; to hang on (à, to) [qqn]. ‖ FAM. Il se raccroche, he won't leave go (ou) give up, he hangs on.

raccrocheur, euse [-ʃœ:r, ø:z] adj. Inviting, enticing.

race [ras] f. Race, ancestry, descent, line, lineage, blood ; de race juive, of Jewish race (ou) descent (ou) blood ; de race noble, of noble race (ou) line (ou) lineage ; questions de race, racial questions. ‖ People, race, nation ; la race entière fut exterminée, the whole race was wiped out. ‖ ZOOL. Race, stock, breed, blood, species (v. ESPÈCE) ; de race, thoroughbred (cheval) ; pedigreed (chien). ‖ LOC. Bon chien chasse de race, what's bred in the bone will come out in the flesh. ‖ FAM. Il chasse de race, he's a chip off the old block ; sale petite race !, naughty little brats !

racé, ée [rase] adj. ZOOL. Pure-bred, thoroughbred. ‖ FAM. Il est très racé, he's a real thoroughbred (ou) a man of breeding.

racémique [rasemik] adj. CHIM. Racemic.

racer [rasœ:r] m. SPORTS. Racing horse. ‖ AUTOM. Racing-car. ‖ NAUT. Racing yacht.

rachat [raʃa] m. Repurchase, buying back. ‖ Ransom (des prisonniers). ‖ COMM. Buying in (de marchandises) ; avec faculté de rachat, with option of repurchase. ‖ ECCLÉS. Redemption (de, of) ; atonement (de, for). ‖ FIN. Redemption (d'une dette) ; surrender (d'une police d'assurance). ‖ NAUT. Ransom (de cargaison).

rachetable [raʃtabl] adj. COMM., FIN. Redeemable. ‖ ECCLÉS. Atoneable, redeemable.

racheter [-te] v. tr. (8b). To repurchase, to buy back (un objet vendu). ‖ To ransom (des prisonniers). ‖ To buy again, to buy more of (un) another (acheter de nouveau). ‖ COMM. To buy in (des marchandises). ‖ ECCLÉS. To redeem, to atone for (des péchés). ‖ FIN. To redeem (une dette) ; to surrender (une police d'assurance). ‖ FIG. To make up for, to make amends for ; to compensate for (une erreur). — v. pr. **Se racheter**, to be repurchased, to be bought back again. ‖ FIN. To cover short sales. ‖ FIG. To redeem oneself.

rachidien, enne [raʃidjɛ̃, ɛn] adj. Rachidian.

rachis [-ʃis] m. BOT., MÉD. Rachis.

rachitique [-ʃitik] adj. MÉD. Rachitic. ‖ FAM. Rickety.

rachitisme [-ʃitism] m. MÉD. Rachitis. ‖ FAM. Rickets.

racial, ale [rasjal] adj. Racial.

racine [rasin] f. BOT., AGRIC. Root. ‖ MÉD. Root (d'un cheveu, d'une dent, d'un ongle). ‖ MATH. Root. ‖ GÉOGR. Foot, base (d'une montagne). ‖ SPORTS. Racine anglaise, silkworm gut. ‖ FIG. Tie, bond (lien) ; root, cause, origin (source) ; couper le mal à la racine, to strike at the root of the evil.

raciner [-ne] v. intr. (1). AGRIC. To root. — v. tr. TECHN. To marble (une reliure) ; to dye with walnut (un textile).

racing-club [rɛsiŋklœb] m. SPORTS. Club.

racinien, enne [rasinjɛ̃, ɛn] adj. Racinian, of (ou) relating to Jean Racine.

racisme [rasim] m. Racialism, U. S. racism.

raciste [-sist] m. Racialist, U. S. racist.

racket [rakɛt] m. FAM. Racket.

racketteur [-tœ:r] m. Racketeer.

raclage [rɑklɑ:ʒ] m. Scraping. ‖ AGRIC. Thinning (d'un taillis) ; raking (de la terre).

racle [rɑ:kl] f. Scraper.

raclée [rɑkle] f. Fam. Hiding, thrashing, licking.

raclement [-kləmɑ̃] m. Scraping.

racler [-kle] v. tr. (1). To scrape; *le fond du navire racla les rochers*, the bottom of the ship grated on the rocks; *se racler la gorge*, to clear one's throat; *un vin qui vous racle le gosier*, a wine that rasps your throat. ‖ Agric. To thin out (un taillis); to rake (la terre). ‖ Fam. To take everything; to clean out (qqn) [au jeu]; *racler les fonds de tiroir*, to scrape the barrel; *l'ennemi les a raclés*, the enemy made a clean sweep of them.
— v. intr. Mus., Fam. *Racler du violon*, to scrape on the fiddle.

raclette [-klɛt] f. Scraper; squeegee (en photographie). ‖ Agric. Hoe.

racleur, euse [-klœ:r, ø:z] s. Scraper. ‖ Fam. *Racleur de violon*, scraper on the fiddle.

racloir [-klwa:r] m. Scraper (de tonnelier); doctor (en typographie).

racloire f. Strickle, strike. ‖ Techn. Spokeshave.

raclure [-kly:r] f. Scrapings.

racolage [rakɔla:ʒ] m. Enlisting (de partisans); accosting, soliciting (par une prostituée). ‖ Comm. Touting (*de*, for). ‖ Milit. Recruiting.

racoler [-le] v. tr. (1). To enlist (des partisans); to accost, to solicit (qqn). ‖ Comm. To tout for (des clients). ‖ Milit. To recruit.

racoleur, euse [-lœ:r, ø:z] adj. Inviting, enticing.
— m. Comm. Tout. ‖ Milit. Recruiting sergeant.

racoleuse [-lø:z] f. Street-walker.

racontable [rakɔ̃tabl] adj. Relatable, tellable.

racontar [-ta:r] m. Fam. Gossip, talk, tittle-tattle.

raconter [-te] v. tr. To tell, to relate, to recount, to narrate; *je vous raconterai tout cela*, I'll tell you all about it; *raconter un voyage à Londres*, to describe a visit to London. ‖ Fam. *On en raconte de belles!*, they tell some fine tales (ou) tall stories!; *on vous a raconté des histoires!*, they've been spinning you a yarn!; *qu'est-ce que tu racontes!*, what on earth are you talking about!

raconteur [-tœ:r] s. Story-teller.

racoon [rakun] m. Zool. Racoon.

racorni, ie [rakɔrni] adj. Shrivelled (cuir); horny (main); wizened (vieillard). ‖ Fig. Hardened (cœur); limited (esprit).

racornir [-ni:r] v. tr. (2). To harden, to make sth. hard (ou) tough (durcir); to shrivel (ratatiner). ‖ To make horny (les mains). ‖ Fig. To harden (le cœur).
— v. pr. Se racornir, to harden, to grow (ou) become hard (ou) tough (ou) horny (durcir); to shrivel up (se ratatiner).

racornissement [-nismɑ̃] m. Hardening, toughening, shrivelling-up.

radar [radar] m. Radar.

radariste [-rist] m. Radar-operator.

rade [rad] f. Naut. Roadstead, roads, anchorage. ‖ Fam. *Rester en rade,* to be brought to a standstill, to stick fast.

radeau [rado] m. Naut. Raft; *radeau de bois,* lumber-raft (ou) -float.

rader [rade] v. tr. (1). Agric. To strike (le grain). ‖ Naut. To bring a ship into the roads.

radiaire [radjɛ:r] adj. Bot. Radiated. (V. Radié.)
— m. Zool. Radiary. ‖ Pl. Radiata.

radial, ale [radjal] adj. Math., Méd. Radial.

radian [radjɑ̃] m. Math. Radian.

radiant, ante [-jɑ̃, ɑ̃:t] adj., m. Astron., Bot., Phys. Radiant.

radiateur [radjatœ:r] m. Autom., Electr. Radiator.

radiation [-sjɔ̃] f. Disbarment (d'un avocat); striking off the rolls (d'un avoué, d'un militaire);

dismissal (d'un fonctionnaire). ‖ Jur. Cancellation (d'une dette); entry of satisfaction (d'hypothèque). ‖ Phys. Radiation.

radical, ale [radikal] adj. Bot., Chim., Math., Fam. Radical. ‖ **Radical-socialisme,** m. Radical-socialism.
— m. Radical (en politique). ‖ Chim. Radical. ‖ Gramm. Root, radical (d'un mot).

radicalement [-lmɑ̃] adv. Radically.

radicalisation [-lizasjɔ̃] f. Toughening (d'un régime politique), hardening (d'une lutte).

radicaliser [-lize] v. tr. (1). To toughen (un régime politique), to harden (une lutte).

radicalisme [-lism] m. Radicalism.

radicelle [radisɛl] f. Bot. Radicle, rootlet.

radiculaire [-kylɛ:r] adj. Méd. Radicular. ‖ Bot. Radicular; *poussée radiculaire,* root pressure.

radicule [-kyl] f. Bot. Radicle.

radié, ée [radje] adj. Zool. Radiated, radiate; rayed.

radier m. Frame, floor, bed; apron (d'un dock); sill (d'écluse); invert (d'égout). ‖ Archit. Foundation raft.

radier v. tr. (1). To erase, to strike (ou) cross out (ou) off. ‖ Jur. *Radier une inscription hypothécaire,* to enter a memorandum of satisfaction of mortgage.
— v. intr. Phys. To radiate, to beam.

radiesthésie [radjɛstezi] f. Radiesthesia.

radiesthésiste [-zist] s. Radiesthesist.

radieux, euse [radjø, ø:z] adj. Dazzling (ciel, sourire); radiant (soleil, sourire, yeux).

radin [radɛ̃] adj. Pop. Stingy.

radiner [radine] v. intr. (1). Pop. To turn up, to roll up.
— v. pr. Se radiner, Pop. To turn up, to roll up.

radinerie [radinri] f. Pop. Stinginess.

radio [radjo] m. Radio (ou) wireless message. ‖ Aviat., Naut. Radio-telegraphist, wireless operator; sparks (fam.).
— f. Radio. Radio (radiodiffusion); *entendre à la radio,* to hear on the radio; *passer à la radio,* to be on the radio (ou) on the air (personne), to be broadcast (programme); *travailler à la radio,* to have a job in radio. ‖ Fam. Radio, radio set (poste); *radio portative,* portable radio. ‖ Aviat., Naut., Milit. Radio, radiotelegraphy, wireless (radiotélégraphie); *envoyer un message radio,* to radio. ‖ Méd. X-ray photograph, X-ray (radiographie); *passer une radio,* to have an X-ray. ‖ **Radio-taxi,** m. Radio-cab.

radioactif, ive [radjoaktif, i:v] adj. Phys. Radioactive; *déchets radioactifs,* radioactive waste.

radioactivité [-aktivite] f. Phys. Radioactivity.

radioalignement [-aliɲmɑ̃] m. Naut., Aviat. Radio range (station, dispositif); radio range finding (action).

radioamateur [-amatœ:r] m. Radio. Radio amateur, radio ham.

radioastronomie [-astrɔnɔmi] f. Astron. Radio astronomy.

radiobalisage [-baliza:ʒ] m. Naut., Aviat. Radio beacon signalling.

radiobalise [-bali:z] f. Naut., Aviat. Radio beacon, radio beacon marker.

radiocarbone [-karbɔn] m. Phys. Radio-carbon; *datation au radiocarbone,* radio-carbon dating.

radiocobalt [-kɔbalt] m. Phys. Radio-cobalt.

radiocommunication [-kɔmynikasjɔ̃] f. Wireless message.

radiocompas [-kɔ̃pɑ] m. Aviat. Radio-compass.

radioconducteur [-kɔ̃dyktœ:r] m. Coherer.

radiodermite [-dɛrmit] f. Méd. X-Ray dermatitis.

radiodiffuser [-difyze] v. tr. (1). To broadcast.

radiodiffusion [-difysjɔ̃] f. Broadcasting.

radioélectricien, enne [-elɛktrisjɛ̃, ɛn] s.

RADIO. Radio engineering. ‖ NAUT. Radio electrician.

radioélectricité [-elɛktrisite] f. RADIO. Radio engineering.

radioélément [-elemɑ̃] m. PHYS. Radio-element.

radiofréquence [-frekɑ̃:s] f. RADIO. Radiofrequency.

radiogoniomètre [-gɔnjɔmɛtr] m. AVIAT., NAUT. Direction-finder, radiogoniometer.

radiogoniométrique [-metrik] adj. AVIAT., NAUT. Beam (navigation).

radiogramme [radjɔgram] m. Wireless message, radiogram.

radiographe [-graf] m. MÉD., PHYS. Radiographer.

radiographie [-grafi] f. MÉD., PHYS. Radiography, X-ray photograph, U. S. X-ray.

radiographier [-grafje] v. tr. (1). MÉD., PHYS. To radiograph, to X-ray.

radioguidage [-gida:ʒ] m. AVIAT. Radio direction-finding; radioguiding.

radioguidé, ée [-gide] adj. Wireless-controlled.

radio-isotope [-izɔtɔp] m. PHYS. Radioisotope.

radiolaires [-lɛ:r] m. pl. ZOOL. Radiolaria.

radiologie [-lɔʒi] f. MÉD. Radiology, X-ray treatment.

radiologue [-lɔg], **radiologiste** [-lɔʒist] m. MÉD. Radiologist.

radiomètre [-mɛtr] m. PHYS. Radiometer.

radionavigant [-navigɑ̃] m. NAUT., AVIAT. Radio officer.

radionavigation [-navigasjɔ̃] f. NAUT., AVIAT. Radio navigation.

radiophare [-fa:r] m. AVIAT. Radiophare, radiobeacon.

radiophonie [-fɔni] f. Radiophony.

radiophonique [-fɔnik] adj. Radio, radiophonic; *jeu radiophonique*, quiz (individuel), panel game (par équipes).

radioreportage [-rəpɔrta:ʒ] m. News broadcast; broadcast account; running commentary (d'un match).

radioreporter [-rəpɔrtɛ:r] m. Radio (ou) wireless commentator.

radioscopie [-skɔpi] f. MÉD. Radioscopy.

radioscopique [-skɔpik] adj. MÉD. Radioscopic.

radiosondage [-sɔ̃da:ʒ] m. Radio-sonde observation.

radiosonde [-sɔ̃:d] f. Radio-sonde.

radiosource [-surs] f. ASTRON. Radio source.

radiotechnique [-tɛknik] adj. RADIO. Radio technological.
— f. RADIO. Radio technology.

radiotélégramme [-telegram] m. Wireless- (ou) radio-telegram.

radiotélégraphie [-telegrafi] f. Wireless- (ou) radio-telegraphy.

radiotéléphonie [-telefɔni] f. Wireless- (ou) radio-telephony.

radiotélescope [-teleskɔp] m. ASTRON. Radio telescope.

radiotélévisé, ée [-televize] adj. RADIO. Broadcast on radio and on television.

radiotélévision [-televizjɔ̃] f. RADIO. Broadcasting.

radiothérapie [-terapi] f. MÉD. X-ray treatment, radiotherapy.

radis [radi] m. BOT. Radish. ‖ FAM. *Ça ne vaut pas un radis*, it's not worth a bean; *ne pas avoir un radis*, to be stony-broke (ou) U. S. dead broke.

radium [radjɔm] m. CHIM. Radium.

radiumthérapie [-terapi] f. Radium-therapy.

radius [radjy:s] m. MÉD. Radius.

radon [radɔ̃] m. PHYS. Radon.

radotage [radɔtaʒ] m. Twaddle, drivel; ramblings (de la vieillesse); *tomber dans le radotage*, to fall into one's dotage (ou) anecdotage.

radoter [-te] v. intr. (1). To talk twaddle (ou) drivel; to go rambling on. ‖ FAM. V. RABÂCHER.

radoteur, euse [-tœ:r, ø:z] s. Driveller, dotard.

radoub [radu] m. NAUT. Refit, repair.

radouber [-be] v. tr. (1) NAUT. To refit, to repair; to put in dry-dock.

radoucir [radusi:r] v. tr. (2). To make milder (ou) softer, to soften (qqch.); to soften, to calm, to mollify (qqn).
— v. pr. **Se radoucir**, to soften down, to mellow (caractère); to get (ou) grow (ou) become milder (temps).

radoucissement [-sismɑ̃] m. Getting gentler, softening, mellowing (du caractère); getting milder (du temps).

rafale [rafal] f. Squall, gust, blast (de vent); *rafale de pluie*, rain-squall, burst of driving rain; *soufflant en rafales*, gusty. ‖ MILIT. Burst, hail, storm (de mitraille).

raffermir [rafɛrmi:r] v. tr. To harden again, to make firmer. ‖ FIN. To strengthen, to restore (le crédit); to steady, to harden (les prix). ‖ MÉD. To improve, to restore (la santé). ‖ FIG. To confirm, to strengthen (l'autorité); to strengthen, to fortify, to steel (le courage); to strengthen (le moral); to steady (les nerfs); to steady, to control (la voix).
— v. pr. **Se raffermir**, to harden, to become harder again. ‖ FIN. To be strengthened (ou) restored (crédit); to steady, to harden (prix). ‖ MÉD. To improve, to get better (santé). ‖ FIG. To get stronger (autorité); to be strengthened (ou) fortified (ou) steeled (courage); to grow steadier (ou) stronger (voix).

raffermissement [-mismɑ̃] m. Hardening, making firmer. ‖ FIN. Hardening, steadying (des prix). MÉD. Improvement (de la santé). ‖ FIG. Strengthening, fortifying (du courage); strengthening, steadying (de la voix).

raffinage [rafina:ʒ] m. Refining.

raffiné, ée [-ne] adj. Refined (pétrole, sucre). ‖ FIG. Subtle, clever (esprit); refined, delicate, nice (goûts); exquisite, refined (plaisirs); polished (style).
— s. Person of refined (ou) delicate taste.

raffinement [-nmɑ̃] m. Refinement. ‖ FIG. Subtlety, nicety (des nuances); refinement (des personnes).

raffiner [-ne] v. tr. (1). To refine (le pétrole, le sucre). ‖ FIG. To refine, to cultivate (le goût); to refine, to polish (le langage).
— v. intr. To be subtle (ou) nice (ou) fastidious.
— v. pr. **Se raffiner**, to become (ou) grow refined (ou) polished.

raffinerie [-nri] f. Refinery (de pétrole, de sucre); *raffinerie de sel*, salt-works.

raffineur [-nœ:r] m. Refiner.

raffoler [rafɔle] v. intr. To be infatuated (de, with); to be excessively fond (de, of). ‖ FAM. To be mad (de, about, on).

raffut [rafy] m. FAM. Row, din, uproar, shindy; *faire du raffut*, to kick up a row (ou) shindy.

rafiot [rafjo] m. NAUT. Skiff. ‖ FAM. *Vieux rafiot*, old tub.

rafistolage [rafistɔla:ʒ] m. FAM. Patching up, tinkering up.

rafistoler [-le] v. tr. (1). FAM. To patch up, to tinker up.

rafle [rɑ:fl] f. Clean sweep, clean-up (par des cambrioleurs); round-up, raid (par la police). ‖ Pair-royal (aux dés). ‖ BOT. Corn-cob (de maïs); stalk (de raisin). ‖ SPORTS. Bird- (ou) fish-net.

rafler [rɑfle] v. tr. (1). To carry off, to sweep off (qqch.); to round up (qqn).
— v. intr. To throw a pair-royal (aux dés).

rafraîchir [rafrɛʃi:r] v. tr. (2). To cool, to freshen (qqch.); to refresh (qqn). ‖ ARCHIT. To renovate (une ruine). ‖ ARTS. To freshen up, to

revive (une couleur); to restore (un tableau). ‖ NAUT. To freshen (une amarre). ‖ FIG. To refresh (la mémoire); *rafraîchir son italien*, to brush up one's Italian. ‖ FAM. To trim (les cheveux).
— v. intr. To cool.
— v. pr. **Se rafraîchir,** to get (ou) grow (ou) become cooler (temps). ‖ To refresh oneself, to have a cooling drink (personne).
afraîchissant, ante [-ʃisɑ̃, ɑ̃:t] adj. Refreshing, cooling. ‖ MÉD. Cooling, laxative.
afraîchissement [-ʃismɑ̃] m. Cooling (d'un liquide, de la température). ‖ Pl. Refreshments. ‖ ARTS. Reviving (d'une couleur); restoring (d'un tableau). ‖ TECHN. *Rafraîchissement par pulvérisation, par ruissellement*, spray-, shower-cooling. ‖ FIG. Refreshing (de la mémoire); brushing-up (d'un sujet).
afraîchissoir [-ʃiswa:r], **rafraîchisseur** [-ʃisœ:r] m. Cooler, refrigerator.
agaillardir [ragajardi:r] v. tr. FAM. To cheer (ou) buck up (qqn).
— v. pr. FAM. **Se ragaillardir,** to cheer up, to buck up, to brace up; to chirk up.
age [ra:ʒ] f. Rage, fury, frenzy; *écumer de rage*, to foam with rage; *faire rage*, to rage (tempête); *la rage au cœur*, seething inwardly. ‖ Passion, mania. ‖ Acute pain (douleur); *rage de dents*, violent toothache. ‖ MÉD. Rabies, hydrophobia.
ageant, ante [raʒɑ̃, ɑ̃:t] adj. FAM. Maddening.
ager [-ʒe] v. intr. (7). To rage, to storm, to fret and fume, to fume, to be in a rage. ‖ FAM. *Ça le fait rager!*, it makes him wild, it gets his goat!
ageur, euse [-ʒœ:r, ø:z] adj. Hot-tempered, choleric, snappish, passionate (personne); snappish, waspish (réponse).
ageusement [-ʒøzmɑ̃] adv. Angrily, passionately, in a temper.
aglan [raglɑ̃] m. Raglan (pardessus).
agondin [ragõdɛ̃] m. Nutria (fourrure).
agot [rago] adj. Stocky, cobby (cheval); dumpy, stumpy, squat, stocky (personne).
— m. ZOOL. Boar in its third year.
agot m. FAM. Gossip, tittle-tattle.
agougnasse [raguɲas] f. Pigswill.
agoût [ragu] m. CULIN. Stew, ragout; *faire cuire en ragoût*, to stew. ‖ FIG. Spice, relish.
agoûtant, ante [-tɑ̃, ɑ̃:t] adj. CULIN. Tempting, inviting, savoury (plat). ‖ FAM. Tempting, inviting, piquant.
agrafer [ragrafe] v. tr. (1). To refasten, to rebuckle, to do up again (une ceinture); to hook (ou) do up again, to refasten (une robe).
— v. pr. **Se ragrafer,** to rebuckle one's belt, to hook up one's dress again.
aguer [rage] v. tr. intr. (1). NAUT. To chafe, to rub.
ahat-loukoum [raatlukum] m. Turkish delight.
ai [rɛ] m. Ray (de lumière); spoke (d'une roue).
aid [rɛd] m. Endurance-test (à cheval, en voiture); long-distance run (en voiture). ‖ MILIT., AVIAT. Raid.
aide [rɛd] adj. Stiff (cadavre, col, membre); straight (cheveux). ‖ Tight (corde). ‖ Steep (escalier); stiff, steep (pente); *vol raide*, swift and straight flight. ‖ FIG. Stiff (attitude); inflexible, unbending (caractère); stiff, starchy (manières); inflexible, severe (morale); *assis raide comme la justice*, sitting bolt upright. ‖ FAM. *C'est un peu raide!*, it's a bit steep (ou) thick!
— adv. *Frapper raide*, to strike hard; *la côte monte très raide*, the hill rises steeply; *parler raide*, to speak harshly; *tomber raide mort*, to drop stone dead; *tuer raide*, to kill outright.
aidement [-dmɑ̃] adv. Stiffly, tensely.

raideur [-dœ:r] f. Stiffness (d'un cadavre, d'un col, d'un membre). ‖ Tenseness, tautness, tightness (d'une corde). ‖ FIG. Inflexibility, severity (du caractère); stiffness, starchiness (des manières); *répondre avec raideur*, to answer stiffly.
raidillon [-dijõ] m. Short steep rise.
raidir [-di:r] v. tr. (2). To tighten, to tauten, to haul taut (une corde); to stiffen, to hold stiffly (un membre); *raidir ses forces*, to brace (ou) steel oneself. ‖ FIG. To make firm (ou) inflexible (l'âme); *raidir sa volonté*, to stiffen one's will.
— v. pr. **Se raidir,** to tighten, to grow taut, to tauten (corde); to grow stiff, to stiffen (membre). ‖ FIG. To grow firm (ou) inflexible (âme); to brace (ou) steel oneself (personne énergique); to become stubborn (personne entêtée).
raidissement [-dismɑ̃] m. Stiffening; tautening (d'une corde).
raidisseur [-disœ:r] m. TECHN. Stretcher, tightener.
raie [rɛ] f. Line, stroke (dans l'écriture). ‖ Streak (dans le marbre); stripe (sur un tissu). ‖ Parting (dans les cheveux). ‖ AGRIC. Furrow (sillon); ridge (entre les sillons). ‖ PHYS. Ray. ‖ ZOOL. Ray, skate; *raie bouclée*, thornback.
raifort [rɛfɔ:r] m. BOT. Horse-radish.
rail [rɑ:j] m. CH. DE F. Rail; *rail conducteur*, live-rail; U. S. third rail; *coordination du rail et de la route*, co-ordination of road and rail transport.
railler [rɑje] v. tr. (1). To laugh at, to jeer at, to scoff at, to mock, to banter, to chaff (*de*, about) [qqn]. ‖ FAM. To chip (*sur*, about) [qqn]; to twit (*sur*, with) [qqn].
— v. pr. **Se railler,** to laugh (*de*, at).
raillerie [-jri] f. Raillery, banter, chaff; *recueillir des railleries*, to be laughed (ou) scoffed at.
railleur, euse [-jœ:r, ø:z] adj. Bantering, scoffing, mocking (personne, ton); *d'un air, d'un ton railleur*, banteringly.
— s. Banterer, scoffer, mocker.
railleusement [-jøzmɑ̃] adv. Banteringly, scoffingly, mockingly.
rainette [rɛnɛt] f. BOT. Rennet, pippin; *rainette grise*, russet. ‖ ZOOL. Tree-frog; green frog.
rainure [rɛny:r] f. MÉD. Groove. ‖ TECHN. Groove, furrow, rabbet, slide, slot; *à rainures*, grooved, slotted, fluted.
rainurer [-nyre] v. tr. (1). To groove.
raire [rɛ:r] v. intr. ZOOL. To bell.
raisin [rɛzɛ̃] m. *Le raisin, du raisin*, grapes; *un raisin*, a bunch of grapes (grappe); a grape (variété); *raisins de Corinthe*, currants; *raisins secs*, raisins; *raisins de Smyrne*, sultanas, U. S. seedless raisins; *raisins de table*, dessert-grapes. ‖ *Grand raisin*, royal (papier). ‖ Lipstick (rouge). ‖ BOT. *Raisin de loup*, black nightshade; *raisin de mer*, bladder-wrack; *raisin d'ours*, arbutus. ‖ ZOOL. *Raisin de mer*, sea-grapes, cuttlefish eggs.
raisiné [-zine] m. Fruit preserved in grape-juice, raisiné.
raison [rɛzõ] f. Reason, intellect (intelligence); *contraire à la raison*, contrary to reason; *elle n'a pas toute sa raison*, she's not in her right mind; *parler raison*, to talk sense; *ramener (ou) rappeler qqn à la raison*, to bring s.o. to his senses; to make s.o. see reason again; *sans rime ni raison*, without rhyme or reason; *vous perdez la raison!*, have you taken leave of your senses! ‖ Reason, cause, ground, motive (motif); *raison de plus*, all the more reason; *raison d'être de*, reason (ou) justification (ou) grounds (ou) object of; *raisons cachées*, hidden motives; *à plus forte raison*, all the more reason, a fortiori; *ce n'est pas une raison*, that doesn't follow; *en raison de mon âge*, on account of my age; *il y a de bonnes raisons pour*, there is much to be said for; *pour des*

raisons de convenance, on grounds of expediency; *pour raison de santé,* on account of ill-health. ‖ Reason, justification; *avec raison,* rightly; *avoir raison,* to be right; *avoir raison de faire,* to be justified in doing; *boire plus que de raison,* to drink more than is good for one; *comme de raison,* as one might expect; *l'événement m'a donné raison,* I was justified in the event; *se faire une raison,* to make the best of a bad job. ‖ Satisfaction, reparation; *avoir raison de,* to get the better of (qqch., qqn); *demander raison de,* to demand satisfaction for; to take the law into one's own hands; *tirer raison de,* to obtain satisfaction from. ‖ Proportion; *varier en raison de la distance,* to vary in proportion to the distance. ‖ Rate (tarif); *à raison de cinq francs le mot,* at the rate of five francs a word. ‖ COMM. *Raison sociale,* name, style, trade-name. ‖ JUR. *Pour valoir ce que de raison,* to be used as thought proper. ‖ ‖ MATH. Ratio. ‖ PHILOS. Reason. ‖ LOC. *La raison du plus fort est toujours la meilleure,* might is right; *le cœur a ses raisons que la raison ne connaît pas,* the heart has a logic of its own (ou) its own reasons.

raisonnable [rɛzɔnabl] adj. Adequate (compensation); reasonable, tolerable, moderate (conditions); reasonable, honest, right, fair (conduite); reasonable, rational (être); reasonable, sensible (personne); reasonable, tolerable, moderate (prix); *à son âge elle pourrait être plus raisonnable,* at her age she should know better.

raisonnablement [-nabləmã] adv. Reasonably; soberly, sanely. ‖ FAM. *Une pièce raisonnablement grande,* a reasonable (ou) fair- (ou) decent-sized room.

raisonné, ée [-ne] adj. Detailed (analyse); reasoned (argument, exposé); *non raisonné,* unreasoning (crainte). ‖ COMM. Descriptive (catalogue). ‖ GRAMM. Rational (grammaire).

raisonnement [-nmã] m. Reasoning (faculté, méthode). ‖ Reasoning, chain of reasoning, argument. ‖ FAM. *Pas de raisonnements!,* don't answer back! (ou) argue!

raisonner [-ne] v. intr. (1). To reason, to be logical (*sur,* about); to argue (*sur,* about); to pursue an argument; to reason, to argue (*avec,* with). ‖ NAUT. V. ARRAISONNER. ‖ FAM. *Ne raisonnez pas tant,* don't be so argumentative.
— v. tr. To consider, to think (ou) reason out (les actions). ‖ To reason with (qqn).
— v. pr. **Se raisonner,** to reason oneself into (ou) out of a particular state of mind.

raisonneur, euse [-nœ:r, ø:z] adj. Reasoning, rational (argumentateur); argumentative (disputailleur).
— s. Reasoner, arguer. ‖ Argumentative person. ‖ FAM. Argufier; *ne faites pas le raisonneur,* don't argue.

rajah [raʒa] m. Rajah.

rajeunir [raʒœni:r] v. intr. (2). To grow young again, to look (ou) get younger.
— v. tr. To make young again (ou) younger, to restore to youth, to rejuvenate (qqn); *cela ne la rajeunit pas,* that doesn't make her look any younger; *le professorat a besoin d'être rajeuni,* the teaching profession needs new blood.
— v. pr. **Se rajeunir,** to make oneself look younger (en apparence); to pretend one is younger than one is (en prétentions).

rajeunissant, -ante [-nisɑ̃, ɑ̃:t] adj. That makes one look younger; youthful.

rajeunissement [-nismɑ̃] m. Rejuvenation, restoring to youth. ‖ Renewal of youth, growing young again.

rajout [raʒu] m. Addition.

rajouter [raʒute] v. tr. (1). To add, to add more of (ou) another.

rajustement [raʒystəmɑ̃] m. Readjustment.

rajuster [-te] v. tr. (1). To readjust, to put in order (ou) right (ou) straight again.
— v. pr. **Se rajuster,** to come back into order, to come right (ou) straight again (chose). ‖ To put one's clothes straight, to adjust one's dress (personne).

râle [rɑ:l] m. Rattle; death-rattle. ‖ MÉD. Râle. ‖ ZOOL. Rail; *râle d'eau, des genêts,* water-rail, land-rail (ou) corn-crake.

râlement [-mɑ̃] m. Rattle; death-rattle. ‖ MÉD. Râle.

ralenti, ie [-ti] adj. Slow, slower (pas, trot).
— m. CINÉM. Slow motion; *film tourné au ralenti,* slow-motion picture. ‖ AUTOM. Idling; *tourner au ralenti,* to tick over, to idle. ‖ COMM. *Marcher au ralenti,* to be slack (affaires). ‖ FIG. *Politique du ralenti,* go-slow policy.

ralentir [ralɑ̃ti:r] v. tr. (2). To slacken (son allure); to lessen, to moderate (son ardeur). ‖ MILIT. *Ralentir le pas,* to step short, to slacken pace. ‖ NAUT. To bank (les feux); *ralentir la marche,* to reduce speed. ‖ FAM. To ease up.
— v. pr. **Se ralentir,** to slacken speed, to slow down (ou) up (voiture). ‖ To relax, to diminish, to decrease, to flag (ardeur).

ralentissement [-tismɑ̃] m. Slackening, slowing down (ou) up (du mouvement). ‖ COMM. Falling off (des affaires). ‖ FIG. Abatement (de l'ardeur).

râler [rɑle] v. intr. (1). To give the death-rattle (mourant). ‖ FAM. To grouse; to bind, to bellyache (pop.).

râleur, euse [rɑlœ:r, ø:z] s. FAM. Grouser.

ralingue [ralɛ̃:g] f. NAUT. Bolt-rope; *tenir les voiles en ralingue,* to keep the sails shivering.

ralinguer [-lɛ̃ge] v. tr. (1). NAUT. To rope.
— v. intr. NAUT. To shiver, to shake in the wind.

ralliement [ralimɑ̃] m. Rallying (action); rally (groupe). ‖ MILT. *Mot de ralliement,* pass-word; *lieu de ralliement,* rallying-place. ‖ FIG. Winning over.

rallier [-lje] v. tr. (1). MILIT. To rally, to assemble, to bring together again (des troupes). ‖ NAUT. *Rallier le bord,* to rejoin one's ship; *rallier la terre,* to stand in for land; *rallier le vent,* to sail close to the wind. ‖ FIG. To win over, to bring round (à, to) [qqn].
— v. pr. **Se rallier,** to rally, to come together again. ‖ FIG. *Se rallier à,* to be won over to, to come round to (un avis); to take sides with, to throw in one's lot with (un parti).

rallonge [ralɔ̃:ʒ] f. Lengthener, lengthening-piece (d'une jupe). ‖ Extension leaf (de bureau); extra leaf (de table); *mettre une rallonge à la table,* to put in another leaf. ‖ AUTOM. Extension-piece. ‖ FAM. *À rallonge,* double-barrelled (nom).

rallongement [-lɔ̃ʒmɑ̃] m. Lengthening.

rallonger [-lɔ̃ʒe] v. tr. (7). To lengthen, to make longer (en général); to let down (une jupe), to put an extra leaf in (une table).
— v. intr. To get longer (jours); *les jupes vont rallonger,* the hemlines will be lowered.

rallumer [ralyme] v. tr. (1). To relight, to rekindle (un feu); to relight, to light again (une lampe). ‖ FIG. To rekindle (l'amour, l'espoir); to rouse again, to rekindle (la colère); to revive, to start again (la guerre).
— v. pr. **Se rallumer,** to be rekindled, to be lighted again (feu, lumière). ‖ FIG. To break out (ou) flare up again (colère, guerre).

rallye [rali] m. AUTOM. Race-meeting. ‖ **Rallye-paper** (pl. *rallye-papers*) m. SPORTS. Paper-chase.

ramadan [ramadɑ̃] m. Ramadan.

ramage [rama:ʒ] m. Floral design; *à ramages,* flowered (étoffe). ‖ Song; carolling, warbling (d'un oiseau).

615 RAMASSAGE — RANCI

ramassage [ramɑsa:ʒ] m. Gathering (du bois); collection (du lait); picking-up, lifting (des pommes de terre); *ramassage à la main*, hand-picking.
ramasse [ramɑs] V. RAMASSER. ‖ **Ramasse-couverts**, m. invar. Plate-basket. ‖ **Ramasse-miettes**, m. invar. Crumb-tray (ou) scoop. ‖ **Ramasse-piétons**, m. invar. Cow-catcher.
ramassé, ée [ramɑse] adj. Squat, stocky, thick-set (personne, taille). ‖ FIG. Compact, condensed (livre, style).
ramasser v. tr. (1). To collect, to gather (des objets épars); to pick up (des objets à terre). ‖ ‖ AGRIC. To lift (des pommes de terre). ‖ FIG. To pick up (des idées). ‖ FAM. To catch it; *se faire ramasser*, to get oneself run in (par la police); to get oneself told off (par qqn); *ramasser une bûche*, to come a cropper.
— v. pr. **Se ramasser**, to gather, to collect together (foule). ‖ To gather oneself together, to crouch (avant un bond); to pick oneself up (après une chute); to double up (en masse pliant).
ramasseur, euse [-sœ:r, ø:z] s. Collector, gatherer.
ramassis [-si] m. Heap, pile, jumble. ‖ FAM. Sweepings (de la société); set, pack (de voleurs).
ramdam [ramdam] m. FAM. Row.
rame [ram] f. AGRIC. Prop, stick.
rame f. NAUT. Oar, scull; *aller à la rame*, to row; *à huit rames*, eight-oared (bateau).
rame f. Ream (de papier). ‖ NAUT. String (de péniches). ‖ CH. DE F. Lift, line (de wagons).
ramé, ée [rame] adj. AGRIC. Trained on sticks.
rameau [ramo] m. BOT. Branch, bough (d'un arbre). ‖ MÉD. Ramification (d'une veine). ‖ ECCLÉS. *Dimanche des Rameaux*, Palm Sunday. ‖ FIG. Branch (d'une famille); sub-division (d'une science).
ramée [rame] f. Green branches (ou) boughs; arbour. ‖ FAM. *Ne pas en ficher une ramée*, not to do a stroke.
ramender [ramɑ̃de] v. tr. NAUT. To mend the meshes of (un filet).
ramener [ramne] v. tr. (5). To take (ou) bring back (qqch., qqn); *ramener qqn chez lui en voiture*, to drive s.o. home. ‖ To pull up, to draw up (en tirant); *ramener son chapeau sur les yeux*, to pull (ou) down one's hat over one's eyes; *ramener ses cheveux en arrière*, to comb one's hair back; *ramener ses couvertures*, to draw (ou) pull up one's blankets. ‖ NAUT. *Ramener à terre*, to bring off from a vessel. ‖ MÉD. *Ramener à la vie*, to bring round, to revive (un malade). ‖ ECCLÉS. To recall (à la foi). ‖ COMM. To bring down (à, to) [un prix]. ‖ MATH. *Ramener à sa plus simple expression*, to reduce to its simplest terms. ‖ PHYS. *Ramené aux conditions normales de température*, corrected for temperature. ‖ FIG. To restore (l'abondance, la paix); to bring (ou) lead back (to, à) [la conversation]; *ramener qqn à une opinion*, to bring s.o. round to an opinion; *ramener tout à une question*, to reduce everything to a single question.
— v. pr. **Se ramener**, to be reduced [à, to]. ‖ To amount, to come down (à, to) [raisonnement]; *se ramener à peu de chose*, to come (ou) boil (ou) narrow down to very little. ‖ FAM. To turn up, to roll along. (V. RAPPLIQUER.)
ramequin [ramkɛ̃] m. CULIN. Ramekin.
ramer [rame] v. tr. (1). AGRIC. To stick, prop, stake (des haricots).
ramer v. intr. (1). NAUT. To row, to scull; to pull on (ou) at an oar.
ramette [-mɛt] f. Ream (de papier à lettres). ‖ TECHN. Chase (pour affiches).
rameur [-mœ:r] m. NAUT. Rower, oarsman; *rameur de couple*, sculler.

rameuter [ramøte] v. tr. (1). To muster (rassembler), to stir up, to rouse (exciter).
rami [rami] m. Rummy (jeu de cartes).
ramier [ramje] m. ZOOL. Wood-pigeon, ring-dove.
ramification [ramifikasjɔ̃] f. BOT. Branching, ramification, ramifying. ‖ MÉD. Ramification (d'une artère, d'un nerf). ‖ GÉOGR. Spur (d'un filon). ‖ CH. DE F. Ramification (d'une voie ferrée). ‖ FIG. Ramification (d'un complot); sub-division, branch (d'une science).
ramifier [-fje] v. tr. (1). To ramify.
— v. pr. **Se ramifier**, to ramify, to branch out.
ramille [rami:j] f. BOT. Twig. ‖ Pl. Small-wood.
ramolli, ie [ramɔli] adj. Softened, made soft (par la chaleur); sodden (par la pluie). ‖ FAM. Soft-headed.
— s. Half-wit. ‖ FAM. Dodderer.
ramollir [-li:r] v. tr. (2). To soften, to make soft (la cire, le cuir). ‖ FIG. To weaken, to enervate, to make soft.
— v. pr. **Se ramollir**, to grow (ou) become soft, to soften (cire, cuir). ‖ FAM. *Il se ramollit*, he is getting soft, he is beginning to dote.
ramollissement [-lismɑ̃] m. Softening, making soft. ‖ MÉD. *Ramollissement cérébral*, softening of the brain.
ramollot [-lo] m. FAM. Dodderer, driveller.
ramonage [ramɔna:ʒ] m. Chimney-sweeping (en général); cleaning (des tuyaux).
ramoner [-ne] v. tr. (1). To sweep (une cheminée); to clear, to rake out (un tuyau). ‖ SPORTS. To climb (en alpinisme).
ramoneur [-nœ:r] m. Chimney-sweep, sweep.
rampant, ante [rɑ̃pɑ̃, ɑ̃:t] adj. BLAS. Rampant. ‖ BOT. Creeping, procumbent (plante). ‖ ZOOL. Crawling, creeping (bête). ‖ ARCHIT. Rampant, sloping (arc, voute). ‖ FIG. Cringing, fawning, grovelling (flagorneur). ‖ FAM., AVIAT. *Personnel rampant*, ground staff, U. S. ground crew.
— m. FAM., AVIAT. Ground wallah, groundling.
rampe [rɑ̃:p] f. Slope, incline, rise. ‖ Gradient. V. CÔTE. ‖ MILIT. *Rampe d'accès*, approach-ramp. ‖ AVIAT. *Rampe d'atterrissage, de lancement*, landing-ramp (ou) U. S. strip, launching-site. ‖ ARCHIT. Banisters, hand-rail (d'escalier); pitch (d'un toit). ‖ AUTOM. *Rampe de graissage*, lubricating-ramp. ‖ THÉÂTR. Footlights, floats; *passer la rampe*, to get across, to come over. ‖ CINÉM. *Rampe de projecteurs*, bank of projectors. ‖ FAM. *Lâcher la rampe*, to kick the bucket.
rampement [rɑ̃pmɑ̃] m. Crawling (d'une bête); creeping (d'une plante); slithering (d'un serpent).
ramper [rɑ̃pe] v. intr. (1). ZOOL. To crawl (bête); to slither (serpent). ‖ BOT. To creep (plante). ‖ ARCHIT. To slope, to ramp. ‖ FIG. To fawn (devant, upon); to grovel (devant, before); to truckle (devant, to); to creep (fam.).
ramponneau [rɑ̃pɔno] m. FAM. Shove. (V. COUP.)
ramure [ramy:r] f. BOT. Branches, boughs, foliage. ‖ ZOOL. Antlers (d'un cerf).
rancard, rancart [rɑ̃ka:r] m. ARG. Information, tip, gen (renseignement). ‖ POP. Rendez-vous, appointment, date.
rancarder [-karde] v. tr. (1). ARG. To give s.o. the gen, to pop up.
— v. pr. **Se rancarder**, to ask around, to find out.
rancart [rɑ̃ka:r] m. *Au rancart*, on the shelf; *mettre au rancart*, to cast aside, to scrap, to shelve (qqch., un projet). ‖ POP. V. RANCARD.
rance [rɑ̃s] adj. Rank, rancid.
— m. *Sentir le rance*, to smell rank (ou) rancid.
ranch [rɑ̃:ʃ] m. Ranch. ‖ Pl. Ranches.
ranci [rɑ̃si] m. Rancid smell (ou) taste; *ça sent le ranci*, it smells rancid.

rancir [rᾱsiːr] v. tr. (2). To become (ou) grow rank (ou) rancid.

rancissement [-sismᾱ] m. Action of becoming rank.

rancissure [-sisyːr] f. Rancidness.

rancœur [rᾱkœːr] f. Rancour; U. S. rancor.

rançon [rᾱsɔ̃] f. Ransom; *mettre à rançon*, to hold to (ou) U. S. for ransom. ‖ Fig. Price to be paid; *la rançon de la célébrité*, the price of fame.

rançonnement [rᾱsɔnmᾱ] m. Action of ransoming.

rançonner [-ne] v. tr. (1). To ransom, to hold to (ou) U. S. for ransom (un individu, une ville); to oppress, to exact money from (un groupe, une ville). ‖ Fam. To fleece (un client).

rançonneur [-nœːr] adj. Extortionate.
— s. Extortioner.

rancune [rᾱkyn] f. Rancour, spite, grudge, malice; *garder rancune à qqn*, to have a grudge (ou) harbour resentment against s.o., to bear s.o. a grudge; *par rancune*, out of spite (ou) malice; *sans rancune*, no offence!, no ill feelings!, let bygones be bygones!

rancuneux, euse [-nø, øːz] adj. Pop. Spiteful.

rancunier, ère [-nje, ɛr] adj. Spiteful, rancorous.
— s. Spiteful (ou) rancorous person; one who bears a grudge.

randonnée [rᾱdɔne] f. Run, outing; *faire une longue randonnée*, to make a long trip. ‖ Milit. *Randonnée offensive*, raid. ‖ Autom. Drive, run, excursion, motor-tour; *en randonnée*, touring, out on a tour. ‖ Sports. Road-race. ‖ Zool. Circuit (d'un cerf).

rang [rᾱ] m. Row, line (d'arbres, d'oignons); row, round (de tricot). [V. RANGÉE.] ‖ Milit. Rank; *avoir rang de*, to hold the rank of; *former, quitter, rompre, serrer les rangs*, to fall in, to fall out, to dismiss, to close up; *en rangs serrés*, in serried ranks; *par rangs de quatre*, four abreast; *par rang de taille*, according to height; *rentrer dans les rangs*, to return to the ranks; *sortir du rang*, to rise from the ranks; *sur deux rangs!* form two deep! ‖ Théâtr. Row (de fauteuils); tier (de loges). ‖ Techn. Row (de touches); *à quatre rangs*, four-bank (machine à écrire). ‖ Fig. Station, rank (v. CLASSE, CONDITION, POSITION); *selon son rang*, according to one's station; *arriver au premier rang*, to come to the front; *avoir (ou) prendre rang avant, après qqn*, to rank before, after s.o.; *de premier rang*, first-class, first-rate, A1 (fam.); *être en bon rang*, to be well up on (sur une liste); *être au premier rang*, to be at the top of the tree (dans une profession); *se mettre sur les rangs*, to enter the lists; *sortir du rang*, to get out of the ruck (fam.); *sur le même rang*, on an equal footing; *tenir son rang*, to keep up one's position.

rangé, ée [rᾱʒe] adj. Steady, tidy, of regular habits (personne); quiet, settled, well-ordered (vie). ‖ Milit. Pitched (bataille).

rangée f. Row, line (d'arbres); array (de chiffres); rope (de perles).

rangement [-ʒmᾱ] m. Setting (ou) placing in order, tidying up.

ranger [-ʒe] v. tr. (7). To range (v. ARRANGER, ORDONNER); to clean (ou) tidy up (une chambre); to put away, to replace, to put back in place, to stow (ou) tidy away, to set in order, to set to rights (des objets). ‖ To classify (des faits). [V. CLASSER, SÉRIER.] To keep back, to keep in its place (la foule). ‖ Milit. To range, to draw up, to marshal (une armée, des troupes). ‖ Naut. To hug (la côte). ‖ Autom. To park (une auto). ‖ Fig. To rank, to set (*parmi*, among) [qqn]; *ranger sous ses lois*, to bring beneath one's sway.
— v. pr. **Se ranger**, to place oneself (se placer).

‖ To get (ou) stand out of the way, to stand back (ou) aside (s'écarter). ‖ Naut. To berth, to come alongside (bateau); to veer round (vent) ‖ Autom. To park; to draw (ou) pull up (le long du trottoir); to pull over to one side. ‖ Fig. To side, to take sides, to fall into line (*à*, with) [une opinion, un parti]; *se ranger à une décision*, to endorse a decision. ‖ Fam. To steady (ou) settle down.

ranimable [ranimabl] adj. Able to be revived

ranimer [-me] v. tr. (1). To revive, to restore to reanimate. ‖ To stir up, to rekindle, to revive (le feu); to revive, to bring back to life (un mort); to resuscitate (un noyé); to bring round, to bring back, to restore to consciousness (une personne évanouie). ‖ Fig. To freshen (une couleur); to revive, to cheer up, to put fresh life into, to re-inspire (qqn).
— v. pr. **Se ranimer**, to revive, to come round to come to life again, to regain consciousness (personne). ‖ To burn up, to burn up again (feu). ‖ Fig. To cheer up, to take fresh heart to buck up (fam.).

raout [raut] m. Reception, party, at-home.

rapace [rapas] adj. Rapacious, predatory (animal); rapacious, greedy, grasping (personne).
— m. pl. Zool. Raptores.

rapacité [-site] f. Rapacity, rapaciousness, pre dacity. (V. CUPIDITÉ.)

râpage [rαpa:ʒ] m. Rasping (du bois); grating (du fromage); wearing threadbare (d'un habit).

rapatrié, ée [rapatrije] adj. Repatriated.
— s. Repatriate.

rapatriement [rapatrimᾱ] m. Repatriation.

rapatrier [-trije] v. tr. (1). To repatriate.

râpe [rɑːp] f. Rasp, rough file; *râpe à fromage à muscade*, cheese, nutmeg-grater. ‖ Bot. Stalk (du raisin).

râpé, ée [rαpe] adj. Rasped (bois); threadbare worn, shabby (vêtement). ‖ Culin. Grated (fromage). ‖ Fig. Shabby.
— m. Rape-wine (vin). ‖ Rappee (tabac).

râper v. tr. (1). To rasp (du bois); to grind (du tabac); to wear threadbare (un vêtement). ‖ Culin. To grate (du fromage).

rapetassage [raptasa:ʒ] m. Fam. Botching-up (action); patched-up work (résultat).

rapetasser [-se] v. tr. (1). Fam. To cobble (des souliers); to patch up (un texte, des vêtements) to botch up (fam.).

rapetissement [raptismᾱ] m. Shrinking (d'une étoffe), shortening (d'un vêtement), foreshortening (des objets vus à distance). ‖ Fig. Dwarfing, belittling (abaissement).

rapetisser [raptise] v. tr. (1). To make smaller to reduce in size (en général); to shrink (une étoffe); to shorten (un vêtement). ‖ Fig. To make look smaller; *cette maison rapetisse les autres* that house dwarfs the others.
— v. intr. To become smaller. ‖ To shrink (étoffe). ‖ Fig. To draw in (jours).
— v. pr. **Se rapetisser**, to become smaller (en général); to shrink (étoffe). ‖ Fig. To stoop (se baisser). ‖ Fig. To draw in (jours).

râpeux, euse [rαpø, øːz] adj. Rough, raspy (langue); harsh (vin); harsh, grating (voix).

raphaélesque [rafaɛlɛsk] adj. Raphaelesque.

raphia [rafja] m. Bot. Raphia-grass; raffia.

rapiat [rapja] adj. Fam. Grasping, stingy.
— s. Fam. Skinflint, U. S. tightwad.

rapiaterie [-tri] f. Fam. Stinginess.

rapide [rapid] adj. Rapid, swift (courant); brisk (pas); fast (train); sharp (trot). ‖ Steep (pente) [V. ABRUPT.] ‖ Sports. Fast (coureur). ‖ Milit *A tir rapide*, quick-firing (fusil). ‖ Techn. High-speed (acier). ‖ Fig. Headlong (chute); rapid

quick (conquête); speedy, expeditious (solution); hurried, hasty (tour).
— m. Rapid (fleuve). ‖ CH. DE F. Express, fast train.

apidement [-dmᾶ] adv. Rapidly, swiftly, briskly, quickly, fast, apace. ‖ Steeply (d'une manière abrupte).

apidité [-dite] f. Speed, pace, swiftness, fleetness, speediness (d'un cheval, d'un sportif); rapidity, quickness (d'un mouvement). [V. VITESSE.] Steepness (d'une pente). ‖ COMM. *Avec toute la rapidité possible,* at your earliest convenience; *rapidité habituelle,* customary dispatch.

apiéçage [rapjesa:ʒ] m. Patching-up, patching (action); patchwork (résultat).

apiécer [-se] v. tr. (6). To patch, to patch up.

apière [rapjɛ:r] f. Rapier.

apin [rapɛ̃] m. FAM. Art student; dauber.

apine [rapin] f. Rapine, plundering; extortion, graft; *habitudes de rapine,* predatory habits; *vivre de rapines,* to live by plunder.

apiner [-ne] v. tr. (1). To plunder.
— v. intr. To pillage, to extort money; to practise graft.

apinerie [-nri] f. Plundering; graft.

aplapla [raplapla] adj. inv. FAM. All in, done in, fagged out, pooped.

aplatir [raplati:r] v. tr. (2). To flatten, to squash.

appareiller [raparɛje] v. tr. (1). To re-match, to find another match for (un cheval, un objet); to make up, to complete (une série).

apparier [rapaje] v. tr. (1). To pair, to pair up, to make the pair of (deux objets); to find the fellow of (un gant); to match, to complete (un service).

appel [rapɛl] m. Recalling; *rappel à l'ordre, à la question,* recalling to order, to the question. ‖ Recalling (d'une impression). ‖ Suspicion, touch, faint smell. (V. SOUPÇON.) ‖ JUR. Recall (d'un ambassadeur). ‖ MILIT. Call-up, recalling to the colours (d'une classe); *battre le rappel,* to call (ou) beat to arms. ‖ ARTS. Recurrent touch (de couleur); *rappel de lumière,* highlights. ‖ THÉÂTR. Curtain call, recall. ‖ SPORTS. Calling-off (des chiens); roping-down, doubled rope, abseiling (en montagne); *en rappel,* on a double rope; *faire une descente en rappel,* to rope down. ‖ FIN. *Rappel de compte, d'échéance,* reminder of amount due, of due date; *rappel de fonds,* calling-in; *rappel de traitement,* back-pay; *toucher le rappel,* to draw arrears of pay. ‖ TECHN. Return (de chariot); *barre de rappel,* drag-link; *bras de rappel,* compensatory arm; *ressort de rappel,* pull-back spring. ‖ MÉD. *Piqûre de rappel,* booster shot (vaccin). ‖ **Rappel-arrière** (pl. *rappels-arrière*), m. Back-spacer.

appelable [raplabl] adj. JUR. Repeatable (décret). ‖ MILIT. Recallable (réserviste).

appelé [-ple] adj. m. MILIT. Recalled.
— s. MILIT. Recalled soldier.

appeler [-ple] v. tr. (8 *a*). To call again (appeler de nouveau). ‖ To call back (faire revenir). ‖ To bring back (ramener); *rappeler qqn à l'ordre,* to call to order; *rappeler à la vie,* to restore to life. ‖ To remind, to call to mind (remémorer); *rappeler d'anciens griefs,* to rake up old scores; *rappelez-moi à son bon souvenir,* remember me kindly to him; *rappelez-moi votre nom,* remind me of your name; *cela me rappelle mon enfance,* that puts me in mind of my youth; *qu'il vaut mieux ne pas rappeler,* best forgotten. ‖ To recover (retrouver); *rappeler son courage,* to summon up one's courage; *rappeler ses esprits,* to recollect oneself. ‖ To ring back (au téléphone). ‖ JUR. To call back, to recall, to summon back (un ambassadeur, un exilé). ‖ MILIT. To recall,

to call up (des réservistes). ‖ THÉÂTR. To call back (un acteur). ‖ ARTS. *Rappeler la lumière,* to distribute the highlights. ‖ COMM. To quote (un numéro); *rappelez la référence A.B.,* reference A.B. ‖ SPORTS. To bring together (les boules au billard); to call off (les chiens à la chasse); to rope down (en montagne). ‖ TECHN. To return (le chariot); to draw back (une pièce).
— v. pr. **Se rappeler,** to recall, to remember, to recollect (qqch.) [V. SE REMÉMORER.]

rappliquer [raplike] v. tr. (1). To re-apply.
— v. intr. FAM. To come up (ou) back; *rappliquer à la maison,* to make tracks for home.

rapport [rapɔ:r] m. Report, statement, account (compte rendu); *au rapport de,* according to; *faire un rapport de,* to give an account of; *faire un rapport de l'état de la question,* to report progress; *faux rapport,* garbled account. ‖ Resemblance (*entre,* between) [analogie]. ‖ Relation, connection (corrélation); *avoir rapport à,* to relate (ou) refer to; *en rapport avec,* in keeping (ou) harmony with; *être en rapport avec,* to square with; *par rapport à,* with regard to, in relation to, compared with; *sans rapport avec,* irrelevant to (ou) without bearing on; *sous le rapport de,* with respect to, in respect of; *sous ce rapport,* in this connection; *sous tous les rapports,* in every way, in all respects. ‖ Pl. Relations, intercourse; *avoir des rapports avec,* to be in contact with; *avoir de bons rapports avec,* to be on good terms with; *se mettre en rapport avec,* to get in touch with. ‖ FIN. Yield, profit, return; *en rapport,* productive (capital); *d'un bon rapport,* profitable (emploi). ‖ COMM. Official report; *rapport de gestion,* annual report. ‖ MATH. Ratio, proportion; *en rapport avec,* proportionate to. ‖ MILIT. *Salle de rapport,* orderly-room. ‖ NAUT. *Rapport de mer,* ship's protest. ‖ AGRIC. Yield; *arbre d'un bon rapport,* good bearer; *en plein rapport,* in full productiveness. ‖ TECHN. *Rapport d'engrenage,* gear-ratio. ‖ ARCHIT. *Maison de rapport,* block of flats; U. S. apartment house. ‖ FAM. *Faire des rapports,* to tell tales out of school. ‖ POP. *Rapport à,* because of.

rapportable [raportabl] adj. Referable (*à,* to).

rapporter [-te] v. tr. (1). To bring (ou) take again; to bring (ou) carry back. ‖ To get, to win (retirer); *en rapporter beaucoup de gloire,* to derive much glory from it. ‖ To report, to relate, to give an account of (relater); *il est rapporté que,* it is on record that. ‖ To repeat (répéter). ‖ To add (ajouter); *manche rapportée,* set-in sleeve. ‖ To refer, to ascribe (attribuer); to attribute (*à,* to) [un effet]; to assign (*à,* to) [un événement]; *rapporter tout à soi,* to consider everything from a selfish point of view. ‖ JUR. To rescind, to revoke (un décret); to call off (un ordre de grève). ‖ AGRIC. To yield, to bear. ‖ SPORTS. To retrieve (le gibier); *chien qui rapporte bien,* good retriever. ‖ FIN. To bring in, to yield, to produce (des bénéfices). ‖ FAM. To tell tales, to sneak.
— v. intr. FIN. To bring in, to yield (placement). ‖ SPORTS. To retrieve (chien). ‖ FAM. *Ça rapporte!,* it pays!
— v. pr. **Se rapporter,** to refer, to relate, to have reference (*à,* to); *les détails qui se rapportent à l'affaire,* the relevant details; *se rapportant à,* relating to. ‖ *S'en rapporter à,* to rely on, to put one's faith in; *je m'en rapporte à vous,* I take your word for it (je vous crois); I leave it to you (je vous confie cela). ‖ † To agree, to tally (*avec,* with).

rapporteur, euse [-tœ:r, ø:z] adj. Tale-bearing, sneaking (fam.).
— s. Tale-bearer, tell-tale, sneak (fam.). [V. CAFARD.]

— m. Reporter, recorder (d'un événement). ‖ Chairman (d'une commission); rapporteur (d'une conférence). ‖ Math. Protractor.

rapprendre [raprɑ̃:dr] v. tr. (80). To learn again, to learn over again (réétudier). ‖ To teach again (enseigner de nouveau).

rapprêter [raprɛte] v. tr. (1). Techn. To dress again, to redress.

rapproché, ée [raprɔʃe] adj. Near in space (de, to); yeux rapprochés, close-set eyes. ‖ Near in time (de, to); à intervalles rapprochés, at short intervals; avenir rapproché, near future. ‖ Similar; espèces rapprochées, closely related species. ‖ Naut. Combat rapproché, close action.

rapprochement [-ʃmɑ̃] m. Bringing together, bringing closer together, bringing nearer (de deux objets). ‖ Rapprochement, re-establishment of good relations (entre deux pays); bringing together, reconciling, re-establishment of good relations, reconciliation (entre deux personnes). ‖ Comparing, comparison, putting side by side (de faits, d'idées); effectuer un rapprochement entre, to bring about a reconciliation between; établir un rapprochement entre, to establish points of similarity between; faire un rapprochement avec, to draw a parallel with. ‖ Closeness, nearness, proximity (de deux objets). ‖ Naut. Closing rate.

rapprocher [-ʃe] v. tr. (1). To bring (ou) put together (deux objets); rapprocher qqch. de, to bring (ou) put (ou) place (ou) set sth. nearer to; rapprocher une chaise du feu, to pull (ou) draw up a chair to the fire. ‖ To compare, to put side by side (des faits, des idées). ‖ To bring together, to join, to unite, to bring (ou) draw closer (deux pays). ‖ To bring together again, to bring closer, to reconcile (deux personnes). ‖ To make... appear closer; une lunette rapproche les objets, field-glasses bring things nearer; l'avion a rapproché les distances, the aeroplane has made the world seem smaller.

— v. pr. **Se rapprocher,** to approach, to draw nearer (de, to) [qqch., qqn]; se rapprocher de la table, to pull up to the table. ‖ To approach, to come near; to approximate (de, to); se rapprocher de la vérité, to approximate to the truth. ‖ To become reconciled (de, with) [qqn]. ‖ To close in (hiver). ‖ Naut. Se rapprocher de la terre, to stand in for shore.

rapprovisionner [raprɔvizjɔne] v. tr. (1). V. réapprovisionner.

rapsodie [rapsɔdi] f. Mus. Rhapsody.

rapt [rapt] m. Kidnapping (d'enfant); rape (d'une femme); abduction (de mineur).

râpure [rɑpy:r] f. Raspings, gratings, filings.

raquer [rake] v. tr. (1). Pop. To shell out, to fork out.

raquette [rakɛt] f. Racquet, racket (de tennis); battledore (de volant). ‖ Snow-shoe. ‖ Bot. Nopal; prickly pear.

raquetteur [-tœ:r] m. Snowshoer.

rare [ra:r] adj. Rare (peu commun); ses visites se font rares, his visits are getting few and far between; un des rares hommes qui, one of the few men who. ‖ Rare, unusual, exceptional (v. exceptionnel, inhabituel); d'une rare beauté, of surpassing beauty; avec un rare courage, with singular courage. ‖ Thin, sparse, scanty (cheveux). ‖ Méd. Feeble, slow (pouls). ‖ Phys. Rare (atmosphère). ‖ Comm. L'argent est rare, money's tight. ‖ Fam. Vous vous faites rare ces temps-ci, you are quite a stranger lately.

raréfaction [rarefaksjɔ̃] f. Phys. Rarefaction.

raréfiable [-fjabl] adj. Phys. Rarefiable.

raréfier [-fje] v. tr. (1). Phys. To rarefy (l'atmosphère). ‖ Comm. To deplete, to make scarce (une denrée).

— v. pr. **Se raréfier,** to rarefy, to become rarefied (atmosphère). ‖ Comm. To become scarce.

rarement [rarmɑ̃] adv. Rarely, seldom.

rareté [-te] f. Rarity, rareness (d'un objet); infrequency (d'une visite). ‖ Scarceness, scarcity, dearth (de l'argent, des denrées). ‖ Singularity, unusualness (d'un phénomène); rare occurrence (fait rare); pour la rareté du fait, as a curiosity. ‖ Rarity, rare object. (V. curiosité.) ‖ Phys. Rarity, tenuity.

rarissime [rarisim] adj. Fam. Exceedingly rare.

ras, ase [rɑ, ɑ:z] adj. Close-shaven (barbe, menton); cropped (tête); short-napped (velours); à poil ras, short-haired (chien). ‖ Full, stricken (mesure). ‖ Bare, blank; en rase campagne, in the open country; faire table rase de, to sweep away; to make a clean sweep of; son esprit est comme une table rase, his mind is a complete blank. ‖ **Ras-le-bol,** m. inv. Pop. Exasperation, sickness; en avoir ras le bol, to have one's fill (de, of), to be pissed off.

— adv. Close; couper les cheveux ras, to cut one's hair close.

— m. Short-napped cloth. ‖ Naut. Reef awash, spit. ‖ À (ou) au ras de, on a level with, flush with; au ras du sol, at zero level; chargé au ras de l'eau, laden to the water-line; remplir un verre à ras du bord, to fill a glass to the brim; voler au ras du sol, to fly close to the ground, to skim the ground.

rasade [razad] f. Brim-full glass; bumper; glassful; brimmer.

rasage [rɑzaːʒ] m. Shaving (du menton); shearing (d'une étoffe).

rasant, ante [-zɑ̃, ɑ̃:t] adj. Level (rayon); skimming, close to the ground (vol); open (vue). ‖ Milit. Low-built, rasant (fortification); grazing (tir). ‖ Fam. Boring, dull, slow (discours); boring, tiresome (personne). [V. barbant.]

rascasse [raskas] f. Zool. Hog-fish.

rase [rɑz]. V. raser. ‖ **Rase-mottes,** m. invar. Aviat. Hedge-hopping; faire du rase-mottes, to skim the ground, to hedge-hop; U. S. to flat-hat.

rasé, ée [-ze] adj. Shaven; entièrement rasé, clean-shaven; rasé de près, close-shaven. ‖ Naut. Dismasted (vaisseau).

raser [-ze] v. tr. (1). To shave (la barbe); to shear (une étoffe); raser qqn, to give s.o. a shave; se faire raser, to have (ou) get a shave. ‖ To graze, to pass close to, to skim over (v. frôler); la balle lui rasa la joue, the bullet grazed his cheek; raser le mur du jardin, to hug the garden-wall; raser le sol, to skim the ground. ‖ To raze (une forteresse); to pull down (une maison); to level to the ground (une ville). ‖ Naut. To raze, to cut down (un vaisseau). ‖ Fam. To bore stiff (v. embêter); ça me rase, it puts years on me.

— v. pr. **Se raser,** to shave; se raser la moustache, to shave off one's moustache. ‖ Fam. To be bored stiff.

raseur, euse [-zœ:r, ø:z] s. Shaver. ‖ Fam. Bore.

rasibus [-ziby:s] adv. Fam. Close.

rasoir [-zwa:r] m. Razor; rasoir à manche, électrique, mécanique (ou) de sûreté, straight, electric, safety razor. ‖ Fam. Bore. (V. raseur.)

rassasiant, ante [rasazjɑ̃, ɑ̃:t] adj. Filling, rich, cloying (nourriture); satisfying (repas).

rassasiement [-zimɑ̃] m. Satisfaction, satisfying (action). ‖ Satiety, surfeit. (V. satiété.)

rassasié, ée [-zje] adj. Satisfied, sated. (V. repu.) ‖ Fig. Cloyed (de plaisirs).

rassasier [-zje] v. tr. (1). To satisfy, to sate (la faim); to satisfy the hunger of (qqn); nourriture qui rassasie, filling food. ‖ To surfeit, to cloy (de, with). ‖ Fam. To satiate (de, with); être rassasié de, to be fed up with.

— v. pr. **Se rassasier,** to eat one's fill; se ras-

sasier de, to gorge oneself with, to take one's
fil: of. ‖ Fig. To gorge oneself (*de*, with) [plai-
sirs] ; to feast (*de*, on) [spectacles] ; *se rassasier le
regard à contempler,* to feast one's eyes on (qqn).

rassemblement [rasᾶbləmᾶ] m. Collecting,
assembling, gathering (d'objets épars). ‖ Crowd,
assemblage, gathering. (V. ATTROUPEMENT.) ‖
Milit. Mustering, falling-in parade (de troupes) ;
sonner le rassemblement, to sound the fall-in.

rassembler [-ble] v. tr. (1). To reassemble, to
bring together again (des objets, des personnes).
‖ Milit. To muster (des troupes). ‖ Sports. To
gather, to collect (un cheval) ; to nurse (les billes,
au billard). ‖ Fig. To gather, to summon up (ses
forces) ; to collect (ses idées).
— v. pr. **Se rassembler,** to re-assemble, to come
together again ; to assemble, to get (ou) flock
together. ‖ Milit. To muster, to fall in.

rasseoir [raswa:r] v. tr. (18). To reseat, to seat
again (qqn) ; to set in place again, to set up
again (un objet renversé). ‖ Fig. To calm, to
compose, to settle (l'esprit, les idées).
— v. pr. **Se rasseoir,** to sit down again, to
resume one's seat (personne). ‖ To settle (vin). ‖
Fig. To calm (ou) settle down.

rasséréner [raserene] v. tr. (5). To clear up,
to clear (le ciel). ‖ Fig. To calm, to restore to
equanimity (qqn) ; *rasséréner les traits,* to compose one's features.
— v. pr. **Se rasséréner,** to clear up (temps). ‖
Fig. To recover one's serenity (personne).

rassis, ise [rasi, i:z] adj. Stale (pain). ‖ Fig. Level-
headed, sedate, sober (v. POSÉ, RÉFLÉCHI) ; *de
sens rassis,* cool and collected.

rassortiment [rasɔrtimᾶ] m. Matching, re-match-
ing (d'objets). ‖ Comm. Re-stocking ; new stock.

rassortir [-ti:r] v. tr. (2). To match, to re-match
(des objets). ‖ Comm. To replenish, to re-stock
(un magasin).
— v. pr. **Se rassortir,** Comm. To lay in a new
stock, to replenish one's stock.

rassurant, ante [rasyrᾶ, ᾶ:t] adj. Reassuring.

rassurer [-re] v. tr. (1). To reassure, to cheer up
(qqn) ; to comfort, to quieten (les esprits).
‖ Archit. To stay, to strengthen (un édifice).
— v. pr. **Se rassurer,** to be reassured, to regain
confidence ; to set one's mind at rest (*au sujet
de,* about).

rasta [rasta], **rastaquouère** [-kwɛ:r] m. Fam.
Flash Harry, flashy adventurer.

rat [ra] m. Zool. Rat ; *rat d'Amérique,* guinea-
pig ; *rat d'eau,* water-vole ; water-rat ; *rat d'égout,*
sewer-rat ; *rat des champs,* field-mouse ; *rat musqué,* musk-rat, musquash. ‖ Théâtr. *Petit rat,*
young ballet-dancer. ‖ Fig. *Rat de bibliothèque,*
bookworm ; *rat de cave,* exciseman, wax-taper ;
rat d'hôtel, hotel thief. ‖ Fam. Stingy (v. RAPIAT).
‖ Loc. *Il est fait comme un rat,* his number's up.
‖ **Rat-de-cave,** m. † Excise officer ; taper (bougie).

rata [rata] m. Pop. Stew.

ratafia [ratafja] m. Ratafia.

ratage [rata:ʒ] m. Fam. Misfire, failure.

rataplan [rataplᾶ] m. Dub-a-dub.

ratatiner v. tr. (1). To shrink, to wrinkle, to
shrivel.
— v. pr. **Se ratatiner,** to become wrinkled
(figure) ; to crinkle (parchemin) ; to become
wizened (personne) ; to shrivel, to become shrivelled (pomme).

ratatouille [ratatu:j] f. Pop. Stew, soup, skilly.

rate [rat] f. Méd. Spleen. ‖ Fam. *Se dilater la
rate,* to split one's sides with laughing ; *ne pas se
fouler la rate,* to take things easy.

rate f. Zool. Female rat.

raté, ée [rate] adj. Abortive (effort) ; ineffective,

ineffectual (personne) ; bungled, botched (travail) ; wasted (vie) ; *affaire ratée,* affair that has
miscarried (ou) come to nothing.
— s. Fam. Failure (personne) ; wash-out (fam.).
— m. Techn. Misfire (de fusil, de moteur).

râteau [rɑto] m. Agric. Rake. ‖ Fam. Big-toothed
comb (peigne).

râtelée [-tle] f. Rakeful.

râteler [-tle] v. tr. (5). To rake. (V. RATISSER.)

râteleur [-tlœ:r] s. Agric. Raker.

râtelier [rɑtəlje] m. Agric. Rack (d'écurie). ‖
Milit. Arms-rack. ‖ Techn. Tool-rack. ‖ Fam.
False teeth, denture (v. DENTIER). ‖ Fam. *Brouter
à plusieurs râteliers,* to derive income from two
sources, to have a foot in both camps.

râtelures [rɑtly:r] f. pl. Agric. Rakings.

rater [rate] v. tr. (1). To miss (v. MANQUER) ; to
fail (un examen) ; to lose (une occasion) ; to miss
(un train). ‖ Sports. *Rater un coup,* to foozle
a shot (au golf) ; to muff a shot (au tennis) ; to
miss the mark (au tir). ‖ Comm. *Rater une affaire,*
to let a piece of business slip through one's
fingers ; *rater une place,* to fail to secure an
appointment. ‖ Culin. To make a mess of (un
plat).
— v. intr. Techn. To miss fire, to fail to go off
(fusil) ; to misfire (moteur). ‖ Fig. To fail (affaire) ;
to miscarry (projet).

ratiboiser [ratibwaze] v. tr. (1). Fam. To filch,
to make away with (qqch.) ; *ratiboiser qqch. à
qqn,* to do s.o. out of something. ‖ Fam. To
fleece (qqn) [au jeu].

ratichon [ratiʃɔ̃] m. Pop. Priest.

ratier [ratje] adj., m. Zool. Ratter.

ratière [-tjɛ:r] f. Rat-trap.

ratificatif, ive [ratifikatif, i:v] adj. Jur. Rati-
fying.

ratification [-kasjɔ̃] f. Approval, confirmation
(d'une décision). [V. CONFIRMATION.] ‖ Jur. Ratification (d'un acte, d'un traité).

ratifier [-fje] v. tr. (1). Jur. To ratify (un acte, un
traité) ; to approve, to confirm (une décision) ;
to sanction (une loi).

ratine [ratin] f. Frieze, ratteen (étoffe).

ratiocination [rasjɔsinasjɔ̃] f. Sophistry,
casuistry, quibbling.

ratiociner [-sine] v. intr. (1). To use sophistry
(ou) casuistry, to quibble.

ration [rasjɔ̃] f. Ration, allowance (portion) ;
ration alimentaire, food intake ; *maigre ration,*
short commons. ‖ Milit. Rations. ‖ Agric. Feed.

rationalisation [rasjɔnalizasjɔ̃] f. Rationalization, rationalizing.

rationaliser [-lize] v. tr. (1). To rationalize.

rationalisme [-lism] m. Philos. Rationalism.

rationaliste [-list] adj. Philos. Rationalist.

rationalité [-lite] f. Rationality.

rationnaire [rasjɔnɛ:r] s. Ration-book holder.

rationnel, elle [-nɛl] adj. Rational (méthode,
système). ‖ Math. Rational (quantité). ‖ Techn.
Pure (mécanique). ‖ Fin. True (escompte).

rationnellement [-nɛlmᾶ] adv. Rationally.

rationnement [-nmᾶ] m. Rationing.

rationner [-ne] v. tr. (1). To ration, to put on
rations (une garnison, un peuple) ; to put on short
commons (qqn). ‖ To ration out (le pain).

ratissage [ratisa:ʒ] m. Agric. Raking. ‖ Culin.
Scraping.

ratisser [-se] v. tr. (1). Agric. To hoe, to rake
(un champ). [V. RÂTELER.] ‖ Culin. To scrape
(un légume). ‖ Sports. To rake in (les mises).
‖ Fam. To nab (une bande de voleurs) ; to fleece
(un joueur) ; *ratissé,* broke to the wide, U. S.
dead broke.

ratissoire [-swa:r] f. Agric. Hoe, rake. ‖ Culin.
Scraper.

RATON — RAVIVER

raton [ratɔ̃] m. Zool. Small rat ; *raton laveur*, racoon. ‖ Fam. Pet, darling.

R.A.T.P. [εratepe] f. Abrév. de *Régie autonome des transports parisiens*, Paris public transport authority, the metro and the buses.

rattachage [rataʃa:ʒ] m. Refastening ; tying up again.

rattachement [-ʃmɑ̃] m. Joining together, union (de deux pays) ; *voter le rattachement à*, to vote for union with.

rattacher [rataʃe] v. tr. (1). To refasten, to retie, to tie up again (un nœud). ‖ To fasten together, to link (deux objets) ; to unite (deux pays). ‖ Fig. To link (à, with) [une idée] ; to link up, to connect (un fait). ‖ Fig. To attach (la vie) [à, to].
— v. pr. **Se rattacher**, to be fastened (à, to) [qqch.]. ‖ To fasten up (vêtement). ‖ Fig. To be bound up (ou) connected (à, with) [qqch.] ; *en ce qui se rattache à*, in respect of, with regard to.

rattrapage [ratrapa:ʒ] m. Recovering, recovery (d'une perte). ‖ Techn. Taking up (de jeu).

rattraper [-pe] v. tr. (1). To catch again, to recapture (un évadé) ; to recover (une occasion) ; to make up for (le temps perdu) ; to catch up with, to overhaul (une voiture) ; *allez devant, je vous rattraperai*, go on ahead, I'll catch up with you (ou) I'll catch you up. ‖ Techn. To take up (le jeu, l'usure). ‖ Fin. To clear off (l'arriéré). ‖ Fig. To catch, to catch out (reprendre) ; *on ne m'y rattrapera plus!*, I shan't be caught like that again ! ‖ Fam. To get one's own back on (revaloir) ; *je vous rattraperai au tournant!*, I'll get you for that !
— v. pr. **Se rattraper**, to make up, to recoup oneself ; *se rattraper de ses pertes*, to make good one's losses. ‖ To be recovered (se retrouver) ; *l'occasion perdue ne se rattrape pas*, the postman only knocks once. ‖ To save oneself (se sauver) ; *se rattraper à qqch.*, to save oneself by clutching at (ou) catching hold of sth. ‖ To catch up again (se remettre à flot).

rattrapeur [-pœ:r] m. Sports. Catcher (au baseball).

raturage [ratyra:ʒ] m. Erasing, scratching out. ‖ Scraping.

rature [-ty:r] f. Erasure (dans un manuscrit). ‖ Scraping (de parchemin).

raturer [-tyre] v. tr. (1). To erase, to scratch out (un mot) ; to scrape (le parchemin).

raucité [rosite] f. Raucity, hoarseness.

rauque [ro:k] adj. Harsh, hoarse, raucous, rough.

ravage [rava:ʒ] m. Devastation, destruction, havoc, ravages ; *faire des ravages*, to make (ou) play (ou) work havoc. ‖ Fig. *Le ravage des ans*, the ravages of time.

ravager [-vaʒe] v. tr. (7). To harry, to lay waste, to ravage (un pays) ; to pillage (une ville). ‖ To line, to wear (un visage) ; *ravagé par la petite vérole*, pitted with smallpox (visage).

ravageur, euse [-vaʒœ:r, ø:z] adj. Pillaging, ravaging (ennemi) ; destructive, devastating (tempête).
— m. Ravager. (V. dévastateur.)

ravalement [ravalmɑ̃] m. Archit. Rough-casting, plastering, re-surfacing (d'une maison) ; recess (dans un pilastre). ‖ Fig. Depravation (v. avilissement) ; disparagement, running-down, snubbing. (V. dénigrement.) ‖ Fam. *Faire le ravalement*, to put on the splash (ou) U. S. war paint.

ravaler [-le] v. tr. (1). To swallow, to swallow again. ‖ Agric. To trim, to cut back (une branche). ‖ Archit. To rough-cast, to plaster, to re-surface (une maison) ; to hollow out a recess in (un pilastre). ‖ Fig. To bottle up (sa colère) ; to choke back (ses larmes) ; to retract (ses paroles) ; to choke down (un sanglot) ; *faire*

ravaler ses paroles à qqn, to make s.o. eat his words. ‖ Fig. To disparage, to run down (dénigrer). ‖ Fig. To reduce to a lower level (rabaisser) ; *ravaler au niveau de*, to set on a level with.
— v. pr. **Se ravaler**, to lower (ou) to debase (ou) to demean oneself.

ravaleur [-lœ:r] m. Archit. Rough-caster.

ravaudage [ravoda:ʒ] m. Darning (de bas) ; cobbling (de souliers) ; mending, patching (de vêtements). [V. raccommodage.] ‖ Arts. Touching up.

ravauder [-de] v. tr. (1). To darn (des bas) ; to cobble (des souliers) ; to mend, to patch (des vêtements). ‖ Arts. To touch up.

ravaudeur, euse [-dœ:r, ø:z] s. Cobbler, patcher, darner, mender.

rave [ra:v] f. Bot. Rape ; *grosse rave*, turnip.

ravet [ravε] m. Zool. Cockroach.

ravi, ie [ravi] adj. Entranced, transported ; delighted, charmed (de, with) [v. enchanté] ; *ravi de vous voir*, glad (ou) delighted to see you.

ravier [ravje] m. Radish-dish.

ravigote [ravigɔt] f. Culin. Ravigote sauce.

ravigoter [-te] v. tr. (1). Fam. To buck up, to put a little pep into. [V. remonter.]
— v. pr. **Se ravigoter**, to pull oneself together ; to perk up a bit.

ravin [ravε̃] m. Ravine, gully ; U. S. gulch.

ravine [ravi:n] f. Ravine ; mountain torrent.

ravinée [ravine] f. Ravine.

ravinement [-nmɑ̃] m. Gully, scoring, hollowing-out.

raviner [-ne] v. tr. (1). To score, to hollow out (le sol). ‖ To furrow, to cut up (une route).

ravioli [ravjoli] m. Culin. Ravioli.

ravir [ravi:r] v. tr. (2). To ravish, to despoil, to snatch (ou) tear away (v. enlever) ; *ravir qqch. à qqn*, to despoil s.o. of sth., to steal sth. from s.o. ; *la mort nous l'a ravi*, death has taken him from us. ‖ Fig. To ravish, to charm, to entrance, to delight (v. enchanter) ; *à ravir*, ravishingly, delightfully, in a charming manner.

raviser (se) [səravize] v. pr. (1). To change one's mind, to think again, to think better of it.

ravissant, ante [ravisɑ̃, ɑ̃:t] adj. Ravening (loup). ‖ Fig. Ravishing (beauté) ; lovely (objet) ; bewitching, delightful, entrancing (personne).

ravissement [-smɑ̃] m. Ravishing, carrying off, rape. (V. rapt.) ‖ Fig. Rapture, delight (v. transport) ; *dans le ravissement*, in an ecstasy.

ravisseur, euse [-sœ:r, ø:z] adj. Predatory (bête) ; ravening (loup).
— m. Ravisher, plunderer. ‖ Kidnapper (d'un enfant) ; abductor (d'une femme).

ravitaillement [ravitɑjmɑ̃] m. Revictualling ; *ministère du ravitaillement*, Ministry of Food. ‖ Milit. Replenishment of stores ; *centre de ravitaillement*, supply base ; *ravitaillement en munitions*, ammunition supply. ‖ Naut. Taking in of stores ; completing.

ravitailler [-je] v. tr. (1). To revictual, to provision (en, with) ; *ravitailler en vivres*, to bring supplies to.
— v. pr. **Se ravitailler**, Naut. To take in fresh stores. ‖ Autom. *Se ravitailler en essence*, to fill up with petrol (ou) U. S. gas.

ravitailleur [-jœ:r] m. Milit. Carrier (de munitions). ‖ Naut. Supply- (ou) depot-ship ; *ravitailleur de sous-marins*, submarine parent-ship. ‖ Aviat. *Ravitailleur d'avion, d'hydravion*, aircraft, seaplane tender.

ravivage [raviva:ʒ] m. Reviving, brightening up (d'une couleur). ‖ Méd. Trimming (d'une plaie).

raviver [-ve] v. tr. (1). To brighten up, to restore (une couleur) ; to revive, to poke up (un feu). ‖ Méd. To trim (une plaie). ‖ Fig. To revive, to rouse (l'espérance) ; to reawaken (un souvenir).
— v. pr. **Se raviver**, to burn up again (feu) ;

to break out again (incendie). ‖ FIG. To revive (espérance) ; to break out again (querelle).

ravoir [ravwa:r] v. tr. (19). To get back, to recover.

rayage [rɛja:ʒ] m. Crossing out (d'un mot) ; striking out, crossing off (d'un nom sur une liste). ‖ MILIT. Rifling (d'un canon). ‖ TECHN. Scoring (d'un cylindre).

rayer [rɛje] v. tr. (9 b). To stripe, to streak (une étoffe) ; to cross out (un mot) ; to cross off, to strike out (un nom sur une liste) ; to rule, to line (du papier) ; to scratch, to mark (une surface). ‖ MILIT. To rifle (un canon). ‖ TECHN. To score, to groove (un cylindre). ‖ FAM. *Rayez cela de vos papiers!*, you need not reckon (ou) U. S. count on that any more!

rayère [rɛjɛ:r] f. ARCHIT. Dream-hole. ‖ TECHN. Head-race.

ray-grass [rɛgra:s] m. AGRIC. Rye-grass.

rayon [rɛjɔ̃] m. Ray, beam (de lumière) ; *rayon de soleil*, sunbeam. ‖ PHYS. Ray ; *rayons X*, X-rays. ‖ MATH. Radius (d'un cercle) ; *dans un rayon de*, within a radius of. ‖ AVIAT., NAUT. Range, radius (d'action) ; *à grand rayon d'action*, long-range. ‖ TECHN. Spoke (d'une roue). ‖ BLAS. Point (d'une étoile). ‖ AGRIC. Small furrow. ‖ FIG. Gleam, ray (d'espoir).

rayon m. Honeycomb (de miel) ; *miel en rayon*, comb-honey. ‖ Shelf (de bibliothèque). ‖ COMM. Department (d'un magasin). ‖ FAM. Line ; *ce n'est pas mon rayon*, that's not my cup of tea (ou) in my line, it's off my beat altogether ; *n'être bon que dans son rayon*, to be good only in one's own alley (ou) line.

rayonnage [rɛjɔna:ʒ] m. Shelving, set of shelves.

rayonnant, ante [-nã, ã:t] adj. PHYS. Radiant (chaleur) ; radiative (puissance). ‖ RADIO. Transmitting (pouvoir). ‖ CHIM. Radio-active. ‖ BOT. Radiating. ‖ ARCHIT., BLAS. Rayonnant. ‖ FIG. Radiant (de, with) ; radiant (beauté) ; beaming, radiant, wreathed in smiles (visage).

rayonne [rɛjɔn] f. Rayon, artificial silk.

rayonnement [rɛjɔnmã] m. Radiance, brightness (d'une étoile). ‖ PHYS. Radiation (de la chaleur). ‖ FIG. Radiance (de la beauté) ; dissemination (de la vérité).

rayonner [-ne] v. intr. (1). To sparkle (étoiles). ‖ To radiate, to spread out (routes). ‖ PHYS. To radiate (chaleur). ‖ RADIO. To howl (dans l'antenne). ‖ FIG. To spread abroad (idée) ; to be radiant, to beam, to shine (visage).

rayure [rɛjy:r] f. Stripe, streak ; *à rayures*, striped (étoffe). ‖ TECHN. Rifling, groove (d'un canon) ; scratch, score (d'un métal).

raz [rɑ] m. Current, race (courant) ; *raz de marée*, tide-race, tidal wave. ‖ FIG. *Raz de marée*, overwhelming victory (aux élections).

razzia [ra(d)zja] f. MILIT. Raid, razzia.

razzier [-zje] v. tr. (1). MILIT. To raid.

ré [re] m. invar. MUS. D, re (note) ; D string (d'un violon).

réa [rea] m. TECHN. Sheave.

réabonnement [reabɔnmã] m. Renewal of subscription (à, to).

réabonner [-ne] v. tr. (1). To renew s.o's subscription (à, to).
— v. pr. **Se réabonner,** to renew one's subscription (à, to) ; to take out a new subscription (à, to).

réabsorber [reapsɔrbe] v. tr. (1). To reabsorb.

réabsorption [-psjɔ̃] f. Reabsorbtion.

réac [reak] adj. FAM. Reactionary, square.
— s. Reactionary, square, old fogey.

réaccoutumer [reakutyme] v. tr. (1). To re-accustom (à, to).
— v. pr. **Se réaccoutumer,** to get (ou) become re-accustomed (à, to).

réactance [reaktã:s] f. ELECTR. Reactance.

réacteur [-tœ:r] m. ELECTR. Reactor ; choke. ‖ AVIAT. Jet plane. ‖ TECHN. Jet engine.

réactif, ive [-tif, i:v] adj. CHIM. Reactive ; *papier réactif,* test-paper.
— m. CHIM. Reagent.

réaction [-sjɔ̃] f. CHIM. Reaction ; *faire la réaction de,* to test for. ‖ RADIO. Howling (dans l'antenne). ‖ MILIT. Kick (d'un fusil). ‖ AVIAT. *Avion à réaction,* jet-propelled aeroplane ; jet (fam.). ‖ TECHN. *Moteur à réaction,* jet engine. ‖ MÉD. *Réaction cutanée,* skin-reaction (ou) test ; afterglow (après un bain). ‖ FIG. Response (à, to).

réactionnaire [-sjɔnɛ:r] adj., s. Reactionary.

réactivation [reaktivasjɔ̃] f. Reactivation, regeneration. ‖ CHIM. Regeneration.

réactiver [-tive] v. tr. (1). To reactivate, to regenerate. ‖ CHIM. To regenerate.

réadaptation [readaptasjɔ̃] f. Adjustment.

réadapter [-te] v. tr. (1). To re-adapt.

réadmettre [readmɛtr] v. tr. (64). To readmit.

réadmission [-misjɔ̃] f. Readmission ; readmittance.

réaffirmer [reafirme] v. tr. (1). To re-affirm.

réagir [reaʒi:r] v. intr. (2). To react (sur, on) [qqch., qqn]. ‖ MÉD. To react (à, to). ‖ FIG. To respond (à, to) ; to react (contre, against) [qqch.].

réajuster [reaʒyste] v. tr. (1). V. RAJUSTER.

réal [real] m. Real.

réalgar [realga:r] m. CHIM. Realgar.

réalisable [realizabl] adj. FIN. Realizable (actif) ; available, convertible into cash (avoir). ‖ FIG. Workable, achievable, feasible (projet).

réalisateur, trice [-zatœ:r, tris] s. FIN. Seller (des actions). ‖ THÉÂTR. Director (de cinéma). ‖ FIG. Realizer (d'un projet).

réalisation [-zasjɔ̃] f. FIN. Selling out (d'actions) ; utilization, availment (en banque). ‖ COMM. *Réalisation du stock,* clearance sale. ‖ FIG. Fulfilment, realization (d'un désir) ; working out, carrying-into effect, realization (d'un projet) ; application (d'une théorie).

réaliser [-ze] v. tr. (1). FIN. To sell out (des actions) ; to effect (une économie) ; to realize (des titres) ; *cours réalisés,* rates obtained. ‖ FIG. To fulfil (un espoir) ; to achieve (une œuvre) ; to carry out, to out (une promesse) ; *ne pas réaliser la perfection,* to fall short of perfection. ‖ FAM. To realize, to understand (v. SE RENDRE COMPTE) ; *réaliser les possibilités d'un projet,* to see the possibilities in a scheme ; *réaliser que,* to grasp the fact that.
— v. pr. **Se réaliser,** to be fulfilled (espérance) ; to materialize (possibilités) ; to be realized, to come to fruition (projet) ; to come true (rêve).

réalisme [realism] m. ARTS, PHILOS. Realism.

réaliste [-list] adj. ARTS. Realistic (peinture). ‖ MUS. *Chanson réaliste,* cabaret song.
— s. ARTS, PHILOS. Realist.

réalité [-lite] f. Reality, actuality, fact ; *réalité et chimère,* fact and fiction ; *en réalité,* really, as a matter of fact ; *fait de demeurer en dessous de la réalité,* understatement ; *loin de la réalité,* wide of the mark.

réaménagement [reamena3mã] m. Refitting.

réaménager [-naʒe] v. tr. (7). To refit.

réanimation [reanimasjɔ̃] f. Resuscitation.

réanimer [-me] v. tr. (1). To resuscitate.

réapparaître [reaparɛ:tr] v. intr. (74). To reappear, to appear again.

réapparition [-risjɔ̃] f. Reappearance.

réapprendre [reaprã:dr] v. tr. (80). V. RAPPRENDRE.

réapprovisionnement [reaprovizjɔnmã] m. Reprovisioning, replenishing of supplies. ‖ COMM. Restocking (d'un magasin).

réapprovisionner [-ne] v. tr. (1). To reprovision, to replenish supplies. ‖ COMM. To restock (un magasin).
— v. pr. **Se réapprovisionner,** to replenish one's supplies. ‖ COMM. To restock.

réargenter [rearʒɑ̃te] v. tr. (1). To resilver, to replate.

réarmement [rearməmɑ̃] m. MILIT. Rearming. ‖ NAUT. Refitting, recommissioning (d'un navire).

réarmer [-me] v. tr. (1). MILIT. To rearm (soldats, troupes, pays). ‖ NAUT. To reequip, to refit (navire). ‖ TECHN. To recock (fusil); to wind on (appareil photo).
— v. intr. MILIT. To rearm.

réarrangement [rearɑ̃ʒmɑ̃] m. Rearrangement. ‖ CHIM. *Réarrangement moléculaire,* molecular rearrangement.

réarranger [-ʒe] v. tr. (7). To rearrange.

réassignation [reasiɲasjɔ̃] f. JUR. Fresh summons.

réassigner [-ɲe] v. tr. (1). JUR. To resummons.

réassortir [reasɔrtir] v. tr. (2). V. RASSORTIR.

réassurance [reasyrɑ̃:s] f. FIN. Reinsurance.

réassurer [-re] v. tr. (1). FIN. To reinsure.

réassureur [-rœ:r] m. FIN. Reinsurer, reinsurance broker.

rebaisser [rəbɛse] v. tr. (1). To lower again.

rebaptisé, ée [rəbatize] adj. Renamed.

rébarbatif, ive [rebarbatif, i:v] adj. Surly (humeur); forbidding, repulsive (mine). [V. RE-VÊCHE.] ‖ Crabbed (style).

rebâtir [rəbɑti:r] v. tr. (2). ARCHIT. To rebuild.

rebattre [rəbatr] v. tr. (20). To beat again, to hammer again (qqch.); to beat again, to re-defeat (qqn); to go over again (une route). ‖ SPORTS. To reshuffle (les cartes). ‖ FAM. To repeat over and over again; *rebattre les oreilles à qqn de qqch.,* to din sth. into s.o.'s ears.

rebattu, ue [-ty] adj. Frequented (chemin). ‖ FIG. Hackneyed, trite (histoire); threadbare, often quoted (vers). [V. USÉ.] ‖ FAM. *En avoir les oreilles rebattues,* to have it dinned into one, to be sick of hearing about it.

rebec [rəbɛk] m. Mus. Rebeck.

rebelle [rəbɛl] adj. Refractory, disobedient (enfant); unruly (esprit); rebellious (personne); *rebelle à la poésie,* insensitive to poetry (personne); ill-suited to poetic treatment (sujet). ‖ MILIT. Insubordinate, mutinous (troupes). ‖ MÉD. Obstinate (maladie). ‖ JUR. Unamenable, contumacious. ‖ TECHN. Unworkable (matière); refractory (minéral).
— s. Rebel.

rebeller (se) [sərəbɛle] v. pr. (1). To rebel, to rise (*contre,* against). [V. RÉVOLTER (SE).]

rébellion [rebɛljɔ̃] f. Rebellion, uprising (V. RÉVOLTE); *en état de rébellion,* insurgent; *en rébellion ouverte,* in open revolt; *faire rébellion à,* to rebel against. ‖ JUR. Contumacy. ‖ FIG. Resistance (*contre,* to).

rebiffer (se) [sərəbife] v. pr. (1). FAM. To bridle, to bristle up, to show one's teeth, to kick over the traces, to jib. ‖ To kick (*contre,* against).

rebiquer [rəbike] v. intr. (1). FAM. To stick up.

reboisement [rəbwazmɑ̃] m. AGRIC. Reafforestation.

reboiser [-ze] v. tr. (1). AGRIC. To reafforest.

rebond [rəbɔ̃] m. Rebound.

rebondi, ie [rəbɔ̃di] adj. Well-filled (bourse); plump (corps); chubby, fleshy (joues); well-rounded (poitrine); *aux formes rebondies,* buxom; *ventre rebondi,* paunch; corporation (fam.).

rebondir [-di:r] v. tr. (2). To rebound, to bounce (ballon); to surge (torrent). ‖ FIG. To start off again, to come to life again (affaire).

rebondissant, ante [-disɑ̃, ɑ̃:t] adj. Rebounding (ballon); surging (torrent).

rebondissement [-dismɑ̃] m. Bounce, rebounding (d'un ballon); surging (d'un torrent). ‖ FIG. Renewal, coming to life again (d'une affaire).

rebord [rəbɔ:r] m. Edge (d'un fossé); rim (d'une soucoupe); lip (d'une tasse); *rebord d'une cheminée, d'une fenêtre,* mantelshelf (ou) mantelpiece, window-sill. ‖ TECHN. Flange (d'un tuyau).

reboucher [rəbuʃe] v. tr. (1). To cork again, to recork (une bouteille); to fill in (ou) up again (un trou); to block up again (un tuyau).

rebours [rəbu:r] m. Wrong way of the nap (d'une étoffe). ‖ FIG. Reverse, opposite.
— loc. adv. **A** (ou) **au rebours,** against the grain (ou) nap; the wrong way; *compliment à rebours,* back-handed compliment; *faire tout à rebours,* to do everything the wrong way round; *marcher à rebours,* to walk backwards; *prendre tout à rebours,* to take everything the wrong way.
— loc. prép. **A** (ou) **au rebours de,** contrary to; *faire tout au rebours de ce qu'il faut,* to do the opposite of what should be done.

rebouter [rəbute] v. tr. (1). MÉD. To set.

rebouteur [-tœ:r], **rebouteux** [-tø] s. MÉD. Bone-setter.

reboutonner [rəbutɔne] v. tr. (1). To rebutton.
— v. pr. **Se reboutonner,** to button up one's clothes again.

rebrousse [rəbru:s]. V. REBROUSSER. ‖ **A rebrousse-poil,** loc. adv. Against the nap; *caresser un chat à rebrousse-poil,* to stroke a cat the wrong way (ou) against the fur; *brosser un tapis à rebrousse-poil,* to brush a carpet against the run of the pile; FIG. *prendre qqch. à rebrousse-poil,* to get things wrong; *prendre qqn à rebrousse-poil,* to rub s.o. up the wrong way.

rebrousser [rəbruse] v. tr. (1). To brush the wrong way (les cheveux); to grain (le cuir); to nap (le drap). ‖ FIG. *Rebrousser chemin,* to turn back, to retrace one's steps; *faire rebrousser chemin à qqn,* to drive s.o. back.

rebuffade [rəbyfad] f. Snub, rebuff.

rébus [reby:s] m. Rebus, picture puzzle.

rebut [rəby] m. Rubbish, scrap, waste material; *de rebut,* cast-off (habits); waste (papier); *mettre au rebut,* to discard (des habits); *viande de rebut,* offal. ‖ Dead letter (lettre); *service central des rebuts,* dead-letter office. ‖ TECHN. *Mettre au rebut,* to scrap (une machine); *pièces de rebut,* rejects. ‖ FIG. Scum (de la société).

rebutant, ante [-tɑ̃, ɑ̃:t] adj. Forbidding (mine); unprepossessing, repulsive, irksome, uncongenial, tedious (travail).

rebuter [-te] v. tr. (1). To rebuff, to repel, to be short with (personne); *son air me rebute,* his manner puts me off. ‖ To dishearten, to dispirit, to weary (travail).
— v. intr. To be displeasing (manières).
— v. pr. **Se rebuter,** to become discouraged, to lose heart; to balk (*devant,* at) [qqch.].

recacheter [rəkaʃte] v. tr. (1). To seal up again.

recalage [rəkala:ʒ] m. FAM. Failure (à un examen).

récalcitrant, ante [rekalsitrɑ̃, ɑ̃:t] adj. Recalcitrant, refractory.
— s. Recalcitrant.

récalcitrer [-tre] v. intr. (1). To recalcitrate, to be refractory, to kick (*contre,* against).

recaler [rəkale] v. tr. (1). To wedge (ou) chock up again (caler de nouveau). ‖ FAM. To fail, to plough (un candidat).

récapitulatif, ive [rekapitylatif, i:v] adj. Recapitulatory, recapitulative.

récapitulation [-lasjɔ̃] f. Recapitulation, summing-up; résumé, summary.

récapituler [-le] v. tr. (1). To recapitulate, to sum up.

recarreler [rəkarle] v. tr. (5). To retile, to repair (une pièce) ; to resole (des souliers).

recaser [rəkɑze] v. tr. (1). FAM. To put back in, to replace (replacer) ; to rehouse (reloger) ; to find a new job for (employer ailleurs).

recauser [rəkoze] v. intr. (1). To have another talk (*de qqch.*, about sth.).

recéder [rəsede] v. tr. (5). *Recéder qqch. à qqn*, to let s.o. have sth. back, to resell sth. to s.o.

recel [rəsɛl] m. JUR. Harbouring (d'un criminel) ; receiving ; fencing (fam.) [d'objets volés].

receler [rəsəle] v. tr. (5). JUR. To harbour (un criminel) ; to receive (des objets volés). ‖ FIG. To contain ; *que de beautés recèle cet ouvrage!* what gems are to be found in that work !

receleur [rəsləœ:r] s. JUR. Receiver of stolen property ; fence (fam.).

récemment [resamɑ̃] adv. Recently, of late.

recensement [rəsɑ̃smɑ̃] m. JUR. Recording (des accidents) ; census (de la population) ; counting (des voix) ; *faire un recensement*, to take a census ; *feuille de recensement*, census paper ; *faire le recensement des voix*, to count the votes. ‖ MILIT. Registration (des soldats). ‖ COMM. Stock-taking ; inventory. ‖ FIG. Review (des événements).

recenser [-se] v. tr. (1). To record (les accidents) ; to take a census of (a population) ; to count (les voix). ‖ MILIT. To register (les soldats). ‖ COMM. To check, to inventory (les stocks).

recenseur [-sœ:r] s. Census-taker (de la population) ; teller (des voix). ‖ COMM. Inventory-taker.

recension [-sjɔ̃] f. Recension (de manuscrits). ‖ Review (compte rendu).

récent, ente [resɑ̃, ɑ̃:t] adj. Recent, new (événement) ; fresh (nouvelle) ; green (souvenir) ; *la piste est toute récente*, the scent is still warm.

récépissé [resepise] m. Receipt.

réceptacle [reseptakl] m. BOT., FIG. Receptacle.

récepteur, trice [-tœ:r, tris] adj. RADIO. Receiving (appareil).
— m. Receiver (du téléphone). ‖ RADIO. Receiving set (ou) station. ‖ TECHN. Driven part (d'une machine).

réceptif, ive [-tif, i:v] adj. Receptive.

réception [-sjɔ̃] f. Receipt (d'une lettre). ‖ Welcome ; *faire une bonne réception à qqn*, to give s.o. a warm welcome. ‖ Graduation (d'un grade universitaire). ‖ Reception (à l'Académie) ; *discours de réception*, speech made by a new member of the Académie. ‖ Reception, levee (à la cour) ; *donner une réception*, to entertain ; *jour de réception*, at-home day ; *salles de réception*, staterooms ; *salon de réception*, reception room. ‖ Reception desk (d'un hôtel) ; *employé à la réception*, reception (ou) U. S. room clerk. ‖ COMM. Taking delivery (de denrées) ; taking over (d'une machine) ; *essais de réception*, official acceptance tests. ‖ THÉÂTR. Acceptance (d'une pièce). ‖ RADIO. Reception.

réceptionnaire [-sjɔnɛ:r] adj. COMM. Receiving ; taking over.
— s. COMM. Reception clerk ; consignee.

réceptionner [-sjɔne] v. tr. (1). COMM. To check and sign for ; to take delivery.

réceptionniste [-sjɔnist] m. COMM. Receptionist.

réceptivité [-tivite] f. Receptivity. ‖ MÉD. Liability to infection.

récessif, ive [resesif, i:v] adj. MÉD. Recessive (gène).

récession [resesjɔ̃] f. Recession.

récessivité [resesivite] f. MÉD. Recessiveness.

recette [rəsɛt] f. FIN. Receipts, returns (d'une entreprise) ; collecting, receiving (de traites) ; collector's office (bureau) ; *garçon de recette*, bank-messenger ; *recettes et dépenses*, incomings and outgoings. ‖ COMM. Receipt ; acceptance. ‖ CULIN.

Recipe, receipt. ‖ NAUT. Taking over. ‖ SPORTS. Gate-money. ‖ THÉÂTR. Takings ; U. S. take ; *faire recette*, to be a draw. ‖ FIG. Tip, wrinkle ; *recettes de métier*, tricks of the trade.

recevabilité [rəsevabilite] f. Receivability. ‖ JUR. Admissibility.

recevable [-vabl] adj. JUR. Receivable, allowable (appel) ; admissible (déposition) ; competent to proceed with a claim (plaignant). ‖ COMM. Fit for acceptance (marchandises).

receveur [-vœ:r] s. *Receveur des postes*, postmaster. ‖ FIN. *Receveur des contributions directes, indirectes*, tax-collector, collector of excise ; *receveur de l'enregistrement*, receiver of registry fees ; *receveur des Finances*, district collector of taxes. ‖ AUTOM. Conductor (d'autobus).

receveuse [-vø:z] f. AUTOM. Conductress ; clippie (fam.) [d'autobus].

recevoir [-vwa:r] v. tr. (3). To get, to receive (un cadeau) ; to meet with (des insultes) ; to take in, to subscribe to (un journal) ; to be in receipt of (une lettre) ; to meet (la mort) ; to be given (un nom) ; to incur (une punition) ; to catch (qqch. en main). ‖ To receive, to entertain (des amis) ; *recevoir à bras ouverts*, to welcome with open arms. ‖ To admit (des élèves) ; to take in, to accommodate (des pensionnaires). ‖ To admit, to give a pass to (un candidat) ; *être reçu à un examen*, to pass an examination ; *être reçu à l'Académie française*, to be made a member of the Académie Française ; *être reçu à la licence ès lettres*, to take an Arts degree ; *être reçu médecin*, to qualify as a doctor ; *être reçu premier*, to be placed first ; to come top (fam.). ‖ To accept (une excuse) ; to admit (une opinion). ‖ FIN. To collect (des impôts). ‖ TECHN. To take. ‖ NAUT. To harbour. ‖ ECCLÉS. To take (les ordres) ; to partake of, to receive (les sacrements).
— v. intr. To receive, to hold a reception ; *recevoir tous les mardis*, to be « at home » on Tuesdays.
— v. pr. **Se recevoir**, to land after a jump (cheval, sauteur).

rechange [rəʃɑ̃:ʒ] m. Replacement ; *des vêtements de rechange*, a change of clothes. ‖ TECHN., AUTOM. *Pièces de rechange, rechanges*, spare parts, spares ; *roue de rechange*, spare wheel. ‖ ÉLECTR. *Pile de rechange*, refill.

rechanger [rəʃɑ̃ʒe] v. tr. (7). To change again.

rechanter [rəʃɑ̃te] v. tr. (1). To sing again.

rechapage [rəʃapa:ʒ] m. AUTOM. Retreading.

rechaper [rəʃape] v. tr. (1). AUTOM. To retread.

réchappé [reʃape] s. Survivor. (V. RESCAPÉ.)

réchapper v. intr. (1). *Réchapper de*, to escape from (un danger) ; to come through (la guerre) ; to get over (la maladie) ; to be saved from (un naufrage) ; *en réchapper*, to get off, to get away with it.

recharge [rəʃarʒ] f. Refill (d'un briquet, d'un stylo). ‖ MILIT. Reload (d'un fusil). ‖ ÉLECTR. Recharging (d'un accu).

rechargement [-ʒəmɑ̃] m. Reloading (d'une voiture). ‖ NAUT. Relading (d'un navire). ‖ MILIT. Reload, reloading (d'un fusil). ‖ ÉLECTR. Recharging (d'un accu). ‖ TECHN. Remetalling (d'une route). ‖ CH. DE F. Reballasting (d'une voie).

recharger [-ʒe] v. tr. (7). To make up (un feu) ; to reburden (qqn) ; to reload (une voiture). ‖ ÉLECTR. To recharge (un accu). ‖ NAUT. To relade (un navire). ‖ MILIT. To charge again (l'ennemi) ; to reload (un fusil). ‖ TECHN. To remetal (une route). ‖ CH. DE F. To reballast (une voie).

réchaud [reʃo] m. Small portable stove ; *réchaud à alcool, à pétrole*, spirit-, oil-stove ; *réchaud à gaz*, gas-ring (à une rampe) ; gas-cooker, U. S. gas-stove (à plusieurs feux). ‖ Hot-plate, plate-warmer, chafing-dish (chauffe-plat). ‖ TECHN. Heater.

réchauffage [-fa:ʒ] m. Re-heating, warming-up again.

réchauffant, ante [-fɑ̃, ɑ̃:t] adj. MÉD. Calefacient.

réchauffé, ée [-fe] m. CULIN. Warmed-up dish. ‖ FIG. Stale news; rehashed literature; *du réchauffé,* a twice-told tale.

réchauffement [-fmɑ̃] m. Warming-up (du temps, du climat).

réchauffer [-fe] v. tr. (1). To warm up, to chafe. ‖ CULIN. To re-heat, to warm up again. ‖ FIG. To stir, to rouse again (un sentiment); to rekindle (le zèle); *réchauffer le cœur,* to warm the cockles of the heart; *réchauffer un serpent dans son sein,* to nourish a viper in one's bosom.
— v. pr. **Se réchauffer,** to warm oneself, to get warm again.

réchauffeur [-fœ:r] m. TECHN. Re-heater.

réchauffoir [-fwa:r] m. CULIN. Hot-plate, plate-warmer.

rechausser [reʃose] v. tr. (1). To put shoes on again, to fit with new shoes (qqn). ‖ ARCHIT. To line the foot of (un mur). ‖ BOT. To pile earth round the foot of (un arbre).
— v. pr. **Se rechausser,** to put one's shoes on again.

rêche [rɛʃ] adj. Rough (surface). ‖ FIG. Rude, rough, crabbed (caractère); sharp, harsh (goût).

recherche [rəʃɛrʃ] f. Search, quest; *aller à la recherche de,* to go in search of; *être à la recherche de,* to be on the look out for. ‖ Research; *faire des recherches sur,* to make researches into; *faire des travaux de recherches,* to do (ou) carry out research work. ‖ JUR. Enquiry (de la police); *droit de recherche,* right of search. ‖ FIG. Pursuit (de la science); *recherche de la vérité,* quest for truth. ‖ FIG. Studied care (ou) elegance; *recherches de cruauté,* refinement of cruelty; *style sans recherche,* unlaboured (ou) natural style.

recherché, ée [rəʃɛrʃe] adj. Much sought after, in great demand (article, personne). ‖ Select, particular (personne); elaborate (toilette); exquisite (travail). ‖ Far-fetched (expression); affected, laboured (style).

rechercher v. tr. (1). To seek, to search for, to look for again (qqch., qqn). ‖ To investigate (les causes); to hunt out (les faits). ‖ To seek after (l'amitié); to court (les faveurs); to seek the acquaintance of (qqn); *rechercher qqn en mariage,* to seek the hand of s.o., to seek s.o. in marriage. ‖ To strive after, to be eager for (une alliance); *rechercher l'esprit,* to make a forced show of wit. ‖ JUR. To try to identify (le criminel).

rechigner [rəʃiɲe] v. intr. (1). To look sour (ou) sullen; *rechigner devant une tâche,* to balk (ou) boggle (ou) jib at a job; *sans rechigner,* with a good face.

rechute [rəʃy:t] f. MÉD. Relapse. ‖ FIG. Backsliding.

rechuter [rəʃyte] v. intr. (1). MÉD. To have a relapse. ‖ FIG. To back-slide.

récidive [residi:v] f. MÉD. Recurrence, reappearance (d'une maladie). ‖ JUR. Second offence; repetition (d'un crime); *vol avec récidive,* theft for the second time. ‖ FIG. Back-sliding, relapse.

récidiver [-dive] v. intr. (1). MÉD. To recur, to reappear. ‖ JUR. To relapse into crime, to commit an offence a second time.

récidiviste [-divist] s. Recidivist, hardened criminal; old lag (fam.). ‖ FIG. Backslider.

récidivité [-divite] f. MÉD. Tendency to recur. ‖ JUR. Recidivity.

récif [resif] m. Reef, submerged reef.

récipiendaire [resipjɑ̃dɛ:r] s. Member elect, newly installed member (d'une Académie).

récipient [-pjɑ̃] m. Container, receptable; storage bin. ‖ PHYS. Bell-jar.

réciprocité [resiprɔsite] f. Reciprocity.

réciproque [-prɔk] adj. Reciprocal (devoir); mutual (sentiment). ‖ MATH. Converse (théorème). ‖ GRAMM. Reciprocal (verbe). ‖ TECHN. Reversible (mouvement).
— f. Like; *rendre la réciproque à qqn,* to pay s.o. back in kind (ou) in his own coin. ‖ MATH. Converse.

réciproquement [-prɔkmɑ̃] adv. Reciprocally, mutually; *se flatter réciproquement,* to flatter one another. ‖ MATH. Conversely.

récit [resi] m. Narrative, recital, story; *faire le récit de,* to give an account of. ‖ MUS. Recitative.

récital [-tal] (pl. **récitals**) m. MUS. Recital.

récitant, ante [-tɑ̃, ɑ̃:t] adj. MUS. Solo (voix); *partie récitante,* recitative.
— s. MUS. Narrator.

récitateur [-tatœ:r] s. Reciter.

récitatif [-tatif] m. MUS. Recitative.

récitation [-tasjɔ̃] f. Recitation (acte, texte); saying (d'une leçon); reciting (de vers). ‖ MUS. Singing of a recitative.

réciter [-te] v. tr. (1). To say (une leçon); to recite (des vers); *faire réciter,* to hear (une leçon). ‖ MUS. To sing.
— v. intr. To recite. ‖ MUS. To sing a recitative.

réclamant [reklamɑ̃] s. Complainer. ‖ JUR. Claimant.

réclamation [-masjɔ̃] f. Complaint, objection; *faire une réclamation,* to lodge a complaint; *registre des réclamations,* suggestion-book; *vives réclamations,* vigorous protests. ‖ JUR. Claim.

réclame [rekla:m] f. Advertising; advertisement; puff (fam.); *faire de la réclame,* to advertise; *mauvaise réclame,* bad publicity; *soigner sa réclame,* to keep in the public eye. ‖ Advertisement sign; *réclame à éclipse, lumineuse,* flashing, illuminated sign. ‖ TECHN. Catchword.

réclamer [reklame] v. tr. (1). To claim (à, from); to lay claim to (revendiquer); *réclamer la parole,* to demand to be heard. ‖ To claim back, to claim the return of (demander le retour); *réclamer de l'argent à,* to dun. ‖ To beg for (solliciter); *réclamer l'indulgence de qqn,* to crave s.o.'s indulgence; *réclamer du secours,* to beg for help. ‖ To call (ou) clamour for (demander instamment); *réclamer le sang d'un tyran,* to call for a tyrant's blood. ‖ To require, to need (exiger); *réclamer les soins d'un médecin,* to require the attention of a doctor. ‖ JUR. To claim (des dommages, un droit). ‖ FIN. *Non réclamé,* unclaimed (dividende). ‖ THÉÂTR. To call for (un acteur). ‖ SPORTS. *Course à réclamer,* selling-plate.
— v. intr. To complain. ‖ To object (contre, to); to protest (contre, against). ‖ JUR. To appeal (contre, against) [une décision].
— v. pr. **Se réclamer de,** to call, to witness (qqn); *se réclamer de l'amitié de qqn,* to claim friendship with s.o.

réclameur [-mœ:r] s. Complainer; objector.

réclamiste [-mist] s. FAM. Forceful advertiser; puff-writer; adman.

reclassement [rəklɑsmɑ̃] m. Reclassification; regrouping. ‖ Regrading (des fonctionnaires).

reclasser [-se] v. tr. (1). To reclassify; to regroup, to rearrange.

reclouer [rəklue] v. tr. (1). To nail (ou) nail up again.

reclus, use [rəkly, y:z] adj. ECCLÉS. Cloistered.
— s. Recluse.

réclusion [reklysjɔ̃] f. Reclusion, seclusion. ‖ JUR. Solitary confinement.

récognitif, ive [rekɔgnitif, iːv] adj. JUR. Recognitive.

récognition [-sjɔ̃] f. PHILOS. Recognition.

recoiffer [rəkwafe] v. tr. (1). To do up s.o.'s hair again (qqn). ‖ To recap (une bouteille).
— v. pr. **Se recoiffer,** to put one's hat on again (se couvrir); to do up one's hair again (se peigner).

recoin [rəkwɛ̃] m. Nook, recess; *tous les coins et recoins,* every nook and cranny. ‖ FIG. Pl. Inmost recesses (de l'âme).

récolement [rekɔlmɑ̃] m. Checking (d'un inventaire). ‖ JUR. Reading over (d'une déposition).

récoler [rekɔle] v. tr. (1). To check (un inventaire). ‖ JUR. To read over (une déposition).

recollage [rəkɔlaːʒ], **recollement** [rəkɔlmɑ̃] m. Sticking together again.

récollection [rekɔlɛksjɔ̃] f. ECCLÉS. Recollection.

recoller [rəkɔle] v. tr. (1). To glue (ou) stick together again (un objet cassé). ‖ FAM. To plough (ou) pluck (ou) U. S. flunk again (un candidat).
— v. pr. **Se recoller,** to stick together again (objet cassé). ‖ MÉD. To knit (os fracturé); to heal up (plaie).

récollet [rekɔlɛ] adj. ECCLÉS. Recollect.

récoltant, ante [rekɔltɑ̃, ɑ̃ːt] adj. AGRIC. *Propriétaire récoltant,* smallholder.
— s. AGRIC. Cropper, smallholder.

récolte [rekɔlt] f. AGRIC. Harvesting, gathering in (du blé); *faire les récoltes,* to bring in the harvest. ‖ Crop; *récolte sur pied,* standing crop; *riche récolte de blé,* good wheat-crop. ‖ FIG. Collecting, gathering (d'objets).

récolter [-te] v. tr. (1). AGRIC. To harvest, to gather in (du blé); to lift (des pommes de terre). ‖ FIG. To collect, to gather; *récolter la haine,* to bring down hatred upon oneself; *récolter la tempête,* to reap the whirlwind.

recommandable [rəkɔmɑ̃dabl] adj. Recommendable (hôtel); praiseworthy (qualité); estimable (personne); advisable (procédé).

recommandation [-dasjɔ̃] f. Recommendation; *lettre de recommandation,* letter of introduction. ‖ Instruction, injunction; *faire des recommandations à,* to instruct (ou) advise; *suivre les recommandations de qqn,* to act upon s.o.'s instructions (ou) advice. ‖ Registration (d'une lettre).

recommandé, ée [-de] V. RECOMMANDER. ‖ Adj. Sent by recorded delivery, U.S. certified (sans indemnisation en cas de perte); registered (avec indemnisation).
— m. Recorded delivery, U. S. certified mail; registered post (ou U.S.) mail.

recommander [-de] v. tr. (1). To recommend (qqch., qqn) [à, to]; *recommander son âme à Dieu,* to commend one's soul to God. ‖ To advise, to enjoin (qqch.); *recommander la discrétion à,* to recommend discretion to, to enjoin discretion on; *recommander à qqn de,* to charge (ou) instruct s.o. to (charger); to advise s.o. strongly to (conseiller); to register, to insure [une lettre].
— v. pr. **Se recommander,** to recommend oneself; *le vrai mérite se recommande tout seul,* true merit is its own recommendation; *se recommander à qqn,* to commend oneself to s.o.; *se recommander de qqn,* to give s.o.'s name as a reference; *se recommander par ses qualités,* to be recommended by one's qualities.

recommencement [rəkɔmɑ̃smɑ̃] m. Recommencement, beginning again.

recommencer [rəkɔmɑ̃se] v. tr. (6). To recommence, to begin again, to start afresh (qqch.); *recommencer à faire qqch.,* to begin to do sth.

again (ou) over again; *recommencer sa vie,* to make a fresh start in life.
— v. intr. To begin again, to start afresh. ‖ To break out again (ou) afresh (guerre); to do it again (personne); to begin again (pluie); to re-open (séance); *recommencer de plus belle,* to start again with renewed vigour.

recomparaître [rekɔ̃parɛːtr] v. tr. (74). JUR. To appear again.

récompense [rekɔ̃pɑ̃ːs] f. Recompense; reward (de, for); *en récompense,* as a reward, in return (de, for). ‖ Prize, award (prix). ‖ Retribution; punishment (d'un crime). ‖ JUR. Compensation.

récompenser [-pɑ̃se] v. tr. (1). To recompense; to reward (une bonne action, qqn); to reward (de, for) [qqn]. ‖ To punish; to pay out (de, for) [un traître].

recomposable [rəkɔ̃pozabl] adj. Able to be recomposed.

recomposer [-ze] v. tr. (1). To recompose (une administration). ‖ CHIM. To recompose, to recombine (un élément). ‖ TECHN. To reset, to set up again (un texte en typographie).

recomposition [-zisjɔ̃] f. Recomposition, recombining. ‖ TECHN. Resetting (en typographie).

recompter [rəkɔ̃te] v. tr. (1). To recount, to count again.

réconciliable [rekɔ̃siljabl] adj. Reconcilable.

réconciliateur, trice [-ljatœːr, tris] s. Reconciler.

réconciliation [-ljasjɔ̃] f. Reconciliation.

réconcilier [-lje] v. tr. (1). To reconcile, to bring together again (deux personnes). ‖ To harmonize, to make compatible (avec, with) [qqch.]. ‖ ECCLÉS. To reconcile.
— v. pr. **Se réconcilier,** to bury the hatchet. ‖ To become friends again, to make it up (avec, with). ‖ ECCLÉS. *Se réconcilier avec Dieu,* to make one's peace with God.

reconductible [rəkɔ̃dyktibl] adj. JUR. Renewable.

reconduction [rəkɔ̃dyksjɔ̃] f. JUR. Renewal.

reconduire [-dɥiːr] v. tr. (85). To escort (ou) see (ou) take s.o. home (qqn chez lui); to accompany (ou) take s.o. back; to see (ou) show out (ou) to the door (un visiteur); *reconduire un intrus à coups de pied,* to kick an intruder out. ‖ MILIT. To drive back (l'ennemi). ‖ JUR. To renew.

reconduite [rəkɔ̃dɥit] f. Taking (ou) seeing (ou) accompanying back (ou) home; seeing out (ou) to the door.

réconfort [rekɔ̃fɔːr] m. Comfort, consolation; help in time of affliction; *apporter du réconfort à,* to bring relief to.

réconfortant, ante [-fɔrtɑ̃, ɑ̃ːt] adj. Stimulating (breuvage); comforting (paroles). ‖ MÉD. Tonic.
— m. Tonic; pick-me-up (fam.).

réconforter [-fɔrte] v. tr. (1). To fortify, to invigorate, to revive. ‖ FIG. To comfort, to cheer up.
— v. pr. **Se réconforter,** to refresh oneself, to take refreshment. ‖ FIG. To cheer up.

reconnaissable [rəkɔnɛsabl] adj. Recognizable (à, by); *à peine reconnaissable,* almost beyond recognition.

reconnaissance [-sɑ̃ːs] f. Recognition (de, of) [qqn]. ‖ Avowal, recognition (d'une faute) [V. AVEU.] ‖ Gratitude, gratefulness (v. GRATITUDE); *avec reconnaissance,* gratefully; *témoigner de la reconnaissance,* to show gratitude. ‖ JUR. Acknowledgment, affiliation (d'un enfant); recognition, acknowledgment (d'un gouvernement). ‖ FIN. Recognizance (d'une dette); *reconnaissance de dette,* acknowledgment of indebtedness; *reconnaissance de mont-de-piété,* pawn-ticket; *signer une reconnaissance,* to write out an I. O. U. (= I owe you). ‖ MILIT. Reconnaissance, reconnoitring (du terrain); *reconnaissance photographique,* photo-reconnaissance; *faire une recon-*

naissance, to make a reconnaissance (ou) a recce. ‖ NAUT. Charting (du littoral). ‖ AVIAT. Aerial reconnaissance. ‖ GÉOGR. Survey, exploration (d'un lieu). ‖ COMM. Note of hand.

reconnaissant, ante [-sã, ã:t] adj. Grateful (*de,* for; *envers,* to); *être reconnaissant à qqn de,* to be obliged (ou) beholden to s.o. for. ‖ Thankful (*de,* for).

reconnaître [rəkɔnɛ:tr] v. tr. (74). To recognize, to know again (qqn); *reconnaître qqn à la voix,* to recognize s.o. by his voice. ‖ To confess to, to avow (un tort); to submit to (un vainqueur); to admit (une vérité). ‖ To be grateful for (une faveur); to reward (un service). ‖ JUR. To recognize, to acknowledge (un enfant, un gouvernement); *reconnu coupable,* found guilty. ‖ NAUT. To make out (un feu); to sight, to make (la terre); to identify (un vaisseau). ‖ FIN. To credit. ‖ MILIT. To reconnoitre (le terrain). ‖ FAM. *Je vous reconnais bien là!,* that's you all over!

— **Se reconnaître,** to recognize oneself, to recognize each other; *se reconnaître dans ses enfants,* to see one's likeness in one's children. ‖ To know where one is; to find one's bearings (trouver son aplomb). ‖ FIG. To admit (ou) acknowledge oneself; *se reconnaître coupable,* to admit that one is guilty. ‖ To repent (se repentir). ‖ FAM. To collect oneself (ou) one's thoughts (ou) one's wits (retrouver ses esprits).

reconnu, e [-ny] adj. Recognized, acknowledged (incontesté).

reconquérir [rəkɔ̃keri:r] v. tr. (13). To reconquer, to win back (un territoire) [*sur,* from]. ‖ FIG. To win back, to regain (l'estime).

reconquête [-kɛ:t] f. Reconquest.

reconsidérer [rəkɔ̃sidere] v. tr. (3). To reconsider.

reconsolidation [rəkɔ̃sɔlidasjɔ̃] f. Reconsolidation.

reconsolider [-de] v. tr. (1). To reconsolidate.

reconstituant [rəkɔ̃stituã] m. MÉD. Restorative, tonic. (V. FORTIFIANT.)

reconstituer [-tɥe] v. tr. (1). ARCHIT. To restore (un édifice). ‖ JUR. To reconstitute, to re-enact (un crime); to reconstruct, to reconstitute (un ministère). ‖ MÉD. To restore (la santé).

— v. pr. **Se reconstituer,** to be reconstituted. ‖ MÉD. To build up one's health (ou) strength again.

reconstitution [-tysjɔ̃] f. ARCHIT. Restoration (d'un édifice). ‖ JUR. Reconstitution, re-enactment (d'un crime); reconstruction, reconstitution (d'un ministère).

reconstruction [rəkɔ̃stryksjɔ̃] f. Reconstruction, rebuilding (des maisons); reconstruction, rehabilitation (des régions dévastées); *ministère de la Reconstruction et de l'Urbanisme,* Ministry of Town and Country Planning.

reconstruire [-trɥi:r] v. tr. (85). To reconstruct, to rebuild.

reconvention [rəkɔ̃vãsjɔ̃] f. JUR. Counter-claim; cross-action.

reconventionnel, elle [-sjɔnɛl] adj. JUR. *Conclusion, demande reconventionnelle,* counter-claim.

reconventionnellement [-sjɔnɛlmã] adv. JUR. As a counter-claim.

reconversion [rəkɔ̃vɛrsjɔ̃] f. Redeployment, readaptation to a new job (de la main-d'œuvre); reconversion, readaptation (des machines).

reconvertir [-tir] v. tr. (2). To redeploy (main-d'œuvre); to reconvert, readapt (machines).

— v. pr. **Se reconvertir,** to readapt (ou) switch over to a new job.

recopier [rəkɔpje] v. tr. (1). To write out (transcrire); to write up, to make a fair copy of (mettre au propre).

recoquiller [rəkɔkije] v. tr. (1). To curl (ou) cockle (ou) bend up.

— v. pr. **Se recoquiller,** to shrivel (feuille); to curl up, to cockle (page).

record [rəkɔ:r] m. SPORTS. Record; *record du monde de distance,* world distance record.

— adj. *Chiffre record,* record figure; *récolte record,* bumper crop.

recordman [rəkɔrdman] (pl. **recordmen;** f. **recordwoman,** pl. **recordwomen)** m. SPORTS. Record-holder.

recorriger [rəkɔriʒe] v. tr. (7). To recorrect, to correct again.

recors [rəkɔ:r] m. JUR. Process-server's assistant.

recoucher [rəkuʃe] v. tr. (1). To put back to bed.

— v. pr. **Se recoucher,** to go back to bed.

recoudre [rəkudr] v. tr. (31). To sew on again (un bouton); to run up (une déchirure); to sew up again (une manche). ‖ FIG. To link up (des souvenirs).

recoupe [rəkup] f. Sharps, middlings (farine). ‖ Cuttings (d'étoffe); chippings (de métal); splinter (de pierre). ‖ Diluted spirits (alcool). ‖ AGRIC. Aftermath.

recoupement [-pmã] m. ARCHIT. Batter. ‖ JUR. Cross-checking (d'un témoignage). ‖ GÉOGR. Intersection.

recouper [-pe] v. tr. (1). To cut again (qqch.); to cut more of (du pain). ‖ To blend (des vins). ‖ To cut again (les cartes). ‖ ARCHIT. To step (un mur). ‖ FIG. To cross-check.

— v. pr. **Se recouper,** FIG. To cross-check.

recouponner [rəkupɔne] v. tr. (1). FIN. To renew the coupons of (un titre).

recourbé, ée [rəkurbe] adj. Bent, curved.

recourbement [-bəmã] m. Bending, curving.

recourber [-be] v. tr. (1). To bend (ou) curve again (qqch.). ‖ To bend back (ou) down (une branche).

— v. pr. **Se recourber,** to bend, to curve.

recourir [rəkuri:r] v. intr. (32). To run again; to run back. ‖ FIG. *Recourir à l'aide de qqn,* to appeal to s.o. for help; *recourir aux armes,* to resort to arms; *recourir à Dieu,* to turn to God; *recourir à la justice,* to take legal proceedings; *recourir au médecin,* to call in the doctor; *recourir à la violence,* to have recourse to violence.

recours [-ku:r] m. Recourse, resort (*à,* to); *avoir recours à,* to have recourse to (qqch.); to turn to (ou) call in (qqn); *en dernier recours,* as a last resort. ‖ Refuge; hope (espoir). ‖ JUR. Redress; *recours en cassation,* appeal; *recours en grâce,* petition for mercy; *voies de recours,* means of redress.

recouvrable [rəkuvrabl] adj. FIN. Collectable (dette); recoverable (somme).

recouvrement [-vrəmã] m. MÉD. Recovery (de la santé). ‖ FIN. Recovering, collection (de dettes); pl. outstanding debts (dettes); *agent de recouvrement,* debt-collector, U.S. bill-collector; *aux fins de recouvrement,* for collection; *faire un recouvrement,* to recover a debt; *service des recouvrements,* debt (ou) U. S. bill collecting department.

recouvrement [-vrəmã] m. Covering up (ou) over. ‖ GÉOGR. Overthrust. ‖ ARCHIT. Lap, overlapping (de tuiles); *planches à recouvrement,* weather-boarding. ‖ TECHN. *A recouvrement,* lapped, lap-jointed.

recouvrer [rəkuvre] v. tr. (1). To retrieve (son bien); to regain (la liberté); to recover (la santé); to get back, to recover (la vue). [V. RETROUVER.] ‖ FIN. To collect, to recover (une dette); *créances à recouvrer,* outstanding debts.

recouvrir [rəkuvri:r] v. tr. (72). To cover again, to re-cover (un parapluie). ‖ To overlay, to cover up (la terre); to cover (*de,* with); *recouvert de nuages,* lowering (ciel); *recouvert de neige,* snow-

capped (pic). ‖ ARCHIT. To reroof (une maison). ‖ FIG. To mask, to hide (un défaut).
— v. pr. Se recouvrir, to cloud over again, to become overcast (ciel). ‖ ARCHIT. To overlap (tuiles).

recracher [rəkraʃe] v. tr. (1). To spit out again.
— v. intr. To spit again.

récréatif, ive [rekreatif, i:v] adj. Light (lecture); entertaining (livre); recreative (occupation).

récréation [-sjɔ̃] f. Recreation. (V. AMUSEMENT.) ‖ Play-time, recess, break (dans une école); cour de récréation, playground; en récréation, at play.

recréer [rəkree] v. tr. (5). To re-create, to create anew.

récréer [rekree] v. tr. (5). To refresh, to enliven (l'esprit); to divert, to entertain (qqn); to delight, to please (les yeux).
— v. pr. Se récréer, to take some recreation.

recrépir [rəkrepi:r] v. tr. (2). ARCHIT. To roughcast again, to apply new stucco to.

recreuser [rəkrøze] v. tr. (1). To dig out again (ou) anew (un fossé). ‖ FIG. To go deeper into (une question).

récrier (se) [sə rekrije] v. pr. (1). To exclaim; to cry out (de, with). ‖ To protest, to expostulate (protester); to cry out, to inveigh (contre, against).

récriminateur, trice [rekriminatœ:r, tris] adj. Recriminative, recriminating.

récrimination [-nasjɔ̃] f. Recrimination.

récriminatoire [-natwa:r] adj. Recriminatory.

récriminer [-ne] v. tr. (1). To recriminate (contre, against).

récrire [rekri:r] v. tr. (44). To rewrite, to write out again.
— v. intr. To write again; to reply by letter.

recroiser [rəkrwaze] v. tr. (1). To recross.

recroître [rəkrwa:tr] v. intr. (34). BOT. To grow again.

recroquevillé, ée [rəkrɔkvije] adj. Curled up, gnarled (doigt); shrivelled (feuille); cockled (parchemin); huddled up (personne).

recroqueviller (se) [sərəkrɔkvije] v. pr. (1). To curl up (doigt); to shrivel up (feuille); to wilt (fleur); to cockle (parchemin); to huddle, to become shrivelled, to shrivel up (personne).

recru, ue [rəkry] adj. Worn out, exhausted; recru de fatigue, dog-tired, dead-tired.

recrû [rəkry] m. BOT. New growth.

recrudescence [rəkrydɛsɑ̃:s] f. Recrudescence, fresh outbreak.

recrudescent, ente [-sɑ̃, ɑ̃:t] adj. Recrudescent.

recrue [rəkry] f. MILIT. Recruit; levy. ‖ FIG. New member (d'un groupe); fresh adherent (à un parti); faire une recrue, to recruit s.o. ‖ FAM. Acquisition.

recrutement [-tmɑ̃] m. Recruitment, appointment (des professeurs). ‖ MILIT. Recruiting; recruitment; de recrutement, recruiting (bureau).

recruter [-te] v. tr. (1). To appoint (des professeurs). ‖ MILIT. To levy, to bring up to strength (un régiment); to enlist (un soldat). ‖ FIG. To recruit, to enlist (des associés).

recruteur [-tœ:r] adj. MILIT. Recruiting (sergent).
— m. COMM. Tout. ‖ MILIT. Recruiting officer.

recta [rɛkta] adv. FAM. Arriver recta, to arrive on the dot; payer recta, to pay on the nail.

rectal, ale [rɛktal] adj. MÉD. Rectal.

rectangle [rɛktɑ̃:gl] adj. MATH. Right-angled.
— m. MATH. Rectangle.

rectangulaire [-tɑ̃gylɛ:r] adj. MATH. Rectangular; right-angled.

recteur, trice [rɛktœ:r, tris] adj. ZOOL. Penne rectrice, tail-feather.
— m. Rector, vice-chancellor (de l'Université). ‖ ECCLÉS. Parish priest (en Bretagne).

rectifiable [rɛktifjabl] adj. Rectifiable.

rectificateur [-fikatœ:r] m. CHIM., ELECTR. Rectifier.

rectificatif, ive [-fikatif, i:v] adj. JUR. Rectifying.
— m. Corrigendum.

rectification [-fikasjɔ̃] f. TECHN. Straightening (du tracé d'une route). ‖ COMM. Adjustment (d'un prix). ‖ MATH., ELECTR., CHIM., FIN., FIG. Rectification. ‖ TECHN. Adjusting, truing.

rectifier [-fje] v. tr. (1). To correct (une erreur); to rectify, to put right (une faute); to amend (une mauvaise habitude). ‖ TECHN. To adjust (un instrument); to straighten (le tracé d'une route). ‖ COMM. To adjust (un prix). ‖ MATH., CHIM., ELECTR., FIN. To rectify. ‖ MILIT. To dress (l'alignement); to correct (le tir). ‖ TECHN. To true; to adjust. ‖ FAM. To adjust (sa cravate).

rectiligne [rɛktiliɲ] adj. MATH. Rectilinear, rectilineal (figure); in a straight line, linear (mouvement). ‖ FAM. One-track (esprit).
— m. MATH. Rectiligne d'un dièdre, dihedral angle.

rectilinéaire [-lineɛ:r] adj. PHYS. Rapid rectilinear.

rection [rɛksjɔ̃] f. GRAMM. Government.

rectitude [rɛktityd] f. Rectitude, uprightness (de caractère); propriety, correctness (de conduite); soundness, honesty (de jugement). [V. DROITURE.]

recto [rɛkto] m. Recto.

rectoral, ale [rɛktɔral] adj. Rectoral.

rectorat [-ra] m. Rectorship, rectorate.

rectum [rɛktɔm] m. MÉD. Rectum.

reçu, ue [rəsy] adj. Received (en général); recognized, admitted (opinion). ‖ Successful (candidat); être reçu à un examen, to pass an exam; être reçu tout juste à un examen, to squeeze through.
— m. COMM. Receipt; au reçu de, on receipt of; reçu pour solde de tout compte, receipt in full.

recueil [rəkœ:j] m. Collection, anthology, miscellany (de poèmes); recueil de morceaux choisis de, selections from. ‖ JUR. Case-book (de jurisprudence); compendium, digest (de lois). ‖ ECCLÉS. Book of prayers.

recueillement [rəkœjmɑ̃] m. Meditation, introversion, contemplation. ‖ ECCLÉS. Recollection.

recueilli, ie [-ji] adj. Conducive to meditation (endroit); thoughtful, meditative, introspective (personne); quiet, contemplative (vie). ‖ ECCLÉS. Recollected.

recueillir [-ji:r] v. tr. (35). To catch (de l'eau de pluie); to collect (des objets). ‖ To select, to collect (des morceaux choisis). ‖ To take in, to give shelter to (un malheureux). ‖ AGRIC. To harvest (du blé); to pick, to gather (des fruits); to garner, to get in (les récoltes). ‖ JUR. To come into (un héritage). ‖ FIG. To succeed to (la couronne); to collect (ses idées); to win (des louanges); to obtain (des nouvelles); to set down (des paroles); to pick up (des renseignements); to take, to count (les voix); recueillir le fruit de son travail, to reap the reward of one's labours.
— v. pr. Se recueillir, to collect one's thoughts, to commune with oneself, to meditate.

recuire [rəkɥi:r] v. tr. (85). CULIN. To bake again (du pain); to cook (ou) roast again (de la viande); recuit, over-cooked, overdone. ‖ TECHN. To anneal (de l'acier, du verre); to rebake (de la céramique).

recuit [rəkɥi] m. TECHN. Annealing (de l'acier, du verre).

recul [rəkyl] m. Backward movement; faire un mouvement de recul, to start back, to retreat. ‖ Backing (d'une charrette). ‖ MILIT. Recoil. ‖ NAUT. Slip (d'une hélice); recession (de la mer).

‖ Sports. Room to move back beyond the baseline (au tennis). ‖ Arts. Perspective. ‖ Méd. Retraction (de la langue).

reculade [-lad] f. Backing (d'une charrette). ‖ Milit. Falling back, retreat (d'une armée). ‖ Fam. Climbing down ; scuttling.

reoulé, ée [-le] adj. Remote, far-off (avenir) ; distant, remote, out-of-the-way (endroit) ; remote (époque). [V. lointain.]

reculement [-lmɑ̃] m. Backing (d'une charrette). ‖ Breeching (d'un harnais). ‖ Archit. Batter (d'un mur). ‖ Fig. Postponement (d'un événement) ; extension (d'une frontière).

reculer [-le] v. tr. (1). To push back (une chaise). ‖ Fig. To postpone, to put off (un événement) ; to extend (une frontière) ; to delay, to defer (un paiement).
— v. intr. To move (ou) step (ou) draw back (personne) ; to back (voiture). ‖ Milit. To recoil (canon) ; to kick (fusil) ; to retreat, to fall back (troupes). ‖ Comm. To fall off (affaires). ‖ Méd. To lose ground (épidémie). ‖ Fig. To be on the downgrade (humanité) ; to back down (personne) ; *ne reculer devant rien*, to stick at nothing ; *reculer à faire qqch.*, to shrink from (ou) to jib at doing sth. ; *reculer devant qqch.*, to hesitate before (ou) to balk at sth ; *reculer pour mieux sauter*, to put off doing sth. one will be bound to do later.
— v. pr. Se reculer, to draw (ou) step (ou) stand back.

reoulons (à) [arəkylɔ̃] loc. adv. Backwards ; *sortir à reculons*, to back out.

récupérable [rekyperabl] adj. Retrievable, recoverable (objets matériels) ; which may be recouped (argent) ; recoverable (créance). ‖ Reclaimable, salvageable (matériaux usés). ‖ Which should be made up for in overtime (congé, heures de travail).

récupérateur, trice [-ratœ:r, tris] adj. Tending to take over (ou) appropriate (ou) usurp (politique, manœuvres). ‖ Techn., Milit. Recuperative (four, ressort).

récupération [-rasjɔ̃] f. Retrieval, recovery (d'un objet perdu ou prêté) ; recoupment (d'argent). ‖ Reclaiming, salvaging (de matériaux usés). ‖ Making up (*de*, for) [d'un congé, d'un pont]. ‖ Taking over, appropriation (d'un mouvement politique). ‖ Rehabilitation (d'un blessé, d'un délinquant). ‖ Jur. Recovery (d'une créance). ‖ Méd. Recuperation (d'un malade).

récupérer [-re] v. tr. (5). To retrieve, to recover (un objet perdu) ; to get back (un objet prêté) ; to recoup (de l'argent). ‖ To reclaim, to salvage (des matériaux usés). ‖ To work overtime in order to make up for (un congé, un pont). ‖ To take over, to appropriate, to usurp (un mouvement politique). ‖ To rehabilitate (un blessé, un délinquant). ‖ Fig. To fetch, to pick up (aller chercher) ; to get (ou) have back (retrouver). ‖ Jur. To recover (une créance). ‖ Méd. To recuperate, to recover (ses forces).
— v. intr. Méd. To recuperate, to recover.

réourage [rekyra:ʒ] m. Cleaning, scouring.

réourer [-re] v. tr. (1). To clean, to scour.

réoureur [-rœ:r] m. Cleaner, scourer.

réourrence [rekyrɑ̃:s] f. Méd. Recurrence.

réourrent, ente [-rɑ̃, ɑ̃:t] adj. Recurrent.

réoursif, ive [-sif, -si:v] adj. Math., Gramm. Recursive.

réousable [rekyzabl] adj. Jur. Exceptionable, challengeable (témoin) ; impugnable (témoignage).

réousant [-zɑ̃] s. Jur. Challenger. ‖ Ecclés. Recusant.

réousation [-zasjɔ̃] f. Jur. Exception, objection (*de*, to) [témoin] ; impugnment (*de*, of) [témoignage].

réouser [-ze] v. tr. (1). Jur. To challenge, to take

exception to, to object to (un témoin) ; to impugn (un témoignage).
— v. pr. Se récuser, to declare oneself incompetent to judge, to decline to give an opinion.

recyolage [rəsikla:ʒ] m. Retraining ; *cours de recyclage*, refresher course. ‖ Techn. Recycling (d'un fluide, d'une matière).

recyoler [-kle] v. tr. (1). To retrain, to give a refresher course to. ‖ Techn. To recycle (un fluide, une matière).
— v. pr. Se recycler, to retrain ; to go to a refresher course.

rédacteur, trice [redaktœ:r, tris] s. Author (d'un article) ; member of the staff (d'un journal) ; drafter (d'un traité) ; *rédacteur en chef*, editor ; *rédacteur militaire*, military correspondent.

rédaotion [-sjɔ̃] f. Composition (d'un article) ; wording (d'une chose rédigée) ; editing (d'un journal) ; drafting, drawing-up (d'un traité). ‖ Editorial staff ; editorship ; *faire partie de la rédaction d'un journal*, to be on the staff of a newspaper. ‖ Offices (d'un journal). ‖ Essay, composition (dans une école).

rédaotionnel, elle [-sjɔnɛl] adj. Editorial.

redan [rədɑ̃] m. Milit. Redan. ‖ Géogr. Jag. ‖ Archit. Foil ; step. ‖ Aviat. Step.

reddition [rɛddisjɔ̃] f. Milit. Surrender. (V. capitulation.) ‖ Fin. Rendering (d'un compte).

redécouverte [rədekuvɛrt] f. Rediscovery.

redécouvrir [-vri:r] v. tr. (72). To rediscover.

redéfaire [rədefɛ:r] v. tr. (50). To undo again.

redemander [rədəmɑ̃de] v. tr. (1). To ask for again (demander de nouveau). ‖ To ask for sth. back again (demander la restitution). ‖ To ask for more of (demander davantage). ‖ To ask for a second helping of (à table).

redémarrer [rədemare] v. intr. (1). To start up (ou) off again (machine, automobile) ; to be given new impetus (affaires, économie).

rédempteur, trice [redɑ̃ptœ:r, tris] adj. Ecclés. Redeeming, redemptive.
— m. Ecclés. Redeemer.

rédemption [-sjɔ̃] f. Ecclés. Redeeming, redemption.

rédemptoriste [-tɔrist] m. Ecclés. Redemptorist.

redent [rədɑ̃] m. V. redan.

redéploiement [rədeplwamɑ̃] m. Redeployment (de l'économie).

redescendre [rədɛsɑ̃:dr] v. tr. (4). To bring down again (des bagages) ; to take down again (un tableau). ‖ To come (ou) go down again (l'escalier) ; to go (ou) sail down again (un fleuve).
— intr. To come (ou) go down again ; to get out again (de voiture). ‖ To fall down again (baromètre). ‖ Naut. To back (vent).

redevable [rədəvabl] adj. Accountable, beholden, indebted (*à*, to) ; *être redevable de qqch. à qqn*, to owe sth. to s.o.
— s. Debtor.

redevance [-vɑ̃:s] f. Fin. Dues ; rent ; fees.

redevenir [rədəvni:r] v. intr. (101). To become again ; *redevenir malade*, to fall ill again.

redevoir [rədəvwa:r] v. tr. (39). Fin. To owe still ; to owe a balance of.

rédhibitoire [-twa:r] adj. Jur. Giving grounds for annulment of sale. ‖ Fig. Redhibitory.

rediffuser [rədifyze] v. tr. (1). To rebroadcast, to repeat (un programme), to rerun (un film à la télévision).

rediffusion [-zjɔ̃] f. Repeat broadcast, repeat (d'un programme), rerun (d'un film).

rédiger [rediʒe] v. tr. (7). To compose, to write (un article) ; to frame (un décret) ; to edit (un journal) ; to draft, to draw up (un traité).

rédimer [redime] v. tr. (1). To buy off, to redeem.
— v. pr. Se rédimer, to redeem oneself ; to get exempt (*de*, from).

redingote [rədɛ̃gɔt] f. Full-length coat (*de femme*); frock-coat (d'homme).

rédintégration [redɛ̃tegrasjɔ̃] f. PSYCH. Redintegration (du souvenir).

redire [rədi:r] v. tr. (40). To say (ou) tell again; to repeat (qqch.).
— v. intr. To find fault; *trouver à redire à*, to carp at, to take exception to; to pick holes in.

rediscuter [rədiskyte] v. tr. (1). To discuss again.

redistribuer [redistribye] v. tr. (1). To redistribute.

redistribution [-bysjɔ̃] f. Redistribution.

redite [rədit] f. Unnecessary repetition.

redondance [rədɔ̃dɑ̃:s] f. Redundancy.

redondant, ante [-dɑ̃, ɑ̃:t] adj. Redundant.

redonner [rədɔne] v. tr. (1). To give again (donner de nouveau); to give more of (donner davantage); to give back, to restore, to return (rendre). ‖ THÉÂTR. To give (ou) produce again (une pièce). ‖ FIG. *Redonner de l'espérance*, to give renewed hope to; *redonner des forces à*, to put fresh life into.
— v. intr. To fall back (*dans*, into) [les excès]; to return (*dans*, to) [une habitude]. ‖ To set in again (froid).
— v. pr. **Se redonner**, to devote oneself anew (à, to).

redorer [rədɔre] v. tr. (1). To regild. ‖ FIG. To light up again (soleil). ‖ FAM. *Redorer son blason*, to marry into money.

redormir [rədɔrmi:r] v. tr. (2). To sleep again.

redoublant, ante [rədublɑ̃, ɑ̃:t] s. Pupil repeating a year (ou) kept down for a year.

redoublé, ée [rəduble] adj. Redoubled; *frapper à coups redoublés*, to rain blows on. ‖ MILIT. *Au pas redoublé*, in quick time, at the double.

redoublement [-bləmɑ̃] m. Redoubling, increase; *avec un redoublement de zèle*, with redoubled zeal. ‖ MUS. Doubling. ‖ GRAMM. Reduplication.

redoubler [-ble] v. tr. (1). To double, to redouble, to increase (une dose); *redoubler le pas*, to double one's pace. ‖ To fold in two (replier) [une couverture]. ‖ To reline (un habit). ‖ *Redoubler une classe*, to be kept back (ou) down for a year, not to get one's remove, to stay down; U. S. to repeat. ‖ FIG. To double (ses efforts, les inquiétudes).
— v. intr. To come on worse than before (pluie). ‖ To stay down, U. S. to repeat (élève). ‖ To be redoubled (efforts); *redoubler d'efforts*, to strive harder than ever; *redoubler de soins*, to take more care.

redoutable [rədutabl] adj. Redoubtable, formidable.

redoute [rədut] f. MILIT. Redoubt.

redouter [rədute] v. tr. (1). To dread, to fear, to stand in fear (ou) dread of. (V. CRAINDRE.) ‖ To be unable to stand (la chaleur).

redoux [rədu] m. Mildening of the weather.

redressé, ée [rədrɛse] adj. ELECTR. Rectified.

redressement [-smɑ̃] m. Straightening out, putting right again (qqch.). ‖ MILIT. Straightening out (d'un front). ‖ NAUT. Righting (d'un bateau). ‖ JUR. *Maison de redressement*, Borstal, approved school; U. S. reform school. ‖ ELECTR. Rectifying (d'un courant). ‖ FIG. Correction, rectifying, rectification (d'une erreur); setting right; relief (d'un tort).

redresser [-se] v. tr. (1). To straighten out (un chemin); to put (ou) set up again (une statue tombée). ‖ MILIT. To straighten out, to re-establish (un front). ‖ NAUT. To right (un bateau); to ease (la barre). ‖ AVIAT. To trim, to lift the nose of (un avion). ‖ ELECTR. To rectify (un courant). ‖ JUR. To reform (les délinquants). ‖ FIG. To correct, to rectify (une erreur); to set (ou) put right (un tort). ‖ FAM. To blow up (qqn).

— v. pr. **Se redresser**, to hold oneself erect, to straighten up; *se redresser sur son séant*, to sit up again. ‖ NAUT. To right itself (bateau). ‖ AVIAT. To flatten out. ‖ FIG. To mend one's ways (s'amender); to swagger (se rengorger); *se redresser fièrement*, to bridle up.

redresseur, euse [-sœ:r, ø:z] adj. Corrective (mesure). ‖ TECHN. Erecting (prisme); *viseur redresseur*, reversal finder.
— s. TECHN. Straightener. ‖ FIG. *Redresseur de torts*, knight-errant.
— m. ELECTR. Rectifier.

réducteur, trice [redyktœ:r, tris] adj. Reducing.
— m. CHIM. Reducing agent. ‖ TECHN. *Réducteur de vitesse*, speed-reducing gear. ‖ LOC. *Réducteur de tête*, head-shrinker.

réductibilité [-tibilite] f. Reductibility.

réductible [-tibl] adj. Reducible.

réductif, ive [-tif, i:v] adj. CHIM. Reducing.

réduction [-sjɔ̃] f. Reduction; decrease (d'une quantité). ‖ Small edition (d'un livre). ‖ COMM. Discount (*sur*, for) [la quantité]. ‖ FIN. Writing-down (de capital); cutting down (des dépenses); reduction (de prix); cut (des salaires). ‖ MILIT. Reduction (d'une forteresse); conquest (d'une province). ‖ MATH. Reduction (de fraction); *compas de réduction*, reducing compass. ‖ PHILOS. *Réduction à l'absurde*, reductio ad absurdum. ‖ MÉD. Setting, reduction (d'une fracture). ‖ JUR. Abatement (d'un legs); mitigation (d'une peine). ‖ CHIM. Reduction (d'un oxyde). ‖ ELECTR. Stepping-down (du voltage). ‖ ARTS. Reduction, small-scale copy (d'une statue). ‖ MUS. *Réduction pour piano*, piano score.

réduire [redyi:r] v. tr. (85). To reduce (*en*, to) [en général]; *réduire du blé en farine*, to grind corn to flour. ‖ To reduce; to curtail (la liberté). ‖ To reduce; to force (à, to) [l'obéissance]; *réduire qqn à faire qqch.*, to constrain s.o. to do sth., to reduce s.o. doing sth. ‖ To drive (à, to) [désespoir]. ‖ MILIT. To reduce (une forteresse); to subjugate (une province). ‖ FIN., COMM. To write down (le capital); to cut down (les dépenses); to reduce, to bring down (un prix). ‖ MATH. To reduce (une fraction). ‖ MÉD. To reduce, to set (une fracture). ‖ CHIM. To reduce (un oxyde). ‖ ELECTR. To step down (le voltage). ‖ TECHN. To relieve (la pression); to slacken (la vitesse). ‖ CULIN. *Réduire par évaporation*, to boil down. ‖ ARTS. To abridge (un ouvrage); to scale down, to reproduce on a smaller scale (une statue). ‖ MUS. To arrange (une partition).
— v. intr. CULIN. To boil down.
— v. pr. **Se réduire**, to confine (ou) limit oneself (à, to) [se borner]. ‖ To amount, to come, to come down, to be reduced (à, to); *son argument se réduit à ceci*, his argument comes to (ou) boils down to this (fam.); *se réduire à peu de chose*, to amount to very little.

réduit [-dyi] m. Retreat, nook; *misérable réduit*, hovel. ‖ MILIT. Redoubt. ‖ NAUT. Casemate; armoured citadel.
— adj. *A prix réduit*, at a reduced price; *à tarif réduit*, low-rate.

réduplicatif, ive [redyplikatif, i:v] adj. GRAMM. Reduplicating (verbe). ‖ BOT. Reduplicate.

réduplication [-sjɔ̃] f. GRAMM. Reduplication.

réécrire [reekri:r] v. tr. (44). V. RÉCRIRE.

réédification [reedifikasjɔ̃] f. Rebuilding, reconstruction.

réédifier [-fje] v. tr. (1). ARCHIT. To rebuild (une maison); to re-erect (un monument). ‖ FIG. To re-establish (une fortune).

rééditer [reedite] v. tr. (1). To republish (un ouvrage). ‖ FIG. To put into circulation again (une anecdote); to rake up again (un scandale).

réédition [-sjɔ̃] f. Republication; re-issue. ‖ Fam. Twice-told tale.

rééducatif, ive [reedykatif, iːv] adj. Méd. Occupational (thérapie).

rééducation [-kasjɔ̃] f. Re-education. ‖ Méd. Rehabilitation.

rééduquer [-ke] v. tr. (1). To re-educate. ‖ Méd. To rehabilitate.

réel, elle [rɛɛl] adj. Real (besoin); substantial (être); actual, positive (fait). ‖ Comm. Cash (offre). ‖ Jur. Real (action); bonded (entrepôt).
— m. Reality, the real.

réélection [reelɛksjɔ̃] f. Re-election; *candidat à la réélection*, candidate for re-election (ou) U. S. to succeed himself.

rééligibilité [-liʒibilite] f. Re-eligibility.

rééligible [-liʒibl] adj. Re-eligible.

réélire [-liːr] v. tr. (60). To re-elect.

réellement [reɛlmɑ̃] adv. Really, actually, in fact.

réembarquer [reɑ̃barke] v. tr., intr. (1). Naut. To re-embark.

réembobinage [reɑ̃bɔbina:ʒ] m. Rewinding.

réémetteur [reemɛtœːr] m. Radio. Relay (ou) repeater station.

réemploi [reɑ̃plwa] m. V. REMPLOI.

réemployer [-plwaje] v. tr. V. REMPLOYER.

réemprunter [reɑ̃prœ̃te] v. tr. V. REMPRUNTER.

réengager [reɑ̃gaʒe] v. tr. V. RENGAGER.

réensemencer [-se] v. tr. (6). Agric. To resow.

rééquilibrer [reekilibre] v. tr. (1). To bring back into balance, to balance again.

réer [ree] v. intr. (1). V. RAIRE.

réescompte [reɛskɔ̃:t] m. Comm., Fin. Rediscount.

réescompter [-kɔ̃te] v. tr. (1). Comm., Fin. To rediscount.

réessayer [reeseje] v. tr. V. RESSAYER.

réévaluation [reevalyasjɔ̃] f. Revaluation, reappraisal. ‖ Fin. *Réévaluation des actifs*, revaluation of assets.

réévaluer [reevalye] v. tr. (1). To revalue, to reappraise.

réexamen [reɛgzamɛ̃] m. Re-examination.

réexaminer [-mine] v. tr. (1). To re-examine.

réexpédier [reɛkspedje] v. tr. (1). To retransmit (une dépêche); to forward (une lettre). ‖ To send back (qqch., qqn). ‖ Comm. To reship (des marchandises).

réexpédition [-disjɔ̃] f. Retransmission (d'une dépêche); forwarding (d'une lettre). ‖ Comm. Reshipment (de marchandises); sending back, returning (à l'expéditeur).

réexportation [reɛkspɔrtasjɔ̃] f. Comm. Re-exportation; re-export.

réexporter [-te] v. tr. (1). Comm. To re-export.

refaçonner [rəfasɔne] v. tr. (1). To reshape, to refashion.

réfaction [refaksjɔ̃] f. Comm. Allowance, rebate.

refaire [rəfɛːr] v. tr. (50). To do again (qqch.). ‖ To write again, to rewrite (un article); to recast (une phrase); to repack (une valise); to make again (un voyage); *c'est à refaire*, it will have to be done again. ‖ To re-adjust (sa coiffure). ‖ Méd. To restore to health (un malade). ‖ Archit. To do up, to repair (une vieille maison). ‖ Fam. To steal (*from*, à) [qqch.]; to trick, to diddle, to do, to swindle (qqn); *on m'a refait de mon portefeuille*, someone has pinched my wallet.
— v. pr. Se **refaire**, to be done over again (tâche). ‖ Méd. To recover one's health, to recuperate. ‖ Comm. To retrieve one's losses, to recoup oneself. ‖ Fig. To change one's nature.

refait, aite [rəfɛ, ɛt] adj. Fam. Duped; stung.

réfection [refɛksjɔ̃] f. Archit. Rebuilding, repairing (d'une maison); remaking, repairing (d'une route). ‖ Méd. Recovery of health and strength.

réfectionner [-sjɔne] v. tr. (1). Archit. To repair.

réfectoire [-twaːr] m. Refectory.

refend [rəfɑ̃] m. Archit. *Bois de refend*, wood sawn into planks; *mur de refend*, internal wall.

refendre [rəfɑ̃:dr] v. tr. (4). To split (une ardoise); to rip, to saw longitudinally (du bois).

référé [refere] m. Jur. Summary procedure (procédure); injunction, provisional order (ordonnance); *juger en référé*, to try a case in chambers.

référence [-rɑ̃:s] f. Reference; *ouvrages de référence*, works of reference, reference books. ‖ Reference, recommendation (d'employé). ‖ Comm. Sample-book, book of patterns (livre); reference number, reference (note).

référencé, ée [-rɑ̃se] adj. Comm. Entered under a reference number.

référendaire [-rɑ̃dɛ:r] adj. Jur. Referendum (campagne, procédure); *conseiller référendaire*, referendary.

référendum [-rɑ̃dɔm] (pl. **référendums**) m. Jur. Referendum.

référent [-rɑ̃] m. Gramm. Referent.

référentiel [-rɑ̃sjɛl] m. Reference frame, frame of reference (gén., math., phys.).

référer [-re] v. tr. (5). To refer, to ascribe, to attribute (*à*, to) [qqn]; to compare (*à*, with) [qqch.]. ‖ Jur. To tender back (*a*, to) [un serment].
— v. intr. Jur. To refer, to appeal (*à*, to); *en référer à*, to submit the matter to.
— v. pr. Se **référer**, to refer (*à*, to); *se référer à qqn*, to ask s.o.'s opinion; *se référer à l'avis de qqn*, to refer (ou) leave the matter to s.o.'s decision; *se référant à*, relating to, re.

refermer [rəfɛrme] v. tr. (1). To close (ou) shut again.
— v. pr. Se **refermer**, to close (ou) shut again. ‖ Méd. To close (ou) heal up again (plaie).

refiler [rəfile] v. tr. (1). Fam. To pass, to pass off (une pièce fausse); to palm off, to foist off, to fob off (qqch.) [*à*, on].

réfléchi, ie [refleʃi] adj. Sober (confiance); well-weighed (décision); considered (opinion); thoughtful, deliberate, serious-minded (personne); carefully thought out (réponse); *tout bien réfléchi*, after careful consideration. ‖ Phys. Reflected. ‖ Gramm. Reflexive.

réfléchir [-ʃiːr] v. tr. (2). To reflect, to throw (ou) bend back (la lumière).
— v. intr. Fig. To reflect, to ponder (*à*, *sur*, on); *cela donne à réfléchir*, that makes you think; *réfléchir avant d'agir*, to reflect before acting; *réfléchissez-y*, think it over.
— v. pr. Se **réfléchir**, to be reflected (lumière); to reverberate (son).

réfléchissant, ante [-ʃisɑ̃, ɑ̃:t] adj. Phys. Reflective.

réfléchissement [-ʃismɑ̃] m. Reflection, reflecting (de la lumière); reverberation (du son).

réflecteur [reflɛktœːr] adj. Reflecting (mirror).
— m. Reflecting mirror; reflector.

reflet [rəflɛ] m. Gleam (des eaux); reflection (d'une image); shimmering (de la lune); *reflet des lumières*, play of lights; *reflet d'or*, golden glint; *reflets irisés*, rainbow effect. ‖ Arts. Accidental light. ‖ Fig. Reflex, reflection.

refléter [-flete] v. tr. (5). To reflect, to throw back (la lumière). ‖ Fig. To show forth (la bonté); to mirror (un intérêt); to reflect, to hold up the mirror to (une influence).
— v. intr. Fig. To be reflected.
— v. pr. Se **refléter**, to be reflected (*sur*, on).

refleurir [rəflœri:r] v. intr. (2). Bot. To bloom (ou) blossom (ou) flower again. ‖ Arts. To flourish anew. ‖ Fig. To blossom out again.

refleurissement [-rismɑ̃] m. Bot. Second flowering; reflorescence. ‖ Fig. Revival (des arts).

reflex [reflɛks] adj. TECHN. Reflex.
— m. TECHN. Reflex camera.

réflexe [reflɛks] adj. MÉD., PHYS. Reflex.
— m. MÉD. Reflex; *réflexe du genou*, knee-jerk.

réflexibilité [-sibilite] f. PHYS. Reflexibility.

réflexible [-sibl] adj. PHYS. Reflexible.

reflexif, ive [-sif, si:v] adj. MATH., PHILOS. Reflexive.

réflexion [-sjɔ̃] f. PHYS. Reflection, reflexion (d'une image). ‖ FIG. Thought (pensée); *à la réflexion*, on second thoughts; *se faire la réflexion que*, to reflect that; *toute réflexion faite*, all things considered. ‖ FIG. Reflection (critique); *faire une réflexion*, to make a remark.

refluement [rəflymɑ̃] m. Reflux, flowing back.

refluer [-flɥe] v. intr. (1). To flow back (eaux); to ebb (marée). ‖ MÉD. To surge (sang). ‖ FIG. To flow back; to pour (*dans*, into).

reflux [-fly] m. Reflux; ebb-tide. ‖ FIG. Surging back (de la foule).

refondre [rəfɔ̃:dr] v. tr. (4). To remelt; to recast (une cloche); to re-fuse (du métal); to remint (des pièces de monnaie). ‖ NAUT. To refit (un navire). ‖ FIG. To recast, to remodel (un ouvrage).

refonte [-fɔ̃:t] f. Recasting (d'une cloche); refusing, remelting (du métal); reminting (des pièces de monnaie). ‖ NAUT. Refitting, refit. ‖ FIG. Recasting, remodelling (d'un ouvrage).

reforger [rəfɔrʒe] v. tr. (7). To reforge.

réformable [reformabl] adj. JUR. Liable to be reversed (jugement). ‖ MILIT. Liable to be discharged (soldat).

reformage [rəforma:ʒ] m. TECHN. Reforming (de l'essence).

réformateur, trice [reformatœ:r, tris] adj. Reforming.
— s. Reformer.

réformation [-sjɔ̃] f. Reform. ‖ ECCLÉS. Reformation.

réformatoire [-twa:r] adj. Reformatory.

réforme [reform] f. Reformation, reform (des abus). ‖ ECCLÉS. *La Réforme*, the Reformation. ‖ MILIT. Casting (d'un cheval); retirement, cashiering (d'un officier); discharge (d'un soldat).

réformé, ée [-me] adj. ECCLÉS. Reformed (religion). ‖ MILIT. Cast (cheval); discharged (soldat).
— s. ECCLÉS. Protestant, member of the Reformed Church. ‖ MILIT. Man invalided out of the service; dismissed officer; *réformés de guerre*, disabled ex-servicemen (ou) U. S. veterans.

reformer [rəfɔrme] v. tr. (1). To re-form. ‖ MILIT. *Reformer les rangs*, to fall in again.
— v. pr. Se reformer, to re-form, to take shape again. ‖ MILIT. To form up again.

réformer [reforme] v. tr. (1). To reform (des abus); to improve (les mœurs). ‖ JUR. To reverse (un jugement). ‖ MILIT. To invalid out of the army (un blessé); to cast (un cheval); to dismiss, to cashier (un officier); to discharge (un soldat).
— v. pr. Se réformer, FIG. To reform.

reforming [rifɔrmiɲ] m. V. REFORMAGE.

réformisme [reformism] m. Reformism.

réformiste [-mist] adj., s. Reformist.

refoulé, ée [rəfule] adj. PSYCH. Repressed (instincts, agressivité).
— m. PSYCH. Repressed instincts (ou) hostility. ‖ FIG. Inhibited (ou) frustrated person.

refoulement [rəfulmɑ̃] m. Stemming (de la marée). ‖ TECHN. Driving in (d'une cheville); fulling (d'une étoffe); compressing (d'un gaz); fullering, hammering (du métal); lift (d'une pompe). ‖ MILIT. Repulsing (d'une attaque); repulsing, driving back (de l'ennemi); ramming home (d'un projectile). ‖ PHILOS. Repression (d'un instinct). ‖ CH. DE F. Backing (d'un train). ‖ MÉD. Inhibition. ‖ FIG. Choking back (d'un sanglot).

refouler [-le] v. tr. (1). To stem (la marée). ‖ NAUT. To stem (un courant). ‖ TECHN. To drive in (une cheville); to deliver (l'eau); to full (une étoffe); to compress (un gaz); to hammer, to fuller (du métal). ‖ MILIT. To repulse (une attaque); to drive back, to repel (l'ennemi); to ram home (un projectile). ‖ PHILOS. To repress (un instinct). ‖ CH. DE F. To back (un train). ‖ FIG. To choke back (un sanglot).
— v. intr. To flow back (foule); to ebb, to be on the ebb (marée).

refouloir [-lwa:r] m. MILIT. Rammer. ‖ TECHN. Hammer; tamping-tool.

réfractaire [refraktɛ:r] adj. Refractory, insubordinate, rebellious (personne). ‖ ECCLÉS. Nonjuring (prêtre). ‖ MÉD. Allergic (*à*, to) [un médicament]; unaffected (*à*, by); proof (*à*, against) [un poison]. ‖ TECHN. Fire-proof; *argile, brique réfractaire*, fire-clay, -brick.
— s. Rebellious (ou) insubordinate person.

réfracté, ée [-te] adj. PHYS. Refracted (rayon). ‖MÉD. Repeated (dose).

réfracter [-te] v. tr. (1). PHYS. To refract.
— v. pr. Se réfracter, to be refracted.

réfracteur [-tœ:r] m. PHYS. Refractor.

réfractif, ive [-tif, i:v] adj. PHYS. Refractive.

réfraction [-sjɔ̃] f. PHYS. Refraction; *indice de réfraction*, refractive index.

refrain [rəfrɛ̃] m. MUS. Refrain, burden (d'une chanson). ‖ FAM. *Toujours le même refrain*, always the same old story (ou) tune.

réfrangible [-ʒibl] adj. PHYS. Refrangible.

refrapper [rəfrape] v. tr. (1). To strike again. ‖ To recoin, to remint (de la monnaie).
— v. intr. To knock again (à la porte).

refrènement [rəfrɛnmɑ̃] m. Curbing.

refréner [-frene] v. tr. (5). To curb, to restrain, to control (ses passions).

réfrigérant, ante [refriʒerɑ̃, ɑ̃:t] adj. Refrigerating (appareil); freezing (mélange). ‖ MÉD. Refrigerant (remède).
— m. Refrigerator. ‖ MÉD. Refrigerant.

réfrigérateur [-ratœ:r] m. Refrigerator; fridge (fam.).

réfrigératif, ive [-ratif, i:v] adj. MÉD. Refrigerative, refrigerant.
— m. MÉD. Refrigerant.

réfrigération [-rasjɔ̃] f. Refrigeration.

réfrigéré, ée [-re] adj. CH. DE F. *Wagon réfrigéré*, refrigerator car. ‖ FAM. Frozen, perished.

réfrigérer [-re] v. tr. (5). To refrigerate.

réfringence [refrɛ̃ʒɑ̃:s] f. PHYS. Refringence, refringency.

réfringent, ente [refrɛ̃ʒɑ̃, ɑ̃:t] adj. PHYS. Refractive, refringent.

refroidir [rəfrwadi:r] v. tr. (2). To chill, to cool (qqch.); to lower, to bring down (la température). ‖ TECHN. *Refroidi par l'air, par l'eau*, air-, water-cooled (moteur). ‖ FIG. To damp, to cool (l'ardeur); .to dash, to kill (l'enthousiasme); to cool (les passions). ‖ POP. To do in, to bump off (qqn).
— v. intr. To grow (ou) become colder (temps). ‖ FIG. To cool down (ou) off (ardeur).
— v. pr. Se refroidir, to grow colder. ‖ MÉD. To catch a chill. ‖ FIG. To cool down (ou) off.

refroidissement [-dismɑ̃] m. Cooling, cooling down; fall (de la température). ‖ TECHN., AUTOM. *A refroidissement par air, par eau*, air-, water-cooled. ‖ MÉD. Chill. ‖ FIG. Cooling down (d'une amitié).

refroidisseur [-disœ:r] m. Cooler.

refuge [rəfy:ʒ] m. Refuge, sanctuary, asylum, retreat. ‖ Alms-house (hospice). ‖ Lay-by, parking place (sur route); street-island, refuge (dans la rue). ‖ FIG. Refuge, resort', expedient.

réfugié, ée [refyʒje] adj., s. Refugee.

réfugier (se) [sərefyʒje] v. pr. (1). To take refuge, to seek shelter; *se réfugier à l'étranger*, to flee abroad. ‖ Fig. To take refuge (*dans*, in); to fall back (*dans*, on); to have recourse (*dans*, to).

refus [rəfy] m. Refusal; *ne pas accepter de refus*, not to take no for an answer. ‖ Milit. *Refus d'obéissance*, insubordination. ‖ Fam. *Ce n'est pas de refus*, I'll not say no to that.

refusable [-sabl] adj. Refusable.

refuser [-se] v. tr. (1). To refuse (une invitation); to decline, to turn down (une offre); to reject (qqch.); to refuse (qqn en mariage); *refuser d'écouter*, to turn a deaf ear to; *refuser de faire*, to decline (ou) refuse (ou) be unwilling to do; *refuser qqch. à qqn*, to deny sth. to s.o.; *refuser sa porte à qqn*, to refuse to receive s.o., not to be at home to s.o.; *refuser toute qualité à un ennemi*, to refuse to see (ou) recognize any good in an enemy. ‖ To fail; to plough, to pluck, U. S. to flunk (fam.) [un candidat]; to reject (un manuscrit à éditer). ‖ Milit. *Refuser le combat*, to decline to give battle.
— v. intr. To refuse. ‖ To refuse, to balk (ou) baulk (cheval). ‖ Naut. To fail to answer to the helm (vaisseau); to veer forward, to haul (vent).
— v. pr. **Se refuser**, to refuse, to deny oneself (qqch.); *se refuser le nécessaire*, to begrudge oneself the necessities of life; *se refuser tout plaisir*, to turn away (ou) aside from all pleasure. ‖ *Se refuser à*, to decline (ou) resist (ou) set one's face against; *se refuser à faire*, to refuse (ou) decline (ou) be unwilling to do.

réfutable [refytabl] adj. Refutable.

réfutation [-tasjɔ̃] f. Refutation; proof to the contrary.

réfuter [-te] v. tr. (1). To refute, to break down (un argument); to refute (des calomnies); to disprove (une théorie).

regagner [rəgɑɲe] v. tr. (1). To recover, to get back (de l'argent); to regain, to win back (l'estime); to win back (qqn); *regagner le temps perdu*, to make up for lost time. ‖ To return to, to go back to (son logis).

regain [rəgɛ̃] m. Agric. Aftermath, aftercrop, second growth. ‖ Comm. Revival (de vente). ‖ Fig. Fresh outburst, recrudescence (d'activité); renewal (de beauté, de jeunesse); improvement (de santé); *regain de vie*, new lease of life.

régal [regal] (pl. **régals**) m. Feast, banquet. (V. festin.) ‖ Culin. Dainty, exquisite dish. ‖ Fig. Treat, pleasure.

régalade [-lad] f. Feasting. ‖ Loc. *Boire à la régalade*, to pour a drink straight down one's throat.

régalant, ante [-lɑ̃, ɑ̃:t] adj. Pleasing, diverting; *cela n'est pas régalant*, it's no joke.

régale [regal] adj. *Eau régale*, aqua regia.

régaler [regale] v. tr. (1). To entertain, to regale, to stand s.o. a treat (qqn). ‖ Fig. To entertain (de, with). ‖ Fam. To pay for the drinks, to stand a round of drinks; *c'est moi qui régale*, this one's on me.
— v. pr. **Se régaler**, to feast (de, on); to treat oneself (de, to). ‖ Fam. To lick one's chops over it.

régalien [regaljɛ̃] adj. m. † Regalian (droit).

regard [rəga:r] m. Look, glance, gaze, expression; *attirer les regards*, to attract attention; *regard appuyé, furieux*, stare, glare; *regard en coulisse*, sidelong glance; *regard dur, interrogateur*, stony, questioning (ou) quizzical look; *regard mort*, dull expression; *yeux sans regard*, lacklustre eyes. ‖ Man-hole (d'un égout); draught-hole (d'un fourneau). ‖ Fig. Attention; eyes (du monde).
— loc. adv., prép. **Au regard de**, compared to, in comparison with; *en regard de*, opposite,

facing; *texte avec traduction en regard*, text with translation on the opposite page.

regardant, ante [-dɑ̃, ɑ̃:t] adj. Niggardly, close-fisted, parsimonious. ‖ Blas. Regardant.

regarder [-de] v. tr. (1). To look at, to watch; *regarder les gens qui passent*, to gaze at the passers-by; *regarder qqch. au microscope*, to look at sth. through a microscope; *regarder à la dérobée*, to steal a glance at; *regarder un match*, to watch a match. ‖ Fig. To consider, to regard; *à y bien regarder*, on thinking it over; *regarder qqn comme un ami*, to look upon s.o. as a friend; *regarder d'un bon œil*, to have a good opinion of, to look with favour on. ‖ To concern; *cela ne vous regarde pas*, that's none of your business. ‖ To consider, to take account of (v. considérer); *il ne regarde que ses propres intérêts*, he is only worried about his own interests. ‖ To face, to look towards; *maison qui regarde le midi*, house facing south.
— v. intr. To look; *regarder à, par la fenêtre*, to look in, at, out of the window; *regarder de plus près*, to take a closer look; *regarder fixement*, to stare; *regarder par le trou de la serrure*, to peep (ou) peek through the keyhole. ‖ Fig. *Regarder à*, to pay attention to, to take account of; *regarder à deux francs*, to worry about the odd halfpenny; *regarder à la dépense*, to spare expense, to sail close to the wind; *sans regarder à la dépense*, regardless of expense; *y regarder à deux fois avant de faire qqch.*, to think twice before doing sth. ‖ Fam. *Tu ne m'as pas regardé, non?*, what do you take me for, a mug (ou) U. S. a fool?
— v. pr. **Se regarder**, to look at oneself; to look at each other; to face each other.

regarnir [rəgarni:r] v. tr. (2). To re-trim (un chapeau, une robe); to re-stock (un garde-manger); to refill, to replenish (un portefeuille). ‖ Comm. To re-stock (un magasin).

régate [regat] f. Regatta. ‖ Sailor-knot tie.

regeler [rəʒəle] v. impers. (8b). To freeze again.
— v. tr. To refreeze, to freeze again.

régence [reʒɑ̃:s] f. Regency.

régénérateur, trice [reʒeneratœ:r, tris] adj. Regenerative, regenerating.
— s. Regenerator.

régénération [-rasjɔ̃] f. Regeneration. ‖ Fig. Moral resurgence.

régénérer [-re] v. tr. (5). To regenerate. ‖ Techn. *Caoutchouc régénéré*, reclaimed rubber. ‖ Fig. To uplift morally.

régénérescence [-rɛssɑ̃:s] f. Rejuvenation.

régent [reʒɑ̃] s. Regent.
— m. † Form-master (dans un collège).

régenter [-te] v. tr. (1). † To teach (une classe). ‖ Fam. To lord it over (qqn).

régicide [reʒisid] m. Regicide (crime, criminel).
— adj. Regicidal.

régie [reʒi] f. Jur. Public corporation; administration (de biens). ‖ Fin. Collection of taxes; excise office. ‖ Théâtr. Stage-management. ‖ Ciném. Production (ou) studio management. ‖ Radio. Control room.

regimber [rəʒɛ̃be] v. intr. (1). To jib, to balk, to baulk (contre, at) [cheval]. ‖ Fam. To kick, to revolt (contre, at, against) [personne].

regimbeur, euse [-bœ:r, ø:z] s. Fam. Refractory, recalcitrant.

régime [reʒim] m. Regime, mode of living. ‖ Organization, administration, management; *régime des hôpitaux, des prisons*, hospital, prison regulations. ‖ Regime, rule, system of government; *l'Ancien Régime*, the Ancien Regime, the regime in France before 1789; *régime monarchique*, monarchical system. ‖ Gramm. Object; *cas régime*, objective case. ‖ Méd. Diet; *se mettre au régime*, to go on a diet; *suivre un régime*, to diet, to follow a special diet. ‖ Jur. Laws; *régime des boissons*, drink-laws; *régime dotal*, dotal (ou) dowry system. ‖ Géogr. Flow, regime (d'un fleuve). ‖ Bot. Bunch, stem (de bananes); cluster (de dattes). ‖ Autom. Speed. ‖ Techn. Speed, normal running (d'un moteur). ‖ Electr. *Régime de charge*, rate of charge (des accus). ‖ Fig. *Elevé au régime du crime*, fed on a diet of crime.

régiment [reʒimɑ̃] m. Milit. Regiment. ‖ Fam. Large number, crowd.

régimentaire [-tɛ:r] adj. Regimental (cadre); regimental (école).

région [reʒjɔ̃] f. Géogr. Region, district, area (d'un continent, d'un pays); *région du coton*, cotton-belt; *région minière*, mining district; *régions polaires*, polar regions. ‖ Phys., Méd. Region. ‖ Fig. Region, sphere.

régional, ale [-ʒjɔnal] adj. Regional.

régionalisation [-ʒjɔnalizasjɔ̃] f. Regionalization, devolution.

régionaliser [-ʒjɔnalize] v. tr. (1). To regionalize.

régionalisme [-ʒjɔnalism] m. Regionalism.

régionaliste [-ʒjɔnalist] adj. Regionalist, devolutionary.
— s. Regionalist.

régir [reʒi:r] v. tr. (2). To govern, to rule (un Etat); to manage (une propriété). ‖ Gramm. To govern (un cas). ‖ Fig. To rule, to govern, to order (un mouvement).

régisseur [-ʒisœ:r] m. Bailiff (d'une ferme); manager, agent, steward (d'une propriété). ‖ Ci-Ném. Assistant director. ‖ Théâtr. Stage-manager.

registration [rəʒistrasjɔ̃] f. Mus. Registration.

registre [-ʒistr] m. Register, record; *registre de l'état civil*, register of births, deaths and marriages. ‖ Comm. Account-book; *registre du commerce*, Trade Register; *registre des délibérations*, minute book. ‖ Mus. Register; stop, stop-knob (d'orgue); compass (de la voix). ‖ Techn. Damper (de cheminée); throttle-valve (de vapeur).

réglable [reglabl] adj. Adjustable.

réglage [-gla:ʒ] m. Adjustment, adjusting, setting (d'un appareil); *réglage de précision*, fine adjustment. ‖ Regulating (d'une montre). ‖ Ruling (du papier). ‖ Radio. Tuning; *changer de réglage*, to tune in to a different station. ‖ Milit. *Tir de réglage*, ranging. ‖ Techn., Autom. Timing (de l'allumage); tuning (du moteur); setting (des soupapes); tuning (de la vitesse).

règle [rɛgl] f. Math. Rule, ruler; *règle à calcul*, slide-rule; *règle de trois*, rule of three. ‖ Sports. Rule, law (d'un jeu). ‖ Méd. Periods; the curse (fam.). ‖ Ecclés. Rule (d'un ordre). ‖ Fig. Rule, custom, guiding principle; *en règle*, in order, correct; *en règle générale*, as a general rule; *dans* (ou) *selon les règles*, according to the rules; *règle d'or*, golden rule; *se faire une règle de*, to make it a rule to; *se mettre en règle avec*, to put oneself right with; *servir de règle*, to serve as an example.

réglé, ée [regle] adj. Ruled (papier). ‖ Regular (mœurs); steady, methodical (personne); well-regulated (vie). ‖ Méd. Regular (pouls). ‖ Fam. *Réglé comme du papier à musique*, as regular as clockwork.

règlement [rɛglmɑ̃] m. Fin. Settlement (d'un compte); *mode de règlement*, method of payment. ‖ Jur. Regulation, order (en général); rule (d'une société); statute (d'une université); *règlement de police*, by-law; *rappeler qqn au règlement*, to call s.o. to order. ‖ Fig. Rule; *se faire un règlement de vie*, to set oneself a rule of life. ‖ Fam. *Règlement de comptes*, squaring of accounts.

réglementaire [regləmɑ̃tɛ:r] adj. According to regulations; appointed (jour); regular (procédure). ‖ Milit. *Tenue réglementaire*, regulation uniform,

service dress. ‖ Naut. *Feux réglementaires*, regulation lights.

réglementairement [-tɛrmɑ̃] adv. In the proper (ou) prescribed manner.

réglementariste [-tarist] adj. Regulationist (pays).

réglementation [-tasjɔ̃] f. Regulating; control (d'une industrie); drawing-up (des règles); *réglementation de la circulation*, traffic control.

réglementer [regləmɑ̃te] v. tr. (1). To regulate, to control.

régler [regle] v. tr. (5). To put in order (ses affaires); to manage, to rule (sa maison). ‖ Fin. To settle, to pay (un compte); to moderate (ses dépenses); *régler ses dépenses sur son revenu*, to cut one's coat according to one's cloth. ‖ To rule (du papier). ‖ Techn. To regulate (une montre). ‖ Milit. *Régler le tir*, to range. ‖ Autom. To time (l'allumage); to tune (le moteur); to set (les soupapes); to govern (la vitesse). ‖ Fig. To settle (un différend, une question). ‖ Fam. *Régler ses comptes avec*, to settle accounts with.
— v. pr. Se régler, to be moderate in one's desires. ‖ *Se régler sur*, to regulate one's life by (qqch.); to take as a pattern (ou) example (qqn).

réglet [reglɛ] m. Archit. Reglet.

réglette [-glɛt] f. Math. Scale, small rule; slide (d'une règle à calcul). ‖ **Réglette-jauge**, f. Autom. Dip-stick.

régleur [-glœ:r] s. Regulator (de mécanisme); ruler (de papier). ‖ Milit. Adjuster.

réglisse [reglis] f. Bot. Liquorice.

régio [reglo] adj. inv. Fam. Straight, square, regular (correct).

réglure [regly:r] f. Ruling.

régnant, ante [reɲɑ̃, ɑ̃:t] adj. Reigning (souverain). ‖ Méd. Prevalent. ‖ Fig. Prevailing (goût).

règne [rɛɲ] m. Reign (d'un souverain); *sous le règne de*, in the reign of. ‖ Bot., Zool. Kingdom. ‖ Fig. Reign (des lois, de la mode, de la paix).

régner [reɲe] v. intr. (5). To reign, to rule, to govern, to hold sway (*sur*, over); *l'art de régner*, the art of kingship. ‖ Méd. To be prevalent (épidémie). ‖ Fig. To reign (abondance, silence); to reign, to prevail (mode).

regonflage [rəgɔ̃fla:ʒ], **regonflement** [-flə-mɑ̃] m. Reinflation, pumping up again (d'un pneu, d'un ballon).

regonfler [rəgɔ̃fle] v. tr. (1). Aviat. To reinflate, to refill (un aérostat). ‖ Autom. To reinflate, to pump up (un pneu).
— v. intr. To swell (ou) rise again (fleuve). ‖ To swell (ou) swell up again. [V. enfler.]
— v. pr. Se regonfler, to swell up again, to become swollen again.

regorgeant, ante [rəgɔrʒɑ̃, ɑ̃:t] adj. Overflowing, crammed (*de*, with).

regorgement [-ʒəmɑ̃] m. Overflowing, flowing back (d'un égout); overflowing, running over (d'un fleuve).

regorger [-ʒe] v. tr. (7). To regurgitate, to throw up, to vomit (sa nourriture). ‖ Fig. To disgorge.
— v. intr. To overflow (égout, fleuve). ‖ Naut. To run (ou) brim over (vaisseau). ‖ To abound (*de*, in); to be full (*de*, of); to be packed (ou) crowded (*de*, with); *regorger de monde*, to swarm with people.
‖ Fig. To be rich, to have possessions in abundance; *regorger de biens*, to be bursting with wealth.

regratter [rəgrate] v. tr. (1). Archit. To scrape, to regrate; to rub down.
— v. intr. Comm. To huckster.

regreffer [rəgrɛfe] v. tr. (1). Agric. To regraft.

régresser [regrɛse] v. intr. (1). To regress; to throw back.

régressif, ive [-sif, i:v] adj. Regressive; *forme régressive*, throw-back.

régression [-sjɔ̃] f. Throw-back. (V. RECUL.) ‖ Recession (de la mer). ‖ COMM. Fall in sales. ‖ PSYCH. Regression.

regret [rəgrɛ] m. Regret, remorse, sorrow (de, for); avoir regret à faire, to feel sorry about doing, to be loth (ou) loath to do; avoir regret de, to regret, to feel sorry about (qqch.); avoir des regrets, to feel regret; être au regret de, to be sorry about.
— loc. adv. A regret, with regret, reluctantly, regretfully; dire, faire qqch. à regret, to be loath (ou) loth to say, to do sth.

regrettable [-tabl] adj. Regrettable, deplorable, to be deplored (erreur); worthy of regret (personne); il est regrettable que, it is a pity that, it is to be regretted that.

regrettablement [-tabləmɑ̃] adv. Regrettably.

regretter [-te] v. tr. (1). To miss (un ami absent); to mourn, to lament, to mourn for (un ami perdu); to wish one had again (ou) back (l'argent dépensé); to regret (qqch., qqn); je regrette de vous avoir dérangé, I'm sorry to have bothered you; regretter amèrement, to rue; regretter d'avoir fait qqch., to be sorry for (ou) to rue having done sth.

regroupement [rəgrupmɑ̃] m. Bringing (ou) gathering together (d'êtres ou de choses dispersés). ‖ Rounding up (d'un troupeau). ‖ Rallying, uniting (de partisans). ‖ Rallying, regrouping (de troupes).

regrouper [-pe] v. tr. (1). To bring (ou) gather together (êtres ou objets dispersés). ‖ To round up (un troupeau). ‖ To rally, to unite (des partisans). ‖ To rally, to regroup (des troupes).
— v. pr. Se regrouper, to get together, to rally, to unite.

régularisation [regylarizasjɔ̃] f. Regularization, regularizing, putting in order (d'affaires); clearing up, putting right (d'une situation). ‖ FIN. Equalization (de dividendes).

régulariser [-ze] v. tr. (1). To regularize, to put in order, to straighten out (une affaire); to correct (sa conduite); to clear up (une situation). ‖ JUR. To put into legal form (un document). ‖ FIN. To equalize (un dividende).

régularité [-te] f. Evenness (d'humeur); orderliness (des mœurs); steadiness (d'un mouvement); equability (de tempérament); regularity (des traits). ‖ Punctuality.

régulateur, trice [regylatœ:r, tris] adj. Regulating (pouvoir). ‖ FIN. Buffer (stocks).
— m. TECHN. Regulator (d'une machine); governor (d'une machine à vapeur); balance-wheel, regulator (d'une montre). ‖ ELECTR. Régulateur de tension, potential regulator.

régulation [-sjɔ̃] f. Regulation, control (d'un processus physiologique, d'un automatisme, du trafic); régulation des naissances, birth control.

régule [regyl] m. Antifriction metal.

régulier, ère [regylje, ɛ:r] adj. Uniform, steady (mouvement). ‖ Regular, methodical (habitude); equable (tempérament); regular (traits); orderly (vie); ce n'est pas régulier, it's not in order. ‖ JUR. Valid (passeport); normal (procédure). ‖ GRAMM., ECCLÉS., MILIT., MATH. Regular. ‖ ARCHIT. Symmetrical, harmonious (édifice). ‖ MÉD. Regular, steady (pouls). ‖ FAM. Il est régulier, he's a regular fellow, he's on the level.
— m. ECCLÉS. Member of the regular clergy. ‖ MILIT. Regular.

régulière [-lje:r] f. POP. Ma régulière, my old dutch, my better half.

régulièrement [-ljɛrmɑ̃] adv. Regularly; uniformly; in accordance with regulations; punctually.

régurgitation [regyrʒitasjɔ̃] f. Regurgitation.

régurgiter [-te] v. tr. (1). To regurgitate.

réhabilitable [reabilitabl] adj. Able to be rehabilitated.

réhabilitation [-tasjɔ̃] f. Rehabilitation. ‖ JUR. Restoration of civil rights; discharge (d'un failli).

réhabilité [-te] s. JUR. Discharged bankrupt.

réhabiliter [-te] v. tr. (1). To rehabilitate (qqn); réhabiliter la mémoire de qqn, to clear s.o.'s name, to clear the good name of s.o. ‖ JUR. To reinstate in his civil rights (un condamné); to discharge (un failli).
— v. pr. Se réhabiliter, to rehabilitate oneself, to re-establish one's good name, to clear one's name. ‖ JUR. To recover (ou) get back one's civil rights (condamné); to obtain one's discharge (failli).

réhabituer [reabitɥe] v. tr. (1). To reaccustom (à, to).
— v. pr. Se réhabituer, to become accustomed, to reaccustom oneself, to get used (à, to).

rehaussement [rəosmɑ̃] m. ARCHIT. Raising, heightening (d'un édifice, d'un mur). ‖ ARTS. Enhancing, touching up, bringing out (des couleurs). ‖ FIN. Appreciation (des monnaies). ‖ COMM. Raising (des prix). ‖ FIG. Enhancing (de la beauté); increasing, bolstering up (du courage).

rehausser [-se] v. tr. (1). ARCHIT. To raise, to heighten (un édifice, un mur). ‖ ARTS. To touch up, to bring out, to enhance (une couleur). ‖ FIN. To appreciate (les monnaies). ‖ COMM. To raise (les prix). ‖ FIG. To enhance (la beauté); to increase, to bolster up (le courage).

rehaut [rəo] m. ARTS. Touch of lighter colour; pl. highlights.

réifier [reifje] v. tr. (1). PHILOS. To reify.

réimperméabiliser [reɛ̃pɛrmeabilize] v. tr. (1). To reproof.

réimporter [-te] v. tr. (1). COMM. To reimport.

réimposer [reɛ̃poze] v. tr. (1). FIN. To tax again (des contribuables); to reimpose (des impôts). ‖ TECHN. To reimpose (en typographie).

réimpression [reɛ̃prɛsjɔ̃] f. Reprinting, reimpression; reprint.

réimprimer [-prime] v. tr. (1). To reprint.

rein [rɛ̃] m. MÉD. Kidney (organe); les reins, the back, the loins, the lumbar region; avoir mal aux reins, to have a stiff back. ‖ ARCHIT. Pl. Extrados, reins. ‖ FIG. Avoir les reins solides, to be sturdy, to have a strong back, to be well-breeched; casser les reins à, to break s.o.'s back; ne pas se casser les reins, not to strain oneself.

réincarcération [reɛ̃karserasjɔ̃] f. Reimprisonment.

réincarcérer [-sere] v. tr. (5). To reimprison, to send back to prison.

réincarnation [reɛ̃karnasjɔ̃] f. Reincarnation.

réincarner [-ne] v. tr. (1). To reincarnate.
— v. pr. Se réincarner, to be reincarnated.

réincorporer [reɛ̃korpore] v. tr. (1). To reincorporate. ‖ MILIT. To re-embody.

reine [rɛn] f. Queen. ‖ SPORTS. Queen (aux échecs). ‖ ZOOL. Reine des abeilles, queen bee. ‖ FIG. Faire la reine, to queen it; reine du bal, belle of the ball. ‖ Reine-claude, f. AGRIC. Greengage. ‖ Reine-des-prés, f. BOT. Meadow-sweet. ‖ Reine-marguerite, f. BOT. China aster. ‖ Reine mère, f. Queen-mother.

reinette [rɛnɛt] f. AGRIC. Rennet, pippin; reinette grise, russet.

réinscription [reɛ̃skripsjɔ̃] f. Reregistration.

réinscrire [-kri:r] v. tr. (44). To put s.o.'s name down again, to reregister.
— v. pr. Se réinscrire, to put one's name down again, to reregister.

réinsérer [reɛ̃sere] v. tr. (5). To reinsert (réintroduire); to rehabilitate (réadapter à la société).

réinsertion [-sɛrsjɔ̃] f. Reinsertion (réintroduction); rehabilitation (réadaptation sociale).

réinstallation [reɛ̃stalasjɔ̃] f. Reinstallation.
réinstaller [-le] v. tr. (1). To reinstall.
— v. pr. Se réinstaller, to settle down again (dans un fauteuil) ; to take up one's abode again (dans une maison).
réinstituer [reɛ̃stitɥe] v. tr. (1). To re-establish.
réintégrable [reɛ̃tegrabl] adj. Able to be reinstated (ou) reintegrated.
réintégration [-grasjɔ̃] f. Reinstatement, readmission (d'un fonctionnaire). ‖ Jur. *Réintégration du domicile conjugal,* return to cohabitation. ‖ Math. Reintegration.
réintégrer [-gre] v. tr. (5). To reinstate (un fonctionnaire) ; to send back to store (ou) U. S. storage (des meubles) ; *réintégrer le domicile conjugal,* to take possession of one's home again ; *réintégrer qqn dans son emploi,* to reinstate s.o. in his employment. ‖ Math. To reintegrate.
réintroduire [reɛ̃trɔdɥi:r] v. tr. (5). To reintroduce.
réinventer [reɛ̃vɑ̃te] v. tr. (1). To invent all over again.
réinvestir [reɛ̃vɛsti:r] v. tr. (1). To reinvest (dans des privilèges, dans une fonction). ‖ Fin. To reinvest (de l'argent), to plough back (des bénéfices).
réinviter [reɛ̃vite] v. tr. (1). To reinvite.
réitérable [reiterabl] adj. Repeatable.
réitératif, ive [-ratif, i:v] adj. Reiterative.
réitération [-rasjɔ̃] f. Reiteration.
réitérer [-re] v. tr. (5). To repeat ; to reiterate.
reître [rɛ:tr] m. Milit. † Reiter. (V. soudard.)
rejaillir [rəʒaji:r] v. intr. (2). To gush, to spirt out (ou) up (liquide) ; to be reflected, to be thrown back (lumière). ‖ Fig. To reflect, to rebound, to recoil (sur, on) ; *les bienfaits de la science rejaillissent sur nous tous,* we all share in the benefits of science.
rejaillissement [-jismɑ̃] m. Spirting, gushing out (ou) up (d'un liquide) ; reflection (de la lumière).
rejet [rəʒɛ] m. Casting up (d'un objet par la mer) ; throwing up (de la terre inutile). ‖ Enjambment (en prosodie). ‖ Jur. Dismissal (d'un pourvoi) ; rejection (d'un projet de loi) ; setting aside (d'une réclamation). ‖ Bot. Shoot. ‖ Fin. Disallowance (d'une dépense).
rejetable [rəʒətabl] adj. Rejectable.
rejeter [rəʒte] v. tr. (8 a). To throw (ou) cast again ; to throw (ou) cast back (qqch.) ; *rejeter des épaves,* to cast up wreckage ; *rejeter son chapeau en arrière,* to tilt one's hat back ; *rejeter ses cheveux en arrière,* to brush (ou) comb one's hair back. ‖ To throw (ou) bring up, to vomit (de la nourriture). ‖ To cast off (des mailles). ‖ Milit. To hurl (ou) throw (ou) fling back, to repulse (l'ennemi). ‖ Jur. To dismiss (un pourvoi) ; to reject, to throw out (un projet de loi) ; to set aside (une réclamation). ‖ Fin. To disallow (une dépense). ‖ Bot. To put out (ou) forth (de surgeons). ‖ Fig. To spurn (un conseil) ; to transfer (la faute) ; to reject, to refuse, to set aside (une offre) ; to turn down (une proposition) ; to repudiate (qqn) ; to shift (la responsabilité) ; *rejeter le blâme sur autrui,* to lay the blame at s.o. else's door, to shift the blame on to s.o. else ; to let s.o. else carry the can (fam.) ; *rejeter dans l'incertitude,* to plunge into doubt.
— v. pr. Se rejeter, to throw oneself back. ‖ Fig. To fall back (sur, on).
rejeton [-tɔ̃] m. Bot. Shoot, sucker, scion. ‖ Fig. Scion, descendant, offspring.
rejoindre [rəʒwɛ̃:dr] v. tr. (59). To rejoin, to join (ou) connect together again, to reunite (réunir). ‖ To rejoin, to catch up with, to overtake (atteindre). ‖ Milit. To rejoin (son régiment).
— v. pr. Se rejoindre, to meet, to join up, to come together again.

rejointoyer [rəʒwɛ̃twaje] v. tr. (9 b). Techn. To repoint (un mur), to regrout (un carrelage).
rejouer [rəʒwe] v. tr. (1). Mus. To play again (un air). ‖ Sports. To replay, to play again (un match). ‖ Théâtr. To play, to act (un rôle) ; to act (ou) give again (une pièce).
réjoui, ie [reʒwi] adj. Jolly, joyous, cheerful, jovial. [V. gai.]
— s. *Un gros réjoui,* a merry old soul.
réjouir [-ʒwi:r] v. tr. (2). To make glad, to warm the cockles of (le cœur) ; to entertain, to divert, to amuse (la compagnie) ; to delight (l'œil) ; to gladden, to please, to cheer up (qqn).
— v. pr. Se réjouir, to rejoice, to be glad (de, of) ; to be delighted (de, at). ‖ To amuse oneself, to be happy, to enjoy, to go' (ou) to be gay.
réjouissance [reʒwisɑ̃:s] f. Rejoicing. ‖ Pl. Festivities, merry-making; *ordonner des réjouissances,* to order public rejoicing. ‖ Comm. Make-weight.
réjouissant, ante [-sɑ̃, ɑ̃:t] adj. Amusing, mirthprovoking (conte) ; cheery, entertaining (personne) ; diverting, amusing, entertaining (pièce).
rejuger [rəʒyʒe] v. tr. (7). To judge again.
relâchant, ante [rəlɑʃɑ̃, ɑ̃:t] adj. Relaxing. ‖ Méd. Laxative.
— m. Fam. Laxative.
relâche [rəlɑ:ʃ] m. Relaxation, rest, respite ; *sans aucune relâche,* uninterruptedly, without respite. ‖ Théâtr. Temporary closing ; *faire relâche,* to close ; « *Relâche* », « Closed », « No performance today ».
relâche f. Naut. Putting in, calling (action) ; port (ou) place of call (lieu) ; *faire relâche à,* to put in at, to call at.
relâché, ée [-lɑʃe] adj. Slack (corde). ‖ Fig. Loose, lax (mœurs). ‖ Fam. Loose (ventre).
relâchement [-lɑʃmɑ̃] m. Slackening, loosening (d'une corde). ‖ Méd. Looseness (de l'intestin). ‖ Fig. Relaxation (of discipline) ; loosening, slackening (des liens) ; slackness (des mœurs) ; looseness, laxity (de la moralité).
relâcher [-lɑʃe] v. tr. (1). To loosen, to slacken (une corde). ‖ Jur. To release, to set free. [V. élargir, libérer.] ‖ Méd. To loosen (l'intestin). ‖ Techn. To release, to slack off (la pression). ‖ Fig. To relax (la discipline) ; to abate, to relax (un effort) ; to allow to become lax (les mœurs) ; to allow to flag (ou) cool (le zèle).
— v. intr. Naut. To put in ; to put (à, into), to call (à, at).
— v. pr. Se relâcher, to slacken, to become loose (ou) slack (corde). ‖ Méd. To become loose. ‖ Fig. To fall off (discipline) ; to ease, to grow less acute (douleur) ; to flag (effort) ; to become lax (mœurs) ; to cool (zèle).
relais [rəlɛ] m. Posting-house, stage. ‖ Relay (de chevaux) ; shift (d'ouvriers). ‖ Sports. *Course à (ou) de relais,* relay-race. ‖ Autom. Filling-station. ‖ Radio. Relay ; U.S. hook-up.
relais [rəlɛ] m. Géogr. Foreshore ; sand-flats.
relance [rəlɑ̃:s] f. Raise (au poker) ; *faire une relance,* to raise the bid. ‖ Fig. New impetus (impulsion donnée) ; new surge, boost (essor pris).
relancement [-lɑ̃smɑ̃] m. Throwing back (ou) again. ‖ Techn. Restarting (d'une machine).
relancer [-lɑ̃se] v. tr. (5). To throw (ou) cast back (ou) again. ‖ Sports. To return, to send back (la balle) ; to start again (le gibier). ‖ Autom. To restart, to start again (le moteur). ‖ Fam. To hunt (ou) rout out, to drop in on (qqn). ‖ Fig. To boost, to give impetus to (l'économie, les affaires).
relaps [rəlaps] adj. Ecclés. Relapsed.
— s. Ecclés. Relapsed heretic.
rélargir [relarʒi:r] v. tr. (2). To widen, to make wider (qqch.) ; to let out (ses vêtements).

relater [rəlate] v. tr. (1). To state (un fait); to relate, to tell, to recount (une histoire).

relateur [-tœ:r] m. Relator; teller.

relatif, ive [rəlatif, i:v] adj. Relative, relating (à, to); connected, in connection (à, with); referring, with reference (à, to); in respect (à, of). ‖ Relative (position, valeur). ‖ GRAMM. Relative (pronom). ‖ MUS. Related, relative (ton).
— m. GRAMM., PHILOS. Relative.

relation [-sjɔ̃] f. Relation (entre, between); connection, reference; avoir relation avec, to have a bearing on (ou) reference to. ‖ Relation, relationship; en relations d'affaires, connected in business; en relations étroites, in close touch; relations d'amitié, friendly terms; se mettre en relation avec, to get in touch with. ‖ Pl. Friends, acquaintances [v. CONNAISSANCES]; avoir de belles relations, to have friends in high places. ‖ Account, narrative, report (récit); relations de voyage, travellers' tales. ‖ Pl. Intercourse (avec, with) [une femme]. ‖ Account, report, statement. [V. COMPTE RENDU.] ‖ CH. DE F. Connection, service (entre deux villes).

relationnel, elle [-sjɔnɛl] adj. PSYCH. Relational.

relativement [rəlativmɑ̃] adv. Relatively, comparatively; in relation (à, to); with reference (à, to).

relativiser [-vize] v. tr. (1). To put in perspective.

relativisme [-vism] m. PHILOS. Relativism.

relativiste [-vist] m. PHILOS. Relativist.

relativité [-vite] f. Relativity.

relaver [rəlave] v. tr. (1). To wash again, to re-wash.

relax(e) [rəlaks] adj. FAM. Relaxed, cool, laid-back (personne); relaxed, informal (atmosphère, vêtement).

relaxation [rəlaksasjɔ̃] f. MÉD. Relaxation.

relaxe [-laks] f. JUR. Release, discharge (d'un prisonnier); reduction (d'une sentence).

relaxer [-lakse] v. tr. (1). MÉD. To relax. ‖ JUR. To release, to discharge.
— v. pr. Se relaxer, FAM. To relax, to unwind.

relayer [rəlɛje] v. tr. (9 b). To relieve, to take turns with. ‖ RADIO. To relay.
— v. intr. To change horses.
— v. récip. Se relayer, to relieve one another, to take it in turns, to work in shifts.

relayeur, euse [-jœ:r, jø:z] s. SPORTS. Relay racer.

relecture [rəlɛkty:r] f. Re-reading, second reading.

relégation [-gasjɔ̃] f. JUR. Relegation.

relégué [rəlege] adj. Isolated (village). ‖ JUR. Relegated (condamné).
— m. JUR. Convict sentenced to transportation.

reléguer [rəlege] v. tr. (1). JUR. To relegate, to transport (un condamné); to banish, to send into exile (qqn). ‖ FIG. To consign (qqch.) [à, dans, to]; reléguer une tradition parmi les fables, to look upon a tradition as an old wives' tale, to relegate a tradition to the legendary sphere.
— v. pr. Se reléguer, to go off, to bury oneself (s'enterrer) [à, in].

relent [rəlɑ̃] m. Musty (ou) stale taste (goût). ‖ Bad odour, stale smell (odeur).

relevable [rəlvabl] adj. AVIAT. Retractable (train).

relevage [-va3] m. Lifting, raising.

relevailles [-va:j] f. pl. Churching; faire ses relevailles, to be churched.

relevant, ante [-vɑ̃, ɑ̃:t] adj. JUR. Dependent (de, on); within the jurisdiction (de, of).

relève [rəlɛ:v] f. MILIT. Relief (d'un factionnaire, de troupes); changing (de la garde); relief force, relieving troops (troupes).

relevé, ée [rəlve] adj. Off-the-face (chapeau); taken up on top of the head (cheveux); stand-up (col); turned-up (manche); held high (tête). ‖ CULIN. Piquant (sauce). ‖ FIG. Exalted, high (condition); noble (sentiment); lofty (style). ‖ FAM. Smart.
— m. Tuck (dans une robe). ‖ Relevé de compteur à gaz, gas-meter reading. ‖ FIN. Statement (de compte). ‖ COMM. Inventory (de stock). ‖ JUR. Summary (des naissances). ‖ AVIAT. Mosaic. ‖ CULIN. Next course; remove.

relevée [rəlve] f. † Afternoon; à deux heures de relevée, at two in the afternoon; two p.m.

relèvement [rəlɛvmɑ̃] m. Setting up, picking up again (d'un objet tombé). ‖ ARCHIT. Raising, rebuilding higher (d'un édifice). ‖ COMM., FIN. Recovery (des affaires); making out (d'un compte); raising (de, of); rise (de, in); increase (des impôts, des prix, des salaires). ‖ TECHN. Resection (en topographie). ‖ MILIT. Relèvement des blessés, picking up of the wounded, collection of casualties. ‖ NAUT. Bearing (d'une côte); raising, lifting (d'un sous-marin); faire un relèvement, to take a bearing. ‖ FIG. Restoration, recovery (de sa fortune); improvement, amelioration (des mœurs); rise, recovery (d'une nation); rise (de la température).

relever [rəlve] v. tr. (5). To raise, to lift, to pick up, to set up again, to set on his (ou) its feet again (qqch., qqn). ‖ To put up (ses cheveux); to roll up (ses manches); to tuck up (sa robe); to turn up (son pantalon); to hold high (la tête); to put up, to raise (son voile). ‖ ARCHIT. To rebuild, to reconstruct, to heighten (un édifice). ‖ FIN. To make out (un compte); to raise, to increase, to put up (le prix); to increase (les salaires). ‖ CULIN. To season, to add seasoning to (une sauce). ‖ MILIT. To pick up (des blessés); to change (la garde); to relieve (une sentinelle). ‖ NAUT. To take a bearing on (un promontoire); to raise (un sous-marin); to refloat, to salve (un vaisseau coulé). ‖ JUR. To take the place of, to take over from, to relieve (qqn); relever de ses fonctions, to relieve of his office, to dismiss. ‖ ECCLÉS. To release (de, from) [un vœu]. ‖ FIG. To enhance, to heighten (la beauté); to set off, to bring into relief (une couleur). ‖ To better, to improve (sa condition); to build up, to revive (une industrie); to reform, to improve (les mœurs). ‖ FIG. To call attention to, to point out (une faute); to retort to (une insulte); relever le gant, to take up the gauntlet, to accept a challenge. ‖ FAM. To take up sharply (qqn).
— v. intr. MÉD. To have just recovered (de, from) [maladie]. ‖ FIG. To be ascribable, to belong (de, to) [qqch.]; to be responsible (ou) answerable (de, to); to be dependent (de, on) [qqn].
— v. pr. Se relever, to rise (ou) get up again; to get to one's feet again. ‖ To rise (température). ‖ NAUT. To right itself (vaisseau). ‖ GÉOGR. To rise (terrain). ‖ FIN. To recover, to revive (affaires). ‖ FAM. To recover (de, from) [une maladie].

releveur, euse [rəlvœ:r, ø:z] adj. MÉD. Levator.
— m. MÉD. Levator. ‖ NAUT. Mine-lifting vessel.

relief [rəljɛf] m. ARTS. Relief, relievo. ‖ RADIO. En relief, stereoscopic (télévision). ‖ GÉOGR. Relief; en relief, relief (carte). ‖ FIG. Contrast, relief; couleurs qui se donnent mutuellement du relief, colours which set each other off. ‖ Prominence; se mettre en relief, to make oneself prominent, to catch the public eye. ‖ Pl. Left-overs (d'un repas).

relier [rəlje] v. tr. (1). To tie (ou) bind (ou) fasten up again (une gerbe); to bind (un livre); to hoop (un tonneau). ‖ To join together, to unite, to connect (réunir). ‖ ELECTR., RADIO.

Relier à la terre, to earth, to connect to earth, to make an earth connection, U. S. to ground. ‖ Fig. To connect (*à*, to); to link (*à*, with).
— v. pr. **Se relier**, to be linked (ou) connected (*avec*, with).
relieur [-ljœ:r] s. Bookbinder.
relieuse [-ljø:z] f. Bookbinding machine.
religieuse [rəliʒjø:z] f. Ecclés. Nun. ‖ Culin. Cake of the eclair variety, double-cream puff.
religieusement [-ʒjøzmɑ̃] adv. Ecclés. Religiously, piously; in piety. ‖ Fig. Scrupulously.
religieux, euse [-ʒjø, ø:z] adj. Ecclés. Religious (cérémonie); sacred (chant); pious (personne, sentiment). ‖ Fig. Scrupulous, punctilious (soin).
— m. Ecclés. Monk.
religion [-ʒjɔ̃] f. Ecclés. Religion; *avoir de la religion*, to be religious; *entrer en religion*, to take the vows; *guerres de Religion*, Wars of Religion, Religious Wars. ‖ Fig. *Se faire une religion de*, to make a religion (ou) a cult of; *surprendre la religion de qqn*, to impose upon s.o.'s good faith.
religiosité [-ʒjozite] f. Religiosity.
reliquaire [rəlikɛ:r] m. Reliquary.
reliquat [rəlika] m. Remainder, residue. ‖ Fin. Balance (d'un compte). ‖ Méd. After-effects (d'une maladie).
relique [rəlik] f. Ecclés. Relic. ‖ Fam. *Garder comme une relique*, to treasure up.
relire [rəli:r] v. tr. (60). To re-read, to read again, to read over again; *lire et relire*, to read over and over again.
— v. pr. **Se relire**, to read what one has written.
reliure [rəljy:r] f. Book-binding (action); binding (résultat); *reliure électrique, en toile*, spring-, cloth binding.
relogement [rələʒmɑ̃] m. Rehousing.
reloger [-lɔʒe] v. tr. (7). To rehouse.
relouer [rəlwe] v. tr. (1). To relet (une maison), to hire again (ou U.S.) to rent again (une voiture) [redonner en location]. ‖ To rent again (une maison), to hire again (ou U.S.) to rent again (une voiture) [reprendre en location].
réluctance [relyktɑ̃:s] f. Electr. Reluctance.
reluire [rəlɥi:r] v. intr. (61). To shine, to glisten, to gleam, to glow; *faire reluire les cuivres*, to polish the brass, to shine up the brasswork. ‖ Fig. To shine.
reluisant, ante [-lɥizɑ̃, ɑ̃:t] adj. Bright (armes); glittering, shining (cuivres); glossy (poil).
reluquer [rəlyke] v. tr. (1). Pop. To ogle, to eye (une femme); to covet (qqch.); to look over, to give the once over (pop.). [V. lorgner.]
relustrer [rəlystre] v. tr. (1). To give a new lustre to; to shine, to shine up (qqch.).
remâcher [rəmɑʃe] v. tr. (1). To chew again. ‖ Fam. To turn over in one's mind, to ruminate (ou) to ponder (ou) to brood over [v. ruminer].
remaillage [rəmɑja:ʒ] m. Mending the meshes (*de*, of) [un filet]; mending the ladders (ou) runs (*de*, in) [un bas].
remailler [rəmɑje] v. tr. (1). To mend the meshes of (un filet) [v. ramender]. ‖ To repair (ou) mend a ladder (ou) run in (un bas).
remailleuse [rəmɑjø:z] f. Ladder-mender; person who mends runs in stockings. ‖ Machine for mending ladders (ou) runs.
remake [rimɛk] m. Ciném. Remake.
rémanence [remanɑ̃:s] f. Electr. Remanence; residual magnetism; retentivity.
rémanent, ente [remanɑ̃, ɑ̃:t] adj. Electr. Remanent; residual.
remanger [rəmɑ̃ʒe] v. tr. (7). To eat again.
— v. intr. To feed again.
remaniable [rəmanjabl] adj. Able to be altered, capable of modification.
remaniement [-nimɑ̃] m. Altering, reshapening,

modifying (d'un ouvrage). ‖ Jur. *Remaniement ministériel*, Cabinet reshuffle.
remanier [-nje] v. tr. (1). To alter, to reshape, to modify (qqch.). ‖ Arts. To recast, to reshape (un livre); to adapt (une pièce).
remanieur [-njœ:r] s. Recaster, adapter.
remaquiller [rəmakije] v. tr. (1). To put make-up back on.
— v. pr. **Se remaquiller**, to make oneself up again, to fix one's make-up.
remarcher [rəmarʃe] v. intr. (1). Fam. To work (ou) go again, to start working again.
remariage [rəmarja:ʒ] m. Remarriage.
remarier [rəmarje] v. tr. (1). To remarry.
— v. pr. **Se remarier**, to remarry, to marry again, to get married again.
remarquable [rəmarkabl] adj. Remarkable, noteworthy.
remarquablement [-bləmɑ̃] adv. Remarkably; *remarquablement doué*, amazingly gifted.
remarque [rəmark] f. Remark, comment; *faire une remarque*, to pass a remark, to comment. ‖ Remark, notice, consideration; *digne de remarque*, noteworthy, worth noticing. ‖ Note, written comment, annotation; *texte accompagné de remarques*, annotated copy, text with notes. ‖ Naut. Landmark.
remarquer [rəmarke] v. tr. (1). To re-mark (du linge). ‖ To remark, to notice, to observe (observer); *faire remarquer qqch. à qqn*, to point out sth. to s.o., to call (ou) draw s.o.'s attention to sth., to bring sth. to s.o.'s attention (ou) notice. ‖ To distinguish; to make out (*dans*, in) [discerner]; *se faire remarquer*, to attract attention, to make oneself conspicuous. ‖ To note (noter).
remballage [rɑ̃bala:ʒ] m. Comm. Repacking; re-baling.
remballer [rɑ̃bale] v. tr. (1). Comm. To repack, to pack up again, to re-bale (des denrées). ‖ Fam. To bully, to snub, to rate (qqn).
rembarquement [rɑ̃barkəmɑ̃] m. Naut. Re-embarking, re-embarkation (de passagers). ‖ Comm. Re-shipping (de denrées).
rembarquer [-ke] v. tr. (1). Naut. To re-embark (des troupes). ‖ Comm. To re-ship (des denrées).
— v. intr. Naut. To re-embark.
— v. pr. **Se rembarquer**, Naut. To re-embark, to go on board again. ‖ Fig. To embark again (*dans*, upon) [une affaire].
rembarrer [rɑ̃bare] v. tr. (1). † To repulse (l'ennemi). ‖ Fam. To snub. [V. rabrouer.]
remblai [rɑ̃blɛ] m. Embankment (de route). ‖ Filling in, banking up (action); filling; spoil heap (terre). ‖ Ch. de f. Embankment.
remblayage [rɑ̃blɛja:ʒ] m. Filling in (d'un trou, d'une mine); banking up (d'une route, d'une voie ferrée).
remblayer [rɑ̃blɛje] v. tr. (9 b). To bank up (une route); to fill in (un terrain). ‖ Ch. de f. To bank up, to embank (une voie ferrée).
remboîtage [rɑ̃bwata:ʒ], **remboîtement** [-tmɑ̃] m. Méd. Reducing, setting (d'un os démis).
remboîter [-te] v. tr. (1). Méd. To set, to reduce.
rembourrage [rɑ̃bura:ʒ] m. Padding, stuffing, upholstering (action); padding, stuffing (matière).
rembourrer [rɑ̃bure] v. tr. (1). To pad, to stuff, to upholster.
remboursable [rɑ̃bursabl] adj. Fin. Repayable, reimbursable, refundable.
remboursement [rɑ̃bursəmɑ̃] m. Fin. Repayment, repaying (une dette); redeeming, redemption (d'une obligation). ‖ Comm. *Livraison contre remboursement*, cash on delivery; C.O.D.
rembourser [rɑ̃burse] v. tr. (1). Fin. To repay, to pay off, to reimburse (un créancier); to repay, to settle (une dette); to redeem (une obligation).

— v. pr. **Se rembourser,** to reimburse oneself ; to get one's money back.

rembrunir [r̃ɑbryni:r] v. tr. (2). To darken, to make darker (qqch.). ‖ FIG. To sadden, to make sad (qqn).

— v. pr. **Se rembrunir,** to grow (ou) become dark, to cloud over, to become overcast (ciel). ‖ FIG. To become gloomy (ou) sad (personne) ; to cloud over (visage).

rembucher [r̃ɑbyʃe] v. tr. (1). SPORTS. To covert.

— v. pr. **Se rembucher,** to return to cover (cerf).

remède [rəmɛd] m. MÉD. Remedy (à, for) ; cure ; *remède de bonne femme,* old wives' cure. ‖ FIG. Remedy, cure ; *sans remède,* beyond remedy.

remédiable [rəmedjabl] adj. Remediable.

remédier [-dje] v. intr. (1). MÉD. *Remédier à,* to cure, to remedy. ‖ FIG. *Remédier à,* to stop (un abus) ; to supply (un défaut) ; to cure (un mal) ; to repair, to make good (une perte).

remêler [rəmɛle] v. tr. (1). To re-mix, to mix again. ‖ To re-shuffle (les cartes).

remembrement [rəm̃ɑbrəm̃ɑ] m. JUR. Reconstitution (d'une propriété) ; regrouping (de terres).

remémoration [-rasjɔ̃] f. Remembrance, recall.

remémorer [-re] v. tr. (1). *Remémorer qqch. à qqn,* to remind s.o. of (ou) about sth.

— v. pr. **Se remémorer,** to remember, to recall, to call to mind.

remener [rəmne] v. tr. (5). To lead (ou) conduct (ou) take back.

remerciement [rəmɛrsim̃ɑ] m. Thanks (à, to) ; acknowledgment ; *un remerciement,* thanks, a thank-you.

remercier [-sje] v. tr. (1) To thank (*for,* de) [qqn] ; *remercier qqn d'un sourire,* to thank s.o. with a smile, to smile one's thanks to s.o. ‖ To decline with thanks (refuser) ; *je l'invitai à dîner, il remercia,* I invited him to dinner, he asked to be excused. ‖ To dismiss, to discharge (v. RENVOYER) ; to fire (fam).

remettre [rəmɛtr] v. tr. (64). To put back, to replace (replacer) ; *remettre son épée au fourreau,* to sheathe (ou) put up one's sword. ‖ To put on again (un vêtement). ‖ To give, to give back, to return, to deliver (livrer) ; *remettre sa démission,* to hand (ou) tender one's resignation ; *remettre une lettre,* to deliver a letter ; *remettre qqn à la police,* to hand (ou) turn s.o. over to the police. ‖ To put on again (mettre à nouveau) ; *remettre en marche,* to restart ; *remettre en question,* to call in question again ; *remettre en usage,* to bring into use again. ‖ To calm, to compose, to reassure (rassurer) ; *cette nouvelle l'a remis,* that news has set his mind at rest. ‖ To reconcile ; to bring together (réconcilier). ‖ To entrust, to hand over (confier) ; *remettre une affaire au jugement de qqn,* to leave a matter to s.o.'s judgment ; *remettre au hasard,* to leave to chance ; *remettre son sort entre les mains de qqn,* to place one's fate in s.o.'s hands. ‖ To defer, to postpone, to put off (différer) ; *remettre une affaire au lendemain, à plus tard,* to put a matter off till next day, till later. ‖ MÉD. To set (un bras cassé) ; to reduce (une épaule démise) ; to restore to health (qqn). ‖ JUR. *Remettre à huitaine,* to adjourn for a week. ‖ COMM. To allow (*sur,* on) [un pourcentage]. ‖ SPORTS. To throw *Remettre le ballon en jeu,* to throw the ball in (au football). ‖ ECCLÉS. To commit (à, to) [son âme] ; to forgive, to pardon (une offense) ; to remit (un péché). ‖ FAM. *Remettez-nous ça!,* same again all round!, set them up again! ‖ FAM. To recognize ; *je vous remets à présent,* I remember you now.

— v. pr. **Se remettre,** to put (ou) place oneself again ; *se remettre à faire qqch.,* to start doing sth. again ; *se remettre au lit,* to go to bed again ; *se remettre au travail,* to set to work again ; *se*

remettre en route, to start off on one's way again. ‖ MÉD. To recover again (*de,* from) ; *se remettre d'une maladie,* to get over an illness, to be on the mend ; *remettez-vous,* pull yourself together. ‖ FIG. *S'en remettre à,* to rely on ; *remettez-vous-en à lui,* leave it to him.

remeubler [rəmœble] v. tr. (1). To refurnish.

Remi [rəmi] m. Remigius.

rémige [remi:ʒ] f. ZOOL. Remex, wing-quill.

remilitariser [rmilitarize] v. tr. (1). To remilitarize.

Remington [remiɲtɔn] m. MILIT. Remington.

réminiscence [reminis̃ɑ:s] f. Reminiscence, vague recollection.

remisage [rəmiza:ʒ] f. AUTOM. Putting up, garaging. ‖ CH. DE F. Putting into a shed.

remise [-mi:z] f. Putting back, putting into its place, replacing (d'un objet). ‖ Delivery (d'une lettre). ‖ Delay, deferment, postponement (retard). ‖ Coach-house (local) ; *voiture de remise,* hired (ou) livery carriage. ‖ Shed (v. HANGAR). ‖ CH. DE F. Engine-shed. ‖ FIN., COMM. Remission (d'une dette) ; remittance (versement) ; *faire une remise,* to remit, to send a remittance. ‖ COMM. Commission (à un agent) ; discount (*de,* of ; *sur,* on) [rabais] ; *remise de 10 p. 100,* 10 per cent discount. ‖ JUR. Adjournment (d'une cause) ; deposition (d'un dossier). ‖ TECHN., AUTOM. *Remise en état,* overhauling, reconditioning ; *remise en marche,* re-starting. ‖ SPORTS. Covert (de gibier) ; *remise en jeu,* throw-in (au football). ‖ MÉD. Setting (d'un os).

— m. Hired (ou) livery carriage.

remiser [-mize] v. tr. (1). To put up, to put away, to put in a coach-house (une voiture). ‖ CH. DE F. To put in a shed. ‖ FAM. To put in his place (qqn).

— v. pr. **Se remiser,** to alight, to come down, to take cover (gibier).

remisier [-mizje] m. FIN. Half-commission man.

rémissibilité [remisibilite] f. Remissibility.

rémissible [-sibl] adj. Remissible.

rémission [-sjɔ̃] f. ECCLÉS., MÉD. Remission. ‖ FIG. *Sans rémission,* unremittingly (sans cesse) ; relentlessly (sans faiblir).

rémittence [remit̃ɑ:s] f. MÉD. Remission.

rémittent, ente [-t̃ɑ, ̃ɑ:t] adj. MÉD. Remittent.

remmaillage [r̃ɑmɑja:ʒ] m. Grafting of a patch.

remmailler [-je] v. tr. (1). To graft a patch into, to stitch together. (V. REMAILLER.)

remmailloter [r̃ɑmɑjɔte] v. tr. (1). To swaddle again.

remmancher [r̃ɑm̃ɑʃe] v. tr. (1). To rehandle.

remmener [r̃ɑmne] v. tr. (5). To take (ou) lead back again.

remodelage [rəmɔdla:ʒ] m. ARCHIT. Redevelopment (d'un quartier). ‖ MÉD. Remodelling (d'un nez).

remodeler [-le] v. tr. (8a). ARCHIT. To redevelop (un quartier). ‖ MÉD. To remodel (un nez).

rémois, oise [remwa, wa:z] Adj. Of (ou) from Reims.

— s. Native (ou) inhabitant of Reims.

remontage [rəm̃ɔta:ʒ] m. Ascending, going up (d'un fleuve). ‖ Rewinding, winding up (d'une horloge) ; *à remontage automatique,* self-winding. ‖ Strengthening with alcohol (d'un vin). ‖ COMM. Re-stocking (d'un magasin). ‖ TECHN. Setting-up, re-assembling (d'une machine).

remontant, ante [-t̃ɑ, ̃ɑ:t] adj. Ascending, going up. ‖ MÉD. Fortifying. ‖ BOT. Remontant.

— m. MÉD. Stimulant, tonic. (V. FORTIFIANT.) ‖ FAM. Pick-me-up.

remonte [rəm̃ɔ:t] f. Ascent (d'un fleuve). ‖ ZOOL. Running (des poissons). ‖ MILIT. Remount (cheval) ; remount service (service). ‖ **Remonte-pente,** m. SPORTS. Ski-lift, ski-tow.

remonté, ée [rəm̃ɔte] adj. High (épaules).

remontée f. Climb (d'une route). ‖ TECHN. Raising (de charbon, de minerais, de mineurs).

remonter v. intr. (1). To go (ou) climb up again; *remonter au sommet d'une colline*, to climb up to the top of a hill again; *remonter en voiture*, to get into a vehicle again; *remonter sur le trône*, to re-ascend the throne; *remonter sur son cheval*, to mount one's horse again, to re-mount. ‖ To ride, to ride (ou) work up (col). ‖ NAUT. To rise (marée); to come round (vent). ‖ COMM. To rise, to go up (prix). ‖ FIG. To rise, to go up (baromètre). ‖ FIG. To go back (dans l'espace); to date back (dans le temps); *remonter à la source de qqch.*, to trace sth. back to its origin; *cette maison remonte aux croisades*, this house dates back to the Crusades.
— v. tr. To ascend (ou) climb again (une colline); to stem (le courant); to go up again (l'escalier); to go (ou) row (ou) sail up (un fleuve); to go (ou) walk up (une rue). ‖ To take (ou) carry up again (qqch.). ‖ To pull up (ses chaussettes); to wind up (une horloge); to roll up (sa manche); to hitch up (son pantalon). ‖ To replenish (une garde-robe); to re-furnish (une maison). ‖ COMM. To re-stock (un magasin). ‖ ARCHIT. To raise (un mur). ‖ MUS. To re-string (un violon). ‖ ARTS. To heighten (une couleur). ‖ THÉÂTR. To put on again (une pièce). ‖ NAUT. *Remonter le vent*, to beat to windward. ‖ MILIT. To remount (un cavalier). ‖ TECHN. To reset (un bijou); to vamp (des chaussures). ‖ FIG. *Remonter le moral de qqn*, to cheer s.o. up, to raise s.o's morale. ‖ FAM. To buck up (v. REVIGORER); *remonter la pendule à qqn*, to egg s.o. on (inciter); to work s.o. up against s.o. else (exciter).
— v. pr. **Se remonter**, to get over it, to rally, to be restored to health, to recover one's spirits. ‖ To replenish oneself.

remonteur [-tœ:r] m. Clock-winder.

remontoir [-twa:r] m. Watch-key, clock-key; *montre à remontoir*, stem-winder, keyless watch. ‖ Key (de jouet).

remontrance [rəmɔ̃trɑ̃:s] f. Expostulation; remonstrance (v. RÉPRIMANDE); *faire des remontrances à*, to remonstrate with.

remontrer [-tre] v. tr. (1). To show again (qqch.). ‖ FIG. To point out (ses torts) [à, to].
— v. intr. To remonstrate. ‖ FAM. *En remontrer à qqn*, to best s.o.

remordre [rəmɔrdr] v. tr. (4). To bite again.
— v. intr. To take another bite (à, at) [un fruit]. ‖ FIG. To have another go (ou) try (à, at) [qqch.]. ‖ FAM. *Y remordre*, to tackle it again; to have another bash (pop.).

remords [rəmɔ:r] m. Remorse (v. REPENTIR); twinge of remorse; *pris de remords*, smitten with remorse; *sans remords*, remorselessly.

remorquage [rəmɔrka:ʒ] m. AUTOM., NAUT. Towing; haulage. ‖ COMM. *Droits, frais de remorquage*, towing fees (ou) dues; towage.

remorque [rəmɔrk] f. NAUT. Tow, towing (action); tow-rope (câble); tow, towed vessel (navire); *à la remorque*, on tow; *prendre en remorque*, to take in tow. ‖ AUTOM. Tow, towing (action); trailer (voiture). ‖ FIG. *Se mettre à la remorque de qqn*, to follow in s.o.'s wake, to tack on to s.o. ‖ **Remorque-roulotte**, f. Caravan, U. S. trailer.

remorquer [-ke] v. tr. (1). AUTOM. To trail (une remorque); to tow (une voiture). ‖ NAUT. To tow, to tug, to haul (un vaisseau). ‖ CH. DE F. To pull, to draw (un train).

remorqueur, euse [-kœ:r, ø:z] adj. AUTOM., NAUT. Towing. ‖ CH. DE F. Relief.
— m. NAUT. Tug, tug-boat.

remoudre [rəmudr] v. tr. (65). To regrind.

remouiller [rəmuje] v. tr. (1). To wet (ou) moisten again. ‖ NAUT. To let go (ou) cast again (l'ancre).

rémoulade [remulad] f. CULIN. Remoulade-sauce.

rémouleur [remulœ:r] m. Knife-grinder.

remous [rəmu] m. Eddy (d'eau, de vent); swirl (de marée); backwash (d'une vague). ‖ NAUT. Wash (d'un bateau). ‖ AVIAT. Slipstream (d'une hélice). ‖ FIG. Public unrest.

rempaillage [rɑ̃paja:ʒ] m. Re-seating, re-bottoming (de chaise).

rempailler [-je] v. tr. (1). To re-seat, to re-bottom.

rempailleur [-jœ:r] s. Chair-mender.

rempaqueter [rɑ̃pakte] v. tr. (1). To wrap (ou) pack up again.

rempart [rɑ̃pa:r] m. ARCHIT. Rampart. ‖ MILIT. Pl. Ramparts, battlements. ‖ FIG. Bulwark (d'une nation).

rempiéter [rɑ̃pjete] v. tr. (5). To re-foot.

rempiler [rɑ̃pile] v. intr. (1). MILIT., FAM. To re-enlist.

remplaçable [rɑ̃plasabl] adj. Replaceable.

remplaçant, ante [-sɑ̃, ɑ̃:t] s. SPORTS. Substitute (dans une équipe). ‖ MÉD. Locum tenens, locum (d'un médecin).

remplacement [-smɑ̃] m. Replacement, substitution; replacing; *en remplacement de*, in place of.

remplacer [-se] v. tr. (6). To replace (*par*, by); *remplacer de vieux meubles par des neufs*, to instal new furniture in place of old. ‖ To deputize for, to fill the place of (qqn) [v. RELAYER, SUPPLÉER]; *remplacer un collègue malade*, to do duty (ou) to substitute for a sick colleague; *se faire remplacer*, to find a substitute. ‖ To supersede (qqch., qqn) [être substitué à].

rempli [rɑ̃pli] m. Tuck.

remplir [-pli:r] v. tr. (2). To fill (sa cave). ‖ To fill (*de*, with); to refill, to fill up (un verre). ‖ To fill in (ou) up (un vide). ‖ To fill (un lieu). ‖ To fill in (ou) up, to complete (une fiche). ‖ To employ fully (ou), to the fill (son temps); to occupy (un siècle). ‖ NAUT. To swamp (un bateau). ‖ FIG. To fulfil (un devoir, ses engagements); to comply with (une formalité); to occupy, to fill (une place); to carry out (une promesse); *remplir des conditions*, to answer requirements.
— v. pr. **Se remplir**, to fill, to be filled; *la cave se remplissait d'eau*, the cellar was filling with water. ‖ POP. *Se remplir le buffet*, to have a good tuck-in (fam.) feed.

remplissage [-plisa:ʒ] m. Filling, filling up (d'un tonneau, d'un verre); filling in (d'un vide). ‖ Padding (dans un texte); filler (texte). ‖ MUS. Filling-in.

remploi [rɑ̃plwa] m. Reuse (de matériaux de construction). ‖ FIN. Reinvestment.

remployer [-je] v. tr. (9 a). To re-employ (qqn); to use (ou) make use of again (qqch.). ‖ FIN. To reinvest (des fonds).

remplumer (se) [sərɑ̃plyme] v. pr. (1). ZOOL. To get (ou) grow new feathers (oiseau). ‖ FAM. To put on weight (grossir); to be in the money again (s'enrichir).

rempocher [rɑ̃pɔʃe] v. tr. (1). To pocket again.

rempoissonnement [rɑ̃pwasɔnmɑ̃] m. Restocking (d'un lac, d'une rivière).

rempoissonner [-sɔne] v. tr. (1). To restock (un lac, une rivière).

remporter [rɑ̃pɔrte] v. tr. (1). To carry (ou) take away (enlever); to carry (ou) take back (rapporter). ‖ SPORTS. To win; to lift (fam.) [la coupe]. ‖ FIG. To carry off (un prix); to achieve (un succès); to win, to gain (une victoire).

rempoter [rɑ̃pɔte] v. tr. (1). AGRIC. To repot.

remprunter [rɑ̃prœ̃te] v. tr. (1). To borrow again.

remuable [remɥabl] adj. Movable.

remuage [-a:ʒ] m. Moving; shaking, stirring up.

remuant, ante [-ɑ̃, ɑ̃:t] adj. Fidgety (enfant); restless, bustling (personne). ‖ FIG. Turbulent.

remue-ménage [-mena:ʒ] m. invar. Moving, moving about (de meubles). ‖ Fig. Upset, commotion, hullabaloo.

remuement [-mã] m. Moving, stirring; removal. ‖ Fig. Disturbance, commotion.

remuer [remɥe] v. tr. (1). To move, to stir (un membre); to shift, to move (un meuble). [V. BOUGER.] ‖ To stir (un liquide). ‖ Fig. To move, to rouse (l'âme); to stir up (les masses); *remuer ciel et terre,* to move heaven and earth, to leave no stone unturned; *ne pas remuer un cil,* not to bat an eyelid (ou) U. S. eye.
— v. intr. To fidget (enfants); to move, to stir (personne). ‖ MÉD. To be loose (dent).
— v. pr. **Se remuer,** to move, to bestir oneself, to bustle about; to be on the go (fam.).

remueur [-œ:r] adj. Active, stirring, restless.
— s. Stirrer, stirring-rod.

remugle [rəmygl] m. Musty smell.

rémunérateur, trice [remyneratœ:r, tris] adj. Remunerative, profitable; U. S. gainful.
— s. Remunerator, rewarder.

rémunération [-rasjõ] f. Remuneration, payment, reward; U. S. compensation; *la juste rémunération de,* a fair return for.

rémunératoire [-ratwa:r] adj. JUR. As a recompense; for services rendered.

rémunérer [-re] v. tr. (5). To remunerate, to pay, to reward (qqn) [*de,* for]. ‖ To pay for, to reward (des services).

renâcler [rənɑkle] v. intr. (1). To snort (cheval). ‖ FAM. To snort, to sniff (personne) [*à,* at]; *renâcler à la besogne,* to fight shy of (ou) to jib at one's work.

renâcleur [-klœ:r] s. FAM. Surly (ou) work-shy person.

renaissance [rənɛsã:s] f. Renaissance, revival (des arts, des lettres); *la Renaissance,* the Renaissance, the Renascence. ‖ Rebirth (du phénix); return (du printemps).
— adj. ARTS. Renaissance (style). ‖ COMM. *Laine renaissance,* shoddy.

renaissant, ante [-sã, ã:t] adj. Renascent, reviving, returning (forces); recurrent (problème). ‖ AGRIC. Coming to life again (végétation).

renaître [rənɛ:tr] v. intr. (68). To be born again. ‖ To rise again (*de,* from). ‖ FIG. To revive, to return, to be restored; *le jour renaît,* a new day is dawning; *renaître à l'espérance,* to take fresh heart; *renaître après une longue maladie,* to ᴅᴇ restored to health after a long illness; *renaître à la vie,* to take on a new lease of life.

rénal, ale [renal] adj. MÉD. Renal (calcul).

renard [rəna:r] m. ZOOL. Fox. ‖ TECHN. Fissure, crack. ‖ FAM. *Un vieux renard,* a sly old fox. ‖ POP. Blackleg, scab, strike-breaker (jaune).

renarde [-nard] f. ZOOL. Vixen.

renardeau [-nardo] m. ZOOL. Fox-cub.

renardière [-nardjɛ:r] f. Fox-hole, fox's earth.

rencaisser [rãkɛse] v. tr. (1). AGRIC. To replace (ou) put back into boxes (ou) tubs (des plantes). ‖ FIN. To receive back (de l'argent). ‖ POP. *Rencaisse tes salades!,* that's enough of your nonsense!

rencard, rencarder. V. RANCARD, RANCARDER.

renchéri, ie [rãʃeri] adj. Fastidious, too particular (personne).
— s. Fastidious, over-particular person; *faire le renchéri,* to be too particular, to put on airs.

renchérir [-ri:r] v. tr. (2). COMM. To make dearer.
— v. intr. COMM. To rise in price, to become dearer, to go up (marchandises). ‖ FIG. To make a higher bid, to go one better; *renchérir sur,* to cap (a citation); to improve on (une histoire); to outdo, to go one better than (qqn).

renchérissement [-rismã] m. Rise in price.

renchérisseur [-risœ:r] s. COMM. Outbidder;

runner up of prices. ‖ FIG. One who tries to outdo other people.

rencogner [rãkɔɲe] v. tr. (1). To push (ou) drive into a corner (qqn).
— v. pr. **Se rencogner,** to crouch (ou) huddle in a corner; to ensconce oneself.

rencontre [rãkõ:tr] f. Meeting, encounter; *aller à la rencontre de qqn,* to go to meet s.o.; *faire une mauvaise rencontre,* to meet with s.o. unpleasant. ‖ Occasion; *à la première rencontre,* at the first opportunity. ‖ Meeting, duel, encounter (de deux duellistes). ‖ Junction (de deux routes); collision (de deux véhicules). ‖ PHYS. Concourse, collision (des atomes). ‖ MILIT. Encounter (de deux armées); *combat de rencontre,* chance skirmish. ‖ COMM. Bargain; snip, U. S. steal (fam.); *de rencontre,* second-hand. ‖ BLAS. Head of a beast caboched.

rencontrer [rãkõtre] v. tr. (1). To meet with (qqch.); to meet (qqn); *rencontrer par hasard,* to happen (ou) chance upon, to run across, to bump into. ‖ To come up against (un obstacle); *la balle a rencontré un os,* the bullet has struck a bone. ‖ MILIT. To encounter (l'ennemi). ‖ NAUT. To meet, to meet with (la barre). ‖ AUTOM. To collide with, to run into (un véhicule). ‖ FIG. To get, to receive.
— v. intr. To guess; *rencontrer juste,* to guess right. ‖ To find what one is looking for; *bien rencontrer,* to be lucky.
— v. pr. **Se rencontrer,** to meet (deux personnes); to join (deux routes); to collide (deux véhicules); *se rencontrer en duel,* to fight a duel. ‖ To occur (événement); to be met with, to be found (objet); to arise, to appear, to be found (personne). ‖ To be of like mind; to think alike (esprits).

rendement [rãdmã] m. AGRIC. Yield, produce (d'une terre); *d'un excellent rendement,* yielding heavy crops. ‖ COMM. Profit (d'une entreprise). ‖ FIN. Return, interest, yield (du capital); *placement à gros rendement,* profitable investment, investment yielding a high interest. ‖ TECHN. Efficiency, useful work, output (d'une machine); work, output, productivity (du personnel); *à plein rendement,* full time, at top speed, full pressure; all out, flat out (fam.); *mauvais rendement,* poor (ou) low output, low productivity.

rendez-vous [rãdevu] m. invar. Rendez-vous, assignation; appointment (*avec,* with); *être au rendez-vous,* to keep an appointment; *sur rendez-vous,* by appointment. ‖ Meeting-place, place of meeting, haunt (lieu). ‖ SPORTS. *Rendez-vous de chasse,* meet.

rendormir [rãdɔrmi:r] v. tr. (41). To put to sleep again; *rendormir un enfant,* to lull a child to sleep again.
— v. pr. **Se rendormir,** to fall (ou) go to sleep again; to drop off to sleep again.

rendre [rã:dr] v. tr. (4). To render, to return, to restore, to give back (restituer). ‖ To give off (une odeur); to emit (un son) [v. ÉMETTRE]; *rendre l'âme,* to give up the ghost. ‖ To throw up (la nourriture). [V. VOMIR.] ‖ To represent (représenter); to express (le sens); *rendre les traits de qqn,* to catch s.o.'s features well; *mal rendre un passage,* to mistranslate a passage. ‖ To pay, to give (donner, faire); *rendre grâce à,* to give thanks to; *rendre hommage à,* to pay homage to; *rendre visite à,* to visit. ‖ To disengage (libérer); *rendre sa parole à qqn,* to release s.o. from (ou) to let s.o. off a promise. ‖ To render (faire devenir); *les voyages en autocar me rendent malade,* travelling by coach (ou) U. S. bus makes me sick; *rendre qqn fou,* to drive s.o. mad; to send s.o. round the bend (fam.); *rendre une tâche plus difficile,* to make a job more diffi-

cult. ‖ MILIT. To lay down (les armes); to surrender, to give up (une forteresse); *rendre coup pour coup*, to return blow for blow. ‖ FIN. To pay back (de l'argent); *rendre la monnaie*, to give change. ‖ FIN. To yield, to bring in (un intérêt). ‖ COMM. To render (un compte); to deliver (des marchandises). ‖ AGRIC. To yield, to produce. ‖ JUR. To pronounce (un arrêt); to dispense (la justice); to bring in (un verdict). ‖ MUS. To render, to give, to play, to perform (un morceau de musique). ‖ MÉD. *Rendre la santé, la vue à qqn*, to restore s.o.'s health, sight. ‖ FAM. *Rendre gorge*, to give up one's ill-gotten gains.
— v. intr. To pay (ou) give back. ‖ To lead (route) [à, to]. ‖ MÉD. To be sick, to vomit. ‖ AGRIC. To be productive (terre). ‖ FIN. To be profitable (placement). ‖ FAM. To work; to run well; *ça rend!*, that does the trick!
— v. pr. Se rendre, to go, to proceed, to make one's way (à, to). ‖ To yield, to accept, to give way (céder); *se rendre à l'avis de qqn*, to fall in with s.o.'s view; *se rendre à l'évidence*, to accept the evidence, to yield to proof; *se rendre à un argument*, to give way to an argument. ‖ To become, to make oneself (devenir); *se rendre maître*, to make oneself master, to get the upper hand; *se rendre utile*, to make oneself useful. ‖ MILIT. To give up, to surrender.

rendu, ue [rɑ̃dy] adj. Arrived; *enfin, nous voilà rendus*, we're there at last. ‖ Rendered, translated (phrase). ‖ FAM. *Rendu de fatigue*, done up, dead beat, knocked up.
— m. COMM. Return, returned article; *faire un rendu*, to return an article. ‖ ARTS. Correct reproduction (d'une couleur); rendering (d'un sujet). ‖ FIG. *Un prêté pour un rendu*, tit for tat.

rendurcir [rɑ̃dyrci:r] v. tr. (2). To harden, to make harder.
— v. pr. Se rendurcir, to become harder.

rêne [rɛ:n] f. Rein. (V. GUIDE.) ‖ FIG. Pl. Reins (du gouvernement).

renégat [rənega] s. Renegade.

reneiger [rənɛʒe] v. impers. (7). To snow again.

renettoyer [rənɛtwaye] v. tr. (9 a). To clean again, to reclean.

renfermé, ée [rɑ̃fɛrme] adj. FIG. Reticent, uncommunicative, close (personne).
— m. *Odeur de renfermé*, stuffy (ou) close (ou) fusty (ou) stale smell (dans une pièce); *sentir le renfermé*, to smell stuffy (ou) close (ou) fusty.

renfermer v. tr. (1). To shut up again (qqch., qqn); to lock up again (un prisonnier). ‖ To contain, to include (contenir); *ce livre renferme de grandes vérités*, there is much truth to be found in this book. ‖ To restrict, to reduce (condenser); *renfermer une pensée en peu de mots*, to reduce a thought to a few words. ‖ FIG. To keep hidden; *renfermer ses chagrins, ses projets*, to keep one's troubles, one's plans to oneself.
— v. pr. Se renfermer, to close (ou) shut oneself up (dans une chambre). ‖ FIG. To withdraw into oneself; *se renfermer dans le silence*, to withdraw into silence; *se renfermer dans son sujet*, to confine oneself to one's subject. ‖ FAM. *Se renfermer dans sa coquille*, to retire into one's shell.

renfiler [rɑ̃file] v. tr. (1). To thread (ou) string again, to restring, to rethread.

renflammer [rɑ̃flame] v tr. (1). To rekindle, to set alight again.
— v. tr. Se renflammer, to catch fire again, to flame (ou) flare up again. ‖ FIG. To be rekindled.

renflé, ée [rɑ̃fle] adj Swollen, swelling up. ‖ ARCHIT. With entasis (colonne). ‖ NAUT. Bluffbowed (navire).

renflement [-fləmɑ̃] m. Swelling, swelling up; bulge. ‖ ARCHIT. Entasis. ‖ BOT. Protuberance.

renfler [-fle] v. tr. (1). To re-inflate.
— v. intr. To swell, to swell up.

renflouage [rɑ̃flua:ʒ], **renflouement** [-mɑ̃] m. NAUT. Refloating.

renflouer [-e] v. tr. (1). NAUT. To refloat, to heave off, to set afloat (un navire). ‖ FIG. To set right, to pull off the rocks (une affaire).

renfoncé, ée [rɑ̃fɔ̃se] adj. Deep-set, sunken (yeux).

renfoncement [-smɑ̃] m. Pushing-in (d'un bouchon); denting (d'un objet). ‖ Recess (dans un caisson); hollow, cavity (dans un mur); dent (dans un objet). ‖ FAM. Bashing in; pulling down (d'un chapeau).

renfoncer [-se] v. tr. (6). To push in (un bouchon); to pull down (un chapeau); to dent (un objet); *renfoncer son chapeau sur ses oreilles*, to pull down one's hat over (ou) about one's ears. ‖ ARCHIT. To set back (une façade); to recess (un mur). ‖ FAM. To choke back (ses larmes).
— v. pr. Se renfoncer, to sink in (dans l'eau). ‖ To draw back, to withdraw (dans un coin).

renforçage [rɑ̃fɔrsa:ʒ] m. ARCHIT. Reinforcing, strengthening. ‖ TECHN. Intensifying (en photo.).

renforçateur [-satœ:r] m. TECHN. Intensifier.

renforcement [-səmɑ̃] m. ARCHIT. Reinforcing, strengthening (d'un édifice); trussing (d'un pont); bracing (d'une poutre). ‖ MILIT. Reinforcing, strengthening (d'une garnison). ‖ PHYS. Intensifying, magnification (d'un son). ‖ TECHN. Intensification (en photo). ‖ FIG. Strengthening, hardening (d'une opinion).

renforcer [-se] v. tr. (6). ARCHIT. To reinforce, to strengthen (un édifice); to truss (un pont); to brace, to stiffen (une poutre). ‖ MILIT. To strengthen, to reinforce (une garnison). ‖ PHYS. To magnify, to intensify (un son). ‖ TECHN. To intensify (en photo). ‖ FIG. To strengthen, to harden (une opinion).
— v. intr. To blow harder (vent).
— v. pr. Se renforcer, to grow (ou) become stronger, to gain in strength.

renforcir [rɑ̃fɔrsir] v. tr. POP. To strengthen.
— v. intr. To grow stronger.

renfort [rɑ̃fɔ:r] m. MILIT. Reinforcement; fresh supply of troops (troupes); reinforce (d'un canon). ‖ TECHN. Strengthening piece, stiffener (pièce); *cheval de renfort*, trace-horse. ‖ LOC. *A grand renfort de*, with a copious supply of.

renfrogné, ée [rɑ̃frɔɲe] adj. Scowling, frowning (mine); surly, crabbed, sullen (personne).

renfrogner (se) [sərɑ̃frɔɲe] v. pr. (1). To scowl, to frown; to wear a sullen look.

rengagé, ée [rɑ̃gaʒe] adj. MILIT. Re-enlisted.
— s. MILIT. Re-enlisted soldier.

rengagement [-ʒmɑ̃] m. MILIT., NAUT. Re-enlistment; re-engagement.

rengager [rɑ̃gaʒe] v. tr. (7). To re-engage (un ouvrier). ‖ To pledge (ou) pawn again (un objet au mont-de-piété). ‖ MILIT. *Rengager le combat*, to renew the struggle.
— v. intr. MILIT., NAUT. To re-enlist.
— v. pr. Se rengager, to take up one's employment again; to sign on again. ‖ MILIT. To re-enlist.

rengaine [rɑ̃gɛ:n] f. FAM. Catch-word, catchphrase; *la même rengaine*, the same old story.

rengainer [rɑ̃gɛne] v. tr. (1). To sheathe, to put up (une épée). ‖ FAM. *Rengainer son compliment*, to refrain from saying what one was about to say.

rengorgement [rɑ̃gɔrʒəmɑ̃] m. ZOOL. Strutting (d'un paon). ‖ FIG. Swaggering; putting on airs.

rengorger (se) [sərɑ̃gɔrʒe] v. pr. (7). ZOOL. To strut (paon). ‖ FIG. To swagger, to put on airs.

rengraisser [rɑ̃grɛse] v. tr. (1). AGRIC. To fatten again.
— v. intr. To put on fat again, to get fat again.

rengrener [rãgrəne] v. tr. (5). To put more corn into (la trémie). ‖ TECHN. To re-engage (un pignon).

reniable [rənjabl] adj. Deniable; able to be disavowed.

reniement [-nimã] m. Disavowal (d'une action); abjuration (de sa foi); repudiation (d'une opinion); denial (de qqn).

renier [-nje] v. tr. (1). To disavow (une action); to repudiate (une opinion); to deny (qqn). ‖ ECCLÉS. To abjure (sa foi); *renier Dieu*, to blaspheme.

reniflement [rənifləmã] m. Sniff; snuffling.

renifler [-fle] v. intr. (1). To sniff, to snuffle. ‖ FAM. To turn one's nose up (*sur*, at).
— v. tr. To sniff at, to smell (une fleur); to sniff (une odeur); to snuff up (du tabac). ‖ FAM. To smell, to scent (le danger).

renifleur [-flœ:r] s. Sniffer.

rennais, aise [rɛnɛ, ɛ:z] adj. GÉOGR. Of (ou) from Rennes.
— s. Native (ou) inhabitant of Rennes.

renne [rɛn] m. ZOOL. Reindeer.

renoircir [rənwarsi:r] v. tr. (2). To blacken (ou) darken again.

renom [rənɔ̃] m. Renown, reputation; *en renom*, renowned, famous; *sans renom*, unknown; *se faire un mauvais renom*, to get oneself a bad name.

renommé, ée [rənɔme] adj. Well-known, renowned.

renommée f. Fame (déesse). ‖ Fame, renoun (célébrité). ‖ Report, rumour, hearsay (ouï-dire). ‖ Reputation; *jouir d'une bonne renommée*, to have a good name.

renommer v. tr. (1). To re-elect.

renonce [rənɔ̃:s] f. SPORTS. Renounce; failure to follow suit (aux cartes); *se, faire une renonce d'une couleur*, to discard a suit.

renoncement [rənɔ̃smã] m. FIG. Renouncement, renouncing, giving up (à, of) [qqch.]; renunciation (abnégation); *renoncement de soi-même*, self-denial, self-sacrifice; *vie de renoncement*, life of renunciation.

renoncer [-se] v. intr. (6). *Renoncer à*, to waive (un droit); to renounce, to give up (une habitude); to abandon, to throw up (un projet); to relinquish (une succession); *renoncer au monde*, to renounce the world; *renoncer au tabac*, to give up smoking; *renoncer à faire*, to give up (ou) over trying to do; *y renoncer*, to give it up as a bad job; to throw up the sponge (fam.). ‖ SPORTS. To drop out (coureur); to renounce (aux cartes).
— v. tr. † To renounce (sa foi); to deny, to disown (qqn). [V. RENIER.]

renonciataire [-sjatɛ:r] s. JUR. Releasee.

renonciateur, trice [-sjatœ:r, tris] s. JUR. Releasor.

renonciation [-sjasjɔ̃] f. JUR. Renunciation, disclaimer (à un droit).

renoncule [rənɔ̃kyl] f. BOT. Ranunculus.

renouement [rənumã] m. Renewal (d'amitié).

renouer [-e] v. tr. (1). To tie up (ses cheveux); to tie again, reknot, to retie (un ruban). ‖ FIG. To take up again (une affaire); to renew (une amitié); to resume (une conversation).
— v. intr. To renew friendship (*avec*, with).

renouveau [rənuvo] m. Springtide, springtime, coming of spring. ‖ FIG. Revival; new lease (de vie).

renouvelable [-vlabl] adj. Renewable.

renouvelant, ante [-vlã, ã:t] s. ECCLÉS. Child renewing his (ou) her first communion.

renouveler [-vle] v. tr. (8 a). To renew (sa garderobe); to renovate (un mobilier); *renouveler son approvisionnement de*, to lay in a fresh stock of. ‖ JUR. To renew (un bail); to reopen (un procès).

‖ AUTOM. To fit a new set of (les pneus). ‖ ECCLÉS. To regenerate (une âme). ‖ COMM. To repeat (un ordre); to renew (son personnel). ‖ FIG. To revive (un chagrin); to reopen (une discussion); to transform, to change (la face du pays); to restore (ses forces); to revive, to bring in again (une mode); *renouveler connaissance avec*, to renew acquaintance with.
— v. pr. **Se renouveler,** to come back, to return (revenir); to be renewed (se rénover). ‖ FIN. To turn over (capital).

renouvellement [-vɛlmã] m. Renovation (d'un mobilier); *renouvellement des tentures d'une pièce*, doing-up a room (fam.). ‖ JUR. Renewal (d'un bail). ‖ ECCLÉS. Regeneration. ‖ FIG. Renewal, restoration (de ses forces); return (des saisons); increase (de tendresse, de zèle); *renouvellement de l'année*, start of a new year.

rénovateur, trice [renɔvatœ:r, tris] adj. Renewing, renovating, restoring.
— s. Renovator, restorer.

rénovation [-vasjɔ̃] f. Renovation, renewal, restoration. ‖ ECCLÉS. *Rénovation des mœurs*, religious revival. ‖ JUR. Renewal (d'un titre).

rénover [-ve] v. tr. (1). To renovate, to restore, to renew. ‖ JUR. To renew (un titre).

renseigné, ée [rãsɛɲe] adj. Informed (*sur*, about); *bien, mal renseigné*, well, ill-informed.

renseignement [rãsɛɲmã] m. Information, indication; piece of information; *aller aux renseignements*, to make enquiries; *avoir de bons renseignements sur*, to have had good reports about; *bureau de renseignements*, information bureau; *donner (ou) fournir des renseignements*, to give (ou) furnish particulars; *prendre des renseignements sur*, to inquire about; *tous renseignements pris*, after full enquiry. ‖ Inquiries, information bureau (bureau). ‖ MILIT. *Officier de renseignements*, intelligence officer; *Service de renseignements*, Intelligence Corps. ‖ FAM. *C'est un vrai bureau de renseignements*, he's a mine of information, he knows it all.

renseigner [-ɲe] v. tr. (1). To inform (*sur*, about) [qqn]; *mal renseigné sur*, misinformed about.
— v. pr. **Se renseigner,** to make inquiries, to inquire, to find out, to obtain information (*sur*, about); to inquire (*sur la façon de*, how to).

rentabiliser [rãtabilize] v. tr. (1). FIN., COMM. To make profitable, to make pay. ‖ FIG. To make pay (ou) worthwhile.

rentabilité [-bilite] f. FIN., COMM. Profitability, profitableness; *rentabilité des investissements*, return on investment; *seuil de rentabilité*, break-even point.

rentable [-bl] adj. FIN., COMM. Profitable, paying (affaire), cost-effective (investissement), which brings in good returns (placement). ‖ FIG. Worthwhile, U.S. juicy (fam.).

rentamer [rãtame] v. tr. (1). To resume, to start again.

rente [rã:t] f. FIN. Revenue, rent, unearned income; *faire une rente à qqn*, to make s.o. an allowance; *rente sur l'État*, government stock (ou) annuity; *rente viagère*, life annuity; *vivre de ses rentes*, to live on a private income.

rentier, ère [rãtje, ɛr] s. FIN. Rentier, stockholder; person living on private (ou) unearned income; *petit rentier*, small investor.

rentoilage [rãtwala:ʒ] m. Relining (de manchettes). ‖ ARTS. Transferring to a new canvas (d'un tableau).

rentoiler [-le] v. tr. (1). To reline (des manchettes). ‖ ARTS. To transfer to a new canvas (un tableau).

rentrage [rãtra:ʒ] m. Housing, cellaring.

rentrant, ante [rãtrã, ã:t] adj. MATH. Re-

entrant (angle). ‖ AVIAT. Retractrable (train d'atterrissage).
— s. SPORTS. Player taking the place of another; new player.
— m. MILIT. Re-entrant, recess.

rentré, ée [rɑ̃tre] adj. Suppressed (rage); hollow, sunken (yeux). ‖ MÉD. Suppressed (scarlatine).

rentrée f. Return, home-coming. ‖ Re-opening, re-assembly; *rentrée des classes,* first day of term (ou) U. S. school, start of a new term (ou) U. S. of the school year. ‖ AGRIC. Bringing (ou) gathering (ou) getting in (des foins). ‖ FIN. Collection, getting in (des effets); receipt, encashment (des fonds); collection, receipt (des impôts). ‖ THÉÂTR. Return, reappearance (d'un acteur); re-opening (d'un théâtre); *faire sa rentrée,* to return to the stage, to make a come-back. ‖ MUS. Re-entry (d'un motif). ‖ NAUT. Tumbling home (d'œuvres mortes); *rentrée au port,* return (ou) putting back to port. ‖ SPORTS. Entry card, re-entry (aux cartes).

rentrer v. intr. (1). To enter, to return, to come (ou) go back; *rentrer dans sa patrie,* to regain one's native land. ‖ To return home, to go (ou) come home; *il est l'heure de rentrer,* it's time to go home; *rentrer chez soi,* to come (ou) go back home; *rentrer souper,* to go home to (ou) for supper; *rentrer se coucher,* to go home to bed. ‖ To go in, to go behind a cloud (soleil). ‖ To recover; *rentrer dans son bien,* to get back (ou) recover one's property; *rentrer dans son droit,* to recover one's rights. ‖ To fit (*dans,* into); *tubes qui rentrent les uns dans les autres,* tubes that fit into one another. ‖ To be part (*dans,* of); to enter (*dans,* into); *cela ne rentre pas dans mes fonctions,* that does not come (ou) fall within my province; *cela n'entre pas dans mes intentions,* that is no part of my plans; *rentrer dans une catégorie,* to fall into a class (ou) category. ‖ To re-open (école); to re-assemble (parlement). ‖ MILIT. *Rentrer dans l'armée,* to re-join the army, to re-enlist. ‖ AVIAT. *Qui n'est pas rentré,* missing. ‖ NAUT. *Rentrer à bord,* to go back on board; *rentrer au port,* to put back to port. ‖ FIN. To come in, to be repaid (argent); *faire rentrer ses fonds,* to call in one's money; *rentrer dans ses frais,* to get back one's outlay. ‖ THÉÂTR. To return to the stage, to appear again (acteur); *rentrer en scène,* to come on again. ‖ MÉD. To go in (maladie éruptive). ‖ SPORTS. To cut in (au jeu de cartes). ‖ FIG. *Rentrer dans les bonnes grâces de qqn,* to get back into s.o's good books; *rentrer dans le néant,* to fall into oblivion; *rentrer en communication avec qqn,* to get into touch (ou) make contact with s.o. again; *rentrer en lice,* to take up the cudgels again; *rentrer en soi-même,* to think deeply, to indulge in serious reflections on one's conduct. ‖ FAM. *Je lui ai rentré dedans,* I pitched into him.
— v. tr. (1). To take (ou) bring (ou) get (ou) carry in. ‖ To draw back (le corps); *rentrer ses griffes,* to draw in (les griffes); to tuck in (les jambes); *rentrer les petits,* to take the children home. ‖ To shorten (raccourcir); *rentrer une robe,* to take a tuck in a dress. ‖ NAUT. To haul in (ou) aboard (l'ancre); to lay in (les avirons); to strike down (les couleurs); to haul up (ou) aboard (une embarcation); *rentrez!,* in oars! ‖ AVIAT. To retract (le train d'atterrissage). ‖ AGRIC. To bring in (des bêtes); to get (ou) gather (ou) bring in (la récolte). ‖ FIG. To restrain, to hold back; to choke back (ses larmes).

rentrouvrir [rɑ̃truvri:r] v. tr. (2). To half-open again.

renvelopper [rɑ̃vlɔpe] v. tr. (1). To wrap up again, to rewrap.

renversable [rɑ̃vɛrsabl] adj. Reversible. ‖ NAUT. Capsizable (canot).

renversant, ante [-sɑ̃, ɑ̃:t] adj. FAM. Amazing, staggering; *c'est renversant,* it's a stunner.

renverse [rɑ̃vɛrs] f. NAUT. Turn (de la marée); shift, change (du vent). ‖ LOC. *Tomber à la renverse,* to fall backwards (ou) on one's back.

renversé, ée [-se] adj. Inverted, reversed (image); inverse (ordre). ‖ NAUT. Hanging (compas). ‖ BLAS. Reversed, renversé. ‖ CULIN. *Crème renversée,* custard mould (ou) shape; U. S. baked custard. ‖ FAM. *C'est le monde renversé!,* I've never seen anything like it!; *en être renversé,* to be taken aback by (ou) at it.

renversement [-səmɑ̃] m. Upsetting, overturning (d'une chaise); spilling, upsetting (d'un liquide); throwing down (d'un mur). ‖ Reversal, inversion (d'une image); *renversement du ruban,* ribbon-reverse. ‖ NAUT. Turn (de la marée); shifting (du vent). ‖ PHYS. Reversal (de polarité). ‖ GÉOGR. Overturn. ‖ MUS., FIN. Inversion. ‖ JUR. Overthrow, subversion (d'un Etat); overthrow, defeat (d'un ministère). ‖ FIG. Confusion, upheaval.

renverser [rɑ̃vɛrse] v. tr. (1). To knock over, to upset (une chaise); to spill, to upset (un liquide); to throw down (un mur); *une voiture l'a renversé,* he's been knocked down by a car. ‖ To reverse, to turn upside down, to invert (une image). ‖ MILIT. To reverse (l'arme). ‖ NAUT. To capsize (un bateau). ‖ TECHN. To reverse (la vapeur). ‖ JUR. To subvert, to overthrow (un Etat); to defeat, to turn out (un ministère); to overthrow (un système). ‖ FIG. To upset, to confuse, to disturb. (V. BOULEVERSER.) ‖ FAM. To astonish, to astound, to stagger (v. STUPÉFIER); *cette nouvelle me renverse,* I can't get over that piece of news.
— v. intr. To overturn (voiture). ‖ NAUT. To capsize (bateau); to turn (marée).
— v. pr. **Se renverser,** to upset, to overturn, to turn over, to capsize; *se renverser dans un fauteuil,* to loll back in an armchair; *se renverser sur le dos,* to roll (ou) turn over on one's back.

renvoi [rɑ̃vwa] m. Returning, throwing back (d'une balle); returning, sending back (d'un cadeau). ‖ Putting off, postponing, postponement (d'un projet). ‖ Dismissal (d'un domestique); expulsion, expelling (d'un élève). ‖ Reference, foot-note; *renvoi en marge,* marginal note. ‖ PHYS. Reflecting, reflection (de la lumière); reverberation (du son). ‖ JUR. Dismissal (d'un ministre); adjournment (d'un procès à plus tard); transfer (d'un procès à une autre juridiction); commitment (d'un projet de loi à une commission). ‖ MÉD. Eructation; belch. ‖ MUS. Repeat, repeat sign. ‖ TECHN. *Arbre de renvoi,* layshaft.

renvoyer [-je] v. tr. (9a). To return, to throw (une balle); to return, to send back (un cadeau); to send back (qqn). ‖ To put off, to postpone (une affaire). ‖ To dismiss (un domestique); to expel (un élève); to turn away (qqn). ‖ To refer; *renvoyer au texte original,* to refer to the original text. ‖ PHYS. To reflect (la lumière); to reverberate (un son). ‖ JUR. To remand (un accusé); to refer (*devant,* to) [une affaire]; to dismiss (un ministre); to commit (un projet de loi); *renvoyer à huitaine,* to adjourn for a week. ‖ MILIT. To discharge, to demobilize (un militaire).

réoccupation [reɔkypasjɔ̃] f. Reoccupation.

réoccuper [-pe] v. tr. (1). To reoccupy.

réopérer [reɔpere] v. tr. (5). MÉD. To operate on again.
— v. intr. MÉD. To operate again.

réorchestration [reɔrkɛstrasjɔ̃] f. MUS. Reorchestration.

réorchestrer [-tre] v. tr. (1). MUS. To reorchestrate.

réorganisateur [reɔrganizatœ:r] adj. Reorganizing.
— s. Reorganizer.
réorganisation [-zasjɔ̃] f. Reórganization.
réorganiser [-ze] v. tr. (1). To reorganize.
réorientation [reɔrjɑ̃tasjɔ̃] f. Redirecting, reorientation. ‖ Redirecting towards a new course of studies (d'un élève, d'un étudiant).
réorienter [-te] v. tr. (1). To redirect, to reorient, to reorientate (le regard, un projecteur, un passant égaré). ‖ To redirect (ou) guide towards a new course of studies (un élève, un étudiant).
— v. pr. **Se réorienter,** to find one's bearings (dans l'espace), to turn (vers, towards), to switch (vers, to) [vers une carrière, une idéologie].
réouverture [reuvɛrty:r] f. Reopening.
repaire [rəpɛ:r] m. Den (de bête féroce). ‖ Haunt, hide-out (de criminels); nest (de pirates); den (de voleurs).
repaître [rəpɛ:tr] v. tr. (86). AGRIC. To feed, to graze (des animaux). ‖ FIG. To fill (de, with) [espérance]; to feast (de, on) [ses yeux].
— v. pr. **Se repaître,** to eat one's fill; se repaître de, to feed on. ‖ FIG. Se repaître de chimères, to feed on empty hopes; se repaître de sang, to wallow in blood.
répandre [repɑ̃:dr] v. tr. (4). To pour out, to spill (de l'eau); to scatter, to strew (des fleurs); to shed (des larmes); to spread, to diffuse (la lumière); to give off (ou) out (une odeur); to sprinkle (du sable, du sel); to shed (du sang). ‖ To spread (des bienfaits); to propagate (une doctrine); to broadcast, to circulate, to spread (une nouvelle).
— v. pr. **Se répandre,** to go out (ou) about (dans le monde). ‖ To spread (sur, over) [liquide]. ‖ To be profuse; se répandre en excuses, to apologize profusely; se répandre en invectives, to let out a torrent of abuse. ‖ FIG. To spread, to become widespread (nouvelle); to gain ground (opinion).
répandu, ue [-pɑ̃dy] adj. Generally accepted, widely held (opinion). ‖ Often seen, widely known (personne); être répandu dans le monde, to go about (ou) move in society.
réparable [reparabl] adj. Reparable, mendable (vêtement). ‖ FIG. Amendable, able to be put right (erreur); retrievable (perte).
reparaître [rəparɛ:tr] v. intr. (74). To reappear, to appear again, to turn up again (personne); to come out again (soleil).
réparateur, trice [reparatœ:r, tris] adj. Restoring, refreshing (sommeil).
— s. Repairer, mender.
réparation [-rasjɔ̃] f. Repair, repairing (d'une machine, d'un pont); en réparation, under repair. ‖ JUR. Réparation civile, compensation. ‖ FIG. Reparation, amends, redress (d'un tort); faire une réparation d'honneur, to make a full apology; refuser réparation à qqn, to refuse s.o. satisfaction; réparation par les armes, duel.
réparatoire [-ratwa:r] adj. Reparative.
réparer [-re] v. tr. (1). To refit (un bateau); to repair, to overhaul (une machine); to repair, to restore (une maison); to mend (des souliers); to patch (des vêtements). ‖ FIG. To make good (un dommage); to correct (une faute); to recruit, to restore (ses forces); to atone for (une offense); to retrieve (des pertes); to make up for (le temps perdu); to redress, to put right (un tort).
reparler [rəparle] v. intr. (1). To speak again (de, of, about); to refer again (de, to). ‖ To speak again (à, to) [qqn]; nous nous reparlons, we are on speaking terms again.
repartager [rəpartaʒe] v. tr. (7). To share out again.

repartie [rəparti] f. Repartee, retort; reparties spirituelles, witty rejoinders.
repartir [rəparti:r] v. intr. (93). To set out (ou) start off again; repartir à zéro, to start from scratch again. ‖ To reply, to retort (répliquer).
répartir [reparti:r] v. tr. (2). To share out, to divide, to distribute. ‖ FIN. To allot (des actions); to distribute (un dividende); to assess (des impôts).
— v. pr. **Se répartir,** to split up, to break up, to be divided.
répartissable [-tisabl] adj. Dividable; assessable; assignable.
répartiteur, trice [-titœ:r, tris] s. Distributor, divider. ‖ FIN. Assessor (d'impôts). ‖ NAUT. Adjuster (d'avaries).
répartition [-tisjɔ̃] f. FIN. Allotment (des actions); distribution (d'un dividende); apportionment, sharing out (des frais); assessment (des impôts). ‖ FIG. Division (du travail).
repas [rəpɑ] m. Meal; repas de noce, wedding breakfast; repas froid, cold snack; faire son repas de, to dine off; heure du repas, meal time.
repassage [rəpɑsa:ʒ] m. Recrossing (d'une rivière). ‖ Ironing (du linge). ‖ Whetting, grinding, sharpening (d'une lame). ‖ Stropping (sur le cuir); honing (à la pierre) [d'un rasoir]. ‖ Going over (ou) running through again (d'une leçon).
repasse [-pɑ:s] f. AGRIC. Coarse flour with bran. ‖ CHIM. Faints.
repasser [-pɑse] v. intr. (1). To repass, to call again, to come (ou) pass again; to drop in again (fam.); je repasserai ce soir, I'll look in again this evening. ‖ FIG. To run through (ou) in; pensée qui me repasse dans la tête, thought that keeps running through my head.
— v. tr. To repass, to pass by again; repasser la mer, to cross the sea again. ‖ To iron (du linge); fer à repasser, iron; planche à repasser, ironing-board. ‖ To sharpen, to whet (un couteau); to strop (un rasoir sur le cuir); to hone (à la pierre). ‖ FIG. To sit again for (un examen); to think over; to turn over (dans, in) [une idée]; to go over (une leçon).
repasseur [-pɑsœ:r] m. Grinder (de couteaux).
repasseuse [-pɑsø:z] f. Ironer (de linge). ‖ Ironing-machine.
repayer [rəpɛje] v. tr. (9b). To pay again, to repay.
repêchage [rəpɛʃa:ʒ] m. Finding out (ou) up again (d'un objet). ‖ SPORTS. Fishing up again. ‖ FAM. Giving a second chance (de, to) [un candidat]; lending (ou) giving a helping hand (de, to) [qqn].
repêcher [rəpɛʃe] v. tr. (1). To fish for again (des poissons). ‖ To fish out (ou) up again (un objet). ‖ FAM. To give a second chance of passing to (un candidat); to lend (ou) give a helping hand to (qqn).
repeindre [rəpɛ̃:dr] v. tr. (59). To paint again (ou) anew, to repaint (des boiseries). ‖ FIG. To depict, to revisualise (un spectacle dans l'esprit).
repenser [rəpɑ̃se] v. intr. (1). To think again; y repenser, to think it over.
repentant, ante [-tɑ̃, ɑ̃:t] adj. Repentant, repenting, penitent.
— s. Penitent.
repenti, ie [-ti] adj. Repentant, penitent. ‖ ECCLÉS. Fille repentie, Magdalen.
— s. Penitent. ‖ Couvent des repenties, Magdalen hospice.
repentir [-ti:r] m. Repentance.
repentir (se) [sərəpɑ̃ti:r] v. pr. (93). To repent; se repentir de, to be sorry for, to repent, to rue.
repérable [rəperabl] adj. Locatable, noticeable; facilement, difficilement repérable, easy, difficult to spot.

repérage [rəpera:ʒ] m. TECHN. Synchronization (d'un film); marking with guide (ou) reference marks (d'un instrument); marking the lay (en typographie). ‖ MILIT. Spotting, locating (d'une batterie); *repérage par le son*, sound-ranging; *appareil de repérage par le son*, sound-detector (ou) -locator.

répercussion [repɛrkysjɔ̃] f. MÉD. Repercussion. ‖ PHYS. Reverberation (du son). ‖ FIG. Pl. Consequences; after-effects.

répercuter [-kyte] v. tr. (1). PHYS. To reflect (la chaleur); to reverberate, to throw back (le son). ‖ FIG. To echo (une opinion).
— v. pr. **Se répercuter,** to be reflected (lumière); to reverberate (son). ‖ FIG. To have repercussions (action).

reperdre [rəpɛ:rdr] v. tr. (80). To lose again.

repère [rəpɛ:r] m. Reference. ‖ GÉOGR. Benchmark, disc; *ligne de repère*, datum line; *point de repère*, landmark. ‖ CINÉM. Synchronizing mark. ‖ TECHN. Lay-mark (en typographie). ‖ FIG. Landmark.

repérer [-pere] v. tr. (5). TECHN. To mark with reference marks (un instrument); to adjust, to fix by guide marks (une machine). ‖ To register (une impression); to mark the lay on (une page). ‖ CINÉM. To synchronize. ‖ MILIT. To locate, to spot (une batterie). ‖ FAM. To spot.
— v. pr. **Se repérer,** to take one's bearings.

répertoire [repɛrtwa:r] m. Index list, catalogue; *appartenant à un répertoire*, repertorial; *répertoire alphabétique*, alphabetical index; *répertoire d'adresses*, address-book. ‖ JUR. Summary. ‖ THÉÂTR. Repertoire, repertory; *du répertoire*, stock. ‖ FIG. Store house of (souvenirs); *répertoire vivant*, mine of information.

répertorier [-tɔrje] v. tr. (1). To index (un article); to make a catalogue of (des volumes).

repeser [rəpəze] v. tr. (5). To re-weigh, to weigh again.

répétailler [repetɑje] v. tr. (1). FAM. To keep on repeating, to repeat ad nauseam.

répéter [repete] v. tr. (5). To repeat, to say again. ‖ To repeat (une calomnie); to relate again (une histoire); to recite, to say again (une leçon). ‖ To repeat, to do again (une action); to carry out again (un exercice). ‖ To reflect (une image); to re-echo (un son). ‖ THÉÂTR. To rehearse (une pièce, un rôle); *répéter de bout en bout*, to act over, to run through.
— v. pr. **Se répéter,** to repeat oneself, to say the same thing again (personne). ‖ To recur (événement).

répétiteur, trice [-titœ:r, tris] s. Assistant lecturer (à l'Ecole polytechnique); assistant master (ou) mistress (dans un lycée). ‖ Private tutor, coach.
— m. NAUT. Repeating ship, repeater. ‖ RADIO. Repeater.

répétitif, ive [-titif, i:v] adj. Repetitive.

répétition [-tisjɔ̃] f. Repetition (d'une action, d'un geste, d'un mot); *montre à répétition*, repeater watch, repeater. ‖ Private lesson; *donner des répétitions*, to do private coaching, to give private lessons. ‖ THÉÂTR. Rehearsal; *en répétition*, in rehearsal; *répétition générale*, dress rehearsal. ‖ MILIT. *Fusil à répétition*, repeating rifle, repeater. ‖ MÉD. *Maladie à répétition*, recurrent illness.

repétrir [rəpetri:r] v. tr. (2). To knead again (de la pâte). ‖ FIG. To mould again (l'esprit).

repeuplement [rəpœpləmɑ̃] m. Restocking (d'un étang); replanting (d'une forêt); repeopling, repopulation (d'un pays).

repeupler [rəpœple] v. tr. (1). To restock (un étang); to replant (une forêt); to repeople, to repopulate (un pays).

repincer [rəpɛ̃se] v. tr. (6). To pinch (ou) nip again. ‖ FAM. To catch again.

repiquage [rəpika:ʒ] m. Repairing, mending (du pavé). ‖ Restitching (d'un vêtement). ‖ AGRIC. Pricking (ou) planting out, bedding (d'une plante). ‖ TECHN. Rerecording (d'un disque), retaping (d'une bande magnétique), retouching (d'une photo).

repiquer [rəpike] v. tr. (1). To prick again. ‖ To repair, to mend (le pavé). ‖ To restitch (un vêtement). ‖ AGRIC. To prick (ou) plant out (une plante); *à repiquer*, bedding. ‖ TECHN. To rerecord (un disque), to retape (une bande magnétique), to retouch (une photo).
— v. intr. FAM. *Repiquer au plat*, to have a second helping; *repiquer au truc*, to get down to it again; to have another bash (pop.).

répit [repi] m. Respite; *ne laisser aucun répit à qqn*, to allow s.o. no breathing-space; *prendre un moment de répit*, to take a breather; *sans répit*, without respite.

replacement [rəplasmɑ̃] m. Replacement, replacing, putting back, returning to its place. ‖ Finding a fresh situation (de, for) [un domestique]. ‖ FIN. Reinvestment (des fonds).

replacer [rəplase] v. tr. (6). To put back, to replace, to return to its place (un objet). ‖ To find a fresh situation for (un domestique). ‖ FIN. To reinvest (des fonds).

replanter [rəplɑ̃te] v. tr. (1). AGRIC. To replant.

replat [rəpla] m. Levelling off (d'une montagne).

replâtrage [rəplɑtra:ʒ] m. ARCHIT. Replastering (d'un mur). ‖ FAM. Short-lived settlement; patched-up peace.

replâtrer [-tre] v. tr. (1). ARCHIT. To carry out temporary repairs; to replaster. ‖ FAM. To settle temporarily; to patch up.

replet, ète [rəplɛ, ɛ:t] adj. Fat, stout, plump.

réplétion [replesjɔ̃] f. Repletion.

repleuvoir [rəplœvwa:r] v. impers. (76). To rain again.

repli [rəpli] m. Crease (dans de l'étoffe); fold (dans du papier). ‖ Coil (d'un serpent). ‖ GÉOGR. Fold, undulation (du terrain). ‖ MILIT. Withdrawal, falling back. ‖ FIG. Pl. Innermost recesses (de l'âme).

repliable [rəplijabl] adj. Foldable; that can be turned up (ou) bent. ‖ NAUT. *Berthon repliable*, collapsible boat.

repliement [rəplimɑ̃] m. Folding; folding back, turning up. ‖ MILIT. Withdrawal, falling back.

replier [rəplije] v. tr. (1). To turn up (le bas d'un pantalon); to bend, to double up (son corps); to fold again, to fold up again, to refold (une feuille de papier); to close (un parapluie); to coil up again (un rouleau de corde). ‖ MILIT. To withdraw (ses troupes).
— v. pr. **Se replier,** to curl up (feuille); to twist, to meander (fleuve); to double up (personne); to twist, to turn (sentier); to coil up (serpent); *se replier sur soi-même*, to retire into one's shell. ‖ MILIT. To withdraw, to fall back. ‖ FIN. To fall back (ou) away, to go back.

réplique [replik] f. Reply, retort, rejoinder; *sans réplique*, unanswerable (argument); *pas de réplique*, don't you dare answer me back! ‖ THÉÂTR. Cue; *donner la réplique à qqn*, to give s.o. his cue. ‖ JUR. Replication. ‖ MUS. Replicate. ‖ AUTOM. Replica.

répliquer [replike] v. intr. (1). To reply, to retort; *répliquer à qqn*, to answer s.o. back.
— v. tr. To answer.

replisser [rəplise] v. tr. (1). To pleat again, to refold.

replonger [rəplɔ̃ʒe] v. tr. (7). To plunge (ou) immerse again; to dip again (dans, into). ‖ FIG. To plunge again (dans, into).
— v. intr. To plunge (ou) dive again.

— v. pr. **Se replonger,** to dive (ou) plunge again. ‖ FIG. To immerse oneself again (*dans*, in).

repolir [rəpɔliːr] v. tr. (2). To repolish, to polish again, to reburnish (un métal). ‖ To touch (ou) furbish up (un ouvrage).

repolissage [-lisaː3] m. Repolishing, reburnishing, burnishing up again.

répondant, ante [repɔ̃dɑ̃, ɑ̃ːt] s. JUR. Surety, guarantor, warrantor; *être le répondant de*, to go bail for.
— m. FAM. *Avoir du répondant*, to be worth a packet, to be a man of means.

répondeur, euse [-dœːr, øːz] adj. Who answers back, argumentative (enfant).
— m. TECHN. Telephone answering machine, Ansafone (nom déposé).

répondre [repɔ̃ːdr] v. tr. (4). To answer, to reply; *répondre une impertinence*, to make a rude (ou) impertinent reply.
— v. intr. To answer, to reply; *bien, mal répondre*, to give a fair, a poor answer; *l'écho répond*, back comes the echo; *répondre en claquant la porte*, to reply by slamming the door. ‖ *Répondre à*, to respond to (un appel); to answer (la porte); to answer (ou) acknowledge (une lettre); to write back, to reply to (qqn). ‖ ECCLÉS. To make the responses (à la messe). ‖ COMM. To come up (à, to) [l'échantillon]. ‖ JUR. *Répondre à une accusation*, to answer a charge. ‖ FIG. *Répondre à*, to return, to requite (l'amour); to meet, to satisfy (un besoin); to answer (un but); to answer, to meet (des conditions); to repay, to meet (un désir); to come up to, to fall short of (une espérance); *pour répondre à l'un des sentiments les plus humains*, to appease a fundamental emotion. ‖ *Répondre de*, to answer for, to hold oneself responsible (ou) answerable for (qqch., qqn); *je vous réponds de sa loyauté*, I guarantee his loyalty; *il est honnête, je vous en réponds*, he is honest, you can take it from me. ‖ *Répondre pour*, to answer for, to stand as surety for, to guarantee (qqn). ‖ To correspond (à, to), to be symmetrical (à, with); *ce pavillon ne répond pas à l'autre*, this pavilion does not match the other. ‖ FAM. *Je vous en réponds!*, You bet! No kidding! ‖ FAM. To talk back (répliquer).

répons [repɔ̃] m. ECCLÉS. Response.

réponse [repɔ̃ːs] f. Answer, reply (à, to) [une question]; *pour toute réponse il tourna les talons*, his only reply was to turn on his heel. ‖ Response (à, to) [un appel, un sentiment]; *rester sans réponse*, to meet with no response. ‖ COMM. *En réponse à*, in reply to; *réponse payée*, reply paid. ‖ JUR. *Droit de réponse*, right of reply.

repopulation [rəpɔpylasjɔ̃] f. Repopulation (d'un pays); restocking (d'une rivière).

report [rəpɔːr] m. Carrying forward (ou) over (en calcul); bringing forward (d'une somme); carry-over (montant); *faire un report*, to carry over, to bring forward; *report à nouveau*, balance to next account. ‖ FIN. Contango, contangoing, continuation (en Bourse); *au taux de report*, contango rate. ‖ TECHN. Transfer (en lithographie); *papier à report*, transfer-paper.

reportable [rəpɔrtabl] adj. FIN. Contangoable, continuable.

reportage [-taːʒ] m. Report, reporting; series of articles (dans un journal); *faire le reportage de*, to cover; *reportage sensationnel et exclusif*, scoop. ‖ RADIO. Running commentary.

reporter [-te] v. tr. (1). To take (ou) carry (ou) bring back (porter de nouveau). ‖ To postpone, to put off (différer). ‖ MATH. To carry over, to bring (ou) carry forward (un total); *à reporter*, carried forward. ‖ FIN. To contango, to carry over, to continue (en Bourse). ‖ TECHN. To trans-

fer (en lithographie). ‖ FIG. To take (ou) carry back in imagination (à, to).
— v. tr., intr. FIN. To contango; to borrow (ou) carry stock.
— v. pr. **Se reporter,** to refer to (à, to) [une autorité]. ‖ FIG. To go back (à, to); to look back (à, on) [une chose passée].

reporter [-tɛ:r] m. Reporter (d'un journal).

reporteur [-tœːr] m. FIN. Taker.

repos [rəpo] m. Repose, rest; peace and quiet; *au repos*, at rest; *avoir la conscience en repos*, to have an easy conscience; *de tout repos*, safe, reliable; *en repos*, at rest, in repose; *prendre un peu de repos*, to take a little time off. ‖ Rest (dans la mort); *champ du repos*, last resting-place. ‖ MILIT. *Au repos*, at half-cock (fusil); standing at ease, off duty (soldat); *repos!*, stand easy!; U. S. at ease! ‖ AGRIC. *Au repos*, lying fallow (terre). ‖ MUS. Pause. ‖ FIN. *Valeur de tout repos*, gilt-edged security. ‖ TECHN. *Au repos*, at rest, not running (machine).

reposant, ante [-zɑ̃, ɑ̃ːt] adj. Restful (lieu); refreshing (sommeil).

repose. V. REPOSER. ‖ **Repose-pied,** m. inv. Foot-rest. ‖ **Repose-tête,** m. inv. Head-rest.

reposé, ée [-ze] adj. Rested, refreshed (air); fresh (teint); *à tête reposée*, at leisure, after due (ou) sufficient time for thought.

reposer [-ze] v. tr. (1). To lay (ou) place (ou) put (ou) set down again; to replace, to put back in place (replacer); *reposer un livre sur la table*, to put a book back on the table, to lay a book down on the table again. ‖ To rest (appuyer); *reposer sa tête sur*, to rest (ou) lay one's head back on. ‖ CH. DE F. To relay (une voie). ‖ FIG. To rest (l'esprit); *reposer les yeux sur*, to rest one's eyes (ou) let one's eyes rest on.
— v. intr. To rest, to repose, to lie; *la maison repose sur le roc*, the house is built upon rock. ‖ To rest (dans la mort); *ici repose*, here lies; *qu'il repose en paix!*, may he rest in peace! ‖ To sleep (dormir); *passer la nuit sans reposer*, to pass a sleepless night. ‖ To stand (liquide); *laisser reposer du vin*, to let wine stand (ou) settle. ‖ FIG. To repose, to be based (sur, on); *ne reposer sur rien de certain*, to be ill-founded (raisonnement).
— v. pr. **Se reposer,** to rest, to take (ou) have a rest (personne); to rest, to come to rest (sur, on) [yeux]. ‖ ZOOL. To settle (ou) alight again (oiseau). ‖ FIG. To rely, to count, to depend (sur, on); to put one's trust (sur, in) [qqch., qqn]; *se reposer sur qqn du soin d'une affaire*, to leave a matter in s.o.'s hands, to entrust a matter to s.o.

reposoir [-zwaːr] m. ECCLÉS. Temporary altar.

reposséder [rəpɔsede] v. tr. (1). To re-possess, to possess again.

repoussage [rəpusaːʒ] m. Repelling, repulsing, driving back. ‖ ARTS. Embossing; repoussé-work.

repoussant, ante [-sɑ̃, ɑ̃ːt] adj. Repellent, repellant, repulsive (air); foul, offensive (odeur).

repousse [rəpus] f. Fresh (ou) second growth.

repoussé, ée [-se] adj. ARTS. Chased (argenterie); embossed (cuir); repoussé (ouvrage).
— m. ARTS. Repoussé; raised (ou) embossed work.

repoussement [-smɑ̃] m. Repulse, repulsing (de qqn). ‖ MILIT. Kick, kick-back, recoil (d'une arme à feu). ‖ FIG. Rejection, voting down (d'une idée); snub, snubbing (de qqn).

repousser [-se] v. tr. (1). To push (ou) shove again; to push (ou) shove back (qqch., qqn); *repousser faute de place*, to crowd out. ‖ To fling back (la porte); to push in (ou) home (un tiroir); to throw back (les volets). ‖ MILIT. To beat off (une attaque); to repel, to drive off (l'ennemi). ‖ BOT. To put out again (des branches); to grow

again (des feuilles). ‖ JUR. To negative (un amendement) ; to deny (une accusation) ; to refuse (une couronne) ; to reject, to throw out (un projet de loi). ‖ FIG. To spurn (des avances) ; to decline, to turn down (une offre) ; to repel, to be repellent to (qqn) ; to put off, to defer, to postpone (un rendez-vous) ; to resist, to put aside (ou) away (la tentation).
— v. intr. To grow again (barbe). ‖ BOT. To sprout again (feuille). ‖ MILIT. To recoil, to kick, to kick back (fusil). ‖ ARTS. To do repoussé work. ‖ FIG. To repel, to be offensive (odeur).

repoussoir [-swa:r] m. TECHN. Driving-bolt, drift. ‖ ARTS. Foreground with high tones. ‖ FAM. Foil ; *servir de repoussoir à qqn*, to act as a foil to s.o. ; to set off s.o.'s merits.

répréhensible [repreɑ̃sibl] adj. Reprehensible.

répréhensif, ive [-sif, i:v] adj. Reprehensive.

répréhension [-sjɔ̃] f. Reprehension.

reprendre [rəprɑ̃:dr] v. tr. (80). To take back (un cadeau). ‖ To re-admit (un élève) ; to take back (ou) on again, to reinstate (un employé). ‖ To put on again, to go back (ou) revert to (ses vêtements d'été). ‖ To pick up (qqn) ; *je viendrai vous reprendre chez vous*, I'll pick you up at your place. ‖ CULIN. To take (ou) have a second helping of (un mets) ; to take more (du pain). ‖ MILIT. To take up again (les armes) ; to reopen (les hostilités) ; to take again, to recapture (un prisonnier évadé) ; to take again, to retake (une ville). ‖ NAUT. *Reprendre la mer*, to put out to sea again ; *reprendre le vent*, to get one's bearings. ‖ THÉÂTR. To revive (une pièce). ‖ MÉD. To catch again (une maladie) ; to recover (ses sens) ; *reprendre froid*, to catch cold again. ‖ ARCHIT. To repair (un mur) ; *reprendre un mur en sous-œuvre*, to underpin a wall. ‖ FIN. To buy (ou) acquire more of (des actions). ‖ SPORTS. To return (un drive) ; to take (une volée). ‖ FIG. To put on (ou) adopt again (un air revêche) ; to adopt (ou) take up again, to re-assume (une attitude) ; to resume (son discours) ; to carry on (la conversation) ; to pluck up (son courage) ; to recover (ses forces) ; to take up again (ses études) ; to recapitulate (les faits) ; to go back to, to revert to (une habitude) ; to take back (sa parole) ; to resume (sa place) ; to resume (une tâche) ; *reprendre le dessus*, to regain the upper hand ; *reprendre la parole*, to go on speaking again, to take up the tale. ‖ FIG. To reprove, to admonish, to find fault with (réprimander) ; to chide (*de*, for) ; *on ne cesse de le reprendre*, he's always being nagged ; they are always getting at him (fam.).
— v. intr. To freeze over again (geler de nouveau). ‖ To set in again (froid). ‖ To come in (ou) back again (mode). ‖ To go on speaking ; *oui, reprit-il*, yes, he went on (ou) replied ; *reprenons !*, let's take it up again. ‖ BOT. To take (ou) strike root (plante). ‖ THÉÂTR. To start to draw the crowd (pièce). ‖ MÉD. To heal up (ou) over (blessure) ; to knit (os) ; to be on the way to recovery (malade) ; to put on flesh (personne amaigrie). ‖ COMM. To improve (affaire).
— v. pr. **Se reprendre,** to recover oneself, to take a hold on oneself, to pull oneself together ; *se reprendre à la vie*, to take on a new lease of life ; *s'y reprendre plusieurs fois avant de réussir*, to have several tries at sth. before succeeding. ‖ To correct oneself in speaking ; *se reprendre à temps*, to catch oneself in time.

représailles [rəprezɑ:j] f. plur. Reprisals (*de*, for) ; *camp de représailles*, punishment camp ; *user de représailles*, to make reprisals.

représentable [rəprezɑ̃tabl] adj. THÉÂTR. Performable.

représentant, ante [-tɑ̃, ɑ̃:t] adj. Representative.

— s. JUR. Representative. ‖ COMM. Representative, agent (v. PLACIER, VOYAGEUR) ; *représentant de commerce*, representative, salesman, commercial traveller, U.S. travelling salesman.

représentatif, ive [-tatif, i:v] adj. Representative.

représentation [-tasjɔ̃] f. Representation. ‖ Production, showing again, exhibition (de titres). ‖ State display ; dignity of official position ; parade (état social). ‖ JUR. Representation (de la nation). ‖ COMM. Representation, agency. ‖ THÉÂTR. Performance (d'une pièce) ; *avoir beaucoup de représentations*, to have a long run ; *droit de représentation*, performing rights ; *représentation au bénéfice d'une œuvre*, charity (ou) U. S. benefit performance. ‖ ARTS. Representation, image. ‖ FIG. Remonstrance, protest, representation ; *faire des représentations à*, to remonstrate with, to make representation to.

représenter [-te] v. tr. (1). To produce, to show, to exhibit (des titres). ‖ To put forward again (un candidat) ; to represent, to sit for (une circonscription). ‖ To represent, to stand (ou) act for (un chef d'Etat). ‖ To introduce again (une personne déjà présentée). ‖ COMM. To represent, to be (ou) act as agents for (une maison de commerce). ‖ THÉÂTR. To take the rôle of, to play the part of (un personnage) ; to stage, to perform, to put on (une pièce). ‖ ARTS. To depict, to portray, to represent (une scène). ‖ FIG. To point out ; *représenter qqch. à qqn*, to represent sth. to s.o., to warn s.o. about sth. ; *représenter à qqn les inconvénients d'une action*, to draw s.o.'s attention to the drawbacks of a course of action. ‖ To recall, to call to mind (rappeler) ; to symbolize (symboliser).
— v. intr. To keep up appearances ; *représenter bien*, to be personable, to be of good appearance, to look distinguished, to have a distinguished air ; *représenter mal*, to be lacking in personal presence, to have a poor personal appearance.
— v. pr. **Se représenter,** to present (ou) introduce oneself again. ‖ To occur (ou) crop up again (occasion) ; to appear (ou) turn up again (personne). ‖ To imagine (se figurer). ‖ THÉÂTR. To be produced (ou) staged (ou) performed (ou) put on again (pièce). ‖ JUR. To stand again (candidat).

répressible [reprɛsibl] adj. Repressible.

répressif, ive [-sif, i:v] adj. Repressive.

répression [-sjɔ̃] f. Repression.

reprêter [rəprɛte] v. tr. (1). To lend again.

réprimable [reprimabl] adj. Repressible.

réprimandable [reprimɑ̃dabl] adj. Reprovable, blameworthy ; deserving reproof.

réprimande [reprimɑ̃d] f. Rebuke, reprimand, censure. (V. REPROCHE.)

réprimander [-mɑ̃de] v. tr. (1). To reprimand, to rebuke, to reprove, to scold.

réprimant, ante [reprimɑ̃, ɑ̃:t] adj. Repressive.

réprimer [-me] v. tr. (1). To repress (en général). ‖ To smother, to strangle, to suppress (un bâillement). ‖ To curb, to keep in check (les passions).

repris, ise [rəpri, iz] adj. Retaken, recaptured (prisonnier). ‖ MÉD. *Etre repris d'une maladie*, to suffer from a recurrence of an illness.
— s. JUR. *Repris de justice*, old offender, habitual (ou) hardened criminal ; old lag (fam.).

reprisage [rəpriza:ʒ] m. Darning, mending.

reprise [rəpri:z] f. Fresh spell (du froid) ; *reprise des classes*, beginning of a term. ‖ Darning, mending ; darn ; *point de reprise*, darning stitch ; *reprise perdue*, invisible darn (ou) mend. ‖ *A deux reprises*, twice, on two successive occasions ; *à maintes reprises*, repeatedly, many times over, over and over again ; *à plusieurs reprises*, on several occasions, several times over ; *à quatre reprises*, four times running ; *faire qqch. par* *reprises,* to do sth. a little at a time. ‖ COMM. Buying in (des effets); taking back, return (des invendus); *reprise des affaires,* recovery of business, trade revival; *reprise en compte, vente en reprise,* U. S. trading in. ‖ JUR. *Reprises matrimoniales,* recovery of belongings; *droit de reprise,* right to recover possession. ‖ THÉÂTR. Revival (d'une pièce). ‖ MUS. Repetition, repeat; re-entry (du sujet). ‖ ARCHIT. Repair, repairing (d'un édifice); resumption, restarting (des travaux). ‖ AUTOM. Acceleration, pick-up (d'un moteur). ‖ AGRIC. Striking (d'une bouture). ‖ SPORTS. Bout; reprise (d'un assaut d'escrime); second half, resumption of play (au football); round (d'un match de boxe). ‖ MILIT. Resumption, renewal (des hostilités); retaking, recapture, recovery (d'une ville). ‖ GRAMM. *Reprise interrogative,* tag question.

repriser [rəprize] v. tr. (1). To darn (un bas); to mend (une robe). [V. RACCOMMODER.]

réprobateur, trice [reprɔbatœːr, tris] adj. Reproachful, reproving, reprobatory.

réprobation [-sjɔ̃] f. Reprobation, disapproval, censure.

reprochable [rəprɔʃabl] adj. Reproachable; deserving of blame. ‖ JUR. Who can be objected to, to whom exception can be taken (témoin).

reproche [rəprɔʃ] m. Reproach, reproof, censure; *à l'abri du reproche,* beyond reproach; *faire des reproches à,* to reproach, to rebuke; *sans reproche,* blameless. ‖ JUR. *Sans reproche,* reliable (témoin).

reprocher [rəprɔʃe] v. tr. (1). *Reprocher qqch. à qqn,* to reproach s.o. with sth., to blame s.o. for sth. (blâmer); *je n'ai rien à me reprocher,* I've nothing to reproach myself with, I am entirely blameless; *reprocher ses défauts à qqn,* to upbraid s.o. for his shortcomings. ‖ *Reprocher qqch. à qqn,* to begrudge (ou) grudge s.o. sth. (trouver à redire à); *reprocher à qqn tous les morceaux qu'il mange,* to grudge s.o. every bite he eats; *reprocher son bonheur à qqn,* to begrudge s.o. his good fortune. ‖ *Reprocher qqch. à qqn,* to remind s.o. reproachfully of sth. (rappeler avec aigreur); *reprocher aux gens les services qu'on leur a rendus,* to reproach people for forgetting services rendered.

reproducteur, trice [rəprɔdyktœːr, tris] adj. MÉD. Reproductive, reproducing (organes). ‖ ZOOL. Kept for breeding purposes (animal).
— m. Animal kept for breeding purposes.

reproductible [-tibl] adj. Reproductible.

reproductif, ive [-tif, iːv] adj. Reproductive.

reproduction [-sjɔ̃] f. MÉD., ZOOL. Reproduction; *organes de la reproduction,* reproductive organs. ‖ COMM. Duplicating, manifolding. ‖ ARTS. Reproduction, copy (d'une œuvre d'art); *droits de reproduction,* copyright.

reproduire [rəprɔdɥiːr] v. tr. (85). To reproduce. ‖ To re-publish (un texte). ‖ ARTS. To reproduce, to copy; *ce tableau est reproduit aux traits sur notre couverture,* this picture is featured on our cover.
— v. pr. **Se reproduire,** MÉD., ZOOL. to reproduce, to multiply, to breed. ‖ FIG. To recur, to happen (ou) occur again (événement); to come out of retirement, to show oneself in society again (personne).

reprographie [rəprɔgrafi] f. TECHN. Reprography.

reprographier [-fje] v. tr. (1). TECHN. To reproduce.

réprouvable [repruvabl] adj. Blameworthy; deserving of blame.

réprouvé, ée [-ve] adj. Rejected, censured (doctrine); disapproved-of by society (personne).
— s. ECCLÉS. One who is damned; *les réprouvés*

et les élus, the damned and the elect. ‖ FAM. Outcast; reprobate.

réprouver [-ve] v. tr. (1). To reject (une doctrine); to disapprove of, to censure (qqn). ‖ ECCLÉS. To reprobate, to damn, to cast off.

reps [rɛps] m. Rep, reps, repp.

reptation [rɛptasjɔ̃] f. ZOOL. Reptation.

reptatoire [-twaːr] adj. ZOOL. Reptatory.

reptile [rɛptil] m. ZOOL. Reptile.

reptilien, enne [-ljɛ̃, ɛn] adj. ZOOL. Reptilian.

repu, ue [rəpy] adj. Full, satiated, sated, glutted.

républicain, aine [repyblikɛ̃, ɛn] adj., s. JUR. Republican.
— m. ZOOL. Weaver-bird.

républicaniser [repyblikanize] v. tr. (1). JUR. To republicanize.

républicanisme [-nism] m. JUR. Republicanism.

republier [rəpyblije] v. tr. (1). To republish.

république [repyblik] f. JUR. Republic. ‖ ZOOL. *République de fourmis,* colony of ants. ‖ FIG. Republic (des lettres).

répudiable [repydjabl] adj. Repudiable.

répudiation [-djasjɔ̃] f. Repudiation (d'une femme). ‖ JUR. Relinquishment, renunciation.

répudier [-dje] v. tr. (1). To repudiate (une femme). ‖ JUR. To renounce, to relinquish (une succession). ‖ FIG. To reject (une croyance).

répugnance [repyɲɑ̃ːs] f. Repugnance; dislike (*pour,* of); aversion (*pour,* to); loathing (*pour,* for); *avoir de la répugnance à,* to be reluctant (ou) loath (ou) loth to; *avec répugnance,* reluctantly, with reluctance.

répugnant, ante [-ɲɑ̃, ɑ̃ːt] adj. Offensive, repugnant (odeur). ‖ FIG. Repugnant, loathsome, sickening (devoir); abject (personne).

répugner [-ɲe] v. intr. (1). To feel repugnance (*à,* to); to feel loathing (*à,* for) [qqch.]; *répugner à faire,* to be loth (ou) loath (ou) reluctant to do. ‖ To be distasteful (ou) repugnant (*à,* to) [qqn]; *répugner à qqn,* to disgust s.o., to fill s.o. with loathing; *cet homme me répugne,* I loathe (ou) detest that man.

répulsif, ive [repylsif, iːv] adj. PHYS. Repulsive, repellent (force). ‖ FIG. Repulsive, repellent.

répulsion [-sjɔ̃] f. PHYS. Repulsion, repellent force (d'un aimant, d'un corps électrisé). ‖ FIG. Repulsion, distaste, aversion (*pour,* for).

réputation [repytasjɔ̃] f. Reputation, repute, name; *avoir la réputation d'un honnête homme,* to be known for one's honesty, to have a reputation for honesty; *connaître qqn de réputation,* to known s.o. by repute; *jouir d'une bonne réputation,* to have a good reputation, to be well spoken of; *perdu de réputation,* without a character; *se faire une réputation,* to make a name for oneself.

réputé, ée [repyte] adj. Well-known; of high repute. ‖ FAM. Reputed (tenu pour).

réputer [repyte] v. tr. (1). To repute, to hold, to consider, to deem; *être réputé avoir dit,* to be reputed to have said, to be accredited with having said; *il est réputé comme un homme de bien,* he is held (ou) considered to be a man of worth; *réputer coupable,* to deem guilty.

requérable [rəkerabl] adj. JUR. Demandable, claimable (rente).

requérant, ante [-rɑ̃, ɑ̃ːt] adj. JUR. Claiming; *partie requérante,* claimant.
— s. JUR. Claimant, plaintiff.

requérir [-riːr] v. tr. (13). To come (ou) go for (aller chercher). ‖ To beg, to ask (prier) [*de,* to]. ‖ To demand, to require (exiger); *requérir qqn de faire qqch.,* to call upon s.o. to do sth. ‖ JUR. To claim, to demand; *requérir l'application d'une peine,* to call for the application of a penalty; *requérir la force armée,* to call upon armed assis-

tance. ‖ Fɪɢ. To require (demander); *requérir une grande application*, to call for considerable application.
— v. intr. Jᴜʀ. To demand a penalty (*contre*, against).

requête [rəkɛ:t] f. Request; *à la requête de*, at the request of. ‖ Jᴜʀ. Petition, address (v. sᴜᴘᴘʟɪᴏ̨ᴜᴇ); *présenter une requête*, to petition, to submit a petition; *requête civile*, appeal against a judgment. ‖ Sᴘᴏʀᴛs. Fresh search (du gibier).

requiem [rekɥiɛm] m. invar. Eᴄᴄʟᴇ́s. Requiem; *messe de requiem*, requiem mass.

requin [rəkɛ̃] m. Zᴏᴏʟ., Fᴀᴍ. Shark.

requinquant [rəkɛ̃kɑ̃] m. Fᴀᴍ. Pick-me-up.
— adj. Fᴀᴍ. Tonic.

requinquer [-ke] v. tr. (1). Fᴀᴍ. To put straight, to set to rights (une pièce); to smarten up (qqn).
— v. pr. **Se requinquer**, Fᴀᴍ. To smarten (ou) spruce oneself up, to tog oneself out (s'attifer); to recover from illness; to perk up (se ravigoter).

requis, ise [rəki, i:z] adj. Required, requisite.
— m. *Requis civil*, labour conscript.

réquisition [rekizisjɔ̃] f. Requisition. ‖ Jᴜʀ. Requisition, demand; *à (ou) sur la réquisition de*, at the demand of; *réquisition illégale*, U. S. moonlight requisition.

réquisitionnaire [-sjɔnɛ:r] m. Mɪʟɪᴛ. Conscript.

réquisitionnement [-sjɔnmɑ̃] m. Requisitioning.

réquisitionner [-sjɔne] v. tr. (1). To requisition, to commandeer.

réquisitoire [-twa:r] m. Jᴜʀ. Requistory; indictment (du ministère public). ‖ Fᴀᴍ. Stream of reproaches.

réquisitorial, ale [-tɔrjal] adj. Jᴜʀ. *Plaidoyer réquisitorial*, indictment.

R.E.R. [ɛrəɛr] m. Abrév. de *Réseau express régional*, underground system serving the Paris region.

resaler [rəsale] v. tr. (1). Cᴜʟɪɴ. To resalt.

rescapé, ée [rɛskape] adj. Rescued, saved from danger (ou) disaster (personne).
— s. Survivor.

rescinder [-de] v. tr. (1). Jᴜʀ. To rescind (un acte); to cancel (une convention).

rescousse [rɛskus] f. Rescue; *à la rescousse*, to the rescue.

rescrit [rɛskri] m. Eᴄᴄʟᴇ́s. Rescript.

réseau [rezo] m. Net, netting, network (filet); hair-net (résille); web (toile d'araignée). ‖ Aʀᴄʜɪᴛ. Tracery. ‖ Mᴇ́ᴅ. Plexus. ‖ Pʜʏs. Diffraction grating. ‖ Gᴇ́ᴏɢʀ. *Réseau fluvial*, system of rivers. ‖ Cʜ. ᴅᴇ ꜰ. Railway network. ‖ Mɪʟɪᴛ. *Réseau de barbelés*, barbed-wire entanglements; *réseau de la Résistance*, resistance group. ‖ Eʟᴇᴄᴛʀ. Mains. ‖ Fɪɢ. Web (d'intrigues).

résection [resɛksjɔ̃] f. Mᴇ́ᴅ. Resection.

réséda [rezeda] m. Bᴏᴛ. Reseda.

réservataire [rezɛrvatɛ:r] adj. Jᴜʀ. *Héritier réservataire*, heir who has a right to part of an inheritance.

réservation [-sjɔ̃] f. Reservation.

réserve [rezɛrv] f. Reserve; *en réserve*, in reserve, put by; *mettre qqch. en réserve*, to put (ou) lay sth. by. ‖ Reserve, reticence, restraint; *accepter sous réserve*, to accept with certain reservations, to qualify one's acceptance; *éloges sans réserve*, unqualified (ou) unstinted praise; *parler avec beaucoup de réserve*, *sans réserve*, to speak very guardedly, without reserve; *se tenir sur la réserve*, to be guarded, to maintain an attitude of reserve. ‖ Cʜ. ᴅᴇ ꜰ. Reservation, reserving, booking (de places). ‖ Fɪɴ. Reserve; provision; pl. accumulations; *fonds de réserve*, reserve funds; *réserve d'or*, gold reserves. ‖ Cᴏᴍᴍ. Storehouse (de magasin). ‖ Jᴜʀ. Written protest (texte); reserve, reservation (à un contrat); *à la réserve de*, with the exception of; *à la réserve que*, except that;

sous réserve, without prejudice; *sous réserve de*, subject to; *sous réserve que*, on condition that; *sous toutes réserves*, without committing oneself. ‖ Mɪʟɪᴛ., Nᴀᴜᴛ. Reserve; *armée, officier de réserve*, reserve army, officer; *cadre de réserve*, reserve of officers. ‖ Nᴀᴜᴛ. *En réserve*, out of commission (navire). ‖ Sᴘᴏʀᴛs. Preserve (de chasse).

réservé, ée [-ve] adj. Reserved (place); *quartier réservé*, brothel (ou) red-lamp (ou) U. S. red-light district. ‖ Reserved, reticent, shy (personne). ‖ Cᴏᴍᴍ. *Tous droits réservés*, all rights reserved. ‖ Eᴄᴄʟᴇ́s. Reserved (cas). ‖ Sᴘᴏʀᴛs. Private (pêche). ‖ Cᴏᴍᴍ. *Cuvée réservée*, special vintage.

réserver [-ve] v. tr. (1). To reserve; to set aside; to keep back; to save; *réserver quelque argent pour*, to set aside some money for; *réserver une danse à*, to save a dance for; *réserver une place*, to reserve (ou) keep a seat; *réserver une part du butin*, to keep back part of the booty. ‖ Fɪɢ. To destine, to hold in store; *à quoi réservez-vous cela?*, for what do you intend that?, what have you in view for that?; *on ne sait jamais ce que le sort nous réserve*, we never know what Fate holds in store for us; *il lui était réservé de mourir jeune*, he was destined (ou) fated to die young.
— v. pr. **Se réserver**, to save (ou) keep (ou) set aside for oneself (qqch.). ‖ To bide one's time; to wait for the opportunity. ‖ *Se réserver de faire qqch.*, to wait for the right time (ou) occasion to do sth.; *se réserver le droit de*, to reserve to oneself full liberty to. ‖ *Se réserver pour*, to save (ou) reserve oneself for.

reservir [rəsɛrvi:r] v. tr., intr. (2). Cᴜʟɪɴ., Mɪʟɪᴛ. To serve again.

réserviste [rezɛrvist] m. Mɪʟɪᴛ. Reservist.

réservoir [rezɛrvwa:r] m. Reservoir, tank; cistern; *réservoir à eau, à essence*, water-, petrol- (ou) U. S. gasoline tank; *réservoir à gaz*, gasholder. ‖ Aᴠɪᴀᴛ. *Réservoir de secours*, reserve tank.

résidant, ante [rezidɑ̃, ɑ̃:t] adj. Residing, resident.
— s. Resident.

résidence [-dɑ̃:s] f. Residence, abode, dwelling (v. ᴅᴇᴍᴇᴜʀᴇ); *obligé à la résidence*, required to reside; *changer de résidence*, to move house, to remove; *établir (ou) fixer sa résidence à*, to take up residence at. ‖ Jᴜʀ. Residentship; residency; *mis en résidence surveillée*, placed under house arrest.

résident [rezidɑ̃] m. Jᴜʀ. Resident.

résidentiel, elle [-dɑ̃sjɛl] adj. Residential.

résider [-de] v. intr. (1). To reside, to dwell, to live, to have one's abode (*dans*, in). [V. ʜᴀʙɪᴛᴇʀ.] ‖ Fɪɢ. To consist, to lie (*en*, in).

résidu [rezidy] m. Cʜɪᴍ. Residue, residuum (*from*, de). ‖ Mᴀᴛʜ. Residue. ‖ Fɪɢ. Residuum.

résiduaire [-dɥɛ:r] adj. Residual. ‖ Waste (eaux).

résiduel, elle [-dɥɛl] adj. Residual. ‖ Mᴇ́ᴅ. Supplemental (air).

résignation [reziɲasjɔ̃] f. Resignation, relinquishment, giving up (d'un emploi). ‖ Fɪɢ. Submission, submissiveness, resignation; *avec résignation*, resignedly, with resignation.

résigné, ée [-ɲe] adj. Resigned (*à*, to). ‖ Humble, submissive.

résigner [-ɲe] v. tr. (1). To resign (un bénéfice); to give up, to relinquish, to resign (ses fonctions).
— v. pr. **Se résigner**, to resign oneself; *se résigner à*, to reconcile oneself to.

résiliable [reziljabl] adj. Jᴜʀ. Able to be cancelled (ou) annulled.

résiliation [-ljasjɔ̃] f. Jᴜʀ. Cancellation.

résilience [-ljɑ̃:s] f. Pʜʏs. Resilience, ductility.

résilier [-lje] v. tr. (1) Jᴜʀ. To cancel, to annul.

résille [rezi:j] f. Hair-net. ‖ ARCHIT. Lattice-work (d'un vitrail).

résinage [rezina:ʒ] m. Resin-tapping.

résine [-zin] f. Resin.

résiné [-zine] m. Retzina (vin).

résiner [-zine] v. tr. (1). To resin (enduire); to tap (extraire).

résineux, euse [-zinø, ø:z] adj. BOT. Resinous (bois); coniferous (forêt). — m. pl. BOT. Conifers.

résipiscence [resipissɑ̃:s] f. Resipicence : *recevoir qqn à résipiscence*, to pardon s.o.'s misdeeds; *venir à résipiscence*, to recognize one's errors.

résistance [rezistɑ̃:s] f. Resistance, opposition (*à*, to); *faire résistance*, to offer (ou) put up resistance. ‖ SPORTS. Stamina, endurance, staying-power (d'un athlète). ‖ TECHN. Toughness, strength, resistance (des matériaux); *à haute résistance*, high-tensile (acier); *limite de résistance*, yield-point; *résistance à la rupture*, breaking-strength. ‖ NAUT., AVIAT. *Résistance à l'avancement*, drag. ‖ ELECTR. Resistance; *boîte de résistance*, resistance box. ‖ RADIO. *Résistance de grille*, grid-leak. ‖ MILIT. Resistance, Resistance (ou) Underground Movement. ‖ CULIN. *Pièce de résistance*, main dish. ‖ FIG. *Pièce de résistance*, main feature, high-light, pièce de résistance.

résistant, ante [-tɑ̃, ɑ̃:t] adj. Able to endure, tough (homme). ‖ Tough (matière); *résistant à la chaleur, au froid*, heat-proof, frost-hardy; *peu résistant*, flimsy (étoffe). ‖ Fast (couleur). — s. MILIT. Member of the Resistance Movement, partisan.

résister [-te] v. intr. (1). To hold out (*à*, against); *résister à trois bombes*, to survive three bombs. ‖ To resist (matière); *résister au marteau*, to withstand the hammer. ‖ To be fast, not to run (couleur). ‖ NAUT. *Résister à une tempête*, to ride out (ou) weather a storm. ‖ FIN. To hold up (ou) firm. ‖ FIG. To resist, to endure; *résister à la douleur*, to stand pain; *résister à la fatigue*, to endure fatigue; *résister à la tentation*, to resist (ou) hold out against temptation; *résister à qqn*, to resist s.o.

résistivité [-tivite] f. ELECTR. Resistivity.

résolu, ue [rezɔly] adj. Resolute, determined.

résolu. V. RÉSOUDRE (87).

résolubilité [rezɔlybilite] f. Resolvability.

résoluble [-lybl] adj. Solvable (problème). ‖ JUR. Cancellable (contrat).

résolument [-lymɑ̃] adv. Resolutely, with determination.

résolutif, ive [-lytif, i:v] adj. MÉD. Resolvent (médicament). ‖ JUR. Avoidance, defeasance.

résolution [-lysjɔ̃] f. Resolution, resolve (dessein). ‖ Resolution, resoluteness, determination, firmness (fermeté). ‖ Resolution (décision); *adopter une résolution*, to adopt a resolution. ‖ JUR. Cancellation, annulment (d'un bail, d'un contrat). ‖ MÉD. Resolution (d'une tumeur). ‖ MATH. Solution (d'une équation); resolution, solving (d'un problème). ‖ CHIM. Solution, resolution (*en*, into).

résolutoire [-lytwa:r] adj. JUR. Resolutory, of avoidance (condition).

résolvais, résolvait, résolvons, résolvez, résolvent. V. RÉSOUDRE (87).

résolvant, ante [rezɔlvɑ̃, ɑ̃:t] adj., s. MÉD. Resolvent.

résonance [rezonɑ̃:s] f. MUS. Resonance (d'un instrument, d'une salle). ‖ PHYS. Resonance, tuning. ‖ FIG. Repercussion.

résonateur [-natœ:r] m. ELECTR. Resonator.

résonnant, ante [-nɑ̃, ɑ̃:t] adj. Resonant, resounding (salle); sonorous (voix).

résonnement [rezonmɑ̃] m. Resounding, resonance, re-echoing, reverberation.

résonner [-ne] v. intr. (1). To resound, to reso-nate, to reverberate, to re-echo (salle). ‖ To twang (corde); to ring, to clang (métal).

resonner [rasɔne] v. tr. To ring for again.
— v. intr. To ring again.

résorber [rezɔrbe] v. tr. (1). MÉD. To resorb, to reabsorb. ‖ FIN. To solve (une crise économique); to get rid of (un déficit); to absorb (les surplus).
— v. pr. **Se résorber**, MÉD. To be resorbing.

résorcine [rezɔrsin] f. CHIM. Resorcin(ol).

résorption [rezɔrpsjɔ̃] MÉD. Resorption, reabsorption.

résoudre [rezu:dr] v. tr. (87). To resolve, to dissolve (*en*, into); reduce (*en*, to) [transformer]. ‖ To decide on, to resolve on (décider) [qqch.]; to resolve, to decide, to make up one's mind (*de*, to); *résoudre qqn à faire*, to determine (ou) induce s.o. to do, to make up s.o.'s mind to do. ‖ JUR. To cancel, to annul, to terminate (un bail, un contrat). ‖ MUS. To resolve (une dissonance). ‖ MÉD. To resolve (une tumeur). ‖ MATH. To solve (une équation). ‖ FIG. To resolve; to clear up, to solve (une difficulté); to guess (une énigme); to settle (une question); to solve (un problème).
— v. pr. **Se résoudre**, to resolve, to be resolved, to dissolve, to be dissolved, to change, to be changed (*en*, into) [se transformer]. ‖ To decide, to resolve, to make up one's mind (*à*, to) [se décider].

respect [rɛspɛ] m. Respect, reverence, regard (v. DÉFÉRENCE); *avoir du respect pour qqn*, to hold s.o. in respect; *manquer de respect à*, to be disrespectful to; *par respect pour*, out of respect for, in deference to; *présenter ses respects à qqn*, to present one's respects to s.o.; *respect humain*, fear of public opinion; *sauf votre respect*, saving your presence, with all due respect; *tenir en respect*, to keep in check.

respectabilité [rɛspɛktabilite] f. Respectability.

respectable [-tabl] adj. Respectable, worthy of respect, worthy (personne). ‖ FAM. Respectable, fair (quantité).

respecter [-te] v. tr. (1). To respect, to esteem, to look up to, to reverence (honorer). ‖ To have regard for, to respect (avoir égard à); *respecter la loi*, to abide by the law; *respecter le sommeil de qqn*, to be careful not to disturb s.o.'s sleep. ‖ FIG. To spare (épargner).
— v. pr. **Se respecter**, to have self-respect.

respectif, ive [-tif, i:v] adj. Respective.

respectivement [-tivmɑ̃] adv. Respectively.

respectueusement [rɛspɛktɥøzmɑ̃] adv. Respectfully, with respect.

respectueux, euse [-tɥø, ø:z] adj. Respectful.

respirable [rɛspirabl] adj. Respirable.

respiration [-rasjɔ̃] f. MÉD. Respiration, breathing. ‖ FIG. *Couper la respiration à qqn*, to take s.o.'s breath away.

respiratoire [-ratwa:r] adj. MÉD. Respiratory.

respirer [-re] v. intr. (1). To breathe. ‖ To live, to give signs of life (vivre). ‖ FIG. To be likelife (paraître vivant). ‖ FAM. To have a breathing-space; *laissez-moi respirer un moment*, give me time to breathe. ‖ FAM. To breathe easy (après un souci).
— v. tr. To breathe, to breathe in, to inhale (de l'air). ‖ FIG. To breathe, to express, to betoken; *respirer la joie*, to be instinct with (ou) to betoken joy; *respirer la santé*, to radiate good health.

resplendir [rɛsplɑ̃di:r] v. intr. (2). To be resplendent, to shine, to be dazzling.

resplendissant, ante [-disɑ̃, ɑ̃:t] adj. Resplendent, shining, dazzling; *resplendissant de santé*, aglow with health.

responsabiliser [rɛspɔ̃sabilize] v. tr. (1). To make aware of one's responsibilities.

responsabilité [rɛspɔ̃sabilite] f. Responsibility;

accountableness, accountability. ‖ Jur. Liability (de, for).

responsable [-sabl] adj. Responsible (de, for; envers, to; à l'égard de, before). ‖ Accountable, answerable. (V. comptable.) ‖ Jur. Liable (de, for) [dommages].

resquille [rɛski:j] f. Fam. Wangling, fiddling; faire de la resquille, to wangle; to gate-crash.

resquiller [-je] v. intr. (1). Fam. To wangle (en général); to gate-crash, to bluff one's way through (pour passer).

resquilleur, euse [rɛskijœ:r, ø:z] s. Fam. Gate-crasher; wangler; wide boy.

ressac [rɛsak] m. Naut. Surf (brisant); undertow (retrait).

ressaisir [rəsɛzi:r] v. tr. (2). To seize again, to recapture, to regain possession of (qqch.). ‖ Jur. Ressaisir le tribunal d'une affaire, to bring a matter before the Court again. ‖ Fig. To recover; to get back into (le pouvoir).
— v. pr. Se ressaisir, to recover oneself, to regain one's self-control, to pull oneself together.

ressasser [rəsase] v. tr. (1). To re-sift (de la farine). ‖ Fam. To repeat ad nauseam, to dwell (ou) harp on; ressasser qqch. à qqn, to din sth. into s.o.'s ears.

ressasseur, euse [-sœ:r, ø:z] s. Person who harps on the same things. (V. rabâcheur.)

ressaut [rəso] m. Archit. Projection, ressaut. ‖ Géogr. Rock-step.

ressauter [rəsote] v. tr. To jump again.

ressayer [resɛje] v. tr. (9b). To try again (qqch.); to try on again (un vêtement).

ressemblance [rəsɑ̃blɑ̃:s] f. Resemblance (avec, to); likeness, similarity; attraper la ressemblance, to catch a likeness; avoir une grande ressemblance, to look much alike.

ressemblant, ante [-blɑ̃, ɑ̃:t] adj. Like, alike, similar; deux frères ressemblants, two brothers who look like each other; portrait ressemblant, good likeness.

ressembler [-ble] v. intr. (1). Ressembler à, to resemble, to look (ou) be like; ce portrait vous ressemble bien, this portrait is a good likeness of you; ressembler beaucoup à son père, to be the image of one's father. ‖ Fam. Ça lui ressemble bien!, that's just like him!
— v. pr. Se ressembler, to be (ou) to look alike; les jours se suivent et ne se ressemblent pas, tomorrow is another day; qui se ressemble s'assemble, birds of a feather flock together; se ressembler comme deux gouttes d'eau, to be alike as two peas.

ressemelage [rəsəmla:ʒ] m. Re-soling.
ressemeler [-le] v. tr. (8 a). To re-sole.
ressemer [rəsəme] v. tr. (5). To re-sow.
ressentiment [rəsɑ̃timɑ̃] m. Resentment; avec ressentiment, resentfully, with resentment.

ressentir [rəsɑ̃ti:r] v. tr. (93). To feel (de l'émotion, de la joie); ressentir vivement, to be deeply affected (ou) moved by, to feel deeply. ‖ To resent (une insulte). ‖ To feel, to experience (un choc).
— v. pr. Se ressentir, to be felt (être perçu). ‖ To feel the effects (ou) after-effects (de, of).

resserre [rəsɛ:r] f. Store-house, store-room, garden-shed. ‖ Storage (entrepôts).

resserré, ée [-sɛre] adj. Narrow, cramped, confined (espace). ‖ Fam. Costive.

resserrement [-sɛrmɑ̃] m. Contraction, compression, tightening, narrowing, constriction. ‖ Heaviness (du cœur); narrowness (de l'esprit); Cutting-down, restriction (des besoins); tightening-up (des restrictions). ‖ Fin. Scarceness, tightness.

resserrer [-sɛre] v. tr. (1). To tighten (un écrou); to draw tighter (un cordon). ‖ To shut (ou) lock up, to put away (renfermer). ‖ To confine, to compress (comprimer); to contract (contracter); to shorten (raccourcir). ‖ Milit. To close up (une ligne de bataille); to close (les rangs). ‖ Méd. To bind, to constipate (le ventre). ‖ Fig. To draw tighter (fortifier); to restrict (restreindre).
— v. intr. Méd. To be binding (ou) constipating.
— v. pr. Se resserrer, to retrench, to restrict oneself. ‖ To shrink (étoffe); to close (pores); to get narrower (vallée).

resservir [rəsɛrvi:r] v. intr. (95). To serve again, to be able to be used again.
— v. tr. Culin. To serve up again.

ressort [rəsɔ:r] m. Springiness, elasticity. ‖ Techn. Spring; grand ressort, main spring; ressort à boudin, helical spring; sans ressort, unsprung. ‖ Ch. de f. Ressort de choc, buffer-spring. ‖ Fig. Incentive, spur; ressort d'une action, motive for an action; avoir du ressort, to be resilient; sans ressort, flat, slack, lacking resilience. ‖ Fam. Faire jouer tous les ressorts, to pull all possible strings.

ressort [rəsɔ:r] m. Jur. Competence, jurisdiction, scope; être du ressort de, to be (ou) fall within the competence of; juger en dernier ressort, to pass judgment without appeal. ‖ Fam. Cela n'est pas de mon ressort, that is not in my power, that does not fall within my province.

ressortir [rəsɔrti:r] v. intr. (2). To come (ou) go out again. ‖ To stand out, to be thrown into relief (mettre en lumière); to be set off (couleur); faire ressortir une couleur, to bring out (ou) set off a colour; faire ressortir les fautes d'autrui, to lay stress on (ou) dwell on (ou) emphasize other people's faults. ‖ To result, to follow, to come out (de, from) [résulter]; il ressort de, it follows from, it appears from.
— v. tr. To bring (ou) take out again (qqch.); ressortir un mouchoir de sa poche, to pull (ou) take a handkerchief out of one's pocket again. ‖ Fam. To drag up (une vieille histoire).

ressortir v. intr. (88). Jur. To be under the jurisdiction (à, of); affaire qui ressortit au juge de paix, case coming before a Justice of the Peace. ‖ Fig. To be amenable (à, to).

ressortissant, ante [-tisɑ̃, ɑ̃:t] adj. Jur. Under the jurisdiction (à, of); ressortissant à la cour d'appel, coming before a court of appeal. ‖ Subject (à, to); belonging (de, to) [un pays].
— m. National, subject (d'un pays).

ressource [rəsu:rs] f. Resource; resourcefulness; homme de ressource, man full of expedients, resourceful man. ‖ Expedience, means, shift (moyen); resort (recours); avoir encore une ressource, to have one string left to one's bow; en dernière ressource, in the (ou) as a last resort; faire ressource de tout, to have recourse to every kind of expedient. ‖ Pl. Resources (en, in); au bout de ses ressources, on one's last legs; sans ressources, without means of support. ‖ Comm., Fin. Funds; resources; ressources personnelles, private means. ‖ Aviat. Pull-out; faire une ressource sur le dos, to bunt.

ressouvenir (se) [sərəsuvni:r] v. pr. (101). To remember, to recall, to remember again; faire ressouvenir de, to remind of; se ressouvenir de qqch., to recall sth. to mind.

ressuer [rəsɥe] v. intr. (1). To sweat (mur).

ressuscité, ée [resysite] adj. Risen (Christ); revived, risen from the dead (personne).

ressusciter v. tr. (1). To resuscitate, to raise, to restore to life (un mort). ‖ Fig. To revive, to renew, to bring back, to resurrect (une mode).
— v. intr. To resuscitate, to return from the dead. ‖ Fam. To regain one's health and strength; to perk up.

ressuyer [rɛsɥije] v. tr. (9 a). To wipe (ou) dry

again (essuyer de nouveau); to dry (v. SÉCHER).
— v. intr. To dry, to dry out.

restant, ante [rɛstɑ̃, ɑ̃:t] adj. Remaining; left over. ‖ *Poste restante,* « poste restante », « to be left till called for », U. S. general delivery.
— s. Survivor, person left behind.
— m. Remainder, remnant, rest (v. RELIQUAT, RESTE); *le restant d'une bouteille,* what is left of (ou) in the bottle.

restaurant, ante [rɛstɔrɑ̃, ɑ̃:t] adj. Restorative, restoring.
— m. COMM. Restaurant; *restaurant de libre service,* cafeteria.

restaurateur [-ratœ:r] m. COMM. Restaurant-keeper. ‖ ARTS. Restorer.

restauration [-rasjɔ̃] f. ARTS, ARCHIT., JUR. Restoration (d'une dynastie, d'un monument, d'un tableau). ‖ FIG. Restoration, re-establishment (de la discipline).

restaurer [-re] v. tr. (1). To restore, to refresh, to set up again (qqn). ‖ ARTS., ARCHIT., JUR. To restore. ‖ FIG. To restore, to re-establish.
— v. pr. **Se restaurer,** to refresh oneself, to take refreshment, to refresh the inner man.

reste [rɛst] m. Rest, remainder (en général); remnant (d'étoffe). ‖ Rest, other part, others; *il n'est pas comme le reste,* he's not like the others. ‖ Pl. Mortal remains (cendres). ‖ CULIN. Pl. Remains of a meal; scraps of the last meal (v. ROGATONS); *manger les restes,* to eat up the scraps. ‖ FIN. Balance (d'une somme); *en reste,* in debt, behindhand with payments. ‖ MATH. Remainder. ‖ MILIT. Remnant (d'une armée). ‖ FIG. Glimmer (d'espoir); *de beaux restes,* traces of beauty; *en reste avec qqn,* indebted to s.o., in s.o.'s debt. ‖ **Au reste, du reste,** moreover, besides, furthermore, what is more. ‖ **Et le reste,** and so on. ‖ **De reste,** surplus, left over.

rester [rɛste] v. intr. (1). To remain, to be left, to be left over (ou) behind; *château dont il ne reste que des ruines,* castle of which only the ruins are left; *il me reste dix francs,* I have ten francs left (ou) over; *il ne reste qu'à attendre,* nothing remains but to wait, all we can do is to wait; *il ne reste que trois maisons,* only three houses survive; *il reste à savoir si, reste à savoir si,* it remains to be seen whether; *il reste beaucoup à faire,* much remains to be done; *tout l'argent qui me reste,* all the money I have left. ‖ To remain, to stay, to dwell, to continue (demeurer); *calomniez hardiment, il en reste toujours qqch.,* if you throw enough mud, some of it will stick; *j'y suis, j'y reste,* here I am and here I stay; *cela doit rester entre nous,* that is strictly between ourselves; *en rester là,* to leave it at that, to proceed no further in the matter; *mots qui restent dans la gorge,* words that stick in one's throat; *où en suis-je resté?,* how far did I get?, where did I leave off?, *rester dîner* (ou) *à dîner,* to stay to dinner, to stay and dine; *rester à la pluie,* to stay out in the rain; *rester amis* (ou) *bien avec,* to remain friends, to keep on good terms with; *rester assis, debout,* to remain seated (ou) sitting, standing; *rester au lit,* to stay in bed, to keep to one's bed; *rester en arrière,* to lag behind; *rester fidèle à ses principes,* to stand by (ou) to remain faithful to one's principles; *rester où l'on est,* to stay where one is, not to move; *rester sur le champ de bataille,* to be killed in action, to fall in battle; *rester tranquille,* to keep quiet; *rester veuve,* to be left a widow. ‖ MATH. *Dix moins huit, reste deux,* ten minus eight leaves two. ‖ FAM. *Rester en carafe* (ou) *en plan,* to be left in the lurch; *y rester,* to be killed. ‖ FAM. To live (habiter).
— impers. *Il reste à,* it remains to.

restituable [rɛstitɥabl] adj. Returnable. ‖ FIN. Repayable.

restituer [-tɥe] v. tr. (1). To restitute, to give (ou) hand back, to restore, to return (qqch.). ‖ To restore (un texte).

restitution [-tysjɔ̃] f. Restitution, return, giving back (de qqch.). ‖ Restoration (d'un texte).

Restoroute [rɛstɔrut] m. (nom déposé). Motorway restaurant.

restreindre [rɛstrɛ̃:dr] v. tr. (59). To restrict (en général); to curtail (une autorité); to cut down (ses dépenses); to limit (ses désirs); to cut down, to restrict (la production); to limit, to confine (le sens).
— v. pr. **Se restreindre,** to cut down expenses, to retrench. ‖ To confine (ou) limit (ou) restrict oneself (à, to).

restreint, einte [-trɛ̃, ɛ̃:t] adj. Narrow, confined (espace); narrow (limites); small, limited (moyens); low, limited (nombre); narrow (sens); limited, restricted (tirage).

restrictif, ive [rɛstriktif, i:v] adj. Restrictive, limitative, limiting. ‖ JUR. Saving (clause).

restriction [-sjɔ̃] f. Restriction, limitation; *restriction mentale,* mental reservation; *sans restriction,* unreservedly.

restringent, ente [rɛstrɛ̃ʒɑ̃, ɑ̃:t] adj., m. MÉD. Astringent, styptic.

restructuration [rəstryktyrasjɔ̃] f. Restructuring, reorganization.

restructurer [-re] v. tr. (1). To restructure, to reorganize.

resucée [rəsyse] f. FAM. Repetition; rehash (d'un livre); *à la troisième resucée,* at the third go. ‖ FAM. Another drink (boisson); *une petite resucée?,* what about another one?

résultant, ante [resyltɑ̃, ɑ̃:t] adj. Resulting, resultant.

résultante [-tɑ̃:t] f. MATH. Resultant.

résultat [-ta] m. Result; consequence; outcome, issue (aboutissement); *avoir pour résultat,* to result in, to lead to; *sans résultat,* without success, vain, fruitless.

résulter [-te] v. impers. (1). To result, to follow, to arise (de, from) [v. S'ENSUIVRE]; *il en résulte que,* it follows that; *personne ne sait ce qui en résultera,* no one knows what will come of it; *résulter d'une enquête,* to be established by an enquiry.

résumé [rezyme] m. Résumé, summary, epitome, abstract (v. ABRÉGÉ); *en résumé,* in a nutshell, in short. ‖ JUR. Summing-up (d'un juge).

résumer v. tr. (1). To sum up, to summarize; *pour résumer les choses,* to make (ou) cut a long story short; *résumer un argument,* to put an argument in a few words. ‖ FIG. To epitomize (des qualités).
— v. pr. **Se résumer,** to sum up; *pour me résumer,* to sum up, to sum it all up. ‖ To be summed up; to amount, to come down (à, to); *son argument se résume en ceci,* his argument boils down to this.

résurgence [rezyrʒɑ̃:s] f. GÉOGR. Resurgence.

resurgir [rəsyrʒi:r] v. intr. (99). To resurge, to rise (ou) spring up again.

résurrection [rezyrɛksjɔ̃] f. Resurrection (des morts). ‖ FIG. Revival (des arts).

retable [rətabl] m. ECCLÉS. Retable, reredos, altar-piece.

rétablir [retabli:r] v. tr. (2). To restore (la discipline, l'ordre, la situation); to restore, to re-estabish (une dynastie); to renew (une habitude). ‖ MILIT. To restore, to retrieve (une bataille). ‖ MÉD. To restore to health (un malade); to recover, to get back (sa santé). ‖ JUR. To bring into force again (une loi). ‖ FIN., COMM. To restore, to

retrieve, to put on a sound footing (les affaires, les finances). ‖ ARTS, ARCHIT. To restore.
— v. pr. Se **rétablir**, to recover one's health; to get well again. ‖ To be restored (discipline); to come back (ou) in again (mode). ‖ COMM. To be looking up (affaires).

rétablissement [-blismɑ̃] m. Recovery; restoration, restoring (de la discipline, de l'ordre); restoration (d'une dynastie); restoration, setting on the throne again (d'un roi). ‖ Restoration (d'un texte). ‖ MÉD. Recovery (de la santé). ‖ FIN. Recovery (des affaires); return to a sound footing (des finances). ‖ ARCHIT. Restoration, repair (d'un monument). ‖ ECCLÉS. Revival (de la religion). ‖ SPORTS. Pull-up; *faire un rétablissement à la barre fixe*, to breast the bar, to do a pull-up.

retailler [rətɑje] v. tr. (1). To cut again, to recut (en général); to resharpen (un crayon). ‖ AGRIC. To reprune, to prune again (un arbre).

rétamage [retama:ʒ] m. Re-silvering (d'un miroir); re-tinning (des ustensiles de cuisine).

rétamer [-me] v. tr. (1). To re-silver (un miroir); to re-tin (des ustensiles de cuisine). ‖ POP. *Rétamé*, stony-broke (sans le sou); tight, cut (ivre).

rétameur [-mœ:r] m. Tinman; tinker; tinsmith.

retapage [rətapa:ʒ] m. FAM. Doing up (d'un chapeau); recovery (d'un malade); touching-up, retouching (d'une pièce de théâtre). ‖ FAM. Ploughing, U. S. plucking (d'un candidat).

retape [-tap] f. POP. Pavement; picking-up; *faire la retape*, to be on the streets, to solicit.

retaper [-tape] v. tr. (1). FAM. To do up (un chapeau); to straighten (un lit); to set on his feet again (un malade); to touch up (une pièce de théâtre). ‖ FAM. To plough (un candidat).
— v. pr. Se **retaper**, to pull oneself together; to perk (ou) buck up. (V. RAVIGOTER [SE].)

retard [rəta:r] m. Delay; lateness; slowness; *avoir du retard*, to be late, to be behind schedule (autobus, train); *avoir du retard à rattraper*, to have leeway to make up; to have to make up for lost time; *être en retard*, to be backward (écolier); to be slow (montre); to be late (personne); *être en retard sur son siècle*, to be behind the times; *ma montre a dix minutes de retard, est en retard sur l'horloge de la gare*, my watch is ten minutes slow, is slow by the station clock; *mettre qqn en retard*, to delay s.o., to make s.o. late; *sans retard*, without delay; *très en retard*, long overdue. ‖ AUTOM. *Retard à l'allumage*, retarded ignition. ‖ FIN., COMM. *En retard*, in arrears. ‖ MUS. Retardation, suspension. ‖ NAUT. Lag (de la marée).

retardataire [rətardatɛ:r] adj. Backward (écolier); late, behind time (personne). ‖ FIN. In arrears (contribuable). ‖ MILIT. Overdue from leave.
— s. Latecomer, loiterer. ‖ FIN. Person in arrears with payment. ‖ MILIT. Soldier who overstays his leave.

retardateur, trice [-tœ:r, tris] adj. CHIM., TECHN. Retarding, retardant. ‖ MILIT. *Action retardatrice*, delaying action.
— m. CHIM., TECHN. Retarder, retardant.

retardé, ée [-de] adj. FAM. Backward, slow (sur le plan scolaire, intellectuel).
— s. FAM. Backward child, simpleton.

retardement [-dəmɑ̃] m. Retardment, delay; putting off, postponing, deferment (d'une action); *esprit à retardement*, belated wit. ‖ MILIT. *A retardement*, delayed-action (bombe).

retarder [-de] v. tr. (1). To delay, to postpone, to put off (qqch.); to delay, to hinder, to impede (qqn). ‖ To put back (une pendule). ‖ MUS. To suspend.
— v. intr. To lose time, to be slow (horloge); to

be behindhand (personne). ‖ NAUT. To lag (marée). ‖ FAM. *Je retarde!*, my watch is slow (sur l'heure); I am behind the times (sur mon temps).

retâter [rətate] v. tr. (1). To feel (ou) touch (ou) handle (ou) finger again.
— v. intr. To have another go (de, at).

reteindre [rətɛ̃:dr] v. tr. (59). To dye again, to redye.

retendre [rətɑ̃:dr] v. tr. (4). To bend again (un arc); to stretch again (une corde); to set again, to reset (un piège). ‖ To stretch out again (le bras); to hold out again (la main). ‖ NAUT. To spread again (une voile).

retenir [rətəni:r] v. tr. (101). To keep, to detain (qqn); *retenir à dîner, à la maison*, to keep for dinner, at home; *retenir au lit*, to confine to bed; *retenir de force*, to detain forcibly, to hold by force. ‖ To keep back, to restrain; to hold (ou) rein in (un cheval); to keep back (la foule). ‖ To restrain (sa colère); to hold back (un cri); to smother (un bâillement); to hold (son haleine); to put a curb on (sa langue); to choke back (ses larmes); to stifle (un sanglot). ‖ To hold in place, to secure (qqch.); to keep (ou) save from falling (qqn) [éviter une chute].‎ To withhold, to keep back; to stop (prélever) [*sur*, out of]. ‖ To book, to reserve (louer); *retenir une chambre à*, to book a room at, U.S. to make a reservation at; *retenir un domestique*, to engage a servant; *retenir un logement*, to take lodgings. ‖ To keep (garder) [une place]. ‖ To retain, to remember (se rappeler); *facile à retenir*, easily remembered. ‖ To retain, to keep (conserver); *retenir une suggestion*, to bear a suggestion in mind. ‖ JUR. *Retenir une cause*, to declare the court competent to try a case. ‖ MATH. To carry (un chiffre). ‖ FIN., COMM. To deduct (l'escompte). ‖ NAUT. *Retenu par la marée*, le vent, tide-, weather-bound.
— v. intr. To hold back.
— v. pr. Se **retenir**, to check (ou) to stop oneself; *se retenir à*, to catch hold of, to clutch at, to cling to, to hold on to. ‖ To restrain oneself, to refrain (de, from). ‖ FAM. To be moderate (sur, in); to go easy (sur, on).

retenter [rətɑ̃te] v. tr. (1). To try again.

rétenteur, trice [retɑ̃tœ:r, tris] adj. Holding back; restraining.

rétention [-sjɔ̃] f. MÉD., JUR. Retention. ‖ MATH. Carrying (d'un chiffre).

retentir [rətɑ̃ti:r] v. intr. (2). To resound (résonner); to sound (klaxon, trompette); to reverberate (son); to ring out (voix); *le monde entier retentit de ses cris*, the whole world is ringing with his cries, his cries re-echo throughout the whole world. ‖ FIG. *Retentir sur*, to affect.

retentissant, ante [-tisɑ̃, ɑ̃:t] adj. Resounding, sonorous (mots); ringing, loud (voix).

retentissement [-tismɑ̃] m. Reverberation (d'un bruit); echoing (de pas); resounding, ringing out (d'une voix). ‖ FIG. Repercussion (d'un événement); *nouvelle qui a eu un grand retentissement*, news that caused considerable stir.

retenue [rətəny] f. Reserve, discretion, restraint; modesty (d'une femme); *avec retenue*, sparingly, with discretion. ‖ Keeping in (dans une école); *mettre en retenue*, to put in detention, to keep in. ‖ MATH. Carrying over (d'un chiffre). ‖ COMM. Retention, withholding (de marchandises). ‖ FIN. Deduction, stoppage (de, of; sur, from). ‖ TECHN. Damming (dam reservoir. (V. BARRAGE.)

réticence [retisɑ̃:s] f. Reticence.

réticent, ente [-sɑ̃, ɑ̃:t] adj. Reticent. ‖ FAM. Hesitant.

réticule [retikyl] m. Hair-net (résille); handbag, reticule (sac). ‖ PHYS. Reticle, cross-hairs.

réticulé, ée [-le] adj. Reticulated.

rétif, ive [retif, i:v] adj. Restive, disobedient (cheval). ‖ FIG. Stubborn, refractory (caractère, esprit). [V. INDOCILE.]
rétine [retin] f. MÉD. Retina.
rétinien, enne [-njɛ̃, ɛn] adj. MÉD. Retinal.
rétinite [-nit] f. MÉD. Retinitis.
retiré, ée [rətire] adj. Secluded, remote, sequestered, quiet (lieu); retired, quiet, solitary (vie); *être retiré des affaires,* to have retired from business.
retirement [-rmɑ̃] m. MÉD. Contraction.
retirer [-re] v. tr. (1). To pull (ou) draw out, to withdraw (enlever); *retirer le bouchon d'une bouteille,* to draw the cork from a bottle; *retirer un enfant du collège,* to take a child away from school; *retirer les mains de ses poches,* to take one's hands out of one's pockets; *retirer qqn de la rivière,* to pull (ou) fish s.o. out of the river. ‖ To pull (ou) draw back, to withdraw (détourner); *retirer la jambe,* to pull in one's leg; *retirer vivement la tête,* to jerk back one's head. ‖ To take away (*from,* à) [ôter]; *retirer sa confiance à qqn,* to cease to have confidence in s.o. ‖ To obtain, to contract (*de,* from) [extraire]. ‖ To draw again (une loterie). ‖ To take back, to withdraw (rétracter); to take back (un mot injurieux, sa parole); to withdraw (une promesse). ‖ THÉÂTR. To withdraw, to take off (une pièce). ‖ FIN. To call in (des billets); to retire (ou) withdraw (un effet). ‖ COMM. To accomplish (un connaissement); *retirer de la douane,* to clear through the custom-house. ‖ JUR. To withdraw (une plainte). ‖ MILIT. To fire again (une arme à feu). ‖ MÉD. To extract (*de,* from) [une balle]. ‖ CH. DE F. To take out, U. S. to check out (des bagages). ‖ TECHN. To reprint (en typographie). ‖ FIG. *Retirer du profit d'un conseil,* to benefit (ou) derive benefit from a piece of advice; *retirer qqn du péché,* to save s.o. from sin, to pluck a brand from the burning.
— v. pr. Se **retirer,** to withdraw; to retire (*into,* à) [la campagne]. ‖ To retire (monter se coucher); to take leave (prendre congé). ‖ To subside (eaux); to ebb (marée); to recede, to go back (mer). ‖ MILIT. To retire, to withdraw (armée). ‖ FIG. To stand down, to withdraw (candidat); *se retirer des affaires,* to retire from business.
retisser [rətise] v. tr. (1). To weave again; to re-weave.
rétivité [retivite] f. Stubbornness, obstinacy.
retombant, ante [rətɔ̃bɑ̃, ɑ̃:t] adj. Drooping (lèvres); walrus, drooping (moustache).
retombée [-be] f. Fall, falling (de draperies); overhang (de lierre). ‖ ARCHIT. Spring, springing (d'une voûte). ‖ PHYS. *Retombées radio-actives,* radioactive fallout. ‖ Pl. Backwash (suites, conséquences); spin-offs (sous-produits).
retomber [-be] v. intr. (1). To fall again, to fall down again; *retomber en pluie,* to fall again as rain. ‖ To fall back; *retomber sur sa chaise,* to fall back into one's chair. ‖ To fall (ou) hang down (*en,* in) [pendre]; *draperies qui retombent,* hanging draperies. ‖ FIG. To fall back (*dans,* into) [des habitudes]; to relapse (*dans,* into) [la misère, le péché]; *retomber dans l'oubli,* to sink into oblivion again. ‖ MÉD. *Retomber malade,* to fall ill again. ‖ FIG. To fall (*sur,* on) [qqn]; *conversation qui retombe sur les mêmes sujets,* conversation that keeps coming round to the same subjects; *faire retomber la faute sur qqn,* to lay the blame at s.o.'s door; *les soupçons retomberont sur lui,* suspicion will fall on him; *tout ça retombera sur moi,* I'll have to carry the can (ou) to stand the racket (ou) to bear the brunt (fam.). ‖ FAM. *Retomber sur ses pieds,* to fall on one's feet, to have a lucky break.

retoquer [rətɔke] v. tr. (1). FAM. To plough, U.S. to pluck (un candidat).
retordre [rətɔrdr] v. tr. (4). To twist (des fils); to wring out (la lessive). ‖ FAM. *Avoir du fil à retordre,* to have one's work cut out; *donner du fil à retordre à qqn,* to be a nuisance to s.o., to give s.o. sth. to think about, to lead s.o. a dance.
rétorquer [retɔrke] v. tr. (1). To retort, to rejoin.
retors, orse [rətɔ:r, ɔ:rs] adj. Twisted (fil, soie). ‖ ZOOL. Hooked, curved (bec). ‖ FIG. Rascally, wily, sharp, crafty, shrewd (personne).
rétorsion [retɔrsjɔ̃] f. JUR. Retortion, retaliation; *par mesure de rétorsion,* in retaliation; *mesures de rétorsion,* reprisals.
retouche [rətuʃ] f. Retouching (d'une photographie); minor alteration (à une robe). ‖ ARTS. Retouch (à un tableau).
retoucher [-ʃe] v. tr. (1). To touch again. ‖ To touch up (un ouvrage); to touch up (une photographie); to make minor alterations to (une robe). ‖ ARTS. To retouch (un tableau).
— v. intr. *Retoucher à,* to touch again (un objet). ‖ ARTS. To touch up.
retoucheur [-ʃœ:r] s. Finisher (en couture). ‖ ARTS. Retoucher.
retour [rətu:r] m. Return, returning; going (ou) coming back; *à mon retour,* on my return, when I come back; *être de retour, sur son retour,* to be back, on the point of returning; *partir sans retour,* to depart for ever; *retour annuel des hirondelles,* the seasonal return of the swallows. ‖ Turn, twist, bend (méandre). ‖ Turn down (d'un drap de lit). ‖ MÉD. *Retour d'âge,* change of life, menopause; *retour atavique,* throwback. ‖ JUR. Reversion (d'un bien). ‖ FIN. Dishonoured bill. ‖ COMM. Return (de marchandises); *vendu avec facilités de retour,* on sale or return. ‖ ARCHIT. Return, bend, angle (d'une façade, d'un mur). ‖ MILIT. *Retour offensif,* counter-attack. ‖ AUTOM. *Retour de flamme,* backfire; *retour de manivelle,* backfire, kick. ‖ CH. DE F. Billet; *billet de retour,* return ticket (ou) half; *train de retour,* up train. ‖ SPORTS. Return (au tennis); *match retour,* return match. ‖ NAUT. *Cargaison de retour,* homeward cargo; *sur le retour,* homeward bound. ‖ MUS. Repetition, recurrence (d'un motif). ‖ CINÉM. Flash-back. ‖ ECCLÉS. *Retour à* (ou) *vers Dieu,* return to God. ‖ TECHN. Blowback (de chaudière); *course de retour,* back-stroke (d'un piston). ‖ ELECTR. *Retour par la terre,* earth return. ‖ FIG. Change, reversal, vicissitude, turn; *retour de la fortune,* turn of fortune; *retour d'opinion,* revulsion of feeling. ‖ FIG. Looking-back (*sur,* over); *faire un retour sur soi-même,* to take stock of oneself. ‖ FIG. Reciprocation (d'un sentiment); return, paying-back (d'un service); *aimer qqn en retour, payer de retour l'amour de qqn,* to requite (ou) return s.o.'s love; *en retour de,* in return for, in consideration of; *sans esprit de retour,* without hoping for anything in return, disinterestedly. ‖ FAM. *Etre sur le retour,* to be on the decline; *retour du travail,* back from work.
retourne [rəturn] f. Turn-up (carte).
retournement [-nəmɑ̃] m. Turning, turning over; turning upside down (ou) inside out. ‖ AVIAT. *Retournement sur l'aile,* wing-over.
retourner [-ne] v. tr. (1). To turn, to turn over, to turn again, to turn upside down; *retourner un gant,* to turn a glove inside out; *retourner un habit,* to turn a coat. ‖ To turn, to turn round; *retourner le bras à qqn,* to twist s.o.'s arm; *retourner la tête,* to look round. ‖ To return, to give (ou) send back (*to,* à) [renvoyer]. ‖ To turn up (une carte). ‖ AGRIC. To turn, to turn over (le foin); to plough up (la terre). ‖ FIN. To return

(un effet). ‖ Culin. To turn (une omelette); to mix (la salade). ‖ Fig. To examine; to turn over (une idée); to thrash out, to ventilate (une question). ‖ Fig. To turn round; to turn (un argument); to return (un compliment). ‖ Fig. To reverse (la situation); *retourner qqn*, to make s.o. change his mind. ‖ Fam. To give a shock to; *ça m'a retourné*, that gave me quite a turn.
— v. intr. To return, to go back (revenir); *retourner à cheval, à pied*, to ride, to walk back; *retourner chez soi* (ou) *dans son pays*, to return home; *retourner en arrière*, to turn back; *retourner sur ses pas*, to retrace one's steps. ‖ To turn up (aux cartes); *il retourne cœur*, hearts are trumps. ‖ Jur. To revert (à, to). ‖ Fig. To return; *retourner à la charge*, to have another try (ou) go; *retourner au travail*, to get down to work again; *retourner sur le passé*, to go back over the past. ‖ Fig. To recoil; to come back (*sur*, on) [par choc en retour].
— v. impers. *De quoi retourne-t-il?* what's it all about, what's going on?
— v. pr. **Se retourner**, to turn round (*vers*, to, towards); *se retourner dans son lit*, to turn over (ou) to toss and turn in bed. ‖ To be turned inside out (gant, parapluie). ‖ Fig. To turn, to veer round; *se retourner contre*, to turn against, to round on. ‖ Fam. *Avoir le temps de se retourner*, to have time to breathe; *on n'a pas assez de place pour se retourner*, there isn't enough room to swing a cat; *savoir se retourner*, to fall on one's feet, to end up (ou) come out on top; *s'en retourner*, to return, to go back.

retracer [rətrase] v. tr. (6). To mark out again (une allée); to retrace (une ligne); to trace again (qqch.). ‖ Fig. To outline again, to draw up again (un plan). ‖ Fig. To recount, to recall (rappeler); to call up (ou) bring to mind (des événements).
— v. pr. **Se retracer**, to be recalled, to come to mind again (événement). ‖ To recall to mind (qqch.); *se retracer l'image de qqch*, to picture sth. to oneself.

rétractation [retraktasjõ] f. Retractation, recantation (v. désaveu); *faire une rétractation publique*, to recant publicly. ‖ Jur. Rescinding (d'un arrêt).
rétracter [-te] v. tr. (1). To retract, to draw (ou) pull in; to draw (ou) pull back (rentrer). ‖ Ecclés. To recant. ‖ Jur. To rescind (un arrêt). ‖ Fig. To recant, to retract, to withdraw (une affirmation, une opinion); *rétracter ses paroles*, to eat one's words.
— v. pr. **Se rétracter**, to shrink (étoffe). ‖ Méd. To retract, to be retracted (muscle). ‖ Ecclés. To recant. ‖ Fig. To retract. (V. se dédire.)
rétractile [-til] adj. Retractile, retractible.
rétractilité [-tilite] f. Retractibility, retractability.
rétraction [-sjõ] f. Contraction, shortening. ‖ Méd. Retraction (d'un muscle).
retraduire [rətradui:r] v. tr. (85). To retranslate, to translate again.
retrait [rətrɛ] m. Shrinking, shrinkage, contraction (du bois); retreat (d'un glacier); running out (de la marée); retirement, withdrawal (de la mer). ‖ Archit. Standing back (d'une maison); recess (d'un mur); *maison bâtie en retrait de la route*, house set back from the road; *panneau en retrait*, recessed (ou) sunk panel. ‖ Fin. Withdrawal, drawing out (d'un dépôt); calling in (de monnaies). ‖ Jur. Redemption (d'un bien); deprivation (d'un emploi); withdrawal (d'un projet de loi).
retraite [rətrɛt] f. Retreat; *maison de retraite*, home, retreat; *vivre dans la retraite*, to live in retirement. ‖ Retirement; superannuation (d'un employé); *caisse de retraite*, superannuation (ou) pension fund; *en retraite*, retired; *demander sa mise à la retraite*, to apply to be retired on pension; *mis à la retraite*, superannuated, pensioned off; *prendre sa retraite*, to retire on

pension. ‖ Pension; *vivre de sa retraite*, to live on one's pension. ‖ Milit. Retirement; *officier en retraite*, officer on the retired list, retired officer. ‖ Milit. Retreat, withdrawal (déroute); *couper la retraite à une armée*, to cut off an army's retreat. ‖ Milit. Tattoo; retreat (sonnerie); *battre la retraite*, to sound a tattoo; *retraite aux flambeaux*, torch-light tattoo. ‖ Naut. Stern quarter; *pièce de retraite*, stern chaser. ‖ Ecclés. Retreat. ‖ Archit. Offset (d'un mur).
retraité, ée [-te] adj. Pensioned off; superannuated (employé, fonctionnaire). ‖ Milit., Naut. On the retired list.
— s. Pensioner.
retraitement [rətrɛtmã] m. Phys., Techn. Reprocessing.
retraiter [-te] v. tr. (1). Phys., Techn. To reprocess.
retranchement [rətrãʃmã] m. Retrenchment; suppression (d'un abus); cutting down (de dépenses); cutting out, excision (d'un mot); stopping (d'une ration). ‖ Milit. Retrenchment, entrenchment. ‖ Fig. *Acculer qqn dans ses derniers retranchements*, to drive s.o. to the last extremity, to leave s.o. without a leg to stand on, to cut the ground from under s.o.'s feet; *poussé dans ses derniers retranchements*, driven into a corner, with one's back to the wall.
retrancher [-ʃe] v. tr. (1). To retrench; to cut out, to excise (un mot); to cut (de, out of) [un passage]; to take away (à, from) [qqch.]. ‖ Milit. To entrench (un camp, une position). ‖ Math. To subtract (un nombre); to deduct (une somme).
— v. pr. **Se retrancher**, to retrench, to cut down one's expenses. ‖ Milit. To entrench oneself; to dig in; *se retrancher derrière*, to take shelter behind. ‖ Fig. To hedge (derrière, behind); *se retrancher derrière sa dignité*, to stand on one's dignity; *se retrancher derrière un prétexte*, to take refuge behind (ou) resort to a pretext.
retranscrire [rətrãskri:r] v. tr. (44). To retranscribe, to copy out again.
retransmetteur [rətrãsmɛtœ:r] m. Radio, Electr. Retransmitter.
retransmettre [-mɛtr] v. tr. (64). Radio. To retransmit.
retransmission [-misjõ] f. Radio. Retransmission.
retravailler [rətravaje] v. tr. (1). To work over again, to touch up (un ouvrage).
— v. intr. To work again, to rework.
retraverser [rətravɛrse] v. tr. (1). To recross.
— v. intr. To cross again.
rétréci, ie [retresi] adj. Narrow, contracted. ‖ Fig. Narrow, limited (esprit).
rétrécir [-si:r] v. tr. (2). To shrink (une étoffe); to narrow (une route); to take in (un vêtement). ‖ Fig. To restrict, to narrow.
— v. intr. To shrink (étoffe); to narrow, to become (ou) get narrow (route).
— v. pr. **Se rétrécir**, to shrink (étoffe); to narrow (route). ‖ Fig. To get narrow, to become restricted (idées).
rétrécissement [-sismã] m. Shrinking (d'une étoffe); narrowing (d'une route). ‖ Narrow part (d'un objet). ‖ Méd. Stricture.
retrempe [rətrã:p] f. Techn. Retempering.
retremper [-trãpe] v. tr. (1). To soak (ou) dip (ou) steep again (du linge). ‖ Techn. To retemper (de l'acier). ‖ Fig. To retemper (l'âme); to strengthen, to fortify (qqn).
— v. pr. **Se retremper**, to gain in strength (ou) fortitude; *se retremper dans*, to gain strength through. ‖ Fam. To immerse oneself again.
rétribuer [retribɥe] v. tr. (1). To pay, to remunerate.
rétributeur [-bytœ:r] m. Remunerator.

rétribution [-bysjɔ̃] f. Remuneration, payment; *sans rétribution*, unpaid, honorary.

rétro [retro] adj. FAM. Imitating a fashion or a style of the recent past; attached to the recent past (personne).
— m. FAM. Style imitating that of the recent past.

rétro m. AUTOM., FAM. Driving (ou) rear-view mirror (rétroviseur). ‖ SPORTS., FAM. Recoil (au billard).

rétroactif, ive [retroaktif, i:v] adj. JUR. Retroactive, retrospective (loi).

rétroaction [-sjɔ̃] f. Retroaction, retrospective effect. ‖ CYBERN. Feedback.

rétroactivement [-tivmã] adv. JUR. Retroactively, retrospectively.

rétroactivité [-tivite] f. JUR. Retroactivity, retrospective effect.

rétrocéder [-sede] v. tr. (5). To yield back. ‖ JUR. To retrocede.

rétrocessif, ive [-sɛsif, iv] adj. JUR. Retrocessive.

rétrocession [-sɛsjɔ̃] f. JUR. Retrocession.

rétroflexe [-flɛks] adj. GRAMM. Retroflex, cacuminal (consonne).
— f. GRAMM. Retroflex consonant, cacuminal.

rétrofusée [retrofyze] f. ASTRON. Retro-rocket.

rétrogradation [retrogradasjɔ̃] f. Retrogression, deterioration. ‖ MILIT. Reduction to a lower rank. ‖ ASTRON. Retrogradation.

rétrograde [-grad] adj. Backward, retrograde (mouvement). ‖ FIG. Retrograde (esprit).
— s. FAM. Back number.

rétrograder [-grade] v. intr. (1). To retrogress, to retire, to move backwards. ‖ ASTRON. To retrograde. ‖ MILIT. To fall back, to give ground. ‖ FIG. To decline, to retrograde.
— v. tr. MILIT. To reduce to a lower rank, to break.

rétrogressif, ive [retrogrɛsif, i:v] adj. Retrogressive.

rétrogression [-sjɔ̃] f. Retrogression.

rétropédalage [retropedala:ʒ] m. SPORTS. Back-pedalling.

rétropédaler [-le] v. intr. (1). To back-pedal.

rétrospectif, ive [retrospɛktif, i:v] adj. Retrospective.

rétrospection [-sjɔ̃] f. Retrospection.

rétrospective [-tiv] f. Retrospect.

rétrospectivement [-tivmã] adv. Retrospectively.

retroussé, ée [rətruse] adj. Turned up (bas de pantalon); tucked up, rolled up (manche); turned-up, snub (nez) [pour un homme]; tip-titled, retroussé [pour une femme]; tucked up (robe).

retroussement [-smã] m. Curling (des lèvres); tucking up (d'une robe).

retrousser [-se] v. tr. (1). To turn up (le bas d'un pantalon); to cock (un chapeau); to curl, to curl up (la lèvre); to tuck (ou) roll up (ses manches); to twist up (sa moustache); to tuck up (une robe).
— v. pr. **Se retrousser**, to tuck up one's dress.

retroussis [rətrusi] m. Top (d'une botte); facing, lappet (d'un uniforme).

retrouvailles [rətruva:j] f. pl. FAM. Reunion, meeting again.

retrouver [rətruve] v. tr. (1). To find again, to rediscover (qqch.). ‖ To meet with again, to find again, to rejoin, to join (qqn); *aller retrouver qqn*, to go and join s.o., to join up with s.o. ‖ MÉD. To regain (ses forces); *retrouver la santé*, to be restored to health. ‖ FIG. To recover, to get back; *retrouver la parole*, to recover one's speech. ‖ FIG. To recognize; *je ne le retrouve plus!*, that's not like him at all! ‖ FIG. To trace (déceler).
— v. pr. **Se retrouver**, to find oneself; to return after an absence. ‖ To meet again; *comme on se retrouve!*, fancy our meeting again!, what a small place the world is! ‖ FIG. To find one's bearings; *je ne m'y retrouve plus*, I feel all at sea. ‖ FAM. To make up one's expenditure.

rétroversion [-vɛrsjɔ̃] f. MÉD. Retroversion.

rétroviseur [-vizœ:r] m. AUTOM. Mirror, driving-mirror.

rets [rɛ] m. Net. ‖ FIG. Pl. Toils; *se laisser prendre dans les rets d'une femme*, to fall into a woman's clutches, to fall prey to a woman's wiles.

réunification [reynifikasjɔ̃] f. Reunification.

réunifier [-fje] v. tr. (1). To reunify.

Réunion [reynjɔ̃] f. GÉOGR. Reunion.

réunion [reynjɔ̃] f. Reunion, reuniting, joining up (ou) together, connection, connecting, bringing together (acte); assembly, gathering, meeting, party (assemblée); *salle de réunion*, assembly room. ‖ MÉD. Reunion, bringing together. ‖ JUR. Union, uniting (d'une province). ‖ MILIT. Juncture, joining up.

réunir [-ni:r] v. tr. (2). To join [à, to, with]; to join together (les deux bouts d'une corde); to concentrate (les rayons du soleil). ‖ MÉD. To bring together (les bords d'une plaie). ‖ MILIT. To gather together, to raise (des troupes). ‖ FIN. To raise, to collect (des fonds). ‖ JUR. To convene (une assemblée); to unite (une province). ‖ FIG. To reconcile (les gens); to combine (des qualités); *l'intérêt réunit les hommes*, mutual interest binds men together; *réunir toutes les conditions*, to satisfy all requirements.
— v. pr. **Se réunir**, to meet, to join, to come together. ‖ MÉD., MILIT. To join. ‖ FIG. To combine (pour, to).

réussi, ie [reysi] adj. Successful, well executed (entreprise); happy (mariage); successful (soirée); *mal réussi*, unsuccessful, badly carried out.

réussir [-si:r] v. intr. (2). To result, to come (ou) work out (aboutir); *mal réussir*, to turn out badly; *ne pas savoir comment un projet réussira*, not to know how a plan will work out. ‖ To succeed, to work out well, to be successful (chose); *l'audace réussit souvent*, boldness often pays; *expédition qui n'a pas réussi*, unsuccessful expedition; *rien ne lui réussit*, everything he touches goes wrong; *tout lui réussit*, everything turns out well for him. ‖ To succeed, to be sucessful (personne); *réussir à*, to succeed in (qqch.); *réussir à faire*, to succeed in doing, to manage to do; *réussir à un examen*, to pass an examination; *réussir dans*, to make a success of; *il réussira*, he'll do well, he'll get on in life. ‖ THÉÂTR. To be a success, to catch on (pièce). ‖ BOT. To thrive (plante).
— v. tr. To make a success of (qqch.); to perform well (ou) with success (ou) successfully (une tâche); *réussir le coup*, to bring it off. ‖ ARTS. To make a success of (un portrait). ‖ CULIN. To make a success of (un plat). ‖ THÉÂTR. To be successful in (un rôle).

réussite [reysit] f. † Result, issue, outcome, upshot (résultat). ‖ Success (v. SUCCÈS). ‖ Patience; *faire des réussites*, to play patience (aux cartes).

revaccination [rəvaksinasjɔ̃] f. MÉD. Revaccination.

revacciner [-ne] v. tr. (1). To revaccinate.

revaloir [rəvalwa:r] v. tr. (103). To return like for like, to pay back in kind; *je vous revaudrai cela!*, I'll pay you out for that, I'll get even with you!

revalorisation [rəvalɔrizasjɔ̃] f. FIN. Revalorization.

revaloriser [-ze] v. tr. (1). FIN. To revalue.

revanchard, arde [rəvãʃa:r, ard] adj., n. Revanchist.

revanche [rəvãʃ] f. Revenge; *prendre sa revanche*, to take one's revenge, to wreak vengeance; to get even, to even the score (fam.);

prendre sa revanche sur, to wreak vengeance on, to get even with. ‖ Requital, something in return ; à charge de revanche, on condition that something similar is done in return ; en revanche, in return, on the other hand. ‖ SPORTS. Return match.

rêvasser [rɛvase] v. intr. (1). To day-dream ; to be wool-gathering.

rêvasserie [-sri] f. Day-dreaming, musing. ‖ FIG. Chim(a)era, fantasy, pipe-dream.

rêvasseur [-sœ:r] s. Day-dreamer.

rêve [rɛ:v] m. Dream (v. SONGE) ; faire de mauvais rêves, to dream bad dreams. ‖ FIG. Dream, day-dream, pipe-dream. ‖ FAM. Ce n'est pas le rêve, it's far from perfect, it's not all one would wish for.

revêche [rəvɛʃ] adj. Rough (étoffe) ; hard to work (pierre) ; harsh (vin). ‖ FIG. Ill-tempered, crabbed, sour, cross-grained (personne).

réveil [revɛ:j] m. Waking, waking up, awakening (v. ÉVEIL) ; à son réveil, on waking up. ‖ Alarm-clock (réveille-matin). ‖ MILIT. Reveille. ‖ ECCLÉS. Revival. ‖ FIG. Awakening (de la nature).

réveille-matin [revɛjmatɛ̃] m. invar. Alarm-clock.

réveiller [revɛje] v. tr. (1). To waken, to awaken, to wake up, to rouse (v. ÉVEILLER). ‖ MILIT., NAUT. To turn out (des hommes). ‖ FIG. To excite, to arouse (l'attention) ; to stir up (le courage) ; to start up again (une douleur) ; to awaken, to rouse (un sentiment) ; to revive (un souvenir). — v. pr. Se réveiller, to wake up, to awake, to awaken. ‖ FIG. To revive (nature) ; to be aroused (sentiment).

réveillon [-jɔ̃] m. Christmas (ou) New Year's Eve party ; faire réveillon, to see the New Year (ou) Christmas in.

réveillonner [-jɔne] v. intr. (1). To go to a réveillon ; to see the New Year in.

révélateur, trice [revelatœ:r, tris] adj. Revealing (circonstance) ; tell-tale (signe). — s. Revealer, discloser. — m. Developer (en photographie).

révélation [-lasjɔ̃] f. Revelation, disclosure ; révélation d'un secret, giving away of a secret. ‖ ECCLÉS. Revelation.

révéler [-le] v. tr. (5). To reveal, to disclose ; to divulge (un secret). ‖ To show, to betoken, to display (de la bonté) ; to betray (de l'embarras) ; les grandes actions révèlent les grands esprits, great actions speak great minds. ‖ To develop (un cliché). ‖ ECCLÉS. Révélé, revealed. — v. pr. Se révéler, to show (ou) reveal oneself. ‖ To be revealed, to come to light, to come out (fait, vérité). ‖ ECCLÉS. To make oneself known, to reveal oneself.

revenant [rəvnɑ̃] m. Ghost ; spook (fam.). ‖ FAM. Mais c'est un revenant !, you are quite a stranger !

revendeur, euse [rəvɑ̃dœ:r, ø:z] s. COMM. Retailer, middleman ; second-hand dealer.

revendicateur, trice [revɑ̃dikatœ:r, tris] s. Protester.

revendicatif, ive [-katif, i:v] adj. Protest.

revendication [-kasjɔ̃] f. Claim, demand, protest ; revendication de salaires, territoriale, wage, territorial claim ; revendications étudiantes, student protest.

revendiquer [-ke] v. tr. (1). To claim, to lay claim to (un territoire, un héritage) ; to assert, to claim (un droit) ; to demand, to put in a claim for (une augmentation de salaire) ; to claim (la responsabilité d'un acte) ; revendiquer la paternité d'un livre, to claim to be the author of a book. — v. intr. To protest.

revendre [rəvɑ̃:dr] v. tr. (4). COMM. To sell again, to resell. ‖ FIN. To sell out (ses titres). ‖ FAM. En revendre à, to put one over on.

revenez-y [rəvnezi] m. invar. FAM. Going back, return ; repetition ; plat qui a un goût de revenez-y, dish that is a bit more-ish ; revenez-y de jeunesse, return to one's youth.

revenir [rəvni:r] v. intr. (101).

---

1. Sens général. — 2. Se renouveler. — 3. MÉD. — 4. CULIN. — 5. FIN. — 6. FIG. Retourner. — 7. Se remettre. — 8. Se résoudre. — 9. Appartenir. — 10. FAM.

---

1. To come back, to return, to come (sens général) ; en revenant, on one's way back ; revenir à pied, à cheval, to walk, to ride back ; revenir en auto, en courant, to drive, to run back ; revenir par avion, par chemin de fer, to fly back, to take a train back (ou) to come back by rail ; revenir sur l'eau, to come to the surface again. ‖ **2.** To return, to come again (se renouveler) ; to come round again, to occur again (anniversaire) ; to come back, to return (mode) ; to return, to come again (printemps) ; to crop up again (question) ; to come out again (soleil) ; to return, to be recalled (souvenir) ; son nom ne me revient pas, I cannot recall his name. ‖ **3.** MÉD. To repeat, to come back (à, on) [aliment] ; to return, to come back (forces) ; revenir à soi, to come round, to recover consciousness ; revenir à la santé, to recover (ou) get back one's health ; revenir de loin, to have been at death's door ; revenir d'une maladie, to recover from (ou) get over an illness. ‖ **4.** CULIN. To soften up (gâteau) ; faire revenir la viande, to brown the meat. ‖ **5.** FIN. To cost ; à combien cela revient-il ?, how much does that come to ? ; revenir à, to come out at (un prix) ; il me revient encore cent francs, there's another hundred francs owing (ou) due to me ; I still have a hundred francs to come. ‖ **6.** FIG. To return (à, sur, to) [retourner] ; revenir à la charge, to return to the charge, to make a fresh effort ; revenir à la question, to get back to the matter in hand ; revenons à nos moutons, let's get back to the point ; revenir sur une opinion, to reconsider an opinion ; revenir sur sa parole, une promesse, to go back on one's word, a promise ; revenir sur une question, to re-examine a question ; revenir sans cesse sur le même sujet, to keep harping on the same string. ‖ **7.** FIG. To recover (se remettre) ; en revenir, to get over it ; je n'en reviens pas !, it beats me ! ; revenir d'une erreur, d'une illusion, to realize one's mistake, to shake off an illusion ; revenir de ses émotions, to get over a shock. ‖ **8.** FIG. To amount, to come (à, to) [se résoudre] ; cela revient à dire que, that amounts (ou) is tantamount to saying that ; cela revient au même, that amounts (ou) comes to the same thing ; tout revient à ceci, it all comes (ou) boils down to this. ‖ **9.** FIG. To fall, to be owing (à, to) [appartenir] ; à chacun ce qui lui revient, give every man his due ; bien qui revient à l'Etat, property which reverts to the State ; honneur qui me revient, honour that falls to me by right. ‖ **10.** FAM. To come round, to make it up ; ils sont revenus ensemble, they have made it up again, they have patched up their quarrel ; revenir après s'être emporté, to cool down after flying into a passion. ‖ FAM. To please ; sa figure me revient, I like the look of him.

revente [rəvɑ̃:t] f. COMM. Resale. ‖ FIN. Selling out (de titres).

revenu [rəvəny] m. FIN. Revenue (de l'Etat) ; income (d'une personne) ; à revenu fixe, fixed-interest (valeur). ‖ TECHN. Drawing, tempering (de l'acier).

rêver [rɛve] v. intr. (1). To dream (de, about) [qqch., qqn]. ‖ To muse, to day-dream, to be wool-gathering (rêvasser) ; to dream (à, of) ; à

quoi rêvez-vous?, what are you dreaming about ?, a penny for your thoughts ; *rêver tout éveillé,* to be in the clouds, to give free rein to one's thoughts ; *vous rêvez!,* you are dreaming ! you are out of your mind ! ‖ To think (*à,* about) [réfléchir]. ‖ To meditate (*sur,* on) ; to ponder (*sur,* over). ‖ To long, to yearn (*de,* for) [désirer].
— v. tr. To dream of ; to see in one's dreams (qqch.) ; *vous l'avez rêvé!* you must have dreamt it. ‖ FIG. To desire ardently ; *c'est la femme rêvée,* she's the wife of one's dreams ; *rêver mariage,* to dream of marriage.

réverbération [revɛrberasjɔ̃] f. Reverberation, reflexion (de la lumière) ; reverberation, re-echoing (du son).

réverbère [-bɛ:r] m. Street-lamp ; reflector. ‖ TECHN. *Four à réverbère,* reverberating furnace.

réverbérer [-bere] v. tr. (5). To reflect, to send back.
— v. pr. **Se réverbérer,** to reflect, to reverberate.

reverdir [rəvɛrdi:r] v. tr. (2). TECHN., ARTS. To paint green again. ‖ BOT. To make verdant again.
— v. intr. BOT. To grow green again, to become verdant again. ‖ FAM. To grow young again (personne).

révérence [reverã:s] f. Reverence, respect. ‖ Bow, curtsy ; *faire la révérence,* to bow, to curtsy, to make a bow, to drop a curtsy. ‖ ECCLÉS. Reverence. ‖ FAM. *Révérence parler,* saving your presence, with all due respect ; *tirer sa révérence,* to take one's leave.

révérenciel, elle [-rãsjɛ] adj. Reverential.

révérencieux, euse [-rãsjø, ø:z] adj. Respectful, reverent ; ceremonious.

révérend, ende [reverã, ã:d] adj. ECCLÉS. Reverend.
— m. FAM. Reverend Father.

révérendissime [-disim] adj. ECCLÉS. Very (ou) Right Reverend.

révérer [revere] v. tr. (5). To revere, to respect, to reverence.

rêverie [rɛvri] f. Reverie, musing, meditation. ‖ Vain illusion, fantastic idea, chimera.

revernir [rəvɛrni:r] v. tr. (2). To revarnish.

revers [rəvɛ:r] m. Reverse, reverse side (v. ENVERS) ; top (d'une botte) ; wrong side (d'une étoffe) ; lapel, revers (d'un habit) ; back (de la main) ; reverse, reverse side, obverse (d'une médaille, d'une pièce) ; other side (d'une page) ; turn-up (de pantalon). ‖ MUS. Other side (d'un disque). ‖ MILIT. Facing (d'un uniforme) ; outside edge (d'une tranchée) ; *prendre à revers,* to take in the rear. ‖ NAUT. *Echelle de revers,* Jacob's ladder. ‖ SPORTS. Back-hand ; *coup de revers,* back-hand stroke ; *en revers,* on the backhand (au tennis). ‖ FIG. Reverse, set-back ; *éprouver des revers de fortune,* to suffer set-backs ; *revers de la médaille,* other side of the medal (ou) picture, seamy side of things.

reverser [rəvɛrse] v. tr. (1). To pour out again ; *reverser à boire,* to pour out another drink. ‖ To pour back ; *reverser du vin dans la bouteille,* to pour wine back into the bottle. ‖ JUR. To transfer (un titre de propriété). ‖ NAUT. To transship. ‖ FIG. To shift (la responsabilité) [*sur,* on).

réversibilité [-sibilite] f. Reversibility.

réversible [-sibl] adj. PHYS. Reversible. ‖ JUR. Revertible (bien, pension). ‖ COMM. Reversible (tissu, vêtement).

réversion [-sjɔ̃] f. JUR. Reversion.

revêtement [rəvɛtmã] m. ARCHIT. Facing, lining, coating, covering. ‖ MILIT. Revetment (d'une tranchée). ‖ NAUT. Skin, skinning (d'un vaisseau). ‖ TECHN. Veneer (de bois) ; metal-cladding (en métal) ; *revêtement calorifuge,* lagging.

revêtir [rəvɛti:r] v. tr. (104). To reclothe, to clothe again (vêtir à nouveau). ‖ To clothe, to

dress (pourvoir). ‖ To put on, to don (un habit). ‖ ARCHIT. To face, to line (un mur). ‖ MILIT. To revet (une tranchée). ‖ NAUT. To skin (un vaisseau). ‖ JUR. *Revêtir un document de sa signature,* to put one's signature to a document. ‖ TECHN. To lag (une chaudière). ‖ FIG. To invest (*de,* with) [une dignité]. ‖ FIG. To take on (un caractère) ; to assume (une forme) ; *revêtir le mal des apparences du bien,* to cloak evil in the semblance of good ; to whitewash a bad case (fam.) ; *revêtir ses pensées d'une forme précise,* to couch one's thoughts in precise terms.
— v. pr. **Se revêtir,** to get dressed again, to put on one's clothes again ; *se revêtir de,* to clothe oneself in, to be covered in.

rêveur, euse [rɛvœ:r, ø:z] adj. Dreamy, dreaming, musing, wool-gathering. (V. MÉDITATIF.)
— s. Dreamer, wool-gatherer.

rêveusement [-vøzmã] adv. Dreamily.

revider [rəvide] v. tr. (1). To re-empty, to empty again.

revient [rəvjɛ̃] m. COMM. *Prix de revient,* cost price, cost of production.

revigorer [rəvigɔre] v. tr. (1). To reinvigorate ; to give fresh vigour to.

revirement [rəvirmã] m. NAUT. Tacking, going about. ‖ FIN. Transfer, making over (d'une dette). ‖ FIG. Sudden change (de fortune) ; veering, changing (d'opinion) ; revulsion (de sentiment).

revirer [-re] v. intr. (1). NAUT. To tack, to go about. ‖ FIG. To change sides, to turn one's coat ; to rat (fam.).

révisable [revizabl] adj. JUR. Revisable.

reviser [-ze] v. tr. (1). To examine again, to go through again (qqch.). ‖ To revise (un texte). ‖ FIN. To audit (un compte). ‖ JUR. To review (un jugement). ‖ AUTOM. To overhaul (une auto).

réviseur [-zœ:r] m. Reviser, revisor, examiner, inspector. ‖ Reader (d'épreuves). ‖ FIN. Auditor.

révision [-zjɔ̃] f. Revision, examination, inspection (de qqch.). ‖ Reading (d'épreuves). ‖ FIN. Audit, auditing (de comptes). ‖ JUR. Review (d'un jugement). ‖ AUTOM. Overhauling (d'une auto). ‖ MILIT. Reviewing board (conseil).

révisionnisme [-zjɔnism] m. Revisionism.

révisionniste [-zjɔnist] adj., n. Revisionist.

revisiter [rəvizite] v. tr. (1). To revisit, to pay another visit to.

revitaliser [rəvitalize] v. tr. (1). To revitalize, to bring new life to.

revivification [rəvivifikasjɔ̃] f. Revivification.

revivifier [-fje] v. tr. (1). To revivify, to revive.

reviviscence [rəvivisã:s] f. Reviviscence.

revivre [rəvi:vr] v. intr. (105). To live again, to come to life again (se ranimer) ; *faire revivre,* to revive, to restore to life. ‖ To gain in strength (se fortifier) ; *se sentir revivre,* to feel a new man. ‖ FIG. To live again (*dans,* in) ; *faire revivre,* to revive (ou) bring back (une coutume).
— v. tr. *Revivre sa vie,* to live one's life over again.

révocabilité [revɔkabilite] f. JUR. Revocability.

révocable [-kabl] adj. JUR. Revocable, subject to appeal (édit) ; removable, subject to dismissal (fonctionnaire).

révocation [-kasjɔ̃] f. JUR. ·Revocation, repeal (d'un édit) ; dismissal (d'un fonctionnaire) ; revocation, annulment (d'un testament).

révocatoire [-katwa:r] adj. JUR. Revocatory.

revoici [rəvwasi] prép. FAM. *Me revoici!,* here I am again !

revoilà [rəvwala] prép. FAM. *Me revoilà!,* there I am again !

revoir [rəvwa:r] v. tr. (106). To see again (qqch., qqn) ; to meet again (qqn). ‖ To visit again, to return to (un pays). ‖ To revise, to re-examine,

to go through again (des comptes, des épreuves, un manuscrit) ; *à revoir,* to be revised.
— v. pr. **Se revoir,** to see (ou) to meet each other again (se rencontrer). ‖ To be seen again.
— m. *Au revoir,* good-bye for the present ; so long, cheerio.

revoler [rəvɔle] v. tr. (1). To steal again (voleur).
revoler [rəvɔle] v. intr. (1). To fly again (ou) back (oiseau). ‖ FIG. To fly (ou) hasten back.
révoltant, ante [revɔltᾶ, ᾶːt] adj. Revolting, disgusting, sickening (spectacle). ‖ Outrageous, disgusting, shocking (procédé).
révolte [revɔlt] f. Revolt, rebellion, insurrection. ‖ FIG. Revolt (de la conscience).
révolté [-te] s. Rebel, insurgent.
révolter [-te] v. tr. (1). To rouse, to stir up (*against,* contre). ‖ FIG. To disgust, to sicken, to revolt (qqn) ; *qui révolte,* shocking (action).
— v. pr. **Se révolter,** to revolt, to rebel, to rise (*contre,* against).
révolu, ue [revɔly] adj. Completed (temps) ; *avoir vingt ans révolus,* to have completed one's twentieth year.
révoluté, ée [revɔlyte] adj. BOT. Revolute (feuille).
révolution [-sjɔ̃] f. MATH. Revolution. ‖ ASTRON. Rotation. ‖ FIG. Upset, change, revolution ; *révolution dans les arts,* artistic revolution.
révolutionnaire [-sjɔnɛːr] adj. Revolutionary.
— s. Revolutionary ; revolutionist.
révolutionnairement [-sjɔnɛrmᾶ] adv. By means of revolution.
révolutionner [-sjɔne] v. tr. (1). To stir up ; *révolutionner un pays,* to cause a country to revolt. ‖ FIG. To revolutionize (les mœurs). ‖ FAM. To upset (qqn) [v. RETOURNER].
revolver [rəvɔlvɛːr] m. Revolver. ‖ Humane killer (aux abattoirs). ‖ TECHN. *Tour à revolver* (ou) *revolver,* turret (ou) capstan lathe.
revolvériser [-vɛrize] v. tr. FAM. To shoot up.
révoquer [revɔke] v. tr. (1). To countermand, to cancel (un ordre). ‖ JUR. To recall (un ambassadeur) ; to revoke, to repeal, to rescind (un édit) ; to dismiss (un fonctionnaire) ; to adeem (un legs). ‖ FIG. *Révoquer en doute,* to call into question.
revoter [rəvɔte] v. intr. (1). To vote again, to revote.
— v. tr. To vote for again.
revouloir [rəvulwaːr] v. tr. (107). To wish (ou) desire again ; to wish for (ou) desire more.
revoyure [rəvwajyːr] f. POP. *A la revoyure,* bye, cheerio, see you.
revue [rəvy] f. Review, examination, inspection ; *passer en revue,* to go through (ses papiers) ; to survey (sa vie). ‖ Review, magazine (journal). ‖ MILIT. Review ; *passer en revue,* to review ; *revue de détail,* detailed kit check. ‖ THÉÂTR. Revue. ‖ FAM. *Etre de revue,* to meet again, to see each other often ; *être encore de la revue,* to be for the high jump, to be in for it again. ‖ **Revue-féerie,** f. THÉÂTR. Pantomime.
revuiste [-ist] s. THÉÂTR. Writer of revues.
révulsé, ée [revylse] adj. Distorted, contracted, twisted (figure) ; turned upwards (yeux).
révulser v. tr. (1). To distort, to contract, to twist (la figure) ; to turn (ou) roll upwards (les yeux).
révulsif, ive [-sif, iːv] adj., m. MÉD. Revulsive.
révulsion [-sjɔ̃] f. MÉD. Revulsion.
rewriting [rərajtiŋ] m. Rewriting.
rez-de-chaussée [redʃose] m. invar. Ground level ; ground floor ; *au rez-de-chaussée,* on the ground floor.
R. F. [ɛrɛf] abrév. de *République française,* the French Republic, France.
rhabillage [rabijaːʒ] m. Dressing (ou) getting dressed again.

rhabiller [rabije] v. tr. (1). To repair, to patch up, to overhaul, to mend (raccommoder). ‖ To reclothe, to provide with new clothing (revêtir). ‖ FIG. To dress up, to put into other words (une idée) ; to gloss over (une faute).
— v. pr. **Se rhabiller,** to get dressed again, to put one's clothes on again. ‖ To buy oneself new clothes.
rhabituer [rabitɥe] v. tr. (1). To reaccustom (*à,* to) ; *rhabituer qqn à qqch.,* to get s.o. accustomed to sth. again.
— v. pr. **Se rhabituer,** to become reaccustomed ; *se rhabituer à,* to reaccustom oneself to.
rhapsode [rapsɔd] m. † Rhapsode, rhapsodist.
rhapsodie [rapsɔdi] f. MUS. Rhapsody.
rhapsodiste [-dist] m. MUS. Rhapsodist.
rhénan, ane [renᾶ, ɑːn] adj. GÉOGR. Rhenish.
Rhénanie [-nani] f. GÉOGR. Rhineland.
rhenium [renjɔm] m. CHIM. Rhenium.
rhéostat [reɔsta] m. ÉLECTR. Rheostat.
rhésus [rezyːs] m. ZOOL. Rhesus (macaque). ‖ MÉD. Rhesus factor.
rhéteur [retœːr] m. Rhetor.
rhétoricien, enne [retɔrisjɛ̃, ɛn] adj. Rhetorical.
— s. Rhetorician.
rhétorique [retɔrik] f. Rhetoric ; *figure de rhétorique,* figure of speech. ‖ † Sixth form, U. S. twelfth class (classe).
rhéto-roman, ane [retɔromᾶ, an] adj. GRAMM. Rhaeto-Romanic.
Rhin [rɛ̃] m. GÉOGR. The Rhine ; *du Rhin,* Rhine (vallée) ; Rhine, Rhenish (vin).
rhinite [rinit] f. MÉD. Rhinitis.
rhinocéros [rinɔserɔs] m. ZOOL. Rhinoceros.
rhinologie [rinɔlɔʒi] f. MÉD. Rhinology.
rhino-pharyngien, enne [-farɛ̃ʒjɛ̃, ɛn] adj. MÉD. Rhinopharyngeal.
rhino-pharyngite [-farɛ̃ʒit] f. MÉD. Rhinopharyngitis, cold, sore throat.
rhinoplastie [-plasti] f. MÉD. Rhinoplasty.
rhinoscopie [-skɔpi] f. MÉD. Rhinoscopy.
rhizome [rizɔːm] m. BOT. Rhizome.
rhodamine [rɔdamin] f. CHIM. Rhodamin(e).
rhodanien, enne [rɔdanjɛ̃, ɛn] adj. GÉOGR. Of the Rhone ; *vallée rhodanienne,* Rhone valley.
Rhodésie [rɔdezi] f. GÉOGR. Rhodesia.
rhodium [rɔdjɔm] m. CHIM. Rhodium.
rhododendron [rɔdɔdɛ̃drɔ̃] m. BOT. Rhododendron.
rhombe [rɔ̃ːb] m. MATH. Rhomb, rhombus.
rhombique [-ik] adj. MATH. Rhombic.
rhomboèdre [rɔ̃bɔɛdr] m. Rhombohedron.
rhomboïde [-id] m. MATH. Rhomboid.
rhubarbe [rybarb] f. BOT. Rhubarb. ‖ LOC. *Passez-moi la rhubarbe et je vous passerai le séné,* you scratch my back and I'll scratch yours, I'll give you a dose of your own medicine.
rhum [rɔm] m. Rum.
rhumatisant, ante [rymatizᾶ, ᾶːt] adj. MÉD. Rheumatic.
— s. MÉD. Rheumatic person.
rhumatismal, ale [-tismal] adj. MÉD. Rheumatic.
rhumatisme [-tism] m. MÉD. Rheumatism ; rheumatics (fam.) ; *rhumatisme articulaire,* rheumatism in the joints, rheumatoid arthritis ; *rhumatisme articulaire aigu,* rheumatic fever ; *rhumatisme musculaire,* fibrositis.
rhumatologie [-tɔlɔʒi] f. MÉD. Rheumatology.
rhumatologue [-tɔlɔg] m. MÉD. Rheumatologist.
rhume [rym] m. MÉD. Cold ; *prendre un rhume,* to catch cold ; *rhume de cerveau, de poitrine,* cold in the head, on the chest ; *rhume des foins,* hay fever. ‖ FAM. *Prendre qqch. pour son rhume,* to get hauled over the coals, to catch it hot.
rhumerie [rɔmri] f. Rum-distillery.
ria [rja] f. GÉOGR. Ria.
riant, ante [rijᾶ, ᾶːt] adj. Cheerful (air) ; smiling

(paysage); pleasant, agreeable (pensée); happy, gay, smiling (personne).

ribambelle [ribɑ̃bɛl] f. FAM. Crowd, swarm, host (d'enfants); volley (d'injures); string (de noms).

ribaud, aude [ribo, o:d] adj., s. † Ribald.

riboflavine [riboflavin] f. MÉD. Riboflavin.

ribonucléique [-nykleik] adj. MÉD. Ribonucleic (acide).

ribote [ribɔt] f. FAM. Drinking bout (v. BOMBE); *en ribote,* on the spree, U. S. on a bender.

ribouis [ribwi] m. POP. Cobbler, snob.

ribouldingue [ribuldɛ̃:g] f. FAM. Spree; razzle-dazzle; U. S. bust.

ricain, aine [rikɛ̃, ɛn] adj. Yankee.
— s. Yank, yankee.

ricanement [rikanmɑ̃] m. Sneering, smirking, snickering, simpering.

ricaner [-ne] v. intr. (1). To sneer, to smirk, to snicker.

ricaneur [-nœ:r] adj. Sneering, derisive (air).
— s. Sneerer, smirker.

richard, arde [riʃa:r, a:rd] s. FAM. Wealthy person (v. RUPIN); *c'est un richard,* he's in the money; he's got bags of lolly; U. S. he's rolling in dough (pop.).

riche [riʃ] adj. Rich, opulent (pays); rich, well-off, wealthy, moneyed (personne); *riche à millions,* rolling in money, rolling in it (pop.); *riche d'un million,* worth a million. ‖ Handsome (cadeau); rich, costly (étoffe); elaborate, splendid, costly (habit). ‖ Rich (de, en, in); crammed (de, en, with); full (de, en, of). ‖ Rich (langue, rime); rich, fruitful, prolific (sujet). ‖ AGRIC. Abundant (moisson); rich, fertile, productive (sol). ‖ MÉD. *Riche en protéine,* rich in protein, with a high protein content. ‖ AUTOM. Rich (mélange). ‖ FAM. *Ce n'est pas riche,* that's not up to much; *riche idée,* grand (ou) first-rate idea, topping wheeze.
— s. Rich person; *nouveau riche,* nouveau riche; *les riches,* the rich.

richelieu [riʃəljø] m. Lace-up shoe.

richement [riʃmɑ̃] adv. Richly, abundantly, sumptuously; *être richement installé,* to live in luxurious surroundings. ‖ FAM. Abundantly.

richesse [riʃɛs] f. Riches, wealth, fortune, opulence; *vivre dans la richesse,* to live in opulence. ‖ Sumptuousness (d'ameublement); richness (d'une étoffe); magnificence (de parure). ‖ Object of value; *musée plein de richesses,* museum full of fine works of art; *la science est une richesse,* science is a boon. ‖ AGRIC. Fertility, productiveness (du sol); luxuriance (de la végétation). ‖ FIG. Richness, vividness (du coloris); richness (de la langue); richness (de la rime); exuberance, fullness, brilliance (du style).

richissime [riʃisim] adj. FAM. Very wealthy; rolling in money.

ricin [risɛ̃] m. BOT. Ricinus, castor-oil plant, palma Christi; *huile de ricin,* castor-oil.

ricocher [rikɔʃe] v. intr. (1). To ricochet, to skip, to bounce, to rebound. ‖ FIG. To rebound; to recoil (sur, on).

ricochet [-ʃɛ] m. Ricochet, rebound; *faire des ricochets,* to play ducks and drakes. ‖ MILIT. Ricochet; *tir à ricochet,* ricochet fire. ‖ FIG. *Par ricochet,* indirectly, in a roundabout way.

ric-rac [rikrak] adv. FAM. Punctually; *payer ric-rac,* to pay on the nail (ou) the dot.

rictus [rikty:s] m. MÉD. Rictus. ‖ FAM. *Rictus moqueur,* mocking grin.

ride [rid] f. Wrinkle, line (sur la figure); ripple, (sur la mer); wrinkle (sur le papier); ridge, ripple (sur le sable). ‖ NAUT. Lanyard (de hauban).

ridé, ée [ride] adj. Wrinkled (figure); rippled mer); ribbed (sable). ‖ BOT. Rugose; shrivelled (pomme) .

rideau [rido] m. Curtain; *rideau de fenêtre, de*

lit, window-, bed-curtain. ‖ Screen, curtain (d'arbres); bank (de brume). ‖ MILIT. Rideau (d'une forteresse); screen, curtain (de troupes); *rideau de fumée,* smoke-screen. ‖ THÉÂTR. Curtain, drop-curtain; *rideau à huit heures,* the curtain goes up at eight o'clock; *rideau de fer,* safety curtain. ‖ JUR. *Rideau de fer,* the Iron Curtain. ‖ COMM. *Rideau ondulé,* rolling shutter. ‖ FIG. *Se tenir derrière le rideau,* to remain behind the scenes; *tirer le rideau sur,* to draw a veil over. ‖ FAM. *Rideau!,* that's enough of that!

ridectomie [ridɛktɔmi] f. MÉD. Face-lifting.

ridelle [ridel] f. Rail (de charrette).

rider [ride] v. tr. (1). To pucker (l'étoffe); to wrinkle, to line (la figure); to ripple, to ruffle (la mer); to wrinkle (du papier); to shrivel, to wrinkle (la peau, une pomme); to rib (du sable). ‖ NAUT. To tighten, to set up (les haubans).
— v. pr. **Se rider,** to wrinkle, to pucker up, to become wrinkled (étoffe, figure); to ripple (mer); to shrivel (peau, pomme).

ridicule [ridikyl] adj. Ridiculous, laughable, absurd, ludicrous; *se rendre ridicule,* to make oneself ridiculous (ou) a laughing-stock.
— m. Ridiculousness, absurdity; *les ridicules de son temps,* the absurdities of one's day. ‖ Ridiculous part (d'une affaire); ridiculous side (d'une situation). ‖ Ridicule; *jeter le ridicule sur,* to heap ridicule on; *tomber dans le ridicule,* to make oneself look ridiculous; *tourner en ridicule,* to hold up to ridicule.

ridiculement [-lmɑ̃] adv. Ridiculously.

ridiculiser [-lize] v. tr. (1). To ridicule, to make look ridiculous, to hold up to ridicule, to poke fun at.

ridoir [ridwa:r] m. NAUT. Turnbuckle.

rien [rjɛ̃] pron.

1. Quelque chose. — 2. Peu. — 3. Aucune chose. — 4. Sports.

1. Anything (quelque chose); *a-t-on jamais vu rien de si beau?,* did you ever see anything so beautiful? ‖ 2. Little (peu); *avoir (ou) obtenir pour rien,* to get for next to nothing, to buy for a song. ‖ 3. Nothing (aucune chose); *cela ne fait rien,* that does not matter, that makes no difference; *cela n'a l'air de rien,* it looks as if there is nothing to it; *cela ne ressemble à rien,* that's neither fish, flesh nor fowl; *cela ne sert à rien,* it's of no use (ou) quite useless; *ce n'est pas rien!,* that's something!; *ce n'est rien,* it's nothing, no harm done; *c'est un homme de rien,* he's a nobody; *comme si de rien n'était,* as if nothing had happened, as if nothing were the matter; *de rien,* don't mention it (pour remercier); *en moins de rien,* in less time than it takes to tell, in next to no time; *il n'a rien d'un héros,* there is nothing of the hero about him; *il ne m'est rien,* he's nothing to me; *il n'en est rien,* such is not the case; *il n'est rien de tel que,* there nothing like; *il ne sait rien de rien,* he's absolutely ignorant; he doesn't know how many beans make five; *il n'y a rien à faire,* it can't be helped, there is nothing to be done about it; *je n'en ferai rien,* I'll do nothing of the sort (ou) kind; *ne ressembler à qqn en rien,* not to be a bit like s.o.; *n'être pour rien dans une affaire,* to have (ou) have had no hand in a matter; *parler pour ne rien dire,* to talk for the sake of hearing one's own voice, to open one's mouth and let one's tongue wag (pop.); *plus rien,* nothing more; *pour rien au monde,* not for worlds, not on any account; *rien d'autre, de nouveau, de moins, de plus,* nothing else, new, less, more; *rien du tout,* nothing at all, absolutely nothing; *rien moins que,* nothing less than, anything but; *rien que,* nothing

but, only, merely; *rien que cela!*, is that all!; *sans rien d'autre que*, with only, with nothing but; *sans rien faire*, without doing anything; *si cela ne vous fait rien*, if you don't mind, if you have no objection, if it's all the same to you; *tout le reste n'est rien*, nothing else matters; *vivre de rien*, to live on nothing (ou) on air. ‖ **4.** SPORTS. Love; *rien partout*, love-all (au tennis).
— adv. POP. Very, not half; *il est rien drôle*, he isn't half a caution, he's really funny.
— m. Nothingness. ‖ Trifle, bagatelle, mere nothing; *ajouter un rien d'eau*, to add the tiniest drop of water; *c'est un rien du tout*, he's lower than the dust, he's quite contemptible; *en un rien de temps*, in the flicker of an eyelid, in one shake of a lamb's tail; *petits riens*, merest trifles (ou) bagatelles; *s'amuser à des riens*, to fritter one's time away; *se fâcher pour un rien*, to get annoyed over nothing; *un rien l'effraye*, the slightest thing scares him.

rieur, euse [rijœ:r, ø:z] adj. Laughing, merry and bright.
— s. Laughter; *mettre les rieurs de son côté*, to have the laugh on one's side.

rififi [rififi] m. ARG. Scrap, aggro.

riflard [rifla:r] m. TECHN. Coarse file (lime); riffler, scraper (palette); jack-plane (rabot).

riflard m. POP. Gamp, brolly. (V. PÉPIN.)

rigaudon [rigodɔ̃] m. V. RIGODON.

rigide [riʒid] adj. Rigid, stiff, unyielding, inflexible. ‖ FIG. Strict, unbending, punctilious (personne); strict, inflexible, rigid (vertu).

rigidement [-dmɑ̃] adv. Rigidly.

rigidifier [-difje] v. tr. (1). To make rigid.

rigidité [-dite] f. Rigidity, stiffness, riginess. ‖ MÉD. *Rigidité cadavérique*, rigor mortis. ‖ FIG. Sternness, harshness, strictness, inflexibility.

rigodon [rigodɔ̃] m. MUS. Rigadoon. ‖ MILIT. Bull's-eye (au tir).

rigolade [rigolad] f. FAM. Laughter, lark; *tout ça, c'est de la rigolade*, that's just tomfoolery.

rigolard, arde [rigola:r, a:rd] adj. POP. Funny, droll (chose); fond of a lark, comic (personne).

rigole [rigɔl] f. Drain, ditch, trench, furrow. ‖ TECHN. Sow-channel (en métallurgie).

rigoler [rigɔle] v. intr. (1). FAM. To laugh, to joke, to have fun, to have a good time.

rigoleur, euse [-lœ:r, ø:z] adj. POP. Laughter-loving, jolly, fond of a joke.
— s. POP. Joker, gay spark.

Rigollot [rigɔlo] m. MÉD. Mustard-plaster.

rigolo, ote [-, ɔt] adj. FAM. Killing, funny, comical, droll, laughable (drôle); rum, queer (étrange); *ce n'était pas rigolo*, it was no joke; *il est rigolo*, he's a card.
— s. FAM. Joker; gay dog. [V. RIGOLEUR.]
— m. FAM. Rod; U. S. gat (revolver).

rigorisme [rigorism] m. Rigorism.

rigoriste [-rist] adj. Rigorous.
— s. Rigorist; hardshell (fam.).

rigoureusement [rigurøzmɑ̃] adv. Rigorously; strictly, harshly (durement). ‖ Exactly (avec précision).

rigoureux, euse [-rø, ø:z] adj. Rigorous. severe (climat); hard (hiver); strict (ordre); stern, harsh, severe, strict (personne); severe, harsh (punition); hard and fast (règle); hard, cruel (sort); *n'être pas trop rigoureux*, to be human.

rigueur [rigœ:r] f. Rigour, U. S. rigor (en général); severity (du climat); harshness, cruelty (du destin); stringency (d'une loi); harshness, sternness, strictness (d'une personne); severity, harshness (d'une punition); oppressiveness (d'un régime); *avec la dernière rigueur*, with the utmost severity; *user de rigueur envers*, to be hard on. ‖ Exactness, precision, preciseness (d'un raisonnement). ‖ Obligation; *de rigueur*, obligatory, indis-

pensable, compulsory; *l'habit est de rigueur*, evening dress is obligatory (ou) de rigueur; *l'habit n'est pas de rigueur*, evening dress optional. ‖ *À la rigueur*, at a pinch, if the worst comes to the worst.

rikiki [rikiki] adj. V. RIQUIQUI.

rillettes [rijɛt] f. pl. CULIN. Rillettes, potted minced pork.

rillons [rijɔ̃] m. pl. CULIN. Greaves, U. S. cracklings.

rimailler [rimɑje] v. intr. (1). To write bad verse (ou) doggerel, to dabble in poetry.

rimailleur [-jœ:r] m. FAM. Rhymester, third-rate (ou) would-be poet.

rimaye [rimɑ:j] f. GÉOGR. Bergschrund.

rime [rim] f. Rhyme; *rimes plates*, rhyming couplets. ‖ FAM. *Sans rime ni raison*, without rhyme or reason.

rimer [-me] v. intr. (1). To make rhymes, to write poetry (ou) verse, to versify (personne). ‖ To rhyme (mot) [*avec*, with]; *rimer pour l'oreille, les yeux*, to rhyme to the ear, the eye. ‖ FAM. *Cela ne rime à rien*, there is neither rhyme nor reason in it.
— v. tr. To rhyme, to put into verse (un conte).

rimeur [-mœ:r] m. Rhymer, versifier.

Rimmel [rimɛl] m. (nom déposé). Mascara.

rinçage [rɛ̃sa:ʒ] m. Rinsing.

rinceau [rɛ̃so] m. ARCHIT. Foliated moulding; foliage. ‖ BLAS. Branch.

rincée [rɛ̃se] f. FAM. Downpour, shower (averse). ‖ POP. Thrashing (raclée).

rincer v. tr. (6). To rinse (du linge); to rinse out (un verre); *se rincer la bouche*, to rinse one's mouth out. ‖ POP. To clean out (mettre à sec); to thrash, to drub (rosser); to drench (tremper); *se faire rincer*, to get a drenching; *se rincer la dalle*, to wet one's whistle; *se rincer l'œil*, to ogle a woman, to eye a woman appreciatively. ‖ **Rince-bouteilles**, m. invar. Bottle-washer, bottle-washing machine. ‖ **Rince-doigts**, m. invar. Finger-bowl.

rincette [-sɛt] f. FAM. Nip, chaser (pousse-café).

rinceur [-sœ:r] s. Rinser, washer.

rinçoir [-swa:r] m. Rinsing-bowl.

rinçure [-sy:r] f. Rinsing-water, slops, rinsings.

ring [riŋ] m. SPORTS. Ring.

ringard, arde [rɛ̃ga:r, ard] adj. FAM. Run down, past its prime.
— s. THÉÂTR. Old thespian.

ringard [rɛ̃ga:r] m. Fire-iron, clinkering-iron, slice-bar (de fourneau); rabble (en métallurgie).

ripaille [ripɑ:j] f. FAM. Feasting, revelry, carousing; *faire ripaille*, to feast, to revel, to carouse.

ripailler [-pɑje] v. intr. (1). FAM. To feast, to revel, to carouse, to guzzle, to stuff oneself.

ripatons [ripatɔ̃] m. pl. POP. Plates, plates of meat, tootsies (pieds); cobblers, U. S. dogs (souliers).

ripe [rip] f. Scraper (de pierre).

riper [ripe] v. tr. (1). To scrape (la pierre). ‖ CH. DE F. To shift. ‖ NAUT. To slip.
— v. intr. To slip (câble); to shift (cargaison); to skid (roue).

Ripolin [ripolɛ̃] m. (nom déposé). Enamel Paint.

ripoliner [-line] v. tr. (1). To paint with enamel paint, to give a coat of enamel paint, to enamel.

riposte [ripɔst] f. SPORTS. Riposte, counter thrust (à l'escrime). ‖ MILIT. Counter-stroke. ‖ FIG. Sharp repartee, retort, pat answer; *prompt à la riposte*, prompt in repartee, U. S. quick to the comeback (fam.).

riposter [-te] v. intr. (1). SPORTS. To riposte (à l'escrime). ‖ FIG. To reply, to retort (à, to).
— v. tr. To retort (qqch.).

ripuaire [ripɥɛ:r] adj., s. Ripuarian.

riquiqui [rikiki] adj. inv. FAM. Weeny, pint-sized.

rire [ri:r] v. intr. (89). To laugh; *cela prête à rire,* it raises a laugh, it invites ridicule ; *faire rire qqn*, to make s.o. laugh ; *rire aux éclats*, to burst out laughing ; *rire aux larmes*, to laugh till one cries ; *rire au nez de qqn*, to laugh in s.o.'s face ; *rire bêtement, bruyamment, cyniquement*, to haw-haw, to guffaw (ou) to cachinnate, to snigger ; *rire dans sa barbe* (ou) *en dedans* (ou) *tout bas*, to chuckle to oneself ; *rire de bon cœur*, to laugh heartily, to grin from ear to ear ; *rire du bout des lèvres*, to give a forced laugh ; *rire jaune*, to give a forced laugh (ou) a sickly smile ; *rire franchement*, to laugh out loud. ‖ To laugh (*de*, at) [ne pas se soucier] ; *rire des menaces de qqn*, to laugh at (ou) make light of s.o.'s threats. ‖ To smile, to be favourable (être favorable) ; *la fortune nous rit aujourd'hui*, fortune is smiling on us today, this is our lucky day. ‖ To jest, to joke (plaisanter) ; *avoir le mot pour rire*, to have a ready wit ; *bataille pour rire*, sham (ou) mock fight ; *dire qqch. pour rire*, to say sth. in jest (ou) for a joke ; *histoire de rire*, for a joke ; *il n'y a pas de quoi rire*, there's nothing to laugh at in that, it's no joke (ou) laughing-matter ; *je ne ris pas*, I'm not joking, I'm in dead earnest ; *journal pour rire*, comic paper ; *n'avoir pas le cœur à rire*, to be in no mood for joking (ou) laughing ; *nous allons rire!*, we shall see some fun ! ; *vous me faites rire!*, you're kidding ! ; don't make me laugh ! ; *vous voulez rire?*, are you kidding ? ‖ Fam. To gape (être déchiré). ‖ Fam. *À crever de rire*, killingly funny ; *c'est pour de rire*, it's just for fun.

— v. pr. **Se rire**, to laugh (*de*, at) ; to make fun (*de*, of).

— m. Laugh, laughing, laughter ; *avoir un accès de fou rire*, to be overcome with uncontrollable laughter ; *gros rire, rire bruyant*, guffaw ; *partir d'un éclat de rire*, to burst out laughing ; *petit rire bête*, titter ; *rire en dessous*, snigger.

ris [ri] m. † Laugh, laughter ; *les Jeux et les Ris*, Sport and Mirth.

ris m. Naut. Reef.

ris m. Culin. *Ris d'agneau, de veau*, sweetbread.

risée [rize] f. Mockery, jeering, derision ; *être un objet de risée, la risée de tous*, to be an object of scorn (ou) derision, a public laughing-stock. ‖ Naut. Squall (de vent).

risette [rizɛt] f. Naut. Cat's-paw. ‖ Fam. Laugh, smile ; *fais risette à maman*, give Mummy a smile.

risible [rizibl] adj. Laughable (comique) ; ludicrous, ridiculous (ridicule).

risiblement [-blamɑ̃] adv. Laughably, funnily, ludicrously.

risotto [rizɔtɔ] m. Culin. Risotto.

risque [risk] m. Risk, hazard ; *à ses risques et .périls*, at one's own risk ; *à tout risque*, at all costs (ou) hazards ; *risques du métier*, occupational hazards. ‖ Risk (v. danger) ; *au risque de*, at the risk of. ‖ Naut. *Risques maritimes*, sea risks, hazards of the sea. ‖ Comm. *Aux risques et périls du destinataire*, at consignee's risk ; *police tous risques*, all-in (ou) all-inclusive policy.

risqué, ée [-ke] adj. Risky, hazardous (affaire). ‖ Fig. Risky, daring (chanson) ; near the knuckle, risqué, U. S. off-color (plaisanterie).

risquer [-ke] v. tr. (1). To risk, to endanger, to imperil. ‖ To jeopardize (son honneur) ; to risk, to endanger (sa vie). ‖ To be in danger (*de*, of) ; *risquer de tomber*, to risk a fall, to be in danger of falling. ‖ Fig. To risk, to chance ; *qui ne risque rien n'a rien*, nothing venture nothing gain. ‖ Fam. *Il risque encore de venir*, he may come yet, he can still come ; *risquer le paquet*, to chance the lot, to go the whole hog. ‖ **Risque-tout**, m. invar. Dare-devil.

— v. pr. **Se risquer**, to take (ou) run a risk ; *se risquer à*, to venture (ou) dare to.

rissole [risɔl] f. Culin. Rissole.

rissoler [-le] v. intr. (1). Culin. To brown ; *faire rissoler*, to brown.

ristourne [risturn] f. Comm., Fin. Refund, rebate, bonus.

ristourner [-ne] v. tr. (1). Comm., Fin. To refund, to repay ; to re-credit.

rital [rital] m. Pop. Wop, Eyetie.

rite [rit] m. Ecclés. Rite.

ritournelle [riturnɛl] f. Mus. Ritornello, ritornelle. ‖ Fam. *Toujours la même ritournelle*, always the same old story. (V. rengaine.)

ritualiser [rituɑlize] v. tr. (1). To ritualize.

ritualisme [rituɑlism] m. Ecclés. Ritualism.

ritualiste [-alist] adj. Ecclés. Ritualistic.

— s. Ecclés. Ritualist.

rituel, elle [-ɛl] adj., m. Ecclés. Ritual.

rivage [riva:ʒ] m. Shore, beach, strand (de la mer) ; bank, side (d'une rivière) ; *bâti sur le rivage* (built on the), water-side, river-side.

rival, ale [rival] adj., s. Rival ; *sans rival*, peerless, unrivalled.

rivaliser [-lize] v. intr. (1). To compete, to vie (*avec*, with) ; *rivaliser avec*, to rival (ou) to emulate (ou) to equal ; *rivaliser avec les meilleurs*, to hold one's own with the best ; *rivaliser d'efforts avec*, to vie with, to match one's efforts with.

rivalité [-lite] f. Rivalry.

rive [ri:v] f. Shore, side (d'un lac) ; shore (de la mer) ; bank, side (d'une rivière). ‖ Lip (d'un four).

rivelaine [rivlɛn] f. Pick (de mineur).

river [rive] v. tr. (1). To clinch (un clou) ; to rivet (des plaques). ‖ Fig. To rivet (ou) bind together. ‖ Fam. *River son clou à qqn*, to shut s.o. up ; to settle s.o.'s hash.

riverain, aine [rivrɛ̃, ɛn] adj. Riparian, riverain, water-side (propriété). ‖ Bordering (*de*, on).

— s. Riparian, riverain ; water-side dweller ; *les riverains de la Tamise*, Thames-side dwellers.

rivet [rivɛ] m. Rivet.

rivetage [rivta:ʒ] m. Riveting.

riveter [-te] v. tr. (8a). To rivet.

riveteuse [-tø:z] f. Riveting-machine.

riveur [rivœ:r] m. Riveter.

rivière [rivjɛ:r] f. Géogr. River, stream. ‖ Fig. River (de feu) ; stream (de sang) ; *rivière de diamants*, diamond rivière.

rixe [riks] f. Brawl, fracas ; set-to (fam.).

riz [ri] m. Rice ; *eau de riz*, rice-water ; *riz glacé*, polished rice. ‖ Culin. *Gâteau de riz*, rice shape ; U.S. rice cake ; *riz au lait*, rice-pudding. ‖ **Riz-pain-sel**, m. invar. Fam. Commissariat, Service Corps.

rizicole [-zikɔl] adj. *Production rizicole*, rice output.

riziculture [-zikylty:r] f. Rice-growing.

rizier, ère [-zje, ɛ:r] adj. *Culture rizière*, rice-growing ; *pays rizier*, rice-producing country.

rizière [-zjɛ:r] f. Rice-field ; rice-plantation ; paddy-field (en Chine).

R.N. [ɛrɛn] f. Abrév. de *route nationale*, main road, A-road.

roadster [rɔdstɛr] m. Two-seater, U. S. roadster.

robe [rɔb] f. Dress, gown, frock (de femme) ; *robe d'après-midi, du soir*, tea-gown, evening dress ; *robe de bal*, dance frock ; U. S. dance dress ; *robe à queue*, gown with a train ; *robe de cérémonie*, State robe ; *robe de chambre*, dressing-gown ; *robe d'intérieur*, house-coat ; *robe de plage*, sun-dress. ‖ Coat (d'un animal) ; outer leaf (d'un cigare) ; husk (d'une fève) ; skin (d'un oignon) ; colour (d'un vin). ‖ Culin. *Pommes de terre en robe des champs* (ou) *de chambre*, potatoes done in their jackets. ‖ Jur. *Gens de robe*, gentlemen of the robe, lawyers ; *noblesse de robe*, nobility recruited from the legal profession.

robinet [rɔbinɛ] m. Tap ; cock ; faucet ; *robinet*

d'arrêt, stop-cock; *robinet d'eau froide*, cold-water tap. ‖ AUTOM. *Robinet d'arrivée d'essence*, petrol-tap, U. S. gasoline tap. ‖ FAM. *Ouvrir le robinet*, to turn on the water-works.

robinetier [rɔbinətje] m. TECHN. Brass-founder, brass-smith.

robinetterie [-nɛtri] f. TECHN. Brass-founding (fabrication); brass-foundry (usine).

robinier [rɔbinje] m. BOT. Robinia; false acacia.

robot [rɔbo] m. Robot. ‖ AVIAT. Pilotless plane.

robotiser [-bɔtize] v. tr. (1). To reduce to an automaton (une personne); to reduce to robot-like gestures (tâche).

robuste [rɔbyst] adj. MÉD. Robust, strong (corps); sturdy, robust, strong (personne); sound (santé). BOT. Hardy (plante). ‖ FIG. Stout, firm (foi).

robustement [-təmɑ̃] adv. Robustly, stoutly.

robustesse [-tɛs] f. Robustness, sturdiness, strength.

roc [rɔk] m. Rock (propre et fig.).

rocade [rɔkad] f. MILIT. *De rocade*, strategic (ligne, voie); *en rocade*, lateral (route).

rocaille [rɔkɑ:j] f. ARCHIT. Rock-work; rubble. ‖ ARTS. Louis XV style, rococo.

rocailleux, euse [-kɑjø, ø:z] adj. Rocky, stony, pebbly. ‖ FIG. Rugged, jarring (style).

rocambeau [rɔkɑ̃bo] m. NAUT. Traveller ring.

rocambole [rɔkɑ̃bɔl] f. BOT. Rocambole, Spanish garlic. ‖ FIG. Stale joke, chestnut.

rocambolesque [-lɛsk] adj. Fantastic, unusual, incredible. (V. INVRAISEMBLABLE.)

rochassier [rɔʃasje] m. SPORTS. Rock-climber.

roche [rɔʃ] f. Rock; boulder. ‖ NAUT. *Fond de roche*, rock-bottom. ‖ FAM. *Clair comme de l'eau de roche*, crystal-clear; *flairer anguille sous roche*, to smell a rat.

rocher [rɔʃe] m. Rock, crag; *bordé de rochers*, rock-bound. ‖ MÉD. Petrosal bone. ‖ FIG. Rock.

rochet [rɔʃɛ] m. ECCLÉS. Rochet.

rochet m. Bobbin (de soie). ‖ TECHN. Ratchet; *roue à rochet*, ratchet-wheel.

rocheux, euse [rɔʃø, ø:z] adj. Rocky. ‖ GÉOGR. *Les montagnes Rocheuses*, the Rocky Mountains; the Rockies.

Roch Hachana [rɔʃaʃana] m. ECCLÉS. Rosh Hashanah.

rock [rɔk], **rock and roll** [rɔkɛndrɔl] m. MUS. Rock, rock and roll, rock 'n' roll.

rocking-chair [rɔkiŋtʃɛ:r] m. Rocking-chair.

rococo [rɔkoko] adj. ARTS. Rococo.
— m. ARTS. Rococo style (ou) period.

rodage [rɔda:ʒ] m. TECHN. Grinding; lapping (du métal). ‖ AUTOM. Running in, U. S. breaking in (d'un moteur); grinding, grinding in (des soupapes); *en rodage*, being run in, U. S. being broken in.

rôdailler [rodɑje] v. intr. (1). To wander (ou) stroll about.

roder [rɔde] v. tr. (1). TECHN. To grind; to lap (du métal). ‖ AUTOM. To run in, U. S. to break in (un moteur); to grind, to grind in (les soupapes).

rôder [rode] v. intr. (1). To prowl, to prowl about, to be on the prowl.

rôderie [rodri] f. Prowling about.

rôdeur [rodœ:r] s. Prowler.
— adj. Prowling.

rodomont [rɔdɔmɔ̃] m. Braggart, blusterer, swashbuckler. (V. BRAVACHE.)

rodomontade [-tad] f. Rodomontade, braggadocio, bluster. (V. FANFARONNADE.)

rogations [rɔgasjɔ̃] f. pl. ECCLÉS. Rogation days; *la semaine des Rogations*, Rogation week.

rogatoire [-twa:r] adj. JUR. Rogatory.

rogaton [rɔgatɔ̃] m. CULIN. Scrap of food.

rognage [rɔɲa:ʒ] m. Trimming (de livres); paring (des ongles); clipping (d'une pièce).

rogne [rɔɲ] f. FAM. Temper, anger; *en rogne*, in a wax, steamed up; *être en rogne*, to have a grouse.

rogner [rɔɲe] v. tr. (1). To trim (un livre); to pare (les ongles); to clip (une pièce de monnaie). ‖ FIG. To clip (les ailes); to cut down (un salaire).
— v. intr. POP. To fume, to rave, to rant and rave. ‖ To cut down (*sur*, on).

rogneur [-ɲœ:r] s. Trimmer (de livres); clipper (de métal).

rogneuse [-ɲø:z] f. TECHN. Trimming machine.

rognon [rɔɲɔ̃] m. CULIN. Kidney.

rognure [rɔɲy:r] f. Cutting (de drap); paring (d'ongles); clipping (de métal); trimming (de papier).

rogomme [rɔgɔm] m. FAM. Drink; *voix de rogomme*, beery voice.

rogue [rɔg] adj. Arrogant; overbearing; brusque.

rogué, ée [rɔge] adj. ZOOL. Roed (hareng).

roi [rwa] m. King (des animaux, d'un pays); *de par le roi*, in the King's name; *jouer au roi*, to king it, to lord it. ‖ King (aux cartes, aux échecs). ‖ ECCLÉS. *Fêter les Rois*, to keep Twelfth Night; *jour des Rois*, Epiphany, Twelfth Night; *galette des Rois*, Twelfth-(night)-cake; *les trois Rois Mages*, the Three Kings; *Roi des rois*, King of Kings. ‖ FAM. *Roi du pétrole*, oil magnate; *roi des resquilleurs*, first-class wangler.

roitelet [-tle] m. Kinglet, petty king (personne). ‖ ZOOL. Wren.

rôle [ro:l] m. Roll, list, catalogue; *à tour de rôle*, by turns, turn and turn about. ‖ Billet (de bois); roll (de tabac). ‖ THÉÂTR. Rôle, part (d'un acteur); *être bien dans son rôle*, to get inside one's part; *premier rôle*, leading part (ou) lead; *rôle secondaire*, minor part (ou) role; *sortir de son rôle*, to overplay one's part. ‖ MILIT. Roster. ‖ NAUT. Muster-roll, ship's articles. ‖ FIN. Register of taxpayers. ‖ JUR. Rôle, list, register; cause-list, U. S. calendar, docket. ‖ FIG. Rôle, part; *jouer* (ou) *remplir un rôle important*, to play (ou) take a prominent part; *jouer un rôle secondaire*, to play second fiddle; *renverser les rôles*, to turn the tables; *le rôle de l'argent*, the part played by money; *sortir de son rôle*, to take too much on oneself.

rollmops [rɔlmɔps] m. CULIN. Rollmop, rollmops.

romain, aine [rɔmɛ̃, ɛn] adj. GÉOGR., MATH., TECHN., FIG. Roman.
— s. GÉOGR. Roman. ‖ FAM. *Travailler comme un Romain*, to work like a slave.

romaine [rɔmɛn] f. Steelyard (balance).

romaine f. CULIN., AGRIC. Cos lettuce, U. S. romaine.

romaïque [rɔmaik] adj., m. Romaic, modern Greek.

roman, ane [rɔmɑ̃, an] adj., m. GRAMM. Romance (langue). ‖ ARCHIT. Norman (en Angleterre); romanesque (en France).

roman [rɔmɑ̃] m. Novel; *lecteur de romans*, reader of fiction; *roman à thèse*, didactic novel, novel with a purpose; *roman d'aventures*, adventure story. ‖ FIG. Fiction, fancy; *cela a l'air d'un roman*, that sounds like pure fiction. ‖ **Roman-cycle**, m. Cyclic novel. ‖ **Roman-feuilleton**, m. Serial story. ‖ **Roman-fleuve**, m. Saga, saga-novel, roman fleuve. ‖ **Roman-photo**, m. Romantic (ou) detective story told in photographs.

romance [rɔmɑ̃:s] f. MUS. Sentimental ballad; love-song; melody.

romancé, ée [-mɑ̃se] adj. In novel form (vie).

romancer [-mɑ̃se] v. tr. (6). To write in (ou) put into novel form (vie).

romanche [rɔmɑ̃:ʃ] m. Romansch.

romancier [rɔmɑ̃sje] s. Novelist.

romand, ande [rɔmɑ̃, ɑ̃d] adj. GÉOGR. *La Suisse romande*, French-speaking part of Switzerland.

romanesque [rɔmanɛsk] adj. Fabulous, like a novel, romantic (aventure); romantic (esprit). — m. Romance.

romanichel, elle [rɔmaniʃɛl] s. Gipsy (v. BOHÉMIEN); vagrant (vagabond).

romanisant, ante [rɔmanizɑ̃, ɑ̃:t] adj. ECCLÉS. Romanizing. — s. ECCLÉS. Romanizer.

romaniser [-ze] v. tr. (1). To Romanize. — v. intr. ECCLÉS. To go over to the Roman Church.

romaniste [-nist] s. ECCLÉS. Romanist. ‖ GRAMM. Specialist in Romance languages.

romantique [rɔmɑ̃tik] adj. Romantic. — s. Romanticist.

romantisme [-tism] m. Romanticism.

romarin [rɔmarɛ̃] m. BOT. Rosemary.

rombière [rɔ̃bjɛ:r] f. POP. *Vieille rombière*, old hag (ou) harridan.

rompre [rɔ̃:pr] v. tr. (90). To break, to snap (une branche); to burst, to break (une digue); to break, to burst (ses liens). ‖ To accustom, to inure (à, to) [qqn]; *rompre qqn aux affaires*, to train s.o. for business. ‖ CULIN. To break, to break into pieces (le pain). ‖ MILIT. To break up, to hold (une attaque); *rompre le pas*, to break step; *rompez les rangs!*, dismiss! fall out! ‖ ELECTR. To break, to open (un circuit). ‖ MÉD. To burst, to rupture (une artère); to trouble, to disturb (le sommeil). ‖ † To break on the wheel (un condamné). ‖ SPORTS. To break in (un cheval). ‖ COMM. To call off (un marché). ‖ TECHN. To upset (l'équilibre); to disturb (le rythme). ‖ FIG. To break off (un mariage); *rompre ses fers*, to free oneself, to regain one's liberty; *rompre le fil d'un discours*, to break the thread of a speech; *rompre une lance avec*, to break a lance with, to cross swords with. ‖ FAM. To break (la glace); *applaudir à tout rompre*, to applaud loud enough to bring the roof down; *rompre les oreilles à qqn*, to deafen s.o. with noise. — v. intr. To break, to snap (bâton, branche). ‖ MILIT. *Rompez!*, dismiss!, fall out! ‖ SPORTS. To break away, to retreat (à la boxe); to break (à l'escrime). ‖ FIG. To break, to cease to be friends (personnes); *rompre avec*, to break (une habitude); to break (ou) fall out with (qqn). — v. pr. **Se rompre**, to break, to snap (bâton, branche); to break (vague). ‖ FIG. To break oneself in, to get used (à, to); *se rompre la tête*, to cudgel (ou) rack one's brains.

rompu, ue [rɔ̃py] adj. Broken, broken up, badly surfaced (chemin). ‖ FIG. *Rompu aux affaires*, experienced in business; *rompu au travail*, inured (ou) used to work. ‖ FAM. *Rompu de fatigue*, worn out, exhausted; all in (fam.). [V. BRISÉ.] — loc. adv. **A bâtons rompus**, in desultory fashion; *conversation à bâtons rompus*, rambling (ou) disjointed conversation; *travailler à bâtons rompus*, to work by fits and starts.

romsteck [rɔmstɛk] m. CULIN. Rump-steak.

ronce [rɔ̃:s] f. BOT. Bramble, blackberry-bush. ‖ TECHN. Curly grain; *ronce de noyer*, figured walnut. ‖ MILIT. *Ronce artificielle*, barbed wire. ‖ FIG. Trials and tribulations (de la vie).

ronceraie [rɔ̃srɛ] f. Patch of brambly ground.

ronceux, euse [-sø, ø:z] adj. Brambly (chemin). ‖ TECHN. Figured (bois).

ronchon [rɔ̃ʃɔ̃] adj. FAM. Grumbling, grumpy, peevish. — s. FAM. Grumbler, grouser.

ronchonnement [rɔ̃ʃɔnmɑ̃] m. FAM. Grousing grumbling; binding, bellyaching (pop.).

ronchonner [-ne] v. intr. (1). FAM. To grouse, to grumble; to bind, to bellyache (pop.).

ronchonneur, euse [-nœ:r, ø:z] s. FAM. Grumbler, grouser.

ronchonot [-no] m. FAM. Grumbler, grouser.

rond, onde [rɔ̃, ɔ̃:d] adj. Unhewn (bois); round (boule, table); full (visage). ‖ FIG. Well-lined (bourse); round, even (compte, nombre); stiff (vent); full (voix); *rond en affaires*, straightforward (ou) straight in business. ‖ FAM. Plump, dumpy (dodu); tight, cut (ivre). — m. Round, circle, ring; *rond de cuir*, round leather chair-cushion (coussin); *rond de jambe*, sweep of the leg; *rond de serviette*, napkin-ring. ‖ TECHN. Washer. ‖ FAM. *Ne pas avoir un rond*, not to have a brass farthing (ou) U. S. nickel. ‖ **Rond-de-cuir** (pl. *ronds-de-cuir*), m. Clerk, penpusher, petty bureaucrat. ‖ **Rond-point**, m. Roundabout, circus; U. S. traffic circle. ‖ **Ronde-bosse**, f. ARTS. Sculpture in the round. — adv. *Tourner rond*, to run true (roue). FAM. To be all right. — loc. adv. **En rond**, in a ring (ou) circle; *danser en rond*, to dance round in a ring; *tourner en rond*, to turn round in a circle.

ronde [rɔ̃:d] f. Round-hand (écriture). ‖ MUS. Round, roundelay; semibreve; U. S. whole note. ‖ MILIT. Round; routine patrol : *faire sa ronde*, to go on one's rounds. ‖ ARCHIT. *Chemin de ronde*, wall-walk, parapet-walk. — loc. adv. **A la ronde**, around; *à dix kilomètres à la ronde*, for a distance (ou) within a radius of ten kilometres all round, within a ten kilometre radius; *boire à la ronde*, to drink in turn; *faire passer la bouteille à la ronde*, to send the bottle round.

rondeau [rɔ̃do] m. Rondeau (poème). ‖ MUS. Rondo. ‖ AGRIC. Roller.

rondel [-dɛl] m. Rondel.

rondelet, ette [rɔ̃dlɛ, ɛt] adj. Plump, roundish (personne); podgy, pudgy (doigts). ‖ Fat, well-lined (bourse); tidy, round (somme).

rondelle [-dɛl] f. Disc (de carton, de métal). ‖ CULIN. Slice (de saucisson). ‖ TECHN. Washer; *rondelle de robinet*, tap washer; *rondelle fusible*, fusible plug. ‖ MILIT. Wad (d'une cartouche); basket-hilted sword (épée).

rondement [-dmɑ̃] adv. FAM. Roundly, smartly, briskly; *il y va rondement*, he goes straight to the point, he doesn't beat about the bush; *marcher rondement*, to walk at a good round pace, *mener une affaire rondement*, to expedite a piece of business.

rondeur [-dœ:r] f. Roundness, plumpness (du bras, de la taille); fullness (de la poitrine); *les rondeurs*, rounded lines, curves. ‖ GÉOGR. Roundness (de la terre). ‖ FIG. Frankness, straightforwardness (de caractère); directness (de manières); roundness (d'une période, du style).

rondin [-dɛ̃] m. Billet, round log (de bois); bar (de fer); *chemin de rondins*, corduroy road. ‖ Fir-tree stripped of bark (sapin).

rondo [rɔ̃do] m. MUS. Rondo.

rondouillard, arde [-duja:r, ard] adj. FAM. Fat, chubby, plump, dumpy. — s. Small fat person.

ronéoter [rɔneɔte], **ronéotyper** [rɔneɔtipe] v. tr. (1). To roneo.

ronflant, ante [rɔ̃flɑ̃, ɑ̃:t] adj. Snoring (personne), booming (voix). ‖ FIG. Pretentious; high sounding, high-falutin' (phrases); high-sounding (promesses); sonorous (titres).

ronflement [-fləmɑ̃] m. Snoring, snore (d'un dormeur). ‖ FIG. Roaring, roar (d'un feu); whir, throb (d'un moteur); booming, pealing (d'un orgue); humming (d'une toupie).

ronfler [-fle] v. intr. (1). To snore. ‖ FIG. To roar (feu); to hum, to whirr, to throb (moteur); to boom, to peal (orgue); to hum (toupie). ‖ POP. *Ça ronfle!*, things are looking up!

ronfleur, euse [-flœ:r, ø:z] s. Snorer.
— m. TECHN. Buzzer.

rongeant, ante [rɔ̃ʒɑ̃, ɑ̃:t] adj. CHIM. Corroding (acide, rouille). ‖ MÉD. Rodent (ulcère). ‖ FIG. Carking, worrying (souci).

ronger [-ʒe] v. tr. (7). To gnaw, to nibble (rat); *se ronger les ongles*, to bite one's nails. ‖ CHIM. To corrode (acide, rouille). ‖ GÉOGR. To erode (mer). ‖ FIG. To sap, to prey upon; *le chagrin le ronge*, he is tormented with grief; *rongé de soucis*, care-worn.
— v. pr. **Se ronger**, to be eaten (ou) worn away (rocher). ‖ FAM. To fret, to chafe (s'énerver); to eat one's heart out (s'inquiéter).

rongeur, euse [-ʒœ:r, ø:z] adj. ZOOL., MÉD. Rodent. ‖ FIG. Carking, worrying.
— m. ZOOL. Rodent.

ronron [rɔ̃rɔ̃], **ronronnement** [rɔ̃rɔnmɑ̃] m. Purring; purr (d'un chat). ‖ AUTOM. Purring, purr; drone; ticking over (d'un moteur).

ronronner [-ne] v. intr. (1). To purr (chat). ‖ AUTOM. To purr, to tick over (moteur).

röntgen [rœntgɛn] m. PHYS. Roentgen, röntgen.

roque [rɔk] m. Castling (aux échecs).

roquefort [rɔkfɔ:r] m. CULIN. Roquefort cheese.

roquer [rɔke] v. intr. (1). To castle (aux échecs).

roquet [rɔkɛ] m. ZOOL., FAM. Pug, mongrel, mutt. ‖ FAM. Whippersnapper; puppy (personne).

roquette [rɔkɛt] f. MILIT., PHYS. Rocket.

rosace [rozas] f. ARCHIT. Rosette, rosace, rose-window.

rosacé, ée [-se] adj. BOT. Rosaceous.

rosacées [-se] f. pl. BOT. Rosaceae.

rosaire [rozɛ:r] m. ECCLÉS. Rosary; *dire son rosaire*, to tell (ou) U. S. say one's beads.

rosat [roza] adj. invar. CHIM. Prepared from roses; *huile rosat*, oil of roses.

rosâtre [rozɑ:tr] adj. Pinkish.

rosbif [rɔsbif] m. CULIN. Roast beef.

rose [ro:z] f. BOT. Rose; *rose de Noël*, hellebore, Christmas rose; *rose moussue*, moss-rose; *rose sauvage*, wild rose; *rose thé*, tea-rose; *rose trémière*, hollyhock. ‖ Rose-diamond (brillant). ‖ ARCHIT. Rose-window; rose. ‖ NAUT. *Rose des vents*, mariner's card. ‖ FIG. *Etre sur un lit de roses*, to be (ou) lie on a bed of roses; *découvrir le pot aux roses*, to get to the bottom of sth.; *à l'eau de rose*, milk-and-water, mushy (histoire); *teint de rose*, rosy complexion; *tout n'est pas rose dans la vie*, life is not a bed of roses. ‖ FAM. *Envoyer sur les roses*, to send to the devil; *ne pas sentir la rose*, to smell bad.
— adj. Pink (couleur); rosy (teint).
— m. Rose colour; pink; *l'aurore aux doigts de rose*, rosy-fingered dawn; *voir la vie en rose*, to look at life through rose-coloured spectacles, to look on the sunny side of life. ‖ **Rose-croix**, m. invar. Rosicrucian.

rosé, ée [roze] adj. Rosy (teint); rosé (vin).

roseau [rozo] m. BOT., FIG. Reed.

rosée [roze] f. Dew; *couvert de rosée*, dewy; *goutte de rosée*, dew-drop. ‖ PHYS. *Point de rosée*, dew-point. ‖ FIG. *Tendre comme rosée*, tender as a new-born babe.

roselet [rozlɛ] m. COMM. Ermine.

roséole [rozeɔl] f. MÉD. German measles, roseola.

roser [-ze] v. tr. (1). To make rosy (ou) pink.

roseraie [-zrɛ] f. AGRIC. Rose-garden, rosery.

rosette [-zɛt] f. Bow (d'un ruban); rosette (de la Légion d'honneur). ‖ CHIM. Red chalk (craie); rosette copper (cuivre); red ink (encre).

rosier [-zje] m. BOT. Rose-tree.

rosière [-zjɛ:r] f. Maiden awarded wreath of roses in recognition of virtuous conduct.

rosiériste [-zjerist] s. AGRIC. Rose-grower.

rosir [-zi:r] v. tr. (2). To make rosy (ou) pink.
— v. intr. To turn (ou) become rosy (ou) pink.

rossard [rɔsa:r] m. POP. Sorry nag (cheval); lazy good-for-nothing (personne).

rosse [rɔs] f. FAM. Old horse, sorry nag (cheval); lazy good-for-nothing (fainéant). ‖ FAM. Beast; *petite rosse*, little bitch.
— adj. FAM. Objectionable, smutty (chanson); low-down, dirty (coup, tour); beastly, nasty (personne); stern, strict (professeur).

rossée [rɔse] f. FAM. Hiding, drubbing, thrashing.

rosser v. tr. (1). FAM. To beat, to thrash; to give a hiding to.

rosserie [rɔsri] f. FAM. Dirty (ou) beastly behaviour (conduite) [ou] story (histoire) [ou] talk (paroles); spiteful remark (remarque); dirty trick (tour); *faire une rosserie à qqn*, to play s.o. a rotten (ou) dirty (ou) scurvy trick, to put one over on s.o.

rossignol [rɔsiɲɔl] m. ZOOL. Nightingale. ‖ COMM. Left-over (ou) unsaleable article; piece of junk; pl. dud stock; *écouler un rossignol*, to sell a pup. ‖ NAUT. Whistle. ‖ TECHN. Skeleton-key (en serrurerie).

rossinante [rɔsinɑ̃:t] f. FAM. Rosinante; sorry-looking nag, worn-out jade.

rostral, ale [rɔstral] adj. ZOOL., ARCHIT. Rostral.

rostre [rɔstr] m. ZOOL., BOT., NAUT. Rostrum.

rostré, ée [rɔstre] adj. Rostrated, rostrate.

rot [ro] m. POP. Belch. (V. RENVOI.)

rôt m. CULIN. Roast meat. (V. RÔTI.)

rotateur, trice [rɔtatœ:r, tris] adj. Rotatory, rotative (force). ‖ MÉD. *Muscle rotateur*, rotator.
— m. MÉD. Rotator.

rotatif, ive [-tif, i:v] adj. Rotary, rotative. ‖ AVIAT. Rotary (moteur). ‖ AUTOM. *Balai rotatif*, rotor.

rotation [-sjɔ̃] f. Rotation (de la terre, d'un moteur). ‖ Frequency of service (d'un bateau, d'un avion). ‖ AGRIC. Rotation (des cultures). ‖ COMM. Turnover (du personnel, des stocks).

rotative [-tiv] f. Rotary printing-press.

rotativiste [-tivist] m. TECHN. Rotary printer.

rotatoire [-twa:r] adj. Rotary.

roter [rɔte] v. intr. (1). POP. To belch.

rôti [roti] m. CULIN. Roast meat, roast (plat); roast-meat course (service); *rôti de bœuf*, joint of roast beef; U. S. roast of beef; *une tranche de rôti*, a cut from the joint, U. S. a slice from the roast.

rôtie f. CULIN. Toast, round of toast.

rotin [rɔtɛ̃] m. BOT. Rattan, calamus. ‖ COMM. Rattan cane (canne).

rotin m. POP. Penny, brass-farthing.

rôtir [roti:r] v. tr. (2). CULIN. To roast (un gigot); to toast (du pain); *pain rôti*, toast; *porc rôti*, roast pork. ‖ FAM. To scorch; to dry up (l'herbe); to sunburn (qqn).
— v. intr. CULIN. To roast (viande). ‖ FAM. To roast, to scorch; *on rôtit ici*, it's scorching hot here.
— v. pr. **Se rôtir**, to roast. ‖ FAM. *Se rôtir au soleil*, to sunbathe, to bask in the sun.

rôtissage [rotisa:ʒ] m. CULIN. Roasting.

rôtisserie [-sri] f. Grill-room.

rôtisseur [-sœ:r] m. † Cook-shop proprietor.

rôtissoire [-swa:r] f. CULIN. Dutch oven.

rotogravure [rɔtɔgravy:r] f. Rotogravure.

rotonde [rɔtɔ̃:d] f. Boot, trunk (de diligence). ‖ ARCHIT. Rotunda, circular building. ‖ CH. DE F. Engine-shed, roundhouse.

rotondité [-tɔ̃dite] f. Rotundity.

rotor [rɔtɔ:r] m. AVIAT., ELECTR. Rotor.

rotule [rɔtyl] f. MÉD. Knee-cap, rotula, patella.

‖ TECHN. Knee-joint, toggle-joint, ball-and-socket joint. ‖ POP. *Sur les rotules,* on one's knees.

rotulien, enne [-ljɛ̃, ɛn] adj. MÉD. Patella; *réflexe rotulien,* knee-reflex.

roture [rɔty:r] f. Plebeian condition. ‖ The common people, the plebs (peuple).

roturier, ère [-tyrje, ɛ:r] adj. Common, plebeian, of the common people.
— s. Commoner, plebeian.

rouage [rua:ʒ] m. TECHN. Wheels, wheel-work, works; mechanism (ensemble); cog, cog-wheel (roue). ‖ FIG. Pl. Wheels (du gouvernement).

rouan, annne [rwɑ̃, an] adj. ZOOL. Roan.

rouanne [rwan] f. TECHN. Auger (de charpentier); rasing-knife (de tonnelier).

roublard, arde [rubla:r, ard] adj. FAM. Crafty, wily, cunning.
— s. FAM. Crafty person; *sacré roublard,* cunning devil.

roublardise [-blardi:z] f. FAM. Sly trick; fast one (action); cunning, craftiness, wiliness (ruse).

rouble [rubl] m. Rouble.

roucoulade [rukulad] f. Billing and cooing (des amoureux).

roucoulant, ante [rukulɑ̃, ɑ̃:t] adj. ZOOL. Cooing. ‖ FAM. Gurgling (rire).

roucoulement [-lmɑ̃] m. Cooing.

roucouler [-le] v. intr. (1). ZOOL. To coo (oiseau). ‖ FAM. To bill and coo (amoureux).
— v. tr. FAM. To coo, to warble (une romance).

roue [ru] f. Wheel; *à deux, à quatre roues,* two-, four-wheeled. ‖ AUTOM. *Roue pleine,* spokeless (ou) disc wheel; *roue de secours,* spare wheel. ‖ CH. DE F. *Roue motrice, porteuse,* driving, carrying wheel. ‖ NAUT. *Roue à aubes,* paddle-wheel; *roue de gouvernail,* steering-wheel, wheel. ‖ SPORTS. *Faire la roue,* to turn cart-wheels. ‖ TECHN. *Roue d'engrenage,* gear-wheel. ‖ ZOOL. *Faire la roue,* to spread its tail (paon). ‖ † Wheel; *condamner à la roue,* to condemn to be broken on the wheel. ‖ FIG. Wheel (de la fortune); *au plus haut de la roue,* at the peak of one's career (or) fortunes; *cinquième roue d'un carrosse,* dead loss (pop.); *faire la roue,* to strut (ou) swagger about, to put on airs (personne); *mettre des bâtons dans les roues de qqn,* to put a spoke in s.o.'s wheel; *pousser à la roue,* to put one's shoulder to the wheel.

roué, ée [rwe] adj. † Broken on the wheel. ‖ FIG. Sly, artful, knowing. (V. RUSÉ.) ‖ FAM. Worn out, exhausted. (V. ROMPU.)
— m. Rake, roué (libertin); cunning (ou) artful person (rusé).

rouelle [rwɛl] f. Fillet (de veau).

rouennais, aise [rwanɛ, ɛ:z] adj. GÉOGR. Of (ou) from Rouen.
— s. Native (ou) inhabitant of Rouen.

rouer [rwe] v. tr. (1). To coil (un câble). ‖ † To break on the wheel (qqn). ‖ FIG. *Rouer de coups,* to thrash, to rain blows on. (V. ROSSER.)

rouerie [ruri] f. Dodge, trick; fast one (fam.) (tour). ‖ Wiliness (ruse).

rouet [rwɛ] m. Spinning-wheel (à filer). ‖ NAUT. Gin. ‖ TECHN. Measuring wheel (d'arpenteur); sheave (de poulie); scutcheon (de serrure).

rouf [ruf] m. NAUT. Deck-house; superstructure.

rouflaquette [ruflakɛt] f. POP. Kiss-curl, U. S. spit-curl (accroche-cœur); Newgate fringe (ou) knocker, U. S. sideburn (favori).

rouge [ru:ʒ] adj. Red; carroty (cheveux); ruddy (joues); rosy (lèvres); *drapeau rouge,* red flag; *fer rouge,* red-hot iron; *rouge ardent,* ruddy; *rouge de colère,* purple (ou) flushed with anger; *rouge de honte,* crimson with shame. ‖ CULIN. Red (chou, viande). ‖ ECCLÉS. *Le chapeau rouge,* the cardinal's hat (chapeau); the cardinalate (fonction). ‖ GÉOGR. *La mer Rouge,* the Red Sea.

‖ **Rouge-gorge,** m. ZOOL. Robin, robin redbreast. ‖ **Rouge-queue,** m. ZOOL. Redstart.
— m. Red, red colour; *rouge d'Andrinople,* Turkey red; *rouge d'Angleterre,* jeweller's rouge. Lipstick (bâton); *se mettre du rouge,* to put on rouge. ‖ FIG. *Avoir le rouge au front,* to flush, to blush. ‖ FAM. Red, Bolshie, Commie (communiste); *le gros rouge,* coarse red wine (vin).
— adv. Red; *se fâcher tout rouge,* to work one-self up into a towering rage; *voir rouge,* to see red.

rougeâtre [-ʒɑ:tr] adj. Reddish.

rougeaud, eaude [-ʒo, od] adj. FAM. Red-faced.
— s. FAM. Red-faced person.

rougeoiement [-ʒwamɑ̃] m. Glow, glare.

rougeole [-ʒɔl] f. MÉD. Measles.

rougeoyant, ante [-ʒwajɑ̃, ɑ̃:t] adj. Reddening, turning red (ciel); glowing, glaring (incendie).

rougeoyer [-ʒwaje] v. intr. (9 a). To redden, to turn (ou) go red (ciel); to glow, to glare (incendie).

rouget [-ʒɛ] m. ZOOL. Harvest bug (aoûtat); red mullet, gurnard (poisson).

rougeur [-ʒœ:r] f. Redness. ‖ MÉD. Flush, blush (coloration); red spot, blotch (tache); *rougeur pudique,* blush of modesty.

rougi, ie [-ʒi] adj. Red; *eau rougie,* wine and water; *rougi au feu,* red-hot.

rougir [-ʒi:r] v. tr. (2). To redden; *eau rougie,* wine and water; *rougir son eau,* to mix water with one's wine; *rougir le fer,* to heat the iron red-hot; *rougir ses mains dans le sang,* to stain one's hands with blood.
— v. intr. To redden, to turn (ou) go red. ‖ To flush, to blush, to colour up (personne); *faire rougir qqn,* to make s.o. blush, to put s.o. to shame; to bring a blush to s.o.'s cheeks; *rougir de colère,* to turn red with anger; *rougir jusqu'aux oreilles,* to blush to the roots of one's hair.

rougissant, ante [-ʒisɑ̃, ɑ̃:t] adj. Reddening, going (ou) turning red. ‖ Blushing, ablush (personne).

roui [rui] m. Retting.

rouille [ru:j] f. Rust; *tache de rouille,* rust-stain, iron-mould. ‖ AGRIC. Rust, mildew, blight. ‖ FIG. Rust (de l'oisiveté).

rouillé, ée [ruje] adj. Rusty (fer). ‖ AGRIC. Rusty, mildewed. ‖ FIG. Rusty (connaissances, personne); out of condition (ou) practice (personne).

rouiller v. tr. (1). To rust, to make rusty (le fer). ‖ AGRIC. To rust, to mildew. ‖ FIG. To make rusty (l'esprit).
— v. intr. To rust, to get (ou) go rusty, to rust up.
— v. pr. Se rouiller, to rust, to get (ou) go rusty, to rust up (fer). ‖ AGRIC. To rust, to mildew, to go mildewed (plante). ‖ FIG. To get rusty (personne).

rouilleux, euse [-jø, ø:z] adj. Rusty.

rouillure [-jy:r] f. Rust, rustiness (sur le fer). ‖ AGRIC. Rust, mildew.

rouir [rui:r] v. tr. (2). To ret, to soak, to steep.

rouissage [ruisa:ʒ] m. Retting. (V. ROUI.)

rouissoir [-swa:r] m. Rettery.

roulade [rulad] f. MUS. Roulade, run (d'un musicien); trill (d'un oiseau).

roulage [rula:ʒ] m. Rolling (action). ‖ Road traffic; *réglementation du roulage,* Traffic Acts. ‖ COMM. Travelling (ou) carriage by road; cartage, haulage (transport); *entreprise de roulage,* haulage firm (ou) undertaking. ‖ AGRIC. Rolling.

roulant, ante [-lɑ̃, ɑ̃:t] adj. Rolling (allure); good, smooth (chemin); moving (escalier); rolling (pierre); smooth-running (voiture). ‖ FIN. *Fonds roulants,* working capital. ‖ CH. DE F. *Matériel roulant,* rolling-stock. ‖ MILIT. *Cuisine roulante,* field-kitchen; *feu roulant,* drumfire. ‖

FIG. *Feu roulant,* running fire (des questions). ‖
FAM. Funny; killing. (V. CREVANT.)
— m. CH. DE F. Train crew.

roulé, ée [rule] adj. Rolled; *pull à col roulé,*
rollneck (ou) polo neck sweater, polo neck. ‖
CULIN. *Épaule roulée,* rolled shoulder; *gâteau
roulé,* Swiss roll, roll. ‖ POP. *Bien roulée,* shapely,
curvaceous.
— m. CULIN. Swiss roll, roll. ‖ **Roulé-boulé,** m.
Roll, somersault.

rouleau [rulo].m. Roller; U. S. curler (de coiffeur); coil (de corde); roll, spool (de film); rouleau (d'or); roll (de papier); twist (de tabac);
rouleau hygiénique, toilet-roll; roll of toilet paper; *rouleau porte-serviettes,* towel-roller. ‖
Squeegee (en .photographie). ‖ TECHN. Platen (de
machine à écrire); beam (de métier à tisser);
power roller (de route); *rouleau compresseur,*
steam-roller. ‖ CULIN. *Rouleau de pâtissier,*
rolling-pin. ‖ AGRIC. *Rouleau brise-mottes,* clod-
crusher. ‖ FAM. *Au bout de son rouleau,* at the
end of one's tether.

roulement [-lmɑ̃] m. Rolling (action) [d'une
balle, d'une voiture]; running (d'une machine);
roll, rolling (d'yeux). ‖ Rolling noise (bruit);
rumbling (d'un camion); rolling, peal (du tonnerre); rattle (d'une voiture). ‖ Rota; rotation;
établir un roulement, to draw up a rota; *par
roulement,* in rotation. ‖ Routine board (tableau
de service). ‖ MUS. Roll (de tambour). ‖ AUTOM.
Bande de roulement, tread (d'un pneu). ‖ AVIAT.
Taxying (d'un avion); *chemin de roulement,* runway. ‖ FIN. *Fonds de roulement,* working capital;
roulement de fonds, turnover, circulation of
capital. ‖ TECHN. Bearing; *chemin de roulement,*
ball-race; *roulements à billes,* ball-bearing.

rouler [-le] v. tr. (1). To roll (*in,* dans) [une boule,
qqn]; to trundle (un tonneau). ‖ To roll (une cigarette); to roll up, to furl (un parapluie); to roll
up (une pièce d'étoffe). ‖ To roll (les yeux).
‖ GRAMM. *Rouler les* r, to roll one's r's. ‖ CULIN.
to roll out (la pâte). ‖ AGRIC. To roll (un champ).
‖ SPORTS. *Faire rouler,* to trundle (une boule
au golf). ‖ CULIN. Roulé, rolled (rôti). ‖ FIG.
Rouler de mauvaises pensées, to think evil
thoughts; *rouler un projet dans sa tête,* to turn
a plan over in one's mind. ‖ FAM. To sting, to
diddle, to swindle, to gull (duper); *rouler sa
bosse,* to knock about the world.
— v. intr. To roll (boule). ‖ To drive, to ride,
to travel (personne); to run, to travel (voiture);
rouler en voiture, to drive (ou) to motor; *rouler
sur une route,* to travel along a road. ‖ To roll,
to peal, to rumble (tonnerre). ‖ To rotate; to take
it in turns (établir un roulement). ‖ CH. DE F.
Roulez!, right away!, U. S. all aboard! ‖
NAUT. To roll (vaisseau). ‖ FIN. To circulate
(argent); to fluctuate (revenu). ‖ AVIAT. To taxi
(avion). ‖ FIG. To turn (*sur,* upon) [conversation];
son discours roula sur la morale, his speech turned
upon morality; *tout roule là-dessus,* everything
depends on that. ‖ FAM. *Ça roule!,* I'm doing
fine!, everything's O.K.!; *rouler dans tous les
pays,* to travel all over the world, to knock about
the world; *rouler sur l'or,* to be rolling in money.
— v. pr. **Se rouler,** to roll (ou) turn over. ‖ To
roll up; *se rouler en boule,* to roll up in a ball.
‖ FAM. To split one's sides with laughter (rire).

rouletabille [-ltabi:j] m. FAM. Rolling stone.

roulette [-lɛt] f. Small wheel, castor; *chaise à
roulettes,* chair on castors. ‖ Pricking-whell (de
cordonnier); roulette (de photograveur); fillet (de
relieur); *roulette à patrons,* tracing-wheel. ‖
MATH. Cycloid, roulette. ‖ SPORTS. Roulette. ‖
MÉD. Dentist's drill. ‖ FAM. *Ça marche comme
sur des roulettes,* things are going swimmingly,
everything is working out smoothly.

rouleur, euse [-lœ:r, ø:z] s. Drawer, trammer,
wheeler (de mine). ‖ FAM. Rolling-stone; *rouleur
de cabarets,* pub-crawler, U. S. barfly.
— m. BOT. Vine-weevil.

rouleuse [-lø:z] f. FAM. Street-walker.

roulier [-lje] adj. Road-haulage carrying, U. S.
trucking.
— m. Haulier, carrier, waggoner, U. S. truck
driver.

roulis [-li] m. NAUT. Roll, rolling, lurch.

roulotte [-lɔt] f. Caravan. ‖ AUTOM. *Circuler
avec une roulotte en remorque,* to caravan; U. S.
to travel with (ou) to pull a trailer.

roulotter [-lɔte] v. tr. (1). To roll a hem on (un
foulard, un rideau).

roulure [-ly:r] f. BOT. Shake (de bois). ‖ POP.
Tart, bag.

roumain, aine [rumɛ̃, ɛn] adj., s. GÉOGR. Rumanian.

Roumanie [rumani] f. GÉOGR. Rumania.

round [raund] m. SPORTS. Round (à la boxe).

roupie [rupi] f. Rupee.

roupie f. POP. Bit of trash.

roupiller [rupije] v. intr. (1). FAM. To snooze, to
doss. (V. PIONCER.)

roupilleur [-jœ:r] s. FAM. Sleeper, snoozer.

roupillon [-jɔ̃] m. FAM. Snooze, doze; *piquer un
roupillon,* to snatch forty winks.

rouquin, ine [rukɛ̃, in] adj. POP. Red (ou) ginger-
(ou) carroty-haired; carroty.
— s. POP. Red-head.

rouquin m. POP. Plonk (vin rouge).

rouscailler [ruskaje] v. intr. (1). FAM. To
grouse; to bellyache. (V. RONCHONNER.)

rouspétance [ruspetɑ̃:s] f. FAM. Protest, recrimination, grousing.

rouspéter [ruspete] v. intr. (1). FAM. To protest,
to recriminate, to kick.

rouspéteur, euse [-tœ:r, ø:z] s. FAM. Protester,
recriminate, grouser; U. S. griper, grouch.
— adj. Obstreperous.

roussâtre [rusɑ:tr] adj. Reddish, rusty-coloured.

rousse [rus] f. POP. *La Rousse,* the bogies, the
busies, the cops.

roussette [rusɛt] f. ZOOL. Flying fox, fox bat
(chauve-souris); spotted dogfish (requin).

rousseur [-sœ:r] f. Redness (des cheveux); *tache
de rousseur,* freckle.

roussi, ie [rusi] adj. Scorched.
— m. Smell of burning. ‖ FIG. *Sentir le roussi,*
to smack of heresy.

roussin [rusɛ̃] m. ZOOL. Cob, strong horse;
roussin d'Arcadie, donkey. ‖ POP. Copper, cop,
bogie, bobby; U. S. flatfoot.

roussir [rusi:r] v. tr. (2). To brown. ‖ To singe
(les cheveux); to scorch (le linge). ‖ CULIN. To
brown (la viande).
— v. intr. To brown (ou) redden; to become
brown (ou) red. ‖ To singe (cheveux); to scorch
(linge).

routard [rutaːr] m. Traveller, rover.

route [rut] f. Road; *route de Douvres,* Dover
road; *route départementale, nationale,* secondary,
main road; *route de ceinture,* ring-road. ‖ Route,
path, way; *barrer la route à,* to bar the way
to; *de route,* travelling (compagnon, frais); *en
route!,* let's be off! off we go!; *en route pour,*
on the way to; *être sur la bonne, la mauvaise
route,* to be on the right, the wrong road; *faire
route avec,* to go along with; *refaire la route à
pied,* to walk back, to return on foot; *se mettre
en route,* to start (ou) set out on one's way;
se remettre en route, to resume one's journey.
‖ MILIT. *Chanson de route,* marching song; *route
militaire, stratégique,* military, strategic road. ‖
NAUT. Course (action); sea route (chemin); *en
route,* on course; *faire route sur,* to steer for, to

make for; *se mettre en route*, to get under way; *tracer la route*, to set the course; *vitesse de route*, sea speed. ‖ Сн. de f. *En route!*. right away; U. S. all aboard! ‖ Aviat. *Route aérienne*, airway. ‖ Arts. *Mettre le moteur en route*, to start up the engine; *mise en route*, starting up. ‖ Fig. *Faire fausse route*, to go the wrong way about sth., to be on the wrong track; *être lent à se mettre en route*, to be a slow starter; *mettre des travaux en route*, to start operations.

routier, ère [-tje, ɛ:r] adj. *Carte routière*, road-map; *gare routière*, bus station; *transports routiers*, road-transport; *voie routière*, carriage-way. ‖ Naut. *Livre routier*, track-chart.
— m. Traveller by road. ‖ Autom. Long-distance driver. ‖ Sports. Road-racer (en cyclisme); Rover (scout). ‖ Naut. Track-chart. ‖ Fig. *Vieux routier*, old hand, old stager (ou) trouper.

routière [-tjɛ:r] f. Autom. Tourer, touring car.

routine [rutin] f. Routine; routinism; *par routine*, by rule of thumb, out of sheer habit; *suivre la routine*, follow the usual routine; *travail de routine*, routine (ou) donkey work.

routinier, ère [-nje, ɛr] adj. Routine, one-track, mechanical (esprit); routine-minded (personne); routine (travail).
— s. Slave to routine.

rouvre [ruvr] adj. Bot. *Chêne rouvre*, robur; Austrian (ou) Russian oak; U. S. British oak.

rouvrir [ruvri:r] v. tr., intr. (72). To open again, to reopen.
— v. pr. **Se rouvrir**, to open again, to reopen.

roux, ousse [ru, us] adj. Reddish-brown, russet, reddish; carroty (cheveux) [fam.]. ‖ *Lune rousse*, April moon. ‖ Culin. Browned (beurre).
— s. Red-haired (ou) sandy-haired person.
— m. Reddish-brown (ou) russet colour. ‖ Culin. Brown sauce.

royal, ale [rwajal] adj. Royal, regal, kingly; *prince royal*, Crown Prince; *Son Altesse Royale (S.A.R.)*, His (ou) Her Royal Highness (H.R.H.). ‖ Naut. Main (pompe).

royale [-ja:l] f. Imperial (barbe).

royalement [-jalmã] adv. Royalty, regally, in royal (ou) kingly fashion.

royalisme [-jalism] m. Royalism.

royaliste [-jalist] adj., s. Royalist. ‖ Fam. *Être plus royaliste que le roi*, to be punctilious to a degree.

royalties [rwajalti] f. pl. Jur. Royalty, royalties (redevance).

royaume [-jo:m] m. Kingdom, realm. ‖ Géogr. *Royaume-Uni*, United Kingdom. ‖ Fig. *Royaume des ombres*, land of shades (ou) shadows.

royauté [-jote] f. Royalty; Kingship.

R.S.V.P. [ɛrɛsvepe] abrév. de *Répondez, s'il vous plaît*, R.S.V.P., please reply.

ru [ry] m. Brook, stream, rivulet.

ruade [ryad] f. Kick, buck (d'un cheval); *décocher une ruade*, to lash out.

Ruanda, Rwanda [ruãda] m. Géogr. Rwanda, Ruanda.

ruban [rybã] m. Ribbon, band; *porter le ruban rouge*, to wear the red ribbon of the Legion of Honour; *ruban de chapeau*, hatband. ‖ Tape (en coton); *ruban adhésif*, adhesive tape, Sellotape, U. S. Scotch tape; *ruban de magnétophone*, recording tape. ‖ Ribbon (de machine à écrire). ‖ Techn. Band (d'acier); *ruban mensurateur*, measuring tape, tape-measure. ‖ Autom. *Ruban de frein*, brake-band. ‖ Archit. Ribbon moulding. ‖ Fig. Stretch (de route). ‖ Pop. Road; *se taper un bon bout de ruban*, to walk a fair step.

rubané, ée [-bane] adj. Ribboned, striped; *canon rubané*, strip-steel gun-barrel.

rubéfaction [rybefaksjõ] f. Méd. Rubefaction.

rubéfiant, ante [-fjã, ã:t] adj., m. Méd. Rubefacient.

rubéole [rybeɔl] f. Méd. Rubella, German measles.

rubescent, ente [-bɛssã, ã:t] adj. Rubescent.

rubicond, onde [-bikõ, õd] adj. Rubicund.

rubidium [-bidjɔm] m. Chim. Rubidium.

rubigineux, euse [-biʒinø, ø:z] adj. Rubiginous (couleur); rusty (métal).

rubis [rubi] m. Ruby; *rubis balais*, balas ruby; *rubis de Bohême*, rose quartz; *rubis du Brésil* burnt topaz; *rubis oriental*, true (ou) oriental ruby. ‖ Chim. *Rubis d'arsenic*, red arsenic. ‖ Fig. *Faire rubis sur l'ongle*, to drain one's glass, to drink to the last drop; *payer rubis sur l'ongle*, to pay on the nail.

rubrique [rybrik] f. Red chalk, red ochre, ruddle (craie). ‖ Heading (de journal); *rubrique des sports*, sports column; *sous la rubrique de*, under the heading of. ‖ Ecclés., Jur. Rubric. ‖ Comm. Item. ‖ Fam. Dodge (truc).

ruche [ryʃ] f. Bee-hive; swarm of bees; *ruche de paille*, skep. ‖ Ruche, ruching (d'une robe). ‖ Fig. Hive.

ruché [ryʃe] m. Ruching, frill, quilting.

ruchée f. Hiveful.

rucher m. Apiary.

rucher v. tr. (1). To ruche, to frill (l'étoffe).

rude [ryd] adj. Rough, uneven (chemin); rough (peau); rugged (pierre); coarse (toile). ‖ Fig. Redoutable, formidable, doughty (adversaire); rough, ungracious (air, manière); heavy, violent (choc, secousse); hard, trying (climat); hard, heavy (coup); severe (épreuve); bitter, hard, severe (hiver); crude (langage, style); hard (maître); hard, arduous (métier); uncouth, crude, rough, primitive (personne); stiff, hard (tâche); harsh, rough (vin); gruff (voix). ‖ Fam. *Un rude lapin*, a tough nut.

rudement [-dmã] adv. Roughly, harshly, sternly (durement). ‖ Fig. *Rudement éprouvé*, sorely (ou) severely tried; *travailler rudement*, to work hard. ‖ Fam. Very (v. bigrement); *j'en suis rudement content*, I am awfully pleased about it; *vous êtes rudement trop bavard*, you're a darned sight too talkative, you're too talkative by half.

rudesse [-dɛs] f. Roughness (de la peau); ruggedness (des traits); gruffness (de la voix). ‖ Coarseness (de la toile); harshness, roughness (d'un vin). ‖ Fig. Severity, coldness (de l'hiver); crudeness (du langage, du style); arduousness (d'une tâche); *traiter avec rudesse*, to browbeat.

rudiment [rydimã] m. Rudiment; element (d'une science). ‖ Méd., Zool. Rudiment.

rudimentaire [-tɛ:r] adj. Rudimentary.

rudoiement [rydwamã] m. Bullying.

rudoyer [-je] v. tr. (9a). To bully, to browbeat.

rue [ry] f. Street; *demeurer rue du Temple*, to live in (ou) U. S. on the Rue du Temple; *grande, petite rue*. main, side street; *rue principale*, main thoroughfare. ‖ Théâtr. Slips. ‖ Fig. *L'homme de la rue*, the man in the street; *nouvelle qui court les rues*, news that is on everybody's lips; *le peuple descend dans la rue*, the populace is coming out on to the streets; *toute la rue est en émoi*, the whole street is buzzing with excitement.

rue f. Bot. Rue.

ruée [rye] f. Rush, onrush; *la ruée vers l'est*, the drive towards the East; *la ruée vers l'or*, the gold rush.

ruelle [ryɛl] f. Narrow street, alley; alley-way, lane. (V. venelle.) ‖ Space between bed and wall (dans une chambre).

ruer [rye] v. intr. (1). To kick, to lash out.
— v. pr. **Se ruer**, to rush, to dash, to hurl oneself (*sur*, at; *vers*, towards).

rueur, euse [rɥœːr, øːz] adj. Kicking (cheval). — s. Kicker.

rufian [ryfjɑ̃] m. Debauchee, libertine; pander.

rugby [rœgbi] m. SPORTS. Rugby, rugby football; rugger (fam.); *rugby à quinze, à treize,* Rugby Union, League.

rugbyman [-man] m. SPORTS. Rugby player.

rugine [ryʒin] f. MÉD. Xyster (de chirurgien); scaler (de dentiste).

ruginer [-ne] v. tr. (1). MÉD. To scrape (un os); to scale (une dent).

rugir [ryʒiːr] v. intr. (2). To roar (lion). ‖ FIG. To roar, to boom (mer); to howl (vent); *rugir de colère,* to roar with anger.
— v. tr. To yell out (des menaces).

rugissant, ante [ryʒisɑ̃, ɑ̃ːt] adj. Roaring (lion). ‖ FIG. Roaring, booming (mer); howling (vent).

rugissement [-smɑ̃] m. Roaring (d'un lion). ‖ FIG. Howling (de la tempête, du vent).

rugosité [rygɔzite] f. Rugosity, roughness, unevenness.

rugueux, euse [-gø, øːz] adj. Rugose, rough. ‖ BOT. Gnarled (arbre, écorce).
— m. MILIT. Striker (de fusée).

ruine [rɥin] f. Ruin, collapse (effondrement). ‖ Pl. Ruins (de, of) [v. DÉCOMBRES]; *amas de ruines,* heap of ruins; *qui tombe en ruine,* dilapidated, tumbledown, falling into ruins (maison). ‖ FIG. Collapse, destruction, downfall, overthrow (d'un Etat); loss (d'une fortune); downfall (d'une personne); *aller* (ou) *courir à la ruine,* to be on the downward path (ou) on the road to ruin; *ce sera votre ruine,* it will be your undoing; *conduire à la ruine,* to bring to ruin.

ruiner [-ne] v. tr. (1). To ruin, to destroy; to demolish (une maison); to lay in ruins (une ville). ‖ ARCHIT. To groove, to notch (une solive). ‖ FIN. To impoverish, to ruin (qqn). ‖ FIG. To blight, to blast (un espoir); to overthrow (un Etat); to demolish (un raisonnement), to blast (une réputation); to ruin, to wreck (la santé); to disprove (une théorie).
— v. pr. **Se ruiner,** to ruin oneself (personne). ‖ To fall into ruin (maison).

ruineusement [-nøzmɑ̃] adv. Ruinously.

ruineux, euse [-nø, øːz] adj. Ruinous (entreprise); costly, ruinous (dépense); disastrous (guerre).

ruisseau [rɥiso] m. Stream, brook, rivulet (cours d'eau). ‖ FIG. Flood (de larmes); river, stream (de sang); lashing (de vin). ‖ FAM. Gutter.

ruisselant, ante [-slɑ̃, ɑ̃ːt] adj. Streaming. ‖ FIG. Streaming, dripping (de, with).

ruisseler [-sle] v. intr. (8 a). To stream, to stream down, to run, to run down (liquide); *le sang ruisselait sur son visage,* blood was streaming down his face. ‖ To run, to drip (surface); *les murs ruisselaient,* the walls were running with water; *ruisseler de sueur,* to be dripping with sweat.

ruisselet [-slɛ] m. Brooklet, streamlet.

ruissellement [-sɛlmɑ̃] m. Streaming, flowing, running, trickling (d'un liquide). ‖ FIG. Flood, stream (de lumière); shimmer (de pierreries).

rumb [rɔːb] m. NAUT. Rhumb.

rumba [rumba] f. Rumba.

rumeur [rymœːr] f. Confused (ou) distant noise; murmur (d'une assemblée); hum (de la circulation); murmur, sighing (des flots); buzz (de voix). ‖ Uproar, din, hubbub, clamour, commotion (mécontentement). ‖ Rumour, report (v. BRUIT); *la rumeur court que,* rumour has it that, it is rumoured that.

ruminant, ante [rymināꞵ, ɑ̃ːt] adj., m. ZOOL. Ruminant.

rumination [-nasjɔ̃] f. Rumination, ruminating.

ruminer [-ne] v. tr. (1). ZOOL. To chew over again (la pâture). ‖ FAM. To ponder, to turn over in one's mind, to ruminate on (ou) over (une idée).
— v. intr. ZOOL. To ruminate, to chew the cud (animal). ‖ FAM. To ruminate, to muse. (V. REMÂCHER.)

rumsteck [rɔmstɛk] m. CULIN. Rump steak.

rune [ryn] f. Rune.

runique [-nik] adj. Runic.

Ruolz [ryɔls] m. Electroplated ware.

rupestre [rypɛstr] adj. BOT. Rupestral, rupicolous. ‖ ARTS. *Art rupestre,* cave art; *dessins rupestres,* rock drawings.

rupicole [rypikɔl] f. ZOOL. Cock-of-the-rock.

rupin, ine [rypɛ̃, in] adj. FAM. Fine, smart (chose); rich (personne).
— m. FAM. Swell, toff.

rupteur [ryptœːr] m. ELECTR. Make-and-break; circuit-breaker.

rupture [-tyːr] f. Rupture; bursting (d'un barrage, d'une digue); parting (d'un câble); breaking (d'une poutre). ‖ MÉD. Rupture (d'une artère). ‖ MILIT. Breaking off (d'un combat); breaking-through, rupture, piercing (du front); *obus de rupture,* armour-piercing shell. ‖ ELECTR. Breaking (du circuit, du courant); *dispositif de rupture,* contact-breaker; *étincelle de rupture,* break spark. ‖ JUR. *Rupture de contrat, de promesse de mariage,* breach of contract, of promise. ‖ TECHN. *Charge, point, tension de rupture,* breaking-load, -point, -stress. ‖ FIG. Breach (d'amitié); loss (d'équilibre); rupture, breaking, breach (de la paix); breaking off (des relations); *il y a rupture entre eux,* they have fallen out; *rupture passagère,* temporary disagreement.

rural, ale [ryral] adj. Rural (facteur); country (vie).
— s. Peasant.

ruse [ryːz] f. Ruse, trick, guile, artifice, dodge; *user de ruse,* to resort to trickery. ‖ MILIT. *Ruse de guerre,* stratagem. ‖ SPORTS. Doubling (du gibier).

rusé, ée [ryze] adj. Artful, cunning, crafty, wily; *avoir un air rusé,* to have a sly look about one.
— s. Artful (ou) cunning (ou) crafty (ou) wily person; dodger; *une petite rusée,* a little baggage (or) minx.

ruser v. intr. (1). To use crafty (ou) cunning methods; to resort to trickery. ‖ SPORTS. To double (gibier).

rush [rœʃ] m. SPORTS. Sprint, spurt. ‖ FIG. Rush.

rushes [rœʃ] m. pl. CINÉM. Rushes.

russe [rys] adj., s. GÉOGR. Russian.
— m. GRAMM. Russian (langue).

Russie [rysi] f. GÉOGR. Russia.

russification [-sifikasjɔ̃] f. Russification, russianization.

russifier [-sifje] v. tr. (1). To russify, to russianize.

russophile [-sɔfil] adj., s. Russophile.

russophobe [-sɔfɔb] adj., s. Russophobe.

rustaud, aude [rysto, od] adj. Rustic, boorish, loutish, oafish (rustre). ‖ Clumsy (gauche).
— s. Boor, lout, bumpkin, oaf. (V. BALOURD.)

rusticité [-tisite] f. Rusticity; uncouthness, boorishness, coarseness (d'une personne); rural character (d'un voisinage). ‖ BOT. Hardiness (d'une plante).

Rustine [rystin] f. AUTOM. Tyre-repair (ou) puncture patch.

rustique [rystik] adj. Rustic, rural, country (travaux). ‖ ARCHIT. Rustic (ordre). ‖ BOT. Hardy (plante). ‖ FIG. Countrified, rustic, uncouth (air, manières); rustic, artless, uncouth (personne).
— m. TECHD. Stone cutter's hammer.

rustiquement [-kmɑ̃] adv. Rustically.

rustre [rystr] m. Peasant. ‖ Bumpkin, boor, lout.

— adj. Rustic, countrified, boorish, loutish, oafish. [V. RUSTAUD.]

rustrerie [-trəri] f. Boorishness, loutishness.

rut [ryt] m. Rut, rutting; *être en rut*, to be in heat (femelle), to rut (mâle).

rutabaga [rytabaga] m. AGRIC. Swedish turnip, swede; U. S. rutabaga.

ruthénium [rytenjɔm] m. CHIM. Ruthenium.

rutilance [rytilɑ̃:s] f. Bright redness, crimson colour (rouge vif). || Gleam, brightness, shininess (éclat).

rutilant, ante [rytilɑ̃, ɑ̃:t] adj. Rutilant (en général); gleaming, red-gold (cheveux); *ciel rutilant,* sky flushed with crimson; *rutilant de médailles,* gleaming with medals.

rutile [rytil] m. CHIM. Rutile.

rutilement [rytilmɑ̃] m. V. RUTILANCE.

rutiler [-le] v. intr. (1). To glow ruddily, to gleam red.

rythme [ritm] m. Rhythm. || Tempo (de production).

rythmé, ée [-me] adj. Rhythmical.

rythmer [-me] v. tr. (1). To suit (ou) submit to a rhythm.

rythmique [-mik] adj. Rhythmic, rhythmical.

— f. SPORTS. Eurhythmics, U.S. eurythmics.

S

s [εs] m. S, s; *en S,* S-shaped (fer); winding (rivière, sentier). || FIG. *Faire des s,* to zigzag.

S. [εs] GÉOGR. Abrév. de *sud,* S, south.

S CHIM. Abrév. de *soufre,* S, sulphur.

sa [sa] adj. poss. V. SON.

S.A. [εsa] f. JUR. Abrév. de *Société anonyme,* Ltd, Limited company.

Saba [saba] m. GÉOGR. Sheba; *la reine de Saba,* the Queen of Sheba.

sabayon [sabajɔ̃] m. CULIN. Sillabub; U. S. zabaglione.

sabbat n. Midnight orgy (ou) revels, sabbath (des sorciers). || ECCLÉS. Sabbath. || FAM. Din, racket, uproar, shindy, row; *un sabbat de tous les diables,* an infernal racket.

sabbatique [-tik] adj. Sabbatical.

sabin, ine [sabε̃, in] adj., s. Sabine; *l'enlèvement des Sabines,* the rape of the Sabines.

sabine [sabin] f. BOT. Savin, savine.

sabir ⌊sabi:r⌋ m. Lingua franca. || FAM. Jargon.

sablage [sɑblaːʒ] m. TECHN. Sand-blasting.

sable [sɑ:bl] m. Sand; *sables mouvants,* quick sands. || NAUT. *Fond de sable,* sandy bottom. || MÉD. Gravel. || FIG. *Bâtir sur le sable,* to build on sand. || FAM. *Le marchand de sable a passé,* the sandman has gone by.

— adj. Sand-coloured.

sable n. Sable (fourrure). || BLAS. Sable, black.

sablé [-ble] n. CULIN. Shortbread (gâteau).

— adj. Sanded, gravelled (allée). || TECHN. Sand-cast (statue); *fontaine sablée,* sand-filter. || FIG. Spotted, speckled; flecked (d'argent).

sabler [-ble] v. tr. (1). To sand, to gravel (une allée). || TECHN. To cast in a sand-mould (couler); to sand-blast (nettoyer). || FIG. To swig, to swill down, to toss off (du champagne).

sableuse [-blø:z] f. TECHN. Sand-blast (machine).

sableux, euse [-blø, ø:z] adj. Sandy.

sablier [-blije] m. † Sand-box (d'un écrivain). || Hour-glass (horloge). || CULIN. Egg-timer. || COMM. Sand-dealer (ou) -merchant.

sablière [-blijɛ:r] f. Sand- (ou) gravel pit. || CH. DE F. Sand-box.

sablon [-blɔ̃] m. Fine sand.

sablonner [-blɔne] v. tr. (1). To scour with sand (écurer); to sand (sabler).

sablonneux, euse [-blɔnø, ø:z] adj. Sandy.

sablonnière [-blɔnjɛ:r] f. Sand-pit.

sabord [sabɔ:r] m. NAUT. Port, port-hole; *sabord de charge,* cargo-port; *sabord de lancement,* port.

sabordage [-daːʒ], **sabordement** [-dəmɑ̃] m. NAUT. Scuttling (d'un navire). || FIG. Wrecking, shutting down (d'une entreprise).

saborder [-de] v. tr. (1). NAUT. To scuttle (un navire). || FIG. To wreck, to shut down (une entreprise).

sabot [sabo] n. Sabot, clog (v. SOQUE). || Slipper-bath (baignoire). || Whipping-top (jouet). || AUTOM. Brake-block (de frein); over-rider (de pare-choc); skid, drag shoe (de roue). || MILIT. Sabot (de projectile). || ZOOL. Hoof (d'un cheval). || ELECTR. Contact-shoe. || COMM. Castor-cup (d'un meuble). || TECHN. Ferrule (d'un poteau). || TECHN. Curved plane (rabot). || FAM. Tub (bateau); dud (billard, instrument); old crock (tacot); botcher (personne); *je vous vois venir avec vos gros sabots,* I can see what you're after; *travailler comme un sabot,* to botch one's work.

sabotage [sabɔtaːʒ] m. Sabot-making (fabrication, métier). || CH. DE F. Chairing. || FIG. Sabotage, wilful destruction, malicious damage; act of sabotage. || FAM. Mangling, murder (d'une chanson); botching (d'un ouvrage).

saboter [-te] v. intr. (1). To make a clatter (faire du bruit). || To make (ou) manufacture sabots. || To botch one's work; to commit acts of sabotage. || SPORTS. To play with a whipping-top.

— v. tr. To sabotage; to do wilful damage to (une machine). || CH. DE F. To chair (les traverses). || TECHN. To shoe (un poteau). || FAM. To murder (une chanson); to botch, to scamp (un ouvrage).

saboterie [-tri] f. Sabot factory.

saboteur, euse [-tœ:r, ø:z] s. Saboteur. || FAM. Botcher, bungler.

sabotier [-tje] m. Sabot-maker.

sabouler [sabule] v. tr. (1). To jostle; to rate.

sabre [sɑ:br] m. MILIT. Sabre; sword. || NAUT. *Sabre d'abordage,* cutlass. || FIG. Sword (force militaire). || FAM. *Sabre de bois!,* hang it! || **Sabre-baïonnette,** m. MILIT. Sword-bayonet.

sabrer [sɑbre] v. tr. (1). MILIT. To sabre, to cut down. || FAM. To make drastic cuts in (un manuscrit); to scamp, to botch (un travail).

sabretache [sɑbrətaʃ] f. MILIT. Sabretache.

sabreur [sɑbrœ:r] m. MILIT. Swordsman, sabreur. || FAM. Slap-dash worker.

saburral, ale [sabyral] adj. Méd. Saburral, coated.

sac [sak] m. Sack, bag ; *sac de blé,* sack of corn ; U. S. bag of wheat ; *sac de camping,* rucksack ; *sac de couchage,* sleeping bag ; *sac de dépêches,* mail bag ; *sac à dos,* knapsack, rucksack ; *sac à main,* handbag ; *sac à outils,* tool-bag ; *sac à ouvrage,* work-bag ; *sac en papier,* paper-bag ; *sac de soirée,* vanity-bag ; U. S. evening bag ; *sac de voyage* travelling-bag ; *porter une robe-sac,* to wear the sack. ‖ Milit. Pack, haversack ; kitbag. ‖ Naut. Belly (d'une voile). ‖ Ecclés. Sackcloth. ‖ Sports. *Course en sac,* sack-race. ‖ Bot. Sac. ‖ Zool. Pouch. ‖ Fig. *Avoir le sac,* to be well off ; *l'affaire est dans le sac,* it's as good as done ; it's in the bag ; *homme de sac et de corde,* gallows-bird ; *prendre la main dans le sac,* to catch red handed ; *vider son sac,* to get it off one's chest ; *sac à vin,* boozer, toper, tippler. ‖ Fam. Belly (ventre). ‖ Loc. *Sac à papier !,* drat it !

sac m. Sacking, sack, pillage ; *mettre à sac,* to ransack (une maison) ; to sack (une ville).

saccade [sakad] f. Jerk, jolt, sharp pull ; *par saccades,* in jerks ; by fits and starts.

saccadé, ée [-de] adj. Jerky, abrupt (mouvement) ; uneven, irregular (respiration) ; jerky (voix). ‖ Fig. Jerky (style) ; *l'aboiement saccadé des mitrailleuses,* the staccato bark of machine-guns.

saccage [saka:ʒ] m. Disorder ; havoc, ravage.

saccagement [-ʒmɑ̃] m. Sacking, pillaging, plundering (d'une ville).

saccager [-ʒe] v. tr. (7). To ransack (une maison) ; to sack, to pillage, to plunder (une ville). ‖ Fam. To play havoc with, to upset, to throw into disorder (une bibliothèque).

saccageur [-ʒœ:r] s. Pillager, plunderer ; ransacker.

saccharate [sakkarat] m. Chim. Saccharate.

sacchareux, euse [-rø, ø:z] adj. Chim. Saccharine, sugary.

saccharide [-rid] m. Chim. Saccharide.

saccharifère [-rifɛ:r] adj. Chim. Sacchariferous.

saccharification [-rifikasjɔ̃] f. Chim. Saccharification.

saccharifier [-rifje] v. tr. (1). Chim. To saccharify.

saccharimètre [-rimɛtr] n. Chim. Saccharimeter.

saccharine [-rin] f. Chim. Saccharin, saccharine.

saccharose [-ro:z] f. Chim. Saccharose.

sacerdoce [sasɛrdɔs] m. Ecclés. Priesthood, church (prêtres) ; priesthood ; ministry (prêtrise).

sacerdotal, ale [-dɔtal] adj. Ecclés. Sacerdotal, priestly.

sache. V. savoir (92).

sachem [saʃɛm] m. Sachem (chef amérindien).

sacherie [-ʃri] f. Sack and bag trade.

sachet [-ʃɛ] m. Small bag ; sachet (à parfums), packet, U. S. package (d'aiguilles). ‖ Milit. Cartridge bag.

sacoche [sakɔʃ] f. Bag (bourse) ; satchel, wallet (serviette). ‖ Wallet (de cycliste). ‖ Milit. Saddlebag. ‖ Autom. Tool-bag.

sacquer [sake] v. tr. (1). Fam. To sack, to give the sack to (licencier) ; to flunk (recaler) ; *se faire sacquer à un examen,* to flunk, to plough in an exam. ‖ Fam. To carpet (réprimander).

sacral, ale [sakral] adj. Sacral.

sacralisation [-lizasjɔ̃] f. Sanctification, making sacred. ‖ Méd. Sacralization.

sacraliser [-lize] v. tr. (1). To sanctify, to make sacred.

sacramentel, elle [-tɛl] adj. Ecclés. Sacramental. ‖ Fam. Binding, decisive, ritual (paroles).

sacramentellement [-tɛlmɑ̃] adv. Sacramentally.

sacre [sakr] m. Ecclés. Consecration (d'un évêque) ; coronation, crowning (d'un roi). ‖ Mus. *Le Sacre du printemps,* the Rite of Spring.

sacre m. † Zool. Saker.

sacré, ée [sakre] adj. Méd. Sacral.

sacré, ée adj. Ecclés. Holy (écriture, ordres) ; sacred, consecrated (livres, vases) ; sacred (voie). ‖ Fig. Sacred (devoir) ; inviolate (loi) ; venerable (personne) ; *pour lui rien n'est sacré,* nothing is sacred to him, he has no respect for anything. ‖ ‖ Fam. *Avoir le feu sacré,* to have one's heart in one's work ; *il n'a pas le feu sacré,* his heart isn't in it. ‖ Pop. Damned, confounded, blasted, cursed (fam.) ; bloody (pop.) ; *sacré imbécile,* you damned fool !, you blithering idiot !, you B. F. ! ; *sacré nom d'un chien !,* damn it all ! ‖ **Sacré-Cœur,** m. invar. Ecclés. Sacred Heart.

— m. The holy, the divine.

sacrebleu, sacredié, sacredieu [sakrəblø, -dje, -djø] interj. Damn it !, confound it !, drat it !

sacrement [-mɑ̃] m. Ecclés. Sacrament ; *les derniers sacrements,* Extreme Unction ; *muni des sacrements de l'Eglise,* fortified with the rites of the Church.

sacrément [sakremɑ̃] adv. Fam. Damned, ever so, awfully, terribly.

sacrer [sakre] v. intr. (1). Fam. To curse and sweat.

— v. tr. Ecclés. To consecrate (un évêque) ; to crown (un roi).

sacrifiable [sakrifjabl] adj. That can be sacrified.

sacrificateur, trice [-fikatœ:r, tris] † Sacrificer.

sacrificatoire [-fikatwa:r] adj. Sacrificial.

sacrifice [-fis] m. Ecclés. Sacrifice (v. holocauste) ; *offrir en sacrifice,* to offer up as a sacrifice ; *le saint sacrifice,* the Holy Sacrament. ‖ Fig. Sacrifice (dépense, renoncement) ; *faire de grands sacrifices,* to make big sacrifices.

sacrificiel, elle [-fisjɛl] adj. Sacrificial.

sacrifié, ée [-fje] adj. Sacrificed, forsaken. ‖ Comm. Rock-bottom, slashed (prix) ; *marchandises sacrifiées,* giveaways.

— s. Sacrificial victim.

sacrifier [-fje] v. tr. (1). Ecclés. To sacrifice, to offer up in sacrifice. ‖ Comm. To sacrifice, to sell at a sacrifice. ‖ Fig. To sacrifice (qqn, un projet) ; to lay down (sa vie) [*à, pour,* for] ; to give up (sa fortune) [*à, to*] ; to devote (son temps) [*à, to*].

— v. intr. Ecclés. To sacrifice, to offer up a sacrifice. ‖ Fig. To make concessions ; *sacrifier à la mode,* to conform to fashion ; *sacrifier à ses passions,* to give free rein to one's passions.

— v. pr. **Se sacrifier,** to sacrify oneself ; to devote oneself (*à, to*).

sacrilège [sakrilɛ:ʒ] adj. Sacrilegious.

— s. Sacrilegious person.

— m. Sacrilege ; *c'est un sacrilège,* it is sacrilege.

sacrilègement [-ʒmɑ̃] adv. Sacrilegiously.

sacripant [sakripɑ̃] m. † Braggart, swaggerer. ‖ Fam. Rascal, rogue, scoundrel, good-for-nothing ; desperado.

sacristain [sakristɛ̃] m. Ecclés. Sacristan.

sacristie [-ti] f. Ecclés. Sacristy, vestry (lieu) ; raiment and vessels (objects).

sacristine [-tin] f. Ecclés. Sacristine, sacristy-nun.

sacro- [sakrɔ] préf. Sacro. ‖ **Sacro-iliaque,** adj. Méd. Sacro-iliac. ‖ **Sacro-lombaire,** adj. Méd. Sacro-lumbal. ‖ **Sacro-saint,** adj. Sacrosanct.

sacrum [sakrɔm] m. Méd. Sacrum.

sadique [sadik] adj. Sadistic.

— m. Sadist.

sadisme [-dism] m. Sadism.

saducéen, éenne [sadyseɛ̃, eɛ̃n] adj. Ecclés. Sadducean.

— s. Ecclés. Sadducee.

safari [safari] m. Safari ; *faire un safari,* to go on safari. ‖ **Safari-photo,** m. Photo-safari.

safran m. Naut. Rudder-blade.

safran [safrɑ̃] adj. invar. Saffron-coloured, yellow.

— m. Bot., Méd., Culin. Saffron.

safrané, ée [safrane] adj. Saffron-coloured; yellow (teint). ‖ Méd. Culin. Saffroned.

safraner v. tr. (1). To saffron; to colour (ou) flavour with saffron.

safranier [-nje] m. Saffron-grower.

safranière [-njɛ:r] f. Agric. Saffron-plantation.

safranine [-nin] f. Chim. Saffranin.

safre [safr] m. Chim. Zaffre, zaffer.

saga [saga] f. Saga.

sagace [sagas] adj. Sagacious, shrewd, acute, perspicacious.

sagacité [sagasite] f. Sagacity, shrewdness (v. Perspicacité); *avec sagacité*, sagaciously.

sagaie [sagɛ] f. Assegai, U. S. assagai.

sage [sa:ʒ] m. Sage, wise man. ‖ Fig. Expert; *comité des sages*, U.S. blue-ribbon committee. — adj. Sage, wise, shrewd (savant). ‖ Judicious, prudent, moderate (modéré); wise, sound (politique); reasonable, sensible (sensé). ‖ Quiet (animal); good (enfant); chaste, modest (femme); *sois sage!*, be good!; *sage comme une image*, as good as gold. ‖ **Sage-femme**, f. Méd. Midwife.

sagement [-ʒmɑ̃] adv. Sagely, wisely. ‖ Prudently (prudemment); quietly (tranquillement); soberly (sobrement).

sagesse [-ʒɛs] f. Wisdom, learning, understanding; *sagesse humaine*, wordly wisdom. ‖ Wisdom; moderation, restraint (retenue); discretion; judgment, sobriety, prudence; *avec sagesse*, wisely, judiciously. ‖ Docility, quietness (d'un animal); good conduct (d'un écolier); good behaviour (d'un enfant); modesty, chastity (d'une femme).

sagittaire [saʒitɛ:r] m. † Archer. ‖ Astron. Sagittarius. — f. Bot. Sagittaire, arrow-head.

sagittal, ale [-tal] adj. Sagittal (en forme de flèche). ‖ Méd. Sagittal (suture, plan).

sagitté, ée [-te] adj. Bot. Sagittate, arrow-shaped.

sagou [sagu] m. Sago.

sagouin [sagwɛ̃] m. Zool. Sagouin (singe). ‖ Fam. Dirty beast, filthy pig (personne).

sagouine [-gwin] f. Fam. Slut, slattern.

sagoutier [sagutje] m. Bot. Sago-tree.

Sahara [saara] m. Géogr. Sahara.

saharien, enne [-rjɛ̃, ɛn] adj. Géogr. Saharan, Saharian, Saharic.

saharienne [-rjɛn] f. Bush jacket, safari jacket.

sahib [saib] m. Sahib.

saie [sɛ] f. † Sagum. ‖ Comm. Woollen lining.

saie f. Techn. Goldsmith's brush.

saignant, ante [sɛɲɑ̃, ɑ̃:t] adj. Bleeding. ‖ Culin. Raw, underdone, U. S. rare.

saignée [-ɲe] f. Méd. Blood-letting, bleeding (action); bend of the arm (pli du bras); blood drawn (quantité); *faire une saignée à*, to bleed. ‖ Agric. Trench, ditch, drain (rigole). ‖ Techn. Groove. ‖ Fig. Drain; *faire une saignée à*, to make inroads into (sa bourse, ses économies); to bleed (qqn); to drain (ses ressources).

saignement [-ɲəmɑ̃] m. Méd. Bleeding; *saignements de nez*, nose-bleeding, U. S. nosebleed.

saigner [-ɲe] v. tr. (1). Méd. To bleed, to let blood from (un malade). ‖ Agric. To stick (un porc); to bleed (un poulet); *saigner à blanc*, to bleed white. ‖ Techn. To tap, to divert (un cours d'eau); to drain (un fossé). ‖ Fig. To bleed, to extort money from; *saigner qqn à blanc*, to bleed s.o. white, to clean s.o. out (fam.). — v. intr. Méd. To bleed; *saigner du nez*, to bleed from the nose, to have a nose-bleed; *faire saigner qqn du nez*, to make s.o.'s nose bleed. ‖ Fig. To bleed; *la plaie saigne encore*, the wound still rankles. — v. pr. Se saigner, Méd. To bleed oneself; *se faire saigner*, to have oneself bled. ‖ Fig. To

bleed oneself, to make sacrifices; *se saigner aux quatre veines*, to bleed oneself white.

Saigon [saigɔ̃] m. Géogr. Saigon.

saillant [sajɑ̃] m. Milit. Salient. — adj. Méd. Projecting (dents); high, prominent (pommettes). ‖ Archit. Projecting, jutting out (corniche). ‖ Milit., Math. Salient. ‖ Fig. Salient, striking, outstanding, conspicuous (trait).

saillie [-ji] f. Bound, spring, leap (bond); spurt, gush (d'eau, de sang); *avancer par saillies*, to advance by leaps and bounds. ‖ Protrusion, projection; *en saillie*, bulging; *faire saillie*, to project, to jut out, to bulge out (avancée); to overhang (toit); to stick out (fam.). ‖ Milit. Sally. ‖ Méd. Protuberance (d'un os). ‖ Archit. Projection; ledge; *en saillie*, projecting (balcon); *fenêtre en saillie*, bay-window. ‖ Arts. Relief; *avoir trop de saillie*, to stand out too much. ‖ Zool. Covering, servicing (d'une femelle). ‖ Fig. Sally, witticism, flash of wit (trait d'esprit).

saillir [-ji:r] v. tr. (91). Zool. To service, to cover. — v. intr. To gush out, to spurt out (eau, sang). ‖ Archit. To project, to jut out, to stand out, to protrude (balcon, pierre); to stick out (fam.). ‖ Milit. To sally, to make a sally. ‖ Arts. To stand out (figure). ‖ Fig. To stand out (traits).

sain, aine [sɛ̃, ɛn] adj. Healthy, bracing (air); sound (bois. fruit); wholesome (nourriture). ‖ Méd. Sound (membre, organe); healthy (personne); hale (vieillard); *sain et sauf*, safe and sound, unscathed; *sain d'esprit*, sound in mind. ‖ Naut. Safe, clear (côte, rade). ‖ Ecclés. Sound, orthodox (doctrine). ‖ Fig. Sound, sane (jugement).

saindoux [sɛ̃du] m. Culin. Lard.

sainement [sɛnmɑ̃] adv. Healthily; wholesomely. ‖ Sanely (judicieusement).

sainfoin [sɛ̃fwɛ̃] m. Bot. Sainfoin.

saint, ainte [sɛ̃, ɛ̃:t] s. Ecclés. Saint (en général); patron saint (protecteur); *mettre au nombre des saints*, to canonize. ‖ Ecclés. *Les saints du dernier jour*, the latter-day saints. ‖ Fam. *Lasser la patience d'un saint*, to try the patience of a saint; *ne savoir à quel saint se vouer*, not to know which way to turn, to be at one's wits' end; *un petit saint*, a little saint (ou) prig. — m. Ecclés. *Le saint des saints*, the Holy of Holies. — adj. Ecclés. Holy (martyr, semaine, trinité, Vierge); *les Saintes Ecritures*, Holy Writ, the Scriptures; *le vendredi saint*, Good Friday. ‖ Ecclés. Saint (devant un nom propre); *saint Pierre*, St. Peter; *la Saint-Pierre*, Saint Peter's day, the feast of St. Peter; *l'église Saint-Pierre*, St. Peter's, St. Peter's church. ‖ Ecclés. Holy, hallowed, consecrated (lieu); *terre sainte*, hallowed ground; *la Terre sainte*, the Holy Land. ‖ Ecclés. Godly, righteous, pious, saintly, good (âme, personne, vie). ‖ **Saint-Ange**, m. *Le fort Saint-Ange*, the Castel of Sant'Angelo. ‖ **Saint-Barthélemy** (la), f. St. Bartholomew's Day; massacre of St. Bartholomew. ‖ **Saint-bernard** m. invar. Zool. St. Bernard (chien). ‖ **Saint-Cyr,** m. invar. Milit. Saint-Cyr military academy (comparable with Sandhurst or West Point). ‖ **Saintcyrien** (pl. *saint-cyriens*), m. Cadet of Saint-Cyr. ‖ **Sainte-barbe,** f. Naut. Powder-magazine; storeroom. ‖ **Sainte-Hélène,** f. invar. Géogr. Saint Helena. ‖ **Sainte nitouche,** f. Smooth hypocrite. ‖ **Saint-Esprit,** m. invar. Ecclés. Holy Ghost. ‖ **Sainte-Touche,** f. invar. Fam. Pay-day. ‖ **Saint-frusquin,** m. invar. Fam. All one's clobber (ou) wordly possessions. ‖ **Saint-glinglin,** n. Fam. *A la saint-glinglin*, for ever and ever. ‖ **Saint-Guy,** m. invar. Méd. *Danse de Saint-Guy*, St-Vitus' dance. ‖ **Saint-honoré** (pl. *saint-honorés*), m. Culin. Cake surrounded with glazed cream buns (or) U. S. puffs and preserved fruit. ‖ **Saint-Jean** (la), f. invar. Midsummer Day; FAM. *employer toutes les herbes de la Saint-Jean,* to leave no stone unturned. ‖ **Saint-Michel** (la), f. Michaelmas. ‖‖ **Saint-père** (le), m. The Holy Father, the Pope. ‖ **Saint-Siège,** m. invar. ECCLÉS. Holy See. ‖ **Saint-simonien** (pl. *saint-simoniens*), adj., s. Saint-Simonian. ‖ **Saint-simonisme,** m. invar. Saint-Simonism, Saint-Simonianism. ‖ **Saint-Sylvestre** (la), f. invar. New-Year's Eve.

saintement [-tmɑ̃] adv. ECCLÉS. Holily, right-eously; *vivre saintement,* to live a godly life.

sainteté [-təte] f. ECCLÉS. Holiness; sanctity (d'un lieu, d'une loi); saintliness, godliness (d'une per-sonne); *Sa, Votre Sainteté,* His, Your Holiness.

sais, sait [sɛ]. V. SAVOIR (92).

saisi, ie [sɛzi] adj. Seized. ‖ V. SAISIR.
— m. JUR. Distrainee.

saisie f. JUR. Seizure, distraint (en général); fore-close (d'une hypothèque); *opérer la saisie de,* to seize. ‖ NAUT. Seizure. ‖ **Saisie-arrêt** (pl. *saisies-arrêts*), f. JUR. Attachment, garnishment. FAM. Execution. ‖ **Saisie-brandon,** f. JUR. Distraint by seizure of crops and fruit. ‖ **Saisie-exécution,** f. JUR. Distress, execution. ‖ **Saisie-gagerie,** f. JUR. Distraint, execution. ‖ **Saisie-revendication,** f. JUR. Seizure under prior claim.

saisine [-zin] f. JUR. Seisin. ‖ NAUT. Lashing.

saisir [-zi:r] v. tr (2). To seize, to grasp, to grab, to lay hold of (prendre vivement); *saisir au collet,* to grab by the collar (fam.); *saisir son épée,* to seize (ou) grasp one's sword; *saisir par le bras,* to seize (ou) grasp by the arm. ‖ To seize, to take possession of (s'emparer de); *saisir le pouvoir,* to seize power. ‖ To seize (ne pas laisser échap-per); *saisir une occasion pour,* to seize (ou) to snatch an opportunity to. ‖ To strike, to sur-prise (frapper, surprendre); *être saisi,* to be stricken (ou) seized (de peur, d'étonnement); *saisi de panique,* panic-stricken; *saisi de peur,* struck with fear; *il fut saisi de le voir en si bonne santé,* he was struck to see him looking so well. ‖ To grasp (comprendre); to seize, to take in (com-prendre, discerner); to catch (entendre); *il n'en saisit pas la signification,* he doesn't grasp its meaning; *je n'ai pas saisi son nom,* I didn't catch his name; *mal saisir qqch.,* to get the wrong idea of sth.; to get the wrong end of the stick (fam.); *saisir une ressemblance,* to catch a likeness. ‖ THÉÂTR. *Saisir un rôle,* to catch the spirit of a part. ‖ CULIN. To cook lightly over a hot flame, to sear (de la viande). ‖ JUR. To inform; *saisir la Chambre d'un projet de loi,* to table a bill; *saisir un tribunal d'une affaire,* to submit (ou) refer a matter to a court, to lay a matter before a court. ‖ JUR. To put in possession (de, of); *saisir qqn d'un héritage,* to vest s.o. with (ou) to put s.o. in posses-sion of an inheritance. ‖ JUR. To seize (des biens. des marchandises de contrebande); to foreclose (une hypothèque); to arrest, to apprehend (un malfaiteur); *saisir un espion,* to catch (ou) to cap-ture a spy; *faire saisir qqn,* to sell s.o. up.
— v. intr. To understand (comprendre); *saisir à demi-mot,* to take the hint; to be quick on the uptake (fam.); *saisir mentalement,* to apprehend.
— v. pr. Se **saisir,** to seize oneself; *Se saisir de,* to seize; to lay hands on (qqn).
— v. récipr. Se **saisir,** to seize each other (ou) one another.

saisissabilité [sɛzisabilite] f. JUR. Liability to attachment (ou) distraint.

saisissable [-sabl] adj. Seizable. ‖ Perceptible, distinguishable (bruit). ‖ JUR. Distrainable (biens); attachable (rente).

saisissant, ante [-sɑ̃, ɑ̃:t] adj. Biting, piercing (froid); thrilling, gripping (histoire, spectacle);

striking, startling (ressemblance). ‖ JUR. Seizing, distraining (partie).
— m. JUR. Distrainor, garnisher.

saisissement [-mɑ̃] m. MÉD. Sudden chill. ‖ FIG. Shock, thrill; *mourir de saisissement,* to die of shock.

saison [sɛzɔ̃] f. Season (de l'année); *la belle sai-son,* the summer months; *saison nouvelle,* spring-tide. ‖ Season, period (époque); *de saison,* season-able, in saison; *hors de saison,* out of season; *saison des semailles,* sowing time. ‖ MÉD. Cure; *faire une saison à Vichy,* to take a cure at Vichy. ‖ COMM. *Morte saison,* dull (ou) slack season. ‖ FIG. *De saison,* opportune (à propos); *hors de saison,* inopportune, unseasonable (déplacé).

saisonnier, ère [-zɔnje, ɛ:r] adj. Seasonal.
— s. Seasonal worker.

sajou [saʒu] m. ZOOL. Sapajou.

saké [sake] m. Saké.

salace [salas] adj. Salacious.

salacité [-site] f. Salacity, salaciousness.

salade [salad] f. CULIN. Salade; *faire la salade,* to mix the salad; *salade de fruits, russe,* fruit, Russian salad. ‖ † Salade, helmet (heaume). ‖ FAM. Medley, mix-up, hotchpotch (méli-mélo).

saladier [-dje] m. Salad-bowl.

salage [-la:ʒ] m. Salting.

salaire [-lɛ:r] m. Salary, wages. ‖ FIG. Reward, recompense (d'une bonne action); retribution (d'un crime).

salaison [-lɛzɔ̃] f. Salting (de harengs, du porc). ‖ CULIN. Salt-provisions (choses salées).

salamalec [salamalɛk] m. Salaam; *faire des sala-malecs à qqn,* to kow-tow to s.o.

salamandre [salamɑ̃:dr] m. ZOOL. Salamander. ‖ TECHN. Slow-combustion stove (poêle).

salami [salami] m. CULIN. Salami.

salanque [salɑ̃:k] f. Salt-marsh.

salant [salɑ̃] adj., m. *Marais salant,* salt-marsh, saline.

salarial, ale [salarjal] adj. Pay, wage, salary (politique, revendication); *masse salariale,* payroll (d'une entreprise), total amount of wages (d'une économie, d'un pays).

salariat [salarja] m. Salaried (ou) wage-earning classes.

salarié, ée [-rje] adj. Salaried, wage-earning.
— s. Wage-earner; salaried employee.

salarier [-rje] v. tr. (1. To pay a wage (ou) salary to.

salaud [salo] m. POP. Swine, filthy beast (mal-propre); dirty-dog, rotter (méprisable).

sale [sal] adj. Dull, dingy (couleur); soiled (linge); dirty, unclean (personne); *eaux sales,* slops. ‖ FAM. Nasty, rotten (affaire); filthy, obscene (pa-role), beastly (temps); dirty (tour).

salé, ée [sale] adj. CULIN. Salted (amandes); salt (beurre, eau). ‖ FAM. Spicy, risqué (conte); exor-bitant, stiff (prix).
— m. CULIN. Salt pork; *petit salé,* pickled pork.

salement [-lmɑ̃] adv. Dirtily, filthily; disgustingly.

saler [-le] v. tr. (1). CULIN. To cure (du lard); to salt, to pickle (du porc); to salt, to put salt in (un ragoût). ‖ FAM. To fleece, to overcharge (un client); *saler la note,* to stick it on the bill. ‖ FAM. *On l'a salé,* they've been tough on him.

saleron [-lrɔ̃] m. Bowl (d'une salière).

saleté [salte] f. Dirtiness, filthiness (état). ‖ Piece of dirt (ou) filth (ordure). ‖ FAM. Obscene (ou) coarse action (ou) word (v. OBSCÉNITÉ); *dire des saletés,* to talk filth.

saleur, euse [salœ:r, ø:z] s. CULIN. Salter, curer, pickler.

salicylate [salisilat] m. CHIM. Salicylate.

salicylique [-lik] adj. CHIM. Salicylic.

salière [saljɛ:r] f. Salt-cellar. ‖ ZOOL. Depression

above the eye-socket (d´un cheval). ‖ Fam. Saltcellar (aux épaules).

salification [salifikasjɔ̃] f. Chim. Salification.

salifier [-fje] v. tr. (1). Chim. To salify.

saligaud, aude [saligo, od] s. Pop. Filthy beast; rotter; swine.

salin, ine [salɛ̃, in] adj. Saline (concrétion); salt, salty (goût).
— m. Salt-marsh.

salinage [-lina:ʒ] m. Salt-mine, salt-works (lieu); concentration of brine (opération); saturated solution of salt (produit).

saline [-lin] f. Salt-mine, salt-works, salina.

salinier [-linje] m. Salter; salt-merchant.

salinité [-linite] f. Saltiness, saltness, salinity.

salique [salik] adj. Jur. Salic (loi).

salir [sali:r] v. tr. (2). To make dirty, to soil, to dirty. ‖ Fig. To sully, to stain, to tarnish (la réputation); to smirch (qqn).
— v. pr. Se salir, to soil (ou) dirty oneself. ‖ Fig. To sully (ou) stain one's reputation.

salissant, ante [-sɑ̃, ɑ̃:t] adj. Easily soiled (ou) dirtied (étoffe). ‖ Soiling, dirtying, dirty (travail).

salissure [salisy:r] f. Stain, defilement.

salivaire [salivɛ:r] adj. Méd. Salivary.

salivard [-va:r] s. Fam. Chatterbox.

salivation [-vasjɔ̃] f. Méd. Salivation.

salive [sali:v] f. Méd. Saliva; spittle. ‖ Fam. *Dépenser beaucoup de salive*, to talk a lot, to natter; *perdre sa salive*, to waste one's breath.

saliver [-ve] v. intr. (1). Méd. To salivate.

salle [sal] f. Hall, room; *salle à manger*, dining-room; *salle de bain(s)*, bathroom; *salle de bal de classe, de conférences, d'études*, ball-, class-, lecture-, school-room; *salle de séjour*, living-room bed-sitting room. ‖ Méd. *Salle d'hôpital*, hospital ward; *salle de garde*, resident students' room; *salle d'opérations*, operating-theatre (ou) U.S. room. ‖ Comm. *Salle des ventes*, sale-room. ‖ Milit. *Salle de police*, guard-room. ‖ Ch. de F. *Salle d'attente*, waiting-room. ‖ Techn. *Salle des chaudières* (ou) *des machines*, boiler-, engine-room. ‖ Jur. *Salle d'audience*, court-room; *salle de conseil*, council-chamber; *salle des pas perdus*, lobby. ‖ Théâtr. Auditorium; *toute la salle applaudit*, the whole house applauded. ‖ Ecclés. *Salle des œuvres*, church (ou) parish hall.

salmigondis [salmigɔ̃di] m. Culin. Salmagundi, ragout. ‖ Fam. Hotchpotch, jumble, farrago.

salmis [salmi] m. Culin. Salmi.

saloir [salwa:r] m. Culin. Salting tub.

salol [salɔl] m. Chim. Salol.

Salomon [salɔmɔ̃] m. Solomon.

salon [salɔ̃] m. Drawing-room, lounge; *salon d'attente*, waiting room; *salon de coiffure*, hairdressing saloon; *salon de thé*, tea room. ‖ Naut. Saloon. ‖ Autom. *Salon de l'automobile*, motor-show. ‖ Arts. Annual art exhibition. ‖ Ch. de F. Saloon-car. ‖ Fig. *Bolchevisme de salon*, parlour (ou) armchair Bolshevism; *fréquenter les salons*, to move in high society; *homme de salon*, ladies' man.

salonnier [salɔnje] m. Arts. Art-critic.

salopard [salɔpa:r] m. Pop. Dirty (ou) unprepossessing person. (V. salaud.)

salope [salɔp] f. Pop. Dirty (ou) slovenly girl (ou) woman; slut, slattern, sloven.

saloper [-pe] v. tr. (1). Pop. To botch, to bungle.

saloperie [-pri] f. Fam. Rubbish, trash (camelote); dirt, filth, filthiness (saleté). ‖ Fam. Smut, dirt, filth; *dire des saloperies*, to talk dirt; *faire une saloperie à*, to play a dirty trick on.

salopette [-pɛt] f. Overalls (d'enfant); overalls, dungarees (d'ouvrier). [V. bleu.]

salpêtre [salpɛ:tr] m. Chim. Saltpetre.

salpêtrer [salpɛtre] v. tr. (1). To treat with

saltpetre (une allée); to cover with saltpetre rot (un mur).

salpêtrerie [-trəri] f. Saltpetre-works.

salpêtreux, euse [-trø, ø:z] adj. Saltpetrous; impregnated with saltpetre.

salpêtrier [-trije] m. Saltpetre worker.

salpêtrière [-trijɛ:r] f. Saltpetre works.

salpêtrisation [-trizasjɔ̃] f. Treating with saltpetre (d'une allée); rotting (d'un mur).

salpingite [salpɛ̃ʒit] f. Méd. Salpingitis.

salsepareille [salsparɛ:j] f. Bot. Sarsaparilla.

salsifis [salsifi] m. Bot. Salsify; oyster plant.

saltatoire [saltatwa:r] adj. Saltatory.

saltimbanque [saltɛ̃bɑ̃:k] m. Juggler, tumbler, showman. ‖ Fig. Charlatan, mountebank.

salubre [saly:br] adj. Salubrious, healthy, health-giving. (V. sain.)

salubrement [-brəmɑ̃] adv. Salubriously, healthily.

salubrité [-brite] f. Salubrity, salubriousness (du climat); cleanliness, wholesomeness (de la nourriture); *salubrité publique*, public health.

saluer [salɥe] v. tr. (1). To greet, to salute, to bow to (qqn); *saluer de la main*, to wave to. ‖ Milit. To salute (un officier); *saluer du drapeau*, to lower the colour. ‖ Naut. To salute (un officier); *saluer un grain*, to shorten sail for a squall; *saluer du pavillon*, to dip the flag; *saluer un navire de vingt coups de canon*, to fire twenty guns in salute to a ship. ‖ Ecclés. *Je vous salue, Marie*, hail, Mary. ‖ Fig. To hail, to acclaim; *saluer l'avènement de la liberté*, to hail the birth of liberty.

salure [saly:r] f. Saltness, saltiness (état); tang (de la mer).

salut [saly] m. Salutation, greeting; *faire un grand salut à qqn*, to bow deeply to s.o.; to make s.o. a deep bow; *faire un salut de la main à qqn*, to wave to s.o.; to give s.o. a wave of the hand. ‖ Welfare, well-being (salubrité). ‖ Safety, security (sécurité); *Comité de salut public*, Committee of Public Safety; *devoir son salut à*, to owe one's safety to; *port de salut*, haven of refuge. ‖ Milit. Salute; *faire le salut militaire*, to salute; *rendre un salut*, to return a salute; *salut du drapeau*, lowering of the colour. ‖ Sports. *Salut des armes*, salute (en escrime). ‖ Ecclés. Saving (des âmes); salvation (bonheur éternel); evening service, Benediction (office); *Armée du Salut*, Salvation Army; *faire son salut*, to find salvation; *travailler à son salut*, to work out one's own salvation.
— interj. Hi! (bonjour); bye!, cheerio!, see you! (au revoir).

salutaire [-tɛ:r] adj. Salutary (conseil); beneficent, good (influence); healthy (respect).

salutairement [-tɛrmɑ̃] adv. Beneficently.

salutation [-tasjɔ̃] f. Salutation, greeting [v. salut]; *faire une profonde salutation*, to make a deep bow; « *veuillez agréer mes respectueuses salutations* », « yours faithfully ».

salutiste [-tist] s. Ecclés. Salvationist; member of the Salvation Army.

Salvador [salvadɔ:r] m. Géogr. El Salvador.

salvateur, trice [salvatœ:r, tris] adj. Saving.

salve [salv] f. Milit. Salvo; *exécuter un feu de salve*, to fire volleys; *tirer une salve*, to fire a salute. ‖ Fig. *Salve d'applaudissements*, burst (ou) round of applause.

samaritain, aine [samaritɛ̃, ɛn] adj., s. Géogr., Ecclés. Samaritan.

samba [sɑ̃ba] f. Mus. Samba.

samedi [samdi] m. Saturday. ‖ Ecclés. *Samedi saint*, Holy Saturday.

samit [samit] m. † Samite.

samizdat [samizdat] m. Samizdat.

samouraï [samurai] m. Samurai.

samovar [samɔva:r] m. Culin. Samovar.

sampan(g) [sãpã] m. Naut. Sampan.

S.A.M.U. [samy] m. Méd. Abrév. de *Service d'aide médicale d'urgence*, system of mobile extensive care units.

sana [sana] m. Méd., Fam. Sanatorium.

sanctifiant, ante [sãktifjã, ã:t] adj. Ecclés. Sanctifying.

sanctificateur, trice [-fikatœ:r, tris] adj. Ecclés. Sanctifying.

— s. Ecclés. Sanctifier; Holy Ghost.

sanctification [-fikasjõ] f. Ecclés. Sanctification (des âmes); observance, keeping (du dimanche).

sanctifier [-fje] v. tr. (1). Ecclés. To observe, to keep (célébrer); to sanctify, to purify (rendre saint); to hallow (révérer); *que votre nom soit sanctifié*, hallowed be Thy Name.

sanction [sãksjõ] f. Assent, approbation, sanction (confirmation); *sanction de l'usage*, sanction of custom; *sanction royale*, royal assent. ‖ Penalty, punishment, sanction (peine); *sanction disciplinaire*, summary punishment, sanction; *sanction pénale*, punitive sanction.

sanctionner [-sjɔne] v. tr. (1). To sanction, to approve, to ratify (confirmer); *usage sanctionné par la pratique*, custom sanctioned by practice.

sanctuaire [sãktɥɛ:r] m. Ecclés. Sanctuary, sacrarium (saint des saints); sanctuary (temple). ‖ Fig. Sanctuary, asylum, refuge. ‖ Fam. Den.

sanctus [-ty:s] m. Ecclés., Mus. Sanctus.

sandale [sãdal] f. Sandal. ‖ Sports. Gym-shoe (ou) plimsoll.

sandalette [-lɛt] f. Sandal.

sandow [sãdɔf] m. Sports. Chest-expander. ‖ Aviat. Shock-absorber.

sandwich [sãdwitʃ] m. Culin. Sandwich; *sandwich au jambon*, ham sandwich. ‖ Comm. *Homme sandwich*, sandwich-man.

sang [sã] m. Blood; *à sang chaud, froid*, warm-, cold-blooded; *être tout en sang*, to be covered with (ou) smothered in blood; *jusqu'au sang*, till the blood comes; *taché de sang*, blood-stained. ‖ Méd. Blood; *écoulement de sang*, bleeding, haemorrhage; *injecté de sang*, bloodshot; *le sang lui monta à la tête*, he reddened (ou) flushed. ‖ Pop. *Bon sang!, bon sang de bon sang!*, curse it! devil take it! ‖ Fig. Blood, relationship, family (famille); *droit du sang*, birthright; *son propre sang*, one's own flesh and blood; *voix du sang*, call of the blood. ‖ Fig. Blood, race (race); *demi-sang, pur-sang*, half-bred, thoroughbred; *sang mêlé*, half-caste, person of mixed blood; *être d'un sang illustre, avoir du sang bleu*, to have blue blood in one's veins; *prince du sang*, prince of the blood. ‖ Fig. Blood, life (vie); *donner son sang pour la patrie*, to give one's life for one's country; *payer une faute de son sang*, to pay for a misdeed with one's life. ‖ Fam. *Avoir le sang chaud*, to be hot-headed (ou) quick-tempered; *avoir du sang dans les veines*, to be a man of mettle; *se faire du mauvais sang*, to worry unduly; *se manger les sangs*, to fret and fume; *suer sang et eau*, to sweat blood; *tourner les sangs à qqn*, to give s.o. a turn (ou) quite a turn; *tout mon sang n'a fait qu'un tour*, my heart came into my mouth. ‖ **Sang-dragon**, m. invar. Dragon's blood. ‖ **Sang-froid**, m. invar. Sang-froid, coolness, self-control; *de sang-froid*, deliberately, in cold blood; *garder son sang-froid*, to keep cool (ou) one's head; *perdre son sang-froid*, to lose one's self-control; to fly off the handle (fam.). ‖ **Sang-mêlé**, s. inv. Half-blood, half-breed.

sanglant, ante [sãglã, ã:t] adj. Bloody (bataille); blood-stained, bloody (épée). [V. ensanglanté.] ‖ Fig. Bitter (affront); violent, cruel (mort); cutting, bitter (reproche).

sangle [sã:gl] f. Strap (en général); webbing (d'un fauteuil); saddle-girth (d'une selle); *lit de sangle*, camp-bed.

sangler [sãgle] v. tr. (1). To girth (un cheval). ‖ To fit with webbing (un fauteuil). ‖ To lace tight (la taille).

sanglier [sãglije] m. Zool. Wild boar.

sanglot [sãglo] m. Sob; *pleurer à gros sanglots*, to sob one's heart out.

sangloter [-glɔte] v. intr. (1). To sob.

sangsue [sãsy] f. Zool., Méd. Leech; *mettre des sangsues à*, to apply leeches to. ‖ Fig. Blood-sucker.

sanguin, ine [sãgɛ̃, in] adj. Méd. Sanguineous (crachat); full-blooded (tempérament); *émission sanguine*, flow of blood; *vaisseau sanguin*, blood-vessel. ‖ Ruddy, red (couleur); *d'un rouge sanguin*, blood-red.

sanguinaire [-ginɛ:r] adj. Sanguinary; bloody (bataille, lutte); bloodthirsty (homme); cruel (loi).

— f. Bot. Blood-root.

sanguine [sãgin] f. Blood-orange (fruit). ‖ Blood-stone (pierre). ‖ Arts. Red chalk (crayon); red chalk drawing (dessin).

sanguinolent [-nɔlã] adj. Sanguinolent, tinged with blood.

sanhédrin [sanedrɛ̃] m. Sanhedrin, sanhedrim. ‖ Fig. Gathering.

sanieux, euse [sanjø, ø:z] adj. Méd. Sanious.

sanitaire [sanitɛ:r] adj. Méd. Sanitary (bureau, cordon); medical (bataillon, formation). ‖ Milit. *Train sanitaire*, ambulance (ou) hospital train. ‖ Aviat. *Avion sanitaire*, flying ambulance.

— m. pl. Sanitary facilities, bathroom.

sans [sã] prép. Without; *cela va sans dire*, it goes without saying; *non sans difficulté*, not without difficulty; *sans faute*, without fail; *sans mentir*, truth to tell, without a word of a lie; *sans moi*, without me; *sans plus*, nothing more; *sans plus tarder*, without further delay, without more ado; *sans rire*, without laughing; *sa question ne fut pas sans me surprendre*, his question came as a surprise to me (ou) was something of a surprise to me; *vous n'êtes pas sans savoir que*, you cannot but know that. ‖ Un-, -less; *sans argent*, penniless; *sans cesse*, unending, ceaseless; *sans chapeau*, hatless, bareheaded; *sans doute*, doubtless, no doubt, for sure; *sans fin*, endless, never-ending; *sans prix*, beyond price (inestimable). ‖ But for; *sans cela, sans quoi*, but for that, had it not been for that; *sans votre aide*, but for (ou) without your help. ‖ **Sans que**, conj. Without, unless; *cela est arrivé sans que je l'aie su*, it happened without my knowing it; *il ne se passe jamais une journée sans qu'il vienne nous voir*, never a day goes by but he comes to see us; *il ne le fera pas sans qu'on le lui demande*, he won't do it unless he is asked. ‖ **Sans-abri**, m. invar. Homeless person. ‖ **Sans-atout**, m. Sports. No trumps; *demander sans-atout*, to go (ou) call no trumps (au bridge). ‖ **Sans-cœur**, s. invar. Heartless person. ‖ **Sans-culotte** (pl. *sans-culottes*), m. Sans-culotte. ‖ **Sans-emploi**, s. inv. Unemployed person. ‖ **Sans-gêne**, m. Off-handedness; s. off-handed person. ‖ **Sans-le-sou**, s. inv. Fam. Penniless person. ‖ **Sans-logis**, s. Homeless person. ‖ **Sans-parti**, s. inv. Independent (en politique). ‖ **Sans-souci**, s. inv. Fam. Easy-going (ou) happy-go-lucky person; adj. Fam. unconcerned, insouciant.

sanscrit [sãskri] adj., m. Sanskrit.

sanscritique [-tik] adj. Sanskritic.

sanscritiste [-tist] s. Sanskritist.

sansonnet [sãsɔnɛ] m. Zool. Starling.

santal [sãtal] (pl. *santals*) m. Bot. Sandal (arbre); sandal-wood (bois).

santé [sãte] f. Méd. Health; *avoir une faible santé*, to suffer from poor health; *en parfaite* *santé,* in perfect health; *ministère de la Santé publique,* Ministry of Health; *respirer la santé,* to be the picture of health; *santé de fer,* iron constitution. ‖ MILIT. *Service de (la) santé,* medical corps. ‖ NAUT. *Agent de santé,* quarantine officer; *conseil de santé,* medical board. ‖ FIG. Health (toast); *à votre santé!,* good health!, cheers! (fam.); *boire à la santé de qqn,* to drink s.o.'s health. ‖ FAM. *Avoir une santé,* to be long-suffering (être patient).

santon [sɑ̃tɔ̃] m. Santon (figurine).

santonine [sɑ̃tɔnin] f. BOT. Santonica. ‖ CHIM. Santonin.

saoudien, enne [saudjɛ̃, ɛn] adj., s. GÉOGR. Saudi, Saudi Arabian.

saoudite [-dit] adj. GÉOGR. *Arabie Saoudite,* Saudi Arabia.

saoul [su], **saoulard, saouler.** V. SOÛL, SOÛLARD, SOÛLER.

sapajou [sapaʒu] m. ZOOL. Sapajou. ‖ FIG. Little monkey.

sape [sap] f. Undermining (d'un mur). ‖ MILIT. Sap (tranchée). ‖ Pl. POP. Gear, duds (vêtements).

sapement [-mɑ̃] m. Sapping, undermining.

sapèque [sapɛk] f. Sapeke.

saper [sape] v. tr. (1). ARCHIT. To undermine (un mur). ‖ MILIT. To mine (une tranchée). ‖ FIG. To sap, to undermine (la morale).
— v. pr. **Se saper,** POP. To get dressed (s'habiller); to put on one's glad rags, to get dolled up (se mettre sur son trente et un).

saperlipopette [sapɛrlipɔpɛt] interj. My aunt!, my sainted aunt!

sapeur [-pœ:r] m. MILIT. Sapper. ‖ **Sapeur-pompier,** m. Fireman; pl. fire-brigade.

saphique [safik] adj. Sapphic; *vers saphiques,* sapphics.

saphir [safi:r] m. Sapphire.

saphisme [safism] m. Sapphism.

sapide [sapid] adj. Sapid. (V. SAVOUREUX.)

sapidité [-dite] f. Sapidity.

sapience [sapjɑ̃:s] f. † Sapience.

sapientiaux [sapjɛ̃sjo] adj. ECCLÉS. Sapiential.
— m. pl. ECCLÉS. Sapiential books.

sapin [sapɛ̃] m. BOT. Fir, fir-tree; *sapin argenté,* silver fir. ‖ FAM. Coffin; *toux qui sent le sapin,* graveyard cough.

sapine [sapin] f. ARCHIT. Movable crane (grue); fir plank (planche).

sapinière [-pinjɛ:r] f. BOT. Fir-plantation.

saponacé, ée [sapɔnase] adj. Saponaceous, soapy.

saponaire [-nɛ:r] f. BOT. Soapwort.

saponifiable [-nifjabl] adj. Saponifiable.

saponification [-nifikasjɔ̃] f. Saponification.

saponifier [-nifje] v. tr. (1). To saponify.

saponine [-nin] f. Saponin, soap-bark.

sapristi [sapristi] interj. Gosh!; damnation!

saprophyte [saprofit] adj. BOT. Saprophytic.
— m. BOT. Saprophyte.

saquer [sake] v. tr. (1). V. SACQUER.

sarabande [sarabɑ̃:d] f. MUS. Saraband.

sarbacane [sarbakan] f. Blow-pipe. ‖ Pea-shooter (d'enfant).

sarcasme [sarkasm] m. Sarcasm; sarcastic remark, taunt, gibe.

sarcastique [-tik] adj. Sarcastic. (V. SARDONIQUE.)

sarcelle [sarsɛl] f. ZOOL. Teal.

sarclage [sarkla:ʒ] m. AGRIC. Weeding.

sarcler [-kle] v. tr. (1). AGRIC. To hoe, to clean (un champ); to weed out, to pull up (les herbes).

sarcleur, euse [-klœ:r, ø:z] s. AGRIC. Weeder.

sarcleuse [-klø:z] f. AGRIC. Weeding-machine.

sarcloir [-klwa:r] m. AGRIC. Hoe.

sarclure [-kly:r] f. AGRIC. Weedings.

sarcologie [sarkɔlɔʒi] f. MÉD. Sarcology.

sarcome [sarko:m] m. MÉD. Sarcoma.

sarcophage [sarkɔfa:ʒ] m. Sarcophagus.

sarcopte [sarkɔpt] m. ZOOL. Sarcoptes.

Sardaigne [sardɛɲ] f. GÉOGR. Sardinia.

sardanapalesque [sardanapalɛsk] adj. Sardanapalian.

sarde [sard] adj. s. GÉOGR. Sardinian.
— m. GRAMM. Sardinian (langue).

sardine [sardin] f. ZOOL. Sardine, pilchard; *sardine anchoitée,* anchovy sardine. ‖ MILIT., FAM. N.C.O.'s stripe; tape.

sardinerie [-nri] f. Sardine-curing station.

sardinier [-nje] s. Sardine-fisher.
— m. Sardine-boat (bateau); sardine-net (filet).

sardoine [sardwan] f. Sard.

sardonique [sardɔnik] adj. Sardonic.

sardoniquement [-mɑ̃] adv. Sardonically.

sargasse [sargas] f. Sargasso, gulf-weed. ‖ GÉOGR. *Mer des Sargasses,* Sargasso Sea.

sari [sari] m. Sari, saree.

sarigue [sarig] f. ZOOL. Opossum.

S.A.R.L. [ɛsaɛrɛl] f. JUR., COMM. Abrév. de *société à responsabilité limitée,* Ltd, Limited company.

sarment [sarmɑ̃] m. BOT. Bine (de plante); vine-shoot (de vigne).

sarmenteux, euse [-tø, ø:z] adj. BOT. Sarmentose, sarmentous.

sarong [sarɔŋ] m. Sarong.

sarrasin, ine [sarazɛ̃, in] adj., s. GÉOGR. Saracen.
— m. AGRIC. Buckwheat.

sarrasine [-zin] f. Portcullis.

sarrau [saro] m. Overall, smock (d'enfant); smock (de paysan).

sarriette [sarjɛt] f. CULIN. Savory.

sarrois, oise [sarwa, wa:z] adj. GÉOGR. Of (ou) from Saarland (ou) the Saar.
— s. Native (ou) inhabitant of Saarland (ou) the Saar.

sas [sɑ] m. Sieve, riddle, screen. (V. TAMIS.) ‖ NAUT. Lock (d'écluse); flooding-chamber (de sous-marin).

sassafras [sasafra] m. BOT. Sassafras.

sasse [sas] f. NAUT. Bailer, bailing-scoop.

sasser [sase] v. tr. (1). To sieve, to sift, to riddle, to screen, to winnow. (V. TAMISER.) ‖ NAUT. To pass through a lock (un bateau).

satané, ée [satane] adj. FAM. Devilish, confounded; *satané menteur.* damned liar.

satanique [-nik] adj. Satanic, fiendish, diabolical.

satanisme [-nism] m. Satanism.

satellisation [satelizasjɔ̃] f. ASTRONAUT. Putting into orbit. ‖ FIG. Reducing (ou) reduction to satellite status.

satelliser [-ze] v. tr. (1). ASTRONAUT. To put into orbit. ‖ FIG. To turn into a satellite, to reduce to satellite status (un pays); *nation satellisée par,* a country that has become a satellite of.

satellite [satellit] m. ASTRON., PHYS. Satellite. ‖ TECHN. Planet-wheel. ‖ FAM. Satellite, henchman; stooge (fam.).

sâti [sa:ti] m., f. Suttee.

satiété [sasjete] f. Satiety, surfeit; *à satiété,* to repletion.

satin [satɛ̃] m. Satin. ‖ BOT. *Bois de satin,* satin-wood. ‖ FIG. *De satin,* smooth, satiny (peau).

satinade [satinad] f. Satinet, satinette.

satinage [-na:ʒ] m. Satining; hot-pressing.

satiné, ée [-ne] adj. Satiny (peau). ‖ *Papier satiné,* satin paper; U. S. glazed paper, coated stock.
— m. Gloss, gloss-finish.

satiner v. tr. (1). To surface, to glaze (du papier); to satin (du tissu).

satinette [-net] f. Satinet, satinette, sateen.

satineur [-nœ:r] m. s. Satiner, glazer.

satire [sati:r] f. Satire (contre, upon).

satirique [-rik] adj. Satiric, satirical.
— m. Satirist.

satiriquement [-rikmᾶ] adv. Satirically.
satiriser [-rize] v. tr. (1). To satirize.
satisfaction [satisfaksjɔ̃] f. Satisfaction, contentment (contentement); *recevoir un témoignage de satisfaction*, to be commended. ‖ Satisfaction, reparation (réparation); *demander satisfaction à*, to demand satisfaction from; *donner satisfaction*, to give satisfaction, to be satisfactory. ‖ EccLÉS. Atonement (*de*, for).
satisfactoire [-twa:r] adj. EccLÉS. Satisfactory, atoning.
satisfaire [satisfɛ:r] v. tr. (50). To meet, to fill, to satisfy (une demande); to meet (un désir); to appease (sa faim); to gratify (ses passions); to satisfy, to give satisfaction to (qqn). ‖ FIN. To pay off (un créancier).
— v. intr. *Satisfaire à*, to fulfil (une condition); to carry out, to fulfil (un devoir); to comply with (une règle). ‖ COMM., FIN. *Satisfaire pour qqn*, to meet s.o.'s liabilities, to pay s.o.'s debts.
— v. pr. **Se satisfaire,** to content oneself (ou) be satisfied (*de*, with).
satisfaisant, ante [-fəzᾶ, ᾶ:t] adj. Satisfying, satisfactory; *peu satisfaisant*, unsatisfactory.
satisfait, aite [-fɛ, ɛt] adj. Satisfied, pleased (*de*, with); *peu satisfait*, dissatisfied (*de*, with).
satisfecit [-fesit] m. invar. Satisfactory report; good mark.
satrape [satrap] m. Satrap.
saturabilité [satyrabilite] f. Saturability.
saturable [-rabl] adj. Saturable.
saturant, ante [-rᾶ, ᾶ:t] adj. Saturating, saturant. ‖ PHYS. Saturated (vapeur).
saturateur [-ratœ:r] m. Humidifier (d'atmosphère); saturator (d'un liquide).
saturation [-rasjɔ̃] f. Saturation.
saturer [-re] v. tr. (1). To saturate (*de*, with). ‖ FIG. To satiate.
saturnales [satyrnal] f. pl. Saturnalia.
Saturne [satyrn] m. ASTRON. Saturn. ‖ CHIM. *Extrait de Saturne*, lead acetate.
saturnien, enne [-njɛ̃, ɛn] adj. Saturnian.
saturnin, ine [-nɛ̃, in] adj. CHIM. Saturnine, lead. ‖ MÉD. *Intoxication saturnine*, lead-poisoning.
saturnisme [-nism] m. MÉD. Lead-poisoning.
satyre [sati:r] m. Satyr. ‖ ZooL. Satyr butterfly.
satyrique [-rik] adj. Satyric.
sauce [so:s] f. CULIN. Sauce; *sauce tomate*, tomato sauce; *sauce au vin*, wine sauce. ‖ ARTS. Black chalk, lamp-black. ‖ FIG. *Accommoder à toutes les sauces*, to serve (ou) dish up in various forms, to dress up in various guises; *ne pas savoir à quelle sauce mettre qqn*, not to know what to make of s.o.; *se mettre à toutes les sauces*, to turn one's hand to anything. ‖ FAM. *Allonger la sauce*, to pad out a book (en écrivant); to expatiate (en parlant).
saucée [sose] f. FAM. Downpour, drenching, sousing, soaking. ‖ PoP. Dressing (ou) U.S. calling-down.
saucer v. tr. (6). To dip (ou) to dunk in the sauce (son pain). ‖ FAM. To drench, to soak to the skin; *se faire saucer*, to get a soaking.
saucier [-sje] m. CULIN. Sauce-cook. ‖ NAUT. Saucer, socket.
saucière [-sjɛ:r] f. CULIN. Sauce-boat.
saucisse [sosis] f. Sausage; *chair à saucisse*, sausage-meat. ‖ MILIT. Observation balloon, blimp. ‖ FIG. *Il n'attache pas son chien avec des saucisses*, he would wring blood out of a stone.
saucisson [-sɔ̃] m. CULIN. Sausage, polony, U. S. boloney (andouille); loaf (pain). ‖ MILIT. Fascine.
saucissonné, ée [-sɔne] adj. FAM. Tied up like a sausage, trussed up.
saucissonner v. tr. (1). FAM. To picnic, to have a picnic.
sauf, auve [sof, o:v] adj. Safe, unscathed; *l'honneur est sauf*, honour is saved; *sain et sauf*, safe

and sound; *s'en tirer avec la vie sauve*, to get off with a whole skin. ‖ **Sauf-conduit** (pl. *sauf-conduits*). m. Safe-conduct, pass.
sauf prép. Save, saving, except; *il a tout vendu, sauf sa maison*, he's sold everything except his house; *sauf accidents*, barring accidents; *sauf erreur ou omission*, errors and omissions excepted; *sauf imprévu*, except for unforeseen circumstances; *sauf de rares exceptions*, with very few exceptions; *sauf votre respect*, saving your presence (ou) reverence. ‖ **Sauf à,** even if (v. QUITTE); *sauf à recommencer*, even if it has to be done over again. ‖ **Sauf que,** conj. Save that, except that. ‖ COMM. *Sauf erreur ou omission*, errors and omissions excepted; E. & O.E.
sauge [so:ʒ] f. BOT., CULIN. Sage.
saugrenu, ue [sograny] adj. Ridiculous, nonsensical; *questions saugrenues*, silly questions.
saulaie [solɛ] f. BOT. Willow-plantation.
saule [so:l] m. BOT. Willow; *saule pleureur*, weeping willow.
saulée [sole] f. BOT. Willow-plantation.
saumâtre [somɑ:tr] adj. Brackish, briny (eau). ‖ FAM. Disagreeable, nasty.
saumon [somɔ̃] m. ZooL. Salmon. ‖ TECHN. Ingot (d'étain); pig (de plomb).
— adj. invar. Salmon-coloured.
saumoné, ée [-mɔne] adj. Salmon-coloured (chair). ‖ ZooL. *Truite saumonée*, salmon-trout.
saumoneau [-mɔno] m. ZooL. Young salmon.
saumurage [somyra:ʒ] m. Pickling in brine.
saumure [somy:r] f. Pickling brine.
saumuré, ée [-re] adj. Pickled in brine; brined.
sauna [sona] m. Sauna.
saunage [sona:ʒ] m. Salt-making season (époque). ‖ Salt-trade, salt-making (fabrication); *faux saunage*, illicit salt-making.
sauner [-ne] v. intr. (1). To manufacture salt.
saunerie [-nri] f. Salt-works; saltern.
saunier [-nje] s. Salt-maker; *faux saunier*, maker of (ou) dealer in contraband salt.
saupiquet [sopikɛ] m. CULIN. Hot sauce.
saupoudrage [sopudra:ʒ] m. Sprinkling, dusting, powdering.
saupoudrer [-dre] v. tr. (1). To sprinkle, to dot, to powder (*de*, with). ‖ FIG. *Saupoudrer son discours de citations latines*, to interlard one's speech with Latin quotations.
saupoudreuse [-drø:z] f. Sprinkler, castor, dredger.
saur [sɔ:r] adj. m. CULIN. Smoke-dried; smoked; *hareng saur*, red (ou) kippered herring.
saura, saurai. V. SAVOIR (92).
saure [sɔr] adj. Brownish-yellow; sorrel (cheval).
saurer [sore] v. tr. (1). CULIN. To smoke-dry, to smoke, to kipper, to bloat.
sauret [-rɛ] adj. CULIN. Lightly-cured (hareng).
saurien [sorjɛ̃] adj., m. ZooL. Saurian.
saussaie [sosɛ] f. Willow-plantation.
saut [so] m. Leap, bound, jump (bond); *au saut du lit*, on getting up, on getting out of bed; *faire un saut*, to jump, to take a leap. ‖ GÉOGR. Cascade, waterfall; *le saut du Niagara*, Niagara Falls. ‖ SPORTS. *Saut à la perche, avec élan, en longueur*, pole, running, long jump; *saut à ski*, ski-jump; *saut de haie*, hurdling; *saut périlleux*, somersault. ‖ Mus. Skip. ‖ FIG. Sudden movement (ou) transition; *faire le saut*, to take the plunge, to give in. ‖ FAM. *Faire un saut chez X*, to pop round to X's, U. S. to drop in on X. ‖ **Saut-de-lit,** m. Dressing-gown. ‖ **Saut-de-loup,** m. Ha-ha, sunken fence. ‖ **Saut-de-mouton,** m. AUTOM., CH. DE F. Flyover, U. S. overpass.
saute [so:t] f. NAUT. Shift (de vent). ‖ PHYS. Rise (de température). ‖ FIG. Sudden change (d'humeur).
saute. V. SAUTER. ‖ **Saute-mouton,** m. Leap-frog.

sauté, ée [sote] adj. CULIN. Sauté.

sauter v. intr. (1). To jump, to leap; *faire sauter*, to blow up (qqch.); to make jump (qqn); *faire sauter la bande d'un journal*, to tear the wrapper off a newspaper; *faire sauter un bouton*, to burst a button; *faire sauter la cervelle à qqn*, to blow s.o.'s brains out; *faire sauter un enfant sur ses genoux*, to dandle a child on one's knees; *sauter à la gorge, au collet de qqn*, to fly at s.o.'s throat; *sauter à terre, en selle*, to jump down, to leap into the saddle; *sauter au bas du lit*, to jump out of bed; *sauter de joie*, to jump for joy. ‖ To come (ou) fly off (bouton); to burst (chaudière); to go off, to explode (mine); to go up, to blow up (poudrière); to start (rivet). ‖ NAUT. To shift (vent). ‖ CULIN. *Faire sauter*, to toss (une crêpe); to fry (des pommes de terre). ‖ ELECTR. To blow out (fusible); *faire sauter les plombs*, to blow a fuse; *le plomb a sauté*, the fuse has blown. ‖ FIN. *Faire sauter la banque*, to break the bank. ‖ SPORTS. *Sauter à la corde, à la perche*, to skip, to pole-vault. ‖ FIG. To jump, to rise suddenly; *faire sauter les écus*, to run through the money; *faire sauter qqn*, to sack (or) fire s.o.; *reculer pour mieux sauter*, to procrastinate only to find one's difficulties increased; *sauter au plafond*, to go up in the air; *sauter aux yeux*, to be obvious; *sauter d'un sujet à un autre*, to jump (ou) dodge from one subject to another; *sauter de la troisième à la première place*, to jump from third to first place; *sauter sur une occasion*, to seize an opportunity. — v. tr. To jump, to leap across (un fossé); to clear, to jump over (une haie). ‖ To drop (une maille); *maille sautée*, drop-stitch. ‖ FIG. To skip (un feuillet); to leave out, to omit (un mot). ‖ **Saute-ruisseau**, m. invar. Office-boy, errand-boy.

sauterelle [sotrɛl] f. ZOOL. Grasshopper; locust.

sauterie [sotri] f. Informal dance; hop (fam.).

sauteur, euse [sotœ:r, ø:z] adj. ZOOL. Jumping (insecte). ‖ FIG. Flighty, unreliable (personne). — s. SPORTS. Jumper (cheval). ‖ FAM. Flighty (ou) unreliable person.

sauteuse [-tø:z] f. CULIN. Shallow pan.

sautillant, ante [sotijã, ã:t] adj. Jumping, hopping, bounding, skipping, dancing (enfant). ‖ FIG. Uneven, jerky (style).

sautillement [-jmã] m. Hopping, skipping, jumping.

sautiller [-je] v. intr. (1). To hop, to skip, to jump.

sautoir [sotwa:r] m. SPORTS. Jump, hurdle (obstacle). ‖ BLAS. Saltire; *en sautoir*, in saltire. ‖ † Watch-chain (de femme). ‖ LOC. *En sautoir*, crosswise; *porter un ordre en sautoir*, to wear an order round one's neck; *porter un sac en sautoir*, to carry a bag with the straps crossed over one's chest.

sauvage [sova:ʒ] adj. BOT. Wild (plante); wild, uncultivated (endroit). ‖ ZOOL. Wild, untamed (animal). ‖ FIG. Shy (ou) unsociable (personne). — m. Wild man (homme). ‖ FIG. Shy (ou) unsociable person.

sauvagement [-ʒmã] adv. Savagely.

sauvageon, onne [-ʒõ, ɔn] s. Little savage. — m. BOT. Wilding, seedling.

sauvagerie [-ʒri] f. Savagery, savageness. ‖ FIG. Unsociability.

sauvagesse [-ʒɛs] f. Wild woman.

sauvagine [-ʒin] f. ZOOL. Waterfowl.

sauvegarde [sovgard] f. Safeguard, safe-keeping, protection. ‖ Safe-conduct (sauf-conduit). ‖ NAUT. Life-line; lanyard, trailing-line (d'aviron); rudder-chain; rudder-pendant (de gouvernail). ‖ FIG. Safeguard, guarantee, defence.

sauvegarder [-de] v. tr. (1). To safeguard, to

protect (qqn, qqch.). ‖ FIG. To save (les apparences, l'honneur).

sauver [sove] v. tr. (1). To save, to preserve (conserver intact); to save, to preserve (les apparences); to save (son honneur); to keep (sa réputation); to retrieve (la situation). ‖ To save, to deliver, to rescue (tirer du péril); *sauver du naufrage*, to save from shipwreck. ‖ MÉD. To save, to pull through (un malade). ‖ ECCLÉS. To save. — v. pr. Se sauver, to run away (ou) off, to make off (fuir). ‖ To escape, to make one's escape (s'échapper); *se sauver de prison*, to get out of prison. ‖ To take refuge (s'abriter). ‖ CULIN. To boil over (liquide). ‖ ECCLÉS. To save oneself (ou) one's soul. ‖ **Sauve-qui-peut**, m. invar. Stampede, headlong (ou) precipitate flight.

sauvetage [-vta:ʒ] m. Rescue, life-saving (d'un homme); *appareil de sauvetage*, life-saving apparatus; *échelle de sauvetage*, fire-escape. ‖ NAUT. Salvage; *bateau de sauvetage*, lifeboat; *remorqueur de sauvetage*, salvage-tug.

sauveteur [-vtœ:r] adj. Saving. ‖ NAUT. *Bateau sauveteur*, lifeboat; salvage-vessel. — m. Saver, rescuer, deliverer.

sauvette (à la) [alasovɛt] loc. adv. On the sly; *vendeur à la sauvette*, unauthorized hawker.

savamment [savamã] adv. Learnedly (avec science). ‖ Knowingly (en connaissance de cause); *j'en parle savamment*, I speak with full knowledge; I know what I'm talking about (fam.).

savane [savan] f. Savanna, savannah.

savant, ante [savã, ã:t] adj. Critical (édition); masterly, learned, scholarly (ouvrage); erudite, learned, well-informed (en, in) [personne]; *chien savant*, performing dog; *femme savante*, blue-stocking. — s. Savant, scholar, scientist, learned (ou) erudite person.

savantissime [-tisim] adj. FAM. Most learned.

savarin [savarɛ̃] m. CULIN. Savarin.

savate [savat] f. Old (ou) worn-out slipper; *traîner la savate*, to be down at heel. ‖ NAUT. Sole-plate. ‖ SPORTS. Foot-boxing. ‖ FAM. Bungler, botcher (bousilleur).

savetier [-vtje] m. Cobbler. ‖ POP. Botcher.

saveur [savœ:r] f. Savour, flavour, taste; *plein de saveur*, fully-flavoured. ‖ FIG. Pungency (d'un ouvrage); *sans aucune saveur*, insipid.

savoir [savwa:r] m. Knowledge, learning, erudition, scholarship.

savoir v. tr. (92). To know (avoir appris); *comment le saurais-je?* how should I know?; *en savoir plus d'une*, to know a thing or two; *n'en savoir rien*, to know nothing about it; *ne savoir rien de rien*, to know nothing about anything, to be a complete ignoramus; *ne savoir que dire, que faire*, not to know what to say, to do; *savoir l'anglais*, to know (ou) to be able to speak English; *savoir sa leçon*, to know (ou) to have learnt one's lesson; *savoir un poème par cœur*, to know a poem by heart. ‖ To know, to be informed of, to be aware of (être informé de); *faire savoir qqch. à qqn*, to tell s.o. sth., to inform s.o. of sth.; to acquaint s.o. with sth., to let s.o. know sth.; *il ne veut rien savoir*, he won't listen; *sans le savoir*, unwittingly; *savoir un secret*, to know a secret; *un je-ne-sais-quoi*, something or other. ‖ To know how; *savoir nager*, to be able to swim; *savoir vivre*, to know how to behave. ‖ To know, to know of (connaître); *savoir un bon médecin*, to know of a good doctor. ‖ Can (pouvoir); *je ne saurais m'en passer*, I cannot do without it. — v. intr. To know; *à savoir, savoir*, namely, to wit; *c'est à savoir*, that remains to be seen; *on ne sait jamais*, one never knows, you never can tell; *pas que je sache*, not that I know of, not to my knowledge; (*pour*) *autant que je sache*, as far as I know, to the best of my knowledge; *reste à savoir si*, it remains to be seen whether (ou) if; *si j'avais su!*, if only I had known! ‖ To know how; *savoir*, *c'est pouvoir*, knowledge is power; *si jeunesse savait, si vieillesse pouvait*, if the young knew how, if the old had the strength. ‖ Fam. *Dieu sait comme!*, Lord knows how! ‖ **Savoir-faire**, m. Savoir-faire, ability, tact. ‖ **Savoir-vivre**, m. Savoir-vivre, knowledge of the world, good manners, etiquette; *manque de savoir-vivre*, breach of manners.

savon [savɔ̃] m. Soap; *eaux de savon*, suds; *savon à barbe*, shaving-soap (ou) -stick; *savon de Marseille*, yellow (ou) household soap; *savon de toilette*, toilet-soap. ‖ Fam. Dressing- (ou) U. S. calling-down, letting-off, rocket; *flanquer* (ou) *passer un savon à qqn*, to haul s.o. over the coals.

savonnage [savɔna:ʒ] m. Washing, soaping.

savonner [-ne] v. tr. (1). To soap, to wash (du linge); to lather (le menton). ‖ Fam. *Savonner la tête à qqn, savonner qqn*, to tell s.o. off.
— v. pr. **Se savonner**, to soap oneself. ‖ To wash (étoffe).

savonnerie [-nri] f. Soap-works; soap-making.

savonnette [-net] f. Cake of soap (pain de savon). ‖ Shaving-brush (blaireau). ‖ Hunter (montre).

savonneux, euse [-nø, ø:z] adj. Soapy (eau). ‖ *Pierre savonneuse*, soapstone.

savonnier, ère [-nje, ɛr] adj. Soap (industrie).
— s. Soap-manufacturer.

savourer [savure] v. tr. (1). To relish, to enjoy. ‖ Fig. To savour, to enjoy (une plaisanterie); to savour, to gloat over (sa vengeance).

savoureusement [-røzmɑ̃] adv. With relish, with gusto.

savoureux, euse [-rø, ø:z] adj. Tasty, savoury (mets). ‖ Fig. Racy (anecdote); pithy (aphorisme); enjoyable (lecture); juicy (texte).

savoyard, arde [savwaja:r, ard] s., adj. Géogr. Savoyard.

saxe [saks] m. Dresden china (porcelaine); piece of Dresden china (objet).

Saxe [saks] f. Géogr. Saxony; *porcelaine de Saxe*, Dresden china.

saxhorn [saksɔrn] m. Mus. Saxhorn.

saxifrage [saksifra:ʒ] m. Bot. Saxifrage.

saxo [sakso] m. Mus. Sax (saxophone); sax player (saxophoniste).

saxon, onne [saksɔ̃, ɔn] adj., s. Géogr. Saxon.

saxophone [saksɔfɔn] m. Mus. Saxophone.

saxophoniste [-fɔnist] s. Mus. Saxophonist.

saynète [sɛnɛt] f. Théâtr. Sketch; short comedy.

sbire [zbi:r] m. Sbirro. ‖ Fam. Cop.

scabieuse [skabjø:z] f. Bot. Scabious, U. S. scabiosa.

scabieux, euse [-bjø, ø:z] adj. Scabious.

scabreux, euse [skabrø, ø:z] adj. Rough, uneven (chemin). ‖ Fig. Risky, dangerous (entreprise); scabrous, improper (récit).

scabrosité [-brozite] f. Scabrousness.

scaferlati [skafɛrlati] m. Tobacco.

scalaire [skalɛ:r] adj. Math. Scalar; *produit scalaire de deux vecteurs*, scalar product (ou) inner product of two vectors.

scalde [skald] m. Skald.

scalène [skalɛ:n] adj. Math. Scalene.

scalp [skalp] m. Scalp.

scalpel [-pɛl] m. Méd. Scalpel.

scalper [-pe] v. tr. (1). To scalp.

scandale [skɑ̃dal] m. Scandal (v. esclandre); *au grand scandale des gens de bien*, to the disgust of decent folk (ou) people; *causer du scandale, faire scandale*, to cause (ou) create a scandal; *c'est un scandale*, it's disgusting (ou) disgraceful!; *crier au scandale*, to cry shame. ‖ Ecclés. Scandal.

scandaleusement [-løzmɑ̃] adv. Scandalously.

scandaleux, euse [-lø, ø:z] adj. Scandalous, disgraceful, shameful.

scandalisateur, trice [-lizatœ:r, tris] s. Scandalizer.

scandaliser [-lize] v. tr. (1). To scandalize, to offend; to shock (par, at, by).
— v. pr. **Se scandaliser**, to be scandalized (ou) shocked; to take offence.

scander [skɑ̃de] v. tr. (1). To scan (des vers). ‖ Fig. To lay stress on; to emphasize (ses paroles) [de, with].

scandinave [skɑ̃dina:v] adj., s. Géogr. Scandinavian.

scanner [skanɛ:r] m. Techn., Méd., Milit. Scanner.

scansion [skɑ̃sjɔ̃] f. Scansion.

scaphandre [skafɑ̃:dr] m. Diving-suit; *casque de scaphandre*, diver's helmet.

scaphandrier [-drije] m. Diver.

scapulaire [skapylɛ:r] adj. Méd. Scapular.
— m. Ecclés. Scapular, scapulary.

scarabée [skarabe] m. Zool. Scarabaeus; beetle.

scarificateur [skarifikatœ:r] m. Agric. Scarifier. ‖ Méd. Scarificator.

scarification [-fikasjɔ̃] f. Agric., Méd. Scarification.

scarifier [-fje] v. tr. (1). Agric., Méd. To scarify.

scarlatine [skarlatin] f. Méd. Scarlatina, scarlet fever.
— adj. Méd. Scarlet (fièvre).

scarole [skarɔl] f. Agric., Culin. Endive, curled endive.

scatologie [skatɔlɔʒi] f. Scatology.

scatologique [-ʒik] adj. Scatological.

sceau [so] m. Seal; *garde des Sceaux*, Keeper of the Seals; *sceau de l'Etat*, Great Seal. ‖ Fig. Stamp (du génie); seal (du secret). ‖ **Sceau-de-Salomon**, m. Bot. Solomon's-seal.

scélérat, ate [selera, at] adj. Nefarious (acte); outrageous (conduite); wicked, villainous (personne).
— s. Scoundrel, villain. ‖ Fam. Rascal.

scélératesse [-tɛs] f. Wickedness, villainy.

scellage [sɛla:ʒ] m. Sealing.

scellé [-le] m. Jur. Official seal; *apposer les scellés*, to affix the seals.

scellement [-mɑ̃] m. Archit. Sealing, setting, bedding.

sceller [-le] v. tr. (1). To set one's seal to (un document); to seal, to close up (une lettre). ‖ Jur. To seal (à, with). ‖ Archit. To plug, to plug in (un clou); to bed, to fix (une poutre). ‖ Fig. To seal, to confirm, to ratify.

scénario [senarjo] m. Théâtr. Scenario (d'un ballet). ‖ Ciném. Script, scenario, screenplay.

scénariste [-rist] s. Ciném. Script- (ou) scenario-writer, U. S. screenwriter.

scène [sɛn] f. Théâtr. Stage, theatre, dramatic art (art); *avoir une parfaite connaissance de la scène*, to know the theatre; *une grande figure de la scène*, a great figure in the theatre; *paraître sur la scène*, to go on the stage. ‖ Théâtr. Scene, action (lieu); *la scène se situe à Rome*, the action takes place in Rome. ‖ Théâtr. Stage (partie du théâtre); *effet de scène*, stage effect; *entrer en scène*, to enter, to come on; *mettre en scène*, to stage, to put on, to stage-manage. ‖ Théâtr. Scene (d'un acte); *scène à faire*, obligatory scene; *acte un, scène trois*, act one, scene three. ‖ Jur. Scene (du crime). ‖ Fig. Scene, sight (spectacle); *scène affligeante*, distressing sight. ‖ Fam. Scene, fuss, row, quarrel (dispute); *faire une scène*, to make a scene; to kick up a fuss (pop.). ‖ **Scène-raccord**, m. Ciném. Insert, inter-cut.

scénique [senik] adj. Théâtr. Scenic, theatrical;

éclairage scénique, stage-lighting; *indications scéniques*, stage directions.
scepticisme [sɛptisism] m. Scepticism.
sceptique [-tik] adj. Sceptical.
— s. Sceptic.
sceptiquement [-tikmɑ̃] adv. Sceptically; with scepticism.
sceptre [sɛptr] m. Sceptre. ‖ Fig. Power, sway, dominion; *sceptre de fer*, despotic government.
schako [ʃako] m. Shako.
schéma [ʃema] m. Scheme, diagram, sketch.
schématique [-tik] adj. Schematic, rough, sketchy (simplifié); oversimplified (simpliste).
schématiquement [-tikmɑ̃] adv. Schematically, roughly, in broad outlines.
schématisation [-tizasjɔ̃] f. Schematization, outline.
schématiser [-tize] v. tr. (1). To schematize, to give the broad outlines of; *trop schématiser*, to oversimplify.
schématisme [-tism] m. Oversimplification, schematism. ‖ Philos. Schematism.
schème [ʃɛm] m. Schema, scheme, pattern. ‖ Philos. Schema.
scherzando [skɛrtzɑ̃do] adv. Mus. Scherzando.
scherzo [skɛrtzo] m. Mus. Scherzo.
schismatique [ʃismatik] adj., s. Schismatic.
schisme [ʃism] m. Ecclés. Schism. ‖ Fig. Schism, break.
schiste [ʃist] m. Schist, shale.
schisteux, euse [-tø, ø:z] adj. Schistose, schistous.
schizo [skizo] adj., n. Fam. Schizo.
schizoïde [skizɔid] adj. Méd. Schizoid.
schizophréne [-zɔfrɛn] adj., n. Méd. Schizophrenic.
schizophrénie [-freni] f. Méd. Schizophrenia.
schlague [ʃlag] f. Milit. † Flogging.
schlitte [ʃlit] f. Wood-sledge.
schlitter [ʃlite] v. tr. (1). To carry on a sledge.
schnaps [ʃnaps] m. Fam. Booze, hooch, U. S. firewater. (V. gnole.)
schnick [ʃnik] m. Pop. Rot-gut.
schnorchel [ʃnɔrkəl] m. Naut. Schnorkel, snorkel.
schooner [ʃunœ:r] m. Naut. Schooner.
schuss [ʃus] m., adv. Sports. Schuss (à ski).
sciage [sja:ʒ] m. Sawing. ‖ Archit. Sawn timber.
sciant, ante [sjɑ̃, ɑ̃:t] adj. Fam. Boring.
sciatique [sjatik] adj. Méd. Sciatic.
— m. Méd. Sciatic nerve.
— f. Méd. Sciatica.
scie [si] f. Saw; *scie à chantourner, à découper, à refendre*, jig- (ou) whip-, fret-, rip-saw; *scie à main, à métaux*, handsaw, hacksaw; *scie à ruban* (ou) *sans fin*, band-saw; *scie circulaire, mécanique*, circular-, power- (ou) buzz-saw; *scie de long*, pit-saw; *trait de scie*, saw-cut, kerf. ‖ Zool. Saw-fish. ‖ Fam. Bore, nuisance (crampon); popular hit (rengaine); catch-phrase (slogan).
sciemment [sjamɑ̃] adv. Knowingly, wittingly.
science [sjɑ̃:s] f. Science, knowledge, learning (connaissance); *puits de science*, well of learning; *science des choses extérieures*, knowledge of exterior things; *science du monde*, knowledge of the world, worldly wisdom. ‖ Science (ensemble de connaissances); *homme de science*, scientist; *sciences exactes*, exact sciences; *sciences naturelles*, natural science. ‖ Ecclés. *Science infuse*, intuition. ‖ **Science-fiction**, f. Science-fiction, S.F., sci-fi.
sciène [sjɛn] f. Zool. Sciaena.
scientificité [sjɑ̃tifisite] f. Scientific character (d'une démarche, d'une théorie).
scientifique [sjɑ̃tifik] adj. Scientific.
— s. Scientist.
scientifiquement [-mɑ̃] adv. Scientifically.
scientisme [sjɑ̃tism] m. Scientism.

scientiste [-tist] adj. Scientistic.
— m. Adept of scientism.
scier [sje] v. tr. (1). To saw, to cut with a saw (du bois); to saw off (une branche). ‖ Pop. *Scier le dos à qqn*, to pester the life out of s.o.
scierie [siri] f. Saw-mill, saw-yard.
scieur [sjœ:r] m. Sawyer; *scieur de long*, pit-sawyer.
scille [sil] f. Bot. Squill.
scindement [sɛ̃dmɑ̃] m. Dividing, splitting up.
scinder [-de] v. tr. (1). To divide, to split up.
— v. pr. **Se scinder**, to divide, to split (parti).
scintigraphie [sɛ̃tigrafi] f. Phys., Méd. Scintigraphy.
scintillant, ante [sɛ̃tijɑ̃, ɑ̃:t] adj. Twinkling (étoile); scintillating, glittering (gemme). ‖ Fig. Sparkling, scintillating (esprit).
scintillateur [-atœ:r] m. Phys. Scintillation counter.
scintillation [-asjɔ̃] f. Astron., Phys., Radio. Scintillation.
scintillement [-jmɑ̃] m. Scintillation, glittering.
scintiller [-je] v. intr. (1). To twinkle (étoile); to scintillate, to glitter (gemme). [V. étinceler.]
scion [sjɔ̃] m. Agric. Scion (rejeton). ‖ Sports. Tip (de canne à pêche).
sciotte [sjɔt] f. Hand-saw.
scission [sisjɔ̃] f. Split, scission.
scissionniste [-sjɔnist] s. Dissident, dissentient; *groupe scissionniste*, splinter group.
scissipare [sisipa:r] adj. Scissiparous.
scissiparité [-parite] f. Scissiparity.
scissure [sisy:r] f. Méd. Scissure.
sciure [sjy:r] f. Dust; *sciure de bois*, sawdust.
scléreux, euse [sklerø, ø:z] adj. Méd. Sclerous.
sclérodermie [-rɔdɛrmi] f. Méd. Sclerodermia.
scléromètre [-mɛtr] m. Phys. Sclerometer.
sclérose [-ro:z] f. Méd. Sclerosis; *sclérose en plaques*, multiple sclerosis. ‖ Fig. Ossification.
sclérosé, ée [-roze] adj. Méd. Sclerotic. ‖ Fig. Ossified, fossilized.
scléroser (se) [səskleroze] v. pr. (1). Méd. To become sclerotic. ‖ Fig. To ossify, to become fossilized.
sclérotique [sklerɔtik] f. Méd. Sclerotic, sclera.
sclérotite [-rɔtit] f. Méd. Sclerotitis.
scolaire [skɔlɛ:r] adj. Scholastic; school (année); educational (réforme); *extra-scolaire*, out-of-school (activités); *travail scolaire*, school-work.
scolarisation [-larizasjɔ̃] f. Provision of educational facilities (d'un pays); sending to school (d'un enfant).
scolariser [-larize] v. tr. (1). To provide with educational facilities (un pays); to send to school (un enfant).
scolarité [-larite] f. School-attendance (à l'école); keeping of terms (à l'université); *frais de scolarité*, school fees; *prolonger la scolarité jusqu'à l'âge de 15 ans*, to raise the school-leaving age to 15; *scolarité obligatoire*, compulsory school-attendance. ‖ † Student status.
scolasticat [skɔlastika] m. Ecclés. Theological college.
scolastique [-tik] adj. Scholastic.
— m. Schoolman.
— f. Philos. Scholasticism.
scoliaste [skɔljast] m. Scholiast.
scoliose [skɔljo:z] f. Méd. Scoliosis.
scolopendre [skɔlɔpɑ̃:dr] f. Bot. Scolopendrium. ‖ Zool. Scolopendra.
sconce [skɔ̃:s] m. Skunk fur; skunk.
scoop [skup] m. Scoop (information en exclusivité).
scooter [skutœ:r, tɛ:r] m. Motor scooter, scooter.
scorbut [skɔrbyt] m. Méd. Scorbutus, scurvy.
scorbutique [-tik] adj., s. Méd. Scorbutic.

score [skɔːr] m. SPORTS. Score.

scorie [skɔri] f. Scoria, slag, dross.

scorpion [skɔrpjɔ̃] f. ZOOL., MILIT., ASTRON. Scorpion.

scorsonère [skɔrsɔnɛːr] f. BOT. Scorzonera, black salsify.

scotch [skɔtʃ] m. Scotch whisky, scotch (boisson). ‖ Sellotape, Scotch tape (ruban adhésif) [noms déposés].

scotcher [-tʃe] v. tr. (1). To sellotape, to scotch tape.

scotomiser [skotomize] v. tr. (1). PSYCH. To screen off, to blank out.

scout [skut] m. Boy-scout, scout.

scoutisme [-tism] m. Boy-scout movement; scouting.

Scrabble [skrabl] m. (nom déposé). Scrabble.

scratch [skratʃ] m. SPORTS. Scratch, scratch-line; *partir scratch*, to be scratch-man, to start at scratch.

scratcher [-ʃe] v. tr. (1). SPORTS. To scratch.

scribe [skrib] m. Scribe. ‖ FAM. Pen-pusher, quill-driver.

scribouillard [-buja:r] m. POP. Pen-pusher, quill-driver.

script [skript] m. CINÉM. Film-script. ‖ **Script-girl**, f. CINÉM. Continuity-girl.

scripte s. CINÉM. Continuity-girl (ou) -man.

scripteur [-tœːr] m. Writer, copier (d'un document). ‖ ECCLÉS. Writer (de bulles).

scriptural, ale [-tyral] adj. ECCLÉS. Scriptural.

scrofulaire [skrɔfylɛːr] f. BOT. Fig-wort.

scrofule [-fyl] f. MÉD. Scrofula; king's evil.

scrofuleux, euse [-fylø, øːz] adj. MÉD. Scrofulous.

scrotal, ale [skrɔtal] adj. MÉD. Scrotal.

scrotum [-tɔm] m. MÉD. Scrotum.

scrupule [skrypyl] m. Scruple (poids). ‖ FIG. Scruple (exactitude); *avec scrupule*, scrupulously, exactly. ‖ FIG. Scruple, qualm (inquiétude); *avoir des scrupules à faire qqch.*, to have scruples (ou) qualms about doing sth.; *sans scrupules*, without scruples, unscrupulous; unscrupulously; *se faire des scrupules*, to have qualms of conscience.

scrupuleusement [-løzmɑ̃] adv. Scrupulously.

scrupuleux, euse [-lø, øːz] adj. Scrupulous, meticulous; *peu scrupuleux*, unscrupulous.

scrupulosité [-lozite] f. Scrupulousness.

scrutateur, trice [skrytatœːr, tris] m. Scrutinizer, investigator. ‖ Teller, scrutineer (aux élections).
— adj. Scrutinizing, searching.

scruter [-te] v. tr. (1). To scrutinize, to examine closely; *scruter qqn du regard*, to give s.o. a searching look. ‖ To search (les écritures).

scrutin [-tɛ̃] m. Ballot, poll; *dépouiller le scrutin*, to count the votes; *scrutin d'arrondissement*, constituency poll; *scrutin de liste*, voting for candidates on a party list; *scrutin découvert, secret*, open, secret vote; *scrutin uninominal*, voting for a single candidate.

sculptage [skylpta:ʒ] m. ARTS. Sculpturing, carving.

sculpter [-te] v. tr. (1). ARTS. To carve (le bois); to sculpture (la pierre).

sculpteur [-tœːr] m. ARTS. Sculptor; *femme sculpteur*, sculptress.

sculptural, ale [-tyral] adj. ARTS. Sculptural (art); statuesque (beauté).

sculpture [-ty:r] f. ARTS. Sculpture; *sculpture sur bois*, wood-carving.

S.D.N. [ɛsdeɛn] f. Abrév. de *Société des nations*, League of Nations.

se [sə] pron. pers. Himself, herself, itself, themselves, oneself.

séance [seɑ̃:s] f. Sitting, session, meeting (session); *en séance*, in session, sitting; *séance ora-* *geuse, publique*, stormy, public (ou) open meeting. ‖ Seat (siège); *prendre séance*, to take one's seat. ‖ Séance (de spiritisme). ‖ CINÉM. Performance (de cinéma). ‖ ARTS. Sitting. ‖ FIG. *Séance tenante*, immediately, on the spot.

séant, ante [seɑ̃, ɑ̃:t] adj. Becoming, fitting, seemly (convenable). ‖ Sitting, in session (en séance).
— m. Bottom; *être sur son séant*, to be in a sitting posture; *se mettre* (ou) *se dresser sur son séant*, to sit up.

seau [so] m. Pail, bucket; *seau à champagne*, ice-bucket; *seau à charbon*, coal-scuttle; *seau à glace*, ice-pail; *seau d'eau*, bucket (ou) pail of water. ‖ Bucketful (plein seau). ‖ FAM. *Il pleut à seaux*, it's coming down in buckets (ou) bucketfuls.

sébacé, ée [sebase] adj. MÉD. Sebaceous.

sébile [sebil] f. Wooden bowl; *tendre la sébile*, to beg for alms.

séborrhée [sebɔre] f. MÉD. Seborrhea.

sébum [sebɔm] m. MÉD. Sebum.

sec, sèche [sɛk, sɛʃ] adj. Dry (en général). ‖ Dry, arid (pays); parched, arid (sol); dry (vent); *mur en pierres sèches*, dry-stone wall; *à pied sec*, dry-shod. ‖ Parched (langue); *avoir la gorge sèche*, to be parched, to feel thirsty. ‖ CULIN. Split (pois); dry (vin); *raisins secs*, raisins; *au pain sec et à l'eau*, on dry bread and water. ‖ AUTOM. *Panne sèche*, failure of the engine through shortage of petrol (ou) U. S. gasoline. ‖ NAUT. Rainless (orage); bare (vergue). ‖ ARTS. Hard (couleur). ‖ TECHN. Face to face (joint). ‖ FIN. Dead (perte). ‖ MÉD. Dry, hacking (toux). ‖ SPORTS. Unguarded (as, roi) [aux cartes]. ‖ FIG. Cool (accueil); sharp (bruit); sharp, smart (coup); sharp, curt, dry (réponse); terse, bald, prosaic (style); incisive (ton); *un merci tout sec*, a bare (ou) mere thank-you; *regarder d'un œil sec*, to look on dry-eyed. ‖ FAM. Dry, prohibitionist (pays). ‖ FAM. Skinny, gaunt, spare, dried-up (personne); *sec comme une allumette* (ou) *une trique*, as thin as a lath (ou) rake; *faire qqch. en cinq sec*, to do sth. in a jiffy (ou) one shake of a lamb's tail.
— m. COMM. « *Mettre au sec* », « out of the wet »; « *tenir au sec* », « keep in a dry place ».
— adv. *Boire sec*, to be a hard drinker, to take one's liquor neat (ou) U. S. straight; *brûler sec*, to burn like tinder; *parler sec*, not to mince one's words; *répondre sec*, to give a curt answer; *rire sec*, to give a dry laugh.
— loc. adv. **A sec**, dry, dried-up; *mettre un étang à sec*, to drain a lake; *puits à sec*, well that has run dry. ‖ NAUT. *A sec de toile*, under bare poles; *haler* (ou) *tirer un bateau à sec*, to haul a boat up on to dry land. ‖ FAM. *A sec*, stony broke, cleaned out, without a bean, hard up (sans argent); *être à sec*, to have run dry (ou) run out of words (ou) ideas (sans idée).

sécable [sekabl] adj. Sectile, divisible.

sécant, ante [sekɑ̃, ɑ̃:t] adj. MATH. Secant.

sécante [-kɑ̃:t] f. MATH. Secant.

sécateur [sekatœːr] m. Pruning-scissors; secateurs.

sécession [sesɛsjɔ̃] f. Secession. (V. DISSIDENCE.) ‖ U. S. *Guerre de Sécession*, Civil war.

sécessionniste [-sjɔnist] adj., s. Secessionist.

séchage [seʃa:ʒ] m. Seasoning (du bois); drying (du linge).

sèche [sɛʃ] f. NAUT. Flat. ‖ POP. Fag (cigarette).

sèche. V. SÉCHER. ‖ Sèche-cheveux, m. inv. Hair drier, drier. ‖ **Sèche-linge**, m. inv. Electric drier, drier. ‖ **Sèche-mains**, m. inv. Hand drier.

sèchement [sɛʃmɑ̃] adv. ARTS. Stiffly. ‖ FIG. *Ecrire sèchement*, to write in a bald style; *répondre sèchement*, to reply in a curt manner, to give a curt reply.

sécher [seʃe] v. tr. (5). To dry, to dry up. (V. DESSÉCHER.) ‖ FIG. To dry (les larmes). ‖ FAM. To cut (un cours). — v. intr. To dry (linge), to dry up (rivière); to become dry; *faire sécher le linge sans le repasser,* to rough-dry. ‖ FIG. *Sécher de chagrin,* to pine away with grief; *sécher sur pied,* to wilt, to wither away. ‖ FAM. To be stumped (à un examen). — v. pr. **Se sécher,** to dry oneself (personne). ‖ To dry (linge); to dry up (rivière).

sécheresse [-ʃrɛs] f. Dryness (de l'air). ‖ AGRIC. Drought (période). ‖ FIG. Coldness, insensibility (du cœur); spareness, leanness (du corps); baldness (du style); barrenness, jejuneness (d'un sujet); curtness (du ton).

sécherie [-ʃri] f. Drying-room, drying-shed.

sécheur [-ʃœːr] m. Drier, drying-apparatus.

sécheuse [-ʃøːz] f. Steam-drier.

séchoir [-ʃwaːr] m. Drying-room, drying-shed (pièce). ‖ Towel-rail (de salle de bains). ‖ Drier (sécheur).

second, onde [səgɔ̃, ɔ̃ːd] adj. Second (v. DEUXIÈME); *au second étage,* on the second (ou) U. S. third floor; *en second lieu,* in the second place; *de second main,* second-hand, at second hand; *de second ordre,* second-class, inferior; *sans second,* peerless; *seconde vue,* second sight. ‖ CHIM. *Eau seconde,* dilute nitric acid. ‖ PHILOS. Secondary (causes). — s. Second (dans un classement); *arriver bon second,* to come in a good second. (V. SECONDE.) — m. Second (dans un duel). ‖ Second (ou) U.S. third floor (étage). ‖ NAUT. First mate; *second maître,* petty officer; *second maître d'équipage,* boatswain's mate. — loc. adv. **En second,** MILIT., NAUT. *Commander en second,* to be second in command. ‖ JUR. *Signer en second,* to countersign.

secondaire [-dɛːr] adj. Secondary (école, enseignement). ‖ Minor, secondary (rôle) [v. ACCESSOIRE]; *question d'intérêt secondaire,* question of minor importance, side-issue. ‖ MÉD. Secondary. ‖ CH. DE F. *Voie secondaire,* side-track. ‖ THÉÂTR. *Intrigue secondaire,* by-plot, sub-plot. ‖ GÉOL. Secondary (ou) Mesozoic (ère). ‖ FIN. Secondary (industries). — m. Secondary school (ou) education. ‖ ÉLECTR. Secondary winding. ‖ GÉOL. Secondary (ou) Mesozoic. ‖ FIN. Secondary industries (ou) sector.

secondairement [-dɛrmɑ̃] adv. Secondarily.

seconde [səgɔ̃ːd] f. Second; *attendez une seconde,* wait a second; half a jiffy (fam.). ‖ Fifth form, U. S. eleventh grade (dans une école française); *élève de seconde,* fifth former, U. S. eleventh grader. ‖ CH. DE F. Second (classe); *voyager en seconde,* to travel second (ou) second-class; *voyageurs de seconde,* second-class passengers. ‖ MUS. Second. ‖ SPORTS. Seconde (en escrime).

secondement [-dmɑ̃] adv. Secondly.

seconder [-de] v. tr. (1). To help, to support, to second; to back up (fam.) [qqn].

secouage [səkwa:ʒ] m. Shaking, jolting.

secouée [-kwe] f. Shaking, shaking up, jolting (action). ‖ FAM. Telling off, blowing up.

secouer [-kwe] v. tr. (1). To shake (un arbre); to plump up (un oreiller); to shake down (des pommes); to shake off (la poussière). ‖ To shake (la tête). ‖ FIG. To shake off (le joug); *secouer la poussière de ses pieds,* to shake the dust from one's feet. ‖ FAM. To wake up, to give a jolt to (exciter); to shake, to upset (bouleverser); to blow up (savonner). — v. pr. **Se secouer,** to shake oneself, to bestir oneself. ‖ FIG. To rouse oneself, to pull oneself together; *secoue-toi,* snap out of it !

secourable [səkurabl] adj. Helpful, willing (ou) ready to help.

secourir [-riːr] v. tr. (32). To succour, to aid, to assist, to help. (V. AIDER.)

secourisme [-rism] m. First aid.

secouriste [-rist] s. Member of a first-aid association.

secours [səkuːr] m. Help, assistance, succour, relief (v. AIDE); *aller au secours de qqn,* to go to s.o.'s assistance; *au secours!,* help!; *crier au secours,* to call (ou) shout for help; *porter (ou) prêter secours à qqn,* to go to s.o.'s assistance. ‖ THÉÂTR. *Sortie de secours,* emergency-exit. ‖ AUTOM. *Roue de secours,* spare wheel. ‖ MÉD. *Premier secours,* first-aid; *équipe de secours,* rescue squad. ‖ AVIAT. *Terrain de secours,* emergency landing-ground. ‖ MILIT. *Poste de secours,* regimental aid post; dressing-station. ‖ MILIT. *Secours militaires,* relief forces. ‖ CH. DE F. *Convoi de secours,* breakdown gang. ‖ FIN. *Caisse de secours,* relief fund; *œuvre de secours,* relief organization; *secours maladie,* sick-benefit; *société de secours mutuels,* mutual benefit society, friendly society. (V. SUBSIDE.) ‖ ECCLÉS. *Chapelle de secours,* chapel of ease.

secousse [səkus] f. Bump (de la route); shake, shaking, jolt, jolting (d'une voiture) [v. SACCADE]; *donner une secousse à,* to jerk; *sans secousse,* smoothly. ‖ MÉD. *Secousse musculaire,* jerk. ‖ FIG. Upset, commotion, shock; *sans secousse,* smoothly, without upset.

secret, ète [səkrɛ, ɛt] adj. Secret, secluded (endroit); secret, hidden, unseen (ennemi); secret, concealed (escalier). ‖ Discreet, reticent (personne).

secret [səkrɛ] m. Secret (chose cachée); *être dans le secret,* to be in the secret, to be in the know (fam.); *garder, trahir un secret,* to keep, to give away (ou) to betray a secret; *mettre qqn dans le secret,* to let s.o. in on a secret; *n'avoir pas de secret pour,* to have no secrets from; *secret de Polichinelle,* open secret; *secret d'État,* State secret; *trahir le secret professionnel,* to commit a breach of confidence. ‖ Secrecy, silence (discrétion); *jurer le secret,* to swear to keep sth. secret; *sous le sceau du secret,* under pledge of secrecy. ‖ Secret, explanation (explication); *avoir le secret de sa conduite,* to know what is behind his actions. ‖ Secret, means, way (procédé); *le secret de l'art d'écrire,* the secret of the writer's art; *trouver le secret de s'enrichir,* to discover the means of getting rich, to find the way to get rich. ‖ TECHN. Secret spring (d'un mécanisme); *faire jouer le secret,* to press the secret spring. ‖ JUR. Solitary confinement (en prison); *mettre au secret,* to put in solitary confinement (ou) in solitary (fam.). — loc. adv. **En secret,** in secrecy, secretly, off the record.

secrétaire [səkretɛ:r] s. Secretary; *secrétaire de direction,* executive secretary, assistant principal; *secrétaire d'État,* Secretary of State; *secrétaire de mairie,* town clerk; *secrétaire à la réception,* secretary-receptionist; *secrétaire de la rédaction,* sub-editor; *secrétaire général,* secretary-general; *secrétaire général du syndicat,* president of the trade union; *secrétaire particulier,* private secretary. — m. Secretaire, writing-desk, davenport, escritoire (meuble).

secrétairerie [-tɛrri] f. Secretary's office, registry (bureau); secretary's staff (employés).

secrétariat [-tarja] m. Secretariat, secretary's office (bureau). ‖ Secretaryship (fonction).

secrètement [səkrɛtmɑ̃] adv. Secretly; in secret.

sécréter [sekrete] v. tr. (5). MÉD. To secrete.

sécréteur, trice [-tœ:r, tris] adj. MÉD. Secretory, secreting.

sécrétion [-sjɔ̃] f. MÉD. Secretion; *glande à sécré-*

tion interne, externe, ductless (ou) endocrine, exocrine gland.

sécrétoire [-twa:r] adj. MÉD. Secretory.

sectaire [sɛktɛ:r] m. Sectary, sectarian.
— adj. Sectarian.

sectarisme [-tarism] m. Sectarianism.

sectateur, trice [-tatœ:r, tris] s. Sectary, votary, member of a sect.

secte [sɛkt] f. Sect. ‖ ECCLÉS. Religion. ‖ FIG. Party; *faire secte à part,* to form one's own party.

secteur [sɛktœ:r] m. ASTRON., MATH. Sector. ‖ TECHN. Quadrant. ‖ MILIT. Sector; zone; *secteur postal,* postal sector. ‖ NAUT., AUTOM. Quadrant. ‖ COMM. Sector; *secteur des affaires,* business sector; *secteur privé,* private sector (ou) enterprise. ‖ ELECTR. Local supply circuit; *branché sur le secteur,* connected with the mains.

sectile [sɛktil] adj. Sectile.

section [sɛksjɔ̃] f. Section, part (d'un chapitre); branch (d'un département). ‖ Section, cutting (d'un tendon); docking (d'une queue). ‖ AUTOM. Stage, fare-stage (en autobus). ‖ ARCHIT. Section, cross-section. ‖ MATH. Section. ‖ MILIT. Platoon; section (d'un peloton).

sectionnel, elle [-sjɔnɛl] adj. Sectional.

sectionnement [-sjɔnmɑ̃] m. Cutting, sectioning; dividing (ou) division into sections.

sectionner [-sjɔne] v. tr. (1). To divide into sections.

sectoriel, elle [sɛktɔrjɛl] adj. Sectorial, restricted to certain sectors.

séculaire [sekylɛ:r] adj. Age-old, century-old (arbre). ‖ Secular (coutume, fête).

séculairement [-lɛrmɑ̃] adv. From century to century; in the course of centuries.

sécularisation [-larizasjɔ̃] f. Secularization.

séculariser [-larize] v. tr. (1). To secularize.

sécularisme [-larism] m. ECCLÉS. Secularism.

sécularité [-larite] f. ECCLÉS. Secularity.

séculier, ère [-lje, ɛr] adj. ECCLÉS. Secular (clergé). ‖ JUR. Secular (bras); temporal, lay, secular (tribunal). ‖ FIG. Worldly (vie).
— m. ECCLÉS. Layman; *les séculiers,* the laity (laïcs); the secular clergy (prêtres).

séculièrement [-ljɛrmɑ̃] adv. Secularly.

secundo [sekɔ̃do] adv. Secondly, in the second place.

sécurisant, ante [sekyrizɑ̃, ɑ̃:t] adj. Comforting, reassuring.

sécuriser [-ze] v. tr. (1). To comfort, to make feel secure.

Securit [sekyrit] adj. *Verre Securit,* safety-glass.

sécurité [-te] f. Security, safety (sûreté); *dispositif de sécurité,* safety-device; *sécurité de la route,* road safety. ‖ Security, secureness, confidence, freedom from anxiety (tranquillité); *connaître la sécurité,* to feel assured of the future. ‖ JUR. *Sécurité sociale,* social security.

sédatif, ive [sedatif, i:v] adj., m. MÉD. Sedative.

sédentaire [sedɑ̃tɛ:r] adj. Sedentary (métier); settled, sedentary (vie).

sédentairement [-tɛrmɑ̃] adv. Sedentarily.

sédentarisation [-tarizasjɔ̃] f. Settling.

sédentariser [-tarize] v. tr. (1). To settle.

sédentarité [-tarite] f. Sedentariness.

sédiment [sedimɑ̃] m. Sediment.

sédimentaire [-tɛ:r] adj. Sedimentary.

sédimentation [-tasjɔ̃] f. Sedimentation.

séditieusement [sedisjøzmɑ̃] adv. Seditiously.

séditieux, euse [-sjø, ø:z] adj. Seditious.
— s. Seditious person; rebel.

sédition [-sjɔ̃] f. Sedition, revolt. (V. ÉMEUTE.)

séducteur, trice [sedyktœ:r, tris] adj. Seductive, tempting, alluring.
— m. Tempter, seducer.

séductible [-tibl] adj. Seducible.

séduction [-sjɔ̃] f. JUR. Seduction, enticement (d'une femme); subornation (d'un témoin). ‖ FIG. Attractiveness, charm (des manières); lure (de la richesse).

séductrice [-tris] f. Temptress, seductress.

séduire [sedɥi:r] v. tr. (85). JUR. To seduce (une femme); to suborn (un témoin). ‖ FIG. To attract, to charm, to captivate, to fascinate (qqn); *ses manières m'ont séduit,* I was much taken by his manners.

séduisant, ante [-zɑ̃, ɑ̃:t] adj. Fascinating, captivating (beauté); seductive, alluring, attractive (femme); winning, taking (manières); tempting, attractive (offre).

segment [sɛgmɑ̃] m. MATH. Segment (de cercle). ‖ AUTOM., TECHN. Segment; *segment de piston,* piston-ring.

segmentaire [-tɛ:r] adj. MATH. Segmentary. ‖ MÉD., ARCHIT. Segmental.

segmentation [-tasjɔ̃] f. Segmentation.

segmenter [-te] v. tr. (1). To segment, to cut into segments.
— v. pr. Se segmenter, to segment.

ségrégatif, ive [segregatif, i:v] adj. Segregative.

ségrégation [-sjɔ̃] f. Segregation; apartheid.

ségrégationnisme [-sjɔnism] m. Segregation, segregationism.

ségrégationniste [-sjɔnist] adj. Segregationist, segregational.
— n. Segregationist.

seiche [sɛʃ] f. ZOOL. Cuttle-fish, sepia; *os de seiche,* cuttle-bone.

seiche, sèche f. Seiche, tidal wave (d'un lac).

séide [seid] s. Thug; henchman.

seigle [sɛ:gl] m. BOT. Rye.

seigneur [sɛɲœ:r] m. Lord, master (suzerain). ‖ Seigneur, lord, noble (aristocrate); *à tout seigneur, tout honneur,* honour to whom honour is due; *seigneurs de la cour,* court nobility. ‖ ECCLÉS. Lord; *le jour du Seigneur,* the Lord's Day; *Notre Seigneur,* Our Lord; *le Seigneur des armées,* the Lord of Hosts. ‖ FIG. *Faire le grand seigneur,* to lord it over people, to put on airs. ‖ FAM. *Le seigneur et maître,* the lord and master (d'une femme).
— interj. *Seigneur!, seigneur Dieu!,* good Lord!

seigneurial, ale [-rjal] adj. † Seigniorial, manorial.

seigneurie [-ri] f. † Domain, manor (domaine). ‖ Lordship, seigniory (titre); *votre Seigneurie,* your Lordship.

seille [sɛ:j] f. Wooden pail. (V. SEAU.)

sein [sɛ̃] m. Breast, bosom (v. GIRON, POITRINE); *presser sur son sein,* to hold to one's breast. ‖ Breast (v. GORGE); *donner le sein à un enfant,* to suckle (ou) breast-feed a child, to give a child the breast; *prendre le sein,* to take the breast. ‖ MÉD. Womb; *elle a porté l'enfant dans son sein,* she carried the child in her womb. ‖ ECCLÉS. Bosom (d'Abraham, de l'Eglise). ‖ FIG. Bosom (âme, cœur); *déposer un secret dans le sein d'un ami,* to confide a secret to a friend. ‖ FIG. Bosom (de la famille); bowels (de la terre); *vivre au sein du luxe,* to live in the lap of luxury.

seine [sɛn] f. Seine (filet).

seiner [sɛne] v. tr. (1). To seine.

seing [sɛ̃] m. † Sign manual. ‖ JUR. *Acte sous seing privé,* private contract (ou) agreement.

séismal [seismal], **séismique** [-mik], etc. V. SISMAL, SISMIQUE.

séisme [seism] m. Seism, earthquake.

seize [sɛ:z] adj. num. invar. Sixteen; *le seize août,* the sixteenth of August, August the sixteenth; U. S. August sixteenth; *Louis seize,* Louis the Sixteenth.
— m. Sixteen.

seizième [sɛzjɛm] adj. num. Sixteenth.
— m. Sixteenth.
seizièmement [-mɑ̃] adv. Sixteenthly, in the sixteenth place.
séjour [seʒuːr] m. Stay, sojourn ; *faire un séjour à la campagne*, to stay in the country ; *frais de déplacement et de séjour*, travelling and hotel expenses. ‖ Resort, abode (lieu).
séjournement [-nəmɑ̃] m. Lying (de l'eau). ‖ Sojourning, staying (d'un voyageur).
séjourner [-ne] v. intr. (1). To lie (eau). ‖ To stay, to sojourn, to stop (voyageur).
sel [sɛl] m. Salt ; *sel de cuisine, de table*, kitchen, table salt ; *sel gemme, marin*, rock-, sea-salt ; *sel pour bains*, bath salts. ‖ Pl. Smelling-salts ; *flacon de sels*, bottle of smelling-salts. ‖ CHIM. *Sel ammoniac*, sal-ammoniac ; *sel d'Angleterre*, Epsom salts, sulphate of magnesium ; *sel de Glauber*, Glauber's salt. ‖ FIG. Salt, piquancy, wit ; *prendre qqch. avec un grain de sel*, to take sth. with a grain of salt ; *sel attique*, Attic salt (ou) wit ; *le sel de la terre*, the salt of the earth.
sélacien [selasjɛ̃] m. ZOOL. Selachian.
séiect [selɛkt] adj. inv. FAM. Select, high-class, smart, exclusive, ritzy.
sélecteur [-tœːr] m. TECHN. Selector, selecting switch.
sélectif, ive [-tif, iːv] adj. Selective.
sélection [-sjɔ̃] f. Selection, choice. (V. CHOIX.) ‖ SPORTS. *Match de sélection*, trial game, trial. ‖ MUS. Selection.
sélectionner [-sjɔne] v. tr. (1). To choose, to select. (V. TRIER.)
sélectionneur, euse [-sjɔnœːr, øːz] s. SPORTS. Selector.
sélectivité [-tivite] f. RADIO. Selectivity.
séléniate [selenjat] m. CHIM. Selenate.
sélénique [-nik] adj. CHIM. Selenic.
sélénium [-niɔm] m. CHIM. Selenium.
self [sɛlf] f. RADIO. Self-induction coil, choking-coil ; *self d'accord*, tuning-coil ; *self d'antenne*, aerial inductance. ‖ **Self-acting**, m. TECHN. Self-acting mule. ‖ **Self-control**, m. Self-control. ‖ **Self-induction**, f. ÉLECTR. Self-induction. ‖ **Self-made man**, m. Self-made man. ‖ **Self-service, self**, m. Self-service restaurant, cafeteria ; self-service shop.
sellage [sɛlaːʒ] m. Saddling.
selle [sɛl] f. Saddle ; *aider à se mettre en selle*, to help into the saddle ; *en selle*, in the saddle ; *selle anglaise*, hunting-saddle ; *selle de bicyclette*, bicycle-saddle ; *selle de dame*, lady's saddle ; side-saddle ; *se mettre, se remettre en selle*, to mount, to remount. ‖ TECHN. Nave-block (de charron) ; table, turn-table (de sculpteur) ; bench (de tonnelier). ‖ MÉD. Stool ; faeces ; *aller à la selle*, to go to stool ; *selles abondantes*, copious stools. ‖ CULIN. Saddle (de mouton). ‖ FAM. *Mettre qqn en selle*, to give s.o. a helping hand (ou) leg up (fam.) ; *être bien en selle*, to be firmly in the saddle.
seller [-le] v. tr. (1). To saddle (un cheval).
sellerie [-lri] f. Saddlery ; saddling trade (industrie). ‖ Harness-room, saddle-room (salle).
sellette [-lɛt] f. Footrest (de décrotteur) ; saddle (de limonier) ; swinging seat, cradle (de maçon). ‖ ARTS. Turn-table (de sculpteur). ‖ JUR. † Stool, bench (de l'accusé). ‖ FIG. *Mettre sur la sellette*, to cross-examine, to cross-question.
sellier [-lje] m. Saddler, harness-maker.
selon [səlɔ̃] prép. According to, having regard to (conformément à) ; *selon ses forces*, according to one's strength. ‖ According to (d'après) ; *selon saint Matthieu*, according to St. Matthew. ‖ According to, in the opinion of (selon l'avis de) ; *selon moi*, in my opinion. ‖ FAM. *C'est selon*, it all depends, that depends.
— loc. conj. **Selon que**, according as.

seltz [sɛls] m. *Eau de Seltz*, seltzer (ou) soda-water.
semailles [səmɑːj] f. pl. AGRIC. Sowing ; *temps des semailles*, sowing-time.
semaine [səmɛn] f. Week ; *dans trois semaines*, in three weeks' time ; *en semaine*, during the week ; *jour de semaine*, week-day. ‖ ECCLÉS. *La semaine sainte*, Holy Week. ‖ FIN. *Prêter à la petite semaine*, to lend at a high rate of interest ; *toucher sa semaine*, to get one's week's wages (ou) pay. ‖ MILIT. *De semaine*, on duty for the week. ‖ FIG. Week's pay (ou) wages ; *faire la semaine anglaise*, to work a five-and-a-half-day week.
semainier, ère [-nje, ɛr] adj. Weekly (rendement). [V. HEBDOMADAIRE.]
— s. Person on duty for the week.
— m. Seven-day razor case (étui). ‖ Time-sheet (d'ouvrier).
semaison [səmɛzɔ̃] f. AGRIC. Sowing-time.
sémantique [semɑ̃tik] adj. Semantic.
— f. Semantics.
sémaphore [semafɔːr] m. Semaphore. ‖ NAUT. Signal-station.
sémaphorique [-fɔrik] adj. Semaphoric.
semblable [sɑ̃blabl] adj. Similar, like, of the same kind (pareil) ; *tout à fait semblables*, exactly alike ; *semblable à*, like, similar to. ‖ Such (tel) ; *ne tenez pas de semblables discours*, don't say such things.
— s. Fellow, like (v. PAREIL) ; *elle n'a point sa semblable*, there is no one like her.
— m. Fellow, like, counterpart ; *aimer ses semblables*, to love one's fellow-men.
semblablement [-bləmɑ̃] adv. Similarly, likewise, in like manner.
semblant [sɑ̃blɑ̃] m. Semblance, appearance ; *faux semblant*, false pretence, sham ; *faire semblant de faire*, to pretend to do, to make a pretence of doing ; *faire un semblant d'opposition*, to put up a show of opposition ; *sans faire semblant de rien*, with an air of apparent indifference ; *semblant d'amitié*, show of friendship.
sembler [-ble] v. intr. (1). To seem, to appear ; *à ce qu'il me semble, ce me semble*, it seems to me, to my mind ; *cela me semble impossible*, it seems impossible to me, it doesn't look possible to me ; *faites comme bon vous semble*, do as you think fit ; *il lui semblait rêver*, it seemed to him (that) he was dreaming ; *il semble que la chose soit possible*, it looks as though the thing is possible, the thing seems to be possible ; *que vous en semble ?*, what do you think of it ? *si bon vous semble*, if you choose to, if you think fit.
séméiologie [semejɔlɔʒi] f. MÉD. Semeiology, semiology, semiotics (symptomatologie).
séméiologique [-lɔʒik] adj. MÉD. Semeiologic, semiologic, semiotic.
semelle [səmɛl] f. Sole ; *semelle de bois*, wooden sole ; *semelle de crêpe*, crêpe sole ; *semelle de feutre, de liège*, felt, cork insole ; *remettre des semelles à*, to re-sole ; *souliers à semelles de caoutchouc*, rubber-soled shoes. ‖ Foot (de bas). ‖ NAUT. Lee-board (de dérive) ; sole-piece (de lancement). ‖ AUTOM. Tread (de pneu). ‖ MILIT. Shoe (d'affût). ‖ ARCHIT. Bed (de béton) ; roof-plate (de comble) ; sole (d'étai) ; flange (de poutre). ‖ TECHN. Bed-plate (de machine) ; face (de rabot). ‖ FIG. *Battre la semelle*, to go on foot ; to hoof it (fam.) ; *ne pas reculer d'une semelle*, not to give way (ou) budge an inch.
semence [səmɑ̃ːs] f. AGRIC. Seed ; *blé de semence*, seed-corn. ‖ MÉD. Semen. ‖ TECHN. Spark (de diamants) ; tack (de tapissier) ; *semence de perles*, seed-pearls. ‖ FIG. *Semence de guerre*, seeds of war.
semer [səme] v. tr. (5). AGRIC. To sow (du blé). ‖ To scatter, to leave about (ses affaires) ; to

squander (de l'argent); to strew (des fleurs); *semé de citations*, sprinkled with quotations; *semé d'étoiles*, star-spangled; *semé de fleurs*, dotted with flowers. ‖ FIG. To sow, to propagate, to spread abroad; *semer la discorde*, to sow the seeds of discord; *semer de faux bruits*, to spread false rumours, to put out false rumours. ‖ SPORTS., FAM. To distance, to leave behind (un concurrent). ‖ FAM. To shed, to shake off, to ditch, to give the slip to (un importun).
— v. intr. *Semer à la volée* (ou) *à tout vent*, to sow broadcast.

semestre [səmɛstr] m. Half-year (de l'année); semester (dans une école); *par semestre*, half-yearly. ‖ FIN. Six months' income (rente); six months' salary (traitement). ‖ MILIT. Six months' leave of absence (congé).

semestriel, elle [-trjɛl] adj. Half-yearly.

semestriellement [-trijɛlmɑ̃] adv. Half-yearly.

semeur [səmœːr] s. AGRIC. Sower (de blé). ‖ FIG. Sower, spreader (de faux bruits).

semi [səmi] préf. Semi. ‖ **Semi-aride**, adj. GÉOGR. Semi-arid. ‖ **Semi-automatique**, adj. Semi-automatic. ‖ **Semi-circulaire**, adj. Semi-circular (gén., méd.). ‖ **Semi-conducteur**, adj. ÉLECTR. Semi-conducting; m. ÉLECTR. Semi-conductor. ‖ **Semi-consonne**, f. GRAMM. Semivowel, glide. ‖ **Semi-fini**, adj. m. *Produit semi-fini*, semi-finished product. ‖ **Semi-lunaire**, adj. Semi-lunar; MÉD. Halfmoon shaped (ganglions). ‖ **Semi-nomade**, adj. Semi-nomadic; s. Semi-nomad. ‖ **Semi-nomadisme**, s. Semi-nomadism. ‖ **Semi-perméable**, adj. PHYS., MÉD. Semi-permeable (membrane). ‖ **Semi-remorque**, f. (ou) m. AUTOM. Articulated lorry, artic (fam.); semi-trailer, semi (fam.). ‖ **Semi-rigide**, adj. AVIAT. Semi-rigid. ‖ **Semi-voyelle**, f. GRAMM. Semivowel.

sémillant, ante [semijɑ̃, ɑ̃:t] adj. Lively, sprightly, gay (enfant); lively (esprit).

séminaire [seminɛːr] m. ECCLÉS. Seminary, Roman Catholic college; *grand séminaire*, seminary, training college; *petit séminaire*, secondary school for seminarists. ‖ FIG. Seminary, training-ground (ou) centre.

séminal, ale [-nal] adj. Seminal, germ, spermary.

séminariste [-narist] m. Seminarist.

séminifère [-nifɛːr] adj. MÉD. Seminiferous.

sémiologie [semjɔlɔʒi] f. GRAMM., MÉD. Semiology, semeiology, semiotics.

sémiologique [-lɔʒik] adj. GRAMM., MÉD. Semiologic, semeiologic, semiotic.

sémiotique [-tik] adj. GRAMM., MATH. Semiotic, semiotical.
— f. GRAMM., MATH. Semiotics.

semis [səmi] m. BOT., AGRIC. Sowing (action); seedling (plant); seed-plot (terrain).

Sémite [semit] s. Semite.

sémitique [-tik] adj. Semitic.

sémitisme [-tism] m. Semitism.

semoir [səmwaːr] m. AGRIC. Seeder, sowing-machine, drill (machine); seed-lip (sac).

semonce [səmɔ̃:s] f. Reprimand, scolding. (V. REPROCHE.) ‖ NAUT. Order to heave to.

semoncer [-mɔ̃se] v. tr. (6). To reprimand, to scold (qqn). ‖ NAUT. To call upon to heave to (un navire).

semoule [səmul] f. CULIN. Semolina.

semper virens [sɛpɛːrvirɛ̃:s] m. inv. BOT. Evergreen.

sempervirent, ente [-rɑ̃, ɑ̃:t] adj. BOT. Evergreen.

sempiternel, elle [sɛ̃pitɛrnɛl] adj. Sempiternal.

sempiternellement [-mɑ̃] adv. Sempiternally.

sénat [sena] m. Senate (assemblée); senate-house (lieu).

sénateur [-tœːr] m. Senator.

sénatorial, ale [-tɔrjal] adj. Senatorial.

séné [sene] m. Senna.

sénéchal [seneʃal] m. Seneschal.

sénéchaussée [-ʃose] f. Seneschalsy (juridiction); seneschal's court (lieu); seneschal's tribunal (tribunal).

seneçon [sensɔ̃] m. BOT. Groundsel.

Sénégal [senegal] m. GÉOGR. Senegal.

sénégalais, aise [-lɛ, ɛz] adj. GÉOGR. Senegalese.

sénégalien, enne [-ljɛ̃, ɛn] adj. GÉOGR. Of Senegal.

sénescence [senɛsɑ̃:s] f. MÉD. Senescence.

sénescent, ente [-sɑ̃, ɑ̃:t] adj. MÉD. Senescent.

senestre [sənɛstr] adj. † Sinistral, left. ‖ BLAS. Sinister.

sénevé [senve] m. BOT. Mustard, mustard-seed.

sénile [senil] adj. Senile.

sénilité [-lite] f. Senility.

senior [senjɔːr] adj. SPORTS. Senior, over eighteen.

senne [sɛn] f. Seine (filet).

sens [sɑ̃:s] m. Direction, way (direction); *couper dans le sens de l'étoffe*, to cut on the straight; *dans le bon sens*, in the right direction; *dans le sens, en sens inverse des aiguilles d'une montre*, clockwise, anti-clockwise; *dans le sens du courant*, with the current (ou) stream; *dans tous les sens*, in all directions; *en sens inverse*, in opposite direction; *retourner qqch. dans tous les sens*, to turn sth. over and over. ‖ Sense (faculté); *reprendre ses sens*, to regain one's senses; *sixième sens*, sixth sense; *sens de l'odorat*, sense of smell. ‖ Pl. Sensuality; *plaisirs des sens*, sensual pleasures. ‖ Sense, understanding, judgment (jugement); *bon sens, sens commun*, common sense; *en dépit du bon sens*, against all sense; *dans son bon sens*, in one's right mind; *homme de sens*, man of sense. ‖ Opinion, point of view (point de vue); *abonder dans le sens de qqn*, to be entirely of s.o.'s opinion; *à mon sens*, in my opinion, to my mind; *parler dans le même sens*, to speak to the same effect. ‖ Sense, appreciation, feeling (sentiment); *sens du beau*, sense of beauty; *sens du coloris*, sense of (ou) feeling for colour; *sens moral*, moral sense. ‖ Sense, meaning, signification (signification); purport (d'une lettre); meaning (d'une phrase); import (d'une remarque); signification (d'un symbole); sense (d'un mot); *mot à double sens*, word with a double meaning, double entendre; *paroles qui n'ont pas de sens*, meaningless words. ‖ GRAMM. *Sens figuré, propre*, figurative, literal sense. ‖ AUTOM. *Sens de la circulation*, direction of traffic; « *sens interdit* », « no thoroughfare »; « *sens unique* », « one-way street ».
— loc. adv. **Sens dessus dessous**, upside down, wrong side-up; *mettre tout sens dessus dessous*, to turn everything topsy-turvy, to set everything to (ou) U. S. at sixes and sevens. ‖ **Sens devant derrière**, the wrong way round, hind-part foremost, back to front.

sensation [sɑ̃sasjɔ̃] f. Sensation, feeling (impression). ‖ FIG. Sensation; *faire sensation*, to make (ou) create a sensation; to cause a stir; *nouvelle à sensation*, sensational news.

sensationnel, elle [-sjɔnɛl] adj. Sensational; *rien de sensationnel*, nothing exciting (ou) sensational; nothing worth writing home about (fam.); *roman sensationnel*, thriller.

sensé, ée [sɑ̃se] adj. Sensible, wise (action); sensible, level-headed (personne).

sensément [-mɑ̃] adv. Sensibly, wisely.

senseur [sɑ̃sœːr] m. TECHN. Sensor, detector.

sensibilisable [sɑ̃sibilizabl] adj. Sensitizable.

sensibilisateur, trice [-zatœːr, tris] adj. Sensitizing.
— m. Sensitizer.

sensibilisation [-zasjõ] f. Sensitization, sensitizing.

sensibiliser [-ze] v. tr. (1). To sensitize.

sensibilité [-te] f. Sensitiveness (d'un appareil, de la peau). ‖ Fig. Sensibility (émotivité); sensitiveness, feeling, compassion; *avoir trop de sensibilité*, to be too tender- (ou) soft-hearted.

sensible [sãsibl] adj. Sensitive, tender, painful (endroit); keen (oreille); sensitive (personne); *être sensible à l'amabilité de qqn*, to be appreciative of s.o.'s kindness; *être sensible à la douleur*, to be susceptible to pain; *être sensible au froid*, to feel the cold; *être sensible à la musique*, to have an ear for music. ‖ Sensitive, impressionable, compassionate (facilement ému); *avoir le cœur sensible*, to be tender- (ou) soft-hearted; *peu sensible*, hard-hearted, callous, unsympathetic; *trop sensible*, too impressionable, soft-hearted. ‖ Sensible. tangible, discernible, appreciable, perceptible (notable); evident, palpable (différence); perceptible (progrès); sensible, tangible (monde); keen, lively (plaisir); *d'une manière sensible*, perceptibly, tangibly, appreciably. ‖ Phys. Sensitive (à, to) [balance]; sensitized (papier). ‖ Mus. Leading (note). ‖ Radio. Sensitive (appareil). ‖ Fam. *Avoir l'épiderme peu sensible*, to have a thick skin.

sensiblement [-bləmã] adv. Perceptibly, noticeably, appreciably (notablement). ‖ Keenly, acutely, deeply (profondément).

sensiblerie [-bləri] f. Sentimentality, mawkishness; sob-stuff, mush (fam.).

sensitif, ive [-tif, i:v] adj. Sensitive (être); sensory (faculté).

sensitive [-ti:v] f. Bot. Sensitive plant. ‖ Fig. Sensitive person.

sensitivité [-tivite] f. Sensitivity.

sensoriel, elle [sãsɔrjɛl] adj. Sensorial, sensory.

sensori-moteur, trice [-rimɔtœ:r, tris] adj. Méd. Sensorimotor.

sensualisme [sãsɥalism] m. Sensualism. ‖ Philos. Sensationalism.

sensualiste [-list] adj., s. Sensualist.

sensualité [-lite] f. Sensuality.

sensuel, elle [sãsɥɛl] adj. Sensual.
— s. Sensualist.

sensuellement [-mã] adv. Sensually.

sentant, ante [sãtã, ã:t] adj. Sentient.

sente [sã:t] f. Footpath.

sentence [sãtã:s] f. Maxim, apophthegm; *rempli de sentences*, sententious. ‖ Jur. Decision, award (décision); sentence (jugement); *sentence arbitrale*, arbitration award; *sentence de mort*, death sentence.

sentencieusement [-sjøzmã] adv. Sententiously, aphoristically, pithily.

sentencieux, euse [-sjø, ø:z] adj. Sententious, oracular, dogmatic.

senteur [sãtœ:r] f. Scent, odour, perfume. (V. odeur.) ‖ Bot. *Pois de senteur*, sweet pea.

senti, ie [sãti] adj. Well-expressed; *bien senti*, heartfelt, well-chosen (parole). ‖ V. sentir.

sentier [sãtje] m. Footpath, path. ‖ Fig. Path (de l'honneur, de la gloire); *sentier de la guerre*, war-path.

sentiment [sãtimã] m. Sense, impression, feeling, consciousness (conscience); *avoir le sentiment d'avoir fait qqch.*, to have a feeling (ou) the impression one has done sth.; *avoir le sentiment de ses droits*, to be aware (ou) conscious of one's rights; *avoir le sentiment de sa force*, to be aware of (ou) to realize one's strength; *sentiment des convenances*, sense of the proprieties (ou) of propriety. ‖ Sentiment, view, opinion (opinion); *changer de sentiment*, to change one's mind (ou) opinion; *partager le sentiment de qqn*, to share

s.o.'s opinion. ‖ Sentiment, feeling (passion); *avec sentiment*, with feeling, feelingly; *avoir un sentiment profond pour*, to be deeply in love with. ‖ Sensation, feeling (impression); *sentiment de soulagement*, feeling of relief. ‖ Sentiment, susceptibility, sensibility (sensibilité); *faire du sentiment*, to sentimentalize; *par sentiment*, out of sentiment, for sentimental reasons.

sentimental, ale [-tal] adj. Sentimental. ‖ Mawkish, namby-pamby (larmoyant, fade).

sentimentalement [-talmã] adv. Sentimentally.

sentimentalisme [-talism] m. Sentimentalism.

sentimentalité [-talite] f. Sentimentality.

sentine [sãtin] f. Naut. Bilge, well. ‖ Fig. Sink of iniquity. (V. cloaque.)

sentinelle [sãtinɛl] f. Milit. Sentry; sentinel (†); *en sentinelle*, on sentry-duty, on guard. ‖ *Faire la sentinelle*, to keep watch (ou) a look-out.

sentir [sãti:r] v. tr. (93). To feel, to appreciate, to be sensitive to (apprécier); *sentir la poésie*, to have a feeling for poetry. ‖ To smack of (avoir l'apparence de); *sentir l'homme du monde*, to have a look of distinction; *sentir le paysan*, to smack of the peasant, to have yokel written all over one. ‖ To feel, to be conscious of (avoir la conscience de); *sentir un danger*, to be conscious of (ou) alive to a danger. ‖ To feel (avoir l'impression); *sentir qu'on a tort*, to have a feeling that one is wrong. ‖ To feel, to experience (éprouver); *faire sentir qqch. à qqn*, to make s.o. feel sth.; *influence qui se fait sentir*, influence which makes itself felt; *sentir le chagrin, le remords*, to feel sorrow, remorse; *sentir la douleur*, to suffer pain; *sentir la faim*, to feel hungry; *sentir grandir son autorité*, to feel one's authority growing. ‖ To smell (ou) taste of, to give off a smell of (exhaler); *sentir le poisson*, to smell (ou) taste of fish, to have a fishy smell (ou) taste; *sentir le renfermé*, to have a fusty smell. ‖ To smell (humer); *sentir une fleur*, to smell a flower. ‖ To touch (toucher); *sentir du doigt*, to touch with the finger, to finger. ‖ To show, to reveal (révéler); *trop sentir le travail*, to give evidence of too much labour. ‖ Fam. *Ne pouvoir sentir qqn*, not to be able to stand (ou) bear s.o., to dislike s.o. intensely; *sentir un petit qqch. pour qqn*, to feel drawn to (ou) attracted towards s.o.
— v. intr. To smell, to stink; *sentir bon*, to smell nice, to have a sweet (ou) pleasant smell; *sentir mauvais*, to smell bad, to have a bad (ou) unpleasant smell, to stink; *viande qui commence à sentir*, meat that is beginning to smell.
— v. pr. Se sentir, to feel the effect (ou) benefit of (se ressentir); *se sentir d'une bonne éducation*, to feel the benefit of a good education. ‖ To feel one's strength (ou) capabilities (reconnaître en soi); *se sentir le courage de faire*, to feel up to (ou) equal to doing. ‖ To feel (se trouver); *ne se sentir pas bien*, to feel unwell, not to feel oneself; *se sentir bien*, to feel fit (ou) well,

seoir [swa:r] v. intr. (94). † To sit. ‖ Fam. *Siedstoi*, sit down. (V. séant, sis.)

seoir [swa:r] v. intr. (94). To suit, to become; *cela vous sied*, that suits you well. (V. seyant.)

séoudite [seudit] adj. Géogr. Saudi (Arabie).

sep [sɛp] m. Agric. Slade (de charrue).

sépale [sepal] m. Bot. Sepal.

séparable [separabl] adj. Separable.

séparateur, trice [-tœ:r tris] adj. Separative.
— m. Separator.

séparatif, ive [-tif, i:v] adj. Separative, separating. ‖ Archit. Dividing (mur).

séparation [-sjõ] f. Separation, parting, dispersal (action). ‖ Partition (chose); *mur de séparation*, partition wall. ‖ Jur. Separation; *séparation de corps et de biens*, judicial separation. ‖ Ecclés. *Séparation de l'Eglise et de l'Etat*, disestablishment of the Church, U. S. separation of Church and State.

séparatisme [-tism] m. Separatism.

séparatiste [-tist] adj., s. Separatist.

séparé, ée [separe] adj. Separate, distinct, different (distinct). ‖ JUR. Separated, living apart.

séparément [-remɑ̃] adv. Separately, apart.

séparer [-re] v. tr. (1). To sever (d'avec, de, from); to cut off, to separate (dissocier); séparer la tête du corps, to sever the head from the body. ‖ To divide (diviser); séparer une chambre en trois, to divide a room into three. ‖ To separate (éloigner); le vent sépara les deux flottes, the wind separated the two fleets. ‖ To separate, to part (empêcher de se battre); séparer deux combattants, to part (ou) separate two fighters. ‖ To separate, to divide (être placé entre); la mer sépare la France et l'Angleterre, France is separated from England by sea; mur qui sépare deux terrains, wall running between (ou) dividing two plots. ‖ To part (partager); séparer les cheveux sur le front, to part the hair on the forehead. ‖ To separate, to set apart (ou) aside (ranger à part); séparer l'ivraie du bon grain, to separate the tares from the wheat. ‖ JUR. To separate judicially (des époux). ‖ FIG. To distinguish, to divide; la raison sépare l'homme des autres animaux. reason sets man apart from the animals.
— v. pr. **Se séparer**, to disperse, to break up (assemblée). ‖ To part, to part company (personnes). ‖ To divide, to branch off (route). ‖ CHIM. To separate, to crystallize out.

sépia [sepja] f. ZOOL. Sepia, cuttle-fish. ‖ ARTS. Sepia; dessin à la sépia, sepia drawing.

sept [sɛt] adj. num. Seven. ‖ Seventh; Charles VII, Charles the Seventh.
— m. Seven (nombre); le sept octobre, the seventh of October; U. S. October seventh. ‖ Seven (aux cartes).

septain [sɛtɛ̃] m. Stanza of seven lines (en prosodie). ‖ Seven-strand rope (corde).

septante [sɛptɑ̃:t] adj. num. † Seventy. ‖ ECCLÉS. La version des Septante, the Septuagint.

septembre [sɛptɑ̃:br] m. September; au mois de septembre, in September, in the month of September.

septembriseur [-brizœ:r] m. Septembrist.

septénaire [septenɛ:r] adj., m. Septenary.

septennal, ale [-tɛnal] adj. Septennial.

septennat [-tɛna] m. Septennate.

septentrion [sɛptɑ̃triɔ̃] m. North. (V. NORD.)

septentrional, ale [-trijɔnal] adj. Northern.
— s. Northerner.

septicémie [sɛptisemi] f. MÉD. Septicaemia.

septicémique [-semik] adj. MÉD. Septicaemic.

septicité [-site] f. MÉD. Septicity.

septième [sɛtjɛm] adj. num. Seventh. ‖ FIG. Au septième ciel, in the seventh heaven.
— m. Seventh (ou) U. S. eighth floor (étage); demeurer au septième, to live on the seventh floor. ‖ Seventh, seventh part (partie).
— f. Top form of lower school, U. S. seventh grade (dans une école). ‖ MUS. Seventh.

septièmement [-mɑ̃] adv. Seventhly.

septime [sɛptim] f. SPORTS. Septime (en escrime).

septique [sɛptik] adj. MÉD. Septic.

septivalent, ente [sɛptivalɑ̃, ɑ̃:t] adj. CHIM. Septivalent.

septuagénaire [sɛptɥaʒenɛ:r] adj., s. Septuagenarian.

Septuagésime [-ʒezim] f. ECCLÉS. Septuagesima.

septuor [sɛptɥɔ:r] m. MUS. Septet.

septuple [sɛptypl] adj., m. Septuple.

septupler [-ple] v. tr., intr. (1). To septuple, to increase sevenfold.

sépulcral, ale [sepylkral] adj. Sepulchral (inscription). ‖ FIG. Sepulchral, cavernous (voix).

sépulcre [-kr] m. Sepulchre. ‖ ECCLÉS. Le Saint Sépulcre, the Holy Sepulchre.

sépulture [-ty:r] f. Burial, sepulture (enterrement). ‖ Burial-place, resting-place, tomb (lieu).

séquanais, aise [sekwanɛ, ɛz] adj. GÉOGR. Of the Seine.

séquelle [sekɛl] f. String, volley (d'injures); crowd, gang, band, set (de personnes). ‖ MÉD. Sequela. ‖ FIG. Pl. Aftermath.

séquence [sekɑ̃:s] f. ECCLÉS., MUS. Sequence. ‖ CINÉM. Sequence; longueur de la séquence, footage.

séquentiel, elle [-kɑ̃sjɛl] adj. Sequential (gén., inform.).

séquestration [sekɛstrasjɔ̃] f. Isolation. ‖ JUR. Sequestration (de biens, de personnes).

séquestre [-kɛstr] m. JUR. Sequestration (acte); sequestrated property (bien); sequestrator, assignee (personne); mettre sous séquestre, to sequestrate; sous séquestre, sequestrated. ‖ MÉD. Sequestrum.
— adj. Sequestrating (tribunal).

séquestrer [-kɛstre] v. tr. (1). JUR. To sequester, to sequestrate (des biens); to confine, to keep in confinement (qqn).
— v. pr. **Se séquestrer**, to sequester oneself, to cut (ou) shut oneself off.

sequin [səkɛ̃] m. Sequin.

séquoia [sekɔja] m. BOT. Sequoia, redwood.

sérac [serak] m. White Swiss cheese. ‖ GÉOL. Serac, ice-pinnacle.

serai, serais, serait. V. ÊTRE (48).

sérail [sera:j] m. Seraglio.

séraphin [serafɛ̃] m. ECCLÉS. Seraph; pl. seraphim.

séraphique [-fik] adj. ECCLÉS. Seraphic (chœur, docteur); Franciscan (ordre). ‖ FIG. Seraphic, angelic.

serbe [sɛrb] adj., s. GÉOGR. Serb, Serbian.

Serbie [sɛrbi] f. GÉOGR. Serbia.

serbo-croate [-bokrɔat] m. GRAMM. Serbo-Croat (langue).

serein [sərɛ̃] m. Evening damp (ou) dew; serein.

serein, eine [-ɛn] adj. Cloudless, clear (ciel); calm, serene (temps). ‖ MÉD. Goutte sereine, amaurosis. ‖ FIG. Calm, serene, unruffled, tranquil (personne).

sereinement [-ɛnmɑ̃] adv. Calmly, serenely, dispassionately.

sérénade [serenad] f. MUS. Serenade; donner une sérénade à, to serenade.

sérénissime [-nisim] adj. Most serene.

sérénité [-nite] f. Serenity, calmness (de l'atmosphère). ‖ Serenity (titre). ‖ FIG. Serenity, calm, calmness; avec sérénité, serenely.

séreux, euse [serø, ø:z] adj. MÉD. Serous.

serf, erve [sɛrf, ɛrv] adj. In bondage; condition serve, serfdom.
— m. Serf; bondman. (V. SERVE.)

serfouette [sɛrfwɛt] f. AGRIC. Hoe.

serfouir [-fwi:r] v. tr. (2). AGRIC. To hoe.

serge [sɛrʒ] f. Serge.

sergé [-ʒe] m. Twill.

sergent [-ʒɑ̃] m. Sergeant; sergent de ville, police-constable, policeman. ‖ † Sergent d'armes, sergeant-at-arms. ‖ MILIT. Sergeant; sergent fourrier, quartermaster-sergeant's assistant; sergent instructeur, drill-sergeant. ‖ Sergent-chef, m. MILIT. Sergeant-major. ‖ Sergent-major, m. MILIT. Quartermaster-sergeant.

sergette [-ʒɛt] f. Sergette.

serial [serjəl] m. Serial (film à épisodes).

séricicole [serisikɔl] adj. Seri(ci)cultural.

sériciculteur [-kyltœ:r] m. Sericulturist, sericiculturist, silkworm-breeder.

sériciculture [-kylty:r] f. Seri(ci)culture.

série [seri] f. Series (de couleurs, de nombres);

succession (de défaites); *en série, par série,* serially, in series. ‖ ELECTR., MATH. Series. ‖ SPORTS. Class, division, series; *série de cinquante,* break of fifty, fifty break (au billard). ‖ NAUT. Set (de pavillons). ‖ COMM. *De série, hors série,* standard, specially manufactured (article); *fabrication en série,* mass-production; *fait en série,* mass-produced; *fin de série,* oddments, remnants; *prix de série,* contract price. ‖ RADIO. *Série d'émissions,* broadcast series. ‖ FAM. *Série noire,* run of bad-luck.

sériel, elle [-rjɛl] adj. Serial (gén., mus.).

sérier [-rje] v. tr. (1). To seriate, to arrange in series (ou) order.

sérieusement [serjøzmɑ̃] adj. Seriously, earnestly, conscientiously; properly (avec application). ‖ Seriously, gravely, grievously (gravement). ‖ Seriously, in earnest, without joking, joking apart, really, sincerely (sans plaisanterie).

sérieux, euse [-rjø, ø:z] adj. Serious, grave (air); serious, weighty (argument); serious, grave, dangerous (maladie); serious, sober, earnest, serious-minded, responsible (personne); serious, real, sincere (promesse). ‖ COMM. Bona-fide, genuine (client); reliable (employé).
— m. Seriousness, solemnity, gravity; *garder son sérieux,* to keep a straight face, to keep one's countenance, to preserve one's gravity; *manque de sérieux,* irresponsibility; *prendre qqch. au sérieux,* to take sth. seriously.

sérigraphie [serigrafi] f. TECHN. Silk-screen painting, serigraphy.

serin, ine [sərɛ̃, in] s. ZOOL. Serin; canary. ‖ FAM. Duffer, nincompoop, twerp.

seriner [sərine] v. tr. (1). To teach to sing (un serin). ‖ FAM. To cram, to drive (ou) drill (qqch.) [à, into].

serinette [-nɛt] f. Bird-organ. ‖ FAM. Person who sings without expression.

seringa [sərɛ̃ga] m. BOT. Syringa.

seringue [sərɛ̃:g] f. MÉD. Syringe; *seringue à lavement,* enema-syringe. ‖ AUTOM. *Seringue à graisse,* grease-gun.

seringuer [-rɛ̃ge] v. tr. (1). To squirt (un liquide). ‖ MÉD. To inject (de la morphine).

sérique [serik] adj. MÉD. Serum (groupe, maladie, accident).

serment [sɛrmɑ̃] m. Oath; *prêter serment,* to take an oath. ‖ JUR. *Faire prêter serment à qqn,* to administer the oath to s.o.; *faux serment,* perjury; *prêter serment,* to be sworn in; *sous serment,* on oath; *témoignage sous serment,* sworn evidence.

sermon [sɛrmɔ̃] m. ECCLÉS. Sermon. ‖ FAM. Sermon, lecture, talking-to.

sermonner [-mɔne] v. tr. (1). To sermonize, to give a lecture to, to preach to (qqn).
— v. intr. To sermonize.

sermonneur, euse [-mɔnœ:r, ø:z] adj. Sermonizing.
— s. Sermonizer.

sérologie [serolɔʒi] f. MÉD. Serology.

sérosité [serozite] f. MÉD. Serosity.

sérothérapie [-terapi] f. MÉD. Serotherapy.

serpe [sɛrp] f. Bill-hook.

serpent [sɛrpɑ̃] m. ZOOL. Serpent, snake; *serpent à lunettes,* cobra; *serpent à sonnettes,* rattle-snake; rattler (fam.); *serpent d'eau, de mer,* grass-, sea-snake. ‖ MUS. Serpent. ‖ FIG. *Réchauffer un serpent dans son sein,* to nourish a viper in one's bosom. ‖ FIN. *Le serpent monétaire,* the snake.

serpentaire [-tɛ:r] m. ZOOL. Serpent-eater, secretary-bird.
— f. BOT. Snake-root.

serpentant, ante [-tɑ̃, ɑ̃:t] adj. Winding (chemin); meandering (ruisseau).

serpente [sɛrpɑ̃:t] adj. *Papier serpente,* tissue paper.

serpenteau [sɛrpɑ̃to] m. Young snake.

serpentement [-tmɑ̃] m. Winding (d'un chemin); meandering (d'un ruisseau).

serpenter [-te] v. intr. (1). To wind (chemin); to meander (ruisseau).

serpentin, ine [-tɛ̃, in] adj. Serpentine, winding (ligne). ‖ *Marbre serpentin,* serpentine, ophite.
— m. Streamer (de papier). ‖ CHIM. Coil, worm (d'alambic).

serpentine [-ti:n] f. Serpentine, ophite (pierre). ‖ BOT. Snake-wood.

serpette [sɛrpɛt] f. AGRIC. Pruning-knife; bill-hook.

serpillière [sɛrpiljɛ:r] f. Canvas apron (tablier); packing-cloth, sacking (toile).

serpolet [sɛrpɔlɛ] m. BOT. Wild thyme.

serrage [sɛra:ʒ] m. Tightening (d'un nœud). ‖ TECHN. Tightening, screwing up (d'un écrou); clamping (d'un joint). ‖ AUTOM. Application des freins).

serre [sɛ:r] f. Pressing (de raisins). ‖ AGRIC. Glass-house, green-house; *cultiver sous serre,* to grow under glass; *serre chaude,* hothouse. ‖ ZOOL. Claw, talon (d'oiseau). ‖ NAUT. Stringer.

serre- [sɛr]. V. SERRER. ‖ **Serre-bosse,** m. invar. NAUT. Shank-painter. ‖ **Serre-file,** m. invar. NAUT. Rear ship; MILIT. Serrefile; *marcher en serre-file,* to bring up the rear. ‖ **Serre-fils,** m. invar. ELECTR. Clamp. ‖ **Serre-freins,** m. invar. CH. DE F. Brakesman. ‖ **Serre-joint,** m. invar. Clamp, cramp. ‖ **Serre-livres,** m. invar. Book-ends. ‖ **Serre-nez,** m. invar. Twitch. ‖ **Serre-papiers,** m. invar. Pigeon-hole (de bureau); paperweight (presse-papiers). ‖ **Serre-tête,** m. invar. Kerchief (coiffe); headbands (ruban); AUTOM. Crash-helmet (de motocycliste).

serré, ée [sɛre] adj. Thick (pluie); close, serried (rangs); tight (soulier, vêtement); close, closely-woven (tissu); *bois de grain serré,* close-grained wood; *les dents serrées,* with clenched teeth; *les lèvres serrées,* with tight (ou) compressed lips; *serrés comme des harengs,* packed like sardines. ‖ SPORTS. *Arrivée serrée,* close finish, photo-finish. ‖ MILIT. *En ligne serrée,* in close order. ‖ ZOOL. *Serré du derrière, du devant,* cow-hocked, knock-kneed (cheval). ‖ FIG. Close (logique, traduction); concise (style); *avoir le cœur serré,* to be sick at heart. ‖ FAM. Close-fisted.
— adv. *Mordre serré,* to bite hard. ‖ SPORTS. *Jouer serré,* to play carefully, to play a cautious game. ‖ FIG. *Jouer serré,* to take no chances, to watch one's step.

serrement [-rmɑ̃] m. Squeezing, pressing; *serrement de main,* handshake. ‖ FIG. *Serrement de cœur,* heartache, pang, tug at one's heartstrings.

serrer [-re] v. tr. (1). To clench, to grit (les dents); to shake, to clasp, to squeeze (la main); to clench (les poings); *serrer la main à qqn,* to shake s.o.'s hand, to shake s.o. by the hand. ‖ To put away (du linge); *serrer qqch. sous clef,* to lock sth. up (ou) away. ‖ To keep close to, to hug, to skirt (un mur). ‖ To tighten (un écrou); to tighten, to pull tight (ou) tighter (un nœud); to tighten, to drive in (une vis). ‖ To pinch, to squeeze (la peau); *serrer les pieds,* to pinch, to be too tight (souliers). ‖ NAUT. To hug (la côte); to haul (le vent); to take in (les voiles); *serrer la terre,* to keep close inshore. ‖ MILIT. *Serrer les rangs,* to close up. ‖ AGRIC. To house (du blé); to get in (une récolte). ‖ AUTOM. To apply, to put on (les freins). ‖ SPORTS. To hamper, to jostle (un coureur); *serrer son jeu,* to play more carefully (ou) with more caution. ‖ FIG. *Serrer le cœur,* to wring one's heart; *serrer son*

style, to write concisely; *serrer le texte de près,* to keep close to the text.
— v. pr. **Se serrer,** to close up, to stand (ou) sit closer together; *se serrer autour,* to press round; *se serrer contre,* to stand (ou) sit close to, to snuggle up to. ‖ To tight-lace (dans un corset). ‖ To tighten (nœud); to clench (poings). ‖ FIG. To sink, to be rent (cœur).

serrure [sɛry:r] f. Lock; *serrure à combinaisons,* combination lock; *trou de la serrure,* key-hole.

serrurerie [-rri] f. Locksmith's shop (lieu); locksmithery, locksmith's trade (métier); ironwork, metalwork (ouvrage).

serrurier [-rje] m. Locksmith.

serte [sɛrt] f. Setting (de pierres fines).

sertir [-ti:r] v. tr. (2). To crimp (une cartouche). ‖ To set (des pierreries).

sertissage [-tisa:ʒ] m. Crimping. ‖ Setting.

sertisseur [-tisœ:r] m. Crimper. ‖ Setter.

sertissure [-tisy:r] f. Crimp. ‖ Setting.

sérum [serɔm] m. MÉD. Serum.

servage [sɛrva:ʒ] m. Serfdom, bondage, thraldom. (V. ESCLAVAGE.)

serval [sɛrval] (pl. **servals**) m. ZOOL. Serval.

servant, ante [sɛrvɑ̃, ɑ̃:t] adj. Serving; *cavalier servant,* squire of dames; *gentilhomme servant,* gentleman-in-waiting. ‖ ECCLÉS. *Frère servant,* lay brother.
— m. MILIT. Gunner; member of a gun-crew. ‖ SPORTS. Server (au tennis).

servante [-vɑ̃:t] f. Servant, maid-servant (personne). ‖ Dumb-waiter (meuble).

serve [sɛrv] f. Bondwoman. (V. SERF.)

serveur [sɛrvœ:r] m. Barman (dans un bar); waiter (dans un restaurant). ‖ SPORTS. Dealer (aux cartes); server (au tennis).

serveuse [-vø:z] f. Barmaid (dans un bar); waitress (dans un restaurant).

serviabilité [-vjabilite] f. Willingness (ou) readiness to help.

serviable [-vjabl] adj. Willing to help; obliging.

service [-vis] m. Service (assistance); *à votre service,* at your service; *offrir ses services,* to offer one's services; *qu'y a-t-il pour votre service?,* what can I do for you? can I be of any assistance?; *rendre un service à qqn,* to do s.o. a favour (ou) a service (ou) a good turn. ‖ Service (d'autobus); *faire le service entre,* to ply (ou) run between; *mettre en service,* to put into service. ‖ Attendance, U.S. service (dans un hôtel); tip, service charge (pourboire); *ajouter 15 p. 100 pour le service,* to add on 15 per cent for attendance (ou) U.S. service. ‖ Service (domesticité); *entrer (ou) se mettre en service,* to go into service. ‖ Teaching duties (ou) hours (d'un professeur). ‖ JUR. Public service (fonction publique); *entreprise de service public,* public utility undertaking; *service diplomatique,* diplomatic service (ou) U.S. corps. ‖ Service (de porcelaine); *service de table,* dinner-service. ‖ CULIN. Course (d'un repas). ‖ MILIT. Service; *bon pour le service,* fit for service; *en service commandé,* on special duty; *être de service,* to be on duty; *faire son service,* to do one's military service; *service actif, obligatoire,* active, compulsory service; *service de santé,* medical corps. ‖ COMM. Department, branch; *chef de service,* head of department, departmental head; *libre service,* self-service (dans une boutique). ‖ FIN., SPORTS. ECCLÉS. Service.

serviette [-vjɛt] f. Feeder, bib (d'enfant). ‖ Napkin, table-napkin, serviette (de table); towel (de toilette); *serviette sans fin,* roller-towel; *serviette hygiénique,* sanitary towel (ou) U.S. napkin. ‖ Portfolio, brief-case (d'avocat, de professeur). ‖ **Serviette-éponge,** f. Terry towel, towel.

servile [-vil] adj. Servile, menial (condition); menial, lowly (métier). ‖ FIG. Mean, base, abject (âme); slavish (imitation).

servilement [-vilmɑ̃] adv. Servilely, slavishly.

servilité [-vilite] f. Servility.

servir [-vi:r] v. tr. (95). To serve, to help, to aid, to assist, to be of service to (aider); *en quoi puis-je vous servir?,* how can I help you?, what can I do to help? ‖ To favour (favoriser). ‖ To serve, to be a servant to, to be in the service of (un maître). ‖ CULIN. To serve, to wait on (un convive); to serve (un plat). ‖ SPORTS. To deal (aux cartes); to bowl (au cricket); to serve (au tennis); to kill (une bête fauve); *servir un sanglier au couteau,* to dispatch a wild boar with the knife. ‖ ECCLÉS. To serve (la messe). ‖ COMM. To serve, to attend to (un client); to supply, to furnish (des denrées). ‖ FIN. To serve, to pay (une rente). ‖ MILIT. To man (une batterie); to serve (un canon, sa patrie).
— v. intr. To wait (à table). ‖ To serve, to be in service, to be a servant (être domestique). ‖ To serve, to be useful, to be of use (être utile); *à quoi cela sert-il?,* what's the use (ou) good of that?; *ne sert à rien,* that's no use (ou) good; *cela peut servir,* it may come in handy; *servir de rien,* to be quite useless. ‖ To serve (*de,* as); to be used (*de,* for); *servir d'exemple,* to serve as an example; *servir de père à qqn,* to be a father to s.o., to take the place of s.o.'s father. ‖ SPORTS. To serve (au tennis).
— v. pr. **Se servir,** to help (ou) serve oneself; *se servir du vin,* to help oneself to wine, to serve oneself with wine. ‖ To use (employer); *se servir de qqch.,* to use sth., to make use of sth. ‖ COMM. To get one's supplies, to buy one's goods (chez un fournisseur).

serviteur [-vitœ:r] m. Servant. (V. DOMESTIQUE.) ‖ FIG. Servant (de Dieu, de l'État); *votre serviteur,* your servant.

servitude [-vityd] f. Servitude. ‖ Bondage, slavery. (V. ESCLAVAGE, SERVAGE.) ‖ JUR. Easement. ‖ NAUT. *Bâtiments de servitude,* harbour craft.

servocommande [sɛrvokɔmɑ̃:d] f. TECHN. Servo-control.

servofrein [-frɛ̃] m. TECHN. Servo-brake.

servomécanisme [-mekanism] m. TECHN. Servo-mechanism, servo-system, servo.

servomoteur [-mɔtœ:r] m. Servo-motor, servo.

ses [sɛ] adj. poss. V. SON.

sésame [sezam] m. BOT. Sesame. ‖ LOC. *Sésame, ouvre-toi!* open, sesame!

sessile [sɛsil] adj. BOT. Sessile.

session [sɛsjɔ̃] f. Session, sitting (du parlement); session, term (d'une université).

sesterce [sɛstɛrs] m. Sesterce.

set [sɛt] m. Table- (ou) place-mat (napperon). ‖ SPORTS. Set. ‖ CINÉM. Set.

sétacé, ée [setase] adj. Setaceous.

setier [sətje] m. † Corn (ou) liquid measure.

séton [setɔ̃] m. MÉD. Seton; *plaie en séton,* flesh-wound.

setter [sɛtɛ:r] m. ZOOL. Setter.

seuil [sœ:j] m. Threshold, doorstep. ‖ PHILOS. Limen. ‖ FIG. Threshold, beginning (de la vie).

seul, e [sœl] adj. Alone (isolé); *avoir l'air seul,* to look lonely (ou) lonesome; *rester tout seul,* to remain alone (ou) by oneself; *tout seul avec vous,* alone with just you; *vivre seul,* to live alone. ‖ Mere (simple); *la seule pensée de la mort m'effraye,* the mere idea of death scares me. ‖ Single, sole, only (unique); *mon seul souci,* my sole (ou) only (ou) one care; *n'avoir pas un seul ami,* not to have a single friend; *un seul Dieu,* one God only, only one God; *la seule et unique occasion,* the one and only time; *se lever comme un seul homme,* to rise like one man. ‖ Single-

handed (sans aide). ‖ Only (seulement); *seul le premier mot prend le pluriel*, only the first word takes the plural ending. ‖ Loc. *Cela ne se fera pas tout seul*, that won't happen (ou) come about of itself; *cela va tout seul*, it's all plain sailing; *parler seul à seul à qqn*, to speak privately with s.o. (ou) with s.o. alone.
— s. Single person (ou) thing; *le gouvernement d'un seul*, absolute government; *il n'en reste plus un seul*, there isn't a single one left; *vous êtes le seul à le savoir*, you are the only one to know.

seulement [sœlmɑ̃] adv. Only, at least (au moins); *si seulement on profitait de l'expérience*, if only one learned from experience. ‖ Only (pas avant); *sa lettre est arrivée seulement ce matin*, his letter came only this morning. ‖ Only, merely, just (rien de plus); *être deux seulement*, to be only two; *laissez-moi seulement vous expliquer*, just let me explain. ‖ Only (toutefois); *il consent, seulement il demande des garanties*, he agrees, only he wants some guarantee. ‖ Only, alone, solely (uniquement); *dites-le-lui seulement*, tell him alone, tell only him. ‖ Even (même); *sans seulement tressaillir*, without even startling.
— loc. adv. **Non seulement ... mais aussi, mais encore**, not only ... but also; *non seulement il est riche, mais il est gentil*, not only is he rich but he is kind too.

seulet, ette [sœlɛ, ɛt] adj. FAM. Alone, lonely, lonesome.

sève [sɛ:v] f. BOT. Sap; *plein de sève*, sappy. ‖ FIG. Vigour, vim.

sévère [sevɛ:r] adj. Severe, hard (climat); stern, hard (juge); severe, harsh (loi); strict, rigid (mœurs); strict, hard (personne); stern, severe (regard); austere, sober (style); *sévère pour*, hard on.

sévèrement [-vɛrmɑ̃] adv. Severely, harshly, sternly, strictly.

sévérité [-verite] f. Strictness (de la discipline); harshness, severity (d'une punition). ‖ Act of severity (acte). ‖ FIG. Severity (du style); *la sévérité des femmes*, disdain employed by women.

sévices [-vis] m. pl. JUR. Maltreatment (*envers*, of); cruelty (*envers*, towards).

sévir [-vi:r] v. intr. (2). To act severely (*contre*, towards); to deal severely (*contre*, with). ‖ MILIT. To rage (guerre). ‖ MÉD. To be rife (épidémie). ‖ FIG. To be bitter (ou) severe (froid).

sevrage [səvra:ʒ] m. Weaning.

sevrer [səvre] v. tr. (5). To wean (un nourrisson). ‖ AGRIC. To separate (une marcotte). ‖ FIG. To deprive (*de*, of).

sèvres [sɛ:vr] m. Sèvres porcelain.

sévrienne [sevrijɛn] f. Student of the Ecole normale supérieure de Sèvres.

sexagénaire [sɛksaʒenɛ:r] adj., s. Sexagenarian.

sexagésimal, ale [-zimal] adj. Sexagesimal.

Sexagésime [-zim] f. ECCLÉS. Sexagesima.

sex-appeal [sɛksapil] m. Sex-appeal.

sexe [sɛks] m. Sex; *les deux sexes*, the two sexes. ‖ Sex organ. ‖ FAM. *Le beau sexe*, the fair sex; *sexe faible, fort*, weaker, strong (ou) male sex.

sexisme [-ism] m. Sexism.

sexiste [-ist] adj., s. Sexist.

sexologie [sɛksɔlɔʒi] f. Sexology.

sexologue [-lɔg] s. Sexologist.

sex-ratio [sɛksrasjo] f. Sex ratio.

sex-shop [-ʃɔp] m. Sex-shop.

sextant [sɛkstɑ̃] m. Sextant.

sexte [sɛkst] f. ECCLÉS. Sext.

sextil, ile [-til] adj. ASTR. Sextile.

sextuor [sɛkstɥɔ:r] m. MUS. Sextet.

sextuple [-typl] adj., m. Sextuple.

sextupler [-typle] v. tr. (1). To sextuple.

sexualiser [sɛksɥalize] v. tr. (1). To sexualize.

sexualisme [sɛksɥalism] m. Sexualism.

sexualité [-lite] f. Sexuality.

sexué, ée [sɛksɥe] adj. Sexed.

sexuel, elle [-ɛl] adj. Sexual; *éducation sexuelle*, sex education.

sexy [sɛksi] adj. FAM. Sexy.

seyant, ante [sɛjɑ̃, ɑ̃:t] adj. Becoming; suitable.

Seychelles [seʃɛl] f. pl. GÉOGR. Seychelles.

S.F. [ɛsɛf] f. Abrév. de *science-fiction*, S.F., sci-fi.

shah [ʃa] m. Shah.

shakehand [ʃɛkhand] m. invar. Handshake.

shaker [ʃɛkœ:r] m. Cocktail-shaker.

shakespearien, enne [ʃɛkspirjɛ̃, ɛn] adj. Shakespearian.

shako [ʃako] m. MILIT. Shako.

shampooing [ʃɑ̃pwɛ̃] m. Shampoo; *faire un shampooing à qqn*, to shampoo (ou) wash s.o.'s hair.

shampouiner [-pwine] v. tr. (1). To shampoo.

shantung [ʃɑ̃tuŋ] m. Shantung (tissu).

shérif [ʃerif] m. Sheriff.

sherpa [ʃɛrpa] m. Sherpa.

sherry [ʃeri] m. Sherry.

shetland [ʃɛtlɑ̃:d] m. Shetland wool. ‖ ZOOL. Shetland pony.

shinto [ʃɛto] m. Shinto.

shintoïsme [-tɔism] m. Shintoism.

shirting [ʃœrtiŋ] m. Shirting.

shock [ʃɔk] m. MÉD. Shock.

shoot [ʃut] m. SPORTS. Shot.

shooter [ʃute] v. intr. (1). SPORTS. To shoot.
— v. pr. **Se shooter**, POP. To fix, to shoot up.

shop(p)ing [ʃɔpiŋ] m. Shopping; *faire du shopping*, to go shopping.

short [ʃɔrt] m. Shorts.

show [ʃo] m. Variety show. ‖ **Show-business**, m. Show business, showbiz.

shrapnel [ʃrapnɛl] m. MILIT. Shrapnel.

shunt [ʃœ̃:t] m. ELECTR. Shunt.

shunter [ʃœ̃te] v. tr. (1). ELECTR. To shunt.

si [si] conj. If (concession); *s'il est jeune, il est cependant intelligent*, if young, he's clever; he may be young but he's clever. ‖ If (condition); *je ne le ferai que si vous êtes d'accord*, I shall only do it if you agree, I shall not do it unless you agree; *il viendra s'il peut*, he will come if he can. ‖ Whether (doute); *je ne sais s'il pourra*, I don't know whether he will be able to. ‖ If (étonnement, indignation); *le connaissez-vous?* — *Si je le connais!*, do you know him? — Of course I know him! ‖ If (hypothèse); *s'il a dit cela, il a eu tort*, if he said that, he was wrong; *et si on buvait du thé?*, what about drinking tea? ‖ If (opposition); *si l'un dit oui, l'autre dit non*, if one of them says yes, the other says no. ‖ If, if only (regret, souhait); *si j'avais su cela*, had I but known that; if only I'd known that; *si seulement on pouvait*, if only one could.
— loc. conj. **Si ce n'est que**, except that, but for the fact that; *si ce n'était qu'il est mon ami*, were he not my friend. ‖ **Si tant est que**, if it be that; *si tant est qu'il soit en danger*, if he really is in danger.
— m. invar. If; *les si et les mais*, ifs and buts.

si [si] adv. So (aussi); *ne courez pas si vite*, don't run so quickly. ‖ Yes (oui); *n'est-il pas encore arrivé?* — *Si*, hasn't he come yet? — Yes, he has; *si fait*, yes indeed; *vous ne gagnerez pas votre procès*. — *Je parie que si*, you won't win your case — I'll bet I do. ‖ So (tellement); *le vent est si fort que*, the wind is so strong that.
— loc. conj. **Si... que**, however; *si heureux qu'on soit*, however happy one may be, be one never so happy. ‖ **Si bien que**, with the result that; *il a travaillé dur, si bien qu'il a fini par*

remporter le prix, he worked hard and so eventually won the prize.
si m. invar. Mus. B ; si.
S.I. [εsi] abrév. de *système international (d'unités),* S.I., international system of units of measurement.
Siam [sjam] m. Géogr. Siam.
siamois [-mwa] adj., s. Géogr. Siamese. ‖ Méd. *Frères siamois, sœurs siamoises,* Siamese twins.
Sibérie [siberi] f. Géogr. Siberia.
sibérien, enne [siberjε̃, εn] adj., s. Siberian.
sibilant, ante [sibilɑ̃, ɑ̃:t] adj. Méd. Sibilant (râle, respiration).
sibylle [sibil] f. Sibyl.
sibyllin, ine [-lε̃, in] adj. Sibylline.
sic [sik] adv. Sic.
sicaire [sikε:r] m. Hired assassin.
siccateur [sikatœ:r] m. Drying-agent, exsiccator, U. S. dessicator.
siccatif, ive [-tif, i:v] adj. Siccative, quick-drying.
— m. Quick-drying substance.
siccité [siksite] f. Dryness.
Sicile [sisil] f. Géogr. Sicily.
sicilien, enne [-ljε̃, εn] adj., s. Géogr. Sicilian.
— m. Gramm. Sicilian (dialecte).
sicilienne [-ljεn] f. Mus. Siciliana.
sicle [sikl] m. Shekel.
side-car [sidka:r] m. Side-car (de moto).
sidéral, ale [sideral] adj. Astron. Sidereal.
sidérant, ante [-rɑ̃, ɑ̃:t] adj. Stunning, stupefying.
sidération [-rasjɔ̃] f. Astron. Sideration. ‖ Méd. Stroke.
sidéré, ée [-re] adj. Blasted, struck by lightning. ‖ Méd. Taken with apoplexy. ‖ Fam. Thunderstruck.
sidérer v. tr. (1). To strike, to strike down. ‖ Fam. To stupefy, to strike dumb.
sidérostat [-rɔsta] m. Astron. Siderostat.
sidérotechnie [siderɔtεkni] f. Metallurgy of iron.
sidérurgie [-ryrʒi] f. Siderurgy, iron metallurgy.
sidérurgique [-ryrʒik] adj. Iron, ironworking.
sidérurgiste [-ryrʒist] s. Steelworker, ironworker (ouvrier); steel (ou) iron manufacturer (industriel).
sidi [sidi] m. Fam. North African.
siècle [sjεkl] m. Century (époque); *au dix-neuvième siècle,* in the (ou) during the nineteenth century; *le grand siècle,* the age of Louis XIV ; *le troisième siècle avant J.-C.,* the third century B.C. ‖ World (monde); *se séparer du siècle,* to renounce the world; *vivre selon le siècle,* to live in worldly fashion. ‖ Ecclés. *Dans tous les siècles des siècles,* world without end. ‖ Fam. *Il y a un siècle que je ne l'ai vu,* I haven't seen him for ages.
siège [sjε:ʒ] m. Seat (d'une chaise); bottom (d'un fauteuil). ‖ Seat, chair; *prenez un siège,* take a seat, sit down. ‖ Comm. *Siège administratif, social,* head, registered office. ‖ Milit. Siege; *proclamer l'état de siège,* to declare (ou) institute martial law; *mettre le siège devant,* to lay siege to. ‖ Jur. Bench (d'un juge); seat (d'un tribunal). ‖ Ecclés. *Siège épiscopal,* see; *Saint-Siège,* Holy See. ‖ Techn. Seat, seating (d'une soupape). ‖ Fig. Seat, centre.
siéger [sjeʒe] v. intr. (7). Jur. To be on the bench (juge); to sit, to be sitting (tribunal). ‖ Comm. To have its head office (société). ‖ Ecclés. To hold his see (évêque). ‖ Fig. To have its seat, to be localized.
sien, enne [sjε̃, εn] adj. poss. His, hers, its, one's; *faire sien,* to accept as one's own; *regarder une chose comme sienne,* to look upon sth.

as his (ou) her (ou) one's own ; *une sienne cousine,* a cousin of his (ou) hers,
— pron. poss. *Le sien, la sienne, les siens, les siennes,* his, hers, one's own ; *ma maison est plus grande que la sienne,* my house is bigger than his (ou) hers.
— m. His own, her own, one's own; *à chacun le sien,* to each his own; *y mettre du sien,* to contribute to sth., to pull one's weight. ‖ Pl. His own (ou) one's own people (famille).
— f. pl. Fam. *Faire des siennes,* to be up to one's old tricks.
Sienne [sjεn] Géogr. Sienna ; *terre de Sienne brûlée, naturelle,* burnt, raw sienna.
sierra [siεra] f. Géogr. Sierra ‖ **Sierra-Leone,** f. Géogr. Sierra Leone.
sieste [sjεst] f. Siesta ; nap (fam.); *faire une petite sieste,* to have forty winks.
sieur [sjœ:r] m. Jur. *Le sieur X,* Mr. X, the said X.
sifflant, ante [siflɑ̃, ɑ̃:t] adj. Whistling, hissing (bruit). ‖ Méd. Wheezy, wheezing (respiration). ‖ Gramm. Sibilant (consonne).
sifflante [-flɑ̃:t] f. Gramm. Sibilant.
sifflement [-fləmɑ̃] m. Whistling, whistle (de qqn, du vent) ; hiss, hissing (d'un serpent) ; hiss (de la vapeur). ‖ Méd. Wheezing. ‖ Milit. Whizz (d'une balle).
siffler [-fle] v. intr. (1). To whistle (qqn, vent) ; to hiss (serpent, vapeur). ‖ Méd. To wheeze. ‖ Milit. To whine, to whizz (balle).
— v. tr. (1). To whistle (un air); to whistle to (un chien). ‖ Théâtr. To hiss, to boo; to give the bird to (fam.) [un acteur, une pièce]. ‖ Fam. To swig, to swill, to toss off (un verre de vin).
sifflet [-fle] m. Whistle; *coup de sifflet,* whistle, blast of the whistle, whistle-blast; *sifflet à vapeur,* steam-whistle. ‖ Naut. Whistle. ‖ Théâtr. Hiss, catcall, boo. ‖ Techn. *En sifflet,* chamfered, slantwise, bevelled. ‖ Pop. *Couper le sifflet à qqn,* to shut s.o. up (faire taire).
siffleur, euse [-flœ:r, ø:z] adj. Wheezy (cheval); whistling (oiseau); hissing (serpent).
— m. Zool. Widgeon.
— s. Whistler. ‖ Théâtr. Booer, hisser.
sifflotement [siflɔtmɑ̃] m. Whistling.
siffloter [-te] v. intr. (1). To whistle softly to oneself, to whistle under one's breath.
— v. tr. To whistle softly (un air).
sigillé [siʒile] adj. Sigillated.
sigillographie [-lɔgrafi] f. Sigillography, sphragistics.
sigisbée [siʒisbe] m. Cicisbeo.
sigle [sigl] m. Sigla ; acronym.
sigma [sigma] m. Sigma.
sigmoïde [-mɔid] adj. Méd. Sigmoid.
signal [siɲal] m. Signal ; *signal d'alarme,* alarm signal; *signal du départ,* signal for departure. ‖ Ch. de f. *Signal avancé,* distant signal. ‖ Autom. *Signaux de route,* road signs. ‖ Naut. *Signaux à bras,* semaphore signals.
signalé, ée [-le] adj. Fig. Signal, noteworthy (service); resounding (victoire).
signalement [-lmɑ̃] m. Jur. Description.
signaler [-le] v. tr .(1). To display (son courage); to draw attention to, to point out, to notify (une faute); to mark, to characterize (un règne) ; to record (un résultat). ‖ Jur. To give a description of (un malfaiteur); to notify (qqch.); to report (à, to) [qqn]. ‖ Naut. To signal (un navire). ‖ Ch. de f. To signal (un train).
— v. pr. **Se signaler,** to distinguish oneself, to make oneself conspicuous.
signalétique [-letik] adj. Jur. Descriptive (état). ‖ Milit. *Feuillet signalétique,* history sheet.
signaleur [-lœ:r] m. Milit. Signaller. ‖ Ch. de f. Signalman.

signalisation [-lizasjɔ̃] f. Signalling. ‖ CH. DE F. Signal-system. ‖ AUTOM. *Signalisation routière*, road signs (signaux).

signaliser [-lize] v. tr. To mark with signs.

signataire [siɲatɛ:r] s. Signatory, signer.

signature [-ty:r] f. Signing (action); signature (nom); *apposer sa signature*, to sign, to set one's hand to; *avoir la signature*, to be authorized to sign for a firm.

signe [siɲ] m. Sign, gesture (geste); *faire signe à qqn*, to nod (ou) beckon to s.o.; *faire un signe d'adieu*, to wave good-bye; *faire signe d'entrer*, to beckon in; *signe de tête*, nod; *signe des yeux*, wink. ‖ Sign (indice); token, mark (d'amitié); sign, indication (de pluie); *signe des temps*, sign of the times; *signes de vie*, signs of life. ‖ Mark, sign (marque). ‖ GRAMM. *Signes de ponctuation*, punctuation marks. ‖ ASTRON. *Signes du zodiaque*, signs of the zodiac. ‖ MÉD. Mark, spot, birthmark (sur le corps); sign, symptom (de maladie). ‖ MATH. Sign, symbol; *signe moins, plus*, minus, plus sign. ‖ ECCLÉS. *Faire le signe de la croix*, to make the sign of the cross, to cross oneself. ‖ MILIT. *Signes de grade*, badges of rank. ‖ JUR. *Signes extérieurs*, external signs; *signes particuliers*, special peculiarities.

signer [-ɲe] v. tr. (1). To sign, to put one's name to (un document); to sign (une lettre); *ne pas savoir signer son nom*, to be unable to write one's own name. ‖ To stamp (de l'argenterie).
— v. intr. To sign; to put one's name (*à*, to).
— v. pr. **Se signer**, ECCLÉS. To make the sign of the cross, to cross oneself.

signet [-ɲɛ] m. Book-mark, tassel.

signifiant [siɲifjɑ̃] m. GRAMM. Signifier, signifiant.

significatif, ive [-fikatif, i:v] adj. Significant, meaning (geste, regard). ‖ MATH. Significant (chiffre).

signification [-fikasjɔ̃] f. Signification, sense, meaning, import. ‖ JUR. Notification, serving, service (d'un acte judiciaire).

significativement [-fikativmɑ̃] adv. Significantly.

signifié [-fje] m. GRAMM. Signified, signifié.

signifier [-fje] v. tr. (1). To signify, to declare, to make known (déclarer); *signifier sa volonté*, to make one's wishes clear. ‖ To signify, to mean (vouloir dire); *cela signifie la ruine pour*, that spells ruin for; *que signifie ce mot-là?*, what does that word mean?, what is the meaning of that word? ‖ JUR. To serve (un exploit); to notify (un jugement).

silence [silɑ̃:s] m. Silence; *garder le silence*, to keep silent, to hold one's peace; *imposer silence à qqn*, to make s.o. keep silent; *passer qqch. sous silence*, to pass over sth. in silence, to ignore sth. ‖ Still, hush, silence (de la nuit). ‖ MUS. Rest.

silencieusement [silɑ̃sjøzmɑ̃] adv. Silently.

silencieux, euse [-sjø, ø:z] adj. Quiet, still, peaceful (lieu). ‖ Noiseless (machine à écrire). ‖ Quiet, silent (personne). [V. TACITURNE.]
— m. AUTOM. Silencer, U. S. muffler.

silésien, enne [silezjɛ̃, ɛn] adj., s. GÉOGR. Silesian.

silex [silɛks] m. Silex, flint.

silhouette [silwɛt] f. Silhouette, outline.

silhouetter [-te] v. tr. (1). To silhouette, to outline.
— v. pr. **Se silhouetter**, to stand out, to be silhouetted (*contre*, against).

silicate [silikat] m. CHIM. Silicate.

silice [silis] f. CHIM. Silica.

siliceux, euse [-sø, ø:z] adj. CHIM. Siliceous.

silicique [-sik] adj. CHIM. Silicic.

silicium [-sjɔm] m. CHIM. Silicon.

siliciure [-sjy:r] m. CHIM. Silicide.

silicone [-kɔn] m. CHIM. Silicone.

silicose [-ko:z] f. MÉD. Silicosis.

silique [silik] f. BOT. Siliqua, silique.

siliqueux, euse [-kø, ø:z] adj. BOT. Siliquose, siliquous.

sillage [sija:ʒ] m. NAUT. Seaway (espace); wake, wash (trace). ‖ AVIAT. Slip-stream (de l'hélice). ‖ TECHN. Continuation of a vein (de charbon). ‖ FIG. Wake; *marcher dans le sillage de qqn*, to follow in s.o.'s wake (ou) footsteps.

sillet [sijɛ] m. MUS. Nut (d'un instrument).

sillomètre [sijɔmɛtr] m. NAUT. Speed indicator.

sillon [sijɔ̃] m. AGRIC. Furrow. ‖ Pl. Furrows, wrinkles, lines (rides). ‖ FIG. Trail (de feu); *creuser son sillon*, to plough one's own furrow.

sillonner [-ɔne] v. tr. (1). AGRIC., NAUT., FIG. To furrow.

silo [silo] m. AGRIC. Silo.

silo-coopérative [silokɔɔperativ] f. Grain-storage Cooperative.

silotage [silɔta:ʒ] m. AGRIC. Ensilage.

siloter [-te] v. tr. To silo, to ensile, to silage.

silure [silyr] m. ZOOL. Silurus.

simagrée [simagre] f. Pretence. ‖ Pl. Affected airs, affectation (v. MINAUDERIE); *faire des simagrées*, to put on airs, to mince.

simarre [simar] f. † Simar (de femme). ‖ JUR. Simar, cassock (de magistrat).

simien [simjɛ̃] m. ZOOL. Simian.

simiesque [simjɛsk] adj. ZOOL. Simian, ape-like.

similaire [similɛ:r] adj. Similar, like.

similairement [-lɛrmɑ̃] adv. Similarly; in like manner.

similarité [-larite] f. Similarity, likeness.

simili [-li] préf. FAM. Imitation, artificial; *similimarbre*, imitation marble; *similipierre*, artificial stone.
— m. FAM. Imitation; *parure en simili*, imitation jewellery.

simili, similigravure [-ligravy:r] f. TECHN. Half-tone engraving.

similiste [-list] m. Half-tone etcher.

similitude [-lityd] f. Similitude, resemblance (de deux objets). ‖ GRAMM. Simile, analogy. ‖ MATH. Similarity.

simoniaque [simɔnjak] adj. Simoniacal.
— m. Simoniac.

simonie [-ni] f. Simony.

simoun [simun] m. Simoom.

simple [sɛ̃:pl] adj. Simple, guileless, naive, innocent (naïf); *un cœur simple*, a simple heart. ‖ Silly (simplet); *simple d'esprit*, half-witted. ‖ Common, simple (ordinaire); plain (nourriture); humble (origine); unpretentious (parure); plain, unvarnished (récit); plain, simple (robe); unaffected, natural (style). ‖ Mere, bare (seul, unique); *c'est une simple question de*, it is only a question (ou) matter of; *pur et simple*, pure and simple; *votre simple parole suffit*, your word alone is enough. ‖ CH. DE F. *Billet simple*, single ticket, single. ‖ ECCLÉS., BOT., GRAMM. Simple. ‖ MILIT. *Simple soldat*, private soldier, private. ‖ NAUT. *Avaries simples*, particular average; *simple matelot*, ordinary seaman. ‖ FIN. Open (cheque). ‖ COMM. Ordinary (facture). ‖ FAM. *Simple comme bonjour*, as easy as winking (ou) as kiss-your-hand; dead easy; « couldn't be simpler ».
— m. Simple; *passer du simple au composé*, to pass from the simple to the compound. ‖ Simple (ou) simple-hearted person (personne). ‖ SPORTS. Single (personne); *simple messieurs*, men's single (ou) singles. ‖ Pl. BOT. Simples.

simplement [-pləmɑ̃] adv. Simply, plainly (sans recherche). ‖ Simply, unaffectedly, naturally, unceremoniously (sans façon). ‖ Simply, purely (uniquement); *purement et simplement*, purely and simply.

simplet, ette [-plɛ, ɛt] adj. Silly, artless; rather stupid.
— m. Fᴀᴍ. Charlie (pop.).
simplicité [-plisite] f. Simplicity (des habits, des mœurs). ‖ Simplicity, simpleness, ingenuousness (v. ɴᴀïᴠᴇᴛᴇ́); naturalness (v. ɴᴀᴛᴜʀᴇʟ); artlessness, silliness. (V. sᴏᴛᴛɪsᴇ.)
simplifiable [sɛ̃plifjabl] adj. Capable of simplification.
simplificateur, trice [-fikatœ:r, tris] adj. Simplifying.
— s. Simplifier.
simplification [-fikasjɔ̃] f. Simplification.
simplifier [-fje] v. tr. (1). To simplify. ‖ Mᴀᴛʜ. To reduce to its lowest terms (une fraction).
— v. pr. Se simplifier, to become simplified.
simplisme [sɛ̃plism] m. Over-simplification.
simpliste [-plist] adj. Over-simple.
— s. Simple-minded person; Simple Simon (fam.).
simulacre [simylakr] m. Simulacrum. (V. ꜰᴀɴᴛᴏ̂ᴍᴇ.) ‖ Fɪɢ. Sham, pretence, semblance.
simulateur, trice [-latœ:r, tris] s. Simulator. ‖ ‖ Mɪʟɪᴛ. Malingerer; lead-swinger (fam.).
— m. Tᴇᴄʜɴ. Simulator.
simulation [-lasjɔ̃] f. Simulation, pretence. ‖ Mɪʟɪᴛ. Malingering, lead-swinging (fam.).
simulé, ée [-le] adj. Mɪʟɪᴛ. Sham (combat); feigned (maladie). ‖ Jᴜʀ. Bogus (acte, vente); counterfeit (contrat).
simuler [-le] v. tr. (1). To simulate (v. ꜰᴇɪɴᴅʀᴇ); *simuler la colère,* to feign anger, to pretend to be angry. ‖ Mɪʟɪᴛ. *Simuler une maladie,* to malinger; to swing the lead (fam.). ‖ Jᴜʀ. To forge, to counterfeit (un document).
simultané, ée [simyltane] adj. Simultaneous. ‖ Tʜᴇ́ᴀ̂ᴛʀ. *Décor simultané,* multiple setting.
simultanéisme [-ism] m. Use of simultaneous action (dans un récit).
simultanéité [-ite] f. Simultaneousness, simultaneity.
simultanément [-mɑ̃] adv. Simultaneously.
sinapisé, ée [sinapise] adj. Mᴇ́ᴅ. *Cataplasme sinapisé,* mustard plaster.
sinapiser v. tr. (1). Mᴇ́ᴅ. To add mustard to.
sinapisme [-pism] m. Mᴇ́ᴅ. Sinapism, mustard plaster.
sincère [sɛ̃sɛ:r] adj. Candid (opinion); sincere, frank, open (personne); sincere, real, genuine (sentiment). [V. ꜰʀᴀɴᴄ.]
sincèrement [-sɛrmɑ̃] adv. Sincerely, frankly, openly, genuinely.
sincérité [-serite] f. Sincerity, frankness, openness (d'une personne); sincerity, genuineness (d'un sentiment). [V. ꜰʀᴀɴᴄʜɪsᴇ.]
sinécure [sineky:r] f. Sinecure.
sine die [sinedje] loc. adv. Sine die.
sine qua non [-kwanɔn] loc. adj. Indispensable, sine qua non; *condition sine qua non,* sine qua non.
Singapour [sɛ̃gapu:r] m. Gᴇ́ᴏɢʀ. Singapore.
singe [sɛ̃:ʒ] m. Zᴏᴏʟ. Monkey, ape. ‖ Mɪʟɪᴛ., Fᴀᴍ. Bully beef. ‖ Fɪɢ. Imitator; ape. ‖ Fᴀᴍ. *Laid comme un singe,* as ugly as sin; *malin comme un singe,* as artful as a box of monkeys. ‖ Pᴏᴘ. Boss, guv'nor (patron).
singer [sɛ̃ʒe] v. tr. (7). To ape, to imitate, to mimic, to take off.
singerie [-ʒri] f. Grimace, antic, monkey-trick, U. S. monkeyshine (grimace). ‖ Copy, imitation (imitation). ‖ Affectation, mincing (simagrée).
singeur, euse [-ʒœ:r, ø:z] adj. Imitating, copying, aping.
— s. Imitator, ape.
single [singəl] m. Single room (dans un hôtel); single compartment (dans un wagon-lit).
singulariser [sɛ̃gylarize] v. tr. (1). To singularize, to make conspicuous, to make stand out.

— v. pr. Se singulariser, to make oneself conspicuous, to make oneself noticed.
singularité [-larite] f. Singularity, oddness, peculiarity.
singulier [-lje] adj. † Single (combat). ‖ Gʀᴀᴍᴍ. Singular (nombre). ‖ Fɪɢ. Peculiar, strange, odd, queer, bizarre (bizarre).
— m. Gʀᴀᴍᴍ. Singular; *au singulier,* in the singular.
singulièrement [-ljɛrmɑ̃] adv. Singularly (beaucoup). ‖ Peculiarly, strangely, oddly, queerly (bizarrement). ‖ Singularly, remarkably, outstandingly (notamment).
sinisant, ante [sinizɑ̃, ɑ̃:t] s. Sinologist.
sinistre [sinistr] adj. Sinister, fatal (événement); sinister, wicked, evil (personnage); sinister (sourire); ominous (symptôme).
— m. Conflagration (incendie). ‖ Disaster, calamity (catastrophe). ‖ Jᴜʀ. Loss, damage (perte).
sinistré, ée [-tre] adj. Damaged, wrecked.
— s. Victim of a disaster.
sinistrement [-trəmɑ̃] adv. Sinisterly.
Sinn-Fein [sinfɛn] m. Sinn Fein.
sinologie [sinɔlɔʒi] f. Sinology.
sinologue [-lɔg] s. Sinologue, sinologist.
sinon [sinɔ̃] conj. Otherwise, if not, or else (autrement, sans quoi). ‖ Except, unless, save (si ce n'est).
sinople [sinɔpl] m. Bʟᴀs. Sinople.
sinué, ée [sinɥe] adj. Bᴏᴛ. Sinuate.
sinueux, euse [-ø, ø:z] adj. Sinuous, winding (chemin); meandering (rivière).
sinuosité [-ozite] f. Sinuosity, winding (d'un chemin); meandering (d'une rivière).
sinus [sinys] m. Mᴇ́ᴅ. Sinus (frontal, maxillaire); antrum (maxillaire supérieur). ‖ Mᴀᴛʜ. Sine.
sinusite [-zit] f. Mᴇ́ᴅ. Sinusitis.
sinusoïdal, ale [-sɔidal] adj. Mᴀᴛʜ. Sinusoidal.
sinusoïde [-sɔid] f. Mᴀᴛʜ. Sinusoid.
sionisme [sjɔnism] m. Zionism.
sioniste [-nist] adj., s. Zionist.
siphoïde [sifɔid] adj. Siphonal, siphoniform.
siphon [sifɔ̃] m. Siphon (d'eau de Seltz). ‖ Trap (d'évier). ‖ Pʜʏs. Siphon.
siphonné, ée [-ne] adj. Pᴏᴘ. Nuts, crackers, loony, off his rocker. (V. ᴅɪɴɢᴜᴇ, ᴛᴏᴏ̨ᴜᴇ́.)
siphonner [-ne] v. tr. (1). To siphon.
sire [si:r] m. † Lord (*de,* of) [seigneur]. ‖ Sire (titre). ‖ Fᴀᴍ. *Un pauvre sire,* a poor specimen.
sirène [sirɛn] f. Siren (femme). ‖ Siren, hooter (d'usine). ‖ Nᴀᴜᴛ. Fog-horn. ‖ Zᴏᴏʟ. Siren. ‖ † Mermaid.
sirocco [sirɔko] m. Sirocco.
sirop [sirɔ] m. Syrup; *sirop de groseille,* redcurrant syrup.
siroter [-te] v. tr. (1). To sip.
sirupeux, euse [sirypø, ø:z] adj. Syrupy.
sis, ise [si, iz] adj. Situated (*à,* in).
sisal [sisal] m. Bᴏᴛ. Sisal; *fibre de sisal,* sisal-hemp (ou) -fibre.
sismal, ale [sismal] adj. Seismal.
sismicité [-misite] f. Seismicity, seismic activity.
sismique [-mik] adj. Seismic.
sismographe [-mɔgraf] m. Seismograph.
sismographie [-mɔgrafi] f. Seismography.
sismologie [-mɔlɔʒi] f. Seismology.
sismomètre [-mɔmɛtr] m. Seismometer.
sistre [sistr] m. Mᴜs. Sistrum.
sitar [sita:r] m. Mᴜs. Sitar.
site [sit] m. Site, spot, landscape. ‖ Mɪʟɪᴛ. *Angle de site,* angle of sight.
sit-in [sitin] m. Sit-in (manifestation).
sitôt [sito] adv. As soon, so soon; *il ne viendra pas de sitôt,* it will be some time before he comes; *sitôt que,* as soon as.
situation [sitɥasjɔ̃] f. Position (attitude, pos-

ture) ; *dans une situation peu confortable,* in an uncomfortable position. ‖ State, condition (condition, état) ; *dans une triste situation,* in a sorry plight ; *roman à situations,* situational novel. ‖ Situation, site, position (position) ; *être en situation de,* to be in a position to. ‖ Position, office, situation, job (poste) ; *chercher une situation,* to look for a job. ‖ Report, statement, return (compte rendu). ‖ Situation (état de choses) ; *l'homme de la situation,* the man for the job ; *mot de la situation,* right (ou) appropriate word. ‖ THÉÂTR. Situation. ‖ FIN. *Situation en banque,* position at the bank ; *situation financière,* financial position ; *dans une bonne situation,* in a strong position. ‖ MILIT. Return, report.

situé, ée [-tɥe] adj. Situated, placed, located.

situer [-tɥe] v. tr. (1). To situate, to site, to place, to locate.
— v. pr. **Se situer,** to be situated.

six [si, sis, siz] adj. num. Six ; *Charles VI,* Charles the Sixth. ‖ **Six-huit,** m. inv. MUS. Six-eight time, six-eight. ‖ **Six-quatre-deux** (à la), loc. adv. FAM. Any old how.
— m. Six ; *le six juin,* the sixth of June. ‖ Six (aux cartes).

sixain [siksɛ̃] m. Sixain, six line stanza (ou) poem.

sixième [sizjɛm] adj. num. Sixth ; *arriver sixième,* to come sixth.
— m. Sixth, sixth part. ‖ Sixth floor (étage) ; *demeurer au sixième,* to live on the sixth floor.
— f. First form (dans un lycée).

sixièmement [-mɑ̃] adv. Sixthly.

six-mâts [sima] m. NAUT. Six-masted vessel ; six-master.

sixte [sikst] f. MUS. Sixth. ‖ SPORTS. Sixte.

sizain [sizɛ̃] m. Sixain, six line stanza (ou) poem.

S. J. [ɛsʒi] abrév. de *Compagnie (ou) Société de Jésus,* S. J., Jesuit.

Skaï [skaj] m. (nom déposé). Leatherette.

skateboard, skate [skɛtbɔrd] m. SPORTS. Skateboard.

skating [sketiɲ] m. SPORTS. Skating-rink (lieu) ; roller-skating (patinage).

sketch [skɛtʃ] (pl. **sketches**] m. THÉÂTR. Sketch, playlet.

ski [ski] m. SPORTS. Ski ; *faire du ski,* to ski, to go ski-ing, to go in for ski-ing ; *ski nautique,* water-ski-ing.

skiable [-abl] adj. SPORTS. Good-ski-ing (neige).

skier [-e] v. intr. (1). To ski.

skieur [-œːr] s. Skier.

skiff [skif] m. NAUT. Skiff.

skip [skip] m. TECHN. Skip.

skipper [skipər] m. NAUT. Skipper (commandant de bord).

skunks [skɔnks] n. ZOOL., COMM. Skunk.

slalom [slalɔm] m. SPORTS. Slalom.

slalomer [-me] v. intr. (1). To slalom.

slalomeur, euse [-mœːr, øːz] s. SPORTS. Slalom racer (ou) specialist.

slave [slav] adj. GÉOGR. Slav, Slavonic.
— s. GÉOGR. Slav.
— m. GRAMM. Slavic, slavonic (langue).

slavisant [-vizɑ̃] s. Slavist.

slavon, onne [-vɔ̃, ɔn] adj., s. Slavonian.

slavophile [-vɔfil] adj., s. Slavophil.

sleeping [slipiɲ] m. CH. DE F. Sleeping-car.

slip [slip] m. Slips (vêtement) ; U. S. briefs (d'homme) ; panties (de femme). ‖ NAUT. Slipway. SPORTS. Slip ; U. S. supporter.

slogan [slɔgɑ̃] m. Slogan, catch-phrase.

sloop [slup] m. NAUT. Sloop.

slovaque [slɔvak] adj., s. GÉOGR. Slovak.

slovène [slovɛn] adj., s. Slovene.

slow [slo] m. Slow fox-trot.

S.M. [ɛsɛm] abrév. de *Sa Majesté,* H.M., Her (ou) His Majesty.

smalah [smala] f. Retinue of Arab chief. ‖ FAM. Large family, brood.

smalt [smalt] m. Smalt.

smaltine [-tin] f. Smaltine.

smash [smaʃ] m. SPORTS. Smash (au tennis).

smasher [smaʃe] v. tr. et intr. (1). SPORTS. To smash (au tennis).

S.M.I.C. [smik] m. Abrév. de *salaire minimum (interprofessionnel) de croissance,* minimum legal wage.

smicard, arde [-kaːr, ard] s. Worker paid minimum legal wage.

smocks [smɔk] m. pl. Smocking (en couture).

smoking [smɔkiɲ] m. Dinner-jacket, U. S. tuxedo.

snack-bar [snakbar] m. Snack-bar.

S.N.C.F. [ɛsɛnseɛf] f. Abrév. de *Société nationale des chemins de fer français,* French railways.

snob [snɔb] adj. Fashionable ; up to the minute ; all the rage ; swell.
— s. Snob ; swanky person. (V. VANITEUX.)

snober [-be] v. tr. (1). To snub, to cut dead, to cut.

snobinard, arde [-binaːr, ard] adj. Snobbish, snobby, snotty, stuck-up.
— s. Snob, snot.

snobisme [-bism] m. Snobbery.

snow-boot [snobut] m. Snow-boot.

sobre [sɔbr] adj. Temperate, abstemious (personne) ; frugal (repas) ; sober (vie). ‖ FIG. Moderate ; *être sobre de louanges,* to be sparing in one's praise.

sobrement [-b.əmɑ̃] adv. Temperately, frugally, soberly.

sobriété [-briete] f. Sobriety, moderation, temperance, abstemiousness. (V. FRUGALITÉ.) ‖ ARTS. Restraint.

sobriquet [sɔbrikɛ] m. Sobriquet ; nickname.

soc [sɔk] m. AGRIC. Ploughshare.

sociabilité [sɔsjabilite] f. Sociability, sociableness.

sociable [-ʒjabl] adj. Sociable ; *il n'est pas sociable,* he's unsociable, he's not a good mixer.

social, ale [sɔsjal] adj. Social (contrat, science) ; *guerre sociale,* class war ; *service social,* social welfare, U. S. social service. ‖ COMM. Trading (année) ; registered (capital) ; *raison sociale,* firm's name (ou) style.

socialement [-lmɑ̃] adv. Socially.

socialisant, ante [-lizɑ̃, ɑ̃:t] adj. Socialistic, with socialist tendencies ; socially orientated.

socialisation [-lizasjɔ̃] f. Socialization.

socialiser [-lize] v. tr. (1). To socialize.

socialisme [-lism] m. Socialism.

socialiste [-list] adj. Socialist, socialistic.
— s. Socialist.

sociétaire [sɔsjeteːr] s. Full member.

sociétariat [-tarja] m. Membership (d'une société).

société [-te] f. Society, gathering, company (compagnie) ; *saluer la société,* to greet the company present ; *société nombreuse,* large gathering. ‖ Society, community (corps social) ; *chaque famille forme une société naturelle,* each family constitutes a natural group ; *devoirs envers la société,* duties towards society (ou) the community ; *vivre en société,* to live in a community. ‖ Society (grand monde) ; *fréquenter la haute société,* to move in fashionable circles. ‖ Society (association) ; *Société des Nations,* League of Nations ; *société de secours mutuels,* friendly society. ‖ COMM. Society, company, firm ; *acte de société,* deed of partnership ; *société anonyme, par actions,* limited, joint-stock company ; *société en participation,* joint enterprise.

socioculturel, elle [sɔsjokyltyrɛl] adj. Socio-cultural.

sociodrame [-dram] m. PSYCH. Sociodrama.

socio-économique [-ekɔnɔmik] adj. Socio-economic.

socio-éducatif, ive [-edykatif, i:v] adj. Educational, cultural.

sociogramme [-gram] m. PSYCH. Sociogram.

sociolinguistique [-lɛ̃gɥistik] f. GRAMM. Socio-linguistics.

sociologie [sɔsjɔlɔʒi] f. Sociology.

sociologique [-lɔʒik] adj. Sociological.

sociologue [-lɔg] s. Sociologist.

sociométrie [-metri] f. PSYCH. Sociometry.

socioprofessionnel, elle [-prɔfɛsjɔnɛl] adj. Socioprofessional; *groupe, statut socioprofessionnel*, group, status as determined by occupation.

socle [sɔkl] m. Pedestal (de statue). ‖ ARCHIT. Footing (de mur). ‖ ELECTR. *Socle isolant*, insulating base. ‖ TECHN. Bed-plate (de machine).

socque [sɔk] m. Clog, patten. ‖ † Sock (d'acteur comique). ‖ FIG. Comedy.

socquette [sɔkɛt] f. Ankle sock, anklet, bobby-sock.

socratique [sɔkratik] adj. Socratic.

soda [sɔda] m. Soda; soda-water.

sodé, ée [sɔde] adj. CHIM. Soda; *chaux sodée*, soda lime. ‖ MÉD. Sodium.

sodique [sɔdik] adj. CHIM. Sodic.

sodium [-djɔm] m. CHIM. Sodium.

sodomie [sɔdɔmi] f. Sodomy.

sodomite [-mit] s. Sodomite.

sœur [sœ:r] f. Sister; *de sœur*, sisterly, sororal; *sœur de lait*, foster-sister; *sœur utérine*, half-sister. ‖ ECCLÉS. Sister, nun. ‖ FIG. Sister; *les neu Sœurs*, the Muses.

sœurette [sœrɛt] f. FAM. Little sister.

sofa [sɔfa] m. Sofa.

software [sɔftwɛ:r] m. INFORM. Software.

soi [swa] pron. pers. Oneself; himself, herself, itself; *à part soi*, to oneself; *chacun pour soi*, everyone for himself; *de soi, en soi*, in itself; *être soi*, to be oneself; *parler de soi*, to talk about oneself; *sur soi*, on one, about one's person; *vivre pour soi seul*, to live for oneself alone. ‖ **Soi-disant**, adj. invar. So-called, self-styled, would-be; alleged, supposed (v. PRÉTENDU); loc. adv. Supposedly; *il est parti soi-disant pour revenir*, he left on the understanding that he would be coming back. ‖ **Soi-même**, pron. Oneself.

soie [swa] f. Silk; *robe de soie*, silk dress; *soie artificielle*, artificial silk, rayon. ‖ Thread (d'araignée). ‖ Tang (de couteau). ‖ Bristle (de porc).

soierie [-ri] f. Silk, silks, silk-goods (étoffe). ‖ Silk-factory (fabrique).

soif [swaf] f. Thirst; *avoir soif*, to be thirsty; *boire à sa soif*, to drink one's fill. ‖ FIG. Thirst, lust; *soif de l'or*, thirst for gold; *soif de revanche*, craving for revenge; *soif du sang*, blood-lust.

soiffard, arde [-fa:r, ard] s. POP. Soaker, boozer, toper.

soigné, ée [swaɲe] adj. Trim, well-groomed (air); well-kept (jardin). ‖ COMM. Soigné, finished. ‖ MÉD. Nursed, doctored; tended. ‖ CULIN. First-rate, well-cooked (repas). ‖ FIG. Polished (style).

soigner v. tr. (1). To care for, to look after, to see to (une bête). ‖ To look after (ses mains); *soigner sa mise*, to dress with care. ‖ COMM. To finish. ‖ MÉD. To nurse, to tend (un malade) [infirmière]; to attend (médecin); to attend to, (sa santé); *se faire soigner*, to have medical treatment. ‖ FIG. To nurse (sa popularité); to polish (son style).
— v. pr. **Se soigner**, to look after oneself, to take care of oneself. ‖ MÉD. To doctor oneself (à, with). ‖ FAM. To coddle oneself (se dorloter).

soigneur [-ɲœ:r] m. SPORTS. Second (de boxeur).

soigneusement [-ɲøzmɑ̃] adv. Carefully.

soigneux, euse [-ɲø, ø:z] adj. Careful, painstaking (ouvrier); meticulous (recherches); *soigneux de sa réputation*, mindful of one's good name.

soin [swɛ̃] m. Care, pains (application, efforts); *avec soin*, carefully; *avoir grand soin de faire*, to take good care to do; *prendre grand soin de qqch.*, to take great care of sth.; *sans soin*, carelessly; *un* (ou) *une sans soin*, a careless (ou) slovenly person. ‖ Pl. Care, attention (sollicitude); *aux bons soins de*, care of, c/o; *être aux petits soins pour qqn*, to wait on s.o. hand and foot, to dance attendance on s.o.; *mettre tous ses soins à faire qqch.*, to do sth. with great care, to be at great pains to do sth.; *par les soins de*, thanks to, through the good offices of. ‖ MÉD. *Soins de beauté*, beauty treatment; *soins médicaux*, medical care (ou) attention; *premiers soins*, first aid; *recevoir des soins à l'hôpital*, to be treated in hospital. ‖ COMM. *Apporter tous ses soins à qqch.*, to give sth. one's best attention.

soir [swa:r] m. Evening, eve; afternoon; *à ce soir*, till this evening, till tonight, see you again this evening (ou) tonight; *demain soir, hier soir*, tomorrow evening, yesterday (ou) last evening; *dix heures du soir*, ten o'clock at night; *du matin au soir*, from morn till night; *robe du soir*, evening dress (ou) gown; *tous les soirs*, every evening; *trois heures du soir*, three o'clock in the afternoon; *un beau soir d'été*, a fine summer's evening. ‖ FIG. Evening (de la vie).

soirée [sware] f. Party, evening party, soirée (réunion); *aller en soirée*, to go to a party; *soirée musicale*, musical evening. ‖ Evening (soir); *pendant la soirée*, during the evening, in the course of the evening. ‖ THÉÂTR. Evening performance.

soissons [swasɔ̃] m. pl. CULIN. Soissons kidney (ou) U. S. Navy beans.

soit [swa, swat] loc. ellipt. *Soit!*, so be it!, very well!, agreed!; *vous aimez mieux cela, soit!*, you prefer that, all right then! (V. ÊTRE).
— conj. *Soit... soit, soit... ou*, either... or, whether... or, *soit l'un, soit l'autre*, either one or the other.
— loc. adv. **Tant soit peu**, ever so little.

soixantaine [swasɑ̃tɛn] f. About sixty, approximately sixty, some sixty; *une soixantaine de francs*, sixty francs or so.

soixante [-sɑ̃:t] adj. num. Sixty; *à la page soixante*, on page sixty.
— m. Sixty.

soixantième [-sɑ̃tjɛm] adj. num., m. Sixtieth.

soja [sɔja] m. BOT. Soya-bean, U. S. soybean.

sol [sɔl] m. Ground, earth. ‖ ELECTR. *Au sol*, earthed; U. S. grounded. ‖ **Sol-air**, adj. invar. MILIT. Ground-to-air (projectile).

sol m. invar. MUS. Sol; G.

solaire [sɔlɛ:r] adj. Sun (cadran, rayon, tache); solar (mythe, système). ‖ MÉD. Solar (plexus).

solanées [sɔlane] f. pl. BOT. Solanaceae.

solarium [sɔlarjɔm] m. Solarium.

soldanelle [sɔldanɛl] f. BOT. Soldanella.

soldat [sɔlda] m. Soldier; *se faire soldat*, to enlist, to join the army; to go for a soldier (pop.); *simple soldat*, private; *soldat de première classe*, lance-corporal. ‖ COMM. *Soldat de plomb*, lead (ou) tin (ou) toy soldier.

soldatesque [-tɛsk] f. Undisciplined soldiery, rabble.
— adj. Barrack-room (manières).

solde [sɔld] f. MILIT., NAUT. Pay; *à la solde de l'ennemi*, in the enemy's pay; *toucher sa solde*, to draw one's pay.

solde m. FIN. Balance. ‖ COMM. Surplus stock; remnant; clearance lines, U. S. broken lots (marchandises); clearance sale (vente).

solder [-de] v. tr. (1). Fin. To pay, to discharge, to settle (un mémoire). ‖ Comm. To sell off, to clear (des marchandises).
— v. pr. **Se solder,** to end (ou) result (*par,* in).
soldeur, euse [-dœ:r, ø:z] s. Comm. Dealer in clearance lines.
sole [sɔl] f. Agric. Field, break, plot.
sole f. Sole (de sabot d'un animal). ‖ Naut. Bottom. ‖ Techn. Sole-plate, base-plate (d'un bâti); sole, bed-plate (de four).
sole f. Zool. Sole (poisson).
soléaire [sɔlee:r] adj. Méd. Soleus (muscle).
solécisme [sɔlesism] m. Gramm. Solecism. ‖ Fig. Blunder, slip, mistake, solecism.
soleil [sɔlɛ:j] m. Sun (astre). ‖ Sunshine (lumière); *au soleil,* out in the sun; *jour de soleil,* sunny day; *sans soleil,* sunless. ‖ Méd. *Coup de soleil,* sunstroke. ‖ Bot. Sunflower. ‖ Ecclés. Monstrance. ‖ Techn. Catherine wheel, pin wheel (feu d'artifice). ‖ Fig. *Le Roi-Soleil,* the Sun-King, Louis XIV; *sous le soleil,* under the sun, on earth. ‖ Fam. *Piquer un soleil,* to blush, to go red.
soleilleux, euse [sɔlɛjø, ø:z] adj. Sunny, sunshiny.
solennel, elle [sɔlanɛl] adj. Solemn (air); solemn, majestic (démarche); solemn, grave (personne); solemn, impressive (silence); solemn, formal (vœu); *d'un ton solennel,* in a solemn (ou) grave tone of voice. ‖ Ecclés. Solemn (messe).
solennellement [-nɛlmɑ̃] adv. Solemnly, impressively.
solennisation [-nizasjɔ̃] f. Solemnization, solemnizing.
solenniser [-nize] v. tr. (1). To solemnize.
solennité [-nite] f. Solemnity, ceremony (cérémonie). ‖ Solemnity (emphase).
solénoïde [sɔlenɔid] m. Electr. Solenoid.
solfège [sɔlfɛ:ʒ] m. Mus. Solfeggio; sol-fa.
solfier [-fje] v. tr. (1). To sol-fa, to solmizate.
solidaire [sɔlidɛ:r] adj. Jur. Liable; answerable (*de,* for); responsible (*de,* for) [personne]; joint and several (responsabilité); *obligation solidaire,* obligation binding on all parties. ‖ Fig. Interdependent.
solidairement [-dɛrmɑ̃] adv. Jointly; *conjointement et solidairement,* jointly and severally.
solidariser [-darize] v. tr. (1). Jur. To render jointly liable. ‖ To join (ou) link together.
— v. pr. **Se solidariser,** Jur. To become jointly responsible. ‖ To join together, to make common cause (*avec,* with).
solidarité [-darite] f. Jur. Joint and several liability. ‖ Fig. Solidarity, fellowship, community of interests.
solide [sɔlid] adj. Solid, strong, well-built (bâtiment); solid (corps); hefty, vigorous (coup de poing); robust (personne). ‖ Fig. Staunch, firm, trusty (ami); sound (argument); sterling (qualité); fast (couleur); substantial (raison).
— m. Math., Phys. Solid, solid body.
solidement [-dmɑ̃] adv. Solidly, vigorously; staunchly; soundly.
solidification [-difikasjɔ̃] f. Solidification.
solidifier [-difje] v. tr. (1). To solidify.
— v. pr. **Se solidifier,** to solidify, to become solid.
solidité [-dite] f. Solidity (en général). ‖ Strength, stability (d'un bâtiment). ‖ Méd. Solidity, compactness, hardness (d'un corps); robustness, strength (d'une personne). ‖ Fig. Staunchness (d'un ami); soundness (d'un argument); fastness (d'une couleur).
soliloque [sɔlilɔk] m. Soliloquy.
soliloquer [-ke] v. intr. (1). To talk to oneself.
solipède [sɔlipɛd] adj. Zool. Whole-hoofed.
— m. Zool. Soliped.
solipsisme [sɔlipsism] m. Philos. Solipsism.

soliste [sɔlist] s. Soloist.
— adj. Solo.
solitaire [sɔlitɛ:r] adj. Lonely, secluded, desolate (lieu); lonely, solitary (personne); *mener une vie solitaire,* to live in seclusion, to live a lonely life. ‖ Bot. Solitary (fleur); lone (pin). ‖ Méd. *Ver solitaire,* tapeworm.
— m. Anchorite, recluse, hermit (anachorète). ‖ Solitaire (diamant). ‖ Zool. Old boar (sanglier).
solitairement [-tɛrmɑ̃] adv. Solitarily, alone; in seclusion.
solitude [sɔlityd] f. Solitude, isolation, loneliness (état). ‖ Solitude, wilderness, desert (lieu).
solivage [sɔliva:ʒ] m. Archit. Joisting.
solive [sɔli:v] f. Archit. Joist, beam; *solive de* (ou) *en fer,* girder.
soliveau [sɔlivo] m. Archit. Small joist. ‖ Fig. Nobody, nonentity, King Log.
sollicitation [sɔllisitasjɔ̃] f. Solicitation, supplication, entreaty. ‖ Jur. Petition, appeal.
solliciter [-te] v. tr. (1). To solicit, to beg, to ask for (demander). ‖ To request, to beseech, to entreat (prier); *solliciter qqn de,* to beg s.o. to. ‖ Jur. To appeal to, to petition (un juge). ‖ Phys. To attract (un corps). ‖ Fig. To provoke (la pitié).
solliciteur [-tœ:r] s. Petitioner; applicant.
sollicitude [-tyd] f. Anxiety, worry (inquiétude). ‖ Care, solicitude (soin).
solo [sɔlo] (pl. **solos, soli**) m. Mus. Solo; *solo de piano,* piano solo.
— adj. invar. Solo; *violon solo,* solo violin.
solstice [sɔlstis] m. Solstice; *solstice d'été, d'hiver,* summer, winter solstice.
solsticial, ale [-sjal] adj. Solstitial.
solubiliser [sɔlybilize] v. tr. (1). To make (ou) render soluble.
solubilité [-te] f. Solubility.
soluble [sɔlubl] adj. Soluble (matière). ‖ Solvable (problème).
soluté [sɔlyte] m. Chim., Méd. Solute, solution.
solution [sɔlysjɔ̃] f. Phys., Math., Méd. Solution. ‖ Jur. Discharge (d'une obligation). ‖ Fig. *Solution de continuité,* gap, break; *recevoir une bonne solution,* to be settled in a satisfactory manner.
solutionner [-sjɔne] v. tr. (1). To solve.
solvabilité [sɔlvabilite] f. Fin. Solvency.
solvable [-vabl] adj. Fin. Solvent.
solvant [-vɑ̃] m. Chim. Solvent.
soma [sɔma] m. Méd. Soma.
Somalie [sɔmali] f. Géogr. Somalia.
somatique [sɔmatik] adj. Méd. Somatic, corporeal, physical; *cellules somatiques,* somatic cells.
sombre [sɔ̃:br] adj. Dull, overcast (ciel); dark, sombre (couleur); dim (lumière). ‖ Fig. Sombre, dark, gloomy (avenir); melancholy, taciturn, gloomy (caractère); gloomy, lugubrious (personne).
sombrement [sɔ̃brəmɑ̃] adv. Sombrely; gloomily; darkly.
sombrer [sɔ̃bre] v. intr. (1). Naut. To founder, to sink (navire). ‖ Fig. To be dashed, to come to nought (espérance); to be engulfed, to be wrecked (fortune); to fail, to be destroyed (raison).
sombrero [sɔ̃brero] m. Sombrero.
sommaire [sɔmɛ:r] adj. Short, succinct, brief, concise (exposé); summary (justice); makeshift (réparation).
— m. Summary, synopsis.
sommairement [-mɑ̃] adj. Summarily; briefly.
sommation [sɔmasjɔ̃] f. Jur. Summons; *faire les trois sommations légales,* to read the riot act. ‖ Fig. Invitation, summons.
sommation f. Math. Summation.
somme [sɔm] f. Load, burden (fardeau); *bête de somme,* beast of burden.
somme f. Sum; *une grosse somme,* a large sum

of money. ‖ Amount; *faire la somme de deux nombres*, to add up two numbers, to add two numbers together; *somme totale*, total amount. ‖ NAUT. Sand-bank (banc de sable). ‖ ECCLÉS. Summa Theologica. ‖ FIG. Sum, total. — loc. adv. *En somme, somme toute*, in short, when all is said and done.

somme m. Nap, doze, short sleep, snooze (fam.); *faire un somme*, to take (ou) have a nap; to have forty winks (fam.).

sommeil [sɔmɛːj] m. Sleep; *avoir sommeil*, to be (ou) feel sleepy; *sans sommeil*, sleepless; *tomber de sommeil*, to be ready to drop. ‖ MÉD. *Maladie du sommeil*, sleeping sickness. ‖ FIG. Sleep; state of inertia (ou) inactivity; *en sommeil*, in abeyance, in a state of suspended animation (entreprise); *sommeil éternel*, eternal rest.

sommeiller [sɔmɛje] v. intr. (1). To sleep, to slumber, to doze, to nod. ‖ FIG. To be dormant.

sommelier [sɔməlje] m. Butler (dans une maison). ‖ Wine-waiter (dans un restaurant).

sommellerie [-mɛlri] f. Butlership (fonction). ‖ Butler's pantry (lieu).

sommer [sɔme] v. tr. (1). MATH. To sum up, to find the sum of (une série).

sommer v. tr. (1). To summon, to call; *sommer qqn de*, to call on s.o. to.

sommes [sɔm]. V. ÊTRE (48).

sommet [sɔmɛ] m. Summit, top. ‖ MATH. Vertex (d'un angle); apex (of a triangle). ‖ FIG. Acme, zenith, top, peak.

sommier [sɔmje] m. Beast of burden, pack-animal (bête de somme). ‖ Mattress (de lit); *sommier élastique*, spring- (ou) box-mattress. ‖ MUS. Wind-chest (d'orgue). ‖ ARCHIT. Lintel, transom (de porte); springer (de voûte). ‖ TECHN. Beam (d'une balance); stock (de cloche); double hoop (de futaille); cross-bar (de grille); bed (de machine).

sommier m. FIN., COMM. Register.

sommité [sɔmite] f. Summit, top. (V. SOMMET.) ‖ FIG. Leader, outstanding person; *une sommité de la littérature*, a leading light in literature.

somnambule [sɔmnãbyl] adj. Somnambulant, somnambulistic. — s. Somnambulist, somnambulant, sleep-walker.

somnambulisme [-lism] m. Somnambulism, sleepwalking; *somnambulisme provoqué*, hypnotism.

somnifère [sɔmnifɛːr] adj. MÉD. Soporific, sleepinducing. ‖ FAM. Boring, dull, tedious. — m. MÉD. Soporific, sleeping-pill.

somnolence [sɔmnɔlãːs] f. Somnolence, sleepiness.

somnolent, ente [-lã, ãːt] adj. Somnolent, sleepy.

somnoler [-le] v. intr. (1). To doze, to drowse.

somptuaire [sɔ̃ptɥɛːr] adj. JUR. Sumptuary.

somptueusement [-øzmã] adv. Sumptuously.

somptueux, euse [-ø, øːz] adj. Munificent, lavish (personne). ‖ Costly, magnificent, sumptuous (repas).

somptuosité [-ozite] f. Sumptuousness.

son [sɔ̃], (f. **sa** [sa]; pl. **ses** [se]) adj. poss. His, her, its, one's.

son m. Sound; ringing (d'une cloche); chink (de l'or); sound, beat, beating (du tambour); sound, blare (de la trompette).

son m. Bran; *eau de son*, bran-water. ‖ MILIT. *Boule de son*, ration loaf. ‖ FAM. *Tache de son*, freckle; *taché de son*, freckled.

sonar [sɔnaːr] m. TECHN., NAUT. Sonar.

sonate [sɔnat] f. MUS. Sonato.

sonatine [-tin] f. MUS. Sonatina.

sondage [sɔ̃daːʒ] m. Boring (action). ‖ Bore-hole, drill hole (trou de sonde). ‖ Poll, survey (enquête); *sondage d'opinion*, opinion poll (ou) survey; *enquête par sondage*, sample survey. ‖ NAUT. Sounding. ‖ MÉD. Probing (d'une plaie).

sonde [sɔ̃ːd] f. Drill, borer (dans une mine). ‖ NAUT. Lead; *grande, petite sonde*, hand-, deepsea lead; *jeter la sonde*, to heave the lead; *naviguer à la sonde*, to navigate by soundings. ‖ MÉD. Probe; *sonde œsophagienne*, probang. ‖ ASTRONAUT. *Sonde spatiale*, space probe. ‖ CULIN. *Sonde à fromage*, cheese taster.

sonder [sɔ̃de] v. tr. (1). NAUT. To sound, to take soundings in. ‖ MÉD. To probe (une plaie). ‖ CULIN. To try, to taste (du fromage). ‖ FIG. To sound, to test; *sonder les dispositions de qqn*, to try to ascertain s.o.'s opinion.

sondeur, euse [-dœːr, øːz] s. Sounder, prober. — m. NAUT. Leadsman.

songe [sɔ̃ːʒ] m. Dream (v. RÊVE); *en songe*, in a dream; *faire un songe*, to have a dream; *le Songe d'une nuit d'été*, Midsummer Night's Dream. ‖ FIG. Dream, illusion. ‖ **Songe-creux**, m. invar. Dreamer, visionary.

songer [sɔ̃ʒe] v. intr. (7). To think of, to intend (avoir l'intention); *songer à se marier*, to think of getting married. ‖ To think over, to consider (considérer); *songez-y bien*, think it over carefully. ‖ To dream, to muse (faire un songe). ‖ To think, to take account (à, of) [penser]; *songer à l'avenir*, to give a thought to the future. ‖ To imagine (s'imaginer); *je ne songeais vraiment pas que*, I never imagined that, little did I think that; *songez un peu!* just fancy!

songerie [-ʒri] f. Dreaming, musing, reverie.

songeur, euse [-ʒœːr, øːz] adj. Dreamy.

sonie [sɔni] f. PHYS. Sone (en acoustique).

sonique [sɔnik] adj. Sound (mur); sonic (vitesse).

sonnaille [-naːj] f. Cow-bell, sheep-bell.

sonnailler [-naje] m. Bell-wether.

sonnailler v. intr. (1). FAM. To be continually ringing. — v. tr. FAM. To ring for continually.

sonnant, ante [-nã, ãːt] adj. Striking; *à huit heures sonnantes*, at eight o'clock precisely; on the stroke of eight; *horloge sonnante*, striking clock. ‖ Sounding, resounding; *espèces sonnantes*, hard cash.

sonné, ée [-ne] adj. Struck, gone (v. RÉVOLU); *il a cinquante ans sonnés*, he's over fifty, he'll never see fifty again; *il est midi sonné*, it's gone twelve. ‖ FAM. Groggy.

sonner [-ne] v. intr. (1). To ring; *sonner à la porte*, to ring at the door. ‖ To peal (carillon); to sound, to peal, to ring (cloche); to toll (glas); to strike (horloge). ‖ To strike (heure); *dix heures sonnent*, it is striking ten; *dix heures viennent de sonner*, it has just struck ten. ‖ ECCLÉS. *La messe sonne*, the bell is ringing for Mass. ‖ FIG. To sound; *faire sonner un mot*, to stress (ou) emphasize a word; *faire sonner une pièce d'argent*, to ring a coin; *sonner creux*, to sound hollow; *sonner faux*, to ring false; *sonner mal à l'oreille*, to offend the ear. — v. tr. To ring (une cloche); to strike (les heures). ‖ To ring for (un domestique). ‖ ECCLÉS. To ring for (la messe). ‖ MILIT. To sound (la charge, la retraite). ‖ POP. *Sonner qqn*, to bang (ou) bash s.o.'s head against sth. ‖ LOC. *Ne sonner mot*, not to say a word; to keep mum.

sonnerie [-nri] f. Chiming, ringing, pealing (de cloches). ‖ Set of bells, chimes (d'une église); *la grosse sonnerie*, full chimes. ‖ Strikingmechanism (de pendule). ‖ *Sonnerie d'alarme, électrique, téléphonique*, alarm-bell, electric bell, telephone bell. ‖ MILIT. Bugle-call, trumpet-call.

sonnet [sɔnɛ] m. ARTS. Sonnet.

sonnette [sɔnɛt] f. Hand-bell, house-bell; *coup de sonnette*, ring; *sonnette électrique*, electric bell. ‖ TECHN. Pile-driver. ‖ ZOOL. *Serpent à sonnettes*, rattle-snake.

sonnettiste [-tist] s. Sonnet-writer, sonneteer.

sonneur [sɔnœ:r] m. Bell-ringer (de cloches);
trumpeter (de trompette).
sono [sɔno] f. FAM. Sound (ou) p. a. system.
sonomètre [sɔnɔmɛtr] m. PHYS. Sonometre.
sonore [sɔnɔ:r] adj. Sonorous, high-sounding
(langage); resonant (métal); resonant, ringing,
sonorous (voix); echoing (voûte). ‖ GRAMM.
Voiced (consonne). ‖ PHYS. *Onde sonore,* sound-
wave. ‖ CINÉM. *Film sonore,* sound-film; *piste
sonore,* sound-track.
sonorisation [sɔnɔrizasjɔ̃] f. Installation of
sound system (*de,* in) [action]. ‖ Sound system,
public address (ou) p. a. system. ‖ GRAMM. Voicing. ‖ CINÉM. Addition of (ou) adding a sound-
track (*de,* to) [d'un film].
sonoriser [sɔnɔrize] v. tr. (1). GRAMM. To voice.
‖ CINÉM. To add the sound-track to (un film).
sonorité [-rite] f. Sonority, sonorousness.
sonothèque [-tɛk] f. Sound archive.
sont [sɔ̃]. V. ÊTRE (48).
sophisme [sɔfism] m. Sophism.
sophiste [-fist] s. Sophist.
— adj. Sophistical.
sophistication [sɔfistikasjɔ̃] f. Sophistication. ‖
Adulteration (du vin).
sophistique [-tik] adj. Sophistical.
— f. Sophistry.
sophistiqué, ée [-ke] adj. Sophisticated (personne, produit) [péjor.].
sophistiquer [-tike] v. intr. (1). To use sophistry.
— v. tr. To adulterate (du vin).
sophistiqueur [-tikœ:r] s. Quibbler. ‖ Adulterator (du vin).
soporatif, ive [sɔpɔratif, i:v]. V. SOPORIFIQUE.
soporeux, euse [-rø, ø:z] adj. MÉD. Comatose.
soporifique [-rifik] adj. Soporific, soporiferous.
— m. Soporific.
sopraniste [sɔpranist] m. MUS. Sopranist.
soprano [-no] m. MUS. Soprano.
sorbe [sɔrb] f. BOT. Sorb-apple.
sorbet [sɔrbɛ] m. CULIN. Sorbet, water-ice;
sherbet.
sorbetière [-bɔtjɛ:r] f. Ice-pail.
sorbier [sɔrbje] m. BOT. Sorb, service-tree; *sorbier sauvage,* rowan-tree, mountain-ash.
sorbonnard [sɔrbɔna:r] m. FAM. Student (or)
professor at the Sorbonne.
sorcellerie [sɔrsɛlri] f. Sorcery.
sorcier [-sje] m. Sorcerer, wizard. ‖ FIG. Wizard.
— adj. FAM. *Ça n'est pas sorcier,* it's not difficult, there's no problem.
sorcière [-sjɛ:r] f. Sorceress, witch. ‖ FAM.
Vieille sorcière, old hag.
sordide [sɔrdid] adj. Base (avarice); filthy, dirty,
squalid (vêtements).
sordidement [-dmɑ̃] adv. Sordidly.
sorgho [sɔrgo] m. AGRIC. Sorghum.
sornette [sɔrnɛt] f. Nonsense, rubbish; twaddle,
tripe (fam.). [V. BALIVERNE.]
sort [sɔ:r] m. Lot, condition (condition); *se
plaindre de son sort,* to complain about one's
lot. ‖ Fate, destiny (destinée); *abandonner qqn
à son sort,* to leave s.o. to his fate. ‖ Chance,
fortune (hasard); *le sort des armes,* the arbitrament of war; *le sort en est jeté,* the die is cast.
‖ Spell, charm (sortilège); *jeter un sort sur,* to
cast a spell on (ou) over.
sortable [sɔrtabl] adj. Suitable.
sortant, ante [-tɑ̃, ɑ̃:t] adj. Going (ou) coming
out (foule); *numéro sortant,* winning number. ‖
JUR. Out-going (député).
— s. Out-goer.
sorte [sɔrt] f. Kind, sort (espèce); *toutes sortes
de bêtes,* all kinds (ou) sorts of animals. ‖ Kind,
stamp, sort (état); *un homme de la sorte,* a man
of that sort, that kind of man. ‖ Manner, way

(façon); *de la sorte,* in that way, like that. ‖
Sort (en typographie).
— loc. adv. En quelque sorte, in a way, as it
were.
— loc. conj. De sorte que, en sorte que, so that,
in such a way that.
sortie [sɔrti] f. Going (ou) coming out (action);
à la sortie de classe, on coming out of school;
examen de sortie, final examination; *faire sa
première sortie après une maladie,* to go out for
the first time after an illness. ‖ Way out, exit
(issue); *maison à deux sorties,* house with two
exits; *sortie de secours,* emergency exit. ‖ COMM.
Export (de marchandises); *droits de sortie,* export
dues. ‖ THÉÂTR. Exit. ‖ MILIT. Sortie, sally. ‖
FIG. Outburst, tirade, diatribe. ‖ Sortie-de-bain,
f. Bathrobe.
sortilège [sɔrtilɛ:ʒ] m. Spell. (V. CHARME.)
sortir [sɔrti:r] v. intr. (93). To go (ou) come
out, to leave; *aller pour sortir,* to make as if
to go, to make a show of leaving; *être sorti,*
to be out; *faire sortir qqn,* to order s.o. out
(ou) to leave (chasser); to bring s.o. out (conduire dans le monde); to take s.o. for a walk,
to take s.o. out (promener); *il ne sort pas de
chez moi,* he is always on my doorstep; *laisser
sortir qqn,* to let s.o. go (ou) come out; *madame
sort d'ici,* the lady has just left; *sortir à la hâte
(ou) précipitamment,* to rush (ou) dash (ou) hurry
out; *sortir de son lit,* to leave one's bed, to get
up; *sortir de la maison,* to leave the house, to go
out; *sortir de prison,* to come out of prison;
sortir en courant, to run out. ‖ To stick out, to
protrude (clou); *les yeux lui sortaient de la tête,*
his eyes were popping out of his head. ‖ To go
(*de,* through); to have been (*de,* at) [une école,
une université]; *il sort de Polytechnique,* he went
through (ou) was trained at « l'Ecole polytechnique ». ‖ To come up (ou) out (numéro); to be
set (question d'examen); *faire sortir un livre,*
to release a book. ‖ To have just come out; *il sort
de table,* he has just dined (ou) just risen from
table; *elle sortait de l'enfance,* she emerged from
childhood. ‖ MILIT. *Faire sortir la garde,* to turn
out the guard; *sortir des rangs,* to step out of the
ranks; *sortir du rang,* to rise from the ranks. ‖
CH. DE F. *Sortir des rails,* to jump the metals (ou)
U. S. rails. ‖ THÉÂTR. *Hamlet sort,* exit Hamlet. ‖
MÉD. *Sortir de l'hôpital,* to be discharged from
(U. S. the) hospital; *sortir de maladie,* to get over
an illness. ‖ BOT., AGRIC. To come up (plante). ‖
FIG. *Sortir d'une bonne famille,* to come of a good
family; *sortir de son caractère,* to do sth. out of
character; *sortir de ses gonds,* to fly off the
handle; *sortir du sujet,* to get off the subject.
— v. tr. To take (ou) bring out (un cheval);
to take out (un enfant); to take out of the
library (un livre emprunté); *sortir les mains de ses
poches,* to take one's hands out of one's pockets.
‖ COMM. To bring out (un nouveau modèle);
to bring out, to publish (un livre publié). ‖ FIG.
Sortir qqn d'embarras, to get s.o. out of a difficulty. ‖ FAM. To turn up (une carte); to throw
out (un importun).
— loc. prép. Au sortir de, on leaving, on coming
out of (un lieu). ‖ FIG. On emerging from (l'enfance); at the end of (l'hiver).
S.O.S. [ɛsoɛs] m. S.O.S.; *lancer un S.O.S.,* to
send out an S.O.S.
sosie [sɔzi] m. Double.
sot, otte [so, ɔt] adj. Stupid, silly, foolish
(v. IMBÉCILE); *rester sot,* to be taken aback.
— s. Simpleton, dolt, fool, ass.
sotie [-ti] f. Farce, burlesque.
sot-l'y-laisse [-lilɛs] m. invar. Parson's (ou)
U. S. pope's nose.
sottement [-tmɑ̃] adv. Foolishly, stupidly.

sottise [-ti:z] f. Stupid (ou) foolish act (action); *faire une sottise,* to do sth. stupid, to commit a blunder, to make a fool of oneself. ‖ Invective, insult (injure); *dire des sottises à,* to abuse (ou) revile. ‖ Stupidity, foolishness (stupidité). ‖ FAM. Nonsense, hokum, tripe, bosh.

sottisier [-tizje] m. Collection of foolish quotations.

sou [su] m. Sou; *affaire de quatre sous,* twopenny-halfpenny business; *cela ne vaut pas quatre sous,* it's not worth twopence (ou) U. S. two cents; *cela vaut mille francs comme un sou,* it's worth a thousand trancs if it's worth a penny; *cent sous,* five francs; *gros sou,* penny piece; *n'avoir pas pour un sou de,* not to have a pennyworth of; *n'avoir pas un sou,* not to have a penny to one's name, to be penniless; *prendre garde à un sou,* to look twice at every penny; *propre comme un sou neuf,* clean as a new penny (ou) pin; *question de gros sous,* matter of pounds, shillings and pence; *sans le sou,* penniless, broke, without a bean.
— loc. adv. **Sou à** (ou) **par sou,** a penny at a time, penny by penny.

soubassement [subɑsmɑ̃] m. ARCHIT. Basement (de bâtiment); stylobate (de colonnade). ‖ Valance (de lit). ‖ Substructure.

soubresaut [subrəso] m. Palpitation, jump (du cœur); start (d'une personne); jolt (d'une voiture).

soubresauter [-te] v. intr. (1). To give a sudden jump (cheval); to start, to jump (personne); to jolt (voiture).

soubrette [subrɛt] f. THÉÂTR. Soubrette.

souche [suʃ] f. AGRIC. Stump (d'arbre); stock (de vigne). ‖ ARCHIT. Stack (de cheminée). ‖ COMM. Counterfoil, stub (d'un carnet de chèques). ‖ ECCLÉS. Stock. ‖ FIG. Founder (d'une famille); stock (origine); *faire souche,* to found a family; *venir de bonne souche,* to come of good stock. ‖ FAM. Blockhead, dolt.

souchet [suʃɛ] m. BOT. Galingale. ‖ ZOOL. Spoonbill, shoveller.

souci [susi] m. Care, worry, anxiety (inquiétude); *avoir des soucis d'argent,* to have money troubles; *c'est là le moindre de mes soucis,* that's the least of my worries; *rongé par les soucis,* careworn; *sans souci,* carefree. ‖ Care, solicitude, concern (soin); *avoir le souci de l'exactitude,* to be a stickler for accuracy; *prendre souci de qqch.,* to have a care for sth.; *sans souci de,* without regard for.

souci m. BOT. Marigold.

soucier [susje] v. tr. (1). To trouble, to give trouble to.
— v. pr. **Se soucier,** to care (de, for); to be concerned (de, about); *ne se soucier de rien,* to care for nothing. ‖ FAM. To want, to be desirous; *je ne me soucie pas qu'il vienne,* I'm not anxious for him to come.

soucieusement [susjøzmɑ̃] adv. Anxiously; with concern.

soucieux, euse [-sjø, ø:z] adj. Careworn, worried (v. INQUIET); *avoir un air soucieux,* to wear a worried look, to look worried. ‖ Anxious, concerned (de, about); *peu soucieux,* careless.

soucoupe [sukup] f. Saucer; *soucoupe volante,* flying saucer.

soudable [sudabl] adj. Weldable; that can be soldered.

soudage [-da:ʒ] m. Soldering, welding.

soudain, aine [sudɛ̃, ɛn] adj. Sudden unexpected.
— adv. Suddenly; all of a sudden.

soudainement [sudɛnmɑ̃] adv. Suddenly.

soudaineté [-nte] f. Suddenness, unexpectedness.

Soudan [sudɑ̃] m. GÉOGR. Sudan.

soudanais, aise [-danɛ, ɛz] adj., s. Sudanese.

soudard [sudaːr] m. Old soldier; ruffianly soldier.

soude [sud] f. BOT. Saltwort. ‖ CHIM. Soda; *cristaux de soude,* washing soda.

souder [-de] v. tr. (1). To solder, to weld; *lampe à souder,* blow-lamp, blow-torch.
— v. pr. **Se souder,** to weld (ou) knit together.

soudeur [-dœːr] s. Solderer, welder.

soudier [-dje] adj. *Industrie soudière,* soda-trade.
— s. Soda-manufacturer.

soudière [-djɛːr] f. Soda-works.

soudoyer [sudwaje] v. tr. (9a). To hire (un assassin); to have in one's pay (des troupes). ‖ To bribe. (V. CORROMPRE.)

soudure [sudyːr] f. Solder (composition); soldered joint, weld (endroit); soldering, welding, brazing (travail). ‖ MÉD. Knitting (des os). ‖ JUR., FIN. *Faire la soudure,* to bridge the gap.

soue [su] f. Pig-sty.

soufflage [sufla:ʒ] m. Glass-blowing. ‖ NAUT. Sheathing, doubling.

soufflant, ante [-flɑ̃, ɑ̃:t] adj. Blowing; *machine soufflante,* blast-engine. ‖ FAM. Breath-taking.

soufflard [-fla:r] m. Blower. ‖ Air-volcano.

souffle [-fl] m. Blast (d'une explosion); *effet du souffle,* blast effect. ‖ Breath, breathing (d'une personne); *à bout de souffle,* out of breath; *au souffle court,* short-winded; *exhaler son dernier souffle,* to breathe one's last; *couper le souffle à,* to wind; *manquer de souffle,* to be short-winded; *retenir son souffle,* to hold one's breath. ‖ Puff, breath (du vent); *souffle glacé,* icy blast. ‖ MÉD. Souffle; *souffle stertoreux,* stertorous breathing. ‖ FIG. Wind, breath (de révolution); *couper le souffle à qqn,* to take s.o.'s breath away; *manquer de souffle,* to lack inspiration; *ne tenir qu'à un souffle,* to hang by a thread.

soufflé, ée [-fle] adj. GRAMM. Unvoiced (consonne). ‖ CULIN. Soufflé (omelette). ‖ MILIT. Destroyed by blast. ‖ FAM. Amazed.
— m. CULIN. Soufflé.

souffler [-fle] v. intr. (1). To blow (personne); *souffler dans ses doigts,* to blow on one's fingers. ‖ To blow (vent); *souffler en ouragan,* to blow a gale. ‖ To take breath (reprendre haleine); *laisser souffler un cheval,* to give a horse a breather. ‖ To pant; to puff, to blow (panteler); *souffler comme un bœuf* (ou) *un phoque,* to puff (ou) blow like a grampus. ‖ FAM. To breathe a word (parler).
— v. tr. To blow out (une bougie); to blow up (le feu); to blow up, to inflate (une vessie). ‖ NAUT. To sheathe (une carène). ‖ THÉÂTR. To prompt (un acteur, une réplique). ‖ TECHN. To blow (du verre). ‖ SPORTS. To huff (un pion) [au jeu de dames]. ‖ MILIT. To blast. ‖ MUS. To blow (l'orgue). ‖ FIG. To stir up (la discorde). ‖ FAM. To trick; *souffler qqch. à qqn,* to do s.o. out of sth.

soufflerie [-fləri] f. Bellows (d'orgue). ‖ AVIAT. Wind-tunnel.

soufflet [-flɛ] m. Bellows (d'appareil photographique). ‖ Hood (de cabriolet); gusset, gore (de robe). ‖ CH. DE F. Vestibule. ‖ MUS. Bellows, swell (d'orgue).

soufflet [-flɛ] m. Box on the ear, slap in the face. (V. GIFLE.) ‖ FIG. Insult, affront.

souffleter [-fləte] v. tr. (8 a). *Souffleter qqn,* to box s.o.'s ears, to slap s.o.'s face. ‖ FIG. To insult, to affront.

souffleteur [-flətœːr] s. Insulter.

souffleur, euse [suflœːr, ø:z] s. MUS. Blower (d'orgue). ‖ TECHN. Blower; *souffleur de verre,* glass-blower. ‖ THÉÂTR. Prompter.

soufflure [-fly:r] f. Flaw, blow-hole (dans la fonte); bubble (dans le verre).

souffrance [sufrɑ̃:s] f. Suffering. (V. DOULEUR.)

‖ Jur. Sufferance. ‖ Comm. *En souffrance,* in suspense. ‖ Fin. *Effet en souffrance,* outstanding bill. ‖ Fig. *Colis en souffrance,* parcel awaiting delivery (ou) waiting to be called for.
souffrant, ante [-frɑ̃, ɑ̃:t] adj. Suffering, in pain. ‖ Méd. Ailing, indisposed; unwell. ‖ Ecclés. *L'Eglise souffrante,* the souls in Purgatory.
souffre-douleur [-frədulœ:r] m. invar. Drudge, whipping-boy, scapegoat.
souffreteux, euse [-frətø, ø:z] adj. Languid (air); puny, sickly (enfant); feeble (vieillard).
souffrir [-fri:r] v. tr. (72). To allow of, to admit, to brook (v. admettre); *cela ne souffre aucun retard,* that admits of no delay. ‖ To suffer, to endure, to undergo (v. endurer); *souffrir la douleur, la faim,* to suffer (ou) feel pain, hunger; *souffrir une perte,* to suffer a loss. ‖ To allow, to permit. (V. permettre.) ‖ To bear, to put up with, to stand (v. supporter); *souffrir le froid,* to stand the cold. ‖ To bear, to stand, to suffer, to tolerate. (V. tolérer.)
— v. intr. To suffer, to suffer (ou) feel pain; *cela me fait souffrir,* that hurts me; *souffrir de la tête,* to have a pain in the head. ‖ Fig. To suffer.
soufisme [sufism] m. Sufism.
soufrage [sufra:ʒ] m. Sulphuring (des allumettes); stumming (du vin).
soufre [sufr] m. Sulphur; *fleur de soufre,* flowers of sulphur.
soufrer [-fre] v. tr. (1). To sulphur (des allumettes); to sulphurate (des laines); to stum (du vin). ‖ Agric. To sulphur, to treat with sulphur (la vigne).
soufroir [-frwa:r] m. Sulphurator.
souhait [swɛ] m. Wish : *souhaits de bonne année,* New Year's greetings.
— loc. adv. **A souhait,** to one's liking, to perfection, as one would wish; *avoir tout à souhait,* to have everything one could wish for; *réussir à souhait,* to succeed to perfection.
souhaitable [-tabl] adj. Desirable, to be wished for; *il est souhaitable que,* it is desirable that, it is to be desired that.
souhaiter [swɛte] v. tr. (1). To wish (le bonjour). ‖ To wish for. (V. désirer.) ‖ Fam. *Je vous en souhaite !,* I hope you get it.
souillard [suja:r] m. Sink-stone (pierre). ‖ Sink-hole (trou).
souiller [-je] v. tr. (1). To soil, to dirty. (V. salir.) ‖ Fig. To sully, to tarnish (sa réputation); *souiller ses mains de sang,* to stain one's hands with blood.
souillon [-jɔ̃] m. Slattern (femme); sloven (homme).
— f. Scullery-wench (servante).
souillure [-jy:r] f. Stain, spot. ‖ Fig. Stain, blemish.
souk [suk] m. Souk (dans les pays arabes). ‖ Fig. Bazaar.
soûl [su] adj. Surfeited, glutted. ‖ Pop. Drunk, tipsy (ivre); gorged, glutted (rassasié); *soûl de musique,* surfeited with music.
— m. Fam. Fill, bellyful; *dormir tout son soûl,* to have one's sleep out; to sleep to one's heart's content; *en avoir tout son soûl,* to have all one wants; *manger son soûl,* to eat one's fill.
soulagement [sulaʒmɑ̃] m. Relief, mitigation.
soulager [-ʒe] v. tr. (7). To relieve, to lighten the load of (qqn); *soulager qqn d'un fardeau,* to relieve s.o. of a burden. ‖ Méd. To relieve, to assuage, to allay. (V. calmer.) ‖ Fig. To help, to succour, to relieve (aider). ‖ Fam. *Soulager qqn de qqch.,* to relieve s.o. of sth., to pinch sth. from. s.o.
— v. pr. **Se soulager,** to relieve oneself (d'un fardeau). ‖ Fig. To relieve oneself, to get a weight off one's mind. ‖ Fam. To relieve oneself.

soûlant, ante [sulɑ̃, ɑ̃:t] adj. Fam. Taxing, tedious, tiresome, irksome.
soûlard, arde [sula:r, ard] **soûlaud, aude** [-lo, od] adj., s. Pop. Drunkard, boozer, tippler.
soûler [-le] v. tr. (1). To intoxicate, to get s.o. drunk (enivrer). ‖ To cram, to stuff, to fill up (gorger). ‖ Fig. To satiate.
— v. pr. **Se soûler,** to gorge (ou) glut oneself (de, with). ‖ To get drunk (s'enivrer).
soûlerie [-lri] f. Orgy, debauch, drinking-bout.
soulèvement [sulɛvmɑ̃] m. Heaving, swell, surging (des flots). ‖ Méd. Heaving, retching (de l'estomac); *soulèvement du cœur,* nausea. ‖ Géogr. Upheaval, upthrust (du sol). ‖ Fig. Revolt, uprising (d'un peuple).
soulever [-lve] v. tr. (5). To lift up, to raise (un fardeau); to raise (la poussière). ‖ Méd., Fam. *Cela soulève le cœur,* it makes one sick, it turns one's stomach. ‖ Fig. To arouse (l'émotion) [chez, in, within]; to rouse, to stir up (le peuple); to raise (une question).
— v. pr. **Se soulever,** to raise oneself. ‖ Fig. To rise up, to revolt (peuple).
souleveur [-lvœ:r] m. Raiser, lifter (d'un poids). ‖ Fig. Instigator (d'une révolte). ‖ Fam. Lady-killer.
soulier [sulje] m. Shoe; *souliers de bal,* evening shoes (de dames), pumps (d'hommes); *souliers Richelieu,* lace-up shoes; *souliers de ski,* ski-boots. ‖ Fig. *Etre dans ses petits souliers,* to feel small; to be ill at ease.
soulignage [suliɲa:ʒ], **soulignement** [-ɲmɑ̃] m. Underlining; stressing.
souligner [-ɲe] v. tr. (1). To underline. ‖ Fig. To underline (le caractère); to stress, to put (ou) lay stress on, to emphasize (un mot).
soûlographie [sulɔgrafi] f. Fam. Boozing; *une soirée de soûlographie,* a drunk, a drinking bout.
soulte [sult] f. Jur. Balance, makeweight.
soumettre [sumɛtr] v. tr. (64). To master, to overcome, to subdue, to subjugate, to tame (maîtriser); *soumettre ses passions,* to keep one's passions in check; *soumettre les rebelles,* to put down the rebels. ‖ To subject (exposer); *soumettre un produit à l'analyse,* to subject a product to analysis. ‖ To submit, to present, to put (présenter); *soumettre une question à,* to submit (ou) refer a question to, to lay a question before. ‖ To subordinate (subordonner); *soumettre la raison à la foi,* to subordinate reason to faith, to put faith above (ou) before reason.
— v. pr. **Se soumettre,** to submit, to give in (à, to); *se soumettre à une décision,* to submit to (ou) comply with a decision.
soumis, ise [sumi, iz] adj. Submissive (air); obedient (enfant); dutiful (fils). ‖ Subject (à, to); *soumis à l'autorité de,* under the sway of.
soumission [-sjɔ̃] f. Submission, submissiveness, obedience. ‖ Comm. Tender, U. S. bid. ‖ Jur. Undertaking, guarantee.
soumissionnaire [-sjɔnɛ:r] m. Comm. Tenderer.
soumissionner [-sjɔne] v. tr. (1). Comm. To tender for, to put in a tender for. ‖ Fin. To underwrite.
soupape [supap] f. Plug (de baignoire). ‖ Electr. *Soupape électrique,* rectifier. ‖ Techn. Valve; *soupape à clapet, à flotteur, à pointeau, de sûreté,* flap-, ball-, needle-, safety-valve. ‖ Fig. Safety-valve.
soupçon [supsɔ̃] m. Suspicion, idea, inkling (idée); *je n'en avais pas le moindre soupçon,* I hadn't the slightest suspicion of it; I didn't suspect it for a moment. ‖ Suspicion, mistrust, distrust, misgiving (méfiance); *avoir quelques soupçons,* to have some misgivings; *éveiller des soupçons,* to arouse suspicions. ‖ Fig. Soupçon, shade, dash (brin); *soupçon de fièvre,* touch of

fever; *soupçon de preuve,* shade (ou) shadow of evidence.
soupçonnable [-sɔnabl] adj. Open to suspicion.
soupçonner [-sɔne] v. tr. (1). To surmise, to suspect, to conjecture (conjecturer). ‖ To suspect, to be suspicious about (suspecter); *soupçonner qqn de qqch.,* to suspect s.o. of sth.
soupçonneur, euse [-sɔnœːr, øːz] s. Suspicious person.
soupçonneusement [-sɔnøzmɑ̃] adv. Suspiciously.
soupçonneux, euse [-sɔnø, øːz] adj. Suspicious.
soupe [sup] f. Soup; *soupe à l'oignon,* onionsoup. ‖ *Soupe populaire,* soup-kitchen. ‖ MILIT. *De soupe,* on cook-house fatigue. ‖ FIG. *S'emporter comme une soupe au lait,* to go off the deep end, to fly off the handle; to flare up very easily; *trempé comme une soupe,* wet to the skin, drenched. ‖ FAM. *Un gros plein de soupe,* a pompous ass; a big-head, a fat-head (pop.).
soupente [supɑ̃ːt] f. Braces (d'un carrosse). ‖ Closet, small room (réduit); *soupente d'escalier,* staircase cupboard.
souper [supe] m. Supper; *sans souper,* supperless.
souper v. intr. (1). To have supper, to sup. ‖ POP. *J'en ai soupé,* I'm fed up (ou) brassed off with it, I've had a bellyful of it.
soupeser [supəze] v. tr. (1). To feel (ou) try the weight of, to weigh in the hand (qqch.).
soupeur [supœːr] s. One who takes supper.
soupière [-pjɛːr] f. Soup-tureen.
soupir [supiːr] m. Sigh; *pousser un soupir,* to sigh, to give a sigh; *soupir de soulagement,* sigh of relief. ‖ Breath (souffle); *rendre le dernier soupir,* to breathe one's last. ‖ MUS. Crotchet-rest; *demi-soupir,* quaver- (ou) U.S. eighth rest; *quart de soupir,* semiquaver- (ou) U.S. sixteenth rest.
soupirail [supiraːj] m. Air-hole, vent, ventilator.
soupirant, ante [-rɑ̃, ɑ̃ːt] m. Suitor, wooer, admirer, lover.
soupirer [-re] v. intr. (1). To sigh, to give (ou) heave a sigh. ‖ FIG. To long, to yearn, to sigh (*après,* for); to hanker (*après,* after).
— v. tr. To sigh out (ses peines).
souple [supl] adj. Supple, pliable, flexible (branche); soft (col); lithe, lissom (corps). ‖ FIG. Tractable, easily moulded (caractère); docile, adaptable (enfant); versatile, adaptable (esprit).
souplement [-pləmɑ̃] adv. Supply, lithely.
souplesse [-plɛs] f. Suppleness, pliability, flexibility (d'une branche); litheness, lissomness (du corps). ‖ FIG. Adaptativeness, adaptability; tractability, docility (du caractère); versatility, adaptability (d'esprit).
souquenille [sukniːj] f. † Smock. ‖ Shabby (ou) worn garment.
souquer [suke] v. tr. (1). NAUT. To haul taut.
— v. intr. NAUT. To pull hard (ou) away (*sur,* at).
source [surs] f. Source, spring (v. FONTAINE); *source de pétrole,* oil-well; *source jaillissante,* gusher. ‖ GÉOGR. Source, head (d'une rivière). ‖ FIG. Source, origin; *remonter à la source de qqch.,* to trace sth. back to its source; *sources de l'histoire,* historical sources; *source du mal,* root of evil; *source de richesses,* source of wealth; *tenir une nouvelle de bonne source,* to have a piece of information from a reliable source (ou) on good authority.
sourcier [-sje] s. Water-diviner, dowser.
sourcil [sursi] m. Eyebrow; *aux sourcils épais, touffus,* beetle-browed, heavy-browed; *froncer les sourcils,* to frown, to knit one's brows.
sourcilier, ère [-lje, ɛr] adj. MÉD. Superciliary.
sourciller [-je] v. intr. (1). To frown, to knit one's brows. ‖ FIG. To blink; *sans sourciller,* without turning a hair, without batting an eyelid.

sourcilleux, euse [-jø, øːz] adj. Supercilious.
sourd, ourde [suːr, uːrd] adj. MÉD. Deaf; hard of hearing; *devenir sourd,* to go deaf. ‖ GRAMM. Voiceless, breathed (consonne). ‖ FIG. Dull, muffled (bruit); dull (couleur); secret, undeclared (guerre); dark (lanterne); underhand (manière); without an echo (pièce); cloudy (pierre); dull, hollow (voix); *faire la sourde oreille,* to turn a deaf ear; *sourd à,* deaf to.
— s. Deaf person; *crier comme un sourd,* to yell, to bellow; *frapper comme un sourd,* to hit out, to lay about one. ‖ **Sourd-muet** (f. **sourde-muette**) adj. Deaf-and-dumb; s. deaf-mute.
sourdement [-dəmɑ̃] adv. Secretly (en secret); in an underhand manner (sournoisement). ‖ Dully, heavily (avec un bruit sourd).
sourdine [-din] f. MUS. Mute; *en sourdine,* muted.
— loc. **En sourdine,** secretly, on the sly.
sourdre [surdr] v. intr. (96). To well, to well up, to spring (eau). ‖ FIG. To arise, to result.
souriant, ante [surjɑ̃, ɑ̃ːt] adj. Smiling.
souriceau [suriso] m. ZOOL. Small mouse.
souricier [-sje] m. ZOOL. Mouser (chat); mouse-catcher (oiseau).
souricière [-sjɛːr] f. Mouse-trap. ‖ FIG. Trap, snare; *se jeter dans la souricière,* to fall into the trap; *tendre une souricière à,* to set a trap for.
sourire [suriːr] v. intr. (89). To smile. ‖ FIG. *Sourire à,* to smile on, to favour (favoriser); to appeal to, to please (plaire).
sourire m. Smile; *garder le sourire,* to keep smiling; *large sourire,* broad smile, grin.
souris f. ZOOL. Mouse; *trou de souris,* mouse-hole. ‖ CULIN. Knuckle-end (d'un gigot).
sournois, oise [surnwa, waz] adj. Sly, deceitful, underhand, artful.
— s. Sneak, sly-boots, cagey fellow.
sournoisement [-zmɑ̃] adv. Slyly, artfully, in an underhand manner.
sournoiserie [-ri] f. Slyness.
sous [su] prép. Under (effet); *sous cette impression,* under that impression; *sous le coup d'une surprise,* under the shock of a surprise. ‖ Under, within (époque); *sous Louis XIV,* under (ou) in the reign of Louis XIV; *sous peu,* soon, in a short while, before long; *sous trois jours,* within three days. ‖ Under (exposé à); *sous le feu de l'ennemi,* under enemy fire. ‖ Under (indication); *sous tel numéro,* under a certain number. ‖ Under, beneath, before, in front of (lieu); *sous ma fenêtre,* beneath my window; *sous les murs du château,* beneath (ou) under the castle walls. ‖ Under, beneath, below (situation); *sous un arbre,* under a tree; *sous enveloppe,* under cover; *sous la pluie,* out in the rain; *sous la table,* under the table. ‖ By (par); *sous le nom de,* by the name of. ‖ On (réserve); *sous cette condition,* on this condition; *sous sa propre responsabilité,* on one's own responsability. ‖ Under (subordination); *sous ses ordres,* under his orders (ou) command. ‖ ELECTR. *Sous caoutchouc, soie,* rubber-, silk-covered. ‖ MILIT. *Sous les armes, le feu,* under arms, fire; *sous les drapeaux,* with the colours. ‖ NAUT. *Sous le vent,* leeward; *sous les voiles,* with sails set. ‖ LOC. *N'avoir rien à se mettre sous la dent,* not to have a bite to eat; *regarder sous le nez,* to look straight in the face; *sous un jour favorable,* in a favourable light; *sous la main,* at hand, handy, close at hand. ‖
Sous-affréter, v. tr. NAUT. To sub-charter. ‖ **Sous-agent,** m. COMM. Sub-agent. ‖ **Sous-aide,** s. Sub-assistant. ‖ **Sous-alimentation,** f. MÉD. Malnutrition. ‖ **Sous-amendement,** m. Amendment to an amendment. ‖ **Sous-arrondissement,** m. Sub-district. ‖ **Sous-bail,** m. Sub-lease. ‖ **Sous-bailleur,** adj. Sub-lessor. ‖ **Sous-barbe,** f. invar. ZOOL. Underjaw (de cheval); NAUT. Bobstay. ‖

Sous-bibliothécaire, s. Sub-librarian. ‖ **Sous-bois**, m. Undergrowth, underwood; ARTS. Painting depicting woodland scene. ‖ **Sous-brigadier**, m. Lance-corporal. ‖ **Sous-chef;** m. COMM. Deputy chief clerk; CH. DE F. Deputy station-master; MUS. Deputy (ou) U. S. assistant conductor. ‖ **Sous-classe**, f. ZOOL., BOT. Subclass. ‖ **Sous-commission**, f. Subcommittee; COMM. subcommission. ‖ **Sous-consommation**, f. Subconsumption. ‖ **Sous-continent**, m. GÉOGR. Subcontinent. ‖ **Sous-couche**, f. TECHN. Undercoat (en peinture). ‖ **Sous-cutané**, adj. MÉD. Subcutaneous. ‖ **Sous-développé**, adj. Underdeveloped. ‖ **Sous-développement**, m. Underdevelopment. ‖ **Sous-diacre**, m. ECCLÉS. Subdeacon. ‖ **Sous-directeur** (f. sous-directrice), s. Assistant manager (en général); vice- (ou) assistant principal (d'école). ‖ **Sous-dominante**, f. MUS. Subdominant. ‖ **Sous-emploi**, m. Underemployment. ‖ **Sous-ensemble**, m. MATH. Subset. ‖ **Sous-entendre**, v. tr. To understand, to imply. ‖ **Sous-entendu**, m. Innuendo, implication. ‖ **Sous-équipé**, adj. Industrially underdeveloped. ‖ **Sous-équipement**, m. Industrial underdevelopment, lack of industry. ‖ **Sous-estimer, sous-évaluer,** v. tr. To underestimate, to underrate, to minimize. ‖ **Sous-exposer**, v. tr. TECHN. To underexpose (un film). ‖ **Sous-exposition**, f. TECHN. Underexposure. ‖ **Sous-faîte**, m. ARCHIT. Ridgeboard. ‖ **Sous-fifre**, m. FAM. Cog, underling. ‖ **Sous-frutescent**, adj. BOT. Suffrutescent. ‖ **Sous-genre**, m. ZOOL., BOT. Subgenus. ‖ **Sous-gorge**, f. inv. Throat lash (de cheval). ‖ **Sous-gouverneur**, m. Vice- (ou) deputy governor. ‖ **Sous-groupe**, m. Subgroup. ‖ **Sous-homme**, m. Sub-man. ‖ **Sous-jacent**, adj. Subjacent, underlying. ‖ **Sous-le-Vent** (îles), f. pl. GÉOGR. Leeward Islands. ‖ **Sous-lieutenant**, m. MILIT. Second-lieutenant. ‖ **Sous-locataire**, s. Subtenant. ‖ **Sous-location**, f. Subletting. ‖ **Sous-louer**, v. tr. To sublet. ‖ **Sous-main**, m. inv. Desk pad; FIG. en sous-main, under the counter. ‖ **Sous-maîtresse**, f. Madam, brothel-keeper. ‖ **Sous-marin**, adj. Submarine (faune, flore); underwater (chasse, pêche); m. NAUT. submarine. ‖ **Sous-marinier**, m. NAUT. Submariner. ‖ **Sous-maxillaire**, m. MÉD. Submaxillary. ‖ **Sous-multiple**, adj., m. MATH. Submultiple. ‖ **Sous-nappe**, f. Under-cloth. ‖ **Sous-normale**, f. MATH. Subnormal. ‖ **Sous-nutrition**, f. Undernutrition, malnutrition. ‖ **Sous-œuvre**, m. ARCHIT. Underpinning. ‖ **Sous-off**, m. MILIT., FAM. Non-commissioned officer, N. C. O.; NAUT. petty-officer. ‖ **Sous-orbitaire**, adj. MÉD. Suborbital. ‖ **Sub-orbital**, adj. ASTRONAUT. Suborbital. ‖ **Sous-ordre**, m. Subordinate, underling; en sous-ordre, subordinately; ZOOL., BOT. suborder. ‖ **Sous-payer**, v. tr. To underpay. ‖ **Sous-peuplé**, adj. Underpopulated. ‖ **Sous-pied**, m. Understrap (de guêtre), trouser-strap (de pantalon). ‖ **Sous-préfectoral**, adj. Sub-prefectoral. ‖ **Sous-préfecture**, f. Sub-prefecture. ‖ **Sous-préfet**, m. Sub-prefect. ‖ **Sous-préfète**, f. Sub-prefect's wife. ‖ **Sous-production**, f. Underproduction. ‖ **Sous-produit**, m. TECHN. By-product; FIG. poor imitation. ‖ **Sous-prolétariat**, m. Underprivileged (ou) downtrodden class, lumpenproletariat. ‖ **Sous-règne**, m. BOT., ZOOL. Subkingdom. ‖ **Sous-secrétaire**, s. Sous-secrétaire d'Etat, undersecretary of State. ‖ **Sous-secrétariat**, m. Undersecretaryship; undersecretary's office. ‖ **Sous-sol**, m. Basement; GÉOGR. subsoil, substratum. ‖ **Sous-soleuse**, f. AGRIC. Subsoil plough. ‖ **Sous-station**, f. ÉLECTR. Substation. ‖ **Sous-tangente**, f. MATH. Subtangent. ‖ **Sous-tasse**, f. Saucer. ‖ **Sous-tendre**, v. tr. To underlie; MATH. to subtend. ‖ **Sous-titrage**, m. Subtitling. ‖ **Sous-titre**, m. Subtitle, caption. ‖ **Sous-titré**, adj. Subtitled, with subtitles. ‖ **Sous-traitance**, f. Subcontracting. ‖ **Sous-traitant**, m. Subcontractor. ‖ **Sous-traiter**, v. tr. To subcontract. ‖ **Sous-ventrière**, f. Belly-band, saddle-girth. ‖ **Sous-verge**, m. inv. Off-horse; FIG. underling. ‖ **Sous-verre**, m. Glass-mount (encadrement); mounted picture (document encadré). ‖ **Sous-vêtement**, m. Undergarment; pl. underwear, underclothes, underclothing.

souscripteur [suskriptœ:r] m. Subscriber (à une publication). ‖ FIN. Drawer (d'un chèque); subscriber (à un emprunt).

souscription [-kripsjɔ̃] f. Signing, execution (action); signature, subscription (signature). ‖ Subscription, contribution (contribution); par souscription publique, by public subscription; verser une souscription, to pay a subscription. ‖ Advance order (commande par souscription). ‖ FIN. Subscription, application (à des actions).

souscrire [-kri:r] v. tr. (44). To take out, to subscribe (un abonnement). ‖ JUR. To execute, to sign (un acte). ‖ FIN. To subscribe, to apply for, to take up (des actions); to draw (un chèque). — v. intr. To subscribe; souscrire pour mille francs, to subscribe a thousand francs. ‖ FIN. To subscribe, to apply (à, for) [des actions]; souscrire à titre réductible, to apply for excess shares. ‖ FIG. To agree (à, to) [un arrangement]; to subscribe (à, to) [une opinion].

soussigné, ée [susiɲe] adj., s. Undersigned; je, soussigné, I, the undersigned; les témoins soussignés, the undersigned witnesses.

soussigner v. tr. (1). To sign, to undersign.

soustractif,ive [sustraktif,i:v] adj. Subtractive.

soustraction [-traksjɔ̃] f. MATH. Subtraction.

soustraire [-trɛ:r] v. tr. (11). To take away, to remove, to purloin (des effets). ‖ MATH. To subtract (de, from). ‖ FIG. To protect, to shield, to preserve (à, from) [qqn]. — v. pr. Se soustraire à, to avoid, to escape (l'attention); to escape (un châtiment); to shirk (un devoir); to elude (la justice).

soutache [sutaʃ] f. Braid.

soutacher [-ʃe] v. tr. (1). To braid.

soutane [sutan] f. ECCLÉS. Cassock; soutane. ‖ FIG. Prendre la soutane, to take holy orders.

soutanelle [-nɛl] f. ECCLÉS. Clerical frock-coat.

soute [sut] f. NAUT. Store-room; soute au biscuit, bread-room; soute à mazout, oil-fuel tank; soute aux poudres, magazine.

soutenable [sutnabl] adj. Bearable (joug); tenable (opinion).

soutenance [-nɑ̃:s] f. Maintaining (d'une thèse).

soutenant [-nɑ̃] m. Maintainer (d'une thèse).

soutènement [sutɛnmɑ̃] m. ARCHIT. Supporting, propping up; mur de soutènement, retaining wall.

souteneur [sutnœ:r] m. Upholder (d'un système). ‖ Pimp, souteneur (d'une prostituée).

soutenir [-ni:r] v. tr. (101). To support, to hold up. ‖ MILIT. To support (une armée). ‖ MUS. Soutenir la voix, to hold a note. ‖ FIG. To resist (une attaque); to support (une cause); to keep up (la conversation); to put up with, to endure (la douleur); to maintain (son droit); to sustain (un effort); to support, to keep, to maintain, to provide for (une famille); to keep (une gageure); to uphold (l'honneur); to support, to maintain (une opinion); to keep up (son rang); soutenir la comparaison avec, to bear comparison with. ‖ FIG. To maintain, to assert; soutenir que, to contend that. — v. pr. Se soutenir, to support oneself, to hold up; se soutenir sur l'eau, to keep afloat. ‖ FIG. To last, to be maintained (durer).

soutenu, ue [-ny] adj. Constant, unflagging (attention); sustained, protracted (effort); lofty, dignified (style). ‖ Sponsored (livre); backed, pushed (personne). ‖ FIN. Steady (marché).

souterrain, aine [sutɛrɛ̃, ɛn] adj. Underground, subterranean; passage souterrain, subway, underground passage. ‖ FIG. Underhand, shady (voie). — m. Subway, underground passage, tunnel.

souterrainement [-rɛnmɑ̃] adv. Underground. ‖ Fɪɢ. Underhandedly, in an underhand manner.

soutien [sutjɛ̃] m. Support, prop (de voûte). ‖ Fɪɢ. Supporter, upholder (v. ᴀᴘᴘᴜɪ); *sans soutien*, unsheltered; *soutien de famille*, breadwinner. ‖ **Soutien-gorge** (pl. *soutiens-gorge*), m. Brassiere; bra (fam.).

soutier [sutje] m. Nᴀᴜᴛ. Coal-trimmer.

soutirage [sutira:ʒ] m. Drawing-off, clarifying, racking (du vin).

soutirer [-re] v. tr. (1). To draw off, to clarify, to rack (du vin). ‖ Fɪɢ. *Soutirer de l'argent à*, to get money out of; *soutirer du tabac à qqn*, to sponge on s.o. for tobacco.

souvenance [suvnɑ̃:s] f. † Recollection.

souvenir [-ni:r] m. Memory, remembrance, recollection (impression); *bon souvenir*, pleasant memory; *souvenir confus*, dim recollection; *souvenir net*, clear memory. ‖ Souvenir, memento, keepsake (objet).

souvenir v. impers. (101). To occur to the mind; *autant qu'il m'en souvienne*, as far as I remember. — v. pr. **Se souvenir de**, to remember, to recall, to bear in mind; *faire souvenir de*, to remind of. ‖ Fᴀᴍ. *Je m'en souviendrai!*, I shan't forget!

souvent [suvɑ̃] adv. Often, frequently (v. ꜰʀÉꟼᴜᴇᴍᴍᴇɴᴛ); *assez souvent*, not infrequently; *peu souvent*, not often, infrequently, seldom.

souverain, aine [suvrɛ̃, ɛn] adj. Sovereign (puissance). ‖ Infallible (remède). ‖ Jᴜʀ. *Cour souveraine*, supreme court. — s. Sovereign (monarque). — m. Fɪɴ. Sovereign (monnaie).

souverainement [-rɛnmɑ̃] adv. Supremely, sovereignly.

souveraineté [-rɛnte] f. Sovereignty.

soviet [sɔvjɛt] m. Soviet.

soviétique [-vjetik] adj. Soviet; *la Russie soviétique*, Soviet Russia.

soviétiste [-vjetist] adj. Soviet. — m. Member of a soviet.

soviétiser [-vjetize] v. tr. (1). To sovietize.

soya [sɔja] m. Bᴏᴛ. Soya-bean, U. S. soybean.

soyeux, euse [swajø, ø:z] adj. Silky. — m. Silk-manufacturer (ou) merchant.

spacieusement [spasjøzmɑ̃] adv. Spaciously, roomily.

spacieux, euse [-sjø, ø:z] adj. Spacious, roomy.

spadassin [spadasɛ̃] m. Swordsman, duellist, bravo (v. ʙʀᴇᴛᴛᴇᴜʀ); *spadassin à gages*, hired ruffian.

spaghetti [spaɡɛti] m. Cᴜʟɪɴ. Spaghetti.

spahi [spai] m. Mɪʟɪᴛ. Spahi.

sparadrap [sparadra] m. Mᴇ́ᴅ. Sticking-plaster.

sparring-partner [spariŋpartnɛ:r] m. Sᴘᴏʀᴛs. Sparring partner (à la boxe).

spartéine [spartein] f. Spartein.

sparterie [spartri] f. Cᴏᴍᴍ. Sparterie, articles made of esparto (articles); esparto factory (fabrique).

spartiate [sparsjat] adj., s. Spartan.

spasme [spasm] m. Mᴇ́ᴅ. Spasm.

spasmodique [-mɔdik] adj. Mᴇ́ᴅ. Spasmodic, spastic.

spasmodiquement [-mɔdikmɑ̃] adv. Spasmodically.

spath [spat] m. Gᴇ́ᴏʟ. Spar; *spath d'Islande*, Iceland spar.

spatial, ale [spasjal] adj. Asᴛʀᴏɴᴀᴜᴛ. Space; *engin spatial*, spacecraft; *vol spatial*, spaceflight. ‖ Mᴀᴛʜ., Pʜʏs. Spatial.

spatio-temporel, elle [-sjotɑ̃pɔrɛl] adj. Spatio-temporal.

spatule [spatyl] f. Mᴇ́ᴅ. Spatula. ‖ Cᴜʟɪɴ. *Spatule à beurre*, butterpat. ‖ Sᴘᴏʀᴛs. Ski-tip.

spatule f. Zᴏᴏʟ. Spoonbill.

spatulé, ée [-le] adj. Spatulate, flat-ended (doigts).

speaker [spikœ:r] (f. **speakerine** [-kərin]) s. Rᴀᴅɪᴏ. Announcer. — m. Speaker (à la Chambre des communes). ‖ Sᴘᴏʀᴛs. Megaphone steward.

spécial, ale [spesjal] adj. Special, particular; *édition spéciale*, extra (ou) special edition; *un parfum spécial à eux*, an aroma of their own. ‖ Mɪʟɪᴛ. Technical (armes). — f. Fᴀᴍ. Higher mathematics class.

spécialement [-lmɑ̃] adv. Specially, especially, particularly.

spécialisation [-lizasjɔ̃] f. Specialization.

spécialiser [-lize] v. tr. (1). To specialize. — v. pr. **Se spécialiser**, to specialize (*dans*, in). ‖ U. S. To major (*dans*, in) [à l'Université].

spécialiste [-list] s. Specialist. (V. ᴛᴇᴄʜɴɪᴄɪᴇɴ.) ‖. Aɢʀɪᴄ. Agricultural expert. ‖ Mɪʟɪᴛ. Tradesman.

spécialité [-lite] f. Speciality, specialty. ‖ Mᴇ́ᴅ. *Spécialités pharmaceutiques*, patent medicines. ‖ Fᴀᴍ. Knack (don); *il a la spécialité de me taper sur les nerfs*, he has a knack of getting on my nerves.

spécieusement [spesjøzmɑ̃] adv. Speciously.

spécieux, euse [-sjø, ø:z] adj. Specious.

spécificatif, ive [spesifikatif, i:v] adj. Specifying.

spécification [-fikasjɔ̃] f. Specification. ‖ Jᴜʀ. Working up.

spécificité [-fisite] f. Specificity; specific character (ou) characteristic.

spécifier [-fje] v. tr. (1). To specify.

spécifique [-fik] adj. Specific, special, peculiar (fonction, qualité). ‖ Pʜʏs., Mᴇ́ᴅ. Specific. — m. Mᴇ́ᴅ. Specific.

spécifiquement [-fikmɑ̃] adv. Specifically.

spécimen [spesimɛn] m. Specimen, sample. — adj. Specimen.

spéciosité [spesjozite] f. Speciousness.

spectacle [spɛktakl] m. Spectacle, sight. (V. sᴄᴇ̀ɴᴇ.) ‖ Tʜᴇ́ᴀ̂ᴛʀ. Play, entertainment, show (v. ʀᴇᴘʀᴇ́sᴇɴᴛᴀᴛɪᴏɴ); *pièce à grand spectacle*, spectacular production; *salle de spectacle*, theatre, auditorium; *taxe sur les spectacles*, entertainment tax.

spectaculaire [-kylɛ:r] adj. Spectacular.

spectateur, trice [-tœ:r, tris] s. Spectator, onlooker. ‖ Tʜᴇ́ᴀ̂ᴛʀ. *Les spectateurs*, the audience.

spectral, ale [spɛktral] adj. Spectral, ghostly. ‖ Pʜʏs. *Couleurs spectrales*, colours of the spectrum. ‖ Cʜɪᴍ. Spectrum (analyse).

spectre [spɛktr] m. Spectre, ghost. (V. ꜰᴀɴᴛᴏ̂ᴍᴇ.) ‖ Pʜʏs. Spectrum. ‖ Fɪɢ. Spectre (de la famine).

spectrographe [spɛktrɔɡraf] m. Spectrograph.

spectromètre [-mɛtr] m. Spectrometer.

spectroscope [-skɔp] m. Spectroscope.

spectroscopie [-skɔpi] f. Spectroscopy.

spectroscopique [-skɔpik] adj. Spectroscopic.

spéculaire [spɛkylɛ:r] adj. Specular. ‖ Mᴇ́ᴅ. Mirror (écriture). ‖ Bᴏᴛ. Specularia. ‖ Tᴇᴄʜɴ. *Fonte spéculaire*, spiegeleisen.

spéculateur, trice [spekylatœ:r, tris] s. Speculator.

spéculatif, ive [-latif, i:v] adj. Speculative. — m. Contemplator, meditator; theorizer.

spéculation [-lasjɔ̃] f. Speculation, meditation; theorizing. ‖ Fɪɴ. Speculation.

spéculativement [-lativmɑ̃] adv. Speculatively.

spéculer [-le] v. intr. (1). To speculate, to meditate, to theorize (*sur*, on, about). ‖ Fɪɴ. To speculate (*sur*, in).

spéculum [-lɔm] m. Mᴇ́ᴅ. Speculum.

speech [spitʃ] m. Speech; *prononcer un speech*, to make a speech in reply to a toast.

spéléologie [speleɔlɔʒi] f. Speleology, spelaeology.

spéléologue [-lɔɡ] s. Speleologist; pot-holer (fam.).

spermaceti [spɛrmaseti] m. Spermaceti.

spermatique [spɛrmatik] adj. MÉD. Spermatic ; *cordon spermatique*, spermatic cord. ·

spermatogenèse [-tɔʒənɛ:z] f. MÉD. Spermatogenesis.

spermatophyte [-tɔfit] m. BOT. Spermatophyte, seed plant.

spermatozoïde[spɛrmatɔzɔid]m.Spermatozoon.

sperme [spɛrm] m. MÉD. Sperm.

spermicide [-misid] adj. Spermicidial.
— m. Spermicid.

sphaigne [sfɛɲ] f. BOT. Sphagnum.

sphénoïdal, ale [sfenɔidal] adj. MÉD. Sphenoidal.

sphénoïde [-nɔid] adj., m. MÉD. Sphenoid.

sphère [sfɛ:r] f. Sphere, globe. ‖ ASTRON. *Sphère céleste*, celestial sphere. ‖ MATH. Sphere. ‖ FIG. Sphere (d'influence) ; *hors de sa sphère*, out of one's sphere (ou) province.

sphéricité [sferisite] f. Sphericity.

sphérique [sferik] adj. MATH. Spherical.
— m. AVIAT. Spherical balloon.

sphériquement [-mɑ̃] adv. Spherically.

sphéroïdal, ale [sferɔidal] adj. MATH. Spheroidal.

sphéroïde [-rɔid] m. MATH. Spheroid.

sphéromètre [-rɔmɛtr] m. Spherometer.

sphérule [sferyl] f. Spherule.

sphincter [sfɛ̃ktɛ:r] m. MÉD. Sphincter.

sphinge [sfɛ̃:ʒ] f. ARTS. Female sphinx.

sphinx [sfɛ̃ks] m. ARTS. Sphinx. ‖ ZOOL. Hawkmoth, sphinx. ‖ FIG. Sphinx.

sphygmographe [sfigmɔgraf] m. MÉD. Sphygmograph.

spica [spika] m. MÉD. Spica.

spider [spidɛ:r] m. AUTOM. Dick(e)y, U. S. trunk. ‖ Dick(e)y seat, U. S. rumble seat.

spina-bifida [spinabifida] m. MÉD. Spina bifida.

spinal, ale [spinal] adj. MÉD. Spinal.

spinelle [spinɛl] adj., m. Spinel.

spinnaker [spinakɛ:r] m. NAUT. Spinnaker.

spinule [spinyl] f. BOT. Spinule.

spiral, ale [spiral] adj. Spiral.
— m. Hair-spring (de montre).

spirale [-ra:l] f. Spiral, helix.
— loc. adv. En spirale, in a spiral, spirally ; *escalier en spirale*, spiral (ou) winding staircase. ‖ AVIAT. *Descente en spirale*, spiral dive.

spiralé, ée [-rale] adj. Spiral, spiraled.

spirant, ante [spirɑ̃, ɑ̃:t] adj. GRAMM. Spirant.

spirante [-rɑ̃:t] f. GRAMM. Spirant.

spire [spi:r] f. Whorl, twirl (d'une coquille) ; single turn (d'une hélice). ‖ ELECTR. Single turn, one winding (d'une bobine).

spirille [spiri] m. Spirillum.

spirillose [-lo:z] f. MÉD. Spirillosis.

spirite [spirit] adj. Spiritualistic.
— s. Spiritualist, spiritist.

spiritisme [-tism] m. Spiritism, spiritualism.

spiritualisation [-tɥalizasjɔ̃] f. Spiritualisation.

spiritualiser [-tɥalize] v. tr. (1). To spiritualize.

spiritualisme [-tɥalism] m. Spiritualism.

spiritualiste [-tɥalist] adj. Spiritualistic.
— s. Spiritualist.

spiritualité [-tɥalite] f. Spirituality.

spirituel, elle [-tɥɛl] adj. Witty (réponse). ‖ ECCLÉS. Spiritual (être, vie) ; *musique spirituelle*, sacred music ; *parents spirituels*, god-parents.
— m. ECCLÉS. Spiritual power.

spirituellement [-tɥɛlmɑ̃] adv. Wittily. ‖ ECCLÉS. Spiritually.

spiritueux, euse [spirityø, ø:z] adj. Spirituous.
— m. Spirituous liquour ; *les spiritueux*, spirits.

spiroïdal, ale [spirɔidal] adj. Spiral, spiroid.

spiromètre [-mɛtr] m. Spirometer.

spleen [splin] m. Spleen, hypochondria, illhumour ; *avoir le spleen*, to be in low spirits.

splendeur [splɑ̃dœ:r] f. Splendour, brilliance, brightness, radiance (du soleil). ‖ FIG. Grandeur, glory (d'un nom) ; magnificence (du trône).

splendide [splɑ̃did] adj. Sumptuous, splendid (repas) ; radiant, brilliant (soleil) ; splendid, magnificent (spectacle) ; glorious (victoire).

splendidement [-mɑ̃] adv. Splendidly, magnificently, gloriously.

splénectomie [splenɛktɔmi] f. MÉD. Splenectomy.

splénique [splenik] adj. MÉD. Splenic.

spoliateur, trice [spɔljatœ:r, tris] s. Despoiler.
— adj. Spoliatory (mesure) ; despoiling (personne).

spoliation [-sjɔ̃] f. Spoliation, despoiling.

spolier [spɔlje] v. tr. (1). To despoil, to plunder, to pillage (piller). ‖ To rob, to deprive (de, of).

spondée [spɔ̃de] m. Spondee.

spongiaire [spɔ̃ʒjɛ:r] m. ZOOL. Spongia, sponge.

spongieux, euse [spɔ̃ʒjø, ø:z] adj. Spongy.

spongiosité [-ʒjozite] f. Sponginess.

spontané, ée [spɔ̃tane] adj. Spontaneous (combustion, mouvement) ; natural, spontaneous (style).

spontanéité [-neite] f. Spontaneity.

spontanément [-nemɑ̃] adv. Spontaneously ; of one's own accord, on one's own account.

sporadicité [spɔradisite] f. Sporadicalness.

sporadique [-dik] adj. Sporadic.

sporadiquement [-dikmɑ̃] adv. Sporadically.

sporange [spɔrɑ̃:ʒ] m. BOT. Sporangium, spore case.

spore [spɔr] f. BOT. Spore.

sport [spɔ:r] m. SPORT. Sport ; *sports athlétiques*, athletics ; *le sport*, sports. ‖ AUTOM. *Grand sport*, sports (modèle).
— adj. inv. Casual (vêtements), sports (veste). ‖ Sporting, sportsmanlike (comportement).

sportif, ive [spɔrtif, i:v] adj. Sporting (journal) ; fond of sport (personne) ; sports (rédacteur).
— m. Sportsman.

sportive f. Sportswoman.

sportivement [-tivmɑ̃] adv. Sportingly.

sportivité [-tivite] f. Sportsmanship. ‖ FIG. *Avoir la sportivité de*, to be sporting enough to.

sportman [spɔrtman] (pl. sportmen) m. Sportsman.

sportwoman [-wuman] (pl. sportwomen). f. Sportswoman.

spot [spɔt] m. Small spotlight, spot (lampe). ‖ Commercial, ad (message publicitaire). ‖ ÉLECTR. Recording (ou) scanning spot, picture element (en télévision).

Spoutnik [sputnik] m. Sputnik.

sprat [sprat] m. ZOOL. Sprat.

spray [sprɛ] m. Spray (atomiseur).

sprint [sprint] m. SPORTS. Sprint.

sprinter [-tœ:r] m. SPORTS. Sprinter.

sprinter [-te] v. intr. (1). SPORTS. To sprint.

squale [skwal] m. ZOOL. Shark, dog-fish.

squame [skwam] f. MÉD., BOT. Squama, scale.

squameux, euse [-mø, ø:z] adj. MÉD., BOT. Squamous, scaly.

square [skwa:r] m. Square with garden.

squatter [-te]. squattériser [-terize] v. tr. (1). To squat in.

squaw [skwo] f. Squaw.

squelette [skəlɛt] m. Skeleton (d'un animal). ‖ NAUT. Carcass, framework, skeleton (d'un navire). ‖ FIG. Skeleton (personne) ; *un vrai squelette*, a living skeleton, a bag of bones. ‖ FAM. Outline, skeleton (d'un roman).

squelettique [-tik] adj. MÉD. Skeletal. ‖ FAM. Thin ; *maigreur squelettique*, extreme thinness, emaciation.

squille [ski:j] f. ZOOL. Squill, squill-fish. ‖ BOT. Squill.

squirre, squirrhe [ski:r] m. Méd. Scirrhus.
squirreux, euse [-rø, ø:z] adj. Méd. Scirrhous.
squirrosité [-rozite] f. Méd. Scirrhosity.
Sri Lanka [srilɑ̃ka] f. Géogr. Sri Lanka.
S.S. [ɛsɛs] abrév. de *Sa Sainteté,* H.H., His Holiness ; abrév. de *Sécurité sociale,* French equivalent of National Health Service.
Sᵗ, Sᵗᵉ abrév. de *saint, sainte,* St., Saint.
stabilisateur, trice [stabilizatœ:r, tris] adj. Stabilizing.
— m. Aviat. Stabilizer.
stabilisation [-zasjɔ̃] f. Stabilization. ‖ Fin. Stabilization (d'une monnaie). ‖ Techn. Annealing, tempering (d'un métal). ‖ Fig. Stabilizing (d'un Etat).
stabiliser [-ze] v. tr. (1). To stabilize. ‖ Fin. To stabilize, to maintain at a fixed value (une monnaie). ‖ Techn. To anneal, to temper (un métal). ‖ Fig. To stabilize (un Etat).
— v. pr. **Se stabiliser,** to become stable, to be stabilized.
stabilité [-te] f. Stability, firmness, steadiness. ‖ Fig. Stability, durability (d'un Etat).
stable [stabl] adj. Stable, firm, solid (édifice) ; *peu stable,* unstable. ‖ Naut. Stiff (navire). ‖ Chim. Stable (corps). ‖ Fig. Secure, assured (paix) ; level-headed (personne).
stabulation [stabylasjɔ̃] f. Agric. Stalling (du bétail) ; stabling (des chevaux). ‖ Méd. Confinement to one's room (d'un malade).
stabuler [-le] v. tr. (1). Agric. To stall (du bétail) ; to stable (des chevaux).
staccato [stakatɔ] adv. Mus. Staccato.
stade [stad] m. Sports. Stadium, sports arena ; athletic club. ‖ Fig. Stadium, stage, period, degree. (V. phase.)
staff [staf] m. Archit. Staff.
stage [sta:ʒ] m. Probationary period, course of instruction ; *faire un stage,* to do a probationary period, to complete a course of training, to be on probation ; to be under instruction. ‖ Fig. Stage, transitory period.
stagiaire [staʒjɛ:r] adj. Probationary (période) ; under instruction, on probation (personne).
— s. Probationer. ‖ Méd. Chemist's assistant (en pharmacie). ‖ Comm. Trainee.
stagnant, ante [stagnɑ̃, ɑ̃:t] adj. Stagnant, standing (eaux). ‖ Fig. Stagnant (affaires).
stagnation [-nasjɔ̃] f. Stagnation, stagnancy (des eaux). ‖ Fig. Stagnation, dullness. (V. marasme.)
stagner [-ne] v. intr. (1). To stagnate.
stakhanovisme [stakanɔvism] m. Stakhanovism.
stalactite [stalaktit] f. Stalactite.
stalag [stalag] m. Stalag.
stalagmite [-lagmit] f. Stalagmite.
stalinien, enne [stalinjɛ̃, ɛn] adj. Stalin (de Staline) ; stalinist (des partisans de Staline).
— n. Stalinist.
stalinisme [stalinism] m. Stalinism.
stalle [stal] f. Stall, box (d'écurie). ‖ Ecclés. Stall. ‖ Théâtr. Seat, stall.
stance [stɑ̃:s] f. Stanza.
stand [stɑ̃:d] m. Stand, stall (à une exposition). ‖ Sports. Stand (aux courses) ; rifle-range, shooting-gallery (au tir).
standard [stɑ̃da:r] m. Comm. Standard. ‖ Electr. Switchboard. ‖ Fig. *Standard de vie,* standard of living.
— adj. Standard.
standardisation [stɑ̃dardizasjɔ̃] f. Standardization.
standardiser [-dize] v. tr. (1). To standardize.
standardiste [-dist] f. Switchboard operator.
standing [stɑ̃diŋ] m. Status, standing.
stannique [stanik] adj. Chim. Stannic.

staphylocoque [stafilokɔk] m. Méd. Staphylococcus.
star [star] f. Star.
starlette [-let] f. Starlet.
starter [startɛ:r] m. Sports. Starter. ‖ Autom. Choke.
starting-block [startiŋblɔk] m. Sports. Starting-block.
stase [stɑ:z] f. Méd. Stasis.
station [stasjɔ̃] f. Resort (lieu) ; *station balnéaire, hivernale,* bathing, winter resort ; *station thermale,* watering place, spa. ‖ Standing position (posture). ‖ Halt, stay, stop (halte) ; *faire une station,* to break one's journey. ‖ Station (d'autobus) ; cab-rank, taxi-rank (ou) U. S. taxi stand (de taxis). ‖ Radio. Station ; *station émettrice, réceptrice,* broadcasting, receiving station. ‖ Ch. de f. Station, halt. ‖ Ecclés. Station (de chemin de croix). ‖ Naut. *Station de sauvetage,* lifeboat-station. ‖ Agric. *Station agronomique,* agricultural research station. ‖ Electr. *Station centrale d'électricité,* power station. ‖ **Station-service** (pl. *stations-service*) f. Autom. Service-station (pour essence) ; repair-station (pour réparations).
stationnaire [-sjɔnɛ:r] adj. Steady (baromètre) ; stationary, fixed (machine) ; stationary (véhicule). ‖ Méd. Stationary (état).
— m. Naut. Guard-ship.
stationnale [-sjɔnal] adj. Ecclés. Stational.
stationnement [-sjɔnmɑ̃] m. Autom. Stopping, waiting, parking ; « *stationnement interdit* », « no parking », « parking forbidden » ; « *stationnement de courte durée* », « no waiting », U. S. « no standing ». ‖ Milit. Quartering, stationing (de troupes).
stationner [-sjɔne] v. intr. (1). To stop, to halt, to stand, to take up one's position. ‖ Autom. To park ; *défense de stationner,* « no parking ».
statique [statik] adj. Static.
— f. Statics.
statisticien [statistisjɛ̃] m. Statistician.
statistique [-tik] adj. Statistical.
— f. Statistics ; *statistiques du mois d'août,* figures for August.
statistiquement [-tikmɑ̃] adv. Statistically.
stator [statɔ:r] m. Electr. Stator.
statoréacteur [statoreaktœ:r] m. Aviat. Ram-jet.
statuaire [statɥɛ:r] adj. Arts. Statuary.
— f. Arts. Statuary (art) ; sculptress (artiste).
— m. Arts. Sculptor.
statue [staty] f. Arts. Statue.
statuer [-tɥe] v. tr. (1). Jur. To order, to decree, to enact (une enquête).
— v. intr. Jur. To pronounce judgment, to give a ruling (*sur,* on).
statuette [-tɥɛt] f. Arts. Statuette.
statufier [-tyfje] v. tr. (1). Fam. To erect a statue to (qqn).
statu quo [statyko] m. Status (in) quo.
stature [staty:r] f. Stature, height. (V. taille.)
statut [staty] m. Comm. Statute, rule, regulation (d'une association) ; charter (d'une société). ‖ Jur. Status, constitution (d'un royaume).
statutaire [-tɛ:r] adj. Statutory, statutable.
statutairement [-tɛrmɑ̃] adv. Statutably ; in accordance with the statutes (ou) articles.
Sᵗᵉ abrév. de *société,* French equivalent of Co., Ltd., U.S. Inc.
steak [stɛk] m. Culin. Steak.
steamer [stimœ:r] m. Naut. Steamer, steamboat.
stéarate [steaʀat] m. Chim. Stearate.
stéarine [-rin] f. Chim. Stearine.
stéarique [-rik] adj. Chim. Stearic.
stéatite [-tit] f. Chim. Steatite, soapstone.
stéatome [-to:m] m. Méd. Steatoma.
stéatose [-to:z] f. Méd. Steatosis.

steeple-chase [stiplətʃɛs] (pl. **steeple-chases**) m. Sports. Steeplechase.

steeple-chaser [-zœ:r] (pl. **steeple-chasers**) m. Sports. Steeplechaser.

stèle [stɛl] f. Stele.

stellage [stɛla:ʒ] m. Fin. Double option.

stellaire [stɛllɛ:r] adj. Astron. Stellar.
— f. Bot. Stellaria, stitchwort.

stencil [stɛsil] m. Stencil.

stendhalien, enne [stɛ̃daljɛ̃, ɛn] adj. Stendhalian, of (ou) relating to Stendhal.

sténo [steno], **sténographe** [-graf] s. Shorthand typist, U.S. stenographer.

sténo, sténographie [-grafi] f. Shorthand, stenography.

sténodactylographier [-grafje] v. tr. (1). To take down in shorthand, to stenograph.

sténogramme [stenɔgram] m. Shorthand report.

sténographe [-graf] s. Stenographer, shorthand-typist.

sténographie [-grafi] f. Stenography, shorthand.

sténographique [-grafik] adj. Stenographic, shorthand.

sténose [steno:z] f. Méd. Stenosis.

sténotype [stenɔtip] m. Stenotype.
— f. Shorthand typewriter.

sténotyper [-pe] v. tr. To stenotype.

sténotypie [-pi] f. Stenotypy.

sténotypiste [-pist] f. Stenotypist.

stentor [stɑ̃tɔ:r] m. Stentor; *de stentor*, stentorian (voix).

stéphanois, oise [stefanwɑ, wɑ:z] adj. Géogr. Of (ou) from Saint-Étienne.
— n. Native (ou) inhabitant of Saint-Étienne.

steppe [stɛp] f. Steppe.

stepper [stɛpœ:r] m. High-stepper (cheval).

stepper [-pe] v. intr. To step high (cheval).

stère [stɛ:r] m. Stere; *bois de stère*, cord-wood.

stéréo [stereo] adj., f. Stereo (stéréophonique, stéréophonie).

stéréobate [stereɔbat] m. Archit. Stereobate.

stéréochimie [-ʃimi] f. Stereochemistry.

stéréomètre [-mɛtr] m. Stereometer.

stéréophonie [-fɔni] f. Stereophony, stereo.

stéréophonique [-fɔnik] adj. Stereophonic, stereo.

stéréoscope [-skɔp] m. Stereoscope.

stéréoscopique [-skɔpik] adj. Stereoscopic.

stéréotype [-tip] m. Techn. Stereotype, stereotyped plate. ‖ Fig. Stereotype, cliché.

stéréotypé, ée [-tipe] adj. Stereotyped, hackneyed.

stéréotypie [-tipi] f. Stereotypy, stereotyping.

stérer [stere] v. tr. (5). To measure by the stere.

stérile [steril] adj. Méd. Sterile (femme); childless (mariage). ‖ Agric. Barren, unproductive (terre); barren (vache). ‖ Fig. Unproductive, sterile (auteur); fruitless (discussion); vain, fruitless (effort); unprofitable (travail).

stérilement [-lmɑ̃] adv. Unfruitfully, fruitlessly, unprofitably.

stérilet [-lɛ] m. Méd. Intra-uterine device, IUD, coil, loop.

stérilisant, ante [-lizɑ̃, ɑ̃:t] adj. Sterilizing.
— m. Sterilizing agent.

stérilisateur [-lizatœ:r] m. Sterilizer.

stérilisation [-lizasjɔ̃] f. Sterilization.

stérilisé, ée [-lize] adj. Sterilized.

stériliser [-lize] v. tr. (1). To sterilize.

stérilité [-lite] f. Sterility, unfruitfulness, barrenness. ‖ Méd. Barrenness.

sterling [stɛrliŋ] adj. invar. Sterling; *livre sterling*, pound sterling.
— m. invar. Sterling.

sternal, ale [stɛrnal] adj. Méd. Sternal.

sterne [stɛrn] m. Zool. Tern.

sternum [stɛrnɔm] m. Méd. Sternum, breast-bone.

sternutation [-sjɔ̃] f. Méd. Sternutation, sneezing.

sternutatoire [-twa:r] adj., m. Méd. Sternutatory.

stéroïde [sterɔid] adj. Méd. Steroidal.

stérol [sterɔl] m. Chim. Sterol.

stertor [stɛrtɔ:r] m. Méd. Stertor.

stertoreux, euse [-tɔrø, ø:z] adj. Méd. Stertorous.

stéthoscope [-skɔp] m. Méd. Stethoscope.

steward [stjuward] m. Naut. Steward.

stewardesse [-dɛs] m. Naut. Stewardess.

sthénique [stenik] adj. Méd. Sthenic.

stick [stik] m. Riding-switch. ‖ Milit. Swagger-cane (ou) -stick.

stigmate [stigmat] m. Méd. Stigma, pock-mark, pit (de la petite vérole). ‖ Ecclés. Pl. Stigmata. ‖ Bot. Stigma. ‖ † Stigma, brand (du fer rouge). ‖ Fig. Stigma, stain (du vice).

stigmatique [-tik] adj. Stigmatic.

stigmatisation [-tizasjɔ̃] f. Stigmatizing, stigmatization.

stigmatisé, ée [-tize] adj. Stigmatized.
— s. Ecclés. Stigmatist.

stigmatiser [-tize] v. tr. (1). Ecclés. To stigmatize. ‖ Méd. To pock-mark. ‖ Fig. To stigmatize, to brand.

stigmatisme [-tism] m. Stigmatism.

stillant, ante [stillɑ̃, ɑ̃:t] adj. Dripping (eau).

stillation [-lasjɔ̃] f. Dripping (de l'eau).

stilligoutte [-ligut] m. Dropper.

stimulant, ante [stimylɑ̃, ɑ̃:t] adj. Stimulating.
— m. Méd. Stimulant. ‖ Fig. Stimulus, incentive.

stimulateur [-latœ:r] m. Méd. *Stimulateur cardiaque*, pacemaker.

stimulation [-lasjɔ̃] f. Stimulation.

stimuler [-le] v. tr. (1). To whet (l'appétit); to stimulate (a digestion); to incite, to spur on (qqn).

stimulus [-lys] m. Méd. Stimulus.

stipe [stip] m. Bot. Stipe, stipes, stem.

stipendiaire [stipɑ̃djɛ:r] adj. Mercenary.
— s. Hireling, mercenary.

stipendié, ée [dje] adj. Hired.
— s. Hireling, mercenary.

stipendier [-dje] v. tr. (1). To hire, to have in one's pay.

stipulation [stipylasjɔ̃] f. Stipulation.

stipule [-pyl] f. Bot. Stipule.

stipulé, ée [-pyle] adj. Bot. Stipuled, stipulate.

stipuler [-pyle] v. tr. (1). To stipulate, to specify, to lay down.

stochastique [stɔkastik] adj. Math. Stochastic.

stock [stɔk] m. Comm. Stock; *stock en magasin*, stock in hand (ou) in warehouse (ou) in trade. ‖ Fin. *Stock d'or*, gold reserve.

stockage [-ka:ʒ] m. Comm. Stocking, keeping in stock (des marchandises). ‖ Fam. Stockpiling.

stocker [-ke] v. tr. (1). Comm. To stock, to keep in stock (des marchandises). ‖ Fam. To stockpile.

stockfisch [stɔkfiʃ] m. Stockfish.

stockiste [stɔkist] m. Comm. Stockist. ‖ Autom. Agent.

stoïcien, enne [stɔisjɛ̃] adj. Stoic, stoical.
— s. Stoic.

stoïcisme [-sism] m. Stoicism.

stoïque [stɔik] adj. Stoic, stoical.
— s. Stoic.

stoïquement [-mɑ̃] adv. Stoically.

stolon [stɔlɔ̃] m. Bot. Stolon.

stomacal, ale [stɔmakal] adj. Méd. Stomachal.

stomachique [-ʃik] adj., m. Méd. Stomachic.

stomate [stɔmat] m. Bot. Stoma.

stomatite [-tit] f. Méd. Stomatitis.

stomatologie [-tɔlɔʒi] f. Méd. Stomatology.

stomatologiste [-tɔlɔʒist] m. Méd. Stomatologist.

stomatoplastie [-tɔplasti] f. Méd. Stomatoplasty.

stop [stɔp] interj. Stop.
— m. Hitching (auto-stop) ; *faire du stop,* to hitch.
‖ Autom. Stop sign (panneau) ; break light (feux arrière).
stoppage [stɔpa:ʒ] m. Stopping (d'un véhicule).
stoppage [-pa:ʒ] m. Invisible mending, fine-darning (d'une déchirure).
stopper [-pe] v. intr. (1). To stop, to come to a stop (train, véhicule).
— v. tr. To stop (un train, un véhicule).
stopper [-pe] v. tr. (1). To mend invisibly, to fine-darn (une déchirure).
stoppeur [-pœ:r] m. Naut. Chain-stopper.
stoppeur, euse [-pœ:r, ø:z] s. Invisible mender, fine-darner. ‖ Fam. Hitcher (auto-stoppeur).
store [stɔ:r] m. Blind, window-blind. U. S. shade.
strabique [strabik] adj. Squinting, squint-eyed.
— s. Squinter.
strabisme [-bism] m. Strabism, strabismus, squint.
stradivarius [stradivarjy:s] m. Mus. Stradivarius ; Strad (fam.).
strangulation [strãgylasjɔ̃] f. Strangulation, strangling, throttling.
strapontin [strapõtɛ̃] m. Théâtr., Autom. Folding-seat, flap-seat ; U. S. jump seat.
strasbourgeois, oise [strasburʒwα, wα:z] adj. Géogr. Of (ou) from Strasbourg.
— s. Native (ou) inhabitant of Strasbourg.
strass [stras] m. Strass ; paste jewellery.
strasse [stra:s] f. Waste silk ; floss-silk.
stratagème [strataʒɛm] m. Stratagem.
strate [strat] f. Géogr. Stratum, layer.
stratège [stratɛ:ʒ] m. Strategus (de l'Antiquité). ‖ Strategist (stratégiste) ; *stratège en chambre,* armchair strategist (ou) U. S. general.
stratégie [-teʒi] f. Strategy (v. tactique) ; *haute stratégie,* grand strategy.
stratégique [-teʒik] adj. Strategic ; *valeur stratégique,* tactical importance.
stratégiquement [-teʒikmã] adv. Strategically.
stratification [stratifikasjɔ̃] f. Stratification.
stratifié, ée [-fje] adj. Stratified. ‖ Techn. Laminated.
stratifier [-fje] v. tr. (1). To stratify.
— v. pr. **Se stratifier,** to stratify.
stratigraphie [stratigrafi] f. Géogr. Stratigraphy.
stratigraphique [-fik] adj. Géogr. Stratigraphic.
strato-cumulus [stratokymylys] m. Strato-cumulus.
stratosphère [-sfɛ:r] f. Astron. Stratosphere.
stratosphérique [-sferik] adj. Stratospheric ; *avion stratosphérique,* strato-cruiser, strato-liner.
stratus [straty:s] m. Stratus.
streptocoque [-kɔk] m. Méd. Streptococcus.
streptomycine [-misin] f. Méd. Streptomycin.
stress [strɛ:s] m. Méd., Psych. Stress.
stressant, ante [strɛsã, ã:t] adj. Méd., Psych. Stressing. ‖ Fig. Stressful.
striation [strijasjɔ̃] f. Striation.
strict, icte [strikt] adj. Strict, severe (personne) ; precise, exact (sens).
strictement [-mã] adv. Strictly, precisely, exactly.
striction [striksjɔ̃] f. Méd. Constriction. ‖ Math. Striction.
stricto sensu [striktosɛ̃sy] loc. adv. Strictly speaking.
stridence [stridã:s] f. Stridency, shrillness.
strident, ente [-dã, ã:t] adj. Strident, shrill.
stridulant, ante [stridylã, ã:t] adj. Stridulant.
stridulation [-lasjɔ̃] f. Stridulation.
striduler [-le] v. tr. (1). To stridulate.
striduleux, euse [-lø, ø:z] adj. Méd. Stridulous.
strie [stri] f. Archit. Stria, fillet. ‖ Géol. Score, scratch, stria ; *strie glaciale,* glacial score. ‖ Streak (de couleur). ‖ Méd. Stria.
strié, ée [-je] adj. Striped, streaked (rayé). ‖

Archit. Fluted, grooved, striated (colonne). ‖ Géol. Striated, scored (rocher).
strier [-je] v. tr. (1). To streak. ‖ Archit. To flute, to groove, to striate (une colonne). ‖ Géol. To striate, to score (un rocher).
strip-tease [striptiz] m. Strip-tease.
strip-teaseuse [-tizø:z] Stripper, strip artist.
striure [strijy:r] f. Striation, scoring, streaking.
stroboscope [strɔbɔskɔp] m. Techn. Stroboscope.
strontiane [strɔ̃sjan] f. Chim. Strontia.
strontium [-sjɔm] m. Chim. Strontium.
strophe [strɔf] f. Stanza, verse (d'un poème) ; strophe (d'une tragédie grecque).
structural, ale [stryktyral] adj. Structural.
structuralement [-tyralmã] adv. Structurally.
structuralisme [-tyralism] m. Philos., Gramm. Structuralism.
structuraliste [-tyralist] adj., s. Philos., Gramm. Structuralist.
structuration [-tyrasjɔ̃] f. Structuring.
structure [-ty:r] f. Archit. Structure, edifice, building (édifice) ; construction (manière de bâtir). ‖ Fig. Construction, structure, arrangement (d'un poème).
structuré, ée [-tyre] adj. Structured.
structurel, elle [-tyrɛl] adj. Structural.
structurer [-tyre] v. tr. (1). To structure.
strychnine [striknin] f. Strychnine.
stuc [styk] m. Archit. Stucco.
stucage [-ka:ʒ] m. Archit. Stucco-work ; stuccoing.
stucateur [-katœ:r] m. Archit. Stucco-worker.
stud [stœd] m. Stud. ‖ **Stud-book,** m. Sports. Stud-book.
studieusement [stydjøzmã] adv. Studiously.
studieux, euse [-djø, ø:z] adj. Studious.
studio [-djo] m. Furniture for one-roomed flat (meubles) ; bedsitting-room (pièce). ‖ Radio. Studio, broadcasting studio. ‖ Ciném. Studio, film-studio. ‖ Arts. Studio (d'artiste).
stupéfaction [stypefaksjɔ̃] f. Stupefaction, amazement.
stupéfait, aite [-fɛ, ɛt] adj. Stupefied, amazed, astounded ; *stupéfait de,* amazed at.
stupéfiant, ante [-fjã, ã:t] adj. Méd. Stupefying, stupefacient. ‖ Fig. Astounding, amazing.
— m. Méd. Narcotic ; drug.
stupéfier [-fje] v. tr. (1). Méd. To stupefy. ‖ Fig. To astound, to amaze.
stupeur [stypœ:r] f. Stupor, lethargy. ‖ Fig. Stupefaction, amazement.
stupide [-pid] adj. Silly, idiotic (air) ; stupid, slow-witted, dull (personne). ‖ Stupefied, stunned (stupéfié).
— s. Stupid person, dolt ; clot (fam.).
stupidement [-pidmã] adv. Stupidly.
stupidité [-pidite] f. Stupidity, foolishness (état). ‖ Piece of stupidity, stupid (ou) foolish action (action) ; stupid (ou) foolish reply (réponse).
stupre [stypr] m. Indecent (ou) shameless act ; rape (acte). ‖ Debauchery (débauche).
style [stil] m. Style, gnomon (de cadran solaire). ‖ Bot. Style. ‖ Mus. *Style d'enregistrement,* record cutter. ‖ Arts. Stylus, style, etching needle (de graveur) ; style (genre) ; *dans le style de,* in the style of ; *style Louis XIV,* in the Louis XIV style. ‖ Gramm. Style ; *style journalistique,* journalesee.
styler [-le] v. tr. (1). To train, to form.
stylet [-lɛ] m. Stiletto, stylet. ‖ Méd. Stylet.
stylisation [-lizasjɔ̃] f. Arts. Stylization.
styliser [-lize] v. tr. (1). Arts. To stylize.
stylisme [-lism] m. Concern for style (en littérature) ; design (dans l'habillement, l'ameublement).
styliste [-list] s. Stylist (écrivain) ; stylist, designer (dessinateur de mode, de mobilier).

stylisticien, enne [-listisjɛ̃, ɛn] s. GRAMM. Stylistics specialist.
stylistique [-listik] adj. GRAMM., ARTS. Stylistic.
— f. GRAMM. Stylistics.
stylo [stilo], **stylographe** [-graf] m. Fountain-pen, pen; *stylo à bille, stylo bille*, ball-pen, ball-point, Biro (nom déposé).
styloïde [stiloid] adj. Styloid.
styptique [stiptik] adj. MÉD. Styptic.
su [sy] m. Knowledge; *au vu et au su de*, to the knowledge of.
— p. p. V. SAVOIR (92).
suaire [sɥɛ:r] m. Winding-sheet, shroud. (V. LINCEUL.) ‖ ECCLÉS. *Le saint suaire*, the Sindon.
suant, ante [sɥɑ̃, ɑ̃:t] adj. Sweating (en sueur).
‖ FAM. Boring, irksome (ennuyeux); *c'est suant*, it's a drag.
suave [sɥav] adj. Suave, bland, smooth (manières); sweet (mélodie); pleasant (parfum); nice, sweet, unctuous (personne).
suavement [-vmɑ̃] adv. Suavely, blandly.
suavité [-vite] f. Suavity, blandness (de manières); sweetness (d'une mélodie); pleasantness (d'un parfum).
subaigu, guë [sybegy] adj. MÉD. Subacute.
subalpin, ine [sybalpɛ̃, in] adj. Subalpine.
subalterne [sybaltɛrn] adj. Subordinate. (V. INFÉRIEUR.) ‖ MILIT. *Officier subalterne*, junior officer.
— s. Subordinate, underling.
subconscience [sybkɔ̃sjɑ̃:s] f. Subconsciousness.
subconscient, ente [-kɔ̃sjɑ̃, ɑ̃:t] adj. Subconscious.
— m. *Le subconscient*, the subconscious.
subcontraire [-kɔ̃trɛ:r] adj. Subcontrary.
subdélégué, ée [-delege] s. Subdelegate.
subdéléguer [-delege] v. tr. (5). To subdelegate.
subdiviser [-divize] v. tr. (1). To subdivide.
subdivision [-divizjɔ̃] f. Subdivision.
subéreux, euse [sybérø, ø:z] adj. BOT. Suberous.
subir [sybi:r] v. tr. (2). To suffer, to meet with (une défaite); to submit to, to put up with (sa destinée); to undergo (un examen); to come under (une influence); to suffer under (un joug); to serve (son jugement); to suffer, to endure (des tortures).
subit, ite [sybi, it] adj. Sudden.
subitement [-tmɑ̃] adv. Suddenly, all of a sudden.
subito [-to] adv. FAM. Suddenly, all of a sudden.
subjectif, ive [syb3ɛktif, i:v] adj. Subjective.
subjectivement [-vmɑ̃] adv. Subjectively.
subjectivisme [-vism] m. Subjectivism.
subjectivité [-vite] f. Subjectivity.
subjonctif, ive [syb3ɔ̃ktif, i:v] adj. GRAMM. Subjunctive.
— m. GRAMM. Subjunctive; *au subjonctif*, in the subjunctive.
subjugation [syb3ygasjɔ̃] f. Subjugation.
subjuguer [-ge] v. tr. (1). To master, to tame, to subdue (un animal); to subjugate, to conquer, to subdue (un pays). ‖ FIG. To master, to subdue (ses passions).
sublimation [syblimasjɔ̃] f. Sublimation.
sublimatoire [-twa:r] adj. CHIM. Sublimatory.
— m. CHIM. Sublimating vessel.
sublime [syblim] adj. Sublime, lofty, noble.
— m. *Le sublime*, the sublime.
sublimé, ée [-me] adj. CHIM. Sublimated.
— m. CHIM. Sublimate.
sublimement [-mmɑ̃] adv. Sublimely.
sublimer [-me] v. tr. (1). CHIM. To sublimate, to sublime.
subliminal, ale [-minal] adj. Subliminal.
sublimité [-mite] f. Sublimity.
sublingual, ale [syblɛ̃gwal] adj. Sublingual.
sublunaire [syblynɛ:r] adj. Sublunar, sublunary.
submerger [sybmɛr3e] v. tr. (7). To flood (une étendue). [V. INONDER.] ‖ To immerse, to put

under water (un objet). ‖ To sink, to swamp (un navire). ‖ FIG. To overwhelm, to overrun; *submergé par l'anarchie*, in the depths of anarchy.
submersible [-sibl] adj. Easily flooded (terrain). ‖ NAUT. Submersible, sinkable (bateau).
— m. NAUT. Submarine.
submersion [-sjɔ̃] f. NAUT. Submersion, submergence; *mourir par submersion*, to die by drowning, to be drowned. ‖ AGRIC. Flooding (d'un terrain).
subodorer [sybɔdɔre] v. tr. (1). To scent (le gibier). ‖ FAM. To get wind of (une affaire).
suborbital, ale [sybɔrbital] adj. ASTRONAUT. Suborbital (syn. SOUS-ORBITAL).
subordination [sybɔrdinasjɔ̃] f. Subordination, subjection. ‖ GRAMM. Subordination.
subordonnant, ante [-nɑ̃, ɑ̃:t] adj. GRAMM. Subordinating.
subordonné, ée [-ne] adj. GRAMM. Subordinate, dependent.
— s. Subordinate, underling, inferior.
subordonner [-ne] v. tr. (1). To subordinate (à, to). ‖ FIG. *Subordonner ses dépenses à son revenu*, to cut one's coat according to one's cloth.
— v. pr. *Se subordonner*, to accept an inferior position, to give way to authority.
subornation [sybɔrnasjɔ̃] f. Subornation, bribery.
suborner [-ne] v. tr. (1). To suborn, to bribe.
suborneur, euse [-nœ:r, ø:z] s. Suborner, briber.
subreptice [sybrɛptis] adj. Surreptitious.
subrepticement [-tismɑ̃] adv. Surreptitiously.
subreption [-sjɔ̃] f. JUR. Subreption.
subrogateur [sybrɔgatœ:r] m. JUR. Surrogate, judge-advocate.
subrogation [-gasjɔ̃] f. JUR. Subrogation.
subrogatoire [-gatwa:r] adj. JUR. *Acte subrogatoire*, act of subrogation.
subrogé, ée [-3e] adj. JUR. Surrogated; *subrogé tuteur*, surrogate guardian.
— s. Surrogate, deputy.
subroger [-3e] v. tr. (7). JUR. To subrogate.
subséquemment [sybsekamɑ̃] adv. Subsequently.
subséquent, ente [-kɑ̃, ɑ̃:t] adj. Subsequent.
subside [sybsid] m. Subsidy.
subsidence [-dɑ̃:s] f. GÉOGR., GÉOL. Subsidence.
subsidiaire [-djɛ:r] adj. Subsidiary.
subsidiairement [-djɛrmɑ̃] adv. Subsidiarily.
subsistance [sybzistɑ̃:s] f. Subsistence, maintenance, sustenance. ‖ Pl. Provisions. ‖ MILIT. *Mis en subsistance*, on the ration strength.
subsistant, ante [-tɑ̃, ɑ̃:t] adj. Subsisting, existing, extant.
— m. MILIT. Soldier on the ration-strength.
subsister [-te] v. intr. (1). To exist, to be in existence; to remain (exister). ‖ To subsist, to live (s'entretenir).
subsonique [sybsɔnik] adj. PHYS., AVIAT. Subsonic.
substance [sybstɑ̃:s] f. Substance, matter, stuff. ‖ COMM. *Substance alimentaire*, food. ‖ FIG. Essence, substance, purport, pith (d'un ouvrage).
— loc. adv. **En substance**, in substance, substantially; essentially.
substantialisme [sybstɑ̃sjalism] m. Substantialism.
substantialité [-sjalite] f. Substantiality.
substantiel, elle [-sjɛl] adj. Substantial, nutritive, nourishing (aliment). ‖ PHILOS. Real, substantial (idée). ‖ FIG. Considerable, weighty (discours).
substantiellement [-sjɛlmɑ̃] adv. Substantially.
substantif, ive [sybstɑ̃tif, i:v] adj., m. GRAMM. Substantive.
substantivement [-tivmɑ̃] adv. Substantively.
substitué, ée [sypstitɥe] adj. JUR. Supposititious (enfant); substituted (héritier).

substituer v. tr. (1). To substitute (*à*, for); to replace (*à*, by).
— v. pr. **Se substituer**, to take the place (*à*, of), to substitute oneself (*à*, for); to act as a substitute (*à*, for).
substitut [-ty] m. Substitute. ‖ JUR. Deputy public prosecutor.
substitution [-tysjɔ̃] f. Substitution (*à*, for; *de*, of). ‖ JUR., MATH. Substitution.
substrat [substra], **substratum** [-tɔm] m. PHILOS., GÉOL. Substratum. ‖ Substrate.
substruction [sypstryksjɔ̃] f. ARCHIT. Substruction; underpinning.
substructure [-ty:r] f. ARCHIT. Substructure.
subterfuge [syptɛrfy:ʒ] m. Subterfuge, shift.
subtil, ile [syptil] adj. Subtle, nice, fine (distinction); subtle, discerning, ingenious (esprit); fine (poussière); subtle, fine-spun (raisonnement); dextrous (tour); subtle, pervasive (venin); clever (voleur); acute, keen (vue).
subtilement [-lmɑ̃] adv. Subtly.
subtilisation [-lizasjɔ̃] f. Subtilization.
subtiliser [-lize] v. tr. (1). To subtilize, to refine (une substance). ‖ FIG. To subtilize (son style). ‖ FAM. To pinch, to make away with (dérober).
— v. intr. To subtilize, to split hairs.
subtiliseur, euse [-lizœ:r, ø:z] s. Subtilizer, hair-splitter.
subtilité [-lite] f. Shrewdness, acuteness (de l'esprit); subtlety (d'un raisonnement). ‖ MÉD. Subtlety, pervasiveness (d'un venin); acuteness, keenness (de la vue).
subtropical, ale [syptropikal] adj. Subtropical.
subulé, ée [sybyle] adj. BOT., ZOOL. Subulate.
suburbain, aine [sybyrbɛ̃, ɛn] adj. Suburban.
subvenir [sybvəni:r] v. intr. (101). To help, to assist; *subvenir à*, to satisfy (un besoin); to relieve (la détresse); to meet (des frais); *subvenir aux besoins de*, to provide for (qqn).
subvention [sybvɑ̃sjɔ̃] f. Subvention, subsidy.
subventionnel, elle [-sjɔnɛl] adj. Subventionary.
subventionner [-sjɔne] v. tr. (1). To subsidize; *subventionné par la commune, l'Etat*, rate-, State-aided.
subversif, ive [sybvɛrsif, i:v] adj. Subversive.
subversion [-sjɔ̃] f. Subversion.
subvertir [-ti:r] v. tr. (2). To subvert.
suc [syk] m. Juice. ‖ MÉD. *Suc gastrique*, gastric juice. ‖ BOT. Sap. ‖ FIG. Essence, quintessence.
succédané, ée [syksedane] adj. Substitute, succedaneous.
— m. Substitute, succedaneum. (V. ERSATZ.)
succéder [syksede] v. intr. (5). *Succéder à*, to succeed, to follow, to come (ou) follow after, to succeed to; *Louis XIII succéda à Henri IV*, Louis XIII succeeded Henry IV; *la tempête succéda au calme*, the calm gave way to a storm. ‖ JUR. *Succéder à un héritage*, to come into an inheritance.
— v. pr. **Se succéder**, to follow (ou) succeed one another; *les victoires se sont succédé*, victory followed upon victory.
succès [syksɛ] m. Success, issue, result (résultat). ‖ Success, favourable result, successful issue (v. RÉUSSITE); *avoir du succès*, to be a success (ou) successful; *roman à grand succès*, best-seller; *sans succès*, without success, unsuccessfully; *succès d'estime*, mild success, « succès d'estime ». ‖ THÉÂTR. *Avoir un succès fou*, to be a huge success, to make a big hit; *pièce à succès*, hit. ‖ MUS. *À succès*, popular (chanson).
successeur [syksesœ:r] m. Successor.
successibilité [-sibilite] f. JUR. Right to succeed (droit); order of succession (ordre).
successible [-sibl] adj. JUR. Entitled to inherit (ou) succeed; *parents successibles*, natural heirs.
successif, ive [-sif, i:v] adj. Successif; *ordre suc-*

cessif, alternation (des jours et des nuits). ‖ JUR. *Droit successif*, right to inherit (ou) succeed.
succession [-sjɔ̃] f. Succession, series, sequence (série); *succession de mésaventures*, chapter of accidents, run of bad luck. ‖ JUR. Estate (biens); succession, transmission (transmission); *droits de succession*, estate duties, death-duties.
successivement [-sivmɑ̃] adv. Successively.
successoral, ale [-sɔral] adj. JUR. Successional, relating to an inheritance.
succin [syksɛ̃] m. Yellow amber.
succinct, incte [syksɛ̃, ɛ̃:t] adj. Succinct, concise.
succinctement [-sɛ̃ktmɑ̃] adv. Succinctly, concisely.
succion [syksjɔ̃] f. MÉD. Suction, sucking.
succomber [sykɔ̃be] v. intr. (1). To succumb; to give way (sous, beneath) [un fardeau]; to yield (sous, to) [le nombre]. ‖ MÉD. To succumb, to die; *succomber à une maladie*, to be carried off by an illness. ‖ FIG. To succumb, to yield (*à*, to) [la tentation].
succube [syky:b] m. Succubus, succuba.
succulence [sykylɑ̃:s] f. Succulence, juiciness.
succulent, ente [-lɑ̃, ɑ̃:t] adj. Succulent, juicy.
succursale [sykyrsal] f. COMM. Branch; *magasin à succursales multiples*, multiple-store, U. S. chain store. ‖ ECCLÉS. Chapel of ease, U. S. mission church.
sucement [sysmɑ̃] m. Sucking.
sucer [-se] v. tr. (6). To suck. ‖ FIG. To absorb, to take in, to imbibe (une doctrine). ‖ FAM. To bleed (qqn).
sucette [-sɛt] f. Dummy, teething-ring (de bébé). ‖ Lollipop; lollie (fam.) [bonbon]; *sucette à la pomme*, toffee-apple, U. S. candied apple. ‖ Sucker (de raffinerie).
suceur, euse [-sœ:r, ø:z] adj. Sucking. ‖ ZOOL. Suctorial.
— m. Sucker. ‖ ZOOL. Pl. Suctoria.
— m. Nozzle (d'aspirateur).
suçoir [-swa:r] m. ZOOL. Sucker.
suçon [-sɔ̃] m. FAM. Mark made by sucking.
suçoter [-sɔte] v. tr. (1). FAM. To keep sucking, to suck away at (un bonbon).
sucrage [sykra:ʒ] m. Sugaring (du vin).
sucrant, ante [-krɑ̃, ɑ̃:t] adj. Sweetening.
sucrase [-krɑ:z] f. CHIM. Invert sugar.
sucrate [-krat] m. Saccharate.
sucre [sykr] m. Sugar; *pain de sucre*, sugar-loaf; *pince à sucre*, sugar-tongs; *sucre candi*, candy-sugar; *sucre de betterave, d'orge*, beet, barley sugar; *sucre de canne*, cane sugar; *sucre cristallisé, en morceaux, en poudre*, granulated, lump, castor (ou) U. S. powdered sugar. ‖ FIG. *En pain de sucre*, sugar-loaf (montagne). ‖ FAM. *Casser du sucre sur le dos de qqn*, to run s.o. down.
sucré, ée [-kre] adj. Sugared, sweetened (café, thé); sweet (fruits). ‖ FIG. Sugary (langage); honeyed (mots).
sucrer v. tr. (1). To sugar, to sweeten, to put sugar in (une boisson).
— v. pr. **Se sucrer**, FAM. To line one's pocket, to take a large slice of the profits.
sucrerie [-krəri] f. Sugar-refinery. ‖ Pl. Sweets, sweetmeats, U. S. dessert.
sucrier, ère [-krije, ɛ:r] adj. Sugar (industrie).
— m. Sugar-basin; U. S. sugar-bowl.
sud [syd] m. South; *au sud*, in the south; *vent du sud*, south wind; *vers le sud*, southwards. ‖ ASTRON. *La Croix du Sud*, the Southern Cross.
— adj. invar. Southern (région); south, southerly (vent). ‖ **Sud-africain**, adj., s. South African. ‖ **Sud-Africaine** (*république*), f. GÉOGR. South Africa. ‖ **Sud-américain**, adj., s. South American. ‖ **Sud-coréen**, adj., s. South Korean. ‖ **Sud-est**, m. South-east; *vent du sud-est*, south-easterly

wind, southeaster; adj. inv. south-eastern (région), south-easterly (vent). ‖ **Sud-ouest,** m. Southwest; adj. inv. south-western (région), southwester (vent).

sudation [sydasjɔ̃] f. MÉD. Sudation.
sudatoire [-twa:r] adj. MÉD. Sudatory.
— m. Sudatorium.
sudiste [sydist] m. Southerner; U. S. FAM. Rebel (dans la guerre de Sécession).
— adj. Southern (armée).
sudorifère [sydɔrifɛ:r] adj. MÉD. Sudoriferous.
sudorifique [-fik] adj., m. MÉD. Sudorific.
sudoripare [-pa:r] adj. MÉD. Sudoriferous.
Suède [sɥɛd] f. GÉOGR. Sweden. ‖ COMM. *De* (ou) *en suède,* suède (gants).
suédine [sɥedin] f. Suede-cloth.
suédois, oise [sɥedwa, wa:z] adj. GÉOGR. Swedish. ‖ COMM. *Allumette suédoise,* safety-match.
— s. GÉOGR. Swede.
— m. GRAMM. Swedish (langue).
suée [sɥe] f. Sweating, sweat. ‖ POP. Fag, grind (corvée); fright, start (peur).
suer v. intr. (1). To sweat, to ooze (mur) [suinter]. ‖ To sweat, to perspire (personne) [transpirer]. ‖ FAM. *Faire suer qqn,* to bore (ou) sicken s.o.
— v. tr. *Suer du sang,* to sweat blood. ‖ FIG. To reek of (la pauvreté); to sweat with (la peur).
sueur [sɥœ:r] f. Sweat, perspiration; *en sueur,* sweating, perspiring; in a sweat. ‖ FIG. *A la sueur de son front,* by the sweat of one's brow.
suffire [syfi:r] v. intr. (97). To suffice, to be sufficient; to be enough (à, for); *cela suffit!, suffit!,* that's enough!, that will do!, stop it! ‖ *Suffire à,* to satisfy, to meet (ses besoins, ses dépenses).
— v. impers. *Il suffit de,* it suffices to; *il suffit que,* it is enough that.
— v. pr. Se suffire, to fend for oneself, to support oneself.
suffisamment [syfizamɑ̃] adv. Sufficiently, enough.
suffisance [-zɑ̃:s] f. Sufficiency; adequate supply, plenty (de, of). ‖ Self-conceit, self-sufficiency, bumptiousness (présomption).
— loc. adv. À (ou) en suffisance, in plenty.
suffisant, ante [-zɑ̃, ɑ̃:t] adj. Sufficient, adequate. ‖ Conceited, self-sufficient, bumptious (personne). ‖ PHILOS., ECCLÉS. Sufficient.
— s. Conceited (ou) bumptious person; prig.
suffisent [-zə]. V. SUFFIRE (97).
suffixal, ale [syfiksal] adj. Suffixal.
suffixation [-ksasjɔ̃] f. Suffixion, suffixation.
suffixe [syfiks] m. Suffix.
— adj. Suffixed.
suffocant, ante [syfɔkɑ̃, ɑ̃:t] adj. Suffocating, choking. ‖ FAM. Startling; stunning.
suffocation [-kasjɔ̃] f. Suffocation, choking.
suffoquer [-ke] v. tr. (1). To choke; *les sanglots le suffoquaient,* he was choking with sobs. ‖ FAM. To take s.o.'s breath away (qqn).
— v. intr. To suffocate; to choke (de, with).
suffragant, ante [syfragɑ̃, ɑ̃:t] adj., m. ECCLÉS. Suffragan.
suffrage [syfra:ʒ] m. Approbation (approbation); *les suffrages du public,* public approbation. ‖ Suffrage, right to vote, vote (droit de voter); vote (voix); *suffrages exprimés,* cast votes; *suffrage universel,* universal suffrage.
suffragette [-ʒɛt] f. Suffragette.
suffragiste [-ʒist] s. Suffragist.
suffusion [syfyzjɔ̃] f. MÉD. Suffusion.
suggérer [sygʒere] v. tr. (5). To suggest, to propose. ‖ JUR. *Suggérer un testament,* to assert undue influence on the matter of a will.
suggestibilité [-ʒɛstibilite] f. Suggestibility.
suggestif, ive [-ʒɛstif, i:v] adj. Suggestive.
suggestion [-ʒɛstjɔ̃] f. Suggestion, suggesting

(action). ‖ Suggestion, thought, idea (idée); *donné à titre de suggestion,* tentative. ‖ MÉD. Suggestion.
suggestionner [-ʒɛstjɔne] v. tr. (1). To influence by means of suggestion (qqn).
suggestivité [-ʒɛstivite] f. Suggestiveness.
suicidaire [sɥisidɛ:r] adj. PSYCH. Suicidal (idées, comportement). ‖ FIG. Suicidal, self-destructive, rash, fatal to one's interests (entreprise).
— s. PSYCH. Suicide prone person.
suicide [sɥisid] m. Suicide, self-murder, self-slaughter. ‖ FIG. *Suicide politique,* political suicide.
suicidé, ée [-de] adj. Suicidal.
— s. Suicide.
suicider (se) [səsɥiside] v. pr. (1). To commit suicide, to take one's life, to do (ou) make away with oneself.
suidés [sɥide] m. pl. ZOOL. Suidae.
suie [sɥi] f. Soot.
suif [sɥif] m. Tallow; *suif de mouton,* mutton-fat. ‖ POP. Telling-off, calling-down.
suiffer [-fe] v. tr. (1). To tallow, to grease.
suiffeux, euse [-fø, ø:z] adj. Tallowy, greasy.
sui generis [sɥiʒeneris] loc. adj. Sui generis.
suint [sɥɛ̃] m. Yolk, suint, wool-oil, wool-grease (de la laine). ‖ Glass gall (du verre).
suintant, ante [-tɑ̃, ɑ̃:t] adj. Oozing, sweating, running, dripping.
suintement [-tmɑ̃] m. Oozing, seeping, trickling (de l'eau); sweating (d'un mur); running (d'une plaie).
suinter [-te] v. intr. (1). To ooze, to trickle, to seep (eau); to sweat (mur). ‖ MÉD. To run (plaie).
— v. tr. To ooze (un liquide). ‖ FIG. To reek of (la misère); to ooze, to exude (la haine).
suis, suit. V. ÊTRE (48), SUIVRE (98).
Suisse [sɥis] f. GÉOGR. Switzerland; *la Suisse alémanique, romande,* German-speaking, French-speaking Switzerland.
suisse adj. Swiss.
suisse, esse [-ɛs] s. Swiss; *les Suisses,* the Swiss. ‖ Hall porter, doorman (portier). ‖ ECCLÉS. Church official. ‖ CULIN. *Petit suisse,* small cream cheese. ‖ LOC. *Faire suisse,* to drink in private, to be a secret drinker.
suite [sɥit] f. Continuation, sequel (continuation); *attendons la suite,* let's wait and see what follows (ou) what happens next; *la suite au prochain numéro,* to be continued in our next; *la suite d'un roman,* sequel to a novel; *par la suite,* later. ‖ Order, connection, coherence (liaison, ordre); *suite dans les idées,* consistency; *sans suite,* incoherent (mots); desultory (lectures). ‖ Suite, retinue, attendants, followers (d'un prince). ‖ Consequence, result, issue (résultat); *les suites d'une affaire,* the consequences of an affair; *donner suite à,* to take appropriate action concerning (une affaire); to carry out (une commande); to give effect to (une décision); to comply with (une requête). ‖ Series, succession, run, sequence (série); *dans la suite des temps,* in the course of time; *suite de malheurs,* series of misfortunes, chapter of accidents; *suite de succès,* run of successes. ‖ COMM. « *Comme suite à* », « further to », « with reference to »; *prendre la suite,* to take over (une maison de commerce); « *sans suite* », « cannot be repeated ». ‖ MUS. Suite. ‖ MATH. Series.
— loc. adv. À la suite de, in deference to (une demande); following, coming after (qqn); *à la suite les uns des autres,* one after another. ‖ De suite, in succession; *et ainsi de suite,* and so on; *pour la troisième nuit de suite,* for the third consecutive night; *trois semaines de suite,* three weeks running; *trois verres de suite,* three glasses in a row (ou) one after the other. ‖ Par suite, consequently, as a natural consequence. ‖ **Tout de suite,** immediately, without delay, at once.

— loc. prép. **En suite de, par suite de,** in consequence of, through, owing to ; *par suite de maladie,* owing to illness.

suitée [-te] adj. f. *Jument suitée,* mare with her foal.

suivant [-vɑ̃] prép. Proportionately to, according to (à proportion de). ‖ Along, in the direction of (dans la direction de). ‖ According to, in the opinion of (selon).
— loc. conj. **Suivant que,** according as.

suivant, ante [-vɑ̃, ɑ̃:t] adj. Following, next ; *le jour suivant,* the next (ou) following day.
— s. Follower.

suivante [-vɑ̃:t] f. Maid. ‖ THÉÂTR. Soubrette.

suiveur [-vœ:r] m. SPORTS. Trainer, manager (ou) journalist following a cycle race. ‖ TECHN. Follower.

suivi, e [-vi] adj. Coherent (raisonnement) ; well-attended (théâtre). ‖ COMM. Regular (affaire).

suivre [-vr] v. tr. (98). To come after, to follow (succéder à). ‖ To follow, to go along (un chemin) ; *lire en suivant les lignes avec son doigt,* to read by tracing the lines with one's finger ; *suivre au galop,* to gallop after ; *suivre qqn des yeux,* to look after s.o., to keep s.o. in sight ; *suivi de,* followed by. ‖ CULIN. *Suivre rigoureusement la recette,* to follow the recipe closely. ‖ SPORTS. To follow, to chase (un lièvre). ‖ COMM. To go on with (un article). ‖ JUR. To conduct (une affaire) ; to shadow (un suspect) ; to run after, to pursue (un voleur). ‖ FIG. To pursue (un but) ; to follow, to act on (un conseil) ; to follow, to take (un cours) ; to yield to (ses goûts) ; to follow, to apply (une méthode) ; to follow, to keep up with (la mode) ; to side with (un parti) ; *cette image me suit partout,* that picture follows me everywhere, I can't get that picture out of my mind ; *suivre son instinct,* to be guided by instinct ; *suivre le mouvement,* to keep in the swim.
— v. intr. To follow, to come after ; *faire suivre une lettre,* to forward a letter ; *prière de faire suivre,* please forward.
— v. pr. **Se suivre,** to be connected (s'enchaîner) ; *ces raisonnements se suivent,* these ideas follow one from the other. ‖ To follow each other (se succéder) ; *les jours se suivent et ne se ressemblent pas,* tomorrow is another day.

sujet, ette [syʒə, ɛt] adj. Subject (à, to) [soumis] ; *sujet aux lois,* subject to the laws. ‖ Subject, prone, inclined, liable (à, to) [susceptible]. ‖ FIN. Liable (à, to) [l'impôt]. ‖ COMM. Subject (à, to) [un droit].
— s. Subject.

sujet m. Subject, cause, motive ; reason (*de,* for) [cause, motif] ; *avoir tout sujet de croire,* to have every reason to believe ; *sujet de plaisanterie,* joking-matter. ‖ Subject (personne) ; *bon sujet,* steady (ou) dependable person ; *mauvais sujet,* hard case, rogue. ‖ Subject, matter (*de,* of) [matière] ; *à ce sujet,* by the way ; concerning this ; *au sujet de,* about, concerning ; *sujet du jour,* talk of the town. ‖ PHILOS. Subject. ‖ MÉD. Subject (cadavre) ; patient (malade). ‖ GRAMM. Subject.

sujétion [syʒesjɔ̃] f. Subjection, servitude, subservience.

sulfamide [sylfamid] m. MÉD. Sulphonamide, sulpha drug.

sulfatage [sylfata:ʒ] m. CHIM. Sulphating. ‖ AGRIC. Treating with copper sulphate.

sulfate [-fat] m. CHIM. Sulphate; *sulfate de cuivre,* copper sulphate.

sulfaté, e [-fate] adj. CHIM. Sulphated.

sulfater [-fate] v. tr. (1). CHIM. To sulphate. ‖ AGRIC. To treat with copper sulphate.
— V. pr. **Se sulfater,** CHIM. To sulphate (accu).

sulfhydrique [-fidrik] adj. CHIM. *Acide sulf-*

hydrique, sulphuretted hydrogen, hydrogen sulphide.

sulfitage [-fita:ʒ] m. Treating with sulphite.

sulfite [-fit] m. CHIM. Sulphite.

sulfurage [-fyra:ʒ] m. CHIM. Sulphuration.

sulfuration [-fyrasjɔ̃] f. CHIM. Sulphuration.

sulfure [-fy:r] m. CHIM. Sulphide.

sulfuré, ée [-fyre] adj. CHIM. Sulphuretted.

sulfurer [-fyre] v. tr (1). CHIM. To sulphurate.

sulfureux, euse [-fyrø, ø:z] adj. CHIM. Sulphurous.

sulfurique [-fyrik] adj. CHIM. Sulphuric.

sulfurisé, ée [-fyrize] adj. *Papier sulfurisé.* butter-paper, imitation parchment-paper.

sultan [syltɑ̃] m. Sultan.

sultanat [-tana] m. Sultanate.

sultane [-tan] f. Sultana.

sumérien, enne [symerjɛ̃, ɛn] adj., s. Sumerian.
— m. GRAMM. Sumerian (langue).

summum [sɔmmɔm] m. Highest degree, acme.

sunlight [sœnlajt] m. CINÉM. Sun-lamp.

sunnite [synnit] m. ECCLÉS. Sunnite, sunni.

super [sypɛ:r] adj. FAM. Super, fantastic, great.
— m. AUTOM., FAM. High-octane (ou) four or five star petrol, premium (syn. SUPERCARBURANT).

superbe [sypɛrb] adj. Proud (air) ; stately, lofty, imposing, superb (bâtiment) ; fine, **magnificent** (femme) ; splendid, fine, glorious (temps).
— f. Arrogance, pride, haughtiness.

superbement [-bəmɑ̃] adv. Superbly, proudly, arrogantly.

superbombe [sypɛrbɔb] f. MILIT. Superbomb.

supercarburant [sypɛrkarbyrɑ̃] m. AUTOM. High-grade (ou) branded petrol; U. S. high-test (ou) -octane gasoline.

supercherie [sypɛrʃəri] f. Fraud, deceit, deception.

superfétatoire [-twa:r] adj. Superfluous.

superficie [sypɛrfisi] f. Surface, surface area. ‖ FIG. Superficial knowledge.

superficiel, elle [-sjɛl] adj. Superficial, slight (blessure), surface-water (eau). ‖ FIG. Shallow (esprit) ; outward (ressemblance).

superficiellement [-sjɛlmɑ̃] adj. Superficially.

superfin, ine [sypɛrfɛ̃, in] adj. Superfine.

superflu, ue [sypɛrfly] adj. Superfluous (ornement) ; useless (regret).
— m. Superfluity, excess.

superfluité [-flɥite] f. Superfluity.

superforteresse [syperfɔrtrɛs] f. AVIAT. Superfortress.

supergrand [sypɛrgrɑ̃] m. FAM. Superpower.

super-huit [sypɛrɥit] m. inv. CINÉM. Super-eight.

supérieur, eure [syperjœ:r] adj. Upper (étage) ; senior (officier) ; higher (offre, température) ; *enseignement supérieur,* higher education. ‖ MÉD. *Lèvre supérieure,* upper lip. ‖ NAUT. *Pont supérieur,* upper deck. ‖ FIG. Superior (talent) ; *supérieur aux événements,* unaffected by events, able to rise above events.
— s. Superior ; better. ‖ ECCLÉS. Superior.

supérieurement [-mɑ̃] adv. Exceedingly well; superlatively ; *supérieurement doué,* exceptionally gifted.

supériorité [syperjɔrite] f. Superiority. ‖ ECCLÉS. Superiorship. ‖ FIG. *Supériorité écrasante,* heavy odds; crushing superiority.

superlatif, ive [sypɛrlatif, i:v] adj. Superlative.
— m. GRAMM. Superlative.
— loc. adv. **Au superlatif,** superlatively.

superlativement [-tivmɑ̃] adv. Superlatively.

supermarché [sypɛrmarʃe] m. Supermarket.

supernova [sypɛrnɔva] f. ASTRON. Supernova.

superphosphate [sypɛrfɔsfat] m. Superphosphate.

superposable [sypɛrpozabl] adj. Superimposable.

superposer [-ze] v. tr. (1). To superimpose, to put one above (ou) on top of the other, to stack; *lits superposés*, bunk-beds. ‖ MATH. To superpose (des figures géométriques).
— v. pr. **Se superposer,** to be superimposed (ou) stacked, to be one above (ou) on top of the other. ‖ MATH. To be superimposed.

superposition [-zisjɔ̃] f. Superimposition. ‖ MATH. Superposition.

superproduction [sypɛrprɔdyksjɔ̃] f. CINÉM. Spectacular; Hollywood epic.

superpuissance [sypɛrpɥisɑ̃:s] f. Superpower.

supersonique [sypɛrsɔnik] adj. AVIAT. Supersonic.

superstitieusement [sypɛrstisjøzmɑ̃] adv. Superstitiously.

superstitieux, euse [-sjø, ø:z] adj. Superstitious.

superstition [-sjɔ̃] f. Superstition.

superstructure [sypɛrstrykty:r] f. ARCHIT., NAUT. Superstructure.

supertanker [sypɛrtɑ̃kœ:r] m. NAUT. Supertanker (en gén.); very large crude carrier, VLCC (pétrolier géant).

superviser [sypɛrvize] v. tr. (1). To supervise, to oversee.

supin [sypɛ̃] m. GRAMM. Supine.

supinateur [sypinatœ:r] adj. m. MÉD. Supinator (muscle).

supination [-sjɔ̃] f. Supination.

supplanter [syplɑ̃te] v. tr. (1). To supplant, to take the place of.

suppléance [sypleɑ̃:s] f. Acting as deputy (ou) substitute (action). ‖ Functions of deputy (ou) substitute (fonction).

suppléant, ante [-ɑ̃, ɑ̃:t] adj. Acting, substitute, deputy (fonctionnaire). ‖ JUR. *Juge suppléant,* surrogate judge.
— s. Deputy, substitute.

suppléer [-e] v. tr. (1). To supply; *suppléer ce qui manque,* to make up what is lacking; *suppléer les lacunes d'un texte,* to fill in the gaps in a text. ‖ To deputize for, to act as substitute for, to take the place of (qqn).
— v. intr. To make up, to compensate (*à,* for).

supplément [-mɑ̃] m. Supplement, addition; *sans supplément,* without extra charge. ‖ Supplement (d'un journal). ‖ CH. DE F. Excess fare. ‖ MATH. Supplement. ‖ MILIT. *Supplément de solde,* extra pay.

supplémentaire [-mɑ̃tɛ:r] adj. Supplementary; additional; *heures supplémentaires,* overtime. ‖ FIN. *Crédit supplémentaire,* extension of credit. ‖ MATH. Supplemental (angles). ‖ MUS. Supplementary (lignes). ‖ CH. DE F. Relief (train).

supplétif, ive [-tif, i:v] adj. GRAMM. Suppletive. ‖ MILIT. Auxiliary.

suppliant, ante [syplijɑ̃, ɑ̃:t] m. Beseeching, supplicating, imploring, entreating.
— s. Suppliant.

supplication [syplikasjɔ̃] f. Supplication.

supplicatoire [-twa:r] adj. Supplicatory.

supplice [syplis] m. Torture, punishment, ill-treatment; *dernier supplice,* death. ‖ ECCLÉS. *Supplices éternels,* eternal torment. ‖ FIG. Torture, pain, agony; *être au supplice,* to be on tenter-hooks; *c'est pour moi un supplice,* it's torture (ou) agony for me.

supplicié, ée [-sje] s. Executed prisoner; person who has been put to death.

supplicier [-sje] v. tr. (1). To execute, to put to death (un prisonnier). ‖ FIG. To torture, to put on the rack (qqn).

supplier [syplije] v. tr. (1). To supplicate, to beg, to implore, to beseech, to entreat.

supplique [-plik] f. Request, petition.

support [sypɔ:r] m. Support, stay, strut, prop. ‖ BLAS. Supporter. ‖ FIG. Support.

supportable [sypɔrtabl] adj. Supportable, endurable, bearable; *cela n'est pas supportable,* that's intolerable.

supporter [-tœ:r, tɛ:r] m. SPORTS. Supporter, follower; fan (fam.).

supporter [-te] v. tr. (1). To support, to bear, to carry, to hold up, to sustain (porter, soutenir). ‖ To stand, to provide for, to pay for (payer); *supporter les frais d'un voyage,* to be responsible for the expenses of a journey. ‖ To suffer, to endure (souffrir); *supporter le froid,* to put up with the cold; *supporter impatiemment les reproches,* to be impatient of blame. ‖ To permit, to stand, to tolerate (tolérer); *ne pas supporter qu'un enfant désobéisse,* not to permit a child to be disobedient, not to tolerate disobedience from a child. ‖ FIG. To stand, to bear (l'examen).

supposable [sypozabl] adj. Supposable.

supposé, ée [-ze] adj. Supposed (auteur); supposititious (enfant); false (nom); forged (testament).
— prep. Supposing.
— loc. adv. **Supposé que,** supposing that.

supposer [-ze] v. tr. (1). To suppose (admettre); *supposons que cela soit vrai,* let us assume (ou) suppose that to be true. ‖ To suppose, to imply (impliquer); *les droits supposent les devoirs,* rights imply duties; *la jeunesse est supposée obéir,* youth is meant to obey. ‖ To suppose, to imagine (imaginer); *je suis bien loin de supposer que,* I don't imagine for a moment that. ‖ JUR. To substitute (un testament).

supposition [-zisjɔ̃] f. Supposition, conjecture, surmise; *pure supposition,* mere conjecture. ‖ JUR. Assumption (de nom); forgery (de titre); *supposition d'enfant,* presentation of a supposititious child.

suppositoire [-zitwa:r] m. MÉD. Suppository.

suppôt [sypo] m. † Servitor. ‖ Henchman, tool, instrument; *suppôt de Satan,* devil, fiend.

suppression [sypresjɔ̃] f. Suppression, destruction (d'un document); abolishing (d'un emploi); suppression, concealment, withholding (d'une nouvelle); deletion, cutting out (d'une phrase); suppression, quelling, putting down (d'une révolte). ‖ CH. DE F. Cancellation (d'un train).

supprimer [-prime] v. tr. (1). To suppress (un document); to abolish (un emploi); to suppress, to withhold, to conceal, to keep back (une nouvelle); to delete, to cut out (une phrase); to suppress, to quell, to put down (une révolte). ‖ FIN. To stop (une subvention). ‖ CH. DE F. To cancel (un train). ‖ FAM. To do away with, to get rid of (qqn).
— v. pr. **Se supprimer,** to do (ou) make away with oneself.

suppurant, ante [sypyrɑ̃, ɑ̃:t] adj. MÉD. Suppurating.

suppuratif, ive [-ratif, i:v] adj., m. MÉD. Suppurative.

suppuration [-rasjɔ̃] f. MÉD. Suppuration.

suppurer [-re] v. intr. (1). To suppurate.

supputation [sypỹtasjɔ̃] f. Calculation, reckoning, computation.

supputer [-te] v. tr. (1). To calculate, to compile, to work out, to reckon (une dépense).

supra [sypra] adv. Supra, above; *voir supra,* see supra (ou) above.

supraconducteur [syprakɔ̃dyktœ:r] adj. PHYS., TECHN. Superconducting, superconductive.
— m. PHYS., TECHN. Superconductor.

supraconduction [-sjɔ̃] f. PHYS., TECHN. Superconductivity.

supranational, ale [-nasjɔnal] adj. Supranational.

suprasensible [-sɑ̃sibl] adj. Supersensible.

supraterrestre [-tɛrɛstr] adj. Superterrestrial.

suprématie [sypremasi] f. Supremacy.

suprême [-prɛːm] adj. Supreme, sovereign (autorité); supreme, crowning (effort); supreme (être); last (honneurs, moments); paramount (importance); *au suprême degré*, in the highest degree. — m. CULIN. Supreme (de, of).

suprêmement [-prɛmmɑ̃] adv. Supremely.

sur [syr] prép. On (à la surface de); *sur l'eau*, on the water. ‖ Over, above (au-dessus); *avoir autorité sur*, to have authority over; *les nuages sur nos têtes*, the clouds above our heads (ou) overhead; *un pont sur le Don*, a bridge on (ou) over the Don. ‖ On (au nom de); *jurer sur l'honneur*, to swear on one's honour. ‖ On, about (au sujet de); *commentaire sur Platon*, commentary on Plato; *se renseigner sur*, to find out about. ‖ On (contre); *frapper sur une enclume*, to strike (on) an anvil. ‖ By, on (d'après); *juger sur les apparences*, to judge by appearances, to go on (ou) by appearances. ‖ On, upon (dessus); *assis sur une chaise*, seated on a chair. ‖ On (du côté de); *marcher sur une ville*, to march on a town; *revenir sur ses pas*, to retrace one's steps. ‖ On (en état de); *sur le qui-vive*, on the qui-vive (ou) alert. ‖ Out of (parmi); *neuf fois sur dix*, in nine cases (ou) times out of ten; *un sur dix*, one out of ten. ‖ After (par répétition de); *faire sottise sur sottise*, to make blunder after blunder, to do one stupid thing after another. ‖ On (tout proche); *ville sur la Seine*, town on the Seine. ‖ FAM. In (dans); *lire qqch. sur le journal*, to read sth. in the paper. ‖ LOC. *Sur l'heure*, without delay; *sur le tard*, towards evening; *sur un ton de reproche*, in a reproachful tone; *sur toute la ligne*, all along the line; *sur toute(s) chose(s)*, above all. ‖ **Sur-le-champ**, adv. At once, right away, immediately.

sur [syːr] adj. Sour, tart.

sûr, ûre [syr, yːr] adj. Sure, reliable, staunch, true (ami); unerring (goût); safe (lieu); sure, unfailing (remède); reliable (renseignement); trustworthy (source); *avoir la main sûre*, to have a steady hand; *avoir le pied sûr*, to be sure-footed; *bien sûr!*, of course!, naturally!; *en lieu sûr*, in a safe place; *en mains sûres*, in safe hands; *sûr de*, sure of, assured of; *jouer au plus sûr*, to play for safety; U. S. to play safe; *peu sûr*, unsafe, uncertain; *le plus sûr*, the safest thing; *sûr de soi*, self-assured; self-confident; *sûr et sûr*, quite sure. ‖ LOC. adv. *A coup sûr, pour sûr*, for certain, assuredly.

surabondamment [syrabɔ̃damɑ̃] adv. Superabundantly.

surabondance [-dɑ̃ːs] f. Superabundance.

surabondant, ante [-dɑ̃, ɑ̃ːt] adj. Superabundant.

surabonder [-de] v. intr. (1). To superabound, to be superabundant (en, in).

suractivité [syraktivite] f. Superactivity.

surah [syra] m. Surah.

suraigu, uë [syrɛgy] adj. Shrill, piercing, high-pitched. ‖ MÉD. Acute.

surajouté [syraʒute] adj. Adjunctive.

surajouter v. tr. (1). To superadd; to superinduce.

suralimentation [syralimɑ̃tasjɔ̃] f. Overfeeding. ‖ MÉD. Feeding up.

suralimenter [-te] v. tr. MÉD. To feed up.

suranné, ée [syrane] adj. Superannuated, faded (beauté); old-fashioned, antiquated (habit); out-of-date (mode).

surarbitre [syrarbitr] m. Deciding umpire.

surbaissé, ée [syrbɛse] adj. ARCHIT. Depressed, segmental, surbased (voûte, arc). ‖ AUTOM. Underslung (châssis).

surbaissement [-smɑ̃] m. ARCHIT. Surbasement.

surbaisser [-se] v. tr. (1). ARCHIT. To depress (une voûte). ‖ AUTOM. To undersling (un châssis).

surboum [syrbum] f. FAM. Party.

surcharge [syrʃarʒ] f. Overloading; overburdening (d'un cheval). ‖ Interlineation (en typographie). ‖ Surcharge (sur un timbre). ‖ CH. DE F. Excess luggage (ou) U. S. baggage. ‖ FIN. Overtax, overcharge. ‖ SPORTS. Weight handicap (d'un cheval de course). ‖ TECHN. *Poids en surcharge*, overload.

surcharger [-ʒe] v. tr. (7). To overload, to overburden (un cheval); to overwork (ses employés). ‖ To interline, to write between the lines of (un manuscrit). ‖ To surcharge (un timbre-poste). ‖ ELECTR. To overcharge (des accus). ‖ FIG. To overelaborate (son style).

surchauffage [syrʃofaːʒ] m. Superheating.

surchauffe [-ʃoːf] f. Superheat, superheating.

surchauffer [-ʃofe] v. tr. (1). To superheat.

surchoix [syrʃwa] m. COMM. First (ou) finest (ou) prime quality.

surclasser [-klase] v. tr. (1). SPORTS. To outclass.

surcompensation [-kɔ̃pɑ̃sasjɔ̃] f. PSYCH. Overcompensation.

surcomposé, ée [-kɔ̃poze] adj. GRAMM. Double compound.

surcomprimé, ée [-kɔ̃prime] adj. AUTOM. Supercharged; blown (fam.).

surcontrer [-kɔ̃tre] v. tr. (1). To redouble (aux cartes).

surcot [syrko] m. † Surcoat.

surcoupe [syrkup] f. Overtrumping (aux cartes).

surcouper [-pe] v. tr. (1). SPORTS. To overtrump.

surcroît [syrkrwa] m. Addition, increase; *par surcroît*, in addition, to boot; *pour surcroît de malheur*, to make matters worse.

surdétermination [syrdetɛrminasjɔ̃] f. PSYCH. Overdetermination, multiple determination.

surdi-mutité [syrdimytite] f. MÉD. Deaf-and-dumbness; deaf-muteness.

surdité [-dite] f. Deafness.

surdoué, ée [syrdue] adj. Specially gifted. — s. Specially gifted child.

sureau [syro] m. BOT. Elder, elder-tree; *baie de sureau*, elder-berry.

surélévation [syrelevasjɔ̃] f. ARCHIT. Heightening, raising (d'un mur). ‖ COMM. Raising, putting up (des prix).

surélever [-lɔve] v. tr. (5). ARCHIT. To heighten, to raise. ‖ COMM. To raise, to put up (les prix).

surelle [syrɛl] f. BOT. Wood-sorrel.

sûrement [syrmɑ̃] adv. Safely, securely, surely (avec sûreté). ‖ Certainly, for sure, assuredly (certainement); surely (très probablement). ‖ Confidently, steadily (sans inquiétude).

suréminent, ente [syreminɑ̃, ɑ̃ːt] adj. Supereminent.

surenchère [syrɑ̃ʃɛːr] f. Outbidding; higher bid.

surenchérir [-ʃeriːr] v. intr. (2). To outbid; *surenchérir sur qqn*, to outbid s.o., to bid higher than s.o.; to go one better than s.o. (fig.).

surenchérissement [-ʃerismɑ̃] m. Outbidding. ‖ COMM. Fresh rise in price.

surenchérisseur, euse [-ʃerisœːr, øːz] adj. Outbidding. — s. Outbidder.

surentraînement [syrɑ̃trɛnmɑ̃] m. SPORTS. Over-training.

surentraîner [-ne] v. tr. (1). To over-train.

suréquipement [syrekipmɑ̃] m. Overequipment.

suréquiper [-pe] v. tr. (1). To overequip.

surestaries [syrɛstari] f. pl. NAUT. Demurrage.

surestimation [syrɛstimasjɔ̃] f. Over-estimation.

surestimer [-me] v. tr. (1). To over-estimate.
suret [syrɛ] adj. Sourish.
sûreté [syrte] f. Sureness, surety, soundness, reliability (certitude) ; *sûreté de mémoire,* retentiveness of memory ; *sûreté de soi,* self-assurance, confidence in oneself. ‖ Security, pledge, guarantee, surety (garantie). ‖ Safety, security (sécurité) ; *en sûreté,* in safety. ‖ Jur. Criminal Investigation Department ; C.I.D. (fam.) ; U. S. Federal Bureau of Investigation ; F.B.I. (fam.).
surévaluation [syrevalɥasjɔ̃] f. Over-estimate.
surévaluer [-lɥe] v. tr. (1). To over-estimate.
surexcitable [syrɛksitabl] adj. Excitable.
surexcitant, ante [-tɑ̃, ɑ̃:t] adj. Exciting.
— m. Méd. Stimulant.
surexcitation [-tasjɔ̃] f. Over-excitement. ‖ Méd. Over-stimulation.
surexciter [-te] v. tr. (1). To over-excite.
surexploiter [syrɛksplwate] v. tr. (1). To over-exploit.
surexposer [syrekspoze] v. tr. (1). To over-expose.
surexposition [syrekspozisjɔ̃] f. Over-exposure.
surf [sœrf] m. Sports. Surfing ; *faire du surf,* to surf.
surface [syrfas] f. Surface ; *la surface de la terre,* the earth's surface. ‖ Math. Surface, surface-area. ‖ Fin., Comm. *Surface financière,* financial standing. ‖ Naut. *Faire surface,* to surface (sous-marin) ; *vitesse de surface,* surface-speed. ‖ Fig. Appearance, surface ; *esprit tout en surface,* shallow (ou) superficial mind ; *s'arrêter à la surface des choses,* to take a superficial view of things. ‖ Comm. *Grande surface,* hypermarket.
surfacer [-se] v. tr. (6). Techn. To surface.
surfaire [syrfɛ:r] v. tr. (50). To overrate, to praise too highly (un auteur, un ouvrage). ‖ Comm. To ask (ou) charge too much for (des marchandises).
— v. intr. Comm. To overcharge.
surfait, aite [-fɛ, ɛ:t] adj. Overrated.
surfalx [syrfɛ] m. Surcingle.
surfil [syrfil] m. Overcast.
surfiler [-le] v. tr. (1). To overcast.
surfin, ine [syrfɛ̃, in] adj. Comm. Superfine.
surfusion [syrfyzjɔ̃] f. Phys. Superfusion.
surgelé, ée [syrʒəle] adj. Agric., Culin. Frozen, deep-frozen, quick-frozen.
— m. Agric., Culin. Frozen (ou) deep-frozen (ou) quick-frozen food.
surgeler v. tr. (8b). Agric., Culin. To freeze, to deep-freeze, to quick-freeze.
surgénérateur [syrʒeneratœ:r] m. V. surré-générateur.
surgeon [syrʒɔ̃] m. Bot. Sucker.
surgir [syrʒi:r] v. intr. (2). To rise, to come up, to come into view, to appear ; *une voile surgit à l'horizon,* a sail loomed up on the horizon. ‖ Fig. To appear ; to arise (difficultés).
surgissement [-ʒismɑ̃] m. Upheaval.
surglacer [syrglase] v. tr. (6). To ice (un gâteau) ; to glaze (du papier).
surhaussé, ée [syrose] adj. Archit. Raised, high-pitched, stilted.
surhausser v. tr. (1). To raise, to heighten (un mur). ‖ Fin. To put (ou) push up, to increase.
surhomme [syrɔm] m. Superman.
surhumain, aine [-ymɛ̃, ɛn] adj. Superhuman.
surimposer [syrɛ̃poze] v. tr. (1). To superimpose ‖ Fin. To overtax.
surimposition [-zisjɔ̃] f. Superimpose. ‖ Fin. Overtaxation.
surimpression [syrɛ̃prɛsjɔ̃] f. Double exposure.
surin [syrɛ̃] m. Pop. Knife, dagger.
Surinam [syrinam] m. Géogr. Surinam.
suriner [syrine] v. tr. Pop. To knife, to stab.

surineur [-nœ:r] m. Pop. Knifer.
surintendance [syrɛ̃tɑ̃dɑ̃:s] f. Superintendent's office (bureau) ; superintendance (charge).
surintendant [-dɑ̃] m. Superintendent.
surintendante [-dɑ̃:t] f. Superintendent's wife. ‖ Principal lady-in-waiting (à la cour). ‖ Woman in charge of welfare (dans une usine).
surir [syri:r] v. intr. (2). To go (ou) turn sour.
surjaler [syrʒale], **surjauler** [-ʒole] v. tr. (1). Naut. To foul (une ancre).
— v. intr. Naut. To become unstocked (ancre).
surjet [syrʒɛ] m. Overcasting ; *point de surjet,* overcast stitch.
surjeter [-ʒte] v. tr. (8a). To overcast.
sur-le-champ [syrləʃɑ̃] loc. adv. V. sur.
surlendemain [syrlɑ̃dmɛ̃] m. Day after the morrow (ou) tomorrow ; *le surlendemain d'un événement,* two days after an event.
surlonge [syrlɔ̃:ʒ] f. Culin. Chuck end of the clod (de bœuf).
surlouer [syrlwe] v. tr. (1). To let (ou) rent at an excessive amount (une maison).
surmenage [syrmǝna:ʒ] m. Overwork, overworking ; *surmenage intellectuel,* mental strain ; brain-fag (fam.).
surmener [-ne] v. tr. (1). To override (un cheval) ; to overwork (qqn).
— v. pr. **Se surmener,** to overwork, to overexert (ou) overstrain oneself.
surmoi [syrmwa] m. Psych. Super-ego.
surmontable [syrmɔ̃tabl] adj. Surmountable.
surmonter [-te] v. tr. (1). To surmount, to crown, to top (couronner). ‖ To rise above, to come up over (passer par-dessus). ‖ Fig. To surmount, to master, to overcome, to get the better of (un obstacle).
— v. pr. **Se surmonter,** to master (ou) control oneself, to get the better of one's feelings.
surmouler [-le] v. tr. (1). To cast from existing mould. ‖ Autom. To retread (les pneus).
surmultiplié [syrmyltiplije] adj. Autom. *Vitesse surmultipliée,* overdrive.
surnager [syrnaʒe] v. intr. (7). To float on the surface. ‖ Fig. To survive.
surnaturel, elle [syrnatyrɛl] adj., m. Supernatural.
surnaturellement [-mɑ̃] adv. Supernaturally.
surnom [syrnɔ̃] m. Surname ; nickname.
surnombre [syrnɔ̃:br] m. Number in excess of that stipulated ; *en surnombre,* supernumerary.
surnommer [syrnɔme] v. tr. (1). To give a surname to ; to nickname.
surnuméraire [syrnymerɛ:r] adj., m. Supernumerary.
suroffre [syrɔfr] f. Fin. Overbid, higher offer.
suroît [syrwa] m. Naut. Sou'wester (chapeau, vent) ; south-west (direction).
surpasser [syrpɑse] v. tr. (1). To surpass, to outdo (excéder) ; *dépense qui surpasse mes moyens,* expense beyond my means (ou) that is too much for my means. ‖ To overtop, to be taller than (dépasser en hauteur). ‖ To go beyond (dépasser) ; *surpasser le diable en diablerie,* to outdevil the devil.
— v. pr. **Se surpasser,** to surpass oneself.
surpaye [syrpɛ:j] f. Overpaying, overpayment (action). ‖ Extra pay, bonus (gratification).
surpayer [-pɛje] v. tr. (9b). To pay too much for (qqch.) ; to overpay (qqn).
surpeuplé, ée [syrpœple] adj. Overpopulated.
surpeuplement [-pləmɑ̃] m. Overpopulation.
surplace [syrplas] m. Sports. *Faire du surplace,* to mark time (dans une course cycliste). ‖ Fig. *Faire du surplace,* to make no progress, to be stuck.
surplis [syrpli] m. Ecclés. Surplice.

surplomb [syrplɔ̃] m. Overhang.
surplombement [-bəmɑ̃] ˙m. Overhang; overhanging.
surplomber [-be] v. tr. (1). To overhang, to hang over.
surplus [syrply] m. Surplus, excess.
— loc. adv. **Au surplus,** moreover; what is more (précédant la proposition); into the bargain (suivant le verbe de la proposition principale).
surpopulation [syrpɔpylasjɔ̃] f. Overpopulation.
surprenant, ante [syrprənɑ̃, ɑ̃:t] adj. Surprising, astonishing, amazing.
surprendre [-prɑ̃:dr] v. tr. (80). To surprise (arriver inopinément); *surprendre un ami chez lui,* to surprise a friend in his home; to drop in on a friend out of the blue. ‖ To catch, to surprise, to take by surprise (prendre à l'improviste); *la pluie nous a surpris,* we were caught out in the rain. ‖ To surprise, to catch in the act (prendre sur le fait). ‖ To surprise, to astonish (étonner); *cette nouvelle m'a surpris,* that news amazed me; *surpris par qqn., par qqch.,* surprised by s.o., at sth. ‖ To overhear (une conversation); to intercept (une lettre) [intercepter]. ‖ To obtain by fraud (obtenir par artifice). ‖ To abuse, to deceive (tromper); *surprendre la bonne foi de qqn,* to abuse s.o.'s good faith.
surpression [syrprɛsjɔ̃] f. Over-pressure.
surprime [syrprim] f. FIN. Extra premium.
surprise [syrpri:z] f. Surprise (action); *par surprise,* by surprise. ‖ Surprise, astonishment (étonnement); *à ma grande surprise,* to my great surprise; *boîte à surprise,* jack-in-the-box; *pochette-surprise,* lucky dip, surprise packet (ou) U. S. package. ‖ **Surprise-partie** ⟨pl. *surprises-parties*⟩ f. Party.
surproduction [syrprɔdyksjɔ̃] f. Overproduction.
surproduire [-dɥi:r] v. tr. (85). To overproduce.
surréalisme [syrrealism] m. ARTS. Surrealism.
surréaliste [-list] adj., s. ARTS. Surrealist.
surrection [syrɛksjɔ̃] f. GÉOL. Uplift (de l'écorce terrestre).
surrégénérateur [syrreʒeneratœ:r] m. PHYS. Breeder reactor, fast reactor.
surrénal, ale [syrenal] adj. MÉD. Suprarenal.
sursaturation [syrsatyrasjɔ̃] f. Supersaturation.
sursaturer [-re] v. tr. (1). To supersaturate.
sursaut [syrso] m. Start, jump; *faire un sursaut,* to start, to give a start (ou) jump.
— loc. adv. **En sursaut,** with a start; *s'éveiller en sursaut,* to wake (ou) to wake up with a start.
sursauter [-te] v. intr. (1). To start, to jump, to give a start (ou) jump.
surséance [syrseɑ̃:s] f. JUR. Stay of execution, suspension.
surseoir [syrswa:r] v. intr. (100). JUR. To postpone, to stay; *surseoir à l'exécution d'un arrêt,* to obtain a stay of execution.
sursis [-si] m. JUR. Postponement, stay of execution. ‖ MILIT. Deferment.
sursitaire [-sitɛ:r] m. MILIT. Deferred conscript.
surtaux [syrto] m. Over-assessment.
surtaxe [syrtaks] f. Over-assessment, excessive tax (taxe excessive). ‖ Supertax, surtax (taxe supplémentaire); *surtaxe d'une lettre,* surcharge on a letter.
surtaxer [-takse] v. tr. (1). To supertax, to surtax; to overtax.
surtension [syrtɑ̃sjɔ̃] f. ELECTR. Over-voltage, voltage-rise, surge.
surtout [syrtu] m. Light cart (charrette). ‖ Overcoat, surtout (manteau). ‖ Table-centre, epergne, U. S. centerpiece (de table).
surtout adv. Above all, especially, particularly.
surveillance [syrvejɑ̃:s] f. Supervision, surveil-

lance, watching; *en surveillance,* under surveillance; *sous la surveillance de la police,* under police supervision. ‖ Invigilation; U. S. proctoring (à l'école). ‖ MÉD. Surveillance.
surveillant, ante [-jɑ̃, ɑ̃:t] s. Supervisor, superintendent. ‖ Invigilator (à l'école); *surveillant des études,* master on duty; U. S. study-hall teacher : *surveillant des travaux,* overseer. ‖ MÉD. *Surveillante de salle,* ward-sister, head nurse.
surveille [syrvɛ:j] f. Two days before.
surveiller [-je] v. tr. (1). To watch over, to look after, to keep an eye on (des enfants); to tend (une machine); to supervize (des travaux); *surveiller de près,* to watch closely, to shadow. ‖ To invigilate (à un examen); U. S. to proctor (à l'école).
— v. pr. **Se surveiller,** to keep a watch on oneself; to watch one's step, to mind one's P's and Q's.
survenance [syrvənɑ̃:s] f. Unexpected arrival. ‖ ‖ JUR. *Survenance d'enfant,* unforeseen birth of issue.
survenant, ante [-nɑ̃, ɑ̃:t] adj. Coming (ou) arriving unexpectedly.
— s. Unexpected arrival, chance-comer.
survendre [syrvɑ̃:dr] v. tr. (4). COMM. To charge too much for.
survenir [-vəni:r] v. intr. (101). To set in (complication); to happen, to take place; to crop up (fam.) [événement]. ‖ To arrive unexpectedly (personne).
survente [-vɑ̃:t] f. COMM. Overcharge, sale at excessive price.
survente f. NAUT. Increase of wind.
surventer [-vɑ̃te] v. intr. (1). NAUT. To increase.
survenue [-vəny] f. Unexpected arrival.
survêtement [syrvɛtmɑ̃] m. Track suit, sweat-suit; *en survêtement,* track-suited.
survie ⎣syrvi] f. Survival. ‖ JUR. Survivorship.
survitrage [-vitra:ʒ] m. TECHN. Double glazing.
survivance [-vivɑ̃:s] f. Survival. ‖ Survivance, reversion ⟨d'une ·charge).
survivant, ante [-vivɑ̃, ɑ̃:t] adj. Surviving.
— s. Survivor.
survivre [-vi:vr] v. intr. (105). *Survivre à,* to survive, to outlive (qqn). ‖ FIG. To survive; *survivre à une perte,* to get over (ou) survive a loss.
— v. pr. **Se survivre,** to live on; to be in one's second childhood.
survol [syrvɔl] m. AVIAT. Flight over, flying over (d'une région). ‖ CINÉM. Panning.
survoler [-le] v. tr. (1). AVIAT. To fly over.
survoltage [syrvɔlta:ʒ] m. ELECTR. Boosting.
survolter [-te] v. tr. (1). ELECTR. To boost. ‖ FIG. To stir to a frenzy; *survolté,* over-excited, het up (personne), explosive (atmosphère).
survolteur [-tœ:r] m. ELECTR. Booster.
sus [sy(s)] adv. *Courir sus à,* to rush upon.
— loc prép. **En sus de,** in addition to, over and above.
— loc. adv. **En sus,** in addition, to boot.
— interj. *Sus à l'ennemi!,* up and at them!
sus [sys] préf. Above. ‖ **Sus-dominante,** f. MUS. Submediant. ‖ **Sus-hépatique,** adj. MÉD. Suprahepatic. ‖ **Sus-jacent,** adj. GÉOL. Overlying. ‖ **Sus-tonique,** adj. MUS. Supertonic.
sus, susse. V. SAVOIR (92).
susceptibilité [sysɛptibilite] f. Susceptibility, sensitiveness; touchiness.
susceptible [-tibl] adj. Susceptible, capable, admitting (de, of); liable (de, to) [apte]; *un livre susceptible de vous intéresser,* a book likely to interest you. ‖ MÉD. Sensitive, delicate (organe). ‖ FIG. Sensitive, thin-skinned, touchy (personne).
suscitation [sysitasjɔ̃] f. Instigation.
susciter [-te] v. tr. (1). To create (faire naître);

Dieu suscita les prophètes, God called forth the prophets. ‖ To provoke, to arouse, to instigate (provoquer); *susciter une querelle,* to provoke a quarrel. ‖ To stir up (soulever); *susciter des ennemis à,* to make enemies for.

suscription [syskripsjɔ̃] f. Superscription.

susdit, ite [sysdi, it] adj., s. JUR. Aforesaid, above-mentioned.

susmentionné, ée [-mãsjɔne] adj., s. JUR. Aforesaid, above-mentioned.

susnommé, ée [-n me] adj., s. JUR. Above- (ou) afore-named.

suspect, ecte [syspɛ, ɛkt] adj. Suspicious, doubtful, questionable; suspect; *suspect de,* suspected of; *tenir qqn pour suspect,* to have suspicions about s.o., to be suspicious of s.o.
— s. Suspect.

suspecter [-pɛkte] v. tr. (1). To suspect, to be suspicious of (qqch., qqn).

suspendre [syspɑ̃:dr] v. tr. (4). To suspend, to hang up (un lustre). ‖ FIG. To hold up, to interrupt (la circulation); to defer, to put off, to suspend (un jugement); to stop, to suspend (un paiement). ‖ To suspend (un fonctionnaire). ‖ FIG. *Être suspendu aux lèvres de qqn,* to hang on s.o.'s words.

suspendu, ue [-pãdy] adj. Suspended (fonctionnaire). ‖ Suspended, hanging (objet); sprung, on springs (véhicule); *jardins suspendus,* hanging gardens; *pont suspendu,* suspension bridge.

suspens [-pã] adj. ECCLÉS. Inhibited (prêtre).
— loc. adv. **En suspens,** in suspense, in doubt, in uncertainty (personne); unsolved (problème); in abeyance (projet).

suspense [-pã:s] f. ECCLÉS. Suspense.

suspense [-pɛns, pɛ̃s] m. CINÉM. Suspense.

suspenseur [-pãsœ:r] adj., m. MÉD. Suspensory.

suspensif, ive [-pãsif, i:v] adj. JUR. Suspensory.

suspension [-pãsjɔ̃] f. Suspension (action). ‖ Hanging-lamp (lampe). ‖ CHIM. Suspension. ‖ FIN. Suspension, stoppage (de paiement). ‖ AUTOM. Suspension, springs, springing (d'une auto). ‖ GRAMM. Abscission (dans une phrase); *points de suspension,* points of suspension.

suspensoir [-pãswa:r] m. MÉD. Suspensory bandage.

suspente [syspã:t] f. NAUT. Sling.

suspicion [syspisjɔ̃] f. Suspicion; *tenir en suspicion,* to suspect, to hold in suspicion.

suspied [sypje] m. Instep strap (d'éperon).

sustentateur, trice [systãtatœ:r, tris] adj. AVIAT. Lifting; *surface sustentatrice,* aerofoil.

sustentation [-tasjɔ̃] f. AVIAT. Lift. ‖ TECHN. *Base de sustentation,* basis of support.

sustenter [-te] v. tr. (1). To sustain, to support.
— v. pr. **Se sustenter,** to take sustenance.

susurration [sysyrasjɔ̃] f. Susurration, susurrus, whispering, murmuring.

susurrement [-rmã] m. Susurration, whispering (murmure); rustling (des feuilles).

susurrer [-re] v. intr. (1). To susurrate, to murmur, to whisper.
— v. tr. To whisper.

susvisé, ée [sysvize] adj. Aforesaid, aforementioned.

sutural, ale [sytyral] adj. MÉD. Sutural.

suture [-ty:r] f. MÉD. Suture.

suturer [-tyre] v. tr. (1). To suture.

suzerain, aine [syzrɛ̃, ɛn] adj. Suzerain, paramount.
— s. Suzerain.

suzeraineté [-rɛnte] f. Suzerainty.

svelte [svɛlt] adj. Svelte, slim, slender.

sveltesse [-tɛs] f. Slimness, slenderness.

S.V.P. [ɛsvepe] abrév. de *s'il vous plaît,* please.

Swaziland [swazilã:d] m. GÉOGR. Swaziland.

sweater [switœ:r] m. Sweater.

sweat-shirt [switʃœ:rt] f. Tee-shirt; U.S. sweat-shirt.

sweepstake [swipstɛk] m. SPORTS. Sweepstake.

sybarite [sibarit] adj. s. Sybarite.

sybaritique [-tik] adj. Sybaritic.

sycomore [sikɔmɔ:r] m. BOT. Sycamore.

sycophant [sikɔfã:t] m. † Sycophant (dans l'Antiquité grecque). ‖ Informer, stool-pigeon (délateur).

syllabaire [sillabɛ:r] m. Syllabary, spelling-book.

syllabe [-lab] f. Syllable.

syllabique [-labik] adj. Syllabic.

syllabisme [-labism] m. Syllabism.

syllabus [-laby:s] m. ECCLÉS. Syllabus.

syllepse [sillɛps] f. Syllepsis.

sylleptique [-lɛptik] adj. Sylleptic.

syllogisme [sillɔ3ism] m. Syllogism.

syllogistique [-3istik] adj. Syllogistic.

sylphe [silf] m. Sylph.

sylphide [-fid] f. Sylph; *taille de sylphide,* sylph-like waist.

sylvain [silvɛ̃] m. Sylvan, silvan.

sylvestre [-vɛstr], **sylvicole** [-vikɔl] adj. Sylvan, silvan. ‖ BOT. Forest.

sylviculteur [-vikyltœ:r] m. Sylviculturist.

sylviculture [-vikylty:r] f. Sylviculture, forestry.

symbiose [sɛ̃bjo:z] f. Symbiosis.

symbole [sɛ̃bɔl] m. Symbol. ‖ ECCLÉS. Creed.

symbolique [-lik] adj. Symbolic, symbolical.
— f. Symbolics.

symboliquement [-likmã] adv. Symbolically.

symbolisation [-lizasjɔ̃] f. Symbolization.

symboliser [-lize] v. tr. (1). To symbolize.

symbolisme [-lism] m. Symbolism.

symboliste [-list] adj. Symbolistic. ‖ Symbolist (mouvement).
— s. Symbolist.

symétrie [simetri] f. Symmetry.

symétrique [-trik] adj. Symmetrical.
— s. Symmetrical point (ou) line (ou) figure.

symétriquement [-trikmã] adv. Symmetrically.

sympa [sɛ̃pa] adj. FAM. Nice, friendly (personne); nice, pleasant (chose).

sympathie [sɛ̃pati] f. Sympathy, fellow-feeling, attraction; *avoir de la sympathie pour qqn,* to feel drawn to s.o.; to like s.o.

sympathique [-tik] adj. Likable, attractive (personne); attractive, sympathetic (personnalité); *savoir se rendre sympathique,* to be a good mixer. ‖ Sympathetic, invisible (encre). ‖ MÉD. Sympathetic (nerf).
— m. MÉD. *Le grand sympathique,* the sympathetic nerve.

sympathiquement [-tikmã] adv. Sympathetically.

sympathisant, ante [-tizã, ã:t] adj. Sympathizing.
— s. Fellow-traveller (communisant).

sympathiser [-tize] v. intr. (1). To have an affinity (avec, for); to be drawn (avec, towards). ‖ To sympathize (avec, with) [partager la peine].

symphonie [sɛ̃fɔni] m. MUS. Symphony.

symphonique [-nik] adj. MUS. Symphonic.

symphoniste [-nist] s. MUS. Composer (compositeur); player in an orchestra (instrumentiste).

symphyse [sɛ̃fi:z] f. MÉD. Symphysis.

symposium [sɛ̃pɔsjɔm] m. Symposium.

symptomatique [sɛ̃ptɔmatik] adj. Symptomatic.

symptomatologie [-tɔlɔ3i] f. m. Symptomatology.

symptôme [sɛ̃pto:m] m. MÉD. Symptom. ‖ FIG. Symptom, sign, indication.

synagogue [sinagɔg] f. Synagogue.

synapse [sinaps] f. MÉD. Synapse, synapsis.

synarchie [sinarʃi] f. Synarchy, joint rule.

synchrocyclotron [sɛkrosiklɔtrɔ̃] m. PHYS. Synchrocyclotron.
synchrone [sɛkrɔn] adj. Synchronous.
synchronie [-ni] f. GRAMM. Synchrony.
synchronique [-nik] adj. Synchronic, synchronous. ‖ GRAMM. Synchronic.
synchronisation [-nizasjɔ̃] f. Synchronization.
synchroniser [-nize] v. tr. (1). To synchronize.
synchroniseur [-nizœ:r] m. TECHN. Synchromesh.
synchronisme [-nism] m. Synchronism.
synchrotron [-trɔ̃] m. PHYS. Synchrotron; *rayonnement synchrotron,* synchrotron radiation.
synclinal, ale [sɛklinal] adj. GÉOL. Synclinal.
— m. GÉOL. Syncline.
syncopal, ale [sɛkɔpal] adj. MÉD. Syncopal.
syncope [sɛkɔp] f. MÉD. Syncope, faint, fainting-fit; *tomber en syncope,* to fall in a faint. ‖ GRAMM. Syncope. ‖ MUS. Syncopation.
syncoper [-pe] v. tr. (1). GRAMM., MUS. To syncopate.
syncrétisme [sɛkretism] m. Syncretism.
syndic [sɛdik] m. Syndic. ‖ FIN., JUR. *Syndic de faillite,* official receiver.
syndical, ale [-kal] adj. Trade union, union (mouvement, section, carte, tarif); *délégué syndical,* union representative, shop steward; *chambre syndicale,* trade association, syndicate (de patrons).
syndicalisme [-kalism] m. Trade-unionism, unionism. ‖ † *Syndicalisme révolutionnaire,* syndicalism.
syndicaliste [-kalist] adj., s. Trade-unionist, unionist.
syndicat [-ka] m. Trade (ou) trades union, union, U. S. labour union (d'ouvriers); trade association, syndicate, federation (de patrons). ‖ *Syndicat d'initiative,* tourist office. ‖ *Syndicat de propriétaires,* association of property owners.
syndicataire [-katɛ:r] adj. FIN., JUR. Of (ou) relating to a syndicate (ou) an association of property owners.
— s. Member of a syndicate (ou) an association of property owners.
syndiqué, ée [-ke] adj. Unionized, belonging to a union; *ouvrier syndiqué,* union member.
— s. Union member.
syndiquer v. tr. (1). To unionize, to organize (des travailleurs).
— v. pr. **Se syndiquer,** to join a union (adhérer à un syndicat); to form a union, to organize (constituer un syndicat ouvrier); to form a trade association (ou) a syndicate (ou) a federation (constituer un syndicat patronal). ‖ FIN. To syndicate.
syndrome [sɛdro:m] m. MÉD. Syndrome.
synecdoque [sinɛkdɔk] f. GRAMM. Synecdoche.
synérèse [sinerɛ:z] f. CHIM., GRAMM. Syneresis.

synergie [sinɛrʒi] f. Synergy.
synesthésie [sinɛstezi] f. PSYCH. Synaesthesia, synesthesia.
synodal, ale [sinodal] adj. Synodal.
synode [sinɔd] m. ECCLÉS. Synod.
synodique [-dik] adj. ECCLÉS. Synodic(al).
synonyme [sinɔnim] adj. Synonymous (*de,* with).
— m. Synonym.
synonymie [-mi] f. Synonymy.
synonymique [-mik] adj. Synonymic.
synopsis [sinɔpsis] m. CINÉM. Synopsis.
synoptique [-tik] adj. Synoptic, synoptical.
— m. pl. ECCLÉS. Synoptic Gospels.
synovial, ale [sinɔvjal] adj. MÉD. Synovial.
synovie [-vi] f. MÉD. Synovia.
syntagmatique [sɛtagmatik] adj. GRAMM. Phrasal, syntagmatic, syntagmic.
syntagme [-tagm] m. GRAMM. Phrase, syntagm; *syntagme nominal, verbal,* noun, verb phrase.
syntaxe [sɛtaks] f. GRAMM. Syntax.
syntaxique [-taksik], **syntactique** [-taktik] adj. GRAMM. Syntactic, syntactical.
synthèse [sɛtɛ:z] f. Synthesis.
synthétique [-tetik] adj. Synthetic, synthetical.
synthétiquement [-tetikmɑ̃] adv. Synthetically.
synthétiser [-tetize] v. tr. (1). To synthetize.
synthétiseur [-tetizœ:r] m. MUS. Synthetizer, Moog synthetizer (nom déposé).
syntonisation [sɛtɔnizasjɔ̃] f. RADIO. Syntonization; tuning.
syntoniser [-ze] v. tr. (1). RADIO. To syntonize, to tune.
syphilis [sifilis] f. MÉD. Syphilis.
syphilitique [-litik] adj. MÉD. Syphilitic.
syriaque [sirjak] m. GRAMM. Syriac (langue).
Syrie [-ri] f. GÉOGR. Syria.
syrien, enne [-rjɛ̃, ɛn] adj., s. GÉOGR. Syrian.
syrinx [sirɛks] f. Syrinx; pipes of Pan.
systématique [sistematik] adj. Systematic, methodical. ‖ FIG. Narrow-minded, hide-bound (étroit); systematic (méthodique).
systématiquement [-tikmɑ̃] adv. Systematically.
systématisation [-tizasjɔ̃] f. Systematization.
systématiser [-tize] v. tr. (1). To systematize.
système [sistɛm] m. System, method, scheme, plan; *esprit de système,* pigheadedness; *par système,* in a stereotyped way; *système féodal,* feudal system. ‖ ASTRON. *Système planétaire,* planetary system. ‖ MATH. *Système métrique,* metric system. ‖ MÉD. *Système nerveux,* nervous system. ‖ FAM. Device, gadget (bidule); *il me tape sur le système,* he gets on my nerves; *système D,* wangling; *employer le système D,* to wangle.
systole [sistɔl] f. MÉD. Systole.
systyle [sistil] adj., m. ARCHIT. Systyle.
syzygie [siziʒi] f. ASTRON. Syzygy.

T

t [te] m. T, t. ‖ TECHN. V. TÉ.
ta [ta] adj. poss. V. TON.
tabac [taba] m. Tobacco; *tabac à chiquer,* chewing tobacco; *tabac à priser,* snuff. ‖ Snuff (prise).

‖ Pl. *Les Tabacs,* State Tobacco Department (administration). ‖ FAM. *C'est le même tabac,* it's much of a muchness; *passage à tabac,* third degree questioning; *passer qqn à tabac,* to give s.o. the third degree (ou) a rough handling; to beat s.o. up; *pot à tabac*, pot-bellied man, dump. — adj. invar. Tobacco- (ou) snuff-coloured.

tabagie [-ʒi] f. Room reeking of stale tobacco-smoke.

tabagisme [-ʒism] m. Nicotinism.

tabasser [tabase] v. tr. FAM. To beat up.

tabatière [tabatjɛ:r] f. Snuff-box (boîte). ‖ *Fenêtre à tabatière*, hinged skylight. (V. LUCARNE.)

tabellion [tabɛljɔ̃] m. JUR. Scrivener. ‖ FAM. Solicitor.

tabernacle [tabɛrnakl] m. ECCLÉS. Tabernacle.

tabès [tabɛs] m. MÉD. Tabes.

tabescence [-sɑ̃:s] f. MÉD. Tabescence.

tabétique [tabetik] adj., s. MÉD. Tabetic.

tablature [tablaty:r] f. MUS. Tablature; fingering chart (d'instrument à vent). ‖ *Donner de la tablature à qqn*, to give s.o. sth. to think about; to lead s.o. a fine dance (ou) a merry chase.

table [tabl] f. Table (meuble); *table à abattants, de chevet* (ou) *de nuit, de jeu, à ouvrage, à rallonges, de salle à manger, de toilette*, gate-legged, bedside, card- (ou) gaming-, work-, extension, dining, dressing table; *table roulante*, dinner wagon, tea trolley, U. S. tea wagon; *la Table ronde*, the Round Table. ‖ Slab (de pierre). ‖ Table, fare (repas); table, board (à repas); *aimer la table*, to be fond of good fare (ou) food; *à table!*, dinner is served (ou) ready!; *bonne table*, good food. ‖ Table (personnes à table). ‖ ECCLÉS. *La sainte table*, the Lord's table. ‖ AVIAT. *Table des commandes*, control panel. ‖ MILIT. *Manger à la même table*, to mess together; *table d'officiers, officers' mess; *table de tir*, range-table. ‖ MÉD. *Table d'opération*, operation-table. ‖ CHIM. *Table de laboratoire*, laboratory bench. ‖ TECHN. Table; flange (de poutre); jigger (à secousses). ‖ ELECTR. Switchboard (téléphonique). ‖ List; catalogue; index (v. INDEX, RÉPERTOIRE); *table des matières*, table of contents. ‖ MATH. Table (de multiplication). ‖ MUS. *Table d'harmonie*, soundboard (de piano); belly (de violon). ‖ POP. *Se mettre à table*, to talk, to spill the beans.

tableau [tablo] m. Board; hoarding (pour affiches); notice-board, U. S. bulletinboard (pour annonces); *tableau noir*, blackboard. ‖ List, table, catalogue. ‖ Promotion list (pour l'avancement). ‖ ARTS. Picture; painting; view. ‖ AUTOM. *Tableau de bord*, dashboard, instrument panel. ‖ AVIAT. Instrument panel. ‖ NAUT. Name-board. ‖ CH. DE F. Train indicator (indicateur). ‖ THÉÂTR. Scene; tableau. ‖ JUR. Rolls (des avocats); panel (des jurés). ‖ ELECTR. Switchboard (de distribution); indicator board (indicateur). ‖ SPORTS. Score-board (au billard); telegraph (aux courses); *tableau de chasse*, bag; *au tableau*, in the bag. ‖ THÉÂTR. *Tableau vivant*, tableau. ‖ FIG. Picture, description. ‖ FAM. *Vieux tableau*, old frump. ‖ LOC. *Miser sur le même tableau*, to put all one's eggs in one basket.

tableautin [-tɛ̃] m. ARTS. Small picture.

tablée [table] f. Tableful of guests; company at table.

tabler v. intr. (1). To sit at table. ‖ FIG. To count, to reckon, to rely (*sur*, on). [V. COMPTER.]

tablette [-blɛt] f. Slide (de bureau); mantelpiece (de cheminée); window-sill (de fenêtre); flat top (de meuble); shelf (rayon). ‖ CULIN. Bar, slab (de chocolat); cube (à potage). ‖ MÉD. Tablet, tabloid, lozenge. ‖ ELECTR. Terminal plate (à bornes). ‖ Pl. Writing-tablets, tablets. ‖ FAM. *Vous pouvez rayer ça de vos tablettes*, you can get that right out of your head.

tablier [tablje] m. Apron; pinafore (d'enfant). ‖ AUTOM. Dashboard. ‖ ARCHIT. Deck, flooring, road (de pont). ‖ TECHN. Register, blower (de cheminée); hearth (de forge). ‖ FAM. *Rendre son*

tablier, to resign; to give notice; to ask for one's card (pop.). ‖ **Tablier-blouse**, f. Overall, U. S. smock.

tabloïd [tablɔid] adj., s. Tabloid.

tabou, oue [tabu] adj. Taboo, tabooed (sacré); *déclarer tabou*, to taboo. ‖ Forbidden, taboo (interdit). — m. Taboo.

tabouret [taburɛ] m. Stool (pour s'asseoir); footstool (pour les pieds). ‖ MUS. Piano stool.

tabulaire [tabylɛ:r] adj. Tabular.

tabulateur [-latœ:r] m. Tabulator (d'une machine à écrire).

tabulatrice [-latris] f. INFORM. Tabulator (pour cartes perforées).

tac [tak] m. SPORTS. *Riposter du tac au tac*, to parry with riposte (à l'escrime); FIG. To give tit for tat.

tache [taʃ] f. Splash (de boue); stain (de boue, de graisse, d'huile, de vin); blob (de couleur); blot (d'encre); bruise (sur un fruit); spot (d'huile); flaw, blemish (dans une pierre précieuse); fleck (de suie); *petite tache*, speck. ‖ ASTRON. *Tache solaire*, sun-spot. ‖ MÉD. *Tache de rousseur*, freckle; *tache de suie*, smut; *tache de vin*, port-wine mark. ‖ FIG. Flaw, blemish; blot, stigma, slur, stain (v. SOUILLURE); *faire tache*, to stand out; *faire tache d'huile*, to spread; *sans tache*, spotless, unblemished, stainless.

tâche [tɑ:ʃ] f. Task; work (besogne). ‖ Piece-work; *ouvrier à la tâche*, jobbing workman; piece-worker; *travailler à la tâche*, to job; to do piece-work. ‖ FIG. Duty (devoir).

tachéomètre [takeɔmɛtr] m. TECHN. Tacheometer, tachymeter.

tachéométrie [-metri] f. Tacheometry.

tacher [taʃe] v. tr. (1). To spot, to stain, to soil, to dirty (un habit); *taché d'encre*, ink-stained. (V. MACULER, SALIR.) ‖ FIG. To soil. — v. pr. **Se tacher**, to get oneself (ou) one's clothes dirty. ‖ To stain, to spot, to get soiled.

tâcher [tɑ:ʃe] v. intr. (1). To try, to endeavour; *tâcher à*, to toil (ou) labour at; *tâcher de*, to try (ou) to attempt to. ‖ POP. *Tâchez moyen de le faire*, have a shot at doing it.

tâcheron [tɑʃrɔ̃] m. Jobbing workman; pieceworker.

tacheté, ée [taʃte] adj. Speckled, mottled, spotted. ‖ ZOOL. Tabby (chat).

tacheter v. tr. (8a). To speckle, to mottle, to fleck.

tachisme [taʃism] m. ARTS. Tachism.

tachiste [-ʃist] adj., s. ARTS. Tachist.

tachycardie [takikardi] f. MÉD. Tachycardia.

tachygraphe [takigraf] m. TECHN. Tachograph.

tachymètre [takimɛtr] m. TECHN. Tacheometer, speedometer, tachymeter.

tacite [tasit] adj. Tacit; implied, implicit; *tacite reconduction*, renewal by tacit agreement.

tacitement [-tmɑ̃] adv. Tacitly.

taciturne [tasityrn] adj. Taciturn; uncommunicative; close-mouthed.

tacot [tako] m. AUTOM., FAM. Old crock, rattletrap, bone-shaker; U. S. jalopy. ‖ CH. DE F. Puffer; local train.

tact [takt] m. Tact; *avec, sans tact*, tactfully, tactlessly; *avoir du tact*, to be tactful; *homme de tact*, tactful man; *manque de tact*, tactlessness; *manquer de tact*, to be tactless. ‖ MÉD. Sense of touch.

tacticien, enne [taktisjɛ̃, ɛn] s. Tactician.

tactile [taktil] adj. Tactile.

tactique [taktik] adj. MILIT. Tactical. — f. MILIT. Tactics.

tael [taɛl] m. Tael.

tænia [tenja] m. ZOOL. Taenia, tapeworm.

taffetas [tafta] m. Taffeta (tissu). ‖ MÉD. *Taffetas gommé*, court- (ou) sticking-plaster, U. S. adhesive tape.
tafia [tafja] m. Tafia.
tahitien, enne [taisjɛ̃, ɛn] adj., s. GÉOGR. Tahitian.
taïaut [tajo] interj. Tally-ho!
taie [tɛ] f. Pillow-case (ou) -slip (d'oreiller). ‖ MÉD. Albugo, leucoma, U. S. leukoma.
taïga [taiga] f. GÉOGR. Taiga.
taillable [tɑjabl] adj. † Talliable. ‖ FIG. *Taillable et corvéable à merci*, entirely at s.o.'s beck and call.
taillade [tɑjad] f. Cut, slash. (V. ENTAILLE.)
taillader [-de] v. tr. (1). To slash, to gash.
taillage [tɑja:ʒ] m. Cutting.
taillandier [-jɑ̃dje] m. Edge-tool maker.
taille [tɑ:j] f. Cutting; pruning (d'un arbre); clipping, cutting, trimming (d'une haie). ‖ Haircut (de cheveux). ‖ Stature, height (d'une personne); *de taille à se défendre*, big enough to look after oneself; *par rang de taille*, in order of height; *quelle est votre taille?*, how tall are you? ‖ Size (des vêtements); *quelle est votre taille?*, what size do you take? *rien à ma taille*, nothing in my size; *grandes tailles*, out-sizes; U. S. oversizes. ‖ Waist (ceinture); *prendre qqn par la taille*, to put an arm round s.o.'s waist; *sortir en taille*, to go out without wearing a coat (ou) jacket. ‖ Cut (coupe) [d'un vêtement]. ‖ Cutting-edge (d'une épée). [V. TRANCHANT.] ‖ MÉD. Lithotomy. ‖ ARTS. *Taille du bois*, woodengraving. ‖ TECHN. Hewing; cutting, dressing (d'une pierre). ‖ AGRIC. *Jeune taille*, coppice. ‖ † Tax (impôt). ‖ **Taille-crayon,** m. Pencilsharpener. ‖ **Taille-douce,** f. Copper-plate engraving. ‖ **Taille-légumes,** m. invar. Vegetableslicer. ‖ **Taille-neige,** m. invar. Snow-plough. ‖ **Taille-racines,** m. invar. AGRIC. Vegetable-cutter.
taillé, ée [tɑje] adj. Cut (cristal, verre). ‖ FIG. *Bien taillé*, well-built; *il n'est pas taillé pour cela*, he's not cut out for that; *taillé à coups de hache*, rough-hewn.
tailler v. tr. (1). To cut (en général); to trim, to clip (une barbe); to cut (les cheveux, un diamant); to sharpen (un crayon); to cut, to slice (le pain); to hew (une pierre); *tailler un chemin dans le roc*, to hew a road out of the rock. ‖ AGRIC. To prune (un arbre); to trim, to clip (une haie); to dress (une vigne). ‖ MILIT. *Tailler en pièces*, to cut to pieces. ‖ COMM. To cut out (un vêtement). ‖ FAM. *On lui a taillé des croupières*, he's had his work cut out for him, they've given him a tough job.
— v. intr. To deal (aux cartes).
— v. pr. **Se tailler**, POP. To hop it, to buzz off; U. S. to scram. ‖ *Se tailler un chemin à travers*, to carve one's way through. ‖ FIG. *Se tailler un succès*, to achieve success.
taillerie [-jri] f. Gem-cutting (action); gemcutter's workshop (atelier).
tailleur [-jœ:r] m. Cutter (de pierres précieuses); hewer (de pierre). ‖ Tailor (v. COUTURIER); *tailleur pour dames*, ladies' tailor; *s'asseoir en tailleur*, to sit cross-legged (ou) tailor-fashion. ‖ Tailor-made costume (costume). ‖ Banker (au casino). ‖ AGRIC. Cutter, pruner (d'arbres). ‖ **Tailleur-pantalon,** m. Trouser-suit, U. S. pantsuit.
tailleuse [-jø:z] f. Tailoress. (V. COUTURIÈRE.)
taillis [taji] m. Copse, coppice.
tailloir [tɑjwa:r] m. Trencher. ‖ ARCHIT. Abacus.
tain [tɛ̃] m. Silvering (de glace). ‖ Tin-bath (bain); tinfoil, foil (feuille).
taire [tɛ:r] v. tr. (75). To say nothing about; to keep secret (un nom); to suppress, to hush up, to keep dark (ou) quiet (la vérité); *taire qqch. à*,

to keep sth. back from; *faire taire*, to silence, to reduce to silence (une batterie, une personne); to stifle (sa douleur); to silence (une opposition); to keep in check (son ressentiment); *faites taire cet enfant*, keep that child quiet; shut that child up (fam.).
— v. pr. **Se taire**, to be kept secret (ou) back (chose, nouvelle); to be hushed up (fam.). ‖ To be silent, to hold one's tongue, to fall silent (personne); to be hushed (voix); *savoir se taire*, to know when to keep silent; *se taire sur qqch.*, to pass sth. over in silence; *taisez-vous!*, hold your tongue!, be quiet!, shut up! (fam.).
Taiwan [taiwan] GÉOGR. Taiwan.
talc [talk] m. CHIM. Talc. ‖ COMM. French chalk. ‖ MÉD. Talcum powder.
talcique [talsik] adj. Talcose, talcous.
talent [talɑ̃] m. Talent (v. APTITUDE, CAPACITÉ, DON); *avoir du talent*, to be talented; *de talent*, gifted, talented; *elle a un joli talent de pianiste*, she is a gifted pianist. ‖ Talent, brain, person of talent (personne). ‖ † Talent (monnaie, poids).
talentueux, euse [-tɥø, ø:z] adj. FAM. Talented.
taler [tale] v. tr. (1). To bruise (des fruits).
talion [taljɔ̃] m. Talion, retaliation; *loi du talion*, law of retaliation, law of « an eye for an eye »; *appliquer la peine du talion à*, to retaliate on.
talisman [talismɑ̃] m. Talisman.
talkie-walkie [tokiwoki] m. Walkie-talkie.
talle [tal] f. AGRIC. Sucker; tiller.
taller [-le] v. intr. (1). AGRIC. To sucker.
Talmud [talmyd] m. Talmud.
talmudique [-dik] adj. Talmudic, Talmudical.
talmudiste [-dist] m. Talmudist.
taloche [talɔʃ] f. Hawk (de plâtrier). ‖ FAM. Cuff, clout. (V. GIFLE.)
talocher [-ʃe] v. tr. (1). FAM. To cuff, to clout.
talon [talɔ̃] m. Heel (de personne, de souliers). ‖ MILIT. Heel (de crosse de fusil); shoulder (de lame d'épée). ‖ NAUT. Heel (de gouvernail, de mât). ‖ AUTOM. Beading, tread (de pneu). ‖ ARCHIT. Ogee-moulding. ‖ MUS. Heel, nut (d'archet). ‖ SPORTS. Stock; talon (aux cartes); butt (de queue de billard). ‖ CULIN. Remnant (de fromage). ‖ FIN. Stub, counterfoil (de souche). ‖ FAM. *Avoir l'estomac dans les talons*, to have an empty feeling; *être toujours sur les talons de qqn*, to dog s.o.'s footsteps; *tourner les talons*, to turn one's back; to turn on one's heels and make off. ‖ LOC. *Talon d'Achille*, heel of Achilles, weak spot; *talon rouge*, aristocrat.
talonner [talɔne] v. tr. (1). To dog; *talonner qqn*, to follow close on s.o.'s heels. ‖ To spur on (un cheval). ‖ MILIT. To press hard (l'ennemi). ‖ SPORTS. To heel out (au rugby). ‖ FIG. To dun (un débiteur); to urge on, to spur on (un élève); to pester, to worry (importuner).
— v. intr. NAUT. To bump, to touch.
talonnette [-nɛt] f. Heel, heel-piece (de bas, de soulier); binding (de pantalon); elevator, heelpad (à l'intérieur d'un soulier).
talpack [talpak] m. MILIT. Busby.
talquer [talke] v. tr. (1). To talc, to use talc on; to sprinkle with chalk.
talqueux, euse [-kø, ø:z] adj. Talcose, talcous.
talure [taly:r] f. Bruise (sur un fruit).
talus [taly] m. Slope; bank; ramp; embankment. (V. REMBLAI.) ‖ MILIT., GÉOL. Talus. ‖ ARCHIT. Batter.
talweg [talvɛg] m. GÉOGR. Thalweg, talweg.
tamanoir [tamanwa:r] m. ZOOL. Great ant-eater.
tamarin [tamarɛ̃] m. BOT. Tamarind-tree (arbre); tamarind (fruit).
tamarin [tamarɛ̃] m. ZOOL. Tamarin.
tamaris [tamaris] m. BOT. Tamarisk.
tambouille [tɑ̃bu:j] f. POP. Cooking, cookery.

tambour [tãbu:r] m. Mus. Drum (instrument); drummer (musicien); *tambour de basque*, tambourine; *tambour de ville*, town-crier. ‖ Techn. Tambour (de broderie); embroidery frame (d'ouvrage à aiguille); *broder au tambour*, to tambour. ‖ Autom. Brake-drum (de frein). ‖ Naut. Paddle-box (de roue à aubes). ‖ Electr. Cylinder, drum (de dynamo). ‖ Archit. Tambour (de porche). ‖ Phys. Vacuum-box (de baromètre). ‖ Techn. Barrel (de montre). ‖ Sports. Drum (de moulinet pour la pêche). ‖ Loc. *Sans tambour ni trompette*, unobtrusively, quietly, on the quiet. ‖ **Tambour-major**, m. Milit. Drum-major.

tambourin [tãburɛ̃] m. Mus. Tambourine (de Provence); tambourine; tabor †. ‖ Sports. Circular bat. ‖ Techn. Cylinder, drum.

tambourinage [-rina:ʒ] m. Drumming (des doigts sur une table, d'un tambour); knocking, tapping (sur une vitre). ‖ Fam. Boosting. (V. battage.)

tambourinaire [-rinɛ:r] m. Mus. Tambourin player.

tambourinement [-rinmã] m. V. tambourinage.

tambouriner [-rine] v. intr. (1). To beat a tattoo, to drum (des doigts). ‖ Mus. To beat the tambourin.
— v. tr. Fig. To broadcast, to shout out, to proclaim (une nouvelle).

tambourineur [-rinœ:r] m. Town-crier. ‖ Mus. Drummer; tambourin player.

tamil [tamil], **tamoul** [-mul] adj., m. Géogr. Tamil.

tamis [tami] m. Sieve, sifter (en général); screen (à charbon); bolter (à farine); sifter (à sable); *passer au tamis*, to sift, to strain. ‖ Fig. *Passer au tamis*, to sift, to examine (ou) look into carefully.

tamisage [-za:ʒ] m. Filtering (de l'air); screening (du charbon); bolting (de la farine); subduing (de la lumière); sifting (du sable).

Tamise [tami:z] f. Géogr. Thames.

tamiser [tamize] v. intr. (1). To filter through.
— v. tr. To filter (l'air); to screen (le charbon); to bolt (la farine); to subdue, to soften (la lumière); to sift (le sable). ‖ Fig. To sift.

tamiseur [tamizœ:r] m. Sifter; screener (de charbon); cinder-sifter (d'escarbilles); bolter (de farine).

tamoul [tamul] adj., m. V. tamil.

tampon [tãpɔ̃] m. Plug, stopper; bath-plug (de baignoire); manhole-cover (d'égout); bung (de liège). ‖ Rubber-stamp; *tampon encreur*, inking-pad. ‖ Techn. Buffer (de choc); pad (pour vernir). ‖ Fam. Milit. Orderly. ‖ Loc. *Coup de tampon*, collision; punch; brawl; *État tampon*, buffer State; *servir de tampon à qqn*, to act as a buffer for s.o. ‖ **Tampon buvard**, m. Hand-blotter.

tamponnement [tãpɔnmã] m. Stopping up, plugging; dabbing. ‖ Méd. Plugging. ‖ Ch. de f., Autom. Collision. ‖ Fam. Drubbing.

tamponner [-ne] v. tr. (1). To stop up, to plug (boucher). ‖ To French-polish (vernir). ‖ To dab (essuyer). ‖ To stamp (timbrer). ‖ To blot (buvarder). ‖ Autom., Ch. de f. To run into, to collide with, to bump into. ‖ Méd. To plug, to tampon (une blessure profonde); to put a wad over (une blessure superficielle). ‖ Fam. To drub, to hammer (qqn).
— v. pr. **Se tamponner**, to collide, to run into each other. ‖ *Se tamponner le front*, to mop one's brow; *se tamponner les yeux*, to dab one's eyes. ‖ Loc. *S'en tamponner*, not to give a damn.

tamponneur, euse [-nœ:r, ø:z] adj. That ran into the other (train). ‖ Autom. *Autos tamponneuses*, dodgems.
— m. Electr. Reactor.

tam-tam [tamtam] (pl. **tam-tams**) m. Tom-tom; gong (chinois). ‖ Fam. *Faire du tam-tam*, to make a great to-do.

tan [tã] m. Tan; U. S. tanbark; *fosse à tan*, tan-pit.

tancer [tãse] v. tr. (6). To rate, to scold.

tanche [tã:ʃ] f. Zool. Tench (poisson).

tandem [tãdɛm] m. Tandem; tandem bicycle. ‖ Techn. *En tandem*, tandem (cylindres).

tandémiste [-demist] s. Tandem rider.

tandis [tãdi] loc. conj. *Tandis que*, whereas, while (au lieu que); while, whilst (pendant que).

tangage [tãga:ʒ] m. Aviat., Naut. Pitching; *angle de tangage*, angle of pitch; *axe de tangage*, lateral axis.

tangence [tãʒã:s] f. Math. Tangency; *point de tangence*, point of contact.

tangent, ente [-ʒã, ã:t] adj. Math. Tangent, tangential. ‖ Fam. *Il a été tangent à son examen*, he was a border-line case.

tangente [-ʒã:t] f. Math. Tangent. ‖ Fig. *S'échapper par (ou) prendre la tangente*, to go off on a side issue, to fly off at a tangent; to wriggle out of a difficulty. ‖ Fam. Porter, usher (appariteur).

tangentiel, elle [-ʒãsjɛl] adj. Math. Tangential. ‖ Techn. Tangent (vis). ‖ Phys. Peripheral.

Tanger [tãʒe] m. Géogr. Tangier, Tangiers.

tangibilité [tãʒibilite] f. Tangibility, tangibleness.

tangible [-ʒibl] adj. Tangible.

tangiblement [-ʒibləmã] adv. Tangibly.

tango [tãgo] adj. invar. Tango; yellow-orange.
— m. Tango (danse).

tanguer [tãge] v. intr. (1). Aviat., Naut. To pitch. ‖ Fig. To reel (personne).

tanière [tanjɛ:r] f. Den, lair (v. antre); hole (de renard); *regagner sa tanière*, to go to ground (renard). ‖ Fig. Den, lair (gîte); hovel (taudis).

tanin [tanɛ̃] m. Chim. Tannin; argol, argal.

taniser [-nize] v. tr. (1). To treat with tannin.

tank [tã:k] m. Milit. Tank.

tanker [tãkœ:r] m. Naut. Tanker.

tankiste [tãkist] m. Member of a tank-crew.

tannage [tana:ʒ] m. Tanning, tannage; dressing (des peaux).

tannant, ante [tanã, ã:t] adj. Tanning; *extraits tannants*, tan liquor. ‖ Fam. Boring.

tannate [tanat] m. Chim. Tannate.

tanné, ée [tane] adj. Tanned. (V. bronzé.)

tannée f. Fam. Tanning. (V. rossée.)

tanner [tane] v. tr. (1). To tan. ‖ Fam. To bore (v. embêter); *je vais lui tanner le cuir*, I'm going to tan his hide for him.

tannerie [-nri] f. Tannery, tan-yard. ‖ Comm. Tanning trade.

tanneur [-nœ:r] m. Tanner.

tannin m., **tanniser** v. tr. V. tanin, taniser.

tan-sad [tãsad] m. Pillion (de moto).

tant [tã] adv. So much (telle quantité); *tant pour cent*, so much per cent; *travailler à tant de l'heure*, to work for so much an hour; ‖ So much, so many (un si grand nombre); so many, as many (une si grande quantité); *je ne savais pas qu'il avait tant d'amis*, I didn't know he had so many friends; *il a tant bu que*, he has drunk so much that; *il a tant d'argent que*, he's got so much money that. ‖ So much (autant). ‖ *il ne travaille pas tant que vous*, he doesn't work as much as you; *mangez tant que vous pouvez*, eat as much as you can. ‖ So long; so often (si longtemps, si souvent); *il est tant resté que*, he stayed so long that; *je l'ai tant vu que*, I have seen so much of him that. ‖ As much, as well (aussi bien); *trait qu'on trouve tant chez les Français que chez les Anglais*, characteristic found as much in the French as in the English. ‖ However (si); *tant honnête qu'il paraisse*, however honest he may appear. ‖ So (tellement); *ce n'est pas la peine de tant vous presser*, you needn't be in such a hurry; *sa femme tant aimée*, his so dearly beloved wife. ‖ Loc. *Tant bien que mal*, somehow or other, after a fashion; *tant de fois*, so often; *tant mieux!*, so much the better!. I'm glad to hear it!; that's a good job!; *tant pis!*, so much the worse!; I'm sorry to hear it!; it can't be helped!, never mind!; *tant et plus*, any amount, ever so much (ou) many; *tant s'en faut*, far from it; *tant s'en faut que je sois de son avis*, I'm far from agreeing with him; *tant que je vivrai*, as long as I live; *tant il est vrai que*, so true it is that; *tant il y a que*, the fact remains that, all the same; *à tant faire que d'acheter une voiture, autant vaut en acheter une bonne*, if it comes to buying a car, one may as well buy a good one; *en tant que*, as (en qualité de); in so far as (selon que); *gagner son tant pour cent de*, to get one's percentage of; *il a tant fait que*, he managed things so well that; *il pleut tant qu'il peut*, it's raining as hard as it can; *médecin tant mieux, tant pis*, optimistic, pessimistic doctor; *puisque vous avez tant fait*, since you have gone so far; *si tant est que*, if indeed; *tous tant que nous sommes*, all of us, everyone of us; every mother's son of us; *vous m'en direz tant!*, you don't say so!; now I understand. ‖ Pop. *Tant qu'à*, as for (quant à); *tant qu'à faire*, if it comes to that.

tantale [tɑ̃tal] m. † Zool. Tantalus.

tantale m. Chim., Electr. Tantalum.

Tantale m. † Tantalus (personnage mythologique); *infliger à qqn un supplice de Tantale*, to tantalize s.o.

tante [tɑ̃:t] f. Aunt-in-law (par alliance); aunt (par le sang). ‖ Fam. *Chez ma tante*, at my uncle's, in pawn, U. S. in hock. ‖ Pop. Pansy (homosexuel); U. S. fairy.

tantième [tɑ̃tjɛm] adj. Given, such a; *la tantième partie d'un tout*, the required part of a whole.
— m. Percentage of profit (des administrateurs).

tantine [tɑ̃tin] f. Fam. Auntie.

tantinet [tɑ̃tinɛ] m. Fam. Bit; shade (v. brin); tiny bit (de pain); wee drop (de vin).
— adv. Somewhat; a wee bit, just a little; *un tantinet trop gros*, a shade too big.

tantôt [tɑ̃to] adv. Soon, presently, by and by (bientôt); after lunch (l'après-midi); *à tantôt!*, so long!, see you this afternoon! ‖ Just now; a little while ago (peu avant). ‖ *Tantôt... tantôt*, now... now, sometimes... sometimes.
— m. Fam. Afternoon (après-midi); *sur le tantôt*, towards evening.

tantrique [tɑ̃trik] adj. Ecclés. Tantric.

tantrisme [-trism] m. Ecclés. Tantrism.

Tanzanie [tɑ̃zani] f. Géogr. Tanzania.

taoïsme [taoism] m. Ecclés. Taoism.

taoïste [-ist] adj., s. Ecclés. Taoist.

taon [tɑ̃] m. Zool. Gad-fly, horse-fly.

tapage [tapa:ʒ] m. Uproar; din; row; *faire du tapage*, to kick up a row. ‖ Jur. *Tapage nocturne*, disturbance of the peace at night. ‖ Fig. Clamour; uproar, hubbub; stir, fuss; *cette nouvelle fera du tapage*, this news will create a sensation (ou) will make quite a stir. ‖ Fam. Touching, U. S. touch (emprunt).

tapageur, euse [-ʒœ:r, ø:z] adj. Noisy, riotous (assistance); boisterous (enfant); noisy, rowdy, obstreperous (personne). ‖ Fig. Boisterous (gaieté); blustering (manière); noisy (manifestation); showy, flashy, loud, gaudy (toilette); flaunting (vanité).
— s. Rowdy, roisterer; obstreperous person. ‖ Jur. Disturber of the peace.

tapageusement [-ʒøzmɑ̃] adv. Noisily; rowdily, uproariously, boisterously (avec bruit). ‖ Showily, flashily, loudly, gaudily (avec éclat).

tapant, ante [tapɑ̃, ɑ̃:t] adj. Fam. Striking (heure); *à l'heure tapante*, on the stroke of the hour; bang on time, on the dot (fam.); *à midi tapant*, sharp on twelve, at twelve sharp.

tape [tap] f. Tap, slap (sur l'épaule); pat (sur la joue). ‖ Fam. Failure, setback.

tapé, ée [tape] adj. Dried (fruits). ‖ Fam. Dotty, cracked, U. S. nuts. (V. cinglé.) ‖ Fam. Smart, straight from the shoulder (réponse); *ça, c'est tapé!*, that's the stuff!

tape-à-l'œil [tapalœ:j] adv. invar. Fam. Gaudy, flashy, showy, loud.
— m. invar. Fam. Shoddy (ou) flashy stuff; eye-wash (frime).

tapecul [tapky] m. Gig; tilbury (voiture); spring less carriage. ‖ Autom. Bone-shaker, rattletrap, U. S. jalopy. ‖ Naut. Jigger (voile). ‖ Sports. See-saw.

tapée [tape] f. Fam. Heaps, bags, tons, pots (de choses); crowds, scores, masses (de gens).

taper v. tr. (1). To tap; to strike (frapper); to hit, to slap, to smack (gifler). ‖ To type, to typewrite (dactylographier). ‖ To bang, to slam (fermer). ‖ Mus. To strum, to thump out (un air). ‖ Arts. To dab on (de la peinture); to lay on (du vernis). ‖ Fam. To touch; *taper qqn de cent francs*, to touch s.o. for a hundred francs.
— v. intr. To tap; to bang (*sur*, on); to knock (*sur*, on); *tapez dessus!*, pitch into him!; *taper du pied*, to stamp one's foot. ‖ Aviat., Milit. *Taper sur*, to paste (bombarder). ‖ Autom. *Taper du 130*, to clock (ou) U. S. to hit 130. ‖ Fig. To blaze hot (soleil); *le soleil nous tapait sur la tête*, the sun was beating down on our heads. ‖ Fam. *Taper sur*, to run down, to slate; *les critiques lui ont tapé dessus*, the critics have gone for him; *taper sur le ventre à qqn*, to poke s.o. in the ribs; *elle lui a tapé dans l'œil*, she has taken his fancy; *il me tape sur les nerfs* (ou) *le système*, he gets on my nerves.
— v. pr. Se taper, to knock oneself; *se taper contre un mur*, to bump into a wall; *se taper sur la cuisse*, to slap one's thigh. ‖ Loc. *Tu peux te taper*, nothing doing, you can whistle for it; *se taper la cloche*, to have a good blow-out; *se taper un bon gueuleton*, to treat oneself to a slap-up meal; *s'en taper* (pop.), not to give a fig, not to care two hoofs.
— v. récipr. Se taper, to hit (ou) knock each other (se heurter).

tapette [tapɛt] f. Fam. Tongue; *avoir une fière tapette*, to be a chatterbox.

tapette f. Mallet (marteau). ‖ Bat, carpet-beater. (V. batte.) ‖ Arts. Dabber, pad (de graveur). ‖ Pop. Pansy, nancy-boy; U. S. fairy.

tapeur [tapœ:r] m. Electr. Tapper.
— s. Fam. Borrower, cadger (emprunteur); piano strummer (pianiste).

tapin [tapɛ̃] m. Pop. *Faire le tapin*, to walk the streets.

tapinois [tapinwa] m. *En tapinois*, slyly, on the sly, stealthily; *partir en tapinois*, to slip away.

tapioca [tapjɔka] m. Comm. Tapioca. ‖ Culin. Tapioca soup.

tapir [tapi:r] m. Zool. Tapir. ‖ Fam. Private pupil.

tapir (se) [sətapi:r] v. pr. (2). To squat; to crouch; to snuggle; to cower. ‖ To take cover, to nestle (lapin, oiseau). ‖ Fig. To nestle, to lie hidden (maison).

tapis [tapi] m. Cover, cloth; *tapis de table*, table cover. ‖ Carpet; *tapis de haute laine*, long-pile carpet; *tapis d'Orient*, *de Smyrne*, Turkey (or) Oriental carpet. ‖ Agric. *Tapis de gazon* (ou) *de verdure*, greensward. ‖ Sports. *Tapis de billard*, billiard-cloth. ‖ Fig. *Etre sur le tapis*, to be on the carpet; *mettre qqch. sur le tapis,* to bring sth. up for discussion; *revenir sur le tapis,* to crop up again; *tapis vert,* gaming table. ‖ **Tapis-brosse** (pl. *tapis-brosses*), m. Door-mat, coir mat.

tapisser [-se] v. tr. (1). To hang with tapestry. ‖ To cover; to paper (une chambre); to line (les rues); *tapissé d'affiches,* plastered with bills; *tapissé de lierre,* ivy-covered.

tapisserie [-sri] f. Tapestry; hangings; upholstery (pour meubles); tapestry-carpet (tapis); *chaise en tapisserie,* chair upholstered with tapestry; *pantoufles en tapisserie,* carpet-slippers. ‖ Wall-paper (papier). ‖ Fig. *Derrière la tapisserie,* behind the scenes; *faire tapisserie,* to be a wallflower.

tapissier [-sje] s. Upholsterer; decorator (décorateur); tapestry-maker (fabricant); tapestry-merchant; wall-paper merchant (marchand).

tapotage [tapɔta:ʒ], **tapotement** [-tmɑ̃] m. Drumming, tapping, thrumming. ‖ Méd. Tapotement.

tapoter [-te] v. tr. (1). To tap; to thrum (des doigts). ‖ To pat (la joue); *se tapoter le visage,* to dab one's face. ‖ Mus. To strum (un air).
— v. intr. To tap (ou) drum (ou) thrum (*sur,* on). ‖ Mus. To strum.

taquet [takɛ] m. Wedge (coin); peg (piquet). ‖ Angle-block (de meuble); catch (de porte). ‖ Ch. de f. Stop-block. ‖ Naut. Rib, whelp (de cabestan); cleat (de hauban).

taquin, ine [takɛ̃, in] adj. Teasing, fond of teasing; *il est très taquin,* he is a big tease.
— s. Tease.

taquiner [takine] v. tr. (1). To tease. ‖ Fam. To worry, to bother (inquiéter); *taquiner le goujon,* to do a bit of fishing, to go fishing.

taquinerie [-nri] f. Teasing disposition (humeur). ‖ Teasing, chaff (acte).

tarabiscoté, ée [tarabiskɔte] adj. Grooved; fluted. ‖ Fam. Finicky, over-elaborate, overloaded.

tarabiscoter v. tr. (1). To groove. ‖ Fam. To overload.

tarabuster [tarabyste] v. tr. (1). Fam. To bother, to badger, to harass (v. Tourmenter); *se tarabuster l'esprit,* to rack one's brains. ‖ Fam. To ill-treat; to bully. (V. Malmener.)

tarare [tara:r] m. Agric. Winnowing machine, winnower.

tarasque [tarask] f. Tarasque.

taratata [taratata] interj. Fam. Nonsense!, fiddlesticks!

taraud [taro] m. Techn. Screw-tap.

taraudage [taroda:ʒ] m. Techn. Screw-cutting.

tarauder [-de] v. tr. (1). Techn. To screw, to tap. ‖ Fam. To pester (ennuyer); to thrash (rosser).

taraudeuse [-dø:z] f. Techn. Tapping-machine, tapper, screw- (ou) thread-cutter.

tard [ta:r] m. *Sur le tard,* late in the day (ou) evening (en fin de journée); late in life (en fin de vie); *il ne viendra que sur le tard,* he won't be here till late.
— adv. Late; *au plus tard,* at the latest (ou) outside; *il se fait tard,* it is getting late; *tard dans la nuit,* late at night; *pas plus tard qu'hier,* only yesterday; *plus tard,* later; later on; afterwards; *trop tard,* too late; *se lever tard,* to get up late. ‖ **Tard-venu** (pl. *tard-venus*) m. Late-comer.

tarder [tarde] v. intr. (1). To delay, to be late, to be long; to put off (différer); *il ne tardera pas à venir,* he won't be long; *sans plus tarder,* without further delay.
— v. impers. *Il me tarde de partir,* I'm anxious to leave; *il lui tarde de la revoir,* he's longing to see her again, he's looking forward to seeing her again.

tardif, ive [-dif, i:v] adj. Late (arbre, heure); backward (fruits). ‖ Fig. Belated (mesures, regrets); tardy (regrets).

tardigrade [tardigrad] adj., m. Zool. Tardigrade.

tardivement [tardivmɑ̃] adv. Tardily, belatedly. ‖ Slowly; *agir tardivement,* to be slow to act.

tardiveté [tardivte] f. Lateness, backwardness, tardiness.

tare [ta:r] f. Comm. Depreciation, loss in value (perte); tare (poids); *faire la tare,* to allow for the tare. ‖ Méd. Taint. ‖ Fig. Blemish; unsoundness; *sans tare,* sound. (V. Défaut.)

taré, ée [tare] adj. Unsound (cheval). ‖ Méd. Degenerate, with a taint. ‖ Fig. Corrupt, depraved; of ill repute.
— s. Pop. Moron, cretin (insulte).

tarentelle [tarɑ̃tɛl] f. Mus. Tarantella.

tarentule [tarɑ̃tyl] f. Zool. Tarantula.

tarer [tare] v. tr. (1). To damage, to spoil. (V. Avarier.) ‖ Comm. To tare, to deduct the tare of, to allow for the weight of (peser). ‖ Fig. To taint (l'esprit); to damage (la réputation).

taret [tarɛ] m. Zool. Teredo, ship-worm.

targe [tarʒ] f. † Targe. (V. Bouclier.)

targette [tarʒɛt] f. Flat bolt.

targuer (se) [sətarge] v. pr. (1). To boast, to be very proud (de, of); to pride (ou) plume oneself (de, on).

tarière [tarjɛ:r] f. Techn. Auger; drill. ‖ Zool. Ovipositor, terebra.

tarif [tarif] m. Tariff; price-list (catalogue); rate, rates (prix); scale of charges; *au tarif des imprimés,* at paper rates, U. S. as printed (ou) third class matter; *au tarif des lettres,* by letter post, U. S. as first-class matter; *tarif postal intérieur,* inland postage, U. S. domestic postage; *tarif préférentiel,* preferential tariff; *tarif des voitures,* taxi-fares. ‖ Ch. de f. Rates; list of fares; *plein tarif,* full tariff (pour marchandises); full fare (pour personnes). ‖ **Tarif-album,** m. Trade-catalogue.

tarifaire [-fɛ:r] adj. Relating to tariffs; tariff.

tarifer [-fe] v. tr. (1). To tariff, to fix the duties on (ou) the price of; *prix tarifé,* list price.

tarification [-fikasjɔ̃] f. Tariffing.

tarin [tarɛ̃] m. Zool. Siskin. ‖ Pop. Snout, hooter. (V. Pif.)

tarir [tari:r] v. intr. (2). To dry up, to run dry; *la source a tari, est tarie,* the spring has dried up, is dry. ‖ Fig. To cease, to stop; to be exhausted; to dry up (fam.); *il ne tarit pas sur ce sujet,* he never stops talking (ou) he's for ever talking about this subject.
— v. tr. To dry up. ‖ Fig. To exhaust; to dry up (fam.).
— v. pr. Se tarir, to dry up, to run dry.

tarissable [-sabl] adj. Liable to run dry.

tarissement [-smɑ̃] m. Drying up, running dry (d'une source); depletion (d'un puits de pétrole).

tarlatane [tarlatan] f. Tarlatan.

tarot [taro] m. Tarot card (carte); tarot pack, tarots (jeu).

tarse [tars] m. Méd. Tarsus.

tarsien, enne [-sjɛ̃, ɛn] adj. Méd. Tarsal.

tarsier [tarsje] m. Zool. Tarsier.

tartan [tartɑ̃] m. Tartan.

tartane [tartan] f. Naut. Tartan, tartane.

tartare [tarta:r] adj., s. Géogr. Tartar.
— m. *Le Tartare,* Tartarus.
— f. Culin. Tartare (sauce); *à la tartare,* dipped in breadcrumbs, broiled and served with cold mustard sauce; *steak tartare,* raw minced beef.

tartarin [tartarɛ̃] m. Fam. Bully. (V. Fanfaron.)

tarte [tart] f. Culin. Tart, flan, U. S. pie; *tarte à la crème, aux pommes,* cream, apple tart (ou) U. S. pie. ‖ Fam. Slap (gifle).
— adj. Fam. Silly, stupid.

tartelette [-lɛt] f. Culin. Tartlet; U. S. tart.

tartempion [tartɑ̃pjɔ̃] m. Fam. What's-his-name (ou) what's-her-name, thingumajig, thingumabob.

tartine [tartin] f. CULIN. Slice of bread and butter; *tartine de confiture*, slice of bread and jam. ‖ FAM. Long winded speech, harangue, U. S. spiel (discours); long and dull article; rigmarole; *il a écrit une tartine là-dessus*, he wrote a long waffle (ou) U. S. rambling article about it.

tartiner [tartine] v. intr. (1). FAM. To be long-winded.
— v. tr. CULIN. To butter (beurrer); to spread (*de*, with) [confiture, foie gras].

tartrate [tartrat] m. CHIM. Tartrate; *tartrate de potassium et d'antimoine*, tartar emetic.

tartre [tartr] m. CHIM., MÉD. Tartar. ‖ TECHN. Fur, scale.

tartré, ée [-tre] adj. CHIM. With the addition of tartar. ‖ MÉD. Coated with tartar (dents). ‖ TECHN. Furry, scaly (chaudière).

tartrique [-trik] adj. CHIM. Tartaric (acide).

tartufe [tartyf] m. Tartufe, Tartuffe.

tartuferie [-fri] f. Tartufism, tartuffism (caractère). ‖ Piece of hypocrisy (action).

tas [tɑ] m. Heap, pile (de bûches, de pierres); *mettre en tas*, to heap up, to pile up. ‖AGRIC. Stook, shock (de blé); *tas de foin*, hay-cock; *tas de fumier*, dunghill, manure heap. ‖ TECHN. *Grève sur le tas*, sit-down strike. ‖ FAM. Heap, heaps, lot, lots, bags, U. S. packs (de choses); lot, crowd, batch (de gens); pack (de mensonges); gang, set, pack (de voleurs); *piquer dans le tas*, to help oneself (à table); to take one's choice (en général).

tasse [tɑːs] f. Cup; *tasse à café*, coffee-cup; *tasse de café*, cup of coffee; *boire dans une tasse*, to drink out of a cup. ‖ FAM. *La grande tasse*, the sea; the drink (fam.); *boire à la grande tasse*, to go to Davy Jones's locker.

Tasse (le) [lɑtas] m. Tasso.

tassé, ée [tɑːse] adj. FAM. Well-filled (assiette); strong, stiff (boisson); closely packed (foule); plentiful (repas); *tassé par l'âge*, shrunk with age.

tasseau [tɑso] m. TECHN. Underprop, bracket (de tablette). ‖ ARCHIT. Brace; batten.

tassée [tɑse] f. Cupful.

tassement [-smɑ̃] m. Cramming together, squeezing together; compression (des objets). ‖ Ramming (de la terre). ‖ Settling, settling down (d'un mur); sinking, subsidence (d'une route). ‖ FIN. Setback. ‖ FAM. Consolidation (de l'opinion publique).

tasser [-se] v. tr. (1). To cram (ou) squeeze together, to compress (des objets); to pack tightly (des choses dans une valise). ‖ To ram, to pack (la terre). ‖ ARTS. To squeeze together (des figures).
— v. pr. Se tasser, to settle, to set (mur); to sink, to subside (route). ‖ To become shorter (ou) smaller, to shrink with age (personne). ‖ To crowd (ou) huddle (ou) squeeze together (gens). ‖ MILIT. To bunch (soldats). ‖ FIN. To weaken (Bourse). ‖ FAM. *Ça se tassera*, things will settle down; it will sort itself out.

taste-vin [tɑstəvɛ̃] m. V. TÂTE-VIN.

tata [tata] f. FAM. Auntie.

tatane [tatan] f. POP. Shoe.

tatar [tataːr] adj. GÉOGR. Tatar, tatarian, tataric.
— s. Tatar.
— m. GRAMM. Tatar (langue).

tâter [-te] v. tr. (1). To feel, to touch, to handle, to finger (une étoffe); to explore (le terrain); *tâter le pavé*, to feel one's way. ‖ MÉD. To feel (le pouls). ‖ MILIT. To probe, to try to draw (l'ennemi). ‖ NAUT. To feel (le fond); to hug (le vent). ‖ FAM. To try to find out (l'opinion); to sound (qqn); *tâter le pouls à qqn*, to sound

s.o.; *tâter le terrain*, to see how the land lies.
— v. intr. *Tâter de*, to try, to taste (un mets).
‖ FIG. To try, to experience; *tâter d'un métier*, to try one's hand at a trade.
— v. pr. Se tâter, to feel oneself. ‖ FAM. To think it over.

tâte-vin [tɑtvɛ̃] m. invar. Wine-taster (coupe); sampling tube (pipette).

tatillon, onne [tatijɔ̃, ɔn] adj. Fussy, finical, finicky, over-particular.
— s. Fussy person; fuss-pot (fam.) [chichiteux]; hair-splitter (pointilleux); caviller (vétilleux).

tatillonner [-jɔne] v. intr. (1). To be fussy, to fuss (faire des embarras). ‖ To split hairs (ergoter).

tâtonnement [tɑtɔnmɑ̃] m. Groping about, feeling one's way. ‖ FIG. Tentative effort; experiment by trial and error.

tâtonner [-ne] v. intr. (1). To grope, to feel one's way. ‖ FIG. To feel one's way. (V. HÉSITER.)

tâtonneur, euse [-nœːr, øːz] s. Groper; fumbler. ‖ FIG. Waverer.

tâtons (à) [atɑtɔ̃] loc. adv. Gropingly; feeling one's way; *chercher à tâtons*, to grope for; *entrer*, *marcher à tâtons*, to grope one's way in, along. ‖ FIG. Gropingly, hesitantly; tentatively.

tatou [tatu] m. ZOOL. Armadillo.

tatouage [tatwaːʒ] m. Tattooing (action); tattoo (dessin).

tatouer [-twe] v. tr. (1). To tattoo.

tatoueur [-twœːr] m. Tattooer, tattooist.

tau [to] m. Tau.

taud [to] m., **taude** [toːd] f. NAUT. Rain awning.

taudis [todi] m. Hovel, squalid house (logement); den (pièce). ‖ Pl. Slums; *lutte contre les taudis*, slum-clearance campaign.

taulard, arde [tolaːr, ard] s. Jailbird, con; *ancien taulard*, old lag.

taule [toːl] f. POP. Clink, jug, quod; U. S. hoosegow; *faire de la taule*, to do a stretch.

taulier [tolje] m. FAM. Proprietor, owner (patron).

taupe [toːp] adj. Taupe (couleur).
— f. ZOOL. Mole. ‖ COMM. Moleskin (peau). ‖ MILIT. *Guerre de taupes*, mine warfare. ‖ FAM. Special mathematics class.

taupé, ée [-pe] adj. Velours (feutre).

taupier [-pje] m. Mole-catcher.

taupière [-pjɛːr] f. Moletrap.

taupin [-pɛ̃] m. MILIT. Sapper. ‖ FAM. Student in special mathematics class.

taupinière [-pinjɛːr] f. Mole-hill.

taure [toːr] f. ZOOL. Heifer. (V. GÉNISSE.)

taureau [toro] m. ZOOL. Bull. ‖ SPORTS. *Course de taureaux*, bull-fight. ‖ ASTRON. Taurus, the Bull. ‖ FIG. *Avoir un cou de taureau*, to be bull-necked; *prendre le taureau par les cornes*, to take the bull by the horns.

taurillon [-rijɔ̃] m. ZOOL. Bull-calf.

taurin, ine [-rɛ̃, in] adj. Of bulls (exposition); bullfighting (jeux).

tauromachie [-rɔmaʃi] f. Bull-fighting, tauromachy.

tauromachique [-rɔmaʃik] adj. Tauromachian.

tautologie [totɔlɔʒi] f. Tautology.

tautologique [-ʒik] adj. Tautological.

taux [to] m. FIN. Rate (d'intérêt, du salaire); *au taux de cinq pour cent*, at the rate of five per cent; *taux de change*, exchange, rate of exchange; *taux de marque*, trade discount. ‖ COMM. Price; *taux du blé*, standard price of wheat; *à un taux trop élevé*, above the established price. ‖ TECHN. Proportion; ratio; *taux de compression*, compression-ratio.

tavelage [tavlaːʒ] m. Spotting, speckling.

tavelé, ée [-le] adj. Spotted, speckled. ‖ ZOOL. Tortoise-shell (chat).

taveler [-le] v. tr. (5). To spot, to speckle.

— v. pr. **Se taveler,** to become spotted (ou) speckled.

tavelure [-ly:r] f. Spots, speckles.

taverne [tavɛrn] f. Café-restaurant. ‖ † Tavern.

tavernier [-nje] s. Tavern-keeper.

taxable [taksabl] adj. Fin. Taxable.

taxateur [taksatœ:r] m. Taxer. ‖ Jur. Taxing official (juge).

taxation [-sjɔ̃] f. Fin. Taxation, valuation, assessment. ‖ Jur. Fixing (des frais).

taxe [taks] f. Official (ou) controlled price (prix officiel); fixed rate. ‖ Jur. Taxing, taxation (des frais). ‖ Fin. Tax, duty, rate; *taxe d'affranchissement,* prepaid rate of postage; *taxe de consommation,* excise-duty (ou) U. S. tax; *taxe de luxe,* luxury tax; *taxe de recommandation,* registration-fee; *taxe de séjour,* visitor's tax; *taxe supplémentaire,* surcharge (sur une lettre); *taxe sur les articles de luxe,* purchase (ou) luxury tax; *taxe à la valeur ajoutée,* value-added tax, VAT.

taxer [-se] v. tr. (1). To fix a controlled price for (le blé); to fix the rate (ou) the scale of (les salaires); *prix taxé,* controlled price. ‖ To surcharge (une lettre); *conversations taxées,* calls charged for overtime (au téléphone). ‖ Jur. To tax (les frais). ‖ Fin. To tax, to put a tax on (un qqn); to tax (qqn). ‖ Fig. To tax (*de,* with); to accuse (*de,* of) [qualifier].

taxi [taksi] m. Autom. Taxi-cab, taxi, cab; *par taxi,* by taxi; *prendre un taxi,* to take a taxi.

taxidermie [taksidɛrmi] f. Taxidermy.

taxidermique [-mik] adj. Taxidermic, taxidermal.

taximètre [taksimɛtr] m. Taximeter; clock (fam.). [V. compteur.]

taxinomie [taksinɔmi] f. Taxonomy.

taxiphone [taksifɔn] m. Public call-box; telephone booth.

taxonomie [taksɔnɔmi] f. V. taxinomie.

tayaut [tajo] interj. Tally-ho!

tayloriser [-rize] v. tr. (1). Techn. To taylorize.

taylorisme [-rism] m. Techn. Taylorism.

Tchad [tʃad] m. Géogr. Chad.

tchadien, enne [tʃadjɛ̃, ɛn] adj., s. Chadian.

tchécoslovaque [tʃekɔslɔvak] adj., s. Géogr. Czecho-Slovak.

Tchécoslovaquie [tʃekɔslɔvaki] f. Géogr. Czecho-Slovakia.

tchèque [tʃɛk] adj., m. Géogr. Czech.

tchernoziom [tʃɛrnɔzjɔm] m. Chernozem.

tchin-tchin [tʃintʃin] interj. Fam. Cheers! (en trinquant).

te [tə] (**t'** before a vowel) pron. pers. You (complément direct); *je te vois,* I see you; *te voilà,* there you are. ‖ To you, you (complément indirect); *il te le dira,* he will tell you; *il t'en parlera,* he will speak to you about it. ‖ (Explétif); *il tè m'a décoché un de ces coups de poing,* he aimed a terrific punch at me. ‖ Yourself (avec un v. pr.) [parfois non traduit]; *tu te fatigues trop,* you are tiring yourself out; *tu t'assieds,* you sit down; *va-t'en,* go away. ‖ † Ecclés. Thee (complément direct); to thee, thee (complément indirect); thyself, thee (avec un v. pr.).

té [te] m. T, t; *en té,* T-shaped. ‖ Arts. T-square, tee-square (à dessin). ‖ Techn. Tee-piece; union-T, tee-joint; *fer en té,* T-iron.

té interj. Fam. Of course! (approbation); why! (étonnement).

technétium [tɛknesjɔm] m. Chim. Technetium.

technicien, enne [tɛknisjɛ̃, ɛn] s. Technician, technicist, engineer.

technicité [-site] f. Technicality.

Technicolor [-kɔlɔr] m. Cinéma. Technicolor.

technique [tɛknik] adj. Techn. Technical.

— m. Technical school (ou) education.

— f. Technique; technics.

techniquement [-kmɑ̃] adv. Techn. Technically.

technocrate [tɛknɔkrat] m. Technocrat.

technocratie [-krasi] f. Technocracy.

technocratique [-kratik] adj. Technocratic.

technologie [tɛknɔlɔʒi] f. Technology.

technologique [-ʒik] adj. Technological.

teck [tɛk] m. Bot., Techn. Teak.

teckel [tekɛl] m. Zool. Dachshund, sausage dog (fam.).

tectonique [tɛktɔnik] adj. Tectonic.

— f. Tectonics; *tectonique des plaques,* plate tectonics.

tectrice [tɛktris] adj. f. *Plume tectrice,* wing-covert, tectrix (pl. tectrices).

Te Deum [tedeɔm] m. Mus. Te Deum.

T.E.E. [teəə] m. Ch. de f. Abrév. de *Trans-Europ-Express,* Trans-Europ-Express.

tee-shirt, t-shirt [tiʃœrt] m. Tee- (ou) t-shirt.

Téflon [teflɔ̃] m. (nom déposé). Teflon.

tégument [tegymɑ̃] m. Tegument.

tégumentaire [-tɛ:r] adj. Tegumentary.

teigne [tɛɲ] f. Zool. Moth, tinea; *teigne de draps,* clothes-moth. ‖ Méd. Tinea; ringworm, scalp-disease. ‖ Bot. Burdock (bardane); scale (sur l'écorce). ‖ Fig. Pest, plague (enfant); shrew (femme).

teigneux, euse [-ɲø, ø:z] adj. Méd. Affected with ringworm (ou) scalp-disease.

— m. Fam. Scurvy fellow.

— s. Méd. Person suffering from ringworm (ou) scalp-disease.

teindre [tɛ̃:dr] v. tr. (59). To dye; to stain, to colour, to tinge; *faire teindre qqch.,* to have sth. dyed; *teindre en rouge,* to dye red; *teindre en pièce,* to piece-dye.

— v. pr. **Se teindre,** to dye one's hair.

teint [tɛ̃] adj., p.p. Dyed; *teint en laine,* dyed in the wool (drap).

— m. Dye, colour; *bon* (ou) *grand teint,* fast colour. ‖ Complexion, colour. (V. carnation.) ‖ Fig. *Partisan bon teint,* staunch supporter.

teinte [tɛ̃:t] f. Tint, hue. (V. couleur.) ‖ Arts. *Teinte plate,* flat tint. ‖ Fig. Tinge, shade, touch, smack. (V. soupçon.)

teinté, ée [tɛ̃te] adj. Tinted; tinged (en général); toned (papier).

teinter v. tr. (1). To tint; to tinge (légèrement).

teinture [-ty:r] f. Dyeing (art, opération); dye (liquide); *teinture en pièce,* piece-dyeing. ‖ Colour, hue, tint (couleur). ‖ Méd. Tincture (d'iode). ‖ Fig. Superficial knowledge, nodding acquaintance, smattering (d'une langue).

teinturerie [-tyrri] f. Dyeing (art); dye-works (atelier); dry-cleaner's, cleaner's (magasin); dyer's-trade (métier).

teinturier [-tyrje] s. Dyer; *teinturier dégraisseur,* dyer and cleaner.

tek [tɛk] m. V. teck.

tel (f. **telle**) [tɛl] adj. indéf. Such (degré, ressemblance); *un tel homme,* such a man; *de tels hommes,* such men; *de telle sorte que,* in such a way that. ‖ Such, so great (si grand); *son pouvoir est tel que tout le monde lui obéit,* his power is such that everyone obeys him. ‖ Such and such (sens vague); *avoir tel ou tel effet,* to have such and such an effect; *à tel endroit,* at such and such a place. ‖ This; *en tel ou tel cas,* in this or that case. ‖ Like; as; *tel père, tel fils,* like father, like son; *tel ... que,* like, such as; as; *voir les hommes tels qu'ils sont,* to see men as they are. ‖ Like, just as (pareil à); *tel un mort,* like a dead man. ‖ *Tel quel,* just as he (ou) it is (dans l'état); ordinary, mediocre; only so-so, not very satisfactory (peu satisfaisant); *laissez les choses telles quelles,* leave things as they are; *sa biblio-*

thèque, telle quelle, vaut une fortune, his library, as it stands, is worth a fortune; *j'ai retrouvé la maison telle quelle,* I found the house just as I had left it. ‖ Comm. *Tel quel,* with all faults; U. S. as is. ‖ Loc. *Il est intelligent, du moins on le prend pour tel,* he is intelligent, or at least people say so; *excellent, ou réputé tel,* excellent, or reputed to be; *je ferai de telle sorte que personne ne me voie,* I shall make sure that no one sees me; *je sais tel petit restaurant où l'on mange bien,* I could name a certain little restaurant where the food is good; *il faut voir les choses telles qu'elles sont,* one must look facts in the face; *il fit telles démarches qu'il crut nécessaires,* he took such steps as he thought necessary; *il n'y a rien de tel qu'un bain chaud,* there's nothing like a hot bath; *c'est à ce moment-là qu'il se montre tel qu'il est,* it's then that he shows himself in his true colours; *une grande ville telle que Paris, par exemple,* a city, like Paris, for example. — pron. indéf. One; some, some people; *tel rit aujourd'hui, qui pleurera demain,* laugh to-day, cry tomorrow. ‖ *Un tel, une telle,* so-and-so; *Monsieur Untel,* Mr. So-and-so.

télamon [telamɔ̃] m. Telamon.

télé [tele] f. Fam. TV, telly, U. S. tele; the box.

télécabine [telekabin] f. Cable-car, gondola.

télécinéma [telesinema] m. Telecine; U. S. movie seen on television.

télécommande [telekɔmɑ̃:d] f. Remote control.

télécommander [-de] v. tr. (1). Electr. To operate by remote control.

télécommunication [telekɔmynikasjɔ̃] f. Electr. Telecommunication.

télédiffuser [-difyze] v. tr. (1). To telecast.

télédistribution [-distribysjɔ̃] f. Cable television, rediffusion.

télé-enseignement [-ɑ̃sɛɲmɑ̃] m. Teaching through radio and TV.

téléférique [-ferik] m. V. téléphérique.

téléfilm [-film] m. Television (ou) TV film.

télégénique [-ʒenik] adj. Telegenic; *être télégénique,* to come over well on television.

télégramme [telegram] m. Telegram; wire (fam.).

télégraphe [-graf] m. Electr. Telegraph; *télégraphe imprimeur,* ticker.

télégraphie [-grafi] f. Electr. Telegraphy; *télégraphie sans fil,* wireless, U. S. radio.

télégraphier [-grafje] v. intr., tr. (1). To telegraph, to wire (à, to). [V. câbler.]

télégraphique [-grafik] adj. Telegraphic (adresse, mandat); telegraph (bureau, fil, poteau); *style télégraphique,* telegraphic style, telegraphese.

télégraphiquement [-grafikmɑ̃] adv. Telegraphically.

télégraphiste [-grafist] s. Telegraphist; telegraph operator, U. S. keyman, telegrapher. ‖ Telegraphboy (facteur).

téléguidage [-gida:ʒ] m. Radio-control.

téléguidé, ée [-gide] adj. Guided (engin).

téléguider [-gide] v. tr. (1). To radio-control.

téléimprimeur [-ɛ̃primœ:r] m. Electr. Teleprinter.

télékinésie [-kinezi] f. Telekinesis.

télématique [-matik] f. Techn. Viewdata processing, Prestel (nom déposé).

télémécanique [-mekanik] adj. Remote controlled. (V. télécommander.)
— f. Electr. Telemechanics.

télémètre [-mɛtr] m. Telemeter. ‖ Milit. Rangefinder.

télémétrer [-metre] v. tr. (5). Techn., Milit. To take the range of.

télémétrie [-metri] f. Tech. Telemetry. ‖ Milit. Range-finding.

télémétrique [-metrik] adj. Techn. Telemetric.

téléobjectif [-ɔbʒɛktif] m. Techn. Telephoto lens.

téléologie [teleɔlɔʒi] f. Philos. Teleology.

télépathe [telepat] adj. Telepathic.
— s. Telepath, telepathist.

télépathie [-pati] f. Telepathy.

télépathique [-patik] adj. Telepathic.

téléphérage [-fera:ʒ] m. Techn. Telpherage, aerial ropeway system.

téléphérer [-fere] v. tr. (5). Techn. To telpher.

téléphérique [-ferik] adj. Techn. Telpher (ligne).
— m. Techn. Telpher; aerial ropeway (ou) cableway; cable-railway; passenger ropeway.

téléphone [-fɔn] m. Electr. Telephone; phone (fam.); *avoir le téléphone,* to be on the phone (fam.); *coup de téléphone,* telephone call; *donner un coup de téléphone à qqn,* to give s.o. a ring (ou) a call; *téléphone intérieur,* inter-communication, intercom (fam.).

téléphoner [-fɔne] v. tr., intr. (1). To telephone, to phone (une nouvelle); *téléphoner à,* to ring, to ring up, to phone (fam.) [qqn].

téléphonie [-fɔni] f. Telephony; *téléphonie sans fil,* wireless telephony, radio-telephony.

téléphonique [-fɔnik] adj. Telephonic; *appel téléphonique,* telephone call; *cabine téléphonique,* telephone booth (ou) kiosk, call-box; *conversation téléphonique,* conversation on the telephone.

téléphoniquement [-fɔnikmɑ̃] adv. Telephonically, by telephone.

téléphoniste [-fɔnist] s. Telephonist, telephone operator.

téléphotographie [-fɔtɔgrafi] f. Telephotography.

téléphotographique [-fɔtɔgrafik] adj. Telephotographic.

télérécepteur [-resɛptœ:r] m. Television set.

télescopage [telɛskɔpa:ʒ] m. Telescoping.

télescope [-kɔp] m. Telescope.

télescoper [-kɔpe] v. tr., intr. (1). To telescope; to crumple up.
— v. pr. **Se télescoper,** to telescope; to crumple up. (V. heurter.)

télescopique [-kɔpik] adj. Telescopic.

téléscripteur [teleskriptœ:r] m. Electr. Teleprinter.

télésiège [-sjɛ:ʒ] m. Chair-lift.

téléski [-ski] m. Teleski; U. S. ski lift.

téléspectateur, trice [-spɛktatœ:r, tris] s. Televiewer, viewer.

télétype [-tip] m. Teletype, teleprinter, U. S. teletypewriter; tape-machine, U. S. ticker (dans les Bourses).

téléviser [-vize] v. tr., intr. (1). Radio. To televise.

téléviseur [-vizœ:r] m. Radio. Television set.

télévision [-vizjɔ̃] f. Radio. Television, T.V.

télex [telɛks] m. Telex.

tellement [tɛlmɑ̃] adv. So, in such a way (ou) manner (de telle sorte). ‖ So, to such a degree (ou) extent (à tel point); *il fait tellement froid que,* it's so cold that; *il a mangé tous les gâteaux, tellement il avait faim,* he ate all the cakes, he was so hungry.

tellure [tɛlly:r] m. Chim. Tellurium.

tellureux, euse [-rø, ø:z] adj. Chim. Tellurous.

tellurien, enne [-rjɛ̃, ɛn] adj. Tellurian.

tellurique [-rik] adj. Phys., Chim., Méd. Telluric. ‖ Electr. Earth.

tellurure [-ry:r] f. Chim. Telluride.

tél(o)ugou [telugu] m. Gramm. Telugu (langue).

téméraire [temerɛ:r] adj. Rash, reckless, daring, headstrong, foolhardy (action, homme); rash (jugement).
— s. Rash (ou) reckless (ou) foolhardy person; dare-devil. (V. hardi.)

témérairement [-rɛrmɑ̃] adv. Rashly, recklessly, daringly.

témérité [-rite] f. Rashness, recklessness, foolhardiness. ‖ Rash action; piece of foolhardiness.

témoignage [temwaɲa:ʒ] m. JUR. Evidence, witness, testimony; *appelé en témoignage,* called as witness; *faux témoignage,* false evidence; *porter témoignage,* to give evidence, to testify; *porter témoignage de,* to bear witness to; *rendre témoignage à,* to testify to, to bear witness to (qqch.); to speak out (ou) to testify in favour of (qqn). ‖ Evidence (preuve); *donner des témoignages de sa valeur,* to give evidence of one's ability. ‖ Statement (déclaration); *d'après son témoignage,* according to his statement. ‖ Evidence (des sens); *ne s'en rapporter qu'au témoignage de ses yeux,* to believe only what one sees. ‖ FIG. Proof, mark, token (d'amitié).

témoigner [-ɲe] v. intr. (1). To testify; to bear witness; *les faits témoignent en sa faveur,* the facts speak in his favour. ‖ JUR. To testify; to give evidence (*contre, en faveur de,* against, for). ‖ *Témoigner de,* to bear witness (ou) testimony to, to testify to, to give evidence (ou) proof of (attester); to be a sign (ou) proof of, to be evidence of (dénoter); to express (exprimer); to prove, to show, to indicate (indiquer); to display (manifester); *je peux témoigner de sa bonne foi,* I can testify to his sincerity. — v. tr. To swear, to testify (jurer). ‖ JUR. To testify, to attest. ‖ FIG. To show, to display; to give proof of (son amitié); to express, to give expression to (sa reconnaissance).

témoin [temwɛ̃] adj. COMM. *Echantillon témoin,* check sample. ‖ ELECTR. *Lampe témoin,* pilot (ou) tell-tale (ou) warning lamp. — m. Witness (v. SPECTATEUR); *témoin ce qui m'est arrivé,* witness what happened to me; *j'ai été témoin de son action,* I saw him do it; *être témoin de,* to witness; *sans témoins,* unseen. ‖ JUR. Witness; *témoin oculaire,* eye-witness; *banc des témoins,* witness-box; *faux témoin,* false witness; *servir de témoin à,* to act as witness at (un mariage). ‖ Witness, evidence, testimony, proof (preuve); *être un témoin du génie de,* to bear witness to the genius of; *prendre à témoin,* to call to witness. ‖ Second (dans un duel). ‖ AUTOM. Wing indicator, capacity indicator (d'une aile). ‖ AGRIC. Tree left standing (arbre); boundary mark (sous une borne). ‖ SPORTS. Stick, baton. ‖ CHIM. Test, check; reference solution. ‖ TECHN. Dog's-ear (en reliure).

tempe [tã:p] MÉD. Temple.

tempérament [tãperamã] m. Temperament, constitution (état physiologique); *par tempérament,* constitutionally, naturally; *tempérament de fer,* iron constitution; *tempérament sanguin,* sanguine temperament. ‖ Temper, temperament, character, disposition, humour (constitution morale); *tempérament violent,* violent temper. ‖ MUS. Temperament. ‖ COMM. *A tempérament,* by instalments, on the instalment (ou) hire-purchase system; U. S. by easy payments; *vente à tempérament,* hire-purchase. ‖ FIG. Moderation, measure, restraint, proportion, middle course (équilibre). ‖ FAM. Amorous temperament; *avoir du tempérament,* to be highly sexed.

tempérance [tãperã:s] f. Temperance, moderation. (V. SOBRIÉTÉ.)

tempérant, ante [-rã, ã:t] adj. Temperate; moderate.

température [tãperaty:r] f. Temperature. ‖ PHYS. *Température d'ébullition, de la glace fondante,* boiling-, freezing-point. ‖ MÉD. *Avoir de la température,* to have a temperature. ‖ FAM. *Prendre la température du public,* to sense public reaction.

tempéré, ée [-re] adj. GÉOGR. Temperate; mild (climat). ‖ MUS. Equally tempered. ‖ FIG. Temperate (v. MODÉRÉ); limited (monarchie); sober, restrained (style); *c'est un esprit tempéré,* he's a moderate-minded man.

tempérer [-re] v. tr. (5). To temper, to moderate (v. MODÉRER). ‖ To soothe; to sober; to have a sobering effect on. (V. ADOUCIR.) — v. pr. **Se tempérer,** to moderate.

tempête [tãpɛ:t] f. Storm, tempest; *tempête de neige,* snow-storm, blizzard; *le vent souffle en tempête,* it's blowing a gale. ‖ NAUT. Storm; hurricane; *battu par la tempête,* storm-tossed (bateau); storm-beaten (côte). ‖ FIG. Storm, outburst (d'applaudissements); row (dispute); *tempête dans un verre d'eau,* storm in a teacup, tempest in a teapot; *laisser passer la tempête,* to let the storm blow over.

tempêter [-pɛte] v. intr. (1). FAM. To storm; to fume, to rant. (V. INVECTIVER, RAGER.)

tempétueusement [tãpetɥøzmã] adv. Stormily, tempestuously.

tempétueux, euse [-tɥø, ø:z] adj. Stormy, tempestuous (mer); wild, boisterous, blustering (vent). ‖ FIG. Stormy, tempestuous, boisterous.

temple [tã:pl] m. ECCLÉS. Temple, place of worship (en général); church (culte protestant). ‖ Temple; *chevaliers du Temple,* Knights Templars.

templier [tãplje] m. Templar, Knight Templar. ‖ LOC. *Jurer comme un templier,* to swear like a trooper.

tempo [tɛmpo] m. MUS. Tempo.

temporaire [tãpɔrɛ:r] adj. Temporary (mesure); provisional (pouvoir). [V. PASSAGER.] ‖ MUS. *Valeur temporaire,* time-value.

temporairement [-rɛrmã] adv. Temporarily; provisionally, for the present, for the time being.

temporal, ale [tãpɔral] adj., m. MÉD. Temporal.

temporalité [tãpɔralite] f. ECCLÉS. Temporality.

temporel, elle [-rɛl] adj. Temporal, secular, of this life (ou) world, worldly (mondain). ‖ Temporal, transient, fleeting (passager). ‖ ECCLÉS. Temporal (pouvoir). — m. ECCLÉS. Temporal power (pouvoir); temporalities (revenu).

temporellement [-rɛlmã] adv. Temporally.

temporisateur, trice [-rizatœ:r, tris] adj. Temporizing. — s. Temporizer; procrastinator. ‖ TECHN. Timer.

temporisation [-rizasjõ] f. Temporization, temporizing.

temporiser [-rize] v. intr. (1). To temporize, to use delaying tactics, to play for time; to procrastinate, to defer action.

temps [tã] m. Time, duration (durée limitée); *bien employer son temps,* to put one's time to good use; *marquer un temps,* to pause; *un temps d'arrêt,* a short pause; *mettre peu de temps à faire qqch.,* not to take long over sth. ‖ Time, while, period; *passer quelque temps chez des amis,* to stay with friends for a time. ‖ Time (délai); *gagner du temps,* to play for time; *le temps de me laver les mains, et je descends,* just a moment while I wash my hands, and I'll be down; *tactique pour gagner du temps,* stalling tactics. ‖ Time, leisure (loisir); *je n'ai jamais le temps de,* I never have time to. ‖ Time, times, age, era, epoch, period, days (époque); *au temps de César,* in the days of Caesar; *le bon vieux temps,* the good old days. ‖ Time, season (saison); *le Temps,* Old Father Time (personnification); *le temps des moissons,* harvest-time. ‖ Times (conditions de vie; époque actuelle); *les temps sont durs,* times are hard; *les modes du temps,* the fashions of the times; today's (ou) present-day fashions; *signe des temps,* sign of the times. ‖ Opportunity, occasion (heure propice); time, hour (moment); *il est grand temps de partir,* it is high time to leave; *le temps* *approche*, the time (ou) the hour is drawing near. ‖ Weather (atmosphérique); *il fait un temps de chien*, the weather is rotten; *par tous les temps*, in all weathers; *quel temps fait-il?*, what's the weather like?; *quelque temps qu'il fasse*, whatever the weather. ‖ NAUT. *Gros temps*, heavy weather. ‖ GRAMM. Tense; *temps composés*, compound tenses; *temps primitifs*, principal parts; *adverbes de temps*, adverbs of time. ‖ MILIT. Time, term, period (de service); *faire temps*, to do one's time. ‖ JUR. *A temps*, for a period of months (ou) years (bannissement); *faire son temps*, to do time (prisonnier); *travaux forcés à temps*, term of penal servitude. ‖ ECCLÉS. *Temps de l'Ascension*, Ascensiontide. ‖ MUS. Time, measure, beat; *temps faible, fort*, up-, down-beat; *mesure à deux, à trois temps*, common (ou) duple, triple time. ‖ SPORTS. *Coup à temps*, time-thrust (en escrime). ‖ MÉD. Stage, phase, step (d'une opération). ‖ ASTRON. Time. ‖ TECHN. Stroke; *à deux temps*, two-stroke (moteur). ‖ LOC. *A temps*, in time (assez tôt); in the nick of time (à point); *au temps jadis*, in the old days; in days of yore (†); *au temps de ma jeunesse*, in my youth, when I was young; *avant le temps*, prematurely; *avec le temps*, in time, in the course of time, in the long run; *avoir bien le temps*, to have plenty of time; *avoir fait son temps*, to be out of date, to have seen its day (livre, opinion); *cela n'aura qu'un temps*, that won't last long; *il y a beau temps que*, it's a long while since; *prendre un peu de bon temps*, to have a good time (s'amuser); to relax (ou) rest for a while (se reposer); *couleur du temps*, sky-blue; *dans le temps*, in the old days, formerly, once; *de temps à autre, de temps en temps*, from time to time, on and off, now and then; *de (ou) en tout temps*, at all times; *du temps où*, when; *en ce temps-là*, at that time; *en son temps*, in due course; *en temps de guerre, de paix*, in war-, peace-time; *en temps et lieu*, at the proper time; *en même temps*, at the same time; *en temps utile (ou) voulu*, in due course (ou) time; *entre-temps*, meanwhile; between times; *être de son temps*, to move with (ou) to keep up with the times; to be up-to-date; *il n'est pas de son temps*, he's behind the times; *il est grand temps de*, it is high time to; *il fut un temps où*, there was once a time when; *par le temps qui court*, as things are; as matters now stand; *perdre son temps*, to waste time; *pour gagner du temps*, to save time; *prendre du temps*, to take time; *prendre son temps*, to take one's time; *tout le temps*, all the time, incessantly; *venir en son temps*, to be timely.

tenable [tənabl] adj. MILIT. Tenable, defensible; *pas tenable*, untenable (poste). ‖ FIG. *Pas tenable*, unbearable (chaleur); uninhabitable (maison).

tenace [tənas] adj. Tenacious; clinging (lierre, odeur); adhesive, sticky (poix). ‖ Tough, hard (fer); stiff (sol). ‖ FIG. Tenacious; stubborn, dogged, obstinate (caractère) [v. TÊTU]; retentive (mémoire); deep-rooted (préjugé); tenacious, persistent (solliciteur).

tenacement [-smã] adv. Tenaciously.

ténacité [tenasite] f. Tenacity, tenaciousness (en général); strength, toughness (du fer); strength (du papier); adhesiveness, stickiness (de la poix); stiffness (du sol). ‖ FIG. Tenacity, tenaciousness; doggedness, firmness, steadfastness (du caractère); retentiveness (de la mémoire); persistency (d'un solliciteur); obstinacy, stubbornness (de la volonté).

tenaille [tənɑ:j] f. TECHN. Pincers (outil); nippers (de cordonnier); tongs (de forgeron). ‖ MILIT. Tenaille; *mouvement en tenaille*, pincer movement.

tenailler [-nɑje] v. tr. (1). † To torture with red-hot pincers. ‖ FIG. To torture, to torment (v. TOURMENTER); to gnaw (faim); to rack (remords).

tenancier [tənɑ̃sje] s. † Freeholder, yeoman. ‖ Lessee (d'un bar, d'un casino); manager (d'un hôtel); keeper (d'une maison de jeu). ‖ AGRIC. Tenant (fermier).

tenancière [-sjɛ:r] f. Manageress (d'un hôtel); Madame, brothel-keeper (d'une maison close).

tenant, ante [tənɑ̃, ɑ̃:t] adj. Attached (col). ‖ LOC. *Séance tenante*, on the spot, at once.
— part. prés. V. TENIR (101).
— m. † Champion. ‖ SPORTS. Holder (d'un record). ‖ FIG. Champion, supporter, upholder, defender (d'une idée, d'une personne); taker (d'un pari). ‖ LOC. *Les tenants et les aboutissants*, boundaries and abuttals; adjoining lands (ou) properties (d'un domaine); ins and outs (d'une question); *d'un seul tenant*, in a single piece.

tendance [tɑ̃dɑ̃:s] f. PHYS. Tendency (to move). ‖ FIN. *Tendance à la baisse, à la hausse*, downward, upward trend (ou) tendency; *tendance soutenue*, steady tone. ‖ FIG. Tendency, propensity, inclination (v. PROPENSION); bent (d'un caractère); leaning (d'un goût); trend (de l'opinion); *à tendance*, tendentious (livre); *les tendances actuelles*, present-day trends of opinion.

tendancieux, euse [-dɑ̃sjø, ø:z] adj. Tendentious. ‖ JUR. Leading (question).

tendant [-dɑ̃] adj. invar. Tending (à, to).

tendelet [tɑ̃dlɛ] m. NAUT. Awning, tilt.

tender [tɑ̃dɛ:r] m. CH. DE F. Tender.

tendeur [tɑ̃dœ:r] s. Layer, setter (de pièges); layer (de tapis); hanger (de tapisseries).
— m. TECHN. Adjuster (de chaîne); belt-tightener (pour courroie); wire-strainer (pour fil de fer). ‖ Boot- (ou) shoe-tree (pour chaussures); trouser-stretcher (pour pantalon). ‖ AUTOM. Tension-rod (de châssis).

tendineux, euse [tɑ̃dinø, ø:z] adj. MÉD. Tendinous. ‖ CULIN. Stringy, sinewy (viande).

tendoir [tɑ̃dwa:r] m. Clothes-lines. ‖ Tenter.

tendon [tɑ̃dɔ̃] m. MÉD. Tendon, sinew.

tendre [tɑ̃:dr] v. tr. (4). To stretch, to strain (tirer). ‖ To tighten (une corde, un fil). ‖ To draw, to bend (un arc); to set (un ressort). ‖ To spread (un filet); to set, to lay (un piège). ‖ To offer (un cadeau, la main). ‖ To crane (le cou); to stretch out, to hold out (la main). ‖ To pitch, to set up (une tente). ‖ To lay (un tapis); to hang (des tapisseries); *tendre une chambre de papier peint*, to paper a room. ‖ NAUT. To unfurl (les voiles). ‖ MUS. To tighten (une corde). ‖ FIG. To strain (l'attention, des rapports); to set, to lay (des pièges); *tendre la joue*, to offer one's cheek; *tendre l'autre joue*, to turn the other cheek; *tendre la main*, to beg; *tendre la perche à qqn*, to give s.o. a helping hand; *tendre l'oreille*, to prick up one's ears.
— v. intr. To lead, to go (chemin, pas); to go, to direct one's steps. ‖ FIG. To tend, to lead (à, to); to be directed (à, to); to have a tendency (à, to); *tendre vers*, to be directed towards.
— v. pr. Se tendre, to stretch, to become taut (corde). ‖ FIG. To become strained (rapports).

tendre adj. Tender. ‖ Tender, sensitive, delicate (peau); soft (pierre). ‖ Delicate (couleur). ‖ Touching (attendrissant). ‖ CULIN. New (pain); tender (viande). ‖ FIG. Tender, soft, kind (cœur); tender, early (enfance); affectionate, fond, loving (paroles); compassionate, tender-hearted, easily moved, sympathetic (personne); *avoir le cœur tendre*, to be tender- (ou) soft-hearted.
— m. FAM. Love.

tendrement [tɑ̃drəmɑ̃] adv. Tenderly, dearly, fondly. ‖ Delicately.

tendresse [tɑ̃drɛs] f. Tenderness, tender affection, love, fondness. ‖ Kindness (bonté); delicacy (délicatesse). ‖ Pl. Tokens of affection; endearments; caresses.

tendreté [-drəte] f. Tenderness.

tendron [tɑ̃drɔ̃] m. BOT. Young shoot. ‖ CULIN. Gristle (de veau). ‖ FAM. Young lass, lassie.

tendu, ue [tɑ̃dy] adj. Strained; tight, taut (corde); *mal tendu*, slack. ‖ Bent (arc). ‖ Spread (filet); set, laid (piège). ‖ *Tendu de noir*, hung with black. ‖ NAUT. Set, spread (voiles). ‖ Held out, outstretched (main). ‖ PHYS. Flat (trajectoire). ‖ FIN. Hard, stiff, firm (prix). ‖ FIG. Tensed (esprit, nerfs); strained (rapports); tense (situation); stilted (style).

ténèbres [tenɛ:br] f. pl. Darkness, gloom (obscurité); shades (de la nuit). ‖ ECCLÉS. Tenebrae. ‖ FIG. Darkness (de l'ignorance); shades (de la mort).

ténébreusement [tenebrøzmɑ̃] adv. Darkly, gloomily. ‖ Mysteriously.

ténébreux, euse [-brø, ø:z] adj. Dark, gloomy, sombre (caverne); forbidding, lowering (ciel). [V. OBSCUR, SOMBRE.] ‖ FIG. Dark (action); mysterious, dark, deep, sinister, shady (projets); obscure (style).
— m. *Beau ténébreux*, hero wrapped in Byronic gloom.

ténesme [tenɛsm] m. MÉD. Tenesmus.

teneur, euse [tənœ:r, ø:z] s. Holder. ‖ COMM. *Teneur de livres*, book-keeper.

teneur f. Tenor, terms (d'un acte); purport (d'un traité). ‖ Grade, assay value (d'un minerai); amount, percentage; content; strength (d'une solution); *teneur en alcool*, alcoholic content; *teneur en eau*, degree of humidity; *de haute teneur*, high-grade (acier).

ténia [tenja] m. MÉD. Taenia, tapeworm.

ténifuge [tenify:ʒ] adj., m. MÉD. Taenifuge.

tenir [təni:r] v. tr. (101).

---

1. Sens général. — 2. Posséder. — 3. Retenir. — 4. Diriger. — 5. Entretenir. — 6. Maintenir. — 7. Renfermer. — 8. Contenir. — 9. Conserver. — 10. Soutenir. — 11. Rester. — 12. Occuper. — 13. Remplir. — 14. Détenir. — 15. Organiser. — 16. Faire honneur à. — 17. Emettre. — 18. Considérer. — 19. Concevoir. — 20. Garder. — 21. NAUT. — 22. AUTOM. — 23. THÉÂTR. — 24. MUS. — 25. SPORTS. — 26. FIN. — 27. COMM. — 28. Tenir de. — 29. En tenir. — 30. Faire tenir.

---

1. To hold (en général) [à la main]; to grip (empoigner); *tenir au collet*, to hold by the scruff of the neck; *tenir qqch. serré*, to keep a tight hold on sth. ‖ 2. To hold, to have, to possess (posséder). ‖ 3. To hold, to retain (retenir) in laisse, to keep on a lead (ou) on the leash; *tenir ses élèves*, to control one's pupils, to have one's pupils in hand; *tenir sa langue*, to hold one's tongue; *tenir au frais*, to keep in a cool place; *tenir qqn de près*, to keep s.o. under control; *tenir en respect*, to hold in respect. ‖ 4. To manage (diriger); to run, U. S. to operate (un hôtel); *tenir la main à*, to see to. ‖ 5. To keep (entretenir); to keep, to look after (un jardin); to keep (une maison); *bien tenu*, well-kept, tidy (jardin). ‖ 6. To hold, to keep (maintenir); *tenir la tête haute*, to hold one's head high. ‖ 7. To hold, to contain, to accommodate, to take, to admit (renfermer); *théâtre qui tient mille personnes*, theatre holding a thousand people (or) with room for a thousand. ‖ 8. To hold, to retain, to keeep in (contenir); *tenir un litre*, to hold a litre. ‖ 9. To hold (conserver); *tenir l'eau*, to hold water, to be water-tight. ‖ 10. To hold up, to keep

up, to support (soutenir); *les contreforts qui tiennent les murs*, the buttresses supporting the walls. ‖ 11. To keep to, to remain in (rester); *tenir le lit*, to stay in bed. ‖ 12. To fill, to take up, to occupy (occuper); *tenir trop de place*, to take up too much room. ‖ 13. To hold, to fill, to occupy (remplir); *tenir un emploi*, to hold a post. ‖ 14. To hold, to occupy (détenir); *tenir une place*, to occupy a seat; *tenir la tête*, to lead, to be in the lead. ‖ 15. To hold (organiser); *tenir une réunion*, to hold a meeting. ‖ 16. To hold, to keep, to carry out (faire honneur à); *tenir sa promesse*, to keep one's promise. ‖ 17. To have, to hold (émettre); to have, to hold (une conversation); to use, to make use of (un langage); to make, to utter (des propos); *tenir des propos désobligeants pour*, to speak disparagingly of. ‖ 18. To hold, to consider, to think, to believe, to maintain, to regard (considérer); to reckon (fam.); *tenir l'affaire comme faite*, to consider the matter settled; *tenir qqch. pour juste*, to believe sth. to be fair and just; *tenir qqn pour honnête*, to regard s.o. as honest; *tenez-le-vous pour dit*, take that once and for all. ‖ 19. To take in, to understand (concevoir). ‖ 20. To take (garder); *tenir compte de*, to take in account; *tenir au courant*, to keep informed. ‖ 21. NAUT. To hug (la côte); to secure (un mât); to keep (le vent); *tenir la mer*, to stay at sea; *capable de tenir la mer*, seaworthy. ‖ 22. AUTOM. To hold (la route); *tenez votre gauche*, keep to the left. ‖ 23. THÉÂTR. To play, to take (un rôle). ‖ 24. MUS. To play, to be at (l'orgue); to take, to sing (une partie). ‖ 25. SPORTS. To control, to keep in hand (un cheval); to take, to take on (un pari). ‖ 26. FIN. To hold, to have charge of; *tenir les livres*, to keep the accounts, to do the book-keeping. ‖ 27. COMM. To keep, to stock (un article). ‖ 28. **Tenir de**, to learn from (apprendre de); to derive from, to owe to, to be indebted to, to get from (être redevable à); *le tenir de bonne source*, to have it on good authority; *tenir sa vivacité de sa mère*, to get one's vivaciousness from one's mother. ‖ 29. **En tenir**, to be winged (oiseau); to have had a nasty knock (personne); FAM. *en tenir un coup*, to be pickled (ivre). ‖ 30. **Faire tenir**, to get into (faire contenir); to send, to forward (une lettre).

— v. intr.

---

1. Rester debout. — 2. Résister. — 3. Durer. — 4. Adhérer. — 5. Rester. — 6. Contenir. — 7. Compter. — 8. Loc. — 9. Tenir à. — 10. Tenir de. — 11. Tenir pour. — 12 En tenir pour.

---

1. To stand (rester debout); *ne plus tenir sur ses jambes*, to be ready (ou) about to drop. ‖ 2. To resist (résister); to hold, to stand the strain (corde); *tenir bon*, to hold fast, to stick to it, to hold out, to make a stand; *tenir envers et contre tout*, to nail one's colours to the mast; *tenir jusqu'au bout*, to stick it out; *à n'y plus tenir*, unbearable; *il ne pouvait plus y tenir*, he couldn't stand it any longer. ‖ 3. To last (durer); to be fast (couleur). ‖ 4. To stick, to adhere (adhérer); *timbre qui ne tient pas*, stamp that won't stay on. ‖ 5. To remain, to stay (rester); *elle ne peut tenir en place*, she can't keep still. ‖ 6. To fit, to be accommodated, to be seated, to find room (contenir); *on tient huit à cette table*, there is room for eight at this table. ‖ 7. To take into account (compter); *il n'y a pas de prudence qui tienne*, it's not a question of being prudent, prudence doesn't enter into it. ‖ 8. LOC. *Tiens!*,

indeed !, why !, you don't say so ! (pas possible) ; *tenez !*, here !, catch !, here you are ! (prenez). ‖ **9. Tenir à,** to be close (ou) next to, to border on to (être contigu à) ; *tenir à la maison voisine,* to adjoin the neighbouring house. ‖ *Tenir à,* to be fixed (ou) attached to (être fixé) ; *miroir qui tient au mur par des clous,* mirror fixed to the wall by nails. ‖ *Tenir à,* to derive (ou) result (ou) come from, to be a result of, to be due to (provenir de) ; *à quoi cela tient-il ?,* what is that due to ? ; *cela tient à votre honnêteté,* that comes of your being honest. ‖ *Tenir à,* to set value (ou) store on, to be attached to, to value, to care for, to prize (priser) ; *tenir à sa peau,* to value one's skin ; *je n'y tiens pas,* I'm not very keen on it ; *un projet auquel je tiens,* a project that means a great deal to me. ‖ *Tenir à,* to be bent (ou) keen on, to be anxious to (ou) for, to be insistent on, to care about, to want (désirer, vouloir) ; *je tiens à y aller,* I am anxious to go ; *il tient à ce que j'y sois à l'heure,* he insists on my being there on time. ‖ *Tenir à,* to depend on (dépendre de) ; *cela ne tient qu'à vous,* that depends entirely on you ; *il ne tient qu'à moi de décider,* the decision rests entirely with me ; *qu'à cela ne tienne !,* never mind that ! ; *sa vie ne tient qu'à un fil,* his life is hanging by a thread ; *s'il ne tient qu'à ça !,* if that's all. ‖ **10. Tenir de,** to be related to, to be connected with, to have sth. in common with, to have sth. of, to savour of, to take after ; *il tient de sa mère,* he takes after his mother ; *cela tient de famille,* it runs in the family ; *cela tient du prodige,* it has a touch of the miraculous about it ; *on tient toujours du lieu d'où l'on vient,* one always smacks of the place one comes from. ‖ **11. Tenir pour,** to side with, to be on the side of, to hold with (être partisan de) ; *tenir la paix,* to be all for peace. ‖ **12. En tenir pour,** to be fond of, to be in love with.
— v. pr. **Se tenir,** to be held (objet). ‖ To take place, to be held (réunion). ‖ To stay, to remain, to keep, to stop (rester) ; to sit (rester assis) ; to stand (rester debout) ; *se tenir debout,* to stand, to stand up ; *se tenir les bras croisés,* to stand idle ; *se tenir à sa place,* to stay in one's place (ne pas bouger) ; to know one's place (garder les distances) ; *se tenir tranquille,* to keep quiet ; *tiens-toi bien,* stand (ou) sit up properly ; behave yourself ! ‖ To be connected, to hold together (être lié) ; *ces arguments se tiennent,* these arguments hold together. ‖ To contrain oneself (se contenir) ; *je n'ai pu me tenir de lui dire ses quatre vérités,* I couldn't resist telling him a few home truths. ‖ FAM. *Se tenir les côtes,* to hold one's sides with laughter. ‖ **Se tenir à,** to hold on to (se cramponner). ‖ *Se tenir à,* to keep at (rester) ; *se tenir au travail,* to keep at work. ‖ **Se tenir pour,** to think (ou) regard (ou) consider oneself as, to look oneself as (se considérer) ; *se tenir pour malheureux,* to think oneself unlucky ; *se le tenir pour dit,* to take it for granted. ‖ **S'en tenir à,** to abide by, to stick to, to be content (ou) satisfied with, to stop at, to limit oneself to (se contenter de) ; *je m'en tiens à ses conseils,* I'll stick to his advice ; *il ne s'en tiendra pas là,* he won't stop at that ; *ne pas savoir à quoi s'en tenir,* not to know what to think (ou) make of it ; *tenons-nous-en là,* we'll let it stand at that.

tennis [tɛnis] m. SPORTS. Tennis, lawn-tennis (jeu) ; tennis-court (terrain) ; *tennis de table,* table-tennis, ping-pong. ‖ Pl. Tennis (ou) gym shoes, plimsolls, sneakers (chaussures de tennis).

tennisman [-man] (pl. **tennismen** [-mɛn]) m. FAM. Tennis-player.

tenon [tənɔ̃] m. TECHN. Tenon ; *à tenon et à mortaise,* mortaise-and-tenon (assemblage).

tenons V. TENIR (101).

ténor [tenɔ:r] m. MUS. Tenor ; *fort ténor,* heroic tenor.

tenorino [tenɔrino] m. MUS. Tenorino ; high- (ou) light-voiced tenor.

ténorisant [-zɑ̃] adj. MUS. High (baryton).

tenseur [tɑ̃sœ:r] adj. MÉD. Tensor (muscle).
— m. MÉD., MATH. Tensor. ‖ TECHN. Tightener.

tensiomètre [tɑ̃sjɔmɛtr] m. MÉD. Sphygmomanometer.

tension [tɑ̃sjɔ̃] f. Tightening (action) ; tightness, tension (d'une corde) ; stress (normale) ; *tension de rupture,* breaking strain. ‖ Flatness (d'une trajectoire). ‖ MÉD. Stretching, straining (des muscles) ; *tension artérielle,* blood pressure ; *avoir trop de tension,* to suffer from high blood pressure. ‖ ELECTR. Tension, voltage ; *chute de tension,* drop in potential ; *fil sous tension,* live wire. ‖ FIG. Tension ; sustained mental effort (d'esprit) ; tenseness, tension (des rapports).

tentaculaire [tɑ̃takylɛ:r] adj. Tentacular, octopus-like.

tentacule [-kyl] m. ZOOL. Tentacle, feeler.

tentant, ante [tɑ̃tɑ̃, ɑ̃:t] adj. Tempting, alluring, attractive (personne) ; inviting, enticing (sujet).

tentateur, trice [tɑ̃tatœ:r, tris] adj. Tempting, alluring, attractive
— m. ECCLÉS., FIG. Tempter.

tentation [-sjɔ̃] f. Temptation.

tentative [-tiv] f. Attempt, try, trial, endeavour. ‖ JUR. *Tentative d'assassinat,* attempted murder.

tentatrice [-tris] f. Temptress. (V. TENTATEUR.)

tente [tɑ̃:t] f. Booth (d'un marché). ‖ SPORTS. Tent ; *tente conique,* bell tent ; *tente individuelle,* bivouac. ‖ NAUT. Awning. ‖ FIG. *Se retirer sous sa tente,* to sulk in one's tent. ‖ **Tente-abri,** f. MILIT. Shelter-tent.

tenter [tɑ̃te] v. tr. (1). To attempt, to undertake (une entreprise). ‖ To make (un effort) ; to try (une expérience). ‖ To tempt (v. ALLÉCHER, SÉDUIRE) ; *c'est une idée qui me tente,* it's an idea that appeals to me ; *laissez-vous tenter,* just for once !, be a devil ! ; *se laisser tenter,* to give way to temptation. ‖ To tempt, to put to the test (mettre à l'épreuve). ‖ ECCLÉS. To tempt ; *tenter Dieu,* to tempt Providence.

tenture [tɑ̃ty:r] f. Hanging (d'une tapisserie). ‖ Wall-paper (papier) ; hangings (rideaux) ; tapestry (tapisserie). ‖ Funeral hangings (de deuil).

tenu, ue [təny] adj. Kept ; *bien tenu,* well-kept, well cared-for (en général). ; tidy (maison) ; *mal tenu,* badly kept, uncared-for ; untidy. ‖ FIN. Firm, hard (valeurs). ‖ FIG. Obliged ; bound, forced (à, de, to). ‖ LOC. *Tenu !,* done ! ‖ V. TENIR (101).

ténu, ue [teny] adj. Tenuous. ‖ Thin, fine, slender (fil). ‖ PHYS. Attenuated (gaz) ; thin (substance). ‖ FIG. Fine, subtle, nice.

tenue [təny] f. Holding (d'une réunion). ‖ Standard (d'un journal). ‖ Keeping, running, managing (d'une maison). ‖ Dress (habillement) ; *tenue estivale,* summer clothes ; *tenue de cérémonie, de soirée,* full, evening dress ; *tenue de ville,* morning dress ; lounge suit ; U. S. business suit. ‖ Behaviour (comportement) ; *avoir de la tenue,* to be well-behaved (ou) mannered ; *de la tenue !,* behave yourself ! ‖ MILIT. Uniform ; *tenue de campagne,* full marching order ; *tenue de corvée,* fatigue-dress ; *tenue de ville,* walking-out dress ; *en grande, petite tenue,* in full dress, in undress. ‖ NAUT. Hold, holding (d'une ancre) ; *tenue à la mer,* sea-going qualities. ‖ AUTOM. *Tenue de route,* road-holding qualities, U. S. roadability. ‖ AVIAT. *Tenue en l'air,* airworthiness, behaviour in the air. ‖ MUS. Sustained (ou) holding note. ‖ JUR. Holding (des assises). ‖ SPORTS. *Avoir une bonne tenue,* to have a good seat (cavalier) ; *avoir de la tenue,* to be a stayer (cheval). ‖ AGRIC. Upkeep (d'une vigne). ‖ COMM. Firmness (d'une étoffe) ; keeping, book-keeping (des livres). ‖ FIN. Firmness, steadiness (des valeurs). ‖ TECHN. Care, maintenance (d'une machine). ‖ LOC. *D'une seule tenue,* all of a piece, adjoining, contiguous. (V. TENANT.)

ténuité [tenɥite] f. Tenuity, tenuousness. ‖ Thinness, fineness, slenderness (d'un fil). ‖ PHYS. Thinness. ‖ FIG. Fineness (v. SUBTILITÉ).

tenure [təny:r] f. † Tenement, holding.

téorbe [teɔrb] m. V. THÉORBE.

ter [tɛ:r] adv. Three times, thrice. ‖ For the third time ; *7 ter,* 7b (numéro). ‖ MUS. Ter.

tératologie [teratɔlɔʒi] f. Teratology.

terbium [tɛrbjɔm] m. CHIM. Terbium.

tercet [tɛrsɛ] m. Tercet, triplet.

térébenthène [terebɑ̃tɛn] m. CHIM. Terebenthene.

térébenthine [-tin] f. Turpentine ; *essence de térébenthine,* turpentine, turps (fam.).

térébinthe [terebɛ̃t] m. BOT. Terebinth, turpentine-tree.

térébrant, ante [terebrɑ̃, ɑ̃:t] adj. ZOOL. Terebrant, boring. ‖ MÉD.. Terebrating.

Tergal [tɛrgal] m. (nom déposé). Tergal.

tergiversateur, trice [tɛrʒiversatœ:r, tris] s. Tergiversator ; shilly-shallier (fam.).

tergiversation [-sasjɔ̃] f. Tergiversation ; shilly-shallying (fam.).

tergiverser [-se] v. intr. (1). To tergiversate, to equivocate ; to beat about the bush, to shilly-shally (fam.). [V. BIAISER.]

terme [tɛrm] m. Term ; word ; expression (mot) ; *terme de métier,* technical term ; *en propres termes,* in so many words ; *dans toute la force du terme,* in the full sense of the expression (ou) word. ‖ Pl. Terms, conditions, wording, stipulations (d'un article, d'un contrat). ‖ Pl. Terms, footing ; *en quels termes êtes-vous avec lui ?,* what are your relations with him ? ; *être en bons termes avec,* to be on good terms (ou) footing with. ‖ Term, end, limit (fin) ; *au terme de,* at the end of ; *mettre un terme à,* to put an end to. ‖ Term (durée) ; *politique à long terme,* long-term policy. ‖ MÉD. Time ; *à terme, avant terme,* in due time, prematurely. ‖ MILIT., NAUT. Service ; *à long terme,* long-service (engagement). ‖ PHILOS. Term (d'un syllogisme). ‖ MATH. Term (d'une équation). ‖ JUR. Time, delay (délai) ; term (d'un bail) ; term, quarter (de loyer) ; quarter-day (jour) ; quarter's rent (loyer). ‖ FIN. Settlement (en Bourse) ; *taux pour les opérations à terme,* forward rates ; *valeurs à terme,* securities dealt in for the account. ‖ FIN. Instalment (versement) ; *achat, vente à terme,* credit purchase, sale ; *acheter, vendre à terme,* to buy, to sell on credit ; *payable en quatre termes,* payable in four instalments. ‖ COMM. Time, date ; *à court, long terme,* short-, long-dated ; *marché à terme,* time transaction (ou) bargain.

terminable [tɛrminabl] adj. Terminable.

terminaison [-nɛzɔ̃] f. Termination, ending ; end. ‖ GRAMM. Termination, ending. (V. DÉSINENCE.)

terminal, ale [-nal] adj. Final, terminal ; *classe terminale,* final year of secondary school, upper sixth form. ‖ MÉD. Terminal.

— m. Terminal (de transports aériens ou routiers, d'un ordinateur) ; terminus (ou) terminal (d'un pipeline).

terminale f. Upper sixth form.

terminer [-ne] v. tr. (1). To bound, to limit. (V. BORNER.) ‖ To terminate, to end, to finish (v. FINIR) ; to conclude, to settle (un accord) ; to bring to an end (ou) a close, to close, to wind up (un discours, une discussion) ; *dire en terminant,* to say in conclusion ; to conclude with. ‖ GRAMM. To end, to terminate (un mot) ; *terminé*

par, ending in. ‖ COMM. To complete (une commande).

— v. intr. To end ; *en terminer,* to make an end ; *terminé ?,* have you finished ?, U. S. are you through ? (fam.) [au téléphone].

— v. pr. **Se terminer,** to end, to be bounded (être borné). ‖ To end, to come to an end, to finish, to conclude, to be over (être achevé). ‖ GRAMM. To end (*en, in*).

terminologie [-nɔlɔʒi] f. Terminology.

terminologique [-nɔlɔʒik] adj. Terminological.

terminus [-ny:s] adj., m. CH. DE F., AUTOM. Terminus (pl. terminuses, termini) ; U. S. end of the line, last stop.

termite [tɛrmit] m. ZOOL. Termite, white ant.

termitière [-tjɛ:r] f. ZOOL. Termitary.

ternaire [tɛrnɛ:r] adj. MATH., CHIM. Ternary. ‖ Mus. Ternary (forme) ; triple (mesure).

terne [tɛrn] adj. Dull ; dim (v. MAT) ; lifeless, drab (couleur) ; tarnished (métal) ; dull, lack-lustre, lustreless (yeux). ‖ FIG. Dull, tame (existence, style) ; drab (ville).

ternir [tɛrni:r] v. tr. (2). To dull, to dim ; to cloud (une glace) ; to deaden (une couleur) ; to tarnish (un métal). ‖ FIG. To sully, to soil, to tarnish, to stain, to besmirch (une réputation).

— v. pr. **Se ternir,** to become dim (ou) dull (couleur) ; to tarnish (métal). ‖ FIG. To be sullied (réputation) ; to grow tame (style).

ternissement [-nismɑ̃] m. **Dulling, fading** (des couleurs), tarnishing (d'un métal). ‖ FIG. Sullying, tarnishing (de la réputation).

ternissure [-nisy:r] f. Dullness ; cloudiness (d'une glace) ; tarnished appearance (d'un métal).

terpinol [tɛrpinɔl] m. CHIM. Terpinol.

terrain [tɛrɛ̃] m. Ground, piece of land ; *terrain à bâtir,* building-plot ; *occuper un vaste terrain,* to occupy a large area. ‖ AGRIC. Ground, land, soil (terre). ‖ GÉOL. Rock-formation. ‖ GÉOGR. Surface, ground ; *terrain accidenté,* hilly ground. ‖ MILIT. Terrain (de campagne) ; drill- (ou) parade-ground (de manœuvres). ‖ AVIAT. Landing-ground, airstrip, U .S. landing field (d'atterrissage). ‖ SPORTS. Ground ; football-field (de football) ; golf-course, golf-links (de golf) ; *terrain de jeu,* playing-field (en général) ; playground (dans un lycée) ; sports ground, U. S. athletic grounds (dans une université). ‖ FIG. Ground ; situation ; position ; *aller sur le terrain,* to fight a duel ; *avancer sur un terrain glissant,* to walk on thin ice ; *connaître le terrain,* to be sure of one's ground ; *être sur son terrain,* to be at home (ou) in one's element ; *ne plus être sur son terrain,* to be out of one's depth ; *gagner, perdre du terrain,* to gain, to lose ground.

Terramycine [-misin] f. (n. dép.). MÉD. Terramycin.

terrassant, ante [tɛrasɑ̃, ɑ̃:t] adj. FAM. Crushing, overwhelming, staggering.

terrasse [tɛras] f. Bank (talus) ; terrace (terre-plein) ; *en terrasse,* terraced (jardin). ‖ Pavement (devant un café) ; *sur la terrasse,* outside the café. ‖ ARCHIT. Balcony (balcon) ; flat roof, platform (toiture). ‖ GÉOL. Terrace.

terrassement [-smɑ̃] m. TECHN. Embanking, earthwork (construction) ; digging (creusage) ; banking (remblayage).

terrasser [-se] v. tr. (1). To throw (s.o.) down, to throw, to down, to floor (renverser). ‖ TECHN. To embank, to bank up (consolider). ‖ MÉD. To lay low (un malade). ‖ FIG. To overcome, to overwhelm, to crush, to dismay (abattre) ; to defeat, to floor, to crush (vaincre).

terrassier [-sje] m. Navvy, labourer. ‖ Earthwork contractor.

terre [tɛ:r] f. Earth, world (planète). ‖ Earth, land (par opposition à la mer) ; *terre ferme,* mainland, continent. ‖ Land, region (contrée) ; people (peuples) ; *hautes terres,* highlands ; *terre inhabitée,* uninhabited region. ‖ Earth, ground (sol) ; *se coucher par terre,* to lie on the ground ; *sous terre,* underground. ‖ Earth (par opposition à l'au-delà) ; *encore sur terre,* still in the land of the living ; *quitter cette terre,* to depart this life ; *mettre en terre,* to bury. ‖ Estate, grounds (domaine) : property ; territory ; *acheter une terre,* to buy an estate. ‖ AGRIC. Earth, soil (terrain) ; land (terrain cultivé) ; *plante de pleine terre,* hardy plant ; *retour à la terre,* back to the land (mouvement). ‖ NAUT. Land, shore ; *arriver en vue de la terre,* to make landfall ; *naviguer terre à terre,* to hug the shore ; *prendre terre,* to land ; *terre!,* land ho! ‖ MILIT. Land, ground, earth ; *armée de terre,* land (ou) ground forces ; *tactique de la terre brûlée,* scorched earth policy. ‖ ECCLÉS. *La Terre sainte,* Holy Land ; *terre sainte,* consecrated ground. ‖ ARTS. Earth, clay ; potter's (ou) modelling clay (glaise) ; *terre cuite,* baked earth, terra-cotta. ‖ ÉLECTR. Earth ; ground ; *mettre à la terre,* to earth, U. S. to ground ; *prise de terre,* earth, earth-wire, U. S. ground wire. ‖ COMM. *Pipe de terre,* clay-pipe ; *terre de pipe,* pipe-clay ; *vaisselle de terre,* earthenware. ‖ CH. DE F. *Voyager par terre,* to travel by land (ou) overland. ‖ FAM. *Avoir les pieds sur terre,* to have both feet firmly on the ground ; to be down-to-earth ; *remuer ciel et terre,* to move heaven and earth ; *terre à terre,* prosaic, unimaginative, matter-of-fact, commonplace, vulgar ; *tomber par terre,* to fall down. ‖ **Terre-neuvas,** m. invar. NAUT. Newfoundland fishing-boat (bateau) ; Newfoundland fisherman (marin). ‖ **Terre-neuve,** m. invar. Newfoundland dog (chien). ‖ **Terre-Neuve,** f. GÉOGR. Newfoundland. ‖ **terre-neuvien** (pl. *terre-neuviens*) adj. GÉOGR. Newfoundland ; s. Newfoundlander ; m. NAUT. V. TERRE-NEUVAS. ‖ **Terre-plein** (pl. *terre-pleins*) m. Earth platform ; strip of flat ground ; MILIT. Terreplein ; CH. DE F. Road-bed ; ARCHIT. Dividing strip, island (dans un boulevard).

terreau [tɛro] m. AGRIC. Vegetable-mould ; compost ; leaf-mould.

terrer [tɛre] v. tr. (1). AGRIC. To earth up (un arbre) ; to earth over (des semis). ‖ TECHN. To clay (du sucre).
— v. pr. **Se terrer,** ZOOL. To burrow (lapin) ; to go to earth (renard). ‖ MILIT. To entrench oneself, to dig oneself in. ‖ FIG. To bury oneself (personne) [*dans,* in].

terrestre [tɛrɛstr] adj. Terrestrial (globe) ; *rotation terrestre,* rotation of the earth. ‖ MILIT. Land (forces). ‖ FIG. Earthly, worldly (pensées). ‖ LOC. *Paradis terrestre,* earthly paradise, Garden of Eden.

terrestrement [-trəmɑ̃] adv. Terrestrially.

terreur [tɛrœːr] f. Terror, fear, dread (v. ÉPOUVANTE) ; *être dans la terreur,* to be in a state of terror ; *pris de terreur,* terror-stricken ; *la Terreur,* the Reign of Terror. ‖ FAM. Terror ; *faire la terreur de,* to be a nightmare to.

terreux, euse [tɛrø, øːz] adj. Earthy (matière). ‖ Dirty, grubby, soiled (mains). ‖ FIG. Dull, muddy (couleur) ; ashen, sallow, unhealthy (visage).

terri [tɛri] m. V. TERRIL.

terrible [tɛribl] adj. Terrible, dreadful, frightful ; *enfant terrible,* problem child ; little pest (ou) terror, plague of a child (fam.). ‖ FAM. Astounding, marvellous (formidable) ; terrific, awful (terrifiant).

terriblement [-bləmɑ̃] adv. Terribly, dreadfully, frightfully. ‖ FAM. Terribly, dreadfully, frightfully, awfully, tremendously. (V. FORMIDABLEMENT.)

terrien, enne [tɛrjɛ̃, ɛn] adj. Terrestrial, living on the earth (population) ; land-owning, landed (propriétaire) ; *esprit terrien,* attachment to the land.

— s. Landowner. ‖ NAUT. Landsman ; landlubber.

terrier [tɛrje] m. Hole, burrow (de lapin) ; earth (de renard) ; *sortir de son terrier,* to break cover. ‖ ZOOL. Terrier (chien).

terrifiant, ante [tɛrifjɑ̃, ɑ̃:t] adj. Terrifying ; frightening. (V. EFFRAYANT.)

terrifier [-fje] v. tr. (1). To terrify · *d'une voix terrifiée,* in a terrified (ou) awed voice.

terril [tɛril] m. Slag-heap.

terrine [tɛrin] f. Earthenware pan ; pot ; terrine. ‖ CULIN. Potted meat, U. S. terrine (pâté).

territoire [tɛritwaːr] m. Territory ; land ; region, district under jurisdiction.

territorial, ale [tɛritɔrjal] adj. GÉOGR., MILIT. Territorial.
— m. MILIT. Territorial, territorial soldier.

territoriale [-rja:l] f. MILIT. Territorial army.

territorialité [-rjalite] f. Territoriality.

terroir [tɛrwaːr] m. AGRIC. Soil ; *goût de terroir,* native (ou) local tang ; *mots de terroir,* local expressions ; *sentir le terroir,* to smack of the soil.

terroriser [tɛrɔrize] v. tr. (1). To terrorize.

terrorisme [tɛrɔrism] m. Terrorism.

terroriste [-rist] s. Terrorist.

tertiaire [tɛrsjɛːr] adj. Tertiary (secteur). ‖ GÉOL. Tertiary, cainozoic, U. S. cenozoic.
— m. Tertiary sector. ‖ GÉOL. Tertiary, Cainozoic, U. S. Cenozoic.

tertio [tɛrsjo] adv. Thirdly.

tertre [tɛrtr] m. Mound, hillock, knoll, hump. (V. BUTTE.) ‖ SPORTS. Tee.

Térylène [terilɛn] m. (nom déposé). Terylene.

tes [te] adj. poss. V. TON.

tessiture [tɛsityːr] f. MUS. Tessitura.

tesson [tɛsɔ̃] m. Fragment, broken piece, potsherd, shard (de bouteille). ‖ Pl. Broken glass (sur un mur).

test [tɛst] m. Test ; *test d'intelligence, d'aptitude, projectif,* intelligence, aptitude, projective test. ‖ ZOOL. Test.

testament [tɛstamɑ̃] m. ECCLÉS. Testament ; *l'Ancien, le Nouveau Testament,* the Old, the New Testament. ‖ JUR. Will, testament ; *ceci est mon testament,* this is my last will and testament.

testamentaire [-mɑ̃tɛːr] adj. JUR. Testamentary ; *dispositions testamentaires,* clauses of a will ; devises ; *exécuteur testamentaire,* executor.

testateur [-tœːr] m. JUR. Testator ; devisor.

testatrice [-tris] f. JUR. Testatrix.

tester [tɛste] v. intr. (1). JUR. To make one's will.

tester v. tr. (1). To test.

testiculaire [tɛstikylɛːr] adj. MÉD. Testicular.

testicule [-kyl] m. MÉD. Testicle ; testis (pl. testes).

testimonial, ale [tɛstimɔnjal] adj. JUR. By witness ; *preuve testimoniale,* oral evidence.

têt [tɛ] m. CHIM. Cupel.

tétanie [tetani] f. MÉD. Tetany.

tétanique [-nik] adj. MÉD. Tetanic.

tétaniser [-nize] v. tr. (1). MÉD. To tetanize.

tétanos [-nos] m. MÉD. Tetanus, lock-jaw.

têtard [tɛtaːr] m. ZOOL. Tadpole, U. S. polliwog (de grenouille) ; chub (poisson). ‖ AGRIC. Pollard.

tête [tɛːt] f. Head ; *donner de la tête contre,* to hit one's head against ; *la tête en bas,* head downwards (personne) ; *la tête la première,* head-first, headlong ; *marcher la tête haute,* to carry one's head high ; *sans tête,* headless ; *tête nue,* bare-headed. ‖ Head, head of hair, hair (chevelure) ; *tête frisée,* curly head. ‖ Head, person ; *allocation tant par tête,* capitation grant ; *par tête,* a head, per person. ‖ Head ; brain (cerveau) ; intellect, intelligence, mind (esprit, intelligence) ; firmness (fermeté) ; *à tête reposée,* at one's leisure ; *avoir un air dans la tête,* to have a tune on the brain ; *avoir qqch. en tête,* to turn sth. over in one's mind; to be up to sth.; *femme de tête,* capable woman; *n'avoir pas de tête pour les chiffres,* to have no head for figures; *ne savoir où donner de la tête,* not to know which way to turn; *se mettre en tête de,* to take it into one's head to. ‖ Temper, nature (caractère); *avoir la tête près du bonnet,* to be hot-headed (ou) quick-tempered (ou) touchy; *en faire à sa tête,* to have one's own way; *forte tête,* strong-minded person; *mauvaise tête,* unmanageable (ou) unruly person; *tenir tête à,* to face up to; to resist, to withstand; *tête de bois,* blockhead; *tête carrée,* square-head, German (Allemand); obstinate person (entêté); *tête chaude,* hot-head; *tête montée,* excitable person; *tête baissée,* blindly; full tilt. ‖ Memory (mémoire); *tête de linotte,* hare-brained person; *de tête,* by (ou) from memory, by rote. ‖ Presence of mind, self-possession (sang-froid); *avoir de la tête,* to be cool-headed (ou) level-headed; *perdre la tête,* to lose one's head (ou) self-control. ‖ Sense, reason (raison); *il a toute sa tête,* he has all his wits about him; *avoir perdu la tête,* to be off one's head; *tomber sur la tête,* to be off one's rocker, to go crackers (fam.). ‖ Head, life (vie); *coûter la tête à qqn,* to cost s.o. his head; *il y va de sa tête,* his life is at stake. ‖ Look, appearance (aspect); expression; *avoir une bonne tête,* to look pleasant; *avoir une drôle de tête,* to be a queer-looking fellow; *avoir une sale tête,* to have a nasty mug; *faire une tête d'une aune,* to pull a long face; *faire la tête à,* to frown at, to look black at; *il a une tête à claques,* I feel I want to smack his face every time I see him. ‖ Head, front (première place); *à la tête de,* at the head of (une armée, une industrie); leading (un cortège); at the top of (une classe); *en tête,* foremost; at the front; leading; *prendre la tête,* to take the lead; *tête de chapitre,* chapter-heading; *tête de ligne,* headline. ‖ Bot. Top, crown, summit (d'un arbre); head (de chou, de salade). ‖ Méd. Head; skull, cranium (crâne); *avoir mal à la tête,* to have a headache; *la tête me tourne,* my head is swimming, I feel giddy; *tête de mort,* death's head, skull. ‖ Milit. Head, vanguard (d'une colonne); *tête mobile,* bolt-head; *tête de pont,* beach-head (sur une côte); bridge-head (au bord d'un fleuve). ‖ Naut. Summit (de roche). ‖ Ch. de f. *Tête de ligne,* terminus, starting-point; rail-head; *voiture de tête,* carriage at the front of the train. ‖ Arts. Head. ‖ Théâtr. *Se faire la tête d'un rôle,* to make up for a part. ‖ Sports. Header (coup); head (longueur); *gagner d'une tête,* to win by a head; *en tête,* leading, in the lead (coureur, équipe); *piquer une tête,* to take a header; *têtes de série,* seeded players (au tennis); *jouer la balle de la tête,* to head the ball. ‖ Agric. *Tête de cuvée,* choice wine. ‖ Culin. *Porter à la tête,* to go to one's head (vin); *qui porte à la tête,* heady (vin). ‖ Zool. Head (d'un animal, d'un poisson). ‖ Techn. Head (d'épingle, de hache, de marteau); *tête de bielle,* big-end. ‖ Fam. *En avoir par-dessus la tête,* to be fed up with it; to be up to the eyes; *laver la tête à qqn,* to give s.o. a dressing-down (ou) a blowing-up (ou) a rocket; *elle se jette à votre tête,* she is rather gushing; *se payer la tête de qqn,* to take a rise out of s.o., to have s.o. on. ‖ **Tête-à-queue,** m. invar. Slew (ou) slue round; *faire un tête-à-queue,* to whip round (cheval); to slew round (voiture). ‖ **Tête-à-tête,** m. invar. Tête-à-tête, private talk (ou) interview (conversation); settee, sociable, U. S. love-seat (meuble); tea-set for two (service à thé); *un dîner en tête à tête,* a tête-à-tête dinner; *en tête à tête,* privately, together. ‖ **Tête-bêche,** adv. Top to bottom; head to tail (animaux); head to foot (personnes). ‖ **Tête-de-loup** (pl. *têtes-de-loup*) f. Pope's-head, Turk's-

head. ‖ **Tête-de-mort,** f. Culin. Dutch cheese; Zool. Death's head moth. ‖ **Tête-de-nègre,** adj., m. invar. Nigger-brown.

tétée [tete] f. Feed; amount of milk taken by a baby at one feed; *l'heure de la tétée,* baby's feeding-time. ‖ Suck (action).

téter v. tr. (5). To suck; *donner à téter à,* to suckle, to give suck to. ‖ Fam. *Téter encore sa mère,* to be still wet behind the ears. — v. intr. To suck; *enfant qui tète encore,* suckling.

téterelle [tetrɛl] f. Méd. Breast-pump.

têtier [tɛtje] m. Naut. Bow (rameur).

têtière [tɛtjɛ:r] f. Cap (pour enfant). ‖ Head-stall (d'une bride). ‖ Antimacassar (de meuble). ‖ Naut. Head.

tétine [tetin] f. Méd. Dug, teat (d'animal); udder (de vache). ‖ Comm. Teat, nipple (de biberon).

téton [-tɔ̃] m. Fam. Titty, tit.

tétracorde [tetrakɔrd] m. Mus. Tetrachord.

tétradactyle [-daktil] adj. Zool. Tetradactyl, four-toed.

tétraèdre [-ɛdr] adj. Math. Tetrahedral. — m. Math. Tetrahedron.

tétraédrique [-edrik] adj. Math. Tetrahedral.

tétraéthyle [-eti:l] adj. Chim. Tetraethyl.

tétragone [tetragɔn] adj. Math. Tetragonal. — m. Math. Tetragon.

tétralogie [tetralɔʒi] f. Tetralogy.

tétrarque [tetrark] m. Tetrarch.

tétrasyllabe [tetrasillab], **tétrasyllabique** [-bik] adj. Tetrasyllabic.

têtu, ue [tɛty] adj. Stubborn, obstinate, mulish; pig-headed (fam.).

teuf-teuf [tœftœf] m. Fam. Puff-puff, puffer, chuffer.

teuton, onne [tøtɔ̃, ɔn] adj. Teutonic. — s. Géogr. Teuton.

teutonique [-tɔnik] adj. Teutonic.

texan, ane [tɛksɑ̃, an] adj., s. Géogr. Texan.

texte [tɛkst] m. Text; *erreur de texte,* textual error; *gravure hors texte,* full-page illustration.

textile [tɛkstil] adj. Textile. — m. Textile industries (industrie); textile (produit); *dans le textile,* in textiles.

textuaire [tɛkstɥɛ:r] adj. Textual, textuary.

textuel, elle [-ɛl] adj. Textual; word-for-word (citation); ‖ Verbatim; sic.

textuellement [-ɛlmɑ̃] adv. Textually, word-for-word; verbatim.

texture [tɛkstyːr] f. Texture (d'une étoffe). ‖ Méd. Texture (de la peau). ‖ Théâtr. Construction, structure (d'une pièce).

T.G.V. [teʒeve] abrév. de *train à grande vitesse,* high-speed train.

thaï [tai] adj. Géogr. Thai, Siamese. — m. Gramm. Thai (langue).

thaïlandais, aise [-lɑ̃dɛ, ɛ:z] adj. Géogr. Thai. — s. Thai, Thaïlander.

Thaïlande [-lɑ̃d] f. Géogr. Thailand, Siam.

thalamus [talamys] m. Thalamus.

thalassémie [talasemi] f. Méd. Thalassemia.

thalassothérapie [-soterapi] f. Méd. Sea water therapy.

thaler [talɛ:r] m. invar. Thaler.

thalidomide [talidɔmid] f. Méd. Thalidomide.

thalle [tal] m. Bot. Thallus.

thallium [taljɔm] m. Chim. Thallium.

thallophyte [talɔfit] f. Bot. Thallophyte, thallogen.

thalweg [talvɛg] m. Géogr. Thalweg, talweg.

thaumaturge [tomatyːrʒ] m. Ecclés. Thaumaturge, miracle-worker.

thé [te] m. Bot. Tea-plant (arbrisseau); tea (feuilles). ‖ Culin. Tea (collation, infusion); tea-

THÉÂTRE — THEATRE

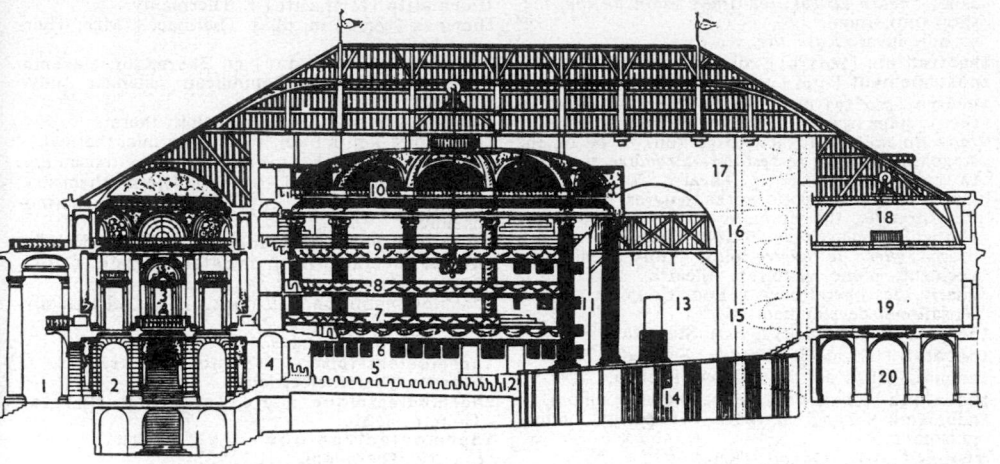

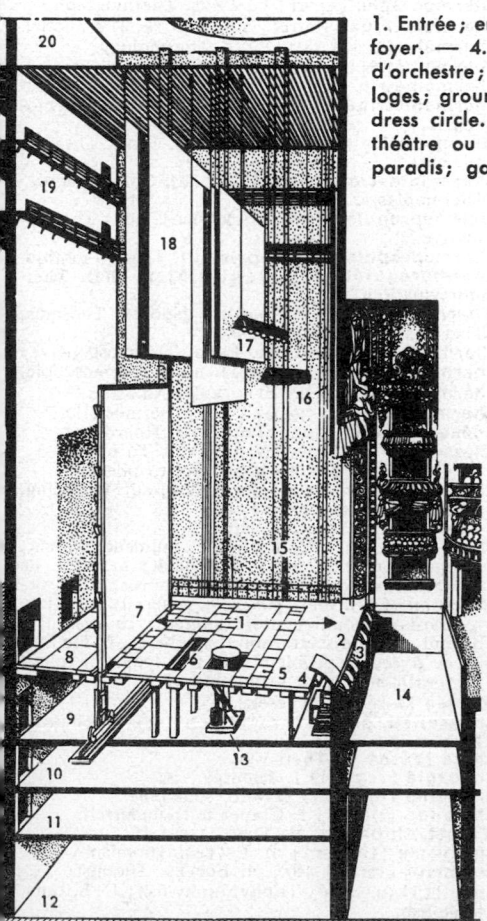

1. Entrée; entrance-hall. — 2. Hall; hall. — 3. Foyer du public; foyer. — 4. Promenoir; promenade, promenoir. — 5. Fauteuils d'orchestre; stalls; (U. S.) orchestra seats. — 6. Baignoires ou loges; ground-floor boxes. — 7. Premier balcon ou mezzanine; dress circle. — 8. Second balcon; upper circle. — 9. Amphithéâtre ou galerie; balcony. — 10. Second amphithéâtre ou paradis; gallery (fam. the gods; U. S. : peanut gallery). — 11. Loge d'avant-scène; stage-box. — 12. Fosse d'orchestre; orchestra-pit. — 13. Scène ou plateau; stage. — 14. Dessous; below-stage. — 15. Coulisses ou dégagements; wings. — 16. Administration; direction. — 17. Magasins des costumes, des accessoires, coiffeur; property-stores, make-up man. — 18. Loge des artistes; dressing-room. — 19. Foyer des artistes, salle des répétitions; green-room. — 20. Entrée des artistes; stage-entrance.

1. Scène; stage. — 2. Avant-scène; proscenium, forestage. — 3. Rampe; footlight. — 4. Trou ou boîte du souffleur; prompt(er's) box. — 5. Trappillons; slots. — 6. Costières; cuts. — 7. Lointain; up stage. — 8. Rue; slips. — 9 à 12. Dessous; below-stage. — 13. Monte-charge pour apparitions; hoist for apparitions. — 14. Fosse d'orchestre; orchestra-pit. — 15. Côté cour (à l'opposé : côté jardin); « O. P. S. » (Opposite Prompt Side) and « P. S. » (Prompt Side). — 16. Rideau de fer (en avant : rideau de scène); iron curtain (in front : stage curtain). — 17. Herses; battens. — 18. Toile de fond ou lointain; back-cloth. — 19. Cintres; flies. — 20. Gril; upper flies.

party (réunion); *thé dansant*, tea-dance, thé dansant; *l'heure du thé*, tea-time; *salon de thé*, teashop (ou) -room.
— adj. invar. *Rose thé*, tea-rose.
théâtral, ale [teɑtral] adj. Theatrical.
théâtralement [-mɑ̃] adv. Theatrically.
théâtre [teɑ:tr] m. THÉÂTR. Theatre, playhouse (lieu); stage (scène). ‖ Theatre, stage (profession); *faire du théâtre*, to act, to go (ou) to be on the stage (ou) boards; *se destiner au théâtre*, to intend to go on the stage. ‖ Theatre; dramatic art (art); drama; dramatic works (œuvres); *le théâtre de Corneille*, the dramatic works of Corneille, Corneille's plays; *le théâtre français*, French drama; *pièce de théâtre*, play. ‖ FIG. Scene (d'un accident, d'une victoire); theatre, seat (de la guerre, des opérations). ‖ LOC. *Coup de théâtre*, sensational development.
théâtreuse [teɑtrø:z] f. FAM. Stage-tart.
thébaïde [tebaid] f. Solitude. ‖ GÉOGR. Thebaid.
thébain [tebɛ̃] adj., s. GÉOGR. Theban.
thébaïque [tebaik] adj. MÉD. Thebaic; opium.
thébaïsme [-ism] m. MÉD. Thebaism, opium-poisoning.
Thèbes [tɛb] f. GÉOGR. Thebes.
théière [tejɛ:r] f. Tea-pot.
théine [tein] f. CHIM. Theine.
théisme [teism] adj. PHILOS. Theism.
théiste [-ist] adj. PHILOS. Theistic.
— s. PHILOS. Theist.
thématique [tematik] adj. Thematic.
thématique f. Themes dealt with.
thème [tɛm] m. Theme; subject; topic; text. ‖ Translation into a foreign language, composition, prose (traduction); *thème latin*, Latin prose. ‖ MILIT. Scheme (de manœuvre). ‖ MUS. Theme; subject. ‖ GRAMM. Stem. ‖ LOC. *Fort en thème*, good at school-work, clever (ou) brainy but unoriginal (adj.).
Thémis [temis] f. Themis.
thénar [tena:r] adj., m. MÉD. Thenar; *éminence thénar*, thenar eminence, ball of the thumb.
théobromine [teɔbromin] f. CHIM. Theobromine.
théocratie [teɔkrasi] f. Theocracy.
théodicée [teɔdise] f. PHILOS. Theodicy.
théodolite [teɔdɔlit] m. TECHN. Theodolite.
théogonie [teɔgɔni] f. Theogony.
théologal, ale [-lɔgal] adj., m. Theologal.
théologie [-lɔʒi] f. Theology; *docteur en théologie*, doctor of divinity, D. D.
théologien, enne [-lɔʒɛ̃, ɛn] s. Theologian.
théologique [-lɔʒik] adj. Theological.
théologiquement [-lɔʒikmɑ̃] adv. Theologically.
théophanie [-fani] f. Theophany.
théorbe [teɔrb] m. MUS. Theorbo.
théorème [teɔrɛm] m. MATH. Theorem.
théoricien, enne [teɔrisjɛ̃, ɛn] s. Theorician, theorist.
théorie [-ri] f. † Theory. ‖ FAM. Procession, line, file, string (de personnes).
théorie [-ri] f. Theory; *en théorie*, in theory; on paper. ‖ MILIT. Theory; training-manual.
théorique [-rik] adj. Theoretic, theoretical.
théoriquement [-rikmɑ̃] adv. Theoretically.
théoriser [-rize] v. tr., intr. (1). To theorize.
théosophe [teɔzɔf] s. Theosophist.
théosophie [-zɔfi] f. ECCLÉS. Theosophy.
théosophique [-zɔfik] adj. Theosophical.
thérapeute [terapø:t] m. MÉD. Therapeutist.
thérapeutique [-pøtik] adj. MÉD. Therapeutic.
. — f. MÉD. Therapeutics, therapy.
thérapie [terapi] m. MÉD. Therapy.
thératron [teratrɔ̃] m. PHYS. Theratron.
thermal, ale [tɛrmal] adj. Thermal (eau); hydropathic (établissement); *station thermale*, spa, watering-place, health resort.

thermalisme [tɛrmalism] m. Balneology.
thermalité [tɛrmalite] f. Thermality.
thermes [tɛrm] m. pl. † Thermae. ‖ MÉD. Thermal baths.
Thermidor [tɛrmidɔr] m. Thermidor, eleventh month in French Republican calendar (july-august).
thermie [tɛrmi] f. Thermal unit, therm.
thermique [-mik] adj. PHYS. Thermic, thermal.
thermocautère [-kotɛ:r] m. MÉD. Thermocautery.
thermochimie [-ʃimi] f. CHIM. Thermochemistry.
thermochimique [-ʃimik] adj. CHIM. Thermochemical.
thermocouple [-kupl] m. ELECTR. Thermocouple.
thermodurcissable [-dyrsisabl] adj. CHIM., TECHN. Thermosetting.
thermodynamique [-dinamik] adj. Thermodynamic.
— f. Thermodynamics.
thermoélectricité [tɛrmoelɛktrisite] f. ÉLECTR. Thermoelectricity.
thermoélectrique [-elɛktrik] adj. ÉLECTR. Thermoelectric.
thermoélectronique [-elɛktrɔnik] adj. ÉLECTR. Thermionic.
thermogène [-ʒɛn] adj. PHYS. Thermogenic, thermogenous. ‖ MÉD. *Ouate Thermogène*, Thermogene, Thermogene (ou) U. S. thermogenic wool.
thermographe [-graf] m. PHYS. Thermograph.
thermoïonique [-jɔnik] adj. ELECTR. Thermionic.
thermologie [-lɔʒi] f. PHYS. Thermology.
thermomètre [-mɛtr] m. PHYS. Thermometer.
thermométrie [-metri] f. PHYS. Thermometry.
thermométrique [-metrik] adj. PHYS. Thermometric.
thermonucléaire [-nyklee:r] adj. PHYS. Thermonuclear.
thermoplastique [-plastik] adj. CHIM., TECHN. Thermoplastic.
thermopropulsé, ée [-prɔpylse] adj. Thermomotive.
thermopropulsion [-prɔpylsjɔ̃] f. Thermo-motion.
thermorégulation [-regylasjɔ̃] f. MÉD. Thermoregulation.
Thermos [tɛrmɔs] f. (nom déposé). Thermos, Thermos (ou) vacuum flask.
thermoscope [-skɔp] m. PHYS. Thermoscope.
thermoscopique [-skɔpik] adj. Thermoscopic.
thermostat [-sta] m. ELECTR. Thermostat.
thermostatique [-statik] adj. Thermostatic.
thésaurisation [tezorizasjɔ̃] f. Hoarding.
thésauriser [tezorize] v. intr. (1). To hoard.
— v. tr. To hoard, to hoard up, to pile up.
thésauriseur, euse [-rizœ:r, ø:z] adj. Hoarding, accumulative, acquisitive.
— s. Hoarder; accumulator.
thèse [tɛ:z] f. Proposition, argument; thesis; attitude, point of view, approach; *la thèse de l'Angleterre sur*, the British approach to the question of; *en thèse générale*, generally speaking. ‖ Thesis (à l'université); *soutenir sa thèse*, to defend one's dissertation (ou) thesis. ‖ THÉÂTR. *Pièce à thèse*, problem play; propaganda play; play with an axe to grind (fam.).
Thésée [teze] m. Theseus.
thessalien, enne [tɛsaljɛ̃, ɛn] adj., s. GÉOGR. Thessalian.
thêta [tɛta] m. Theta.
théurgie [teyrʒi] f. Theurgy.
thiamine [tjamin] f. MÉD. Thiamine.
thibaude [tibo:d] f. Carpet felt; underfelt.
Thibet, thibétain. V. TIBET, TIBÉTAIN.
thomisme [tɔmism] m. ECCLÉS. Thomism.
thomiste [-mist] adj., m. ECCLÉS. Thomist.
thon [tɔ̃] m. ZOOL. Tunny, tunny-fish; U. S. tuna, tuna fish.

thonier [tɔnje] m. NAUT. Tunny- (ou) U. S. tuna-fishing-boat (bateau).

thoracique [tɔrasik] adj. MÉD. Thoracic.

thorax [-raks] m. MÉD. Thorax, chest. ‖ ZOOL. Thorax.

thorite [tɔrit] f. Thorite.

thorium [tɔrjɔm] m. CHIM. Thorium.

thrène [trɛn] m. Threnody, dirge.

thriller [trilœːr] m. Thriller, whodunnit, spine-chiller.

thrombocyte [trɔbosit] m. MÉD. Thrombocyte, blood platelet.

thrombose [trɔboːz] f. MÉD. Thrombosis.

thrombus [-byːs] m. MÉD. Thrombus.

thulium [tyljɔm] m. CHIM. Thulium.

thune [tyn] f. POP. Five-franc piece.

thuriféraire [tyrifereːr] m. ECCLÉS. Thurifer. ‖ FIG. Sycophant; fawner.

thuya [tyja] m. BOT. Thuya, arbor vitæ; *bois de thuya*, citron-wood.

thym [tɛ̃] m. BOT. Thyme.

thymique [timik] adj. MÉD. Thymic.

thymol [timɔl] m. MÉD. Thymol.

thymus [timyːs] m. MÉD. Thymus, thymus gland.

thyratron [tiratrɔ̃] m. Thyratron.

thyroïde [tirɔid] adj., f. MÉD. Thyroid.

thyroïdien, enne [-djɛ̃, ɛn] adj. MÉD. Thyroidean, thyroidal.

thyroxine [tirɔksin] f. MÉD. Thyroxine.

thyrse [tirs] m. † BOT. Thyrsus.

tiare [tjaːr] f. Tiara. ‖ FIG. Papacy.

Tibet [tibɛ] m. GÉOGR. Tibet.

tibétain, aine [tibetɛ̃, ɛn] adj., s. GÉOGR. Tibetan.

tibia [tibja] m. MÉD. Tibia, shin-bone; shin.

Tibre [tibr] m. GÉOGR. Tiber.

tic [tik] m. MÉD. Tic, twitch, twitching; *tic douloureux*, facial neuralgia. ‖ ZOOL. Vicious habit (d'un cheval). ‖ FIG. Trick, habit, way, mannerism.

ticket [tikɛ] m. Ticket; check. ‖ Coupon, unit (de carte d'alimentation); voucher, ticket, U. S. chit (de repas). ‖ CH. DE F. *Ticket de quai*, platform ticket.

tic-tac [tiktak] m. invar. FAM. Pit-a-pat (du cœur); click-clack (d'un moulin); tick, ticking, tick-tock (d'une pendule).

tictaquer [tiktake] v. intr. (1). FAM. To go pit-a-pat (cœur); to go click-clack (moulin); to tick, to go tick-tock (pendule).

tiédasse [tjedas] adj. FAM. Lukewarmish.

tiède [tjɛd] adj. Tepid, lukewarm (bain, eau); mild, warm (vent). ‖ ECCLÉS. Lukewarm. ‖ FIG. Indifferent; lukewarm.

— adv. *Boire tiède*, to take the chill off one's drink.

tièdement [-dmɑ̃] adv. Tepidly, lukewarmly.

tiédeur [tjedœːr] f. Tepidity, tepidness, lukewarmness (d'un bain); mildness (du vent). ‖ FIG. Lukewarmness, indifference; *agir avec tiédeur*, to act half-heartedly.

tiédir [-dir] v. intr. (2). To become tepid (ou) lukewarm (eau). ‖ FIG. To cool off (amitié).

— v. tr. To make tepid (ou) lukewarm, to take the chill off (eau).

tien, tienne [tjɛ̃, tjɛn] adj. poss. †, ECCLÉS. Thine. ‖ LOC. *Un tien ami*, a friend of yours.

— pron. poss. *Le tien* (f. *la tienne*; pl. *les tiens, les tiennes*). ECCLÉS., † Thine. ‖ Yours; *voici mon livre, voilà le tien*, this is my book, and that is yours. ‖ FAM. *A la tienne!*, here's to you!, cheers!, cheerio!

— m. ECCLÉS., † Thine own. ‖ Your own; *il faut y mettre du tien*, you must do your share (ou) bit. ‖ Pl. Your own; your own folk (ou) family (ou) people; *toi et les tiens*, you and your people.

— f. pl. FAM. Pranks, escapades; *tu fais encore des tiennes*, you're up to your old tricks again.

tiendrai [tjɛ̃dre]. V. TENIR (101).

tiens interj. Hullo!

— indic. prés. V. TENIR (101).

— m. *Un tiens*, something that you possess; *un tiens vaut mieux que deux tu l'auras*, a bird in the hand is worth two in the bush.

tierce [tjɛrs] adj. f. V. TIERS.

— f. MATH., ASTRON., MUS. Third. ‖ ECCLÉS., SPORTS. Tierce. ‖ TECHN. Final (ou) press proof (en imprimerie).

tiercé, ée [-se] adj. BLAS. Tierced. ‖ LOC. *Rimes tiercées*, terza rima.

— m. SPORTS. Three-horse combination bet.

tiercelet [-slɛ] m. ZOOL. Tercelet, tercel.

tiercer [-se] v. tr. (5). AUTOM. To space (les segments). ‖ AGRIC. To plough for the third time.

tiers, tierce [tjɛːr, tjɛrs] adj. Third (personne); *tiers arbitre*, referee; *le tiers état*, the third estate, the commonalty. ‖ ECCLÉS. *Tiers ordre*, Third Order. ‖ JUR. Third; *tierce opposition*, opposition by a third party. ‖ MÉD. Tertian (fièvre). ‖ MATH. *N tierce* (*n‴*), N triple prime. ‖ FIN. *Tiers porteur*, holder in due course. ‖ **Tiers-point** (pl. *tiers-points*) m. TECHN. Triangular file (lime). ‖ ARCHIT. Tierce-point; *en tiers-point*, equilateral (arc). ‖ **Tiers monde**, m. Third World.

— m. Third, third part (partie). ‖ Third person (ou) party (personne); *être en tiers*, to make a third; to be odd man out. ‖ FIN. *Tiers provisionnel*, instalment on yearly income tax; *assurance au tiers*, third party insurance. ‖ MATH., PHILOS. *Principe du tiers exclu*, law of the excluded middle. ‖ FAM. *Il se moque du tiers comme du quart*, he doesn't give a damn for anybody or anything.

tifs [tif] m. pl. FAM. Thatch (cheveux).

tige [tiːʒ] f. BOT. Trunk, bole (d'arbre); stem, stalk (de plante). ‖ AUTOM. Rod. ‖ ARCHIT. Shaft, body (de colonne). ‖ ZOOL. Body (de plume). ‖ COMM. Leg, upper (de botte); *bottes à tiges*, top-boots. ‖ TECHN. Shank (de clou); *tige du piston*, piston-rod.

tigelle [tiʒɛl] f. BOT. Tigelle, tigella, tigel.

tignasse [tiɲas] f. FAM. Shock of tousled hair, mop, mane.

tigre [tigr] m. ZOOL. Tiger. ‖ GÉOGR. Tigris.

tigré, ée [-gre] adj. Speckled; tabby (chat); leopard-spotted (cheval); striped (fourrure).

tigresse [-grɛs] f. ZOOL. Tigress.

tilbury [tilbyri] m. Tilbury.

tilde [tild] m. Tilde.

tildé, ée [-de] adj. With a tilde : *n tildé*, n tilde, ñ.

tillac [tijak] m. NAUT. Deck.

tille [tiːj] f. NAUT. Cuddy.

tille f. TECHN. Adze.

tilleul [tijœl] m. BOT. Lime- (ou) linden-tree, U. S. basswood (arbre); lime blossom (fleur). ‖ MÉD. Lime-blossom tea (infusion).

tilt [tilt] m. FAM. *Faire tilt*, to ring a bell, to set one thinking.

timbale [tɛ̃bal] f. Metal cup (ou) mug, tin drinking mug (gobelet). ‖ MUS. Kettledrum; *les timbales*, the timpani (dans un orchestre). ‖ CULIN. Deep round dish (ou) mould (moule); timbale, raised pie (plat); *macaroni en timbale*, macaroni cheese, U. S. baked macaroni. ‖ SPORTS. Battledore. ‖ FIG. *Décrocher la timbale*, to carry off the prize.

timbalier [-lje] m. MUS. Kettledrummer; timpanist.

timbrage [tɛ̃braːʒ] m. Stamping.

timbre [tɛ̃ːbr] m. Bell (de bicyclette); gong (de pendule); *timbre électrique*, electric bell (ou) gong. ‖ Stamp office (bureau); stamp-duty (droit). ‖ Stamp (sur un document); postage-stamp (sur une lettre); *timbre du jour*, date; *timbre de la poste*, post-mark. ‖ Stamp (instrument); *timbre à date*, date-stamp; *timbre humide*, pad (ou) rubber stamp; *timbre sec,* embossing press. ‖ Mus. Timbre, quality, tone (d'un son, d'une voix); ring (d'unc voix). ‖ **Timbre-épargne** (pl. *timbres-épargne*) m. Savings-stamp. ‖ **Timbre-poste** (pl. *timbres-poste*) m. Postage-stamp. ‖ **Timbre-quittance** (pl. *timbres-quittance*) m. Receipt-stamp. ‖ **Timbre-retraite** (pl. *timbres-retraite*) m. Old-age pension stamp. ‖ **Timbre-taxe** (pl. *timbres-taxe*) m. Postage-due stamp.

timbré, ée [tɛbre] adj. Ringing, sonorous (voix). ‖ Stamped (papier). ‖ FAM. Cracked, crackers, crazy, dotty, daft, touched, round the bend; U. S. nuts. (V. CINGLÉ.)

timbrer v. tr. (1). To stamp (une lettre par l'expéditeur); to post-mark (par la poste). ‖ To stamp (du papier).

timbreur [-brœ:r] m. TECHN. Stamper.

timide [timid] adj. Shy, retiring (caractère); shy, timide, bashful (enfant); bashful (jeune fille); *d'aspect timide,* shy-looking; *faussement timide,* coy. ‖ Timid, timorous, shy (animal). ‖ Diffident, hesitant; weak, nerveless (style).
— s. Shy (ou) retiring person; *c'est un grand timide,* he's very shy.

timidement [-dmɑ̃] adv. Timidly; apprehensively (avec appréhension); shyly, bashfully, coyly; diffidently (avec défiance); timorously, fearfully (avec peur).

timidité [-dite] f. Timidity; shyness, bashfulness, coyness, diffidence (réserve). ‖ Timorousness (crainte).

timon [timɔ̃] m. Beam (de charrue); pole (de voiture). ‖ NAUT. Tiller. ‖ FIG. Helm.

timonerie [timɔnri] f. NAUT. Steering (ou) steerage (d'un navire); *kiosque de timonerie,* wheel-house. ‖ NAUT. Signalling; *maître de timonerie,* yeoman of signals, signalman; *poste de timonerie,* signal station. ‖ AUTOM., CH. DE F. Brake- (ou) steering-gear.

timonier [-nje] m. Wheel-horse (cheval). ‖ NAUT. Helmsman, man at the wheel, steersman (homme de barre); signalman (signalisateur); lookout (vigie); *timonier coureur,* messenger.

timoré, ée [timɔre] adj. Timorous, timid, pusillanimous, easily alarmed; *d'un air timoré,* timorously. ‖ Over-scrupulous (conscience).

tin [tɛ̃] m. Barrel-chock (pour tonneaux). ‖ NAUT. Chock, block.

tinctorial, ale [tɛktɔrjal] adj. Dye (bois); tinctorial (plante).

tine [tin] f. Butt; tub (baste).

tine f. Tin, biscuit-tin, U. S. cracker box (boîte).

tinette [tinɛt] f. Firkin, tub (pour beurre). ‖ Soil-tub (pour la vidange). ‖ Pl. FAM. Latrines.

tins, tînt. V. TENIR (101).

tintamarre [tɛtama:r] m. Uproar; din, row, racket, hubbub, hullabaloo (fam.). ‖ FIG. Noise, publicity, U. S. ballyhoo.

tintamarresque [-rɛsk] adj. FAM. Loud, noisy.

tintement [tɛtmɑ̃] m. Ringing (d'une cloche); *tintement funèbre,* tolling. ‖ Jingle, jingling (de clefs, de clochettes); chink, chinking (de pièces); tinkle, tinkling (d'un timbre); clink, clinking (de verres). ‖ MÉD. Buzzing, singing, ringing, tingling (d'oreille).

tinter [-te] v. intr. (1). To ring, to toll (cloche). ‖ To jingle (clefs, clochettes); to chink (pièces); to clink, to tinkle (timbre); to clink (verres); *faire tinter les verres,* to clink glasses. ‖ MÉD. To buzz, to sing, to ring, to tingle (oreilles). ‖ FAM. *Les oreilles ont dû vous tinter,* your ears must have burned.
— v. tr. To ring, to toll (une cloche). ‖ ECCLÉS. To ring, to sound (l'angélus).

tintinnabuler [tɛtinabyle] v. intr. (1). To jingle, to tinkle, to ring.

tintouin [tɛtwɛ̃] m. FAM. Worry, trouble, bother; *donner du tintouin à qqn,* to give s.o. trouble.

tipule [tityl] f. ZOOL. Tipula; daddy-long-legs.

tique [tik] f. ZOOL. Tick.

tiquer [tike] v. intr. (1). MÉD. To twitch. ‖ ZOOL. To have a vicious habit; to crib (cheval). ‖ FAM. To wince, to show surprise (ou) dissatisfaction; to start; *ce mot l'a fait tiquer,* that word shook him, that word made him raise his eyebrows; *sans tiquer,* without turning a hair.

tiqueté, ée [tikte] adj. Mottled, speckled.

tir [tir] m. Shooting. ‖ Shooting-gallery (à une foire). ‖ MILIT. Shooting, fire, firing (acte); musketry, gunnery (art); shooting-match (concours); rifle-range (endroit); fire (résultat); *tir à la cible,* target practice; *tir aux pigeons,* pigeon-shooting; *tir à volonté,* individual fire; *tir de la D.C.A.,* A-A fire, ack-ack, flak; *à tir rapide,* quick-firing; *s'exercer au tir,* to practise shooting; *être habile au tir,* to be a good shot; *habileté au tir,* marksmanship; *ligne de tir,* line of fire.

tirade [tirad] f. THÉÂTR. Tirade, declamatory speech. ‖ MUS. Tirade, run. ‖ FAM. Tirade; diatribe; volley, string (d'insultes).

tirage [tira:ʒ] m. Pulling, dragging, drawing (acte); towing (d'un bateau); hauling (d'un fourgon). ‖ Tow-path (chemin de halage). ‖ Draw, drawing (de loterie); *sorti au tirage,* drawn (bons); *tirage au sort,* drawing lots. ‖ Draught (d'une cheminée). ‖ AUTOM. Pull (d'un moteur). ‖ FIN. Drawing, making out (d'un chèque); *par voie de tirage,* by lot. ‖ TECHN. Printing, printing off (en imprimerie, en photographie); impression; circulation (d'un journal); number of copies printed (d'un livre); *à gros tirage,* with a large circulation (journal); *tirage limité,* limited edition; *tirage à part,* off-print, separate reprint. ‖ TECHN. Wire-drawing (du fil de fer). ‖ FAM. Difficulty; *il y a du tirage entre eux,* there's friction between them.

tiraillement [tirɑjmɑ̃] m. Pulling, tugging (sur une corde). ‖ MÉD. *Tiraillements d'estomac,* gnawing pain in the stomach. ‖ FAM. Pl. Pricking, pangs (de conscience); friction (tirage).

tirailler [-je] v. intr. (1). MILIT. To fire wildly (ou) aimlessly, to blaze away, to fire away; to pot (fam.) [*contre,* at].
— v. tr. To pull about (*par,* by). ‖ FIG. To tear (*entre,* between).
— v. récipr. Se tirailler, to pull each other about.

tiraillerie [-jri] f. FAM. Friction, wrangling.

tirailleur [-jœ:r] m. MILIT. Rifleman, sharp-shooter, tirailleur; *tirailleurs algériens,* native Algerian light infantry; *en tirailleurs,* in extended order. ‖ FAM. Free-lance (journaliste).

tirant, ante [tirɑ̃, ɑ̃:t] adj. Heavy (chemin).
— m. Purse-string (de bourse); boot- (ou) shoe-string (de soulier). ‖ CULIN. Sinew (de viande). ‖ ARCHIT. Tie, tie-beam, tie-rod, truss, clamp. ‖ NAUT. Draught (d'eau); *avoir douze pieds de tirant d'eau,* to draw twelve feet of water.

tire [ti:r] f. *Vol à la tire,* pocket-picking; U. S. pickpocketing; *voleur à la tire,* pickpocket. ‖ **Tire-au-flanc,** m. invar. FAM. Shirker, lead-swinger, malingerer; slacker; U. S. goldbricker. ‖ **Tire-balle,** m. MÉD. Crow-bar; bullet-forceps; MILIT. Bullet-extractor. ‖ **Tire-bonde,** m. Bung-drawer. ‖ **Tire-botte,** m. Boot-jack (pour ôter les bottes); boot-hook (pour mettre les bottes). ‖ **Tire-bouchon,** m. Corkscrew (outil). ‖ FAM. Cork-screw curl (cheveux); *en tire-bouchon,* twisted, corkscrew. ‖ **Tire-bouchonnant,** adj. Twisted; corkscrew; twisting (serpentant). ‖ **Tire-bouchonner,** v. intr. (1). To spiral (ou) curl up; v. tr. To twist into a corkscrew (ou) spiral; to screw up (un mouchoir). ‖ **Tire-bourre,** m. invar. MILIT. Wad-extractor; TECHN. Packing-extractor. ‖ **Tire-bouton,** m. Buttonhook. ‖ **Tire-braise,** m. invar.

Oven rake. ‖ **Tire-cartouche**, m. MILIT. Cartridge-extractor. ‖ **Tire-clou**, m. Nail-puller (ou) -wrench ; claw-hammer. ‖ **Tire-d'aile (à)**, loc. adv. Swiftly. ‖ **Tire-feu**, m. invar. MILIT. Lanyard. ‖ **Tire-fond**, m. invar. CH. DE F. Sleeper-screw ; TECHN. Hook, ring (anneau) ; wood screw. ‖ **Tire-jus**, m. invar. POP. Nose-wiper, snot-rag. ‖ **Tire-laine**, m. invar. † Coat-snatcher, footpad, robber. ‖ **Tire-lait**, m. invar. MÉD. Breast-pump. ‖ **Tire-larigot (à)**, loc. adv. Abundantly ; *boire à tire-larigot*, to drink like a fish. ‖ **Tire-ligne**, m. Drawing-pen ; *compas à tire-ligne*, pen-compass ; scribing-tool (de plombier). ‖ **Tire-l'œil**, m. invar. Showy object ; adj. *Titre tire-l'œil*, eyecatching headline. ‖ **Tire-pied**, m. invar. Stirrup (de cordonnier). ‖ **Tire-point**, m. TECHN. Stabbing-awl, pricker.

tiré, ée [tire] adj. Pulled, stretched, drawn ; *broderie à fils tirés*, drawn-thread work. ‖ Drawn, worn, haggard (traits). ‖ LOC. *Tiré par les cheveux*, far-fetched ; *tiré à quatre épingles*, dressed to kill (ou) U. S. to the teeth ; U. S. all dolled up. ‖ **Tiré-à-part** (pl. *tirés-à-part*) m. Off-print, separate reprint. — m. SPORTS. Shoot (gibier) ; shooting-preserve (taillis). ‖ COMM. Drawee.

tirée f. SPORTS. Pull-up (en alpinisme).

tirelire [tirli:r] f. Money-box.

tirer [tire] v. tr. (1).

---

1. Sens général. — 2. Allonger. — 3. Oter. — 4. Extraire. — 5. Obtenir. — 6. Faire sortir. — 7. Dresser. — 8. A la loterie. — 9. GRAMM. — 10. SPORTS. — 11. MILIT. — 12. NAUT. — 13. AGRIC. — 14. MÉD. — 15. THÉÂTR. — 16. ARCHIT. — 17. FIN. — 18. TECHN. — 19. FAM.

---

1. To pull, to draw (en général) ; to haul (hâler) ; to tug, to drag (traîner) ; *tirer la jambe*, to limp ; *tirer qqn par le bras*, to pull s.o. by the arm ; *tirer qqn par la manche*, to pluck s.o.'s sleeve ; *tirer qqn de son lit*, to pull s.o. out of bed ; *tirer les rideaux, le verrou*, to draw the curtains, the bolt. ‖ **2.** To pull ; to lengthen (allonger) ; to pull up (ses chaussettes) ; to stretch (une courroie, des draps) ; *tirer une affaire en longueur*, to spin out an affair ; *tirer la langue*, to hang out its tongue (chien) ; to put one's tongue out (personne). ‖ **3.** To pull off (ôter) ; to take off (*devant*, to) [son chapeau] ; to take off (ses souliers). ‖ **4.** To extract (extraire) ; to take out ; to draw (de l'eau, du vin) ; to pull out (une épine) ; *tirer ses gants de sa poche*, to pull one's gloves out of one's pocket. ‖ **5.** To obtain, to get (obtenir) ; to draw (une conclusion) ; to deduce (des preuves) ; *tirer des larmes des yeux de qqn*, to draw tears from s.o.'s eyes ; *tirer un mot de*, to get a word out of ; *tirer parti de*, to take advantage of ; *tirer plaisir de*, to derive pleasure from ; *tirer satisfaction de*, to obtain satisfaction for. ‖ **6.** To draw (faire sortir) ; to drag away (*de*, from) ; to get out (*de*, of) ; *tirer d'affaire*, to pull through (un malade) ; to get out of a mess (qqn) ; *tirer de prison*, to get out of prison ; *tirer qqn de son sommeil*, to arouse s.o. from his sleep ; *tirer qqn de son travail*, to tear s.o. away from his work. ‖ **7.** To make, to draw up (dresser) [ses plans] ; *tirer une affaire au clair*, to clear a matter up ; *tirer son origine* (ou) *sa source de*, to come of, to derive from, to spring from. ‖ **8.** To draw (une loterie) ; *tirer les cartes*, to tell fortunes ; *tirer le bon numéro*, to draw the lucky number. ‖ **9.** GRAMM. To take, to borrow (emprunter) ; *mot tiré du latin*, word borrowed from Latin. **10.** SPORTS. To shoot at (un animal) ; to pull (la balle, un coup). ‖ **11.** MILIT. To shoot, to fire

(un canon) ; to let fly (une flèche) ; to shoot, to fire, to let off, to discharge (un fusil) ; to fire (une salve) ; *tirer un coup de revolver à qqn*, to shoot at s.o. with a revolver. ‖ **12.** NAUT. To draw, to have a draught of ; *bateau qui tire dix pieds*, boat with a draught of ten feet. ‖ **13.** AGRIC. To milk. (V. TRAIRE.) ‖ **14.** MÉD. To draw, to pull out (une dent) ; *tirer du sang à qqn*, to bleed s.o. ; to take a blood specimen. ‖ **15.** THÉÂTR. To draw, to take ; *pièce tirée d'un roman*, play adapted from a novel. ‖ **16.** ARCHIT. To draw (une ligne, un plan) ; to make (un plan). ‖ **17.** FIN. To draw, make out (un chèque) ; to draw (une lettre de change). ‖ **18.** TECHN. To extract (du charbon, de l'or) ; to quarry, to extract (de la pierre). ‖ TECHN. To draw (des fils métalliques). ‖ TECHN. To print, to print off (en imprimerie, en photographie) ; to run off (en imprimerie) ; to take (une épreuve). ‖ **19.** FAM. *Encore une heure à tirer*, still another hour to go ; *il tire son temps*, he's doing his stretch ; *tirer de la prison*, to do time ; *tirer le portrait de qqn*, to take s.o.'s picture (ou) photograph, to snap s.o.

— v. intr. To pull ; to pull (*sur*, at, on) ; to tug (*sur*, at, on) ; *tirer sur sa cigarette*, to draw on one's cigarette ; *tirer sur une corde*, to pull on a rope ; *tirer sur sa pipe*, to pull at one's pipe, to suck one's pipe ; *cheval qui tire bien*, good puller. ‖ To tend, to incline (*à, sur*, to) ; to verge (*à, sur*, on) ; *tirer à sa fin*, to draw to a close (histoire, jour) ; to run low, to give out (stock) ; *tirer sur le jaune*, to border on (ou) to incline to (ou) to shade off to yellow. ‖ **16.** ARCHIT. To draw (cheminée). ‖ To draw ; *tirer au sort*, to draw lots. ‖ AUTOM. To pull (*vers*, to). ‖ NAUT. *Tirer au large*, to stand out to sea. ‖ MILIT. To shoot, to fire (*sur*, at, on) ; *tirer bien*, to be a good shot ; *s'exercer à tirer au revolver*, to practise revolver-shooting. ‖ SPORTS. To fence (à l'escrime). ‖ COMM., FIN. To draw (*sur*, on) ; *tirer à découvert*, to overdraw one's account. ‖ FAM. *Tirer au flanc*, to swing the lead, to dodge the column, U. S. to goof off, to goldbrick ; *tirer au large*, to clear off, to hop it, U. S. to beat it, to scram ; *tirer à la ligne*, to pad (ou) spin out an article ; *tirer en longueur*, to drag on, to protract.

— v. pr. *Se tirer*, to extricate oneself (*de*, from), to get out (*de*, of) ; to pull oneself out (d'un bourbier) ; to get clear (d'un danger) ; *se tirer d'affaire*, to get out of trouble ; *s'en tirer bien*, to come off well ; *s'en tirer avec une excuse*, to get away with an excuse ; *s'en tirer tout juste*, to escape by the skin of one's teeth (s'en sortir) ; to scrape along (vivoter). ‖ To acquit oneself ; *il s'est bien tiré de l'oral*, he put up a good show in the viva (ou) U. S. at the orals. ‖ To be drawn (loterie). ‖ To be stretched ; *ses traits commencent à se tirer*, he is beginning to look drawn (ou) haggard. ‖ FAM. *Ça se tire*, the end is in sight, it's nearly finished. ‖ POP. To be off, to make tracks ; *se tirer en vitesse*, to hop it, U. S. to beat it.

tiret [-rɛ] m. Dash (trait). ‖ hyphen (trait d'union).

tirette [-rɛt] f. Curtain cord (de rideau). ‖ Slide (de bureau).

tireur [-rœ:r] s. Drawer (sens général). ‖ Drawer (de vin). ‖ SPORTS. Fencer (à l'épée) ; marksman (au fusil) ; *c'est un bon, mauvais tireur*, he's a good, bad shot. ‖ MILIT. Marksman ; *tireur embusqué* (ou) *isolé*, sniper. ‖ COMM. Drawer (de chèque, de lettre de change). ‖ TECHN. Puller (d'épreuves d'imprimerie) ; printer (d'épreuves photographiques) ; drawer (de fils). ‖ FAM. *Tireur-au-flanc*, v. TIRE-AU-FLANC.

tireuse [-rø:z] f. Markswoman (au concours de tir). ‖ *Tireuse de cartes*, fortune-teller. ‖ TECHN. Printer, printing-box (en photographie).

tiroir [tirwa:r] m. Drawer (d'un meuble). ‖ THÉÂTR. *Pièce à tiroirs*, episodic play. ‖ TECHN. Slide, slide-valve. ‖ **Tiroir-caisse**, m. COMM. Till.

tisane [tizan] f. Infusion, decoction, herb-tea; *tisane d'orge*, barley-water. ‖ FAM. Cat-lap, wishwash, U. S. bellywash (boisson).

tison [tizɔ̃] m. Brand, ember, smouldering log. ‖ Fusee (allumette).

tisonner [tizɔne] v. intr. (1). To poke (ou) stir the fire.
— v. tr. To poke, to stir (le feu). ‖ FIG. To stir up, to fan.

tisonneur, euse [-nœ:r, ø:z] s. Person who is always poking the fire.

tisonnier [-nje] m. Poker.

tissage [tisa:ʒ] m. Weaving (acte); cloth-mill (usine).

tisser [tise] v. tr. (1). To weave. ‖ ZOOL. To spin (une toile d'araignée).

tisserand [-sərɑ̃] s. Weaver.

tisseur, euse [-sœ:r, ø:z] s. Weaver.

tissu, ue [-sy] adj. FIG. Made up, composed.
— m. Texture (d'une étoffe); *étoffe d'un tissu serré*, closely woven material. ‖ Fabric (en général); material (cotonnade, Nylon, soirie); cloth (lainage); tissue (lamé); *tissu métallique*, wire gauze. ‖ MÉD. Tissue. ‖ FIG. Tissue, pack (de mensonges). ‖ **Tissu-éponge**, m. Towelling, sponge-cloth; U. S. terry cloth.

titan [titɑ̃] m. Titan; *de titan*, titanic; gigantic.

titane [titan]m. CHIM. Titanium.

titané, ée [-ne] adj. CHIM. Titaniferous.

titanesque [titanɛsk] adj. Titanesque, titanic.

titanique [-nik] adj. CHIM. Titanic.

titanite [titanit] f. CHIM. Titanite, sphene.

Tite-Live [titli:v] m. Livy.

titi [titi] m. FAM. Smart (ou) cheeky urchin; street-arab.

titillation [titillasjɔ̃] f. Titillation, tickling.

titiller [-le] v. tr. (1). To titillate, to tickle.
— v. intr. To tickle.

titrable [titrabl] adj. TECHN. Assayable (métal).

titrage [titra:ʒ] m. CHIM. Assaying (d'un minerai); titration, titrating (d'une solution); ascertaining of the strength (d'un vin). ‖ CINÉM. Insertion of the titles.

titre [ti:tr] m. Heading (de chapitre); section (du code civil); headline (de journal); title (de livre, d'une œuvre); *titre courant*, headline, running title (ou) U. S. head; *gros titres*, large (ou) big headlines. ‖ Title (d'un personnage); *titre de duc*, title of duke; *avoir un titre de noblesse*, to have a title, to be titled; *se donner le titre de*, to style oneself. ‖ Title, name (nom). ‖ Title; right (droit); claim (juridique); *titres de gloire*, titles to fame; *ses titres à*, one's claims to; *à titre de*, by virtue of, by way of, as a; *à titre d'ami*, as a friend; *à titre d'essai*, as a trial measure; experimentally; on trial (ou) approval; *à titre gratuit*, as a favour; *à juste titre*, justly, rightly; *au même titre*, for the same reason; *à plus d'un titre*, for more than one good reason; *à titre provisoire*, provisionally; *à quel titre le dites-vous?*, by what right (ou) on what grounds do you say so? ‖ Qualification (à, for); *recruter sur titres*, to appoint according to qualifications. ‖ Office; position; *en titre*, titular; by appointment; *la maîtresse en titre du roi*, the King's acknowledged mistress; *professeur en titre*, titular professor; *sans titre officiel*, without any official status. ‖ Certificate, diploma; degree (universitaire); *qui a tous ses titres*, fully-qualified. ‖ MILIT. *Titre de permission*, pass, leave-pass; leave-chit (fam.). ‖ CH. DE F. *Titre de transport*, ticket. ‖ JUR. Title, title-deed; *titre de créance*, proof of debt; *titre de mouvement*, removal warrant; *titres de propriété*, title-deeds; *possession vaut titre*, possession is nine points of the law. ‖ FIN. Certificate; bond; warrant; pl. securities, stocks and shares (ou) U. S. bonds; *titres nominatifs*, registered securi-

ties; *titre au porteur*, bearer bond; *titre de rente*, government bond. ‖ CHIM. Title (de l'or); title, strength (d'une solution); *or au titre*, standard gold; *titre d'alcool*, degree of alcohol.

titré, ée [titre] adj. Titled (noble). ‖ Certificated, qualified (professeur). ‖ CHIM. Titrated, standard.

titrer v. tr. (1). To title. ‖ CINÉM. To insert the titles of (un film). ‖ CHIM. To determine the strength of (de l'alcool, du vin); to assay (un minerai); to titrate, to standardize (une solution); *ce minerai titre une forte proportion d'or*, this ore assays high in gold.
— v. intr. To splash; *titrer en manchettes énormes*, to print in enormous headlines.

titreur [titrœ:r] m. CINÉM. Title writer.

titubant, ante [titybɑ̃, ɑ̃:t] adj. Reeling, staggering, lurching, tottering. ‖ MÉD. Titubant.

titubation [-basjɔ̃] f. Staggering, tottering. ‖ MÉD. Titubation.

tituber [-be] v. intr. (1). To reel, to stagger, to lurch, to totter; *entrer en titubant*, to stagger in.

titulaire [titylɛ:r] adj. Titular; regular (juge); full (professeur). ‖ ECCLÉS. Titular (évêque).
— s. Holder (d'un certificat, d'un document); holder (d'une décoration, d'une dignité); titular, holder (d'un office); bearer (d'un passeport); occupant (d'un poste). ‖ MILIT. *Titulaire d'un commandement*, holding a command. ‖ FAM. *Etre titulaire de plusieurs condamnations*, to have several convictions to one's name.
— m. ECCLÉS. Titular bishop (d'un évêché); incumbent (d'une paroisse).

titularisation [-larizasjɔ̃] f. Confirmation in one's appointment; granting of tenure to (d'un enseignant).

titulariser [-larize] v. tr. (1). To confirm in his appointment; to put on the establishment; to appoint to the permanent staff; to grant tenure to (un enseignant).

tmèse [tmɛ:z] f. GRAMM. Tmesis.

T.N.T. [teɑ̃te] m. Abrév. de *trinitrotoluène*, T. N. T., trinitrotoluene.

toast [tɔst] m. Toast; *porter un toast*, to propose a toast; *porter un toast à*, to toast, to drink to. ‖ CULIN. Toast. (V. RÔTIE.)

toaster [-te] v. intr. (1). To propose a toast.

toboggan [tɔbɔgɑ̃] m. Toboggan.

toc [tɔk] adj. invar. POP. Crazy, cracked, dotty (fou); ugly (laid); worthless (sans valeur).
— m. Tap, rap (à la porte). ‖ FAM. Sham (ou) imitation (ou) fake (ou) U. S. costume jewelry, pinchbeck (bijou); faked stuff; rubbishy (ou) trashy (ou) sham (ou) flashy (ou) brummagem goods (camelote); *c'est du toc*, it's sham.
— interj. Tap; *toc, toc!*, tap, tap!, rap, rap!

tocante [tɔkɑ̃:t] f. V. TOQUANTE.

tocard, arde [tɔka:r, ˈardə] adj. POP. Worthless, rubbishy, trashy (de camelote). ‖ Gaudy, showy (voyant).
— m. FAM. Rank outsider, also-ran (cheval); also-ran, non-starter, dead loss (personne).

toccata [tɔkkata] (pl. **toccate**) f. MUS. Toccata.

tocsin [tɔksɛ̃] m. Tocsin; alarm bell.

toge [tɔ:ʒ] f. Toga (des Romains). ‖ Gown, robe (d'avocat, de juge); gown (de professeur).

Togo [tɔgo] m. GÉOGR. Togo.

togolais, aise [tɔgɔlɛ, ɛ:z] adj., s. GÉOGR. Togolese.

tohu-bohu [tɔybɔy] m. invar. FIG. Confusion, hubbub.

toi [twa] pron. pers. invar. † Thou (sujet); thee (compliment) [style biblique et poétique]. ‖ You; *c'est toi*, it's you; *c'est toi qui l'as fait*, you're the one who did it; *un ami à toi*, a friend of yours; *ce livre est à toi*, this book is yours; *c'est à toi de jouer*, it's your turn to play; *de toi à moi*, between ourselves; *je n'ai pas eu de nouvelles de toi*, I have had no news of you; *lire qqch. de toi*, to read sth. of yours; *toi et moi*, you and I. ‖ **Toi-même**, pron. pers. invar. Thyself (†, ecclés.); yourself; *tu l'as fait toi-même*, you did it yourself.

toile [twal] f. Linen, linen cloth; cloth (en général); shirting (à chemises); sheeting (pour draps); *toile cirée*, oilcloth, American cloth; *toile imprimée* (ou) *peinte*, print; *toile à matelas*, tick; U. S. ticking; *toile à sac*, sacking, sackcloth; *toile de coton*, calico; *toile d'emballage*, packing-sheet; *toile de Jouy*, cretonne print; *toile métallique*, wire netting; *drap de toile*, linen sheet; *relié toile*, cloth-bound (livre). ‖ ZooL. Web, cobweb (d'araignée). ‖ SPORTS. *Village de toile*, canvas town. ‖ MILIT. Canvas, tent; *coucher sous la toile*, to sleep under canvas. ‖ NAUT. Screen (de passerelle); sail, canvas (voile). ‖ AUTOM. Canvas (d'un pneu). ‖ ARTS. Canvas (à tableau); canvas, oil painting (tableau). ‖ THÉÂTR. Curtain; *toile de fond*, backcloth, U. S. backdrop. ‖ FIG. Pl. Toils (piège).

toilé, ée [-le] adj. Linen, linen-faced, linen-finished (papier).

toilerie [-lri] f. Linen-trade; textile trade (commerce); linen (ou) textile manufactory (fabrique); linen drapery, linen store (magasin); cloth; linen; linen (ou) cotton goods (tissu).

toilettage [twalɛta:ʒ] m. Grooming (d'un animal).

toilette [twalɛt] f. Dressing-table (coiffeuse), wash-stand (lavabo); toilet-table (table); *garniture de toilette*, toilet-service (ou) -set. ‖ Toilet, dressing, washing (action) : *faire un brin de toilette*, to have a wash and brush up; to tidy oneself up; *faire la toilette d'un mort*, to lay out a corpse; *faire sa toilette*, to dress, to wash; *objets de toilette*, toilet accessories. ‖ Dress (tenue); *aimant la toilette*, dressy; *en toilette*, dressed up; *en grande toilette*, in full dress; *marchande à la toilette*, wardrobe-dealer. ‖ Lavatory (cabinet d'aisances); cloakroom, toilet, U. S. powder room (euphémismes). ‖ Wrapper (de couturière, de tailleur). ‖ CULIN. Caul (de mouton).

toiletter [-lɛte] v. tr. (1). To groom (un animal).

toilier, ère [-lje, ɛ:r] adj. Linen (industrie).
— s. Linen manufacturer (fabricant); linen dealer (marchand).

toise [twa:z] f. Fathom (mesure). ‖ Measuring apparatus (appareil); *passer à la toise*, to be measured. ‖ FIG. Standard. (V. AUNE.) ‖ FAM. *Long d'une toise*, as long as your arm.

toiser [twaze] v. tr. (1). To measure. ‖ ARCHIT. To survey for quantities. ‖ FIG. To look up and down, to eye from head to foot, to eye all over, to give the once-over to (qqn).

toison [twazɔ̃] f. Fleece. ‖ FAM. Mop, mane. (V. TIGNASSE.) ‖ LOC. *Toison d'or*, Golden Fleece.

toit [twa] m. Roof; *toit de chaume, de tuiles*, thatched, tiled roof; *habiter sous les toits*, to live in a garret (ou) an attic. ‖ House, dwelling (maison); *le toit paternel*, the home, the paternal roof. ‖ Roof (d'une voiture); *toit ouvrant*, sunshine roof. ‖ TECHN. Hanging wall (d'un filon); top head (d'une galerie). ‖ FIG. *Crier sur les toits*, to shout from the house-tops.

toiture [-ty:r] f. Roof, roofing.

tokay [tɔkɛ], **tokaï** [tɔka:j] m. Tokay.

tôlage [tola:ʒ] m. Covering with sheet metal.

tôlard [tola:r] s. V. TAULARD.

tôle [to:l] f. Sheet iron; *tôle d'acier*, sheet steel; *tôle galvanisée, ondulée*, galvanized, corrugated iron; *tôle de blindage*, armour-plate. ‖ FAM. Clink. (V. TAULE.)

Tolède [tɔlɛd] m. GÉOGR. Toledo.

tôlée [tole] adj. f. *Neige tôlée*, crusted snow.

tolérable [tɔlerabl] adj. Tolerable, bearable. ‖ TECHN. Permissible.

tolérablement [-rabləmɑ̃] adv. Tolerably, bearably.

tolérance [-rɑ̃:s] f. Tolerance, toleration; *maison de tolérance*, licensed brothel; *par tolérance*, on sufferance. ‖ ECCLÉS. Toleration. ‖ JUR. Allowance (à la douane); *il y a une tolérance de 200 cigarettes*, up to 200 cigarettes may be imported duty-free. ‖ MÉD., FIN., TECHN. Tolerance.

tolérant, ante [-rɑ̃, ɑ̃:t] adj. Tolerant.

tolérantisme [-rɑ̃tism] m. ECCLÉS. Religious toleration, latitudinarianism.

tolérer [-re] v. tr. (5). To tolerate (supporter); to endure, to bear, to put up with (une personne); to allow, to admit (un point de vue). ‖ To allow (permettre); to wink at, to turn a blind eye to (des abus). ‖ MÉD. To tolerate (une drogue).

tôlerie [tolri] f. Sheet-metal manufacture (industrie). ‖ Sheet-metal manufactory, rolling-mills (fabrique). ‖ Sheet-metal goods (marchandises).

tolet [tɔlɛ] m. NAUT. Rowlock, thole. ‖ TECHN. Fulcrum, swivel.

tôlier, ère [tolje, ɛr] adj. Sheet-metal.
— m. Sheet-metal manufacturer (fabricant); sheet-metal dealer (marchand); sheet-metal worker (ouvrier). ‖ FAM. V. TAULIER.

tollé [tɔle] m. Outcry; cry of indignation; *soulever un tollé général contre*, to raise a general outcry against.

toluène [tɔlɥɛn] m. CHIM. Toluene, methyl benzene.

T.O.M. [tɔm] m. Abrév. de *territoire d'outre-mer*, French territory overseas.

tomahawk [tɔmaɔk] m. Tomahawk.

tomaison [tɔmɛzɔ̃] f. Volume number.

tomate [tɔmat] adj. invar., f. BOT., CULIN. Tomato.

tombal, ale [tɔbal] adj. *Pierre tombale*, gravestone, tombstone.

tombant, ante [tɔbɑ̃, ɑ̃:t] adj. Falling; *à la nuit tombante*, at nightfall. ‖ Flowing (cheveux); drooping, sloping (épaules); drooping, walrus (moustache). ‖ BOT. Drooping (branche, tige).
— m. Fringe (d'épaulette). ‖ Hang (de pantalon).

tombe [tɔ̃:b] f. Tomb, grave (lieu); tombstone, gravestone (pierre); *au bord de la tombe*, at death's door. ‖ FIG. *Muet comme la tombe*, silent as the tomb.

tombé, ée [tɔbe] adj. Fallen; *fruits tombés*, windfalls. ‖ SPORTS. *Coup de pied tombé*, drop-kick.

tombeau [-bo] m. Tomb; monument; vault (de famille); barrow (préhistorique); *mise au tombeau*, entombment. ‖ LOC. *Il me conduira au tombeau*, he'll be the death of me; *rouler à tombeau ouvert*, to drive at breakneck speed, to blind along.

tombée [-be] f. Fall (de pluie). ‖ LOC. *A la tombée du jour, de la nuit*, at close of day, at nightfall.

tomber [tɔbe] v. intr. (1).

> 1. Choir. — 2. S'effondrer. — 3. Se jeter. — 4. Pendre. — 5. Décliner. — 6. Dégénérer. — 7. Se démoder. — 8. S'anéantir. — 9. Devenir. — 10. Arriver. — 11. Echoir. — 12. MILIT. — 13. NAUT. — 14. AVIAT. — 15. MÉD. — 16. JUR. — 17. THÉÂTR. — 18. SPORTS. — 19. MATH. — 20. FAM. — 21. Tomber dans. — 22. Tomber en. — 23. Tomber sur. — 24. Faire tomber. — 25. Laisser tomber.

1. To fall, to fall down (choir); to fall, to come down (arbre); to fall, to tumble, to tumble down (enfant); to come off (feuilles, fruits); to strike (foudre); to drop (livre); *tomber de bicyclette*, to fall off one's bicycle; *tomber de cheval*, to fall off a horse; *mes cheveux commencent à tomber*, my hair is beginning to come out; *tomber mort*, to fall dead; *la pluie tombe*, it is raining. ‖ **2.** To fall, to collapse (s'effondrer) ; *tomber de fatigue,* to be ready to drop, to be dead tired. ‖ **3.** To fall (se jeter) ; *tomber aux pieds de qqn,* to fall (ou) throw oneself at s.o's feet. ‖ **4.** To fall, to hang, to hang down (pendre) ; *les cheveux lui tombent sur les épaules,* her hair falls about her shoulders ; *manteau qui tombe bien,* coat that hangs well. ‖ **5.** To decrease (décliner) ; to fall, to subside, to abate (colère, vent) ; to flag (conversation) ; to die down (ou) out (feu) ; to decline (force) ; to close, to draw in (jour) ; to fall (nuit) ; *tomber à plat,* to fall flat. ‖ **6.** To degenerate, to sink low (dégénérer) ; to fall (moralement) ; to decline (physiquement). ‖ **7.** To go out of fashion (se démoder) ; to go out (mode). ‖ **8.** To die away (s'anéantir) ; to be lost (illusions) ; *tomber à rien,* to come to nothing ; *tomber de haut,* to come down to earth with a bump ; *tomber de la lune* (ou) *des nues,* to be staggered. ‖ **9.** To fall (devenir) ; *tomber amoureux de,* to fall in love with ; *tomber d'accord,* to agree, to reach agreement ; *tomber malade,* to fall (ou) to be taken ill ; *tomber sous le sens,* to make sense, to be clear. ‖ **10.** To come, to turn up, to appear, to arrive (arriver) ; to fall ; to happen (avoir lieu) ; *tomber le jeudi,* to fall on a Thursday (fête) ; *tomber bien,* to happen at the right moment (événement) ; *tomber juste,* to hit the nail on the head (en tirant une déduction) ; *tomber chez qqn,* to drop in on s.o. ; *vous tombez bien, mal,* you have come just at the right, wrong moment (arriver) ; you are lucky, unlucky (réussir) ; you have applied to the right, wrong person (s'adresser). ‖ **11.** To fall, to come (échoir, parvenir) ; *tomber aux mains, au pouvoir de qqn,* to fall into s.o.'s hands, power. ‖ **12.** MILIT. To fall (sur le champ de bataille). ‖ **13.** NAUT. To fall off (bateau) ; to go down (marée) ; *laisser tomber l'ancre,* to drop the anchor ; *tomber sous le vent,* to drop to leeward ; *tomber sur,* to foul (un navire). ‖ **14.** AVIAT. To crash (avion). ‖ **15.** MÉD. To descend (décliner) ; to die (mourir) ; *son rhume lui est tombé sur la poitrine,* his cold has gone down on to his chest. ‖ **16.** JUR. To fall, to be overthrown (gouvernement). ‖ **17.** THÉÂTR. To fall flat, to be a failure (ou) a flop, to flop, U. S. to be a turkey (pièce). ‖ **18.** SPORTS. *Faire tomber le roi,* to drop the king (aux cartes). ‖ **19.** MATH. To work out right (calcul). ‖ **20.** FAM. *Les bras m'en tombent,* I'm flabbergasted (ou) dumbfounded ; *prenez cette rue et vous tomberez dans la rue du Bac,* follow this street and it will take you to the Rue du Bac ; *laisser tomber qqn,* to drop s.o., to leave s.o. in the lurch. ‖ **21. Tomber dans,** to fall into ; *tomber dans l'erreur, l'oubli,* to fall into error, oblivion ; *tomber dans un piège,* to fall into a trap ; *tomber dans le ridicule,* to make a fool of oneself. ‖ **22. Tomber en,** to fall into ; *tomber en décadence, disgrâce,* to fall into decline, disgrace ; *tomber en ruine,* to fall in ruins ; *tomber en lambeaux,* to crumble away ; *tomber en poussière,* to turn to dust. ‖ **23. Tomber sur,** to fall on, to pitch into (attaquer) ; to meet, to meet with, to run into (ou) across (rencontrer) ; to bump into (fam.) ; to fall on, to turn to (se porter sur) ; to fall upon (l'ennemi) ; *tomber sur un mot,* to come across a word ; *la conversation tomba sur lui,* the conversation turned to him ; *son regard tomba sur la bague,* his gaze fell (ou) alighted on the ring. ‖ **24. Faire tomber,** to bring down (faire baisser) ; to trip up (faire un croc-en-jambe à) ; to knock (ou) push over (renverser) ; *faire tomber la conversation,* to bring round the conversation ; *faire tomber le gouvernement,* to bring about the fall of the government ; *faire tomber un vase d'une table,* to knock a vase off a table. ‖ **25. Laisser tomber,** to drop (sens général) ; to

discard, to give up (un projet) ; to let fall (un regard) ; to drop (la voix) ; *se laisser tomber dans un fauteuil,* to drop (ou) sink into an armchair ; *laisser tomber le feu,* to let the fire die down.
— v. impers. *Il m'est tombé sous la main une lettre de lui,* a letter of his has come into my hands, I have come across a letter of his ; *il tombe de la pluie,* it is raining. ‖ FAM. *Qu'est-ce qu'il va tomber !,* it's going to pour with rain !
— v. tr. FAM. To bring down, to cause the fall of ; to throw (un adversaire) ; to overthrow (le gouvernement). ‖ FAM. To take off (la veste).

tombereau [tɔ̃bro] m. Tip-cart ; dumpcart ; *tombereau à ordures,* dust- (ou) refuse- (ou) dung-cart ; U. S. garbage cart ; *emporter, porter dans un tombereau,* to cart away, to cart. ‖ Cart-load (de, of) [plein tombereau]. ‖ † Tumbril, tumbrel (de la Révolution).

tombeur [tɔ̃bœːr] m. House-breaker, U. S. house-wrecker (ouvrier). ‖ SPORTS. Wrestler (lutteur). ‖ FAM. Seducer (de femmes).

tombola [tɔ̃bɔla] f. Tombola ; *tirer une tombola,* to draw a lottery.

tome [toːm, tɔm] m. Volume, book.

tom(m)e [tɔm] f. Cheese.

tom(m)ette [tɔmɛt] f. Hexagonal floor tile.

tom-pouce [tɔmpus] (pl. **tom-pouces**) m. Tom Thumb, dwarf, midget (nain). ‖ Chubby (ou) short umbrella (parapluie).

ton [tɔ̃] (f. **ta** [ta], pl. **tes** [tɛ]) adj. poss. Thy († ECCLÉS.). ‖ Your ; *ton ami, ton amie,* your friend ; *ton frère et ta sœur,* your brother and sister ; *tes père et mère,* your father and mother ; *à ta santé !,* your health !

ton m. Tone, intonation (de la voix) ; *faire baisser le ton à qqn,* to make s.o. sing small ; to take s.o. down a peg ; *ce n'est pas ce qu'il dit mais le ton dont il le dit,* it's not what he says but the way he says it ; *il l'a pris sur un ton !,* he went up in the air ; U. S. he hit the ceiling ; *sur un ton amical,* in a friendly tone ; *sur le ton de la plaisanterie,* in a humorous tone (ou) vein (ou) style. ‖ Fashion (mode) ; *donner le ton,* to set the fashion. ‖ Manners, tone, breeding, form ; *il est de bon ton de,* it is considered good form to. ‖ GRAMM. Pitch accent (en linguistique). ‖ MÉD. Tone (énergie) ; *donner du ton à,* to tone up, to brace up. ‖ MUS. Tone (d'un instrument) ; key (de ré) ; *donner le ton,* to give the pitch ; *hauteur de ton,* pitch ; *ton d'église,* church mode. ‖ ARTS. Tone, colour, tint, shade ; *ton chaud,* warm tint ; *ton sur ton,* self-coloured.

tonal, ale [tɔnal] (pl. **tonals**) adj. Tonal.

tonalité [-lite] f. MUS., RADIO. Tonality.

tondeur [tɔ̃dœːr] s. Clipper (d'animaux) ; shearer (de drap, de moutons).

tondeuse [-døːz] f. TECHN. Shearing-machine (mécanique) ; clippers (pour chevaux, pour cheveux) ; shears (pour drap, pour moutons). ‖ AGRIC. Lawn-mower (de gazon).

tondre [tɔ̃dr] v. tr. (4). To clip (un cheval, des cheveux) ; to shear (des moutons) ; *tondre qqn,* to clip (ou) crop s.o.'s hair. ‖ ZOOL. To crop (brouter). ‖ AGRIC. To mow (le gazon). ‖ TECHN. To shear, to crop (du drap). ‖ FAM. To fleece, to skin (s.o.) ; *il tondrait un œuf,* he's a real skin-flint.

tondu, ue [tɔ̃dy] adj. Clipped (cheval, cheveux, haie) ; cropped (drap) ; shorn (drap, moutons) ; mown (gazon).
— m. ECCLÉS. Monk. ‖ FAM. *Le Petit Tondu,* Napoleon Bonaparte ; *il y avait quatre pelés et un tondu,* there were only a few nonentities (ou) odd bods (ou) odds and sods (pop.) there.

tonicité [tɔnisite] f. MÉD. Tonicity.

tonifiant, ante [-fjɑ̃, ɑ̃:t] adj. Tonic. ‖ Bracing, invigorating (air).
— m. MÉD. Tonic.

tonification [-fikasjɔ̃] f. Toning up, bracing.
tonifier [-fje] v. tr. (1). To tone up, to brace, to invigorate (qqn). ‖ To give tone to (la peau).
— v. intr. To brace up.
tonique [tɔnik] adj. Tonic (accent); stressed, accentuated (syllabe); *l'accent tonique tombe sur,* the stress falls on. ‖ MÉD., MUS. Tonic.
— m. MÉD. Tonic
— f. MUS. Tonic, key-note.
tonitruant, ante [tɔnitryɑ̃, ɑ̃:t] adj. Thundering, thunderous. ‖ Blustering, violent (vent); of thunder (voix).
tonitruer [-trye] v. intr. (1). FAM. To thunder.
Tonkin [tɔkɛ̃] m. GÉOGR. Tonking, Tongking.
tonkinois, oise [tɔ̃kinwa, waz] adj., s. GÉOGR. Tonkinese, Tongkinese.
tonnage [tɔna:ʒ] m. NAUT. Tonnage; displacement; *tonnage marchand,* shipping.
tonnant, ante [tɔnɑ̃, ɑ̃:t] adj. Thundering; *Jupiter tonnant,* Jupiter Tonans. ‖ FIG. Thundering; *donner un ordre d'une voix tonnante,* to thunder out an order; *voix tonnante,* voice of thunder.
tonne [tɔn] f. Tun, cask (tonneau). ‖ Ton (poids). ‖ FAM. Ton. (V. TAS.)
tonneau [tɔno] m. Barrel, tun, cask (v. BARIL, BARRIQUE); keg (barillet); butt (à eau); *bière au tonneau,* draught beer; U. S. beer on tap. ‖ Barrel, cask (de, of) [contenu]. ‖ NAUT. Ton (poids). ‖ Governess-cart (voiture). ‖ AUTOM. Tonneau. ‖ AVIAT. Barrel-roll; *descente en tonneau,* flat-spin. ‖ SPORTS. Tonneau (game). ‖ FAM. *Du même tonneau,* out of the same basket.
tonnelage [-nla:ʒ] m. Cooperage; *marchandises de tonnelage,* goods in barrels.
tonnelet [-nlɛ] m. Small cask; keg.
tonnelier [-nəlje] m. Cooper.
tonnelle [tɔnɛl] f. Bower, arbour. (V. BOSQUET.) ‖ SPORTS. Tunnel-net (filet). ‖ ARCHIT. Round arch; barrel-vault.
tonnellerie [tɔnɛlri] f. Cooperage, coopery. ‖ Cooper's workshop (lieu).
tonner [tɔne] v. intr. (1). To thunder (orage). MILIT. To boom (canons). ‖ FIG. To thunder (*contre,* against); to inveigh (*contre,* against).
— v. impers. To thunder; *il tonne,* it is thundering.
tonnerre [tɔnɛ:r] m. Thunder; thunderbolt (foudre); *un coup de tonnerre,* a clap (ou) peal of thunder, a thunderclap. ‖ FIG. Booming (de la mer); *voix de tonnerre,* voice of thunder. ‖ FAM. *Elle est du tonnerre,* she's terrific; *repas du tonnerre,* thundering good meal, U. S. bang-up feed.
— interj. *Tonnerre!, tonnerre de chien!, mille tonnerres!,* by thunder!, by Jove!
tonsure [tɔ̃sy:r] f. ECCLÉS. Tonsure; *recevoir la tonsure,* to enter the priesthood.
tonsuré, ée [tɔ̃syre] adj. Shaven (tête). ‖ ECCLÉS. Tonsured (clerc).
— m. ECCLÉS. Cleric, priest.
tonsurer v. tr. (1). ECCLÉS. To tonsure.
tonte [tɔ̃:t] f. Sheep-shearing, shearing (action); clip (quantité de laine); shearing-time (saison) [pour les moutons]. ‖ Clipping (d'une haie); mowing (du gazon). ‖ Shearing (du drap).
tontine [tɔ̃tin] f. FIN. Tontine.
tonton [tɔ̃tɔ̃] m. FAM. Uncle.
tonus [tɔny:s] m. MÉD. Tonicity; tonus.
top [tɔp] m. RADIO. Pip (de l'horloge parlante); top (de radio-phare).
topaze [tɔpa:z] f. Topaz; *topaze brûlée,* pink topaz.
tope! [tɔp] interj. FAM. Done!, agreed!, shake on it!, all right!
toper [-pe] v. intr. (1). To accept (ou) take on a bet. ‖ FAM. To agree; *tope là,* agreed!
topette [tɔpɛt] f. Phial.

topinambour [tɔpinɑ̃bu:r] m. BOT. Jerusalem artichoke.
topique [tɔpik] adj. Pertinent, apposite, to the point (argument); local (divinité). ‖ MÉD. Topical, local (maladie, remède).
— m. MÉD. Local (ou) topical remedy. ‖ GRAMM., PHILOS. Commonplace.
topique f. PSYCH. Mental topography.
topiquement [-mɑ̃] adv. Pertinently, to the point.
topo [tɔpo] m. FAM. Article (dans un journal); exposition, essay, paper, lecture, talk (dans un lycée); *faire un topo sur,* to hold forth on. ‖ FAM. Plan, outline.
topographe [tɔpɔgraf] m. Topographer.
topographie [-fi] f. Topography. ‖ Topographical map.
topographique [-fik] adj. Topographic, topographical; ordnance (carte); surveying (instruments); *croquis topographique,* area sketch, sketch map; *service topographique,* Ordnance Survey.
topologie [tɔpɔlɔʒi] f. MATH. Topology.
topologique [-ʒik] adj. MATH. Topological.
toponyme [tɔpɔnim] m. Place-name, toponym.
toponymie [tɔpɔnimi] f. Toponymy.
toquade [tɔkad] f. FAM. Fancy, craze, infatuation; *avoir une toquade pour,* to have fallen for.
toquante [tɔkɑ̃:t] f. FAM. Ticker.
toquard [tɔka:r] adj., m. V. TOCARD.
toque [tɔk] f. Toque (de femme); cap (de jockey, de juge, de professeur).
toqué, ée [tɔke] adj. FAM. Crazy, cracked, daft, dotty, balmy, batty, U. S. nuts. (V. CINGLÉ.) ‖ FAM. Mad (de, on); crazy (de, about) [entiché].
— s. FAM. Crazy (ou) cracked (ou) daft (ou) dotty person.
toquer v. intr. (1). To rap (ou) tap (taper).
— v. pr. Se toquer, FAM. To become crazy, to go mad (de, about). [V. S'ENTICHER.]
torche [tɔrʃ] f. Torch (flambeau). ‖ Straw-twist (bouchon). ‖ Head-pad (pour fardeaux). ‖ AVIAT. *Se mettre en torche,* to snake, to bail out (parachute). ‖ ELECTR. Torch.
torche. V. TORCHER. ‖ **Torche-cul,** m. POP. Bumf, U. S. bum-wad. ‖ **Torche-pinceau,** m. Paint-rag.
torcher [tɔrʃe] v. tr. (1). ARCHIT. To daub (un mur). ‖ FAM. To wipe, to wipe clean; to clean (nettoyer); *torcher un enfant,* to wipe a child's bottom. ‖ FAM. To polish off, to hurry (ou) rush through (son ouvrage); *mal torché,* badly done, scamped, botched, slipshod.
— v. pr. Se torcher, FAM. To wipe oneself.
torchère [tɔrʃɛ:r] f. † Cresset (vase). ‖ Candelabrum. ‖ ELECTR. Standard-lamp.
torchis [tɔrʃi] m. ARCHIT. Cob, daub; *mur en torchis,* cob-wall.
torchon [tɔrʃɔ̃] adj. Torchon (papier).
— m. Twist (ou) mat of straw (paille). ‖ Duster (à meuble); dish-cloth (à vaisselle). ‖ FAM. Trollop, slattern (souillon). ‖ FAM. *Coup de torchon,* row, scrap; *le torchon brûle chez eux,* they're always nagging each other
torchonner [-ʃone] v. tr. (1). To rub, to dry (la vaisselle). ‖ FAM. To scamp, to botch, to dash off (un ouvrage).
tord [tɔr]. V. TORDRE. ‖ **Tord-boyaux,** m. invar. FAM. Rot-gut. ‖ **Tord-nez,** m. invar. Twitch.
tordant, ante [tɔrdɑ̃, ɑ̃:t] adj. FAM. Killing, screamingly funny. (V. CREVANT.)
tordeur, euse [tɔrdœ:r, ø:z] s. Twister (de fil, de laine); throwster (de soie).
tordeuse [-dø:z] f. TECHN. Cable-twisting machine.
tordoir [tɔrdwa:r] m. Rope-twister (ou) -tightener. ‖ Mangle, wringer (de blanchisseur). ‖ TECHN. Cable-twisting machine.
tordre [tɔrdr] v. tr. (4). To twist (une corde, du

fil) ; to wring (du linge). ‖ To twist (un bras) ; *tordre le cou à qqn,* to wring s.o.'s neck.
—v. pr. **Se tordre,** to twist, to writhe, to writhe about ; to wriggle (enfant, ver) ; *se tordre la cheville,* to twist (ou) wrench one's ankle ; *se tordre les mains,* to wring one's hands. ‖ To become twisted (arbre) ; to buckle (plaque de métal). ‖ FAM. *A se tordre,* side-splitting ; *se tordre de rire,* to split one's sides with (ou) to be convulsed with laughter.

tordu, ue [tɔrdy] adj. Twisted. ‖ Crooked (jambes, nez) ; distorted (membre). ‖ TECHN. Bent (châssis) ; buckled (plaque de métal).
— s. POP. Freak ; *eh! va donc, tordue!,* go on, you old hag!

tore [tɔ:r] m. ARCHIT. Torus. ‖ MATH. Tore.

toréador [tɔreadɔ:r] m. Toreador, bullfighter.

toréer [tɔree] v. intr. (1). SPORTS. To fight in the bull-ring.

torero [tɔrero] m. Torero, bullfighter.

torgnole [tɔrɲɔl] f. FAM. Slap, smack, wallop, slosh, cuff.

toril [tɔril] m. Bull pen.

torique [tɔrik] adj. MATH. Toric.

tornade [tɔrnad] f. Tornado. (V. BOURRASQUE.)

toron [tɔrɔ̃] m. TECHN. Strand (d'une corde) ; wisp (de paille).

toron m. ARCHIT. Lower torus.

torpédo [tɔrpedo] f. AUTOM. Open tourer, roadster.

torpeur [tɔrpœ:r] f. Torpor.

torpide [-pid] adj. Torpid.

torpillage [tɔrpijaːʒ] m. NAUT. Torpedoing.

torpille [-piːj] adj. Barrel-shaped (sac).
— f. NAUT., AVIAT. Torpedo ; *attaquer à la torpille,* to make a torpedo attack on ; *atteindre d'une torpille,* to torpedo. ‖ ZOOL. Torpedo.

torpiller [-pije] v. tr. (1). NAUT., FIG. To torpedo.

torpillerie [-pijəri] f. NAUT. Torpedo-store (magasin) ; torpedo-gear (matériel).

torpilleur [-pijœ:r] adj. NAUT. Torpedo.
— m. NAUT. Torpedo-boat, destroyer (bateau) ; torpedo man (ou) officer (marin).

torque [tɔrk] m. † Torque (collier).
— f. Coil, twist (de fil de fer, de tabac).

torréfacteur [tɔrrefaktœ:r] m. Coffee-roaster.

torréfaction [-faksjɔ̃] f. Torrefaction, coffee-roasting.

torréfier [-fje] v. tr. (1). To torrefy ; to roast (du café). [V. GRILLER.]

torrent [tɔrrɑ̃] m. Torrent ; *il pleut à torrents,* the rain is coming down in torrents. ‖ FIG. Torrent, stream (d'injures) ; flood (de larmes).

torrentiel, elle [-sjɛl, ɛ:l] adj. Torrential ; teeming (pluie).

torrentiellement [-sjɛlmɑ̃] adv. Torrentially.

torrentueux, euse [-tɥø, ø:z] adj. Torrent-like, rushing (rivière).

torride [tɔrrid] adj. GÉOGR. Torrid (zone). ‖ FAM. Tropical, scorching (chaleur).

tors [tɔ:r] (f. **torse** [tɔrs], **torte** [tɔrt]) adj. Twisted (fils) ; thrown (soie). ‖ MÉD. Twisted, crooked (membres) ; *jambes tortes,* crooked legs. ‖ ARCHIT. Twisted, wreathed (colonne).
— m. Twist (de corde) ; twisted cord (de tapissier).

torsade [tɔrsad] f. Twisted cord (ou) fringe. ‖ Twist (ou) coil (de cheveux) ; *en torsade,* twisted, coiled. ‖ ARCHIT. Rope-moulding. ‖ TECHN. Twist-joint (de fils). ‖ Pl. MILIT., NAUT. Thick bullion (d'épaulette).

torsadé, ée [-de] adj. ELECTR. Twin (fil).

torsader [-de] v. tr. (1). To twist (together).

torse [tɔrs] m. Torso, trunk (de personne) ; *le torse nu,* stripped to the waist. ‖ ARTS. Torso. ‖ FAM. Chest (poitrine) ; *faire des effets de torse,* to strike a pose.

torsion [tɔrsjɔ̃] f. Twisting (d'une corde). ‖ PHYS., TECHN. Torsion. ‖ AUTOM. *Barre de torsion,* torsion bar.

tort [tɔ:r] m. Harm, hurt, injury, damage, detriment (v. PRÉJUDICE) ; *tort léger,* minor offence ; *faire tort à qqn de,* to defraud s.o. of ; *faire un tort irréparable à une cause,* to do a cause irreparable harm ; *faire du tort au jardin,* to do some damage to the garden ; *faire tort à qqn de deux cents francs,* to cheat s.o. of two hundred francs. ‖ Wrong, error, fault ; *avoir tort,* to be wrong ; *donner tort à,* to lay the blame on ; *être, se mettre dans son tort,* to be, to put oneself in the wrong ; *il a eu le tort de ne pas dire toute la vérité,* he made the mistake of not telling the whole truth ; *vous avez tort de lui parler sur ce ton,* you shouldn't speak to him in that tone of voice ; *vous ne dansez jamais? vous avez tort!,* you never dance? you ought to.
— loc. adv. **A tort,** wrongly ; wrongfully, unjustly ; *à tort ou à raison,* rightly or wrongly ; *à tort et à travers,* at random ; anyhow ; without rhyme or reason.

torte [tɔrt] adj. f. V. TORS.

torticolis [tɔrtikɔli] m. MÉD. Torticollis ; crick in the neck ; stiff neck ; wryneck.

tortil [tɔrtil] m. BLAS. Baron's coronet.

tortillage [tɔrtijɑ:ʒ] m. FAM. Quibbling, beating around the bush ; rigmarole of words (v. AMBAGES) ; trickery, underhand intrigue (tours).

tortillard, arde [-ja:r, ard] adj. Twisted. ‖ BOT. Knotty (orme).
— m. CH. DE F. Stopping train ; U. S. jerkwater.

tortillement [-jmɑ̃] m. Twisting (action) ; twist (état). ‖ Wriggling (d'un ver). ‖ FAM. Wriggling.

tortiller [-je] v. intr. (1). FAM. To wriggle ; *tortiller des hanches,* to swing one's hips. ‖ FAM. To shilly-shally, to beat about the bush (hésiter) ; *il n'y a pas à tortiller,* there's no getting out of it (ou) away from it ; there's no denying it.
— v. tr. To twist, to kink (une corde) ; to twist up (du papier) ; to twirl, to twiddle, to fiddle with (sa moustache).
— v. pr. **Se tortiller,** to twist (serpent) ; to wriggle (ver). ‖ To wriggle (enfant). ‖ To writhe, to squirm (de douleur).

tortillon [-jɔ̃] m. Head-pad (coussinet). ‖ Wisp (de paille) ; twist (de papier).

tortionnaire [tɔrsjɔnɛ:r] adj. Of torture (appareil). ‖ JUR. Iniquitous.
— m. Torturer.

tortu, ue [tɔrty] adj. Crooked, twisted (arbre) ; twisting, winding (chemin). ‖ FIG. Crooked ; tortuous (esprit, raisonnement).

tortue [tɔrty] f. ZOOL. Tortoise ; *tortue de mer,* turtle. ‖ † MILIT. Testudo. ‖ CULIN. *Soupe à la tortue,* turtle soup ; *tête de veau tortue,* mock-turtle. ‖ FAM. *A pas de tortue,* at a snail's pace.

tortueusement [tɔrtɥøzmɑ̃] adv. Tortuously, crookedly.

tortueux, euse [-tɥø, ø:z] adj. Meandering (rivière) ; twisting, tortuous, winding (rue). ‖ FIG. Underhand (conduite) ; roundabout, crooked (moyen) ; crafty, wily, scheming (personne) ; involved (style).

tortuosité [-tɥozite] f. Tortuosity. ‖ Winding, meandering (d'une rivière). ‖ FIG. Crookedness.

torturant, ante [tɔrtyrɑ̃, ɑ̃:t] adj. Torturing (er général) ; gnawing (remords).

torture [-ty:r] f. Torture. ‖ FIG. Torture, torment (v. SUPPLICE) ; *mettre à la torture,* to torture ; *se mettre l'esprit à la torture,* to rack one's brains

torturer [-tyre] v. tr. (1). To torment (un animal) ; to torture (une personne). ‖ FIG. To torture, to twist (un texte).
— v. pr. **Se torturer,** to torture oneself ; *se torturer l'esprit,* to rack (ou) cudgel one's brains.

torve [tɔrv] adj. Grim, forbidding, scowling (menaçant); black, stony (sombre); *jeter un regard torve à*, to look askance at.

tory [tɔri] (pl. **tories**) adj., m. Tory.

toscan, ane [tɔskɑ̃, an] adj., s. GÉOGR. Tuscan.

tôt [to] adv. Soon (bientôt); soon, quickly (vite); *tôt après*, soon after; *tôt ou tard*, sooner or later; *au plus tôt*, at the earliest; *le plus tôt possible*, as soon as possible; *le plus tôt sera le mieux*, the sooner the better. ‖ Early (de bonne heure); *se coucher tôt*, to go to bed early. ‖ FAM. *Ce n'est pas trop tôt!*, and about time too!

total, ale [tɔtal] adj. Total, entire, whole. ‖ Complete (destruction, échec, perte); utter (ruine); *somme totale*, sum total. ‖ ASTRON. Total (éclipse).
— m. Total, whole; sum total; full amount; *faire le total de*, to add up, to tot up (fam.).
— loc. adv. *Au total*, on the whole, all things considered.

totalement [-lmɑ̃] adv. Totally, entirely, wholly (entièrement). ‖ Completely, utterly (détruit).

totalisateur, trice [-lizatœːr, tris] adj. Adding (appareil).
— m. Adding-machine. ‖ SPORTS. Totalizator, tote (fam.).

totalisation [-lizasjɔ̃] f. Totalization; adding up, summing up, totting up.

totalisatrice [-lizatris] f. COMM. Cash register.

totaliser [-lize] v. tr. (1). To totalize, to total up, to tot up.

totalitaire [tɔtalitɛːr] adj. Totalitarian.

totalitarisme [-tarism] m. Totalitarianism.

totalité [-te] f. Totality, total, entirety, whole; *en totalité*, totally, completely, wholly; *la presque totalité de ses dents*, almost all his teeth; *pris dans sa totalité*, taken as a whole.

totem [tɔtɛm] m. Totem.

totémisme [-temism] m. Totemism.

totémique [-temik] adj. Totem, totemic.

toto [toto] m. FAM. Louse.

toton [tɔtɔ̃] m. Teetotum; small top. ‖ FAM. *Faire tourner qqn comme un toton*, to twist s.o. round one's little finger; to keep s.o. up to scratch.

touage [tua:ʒ] m. NAUT. Chain-towing (à la chaîne); warping, kedging (à la corde). ‖ NAUT. Chain-towage dues (prix).

touaille [twa:j] f. Roller-towel.

touareg [twarɛg] adj., s. pl. Tuareg.

toubib [tubib] m. MILIT., FAM. Medical officer, M. O. ‖ FAM. Doc, medico.

toucan [tukɑ̃] m. ZOOL. Toucan.

touchable [tuʃabl] adj. Touchable. ‖ FIN. Cashable, payable (chèque); collectable (effets).

touchant, ante [-ʃɑ̃, ɑ̃:t] adj. Touching, moving, affecting. (V. ÉMOUVANT.)
— m. Touching side, pathetic part.
— prép. Touching, concerning, with regard to, as regards, about. (V. CONCERNANT.)

touche [tuʃ] f. Touch, touching (action); test, testing (essai, moyen); *pierre de touche*, touch-stone. ‖ Tab (de fichier); thumb-index (de livre à référence). ‖ MUS. Key (d'un clavier); fret (d'une guitare); finger-board (d'un violon). ‖ ARTS. Style (d'un écrivain); manner, touch (d'un peintre). ‖ SPORTS. Touch; hit (au billard, à l'escrime); bite, nibble (à la pêche). ‖ TECHN. Key (de machine à écrire); *touche de blocage, de manœuvre*, shift-lock, -key. ‖ AGRIC. Goad (de bouvier); herd, drove (troupeau). ‖ FAM. Appearance, look; *quelle touche!*, *il a une drôle de touche*, he's a queer-looking chap. ‖ POP. *Faire une touche*, to catch s.o.'s eye; *j'ai fait une touche*, I've clicked, I've got off.

touche-à-tout [-ʃatu] adj. invar. Meddlesome, meddling.

— s. invar. Meddler; meddlesome person (indiscret). ‖ Jack-of-all-trades (bricoleur).

toucher [-ʃe] v. tr. (1).

---

1. Palper. — 2. Blesser. — 3. Manier. — 4. Atteindre. — 5. Etre en rapport avec. — 6. Prendre contact avec. — 7. Emouvoir. — 8. Concerner. — 9. Faire allusion à. — 10. Dire. — 11. AGRIC. — 12. MILIT. — 13. NAUT. — 14. SPORTS. — 15. FIN. — 16. MATH. — 17. FAM.

---

1. To touch (palper); *toucher la main à*, to shake hands with. ‖ 2. To touch; to wound (blesser); to damage (endommager); to strike, to hit (frapper); to graze (frôler). ‖ 3. To touch, to handle (manier). ‖ 4. To touch, to reach (atteindre); *ma lettre l'a touché*, my letter has reached him; *toucher le plafond*, to touch the ceiling. ‖ 5. To be related to, to be connected with (être en rapport avec); *il me touche de près*, he is related (ou) closely connected to me. ‖ 6. To touch, to come into contact with, to contact (prendre contact avec). ‖ 7. To touch, to affect, to move (émouvoir); to have an effect on; *qui touche profondément*, deeply moving; *cette critique ne risque pas de le toucher*, that criticism is not likely to have any effect on him. ‖ 8. To touch, to affect, to concern (concerner); *en ce qui me touche*, as far as it concerns me. ‖ 9. To touch on, to allude to (faire allusion à); to deal with, to manage, to handle (traiter). ‖ 10. To say (dire); *je lui en toucherai quelques mots*, I'll have a word with him about it. ‖ 11. AGRIC. To drive, to goad (des bœufs); *toucher du fouet*, to whip up, to touch up (un cheval). ‖ 12. MILIT. To hit (le but); to draw (des rations). ‖ 13. NAUT. To strike (le fond, un rocher); *toucher terre*, to touch land. ‖ 14. SPORTS. To handle (le ballon); to touch, to hit (en escrime); *touché!*, a hit. ‖ 15. FIN. To receive, to draw (de l'argent); to cash (un chèque); to draw (un chèque, des dividendes, son salaire). ‖ 16. MATH. To touch; to be tangent to. ‖ 17. FAM. *Touchez du bois*, touch wood.

— v. intr.

---

1. Atteindre. — 2. Tripoter. — 3. Se mêler. — 4. Modifier. — 5. Goûter. — 6. Concerner. — 7. Etre contigu. — 8. Etre apparenté ou en rapport. — 9. NAUT. — 10. MUS. — 11. SPORTS. — 12. FIN. — 13. FAM.

---

1. *Toucher à*, to touch, to reach (atteindre). ‖ 2. *Toucher à*, to touch (tripoter); *enfant qui touche à tout*, meddlesome child; *n'y touchez pas!*, don't touch it!, leave it alone. ‖ 3. *Toucher à*, to meddle with, to tamper with, to interfere with (se mêler); *toucher à des sujets délicats*, to tread on dangerous ground; *toucher à des droits acquis*, to interfere with vested interests. ‖ 4. *Toucher à*, to change (modifier); to alter (des lois). ‖ 5. *Toucher à*, to touch (goûter) [un plat]; *il n'a pas touché au saumon*, he left the salmon untasted. ‖ 6. *Toucher à*, to touch, to concern, to have to do with (concerner); *toucher à une question*, to be connected with a question. ‖ 7. *Toucher à*, to be close to, to be near; to be close on, to verge on, to abut on, to border on (être contigu à); *toucher au but*, to be near one's goal; *toucher à sa fin (ou) à son terme*, to draw (ou) come to its end. ‖ 8. *Toucher à*, to be close to; to be related to (être apparenté à); to be in touch with (être en rapport avec); *toucher de près à*, to be in close touch with. ‖ 9. NAUT. *Toucher à*, to call (ou) put in at (un

port). ‖ **10.** Mus. *Toucher du,* to play on (clavecin, piano). ‖ **11.** Sports. *Toucher dans les buts,* to touch down. ‖ **12.** Fin. To be paid. ‖ **13.** Fam. *Touchez là,* shake!, done!, your hand on it ; *il n'a pas l'air d'y toucher,* he looks as if butter wouldn't melt in his mouth.
— v. pr. **Se toucher,** to touch oneself. ‖ To be touched (sens passif).
— v. récipr. **Se toucher,** to touch each other. ‖ To touch, to adjoin (jardins) ; to border on each other (pays). ‖ Math. To touch ; to meet (lignes).
— m. Touch, feeling, sense of touch (sens) ; *reconnaître qqch. au toucher,* to recognize sth. by the feel of it ; *c'est chaud au toucher,* it feels hot. ‖ Feel (d'une étoffe). ‖ Mus. Touch.

touchette [tuʃɛt] f. Mus. Fret (d'une guitare).

toucheur [-ʃœ:r] m. Agric. Drover, cattle-drover.

toue [tu] f. Naut. Warping, kedging (action) ; chain-ferry (bac) ; flat-bottomed boat (barque).

touée [-e] f. Naut. Warping, kedging (action) ; warp, warping-rope (corde) ; scope (longueur).

touer [-e] v. tr. (1). Naut. To warp, to kedge ; to chain-tow.

toueur [-œ:r] adj. Naut. Kedge (ancre) ; warping (bateau).
— m. Naut. Tug (bateau) ; warper (marinier).

touffe [tuf] f. Cluster ; clump (d'arbres) ; bunch (de fleurs) ; tuft (d'herbes, de poils).

touffeur [tufœ:r] f. Fug ; suffocating heat.

touffu, ue [-fy] adj. Bushy (barbe) ; thick, shaggy, bushy (cheveux). ‖ Thick (bois) ; thickly wooded (colline). ‖ Fig. Solid (étude) ; heavy (roman) ; involved (style).

touillage [tuja:ʒ] m. Fam. Stirring, stirring up.

touiller [-je] v. tr. (1). Fam. To stir, to stir up.

toujours [tuʒu:r] adv. Always, for ever (à jamais) ; *à (ou) pour toujours,* for ever. ‖ Always, at all times (tout le temps) ; *je l'ai toujours admiré,* I have always admired him. ‖ Still (encore) ; *il fait toujours aussi froid,* it's as cold as ever ; *il vit toujours,* he is still alive. ‖ Always, some day (un jour) ; *ça peut toujours vous rendre service,* it may be useful to you some day. ‖ Nevertheless, anyhow, anyway, all the same, at all events, in any case (de toute façon, néanmoins) ; *toujours est-il que,* the fact remains that, anyhow ; *dites toujours,* go on ; *on peut toujours aller voir,* one can at least go and see ; *on peut toujours essayer,* one can but try ; *il en restera toujours qqch.,* there's bound to be sth. left over.

toulousain, aine [tuluzɛ̃, ɛn] adj. Géogr. Of (ou) from Toulouse.
— s. Native (ou) inhabitant of Toulouse.

toundra [tundra] f. Tundra.

toupet [tupɛ] m. Forelock (d'un cheval) ; forelock, calf-lick, U. S. cow-lick (sur le front) ; tuft (de poils) ; *faux toupet,* toupet, toupee. ‖ Fam. Cheek, neck, nerve, sauce (v. Culot) ; *il a du toupet!,* he's got a cheek (ou) nerve! ; *payer de toupet,* to brazen it out.

toupie [tupi] f. Top, spinning-top (en général) ; humming-top (d'Allemagne). ‖ Techn. Moulding-lathe ; vertical cutter (de menuisier) ; turnpin (de plombier). ‖ Fam. Flighty person ; *vieille toupie,* old frump (ou) trout.

touque [tuk] f. Jerrycan (de pétrole).

tour [tu:r] f. Archit. Tower ; *tour Eiffel,* Eiffel Tower ; *tour de Babel,* tower of Babel ; *tour de guet,* watch-tower. ‖ Castle, rook (aux échecs).

tour m. Turn, revolution (de roue) ; turn (de vis) ; *fermer à double tour,* to double-lock. ‖ Circuit, going round (action) ; *faire le tour du monde, des remparts, de la ville,* to go round the world, the ramparts, the town ; *faire le tour du quartier,* to go all round the neighbourhood ; *faire le grand tour,* to come the long way round. ‖ Circumference ; distance round (mesure) ; *tour*

de poitrine, bust measurement (de femme) ; chest measurement (d'homme) ; *tour de taille,* waist measurement ; *tour de tête,* size in hats. ‖ Turning, winding, twisting (méandre). ‖ Walk, stroll (promenade) ; *faire un petit tour,* to go for a stroll. ‖ Turn ; *à, avant son tour,* in, out of one's turn ; *avoir un tour de faveur,* to get preferential treatment ; *c'est à votre tour,* it's your turn, *à qui le tour?,* who's next?, whose turn is it? ; *son tour est venu,* his number's up (fam.) ; *tour à tour, à tour de rôle,* in turn, by turns ; *faire qqch. tour à tour,* to take turns at doing sth. ‖ Trick (trait) ; *mauvais, sale tour,* nasty, dirty trick ; *le tour est joué,* the trick has worked ; *avoir plus d'un tour dans son sac,* to have more than one trick up one's sleeve. ‖ Trick, feat, knack, skill (habileté) ; *tour d'adresse,* feat of skill ; *tour de force,* tour de force, feat of strength ; *tour de main,* knack ; skill. ‖ Turn (orientation) ; turn, twist (de la pensée) ; *tour d'esprit,* turn of mind ; *tour gracieux, original,* felicitous, original touch. ‖ Turn, course (allure) ; *prendre meilleur tour,* to look up (affaires) ; to take a better turn (négociations). ‖ Shape, outline (du visage). ‖ Row (en tricot). ‖ Milit. Turn, spell (de service). ‖ Naut. Turn (d'amarre) ; elbow (de chaîne) ; swinging, sweep (circuit). ‖ Ecclés. Turning-box (d'un couvent). ‖ Méd. Wrench, twist, sprain, strain ; *se donner un tour de reins,* to strain one's back. ‖ Sports. Circuit, lap (de piste) ; *le Tour de France,* the round-France cycle race. ‖ Comm. *Tour de main,* tricks of the trade. ‖ Techn. Wheel (de potier) ; lathe (de tourneur) ; *fait au tour,* turned ; *travail au tour,* lathe-work. ‖ Mus. *Tour de chant,* vocal number. ‖ Fig. *Tour d'horizon,* survey. ‖ Fam. *A tour de bras,* hammer and tongs, with might and main ; *jambe faite au tour,* shapely leg ; *mon sang n'a fait qu'un tour,* I flared up at once it gave me quite a turn (pop.) ; *en un tour de main,* in a flash (ou) trice (ou) jiffy (fam.).

Tour-de-cou (pl. *tours-de-cou*) m. Neckband (de chemise) ; comforter (cache-nez) ; tippet (écharpe en fourrure) ; scarf (foulard).

tourangeau, elle [turɑ̃ʒo, ɛl] adj. Géogr. Pertaining to Tours ; of Touraine.
— s. Géogr. Native (ou) inhabitant of Tours (ou) Touraine.

tourbe [turb] f. Mob, rabble. (V. Populace.)

tourbe f. Peat (combustible).

tourbeux, euse [-bø, ø:z] adj. Peaty (sol) ; *marais tourbeux,* turf-moor.

tourbière [-bjɛ:r] f. Peat-bog ; turf-moor.

tourbillon [turbijɔ̃] m. Whirlwind. (V. Bourrasque.) ‖ Eddy, swirl, swirling cloud (de fumée, de neige, de poussière) ; *monter en tourbillon,* to swirl up. ‖ Eddy (d'eau) ; whirlpool (masse d'eau). ‖ Phys. Vortex. ‖ Fig. Bustle, whirl (des affaires) ; round (des plaisirs).

tourbillonnant, ante [-jɔnɑ̃, ɑ̃:t] adj. Whirling. ‖ Sports. Spinning (ballon).

tourbillonnement [-jɔnmɑ̃] m. Wirling, swirling, eddying. ‖ Fig. Bustle, whirl.

tourbillonner [-jɔne] v. intr. (1). To whirl round, to whirl, to swirl, to eddy ; *monter en tourbillonnant,* to spiral up.

tourelle [turɛl] f. Archit. Turret ; *tourelle en encorbellement,* bartizan. ‖ Naut., Techn. Turret. ‖ Aviat. Gun-turret.

touret [turɛ] m. Techn. Reel (de cordier) ; polishing-lathe (de graveur) ; drum (de tour). ‖ Naut. Thole-pin. ‖ Sports. Reel (de canne à pêche). ‖ Electr. Cable-drum.

tourie [turi] f. Carboy.

tourier, ère [turje, ɛr] adj. Ecclés. *Frère tourier,* monk on duty at the turning-box ; *sœur tourière,* turn (ou) extern (ou) out sister.

tourillon [turijɔ̃] m. TECHN. Spindle; pivot, pin (de grille, de porte). || MILIT. Trunnion (de canon).

tourisme [turism] m. Tourism; *agence de tourisme*, travel (ou) tourist agency. || AUTOM. *Voiture de tourisme*, private car (torpédo); touring-car (personnelle).

touriste [-rist] s. Tourist; tripper.

touristique [-ristik] adj. Touristic, travel; tourist.

tourlourou [turluru] m. FAM. Foot-slogger.

tourmaline [turmalin] f. Tourmaline.

tourment [turmɑ̃] m. Torment, torture. || FIG. Torment; torture, agony; anxiety; anguish. || Pl. Pangs (de la faim, de la jalousie).

tourmente [-mɑ̃:t] f. Gale, storm (v. TEMPÊTE); *tourmente de neige*, blizzard, snowstorm. || FIG. Storm, upheaval, turmoil.

tourmenté, ée [-mɑ̃te] adj. Tormented, tortured; racked (par la douleur, le remords). || Tormented, tortured, uneasy (esprit); worried, anxious (personne); harassed (visage). || Turbulent, angry, rough (mer); broken (rivage); rough (sol). || Exaggerated (couleurs); over-elaborate (style).

tourmenter [-mɑ̃te] v. tr. (1). To torment, to torture (faire souffrir). || To torment, to worry, to bother (inquiéter). || To torment, to bother, to pester, to plague (harceler, importuner); to dun (créanciers). || FIG. To over-elaborate (son style).
— v. pr. Se **tourmenter**, to be anxious (ou) uneasy, to worry, to fret (v. SE SOUCIER); *ne vous tourmentez pas,* don't worry (ou) bother. || TECHN. To warp (bois).
— v. récipr. Se **tourmenter**, to bother (ou) pester (ou) plague each other.

tourmenteur, euse [-mɑ̃tœ:r, ø:z] adj. Tormenting.
— m. † Torturer. (V. BOURREAU.) || Tormenter.

tournage [turna:ʒ] m. CINÉM. Shooting. || NAUT. Belaying-cleat. || TECHN. Turning (au tour).

tournailler [-nɑje] v. intr. (1). FAM. To go round and round; to prowl about; *tournailler autour d'une femme*, to hang round a woman.

tournant, ante [-nɑ̃, ɑ̃:t] adj. Turning (en général); winding (allée, route); spiral (escalier); revolving (plateau). || MILIT. Outflanking (mouvement). || CH. DE F. *Plaque tournante*, turn-table. || TECHN. Live (essieu); *pont tournant*, swing-bridge. || ELECTR. Rotating (champ). || LOC. *Les tables tournantes*, table-turning.
— m. Corner, street corner (coin de rue); turn, bend (de rivière). || AUTOM. Turn, bend (sur route); turning-space (de voiture); *tournant brusque*, sharp bend, dangerous corner; *prendre un tournant à la corde*, to cut a corner close. || NAUT. Whirlpool (tourbillon). || TECHN. Water-wheel (de moulin). || FIG. Pl. Turning-points de l'histoire).

tourne [turn] f. CULIN. Turning, turning sour (du lait). || **Tourne-disque**, m. Turn-table, record-player. || **Tourne-feuille**, m. Leaf-turner.

tourné, ée [-ne] adj. Turned; *pieds tournés en dedans*, in-toed (ou) turned-in feet; *avoir les pieds tournés en dedans*, to be pigeon-toed. || CULIN. Sour (lait, vin). || ECCLÉS. Oriented (église). || TECHN. Turned, shaped (au tour). || FIG. Turned; *avoir l'esprit mal tourné*, to be perverse; *avoir la tête tournée*, to be off one's head; *bien tourné*, shapely (jambe); well (ou) neatly turned (phrase).

tournebouler [-nbule] v. tr. (1). FAM. *Tournebouler la cervelle à qqn*, to make s.o. lose his head.

tournebride [-nəbrid] m. Roadside inn.

tournebroche [-nəbrɔʃ] m. CULIN. Roasting-jack.

tournedos [-nədo] m. CULIN. Tournedos; fillet steak; U. S. filet mignon.

tournée [-ne] f. Tour (d'un conférencier, d'un fonctionnaire, d'inspection); round (d'un facteur); circuit (d'un juge); round of visits (d'un médecin); *en tournée*, on tour (acteurs); away on business (commerçant); *faire la tournée des magasins*, to go round the shops; *faire une tournée*, to be on tour. || SPORTS. Round (de golf). || FAM. Round of drinks (boissons); *c'est ma tournée*, it's my round; *payer une tournée*, to stand a round of drinks. || FAM. Walk, stroll (à pied); trip (en voiture). || FAM. Thrashing, walloping. (V. RACLÉE.)

tournemain [-nəmɛ̃] m. *En un tournemain*, in the twinkling of an eye, in a flash (ou) trice.

tourner [-ne] v. tr. (1).

---
1. Sens général. — 2. Eluder. — 3. Présenter. — 4. Interpréter. — 5. Transformer. — 6. Diriger. — 7. Etudier. — 8. MILIT. — 9. NAUT. — 10. THÉÂTR. — 11. CULIN. — 12. TECHN. — 13. FAM.
---

1. To turn (une broche, une clé, une manivelle); to turn, to revolve, to rotate (une roue). || To turn (à, on) [le dos]; to turn, to wind, to twist (la main, une page); to turn (la tête); *tourner les pieds en dedans, en dehors*, to turn one's toes in, out. || To turn (un coin de rue). || 2. To get round; to turn (une difficulté); to evade (la loi). || 3. To turn (une lettre, une phrase); *il sait bien tourner une lettre*, he can write a good letter. || 4. To interpret (une parole); *tourner tout en bien, en mal*, to put a good, bad construction on everything. || 5. To turn, to convert (en, into), *tourner qqch., qqn en ridicule*, to ridicule sth., s.o. || 6. To turn, to direct (ses efforts, ses pensées); *tourner le regard vers*, to cast one's eyes upon. || To turn (qqn); *elle le tourne à son gré*, she twists him round her little finger; *tourner la tête à qqn*, to turn s.o.'s head. || 7. To turn over, to consider, to think about, to go into, to examine (une question); *tourner et retourner dans tous les sens*, to turn over and over. || 8. MILIT. To outflank (l'ennemi); to turn (le flanc de l'ennemi); *tourner le dos*, to turn tail. || 9. NAUT. To weather (un cap). || 10. THÉÂTR. To make (un film); to shoot (une scène) [cinéaste]; to play in, to star in (un film) [vedette]. || 11. CULIN. To toss (une crêpe); to stir (une sauce). || 12. TECHN. To turn, to shape, to fashion (au tour). || 13. FAM. *Tourner l'estomac à qqn*, to turn s.o.'s stomach; *à vous tourner le sang*, blood-curdling.
— v. intr.

---
1. Sens général. — 2. Changer de direction. — 3. Aller. — 4. Tendre à. — 5. Devenir. — 6. S'altérer. — 7. Mûrir. — 8. Dépendre. — 9. Tourner autour. — 10. Tourner contre. — 11. ASTRON. — 12. NAUT. — 13. AUTOM. — 14. MÉD. — 15. THÉÂTR. — 16. FAM.
---

1. To turn (clé, personne); to swing (porte); to turn, to rotate, to revolve, to go round (roue); to spin (toupie); *tournez à gauche*, turn left; *la route tourne à gauche*, the road bends (ou) bears (ou) turns to the left. || 2. To turn (changer de direction); *sa chance a tourné*, his luck has changed; *tourner du côté de*, to side with; *tourner à tout vent*, to turn like a weathercock; to dance to every fiddle; *le vent a tourné*, the situation has changed. || 3. To turn (aller); *tourner bien (ou) rond*, to shape (ou) go well (affaire); to do well (personne); to turn out well (situation); *tourner court*, to come to a sudden end

(cesser); to break off (cesser de parler); *tourner mal,* to shape up (ou) go badly (affaire); to go to the bad (ou) the dogs (fam.); to turn out badly (situation). ‖ **4.** To turn (avoir une tendance vers); *vert qui tourne au bleu,* green verging on blue; *tourner à la religion,* to turn to religion; *tourner au tragique,* to take on a tragic turn. ‖ **5.** To turn, to change (devenir); *tourner à l'aigre,* to grow bitter (discussion): to turn sour (vin). ‖ **6.** To turn (s'altérer); *le lait, le vin a tourné,* the milk, wine has turned sour. ‖ **7.** To ripen (mûrir). ‖ **8.** To turn, to depend (*autour de, sur, on*) [dépendre]. ‖ **9. Tourner autour,** to turn round; *tourner autour d'une femme,* to hang round a woman; *tourner autour du pot,* to beat about (ou) around the bush; *tourner autour de la terre,* to orbit the earth (satellite artificiel). ‖ **10. Tourner contre,** to turn against. ‖ **11.** ASTRON. To revolve (terre). ‖ **12.** NAUT. To veer (ou) to turn round (vent). ‖ **13.** AUTOM. To turn; *tourner trop court,* to corner (ou) to turn too sharply; *tourner rond,* to run well (moteur). ‖ **14.** MÉD. To turn over, to twist (pied); to turn (tête); *le pied m'a tourné,* I've twisted my ankle; *j'ai la tête qui tourne, la tête me tourne,* I feel giddy, my head is swimming (ou) going round. ‖ **15.** THÉÂTR. To film; to act, to play, to star, to feature (jouer). ‖ **16.** FAM. *Tourner de l'œil,* to faint (s'évanouir); *elle lui a fait tourner la tête,* she has turned his head; *faire tourner qqn en bourrique,* to drive s.o. crazy.
— v. pr. **Se tourner,** to be turned (ou) rotated (roue). ‖ To turn (*vers,* to); to turn round (se diriger); *de quelque côté qu'on se tourne,* whichever way one turns. ‖ To turn, to change (*à, en, to, into*) [se transformer].

tournesol [turnəsɔl] m. BOT. Sunflower, turnsole; heliotrope. ‖ CHIM. Litmus (papier).

tourneur, euse [-nœ:r, ø:z] adj. Dancing (derviche). ‖ TECHN. *Ouvrier tourneur,* turner, latheworker (menuisier); thrower (potier).
— m. TECHN. Turner; lathe-worker; thrower.

tournevent [-nəvɑ̃] m. invar. TECHN. Chimneycowl.

tournevis [-nəvis] m. TECHN. Screw-driver.

tournicoter [-nikɔte] v. intr. (1). FAM. To wander (ou) drift about.

tournière [-njɛ:r] f. AGRIC. Headland.

tourniole [-njɔl] m. MÉD. Whitlow, felon.

tourniquer [-nike] v. intr. (1). FAM. To wander (ou) drift about; to hang around.

tourniquet [-nikɛ] m. Turnstile (barrière). ‖ Lottery-wheel (disque tournant). ‖ MÉD. Tourniquet. ‖ TECHN. Sprinkler (arrosoir); catch (de volet). ‖ PHYS. *Tourniquet électrique,* electric vane; *tourniquet hydraulique,* reaction wheel. ‖ FAM., MILIT. *Passer au tourniquet,* to be court-martialled.

tournis [-ni] m. MÉD. Staggers (des agneaux). ‖ LOC. *Avoir, donner le tournis,* to be, to make dizzy (ou) giddy.

tournoi [-nwa] m. Tournament.

tournoiement [-nwamɑ̃] m. Turning round. ‖ Swirling, eddying (de l'eau); spinning, twirling, whirling (des feuilles); wheeling (des oiseaux). ‖ MÉD. Giddiness, dizziness (de tête).

tournoyant, ante [-nwajɑ̃, ɑ̃:t] adj. Turning. ‖ Twisting (corde); swirling, eddying (eau); spinning, twirling, whirling (feuilles); wheeling (oiseaux). ‖ AVIAT. *Combat tournoyant,* dogfight.

tournoyer [-nwaje] v. intr. (9 a). To turn round. ‖ To twist (corde); to swirl, to eddy (eau); to spin, to twirl (feuilles); to wheel (oiseaux); *les feuilles descendent en tournoyant,* the leaves come twisting (ou) spiralling down. ‖ FIG. To be in a whirl (pensées).

tournure [-ny:r] f. Turn, course, direction; *donner une autre tournure à,* to give a fresh turn to; *prendre une bonne, une mauvaise tournure,* to go well, badly; *prendre une meilleure tournure,* to look up (affaires); to take a turn for the better (situation); *tournure nouvelle,* new development; *tournure d'esprit,* turn of mind. ‖ Shape, figure, appearance (forme); *avoir une jolie tournure,* to have a nice figure; *prendre tournure,* to take shape. ‖ GRAMM. Construction; turn of phrase, expression. ‖ TECHN. Turning (déchet métallique); pl. turnings, shavings.

touron [turɔ̃] m. CULIN. Almond paste.

tourte [turt] f. CULIN. Pie; covered tart (aux fruits); round loaf (pain). ‖ FAM. Duffer (sot).

tourteau [-to] m. CULIN. Round loaf. ‖ AGRIC. Cattle-cake. ‖ ZOOL. Edible crab.

tourtereau [turtəro] m. ZOOL. Young turtle-dove. ‖ FAM. Lover; *comme deux tourtereaux,* like two turtle-doves.

tourterelle [-rɛl] f. ZOOL. Turtle-dove.

tourtière [turtjɛ:r] f. CULIN. Pie-dish, baking-tin; U. S. pie plate, piepan.

tous [tu, tus] v. TOUT.

Toussaint (la) [latusɛ̃] f. ECCLÉS. All Saints' Day, All Hallows' day; *la veille de la Toussaint,* Hallowe'en.

tousser [tuse] v. intr. (1). To cough; to hem; *il toussa pour m'avertir,* he gave me a warning cough.

toussotement [-sɔtmɑ̃] m. Slight cough (ou) coughing.

toussoter [-sɔte] v. intr. (1). To have a slight cough; to cough slightly.

tout [tu] (f. **toute,** pl. **tous, toutes** [tut, tu, tut]) adj. All, whole (total); *il a lu tout Balzac,* he has read the whole of Balzac; *une robe de toute beauté,* a perfectly lovely dress; *de tout mon cœur,* with all my heart; *de toute évidence,* evidently, obviously; *toute la famille,* the whole family; *c'est toute une histoire,* it's quite a business; it's a long story; *travailler toute la journée,* to work all day long; *tout le monde,* everybody, everyone; *c'est tout ce qu'il y a à manger,* that's all there is to eat; *c'est tout ce qu'il y a de plus simple,* it's the simplest thing in the world; *faire tout son possible,* to do one's utmost; *tout Rome y assistait,* all Rome was present; *il est tout le temps à se plaindre,* he's always complaining; *pendant toute la soirée,* throughout the evening; *somme toute,* on the whole. ‖ All, sole, only, one and only (seul); *pour toute réponse il ferma la porte,* his only reply was to shut the door. ‖ Any, every (chaque); *toute autre chose,* anything else; *tout autre que vous,* anyone but you; *tout homme qui se respecte,* every self-respecting man; *toute personne qui traversera la rue,* any person crossing the street; *nous avons toute raison de croire que,* we have every reason to believe that; *en tout temps,* at all times. ‖ Pl. All; *de tous côtés,* on all sides; *toutes les fois que,* whenever; *tous les deux jours,* every other day; *nous avons eu toutes les peines du monde,* we have had all the trouble in the world; *je les ai vus tous deux, tous trois,* I saw them both, I saw all three of them. ‖ **Tout-à-l'égout,** m. invar. TECHN. Main drainage, sewage system. ‖ **Toute-puissance,** f. invar. Omnipotence. ‖ **Tout-le-monde,** m. invar. *M. Tout-le-monde,* Mr. Average Man. ‖ **Tout-Paris,** m. invar. Fashionable Paris, the Parisian smart set (ou) socialites. ‖ **Tout-petit** (pl. *tout-petits*), m. Baby, tiny tot; *les tout-petits,* the very young. ‖ **Tout-puissant** (f. *toute-puissante,* pl. *tout-puissants, toutes-puissantes*), adj. Omnipotent, all-powerful, almighty; ECCLÉS. *le Tout-Puissant,* the Almighty. ‖ **Tout-terrain,** adj. Cross-country. ‖ **Tout-venant,** m. Ungraded

product; unscreened coal (houille); FIG. run of the mill, ragbag (v. VENANT).
— pr. indéf. (invariable au sing.; pl. m. **tous** [tus], f. **toutes** [tut]). All, everything; *après tout*, after all; *tout est bien qui finit bien*, all's well that ends well; *c'est facile comme tout*, it's as easy as anything; *c'est tout*, that's all; *c'est tout dire*, that's the long and the short of it; *c'est tout ce qu'il y a de plus amusant*, it's the funniest thing in the world; *je vais tout vous dire*, I'm going to tell you everything; *et tout et tout*, and all the rest of it; *je lui ai écrit trois fois en tout*, I wrote to him three times in all; *j'ai fait un peu de tout*, I have tried my hand at everything; *un homme à tout faire*, a handy man; a jack-of-all-trades; an all-round man; *il est capable de tout*, he is capable of anything, he will stick at nothing; *il a tout du campagnard*, he's the complete (ou) a thorough countryman, he's a countryman through and through; *il a tout de son père*, he's just like his father; *il mange de tout*, he will eat anything; *à tout prendre*, on the whole. ‖ Pl. All; *une bonne fois pour toutes*, once and for all; *ils sont tous partis*, they have all left; *nous, vous tous*, all of us, of you; *sortez tous!*, get out all of you!; *sortons tous!*, let's all get out!
— m. **Le tout**, all, the whole, the lot; everything; *le tout est de réussir*, the main thing is to succeed; *risquer le tout pour le tout*, to risk everything (ou) one's shirt (fam.); *ce n'est pas le tout que d'être riche*, being rich is not everything. ‖ Whole (aux charades). ‖ MATH. Whole.
— adv. Quite, wholly, entirely, completely, all, altogether, utterly; *elle est tout aimable, tout heureuse, toute belle*, she is very pleasant, happy, beautiful; *il est tout à son travail*, he is absorbed in his work; *tout autre chose*, quite another thing; *tout en blanc*, all in white; *tout chaud*, all hot; piping-hot (plat); *tout comme nous autres*, the same as (ou) just like the rest of us; *tout content*, perfectly happy; *tout à coup*, suddenly; all at once; *tout d'un coup*. in a moment; at a draught (en buvant); *tout doux!*, gently!, quietly!; *marcher tout droit*, to walk straight ahead; *se tenir tout droit*, to hold oneself very erect (ou) bolt upright; *tout en bas de, en haut de*, right at the bottom, top of; *tout éveillé*, wide awake; *tout fait*, ready-made (complet); already done (travail); *tout à fait*, quite, wholly, thoroughly, entirely, altogether, absolutely; exactly; dead (certain, sûr); *tout haut*, aloud; *tout à l'heure*, presently, directly, by and by (sens futur); just now (sens passé); *à tout à l'heure!*, see you soon!; cheerio for now!; *tout juste*, just so; *tout juste à temps*, in the nick of time; *tout en larmes*, weeping bitterly; *tout le long de*, all along; *tout de même*, all the same; *tout au moins*, at the least; *tout neuf*, brand-new; *tout nu*, stark naked; *un tout petit peu*, just a very little; *il y avait tout plein de boue*, there was mud everywhere; *tout au plus*, at the very most (ou) outside; *il le dirait tout le premier*, he would be the first to say so; *les tout premiers venus*, the very first arrivals (ou) comers; *de tout premier ordre*, of the very first order (ou) rank; *nous étions tout seuls*, we were all alone; *tout de suite*, at once; right away; *c'est tout un*, it's all the same; *tout à vous*, yours very truly (dans une lettre). ‖ While (en même temps que); *tout en parlant il termina la lettre*, he finished the letter while speaking. ‖ Although (bien que); *il s'engagea dans la rue tout en se rendant compte qu'il s'était trompé de chemin*, he turned down the street although he realized that he had lost his way. ‖ **Tout ... que**, although, though; *tout intelligent qu'il est*, intelligent though he is (ou) may be.

— loc adv. **Du tout au tout**, utterly, entirely. ‖ **En tout**, entirely; *les détails manquent en tout*, the details are wholly lacking. ‖ **Pas du tout, du tout**, not at all; by no means; not in the least (ou) slightest.
toutefois [tutfwa] adv. However, still, yet, nevertheless.
toutou [tutu] m. FAM. Doggie, bow-wow.
toux [tu] f. MÉD. Cough.
toxémie [tɔksemi] f. MÉD. Toxaemia, toxemia.
toxicité [-sisite] f. MÉD. Toxicity, poisonousness.
toxicologie [tɔksikɔlɔʒi] f. MÉD. Toxicology.
toxicologique [-lɔʒik] adj. MÉD. Toxicological.
toxicologue [-lɔg] s. MÉD. Toxicologist.
toxicomane [-man] s. MÉD. Drug addict.
toxicomanie [-mani] f. MÉD. Drug addiction.
toxine [tɔksin] f. MÉD. Toxin.
toxique [-sik] adj. MÉD. Toxic, poisonous. ‖ MILIT. Poison (gaz).
— m. MÉD. Poison.
trac [trak] m. Speed (d'une bête de somme). ‖ Track (du gibier). ‖ LOC. *Tout à trac*, thoughtlessly, heedlessly, without thinking.
trac m. FAM. Trepidation, funk (peur); examination nerves (à un examen); *avoir le trac*, to have the wind up, to be in a funk. ‖ THÉÂTR. Stage-fright.
traçage [trasaʒ] m. Tracing (d'un dessin); laying-out (d'un jardin); marking-out (d'un terrain de football).
traçant, ante [-sɑ̃, ɑ̃:t] adj. BOT. Running, creeping (racine). ‖ MILIT. *Balle traçante*, tracer-bullet.
traçante [-sɑ̃t] f. MILIT. Tracer-bullet, tracer.
tracas [trakɑ] m. Bother, bustle, confusion (d'un déménagement). ‖ Worry, bother, trouble, anxiety; *le tracas des affaires*, business worries. ‖ TECHN. Hoist-hole (dans une fabrique).
tracassant, ante [-sɑ̃, ɑ̃:t] adj. Worrying, bothersome.
tracassement [-smɑ̃] m. Worrying, bothering.
tracasser [-se] v. tr. To worry, to bother (inquiéter); to bother, to plague, to badger (tourmenter).
— v. pr. Se tracasser, to worry, to bother.
tracasserie [-ri] f. Teasing; worrying, bothering, pestering (action). ‖ Pl. Cares, anxieties, worries.
tracassier, ère [-sje, ɛ:r] adj. Fussy; pestering, interfering, badgering (personne); annoying, vexatious (restrictions).
— s. Busybody; harasser; fuss-pot (fam.).
trace [tras] f. Trace; trail, track, spoor (d'une bête); trial, footprint (de qqn); track, tyre- (ou) wheel-mark (d'une voiture); *marcher sur les traces de*, to follow in the footsteps of; *perdre, retrouver la trace*, to lose, to pick up the scent (ou) trail; *suivre qqn à la trace*, to follow s.o.'s trail. ‖ Sign; mark, scar, weal (d'une brûlure); *traces de fatigue*, signs of weariness. ‖ Trace (petite quantité); *traces de sang*, traces of blood. ‖ MÉD. Trace (d'albumine). ‖ SPORTS. *Faire la trace*, to lead the way; U. S. to blaze a trail. ‖ FIG. *Trace profonde*, deep impression.
tracé [-se] m. Tracing (d'un dessin); laying-out (d'un jardin, d'une route); marking-out (d'un terrain de football); *faire le tracé de*, to lay out, to mark out. ‖ Lay-out (du métro, d'une ville); lie (d'une route). ‖ MATH. Plotting, graph (d'une courbe); *faire le tracé de*, to plot.
tracer [trase] v. intr. (6). BOT. To run (plante). ‖ ZOOL. To burrow (taupes).
— v. tr. To draw (des caractères, une ligne); to draw, to trace out, to outline (un dessin, un plan); to lay out (un jardin, une voie); to map out (une route); to mark out (un terrain de football). ‖ NAUT. *Tracer la route*, to set the course. ‖ MATH. To plot (une courbe). ‖ FIG. To depict; *tracer le tableau de ses malheurs*, to tell the

story of one's misfortunes. ‖ Fig. To show, to indicate ; *tracer une ligne de conduite à*, to map out a policy for.

traceret [-srɛ] m. Techn. Scriber (outil).

traceur [-sœ:r] adj., m. Milit. Tracer.

trachéal, ale [trakeal] adj. Méd. Tracheal.

trachée [-ʃe] f. Bot., Zool., Méd. Trachea. ‖ Trachée-artère, f. Méd. Trachea, windpipe.

trachéen, enne [-keɛ̃, ɛn] adj. Zool. Tracheal.

trachéite [-keit] f. Méd. Tracheitis.

trachéotomie [-keotɔmi] f. Méd. Tracheotomy.

trachome [trako:m] m. Méd. Trachoma.

traçoir [traswa:r] m. Techn. Scriber.

tract [trakt] m. Tract. ‖ Milit. Propaganda leaflet ; *distribution de tracts par air*, leaflet raid (ou) U. S. drop.

tractabilité [traktabilite] f. Pliancy, ductility.

tractation [-sjɔ̃] f. Comm. Bargaining, dealing, deal ; negotiation.

tracté, ée [-te] adj. Tractor-drawn.

tracter v. tr. (1). To tow.

tracteur [-tœ:r] m. Tractor ; traction-engine.

tractif, ive [-tif, i:v] adj. Techn. Tractive. ‖ Aviat. Tractor (hélice).

traction [-sjɔ̃] f. Traction, pulling, drawing ; draught ; *force de traction*, tractive force ; *résistance à la traction*, tensile strength ; *système de traction*, haulage system ; *voiture à traction hippomobile, motrice*, horse-drawn, motor vehicle. ‖ Aviat. Thrust (de l'hélice). ‖ Ch. de f. Rolling-stock department. ‖ Sports. *Faire une traction*, to pull up to the bar ; *lutte à la corde de traction*, tug-of-war. ‖ Méd. Traction (de la langue). ‖ Traction-avant, f. Autom. Car with front-wheel drive ; *des gangsters en traction*, gangsters in a fast car.

tractus [-tys] m. Méd. Tract.

tradescantia [tradɛskɑ̃sja] m. Bot. Tradescantia, spiderwort, wandering Jew.

tradition [tradisjɔ̃] f. Tradition ; *de tradition*, traditional. ‖ Jur. Delivery ; handing over.

traditionalisme [-sjɔnalism] m. Traditionalism.

traditionaliste [-sjɔnalist] s. Traditionalist.

traditionnel, elle [-sjɔnɛl] adj. Traditional. ‖ Habitual, usual, customary. ‖ Standing (sujet de plaisanterie).

traditionnellement [-sjɔnɛlmɑ̃] adv. Traditionally.

traducteur, trice [tradyktœ:r, tris] s. Translator.

traduction [-sjɔ̃] f. Translating, translation (action). ‖ Translation (v. version) ; *tentative de traduction*, proposed rendering ; *traduction juxtalinéaire*, crib, U. S. trot (fam.). ‖ Interpretation.

traduire [tradɥi:r] v. tr. (85). To translate (*de*, from ; *en*, into) ; *impossible à traduire*, untranslatable. ‖ To explain, to interpret, to express (exprimer) ; *vous traduisez mal mon idée*, you misinterpret (ou) misconstrue me ; *son visage traduit son chagrin*, his face reveals his sorrow. ‖ Jur. *Traduire en justice*, to prosecute, to sue, to indict. ‖ Radio. To decode (une dépêche). — v. pr. **Se traduire**, to be translated ; *qui se traduit facilement*, easily translated (ou) translatable. ‖ To be shown (ou) expressed (*par*, in) [s'exprimer]. ‖ To come (ou) amount (*par*, to) [aboutir à].

traduisible [-zibl] adj. Translatable. ‖ Jur. *Traduisible en justice*, liable to prosecution.

Trafalgar [trafalgar] m. Géogr. Trafalgar. ‖ Fam. *Coup de Trafalgar*, sudden calamity.

trafic [trafik] m. Comm. Traffic ; *le trafic des armes*, arms traffic ; *faire le trafic de*, to traffic in. ‖ Ch. de f. Traffic ; *trafic marchandises, voyageurs*, goods, passenger traffic. ‖ Fig. Traffic ; *trafic d'influences*, corrupt practices.

traficoter [-kɔte] v. tr. (1). Fam. To tamper

with, to doctor (un vin, un moteur). ‖ Fam. To be up to.

trafiquant, ante [-kɑ̃, ɑ̃:t] s. Trafficker, racketeer ; *trafiquant en stupéfiants*, dope-peddler.

trafiquer [-ke] v. intr. Comm. To traffic. (V. spéculer.) ‖ Fig. To make money (*de*, out of) ; *trafiquer de son honneur*, to sell (ou) barter away one's honour. — v. tr. Fam. To tamper with, to doctor (un vin, un moteur). ‖ Fam. To be up to.

tragédie [traʒedi] f. Théâtr. Tragedy, tragic art, art of tragedy (art) ; tragedy (genre, pièce). ‖ Fig. Tragic event.

tragédien, enne [-djɛ̃, ɛn] s. Théâtr. Tragedian, tragic actor.

tragédienne [-djɛn] f. Théâtr. Tragedienne.

tragi-comédie [traʒikɔmedi] (pl. **tragi-comédies**) f. Théâtr. Tragi-comedy.

tragi-comique [-mik] (pl. **tragi-comiques**) adj. m. Tragi-comic.

tragique [traʒik] adj. Théâtr. Tragic. ‖ Fig. Tragic, tragical. — m. Tragic actor (acteur) ; tragic poet, writer of tragedies (auteur) ; tragedy, tragic art (genre). ‖ Fam. Tragic side, tragicalness (d'une histoire, d'une situation) ; *prendre les choses au tragique*, to take things too seriously ; to fly into a panic (ou) flap (fam.) ; *tourner au tragique*, to become serious.

tragiquement [-mɑ̃] adv. Tragically.

tragus [tragy:s] m. Méd. Tragus.

trahir [trai:r] v. tr. (2). To betray, to be false to, to abandon, to desert, to let down, to go back on (un ami) ; to betray (la confiance) ; to fail in, to fall short of (son devoir) ; to betray (son pays) ; to go against (ses sentiments) ; to violate, to be false to (ses serments) ; *ses forces le trahissent*, his strength is failing him. ‖ To betray, to show up, to reveal (divulguer) ; to give away (un secret) ; to reveal (sa pensée) ; *sa figure le trahit*, his face gives him away. ‖ To misrepresent (déformer) ; *l'expression a trahi sa pensée*, his words did not accurately express his thoughts. — v. pr. **Se trahir**, to betray oneself ; to give oneself away (fam.). ‖ To show, to appear (se manifester). — v. récipr. **Se trahir**, to betray (ou) deceive each other, to give each other away ; to let each other down (fam.).

trahison [traizɔ̃] f. Betrayal, betraying. ‖ Jur. Treason ; *haute trahison*, high treason. ‖ Fam. Treachery, perfidy, deceit, deception.

traille [trɑ:j] f. Naut. Trail-ferry (bac) ; trawl (chalut).

train [trɛ̃] m. Drove (de bœufs) ; procession (de voitures) ; *train de bois*, raft, float. ‖ Speed, pace, rate (v. allure) ; gait (d'un cheval) ; *à fond de train*, at full speed (ou) tilt ; *aller à un train d'enfer*, to go like the devil ; *aller bon, grand train*, to go at a good, cracking pace (ou) U. S. clip ; *aller son petit train*, to jog along ; *au train dont il va*, at the rate he's going ; *mener qqn bon train*, to keep s.o. on the move, to hustle s.o. about. ‖ Style (ou) manner (ou) mode (ou) way of living (mode de vie) ; *train de maison* (ou) *de vie*, style of living ; *mener grand train*, to live in style. ‖ Way, course, process (action) ; *en train de*, in the act (ou) process of ; *il était en train de lire*, he was reading ; *être en train*, to be under way ; *mettre qqch. en train*, to set sth. going, to start sth. off ; *mise en train*, starting off ; warming-up ; *les affaires vont leur train*, things are taking their normal course. ‖ Mood (humeur) ; *en train*, in good spirits (ou) form ; *être mal en train*, to feel out of sorts, not to feel up to the mark. ‖ Noise, row (bruit) ; din, uproar, shindy (tapage) ;

mener un train du tonnerre, to kick up a row. ‖ † Suite, retinue, attendants. ‖ Aᴜᴛᴏᴍ. Set (de pneus). ‖ Aᴠɪᴀᴛ. *Train d'atterrissage*, under-carriage, landing-gear. ‖ Cʜ. ᴅᴇ ꜰ. Train; *train de luxe*, Pullman-car express; *train de marchandises, de plaisir, de voyageurs*, goods (ou) U. S. freight, excursion, passenger train. ‖ Mɪʟɪᴛ. *Train des équipages*, Royal Army Service Corps, Supply Services. ‖ Sᴘᴏʀᴛs. Pace (allure); field (aux courses de chevaux); *mener le train*, to set the pace. ‖ Zᴏᴏʟ. *Train de derrière, de devant*, hind-quarters, fore-quarters (d'un cheval). ‖ Rᴀᴅɪᴏ. Train (d'ondes). ‖ Tᴇᴄʜɴ. *Train baladeur*, sliding gear; *train de laminoir*, rolling-mill; *mise en train*, setting up (en typographie). ‖ Fɪɢ. *Être dans le train*, to be up-to-date, to be abreast of the times; *manquer le train*, to miss the boat (ou) bus (rater une occasion); *prendre le train onze*, to go by Shanks's pony, to foot it, U. S. to hoof it. ‖ **Train-auto**, n. Cʜ. ᴅᴇ ꜰ. Car-sleeper. ‖ **Train-poste** (pl. *trains-poste* ou *-postes*), m. Cʜ. ᴅᴇ ꜰ. Mail-train. ‖ **Train-train**, m. invar. Fᴀᴍ. Routine; monotonous (ou) humdrum business (ou) existence; jogtrot; *le train-train de la vie*, the same old humdrum life; *aller son petit train-train*, to jog along.

traînage [trɛna:ʒ] m. Hauling. ‖ Sleigh transport; sledging (par traîneau). ‖ Aᴠɪᴀᴛ. Trail. ‖ Cʜ. ᴅᴇ ꜰ. Haulage. ‖ Rᴀᴅɪᴏ. Streaking (en T. V.).

traînailler [-nɑje] v. intr. (1). V. ᴛʀᴀÎɴᴀssᴇʀ.

traînance [-nɑ̃:s] s. Aᴠɪᴀᴛ. Drag.

traînant, ante [-nɑ̃, ɑ̃:t] adj. Dragging. ‖ Trailing (robe). ‖ Fɪɢ. Slow, sluggish, slouching, shambling, shuffling (démarche); droning (musique); dull, lifeless (style); drawling (voix); *il entra à pas traînants*, he shambled (ou) shuffled in.

traînard, arde [trɛna:r, ard] adj. Fᴀᴍ. Straggler, dawdler, laggard (retardataire); slowcoach, U. S. slowpoke (lambin).

traînasser [-nase] v. intr. (1). Fᴀᴍ. To loiter (ou) dawdle (ou) hang about; *traînasser dans les rues*, to loaf about the streets.
— v. tr. Fᴀᴍ. To spin out (une affaire); to drag out (une existence).

traîne [trɛ:n] f. Train (d'une robe). ‖ Seine- (ou) drag-net (filet). ‖ Drag (de cordier). ‖ Lᴏᴄ. *À la traîne*, being dragged (ou) pulled; in tow (bateau); behind (en arrière); *avoir qqch. à la traîne*, to have sth. dragging behind one; *laisser qqn à la traîne*, to leave s.o. in the lurch. ‖ **Traîne-savates**, m. inv. Loafer, loiterer, bum.

traîneau [trɛno] m. Sledge, sleigh, sled; *traîneau automobile*, motor sledge; *chien de traîneau*, husky, sledge dog; *se promener en traîneau*, to go sledging (ou) sleighing. ‖ Seine- (ou) drag-net (filet).

traînée [-ne] f. Trail (de fumée, de sang); streak, splash (de lumière); train (de poudre) [v. ᴛʀᴀᴄÉ]; *se répandre comme une traînée de poudre*, to spread like wildfire. ‖ Aᴠɪᴀᴛ. Drag (d'un avion); lag (d'une bombe). ‖ Pᴏᴘ. Trollop, drab (femme).

traînement [-nmɑ̃] m. Trailing, dragging (action); drawling (de la voix).

traîner [-ne] v. tr. (1). To drag (un canon, une charrette, un filet); to haul (un fardeau); to draw, to pull (des wagons). ‖ To lead away, to carry off, to drag along (qqn); *traîner qqn en prison*, to haul s.o. off to prison. ‖ To carry away (v. ᴄʜᴀʀʀɪᴇʀ); *rivière qui traîne du sable*, river that brings (ou) carries sand down with it. ‖ To be accompanied (ou) attended (avec, by); to bring; *traîner qqn partout avec soi*, to take s.o. about everywhere with one. ‖ To drag out (une existence morne). ‖ To drawl out (les mots); to drag (les pieds); *traîner la jambe*, to limp, to hobble; to be lame. ‖ To protract, to drag out, to spin out (une affaire, un discours); *traîner une*

affaire en longueur, to keep putting a matter off; to spin (ou) U. S. to drag a matter out. ‖ Nᴀᴜᴛ. To tow (en remorque). ‖ Zᴏᴏʟ. To drag. ‖ Fᴀᴍ. *Traîner la patte*, to limp along (boiter); to lag behind, to straggle (s'attarder).
— v. intr. To drag. ‖ To hang down (cheveux); to trail (manteau, robe). ‖ To shuffle along (marcheur). ‖ To fall back, to lag behind, to straggle (coureur); to trail behind (enfant). ‖ To loiter, to hang about, to dawdle about, to loaf about (v. ʟᴀᴍʙɪɴᴇʀ); *traîner dans les cafés, les rues*, to hang about the cafés, the streets; *traîner sur les mots*, to drawl out words. ‖ To lie about, to be scattered about; to knock about (fam.) [objet]; *laisser traîner ses clés*, to leave one's keys lying about (ou) around; *tout traîne dans cette maison*, things are lying about everywhere in this house; *cela traîne partout*, you can find that anywhere. ‖ To languish, to flag; to drag on, to hang fire (affaire); to drag, to be tedious, to be heavy going (discours, livre, pièce); *cela n'a pas traîné*, it didn't take long; *laisser traîner ses dettes*, to leave one's debts unpaid; *traîner en longueur*, to drag on. ‖ Mᴇᴅ. To linger on (maladie); to be in poor health (personne). ‖ Zᴏᴏʟ. *Traîner de l'aile*, to drag its wing.
— v. pr. **Se traîner**, to be dragged (ou) pulled (ou) trailed along (sens passif). ‖ To crawl (enfant); to drag oneself along (personne); *je ne peux pas me traîner plus loin*, I can't drag myself a step farther; *se traîner aux genoux de qqn*, to throw oneself at s.o.'s feet. ‖ Fɪɢ. To drag, to drag on (existence); to be slow (ou) tedious (pièce, roman); to hang heavy (temps).

traînerie [trɛnri] f. Slowness, delay; dawdling.

traîneur [-nœ:r] s. Trailer, dragger. ‖ Sledge- (ou) sleigh-driver (de traîneau). ‖ Dawdler, straggler (traînard).
— m. Straggler (traînard). ‖ Tᴇᴄʜɴ. Hauler (de wagonnets). ‖ Fᴀᴍ. *Traîneur de sabre*, swashbuckler (bretteur); old sweat (vétéran).

training [trɛniŋ] m. Sᴘᴏʀᴛs. Training (entraînement); sweat-shirt (pull), track- (ou U. S.) sweatsuit (survêtement); gym (ou) training shoe (chaussure).

traire [trɛ:r] v. tr. (11). Aɢʀɪᴄ. To draw (le lait); to milk (une vache).

trait [trɛ] adj. Tᴇᴄʜɴ. Wire-drawn (métal).

trait [trɛ] m. Drawing, pulling; pull (traction). ‖ Projection, throwing (lancement). ‖ Trace (longe). ‖ Gulp, draught (gorgée); *d'un trait*, at a draught, in one gulp; *à longs traits*, in long draughts. ‖ Stroke; mark; line; dash (ligne); *d'un trait de plume*, with a stroke of the pen. ‖ Flash (de lumière); ray (rayon). ‖ Piece (de médisance); shaft (de satire); *lancer un trait à qqn*, to have a dig at s.o. ‖ Deed, act (fait); episode; *trait d'histoire*, historic deed. ‖ Stroke, touch; *trait d'esprit*, flash of wit, witticism; *trait de génie*, stroke of genius. ‖ Reference; *avoir trait à*, to have a connection with, to be connected with, to have a bearing on, to refer to; *n'avoir aucunement trait à*, to have nothing to do with. ‖ Trait, characteristic, feature; *trait de caractère*, characteristic. ‖ Pl. Mᴇᴅ. Traits, features (du visage). ‖ Mɪʟɪᴛ. Arrow (flèche); dart, javelin (javelot); *partir comme un trait*, to be off like a shot. ‖ Gʀᴀᴍᴍ. *Trait d'union*, hyphen. ‖ Mᴜs. Run; brilliant passage. ‖ Aʀᴛs. Line; outline; contour; *trait pour trait*, line for line; *dessin au trait*, outline drawing; *gravure au trait*, line engraving. ‖ Sᴘᴏʀᴛs. First move (aux échecs). ‖ Tᴇᴄʜɴ. Cut (de scie). ‖ Fɪɢ. *Décrire une situation à grands traits*, to give a general (ou) rough outline of a situation; *peindre l'amitié en traits touchants*, to portray friendship in touching terms; *trait d'union*, link.

traitable [trɛtabl] adj. Accommodating, understanding (caractère); tractable, manageable (personne). ‖ Treatable (sujet); *difficilement traitable,* hard to tackle (ou) to deal with. ‖ TECHN. Tractable, malleable, ductile (matière).

traitant, ante [-tɑ̃, ɑ̃:t] adj. *Médecin traitant,* medical practitioner.

traite [trɛt] f. Stretch (de chemin); stage (de voyage); *faire une longue traite,* to cover a long distance. ‖ Tradc, trading (vente); *traite des blanches,* white slave trade (ou) traffic; *traite de l'ivoire,* ivory trade; *traite des noirs,* slave-trade. ‖ FIN. Bill, draft; *traite à vue,* sight draft; *faire traite sur,* to draw on. ‖ AGRIC. Milking (action); milk (lait). ‖ LOC. *Tout d'une traite,* at a stretch; in one stage; at a sitting; straight off.

traité [trɛte] m. Treatise (livre). ‖ JUR. Treaty, agreement (entre gouvernements); *traité de paix,* peace treaty. ‖ COMM. Agreement; contract; *être en traité avec qqn pour,* to be negotiating with s.o. for.

traitement [-tmɑ̃] m. Treatment; *traitement brutal,* rough handling; *subir de mauvais traitements,* to be ill-treated. ‖ Salary (d'un fonctionnaire); *sans traitement,* unpaid, unsalaried. ‖ MÉD. Treatment; *en traitement,* under treatment. ‖ TECHN. Processing (des matières premières).

traiter [-te] v. tr. (1). To treat, to deal with, to behave towards (agir avec); to welcome, to receive (recevoir); *traiter mal qqn,* to treat s.o. badly, to be unkind to s.o. ‖ To treat, to feed, to entertain (régaler); *l'aubergiste nous a bien traités,* the innkeeper did us well (ou) U. S. did well by us. ‖ To treat, to handle, to tackle, to deal with, to discuss (une question); *traiter Shelley comme un poète de l'amour,* to discuss Shelley as a poet of love. ‖ To handle, to deal with, to attend to, to negotiate, to transact (une affaire); to arrange (un mariage). ‖ To call; *traiter qqn de voleur,* to call s.o. a thief. ‖ MÉD. To treat (un malade, une maladie); *on la traite pour ses rhumatismes,* she is being treated for her rheumatism. ‖ TECHN. To treat, to process (un minerai).
— v. intr. To negotiate, to deal (*avec,* with; *de,* for) [négocier]. ‖ To treat (*de,* of); to deal (*de,* with) [concerner].
— v. pr. **Se traiter,** to look after oneself; *se traiter bien,* to do oneself well; U. S. to do well by oneself. ‖ To be discussed (question). ‖ MÉD. To be treated. ‖ COMM. To be negotiated.
— v. récipr. **Se traiter,** to behave towards each other. ‖ To treat each other (s'offrir). ‖ To call each other (s'appeler); *se traiter de voleurs,* to call each other thieves.

traiteur [-tœ:r] m. Eating-house (ou) restaurant keeper.

traître, esse [trɛ:tr, ɛs] adj. Vicious, dangerous (animal); traitorous, treacherous, perfidious, false (personne). ‖ Treacherous, dangerous (escalier); false, insidious (paroles); insidious (vin). ‖ LOC. *Il n'en a pas dit un traître mot,* he didn't breathe a word about it.
— m. Traitor (homme); betrayer; *en traître,* treacherously. ‖ THÉÂTR. Villain.

traîtresse [-trɛs] f. Traitress; betrayer.

traîtreusement [-trøzmɑ̃] adv. Treacherously.

traîtrise [-tri:z] f. Treachery, treacherousness, traitorousness. ‖ Piece of treachery, traitorous deed (acte).

trajectoire [traʒɛktwa:r] adj. MATH. *Ligne trajectoire,* trajectory.
— f. Trajectory; path.

trajet [traʒɛ] m. Journey, way (v. CHEMIN, PARCOURS); *un trajet de cinq heures,* a five hours' journey; *faire une partie du trajet à pied,* to walk part of the way; *pendant le trajet,* on the way; *sur le trajet de,* on the way to. ‖ NAUT. Passage,

voyage, crossing. ‖ MILIT. Path, course (d'un projectile). ‖ AUTOM. Journey, drive, ride, run. ‖ AVIAT. Flight. ‖ CH. DE F. Journey. ‖ MÉD. Course (d'un nerf).

tralala [tralala] m. Tra-la-la (refrain). ‖ FAM. *En grand tralala,* all togged (ou) dolled up, dressed up to the nines; *faire du tralala,* to make a big fuss (ou) to-do.

tram [tram] m. V. TRAMWAY.

tramail [trama:j] m. Trammel net, trammel.

trame [tra:m] f. Plot, intrigue, conspiracy (complot). ‖ RADIO. Frame (en télévision). ‖ TECHN. Cross-ruled screen (en photographie). ‖ TECHN. Woof (en textile); tram (soie). ‖ FIG. Texture (d'un roman); web; thread (de la vie).

tramer [trame] v. tr. (1). TECHN. To weave (un tissu). ‖ FIG. To weave, to hatch (un complot).
— v. pr. **Se tramer,** to be hatched, to brew.

trameur [-mœ:r] s. Weft-winder (de textile).

trameuse [-mø:z] f. TECHN. Weft-winding machine.

traminot [tramino] m. Tramways employee, U. S. streetcar (ou) trolley car employee.

tramontane [tramɔtan] f. Tramontane, north wind (vent).

tramp [trɑ:p] m. NAUT. Tramp steamer.

tramway [tramwɛ] m. Tramway (voie); tramcar, U. S. streetcar, trolley car, cable car (voiture).

tranchage [trɑ̃ʃa:ʒ] m. TECHN. Cutting.

tranchant, ante [-ʃɑ̃, ɑ̃:t] adj. Sharp, keen (couteau); cutting (outil); *écuyer tranchant,* gentleman carver. ‖ Violently contrasting; glaring (couleurs). ‖ FIG. Trenchant (argument); decisive (paroles); cutting, sharp, peremptory (ton). ‖ FIG. Self-assertive; dogmatic, downright (personne).
— m. Cutting edge, edge (d'un couteau); *à deux tranchants,* two-edged. ‖ FIG. *Argument à double tranchant,* double-edged argument, argument that cuts both ways.

tranche [trɑ̃:ʃ] f. Slab (de marbre). ‖ CULIN. Rasher (de bacon); round (de bœuf); slice (de pain); *en tranches,* in slices, sliced; *couper en tranches,* to slice, to cut into slices; *couper par tranches,* to cut slices off; *tranche napolitaine,* Neapolitan ice-cream. ‖ MILIT. Face (d'un canon). ‖ CH. DE F. *Tranche de voitures,* portion. ‖ FIN. Sum (d'argent); portion, block (d'émission); instalment (d'emprunt). ‖ MATH. Group (de chiffres); section (verticale). ‖ AGRIC. Ridge (de sillon); slice of earth (terre). ‖ TECHN. Chisel, set (outil). ‖ TECHN. Edge (de livre, de pièce de monnaie, de planche); *doré sur tranche,* gilt-edged. ‖ COMM. Batch; *par tranches de,* in batches of. ‖ FIG. Slice, cross-section (de vie). ‖ FAM. *S'en payer une tranche,* to have fun, to have one's fling.

tranché, ée [trɑ̃ʃe] adj. Distinct, clear-cut, well defined.

tranchée f. MILIT. Trench; entrenchment (v. BOYAU); *guerre de tranchées,* trench warfare. ‖ CH. DE F. Cutting. ‖ AGRIC. Trench, drain; clearing, cutting (dans une forêt). ‖ MÉD. Gripes, colic (v. COLIQUE); *tranchées utérines,* after-pains. ‖ **Tranchée-abri,** f. MILIT. Shelter-trench.

tranchefile [-ʃfi:l] f. Headband.

trancher [-ʃe] v. tr. (1). To cut; to cut off, to sever (couper); *on lui trancha la tête,* his head was cut off (ou) chopped off. ‖ To slice (du pain). ‖ FIG. To settle, to solve (une difficulté); to cut short (une discussion); to cut short (ses jours); *trancher le mot,* to speak bluntly (ou) plainly.
— v. intr. To cut (outil, rasoir). ‖ MÉD. *Trancher dans le vif,* to cut into the flesh. ‖ FIG. To contrast sharply (caractères); to stand out clearly (couleurs); to be dogmatic (ou) positive; to lay down the law (personne); *trancher du bel esprit,* to set up as (ou) for a wit; *trancher du grand seigneur,*

to give oneself lordly airs; *trancher dans le vif,* to take drastic measures.

tranchet [-ʃɛ] m. TECHN. Paring-knife (de cordonnier); anvil-cutter (d'enclume).

trancheur [-ʃœːr] m. Cutter.

tranchoir [-ʃwaːr] m. CULIN. Carving-knife (couteau); trencher (plateau). ‖ ZOOL. Moorish idol.

tranquille [trɑ̃kil] adj. Still (air); still, placid (eau); calm (mer); quiet, peaceful (quartier, rue, ville). ‖ Tranquil, peaceful, serene, untroubled, undisturbed (âme, conscience); easy (conscience); quiet (vie); *dormir tranquille,* to sleep in peace; *je n'ai pas l'esprit tranquille,* I'm uneasy in my mind; *laissez-moi tranquille,* leave me alone; *soyez tranquille à ce sujet,* don't worry about that. ‖ Quiet (gens); *personne qui ne peut pas rester tranquille,* fidget, fidgety person; *tenez-vous tranquille,* keep quiet (ou) still.

tranquillement [-lmɑ̃] adv. Tranquilly, quietly.

tranquillisant, ante [-lizɑ̃, ɑ̃ːt] adj. Tranquillizing; soothing, calming (effet); reassuring (nouvelle).
— m. MÉD. Tranquillizer.

tranquilliser [-lize] v. tr. (1). To tranquillize. ‖ To soothe, to calm, to quieten (l'esprit); to reassure (qqn). [V. APAISER, RASSURER.]
— v. pr. **Se tranquilliser,** to calm down (mer). ‖ To be reassured, to set one's mind at rest (personne).

tranquillité [-lite] f. Tranquillity; quietness, peace, calm; stillness (de l'air, du soir); calmness (de la mer); calm, calmness (de qqn). ‖ Tranquillity, serenity, peace (de l'esprit).

transaction [trɑ̃saksjɔ̃] f. JUR. Compromise, arrangement, settlement. ‖ COMM. Transaction, deal; business.

transactionnel, elle [-sjɔnɛl] adj. Having the nature of a compromise.

transafricain, aine [trɑ̃zafrikɛ̃, ɛn] adj. GÉOGR. Trans-African.

transalpin, ine [trɑ̃zalpɛ̃, in] adj. GÉOGR. Transalpine.

transaméricain, aine [trɑ̃zamerikɛ̃, ɛn] adj. GÉOGR. Trans-American.

transaminase [trɑ̃samina:z] f. MÉD. Transaminase.

transat [trɑ̃zat] m. V. TRANSATLANTIQUE.

transatlantique [trɑ̃zatlɑ̃tik] adj. GÉOGR. Transatlantic.
— m. Deck-chair (fauteuil). ‖ NAUT. Atlantic (ou) ocean liner.

transbahuter [trɑ̃sbayte] v. tr. (1). FAM. To hump, to cart.
— v. pr. **Se transbahuter,** FAM. To trek, to traipse.

transbordement [trɑ̃sbɔrdəmɑ̃] m. Ferrying across (d'une rive à l'autre). ‖ NAUT. Trans-shipment, transhipment. ‖ CH. DE F. Transfer.

transborder [-de] v. intr. (1). NAUT. To trans-ship, to tranship.
— v. tr. To ferry across (d'une rive à l'autre). ‖ NAUT. To tranship. ‖ CH. DE F. To transfer.

transbordeur [-dœːr] m. Transporter bridge (pont). ‖ NAUT. Train-ferry (bac).

transcanadien, enne [trɑ̃skanadjɛ̃, ɛn] adj. Trans-Canada.

transcaucasien, enne [-zjɛ̃, ɛn] adj. GÉOGR. Transcaucasian.

transcendance [trɑ̃ssɑ̃dɑ̃ːs] f. Transcendence, transcendency.

transcendant, ante [-dɑ̃, ɑ̃ːt] adj. Transcendent. ‖ MATH. Transcendental.

transcendantal, ale [-dɑ̃tal] adj. Transcendental.

transcendantalisme [-dɑ̃talism] m. PHILOS. Transcendentalism.

transcender [-de] v. tr. (1). To transcend.

transcodage [trɑ̃skɔda:ʒ] m. Code conversion, conversion.

transcoder [-kɔde] v. tr. (1). To convert.

transcontinental, ale [trɑ̃skɔ̃tinɑ̃tal] adj. Transcontinental.

transcripteur [trɑ̃skriptœːr] m. Transcriber.

transcription [-sjɔ̃] f. Transcription; transcribing. ‖ JUR. Recording, registration. ‖ FIN. Posting.

transcrire [trɑ̃skriːr] v. tr. (44). To transcribe, to copy. ‖ To write out (des notes). ‖ MUS. To transcribe. ‖ JUR. To record, to register. ‖ FIN. To post, to post up (au grand livre).

transe [trɑ̃ːs] f. MÉD. Trance. ‖ Pl. Fear, dread, fright, mortal anxiety; apprehension; *être dans les transes,* to be shivering (ou) quaking in one's shoes (fam.).

transept [trɑ̃sɛpt] m. ARCHIT. Transept.

transférable [trɑ̃sferabl] adj. Transferable.

transfèrement [-fɛrmɑ̃] m. Transfer, transference.

transférer [-fere] v. tr. (5). To transfer, to transport, to remove, to convey (à, to; de, from) [déplacer]. ‖ ECCLÉS. To translate. ‖ JUR. To assign, to make over (ses biens); to convey (une propriété). ‖ FIN. To transfer. ‖ COMM. *Transféré à,* removed to.

transfert [-fɛːr] m. Transfer, transference. ‖ JUR. Assignment (de biens); transfer (de propriété). ‖ ECCLÉS. Translation. ‖ FIN. Transfer. ‖ COMM. Removal. ‖ TECHN. *Papier de transfert,* transfert paper (en photographie). ‖ PSYCH. Transference.

transfiguration [trɑ̃sfigyrasjɔ̃] f. Transfiguration.

transfigurer [-re] v. tr. (1). To transfigure.
— v. pr. **Se transfigurer,** to be (ou) become transfigured.

transfiler [trɑ̃sfile] v. tr. (1). NAUT. To lace.

transfo [trɑ̃sfo] m. ÉLECTR., FAM. Transformer.

transformable [trɑ̃sfɔrmabl] adj. Transformable. ‖ AUTOM. Convertible.

transformateur, trice [-matœːr, tris] adj. ÉLECTR. Transforming.
— m. ÉLECTR. Transformer.

transformation [-masjɔ̃] f. Transformation. ‖ PHILOS. Conversion. ‖ MATH., TECHN. Transformation. ‖ THÉÂTR. Transformation, wig (perruque); *acteur à transformations,* quick-change artist. ‖ ZOOL. Metamorphosis (des insectes). ‖ TECHN. Alteration (modification).

transformationnel, elle [-masjɔnɛl] adj. GRAMM. Transformational.

transformer [-me] v. tr. (1). To transform, to convert, to change, to turn (en, into); to alter (en, to). ‖ To make over (une robe). ‖ PHILOS. To convert. ‖ MATH. To transform. ‖ SPORTS. To convert (un essai).
— v. pr. **Se transformer,** to be transformed, to change, to turn (en, into); to turn (en, to, into).

transformisme [-mism] m. Transformism.

transformiste [-mist] adj. PHILOS. Transformist.
— s. PHILOS. Transformist. ‖ THÉÂTR. Quick-change artist.

transfuge [trɑ̃sfy:ʒ] m. MILIT. Deserter to the enemy. ‖ FIG. Deserter, runaway (fuyard); turncoat (renégat).

transfuser [trɑ̃sfyze] v. tr. (1). To transfuse, to decant (transvaser). ‖ MÉD. To transfuse (du sang). ‖ FIG. To instil (à, into).

transfusion [-zjɔ̃] f. MÉD. Transfusion.

transgresser [trɑ̃sgrese] v. tr. (1). To transgress, to infringe, to contravene, to trespass against, to break (la loi).

transgresseur [-sœːr] m. Transgressor.

transgressif, ive [-sif, iːv] adj. Transgressive.

transgression [-sjɔ̃] f. Transgression.

transhumance [trɑ̃zymɑ̃:s] f. Transhumance.

transhumant, ante [-mɑ̃, ɑ̃:t] adj. AGRIC. Transhumant, on the move.

transhumer [-me] v. tr., intr. (1). AGRIC. To transhume, to move to another pasturage.

transi, ie [trãsi] adj. Perished, chilled to the bone (de froid). ‖ FIG. Paralysed, transfixed (de peur); bashful, faint-hearted (de timidité).

transiger [trãziʒe] v. intr. (7). To compromise, to compound, to come to an understanding (ou) agreement, to come to terms (avec, with). ‖ FIG. To compound (avec, with).

transir [trãsi:r] v. tr. (2). To chill, to benumb (de froid). ‖ FIG. To paralyze, to transfix (de peur). — v. intr. To be chilled (ou) benumbed (de froid). ‖ FIG. To be paralyzed (ou) transfixed (de peur).

transistor [trãzistɔr] m. ÉLECTR. Transistor. ‖ RADIO. Transistor radio, transistor.

transistoriser [-rize] v. tr. (1). ÉLECTR. To transistorize.

transit [trãzit] m. COMM. Transit; de transit, transit; en transit, in transit. ‖ CH. DE F. Through traffic.

transitaire [-tɛ:r] adj. COMM. Pertaining to the transit of goods (commerce); through which goods pass in transit (pays). — m. COMM. Forwarding agent.

transiter [-te] v. intr. (1). COMM. To be in transit. — v. tr. COMM. To send (ou) convey in transit; to forward.

transitif, ive [-tif, i:v] adj. GRAMM. Transitive. ‖ GÉOL. Transitional.

transition [-sjɔ̃] f. Transition; faire une transition, to effect a transition. ‖ MUS. Modulation. ‖ GÉOL. De transition, transitional.

transitivement [-tivmã] adv. Transitively.

transitivité [-tivite] f. GRAMM., MATH. Transitiveness, transitivity.

transitoire [-twa:r] adj. Transitory, transient, fleeting, ephemeral (passager). ‖ JUR. Transitional, temporary, provisional (loi, mesure).

transitoirement [twarmã] adv. Transitorily.

Transjordanie [trãsʒɔrdani] f. GÉOGR. Transjordania.

translateur [trãslatœ:r] m. RADIO. Translator, repeater.

translatif, ive [-tif, i:v] adj. JUR. Translative; acte translatif, transfer, conveyance.

translation [-sjɔ̃] f. Transfer. ‖ ECCLÉS., TECHN. Translation. ‖ JUR. Transferring, conveying (de biens). ‖ RADIO. Relaying.

translit(t)ération [trãsliterasjɔ̃] f. Transliteration.

translucide [trãslysid] adj. Translucent.

translucidité [-dite] f. Translucence, translucency.

transmetteur [trãsmɛtœ:r] adj. RADIO. Transmitting. ‖ NAUT. Signals. — m. RADIO. Transmitter. ‖ NAUT. Ship's telegraph; transmitter.

transmettre [-mɛtr] v. tr. (64). To forward (une lettre); to transmit, to convey, to pass on (un ordre). ‖ JUR. To hand down (ou) on (un héritage, un nom); to transfer, to convey (une propriété). ‖ RADIO. To transmit, to send, to relay, to broadcast (un message). ‖ PHYS. To transmit (la lumière, les sons). ‖ MÉD. To transmit, to pass on (une maladie). — v. pr. Se transmettre, MÉD. To be transmitted (ou) passed on, to spread (maladie).

transmigration [trãsmigrasjɔ̃] f. Transmigration.

transmigrer [-gre] v. intr. (1). To transmigrate.

transmissibilité [trãsmisibilite] f. Transmissibility. ‖ JUR. Transferability.

transmissible [-sibl] adj. Transmissible, transmittable. ‖ JUR. Transferable; biens transmissibles, hereditaments.

transmission [-sjɔ̃] f. Forwarding (d'une lettre); transmission, conveying, passing on (d'un ordre).

‖ MILIT., NAUT. Pl. Signals; officier des transmissions, signals officer. ‖ JUR. Handing down (ou) on (d'un héritage); transfer, conveyance; assignment (d'une propriété); transmission des pouvoirs, handing over. ‖ MÉD. Transmission (d'une maladie). ‖ RADIO. Transmission, transmitting, sending, relaying, broadcasting (d'un message). ‖ PHYS. Transmission (de la lumière, des sons). ‖ TECHN. Transmission (du mouvement); driving-belt (courroie); transmission gear, gearing, drive (mécanisme); arbre, engrenage de transmission, driving-shaft, -gear. ‖ FIG. Handing down (ou) on (d'une expérience, d'une tradition); transmission (de pensée).

transmuable [trãsmɥabl] adj. Transmutable.

transmuer [-e] v. tr. (1). To transmute (en, into).

transmutation [trãsmytasjɔ̃] f. Transmutation.

transocéanique [trãsɔseanik] adj. Transoceanic.

transparaître [trãsparɛ:tr] v. intr. (74). To show through.

transparence [-rã:s] f. Transparency.

transparent, ente [-rã, ã:t] adj. Transparent. (V. TRANSLUCIDE.) ‖ FIG. Clear, obvious (allusion). — m. Transparency (tableau). ‖ Underlines, black lines (feuille).

transpercement [trãspɛrsəmã] m. Transpiercing; transfixion.

transpercer [-se] v. tr. (5). To transpierce; to transfix. ‖ To shoot through (d'une balle); to run through (d'une épée); to stab (d'un poignard); la pluie le transperça, the rain drenched him; tunnel qui transperce une montagne, tunnel which runs through a mountain.

transpiration [trãspirasjɔ̃] f. MÉD. Perspiring, sweating (action); perspiration, sweat (sueur); en transpiration, in a sweat. ‖ BOT. Transpiration. ‖ FIG. Transpiring, coming to light, leaking out.

transpirer [-re] v. intr. (1). MÉD. To perspire, to sweat (v. SUER); il transpire des pieds, his feet perspire; he has sweaty feet (fam.). ‖ BOT. To transpire. ‖ FIG. To transpire, to come to light, to leak out (v. PERCER).

transplant [trãsplã] m. MÉD. Transplant.

transplantable [-tabl] adj. AGRIC., MÉD., FIG. Transplantable.

transplantation [-tasjɔ̃] f. AGRIC., MÉD., FIG. Transplantation, transplanting (action). ‖ MÉD. Transplant (greffe).

transplanter [-te] v. tr. (1). AGRIC., MÉD., FIG. To transplant. — v. pr. Se transplanter, to move (ou) settle elsewhere.

transport [trãspɔ:r] m. Transport, conveyance, carriage, removal (v. TRANSFERT); capacité de transport, carrying capacity; compagnie de transport, forwarding company; frais de transport, freight charges; moyens de transport, transport. ‖ NAUT. Transport (navire); transport de troupes, troop transport, troop-ship. ‖ JUR. Assignment (de dettes); transfer (d'une rente); transport sur les lieux, visit to the scene. ‖ MÉD. Transport au cerveau, stroke (attaque); delirium, brain-storm (délire). ‖ GÉOL. Terrain de transport, alluvial deposit. ‖ FIN. Balance brought forward; transfer (d'un compte). ‖ ÉLECTR. Conveyance (d'énergie). ‖ TECHN. Courroie de transport, conveyor belt. ‖ FIG. Burst, outburst, fit, paroxysm (de colère); transport, ecstasy, rapture, paroxysm (de joie); enthusiastically. ‖ Transport-hôpital (pl. transports-hôpitaux) m. NAUT. Hospital-ship.

transportable [trãspɔrtabl] adj. Transportable; able (ou) fit to be moved (malade).

transporté [-te] s. JUR. Transported convict. — adj. Transported; carried; transporté par air, flown to. ‖ FIG. Transported; carried away, beside oneself (de colère, de joie).

transporter [-te] v. tr. (1). To transport, to

transfer, to convey, to carry, to remove, to take. ‖ Aviat. *Transporter par avion*, to fly. ‖ Jur. To transfer, to make over. ‖ Fin. To carry over; to transfer. ‖ Théâtr. *Transporter sur la scène*, to stage. ‖ Fig. To transport, to enrapture, to thrill; to carry away (de colère, de joie); *transporter qqn en un pays féerique*, to carry s.o. off (ou) away to an enchanted land.
— v. pr. Se **transporter**, to go, to take oneself, to travel, to repair. ‖ Jur. *Se transporter sur les lieux*, to visit the scene. ‖ Fig. To project oneself (dans l'avenir); to take oneself back (dans le passé).

transporteur [-tœ:r] adj. Techn. Conveying. ‖ Naut. Transport (navire).
— m. Transporter, carrier, forwarding agent. ‖ Techn. Conveyor; *transporteur aérien*, cableway, aerial ropeway.

transposable [trãspozabl] adj. Transposable.

transposer [-ze] v. pr. (1). To transpose.

transpositeur, trice [-zitœ:r, tris] adj. Mus. Transposing.
— Mus. Transposer.

transpositif, ive [-zitif, i:v] adj. Transpositive.

transposition [-zisjɔ̃] f. Transposition. ‖ Ciném. Dubbing (d'un film).

transpyrénéen, enne [trãspirenɛ̃, ɛn] adj. Géogr. Trans-Pyrenean.

transrhénan, ane [-renã, an] adj. Géogr. Trans-rhenane, beyond the Rhine.

transsaharien, enne [-saarjɛ̃, ɛn] Géogr. Trans-Saharan.

transsexualisme [-sɛksyalism] m. Psych. Trans(s)exualism.

transsibérien, enne [-siberjɛ̃, ɛn] adj. Géogr. Trans-Siberian.

transsonique [trãssɔnik] adj. Aviat. Transonic.

transsubstantiation [trãssypstãsjasjɔ̃] f. Ecclés. Transubstantiation.

transsubstantier [-sje] v. tr. (1). Ecclés. To transubstantiate.

transsudation [trãssydasjɔ̃] f. Transudation.

transsuder [-de] v. tr., intr. (1). To transude.

transuranien [trãsyranjɛ̃] adj. Transuranic.

transvasement [trãsvazmã] m. Decanting.

transvaser [-ze] v. tr. (1). To decant.
— v. pr. Se **transvaser**, to siphon.

transversal, ale [trãsvɛrsal] adj. Cross, transverse (rayure, barre, coupe); cross-country (route, ligne de chemin de fer); cross-town (ligne de métro); side (rue). ‖ Math. Transversal (droite). ‖ Méd. Transverse (artère).

transversale f. Cross-country link; cross-town line. ‖ Math. Transversal.

transversalement [-salmã] adv. Cross-wise, across, transversely.

transverse [trãsvɛrs] adj., m. Méd., Math. Transverse.

transvestisme [trãsvɛstism] m. V. Travestisme.

trapèze [trapɛ:z] adj. Méd. Trapezius (muscle); trapezium (os).
— m. Math. Trapezium. ‖ Méd. Trapezius. ‖ Sports. Trapeze.

trapéziforme [trapeziform] adj. Math. Trapeziform.

trapéziste [-zits] s. Sports. Trapezist, trapeze-artist, U. S. aerialist.

trapézoïdal, ale [-zoidal] adj. Trapezoidal.

trapézoïde [-zoid] m. Techn. Trapezoid.

trappe [trap] f. Trap, trap-door. ‖ Hatchway, sliding-door (porte à coulisse). ‖ Trap, pitfall (piège).

Trappe f. Ecclés. Trappist monastery (monastère); Trappist order (ordre).

trappeur [-pœ:r] m. Trapper.

trappillon [-pijɔ̃] m. Trap-door. ‖ Théâtr. Slot.

trappiste [-pist] adj., m. Ecclés. Trappist.

trappistine [-pistin] f. Ecclés. Trappistine.

trapu, ue [trapy] adj. Thickset, squat, stocky, dumpy; stubby (fam.).

traquenard [trakna:r] m. Trap; booby-trap. ‖ Zool. Racking gait (allure); racker (cheval). ‖ Fig. Pitfall; *être pris dans son propre traquenard*, to be hoist with one's own petard, to fall into one's own trap.

traquer [trake] v. tr. (1). To hem in (entourer); to track down, to pursue, to run to earth (serrer de près); *regard de bête traquée*, hunted look.

traquet [trakɛ] m. Mill-clapper (de moulin). ‖ Zool. Stonechat (oiseau).

traqueur [trakœ:r] m. Beater. ‖ Tracker (en Afrique).

trauma [troma] m. Psych. Trauma (choc émotif).

traumatique [tromatik] adj. Méd. Traumatic.

traumatisant, ante [-tizã, ã:t] adj. Fig. Traumatic (expérience).

traumatiser [-tize] v. tr. (1). Méd., Psych. To traumatize.

traumatisme [-tism] m. Méd., Psych. Trauma (choc, blessure); traumatism (troubles résultant d'un choc).

traumatologie [-tɔlɔʒi] f. Méd. Traumatology.

travail [trava:j] (pl. **travaux** [travo]) m. Work; toil; labour (labeur); *travail intellectuel, manuel*, brain-, manual work; *travail à la pièce*, piece-work; *travail en série*, mass production; *travail d'équipe*, team-work; *avoir le travail facile*, to work easily; *vêtements de travail*, working-clothes; *ne vous tuez pas au travail*, don't work yourself to death. ‖ Work, job, occupation; *cesser le travail*, to down tools, to go on strike (grévistes); *être sans travail*, to be out of work; *les sans-travail*, the out-of-work, the unemployed. ‖ Piece of work (ouvrage); *un travail délicat*, a delicate piece of work. ‖ Workmanship (art); *bijou d'un beau travail*, jewel of fine workmanship. ‖ Exercise, practice (pratique); *coup qui demande beaucoup de travail*, stroke requiring a lot of practice. ‖ Shrinking (du bois); working (du vin). ‖ Work, undertaking (entreprise); *travaux publics*, public works; *ministère des Travaux publics*, Ministry of Works; U. S. Public Works Administration; *travaux de recherche*, research work; *les travaux sont bien avancés*, the work is making good headway. ‖ Labour; *Bureau international du travail*, International Labour Office; *Inspecteur du travail*, factory inspector; *ministère du Travail*, Ministry of Labour. ‖ Business, transactions, proceedings (d'une commission); *séance de travail*, business meeting. ‖ Work (étude écrite); *travaux pratiques*, tutorial(s) (à l'Université). ‖ Agric. *Travaux de la campagne*, farm-work. ‖ Méd. Labour, childbirth, travail; *femme en travail*, woman in labour. ‖ Jur. Labour; *travaux forcés à perpétuité*, penal servitude for life. ‖ Techn. Power. ‖ Loc. *Les travaux d'Hercule*, the labours of Hercules.

travail [trava:j] (pl. **travails** [trava:j]) m. Frame, sling.

travaillé, ée [travaje] adj. Worked. ‖ Tormented (par une idée); exhausted (par une maladie). ‖ Techn. Wrought (fer). ‖ Géogr. Weathered (rocher). ‖ Agric. Cultivated; ploughed (terre). ‖ Fig. Worked up (opinion); elaborate, highly polished (style).

travailler v. tr. (1). To work at, to study (une langue). ‖ To bestow care on, to polish (son style, ses vers). ‖ To work, to shape, to fashion (du bois, du métal). ‖ Mus. To practise (le piano). ‖ Culin. To knead (la pâte). ‖ Agric. To work, to till, to cultivate, to plough (la terre). ‖ Zool. To exercise (un cheval). ‖ Techn. To work up

(un cliché) ; *travailler au marteau,* to beat out, to hammer out (un métal). ‖ FIG. To work up, to stir up, to work upon (le peuple) ; to tamper with (des témoins). ‖ FAM. To trouble, to upset ; to worry, to obsess (tourmenter) ; *il y a une chose qui me travaille,* there is something bothering me ; *la fièvre le travaille,* he is racked with fever.
— v. intr. To work, to toil ; to labour ; *travailler tard dans la nuit,* to work late into the night, to burn the midnight oil. ‖ To work, to have a job, to be employed (être employé). ‖ To warp, to shrink (bois) ; to stretch, to give (corde) ; to fade (couleur) ; to sag (poutre) ; to work, to ferment (vin). ‖ To work (*à,* at, on) [un ouvrage]. ‖ To work (*à, pour,* for ; *contre,* against) ; *travailler à la perte de,* to work for the destruction of. ‖ NAUT. To strain (navire). ‖ FIN. To produce interest (argent) ; *être travaillé,* to be dealt in (titre) ; *faire travailler son argent,* to put one's money out at interest (ou) U. S. to work. ‖ TECHN. To work. ‖ FIG. To be active (esprit). ‖ FAM. *Travailler du chapeau,* to have bats in the belfry, to have a screw loose. ‖ LOC. *Travailler pour le roi de Prusse,* to work for love.
— v. pr. Se travailler, to be worked (sens passif).
travailleur, euse [-jœ:r, ø:z] adj. Hard-working, industrious.
— m. Worker ; workman, labourer (v. OUVRIER) ; *travailleur de force,* heavy worker ; *travailleurs de la mer,* toilers of the deep. ‖ Worker ; *bon travailleur,* hard-working man, hard worker.
travailleuse [travajø:z] f. Worker, work-woman (femme). ‖ Work-table (table).
travaillisme [-jism] m. Labour, Labour Party.
travailliste [-jist] adj. Labour (député, parti).
— m. Member of the Labour Party. ‖ Labour member (député).
travée [-ve] f. ARCHIT. Bay ; span (de pont). ‖ AVIAT. Rib.
travelling [travəliŋ] m. CINÉM. Travelling platform (d'une caméra) ; *travelling avant,* approach shot.
travelo [travlo] m. POP. Transvestite, drag queen.
travers [travɛ:r] m. Breadth ; *travers de doigt,* finger's breadth. ‖ ARCHIT. Irregularity (d'un bâtiment) ; lintel (d'une cheminée). ‖ NAUT. Broadside, beam ; *être par le travers de,* to be abeam (ou) abreast of ; *présenter le travers à,* to turn broadside on to. ‖ SPORTS. Cross-string (d'une raquette). ‖ FIG. Wrong direction ; *donner dans le travers,* to go astray. ‖ FIG. Bad habit ; eccentricity ; fault, failing, defect (défaut) ; *malgré ses travers,* in spite of his faults.
— loc. adv. Au travers, through ; *passer au travers,* to get through. ‖ De travers, awry, askew, crooked ; amiss ; the wrong way ; *aller de travers,* to go wrong ; *avoir l'esprit de travers,* to have queer ideas ; to be wrong-headed ; *avoir le nez de travers,* to have a crooked nose ; *entendre de travers,* to misunderstand ; *prendre de travers,* to take amiss ; *regarder de travers,* to scowl at. ‖ En travers, across, crosswise, athwart.
— loc. prép. À travers, through ; *à travers champs,* through the fields. ‖ Au travers de, through ; *passer au travers de l'ennemi,* to cut one's way through the enemy. ‖ En travers de, across, athwart ; *se mettre en travers des projets de qqn,* to thwart s.o.
traversable [-vɛrsabl] adj. Fordable (rivière) ; traversable (rue).
traverse [travɛrs] f. Cross-street (rue) ; *chemin de traverse,* short cut, cross-road. ‖ Rung (d'une échelle) ; rail (d'une porte). ‖ ARCHIT. Cross-beam (poutre). ‖ AUTOM., AVIAT. Cross-member. ‖ MILIT. Cross-bar. ‖ NAUT. Bar (d'un fleuve). ‖ CH. DE F. Sleeper. ‖ FIG. Obstacle, hindrance,

reverse, setback ; hitch (fam.) ; *essuyer bien des traverses,* to meet with many setbacks.
traversée [-se] f. Crossing (action). ‖ NAUT. Crossing, passage ; *faire la traversée de la Manche,* to cross the Channel ; *mauvaise traversée,* rough crossing. ‖ CH. DE F. *Traversée de voie,* crossover, railway crossing. ‖ AUTOM. *Faire la traversée d'une ville,* to pass through a town. ‖ SPORTS. Traverse (en alpinisme).
traverser [-se] v. tr. (1). To go across (v. FRANCHIR) ; to go through, to make one's way through (une foule) ; to traverse (une région) ; to cross (une rivière, la rue) ; *traverser en auto,* to drive through ; *traverser en avion, en bateau, à la nage,* to fly, to sail, to swim across ; *pont qui traverse une rivière,* bridge that crosses (ou) spans a river ; *rivière qui traverse une ville,* river that runs through a town. ‖ To run through, to transpierce (transpercer) ; *la pluie a traversé mes habits,* the rain has soaked through my clothes. ‖ FIG. To pass through (une époque) ; to cross, to flash across (l'esprit). ‖ FIG. To thwart (les projets de qqn).
traversier [-sje] adj. Cross, crossing. ‖ NAUT. Cross (barres) ; leading (vent) ; *barque traversière,* ferry-boat. ‖ MUS. Transverse, German (flûte).
traversin [-sɛ̃] m. Bolster (de lit). ‖ Beam (de balance). ‖ NAUT. Cross-tree.
traversine [-sin] f. NAUT. Gang-plank, plank. ‖ TECHN. Cross-piece.
travertin [travɛrtɛ̃] m. GÉOL. Travertine, calcsinter.
travesti, ie [travɛsti] adj. Disguised ; *bal travesti,* fancy-dress ball. ‖ THÉÂTR. *Rôle travesti,* female part (pour acteur) ; male part (pour actrice).
— m. Fancy dress (habit). ‖ Transvestite, man in drag (homme). ‖ THÉÂTR. Female part (pour un acteur) ; male part (pour une actrice).
travestir [-ti:r] v. tr. (2). To disguise, to dress (ou) get up (*en,* as). ‖ FIG. To travesty, to burlesque, to parody, U. S. to take off (fam.) [un ouvrage] ; to misrepresent (une pensée).
— v. pr. Se travestir, to disguise oneself.
travestisme [-tism] m. PSYCH. Transvestism.
travestissement [-tismɑ̃] m. Disguise ; disguising (action). ‖ Travesty ; U. S. take off (fam.) [d'un ouvrage]. ‖ FIG. Misrepresentation (d'une pensée) ; travesty (de la vérité).
travestisseur [-tisœ:r] adj. Parodying.
— s. Parodist.
traviole (de) [dətravjɔl] loc. adv. FAM. Awry, askew, crooked.
trayeur [trɛjœ:r] m. AGRIC. Milker.
trayeuse [-jø:z] f. AGRIC. Milking-machine (appareil) ; milkmaid (femme).
trayon [-jɔ̃] m. ZOOL. Dug, teat. (V. TÉTINE.)
trébuchant, ante [trebyʃɑ̃, ɑ̃:t] adj. Tottering, staggering, stumbling (chancelant). ‖ JUR. Of full weight (pièce de monnaie) ; *espèces sonnantes et trébuchantes,* hard cash.
trébucher [-ʃe] v. tr. (1). JUR. To test for weight.
— v. intr. To totter, to reel, to stumble (v. BUTER) ; *trébucher sur une pierre,* to trip over a stone. ‖ JUR. To turn (ou) tip the scale (pièce de monnaie). ‖ FIG. To stumble, to trip.
trébuchet [-ʃɛ] m. Bird-trap, trap (piège). ‖ TECHN. Precision balance. ‖ † Trebuchet (engin).
tréfilage [trefila:ʒ] m. TECHN. Wire-drawing.
tréfiler [-le] v. tr. (1). TECHN. To wire-draw.
tréfilerie [-lri] f. TECHN. Wire-drawing (action) ; wire-mill (atelier).
tréfileur [-lœ:r] m. Wire-drawer (ou) -maker.
trèfle [trɛfl] m. BOT. Trefoil, clover ; *trèfle blanc,* white clover, shamrock ; *trèfle à quatre feuilles,* four-leaved clover. ‖ Clubs (aux cartes). ‖ ARCHIT. Trefoil, ball-flower.
tréflière [trefliɛ:r] f. AGRIC. Clover-field.

tréfonds [trefɔ̃] m. Subsoil (terre). ‖ Fig. *Le tré-fonds de notre âme,* the very depths of our soul, our innermost being; *dans le tréfonds de mon cœur,* in my heart of hearts; *le fonds et le tréfonds d'une affaire,* the ins and outs of a matter.

treillage [trɛja:ʒ] m. Trellis, trellis-work; lattice-work (en bois); wire-netting (en fil de fer).

treillager [-jaʒe], **treillisser** [-jise] v. tr. (1). To trellis, to lattice (en bois); to enclose with wire-netting (en fer); *fenêtre treillagée,* lattice- window.

treille [trɛ:j] f. Vine-arbour (berceau). ‖ Bot. Climbing vine (sur un mur); *le jus de la treille,* the juice of the grape.

treillis [trɛji] m. Trellis, trellis-work; lattice (de bois); wire netting (de fer). ‖ Grating; grid (à copier). ‖ Ticking (pour matelas); sacking (pour sacs); canvas (pour vêtements). ‖ Milit. Fatigue dress.

treize [trɛ:z] adj., m. invar. Thirteen; *treize à la douzaine,* a baker's dozen. ‖ Thirteenth; *le treize du mois,* the thirteenth of the month; *Louis Treize,* Louis the Thirteenth.

treizième [trɛzjɛm] adj., s. Thirteenth.
— m. Math. Thirteenth, thirteenth part.
— f. Mus. Thirteenth.

treizièmement [-mɑ̃] adv. Thirteenthly, in the thirteenth place.

trekking [trɛkiŋ] m. Trek; *faire du trekking,* to go trekking.

tréma [trema] m. Diaeresis (pl. diaereses).

trémail [trema:j] m. V. tramail.

tremblant, ante [trɑ̃blɑ̃, ɑ̃:t] adj. Flickering (lumière). ‖ Trembling, shaking (main); quivering (visage); trembling, faltering, quavering, quaking, shaking, shaky (voix). ‖ Shaking, quivering (de, with) [colère]; shivering (de, with) [froid, peur]; *tout tremblant,* all of a tremble.
— m. Mus. Tremolo, tremolo stop (d'un orgue).

tremble [trɑ̃:bl] m. Bot. Aspen.

tremblé, ée [trɑ̃ble] adj. Shaky (écriture); tremulous (son). ‖ Mus. Tremolo (note). ‖ Techn. Waved, wavy (filet).
— m. Techn. Waved line.

tremblement [-blǝmɑ̃] m. Tremor (de colère); shiver, shivering (de froid, de peur); shudder (d'horreur). ‖ Flickering (de la lumière). ‖ Trembling, shaking (de la main); trembling, falter, quaver, quavering (de la voix). ‖ Mus. Tremolo. ‖ Méd. Tremor; *tremblement de fièvre,* fit of ague, chill. ‖ Géogr. *Tremblement de terre,* earth tremor, earthquake. (V. séisme.) ‖ Fam. *Tout le tremblement,* the whole boiling (ou) caboodle (ou) U. S. works, the whole bag of tricks, the whole blessed lot.

trembler [-ble] v. intr. (1). To rock (bâtiment); to rattle (fenêtre); to shake, to shudder (plancher). ‖ To waver (flamme); to flicker (lumière). ‖ To tremble, to shake (main); to quaver, to quiver, to falter (voix). ‖ *Trembler de,* to quiver with (colère); to shiver with (froid); to shudder with (horreur); to shake (ou) to quake with (peur). ‖ Fig. To tremble; to fear, to be afraid (ou) alarmed, to dread (avoir peur); *trembler de faire qqch.,* to tremble at the thought of doing sth.; *en tremblant,* tremulously; *je tremble qu'il n'arrive trop tôt,* I'm terrified lest he should arrive too soon; *ça me fait trembler rien que d'y penser,* the very thought of it gives me the shivers.

trembleur, euse [-blœ:r, ø:z] adj. Trembling.
— s. Trembler; funk (fam.). [V. froussard.] ‖ Ecclés. Pl. Quakers, Shakers. ‖ Electr. Trembler, vibrator; buzzer.

tremblotant, ante [-blɔtɑ̃, ɑ̃:t] adj. Trembling. ‖ Fluttering (ailes); quivering, shivering, shaking (corps); shaky (main); doddering (vieillard); quavering, faltering (voix). ‖ Flickering, unsteady, twinkling (lumière).

tremblote [-blɔt] f. Fam. *Avoir la tremblote,* to have the shivers.

tremblotement [-blɔtmɑ̃] m. Quivering, shivering (du corps); quavering (de la voix). ‖ Flickering (de lumière).

trembloter [-blɔte] v. intr. (1). To flutter (ailes); to quiver, to shiver, to shake (corps); to dodder, to totter (vieillard); to quaver, to falter, to be tremulous (voix). ‖ To flicker, to twinkle (lumière).

trémie [tremi] f. Techn. Hopper. ‖ Agric. Feeding-box (mangeoire).

trémière [tremjɛ:r] adj. Bot. *Rose trémière,* hollyhock.

trémolo [tremɔlo] m. Mus. Tremolo (effet); tremolo stop (d'orgue). ‖ Fam. *Un trémolo dans la voix,* a quaver in one's voice.

trémoussement [tremusmɑ̃] m. Jumping (ou) bobbing up and down; jerking, shaking. ‖ Fluttering (d'ailes).

trémousser [-se] v. intr. To flutter about (oiseau); *trémousser de l'aile,* to flutter its wings.
— v. pr. **Se trémousser,** to dance about; to bob up and down; to fidget about (sur sa chaise). ‖ To frisk about (chien); to flutter about (oiseau). ‖ To get a move on, to look sharp (se dépêcher).

trempage [trɑ̃pa:ʒ] m. Soaking.

trempe [trɑ̃:p] f. Steeping, soaking. ‖ Techn. Damping (du papier). ‖ Techn. Temper, tempering, hardening (procédé); *de bonne trempe,* well-tempered. ‖ Fig. Stamp, calibre, character; grit; *un homme de sa trempe, d'une tout autre trempe,* a man of his stamp, of quite a different calibre. ‖ Fam. Thrashing, hiding, walloping (v. raclée).

trempé, ée [trɑ̃pe] adj. Soaked, wet. ‖ Sodden (terrain) ‖ Bathed (de, in) [sueur]; *trempé comme une soupe,* like a drowned rat; *trempé jusqu'aux os,* drenched (ou) soaked to the skin. ‖ Techn. Tempered, hardened (acier); damped (papier). ‖ Fig. Well-tempered (esprit); energetic, strong (personne).

tremper v. intr. (1). To steep, to soak. ‖ To be dipped (mains). ‖ Fig. To harden (la volonté). ‖ Fam. To be involved, to have a hand (dans, in); to be a party (dans, to).
— v. tr. To steep, to soak; to dip. (V. baigner, mouiller.) ‖ To drench (pluie). ‖ To dip (sa plume). ‖ Culin. To soak (du pain); *tremper une mouillette,* to dunk one's bread; *tremper la soupe,* to pour the soup on to the bread. ‖ Techn. To temper, to harden (de l'acier); to damp (du papier). ‖ Fig. To temper (le caractère); *tremper ses mains dans le sang,* to steep one's hands in blood.
— v. pr. **Se tremper,** to soak (ou) dip oneself. ‖ Techn. To be tempered (ou) hardened (acier).

trempette [-pɛt] f. Sippet (de pain); *faire la trempette,* to dip (ou) to dunk one's bread (ou) biscuit. ‖ Fam. *Faire trempette,* to have a dip.

trempeur [-pœ:r] adj., m. Wetting. ‖ Tempering.
— m. Dipper. ‖ Techn. Wetter (de papier). ‖ Techn. Temperer, hardener (d'acier).

tremplin [trɑ̃plɛ̃] m. Sports. Diving-board (de piscine); spring-board (de saut); ski-jump (de ski). ‖ Fig. Stepping-stone (pour, to); *servir de tremplin à qqn,* to serve s.o. as a stepping-stone to advancement.

trémulation [tremylasjɔ̃] m. Méd. Tremor.

trench-coat [trɛnʃkot] m. Trench coat.

trentaine [-tɛn] f. About thirty; thirty or so; *une bonne trentaine de personnes,* a good thirty people; *dépasser la trentaine,* to be over thirty, to be in one's thirties.

trente [trɑ̃:t] m. invar. Thirty.
— adj. invar. Thirty; *trente et un,* thirty-one; *trente-deux,* thirty-two. ‖ Thirtieth; *le trente mai,* the thirtieth of May, May the thirtieth, May 30th. ‖ Sports. *Trente et un,* trente et un; *trente*

partout !, thirty all! (au tennis). ‖ Loc. *Se mettre sur son trente et un*, to put on one's Sunday best (ou) one's glad rags, to tog oneself up. ‖ **Trente-six**, adj., m. invar. Thirty-six; thirty-sixth; FAM. Umpteen, dozens, hundreds; *voir trente-six chandelles*, to see stars; *il n'y va pas par trente-six chemins*, he doesn't beat about the bush; *je te l'ai dit trente-six fois*, I've told you dozens of times; *il n'y a pas trente-six façons de le faire*, there are no two ways of doing it; *tous les trente-six du mois*, once in a blue moon.

trentième [trɑ̃tjɛm] adj., s. Thirtieth.
— m. MATH. Thirtieth, thirtieth part.

trépan [trepɑ̃] m. MÉD. Trepan, trephine (instrument); trepanning, trephining (opération). ‖ TECHN. Boring-bit, drill-bit (de menuisier); rock-drill (de mineur).

trépanation [trepanasjɔ̃] f. MÉD. Trepanning, trephining.

trépaner [-ne] v. tr. (1). MÉD. To trepan, to trephine. ‖ TECHN. To drill, to bore.

trépas [trepɑ] m. Death, decease (v. DÉCÈS); *passer de vie à trépas*, to depart this life.

trépassé, ée [-pase] adj. Dead, deceased.
— s. Dead, deceased (v. DÉCÉDÉ); *les trépassés*, the dead, the departed. ‖ ECCLÉS. *La fête des Trépassés*, All Souls' Day.

trépasser [-pase] v. intr. (1). To die, to pass away. (V. MOURIR.)

trépidant, ante [trepidɑ̃, ɑ̃:t] adj. Vibrating, quivering, shaking (secoué). ‖ FIG. Busy (rue); hectic (vie).

trépidation [-dasjɔ̃] f. Trembling, vibrating, quivering, shuddering, shaking, vibration, tremor. ‖ Rattling (des vitres). ‖ MÉD. Clonus. ‖ FIG. Flurry.

trépider [-de] v. intr. (1). To vibrate, to quiver, to shudder, to shake. ‖ FIG. To be in a state of trepidation; to tremble with agitation.

trépied [trepje] m. Tripod. ‖ CULIN. Trivet. ‖ MILIT. Tripod mounting. ‖ TECHN. Tripod stand.

trépignement [trepiɲmɑ̃] m. Prancing, dancing; stamping (des pieds).

trépigner [-ɲe] v. tr. (1). To trample (ou) tread down.
— v. intr. To dance (ou) prance about; *trépigner de colère*, to hop about with rage, to be hopping mad (fam.); *trépigner d'impatience*, to stamp with impatience; *trépigner de joie*, to jump for joy.

trépointe [trepwɛ̃:t] f. Welt (de soulier).

tréponème [trepɔnɛm] m. MÉD. Treponema.

très [trɛ] adv. Very; much, very much; *très apprécié*, greatly (ou) highly appreciated; *très connu*, very well known; *très estimé*, much esteemed; *très lu*, widely read; *elle est très femme*, she is very much of a woman, she is very womanly. ‖ **Très-Haut** (le), m. invar. ECCLÉS. The Almighty, the Most High.

trésor [trezɔr] m. Treasure. ‖ Treasure-chest, treasure-house (lieu). ‖ Pl. Treasures; riches, wealth; *dépenser des trésors*, to spend a fortune. ‖ ECCLÉS. Treasure (d'église). ‖ JUR. Treasure-trove. ‖ FIN. Treasury; *le trésor public*, the Treasury, public funds. ‖ GRAMM. Thesaurus (d'une langue). ‖ FAM. Treasure; *c'est un trésor*, he is a treasure; *mon trésor !*, my precious!

trésorerie [-rri] f. Treasury; tresorier's office. ‖ Treasurership (fonctions). ‖ FIN. *Trésorerie publique*, Treasury, Exchequer; U. S. Treasury Department. ‖ COMM. Funds (capitaux).

trésorier [-rje] m. Treasurer, paymaster. ‖ MILIT., NAUT., FIN. Paymaster.

trésorière [-rjɛ:r] f. Treasurer; paymistress.

tressage [trɛsa:ʒ] m. Tressing, plaiting, braiding.

tressaillant, ante [trɛsajɑ̃, ɑ̃:t] adj. Thrilling (de joie); shivering, quivering, shuddering (de peur).

tressaillement [-jmɑ̃] m. Thrill (de joie); shiver, shudder (de peur).

tressaillir [-ji:r] v. intr. (17). To thrill (de, with) [joie]; to shiver, to shudder (de, from, with) [peur]; to shiver (de, with) [surprise]; *tressaillir de douleur*, to wince; *il m'a fait tressaillir*, he made me jump, he startled me. ‖ To tremble, to shudder (sous un choc). ‖ MÉD. To bound, to throb (cœur).

tressaut [trɛso] m. Start, jump. ‖ Jolt (cahot).

tressauter [-te] v. intr. (1). To start, to jump (tressaillir). ‖ To jolt (cahoter).

tresse [trɛs] f. Braid (galon). ‖ Tress, plait, braid (de cheveux); plait (de paille); *à tresse*, plaited, braided. ‖ Thick brown paper (papier). ‖ NAUT. Sennit. ‖ ELECTR. *Sous tresse*, braided (fil). ‖ ARCHIT. Strap-work.

tresser [-se] v. tr. (1). To braid; to tress, to plait (des cheveux); to weave (une guirlande); to plait (de la paille). ‖ ELECTR. To braid (des fils).

tréteau [treto] m. Trestle, stand, support. ‖ Pl. THÉÂTR. Stage.

treuil [trœ:j] m. TECHN. Winch, windlass; draw works.

trêve [trɛ:v] f. Truce (en général). ‖ FIG. Respite; rest (repos); *trêve de plaisanteries*, no nonsense, no more joking; *sans trêve*, relentlessly, unceasingly, without a break.

trévire [trevi:r] f. NAUT. Parbuckle.

tri [tri] m. Sorting; *faire le tri*, to sort.

triable [-abl] adj. Sortable; worth sorting out.

triacide [triasid] m. CHIM. Triacid.

triade [trijad] f. Triad.

triage [trija:ʒ] m. Sorting (des lettres). ‖ Choosing, selecting, picking (action); choice, pick (choix). ‖ CH. DE F. Marshalling; *voie de triage*, siding; *gare de triage*, marshalling yard(s).

triangle [trijɑ̃:gl] m. MATH., MUS., ASTRON. Triangle. ‖ ARTS. Set square (en dessin). ‖ NAUT. Triangular formation (disposition); triangular flag (pavillon).

triangulaire [trijɑ̃gylɛ:r] m. MÉD. Triangularis.
— adj. MATH. Triangular. ‖ TECHN. Three-square (outil). ‖ *Élection triangulaire*, three-cornered fight (en politique).

triangulairement [-lɛrmɑ̃] adv. Triangularly.

triangulation [-lasjɔ̃] f. TECHN. Triangulation.

trianguler [-le] v. tr. (1). TECHN. To triangulate.

trias [trijɑs] m. GÉOL. Trias, Triassic.

triasique [-jazik] adj. GÉOL. Triassic.

triatomique [triatɔmik] adj. CHIM. Triatomic.

tribal, ale [tribal] adj. Tribal.

tribalisme [-lism] m. Tribalism.

triboélectricité [triboelɛktrisite] f. PHYS. Tribo-electricity.

triboluminescence [-lyminɛsɑ̃:s] f. PHYS. Tribo-luminescence.

tribomètre [tribɔmɛtr] m. PHYS. Tribometer.

tribométrie [-metri] f. PHYS. Tribometry.

tribord [tribɔ:r] m. NAUT. Starboard; *à* (ou) *par tribord*, to starboard; *la barre toute à tribord !*, hard a-starboard!

tribraque [tribrak] m. Tribrach.

tribu [triby] f. Tribe; *membre d'une tribu*, tribes-man; *vie de la tribu*, tribal life.

tribulation [tribylasjɔ̃] f. Tribulation. ‖ Pl. Troubles, trials.

tribun [tribœ̃] m. † Tribune. ‖ Popular orator (ou) leader; champion of popular rights.

tribunal [-bynal] m. † Tribunal (siège). ‖ JUR. Law-court, court of justice (lieu); magistrates (magistrats); bench, judge's seat (siège); *tribunal pour enfants*, juvenile court; *tribunal de simple police*, police-court.

tribune [-byn] f. Tribune; rostrum, speaker's platform (v. ESTRADE); *éloquence de la tribune*, parliamentary eloquence; *monter à la tribune*, to address the House (à la Chambre). ‖ Ecclés. Organ-loft (à l'orgue); pulpit (chaire). ‖ Archit. Gallery (balcon). ‖ Sports. Grand-stand; stand.

tribut [triby] m. † Tribute, tribute-money (argent); duty, tax (impôt); *lever un tribut*, to raise a tax; *payer tribut*, to pay tribute. ‖ Reward, recompense (rétribution). ‖ Contribution (apport). ‖ Loc. *Payer son tribut à la nature*, to pay the debt of nature.

tributaire [-tɛ:r] adj. Tributary (peuple, rivière). ‖ Fig. Dependent (*de*, upon).

tricar [trikar] m. Three-wheeler (fam.).

tricentenaire [trisãtnɛ:r] adj., m. Tercentenary.

tricéphale [trisɛfal] adj. Tricephalous, three-headed.

triceps [trisɛps] m. Méd. Triceps.

triche [triʃ] f. Fam. Cheating.

tricher [-ʃe] v. intr., tr. (1). To trick, to cheat.

tricherie [-ʃri] f. Cheating (au jeu).

tricheur, euse [-ʃœ:r, ø:z] adj. Given to cheating.
— s. Cheat (au jeu).

trichine [trikin] f. Zool. Trichina.

trichocéphale [trikɔsɛfal] m. Méd. Trichocephalus.

trichrome [trikro:m] adj. Techn. Trichromatic, three-colour.

trichromie [-krɔmi] f. Techn. Trichromatism, three-colour process.

trick [trik] m. Trick (aux cartes).

tricolore [trikɔlɔ:r] adj. Tricolour, tricoloured; *le drapeau tricolore*, the Tricolour, the French flag. ‖ Sports. French (équipe).
— m. pl. Sports. *Les Tricolores*, the French.

tricorde [-kɔrd] adj. Mus. Trichord, three-stringed.

tricorne [-kɔrn] adj. Three-cornered. ‖ Zool. Three-horned (animal).
— m. Tricorn, three-cornered hat.

tricot [triko] m. Knitting (action); *faire du tricot*, to knit. ‖ Knitted wear; jumper, jersey; tricot; sweater, pull-over (vêtement); *tricot de corps* (under)vest, U. S. undershirt.

tricotage [trikɔta:ʒ] m. Knitting (acte, tricot).

tricoter [-te] v. tr. (1). To knit (des bas); to make (de la dentelle); *aiguilles à tricoter*, knitting-needles.
— v. intr. To knit. ‖ Fam. To dance (danser); to take to one's heels (fuir); to leg it (marcher).

tricoteur, euse [-tœ:r, ø:z] s. Knitter.

tricoteuse [-tø:z] f. Techn. Knitting-machine.

trictrac [triktrak] m. Backgammon board (damier); backgammon (jeu).

tricycle [trisikl] m. Tricycle; three-wheeled vehicle (voiture).

tricycliste [-klist] s. Tricyclist.

tridactyle [tridaktil] adj. Zool. Tridactyl(ous).

trident [tridã] m. Trident. ‖ Agric. Three-pronged pitchfork.

tridenté, ée [-te] adj. Tridental.

tridimensionnel, elle [tridimãsjɔnɛl] adj. Tridimensional, three-dimensional.

trièdre [triɛdr] adj., m. Math. Trihedral.

triennal, ale [triɛnnal] adj. Triennial.

triennat [-na] m. Triennium (temps). ‖ Three-years' spell of office (exercice).

trier [trije] v. tr. (1). To sort (des lettres). ‖ To pick (de la laine). ‖ To select, to choose (v. sélectionner); *trier à la main*, to hand-pick. ‖ Ch. de f. To marshal (des wagons). ‖ Sports. To seed (des joueurs).

trière [-jɛ:r] f. Naut. Trireme.

trieur [-jœ:r] m. Sorter (de lettres); *trieur de laine*, wool-picker. ‖ Techn. Separator, screening machine.

trieuse [-jø:z] f. Sorter (de lettres). ‖ Techn. *Trieuse de laine*, wool-picking machine.

trifolié, ée [-fɔlje] adj. Bot. Trifoliate, three-leaved.

triforium [trifɔrjɔm] m. Archit. Triforium.

trifouillage [trifuja:ʒ] m. Fam. Rummaging (ou) fumbling about.

trifouiller [-je] v. intr. (1). Fam. To rummage (ou) fumble about (*dans*, in).
— v. tr. Fam. To meddle with, to tamper with (un mécanisme).

triglyphe [triglif] m. Archit. Triglyph.

trigone [trigɔn] adj. Trigonal.
— m. Trigon.

trigonométrie [trigɔnɔmetri] f. Math. Trigonometry.

trigonométrique [-trik] adj. Math. Trigonometric, trigonometrical.

trigonométriquement [-trikmã] adv. Math. Trigonometrically.

trigrille [trigri:j] f. Radio. Five-electrode valve (ou) U. S. tube.

trihebdomadaire [triɛbdɔmadɛ:r] adj. Tri-weekly, thrice weekly.

trijumeau [triʒymo] adj. Méd. Trigeminal.
— m. Méd. Trigeminal (ou) trifacial nerve.

trilatéral, ale [-lateral] adj. Trilateral, three-sided.

trilinéaire [-lineɛ:r] adj. Math. Trilinear.

trilingue [-lɛ̃:g] adj. Trilingual.

trille [tri:j] f. Mus. Trill, shake.

triller [trije] v. intr., v. tr. (1). Mus. To trill.

trillion [triljɔ̃] m. Trillion (10¹⁸); U. S. quintillion. ‖ (before 1948) Billion (10¹²); U. S. trillion.

trilobé, ée [trilɔbe] adj. Trilobate. ‖ Archit. Trefoiled.

trilogie [trilɔʒi] f. Trilogy.

trimaran [trimarã] n. Naut. Trimaran.

trimarder [trimarde] v. intr. (1). Pop. To be on the tramp. ‖ Fam. To toil (v. trimer).

trimardeur [-dœ:r] m. Pop. Tramp, U. S. hobo, bum.

trimbalage [t-ɛ̃bala:ʒ] m., **trimbalement** [-ləmã] m. Fam. Lugging (ou) dragging (ou) carting about.

trimbaler [-le] v. tr. (1). Fam. To lug (ou) drag (ou) cart about (v. traîner); to drag, to tow (ses gosses)
— v. pr. Se trimbaler, Fam. To drag oneself along.

trimer [trime] v. intr. Pop. To toil, to slog away; to grub along.

trimestre [trimɛstr] m. Quarter, three months; trimester; *par trimestre*, quarterly. ‖ Quarter's rent (loyer); quarter's salary (salaire). ‖ Term (études); term's fees (frais) [à l'école].

trimestriel, elle [-trjɛl] adj. Quarterly; trimestrial; *bulletin trimestriel*, end-of-term report.

trimestriellement [-trjɛlmã] adv. Quarterly, every three months.

trimètre [trimɛtr] m. Trimeter.

trimoteur [trimɔtœ:r] adj. Aviat. Three-engined.
— m. Aviat. Three-engined aeroplane.

tringlage [trɛ̃gla:ʒ] m. System of rods.

tringle [trɛ̃:gl] f. Rod; *tringle d'escalier*, stair-rod; *tringle de rideau*, curtain-rod, tringle. ‖ Autom. Wire (de pneu). ‖ Archit. Tringle, square moulding. ‖ Pop. *Se mettre la tringle*, to go without.

tringlot [trɛ̃glo] m. Milit., Pop. Soldier in the French Army Service Corps.

trinitaire [trinitɛ:r] s. Ecclés. Trinitarian.

Trinité [-te] f. Ecclés. Trinity (Dieu); Trinity Sunday (fête). ‖ Géogr. *La Trinité*, Trinidad.

trinitrotoluène [trinitrɔtɔlɥɛn] m. Chim. Trinitrotoluene, T.N.T.

trinôme [trino:m] adj., m. Math. Trinomial.

trinquer [trɛ̃ke] v. intr. (1). To clink (ou) chink glasses (*avec*, with). ‖ Fam. To have a drink (*avec*, with) [boire]. ‖ Fam. To stand the loss, to get the worst of it, to come off badly (souffrir).

trinquet [-kɛ] m. Naut. Foremast.

trinquette [-kɛt] f. Naut. Fore-topmast staysail.

trio [trijo] m. Trio. ‖ Techn. Three-cylindered rolling-mill (laminoir). ‖ Mus. Trio.

triode [triɔd] adj., f. Radio. Triode.

triolet [trijɔlɛ] m. Triolet (vers). ‖ Mus. Triplet.

triomphal, ale [trijɔfal] adj. Triumphal.

triomphalement [-falmɑ̃] adv. Triumphantly.

triomphalisme [-falism] m. Triumphant attitude, crowing, boastfulness.

triomphant, ante [-fɑ̃, ɑ̃:t] adj. Triumphant.

triomphateur, trice [-fatœːr, tris] adj. Triumphing; victorious (nation).
— m. † Triumpher. ‖ Fam. Victor; triumpher; conquering hero.

triomphe [trijɔ:f] f. Triumph (jeu).

triomphe m. Triumph; *arc de triomphe,* triumphal arch; *porter en triomphe,* to bear in triumph, to carry shoulder-high, to chair. ‖ Fig. Triumph; exultation; *jour de triomphe pour,* triumphal (ou) great day for.

triompher [trijɔfe] v. intr. (1). † To triumph. ‖ To be triumphant, to prevail (dans une discussion); *triompher de,* to overcome (une difficulté); to master (ses passions); to triumph over (qqn); to conquer (sa timidité). ‖ To excel (*dans,* in) [un art]. ‖ Fam. To boast (s'enorgueillir); to triumph, to exult (se réjouir); *triompher du malheur d'autrui,* to gloat over another's misfortune.

tripaille [tripɑ:j] f. Fam. Guts; offal.

tripale [tripa:l] adj. Aviat. Three-bladed (hélice).

triparti, e [triparti] adj. V. tripartite.

tripartisme [tripartism] m. Three-party government.

tripartite [-tit] adj. Tripartite (accord); three-power (pacte).

tripartition [-tisjɔ̃] f. Tripartition.

tripatouillage [tripatuja:ʒ] m. Fam. Tinkering, tampering; cooking (des comptes); rummaging (dans un tiroir). ‖ Mus. Tasteless arrangement; re-hash.

tripatouiller [-je] v. intr. (1). Fam. To rummage.
— v. tr. Fam. To tinker with, to tamper with; to cook (des comptes); to garble (un récit).

tripe [trip] f. (généralement pl.). Culin. Tripe; *tripes à la mode de Caen,* stewed tripe. ‖ Comm. Filling (d'un cigare). ‖ Fam. Tripes, bowels, guts; *rendre tripes et boyaux,* to be as sick as a dog.

triperie [-pri] f. Comm. Tripery, tripe-shop (boutique); tripe trade (commerce).

tripette [-pɛt] f. Fam. *Cela ne vaut pas tripette,* that's not worth a scrap.

triphasé, ée [trifaze] adj. Electr. Triphase, three-phase.

triphtongue [triftɔ:g] f. Triphthong.

tripier [tripje] s. Comm. Tripe-dealer (ou) -seller.

triplace [triplas] adj., m. Three-seater.

triplan, ane [-plɑ̃, an] adj., m. Aviat. Triplane.

triple [tripl] adj. Triple, treble, three-fold; *à triple étage,* three-storeyed (bâtiment); *en triple exemplaire,* in triplicate. ‖ Mus. *Triple croche,* demisemiquaver, U. S. thirty-second note. ‖ Math., Chim., Astron. Triple. ‖ Fig. Complete, utter; out-and-out (sot).

triplé, ée [-ple] adj. Math. Triplicate.
— s. Triplet (enfant).

triplement [-pləmɑ̃] adv. Trebly; threefold.
— m. Tripling, trebling, threefold increase.

tripler [-ple] v. intr., v. tr. (1). To triple, to treble, to increase threefold.

triplet [-plɛ] m. Archit., Techn. Triplet.

triplette [-plɛt] f. Three-seater (bicyclette).

Triplex [triplɛks] adj. invar. Triplex (verre).

tripode [tripɔd] adj., m. Tripod.

triporteur [tripɔrtœːr] m. Comm. Carrier-tricycle.

tripot [tripo] m. Gambling-den (maison de jeu). ‖ Bawdy house; dive (bouge).

tripotage [tripɔta:ʒ] m. Mess (mélange). ‖ Messing (ou) pottering (ou) fiddling about (arrangements). ‖ Fam. Jobbery (malversations); intrigue, shady dealings (manœuvres); *il y a du tripotage là-dedans,* there's something fishy about it all; *tripotage de comptes,* cooking (ou) manipulation of accounts.

tripotée [-te] f. Fam. Thrashing, drubbing, beating up, licking, hiding. (V. volée.) ‖ Fam. Lots, bags, heaps, masses, loads, piles (tas); swarms, crowds, hordes (d'enfants); oodles (de nourriture).

tripoter [-te] v. tr. (1). To meddle with, to mess about with. ‖ To toy with, to finger (ses breloques, son collier); to potter about with, to tinker with (un mécanisme); to paw (qqn). ‖ Fam. To gamble away, to misappropriate (l'argent d'autrui).
— v. intr. To mess about; to dabble (dans l'eau); to tinker, to potter about, to do odd jobs (dans la maison); to muck about (dans la terre); to rummage (dans un tiroir). ‖ To engage in underhand dealings (v. trafiquer); *tripoter dans la caisse,* to meddle (ou) tamper with the cash; *tripoter sur les blés,* to speculate in wheat.

tripoteur, euse [-tœːr, ø:z] s. Meddler; mischief (enfant). ‖ Shady speculator; peculator.

triptyque [triptik] m. Arts. Triptych. ‖ Autom. Triptyque; pass sheet.

trique [trik] f. Cudgel; *donner des coups de trique à,* to cudgel. ‖ Fam. Big stick methods; *mener sa famille à la trique,* to rule one's family with a rod of iron.

triquer [-ke] v. tr. (1). To cudgel. ‖ Naut. To square. ‖ Techn. To sort.

triquet [trike] m. Sports. Tennis-bat, racket. ‖ Techn. Trestle (échafaud); pair of steps (échelle).

trirectangle [trirɛktɑ̃:gl] adj. Math. Trirectangular.

trirème [trirɛm] f. Naut. Trireme.

trisaïeul [trizajœl] m. Great-great-grandfather.

trisaïeule [-jœːl] f. Great-great-grandmother.

trisannuel, elle [trizanɥɛl] adj. Triennial.

trisecteur, trice [trisɛktœːr, tris] adj. Trisecting.
— m. Math. Trisector.

trisection [-sjɔ̃] f. Math. Trisection.

trismus [trismys] m. Méd. Trismus, lockjaw.

trisoc [trisɔk] m. Agric. Three-shared plough.

trisomie [trizomi] f. Méd. Trisomy.

trisser [trise] v. intr. (1). Zool. To twitter.

trisser v. intr. (1). Théâtr. To call for a second encore.
— v. tr. Théâtr. To encore twice.

trisser (se) [sətrise] v. pr. (1). Pop. To clear off, to split (v. décamper).

trissyllabe [trisilab] adj. Trisyllabic.
— m. Gramm. Trisyllable.

trissyllabique [-bik] adj. Gramm. Trisyllabic.

triste [trist] adj. Downcast, dejected (abattu); sad, sorrowing, sorrowful, mournful, grieving (chagriné); melancholy, gloomy (mélancolique). ‖ Unenthusiastic (accueil); sorrowful, doleful, woeful, woebegone, dejected, downcast (air); sad, wan (sourire); *faire une triste figure, être triste comme un bonnet de nuit,* to pull a long face. ‖ Sad, melancholy, grievous (nouvelle); *triste à pleurer,* dull as ditchwater. ‖ Sad, sombre (cérémonie, occasion); depressing, dismal, dreary, gloomy, cheerless, dull (lieu, temps, vie); *avoir le vin triste,* to be maudlin in one's cups. ‖ Painful, unhappy (devoir, souvenir). ‖ Dark, gloomy (chambre); dismal, cheerless (couleur). ‖ Bad, unfortunate (fin); *c'est une triste affaire,* it's a bad business (ou) show (fam.). ‖ Poor, sorry, wretched, pathetic, dismal, pitiful (auteur, dîner); *triste sire,* sorry creature, poor specimen, pathetic individual; *faire triste figure,* to cut a sorry figure.

tristement [-təmã] adv. Sadly, sorrowfully, mournfully (avec douleur). ‖ Gloomily, dismally, dully, cheerlessly (avec mélancolie). ‖ Wretchedly, miserably, poorly, sorrily (pitoyablement).

tristesse [-tɛs] f. Sadness, gloom, melancholy; *avec tristesse*, sadly. ‖ Dullness, dreariness, cheerlessness (de l'existence). ‖ Gloominess, dismalness, cheerlessness (d'une maison).

tristounet, ette [-tunɛ, ɛt] adj. FAM. Glum, bleak (v. MORNE, MAUSSADE).

trisyllabe [trisilab] adj., m. V. TRISSYLLABE.

tritium [tritjɔm] m. CHIM. Tritium.

triton [tritɔ̃] m. † Triton. ‖ ZOOL. Newt (batracien); Triton's shell, U. S. triton (mollusque). ‖ PHYS. Triton.

triturateur [trityratœ:r] m. TECHN. Triturator.

trituration [-rasjɔ̃] f. TECHN. Trituration.

triturer [-re] v. tr. (1). To knead (la pâte), to grind (la poudre). ‖ TECHN. To triturate (la poudre, les aliments). ‖ To fiddle with; *se triturer les méninges* (fam.), to rack one's brain.

triumvir [triɔmvi:r] m. † Triumvir.

triumvirat [-vira] m. † Triumvirate.

trivalence [trivalã:s] f. CHIM. Trivalence, trivalency.

trivalent, ente [-lã, ã:t] adj. CHIM. Trivalent.

trivial, ale [trivjal] m. Commonplace. ‖ Vulgarity, coarseness.
— adj. Common, commonplace, hackneyed, trite, everyday (rebattu); vulgar, coarse, low (vulgaire).

trivialement [-lmã] adv. Vulgarly.

trivialiser [-lize] v. tr. (1). To vulgarize.

trivialité [-lite] f. Triteness; commonplace (banalité). ‖ Vulgarity; vulgarism (vulgarité).

troc [trɔk] m. Barter, exchange; swap, swapping.

trocart [trɔka:r] m. MÉD. Trocar.

trochaïque [trɔkaik] adj., m. GRAMM. Trochaic.

trochanter [trɔkãtɛ:r] m. MÉD. Trochanter.

trochée [trɔʃe] m. GRAMM. Trochee.

troène [trɔɛn] m. BOT. Privet.

troglodyte [trɔglɔdit] m. Troglodyte.

troglodytique [-tik] adj. Troglodytic.

trogne [trɔɲ] f. Bloated face.

trognon [-ɲɔ̃] m. Stump (de chou); core (de pomme). ‖ POP. Darling, pet.

Troie [trwa] f. GÉOGR. Troy.

tro ka [trɔika] f. Troika (pr., fig.).

trois [trwɑ] adj. invar. Three; *trois hommes*, three men. ‖ Third; *Henri trois*, Henry the Third; *le trois mai*, the third of May, May the third. ‖ LOC. *Les trois quarts du temps*, most of the time.
— m. Three; *un trois mal fait*, a badly formed three. ‖ MATH. *Règle de trois*, rule of three. ‖ FIN. *Le trois pour cent*, three per cent bonds (valeur). ‖ LOC. *Les Trois Grands*, the Big Three; *la vie à trois*, the eternal triangle. ‖ **Trois-étoiles**, m. invar. COMM. Three-star (cognac); FAM. *Madame trois-étoiles*, *Mᵐᵉ ****, Mrs. X. ‖ **Trois-huit**, m. invar. MUS. Three-eight time (mesure); piece in three-eight time (morceau). ‖ **Trois-mâts**, m. invar. NAUT. Three-master. ‖ **Trois-ponts**, m. invar. NAUT. Three-decker. ‖ **Trois-quarts**, m. invar. SPORTS. Three-quarter; MUS. Small violin; COMM. Three-quarter-length coat (manteau). ‖ **Trois-quatre**, m. invar. MUS. Three-four time (mesure); piece in three-four time (morceau). ‖ **Trois-six**, m. invar. Proof spirit.

troisième [-zjɛm] adj. Third.
— m. Third (personne). ‖ Third floor (étage); *habiter au troisième*, to live on the third floor. ‖ MATH. Third. ‖ SPORTS. *Arriver troisième*, to come in third.
— f. Third (personne). ‖ Fourth form (au lycée); U. S. tenth grade. ‖ CH. DE F. Third class; *voyager en troisième*, to travel third.

troisièmement [-zjɛmmã] adv. Thirdly.

trôle [tro:l] f. Furniture-hawking (ou) U. S. peddling.

troll [trɔl] m. Troll (gnome).

trolley [trɔlɛ] m. Trolley (dispositif); trolley-pole (perche); *tramway à trolley*, trolley tramcar.

trolleybus [-bys] m. AUTOM. Trolleybus.

trombe [trɔ̃:b] f. Waterspout. ‖ FIG. *Entrer, sortir en trombe*, to burst (ou) dash in, out.

trombine [trɔ̃bin] f. POP. Dial, mug, U. S. pan.

tromblon [trɔ̃blɔ̃] adj. Broad-topped (chapeau).
— m. MILIT. Grenade-sleeve (cylindre); blunderbuss (fusil). ‖ FAM. Broad-topped hat (chapeau).

trombone [trɔ̃bɔn] m. MUS. Trombone (instrument); trombone-player (musicien); posaune (d'orgue); *trombone à coulisse, à pistons*, slide-, valve-trombone. ‖ COMM. Paper-clip.

tromboniste [-nist] m. MUS. Trombonist, trombone-player.

trommel [trɔmɛl] m. TECHN. Rotary screen.

trompe [trɔ̃:p] f. Horn, trump; *trompe de chasse*, hunting-horn; *publier à son de trompe*, to trumpet abroad. ‖ AUTOM. Horn, hooter. ‖ NAUT. Foghorn (de brume). ‖ MÉD. Tube; *trompe d'Eustache*, Eustachian tube. ‖ ARCHIT. Squinch. ‖ ZOOL. Trunk (d'éléphant); proboscis, probe (d'insecte). ‖ TECHN. Aspirator; blast-pump.

trompe-la-mort [trɔ̃plamɔ:r] s. invar. FAM. Person looking like death warmed up (ou) over (malade); death-dodger (vieillard).

trompe-l'œil [trɔ̃plœ:j] m. invar. ARTS. Trompe-l'œil (tableau). ‖ ARCHIT. Dummy window (ou) door. ‖ FIG. Illusion, deception, camouflage; bluff; dummy. ‖ FAM. Eye-wash (tape-à-l'œil).

tromper [trɔ̃pe] v. tr. (1). To deceive, to delude; to take in; to cheat (un client); *se laisser tromper*, to be taken in. ‖ To betray, to be unfaithful to (sa femme, son mari). ‖ To deceive, to mislead (*sur*, about) [qqn]. ‖ To frustrate; to run counter to (les calculs); to disappoint (les espérances); to foil, to elude, to escape (la mort, la vigilance). ‖ To beguile (le chagrin, l'ennui); to stave off (la faim); to while away (le temps).
— v. pr. Se tromper, to deceive (ou) delude oneself. ‖ To be mistaken, to make a mistake, to be wrong (faire une erreur); to be out (dans ses calculs); *se tromper de chemin*, to take the wrong road, to miss one's way; *se tromper d'heure*, to mistake the time; *se tromper de porte*, to go to the wrong door; *si je ne me trompe*, unless I'm mistaken; *que l'on ne s'y trompe pas*, let there be no mistake about it (ou) no misunderstanding.
— v. récipr. Se tromper, to deceive (ou) cheat each other (ou) one another.

tromperie [-pri] f. Deceit, deceiving, deception; cheating; fraud; imposture.

trompeter [trɔ̃pəte] v. intr. (8 a). To sound the trumpet. ‖ ZOOL. To scream (aigle); to trumpet (cygne).
— v. tr. To trumpet (ou) blazen abroad (une nouvelle). ‖ To publish by trumpet (un arrêté).

trompeteur [-tœ:r] m. MUS. Trumpet-player. ‖ MÉD. Buccinator.

trompette [trɔ̃pɛt] f. MUS. Trumpet (instrument, jeu d'orgues); *trompette d'harmonie, à pistons*, orchestral, valve trumpet; *trompette marine*, one-string fiddle; *jouer, sonner de la trompette*, to play, to sound the trumpet. ‖ ZOOL. Trumpet-shell (coquillage). ‖ FAM. *Avoir le nez en trompette*, to have a turned-up nose; *déloger sans tambour ni trompette*, to leave on the quiet, to slink off; *emboucher la trompette*, to adopt a heroic (ou) pompous style; *la trompette du jugement dernier*, the last trump, the trump of doom; *la trompette du quartier*, the local newsmonger (ou) gossip. ‖ **Trompette-des-morts**, f. BOT. Horn of plenty.
— m. MILIT. Trumpeter. ‖ **Trompette-major**, m. MILIT. Trumpet-major.

trompettiste [-tist] m. Mus. Trumpet-player.
trompeur, euse [trɔ̃pœ:r, ø:z] adj. Deceptive, misleading (apparence); deceitful (paroles, personne).
— s. Deceiver; cheat; *le trompeur trompé,* beaten at his own game; the biter bit.
trompeusement [-pøzmã] adv. Deceitfully; deceptively.
tronc [trɔ̃] m. Bot. Trunk, bole. ‖ Méd. Trunk. ‖ Ecclés. Collection-box; alms-box, poor-box. ‖ Math. Frustum (de cône, de prisme). ‖ Archit. Trunk, drum. ‖ Fig. Stem, stock (souche).
tronche [trɔ̃:ʃ] f. Log, block (bille de bois). ‖ Pop. Mug (visage).
tronçon [trɔ̃sɔ̃] m. Stump, stub, piece, end; broken length; *tronçon de bois,* log; *tronçon d'une queue de cheval,* dock of a horse. ‖ Ch. de f. Section.
tronconique [trɔ̃kɔnik] adj. Math. In the shape of a truncated cone.
tronçonnage [trɔ̃sɔna:ʒ], **tronçonnement** [-sɔnmã] m. Cutting up.
tronçonner [trɔ̃sɔne] v. tr. (1). To cut into sections (ou) lengths; to cut up.
tronçonneuse [-nø:z] f. Techn. Chain-saw.
trône [tro:n] m. Throne; *monter sur le trône,* to ascend the throne. ‖ Pl. Ecclés. Thrones (anges). ‖ Fam. Throne (w.-c.).
trôner [trone] v. intr. (1). To sit enthroned (ou) on the throne. ‖ Fam. To reign supreme; to lord it (fam.) [dominer]; to sit in state (à la caisse).
tronqué, ée [trɔ̃ke] adj. Math., Archit. Truncated. ‖ Fig. Mutilated (texte).
tronquer [trɔ̃ke] v. tr. Archit. To truncate. ‖ Fig. To mutilate, to cut down (un texte).
trop [tro] adv. Too, over- (avec un adj.); *vous êtes trop aimable,* it is too kind of you; *de trop bonne heure,* too early; *trop connu,* too well known; *trop fatigué pour manger,* too tired to eat; *trop forte dose,* overdose; *trop plein,* overfull; *il est trop tard pour que nous arrivions ce soir,* it's too late for us to arrive this evening. ‖ Too (avec un adv.); *trop peu,* too few (nombre); too little (quantité). ‖ Too much, over-much, unduly (avec un verbe); *trop appuyer, travailler,* to lean, to work too hard; *trop boire,* to drink too heavily; *trop parler,* to talk too much, to be too talkative; *c'en est trop,* it's too much of a good thing, it's going too far; *je n'en sais trop que dire,* I don't quite know what to say; *je ne le sais que trop,* I know it only too well; *je n'en sais trop rien,* I'm not too sure. ‖ Too many (nombre); too much (quantité); *trop d'argent,* too much money; *trop de voitures,* too many cars. ‖ **De trop,** too many (nombre); too much (quantité); in excess; *avoir de l'argent de trop,* to have money to spare; *avoir bu un verre de trop,* to have had one too many (ou) one over the eight; *une fois de trop,* once too often; *nous sommes de trop,* we are not wanted; we are in the way (ou) « de trop ». ‖ **Par trop,** too, far too; *par trop difficile, facile,* far too hard, much too easy; *c'est par trop fort,* it's going too far; it's a bit much (fam.).
— m Excess. ‖ **Trop-perçu** (pl. *trop-perçus*). Fin. Overcharge, excess charge; *rembourser le trop-perçu,* to repay overpaid tax (impôts). ‖ **Trop-plein** (pl. *trop-pleins*) m. Techn. Overflow; waste- (ou) overflow-pipe (tuyau).
trope [trɔp] m. Gramm., Mus. Trope.
trophée [trɔfe] m. Trophy.
tropical, ale [trɔpikal] adj. Tropical.
tropique [-pik] adj. Tropical.
— m. Géogr. Tropic; *Tropique du Cancer, du Capricorne,* Tropic of Cancer, of Capricorn. ‖ Pl. Géogr. Tropics; *sous les tropiques,* in the tropics.
tropisme [trɔpism] m. Bot., Zool. Tropism.
troposphère [trɔpɔsfɛ:r] f. Troposphere.

troquer [trɔke] v. tr. (1). To barter, to exchange; to swap (fam.). ‖ Loc. *Troquer son cheval borgne contre un aveugle,* to exchange bad for worse.
troquet [trɔkɛ] m. Fam. Pub; *le troquet du coin,* the local.
trot [tro] m. Trot; *aller au trot,* to trot; *au petit trot,* at an easy trot; at a jog-trot (fam.); *partir au trot,* to trot off; *prendre le trot,* to break into a trot. ‖ Fam. *Au trot,* quickly, double-quick; *mener une affaire au trot,* to push a thing through smartly (ou) quickly; *tire-toi de là, et au trot!,* clear off, and sharp about it!; hop it!; scram!
trotskyste [trɔtskist] m. Trotskyist.
trottable [trɔtabl] adj. Suitable for trotting.
trotte [trɔt] f. Distance, way, stretch, walk, run; *une bonne trotte,* a good way.
trotte-menu [-məny] adj. invar. Scampering, pitter-patter (souris); *la gent trotte-menu,* the mouse-tribe.
trotter [trɔte] v. tr. (1). To trot (un cheval).
— v. intr. To trot (cheval); to scamper (souris). ‖ To toddle (enfant); to run about (ou) around, to be on the go (personne). ‖ Fig. To haunt; *cet air me trotte dans la tête,* I've got that tune on the brain, that tune is running through my head.
— v. pr. **Se trotter,** Fam. To be off, to make tracks.
trotteur, euse [-tœ:r, ø:z] adj. Walking (costume).
— s. Trotter (cheval). ‖ Fam. Fast walker (personne).
trotteuse [-tø:z] f. Second hand (aiguille).
trottin [-tɛ̃] m. Errand-girl. (V. midinette.)
trottinement [-tinmã] m. Trotting (d'un cheval); scampering (de souris). ‖ Toddling about (d'une personne).
trottiner [-tine] v. intr. (1). To trot short (cheval). ‖ To trot about; to toddle (enfant, vieille femme); to pit-a-pat, to patter (pieds).
trottinette [-tinɛt] f. Sports. Scooter.
trotting [-tiŋ] m. Sports. Trotting race.
trottoir [-twa:r] m. Pavement, footpath, U. S. sidewalk; *trottoir cyclable,* cycle path. ‖ *Faire le trottoir,* to walk the streets; *fille de trottoir,* street-walker. ‖ Ch. de f. Platform (quai).
trou [tru] m. Hole (en général); gap (brèche); *boucher un trou,* to stop up a hole; *tomber dans un trou,* to fall down a hole. ‖ Autom. Pot-hole (nid de poule). ‖ Aviat. *Trou d'air,* air-pocket. ‖ Milit. Crater (de bombe, d'obus). ‖ Naut. *Trou de chat,* lubber's hole. ‖ Théâtr. *Trou du souffleur,* prompter's box. ‖ Zool. Hole (d'un animal); *trou de souris,* mouse-hole. ‖ Géol. Cave (grotte). ‖ Techn. *Trou d'aération,* vent; *trou d'homme,* man-hole. ‖ Techn. Eye (d'une aiguille); *trou de serrure,* key-hole. ‖ Fig. Gap (dans un récit). ‖ Fam. Hole, out-of-the-way spot (hôtel, village); hole (logement); dump, dead-and-alive hole. ‖ Fam. *Boire comme un trou,* to drink like a fish; U. S. to have a hollow leg; *boucher un trou,* to pay off a debt, to settle up; *faire son trou,* to get on in the world, to make one's name; *faire un trou à la lune,* to abscond, to make off without paying one's debts. ‖ **Trou-trou** (pl. *trou-trous*) m. Comm. Ribbon-leading (ou) U. S. holes.
troubadour [trubadu:r] m. Troubadour.
troublant, ante [trublã, ã:t] adj. Disturbing, disquieting, disconcerting, troubling, worrying, unsettling (pensées). ‖ Alluring, fascinating, disturbing (femme); heady (parfum).
trouble [trubl] adj. Murky, overcast (ciel); muddy, turgid (eau); dim (lumière, œil, verre); misty, blurred (lunettes); unsettled (temps); cloudy (vin). ‖ Méd. *Avoir la vue trouble,* to be dim-sighted, to see things through a haze. ‖ Fig. Shady, questionable, suspicious (attitude); uneasy (esprit); confused (situation); *pêcher en eau trouble,* to fish in troubled waters.

— adv. Dimly; *voir trouble*, to be dim-sighted.
— m. Discord, discussion, quarrel; upset (fam.). ‖ Disorder, commotion, tumult, turmoil (brouhaha). ‖ Pl. Troubles, riots, disturbances (émeutes). ‖ Murkiness (du ciel). ‖ Méd. Disorder (de l'estomac); thickness (dans la voix); trouble (des yeux). ‖ Jur. *Trouble de jouissance*, disturbance of possession. ‖ Fig. Trouble (du cœur); anxiety, agitation, perturbation, confusion, trouble (de l'esprit); disorder, confusion (dans les idées).
— v. V. TROUBLER. ‖ **Trouble-fête**, m. invar. Wet blanket, kill-joy, spoil-sport. ‖ **Trouble-ménage**, m. invar. Creator of discord, mischief-maker.

troubler [-ble] v. tr. (1). To make muddy (l'eau); to disturb, to ruffle (la surface de l'eau); to cloud, to make cloudy (le vin). ‖ To disturb (la nuit, le silence, le sommeil). ‖ To disturb, to interrupt (un entretien); to trouble, to disturb, to mar (une fête, une soirée). ‖ To cause dissension in (un ménage). ‖ To trouble; to mar, to spoil (le bonheur); to worry, to bother (la conscience); to disturb, to confuse, to perplex (l'esprit); to dim (la mémoire); to unsettle (la raison). ‖ To confuse, to disconcert (déconcerter); to excite, to stir (exciter); to intimidate (intimider); to irritate, to upset, to annoy (irriter); *la présence de la jeune fille le troublait*, the presence of the girl disturbed him (ou) sent a thrill through him. ‖ Méd. To derange, to upset (l'estomac); to blur, to dim (les yeux). ‖ Jur. To disturb (v. PERTURBER); *troubler l'ordre public*, to break the peace.
— v. pr. **Se troubler**, to cloud over, to become cloudy (ou) overcast (ciel); to become cloudy (ou) muddy (liquide). ‖ To get confused (esprit); to waver, to falter, to break (voix); to grow dim (ou) blurred (vue). ‖ To falter; to get confused (ou) flustered (ou) flurried (personne).

troué, ée [true] adj. Holed; in holes (chaussettes); *troué aux coudes, aux genoux*, out at the elbows, knees.

trouée f. Gap, opening, hole. ‖ Milit. Breach (dans les lignes); gap (dans les rangs); breakthrough (pénétration). ‖ Géogr. *La trouée de Belfort*, the Belfort Gap.

trouer v. tr. (1). To make a hole (ou) holes in. ‖ To make gaps in (une haie); to perforate (de la tôle). ‖ Milit. To make a breach in (les lignes).
— v. pr. **Se trouer**, to wear into holes (vêtement). ‖ To bore (bois). ‖ Milit. To be breached (lignes).

troufion [trufjɔ̃] m. Milit., Fam. Footslogger.

trouillard, arde [truja:r, a:rd] s. Pop. **Funk**, big coward.

trouille [tru:j] f. Fam. Funk; U. S. scare; *avoir la trouille*, to have the jitters (ou) the wind up, to be funky (ou) jittery; *ça me flanque la trouille*, that puts the wind up me, that gives me the jitters; U. S. that scares the pants off me.

troupe [tru:p] f. Troop, company, band, throng (de gens); bevy (de jeunes filles); gang, set (de voleurs); *aller en troupe*, to go about in bands. ‖ Zool. Troop; herd (de buffles); bevy (de cailles); swarm (de frelons, de mouches); pride (de lions); flock (de moutons, d'oies); flight (d'oiseaux); *vivre en troupe*, to herd together. ‖ Ecclés. *Troupe céleste*, heavenly host. ‖ Milit. Troop; body of troops; soldiers, men; pl. troops, forces; *les officiers et la troupe*, officers and men. ‖ Théâtr. Troop, company.

troupeau [trupo] m. Agric. Herd, drove (de bœufs); flock (de moutons, d'oies); gaggle (d'oies). ‖ Pack, herd, crowd, mob (d'hommes). ‖ Ecclés. Flock.

troupier [-pje] m. Milit., Fam. Soldier, private.
— adj. *Comique troupier*, barracks humour.

troussage [trusa:ʒ] m. Culin. Trussing. ‖ Techn. Strickling.

trousse [tru:s] f. Bundle, package, roll (de linge).

‖ Pencil-case (ou) -wallet (d'écolier). ‖ Dressing-case, toilet-case (de toilette). [V. NÉCESSAIRE.] ‖ Milit. *Trousse de couture*, housewife. ‖ Méd. Instrument-case. ‖ Techn. Tool-bag, tool-kit (à réparation). ‖ Pl. Trunk-hose (chausses); *avoir la police à ses trousses*, to have the police on one's tail (ou) at one's heels.

troussé, ée [truse] adj. † Arrayed (habillé). ‖ Culin. Trussed. ‖ Fam. Built (bâti); made (fait); *bien troussé*, well-turned (compliment); well-built (gaillard).

trousseau [-so] m. Bundle; bunch (de clefs). ‖ Outfit; school-outfit (d'enfant); trousseau, bottom-drawer, U. S. hope-chest (fam.) [de mariée].

trousse-queue [-skø] m. invar. Tail leather.

troussequin [truskɛ̃] m. V. TRUSQUIN.

trousser [-se] v. tr. (1). To tuck up, to pin up (sa jupe); to turn up, to roll up (son pantalon); *trousser un enfant*, to turn up (ou) pull up a child's clothes. ‖ Culin. To truss (une volaille). ‖ Techn. To strickle (un moule). ‖ Fam. To get quickly through (une affaire); to polish off, to whip through (fam.).
— v. pr. **Se trousser**, to tuck up one's clothes.

troussis [-si] m. Tuck (pli).

trouvable [truvabl] adj. Findable, to be found.

trouvaille [-va:j] f. Find, lucky find, happy discovery. ‖ Fig. Felicity (de style); brain-wave (idée).

trouvé, ée [-ve] adj. Found; *bureau des objets trouvés*, lost property office; U. S. lost and found department; *enfant trouvé*, foundling. ‖ Fig. Found; *expression trouvée*, happy turn of phrase; felicitous expression; *tout trouvé*, right at hand.

trouver [-ve] v. tr. (1). To find; *je ne trouve pas mon stylo*, I can't find my pen. ‖ To find, to discover, to come across, to stumble across (ou) on, to hit on (par hasard). ‖ To find; to see; *aller trouver*, to go and see (ou) find; *venez me trouver ce soir*, come and see me this evening. ‖ To find out, to discover (découvrir, inventer); *trouver moyen de faire*, to find a way of doing. ‖ To find, to get, to obtain (obtenir); *trouver un emploi*, to find a job. ‖ To meet with (recevoir, rencontrer); *trouver bon accueil*, to meet with a warm welcome; *trouver la mort*, to meet one's death. ‖ To find, to show, to point to (ou) out (indiquer); *je vous trouverai une place*, I'll find you a seat. ‖ To find, to see, to observe, to notice (constater); to think (estimer, juger); *je n'y trouve rien d'anormal*, I find nothing unusual in that; *je ne lui trouve pas bonne mine*, I don't think he's looking very well; *il trouve ce roman bien fait*, he thinks this novel is well written; *vous trouvez?*, do you think so?; *comment la trouvez-vous?*, how do you like her?, what do you think of her?; *il a trouvé bon de*, he thought fit to; *il trouve mauvais que je sois impliqué là-dedans*, he doesn't like my being implicated in it. ‖ **Trouver à**, to find means of (trouver le moyen de); to find grounds for (trouver des raisons pour); *trouver à redire à*, to find fault with; *trouver à qui parler*, to meet one's match. ‖ Fam. *Je la trouve mauvaise*, I'm not having it; it's not at all funny.
— v. pr. **Se trouver**, to be; to be present (à un incident); to find oneself (dans une situation); *trouvez-vous là à une heure*, be there at one o'clock. ‖ To feel (se sentir); *se trouver mal*, to feel ill (être souffrant); to faint (s'évanouir); *je me trouve très bien*, I'm very comfortable; *je me trouve mieux*, I'm feeling better. ‖ To think (ou) consider (ou) regard oneself as (beau, intelligent). ‖ To be, to exist; to be met with (se rencontrer); *plante qui se trouve partout*, plant which one comes across everywhere. ‖ To be, to be found (être placé); *la maison se trouve au coin*, the house stands on the corner; *son numéro se trouve*

dans l'annuaire, his number is in the directory; *publication qui se trouve chez tous les libraires*, publication which is obtainable from (ou) is on sale at all booksellers' (ou) U. S. bookstores. ‖ To happen (arriver); *je me trouve avoir une heure de libre*, I happen to have a free hour. ‖ *Il se trouve*, there is (il y a); *il se trouve que*, it happens that, it turns out that; *il se trouve que vous avez raison*, you happen to be right.

trouvère [-vɛ:r] m. † Trouvere, minstrel. ‖ THÉÂTR. *Le Trouvère*, « Il Trovatore » (opéra).

trouveur, euse [-vœ:r, ø:z] s. Finder, discoverer, inventor.

troyen, enne [trwajɛ̃, ɛn] adj. GÉOGR. Trojan (de Troie); from Troyes (de Troyes).
— s. GÉOGR. Trojan (de Troie); native of Troyes (de Troyes).

truand, ande [tryɑ̃, ɑ̃d] s. † Wandering beggar. ‖ Crook, swindler.

truander [-de] v. tr. (1). POP. To cheat, to swindle; *se faire truander*, to be conned (ou) had.

truanderie [-dri] f. † Vagabondage (acte); vagabonds (ensemble). ‖ FAM. Gang.

truble [trybl] f. Hoop-net (de pêcheur).

trublion [trybljɔ̃] m. Mischief- (ou) trouble-maker.

truc [tryk] m. Trick, dodge; knack; *connaître les trucs du métier*, to know the tricks of the trade; *j'ai trouvé le truc*, I've got the knack (ou) hang of it. ‖ Trick, device (en littérature). ‖ FAM. Thing, thingummy, what-not, what's-his-name, do-da, doings (chose, personne); thing, gadget, jigger, contraption, U. S. gimmick, doodad (outil).

truc [tryk] m. CH. DE F. Truck.

trucage [tryka:ʒ] m. Fake. ‖ Faking (de bijoux, de meubles); cooking (de comptes); gerrymandering (d'élections). ‖ CINÉM. Effects. ‖ MILIT. Camouflage.

truchement [tryʃmɑ̃] m. Interpreter; dragoman (†). ‖ Go-between; spokesman; *servir de truchement à qqn*, to act as spokesman for s.o.

trucider [tryside] v. tr. (1). FAM. To bump off.

truck [tryk] m. CH. DE F. Truck.

truculence [trykylɑ̃:s] f. Earthy realism; earthiness, broadness.

truculent, ente [-lɑ̃, ɑ̃:t] adj. Broad, earthy (langage); ruddy, rubicund (visage).

truelle [tryɛl] f. TECHN. Trowel. ‖ CULIN. Fish-slice.

truellée [tryɛle] f. Trowelful.

truffage [tryfa:ʒ] m. CULIN. Stuffing with truffles. ‖ FAM. Grangerizing (d'un livre).

truffe [tryf] f. BOT. Truffle. ‖ ZOOL., FAM. Nose, muzzle (d'un chien). ‖ FAM. Snout (trogne).

truffé, ée [-fe] adj. CULIN. Stuffed (dinde). ‖ FIG. Stuffed, crammed (bondé); riddled (de balles).

truffer [-fe] v. tr. (1). CULIN. To stuff with truffles. ‖ TECHN. To grangerize (en imprimerie). ‖ FAM. To riddle (de, with) [bullets].

trufficulteur [-fikyltœ:r] m. Truffle-grower.

trufficulture [-fikylty:r] f. Truffle-growing.

truffier [-fje] m. AGRIC. Truffle-hunter (chercheur); truffle-grower (producteur).
— adj. AGRIC. Pertaining to truffles; truffle-producing (région); *chien truffier*, truffle-hound.

truffière [-fjɛ:r] f. AGRIC. Truffle-bed.

truie [tryi] f. ZOOL. Sow; *truie de mer*, hog-fish.

truisme [tryism] m. Truism.

truite [tryit] f. ZOOL. Trout (invariable au pluriel); *truite arc-en-ciel, saumonée*, rainbow, salmon trout; *truite de rivière*, brown trout.

truité, ée [-te] adj. Trout-coloured; spotted (chien); mottled (fonte); crackled (poterie).

truiton [-tɔ̃] m. ZOOL. Troutlet, small trout.

trumeau [trymo] m. ARCHIT. Pier-glass (glace); pier; chimney-breast (mur). ‖ CULIN. Shin (de bœuf). ‖ FAM. Old hag (femme).

truquage [tryka:ʒ] m. V. TRUCAGE.

truquer [tryke] v. tr. (1). To fake (des bijoux, des meubles); to cook (des comptes); to gerrymander (une élection); *truqué*, trumped-up (résultats).
— v. intr. FAM. To cheat; to use trickery.

truqueur [-kœ:r] s. Faker.

trusquin [⁺ryskɛ̃] m. TECHN. Marking-gauge, scriber.

trusquiner [⁻kine] v. tr. (1). TECHN. To scribe.

trust [trœst] m. FIN. Trust; *trust de valeurs*, holding company.

truster [-te] v. tr. (1). FIN. To monopolize.
— v. intr. FIN. To trust.

trusteur [-tœ:r] m. Truster.

trypanosome [tripanozo:m] m. MÉD. Trypanosome.

trypsine [tripsin] f. CHIM. Trypsin.

tsar [tsa:r] m. Tsar, czar.

tsarévitch [tsarevitʃ] m. Tsarevitch, czarevitch.

tsarine [-rin] f. Tsarina, czarina.

tsarisme [-rism] m. Tsarism, czarism.

tsariste [-rist] adj., s. Tsarist, czarist.

tsé-tsé [tsetse] adj. invar. ZOOL. Tsetse.
— f. invar. ZOOL. Tsetse-fly.

T.S.F. [teesɛf] f. Abrév. de *Télégraphie sans fil*, † wireless.

tsigane [tsigan] adj., s. Tzigane.

tu [ty] pron. pers. † Thou (style biblique et poétique). ‖ You; *à tu et à toi avec*, on familiar terms with; hail-fellow-well-met with.

tu p.p. V. TAIRE.

tuable [tɥabl] adj. Fit for slaughter (animal).

tuant, ante [tɥɑ̃, ɑ̃:t] adj. FAM. Killing, back-breaking (métier); exasperating; fatiguing (personne).

tub [tœb] m. Tub, sponge-bath; *prendre un tub*, to have a tub, to tub oneself.

tuba [tyba] m. MUS. Tuba.

tubage [tyba:ʒ] m. TECHN. Tubing; tubes; casing (de sondages). ‖ MÉD. Tubing.

tubaire [-bɛ:r] adj. MÉD. Tubal.

tubard, arde [tyba:r, ard] adj. FAM. Tuberculous, consumptive.
— s. FAM. T. B. patient, consumptive.

tube [tyb] m. Tube (de vaseline). ‖ MILIT., BOT. Tube. ‖ NAUT. Torpedo-tube. ‖ MÉD. Tube, duct. ‖ ÉLECTR., RADIO. Valve, U. S. tube; *tube électronique, à vide*, electron, vacuum tube (ou) valve. ‖ CHIM., PHYS. Tube; *tube à essai*, test tube. ‖ TECHN. Tube, pipe; *à tubes*, tubular (chaudière); *tube d'alimentation*, feed pipe. ‖ FAM. † Top-hat, topper (chapeau). ‖ FAM. Hit (chanson, disque).

tuber [-be] v. tr. (1). TECHN. To tube; to case (des sondages). ‖ MÉD. To tube.

tubercule [tybɛrkyl] m. BOT. Tuber. ‖ MÉD. Tubercle.

tuberculé, ée [-le] adj. Tubercled, tuberculate.

tuberculeux, euse [-lø, ø:z] adj. BOT. Tubercular. ‖ FAM. Tuberculous.
— s. MÉD. Tubercular (ou) T.B. patient; consumptive.

tuberculination [-linaʒɔ̃], **tuberculisation** [-lization] f. MÉD. Tuberculization.

tuberculine [-lin] f. MÉD. Tuberculine.

tuberculiner [-line], **tuberculiser** [-lize] v. tr. (1). MÉD. To tuberculize, to tuberculize.

tuberculisable [-lizabl] adj. MÉD. Subject to tuberculosis.

tuberculose [-lo:z] f. MÉD. Tuberculosis.

tubéreuse [-røz] f. BOT. Tuberose, polianthes.

tubéreux, euse [tyberø, ø:z] adj. BOT. Tuberous, tuberose.

tubulaire [tybylɛ:r] adj. Tubular.

tubulé, ée [-le] adj. Tubular. ‖ CHIM. Tubulated.

tubuleux, euse [-lø, ø:z] adj. BOT. Tubulous.

tubulure [-ly:r] f. TECHN. Tubulure, tubulature;

neck; *à trois tubulures,* three-neck (flacon). ‖ Techn. Manifold (d'échappement).

tudesque [tydɛsk] adj. Teutonic, Germanic.

tudieu! [tydjø] interj. † S'death!, zounds!

tue [ty]. V. Tuer. ‖ **Tue-mouches,** m. invar. Fly-swatter (palette); fly-paper (papier). ‖ **Tue-tête (à),** loc. adv. At the top of one's voice.

tué [tɥe] s. *Les tués,* the dead (personnes); the fallen (soldats).

tuer v. intr. To kill (boucher).
— v. tr. To kill, to slaughter (à l'abattoir). ‖ To kill, to destroy (une plante). ‖ To kill, to slay (un homme); *tuer qqn à coups de fusil, de poignard,* to shoot s.o. dead, to stab s.o. to death; *tué à l'ennemi,* killed in action; *tué raide, sur le coup,* killed outright, on the spot; *ses excès le tueront,* his excesses will kill him (ou) will be the end of him; *se faire tuer,* to be (ou) get killed. ‖ Fig. To kill (le temps). ‖ Fam. To bore to death (ennuyer); to tire out (éreinter); to worry to death (importuner).
— v. pr. **Se tuer,** to be (ou) to get killed (par accident). ‖ To kill oneself, to commit suicide (se suicider). ‖ Fig. To wear oneself out (au travail); to rack one's brains (se creuser la tête); *je me tue à le lui dire,* I'm sick and tired of telling him, I've told him so till I'm blue in the face.

tuerie [tyri] f. Carnage, massacre, slaughter, butchery.

tueur, euse [tɥœ:r, ø:z] s. Killer, slayer (meurtrier).
— m. Butcher, slaughterman (à l'abattoir).

tuf [tyf] m. Géogr. Tufa, subsoil (calcaire); tuff (volcanique). ‖ Fin. Rock-bottom.

tuile [tɥil] f. Techn. Tile; *tuile creuse, faîtière,* gutter-, ridge-tile; *tuile flamande,* pantile; *couvert de tuiles,* tiled. ‖ Fam. Nasty blow, bad (ou) tough luck; *quelle tuile!,* what a crusher!, what a nasty blow!

tuilerie [-lri] f. Tile-works, tile-field. ‖ Pl. The Tuileries (à Paris).

tuilier [-lje] adj. Tile-making.
— m. Tiler, tile-maker (ouvrier). ‖ Owner of a tile-works (exploitant).

tulipe [tylip] f. Bot. Tulip. ‖ Electr. Tulip-shaped shade.

tulipier [-pje] m. Bot. Tulip-tree.

tulle [tyl] m. Comm. Tulle, net.

tullerie [-lri] f. Comm. Tulle-making (commerce); tulle-factory (fabrique).

tuméfaction [tymefaksjõ] f. Tumefaction.

tuméfier [-fje] v. tr. (1). Méd. To tumefy, to cause to swell. (V. Gonfler.)
— v. pr. **Se tuméfier,** Méd. To tumefy, to swell.

tumescence [tymɛsɑ̃:s] f. Méd. Tumescence.

tumescent, ente [-sɑ̃, ɑ̃:t] adj. Méd. Tumescent.

tumeur [tymœ:r] f. Méd. Swelling (bénigne); tumour (en général).

tumoral, ale [-mɔral] adj. Méd. Tumorous, tumoral.

tumulaire [tymylɛ:r] adj. Tumular, sepulchral; *pierre tumulaire,* tombstone, gravestone.

tumulte [tymylt] m. Tumult; uproar, commotion, hubbub. ‖ Bustle, rush (des affaires); thunder, storm (des applaudissements); clash (des armes); turmoil (de la vie politique); *en tumulte,* in disorder, riotously (en désordre); in a riotous mob (en foule); *loin du tumulte du monde,* far from the madding crowd.

tumultueusement [-tɥozmɑ̃] adv. Tumultuously, boisterously, noisily.

tumultueux, euse [-tɥø, ø:z] adj. Tumultuous; boisterous. ‖ Riotous, noisy (réunion). ‖ Fig. Tumultuous; stormy (vie).

tumulus [tymyly:s] m. Barrow, tumulus.

tuner [tjunœ:r] m. Radio. Tuner (d'une chaîne haute fidélité).

tungstène [-stɛn] m. Chim. Tungsten.

tungstique [-stik] adj. Chim. Tungstic.

tunique [tynik] f. † Tunic (des Anciens). ‖ Milit., Méd., Bot. Tunic. ‖ Ecclés. Tunicle.

Tunisie [tynizi] f. Géogr. Tunisia.

tunisien, enne [tynizjɛ̃, ɛn] adj., s. Géogr. Tunisian.

tunnel [tynɛl] m. Tunnel; *percer un tunnel sous,* to tunnel through; *sous le tunnel,* in the tunnel. ‖ Aviat. *Tunnel aérodynamique,* wind tunnel.

turban [tyrbɑ̃] m. Turban (coiffure).

turbané, ée [-bane] adj. Turbaned.

turbidité [tyrbidite] f. Turbidity, turbidness, cloudiness.

turbin [tyrbɛ̃] m. Fam. Swotting, U. S. grind (d'écolier); slog, grind (de travailleur); *faire le turbin promis,* to deliver the goods.

turbinage [-binaʒ] m. Techn. Feeding into the turbine. ‖ Fam. Slogging, grinding.

turbine [-bin] f. Techn. Turbine.

turbiner [-bine] v. intr. (1). Fam. To swoot, U. S. to grind (à l'école); to slog, to grind (en général).

turbineur [-binœ:r] m. Fam. Slogger, grinder.

turbith [tyrbit] m. Méd. Turpeth.

turbo– [tyrbo] préf. Turbo-. ‖ **Turbo-alternateur,** m. Electr. Turbo-alternator. ‖ **Turbocompresseur,** m. Techn. Turbo-compressor (ou) -supercharger. ‖ **Turbodynamo,** f. Electr. Turbo-dynamo. ‖ **Turbo-électrique,** adj. Electr. Turbo-electric. ‖ **Turbogénérateur,** m. Techn. Turbo-generator. ‖ **Turbomoteur,** m. Techn. Turbo-motor, turbine. ‖ **Turbopompe,** f. Techn. Turbo-pump. ‖ **Turbopropulseur,** m. Aviat. Propeller turbine, turbo-prop engine; *avion à turbopropulseur,* turbo-prop, prop-jet. ‖ **Turboréacteur,** m. Aviat. Turbo-jet. ‖ **Turbosoufflante,** f. Tech. Turbo-blower. ‖ **Turbotrain,** m. Ch. de f. Turbotrain.

turbot [tyrbo] m. Zool. Turbot.

turbotière [-tjɛ:r] f. Culin. Turbot-kettle.

turbulence [tyrbylɑ̃:s] f. Turbulence (agitation); unruliness, disorderliness (indiscipline); boisterousness (tapage). ‖ Phys. Turbulence.

turbulent, ente [-lɑ̃, ɑ̃:t] adj. Turbulent; unruly, wild, disorderly, boisterous (enfants); troubled (époque); restless, unruly (esprit, gens); stormy (vie).
— m. Techn. Drum.

turc [tyrk] (f. **turque**) adj. Turkish; *à la turque,* in the Turkish fashion (ou) way (ou) style; *assis à la turque,* sitting cross-legged.
— m. Turkish (langue).
— s. Géogr. Turk. ‖ Fam. *Tête de Turc,* try-your-strength machine (dans les foires); scapegoat, butt (personne); *fort comme un Turc,* as strong as a horse; *je m'en moque comme du Grand Turc,* I don't care a tinker's cuss.

turcoman [tyrkɔmɑ̃] m. Turcoman, turkoman.

turf [tyrf] m. Sports. Racing (course); race-course (terrain).

turfiste [tyrfist] s. Sports. Race-goer.

turgescence [tyrʒɛsɑ̃:s] f. Méd. Turgescence.

turgescent, ente [-sɑ̃, ɑ̃:t] adj. Méd. Turgescent.

turgide [tyrʒid] adj. Swollen. (V. Enflé.)

turlupinade [tyrlypinad] f. Piece of low tomfoolery. ‖ Low pun (calembour).

turlupinage [-naʒ] m. Buffoonery, tomfoolery, low punning. ‖ Fam. Worry.

turlupiner [-ne] v. intr. (1). To act the buffoon.
— v. tr. Fam. To bother, to worry (agacer).
— v. pr. **Se turlupiner,** to worry, to fuss, to bother (*pour,* about).

turlutaine [tyrlytɛn] f. Fam. Pet theme (ou) idea; *c'est sa turlutaine,* he's always harping on that.

turlututu [tyrlytyty] m. FAM. Flute.
— interj. Fiddle-de-dee! stuff and nonsense!

turne [tyrn] f. FAM. Hovel (maison). ‖ FAM. Digs (chambre meublée); den (chez soi); hole (péjoratif). ‖ FAM. Room, study (à Normale Supérieure).

turnep(s) [tyrnεp] m. AGRIC. Kohl-rabi.

turpitude [tyrpityd] f. Turpitude; baseness; base deed.

turque [tyrk]. V. TURC.

Turquie [-ki] f. GÉOGR. Turkey; *Turquie d'Asie, d'Europe,* Turkey in Asia, in Europe; *tapis de Turquie,* Turkish (ou) Turkey carpet, U. S. Oriental rug.

turquoise [tyrkwa:z] adj. invar., f. Turquoise.

tussor [tysɔ:r] m. COMM. Tussore, tussore silk.

tutélaire [tylelε:r] adj. Tutelary. ‖ ECCLÉS. Guardian. ‖ JUR. *Gestion tutélaire,* guardianship.

tutelle [-tεl] f. JUR. Tutelage, guardianship; *en tutelle,* under guardianship. ‖ FIG. Protection (des lois); supervision (surveillance); trusteeship (en politique); *prendre qqn sous sa tutelle,* to take s.o. under one's wing.

tuteur, trice [-tœ:r, tris] s. JUR. Guardian, tutor. ‖ FIG. Protector.
— m. AGRIC. Stake, prop, support.

tuteurer [-tœre] v. tr. (1). AGRIC. To stake, to prop, to support.

tutoiement [tytwamɑ̃] m. Use of *tu* and *toi.*

tutoyer [-je] v. tr. (9a). To address as *tu* and *toi;* to be on familiar terms with (qqn). ‖ FAM. To insult.

tutoyeur, euse [-jœ:r, ø:z] s. Person fond of using *tu* and *toi,* when addressing others. ‖ Overfamiliar person.

tutti [tytti, tutti] m. invar. MUS. Tutti. ‖ LOC. *Tutti quanti,* all the rest.

tutu [tyty] m. THÉÂTR. Ballet-skirt, tutu.

tuyau [tɥijo, tyjo] m. Tube, pipe; *tuyau acoustique,* speaking-tube; *tuyau d'arrosage,* hose; *tuyau de cheminée,* chimney-flue; *tuyau d'eau,* water-pipe; *tuyau d'incendie,* fire-hose; *tuyau de poêle,* stove-pipe; *tuyau principal,* main. ‖ AUTOM. *Tuyau d'échappement,* exhaust-pipe. ‖ MUS. Pipe (d'orgue). ‖ COMM. Fluting (plis). ‖ ZOOL. Quill (de plume). ‖ FAM. *Tuyau de poêle,* stove-pipe, topper (chapeau); *pantalon en tuyau de poêle,* drain-pipe trousers. ‖ FAM. Tip, inside information, hint, pointer, wrinkle; U. S. *un tuyau sérieux,* a good tip; *avoir des tuyaux,* to be in the know. ‖ LOC. *Dire qqch. à qqn dans le tuyau de l'oreille,* to whisper sth. in s.o.'s ear.

tuyautage [-ta:ʒ] m. TECHN. Piping, tubing; system of pipes (ou) tubes. ‖ COMM. Fluting, goffering (du linge). ‖ FAM. Tipping, tipping-off.

tuyauté [-te] m. Fluting, goffering (du linge).

tuyauter v. tr. (1). COMM. To flute, to goffer (du linge); *fer à tuyauter,* goffering-iron. ‖ FAM. To tip off, to give a tip to; *être bien tuyauté,* to be in the know, to have all the gen; *tuyauter qqn sur,* to put s.o. up to.

tuyauterie [-tri] f. Pipe and tube trade (commerce); pipe and tube works (fabrique). ‖ TECHN. Piping, tubing; plumbing; system of pipes (ou) tubes.

tuyauteur [-tœ:r] m. FAM. Tipster.

tuyère [tɥijε:r] f. TECHN. Nozzle; blast-pipe. ‖ AVIAT. *Tuyère d'éjection,* outlet jet, U. S. jet outlet.

T. V. A. [teveα] f. Abrév. de *taxe à la valeur ajoutée,* VAT, value-added tax.

tweed [twi:d] m. COMM. Tweed.

twill [twil] m. COMM. Twill.

twist [twist] m. Twist (danse).

tympan [tɛ̃pɑ̃] m. MÉD. Tympanum, drum, ear-drum. ‖ ARCHIT. Tympanum. ‖ TECHN. Pinion (pignon); scoop-wheel (roue hydraulique). ‖ FIG. *Casser le tympan à qqn,* to split s.o.'s ears.

tympanal, ale [-panal] adj. Tympanal.

tympanique [-panik] adj. MÉD. Tympanic. ‖ MUS. Percussive.
— f. MUS. Art of percussion-playing.

tympanon [-panɔ̃] m. MUS. Dulcimer.

type [tip] m. Type; model, pattern (modèle). ‖ Type, characteristics; *il a un peu le type anglais,* there is something English about him. ‖ COMM. Pattern, sample (échantillon); standard design (ou) pattern (d'un produit). ‖ ZOOL. Type. ‖ TECHN. Type (en imprimerie). ‖ FAM. Eccentric person, character (numéro); fellow, type, chap (personnage); *un brave type,* a decent sort of chap; *un chic type,* a grand chap, a brick; U. S. a swell guy; *un drôle de type,* a queer fish; *c'est un vrai type,* he's a real character; *quel est ce type-là?* who's that chap (ou) bloke (pop.)?
— adj. Specimen; *c'est l'Anglais type,* he's typically English.

typé, ée [-pe] adj. Characteristic, particular (visage, personnalité); *bien typé,* well characterized (personnage).

typesse [-pεs] f. POP. Female, U. S. dame.

typhique [tifik] adj. MÉD. Typhous.
— s. MÉD. Patient suffering from typhus (ou) typhoid fever.

typhlite [tiflit] f. MÉD. Typhlitis.

typhoïde [tifɔid] adj., f. MÉD. Typhoid.

typhoïdique [-dik] adj. MÉD. Typhoidal.

typhon [tifɔ̃] m. Typhoon.

typhus [tify:s] m. MÉD. Typhus.

typique [tipik] adj. Typical; true-to-type. ‖ Symbolical (sens). ‖ FAM. *C'est typique!,* that's typical!; that's just like him!

typiquement [-mɑ̃] adv. Typically.

typo [tipo], **typographe** [-graf] adj. *Ouvrier typographe,* printer.
— s. Typographer, printer.

typo [tipo], **typographie** [-grafi] f. Typography.

typographique [-grafik] adj. Typographical; *erreur typographique,* printer's error, misprint.

typographiquement [-grafikmɑ̃] adv. Typographically.

typolithographie [-litɔgrafi] f. TECHN. Typolithography.

typomètre [-mεtr] m. TECHN. Typometer.

typotélégraphie [-telegrafi] f. TECHN. Typotelegraphy.

tyran [tirɑ̃] m. Tyrant; *faire le tyran,* to play the tyrant. ‖ ZOOL. Tyrant-bird.

tyranneau [tirano] m. Petty tyrant.

tyrannicide [-nisid] m. Tyrannicide.

tyrannie [-ni] f. Tyranny.

tyrannique [-nik] adj. Tyrannical, tyrannous.

tyranniquement [-nikmɑ̃] adv. Tyrannically, tyrannously.

tyranniser [-nize] v. tr. (1). To tyrannize; to rule with a rod of iron; to oppress; to bully.

Tyrol [tirɔl] m. GÉOGR. Tyrol.

tyrolien, enne [-ljɛ̃, εn] adj., s. GÉOGR. Tyrolese.

tyrolienne [-ljɛn] f. MUS. Tyrolienne, yodel-song; *chanter la tyrolienne,* to yodel, to yodle.

tzar [tza:r] m. V. TSAR.

tzigane [tzigan] adj., s. Tzigane.

U

u [y] m. U, u; *fer en U*, U-girder.

ubac [ybak] m. Géogr. Ubac, mountain slope shaded from the sun.

ubiquité [ybikцite] f. Ubiquity; *avoir le don d'ubiquité*, to be ubiquitous.

ubuesque [ybyɛsk] adj. Grotesque in the manner of A. Jarry's Ubu.

U.E.R. [yaɛːr] f. Abrév. de *Unité d'enseignement et de recherche*, university department in French educational system.

uhlan [ylɑ̃] m. Milit. Uhlan.

ukase [ykɑːz] m. Ukase.

Ukraine [ykrɛn] f. Géogr. The Ukraine.

ukrainien, enne [-ɛnjɛ̃, jɛn] adj., s. Géogr. Ukrainian.
— m. Gramm. Ukrainian (langue).

ukulélé [ykylele] m. Mus. Ukulele.

ulcérant, ante [ylserɑ̃, ɑ̃ːt] adj. Fig. Rankling.

ulcération [-rasjɔ̃] f. Méd. Ulceration.

ulcère [ylsɛːr] m. Méd. Ulcer.

ulcéré, ée [ylsere] adj. Méd. Ulcerated. ‖ Fig. Deeply wounded; *il en était ulcéré*, it rankled with him.

ulcérer v. tr. (5). Méd. To ulcerate. ‖ Fig. To wound, to embitter (v. blesser); *cela l'a ulcéré*, it rankles in his mind.

ulcéreux, euse [-rø, øːz] adj. Méd. Ulcerous.

uléma [ylema] m. Ulema.

uliginaire [yliʒinɛːr], **uligineux, euse** [-nø, øːz] adj. Swampy (terrain). ‖ Bot. Uliginous.

ulmine [ylmin] f. Chim. Ulmin.

ulnaire [ylnɛːr] adj. Méd. Ulnar.

Ulster [ylster] m. Ulster. ‖ Géogr. Ulster.

ultérieur, eure [ylterjœːr] adj. Ulterior, later; *à une date ultérieure*, on (ou) at a later date.

ultérieurement [-mɑ̃] adv. Ulteriorly.

ultimatum [yltimatɔm] m. Ultimatum.

ultime [yltim] adj. Ultimate, last. (V. dernier, final.) ‖ Ultimate. (V. essentiel, fondamental.) ‖ Fig. *Ultime déclaration*, dying declaration.

ultra [yltra] m. Ultra (en politique.) [V. extrémiste.]

ultracentrifugeuse [-sɑ̃trify ʒøːz] f. Phys., Chim. Ultracentrifuge.

ultracourt, ourte [-kuːr, urt] adj. Phys. Ultrashort (ondes).

ultramicroscope [-mikrɔskɔp] m. Phys. Ultramicroscope.

ultramoderne [-mɔdɛrn] adj. Ultramodern, right up-to-date.

ultramontain, aine [-mɔ̃tɛ̃, ɛn] adj., s. Géogr. † Ultramontane. ‖ Ecclés. Ultramontane, ultramontanist.

ultraroyaliste [-rwajalist] adj., s. Ultraroyalist, ultra.

ultrasensible [-sɑ̃sibl] adj. Hypersensitive (personne). ‖ Ciném. High-speed (pellicule).

ultrason [-sɔ̃] m. Phys. Ultrasonic wave.

ultrasonore [-sɔnɔːr] adj. Phys. Ultrasonic.

ultraviolet, ette [-vjɔlɛt, ɛt] adj. Phys. Ultraviolet.
— m. Phys. Ultraviolet ray.

ultravirus [-viryːs] m. Méd. Ultravirus.

ululement [ylylmɑ̃] m. Ululation, howling, hooting; to-whit, to-whoo.

ululer [-le] v. intr. (1). To ululate, to hoot, to to-whoo.

umbre [ɔ̃ːbr] m. Zool. Umbra, mud-minnow.

un [œ̃] (f. **une** [yn]) adj. num. invar. One; *une*

chose *à la fois*, one thing at a time; *une fois*, once; *un jour sur deux*, every other day; *une pomme*, one apple; *avoir un an*, to be one year old; *encore une question*, one further (or) more question; *trente et un jours*, thirty-one days; *mille et un ennuis*, a thousand and one troubles. ‖ One, first (premier); *page un*, page one, first page. ‖ One (indivisible); *Dieu est un*, God is One; *ils ne font qu'un*, they are one man; *leurs pensées ne font qu'un*, their thoughts are one; *ne faire qu'un*, to be rolled into one.
— s. One; *le un*, the first (dans une charade); *la une*, the first page (d'un journal); *habiter au un*, to live at number one. ‖ Comm. *Vingt francs l'un*, twenty francs apiece (ou) each. ‖ Théâtr. *Le un*, the first act, Act One. ‖ Fam. *Il était moins une*, it was a close thing.; you had a narrow escape; *ne faire ni une ni deux*, not to think twice, to make no bones about it, not to give a second thought to it.
— art. indéf. A (devant consonne, h aspirée, *one* et le son [ju]); an (devant voyelle, h muette); *une guerre*, a war; *une heure*, an hour; *un moyen*, a means; *un œuf*, an egg; *un usage*, a use; *un tel*, such a one. ‖ A (sens collectif); *un petit garçon doit obéir*, a little boy must obey (ou) do what he is told (fam.). ‖ A (devant les noms abstraits strictement déterminés); *il a montré une sagesse que tout le monde a admirée*, he showed a discretion which everybody admired. ‖ A (emphatique); *un Churchill*, a Churchill. ‖ One (un certain); *un M. Jones*, one (ou) a certain Mr. Jones; *un jour de la semaine dernière*, one day last week. ‖ (Non traduit devant les noms abstraits qualifiés); *avec une grande prudence*, with great prudence; *montrer un grand courage*, to show great courage. ‖ (Non traduit devant les noms de matière indivisible); *d'un bois dur*, in hard wood. ‖ Loc. *Un jour ou l'autre*, some day or other; *un père de famille*, the father of a family, a family man; *un tronc d'arbre*, a tree-trunk, the trunk of a tree.
— pron. indéf. One (au sing.); *un à un*, one by one; *un de ces jours*, one of these days; *un qui a de la chance*, a lucky man, a lucky one; *l'un d'eux*, one of them; *l'un.... l'autre*, one... the other; *l'un après l'autre*, one after the other; *se regarder l'un l'autre*, to look at each other (v. autre); *donnez-m'en un quelconque*, give me any one; *donnez-m'en un*, give me one; *pas un*, not one; *tout un*, all the same thing. ‖ Some (au pluriel); *les uns sont fiers, les autres sont humbles*, some are proud, the others are humble.

unanime [ynanim] adj. Unanimous, of the same mind.

unanimement [-nimmɑ̃] adv. Unanimously.

unanimité [-nimite] f. Unanimity; *à l'unanimité*, with one voice (ou) accord, unanimously, as one man, one and all, without a dissentient (ou) dissenting voice, en bloc.

Unesco [ynɛskɔ] m. Unesco (United Nations Educational, Scientific and Cultural Organization).

unguéal, ale [ɔ̃gɥeal] adj. Méd. Ungual.

unguifère [ɔ̃gɥifɛːr] adj. Unguiferous, clawed.

uni, ie [yni] adj. United (amis, États, famille, royaume). ‖ Plain (couleur, tissu); self-coloured (tissu). ‖ Even, smooth (terrain). ‖ Plain, simple (style); even, uneventful (vie).
— m. Plain material (tissu).

Unicef [ynisɛf] m. Unicef (United Nations Children's Fund).

unicellulaire [yniselylɛ:r] adj. MÉD. Unicellular.

unicité [ynisite] f. Oneness.

unicolore [ynikɔlɔ:r] adj. Unicoloured, one-coloured.

unicorne [-kɔrn] adj. Unicornous, single-horned. — m. Unicorn. (V. LICORNE.)

unidirectionnel, elle [-dirɛksjɔnɛl] adj. TECHN. Unidirectional.

unième [ynjɛm] adj. num. First; *vingt et unième,* twenty-first.

unièmement [-mã] adv. Firstly; *vingt et unième-ment,* twenty-firstly.

unificateur, trice [ynifikatœ:r, tris] adj. Unifying. — s. Unifier.

unification [ynifikasjõ] f. Unification. ‖ COMM. Standardization. ‖ FIN. Consolidation.

unifié, ée [-fje] adj. Unified. ‖ COMM. Standardized. ‖ FIN. Consolidated.

unifier [-fje] v. tr. (1). To unify. ‖ COMM. To standardize. ‖ FIN. To consolidate. — v. pr. **S'unifier,** to unify.

uniflore [yniflɔ:r] adj. BOT. Uniflorous.

uniforme [-fɔrm] adj. Uniform (en général); even, equable (geste, température); regular, uniform (vitesse). [V. ÉGAL.] ‖ Smooth, even (terrain). ‖ Even, uniform (couleur). ‖ Uniform, consistent, regular (conduite, vie); featureless, monotonous (spectacle). [V. MONOTONE.] — m. Uniform; *grand uniforme,* full uniform. ‖ MILIT. Uniform, regimentals; *en uniforme,* uniformed, in uniform; *endosser l'uniforme,* to join the army.

uniformément [-memã] adv. Uniformly; evenly.

uniformisation [-fɔrmizasjõ] f. Standardization.

uniformiser [-mize] v. tr. (1). To standardize, to make uniform.

uniformité [-mite] f. Uniformity (en général). ‖ Evenness, equability (des gestes, de la température); regularity, uniformity (de la vitesse). ‖ Evenness, smoothness (du terrain). ‖ Evenness, uniformity, flatness (des couleurs). ‖ Uniformity, consistency, regularity (de la conduite, de la vie); sameness (d'un spectacle).

unigraphie [ynigrafi] f. FIN. Single entry bookkeeping.

unijambiste [-zãbist] s. One-legged person.

unilatéral, ale [-lateral] adj. Unilateral. ‖ FIG. One-sided.

unilatéralement [-lateralmã] adv. Unilaterally.

unilingue [-lɛ̃:g] adj. Unilingual.

uniment [-mã] adj. Evenly. ‖ Plainly.

uninominal, ale [-nɔminal] adj. Uninominal.

union [ynjõ] f. Union, junction (des choses). ‖ Marriage, union (de deux personnes). ‖ Union, association (d'associés). ‖ Union, alliance, league (de nations); *Union américaine, française,* American, French Union; *Union postale,* Postal Union. ‖ Union, coalition (des partis). ‖ FIG. Unity, concord, agreement (des cœurs, des idées, des forces); *en union avec,* in unity with.

unionisme [ynjɔnism] m. Unionism.

unioniste [-nist] s. Unionist.

unipare [ynipa:r] adj. Uniparous.

unipétale [-petal] adj. BOT. Unipetalous.

uniphasé, ée [-fɑze] adj. ELECTR. Monophase, single-phase.

unipolaire [-pɔlɛ:r] adj. PHYS. Unipolar.

unipolarité [-pɔlarite] f. PHYS. Unipolarity.

unique [ynik] adj. Only, sole, single (v. SEUL); *son unique espoir,* his one (ou) last hope; *fils unique,* only son; *seul et unique,* one and only.

‖ ECCLÉS. *Fils unique du Père,* Only Begotten of the Father. ‖ MILIT. United (front). ‖ AUTOM. *Sens unique,* one-way street. ‖ FIG. Unique, unmatched, unequalled (sans pareil). ‖ FAM. *Il est unique!,* he's priceless!, he is a one!

uniquement [-mã] adv. Solely, uniquely. ‖ Merely, simply (simplement).

unir [yni:r] v. tr. (2). To unite (en général) [à, avec, to]. ‖ To couple, to join in wedlock (marier) [à, to]. ‖ To join, to connect (deux pays). ‖ To combine (des actes, des forces, des qualités) [à, with]; to link (ou) to bind together (des faits); *unir le geste à la parole,* to suit the action to the word. ‖ To smooth, to make even (un terrain). ‖ COMM. To merge, to amalgamate (des sociétés). — v. pr. **S'unir,** to marry (se marier). ‖ To unite, to join forces (avec, with) [personnes]. ‖ To combine, to unite (choses).

unisexe [ynisɛks] adj. Unisex (coiffure, mode).

unisexué, ée [ynisɛksɥe] adj. Unisexual.

unisson [-sõ] m. MUS. Unison; *à l'unisson de,* in unison with. ‖ FIG. Harmony; *à l'unisson de,* attuned to, in keeping with, chiming (in) with.

unissonance [-sɔnã:s] f. Unisonance.

unissonant, ante [-sɔnã, ã:t] adj. Unisonant.

unitaire [-tɛ:r] adj. Unitarian. ‖ CHIM., MATH. Unitary. ‖ TECHN. *Charge unitaire,* basic load.

unitarien, enne [-tarjɛ̃, ɛn] adj., s. ECCLÉS. Unitarian.

unitarisme [-tarism] m. ECCLÉS. Unitarianism.

unité [ynite] f. MATH. Unit (de mesure); unity, one (chiffre). ‖ MILIT. Unit. ‖ NAUT. Ship; *grosse unité,* capital ship. ‖ COMM. One (article); *prix de l'unité,* unit-price. ‖ ECCLÉS. Oneness (de Dieu). ‖ GRAMM. Unity (de lieu, de temps). ‖ FIG. Unity, consistency (de la conduite); unity, cohesion (des efforts); unity (de l'œuvre). ‖ FAM. *Une unité,* one million francs.

univalence [ynivalã:s] f. CHIM. Univalence, univalency.

univalent, ente [-valã, ã:t] adj. CHIM. Univalent.

univalve [-valv] adj. ZOOL. Univalve. ‖ BOT. Univalved.

univers [ynivɛ:r] m. Universe. (V. MONDE.) ‖ FIG. *Avoir l'univers devant soi,* to have the world before one.

universalisation [-salizasjõ] f. Universalization.

universaliser [-salize] v. tr. (1). To universalize.

universalisme [-salism] m. PHILOS. Universalism.

universaliste [-salist] s. PHILOS. Universalist.

universalité [-salite] f. Universality.

universaux [-so] m. pl. PHILOS. Universals.

universel, elle [-sɛl] adj. Universal (en général). ‖ MILIT. World (guerre). ‖ JUR. Residuary (légataire). ‖ TECHN. Universal (clé). ‖ PHILOS. Universal (proposition). ‖ ECCLÉS. Catholic (église). ‖ MÉD. *Remède universel,* panacea. ‖ FIG. Unanimous (avis); world-wide (renommée); all-embracing (savoir); *il est universel,* he is a walking encyclopaedia. — m. PHILOS. Universal.

universellement [-sɛlmã] adv. Universally (mondialement). ‖ Unanimously. (V. UNANIMITÉ [À L'].)

universitaire [-sitɛ:r] adj. University (concours, éducation, études, ville). — s. Member of the teaching profession; *les universitaires,* academic people.

université [-site] f. University; varsity (fam.).

univocité [-vɔsite] f. Univocity, unambiguity, unmistakableness.

univoque [-vɔk] adj. Univocal, unambiguous, unmistakable.

untel [œ̃tɛl], **unetelle** [yntɛl] s. *M. Untel,* Mme *Unetelle,* Mr, Mrs So-and-so.

uppercut [ypɛrkyt] m. SPORTS. Upper-cut.

uranifère [yranifɛ:r] adj. CHIM., GÉOGR. Uraniferous.

uranique [yranik] adj. CHIM. Uranic.

uranisme [-nism] m. MÉD. Uranism.

uraniste [-nist] s. MÉD. Uranist.

uranium [-njom] m. CHIM. Uranium.

uranographie [-nɔgrafi] f. Uranography.

uranométrie [-nɔmetri] f. Uranometry.

Uranus [yranys] m. ASTRON. Uranus.

urbain, aine [yrbɛ̃, ɛn] adj. Urban (administration, centre, population) ; town (maison).

urbanisation [yrbanizasjɔ̃] f. Urbanization.

urbaniser [-ze] v. tr. (1). To urbanize, to develop, to build on ; *zone urbanisée,* urbanized (ou) built-up area.

— v. pr. **S'urbaniser,** to become urbanized.

urbanisme [-nism] m. Town-planning, U. S. city planning.

urbaniste [-nist] m. Town-planner, U. S. city planner.

— adj. Town-planning, planning.

urbanistique [-nistik] adj. Town-planning, planning.

urbanité [-nite] f. Urbanity. (V. COURTOISIE.)

urdu [urdu] m. GRAMM. Urdu (langue).

urée [yre] f. MÉD. Urea.

urémie [-mi] f. MÉD. Uraemia.

urémique [-mik] adj. MÉD. Uraemic.

uréomètre [-ɔmɛtr] m. MÉD. Ureometer.

urétéral, ale [-teral] adj. MÉD. Ureteral.

uretère [yrətɛ:r] m. MÉD. Ureter.

urétral, ale [yretral] adj. MÉD. Urethral.

urètre [yrɛ:tr] m. MÉD. Urethra ; *le canal de l'urètre,* the canal, the passage (fam.).

urétrite [yretrit] f. MÉD. Urethritis.

urgence [yrʒɑ̃:s] f. Urgency, emergency ; pressure ; *d'urgence,* urgently, immediately, without loss of time ; *en cas d'urgence,* in case of emergency ; in an emergency ; *il y a urgence,* the case is pressing ; *mesures d'urgence,* emergency measures. ‖ MÉD. *Une urgence,* an emergency ; *état d'urgence,* state of emergency.

urgent, ente [-ʒɑ̃, ɑ̃:t] adj. Urgent (en général). [V. PRESSANT.] ‖ Urgent, instant (besoin) ; urgent (colis, lettre). ‖ MÉD. *Cas urgent,* emergency.

urger [-ʒe] v. intr. (7). FAM. To be urgent.

urinaire [yrinɛ:r] adj. MÉD. Urinary ; *voies urinaires,* urinary system.

urinal [-nal] m. MÉD. Urinal.

urine [yrin] f. Urine.

uriner [-ne] v. tr. (1). To urinate, to make water.

urineux, euse [-nø, ø:z] adj. Urinous.

urinoir [-nwa:r] m. Urinal. (V. VESPASIENNE.)

urique [yrik] adj. MÉD. Uric (acide).

urne [yrn] f. Urn ; *urne funéraire,* cinerary urn. ‖ Urn, ballot-box (électorale) ; *aller aux urnes,* to go to the polls.

urogénital, ale [yrɔʒenital] adj. MÉD. Urogenital.

urologie [yrɔlɔʒi] f. MÉD. Urology.

urologue [-lɔg] s. MÉD. Urologist.

U. R. S. S. [yrs] f. U. S. S. R.

Ursuline [yrsylin] f. ECCLÉS. Ursuline.

urticaire [yrtikɛ:r] f. MÉD. Urticaria, nettle-rash.

urticant, ante [-kɑ̃, ɑ̃:t] adj. Urticating.

urubu [yryby] m. ZOOL. Urubu.

Uruguay [yrygwɛ] m. GÉOGR. Uruguay.

uruguayen, enne [-gwɛjɛ̃, ɛn] adj., s. GÉOGR. Uruguayan.

urus [yrys] m. ZOOL. Urus.

us [ys] m. pl. Usages ; *us et coutumes,* manners and customs.

usable [yzabl] adj. Liable to deteriorate through wear.

usage [yza:ʒ] m. Use (v. EMPLOI) ; *à l'usage de,* intended for, for the use of ; *d'usage courant,* in common use ; *en usage,* in use ; *faire usage de,* to use ; *faire bon, mauvais usage de qqch.,* to make good, bad use of sth., to put sth. to good,

bad use ; *hors d'usage,* useless, disused ; *s'améliorer à l'usage,* to improve with use. ‖ Wear, service ; *faire de l'usage,* to wear well, to do service ; *des chaussures d'usage,* hard-wearing boots. ‖ Usage, use, practice, custom (coutume) ; *d'usage,* usual, customary ; *contraire à l'usage,* contrary to common practice ; *l'usage du pays,* the custom of the country ; *passer en usage,* to become the custom ; *selon les usages,* in accordance with usual practice. ‖ Practice (pratique) ; *avoir l'usage de,* to be experienced in ; *avoir l'usage du monde,* to be accustomed to the ways of society ; *manquer d'usage,* to lack breeding. ‖ JUR. Use, user ; *avoir l'usage de,* to enjoy, to have the enjoyment of ; *droit d'usage,* right of user. ‖ MÉD. *Usage externe,* for external use. ‖ GRAMM. *Hors d'usage,* obsolete, out of use (expression) ; *le bel usage,* correct English, the king's English ; *orthographe d'usage,* dictionary spelling ; *l'usage d'une langue,* the practice of a language.

usagé, ée [yzaʒe] adj. Worn, second-hand, used.

usager, ère [-ɛ:r] adj. For personal use (objet).
— m. User (*de,* of) ; *les usagers du métro,* tube-travellers, U. S. subway-riders. ‖ JUR. Commoner.

usance [yzɑ̃:s] f. COMM. Usance.

usant, ante [yzɑ̃, ɑ̃:t] adj. CHIM. Abrading. ‖ FAM. Wearing (travail).

usé, ée [yze] adj. Worn (objet, vêtement) ; *usé jusqu'à la corde,* threadbare. ‖ AGRIC. Exhausted (terrain). ‖ FIG. Worn out (personne) ; hackneyed, stale (sujet) ; *usé par le chagrin, le temps,* care-, time-worn.

user v. intr. (1). To use ; *user de,* to use, to make use of, to employ (v. EMPLOYER, UTILISER) ; *user de son autorité,* to exert one's authority ; *user d'un droit,* to exercise a right ; *user d'une permission,* to avail oneself of permission ; *user de moyens illégitimes,* to resort to illegitimate means ; *bien, mal user de,* to make good, bad use of ; *en bien, mal user avec qqn,* to treat s.o. well, badly ; *en user avec,* to deal with, to act towards.

— v. tr. To use, to use up ; *user du gaz,* to burn gas. ‖ To wear, to wear out (un objet, ses vêtements). ‖ CHIM. To abrade ; to eat. ‖ FIG. To play out (son influence) ; to fret (ses nerfs) ; to undermine (sa santé) ; to waste (son temps) ; *user d'expédients,* to resort to expedients.

— v. pr. **S'user,** to wear, to wear away (objet, vêtement). ‖ To play out (influence) ; to wear out (patience). ‖ To be strained (nerfs) ; to wear out (personne) ; *s'user les yeux à pleurer,* to spoil one's eyes by weeping.

— m. Usage. (V. USAGE.) ‖ Practice, experience.

usinage [yzina:ʒ] m. TECHN. Machining, manufacturing.

usine [yzi:n] f. TECHN. Factory, manufactory (v. FABRIQUE, MANUFACTURE) ; works, mill ; *usine à gaz,* gas-works ; *usine électrique,* power-house ; *usine de laminage,* rolling-mill ; *usine pilote,* pilot-factory.

usiner [-ne] v. tr. (1). TECHN. To machine, to tool, to machine-finish.

usinier [-nje] m. Manufacturer, mill-owner.

usité, ée [yzite] adj. In use, used, current (v. COURANT) ; *non usité,* out of use, obsolete ; *très usité,* in common use.

ustensile [ystɑ̃sil] m. Utensil, implement. ‖ CULIN. Kitchen utensil.

usuel, elle [yzɥɛl] adj. Usual. (V. COUTUMIER, HABITUEL.) ‖ Ordinary. (V. COMMUN.) ‖ Everyday (langue).
— m. Reference work, book on the open shelf.

usuellement [-mɑ̃] adv. Usually.

usufruit [-frɥi] m. JUR. Usufruct.

usufruitier, ère [-frɥitje, ɛr] adj., s. JUR. Usufructuary, beneficial owner.

usuraire [yzyrɛ:r] adj. Usurious.
usurairement [-rɛrmɑ̃] adv. Usuriously.
usure [yzy:r] f. JUR. Usury. ‖ FIG. Usury, interest ; *rendre avec usure,* to repay with interest.
usure f. Wear, wear and tear (des objets, des vêtements). ‖ MILIT. *Guerre d'usure,* war of attrition. ‖ GÉOL., GRAMM. Erosion.
usurier [yzyrje] s. Usurer.
usurpateur, trice [yzyrpatœ:r, tris] s. Usurper. — adj. Usurping.
usurpation [-pasjɔ̃] f. Usurpation.
usurpatoire [-patwa:r] adj. Usurpatory.
usurper [-pe] v. tr. (1). To usurp.
ut [yt] m. inv. MUS. C.
utérin, ine [yterɛ̃, in] adj. MÉD., JUR. Uterine.
utérus [-rys] m. MÉD. Uterus.
utile [ytil] adj. Useful, of use, serviceable ; *être utile à,* to be of use to ; *en quoi peut-il vous être utile ?,* what can he do to help you ? ‖ Useful, advantageous (v. PROFITABLE) ; *est-il utile de faire ?,* is it a good thing to do ?, is it any use doing ? ; *ne pas juger utile de,* to see no good in. ‖ Necessary (v. NÉCESSAIRE, VOULU) ; *les mesures utiles,* the necessary arrangements. ‖ Due (v. OPPORTUN) ; *en temps utile,* duly, within the prescribed time. ‖ TECHN. *Charge utile,* live (ou) useful load, carrying capacity.
— m. Useful ; *l'utile et l'agréable,* pleasure and profit, business and pleasure.

utilement [-lmɑ̃] adv. Usefully. ‖ Avantageously.
utilisable [-lizabl] adj. Usable, utilizable.
utilisateur, trice [-lizatœ:r, tris] adj. Using ; *industries utilisatrices de pétrole,* oil using industries.
— s. User ; *les utilisateurs du métro,* underground users.
utilisation [-lizasjɔ̃] f. Use, utilization.
utiliser [-lize] v. tr. (1). To use, to make use of, to utilize. (V. EMPLOYER, USER.)
utilitaire [-litɛ:r] adj. m. Utilitarian. ‖ AUTOM. Commercial (voiture). ‖ COMM. *Articles utilitaires,* utility goods.
utilitairement [-litɛrmɑ̃] adv. From a utilitarian point of view.
utilitarisme [-litarism] m. Utilitarianism.
utilitariste [-litarist] adj., s. Utilitarian.
utilité [-lite] f. Utility, usefulness (v. PROFIT) ; *d'une grande utilité,* of great use ; *sans utilité,* useless ; *voir l'utilité de,* to see the use of. ‖ THÉÂTR. Utility-man (acteur) ; small part (rôle).
utopie [ytɔpi] f. Utopia.
utopique [-pik] adj. Utopian.
utopiste [-pist] adj., s. Utopian.
utricule [ytrikyl] m. MÉD. Utricle.
uva [yva] m. BOT. Uva.
uval [yval] adj. Of grapes ; *cure uvale,* grape-cure.
uvulaire [yvylɛ:r] adj. MÉD. Uvular. ‖ BOT. Uvularia.
uvule [yvyl] f. MÉD. Uvula.

v [ve] m. V, v ; *double v,* W, w ; *en forme de V,* V-shaped.
va [va]. V. ALLER. ‖ **Va-comme-je-te-pousse (à la),** loc. adv. In a slapdash manner. ‖ **Va-et-vient,** m. invar. Backward and forward motion ; to and fro motion ; swinging (d'un balancier) ; coming and going, hurrying to and fro (des gens) ; bustle (de la rue) ; ELECTR. Two-way wiring ; two-way switch (commutateur) ; NAUT. Plying (d'un bac) ; hauling line. ‖ **Va-nu-pieds,** m. invar. Ragamuffin, street-arab, urchin, guttersnipe (enfant) ; barefoot tramp (vagabond). ‖ **Va-tout,** m. invar. All one has, one's all ; *jouer son va-tout,* to stake one's shirt (ou) one's last farthing. ‖ **Va-vite (à la),** loc. adv. Hastily, hurriedly, in a rush, carelessly.
vacance [vakɑ̃:s] f. Vacancy (fait) ; vacant post (poste). ‖ Pl. Vacation, holidays (congé) ; *un jour de vacances,* a day's holiday ; *les grandes vacances,* the summer holidays ; the long vacation (à l'université) ; *en vacances,* on holiday, U. S. on vacation ; *passer ses vacances au travail,* to take a busman's holiday. ‖ JUR. pl. Recess (des tribunaux).
vacancier, ère [-kɑ̃sje, ɛ:r] s. Holiday-maker, U. S. vacationer.
vacant, ante [-kɑ̃, ɑ̃:t] adj. Vacant ; unoccupied, tenantless (maison) ; empty (place) ; unfilled (poste). [V. INOCCUPÉ, LIBRE.] ‖ JUR. *Succession vacante,* estate in abeyance.
vacarme [vakarm] m. Uproar, row, racket, hubbub, din, shindy. (V. TAPAGE.)

vacataire [vakatɛ:r] s. Temporary employee.
vacation [vakasjɔ̃] f. JUR. Abeyance (de droit, d'héritage) ; sitting, attendance, session, meeting (d'experts) ; sale, clearance (vente). ‖ Pl. Fees (émoluments) ; vacation, recess (des tribunaux).
vaccin [vaksɛ̃] m. MÉD. Vaccine.
vaccinable [vaksinabl] adj. Fit (ou) able to be vaccinated.
vaccinal, ale [-nal] adj. MÉD. Vaccinal ; *pustule vaccinale,* pustule of vaccinia.
vaccinateur [-natœ:r] m. MÉD. Vaccinator.
vaccination [-nasjɔ̃] f. MÉD. Vaccination ; *vaccination préventive,* protective inoculation.
vaccine [vaksin] f. Vaccinia ; horse-pox (du cheval) ; cow-pox (de la vache).
vacciner [-ne] v. tr. To vaccinate ; to immunize ; *se faire vacciner,* to be vaccinated. ‖ FIG. To make impervious (*contre,* to).
vachard, arde [vaʃa:r, ard] adj. POP. Nasty, rotten, bitchy (remarque) ; lousy (question, problème).
vache [vaʃ] f. ZOOL. Cow (animal) ; milch-cow (laitière). ‖ COMM. Cow-hide, leather (cuir). ‖ FAM. *Manger de la vache enragée,* to have a hard time of it ; *parler français comme une vache espagnole,* to talk horridly bad French ; *le plancher des vaches,* terra firma. ‖ POP. Cow, bitch (femme) ; beast, swine (homme) ; cop, U. S. flatfoot, bull (policier) ; *mort aux vaches !,* down with the cops ! ; *oh ! la vache !,* damn it !
— adj. POP. Darned difficult (personne) ; awkward (question).

vachement [-mɑ̃] adv. Pop. Tremendously, terrifically.

vacher, ère [-ʃe, ɛr] s. Cowherd; cow-keeper.

vacherie [-ʃri] f. Cow-house (étable); dairy-farm (ferme). ‖ Pop. Nastiness, obnoxiousness, bitchiness (méchanceté); catty (ou) bitchy (ou) nasty remark (parole méchante); dirty (ou) nasty trick (acte méchant); a real bastard (ou) bitch (tâche, travail).

vacherin [-ʃrɛ] m. Vacherin (gâteau, fromage).

vachette [-ʃɛt] f. Zool. Young cow. ‖ Techn. Calfskin, kipskin, kip.

vacillant, ante [vasijɑ̃, ɑ̃:t] adj. Vacillating; reeling, staggering, tottering (démarche); flickering (lumière); shaky (main); unsteady, wobbly (meuble). ‖ Fig. Hesitant, undecided (esprit); wavering, erratic (raison); uncertain (santé).

vacillation [-jasjɔ̃] f. Vacillation; unsteadiness; flickering (d'une flamme); wobbling (d'un meuble). ‖ Naut. Rocking, swaying (d'un bateau). ‖ Fig. Vacillation; fluctuation, wavering (de l'opinion).

vacillatoire [-latwa:r] adj. Vacillatory; erratic; wavering; unsteady (chancelant); fluctuating (fluctuant); vacillating.

vacillement [-jmɑ̃] m. Vacillation.

vaciller [-je] v. tr. (1). To vacillate, to fluctuate. ‖ To flicker (lumière); to wobble (meuble). ‖ To stagger, to reel, to sway (chanceler). ‖ Naut. To rock, to be unsteady (bateau). ‖ Fig. To hesitate; to be shaky (mémoire); to waver (opinion).

vacuité [vakɥite] f. Vacuity, emptiness.

vacuole [vakɥɔl] f. Méd. Vacuole.

vade-mecum [vademekɔm] m. invar. Vademecum.

vadrouille [vadru:j] f. Naut. Mop; swab. ‖ Pop. Spree, bender; pub-crawl; *en vadrouille,* on the spree (ou) the loose.

vadrouiller [vadruje] v. tr. (1). Pop. To gallivant, to gad about (galvauder); to pub-crawl (godailler); to go on the spree (ou) on a bender (nocer). ‖ Fam. To roam, to wander about (errer).

vadrouilleur, euse [-jœ:r, ø:z] adj. Pop. Gallivanting.
— s. Gadabout; gallivanter; pub-crawler; U. S. bar-fly.

vagabond, onde [vagabɔ̃, ɔ̃:d] adj. Vagabond, vagrant (personne); roaming, nomadic (tribu); roving, wandering (vie). ‖ Fig. Wandering (attention, pensées); roving, wayward, flighty, capricious (imagination).
— s. Vagabond; vagrant, tramp.

vagabondage [-da:ʒ] m. Vagabondage, vagrancy. ‖ Jur. *Vagabondage spécial,* living on immoral earnings.

vagabonder [-de] v. intr. (1). To be a vagabond. ‖ To rove about, to wander about (errer); to loaf about (flâner). ‖ To play truant (s'absenter). ‖ Fig. To rove, to roam; to wander (imagination).

vagin [vaʒɛ̃] m. Méd. Vagina.

vaginal, ale [vaʒinal] adj. Méd. Vaginal.

vaginite [-nit] f. Méd. Vaginitis.

vagir [vaʒi:r] v. intr. (2). To wail, to cry (enfant). ‖ Zool. To squeak (lièvre).

vagissant, ante [vaʒisɑ̃, ɑ̃:t] adj. Wailing, crying (enfant); squeaking (lièvre). ‖ Fig. In its infancy; still undeveloped.

vagissement [-smɑ̃] m. Wail, wailing, cry (d'un enfant); squeak, squeaking (d'un lièvre).

vague [vag] adj. Vacant, empty (regard); *regarder d'un air vague,* to stare vacantly at; *terrain vague,* waste ground, U. S. vacant land. ‖ Vague; sketchy (connaissance); indeterminate (couleur); doubtful, indefinite (forme); hazy, dim, faint (idée); uncertain (lumière); loose (terme). ‖ Fam. *Quelque vague poète,* some poet or other.
— m. Vacant (ou) empty space (vide); *le vague*

---

des airs, the vacant air; *regard perdu dans le vague,* far-away look. ‖ Méd. Vagus. ‖ Fig. Vagueness, uncertainty (indécision); *avoir du vague à l'âme,* to have vague longings, to be unsettled.

vague [vag] f. Wave, billow (en général); breaker, comber (déferlante). ‖ Electr. Surge (de courant). ‖ Milit. Wave (d'assaut). ‖ Fig. Wave, surge (de colère); ripple (de rire); *vague de chaleur,* heat-wave.

vaguelette [-lɛt] f. Small wave, wavelet.

vaguement [vagmɑ̃] adv. Vaguely, indefinitely, dimly, hazily; loosely; *penser vaguement,* to have a vague idea (que, that); to have half a mind (à, to).

vaguemestre [vagmɛstr] m. Milit. Post-orderly, U. S. mail clerk. ‖ Naut. Postman.

vaguer [vage] v. intr. (1). To wander, to wander about. (V. errer.)

vahiné [vaine] f. Tahitian maiden.

vaigrer [vɛgre] v. tr. (1). Naut. To put in the ceiling of.

vaillamment [vajamɑ̃] adv. Valiantly, gallantly, stoutly.

vaillance [vajɑ̃:s] f. Valour, gallantry. (V. bravoure, courage.) ‖ Fortitude (force d'âme).

vaillant, ante [vajɑ̃, ɑ̃:t] adj. Valiant. (V. brave, courageux.) ‖ Stout (cœur); spirited (défense); gallant (soldat). ‖ Fam. In good (ou) fine fettle, up to the mark, U. S. up to scratch.
— s. Valiant (ou) brave person.

vaillant part. prés. *N'avoir pas un sou vaillant,* not to be worth a penny, not to have a bean (ou) U. S. a red cent (fam.).

vaille [vaj] V. valoir (103).

vain, aine [vɛ̃, ɛn] adj. Vain, conceited, vainglorious (personne). ‖ Vain, futile, trivial (amusements); fruitless, ineffectual, useless, unavailing (efforts); idle, empty (paroles); hollow (promesses); *vaine gloire,* vainglory. ‖ Agric. Uncultivated; *vaine pâture,* common land.
— loc adv. **En vain,** vainly, in vain, fruitlessly (sans résultat); uselessly, to no purpose (sans utilité).

vaincre [vɛ̃:kr] v. tr. (102). To master (un cheval); to beat, to outdo, to get the better of, to surpass (un rival). ‖ Milit. To vanquish, to defeat, to conquer, to beat, to overpower. ‖ Sports. To beat. ‖ Fig. To surmount (une difficulté, un obstacle); to overcome, to sweep away (l'opposition, des préjugés); *vaincre en générosité,* to outdo in generosity; *se laisser vaincre par l'émotion,* to give way to one's feelings.

vaincu, ue [vɛ̃ky] adj. Vanquished, defeated, conquered, beaten, overcome; *s'avouer vaincu,* to admit defeat. ‖ Fig. Carried away (par l'émotion).
— m. Vanquished (ou) conquered person; *les vaincus,* the conquered, the vanquished.
— p.-p. V. vaincre (102).

vainement [vɛnmɑ̃] adv. Vainly, in vain; fruitlessly; uselessly; to no purpose.

vainque, vainquis. V. vaincre (102).

vainqueur [vɛ̃kœ:r] adj. Victorious, conquering. (V. victorieux.) ‖ Triumphant; *air vainqueur,* air of victory, conquering air; arrogant air.
— m. Victor, vanquisher, conqueror. ‖ Sports. Winner.

vair [vɛ:r]. m. Comm. Squirrel fur (fourrure). ‖ Blas. Vair.

vairé, ée [-re] adj. Trimmed with squirrel fur. ‖ Blas. Vairy.

vairon [vɛrɔ̃] adj. m. Wall-eyed (cheval); of different colours (yeux).
— m. Zool. Minnow (poisson).

vais [vɛ]. V. aller (15).

vaisseau [vɛso] m. Vessel, receptacle. (V. récipient.) ‖ Archit. Nave (d'une église). ‖ Bot.

Sheath. ‖ Méd. Vessel, canal, duct; *vaisseau sanguin*, blood-vessel. ‖ Naut. Vessel, ship (v. BATEAU); *vaisseau amiral*, flagship; *vaisseau rasé*, hulk. ‖ Fig. *Brûler ses vaisseaux*, to burn one's boats; *le vaisseau de l'Etat*, the ship of State. ‖ **Vaisseau-école**, m. invar. Naut. Training-ship.

vaisselier [vɛsəlje] m. Dresser (meuble).

vaisselle [vɛsɛl] f. Plates and dishes; table-service; table-ware; china (de porcelaine); crockery (de terre); *eau de vaisselle*, dish-water; *faire la vaisselle*, to wash up, U. S. to wash the dishes.

vaissellerie [-ri] f. Manufacture of kitchen- (ou) table-ware. ‖ Kitchen- (ou) table-ware.

val [val] (pl. **vaux**) m. Valley, vale, dale. ‖ Loc. *Par monts et par vaux*, up hill and down dale.

valable [valabl] adj. Valid, good, sound. ‖ Cogent (raison). ‖ Ch. DE F. Valid, available, good (billet). ‖ Jur. Live (créances); valid (testament, titres).

valablement [-bləmɑ̃] adv. Validly.

valdinguer [valdɛ̃ge] v. intr. (1). Pop. To go flying, to come a cropper; *envoyer valdinguer*, to send flying (objet), to chuck up (travail, amis).

valence [valɑ̃:s] f. Chim. Valence, valency. ‖ Géogr. Valencia (en Espagne); Valence (en France).

valenciennes [valɑ̃sjɛn] f. Valenciennes lace.

Valentin [valɑ̃tɛ̃] m., **Valentine** [-tin] f. Valentine.

valérianate [valerjanat] m. Chim. Valerate, valerianate.

valériane [-rjan] f. Bot. Valerian.

valet [valɛ] m. Man-servant; *valet de chambre, d'écurie, de ferme, de pied*, valet, groom (ou) lad (ou) stable-lad (ou) ostler, farm-hand, footman. ‖ Techn. Stand, support, rest, ring (de laboratoire); holdfast, dog, clamp (de menuisier); counterweight (de porte). ‖ Fig. Toady, groveller, fawner, sycophant (flatteur); *âme de valet*, servile nature.

valetaille [-ltɑ:j] f. † Menials, flunkeys.

valétudinaire [valetydinɛ:r] adj. Valetudinary. — s. Valetudinarian.

valeur [valœ:r] f. Value, worth; *de valeur*, valuable (tableau); *objets de valeur*, valuables; *sans valeur*, of no value, worthless, valueless. ‖ Equivalent; *la valeur de deux verres*, about two glasses full. ‖ Milit. *Valeur militaire*, fighting qualities. ‖ Naut. *Valeur nautique*, seaworthiness. ‖ Mus. Value, length, duration (d'une note). ‖ Arts. Value (des tons). ‖ Fin. Value; asset, security, stock, share, draft, bill, bond; *valeur d'achat*, cost; *valeurs actives*, assets; *valeur le 20 courant*, payable on the 20th instant; *valeur en espèces*, cash; *valeur à lots*, lottery bond; *valeur marchande, nominale*, market, face value; *valeurs mobilières*, stocks and shares (ou) U. S. bonds; *valeur à vue*, sight draft; *en valeur déclarée*, insured (colis). ‖ Math., Philos. Value. ‖ Agric. Yield, output, productiveness; *mettre en valeur*, to reclaim (un marais); to exploit, to improve, to develop (des terres); *région à mettre en valeur*, development area. ‖ Fig. Value, force, weight (d'un argument); importance, consequence; import, meaning (signification); valour (v. Vaillance); ability, worth (valeur personnelle ou morale); *artiste de valeur*, gifted artist; *mettre en valeur*, to show in a favourable light (en général); to enhance (la beauté); to emphasize (un mot).

valeureusement [valœrøzmɑ̃] adv. Valorously.

valeureux, euse [-rø, ø:z] adj. Valorous.

valez [valɛ]. V. VALOIR (103).

validation [validasjɔ̃] f. Validation.

valide [valid] adj. Valid; fit, sound, able-bodied (homme); good, sound (santé). ‖ Milit. Fit for

service. ‖ Jur. Valid (contrat). ‖ Ch. DE F. Valid, available (billet).

validement [-dmɑ̃] adv. Validly.

valider [-de] v. tr. (1). To validate (une élection); to ratify (une loi).

validité [-dite] f. Validity. ‖ Jur. *Etablir la validité d'un testament*, to prove a will. ‖ Ch. DE F. Availability (d'un billet); period for which a ticket is valid (durée).

valise [vali:z] f. Suit-case (petite malle); valise, grip, bag (sac).

vallée [vale] f. Géogr. Valley. (V. VAL.) ‖ Fig. *Vallée de larmes*, vale of tears.

vallon [valɔ̃] m. Géogr. Small valley; vale, dale, dell (v. VAL); glen (en Ecosse). ‖ Fig. Vale.

vallonné, ée [-lɔne] adj. Undulating, rolling; broken up by small valleys.

vallonnement [-lɔnmɑ̃] m. Géogr. Foothill; undulation. ‖ Laying out in dells (d'un terrain).

vallonner v. tr. To lay out in dells.

valoir [valwa:r] v. intr. (103). To be worth (avoir une valeur commerciale ou réelle); *cela ne vaut pas cher* (ou) *grand-chose*, it is not up to (ou) worth much; *une montre qui vaut cinq mille francs*, a watch worth five thousand francs; *rien qui vaille*, nothing of value. ‖ To be worth, to be worth as much as, to be equivalent to (être égal ou équivalent à); *huit kilomètres valent cinq milles*, eight kilometres are equivalent to five miles; *l'un vaut l'autre*, there is nothing to choose between them; *une réponse qui en vaut une autre*, as good a reply as any. ‖ To be worth, to deserve, to merit (mériter); *cela vaut la peine*, it's worth while (ou) worth the trouble; *ce film vaut la peine d'être vu*, this film is worth seeing; *un service en vaut un autre*, one good turn deserves another. ‖ To remain valid (conserver sa valeur); *cela vaudra toujours*, that will always prove true (ou) hold good. ‖ To be profitable to (être profitable à); *cette liqueur ne vous vaut rien*, that liqueur is not good for you. ‖ *Faire valoir*, to turn to account, to make the most of; to set off, to enhance (la beauté); to insist on, to assert, to enforce (ses droits); to emphasize (un mot); to put forward (des raisons); *se faire valoir*, to make the most of oneself (se perfectionner); to push oneself forward, to show off (se vanter). ‖ Fin. *A valoir*, on account (sur, of); *un à valoir*, a sum on account; *faire valoir*, to invest profitably (son argent). ‖ Agric. *Faire valoir*, to farm, to exploit, to develop, to make productive (des terres). ‖ Fig. To be worth, to be as good as (avoir autant de valeur morale que); *il ne vaut pas son frère*, he can't compare with his brother, he is not a patch on his brother (fam.). ‖ Fam. *Ça vaut le coup*, it's worth trying. ‖ Loc. *Vaille que vaille*, however things turn out; for better or for worse; come what may.
— v. impers. *Il vaut mieux* (ou) *mieux vaut rester à la maison*, it is better to stay indoors; *mieux vaut tard que jamais*, better late than never; *autant vaut dormir*, one might as well sleep; *c'est une affaire faite ou autant vaut*, it's as good as done.
— v. tr. To bring in, to fetch, to produce, to yield (de l'argent). ‖ Fig. To gain, to obtain, to win (un honneur); *la gloire que lui ont value ses exploits*, the glory that his exploits have won him.
— v. pr. **Se valoir**, to be much about the same; *cela se vaut*, that (ou) it amounts to the same.
— v. récipr. **Se valoir**, to be as good (ou) bad as the other.

valorisant, ante [valɔrizɑ̃, ɑ̃:t] adj. Good for one's image (ou) standing.

valorisation [-zasjɔ̃] f. Increase in the value of (d'un fonds de commerce, d'un terrain); development (d'une région). ‖ High value set on (de l'effort, du travail) ; improvement of the image (ou) standing (d'une personne). ‖ Fin. Valorization (d'une denrée, d'une monnaie) ; valuing (d'un chèque).

valoriser [-ze] v. tr. (1). To increase the value of (un fonds de commerce, un terrain) ; to develop (une région). ‖ To set a high value on (l'effort, le travail) ; to improve the image (ou) the standing (une personne). ‖ Fin. To valorize (une denrée, une monnaie) ; to value (un chèque).

valse [vals] f. Mus. Waltz. ‖ **Valse-hésitation,** f. Hemming (ou) humming and hawing, shilly-shallying, dithering.

valser [-se] v. intr. (1). Mus. To waltz ; *faire valser*, to dance with. ‖ Fam. *Faire valser l'argent*, to make the money fly, to spend money like 'water ; *faire valser qqn*, to lead s.o. a dance (lui en faire voir) ; to kick s.o. out (le renvoyer). — v. tr. Mus. To waltz.

valseur, euse [-sœ:r, ø:z] adj. Waltzing. — s. Waltzer.

valu [valy] p. p. V. valoir (103).

valve [valv] f. Méd., Bot., Zool., Electr. Valve. ‖ Autom. Tyre-valve.

valvulaire [-vylɛ:r] adj. Valvular ; valvulate.

valvule [-vy:l] f. Méd. Valvula, valve.

vamp [vãp] f. Fam. Vamp.

vamper [-pe] v. tr. (1). Fam. To vamp, to seduce.

vampire [vãpi:r] m. Zool. Vampire, vampire-bat. ‖ Fig. Vampire, blood-sucker, extortioner.

vampirique [-rik] adj. Vampiric, blood-sucking.

vampirisme [-rism] m. Vampirism. ‖ Fig. Blood-sucking, extortion.

van [vã] m. Agric. Winnowing-basket (en osier) ; winnowing-machine, aspirator (mécanique) ; fan (tarare) ; *passer au van*, to winnow. ‖ Techn. Van, vanning-shovel (de mines).

van [vã] m. Horse-van (voiture).

vanadium [vanadjɔm] m. Chim. Vanadium.

vandale [vãdal] s. Vandal.

vandalisme [vãdalism] m. Vandalism.

vandoise [vãdwa:z] f. Zool. Dace.

vanesse [vanɛs] f. Zool. Vanessa.

vanille [vani:j] f. Culin. Vanilla ; *glace à la vanille*, vanilla ice.

vanillé, ée [vanije] adj. Culin. Vanilla-flavoured.

vanillerie [-jri] f. Vanilla-plantation.

vanillier [-lje] m. Bot. Vanilla-plant.

vanilline [-lin] f. Chim. Vanillin.

vanité [vanite] f. Vanity, futility, emptiness, triviality, worthlessness (vide) ; *tout est vanité,* all is vanity. ‖ Vanity, vainglory, self-admiration, self-sufficiency, conceitedness, petty pride (suffisance) ; *par vanité,* out of vanity ; *sans vanité,* in all due modesty ; *tirer vanité de,* to pride oneself on.

vaniteusement [-tøzmã] adv. Vainly, conceitedly ; vaingloriously.

vaniteux, euse [-tø, ø:z] adj. Vain, conceited ; vainglorious. (V. prétentieux, suffisant.) — s. Vain (ou) conceited person.

vannage [vana:ʒ] m. Agric. Winnowing. ‖ Techn. Vanning. ‖ Fam. Exhaustion.

vannage m. Techn. Sluicing (d'une écluse) ; gating (d'une turbine). ‖ Sluices, sluice-gates (vannes).

vanne [van] f. Sluice, sluice-gate ; flood-gate, overflow weir (de décharge) ; *lever les vannes,* to open the sluice-gates. ‖ Naut. Cock. ‖ Techn. Gate (de turbine) ; *vanne d'eau,* water valve. ‖ Pl. Zool. Wing-feathers.

vanne f. Fam. Dig, gibe, taunt ; *lancer des vannes à qqn,* to gibe at, to taunt s. o.

vanneau [vano] m. Zool. Lapwing, peewit.

vannelle [vanɛl] f. Techn. Sluice-valve.

vanner [vane] v. tr: Techn. To sluice (une écluse) ; to gate (une turbine).

vanner v. tr. Agric. To winnow, to sift, to fan

(le blé). ‖ Techn. To van (le minerai). ‖ Fam. To tire out, to exhaust (v. éreinter) ; *être vanné,* to be dead-beat (ou) all-in (ou) U. S. all-shot.

vannerie [-nri] f. Basket-making, basket-trade (métier) ; basket-work, wicker-work (ouvrage).

vanneur [-nœ:r] m. Agric. Winnower, sifter. ‖ Techn. Vanner.

vanneuse [-nø:z] f. Agric. Winnowing-machine.

vannier [-nje] m. Basket-maker, basket-worker.

vannure [-ny:r] f. Agric. Husks, chaff.

vantail [vãta:j] (pl. **vantaux** [vãto]) m. Leaf (d'une porte, d'un volet) ; folding-panel (d'un triptyque) ; *à deux vantaux,* folding (porte).

vantard, arde [vãta:r, ard] adj. Boasting, boastful, bragging. (V. hâbleur.) — s. Braggart, boaster.

vantardise [-di:z] f. Boating, boastfulness, bragging ; brag, boast, piece of bluff. (V. hâblerie.)

vanter [vãte] v. tr. (1). To praise, to praise up, to speak highly of ; to crack up (fam.). — v. pr. **Se vanter,** to brag, to boast (de, of) ; to pride oneself (de, on) ; *il n'y a pas de quoi se vanter,* it's nothing to boast about ; *se vanter de faire,* to undertake to do.

vanterie [-tri] f. Boasting, bragging ; boast, brag.

vapes [vap] f. pl. Pop. *Tomber dans les vapes,* to pass out, to faint ; *être dans les vapes,* to be dopey (ou) muzzy (ou) U.S. woozy.

vapeur [vapœ:r] m. Naut. Steamer, steamship ; screw-steamer (à hélices) ; paddle-steamer (à roues) ; *vapeur charbonnier,* steam collier. — f. Vapour, U. S. vapor (d'eau) ; steam (d'eau bouillante) ; fumes (de l'encens, du vin) ; mist, haze (du matin). ‖ Ch. de f. *Machine à vapeur,* steam-engine. ‖ Naut. *Bateau à vapeur,* steamer, steamship ; *à toute vapeur,* full steam ahead. ‖ Pl. Méd. Vapours. ‖ Fam. *A toute vapeur,* at full speed.

vapocraquage [vapokraka:ʒ] m. Techn. Steam cracking.

vaporeusement [vaporøzmã] adv. Vaporously.

vaporeux, euse [-rø, ø:z] adj. Vaporous, vapourish (v. flou) ; steamy (atmosphère) ; hazy, misty (lumière). ‖ Fig. Hazy, vague (idées) ; vapourish (personne) ; nebulous (style) ; light, filmy (tissu).

vaporisable [vaporizabl] adj. Vaporisable.

vaporisateur [-ratœ:r] m. Vaporizer, atomizer (pulvérisateur) ; scent-spray, U. S. perfume atomizer (de toilette). ‖ Techn. Evaporator.

vaporisation [-rizasjõ] f. Vaporization, atomization. (V. pulvérisation.)

vaporiser [-rize] v. tr. (1). To vaporize, to volatilize (volatiliser). ‖ To atomize, to spray (un liquide). — *.* pr. **Se vaporiser,** to vaporize, to become vaporized (liquide) ; to spray oneself (personne).

vaquer [vake] v. intr. (1). To be vacant (situation). ‖ Jur. To be in vacation, not to sit, not to be sitting (tribunaux). ‖ **Vaquer à,** to attend to, to concern oneself with, to see to, to look to (en général) ; to go about (ses affaires) ; to be busy with (son ouvrage).

varaigne [varɛɲ] f. Tide-gate.

varangue [varã:g] f. Naut. Floor-frame, floor-timber ; floor-rider.

varappe [varap] f. Sports. Rock climbing.

varappeur, euse [-pœ:r, ø:z] s. Sports. Rock climber, climber.

varech [varɛk] m. Wrack, seaweed.

vareuse [varø:z] f. Jumper (de femme) ; close-fitting jacket (d'homme). ‖ Milit. Tunic (d'officier) ; blouse, fatigue jacket (de soldat). ‖ Naut. Jersey, jumper (de marin) ; pilot-coat, pea-jacket.

variabilité [varjabilite] f. Variability. ‖ Changeableness (du temps).

variable [-djabl] adj. Variable. ‖ Unsteady (baromètre) ; « change » (indication du baromètre) ;

changeable, unsettled (temps). ‖ Méd. Unequal (pouls). ‖ Math., Electr. Variable. ‖ Fin. *Valeurs à revenu variable*, variable yield securities. ‖ Fig. Capricious, fickle (humeur). [V. changeant, versatile.]
— m. *Au variable*, at « change ».
— f. Math. Variable.
variablement [-rjabləmᾶ] adv. Variably.
variance [-rjᾶːs] f. Math. Variance.
variante [-rjᾶːt] f. Variant, different reading.
variateur [-rjatœːr] m. Techn. *Variateur de vitesse*, variable speed-drive.
variation [-rjasjɔ̃] f. Variation (v. changement); change (du temps). ‖ Milit. Change (de hausse). ‖ Naut. Error (du compas); *compas à variation*, variation compass. ‖ Mus., Zool. Variation. ‖ Astron. Deviation (d'un astre). ‖ Electr. Variation (du courant); drop (de potentiel). ‖ Fin. Fluctuation (des cours). ‖ Fig. Variation (de l'esprit).
varice [varis] f. Méd. Varix (pl. *varices*).
varicelle [varisɛl] f. Méd. Varicella, chicken-pox.
varicocèle [-kɔsɛl] f. Méd. Varicocele.
varié, ée [varje] adj. Varied; variegated, mixed (couleurs); miscellaneous (nouvelles); varying, diversified (types). ‖ Mus. *Air varié*, theme with variations. ‖ Techn. Variable (mouvement). ‖ Fig. Chequered (existence).
varier v. intr. (1). To change (temps, vent). ‖ To vary, to differ (se modifier). ‖ To vary, to deviate, to be inconsistent (fluctuer). ‖ To vary, to be at variance, to disagree (différer). ‖ Fin. To fluctuate.
— v. tr. To variegate (les couleurs); to diversify (ses expressions); to vary (les plats, son style). ‖ Mus. To make variations on.
variété [-rjete] f. Variety; wide range (de lectures); diversity (d'opinions); variedness (du paysage); *donner de la variété à*, to lend variety to. ‖ Théâtr. Pl. Variety theatre. ‖ Comm. Range (de rayons). ‖ Bot. Variety (d'une fleur).
variole [varjɔːl] f. Méd. Variola, smallpox. ‖ Sheep-pox (des moutons); cow-pox (des vaches).
variolé, ée [varjɔle] adj. Pock-marked.
varioleux, euse [-lœ, øːz] adj. Méd. Variolous.
— s. Smallpox patient.
variolique [-lik] adj. Méd. Variolous.
variomètre [varjɔmɛtr] m. Electr. Variometer.
variqueux, euse [varikø, øːz] adj. Méd. Varicose.
varlope [varlɔp] f. Techn. Trying (ou) jointing-plane.
varloper [-pe] v. tr. (1). Techn. To plane down, to plane.
Varsovie [varsɔvi] f. Géogr. Warsaw.
vasculaire [vaskylɛːr] adj. Bot., Méd. Vascular.
vascularisation [-larizasjɔ̃] f. Bot., Méd. Vascular meshwork; vascularization.
vascularisé, ée [-larize] adj. Bot., Méd. Vascularized.
vase [vɑːz] m. Vase (à fleurs). ‖ Vessel, receptacle (v. récipient); *vase de nuit*, chamber-pot. ‖ Archit. Bell, vase (de chapiteau). ‖ Ecclés. *Vase d'élection*, chosen vessel; *vases sacrés*, consecrated vessels. ‖ Bot. Vase, calyx (de tulipe). ‖ Phys. *Vase clos*, retort; *vases communicants*, communicating vessels; *vase évaporateur*, evaporating basin. ‖ Fig. *Vase clos*, isolation.
vase f. Mud, mide, slime, ooze, silt, sludge.
vasectomie [vazɛktɔmi] f. Méd. Vasectomy.
vaseline [vazliːn] f. Petroleum jelly, Vaseline; *enduire de vaseline*, to Vaseline.
vaseliner [-line] v. tr. (1). To Vaseline.
vaseux, euse [vazø, øːz] adj. Slimy, muddy. (V. bourbeux.) ‖ Fig. Dirty, filthy. ‖ Fam. Poorish, pretty weak (explication); woolly (idées); seedy, not up to much, out of sorts, off-colour, bleary

(personne); *il a l'air vaseux*, he looks a bit under the weather (ou) washed out.
vasistas [vazistɑːs] m. Ventilator (d'une fenêtre, d'une porte); fan-light, U. S. transom (d'une porte).
vasoconstricteur, trice [vazokɔ̃striktœːr, tris] adj. Méd. Vaso-constrictive, vaso-constrictor.
— m. Méd. Vaso-constrictor.
vasoconstriction [-kɔ̃striksjɔ̃] f. Méd. Vasoconstriction.
vasodilatateur, trice [-dilatatœːr, tris] adj. Méd. Vaso-dilating, vaso-dilator.
— m. Méd. Vaso-dilator.
vasodilatation [-dilatasjɔ̃] f. Méd. Vaso-dilatation.
vasomoteur, trice [-mɔtœːr, tris] adj. Méd. Vaso-motor.
vasouiller [vazuje] v. intr. (1). Fam. To get bogged down, to flounder.
vasque [vask] f. Bassin (d'une fontaine); bowl (de table).
vassal, ale [vasal] adj., s. Vassal.
vassalité [vasalite] f., **vasselage** [vasla:ʒ] m. Vassalage; bondage.
vaste [vast] adj. Vast, huge (v. ample, spacieux); enormous (bâtiment); wide, spreading (campagne); vast, far-flung (empire); broad (étendue); boundless (océan). ‖ Milit. Great, mighty (armée). ‖ Fig. Vast, huge; extensive, comprehensive, far-reaching, all-embracing (connaissances); gigantic (entreprise). ‖ Fam. Awful, gigantic (erreur).
— m. Méd. Vastus (muscle).
vastement [-temᾶ] adv. Vastly; widely.
Vatican [vatikᾶ] m. Vatican.
vaticane [-kan] adj. Pertaining to the Vatican; Vatican (bibliothèque).
— f. *La Vaticane*, the Vatican Library.
vaticinateur, trice [vatisinatœːr, tris] adj. Vaticinal.
— s. Vaticinator.
vaticination [-nasjɔ̃] f. Vaticination.
vaticiner [-ne] v. intr. (1). To vaticinate.
vauclusien, enne [voklyzjɛ̃, ɛn] adj. Géogr. Of (ou) from the department of Vaucluse. ‖ Géol. *Source vauclusienne*, resurgent water.
vaudeville [vodvil] m. Théâtr. Vaudeville, light comedy; bedroom farce (fam.).
vaudevillesque [-lɛsk] adj. Comical, Gilbertian, farcical, worthy of a vaudeville.
vaudevilliste [-list] s. Vaudevillist.
vaudois, oise [vodwa, aːz] adj. Géogr. Vaudois, of (ou) from the Swiss canton of Vaud.
— s. Géogr. Vaudois, inhabitant of Vaud. ‖ Ecclés. Vaudois, member of the Waldenses.
vaudou [vodu] m. Voodoo.
vaudra, vaudrai, vaudrait. V. valoir (103).
vau-l'eau (à) [avolo] loc. adv. Down-stream, with the stream (ou) the current. ‖ Fig. Adrift; *aller à vau-l'eau*, to be left to drift (affaires); to go to rack and ruin, to drift; to go to the dogs, to go to pot (fam.).
vaurien [vorjɛ̃] m. Worthless individual, good-for-nothing, ne'er-do-well (bon à rien). ‖ Rascal, scamp (gamin). ‖ Scoundrel, rogue, blackguard; rotter (fam.) [canaille].
vaurienne [-rjɛn] f. Worthless woman; bad lot.
vaut [vo]. V. valoir.
vautour [votuːr] m. Zool. Vulture.
vautre [voːtr] m. Zool. Boar-hound.
vautrer (se) [səvotre] v. pr. To wallow (dans, in) [la boue]; to loll (dans, in) [un fauteuil]; to sprawl (sur, on) [le sol]. ‖ Fig. To wallow (dans, in) [le vice].
Vauvert [vovɛːr] m. *Aller au diable Vauvert*, to go miles away; *c'est au diable Vauvert*, it's a deuce of a way, it's at the back of beyond.
vaux [vo] m. pl. V. val.

vavassal [vavasal], **vavasseur** [-sœ:r] m. Vava-sour.

veau [vo] m. ZOOL. Calf (animal); *veau de lait*, suckling calf; *veau gras*, fatted calf; *veau marin*, seal, sea-calf. ‖ COMM. Calf, calf-skin, calf leather (cuir). ‖ CULIN. Veal; *gelée de pied de veau*, calves-foot jelly; *tête de veau*, calf's head. ‖ FIG. *Adorer le veau d'or*, to worship the golden calf. ‖ FAM. *Faire le veau*, to loll, to sprawl; *pleurer comme un veau*, to blubber, to cry like a baby; *tête de veau*, bald-head. ‖ POP. Ninny, noodle (imbécile); lump, clod (mou).

vecteur [vɛktœ:r] adj. Carrier. ‖ MATH. *Rayon vecteur*, radius vector.
— m. MATH. Vector.

vectoriel, elle [-tɔrjɛl] adj. MATH. Vectorial.

vécu, ue [veky] p.p. V. VIVRE (105).
— adj. Lived. ‖ FIG. Authentic, founded on fact, that really happened (incident); realistic, true, true to life (personnage); *aventure vécue*, real adventure (récit).
— m. Personal experience; real life.

vedettariat [vədɛtarja] m. Stardom (rang, état); star system (système).

vedette [-dɛ:t] f. MILIT. Vedette, mounted sentry; *en vedette*, on vedette duty. ‖ NAUT. Vedette-boat, patrol-boat, scout (bâtiment de guerre); motor boat, launch (embarcation à moteur); police-launch (de la police); *vedette lance-torpilles*, motor torpedo boat, E-boat (allemande), M.T.B. (anglaise). ‖ AVIAT. *Vedette aérienne*, blimp. ‖ TYPOGR. *En vedette*, on a separate line (détaché); in bold type (en gras). ‖ SPORTS. Star; *club vedette*, star club. ‖ THÉÂTR., CINÉM. Star; film (ou) U. S. movie star; lead (au cinéma); leading man (ou) lady (au théâtre); *être en vedette*, to star, to head the bill. ‖ FIG. Leading light; *être en vedette*, to be in the forefront (ou) in the limelight; *donner la vedette à*, to headline, U. S. to feature (une nouvelle).

védique [vedik] adj. Vedic.
— m. GRAMM. Vedic (langue).

védisme [-dism] m. Vedaism.

végétabilité [veʒetabilite] f. Vegetability.

végétal, ale [-tal] adj. BOT. Plant; vegetable (règne); *terre végétale*, loam. ‖ CULIN. Vegetable (beurre, graisse).
— m. BOT. Plant.

végétalisme [-talism] m. Veganism, strict vege-tarianism.

végétarianisme [-tarjanism], **végétarisme** [-ta-rism] m. Vegetarianism.

végétarien, enne [-tarjɛ̃, ɛn] adj., s. Vegetarian.

végétatif, ive [-tatif, i:v] adj. Vegetative.

végétation [-tasjɔ̃] f. Vegetation; *en pleine végé-tation*, in full growth. ‖ MÉD. Pl. Vegetations; adenoid growths.

végéter [-te] v. intr. (5). To vegetate, to grow. ‖ FIG. To vegetate; to live an uninteresting (ou) inactive life. (V. VIVOTER.)

végéto- [-to] préf. Vegeto-. ‖ **Végéto-animal,** adj. Vegeto-animal. ‖ **Végéto-minéral,** adj. Vegeto-mineral.

véhémence [veemɑ̃:s] f. Vehemence (v. FOUGUE); *avec véhémence*, vehemently.

véhément, ente [-mɑ̃, ɑ̃:t] adj. Vehement.

véhémentement [-mɑ̃tmɑ̃] adv. Vehemently, passionately, violently.

véhiculaire [veikylɛ:r] adj. Vehicular.

véhicule [-kyl] m. Vehicle, conveyance, carriage (v. VOITURE); *véhicules utilitaires*, commercial vehicles. ‖ MÉD. Vehicle, medium (d'une drogue); carrier (d'une maladie). ‖ FIG. Vehicle, medium (du son).

véhiculer [-kyle] v. tr. (1). To convey, to trans-port, to carry (dans une camionnette); to cart (dans une charrette).

veille [vɛ:j] f. Sitting up, staying up, late nights (privation de sommeil); keeping awake; watch-fulness (état de veille). ‖ Vigil (de fête); night before, eve, day before (jour précédent); *la veille du jour de l'An, de Noël*, New Year's, Christmas Eve. ‖ Pl. Staying up at night; sleepless nights (insomnie); night-work, lucubrations, midnight oil (travaux); *il a été pour moi la cause de bien des veilles*, he has caused me many a sleepless night. ‖ MILIT. Watch, night watch. ‖ NAUT. Lookout. ‖ FIG. Point, brink, verge; *à la veille de*, on the eve of, close to.

veillée [vɛje] f. Evening (soirée). ‖ Evening, evening meeting, party (réunion). ‖ ECCLÉS. Vigil, watching (d'un corps); *veillée du corps*, wake. ‖MÉD. Sitting up; night-attendance, night-nurs-ing. ‖ MILIT. *Veillée d'armes*, armed vigil.

veiller v. intr. (1). To stay awake, to sit up, to stay up (debout); to lie awake (au lit); *veiller auprès d'un malade*, to sit up with a sick person; *veiller tard*, to sit up late, to burn the midnight oil; *veiller jusqu'à ce que qqn rentre*, to wait up for s.o. ‖ MILIT. To keep watch, to be on guard; to stand by. ‖ NAUT. To be on the watch (ou) on the lookout; to stand by. ‖ JUR. To watch; *veiller aux intérêts de qqn*, to hold a watching brief for s.o. ‖ **Veiller à,** to look after; to see to; to attend to; *veillez à la besogne*, see to the work, keep an eye on the work; *veillez à ce que la porte soit fermée*, see that the door is shut, make sure the door is closed; *veiller à faire qqch.*, to be careful to do sth. ‖ **Veiller sur,** to watch over, to keep watch over; to take care of; to look after. (V. SURVEILLER.) ‖ FAM. *Veiller au grain*, to look out for squalls.
— v. tr. To sit up with, to look after, to attend to, to watch over (un malade); *veiller un mort*, to watch by (ou) to sit up with a dead body, to wake a corpse.

veilleur [-jœ:r] m. Watcher; watchman; *veilleur de nuit*, night-watchman.

veilleuse [-jø:z] f. Night-light (lampe). ‖ Pilot-light (de bec de gaz); by-pass (de brûleur de gaz); *mettre en veilleuse*, to turn low (l'électricité); to damp down (un haut fourneau); to turn down (le gaz). ‖ AUTOM. Dimmer-bulb; *mettre en veil-leuse*, to dim (les phares). ‖ FIG. *Mettre une entre-prise en veilleuse*, to reduce output to a minimum, to keep the wheels just turning.

veinage [vɛna:z] m. Veining, graining.

veinard, arde [vɛna:r, ard] adj. FAM. Lucky.
— s. FAM. Lucky person; *c'est un veinard*, he's a lucky fellow (ou) devil (ou) dog, he has all the luck. (V. CHANCEUX.)

veine [vɛn] f. MÉD. Vein; *veine cave*, vena cava. ‖ BOT. Vein. ‖ TECHN. Grain (du bois, de la pierre); vein (du bois, du marbre); seam (de houille); marbling (sur la tranche d'un livre); lode (de mineral). ‖ FIG. Vein, humour, mood, inspiration; bent; *veine poétique*, poetic vein; *il n'est pas en veine de plaisanter*, he's in no mood for joking. ‖ FAM. Good luck (v. CHANCE); run of good luck (filon); *il a de la veine*, he's in luck; *c'est bien ma veine*, just my luck; *coup de veine*, stroke of luck; fluke; *quelle veine!*, what a stroke of luck!; *pas de veine!*, bad (ou) hard (ou) rotten luck!

veiné, ée [-ne] adj. Veined (arbre); grained (sur-face).

veiner v. tr. (1). To vein, to grain.

veineux, euse [-nø, ø:z] adj. MÉD. Venous (sang, système). ‖ BOT. Veiny, venous (bois, feuille).

veinule [-nyl] f. MÉD. Veinlet, veinule.

veinure [-nyr] f. Veining (du marbre); graining (d'une porte).

vêlage [vɛla:ʒ] m. Calving (d'une vache).

vélaire [vɛlɛ:r] adj. GRAMM. Velar; back (consonne, voyelle); *r vélaire,* uvular r.
— f. Velar guttural; back consonant; back vowel.

vêlement [vɛlmɑ̃] m. Calving (d'une vache).

vêler [vɛle] v. intr. To calve (vache).

vélin [velɛ̃] adj. Vellum; *papier vélin,* wove paper.
— m. Vellum. ‖ Fine Alençon lace (dentelle).

vélite [velit] m. MILIT. † Velites.

velléitaire [vɛleitɛ:r] adj. Erratic, impulsive; full of whims.
— s. Erratic (ou) impulsive person; trifler.

velléité [-te] f. Slight desire, inclination, fancy, slight impulse, whim; *avoir quelque velléité de,* to have half a mind to, to toy with the idea of; *avoir des velléités de résistance,* to put up a resistance of sorts (ou) a show of resistance.

vélo [velo] m. FAM. Bike, cycle; *aller à vélo,* to bike, to cycle; *faire du vélo,* to go in for cycling. ‖ **Vélo-pousse** (pl. *vélos-pousse*), m. Bicycle rickshaw, U. S. pedicab.

vélocar [veloka:r] m. Pedal-car.

véloce [velɔs] adj. Swift, fleet, fast (coureur).

vélocimane [velɔsiman] m. Horse on wheels.

vélocipède [-sipɛd] m. † Velocipede.

vélocité [-site] f. Velocity, speed, swiftness (v. RAPIDITÉ); fleetness (d'un coureur).

vélodrome [-drɔ:m] m. Cycle-racing track (piste); U. S. velodrome (édifice).

vélomoteur [-mɔtœ:r] m. Motor-assisted bicycle; light motor-cycle; moped (fam.).

vélotaxi [-taksi] m. Bicycle with passenger trailer, U. S. pedicab. (V. VÉLO-POUSSE.)

velours [vəlu:r] m. Velvet (en général); corduroy (à côtes); velveteen (de coton); figured velvet (façonné); shot velvet (glacé); velours, plush (de laine); short-nap velvet (ras); *de velours,* velvet. ‖ COMM. Pl. Velvetings. ‖ Bloom (duvet). ‖ FIG. *Faire patte de velours,* to draw in its claws (chat); to show the velvet glove (personne); *jouer sur le velours,* to be on velvet.

velouté, ée [vəlute] adj. Velvety; velvet-like (d'aspect); soft, soft as velvet (au toucher). ‖ Downy (joues, pêche). ‖ TECHN. Velvet-surface (papier). ‖ FIG. Soft, caressing (regard); rich, mellow, velvety (vin).
— m. Velvetiness, softness (d'une étoffe); bloom (d'une pêche); rich colour (d'une pierre précieuse). ‖ *Velouté de laine,* velours, velvet braid. ‖ CULIN. Velouté.

velouter v. tr. (1). To give a velvety appearance (ou) finish to.

velouteux, euse [-tø, ø:z] adj. Velvety, downy.

veloutine [-tin] f. Soft flannelette.

Velpeau [vɛlpo] m. MÉD. *Bande Velpeau,* crape (ou) U. S. crepe bandage.

velu, ue [vəly] adj. Hairy, shaggy. (V. POILU.) ‖ BOT. Pubescent; villous (feuille).

vélum [velɔm] m. Awning.

venaison [vənɛzɔ̃] f. CULIN. Venison.

vénal, ale [venal] adj. Venal, purchasable (charge). ‖ COMM. Usual selling (poids); market (valeur). ‖ FIG. Venal, mercenary (personne).

vénalement [-lmɑ̃] adv. Venally.

vénalité [-ilte] f. Venality, mercenariness, money-mindedness.

venant, ante [vənɑ̃, ɑ̃:t] adj. Coming; *bien venant,* thriving, growing, coming on (arbre, enfant). ‖ FIN. Regular, paid regularly (rente).
— m. Comer; *les allants et venants,* comers and goers; passers-by; *à tout venant,* to anyone, to all and sundry, to all comers.

vendable [vɑ̃dabl] adj. COMM. Saleable, marketable; *difficilement vendable,* hard to sell, unsaleable, not in demand. ‖ JUR. Vendible.

vendange [vɑ̃dɑ̃:ʒ] f. AGRIC. Grape harvest, crop of grapes (raisins); vintage, vintaging, grape-harvesting, grape-gathering (récolte); vintage, vintage-season (temps). ‖ FIG. Profit. ‖ LOC. *Adieu paniers, vendanges sont faites,* it's all over and done with.

vendanger [-ʒe] v. intr. To vintage, to gather the grapes, to harvest grapes.
— v. tr. To vintage, to gather the grapes of. ‖ FIG. To sweep away, to destroy (détruire); to make off with (s'approprier).

vendangeur [-ʒœ:r] s. Vintager, grape-gatherer (ou) -picker (ou) -harvester.

vendéen, enne [vɑ̃deɛ̃, ɛn] adj., s. GÉOGR. Vendean.

vendémiaire [vɑ̃demjɛ:r] m. Vendémiaire, first month in French Republican calendar (september-october).

venderesse [vɑ̃drɛs] f. JUR. Vendor.

vendetta [vɛ̃dɛtta] f. Vendetta, feud.

vendeur [vɑ̃dœ:r] m. Seller. ‖ COMM. Vendor; Salesman; shopman; shop-assistant, counterhand; U. S. salesclerk. ‖ JUR. Vendor.

vendeuse [-dø:z] f. Seller. ‖ COMM. Vendor; saleswoman, salesgirl; shopwoman, shop-girl; shop-assistant, counter-hand; U. S. salesclerk.

vendre [vɑ̃:dr] v. tr. (4). To sell; *je lui ai vendu ma montre,* I sold him my watch, I sold my watch to him; *vendre au kilo,* to sell by the kilo. ‖ COMM. *A vendre,* to be sold, for sale; *maison à vendre,* house for sale; *faire vendre,* to sell up (qqn pour dette); *vendre moins cher que qqn,* to undersell s.o. ‖ FIG. To sell (sa conscience, son honneur); to barter away (sa liberté); *vendre cher sa vie,* to sell one's life dearly. ‖ FIG. To give away, to denounce, to inform against, to sell (fam.) [un complice]; to betray, to give away (un secret); *vendre un copain,* to rat on a pal (fam.).
— v. pr. **Se vendre,** to sell, to be sold; *se vendre cher,* to fetch (ou) U. S. to bring a high price; *se vendre comme des petits pains,* to sell like hot cakes; *se vendre pour un morceau de pain,* to go for a song.
— v. récipr. **Se vendre,** to sell (ou) to betray each other, to give each other away.

vendredi [vɑ̃drədi] m. Friday; *le vendredi saint,* Good Friday.

vendu, ue [vɑ̃dy] adj. Sold. ‖ FIG. *Homme vendu au gouvernement,* minion of the government.
— m. Traitor; minion; stooge; *les vendus de la politique,* corrupt politicians.

venelle [vənɛl] f. † Narrow street, alley.

vénéneux, euse [venenø, ø:z] adj. Poisonous.

vénérabilité [venerabilite] f. Venerability, venerableness.

vénérable [-rabl] adj. Venerable.
— m. Grand Master (d'une loge maçonnique).

vénérablement [-rabləmɑ̃] adv. Venerably.

vénérateur, trice [-ratœ:r, tris] s. Venerator.

vénération [-rasjɔ̃] f. Veneration, reverence.

vénérer [-re] v. tr. (5). To venerate, to revere, to reverence, to respect. ‖ ECCLÉS. To venerate.

vénerie [venri] f. SPORTS. Venery; hunting (art); administration of the Royal Hunt (bureau).

vénérien, enne [venerjɛ̃, ɛn] adj. MÉD. Venereal.

venette [vənɛt] f. POP. Funk. (V. FROUSSE.)

veneur [vənœ:r] m. Huntsman; *Grand Veneur,* Master of the Royal Hunt.

Venezuela [venezɥela] m. GÉOGR. Venezuela.

vénézuélien [-ljɛ̃] adj., s. GÉOGR. Venezuelan.

vengeance [vɑ̃ʒɑ̃:s] f. Vengeance, revenge; *esprit de vengeance,* vengefulness; *par vengeance,* out of revenge; *tirer vengeance de,* to be revenged for (une offense); to take vengeance on, to be avenged upon, to wreak vengeance (ou) revenge on (qqn). ‖ ECCLÉS. *La vengeance du ciel,* divine retribution.

venger [-ʒe] v. tr. (7). To vindicate (son honneur) ; to avenge (une offense) ; to revenge, to avenge (une personne).

— v. pr. **Se venger,** to revenge oneself, to be revenged for, to have one's revenge ; *se venger de,* to revenge oneself for, to take vengeance for (une offense) ; to be revenged on, to take vengeance on, to avenge oneself on (une personne).

vengeur, eresse [-ʒœ:r, ərɛs] adj. Avenging, vengeful, revengeful.

— s. Avenger, revenger.

véniel, elle [venjɛl] adj. Venial.

véniellement [-mɑ̃] adv. Venially.

venimeux, euse [vənimø, ø:z] adj. Venomous, poisonous (animal) ; poisonous (morsure). ‖ FIG. Malignant, spiteful, malicious (critique, langue) ; envenomed (parole).

venimosité [-mozite] f. Venomousness.

venin [vənɛ̃] m. Venom, poison. ‖ FIG. Venom, malice, spite, virulence ; *jeter tout son venin,* to vent all one's spleen.

venir [vəni:r] v. intr. (101).

---

1. Sens général. — 2. Arriver. — 3. Se développer. — 4. Se présenter. — 5. Provenir. — 6. Etre tiré. — 7. Parvenir. — 8. Atteindre. — 9. Etre accueilli. — 10. Couler. — 11. *Venir* suivi de l'infinitif. — 12. NAUT. — 13. TECHN. — 14. **Venir à.** — 15. **Venir de.** — 16. **Venir de ce que.** — 17. **En venir à.** — 18. **Faire venir.** — 19. **Voir venir.**

---

1. To come, to be coming, to come along (*avec,* with) [sens général] ; *venez par ici,* come this way. ‖ 2. To come, to arrive (arriver) ; *elle est venue en voiture,* she came by car, she drove here ; *je ne fais qu'aller et venir,* I shall be back at once ; U. S. I'll be right back ; *prendre les choses comme elles viennent,* to take things as they come ; *le printemps viendra,* spring will soon be here ; *l'année qui vient,* next year ; *dans les années à venir,* in years to come ; *son bonheur à venir,* his future happiness ; *venir au monde,* to be born, to come into the world. ‖ 3. To come on, to develop (se développer) ; to shape (affaire) ; to come out (détail) ; to grow up (enfant) ; to grow, to come up (plante) ; to take shape (tableau) ; *bien venir,* to thrive (plante) ; *être bien venu,* to be successful ; to be well produced (édition) ; to come out well (photographie) ; *mal venu,* weedy (jeune homme) ; stunted (sujet) ; *venir à maturité,* to reach maturity. ‖ 4. To come, to occur (se présenter) ; *l'idée me vient que,* it comes to my mind that, it occurs to me that, the thought strikes me that ; *la première solution venue,* the first solution that comes to mind. ‖ 5. To come, to come into one's possession (provenir) ; *d'où cela vient-il?,* where does that come from ?, what's the reason for that ? ; *d'où lui vient sa fortune?,* where does his fortune come from ? ; *cette pendule lui vient de son père,* he inherited this clock from his father. ‖ 6. To come, to be derived, to issue, to be descended, to be drawn (être tiré) ; to spring (source) ; *mot qui vient du latin,* word derived from Latin ; *il vient de Londres,* he comes from (ou) he hails from London ; *thé qui vient de Chine,* tea from China ; *il vient de bonne souche,* he comes of good stock. ‖ 7. To come, to reach (parvenir) ; to come, to be handed down (tradition). ‖ 8. To come, to reach, to attain (atteindre) ; *elle ne me vient pas à l'épaule,* she doesn't come up to my shoulder ; *venir à bien,* to prosper, to succeed ; *venir à bout de qqch.,* to succeed in doing sth., to manage to do sth. ; *je n'en viendrai jamais à bout,* I shall never

manage it ; *venir à rien,* to come to nothing. ‖ To come about, to happen, to occur (avoir lieu) ; *un malheur ne vient jamais seul,* misfortunes never happen singly. ‖ 9. To come, to be received (être accueilli) ; *être bien venu* (ou) *mal venu,* to be welcome (ou) unwelcome ; *vous êtes mal venu à m'en parler,* it's not for you to tell me about it (ce n'est pas votre affaire) ; this is no time to tell me about it (ce n'est pas le moment). ‖ 10. To come, to run, to flow (couler) ; *l'eau commence à venir,* water is beginning to flow. ‖ 11. To come and, to come to (suivi de l'infinitif) ; *venez me voir demain;* come and see me tomorrow ; *il est venu me voir,* he came and saw me (action) ; he came to see me (but) ; *venir prendre qqn,* to come and fetch s.o., to call for s.o. ‖ 12. NAUT. To come, to change course ; *venir sur bâbord,* to alter course to port ; *venir dans le vent,* to come round. ‖ 13. TECHN. To come out. ‖ 14. **Venir à** (suivi de l'infinitif), to happen to, to chance to ; *si je venais à mourir,* if I should happen to die, if I should die. ‖ 15. **Venir de** (suivi de l'infinitif), to have just ; *il vient de partir,* he has just left ; *il venait de le faire,* he had just done it. ‖ 16. **Venir de ce que,** to result from, to be the result of, to be due to. ‖ 17. **En venir à,** to come to, to reach, to go as far as (aller jusqu'à) ; to be reduced to ; to bring oneself to, to have recourse to (être réduit à) ; to come round to (un point de vue) ; *en venir aux coups,* to come to blows ; *les choses en sont là,* that is how matters stand, matters have come to that ; *je vois où il veut en venir,* I see what he's driving at (ou) what he's getting at ; *en venir aux faits,* to get down to business (ou) brass tacks (fam.). ‖ 18. **Faire venir,** to cause to come ; to raise, to grow, to produce (du blé) ; to send for (envoyer chercher) ; to order, to get in (des provisions) ; *faire venir les larmes aux yeux,* to bring tears to the eyes ; *se faire bien venir de qqn,* to get into s.o.'s good books. ‖ 19. **Voir venir,** to watch coming ; FIG. *je vous vois venir,* I see what you are driving at (ou) getting at, I see your little game.

— v. impers. To come (arriver) ; *il est venu qqn,* s.o. has called (ou) been. ‖ To come ; *il me vient l'idée que* (ou) *il me vient à l'esprit que,* the thought strikes me that, it occurs to me that ; *il lui est venu une tumeur,* he has developed a tumour. ‖ To come, to happen (se passer) ; *d'où vient-il que...?,* how is it that...?

— v. pr. **S'en venir,** to make one's way ; to return.

Venise [vəni:z] f. GÉOGR. Venice. ‖ COMM. *Dentelle de Venise,* Venetian lace.

vénitien, enne [venisjɛ̃, ɛn] adj., s. Venetian. ‖ *Blond vénitien,* Titian red.

vénosité [venozite] f. MÉD. Venosity.

vent [vɑ̃] m. Wind ; *vent du nord,* north wind ; *il fait du vent,* it is windy ; *exposé au vent,* windy ; *à l'abri du vent,* out of (ou) sheltered from the wind ; *en plein vent,* in the open air. ‖ Air ; *ballon plein de vent,* balloon full of air. ‖ NAUT. Wind ; breeze ; weather ; *vent fort,* high wind ; gale ; *vent frais,* strong (ou) fresh breeze ; *avoir bon vent,* to have a fair wind ; *contre le vent,* in the teeth of the wind ; *côté du vent,* weatherside ; *être sous le vent,* to be to leeward ; *passer au vent de,* to keep to windward of. ‖ MILIT. Windage. ‖ AVIAT. *Vent de l'hélice,* slipstream. ‖ MUS. *A vent,* wind (instrument). ‖ SPORTS. Wind, scent (en vénerie) ; *avoir vent de,* to have the wind of. ‖ TECHN. Vent ; *donner vent à,* to make a vent in (un tonneau). ‖ TECHN. Blast (d'un four). ‖ MÉD. Wind, flatulence (v. PET) ; *lâcher un vent,* to break wind, to fart (pop.). ‖ FIG. Wind ; influence ; impulse ; air ; *le vent de l'adversité,* the chill wind of adversity. ‖

FAM. Hot air (frime); *c'est du vent*, it's all eyewash (ou) bunkum (ou) U. S. hooey. ‖ FAM. *Avoir du vent dans les voiles*, to be three sheets in the wind, to be rolling drunk; *vous perdez votre vent*, you're wasting your breath. ‖ LOC. *Aller comme le vent*, to go like the wind; *aller selon le vent*, to drift with the tide; *avoir vent de*, to get wind of; to have an inkling of; *autant en emporte le vent*, gone with the wind (titre de roman); *entrer en coup de vent*, to burst (ou) dash in; *être logé aux quatre vents*, to live in a draughty place; *prendre le vent*, to see how the land lies; to see which way the wind is blowing; *quel bon vent vous amène?*, what good fortune brings you here, how nice to see you; *selon le vent la voile*, trim your sails to the wind.

ventage [vɑ̃ta:ʒ] m. AGRIC. Winnowing.

ventail [vɑ̃ta:j] (pl. **ventaux**) m. f. † Ventail.

vente [vɑ̃:t] f. Sale. ‖ Bazaar, charity bazaar, sale of work (de charité). ‖ COMM. *Vente à l'amiable*, sale by private treaty; *vente au déballage*, hawking; *vente aux enchères*, sale by auction, auction-sale; *en vente*, on sale (en général); out, published (livre); *en vente chez*, sold by, obtainable from, to be had from; *mettre en vente*, to publish (un livre); to put up for sale, to offer for sale (un objet); *mise en vente*, publication, publishing (d'un livre); putting on sale (d'un objet); *en vente libre*, off the ration; *mettre en vente libre*, to de-ration; *mise en vente libre*, de-rationing; *possibilité de vente*, saleability; *salle de vente*, sale-room, U. S. sales-room; *salle des ventes*, auction-room. ‖ JUR. *Vente judiciaire*, sale by order of the court. ‖ AGRIC. Felling (d'arbres); timber felled (bois).

venté, ée [vɑ̃te] adj. Wind-bent, twisted by the wind (arbre); wind-driven (marée).

venteaux [-to] m. pl. Air-holes.

venter [-te] v. intr. (1). To blow. (V. SOUFFLER.)
— v. impers. To blow; *il vente fort*, it is very windy, it is blowing hard.
— v. tr. To blow about, to toss, to drive.

venteux, euse [-tø, ø:z] adj. Windy (région, saison, temps); wind-swept (pays).

ventilateur [vɑ̃tilatœ:r] m. Ventilator; ventilation hole; *ventilateur électrique*, electric fan; *ventilateur soufflant*, blower.

ventilation [-sjɔ̃] f. Ventilation; *puits de ventilation*, ventilating shaft. ‖ JUR. Separate valuation. ‖ FIN. Apportionment (en comptabilité).

ventilé, ée [vɑ̃tile] adj. Ventilated, aired; *mal ventilé*, stuffy (salle).

ventiler v. tr. To ventilate, to air. (V. AÉRER.) ‖ JUR. To value separately. ‖ FIN. To apportion (en comptabilité). ‖ FIG. To air (une question).

ventôse [vɑ̃to:z] m. Ventôse, sixth month in French Republican calendar (february-march).

ventouse [vɑ̃tu:z] f. MÉD. Cupping-glass; *appliquer des ventouses à*, to cup. ‖ NAUT. Air-scuttle. ‖ ZOOL. Sucker (de sangsue). ‖ TECHN. Vent, ventilator, air-hole (évent); air-valve; nozzle, mouthpiece (d'aspirateur); *cendrier à ventouse*, suction-grip ash-tray.

ventral [vɑ̃:tral] adj. Ventral.

ventre [vɑ̃:tr] m. Abdomen, belly; *avoir du ventre*, to be stout; to be pot-bellied, to have a corporation; *prendre du ventre*, to grow stout; *se jeter à plat ventre*, to fall flat on one's face. ‖ Stomach, paunch (v. BEDAINE); tummy (fam.); *avoir le ventre creux*, to have an empty stomach; *faire un dieu de son ventre*, to worship one's belly. ‖ Womb (v. SEIN); *le ventre de ma mère*, my mother's womb. ‖ MÉD. Abdomen; *avoir mal au ventre*, to have the belly-ache (ou) stomach-ache (ou) tummy-ache; *ventre aigu chirurgical*, acute abdomen, acute abdominal condition. ‖ NAUT. Belly (de navire); sag (de voile). ‖ AVIAT.

Underbelly (d'hélicoptère); *atterrissage sur le ventre*, belly-landing. ‖ ELECTR. Loop (de potentiel). ‖ TECHN. Bulge (de mur); swell, sagging; *faire ventre*, to bulge out (mur). ‖ FAM. *Il lui tape sur le ventre*, he's very hail-fellow-well-met with him; *il a qqch. dans le ventre*, there's sth. in him; U. S. he has sth. on the ball; *il n'a rien dans le ventre*. he's got no guts (courage); he has nothing in him (qualités); *il a les yeux plus gros que le ventre*, his eyes are bigger than his stomach, he bites off more than he can chew; *la reconnaissance du ventre*, cupboard love. ‖ LOC. *A ventre déboutonné*, gluttonously; *ventre à terre*, at full speed, flat-out, lickety-split (fam.); *se mettre à plat ventre devant*, to grovel before, to cringe to.
— adj. *Ventre-de-biche*, fawn (couleur).

ventrebleu [-trəblø] interj. † Gadzooks! (†).

ventrée [-tre] f. ZOOL. Litter. ‖ POP. Bellyful.

ventriculaire [vɑ̃trikylɛ:r] adj. MÉD. Ventricular.

ventricule [-kyl] m. MÉD. Ventricle.

ventrière [-jɛ:r] f. Sling, girth.

ventriloque [-lɔk] adj. Ventriloquous.
— s. Ventriloquist.

ventriloquie [-lɔki] f. Ventriloquy, ventriloquism.

ventripotent, ente [pɔtɑ̃, ɑ̃:t] adj. Ventripotent.

ventru, ue [vɑ̃try] adj. FAM. Big-bellied, pot-bellied. (V. PANSU.)

venu, ue [vəny] p. p., adj. V. VENIR.
— s. Comer; *le dernier venu*, the latest comer (le dernier arrivé); a mere nobody, any Tom, Dick or Harry (fam.) [un piètre individu]; *les nouveaux venus*, the newcomers; *le premier venu*, the first comer (le premier arrivé); anyone, anybody (n'importe qui).

venue f. Coming; arrival; *à ma venue*, on my arrival; *allées et venues*, coming and going; bustle, running about. ‖ Growth (d'un arbre); *d'une belle venue*, well-grown; *tout d'une venue*, shapeless. ‖ Approach (de l'hiver).

Vénus [veny:s] f. Venus (déesse, étoile). ‖ ZOOL. Venus, clam.

vêpres [vɛ:pr] f. pl. ECCLÉS. Vespers, evensong.

ver [vɛ:r] m. Worm; lug-worm (des pêcheurs); earth-worm (de terre). ‖ Larva; grub (blanc); wood-worm (du bois); moth (des étoffes); glow-worm (luisant); maggot (du fromage, de la viande); silk-worm (à soie); *piqué des vers*, worm-eaten. ‖ MÉD. Worm (en général); tapeworm (solitaire); *avoir des vers*, to have worms. ‖ FAM. *Tirer les vers du nez à*, to worm secrets out of, to pump; *tuer le ver*, to have a pick-me-up before breakfast.

vérace [veras] adj. Veracious.

véracité [-site] f. Veracity, truthfulness. (V. FRANCHISE.) ‖ Truth, accuracy, correctness (d'une affirmation); veracity (d'un fait).

véranda [verɑ̃da] f. Veranda, verandah; U.S. porch, piazza.

vératrine [veratrin] f. CHIM. Veratrine, veratria.

verbal, ale [vɛrbal] adj. Verbal, by word of mouth (v. ORAL); *note verbale*, verbal note. ‖ GRAMM. Verbal. ‖ JUR. *Convention verbale*, simple contract, verbal agreement.

verbalement [-lmɑ̃] adv. Verbally, by word of mouth. (V. ORALEMENT.)

verbalisateur [-lizatœ:r] m. JUR. Policeman taking down particulars.

verbalisation [-lizasjɔ̃] f. JUR. Taking down of particulars (ou) of s.o.'s name and address; making of a report.

verbaliser [-lize] v. intr. (1). JUR. To draw up an official report; to make a statement; *verbaliser contre qqn*, to take down s.o.'s name and address (ou) particulars.
— v. tr. To verbalize, to put into words.

verbalisme [-lism] m. Verbalism.

verbe [vɛrb] m. Speech; tone of voice; way of speaking; *avoir le verbe haut,* to be loud-mouthed. ‖ GRAMM. Verb. ‖ ECCLÉS. Word. ‖ FIG. *Avoir le verbe haut,* to be arrogant (ou) dictatorial (ou) peremptory.

verbeux, euse [-bø, ø:z] adj. Verbose, long-winded, prosy, wordy. (V. DIFFUS, PROLIXE.)

verbiage [-bja:ʒ] m. Verbiage; wordiness; all talk, just words (fam.).

verbosité [-bozite] f. Verbosity, long-windedness.

verdâtre [vɛrdɑ:tr] adj. Greenish.

verdelet, ette [-dəlɛ, ɛt] adj. Greenish (couleur); slightly acid, rather tart (vin). ‖ FAM. Hale and hearty, spry (vieillard).

verdeur [-dœ:r] f. Greenness (du bois); greenness, unripeness, immaturity (des fruits); acidity, tartness, sourness (du vin). ‖ FIG. Greenness (de l'âge); freedom, licentiousness (d'un propos); vigour, spryness, vitality, liveliness (d'un vieillard).

verdi, ie [-di] adj. Green; turned green. ‖ Verdigrised (métal).

verdict [vɛrdikt] m. Verdict; judgment (de l'opinion publique). ‖ JUR. Verdict, finding of the jury; *verdict d'acquittement,* verdict of not guilty; *rendre son verdict,* to return a verdict.

verdier [vɛrdje] m. ZOOL. Greenfinch, green linnet.

verdir [vɛrdi:r] v. intr. (2). To become (ou) to turn (ou) to grow green (végétation). [V. VERDOYER.] ‖ To become covered with verdigris (métal).
— v. tr. To colour green, to make green (un objet); to paint green (par la peinture).

verdissant, ante [-disɑ̃, ɑ̃:t] adj. Becoming (ou) turning (ou) growing green.

verdoiement [-dwamɑ̃] m. Turning green, becoming verdant.

verdoyant, ante [-dwajɑ̃, ɑ̃:t] adj. Greenish (colour); verdant, green (pré).

verdoyer [-dwaje] v. intr. (9 a). To be (ou) to become green.

verdunisation [vɛrdynizasjɔ̃] f. Chlorination.

verduniser [-ze] v. tr. (1). To chlorinate.

verdure [vɛrdy:r] f. Foil (pour bouquets). ‖ BOT. Greenness, verdure (couleur); green vegetation, greenery (plantes); *tapis de verdure,* green sward. ‖ THÉÂTR. *Théâtre de verdure,* open-air theatre. ‖ CULIN. Green-stuff, greens. ‖ ARTS. Tapestry representing trees and foliage.

verdurier [-dyrje] s. Greengrocer.

véreux, euse [verø, ø:z] adj. Worm-eaten (bois); maggoty (fromage, viande); worm-eaten, wormy, maggoty (fruit). ‖ FIG. Doubtful, fishy (affaire); doubtful, shady, of dubious character (homme d'affaires).

verge [vɛ:rʒ] f. Stick, cane, switch, rod (baguette); *battre de verges,* to birch; *faire passer qqn par les verges,* to make s.o. run the gauntlet; *poignée de verges,* birch. ‖ Wand (d'escamoteur). ‖ Verge; rod, staff (d'huissier); *huissier à verge,* tipstaff. ‖ ECCLÉS. Rod (de Moïse). ‖ NAUT. Shank (d'ancre). ‖ MÉD. Penis. ‖ TECHN. Rod (d'arpenteur, de piston); beam (de balance); foot-rule (de charpentier); stick (de fusée); spindle (de girouette). ‖ FIG. Power, domination, sway (v. FÉRULE); *verge de fer,* rod of iron.

vergé, ée [vɛrʒe] adj. Streaky, badly dyed (étoffe); laid (papier).
— m. Laid paper; *vergé blanc,* cream-laid paper.

verger m. Orchard.

vergeté, ée [-ʒəte] adj. Streaky. ‖ BLAS. Paly.

vergette [-ʒɛt] f. Small rod (ou) stick (ou) cane (verge). ‖ Clothes-brush (brosse). ‖ MUS. Hoop (de tambour). ‖ BLAS. Pallet.

vergeture [-ʒəty:r] f. Weal, red mark. ‖ MÉD. Vibex, stria.

verglacé, ée [vɛrglase] adj. Slippery, icy.

verglacer v. impers. (6). To be slippery (ou) icy.

verglas [-glɑ] m. Silver thaw, glazed frost; frozen rain; sleet; *il y a du verglas,* the roads are slippery.

vergne [vɛrɲ] m. BOT. Alder, alder-tree.

vergogne [vɛrgɔɲ] f. Shame; *sans vergogne,* shameless (adj.); shamelessly (adv.).

vergue [vɛrg] f. NAUT. Yard; *grande vergue,* main yard; *vergue de grand cacatois, de hunier, de misaine, de perroquet,* main royal, topsail, fore-, topgallant yard; *avoir vent sous vergue,* to run (ou) scud before the wind.

véridique [veridik] adj. Veracious, truthful, trustworthy.

véridiquement [-mɑ̃] adv. Veraciously, truthfully.

vérifiable [verifjabl] adj. Verifiable.

vérificateur, trice [-fikatœ:r, tris] adj. Testing (appareil); verifying (expert).
— m. Verifier; inspector, checker, tester, examiner. ‖ COMM. *Vérificateur comptable,* auditor. ‖ TECHN. Testing apparatus; calipers (compas). ‖ AUTOM. Tyre pressure-gauge (pour pneus).

vérificatif, ive [-fikatif, i:v] adj. Verificatory.

vérification [-fikasjɔ̃] f. Verification (d'une affirmation); scrutiny (des suffrages); inspection, checking, testing, examination (des travaux). ‖ FIN. Auditing, checking (des comptes). ‖ JUR. Proving (en général); scrutiny (des votes); *vérification en douane,* customs examination; *vérification d'un testament,* probate. ‖ TECHN. Testing (des connexions); overhauling, U. S. tuning up (d'un moteur).

vérifier [-fje] v. tr. (1). To verify, to prove, to confirm (une affirmation); to ascertain, to make sure of (un fait); to take up (des références); to inspect, to check, to test, to examine (un travail). ‖ JUR. To scrutinize (les votes). ‖ FIN. To audit (les comptes). ‖ TECHN. To test (des connexions); to overhaul, U. S. to tune up (un moteur).

vérin [verɛ̃] m. TECHN. Jack (cric); hydraulic jack (à eau); screw-jack (à vis).

vérine [verin] f. NAUT. Hook-rope, chain-hook.

véritable [veritabl] adj. True (histoire, religion). [V. VRAI.] ‖ Veritable; true, good (ami); genuine, real (antiquités, artiste); thorough, regular, down-right (coquin); true, exact, actual, real (raison); correct, authentic, truthful (récit). ‖ FIN. Actual (bénéfice); true, real (prix, valeur).

véritablement [-bləmɑ̃] adv. Veritably, truly; really; indeed; actually; in reality.

Veritas [veritɑ:s] m. NAUT. Lloyd's (bureau); Lloyd's List (répertoire).

vérité [-te] f. Verity, truth (d'une affirmation); *dire la vérité,* to speak the truth; *celui qui dit la vérité,* truth-teller; *la vérité pure et simple,* the plain (ou) the honest truth; *la vérité vraie,* an actual fact, the honest truth; *à la vérité,* to tell the truth, as a matter of fact; *en vérité,* truly, really, actually. ‖ Truth, fact, principle (scientifique); *c'est la vérité,* it's a fact. ‖ Truthfulness, sincerity; *avec un accent de vérité,* with a note of sincerity. ‖ FAM. *Dire à qqn ses quatre vérités,* to tell s.o. a few home truths; U. S. to straighten s.o. out.

verjus [vɛrʒy] m. Verjuice; *aigre comme du verjus,* as sour as vinegar.

verjuté, ée [-te] adj. Verjuiced. ‖ Acid, vinegary, sour. ‖ FIG. Sour.

vermeil, eille [vɛrmɛ:j] adj. Vermilion, bright red. ‖ Mellow (fruit); rosy (joues); ruby (lèvres).
— m. Vermeil, silver gilt, gilt bronze.

vermicelle [vɛrmisɛl] m. CULIN. Vermicelli.

vermiculaire [-kyle:r] adj. Vermicular, worm-shaped. ‖ MÉD. Vermiform (appendice); vermicular (mouvement); faint and irregular (pouls).

vermiculé, ée [-kyle] adj. ARCHIT. Vermiculated. ‖ ZOOL. Vermiculate.

vermiculure [-kyly:r] f. Archit. Vermiculation.

vermiforme [-fɔrm] adj. Vermiform.

vermifuge [-fy:ʒ] ad., s. Méd. Vermifuge.

vermillon [vɛrmijɔ̃] adj. Vermilion, bright red. — m. Vermilion; cinnabar. ‖ Vermilion, bright red (couleur); rosy colour (des joues).

vermillonner [-jɔne] v. tr. To vermilion; to paint bright red; to rouge.

vermine [vɛrmin] f. Zool. Vermin; *couvert de vermine*, alive (ou) crawling with vermin; verminous. ‖ Fig. Vermin, riff-raff, rabble.

vermineux, euse [-nø, ø:z] adj. Méd. Caused by worms (maladie); verminous (pouilleux).

vermisseau [-so] m. Zool. Small earth-worm.

vermoulu, ue [vɛrmuly] adj. Worm-eaten (bois). ‖ Fam. Decrepit; out-of-date, outworn, moth-eaten (idées); tottering, shaky (régime).

vermoulure [-ly:r] f. Wood dust (poudre); worm-hole (trou).

vermouth [vɛrmut] m. Vermouth.

vernaculaire [vɛrnakylɛ:r] adj. Vernacular.

vernal, ale [vɛrnal] adj. Vernal.

verni, ie [vɛrni] adj. Varnished (bois); patent (cuir, souliers). ‖ Fam. Lucky (v. veinard); *être verni*, to have (ou) to lead a charmed life.

vernier [vɛrnje] m. Math. Vernier.

vernir [vɛrni:r] v. tr. (2). To polish (du bois); to japan (du cuir); to glaze (la poterie); to varnish (un tableau); *vernir au tampon*, to French-polish.

vernis [-ni] m. Polish (sur un meuble); glaze (sur une poterie); varnish (sur un tableau). ‖ Spirit varnish (à l'alcool); turpentine varnish (à l'essence); oil varnish (gras); japan (japonais); French-polish (au tampon). ‖ Bot. *Vernis du Japon*, lacquer-tree, varnish-tree. ‖ Fig. Polish; veneer (de connaissances, de politesse); gloss (sens péjoratif). ‖ **Vernis-émail** (pl. *vernis-émaux*) m. Japan enamel.

vernissage [-nisa:ʒ] m. Japanning (du cuir); polishing (d'un meuble); glazing (d'une poterie); varnishing (d'un tableau); French-polishing (au tampon). ‖ Arts. Vernissage, varnishing-day, private view.

vernissé, ée [-nise] adj. Glazed.

vernisser v. tr. To glaze (la poterie).

vernisseur [-nisœ:r] s. Varnisher, polisher (en général); glazer (de poterie); French-polisher (au tampon).

vernissure [-nisy:r] f. Varnishing; glazing (action); varnish; glaze (vernis).

vérole [verɔl] f. Méd. *Petite vérole*, smallpox; *marques de la petite vérole*, pock-marks. ‖ Pop. Pox (syphilis).

vérolé, ée [verɔle] adj. Pop. Poxed.

Véronal [verɔnal] m. Méd. Veronal; barbitone; U. S. barbital.

véronique [verɔnik] f. Bot., Ecclés. Veronica.

verrai [vɛre]. V. voir (106).

verrat [vɛra] m. Zool. Boar.

verre [vɛ:r] m. Glass; *verre à bouteille*, bottle glass; *verres-dalles*, pavement lights; *verre de lampe, de montre*, lamp-, watch-glass; *verre soluble*, water-glass; *articles en verre*, glass-ware; *sous verre*, under glass, in a glass case. ‖ Glass, drinking-glass (à boire); tumbler (sans pied); *verre à dégustation, à liqueur, à Madère, à vin*, balloon, liqueur-, sherry-, wine-glass. ‖ Glass, glassful (de vin); *boire un petit verre*, to have a nip (ou) a short; *boire à plein verre*, to drink by the glassful. ‖ Bottle (emballage). ‖ Méd. *Verre à dents*, tooth-glass. ‖ Chim. *Verre d'antimoine*, glass of antimony. ‖ Phys. *Verre grossissant, d'optique*, magnifying, optical glass. ‖ Fam. *Avoir un verre de trop*, to have had one over the eight (ou) one too many; *se noyer dans un verre d'eau*,

to make a mountain out of a molehill; *verre de montre*, backside, rear, bottom (derrière).

verré, ée [vɛre] adj. *Papier verré*, glass- (ou) sand-paper.

verrée f. Glassful.

verrerie [-rri] f. Glass-making (art); glass-ware (articles); glass-works (usine); *verrerie allant au four*, oven-glass, Pyrex.

verrier [-rje] adj. Glass (marché); *peintre verrier*, artist in stained glass. — m. Glass-blower, glass-maker (artisan); glass-basket (ou) -rack (ou) -stand (panier).

verrière [-rjɛ:r] f. Ecclés. Stained glass window. ‖ Ch. de f. Glass roof. ‖ Aviat. Canopy.

verrine [-rin] f. Glass casing. ‖ Naut. Lantern.

verroterie [-rɔtri] f. Small glass-ware; glass trinkets; glass beads.

verrou [vɛru] m. Bolt, bar; *fermer au verrou*, to bolt; *tirer les verrous de*, to unbolt (pour ouvrir). ‖ Milit. Bolt (de fusil). ‖ Ch. de f. Switch-lock. ‖ Jur. *Sous les verrous*, under lock and key, in safe custody.

verrouillage [-ja:ʒ] m. Bolting, locking; locking mechanism.

verrouiller [-je] v. tr. (1). To bolt (une porte); to bolt in, to lock up (qqn). ‖ Milit. To lock (la culasse). ‖ Techn. To lock. — v. pr. **Se verrouiller**, to bolt oneself in.

verrucosité [vɛrykozite] f. Méd. Warty swelling.

verrue [vɛry] f. Méd. Wart, verruca.

vers [vɛ:r] m. Verse, line of poetry; pl. verse, poetry; *vers blancs*, blank verse; *méchants vers*, doggerel; *petits vers*, light verse; *vers de circonstance, de salon*, occasional, saloon verse; *vers au rythme large*, free swinging verse; *faire des vers*, to write poetry (ou) verse.

vers pr ... Towards, to (direction); *vers le but*, towards the goal; *aller vers la maison*, to go homewards; *tourner les yeux vers le ciel*, to look up to heaven. ‖ Towards; about (temps); *vers la fin du siècle*, towards the end of the century; *vers midi*, about twelve, around noon. ‖ † To (auprès de); to, towards (envers).

versage [vɛrsa:ʒ] m. Agric. First ploughing. ‖ Techn. Tipping, emptying (d'une benne).

versant [-sɑ̃] m. Géogr. Versant, slope (pente), bank (de digue); *versant de colline*, hillside. ‖ Fig. Decline, down grade; wrong side (de la cinquantaine).

versatile [vɛrsatil] adj. Fickle, inconstant, unstable, unsteady, volatile. (V. changeant.)

versatilité [-lite] f. Fickleness, inconstancy, instability, unsteadiness, changeableness. ‖ Zool. Versatility.

verse [vɛrs] adj. Math. Versed (sinus).

verse (à) [avɛrs] loc. adv. In torrents; *il pleut à verse*, it's pouring with rain, it's raining buckets (ou) cats and dogs.

versé, ée [vɛrse] adj. Well versed, experienced, practised, well up, skilled (dans, in); conversant (dans, with).

Verseau (le) [ləvɛrso] m. Astron. Aquarius, the Water-bearer.

versement [vɛrsəmɑ̃] m. Pouring forth (ou) out (d'un liquide). ‖ Fin. Paying in, payment, deposit; *versement partiel*, instalment; *en versements échelonnés*, by instalments, on the instalment plan; *versement de libération*, final instalment; *bulletin de versement*, pay-in (ou) U. S. deposit slip; *carne de versement*, pay-in book; U. S. bank-book; *faire un versement à un compte*, to pay in money to an account. ‖ Milit. Issue.

verser [-se] v. intr. To tip over, to overturn, to upset (voiture). ‖ Agric. To be blown over, to be laid flat, to be beaten flat, to be flattened, to be laid (blé). ‖ Fig. *Verser dans*, to take to, to turn to (avoir recours à); to drift into (prendre l'habitude de); to fall a prey to (tomber en proie à). — **v. tr.** To pour, to pour out (de l'eau); to shed (des larmes, du sang) [v. RÉPANDRE]; *verser à boire à qqn,* to pour s.o. out a drink. ‖ To upset, to overturn, to tip over (une voiture). ‖ FIN. To pay, to pay in, to deposit; *capitaux versés,* paid-up capital; *verser un chèque à son compte,* to pay in (ou) U. S. to deposit a cheque to one's account; *verser des fonds dans une affaire,* to invest capital in an undertaking. ‖ MILIT. To draft (*dans,* into); to transfer (*dans,* to); to issue (du matériel). ‖ AGRIC. To lay, to beat down, to flatten (le blé). ‖ TECHN. To tip (une benne); to tip, to shoot (des décombres). ‖ FIG. To shed (de la lumière). — **v. pr. Se verser,** to be poured out (liquide). ‖ FIN. To be paid (ou) deposited (ou) banked.

verset [-sɛ] m. Versicle. ‖ ECCLÉS. Verse. ‖ MUS. Verset.

verseur [-sœ:r] adj. m. *Bec verseur,* spout, pouring lip; *bouchon verseur,* pour-through stopper.

verseuse [-sø:z] f. Coffee-pot.

versicolore [vɛrsikɔlɔ:r] adj. Versicoloured, variegated; changeable in colour.

versificateur, trice [vɛrsifikatœ:r, tris] s. Versifier.

versification [-fikasjɔ̃] f. Versification.

versifier [-fje] v. intr., tr. (1). To versify.

version [vɛrsjɔ̃] f. Translation (into the mother tongue) [par un écolier]. ‖ Version, translation (d'un ouvrage). ‖ Version, account (d'un fait). ‖ MÉD. Version.

verso [-so] m. Verso, reverse, back (d'une feuille); left-hand page (d'un livre); *voir au verso,* turn over; see on the back (d'une carte); see overleaf (d'une feuille). ‖ FIN. *Voir au verso,* as per back.

versoir [-swa:r] m. AGRIC. Mould-board.

verste [vɛrst] f. Verst.

vert, erte [vɛ:r, ɛ:rt] adj. Green (couleur); *vert bouteille,* bottle-green; *vert d'eau,* sea-green. ‖ Verdant (pré); *plantes vertes,* evergreens; *vert comme pré,* as green as grass. ‖ Green; unseasoned (bois); raw (cuir); unripe (fruit); fresh-hewn (pierre); new, young, sharp (vin). ‖ GÉOGR. *Le cap Vert,* Cape Verde. ‖ TECHN. Green (terre); *fonte verte,* brass; gun-metal. ‖ CULIN. Unroasted (café); *chou vert,* colewort; *haricots verts,* French (ou) string beans; *légumes verts,* greens. ‖ FIG. Biting, caustic, sharp, severe, tart (semonce); vigorous, flourishing, spry, brisk, hale and hearty (vieillard). ‖ FIG. Spicy, smutty (histoire); *langue verte,* slang. ‖ LOC. *Ils sont trop verts!,* sour grapes! — m. Green (couleur). ‖ Greenery, verdure, green grass, fresh vegetation; *mettre au vert,* to turn out to grass (ou) graze (un animal); *se mettre au vert,* to go to stay (ou) live in the country (personne). ‖ Sharpness, newness (du vin). ‖ BOT. *Vert des feuilles,* chlorophyll. ‖ SPORTS. Putting-green (au golf). ‖ FIG. *Prendre qqn sans vert,* to catch s.o. napping. ‖ **Vert-de-gris,** m. invar. Verdigris. ‖ **Vert-de-grisé,** adj. Verdigrised, coated with verdigris. ‖ **Vert-de-griser (se),** v. pr. To become coated with verdigris.

verte [vɛrt] f. FAM. Glass of absinthe. ‖ FAM. Spicy (ou) smutty story (histoire).

vertébral, ale [vɛrtebral] adj. MÉD. Vertebral; *colonne vertébrale,* backbone, spinal column, vertebral column.

vertèbre [-tɛ:br] f. MÉD. Vertebra (pl. vertebrae).

vertébré [-tebre] adj., m. ZOOL. Vertebrate.

vertement [vɛrtəmɑ̃] adv. Sharply, smartly; sternly (v. SÉVÈREMENT); *tancer qqn vertement,* to give s.o. a sharp dressing-down.

vertex [vɛrtɛks] m. MÉD. Vertex (pl. vertices).

vertical, ale [vɛrtikal] adj. Vertical. (V. PERPENDICULAIRE.) ‖ Overhead (éclairage).

verticale [-ka:l] f. MATH. Vertical.

verticalement [-kalmɑ̃] adv. Vertically.

verticalité [-kalite] f. Verticality.

verticillé, ée [vɛrtisille] adj. BOT. Verticillate.

vertige [vɛrti:ʒ] m. MÉD. Vertigo; dizziness, giddiness, swimming of the head (v. ÉTOURDISSEMENT); *avoir le vertige,* to feel dizzy (ou) giddy; *avoir des vertiges,* to have fits of giddiness; *cela me donne le vertige,* it makes me dizzy (ou) giddy, it makes my head go round (ou) swim. ‖ Fear of heights (en ascension). ‖ FIG. Turning of the head.

vertigineusement [-ʒinøzmɑ̃] adv. Vertiginously.

vertigineux, euse [-ʒinø, ø:z] adj. Vertiginous; dizzy, giddy (hauteur, vitesse). ‖ MÉD. Causing staggers.

vertigo [-tigo] m. MÉD. Staggers.

vertu [vɛrty] f. Virtue; *faire de nécessité vertu,* to make a virtue of necessity; *vivre dans la vertu,* to live a life of virtue. ‖ Virtue, chastity; *femme de petite vertu,* woman of easy virtue. ‖ Virtuous woman; *ce n'est pas une vertu,* she's no saint. ‖ Virtue, quality, property, power (v. PROPRIÉTÉ); *plante qui a la vertu de guérir,* plant that has healing properties. ‖ ECCLÉS. Virtue. ‖ † Courage, valour. ‖ **En vertu de,** by virtue of, in pursuance of, under (un jugement, une loi, pouvoirs); because of, in consequence of (sa réputation, sa vitesse); under the terms of (un traité).

vertueusement [-tɥøzmɑ̃] adv. Virtuously.

vertueux, euse [-tɥø, ø:z] adj. Virtuous. ‖ Chaste (femme).

vertugadin [vɛrtygadɛ̃] m. Farthingale.

verve [vɛrv] f. Verve; animation, zest, life, high spirits, go, U. S. zip (fam.); breeziness (d'un discours); *en verve,* in great form.

verveine [vɛrvɛ:n] f. BOT., MÉD. Vervain, verbena.

verveux, euse [vɛrvø, ø:z] adj. Animated, lively, high-spirited, racy.

verveux m. Hoop-net (filet).

vesce [vɛs] f. BOT. Vetch, tare.

vésical, ale [vezikal] adj. MÉD. Vesical.

vésicant, ante [-kɑ̃, ɑ̃:t] adj. MÉD. Vesicant, vesicatory; blistering (cataplasme). ‖ MILIT. Blistering (gaz).

vésicatoire [-katwa:r] adj., m. MÉD. Vesicatory.

vésiculaire [-kylɛ:r] adj. MÉD. Vesicular.

vésicule [-kyl] f. MÉD. Vesicle; *vésicule biliaire,* gall-bladder. ‖ TECHN. Blister.

vésiculeux, euse [-kylø, ø:z] adj. Vesiculose, vesicular.

vesou [vəzu] m. Cane-juice.

vespasienne [vɛspazjɛn] f. Street urinal.

vespéral, ale [vɛsperal] adj. Vespertine. — m. ECCLÉS. Vesperal.

vesse [vɛ:s] f. POP. Silent fart.

vesse-de-loup [vɛsdəlu] (pl. **vesses-de-loup**) f. BOT. Puff-ball.

vessie [vɛsi] f. MÉD. Bladder; *vessie à glace,* icebag. ‖ SPORTS. Bladder (de ballon). ‖ FAM. *Prendre des vessies pour des lanternes,* to think that the moon is made of green cheese; *faire prendre à qqn des vessies pour des lanternes,* to pull the wool over s.o.'s eyes.

vestale [vɛstal] f. Vestal. ‖ FIG. Virtuous girl.

veste [vɛst] f. Jacket, coat. ‖ SPORTS. Fencing-jacket (d'escrime); *veste de sport,* sports jacket, blazer. ‖ FAM. *Remporter une veste,* to fail, to be unsuccessful (en général); to plough, U. S. to flunk (à un examen); *retourner sa veste,* to turn one's coat, to change sides; *tomber la veste,* to take one's coat off.

vestiaire [vɛstjɛ:r] m. Wardrobe-room, U. S. coatroom (dans une école). ‖ Hat-and-coat rack (meuble). ‖ THÉÂTR. Cloak-room, U. S. check-

room. ‖ Jur. Robing-room. ‖ Sports. Dressing-room. ‖ Fam. Hat and coat, things (objets déposés).
vestibule [vɛstibyl] m. Vestibule, hall, lobby, passage. ‖ Méd. Vestibule.
vestige [vɛsti:ʒ] m. Footprint, trace, mark. ‖ Fig. Vestige, trace, remains (d'une civilisation); relics (du passé); *derniers vestiges*, last remnants.
vestimentaire [vɛstimɑ̃tɛ:r] adj. Vestimentary; *d'une grande élégance vestimentaire*, well-tailored, well- (ou) smartly-dressed.
veston [vɛstɔ̃] m. Jacket, coat; lounge-coat; *complet veston*, lounge (ou) U. S. business suit; *il est en veston*, he is in (ou) he is wearing a lounge (ou) U. S. business suit.
Vésuve [vezy:v] m. Géogr. Vesuvius.
vêtement [vɛtmɑ̃] m. Garment. ‖ Pl. Clothes, clothing, dress (v. habits); togs, things (fam.) [v. affaires, effets]; raiment (†); *vêtements de dessous*, underwear; *vêtements de deuil*, mourning. ‖ Ecclés. *Vêtements sacerdotaux*, canonicals. ‖ Comm. Clothing trade (industrie).
vétéran [veterɑ̃] m. Milit. Veteran; old campaigner (ou) soldier. ‖ Naut. Old hand. ‖ Fam. Pupil repeating a course (au lycée); pl. older (ou) senior boys. ‖ Loc. *Vétérans de la politique*, elder statesmen.
vétérinaire [veterinɛ:r] adj. Veterinary.
— m. Méd. Veterinary surgeon; vet (fam.); U. S. veterinarian.
vétille [veti:j] f. Bagatelle, trifle, mere nothing.
vétiller [vetije] v. intr. (1). To trifle (badiner). ‖ To quibble, to niggle, to split hairs (ergoter).
vétilleur [-jœ:r] s. Trifler (badineur). ‖ Quibbler, niggler, hair-splitter, caviller (ergoteur).
vétilleux, euse [-jø, ø:z] adj. Trifling. ‖ Finicky, delicate, ticklish (affaire); finicky, fastidious, particular, punctillous (personne).
vêtir [vɛti:r] v. tr. (104). To clothe, to dress, to attire (de, in) [habiller]. ‖ To put on, to dress oneself in, to don (mettre sur soi).
— v. pr. Se vêtir, to dress, to put on one's clothes (s'habiller); to clothe (ou) dress oneself (de, in).
veto [veto] m. invar. Veto; *avoir le droit de veto*, to have the power of veto; *droit de veto*, right of veto; *mettre son veto à*, to veto.
vêtu, ue [vɛty] p. p., adj. Clothed, clad. ‖ V. vêtir.
vêture [-ty:r] f. Ecclés. Taking of the veil (pour une religieuse); taking of the habit (pour un religieux). ‖ Jur. Providing of clothing.
vétuste [vetyst] adj. Decrepit, decayed (v. vieux); worn-out (habit).
vétusté [-te] f. Decrepitude, decay; old age; *tomber de vétusté*, to fall to pieces with age.
veuf, euve [vœf, œ:v] adj. Widowed. ‖ Fig. Deprived, bereft (de, of) [privé].
— m. Widower (réellement). ‖ Fam. Grass widower (par absence de la conjointe, U. S. par divorce).
veuille [vœ:j]. V. vouloir (107).
veule [vø:l] adj. Dull, drab, flat, empty (existence); weak, feeble, flabby, spineless (personne); toneless (voix).
veulerie [vølri] f. Dullness, drabness, emptiness (de l'existence); inertia, flabbiness, spinelessness, weakness, slackness, listlessness (d'une personne); tonelessness (d'une voix).
veut, veux [vø:]. V. vouloir (107).
veuvage [vœva:ʒ] m. Widowhood (d'une femme); widowerhood (d'un homme).
veuve [vœ:v] f. Widow (réellement); grass widow (par absence du conjoint, U. S. par divorce); *vêtements de veuve*, widow's weeds. ‖ Bot. Sweet scabious. ‖ Zool. Widow-bird, whidah-bird. ‖ Fam. Guillotine.
vexant, ante [vɛksɑ̃, ɑ̃:t] adj. Vexing, annoying, provoking.
vexateur, trice [-satœ:r, tris] adj. Vexatious.
— s. Vexer.

vexation [-sasjɔ̃] f. Harassing, troubling, plaguing (fam.). ‖ Vexatious measure.
vexatoire [-satwa:r] adv. Vexatious.
vexer [-se] v. tr. (1). To vex, to worry, to harass, to plague (tourmenter). ‖ To vex, to annoy, to provoke, to irritate.
— v. pr. Se vexer, to get vexed (ou) annoyed (ou) irritated (de, at). [V. se froisser.]
via [via] prép. Via, by way of.
viabiliser [vjabilize] v. tr. (1). Techn. To lay on services to (un terrain).
viabilité [-te] f. Viability (d'un enfant); viability, feasibility (d'un projet). ‖ Autom. Practicability (d'une route). ‖ Techn. Laying on of services (d'un terrain).
viable [vjabl] adj. Viable, capable of living (enfant). ‖ Fig. Durable, likely to last (ministère); feasible (projet).
viaduc [vjadyk] m. Viaduct.
viager, ère [-vjaʒe, ɛ:r] adj. Jur. Life-, for life; *bien viager*, life estate; *rente viagère*, life annuity, life interest; *rentier viager*, annuitant.
— m. Jur. Life annuity, life interest; *mettre son avoir en viager*, to buy an annuity, to invest one's money in a life annuity.
viande [vjɑ̃:d] f. Meat, flesh; *viande de cheval*, horse-flesh; *viande fraîche, frigorifiée*, fresh, chilled (ou) frozen meat. ‖ † Meat, food (nourriture). ‖ Fam. Substance, matter.
viatique [vjatik] m. Travelling expenses; provisions for a journey. ‖ Ecclés. Viaticum; last sacrament.
vibrant, ante [vibrɑ̃, ɑ̃:t] adj. Vibrant, vibrating; *vibrant d'émotion*, quivering (ou) ringing with emotion. ‖ Méd. Throbbing (pouls). ‖ Fig. Rousing, stirring (appel, paroles); eager (public).
vibraphone [vibrafɔn] m. Mus. Vibraphone.
vibrateur [vibratœ:r] m. Electr. Vibrator, buzzer.
vibratile [-til] adj. Vibratile.
vibration [-sjɔ̃] f. Vibration. ‖ Resonance (de la voix). ‖ Aviat. Vibration; flutter, fluttering (des ailes). ‖ Fig. Sensation.
vibrato [-to] m. Mus. Vibrato. ‖ Fig. Tremor (dans la voix).
vibratoire [-twa:r] adj. Vibratory, vibrating. ‖ Méd. *Massage vibratoire*, vibro-massage. ‖ Electr. Oscillatory, oscillating (circuit).
vibré, ée [vibre] adj. Électr. *Appel vibré*, buzzer call.
vibrer v. intr. To vibrate; *faire vibrer qqch.*, to make sth. vibrate, to vibrate sth., to shake sth. ‖ Fig. *Faire vibrer la corde sensible*, to play on s.o.'s heart-strings.
vibreur [vibrœ:r] m. Électr. Vibrator; buzzer.
vibrion [vibrjɔ̃] m. Méd. Vibrio.
vibromasseur [vibromasœ:r] m. Méd. Vibrator.
vibroscope [-skɔp] m. Électr. Vibroscope.
vicaire [vikɛ:r] adj. Vicarious.
— m. † Deputy, substitute. ‖ Ecclés. Assistant priest, curate; *grand vicaire*, vicar-general; *le vicaire de Jésus-Christ*, the Vicar of Christ, the Pope.
vicarial, ale [vikarjal] adj. Vicarial. ‖ Ecclés. Pertaining to a curate.
vicariat [-rja] m. Ecclés. Vicariate; curacy.
vice [vis] m. Vice, corruption, depravity (dépravation); immorality, debauchery (libertinage). ‖ Defect, imperfection, flaw, blemish, fault (v. défaut); *vice de conformation*, malformation; *vice propre*, inherent defect. ‖ Jur. *Vice de forme*, faulty drafting (dans un acte); irregularity (dans un jugement); flaw (dans un procès). ‖ Méd. Impurity (du sang). ‖ Fam. *Il a tous les vices*, he's a thorough bad lot; *il a du vice*, he's a sly dog, there are no flies on him.
vice- préfixe invar. Vice-, deputy. ‖ **Vice-amiral,** m.

NAUT. Vice-admiral (officier); vice-admiral's flagship (vaisseau). ‖ **Vice-amirauté**, f. NAUT. Vice-admiralty. ‖ **Vice-chancelier**, m. Vice-chancellor. ‖ **Vice-consul**, m. Vice-consul. ‖ **Vice-doyen**, m. Sub-dean. ‖ **Vice-gérance**, f. Vice-managership. ‖ **Vice-gérant**, m. Vice-manager, acting manager. ‖ **Vice-légat**, m. Vice-legate. ‖ **Vice-présidence**, f. Vice-presidency; vice-chairmanship. ‖ **Vice-président**, m. Vice-president; vice-chairman. ‖ **Vice-recteur**, m. Vice-rector. ‖ **Vice-reine**, f. Vice-reine. ‖ **Vice-roi**, m. Viceroy. ‖ **Vice-royauté**, f. Viceroyalty.

vicennal, ale [visɛnnal] adj. Vicennial.

vicésimal, ale [visezimal] adj. MATH. Vicenary; vigesimal.

vice versa [visevɛrsa] loc. adv. Vice versa conversely.

Vichy [viʃi] m. GÉOGR. Vichy; *le gouvernement de Vichy*, the Vichy government. ‖ COMM. Vichy water (eau); Vichy cotton (toile).

vichyssois, oise [-ʃiswa, waːz] adj. Pertaining to Vichy; *le gouvernement vichyssois*, the Vichy government.
— s. Native of Vichy (en général); Vichyist; Vichy-ite (en politique).

violation [visjasjɔ̃] f. Vitiation; contamination (de l'air); corruption (du goût). ‖ JUR. Vitiation.

vicié, ée [-sje] adj. Vitiated, polluted, stale (air). ‖ Vitiated, warped (raisonnement). ‖ JUR. Vitiated (acte).

vicier [-sje] v. tr. (1). To vitiate; to make impure (ou) foul, to taint, to poison. (V. CONTAMINER, POLLUER.) ‖ JUR. To vitiate, to make void, to invalidate. ‖ FIG. To spoil; to corrupt; to debase.
— v. pr. **Se vicier**, to become vitiated (ou) corrupted (ou) tainted.

vicieusement [-sjøzmɑ̃] adv. Imperfectly, defectively, faultily.

vicieux, euse [-sjø, øːz] adj. Vicious (cercle); defective, faulty, imperfect (conformation); incorrect (locution, usage); wrong (méthode); vicious (personne, raisonnement). ‖ Bad-tempered, restive (cheval). ‖ JUR. Vicious, having a flaw.
— s. Vicious (ou) depraved person.

vicinal, ale [visinal] adj. *Chemin vicinal*, by-road, local road, U. S. back road; *ingénieur du service vicinal*, road-surveyor.

vicinalité [-lite] f. Local status; *chemin de grande vicinalité*, important local road.

vicissitude [visisityd] f. Vicissitude, mutability (de la fortune). ‖ Pl. Ups and downs (de la vie).

vicomtal, ale [vikɔ̃tal] adj. Pertaining to a viscount.

vicomte [-kɔ̃t] m. Viscount.

vicomté [-kɔ̃te] f. Viscountcy, viscountship. ‖ Viscounty (juridiction).

vicomtesse [-kɔ̃tɛs] f. Viscountess.

victime [vikti:m] f. Victim, sacrifice (offrande). ‖ Victim, sufferer; *être victime de*, to be swindled by (un escroc); to be down with (la grippe); to labour under (une illusion); to be victimized by (un maître chanteur); *victimes civiles*, casualties.

victoire [viktwa:r] f. Victory; triumph; *chanter victoire*, to triumph, to crow (fam.); *remporter la victoire*, to gain the victory, to win the day; *victoire à la Pyrrhus*, Pyrrhic victory.

victoria [viktɔrja] f. Victoria (voiture).
— m. BOT. Victoria (nénuphar).

victorien, enne [-rjɛ̃, ɛn] adj. Victorian.

victorieusement [-rjøzmɑ̃] adv. Victoriously.

victorieux, euse [-rjø, øːz] adj. Victorious (de, over). ‖ FIG. Triumphant (air); decisive (preuve).

victuailles [viktɥa:j] f. pl. Victuals, eatables.

vidage [vida:ʒ] m. Emptying. ‖ CULIN. Cleaning, gutting (d'un poisson); drawing (d'une volaille). ‖ TECHN. Embankment, bank. ‖ FAM. Dismissal, throwing out (expulsion).

vidame [vidam] m. Vidame.

vidange [vidɑ̃:ʒ] m. Emptying, draining; clearing (ou) cleaning out (d'une fosse d'aisances). ‖ Dry ullage, ullage; *en vidange*, opened (bouteille); broached, tapped (tonneau). ‖ Pl. Night-soil (matières); sludge (de chaudière). ‖ TECHN. Emptying, blowing out (d'une chaudière); draining (d'un radiateur); *robinet de vidange*, drain cock. ‖ NAUT. Bilge-water (de cale).

vidanger [-dɑ̃ʒe] v. tr. (7). To clear out; to blow off (une chaudière); to clean out (une fosse d'aisances); to drain (un radiateur).

vidangeur [-dɑ̃ʒœ:r] m. Nightman.

vide [vi:d] adj. Empty (bourse, estomac); blank (espace); unoccupied, vacant (maison, place, poste); waste, desolate (région); *emballages vides*, empties; *espace vide*, blank. ‖ FIG. Empty; hollow, vain (phrases); *vide d'intérêt*, devoid of interest; *avoir le cerveau vide*, to feel light-headed; *avoir la tête vide*, to be empty-headed (ou) brainless; *revenir les mains vides*, to return empty-handed.
— m. Empty space; void; gap; *combler le vide*, to fill the gap. ‖ Room (dans une valise). ‖ Spare time, unoccupied moments (dans l'emploi du temps). ‖ Blank (dans un document); ullage (dans un tonneau). ‖ MILIT. Pl. Empty ranks; *combler les vides*, to make good the losses (ou) the casualties. ‖ TECHN. Vacuum; *dans le vide*, in a vacuum; *à vide*, vacuum (frein, pompe); *nettoyage par le vide*, vacuum cleaning. ‖ FIG. Emptiness; nothingness; vanity; *faire le vide autour de*, to isolate; *frapper dans le vide*, to beat the air; *sa mort a fait un grand vide*, his death has left a gap; *regarder dans le vide*, to stare into vacancy (ou) empty space.
— loc. adv. **A vide**, empty; without a load; *emballer un moteur à vide*, to race an engine; *marcher à vide*, to run light; *poids à vide*, weight when empty; *tourner à vide*, to tick over, to idle. ‖ ELECTR. *Accus à vide*, discharged battery.

vide [vi:d]. V. VIDER. ‖ **Vide-citron**, m. (pl. *vide-citrons*). Lemon squeezer. ‖ **Vide-ordures**, m. invar. Rubbish-shoot, refuse chute. ‖ **Vide-poches**, m. invar. Dressing-room tidy. ‖ **Vide-pomme**, m. invar. Apple-corer. ‖ **Vide-vite**, m. invar. AVIAT. Escape-hatch.

vidé, ée [vide] adj. Emptied (vide). ‖ FAM. Exhausted; played out, worn out, done up (personne); settled; discussed (question).

vidéo [video] adj. Video (signal, bande).
— f. Video tape recording.

vidéocassette [-kasɛt] f. Video cassette.

vidéodisque [-disk] m. Video disc.

vider v. tr. To empty (une bouteille, un sac); to drain (un tonneau, un verre); *videz vos verres*, drink up. ‖ To drain off (un étang); to clear out (une salle); to clean out (un tiroir); *vider les lieux*, to clear out. ‖ CULIN. To blow (un œuf); to clean, to gut (un poisson); to core (une pomme); to draw, to clean (une volaille). ‖ TECHN. To blow off (une chaudière). ‖ FIG. To exhaust (l'esprit); to settle (une querelle, une question). ‖ FAM. To tire out, to wear out, to play out (éreinter); to ruin, to bleed, to squeeze dry (ruiner). ‖ FAM. To dismiss, to sack, to throw out (renvoyer); *il fut vidé de l'auto*, he was thrown clear of the car. ‖ LOC. *Vider les arçons*, to be thrown; *vider son sac*, to get it off one's chest, to speak one's mind.
— v. pr. **Se vider**, to empty; to become empty.

videur, euse [vidœ:r, øz] s. Emptier; *videur de poches*, pickpocket. ‖ CULIN. Gutter (de poissons); drawer (de volaille).
— m. FAM. Bouncer (dans une boîte de nuit).

viduité [vidɥite] f. Viduage, widowhood.

vidure [vidy:r] f. Guts (d'une volaille). ‖ Open-work (en couture).

vie [vi] f. Life (v. EXISTENCE); *accorder la vie à*, to spare (un ennemi); *avoir la vie dure*, to be tough, to be hard to kill; *donner la vie à*, to beget, to give birth to (un enfant, un projet); *enseigner à qqn les mystères de la vie*, to tell s.o. the facts of life; *entre la vie et la mort*, hovering between life and death; *être en vie*, to be alive (ou) living; *rappeler à la vie*, to bring back to life; *redonner la vie à*, to put new life into; *sans vie*, lifeless; *il y va de la vie*, it's a matter of life and death, s.o.'s life is at stake. ‖ Life, spirit, animation (entrain); *déborder de vie*, to bubble over with vitality; *donner de la vie à*, to enliven, to liven up. ‖ Life, way (ou) mode of living (manière de vivre); *la vie américaine*, the American way of life; *la vie rose*, a honeyed life; *vie de bâton de chaise, de chien*, wild, dog's life; *c'est la vie*, such is life; *changer de vie*, to turn over a new leaf; *connaître la vie*, to see life; *enterrer sa vie de garçon*, to give a farewell bachelor party; *femme de mauvaise vie*, loose woman; *mauvaise vie*, loose living; *mener joyeuse vie*, to lead a gay life; *régime de vie*, mode of life; *rendre la vie dure à qqn*, to give s.o. a hard time of it. ‖ Life, lifetime (durée de la vie); *amis à la vie, à la mort*, friends for life, lifelong friends; *de toute ma vie*, in all my life (ou) born days; *jamais de la vie*, never, not on your life; *nommé à vie*, appointed for life; *pension à vie*, life-pension; *une fois dans la vie*, once in a lifetime; *pour la vie*, for life, for good and all; *plus tard dans la vie*, in after life. ‖ Living, livelihood (moyens d'existence); *allocation de vie chère*, cost-of-living allowance; *coût de la vie*, cost of living; *gagner sa vie*, to earn one's living; *niveau de vie*, standard of living. ‖ Life (v. BIOGRAPHIE); *écrire la vie de qqn*, to write s.o.'s life. ‖ FAM. *Faire une vie*, to kick up a row; *faire la vie*, to live a fast (ou) gay life.

vieil [vjɛːj] adj. V. VIEUX.

vieillard [vjɛjaːr] m. Old man, greybeard. ‖ Pl. The aged, old (ou) elderly people.

vieille [vjɛːj] f. (V. VIEUX.) Old woman, old crone. ‖ FAM. *La vieille*, mother; *dis donc, ma vieille!*, I say old girl!

vieillerie [vjɛjri] f. Old thing; old rubbish (ou) stuff. ‖ Worn-out idea.

vieillesse [-jɛs] f. Old age, age. ‖ FIG. Oldness (d'une coutume); *son bâton de vieillesse*, the staff of his old age.
— adj. JUR. *Fonds vieillesse*, old-age pensions.

vieilli, ie [-ji] adj. Grown old; out of date, obsolete (idées); antiquated (style). [V. DÉSUET.]

vieillir [-jiːr] v. intr. (2). To grow old, to reach old age (prendre de l'âge). ‖ To age, to look old (ou) older (perdre sa fraîcheur). ‖ To become antiquated (ou) old-fashioned (ou) out of date (ou) obsolescent (ou) obsolete; to go out of fashion (se démoder).
— v. tr. To age; *vieillir qqn*, to make s.o. look older; to make s.o. out to be older than he is.
— v. pr. **Se vieillir**, to make oneself look old (ou) older (se donner l'apparence de la vieillesse). ‖ To make oneself out to be older than one is (se faire plus vieux qu'on est).

vieillissant, ante [-jisɑ̃, ɑ̃ːt] adj. Ageing, growing old (personne). ‖ Becoming antiquated, falling behind the times, getting old-fashioned (idées).

vieillissement [-jismɑ̃] m. Ageing, growing old (des personnes). ‖ Becoming antiquated, getting old-fashioned (des idées); obsolescence (d'une locution). ‖ Artificial ageing (des meubles).

vieillot, otte [-jo, ɔt] adj. Oldish; oldish-looking. ‖ Old-looking (enfant); wizened (visage). ‖ FIG. Antiquated, old-fashioned (idées).
— s. Little old man (ou) woman.

vièle [vjɛl] f. MUS. Vielle (à archet).

vielle f. MUS. Hurdy-gurdy (à roue).

vieller [-le] v. intr. (1). MUS. To play the hurdy-gurdy (ou) vielle.

vielleur [-lœːr] s. MUS. Hurdy-gurdy player (ou) grinder; vielle-player.

Vienne [vjɛn] f. GÉOGR. Vienna (en Autriche); Vienne (en France).

viennois, oise [vjɛnwa, waz] adj., s. GÉOGR. Viennese.

viens [vjɛn]. V. VENIR.

vierge [vjɛrʒ] adj. Virginal, pure (personne). ‖ Virgin (forêt); unbroken (terre). ‖ Unexposed (film); blank (page). ‖ FIG. Untarnished, unsullied (réputation).
— f. Virgin, maiden, maid. ‖ ECCLÉS. *Chapelle de la Vierge*, Lady Chapel; *la Sainte Vierge*, the Blessed Virgin. ‖ ASTRON. Virgo.

Viêt-nam [vjɛtnam] m. GÉOGR. Vietnam.

vietnamien, enne [-namjɛ̃, ɛn] adj., s. GÉOGR. Vietnamese.
— m. GRAMM. Vietnamese (langue).

vieux [vjø] (f. vieille [vjɛːj]) [m. vieil before a vowel or a mute h] adj. Old, aged, elderly (v. ÂGÉ); *devenir vieux*, to grow old; *se faire vieux*, to grow old, to get on in years; *se faire plus vieux qu'on n'est*, to make oneself out to be older than one is; *une vieille folle*, a silly old woman; *un vieux monsieur*, an elderly (ou) old gentleman. ‖ Old (chose); worn-out, worn, shabby (habit); obsolete (locution); ancient (monument); stale (nouvelles, pain); *vieux papiers*, waste paper. ‖ Old, old-fashioned, antique, antiquated (idées, mode). ‖ Old (d'autrefois); *un diplomate de la vieille école*, a diplomat of the old school; *le bon vieux temps*, the good old days. ‖ Old, of long standing (amitié, service); *vieil ami*, old friend; *vieille fille*, old maid, spinster. ‖ LOC. *Vieux jeu*, old-fashioned, antiquated, out of date, outworn; U. S. old-hat (pop.) [idées]; *il est très vieux jeu*, he's a back-number (ou) a stick-in-the-mud (ou) an old fogey.
— m. Old man (vieillard). ‖ FAM. Old man, governor (patron, père); *mes vieux*, my parents (ou) old folk (ou) old people; *dis donc, mon vieux*, I say old chap (ou) fellow (ou) man. ‖ LOC. *Un vieux de la vieille*, one of the old brigade, a die-hard.
— adv. *S'habiller trop vieux*, to dress too old for one's age.

vif, ive [vif, iːv] adj. Alive, living, live (vivant); *brûlé vif*, burnt alive; *mort ou vif*, dead or alive. ‖ Lively, active, quick, brisk (alerte); vivacious; sprightly, nimble (personne). ‖ Hasty, quick-tempered (emporté). ‖ Lively, active, quick, nimble, sharp, smart, keen (esprit); strong (foi); lively, vivid (imagination). ‖ Violent (douleur); keen (plaisir); lively (satisfaction). ‖ Sharp (attaque, paroles); hearty, sincere, heartfelt (remerciements); biting, bitter (reproche); energetic (riposte). ‖ Biting, bitter, keen, sharp, bracing (air, froid, vent); intense (chaleur); cutting (vent). ‖ Bright, brilliant, vivid, intense (couleur); dazzling (éclat); blazing, flaming, glowing (feu); sparkling (œil). ‖ Mettlesome, spirited (cheval). ‖ Spring, running (eau); *eaux vives*, spring tide. ‖ Sharp (arête); living (bois); quickset (haie); solid (roc); *chaux vive*, quicklime. ‖ LOC. *A vive allure*, at a brisk pace; at high speed (voiture); *de vive force*, by sheer strength, by main force; *de vive voix*, viva voce; by word of mouth; orally. ‖ **Vif-argent**, m. Quicksilver, mercury; *avoir du vif-argent dans les veines*, to be full of vitality, to be always on the go.
— m. Living person (vivant); *les morts et les vifs*, the quick and the dead. ‖ Life (vie); *peindre au vif*, to paint from life. ‖ Living flesh, quick (chair). ‖ JUR. *Entre vifs*, inter vivos; *le mort saisit le vif*, the heir-at-law inherits as of right. ‖ FIG. *Entrer dans le vif du sujet*, to come to the

heart of the matter; *piquer au vif,* to sting to the quick.

vigie [viʒi] f. NAUT. Danger-buoy (balise); lookout, lookout man (marin); lookout (veille); *être de vigie,* to be on the lookout. ‖ CH. DE F. Observation box.

vigilamment [viʒilamɑ̃] adv. Vigilantly, watchfully.

vigilance [-lɑ̃:s] f. Vigilance; watchfulness; *surprendre la vigilance de qqn,* to catch s.o. napping (ou) off his guard.

vigilant, ante [-lɑ̃, ɑ̃:t] adj. Vigilant, watchful, alert; on one's guard (personne). ‖ Watchful, incessant (soins).

vigile [viʒil] f. ECCLÉS. Vigil.

vigne [vi:ɲ] f. BOT. Vineyard (lieu); vine (plante); *vigne vierge,* Virginia creeper, U. S. woodbine. ‖ ECCLÉS. *Travailler à la vigne du Seigneur,* to work in the Lord's vineyard. ‖ FAM. *Dans les vignes du Seigneur,* tipsy.

vigneau [viɲo] m. ZOOL. Winkle, periwinkle (bigorneau).

vigneron [viɲrɔ̃] m. Vine-grower; vine-dresser.

vignette [viɲɛt] f. ARTS. Vignette. ‖ TECHN. Head-and-tail-piece; ornamental border; cut, engraving (en imprimerie). ‖ COMM. Inland-revenue band, U. S. Internal Revenue stamp (sur un paquet de cigarettes). ‖ MÉD. National Health label (en pharmacie). ‖ AUTOM. Road-fund licence, tax disc.

vignettiste [-tist] s. Vignettist, vignette-engraver.

vignoble [viɲɔbl] m. Vineyard.

vignot [viɲo] m. V. VIGNEAU.

vigogne [vigɔɲ] f. Vicuña (lama, tissu).

vigoureusement [vigurøzmɑ̃] adv. Vigorously.

vigoureux, euse [-rø, ø:z] adj. Vigorous; sturdy (enfant); strong, powerful (homme); hardy (plante); sound (santé); robust (vieillard). ‖ Vigorous; powerful (coup); spirited (défense); forceful, impassioned (discours); strenuous (efforts); energetic (opposition). ‖ ARTS. Spirited, bold (coloris); forceful, vigorous (style); firm (trait).

vigueur [vigœ:r] f. Vigour; strength, force (morale, physique); energy (de la pensée); *donner de la vigueur à,* to invigorate; *retrouver sa vigueur,* to regain strength; *sans vigueur,* spiritless, unenergetic (personne); tame (style); *vigueur intellectuelle,* strength of intellect. ‖ Force; effect (effet); *en vigueur,* in force; *cesser d'être en vigueur,* to lapse; *entrer en vigueur,* to take effect, to come into force; *mettre en vigueur,* to bring into force, to enforce; *remettre en vigueur,* to re-instate.

Viking [vikiŋ] m. Viking.

vil, ile [vil] adj. Cheap (marchandises); *à vil prix,* dirt cheap. ‖ Low, lowly (condition); base (métal). ‖ Vile, ignoble (action); despicable (mensonge); mean, base (motif, personne). [V. BAS.]

vilain, aine [vilɛ̃, ɛn] adj. Ugly (figure); unsightly (maison); low, sordid (quartier). [V. LAID.] ‖ Mean, shabby (action); nasty (affaire, blessure, caractère, maladie); ugly (bruits, histoires); low, vile (métier); bad, naughty (parole); unpleasant, nasty (pensées); vile, nasty, mean, objectionable (personnage); dirty, nasty, filthy (temps); dirty, rotten, mean, scurvy (tour); *le vilain côté de la vie,* the seamy side of life; *il fait vilain,* it's beastly (ou) nasty weather; *le vilain petit garçon!,* you naughty boy!
— s. † Villein (serf). ‖ Villain; scoundrel, rogue, scamp, naughty boy (ou) girl (enfant). ‖ FAM. Trouble, row; *il va y avoir du vilain,* there's going to be trouble.

vilainement [-lɛnmɑ̃] adv. Scurvily, basely, meanly, nastily.

vilebrequin [vilbrəkɛ̃] m. TECHN. Brace; brace and bit.

vilement [vilmɑ̃] adv. Vilely, despicably, meanly.

vilenie [vilni] f. Low (ou) mean action; foul deed (action vile); rotten (ou) low-down trick (mauvais tour).

vilipender [vilipɑ̃de] v. tr. (1). To vilipend, to vilify; to run down, to speak disparagingly of.

villa [villa] f. Villa; cottage; country house.

village [vila:ʒ] m. Village. ‖ FAM. *Il est bien de son village,* he is a real country bumpkin, he is as green as grass.

villageois, oise [-ʒwa, wa-z] adj. Village, country, rustic (coutume); awkward, clownish, uncouth (manières).
— m. Villager; countryman. ‖ Yokel (rustre).

villageoise [-ʒwaz] f. Villager; countrywoman; country wench.

ville [vil] f. Town; city (grande ville); *en ville,* in town; « local » (sur une adresse); *aller en ville,* to go to (ou) into town; *dîner en ville,* to dine out; *tenue de ville,* lounge (ou) U. S. business suit; *toilette de ville,* outdoor dress; *ville d'eaux,* watering-place; spa; *la ville lumière,* Paris; *la ville et la province,* town and country. ‖ LOC. *La ville, s'il vous plaît,* exchange (ou) U. S. operator, please (au téléphone). ‖ **Ville-champignon,** f. Boom (ou) mushroom town. ‖ **Ville-dortoir,** f. Dormitory town (ou) suburb. ‖ **Ville-satellite,** f. Satellite town, overspill town.

villégiature [vileʒjaty:r] f. Stay (on holiday) in the country; *être en villégiature,* to be staying in the country; to be on holiday. ‖ POP. *En villégiature,* in prison.

villégiaturer [-tyre] v. intr. (1). FAM. To stay in the country; to be on holiday.

villégiaturiste [-tyrist] s. Holiday-maker, U. S. vacationist, vacationer. (V. VACANCIER.)

villosité [villozite] f. MÉD. Villosity.

vin [vɛ̃] m. Wine; *vin fin* (ou) *de marque,* vintage wine; *les grands vins,* the famous vintage wines; *vin ordinaire,* dinner (ou) table wine; *vin du Rhin,* hock; U. S. Rhine wine; *vin en fût,* wine in the wood; *vin d'honneur,* official reception; *négociant en vin,* wine merchant. ‖ LOC. *Avoir le vin gai,* to be merry in one's cups; *entre deux vins,* half-seas over; *porter bien le vin,* to carry one's liquor well; *pris de vin,* intoxicated; *sac à vin,* wine-bibber, boozer. ‖ FIG. *Quand le vin est tiré, il faut le boire,* one must face the consequences.

vinage [vina:ʒ] m. Fortifying (de vins).

vinaigre [vinɛ:gr] m. Vinegar; *vinaigre de vin,* wine vinegar.

vinaigrer [vinɛgre] v. tr. (1). CULIN. To season with vinegar. ‖ FIG. To give an acid flavour to.

vinaigrerie [-grəri] f. Vinegar trade (commerce); vinegar-making (fabrication); vinegar factory (usine).

vinaigrette [-grɛt] f. CULIN. Vinegar sauce, vinaigrette; *à la vinaigrette,* with vinegar sauce. ‖ † Vinaigrette, two-wheeled sedan chair (voiture).

vinaigrier [-grije] m. Vinegar-maker (fabricant); vinegar-merchant (marchand). ‖ Vinegar cruet (burette).

vinasse [vinas] f. Vinasse. ‖ FAM. Washy wine.

vindicatif, ive [vɛ̃dikatif, i:v] adj. Vindictive, spiteful, revengeful.

vindicte [-dikt] f. JUR. Punishment, prosecution. ‖ FAM. *Vindicte publique,* public contumely.

vinée [vine] f. Vintage.

viner v. tr. (1). To add alcohol to, to fortify.

vineux, euse [-nø, ø:z] adj. Full-bodied (vin). ‖ Rich in wine (région); *année vineuse,* good vintage year. ‖ Vinous (goût); wine-flavoured (pêche). ‖ Wine-coloured (étoffe).

vingt [vɛ̃] adj. invar. Twenty; *vingt et un,* twenty one; *vingt-deux,* twenty two; *vingt mille francs,* twenty thousand francs; *il n'a pas encore vingt ans,*

he is still in his teens; *dans les vingt-quatre heures,* within twenty-four hours. ‖ Twenty, twentieth; *le vingt mai,* the twentieth of May, U. S. May twentieth; *j'y suis allé le vingt mai,* I went there on the twentieth of May; *chapitre vingt,* chapter twenty. ‖ MILIT. *Faire ses vingt-huit jours,* to put in one's four weeks' training in the reserve. ‖ SPORTS. *Vingt-et-un,* vingt et un, pontoon. ‖ FAM. *Je vous l'ai dit vingt fois,* I've told you scores of times; *vingt-deux!,* look out!, cave! (attention!); the cops! (devant la police).
— m. invar. Twenty.

vingtaine [vɛ̃tɛn] f. Twenty; score; about twenty, twenty or so.

vingtième [vɛ̃tjɛm] adj. Twentieth.
— m. Twentieth, twentieth part.

vingtièmement [-mɑ̃] adv. Twentiethly, in the twentieth place.

vinicole [vinikɔl] adj. Wine-growing, vinicultural; wine (industrie).

vinifère [-fɛːr] adj. AGRIC. Vine-bearing.

vinification [-fikasjɔ̃] f. Vinification.

vinique [vinik] adj. Vinic.

vinyle [vinil] m. CHIM. Vinyl.

vinylique [vinilik] adj. CHIM. *Composés vinyliques,* vinyl compounds.

viol [vjɔl] m. Rape, violation.

violacé, ée [vjɔlase] adj. Violaceous; purplish-blue; *violacé par le froid,* blue with cold.

violacée f. BOT. Violaceous plant.

violacer v. intr. (6). To become violaceous, to turn purplish-blue.

violateur, trice [vjɔlatœːr, tris] s. Violator; transgressor, infringer (d'un droit); profaner (d'une église); ravisher (d'une femme).

violation [-sjɔ̃] f. Violation; infringement, transgression. ‖ Breach (de la foi, d'une loi); breaking (des règles); desecration, profanation (d'un temple). ‖ JUR. *Violation de domicile,* unlawful entry; *violation de secret professionnel,* violation of professional secrecy; *violation de sépulture,* desecration of a grave.

violâtre [vjɔlɑːtr] adj. Purplish.

viole [vjɔl] f. MUS. Viol; *viole d'amour, de gambe,* viola d'amore, da gamba; *jeu de violes,* consort of viols.

violemment [vjɔlamɑ̃] adv. Violently.

violence [-lɑ̃ːs] f. Violence (en général); force; severity (de la douleur); stress (du temps); boisterousness, fury (du vent). ‖ Outrage, injury. ‖ JUR. Duress. ‖ LOC. *Faire violence à,* to do violence to; to violate, to rape (une femme); to stretch (la loi); *se faire violence,* to do violence to one's feelings.

violent, ente [-lɑ̃, ɑ̃ːt] adj. Violent; furious (attaque); fiery, ungovernable (caractère); severe (douleur); fierce (lutte); pungent (parfum); hot-tempered, fiery (personne); high, furious, boisterous (vent); *mourir de mort violente,* to die a violent death. ‖ FAM. *C'est un peu violent!,* that's a bit thick!, it's beyond a joke!

violenter [-lɑ̃te] v. tr. (1). To do violence to; to constrain by force; to compel. (V. FORCER.) ‖ To ravish (une femme).
— v. pr. **Se violenter,** to do violence to oneself, to force oneself.

violer [-le] v. tr. (1). To violate; to infringe, to break, to transgress (la loi); to break (sa parole, une promesse). ‖ To violate; to desecrate, to profane (un lieu saint); to enter unlawfully (une maison); to despoil (un tombeau). ‖ To violate, to rape, to outrage, to ravish (une femme).

violet, ette [vjɔlɛ, ɛt] adj. Violet, purple; *violet de colère,* black in the face (ou) purple with rage; *violet de froid,* blue with cold. ‖ PHYS. Violet (rayons).
— adj. invar. *Des rubans violet évêque,* bishop's-purple ribbons.
— m. Violet (couleur).

violette [-lɛt] f. BOT. Violet; *violette de Parme,* Parma violet.

violeur, euse [vjɔlœːr, øːz] s. Rapist.

violine [vjɔlin] adj. Purple (couleur).

violon [vjɔlɔ̃] m. MUS. Violin; fiddle (fam.) [instrument]; violin, violinist [instrumentiste]; *jouer du violon,* to play the violin; *premier violon,* first violin. ‖ FAM. Lock-up, cells; U. S. hoosegow; *au violon,* in quod, U. S. jugged. ‖ LOC. *Violon d'Ingres,* pet hobby, U. S. avocation; *payer les violons,* to pay the piper.

violoncelle [-lɔ̃sɛl] m. MUS. Violoncello, 'cello (instrument); 'cello, 'cellist (instrumentiste).

violoncelliste [-lɔ̃sɛlist] s. MUS. Violoncellist, 'cellist.

violoneux [-lɔnø] m. MUS. Fiddler.

violoniste [-lɔnist] s. MUS. Violinist.

viorne [vjɔrn] f. BOT. Viburnum.

vipère [vipɛːr] f. ZOOL. Viper; adder; *vipère aspic,* asp. ‖ FIG. *Langue de vipère,* viperish tongue; *vipère lubrique,* insidious vermin.

vipereau [vipro] m. ZOOL. Young viper.

vipérin, ine [vipeʀɛ̃, in] adj. Viperine. ‖ FIG. Viperous, venomous (langue).

vipérine [viperin] f. BOT. Viper's bugloss. ‖ ZOOL. Viperine snake.

virage [viraːʒ] m. Turning round; slewing round; cornering, turning (action) [d'une auto]; swinging round [d'une grue]. ‖ AVIAT. Banking. ‖ NAUT. Tacking, going about. ‖ AUTOM. Bend, corner, turn; sharp curve (de la route); banked corner (d'un vélodrome); *prendre un virage,* to take a corner, to corner; *virage en épingle à cheveux,* hairpin bend (ou) turn; *virage à visibilité réduite,* blind corner. ‖ TECHN. Changing of colour (d'une étoffe); toning (en photographie); *bain de virage,* toning-bath. ‖ **Virage-fixage,** m. Combined toning and fixing.

virago [virago] f. Virago. (V. MARITORNE.)

viral, ale [viral] adj. MÉD. Viral.

vire [viːr] f. Ledge (en montagne).

virée [vire] f. Turn; *tournées et virées,* comings and goings. ‖ FAM. Joy-ride, ride, trip, run (ballade); spree, binge, bender (noce).

virelai [virlɛ] m. Virelay.

virement [virmɑ̃] m. Turn, turning. ‖ FIN. Transfer (à, to); *comptoir général de virement,* banker's clearing-house; *mandat de virement,* order to transfer; *faire un virement de dix mille francs à un compte,* to transfer ten thousand francs to an account.

virer [-re] v. intr. (1). To turn, to turn round. (V. TOURNER.) ‖ To swing round (grue). ‖ AUTOM. To turn, to corner, to take a corner (ou) a bend (voiture); *virer court,* to corner sharply; *virer trop large,* to take a corner too wide; *virer sur place,* to turn in one's own length. ‖ AVIAT. To bank (sur l'aile). ‖ NAUT. To heave (haler); *virer de bord,* to tack, to come about. ‖ TECHN. To change colour, to turn colour (étoffe); to tone (épreuve photographique). ‖ FIG. *Tourner et virer,* to shilly-shally (barguiner); *virer à tout vent,* to be always chopping and changing; *virer de bord,* to change sides, to rat.
— v. tr. To turn. ‖ CULIN. To toss (une crêpe). ‖ FIN. To transfer. ‖ NAUT. *Virer le cap à l'ouest,* to turn her head to the west. ‖ TECHN. To tone (une épreuve). ‖ FAM. *Tourner et virer qqn,* to put s.o. through a searching examination.

vireur [-rœːr] m. TECHN. Turning-gear.

vireux, euse [virø, øːz] adj. Virose, virous (plante); virose, rank (odeur).

virevolte [virvɔlt] f. Swift turning round. ‖ FIG. Sudden changing (de l'opinion).

virevolter [-te] v. intr. (1). To turn round swiftly (cheval); to spin round, to twirl round (personne).

Virgile [virʒil] m. Virgil, Vergil.

virgilien, enne [-ljɛ̃, ɛn] adj. Virgilian, Vergilian.

virginal, ale [virʒinal] adj. Virginal ; maidenly. ‖ Pure white (lys).

virginal m. Mus. Virginal, virginals.

virginaliste [-list] s. Mus. Virginal player.

virginité [virʒinite] f. Virginity ; maidenhood.

virgule [virgyl] f. Comma ; *point et virgule,* semicolon. ‖ Math. Decimal point ; *deux virgule cinq (2,5),* two point five (2.5). ‖ Méd. *Bacille virgule,* comma bacillus. ‖ Fig. *Observer les points et les virgules,* to be meticulous over details (ou) in little things, to be punctilious.

viril, ile [viril] adj. Virile ; manly (action) ; male (sexe) ; *l'âge viril,* manhood. ‖ Jur. *Portion virile,* lawful share. ‖ Méd. *Membre viril,* penis ; *parties viriles,* genitals.

virilement [-lmɑ̃] adv. Like a man, in a manly fashion.

viriliser [-lize] v. tr. (1). To instil manliness into, to make a man of.

virilité [-lite] f. Virility ; manhood ; manliness.

viro-fixage [virɔfiksa:ʒ] m. Toning and fixing.

viro-fixateur [-satœ:r] (pl. **viro-fixateurs**) m. Toning and fixing bath.

virole [virɔl] f. Ferrule (d'une canne). ‖ Techn. Collar, binding-ring, sleeve (de manche) ; thimble-joint (de tuyaux) ; ring-die (moule d'acier). ‖ ‖ Milit. Locking-ring (de baïonnette). ‖ Blas. Virole.

viroler [-le] v. tr. (1). To ferrule. ‖ To place in the ring-die.

virolet [-lɛ] m. Techn. Roller.

virtualité [virtɥalite] f. Virtuality.

virtuel, elle [-tɥɛl] adj. Virtual.

virtuellement [-tɥɛlmɑ̃] adv. Virtually ; practically, to all intents and purposes ; potentially.

virtuose [virtɥo:z] s. Mus. Virtuoso. ‖ Fam. First-rater.

virtuosité [-ozite] f. Virtuosity.

virulence [virylɑ̃:s] f. Virulence. ‖ Fig. Virulence; malignity, malevolence ; poisonousness.

virulent, ente [-lɑ̃, ɑ̃:t] adj. Virulent. ‖ Fig. Virulent, malignant ; scathing (critique).

virus [viry:s] m. Méd. Virus ; *maladie à virus,* virus disease.

vis [vi]. V. Vivre (105) et Voir (106).

vis [vis] f. Screw ; *vis d'Archimède,* Archimedean screw ; *vis de rappel,* adjusting screw ; *vis sans fin,* worm, endless screw ; *escalier à vis,* spiral staircase. ‖ Fam. *Serrer la vis à,* to put the screw on. ‖ **Vis-butoir** (pl. *vis-butoirs),* f. Stop-screw.

visa [viza] m. Visa, visé (sur un passeport). ‖ Signature ; initials (paraphe) ; certification. ‖ Sighting (d'une lettre de change). ‖ Ch. de f. Stamping (d'un billet). ‖ Milit. *Avec le visa militaire,* approved by the military authorities.

visage [viza:ʒ] m. Face ; visage ; *à deux visages,* double-faced (aspect) ; two-faced (hypocrisie) ; *au visage agréable,* pleasant-faced ; *les visages pâles,* pale-faces. ‖ Countenance ; look (allure) ; *avoir bon, mauvais visage,* to look well, ill ; *changer de visage,* to change countenance ; *faire bon, mauvais visage à qqn,* to give s.o. a warm, cool welcome. ‖ Loc. *A visage découvert,* barefacedly, openly ; *trouver visage de bois,* to find nobody in.

visagiste [vizaʒist] s. V. Esthéticienne.

vis-à-vis [vizavi] loc. adv. Opposite ; *assis vis-à-vis,* sitting face to face ; *la maison vis-à-vis,* the house opposite (ou) over the way ; *places en vis-à-vis,* seats facing each other.

— loc. prép. **Vis-à-vis,** opposite, facing (face à) ; in presence of (en face de) ; *vis-à-vis de la mairie,* opposite the town hall ; *l'un vis-à-vis de l'autre,* facing each other. ‖ Towards, in regard to, with respect to, in relation to (envers) ; *sincère vis-à-vis de soi-même,* sincere with oneself.

— m. Person opposite (en général) ; partner (aux cartes) ; vis-à-vis (à une danse). ‖ Vis-à-vis (canapé, voiture).

viscéral, ale [viseral] adj. Visceral.

viscère [-sɛ:r] m. Méd. Internal organ. ‖ Pl. Viscera.

viscose [visko:z] m. Techn. Viscose (textile).

viscosité [viskozite] f. Viscosity, viscidity ; stickiness, glutinousness.

visé [vize] m. Aimed shot.

visée f. Aim (v. but). ‖ Milit. Aiming, sighting ; *appareil de visée,* sighting apparatus ; *ligne de visée,* line of sight ; *prendre sa visée,* to take aim. ‖ Naut. *Appareil de visée,* director (de torpille). ‖ Fig. Pl. Aims, designs ; ambitions ; plans ; *avoir de hautes visées,* to aim high.

viser v. intr. (1). To aim (*à,* at) ; *viser au cœur,* to aim at the heart ; *viser juste,* to aim straight ; *bien viser,* to take good aim. ‖ Fig. *Viser à,* to aim at ; to aspire to ; *viser à des buts nobles,* to pursue noble aims ; *viser à l'effet,* to aim at effect ; *à quoi vise tout cela?,* what is the end in view?, where is it all leading?

— v. tr. To aim at, to take aim at ; to take a sight on. ‖ Sports. To address (la balle). ‖ Fig. To affect (affecter) ; to relate to ; to refer to ; to allude to (concerner) ; to have in view (ou) in mind (tendre à) ; *être visé par une décision,* to be affected by a decision ; *je ne vise personne,* I am not alluding to anyone in particular ; *il se sentait visé par la critique,* he felt that the criticism was directed against him. ‖ Fam. To look at (regarder) ; to watch (surveiller).

viser v. tr. (1). To certify (un chèque) ; to countersign, to initial (un document) ; to visa, to visé (un passeport). ‖ Ch. de f. To stamp (un billet).

viseur [-zœ:r] m. Aimer (personne). ‖ Techn. Viewfinder (d'appareil photographique) ; sighting-tube ; *viseur optique,* telescopic sight. ‖ Milit. Sight-vane ; *viseur automatique,* predictor. ‖ Aviat. Bomb-sight (de lancement).

visibilité [vizibilite] f. Visibility ; *mauvaise visibilité,* poor (ou) low visibility ; *sans visibilité,* blind (atterrissage, tournant). ‖ Aviat. *Voler sans visibilité,* to fly blind.

visible [-bl] adj. Visible ; perceptible. (V. Apparent, perceptible.) ‖ Visible, obvious (v. évident, manifeste) ; patent (indifférence). ‖ Open to the public (collection, musée) ; disengaged, ready to receive company, at home to visitors (personne) ; *elle n'est pas visible ce soir,* she cannot see anyone this evening.

visiblement [-bləmɑ̃] adv. Visibly, perceptibly, noticeably. ‖ Obviously, evidently, clearly, manifestly ; conspicuously.

visière [vizjɛ:r] f. Visor, vizor (de casque) ; peak (de casquette). ‖ Autom. Eye-shade. ‖ Milit. Sight. ‖ Loc. *Rompre en visière avec,* to quarrel openly with.

vision [vizjɔ̃] f. Vision ; sight ; eye-sight ; perception ; seeing ; *vision momentanée,* glimpse. ‖ Vision, imagination (chimère). ‖ Apparition, ghost. ‖ Ciném. *En première vision,* first showing.

visionnaire [vizjɔnɛ:r] adj. Visionary.

— s. Visionary, seer.

visionner [-ne] v. tr. (1). Ciném. To pre-view.

visionneuse [-nø:z] f. Viewer.

visitandine [vizitɑ̃din] f. Ecclés. Nun of the Order of the Visitation.

Visitation [-tasjɔ̃] f. Ecclés. Visitation.

visite [vizit] f. Visit, call ; *rendre visite à,* to visit (ou) to call on ; *visite de cérémonie, de politesse,* formal, duty call ; *en visite chez,* on a visit to, paying a call on ; *heures de visite,* calling hours (chez qqn) ; visiting hours (à l'hôpital). ‖ Visitor, caller ; *attendre des visites,* to expect callers. ‖

Visit ; examination, inspection. ‖ JUR. Examination (par la douane) ; search (par la police) ; *visite des lieux*, search of the premises. ‖ MÉD. Visit, attendance (d'un médecin) ; *passer une visite médicale*, to undergo a medical examination, U. S. to take a physical examination. ‖ ECCLÉS. Visitation (par un évêque). ‖ MILIT. *Passer la visite*, to come before the medical officer. ‖ NAUT. Survey (d'un navire) ; *droit de visite*, right of search. ‖ TECHN. Servicing (d'une auto) ; overhauling (d'un moteur).

visiter [-te] v. tr. (1). To visit (les malades, les pauvres). ‖ To view, to inspect, to see over, to look over, to go over (une maison) ; to visit (un monument) ; to go round, to look round (un musée) ; *il me fit visiter la maison*, he showed me over the house. ‖ ECCLÉS. To visit (évêque) ; *visiter les pauvres*, to do district visiting. ‖ MÉD. To visit, to attend (médecin). ‖ JUR. To inspect, to examine ; to search (des bagages, une maison) ; to visit (un navire). ‖ NAUT. To survey (un navire). ‖ TECHN. To service (une auto) ; to overhaul (un moteur).

visiteur, euse [-tœ:r, ø:z] s. Visitor, caller. ‖ Visitor (d'un château). ‖ ECCLÉS. District visitor (des pauvres). ‖ JUR. Inspector ; searcher (douanier). ‖ NAUT. Surveyor (d'un navire). ‖ SPORTS. Pl. Visiting team (équipe).

vison [vizɔ̃] m. ZOOL. Vison, American mink. ‖ COMM. Mink (fourrure).

visqueux, euse [viskø, ø:z] adj. Viscous, sticky, gluey ; slimy ; tacky. (V. GLUANT, POISSEUX.) ‖ Thick (huile) ; clammy (peau).

vissage [visa:ʒ] m. Screwing.

visser [-se] v. tr. (1). To screw, to screw on (ou) in (ou) up (ou) down. ‖ FAM. To put the screw on, to clamp down on (qqn).
— v. pr. Se **visser**, to be screwed on (ou) in (ou) up (ou) down. ‖ FAM. To attach oneself firmly ; *se visser sur sa chaise*, to sit tight on one's chair.

visu (de) [devizy] loc. adv. With one's own eyes, for oneself.

visualisation [vizɥalizasjɔ̃] f. Visualization. ‖ TECHN. *Écran de visualisation*, visual display unit, VDU.

visualiser [-alize] v. tr. (1). To visualize.

visuel, elle [-ɛl] adj. Visual ; *champ visuel*, field of vision.

visuellement [-ɛlmɑ̃] adj. Visually.

vit [vi]. V. VIVRE (105) et VOIR (106).

vital, ale [vital] adj. Vital ; necessary to life ; *parties vitales*, vitals. ‖ FIG. Vital, fundamental.

vitalisme [-lism] m. PHILOS. Vitalism.

vitalité [-lite] f. Vitality.

vitamine [vitamin] f. MÉD. Vitamin.

vitaminé, ée [-mine] adj. Vitamin rich, with added vitamins, vitaminized.

vitaminique [-minik] adj. MÉD. Vitaminic.

vite [vit] adv. Fast, quickly, swiftly, rapidly ; *allez vite*, go quickly (sans attendre) ; go fast (rapidement) ; *au plus vite*, as fast as possible ; *aller vite en besogne*, to be a quick worker ; *vous allez trop vite pour moi*, you are going too fast for me ; I can't keep up with you (prop. et fig.) ; I think you are taking too much for granted (vous vous illusionnez) ; *le temps passe vite*, time flies (ou) goes by quickly. ‖ Quickly, hastily (hâtivement) ; *j'ai agi trop vite*, I was too hasty. ‖ Quickly, soon (tôt) ; *il vient aussi vite que possible*, he is coming as soon as he can ; *c'est vite fait*, it doesn't take long ; *il eut vite fait de déjeuner*, he got his lunch over quickly ; *on a vite fait de dire*, it's easy to say.
— interj. Make haste !, be quick ! ; *faites vite*, hurry up, buck up, look sharp, look alive.
— adj. SPORTS. *Les coureurs les plus vites*, the fastest (ou) swiftest runners.

vitellin, ine [vitɛllɛ̃, in] adj. Vitelline.

vitesse [-tɛs] f. Speed ; rate ; rapidity, quickness

(en général) ; swiftness, fleetness (d'un cheval, d'un coureur) ; velocity (d'un projectile) ; *à toute vitesse*, at top (ou) full speed, all out (fam.) ; *vitesse acquise*, impetus ; momentum ; *vitesse folle*, breakneck speed ; *vitesse initiale*, muzzle velocity (d'un projectile) ; *vitesse de régime*, normal running speed (d'un moteur) ; *faire de la vitesse*, to speed ; *forcer la vitesse*, to force the pace ; *gagner qqn de vitesse*, to overtake (ou) outstrip s.o. ; *indicateur de vitesse*, speedometer ; *lutter de vitesse avec*, to race against, to run a race with ; *prendre de la vitesse*, to gather speed. ‖ AVIAT. *Vitesse aérodynamique*, air speed ; *vitesse à l'atterrissage*, landing speed ; *vitesse minimale de sustentation*, stalling speed ; *perdre de la vitesse*, to stall. ‖ CH. DE F. *Train de grande vitesse*, express passenger train ; *expédier un colis en grande vitesse*, to express a parcel ; *en petite vitesse*, by goods (ou) U. S. freight train. ‖ AUTOM. *Boîte de vitesses*, gear-box ; *passer les vitesses*, to go through the gears ; *première vitesse*, first (ou) low (ou) bottom gear ; *à quatre vitesses*, four-gear, with four gears. ‖ FIG. *Gagner de vitesse*, to forestall (s.o.). ‖ FAM. *En quatrième vitesse, à une vitesse grand V*, at top speed ; *partir en vitesse*, to rush away.

viticole [vitikɔl] adj. Viticultural.

viticulteur [-kyltœ:r] m. AGRIC. Viticulturalist, wine-grower. (V. VIGNERON.)

viticulture [-kylty:r] f. AGRIC. Viticulture, vine- (ou) wine-growing.

vitrage [vitra:ʒ] m. Glazing (action). ‖ Windows, glass-work (vitres). ‖ Glass door (porte) ; glass partition (séparation). ‖ Vitrage-curtain (rideau).

vitrail [vitra:j] (pl. **vitraux** [vitro]) m. Leaded glass window. ‖ ECCLÉS. Stained glass window.

vitre [vitr] f. Window-pane, pane of glass.

vitré, ée [vitre] adj. Glazed ; glass (porte). ‖ MÉD., ELECTR. Vitreous.

vitrer v. tr. (1). To glaze, to put glass in, to fit with glass.

vitrerie [-trəri] f. Glaziery.

vitreux, euse [-trø, ø:z] adj. Vitreous ; glassy. ‖ Glassy, glazed (yeux).

vitrier [-trije] m. Glazier. ‖ Window-glass maker (fabricant).

vitrifiable [vitrifjabl] adj. Vitrifiable.

vitrification [-fikasjɔ̃] f. Vitrification, vitrifaction. ‖ Vitrified object.

vitrifier [-fje] v. tr. (1). To vitrify ; to fuse (par fusion).
— v. pr. Se **vitrifier**, to vitrify.

vitrine [vitrin] f. Shop- (ou) show-window, window (devanture). ‖ Show-case (montre). ‖ Glass case, glass cabinet (armoire) ; *vitrine d'exposition*, exhibit case ; *sous vitrine*, under glass.

vitriol [vitrijɔl] m. CHIM. Vitriol. ‖ FIG. *Au vitriol*, vitriolic, caustic, biting (paroles).

vitriolage [-la:ʒ] m. Vitriol-throwing. ‖ TECHN. Souring (des toiles).

vitriolé, ée [-le] adj. Vitriolized.
— s. Victim of vitriol-throwing.

vitrioler [-le] v. tr. (1). To throw vitriol at, to vitriolize.

vitrioleur [-lœ:r] s. Vitriol-thrower.

vitupérateur, trice [vityperatœ:r, tris] adj. Vituperating, abusing.

vitupération [-rasjɔ̃] f. Vituperation, abuse.

vitupérer [-re] v. tr. (1). To vituperate ; to rail.

vivable [vivabl] adj. FAM. Livable-with ; *cet homme n'est pas vivable*, that man is impossible to get on with.

vivace [vivas] adj. Long-lived. ‖ BOT. Hardy. ‖ FIG. Inveterate (haine, préjugé) ; enduring (remords) ; green (souvenir).

vivace [vivatʃe] adj. invar. MUS. Vivace.

vivacité [-site] f. Promptness (promptitude) ;

quickness, swiftness (rapidité); alertness. ‖ Hastiness; outburst of temper (emportement); hasty
action (dans l'action); hasty utterance (dans la
parole). ‖ Sharpness (d'une attaque); petulance
(du caractère); fury, heat (d'un combat); vividness, brilliancy (d'une couleur); warmth, heat
(d'une discussion); intensity (d'une passion);
acuteness (d'une sensation). ‖ Vivacity, sprightliness; vivaciousness (animation); readiness (de
l'esprit); brightness (du regard); liveliness (du
style); *avec vivacité,* vivaciously; *avoir de la
vivacité,* to be vivacious.

vivandier [vivãdje] m. Sutler; canteen-keeper.
vivandière [-djɛ:r] f. Vivandière.
vivant, ante [vivã, ã:t] adj. Alive, living; *il l'a
connu vivant,* he knew him when he was alive;
animal vivant, live animal; *êtres vivants,* living
creatures. ‖ FIG. Living; lively (animé); live
(pièce); animated (quartier, scène); vivid, spirited
(récit); *une bibliothèque vivante,* a walking ency-
clopedia; *les langues vivantes,* modern languages;
portrait vivant, living image (personne); lifelike
portrait (tableau).
— m. Living person; *les morts et les vivants,* the
quick and the dead. ‖ LOC. *Bon vivant,* man who
enjoys good living; easy-going person; jolly
fellow; *du vivant de mon père,* in my father's day
(ou) lifetime, when my father was alive; *de son
vivant,* in his day, during his lifetime.
vivarium [vivarjɔm] m. Vivarium.
vivat [viva] m., interj. Hurrah; cheer; *pousser
des vivats,* to cheer, to shout hurrah.
vive [vi:v] f. ZOOL. Weever, sting-fish (poisson).
vive! interj Long live, up with, hail; *vive (ou)
vivent les vacances!,* hurrah for the holidays!
vivement Lvivmã] adv. Quickly, smartly, sharply,
briskly (remuer); sharply, warmly (répondre). ‖
Warmly (applaudir, remercier); severely (blesser); deeply, profoundly (émouvoir); acutely,
keenly (sentir); very much (souhaiter); *s'intéresser vivement à,* to take a lively interest in.
— interj. I wish that, I'll be glad when; *vivement
les vacances,* I wish it were holiday time already,
roll on the holidays; *vivement que ce soit fini,* I'll
be glad when it's over.
viveur [vivœ:r] m. One of the fast set; gay dog,
rake, libertine. (V. DÉBAUCHÉ, NOCEUR.)
vivier [vivje] m. Fish-pool, fish-pond (étang);
fish-preserve. ‖ Well, fish-well (d'un bateau). ‖
FIG. Breeding ground.
vivifiant, ante [vivifjã, ã:t] adj. Vivifying;
enlivening; bracing, invigorating, tonic (air, climat). ‖ ECCLÉS. Quickening.
vivificateur, trice [vivifikatœ:r, tris] adj. Vivifying.
vivification [-fikasjɔ̃] f. Vivification; reviving.
vivifier [-fje] v. tr. (1). To vivify; to vitalize; to
endue with life. ‖ To invigorate, to brace, to
fortify (revigorer). ‖ To put new life into (une
entreprise); to revive (l'industrie).
vivipare [vivipa:r] adj. ZOOL. Viviparous.
— m. ZOOL. Viviparous animal.
viviparité [-parite] f. ZOOL. Viviparity, vivipa-
rousness.
vivisecteur [visisɛktœ:r] m. MÉD. Vivisector;
vivisectionist.
vivisection [-sjɔ̃] f. MÉD. Vivisection.
vivoter [vivɔte] v. intr. (1). FAM. To live sparely,
to rub (ou) get along somehow; U. S. to live
close to the line. (V. VÉGÉTER.)
vivre [vi:vr] v. intr. (105). To live, to be alive
(être vivant); *cesser de vivre,* to die, to expire;
il n'y avait pas âme qui vive, there was not a
living soul; *les soixante ans qu'il avait vécu,* the
sixty years of his life. ‖ To live, to spend one's
life (passer sa vie); *il fait bon vivre ici,* life is
pleasant here; *vivre avec une femme,* to live (ou)
to cohabit with a woman; *vivre à Londres,* to live

in London; *vivre saintement,* to live a godly life;
savoir vivre, to be well-bred (ou) well-mannered;
vivre dans la terreur, to live in a state of terror.
‖ To live, to subsist, to exist (subsister); *gagner
juste de quoi vivre,* to earn just enough to live on;
vivre bien, to live in comfort; *vivre au jour le
jour,* to live from hand to mouth; *vivre de
légumes,* to live on vegetables; *vivre de ses
rentes,* to live on a private income; *travailler
pour vivre,* to work for a living. ‖ MILIT. *Qui
vive?,* who goes there? ‖ FIG. To live, to exist;
to last, to endure, to survive (durer, survivre);
sa gloire vivra toujours, his glory will live for
ever. ‖ FAM. *Apprendre à vivre à qqn,* to teach
s.o. manners; *avoir beaucoup vécu,* to have seen
life; *être difficile à vivre,* to be difficult to get on
with; *se laisser vivre,* to take it easy. ‖ LOC. *Qui
vivra verra,* live and learn; time will show (ou) tell.
— v. tr. To live; *vivre sa vie,* to live one's life;
les expériences que nous avons vécues, the experiences that we have lived through.
— m. Living. ‖ Food; *le vivre et le couvert,*
board and lodging. ‖ MILIT. Pl. Rations. ‖ Pl.
Provisions, supplies; *vivres de réserve,* iron
(ou) U. S. emergency rations. ‖ FIG. *Couper les
vivres à qqn,* to stop s.o.'s allowance.
vivrier, ère [vivrije, ɛ:r] adj. AGRIC. Food-
producing.
vizir [vizi:r] m. Vizier.
vlan! [vlã] interj. Slap!, whack!, hang!; *vlan!
en plein dans la figure,* smack in the face.
vocable [vɔkabl] m. Vocable. (V. MOT.) ‖ ECCLÉS.
Name-patronage (d'un saint); *sous le vocable de,*
dedicated to.
vocabulaire [-bylɛ:r] m. Vocabulary, word-book,
word-list (lexique); vocabulary (nombre de mots).
vocal, ale [vɔkal] adj. Vocal.
vocalement [-lmã] adv. Vocally.
vocalique [-lik] adj. Vocalic, vowel.
vocalisateur [-lizatœ:r] m. Vocalizer.
vocalisation [-lizasjɔ̃] f. Vocalization.
vocalisatrice [-lizatris] f. Vocalizer. ‖ MUS.
Coloratura soprano.
vocalise [-li:z] f. MUS. Vocalizing; exercise in
vocalization.
vocaliser [-lize] v. tr., intr. (1). MUS., GRAMM.
To vocalize.
vocalisme [-lism] m. GRAMM. Vocalism; vowel-
system (d'une langue); vowels (d'un mot).
vocatif [vɔkatif] m. GRAMM. Vocative.
vocation [vɔkasjɔ̃] f. Vocation; calling, bent,
inclination (v. PENCHANT); *avoir la vocation de,*
to have a vocation for, to be cut out for; *manquer sa vocation,* to miss one's calling. ‖ ECCLÉS.
Vocation, call, calling.
vociférant, ante [vɔsiferã, ã:t] adj. Vociferous,
vociferant, clamorous.
vociférateur, trice [-ratœ:r, tris] s. Vociferator.
vociférations [-rasjɔ̃] f. pl. Vociferations; shouts,
yells; bawling.
vociférer [-re] v. intr., tr. (5). To shout, to yell,
to bawl (v. BRAILLER); to vociferate (contre,
against).
vodka [vɔdka] f. Vodka.
vœu [vø] m. Vow (promesse); *faire vœu de,* to
make a vow to, to vow to, to swear to. ‖ Wish,
vow (désir); wish (souhait); *émettre un vœu,* to
express a wish; *meilleurs vœux, tous mes vœux,*
best wishes. ‖ Motion, resolution (à l'Assemblée).
‖ ECCLÉS. Vow; *prononcer ses vœux,* to take
one's vows.
vogue [vɔg] f. Vogue, fashion (v. MODE); *c'est
la grande vogue d'aujourd'hui,* it's all the rage
today; *entrer en vogue,* to come into vogue; *être
en vogue,* to be popular (ou) fashionable (ou) in
fashion; *mettre en vogue,* to bring into fashion,
to popularize.

voguer [vɔge] v. intr. (1). NAUT. To be rowed (galère); to sail (navire). ‖ FIG. To drift; to scud (nuages); to wander (pensées). ‖ LOC. *Vogue la galère*, come what may; let's chance it; here goes! (fam.).

voici [vwasi] prép. Here is (ou) are; *voici ce dont il s'agit*, this is what it is all about; *voici comment*, this is how; like this; *le voici qui vient*, here he comes; *me voici*, here I am; *nous voici bientôt arrivés*, we shall soon be there; *nous voici enfin arrivés*, here we are at last; *voici pourquoi*, for this (ou) for the following reason; this is the reason why; *voici qui vous étonnera*, this will astonish you. ‖ Here is, this is, here are, there are; *voici mon livre, voilà le sien*, this is my book, that is his. ‖ For (il y a); *voici dix ans que je ne l'ai pas vu*, I haven't seen him for ten years; *voici trois semaines que j'attends une réponse*, I've been waiting for a reply for three weeks. ‖ LOC. *Voici venir*, here is (ou) are, here comes (ou) come; *voici venir l'automne*, autumn is drawing near.

voie [vwa] f. Way, road; path (v. ROUTE); street (v. RUE); *voie fluviale*, waterway; *par voie de terre*, by land; *voie publique*, public thoroughfare; highway. ‖ Load (de bois); sack (de charbon). ‖ JUR. *Voies de droit*, legal proceedings; *voies de fait*, assault and battery; *par voie diplomatique*, through diplomatic channels. ‖ ECCLÉS. *Les voies de Dieu*, the ways of God; *la voie étroite*, the strait and narrow path. ‖ NAUT. *Faire une voie d'eau*, to spring a leak; *voie d'eau*, leak. ‖ AVIAT. *Voie aérienne*, airway, air-route; *voie de départ*, runway. ‖ AUTOM. Gauge (des roues). ‖ CH. DE F. Railway, U. S. railroad; *à deux voies*, double-track (ligne); *à voie étroite*, narrow-gauge; *par voie ferrée*, by rail. ‖ SPORTS. Track, scent (à la chasse). ‖ MÉD. Duct (biliaire); tract (respiratoire); passage (urinaire). ‖ ELECTR. Circuit. ‖ ASTRON. *Voie lactée*, Milky Way. ‖ FIG. Course (ligne d'action); way, means, course, method (moyens); *en bonne voie*, going well, well on the way; *être dans la bonne voie*, to be on the right track; *s'engager dans une voie dangereuse*, to enter upon a dangerous course; *mettre qqn sur la voie*, to put s.o. on the track. ‖ FIG. Vocation; *trouver sa voie*, to find oneself (ou) one's feet. ‖ LOC. **En voie de**, in process of; *en voie de réparation*, under repair. [V. CLAIRE-VOIE.]

voilà [vwala] prép. There is (ou) are; *voilà mon affaire*, that just suits me; *voilà qui est bien, bizarre*, that's good, strange; *en voilà assez*, that's enough; *la maison que voilà*, that house, the house over there; *les voilà*, there they are; *le voilà qui sort*, there he is going out; *et voilà qu'il se met en colère*, and now he's getting angry. ‖ There is (ou) are; that is, those are; *voici mon livre, voilà le sien*, this is my book, that is his. ‖ (Voici); *voilà ce qu'il fallait dire*, that's what you should have said; *me voilà*, here I am. ‖ For (il y a); *voilà deux jours que je le cherche*, I have been looking for it for two days; *voilà cinq ans qu'il est parti*, he went away five years ago. ‖ FAM. *En voilà-t-il!*, what a lot! ; *voilà que ça recommence*, blow me if it's not beginning again; *voilà-t-il pas que j'ai perdu ma clé*, well, if I haven't gone and lost my key; *voilà ce que c'est que de mentir*, that's what you get by (ou) for telling lies.
— interj. Coming! ; here! ; there you are!

voilage [vwala:ʒ] m. Net curtain (rideau); veiling (étoffe).

voile [vwal] f. NAUT. Sail, canvas (toile); sailing-boat (voilier); *voiles basses, hautes*, lower, upper sails; *grand-voile*, main sail; *bateau à voiles*, sailing boat, U. S. sailboat; *faire voile, mettre à la voile*, to set sail (pour, for); *naviguer à la voile*, to sail; *sous voile*, under sail (ou) canvas. ‖ FIG. *Mettre toutes voiles dehors*, to make the best show one can; to put on one's smartest clothes. ‖ FAM. *Mettre les voiles*, to clear out. (V. DÉCAMPER.)

voile m. Veil (de tête). ‖ Antimacassar (de fauteuil). ‖ Voile (étoffe). ‖ ECCLÉS. Veil; *prendre le voile*, to take the veil. ‖ MÉD. Blur, mist (devant les yeux); *voile du palais*, soft palate. ‖ TECHN. Fog (en photographie); warping; buckle (d'une roue). ‖ FIG. Screen; cloak, veil, guise, mask; *jeter un voile sur*, to cast a veil over; *sous le voile de*, under the cloak (ou) mask of; *les voiles de la nuit*, the shades of night.

voilé, ée [vwale] adj. Hazy; overcast (ciel); dim, veiled (lumière); dull (regard); muffled (tambour); slightly husky (voix); *visage voilé de tristesse*, face overcast with sorrow; *yeux voilés de larmes*, eyes dimmed with tears. ‖ Veiled (termes); *en termes peu voilés*, in thinly veiled terms, in no uncertain way. ‖ MUS. Veiled (voix). ‖ TECHN. Warped (planche); fogged (plaque); buckled (roue).

voilement [vwalmɑ̃] m. TECHN. Warping (d'une planche), buckling, bending (d'une roue).

voiler v. tr. (1). NAUT. To rig with sails.

voiler v. tr. (1). To veil (le visage). ‖ To obscure, to hide, to cover (les étoiles); to dim, to veil (la lumière); to dim (le regard); to muffle (un tambour); to make slightly husky, to veil (la voix). ‖ TECHN. To twist, to send out of true; to warp (une planche); to fog (une plaque); to buckle, to bend (une roue). ‖ FIG. To screen (ses fautes); to cloak, to mask (ses intentions, ses pensées).
— v. intr. TECHN. To twist, to go out of true; to warp (planche); to buckle (roue).
— v. pr. **Se voiler**, to cloud over, to become overcast (ciel); to dim (lumière); to grow husky (voix). ‖ TECHN. To twist, to go out of true; to warp (planche); to buckle (roue).

voilerie [-lri] f. NAUT. Sail-loft.

voilette [-lɛt] f. Veil, hat-veil.

voilier [-lje] adj. NAUT. Sailing; *bâtiment bon voilier*, good sailer. ‖ AVIAT. Flying (qualités). ‖ ZOOL. Long-flight (oiseau).
— m. NAUT. Sailing-boat (ou) ship; U. S. sailboat. ‖ TECHN. Sail-maker.

voilure [-ly:r] f. NAUT. Sails; *réduire la voilure*, to shorten sail. ‖ AVIAT. Wings, flying-surface.

voir [vwa:r] v. tr. (106).

---

1. Percevoir. — 2. Distinguer, observer. — 3. Lire. — 4. Examiner. — 5. Visiter. — 6. Connaître. — 7. Découvrir, savoir. — 8. Comprendre. — 9. Prévoir. — 10. Concevoir. — 11. Apprécier. — 12. Essayer. — 13. Expérimenter. — 14. MÉD. — 15. FAM. — 16. LOC. — 17. Voir à. — 18. Voir venir. — 19. Faire voir. — 20. Laisser voir.

---

1. To see, to perceive (percevoir); *voir c'est croire*, seeing is believing; *il ne voit pas plus loin que son nez*, he can't see farther than the end of his nose. ‖ 2. To see, to notice, to remark; to distinguish, to observe (distinguer, observer); *je vois que vous avez grossi*, I see you have put on weight; *je l'ai vu de mes propres yeux*, I saw it with my own eyes; *on ne voit que ça*, you see it everywhere; *voir page deux*, see page two. ‖ 3. To read (lire); *je l'ai vu dans le journal*, I read (ou) saw it in the paper. ‖ 4. To see (ou) about, to examine, to look into (examiner); *voir de plus près*, to have a closer look; *voir qqch. à fond*, to look into sth. thoroughly; *nous verrons ça*, we'll see all about that. ‖ 5. To see, to visit (une expo-

sition, un musée, un pays) ; to meet with, to visit, to receive (qqn) ; *aller voir qqn*, to go and see s.o., to look s.o. up (fam.) ; *je l'ai vu hier à Londres*, I met him in London yesterday ; *il a vu du pays*, he's been around a bit ; *il ne voit jamais personne*, he never sees (ou) receives anybody ; *on ne vous voit plus*, you are quite a stranger. ‖ **6.** To see, to witness (connaître) ; *je n'ai jamais vu le pareil*, I have never seen anything like it. ‖ **7.** To see, to find out (découvrir, savoir) ; *je vais voir s'il y a qqn*, I'll go and see if there is anyone there ; *vous verrez qu'il a raison*, you'll see that he's right ; *viendra-t-elle demain ? c'est à voir*, will she come tomorrow ? that remains to be seen. ‖ **8.** To see, to grasp, to understand (comprendre) ; *je ne vois pas ce que vous voulez dire*, I don't see what you mean. ‖ **9.** To see, to foresee (prévoir) ; *je ne vois pas la fin de nos problèmes*, I can't see any end to our difficulties ; *voir les choses de loin*, to have plenty of foresight ; to be prudent. ‖ **10.** To see, to imagine, to conceive (concevoir) ; *à ce que je vois*, from what I see ; *je ne le vois pas homme d'affaires*, I can't imagine him as a business man. ‖ **11.** To see, to consider, to judge, to regard, to appreciate (apprécier) ; *sa façon de voir les choses*, his way of seeing things ; *se faire bien, mal voir*, to get into s.o.'s good, bad books ; *nous ne voyons pas les choses du même œil*, we don't see eye to eye ; *voyez vous-même*, see (ou) judge for yourself. ‖ **12.** To see, to try (essayer) ; *je vais voir un peu si je peux le faire*, I am going to see if I can do it, I'm going to have a try at doing it. ‖ **13.** To undergo, to go through, to experience (expérimenter) ; *il a vu bien des malheurs*, he has been through a lot of misfortune. ‖ **14.** MÉD. To see, to attend (un malade) ; to see, to consult (un médecin). ‖ NAUT. To sight (un navire). ‖ **15.** FAM. To tolerate, to put up with (supporter) ; *ne pas pouvoir voir qqn*, not to be able to stand s.o. ‖ FAM. *Dites voir*, let's hear it ; *écoutez voir*, just listen ; *essayez voir*, just have a try ; *essayez voir si ça va*, try it to see if it's all right ; *il ferait beau voir qu'il ne veuille pas*, I'd just like to see him say no, I can just imagine him refusing ; *je l'ai fait pour voir*, I did it just to see what would happen ; *montrez voir*, show us ; *regardez voir*, have a look ; *voyons voir*, let's see. ‖ **16.** LOC. *N'avoir rien à voir à* (ou) *avec*, to have nothing to do with ; *il n'a rien à y voir*, it's no business of his. ‖ **17.** *Voir à*, to see, to see to it, to make sure, to take care ; to do one's best ; *voyez à y être à l'heure*, see (to it) that you are there on time. ‖ **18.** *Voir venir*, to wait and see ; *je le vois venir*, I see him coming ; I see what he's driving (fig.). ‖ **19.** *Faire voir*, to show ; to display (du courage) ; to prove (une erreur) ; to take (un malade au médecin) ; *faites voir, faites-moi voir ça*, show me, show it to me ; FAM. *se faire voir par le médecin*, to get examined, U. S. to have a physical. ‖ **20.** *Laisser voir*, to show, to reveal ; FIG. To betray ; *son visage laissait voir sa colère*, his face betrayed his anger.

— v. pr. Se voir, to see oneself (se regarder). ‖ To be seen ; to show itself (sens passif) ; *cela se voit tous les jours*, that happens every day ; you can see that every day ; *il n'est pas content, cela se voit*, he's not very pleased, that's obvious. ‖ FIG. To see (ou) find oneself ; *se voir dans l'obligation de*, to find oneself bound to.

— v. récipr. Se voir, to see each other. ‖ To visit each other ; to be on friendly terms (se fréquenter).

voire [vwa:r] adv. † In truth, in sooth. ‖ Nay, even, indeed ; *surpris, voire étonné*, surprised, nay, astonished.

voirie [vwari] f. † Garbage-heap (d'un abattoir) ; refuse-dump (d'une ville). ‖ Roads ; *travaux de voirie*, road works ; *entretien de la voirie*, road maintenance. ‖ Roads Department, U. S. Highway Division (administration).

vois [vwa]. V. VOIR (106).

voisé, ée [vwaze] adj. GRAMM. Voiced.

voisement [vwazmɑ̃] m. GRAMM. Voicing.

voisin, ine [vwazɛ̃, in] adj. Neighbouring ; in the neighbourhood ; near, nearby (proche) ; *habiter la maison voisine*, to live next door ; *la maison voisine*, the next house. ‖ Adjacent ; *deux maisons voisines*, two adjoining houses. ‖ Preceding (dans le passé). ‖ FIG. Allied, closely related (espèces) ; kindred (esprits, idées) ; akin (*de*, to) ; bordering (*de*, on).

— s. Neighbour ; *agir en bon voisin*, to act in a neighbourly way ; *les voisins*, the neighbours ; the people next door ; *mon voisin d'à côté*, my next-door neighbour.

voisinage [-zina:ʒ] m. Neighbourhood, surrounding district (v. ALENTOUR) ; *dans le voisinage*, in the neighbourhood ; near here. ‖ Proximity, nearness, vicinity (proximité). ‖ Neighbours ; neighbourhood (personnes) ; *il est connu de tout le voisinage*, the whole neighbourhood knows him, he is well known in the district. ‖ Neighbourly relations (rapports) ; *rapports de bon voisinage*, neighbourly terms, neighbourliness.

voisiner [-zine] v. intr. (1). To visit one's neighbours ; to be on friendly terms with the neighbours ; to be neighbourly (personnes). ‖ To be adjacent, to adjoin, to be placed side by side (objets) ; *voisiner avec*, to be next (ou) close to.

voiturage [vwatyra:ʒ] m. Carriage, cartage, conveyance (transport). ‖ Cost of conveyance ; fare (tarif).

voiture [-ty:r] f. Vehicle, carriage, conveyance (v. VÉHICULE) ; *voiture de place*, hackney carriage ; *voiture publique*, public conveyance. ‖ Donkey-cart (à âne) ; barrow, hand-cart (à bras) ; prison van (cellulaire) ; perambulator, pram (fam.), U. S. baby carriage (d'enfant) ; delivery van (de livraison) ; invalid (ou) wheel chair (de malade) ; waggon (de roulier) ; tram-car (de tramway) ; *petite voiture des quatre-saisons*, apple-cart, street-barrow, U. S. street-wagon. ‖ Cost of conveyance, carriage ; fare. (V. VOITURAGE.) ‖ Load ; cartload (de marchandises) ; car-load, carriageful (de voyageurs). [V. VOITURÉE.] ‖ AUTOM. Motor, motor car ; *voiture de sport, de tourisme*, sports, touring car ; *voiture pie*, police traffic-control car ; *aller en voiture*, to drive ; *venir en voiture*, to come by car. ‖ CH. DE F. Coach, carriage, U. S. car ; goods truck, U. S. freight car (à marchandises) ; *en voiture !*, take your seats !, mind the doors !, U. S. all aboard ! ‖ COMM. Transportation, carriage, conveyance ; *lettre de voiture*, way-bill, consignment note. ‖ **Voiture-atelier**, f. MILIT. Travelling workshop. ‖ **Voiture-école**, f. AUTOM. « School of Motoring », « L » (= « Learner ») ; « Driver under instruction ». ‖ **Voiture-radio** (pl. *voitures-radio*), f. Radio-car.

voiturée [-tyre] f. Load ; cartload (de marchandises) ; carriageful, car-load (de voyageurs).

voiturer [-tyre] v. tr. (1). To cart (des marchandises) ; to transport, to convey, to carry, to take (des marchandises, des personnes).

voiturette [-tyrɛt] f. Trap. ‖ AUTOM. Light car. ‖ MILIT. Scout-car, armoured car.

voiturier, ère [-tyrje, ɛr] adj. Carriage.

— m. Carrier, carter.

voix [vwa] f. Voice ; *à voix basse*, in a low voice, in a whisper ; *à haute voix*, aloud, out loud, loudly ; *avoir une extinction de voix*, to have lost one's voice ; *de vive voix*, by word of mouth ; *donner de la voix*, to give tongue ; *élever la voix*, to raise one's voice; to speak out; *faire la grosse voix*, to speak gruffly. ‖ Speech; *sans voix*, speechless. ‖ Mus. Voice (organe); part (partition); singer (personne); *voix de fausset*, falsetto; *voix humaine*, vox humana (de l'orgue); *voix de poitrine, de tête*, chest-, head-voice; *voix de soprano, de ténor*, soprano, tenor voice; *à trois voix*, three-part (chant); *être en voix*, to be in voice; *placer la voix dans le masque*, to pitch the voice forward; *pose de la voix*, voice production. ‖ Gramm. Voice. ‖ Jur. Vote; *aller aux voix*, to vote; *mettre aux voix*, to put to the vote. ‖ Fig. Sound; voice (d'une cloche); thunder, roar (des flots); roll (de tonnerre). ‖ Fig. Word; speech; voice (de la conscience, de la raison); call (de la nature). ‖ Fig. Opinion; *la voix publique*, vox populi, public opinion; *avoir voix au chapitre*, to have a say in the matter; *élever la voix en faveur de*, to speak in favour of.

vol [vɔl] m. Flight, flying (action); *en plein vol*, in full flight; *prendre son vol*, to take wing; *oiseau au vol*, bird on the wing. ‖ Flight, flock (d'oiseaux); covey (de perdreaux); swarm (de sauterelles). ‖ Flight (distance). ‖ Wingspread (envergure). ‖ Aviat. Flight; pl. sorties (départs); *heures de vol*, flying time; *prendre son vol*, to take off (avion); *vol de nuit*, night-flying; nightflight; *vol en piqué*, dive; *vol à voile*, gliding; *faire du vol plané*, to volplane. ‖ Fig. Flight, soaring (de l'esprit, de l'imagination); flight, fleeting (du temps). ‖ Loc. *A vol d'oiseau*, as the crow flies; *Paris à vol d'oiseau*, bird's-eye view of Paris; *saisir au vol*, to snatch up, to catch on the wing (ou) U. S. fly. ‖ **Vol-au-vent**, m. invar. Culin. Vol-au-vent.

vol m. Jur. Thieving, stealing, robbery (action); larceny, theft (résultat); confidence trick (à l'américaine); highway robbery (de grand chemin); burglary (avec effraction); shop-lifting (à l'étalage); armed robbery, robbery with violence (à main armée); article stolen; stolen goods (produits du vol).

volable [-labl] adj. Easy to rob (personne). ‖ Worth stealing (effets).

volage [vɔla:ʒ] adj. Fickle, inconstant.

volaille [vɔla:j] f. Zool. Poultry, fowls; *marchand de volaille*, poulterer. ‖ Culin. Fowl.

volailler [-laje], **volailleur** [-lajœ:r] m. Poulterer, poultryman (marchand de volaille); poulterer, chicken farmer (éleveur).

volant, ante [vɔlɑ̃, ɑ̃:t] adj. Flying; *fusée volante*, sky-rocket; *poisson volant*, flying fish. ‖ Flowing, floating (robe); fluttering (rubans). ‖ Fly (ou) loose (câble, feuille); light (chaise); movable (cloison); occasional (table). ‖ Milit. *Bombe volante*, flying bomb, V1, doodle-bug. ‖ Naut. Portable (cabestan); flying (escadron). ‖ Aviat. Flying (aile, soucoupe); *non volant*, non-flying (personnel). ‖ Archit. Flying (pont). ‖ Electr. *Fiche volante*, wander-plug. ‖ Sports. Temporary, flying (camp).
— m. Flounce (d'une robe). ‖ Sports. Shuttlecock; *jouer au volant*, to play battledore and shuttlecock. ‖ Autom. Steering-wheel; *se mettre au volant*, to take the wheel; *tenir le volant*, to drive. ‖ Aviat. Control-wheel; U. S. yoke. ‖ Naut. Upper top-sail. ‖ Techn. Flywheel; fly (en horlogerie); hand-wheel (de manœuvre). ‖ Fin. *Volant de sécurité*, reserve fund (ou) supply, reserves; margin.

volapük [vɔlapyk] m. Gramm. Volapük. ‖ Fig. Gibberish.

volatil, ile [vɔlatil] adj. Chim., Fig. Volatile.

volatile [vɔlatil] m. Zool. Winged creature; bird; fowl (volaille).

volatilisable [-lizabl] adj. Volatilizable.

volatilisation [-lizazjɔ̃] f. Volatilization.

volatiliser [-lize] v. tr. (1). To volatilize.
— v. pr. **Se volatiliser**, to volatilize. ‖ To burn up (fusée). ‖ Fig. To go into thin air.

volatilité [-lite] f. Volatility.

volcan [vɔlkɑ̃] m. Volcano. ‖ Loc. *Danser sur un volcan*, to sit on a volcano.

volcanique [-nik] adj. Volcanic (propr. et fig.).

volcaniser [-nize] v. tr. (1). To volcanize.

volcanisme [-nism] m. Volcanism.

volcanologie [-nɔlɔʒi] f. Volcanology, vulcanology.

volcanologue [-nɔlɔg] s. Volcanologist, vulcanologist.

vole [vɔl] f. Vole, slam (aux cartes); *faire la vole*, to win all the tricks, to make a slam.

volée [vɔle] f. Flight (d'un oiseau, d'un projectile); *prendre sa volée*, to take wing. ‖ Flight (en général); bevy (d'alouettes); flock (de moineaux); covey (de perdrix); brood (de pigeons). ‖ Volley, peal (de cloches). ‖ Shower (de coups) [v. raclée]; *donner une bonne volée à qqn*, to give s.o. a good thrashing. ‖ Milit. Volley. ‖ Naut. Broadside. ‖ Archit. Flight (d'escalier). ‖ Sports. Volley (au tennis); *volée haute*, smash; *prendre une balle entre bond et volée*, to half-volley a ball. ‖ Techn. Jib (d'une grue); throw (d'un piston); trace-block, splinter-bar (d'une voiture); *cheval de volée*, leader. ‖ Fig. Rank, high standing; quality; *de haute volée*, of high ranking, of good standing; of the first rank (fam.) first-rate; *la haute volée*, the upper ten, high society. ‖ Fam. Band, collection, company (troupe); bevy (de jeunes filles). ‖ **À la volée**, in flight; on the wing (oiseau); at random; *renvoyer une balle à la volée*, to volley a ball; *saisir à la volée*, to snatch up; *semer à la volée*, to sow broadcast. ‖ **À toute volée**, in full swing (à tire d'aile); vigorously; in good earnest (avec vigueur); *sonner à toute volée*, to ring a full peal.

voler [vɔle] v. intr. (1). To fly; to wing one's way (oiseau). ‖ To fly (objet); *voler en éclats*, to burst, to fly (ou) to shiver into pieces; *faire voler qqch.*, to send sth. flying; to knock sth. (de, out of, off). ‖ Aviat. To fly; *voler à voile*, to glide. ‖ Fig. To fly, to go fast (courir); *il vola à sa rencontre*, he rushed (ou) dashed to meet her; *voler de ses propres ailes*, to stand on one's own feet; to fend for oneself. ‖ Fig. To soar (imagination); to fly (temps). ‖ Fam. *On aurait pu entendre voler une mouche*, you could have heard a pin drop.

voler v. tr. (1). To steal (dérober); to usurp (un titre); *voler qqch. à qqn*, to rob s.o. of sth., to steal sth. from s.o.; *on m'a volé mon portefeuille*, my wallet has been stolen. ‖ To rob (qqn); to cheat, to swindle, to do (fam.) [rouler]; *il s'est fait voler*, he's been had (ou) done. ‖ Fam. *Il ne l'a pas volé!*, serve him right!
— v. intr. To commit robbery.

volet [vɔlɛ] m. Sorting-board (à trier). ‖ Shutter (d'une boutique, d'une fenêtre); *enlever, mettre les volets*, to take down, to put up the shutters. ‖ Ecclés. Palla, U. S. pall (du calice); volet (d'un triptyque). ‖ Aviat. Tab (de centrage); flap (de commande). ‖ Autom. Butterfly-valve (de carburateur); *volets thermiques*, radiator shutters. ‖ Electr. *Indicateur à volets*, drop indicator; *volet d'appel*, disc, U. S. call indicator. ‖ Techn. Shutter (en photographie); paddle (de roue hydraulique). ‖ Fig. *Trié sur le volet*, hand-picked, select, carefully chosen (ou) selected (en général); screened (candidats).

voleter [vɔlte] v. intr. (8a). To flutter; to flutter about; to flit. ‖ Fig. To flit, to skip (esprit).

volette [-lɛt] f. Fly-net (de cheval). ‖ Culin. Pastry-stand.

volettement [-lɛtmɑ̃] m. Flutter, fluttering (d'ailes); flitting (vol çà et là).

voleur, euse [vɔlœːr, øːz] adj. Thieving (en général); dishonest (commerçant); pilfering (enfants); thievish, thieving (pie).
— s. Thief; robber, stealer (en général); burglar (cambrioleur); highwayman, footpad (de grand chemin); shop-lifter (à l'étalage); pickpocket (à la tire); *au voleur!*, stop thief!

volière [vɔljɛːr] f. Aviary; bird-cage.

volige [vɔliːʒ] f.. ARCHIT. Roofing-strip, slatelath; batten.

volitif, ive [vɔlitif, iːv] adj. Volitive, volitional.

volition [-sjɔ̃] f. Volition.

volley-ball [vɔlɛbol] m. SPORTS. Volley-ball.

volleyeur, euse [vɔlɛjœːr, øːz] s. SPORTS. Volley-ball player (joueur de volley-ball); volleyer (au tennis).

volontaire [vɔlɔ̃tɛːr] adj. Voluntary; intentional; deliberate; spontaneous (acte). ‖ Self-willed; stubborn; obstinate; wilful; ' headstrong (personne). ‖ MILIT. *Engagé volontaire*, volunteer.
— m. MILIT. Volunteer; *s'engager comme volontaire*, to volunteer.

volontairement [-tɛrmɑ̃] adv. Voluntarily, spontaneously, of one's own free will (spontanément, volontiers). ‖ Purposely, on purpose; wilfully (exprès). ‖ Stubbornly, obstinately, doggedly (avec obstination).

volontariat [-tarja] m. MILIT. Voluntary military service.

volontarisme [-tarism] m. PHILOS. Voluntarism, voluntaryism. ‖ FIG. Will-power.

volonté [-te] f. Will, volition (vouloir); willpower (force); purpose (intention); *volonté de fer*, iron will; *de forte volonté*, strong-willed; *faire appel à toute sa volonté*, to summon up all one's will-power; *manque de volonté*, lack of will; *montrer de la bonne, de la mauvaise volonté*, to show willingness, unwillingness; *travailler de bonne volonté*, to work with a will. ‖ Will, wish; desire, pleasure (désir); *la volonté de Dieu*, the will of God; *les dernières volontés de*, the last will and testament of; *en faire à sa volonté*, to have one's own way; to do just what one pleases; *de sa propre volonté*, of one's own accord (ou) free will, spontaneously. ‖ Pl. Whims, fancies (fantaisies); *faire ses quatre volontés*, to act according to one's own sweet will. ‖ À volonté, ad lib.; at pleasure; at will; at discretion; *payable à volonté*, payable on demand; *prenez-en à volonté*, take as much as you like.

volontiers [vɔlɔ̃tje] adv. Willingly, gladly, readily, with pleasure (de bon gré). ‖ Readily, easily (facilement); *on croit volontiers que*, people are apt to think that.

volt [vɔlt] m. ELECTR. Volt.

voltage [-taːʒ] m. ELECTR. Voltage.

voltaïque [-taik] adj. ELECTR. Voltaic.

voltaire [vɔltɛːr] m. High-backed armchair.

voltairianisme [-rjanism] m. Voltairianism.

voltairien, enne [-rjɛ̃, ɛn] adj., s. Voltairian.

voltamètre [vɔltamɛtr] m. ELECTR. Voltameter.

voltampère [-tɑ̃pɛːr] m. ELECTR. Voltampere.

volte [vɔlt] f. Vaulting (en gymnastique). ‖ SPORTS. Volte (du cheval, à l'escrime). ‖ Volte-face, f. invar. Volte-face; *faire volte-face*, to wheel round, to face about (au propre); to reverse one's opinions (ou) policy; to change sides (au figuré).

volter [-te] v. intr. (1). SPORTS. To volt.

voltige [-tiːʒ] f. SPORTS. Trick-riding (en équitation); slack rope (corde); slack-rope exercises; exercises on the flying trapeze (en gymnastique).

voltigeant, ante [-tiʒɑ̃, ɑ̃ːt] adj. Fluttering, flitting.

voltigement [-tiʒmɑ̃] m. Fluttering; flitting.

voltiger [-tiʒe] v. intr. (7). To fly; to flit (v. VOLETER); to flutter (papillon); *voltiger de fleur en fleur*, to flit from flower to flower. ‖ SPORTS. To do trick-riding (en équitation); to perform on the slack-rope; to perform on the flying trapeze (en gymnastique). ‖ FIG. To flutter about; to flit; to fly; to be inconstant (personne); to hover (sourire).

voltigeur [-tiʒœːr] m. MILIT. Voltigeur; light-infantryman; pl. the light infantry.
— s. Acrobat; performer on the flying trapeze.

voltmètre [vɔltmɛtr] m. ELECTR. Voltmeter.

volubile [vɔlybil] adj. Voluble, glib. ‖ BOT. Voluble, twining, twisting.

volubilis [-lis] m. BOT. Morning-glory.

volubilité [-lite] f. Volubility; glibness; garrulity, garrulousness.

volume [vɔly:m] m. Volume, tome; *en deux volumes*, in two volumes. ‖ Volume, mass, bulk (d'un solide); volume (d'un son, de la voix). ‖ **Volume-contrôle** (pl. *volumes-contrôles*) m. Volume-control.

volumétrique [-metrik] adj. Volumetric, volumetrical.

volumineux, euse [-minø, øːz] adj. Voluminous (en général); bulky (paquet). ‖ FIG. Voluminous.

volupté [vɔlypte] f. Delight, pleasure. ‖ Sensual delight.

voluptueusement [-tɥøzmɑ̃] adv. Voluptuously.

voluptueux, euse [-tɥø, øːz] adj. Voluptuous.
— s. Voluptuary, sensualist.

voluptuosité [-tɥɔzite] f. Voluptuosity.

volute [vɔlyːt] f. Volute, whorl (coquille). ‖ ARCHIT. Volute, scroll. ‖ FIG. Spiral, twirl, wreath, curl, twist (de fumée); curl (d'une vague).

voluté, ée [-te] adj. ARCHIT. Voluted, scrolled.

volve [vɔlv] f. BOT. Volva.

vomer [vɔmɛːr] m. MÉD. Vomer. ‖ ZOOL. Moon-fish.

vomique [vɔmik] adj. BOT., MÉD. *Noix vomique*, nux vomica.

vomiquier [-kje] m. BOT. Nux vomica (arbre).

vomir [vɔmiːr] v. tr. (2). To vomit (v. RENDRE); *avoir envie de vomir*, to feel sick, U. S. to feel like vomiting; *faire des efforts pour vomir*, to retch. ‖ FIG. To vomit, to belch forth (de la fumée). ‖ FAM. *C'est à faire vomir*, it's enough to make one sick.
— v. intr. MÉD. To vomit, to be sick, to spew.

vomissement [vɔmismɑ̃] m. Vomiting (action); vomit (matières); *avoir des vomissements*, to vomit.

vomissure [-syːr] f. Something vomited, vomit.

vomitif, ive [-tif, iːv] adj., m. MÉD. Vomitive, vomitory. (V. ÉMÉTIQUE.)

vont [vɔ̃]. V. ALLER (15).

vorace [vɔras] adj. Voracious.

voracement [-smɑ̃] adv. Voraciously.

voracité [-site] f. Voracity, voraciousness; *avec voracité*, voraciously.

vortex [vɔrtɛks] m. Vortex; vortex-ring; whorl.

vos [vo] adj. poss. V. VOTRE.

vosgien, enne [voʒjɛ̃, ɛn] adj. GÉOGR. Of (ou) from the Vosges.
— s. Native (ou) inhabitant of the Vosges.

votant, ante [vɔtɑ̃, ɑ̃ːt] adj. Voting (assemblée); voting, having a vote, entitled to vote (personne).
— s. Voter; *liste des votants*, electoral roll, parliamentary register.

vote [vɔt] m. Vote; voting; ballot, poll (aux élections); *bureau, centre, section de vote*, polling-booth, -station, -district; *droit de vote*, franchise. ‖ Vote; division; passing (d'un projet de loi); *vote de confiance*, vote of confidence; *provoquer un vote*, to challenge a division. ‖ Vote, result of a vote, decision (résultat); *le vote est pour, contre*, the ayes, the noes have it.

voter [-te] v. intr. (1). To vote (Communes); *voter blanc*, to return a blank voting paper;

voter à main levée, to vote by a show of hands. ‖ To divide (à la Chambre).

— v. tr. To vote (des crédits); to carry, to pass (un projet de loi, une résolution); *voter des remerciements à,* to pass a vote of thanks to.

votif, ive [-tif, i:v] adj. Votive.

votre [vɔtr] (pl. **vos** [vo]) adj. poss. Your; *votre tante,* your aunt; *vos père et mère,* your father and mother; *un de vos amis,* a friend of yours.

vôtre [vo:tr] adj. poss. Yours; *je suis tout vôtre,* I am entirely at your service.

— pron. poss. **Le vôtre** (f. *la vôtre;* pl. *les vôtres).* Yours; *voici mon livre, voilà le vôtre,* this is my book, and that is yours. ‖ FAM. *A la vôtre, à la bonne vôtre,* cheerio!, cheers!, here's to you!

— m. Your own; *il faut y mettre du vôtre,* you must do your share (ou) bit. ‖ Pl. Your own; your own folk (ou) family (ou) people. ‖ Pl. FAM. Pranks, escapades; *vous faites encore des vôtres,* you're up to your old tricks again; you're having another fling.

voudrai [vudre]. V. VOULOIR (107).

voué, ée [vwe] adj. Dedicated, devoted. (V. CONSACRÉ.) ‖ Addicted; pledged. (V. ADONNÉ.) ‖ Doomed (à l'oubli).

vouer v. tr. (1). To dedicate, to devote, to give up (sa vie); *vouer obéissance,* to vow obedience. ‖ ECCLÉS. To vow, to consecrate, to dedicate.

— v pr. Se vouer, to devote (ou) dedicate oneself; to devote one's life; to pledge oneself. ‖ FAM. *Ne pas savoir à quel saint se vouer,* not to know which way to turn, to be at one's wit's end.

vouloir [vulwa:r] v. tr. (107).

---

1. Sens général. — 2. Viser à. — 3. Exiger. — 4. Désirer. — 5. Avoir l'intention. — 6. Consentir. — 7. Essayer. — 8. Avoir besoin. 9. Demander. — 10. Avouer; penser. — 11. *Vouloir* dans une subordonnée. — 12. GRAMM. — 13. LOC. — 14. En vouloir à. — 15. Vouloir dire.

---

1. To will; *vouloir c'est pouvoir,* where there's a will, there's a way; *Dieu veuille que,* God grant that; *ne pas savoir vouloir,* to have no will-power. ‖ **2.** To want, to aim at, to be bent on (viser à). ‖ **3.** To want, to demand, to insist on, to require, to need (exiger); *je veux que ce soit bien fait,* I want it well done; *il veut absolument que vous partiez,* he insists on your leaving. ‖ **4.** To wish, to want (désirer); to wish for (qqch.); to like (au conditionnel); *vouloir du bien, du mal à qqn,* to wish s.o. good, ill; *j'aurais voulu rester chez moi,* I wish I had stayed at home; *je voudrais le voir me parler sur ce ton,* I'd like to see him speaking to me in that tone of voice; *je voudrais vous voir demain,* I should like to see you tomorrow; *il ne veut pas que je le fasse,* he doesn't want me to do it; *il ne veut pas de moi comme collègue,* he doesn't want me for a colleague; *lequel voudriez-vous?,* which one would you like (ou) choose?; *nous ne l'avons pas voulu,* it's not our fault; we didn't expect that; *que voulez-vous?,* what do you expect?; *que voulez-vous!,* it can't be helped!; *que voulez-vous que cela me fasse?,* what difference do you think that makes to me?; *que voulez-vous que j'y fasse?,* what can I do about it?; *que voulez-vous de moi?,* what do you want me for?; what do you want of me?; *si vous vouliez y aller, je pourrais vous y emmener en voiture,* if you wanted to go, I could drive you; *voulez-vous une cigarette?,* would you like a cigarette?; *voulez-*

vous que je vous y conduise?, would you like me to take you there?; *vous l'avez voulu!,* it serves you right; *vous l'aurez voulu!,* it'll be your fault! ‖ **5.** To want, to intend, to mean, to purpose (avoir l'intention de); *sans le vouloir,* without meaning it, unintentionally; *vouloir sans le vouloir,* to have a sneaking desire; *le sort veut que,* fate decrees that; *le destin n'a pas voulu que,* fate has not willed that. ‖ **6.** To agree to, to be willing to, to consent to, to be prepared to, to be ready to (consentir); to be able (en parlant des choses); *je viendrai demain, si vous le voulez bien,* I'll come tomorrow, if you don't mind (ou) if that suits you (ou) if it is all right with you; *je vous prie de bien vouloir faire,* be so kind as to do, will you be good enough to do; *quand il veut, il est charmant,* when he wants to (ou) when he feels like it, he can be charming; *veuillez agréer mes salutations distinguées,* yours truly, yours faithfully; *veuillez me dire,* please tell me; *veuillez transmettre mes meilleurs vœux à,* give my best wishes to; *voulez-vous bien reculer un peu?,* would you mind moving back a little?; *la voiture ne veut pas marcher,* the car won't go, the car refuses to go. ‖ **7.** To want, to try (essayer) [au passé historique]; *il voulut attraper la balle,* he tried to catch the ball. ‖ **8.** To want, to require, to need (avoir besoin de); *cette plante veut de l'eau,* that plant needs water. ‖ **9.** To want, to ask (demander); *combien en voulez-vous?,* how much are you asking for it? ‖ **10.** To allow, to admit (avouer); to insist, to be convinced (être convaincu que); to think, to hold, to maintain (penser); *je veux bien que vous ayez raison, mais...,* I'm prepared to admit that you are right, but...; *on veut qu'il soit artiste, mais je ne suis pas de cet avis,* they maintain that he's an artist, but I don't agree with them. ‖ **11.** To want, to wish, to like, to choose, to please (dans une proposition subordonnée); *faites comme vous voudrez,* do as you please; *il sait ce qu'il veut,* he has a will of his own; *il ne sait pas ce qu'il veut,* he doesn't know his own mind; *nous y irons, qu'il le veuille ou non,* we shall go, whether he likes it or not. ‖ **12.** GRAMM. To take; *vouloir l'accusatif,* to take the accusative. ‖ **13.** LOC. *En veux-tu en voilà,* lots, as much as you like; *il y en avait à bouche que veux-tu,* there was any amount. ‖ **14.** En vouloir à, to have a grudge against; to be vexed with, to be set against (qqn); to have designs on (qqch.); *il m'en veut,* he has a grudge against me; he holds it against me; *il m'en veut à mort,* he's mad at me. ‖ **15.** Vouloir dire, to mean to say, to intend to say (avoir l'intention de dire); to mean (signifier); *qu'est-ce que cela veut dire?,* what does that mean?

— v. pr. Se vouloir, to wish oneself. ‖ S'en vouloir, to be angry (ou) vexed with oneself (ou) each other; *je m'en voulais de ma stupidité,* I could have kicked myself for being so stupid; *un rire qui se voulait féroce,* a would-be ferocious laugh.

— m. Will; *le vouloir de Dieu,* the will of God; *bon, mauvais vouloir,* good-will, ill-will; *de son bon vouloir,* of one's own accord.

voulu, ue [vuly] adj. Required; necessary, prescribed; imposed. ‖ Requisite (formalités); proper (heure, moment); *en temps voulu,* in due time. ‖ Deliberate, intentional, wilful; studied (négligence). ‖ Premeditated. ‖ V. VOULOIR (107).

vous [vu] pron. pers. invar. You. ‖ You (sujet); *vous le voyez,* you see him; *le voyez-vous?,* do you see him? ‖ You (complément direct); *il vous voit,* he sees you. ‖ You, to you (complément indirect); *ce livre est à vous,* this book is yours; *c'est à vous de jouer,* it's your turn to play; *de vous à moi,* between ourselves; *je n'ai pas eu de* *nouvelles de vous,* I have had no news of you; *il vous le dira,* he will tell you; *il vous en parlera,* he will speak to you about it. ‖ You, one (indéfini); *quand le temps vous empêche de sortir, on reste au coin du feu,* when the weather prevents you from going out, you sit by the fire. ‖ Yourself; pl. yourselves (avec un v. pr.); *vous vous fatiguez trop,* you are tiring yourself out; *vous vous êtes blessé,* you have hurt yourself. ‖ Each other, one another (avec un v. récipr.); *vous vous connaissez,* you know one another. ‖ You (emphatique); *vous autres Anglais,* you English. ‖ Loc. *Si j'étais que de vous,* if I were in your shoes. ‖ **Vous-même,** pron. pers. (pl. *vous-mêmes*). Yourself; pl. yourselves.

voussé, ée [vuse] adj. ARCHIT. Arched (porte d'entrée); vaulted (toit).

vousseau [-so], **voussoir** [-swa:r] m. ARCHIT. Voussoir, arch-stone.

voussure [-sy:r] f. ARCHIT. Arching (d'une baie); coving (d'un plafond); curve, bend (d'une voûte).

voûte [vut] f. ARCHIT. Vault; arch; archway; *voûte en berceau, en ogive, à plein cintre,* barrel, ogival, semi-circular vault. ‖ MÉD. Dome (du crâne); roof (du palais). ‖ TECHN. Vault, dome (d'un fourneau). ‖ Loc. *La voûte céleste,* the vault (ou) canopy of heaven.

voûté, ée [-te] adj. ARCHIT. Vaulted; arched. ‖ MÉD. Bent; round-shouldered (personne); *être voûté,* to be round-shouldered, to have a stoop.

voûtelette [-tlɛt] f. Small arch.

voûter [-te] v. tr. (1). To vault, to vault over; to arch. ‖ FIG. To bow (la taille).

— v. pr. **Se voûter,** to vault, to arch. ‖ FIG. To become bent (ou) bowed (choses); to get round-shouldered, to develop a stoop (personnes).

vouvoiement [vuvwamã] m. Use of *vous* in conversation.

vouvoyer [-je] v. tr. (9 a). To address s.o. as *vous*.

voyage [vwaja:ʒ] m. Journey; trip, run (d'agrément); flight (en avion); voyage (sur mer); tour; travel, travelling; running about (petits déplacements); *voyage en auto, en autocar, en chemin de fer,* car, coach, railway journey; U. S. car, bus, train trip; *voyage autour du monde,* world tour; *voyage d'essai, de noces,* trial trip, honeymoon; *voyage en Russie,* visit to Russia; *aimer les voyages,* to be fond of travel; *bon voyage!,* goodbye!, pleasant journey!; *agence de voyage,* tourist agency; U. S. travel bureau; *être en voyage,* to be travelling; *frais de voyage,* travelling expenses; *partir en voyage,* to go on (ou) to set out on a journey. ‖ NAUT. Voyage; *premier voyage,* maiden voyage. ‖ FIG. *Faire le grand voyage,* to go on one's last journey.

voyager [-ʒe] v. intr. (7). To travel, to journey, to make a journey (ou) trip; to voyage (par mer); *il a beaucoup voyagé,* he has travelled widely; *voyager aux Etats-Unis,* to travel to (ou) in the United States. ‖ COMM. To travel; to be a traveller (personne); to be transported (produits).

voyageur, euse [-ʒœ:r, ø:z] adj. Travelling. ‖ ZOOL. Migratory (oiseau); carrier (pigeon).

— s. Traveller; passenger (par le bateau, le car, le train); strap-hanger (debout); fare (dans un taxi). ‖ COMM. Commercial traveller.

voyance [vwajã:s] f. Clairvoyance.

voyant, ante [-jã, ã:t] adj. Showy, conspicuous (en général). ‖ Gifted with sight, seeing (personne). ‖ Clairvoyant. ‖ Gaudy, loud, garish, glaring (couleur).

— m. Person who can see. ‖ Clairvoyant. ‖ NAUT. Sphere (de bateau-feu); top-mark (de bouée). ‖ ARCHIT. Slide-vane, sighting-board. ‖ AUTOM. Direction roller (d'autobus). ‖ TECHN. Signal.

voyante [-jã:t] f. Clairvoyant.

voyelle [vwajɛl] f. Vowel.

voyer [vwaje] adj. *Agent voyer,* road-surveyor.

— m. FAM. Road-surveyor.

voyeur [vwajœ:r] m. Voyeur; Peeping Tom (fam.).

voyeurisme [-jœrism] m. Voyeurism.

voyou [vwaju] adj. Gutter, coarse (langage).

— m. Gutter-snipe; street-arab; hooligan; blackguard, U. S. hoodlum. (V. VAURIEN.)

voyoucratie [-krasi] f. Hooligan rule.

vrac [vrak] m. *En vrac,* loose, in bulk; *jeter en vrac,* to throw higgledy-piggledy; *marchandises en vrac,* loose (ou) unpacked goods; bulk cargo.

vrai, aie [vrɛ] adj. True (en général); sincere, real, staunch, loyal (ami); truthful, correct (assertion); life-like (couleurs); arrant, regular, downright (coquin); genuine, real (diamant); authentic (fait); realistic (style); sheer, absolute (supplice); *un vrai Anglais,* a real Englishman. ‖ NAUT. True (longitude, nord, temps).

— m. Truth; *le vrai de l'affaire,* the truth of the matter; *être dans le vrai,* to be right. ‖ FAM. *Un vrai de vrai,* one of the lads, the real McCoy.

— adv. Truly; *dire vrai,* to tell the truth; *à vrai dire,* to tell the truth; as a matter of fact; actually; strictly speaking; *voici au vrai ce qui s'est passé,* this is what actually happened; *pour de vrai,* for good, once and for all.

— interj. Really, truly; honestly; *vrai de vrai!,* really and truly.

vraiment [-mã] adv. Really, truly; *il est vraiment trop tard,* it's really too late. ‖ Really, indeed; is that so?; *j'aime aller au théâtre — vraiment?,* I like going to the theatre — do you?; *je n'y suis jamais allé — vraiment?,* I've never been there — haven't you?

vraisemblable [vrɛsãblabl] adj. Probable, likely, conceivable, credible (v. PLAUSIBLE); true to life (pièce, roman); *peu vraisemblable,* unconvincing, unlikely, improbable (histoire); hardly credible (nouvelle).

— m. What is probable (ou) likely; *au-delà du vraisemblable,* beyond the bounds of probability.

vraisemblablement [-blabləmã] adv. Probably, very likely.

vraisemblance [-blã:s] f. Verisimilitude; probability, likelihood; *selon toute vraisemblance,* in all probability. ‖ ARTS. Verisimilitude.

vrille [vri:j] f. BOT. Tendril. ‖ AVIAT. Tail spin; *vrille à plat,* flat spin; *chute en vrille,* spin fall; *monter en vrille,* to corkscrew; *tomber en vrille,* to get into a spin. ‖ TECHN. Gimlet, borer. ‖ FIG. *Des yeux en vrille,* gimlet eyes.

vrillé, ée [vrije] adj. Bored (bois). ‖ Twisted, kinked (corde, ficelle, fil). ‖ BOT. Tendrilled.

vriller v. tr. (1). To bore with a gimlet.

— v. intr. To spiral up; to ascend in a spiral. ‖ To twist, to kink (corde, ficelle, fil); to snarl (textile).

vrillerie [-jri] f. Auger-making; auger-factory. ‖ Set of boring (ou) piercing tools.

vrillonner [-jone] v. intr. (1). To twist, to kink.

vrombir [vrõbi:r] v. intr. (2). To hum (avion, moteur, toupie); to throb, to purr (moteur); to buzz (mouche); to whizz (obus).

vrombissement [-bismã] m. Humming (d'un avion, d'un moteur, d'une toupie); throbbing, purring (d'un moteur); buzzing (de mouches); whizzing (d'obus).

V.R.P. [veɛrpe] m. Abrév. de *voyageur, représentant, placier,* rep, representative, commercial traveller, U. S. traveling salesman.

vu, ue [vy] adj. Regarded, considered; *être bien vu,* to be well thought of; *être mal vu,* to be thought poorly of; *ni vu ni connu,* no one is any the wiser; keep it dark; *vu de près,* close-up (détail). [V. VOIR.]

— prép. Considering; owing to; in view of.

— loc. conj. **Vu que,** considering (ou) seeing that, since ; whereas (jur.).
— m. Sight ; examination ; *au vu de tous,* openly, in everyone's sight ; *au vu et au su de tous,* to everyone's knowledge ; as everyone knows ; *cela me fait l'effet du déjà vu,* that strikes me as familiar. ‖ JUR. *Au vu de,* upon presentation of.

vue [vy] f. Sight (faculté, sens) ; *avoir la vue courte,* to be short-sighted ; *se gâter la vue,* to strain one's eyes, to ruin one's sight. ‖ Eyes (yeux) ; *tourner la vue vers,* to turn one's eyes towards. ‖ Look, sight, appearance (aspect) ; *la vue de la maison l'impressionna,* the appearance of the house impressed him. ‖ Sight (observation) ; *à la vue de tous,* in sight of everybody ; *à perte de vue,* as far as the eye can see ; *à première vue,* at first sight ; *connaître de vue,* to know by sight ; *garder à vue,* to keep a close watch on ; *hors de vue,* out of sight ; *perdre de vue,* to lose sight of. ‖ Vista (échappée) ; view (perspective) ; *boucher la vue à qqn,* to block s.o.'s view ; *prendre vue sur la rue,* to look on to the street ; *vue d'ensemble,* general view. ‖ Light, window (ouverture) ; *condamner les vues,* to block up the windows. ‖ View ; purpose, aim, object, intention (objet) ; pl. designs, plans ; *avoir des vues sur,* to have designs on ; *avoir en vue,* to have in mind ; *en vue de l'avenir,* with an eye to the future. ‖ View, idea, notion ; conception ; opinion ; consideration ; *avoir des vues très avancées,* to hold very advanced views ; *au point de vue de son utilité,* as regards its usefulness ; *point de vue,* point of view. ‖ JUR. *Droit de vues,* ancient lights. ‖ ART. View (dessin) ; *vues de Paris,* views (ou) pictures of Paris ; *dessin à vue,* free-hand drawing. ‖ CINÉM. Lantern-slide (pour projecteurs) ; *faire les prises de vues,* to be on location ; *prendre les vues,* to shoot the film ; *prise de vues,* film-shooting. ‖ MUS. *Déchiffrer à vue,* to sight-read. ‖ FIG. *En vue,* conspicuous, prominent ; *mettre en vue,* to bring to the fore ; *perdre de vue,* to overlook (une demande) ; to lose touch with (qqn). ‖ FAM. *A vue de nez,* at a rough guess ; *à vue d'œil,* judging by appearances ; *en mettre plein la vue à,* to bluff.

Vulcain [vylkɛ̃] m. Vulcan.
vulcain m. ZOOL. Red admiral (papillon).
vulcanisation [vylkanizasjɔ̃] f. Vulcanization.
vulcanisateur [-zatœ:r] m. Vulcanizer.
vulcaniser [-ze] v. tr. (1). To vulcanize.
vulcanisme [vylkanism] m. Vulcanism.
vulcanite [-nit] f. Vulcanite, ebonite.
vulcanologie [-nɔlɔʒi] f. V. VOLCANOLOGIE.
vulgaire [vylgɛ:r] adj. Everyday (coutume) ; common, general, vulgar (opinion) ; *langue vulgaire,* vernacular. ‖ Vulgar, coarse, low, common (trivial) ; cheap (personne).
vulgairement [-gɛrmɑ̃] adv. Vulgarly, generally, commonly. ‖ Vulgarly, crudely, coarsely.
vulgarisateur, trice [vylgarizatœ:r, tris] adj. Popularizing.
— s. Popularizer ; popular exponent.
vulgarisation [-rizasjɔ̃] f. Popularization ; *cours de vulgarisation,* extension courses (pour adultes) ; public lectures (au Collège de France) ; *ouvrage de vulgarisation,* popular work ; *services de vulgarisation,* advisory services, U. S. extension services.
vulgariser [-rize] v. tr. (1). To popularize (les sciences). ‖ To vulgarize, to make vulgar, to cheapen, to coarsen.
— v. pr. **Se vulgariser,** to become vulgar.
vulgarisme [-rism] m. Vulgarism.
vulgarité [-rite] f. Vulgarity.
Vulgate [vylgat] f. ECCLÉS. Vulgate.
vulgum pecus [vylgɔmpekys] m. FAM. Hoi polloi, common herd.
vulnérabilité [vylnerabilite] f. Vulnerability.
vulnérable [-rabl] adj. Vulnerable.
vulnéraire [vylnerɛ:r] adj., m. MÉD. Vulnerary.
vulnérant, ante [vylnerɑ̃, ɑ̃:t] adj. Wounding.
vulpin [vylpɛ̃] m. BOT. Foxtail.
vulvaire [vylvɛ:r] adj. MÉD. Vulvar, vulval.
— f. BOT. Stinking goose-foot.
vulve [vylv] f. MÉD. Vulva.
vulvite [-vit] f. MÉD. Vulvitis.
vulvo-vaginite [-vaʒinit] f. MÉD. Vulvo-vaginitis.

W·X·Y·Z

W, w [dublave] m. W, w.
wagon [vagɔ̃] m. ARCHIT. Flue. ‖ CH. DE F. Truck, wagon, waggon, U. S. car (de marchandises) ; carriage, U. S. coach (de voyageurs) ; *wagon à bestiaux,* cattle-van, U. S. cattle car. ‖ **Wagon-citerne,** m. Tank-car. ‖ **Wagon-couloir,** m. Corridor-carriage. ‖ **Wagon détaché,** m. Slip-coach. ‖ **Wagon-écurie,** m. Horse-box ; U. S. horse car. ‖ **Wagon frigorifique,** m. Refrigerator-car. ‖ **Wagon-glacière,** m. Ice-waggon. ‖ **Wagon-lit,** m. Sleeping-car, sleeper (fam.). ‖ **Wagon-poste,** m. Mail-van ; U. S. mail-car. ‖ **Wagon-réservoir,** m. Tank-car. ‖ **Wagon-restaurant,** m. Dining-car, luncheon-car. ‖ **Wagon-salon,** m. Saloon-car ; U. S. club-car. ‖ **Wagon-tabagie,** m. FAM. Smoking-compartment.
wagnérien, enne [vagnerjɛ̃, ɛn] adj., s. Wagnerian.

wagonnet [vagɔnɛ] m. Tip-truck.
wagonnette [-nɛt] f. Waggonnette.
wallon, onne [walɔ̃, ɔn] adj., s. GÉOGR. Walloon.
wapiti [wapiti] m. ZOOL. Wapiti, elk, moose.
warrant [varɑ̃:t] m. JUR. Warrant. ‖ COMM. Warehouse ; warrant, dock-warrant.
warrantage [-ta:ʒ] m. COMM. Issuing of a warehouse-warrant.
warranté, ée [-te] adj. COMM. Covered by a warehouse-warrant.
warranter [-te] v. tr. (1). COMM. To cover by a warehouse-warrant.
water-ballast [watɛrbalast] m. NAUT. Water-ballast.
water-closets [-klɔzɛt], **waters** m. pl. Water-closet, w.-c., toilet.
water-polo [-polo] m. SPORTS. Water-polo.
waterproof [-pruf] m. Waterproof, mackintosh.

watt [wat] m. ELECTR. Watt.
watté, ée [-te] adj. ELECTR. Watt (composante).
wattheure [watœ:r] m. ELECTR. Watt-hour.
wattman [watman] (pl. **wattmen**) m. Driver, U. S. motorman (de motrices, de tramway).
wattmètre [-mɛtr] m. ELECTR. Wattmeter.
wattseconde [-səgɔ̃d] m. Watt-second.
W.-C. [dubləvese] m. pl. V. WATER-CLOSETS.
week-end [wikɛnd] m. Week-end.
western [wɛstɛrn] m. CINÉM. Western.
wharf [warf] m. Wharf.
whig [wig] adj., m. Whig.
whisky [wiski] m. Whisky (écossais); whiskey (irlandais, américain).
whist [wist] m. Whist.
white-spirit [wajtspirit] m. White spirit, turpentine substitute.
wicket [wikɛt] m. SPORTS. Wicket (de criquet).
wigwam [wigwam] m. Wigwam.
wisigoth [vizigo] adj. Visigothic.
— s. GÉOGR. Visigoth.
wisigothique [-gɔtik] adj. Visigothic.
wormien [vɔrmjɛ̃] adj. MÉD. Wormian (os).

X

X, x [iks] m. X, x; *entrer à l'X,* to enter the Ecole polytechnique (à Paris). ‖ MÉD. *Passer aux rayons X,* to X-ray; *rayon X,* X-ray.
xanthoderme [gzɑ̃tɔdɛrm] adj. *Race xanthoderme,* xanthoderm (ou) yellow (ou) Mongoloid race.
xénon [gzenɔ̃] m. CHIM. Xenon.
xénophile [ksenofil] adj., s. Xenophil.
xénophobe [-fɔb] adj., s. Xenophobe.
xénophobie [-fɔbi] f. Xenophobia.
xérès [kserɛs] m. Sherry (vin). ‖ GÉOGR. Jerez.
xérophtalmie [-ftalmi] f. MÉD. Xerophthalmia.
xylographe [ksilograf] m. Xylographer.
xylographie [-grafi] f. Xylography.
xylographique [-grafic] adj. Xylographic(al).
xylophone [-fɔn] m. MUS. Xylophone.

Y

Y, y [igrek] m. Y, y.
y [i] adv. There; *je lui ai dit que j'y serais,* I told him I should be there; *je voulais la voir, mais elle n'y était pas,* I wanted to see her, but she was not in (ou) at home (ou) there; *M. Brown y est-il?,* is Mr. Brown at home (ou) in?; *n'y être pour personne,* not to be at home to anyone; *j'y suis, j'y reste,* here I am and here I stay; *proposer d'y aller tout de suite,* to propose to go at once.
— pron. It, them (se rapportant à des choses); *il y pense toujours,* he always thinks of it (ou) of them; *y trouver du plaisir,* to find pleasure in it. ‖ Him, her, them (se rapportant à des personnes) : *c'est un homme honnête, on peut s'y fier,* he is an honest man and you can trust him; *je connais cette vieille femme, et j'y pense souvent,* I know this old woman, and often think of her. ‖ (Se rapportant à une proposition); *elle est aimable, mais il ne faut pas s'y laisser prendre,* she is kind but you must not let yourself be taken in by it; *sans que je m'y attende,* without my expecting it. ‖ LOC. *Y aller carrément,* to go right at it; *vas-y,* let him have it!, have a go! (à un boxeur); go (ou) come on! (à un coureur); *j'y suis!,* I've go it; *y compris mes parents,* my parents included, including my parents; *y être,* to catch on, to understand (comprendre); to be ready (être prêt); *ne pas y être, n'y rien comprendre,* to be all at sea; *y être pour beaucoup,* to have had a lot to do with it, to have had a hand in it;

to be responsible to a great extent for; *n'y être pour rien,* to have had nothing to do with it (ou) no part in it; *y voir clair,* to see through something; *y voir encore,* to be still able to see; *s'y connaître,* to be an expert in the matter; *ça y est!,* there!, that's it; *cela n'y fait rien,* that makes no difference; *il y est,* he is at it (il y travaille); *il lui tarde de s'y mettre,* he is longing to be at it; *je n'y peux rien,* there's nothing I can do about it; *pendant que j'y pense,* by the way, by the by; *while I think of it; pendant que nous y sommes,* while we are about it; *que je t'y repince!,* let me catch you at it again!
yacht [jak, jɔt] m. NAUT. Yacht.
yachting [jotiŋ] m. SPORTS. Yachting.
yachtman [-man] m. Yachtman; yachting man (ou) enthusiast.
yack [jak] m. ZOOL. Yak.
Yang-tseu [jɑ̃gtsø], **Yangzi** [-zi] m. GÉOGR. Yangtze (River).
Yankee [jɑ̃ki] m. Yankee, Yank.
yaourt [jaurt] m. Yog(h)urt, yaourt.
yard [jard] m. Yard.
yatagan [jatagɑ̃] m. Yataghan.
yearling [jœ:rliŋ] m. Yearling.
Yémen [jemɛn] m. GÉOGR. Yemen.
yéménite [-menit] adj., s. GÉOGR. Yemeni.
yen [jɛn] m. Yen.
yeuse [jø:z] f. BOT. Ilex, holm-oak.
yeux [jø:] m. pl. V. ŒIL.
yé-yé [jeje] adj. FAM. Teeny bopper; swinging, trendy (mode, musique, attitude).
— s. Teeny bopper.
— m. MUS. *Le yé-yé,* sixties pop.
yiddish [jidiʃ] adj., m. Yiddish.
ylang-ylang [ilɑ̃g-ilɑ̃g] m. BOT. Ylang-ylang.
yod [jɔd] m. GRAMM. Yod.
yodler [jɔdle] v. intr. (1). To yodel.
yoga [jɔga] m. PHILOS. Yoga.
yogi [-gi] m. Yogi.
yogourt [jɔgurt] m. V. YAOURT.
yole [jɔl] f. NAUT. Yawl.
Yom Kippour [jɔmkipu:r] m. ECCLÉS. Yom Kippur.
yougoslave [jugoslav] adj. Jugoslav, Yugoslav.
— s. Jugoslav, Yugoslav.
Yougoslavie [jugoslavi] f. GÉOGR. Jugoslavia, Yugoslavia.
youpin, ine [jupɛ̃, in] s. POP. Yid (péj.).
youyou [juju] m. NAUT. Dinghly; *youyou pliant* (ou) *Berthen,* rubber dinghy.
yo-yo [jojo] m. Yo-yo.
yourte [jurt] f. Yurt.
ypérite [iperit] f. CHIM. Mustard-gas; yperite.
ytterbium [itɛrbiɔm] m. CHIM. Ytterbium.
yttria [itria] m. CHIM. Yttria, yttrium-oxide.
yttrifère [itrifɛ:r] adj. Yttriferous.
yttrium [itriɔm] m. CHIM. Yttrium.
yttrotantalite [itrotɑ̃talit] m. CHIM. Yttrotantalite.
yucca [juka] m. BOT. Yucca.

Z

z [zɛd] m. Z, z; *fer en Z,* Z-bar.
Z.A.C. [zak] f. Abrév. de *zone d'aménagement concerté,* zone whose development is promoted by the government.
zain [zɛ̃] adj. m. Whole-coloured, U. S. zain.
Zaïre [zai:r] m. GÉOGR. Zaïre.
Zambèze [zɑ̃bɛ:z] m. GÉOGR. Zambezi, Zambese.
Zambie [zɑ̃bi] f. GÉOGR. Zambia.
zan(n)i [zani] (pl. **zanni**) m. THÉÂTR. Zany.
zazou [zazu] m. FAM. Teddy-boy; U. S. zoot suiter; cool cat (pop.).
zèbre [zɛbr] m. ZOOL. Zebra. ‖ FAM. Bloke, chap,

U. S. guy (type) ; *courir comme un zèbre,* to be a fast runner.
zébrer [zebre] v. tr. (1). To stripe (ou) streak (*de,* with).
zébrure [-bry:r] f. Stripe, streak ; pl. striped markings.
zébu [zeby] m. ZOOL. Zebu.
zélateur, trice [zelatœ:r, tris] m. Zealot, fanatic.
zèle [zɛ:l] m. Zeal, fervour, ardour, enthusiasm. ‖ FAM. *Faire du zèle,* to be overzealous, to overdo it.
zélé, ée [zele] adj. Zealous, fervent, ardent, passionate, enthusiastic.
zélote [zelɔt] m. Zealot.
zélotisme [-tism] m. Zealotism, zealotry.
zen [zɛn] adj., m. PHILOS., ARTS. Zen.
zend [zɛd] adj., m. Zend.
zénith [zenit] m. ASTRON. Zenith.
zénithal, ale [-tal] adj. ASTRON. Zenithal ; *distance zénithale,* zenith-distance.
zéolithe [zeolit] f. GÉOL. Zeolite.
zéolithique [-tik] adj. GÉOL. Zeolitic.
zéphyr [zefi:r] m. Zephyr (en mythologie). ‖ Zephyr, gentle breeze, soft (ou) balmy wind (vent). ‖ Zephyr (étoffe).
zéphyrien, enne [-rjɛ̃, ɛn] adj. Zephyr-like.
zeppelin [zɛplɛ̃] m. MILIT. Zeppelin, zcpp (fam.).
zéro [zero] m. Zero, nought, naught, cipher. ‖ SPORTS. *Trois à zéro,* three love (tennis). ‖ FIG. *Partir de zéro,* to start from scratch.
zeste m. Peel (de citron, d'orange) ; skin of walnut-kernel (de noix).
zêta [dzɛta] m. Zeta (lettre).
zeugma [zøgma] m. Zeugma (lettre).
Zeus [zø:s] m. Zeus.
zézaiement [zezɛmã] m. Lisp, lisping.
zézayer [-je] v. tr. (9 *b*). To lisp.
Z.I. [zɛdi] abrév. de *zone industrielle,* industrial estate (ou) U.S. park.
zibeline [ziblin] f. ZOOL., COMM. Sable (animal, fourrure).
zieuter [zjøte] v. tr. (1). POP. To have a look (ou) a butcher's at (jeter un coup d'œil) ; to ogle (reluquer).
zig, zigue [zig] m. POP. Bloke, guy ; *drôle de zig,* odd (ou) strange character, odd fish, U. S. oddball.
zigoto [zigɔtɔ] m. FAM. Queer customer ; *faire le zigoto,* to play the fool.
zigouiller [ziguje] v. tr. (1). POP. To slit the throat of (égorger) ; to knock (ou) bump off, to do in, to make cold meat of (tuer).
zigzag [zigzag] m. Zigzag ; *en zigzag,* zigzag.
zigzaguer [-ge] v. tr. (1). To zigzag, to walk (ou) run zigzag. ‖ AUTOM. To drive erratically.
Zimbabwe [zimbabwe] m. GÉOGR. Zimbabwe.
zinc [zɛ̃:g] m. CHIM. Zinc. ‖ FAM. Counter, bar.
zinguer [zɛ̃ge] v. tr. (1). To zinc, to galvanize, to coat (ou) lay with zinc (du fer) ; to zinc, to cover with zinc (un toit).
zinguerie [-gri] f. Zinc-ware (articles) ; zinc-trade (commerce) ; zinc-works (ou) -shop (fabrique).
zingueur [-gœ:r] m. Zinc-worker (ou) -roofer.
zinnia [zinja] m. BOT. Zinnia.
zinzin [zɛ̃zɛ̃] adj. FAM. Loony, nuts, crackers (v. DINGUE).
— m. FAM. Do-da, doings, gizmo (v. TRUC).
zircon [zirkɔ̃] m. Zircon.
zircone [zirkɔn] f. CHIM. Zirconia.
zist [zist] m. Pith.
zizanie [zizani] f. BOT. Zizania, Indian (ou) Canadian (ou) wild rice. ‖ FAM. Discord, dissension, variance, wrangling.

zizi [zizi] m. FAM. Willy.
zoanthaires [zoɑ̃tɛ:r] m. pl. ZOOL. Zoantharia.
zodiacal, ale [zɔdjakal] adj. ASTRON. Zodiacal.
zodiaque [-djak] m. ASTRON. Zodiac.
Zoïle [zoil] m. Zoilus. ‖ FAM. Carping critic.
zoïsme [zoism] m. Zoism.
zombie [zɔ̃bi] m. Zombie.
zona [zɔna] m. MÉD. Zona, shingles.
zonal, ale [-nal] adj. Zonal.
zone [zo:n] f. Zone (frontière, postale). ‖ MILIT. Zone ; *zone d'action,* area ; *zone des armées, de combat,* war, battle zone. ‖ ASTRON. Zone ; *zone de dépression,* trough. ‖ GÉOGR. Zone ; *zone glaciale, tempérée, torride,* frigid, temperate, torrid zone. ‖ GÉOM. Zone. ‖ BOT., ZOOL. Zone, zona belt. ‖ FAM. *De deuxième zone,* non-vintage (vin). ‖ FIG. Slum belt (autour d'une ville).
zoné, ée [zɔne] adj. BOT., ZOOL. Zoned, zonate.
zoo [zɔɔ] m. Zoo.
zoobiologie [zɔɔbiɔlɔʒi] f. Zoobiology.
zoobiotique [-tik] adj. ZOOL. Zoobiotic.
zoochimie [zɔɔʃimi] f. Zoochemistry.
zoogénie [-ʒeni] f. Zoogeny.
zoogéographie [-ʒeɔgrafi] f. Zoogeography.
zoographe [-graf] m. Zoographer, zoographist.
zoographie [-grafi] f. Zoography.
zoolithe [zɔɔlit] m. Zoolite.
zoologie [zɔɔlɔʒi] f. Zoology.
zoologique [-ʒik] adj. Zoological.
zoologiste [-ʒist] m. Zoologist.
zoom [zu:m] m. TECHN. Zoom lens, zoom.
zoomorphie [-mɔrfi] f Zoomorphy.
zoomorphisme [-mɔrfism] m. Zoomorphism.
zoophile [-fil] adj. Zoophilous.
— s. Zoophile.
zoophobe [-fɔb] adj. Zoophobous.
— s. Zoophobe.
zoophyte [-fit] m. Zoophyte.
— m. pl. Zoophyta.
zooplancton [-plɑ̃ktɔ̃] m. Zooplankton.
zoosporange [-spɔrɑ̃:ʒ] m. Zoosporangium.
zoospore [-spɔ:r] f. Zoospore.
zootechnicien, enne [-teknisjɛ̃, ɛn] s. Zootechnician.
zootechnie [-tekni] f. Zootechny, zootechnics.
zootechnique [-teknik] adj. Zootechnical.
zootrope [-trɔp] m. Zootrope.
zootype [-tip] m. Zootype.
zoroastrien, enne [zɔrɔastrjɛ̃, ɛn] adj. Zoroastrian.
— s. Zoroastrian.
zoroastrisme [-trism] m. Zoroastrianism.
zouave [zwa:v] m. MILIT. Zouave.
Zoulou [zulu] m. GÉOGR. Zulu.
zozoter [zozɔte] v. intr. To lisp.
Z.U.P. [zyp] f. Abrév. de *zone à urbaniser en priorité,* zone scheduled for urban development.
zut ! [zyt] interj. POP. Dash it !, darn it !
zwinglien, enne [zvɛ̃gljɛ̃, ɛn] adj., s. Zwinglian.
zygodactyle [zigɔdaktil] adj. ZOOL. Zygodactyl.
zygomatique [zigɔmatik] adj. MÉD. Zygomatic (fosse, muscle).
zygomorphe [-mɔrf] adj. BOT. Zygomorphic, zygomorphous.
zygospore [-spɔ:r] m. BOT. Zygospore.
zygote [zigɔt] m. Zygote.
zymase [-ma:z] f. Zymase.
zymogène [zimoʒɛn] adj. CHIM. Zymogenic.
zymosimètre [-zimɛtr] m. PHYS. Zymometer, zymosimeter.

Chez le même éditeur :

collection "Dictionnaires du langage"

Une série d'ouvrages qui éclairent les différents aspects
particuliers de la langue.

Chaque volume relié (13,5 × 20 cm).

DICTIONNAIRE DES ANGLICISMES*
(M. Höfler)

et :

NOUVEAU DICTIONNAIRE ANALOGIQUE*
(G. Niobey)

DICTIONNAIRE DE L'ANCIEN FRANÇAIS*
(A.-J. Greimas)

DICTIONNAIRE DES CITATIONS FRANÇAISES ET ÉTRANGÈRES

DICTIONNAIRE DES DIFFICULTÉS DE LA LANGUE FRANÇAISE*
(A.-V. Thomas) (couronné par l'Académie française)

NOUVEAU DICTIONNAIRE ÉTYMOLOGIQUE*
(A. Dauzat, J. Dubois et H. Mitterand)

DICTIONNAIRE DU FRANÇAIS CLASSIQUE
(J. Dubois, R. Lagane et A. Lerond)

DICTIONNAIRE DE LINGUISTIQUE
(J. Dubois, M. Giacomo, L. Guespin, Ch. et J.-B. Marcellesi, J.-P. Mével)

DICTIONNAIRE DES LOCUTIONS FRANÇAISES
(M. Rat)

DICTIONNAIRE DES NOMS ET PRÉNOMS DE FRANCE*
(A. Dauzat)

DICTIONNAIRE DE LA PRONONCIATION
(A. Lerond)

DICTIONNAIRE DES PROVERBES, sentences et maximes*
(M. Maloux) (couronné par l'Académie française)

DICTIONNAIRE DES RIMES orales et écrites
(L. Warnant)

NOUVEAU DICTIONNAIRE DES SYNONYMES*
(E. Genouvrier, Cl. Désirat et Tr. Hordé)

DICTIONNAIRE DES VERBES FRANÇAIS
(J.-P. et J. Caput)

et aussi :

NOUVEAU DICTIONNAIRE DES MOTS CROISÉS*

DICTIONNAIRE DU SCRABBLE ET JEUX DE LETTRES*
(M. Pialat)

(*) Cet ouvrage existe dans la collection «Dictionnaires de poche de la langue française»,
ainsi que le Dictionnaire des Citations françaises (1re partie des Citations françaises et étrangères).
Chaque volume broché (12,5 × 17,5 cm).

LAROUSSE DE LA LANGUE FRANÇAISE - Lexis

sous la direction de Jean Dubois, professeur à l'université de Paris X.

un dictionnaire unique

• par sa richesse en mots : plus de 76 000 mots des domaines courant, classique et littéraire, technique et scientifique, néologismes, locutions...

• par sa richesse en renseignements sur les mots : étymologie et datation, sens et utilisations, définitions, exemples, citations contemporaines et classiques, constructions usuelles...

• par la clarté de classement du vocabulaire : regroupement et dégroupement selon les différents sens ;

• par la construction raisonnée des articles : mise en ordre systématique des acceptions, indication des synonymes et contraires après chaque sens, présentation méthodique de l'analogie, séparation claire entre les sens actuels et les sens classiques et littéraires ;

• par l'introduction, pour la première fois dans un dictionnaire, d'une grammaire complète, traitée sous forme de tableaux synthétiques et comparatifs ;

• par l'actualité de son information, due aux sources scientifiques les plus récentes, à la large place accordée aux termes nouveaux, à la représentativité bien réelle des auteurs auxquels sont empruntées les citations contemporaines.

Un volume relié (15,5 × 23 cm), 2126 pages, dont 64 de grammaire.

DICTIONNAIRE ENCYCLOPÉDIQUE LAROUSSE
un volume en couleurs

A la fois grand dictionnaire par son format et par la qualité de son illustration, et ouvrage de consultation aisée parce qu'il est en un seul volume réunissant noms communs et noms propres,

• il fait connaître tout le vocabulaire employé aujourd'hui dans la langue courante, dans les médias et dans les grands domaines de la culture contemporaine ;

• il fait comprendre les réalités du monde moderne par des explications « encyclopédiques » particulièrement développées ;

• il fait voir par l'illustration, essentiellement en couleurs, qui renforce et complète définitions et explications.

Un volume relié (23 × 29 cm), 1536 pages, près de 4300 illustrations.

DICTIONNAIRE

ANGLAIS FRANÇAIS

COLLECTION SATURNE

par Marguerite-Marie Dubois
Docteur ès lettres
professeur à l'université de Paris-IV

AVEC LA COLLABORATION DE
Charles Cestre †
professeur honoraire à la Sorbonne

Barbara Shuey
M.A. (University of California)

Denis J. Keen
M.A. (Cantab.)
Maître-assistant à l'université de Paris-III

W. Ian James
B.A. Hons. (London)
Licencié ès lettres
Senior Modern Languages Master
King Edward VI Grammar School Chelmsford

RÉVISEUR GÉNÉRAL
William Maxwell Landers
B.A., Ph. D.
Sub Dean. King's College. London.

RÉVISEURS ASSISTANTS
Roger Shattuck
B.A. (Yale)
Society of Fellows (Harvard),
Associate Professor of Romance Languages
University of Texas

Margaret G. Cobb
Editorial Consultant (New York)

**nouvelle édition
augmentée
de 10 000 termes**

Michèle Beaucourt
Jacqueline Blériot
David Jones

LIBRAIRIE LAROUSSE

17, rue du Montparnasse, 75006 Paris.

USERS' GUIDE

WORD-ORDER

a) Words are given in strictly alphabetical order. Head-words having the same meaning and closely related spellings may be found grouped under the same entry (e.g. : **autonomic** and **autonomous**). If they exist in two forms, the variable part of the word is, wherever possible, placed between brackets : thus **rhythmic(al)** means that the forms *rhythmic* and *rhythmical* are both found. If two head-words spelt identically differ in etymology, they are glossed as separate entries (e.g. : **perche** [fish] and **perche** [pole]).

b) Hyphenated compound words will be found entered alphabetically under their first element (thus **couvre-chef** is to be found under **couvre** and **axle-arm** under **axle**). Compounds written as one word are treated as headwords and will be found at their alphabetical place (thus **adman** is not under **ad**). However, as English usage varies considerably as to whether the two elements of a compound are hyphenated or merged into a single word, if a compound word is not to be found under its first element, it is advisable to look it up in its alphabetical place.

c) French pronominal (reflexive) verbs used also in a simple, non-pronominal form, are glossed after their simple verb forms (e.g. : **se perdre** is to be found under **perdre**). Exclusively pronominal French verbs are entered in the alphabetical order of the simple verb (e.g. : *s'évanouir* is to be found under **évanouir [s']**).

d) English verbs, followed by postpositions and differing in meaning from the simple verb, are glossed after the simple verb entry (e.g. : **to go about** is to be found under **go**).

PHONETIC TRANSCRIPTION

The pronunciation, shown between square brackets immediately after the head-word, is given in the phonetic transcription of the International Phonetic Association. (See I et II, p.XIII-XIV, for explanatory tables.)

GRAMMATICAL INFORMATION

a) The grammatical function of the head-word is made clear by an abbreviation placed after it. (See list on I, p. VI.) Note that n. (noun) is used for all the generally neuter English nouns, whereas, in the case of French nouns, m. corresponds to the masculine, f. to the feminine, and s. to both masculine and feminine genders. The inclusion of a grammatical summary (see I, p. VII for the French, and II, p. VII for the English sections) has made it unnecessary to show regular variations in gender and number in French head-words. For this reason only the masculine singular of the noun is given when the feminine and plural forms are regular (thus **voleur** presupposes the feminine *voleuse;* **cheval** presupposes the plural *chevaux*). On the other hand, irregular feminine and plural forms are always given (e.g. : *directrice, chacals*). However, to simplify matters for the less experienced, both masculine and feminine forms of adjectives in the French-English part have been indicated. Similarly we have shown the genders of French words translating English head-words.

b) The regular plural of French compound nouns, i.e. when both elements are affected (e.g. : *des petits-enfants*), is not given. On the other hand, irregular forms are indicated in the text (e.g. **en-tête**, pl. **en-têtes**).

GUIDE D'EMPLOI

ORDRE DES MOTS

a) Les mots-souches se présentent toujours dans l'ordre alphabétique. Toutefois, si deux mots-souches ont le même sens et des orthographes très voisines, ils peuvent être groupés (ex. : **autonomic** et **autonomous**). S'ils possèdent une double forme, la partie variable du mot peut être placée entre parenthèses : [**rhythmic(al)** signifie qu'on emploie *rhythmic* ou *rhythmical*]. Si deux mots-souches homonymes ont des étymologies différentes, ils font l'objet d'articles différents (ex. : **perche** [poisson] et **perche** [gaule]).

b) Les mots composés écrits avec un trait d'union sont traités à la fin du mot simple dont ils dérivent (ainsi **couvre-chef** est à chercher à **couvre ; axle-arm** à **axle**). Les «mots composés» écrits en un seul mot sont à leur ordre alphabétique (ainsi **adman** est à son ordre, il n'est pas avec **ad**). Étant donné le flottement dans l'usage orthographique anglais concernant l'emploi du trait d'union, on aura intérêt, quand on aura cherché en vain un terme composé sous son premier élément, à se reporter à l'ordre alphabétique.

c) Les verbes français accidentellement pronominaux, dépendant d'un verbe simple, sont donnés à la suite du verbe simple (cherchez **se perdre** à **perdre**). Les verbes français essentiellement pronominaux, ne dépendant d'aucun verbe simple, sont traités comme des mots-souches à l'ordre alphabétique du verbe (cherchez *s'évanouir* à **évanouir [s']**).

d) Les verbes anglais suivis d'une postposition, présentant des sens qui les différencient du verbe simple, sont traités à la suite de ce verbe simple (cherchez **to go about** à **go**).

PRONONCIATION FIGURÉE

La prononciation figurée, placée entre crochets à la suite du mot-souche, est indiquée selon la méthode universellement connue de l'Association phonétique internationale. (Pour son utilisation pratique, consultez les tableaux détaillés I et II, p. XIII-XIV.)

INDICATIONS GRAMMATICALES

a) La nature morphologique du mot-souche est indiquée par une abréviation très claire. (Voir la liste I, p. VI.) Notez que n. (noun) désigne tous les substantifs anglais généralement neutres, alors qu'en français m., f., s. correspondent au masculin, au féminin, aux deux genres. L'emploi du précis grammatical (pour le français voir I, p. VII et pour l'anglais, II, p. VII) rend inutile l'indication des variantes régulières de genre et de nombre pour les mots-souches français. C'est pourquoi le masculin singulier du substantif est seul indiqué lorsque le féminin et le pluriel sont réguliers (**voleur** suppose le féminin *voleuse;* **cheval** suppose le pluriel *chevaux*). En revanche, le féminin et le pluriel irréguliers sont toujours mentionnés (*directrice, chacals*). Toutefois, afin de faciliter la tâche des lecteurs les moins avertis, le double genre des adjectifs français a été uniformément signalé. De même, on a précisé avec soin le genre des mots français traduisant des mots-souches anglais.

b) Le pluriel régulier des mots composés français, c'est-à-dire portant sur les deux termes (ex. : *des petits-enfants*), n'est jamais indiqué. En revanche, des précisions sont fournies pour les emplois irréguliers (ex. : **en-tête**, pl. **en-têtes**).

c) When the same head-word has several grammatical functions, they are treated under the same entry in separate paragraphs (e.g. : under **personne**, the noun is followed by the pronoun; under **personnel**, the adjective is followed by the noun).

d) The conjugations of French and English verbs are given by a bracketed number placed after the abbreviation showing their grammatical function (e.g. : **faire**, v. tr. [50]; **cast**, v. tr. [32]). These numbers refer back to the appropriate section of the grammatical summary. (See I, p. XI for the French section, II, p. XII for the English section.)

DIFFERENTIATION OF MEANINGS

Translations are grouped according to meaning, the groups being separated by the sign ‖. Each acceptation is carefully distinguished, so that the user may readily find the desired shade of meaning without having to read through the whole entry. If a word has a great variety of meanings, a table with numbered references summarizing the meanings is inserted at the beginning of the entry (see **faire**). The usual meanings are given first, followed by those classified under abbreviations (see list on p. IV); figurative and familiar meanings are then listed, and finally, expressions. We have distinguished three categories of familiar speech, in order to guard against the use of unsuitable expressions in translation. FAM. corresponds to "familiar but accepted", POP. to "popular and vulgar", and ARGOT to "very vulgar or even indecent". For stylistic reasons, familiar expressions have, as far as possible, been translated by a familiar equivalent. It is to be noted that the abbreviation FAM., preceding the translation, applies to the head-word used in that sense (e.g. under **chap**, the translation "FAM. type" means that *chap* is an English familiar word); but when (fam.) follows the translation, it applies solely to the translation [e.g. under **individual**, the equivalent of which is "individu", the translation "type (fam.)" means that "type" is a familiar French word which can be used to translate *individual*].

CLARIFICATION OF MEANINGS

For the sake of easy and accurate reference, shades of meaning are made clear by words, illustrating usage, placed in brackets immediately after the proposed translations; thus under **pernicieux** are to be found : pernicious (action); noxious (effect); baneful (influence), etc. Such examples of usage help the user in his choice of words, and reduce the risks of mistranslation to a minimum.

EXAMPLES

The examples, arranged in alphabetical order, are short, and generally given in an idiomatic form so as to offer the user a wide range of ready-made expressions and common phrases. When there is a choice of several terms, the indications (ou) in the French-English part, and (or) in the English-French part, save unnecessary repetition of a phrase : thus *to look ill* (ou) *unwell* means that one may use *to look ill* or *to look unwell*. In the same way, similar forms have been grouped together : thus *marché aux fleurs, au poisson, à la volaille,* " flower, fish, poultry market ", means that *marché au poisson* is translated by " fish market ".

AMERICANISMS

The growth of American as an independent language has led to the inclusion in this work of characteristic forms of American English. Americanisms are preceded by the abbreviation U. S., wherever they have not been completely adopted by British English. Variations in American spelling are dealt with in general terms on II, p. XII; variants are included in the dictionary when their alphabetical place is too far from that of the corresponding English form.

ABBREVIATIONS AND ACRONYMS

The most common abbreviations and acronyms are included in their alphabetical place. In the French section their gender is shown (thus **H. L. M.** is followed by the mention «*m.* or *f.*»). The phonetic transcription indicates whether they are pronounced as a single word (as with **U. N. E. S. C. O.** [ju'neskou]) or whether each letter is pronounced separately.

WORD-LISTS

Full-page word-lists group together the essential vocabulary of a number of specialized subjects, e.g. car and machines.

ILLUSTRATIONS

Accurate illustrations provide the user with an effective and interesting method of associating words and images, and of enlarging his vocabulary.

My warmest thanks are due in the first place to my English, American and French colleagues who have shown the very greatest spirit of co-operation in composing part of the text, and whose competence and scholarship have made this dictionary a sound and reliable work of reference. In this respect, special mention must be made of the invaluable contribution of Dr. Landers who has read through the entire work both in manuscript- and proof-form; while for the American side of the dictionary we are particularly indebted to Prof. R. Shattuck, to Miss Shuey and to Mrs. Cobb. The long experience of M. Cestre, the subtle mind of Mr. Keen, and Mr. James's predilection for accuracy, have helped to make this work one filled with useful linguistic information, and rich in shades of meaning. I also wish to thank a very large number of teachers and students for their assistance and suggestions, especially Dr. King, of London University and Mr. J. C. Palmes, Librarian of the Royal Institute of British Architects.

M.-M. DUBOIS

AMÉRICANISMES

Le développement de l'américain en tant que langue indépendante nous a conduits à introduire dans cet ouvrage les formes propres à l'anglais d'Amérique. Les américanismes sont précédés de la mention U. S., dans la mesure où ils ne sont pas encore entièrement adoptés par l'anglais insulaire. Les variantes orthographiques américaines font l'objet d'un paragraphe général, II, p. XII; certaines sont indiquées à l'intérieur du dictionnaire, quand elles sont très éloignées, dans l'ordre alphabétique, de la forme anglaise correspondante.

ABRÉVIATIONS ET SIGLES

Les abréviations et sigles les plus usuels ont été classés à leur ordre alphabétique. Dans la partie française, on a indiqué leur genre (ainsi **H. L. M.** est noté «*m.* ou *f.*»). La transcription phonétique indique s'ils se prononcent en un seul mot (comme **U. N. E. S. C. O.** [ju'neskou]) ou en détachant chaque lettre.

TABLEAUX

Des tableaux hors texte offrent au lecteur soucieux de synthèse de vastes centres d'intérêt où se trouvent groupés les principaux éléments du vocabulaire concernant une notion maîtresse (telle que automobile, machine).

ILLUSTRATIONS

Des illustrations, effectuées avec le plus grand soin, permettent enfin d'associer l'image au mot et constituent le plus heureux des moyens mnémotechniques.

Ma reconnaissance la plus vive va tout d'abord à mes collaborateurs anglais, américains et français qui ont rédigé une partie de cet ouvrage dans un inappréciable esprit d'équipe et dont la haute compétence confère à ce volume un caractère de sérieux et de sécurité. A cet égard, l'apport du Dr Landers, qui a revu l'ensemble du travail, apparaît comme primordial, tandis qu'au professeur R. Shattuck, à Miss Shuey et à Mrs. Cobb est dû plus particulièrement l'aspect américain du dictionnaire. L'expérience du regretté M. Cestre, la subtilité de Mr. Keen, la précision de Mr. James ont abouti à des pages denses et nuancées. Je remercie également les nombreux professeurs et étudiants qui m'ont apporté leur concours ou leurs suggestions, tout spécialement le Dr. King, professeur à l'Université de Londres et Mr. J. C. Palmes, Librarian of the Royal Institute of British Architects.

M.-M. DUBOIS

ABBREVIATIONS

abrév.	abréviation	abbreviation	n.	nom anglais	noun
adj.	adjectif	adjective	pers.	personnel	personal
adv.	adverbe	adverb	pl.	pluriel	plural
art.	article	article	poss.	possessif	possessive
aux.	auxiliaire	auxiliary	p.p.	participe passé	past participle
comp.	comparatif	comparative	p.pr.	participe présent	present participle
cond.	conditionnel	conditional	pr.	présent	present
conj.	conjonction	conjunction	préf.	préfixe	prefix
déf.	défini	definite	prép.	préposition	preposition
défect.	défectif	defective	pron.	pronom, pronominal	pronoun, pronominal
démonstr.	démonstratif	demonstrative	prop.	propre	proper, literal
dimin.	diminutif	diminutive	qqch.	quelque chose	something
f.	féminin	feminine	qqn	quelqu'un	someone
imp.	imparfait	imperfect	réfl.	réfléchi	reflexive
imper.	impératif	imperative	rel.	relatif	relative
impers.	impersonnel	impersonal	s.	substantif français masculin ou féminin	substantive
ind.	indicatif	indicative			
indéf.	indéfini	indefinite	s.o.	quelqu'un	someone
interj.	interjection	interjection	sth.	quelque chose	something
interrog.	interrogation	interrogation	sup.	superlatif	superlative
intr.	intransitif	intransitive	tr.	transitif	transitive
invar.	invariable	invariable	U.S.	Etats-Unis	United States
m.	masculin	masculine	v.	verbe	verb

LABELS

AGRIC.	Agriculture, économie rurale.	Agriculture, husbandry.	GRAMM.	Grammaire, linguistique.	Grammar, linguistics.
ARCHIT.	Architecture, construction.	Architecture, building.	INFORM.	Informatique.	Data processing.
ARGOT	Argot, termes indécents.	Slang; not in decent use.	JUR.	Jurisprudence, administration, politique, sociologie.	Jurisprudence, administration, politics, sociology.
ARTS	Arts.	Arts.			
ASTRON.	Astronomie.	Astronomy.	LOC.	Locution.	Phrase.
ASTRONAUT.	Astronautique.	Astronautics.	MATH.	Mathématiques.	Mathematics.
AUTOM.	Automobilisme.	Automobilism.	MÉD.	Médecine, biologie, hygiène, pharmacie, art vétérinaire.	Medicine, biology, hygiene, pharmacy, veterinary science.
AVIAT.	Aviation, aéronautique.	Aviation, aeronautics.			
BLAS.	Blason.	Heraldry.	MILIT.	Militaire.	Military.
BOT.	Botanique.	Botany.	MUS.	Musique.	Music.
CH. DE F.	Chemin de fer.	Railways.	NAUT.	Art nautique, marine.	Nautical, navy.
CHIM.	Chimie.	Chemistry.	PHILOS.	Philosophie.	Philosophy.
CINEM.	Cinématographie.	Cinematography.	PHYS.	Physique.	Physics.
COMM.	Commerce.	Commerce, trade.	POP.	Populaire.	Popular.
CULIN.	Art culinaire, nourriture.	Culinary.	PSYCH.	Psychologie, psychiatrie, psychanalyse.	Psychology, psychiatry, psychoanalysis.
ECCLES.	Église, religion.	Ecclesiastical.	RADIO.	Radiophonie, télévision.	Radiophony, television.
ELECTR.	Électricité, électronique.	Electricity, electronics.	SPORTS	Sports, jeux.	Sports, games.
FAM.	Familier.	Familiar, colloquial.	TECHN.	Technologie, mécanique, industrie.	Technology, mechanics, industry.
FIG.	Figuré.	Figuratively.			
FIN.	Finances.	Finance.	THEATR.	Théâtre.	Theatre.
GEOGR.	Géographie.	Geography.	†	Vieux. Histoire.	Archaism. History.
GÉOL.	Géologie.	Geology.	ZOOL.	Zoologie.	Zoology.

L'ESSENTIEL DE LA GRAMMAIRE ANGLAISE

L'ARTICLE

L'article **défini** *the* est invariable. Ex. : le garçon, *the boy;* la fille, *the girl;* les rois, *the kings.* Il se prononce [ði:] devant une voyelle ou un h muet, et quand il est seul ou fortement accentué. Dans tous les autres cas, on le prononce [ðə].

L'article défini ne s'emploie pas, dans le sens général, devant : 1° les noms pluriels; 2° les noms abstraits; 3° les noms de couleur; 4° les noms de matière (pain, vin, bois, etc.) ; 5° les noms de langage; 6° *man* et *woman*. Ex. : les chats, *cats;* la colère, *anger;* le rouge, *red;* le pain, *bread;* l'anglais, *English.* Mais il faut toujours l'employer, comme en français, quand le sens n'est pas général. Ex. : l'homme que je vois, *the man that I see.*

L'article **indéfini** a deux formes : 1° devant les consonnes (y compris *w, h*, et *y* initial, et toute voyelle ou tout groupe de voyelles ayant le son [ju:]), on emploie la forme **a**. Ex. : un homme, *a man;* une dame, *a lady;* une maison, *a house;* un usage, *a use;* 2° devant une voyelle ou un *h* muet, on emploie **an**.

L'article indéfini n'a pas de pluriel. (V. QUELQUE.)

L'article indéfini s'emploie devant tout nom concret non précédé d'un autre article, d'un possessif ou d'un démonstratif. Ex. : mon père, officier de marine, était veuf, *my father, a naval officer, was a widower;* sans foyer, *without a home.* [V. article A.]

LE NOM

Pluriel. — On le forme en ajoutant s au singulier (cet s se prononce).

Exceptions. — Les noms terminés en o, s, x, z, sh ajoutent es. Ex. : box (boîte), *boxes;* potato (pomme de terre), *potatoes.* (Exceptions : *pianos, albinos,* etc.)

Les noms terminés par ch ajoutent es, sauf lorsque le ch se prononce [k]. Ex. : church, *churches;* monarch, *monarchs.*

Les noms terminés en y forment leur pluriel : 1° en *ys* quand l'*y* est précédé d'une voyelle ; 2° en *ies* quand l'*y* est précédé d'une consonne. Ex. : boy, *boys;* fly, *flies;* lady, *ladies.*

Les noms terminés par fe et certains noms terminés par f (*calf, half, leaf, loaf, sheaf, shelf, thief, wolf, elf, self*) forment leur pluriel en ves. Ex. : knife, *leaf, self;* pl. *knives, leaves, selves.*

Man, woman, child, ox font *men, women, children, oxen.* **Foot, tooth, goose** font *feet, teeth, geese.* **Mouse** et **louse** font *mice* et *lice.* **Deer, salmon, sheep, trout, swine** et **grouse** sont invariables.

Genre des noms. — La plupart des noms anglais sont du masculin quand ils désignent un homme ou un être mâle, du féminin quand ils désignent une femme ou un être femelle, du neutre dans tous les autres cas. *Parent* désigne le père ou la mère, *cousin* un cousin ou une cousine. Les mots en *er*, comme *reader*, sont du masculin (*lecteur*), du féminin (*lectrice*) ou du neutre (*livre de lecture*).

Les principales exceptions sont : *child* et *baby*, généralement neutres, *ship, engine, aeroplane, car*, généralement féminins.

Formation du féminin. — Comme en français, le féminin se forme de trois façons : 1° par un mot différent (ex. : *father, brother, son, boy* ont pour féminin *mother, sister, daughter, girl*) ; 2° par un mot composé (ex. : *milkman* a pour féminin *milkmaid*) ; 3° par une désinence (ex. : *lion, actor, prince* font au féminin *lioness, actress, princess;* *widow* [veuve] fait au masculin *widower* [veuf]).

Le cas possessif. — Le cas possessif ne peut s'employer que lorsque le possesseur est une personne ou un nom de mesure. On le forme en plaçant le nom possesseur suivi d'une apostrophe et d'un s, devant le nom de l'objet possédé (dont l'article est supprimé). Ex. : le livre de Bob, *Bob's book;* une promenade d'une heure, *an hour's walk.* Les noms pluriels terminés par s prennent seulement l'apostrophe. Ex. : les livres des élèves, *the pupils' books.*

L'ADJECTIF

L'adjectif est invariable et se place **avant** le nom qu'il qualifie. Ex. : un bon garçon, *a good boy;* une bonne fille, *a good girl;* des dames aimables, *kind ladies.*

Le **comparatif** et le **superlatif** des adjectifs de plus de deux syllabes se forment avec les adverbes **more** (plus) et **the most** (le plus). Ex. : plus actif, *more diligent;* la plus élégante, *the most elegant.*

Les adjectifs d'une syllabe font leur comparatif en prenant la désinence **er** et leur superlatif en prenant la désinence **est**. Ex. : petit, *small;* plus petit, *smaller;* le plus petit, *the smallest.*

La consonne finale d'un adjectif d'une syllabe doit être doublée devant une désinence commençant par une voyelle (-er, -est, -ish, -y). Ex. : red, *redder, the reddest;* reddish.

La plupart des adjectifs de deux syllabes, et notamment tous ceux terminés par *y*, forment leur comparatif et superlatif comme ceux d'une syllabe. Ex. : narrow, *narrower, narrowest.* (Ceux en *y* prennent *ier* et *iest* : lazy, *lazier, laziest.*)

Comparatifs et superlatifs irréguliers. — *Good* (bon), *better* (meilleur), *the best* (le meilleur)*; bad* (mauvais), *worse* (pire), *the worst* (le pire) ; *little* (petit), *less, lesser* (moindre), *the least* (le moindre) ; *far* (éloigné), *farther, the farthest; old* (vieux) fait *older* et *the oldest* dans le sens général, mais *elder* et *the eldest* dans le sens de aîné; *fore* (antérieur) donne *former* (premier de deux, opposé à *latter*, dernier) et *the first* (le premier de tous, opposé à *last*, dernier).

Adjectif numéral cardinal. — *One, two, three, four, five, six, seven, eight, nine, ten, eleven, twelve, thirteen, fourteen, fifteen, sixteen, seventeen, eighteen, nineteen, twenty, twenty-one, thirty, forty, fifty, sixty, seventy, eighty, ninety, one hundred, one hundred and one, two hundred..., one thousand..., two thousand..., one million...* Mais on dit *a thousand men*, dans le sens général, quand il ne s'agit pas d'un chiffre exact.

Dozen, score (vingtaine), *hundred, gross, thousand* et *million* prennent un s au pluriel quand on les emploie comme substantifs.

Adjectif numéral ordinal. — *First, second, third, fourth, fifth, sixth, seventh, eighth, ninth, tenth, eleventh, twelfth, thirteenth, fourteenth, fifteenth, sixteenth, seventeenth, eighteenth, nineteenth, twentieth, twenty-first... thirtieth, fortieth, fiftieth, sixtieth, seventieth, eightieth, ninetieth, hundredth..., thousandth,..., millionth.*

Adjectifs démonstratifs et possessifs. — V. LE PRONOM.

Quelque se traduit par *some* ou *any*. *Some* s'emploie surtout dans les phrases affirmatives. Ex. : j'ai quelque livres, *I have some books*.

Le véritable sens de *any* étant « n'importe quel », on s'en sert surtout dans les phrases interrogatives, négative et dubitatives. Ex. : je lis n'importe quel livre, *I read any book;* il ne lit aucun livre, *he does not read any boo* (*he does not read some books* voudrait dire : il y a des livres qu'il ne lit pas).

L'article partitif se traduit souvent par *some* ou *any*. Ex. : Voulez-vous du pain? *Will you have some bread*

Quelqu'un : *somebody;* quelques-uns : *some*.

Personne : *nobody, not... anybody*.

Quelque chose : *something* (rien : *nothing, not... anything*).

Beaucoup de se traduit par *much* au singulier et *many* au pluriel.

Peu de se traduit par *little* au singulier et *few* au pluriel.

Un peu de : *a little* (sing.), *a few* (pl.).

LE PRONOM

Pronoms personnels (sujets). — *I, you, he* (m.), *she* (f.), *it* (neutre) ; *we, you, they*. Le pronom *thou* (tu n'est guère employé que pour s'adresser à Dieu; même dans l'intimité, les Anglais se disent *you*.

Pronoms personnels (compléments). — *Me, you, him* (m.), *her* (f.), *it* (n.) ; *us, you, them* (*thee* [toi] ne s dit qu'à Dieu).

Adjectifs possessifs. — *My* (mon, ma, mes), *your, his* (m.), *her* (f.), *its* (n.) ; *our, your, theirs;* (tutoie ment : *thy*).

A la troisième personne, l'adjectif possessif, comme le pronom, s'accorde avec le possesseur. Ex. : son chapea (de Jean), *his hat;* (de Jeanne), *her hat;* son toit (de la maison, neutre), *its roof;* ses livres (de Jean), *his books* (de Jeanne), *her books*.

Pronoms possessifs. — *Mine* (le mien, la mienne, les miens, les miennes), *yours, his, hers, its own; ours theirs* (tutoiement : *thine*).

On emploie le pronom possessif pour traduire l'expression « à moi, à toi, etc. ». Ex. : ce chat est à toi *this cat is yours*.

Pronoms réfléchis. — *Myself* (moi-même), *yourself; himself* (m.), *herself* (f.), *itself* (n.) ; *ourselves, yourselves themselves*. Toutes les fois que le pronom complément exprime la même personne que le sujet, on le traduit par l pronom réfléchi. Ex. : il se flatte, *he flatters himself;* parle pour toi, *speak for yourself*.

Adjectifs et pronoms démonstratifs. — *This* (pl. *these*) correspond à « ce...-ci » et indique un objet trè proche. Ex. : *this day*, ce jour-ci (aujourd'hui) ; *these books*, ces livres(-ci) ; *this*, pronom, veut dire « ceci » *That* (pl. *those*) correspond à « ce...-là », et comme pronom à « cela ». Ex. : *those people*, ces gens-là ; *on that day* ce jour-là.

Celui de, ceux de... se traduisent par *that of, those of...*

Celui qui, ce que. V. PRONOMS RELATIFS.

Pronoms relatifs. — Le pronom relatif *that* est invariable. Ex. : l'homme (la femme) qui parle, *the ma* (*the woman*) *that speaks;* le livre (les livres) que je vois, *the book* (*the books*) *that I see*.

Le pronom *that* ne peut s'employer que lorsqu'il introduit une subordonnée déterminative, indispensable au sen de la phrase. L'autre pronom relatif, qu'on peut employer dans presque tous les cas, a quatre formes : *who* (sujet m. f., sing. et pl.), *whom* (compl. m., f., sing. et pl.), *whose* (cas possessif; v. DONT) et *which* (neutre sing. et pl.) Ex. : l'homme (la femme) qui vient, que je vois, *the man* (*the woman*) *who comes, whom I see;* les livres qui son là, que je vois, *the books which are here, which I see*.

Ce qui, ce que se traduisent par *what* quand « ce » appartient grammaticalement à la proposition principal et « qui » ou « que » à la subordonnée, par *which* quand tout le groupe « ce que, ce qui » appartient à la subordonnée Ex. : je sais ce que je dis, *I know what I say;* ce qu'il dit est très intéressant, *what he says is very interesting* je sais ma leçon, ce qui vous surprend, *I know my lesson, which surprises you*.

Quoi se traduit comme « ce qui, ce que ».

Celui qui, celle qui, etc., se traduisent pour les personnes par *he* (m.) ou *she* (f.), *him* (m. compl.) *her* (f. compl.), *they* (pl.), *them* (pl. compl.) suivis de *who* (sujet) ou *whom* (compl.) ; pour les choses, par *the on which* (pl. *the ones which*). Ex. : celui que vous voyez, *he whom you see;* prenez celui (le livre, neutre) que vou voudrez, *take the one* (*which*) *you like*.

Dont (et **de qui, duquel, de laquelle, desquels, desquelles**) se traduit par *whose* toutes les fois qu'il exprim un rapport de possession et que le possesseur est une personne. Dans les autres cas, il faut décomposer « dont » e « de qui » et traduire séparément les deux mots. Ex. : l'homme dont je lis le livre, *the man whose book I read;* l'homm dont je parle, *the man of whom I speak*.

On se traduit le plus souvent par le passif. Ex. : on m'a puni, *I was punished;* on dit que vous êtes riche *you are said to be rich*.

Autres façons de traduire *on* : on frappe à la porte, *somebody is knocking at the door;* on pourrait dire, *on might say;* en France on boit du vin, en Angleterre, on boit de la bière, en Chine, on boit du thé (dit par un Français à un Anglais), *in France we drink wine, in England you drink beer, in China they drink tea*.

En, y se traduisent de différentes façons selon qu'ils sont pronoms ou adverbes. Ex. : j'en parlais, *I wa speaking of it;* j'en viens, *I have just come from there;* donnez-m'en, *give me some;* j'en ai assez, *I have enoug* (*of it*) ; j'y songe, *I think of it;* vas-y, *go there*.

Pronoms interrogatifs. — *Who* (qui?, qui est-ce qui?) est employé comme sujet; *whom* (qui?, qui est-ce que?) comme complément; au neutre le sujet est *what* (quoi?, qu'est-ce qui?), le complément est *what* (quoi?, que? qu'est-ce que?).

L'ADVERBE

L'adverbe anglais se forme en ajoutant *ly* à l'adjectif. Ex. : *poor*, pauvre; *poorly*, pauvrement. Les adjectifs terminés par *y* (sauf ceux en *ly*) forment leur adverbe en *ily*. Ex. : *happy*, heureux; *happily*, heureusement.

Les adjectifs terminés en *ly* sont aussi employés comme adverbes.

LE VERBE

Les verbes anglais n'ont que trois désinences : **s** pour la troisième personne du singulier de l'indicatif, **ed** pour le passé simple et le participe passé (toujours invariable), **ing** pour le participe présent. Ex. : je travaille, *I work;* il travaille, *he works;* il travailla, *he worked;* travaillé, *worked;* travaillant, *working*.

L'imparfait français se traduit parfois par le passé simple (ou prétérit), mais le plus souvent par la forme progressive (v. plus loin) quand il indique la continuation, ou par la forme fréquentative (v. plus loin) quand i indique l'habitude.

Le **passé simple** (ou prétérit) se forme en ajoutant *ed* à l'infinitif : il a la même forme à toutes les personnes : *I worked, you worked*, etc. Il s'emploie pour traduire le passé simple français dans tous les cas, et le passé composé lorsque celui-ci exprime une action complètement passée dans un temps qui exclut le présent. Ex. : ma montre s'arrêta (ou s'est arrêtée) hier, *my watch stopped yesterday*.

Le **passé composé** se forme comme en français avec l'auxiliaire *avoir* et le participe passé, mais il ne s'emploie que pour indiquer une action qui se continue dans le présent ou qui embrasse une période comprenant le présent. Ex. : j'ai reçu beaucoup de lettres cette année, *I have received many letters this year*.

Le présent français suivi de « depuis » ou précédé de « il y a... que » se traduit par un passé composé en anglais. Ex. : j'habite Londres depuis six mois, il y a six mois que j'habite Londres, *I have been living in London for six months*.

Le **futur** anglais se forme au moyen de deux auxiliaires (*will* et *shall*) et de l'infinitif. D'ordinaire, on emploie *shall* pour la première personne et *will* pour la seconde et la troisième. Ex. : je viendrai, *I shall come*; tu iras, vous irez, *you will go*; elle vous verra, *she will see you*.

A la première personne, *will* indiquerait la volonté; aux autres personnes, *shall* indiquerait le commandement, l'obligation, la promesse ou la menace. (V. VERBES DÉFECTIFS.)

L'**impératif** anglais se forme au moyen de l'auxiliaire *let* (laisser), du pronom personnel complément et de l'infinitif, sauf à la deuxième personne, où l'on emploie seulement l'infinitif sans *to*. Ex. : qu'il parle, *let him speak*; parlons, *let us speak*; parle, parlez, *speak*.

Le **conditionnel** se forme au moyen de deux auxiliaires : *should* pour la première personne, *would* pour la deuxième et la troisième. Ex. : il viendrait, *he would come*; j'irais, *I should go*.

Le **subjonctif** est très rarement employé en anglais. Il ne diffère de l'indicatif qu'au présent et seulement à la troisième personne du singulier (qui ne prend pas d's). On traduit le subjonctif français tantôt par l'*indicatif* (notamment après « quoique », « avant que » et « jusqu'à ce que »), tantôt par *should* et l'*infinitif* (après « de peur que »), ou par *may* (passé *might*) et l'*infinitif* (après « afin que »), parfois par l'*infinitif*. Ex. : je veux qu'il travaille, *I want him to work*.

L'**infinitif** anglais est généralement précédé de *to*. Principales exceptions : on n'emploie pas *to* après les verbes défectifs (sauf *I am, I have*, et *I ought*) et après les verbes de perception (voir, entendre, etc.).

L'infinitif français se traduit généralement par l'infinitif. On le traduit par le *participe présent* : 1º après toutes les prépositions; 2º après les verbes de commencement, de continuation ou de fin; 3º quand l'infinitif joue le rôle d'un nom. Ex. : avant de parler, *before speaking*; il cessa de chanter, *he stopped singing*; nager est très sain, *swimming is very healthy*.

Le **passif** se conjugue comme en français avec le verbe *être* et le *participe passé*. Ex. : tu es aimé, *you are loved*.

Le **verbe « être »**. — Ind. pr. : *I am, he is, we are, you are, they are*. P. simpl. : *I was, he was, we were, you were, they were*. P. comp. : *I have been, he has been*... Pl.-q.-p. : *I had been*... Fut. : *I shall be, you will be*... Fut. ant. : *I shall have been, you will have been*... Cond. pr. : *I should be, you would be*... Cond. prét. : *I should have been, you would have been*... Subj. : *I be, you be, he be*... Subj. prét. : *I were, he were, you were*... Inf. : *to be*. P. pr. : *being*. P. p. : *been*.

Le verbe **avoir** se traduit en anglais par *to have*, qui garde la même forme (*have*) à toutes les personnes au présent de l'indicatif, sauf à la troisième du singulier (*has*). Le verbe *to have* sert d'auxiliaire du passé à tous les verbes, même neutres et réfléchis. Ex. : il est venu, *he has come*; elle s'était flattée, *she had flattered herself*.

Verbes défectifs. — Ils sont fréquemment employés comme auxiliaires.

Pouvoir se traduit par le défectif *can* lorsqu'il indique la capacité personnelle, par *may* quand il indique la permission ou la possibilité.

Devoir se traduit par *ought to* quand il indique l'obligation de la conscience, par *must* quand il indique l'obligation extérieure ou la nécessité.

Le futur, on l'a vu, se sert de *will* (volonté personnelle) et de *shall* (obligation extérieure).

Les verbes défectifs n'ont que deux formes au plus : *can* fait au passé *could*; *may* donne *might*; *would* (passé de *will*) et *should* (passé de *shall*) forment l'auxiliaire du conditionnel; *ought* et *must* n'ont qu'une forme.

Aux temps qui leur manquent, les verbes défectifs sont remplacés : *can* par *to be able*, *may* par *to be permitted*, *must* par *to be obliged to*. On supplée souvent au conditionnel passé en faisant suivre le verbe de l'infinitif passé. Ex. : elle aurait pu dire, *she might have said* (elle pourrait avoir dit).

Conjugaison négative. — Un verbe négatif doit toujours contenir un auxiliaire (sauf aux cas 3º et 4º).

1º Pour conjuguer négativement un verbe auxiliaire, on place *not* après ce verbe. Ex. : je veux, *I will*; je ne veux pas, *I will not*.

2º Pour conjuguer négativement un verbe non auxiliaire, on fait précéder l'infinitif de *do not* au présent de l'indicatif (*does not* à la 3e personne du singulier) et de *did not* au passé simple (tous les autres temps se conjuguent avec les auxiliaires). Ex. : il parle, *he speaks*, il ne parle pas, *he does not speak*; il s'arrêta, *he stopped*, il ne s'arrêta pas, *he did not stop*.

3º A l'infinitif ou au participe, on place *not* devant le verbe. Ex. : ne pas dire, *not to tell*; ne voyant pas, *not seeing*.

4º Quand la phrase contient un mot négatif autre que *not* (c.-à-d. *nobody, nothing, nowhere*, etc.), le verbe reste affirmatif. Ex. : il voit quelqu'un, *he sees somebody*; il ne voit personne, *he sees nobody*.

5º L'infinitif négatif en français est parfois traduit par l'impératif : ne pas se pencher au dehors, *do not lean out*.

Conjugaison interrogative. — Un verbe interrogatif doit toujours contenir un auxiliaire (sauf lorsque le pronom interrogatif est sujet : qui va là? *who goes there?*).

1º Pour conjuguer interrogativement un verbe auxiliaire ou un verbe à un temps composé, on place le sujet après l'auxiliaire. Ex. : êtes-vous bien? *are you well?*; votre père le saura-t-il? *will your father know it?*; avait-il parlé? *had he spoken?*

2º Pour conjuguer interrogativement un verbe non auxiliaire, au présent ou au passé simple, on retiendra la formule *D.S.I.* : *D* représentant **do** pour le présent (*does* pour la troisième personne du singulier ou *did* pour le passé), *S* représentant le **sujet**, *I* représentant l'**infinitif** du verbe. Ex. : savez-vous? (*D* : do; *S* : you; *I* : know) *do you know?*; votre père voit-il cela? (*D* : does; *S* : your father; *I* : see), *does your father see this?*

Verbes réfléchis. — Les verbes réfléchis se forment avec le verbe et le pronom réfléchi. Ex. : elle se flatte, *she flatters herself*. Beaucoup de verbes réfléchis français se traduisent par des verbes neutres en anglais. Ex. : Il s'arrêta, *he stopped*.

Verbes réciproques. — On les forme avec les pronoms *each other* (ou *one another*). Ex. : Ils se flattent (mutuellement), *they flatter each other*.

La **forme progressive**, particulière à l'anglais, consiste à employer le verbe « être » avec le participe présent (dans le sens de « être en train de »). Ex. : fumez-vous? *are you smoking?* (*do you smoke?* signifie : fumez-vous d'habitude, êtes-vous fumeur?).

La forme progressive est commode pour traduire l'imparfait (de continuation). [V. IMPARFAIT.] On l'emploie aussi dans l'expression « il y a... que ». Ex. : il y a six mois que j'apprends l'anglais, *I have been learning English for six months*.

La **forme fréquentative** consiste à employer *would* (ou *used to*) devant l'infinitif pour indiquer *l'habitude*. (V. IMPARFAIT.) Ex. : je fumais un cigare de temps en temps, *I would smoke a cigar now and then* (*used to* indiquerait une habitude plus régulière).

Particularités de prononciation. — *a*) La terminaison *ed* du prétérit et du participe passé se prononce :

1º Comme [d] lorsque la consonne terminale du radical est sonore ou après un son vocalique : *filled, loved, moved, called, spared, buzzed; hewed, rued, sawed, freed*;

2º Comme [t] lorsque la consonne terminale du radical est sourde : *licked, brushed, scoffed, placed, remarked, passed, reached, pitched;*

3º Comme une syllabe supplémentaire [id] après les dentales (*t* ou *d*) : *glided, flitted, rated, melted, corroded.*

N. B. — Il existe un certain nombre d'adjectifs en *ed* (prononcer [id]) : *aged, beloved, blessed, learned, naked, ragged, rugged, wicked, wretched.*

b) Les verbes dont l'infinitif se termine par -*ce*, -*se*, -*ge* se prononcent avec une syllabe supplémentaire [iz] à la troisième personne du singulier de l'indicatif présent : *dances, fences, cleanses, changes.*

c) Les verbes dont l'infinitif se termine par -*ss*, -*x*, -*z*, -*sh* et -*ch* forment la troisième personne du singulier de l'indicatif présent en -*es* avec une syllabe supplémentaire dans la prononciation [iz] : *passes, misses, fixes, reaches, fizzes, crushes.*

d) Lorsqu'un verbe d'origine romane a la même forme que le substantif ou l'adjectif correspondant, le verbe s'accentue d'ordinaire sur la dernière syllabe, et le substantif ou l'adjectif sur la première.

ACCENT (n.) ['æksənt]; (v.) [æk'sent];
CONDUCT (n.) ['kɔndəkt]; (v.) [kən'dʌkt];
DESERT (n.) ['dezət]; (v.) [di'zə:t];
INCENSE (n.) ['insens]; (v.) [in'sens], etc.

Il existe des exceptions à cette règle : *comfort* (n. et v.) ['kʌmfət]; *profit* (n. et v.) ['prɔfit]; *purpose* (n. et v.) ['pə:pəs], etc.

Noter que pour *use, refuse* l's du substantif est dur [s] et celui du verbe doux [z].

TABLEAU DES PARTICULARITÉS VERBALES

N. B. — Les numéros placés en tête des paragraphes ci-dessous se retrouvent dans le courant du dictionnaire, à la suite du verbe qui obéit à la règle correspondante.

1. **Le redoublement de la consonne finale** d'un verbe monosyllabique a lieu si elle est précédée d'une seule voyelle, devant toute désinence commençant par une voyelle. Ex. : *stop, stopped.*

La consonne finale d'un mot de deux syllabes suit la même règle, si l'accent porte sur la dernière syllabe. Ex. : *to prefer*, préférer [pri'fə*]; *preferred;* mais : *to offer*, offrir ['ɔfə*], *offered.*

La consonne finale d'un mot de plusieurs syllabes suit la même règle, si la dernière syllabe porte un accent.

Exceptions : 1º Tous les verbes polysyllabiques terminés par une voyelle suivie de *l* (sauf *parallel*) redoublent le *l* final. Ex. : *To travel*, *travelled; to carrol, carrolled.*

2. Les **verbes terminés en « y »** précédé d'une consonne forment leur troisième personne du singulier de l'indicatif présent en *ies* et leur passé en *ied.* Ex. : *to study*, étudier; *he studies; studied.*

Les verbes dont l'infinitif se termine en -*y* précédé d'une voyelle forment la 3e pers. du sing. à l'ind. pr. en -*ys* et du p. pr. en *ying.* Ex. : *to play*, jouer; *plays; playing.*

3. Les **verbes monosyllabiques terminés en « ie »** font leur participe présent en *ying.* Ex. : *to die*, mourir; *died; dying.*

4. Les **verbes terminés en « o »** ajoutent la désinence directement à la voyelle finale. Ex. : *to halo*, auréoler; *haloed.*

LISTE DES VERBES DITS IRRÉGULIERS

N. B. — On donne l'infinitif, le prétérit, le participe passé et le sens.

5. *To abide;*	*abode;*	*abode.*	Demeurer.
6. *To arise;*	*arose;*	*arisen.*	Se lever.
7. *To awake;*	*awoke;*	*awaked, awaken.*	S'éveiller.
8. *To be;*	*was;*	*been.*	Etre.
9. *To bear;*	*bore;*	*borne (born = né).*	Porter.
10. *To beat;*	*beat;*	*beaten.*	Battre.
11. *To become;*	*became;*	*become.*	Devenir.
12. *To befall;*	*befell;*	*befallen.*	Arriver à.
13. *To beget;*	*begot;*	*begotten.*	Engendrer.
14. *To begin;*	*began;*	*begun.*	Commencer.
15. *To behold;*	*beheld;*	*beheld.*	Contempler.
16. *To bend;*	*bent;*	*bent.*	Courber.
17. *To bereave;*	*bereft, bereaved;*	*bereft, bereaved.*	Priver.
18. *To beseech;*	*besought;*	*besought.*	Supplier.
19. *To bespeak;*	*bespoke;*	*bespoken.*	Commander, retenir.
20. *To bid;*	*bade, bid;*	*bidden, bid.*	Ordonner.
21. *To bind;*	*bound;*	*bound.*	Lier, relier.
22. *To bite;*	*bit;*	*bitten.*	Mordre.
23. *To bleed;*	*bled;*	*bled.*	Saigner.
24. *To blow;*	*blew;*	*blown.*	Souffler.
25. *To break;*	*broke;*	*broken.*	Briser.
26. *To breed;*	*bred;*	*bred.*	Elever.
27. *To bring;*	*brought;*	*brought.*	Apporter.
28. *To build;*	*built.*	*built.*	Construire.
29. *To burn;*	*burnt;* U. S. burned;	*burnt;* U. S. burned.	Brûler.
30. *To burst;*	*burst;*	*burst.*	Eclater.
31. *To buy;*	*bought;*	*bought.*	Acheter.
32. *To cast;*	*cast;*	*cast.*	Jeter.
33. *To catch;*	*caught;*	*caught.*	Attraper.
34. *To chide;*	*chid;*	*chidden, chid.*	Gronder.
35. *To choose;*	*chose;*	*chosen.*	Choisir.
36. *To cleave;*	*cleft, cleaved;*	*cleft, cleaved.*	Fendre.
37. *To cling;*	*clung;*	*clung.*	S'accrocher.
38. *To clothe;*	*clothed, clad;*	*clothed, clad.*	Vêtir.
39. *To come;*	*came;*	*come.*	Venir.
40. *To cost;*	*cost;*	*cost.*	Coûter.
41. *To creep;*	*crept;*	*crept.*	Ramper.
42. *To crow;*	*crowed, crew;*	*crowed.*	Chanter (coq)
43. *To cut;*	*cut;*	*cut.*	Couper.
44. *To dare;*	*dared, durst;*	*dared.*	Oser.
45. *To deal;*	*dealt;*	*dealt.*	Distribuer.

46. *To dig ;*	*dug ;*	*dug.*	Creuser.
47. *To do ;*	*did ;*	*done.*	Faire.
48. *To draw ;*	*drew ;*	*drawn.*	Tirer.
49. *To dream ;*	*dreamed, dreamt ;*	*dreamed, dreamt.*	Rêver.
50. *To drink ;*	*drank ;*	*drunk.*	Boire.
51. *To drive ;*	*drove ;*	*driven.*	Conduire.
52. *To dwell ;*	*dwelt ;*	*dwelt.*	Demeurer.
53. *To eat ;*	*ate ;*	*eaten.*	Manger.
54. *To fall ;*	*fell ;*	*fallen.*	Tomber.
55. *To feed ;*	*fed ;*	*fed.*	Nourrir.
56. *To feel ;*	*felt ;*	*felt.*	Sentir.
57. *To fight ;*	*fought ;*	*fought.*	Combattre.
58. *To find ;*	*found ;*	*found.*	Trouver.
59. *To flee ;*	*fled ;*	*fled.*	Fuir.
60. *To fling ;*	*flung ;*	*flung.*	Lancer.
61. *To fly ;*	*flew ;*	*flown.*	Voler.
62. *To forbear ;*	*forbore ;*	*forborne.*	S'abstenir.
63. *To forbid ;*	*forbade ;*	*forbidden.*	Défendre.
64. *To forget ;*	*forgot ;*	*forgotten.*	Oublier.
65. *To forgive ;*	*forgave ;*	*forgiven.*	Pardonner.
66. *To forsake ;*	*forsook ;*	*forsaken.*	Abandonner.
67. *To freeze ;*	*froze ;*	*frozen.*	Geler.
68. *To get ;*	*got ;*	*got ;* U. S. gotten.	Obtenir.
69. *To gild ;*	*gilded, gilt ;*	*gilded, gilt.*	Dorer.
70. *To gird ;*	*girded, girt ;*	*girded, girt.*	Ceindre.
71. *To give ;*	*gave ;*	*given.*	Donner.
72. *To go ;*	*went ;*	*gone.*	Aller.
73. *To grind ;*	*ground ;*	*ground.*	Moudre.
74. *To grow ;*	*grew ;*	*grown.*	Croître.
75. *To hang ;*	*hung ;*	*hung.*	Suspendre, pendre.
	hanged ;	*hanged.*	Pendre (au gibet).
76. *To have ;*	*had ;*	*had.*	Avoir.
77. *To hear ;*	*heard ;*	*heard.*	Entendre.
78. *To heave ;*	*heaved,* NAUT. *hove ;*	*heaved, hove.*	Se soulever.
79. *To hew ;*	*hewed ;*	*hewed, hewn.*	Tailler.
80. *To hide ;*	*hid ;*	*hidden, hid.*	Cacher.
81. *To hit ;*	*hit ;*	*hit.*	Frapper, atteindre.
82. *To hold ;*	*held ;*	*held.*	Tenir.
83. *To hurt ;*	*hurt ;*	*hurt.*	Blesser.
84. *To keep ;*	*kept ;*	*kept.*	Garder.
85. *To kneel ;*	*knelt ;*	*knelt.*	S'agenouiller.
86. *To knit ;*	*knit ;*	*knit.*	Tricoter.
87. *To know ;*	*knew ;*	*known.*	Connaître.
88. *To lade ;*	*laded ;*	*laden.*	Charger.
89. *To lay ;*	*laid ;*	*laid.*	Poser.
90. *To lead ;*	*led ;*	*led.*	Conduire.
91. *To lean ;*	*leant, leaned ;*	*leant, leaned.*	Se pencher.
92. *To leap ;*	*leapt ;*	*leapt.*	Bondir.
93. *To learn ;*	*learnt ;*	*learnt, learned.*	Apprendre.
94. *To leave ;*	*left ;*	*left.*	Laisser.
95. *To lend ;*	*lent ;*	*lent.*	Prêter.
96. *To let ;*	*let ;*	*let.*	Laisser.
97. *To lie ;*	*lay ;*	*lain.*	Etre couché.
98. *To light ;*	*lighted, lit ;*	*lighted, lit.*	Allumer.
99. *To lose ;*	*lost ;*	*lost.*	Perdre.
00. *To make ;*	*made ;*	*made.*	Faire.
01. *To mean ;*	*meant ;*	*meant.*	Signifier.
02. *To meet ;*	*met ;*	*met.*	Rencontrer.
03. *To mistake ;*	*mistook ;*	*mistaken.*	Se tromper.
04. *To mow ;*	*mowed ;*	*mown, mowed.*	Faucher.
05. *To pay ;*	*paid ;*	*paid.*	Payer.
06. *To pen ;*	*penned, pent ;*	*penned.*	Parquer.
07. *To put ;*	*put ;*	*put.*	Mettre.
08. *To read ;*	*read ;*	*read.*	Lire.
09. *To rend ;*	*rent ;*	*rent.*	Déchirer.
10. *To rid ;*	*rid ;*	*rid.*	Débarrasser.
11. *To ride ;*	*rode ;*	*ridden.*	Chevaucher.
12. *To ring ;*	*rang ;*	*rung.*	Sonner.
13. *To rise ;*	*rose ;*	*risen.*	Se lever.
14. *To run ;*	*ran ;*	*run.*	Courir.
15. *To saw ;*	*sawed ;*	*sawn, sawed.*	Scier.
16. *To say ;*	*said ;*	*said.*	Dire.
17. *To see ;*	*saw ;*	*seen.*	Voir.
18. *To seek ;*	*sought ;*	*sought.*	Chercher.
19. *To seethe ;*	*seethed ;* † *sod ;*	*seethed ;* † *sodden.*	Bouillir.
20. *To sell ;*	*sold ;*	*sold.*	Vendre.
21. *To send ;*	*sent ;*	*sent.*	Envoyer.
22. *To set ;*	*set ;*	*set.*	Placer.
23. *To shake ;*	*shook ;*	*shaken.*	Secouer.
24. *To shear ;*	*shore, sheared ;*	*shorn.*	Tondre.
25. *To shed ;*	*shed ;*	*shed.*	Verser.
26. *To shine ;*	*shone ;*	*shone.*	Briller.
27. *To shoe ;*	*shod ;*	*shod.*	Chausser.
28. *To shoot ;*	*shot ;*	*shot.*	Tirer (un projectile).
29. *To show ;*	*showed ;*	*shown.*	Montrer.
30. *To shred ;*	*shred, shredded ;*	*shred, shredded.*	Lacérer.
31. *To shrink ;*	*shrank ;*	*shrunk.*	Se rétrécir.
32. *To shrive ;*	*shrove ;*	*shriven.*	Confesser.
33. *To shut ;*	*shut ;*	*shut.*	Fermer.
34. *To sing ;*	*sang ;*	*sung.*	Chanter.
35. *To sink ;*	*sank ;*	*sunk.*	Enfoncer.
36. *To sit ;*	*sat ;*	*sat.*	Etre assis.

137. *To slay;*	*slew;*	*slain.*	Tuer.
138. *To sleep;*	*slept;*	*slept.*	Dormir.
139. *To slide;*	*slid;*	*slid, slidden.*	Glisser.
140. *To sling;*	*slung;*	*slung.*	Lancer.
141. *To slink;*	*slunk;*	*slunk.*	Se glisser.
142. *To slit;*	*slit;*	*slit.*	Fendre.
143. *To smell;*	*smelt;* U. S. smelled;	*smelt;* U. S. smelled.	Sentir.
144. *To smite;*	*smote;*	*smitten.*	Frapper.
145. *To sow;*	*sowed;*	*sown.*	Semer.
146. *To speak;*	*spoke;*	*spoken.*	Parler.
147. *To speed;*	*sped;*	*sped.*	Se hâter.
148. *To spell;*	*spelt;*	*spelt.*	Epeler.
149. *To spend;*	*spent;*	*spent.*	Dépenser.
150. *To spill;*	*spilt;* U. S. spilled;	*spilt;* U. S. spilled.	Répandre.
151. *To spin;*	*spun, span;*	*spun.*	Filer, tourner.
152. *To spit;*	*spit, spat;*	*spit.*	Cracher.
153. *To split;*	*split;*	*split.*	Fendre (en éclats).
154. *To spoil;*	*spoilt;* U. S. spoiled;	*spoilt;* U. S. spoiled.	Gâter.
155. *To spread;*	*spread;*	*spread.*	Etendre.
156. *To spring;*	*sprang;*	*sprung.*	S'élancer.
157. *To stand;*	*stood;*	*stood.*	Se tenir debout.
158. *To stay;*	*stayed;*	*stayed.*	Séjourner.
159. *To steal;*	*stole;*	*stolen.*	Voler (dérober).
160. *To stick;*	*stuck;*	*stuck.*	Coller.
161. *To sting;*	*stung;*	*stung.*	Piquer.
162. *To stink;*	*stank;*	*stunk.*	Puer.
163. *To strew;*	*strewed;*	*strewn.*	Joncher.
164. *To stride;*	*strode;*	*stridden.*	Marcher à grands pas.
165. *To strike;*	*struck;*	*struck, stricken.*	Frapper.
166. *To string;*	*strung;*	*strung.*	Enfiler.
167. *To strive;*	*strove;*	*striven.*	S'efforcer.
168. *To swear;*	*swore;*	*sworn.*	Jurer.
169. *To sweat;*	*sweat;*	*sweat.*	Suer.
170. *To sweep;*	*swept;*	*swept.*	Balayer.
171. *To swell;*	*swelled;*	*swollen.*	Enfler.
172. *To swim;*	*swam;*	*swum.*	Nager.
173. *To swing;*	*swung;*	*swung.*	Balancer.
174. *To take;*	*took;*	*taken.*	Prendre.
175. *To teach;*	*taught;*	*taught.*	Enseigner.
176. *To tear;*	*tore;*	*torn.*	Déchirer.
177. *To tell;*	*told;*	*told.*	Dire.
178. *To think;*	*thought;*	*thought.*	Penser.
179. *To thrive;*	*throve;*	*thriven.*	Prospérer.
180. *To throw;*	*threw;*	*thrown.*	Jeter.
181. *To thrust;*	*thrust;*	*thrust.*	Lancer.
182. *To tread;*	*trod;*	*trodden, trod.*	Fouler (aux pieds).
183. *To understand;*	*understood;*	*understood.*	Comprendre.
184. *To undo;*	*undid;*	*undone.*	Défaire.
185. *To upset;*	*upset;*	*upset.*	Renverser.
186. *To wear;*	*wore;*	*worn.*	Porter, user.
187. *To weave;*	*wove;*	*woven.*	Tisser.
188. *To weep;*	*wept;*	*wept.*	Pleurer.
189. *To win;*	*won;*	*won.*	Gagner.
190. *To wind;*	*wound;*	*wound.*	Enrouler.
191. *To withdraw;*	*withdrew;*	*withdrawn.*	Retirer.
192. *To withstand;*	*withstood;*	*withstood.*	Résister à.
193. *To work;*	*worked, wrought;*	*worked, wrought.*	Travailler.
194. *To wring;*	*wrung;*	*wrung.*	Tordre.
195. *To write;*	*wrote;*	*written.*	Ecrire.
196. *To writhe;*	*writhed;*	*writhen, writhed.*	Se tordre.

ORTHOGRAPHE AMÉRICAINE

L'orthographe américaine diffère parfois de l'orthographe anglaise :

a) Notez les graphies suivantes :

Br. -our; U. S. -or. Ex. : *honour, honor.*

Br. -re; U. S. -er. Ex. : *centre, center* (exceptions : *ogre* et les mots terminés par *-cre*, comme *massacre*)

Br. -ce; U. S. -se. Ex. : *defence, defense.*

Br. -ou-; U. S. -o-. Ex. : *mould, mold.*

b) Dans un certain nombre de mots où l'anglais redouble la consonne, l'américain emploie une consonne simple Ex. : Br. *travelled, worshipper, waggon;* U. S. *traveled, worshiper, wagon,* etc.

c) Au préfixe anglais **em-,** l'américain préfère parfois le préfixe **im-.** Ex. : Br. *empanel,* à côté de U. S. *impanel,* etc.

d) Dans certains mots, le e muet qui existe en anglais disparaît en américain. Ex. : Br. *storey, good-bye,* U. S. *story, good-by,* etc.

e) Dans quelques emprunts français dont l'anglais conserve l'orthographe d'origine, l'américain supprime la terminaison inaccentuée. Ex. : Br. *catalogue, programme;* U. S. *catalog, program,* etc.

f) A la graphie savante ae, oe, conservée en anglais, l'américain substitue fréquemment e. Ex. : Br. *anaemia diarrhoea;* U. S. *anemia, diarrhea.*

g) Remarquez en outre quelques cas spéciaux. Ex. : Br. *plough, grey, tyre, instalment, gaol, kerb, skilful,* U. S. *plow, gray, tire, installment, jail, curb, skillful,* etc.

SONS ANGLAIS

CONSONNES

SIGNES	MOTS TYPES
[b]	bat [bæt]
[d]	dot [dɔt], begged [begd]
[dʒ]	jam [dʒæm], edge [edʒ]
[f]	fat [fæt], phrase [freiz], laugh [lɑ:f]
[g]	goat [gout], ghastly ['gɑ:stli], guard [gɑ:d]
[gw]	language ['læŋgwidʒ]
[gz]	exact [ig'zækt]
[ʒ]	measure ['meʒə*], azure ['eiʒə*], garage ['gærɑ:ʒ], bijou ['bi:ʒu:]
[h]	hat [hæt]
[k]	cat [kæt], keen [ki:n], Christmas ['krisməs], antique [æn'ti:k]
[ks]	taxi ['tæksi], access ['ækses], eczema ['eksimə]
[kw]	quack [kwæk]
[l]	lap [læp]
[l̩]	people ['pi:pl̩], pistol ['pistl̩], colonel ['kə:nl̩]
[m]	mat [mæt]
[m̩]	realism ['riəlizm̩]
[n]	natter ['nætə*]
[n̩]	fatten ['fætn̩]
[ʃ]	shame [ʃeim], wish [wiʃ]
[t]	tatter ['tætə*], fixed [fikst], thyme [taim]
[tʃ]	chat [tʃæt], match [mætʃ], nature ['neitʃə*]
[θ]	thatch [θætʃ]
[ð]	that [ðæt], father ['fɑ:ðə*]
[v]	vat [væt], Stephen ['sti:vn̩]
[z]	haze [heiz], disease [di'zi:z], scissors ['sizəz], xebec ['zi:bek]

SEMI-VOYELLES

SIGNES	MOTS TYPES
[j]	yet [jet], onion ['ʌnjən], extraneous [eks'treinjəs]
[w]	war [wɑ:*], quite [kwait] ; (cf. [kw], [gw])

SEMI-VOYELLES ET VOYELLES

SIGNES	MOTS TYPES
[ju:]	unit ['ju:nit], new [nju:], suit [sju:t], adieu [ə'dju:], beauty ['bju:ti], yule [ju:l], yew, you [ju:], deuce [dju:s]
[juə]	fewer ['fjuə*], pure ['pjuə*]
[wʌ]	one, won [wʌn]; (cf. [w], [kw], [gw])

VOYELLES

SIGNES	MOTS TYPES
[æ]	cat [kæt], plait [plæt]
[e]	hen [hen], head [hed], any [eni], bury ['beri], leisure ['leʒə*], said [sed], leopard ['lepəd], friend [frend]
[i]	pig [pig], English ['iŋgliʃ], women ['wimin], palace ['pælis], business ['bizinis], pyx [piks], barley ['bɑ:li], sieve [siv], build [bild], carriage ['kæridʒ], Greenwich ['grinidʒ], captain ['kæptin], Sunday ['sʌndi], foreign ['fɔrin], forehead ['fɔrid]
[ɔ]	cock [kɔk], wash [wɔʃ], because [bi'kɔz], Gloucester ['glɔstə*], knowledge ['nɔlidʒ]
[u]	bull [bul], book [buk], wolf [wulf], could [kud], worsted ['wustid]
[ʌ]	duck [dʌk], come [kʌm], courage ['kʌridʒ], blood [blʌd]
[ə]	again [ə'gein], verandah [və'rændə], bacon ['beikən], tortoise ['tə:təs], famous ['feiməs], suggest [sə'dʒest], collar ['kɔlə*], cover ['kʌvə*], tapir ['teipə*], motor ['moutə*], cupboard ['kʌbəd], vigour ['vigə*], chauffeur ['tʃɔ:fə*], figure ['figə*], litre ['litə*]
[ə:]	bird [bə:d], hermit ['hə:mit], earn [ə:n], amateur ['æmətə:*], word [wə:d], courteous ['kə:tiəs], nurse [nə:s], myrtle ['mə:tl̩], colonel ['kə:nl̩]
[ɑ:]	calf [kɑ:f], far [fɑ:*], farm [fɑ:m], aunt [ɑ:nt], clerk [klɑ:k], heart [hɑ:t]
[i:]	sheep [ʃi:p], tea [ti:], scene [si:n], seize [si:z], litre [li:tr], fiend [fi:nd], Caesar ['si:zə*], quay [ki:], people ['pi:pl̩]
[ɔ:]	lawn [lɔ:n], off [ɔ:f], caught [kɔ:t], war [wɔ:*], broad [brɔ:d], born [bɔ:n], thought [θɔ:t], source [sɔ:s], all [ɔ:l], more [mɔ:*], floor [flɔ:*], boar [bɔ:*], your [jɔ:*]
[u:]	goose [gu:s], rule [ru:l], who [hu:], wound [wu:nd], blue [blu:], juice [dʒu:s], screw [skru:], shoe [ʃu:], manœuvre [mə'nu:və*]

DIPHTONGUES

SIGNES	MOTS TYPES
[ai]	ice [ais], fly [flai], aye, eye [ai], height [hait], pie [pai], rye [rai], buy [bai], island ['ailənd], light [lait]
[ei]	snake [sneik], maid [meid], play [plei], veil [veil], great [greit], phaeton ['feitn̩], gauge [geidʒ], gaol [dʒeil], grey [grei], weigh [wei]

SIGNES	MOTS TYPES
DIPHTONGUES	
[ɔi]	coin [kɔin], joy [dʒɔi], Reuter ['rɔitə*], buoy [bɔi]
[au]	mouse [maus], cow [kau], plough [plau]
[ou]	go [gou], goat [gout], doe [dou], soul [soul], blow [blou], brooch [broutʃ], mauve [mouv], bureau [bjuə'rou], yeoman ['joumən], sew [sou], dough [dou], owe [ou]
[ɛə]	bear [bɛə*], care [kɛə*], pair [pɛə*], there [ðɛə*], Ayr [ɛə*], prayer ['prɛə*], mayor [mɛə*], aerial ['ɛəriəl], heir [hɛə*], vary ['vɛəri]
[iə]	deer [diə*], here [hiə*], tier [tiə*], beard [biəd], weird [wiəd], theory ['θiəri], Ian [iən], idea ['aidiə]
[uə]	poor [puə*], sure [suə*], tour [tuə*], pleurisy ['pluərisi], cruel [kruəl], Boer [buə*]

TRIPHTONGUES

SIGNES	MOTS TYPES
[aiə]	science ['saiəns], via ['vaiə], liar ['laiə*], tier ['taiə*], lion ['laiən], pious ['paiəs], higher ['haiə*], fire ['faiə*], choir ['kwaiə*], buyer ['baiə*], dryer ['draiə*], pyre ['paiə*]
[auə]	flower [flauə*], vowel ['vauəl], hour [auə*], coward ['kauəd]

Symboles. — Les symboles employés sont ceux de l'alphabet de phonétique internationale (méthode D. Jones).

Accent tonique. — L'accent tonique principal est indiqué par l'apostrophe ('), qui précède la syllabe accentuée; l'accent secondaire est indiqué par la virgule (,).

N. B. — La prononciation américaine diffère souvent de la prononciation anglaise. Faute de place, nous n'avons donné que la prononciation anglaise, parce qu'elle est la plus fréquente.

ALPHABET ANGLAIS

SIGNE majuscule et minuscule	PRONONCIATION	SIGNE majuscule et minuscule	PRONONCIATION
A, a	[ei]	N, n	[en]
B, b	[bi:]	O, o	[ou]
C, c	[si:]	P, p	[pi:]
D, d	[di:]	Q, q	[kju:]
E, e	[i:]	R, r	[ɑ:*]
F, f	[ef]	S, s	[es]
G, g	[dʒi:]	T, t	[ti:]
H, h	[eitʃ]	U, u	[ju:]
I, i	[ai]	V, v	[vi:]
J, j	[dʒei]	W, w	['dʌblju:]
K, k	[kei]	X, x	[eks]
L, l	[el]	Y, y	[wai]
M, m	[em]	Z, z	[zed]

DIVISION SYLLABIQUE DES MOTS ANGLAIS

1. On ne peut couper les mots ou parties de mot qui se prononcent en une seule syllabe : times [taimz], stopped [stɔpt], late [leit], bur-lesque [bə:'lesk].

2. On divise les composés et les dérivés par éléments de composition ou de dérivation : en-joy-ment, an-oth-er, lov-ed, tail-ing, knick-er-bock-er, grump-i-ness.

3. Dans les autres cas, on coupe selon le rythme qu'imposent les accents forts et faibles des mots : leth-ar-gy, grum-ble, dis-qual-i-fi-ca-tion, knight-er-rant-ry, ar-chi-pel-a-go.

4. La meilleure règle pour diviser les syllabes est d'ailleurs de... s'en abstenir.

MONNAIES, POIDS ET MESURES ANGLAIS ET AMÉRICAINS

Monnaies.

Grande-Bretagne.
£ 1 : a pound (ARGOT a quid [kwid]) = 100 pence.

PIÈCES	VALEUR
1/2 p : a halfpenny	a halfpenny ['heipni]
1 p : a penny	a penny : FAM. one p [pi:]
2 p : a twopenny ['tʌpni] piece	twopence ['tʌpns] : FAM. two p [pi:]
5 p : a fivepenny piece	five pence
10 p : a tenpenny piece	ten pence
50 p : a fifty pence piece	fifty pence

BILLETS : £ 1. £ 5. £ 10. £ 20.

La « guinée » (guinea, abrév. gns) est une monnaie de compte, utilisée pour indiquer le montant des honoraires, le prix de certains articles de luxe, etc., et vaut 105 pence.

Avant l'adoption du système monétaire décimal (15 février 1971), la livre était divisée en 20 shillings, le shilling en 12 pence.

États-Unis.
$ 1 : a dollar (ARGOT a buck) = 100 cents.

PIÈCES	VALEUR
1 ¢ : a penny	a cent
5 ¢ : a nickel	five cents
10 ¢ : a dime	ten cents
25 ¢ : a quarter	twenty-five cents
50 ¢ : a half-dollar	half a dollar

BILLETS : $ 1. $ 5. $ 10. $ 20.

Australie, Canada, Nouvelle-Zélande.
Même système qu'aux États-Unis : $ 1 = 100 cents.

Poids. *(Système avoirdupois.)*

Grain (gr.)		0,64 g	Hundredweight (cwt) .	112 lb.	50,8	kg
Dram (dr.)	27 grains	1 772 g	Ton (t.)	20 cwts.	1 017	kg
Ounce (oz.)		28,35 g	U. S. 25 pounds . . .		11,34	kg
Pound (lb.)	16 oz.	453,592 g	U. S. 100 pounds . . .		45,36	kg
Stone (st.)	14 lb.	6,350 kg	U. S. short ton. . . .		907,18	kg
Quarter (Qr.) . . .	28 lb.	12,695 kg	U. S. Quintal . . .		45,36	kg

(Système troy pour les matières précieuses.)

Grain (gr.)		0,064 g	Ounce troy	20 dwts	31,10	g
Pennyweight (dwt) . .	24 grains	1,555 g	Pound troy	12 oz.	373,23	g

Mesures de longueur.

Inch (in.)	12 lines	0,0254 m	Pole, rod, perch . . .	5,5 yards	5,0292	m
Foot (ft.)	12 inches	0,3048 m	Chain	4 poles	20,116	m
Yard (yd.)	3 feet	0,9144 m	Rood, furlong	40 poles	201,16 8	m
Fathom (fthm.) . . .	6 feet	1,8288 m	Mile (m.).	8 furlongs	1 609,344	m

Nautical mile . . . . . 2 025 yards . . . . . 1 853 m

Mesures de superficie.

Square inch	6,451 cm²	Square yard.	0,8361 m²
Square foot	929 cm²	Rood	10,11 ares
Acre	40,46 ares	Square mile	259 ha

Mesures de volume.

Cubic inch	16,387 cm³	Cubic foot . . . . 28,315 dm³

Cubic yard . . . . 764 dm³

Mesures de capacité.

Pint (pt.)		0,567 litre	U. S. Peck (pk.) . . .	8,81	litres
Quart (qt.)	2 pints	1,135 —	U. S. Bushel	35,24	—
Gallon (gal.)	4 quarts	4,543 litres	U. S. Liquid gill. . .	0,118	litre
Bushel (bu.)	8 gallons	36,347 —	U. S. Liquid pint . .	0,473	—
Quarter.	8 bushels	290,780 —	U. S. Liquid quart . .	0,946	—
U. S. Dry pint. . .		0,551 litre	U. S. Liquid gallon. .	3,785	litres
U. S. Dry quart . . .		1,11 —	U. S. Barrel. . . .	119	—
U. S. Dry gallon . .		4,41 litres	U. S. Barrel petroleum.	158,97	—

WORD-LISTS AND ILLUSTRATIONS

The words followed by the symbol ● are illustrated; the Roman numeral I refers to the French-English section and II refers to the English-French section; the Arab numerals give the number of the page to look up.

A

[ei] n. A, a m.; *not to know A from B*, ne savoir ni *A* ni *B*. ‖ Premier (first); *A-1*, de première qualité. ‖ CHIM. Argon. ‖ MUS. La. ‖ **A-bomb**, n. MILIT. Bombe atomique *f*. ‖ **A-level**, n. En Grande-Bretagne, examen (*m.*) de fin d'études secondaires. ‖ **A-road**, n. AUTOM. Route nationale, grande route *f*.

([ei, ə] before a consonant, a sounded *h*, one [ju] sound; **an** [æn] before a vowel, a mute *h*) indef. art. Un, une; *an egg*, un œuf; *a ewe*, une brebis; *a house*, une maison; *an hour*, une heure; *a use*, un usage; *a war*, une guerre; *so great a man*, un si grand homme; *such a one*, un tel; *too cautious a man*, un homme trop circonspect. ‖ Un certain, un; *a Mr. Jones*, un certain M. Jones. ‖ Le, la, les; *to have a broken leg*, avoir la jambe cassée; *to set an example*, donner l'exemple. ‖ Le (ou) la même; *to be of an age*, être du même âge. ‖ Du, de la; *to have a taste for*, avoir du goût pour; *to make a noise*, faire du bruit. ‖ (Omitted in French); *as a tax-payer*, en tant que contribuable; *his father is a doctor*, son père est médecin; *my friend, a teacher of languages*, mon ami professeur de langues; *what a surprise you gave me!*, quelle surprise vous m'avez faite! ‖ (With few, many); *a great many people*, un grand nombre de personnes; *in a few minutes*, dans quelques minutes.

[ə] prep. Par, de, à; *twice a day*, deux fois par jour; *two shillings a head*, deux shillings par tête. ‖ † *My days are gone a-wandering*, mes jours s'en sont allés errants; *to go a-hunting*, aller à la chasse.

A. [eiei] abbr. *Automobile Association*, association automobile britannique. ‖ U.S. Abbr. *Alcoholics Anonymous*, Alcooliques Anonymes, association dont le but est de venir en aide aux alcooliques.

aardvark [ˈɑːdvɑːk] n. ZOOL. Oryctérope, cochon de terre *m*.

aaron [ˈɛərən] n. Aaron (patriarch). ‖ BOT. *Aaron's beard*, millepertuis; *Aaron's rod*, molène médicinale.

aback [əˈbæk] adv. † En arrière. ‖ NAUT. Coiffé, masqué; *to be aback*, avoir le vent dessus. ‖ FIG. *Taken aback*, décontenancé, interloqué.

abacus [ˈæbəkəs] n. Boulier compteur m. ‖ TECHN. Augette *f*. ‖ ARCHIT. Abaque *m*.
— N. B. Deux pluriels : *abacuses, abaci*.

abaft [əˈbɑːft] adv. Vers l'arrière.
— prep. NAUT. Sur l'arrière, en arrière.

abalone [ˌæbəˈlouni] n. ZOOL. Ormeau m.; oreille de mer, haliotide *f*.

abandon [əˈbændən] n. Laisser-aller; abandon, relâchement m. ‖ Détente, désinvolture *f*.
— v. tr. Abandonner, délaisser, quitter; *to abandon oneself to*, s'abandonner à, se laisser aller à. ‖ NAUT. Faire délaissement de (a cargo); évacuer (a ship). ‖ JUR. Renoncer à (a prosecution).

abandoned [-d] adj. Abandonné, délaissé. ‖ FIG. Débauché, dévoyé.

abandonment [-mənt] n. Abandon m. (condition, fact). ‖ Détente *f.*; laisser-aller m. ‖ JUR. Cession *f.*; désistement m. ‖ NAUT. Délaissement m.

abase [əˈbeis] v. tr. Mortifier, humilier. (See HUMILIATE.) ‖ Abaisser, ravaler, dégrader (to lower); *to abase oneself so far as to*, s'abaisser (or) se commettre jusqu'à.

abasement [-mənt] n. Abaissement, avilissement m. ‖ Humiliation *f*. ‖ Déchéance, dégradation *f*.

abash [əˈbæʃ] v. tr. Confondre, troubler, déconcerter, dérouter; démonter (fam.).

abashment [-mənt] n. Confusion *f*.

abate [əˈbeit] v. tr. † Abattre. ‖ COMM. Diminuer, déduire, rabattre (of, sur). ‖ JUR. Annuler, remettre. ‖ FIG. Affaiblir, amoindrir.
— v. intr. S'affaiblir, diminuer. ‖ Baisser (flood); s'apaiser (storm). ‖ JUR. Devenir caduc (claim). ‖ MÉD. S'apaiser (pain); décroître (epidemic, fever). ‖ FIN. Baisser (rent). ‖ NAUT. Mollir (wind). ‖ FIG. S'affaiblir, diminuer (courage).

abatement [-mənt] n. Diminution, réduction *f*. ‖ Abolition *f*. ‖ COMM. Rabais, abattement m.; remise *f*. ‖ JUR. Annulation; remise *f*. (of a fine); réduction *f* (of a legacy). ‖ MÉD. Décours m.; rémission *f*. (of illness).

abater [-ə*] n. Personne *f*. qui réduit (or) diminue. ‖ MÉD. Calmant m.

abatis [ˈæbətis] n. MILIT. Abattis m.

abattoir [ˈæbətwɑː*] n. Abattoir m.

abb [æb] n. Fil de trame m. ‖ Déchets de laine m.

abbacy [ˈæbəsi] n. ECCLES. Abbatiat m.

abbatial [æˈbeiʃəl] adj. ECCLES. Abbatial.

abbess [ˈæbis] n. ECCLES. Abbesse *f*.

abbey [ˈæbi] n. Abbatiale *f*. (church); abbaye *f*. (minster).

abbot [ˈæbət] n. ECCLES. Abbé, supérieur m. (of a monastery).

abbreviate [əˈbriːvieit] v. tr. Abréger, raccourcir. (See SHORTEN.) ‖ MATH. Réduire.
— n. JUR. Extrait, intitulé m.

abbreviation [əˌbriːviˈeiʃən] n. Abréviation *f*. ‖ MATH. Réduction *f*.

ABC [eibiːsiː] n. Alphabet m.; *as easy as ABC*, simple comme bonjour. ‖ ABC m. (rudiments of a subject). ‖ Abécédaire m.

abdicate [ˈæbdikeit] v. tr. Abdiquer (one's authority); se démettre de (a function) [see RESIGN]; *to abdicate the throne*, déposer la couronne. ‖ Renoncer à (one's rights). ‖ JUR. Déshériter (children).
— v. intr. Abdiquer.

abdication [ˌæbdiˈkeiʃən] n. Abdication; démission *f*. ‖ Désistement m.; renonciation *f*. ‖ JUR. Désaveu m. (of fatherhood).

abdicator ['æbdikeitə*] n. Abdicataire *m.* (king). ‖ Renonciateur *m.*
abdomen ['æbdəmən] n. MED. Abdomen *m.*
abdominal [æb dominl] adj. MED. Abdominal.
abdominous [-əs] adj. MED. Abdominal. ‖ FAM. Ventru, pansu.
abducent [æb'dju:snt] adj. MED. Abducteur.
abduct [æb'dʌkt] v. tr. JUR. Enlever (to kidnap) ; détourner (s.o.). ‖ MED. Faire mouvoir, dévier.
abduction [-ʃən] n. JUR. Enlèvement, rapt *m. ;* détournement *m.* de mineure. ‖ MED. Abduction *f.* ‖ GRAMM., PHILOS. Apagogie *f.*
abductor [-tə*] n. JUR. Ravisseur ; détourneur *m.* ‖ MED. Muscle abducteur *m.*
abeam [ə'bi:m] adv. NAUT. Par le travers, de flanc ; *to shoot abeam,* tirer en belle.
abearance [ə'bɛərəns] n. Comportement *m.*
abecedarian [,eibisi'dɛəriən] adj. Abécédaire ; élémentaire.
— n. Elève (ou) maître d'une classe élémentaire.
abed [ə'bed] adv. Au lit.
aberrance [æ'berəns] n. Aberrance *f.* ‖ Déviation *f.*
aberrant [-ənt] adj. Aberrant ; dévié. ‖ Anormal.
aberration [,æbə'reiʃən] n. Déviation, divergence *f.* ‖ Anomalie *f.* ‖ MED. Dérangement mental *m.* ‖ OPT., ASTRON., FIG. Aberration *f.*
abet [ə'bet] v. tr. Inciter, stimuler, pousser (pej.). ‖ JUR. *To aid and abet,* être complice de.
abetment [-mənt] n. Instigation, incitation *f.* ‖ JUR. Complicité *f.*
abettor [-ə*] n. Incitateur *m.* ‖ JUR. Complice *m.*
abeyance [ə'beiəns] n. Suspension temporaire *f.* ‖ JUR. Vacance, deshérence *f. ; in abeyance,* en désuétude ; en suspens.
abhor [əb'hɔ:*] v. tr. Abhorrer, exécrer.
abhorrence [-rəns] n. Horreur, aversion *f.*
abhorrent [-rənt] adj. Exécrable, détestable. ‖ En désaccord (ou) contradiction (*from, to,* avec) ; opposé (*from, to,* à).
abidance [ə'baidəns] n. Conformité *f.* (*by,* à) ; respect *m.* (*by,* de). ‖ Persistance *f.* (*in,* dans).
abide [ə'baid] v. intr. (5). † Demeurer, habiter, séjourner (*at, in,* dans). ‖ Durer, continuer, se maintenir (to go on being) ; *abiding,* persistant, durable. ‖ *To abide by,* se soumettre à (a decision) ; rester fidèle à (a promise) ; s'en tenir à (a resolution) ; respecter (the rules).
— v. tr. Attendre (to await). ‖ † Faire face à (terrors) ; souffrir, supporter (s.o.) ; *to abide it dearly,* le payer cher.
abiding [-iŋ] adj. Durable ; *law abiding,* respectueux des lois.
abigail ['æbigeil] n. Soubrette, suivante *f.*
ability [ə'biliti] n. Pouvoir d'action *m. ;* aptitude *f.* (*to,* à). ‖ Efficience, compétence, capacité *f.* ‖ Habileté *f. ;* talent *m.* ‖ Pl. Talents *m. ;* possibilités *f. pl.* ‖ JUR. Capacité légale *f.* ‖ FIN. Pl. Disponibilités *f.*
ab initio [æbi'niʃiou] adv. Dès l'origine, dès le départ.
abirritant [æ'biritənt] adj., n. MED. Adoucissant *m.*
abject ['æbdʒekt] adj. Abject, méprisable, vil (person) ; noir, misérable, sinistre (poverty).
abjection [æb'dʒekʃən] n. Abjection *f.*
abjectly ['æbdʒektli] adv. Bassement, avec abjection.
abjuration [,æbdʒu'reiʃən] n. ECCLES. Abjuration *f.* ‖ JUR. *Abjuration of the realm,* serment de quitter le royaume.
abjure [əb'dʒuə*] v. tr. Renoncer à (one's rights). ‖ Rétracter, revenir sur (one's opinions). [See RECANT.] ‖ JUR. *To abjure the realm,* jurer de s'expatrier. ‖ ECCLES. Abjurer ; *to abjure one's faith,* apostasier.
— v. intr. Abjurer.
ablactation [æb,læk'teiʃən] n. MED. Ablactation *f.*

ablation [æb'leiʃən] n. Ablation *f.*
ablative ['æblətiv] n. GRAMM. Ablatif *m.*
— adj. GRAMM. A l'ablatif.
ablaut ['æblaut] n. GRAMM. Apophonie *f.*
ablaze [ə'bleiz] adv. En feu.
— adj. Enflammé (*with,* de).
able ['eibl] adj. Capable ; *to be no longer able t* n'être plus en état de. ‖ Capable, habile, compéten ‖ De talent ; talentueux (fam.) [orator] ; bien fa (work). ‖ MED. Sain. ‖ **Able to,** capable de, qualif pour, propre à, apte à ; *to be able to,* pouvoir. **Able-bodied,** adj. Fort, solide, costaud ; MILI Bon pour le service ; NAUT. Breveté (seaman). **Able-minded,** adj. Intelligent.
ablepsy [ə'blepsi] n. MED. Cécité *f.*
ablet ['æblet] n. ZOOL. Ablette *f.*
abloom [ə'blu:m] adv. En fleurs, épanoui.
abluent [əb'luənt] n. Détergent *m.*
ablush [ə'blʌʃ] adj. Rougissant.
ablution [əb'blu:ʃən] n. ECCLES. Ablution *f.*
ably ['eibli] adv. Habilement, avec talent.
abnegate ['æbnigeit] v. tr. Renoncer à. ‖ ECCLE Renier.
abnegation [æbni'geiʃən] n. Reniement, désave déni *m.* ‖ Renoncement *m.* (of rights) ; *self-abn gation,* abnégation.
abnegator ['æbnegeitə*] n. Renonciateur, dén gateur *m.*
abnormal [æb'nɔ:məl] adj. Anormal, insolite. MED. Anormal ; *abnormal psychology,* psycholog des anormaux.
abnormality [æbnɔ:'mæliti] n. Anomalie *f* caractère exceptionnel *m.* ‖ MED. Difformité, ma formation *f.*
abnormally [æb'nɔ:məli] adv. Anormalement. Extraordinairement ; exceptionnellement.
abnormity [-iti] n. Anomalie *f.* ‖ Monstruosité ‖ Monstre *m.*
abo ['æbou] adj., n. POP. Aborigène *adj., s.* (i Australia).
aboard [ə'bɔ:d] adv. NAUT. A bord ; *to go aboar* s'embarquer ; *to take aboard,* embarquer. ‖ Cont le bord ; *to keep the land aboard,* longer la côt ‖ U. S. *All aboard !,* en voiture !
— prép. NAUT. A bord de (a ship). ‖ CH. DE FE U. S. Dans (a train).
abode. See ABIDE.
abode [ə'boud] n. Habitation, résidence *f. ; to ta* up one's abode, élire domicile. ‖ Séjour *m.* (sojourn
abolish [ə'bɔliʃ] v. tr. Abolir. ‖ JUR. Annule abroger.
abolishable [-əbl] adj. Abolissable, abrogeable.
abolishment [-mənt] n. Abolissement *m.*
abolition [,æbo'liʃən] n. Abolition *f.*
abolitionism [-izm] n. Abolitionnisme *m.*
abolitionist [-ist] n. Abolitionniste *s.*
abomasum [æbo'meisəm] n. Caillette *f.*
abominable [ə'bɔminəbl] adj. Abominable, odieu (loathsome). ‖ Déplaisant, désagréable, exécrab (nasty).
abominate [ə'bɔmi,neit] v. tr. Abominer, abho rer, avoir en horreur ; détester (by exaggeration).
abomination [ə,bɔmi'neiʃən] n. Abominatic (action, object) ; *to be an abomination to,* être e abomination à.
aboriginal [,æbə'ridʒinəl] adj., n. Aborigène *m.*
aborigines [-ni:z] n. pl. Aborigènes *m. pl.*
abort [ə'bɔ:t] v. intr. MED., FIG. Avorter.
— v. tr. MED. Faire avorter (a disease, woman).
abortifacient [,æbɔrti'feiʃənt] adj., n. MÉ Abortif *m.*
abortion [ə'bɔ:ʃən] n. MED. Avortement *f. ; to pr cure abortion,* faire avorter. ‖ Avorton *m. ;* œuv manquée *f.*
abortionist [-ist] n. Avorteuse ; faiseuse d'anges (fam.) ; médecin avorteur *m.*
abortive [ə'bɔ:tiv] adj. MED. Abortif. ‖ FIG. Impa

fait, incomplet (rudimentary) ; avorté, raté (unsuccessful).

aboulia [æ'bu:liə] n. MED. Aboulie *f.*

aboulic [-lik] adj. MED. Aboulique.

abound [ə'baund] v. intr. Abonder (*in*, en) ; regorger, grouiller (*with*, de).

about [ə'baut] adv. Autour, à la ronde (all around) ; *to look about*, regarder autour de soi ; *round about*, tout autour. ‖ Près (near) ; *somewhere about*, quelque part par là. ‖ De tous côtés, çà et là ; de-ci de-là (here and there) ; *to travel about*, voyager dans toutes les directions. ‖ Environ, à peu près, presque (approximately) ; *about three thousand men*, dans les trois mille hommes. ‖ Vice versa, à l'envers, à rebours (to a reversed position) ; *to send s. o. to the right about*, envoyer qqn dans le sens opposé. ‖ NAUT. *About ship!*, envoyez! ‖ FAM. Presque (almost) ; *just about ready*, tout juste prêt ; *that's about right*, c'est à peu près juste.
— adj. En mouvement (astir) ; *he is about again*, il est de nouveau sur pied. ‖ En action (prevalent) ; *polio is about*, la polio est dans l'air.
— prep. Autour de (around) ; *about the garden*, autour du jardin. ‖ A travers, parmi ; *about the streets*, par les rues. ‖ Aux alentours de, vers, dans le voisinage de (near to) ; *round about Cork*, près de Cork. ‖ En, dans (here and there in) ; *about the house*, quelque part dans la maison. ‖ Sur (on, with) ; *to have a handkerchief about one*, avoir un mouchoir sur soi. ‖ Au sujet de, à propos de, concernant ; *he told me all about it*, il m'a mis absolument au courant ; *what is it about?*, de quoi s'agit-il ? ; *what about that tea, waiter?*, et ce thé, garçon ? ‖ Approximativement ; *about four o'clock*, vers quatre heures ; *about my height*, à peu près de ma taille. ‖ Occupé ; *to set about one's task*, se mettre au travail ; *what are you about?*, qu'est-ce que vous faites ? (or) fabriquez ? (fam.). ‖ **About to**, sur le point de ; *about to die*, près de mourir. ‖ **About-face**, n. Volte-face ; FIG. Pirouette *f.* ; v. intr. faire volte-face (ou) demi-tour. ‖ **About-ship**, v. intr. NAUT. Virer de bord ; envoyer. ‖ **About-sledge**, n. Masse de forgeron.

above [ə'bʌv] adv. Au-dessus, en haut ; *view from above*, vue plongeante ; *from above*, d'en haut, du ciel. ‖ De plus, davantage ; *over and above*, en sus de, outre. ‖ Ci-dessus. ‖ **Above-mentioned**, adj. Susmentionné. ‖ **Above-named**, adj. Susnommé. ‖ **Above-said**, adj. Susdit.
— prep. Au-dessus de ; *above all*, par-dessus tout ; *above measure*, hors de mesure, d'une manière outrée ; *nature is above art*, la nature surpasse l'art. ‖ En amont de ; *above the lock*, en amont de l'écluse. ‖ Plus haut que (beyond, past) ; *the road above the village*, la route passé le village. ‖ Supérieur à (superior to) ; *above the average*, au-dessus de la moyenne. ‖ Plus de (more than) ; *above thirty*, plus de trente. ‖ **Above-board**, adj. Loyal, franc, ouvert ; adv. *to play above-board*, jouer cartes sur table. ‖ **Above-ground**, adj. TECHN. Extérieur ; au jour (work) ; adv., adj. U. S. Sur terre, bien vivant.
— adj. Ci-dessus mentionné, précité.

abracadabra [,æbrəkə'dæbrə] n. Abracadabra ; formule magique *f.* (incantation). ‖ Jargon *m.*

abrade [ə'breid] v. tr. Gratter, effacer (or) user en frottant. ‖ MED. Ronger. ‖ GEOL. Eroder.

abrasion [ə'breiʒən] n. GEOGR. Erosion *f.* ‖ MED. Ecorchure *f.* ‖ TECHN. Abrasion *f.*

abrasive [ə'breiziv] n., adj. Abrasif *m.* ; *abrasive cloth*, toile émeri.

abreaction [,æbri'ækʃən] n. PSYCH. Abréaction *f.*

abreast [ə'brest] adv. De front, côte à côte, l'un à côté de l'autre ; *four abreast*, par rangs de quatre. ‖ *Abreast of* (or) *with*, parallèlement à, en ligne avec (not behind) ; *to keep abreast of*, se tenir au courant de, suivre les progrès de, suivre.

— adj. ELECTR. *Abreast connection*, couplage en parallèle.

abridge [ə'bridʒ] v. tr. Abréger, résumer ; *abridged account*, résumé, raccourci. ‖ Limiter, diminuer, restreindre (rights). ‖ Priver (s.o.) [*of*, de]. ‖ MATH. Simplifier.

abridgment [-mənt] n. Résumé, abrégé *m.* (abstract). ‖ Diminution, réduction *f.* ‖ JUR. Privation *f.* (of rights). ‖ MATH. Simplification *f.*
— SYN. : ABSTRACT, BRIEF, DIGEST, EPITOME, SUMMARY.

abroach [ə'broutʃ] adv. En perce (cask). ‖ FIG. † En train.

abroad [ə'brɔ:d] adv. Au loin (far and wide) ; *to scatter abroad*, éparpiller aux quatre vents. ‖ En circulation ; *a report is abroad that*, le bruit court que. ‖ Dehors, hors de chez soi (outdoors) ; dehors, à l'extérieur (outside) ; à l'étranger, U. S. en Europe (outside one's own country).

abrogate ['æbrogeit] v. tr. Abroger.

abrogation [,æbro'geiʃən] n. Abrogation *f.*

abrupt [ə'brʌpt] adj. Abrupt, escarpé (steep). ‖ FIG. Décousu (jerky) ; brusque, bourru (gruff) ; brusqué, précipité (hasty).

abruptly [-li] adv. A pic. ‖ FIG. D'une façon abrupte ; brusquement ; avec brusquerie.

abscess ['æbsis] n. MED. Abcès *m.* ‖ FIG. *To pierce the abscess*, crever l'abcès.

abscissa [æb'sisə] (pl. **abscissæ** [-i:]) n. MATH. Abscisse *f.*

abscond [əb'skɔnd] v. intr. JUR. S'enfuir secrètement, déguerpir (*from*, de) ; lever le pied (*with*, avec).

absconder [-ə*] n. Fugitif *s.* ‖ JUR. Contumax, défaillant *m.*

abseil ['æbsail] n. SPORTS. Rappel *m.*
— v. intr. SPORTS. Descendre en rappel.

absence ['æbsns] n. Absence *f.* (action, time) ; éloignement *m.* ; *during the absence of*, en l'absence de. ‖ MILIT. *On leave of absence*, en permission. ‖ JUR. Défaut *m.*, non-comparution *f.* ; *in his absence*, par défaut, par contumace. ‖ FIG. Manque, défaut *m.* ; *absence of mind*, distraction, absence ; *in the absence of*, à défaut de, faute de.

absent [-nt] adj. Absent (not present). ‖ Manquant, défaillant (lacking) ; distrait (not attentive). ‖ **Absent-minded**, adj. Distrait, absent ; absorbé, préoccupé.
— v. tr. *To absent oneself*, s'absenter (*from*, de). ‖ JUR. *To absent oneself*, refuser de comparaître.

absentee [æbsn'ti:] n. Absent *s.* (from school, work) ; manquant *s.* ‖ MILIT. Insoumis *m.* ‖ JUR. Absentéiste *s.*
— adj. *Absentee voter*, électeur par correspondance.

absenteeism [-izm] n. Absentéisme *m.*

absently ['æbsntli] adv. Distraitement.

absinth(e) ['æbsinθ] n. BOT., COMM. Absinthe *f.*

absolute ['æbsəlu:t] adj. Absolu, total : *absolute necessity*, force majeure. ‖ Impérieux, entier, autoritaire ; *absolute judgment*, jugement absolu. ‖ Complet, total, parfait ; *absolute idiot*, parfait crétin. ‖ Illimité, souverain ; *absolute power*, pouvoir absolu. ‖ Réel ; *absolute truth*, vérité absolue. ‖ JUR. Irrévocable ; *decree absolute*, jugement définitif. ‖ CHIM. Pur, absolu (alcool). ‖ PHYS., MUS. Absolu. ‖ AVIAT. Absolu (altitude, ceiling). ‖ GRAMM. *Ablative absolute*, ablatif absolu.
— n. PHILOS. Absolu *m.*

absolutely [-li] adv. Absolument. ‖ Entièrement, totalement (quite). ‖ Complètement, formellement (expressly). ‖ JUR. *Absolutely void*, radicalement nul. ‖ GRAMM. Absolument.

absolution [,æbsə'lu:ʃən] n. Rémission *f.* (of penalty). ‖ JUR. Acquittement *m.* ‖ ECCLES. Absoute *f.* (of the dead) ; absolution *f.* (of sins).

absolutism ['æbsəlu:tizm] n. PHILOS., JUR. Absolutisme *m.* ‖ ECCLES. Prédestination *f.*

absolutory [,æbsə'lu:təri] adj. Absolutoire.

absolve [əb'zɔlv] v. tr. Absoudre (of, de) [a crime]. ‖ Délier, relever (from, de) [an oath]. ‖ JUR. Absoudre, acquitter (s.o.); décharger (from, de) [a penalty].

absonant [əb'sounənt] adj. MUS. Dissonant. ‖ FIG. En désaccord (from, to) avec).

absorb [əb'sɔ:b] v. tr. Absorber (food, water). ‖ AUTOM. Amortir (a shock). ‖ PHYS., JUR. Absorber. ‖ FIG. Absorber (s.o.); to become absorbed in, s'absorber dans.

absorbable [-əbl] adj. Absorbable.

absorbed [-d] adj. Absorbé (sucked up). ‖ FIG. Absorbé (in, dans); pris (in, par).

absorbedly [-dli] adv. D'un air absorbé, avec concentration.

absorbefacient [əb,sɔ:bi'feiʃənt] adj. MED. Résorbant.

absorbent [əb'sɔ:bənt] adj. MED. Absorbant; absorbent cotton, coton hydrophile.
— n. MED. Absorbant.

absorber [əb'sɔ:bə*] n. PHYS., CHIM. Absorbeur m. ‖ AUTOM. Amortisseur m.

absorbing [-iŋ] adj. Absorbant. ‖ Passionnant (novel).

absorption [əb'sɔ:pʃən] n. MED., PHYS. Absorption f. ‖ AUTOM. Amortissement m. (of shocks). ‖ FIG. Concentration f.; absorbement m.

absorptive [-tiv] adj. Absorbant m.

absquatulate [əbs'kwɔtjuleit] v. intr. FAM. Déguerpir, détaler, décamper.

abstain [əbs'tein] v. intr. S'abstenir (from, de); to abstain from meat, faire maigre. ‖ S'abstenir de boissons alcoolisées.

abstainer [-ə*] n. Abstinant, abstème m.

abstaining [-iŋ] n. Abstention f. (from, de). ‖ JUR. Abstention f. (from voting).

abstemious [æb'sti:miəs] adj. Sobre, frugal, abstinent (temperate).

abstemiousness [-nis] n. Sobriété, frugalité, tempérance f.

abstention [æb'stenʃən] n. Abstention f. (from voting). ‖ Abstinence f. (from drinking). ‖ JUR. Renonciation f. (from an inheritance).

abstentionist [-ist] n. JUR. Abstentionniste m.

abstergent [æb'stə:dʒənt] adj., n. Détersif.

abstersion [-ʃən] n. Détersion f.

abstersive [-siv] adj. Détersif. (See ABSTERGENT.)

abstinence ['æbstinəns] n. ECCLES., FIG. Abstinence f. (from, de).

abstinency [-ənsi] n. Habitude de frugalité f.

abstinent [-ənt] adj. Abstinent, tempérant.

abstract ['æbstræct] adj. ARTS, GRAMM., FIG. Abstrait). ‖ FAM. Abstrus (abstruse); théorique (not practical).
— n. Abstrait m.; in the abstract, dans l'abstrait, en théorie. ‖ Abstraction f.; terme abstrait m. ‖ Résumé, abrégé, extrait m. (abridgment). ‖ JUR. Abstract of title, intitulé.
— [æbs'trækt] v. tr. Abstraire (from, à); to abstract fraudulously, soustraire, détourner. ‖ Distraire (from, de) [one's mind]. ‖ Faire abstraction de (an idea). ‖ CHIM. Extraire en distillant, isoler.

abstracted [æbs'træktid] adj. Dégagé, abstrait (from, de). ‖ Distrait (absent-minded); pensif, absorbé (preoccupied); dans la lune (fam.).

abstractedly [-idli] adv. Abstractivement, dans l'abstrait, en théorie. ‖ Distraitement; d'un air distrait.

abstraction [æbs'trækʃən] n. JUR. Soustraction f., détournement m. (of funds). ‖ CHIM. Extraction f. ‖ PHYS. Perte (of heat). ‖ PHILOS., GRAMM. Abstraction f. ‖ FIG. Distraction, préoccupation f.

abstractionist [-ist] n. ARTS. Peintre abstrait m.

abstruse [æbs'tru:s] adj. Abstrus, abscons.

abstruseness [-nis] n. Caractère abstrus, m.

absurd [əb'sə:d] adj. Absurde, stupide, déraison‖ nable. ‖ Ridicule, risible (laughable).

absurdity [-iti] n. Absurdité f.; absurde m. ‖ P‖ Insanité, stupidité f.

absurdly [-li] adv. Absurdement, stupidement.

abundance [ə'bʌndəns] n. Abondance, profusion (plenty); flowers in abundance, une abondance c fleurs. ‖ Foisonnement m.; foule f. (of people). ‖ Abondance, richesse, opulence f. (wealth). ‖ FI‖ Abondance (of heart).

abundant [-ənt] adj. Abondant (plentiful); copieu‖ foisonnant (in, en). ‖ Opulent, riche (in, en); abu‖ dant year, année d'abondance. ‖ JUR. Abondax (proof).

abundantly [-əntli] adv. Abondamment.

aburton [ə'bə:tən] adv. NAUT. En breton.

abuse [ə'bju:z] v. tr. Mésuser de, faire mauva‖ usage de (to misuse). ‖ Dénigrer, médire de, débi‖ ner (fam.) [to disparage]. ‖ Insulter; to abuse s.‖ right and left, accabler qqn d'injures. ‖ Trompe‖ to be abused, faire erreur. ‖ Profaner (one's talen‖ ‖ JUR. Abuser de, violer (a woman).
— [ə'bju:s] m. Abus m.; to remedy abuses, répr‖ mer les abus. ‖ Insulte, injure f.; outrage m. ‖ Dénigrement m.; médisance f. (disparaging). ‖ JU‖ Dommages m. pl.; dégradations f. pl. (to the hig‖ way); viol m. (of a woman). ‖ GRAMM. Empl‖ abusif m.; catachrèse f.; much abused word, m‖ trop souvent mal employé.

abuser [-ə*] n. Personne (f.) qui abuse. ‖ Médisan‖ détracteur (disparager); insulteur m. (reviler). ‖ Séducteur, ravisseur m. (seducer). ‖ † Imposteur r‖ (deceiver).

abusive [ə'bju:siv] adj. Abusif. ‖ Insultant, inj‖ rieux, offensant (language); grossier (person). ‖ GRAMM. Impropre. ‖ † Trompeur.

abusively [-li] adv. Abusivement. ‖ Grossièremer

abusiveness [-nis] n. Grossièreté f.; outrage m.

abut [ə'bʌt] v. intr. (1). Donner (on, sur); about (on, à). ‖ Se toucher, être contigu. ‖ S'appuy‖ (against, contre, sur).
— v. tr. Etre contigu à (or) limitrophe de; to ab‖ the church, s'adosser à l'église. ‖ TECHN. Aboute

abutment [-mənt] n. ARCHIT. Pied-droit m. (of ‖ arch); culée, butée f. (of a bridge); contrefort r‖ (of a church); point m. de poussée (of a vault).

abutter [-ə*] n. JUR. Propriétaire limitrophe; riv‖ rain m.

abuzz [ə'bʌz] adv., adj. Bourdonnant.

abysmal [ə'bizməl] adj. FIG. Insondable.

abyss [ə'bis] n. Abîme, gouffre m. ‖ GEO‖ Abysse m. (ocean depths).

abyssal [-l] adj. ZOOL., GEOL. Abyssal. ‖ FIG. Sa‖ fond.

A.C. [ei'si:] abbr. Alternating current, coura‖ alternatif m.

acacia [ə'keiʃə] n. BOT. Acacia m. ‖ U. S. Gomm‖ arabique f.

academic [ækə'demik] adj. Académique (schola‖ tic). ‖ Spéculatif, théorique, conventionnel (n‖ practical). ‖ Compassé, pédant (formal). ‖ Unive‖ sitaire; classique; academic year, année scolaire. ‖ ARTS. Académique.
— n. Académicien; membre d'une société savant‖ ‖ Universitaire m. ‖ Pl. Arguments académiqu‖ m. pl.; discussions théoriques f. pl. (arguties). ‖ PHILOS. Platonicien m.

academical [-əl] adj. Universitaire.
— n. pl. Costume académique m.

academically [-əli] adv. Académiquement.

academician [ə,kædə'miʃən] n. Académicie‖ membre m. d'une académie.

academy [ə'kædəmi] n. Académie, société f‖ Royal Academy, Académie royale; Salon d‖ Beaux-Arts. ‖ Ecole f.; collège m. ‖ U. S. Pensio‖ nat m. ‖ MILIT., NAUT. Military, Naval Academ‖

Ecole militaire, navale. ‖ Arts. *Academy figure*, académie, nu. ‖ Philos. Ecole platonicienne *f.* ‖ Mus. Conservatoire *m.* (of Music).

canthus [ə'kænθəs] n. Bot., Archit. Acanthe *f.*

carid ['ækərid] n. Zool. Acarien *m.*

carpous [ə'kɑːpəs] adj. Bot. Acarpe.

caulous [ə'kɔːləs] adj. Bot. Acaule.

ccede [æk'siːd] v. intr. Accéder, parvenir, atteindre (*to*, à); entrer en possession (*to*, de) [a post]. ‖ Consentir, donner son adhésion, faire droit, souscrire (*to*, à) [a proposal]. ‖ Se joindre, s'agréger (*to*, à) [a party].

ccelerant [æk'selərənt] n. Techn. Accélérant *m.* ‖ Chim. Catalyseur *m.*

ccelerate [-eit] v. tr. Autom., Techn., Med. Accélérer, activer, hâter, précipiter (movement). — v. intr. S'accélérer (motion). ‖ Fig. S'accentuer (deterioration).

ccelerative [-ətiv] adj. Accélérateur.

cceleration [æk,selə'reiʃən] n. Accélération *f.*; *negative acceleration*, ralentissement. ‖ Autom. Reprise *f.* ‖ Jur. Réduction *f.* de délai d'exécution.

ccelerator [æk'seləreitə*] n. Autom. Accélérateur; champignon *m.* (fam.).

ccelerometer [æk,selə'rɔmitə*] n. Accéléromètre *m.*

ccent ['æksənt] n. Accent tonique *m.* (emphasis); accent *m.* (manner of pronouncing). ‖ Accent *m.* (tone); *an accent of displeasure*, un ton de mécontentement; *in broken accents*, d'une voix entrecoupée. ‖ Accent, temps *m.* (rhythmic stress). ‖ Manière (or) marque distinctive; *accent of cruelty*, élément de cruauté. ‖ Mus., Arts, Gramm. Accent *m.*
— [æk'sent] v. tr. Accentuer (to emphasize). ‖ Gramm. Mettre des accents. ‖ Fig. Intensifier, augmenter.

ccentual [æk'sentjuəl] adj. Appuyé sur l'accent (or) l'accentuation; rythmique. ‖ Accentuel (poetry).

ccentuate [-eit] v. tr. Accentuer, souligner, faire ressortir (a detail). ‖ Augmenter (an effect). ‖ U. S. Accentuer (a word).

ccentuation [æk,sentju'eiʃən] n. Accentuation *f.* ‖ Fig. Aggravation, augmentation.

ccept [ək'sept] v. tr. Accepter; agréer; recevoir favorablement. ‖ Se soumettre à; se plier à; se résigner à (one's fate). ‖ Se charger de; assumer (a responsibility). ‖ Admettre, accueillir, accepter (s.o.'s apology). ‖ Comm. Accepter (a bill); prendre livraison de (goods). ‖ Jur. Adopter, approuver (a report). ‖ Eccles. *To accept persons*, faire acception des personnes.

cceptable [-əbl] adj. Acceptable, convenable; notable, possible (fam.). ‖ Agréable (*to*, à). ‖ Opportun, bienvenu; *your offer is very acceptable*, votre offre vient fort à propos.

cceptably [-əbli] adv. D'une manière acceptable (or) agréable.

cceptance [-əns] n. Acceptation (of appointment); admission *f.* (of a piece of work, of s.o.); *acceptance test*, épreuve d'admissibilité; essai de réception; *to qualify one's acceptance*, accepter sous réserve; *to secure acceptance of sth.*, faire accepter qqch. ‖ Agrément, consentement *m.*; approbation *f.* (approval); *to find acceptance*, trouver créance; *to meet with acceptance*, rallier les suffrages. ‖ Comm. Acceptation (of a bill); *acceptance house*, banque d'escompte des effets étrangers. ‖ Jur. *Acceptance of a judgment*, acquiescement à un jugement; *acceptance of persons*, acception de personnes. ‖ Theatr. Réception (of a play).

cceptation [,æksep'teiʃən] n. † Acceptation *f.* ‖ Gramm. Acception *f.*

ccepted [ək'septid] adj. Accepté, reçu, admis.

cceptor [-ə*] n. Comm. Accepteur *m.* (see drawee); *acceptor for honour*, intervenant, avaliseur, avaliste.

ccess ['ækses] n. Accès, abord *m.*; *difficult of*

access, d'un abord difficile, peu abordable (person); d'accès difficile (place); *to desire access to*, désirer accéder auprès de; *to give access to*, donner accès à, commander l'accès à. ‖ Med. Accès *m.*; crise, attaque *f.* (lit. and fig.). ‖ Jur. Droit *m.* de passage (right of way); relations sexuelles *f. pl.* (sexual intercourse). ‖ Fig. Accès (of anger); élan (of patriotism).

accessary [æk'sesəri] n. Jur. Complice, co-auteur *s.*; malfaiteur (*s.*) par accessoire; *accessary before an offence*, complice d'un crime, d'un délit; *accessary after an offence*, coupable de recel (or) d'assistance à malfaiteur.
— adj. Jur. Complice.

accessibility [æk,sesi'biliti] n. Accessibilité *f.*; facilité *f.* d'accès.

accessible [æk'sesibl] adj. Abordable (person); accessible (place). ‖ Fig. Ouvert, accessible (*to*, à).

accession [æk'seʃən] n. Accès *m.*; admission *f.* (*to*, auprès de). ‖ Entrée en jouissance *f.* (to an estate). ‖ Avènement (of a king); accession *f.* (to power); *accession to manhood*, arrivée à l'âge d'homme. ‖ Accroissement *m.* (increase); augmentation, addition *f.*; *accessions book*, registre des additions (in a library); *accession to territory*, accroissement de territoire. ‖ Adhésion *f.* (to a party). ‖ Techn. Admission *f.* (of air). ‖ Fig. Assentiment *m.*

accessorily [æk'sesərili] adv. Accessoirement.

accessory [-əri] adj. Accessoire, subsidiaire (*to*, à); auxiliaire, secondaire (additional). ‖ Subordonné (*to*, à).
— n. Techn., Autom. Accessoire, appareillage, *m.*; *automobile accessories*, accessoires d'automobile. ‖ Comm. Accessoire *m.*; *toilet accessories*, objets de toilette. ‖ Jur. Complice *m.* (*to*, de) [a crime]; promoteur *m.*; *accessory before the fact*, complice par instigation.

accidence ['æksidəns] n. Gramm. Morphologie *f.* ‖ Fig. Rudiments *m. pl.*

accident [-ənt] n. Evénement *m.* (unexpected happening). ‖ Accident *m.* (mishap); *accident to a third party*, accident causé à un tiers; *to meet with an accident*, avoir un accident. ‖ Hasard *m.*; chance *f.*; *by accident*, accidentellement; *by a mere accident*, par un pur hasard. ‖ Geogr., Geol., Eccles., Mus. Accident. ‖ Autom. *Motoring, road accident*, accident de voiture, de la circulation. ‖ Aviat. *Aircraft accident*, accident d'avion. ‖ Naut. *Accidents at sea*, fortunes de mer; *accident to the engines*, avarie aux machines.

accidental [,æksi'dentl] adj. Accidentel; fortuit (circumstances). ‖ Occasionnel (incidental). ‖ Accessoire, secondaire, subsidiaire (non essential). ‖ Mus. Accidentel. ‖ Arts. *Accidental lights*, contre-jour, reflets, effets de lumière secondaires.
— n. Mus. Accident *m.*

accidentally [-əli] adv. Accidentellement; fortuitement; incidemment; par hasard.

acclaim [ə'kleim] v. tr. Acclamer (to applaud). ‖ Proclamer (to hail as).
— n. Acclamation *f.*

acclaimer [-ə*] n. Acclamateur *m.*

acclamation [,æklə'meiʃən] n. Acclamation *f.*

acclimatation [ə,klaimə'teiʃən] n. Acclimatement *m.*

acclimate [ə'klai,mit] v. U. S. Acclimater.

acclimatization [ə,klaimətai'zeiʃən], U. S. **acclimation** [əkli'meiʃən] n. Acclimatation *f.*; accoutumance *f.* (*to*, à).

acclimatize [ə'klaimətaiz] v. intr. Acclimater (*to*, à); *to become acclimatized*, s'acclimater. — v. tr. S'accoutumer à, s'acclimater à,

acclivity [ə'kliviti] n. Montée, côte *f.*

acclivous [-əs] adj. Montant, en côte.

accolade [,æko'leid] n. Accolade *f.*

accommodate [ə'kɔmədeit] v. tr. Accommoder,

conformer, ajuster, adapter (to, à); *to accommodate oneself to*, s'adapter (or) s'accommoder à. ‖ Harmoniser, mettre d'accord, concilier; *the dispute has been accommodated*, le différend a été réglé; *to accommodate matters*, arranger les choses. ‖ Equiper, fournir (with, de); *to accommodate s.o. with dinner*, servir à dîner à qqn. ‖ Rendre service à; *to accommodate a friend with a loan*, obliger un ami en lui prêtant de l'argent. ‖ Loger, abriter; caser (fam.) [to lodge].

accommodating [-iŋ] adj. Obligeant, serviable (obliging). ‖ Accommodant, arrangeant, coulant (person). ‖ Complaisant (husband); facile (morale).

accommodatingly [-iŋli] adv. Avec complaisance.

accommodation [ə,kɔmə'deiʃən] n. Accommodation *f.*; ajustement *m.* (to, à). ‖ Complaisance *f.*: *spirit of accommodation*, esprit d'accommodement. ‖ Arrangement, compromis *m.*; *to come to an accommodation with*, aboutir à un accord avec. ‖ Commodités, facilités *f. pl.*; *it would be a great accommodation for him*, cela l'arrangerait bien. ‖ Pl. Logement, hébergement *m.*; place *f.*; *accommodations for visitors*, facilités de logement pour visiteurs; *book accommodation at the hotel*, retenez une chambre à l'hôtel; *assistance and accommodation*, secours et abri. ‖ Installation *f.* ‖ NAUT. Aménagements *m. pl.*; *accommodation ladder*, échelle de coupée. ‖ JUR. *Accommodation land*, terrain acquis en vue d'améliorer le terrain contigu; *accommodation party*, avaliseur. ‖ COMM. *Accommodation bill*, effet de complaisance. ‖ FIN. Prêt d'argent *m.*; avances *f. pl.* ‖ CH. DE F. U. S. *Accommodation train*, train omnibus. ‖ MED. Accommodation (of the eye). ‖ **Accommodation-unit**, n. Bloc-logement *m.*

accompaniment [ə'kʌmpənimənt] n. Accompagnement *m.* ‖ MUS. Accompagnement; *to sing to one's own accompaniment*, chanter en s'accompagnant. ‖ BLAS. Accompagnement.

accompanist [-ist] n. MUS. Accompagnateur *m.*; accompagnatrice *f.*

accompany [-i] v. tr. Accompagner, suivre (to attend). ‖ Faire suivre, accompagner (with, de); compléter (with, par). ‖ MUS. Accompagner (à, on).

accomplice [ə'kʌmplis] n. JUR. Complice *m.* ‖ Compère (of a conjurer).

accomplish [ə'kʌmpliʃ] v. tr. Accomplir, exécuter, remplir (a promise). ‖ Réaliser (a desire, a prediction). ‖ Atteindre, aboutir à (an end); *to accomplish one's object*, arriver à ses fins. ‖ Parcourir (a mile). ‖ Achever, terminer (a task).

accomplished [-t] adj. Accompli (fact, years); accompli, achevé (task). ‖ Accompli (young person).

accomplishment [-mənt] n. Accomplissement *m.*; exécution, réalisation *f.*; *difficult of accomplishment*, d'exécution difficile. ‖ Chose réalisée, œuvre accomplie *f.* (achievement). ‖ Pl. Talents, arts d'agrément *m.*

accord [ə'kɔ:d] v. tr. Accorder; concéder; octroyer (to, à); *to accord a request*, faire droit à une requête. ‖ † Mettre d'accord; arranger (the material).
— v. intr. S'accorder; concorder; être d'accord (with, avec, sur).
— n. Accord; consentement *m.*; entente *f.*; *in accord with*, d'accord avec; *of my own accord*, de mon plein gré; spontanément; *out of accord with*, en désaccord avec; *with one accord*, d'un commun accord. ‖ Pacte, traité *m.* ‖ ARTS, MUS. Harmonie *f.*; accord *m.* ‖ JUR. Novation *f.*

accordance [-əns] n. Accord *m.*; conformité *f.* (with, avec); *in accordance with*, conformément à, en harmonie avec, suivant. ‖ Octroi *m.*; concession *f.* (to, à).

accordant [-ənt] adj. Concordant. ‖ D'accord (with, avec); conforme (with, to, à).

according [-iŋ] adv. **According as**, selon que, suivant que, dans la mesure où. ‖ **According to**, conformément à; suivant, selon, d'après; à en juger par.

accordingly [-iŋli] adv. En conséquence (therefore). ‖ Conformément; en correspondance avec, à l'avenant (correspondingly); *she was grateful t him accordingly*, elle lui témoignait une reconnaissance en rapport avec ses bienfaits.

accordion [ə'kɔ:diən] n. MUS. Accordéon *m.* **Accordion-player**, n. MUS. Accordéoniste *s.* **Accordion-pleated**, adj. Plissé soleil.

accordionist [-ist] n. MUS. Accordéoniste *s.*

accost [ə'kɔst] v. tr. Accoster; approcher; aborder; s'adresser à. ‖ Racoler (prostitute).
— n. Abord *m.* (action). ‖ Racolage *m.*

accouchement [ə'ku:ʃmã] n. MED. Accouchement *m.*

accoucheur [,æku:'ʃə*] n. MED. Accoucheur *m*

accoucheuse [-'ʃə:z] n. MED. Sage-femme, accoucheuse *f.*

account [ə'kaunt] v. tr. Estimer, considérer comme, prendre pour; *to account oneself lucky*, s'estime heureux; *to be accounted rare*, passer pour rare
— v. intr. **To account for**, rendre compte de, just fier de; *to account for one's stewardship*, rendr compte d'une gestion; *to account for a cash credi* justifier de l'utilisation du crédit. ‖ Expliquer *I cannot account for it*, je ne me l'explique pa je n'y comprends rien, j'y perds mon latin. ‖ SPORTS. Avoir au tableau (or) à son actif (hea of game). ‖ FAM. **To account for**, régler son compt à (s.o.). ‖ † *To account of*, estimer, faire cas d
— n. MATH. Calcul *m.*; *taking everything int account*, tout calculé. ‖ FIN. Compte *m.*; *account payable*, dettes passives; *account stated*, arrêté d comptes; *bank account*, compte en banque; *cas account*, compte de caisse; *dealing for the accoun* négociations à terme; *falsification of accounts*, fa sification d'écritures comptables; *in account with* en compte avec; *to keep the accounts*, tenir la comptabilité (or) les comptes; *to keep a stric account*, tenir un compte rigoureux. ‖ FIN., COMM Note *f.*; état *m.*; *stock-record account*, état de marchandises en magasin; *to settle an accoun* régler une note; *to take into account*, faire état d (sth.). ‖ FIN. Acompte *m.*; *twelve pounds o account*, un acompte de douze livres, douze livre à valoir. ‖ Récit, exposé *m.*; relation, descriptic *f.*; *by his own account*, à l'en croire, d'après s dires; *by all accounts*, au dire de tous, de l'av général; *to give an account of*, faire un expos (or) un compte rendu (or) la relation de. ‖ Règle ments (m.) de comptes; *to call to account*, demande des comptes à. ‖ Estime *f.*; égard *m.*; *on accou of*, à cause de, en considération de, sous le chef d *on every account*, sous tous les rapports; *on n account*, en aucun cas, sous aucun prétexte; *on many accounts*, à divers titres; *to make litt account of*, faire peu de cas de; *to take into account*, avoir égard à. ‖ Profit *m.*; *for the accou of*, pour le compte de; *to give a good account o oneself*, donner une bonne idée de soi, s'en tir à son avantage, bien se défendre; *to turn account*, tirer parti de, mettre à profit. ‖ Impo tance, valeur *f.*; *man of no account*, homme sa importance, quantité négligeable; *of some accoun* notable, qui compte.

accountability [ə,kauntə'biliti] n. Responsabilité

accountable [ə'kauntəbl] adj. Responsable; com table (for, de; to, vis-à-vis, envers, devant, à l'égar de). ‖ Explicable. ‖ FIN., COMM. *Accountab receipt*, quittance comptable, reçu certifié.

accountancy [-ənsi] n. FIN. Comptabilité *f.*; cha tered accountancy, expertise comptable.

accountant [-ənt] n. FIN. Comptable, agent com table; *accountant general*, trésorier-payeur gén ral; *chief accountant*, chef comptable; *chartered accountant*, *U. S. certified public accountant (C. P. A.)*, expert comptable.

ccounting [-iŋ] n. FIN. Comptabilité *f.*; *accounting period*, exercice.

ccoutre [ə'ku:tə*] v. tr. Accoutrer. ‖ MILIT. Equiper (*with*, de).

ccoutrement [-mənt] n. Accoutrement *m.* ‖ MILIT. Equipement, fourniment *m.*

ccredit [ə'kredit] v. tr. Accréditer (*to*, auprès de) [s.o., sth.]. ‖ Mettre sur le compte de; *to accredit sth. to s.o. (or) s.o. with sth.*, attribuer qqch. à qqn; *to be accredited with having said*, être réputé (or) censé avoir dit.

ccredited [-id] adj. Accrédité (person); sous contrat (educational institution). ‖ Accrédité, répandu, couramment admis (belief). ‖ AGRIC. Garanti par l'inspection sanitaire (milk, cattle).

ccrete [ə'kri:t] v. intr. S'accroître par addition (or) concrétion. ‖ Adhérer, s'attacher (*to*, à). ‖ JUR. *Accreted land*, accrue.
— v. tr. Attirer; grouper; enrôler (s.o.).

ccretion [ə'kriʃən] n. Accroissement *m.*; concrétion *f.* ‖ Additions progressives *f. pl.* (*to*, à). ‖ JUR. Accrue *f.* (land); majoration *f.* (increase). ‖ MED. Soudure *f.*

ccrue [ə'kru:] v. intr. Revenir, échoir (*to*, à) [advantages]. ‖ Provenir, dériver (*from*, de). ‖ FIN. S'accroître, s'accumuler.

ccruing [-iŋ] adj. Afférent (*to*, à).

ccumulate [ə'kju:mjuleit] v. tr. Accumuler, amonceler, entasser. ‖ ELECTR. Emmagasiner.
— v. intr. S'accumuler, s'entasser.

ccumulation [ə,kju:mju'leiʃən] n. Accumulation *f.*; entassement, amoncellement *m.* (action); amas, tas *m.* (heap). ‖ FIN. Accroissement *m.* (of capital); thésaurisation *f.*; *improper accumulations*, réserves abusives. ‖ ELECTR. Emmagasinage *m.* ‖ JUR. Cumul *m.* ‖ MED. Dépôt *m.* (of pus).

ccumulative [ə'kju:mjuleitiv] adj. Thésauriseur (person); qui s'accumule; accumulé (thing). ‖ JUR. *Accumulative sentence*, cumul de peines.

ccumulator [-ə*] n. Thésauriseur *m.* ‖ ELECTR. Accumulateur, accu *m.* ‖ **Accumulator-capacity indicator**, n. Accumètre *m.*

ccuracy ['ækjurəsi] n. Exactitude, précision *f.* ‖ MILIT., MUS. Justesse *f.*

ccurate [-it] adj. Exact, précis. ‖ Rigoureux (demonstration); fidèle (memory, translation); attentif (reader); net (view); *accurate eye*, coup d'œil juste.

ccurately [-itli] adv. Avec précision (or) justesse; exactement; fidèlement.

ccursed [ə'kə:sid] adj. Maudit. ‖ Détestable, haïssable (odious).

ccusable [ə'kju:zəbl̩] adj. Accusable (*of*, de).

ccusal [ə'kju:z1] n. Accusation *f.*

ccusation [,ækju'zeiʃən] n. Accusation, incrimination *f.*; acte (*m.*) d'accusation.

ccusative [ə'kju:zətiv] adj., n. GRAMM. Accusatif *m.*; *in the accusative*, à l'accusatif.

ccusatorial [,əkju:zətɔ:riəl] adj. JUR. Accusatoire.

ccusatory [ə'kju:zətəri] adj. Accusateur, accusatrice. ‖ Accusatoire.

ccuse [ə'kju:z] v. tr. Accuser, taxer, inculper, incriminer (*of*, de); *to accuse oneself of*, s'accuser de.

ccused [-d] n. JUR. Accusé, inculpé, prévenu *s.*

ccuser [-ə*] n. Accusateur *m.*; accusatrice *f.*

ccustom [ə'kʌstəm] v. tr. Accoutumer, habituer (*to*, à); *to accustom oneself to*, s'accoutumer (or) s'habituer (or) se faire à; se familiariser avec, s'aguerrir contre.

ccustomed [-d] adj. Accoutumé, habitué, fait (*to*, à); *to become (or) get accustomed to*, se faire à, être habitué à. ‖ Coutumier, habituel.

ace [eis] n. As *m.* (at cards); un *m.* (indice, dominoes, tennis). ‖ Quantité minime *f.*; brin, atome *m.*; *an ace lower*, un rien plus bas; *within an ace of*, à deux doigts de, au bord de. ‖ AVIAT. As *m.* ‖ FIG. *To have an ace up one's sleeve*, avoir un atout dans sa manche; *to play one's ace of trumps*, jouer sa meilleure carte.
— adj. FAM. Epatant, formidable.

acephalous [ə'sefələs] adj. ZOOL. Acéphale.

acerb(ic) [ə'sə:b(ik)] adj. Acide, âcre, âpre (taste); acerbe (speech, manner).

acerbity [ə'sə:biti] n. Acreté, âpreté *f.* ‖ FIG. Aigreur, acerbité *f.*

acervate ['æsəveit] v. tr. Accumuler, entasser.
— [-it] adj. BOT. En grappe, en bouquet.

acescent [ə'sesn̩t] adj. Acescent, aigrissant.

acetabulum [,æse'tæbjuləm] (pl. **acetabula** [-ə]) n. † Acétabule *m.* ‖ ZOOL. Suçoir *m.*; ventouse *f.* ‖ MED. Cotyle *f.*

acetaldehyde [,æsi'tældi,haid] n. CHIM. Acétaldéhyde *m.*, aldéhyde acétique *m.*

acetamide [ə'sɛtəmaid] n. CHIM. Acétamide *m.*

acetate ['æsiteit] n. CHIM. Acétate *m.*

acetic [ə'setik] adj. CHIM. Acétique.

acetification [ə,setifi'keiʃən] n. CHIM. Acétification *f.*

acetify [ə'setifai] v. tr. (2). CHIM. Acétifier.
— v. intr. Aigrir.

acetone ['æsitoun] m. CHIM. Acétone *m.*

acetous [-əs] adj. CHIM. Acéteux.

acetyl ['æsi,tail] n. CHIM. Acétyle *m.*
— adj. TECHN. *Acetyl silk*, acétate (fabric).

acetylcholine [,æsitail'kouli:n] n. MED. Acétylcholine *f.*

acetylene [ə'setili:n] n. CHIM. Acétylène *m.*

ache [eik] v. tr. Faire mal, faire souffrir, être douloureux; *my head aches*, j'ai mal à la tête. ‖ FAM. *To be aching to*, brûler de, avoir envie de.
— n. Douleur *f.*; mal *m.* ‖ FIG. Peine *f.*

achievable [ə'tʃi:vəbl] adj. Faisable, réalisable.

achieve [ə'tʃi:v] v. tr. Accomplir, exécuter, mener à bien (to accomplish); réaliser (an enterprise, a wish). ‖ Atteindre (an end); parvenir à (fame); se faire (a good reputation); obtenir (success); acquérir (wealth). ‖ MILIT. Remporter (a victory).

achievement [-mənt] n. Accomplissement *m.*; exécution *f.* (achieving). ‖ Œuvre remarquable, réussite *f.*; travail remarquable *m.* (masterpiece). ‖ Hauts faits *m. pl.* (feat). ‖ PHILOS., MED. *Achievement quotient*, coefficient mental.

Achilles [ə'kili:z] n. Achille (hero); *Achilles' heel*, talon d'Achille (med., fig.); *Achilles' tendon*, tendon d'Achille.

aching ['eikiŋ] n. MED. Douleur *f.*
— adj. Douloureux (void); *aching all over*, tout moulu, perclus de douleurs.

achromatic [,ækro'mætik] adj. Achromatique.

achromatism [ə'kroumətizm] n. Achromatisme *m.*

achromatopsy [ə'kroumə,tɔpsi] n. MED. Achromatopsie *f.* (See DALTONISM.)

achy ['eiki] adj. Souffrant, mal fichu (fam.); *my head, my throat is achy*, j'ai mal à la tête, à la gorge.

acid ['æsid] adj. Acide (taste); *acid drop*, bonbon acidulé. ‖ Acide (tone of voice); mordant (remark).
— n. CHIM. Acide *m.* ‖ FAM. Acide *m.* (L.S.D.). ‖ FIG. *To give the acid test to sth.*, mettre qqch. à l'épreuve. ‖ **Acid-head**, n. FAM. Habitué (*s.*) du L.S.D. ‖ **Acid-proof**, adj. Inattaquable par les acides.

acidic [-ə'sidik] adj. CHIM. Acide.

acidification [ə,sidifi'keiʃən] n. Acidification *f.*

acidify [ə'sidifai] v. tr. (2). Acidifier.

acidity [-ti] n. Acidité *f.*

acidize ['æsidaiz] v. tr. CHIM. Acidifier.

acidosis [,æsi'dousis] n. MED. Acidose *f.*

acidulate [ə'sidjuleit] v. tr. Aciduler.
acidulous [-əs] adj. Acidulé (lit. and fig.).
acierage ['æsiəridʒ] n. TECHN. Aciérage m.
ack-ack ['æk'æk] n. MILIT., FAM. Défense (f.) antiaérienne (or) contre avions, D. C. A.; *ack-ack guns,* canons antiaériens.
acknowledge [,ək'nɔlidʒ] v. tr. Reconnaître, admettre, convenir de (to admit); avouer (to avow); *to acknowledge one's guilt,* se reconnaître coupable. ‖ Manifester sa gratitude pour; *to acknowledge a gift,* remercier d'un cadeau et y répondre; *how to acknowledge your kindness,* comment m'acquitter envers vous. ‖ Accuser réception de (a letter). ‖ JUR. Reconnaître (a child).
acknowledged [-d] adj. Reconnu, notoire.
acknowledgment [-mənt] n. Reconnaissance f. (of a fact, an obligation). ‖ Remerciement m., reconnaissance f. (of, pour) [s.o.'s help]. ‖ Aveu m. (of a misdeed). ‖ COMM. Reçu, récépissé m.; quittance f.; *acknowledgment of receipt,* accusé de réception; *acknowledgment of indebtedness,* reconnaissance de dette.
aclinic [ə'klinik] adj. PHYS. Aclinique.
acme ['ækmi] n. Point culminant, comble, faîte m.; apogée m. (see CULMINATION); *the acme of perfection,* la perfection même.
acne ['ækni] n. MED. Acné m.
acolyte ['ækɔlait] n. ECCLES., FIG. Acolyte m.
aconite ['ækɔnait] n. BOT. Aconit m.
acorn ['eikɔ:n] n. BOT. Gland m. (of an oak). ‖ **Acorn-crop,** n. Glandée f. ‖ **Acorn-cup,** n. BOT. Cupule f.
acoustic [ə'kustik] adj. PHYS., MED. Acoustique.
acoustics [-s] n. pl. PHYS. Acoustique f.
acquaint [ə'kweint] v. tr. Informer, aviser, instruire (with, de); renseigner (with, sur); *to acquaint s.o. with a fact,* faire part d'un fait à qqn; *to acquaint s.o. with his duties,* mettre qqn au courant de ses fonctions (or) obligations. ‖ *To be acquainted with,* connaître (s.o., sth.); être au courant de (sth.); *to become acquainted with,* faire la connaissance de (s.o.); prendre connaissance de, être informé de (sth.); *to make two persons acquainted,* mettre deux personnes en relation; *they have long been acquainted,* il y a longtemps qu'ils se connaissent.
acquaintance [-əns] n. Connaissance f. (with, de); *further acquaintance,* plus ample connaissance; *old acquaintances,* de vieilles connaissances; *to make s.o.'s acquaintance,* faire la connaissance de qqn; *to make acquaintance with,* faire connaissance avec (s.o.); *to improve upon acquaintance,* gagner à être connu. ‖ Relations f. pl. (with, avec); *a wide acquaintance,* des relations très étendues. ‖ Familiarité f. (with, avec); connaissance f. (with, de) [art, politics].
acquaintanceship [-ənsʃip] n. Fait d'être en relations. ‖ Relations f. pl.
acquest [ə'kwest] n. Acquisition f. ‖ JUR. Acquêt m.
acquiesce [ækwi'es] v. intr. Acquiescer; consentir; donner son assentiment (in, à) [to consent]. ‖ Accepter, se soumettre, se plier (in, à) [to assent].
acquiescence [-ņs] n. Acquiescement, assentiment m. (in, à) [agreement]; soumission f. (in, à) [assent]; consentement tacite m. (consent); ratification f.
acquiescent [-ņt] adj. Consentant. ‖ Accommodant, conciliant.
acquire [ə'kwaiə*] v. tr. Gagner (money); acquérir (by, par; for, pour) [wealth]. ‖ Entrer en possession de. ‖ Contracter, prendre (a habit); *acquired characteristic,* caractère acquis; *to acquire a taste for,* prendre goût à. ‖ Apprendre (a language).
acquirement [-mənt] n. Acquisition f. (of, de). ‖ Connaissances f. pl.; *a man of great acquirements,* un homme qui a beaucoup d'acquis.

acquirer [-ə*] n. COMM. Acquéreur m.
acquisition [,ækwi'ziʃən] n. Acquisition f. (act; thing). ‖ FAM. Recrue f. (to, pour).
acquisitive [ə'kwizitiv] adj. Apre au gain, thésau riseur. (See GREEDY.)
acquisitiveness [-tivnis] n. Apreté (f.) au gain.
acquit [ə'kwit] v. tr. (1). Acquitter; payer; régle (a debt). ‖ Absoudre (of, de) [s.o.]. ‖ Acquitter exonérer, décharger, dégager (of, de) [obligation]. ‖ Accomplir, s'acquitter de (a promise); *to acqu oneself well of,* bien se tirer de. ‖ JUR. Acquitte par manque de preuve; décharger (of, de).
acquittal [-l] n. Acquittement m. (of a debt). ‖ Exé cution f.; accomplissement m. (of a duty). ‖ COMM Acquit; quitus m. ‖ JUR. Acquittement m.
acquittance [-əns] n. COMM., FIN. Acquittement m (act); décharge; quittance f.; acquit m. (receipt).
acre ['eikə*] n. AGRIC. Acre f.; arpent m. ‖ † Cham m.; *God's acre,* cimetière; *ancestral acres,* terr ancestrale, bien de famille.
acrid ['ækrid] adj. Acre. ‖ FIG. Acerbe, caustique
acridity [ə'kriditi] n. Acreté, f. ‖ Pl. Remarque acerbes f.
acridness ['ækridnis] n. FIG. Acrimonie f.
acrimonious [,ækri'mounjəs] adj. Acrimonieux.
acrimony ['ækriməni] n. Acrimonie (bitterness) parole acrimonieuse f. (speech).
acrobat ['ækrəbæt] n. SPORTS. Acrobate s.
acrobatic [,ækrə'bætik] adj. SPORTS. Acrobatique
acrobatics [-s] n. pl. SPORTS, FIG. Acrobatie f.
acromegaly [,ækrou'megəli] n. MED. Acroméga lie f.
acronym ['ækrənim] n. Sigle m.
acrophobia [,ækrə'foubiə] n. PSYCH. Acropho bie f.
acropolis [ə'krɔpəlis] n. ARCHIT. Acropole f.
across [ə'krɔ:s] prép. En travers de; au travers de *across the fields,* à travers champs; *to walk acro the hall,* traverser le vestibule. ‖ D'un côté à l'autr par le travers; *across the street,* de l'autre côté d la rue; *a bridge across the Seine,* un pont sur l Seine. ‖ A la rencontre de, en contact avec; *to com across s.o.,* rencontrer qqn par hasard; *it just cam across my mind,* cela venait de me traverser l'espri ‖ **Across-the-board,** adj. Général, généralisé, pou tout le monde.
— adv. En travers; de l'autre côté; *to come acros.* traverser.
acrostic [ə'krɔstik] n. Acrostiche m.
acrylic [ə'krilik] adj. CHIM. Acrylique.
act [ækt] n. Action f.; acte m.; *act of justic of war,* acte de justice, de guerre; *caught in th very act,* pris sur le fait; *in the act of,* sur le poir de, prêt à. ‖ Loi f.; *Act of Parliament,* loi (o décret adopté par le Parlement; *act of State,* act de gouvernement. ‖ JUR. Acte; *act of God,* cas d force majeure, cause naturelle; *act of bankruptc; dépôt de bilan, déclaration d'insolvabilité; *act o petition,* procédure de référé. ‖ THEATR. Acte n (of a play); numéro m. (in circus). ‖ FAM. Comédie allure affectée f.
— v. intr. Agir; prendre des mesures; se compo ter; *to act one's age,* se conduire selon son âge *to act for the best,* faire pour le mieux. ‖ Fair office, exercer les fonctions (as, de). ‖ Agir (o sur; upon, d'après); *to act for,* agir au nom d représenter (s.o.); *to act up to,* agir conformémer à. ‖ TECHN. Fonctionner, marcher. ‖ THEATR. Jouc (in, dans); *to act out,* jouer jusqu'au bout; *to a over,* répéter de bout en bout. ‖ FAM. U. S. T *act up,* se conduire avec gaminerie (or) mal.
— v. tr. Exécuter, réaliser (a project). ‖ THEAT Jouer, tenir (a part); *to act the king,* tenir le rô du roi. ‖ FIG. Simuler, feindre; *to act a part,* joue la comédie; *to act the fool,* faire l'idiot.
acting [-iŋ] adj. Faisant fonction de; suppléan intérimaire; provisoire; *acting manager,* admini

trateur gérant ; *acting order*, délégation de pouvoir. || En fonction, en exercice (functioning). || Agissant, efficace. || Techn. *Single-acting*, à simple effet. || Theatr. Jouable (version) ; *acting company*, troupe de comédiens.
— n. Fait d'agir *m.*, action *f.* || Theatr. Jeu *m.* (act, art). || Fig. Comédie, simulation *f.*

actinia [æk'tiniə] n. Zool. Actinie *f.*
— N. B. Notez les deux pluriels : *actiniæ, actinias.*

actinic [-k] adj. Phys. Actinique.

actinium [-əm] m. Chim. Actinium *m.*

actinometer [‚ækti'nɔmitə*] n. Phys. Actinomètre *m.*

action ['ækʃən] n. Action *f.; line of action*, ligne de conduite, plan d'action. || Activité *f.; to take action*, prendre une initiative, intervenir. || Acte *m.; illegal action*, acte illégal ; *splendid action*, magnifique exploit, haut fait. || Action, influence *f.; to have an action on*, influer sur, avoir une action sur ; *double-action*, à double effet. || Allure *f.; high-action*, allure relevée. || Mesure *f.; disciplinary action*, mesure disciplinaire ; *to take action*, prendre des mesures effectives. || Mouvement *m.;* action *f.; to put in action*, mettre en mouvement. || Theatr. Action, intrigue *f.* || Techn. Marche *f.;* mécanisme, mouvement *m.; in full action*, en pleine marche ; *out of action*, hors de service (or) d'usage ; *to put out of action*, détraquer. || Jur. Action (*against*, contre ; *upon*, prise à la suite de) ; litige *m.; brought to action*, poursuivi en justice ; *rights of action*, droit d'ester ; *to bring the law into action*, faire intervenir la loi, mettre la justice en branle ; *to institute an action*, introduire une instance ; *to take action against*, citer, poursuivre, attaquer en justice, entamer des poursuites contre. || Milit. Action *f.; action stations*, positions de combat ; *to be in action*, opérer ; *to come into action*, engager le combat ; *to go into action*, aller au feu ; *to see action*, prendre part au combat ; *killed in action*, tué à l'ennemi.
— v. tr. Jur. Actionner, intenter un procès à.

actionable [-əb] adj. Jur. Actionnable.

actionless [-lis] adj. Chim. Inerte.

activate ['æktiveit] v. tr. Activer, accélérer. || Milit. Organiser. || Phys. Activer.

activation [‚ækti'veiʃən] n. Phys. Activation *f.*

active [-iv] adj. Actif (life, person) ; diligent (person) [see BUSY]. || Actif (forces) ; *to be an active party to*, prendre une part active à. || Milit. Effectif ; actif ; *active duty*, activité de service ; *active list*, cadres de l'active. || Jur. *Active consideration*, examen approfondi ; *in active employment*, en service actif. || Med. *Active immunity*, immunité par les anticorps ; *active poison*, poison rapide. || Gramm. Actif. || Techn. *Active cell*, élément d'accu chargé, pile amorcée. || Fin. Actif (debt, funds, market). || **Active-minded**, adj. A l'esprit actif.

activity [æk'tiviti] n. Activité f. (quality). || Pl. Activités, occupations ; menées *f.; within his activities*, dans le cadre de ses fonctions (or) de ses activités. || Fin., Aviat. Activité *f.*

activism ['æktivizm̩] n. Activisme *m.*

activist [-ist] n. Activiste *s.*

actor ['æktə*] n. Theatr. Acteur *m.; film* (ou) U. S. *movie actor*, acteur de cinéma ; *tragic actor*, tragédien. || Fam. U. S. *Bad actor*, mauvais sujet.

actress [-ris] n. Theatr. Actrice *f.*

actual ['æktjuəl] adj. Effectif, réel, positif, de fait (see FACTUAL, REAL) ; concret (case) ; réel (damage, life, value) ; positif (fact) ; direct (knowledge) ; *actual possession*, possession de fait ; *actual provisions*, dispositions expresses. || Même ; *the actual book, thing*, le livre, la chose même. || Actuel, contemporain (present). || Eccles. Actuel (sin). || Jur. *Actual notice*, notification en personne. || Electr. Réel, actif (power).

actuality [‚æktju'æliti] n. Réalité *f.;* fait *m.;*

to give actuality to, donner de la réalité à, rendre pratique. || Pl. Réalités, conditions actuelles *f.; historical actualities*, les circonstances historiques actuelles.

actualization [‚æktjuəlai'zeiʃən] n. Philos. Actualisation *f.*

actualize ['æktjuəlaiz] v. tr. Réaliser (possibilities). || Décrire avec réalisme ; actualiser ; faire vivre (an imaginative situation).

actually [-li] adv. Réellement, positivement, de fait, véritablement (really) ; *actually present*, bel et bien présent ; *actually paid*, effectivement payé. || Mais oui, et même ; *he actually wept*, il se laissa aller à pleurer. || A l'heure actuelle (now).

actuary [-əri] n. Jur. Actuaire *m.*

actuate [-eit] v. tr. Techn. Actionner (an engine). || Fig. Faire agir, inciter (s.o.) ; *actuated by*, poussé (or) mû par, animé de.

acuity [ə'kju:ti] n. Acuité *f.*

acumen [-men] n. Pénétration, perspicacité *f.; critical acumen*, sens critique. || Bot. Pointe *f.*

acuminate [-minit] adj. Bot. Acuminé.
— [-mineit] v. tr. U. S. Aiguiser, appointer.

acupunctor [‚ækju'pʌŋktə*] n. Med. Acuponcteur *m.*

acupuncture [-ʃə*] n. Med. Acuponcture *f.*
— v. tr. Med. U. S. Traiter à l'acuponcture.

acute [ə'kju:t] adj. Aigu ; pointu (sharp). || Math. Aigu (angle). || Med. Aigu (disease) ; aigu, vif (pain) ; *acute abdomen*, U. S. *acute abdominal condition*, ventre chirurgical. || Gramm. Aigu (accent). || Fig. Pénétrant, avisé ; *acute observer*, observateur perspicace. || U. S. Avisé, entendu (businessman). || **Acute-angled**, adj. Math. A angles aigus.

acutely [-li] adv. Vivement, intensément. || Fig. Avec perspicacité.

acuteness [-nis] n. Math. Acuité *f.* || Med. Forme aiguë *f.* (of a disease) ; acuité, intensité *f.* (of a pain). || Mus. Finesse *f.* (of ear) ; acuité *f.* (of sight). || Fig. Pénétration, perspicacité *f.*

acyclic [ə'saiklik] adj. Chim. Acyclique.

acyl ['eisail] n. Chim. Acyle *m.*

ad [æd] n. Fam. Publicité, pub *f.* (fam.), message (or) spot publicitaire *m.; small* (or) *classified ads*, petites annonces.

A.D. [ei'di:] abbr. *Anno Domini*, A. D., de l'ère chrétienne, apr. J.-C.

adage ['ædidʒ] n. Adage *m.*

Adam ['ædəm] n. Adam *m.; not to know from Adam*, ne connaître ni d'Eve ni d'Adam. || Med. *Adam's apple*, pomme d'Adam. || Fam. *Adam's ale*, la flotte, château-la-pompe (water).

adamant ['ædəmənt] n. Diamant *m.* (diamond). || Substance infrangible *f.* || † Aimant *m.*
— adj. U. S. Infrangible. || Fig. Inflexible.

adamantine [‚ædə'mæntain] adj. Adamantin. || Infrangible (unbreakable). || Fig. Inflexible ; inexorable.

adamsite ['ædəmzait] n. Diphénylaminechlorarsine *f.*

adapt [ə'dæpt] v. tr. Adapter (*to*, à ; *for*, pour) ; ajuster, accommoder ; *to adapt oneself to*, se mettre à la portée de (one's audience) ; s'adapter à, se conformer à, se faire à, s'accommoder de (sth.). || Theatr. Adapter (*for*, pour ; *from*, de). || Radio. *To adapt for broadcasting*, mettre en ondes.

adaptability [ə‚dæptə'biliti] n. Faculté d'adaptation *f.* (*of*, de ; *to*, à) ; souplesse *f.*

adaptable [ə'dæptəb] adj. Adaptable. || Capable de s'adapter, souple.

adaptation [‚ædæp'teiʃən] n. Adaptation *f.* (*to*, à ; *for*, pour, à destination de) [fact, result]. || Theatr. Adaptation ; arrangement *m.* || Med. Accommodation *f.* (of the eye).

adapter, adaptor [ə'dæptə*] n. Techn. Adaptateur, raccord m. ‖ ELECTR. Prise multiple f. (plug.). ‖ CINEM. Adaptateur m.; adaptatrice f.

adaptiveness [-ivnis] n. Faculté d'adaptation, souplesse f.

add [æd] v. tr. Ajouter (to, à); to add to s.o.'s grief, augmenter la peine de qqn; there is nothing to add, c'est tout dire. ‖ To add in, inclure (or) comprendre dans. ‖ To add together, joindre, additionner. ‖ To add up, additionner, totaliser; to add up to, s'élever à, se monter à (total); signifier (to mean) [fam.]; se résumer à (fam.).

addendum [ə'dendəm] n. Addendum m.

adder ['ædə*] n. † Basilic m. ‖ ZOOL. Vipère f.; U. S. orvet m.; flying adder, libellule. ‖**Adder-spit,** n. BOT. Fougère f.

addict [ə'dikt] v. tr. Vouer, consacrer (to, à); to addict oneself to, s'adonner à, se livrer à.
— ['ædikt] n. MED. Intoxiqué s.; drug addict, toxicomane; morphia (or) morphine addict, morphinomane. ‖ SPORTS. Fanatique s.

addictedness [-nis], **addiction** [ə'dikʃən] n. Penchant, goût m. (to, pour). ‖ MED. Manie pathologique, intoxication f.

addictive [ə'diktiv] adj. MED. Qui crée une assuétude (or) une dépendance.

addition [ə'diʃən] n. Addition; augmentation f. (increase); accroissement, surcroît m.; in addition, en outre, en supplément, de plus; in addition to, en plus de, en sus de, outre. ‖ MATH. Addition f. ‖ BLAS. Brisure f. ‖ TECHN. Vectorial (ou) U. S. vector addition, composition de forces. ‖ JUR. Titre identificateur m. ‖ ARCHIT. Rajout m.

additional [-l] adj. Additionnel. ‖ Supplémentaire (allowance).

additionally [-əli] adv. En plus, en outre, en sus (to, de).

additive ['æditiv] adj., s. Additif adj., m.

addle ['ædl] adj. Pourri (egg); croupissant (pool). ‖ Creux, vide (brain); brouillé, confus (mind). ‖ **Addle-brained,** adj. Brouillon, écervelé. ‖ **Addlehead, addle-pate,** n. FAM. Tête folle f.; songecreux m.
— v. intr. Se pourrir (egg).
— v. tr. Troubler, brouiller (mind). ‖ Rendre stérile, pourrir, gâcher (a victory).

addled ['ædld] adj. Pourri (egg). ‖ Brouillé, confus, dérangé (mind).

address [ə'dres] v. tr. Adresser (to, à) [criticisms, prayers]. ‖ Mettre (or) écrire l'adresse sur (a letter). ‖ S'adresser à; faire un discours à, haranguer (a crowd); to address the House, prendre la parole à la Chambre, monter à la tribune. ‖ Aborder, accoster (a passer-by). ‖ Apostropher; to address s.o. as Mylord, donner du Monseigneur à qqn. ‖ To address oneself to, se mettre à, s'attaquer à. ‖ NAUT. Consigner (to, à) [a ship]. ‖ SPORTS. To address the ball, viser (in golf).
— n. Adresse, suscription f. (of a letter); domicile m. (of s.o.). ‖ Adresse f.; of (or) U. S. with no address, sans domicile connu; to your home address, à votre adresse particulière. ‖ Abord, aspect m.; lady of great address, dame de grand air. ‖ Requête, pétition f.; Address to the queen, supplique à la reine. ‖ Discours m.; allocution f. (speech). ‖ Adresse, habileté f. (in, en) [skill]. ‖ Pl. Galanterie, cour f. ‖ **Address-book,** n. Carnet (m.) d'adresses.

addressee [,ædre'si:] n. Destinataire m.

addresser [ə'dresə*] n. Expéditeur m.; expéditrice f. (sender). ‖ Pétitionnaire m. (petitioner).

addressograph [ə'dresou,grɑ:f] n. Machine (f.) à adresser, adressographe m.

adduce [ə'dju:s] v. tr. Alléguer, invoquer, citer (an authority); produire (claim, evidence, reason); apporter, fournir (proof).

adducent [-nt] adj. MED. Adducteur.

adduction [ə'dʌkʃən] n. MED. Adduction f. ‖ JUR. Allégation f.

adductor [-tə*] n. MED. Adducteur m.

adenitis [,ædi'naitis] n. MED. Adénite f.

adenoids ['ædinɔidz] n. pl. MED. Adénoïdes, végétations f. pl.

adenoma [,ædi'noum] n. MED. Adénome m.

adept ['ædept] n. Initié, adepte m. ‖ Expert m (in, en).
— adj. Expert, versé (in, dans, en).

adequacy ['ædikwəsi] n. Exactitude (of an idea) justesse f. (of a word). ‖ Suffisance f. (of a reward). ‖ JUR. Compétence (of a judge).

adequate [-kwit] adj. Adéquat, suffisant, acceptable. ‖ Proportionné, correspondant, adapté (to à); à la hauteur (to, de). ‖ JUR. Raisonnable (compensation); compétent (judge).

adequately [-kwitli] adv. Congrûment, de façon adéquate; convenablement.

adhere [əd'hiə*] v. intr. Adhérer, coller (to, à) these labels adhere well, ces étiquettes tiennen bien. ‖ Donner son adhésion, adhérer (to, à) [a party]. ‖ Persister (to, dans); to adhere to one' resolution, maintenir sa résolution.

adherence [-rəns] n. Adhérence f. ‖ FIG. Adhésio f.; attachement m. (to, à) [cause, party, person].

adherent [-rənt] adj. Adhérent, collé (to, à) [a paper]. ‖ FIG. Inhérent (to, à) [a position].
— n. Adhérent, adepte, partisan m.

adhesion [əd'hi:ʒən] n. Adhérence f. (of a stamp) ‖ Adhésion f. (to a party). ‖ Attachement m. (to, à) ‖ MED. Adhérence f.

adhesive [əd'hi:siv] adj. Adhésif, collant, adhéren (sticky); gommé (envelope); adhesive tape, taffeta gommé (or) anglais. ‖ PHYS. Moléculaire (attrac tion). ‖ FIG. Persévérant, tenace.

adiabatic [,ædiə'bætik] adj. PHYS. Adiabatique.

adiantum [,ædi'æntəm] n. BOT. Capillaire m.

adiaphoria [,ædiə'fɔ:riə] n. CHIM. Neutralité f.

adieu [ə'dju:] interj., n. Adieu m.

ad infinitum [æd,infi'naitəm] adv. A l'infini etc., et ainsi de suite.

ad interim [æd'intərim] adv. Temporairement par intérim.
— adj. Temporaire, provisoire, intérimaire.

adipose ['ædipous] adj. Adipeux.
— n. Graisse animale f.

adiposity [,ædi'pɔsiti] n. Adiposité f.

adit ['ædit] n. Accès m.; entrée f. ‖ TECHN. Galeri (f.) d'accès (into a mine).

adjacency [ə'dʒeisənsi] n. Proximité f. ‖ U. S Chose voisine f. ‖ MATH. Adjacence f.

adjacent [-ənt] adj. Adjacent, attenant (to, à). JUR. Adjacent ownew, riverain.

adjectival [,ædʒek'taivəl] adj. GRAMM. Adjectif.

adjective ['ædʒektiv] adj., n. GRAMM. Adjectif m

adjectively [-li] adv. GRAMM. Adjectivement.

adjoin [ə'dʒɔin] v. tr. Adjoindre, joindre (to, à). Toucher, attenir (to, à).
— v. intr. Se toucher.

adjoining [-iŋ] adj. Adjacent à, limitrophe de attenant à. (See ADJACENT.)

adjourn [ə'dʒə:n] v. tr. Ajourner, différer, ren voyer, remettre (to, à). [See POSTPONE.] ‖ JUR Adjourned summons, renvoi, remise; to adjourn . session, lever la séance, clore les débats.
— v. intr. S'ajourner; suspendre la séance. ‖ S déplacer; to adjourn to the smoking-room, passe au fumoir; to adjourn to the theatre, s'en alle passer la soirée au théâtre.

adjournment [-mənt] n. Ajournement m. (for, à) remise f.; renvoi (m.) à la suite. ‖ Suspension d séance, prorogation de session f.

adjudge [əˈdʒʌdʒ] v. tr. Attribuer, décerner (a prize). ‖ Jur. Accorder (to give); condamner (to condemn); juger (to judge); *to adjuge a question*, prononcer sur une question.

adjudgment [-mənt] n. Jur. Jugement, arrêt *m*.

adjudicate [əˈdʒuːdikeit] v. tr. Jur. Juger; *to adjudicate s.o. bankrupt*, déclarer qqn en faillite. — v. intr. Rendre un arrêt; se prononcer (*in, on, upon*, sur).

adjudication [ə,dʒuːdiˈkeiʃən] n. Jur. Décision (*f.*) du tribunal; prononcé (*m.*) de jugement.

adjudicator [əˈdʒuːdikeitə*] n. Jur. Juge *m*.

adjunct [ˈædʒʌŋkt] adj. Adjoint (*to*, à). ‖ Auxiliaire; U. S. *adjunct professor*, professeur adjoint. ‖ Lié (*to*, à). — n. Adjoint *s*. ‖ Gramm. Mot accessoire, complément *m*.

adjunction [-ʃən] n. Adjonction *f.* (*to*, à).

adjunctive [-tiv] adj. Accessoire, ajouté, surajouté (*to*, à).

adjuration [,ædʒuəˈreiʃən] n. Adjuration *f*.

adjure [əˈdʒuə*] v. tr. Adjurer, supplier (*by*, par, au nom de).

adjust [əˈdʒʌst] v. tr. Adapter, ajuster (*to*, à); *to adjust oneself to*, s'adapter à. ‖ Ajuster, arranger (one's clothes). ‖ Techn. Ajuster, mettre au point; régler; *to adjust oneself to*, s'encastrer dans. ‖ Naut. Répartir (an average); rectifier; compenser (compass). ‖ Fig. Arranger, régler (a difference); vider (a quarrel).

adjustable [-əbl] adj. Réglable, ajustable. ‖ Techn. A molette (spanner, U. S. wrench).

adjuster [-ə*] n. Ajusteur *m*. ‖ Techn. Régleur *m.*; *chain adjuster*, tendeur de chaîne. ‖ Naut. *Adjuster of averages*, dispacheur.

adjustment [-mənt] n. Techn. Ajustage, réglage *m.*; mise au point *f*. ‖ Milit. *Adjustment of fire*, réglage du tir. ‖ Naut. *Average adjustment*, dispache. ‖ Fig. Ajustement, arrangement; règlement *m.* (of a difference). ‖ Fig. Adaptation *f.*; accord harmonieux *m.*; *the lack of adjustment between her temperament and his*, l'incompatibilité d'humeur entre elle et lui; *social adjustment*, adaptation au milieu social.

adjutancy [-ənsi] n. Milit. Fonction (*f.*) et grade (*m.*) d'adjudant-major. ‖ Fig. Assistance *f*.

adjutant [-ənt] n. Assistant, aide *m*. ‖ Milit. Adjudant major *m.*; *Adjutant General*, chef du service d'administration de l'Etat-Major. ‖ Zool. Marabout *m*.

adjuvancy [ˈædʒuvənsi] n. Aide *m*.

adjuvant [-ənt] adj., n. Auxiliaire *s*. ‖ Med. Adjuvant *m*.

ad-lib [,ædˈlib] v. tr., intr. Theatr., Fam. U. S. Improviser. — adj. Fam. Spontané. — adv. Fam. A volonté, à discrétion.

adman [ˈæd,mæn] (pl. **admen**) n. Publicitaire, publiciste *s.*, agent (*m.*) de publicité; *he is an adman*, il travaille dans la pub (fam.).

admass [ˈædmæs] n. Gros du public *m.*, masse *f*.

admeasure [ədˈmeʒə*] v. tr. Effectuer un partage.

admin [ˈædmin] n. Fam. Direction *f.* (management); personnel administratif *m.* (office staff); *admin measures*, mesures directoriales; *admin block* (or) *buildings*, bâtiments administratifs.

administrate [ədˈministə*], U. S. **administrate** [-treit] v. tr. Administrer, distribuer (*to*, à). ‖ Fin. Administrer, gérer (the finances). ‖ Eccles. Administrer (sacraments). ‖ Jur. Rendre (justice); déférer (an oath); produire (proofs); *to administer an oath to*, faire prêter serment à. ‖ Med. Administrer (a remedy). — v. intr. Administrer. ‖ Pourvoir, subvenir (*to*, à).

administration [əd,minisˈtreiʃən] n. Administra-

tion *f.* (*of*, de); gestion *f.* (management). ‖ Administration; U. S. government *m*. ‖ Distribution, dispensation *f*. ‖ Jur. Curatelle *f.*; *administration of assets*, liquidation d'actif; *administration of an agreement*, application d'un accord; *administration of the oath*, prestation de serment. ‖ Med. Administration (of a remedy).

administrative [ədˈministrətiv] adj. Administratif.

administrator [-treitə*] n. Administrateur, gérant *m*. ‖ Jur. Curateur; conseil judiciaire *m*.

administratorship [-treitə,ʃip] n. Fonctions (*f.*) d'administrateur (or) de curateur. ‖ Gestion *f*.

administratrix [-treitriks] (pl. **administratrices**) n. Gérante, gestionnaire *f*. ‖ Jur. Curatrice *f*.

admirable [ˈædmirəbl] adj. Admirable. ‖ Fam. Excellent.

admirably [-bli] adv. Admirablement; à merveille.

admiral [ˈædmirəl] n. Naut. Amiral *m.* (person); vaisseau amiral *m.* (ship); *Admiral Superintendent*, préfet maritime. ‖ Zool. Vanesse *f.; Red Admiral*, Vulcain.

admiralship [-ʃip] n. Naut. Fonctions (*f. pl.*) [or] titre (*m.*) d'amiral.

admiralty [-ti] n. Naut. Amirauté *f*. ‖ Ministère (*m.*) de la Marine; *Board of Admiralty*, Conseil de la Marine.

admiration [,ædmiˈreiʃən] n. Admiration *f.; to admiration*, à merveille; *to be the admiration of*, faire l'admiration de.

admire [ədˈmaiə*] v. tr. Admirer. ‖ Etre amoureux de (to be in love with). ‖ Estimer, honorer (to esteem). ‖ † S'émerveiller devant. — v. intr. Etre en admiration (*at*, devant).

admirer [-rə*] n. Admirateur *m.*; admiratrice *f*. Amoureux *m.* (lover).

admiring [-riŋ] adj. Admiratif.

admissibility [əd,misiˈbiliti] n. Admissibilité; acceptabilité; recevabilité *f*.

admissible [ədˈmisibl] adj. Admissible; acceptable. ‖ Techn. Admis (play). ‖ Jur. Recevable, valable.

admission [ədˈmiʃən] n. Admission *f.*; accès *m.* (*to*, à); *free admission*, entrée gratuite; *to gain admission to*, trouver accès auprès de. ‖ Jur. Admission, acceptation *f.* (of evidence); aveu *m.*; *by his own admission*, de son propre aveu. ‖ Techn. Admission, adduction *f.*; *admission pipe*, conduite d'amenée. ‖ U. S. *Admission Day*, fête légale célébrant l'admission d'un Etat dans l'Union.

admit [ədˈmit] v. tr. (1). Admettre, laisser entrer (*to, into*, dans); recevoir (*to*, à); donner accès (*to, into*, à) [to let in]. ‖ Permettre d'entrer, laisser passer (to entitle to enter); *this ticket admits two to the museum*, ce ticket donne droit à deux entrées au musée. ‖ Contenir (to have room for). ‖ Reconnaître, convenir de (to acknowledge); admettre, concéder (to concede); *it must be admitted that*, il faut avouer que. — v. intr. Admettre (to concede). ‖ **To admit of**, admettre, laisser place; *to admit of no hesitation*, ne permettre aucune hésitation.

admittable [-əbl] adj. Admissible.

admittance [-əns] n. Admission *f.*; droit (*m.*) d'entrée; accès *m.* (*to*, auprès de); *no admittance*, entrée interdite. ‖ Electr. Admittance *f*. ‖ Jur. Remise en possession d'un bien foncier.

admittedly [-ədli] adv. De l'aveu général; de l'aveu de l'intéressé.

admix [ədˈmiks] v. tr. Mélanger (*with*, avec). — v. intr. Se mélanger (substances).

admixture [ədˈmikstʃə*] n. Mélange, dosage *m*. ‖ Med. Admixtion *f*.

admonish [ədˈmɔniʃ] v. tr. Admonester. ‖ Conseiller (*to*, de); exhorter (*to*, à). ‖ Avertir, prévenir (*of*, de) [to inform].

admonishment [-mənt], **admonition** [ədmoˈniʃən]

n. Admonestation, admonition, remontrance *f.* ‖ Jur. Avertissement *m.*

admonitory [əd'mɔnitəri] adj. D'avertissement, de reproches.

ad nauseam [æd'nɔːziˌæm] adv. Jusqu'à l'écœurement, à satiété.

ado [a'du] n. Difficulté, peine *f.; mal m.* (difficulty). ‖ Affairement, embarras *m.; much ado about nothing,* beaucoup de bruit pour rien; *without further ado,* sans plus de cérémonies (or) d'histoires (fam.).

adobe [ə'doubi] n. Adobe *m.*

adolescence [ædo'lesns] n. Adolescence *f.*

adolescent [-nt] n., adj. Adolescent *s.*

Adonis [ə'dounis] n. Adonis *m.* (handsome young man). ‖ Zool. *Adonis blue,* adonis (butterfly).

adopt [ə'dɔpt] v. tr. Jur. Adopter (a child, a motion); *adopted child,* enfant adoptif; *adopted country,* pays d'adoption. ‖ Fig. Choisir (a course); adopter (an idea, a word).

adoptee [ədɔp'tiː] n. Jur. Adopté *s.*

adoptedly [ə'dɔptidli] adv. Jur. Par adoption.

adopter [-ə*] n. Jur. Adoptant *s.*

adoption [ə'dɔpʃən] n. Jur., Fig. Adoption *f.*

adoptive [-tiv] adj. Adopté (child); adoptif (father).

adorable [ə'dɔːrəbl] adj. Adorable.

adorably [-əbli] adv. Adorablement.

adoration [ædo'reiʃən] n. Eccles., Fig. Adoration *f.*

adore [ə'dɔːr] v. tr. Eccles. Adorer.

adorer [-ə*] n. Eccles. Adorateur *m.;* adoratrice *f.* ‖ Fam. Soupirant *m.*

adoringly [-iηli] adv. Avec adoration.

adorn [ə'dɔːn] v. tr. Orner, parer (with, de).

adornment [-mənt] n. Ornement *m.;* parure *f.*

adown [ə'daun] adv. See down.

ADP [eidiːpiː] abbr. *Automatic Data Processing,* Inform. Traitement *(m.)* automatique des données, informatique *f.*

adrenal [ə'driːnəl] adj. Med. Surrénal.
— n. Med. Surrénale *f.*

adrenalin [-in] n. Med. Adrénaline *f.*

adrift [ə'drift] adv., adj. A la dérive. ‖ Naut., Fam. *To be adrift,* tirer une bordée sans permission. ‖ Fig. *To be all adrift,* dévier, dérailler; *to cut adrift,* laisser aller à vau l'eau.

adroit [ə'drɔit] adj. Adroit.

adroitness [-nis] n. Adresse *f.*

adscititious [ædsi'tiʃəs] adj. Additionnel.

adsorb [əd'sɔːb] v. tr. Phys. Adsorber.

adsorption [-pʃən] n. Phys. Adsorption *f.*

adsum ['ædsəm] interj. Présent!; *to say « adsum »,* répondre à l'appel.

adulate ['ædjuleit] v. tr. Aduler, flagorner.

adulation [ˌædju'leiʃən] n. Adulation *f.*

adulator ['ædjuleitə*] n. Flagorneur, adulateur *m.*

adulatory [-təri] adj. Adulateur *m.;* adulatrice *f.*

adult [ə'dʌlt] n. Adulte *s.*
— adj. Adulte. ‖ Pour les adultes (education, film).

adulterant [ə'dʌltərənt] adj., n. Adultérateur *m.*

adulterate [-it] adj. Comm. Frelaté, falsifié (goods). ‖ Jur. Adultérin (child); adultère (wife).
— [-eit] v. tr. Adultérer, falsifier; *adulterated milk,* lait baptisé (fam.).

adulteration [əˌdʌltə'reiʃən] n. Comm. Altération, falsification *f.;* frelatage *m.* ‖ U. S. Substance adultérée *f.*

adulterator [-'reitə*] n. Falsificateur *m.*

adulterer [ə'dʌltərə*], **adulteress** [-is] n. Jur. Adultère *s.*

adulterine [-ain] adj. Jur. Adultérin (child). ‖ Comm. Frelaté (goods).

adulterous [-əs] adj. Jur. Adultère.

adultery [-i] n. Adultère *m.* (act).

adumbrate ['ædʌmbreit] v. tr. Esquisser (a pro-

ject). ‖ Ombrager, obscurcir (to overshadow). ‖ U. S. Faire pressentir (to foreshadow).

adumbration [ˌædʌm'breiʃən] n. Ebauche, esquisse *f.* (sketch). ‖ Obscurcissement *m.* ‖ U. S. Signe précurseur *m.*

adust [ə'dʌst] adj. † Aduste. ‖ Mélancolique, maussade (gloomy).

advance [əd'vɑːns] v. tr. Avancer, progresser. Faire progresser, faire avancer; *to advance a friend,* pousser un ami. ‖ Avancer, émettre (an opinion). ‖ Fin. Avancer, prêter (money); augmenter, faire monter (prices).
— v. intr. S'avancer (towards, vers) [to move ahead]. ‖ Progresser, gagner du terrain (to make progress); *to advance on,* se porter sur. ‖ Fin. S'élever, monter (prices).
— n. Avance, marche en avant, progression *f.* Milit. Avance, progression *f.; advance post, work* poste, ouvrage avancé; *advance to contact,* marche d'approche. ‖ Comm. *Advance orders,* commandes avant parution. ‖ Fin. Avance *f. (to,* à) [of funds] hausse, augmentation *f.* (in price); *advance payment,* paiement anticipé. ‖ Autom. *Advance of the ignition,* U. S. *spark advance,* avance à l'allumage. ‖ Techn. *Advance sheets,* bonnes feuilles. Fig. Avances *f. pl.; to make the first advances to* faire les premiers pas vers. ‖ Loc. *In advance, en* avance; d'avance; par avance; *to be in advance of one's time,* devancer son époque. ‖ **Advance booking,** n. Réservation, location *f.* ‖ **Advance copy,** n. Exemplaire *m.)* de presse (of book); texte polyco pié *m.* (of speech). ‖ **Advance guard,** n. Milit Avant-garde *f.*

advanced [-t] adj. Milit. Avancé (post). ‖ Fin Avancé (money); *sums advanced,* avances, provi sions. ‖ Fig. Avancé (idea, hour, season, students) supérieur (studies). ‖ **Advanced-level,** n. E Grande-Bretagne, examen de fin d'études secon daires.

advancement [-mənt] n. Avance *f.* (advancing). Avancement *m.;* promotion *f.* ‖ Progrès *m.* (improvement). ‖ Jur. Avance d'hoirie *f.*

advantage [əd'vɑːntidʒ] n. Avantage *m.,* supério rité *f. (of, over,* sur); *to take advantage of,* profite de, abuser de. ‖ Avantage *m.;* circonstance prof table *f.; to turn to advantage,* tirer parti de. ‖ Profit bénéfice *m.; for whose advantage?,* au profit d qui?; *to find it to one's advantage,* y trouver so compte. ‖ Comm. Profit *m.; to good advantage,* à prix avantageux. ‖ Sports. Avantage *m.* (in ten nis). ‖ Techn. Multiplication *f.*
— v. tr. Etre avantageux à, profiter ‖ Favoriser aider, avantager.

advantageous [ˌædvən'teidʒəs] adj. Favorable avantageux, profitable.

advantageously [-li] adv. Avantageusement.

Advent ['ædvent] n. Eccles. Avent *m.; Secon Advent,* parousie. ‖ Venue, arrivée *f.;* avènement *m*

Adventist ['ædventist] n. Eccles. Adventiste *s.*

adventitious [ædven'tiʃəs] adj. Bot., Fig. Adver tice. ‖ Jur. Accessoire; adventif (property).

adventure [əd'ventʃə*] n. Aventure *f.; to mee with an adventure,* avoir une aventure. ‖ Aventure risque *m.; to be full of adventure,* avoir des goût aventureux. ‖ Evénement périlleux *m.;* péripétie aventure *f.* ‖ Hasard *m.; by adventure,* par hasard
— v. tr. Aventurer, risquer (to risk).
— v. intr. S'aventurer; prendre des risques; s hasarder (in, into, dans).

adventurer [-rə*] n. Aventurier, homme aventu reux *m.* ‖ Aventurier, chevalier *(m.)* d'industrie. Milit. Soldat *(m.)* de fortune.

adventuresome [-səm] adj. Aventureux.

adventuress [-ris] n. Aventurière *f.*

adventurism [-rizm] n. Aventurisme *m.*

adventurist [-rist] n. Aventuriste *s.*

adventurous [-rəs] adj. Aventureux, audacieux (daring). ‖ U. S. Aventureux, risqué (risky).
adverb ['ædvə:b] n. GRAMM. Adverbe *m.*
adverbial [əd'və:biəl] adj. GRAMM. Adverbial.
adverbially [-i] adv. GRAMM. Adverbialement.
adversary ['ædvəsəri] n. Adversaire *m.* (See OPPONENT.) ‖ ECCLES. Satan *m.*
adversative [əd'və:sətiv] adj. GRAMM. Adversatif.
adverse ['ædvə:s] adj. Hostile, adverse, ennemi. ‖ Contraire, défavorable ; *adverse days,* jours d'adversité. ‖ Opposé (opposite). ‖ BOT., MILIT., JUR. Adverse.
adversity [əd'və:siti] n. Adversité *f.* ‖ Malheur *m.*
advert [æd'və:t] v. intr. Se référer, faire allusion (*to,* à).
advert n. FAM. Annonce *f.* (See AD.)
advertise ['ædvətaiz] v. tr. Faire de la réclame (or) publicité pour (things for sale). ‖ Afficher, diffuser ; *to advertise a house for sale,* afficher la vente d'une maison. ‖ Faire du battage sur (a fact). ‖ NAUT. *Advertised to sail on the,* annoncé comme devant partir le.
— v. intr. Mettre une annonce, faire de la publicité. ‖ **To advertise for,** demander par voie d'annonce.
advertisement [əd'və:tismənt] n. Annonce (see AD) ; *classified advertisements,* petites annonces.
advertiser ['ædvətaizə*] n. Annonceur *m.*
advertising [-iŋ] n. Annonce, réclame, publicité *f.;* *advertising manager, medium,* chef, organe de publicité.
advice [əd'vais] n. Avis, conseils *m. pl.* (see COUNSEL) ; *to seek advice,* demander conseil ; *a piece of advice,* un avis (or) conseil. ‖ Nouvelle *f.;* *diplomatic advices,* nouvelles diplomatiques. ‖ MED. *To take medical advice,* consulter un médecin. ‖ COMM. Avis ; *as per advice from,* suivant avis de. ‖ **Advice-boat,** n. NAUT. Aviso *m.*
advisability [əd'vaizə'biliti] n. Opportunité *f.*
advisable [əd'vaizəbl] adj. Judicieux, sage, recommandable, prudent. ‖ Opportun, à propos, bon (*to,* de).
advise [əd'vaiz] v. tr. Conseiller. (See COUNSEL.) ‖ Recommander à (*to,* de] ; engager (*to,* à) [s.o.] ; *to advise s.o. against sth.,* déconseiller qqch. à qqn. ‖ Aviser, informer, notifier à, faire part à (s.o.) [*of,* de].
— v. intr. **To advise with,** consulter,. prendre l'avis de (s.o.).
advised [-d] adj. Avisé. ‖ Délibéré, réfléchi, fait en connaissance de cause (planned).
advisedly [-idli] adv. Délibérément, en pleine connaissance de cause.
adviser [-ə*] n. Conseiller *m.* ‖ JUR. *Legal adviser,* conseiller juridique.
advisory [-əri] adj. Consultatif ; *Business Advisory Committee,* Comité consultatif ; *in an advisory capacity,* à titre consultatif. ‖ De diffusion, de vulgarisation (services).
advocacy ['ædvəkəsi] n. JUR. Profession (*f.*) d'avocat. ‖ Plaidoyer (*of,* pour).
advocate [-it] n. Avocat, défenseur *m.* (of a cause) ; *to become the advocate of,* se faire le champion de. ‖ JUR. Avocat *m.* (in Scotland).
— [-eit] v. tr. Recommander, préconiser, soutenir.
advowson [əd'vauzən] n. ECCLES. Collation (*f.*) d'un bénéfice.
adz(e) [ædz] n. TECHN. Herminette, doloire *f.*
— v. tr. TECHN. Dresser (wood).
aedile ['i:dail] n. Edile *m.*
Ægean [i'dʒi:ən] adj. GEOGR. Egéen ; *Ægean Sea,* mer Egée.
aegis ['i:dʒis] n. Egide, protection *f.*
Æneas [i:'ni:əs] n. Enée.
aeolian [i:'ouliən] adj. MUS. Eolien.
aeon ['i:ən] n. Milliers (*m.*) d'années.
aerate ['eiəreit], ['ɛəreit] v. tr. Aérer. ‖ MED.

Oxygéner (blood). ‖ COMM. Gazéifier (water) ; *aerated water,* eau gazeuse.
aeration [,eiə'reiʃən], [,ɛə'reiʃən] n. Aération *f.* ‖ MED. Oxygénation *f.* ‖ COMM. Gazéification *f.*
aerial ['ɛəriəl] adj. Aérien, léger (light). ‖ Irréel (imaginary). ‖ Aérien, très haut (high up). ‖ AVIAT. Aérien (map, railway, torpedo).
— n. RADIO. Antenne *f.;* *umbrella aerial,* antenne-parapluie.
aerialist ['eiriəlist] n. U. S. Trapéziste *s.*
aerie ['i:əri] n. Aire *f.* (of an eagle). ‖ ZOOL. Nichée *f.* (of eaglets). ‖ FIG. Nid (*m.*) d'aigle.
aeriferous ['ɛə'rifərəs] adj. Aérifère.
aerify ['ɛərifai] v. tr. Aérifier.
aerium ['ɛəriʌm] n. MED. Aérium *m.*
aerobatics [,eiro'bætiks] n. AVIAT. Acrobaties aériennes *f.*
aerobe ['ɛəroub] n. MED. Aérobie *m.*
aerocartography ['ɛərokɑ:'tɔɡrafi] n. Aérocartographie *f.*
aerodrome ['ɛərədroum] n. AVIAT. Aérodrome *m.*
aerodynamic ['ɛərodai'næmik] adj. Aérodynamique.
aerodynamics [-s] n. Aérodynamique *f.*
aerodyne ['ɛərədain] n. AVIAT. Aérodyne *m.*
aero-engine ['ɛərou,endʒin] n. AVIAT. Moteur (*m.*) d'avion.
aerofoil ['ɛərou,fɔil] n. AVIAT. Surface portante (or) de sustentation *f.;* *aerofoil section,* profil aérodynamique.
aerograph ['ɛərəɡrɑ:f] n. AVIAT. Aérographe *m.*
aerogram [-græm] n. Radiotélégramme *m.*
aerolite [-lait] n. ASTRON. Aérolithe *m.*
aerology [ɛə'rɔlədʒi] n. AVIAT. Aérologie *f.*
aeromarine ['ɛəromæ'ri:n] adj. Aéromaritime.
aerometer [ɛə'rɔmitə*] n. Aéromètre *m.*
aeromodelling [,ɛəro'mɔdliŋ] n. AVIAT. Aéromodélisme *m.*
aeronaut ['ɛərənɔ:t] n. AVIAT. Aéronaute *m.*
aeronautic [,ɛəro'nɔ:tik] adj. Aéronautique.
aeronautics [-s] n. AVIAT. Aéronautique *f.*
aeronaval [,ɛəro'neivəl] adj. Aéronaval.
aerophagia [-feidʒiə] n. MED. Aérophagie *f.*
aerophotography [,ɛərofə'tɔɡrafi] n. Aérophotographie *f.*
aeroplane ['ɛəroplein] n. Aéroplane, avion *m.*
aerosol ['ɛərosɔl] n. Aérosol *m.;* *aerosol bomb,* vaporisateur à insecticide.
aerospace [-speis] n. AVIAT., ASTRONAUT. Espace (*m.*) atmosphérique (or) extra-atmosphérique ; *aerospace industry,* industrie aérospatiale.
aerostat ['ɛərostæt] n. AVIAT. Aérostat *m.*
aerostatic [,ɛəro'stætik] adj. Aérostatique.
aerostatics [-s] n. Aérostatique *f.*
aerostation [,ɛəro'steiʃən] n. Aérostation *f.*
aeruginous [iə'ru:dʒinəs] adj. Vert-de-grisé.
aesthete ['i:sθi:t] n. Esthète *m.*
aesthetic(al) [is'θetik(əl)] adj. Esthétique.
aesthetically [-əli] adv. Esthétiquement.
aestheticism [is'θeti,sizm] n. Esthétisme *m.*
aesthetics [is'θetiks] n. Esthétique *f.*
aestival [i:s'taivəl] adj. Estival.
aestivate ['i:stiveit] v. intr., tr. Estiver.
aestivation [i:sti'veiʃən] n. Estivation *f.*
aetiology [,i:ti'ɔlədʒi] n. Etiologie *f.*
afar [ə'fɑ:] adv. Loin, à distance ; *from afar,* de loin.
affability [,æfə'biliti] n. Affabilité *f.*
affable ['æfəbl] adj. Affable. (See AMIABLE.)
affably [-əbli] adv. Avec affabilité.
affair [ə'fɛə*] n. Affaire, occupation *f.* (business) ; *that is his affair,* c'est son affaire, cela le regarde. ‖ Affaire, question *f.* (matter) ; *family affairs,* affaires de famille. ‖ Duel *m.;* *affaire* (*f.*) *d'honneur.* ‖ Affaire (*f.*) de cœur ; liaison *f.* (amour). ‖ COMM. Affaire, spéculation, transaction *f.* (deal) ; pl. affaires

(matters of business). ‖ Pl. Jur. Affaires *f. pl.* (public affairs); *Foreign Affairs*, Affaires étrangères. ‖ Fam. Affaire *f.*; fourbi *m.*; *that's another affair altogether!*, c'est une autre question (or) paire de manches!

affect [əˈfekt] v. tr. Affecter, atteindre, avoir une action sur; retentir sur (to have an effect on); influencer, influer sur (see INFLUENCE); *to be affected*, se ressentir. ‖ Affecter, modifier, transformer (to produce a change in). ‖ Toucher, concerner (to concern). ‖ Emouvoir, affecter, toucher. (See MOVE.) ‖ Med. Affecter (health); intéresser (an organ). ‖ Jur. Affecter (an estate).
— [ˈæfekt] n. Psych. Affect *m.*

affect v. tr. Affecter, prendre (a shape). ‖ Aimer, affectionner (a garment). ‖ Affecter, feindre (indifference). [See FEIGN.]

affectation [ˌæfekˈteiʃən] n. Affectation, feinte *f.* (pretence). ‖ Affectation *f.*; maniérisme *m.* (pose).

affected [əˈfektid] adj. Affecté, influencé. ‖ Affecté, ému, touché, remué (moved). ‖ Disposé (*to, towards*, à l'égard de, envers). ‖ Med. Affecté (*with*, par); atteint (*with*, de).

affected [əˈfektid] adj. Affecté, simulé, feint. ‖ Artificiel, affecté, affété, maniéré.

affectedly [-idli] adv. Avec affectation (or) simulation.

affecting [-iɳ] adj. Emouvant, touchant.

affection [əˈfekʃən] n. Etat (*m.*) d'âme; sentiment *m.*; disposition *f.* ‖ Affection, tendresse *f.* (*for, towards*, pour); *to win affection*, se faire aimer. ‖ Philos. Attribut *m.*; propriété *f.* ‖ Med. Affection, maladie *f.*

affectionate [-it] adj. Affectueux, tendre, aimant.

affectionately [-itli] adv. Affectueusement.

affective [əˈfektiv] adj. Affectif.

affectivity [ˌæfekˈtiviti] n. Psych. Affectivité *f.*

afferent [ˈæfərənt] adj. Med. Afférent.

affiance [əˈfaiəns] n. † Confiance, foi *f.* (*in*, en). ‖ Promesse (*f.*) de mariage, fiançailles *f.* (betrothal).
— v. tr. Fiancer (*to*, avec); *to become affianced to*, se fiancer avec.

affidavit [ˌæfiˈdeivit] n. Jur. Affidavit *m.*; déclaration (*f.*) sous serment; *affidavit by process-server*, constat d'huissier.

affiliate [əˈfilieit] v. tr. Affilier (*to, with*, à); *to affiliate oneself to*, s'affilier à. ‖ Jur. Faire reconnaître (a child) [*upon, to*, par]. ‖ Fig. Chercher les sources (of a language); attribuer (a piece of work) [*to*, à].

affiliation [əˌfiliˈeiʃən] n. Affiliation *f.* ‖ Jur. Légitimation *f.*; *action for affiliation*, procédure en recherche de paternité.

affinitive [əˈfinitiv] adj. Apparenté; qui a des liens d'affinité.

affinity [-ti] n. Affinité *f.*; parenté par alliance *f.* (*to, with*, avec). ‖ Affinité, attraction *f.* (*between*, entre). ‖ Contact, rapport *m.*; ressemblance *f.* (*between*, entre) [languages, species]. ‖ Chim. Affinité (*with*, pour). ‖ U. S. Béguin *m.* (person).

affirm [əˈfəːm] v. tr. Affirmer, déclarer, assurer. (See ASSERT.) ‖ Jur. Confirmer, homologuer, ratifier.
— v. intr. Jur. Affirmer solennellement.

affirmation [ˌæfəˈmeiʃən] n. Affirmation, assurance, assertion *f.* ‖ Jur. Affirmation solennelle.

affirmative [əˈfəːmətiv] adj. Affirmatif.
— n. Affirmative *f.*

affirmatively [-tivli] adv. Affirmativement.

affirmatory [-təri] adj. Affirmatif.

affix [əˈfiks] v. tr. Joindre, annexer, attacher (*to*, à) [a document]. ‖ Apposer (*to*, sur) [a seal]. ‖ Afficher (a notice).
— [ˈæfiks] n. Annexe, addition *f.* ‖ Gramm. Affixe *m.*

afflatus [əˈfleitəs] n. Eccles., Fig. Inspiration *f.*

afflict [əˈflikt] v. tr. Affliger (*by*, par); *to be*

afflicted, s'affliger. ‖ Med. Atteindre, affliger (*with*, de).

affliction [əˈflikʃən] n. Affliction, peine *f.* ‖ Tribulation, catastrophe, calamité *f.* ‖ Pl. Med. Affections, infirmités *f.*

afflictive [-tiv] adj. Affligeant, attristant.

affluence [ˈæfluəns] n. Affluence *f.*; afflux (*m.*) de gens (influx). ‖ Opulence, fortune *f.* (wealth).

affluent [-ənt] adj. Med. Affluent. ‖ Fig. Foisonnant; opulent.
— n. Géogr. Affluent *m.*

afflux [ˈæflʌks] n. Afflux *m.* ‖ Affluence *f.*

afford [əˈfɔːd] v. tr. *Can afford*, pouvoir, avoir les ressources pour, être à même de; *he cannot afford the expense*, il ne peut assumer cette dépense, ses moyens ne lui permettent pas de faire cette dépense; *he can afford to speak frankly*, il peut se permettre (or) se payer le luxe de parler net. ‖ Fournir, donner (nourishment, supply). ‖ Fig. Fournir, causer, procurer, offrir (facilities, pleasure, opportunities).

afforest [æˈfɔrist] v. tr. Agric. Planter, boiser.

afforestation [æˌfɔristˈteiʃən] n. Agric. Afforestation *f.*

affranchise [æˈfræntʃaiz] v. tr. Affranchir.

affray [əˈfrei] n. Echauffourée; rixe, bagarre *f.*

affricate [ˈæfrikit] n. Gramm. Affriquée *f.*

affright [əˈfrait] v. tr. † Effrayer, épouvanter, terrifier.
— n. † Effroi *m.*

affront [əˈfrʌnt] v. tr. Insulter, outrager (to slight). ‖ Affronter, braver, défier (to brave).
— n. Affront, outrage *m.*; insulte *f.*; *to submit s.o. to an affront, to offer an affront to s.o.*, infliger un affront à qqn, faire affront à qqn.

affusion [əˈfjuːʒən] n. Affusion *f.*

afghan [ˈæfgæn] adj. Géogr. Afghan. ‖ Zool. *Afghan hound*, lévrier afghan.
— n. Géogr. Afghan *s.* ‖ Comm. Veste afghane *f.*

Afghanistan [æfˈgænis,tɑːn] n. Géogr. Afghanistan *m.*

aficionado [əˌfiʃjəˈnɑːdou] n. Aficionado *m.*

afield [əˈfiːld] adv. Aux champs (on, to the fields); sur le champ de bataille (on, to the battlefield). ‖ Fig. Loin; *far afield*, au loin, bien loin; *further afield*, plus loin, plus avant.

afire [əˈfaiə*] adv. En feu.

aflame [əˈfleim] adv. En flammes. ‖ Fig. Embrasé.

A.F.L.-C.I.O. [eiefelsiːaiou] abbr. *American Federation of Labour and Congress of Industrial Organizations*, A. F. L.-C. I. O., centrale syndicale américaine.

afloat [əˈflout] adv. Naut. Flottant, à flot sur l'eau; *to set afloat*, mettre à l'eau, renflouer. ‖ Naut. A bord. ‖ Fin. A flot; *to keep afloat*, se maintenir à flot, demeurer solvable. ‖ Fig. Répandu, en circulation (idea, rumour); *to be afloat again*, revenir sur le tapis. ‖ Fig. A la dérive; *to be all afloat*, aller à vau l'eau (affairs).

afoot [əˈfut] adv. A pied, pédestrement. ‖ Med. *To be afoot*, être remis sur pied. ‖ Fig. En route, en marche, en train.

afore [əˈfɔː*] adv. Naut. A l'avant.
— prép. Naut. A l'avant de.

aforementioned [əˈfɔː,mɛnʃnd] adj. Susmentionné, ci-dessus désigné.

aforenamed [əˈfɔː,neimd] adj. Susnommé, ci-dessus nommé.

aforesaid [-,sed] adj. Susdit, précité.

aforethought [-ˈθɔːt] adj. Prémédité.

afoul [əˈfaul] adv., adj. En collision; *to run afoul of*, aborder, heurter, entrer en collision avec (a boat); emboutir (a car).

afraid [əˈfreid] adj. Apeuré, effrayé (see FEARFUL); *to be afraid of, lest*, avoir peur de, que. ‖ Hésitant; *to feel afraid to speak*, ne pas oser parler. ‖ Fam.

Au regret de ; *I'm afraid I can't go*, je crains de ne pouvoir y aller.

afresh [ə'freʃ] adv. De (or) à nouveau.

Africa ['æfrikə] n. GEOGR. Afrique *f.*

African [-ən] adj., n. Africain.

Afrikaans [,æfri'kɑːns] n. GRAMM. Afrikaans *m.*

Afrikaner [,æfri'kɑːnə*] n. GEOGR. Afrikaner *s.*

Afro- ['æfrou] pref. Afro-. ‖ **Afro-American,** adj., n. Afro-américain *adj., s.* ‖ **Afro-Asian** (or) **-Asiatic,** adj., n. Afro-asiatique *adj., s.* ‖ **Afro** adj. Afro (hairstyle).

aft [ɑːft] adv. NAUT. A l'arrière ; sur l'arrière.

after [ɑː'ftə*] adv. Après, derrière (behind) ; après, plus tard (later) ; après, ensuite (next). ‖ **After-dinner,** n. Après-dîner *m. ;* adj. d'après dîner. ‖ **After-mentioned,** adj. Ci-après mentionné, plus bas. ‖ **After-school,** adj. Post-scolaire ; ayant lieu après les cours.
— prép. Derrière, après (behind) ; *just after the church*, aussitôt passé l'église. ‖ En quête de, après (in search of) ; *to try after a job*, essayer de trouver du travail ; *to whistle after one's dog*, siffler son chien. ‖ Plus tard que, après (later than) ; *it was after ten when he came*, il était plus de dix heures quand il vint. ‖ A la suite de ; *after what has happened*, après ce qui est arrivé. ‖ En dépit de, malgré ; *after all I have done*, après tout ce que j'ai fait. ‖ Après, au-dessous de ; *to place X after Y*, placer X après Y. ‖ D'après ; à la manière de ; *after his manner*, à sa façon ; *after the pattern*, selon le modèle. ‖ En souvenir de ; en l'honneur de ; *to be christened after one's grandfather*, recevoir au baptême le nom de son grand-père. ‖ Au sujet de, après ; *to ask after s.o.*, s'informer de la santé de qqn. ‖ Après, vers ; *to languish after s.o.*, languir après qqn. ‖ Sur, vis-à-vis ; *to look after s.o.*, veiller sur qqn.
— conj. Après que (later than).
— adj. Ultérieur, postérieur ; futur (ages). ‖ NAUT. Arrière, de l'arrière. ‖ **After-damp,** n. Mofette *f.* ‖ **After-grass,** n. AGRIC. Regain *m.* ‖ **After-hold,** n. NAUT. Cale arrière *f.* ‖ **After-image,** n. Persistance rétinienne *f.* ‖ **After-life,** n. Reste (*m.*) de la vie ; vie future *f.* ‖ **After-sensation,** n. PHILOS. Image consécutive *f.* ‖ **After-taste,** n. Arrière-goût *m.* ‖ **After-war,** adj. D'après guerre ; *after-war period*, après-guerre. ‖ **After-wit,** n. Esprit (*m.*) de l'escalier ; illumination (*f.*) après coup. ‖ **After-word,** n. Postface *f.* ‖ **After-world,** n. Monde futur, au-delà *m.*

afterbirth ['ɑː'ftəbəː θ] n. MED. Placenta *m.* ‖ JUR. Naissance posthume *f.*

aftereffect ['ɑː'ftəri,fekt] n. Répercussion, incidence *f. ;* contrecoup, effet à retardement *m.*

afterglow [-glou] n. Réaction *f.* (after a bath). ‖ Derniers reflets *m. pl.* (after sunset). ‖ Phosphorescence *f.*

afterlight [-lait] n. Illumination tardive *f. ;* lumière (*f.*) des événements.

aftermath [-mæθ] n. AGRIC. Regain *m.* ‖ FIG. Suites fâcheuses, séquelles *f. pl.*

aftermost [-moust] adj. NAUT. Le plus en arrière.

afternoon ['ɑː'ftə'nuːn] n. Après-midi *m.*

afterpiece ['ɑːftəpiːs] n. Baisser (*m.*) de rideau.

afters ['ɑːftəz] n. pl. FAM. Dessert *m.*

aftershave ['ɑːftə,ʃeiv] n. After-shave *m.*
— adj. *After-shave lotion*, lotion après-rasage.

afterthought [-θɔːt] n. Explication ultérieure *f.* ‖ Illumination (*f.*) après coup. (See AFTER-WIT.)

afterwards [-wədz] M., U.S. **afterward** [-wəd] adv. Après, ensuite.

aga ['ɑː:gə] n. Ag(h)a *m. ; Aga Khan*, Agha Khan.

again [ə'gein] adv. De nouveau ; encore, une fois de plus (anew) ; *to say again and again*, ne cesser de dire ; *to wish oneself young again*, vouloir redevenir jeune. ‖ En outre, de plus ; par dessus le marché (fam.) ; *now and again*, de temps à autre. ‖

En retour ; *to answer again*, riposter. ‖ En plus ; *as much again*, deux fois plus ; *half as short again*, de moitié plus court, raccourci de moitié. ‖ FAM. Déjà ; *what's your name again?*, comment vous appelez-vous déjà ?

against [-st] prep. Contre ; *to go against s.o.*, être hostile à qqn. ‖ Contre, sur ; *to run against a rock*, donner contre un rocher. ‖ A l'opposé de ; contre (the stream) ; *against the nap*, à rebrousse-poil. ‖ Contre, sur, en contraste avec ; *as against this*, en contre-partie. ‖ Près, contre ; *close against the hospital*, tout près (or) contre l'hôpital. ‖ En face de, vis-à-vis de ; *over against the church*, face à l'église. ‖ En vue de, en cas de, contre ; *against adverse days*, en prévision de l'adversité.
— conj. Pour quand.

agamic [ə'gæmik] adj. BOT., ZOOL. Agame.

agape [ə'geip] adj., adv. Bouche bée, la bouche ouverte, béant (gaping).

agape ['ægəpi] n. ECCLES. Agape *f.* (feast).

agar-agar ['eigɑː:'eigɑː:] n. Agar-agar *m.*

agaric ['ægərik] n. BOT. Agaric *m.*

agate ['ægət] n. Agate *f.* (stone, tool). ‖ U. S. Corps 5,5 (typogr.).

agave [ə'geivi] n. BOT. Agave *m.*

age [eidʒ] n. Age *m.* (of a person) ; *of doubtful age*, entre deux âges ; *to be thirty years of age*, avoir trente ans ; *to be over age*, avoir dépassé la limite d'âge. ‖ Majorité *f. ; to come of age*, atteindre sa majorité ; *under age*, mineur. ‖ Vieillesse *f. ; bowed with age*, courbé par les ans. ‖ Age *m. ;* époque *f.* (see PERIOD). ‖ *Atomic Age*, ère atomique ; *Ice Age*, âge des glaciers ; *Elizabethan age*, période élisabéthaine. ‖ FAM. Siècle *m.*, éternité *f.* ‖ **Age-group,** n. Classe (*f.*) d'âge ; MILIT. Classe. ‖ **Age-old,** adj. Séculaire.
— v. tr., intr. Vieillir. ‖ U.S. Faisander.

aged [-id] adj. Agé, vieux ; *the aged*, les gens âgés. ‖ ZOOL. Hors d'âge (cheval).
— [-d] adj. Agé de ; *aged six*, ayant six ans.

ageless [-lis] adj. Toujours jeune. ‖ Sans âge, séculaire (age-old).

agency ['eidʒənsi] n. Action *f. ; free agency*, libre action. ‖ Agent *m. ; natural agency*, agent naturel. ‖ Entremise *f. ; through s.o.'s agency*, par l'intermédiaire (or) l'organe de qqn. ‖ COMM. Agence *f. ; business agency*, bureau d'affaires ; *real estate agency*, agence immobilière. ‖ FIN. Agence, succursale *f.* (of a bank).

agenda [ə'dʒendə] n. pl. Ordre du jour *m.* (of a meeting). ‖ Agenda *m.* (memorandum book).

agent ['eidʒənt] n. Agent *m. ; business, press agent*, agent d'affaires, de presse ; *literary agent*, agent littéraire. ‖ Agent *m.* (see FACTOR) ; *chemical agent*, agent chimique. ‖ COMM. Agent, représentant *m.* ‖ MILIT. *Agent provocateur*, agent provocateur ; *secret agent*, agent secret.

agentive [-iv] adj. GRAMM. D'agent (affix).

agglomerate [ə'glɔmɔreit] v. tr. Agglomérer.
— v. intr. S'agglomérer.
— [-it] adj. Aggloméré.
— n. Aggloméra̱t *m.*

agglomeration [ə,glɔme'reiʃən] n. Agglomération *f.* (act, condition).

agglutinate [ə'gluː:tineit] v. tr. Agglutiner.
— [-it] adj. Agglutiné. ‖ GRAMM. Agglutinant (language).

aggrandize [ə'grændaiz] v. tr. Agrandir (a state). ‖ Exagérer, enfler (an incident) ; augmenter (s.o.'s power).

aggrandizement [-izmənt] n. Agrandissement, développement *m.*

aggravate ['ægrəveit] v. tr. Aggraver, empirer. (See INTENSIFY.) ‖ FAM. Agacer, exaspérer.

aggravating [-iŋ] adj. Aggravant. ‖ FAM. Agaçant.

aggravation [,ægrə'veiʃən] n. Aggravation *f.* ‖

Circonstance aggravante *f*. ‖ JUR. Majoration *f*. ‖ FAM. Agacement *m.;* irritation *f*.

aggregate ['ægrigit] n. Total, tout *m.;* masse *f.; in the aggregate,* l'un dans l'autre, dans l'ensemble. ‖ PHYS., BOT. Agrégat *m*.
— adj. Global, collectif, total. ‖ JUR. Agrégé. ‖ BOT. En bouquet.
— [-eit] v. tr. Agréger, rassembler. ‖ Agréger, associer, incorporer *(to,* à) [s.o.].
— v. intr. FAM. Se monter à, s'élever à, totaliser.

aggregation [,ægri'geiʃən] n. Agrégation *f*. ‖ Assemblage *m*.

aggregative ['ægrigeitiv] adj. PHYS. Agrégatif.

aggression [ə'greʃən] n. Agression *f*.

aggressive [ə'gresiv] adj. Agressif, combatif. ‖ MILIT. Offensif. ‖ U. S. Entreprenant.

aggressively [-ivli] adv. Agressivement.

aggressiveness [-ivnis] n. Agressivité *f.*

aggressor [-ə*] n. Agresseur *m*.

aggrieve [ə'gri:v] v. tr. Peiner, chagriner. ‖ JUR. Léser.

aggro ['ægrou] n. POP. Bagarre, rixe, échauffourée *f.*

aghast [ə'gɑ:st] adj. Epouvanté, horrifié. ‖ Sidéré (fam.).

agile ['ædʒail] adj. Agile, alerte.

agility [ə'dʒiliti] n. Agilité *f.*

agio ['ædʒiou] n. FIN. Agio *m*.

agiotage [ˈædʒətidʒ] n. FIN. Agiotage *m*.

agitate ['ædʒiteit] v. tr. Agiter, secouer. ‖ MED. Agiter. ‖ FIG. Agiter, discuter, débattre.
— v. intr. Faire de l'agitation; ameuter (or) soulever l'opinion *(against,* contre; *for,* en faveur de).

agitation [,ædʒi'teiʃen] n. Agitation *f*. ‖ Emotion, excitation *f*. (excitement). ‖ Discussion *f.,* débat *m*. ‖ Campagne *f*. (of an agitator).

agitator [ˈædʒiteitə*] n. CULIN. Mixer *m*. ‖ FIG. Agitateur *m*.

aglet ['æglit] n. Ferret *m*. (of a lace). ‖ MILIT. Aiguillette *f*. ‖ BOT. Chaton *m*. (of birch, hazel).

aglow [ə'glou] adj. Embrasé, rougeoyant. ‖ FIG. Pourpre.

agnail ['ægneil] n. MED. Envie *f*. (See HANGNAIL.)

agnate ['ægneit] adj. Agnat, consanguin. ‖ De même race. ‖ FIG. Apparenté.
— n. Agnat *m*.

agnation [ə'gneiʃən] n. Consanguinité *f*. ‖ Identité raciale *f.*

agnostic [æg'nɔstik] adj., n. Agnostique *s*.

agnosticism [-tisizm] n. Agnosticisme *m*.

ago [ə'gou] adv. Autrefois; *long ago,* il y a un longtemps; *not long ago,* depuis peu.
— adj. Ecoulé (past); *two years ago,* voici deux ans, il y a deux ans.

agog [ə'gɔg] adj. Impatient, brûlant *(to,* de); *to set agog,* mettre en mouvement; *to set s.o. agog for,* attiser l'envie de qqn pour.

agonize ['ægənaiz] v. intr. Lutter, faire des efforts désespérés pour. ‖ Souffrir horriblement; se tordre de douleur.
— v. tr. Torturer.

agonizing [-iŋ] adj. Douloureux, angoissant, torturant.

agonizingly [-iŋli] adv. Effroyablement, épouvantablement.

agony [-ni] n. Angoisse, détresse *f.: agony column,* rubrique (or) annonce pour recherche de disparus. ‖ Douleur intense *f.;* supplice moral *m; to suffer agonies,* endurer un vrai martyre. ‖ Paroxysme *m.;* délire *m*. (of joy); *in an agony of terror,* au comble de l'épouvante. ‖ MED. Agonie *f*.

agoraphobia [,ægərə'foubiə] n. Agoraphobie *f*.

agouti [ə'gu:ti] n. ZOOL. Agouti *m*.

agrapha ['ægrəfə] n. pl. ECCLES. Agrapha *f. pl.,* paroles (*f. pl.*) attribuées à Jésus.

agrarian [ə'grɛəriən] adj. Agraire.
— n. Agrarien *m*.

agree [ə'gri:] v. intr. Consentir, se prêter *(to,* à); *to agree to a proposal,* accepter une proposition. ‖ S'entendre, s'accorder, concorder *(about,* sur; *with,* avec). ‖ Etre d'accord, convenir, reconnaître *(that,* que); *it is agreed,* c'est entendu. ‖ Etre d'accord *(with,* avec); être de l'avis *(with,* de). ‖ Convenir, réussir *(with,* à); *the climate doesn't agree with him,* ce climat ne lui vaut rien. ‖ GRAMM. S'accorder *(with,* avec). ‖ COMM. *Agreed fair price,* prix imposé.

agreeable [-əbl] adj. Plaisant, aimable, agréable. (See PLEASANT.) ‖ Consentant *(to,* à); *you're agreeable?,* vous voulez bien? ‖ Conforme *(to,* à).

agreeableness [-əblnis] n. Amabilité *f.;* charme *m*. ‖ Concordance *f*. ‖ Consentement *m*. ‖ Conformité *f*. *(to,* à).

agreeably [-əbli] adv. Agréablement. ‖ Conformément *(to,* à). ‖ De bon gré, volontiers.

agreement [-:mənt] n. Harmonie, concordance *f.; in agreement,* de conserve. ‖ Entente *f.;* accord *m*. (arrangement). ‖ Contrat *m.;* convention *f.; collective agreement,* contrat collectif; *stated parole agreement,* convention verbale expresse. ‖ COMM. *As per agreement,* comme convenu. ‖ GRAMM. Accord.

agrestic [ə'grestik] adj. Agreste, rustique.

agricultural [,ægri'kʌltʃərəl] adj. Agricole.

agriculture [-tʃə*] n. AGRIC. Agriculture *f*.

agriculturist [,ægri'kʌltʃərist] n. AGRIC. Agriculteur *m*.

agronomist [æg'rɔnəmist] n. AGRIC. Agronome *m*.

agronomy [-mi] n. AGRIC. Agronomie *f*.

aground [ə'graund] adv. NAUT. A la côte, à sec; *to run aground,* s'échouer (ship).

ague ['eigju:] n. MED. Fièvre récurrente *f*. (fever); frisson *m*. (fit of shivering).

agued [-d] adj. MED. Fébrile; frissonnant.

ah! [ɑ:] interj. Ah!, oh!

aha! [ɑ:'hɑ:] interj. Ah ah!

ahead [ə'hed] adv. En avant; *to get ahead,* prendre de l'avance; *to go ahead,* aller de l'avant. ‖ NAUT. En avant, sur l'avant. ‖ SPORTS. *To draw (or) to get ahead,* décoller, se détacher (cyclist). ‖ *Ahead of,* en avant de, devant; *to get ahead of,* surpasser.

aheap [ə'hi:p] adv. En bloc, en tas.

ahem! [hm] interj. Hum!

ahistoric(al) [,eihis'tɔrikəl] adj. Anhistorique.

ahoy [ə'hɔi] interj. NAUT. Ohé!

aid [eid] v. tr. Aider *(to,* à); *to aid one another,* s'entraider. ‖ MED. Contribuer à (s.o.'s recovery).
— n. Aide *f.;* secours *m*. (See HELP.) ‖ Aide, assistance *f.; to lend one's aid to,* prêter son concours à. ‖ Aide, assistant *m*. (helper). ‖ MED. Secours *m.; first aid,* secours aux blessés; *first-aid station,* poste de secours.

aide-de-camp ['eiddə'kɔŋ] n. MILIT. Aide-de-camp *m*.

aide-mémoire ['eidmem'wɑ:*] n. Aide-mémoire *m. inv*. ‖ JUR. Mémorandum *m*.

aidman [-mən] n. U. S. Infirmier militaire *m*.

aigrette [ei'gret] n. Aigrette *f*.

aiguille ['eigwil] n. GEOGR. Aiguille *f*.

aiguillette [,eigwi'let] n. MILIT. Aiguillette *f*.

ail [eil] v. tr. Faire souffrir.
— v. intr. Souffrir.

aileron ['eilərɔn] n. AVIAT. Aileron *m*.

ailing ['eiliŋ] adj. MED. Souffrant.

ailment [-mənt] n. MED. Indisposition *f.;* malaise *m*.

aim [eim] v. tr. Allonger (a blow). ‖ MILIT. Pointer *(at,* contre) [a weapon]. ‖ FIG. Diriger *(at,* vers) [one's efforts]; décocher (a remark); *to aim one's shafts at,* prendre pour cible.
— v. intr. MILIT. *To aim at,* viser (s.o., sth.). ‖ FIG. Viser, tendre *(at,* à); s'efforcer *(at,* de).

— n. MILIT. Visée *f.*; pointage *m.* (act); but *m.* (of a missile); *to take aim at,* coucher en joue. ‖ FIG. Dessein *m.*; visées *f. pl.* (see INTENTION); *with the aim of,* visant à.

aimer [-ə*] n. MILIT., AVIAT. Viseur *m.*

aimless [-lis] adj. Sans but.

ain't [eint] POP. Representation of *am not, is not, are not, has not, have not.*

air ⌊εə*⌋ n. Air, aspect *m.*; *to have an air,* avoir de la gueule (fam.); *to put on an air,* enfler le jabot (fam.). ‖ Pl. Airs *m.*; mines *f.*; *to give oneself airs, to put on airs,* se donner des airs.

air adj. De l'air, aérien. ‖ AVIAT. Aérien (attack, base, defence); *air crew,* équipage d'un avion; *air force,* forces aériennes, aviation; *Fleet Air Arm,* Aéronavale. ‖ PHYS. Atmosphérique (flow, pressure).

— n. Air *m.*; *in the air,* en l'air, dans les airs; *to take the air,* prendre l'air (or) le frais. ‖ Air *m.* (wind); *a breath of fresh air,* un souffle d'air frais. ‖ RADIO. *To be on the air,* parler à la radio; *to be put on the air,* être radiodiffusé. ‖ MUS. Air *m.* ‖ AVIAT. Air; vol *m.*; sortie *f.*; *to take the air,* prendre l'air (plane). ‖ FIG. Air, cours *m.*; *in the air,* en circulation (ideas); *all in the air,* en l'air (projects). ‖ FIG. Atmosphère *f.* (of luxury). ‖ FAM. *Hot air,* des phrases, du vent, du blablabla; *to give s.o. the air,* montrer la porte à qqn; *to live on air,* vivre de l'air du temps; *to walk on air,* ne pas toucher terre; U. S. *up in the air,* très monté (angry). ‖ **Air-balloon,** n. Ballon (toy). ‖ **Air-bed,** n. Matelas pneumatique *m.* ‖ **Air-bladder,** n. Vessie natatoire *f.* ‖ **Airborne,** adj. AVIAT. Aéroporté. ‖ **Air-brake,** n. TECHN. Frein à air comprimé *m.* ‖ **Air-bridge,** n. AVIAT. Parcours aérien *m.* ‖ **Air-chamber,** n. AUTOM., PHYS. Chambre (*f.*) à air. ‖ **Air-condition,** v. tr. Climatiser. ‖ **Air-conditioner,** n. Conditionneur d'air *m.* ‖ **Air-conditioning,** n. Climatisation *f.* ‖ **Air-conveyance,** n. Transport par air *m.* ‖ **Air-cooled,** adj. TECHN. Refroidi par circulation d'air. ‖ **Air-cover, air-umbrella,** n. AVIAT. Force de protection aérienne *f.* ‖ **Air-cushion,** n. Coussin pneumatique; matelas d'air *m.* ‖ **Air-duct,** n. AVIAT. Canalisation (*f.*) d'air. ‖ **Air-ferry,** n. AVIAT. Service d'avions transbordeurs. ‖ **Air-frame,** n. AVIAT. Cellule d'avion; *air-frame components,* éléments de cellule. ‖ **Air-gun,** n. Pistolet à air comprimé *m.* ‖ **Air-hole,** n. Event *m.* ‖ **Air-hostess,** n. AVIAT. Hôtesse (*f.*) de l'air. ‖ **Air-jacket,** n. Gilet de sauvetage *m.* ‖ **Air-lift,** n. AVIAT. Pont aérien *m.* ‖ **Air-lock,** n. Poche (*f.*) d'air. ‖ **Air-mail,** n. Poste aérienne *f.*; *by air-mail,* par air; v. tr. envoyer par avion. ‖ **Air-mass,** n. Masse (*f.*) d'air. ‖ **Air-mattress,** n. Matelas pneumatique *m.* ‖ **Air-minded,** adj. Intéressé par l'aviation. ‖ **Air-pocket,** n. AVIAT. Trou d'air *m.* ‖ **Air-proof,** adj. Etanche à l'air. ‖ **Air-pump,** n. TECHN. Compresseur *m.*; machine pneumatique *f.* ‖ **Air-raid,** n. AVIAT. Raid aérien *m.*; *air-raid precautions,* défense antiaérienne (or) passive. ‖ **Air-route,** n. AVIAT. Aéroroute. ‖ **Air-scoop,** n. AVIAT., NAUT. Manche à air *m.* ‖ **Air-shed,** n. AVIAT. Hangar *m.* ‖ **Air-show,** n. AVIAT. Meeting d'aviation. ‖ **Air-sick,** adj. MED. Atteint du mal de l'air. ‖ **Air-sickness,** n. MED. Mal de l'air *m.* ‖ **Air-speed,** n. Vitesse relative *f.*; *air-speed indicator,* badin. ‖ **Air-stop,** n. AVIAT. Centre d'hélicoptères *m.* ‖ **Air-superiority,** n. AVIAT. Supériorité aérienne *f.* ‖ **Air-terminal,** n. AVIAT. Aérogare *f.* ‖ **Air-threads,** n. BOT. Fils (*m. pl.*) de la Vierge. ‖ **Air-tight,** adj. Etanche à l'air. ‖ **Air-to-air,** adj. AVIAT. Avion-avion. ‖ **Air-to-ground,** adj. AVIAT. Avion-terre. ‖ **Air-track,** n. AVIAT. U. S. Pilotage (*m.*) sans visibilité.

— v. tr. Aérer, ventiler (a room); *to air oneself,* prendre l'air. ‖ Sécher à l'air (linen). ‖ Bassiner (a bed). ‖ FIG. Exhaler (one's anger); donner libre

cours à (one's feelings); étaler (one's knowledge); afficher (one's opinions); ventiler (a question).

aircraft ['εə,krɑ:ft] n. AVIAT. Avion, appareil; aéronef *m.*; *aircraft carrier,* porte-avions.

aircraftman [-mən] (pl. **aircraftmen**) n. AVIAT. Aviateur, aéronaute *m.*

airdrome ['εədroum] n. U. S. AVIAT. Aérodrome *m.*

Airedale ['εə,deil] n. ZOOL. Airedale *m.* (dog).

airfield [-fi:ld] n. AVIAT. Champ d'aviation *m.*

airflow [-flou] adj. AUTOM. *Airflow body,* carénage aérodynamique.

airfoil [-fɔil] n. U. S. See AEROFOIL.

airily [-rili] adv. D'un air dégagé, légèrement.

airiness [-rinis] n. Situation aérée *f.* ‖ Ventilation, aération *f.* ‖ FIG. Frivolité, légèreté *f.*

airing [-riŋ] n. Aération *f.* (of linen). ‖ Bassinement *m.* (of a bed). ‖ Petit tour *m.*; *to give oneself an airing,* faire un tour, se donner un peu d'air.

airless [-lis] adj. Mal aéré, qui manque d'air (room); sans un souffle d'air (day, evening).

airline [-,lain] n. AVIAT. Ligne aérienne *f.*

airliner [-,lainə*] n. AVIAT. Avion de ligne *m.*

airman [-mən] (pl. **airmen**) n. AVIAT. Aviateur *m.*

airplane [-plein] n. AVIAT. Aéroplane, avion *m.*

airport [-,pɔ:t] n. AVIAT. Aéroport *m.*

airscrew [-,skru:] n. AVIAT. Hélice *f.*

airship [-ʃip] n. AVIAT. Dirigeable *m.*

airspace [-,speis] n. AVIAT., JUR. Espace aérien *m.*

airstrip [-strip] n. AVIAT. Terrain d'atterrissage *m.*

airway [-wei] n. AVIAT. Route aérienne *f.* ‖ TECHN. Galerie d'aération *f.* (in mine).

airwoman [-,wumən] (pl. **airwomen** [-wimin]) n. AVIAT. Aviatrice *f.*

airworthiness ['εə'wə:ðinis] n. AVIAT. Navigabilité aérienne *f.*

airworthy [-,wə:ði] adj. AVIAT. En état de tenir l'air, navigable.

airy ['εəri] adj. Aérien. ‖ Eventé, aéré (breezy). ‖ FIG. Superficiel, léger (flippant); gracieux (graceful); vif, gai (sprightly); chimérique, sans consistance (unsubstantial). ‖ FAM. U. S. maniéré (affected).

aisle [ail] n. ARCHIT. Bas-côté (*m.*) d'une église; nef latérale *f.* ‖ U. S. Passage entre des sièges; couloir central, corridor *m.*

aitch [eitʃ] n. H (letter); *to drop one's aitches,* oublier d'aspirer les h.

aitchbone ['eitʃ:boun] n. CULIN. Culotte (*f.*) de bœuf.

ajar [ə'dʒɑ:*] adv. Entrebâillé.

akimbo [ə'kimbou] adv. *Arms akimbo,* les poings sur les hanches.

akin [ə'kin] adj. Apparenté, allié (to, à). ‖ FIG. Proche, voisin (to, de).

alabaster ['æləbɑ:stə*] n. Albâtre *m.*

— adj. Blanc, d'albâtre.

alack! [ə'læk] interj. Hélas!

alacrity [ə'lækriti] n. Alacrité *f.*

alar ['eilə*] adj. AVIAT. Alaire. ‖ MED. Axillaire.

alarm [ə'lɑ:m] n. Alarme *f.*; *alarm bell,* tocsin; *alarm clock,* réveille-matin; *alarm signal,* signal d'alarme; *burglar alarm,* sonnerie d'alarme en cas de cambriolage. ‖ Alarmes, craintes *f. pl.*

— v. tr. Alerter, donner l'alarme (to warn). ‖ Alarmer, apeurer (to frighten).

alarming [-iŋ] adj. Alarmant; *alarming nature,* caractère de gravité.

alarmingly [-iŋli] adv. D'une manière alarmante.

alarmist [-ist] n. Alarmiste; paniquard *m.* (fam.).

alas [ə'lɑs] interj. Hélas!

Alaska [ə'læskə] n. GEOGR. Alaska *m.* ‖ CULIN. *Baked Alaska,* omelette norvégienne.

alate ['eileit] adj. Ailé.

alb [ælb] n. ECCLES. Aube.

Albania [æl'beiniə] n. GEOGR. Albanie *f.*

Albanian [-n] adj., n. GEOGR. Albanais *s.*

albata [æl'beitə] n. Maillechort *m.*

albatross ['ælbatrɔs] n. ZOOL. Albatros *m.*

AIRPLANES — AVIONS

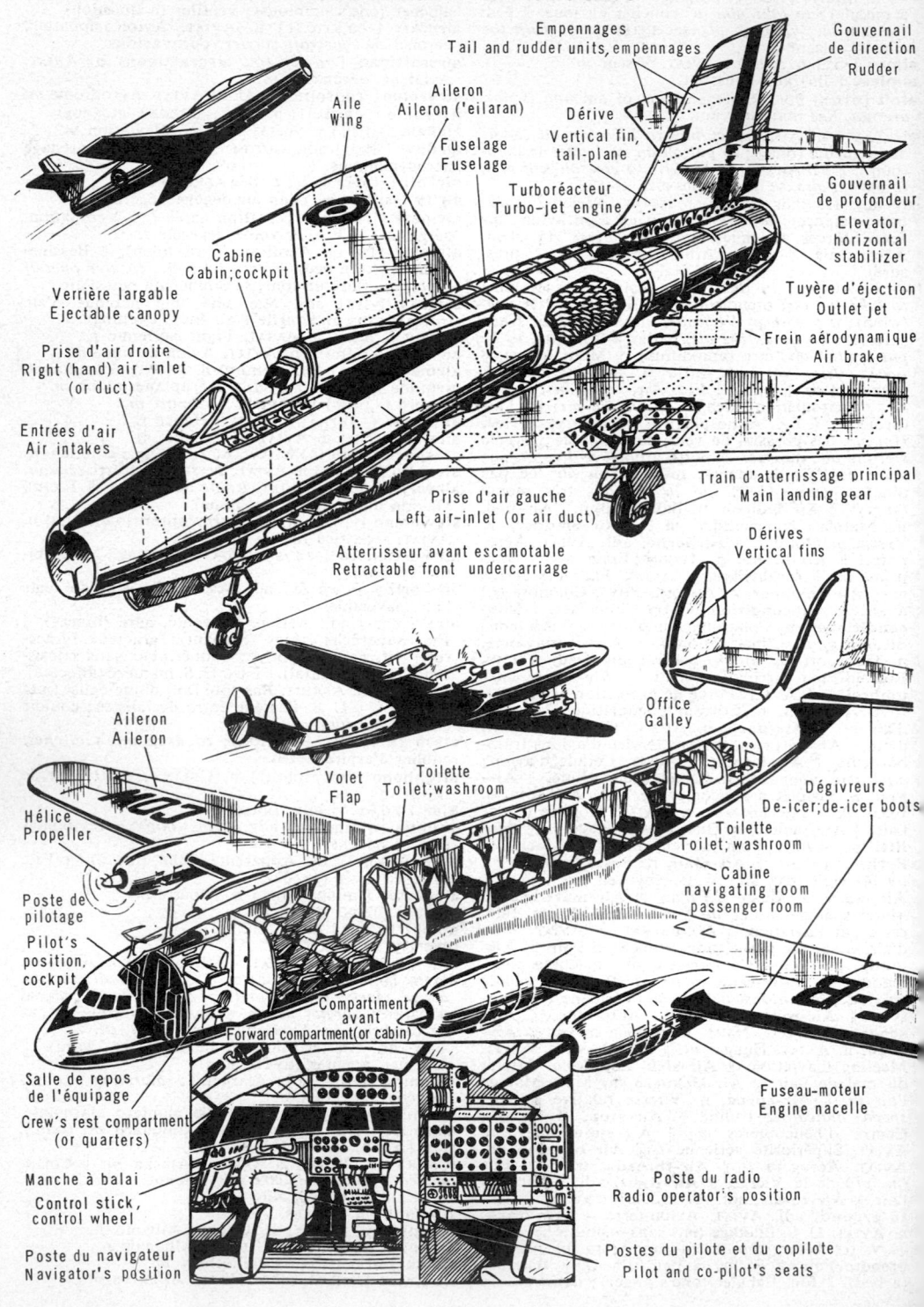

Empennages
Tail and rudder units, empennages

Gouvernail de direction
Rudder

Aile
Wing

Aileron
Aileron ('eilaran)

Dérive
Vertical fin, tail-plane

Fuselage
Fuselage

Turboréacteur
Turbo–jet engine

Gouvernail de profondeur
Elevator, horizontal stabilizer

Cabine
Cabin; cockpit

Tuyère d'éjection
Outlet jet

Verrière largable
Ejectable canopy

Frein aérodynamique
Air brake

Prise d'air droite
Right (hand) air –inlet (or duct)

Entrées d'air
Air intakes

Train d'atterrissage principal
Main landing gear

Prise d'air gauche
Left air–inlet (or air duct)

Dérives
Vertical fins

Atterrisseur avant escamotable
Retractable front undercarriage

Aileron
Aileron

Office
Galley

Volet
Flap

Toilette
Toilet; washroom

Dégivreurs
De-icer; de-icer boots

Hélice
Propeller

Toilette
Toilet; washroom

Poste de pilotage

Cabine
navigating room
passenger room

Pilot's position, cockpit

Compartiment avant
Forward compartment (or cabin)

Salle de repos de l'équipage

Crew's rest compartment (or quarters)

Fuseau–moteur
Engine nacelle

Manche à balai

Control stick, control wheel

Poste du radio
Radio operator's position

Poste du navigateur
Navigator's position

Postes du pilote et du copilote
Pilot and co-pilot's seats

albeit ['ɔ:l'bi:it] conj. † Bien que, quoique.
albinism ['ælbi,nizm̩] n. MED. Albinisme *m*.
albino [æl'bi:nou] (pl. **albinos** [-z]) n. Albinos *s*.
album ['ælbəm] n. Album *m*.
albumen [æl'bju:min] n. Albumen *m*.
albumenize [æl'bju:minaiz] v. tr. Albuminiser.
albumin [-min] n. MED. Albumine *f*.
albuminoid [-nɔid] adj., n. Albuminoïde *m*.
albuminous [-nəs] adj. Albumineux.
albuminuria [æl,bju:mi:'njuəriə] n. MED. Albuminurie *f*.
alburnum [æl'bə:nəm] n. BOT. Aubier *m*.
alcaide [æl'kældi] n. Alcade *m*.
alcarraza [ælkɑ'rɑ:zə] n. Alcarazas *m*.
alchemist ['ælkimist] n. Alchimiste *m*.
alchemize [-maiz] v. tr. Transmuter (elements).
alchemy [-mi] n. Alchimie *f*.
alcohol ['ælkəhɔl] n. Alcool *m*.
alcoholate [-it] n. CHIM. Alcoolat *m*.
alcoholic [,ælkə'hɔlik] adj. Alcoolique.
alcoholism ['ælkəhɔlizm̩] n. Alcoolisme *m*.
alcoholize [-aiz] v. tr. Alcooliser.
alcoholometer [,ælkəhɔ'lɔmitə*] n. CHIM. Alcoomètre *m*.
Alcoran [,ælkɔ'rɑ:n] n. Coran *m*.
alcove ['ælkouv] n. Renfoncement *m*. (nook); alcôve *f*. (recess). || Tonnelle *f*. (summer house).
aldehyde [ældihaid] n. CHIM. Aldéhyde *m*.
alder ['ɔ:ldə*] n. BOT. Aune *m*.
alderman ['ɔ:ldəmən] (pl. **aldermen**) n. Conseiller municipal, alderman *m*.
Alderney ['ɔ:ldəni] n. GEOGR. Aurigny (Channel island). || ZOOL. Vache laitière (*f*.) de race alderney.
— adj. ZOOL. De race alderney.
ale ['eil] n. Bière, ale *f*. || FIG. Beuverie *f*. || FAM. *Adam's ale*, flotte. || **Ale-house**, n. Cabaret *m*., brasserie *f*.
aleatoric [,eiliə'tɔrik], **aleatory** ['eiliətəri] adj. Aléatoire (gen., mus.).
alee [ə'li:] adv. NAUT. Sous le vent.
alegar ['eiligə*] n. CULIN. Vinaigre (*m*.) de bière.
Alemannian [ælə'mænjən] adj. GEOGR. Alémanique.
alembic [ə'lembik] n. PHYS. Alambic *m*. || FIG. Creuset *m*. (of fancy).
alembicated [-itid] adj. FAM. Alambiqué.
alert [ə'lə:t] adj. Vigilant, éveillé (watchful). || Alerte, agile (nimble).
— n. Alerte *f*.; *on the alert*, en alerte, en éveil. || MILIT. Alerte; *gas alert*, alerte aux gaz.
— v. tr. Alerter.
alexandrine [,æleg'zɑ:ndrain] n., adj. Alexandrin.
alexipharmic [ə,leksi'fɑ:mik] adj., n. Antidote.
alfa ['ælfə] n. BOT. Alfa *m*.
alfalfa [æl'fælfə] n. BOT. Luzerne *f*.
alfresco [æl'freskou] adj., adv. En plein air, dehors.
alga ['ælgə] (pl. **algae** ['æld3i:]) n. BOT. Algue *f*.
algebra ['æld3ibrə] n. MATH. Algèbre *f*.
algebraic [,æld3i'breiik] adj. MATH. Algébrique.
algebraically [-əli] adv. MATH. Par l'algèbre.
algebraist ['æld3ibreiist] n. MATH. Algébriste *m*.
Algeria [æl'd3iəriə] n. GEOGR. Algérie *f*.
algesia [æl'd3i:zjə] n. MED. Algésie *f*.
algid ['æld3id] adj. MED. Algide.
Algol ['ælgɔl] n. INFORM. Algol *m*.
algorithm ['ælgə,riðm̩], **algorism** [-zm̩] n. MATH. Algorithme *m*.
algorithmic [,ælgə'riðmik] adj. MATH. Algorithmique.
alias ['eiliæs] adv. Alias.
— n. Nom d'emprunt *m*.
alibi ['ælibai] n. Alibi *m*. || FAM. Excuse *f*.
alien ['eiliən] adj. Etranger (*from*, à). || Contraire, hostile, répugnant (*to*, à).
— n. Etranger *s*. (See FOREIGNER, STRANGER.)

alienable [-əbl̩] adj. JUR. Aliénable.
alienate [-eit] v. tr. JUR. Aliéner. || FIG. S'aliéner, détacher de soi.
alienation [,eiliə'neiʃən] n. Désaffection *f*. (*from*, de); aversion *f*. (*from*, pour). || JUR. Aliénation *f*. (of an estate). || MED. Démence *f*.; *mental alienation*, aliénation mentale. || THEATR. Distanciation *f*.
alienator ['eiliəneitə*] n. JUR. Aliénateur *m*.; aliénatrice *f*.
alienee [,eiliə'ni:] n. JUR. Aliénataire *s*.
alienist ['eiliənist] n. MED. Aliéniste *m*.
alight [ə'lait] v. intr. Mettre pied à terre; *to alight from*, descendre de (carriage, horse). || Se poser (birds). || AVIAT. Atterrir (on the ground); amerrir (on the sea).
alight adj. Allumé (kindled); éclairé (lighted up); embrasé, en feu (on fire); *to blow the fire alight again*, rallumer le feu en soufflant.
align [ə'lain] v. tr. Aligner; *to align oneself with*, s'aligner sur (s.o.). || FIN. Aligner (currency) [*on*, sur]. || TECHN. Dégauchir.
— v. intr. MILIT. Se mettre en ligne.
alignment [-mənt] n. Alignement *m*. || AUTOM. U. S. *Wheel alignment*, pincement des roues.
alike [ə'laik] adj. Pareil, semblable; *they are all alike*, ils se ressemblent tous. || Egal, indifférent; *it's all alike to me*, ça m'est égal.
— adv. De la même façon, de même, identiquement; *we think alike*, nous sommes du même avis. || Egalement, aussi bien; indistinctement, indifféremment; *winter and summer alike*, été comme hiver.
aliment ['ælimənt] n. Aliment *m*.
alimental [,æli'mentl̩] adj. Nutritif. || JUR. Alimentaire.
alimentary [-əri] adj. Alimentaire; nourrissant. || MÉD. *Alimentary canal*, tube digestif. || JUR. Alimentaire.
alimentation [,ælimen'teiʃən] n. Alimentation *f*.
alimony ['æliməni] n. JUR. Pension alimentaire *f*.
aliped ['æliped] adj., n. ZOOL. Chiroptère *m*.
aliphatic [,æli'fætik] adj. CHIM. Aliphatique.
aliquot ['ælikwɔt] adj., n. MATH. Aliquote *m*.
alive [ə'laiv] adj. Vivant, vif (see LIVING); *to come alive again*, renaître à la vie. || Au monde, en vie; *any man alive*, n'importe qui, tout être au monde. || Plein de vie (or) d'allant, vivant, éveillé; *look alive!*, dépêchez-vous! || Grouillant, fourmillant (*with*, de). [See SWARMING.] || Ouvert (*to*, à) [an idea]; sensible (*to*, à) [praise]. || Attentif (*to*, à), soucieux (*to*, de) [one's interests]. || Conscient (*to*, de); *to be alive to the fact that*, n'être pas sans savoir que. || FAM. *Man alive!*, Seigneur!
alkalescent ['ælkə'lɛsn̩t] adj. CHIM. Alcalescent.
alkali ['ælkəlai] n. CHIM. Alcali *m*.
alkalify [-lifai], **alkalize** [-laiz] v. tr. Alcaliser.
alkaline [-lain] adj. CHIM. Alcalin.
alkaloid [-lɔid] n. CHIM. Alcaloïde *m*.
all [ɔ:l] adj. Tout; *all China*, toute la Chine; *all the others*, tous les autres. || Tout, n'importe quel (any whatever); *at all hours*, à toute heure. || Total, tout (the greatest possible); *in all sincerity*, en toute sincérité. || Tout, en totalité; *life is not all pleasure (or) roses*, vivre n'est pas tout rose. || Entièrement d'avis; *to be all for*, ne pas demander mieux que.
— n. Tout *m*.; totalité, entièreté *f*.; *give your all*, donnez tout ce que vous avez.
— pron. Tous, tout le monde (everybody); *all of us*, nous tous; *all must die*, tout le monde doit mourir. || Tout (everything); *all is over between them*, tout est fini entre eux. || Tout (every part); *all of it is burnt*, tout a brûlé. || Loc. *Above all*, surtout; *after all*, après tout, somme toute; *all but*, presque; *all in all*, absolument tout, tout considéré; *all one*, tout un; *all that*, tout cela; tout ce qui (or) ce que; *all who*, tous ceux qui; *all very fine, but*, tout ça c'est bien bon, mais; *and all that*, et

tout et tout ; *first of all*, tout d'abord, avant tout ; *in all*, en tout ; *most of all*, surtout, plus encore ; *not at all*, pas du tout ; *that's all*, c'est tout ; je ne vous dis que ça.
— adv. Tout, entièrement, tout à fait ; *all covered with dust*, tout couvert de poussière. ‖ Partout, à égalité ; *five all*, cinq à cinq (score). ‖ Loc. *All alone*, tout seul ; *all at once*, tout d'un coup ; *all one*, tout un ; *all out*, de toutes ses forces ; *all over*, entièrement, d'un bout à l'autre ; achevé, fini ; *all the better*, *all the worse for*, tant mieux, tant pis pour ; *all the same*, malgré tout, n'empêche que ; *all the same to*, égal (or) indifférent à. ‖ Fam. *All in*, éreinté ; *all right*, ça va, bon, très bien ; *he isn't quite all there*, il déménage quelque peu, il n'a pas toute sa tête. ‖ **All-bountiful**, adj. Infiniment bon. ‖ **All-clear**, n. Milit. Fin d'alerte *f.* ‖ **All-fours**, n. pl. Quatre pattes ; *to go on all-fours*, marcher à quatre pattes ; Fig. *to be on all-fours with*, être de plein niveau avec, cadrer parfaitement avec. ‖ **All-in**, adj. Electr. Mixte (agreement) ; *all tous-risques* (policy) ; Comm. tout compris (price) ; U. S. Fam. Epuisé. ‖ **All-included**, adj. Tout compris. ‖ **All-inclusive**, adj. Qui englobe tout ; U. S. See ALL-IN. ‖ **All-India**, adj. Geogr. Pan-Indien. ‖ **All-in-wrestling**, n. Sports. Catch *m.* ‖ **All-mains**, adj. Radio. Tous courants. ‖ **All-of-a-sudden**, adj. Primesautier, tout de go. ‖ **All-out**, adj. Maximum (effort) ; *all-out war*, guerre à outrance. ‖ **All-purpose**, à tout usage, propre à tout. ‖ **All-red**, adj. Entièrement sur territoire britannique (route). ‖ **All-round**, adj. Fam. Universel (person) ; global (price). ‖ **All-rounder**, n. Fam. Esprit universel *m.* ‖ **All-star**, adj. Theatr. Joué exclusivement par des vedettes. ‖ **All-time**, adj. De tous les temps ; *an all-time low*, un record de médiocrité, le point le plus bas jamais atteint. ‖ **All-up**, adj. Aviat. En vol ; *all-up weight*, poids global en vol. ‖ **All-weather**, adj. Tout-temps.
allay [ə'lei] v. tr. Calmer, apaiser (fears) ; alléger (grief) ; diminuer (pleasure). [See RELIEVE.] ‖ Med. Soulager (pain).
allegation [,æli'geiʃən] n. Allégation *f.* ‖ Jur. Articulation *f.* de faits.
allege [ə'ledʒ] v. tr. Alléguer, prétendre. ‖ Jur. Plaider (insanity) ; exciper de (one's good faith) ; *alleged thief*, voleur présumé.
allegiance [ə'li:dʒəns] n. † Allégeance *f.* ‖ Fidélité, soumission *f.*
allegoric(al) [,æli'gɔrikəl] adj. Allégorique.
allegorically [-i] adv. Allégoriquement.
allegorist ['æligɔrist] n. Allégoriste *m.*
allegory [-i] n. Allégorie *f.*
alleluia, alleluya [,æli'lu:jə] n. Eccles., Mus. Alléluia *m.*
allergen ['ælə:dʒin] n. Med. Allergène *m.*
allergic [ə'lə:dʒik] adj. Med. Allergique. ‖ Fam. Réfractaire, répugnant (to, à).
allergy ['ælədʒi] n. Med. Allergie *f.*
alleviate [ə'li:vieit] v. tr. Soulager, alléger.
alleviation [ə,li:vi'eiʃən] n. Soulagement *m.*
alleviative [ə'li:vieitiv] adj., n. Med. Calmant, lénitif *m.*
alleviator [-ə*] n. Med. Anodin *m.* ‖ Fig. Personne *f.* qui soulage.
alley ['æli] n. Allée *f.* (in a park). ‖ Ruelle *f.* ; *blind alley*, cul-de-sac.
alleyway ['æliwei] n. U. S. Ruelle *f.*
alliaceous [,æli'eiʃəs] adj. Bot., Culin. Alliacé.
alliance [ə'laiəns] n. Alliance *f.* (by marriage). ‖ Alliance *f.* (of nations, political parties) [with, avec] ; *electoral alliance*, apparentement.
alligator ['æligeitə*] n. Zool. Alligator *m.* (See CROCODILE.) ‖ Comm. Croco *m.* (leather). ‖ Bot. *Alligator pear*, poire avocat. (See AVOCADO.)
alliterate [ə'litəreit] v. intr. Gramm. Allitérer.
alliteration [ə,litə'reiʃən] n. Allitération *f.*

allocate ['ælokeit] v. tr. Assigner, attribuer (an amount). ‖ Fin. Allouer, affecter (funds). ‖ U. S. Localiser.
allocatee [,æləkei'ti:] n. Allocataire *s.*
allocation [,ælo'keiʃən] n. Allocation *f.* (of supplies). ‖ Répartition (of shares). ‖ Part *f.*
allocution [,ælo'kju:ʃən] n. Allocution *f.*
allodium [ə'loudiəm] n. † Alleu *m.*
allomorph ['ælomɔ:f] n. Gramm. Allomorphe *m.*
allopath ['ælopæθ], **allopathist** [æ'lɔpəθist] n. Med. Allopathe *s.*
allopathic [,ælo'pæθik] adj. Med. Allopathique.
allopathy [ə'lɔpəθi] n. Med. Allopathie *f.*
allophone ['ælofoun] n. Gramm. Allophone *m.*
allot [ə'lɔt] v. tr. (1). Lotir, répartir. ‖ Accorder, allouer, assigner (a share) [to, à].
allotment [-mənt] n. Répartition *f.* ; *on allotment*, lors du partage. ‖ Part *f.* ‖ Agric. Lotissement, terrain loti *m.* ‖ Milit. Délégation de solde *f.*
allotrope ['ælotroup] n. Chim. Variété allotropique *f.*
allotropic(al) [,ælo'trɔpik(əl)] adj. Chim. Allotropique.
allotropy [ə'lɔtrəpi] n. Chim. Allotropie *f.*
allow [ə'lau] v. tr. Admettre, accorder, concéder, convenir (to admit) ; *to admit sth. to be true*, admettre la véracité d'un fait, reconnaître qu'une chose est vraie. ‖ Permettre, autoriser ; *to allow smoking*, permettre de fumer ; *to allow s.o. sth.*, permettre qqch., à qqn ; *to allow s.o. to do sth.*, autoriser qqn à faire qqch. ; *to allow oneself*, se permettre, s'accorder. ‖ Jur. Admettre (a request) ; impartir (a delay). ‖ Fin., Comm. Consentir (a discount) ; allouer (a sum) ; *to allow 5 per cent for damages*, déduire 5 pour 100 pour avaries.
— v. intr. **To allow for**, tenir compte de ; *allowing for*, eu égard à. ‖ **To allow of**, souffrir, tolérer, admettre.
allowable [-əbl] adj. Admissible, autorisable.
allowance [-əns] n. Permission, autorisation *f.* ‖ Ration *f.* ‖ Argent *m.* de poche (of a child). ‖ Jur. Pension, rente *f.* ; *family allowance fund*, caisse d'allocations familiales. ‖ Fin. Indemnité, allocation *f.* ‖ Milit. Enlistment allowance, prime d'engagement. ‖ Jur. Prestation *f.* ‖ Comm. Remise, réduction *f.* ; abattement *m.* ‖ Techn. Tolérance *f.* ‖ Fig. *To make allowance for*, faire la part de, tenir compte de ; *to make allowances*, faire la part des choses, en rabattre.
— v. tr. Rationner (s.o.). ‖ Jur. Pensionner.
alloy [ə'lɔi] n. Alliage *m.* (of two metals). ‖ Aloi *m.* (of gold).
— v. tr. Faire un alliage de, combiner. ‖ Fig. Déprécier, diminuer.
— v. intr. S'allier (metals).
allspice ['ɔ:lspais] n. Culin. Quatre épices *m.*
allude [ə'lju:d] v. intr. Faire allusion (to, à).
allure [ə'ljuə*] v. tr. Attirer, allécher (to attract) ; fasciner, aguicher, séduire (to seduce) [by, par]. ‖ Détourner (from, de) [one's duty].
allurement [-mənt] n. Attrait *m.* ; fascination, séduction *f.* ‖ Pl. Charmes *m. pl.* (of a woman).
alluring [-riŋ] adj. Attrayant ; fascinant, séduisant, aguichant, désirable.
allusion [ə'lju:ʒən] n. Allusion, mention *f.*
allusive [-siv] adj. Allusif. ‖ Blas. Parlantes (arms).
alluvial [ə'lju:viəl] adj. Alluvial, alluvionnaire ; limoneux.
alluvion [-ən] n. Action (f.) de l'eau baignant la rive. ‖ Geol. Alluvion *f.*
alluvium [-iəm] n. Geol. Alluvion *f.*
— N. B. Deux pluriels : *alluvia, alluviums.*
ally [ə'lai] v. tr. (2). Allier (to, with, à, avec) ; unir (by marriage). ‖ Gramm., Bot. *Allied to*, apparenté à.
— v. intr. S'allier.
— ['ælai] n. Allié *s.*

almah, U. S. **alma** ['ælmə] n. Almée f.
almanac ['ɔ:lmənæk] n. Almanach, calendrier m.
almighty [ɔ:l'maiti] adj. ECCLES. Tout-puissant. ‖ FAM. Formidable.
— adv. FAM. Formidablement.
almond ['ɑ:mənd] n. BOT. Amande f.; almond tree, amandier. ‖ CULIN. Almond paste, pâte d'amandes; sugared almond, dragée. ‖ MED. Glande f. ‖ **Almond-eyed,** adj. Aux yeux en amande. ‖ **Almond-shaped,** adj. En amande.
almoner ['ælmənə*] n. Aumônier m.
almost ['ɔ:lmoust] adv. Presque, à peu près.
— adj. FAM. Quasi.
alms [ɑ:mz] n. sg (or) pl. Aumône f.; to give alms, faire la charité. ‖ † Œuvre de charité f. ‖ **Alms-box,** n. Tronc. ‖ **Alms-folk,** n. Vieillards (m. pl.) de l'hospice. ‖ **Alms-giving,** n. Action (f.) de faire la charité. ‖ **Alms-house,** n. MED. Hospice, asile m.; maison de retraite f.
almsman [-mən] (pl. **almsmen**) n. Vieillard assisté m.
aloe ['ælou] n. BOT. Aloès m.
aloft [ə'lɔ:ft] adv. NAUT. En haut. ‖ AVIAT. En vol (plane). ‖ FAM. En l'air.
alogical [ei'lɔdʒikəl] adj. Alogique.
alone [ə'loun] adj. Seul; all alone, tout seul; he alone would talk like that, lui seul parlerait ainsi. ‖ FAM. De côté; to leave (or) let s.o. alone, laisser qqn tranquille; let alone, sans compter, mis à part; let well alone, le mieux est l'ennemi du bien.
— adv. Seulement.
along [ə'lɔŋ] adv. Dans le sens de la longueur; all along, toujours, constamment. ‖ En avant; to move along, avancer. ‖ Sur (or) avec soi; he took his umbrella along, il prit son parapluie. ‖ **Along with,** de conserve avec; to go along with s.o., accompagner qqn. ‖ FAM. Go along with you!, tirez-vous de là!; pour qui me prenez-vous!
— prép. Le long de; along the river, le long de la rivière. ‖ Sur. ‖ POP. Along of, avec. ‖ **Along-shore,** adv. Le long de la côte.
alongside [-'said] adv. NAUT. Bord à bord; to come alongside, accoster.
— prép. A côté de, le long de.
aloof [ə'lu:f] adv. A distance; to keep aloof from, se tenir à l'écart de; to remain aloof, se tenir sur son quant-à-soi. ‖ NAUT. Au large.
— adj. Eloigné, isolé (removed). ‖ FIG. Distant peu abordable.
aloofness [-nis] n. Froide réserve, attitude distante f. (from, envers).
alopecia [ælə'pi:ʃiə] n. MED. Alopécie f.
aloud [ə'laud] adv. Haut, à haute voix.
Alp [ælp] n. Alpe f. ‖ Pl. GEOGR. Alpes f. pl.
alpaca [æl'pækə] n. ZOOL., COMM. Alpaga m.
alpenhorn ['ælpənhɔ:n] n. MUS. Alpenhorn m.
alpenstock ['ælpənstɔk] n. Alpenstock m.
alpha ['ælfə] n. Alpha m. (letter). ‖ PHYS. Alpha (rays, particles). ‖ ASTRON. Etoile (f.) alpha. ‖ FAM. Alpha plus, excellente note.
alphabet [-bet] n. Alphabet m.
alphabetical [ælfə'betikəl] adj. Alphabétique.
alphabetically [-i] adv. Alphabétiquement.
alphabetize ['ælfəbətaiz] v. tr. Classer par ordre alphabétique.
Alpine ['ælpain] adj. Alpin, alpestre. ‖ MILIT. Alpine troops, chasseurs alpins.
alpinist ['ælpinist] n. Alpiniste s.
already [ɔ:l'redi] adv. Déjà; d'ores et déjà.
Alsatian [æl'seiʃən] adj., n. GEOGR. Alsacien s. ‖ ZOOL. Berger allemand m.
also ['ɔ:lsou] adv. Aussi, de plus, en outre (moreover). ‖ Aussi, également (too).
alt [ælt] n. MUS. Contraigu m.; C in alt, contre-ut.
altar ['ɔ:ltə*] n. ECCLES. Autel m. (platform); table de communion f. (table). ‖ Altar-boy, n. ECCLES.

Enfant de chœur m. ‖ **Altar-cloth,** n. ECCLES. Nappe (f.) d'autel. ‖ **Altar-curtain,** n. ECCLES. Custode (f.) d'autel. ‖ **Altar-frontal,** n. ECCLES. Devant d'autel m. ‖ **Altar-piece,** n. ARTS. Retable m.
alter ['ɔ:ltə*] v. tr. Changer, modifier (s.o., a word). ‖ Retoucher (a garment). ‖ FAM. To alter one's tune, déchanter.
— v. intr. Changer, se transformer (see CHANGE); to alter for the worse, s'altérer, empirer.
alterability [,ɔ:ltərə'biliti] n. Variabilité f.
alterable ['ɔ:ltərəbl] adj. Variable; modifiable.
alteration [,ɔl:tə'reiʃən] n. Modification, transformation f.; changement m. (action, result). ‖ Remaniement m.; retouche f. (to, à). ‖ JUR. Falsification f. (of public records).
alterative ['ɔ:ltərətiv] adj. Modificateur. ‖ MED. Altératif.
— n. MED. Altérant m.
altercate ['ɔ:ltə:keit] v. intr. Se quereller.
altercation [,ɔ:ltə:'keiʃən] n. Altercation f.
alternant [ɔ:l'tə:nənt] adj. GEOL. Alternant.
alternate [-nit] adj. Alternatif, pendulaire (movement); alternées (questions); croisées (rimes). ‖ MATH., BOT. Alterne.
— n. Substitut, intérimaire, remplaçant, suppléant m.
— [-neit] v. tr. Alterner, faire alterner.
— v. intr. Alterner (with, avec). ‖ Se succéder. ‖ FIG. Osciller (between, entre).
alternately [-nitli] adv. Tour à tour.
alternating ['ɔ:ltəneitiŋ] adj. ELECTR. Alternatif (current).
alternation [,ɔ:ltə:'neiʃən] n. Alternance f.
alternative [ɔ:l'tə:nətiv] adj. Alternatif. ‖ Autre, au choix (route). ‖ Nouveau (extract). ‖ MILIT. De repli (position). ‖ TECHN. De rechange.
— n. Alternative f.; he had no other alternative, il n'y avait pas pour lui d'autre solution possible.
alternatively [-li] adv. Alternativement. ‖ Avec l'alternative de.
alternator ['ɔ:ltə:,neitə*] n. ELECTR. Alternateur m.
although [ɔ:l'ðou] conj. Bien que, quoique, en dépit de ce que. ‖ Quand bien même. (See THOUGH.)
altimeter [æl'timətə*] n. AVIAT. Altimètre m.
altitude ['æltitju:d] n. GEOGR., AVIAT. Altitude f. ‖ MATH., ASTRON. Hauteur f. ‖ FIG. Eminence; hauteur f.
alto ['æltou] n. MUS. Alto (instrument, part); contralto (female voice, singer); haute-contre (male voice). ‖ **Alto-relievo,** n. ARTS. Haut-relief.
altocumulus [,æltou'kju:mjuləs] n. Altocumulus m.
altogether [,ɔ:ltu'geðə*] adv. Somme toute; tout compris, au total (on the whole); entièrement, absolument (wholly).
— n. FAM. In the altogether, nu.
altostratus [,æltou'streitəs] n. Altostratus m.
altruism ['æltruizm] n. Altruisme m.
altruist [-st] n. Altruiste s.
altruistic [,æltru'istik] adj. Altruiste.
alum ['æləm] n. CHIM. Alun m. ‖ **Alum-stone,** n. Alunite f.
— v. tr. CHIM. Aluner.
alumina [ə'lju:minə] n. CHIM. Alumine f.
aluminize [ə'lju:mi,naiz] v. tr. TECHN. Aluminiser (glass); procéder à l'aluminiage de (metal); revêtir d'aluminium, caloriser (steel).
aluminium [,əlju'minjəm], U. S. **aluminum** [,əlju'minəm] n. Aluminium m.
aluminous [ə'lju:minəs] adj. Alumineux.
alumnus [ə'lʌmnəs] (pl. **alumni** [-ai]) n. Ancien élève, ancien, labadens m.
alundum [ə'lʌndəm] n. CHIM. Alundum m.
alunite ['æljunait] n. Alunite f.
alveolar [æl'violə*] adj. Alvéolaire.
alveolate ['ælviolit] adj. Alvéolé.

alveolus [-ləs] (pl. **alveoli** [-lai]) n. Bot., Med. Alvéole *m*.
always ['ɔ:lweiz] adv. Toujours.
A. M. [eiem] abbr. *Amplitude modulation*, Radio. A. M., modulation d'amplitude.
a. m. abbr. *Ante meridiem*, avant midi, du matin; *at 7 a. m.*, à 7 heures (du matin).
amalgam [ə'mælgəm] n. Amalgame *m*.
amalgamate [-eit] v. tr. Amalgamer.
— v. intr. S'amalgamer.
amalgamation [ə,mælgə'meiʃən] n. Chim., Fin., Jur. Amalgamation *f*. ‖ U. S. Métissage *m*.
amanuensis [ə,mænju'ensis] (pl. **amanuenses**) [-i:z] n. Secrétaire *m*. (person).
amaranth ['æmərænθ] n. Bot. Amarante *f*. ‖ Amarante (colour).
amaryllis [,æmə'rilis] n. Bot. Amaryllis *f*.
amass [ə'mæs] v. tr. Amasser.
amateur ['æmətə:*] n. Amateur *m*.
amateurish [,æmə'tə:riʃ] adj. D'amateur.
amateurism [-'tə:rizm] n. Amateurisme *m*.
amative ['æmətiv] adj. Passionné, qui a du tempérament.
amatory [-təri] adj. Amoureux (feeling); d'amour (letter); érotique (poem).
amaurosis [,æmo'rousis] n. Med. Amaurose *f*.
amaze [ə'meiz] v. tr. Stupéfier. ‖ Fam. Renverser, épater, époustoufler.
amazement [-mənt] n. Stupéfaction; stupeur *f*.
amazing [-iŋ] adj. Stupéfiant; renversant; clouant, ébouriffant (fam.).
amazon ['æməzən] n. † Amazone *f*. ‖ Zool. *Amazon ant*, fourmi esclavagiste. ‖ Fam. Gendarme *f*. (virago).
ambages [æm'beidʒi:z] n. pl. Ambages *m. pl.*
ambassador [æm'bæsədə*] n. Ambassadeur *m*.
ambassadress [-dris] n. Ambassadrice *f*.
amber ['æmbə*] n. Ambre *m*.
— adj. D'ambre.
— v. tr. Ambrer.
ambergris [-gri:s] n. Ambre gris *m*.
ambiance ['ɑbjɑs] n. Ambiance *f*.
ambidexter [,æmbi'dekstə*] n. Ambidextre *s*.
ambidextrous [-strəs] adj. Ambidextre.
ambient ['æmbiənt] adj. Ambiant.
ambiguity [,æmbi'gjuiti] n. Ambiguïté *f*.
ambiguous [æm'bigjuəs] adj. Ambigu. (See equivocal.) ‖ Vague, indéfini.
ambit ['æmbit] n. Limites *f. pl.* (of a land); enceinte *f*. (of a town).
ambition [æm'biʃən] n. Ambition *f*.
ambitious [-əs] adj. Ambitieux (attempt, person); *to be ambitious to*, ambitionner de.
ambitiously [-əsli] adv. Ambitieusement.
ambivalence [æm'bivələns] n. Ambivalence *f*.
ambivalent [-lənt] adj. Ambivalent.
ambiversion [,æmbi'və:ʃən] n. Psych. État (*m*.) d'équilibre entre l'introversion et l'extraversion, ambiversion *f*.
ambivert ['æmbi,və:t] n. Psych. Personnalité (*f*.) équilibrée entre l'introversion et l'extraversion.
amble ['æmbl] v. intr. Ambler, aller l'amble (horse, rider). ‖ Déambuler (person).
— n. Sports. Amble *m*.
ambo ['æmbou] n. Archit. Ambon *m*.
ambrosia [æm'brouziə] n. Ambroisie *f*.
ambrosial [-əl] adj. Ambrosiaque.
ambulance ['æmbjuləns] n. Med. Ambulance *f*. ‖ Milit. Hôpital militaire *m*.; *motor surgical ambulance*, autochir. ‖ Aviat. *Flying ambulance*, avion sanitaire, aérochir. ‖ Ch. de f. *Ambulance train*, train sanitaire.
ambulant [-ənt] adj. Med. Ambulatoire.
ambulatory [-ətəri] adj. Ambulatoire. ‖ Jur. Eventuellement révocable (will).
— n. Archit. Déambulatoire *m*.

ambuscade [,æmbəs'keid] n. Embuscade *f*.
— v. tr. Embusquer.
— v. intr. S'embusquer.
ambush ['æmbuʃ] n. Milit. Embuscade *f*. (action, place, troops). ‖ Fig. Embûche *f*.
— v. tr. Milit. Embusquer.
— v. intr. Milit. S'embusquer.
ameba [ə'mi:bə] n. U. S. See amoeba.
ameer [ə'miə*] n. See amir.
ameliorate [ə'mi:liəreit] v. tr. Améliorer.
— v. intr. S'améliorer. (See improve.)
amelioration [ə'mi:liə'reiʃən] n. Amélioration *f*.
amen [,ei'men] n., interj. Amen *m. inv.; to say amen to*, dire amen à.
amenable [ə'mi:nəbl] adj. Souple, docile, soumis (*to*, à). ‖ Responsable (*to*, envers). ‖ Jur. Justiciable, relevant (*to*, de) [a court]; passible (*to*, de) [a fine].
amend [ə'mend] v. tr. Amender; améliorer (to improve). ‖ Modifier (to alter).
— v. intr. S'amender.
amendment [-mənt] n. Amélioration *f*. ‖ Correction *f*. ‖ Jur. Amendement *m*.
amends [-z] n. pl. Jur. Dédommagement *m.; to make amends for*, dédommager de; compenser. ‖ Fig. Compensation, réparation *f.; to make amends for*, réparer, faire oublier.
amenity [ə'mi:niti] n. Aménité, amabilité *f*. (of a person); charme, agrément *m*. (of a place). ‖ Pl. Commodités *f.;* confort *m*. (of life). ‖ Pl. Civilités, amabilités *f.;* ressources *f.; educational amenities*, ressources intellectuelles et artistiques.
ament [ə'ment] n. Med. Faible (*s*.) d'esprit; idiot (*s*.) de naissance.
amentia [ə'menʃə] n. Med. Idiotie congénitale *f*.
amerce [ə'mə:s] v. tr. Jur. Pénaliser.
America [ə'merikə] n. Geogr. Amérique *f*.
American [-ən] adj. Geogr., Comm., Gramm. Américain; *American cloth*, toile cirée; *American English*, l'anglais d'Amérique.
— n. Geogr. Américain *s*.
Americanism [-ənizm] n. Américanisme *m*.
Americanist [-ənist] n. Américaniste *s*. ‖ U. S. Amérindianiste *s*.
Americanize [-ənaiz] v. tr. Américaniser.
— v. intr. S'américaniser.
americium [ə,mə:r'iʃiəm] n. Chim. Américium *m*.
Amerind ['æmərind] n. Geogr. Amérindien *s*.
Amerindian [æmə'rindjən] adj., n. Geogr. Amérindien *s*.
amethyst ['æmiθist] n. Améthyste *f.; oriental amethyst*, saphir violet.
— adj. Améthyste, violet (colour). ‖ D'améthyste.
amiability [,eimjə'biliti] n. Amabilité, affabilité *f*.
amiable ['eimjəbl] adj. Aimable, affable.
amiably [-bli] adv. Aimablement.
amianthus [,æmi'ænθəs] n. Amiante *m*.
amicable ['æmikəbl] adj. Amical. ‖ Jur. Amiable; à l'amiable (arrangement).
amicability [,æmikə'biliti] n. Cordialité, attitude amicale *f*.
amicably ['æmikəbli] adv. Amicalement. ‖ Jur. A l'amiable.
amice ['æmis] n. Eccles. Amict *m*. (white linen); aumusse *m*. (tippet).
amid(st) [ə'mid(st)] prep. Parmi, entre, au milieu de.
amide ['æmaid] n. Chim. Amide *m*.
amidships [ə'midʃips] adv. Naut. Au milieu (or) par le milieu du navire.
amine [ə'main] n. Chim. Amine *f*.
amino-acid [ə'mainou,æsid] n. Med. Amino-acide, acide aminé *m*.
amir [ə'miə*] n. Emir *m*.
amirate [ə'miərit] n. Emirat *m*.

amiss [ə'mis] adv. Mal à propos, inopportunément (untowardly) ; mal, de travers (wrongly). — adj. Détraqué (out of order) ; *not amiss,* pas mal, bien torché (fam.) ; *there's sth. amiss,* ce n'est plus ça, il y a qqch. qui cloche, ça ne tourne pas rond (fam.) ; *what's amiss with you ?,* qu'est-ce qu'il y a qui ne va pas ?, qu'est-ce qui vous chiffonne?

amity ['æmiti] n. Relations amicales *f. pl. ;* bonne intelligence *f.*

ammeter ['æmitə*] n. ELECTR. Ampèremètre *m.*

ammo ['æmou] n. MILIT., FAM. Munitions *f. pl.*

ammonia [ə'mounjə] n. CHIM. Ammoniaque *m.* (gas) ; alcali *m.* (solution).

ammoniac [-æk] adj. CHIM. Ammoniac.

ammoniacal [,æmo'naiəkəl] adj. Ammoniacal.

ammoniated [ə'mounieitid] adj. Ammoniacé.

ammonium [ə'mouniəm] n. CHIM. Ammonium *m.*

ammunition [,æmju'niʃən] n. MILIT. Munitions *f. pl. ; ammunition belt,* bande de munitions ; *ammunition boots,* brodequins. ‖ FIG. Moyen (*m.*) de défense.

amnesia [æm'ni:ʒiə] n. MED. Amnésie *f.*

amnesic [-sik] adj., n. MED. Amnésique *s.*

amnesty ['æmnisti] f. Amnistie *f.* — v. tr. (2). Amnistier.

amoeba [ə'mi:bə] n. MED. Amibe *f.*

amoebic [-ik] adj. MED. Amibien.

amok [ə'mɔk] See AMUCK.

among(st) [ə'mʌŋ(st)] prep. Entre ; *divided among us,* partagé entre nous. ‖ Entre, parmi ; *among many friends,* parmi beaucoup d'amis. ‖ Entre, au nombre de ; *among other things,* entre autres. ‖ Entre, sur ; *one among a thousand,* un sur mille. ‖ Entre ; *they don't agree among themselves,* ils ne s'entendent pas entre eux. ‖ Au milieu de ; *to pass among the crowd,* passer dans la foule. ‖ Chez, parmi ; *popular among lawyers,* populaire chez les gens de robe.

Amontillado [ə,mɔnti'lɑ:dou] n. Amontillado *m.,* vin (*m.*) de Xérès.

amoral [æ'mɔrəl] adj. Amoral.

amorous ['æmərəs] adj. Porté à l'amour ; concupiscent. ‖ Erotique (verse).

amorously [-li] adv. Amoureusement.

amorphism [ə'mɔ:fizm̩] n. Amorphisme *m.*

amorphous [-əs] adj. Amorphe.

amortization [ə,mɔ:ti'zeiʃən] n. FIN. Amortissement *m.*

amortize [ə'mɔ:taiz] v. tr. FIN. Amortir. ‖ JUR. Aliéner en mainmorte.

amount [ə'maunt] v. intr. S'élever, se monter (*to,* à) [sum] ; *amounting to twenty,* au nombre de vingt. ‖ Equivaloir ; se ramener, se réduire, se résumer (*to,* à). — n. Montant, total *m. ;* somme *f. ; to the amount of,* jusqu'à concurrence de. ‖ COMM. *Amount due,* débit. ‖ JUR. *Amount in controversy,* somme en litige. ‖ FIG. Valeur, signification, substance *f.* (of a promise) ; somme *f.* (of resistance, work).

amour [ə'muə*] n. Affaire (*f.*) d'amour ; intrigue, liaison *f.*

amourette ['æmurɛt] n. Amourette *f.*

amp [æmp] n. ELECTR., FAM. Ampère *m.* ‖ TECHN., FAM. Ampli *m.* (amplifier).

amperage ['æmpəridʒ] n. ELECTR. Ampérage *m.*

ampere ['æmpɛə*] n. ELECTR. Ampère *m.* ‖ **Ampere-hour,** n. ELECTR. Ampèreheure *m.*

ampersand ['æmpəsænd] n. Esperluète *f.*

amphetamine [æm'fetə,mi:n] n. MED. Amphétamine *f.*

amphibian [æm'fibiən] adj. MILIT., ZOOL. Amphibie (tank, animal). — n. ZOOL. Amphibien *m.* (animal).

amphibious [æm'fibiəs] adj. ZOOL., MILIT., AVIAT. Amphibie. ‖ FIG. U. S. Qui a deux natures.

amphibological [,æmfibo'lɔdʒikəl] adj. Amphibologique.

amphibology [,æmfi'bɔlədʒi] n. Amphibologie *f.*

amphitheatre ['æmfi,θi:ətə*] n. Amphithéâtre *m.* ‖ FIG. Arène *f.*

amphitryon [æm'fitriən] n. Amphitryon, hôte *m.*

amphora ['æmfərə] n. Amphore *f.* — N. B. Notez les pluriels : *amphorae, amphoras.*

ample ['æmpl] adj. Ample, large ; spacieux, étendu (spacious). ‖ Abondant, copieux (copious) ; *ample means,* de gros moyens. ‖ Suffisant ; *to have ample time,* avoir largement le temps.

ampleness [-nis] n. Ampleur *f.* ‖ Abondance, richesse *f.*

ampliative ['æmpliətiv] adj. Ampliatif.

ampliation [,æmpli'eiʃən] s. Ampliation *f.* ‖ JUR. Prorogation (*f.*) de délai ; ajournement *m.*

amplification [,æmplifi'keiʃən] n. Amplification, extension *f.* ‖ RADIO. Amplification *f.*

amplifier ['æmplifaiə*] n. RADIO. Amplificateur ; haut-parleur *m.*

amplify [-fai] v. tr. (2). Augmenter, développer (one's authority) ; amplifier (an idea, a story) ; développer (a statement). ‖ ELECTR. Amplifier. — v. intr. S'amplifier, se développer (authority, idea). ‖ Développer longuement, détailler ; allonger la sauce (fam.). [See EXPATIATE.]

amplitude [-tju:d] n. Etendue, largeur f. ‖ ASTRON., PHYS., RADIO. Amplitude *f.* ‖ FIG. Ampleur *f.* (of intellect, mind) ; étendue *f.* (of thought).

amply ['æmpli] adv. Amplement ; abondamment.

ampoule [æm'pu:l] n. MED. Ampoule *f.* (to be injected).

ampulla [æm'pʌlə] n. † ECCLES. Ampoule. ‖ MED. Ampoule *f.* (of a canal). — N. B. Notez les pluriels : *ampullae, ampullas.*

ampullaceous [,æmpu'leiʃəs] adj. MED. Turgescent. ‖ BOT. Ampulacé.

amputate ['æmpjuteit] v. tr. MED. Amputer.

amputation [,æmpju'teiʃən] n. MED. Amputation *n.*

amputee [æmpju'ti:] n. MED. Amputé *m.*

amuck [æ'mʌk] adv. En furie ; *to run amuck,* courir comme un fou furieux. ‖ FIG. *To run amuck,* voir rouge.

amulet ['æmjulit] n. Amulette *f.*

amuse [ə'mju:z] v. tr. Amuser, divertir (*by,* en ; *with,* par) ; *to amuse oneself,* s'amuser, se récréer ; *to be amused at* (or) *by* (or) *with,* s'amuser de. ‖ Charmer (one's leisure). ‖ Amuser, faire rire, distraire ; *to keep people amused,* amuser la galerie (fam.). ‖ † Amuser, abuser, leurrer, tromper (to deceive) [*with, par*].

amusement [-mənt] n. Amusement, divertissement *m. ;* récréation, distraction *f.* ‖ Amusement *m. ;* envie (*f.*) de rire ; *look of amusement,* regard amusé. ‖ Attraction *f. ; amusement park,* parc des attractions. ‖ FIN. *Amusement tax,* taxe sur les spectacles.

amusing [-iŋ] adj. Amusant, distrayant, divertissant. ‖ Plaisant.

amyl ['æmil] n. CHIM. Amyle *m.*

amylaceous [,æmi'leiʃəs] adj. CHIM. Amylacé.

amylic [ə'milik] adj. CHIM. Amylique.

an [æn] See A.

an conj. † Si.

ana ['einə] n. Ana *m.*

Anabaptist [,ænə'bæptist] n. Anabaptiste *s.*

anabasis [ə'næbəsis] n. Retraite (*f.*) des Dix-Mille.

anabolism [ə'næbə,lizm̩] n. MED. Anabolisme *m.*

anacard ['ænəkɑ:d] n. BOT. Anacarde *m.*

anachronic [,ænə'krɔnik], **anachronistic** [,ænækrə'nistik] adj. Anachronique.

anachronism [ə'nækrənizm̩] n. Anachronisme *m.* ‖ ARCHIT. Bâtiment de style anachronique *m.*

anacoluthon [,ænəkə'lju:θən] (pl. **anacolutha** [-ə]) n. GRAMM. Anacoluthe *f.*

anaconda [,ænə'kɔndə] n. ZOOL. Anaconda *m.*

AMERICANISMS — AMÉRICANISMES

AMERICAN	ENGLISH	FRENCH
airfield	aerodrome	aérodrome
airplane	aeroplane	avion
aisle	corridor	corridor, couloir (train)
aluminum	aluminium	aluminium
all aboard!	take your seats!	en voiture!
apartment	flat	appartement
automobile	car	automobile, voiture
baby carriage	perambulator, pram	voiture d'enfant
baggage	luggage	bagages
bakery	baker's shop	boulangerie
bartender	barman	barman
bathrobe	dressing-gown	peignoir, robe de chambre
bathtub	bath	baignoire
beach (on the)	seaside [at the]	au bord de la mer
bellboy, bellhop	page, page-boy	groom, chasseur
bill [commerce]	invoice	facture
bill [money]	note	billet
bookstore	book-shop	librairie
business suit	lounge suit	complet veston
can	tin	boîte de conserve
can opener	tin-opener	ouvre-boîtes
candy, candies	sweet, sweets	bonbon, sucreries
candy box	sweetmeat box	bonbonnière
carom (to)	cannon (to)	caramboler
check	cheque	chèque
checkbook	cheque-book	carnet de chèques
checkers	draughts	jeu de dames
checkroom	cloak-room, left-luggage office	consigne
chief of police	police superintendant	commissaire de police
cigar store	tobacconist's	bureau de tabac
comforter	eiderdown	édredon
conductor [of a train]	guard	chef de train
cookbook	cookery book	livre de cuisine
corn	maize	maïs
cozy	cosy	à l'aise, confortable
cracker	biscuit	biscuit
custom-made	bespoke	fait sur commande
cutaway	tail-coat	jaquette
daylight-saving time	summer-time	heure d'été
deck	pack [of cards]	jeu [de cartes]
derby	bowler [hat]	melon (chapeau)
dessert	sweet, dessert	dessert
dicker, to (fam.)	to haggle	marchander
dollar bill	one-dollar note	billet d'un dollar
draft [of air]	draught [of air]	courant d'air
druggist	chemist	pharmacien
drugstore	chemist's [shop]	pharmacie
elevator	lift	ascenseur
endive	chicory	endive
fall	autumn	automne
fender	wing, mud-guard	garde-boue, aile
fire department	fire-brigade	pompiers
first floor	ground floor	rez-de-chaussée
garbage can	dust-bin	poubelle
garters	suspenders	jarretières
gasoline, gas	petrol	essence [automobile]
Good for you!	Well done!	Bravo!
government worker, civil service employee	civil servant	fonctionnaire
grade-crossing	level crossing	passage à niveau
guest room	spare room	chambre d'ami
hallway	hall, passage	antichambre, hall
hardware store	ironmonger's shop	quincaillerie
hood [of a car]	bonnet [of a car]	capot [d'une automobile]
homely [girl]	plain, ugly	laide [jeune fille]
Indian corn	maize	maïs
Information Bureau	Enquiry Office	bureau de renseignements
intermission	interval	entracte
life preserver	life-belt	bouée de sauvetage
line	queue	queue, file d'attente
line up, to	to queue up	faire la queue
low gear	first speed	première vitesse
mail, to	to post	mettre à la boîte
mailbox	letter-box, pillar-box	boîte aux lettres
mailman, letter carrier	postman	facteur
maybe [plus fréquent aux U. S.]	perhaps [plus fréquent en G.-B.]	peut-être
monkey wrench	adjustable spanner, screw-wrench	clé anglaise, clé à molette
movies, moving pictures	cinema; pictures	cinéma
mustache	moustache	moustache
newsdealer	newsagent	marchand de journaux

N. B. — L'abréviation « U. S. », précédant un mot, indique que ce mot appartient à l'anglais d'Amérique plutôt qu'à l'anglais insulaire. Mais elle n'implique ni restriction ni limitation; il serait faux d'en déduire que le mot ainsi désigné est le meilleur, encore moins l'unique, utilisé en américain.

AMERICAN	ENGLISH	FRENCH
oatmeal	porridge	bouillie d'avoine
one-way ticket	single ticket	aller simple
pack [of cigarets]	packet [of cigarettes]	paquet [de cigarettes]
package	parcel	paquet, colis
pajamas	pyjamas	pyjama
pantry	larder	garde-manger
parking space	car-park	parc à autos
pie (apple)	tart (apple)	tarte [aux pommes]
pitcher	jug	carafe, cruche
potato chips	potato crisps	pommes chips
price tag	label	étiquette
program	programme	programme
purse	hand-bag [ladies'-]	sac à main
race track	race-course	champ de courses
railroad	railway	chemin de fer
raise [in wages]	rise [in wages]	augmentation [de salaire]
refueling	refuelling	réalimentation [en essence]
rent (house for)	house to let	maison à louer
rent (boat for)	boat for hire	bateau à louer
restroom	toilet ; lavatory	toilettes
right away	straight away	tout de suite
right here	at this very place	ici même
right now	just now, at the moment	au moment même, tout de suite
roadster	two-seater	voiture de sport [à 2 places]
roast	joint	rôti
roller-coaster	switchback	montagnes russes
room-clerk (hotel)	reception-clerk	employé à la réception
roomer	lodger	locataire
round trip [by train]	return ticket	retour (aller et)
run (in a stocking)	ladder	échelle (dans un bas)
sailboat	sailing-boat	bateau à voile
sales girl	shop-girl	vendeuse
schedule (pron. skèd)	schedule (pron. shèd)	plan, prévision
scratchpad	scribbling-block	bloc-notes
second floor	first floor	premier étage
sedan	saloon	limousine
shine (to) [shoes]	black (to)	cirer (chaussures)
sidewalk	pavement	trottoir
skeptic	sceptic	sceptique
So long! (fam.)	Cheerio!	Au revoir!
specialty	speciality	spécialité
sporting goods	sports requisites (ou) equipment	articles de sport
stickpin	tie-pin	épingle de cravate
stock	share	action
stockholder	shareholder	actionnaire
store	shop	magasin, boutique
storekeeper	shopkeeper	commerçant, boutiquier
story [= floor]	storey	étage
streetcar	tramcar, tram	tramway
street floor (1)	ground floor	rez-de-chaussée
string beans	French beans	haricots verts
stub [of check, etc.]	counterfoil	souche, talon
subway	tube, Underground	métro
sugar bowl	sugar-basin	sucrier
sundown ; sunup	sunset ; sunrise	coucher, lever du soleil
suspenders	braces	bretelles
telephone booth	call-box	cabine téléphonique
tenpin	ninepin, skittle	quille
terminal	terminus	terminus
theater	theatre	théâtre
thumbtack	drawing-pin	punaise
ticket office	booking-office	guichet des billets
tire	tyre	pneu
top coat	overcoat	manteau
trailer	caravan	remorque-caravane
trash	rubbish, litter	ordures, déchets
traveling salesman	commercial traveller	représentant de commerce
trolley [car]	tramcar	tramway
truck	lorry	camion
tuxedo (Abbrev. tux)	dinner-jacket	smoking
underpass	subway	passage souterrain
undershirt	vest	tricot, maillot de corps
vacation [plus commun aux U. S. A.]	holiday [plus commun en G.-B.]	vacances
vacationist	holiday-maker	estivant
vest	waistcoat	gilet
walk-up	house without a lift	maison sans ascenseur
wash room	lavatory	W.-C., toilettes
waste basket	waste-paper basket	corbeille à papier
Watch [your feet]!	Mind [your feet]!	Attention à [vos pieds]!
water heater	geyser (gas), immersion heater	chauffe-eau, chauffe-bain
wheat	corn	blé
windshield	wind-screen	pare-brise
windshield wiper	screen-wiper	essuie-glace
zee	zed	la lettre z

N. B. — The abbreviation « U. S. », preceding a word, shows that the word belongs to American English rather than to British English. But the said abbreviation does not imply that the term is restricted to American use; and it should not be infered from it that the mentioned word is the best, even less the only one, used in the American language.

anacrusis [,ænə'kru:sis] n. Mus., Gramm. Anacruse f.

anaemia [ə'ni:miə] n. Med. Anémie f.

anaemic [-ik] adj. Med. Anémique, anémié.

anaerobe [ən'ɛərou:b] n. Med. Anaérobie f.

anaesthesia [,ænis'θi:zjə] n. Med. Anesthésie f.

anaesthetic ['ænis'θetik] adj. Med. Insensibilisateur m.; insensibilisatrice f.
— n. Med. Anesthésique m.

anaesthetist [ə'ni:sθətist] n. Med. Anesthésiste s.

anaesthetize [-taiz] v. tr. Med. Anesthésier.

anagram ['ænəgræm] n. Anagramme m.

anagrammatist [,ænə'græmətist] n. Faiseur d'anagrammes m.

anagrammatize [-taiz] v. tr. Mettre sous forme d'anagramme.

anal ['einəl] adj. Med. Anal; artificial anal opening, anus artificiel.

analecta [,ænə'lɛktə], analects ['ænələkts] n. Analectes m. pl.

analgesia [,ænæl'dʒi:ziə] n. Med. Analgésie f.

analgesic [-sik] adj., n. Med. Analgésique m.

analogic(al) [,ænə'lɔdʒik(əl)] adj. Analogique.

analogically [-əli] adv. Analogiquement.

analogize [ə'nælədʒaiz] v. tr. Représenter (or) expliquer par analogie.
— v. intr. Raisonner par analogie. ‖ Etre en analogie (with, avec).

analogous [ə'næləgəs] adj. Analogue.

analogue ['ænəlɔg] n. Analogue m.

analogy [ə'nælədʒi] n. Analogie f. (between, entre; with, avec); on the analogy of, par analogie avec.

analysable ['ænəlaizəbl] adj. Analysable.

analyse, U. S. analyze [-laiz] v. tr. Analyser.

analysis [ə'næləsis] (analyses [-i:z]) n. Math., Phys., Chim. Analyse f.; electrolytic analysis, electroanalyse; stress analysis, calcul statique. ‖ Gramm. Close analysis, explication de texte; sentence analysis, analyse logique. ‖ Fig. Analyse f.

analyst ['ænəlist] n. Chim. Analyste s. ‖ U. S. Psychanalyste m.

analytic [,ænə'litik] adj. Math. Analytique.

analytical [-əl] adj. Gramm., Philos. Analytique.

ananas [ə'nɑ:nəs] n. Bot. Ananas m.

anandrous [ə'nændrəs] adj. Bot. Sans étamine.

anapaest ['ænəpi:st] n. Gramm. Anapeste m.

anaphora [ə'næfərə] n. Gramm. Anaphore m.

anaphoric [,ænə'fɔrik] adj. Gramm. Anaphorique.

anaphylactic [æn,əfə'læktik] adj. Med. Anaphylactique.

anaphylaxis [-'læksis] n. Med. Anaphylaxie f.

anarchic [æ'nɑ:kik] adj. Anarchique.

anarchically [-əli] adv. Anarchiquement.

anarchism ['ænəkizm] n. Anarchisme m.

anarchist [-ist] n. Anarchiste s.

anarchy [-i] n. Anarchie f.

anasarca [,ænə'sɑ:kə] n. Med. Leucophlegmasie f.

anastatic [,ænə'stætik] adj. Techn. En relief.

anastigmat [ə'næstigmæt] n. Phys. Anastigmat m.

anastigmatic [ænəstig'mætik] adj. Phys. Anastigmatique.

anastomosis [ə,næstə'mousis] n. Med., Bot. Anastomose f.

anathema [ə'næθimə] n. Eccles. Anathème m.

anathematize [-ətaiz] v. tr. Eccles. Anathématiser.

anatomic(al) [,ænə'tɔmikəl] adj. Med. Anatomique.

anatomically [-əli] adv. Med. Anatomiquement.

anatomist [ə'nætəmist] n. Med. Anatomiste s. ‖ Fig. Analyste m.

anatomize [-maiz] v. tr., intr. Anatomiser, disséquer. ‖ Analyser.

anatomy [-mi] f. Med. Dissection f. (dissecting); anatomie f. (science, structure).

ancestor ['ænsestə*] n. Ancêtre, aïeul, ascendant m.

ancestral [æn'sestrəl] adj. Ancestral.

ancestry ['ænsistri] n. Ancêtres, aïeux m. pl. (ancestors); lignée f. (lineage).

anchor ['æŋkə*] n. Naut. Ancre f.; to cast, to drop, to weigh anchor, jeter, mouiller, lever l'ancre; to lie (or) ride at anchor, être à l'ancre. ‖ Fig. Planche (f.) de salut; to come to anchor, s'accrocher, s'ancrer. ‖ Anchor-plate, n. Archit. Plaque (f.) d'ancrage. ‖ Anchor-ring, n. Naut. Organeau m.
— v. tr. Naut., Fig. Ancrer.
— v. intr. Naut. Jeter l'ancre. ‖ Fig. S'ancrer.

anchorage [-ridʒ] n. Naut. Ancrage, mouillage m. ‖ Jur. Droits d'ancrage m. ‖ Fig. Point (m.) de fixation; havre (m.) de sécurité.

anchoress ['æŋkəris] n. Eccles. Recluse f.

anchoret [-ret] n. Eccles. Anachorète m.

anchovy ['æntʃəvi] n. Zool., Culin. Anchois m. ‖ Anchovy-paste, n. Culin. Beurre (m.) d'anchois. ‖ Anchovy-sardine, n. Sardine anchoitée f. ‖ Anchovy-toast, n. Culin. Sandwich (or) pain tartiné (m.) aux anchois.

anchylose ['æŋkilouz] v. tr. Ankyloser.
— v. intr. S'ankyloser.

anchylosis [,æŋkai'lousis] n. Med. Ankylose f.

ancien régime [ãsjɛ̃reʒim] n. † Ancien Régime m. (lit., fig.).

ancient ['einʃənt] adj. Ancien (document, history); antique (world); ancient days, le temps jadis.
— n. Ancien, vieillard m. (old man). ‖ Pl. Anciens m. pl. (people, writers). ‖ Eccles. The Ancient of Days, l'Eternel.

anciently [-li] adv. Anciennement.

ancientness [-nis] n. Ancienneté; antiquité f.

ancientry [-ri] n. Ancienneté f. ‖ Antiquaille, vieillerie f. ‖ Temps passé, m.

ancillary [æn'siləri] adj. Ancillaire. ‖ Subordonné (to, à). ‖ Auxiliaire (undertaking).

and [ænd, ənd] conj. Et; there are friends and friends, il y a amis et amis; stir and you are a dead man, un seul mouvement et vous êtes mort. ‖ A; to walk two and two, marcher deux à deux. ‖ En; better and better, de mieux en mieux; now and then, de temps en temps. ‖ (Omitted in French); two hundred and thirty, deux cent trente; try and come, essayez de venir.

Andalusian ['ændə'lu:ziən] adj., n. Andalou s.

Andean [æn'di:ən] adj. Geogr. Andin.

andiron ['ændaiən] n. Chenet m.

Andorra [æn'dɔ:rə] n. Geogr. Andorre f.

androgen ['ændrədʒən] n. Med. Androgène m.

androgenic [,ændrə'dʒenik] adj. Med. Androgène.

androgyne ['ændrədʒin] n. Androgyne s.

androgynous [æn'drɔdʒinəs] adj. Androgyne.

android ['ændrɔid] n. Androïde m.

anecdotage ['ænɛkdoutidʒ] n. Collection (f.) d'anecdotes. ‖ Fam. Radotage m.; sénilité f.

anecdote [-dout] n. Anecdote f.

anecdotic [,ænək'dɔtik], anecdotal [-'doutəl] adj. Anecdotique.

anecdotist ['ænekdoutist] n. Anecdotier m.

anemograph [æ'nemogrɑ:f] n. Anémographe m.

anemometer [,æni'mɔmitə*] n. Anémomètre m.

anemone [æ'nemɔni] n. Bot. Anémone f. ‖ Zool. Sea anemone, actinie.

anent [ə'nent] prep. Relatif à, concernant (in Scotland).

aneroid ['ænərɔid] adj., n. Phys. Anéroïde m.

anesthesia [,ænis'θi:zjə] U. S. See ANAESTHESIA.

aneurism ['ænjuərizm] n. Med. Anévrisme m.

anew [ə'nju:] adv. De nouveau, encore (again); sous une nouvelle forme, à nouveau (in a new way). ‖ A neuf (as good as new).

anfractuosity [æn,fræktju'ɔsiti] n. Anfractuosité

f. ‖ MED. Pl. Anfractuosités *f. pl.* (of the brain). ‖ Pl. Sinuosités *f. pl.*

angel ['eindʒəl] n. ECCLES. Ange *m.; to entertain an angel unawares,* abriter un ange sans le savoir, rendre service à un noble inconnu. ‖ FIN. Angelot, noble à l'ange *m.* (coin). ‖ CULIN. *Angels on horse-back,* fricassée d'huîtres au bacon. ‖ U. S. FAM. Commanditaire *m.* ‖ FAM. Ange, amour *m.* (child, person); *an angel flew through the room,* un ange passa.
— adj. Angélique, d'ange.
— v. tr. U. S. FAM. Commanditer.

angelic(al) [æn'dʒelik(əl)] adj. Angélique.
angelica [-ə] n. BOT., CULIN. Angélique *f.*
angelus ['ændʒiləs] n. ECCLES. Angélus *m.* (ave-bell, prayer).
anger ['æŋgə*] n. Colère *f.;* courroux, emportement *m.*
— v. tr. Mettre en colère, courroucer. (See ENRAGE.)
Angevin ['ændʒəvin] adj., n. GEOGR. Angevin.
angina [æn'dʒainə] n. MED. Angine *f.; angina pectoris,* angine de poitrine.
angiology [æn,dʒi'ɔlədʒi] n. MED. Angiologie *f.*
angle ['æŋgl] n. MATH., AVIAT., MILIT. Angle *m.* ‖ RADIO. *Angle of phase-difference,* angle de déphasage; *viewing angle,* angle de vision. ‖ PHYS. *View angle,* angle de champ. ‖ MED. *Visual angle,* angle visuel. ‖ FIG. Angle, aspect *m.;* face *f.* (of a question). ‖ **Angle-iron,** n. TECHN. Cornière *f.* ‖ **Angle-wise,** adj. A un angle.
— v. tr. U. S. Former en angle. ‖ FAM. U. S. Présenter sous un certain angle (a report).
angle v. intr. SPORTS. *To angle for,* pêcher à la ligne (fish). ‖ FIG. *To angle for,* chercher à accaparer (s.o.'s attention); quêter (compliments); amorcer, essayer de pêcher (a husband).
angled [-d] adj. MATH. Angulaire.
angler [-ə*] n. SPORTS. Pêcheur (*m.*) à la ligne. ‖ ZOOL. Baudroie *f.*
Anglican ['æŋglikən] adj., n. ECCLES. Anglican *s.*
Anglicanism [-izm] n. Anglicanisme *m.*
Anglicism ['æŋglisizm] n. Anglicisme *m.*
Anglicist [-ist] n. Angliciste *s.*
Anglicize [-aiz] v. tr. Angliciser.
Anglo– ['æŋglo-] pref. Anglo-. ‖ **Anglo-catholic,** adj., n. ECCLES. Anglo-catholique *s.* ‖ **Anglo-French,** adj. Franco-britannique. ‖ **Anglo-Indian,** adj., n. Anglais (*s.*) des Indes. ‖ **Anglo-Norman,** adj., s. Anglo-Normand *s.* ‖ **Anglo-saxon,** adj., n. Anglo-Saxon *s.*
Anglomania ['æŋglo'meiniə] n. Anglomanie *f.*
Anglophile [-'fail] adj., n. Anglophile *s.*
Anglophilia [-'filiə] n. U. S. Anglophilie *f.*
Anglophobe [-'foub] adj., n. Anglophobe *s.*
Anglophobia [-'foubiə] n. Anglophobie *f.*
anglophone [-'foun] adj., n. Anglophone *s.*
Angola [æŋ'goulə] n. GEOGR. Angola *m.*
angora [æŋ'gɔ:rə] adj., n. ZOOL., COMM. Angora (cat, wool).
angostura [,æŋgə'stjuərə] n. *Angostura bark,* écorce d'angustura; *angostura bitters,* angustura.
angrily ['æŋgrili] adv. En colère; avec emportement.
angry [-i] adj. En colère, fâché, irrité, furieux (*at, about,* à cause [or] à propos de; *at, with,* contre). ‖ Courroucé (letter, look, reply); en courroux, en furie (sea); furieux (wind). ‖ MED. Enflammé (wound).
angst [æŋst] n. Angoisse *f.* ‖ **Angst-forming,** adj. Anxiogène.
angström ['æŋstrəm] n. PHYS. Angstrœm *m.*
anguine ['æŋgwin] adj. Anguiforme.
anguish ['æŋgwiʃ] n. MED. Douleur, souffrance, angoisse *f.* ‖ FIG. Angoisse *f.*
anguished [-t] adj. Angoissé, tourmenté (conscience); d'angoisse (cries, shriek).
anguishing [-iŋ] adj. Angoissant, déchirant.

angular ['æŋgjulə*] adj. Angulaire (distance). ‖ FAM. Anguleux (disposition, elbow, face); maigre, sec (person).
angularity [,æŋgju'læriti] n. Forme angulaire *f.*
anhydride [æn'haidrid] n. CHIM. Anhydride.
anhydrous [-drəs] adj. CHIM. Anhydre.
anil ['ænil] n. BOT. Indigotier. ‖ COMM. Indigo.
anile ['ænail] adj. De vieille, sénile. ‖ Imbécile.
aniline ['ænilain] n. CHIM. Aniline *f.*
— adj. CHIM. Azoïque.
anility ['æniliti] n. Radotage (*m.*) de vieille femme.
anima ['ænimə] n. PSYCH. Anima *f.*
animadversion [.ænimæd'və:ʃən] n. Critique, censure, désapprobation *f.;* blâme *m.*
animadvert [-'və:t] v. intr. *To animadvert on* (or) *upon,* critiquer, blâmer.
animal ['æniməl] n. ZOOL. Animal *m.* (See BEAST.) ‖ FIG. Animalité *f.;* instinct bestial *m.* ‖ FAM. Brute *f.* (person).
— adj. Animal (kingdom, life); animé; *animal spirits,* entrain, vie. ‖ AGRIC. *Animal husbandry,* soins du bétail.
animalcule [,æni'mælkju:l] n. Animalcule *m.*
animalist ['æniməlist] n. ARTS. Animalier *m.*
animality [,æni'mæliti] n. Animalité *f.*
animalize ['æniməlaiz] v. tr. Animaliser.
animate [-mit] adj. Animé (living, lively).
— [-meit] v. tr. Animer, vivifier (the body); *animated cartoon,* dessins animés. ‖ Animer, faire frémir (the leaves). ‖ FIG. Animer, exciter, stimuler (courage, zeal); animer, échauffer (a discussion); pousser, encourager, stimuler (s.o.) [*to, à*].
animation [,æni'meiʃən] n. Animation *f.*
animator ['ænimeitə*] n. Animateur *m.;* animatrice *f.*
animism [-izm] n. PHILOS. Animisme *m.*
animosity [,æni'mɔsiti] n. Animosité *f.*
animus ['æniməs] n. Force vive *f.* ‖ Intention *f.* ‖ Animosité *f.* ‖ PHILOS. Animus *m.*
anion ['ænjən] n. CHIM., ELECTR. Anion *m.*
anise ['ænis] n. BOT. Anis *m.* ‖ **Anise-flavoured,** adj. CULIN. Parfumé à l'anis.
aniseed [-i:d] n. Graine (*f.*) d'anis; *an aniseed ball,* un anis.
anisette [,æni'zet] n. Anisette *f.*
anisotropic [æn,aisə'trɔpik] adj. Anisotrope.
anisotropy [æ-i:] n. BOT., PHYS. Anisotropie *f.*
anker ['æŋkə*] n. Quartaut *m.*
ankle ['æŋkl] n. MED. Cheville *f.* ‖ **Ankle-deep,** adv. Jusqu'à la cheville. ‖ **Ankle-sock,** n. Socquette *f.* ‖ **Ankle-strap,** n. Barrette *f.* (of shoes).
anklet [-lit] n. Bracelet *m.* de cheville (ring). ‖ Socquette *f.* (sock).
ankylosis [,æŋkai'lousis] n. U. S. Ankylose *f.*
annalist ['ænəlist] n. Annaliste *m.*
annals ['ænlz] n. pl. Annales *f. pl.*
Annamese [,ænə'mi:z] adj., n. GEOGR. Annamite *s.*
anneal [ə'ni:l] v. tr. Recuire (glass); détremper (metal).
annelida [ə'nelidə] n. pl. ZOOL. Annélides *m. pl.*
annex [ə'neks] v. tr. Annexer (*to, à*).
— ['æneks] n. Annexe *f.* (building, document).
annexation [,ænek'seiʃən] n. Annexion *f.* (*of, de*); mainmise *f.* (*of, sur*).
annihilable [ə'naiiləb] adj. Annihilable.
annihilate [-leit] v. tr. Annihiler. (See DESTROY.) ‖ MILIT. Exterminer (troops).
annihilation [ə,naii'leiʃən] n. Annihilation *f.;* anéantissement *m.*
anniversary [,æni'və:səri] n. Anniversaire *m.*
Anno Domini ['ænou'dɔmi,nai] adv. De l'ère chrétienne, apr. J.-C., Anno Domini.
— n. FAM. Poids des ans, âge *m.;* *to be suffering from Anno Domini,* souffrir de la maladie de vieillesse.

annotate [ˈænoteit] v. tr. Annoter.
— v. intr. Porter des annotations (on, sur).
annotation [ˌænoˈteiʃən] n. Annotation, note ƒ.
annotator [ˈænoteitə*] n. Annotateur m.
announce [əˈnauns] v. tr. Annoncer, publier, proclamer; faire connaître.
— v. intr. RADIO. Parler comme speaker.
announcement [-mənt] n. Annonce, proclamation ƒ. ‖ Annonce; avis m. ‖ RADIO. Annonce par radio; émission ƒ. ‖ JUR. Avis judiciaire m.
announcer [-ə*] n. RADIO. Speaker m.; lady announcer, speakerine.
annoy [əˈnɔi] v. tr. Ennuyer, énerver, contrarier, agacer (to irritate); importuner, gêner, incommoder, lasser (to plague). ‖ MILIT. Harceler (the enemy).
annoyance [-əns] n. Ennui, désagrément, inconvénient m. ‖ Contrariété ƒ.; tracas m. ‖ Vexation, molestation ƒ.
annoying [-iŋ] adj. Ennuyeux, agaçant, contrariant, énervant (irritating). ‖ Importun, gênant, fâcheux (bothersome); annoying requirements, exigences tracassières.
annual [ˈænjuəl] adj. Annuel. ‖-JUR. Annual instalment, annuité.
— n. Publication annuelle ƒ.; annuaire m. (book). ‖ BOT. Plante annuelle ƒ. ‖ ECCLES. Messe (ƒ.) de bout de l'an.
annuitant [əˈnjuitənt] n. FIN. Pensionné; rentier, viager m.
annuity [-i] n. FIN. Rente, pension ƒ. (investment); annuité ƒ. (yearly payment).
annul [əˈnʌl] v. tr. (1). Résilier (a contract); abroger (a law), casser, infirmer (a judgment; annuler (a marriage); dénoncer (a treaty); annihiler (a will).
annular [ˈænjulə*] adj. MED., ASTRON., TECHN. Annulaire.
annulate [-leit] adj. Annelé.
annulet [-et] n. ARCHIT. Filet m.; armille ƒ.
annulment [æˈnʌlmənt] n. Résiliation ƒ. (of a contract); abrogation ƒ. (of a law); cassation ƒ. (of a judgment); annulation ƒ. (of a marriage); dénonciation ƒ. (of a treaty); annihilation ƒ. (of a will).
annulose [ˈænjulous] adj. ZOOL. Annelé.
annulus [-əs] n. BOT. Bague, collerette ƒ. (of a mushroom). ‖ MATH. Tore m.
annunciate [əˈnʌnʃieit] v. tr. Annoncer.
annunciation [əˌnʌnsiˈeiʃən] n. Annonce ƒ. ‖ ECCLES. Annonciation ƒ.
annunciator [əˈnʌnʃieitə*] n. Annonciateur m. ‖ ELECTR. Tableau annonciateur m.
anode [ˈænoud] n. ELECTR. Anode ƒ.
anodic [əˈnɔdik] adj. ELECTR. Anodique.
anodize [ˈænəˌdaiz] v. tr. TECHN. Anodiser.
anodyne [ˈænəˌdain] adj. MED., FIG. Calmant, apaisant.
— n. MED. Calmant, analgésique m. ‖ FIG. Apaisement m., consolation ƒ.
anoint [əˈnɔint] v. tr. Oindre (with, de). ‖ ECCLES. Oindre; sacrer.
anomalous [əˈnɔmələs] adj. BOT., MED., GRAMM. Anomal. ‖ FAM. Anormal.
anomalously [-ləsli] adv. Irrégulièrement. ‖ Anormalement.
anomaly [-li] n. ASTRON., FIG. Anomalie ƒ.
anon [əˈnɔn] adv. † Tout de suite, sans retard, aussitôt, immédiatement. ‖ Parfois; ever and anon, de temps en temps. ‖ Tout à l'heure, bientôt.
anonym [ˈænonim] n. Anonyme m.
anonymity [ˌænoˈnimiti] n. Anonymat m.
anonymous [əˈnɔniməs] adj. Anonyme.
anopheles [əˈnɔfiliːz] s. ZOOL. Anophèle m.
anorak [ˈænɔræk] n. Anorak m.
anorexia [ˌænəˈreksiə] n. MED. Anorexie ƒ.

anosmia [ænˈɔzmiə] n. MED. Anosmie ƒ.
another [əˈnʌðə*] adj. Un autre, un de plus, encore un (additional); do eat another apple, mangez donc une autre pomme; give me another twenty, donnez-m'en encore vingt. ‖ Un autre (different); that's another matter, c'est une autre question (or) affaire. ‖ Un autre (similar); another Caesar, un second (or) un autre César.
— pron. Un autre; encore un; many another, beaucoup d'autres, maint autre. ‖ Un autre (a different one); another came before you, il en est venu un autre avant vous. ‖ Un autre (one of the same kind); such another, un du même genre. ‖ LOC. One another, les uns les autres, réciproquement; to help one another, s'entraider.
anoxemia [ænɔkˈsiːmiə] n. MED. Anoxémie ƒ.
ansate [ˈænseit] adj. TECHN. Emmanché.
anserine [ˈænsərain] adj. ZOOL. D'oie. ‖ FAM. Bête comme une oie.
answer [ˈɑːnsə*] n. Réponse ƒ. (to, à); to give an answer, faire (or) formuler une réponse, répondre. ‖ Réplique, riposte ƒ.; to have an answer to everything, avoir réponse à tout. ‖ JUR., Réfutation ƒ.; answer to a charge, réplique du défendeur. ‖ MILIT., SPORTS. Parade ƒ. ‖ MATH. Solution ƒ. (of a problem); answer book, livre du maître. ‖ COMM. In answer to, en réponse à, comme suite à (a letter). ‖ MUS. Réplique, réponse ƒ. ‖ LOC. The answer to a maiden's prayer, le rêve, la solution idéale.
— v. intr. Répondre (to, à) [by an action or in words]; don't you dare answer me back, pas de réplique!; ne répliquez pas! ‖ Répondre (to, à) [à name]. ‖ Répondre (to, à) [a stimulus]; to answer to the spur, obéir à l'éperon. ‖ Répondre, correspondre (to, à) [a description, an effort]. ‖ Faire l'affaire; réussir, aboutir (to succeed); that won't answer, ça ne servira à rien; ça ne rendra pas (fam.). ‖ Répondre, se porter garant (for, de) [s.o., sth.]. ‖ Répondre (for, de); payer (for, pour); to answer for a crime with one's head, payer un crime de sa tête.
— v. tr. Répondre (sth.); not to answer a word, ne pas répondre un mot, ne pas souffler (or) piper mot. ‖ Répondre à (an argument, a call, a letter, s.o., sth.); répondre à, répliquer à (criticism); répondre à, obéir à (the spur); to answer the bell, aller ouvrir. ‖ Répondre à, correspondre à (a description); répondre à (a hope); répondre à, résoudre (a puzzle). ‖ Etre utile à; to answer the purpose, remplir le but, faire l'affaire, convenir. ‖ JUR. Répondre à, réfuter (a charge).
answerable [-rəbl] adj. Réfutable (objection); qui admet une réponse, à quoi l'on peut répondre (question). ‖ Relevant, dépendant, solidaire (to, de) [dependent]. ‖ Responsable, comptable, garant (for, de; to, envers) [responsible]. ‖ JUR. Réfutable (charge). ‖ MATH. Soluble (problem). ‖ † Correspondant (to, à).
answerer [-rə*] n. JUR. Répondant m.
ant [ænt] n. ZOOL. Fourmi ƒ.; red ant, fourmi rouge; white ant, termite. ‖ **Ant-bear**, n. ZOOL. Tamanoir m. ‖ **Ant-eater**, n. ZOOL. Fourmilier m. ‖ **Ant-eggs**, n. pl. ZOOL. Œufs (m. pl.) de fourmi. ‖ **Ant-fly**, n. ZOOL. Fourmi ailée ƒ. ‖ **Ant-hill**, n. ZOOL. Fourmilière ƒ.
anta [ˈæntə] (pl. antae [-iː]) n. ARCHIT. Ante ƒ.
antacid [ˈæntˈæsid] adj., n. CHIM. Alcalin m.
antagonism [ænˈtægənizm] n. Antagonisme m. (between, entre); opposition (with, avec).
antagonist [-nist] n. Antagoniste, adversaire, opposant m. ‖ MED. Muscle antagoniste m.
antagonistic [ænˌtægəˈnistik] adj. Antagonique, opposé, contraire (to, à).
antagonistically [-əli] adv. En antagonisme.
antagonize [ænˈtægənaiz] v. tr. Tendre à neutraliser, contrarier, s'opposer à (a force). ‖ Soulever

l'opposition (or) l'inimitié de, éveiller l'hostilité de, indisposer (s.o.).

antalgic [æn'tældʒik] adj. MED. Antalgique.

Antarctic [ænt'ɑ:ktik] adj., n. Antarctique *m.*

ante ['ænti] n. Mise *f.* (in poker). ‖ FIG. Mise, participation financière *f.; to raise the ante,* augmenter la mise.
— v. tr. Miser, mettre en jeu (lit., fig.). ‖ **To ante up,** U. S. Casquer, abouler l'argent.

antecedence [,ænti'si:dəns] n. Priorité, antériorité *f.* ‖ ASTRON. Antécédence *f.*

antecedent [-ənt] adj. Antérieur *(to,* à). [See PREVIOUS.] ‖ Présumé (presumptive).
— n. PHILOS., MATH., GRAMM., MED. Antécédent *m.* ‖ JUR. Précédent *m.* ‖ Pl. Antécédents *m. pl.*

antecedently [-tli] adv. Antérieurement.

antechamber ['ænti,tʃeimbə*] n. Antichambre *f.*

antedate ['ænti'deit] n. Antidate f.
— v. tr. Antidater (a document). ‖ Anticiper sur. ‖ Prévenir, précéder, devancer (an event). ‖ MED. Avancer le terme de (a delivery).

antediluvian ['æntidi'lju:vjən] adj. Antédiluvien.
— n. Etre préhistorique *m.* ‖ FAM. Fossile *m.*

antelope ['æntiloup] n. ZOOL. Antilope *f.*

antemundane ['ænti'mʌndein] adj. Préexistant au monde.

antenatal [-neitl̩] adj. Prénatal.

antenna [æn'tenə] n. (pl. **antennae** [-i:]) n. ZOOL. Antenne *f.* (of insects); corne *f.* (of snails). ‖ RADIO. Antenne *f.*

antenuptial [ænti'nʌpʃəl] adj. Prénuptial.

antepalatal [-'pælətəl] adj. GRAMM. Prépalatal.

antependium [-'pendjəm] n. ECCLES. Devant d'autel *m.*

antepenultimate ['ænti'nʌltimit] adj., n. GRAMM. Antépénultième *f.*

anterior [æn'tiəriə*] adj. Antérieur *(to,* à).

anteriority [æn,tiəri'ɔriti] n. Antériorité *f.*

anteriorly [-li] adv. Antérieurement.

ante-room ['ænti,ru:m] n. Antichambre *f.* ‖ MILIT. Salon *(m.)* du mess des officiers.

anthelmintic [,ænθel'mintik] adj., n. MED. Vermifuge *m.*

anthem ['ænθəm] n. Hymne *m.* ‖ ECCLES. Antienne *f.* ‖ † Chant *(m.)* de réjouissance.

anther ['ænθə*] n. BOT. Anthère *f.*

anthology [æn'θɔlədʒi] n. Anthologie *f.*

anthozoa [ænθo'zouə] n. pl. ZOOL. Anthozoaires *m. pl.*

anthracene ['ænθrəsi:n] n. CHIM. Anthracène *m.*

anthracite [-sait] n. Anthracite *m.*

anthrax ['ænθræks] n. MED. Anthrax *m.* (carbuncle); charbon *m.* (of cattle).

anthropocentrism [,ænθrəpə'sentrizm̩] n. PHILOS. Anthropocentrisme *m.*

anthropoid ['ænθrəpɔid] adj., n. ZOOL. Anthropoïde *m.*

anthropologist [,ænθrə'pɔlədʒist] n. Anthropologiste *s.*

anthropology [-dʒi] n. Anthropologie *f.*

anthropometric [,ænθrəpə'metrik] adj. Anthropométrique.

anthropometry [-'mitri] n. Anthropométrie *f.*

anthropomorphic [,ænθrəpə'mɔ:fik] adj. Anthropomorphique.

anthropomorphism [,ænθrəpə'mɔ:fizm] m. Anthropomorphisme *m.*

anthropomorphist [-ist] n. Anthropomorphiste *m.*

anthropomorphous [-əs] adj. Anthropomorphe.

anthropophagous [,ænθrə'pɔfəgəs] adj. Anthropophage.

anthropophagy [-dʒi] n. Anthropophagie *f.*

anthropopithecus [,ænθrəpəpi'θi:kəs] n. Anthropopithèque *m.*

anti [ænti] pref. Contre. ‖ **Anti-aircraft,** adj. MILIT. Antiaérien. ‖ **Anti-g,** adj. AVIAT., ASTRO-

NAUT. Anti-g. ‖ **Anti-hero,** n. Anti-héros *m.* ‖ **Anti-icer,** n. AVIAT. Antigivrant *m.* ‖ **Anti-personnel,** adj. MILIT. Antipersonnel. ‖ **Anti-Semite,** adj., n. Antisémite *adj., s.* ‖ **Anti-semitic,** adj. Antisémite. ‖ **Anti-Semitism,** n. Antisémitisme *m.*

antibiotic [,æntibai'ɔtik] n. MED. Antibiotique *m.*

antibody ['æntibɔdi] n. MED. Anticorps *m.*

antic [æntik] adj. Grotesque.
— n. Cabriole, gambade *f.* (caper); singerie *f.* (grimace).
— v. intr. U. S. Faire des singeries (or) des cabrioles.

anticathode [,ænti'kæθoud] n. ELECTR. Anticathode *f.*

antichrist ['æntikraist] n. ECCLES. Antéchrist *m.*

anticipate [æn'tisipeit] v. tr. Prévenir, devancer, aller au devant de (desires, objections, orders); envisager, prévoir, pronostiquer (a difficulty); s'attendre à (an event); souffrir à l'avance (a grief); savourer à l'avance, se promettre (a pleasure); escompter (a result, success); *as anticipated,* comme prévu. ‖ FIN. Anticiper sur (one's income); anticiper (a payment); escompter (profits).

anticipation [æn,tisi'peiʃən] n. Anticipation *f.; thanking you in anticipation,* avec mes remerciements anticipés. ‖ Prévision *f.; to be beyond all anticipation,* dépasser toutes les prévisions. ‖ Attente *f.; in anticipation of the pleasure of,* dans l'attente du plaisir de. ‖ Appréhension *f.* (of a pain); avant-goût *m.* (of a pleasure). ‖ MUS. Anticipation *f.* (of one's rights).

anticipative [æn'tisipeitiv] adj. Anticipé. ‖ *Anticipative of,* exprimant (or) ressentant à l'avance, s'attendant à.

anticipator [-ə*] n. Personne *(f.)* qui anticipe.

anticipatory [-əri] adj. Anticipatif.

anticlerical [ænti'klerikəl] adj. Anticlérical.

anticlericalism [-izm] n. Anticléricalisme *m.*

anticlimax ['ænti'klaimæks] n. GRAMM. Anticlimax *m.* ‖ FAM. Chute *(f.)* dans le trivial; dégringolade *f.*

anticlinal [,ænti'klainl̩] adj. GEOL. Anticlinal.

anticline ['ænti,klain] n. GEOL. Anticlinal *m.*

anticlockwise [,ænti'klɔk,waiz] adj., adv. Dans le sens inverse des aiguilles d'une montre.

anticoagulant [,æntikou'ægjulənt] adj., n. MED. Anticoagulant *adj., m.*

anticonstitutional [ænti,kɔnsti'tju:ʃənəl] adj. Anticonstitutionnel.

anticonvulsant [,æntikən'vʌlsənt] adj., n. MED. Anticonvulsif *adj., s.*

anticyclone ['ænti'saikloun] n. Anticyclone *m.*

antidotal ['æntidoutl̩] adj. MED. Antivénéneux; agissant comme antidote.

antidote [-dout] n. MED. Contrepoison; antidote *m.* ‖ FIG. Antidote *m.* *(against, for, to,* contre).

antifading ['ænti'feidiŋ] adj. RADIO. Antifading.

antifebrile [-'fi:brəl] adj., n. MED. Antifébrile, fébrifuge *m.* (See ANTIPYRETIC.)

antifreeze ['ænti,fri:z] n. AUTOM., AVIAT. Antigel *m.*

antifriction [-'frikʃən] adj. TECHN. Antifriction.

antigen ['æntidʒen] n. MED. Antigène *m.*

antihistamine ['ænti'histəmi:n] n. MED. Antihistaminique *m.*

antihistaminic [-'histəminik] adj. MED. Antihistaminique.

antiknock [,ænti'nɔk] n. AUTOM. Produit antidétonant *m.*

antiliberal [-'libərəl] adj. Antilibéral.

antilogarithm [-'lɔgəriθm] n. MATH. Antilogarithme *m.*

antilogy [æn'tilədʒi] n. GRAMM. Antilogie *f.*

antimacassar [,æntimə'kæsə*] n. Voile de fauteuil *m.*

antimagnetic ['ænti,mæg'netik] adj. PHYS. Antimagnétique.

antimatter ['ænti,mætə*] n. Phys. Antimatière *f.*
antimilitarism [-'militərizm] n. Antimilitarisme *m.*
antimilitarist [-'militərist] adj. Antimilitariste.
antimonarchical [,æntimo'nα:kikəl] adj. Antimonarchique.
antimony ['æntiməni] n. Chim. Antimoine *m.*
antinational [ænti'næ,ɾənl] adj. Antinational.
antineuralgic [,æntinju'rældʒik] adj. Med. Antinévralgique.
antinomy [æn'tinəmi] n. Antinomie *f.*
antiparticle ['ænti,pɑ:tikl] n. Phys. Antiparticule *f.*
antipathetic(al) [,æntipə'θetik(əl)] adj. Antipathique (*to*, à).
antipathy [æn'tipəθi] n. Antipathie *f.* (*against, to, pour*).
antiperistalsis ['æntiperi'stælsis] n. Med. Contractions antipéristaltiques *f. pl.*
antiperspirant [,ænti'pə:spərənt] adj. Contre la transpiration, déodorant.
— n. Déodorant *m.*
antiphlogistic ['æntiflo'dʒistik] adj., n. Med. Antiphlogistique *m.*
antiphon ['æntifən] n. Eccles., Mus. Antienne *f.*
antiphonary [æn'tifənəri] n. Eccles. Antiphonaire *m.*
antiphony [æn'tifəni] n. Mus. Antiphonie *f.*
antiphrasis [æn'tifrəsis] n. Gramm. Antiphrase *f.*
antipodal [æn'tipədl] adj. Geogr. Antipodal. || Fig. Situé aux antipodes, diamétralement opposé.
antipodes [æn'tipoudi:z] n. Geogr., Fig. Antipodes *m. pl.*
antipope ['æntipoup] n. Eccles. Antipape *m.*
antiprohibitionism [,æntiprohi'biɾənizm] n. Antiprohibitionnisme *m.*
antiprohibitionist [-ist] n. Antiprohibitionniste *s.*
antiproton ['ænti,proutɔn] n. Phys. Antiproton *m.*
antipsychiatry [,æntisai'kaiətri] n. Psych. Antipsychiatrie *f.*
antipyretic [,æntipai'retik] adj., n. Med. Antipyrétique, fébrifuge *m.*
antipyrin [,ænti'paiərin] n. Med. Antipyrine *f.*
antiquarian [,ænti'kwɛəriən] adj. D'antiquaire.
— n. Antiquaire *s.* || Double grand aigle *m.* (format).
antiquary ['æntikwəri] n. Antiquaire, archéologue *s.*
antiquated ['æntikweitid] adj. Vétuste (building); démodé (dress); vieillot (ideas); suranné (manners); vieux jeu (person); archaïque, désuet, vieilli (phrase); rococo (style).
antique [æn'ti:k] adj. Antique, ancien; de l'antiquité. || Désuet, archaïque (obsolete).
— n. Arts. Antique *m.* (ancient style); antique *f.* (work of art). || Techn. Antique *f.* (type).
antiqueness [-nis] n. Antiquité *f.*
antiquity [æn'tikwiti] n. Antiquité *f.* (monument, period, quality).
antirachitic [æntira'kitik] adj. Med. Antirachitique.
antiradar [ænti'reidɑ:*] adj. Aviat. Antiradar.
antirational [-'ræ,ɾnl] adj. Antirationnel.
antireligious [,æntiri'lidʒəs] adj. Antireligieux.
antirevolutionary ['ænti,revɔ'lu:,ɾənəri] adj., n. Antirévolutionnaire *s.*
antirrhinum [,ænti'rainəm] n. Bot. Antirrhinum, muflier *m.*
antiscorbutic [-'skɔ:bjutik] adj., n. Med. Antiscorbutique *m.*
antisepsis [-'sepsis] n. Med. Antisepsie *f.*
antiseptic [-'septik] adj., n. Antiseptique *m.*
antiserum [-'si:ərəm] n. Med. Antisérum *m.*
antislavery [-'sleivəri] adj. Antiesclavagiste.
antisocial [-'souɾəl] adj. Antisocial.
antispasmodic ['ænti,spæs'mɔdik] adj., n. Med. Antispasmodique.

antistatic [,ænti'stætik] adj. Antistatique.
antitank [-'tæŋk] adj. Milit. Antichar, antiblindé.
antitetanic ['æntitə'tænik] adj. Med. Antitétanique.
antithesis [æn'tiθəsis] (pl. **antitheses** [-i:s]) n. Gramm. Antithèse *f.* || Fig. Opposition, antithèse *f.*; contraire *m.*
antithetic(al) [,ænti'θetik(əl)] adj. Gramm. Antithétique.
antithetically [-əli] adv. Gramm. Par antithèse.
antitoxic ['ænti'tɔksik] adj. Med. Antitoxique.
antitoxin [-'tɔksin] n. Med. Antitoxine *f.*
antitrust [-'trʌst] adj. Fin. Antitrust.
antitubercular ['æntitju'bə:kjulə*] adj. Med. Antituberculeux.
antitype ['ænti,taip] n. Antitype *m.*; chose figurée *f.*; contrepartie *f.*
antiviral [-'vairəl] adj. Med. Antiviral.
antivivisectionism [-,vivi'sekɾənizm] n. Campagne (*f.*) contre la vivisection.
antler ['æntlə*] n. Andouiller *m.*
antonym ['æntənim] n. Gramm. Antonyme *m.*
antonymy [æn'tɔnimi] n. Gramm. Antonymie *f.*
antrum ['æntrəm] n. Med. Sinus, antre *m.*
anuclear ['einju:kliə*] adj. Phys. Anucléaire.
anus ['einəs] n. Med. Anus *m.*
anvil ['ænvil] n. Techn., Med. Enclume *f.* || Fig. *On the anvil*, sur le chantier.
anxiety [æŋ'zaiəti] n. Anxiété, appréhension, inquiétude *f.* || Anxiété *f.*; désir anxieux *m.* (*for, to*, de).
anxious ['æŋkɾəs] adj. Anxieux, soucieux, inquiet, tourmenté, angoissé (*about*, au sujet de, à propos de). || Inquiétant, préoccupant (business); *anxious moment*, moment d'inquiétude, mauvais quart d'heure. || Désireux, anxieux, soucieux (*for, to*, de); *anxious for glory*, avide de gloire; *he is anxious to start*, il lui tarde de partir; *to be anxious for s.o.'s return*, attendre avec impatience le retour de qqn.
anxiously [-li] adv. Anxieusement, avec anxiété (apprehensively); avec impatience (or) fébrilité (eagerly).
any ['eni] adj. N'importe quel; *any doctor will tell you*, n'importe quel médecin vous le dira. || Tout; *at any moment*, à tout moment. || De, de la, des (in interrogative and negative sentences); *have you any pears?*, avez-vous des poires? || Le moindre; *there is not any doubt*, il n'y a pas le moindre doute; *there isn't any wine in the bottle*, il n'y a pas une goutte de vin dans la bouteille. || Aucun; *she hasn't any reason to cry*, elle n'a aucune raison de pleurer. || Quelconque; *a business of any real importance*, une affaire tant soit peu importante (or) d'une importance quelconque.
— pron. N'importe lequel; *any of these rooms*, n'importe laquelle de ces pièces. || Aucun; *less than any of us*, moins qu'aucun de nous. || Quiconque; *any who wish to come*, quiconque veut venir. || En; *have you any money?, I haven't any*, avez-vous de l'argent? je n'en ai pas.
— adv. Un peu, si peu que ce soit; *is she any better this evening?* est-elle un tout petit peu mieux ce soir? || Aucunement; en aucune façon; *he cannot go any further*, il ne peut vraiment pas aller plus loin.
anybody [-bɔdi] pron. N'importe qui, qui que ce soit; *anybody can do that*, n'importe qui peut en faire autant. || Personne; *I don't know anybody*, je ne connais personne. || Quelqu'un; *has anybody been here?*, quelqu'un est-il venu? || Fam. Quelqu'un; *if I wish to be anybody*, si je veux devenir quelqu'un.
— n. Fam. Type quelconque; quidam *m.*
anyhow [-hau] adv. N'importe comment; de n'importe quelle manière (in any manner). || N'importe

comment, sans soin; à la va-comme-je-te-pousse, au petit bonheur (fam.); *to be all anyhow,* être tout chose (person); être en pagaïe (things).
— conj. De toute façon (or) manière, en tout cas (at any rate).

anyone [-wʌn] pron. See ANYBODY.

anyplace [-pleis] U. S. See ANYWHERE.

anything [-θiŋ] pron. N'importe quoi, tout; *anything but that,* tout mais pas ça!; *to eat anything,* manger de tout. ‖ Quelque chose; *anything else?,* et avec ça?, c'est tout ce qu'il vous faut?; *if he has anything to say,* s'il a qqch. à dire. ‖ Rien; *he has not seen anything,* il n'a rien vu. ‖ Loc. *Anything but,* rien moins que; *as* (or) *like anything,* comme tout.
— n. Quelque chose.

anyway [-wei] adv. See ANYHOW. ‖ U. S. En fait, en somme, en fin de compte.

anywhere [-wɛə*] adv. En n'importe quel endroit, en quelque lieu que ce soit, n'importe où; *anywhere but here,* n'importe où ailleurs qu'ici. ‖ Partout; *anywhere else,* partout ailleurs. ‖ Quelque part; *are you going anywhere?,* allez-vous quelque part? ‖ Nulle part; *I didn't see him anywhere,* je ne l'ai vu nulle part.

anywise [-waiz] adv. D'une façon quelconque (in any manner). ‖ Aucunement; en aucun⸴ façon.

aorist ['ɛərist] n. GRAMM. Aoriste *m.*

aorta [ei'ɔ:tə] n. MED. Aorte *f.*

aortic [-tik] adj. MED. Aortique.

apace [ə'peis] adv. Rapidement, vite.

apache [ə'pætʃi] n. Apache *m.* (Indian).
— [ə'pæʃ] n. Apache *m.* (ruffian).

apagogy [æpə'goudʒi] n. PHILOS., MATH. Apagogie *f.*

apanage ['æpənidʒ] n. Apanage *m.*

apart [ə'pɑ:t] adv. De côté; *to set apart,* mettre de côté; réserver. ‖ Séparément; *to come, to move apart,* se désunir, se séparer. ‖ A part; *viewed apart,* examiné à part. ‖ En pièces, en morceaux; *to take apart,* démonter. ‖ A distance; *they are ten kilometres apart,* ils sont à dix kilomètres l'un de l'autre. ‖ Indépendamment, en dehors (*from,* de) [considerations]; à l'écart (*from,* de) [a place].

apartheid [ə'pɑ:thait] n. Apartheid *m.*

apartment [ə'pɑ:tmənt] n. Pièce *f.; pl.* appartement *m.* ‖ U. S. Appartement *m.; apartment house,* maison meublée.

apathetic [æpə,θetik] adj. Apathique. ‖ Indifférent.

apathetically [-əli] adv. Nonchalamment; avec indifférence.

apathy ['æpəθi] n. Apathie *f.*

ape [eip] n. ZOOL., FIG. Grand singe *m.*
— v. tr. Singer. (See IMITATE.)

apeak [ə'pi:k] adv. NAUT. A pic (anchor); en pantenne (yard-arms).

Apennines ['æpenainz] n. pl. GEOGR. Apennins *m. pl.*

aperçu [æpə:'sju] n. Aperçu *m.*

aperient [ə'piəriənt] adj., n. MED. Laxatif *m.*

aperiodic [,eipiəri'ɔdik] adj. PHYS. Apériodique.

aperitif [ə'peritif] n. Apéritif *m.*

aperitive [-tiv] adj., n. MED. Laxatif *m.*

aperture ['æpətʃuə*] n. Ouverture *f.* ‖ ARCHIT. Jour, regard m.

apery ['eipəri] n. Singerie *f.*

apetalous [ə'petələs] adj. BOT. Apétale.

apex ['eipeks] n. MATH., MED. Sommet *m.* ‖ ASTRON. Apex *m.* ‖ FIG. Apogée, zénith *m.*

aphasia [æ'feiziə] n. MED. Aphasie *f.*

aphasi(a)c [-i(ə)k] n. MED. Aphasique *s.*

aphelion [æ'fi:liən] n. ASTRON. Aphélie *f.*

aphesis ['æfəsis] n. GRAMM. Aphérèse *f.*

aphidian [ei'fidiən] adj., n. ZOOL. Aphidien *m.*

aphis ['æfis] (pl. **aphides** [-idi:z]) n. ZOOL. Puceron *m.*

aphonic [ə'fɔnik] adj. MED. Aphone.

aphonia [ə'founiə] n. MED. Aphonie *f.*

aphorism ['æforizm] n. Aphorisme *m.*

aphoristically [,æfə'ristikəli] adv. Sentencieusement.

aphrodisiac ['æfro'diziək] adj., n. Aphrodisiaque *m.*

aphthae ['æfθi:] n. pl. MED. Aphte *m. pl.*

aphthous [-θəs] adj. MED. Aphteux.

apiarian [eipi'ɛəriən] adj. Apicole.

apiarist ['eipiərist] n. AGRIC. Apiculteur *m.*

apiary [-i] n. Rucher *m.*

apiculture ['eipikʌltʃə*] n. AGRIC. Apiculture *f.*

apidae ['æpidi:] n. pl. ZOOL. Apidés *m. pl.*

apiece [ə'pi:s] adv. Par personne, par tête, chacun (person); la pièce, chacun (thing).

apish ['eipiʃ] adj. Simiesque. ‖ FIG. Grimacier (affected); contrefaisant, de singe (imitative); *apish prank,* singerie.

apishly [-li] adv. De manière simiesque (or) grimacière.

aplomb ['ʌplɔ̃] n. FIG. Assurance *f.*

apnœa, U. S. **apnea** [ə'pni:ə] n. MED. Apnée *f.*

apocalypse [ə'pokəlips] n. ECCLES. Apocalypse *f.*

apocalyptic [ə,pokə'liptik] adj. Apocalyptique.

apocope [ə'pokəpi] n. GRAMM. Apocope *f.*

Apocrypha [ə'pokrifə] n. Apocryphes *m. pl.*

apocryphal [-əl] adj. Apocryphe.

apod ['æpɔd] n. ZOOL. Apode *m.*

apodal [-əl] adj. ZOOL. Apode.

apogee [-əpodʒi] n. ASTRON. Apogée *m.*

apolitical [,eipə'litik] adj. Apolitique.

Apollo [ə'pɔlou] n. Apollon *m.*

Apollyon [ə'pɔljən] n. Lucifer, Satan *m.*

apologetic(al) [ə,pɔlə'dʒetik(əl)] adj. D'excuse; *an apologetic air,* un air de s'excuser. ‖ Apologétique (book).

apologetics [-s] n. sg. ECCLES. Apologétique *f.*

apologia [,æpə'loudʒiə] n. Apologie *f.*

apologist [ə'pɔlədʒist] n. Apologiste *m.*

apologize [-iʒaiz] v. intr. S'excuser (*for,* de; *to,* auprès de); faire des excuses (*to,* à).

apologue ['æpəlɔg] n. Apologue *m.*

apology [ə'pɔlədʒi] n. Apologie, justification *f.* ‖ Amende honorable *f.; to make apology for,* faire amende honorable pour, s'excuser platement de. ‖ Mauvais spécimen (or) substitut m. (*for,* de); *apology for a hat,* semblant de chapeau; *sorry apology for an actor,* triste doublure d'acteur.

apophthegm ['æpoθem] n. Apophtegme *m.*

apophysis [ə'pɔfisis] n. MED. Apophyse *f.*

apopletic [,æpo'plektik] adj. MED. Apoplectique (person); d'apoplexie (stroke).

apoplexy ['æpəpleksi] n. MED. Apoplexie *f.*

apostasy [ə'pɔstəsi] n. Apostasie *f.*

apostate [ə'pɔstit] adj., n. Apostat *s.*

apostatize [-tetaiz] v. intr. Apostasier.

a posteriori [eipɔs,teri'ɔ:rai] adj., adv. A posteriori.

apostil [ə'pɔstil] n. Apostille, note marginale *f.*

apostle [ə'pɔsl] n. ECCLES., FIG. Apôtre *m.*

apostleship [-ʃip], **apostolate** [ə'pɔstəlit] n. ECCLES., FIG. Apostolat *m.*

apostolic [,æpəs'tɔlik] adj. ECCLES. Apostolique.

apostolically [-əli] adv. ECCLES. Apostoliquement.

apostrophe [ə'pɔstrəfi] n. Apostrophe *f.* (address, sign).

apostrophize [-ʃaiz] v. tr. Apostropher.

apothecary [ə'pɔθikəri] n. MED. Apothicaire *m.*

apotheosis [ə,pɔθi'ousis] n. Apothéose *f.*

apotheosize [ə:'pɔθiəsaiz] v. tr. Déifier (to deify); glorifier (to glorify); idéaliser (to idealize).

appal, U. S. **appall** [ə'pɔ:l] v. tr. (1). Terrifier, frapper d'épouvante, horrifier.

Appalachian [,æpə'leitʃiən] adj. GEOGR. *Appalachian Mountains,* Appalaches.
— n. pl. GEOGR. Appalaches *f. pl.*

appalling [-iŋ] adj. Epouvantable, terrifiant.
appallingly [-iŋli] adv. Epouvantablement.
appanage ['æpənidʒ] n. See APANAGE.
apparat [apə'rɑ:t] n. Appareil (*m.*) [or] machine (*f.*) du parti.
apparatchik [-ʃik] n. Apparatchik *m.*
apparatus [,æpə'reitəs] (pl. **apparatuses** [-iz]) n. Appareil *m.; critical apparatus,* appareil critique (or) scientifique. ‖ MED. *Breathing* (or) *respiratory apparatus,* appareil respiratoire.
apparel [ə'pærəl] n. Vêtements *m.;* mise *f.* ‖ Appareil *m.;* parure *f.;* ornement *m.* ‖ ECCLES. Parements *m. pl.*
— v. tr. (1). Vêtir, revêtir (to clothe). ‖ Parer, orner (to adorn).
apparent [ə'pærənt] adj. Visible, apparent (readily seen). ‖ Evident, manifeste, ostensible (obvious). ‖ Apparent, de surface (not real). ‖ JUR. *Heir apparent,* héritier présomptif.
apparently [-li] adv. Visiblement, manifestement (obviously); en apparence (seemingly).
apparition [æpə'riʃən] n. Apparition *f.* (act, ghost).
apparitor [ə'pæritə*] n. JUR. Appariteur *m.*
appeal [ə'pi:l] v. intr. Faire appel (*to,* à); lancer un appel (*for,* en faveur de). ‖ S'adresser, faire appel, avoir recours (*for,* pour; *to,* à) [to resort]. ‖ JUR. Faire (ou) interjeter appel; se pourvoir; *to appeal against,* réclamer contre (an order); *to appeal to the country,* en appeler au pays. ‖ **To appeal to,** intéresser, allécher, séduire; *if it appeals to you,* si cela vous sourit (or) chante, si le cœur vous en dit, si cela vous tente.
— n. Appel (*to,* à); *appeal for funds,* appel de fonds. ‖ Attrait, intérêt *m.* ‖ JUR. Appel, pourvoi *m.; court of appeal,* cour d'appel; *right of appeal,* droit de recours; *without appeal,* en dernier ressort, sans appel.
appealing [-iŋ] adj. Séduisant, attirant.
appear [ə'piə*] v. intr. Apparaître, paraître, se manifester (to become visible). ‖ Paraître, être publié, sortir (to be published). ‖ Sembler, paraître, avoir l'air (to seem); *so it appears,* il semble que oui, à ce qu'il paraît. ‖ Etre évident (or) notoire, paraître; *to make it appear that,* laisser voir (or) manifester que, faire apparaître que. ‖ THEATR. Paraître, jouer (*in,* dans); *to appear on the stage,* entrer en scène. ‖ JUR. Apparoir; *as it appears from,* ainsi qu'il appert (ou) ressort de. ‖ JUR. Comparoir, comparaître; se présenter (*against,* contre); plaider (*for,* pour); *to fail to appear,* faire défaut.
appearance [-rəns] n. † Apparition *f.* (ghost). ‖ Apparition, arrivée *f.; to put in an appearance,* se montrer, faire acte de présence, faire une apparition. ‖ Parution, apparition (of a book). ‖ Apparence, mine, tournure *f.;* aspect, air *m.; youthful in appearance,* jeune d'aspect. ‖ Abord, dehors, extérieur *m.; at first appearance,* au premier abord, à première vue; *deceitful appearances,* dehors trompeurs. ‖ Effet *m.; to make a splendid appearance,* faire un effet splendide. ‖ Apparence *f.;* air, semblant *m.; to put on an appearance of,* se donner l'air de, faire semblant de. ‖ Apparence, probabilité *f.; to all appearances,* selon toute vraisemblance. ‖ Pl. Apparences; *to judge by appearances,* juger d'après les apparences. ‖ THEATR. *First appearance,* début; *in order of appearance,* par ordre d'entrée en scène. ‖ COMM. Présentation *f.* ‖ JUR. Comparution *f.* (before a court); constitution (*f.*) d'avoué.
appeasable [ə'pi:zəbl] adj. Qui peut être apaisé; qu'on peut calmer.
appease [ə'pi:z] v. tr. Apaiser; calmer, assouvir, satisfaire (hunger, thirst). ‖ Apaiser, calmer (anger); pacifier (mind); assouvir (passion); apaiser (quarrel). ‖ Apaiser, calmer, adoucir, rasséréner (a person); apaiser par des concessions, chercher à se

concilier (a potential aggressor). ‖ MED. Apaiser, soulager (pain).
appeasement [-mənt] n. Assouvissement *m.* ‖ Apaisement *m.* ‖ Conciliation *f.; appeasement policy,* politique de conciliation.
appeaser [-ə*] n. Conciliateur *m.*
appellant [ə'pelənt] adj., n. JUR. Appelant *m.*
appellate [-it] adj. U. S. JUR. D'appel (Court).
appellation [,æpə'leiʃən] n. Appellation, dénomination *f.;* nom *m.*
appellative [ə'pelətiv] adj. GRAMM. Commun.
— n. GRAMM. Nom commun *m.*
append [ə'pend] v. tr. Annexer, joindre (a document); ajouter (notes); apposer (one's signature).
appendage [-idʒ] n. Addition *f.;* accessoire *m.* ‖ ARCHIT. Annexe, dépendance *f.;* appendice *m.* ‖ BOT., MED. Appendice *m.*
appendant [-ənt] adj. Annexé, accessoire. ‖ Attaché (*to,* à); dépendant (*to,* de).
— n. Dépendance (*to,* de); annexe *f.* (*to,* à) [thing]. ‖ Subordonné *m.* (*to,* à) [person].
appendicitis [ə,pendi'saitis] n. Appendicite *f.*
appendicular [æpen'dikjulə*] adj. MED. Appendiculaire.
appendix [ə'pendiks] (pl. **appendices** [-isi:z], **appendixes** [-iksiz]) n. Appendice *m.* (to a book). ‖ MED. Appendice *m.*
appertain [æpə'tein] v. intr. Appartenir (*to,* à). ‖ Incomber, être attaché (or) dévolu (*to,* à); faire partie (*to,* de).
appetence ['æpitəns], **appetency** [-ənsi] n. Désir, appétit *m.* (*of, for,* de) [craving]. ‖ Attirance, affinité *f.* (*for,* pour). ‖ Tendance, propension (*for,* à) [propensity]. ‖ MED. Appétence *f.*
appetent [-tənt] adj. Brûlant, avide (*after, of,* de).
appetite [-tait] n. Appétit *m.; to eat with an appetite,* manger à belles dents. ‖ FIG. Appétit, désir *m.;* convoitise (*for,* de); avidité *f.* (*for,* pour).
appetizer [-taizə*] n. Apéritif *m.* (drink); amuse-gueule *m.* (fam.) [food].
appetizing [-taiziŋ] adj. Appétissant.
applaud [ə'plɔ:d] v. intr. Applaudir.
— v. intr. Applaudir. ‖ FIG. Applaudir à; louer, approuver.
applauder [-ə*] n. Applaudisseur, approbateur *m.*
applause [ə'plɔ:z] n. invar. Applaudissements *m. pl.* ‖ FIG. Approbation *f.*
apple ['æpl] n. BOT. Pomme *f.; table* (or) *eating apple,* pomme au couteau. ‖ MED., FIG. Prunelle (of the eye). ‖ **Apple-brandy,** U. S. **Apple-jack,** n. Eau-de-vie (*f.*) de cidre, calvados *m.* ‖ **Apple-cart,** n. Voiture des quatre-saisons, petite voiture, baladeuse *f.* ‖ **Apple-dumpling,** n. CULIN. Pomme enrobée *f.* ‖ **Apple-fritter,** n. CULIN. Beignet (*m.*) aux pommes. ‖ **Apple-loft,** n. Fruitier *m.* ‖ **Apple-pie,** n. CULIN. Tourte aux pommes *f.;* adj. FAM. *en portefeuille* (bed); sans fondement (excuses); parfait (ordre). ‖ **Apple-polish,** v. tr. U. S. FAM. Faire de la lèche à, lécher les bottes de. ‖ **Apple-polisher,** n. U. S. FAM. Lèche-bottes *m.* ‖ **Apple-sauce,** n. CULIN. Compote de pommes *f.;* FAM. flagornerie *f.;* U. S. boniments (*m. pl.*) à la noix. ‖ **Apple-tree,** n. BOT. Pommier (*m.*) ‖ **Apple-turn-over,** n. CULIN. Chausson (*m.*) aux pommes.
appliance [ə'plaiəns] n. Appareil, dispositif, instrument *m.; home appliances,* appareils électro-ménagers. ‖ MILIT. Engin *m.* ‖ Pl. Accessoires *m.*
applicability [,æplikə'biliti] n. Applicabilité *f.*
applicable ['æplikəbl] adj. Applicable (*to,* à).
applicant [-ənt] n. Postulant, candidat (*for,* à). ‖ FIN. Souscripteur *m.* ‖ JUR. Requérant; pétitionnaire *s.*
application [,æpli'keiʃən] n. Application (*to,* sur) ‖ Application, utilisation *f.* (*of,* de; *to,* à); *in application of,* en vertu de, conformément à. ‖ Sollicitation, demande *f.; application for a job,* demande

d'emploi, candidature ; *on application,* sur demande. ‖ Application, attention *f.* (concentration).

applicator ['æplikeitə*] n. MED. Applicateur *m.*

applied [ə'plaid] adj. Appliqué (art, science).

appliqué [æ'pli:kei] n. Broderie, application *f.*

apply [ə'plai] v. tr. (2). Appliquer (glue, paint) [*to,* à, sur]. ‖ Mettre en pratique (a theory). ‖ Infliger (criticisms) ; appliquer (epithets) [*to,* à]. ‖ Appliquer, fixer (one's mind) ; orienter (one's studies) ; *to apply oneself to,* s'appliquer à, se donner à, s'attaquer à, s'occuper de (a task). ‖ FIN. Appliquer, affecter, employer (funds) [*to,* à] ; souscrire (*for,* à). ‖ JUR. Appliquer (law, rule). ‖ MED. Appliquer (a remedy). ‖ TECHN. Actionner (the brakes).
— v. intr. S'appliquer ; être applicable. ‖ S'appliquer, se rapporter ; se référer (*to,* à) [a case, a question]. ‖ S'adresser (*at, to,* à ; *for,* au sujet de) ; *to apply for a job,* faire une demande d'emploi, postuler (*to,* solliciter un emploi (*to,* auprès de).

appoint [ə'point] v. tr. Nommer, désigner, préposer (s.o.) [*to,* à]. ‖ Fixer, désigner, assigner (a date, a place) ; *at the appointed time,* à l'heure dite (or) convenue. ‖ Equiper, organiser, installer (a home). ‖ JUR. Instituer (an heir). ‖ COMM. *Appointed agent,* agent attitré.
— v. intr. Décider, disposer.

appointee [əpoin'ti:] n. Délégué *s.*

appointment [ə'pointmənt] n. Rendez-vous *m.* ; *by appointment,* sur rendez-vous ; *to make an appointment with,* donner (or) fixer un rendez-vous à. ‖ Nomination, désignation *f.* (*as,* au poste de ; *of,* de ; *to,* à) ; emploi, poste *m.* ‖ Recrutement *m.* (of new teachers). ‖ Pl. Installation *f.* ; aménagements *m. pl.* (of a house). ‖ Pl. Appointements *m. pl.* (salary). ‖ MILIT. Équipement *m.* (of troops). ‖ JUR. Institution *f.* (of an heir). ‖ COMM. *By Appointment to H. M. the Queen,* fournisseur de Sa Majesté la Reine.

apportion [ə'po:ʃən] v. tr. Répartir (a sum). ‖ Lotir (an estate). ‖ Allouer, assigner (*to,* à). [See ALLOT.] ‖ FIN. Ventiler (expenses).

apportionment [-mənt] n. Répartition *f.* ‖ Lotissement *m.* ‖ FIN. Ventilation *f.*

apposite ['æpozit] adj. Approprié, juste, bien venu.

appositely [-li] adv. Avec à-propos.

appositeness [-nis] n. A-propos *m.* ; justesse *f.*

apposition [,æpo'ziʃən] n. Apposition, application *f.* ‖ GRAMM. Apposition *f.*

appositive [ə'pozitiv] adj. GRAMM. En apposition.

appraisal [ə'preizəl] n. Estimation, évaluation *f.*

appraise [ə'preiz] v. tr. Evaluer, estimer, apprécier.

appraiser [-ə*] n. Estimateur *m.* ; *official appraiser,* commissaire-priseur, expert.

appreciable [ə'pri:ʃjəbl] adj. Appréciable.

appreciate [-ʃieit] v. tr. Evaluer, estimer (to estimate). ‖ Apprécier, priser, faire cas de (to esteem). ‖ U. S. Etre reconnaissant de ; être conscient de. ‖ FIN. Augmenter la valeur de.
— v. intr. Monter, augmenter (goods).

appreciation [ə,pri:ʃi'eiʃən] n. Appréciation, estime *f.* ; *to send a message of appreciation,* envoyer ses félicitations ; *to smile one's appreciation,* remercier d'un sourire. ‖ Critique *f.* ‖ U. S. Reconnaissance *f.* (of benefits). ‖ FIN. Hausse, augmentation *f.*

appreciative [ə'pri:ʃietiv] adj. Appréciateur, appréciatif. ‖ U. S. Reconnaissant.

appreciatory [-təri] adj. Appréciateur.

apprehend [,æpri'hend] v. tr. Appréhender, craindre (to dread). ‖ Saisir, comprendre, percevoir (to understand). ‖ JUR. Appréhender, arrêter.

apprehensible [-sibl] adj. Compréhensible, perceptible, saisissable.

apprehension [-ʃən] n. Appréhension, crainte *f.* ‖ Compréhension, perception *f.,* entendement *m.* ‖ JUR. Arrestation *f.*

apprehensive [-siv] adj. Anxieux, craintif, plein d'appréhension ; *to be apprehensive of,* appréhender. ‖ Compréhensif, perceptif, d'intelligence prompte, d'esprit vif.

apprehensively [-sivli] adv. Avec appréhension. ‖ Avec vivacité (ou) intelligence.

apprehensiveness [-sivnis] n. Timidité, inquiétude (*f.*) d'esprit. ‖ Compréhension, perception *f.*

apprentice [æ'prentis] n. Apprenti *s.* ‖ FAM. Débutant, novice *s.*
— v. tr. Mettre en apprentissage (*to,* chez).

apprenticeship [-ʃip] n. Apprentissage *m.* ; *to serve one's apprenticeship with,* faire son apprentissage chez (s.o.).

apprise [ə'praiz] v. tr. Informer, mettre au courant (*of,* de).

appro ['æprou] n. COMM., FAM. *On appro,* à condition, à l'essai.

approach [ə'proutʃ] v. intr. S'approcher, approcher (to go near). ‖ FIG. *To approach to,* se rapprocher de, friser, côtoyer.
— v. tr. Approcher de (a place). ‖ Aborder (a position, question) ; approcher, aborder, s'approcher de (s.o.). ‖ Se rapprocher de, être à la limite de (to border). ‖ NAUT. Arraisonner (a ship).
— n. Approche, arrivée *f.* ; *on nearer approach,* vu de plus près. ‖ Voie (*f.*) d'accès ; *the approach to the castle,* l'avenue qui conduit au château. ‖ Accès *m.* ; *to open a way of approach,* ouvrir accès auprès de. ‖ Abord *m.* ; *difficult of approach,* d'abord difficile. ‖ Allure, attitude *f.* ‖ Façon (*f.*) de prendre contact avec ; *approach to a problem,* manière d'aborder un problème. ‖ Semblant *m.* ; *some approach to cheerfulness,* quelque apparence de gaieté. ‖ Pl. Approches ; avances *f. pl.* (*to,* à). ‖ MILIT. Cheminement *m.* ; pl. travail (*m.*) d'approche. ‖ NAUT. *Approach to land,* atterrage. ‖ AVIAT. *Approach aids,* aide à l'atterrissage. ‖ MATH. Approximation *f.* ‖ FIG. *Approach works,* travaux d'approche.

approachable [-əbl] adj. Approchable, accessible (place) ; abordable (person).

approaching [-iŋ] adj. Prochain, avoisinant. ‖ Approchant.

approachless [-lis] adj. Inapprochable, inaccessible (place) ; inabordable (person).

approbate ['æprobeit] v. tr. U. S. Approuver.

approbation [æprə'beiʃən] n. Approbation *f.* ‖ COMM. *On approbation,* à condition, à l'essai.

approbative ['æprobeitiv], **approbatory** [,æpro'beitəri] adj. Approbatif.

appropriate [ə'proupriit] adj. Bien venu, juste, opportun (remark) ; propre, adéquat, idoine (word). ‖ Approprié, propre, convenable (*for, to,* à).
— [-eit] v. tr. S'approprier, s'attribuer, s'arroger. ‖ Destiner, affecter, consacrer (*for, to,* à).

appropriately [-itli] adv. Convenablement, à propos ; à juste titre.

appropriateness [-itnis] n. Justesse *f.* (of a remark) ; propriété *f.* (of a word).

appropriation [ə,proupri'eiʃən] n. Appropriation, prise de possession *f.* ‖ FIN. Attribution, affectation, imputation *f.* (of funds) ; crédit budgétaire *m.* ; *appropriation bill,* projet de loi de finances. ‖ JUR. Détournement *m.* (of funds).

appropriator [ə'prouprieitə*] n. Malversateur ; usurpateur *m.*

approval [ə'pru:vəl] n. Approbation *f.* ; *sent on approval,* envoyé en communication (book). ‖ COMM. *To buy on approval,* acheter à condition.

approve [ə'pru:v] v. tr. Approuver ; *to be approved by,* recueillir l'approbation de. ‖ Agréer (a request). ‖ Prouver, manifester, démontrer (one's quality) ; *to approve oneself,* se montrer.
— v. intr. **To approve of,** approuver, être partisan de, être d'avis de.

approved [-d] adj. Admis, approuvé. ‖ Classique (method). ‖ JUR. Agréé, approuvé, homologué ;

approved school, maison d'éducation surveillée (or) de correction. ‖ Fin. Accrédité.

approver [-ə*] n. Approbateur *m.;* approbatrice *f.* ‖ Jur. Complice *m.*

approving [-iŋ] adj. Approbateur *m.*, approbatrice *f.;* approbatif.

approvingly [-iŋli] adv. Avec approbation.

approximate [ə'prɔksimïit] adj. Proche, avoisinant, rapproché (near). ‖ Ressemblant (*to*, à); approchant (*to*, de) [much like]. ‖ Approximatif (fairly correct).
— [-eit] v. intr. To approximate to, s'approcher de, se rapprocher de (in number, quantity, value).
— v. tr. Rapprocher (*to*, de). ‖ Math. Forcer (a decimal).

approximately [-itli] adv. Approximativement.

approximation [,əprɔksi'meiʃən] n. Rapprochement *m.* (*to*, avec, de). ‖ Approximation *f.;* résultat approximatif *m.*

approximative [ə'prɔksimətiv] adj. Approximatif.

appui [æ'pwi:] n. Milit. Appui *m.*
— v. tr. Milit. Appuyer.

appurtenance [ə'pə:tinəns] n. Archit. Dépendance *f.* ‖ Jur. Servitude immobilière *f.* ‖ Pl. Attirail *m.;* affaires *f. pl.*

appurtenant [-ənt] adj. Appartenant (*to*, à); dépendant (*to*, de).

après-ski [,æprei'ski:] n. Loisirs (*m. pl.*) après le ski.
— adj. Pour l'après-ski.

apricot ['eiprikət] n. Bot. Abricot *m.* ‖ **Abricot-tree**, n. Bot. Abricotier *m.*

april ['eipril] n. Avril *m.* ‖ **April-fool**, n. Victime (*f.*) d'un poisson d'avril; *April-fool* (or) U. S. *April Fools' day*, premier avril; *to make an April-fool of*, faire un poisson d'avril à; *April-fool hoax* (or) *joke* (or) U. S. *gag*, poisson d'avril.

a priori [eiprai'ɔ:rai] adj., adv. A priori; *a priori judgement*, a priori *m.*

apriorism [ei'praiə,rizm̦] n. Philos. Apriorisme *m.*

apron ['eiprən] n. Tablier *m.* (garment). ‖ Theatr. Avant-scène *f.* ‖ Autom. Tablier *m.* ‖ Aviat. Aire de manœuvre *f.* ‖ Naut. Contre-étrave *f.* ‖ **Apron-string**, n. Cordon de tablier *m.;* Fam. *tied to s.o.'s apron-strings*, suspendu aux jupes de qqn.

apropos [æprə'pou] adv. Opportunément; à propos.
— adj. Opportun. (See relevant.)
— n. A-propos *m.*

apse [æps] n. Archit. Abside *f.*

apsidal [-idl̦] adj. Archit. Absidal; *apsidal chapel*, absidiole.

apsis [-sis] (pl. **apsides** [æp'saidi:z] n. Astron. Apside *f.*

apt [æpt] adj. Approprié, juste, adéquat. (See relevant.) ‖ Prompt, disposé; enclin, porté (*to*, à) [inclined]. ‖ Sujet, exposé (*to*, à); susceptible (*to*, de); doué, fait (*at*, pour) [gifted].

aptitude [-itju:d] n. Aptitude *f.* (*for*, à); capacité, facilité *f.* (*for*, pour). ‖ Inclination, disposition *f.* (*for*, pour).

aptly [-li] adv. Avec à-propos (or) justesse. ‖ Habilement, facilement.

aptness [-nis] n. A-propos *m.;* justesse *f.* ‖ Aptitude, facilité *f.* ‖ Disposition, tendance *f.*

aquacade [æ'kwəkeid] n. U. S. Fête nautique *f.*

aquaculture ['ækwə,kʌltʃə*] n. Aquaculture, aquiculture *f.*

aquafortis ['ækwə'fɔ:tis] n. Eau-forte *f.*

aquafortist [-ist] n. Arts. Aquafortiste *s.*

aqualung ['ækwə,lʌŋ] n. Sports. Appareil (*m.*) de plongée sous-marine.
— v. intr. Sports. Faire de la plongée sous-marine.

aquamarine ['ækwəmə'ri:n] n. Aigue-marine *f.*

aquanaut ['ækwənɔ:t] n. Sports., Naut. Plongeur sous-marin *m.*, homme-grenouille *m.*

aquaplane [æ'kwəplein] n. Aquaplane *f.*

— v. intr. Sports. Faire de l'aquaplane. ‖ Autom. Faire de l'aquaplaning.

aquarelle [.ækwə'rel] n. Arts. Dessin aquarelle *m.;* aquarelle *f.*

aquarium [ə'kwɛəriəm] n. Aquarium.

Aquarius [-iəs] n. Astron. Verseau *m.*

aquatic [ə'kwɔtik] adj. Bot., Sports. Aquatique
— n. Zool. Animal aquatique *m.* ‖ Bot. Plante aquatique *f.*

aquatics [-s] n. Sports. Sports aquatiques *m. pl.*

aquatint ['ækwə,tint] n. Arts. Aquatinte *f.*

aqueduct ['ækwidʌkt] n. Aqueduc *m.*

aqueous ['eikwiəs] adj. Aqueux. ‖ Geol. Sédimentaire (rock).

aquiline ['ækwilain] adj. D'aigle. ‖ Aquilin (nose)

aquosity [æ'kwɔsiti] n. Aquosité *f.*

Arab ['ærəb] n. Geogr. Arabe *s.* ‖ Zool. Arabe *m* (horse). ‖ Fam. Gosse *m.; street Arab*, gavroche poulbot, titi.
— adj. Geogr. Arabe (League).

arabesque [,ærə'besk] n. Arts, Archit., Mus Arabesque *f.*
— adj. Geogr. Arabe. ‖ Archit. Arabesque. Fam. Fantastique, enchevêtré.

Arabia [ə'reibiə] n. Geogr. Arabie *f.*

Arabian [-ən] adj. Geogr. D'Arabie (desert); Ara bique (gulf); arabe (people); *Arabian Nights*, le Mille et Une Nuits.
— n. Arabe *s.*

Arabic ['ærəbik] adj. Arabique (gum); arabe (lan guage, numerals).
— n. Arabe *m.* (language).

Arabist [-ist] n. Arabisant *s.*

arable ['ærəb] adj. Agric. Arable. (See tillable
— n. Agric. Terre arable *f.*

arachis ['ærəkis] n. Arachide *f.*

arachnid [ə'ræknid] n. Zool. Arachnide *m.*

arachnoid [ə'ræknɔid] n. Med. Arachnoïde *f.*

arak ['ærək] n. Arak *m.*

Aramaic [,ærə'meiik] n. Araméen *m.* (language).

Aramean [-'mi:ən] adj., n. Geogr. Araméen *s.*

araucaria [ærɔ:'kɛəriə] n. Bot. Araucaria *m.* (Se monkey-puzzle).

arbalest ['ɑ:bəlist] n. Arbalète *f.*

arbiter ['ɑ:bitə*] n. Arbitre, médiateur *m.; Arb ter elegantiarum*, arbitre des élégances.

arbitrage [,ɑ:bi'tridʒ] n. Fin. Arbitrage *m.*

arbitral ['ɑ:bitrəl] adj. Arbitral.

arbitrament [-trəmənt] n. Arbitrage *m.*

arbitrarily [-trərili] adv. Arbitrairement.

arbitrariness [-trərinis] n. Caractère arbitraire *n*

arbitrary [-trəri] adj. Arbitraire, capricieux. Despotique. ‖ Jur. Discrétionnaire.

arbitrate [-treit] v. tr., intr. Arbitrer.

arbitration [,ɑ:bi'treiʃən] n. Arbitrage *m.; labor arbitration*, arbitrage des conflits du travail; *to g to arbitration*, recourir à l'arbitrage. ‖ Jur. Arb tration clause*, clause compromissoire.

arbitrator ['ɑ:bitreitə*] n. Jur. Arbitre bénévol arbitre-juge *m.*

arbitress [-tris] n. Arbitre *f.*

arbor ['ɑ:bə*] n. Techn. Arbre, mandrin *m.*

arbo(u)r ['ɑ:bə*] n. Tonnelle, charmille *f.;* be ceau (m.) de verdure.

arboreal [ɑ:'bɔ:riəl] adj. Zool., Agric. Arb ricole.

arboreous [-əs] adj. Boisé (wooded). ‖ Arborescen

arborescence [ɑ:bɔ'resns] n. Arborescence *f.*

arborescent [-nt] adj. Arborescent.

arboretum [,ɑ:bə'ri:təm] (pl. **-tums, -ta** [-təm -tə]) n. Bot. Arboretum *m.*

arboriculture [,ɑ:bɔri'kʌltʃə*] n. Agric. Arbor culture *f.*

arboriculturist [-tʃərist] n. Agric. Arboriculteu pépiniériste *m.*

arborization [ɑ:bɔri'zeiʃən] n. Arborisation *f.*

arbutus [ɑ:'bju:təs] n. Bot. Arbousier *m.* ‖ U.

Trailing arbutus, plante épigée rampante. ‖ **Arbutus-berry**, n. Bot. Arbouse *f.*

arc [ɑ:k] n. Math. Arc *m.* (of a circle). ‖ Electr. Arc *m.* ‖ Milit. Champ de tir *m.* ‖ Astron. Limbe *m.* ‖ **Arc-brazing**, n. Electr. Soudo-brasage à l'arc *m.* ‖ **Arc-lamp** n. Electr. Lampe (*f.*) à arc. ‖ **Arc-weld**,v. tr. Techn. Souder à l'arc.

arcade [ɑ:'keid] n. Passage couvert *m.; galeries f. pl.* ‖ Archit. Arcade *f.*

Arcadia [ɑ:'keidiə] n. Geogr. Arcadie *f.*

Arcadian [-iən] n., adj. Geogr. Arcadien, *s., adj.*

arcane [ɑ:'kein] adj. Mystérieux ; occulte.

arcanum [ɑ:'keinəm] (pl. **arcana** [-ə]) n. Arcane *m.* ‖ Fig. Secret, mystère *m.*

arch [ɑ:tʃ] n. Archit. Arc, cintre *m.; arche, voûte f.* ‖ Med. Arcade *f.* (dental, orbital) ; cambrure *f.* (of the foot). ‖ Sports. Courbure *f.* (of the ski). — v. tr. Arquer, bomber. ‖ Archit. Cintrer. — v. intr. S'arquer ; former voûte.

arch adj. Malicieux, malin, espiègle (look, smile).

arch adj. Insigne, remarquable, éminent. ‖ Fam. Fieffé, achevé. ‖ **Arch-enemy, arch-fiend**, n. Ennemi (*m.*) numéro un ; Satan. ‖ **Arch-flatterer**, n. Flatteur insigne *m.* ‖ **Arch-foe**, n. See Arch-enemy. ‖ **Arch-liar**, n. Fieffé menteur *s.* — pref. Archi-. ‖ **Arch-priest**, n. Eccles. Archiprêtre, *m.*

archaeologic(al) [,ɑ:kiə'lɔdʒikəl] adj. Archéologique.

archaeologist [,ɑ:ki'ɔlədʒist] n. Archéologue *s.*

archaeology [-dʒi] n. Archéologie *f.*

archaic [ɑ:'keiik] adj. Archaïque.

archaism [-izm] n. Archaïsme *m.*

archaize [-aiz] v. tr. Rendre archaïque. — v. intr. Archaïser.

archangel ['ɑ:k,eindʒəl] n. Eccles. Archange *m.*

archbishop ['ɑ:tʃ'biʃəp] n. Eccles. Archevêque *m.*

archbishopric [-rik] n. Eccles. Archevêché *m.* (province) ; archiépiscopat *m.* (duties, office, rank).

archdeacon ['ɑ:tʃ'di:kən] n. Eccles. Archidiacre *m.*

archdeaconry [-ri] n. Eccles. Archidiaconé *m.*

archdeaconship [-ʃip] n. Eccles. Archidiaconat *m.*

archdiocese [,ɑ:tʃ'daiə,sis] n. Eccles. Archidiocèse *m.*

archducal ['ɑ:tʃ'dju:kəl] adj. Archiducal.

archduchess [-'dʌtʃis] n. Archiduchesse *f.*

archduchy [-'dʌtʃi] n. Archiduché *m.*

archduke ['ɑ:tʃ'dju:k] n. Archiduc *m.*

archer ['ɑ:tʃə*] n. Archer *m.* ‖ Astron. Sagittaire *m.*

archery [-ri] n. Tir à l'arc *m.*

archetype ['ɑ:kitaip] n. Archétype, prototype *m.*

archiepiscopal [ɑ:kie'piskɔpəl] adj. Eccles. Archiépiscopal.

archiepiscopate [-pit] n. Archiépiscopat *m.*

archimandrite [ɑ:ki'mændrait] n. Archimandrite *m.*

archipelago [,ɑ:ki'peləgou] n. Geogr. Archipel *m.* (†) ; mer Egée *f.*

architect ['ɑ:kitekt] n. Architecte *m.; U. S. landscape architect*, architecte paysagiste. ‖ Fig. Artisan *m.*

architectonic [,ɑ:kitek'tɔnik] adj. Architectonique.

architectonics [-iks] n. Archit. Architectonique *f.* ‖ Fig. Structure *f.*

architectural [,ɑ:kitekt'ʃərəl] adj. Archit. Architectural.

architecture ['ɑ:kitektʃə*] n. Architecture *f.*

architrave [-treiv] n. Archit. Architrave *f.*

archives ['ɑ:kaivz] n. pl. Archives *f. pl.*

archivist ['ɑ:kivist] n. Archiviste *s.*

archivolte ['ɑ:kivoult] n. Archit. Archivolte *f.*

archly ['ɑ:tʃli] adv. Malicieusement.

archness [-nis] n. Malice, espièglerie *f.*

archway ['ɑ:tʃwei] n. Voûte *f.; passage voûté m.*

Arctic ['ɑ:ktik] adj. Geogr. Arctique.

ardent ['ɑ:dənt] adj. Brûlant, ardent (heat) ; *ardent spirits*, spiritueux. ‖ Fig. Ardent, fervent.

ardently [-li] adv. Ardemment.

ardo(u)r ['ɑ:də*] n. Chaleur intense *f.* ‖ Fig. Ardeur ; ferveur *f.* (See fieriness.)

arduous ['ɑ:djuəs] adj. Ardu, escarpé (way). ‖ Ardu, dur, ingrat, laborieux (work). ‖ Acharné (effort).

arduousness [-nis] n. Difficulté *f.*

are [ɑ:] See be.

are [ɑ:] n. Are *m.* (unit of measure).

area ['ɛəriə] n. Aire, étendue, superficie ; surface couverte *f.* ‖ Territoire *m.; industrial area*, région industrielle. ‖ Cour basse *f.* (yard). ‖ Milit. Secteur *m.; zone f.; hostile aera*, territoire ennemi. ‖ Naut. *In the western area of the Channel*, dans les eaux occidentales de la Manche ; *outer harbour area*, avant-port, rade. ‖ Aviat. *Area bombing*, pilonnage ; *air area*, secteur de reconnaissance aérienne ; *wing area*, surface portante. ‖ Jur. *Judicial area*, ressort judiciaire.

areaway [-'wei] n. Passage *m.* (between buildings).

arena [ə'ri:nə] n. Arène *f.*

areola [ɛə'ri:ələ] n. Med. Aréole *f.* (of the nipple) ; zone rouge *f.* (of vaccination). ‖ Bot. Aréole *f.*

areometer [,æri'ɔmitə*] n. Aréomètre *m.*

Areopagus [-əs] n. Aréopage *m.*

arête [æ'reit] n. Geogr. Arête *f.* (of mountain).

argent ['ɑ:dʒənt] n., adj. Blas. Argent.

argentiferous [,ɑ:dʒən'tifərəs] adj. Argentifère.

Argentina [ɑ:dʒən'ti:nə] n. Geogr. Argentine *f.*

Argentine ['ɑ:dʒən'tain] adj., n. Argentin *s.*

argil ['ɑ:dʒil] n. Argile *f.*

argillaceous [,ɑ:dʒi'leiʃəs] adj. Argileux.

argle-bargle ['ɑ:gl'bɑ:gl] n. Fam. Ergotage *m.* — v. intr. Ergoter ; discuter le coup (fam.).

argol ['ɑ:gɔl] n. Tanin *m.* (of wine).

argon ['ɑ:gɔn] n. Chim. Argon *m.*

Argonaut ['ɑ:gənɔ:t] n. Argonaute *m.*

argosy ['ɑ:gəsi] n. Naut. Caraque *f.*

argot ['ɑ:gou] n. Argot professionnel, parler, jargon *m.*

arguable ['ɑ:gjuəbl] adj. Discutable, contestable (debatable). ‖ Défendable (tenable) ; *it is arguable that*, on peut prétendre que.

arguably [-bli] adv. Sans doute, peut-être.

argue ['ɑ:gju:] v. intr. Faire des objections (or) des raisonnements, discuter. ‖ Discuter, argumenter, disputer (*about*, au sujet de ; *against*, contre ; *with*, avec). ‖ Plaider, témoigner (*against*, contre ; *for*, en faveur de) ; *it argues well for him*, cela prouve en sa faveur. ‖ Tirer argument (*from*, de). — v. tr. Prouver, dénoter ; *it argues him to be a rogue*, cela démontre qu'il est un coquin. ‖ Soutenir, affirmer (*that*, que) [to maintain]. ‖ Persuader ; *to argue s.o. into* (or) *out of doing sth.*, réussir à convaincre qqn de faire (or) de ne pas faire qqch. ‖ Fam. *To argue the toss*, discutailler.

arguer [-ə*] n. Ergoteur, raisonneur, discutailleur, faiseur (s.) de raisonnements.

argufy [-fai] v. intr. Fam. Ergoter.

argument [-mənt] n. Argument *m.* (*against*, contre ; *for*, pour). ‖ Argumentation *f.; raisonnement m.* ‖ Discussion, controverse *f.; débat m.; it is beyond argument*, c'est indiscutable. ‖ Sommaire *m.* (summary). ‖ Jur. Plaidoyer *m.; thèse f.*

argumentation [,ɑ:gjumen'teiʃən] n. Argumentation *f.* (reasoning). ‖ Discussion *f.; débat m.*

argumentative [,ɑ:gju'mentətiv] adj. Ergoteur, raisonneur (person) ; raisonné (work).

argute [ɑ:'gju:t] adj. Aigu, perçant (sound). ‖ Fig. Avisé, pénétrant, fin (person).

argy-bargy ['ɑ:dʒi'bɑ:dʒi] n., v. intr. (2). See argle-bargle.

aria ['ɑ:riə] n. Mus. Aria *m.*

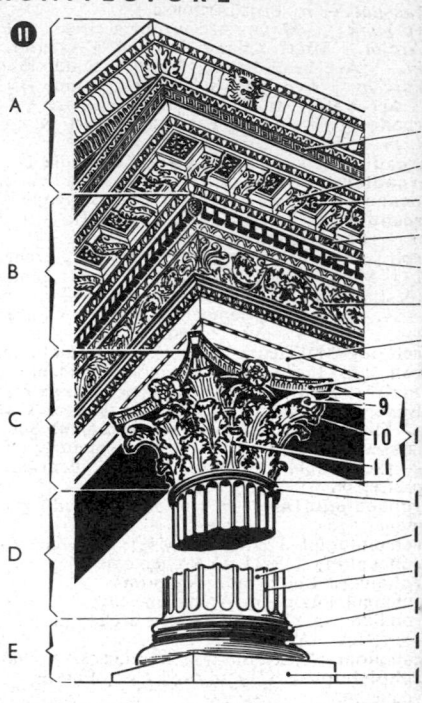

I. A. *Toscan* (ordre) ; Tuscan (order). — B. *Dorique ;* Doric. — C. *Ionique ;* Ionic. — D. *Corinthien,* Corinthian. -
E. *Composite ;* composite.
II. A. *Corniche ;* Cornice. — B. *Architrave ;* Architrave. — C. *Chapiteau ;* capital. — D. *Fût ;* Shaft. — E. *Base ;* Bas
1. *Cimaise* (grecque) ; Cyma (Greek). — 2. *Modillon ;* Modillon. — 3. *Caissons ;* Coffers, lacunars. — 4. *Rais-de-cœur*
Rai-de-cœur, Doucine finials. — 5. *Denticules ;* Denticules ; (U. S.) Dentils. — 6. *Frise de rinceaux ;* Ornamental frieze. -
7. *Bandeau ;* String-course. — 8. *Abaque ou tailloir ;* Abacus. — 9. *Volute ;* Volute, scroll. — 10. *Caulicoles ;* Cauliculi. –
11. *Feuille d'acanthe ;* Acanthus leaf. — 12. *Echine ;* Echinus. — 13. *Astragale ;* Astragal. — 14. *Cannelure ;* Flut
fluting. — 15. *Méplat ;* Flat. — 16. *Tore ;* Torus. — 17. *Scotie ;* Scotia. — 18. *Plinthe ;* Plinth.

Ariadne [ˌæriˈædni] n. Ariane *f.*
Arian [ˈɛəriən] n., adj. ECCLES. Arien *s.*
arid [ˈærid] adj. Aride, sec. (See DRY.) ‖ FIG. Aride.
aridity [əˈriditi] n. Aridité *f.*
Aries [ˈɛəriiːz] n. ASTRON. Bélier *m.*
arietta [ˌæriˈetə] n. MUS. Ariette *f.*
aright [əˈrait] adv. Bien, correctement, juste.
arise [əˈraiz] v. intr. (6). S'élever (building). ‖ Se
lever (person, sun) ; surgir, paraître (person). ‖
S'élever (cry) ; s'élever, survenir, surgir, se produire
(difficulties) ; se poser, se présenter (problem, question). ‖ Résulter, provenir (*from,* de) ; être dû
(*from,* à).
aristocracy [ˌærisˈtɔkrəsi] n. Aristocratie *f.*
aristocrat [ˈæristəkræt] n. Aristocrate *s.*
aristocratic [ˌæristəˈkrætik] adj. Aristocratique.
aristocratically [-əli] adv. Aristocratiquement.
Aristotelian [ˌæristəˈtiːliən] adj., n. Aristotélicien *adj., s.*
Aristotle [ˈæristɔtl] n. Aristote *m.*
arithmetic [əˈriθmətik] n. MATH. Arithmétique *f.*
Arithmetic-book, n. Arithmétique *f.*
arithmetical [æriθˈmetikəl] adj. MATH. Arithmétique.
arithmetically [-əli] adv. MATH. Arithmétiquement,
par l'arithmétique.
arithmometer [æriθˈmɔmitə*] n. Arithmographe,
arithmomètre *m.*
ark [ɑːk] n. Arche *f.* ‖ ECCLES. *Ark of the covenant,* Arche d'alliance ; *Noah's ark,* arche de Noé.
‖ FAM. *Sth. out of the ark,* qqch. qui remonte au
déluge.

arm [ɑːm] n. MED. Bras *m. ; in one's arms,* da
les bras ; *on one's arm,* au bras ; *to make a lor
arm for,* allonger le bras vers. ‖ Manche *f.* (sleeve
‖ TECHN. Bras (of a balance) ; rayon *m.* (of
wheel). ‖ MILIT. Mâchoire *f.* (of a pincer mov
ment). ‖ NAUT. Patte *f.* (of anchor). ‖ GEOGR. Bra
(of a river, of the sea). ‖ JUR. *Secular arm,* bra
séculier. ‖ AUTOM. Bras *m.* ‖ FIG. *To keep s.o.*
arm's length, tenir qqn à distance. ‖ FAM. *To hav
a long arm,* avoir le bras long ; *he'd cut off h
right arm for her,* il se couperait en petits morceau
pour elle. ‖ **Arm-chair,** n. Fauteuil *m. ;* FAM. *Arm
chair strategist,* stratège du café du commerce.
Arm-hole, n. Emmanchure *f.* ‖ **Arm-in-arm,** ad
Bras dessus bras dessous. ‖ **Arm-rest,** n. Appui
bras, accoudoir *m.*
arm n. Arme *f. ; in arms,* armé ; *under arms,* sou
les armes. ‖ MILIT. Arme *f.* (branch) ; pl. carriè
(*f.*) des armes. ‖ BLAS. Armes, armoiries *f. pl. ; co
of arms,* blason, écu. ‖ FAM. *Up in arms agains
en rébellion ouverte contre.
— v. tr. Armer (a nation, s.o.) ; *to arm onese
with,* s'armer de. ‖ TECHN. Armer (a fuse,
magnet). ‖ ARCHIT. Renforcer (a beam). ‖ NAU
Armer (a ship).
— v. intr. S'armer (*against,* contre).
Armada [ɑːˈmɑːdə] n. NAUT. Armada *f.*
armadillo [ɑːməˈdilou] n. ZOOL. Tatou *m.*
Armageddon [ˌɑːməˈgedn̩] n. Bataille apocaly
tique *f.*
armament [ˈɑːməmənt] n. MILIT. Armement (ac
equipment) ; troupe armée *f.* (forces) ; matériel (*m*

de guerre (guns). ‖ Naut. Artillerie *f.* (guns); flotte armée *f.* (forces).

armature ['ɑːmətjuə*] n. Techn., Archit., Electr. Armature *f.*

Armenia [ɑːˈmiːnjə] n. Geogr. Arménie *f.*

Armenian [-ən] adj., n. Geogr. Arménien *s.* ‖ Med. *Armenian bole*, bol d'Arménie.

armful ['ɑːmful] n. Brassée *f.*

armistice ['ɑːmistis] n. Milit. Armistice *m.*

armlet ['ɑːmlit] n. Brassard *m.* ‖ Geogr. Petit bras (*m.*) de rivière (or) de mer.

armo(u)r ['ɑːmə*] n. Armure *f.* ‖ Milit. Blindage *m.* (steel plates); blindés, chars *m. pl.* (vehicles). ‖ Naut. Scaphandre *m.* ‖ Blas. Armoiries *f. pl.* ‖ **Armour-clad,** adj. Milit. Blindé, cuirassé. ‖ **Armour-piercing,** adj. Milit. De rupture (bomb). ‖ **Armour-plate,** n. Milit. Plaque (*f.*) de blindage. — v. tr. Milit., Naut. Blinder, cuirasser.

armorial [ɑːˈmɔːriəl] adj., n. Armorial *m.*

armory ['ɑːməri] n. Science héraldique *f.*

armoured [-d] adj. Milit. Blindé, cuirassé; *armoured car*, automitrailleuse.

armourer [-rə*] n. Armurier *m.*

armoury [-ri] n. Milit. Arsenal *m.;* armurerie *f.* ‖ U. S. Fabrique d'armes *f.* ‖ Fig. Arsenal *m.*

armpit ['ɑːmpit] n. Med. Aisselle *f.*

army ['ɑːmi] n. Armée *f.* (military profession, troops). ‖ Fig. Armée, foule *f.* (crowd). ‖ Loc. *Salvation Army,* armée du Salut. ‖ **Army-corps,** n. Milit. Corps (*m.*) d'armée.

arnica ['ɑːnikə] n. Bot., Med. Arnica *m.*

aroint [əˈrɔint] interj. Arrière!

aroma [əˈroumə] n. Arôme *m.*

aromatic [əroˈmætik] adj. Aromatique.

aromatize [əˈroumətaiz] v. tr. Aromatiser.

arose [əˈrouz]. See arise.

around [əˈraund] adv. Autour, alentour. ‖ De tous côtés (on all sides). ‖ Fam. Par là; *stay around,* rester par là; *to have been around,* s'être déluré. — prep. Autour de (round). ‖ A la périphérie de (on the border of). ‖ Fam. *To get around s.o.,* entortiller qqn. ‖ Fam. U. S. *Around six pounds,* six livres environ; *around 1900,* aux alentours de 1900.

arouse [əˈrauz] v. tr. Eveiller, réveiller (to wake). ‖ Fig. Eveiller; provoquer, stimuler, exciter.

arpeggio [ɑːˈpɛdʒiou] n. Mus. Arpège *m.*

arquebus ['ɑːkwibəs] n. Arquebuse *f.*

arrack ['ærək] n. Arack *m.*

arraign [əˈrein] v. tr. Attaquer, critiquer (an opinion, s.o.); mettre en doute (a statement). ‖ Jur. Accuser, mettre en accusation (s.o.).

arraignment [-mənt] n. Censure *f.* ‖ Jur. Mise en accusation *f.;* réquisitoire *m.*

arrange [əˈreindʒ] v. tr. Ranger (pieces of furniture); arranger, aménager (a room). ‖ Arranger, ajuster (one's hair). ‖ Arranger, organiser, fixer (a marriage, a meeting). ‖ Arranger, ajuster (a difference). ‖ Math. Ordonner (terms). ‖ Mus. Adapter (a piece). ‖ Jur. Préparer, conclure (a treaty). — v. intr. Prendre des dispositions, s'arranger (*for, pour*). ‖ S'arranger, s'entendre (*with, avec*).

arrangement [-mənt] n. Arrangement, aménagement *m.* ‖ Arrangement *m.;* convention *f.* ‖ Règlement *m.* (of a dispute). ‖ Jur. *Pooling (or) linking arrangement,* apparentements politiques. ‖ Pl. Arrangements; mesures *f. pl.* ‖ Mus. Adaptation. ‖ Techn. Dispositif *m.* ‖ Fam. Fourbi, machin *m.*

arrant ['ærənt] adj. Fieffé, notoire, avéré.

arras ['ærəs] n. † Tapisserie, tenture *f.*

array [əˈrei] v. tr. Parer, orner (*in, de*). ‖ Milit. Dresser, déployer (forces). ‖ Jur. Dresser le tableau des jurés. — n. Appareil *m.;* atours *m. pl.* ‖ Milit. Rang *m.; in battle array,* en ordre de bataille. ‖ Jur. Tableau (*m.*) des jurés. ‖ Fig. Etalage *m.*

arrear [əˈriə*] n. † Arrière *m.* ‖ Fin. Pl. Arriéré *m.* ‖ Fig. Pl. *In arrears with,* en retard pour.

arrearage [-ridʒ] n. Retard *m.* ‖ Pl. Dettes *f. pl.;* arrérages *m. pl.*

arrest [əˈrest] v. tr. Arrêter (a motion). ‖ Jur. Surseoir à (a judgment); arrêter (s.o.). ‖ Fig. Retenir, arrêter (s.o.'s attention, sight). — n. Arrêt *m.* (stoppage). ‖ Jur. Surséance *f.* (of judgment); arrestation *f.* (of s.o.). ‖ Milit. Arrêts *m. pl.; to put under close, open arrest,* mettre aux arrêts de rigueur, simples.

arrester [-ə*] n. Electr. Limiteur (*m.*) de tension; *lightning-arrester,* paratonnerre. ‖ **Arrester-hook,** n. Aviat. Dispositif de freinage à la descente.

arresting [-iŋ] adj. Attrayant, captivant, frappant. — n. Arrestation *f.*

arris ['æris] n. Archit. Arête *f.*

arrival [əˈraivəl] n. Arrivée *f.* (act); arrivant *m.* (person); *on arrival,* à l'arrivée, au débarqué, au débotté. ‖ Comm. Arrivage *m.*

arrive [əˈraiv] v. intr. Arriver (*at, in,* à). ‖ Fig. Arriver; atteindre, parvenir (*at,* à).

arrivisme [ˌæriːˈvizmə] n. Arrivisme *m.*

arriviste [-ˈvist] n. Arriviste *s.*

arrogance ['ærəgəns] n. Arrogance *f.*

arrogant [-ənt] adj. Arrogant.

arrogantly [-əntly] adv. Avec arrogance.

arrogate ['ærogeit] v. tr. Revendiquer sans droit; *to arrogate to oneself,* s'arroger.

arrow ['ærou] n. Flèche *f.* ‖ Techn. Fiche *f.* (of surveyor). ‖ Fig. *Returning arrow,* choc en retour. ‖ **Arrow-headed,** adj. Gramm. Cunéiforme (character). — v. tr. Flécher (a direction, a road).

arrowroot [-ruːt] n. Bot. Arrow-root *m.*

arse [ɑːs] n. Pop. Cul *m.* ‖ **Arse-crawler, arse-creeper,** n. Pop. Lèche-cul *m.*

arsenal ['ɑːsinl] n. Milit. Arsenal *m.*

arseniate [ɑːˈsenieit] n. Chim. Arséniate *m.*

arsenic ['ɑːsnik] m. Chim. Arsenic *m.* — adj. Chim. Arsénique.

arsenical [ɑːˈsenikəl] adj. Chim. Arsenical.

arsenide ['ɑːsnaid] n. Chim. Arséniure *m.*

arsenious [ɑːˈsiːnjəs] adj. Chim. Arsénieux.

arsine ['ɑːsiːn] n. Chim. Arsine *f.*

arson ['ɑːsn] n. Jur. Crime d'incendie volontaire *m.*

art [ɑːt]. See be.

art n. Art *m.;* adresse *f.* (skill). ‖ Artifice *m.;* ruse *f.* (cunning). ‖ Métier *m.;* connaissances *f. pl.; Arts and Crafts,* arts et métiers; *Bachelor of Arts,* licencié ès lettres; *black art,* magie noire. ‖ Arts. *Art for art's sake,* l'art pour l'art; *fine arts,* Beaux-Arts. ‖ Techn. Procédé *m.;* technique *f.* (in a patent). ‖ Jur. *To have art and part in a crime,* être fauteur et complice d'un crime. ‖ **Art-critic,** n. Arts. Critique d'art *m.* ‖ **Art deco,** adj., n. Art déco *adj., m.* ‖ **Art-form,** n. Arts. Forme artistique *f.;* moyen (*m.*) d'expression artistique. ‖ **Art nouveau,** n. Techn. Art nouveau, modern style *m.*

artefact ['ɑːtiˌfækt] n. Artefact *m.* (in biology). ‖ Objet fabriqué *m.* (in archaeology).

arterial [ɑːˈtiəriəl] adj. Med. Artériel. ‖ Fig. National (road).

arterialize [-aiz] v. tr. Med. Artérialiser.

arteriole [ɑːˈterioul] n. Med. Artériole *f.*

arteriosclerosis [ɑːˈtiəriɔskliəˈrousis] n. Med. Artériosclérose *f.*

arteritis [ɑːtəˈraitis] n. Med. Artérite *f.*

artery ['ɑːtəri] n. Med., Fig. Artère *f.*

artesian [ɑːˈtiːʒən] adj. Artésien (well).

artful ['ɑːtful] adj. Adroit, habile, ingénieux (clever); artificieux, astucieux, rusé, malin (cunning); ‖ Artificiel.

artfully [-i] adv. Habilement (cleverly); avec astuce (cunningly).

artfulness [-nis] n. Habileté, adresse, ingéniosité *f.* (cleverness); astuce, ruse *f.* (craft).

arthralgia [ɑːˈθrældʒiə] n. Med. Arthralgie *f.*

arthritic [ɑːˈθritik] adj. Arthritique.

arthritis [ɑ:'θraitis] n. MED. Arthrite *f* : *rheumatoid arthritis*, rhumatisme articulaire.
arthropod ['ɑ:θrə,pɔd] n. ZOOL. Arthropode *m.*
arthrosis [ɑ:'θrousis] n. MED. Arthrose *f.*
Arthurian [ɑ:'θjuəriən] adj. Arthurien.
artic [ɑ:'tik] n. AUTOM., FAM. Semi-remorque *m.*
artichoke ['ɑ:tit,ʃouk] n. BOT., CULIN. Artichaut *m.; Jerusalem artichoke,* topinambour.
article ['ɑ:tikl] n. Article *m.* (in a newspaper). ‖ JUR. Article *m.; clause f.; articles of apprenticeship,* contrat d'apprentissage; *articles and conditions,* cahier des charges; *articles of incorporation,* statuts d'une société commerciale. ‖ MILIT. *Articles of war,* code de justice militaire. ‖ NAUT. *Ship's articles,* rôle de l'équipage. ‖ ECCLES. Article *m.* (of faith, of religion). ‖ GRAMM. Article *m.* ‖ COMM. Article *m.; article of clothing,* objet d'habillement. ‖ FIG. Sujet, point *m.* ‖ FIG. Moment; article *m.* (of death). ‖ U. S. FAM. Numéro *m.* (guy).
— v. tr. Articuler, formuler, stipuler. ‖ Mettre en apprentissage. ‖ JUR. Accuser (*for*, de).
articular [ɑ:'tikjulə*] adj. MED. Articulaire.
articulate [ɑ:'tikjulit] adj. Parlant bien, s'exprimant avec aisance (person). ‖ Bien articulé (word, speech). ‖ ZOOL., BOT. Articulé.
— v. tr. [-leit] Exprimer clairement. ‖ Bien articuler.
articulated [-leitid] adj. Articulé. ‖ AUTOM. *Articulated lorry,* semi-remorque *m.*
articulation [ɑ:,tikju'leiʃən] n. Articulation *f.*
artifact ['ɑ:ti,fækt] n. U. S. See ARTEFACT.
artifice ['ɑ:tifis] n. Artifice, expédient habile, stratagème *m.; ruse f.* (trickery). ‖ Ingéniosité, adresse, habileté *f.* (skill).
artificer [-ə*] n. TECHN. Artisan *m.* ‖ NAUT. Mécanicien *m.* ‖ MILIT. Artificier *m.*
artificial [ɑ:ti'fiʃəl] adj. Artificiel (ice, flower, light); *artificial wood,* simili-bois. ‖ MED. Artificiel (insemination, respiration); artificiel, faux (teeth). ‖ COMM. Ersatz, synthétique, artificiel. ‖ AGRIC. Chimique (manure); artificiel (meadow). ‖ FIG. Artificiel, étudié, factice (manner, style); forcé (smile).
artificiality [,ɑ̃:tifiʃi'æliti] n. Artifice, caractère artificiel *m.*
artificially [,ɑ:ti'fiʃəli] adv. Artificiellement.
artillery [ɑ:'tiləri] n. MILIT., FIG. Artillerie *f.*
artilleryman [-mən] (pl. **artillerymen**) n. MILIT. Artilleur *m.*
artisan [,ɑ:ti'zæn] n. Artisan *s.*
artist ['ɑ:tist] n. ARTS. Artiste *s.*
artiste [ɑ:'ti:st] n. MUS., THEATR., FIG. Artiste *s.*
artistic [ɑ:'tistik] adj. Artistique.
artistically [-ikəli] adv. Artistement, artistiquement, avec art.
artistry ['ɑ:tistri] n. Art *m.,* qualité artistique *f.* (workmanship, skill).
artless ['ɑ:tlis] adj. Sans art, peu artistique. ‖ Sans culture (ignorant); gauche, malhabile (unskilful). ‖ Ingénu, candide (naïve); sans artifice, naturel (simple).
artlessly [-li] adv. Sans art. ‖ Sans artifice. ‖ Naïvement, avec ingénuité.
artlessness [-nis] n. Candeur, ingénuité, naïveté *f.*
artwork ['ɑ:t,wə:k] n. Iconographie, illustration *f.; graphisme m.*
arty ['ɑ:ti] adj. FAM. Qui a des prétentions artistiques. ‖ **Arty-crafty,** adj. Plus artistique que confortable (furniture); bohème, affichant le genre artiste (person).
arum ['ɛərəm] n. BOT. Arum *m.*
aryan ['ɛəriən] adj., n. GEOGR. Aryen *s.*
as [æz] adv. Autant, aussi (equally). ‖ Comme, par exemple (for instance). ‖ **As ... as,** aussi ... que, *as courageous as you,* aussi courageux que vous; *as much* (or) *many ... as,* autant (or) autant de ... que; pas moins de. jusqu'à.

— conj. Comme, ainsi que; *as in a boat,* comme dans un bateau; *born actor as he was,* acteur né qu'il était; *disguised as a woman,* déguisé en femme. ‖ Comme, alors que, au moment où, tandis que (while); *he arrived as you were leaving,* il est arrivé comme vous partiez. ‖ Puisque, étant donné que, parce que (because); *as he objects, I won't read,* je ne lirai pas puisqu'il s'y oppose. ‖ Quoique, bien que, comme (though); *intelligent as he was,* intelligent comme il était, bien qu'il fût intelligent, pour intelligent qu'il fût, tout (or) si (or) quelque intelligent qu'il fût; *despise him as she might,* si peu d'estime qu'elle lui portât. ‖ COMM. *As is,* tel quel; *as and when received,* au fur et à mesure des rentrées. ‖ **As if, as though,** comme si; *as if the funds were inexhaustible,* comme si les fonds étaient inépuisables. ‖ **As ... so,** de même que ... de même; *as I helped you, so you ought to help my son,* tout comme je vous ai aidé, vous devriez aider mon fils.
— prep. En tant que; comme; *famous as an orator,* célèbre comme orateur; *to act as a friend,* agir en ami. ‖ **As for, as to,** quant à; *as for translating that,* quant à traduire cela; *he hesitated as to whether he would accept or not,* il hésita pour savoir s'il accepterait ou non; *there is no guessing as to the conclusion,* il n'y a pas moyen de deviner quelle sera la conclusion. ‖ **So ... as to,** si ... que, assez... pour; *can anyone be so silly as to believe this?,* peut-on être assez sot pour y croire? ‖ **So as to,** afin de, de façon à; *so as to be sure,* afin d'être sûr.
— pron. Ainsi que, de même que; *she is beautiful as anyone can see,* elle est belle, comme tout le monde peut le voir. ‖ Que; *in proportion as,* à mesure que; *not so good as you,* pas si bon que vous.
as [æs] n. As *m.* (coin, weight).
asafoetida [æsə'fi:tidə] n. MED. Assa-fœtida *f.*
asbestos [æz'bestɔs] n. Asbeste, amiante *m.; asbestos cement,* fibro-ciment.
ascend [ə'send] v. intr. Monter, s'élever (*to,* à) [to rise]. ‖ Monter, grimper (to slope). ‖ Remonter (towards, vers). ‖ MUS. Monter (sound). ‖ FIG. S'élever (in rank).
— v. tr. Monter à (a ladder); monter sur (a throne). ‖ Remonter (a river). ‖ ECCLES. *To ascend the pulpit,* monter en chaire. ‖ SPORTS. Gravir (a mountain).
ascendancy [-ənsi] n. FIG. Ascendant *m.; influence f.* (over, sur).
ascendant [-ənt] n. JUR., ASTRON. Ascendant *m., in the ascendant,* à l'ascendant. ‖ FIG. Ascendant *m.* ‖ LOC. *In the ascendant,* à l'apogée.
— adj. Montant. ‖ ASTRON. Ascendant. ‖ FIG. Dominant.
ascension [ə'senʃən] n. Ascension *f.* ‖ **Ascension-day,** n. ECCLES. Jour (*m.*) de l'Ascension.
ascensionnal [-l] adj. Ascensionnel.
ascensive [ə'sensiv] adj. Montant, progressif. ‖ GRAMM. Intensif.
ascent [ə'sent] n. Côte, montée, inclinaison *f* (slope). ‖ SPORTS. Ascension *f.* ‖ FIG. Ascension *f.* (in rank); remontée *f.* (in time).
ascertain [,æsə'tein] v. tr. Constater, se rendre compte, vérifier. ‖ S'informer de (from, auprès de). ‖ S'assurer; acquérir la certitude (that, que).
ascertainable [-əbl] adj. Vérifiable.
ascertainment [-mənt] n. Constatation, vérification *f.* ‖ JUR. Fixation *f.* (of indemnity).
ascetic [ə'setik] adj. Ascétique.
— n. Ascète *s.*
asceticism [-isizm] n. Ascétisme *m.; ascèse f.*
ascidium [ə'sidiəm] n. BOT. Ascidie *f.*
ascorbic [ə'skɔ:bik] adj. CHIM. *Ascorbic acid,* acide ascorbique.
ascribable [ə'skraibəbl] adj. Imputable, attribuable.

ascribe [ə'skraib] v. tr. Imputer, attribuer.
ascription [ə'skripʃən] n. Imputation, attribution f. (of, de; to, à).
asdic ['æzdik] n. TECHN., NAUT. Asdic m.
asepsis [ə'sepsis] n. MED. Asepsie f.
aseptic [-tik] adj., n. MED. Aseptique m.
asepticize [-tisaiz] v. tr. MED. Aseptiser.
asexual [æ'seksjuəl] adj. Asexué.
ash [æʃ] n. BOT. Frêne m.
ash n. Cendre f.; to burn to ashes, réduire en cendres. ‖ Pl. Cendres (human remains). ‖ ECCLES. Ash Wednesday, mercredi des Cendres. ‖ **Ash-bin**, U. S. **ash-can**, n. Cendrier m.; boîte à ordures f. ‖ **Ash-blond**, adj. Blond cendré. ‖ **Ash-coloured** (or) **-grey**, adj. Cendré, gris cendré. ‖ **Ash-fire**, n. CHIM. Feu couvert m. ‖ **Ash-tray**, n. Cendrier m.
ashamed [ə'ʃeimd] adj. Honteux, confus (of, to, de); to be ashamed of, avoir honte de.
ashen ['æʃn] adj. BOT. De frêne.
ashen adj. Cendré, couleur de cendre. ‖ Blême, terreux (pale).
ashlar ['æʃlə*] n. ARCHIT. Moellon m.
ashore [ə'ʃɔː*] adv. NAUT. Echoué, à la côte (ship). ‖ NAUT. A terre; to set passengers ashore, débarquer des passagers.
ashy ['æʃi] adj. Cendré, couleur de cendre (ashen); cendreux (covered with ashes).
Asia ['eiʃə] n. GEOGR. Asie f.
Asian [-n], **Asiatic** [eiʃi'ætik] adj., n. Asiatique s.
aside [ə'said] adv. De côté, à part; to turn aside from, se détourner de. ‖ U. S. En plus de (in addition to). ‖ THEATR. En aparté.
— m. THEATR. Aparté m.
asinine ['æsinain] adj. ZOOL. Asine (race). ‖ FAM. Sot; d'âne.
ask [ɑːsk] v. tr. Interroger; to ask s.o. about sth., interroger qqn au sujet de qqch., s'informer de qqch. auprès de qqn. ‖ Demander, solliciter (favour); to ask s.o. sth. (or) s.o. for sth. (or) sth. of s.o., demander qqch. à qqn; to ask s.o. to do sth., demander à qqn (or) solliciter qqn de faire qqch.; to ask to be allowed to speak, demander la parole. ‖ Inviter, convier (to, à) [s.o.]. ‖ Poser, formuler (a question). ‖ JUR. Publier (the banns). ‖ COMM. Demander (a price). ‖ FIG. Demander, exiger (attention); demander, prendre (time).
— v. intr. To ask about, s'informer de, s'enquérir de, se renseigner sur (s.o., sth.). ‖ To ask after, demander des nouvelles de; demander après (fam.) [s.o.]. ‖ To ask for, demander (s.o., sth.). ‖ FAM. To ask for the moon, demander la lune; to be asking for trouble, chercher les embêtements.
askance [əs'kæns] adv. Du coin de l'œil; to look askance at, regarder de travers (or) avec méfiance.
askew [əs'kjuː] adv. De côté; de guingois.
asking ['ɑːskiŋ] n. Action (f.) de demander; it is to be had for the asking, il n'y a qu'à le demander.
aslant [ə'slɑːnt] adv. Obliquement, de biais.
— prep. En travers de.
asleep [ə'sliːp] adv. Endormi; to fall asleep, s'endormir. ‖ Engourdi, endormi (numb). ‖ FAM. Inactif, endormi.
aslope [ə'sloup] adv. En pente.
asocial [ei'souʃəl] adj. Asocial.
asp [æsp] n. BOT. Tremble m.
asp [ɑsp] n. ZOOL. Aspic m.
asparagus [əs'pærəgəs] n. BOT. Asperge f. ‖ CULIN. Asperges f. pl. ‖ **Asparagus-fern**, n. BOT. Asparagus m.
aspect ['æspekt] n. Aspect m. (see APPEARANCE); of good aspect, d'aspect favorable. ‖ Air m.; to wear quite another aspect, changer tout à fait de mine (or) d'allure. ‖ Angle, aspect m.; in all its aspects, sous toutes ses faces. ‖ Exposition, orientation f. (of a house); with eastern aspect, orienté au

levant. ‖ ASTRON., GRAMM. Aspect m. ‖ **Aspect-ratio**, n. AVIAT. Allongement m.
aspen ['æspən] adj. BOT. De tremble. ‖ FAM. Tremblant.
— n. BOT. Tremble m.
aspergillum [ˌæspə'dʒiləm] n. Goupillon m.
asperity [æs'periti] n. Aspérité f. ‖ FIG. Sévérité, âpreté f. (of a person); rigueur f. (of weather).
asperse [əs'pəːs] v. tr. Asperger (with, de). ‖ FIG. Entacher, porter atteinte à (s.o.'s reputation); calomnier, diffamer, salir (s.o.).
aspersion [-pə'ʃən] n. Aspersion f. ‖ FIG. Calomnie f.
aspersive [-pə'siv] adj. FIG. Calomnieux.
aspersorium [æspə'sɔːrjəm] n. Bénitier; goupillon m.
asphalt ['æsfælt] n. Asphalte m.
— v. tr. Asphalter.
asphodel ['æsfɔdel] n. BOT. Asphodèle m.
asphyxia [æs'fiksiə] n. MED. Asphyxie f.
asphyxiate [-eit] v. tr. Asphyxier.
asphyxiation [ˌæsfik'sieiʃən] n. MED. Suffocation, asphyxie f.
aspic ['æspik] n. ZOOL. Aspic m.
aspic n. CULIN. Aspic m.
aspidistra [æspi'distrə] n. BOT. Aspidistra m.
aspirant [əs'paiərənt] n. Aspirant s.
— adj. Ambitieux.
aspirate ['æspəreit] v. tr. MED., GRAMM. Aspirer.
— [-it] adj. Aspiré.
— n. GRAMM. Aspirée f.
aspiration [ˌæspi'reiʃən] n. MED., GRAMM., FIG. Aspiration f.
aspirator ['æspireitə*] n. TECHN., MED. Aspirateur m. ‖ AGRIC. Tarare m.
aspire [əs'paiə*] v. intr. Aspirer (after, at, to, à). ‖ FIG. S'élever, se porter (ambition, thought).
aspirin ['æspirin] n. MED. Aspirine f. ‖ FAM. Comprimé (m.) d'aspirine.
aspiring [əs'paiəriŋ] adj. Ambitieux.
asquint [ə'skwint] adv. De côté, du coin de l'œil; to eye s.o. asquint, loucher vers qqn.
ass [æs] n. ZOOL. Ane m.; ass's foal, ânon; ass's milk, lait d'ânesse; wild ass, onagre. ‖ MATH. Asses' bridge, pont aux ânes. ‖ FAM. Ane m.; bourrique f.; imbécile s. ‖ U. S. POP. Cul m.
assagai ['æsigai] n. Sagaie f.
assail [ə'seil] v. tr. Assaillir, attaquer (s.o.). ‖ Assaillir, accabler (with, de) [arguments, questions]. ‖ Faire face à, s'attaquer à (a difficulty).
assailable [-əbl] adj. Susceptible d'être assailli, attaquable.
assailant [-ənt], **assailer** [-ə*] n. Assaillant, agresseur m. ‖ FIG. Adversaire m. (of a doctrine).
assassin [ə'sæsin] n. Assassin m.
assassinate [-eit] v. tr. Assassiner.
assassination [əˌsæsi'neiʃən] n. Assassinat m.
assault [ə'sɔːlt] n. JUR. Agression f.; assault and battery, menaces et voies de fait; aggravated assault, coups et blessures; criminal assault, tentative de viol; indecent assault, attentat à la pudeur. ‖ MILIT. Assaut m.; attaque brusquée f.; bayonet assault, attaque à la baïonnette; to make an assault, donner l'assaut. ‖ SPORTS. Assaut (in fencing). ‖ FIG. Attaque f. (upon, contre).
— v. tr. Attaquer, assaillir (s.o.). ‖ JUR. Se livrer à des voies de fait sur (s.o.); violenter (a woman). ‖ MILIT. Attaquer.
assaulter [-ə*] n. Assaillant, agresseur m.
assay [æ'sei] n. TECHN. Essai m. (of metals); métal analysé m. (metal); assay value, teneur.
— v. tr. TECHN. Essayer. ‖ FIG. Essayer, tenter (to, de).
— v. intr. TECHN. Titrer.
assegai ['æsigai] n. Sagaie f.

assemblage [ə'semblidʒ] n. Assemblage; rassemblement m.

assemble [-ļ] v. tr. Assembler, rassembler. ‖ TECHN. Monter (a machine). ‖ JUR. Convoquer (the Parliament).

assembly [-li] n. Assemblée, réunion f. ‖ JUR. Assemblée législative f. ‖ TECHN. Assemblage, montage m. ‖ MILIT. Rassemblement m. (call). ‖ **Assembly-area,** n. MILIT. Zone (f.) de rassemblement. ‖ **Assembly-line,** n. TECHN. Ligne (f.) de montage; assembly-line work, travail à la chaîne. ‖ **Assembly-room,** n. Salle (f.) des fêtes ; TECHN. Atelier de montage m. ‖ **Assembly-shop,** n. TECHN. Atelier de montage m.

assent [ə'sent] v. intr. To assent to, consentir à, acquiescer à (to acquiesce) ; admettre, approuver (to admit).
— n. Assentiment, acquiescement, consentement m. ; to nod assent, opiner, acquiescer d'un signe de tête, faire signe que oui. ‖ JUR. Agrément m.

assentation [,æsən'teiʃən] n. Approbation servile ; adulation f.

assenter [ə'sentə*] n. Approbateur ; béni-oui-oui m. (fam.). [See YES-MAN.]

assentient [ə'senʃiənt] adj., n. Approbateur m., approbatrice f.

assert [ə'sə:t] v. tr. Faire valoir, revendiquer, défendre (one's rights) ; to assert oneself, s'affirmer, s'imposer ; se mettre en avant. ‖ Affirmer, prétendre, soutenir (sth.) ; protester de (one's innocence).

assertion [ə'sə:ʃən] n. Revendication, défense f. (of a right). ‖ Assertion, affirmation f.

assertive [ə'sə:tiv] adj. Affirmatif. ‖ Péremptoire, cassant, tranchant.

assertor [-ə*] n. Champion, défenseur, avocat m. (of a cause). ‖ Personne (f.) qui affirme.

assess [ə'ses] v. tr. FIN. Estimer la valeur locative de (a building) ; établir, déterminer le montant de (damages, fine, taxes) ; répartir (expenses) ; taxer, imposer (persons, property) ; évaluer, estimer, coter (rental value) ; assessed taxes, cote mobilière.

assessable [-əbļ] adj. FIN. Imposable.

assessment [-mənt] n. FIN. Fixation, détermination f. (of damages, fine, taxes) ; taxation, imposition f. (of persons, properties) ; évaluation, estimation f. (of rental value) ; assiette f. (of taxes) ; discretionary assessment, taxation d'office ; empirical assessment, imposition forfaitaire. ‖ Impôt m. ; cote f. ; reduction of assessment, dégrèvement fiscal.

assessor [-ə*] n. FIN. Répartiteur-contrôleur m. (of taxes). ‖ JUR. Assesseur m.

asset ['æsit] n. FIG. Avantage, atout, apport, capital m. ‖ Pl. FIN. Biens, avoirs m. pl. ; liquid assets, valeurs disponibles ; personal, real assets, biens meubles, immobiliers. ‖ JUR. Pl. Masse active f. ‖ COMM. Pl. Actif m.

asseverate [ə'sevəreit] v. tr. Affirmer avec véhémence, protester de. (See ASSERT.)

asseveration [ə,sevə'reiʃən] n. Assurance, protestation f.

assiduity [,æsi'djuiti], **assiduousness** [ə'sidjuəsnis] n. Assiduité, diligence f. (in, à). ‖ Pl. Attentions, prévenances f. pl. (to, envers).

assiduous [ə'sidjuəs] adj. Assidu (person, work).

assign [ə'sain] v. tr. Assigner, fixer (a cause, a date) ; attribuer, attacher (a meaning) ; attribuer, alléguer (a reason) ; assigner (an office, a task) ; attribuer (a room). ‖ Affecter, désigner, nommer [to, à] (s.o.). ‖ FIN. Assigned to, destiné à (sum).
— n. JUR. Ayant droit, ayant cause m.

assignable [-əb] adj. Attribuable, afférent, assignable (to, à). ‖ JUR. Cessible.

assignation [,æsig'neiʃən] n. Attribution, affectation, désignation f. ‖ Rendez-vous galant m. ‖ JUR. Cession f. ; transfert m.

assignee [,æsi'ni:] n. JUR. Ayant cause m. ; syndic, séquestre m. ; assignee in bankruptcy, syndic de faillite. ‖ Mandataire m.

assignment [ə'sainmənt] n. Assignation, attribution, affectation f. (act) ; tâche assignée f., mission f. (task). ‖ JUR. Cession f. ; transfert m. ‖ MILIT. Assignment of pay, délégation de solde.

assimilable [ə'similəb] adj. Assimilable.

assimilate [-eit] v. tr. Assimiler (to, à). ‖ Comparer (to, à) ; rapprocher (to, de). ‖ MED., FIG. Assimiler.
— v. intr. MED., FIG. S'assimiler.

assimilation [ə,simi'leiʃən] n. MED., GRAMM., FIG. Assimilation.

assimilative [ə'similətiv] adj. Assimilatif.

assimilatory [-təri] adj. Assimilateur, assimilatrice.

assist [ə'sist] v. tr. Aider, seconder, assister [in, à] (s.o.) ; assisted by, avec le concours de. ‖ Aider à, faciliter (sth.).
— v. intr. Aider (to help). ‖ To assist at, assister à, être présent à.

assistance [-əns] n. Aide, assistance f. ; secours m. ; to render assistance, prêter main-forte.

assistant [-ənt] adj. Auxiliaire, assistant, adjoint. ‖ THEATR. Assistant director, régisseur. ‖ U. S. Assistant professor, professeur- (or) maître-assistant.
— n. Auxiliaire, aide s. ‖ Assistant s. (in schools). ‖ JUR. Adjoint, suppléant, assesseur m. ‖ MED. Chemist's assistant, stagiaire en pharmacie. ‖ MED. Non-resident assistant, externe.

assize [ə'saiz] n. COMM. Barème, prix tarifié m. ‖ JUR. Jury ; jugement par jury m. ‖ Pl. JUR. Assises f. pl.

associable [ə'souʃiəb] adj. Associable (with, avec).

associate [-it] adj. Uni, associé. ‖ JUR. Assesseur (justice). ‖ U. S. Adjoint ; Associate Professor, maître de conférences.
— n. Collègue, camarade s. ‖ Membre associé m. (of a society). ‖ JUR. Complice s. (See ACCOMPLICE.) ‖ Pl. Consorts m. pl.
— [-eit] v. tr. (Associer (in, à) [sth.]. ‖ Mettre en contact (with, avec) ; associer (with, à) [s.o.].
— v. intr. To associate with, fréquenter, frayer avec (to frequent) ; s'associer à, s'allier à (to join)

association [ə'sousi'eiʃən] n. Association, société, amicale f. ‖ Relations f. pl. ; fréquentation f. (with, de). ‖ PHILOS. Association f. (of ideas). ‖ SPORTS. Association football, football.

assoil [ə'sɔil] v. tr. † Absoudre.

assonance ['æsənəns] n. Assonance f.

assort [ə'sɔ:t] v. tr. Assortir (with, à). ‖ Classifier, ranger, grouper (with, parmi). ‖ COMM. Assortir, monter (a shop, a warehouse).
— v. intr. To assort with, s'assortir avec, s'harmoniser avec (sth.) ; fréquenter, s'entendre avec (s.o.).

assorted [-id] adj. Assorti ; well-, ill-assorted, bien, mal assorti. ‖ Divers, de toutes sortes.

assortment [-mənt] n. Classification f. ‖ Assortiment m.

assuage [ə'sweidʒ] v. tr. Assouvir, satisfaire (hunger) ; étancher (thirst). ‖ MED. Soulager (pain) ; to be assuaged, se calmer. ‖ FIG. Apaiser (anger) ; satisfaire (désir).

assuagement [-mənt] n. Adoucissement, soulagement m.

assumable [ə'sju:məb] adj. Supposable, présumable. ‖ Qu'on peut assumer (responsibility).

assume [ə'sju:m] v. tr. Assumer, revêtir, prendre (an appearance) ; assumer, endosser (responsibilities, risks). ‖ Emprunter (a name) ; s'arroger, s'attribuer (control, right). ‖ Affecter, feindre (a virtue). ‖ Présumer, supposer, admettre ; assuming that it is true, en supposant que ce soit vrai ; he was assumed to be honest, on le croyait honnête.

assumed [-d] adj. Supposé, prétendu, d'emprunt (name) ; feint, simulé (virtue). ‖ Admis.

assuming [-iŋ] adj. Présomptueux.

assumption [ə'sʌmpʃən] n. Fait d'assumer m. ‖ Appropriation, usurpation f. (of power). ‖ Admission f. (of a fact); on the assumption that, en supposant que. ‖ Prétention, présomption f. ‖ PHILOS., ECCLES. Assomption f.

assumptive [-tiv] adj. Admis (fact). ‖ Présomptueux; arrogant.

assurance [ə'ʃuərəns] n. Assurance, protestation f. (affirmation). ‖ Assurance, certitude, conviction f. (See CERTAINTY.) ‖ Assurance, garantie f. (guarantee); to make assurance doubly sure, par surcroît de précaution. ‖ Effronterie, audace f. (impudence); assurance, confiance en soi f. (self-confidence). ‖ JUR. Assurance f. (See INSURANCE.)

assure [ə'ʃuə*] v. tr. Assurer, convaincre (of, de) [to convince]; to assure oneself, s'assurer. ‖ Assurer, affirmer (to declare); certifier, garantir (to guarantee). ‖ Rassurer (to reassure). ‖ JUR. Assurer (to insure). ‖ † Fiancer.

assuredly [-ridli] adv. Assurément, certainement.

assuredness [-ridnis] n. Assurance, conviction f.

Assyrian [ə'siriən] adj., n. GEOGR. Assyrien s.

Assyriology [ə,siri'ɔlədʒi] n. Assyriologie f.

astable [ei'steibl] adj. Instable. ‖ ELECTR. Astable.

astatic [æ'stætik] adj. PHYS. Astatique.

astatine ['æstə,ti:n] n. CHIM. Astate m.

aster ['æstə*] n. BOT. Aster m.

asterisk ['æstərisk] n. Astérisque m.

astern [əs'tə:n] adv. NAUT. A l'arrière, sur l'arrière, en poupe; en arrière, d'arrière; to come astern, culer.
— prep. Astern of, sur l'arrière de.

asteroid ['æstərɔid] adj. En étoile.
— n. Etoile f. (of firework). ‖ ASTRON. Astéroïde m. ‖ ZOOL. Astérie f.

asthenia [æs'θi:niə] n. MED. Asthénie f.

asthenic [-θenik] adj., n. MED. Asthénique s.

asthma ['æsmə] n. MED. Asthme m.

asthmatic [æs'mætik] adj., n. MED. Asthmatique s.

astigmatic [,æstig'mætik] adj. MED. Astigmate.

astigmatism [æs'tigmətizm] n. MED. Astigmatisme m.

astir [əs'tə:*] adj., adv. Levé, debout (out of bed). ‖ En mouvement, animé (in motion). ‖ Excité, agité (in excitement).

astonish [əs'tɔniʃ] v. tr. Etonner. (See SURPRISE.)

astonishing [-iŋ] adj. Etonnant; it's astonishing to me, cela me surprend.

astonishingly [-iŋli] adv. Etonnamment.

astonishment [-mənt] n. Etonnement m.; to be lost in astonishment, ne pas en revenir.

astound [əs'taund] v. tr. Stupéfier, abasourdir; sidérer, renverser (fam.). ‖ Atterrer, consterner.

astounding [-iŋ] adj. Stupéfiant, abasourdissant (amazing); consternant (calamitous).

astraddle [əs'trædl] adv., adj. A califourchon, à cheval (on, sur).

astragal ['æstrəgəl] n. ARCHIT., MILIT. Astragale m.

astragalus [əs'trægələs] n. MED., BOT. Astragale m.

astrakhan [,æstrə'kɑ:n] n. ZOOL., COMM. Astrakan m.

astral ['æstrəl] adj. ASTRON., PHILOS. Astral.

astray [əs'trei] adv. Hors du bon chemin, égaré, perdu; to go astray, se détourner de son chemin, se dérouter. ‖ FIG. Egaré; to lead astray, dévoyer; détourner.

astriction [əs'trikʃən] n. Astriction f.

astrictive [-tiv] adj. Astrictif, astringent.

astride [əs'traid] adv., adj. A califourchon, à cheval (astraddle). ‖ Jambes écartées; le compas ouvert (fam.).
— prep. A califourchon (or) à cheval sur, chevauchant.

astringe [əs'trindʒ] v. tr. Resserrer, contracter (to constrict). ‖ Lier ensemble (to bind). ‖ MED. Constiper.

astringency [-ənsi] n. Astringence f.

astringent [-ənt] adj. Astringent. ‖ FIG. Austère.
— n. MED. Astringent m.

astrobiology ['æstro,bai'ɔlɔdʒi] n. PHILOS. Astrobiologie f.

astrodome ['æstrodoum] n. AVIAT. Coupole vitrée avant f.

astrogate [-geit] v. intr. Faire de la navigation interplanétaire.

astrolabe [-leib] n. ASTRON. Astrolabe m.

astrologer [æs'trɔlɔdʒə*] n. Astrologue s.

astrologic(al) [,æstrə'lɔdʒik(əl)] adj. Astrologique.

astrology [æs'trɔlədʒi] n. Astrologie f.

astronaut ['æstrənɔ:t] n. AVIAT. Astronaute s.

astronautics [æstrə'nɔ:tiks] n. Astronautique f.

astronomer [æs'trɔnəmə*] n. Astronome m.

astronomic(al) [,æstrə'nɔmik(əl)] adj. ASTRON., FAM. Astronomique.

astronomically [-əli] adv. Astronomiquement.

astronomy [æs'trɔnəmi] n. ASTRON. Astronomie f.

astrophysics [æstro'fiziks] n. sg. Astrophysique f.

Asturias [æs'tjuəriəs] n. GEOGR. Asturies f. pl.

astute [əs'tju:t] adj. Astucieux, rusé. (See SHREWD.)

astutely [-li] adv. Astucieusement.

astuteness [-nis] n. Astuce, ruse f.

asunder [ə'sʌndə*] adv. En deux; to break asunder, se casser en deux. ‖ A part; to come asunder, se désunir.

asylum [ə'sailəm] n. Asile, abri, refuge m. (See SHELTER.) ‖ MED. Asile m.

asymmetrical [,æsi'metrikəl] adj. Asymétrique.

asymmetry [æsi'mitri] n. Asymétrie f.

asymptote ['æsimptout] n. MATH. Asymptote f.

asynchronous [ə'siŋkrənəs] adj. Asynchrone.

at [æt] prep. A; at any cost, à n'importe quel prix; at full speed, à toute allure; at Reading, à Reading; to play at cards, jouer aux cartes. ‖ A propos de; what is he laughing at?, de quoi rit-il? ‖ Chez; at the chemist's, chez le pharmacien. ‖ Contre; angry at, fâché contre; she is at me again, la voilà encore après moi! ‖ Dans; at a loss, dans l'embarras. ‖ De; at a distance, de loin; at a stretch, d'une traite; attempt at escape, tentative d'évasion. ‖ Devant; to dry oneself at the fire, se sécher devant le feu; to hesitate at nothing, n'hésiter devant rien. ‖ En; at any rate; en tout cas; at peace with, en paix avec; child at nurse, enfant en nourrice. ‖ En train de; to be at play, être en train de jouer. ‖ Par; annoyed at, contrarié par; to go in at one door and come out at the other, entrer par une porte et sortir par une autre. ‖ Selon, suivant; at your request, sur votre demande. ‖ Sur; at sea, sur mer; to dash at, se précipiter sur; I was shot at, on m'a tiré dessus. ‖ LOC. At it, y; he is at it, il y travaille, il y est, il s'y est mis; he is longing to be at it, il lui tarde de s'y mettre; let me see you at it again!, que je t'y reprenne (or) repince! (fam.); to be always at it, être toujours à l'attache (working). ‖ At that, tel quel (at that estimate); par-dessus le marché (into the bargain); là-dessus (thereupon). ‖ At-home, n. Réception f.; at-home day, jour de réception.

ataraxy [ætə'ræksi] n. PHILOS. Ataraxie f.

atavism ['ætəvizm] n. Atavisme m.

atavistic [ætə'vistik] adj. Atavique.

ataxic [ə'tæksik] adj. MED. Ataxique.

ataxy [-si] n. MED. Ataxie f.

ate [et] pret. See EAT.

atelier ['ætɔljei] n. ARTS. Atelier, studio m.

athanasia [,æθə'neizjə] n. Immortalité f.

atheism ['eiθiizm] n. Athéisme m.

atheist [-ist] n. Athée s.

atheistic [,eiθi'istik] adj. Athée.
Athenaeum [,æθi'ni:əm] n. Athénée *m.* ‖ Cercle littéraire *m.* (club).
Athenian [ə'θi:niən] adj., n. GEOGR. Athénien, *adj., s.*
Athens ['æθenz] n. GEOGR. Athènes *f.*
athermanous [ə'θə:mənəs] adj. PHYS. Athermane.
athirst [ə'θə:st] adj. FIG. Altéré, assoiffé (*for,* de).
athlete ['æθli:t] n. SPORTS. Athlète, sportif *m.* ‖ MED. *Athlete's heart,* cardiectasie *f.;* cœur claqué (fam.). ‖ MED. *Athlete's foot,* épidermophytie plantaire *f.;* pied d'athlète *m.* (fam.).
athletic [æθ'letik] adj. SPORTS. Athlétique (exercices); sportif (meeting).
athleticism [-isizm̥] n. SPORTS. Athlétisme *m.;* culte du sport *m.*
athletics [-iks] n. sg. (or) pl. SPORTS. Athlétisme *m.;* sports *m. pl.*
athwart [ə'θwɔ:t] adv. De (or) en travers. ‖ NAUT. Par le travers.
— prep. En travers de. ‖ NAUT. Par le travers de.
atilt [ə'tilt] adv. † Lance basse (or) en arrêt. ‖ De côté, incliné.
Atlas ['ætləs] n. † Atlas (Titan). ‖ GEOGR. Atlas *m.* (book, mountain). ‖ MED. Atlas (vertebra). ‖ TECHN. Colombier *m.* (size of paper).
atmosphere ['ætməsfiə*] n. PHYS., FIG. Atmosphère *f.*
atmospheric(al) [,ætməs'ferik(əl)] adj. Atmosphérique.
atmospherics [-iks] n. pl. RADIO. Parasites *m. pl.*
atoll [ə'tɔl] n. GEOGR. Atoll *m.;* île (*f.*) de corail.
atom ['ætəm] n. PHYS., CHIM. Atome *m.* ‖ MILIT. *Atom bomb,* bombe atomique; *to atom-bomb,* détruire à la bombe atomique. ‖ FIG. Atome, grain; iota *m.* ‖ **Atom-free,** adj. Dénucléarisé (zone).
atomic [ə'tɔmik] adj. PHYS., CHIM., MILIT. Atomique.

ATOM — ATOME

atomiste	nuclear physicist
atomistique (l')	nucleonics
barre de réglage	control rod
berkélium	berkelium
bombe à hydrogène	hydrogen bomb, H bomb
bombe atomique	atomic bomb, A bomb
bore	boron
centrale atomique	atomic power station
cobalt (bombe au)	cobalt (bomb)
cœur [de la pile]	core (of the reactor)
curie (unité)	curie
cyclotron	cyclotron
désintégration	splitting, disintegration
détecteur à scintillations	scintillation counter
eau lourde	heavy water
écran biologique	biological shield
électron	electron
énergie atomique	nuclear energy
ère atomique	Atomic age
fissile (matière)	fissionable (material)
fission nucléaire	nuclear fission
fusion nucléaire	nuclear fusion
Geiger (compteur de)	Geiger (counter)
isotope	isotope
méson, mésotron	meson, mesotron
modérateur	moderator
noyau	nucleus (plur. nuclei)
nucléons (protons + neutrons)	nucleons (protons + neutrons)
nucléonique (la)	nucleonics
pile atomique	atomic reactor (ou) pile
radio-actif, -ivité	radioactive, -ivity
ralentisseur	moderator
réaction en chaîne	chain reaction
transuraniens (éléments)	transuranic (elements)
uranium	uranium
usine atomique	atomic energy plant
xénon	xenon

---

atomicity [,ætə'misiti] n. CHIM. Atomicité *f.*
atomism ['ætəmizm̥] n. PHILOS. Atomisme *m.*
atomist [-ist] n. PHILOS. Atomiste *m.*
atomistic [,ætoʊ'mistik] adj. PHILOS. Atomistique.
atomize ['ætəmaiz] v. tr. Atomiser, pulvériser.
atomizer [-ə*] n. Vaporisateur *m.* ‖ MED. Pulvérisateur *m.*
atonal [ei'tounl̥] adj. MUS. Atonal.
atonality [ætoʊ'næliti] n. MUS. Atonalité *f.*
atone [ə'toun] v. intr. *To atone for,* racheter, expier (*by,* en, par); *to atone with,* se réconcilier avec.
— v. tr. † Réconcilier (enemies).
atonement [-mənt] n. Réparation, expiation f. (*for,* de); *Day of Atonement,* Jour des Propitiations. ‖ ECCLES. Rachat *m.;* Rédemption *f.; to make atonement,* satisfaire, expier.
atonic [æ'tɔnik] adj. MED. Atonique. ‖ MED., GRAMM. Atone.
atony [-ni] m. Atonie *f.*
atop [ə'tɔp] adv. Au sommet, en haut (*de,* of).
atrabilious ['ætrə'biljəs] adj. Atrabilaire. (See HYPOCHONDRIAC.)
atrabiliousness [-nis] n. Hypocondrie, humeur noire *f.*
atrip [ə'trip] adj. adv. NAUT. Dérapé (anchor).
atrium ['ɑ:triəm] n. Atrium *m.* ‖ MED. Oreillette *f.* (of the heart).
atrocious [ə'trouʃəs] adj. Atroce. ‖ FAM. Affreux (dress); exécrable (pun).
atrociously [-li] adv. Atrocement.
atrociousness [-nis] n. Atrocité *f.* (of an act).
atrocity [ə'trɔsiti] n. Atrocité *f.* (act, behaviour). ‖ FAM. Atrocité, horreur *f.*
atrophy ['ætrəfi] n. MED., FIG. Atrophie *f.*
— v. tr. MED., FIG. Atrophier.
— v. intr. MED., FIG. S'atrophier.
atropine ['ætroʊpi:n] n. MED., CHIM. Atropine *f.*
attaboy ['ætə,bɔi] interj. U. S. Vas-y, petit gars! (expressing encouragement); bravo, mon grand! (expressing admiration).
attach [ə'tætʃ] v. tr. Attacher, lier, fixer (*to,* à) [sth.]. ‖ Attacher, attribuer (*to,* à) [importance, value]; *to attach credence to,* ajouter foi à. ‖ Attacher, appliquer (*to,* à) [an epithet]. ‖ Attacher (s.o.); *to attach oneself to,* s'attacher à (s.o.). ‖ JUR. Saisir (goods); mettre opposition sur (salary); arrêter (s.o.). ‖ MILIT. Attacher, affecter (troops).
— v. intr. **To attach to,** être attaché (or) attribué (or) imputé à, s'attacher à, être afférent à; *no blame attaches to him,* nul blâme ne lui est imputable.
attachable [-əbl̥] adj. Fixable, qu'on peut attacher. ‖ Qu'on peut s'attacher. ‖ JUR. Saisissable (goods, salary); appréhendable (person).
attaché [ə'tæʃei] n. Attaché (*m.*) d'ambassade. ‖ MILIT. Attaché. ‖ **Attaché-case,** n. Valise *f.*
attachment [ə'tætʃmənt] n. Action (*f.*) d'attacher, fixation *f.* ‖ Attache *f.;* lien *m.* ‖ TECHN. Accessoire *m.* ‖ CH. DE F. *Tongue attachment,* patte d'attache. ‖ JUR. Saisie-arrêt, opposition *f.* (*on,* sur). ‖ FIG. Attachement *m.;* affection *f.* (*for,* pour).
attack [ə'tæk] v. tr. Attaquer (s.o.); s'attaquer à (a person, problem, task). ‖ MED. *To be attacked by,* être atteint par. ‖ CHIM. Attaquer, corroder. ‖ MUS., MILIT. Attaquer.
— n. MILIT. Attaque *f.* (*on,* sur); *renewed attack,* retour offensif; *surprise attack,* attaque par surprise, coup de main. ‖ MUS., MED., FIG. Attaque *f.* ‖ FAM. *To have an attack,* piquer une crise.
attain [ə'tein] v. tr. Atteindre, arriver à. (See REACH.) ‖ FIG. Parvenir à (an age); atteindre à (happiness); acquérir (knowledge); atteindre, s'élever à (a rank).
— v. intr. **To attain to,** atteindre à, parvenir à (perfection).
attainable [-əbl̥] adj. Accessible; *attainable by all men,* à la portée de tout le monde.
attainder [-də*] n. JUR. Mort civile *f.*

attainment [-mənt] n. Réalisation, obtention, acquisition *f.;* aboutissement *m.; difficult of attainment,* difficile à acquérir. ‖ Pl. Connaissances *f. pl.;* acquis *m.; classical attainments,* culture classique.

attaint [ə'teint] v. tr. JUR. Frapper de mort civile. ‖ MED. Atteindre, affecter. ‖ FIG. Flétrir.

attar ['ætə*] n. CHIM. Essence (*f.*) de roses.

attemper [ə'tempə*] v. tr. Tempérer, mitiger, atténuer, adoucir. ‖ Rendre propre (*to,* à). ‖ TECHN. Tremper (metals).

attempt [ə'tempt] v. tr. Tenter, essayer (to try). ‖ Entreprendre, s'attaquer à (a piece of work). ‖ MILIT. S'attaquer à (a fortress). ‖ JUR. Attenter à (s.o.'s life); *attempted murder,* tentative d'assassinat. — n. Tentative *f.;* essai *m.* (*at, to,* de) [see ESSAY]; *first attempt,* coup d'essai; *to make an attempt at doing,* s'essayer à faire. ‖ Atteinte *f.* (*upon,* à); *constituting an attempt upon,* attentatoire à. ‖ JUR. Attentat *m.* (*upon,* contre).

attend [ə'tend] v. tr. Accompagner, suivre, escorter. (See ACCOMPANY.) ‖ Assister à, suivre (lectures); *to attend church,* fréquenter l'église. ‖ Servir, être au service de; *attended by a maid,* servi par une bonne. ‖ MED. Soigner; *to attend the family,* être le médecin de famille. ‖ FIG. Accompagner, entourer; résulter de. — v. intr. **To attend at,** assister à; *I didn't attend,* je n'étais pas présent. ‖ **To attend to,** s'occuper de, vaquer à (one's business); remplir (one's duties); veiller à (one's interests); faire attention à, écouter; prêter l'oreille à (a proposition); tenir compte de; avoir égard à (a recommendation); veiller sur, s'occuper de (s.o.). ‖ **To attend upon,** se rendre chez, être de service auprès de (s.o.). ‖ COMM. **To attend to,** servir, s'occuper de (a customer); exécuter (an order). ‖ THEATR. *Well attended play,* spectacle couru. ‖ FAM. *Now children, attend!,* maintenant, mes enfants, attention! (or) écoutez!

attendance [-əns] n. Fait d'accompagner (or) d'escorter *m.* (accompanying). ‖ Présence, assistance *f.* (*at,* à); *regular attendance at,* assiduité à. ‖ Assistance *f.;* auditoire *m.* (at a class, meeting). ‖ Attente *f.; cabs in attendance,* taxis en stationnement; *to dance attendance,* faire antichambre (*on,* chez); faire le pied de grue, croquer le marmot, droguer (fam.). ‖ Service *m.* (*on,* auprès de); *to dance attendance on,* être aux petits soins de, faire l'empressé auprès de (to fuss over); être toujours suspendu aux basques de (to run after). ‖ COMM. Service *m.* ‖ MED. Soins (*on,* à).

attendant [-ənt] adj. Coexistant, concomitant; *life and its attendant difficulties,* la vie et son cortège de difficultés. ‖ Au service, dépendant (*on,* de). ‖ Présent, assistant. — n. Membre (*m.*) de la suite (or) de l'escorte; *to be a constant attendant on,* être assidu auprès de. ‖ Assistant *s.* (*at,* à) [person present]. ‖ THEATR. Ouvreuse *f.* ‖ MED. *Medical attendant,* médecin.

attention [ə'tenʃən] n. Attention *f.; attention of Mr. Jones,* à l'attention de M. Jones; *to call attention to,* attirer l'attention sur; *to pay attention to,* faire attention à. ‖ Pl. Attentions, prévenances *f. pl.* (*to,* pour); *to pay one's attentions to,* faire la cour à. ‖ MILIT. Garde-à-vous *m.; to come to, to stand at attention,* se mettre, être au garde-à-vous. ‖ COMM. *Our best* (or) *full attention,* tous nos soins; *best and prompt attention,* tous soins et diligence. ‖ FAM. *To be all attention,* être tout oreilles.

attentive [ə'tentiv] adj. Attentif (*to,* à) [a remark]. ‖ Soucieux (*to,* de) [one's interests]. ‖ Attentif (*to, envers*); prévenant (*to,* pour); empressé (*to,* auprès de).

attentively [-li] adv. Attentivement.

attentiveness [-nis] n. Attention *f.*

attenuate [ə'tenjueit] v. tr. Amincir, affiner (a thread), atténuer (one's words). ‖ MED. Atténuer,

affaiblir (a virus). ‖ CHIM. Raréfier (a gas). — [-it] adj. Aminci. ‖ Atténué.

attenuation [ə,tenju'eiʃən] n. Amincissement *m.* ‖ Atténuation *f.* (of a statement). ‖ MED. Amaigrissement *m.* (of a person); affaiblissement *m.* (of a virus). ‖ RADIO. Affaiblissement *m.*

attest [ə'test] v. tr. Attester, assurer, certifier (to certify); témoigner de, démontrer, prouver (to demonstrate). ‖ JUR. Certifier (a copy); légaliser (a signature). ‖ MILIT. Faire prêter serment à (recruits). — v. intr. **To attest to,** porter témoignage pour, témoigner de.

attestation [,ætes'teiʃən] n. Attestation formelle *f.* ‖ JUR. Attestation, légalisation *f.;* témoignage *m.* ‖ MILIT. Assermentation *f.;* prestation (*f.*) de serment.

Attic ['ætik] adj. GEOGR., ARCHIT., GRAMM. Attique.

attic n. Grenier *m.;* mansarde *f.* ‖ ARCHIT. Attique *m.*

attire [ə'taiə*] v. tr. vêtir, revêtir (to clothe); parer, orner (to dress up); *to attire oneself in,* se parer de. — n. Vêtement, habillement *m.;* toilette *f.*

attitude ['ætitju:d] n. Attitude, position *f.; fencing attitude,* attitude de l'escrimeur. ‖ Pose *f.; to strike an attitude,* poser, prendre une pose théâtrale. ‖ AVIAT. Position *f.; steep attitude,* vol cabré. ‖ FIG. Attitude, disposition *f.; attitude of mind,* état d'esprit.

attitudinize [,æti'tju:dinaiz] v. intr. Poser.

attorney [ə'tə:ni] n. Mandataire, représentant *m.; power of attorney,* délégation de pouvoir. ‖ JUR. Avoué *m.; Attorney General,* procureur général; U. S. Ministre de la Justice, garde des Sceaux.

attorneyship [-ʃip] n. Procuration *f.* ‖ JUR. Charge (*f.*) d'avoué.

attract [ə'trækt] v. intr. Attirer (*to,* à, vers); *to attract one another,* s'attirer. ‖ Attirer (admiration, attention); attirer, séduire (s.o.); *he was attracted to her,* elle lui plut.

attractable [-əbl] adj. Attirable.

attraction [ə'trækʃən] n. PHYS. Attraction *f.; attraction of gravity,* attraction universelle. ‖ MED. *Attraction sphere,* sphère d'attraction. ‖ Pl. Attractions. ‖ FIG. Attrait, charme *m.;* attraction, séduction, attirance *f.*

attractive [ə'træktiv] adj. PHYS. Attractif. ‖ COMM. Intéressant (prices). ‖ FIG. Attrayant, séduisant (offer, person); riant, alléchant (*to,* pour) [prospect].

attractively [-li] adv. D'une façon attrayante.

attractiveness [-nis] n. Nature attrayante *f.;* attrait *m.*

attractivity [ətræk'tiviti] n. PHYS. Attractivité *f.*

attributable [ə'tribjutəbl] adj. Attribuable.

attribute ['ætribju:t] n. Attribut *m.* ‖ GRAMM. Epithète *f.* — [ə'tribju:t] v.tr. Attribuer (*à,* to). [See ASCRIBE.]

attribution [,ætri'bju:ʃən] n. Attribution *f.* (*to,* à). ‖ Affectation *f.* (assignment). ‖ Pl. Attributions.

attributive [ə'tribjutiv] adj. Attributif. ‖ GRAMM. Qualificatif. — n. GRAMM. Epithète *f.*

attrite [ə'trait], **attrited** [-id] adj. Usé par friction.

attrition [ə'triʃən] n. Frottement *m.;* attrition *f.* (See ABRASION.) ‖ MILIT. *War of attrition,* guerre d'usure. ‖ ECCLES. Attrition *f.*

attune [ə'tju:n] v. tr. MUS. Accorder. ‖ FIG. Harmoniser, mettre à l'unisson, accorder (*to,* avec).

atwist [ə'twist] adj. Tordu, déjeté.

atypical [ei'tipikl] adj. Atypique.

aubergine ['oubəʒi:n] n. BOT. Aubergine *f.*

aubrietia, aubretia [ɔ:'bri:ʃjə] n. Bot. Aubrietia m.

auburn ['ɔ:bən] adj. Châtain clair, auburn.

au courant [okurɑ̃] adj. Au courant (with, of, de); au courant, bien informé.

auction ['ɔ:kʃən] n. Enchères f. pl.; vente aux enchères (or) à la criée f.; encan m.; auction bridge, bridge aux enchères; auction market, hôtel des ventes; Dutch auction, adjudication au rabais; to put up to (or) U. S. at auction, mettre aux enchères; to sell by auction, vendre à l'encan.

auctioneer [,ɔ:kʃə'niə*] n. Commissaire-priseur, adjudicateur m.
— v. intr. Conduire une vente aux enchères.
— v. tr. Vendre aux enchères.

audacious [ɔ:'deiʃəs] adj. Audacieux, hardi (daring). || Insolent, effronté, hardi (impudent).

audaciously [-li] adv. Audacieusement.

audaciousness [-nis] n. Audace f.

audacity [ɔ:'dæsiti] n. Audace, intrépidité, hardiesse f. (See TEMERITY.) || Effronterie, audace f.; toupet m. (fam.). || Pl. Hardiesses f. pl.

audibility [ɔ:di'biliti] n. Audibilité f.

audible ['ɔ:dibl] adj. Audible; in an audible voice, à haute et intelligible voix; there were audible cries, des cris se firent entendre. || Phys. Above the audible range, ultra-sonore.

audibly [-bli] adv. Intelligiblement, distinctement.

audience ['ɔ:djəns] n. Action (f.) d'écouter (act). || Audience f. (of, de; to, à); audience room, salle d'audience. || Assistance f.; auditoire m. (of a lecturer); public m.; lecteurs m. pl. (of a writer). || Mus. Auditeurs m. pl. || Theatr. Spectateurs m. pl. || Radio. Auditeurs; téléspectateurs m. pl.

audio [ɔ:diou] pref. Audio-. || **Audio-frequency,** n. Fréquence téléphonique, audio-fréquence f. || **Audio-visual,** adj. Audio-visuel.

audiology [,ɔ:di'ɔlədʒi] n. Méd., Phys. Audiologie f.

audiometer [-'ɔmitə*] n. Phys. Audiomètre m.

audiphone ['ɔ:difoun] n. Audiophone m.

audit ['ɔ:dit] n. Jur. Apurement m. (or) vérification (f.) des comptes; Audit Office, Cour des comptes; Commissioner of Audit, auditeur à la Cour des comptes; || **Audit-room,** n. Eccles. Salle (f.) du chapitre.
— v. tr. Jur. Apurer, vérifier (the accounts). || U. S. Assister en auditeur libre à (a class).

audition ['ɔ:diʃən] n. Audition f.
— v. tr., intr. Theatr., Mus. Auditionner.

auditive [-tiv] adj. Auditif.

auditor [-tə*] n. Auditeur m. || Jur. Commissaire aux comptes m. || Comm. Expert comptable m.

auditorium [,ɔ:di'tɔ:riəm] n. Mus. Auditorium m. || Theatr. Salle f. || Eccles. Vaisseau m. (of a church); parloir m. (of a convent).

auditory ['ɔ:ditəri] adj. Méd. Auditif; de l'ouïe.
— n. Auditoire m. (audience); salle de conférences f. (auditorium).

A.U.E.W. [eiju:i:'dʌblju:] abbr. Amalgated Union of Engineering Workers, syndicat britannique des travailleurs de l'industrie.

au fait [ou'fei] adj. Au courant, au fait (with, de); to put, to make au fait with, mettre au fait de, tenir au courant de.

Augean [ɔ:'dʒiən] adj. D'Augias (stables). || Fig. Immonde, infect.

auger [ɔ:'gə*] n. Techn. Foret m.; tarière f.
— v. intr. U. S. Fam., Aviat. To auger in, casser du bois.

aught [ɔ:t] n. Quelque chose, quoi que ce soit; are afflictions aught but blessings in disguise?, l'adversité est-elle autre chose qu'un mal pour un bien?; for aught I know, à ma connaissance, autant que je sache.

augment ['ɔ:gmənt] n. Gramm. Augment m.

— [ɔ:g'ment] v. tr. Augmenter, accroître. || Gramm. Ajouter un augment à.
— v. intr. Augmenter, grandir, croître, s'accroître.

augmentation [,ɔ:gmen'teiʃən] n. Augmentation, addition f.; accroissement m. || Mus. Augmentation f.

augmentative [ɔ:g'mentətiv] adj., n. Augmentatif.

augur ['ɔ:gə*] n. Augure m. (person).
— v. tr., intr. Augurer, prédire, prévoir; to augur ill of, augurer mal de. || Présager; to augur well for, être de bon augure pour.

augural ['ɔ:gjurəl] adj. Augural.

augury [-i] n. Divination f. (art); augure, présage m. (omen).

August ['ɔ:gəst] n. Août m.

august [ɔ:'gʌst] adj. Auguste, majestueux, imposant, vénérable.

Augustan [-ən] adj. D'Auguste (age); d'Augsbourg (confession).

Augustine [ɔ:'gʌstin] n. Eccles. Augustin s.

Augustinian [,ɔ:gəs'tiniən] adj., n. Eccles., Philos. Augustinien, adj., s.

auk [ɔ:k] n. Zool. Pingouin m.

auld ['ɔ:ld] adj. Vieux (en écossais).

aulic ['ɔ:lik] adj. Aulique.

aunt [ɑ:nt] n. Tante f. || Fam. Aunt Sally, jeu de massacre. || **Aunt-in-law,** n. Tante par alliance f.

auntie [-i] n. Fam. Tantine f.

au pair [ou'pɛə*] adj. Au pair.
— n. Jeune fille (f.) au pair.

aura ['ɔ:rə] n. Effluve m. || Méd., Philos. Aura f.

aural ['ɔ:rəl] adj. Méd. Auriculaire.

aureate [ɔ:'rieit] adj. Doré, d'or.

aureola, aureole [ɔ:'riələ] n. Eccles. Auréole f. (See GLORY, HALO.) || Astron. Halo m.

aureomycin [,ɔ:riou'maisin] n. Méd. Auréomycine f.

auric ['ɔ:rik] adj. D'or. || Chim. Aurique.

auricle ['ɔ:rikl] adj. Méd. Auricule f. (ear); oreillette f. (of the heart).

auricled [-d] adj. Auriculé.

auricular [ɔ:'rikjulə*] adj. Méd. Auriculaire (duct); des oreillettes. || Eccles., Jur. Auriculaire.
— n. Méd. Auriculaire m. (finger). || Zool. Pl. Auricules f. pl.

auriferous [ɔ:'rifərəs] adj. Aurifère.

aurist ['ɔ:rist] n. Méd. Auriste, otologiste m.

aurochs ['ɔ:rɔks] n. Zool. Aurochs m.

aurora [ɔ:'rɔ:rə] n. Aurore f.; aurora australis, borealis, aurore australe, boréale.

aurous ['ɔ:rəs] adj. Chim. Aureux.

auscultate ['ɔ:skʌlteit] v. tr. Méd. Ausculter.

auscultation [,ɔ:skəl'teiʃən] n. Méd. Auscultation f. (See SOUNDING.)

auspex ['ɔ:speks] n. Auspice m. (priest).

auspicate ['ɔ:spikeit] v. tr. Inaugurer (to inaugurate).
— v. intr. Présager (to augurate).

auspice ['ɔ:spis] n. Auspice, présage m. (omen). || Pl. Auspices m. pl.; patronage m.; protection f.

auspicious [ɔ:s'piʃəs] adj. Propice, favorable (hour, wind); de bon augure (sign). [See FAVOURABLE.] || Prospère, fortuné (age, person).

auspiciously [-li] adv. Favorablement, sous d'heureux auspices.

auspiciousness [-nis] n. Heureux auspices m. pl.; caractère propice m.

Aussie ['ɔzi] adj. Fam. Australien.
— n. Fam. Australie f.; Australien s.

austere [ɔ:s'tiə*] adj. † Apre, amer. || Fig. Austère, ascétique (ascetic); austère, dépouillé (plain); austère, grave (sober); austère, sévère (strict).

austerely [-li] adv. D'une façon austère.

austerity [ɔ:s'teriti] n. Austérité f.; days of austerity, temps des restrictions.

austral ['ɔ:strəl] adj. Austral.

Australasia [ˌɔ:strə'leiʒjə] n. GEOGR. Australasie f.

Australia [ɔ:s'treiljə] n. GEOGR. Australie f.

Australian [ɔ:s'treiljən] adj., n. Australien s.

Austria ['ɔ:striə] n. GEOGR. Autriche f.

Austrian [-n] adj., n. Autrichien s.

autarchy ['ɔ:tɑ:ki] n. Autarchie ; U. S. autarcie f.

autarky n. Autarcie f.

authentic [ɔ:'θentik] adj. Authentique.

authentically [-əli] adv. Authentiquement.

authenticate [-eit] v. tr. Authentiquer, établir l'authenticité de. ‖ JUR. Certifier, légaliser, valider, homologuer.

authentication [ɔ:ˌθenti'keiʃən] n. Authentification f. ‖ JUR. Certification, légalisation, validation, homologation f.

authenticity [ˌɔ:θen'tisiti] n. Authenticité f.

author ['ɔ:θə*] n. Auteur, créateur, instigateur m. (of, de). ‖ Auteur, écrivain m. (writer). ‖ FAM. Auteur m., ouvrages m. pl. (writings).

authoress [-ris] n. Femme (f.) auteur.

authoritarian [ɔ:ˌθɔri'tɛəriən] adj. Autoritaire (state, person).

authoritarianism [ɔ:ˌθɔri'tɛəriənizm̩] n. Autoritarisme m.

authoritative [ɔ:'θɔritətiv] adj. Autoritaire (disposition); impératif, impérieux (tone). ‖ Qui fait autorité (book, document); autorisé (source).

authoritatively [-li] adv. Avec autorité. ‖ Impérieusement. ‖ Avec compétence; de source certaine.

authority [ɔ:'θɔriti] n. Autorité f.; pouvoir m.; abuse of authority, abus de pouvoir. ‖ Autorisation f.; délégation (f.) de pouvoir; pouvoir, mandat m. (to, pour); on my own authority, de ma propre autorité, de mon chef; to act on the authority of, agir par délégation de; without authority, sans autorisation. ‖ Autorité, influence f.; to exercise authority over, avoir de l'ascendant sur. ‖ Autorité, créance f.; his authority is beyond exception, son autorité est hors de doute. ‖ Autorité, personne compétente f. (on, en); to apply to the proper authority, s'adresser à qui de droit. ‖ Autorité, source autorisée f.; on good authority, de bonne source; to quote one's authorities, citer ses références. ‖ Pl. Autorités f. pl.; corps constitués m. pl. ‖ JUR. Jurisprudence f.; précédent juridique m.; authority of father, puissance paternelle; having authority, faisant foi (document).

authorization [ˌɔ:θərai'zeiʃən] n. Autorisation f. ‖ Pouvoir, mandat m.

authorize ['ɔ:θəraiz] v. tr. Autoriser, permettre. (See PERMIT.) ‖ Donner pouvoir (or) mandat à; to be authorized to, avoir qualité pour. ‖ Sanctionner (by, par). ‖ Justifier, autoriser (to justify).

authorless ['ɔ:θəlis] adj. Anonyme, d'auteur inconnu.

authorship [-ʃip] n. Profession (f.) d'écrivain; to take to authorship, se mettre à écrire. ‖ Paternité f. (of a book, an idea); of unknown authorship, d'auteur inconnu.

autism ['ɔ:tizm̩] n. PSYCH. Autisme m.

autistic [-tistic] adj. PSYCH. Autiste, autistique.

auto ['ɔ:to] n. AUTOM., FAM. Auto f.
— pref. Auto-. ‖ **Auto-cycle**, n. AUTOM. Cyclomoteur, vélomoteur m. ‖ **Auto-eroti(ci)sm**, n. Autoérotisme m. ‖ **Auto-immune**, adj. MED. Auto-immune (diseases); auto-immunitaire (process). ‖ **Auto-immunity**, n. MED. Auto-immunité f. ‖ **Auto-intoxication**, n. Auto-intoxication, f. ‖ **Auto-suggestion**, n. Autosuggestion f. ‖ **Auto-vaccine**, n. MED. Auto-vaccin m.

autobiographer [ˌɔ:tobai'ɔgrəfə*] n. Autobiographe m.

autobiographic(al) [ˌɔ:toˌbaio'græfik(əl)] adj. Autobiographique.

autobiography [ˌɔ:tobai'ɔgrəfi] n. Autobiographie f.

autocade ['ɔ:to,keid] n. U. S. Cortège (m.) de voitures.

autocar ['ɔ:tokɑ:*] n. † Auto f. ‖ Autocar m.

autochthon [ɔ:'tɔkθən] n. Autochtone m.

autochthonous [-əs] adj. Autochtone.

autoclave ['ɔ:tokleiv] adj., n. CHIM., CULIN. U. S. Autoclave m.
— v. tr. Passer à l'autoclave.

autocracy [ɔ:'tɔkrəsi] n. Autocratie f.

autocrat ['ɔ:tɔkræt] n. Autocrate m.

autocratic(al) [ˌɔ:tɔ'krætik(əl)] adj. Autocratique.

autocross ['ɔ:to,krɔs] n. SPORTS., AUTOM. Course automobile (f.) tous terrains.

auto-da-fé [ˌɔ:todə'fei] n. Autodafé m.

autogenous [ɔ:'tɔdʒənəs] adj. Autogène.

autogiro ['ɔ:to'dʒairou] n. Autogire m.

autognosis [ˌɔ:tɔg'nousis] n. PHILOS. Connaissance (f.) de soi-même.

autograph ['ɔtəgrɑ:f] n. Autographe m. (for an admirer). ‖ Copie autographiée f. ‖ Signature f.
— v. tr. Ecrire de sa main. ‖ Revêtir de sa signature. ‖ Autographier.

autographic(al) [ˌɔ:to'græfik(el)] adj. Autographique (copy); autographe (letter).

autography [ɔ:'tɔgrəfi] n. Autographie f.; écriture autographe f.

autogyro [ˌɔ:to'dʒairou] n. See AUTOGIRO.

autokinetic [ˌɔ:tɔkai'ni:tik] adj. Automobile.

autolysis [ɔ:'tɔlisis] n. MED. Autolyse f.

automat ['ɔ:tɔmæt] n. U. S. Restaurant (m.) à service automatique.

automate ['ɔ:to,meit], **automatize** [ɔ:'tɔmə,taiz] v. tr. Automatiser.

automatic(al) [ˌɔto'mætik(əl)] adj. Automatique.

automatically [-əli] adv. Automatiquement.

automaticity [ˌɔ:tɔmə'tisiti] n. Automaticité f.

automation [ˌɔ:to'meiʃən] n. TECHN. Automatisation f. (principe); automatique, automation f. (science).

automatism [ɔ:'tɔmətizm̩] n. Automatisme m.

automatize [ɔ:'tɔmə,taiz] v. tr. TECHN. Automatiser.

automaton [-ən] (pl. **automata** [-ə]) n. Automate m.

automobile ['ɔ:tomɔbi:l] n. AUTOM. Automobile f.
— adj. U. S. Automobile (business).

automotive [ɔ:to'motiv] adj. Automobile.

autonomic [ɔ:'tɔnəmik], **autonomous** [-məs] adj. Autonome.

autonomy [-mi] n. Autonomie f.

autopilot [ˌɔ:tə'pailət] n. AVIAT. Pilote automatique m.

autoplasty ['ɔto,plæsti] n. MED. Autoplastie f.

autopsy ['ɔ:tɔpsi] n. MED. Autopsie f.

autostrada [ˌɔto'strɑ:də] n. Autostrade f.

autosuggestion [ˌɔ:tosʌ'dʒetʃən] n. autosuggestion f.

autotype ['ɔ:totaip] n. Fac-similé m.; reproduction f. ‖ Autotypie f. (process).

autumn ['ɔ:təm] n. Automne m.

autumnal [-nəl] adj. D'automne, automnal; d'arrière-saison.

auxiliary [ɔ:g'ziljəri] adj. Auxiliaire, subsidiaire, secondaire.
— n. Auxiliaire, aide s.

avail [ə'veil] v. intr. Servir, être profitable (or) utile (or) efficace; nothing avails against death, on ne peut rien contre la mort.
— v. tr. Servir à, profiter à. ‖ To avail oneself of, donner suite à (an offer); profiter de, tirer parti de (an opportunity); se prévaloir de, user de (a right); utiliser (a service).
— n. Utilité, efficacité f.; avantage, profit m.; of what avail is it?, à quoi bon?; to be of little avail, ne pas servir à grand-chose; without avail, sans effet, inutilement.

availability [ə,veilə'biliti] n. Utilité, efficacité *f.* ‖ Disponibilité *f.* (*for*, pour). ‖ CH. DE F. Validité *f.*

available [ə'veiləbḷ] adj. Utilisable (*for*, pour); *by all available means*, par tous les moyens possibles. ‖ Disponible, qu'on a sous la main; *to make available to*, mettre (or) placer à la disposition de. ‖ CH. DE F. Valable, valide, bon (*for*, pendant) [ticket]; accessible (*for*, à) [train]. ‖ FIN. Réalisable (assets); *available funds*, disponibilités.

availably [-əbli] adv. Utilement, efficacement, avantageusement.

availment [-mənt] n. FIN. Réalisation *f.*

avalanche ['ævəlɑ:nʃ] n. Avalanche *f.* ‖ FIG. Avalanche, averse *f.*

avania [,ævə'niə] n. FIN. Imposition forcée *f.*

avant-garde [,ævɔŋ'gɑ:d] adj. D'avant-garde, avant-gardiste.
— n. Avant-garde *f.*

avant-gardism [-izm] n. Avant-gardisme *m.*

avant-gardist [-ist] n. Avant-gardiste *s.*; artiste (*s.*) d'avant-garde.

avarice ['ævəris] n. Avarice, cupidité *f.*

avaricious [,ævə'riʃəs] adj. Avare, avaricieux.

avariciously [-li] adv. Avaricieusement.

avariciousness [-nis] n. Avarice, nature cupide *f.*

avast! [ə'vɑ:st] interj. NAUT. Tenez bon!

avatar [,ævə'tɑ:r] n. Avatar *m.* ‖ FAM. Manifestation, matérialisation *f.*

avaunt [ə'vɔ:nt] interj. Arrière!, hors d'ici!

ave ['ɑ:vi] n. ECCLES. Avé *m.* ‖ **Ave-bell,** n. ECCLES. Angélus *m.*
— interj. Salut!

avenge [ə'venʒ] v. tr. Venger (s.o., sth.); *to be avenged of*, prendre sa revanche sur; *to avenge oneself*, se revancher.

avenger [-ə*] n. Vengeur *m.*

avenging [-iŋ] adj. Vengeur *m.*; vengeresse *f.*

aventurine [ə'ventjurin] n. Aventurine *f.*

avenue ['ævinju:] n. Allée (or) route (*f.*) bordée d'arbres. ‖ U. S. Avenue, artère, rue principale *f.* ‖ FIG. Voie (*f.*) d'accès.

aver [ə'və:*] v. tr. (1). Assurer, affirmer. ‖ JUR. Etablir la preuve de.

average ['ævəridʒ] n. Moyenne *f.* (see NORM); *on the average*, en moyenne; *to strike, to take an average*, établir, faire la moyenne. ‖ NAUT. Avarie *f.*; *average adjustment*, dispache; *average adjuster*, dispacheur.
— adj. TECHN., COMM., FIN. Moyen. ‖ FIG. Moyen, ordinaire, courant.
— v. tr. Etablir (or) prendre la moyenne de. ‖ S'élever en moyenne à; *the children average ten years of age*, les enfants ont dix ans en moyenne. ‖ Atteindre la moyenne de; *he averages ten hours of work a day,* il travaille en moyenne dix heures par jour. ‖ U. S. Répartir proportionnellement (*among*, entre).
— v. intr. *To average up to,* s'élever en moyenne à.

averment [ə'və:mənt] n. Allégation, affirmation, protestation *f.* (assurance). ‖ JUR. Preuve *f.* (of an assertion).

averruncate [,ævərʌŋ'keit] v. tr. AGRIC. Echeniller.

averruncator [-ə*] n. AGRIC. Echenilloir *m.*

averse [ə'və:s] adj. Opposé, peu disposé, répugnant (*to*, à); adversaire, ennemi (*to*, de); *to be averse to,* répugner à.

averseness [-nis] n. Répugnance *f.*

aversion [ə'və:ʃən] n. Aversion, répugnance *f.*; dégoût *m.* (*for, from, to,* pour); *to feel an aversion to lying,* répugner à mentir; *to take an aversion to s.o.,* prendre qqn en grippe, ne pas pouvoir souffrir qqn, se dégoûter de qqn. ‖ Objet (*m.*) d'aversion; *pet aversion,* bête noire.

avert [ə'və:t] v. tr. Détourner (*from,* de). ‖ FIG. Détourner, écarter, conjurer (danger); détourner (suspicions).

aviary ['eiviəri] n. Volière *f.*

aviate [-eit] v. intr. AVIAT. Voler.

aviation [,eivi'eiʃən] n. AVIAT. Aviation *f.; Naval Aviation,* aéronavale.

aviator ['eivieitə*] n. AVIAT. Aviateur *m.*

aviatrix [-triks] n. AVIAT. Aviatrice *f.*

avid ['ævid] adj. Avide (*for,* de). [See EAGER.]

avidity [ə'viditi] n. Avidité, voracité *f.* ‖ FIG. Avidité, cupidité *f.* (for money); avidité, ardeur *f.* (for study).

avidly ['ævidli] adv. Avec avidité, avidement.

avifauna [,eivi'fɔ:nə] n. ZOOL. Avifaune *f.*

avionics [,eivi'ɔniks] n. AVIAT., ELECTR. Avionique *f.*

aviso [ə'vaizou] n. NAUT. Aviso *m.*

avitaminosis [ə'vitəminousis] n. MED. Avitaminose *f.*

avocado [ævə'kɑ:do] n. BOT. Avocat *m.* (fruit); avocatier *m.* (tree).

avocation [,ævo'keiʃən] n. Dérangement *m.; distraction *f.* (*from,* de). ‖ Distraction, occupation secondaire *f.;* violon d'Ingres *m.* (pet hobby). ‖ Profession *f.;* métier *m.* (vocation).

avoid [ə'vɔid] v. tr. Eviter (s.o.); échapper à, esquiver (sth.); *he couldn't avoid mentioning it,* il ne put moins faire (or) ?aire autrement que d'en parler ‖ S'esquiver, se soustraire à, se détourner de; *I can't very well avoid asking him to stay to dinner,* il m'est difficile de ne pas le retenir à dîner. ‖ AVIAT. *To take avoiding action,* s'esquiver, se dérober. ‖ JUR. Annuler, résilier.

avoidable [-əbḷ] adj. Evitable. ‖ JUR. Annulable, résoluble.

avoidance [-əns] n. Action (*f.*) d'éviter; *his avoidance of his cousins,* le soin qu'il prend pour éviter ses cousins. ‖ JUR. Annulation, résiliation *f.; condition of avoidance,* condition résolutoire. ‖ ECCLES. Vacance *f.* (of benefice).

avoirdupois [,ævədə'pɔiz] adj. Au poids commercial.
— n. Poids commercial *m.;* système (*m.*) anglais des poids et mesures.

avouch [ə'vautʃ] v. tr. Affirmer, déclarer, assurer, proclamer. ‖ Reconnaître, avouer (to avow).
— v. intr. Assurer. ‖ Se porter garant (*for,* de).

avouchment [-mənt] n. Affirmation, assurance, garantie *f.* ‖ Aveu *m.;* reconnaissance *f.* (of s.o.'s action).

avow [ə'vau] v. tr. Avouer, confesser, admettre; *to avow oneself,* s'avouer, se déclarer. ‖ JUR. Reconnaître (*as,* pour).

avowable [-əbḷ] adj. Avouable.

avowal [-əl] n. Aveu *m.*

avowed [-d] adj. Avoué, notoire, avéré.

avowedly [-idli] adv. Franchement (admittedly); de son propre aveu (by avowal).

avulsion [ə'vʌlʃən] n. † Arrachement *m.* ‖ JUR. Avulsion *f.*

avuncular [ə'vʌŋkjulə*] adj. Avunculaire.

aw [ɔ:] interj. Oh! (expressing commiseration, disappointment).

await [ə'weit] v. tr. Attendre (sth.) [to wait for]; *awaiting,* dans l'attente de, en instance de. ‖ COMM. *Awaiting delivery,* en souffrance (parcels). ‖ FIG. Etre réservé à, être préparé pour, attendre.

awake [ə'weik] v. intr. (7). S'éveiller, se réveiller; *to awake from sleep,* sortir du sommeil. ‖ Se retrouver; *to awake to the place with surprise,* être surpris de se retrouver en ce lieu. ‖ FIG. *To awake from,* revenir de, s'arracher à; *to awake to,* s'éveiller à, se rendre compte de, prendre conscience de, commencer à percevoir.
— v. tr. Eveiller, réveiller (s.o.). ‖ U. S. Activer,

réveiller. ‖ FIG. Eveiller, faire naître (curiosity, hope, passion); éveiller (intelligence, remorse); réveiller (fear, memories); mettre en éveil (s.o.). — adj. Eveillé, réveillé; *to keep awake*, tenir éveillé, empêcher de dormir. ‖ FIG. Eveillé, vigilant, en éveil; *to be awake to*, être conscient de; avoir l'œil sur; *wide awake*, avisé; dégourdi (fam.).

awaken [-ən] v. tr. Eveiller, réveiller.
— v. intr. Se réveiller.

awakening [-iŋ] n. Réveil (lit. and fig.).

award [ə'wɔːd] v. tr. Adjuger, attribuer, allouer, décerner. ‖ JUR. Accorder (damages).
— n. Récompense, distinction honorifique f. ‖ JUR. Décision, sentence arbitrale f.; dommages-intérêts m. pl.; indemnités f. pl. ‖ U. S. Bourse f. (scholarship).

awarding [-iŋ] n. Attribution f. (of, de).

aware [ə'wɛə*] adj. Conscient; avisé, averti, informé, au courant (of, de); *as far as I am aware*, autant que je sache, à ma connaissance; *to be aware of*, s'apercevoir de, se rendre compte de, avoir conscience de, sentir, percevoir.

awash [ə'wɔʃ] adj. A fleur d'eau. ‖ Flottant, surnageant (floating).

away [ə'wei] adv. Au loin; *far away*, au loin; *to entice s.o. away*, persuader à qqn de partir; *to leap away*, s'enfuir en bondissant; *I must away*, il faut que je parte. ‖ Loin; *away behind*, loin derrière. ‖ A l'écart; *to look away*, détourner son regard; *to put away*, mettre de côté (money); *to stand away from*, s'écarter de; *A distance*; *a mile away*, à un mille de là. ‖ En mourant; *to die away*, s'éteindre, disparaître; *to make away with*, détruire. ‖ En perdant; *to gamble away*, perdre au jeu; *to talk one's breath away*, parler à en perdre le souffle. ‖ Sans arrêt (or) interruption, continuellement; *to work away*, continuer à travailler, poursuivre son travail; travailler sans débrider (or) souffler (fam.). ‖ Aussitôt, sur-le-champ, sans tergiverser; *fire away*, allez-y!, racontez donc! ‖ Rapidement; *right away*, tout de suite, sur-le-champ; *to eat away*, dévorer.
— adj. Absent, parti; *to be away from home*, ne pas être chez soi; *to stay away*, s'absenter. ‖ SPORTS. *Away ground*, terrain adverse; *away match*, match aller.
— interj. Arrière!, hors d'ici!; *away with you!*; allez-vous-en!, sortez!; *to horse and away!*, à cheval et hue cocotte!; *right away!*, en route! ‖ A bas!; *away with X!*, conspuez X!

awe [ɔː] n. TECHN. Aube f. (of paddle-wheel).

awe [ɔː] n. Crainte révérentielle; sainte frousse f. (fam.); *to keep in awe*, en imposer à; *to stand in awe of*, être intimidé (or) glacé par; *to strike with awe*, inspirer de la crainte à. ‖ **Awe-commanding** (or) **-inspiring**, adj. Impressionnant, terrifiant.
— v. tr. Terrifier, inspirer de la crainte à; *with an awed voice*, d'une voix terrifiée.

awesome ['ɔːsəm] adj. Impressionnant, imposant, terrifiant (awe-inspiring); terrifié, frappé de terreur (awestruck).

awestruck ['ɔː'strʌk] adj. Frappé de terreur; très impressionné.

awful ['ɔːful] adj. Imposant, impressionnant, majestueux, solennel. ‖ Terrifiant, redoutable, terrible, épouvantable. ‖ FAM. Terrible (bore); affreux (coat); carabiné (cold); formidable (din); fameux (fool); détestable (joke, weather); épouvantable (scrawl).

awfully [-li] adv. Terriblement, affreusement, de façon terrifiante. ‖ FAM. Bigrement, fameusement, rudement; *awfully nice*, tout plein gentil; *awfully shrewd*, malin en diable.

awhile [ə'wail] adv. Un moment, un instant, pendant quelque temps; *not yet awhile*, pas de sitôt.

awkward ['ɔːkwəd] adj. Malaisé (corner, path); peu commode (or) maniable (tool). ‖ Ingrat (age); fâcheux, inopportun (moment); embarrassant (question); gêné, embarrassé (silence); gênant, faux, délicat (situation); gauche, lourd (style). ‖ Gauche, maladroit, inhabile; emprunté, empoté (fam.) [person]. ‖ FAM. Pas facile; *awkward customer*, type pas commode.

awkwardly [-li] adv. Avec gêne. ‖ D'une façon embarrassante. ‖ Gauchement, maladroitement.

awkwardness [-nis] n. Incommodité f. (of a tool). ‖ Caractère gênant m.; délicatesse, difficulté f. (of a situation). ‖ Gêne f.; embarras m. ‖ Gaucherie, maladresse f. (clumsiness).

awl [ɔːl] n. TECHN. Alène f.

awn [ɔːn] n. BOT. Barbe f.

awning ['ɔːniŋ] n. Tente f.; bâche (of cart); banne (of shop). ‖ Marquise f. (at hotel-door). ‖ CH. DE F. Marquise f. ‖ NAUT. Tente f.; tendelet m.; rain-awning, taud. ‖ **Awning-deck**, n. NAUT. Pont-abri m. ‖ **Awning-rope**, n. Ralingue f.

awry [ə'rai] adj., adv. De travers, de guingois (askew). ‖ De travers (amiss).

axe [æks] n. Hache f.; *felling axe*, cognée. ‖ MILIT. *Battle-axe*, hache d'armes. ‖ FIG. Coupe sombre f.; *to apply the axe to*, porter la hache dans. ‖ FAM. *To have an axe to grind*, prêcher (or) travailler pour son saint; *to put the axe in the helve*, trouver le joint. ‖ FAM. U. S. *To get the axe*, passer au couperet. ‖ **Axe-hammer**, n. TECHN. Laie f.
— v. tr. FAM. Faire des coupes sombres dans (expenditure, personnel).

axial ['æksiəl] adj. Axial.

axil ['æksil] n. BOT. Aisselle f.

axilla [æk'silə] n. MED. Aisselle f. (See ARMPIT.)

axillary [-ri] adj. MED., BOT. Axillaire.

axiom ['æksiəm] n. Axiome m.

axiomatic [,æksiə'mætik] adj. Axiomatique. ‖ FAM. Evident.

axis ['æksis] (pl. **axes** [-iːz]) n. GEOGR., MILIT., AVIAT., PHYS., FIG. Axe m. ‖ MED. Axis m.

axle ['æksl] n. TECHN. Arbre, axe, essieu m. (of a wheel). ‖ CH. DE F. *Driving axle*, pont. ‖ AUTOM. *Rear axle*, pont arrière. ‖ **Axle-arm**, n. TECHN. Fusée f. ‖ **Axle-box**, n. TECHN. Boîte à graisse f. ‖ **Axle-journal**, n. TECHN. Tourillon m. ‖ **Axle-pin**, n. TECHN. Esse f. ‖ **Axle-tree**, n. TECHN. Essieu m.

ay(e) [ai] interj. Oui, bien. (See YEA, YES.)
— n. Oui; *ayes and noes*, voix pour et contre; *the ayes have it*, les « oui » l'emportent.

ay(e) [ei] adv. Toujours; *for ay*, à jamais.

ayatollah [æjæ'tɔlɑ:] n. Ayatollah m.

azalea [ə'zeiliə] n. BOT. Azalée f.

azimuth ['æziməθ] n. ASTRON., MILIT. Azimut m.
— adj. Azimutal (circle).

azimuthal [,æzi'mjuːθəl] adj. ASTRON. Azimutal.

azoic [ə'zouik] adj. GEOL. Azoïque.

Azores [ə'zɔːz] n. pl. GEOGR. Açores f. pl.

azote [ə'zout] n. CHIM. Azote m. (See NITROGEN.)

azotic [ə'zɔtik] n. CHIM. Azotique. (See NITRIC.)

azotize [ə'zoutaiz] v. tr. CHIM. Azoter.

azotous [ə'zoutəs] adj. CHIM. Azoteux.

azure ['eiʒə*] n. Azur m.
— adj. D'azur, azuré, bleu-ciel (sky-blue).
— v. tr. Azurer.

azurine ['eiʒjurain] n. Azurine f.

azurite [-ait] n. Azurite f.

azygous ['æzigəs] adj. MED. Azygos.

B

b [bi:] n. B, b *m.* ‖ B, second (in a series). ‖ Mus. Si *m.* ‖ **B-girl,** n. Fam. Entraîneuse *f.*

B. A. [bi:ei] abbr. *Bachelor of Arts,* licence ès lettres (degree); licencié ès lettres (graduate).

baa [bɑ:] n. Bêlement *m.* ‖ **Baa-lamb,** n. Fam. Agneau *m.*
— v. intr. Bêler.

babbitt ['bæbit] v. tr. Techn. Réguler. ‖ **Babbitt-metal,** n. Techn. Métal blanc antifriction *m.*

babble ['bæbl̩] v. intr. Babiller, gazouiller, jaser (baby, brook); clabauder (hound); bavarder, jaboter (person). ‖ Jaser (to reveal secrets).
— v. tr. Bafouiller. ‖ Débiter, dire à tort et à travers. ‖ Révéler, divulguer (a secret).
— n. Babil, babillage *m.* ‖ Jabotage, bavardage, caquetage *m.* ‖ Gazouillis, murmure *m.* (of a brook). ‖ Techn. Diaphonie multiple *f.*

babbler [ə*] n. Babillard, bavard *s.* ‖ Bavard, jaseur *s.* ‖ Clabaud *m.* (hound).

babe [beib] n. Bébé, bambin *m.* ‖ Fam. Enfant *m.* (naive person). ‖ Pop. U. S. Pépée *f.* (girl).

Babel ['beibəl] n. Tour (*f.*) de Babel (lit. and fig.). ‖ Fig. Projet extravagant *m.*

baboon [bə'bu:n] n. Zool. Babouin *m.*

babouche [bə'bu:ʃ] n. Babouche *f.*

baby ['beibi] n. Bébé *m.* ‖ Enfant, gosse *m.* ‖ Fam. *To hold the baby,* payer les pots cassés; *now he is holding the baby,* maintenant c'est sur lui que ça retombe; *to pass the baby,* renvoyer la balle. ‖ **Baby-carriage,** n. U. S. Voiture (*f.*) d'enfant, poussette *f.* ‖ **Baby-doll,** n. Poupard *m.* ‖ **Baby-farm,** n. Pouponnière, garderie *f.* ‖ **Baby-farmer,** n. Personne (*f.*) qui prend des enfants en nourrice. ‖ **Baby-linen,** n. Layette *f.* ‖ **Baby-sitter,** n. Gardienne (*f.*) d'enfants; garde-bébé *s.* ‖ **Baby-sitting,** n. Garde (*f.*) d'enfants; service biberon *m.* ‖ **Baby-snatching,** n. Kidnapping *m.;* Fam. Détournement (*m.*) de mineur. ‖ **Baby-walker,** n. Chariot d'enfant, « Bébétrott » *m.* ‖ **Baby-weighing scales,** n. Pèse-bébé *m.*
— adj. De bébé; *baby talk,* babil enfantin; *baby girl,* toute petite fille. ‖ Petit; *baby camera,* kodak de poche. ‖ Autom. *Baby car,* voiturette. ‖ Mus. *Baby grand,* piano demi-queue, crapaud.
— v. tr. U. S. Dorloter, cajoler.

babyhood [-hud] n. Prime enfance *f.*

babyish [-iʃ] adj. De bébé, enfantin. ‖ Puéril.

Babylon ['bæbilən] n. Babylone *f.*

Babylonian [,bæbi'lounjən] adj., n. Babylonien.

baccalaureate [,bækə'lɔ:riit] n. Baccalauréat *m.*

baccarat ['bækərɑ:] n. Baccara *m.* (game).

baccate ['bækeit] adj. Baccifère; bacciforme.

bacchanal ['bækənl] n. Bacchante *f.* ‖ Ivrogne, noceur *m.* (carouser). ‖ Bacchanale, orgie *f.*

Bacchanalia [,bækə'neiljə] n. pl. Bacchanales *f. pl.*

bacchanalian [-ən] adj. Bachique. ‖ Orgiaque.
— n. Noceur *m.*

bacchante [bə'kænti] n. Bacchante *f.*
— adj. Bachique.

Bacchic [-ik] adj. Bachique.

baccy ['bæki] n. Fam. Pétun *m.*

bach [bætʃ] v. tr. U. S. Fam. *To bach it,* vivre en célibataire.

bachelor ['bætʃələ*] n. † Bachelier *m.* ‖ Licencié *s.; Bachelor of Arts, of Science, of Law,* Licencié ès lettres, ès sciences, en droit. ‖ Célibataire *s.; bachelor room,* garçonnière *f.; old bachelor,* vieux garçon. ‖ Bot. *Bachelor's button,* bouton d'or.

— adj. De célibataire, célibataire; *bachelor girl,* jeune fille célibataire et indépendante; *in my bachelor days,* quand j'étais garçon.

bachelorhood [-hud] n. Célibat *m.*

bachelorship [-ʃip] n. Baccalauréat *n.* ‖ Célibat *m.*

bacillar(y) [bə'siləri] adj. Méd. Bacillaire.

bacilliform [-ifɔ:m] adj. Méd. Bacilliforme.

bacillus [-əs] (pl. **bacilli** [-ai]) n. Méd. Bacille *m.*

back [bæk] n. Dos *m.; reins m. pl.; to break one's back,* se casser les reins; *to fall on one's back,* tomber à la renverse; *to lend a back to,* faire la courte échelle à; *to stand with one's back to,* tourner le dos à. ‖ Dos *m.* (of book, door, knife); dossier *m.* (of a chair); envers *m.* (of a fabric); revers, dessus *m.* (of hand); derrière *m.* (of head, house); revers *m.* (of a medal); fond *m.* (of a room); verso *m.* (of a sheet). ‖ Fin. Dos *m.* (of a cheque). ‖ Geogr. Croupe *f.* (of a hill). ‖ Naut. Coque *f.* ‖ Sports. Arrière *m.* ‖ Fig. *To have a broad back,* avoir bon dos; *to have s.o. at one's back,* avoir qqn derrière soi, être épaulé par qqn; *to have s.o. on one's back,* avoir qqn sur le dos; *to get one's back up,* se hérisser, se rebiffer, prendre la mouche, montrer les dents; *to turn one's back on,* tourner le dos à; tourner les talons devant; *with one's back to the wall,* le dos au mur, au pied du mur, acculé. ‖ Fam. *At the back of beyond,* au fin fond de la cambrouse, au diable vauvert, en plein bled, au-delà des poules; *there's sth. at the back of it,* il y a quelque chose là-dessous; *to be on one's back,* être sur le flanc; *to break one's back,* s'éreinter, s'échiner; *to put one's back into it,* y mettre sa force, donner un coup de collier, en mettre un coup. ‖ **Back-ache,** n. Méd. Mal de dos *m.* ‖ **Back-breaking,** adj. Fam. Éreintant. ‖ **Back-scratcher,** n. Gratte-dos *m.;* Fam. Lèche-bottes *m.* ‖ **Back-slapper,** n. Personne démonstrative et exubérante *f.*
— adj. De derrière, d'arrière, arrière, en arrière; *back apartment,* pièce sur la cour; *back hair,* chignon; *back shop,* arrière-boutique; *back street,* rue écartée; rue pauvre. ‖ Arriéré, d'autrefois; *back number,* ancien numéro (of a magazine). ‖ De retour; *back fare,* tarif retour. ‖ Autom. *Back axle, seat,* pont, siège arrière. ‖ Fin. *Back interest,* arrérage; *back pay,* rappel de traitement. ‖ Gramm. D'arrière (vowel). ‖ Fam. *Back number,* vieille baderne, rétrograde; *back seat,* second plan, position subalterne. ‖ **Back bench,** n. Banc (*m.*) des députés sans portefeuille. ‖ **Back-chat,** n. Réplique impertinente *f.* ‖ **Back-cloth,** n. Theatr. Toile (*f.*) de fond. ‖ **Back-current,** n. Electr. Contre-courant *m.* ‖ **Back-date,** v. tr. Antidater. ‖ **Back-end,** n. Arrière-saison *f.* ‖ **Back-fire,** n. Techn. Retour (*m.*) de flamme; Autom. Pétarade *f.;* U.S. Contre-feu *m.;* v. intr. Techn. Avoir des retours de flamme; Autom. Pétarader. ‖ **Back-formation,** n. Gramm. Dérivation rétrograde *f.* ‖ **Back-kitchen,** n. Culin. Arrière-cuisine *f.* ‖ **Back-marker,** n. Sports. Scratch *s.* ‖ **Back-pedalling,** adj. A rétropédalage. ‖ **Back-room,** n. Pièce (*f.*) de derrière; Fam. *Back-room boys,* savants employés à des recherches secrètes. ‖ **Back-sight,** n. Milit. Cran (*m.*) de mire. ‖ **Back-stroke,** n. Contrecoup *m.;* Sports. Brasse (*f.*) sur le dos; Techn. Retour *m.* (of a piston). ‖ **Back-talk,** n. Fam. U. S. Réplique impertinente *f.* ‖ **Back-type,** adj. Aviat. Dorsal (parachute). ‖ **Back-yard,** n. Arrière-cour *f.*

— adv. En arrière, vers l'arrière, à l'arrière; *back from*, en retrait de (position); *to stand back*, se tenir en arrière, reculer, s'écarter. ‖ En sens inverse; *to make one's way back*, s'en retourner; *to walk back*, revenir à pied; rebrousser chemin. ‖ En retour; *to answer back*, rétorquer; *to bow back to*, rendre son salut à. ‖ Plus tôt; *two years back*, il y a deux ans, deux ans auparavant, en remontant à deux ans en arrière. ‖ De retour; *just back from London*, tout juste revenu de Londres; *he's back*, il est de retour.

— prep. Back of, derrière, en arrière de.

— v. tr. Faire reculer. ‖ AUTOM. Faire faire marche arrière à. ‖ CH. DE F. Faire faire machine arrière à. ‖ NAUT. Empenneler (an anchor); coiffer (a sail); *to back water*, nager à culer. ‖ SPORTS. Parier pour, jouer (to bet on); monter (to mount) [a horse]. ‖ TECHN. Endosser (a book). ‖ FIN. Endosser (a cheque); financer (s.o.). ‖ COMM. Avaliser (a bill). ‖ JUR. Contresigner (a document). ‖ FIG. Epauler, soutenir (to support); *to back up*, seconder, appuyer. ‖ FIG. Servir de fond à (to form the back of).

— v. intr. Reculer (*into*, contre); marcher à reculons (to go backwards); *to back out*, sortir à reculons. ‖ NAUT. Ravaler (wind). ‖ AUTOM., CH. DE F. Faire marche arrière. ‖ FIG. *To back down*, abandonner, lâcher la partie; *to back out of*, se retirer de, se soustraire à.

back [bæk] n. Bac *m*. (tub).
backband [-bænd] n. Dossière *f*.
backbite [-bait] v. tr. Médire de, dénigrer par-derrière; débiner (fam.)
backbiter [-baitə*] n. Médisant, dénigreur *s*.
backbiting [-baitiŋ] n. Médisance *f*.; dénigrement *m*.
backboard [-bɔːd] n. Dossier *m*. ‖ MED. Planche (*f*.) à dos.
backbone [-boun] n. MED. Colonne vertébrale, épine dorsale *f*. ‖ FIG. Caractère, cran *m*.; *he has no backbone*, c'est un invertébré (ou) une chiffe (ou) un mollusque. ‖ FIG. Point d'appui, pivot *m*.
backdoor ['dɔː*] n. Porte (*f*.) de derrière. ‖ FIG. Petite porte *f*.
backer ['bækə*] n. Partisan, soutien, supporter *m*. ‖ SPORTS. Parieur *s*. ‖ COMM. Avaliste *m*. ‖ FIN. *Financial backer*, bailleur de fonds *m*.) ‖ U. S. THEATR. Commanditaire *m*.
backgammon [bæk'gæmən] n. Trictrac *m*.
background ['bækgraund] n. ARTS. Fond; arrière-plan *m*. ‖ MUS., THEATR. Fond sonore *m*. ‖ FIG. Arrière-plan, second plan *m*. ‖ FIG. Données de base *f. pl.*; éléments *m. pl.* (of a problem). ‖ FIG. Fonds, acquis *m*. (experience).
backhand(ed) ['bæk'hænd(id)] adj. Renversé (writing). ‖ SPORTS. De revers. ‖ FIG. Equivoque; à rebours (compliment); en arrière de la main (fam.). ‖ U. S. Maladroit (clumsy).
backhander [-ə*] n. SPORTS. Coup de revers *m*. ‖ FAM. Dessous (*m*.) de table. ‖ FAM. Mornifle *f*. ‖ FIG. Riposte déloyale *f*.
backing ['bækiŋ] n. Soutien, renforcement *m*. ‖ Recul *m*. ‖ TECHN. Endossage *m*. (of a book). ‖ ARTS. Rentoilage (of a picture). ‖ NAUT. Empennelage (of an anchor); renversement (of the wind).
backlash ['bæk'læʃ] n. TECHN. Saccade *f*. (jar); jeu *m*. (play); contrecoup *m*. (of an explosion). ‖ U. S. Brusque recul *m*. (recoil).
backlog [-'lɔg] n. Bûche maîtresse *f*. ‖ FIG. Accumulation *f*.
backpedal [-'pedl] v. intr. Contre-pédaler.
backset ['bækset] n. Contre-courant *m*.
backsheesh [bæk'ʃiːʃ] n. See BAKSHEESH.
backside [-said] n. Derrière, postérieur *m*.
backslide ['bæk'slaid] v. intr. (139). Rechuter, récidiver. ‖ ECCLES. Etre relaps.
backslider [-ə*] n. Récidiviste *s*. ‖ ECCLES. Relaps.

backsliding [-iŋ] n. Récidive *f*.
backstairs ['bæk'stɛəz] n. pl. Escalier de service *m*.; escalier dérobé *m*. ‖ FIG. Intrigue *f*.
— adj. Occulte, secret.
backstay ['bækstei] n. NAUT. Galhauban *m*.
backstitch [-stitʃ] n. Point arrière *m*.
backstroke [-strouk] n. Coup de revers *m*.
— v. tr. Frapper d'un coup de revers.
— v. intr. Donner un- coup de revers.
backsword [-sɔːd] n. SPORTS. Sabre *m*. (broadsword);˙ bâton *m*. (singlestick).
backward ['bækwəd] adj. En arrière; *backward look*, regard en arrière. ‖ A rebours; *backward flow*, contre-courant, remous. ‖ En retard; retardataire (behind time). ‖ Retardé, arriéré (retarded). ‖ MED. Arriéré (child). ‖ *Backward in*, peu disposé à (reluctant); timide pour (shy); lent à (slow). ‖ *Backward and forward*, de va-et-vient (movement).
backward(s) [-z] adv. En arrière; *backwards and forwards*, de long en large, d'avant en arrière et d'arrière en avant; en faisant la navette. ‖ A rebours; à l'envers; *to stroke the cat backwards*, caresser le chat à rebrousse-poil. ‖ Vers le passé; en arrière (into the past). ‖ En pis; *to go backwards*, rétrograder. ‖ FAM. *To lean over backwards to*, se décarcasser pour, y mettre beaucoup du sien pour.
backwardation [,bækwə'deiʃən] n. FIN. Déport *m*.
backwardness ['bækwədnis] n. AGRIC. Tardiveté *f*.; retard *m*. ‖ MED. Lenteur (*f*.) d'esprit; arriération mentale *f*. ‖ FIG. Répugnance *f*.; défaut (*m*.) d'empressement (*in*, à).
backwash ['bækwɔʃ] n. NAUT., AVIAT., FIG. Remous *m*.
backwater ['bæk,wɔːtə*] n. Bras (*m*.) de décharge (of a river); accul *m*. (of the sea); ressac *m*. (of the waves). ‖ Eau arrêtée (or) stagnante *f*. ‖ FIG. Marécage, marais *m*.; eaux stagnantes *f. pl.*
— v. intr. NAUT. Nager à culer, ramer à rebours.
backway [-,wei] n. Chemin détourné *m*.
backwoods ['bækwudz] n. pl. Forêt(s) vierge(s) *f*. (*pl*.). ‖ FAM. U. S. Brousse *f*.
bacon ['beikən] n. Lard *m*. ‖ FAM. *To bring home the bacon*, gagner sa croûte (to earn a living); remporter la timbale (to succeed); *to save one's bacon*, sauver sa peau. ‖ U. S. POP. Gâteau *m*. (booty).
Baconian [bei'kouniən] adj. Baconien, de Bacon.
-- n. Baconiste *m*.
bacony ['beikəni] adj. Graisseux.
bacteriological [bæk,tiəriə'lɔdʒikəl] adj. MED. Bactériologique.
bacteriology [bæk,ti:əri'ɔlədʒi] n. MED. Bactériologie *f*.
bacteriolysis [-'ɔlisis] n. MED. Bactériolyse *f*.
bacteriophage [bæk'ti:əriəfeidʒ] n. MED. Bactériophage *m*.
bacterium [bæk'tiəriəm] (pl. **bacteria** [-iə]) n. MED. Bactérie *f*.
baculine ['bækjulain] adj. Frappant (argument).
bad [bæd] adj. Mauvais, méchant (action, habit, person); corrompu (air); grossier (language). ‖ Mauvais (smell, weather). ‖ Mauvais (argument, grace, opinion, pronunciation, reputation, work); gros (blunder); fâcheux, mauvais (news); défavorable, péjoratif (sense); *bad form*, mauvaise tenue. ‖ Mauvais (*for*, pour); *to be bad for*, ne rien valoir à; ne pas réussir à. ‖ CULIN. Avancé (fish); insuffisant, mauvais (food); gâté (fruit); avarié (meat); *to go bad*, se gâter, s'avarier; tourner (fam.). ‖ AGRIC. Mauvais (land). ‖ MED. Grave (accident); vicié (blood); gros (cold); sérieux (disease); fort (headache); malade (leg); *to be bad*, être mal fichu; *to have a bad leg*, avoir mal à une jambe. ‖ JUR. Faux (coin); dévié, faussé, mal compris (law). ‖ FIN. Irrécouvrable (debt). ‖ MILIT. Cruel (defeat); raté (shot). ‖ FAM. *Bad egg* (or *hat*,

mauvais garçon, canaille, sale coco ; *bad job*, mauvaise affaire ; *in a bad way*, en fichue posture, dans un beau pétrin ; *too bad !*, dommage !, tant pis !, c'est le bouquet !
— adv. U. S., Pop. Vachement, méchamment ; *to want sth. bad*, avoir vachement envie de qqch.
— m. Mauvais *m.* ; *the bad and the good*, le bon et le mauvais. ‖ Mal *m.* ; *from bad to worse*, aller de mal en pis ; *to go to the bad*, tourner mal. ‖ Fin. *To be ten thousand pounds to the bad*, être en déficit de dix mille livres.

baddish [-iʃ] adj. Fam. Plutôt mal, pas brillant.

bade [beid, bæd] pret. See BID.

Baden ['bɑːdn̩] n. Geogr. Bade.

badge [bædʒ] n. Insigne *m.* ‖ Croix *f.* (at school). ‖ Plaque *f.* (of an order, a policeman). ‖ Med. *Red Cross badge*, brassard de la Croix-Rouge. ‖ Milit. Insigne *m* (of rank) ; écusson *m.* (of a regiment).

badger [-ə*] n. Zool., Comm. Blaireau *m.* (animal, shaving brush).
— v. tr. Harceler ; casser les pieds à (fam.).

badgering [-riŋ] adj. Fam. Tracassier.

badinage ['bædinɑːʒ] n. Badinage *m.*

badly ['bædli] adv. Mal ; *badly done*, mal fait. ‖ Med. Gravement, sérieusement, grièvement. ‖ Fam. Joliment, diablement, bigrement.

badminton ['bædmintən] n. Badminton *m.* (game). ‖ Culin. Vin sucré au citron *m.*

badness ['bædnis] n. Méchanceté *f.* (of a person). ‖ Sévérité *f.* (of the climate) ; rigueur *f.* (of the weather). ‖ Mauvais état *m.* (of a road). ‖ Comm. Mauvaise qualité *f.*

Baedeker ['beidikə*] n. Guide (*m.*) touristique Baedeker. ‖ Milit. *Baedeker raids*, raids de représailles allemands, en 1942, contre les centres historiques et culturels de l'Angleterre.

baffle ['bæfl] v. tr. Confondre, dérouter (to confound). ‖ Frustrer, décevoir (to balk). ‖ Déjouer, faire échouer, mettre en échec ; *to baffle all description*, échapper à (or) défier toute description. ‖ Etablir des chicanes dans (to hinder).
— m. Chicane *f.* ‖ Contre-porte *f.* ‖ Radio. Baffle *m.* ‖ **Baffle-board**, m. Revêtement insonorisant *m.* ‖ **Baffle-plate**, n. Cloison, séparation *f.* ‖ **Baffle-wall**, n. Contre-mur, mur insonore *m.*

baffling [-iŋ] adj. Naut. *Baffling winds*, brises folles. ‖ Fig. Déconcertant.

baffy ['bæfi] n. Sports. Club de golf en bois *m.*

bag [bæg] n. Sac *m.* ; *diplomatic bag*, valise diplomatique ; *money bag*, sacoche ; *sleeping bag*, sac de couchage. ‖ Poche *f.* (at the knee). ‖ Zool. Pis *m.* (of a cow) ; *poison bag*, poche à venin. ‖ Med. Poche *f.* (of waters, under the eyes). ‖ Sports. Chasse *f.*, tableau (*m.*) de chasse. ‖ Aviat. *In the bag*, au tableau. ‖ Ecclec. Bourse *f.* ‖ Pl. Fam. Falzar, grimpant *m.* (pants). ‖ Fam. *A bag of bones*, un vrai squelette, un paquet d'os ; *in the bottom of one's bag*, au fond de sa poche, comme dernier atout ; *to get the bag*, recevoir son paquet ; *to get away with bag and baggage*, filer avec armes et bagages, prendre ses cliques et ses claques ; *to give s.o. the bag to hold*, laisser qqn se tirer des flûtes ; *to let the cat out of the bag*, vendre la mèche. ‖ Pop. Putain *f.* (woman). ‖ **Bag-sleeve**, n. Manche bouffante (*f.*) serrée au poignet.
— v. tr. (1). Ensacher, mettre en sac. ‖ Sports. Tuer à la chasse. ‖ Fam. Empocher, choper ; mettre le grapin sur ; *bags I that !*, pour bibi ça !
— v. intr. (1). Bouffer (garment, sleeve) ; faire la poche (trousers). ‖ Naut. Faire le sac (sail) ; tomber sous le vent (ship).

bagasse [bæ'gæs] n. Bagasse *f.* (See CANE-TRASH.)

bagatelle [,bægə'tel] n. Bagatelle *f.* (See TRIFLE.) ‖ Mus. Divertissement musical *m.* ‖ Sports. Jeu de billard anglais *m.*

baggage ['bægidʒ] n. U. S., Milit. Bagages *m.* pl. ‖ Fam. Friponne *f.* ‖ Pop. U. S. Traînée *f.* (prostitute). ‖ **Baggage-check**, n. U. S. Bulletin de bagages *m.* ‖ **Baggage-master**, n. U. S. Préposé aux bagages *m.* ; Milit. Vaguemestre *m.* ‖ **Baggage-room**, n. U. S. Ch. de F. Consigne *f.*

bagging ['bægiŋ] n. Mise (*f.*) en sac (sacking). ‖ Toile (*f.*) à sac (cloth).

baggy [-i] adj. Bouffant (garment) ; formant poche (trousers). ‖ Med. *Baggy cheeks*, bajoues.

bagman [-mən] (pl. **bagmen**) n. Comm. Commis voyageur *m.*

bagnio ['bænjou] n. † Etablissement de bains *m.* ‖ Prison *f.* ‖ Bordel *m.*

bagpipe ['bægpaip] n. Mus. Cornemuse *f.*

bagpiper [-ə*] n. Mus. Joueur (*s.*) de cornemuse.

bah ! [bɑː] interj. Bah ! (surprise). ‖ Pooh ! (contempt, disgust).

Bahamas [bə'hɑːməz] n. pl. Geogr. Bahamas *f.* pl.

Bahrain [bɑː'rein] n. Geogr. Bahreïn *m.*

baignoire ['beinwɑː*] n. Theatr. Baignoire *f.*

bail n. Archit. Lice *f.* (of a castle). ‖ Agric. Bat-flanc *m.* (in a stable). ‖ Sports. Bâtonnet, bail *m.* (in cricket).

bail n. Cerceau, arceau *m.* (of a canopy). ‖ Anse *f.* (of a bucket).

bail n. Naut. Ecope *f.*
— v. tr. Naut. Ecoper.

bail n. Jur. Cautionnement *m.* ; caution *f.* (money) ; caution ; garant, répondant *m.* (person) ; *to go bail for*, cautionner, se porter garant de, répondre de. ‖ Jur. Mise en liberté provisoire sous caution *f.*
— v. tr. Déposer, confier (goods). ‖ Jur. Cautionner, se porter caution pour ; *to bail s.o. out*, obtenir sous caution la mise en liberté de qqn.

bailable [-əbl] adj. Jur. Admis à fournir caution ; admettant l'élargissement (*s.*) sous caution.

bailee [bei'liː] n. Jur. Dépositaire de biens *m.*

bailey ['beili] n. Archit. Mur (*m.*) d'enceinte. ‖ Jur. *Old Bailey*, cour d'assises à Londres. ‖ Milit. *Bailey bridge*, pont Bailey (or) de secours *m.*

bailiff ['beilif] n. Bailli *m.* ‖ Gouverneur *m.* ‖ Agric. Régisseur, intendant *m.* ‖ Jur. *Sheriff's bailiff*, huissier.

bailment ['beilmənt] n. Jur. Consignation, caution *f.* ‖ Jur. Elargissement *m.* sous caution.

bailor [-ə*] n. Jur. Caution *f.* ; déposant, prêteur *m.*

bain-marie [,bɛmæ'ri] n. Culin. Bain-marie *m.*

bairn [bɛən] n. Enfant *m.*

bait [beit] v. tr. Donner à manger à (a horse). ‖ Appâter, amorcer (a hook) ; acharner (a trap). ‖ Attaquer, mordre (dogs). ‖ Fam. Harceler, asticoter, tisonner.
— v. intr. Faire halte pour se restaurer.
— n. Appât *m.* ; amorce *f.* ‖ Halte (*f.*) pour se restaurer. ‖ Fig. Leurre *m.* ; *to swallow the bait*, mordre à l'hameçon.

baize [beiz] n. Feutrine *f.* ; *green baize*, tapis vert.

bake [beik] v. tr. Arts, Culin. Cuire au four. ‖ Agric. Mûrir au soleil (fruit). ‖ Fig. Bronzer, se bronzer (person, skin) ; durcir à la chaleur (soil). ‖ Fam. *Will it bake bread ?*, est-ce que ça nous donnera de quoi croûter ?
— v. intr. Culin. Cuire. ‖ Fig. Se durcir, se dessécher (soil).

bakehouse ['-haus] n. Fournil *m.* ‖ Boulangerie *f.*

Bakelite ['beikəlait] n. (trade mark). Chim. Bakélite *f.*

baker ['beikə*] n. Boulanger *m.* ; *baker's boy, wife*, mitron, boulangère ; *baker's dozen*, treize à la douzaine.

bakery ['-əri] n. U. S. Boulangerie *f.*

bakestone ['beikstoun] n. Plaque (*f.*) de four.

baking [-iŋ] n. Culin. Cuisson *f.* ‖ **Baking-apple**, n. Pomme (*f.*) à cuire. ‖ **Baking-dish**, n. Culin. Plat allant au four *m.* ‖ **Baking-powder**, n. Culin.

Levure *f.* ‖ **Baking soda,** n. U. S. Bicarbonate (*m.*) de sodium.

baksheesh [bæk'ʃiːʃ] n. Bakchich *m.*

Balaam ['beiləm] n. Balaam *m.* ‖ Fig. Prophète décevant *m.* ‖ Fam. Pesée *f.*; bidon *m.* (journalese).

Balaclava [,bælə'klɑːvə] n. Geogr. Balaklava; *Balaclava helmet,* passe-montagne.

balalaika [bælə'laikə] n. Mus. Balalaïka *f.*

balance ['bæləns] n. Balance *f.* (scales); *analytical balance,* balance de précision. ‖ Balancier *m.* (of a clock). ‖ Fin. Balance *f.*; *balance in hand, due,* solde créditeur, débiteur; *balance of trade,* balance du commerce extérieur; *balance sheet,* bilan d'inventaire; *balance to next account,* report à nouveau. ‖ Fig. Equilibre *m.*; *off one's balance,* déséquilibré; *to hold the balance even between,* tenir la balance égale entre. ‖ Fam. Hésitation *f.*; *to hang in the balance,* être en balance. ‖ **Balance-beam,** m. Fléau (*m.*) de balance. ‖ **Balance-weight,** n. Contrepoids *m.* ‖ **Balance-wheel,** n. Balancier *m.* (of a watch).
— v. tr. Faire pencher (the scales). ‖ Tenir en équilibre (*on,* sur). ‖ Peser (chances, questions); comparer (propositions). ‖ Equilibrer, compenser (*by, with,* par); *to balance the matter,* pour faire compensation. ‖ Faire contrepoids à, contrebalancer (s.o.'s power). ‖ Balancer (a sentence). ‖ Comm. Balancer (accounts); équilibrer (le budget). ‖ Med. *Balanced diet,* régime équilibré.
— v. intr. Balancer, osciller. ‖ Se faire équilibre, s'équilibrer. ‖ Etre en balance (or) rapport (*with,* avec). ‖ Comm. Se balancer (accounts). ‖ Arts. Balancer (in dancing).

balas ['bæləs] n. Rubis balais *m.*

balcony ['bælkəni] n. Archit. Balcon *m.*, galerie *f.* ‖ Theatr. Deuxième balcon *m.*

bald [bɔːld] adj. Chauve (head, person). ‖ Zool. *Bald horse,* cheval belle-face. ‖ Fig. Maigre (statement); sec (style); dénudé, nu, dépouillé (tree). ‖ **Bald-coot,** n. Zool. Foulque *f.* ‖ **Bald-head,** n. Fam. Caillou *m.* (head); déplumé *s.* (person). ‖ **Bald-headed,** adv. Fam. Tête baissée; adj. Chauve.

baldachin ['bældəkin] n. Baldaquin *m.*

balderdash ['bɔːldədæʃ] n. Balivernes, calembredaines, fariboles *f. pl.*

baldly ['bɔːldli] adv. A nu. ‖ Fig. Sèchement.

baldness [-nis] f. Calvitie *f.* ‖ Fig. Nudité *f.* (of a mountain, tree); sécheresse *f.* (of style).

baldric ['bɔːldrik] n. Baudrier *m.*

bale [beil] n. † Calamité; douleur *f.*

bale n. Balle *f.* (of cotton); ballot *m.* (of goods).

bale v. tr. Naut. Ecoper. ‖ Aviat. *To bale out,* sauter en parachute.

baleen [bə'liːn] n. Baleine *f.* (See whalebone.)

balefire ['beil,faiə*] n. Feu (*m.*) de joie (bonfire). ‖ Feu (*m.*) de signalisation (beacon-fire). ‖ Bûcher funéraire *m.*

baleful ['beilful] adj. Nuisible, pernicieux, funeste.

balk [bɔːk] n. Archit. Solive *f.* ‖ Agric. Billon *m.* ‖ Fig. Obstacle, contretemps *m.*
— v. tr. Frustrer (*of,* de). ‖ Fuir, éviter, se dérober à (to evade); laisser passer, manquer (to miss). ‖ Entraver, gêner (to hinder); contrarier, contrecarrer (to thwart).
— v. intr. Se dérober (horse). ‖ Fam. *To balk at a difficulty,* caler devant une difficulté; *to balk at the work,* rechigner au travail.

ball [bɔːl] n. Pompon (of a fringe); boule (of snow); pelote (of string, wool); peloton (of thread). ‖ Astron. Globe *m.*; sphère *f.* ‖ Sports. Bille *f.* (billiards); boule *f.* (croquet, hockey); ballon *m.* (football); balle *f.* (golf, tennis). ‖ Milit. Boulet *m.* (of cannon); balle *f.* (of rifle); *to fire ball cartridge,* tirer à balle. ‖ Med. Prunelle *f.*; globe *m.* (of the eye); *ball of the foot,* éminence métatarsienne; *ball of the thumb,* éminence thénar. ‖ Culin. Boulette *f.*

(of meat); U. S. *sour balls,* bonbons acidulés. ‖ Techn. *Ball and socket joint,* joint à rotule. ‖ Jur. Boule (*f.*) de vote. ‖ Fam. *To be on the ball,* être toujours là pour un coup; être dégourdi (or) dessalé; U. S. *to drop the ball,* faire un pas de clerc; *to have the ball at one's feet,* avoir la partie belle; U. S. *to have sth. on the ball,* avoir qqch. dans le ventre; *to keep up the ball, to keep the ball rolling,* animer la conversation, renvoyer la balle; *to play ball,* coopérer; être en tandem (or) en cheville avec qqn. ‖ Arg. Pl. Couilles *f. pl.*; connerie *f.* ‖ **Ball-bearings,** n. Techn. Roulement (*m.*) à billes. ‖ **Ball-cock** (or) **-tap,** n. Robinet à flotteur *m.* ‖ **Ball-firing,** n. Milit. Tir (*m.*) à balles. ‖ **Ball-flower,** n. Archit. Trèfle *m.* ‖ **Ball-point,** n. Pointe-bille *f.*; *ball-point pen,* stylo à bille.
— v. tr. (1). Peloter, mettre en pelote (thread, wool). ‖ Agglomérer en boule (snow).
— v. intr. (1). S'agglomérer, se botter (snow). ‖ *To ball up,* embrouiller, emberlificoter; *to be balled up,* vasouiller (speaker) [fam.].

ball [bɔːl] n. Bal *m.*; *fancy dress ball,* bal costumé. ‖ U. S. Fam. *To have a ball,* rigoler. ‖ **Ball-room,** n. Salle (*f.*) de bal.

ballad [bæ'læd] n. Ballade; légende (*f.*) en vers. ‖ Mus. Romance *f.*

ballast ['bæləst] n. Naut., Aviat. Lest *m.* ‖ Ch. de f. Ballast *m.* ‖ Fam. Pondération *f.*; plomb *m.*
— v. tr. Naut., Aviat. Lester. ‖ Ch. de f. Ballaster. ‖ Techn. Empierrer (a road). ‖ Fam. Mettre du plomb dans la tête à.

ballerina [bælə'riːnə] n. Theatr. Ballerine *f.*; *prima ballerina,* danseuse étoile.

ballet ['bælei] n. Theatr. Ballet *m.* ‖ **Ballet-girl,** n. Danseuse, ballerine *f.* ‖ **Ballet-skirt,** n. Tutu *m.*

balletomane [,bælətə'mein] n. Fam. Fanatique de ballet *m.*

ballistic [bə'listik] adj. Milit. Balistique (wave). **ballistics** [-tiks] n. sg. Milit. Balistique *f.*

ballocks ['bæləks] n. pl. Arg. Couilles *f. pl.* ‖ Fig., Arg. Connerie, couillonnade *f.* (nonsense); merdier *m.* (muddle); *to make a ballocks of,* faire un gâchis de. ‖ **Ballocks-up,** n. Arg. Merdier *m.*
— v. tr. Arg. Faire un gâchis de, saloper.
— interj. Arg. Merde!

ballonet ['bælənet] n. Aviat. Ballonnet compensateur *m.*

balloon [be'luːn] n. Aviat. Ballon, aérostat *m.*; *meteorological balloon,* radiosonde, ballon-sonde; *observation balloon,* éclaireur. ‖ Chim. Ballon *m.* ‖ Archit. Boule *f.* ‖ Ballon *m.* (typogr.).
— adj. Ballon, à dégustation (glass). ‖ Autom. *Balloon tyre,* pneu confort. ‖ **Balloon-maker,** n. Ballonnier *m.*
— v. intr. Aviat. Monter en ballon. ‖ Med. Se ballonner.
— v. tr. Med. Ballonner.

balloonist [-ist] n. Aviat. Aérostier, stratonaute *m.*

ballot ['bælət] n. Aviat. Boule (*f.*) [or] bulletin (*m.*) de vote. ‖ Scrutin *m.*; *by ballot,* au scrutin secret; *second ballot,* ballottage, second tour. ‖ Tirage au sort *m.* ‖ **Ballot-box,** n. Urne *f.* ‖ **Ballot-paper,** n. Bulletin de vote *m.*
— v. intr. Voter au scrutin secret; *to ballot for,* tirer au sort (precedence).

bally ['bæli] adj. Fam. Sacré, satané, fichu.

ballyhoo [bæli'huː] n. Pop. Battage *m.*; réclame *f.* ‖ Bourrage de crâne; baratin *m.*

ballyrag ['bæliræg] v. tr., intr. (1). Fam. Blaguer.

balm [bɑːm] n. Med., Fig. Baume *m.* ‖ Fig. Dictame *m.* ‖ **Balm-cricket,** n. Zool. Cigale *f.*

balmoral [bæl'mɔrəl] n. Balmoral *m.* (bonnet, boot, petticoat).

balmy ['bɑːmi] adj. Calmant, adoucissant (soothing). ‖ Embaumé, parfumé (fragrant). ‖ Produisant du baume. ‖ Fam. Toqué.

balneology ['bælniɔ'lɔdʒi) n. Thermalisme *m*.

balneotherapy ['bælniɔ'θerəpi] n. MED. Balnéothérapie *f*.

baloney [bə'louni] n. U. S. POP. Blague, foutaise *f*.; chiqué, boniment *m*.

balsa ['bɔːlsə] n. Radeau *m*. (raft). ‖ BOT. Balsa *m*. (tree, wood).

balsam ['bɔːlsəm] n. MED., FIG. Baume, *m*. ‖ CHIM. Oléorésine *f*. ‖ BOT. *Balsam fir*, sapin baumier; *garden balsam*, balsamine.

balsamic [bɔːl'sæmik] adj. Balsamique.

Baltic ['bɔːltik] adj., n. GEOGR. Baltique *f*.

baluster ['bæləstə*] n. ARCHIT. Balustre *m*. ‖ Pl. Rampe *f*. (of a staircase).

balustrade [,bæləs'treid] n. Balustrade *f*.

bambino [bæm'biːnou] n. ARTS. Enfant Jésus *m*. ‖ FAM. Bambino, bambin *m*.

bamboo [bæm'buː] n. BOT. Bambou *m*.

bamboozle [bæm'buːzl̩] v. tr. FAM. Embobeliner, empaumer, entortiller. ‖ POP. Mystifier; *to bamboozle s.o. out of sth*., soutirer qqch. en lui bourrant le crâne.

ban [bæn] v. tr. (1). † Maudire. ‖ Interdire, prohiber. ‖ FIG. Mettre au ban.
— n. ECCLES. Interdit *m*. ‖ JUR. Bannissement *m*.; proscription *f*. ‖ FIG. Ostracisme général *m*.; *under a ban*, mis au ban de la société.

banal ['beinl̩] adj. Banal.

banality [bə'næliti] n. Banalité *f*.

banana [bə'nɑːnə] n. BOT. Banane *f*. (fruit); bananier *m*. (tree). ‖ **Banana-plantation**, n. BOT. Bananeraie *f*.

banco ['bæŋko] adj. Banco; *to go banco*, faire banco.

band [bænd] n. Bande *f*. (of leather, material, metal, paper); ruban *m*. (of cloth, rubber); *arm band*, brassard; *elastic band*, élastique; *hat band*, ruban de chapeau. ‖ Bande, troupe *f*. (of armed men, robbers). ‖ Ligue *f*. (of Hope). ‖ ECCLES., JUR. Rabat *m*. ‖ ARCHIT. Cordon *m*. ‖ TECHN. Courroie *f*.; *steel band*, jante en acier. ‖ NAUT. *Reef-band*, bande de ris. ‖ MILIT. *Cartridge band*, bande de cartouches; *driving band*, ceinture conductrice. ‖ AVIAT. *Trajectory band*, ralingue ? ‖ MUS. Orchestre *m*.; fanfare *f*. (orchestra); plage *f*. (of record); *military band*, musique militaire. ‖ RADIO. *Frequency band*, bande de fréquence. ‖ **Band-brake**, n. TECHN. Frein à collier *m*. ‖ **Band-saw**, n. TECHN. Scie sans fin *f*. ‖ **Band-waggon**, n. Voiture de parade *f*.; FAM. *To climb on the band-waggon*, se mettre du côté du manche. ‖ **Band-wheel**, n. TECHN. Roue de transmission.
— v. tr. Marquer de bandes colorées. ‖ Bander. ‖ Réunir en bandes, grouper. ‖ Liguer; *to band together*, se liguer. ‖ Baguer (a pigeon).

bandage ['bændidʒ] n. Bandeau *m*. ‖ MED. Pansement *m*. (for wound); *first-aid bandage*, pansement individuel. ‖ MED. Bandage *m*. (for fracture); *crepe bandage*, bande Velpeau.
— v. tr. MED. Bander; mettre un pansement à; *bandaged finger*, nonnette (fam.).

bandanna [bæn'dænə] n. Foulard *m*.

b. and b. [biːənd'biː] abbr. *Bed and breakfast*, chambre avec petit déjeuner; chambre chez l'habitant.

bandbox ['bændbɔks] n. Carton à chapeau *m*.; boîte (*f*.) à rubans. ‖ FAM. *To look as if one came out of a bandbox*, avoir l'air de sortir d'une boîte.

bandeau ['bændou] n. Bandeau *m*., serre-tête *m. inv*.

banderole ['bændəroul] n. NAUT., ARCHIT. Banderole *f*.

bandit ['bændit] n. Bandit *m*.

bandmaster ['bænd,mɑːstə*] n. MUS. Chef (*m*.) de musique.

bandog ['bændɔg] n. ZOOL. Mâtin, chien (*m*.) de garde.

bandolier [,bændə'liə*] n. Bandoulière, cartouchière *f*.

bandoline ['bændoliːn] n. Brillantine, Gommina *f*.

bandsman ['bændzmən] (pl. **bandsmen**) n. MUS. Musicien *m*.

bandy ['bændi] v. tr. (2). Echanger (*with*, avec); se renvoyer (blows, jokes). ‖ Faire circuler (a tale).

bandy adj. Ecarté. ‖ **Bandy-legged**, adj. Bancal.

bane [bein] n. Poison *m*.; *rat's bane*, mort-auxrats. ‖ FIG. Fléau *m*.; ruine *f*.; *to be the bane of s.o.'s life*, empoisonner la vie de qqn.

baneful [-ful] adj. Empoisonné. ‖ FIG. Pernicieux.

bang [bæŋ] v. tr. Claquer (the door); poser (or) jeter brusquement; *to bang down the receiver*, raccrocher d'un geste brusque. ‖ Rosser, cogner sur (to thrash).
— v. intr. Claquer avec fracas.
— n. Claquement, coup sec *m*.; *to fall with a bang*. tomber avec fracas. ‖ Détonation *f*. (of a gun). ‖ AVIAT. *Supersonic bang*, bang.
— interj. Paf! Pan! (shot).
— adv. Avec brusquerie et violence (abruptly); *he went bang at him*, il lui est rentré pile dedans. ‖ Avec fracas (noisily). ‖ FAM. *Bang on!*, au poil!

bang v. tr. Couper en frange (hair).
— n. Frange *f*. ‖ **Bang-tailed**, adj. Ecourté (horse).

Bangladesh [,bɑːŋglə'deʃ] n. GEOGR. Bangladesh *m*.

bangle [,bæŋgl̩] n. Bracelet (*m*.) de poignet ou de cheville. (See ANKLET.)

banian ['bæniən] n. Banian *m*. (gown, person). ‖ NAUT. Maigre (day).

banish ['bæniʃ] v. tr. Bannir, exiler (*from*, de). ‖ FIG. Expulser, chasser, proscrire.

banishment [-mənt] n. Bannissement, exil *m*.; *local banishment*, interdiction de séjour.

banister ['bænistə*] n. Rampe *f*. (of a staircase).

banjo ['bændʒou] n. MUS. Banjo *m*.

banjoist [-ist] n. MUS. Joueur de banjo *m*.

bank [bæŋk] n. Talus, remblai *m*.; levée *f*. (of earth). ‖ Berge, rive *f*.; bord *m*. (of a river). ‖ Amoncellement *m*. (of cloud, fog, snow). ‖ TECHN. Carreau *m*. (in mining); rang (*m*.) de touches (in typewriting). ‖ NAUT. Banc *m*. ‖ AVIAT. Virage (*m*.) sur l'aile. ‖ THEATR. Rampe *f*. (of projection).
— v. tr. Remblayer; enfermer entre des talus. ‖ Endiguer (a river). ‖ Amonceler, entasser; *to bank up the fire*, couvrir le feu. ‖ TECHN. *To bank a road at a corner*, relever un virage.
— v. intr. S'amonceler, s'accumuler (clouds, fog, snow). ‖ TECHN. Buter. ‖ AVIAT. Virer sur l'aile.

bank n. FIN. Banque *f*.; U. S. *bank references*, références bancaires. ‖ SPORTS. *To break the bank*, faire sauter la banque. ‖ MED. *Blood, eye bank*, banque du sang, des yeux. ‖ FAM. Réserve *f*.; *as safe as the Bank of England*, de l'or en barre. ‖ **Bank-book**, n. FIN. Carnet (*m*.) de banque. ‖ **Bank-clerk**, n. Employé (*s*.) de banque. ‖ **Bank-credit**, n. FIN. Crédit bancaire *m*. ‖ **Bank-holiday**, n. Jour férié *m*.; fête légale, *f*. ‖ **Bank-night**, n. U. S. Gala cinématographique (*m*.) avec loterie. ‖ **Bank-note**, n. FIN. Billet (*m*.) de banque. ‖ **Bank-rate**, n. FIN. Taux d'escompte *m*.
— v. tr. FIN. Déposer en banque. ‖ Changer, convertir en espèces.
— v. intr. FIN. Etre banquier; *to bank with*, avoir pour banquier. ‖ Tenir la banque (gaming). ‖ MED. Entreposer, conserver (blood). ‖ FIG. *To bank on*, miser (or) tabler sur, escompter.

bank n. NAUT. Banc de rameurs *m*. (in a galley); rangée (*f*.) d'avirons (oars). ‖ Rangée de clefs *f*. (on a keyboard). ‖ MUS. Clavier *m*. ‖ ELECTR. Batterie *f*.; groupe *m*.

bankable [-əbl̩] adj. Fin. Bancable, négociable en banque. ‖ Fig. Sûr, fiable.

banker [-ə*] n. Techn. Terrassier *m.* ‖ Naut. Morutier *m.* ‖ Sports. Cheval (*m.*) qui saute les banquettes. ‖ Ch. de f. Machine (*f.*) de renfort.

banker n. Fin., Sports. Banquier *m. ; banker's references,* références bancaires.

banking [-iŋ] n. Fin. Opérations (*f. pl.*) de banque, activité (*f.*) bancaire. ‖ Techn. Relèvement *m.* (at a bend).

bankrupt [-rʌpt] n. Failli *m. ; bankrupt's certificate,* concordat ; *fraudulent bankrupt,* banqueroutier ; *to be adjudicated bankrupt,* être déclaré (or) mis en faillite. ‖ Med. *Mental bankrupt,* déficient mental.
— adj. Failli, en faillite ; *to become bankrupt,* faire faillite. ‖ Insolvable. ‖ Fig. Privé (*of,* de).
— v. tr. Réduire à la faillite.

bankruptcy [-rʌptsi] n. Faillite *f. ; fraudulent bankruptcy,* banqueroute. ‖ Insolvabilité *f.* ‖ Fig. Faillite *f.*

banksman [-smən] (pl. **banksmen**) n. Techn. Porion *m.* (in mining).

banner ['bænə*] n. Milit., Eccles., Fig. Bannière *f.*
— adj. Exceptionnel ; *banner headline,* titre flamboyant (in newspaper).
— v. intr. U. S. Titrer en manchettes énormes.

banneret [-rit] n. Banneret *m.*

bannerol [-rɔl] n. Banderole *f.*

bannock ['bænək] n. Culin. Galette écossaise *f.*

banns [bænz] n. pl. Bans *m. pl.*

banquet ['bæŋkwit] n. Banquet *m.*
— v. intr. Banqueter.
— v. tr. Régaler, offrir un festin à.

banquette [bæŋ'ket] n. Milit. Banquette (*f.*) de tir. ‖ U. S. Trottoir *m.* (streetwalk).

banshee [bæn'ʃi:] n. Dame blanche *f.*

bantam ['bæntəm] n. Zool. Bantam, coq nain *m.* ‖ Fam. Coq *m.* (person). ‖ **Bantam-weight,** *n.* Sports. Poids coq *m.*

banter ['bæntə*] n. invar. Plaisanterie, badinerie, raillerie plaisante *f.*
— v. tr., intr. Plaisanter (*with,* avec) ; railler.

banting [-iŋ] n. Med. Régime amaigrissant *m.*

bantling [-liŋ] n. Gosse *m.* (See BRAT.)

baobab ['beiobæb] n. Bot. Baobab *m.*

bap [bæp] n. Culin. Miche (*f.*) de pain mou.

baptism ['bæptizm̩] n. Eccles. Baptême *m.* ‖ Milit. *Baptism of fire,* baptême du feu.

baptismal [bæp'tizməl] adj. Eccles. Baptismal, du baptême.

Baptist ['bæptist] n. Eccles. Baptiste *m.* ‖ Anabaptiste *m.*

baptistery [-ri] n. Eccles. Baptistère *m.*

baptize [bæp'taiz] v. tr. Eccles., Fam. Baptiser.

bar [bɑ:*] n. Barre *f.* (of chocolate, metal, soap, wood) ; barreau *m.* (of a gate, window). ‖ Barrière *f.* (barrier). ‖ Bar *m. ; buvette f. ; in the bar,* au bar. ‖ Sports. Barre *f. ; horizontal bar,* barre fixe. ‖ Techn. *Tension bar,* barre de tension. ‖ Mus. Barre ; mesure *f.* ‖ Naut. Barre. ‖ Milit. Barrette *f.* (of a medal). ‖ Jur. Barreau *m. ; basoche f. ; Bar Council,* Conseil de l'ordre ; *to be called to the bar,* être reçu avocat ; *to read for the bar,* faire son droit. ‖ Jur. Barre *f. ;* banc (*m.*) de la défense (or) des accusés ; *at the bar,* devant le tribunal. ‖ Jur. Empêchement *m. ;* exception *f.* ‖ Blas. Burèle *f.* ‖ Fig. Obstacle *m. ; in bar of,* pour faire obstacle à. ‖ Fig. Tribunal *m.* ‖ **Bar-girl,** n. U. S. Entraîneuse *f.* ‖ **Bar-happy,** adj. U. S. Emêché, gai. ‖ **Bar-keeper,** n. Cabaretier, buvetier *m.*
— v. tr. (1). Barricader (a door). ‖ Griller, grillager (a window). ‖ Barrer, rayer, raturer (a text). ‖ Fermer (an entrance) ; barrer (the way). ‖ † Priver de. ‖ Jur. Interdire ; opposer une fin de non-recevoir à (an action) ; défendre (a cause). ‖ Fig.

Exclure ; *to bar s.o. from a career,* barrer une carrière à qqn.
— prep. Sauf, excepté. (See BARRING.)

bar n. Phys. Bar *m.*

bar n. Zool. Bar *m.*

barb [bɑ:b] n. Barbelure *f.* (of an arrow). ‖ Barbe *f.* (of a feather, fish-hook, harpoon). ‖ Bot. Barbe (of corn). ‖ Zool. Barbillon *m.* (of fish). ‖ Eccles. Barbette *f.* (of a nun). ‖ Fig. Traits *m. pl.* (of wit).
— v. tr. Garnir de barbelures.

barb n. Zool. Barbe *m.* (horse).

Barbados [bɑ:'beidous] n. Geogr. Barbade (la) [*f.*].

barbarian [bɑ:'bɛəriən] adj., n. Barbare *s.* ‖ Fam. Béotien *s.*

barbaric [[bɑ:'bærik] adj. Barbare, de barbare.

barbarism ['bɑ:bərizm̩] n. Manque (*m.*) de culture. ‖ Gramm. Barbarisme *m.*

barbarity [bɑ:'bæriti] n. Barbarie, sauvagerie, cruauté *f.* ‖ Acte (or) goût barbare *m.*

barbarize ['bɑ:bəraiz] v. tr. Ramener à l'état barbare (a people). ‖ Gramm. Corrompre (a language).
— v. intr. Retourner à la barbarie. ‖ Gramm. Faire des barbarismes.

barbarous [-əs] adj. Barbare, de barbare ; de sauvage. ‖ Cruel, barbare.

barbarously [-əsli] adv. Avec barbarie.

barbate ['bɑ:beit] adj. Bot. Barbu.

barbecue ['bɑ:bikju:] n. Culin. Boucan, gril *m. ;* animal entier rôti *m.* ‖ Repas en plein air *m.*
— v. tr. Culin. Préparer, rôtir en « barbecue ».

barbed ['bɑ:bd] adj. Barbelé (arrow) ; *barbed wire,* fil de fer barbelé. ‖ Fig. Acéré (words).

barbel ['bɑ:bəl] n. Zool. Barbillon *m.* (barb) ; barbeau *m.* (fish).

barber ['bɑ:bə*] n. Barbier † ; coiffeur *m.*
— v. tr. Coiffer, raser. ‖ U. S. Jacasser.

barberry ['bɑ:bəri] n. Bot. Epine-vinette *f. ;* béris *m.*

barbershop ['bɑ:bə,ʃɔp] n. U. S. Salon (*m.*) de coiffure pour hommes.

barbette [bɑ:'bet] n. Milit. Barbette *f.*

barbican ['bɑ:bikən] n. Milit. Barbacane *f.*

barbiturate [bɑ:bi'tjuəreit] n. Chim. Barbiturique *m.*

barbituric [-rik] adj. Chim. Barbiturique.

barcarolle ['bɑ:kəroul] n. Mus. Barcarolle *f.*

bard [bɑ:d] n. Barde *m.* (poet).

bard n. Barde *f.* (armour).
— v. tr. Culin. Barder. ‖ **Barding-needle,** n. Lardoire *f.*

bare [bɛə*] adj. Nu, dénudé (arm, mountain, tree) ; nu, vide, dégarni (room) ; nu, dégainé, tiré (sword). ‖ Nu, non protégé ; *he killed the wolf with his bare hands,* il tua le loup à mains nues. ‖ Vide, dépourvu (*of,* de). ‖ Electr. Dénudé (wire). ‖ Fig. Simple, sec, à peine suffisant ; *bare living,* portion congrue, strict minimum ; *bare thanks,* un merci sans chaleur. ‖ **Bare-back,** adv. A cru, à poil (riding). ‖ **Bare-headed,** adj. Nu-tête. ‖ **Bare-midriff dress,** n. Deux-pièces, maillot deux pièces *m.*
— v. tr. Dénuder, dépouiller, mettre à nu ; *to bare the neck,* dégager le cou. ‖ Dégainer (a sword). ‖ Fig. Révéler.

barefaced [-feist] adj. Glabre (without beard). ‖ A visage nu (unmasked). ‖ Fig. Ehonté, effronté (shameless).

barefacedly [-feisidli] adv. A découvert, ouvertement (openly). ‖ Fig. Effrontément, cyniquement.

barefoot [-fut] adv. Nu-pieds, pieds nus.

barefooted [-futid] adj. Nu-pieds. ‖ Eccles. Déchaux.

barely [-li] adv. A peine, tout juste.

bareness [-nis] n. Nudité *f.* ‖ Fig. Dénuement *m. ;* sécheresse *f.*

barfly ['bɑ:flai] n. U. S. Fam. Pilier (*m.*) de bar.

bargain ['bɑ:gin] n. Comm. Marché *m. ; into the*

bargain, par-dessus le marché; *it's a bargain,* marché conclu. ‖ Comm. Affaire, occasion *f.; a good bargain,* une bonne affaire (or) emplette. ‖ Fig. *The worst of the bargain,* le plus mal partagé; *to make the best of a bad bargain,* tirer le meilleur parti d'une mauvaise affaire. ‖ **Bargain counter** (or) **basement,** n. U. S. Comm. Rayon (*m.*) des soldes.
— v. intr. Marchander. (See HAGGLE.) ‖ Négocier, traiter (*for,* de; *with,* avec). ‖ Fam. *To bargain for,* s'attendre à, compter sur; *to get more than one bargained for,* avoir affaire à plus forte partie qu'on ne croyait.
— v. tr. *To bargain away,* vendre à perte; bazarder, liquider (fam.).
bargaining [-iŋ] n. Marchandage *m.* ‖ Jur. *Collective bargaining,* convention collective.
barge ['bɑ:dʒ] n. Naut. Péniche, allège, gabare *f.;* chaland *m.* (freight-boat); barge de parade *f.* (house-boat); canot *m.* (admiral's). ‖ **Barge-pole,** n. Gaffe *f.;* Fam. *I wouldn't touch it with a barge-pole,* il n'est pas à prendre avec des pincettes.
— v. tr. U. S. Transporter par péniche.
— v. intr. Fam. *To barge in,* mettre les pieds dans le plat, piétiner les bégonias; *to barge into sth.,* se cogner contre qqch.
bargee [-i:] n. Naut. Marinier *m.* ‖ Fam. *To swear like a bargee,* jurer comme un charretier.
bargeman [-mən] n. Naut. Marinier *m.*
baritone ['bæritoun] see BARYTONE.
barium ['bɛəriəm] n. Chim. Baryum *m.*
bark [bɑ:k] n. Bot. Ecorce *f.* ‖ Tan *m.* ‖ Med. *Peruvian bark,* quinine. ‖ Fam. Cuir *m.* (skin).
— v. tr. Ecorcer (a tree). ‖ Tanner (leather). ‖ Encroûter. ‖ Fam. S'écorcher.
bark n. Naut. Trois-mâts barque *m.* ‖ Barque *f.*
bark n. Aboiement *m.* (of a dog). ‖ Fam. *His bark is worse than his bite,* il fait plus de bruit que de mal.
— v. intr. Aboyer (*at,* après, contre). ‖ Fam. Aboyer, glapir (person); *to bark up the wrong tree,* se tromper de but, prendre le mauvais train, suivre la mauvaise piste. ‖ Pop. Tousser.
barker [-ə*] n. Aboyeur *m.* (dog, person). ‖ Comm. Aboyeur, bonimenteur *m.* ‖ Pop. Pétard *m.* (firearm).
barley ['bɑ:li] n. Bot. Orge *f.; pearl, peeled barley,* orge perlé, mondé. ‖ **Barley-broth,** n. Fam. Bière *f.* ‖ **Barley-sugar,** n. Sucre (*m.*) d'orge.
barleycorn [-kɔ:n] n. Grain (*m.*) d'orge. ‖ Fam. *John Barleycorn,* whisky.
barm ['bɑ:m] n. Levure de bière *f.*
barmaid [-meid] n. Barmaid *f.*
barman [-mən] (pl. **barmen**) n. Barman *m.*
bar mitzvah [bɑ:'mitsvə] n. Eccles. Bar-mitsva *f.*
barmy [-mi] adj. Ecumeux. ‖ Fam. Toqué, fêlé.
barn [bɑ:n] n. Agric. Grange *f.* ‖ U. S. Etable *f.* (stable); hangar *m.* (storage place). ‖ **Barn-floor,** n. Aire *f.* ‖ **Barn-owl,** n. Zool. Effraie *f.* ‖ **Barn-stormer,** n. Theatr. Acteur ambulant *m.;* U. S. Orateur électoral *m.* ‖ **Barn-yard,** m. Basse-cour *f.*
barnacle ['bɑ:nəkl̩] n. Zool. Bernacle, oie sauvage *f.* (goose); anatife *m.;* barnacle *f.* (shellfish). ‖ Fam. Crampon; pot (*m.*) de colle.
barograph ['bærogrɑ:f] n. Phys. Barographe *m.*
barometer [bə'rɔmitə*] n. Phys. Baromètre *m.*
barometric [,bæro'metrik] adj. Barométrique.
baron ['bærən] n. Baron *m.* ‖ Culin. Double aloyau *m.* (of beef). ‖ Fam. Roi *m.*
baronage [-idʒ] n. Baronnage *m.* (class, domain, rank). ‖ Gotha *m.* (book).
baroness [-is] n. Baronne *f.*
baronet [-it] n. Baronnet *m.*
— v. tr. Créer baronnet.
baronetage [-itidʒ] n. Nobiliaire, Gotha *m.*

baronial [bə'rouniəl] adj. De baron. ‖ Fam. *Baronial hall,* vaste maison, castel.
barony ['bærəni] n. Baronnie *f.*
baroque [bə'rouk] adj. Arts, Fig. Baroque.
baroscope ['bærəskoup] n. Phys. Baroscope *m.*
barouche [bə'ru:ʃ] n. Calèche *f.;* landau *m.*
barque [bɑ:k] n. Naut. Trois-mâts barque *m.*
barquentine ['bɑ:kənti:n] n. Naut. Goélette *f.*
barrack ['bærək] n. Baraque *f.;* baraquement *m.* ‖ Pl. Milit. Caserne *f.; disciplinary barracks,* locaux disciplinaires. ‖ Fam. Caserne, grande baraque *f.* ‖ **Barrack-room,** n. Milit. Chambrée *f.; barrack-room joke,* plaisanterie de corps de garde.
— v. tr. Milit. Caserner. ‖ Sports, Fam. Chahuter, conspuer.
barracuda [,bærə'kju:də] n. Zool. Barracuda *m.,* bécune *f.*
barrage ['bærɑ:ʒ] n. Barrage *m.* (See DAM.) ‖ Milit. Barrage *m.; balloon barrage,* réseau de ballons de protection. ‖ Fam. Nuée *f.* (of questions); flot *m.* (of words).
— adj. Milit. De protection (ballon).
barrator ['bærətə*] n. Jur. Procédurier *m.* ‖ Fam. Chicaneur *m.*
barratry [-ri] n. Esprit (*m.*) de chicane. ‖ Jur. Baraterie *f.*
barred [bɑ:d] adj. Barré. ‖ Naut. Ensablé.
barrel ['bærəl] n. Baril *m.;* demi-pièce *f.* (of wine) ‖ Caque *f.* (of herrings); gonne *f.* (of tar). ‖ Mus. Caisse *f.* (of a drum). ‖ Milit. Canon *m.* (of a gun). ‖ Naut. Cloche *f.* (of a capstan). ‖ Zool. Tuyau *m.* (of a feather); tronc *m.* (of a horse). ‖ Techn. Réservoir *m.* (of a fountain-pen); canon *m.* (of a key); corps *m.* (of a pump); barillet *m.* (of a watch); tambour *m.* (of a windlass). ‖ Med. *Barrel of the ear,* caisse du tympan. ‖ Fam. U. S. *Pork-barrel,* assiette au beurre. ‖ **Barrel-chair,** n. Fauteuil-tonneau *m.* ‖ **Barrel-organ,** n. Mus. Orgue (*m.*) de barbarie. ‖ **Barrel-road,** n. Chaussée bombée. ‖ **Barrel-roll,** n. Aviat. Tonneau *m.* ‖ **Barrel-vault,** n. Archit. Voûte (*f.*) en berceau.
— v. tr. (1). Embariller.
— v. intr. Fam. U. S. *To barrel along,* aller à fond de train (in a vehicle).
barrelled [-d] adj. Embarillé. ‖ Milit. *Double-barrelled,* à deux coups (gun).
barren ['bærən] adj. Med., Zool., Bot. Stérile. ‖ Fig. Stérile, improductif (efforts); aride, sec (style).
— n. Lande *f.*
barrenly [-li] adv. Stérilement.
barrenness [-nis] n. Med., Zool., Bot. Stérilité *f.* ‖ Fig. Stérilité (of efforts); aridité *f.* (of a matter); sécheresse *f.* (of style).
barret ['bærit] n. Eccles. Barrette *f.*
barricade [,bæri'keid] n. Barricade *f.* ‖ Fig. Barrière *f.*
— v. tr. Barricader.
barrier ['bæriə*] n. Barrière *f.* ‖ Ch. de f. Portillon *m.* ‖ Aviat. *Sound barrier,* mur du son. ‖ Fig. Obstacle *m.*
— v. tr. Mettre obstacle à.
barring ['bɑ:riŋ] prep. Sauf, excepté. (See EXCEPT.)
barrister ['bæristə*] n. Jur. Avocat *m.; consulting barrister,* avocat conseil; *revising barrister,* contrôleur des listes électorales. ‖ **Barrister-at-law,** n. Jur. Avocat (*m.*) à la cour.
barrow ['bærou] n. Bard *m.* (handbarrow). ‖ Brouette *f.* (wheel-barrow); *coster's barrow,* voiture des quatre-saisons. ‖ Med. Brancard *m.;* civière *f.* ‖ **Barrow-boy,** n. Comm. Marchand (*m.*) des quatre saisons.
barrow n. Tumulus *m.* ‖ Geogr. Colline *f.*
barry ['bæ:ri] adj. Blas. Fascé, barré.
bartender ['bɑ:,tendə*] n. U. S. Barman *m.*
barter ['bɑ:tə*] v. tr. Echanger, troquer (*for,* contre). ‖ *To barter away,* bazarder, liquider.

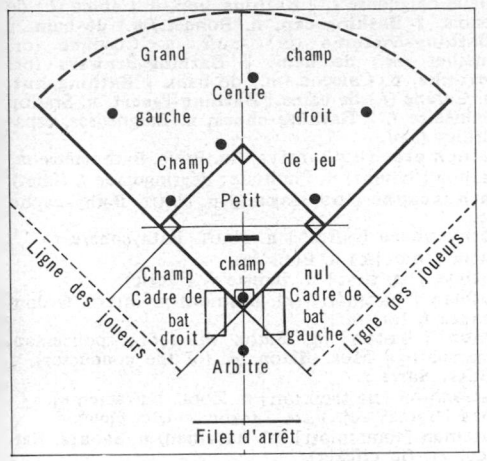

Grand champ
Centre
gauche droit
Champ de jeu
Petit
Champ champ nul
Cadre de Cadre de
bat bat
droit gauche
Arbitre
Ligne des joueurs
Filet d'arrêt

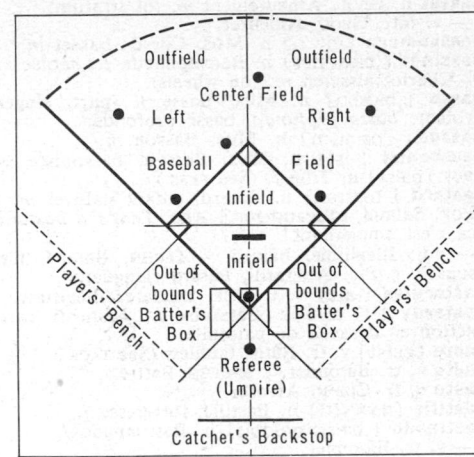

Outfield Outfield
Center Field
Left Right
Baseball Field
Infield
Infield
Out of Out of
bounds bounds
Batter's Batter's
Box Box
Players' Bench
Referee
(Umpire)
Catcher's Backstop

— v. intr. Faire du troc.
— n. Troc, échange *m.* ‖ COMM. *Barter agreement,* accord de compensation. ‖ FIG. Echange (of talk).
bartizan [ˌbɑːˈtiˈzæn] n. ARCHIT. Echauguette *f.* ‖ Parapet crénelé *m.*
barton [ˈbɑːtn̩] n. AGRIC. Ferme *f.* (of a manor); cour de ferme *f.* (farmyard).
barye [ˈbæriː] n. PHYS. Barye *f.*
baryon [ˈbæriˌɔn] n. PHYS. Baryon *m.*
barysphere [ˈbæriˌsfiə*] n. GEOGR. Barysphère *f.*
baryta [bæˈriːtə] n. CHIM. Baryte *f.*
barytes [-tiːz] n. CHIM. Barytine *f.*
barytone [ˈbæritoun] n. MUS., GRAMM. Baryton *m.*
barytron [ˈbæritrɔn] n. PHYS. Méson *m.*
basal [ˈbeisl̩] adj. Fondamental. ‖ MED. Basal (metabolism).
basalt [ˈbæsɔːlt] n. Basalte *m.*
basan [ˈbæsn̩] n. Basane *f.*
bascule [ˈbæskyul] n. Bascule *f.*
base [beis] n. Base, assise, fondation *f.;* fondement *m.* (foundation). ‖ Pied *f.* (of a column); base *f.* (of the thumb). ‖ AVIAT. Base *f.; launching base,* rampe de lancement. ‖ MATH., MILIT., CHIM., SPORTS. Base *f.* ‖ NAUT. *Submarine base,* nid de sous-marins. ‖ GRAMM. Radical *m.* ‖ FIG. Base *f.* (of a system). ‖ FAM. U. S. *To get to first base,* parvenir à la première étape, gagner la première manche.
—adj. De base.
— v. tr. Fonder, asseoir, établir; baser (fam.) [*on, sur*]. ‖ AVIAT., MILIT. Baser.
base adj. Vil, de mauvais aloi (coin); vil, sans valeur (metal). ‖ FIG. Bas, abject, vil (action); servile (task). ‖ GRAMM. Bas. ‖ **Base-born,** adj. De basse extraction (of low birth); bâtard (illegitimate). ‖ **Base-court,** n. Cour (*f.*) de derrière. ‖ **Base-fee,** II. JUR. Propriété conditionnelle *f.* ‖ **Base-minded,** adj. A l'âme vile. ‖ **Base-spirited,** adj. Pusillanime.
baseball [-ˈbɔːl] n. SPORTS. Base-ball *m.; baseball player,* baseballer.
baseless [-lis] adj. Sans fondement (groundless).
basely [-li] adv. Bassement.
basement [-mənt] n. ARCHIT. Fondations *f.* pl.; soubassement *m.* pl.; *in the basement,* au sous-sol.
baseness [-nis] n. Illégitimité *f.* (of birth). ‖ FIG. Bassesse *f.*
bash [bæʃ] v. tr. FAM. Cogner; porter un coup violent à; *to bash in,* enfoncer (a door); cabosser (a hat).

— n. Coup violent; gnon. ‖ POP. *To have a bash,* tenter le coup; y aller-à son tour; en mettre un coup.
bashful [-ful] adj. Timide (see COY, SHY); *bashful lover,* amoureux transi. ‖ Pudibond, pudique.
bashfully [-fuli] adv. Timidement.
bashfulness [-fulnis] n. Timidité, fausse honte *f.*
bashing [-iŋ] n. FAM. Volée, raclée *f.*
basic [ˈbeisik] adj. CHIM. Basique. ‖ GRAMM. De base, élémentaire (vocabulary). ‖ COMM. *Basic pay,* salaire de base. ‖ U. S. *Basic dress,* robe à transformations à porter avec accessoires.
— n. FAM. Anglais (*m.*) de base.
basicity [beiˈsisiti] n. CHIM. Basicité *f.*
basil [ˈbæzl̩] n. BOT. Basilic *m.*
basilic [bəˈzilik] adj. MED. Basilique (vein).
basilica [-ə] n. ARCHIT., ECCLES. Basilique *f.*
basilisk [ˈbæzilisk] n. Basilic *m.*
basin [ˈbeisn̩] n. Bassin *m.;* cuvette *f.* (wash-bowl). ‖ Bol *m.* (bowl); *sugar basin,* sucrier. ‖ GEOGR. Bassin (of a river); port naturel *m.* (landlocked harbour); cuvette (valley). ‖ NAUT. Bassin de port *m.*
basinet [ˈbæsinet] n. Bassinet *m.* (helmet).
basinful [ˈbeisnful] n. Bolée *f.* (milk); pleine cuvette *f.* (of water). ‖ POP. *To have had a basinful,* en avoir marre (or) soupé.
basis [ˈbeisis] (pl. **bases** [-iːz]) n. MILIT. Base *f.* ‖ FIG. Base *f.;* fondement *m.*
bask [bɑːsk] v. intr. Se chauffer; *to bask in the sun,* prendre un bain de soleil; se chauffer au soleil; lézarder (fam.).
basket [ˈbɑːskit] n. Panier *m.;* corbeille *f.* ‖ Banne *f.* (for coal); bourriche *f.* (for fish or game). ‖ Hotte *f.* (carried on the back). ‖ Panier-arrière *m.* (of a stage-coach); plein panier *m.;* pleine corbeille *f.* (basketful). ‖ ARCHIT. Corbeille *f.* ‖ CH. DE F. *Luncheon basket,* panier-repas. ‖ **Basketball,** n. SPORTS. Basket-ball, basket *m.* ‖ **Basket-lunch,** n. U. S. Pique-nique *m.* ‖ **Basket-maker,** n. Vannier *m.* ‖ **Basket-trunk,** n. Malle (*f.*) en osier. ‖ **Basket-work,** n. Vannerie *f.*
Basque [bæsk] adj. GEOGR. Basque.
— n. Basque *m.* (language).
basque n. Basque *f.* (of a tunic).
bas-relief [ˈbæsriˌliːf] n. ARCHIT. Bas-relief *m.*
bass [bæs] n. ZOOL. Perche *f.* (fish); bar *m.* (sea-bass).
bass n. Teille, fibre (*f.*) de tilleul.
bass [beis] adj. MUS. Grave, de basse. ‖ **Bass-viol,** n. MUS. Violoncelle *m.*
— n. MUS. Basse *f.* (part, singer).

basset ['bæsit] n. ZOOL. Basset *m* (dog).
basset n. GEOL. Affleurement *m*. (of stratum).
— v. intr. GEOL. Affleurer.
basset-horn [-hɔːn] n. MUS. Cor de basset *m*.
bassinet [,bæsi'net] n. Bercelonnette *f.*; moïse *m*. ‖ Chariot alsacien *m*. (on wheels).
basso [,bæsou] n. MUS. Basse *f*. (part, singer, voice); *basso profundo,* basse profonde.
bassoon [ba'suːn] n. MUS. Basson *m*.
bassoonist [-ist] n. MUS. Basson, bassoniste *m*.
bast [bæst] n. Tille *f*. (See BASS.)
bastard ['bæstəd] n. Bâtard, enfant naturel *m*. ‖ POP. Salaud, saligaud *m*. ‖ ARG. *That's a bastard,* ça c'est emmerdant !
— adj. Illégitime, bâtard. ‖ TECHN. Bâtard (file, sugar). ‖ FIG. Abâtardi, bâtard (language).
bastardize [-aiz] v. tr. JUR. Déclarer illégitime.
bastardy [-i] n. JUR. Bâtardise *f.*; *bastardy case,* action en désaveu de paternité.
baste [beist] v. tr. Bâtir, faufiler. (See TACK.)
baste v. tr. CULIN. Arroser.
baste v. tr. Bâtonner.
bastille [bæs'tiːl] n. Bastille, forteresse *f*.
bastinado [,bæsti'neidou] n. Bastonnade *f*.
— v. tr. Bâtonner.
bastion ['bæstiən] n. MILIT., FIG. Bastion *m*.
bat [bæt] n. ZOOL. Chauve-souris *f*. ‖ FAM. *To have bats in the belfry,* avoir une araignée au plafond.
bat n. SPORTS. Batte *f*. (in baseball, cricket); palette, raquette *f*. (in table-tennis); batteur *m*. (batsman). ‖ Battoir *m*. (of washerwoman). ‖ U. S. Coup *m*. (blow). ‖ FAM. *He did it off his own bat,* il a pris ça sous son bonnet.
— v. intr. (1). SPORTS. Manier la batte. ‖ FAM. U. S. *To bat around,* disputailler au sujet de (an idea, a plan).
bat v. tr. (1). FAM. U. S. Cligner ; *not to bat an eyelid* (or) U. S. *an eye,* ne pas sourciller (or) broncher.
bat n. FAM. Allure *f ; at a rare bat,* en quatrième vitesse. ‖ U. S. POP. Noce, bringue *f*.
batata [bət'ɑːtə] n. BOT. Patate douce *f*.
Batavian [bə'teiviən] adj., n. GEOGR. Batave *s*.
batch [bætʃ] n. Fournée *f*. (of loaves). ‖ Liasse *f.*; tas *m*. (of letters). ‖ COMM. Lot *m*. (of goods). ‖ FAM. Fournée *f*. (of prisoners).
bate [beit] v. tr. COMM. Rabattre (a shilling). ‖ FIG. Baisser ; *with bated breath,* dans un murmure. ‖ FIG. Abandonner (hope).
— v. intr. Décroître, baisser.
bate n. TECHN. Bain alcalin, confit *m*.
— v. tr. TECHN. Chiper (hides).
bath [bɑːθ] n. Bain *m*. (in a bath-tub). ‖ Baignoire *f.*; tub *m*. (bath-tub). ‖ Pl. Thermes *m. pl.*; *public baths,* établissement de bains *m*. ‖ Ville d'eaux *f*. (spa). ‖ Ordre du Bain *m*. (order). ‖ TECHN., CHIM. Bain *m*. ‖ U. S. *Room with bath,* chambre avec salle de bains. ‖ FIG. Bain *m*. (of blood). ‖ **Bath-attendant** (or) **-keeper,** n. Baigneur *s*. ‖ **Bath-chair,** n. MED. Fauteuil roulant *m*. ‖ **Bath-house,** n. U. S. Establissement de bains *m*. (public baths); cabine (*f*.) de bains (bathing box). ‖ **Bath-mat,** n. Descente (*f*.) de bain. ‖ **Bath-robe,** n. U. S. Baigneuse *f.,* peignoir (*m*.) de bain. ‖ **Bathroom,** n. Salle (*f*.) de bains. ‖ **Bath-tub,** n. Baignoire *f*. ‖ **Bath-wrap,** n. Peignoir (*m*.) de bain.
— v. tr. Baigner, donner un bain à (a child, an invalid).
— v. intr. Se baigner, prendre des bains.
bathe [beið] v. tr. Baigner (*in,* dans) [s.o., sth.]; *to bathe one's arm,* se baigner le bras. ‖ MED. Baigner, bassiner (one's eyes); laver (a wound). ‖ GEOGR. Baigner, arroser. ‖ FIG. Baigner.
— v. intr. Se baigner, prendre un bain (in sea).
— n. Bain *m.*; baignade *f*. (in river, sea).
bather [-ə*] n. Baigneur *s*. (taker of a bath).
bathing [-iŋ] n. Baignades *f. pl.*; *sea bathing,* bains

de mer. ‖ MED. Bassinage *m*. ‖ **Bathing-beauty,** n. Belle baigneuse *f*. ‖ **Bathing-box,** n. Cabine (*f*.) de bains. ‖ **Bathing-cap,** n. Bonnet (*m*.) de bain. ‖ **Bathing-costume** (or) **-suit,** n. Costume (or) maillot (*m*.) de bain. ‖ **Bathing-drawers** (or) **-trunks,** n. Caleçon (*m*.) de bain. ‖ **Bathing-hut,** n. Cabine (*f*.) de bains. ‖ **Bathing-resort,** n. Station balnéaire *f*. ‖ **Bathing-shoes,** n. Baigneuses, espadrilles *f. pl.*
bathometer [bə'θɔmitə*] n. PHYS. Bathymètre *m*.
bathos ['beiθɔs] n. Platitude ; dégringolade *f*. (fam.).
bathyscaphe ['bæθiskæf] n. NAUT. Bathyscaphe *m*.
bathysphere [-sfiːə*] n. NAUT. Bathysphère *f*.
batik ['bætik] n. Batik *m*.
batiste [bæ'tiːst] n. Batiste *f*. (fabric).
batman ['bætmən] (pl. **batmen**) n. MILIT. Ordonnance *f*. (or) *m*.
baton ['bætən] n. Bâton *m*. (of a policeman, marshal). ‖ MUS. Bâton *m*. (of the conductor). ‖ BLAS. Barre *f*.
batrachian [bə'treikiən] n. ZOOL. Batracien *m*.
bats [bæts] adj. FAM. Dingue, cinglé, piqué.
batsman ['bætsmən] (pl. **batsmen**) n. SPORTS. Batteur *m*. (in cricket).
battalion [bə'tæl̩ən] n. MILIT., FIG. Bataillon *m*.
batten ['bætn] n. Planche *f*. (for flooring). ‖ Latte de traverse (or) de claire-voie *f*. ‖ NAUT. Latte ; étrésillon *m*.
— v. tr. Planchéier (a floor). ‖ Latter. ‖ NAUT. *To batten down,* coincer (the hatches).
batten v. intr. S'engraisser (*on,* aux dépens de).
batter ['bætə*] v. tr. Cabosser (a hat); abîmer, défoncer (the furniture); rouer (s.o.). ‖ TECHN. Battre (metal). ‖ MILIT. Battre en brèche. ‖ *To batter about,* maltraiter, rosser. ‖ *To batter down,* démolir, abattre (a wall). ‖ *To batter in,* enfoncer (a door); défoncer (the skull).
— n. CULIN. Pâte (*f*.) à crêpes (or) à frire. ‖ TECHN. Caractère typographique écrasé *m*.
batter n. ARCHIT. Talus *m*. (of an embankment); fruit *m*. (of a wall).
— v. tr. ARCHIT. Taluter (an embankment); donner du fruit à (a wall).
battering [-iŋ] n. Action (*f*.) de battre en brèche. ‖ **Battering-ram,** n. MILIT. Bélier *m*. ‖ **Battering-train,** n. MILIT. Artillerie (*f*.) de siège.
battery ['bætəri] n. MILIT., NAUT. Batterie *f*. ‖ ELECTR. Batterie *f.*; *electric battery,* pile. ‖ JUR. *Assault and battery,* voies de fait. ‖ FIG. *To turn a man's battery against himself,* battre qqn avec ses propres armes.
batting ['bætiŋ] n. Ouate en feuille *f*.
battle ['bætl] n. MILIT. Bataille *f.*; combat *m.*; *killed in battle,* tué à l'ennemi ; *to give battle,* livrer bataille. ‖ MILIT. Victoire *f.*; *soldier's battle,* victoire due à la vaillance des troupes. ‖ **Battle-axe,** n. Hache d'armes *f*. (weapon) ; FAM. Virago *f*. (woman). ‖ **Battle-cruiser,** n. NAUT. Croiseur (*m*.) de bataille. ‖ **Battle-dress,** n. MILIT. Tenue de campagne. ‖ **Battle-field,** n. MILIT. Champ (*m*.) de bataille. ‖ **Battle-piece,** n. Tableau (*m*.) de bataille.
— v. intr. Lutter (*against,* contre ; *with,* avec). ‖ FIG. Lutter, batailler.
battledore [-dɔː*] n. Battoir *m*. (of washerwoman). ‖ Pelle (*f*.) à enfourner (in baking). ‖ SPORTS. Raquette *f*. (bat); *battledore and shuttlecock,* jeu de volant.
battlement [-mənt] n. ARCHIT. Créneau *m.*; pl. remparts *m. pl.*; *battlemented,* crénelé.
battleship [-ʃip] n. NAUT. Cuirassé *m.*; *pocket battleship,* cuirassé de poche.
battlewagon [-wægən] n. U. S. FAM. Cuirassé *m*.
battleworthy ['bætl'wəːði] adj. MILIT. Fort, en état de se battre.

battue [bæ'tju:] n. Sports. Battue *f.* ‖ Fam. Hécatombe *f.*

batty ['bæti] adj. Fam. Cinglé, toqué, timbré. (See
CRACKED.)

bauble ['bɔ:bl̩] n. Marotte *f.* (of a jester). ‖ Fig.
Babiole *f.*

baulk [bɔ:k]. See BALK.

bauxite ['bɔ:ksait] n. Bauxite *f.*

Bavarian [bə'vɛəriən] adj., n. Geogr. Bavarois *s.*
‖ Culin. *Bavarian cream,* bavaroise.

bawbee [bɔ:'bi:] n. Demi-penny, sou *m.* (in Scotland).

bawd [bɔ:d] n. Proxénète *s.; entremetteuse *f.* ‖
Poissarde *f.*

bawdy [-i] adj. Obscène, ordurier, de poissarde
(talk). ‖ **Bawdy-house,** n. Maison close *f.*

bawl [bɔ:l] v. intr. Brailler (*at,* contre). ‖ Clabauder
(dog). ‖ Fam. U. S. Bramer (to weep).
— v. tr. Brailler, beugler, hurler (an order, a song).
‖ Fam. U. S. *To bawl s.o. out,* engueuler qqn.

bay [bei] n. Bot. Laurier *m.; bay rum,* eau de toilette au laurier. ‖ Culin. *Bay leaf,* feuille de laurier. ‖ Fig. Pl. Honneurs, lauriers *m. pl.; gloire *f.*

bay n. Geogr. Baie, anse *f.; golfe *m.* ‖ **Bay-salt,**
n. Culin. Sel gris *m.*

bay n. Architt. Culée *f.* (of a bridge); travée *f.* (of
a roof); baie *f.* (window). ‖ **Bay-window,** n. Baie *f.;*
fenêtre en saillie *f.;* U. S. Pop. Brioche *f.* (paunch).

bay n. Aboiement, aboi *m.* (of dogs). ‖ Fig. Abois
m. pl.; to be at bay, être aux abois; *to bring to bay,*
acculer; *to keep at bay,* tenir en échec.
— v. intr. Aboyer [*at,* à, après].
— v. tr. Aboyer à.

bay adj. Bai (horse).

bayadere [bejə'di:ə*] n. Bayadère *f.* (dancing girl,
fabric).

bayonet ['beiənit] n. Milit. Baïonnette *f.; fixed
bayonet,* baïonnette au canon. ‖ Milit. Pl. Infanterie *f.*
— v. tr. Milit. Passer à la baïonnette.

bazaar [bə'zɑ:*] n. Bazar *m.* (market, shop). ‖
Vente de charité *f.*

bazooka [bə'zu:kə] n. Milit. Bazooka *m.*

B.B.C. [bi:bi:si:] abbr. *British Broadcasting Corporation,* B. B. C.

B.C. [bi:si:] abbr. *Before Christ,* av. J.-C., avant
Jésus-Christ.

be [bi:] v. intr. (8). Etre, exister; *as things are,*
dans l'état actuel des choses; *for the time being,*
pour l'instant; *that may be,* cela se peut, peut-être
bien. ‖ Aller, se porter; *how are you?,* comment
allez-vous? ‖ Aller, venir, arriver; *have you been
to London?,* êtes-vous allé à Londres?; *has anyone
been?,* est-ce que quelqu'un est venu?; *we shall be
too late,* nous arriverons trop tard. ‖ Advenir; *woe
is me!,* malheur à moi! ‖ Avoir; *there will be only
one fire in the house,* il n'y aura qu'un feu à la
maison. ‖ Se produire; *it may well be that,* il peut
se faire que; *when will the ceremony be?,* à quel
moment aura lieu la cérémonie? ‖ Se trouver, être
placé; *here is Mr. Smith,* voici M. Smith; *there
are your shoes,* voilà vos souliers; *near the town
hall is the church,* près de la mairie se trouve
l'église. ‖ Rester; *will she be here long?,* restera-
t-elle longtemps? ‖ **To be at,** être occupé à; *they're
always at it,* ils ne font que ça. ‖ **To be for,** être
partisan de; *I am for the reform,* je suis pour la
réforme. ‖ **To be to,** avoir l'intention de, devoir;
être destiné à; *I am to tell you,* je dois vous dire;
I am to write, il faut que j'écrive; *he was to die a
week later,* il devait mourir une semaine après. ‖
To be to, venir à; *if the fire were to go out,* si le
feu venait à s'éteindre. ‖ **To be upon,** s'occuper
de; avoir en vue.
— v. copul. Etre; *are you happy?, I am,* êtes-vous
heureux?, oui; *he is a fool!, so he is,* c'est un imbé-

cile!, oui certes; *she is ill. Is she?,* elle est malade.
Vraiment?; *you are happy, aren't you?,* vous êtes
heureux, n'est-ce pas? (or) non? (fam.). ‖ Avoir;
to be afraid, cold, hungry, sleepy, wrong, avoir
peur, froid, faim, sommeil, tort; *to be sixty,* avoir
soixante ans. ‖ Appartenir; *it's mine,* c'est à moi,
c'est mon bien, cela m'appartient. ‖ Comm. Valoir;
to be ten pounds, valoir dix livres, être à dix livres.
‖ Math. Faire; *twice three is six,* deux fois trois
font six.
— v. aux. Etre; *I am told that,* on me dit que;
to be killed, être tué. ‖ Etre en train de; *the church
is being built,* on est en train de construire l'église,
l'église est en construction. ‖ Mettre, passer; *to be
two hours in writing a chapter,* mettre deux heures
à écrire un chapitre.
— v. impers. Etre; *as it were,* pour ainsi dire; *had
it not been for,* n'eût été, sans, mis à part; *it is
said that,* on dit que; *it was winter,* c'était l'hiver;
let it be so, soit; *so be it,* ainsi soit-il; *were it not
that,* si ce n'était que. ‖ Avoir; *it is four miles to,*
il y a quatre milles jusqu'à; *it is a month since,*
il y a un mois que. ‖ Faire; *it is cold,* il fait froid.

beach [bi:tʃ] n. Grève, plage *f.; beach umbrella,*
parasol. ‖ Galets *m. pl.* (pebbles). ‖ **Beach-comber,**
n. Vague déferlante *f.; Fig. Propre à rien *m.* ‖
Beach-head, n. Milit. Tête (*f.*) de pont. ‖ **Beach-
mariner,** n. Fam. Marin (*m.*) d'eau douce.
— v. tr. Naut. Echouer (a ship).

beacon ['bi:kən] n. Signal lumineux; fanal *m.* ‖
Naut. Balise *f.* ‖ Aviat. Phare *m.; aerial beacon,*
aérophare. ‖ Fig. Flambeau *m.*
— v. tr. Naut., Aviat. Baliser. ‖ Fig. Guider,
éclairer.

bead [bi:d] n. Grain *m.;* perle *f.; string of beads,*
collier. ‖ Goutte *f.* (of sweat); *to stand out in
beads,* perler (sweat); *to tell
(or) U. S. to say one's beads,* dire son chapelet. ‖
Autom. Bourrelet *m.* (of a tyre). ‖ Milit. Mire *f.;*
guidon *m.* ‖ Architt. Moulure, baguette *f.*
— v. tr. Enfiler. ‖ Emperler.
— v. intr. Perler.

beading ['bi:diŋ] n. Ornement (*m.*) de perles. ‖
Architt. Moulure, baguette *f.*

beadle ['bi:dl̩] n. Jur. Huissier, appariteur *m.* ‖
Eccles. Bedeau *m.*

beadledom [-dɔm] n. Bureaucratie *f.*

beady ['bi:di] adj. En vrille (eye). ‖ Emperlé
(liquid).

beagle ['bi:gl̩] n. Zool. Bigle, briquet *m.* (dog).

beak [bi:k] n. Zool. Bec *m.* (of birds, turtles). ‖
Bec (of a pitcher). ‖ Naut. Eperon *m.* ‖ Techn.
Bigorne *f.* (of anvil). ‖ Fam. Nez crochu *m.* ‖ Pop.
Chat fourré *m.* (magistrate).

beaker [-ə*] n. Coupe *f.* ‖ Chim. Vase à bec *m.*

beam [bi:m] n. Rayon *m.* (of light); faisceau *m.*
(of searchlight). ‖ Architt. Poutre *f.* ‖ Agric. Timon
m. (of a carriage, plough). ‖ Techn. Balancier *m.*
(of engine); rouleau *m.* (of a loom); fléau *m.* (of
scales). ‖ Electr. *Electron beam,* faisceau électronique. ‖ Naut. Bau *m.* (of anchor); *on the beam,*
par le travers. ‖ Radio. *Beam navigation,* navigation radiogoniométrique. ‖ Autom. U. S. *High
beams,* éclairage route; *low beams,* feux de croisement. ‖ Fig. Rayonnement; sourire lumineux *m.* ‖
Fam. *To be off the beam,* dérailler. ‖ **Beam-ends,**
n. pl. Naut. *To be on her beam-ends,* être engagé;
Fam. *To be on one's beam-ends,* être à la côte.
— v. intr. Briller, rayonner. ‖ Avoir un sourire
rayonnant.
— v. tr. Emettre (light, warmth); darder (rays). ‖
Radio. Emettre; *beamed in,* dirigé vers (broadcasting). ‖ Fig. Rayonner de (delight).

beamy [-i] adj. Naut. Large. ‖ Techn. Massif.

bean [bi:n] n. Bot. Haricot *m.; fève *f.; French* (or)
U. S. *string beans,* haricots verts; *kidney beans,*
haricots blancs, flageolets. ‖ Bot. Grain *m.* (of

coffee). ‖ FAM. *To be full of beans*, péter du feu ; *to be without a bean*, n'avoir pas un radis ; *to give s.o. beans*, flanquer un poil à qqn ; *to spill the beans*, vendre la mèche ; manger le morceau ; *not to be worth a bean*, ne pas valoir les quatre fers d'un chien. ‖ **Bean-feast**, n. FAM. Gueuleton *m*. ‖ **Bean-king**, n. Roi *m*. (on Twelfth-Night).

bear [bɛə*] n. ZOOL. Ours *m.; bear's cub* (or) *whelp*, ourson ; *she-bear*, ourse. ‖ ASTRON. *Great, Little Bear*, Grande, Petite Ourse. ‖ FIN. Baissier *m*. ‖ FAM. Ours *m*. (person) ; *like a bear with a sore head*, d'une humeur de dogue ; *to be a bear for punishment*, savoir encaisser. ‖ **Bear-baiting**, n. Combat (*m*.) d'ours et de chiens. ‖ **Bear-garden**, n. FAM. Foire *f*. (noisy place). ‖ **Bear-leader**, n. Montreur (*m*.) d'ours ; FAM. Cornac *m*.
— v. intr. FIN. Spéculer à la baisse.
— v. tr. FIN. Faire baisser.

bear v. tr. (9). Porter (a name, title, weight) ; *to bear company*, tenir compagnie. ‖ Conserver ; *to bear in mind*, garder en mémoire. ‖ Présenter, offrir (an analogy, aspect, expression, a meaning, relation) ; *to bear reference to*, se rapporter à. ‖ Eprouver, ressentir (hatred, love) ; *to bear a grudge against*, en vouloir à, garder rancune à. ‖ Jouer (a part) ; exercer (power) ; jouir de (reputation). ‖ Supporter, souffrir, endurer, tolérer ; *I can't bear him*, je ne peux pas le souffrir ; *to bear comparison*, soutenir la comparaison ; *to bear inspection*, supporter l'examen ; *to bear quotation*, mériter d'être cité ; *to bear oneself*, se comporter, agir. ‖ MED. Porter, enfanter (a child) ; *born of*, *borne by*, né de ; *she bore him six children*, elle lui a donné six enfants ; *she was born in 1900*, elle est née en 1900. ‖ BOT. Porter, produire (fruit). ‖ FIN. Supporter, payer (the charges) ; porter, rapporter (interest) ; atteindre (a price). ‖ JUR. Porter, être revêtu de (a signature) ; *to bear witness*, porter témoignage. ‖ MILIT. Porter (arms). ‖ **To bear away** (or) **off**, emmener (s.o.) ; emporter, transporter (sth.) ; FIG. Remporter (a prize). ‖ **To bear down**, accabler, rabaisser, renverser, vaincre (an enemy, opposition). ‖ **To bear out**, emporter, enlever (s.o., sth.) ; appuyer, confirmer (a statement) ; *to bear s.o. out*, soutenir qqn. ‖ **To bear up**, soutenir, soulever (s.o., sth.).
— v. intr. Souffrir ; endurer avec patience. (See ENDURE, SUFFER.) ‖ Avoir la force de soutenir ; être assez solide. ‖ Porter, appuyer, reposer (*on*, sur). ‖ Avoir de la patience (*with*, pour) ; *to bear with s.o.*, supporter qqn, se montrer patient envers qqn. ‖ Se diriger (*to*, vers) ; *to bear to the left*, appuyer à gauche. ‖ Porter, faire de l'effet (argument, idea) ; *to bring to bear*, mettre en action. ‖ Agir (*upon*, sur) ; porter (*on*, sur) ; se rapporter, avoir trait (*on*, à) ; *to bring one's mind to bear on*, porter son attention sur. ‖ NAUT. Laisser, porter ; *bearing north*, gisant au nord. ‖ BOT. Produire, donner (tree). ‖ **To bear away**, NAUT. Laisser porter. ‖ **To bear down**, se précipiter ; courir, foncer (*on*, *upon*, sur). ‖ **To bear in**, s'implanter ; *it was borne in upon him that*, l'idée lui était venue que ; NAUT. *To bear in with*, se diriger vers. ‖ **To bear off**, NAUT. Prendre le large. ‖ **To bear up**, NAUT. Laisser porter (*for*, sur) ; FIG. Tenir bon, avoir du ressort, se montrer courageux ; *to bear up against*, tenir tête à, réagir contre.

beard [bi:əd] n. Barbe *f.; to wear a full beard*, porter toute sa barbe. ‖ BOT. Barbe, arête *f*. ‖ ZOOL. Barbe *f*. (of goat). ‖ TECHN. Barbe *f*. (of hook, paper). ‖ FAM. *The beard won't pay for the shaving*, le jeu n'en vaut pas la chandelle.
— v. tr. Tirer par la barbe. ‖ FIG. Défier, braver, narguer.

bearded [-id] adj. Barbu (animal, man). ‖ Barbelé (arrow). ‖ BOT. Aristé (wheat).

bearer ['bɛərə*] n. Porteur *s*. (of coffin, letters,

weight). ‖ FIN. Porteur *m*. (of cheque) ; titulaire *m*. (of passport). ‖ TECHN. Support *m*. ‖ BOT. Arbre (*m*.) [or] plante (*f*.) de bon rapport. ‖ **Bearer-bond**, n. FIN. Titre au porteur *m*. ‖ **Bearer-cheque**, n. FIN. Chèque au porteur *m*.

bearing [-iŋ] n. Port, transport *m*. (of a weight). ‖ Port *m.; allure f*. (see CARRIAGE) ; comportement *m*. (see DEPORTMENT). ‖ Portée *f*. (of an argument, a question) ; aspect, angle *m*., face *f*. (of a question). ‖ Rapport *m.; relation f*. (*on*, avec). ‖ Endurance, patience *f.; beyond all bearing*, intolérable. ‖ ARCHIT. Appui *m.; portée f*. ‖ TECHN., AGRIC. Rapport *m.; production f*. ‖ MED. Enfantement *m*. (of a child). ‖ BLAS. Pièce honorable *f.; pl*. armoiries *f. pl*. ‖ RADIO. *Radio bearing station*, phare radiogoniométrique. ‖ NAUT. Relèvement *m.; position f.; to take the ship's bearings*, faire le point. ‖ FAM. *To lose one's bearings*, s'égarer, perdre la boussole ; *to take one's bearings*, se repérer.

bearskin ['bɛə:skin] n. Peau (*f*.) d'ours. ‖ MILIT. Bonnet à poil *m*.

beast [bi:st] n. ZOOL. Bête *f*. ‖ AGRIC. Pl. Bétail *m*. ‖ FIG. Brute *f*. ‖ FAM. Abruti *m.; brute, vache f.; chameau m*.

beastliness [-linis] n. Bestialité *f*. (act, quality). ‖ Obscénité *f*. ‖ FAM. Saloperie, cochonnerie *f*. (food).

beastly [-li] adj. Brutal, bestial. ‖ FIG. Dégoûtant, répugnant. ‖ FAM. Infect, abominable, ignoble ; *beastly weather*, temps à ne pas mettre un chien dehors, sale temps.
— adv. FAM. Bigrement, bougrement.

beat [bi:t] v. tr. (10). Battre, frapper, rosser ; *to beat black and blue*, battre comme plâtre. ‖ Battre (a carpet) ; marteler (a nail) ; *to beat a nail into*, enfoncer un clou dans. ‖ Battre (the bushes, the countryside, the woods) ; battre, fouler (the ground). ‖ Battre, vaincre (to defeat) ; *to beat at every point*, battre sur toute la ligne. ‖ TECHN. Battre (gold). ‖ ZOOL. *To beat its wings*, battre des ailes. ‖ MILIT. *To beat a retreat*, battre en retraite. ‖ MUS. *To beat a drum, time*, battre du tambour, la mesure. ‖ CULIN. Battre, fouetter (eggs) ; battre (meat). ‖ FAM. *That beats it!*, c'est le bouquet ! ça enfonce tout ! ; il ne manquait plus que ça ! ; *that beats cockfighting*, c'est plus fort que de jouer au bouchon ; *that beats me*, ça me renverse ; *to beat it*, ficher le camp. ‖ **To beat back**, MILIT. Repousser, faire battre en retraite. ‖ **To beat down**, frapper, tomber (upon, sur) ; abattre, rabattre ; AGRIC. Coucher (the corn) ; FIN. Faire baisser (a price) ; faire baisser ses prix (s.o.) ; FIG. Abattre, déprimer. ‖ **To beat in**, enfoncer, défoncer (a door). ‖ **To beat off**, repousser ; SPORTS. Distancer. ‖ **To beat out**, frayer, ouvrir, tracer (path) ; TECHN. Etaler, marteler, battre (gold, iron) ; MUS. Marquer (rhythm). ‖ **To beat up**, CULIN. Battre, fouetter (cream, eggs) ; FAM. Tabasser (s.o.) ; *to beat it up*, faire la bringue (to booze).
— v. intr. Taper, cogner, frapper (at the door). ‖ Battre (against, contre) [rain, waves]. ‖ MED. Battre (heart, pulse) ; *to beat wildy*, battre la chamade. ‖ MUS. Battre (drum). ‖ SPORTS. Faire une battue (for game). ‖ **To beat about**, NAUT. Louvoyer ; FAM. *To beat about the bush*, tourner autour du pot.
— adj. FAM. Crevé, claqué, éreinté.
— n. Secteur *m.; ronde f*. (of a policeman). ‖ MED. Battement *m.; pulsation f*. ‖ MUS. Temps *m.; battement (m.)* de la mesure ; batterie *f*. (of drum). ‖ PHYS., ELECTR., RADIO. Battement *m*. ‖ SPORTS. Battue *f*. ‖ FAM. *That's off my beat*, ce n'est pas de mon rayon. ‖ U. S. Primeur d'une nouvelle sensationnelle *f*. (See SCOOP.)

beaten [-n] adj. Battu (earth) ; *beaten track*, sentier battu. ‖ MILIT. Battu, vaincu. ‖ TECHN. Battu, martelé (gold, iron). ‖ FIG. Rebattu ; *to be off the* *beaten track*, sortir de l'ordinaire. ‖ Fam. Ereinté, esquinté.

beater [-ə*] n. Techn. Battoir, batteur ; pilon *m.* ‖ Sports. Rabatteur *m.* (in shooting).

beatific [biə'tifik] adj. Béatifique.

beatification [bi,ætifi'kei ʃ ən] n. Eccles. Béatification *f.*

beatify [bi'ætifai] v. tr. Eccles. Béatifier.

beating ['bi:tiŋ] n. Battement *m.* (of wings). ‖ Med. Battement *m.* ‖ Sports. Rabattage *m.* (of game). ‖ Naut. Louvoyage *m.* ‖ Fam. Pile *f.* (defeat) ; tournée, dégelée (thrashing).

beatitude [bi'ætitju:d] n. Béatitude *f.*

beatnik ['bi:tnik] n. Beatnik *m.*

beau [bou] (pl. **beaus, beaux**) n. Dandy ; bellâtre *m.; old beau*, vieux beau. ‖ Amoureux, soupirant *m.* (sweetheart).
— adj. *Beau geste*, beau geste ; *beau ideal*, beauté idéale ; *beau monde*, beau monde, gens à la mode.

Beaufort scale ['boufət'skeil] n. Naut. Échelle (*f.*) de Beaufort.

beauteous ['bju:tiəs] adj. Beau. (See beautiful.)

beautician [bju:'ti ʃ ən] n. U. S. Esthéticienne *f.*

beautifier ['bju:tifaiə*] n. Embellisseur *m.*

beautiful [-ful] adj. Beau, belle ; splendide (person, thing). ‖ Fam. Beau, remarquable, admirable (organisation, quality).
— n. Beau *m.*

beautify [-fai] v. tr. Embellir.

beauty ['bju:ti] n. Beauté *f.; beauty cream, preparations, treatment*, crème, produits, soins de beauté ; *beauty parlour* (or) *shop*, institut de beauté ; *beauty sleep*, sommeil d'avant minuit ; *beauty specialist*, esthéticienne. ‖ Beauté *f.* (person) ; *she is a beauty*, c'est une beauté. ‖ Fam. Joli côté *m.; that's a beauty!*, ça c'est un poème! ; *that's the beauty of it*, voilà le beau de l'affaire. ‖ **Beauty-spot**, n. Grain (*m.*) de beauté (mole) ; mouche *f.* (patch).

beaver ['bi:və*] n. Zool., Comm. Castor *m.*

beaver n. † Visière *f.* (of a helmet).

be-bop ['bi:bɔp] n. Mus. Be-bop.

becalm [bi'kɑ:m] v. tr. Calmer. ‖ Naut. Déventer.

because [bi'kɔz] conj. Parce que (in general). ‖ Que (after a comparative) ; *the more powerful because*, d'autant plus puissant que. ‖ *Because of*, à cause de, en raison de, de par.

beccafico [,bekə'fi:kou] n. Zool. Becfigue *m.*

bechamel ['be ʃ əmel] n. Culin. Béchamel *f.*

bêche-de-mer [,be ʃ də'mer] n. Zool., Gramm. Bêche-de-mer *f.*

beck [bek] n. Petit ruisseau *m.*

beck n. Signe, appel *m.* ‖ Fam. *To be at s.o.'s beck and call*, être aux ordres (or) à la dévotion de qqn, obéir à qqn au doigt et à l'œil.
— v. intr. Faire un signe.
— v. tr. Appeler d'un signe de tête.

becket ['bekit] n. Naut. Garcette, patte *f.*

beckon ['bekən] v. intr. Faire signe (*to*, à).
— v. tr. Faire signe à ; *to beckon s.o. out*, faire signe à qqn de sortir.

becloud [bi'kloud] v. tr. Ennuager, assombrir.

become [bi'kʌm] v. intr. (11). Devenir ; *to become old, red, visible, rougir* ; *to become obstructed*, se boucher. ‖ Se faire ; *to become a soldier*, se faire soldat ; *to become inured to fatigue*, se faire à la fatigue. ‖ Commencer à ; *to become anxious, known*, commencer à s'inquiéter, à être connu. ‖ *To become of*, advenir de ; devenir. (See happen.)
— v. tr. Aller bien à ; seoir †. (See suit.) ‖ Fig. Convenir à.

becoming [-iŋ] adj. Seyant, qui va bien (blouse, hat). ‖ Fig. Bienséant, convenable (*to*, pour) ; approprié (*to*, à) ; digne (*of*, de).
— n. Philos. Devenir *m.*

becomingly [-iŋli] adv. Elégamment. ‖ Fig. Convenablement.

bed [bed] n. Lit *m.; couche f.; double bed*, lit à deux places ; *in bed*, au lit ; *to get into bed*, se mettre au lit ; *to go to bed*, se coucher, aller au lit ; *to make one's bed*, faire son lit ; *to put to bed*, mettre au lit, coucher ; *to turn down the bed*, faire la couverture. ‖ Matelas *m.; air bed*, matelas pneumatique. ‖ Assiette *f.* (of roads) ; lit *m.* (of a river). ‖ Lit *m.; couche f.* (of dust, sand, stones). ‖ Logement *m.; bed and board*, logement et nourriture, gîte et couvert. ‖ Med. *To be brought to bed*, accoucher (*of*, de) ; *to keep to one's bed*, garder le lit ; *to take to one's bed*, s'aliter. ‖ Geol. Couche *f.* (of clay) ; gisement *m.* (of ore). ‖ Agric. Plate-bande *f.; parterre m.* (for flowers) ; *hot bed*, couche de fumier. ‖ Archit. Assises *f. pl.* (of a building) ; bain *m.* (of mortar). ‖ Techn. Sommier *m.* (of an engine) ; banc *m.* (of lathe). ‖ Milit., Aviat. Berceau *m.* ‖ Naut. Souille *f.; carré m.* ‖ Jur. Lit *m.; child of the second bed*, enfant du second lit ; *divorce from bed and board*, séparation de corps et de biens. ‖ Fam. *To get out of bed on the wrong side*, se lever du pied gauche (ou) de mauvais poil. ‖ **Bed-boards**, n. Châlit *m.* ‖ **Bed-bug**, n. Zool. Punaise *f.* ‖ **Bed-cover**, n. Dessus-de-lit *m.* ‖ **Bed-frame**, n. Bois de lit *m.* ‖ **Bed-head**, n. Chevet *m.* ‖ **Bed-jacket**, n. Liseuse *f.* ‖ **Bed-pan**, n. Med. Bassin *m.* ‖ **Bed-plate**, n. Techn. Plaque d'assise *f.* ‖ **Bed-post**, n. Colonne (*f.*) de lit. ‖ **Bed-rock**, n. Geol. Soubassement rocheux *m.;* Fig. Base *f.;* fondement *m.;* adj. dernier, ultime, le plus bas (price) ; adv. Fig. au fond des choses. ‖ **Bed-settee**, n. Canapé-lit *m.* ‖ **Bed-sitting-room**, n. Studio *m.;* salle (*f.*) de séjour. ‖ **Bed-spread**, n. Couvre-lit *m.* ‖ **Bed-vein**, n. Geol. Filon *m.* ‖ **Bed-warmer**, n. Chauffe-lit *m.* ‖ **Bed-wetting**, adj. Med. Incontinent, qui mouille son lit ; n. Med. incontinence nocturne *f.*
— v. tr. (1). Coucher (*with*, avec). ‖ Disposer en couche. ‖ Agric. Planter, repiquer (in bed of earth) ; disposer en plate-bande (earth). ‖ Archit. Asseoir (foundations). ‖ Fam. Enfoncer.
— v. intr. Se coucher. ‖ Geol. Former couche. ‖ Archit. S'asseoir (foundations). ‖ Fam. S'enfoncer.

B. Ed. [bi:'ed] abbr. *Bachelor of Education*, diplôme de sciences de l'éducation (degree) ; diplômé en sciences de l'éducation (graduate).

bedaub [bi'dɔ:b] v. tr. Barbouiller. ‖ Enjoliver, chamarrer.

bedchamber ['bed,t ʃ eimbə*] n. Chambre *f.* (of the king).

bedclothes [-klou ð s] n. pl. Draps (*m. pl.*) et couvertures (*f. pl.*).

bedding [-iŋ] n. Literie f. ‖ Agric. Massif m. (for flowers) ; litière *f.* (for horses). ‖ Geol. Stratification *f.* ‖ Archit. Assiette *f.*
— adj. Agric. A repiquer (plant).

bedeck [bi'dek] v. tr. Orner (*with*, de).

bedevil [bi'devl] v. tr. (1). Agacer, harceler, endiabler (to harass) ; tourmenter, violenter (to torment). ‖ Posséder, envoûter (to bewitch). ‖ Abîmer ; gâter (to spoil). ‖ Fam. Vouer au diable.

bedevilment [-mənt] n. Possession *f.;* envoûtement, ensorcellement *m.* ‖ Désordre *m.;* confusion *f.*

bedew [bi'dju:] v. tr. Humecter (*with*, de).

bedfellow ['bed,felou] n. Compagnon de lit *m.*

bedgown [bi'gaun] n. Robe (ou) chemise de nuit *f.*

bedight [bi'dait] adj. Orné (*with*, de).

bedim [bi'dim] v. tr. (1). Obscurcir, voiler.

bedizen [bi'daizn] v. tr. Affubler, attifer.

Bedlam ['bedləm] n. Med. Sainte-Anne *f.;* Charenton *m.;* maison (*f.*) de fous. ‖ Chahut, tohu-bohu *m.*

bedlamite [-ait] n. Fam. Echappé (*s.*) de Sainte-Anne (or) de Charenton.

bedmate ['bedmeit] n. Compagnon de lit *m.*

bedraggle [bi'drægl] v. tr. Crotter, tacher de boue.

bedridden ['bed,ridṇ] adj. MED. Cloué au lit, alité.

bedroom ['bedrum] n. Chambre (f.) à coucher. ‖ THEATR. *Bedroom farce*, vaudeville.

bedside [-said] n. Chevet m.
— adj. De chevet (table). ‖ MED. *Bedside manner*, comportement au chevet d'un malade.

bedsore [-sɔ:*] n. MED. Escarre f.

bedspring [-spriŋ] n. Sommier m.

bedstead [-stid] n. Châlit, bois de lit ; lit m.

bedtick [-tik] n. Toile (f.) à matelas. ‖ U. S Punaise f.

bedtime [-taim] n. Heure (f.) de se coucher.
— adj. *Bedtime stories*, contes de nourrice.

bed(o)uin ['beduin] adj., n. Bédouin adj., s.

bee [bi:] n. ZOOL. Abeille f ; *bumble bee*, bourdon ; *working bee*, ouvrière. ‖ U. S. Réunion active. f. ; *spelling bee*, concours d'orthographe. ‖ FAM. *To have a bee in one's bonnet*, avoir une marotte. ‖ **Bee-bread**, n. Pollen m. ‖ **Bee-eater**, n. ZOOL. Guêpier m. ‖ **Bee-keeper** (or) **master**, n. AGRIC. Apiculteur m. ‖ **Bee-keeping**, n. AGRIC. Apiculture f. ‖ **Bee-line**, n. Ligne (f.) à vol d'oiseau ; *to make a bee-line for*, se diriger tout droit vers. ‖ **Bee-skep**, n. Ruche en paille f.

beech Lbi:tʃ] n. BOT. Hêtre m. ‖ **Beech-nut**, n. BOT. Faine f.

beechen [-ṇ] adj. De hêtre.

beechmast [-mɑ:st] n. Faines f. pl.

beef [bi:f] n. CULIN. Bœuf m ; *bully beef*, singe (fam.) ; *corned beef*, bœuf en conserve. ‖ U. S. Bœuf de boucherie m. ; *beef cuts*, parties du bœuf. ‖ FAM. Muscle m. ; viande f. ‖ **Beef-tea**, n. CULIN. Consommé m.
— N. B. Au sens de viande, *beef* est invariable ; au sens de bœuf gras, il fait *beeves* au pl.
— v. intr. U. S. POP. Râler (to protest).

beefeater [-i:tə*] n. MILIT. Hallebardier m. ‖ U. S. Costaud, rougeaud m.

beefsteak [-steik] n. CULIN. Bifteck m.

beefy [-i] adj. FAM. Rougeaud (cheek) ; costaud, râblé (person).

beehive ['bi:haiv] n. Ruche f. (lit. and fig.).

been [bi:n]. See BE.

beer [biə*] n. Bière f. (ale) ; *ginger beer*, limonade au gingembre. ‖ FAM. *Beer and skittles*, tout rose ; *to think no small beer of oneself*, ne pas se prendre pour de la petite bière. ‖ **Beer-engine**, n. Pompe à bière f. ‖ **Beer-glass**, n. Bock m. ; chope f. ‖ **Beer-house**, n. Brasserie f.

beery [-ri] adj. Qui sent la bière. ‖ FAM. Gris, parti, paf (tipsy).

beeswing ['bi:zwiŋ] n. Dépôt du vin, tanin déposé m.

beet [bi:t] n. BOT. Betterave f. ‖ **Beet-grower** (or) -**worker**, n. Betteravier m.
— adj. Betteravier (industry) ; de betterave (sugar).

beetle ['bi:tḷ] n. Maillet m. ; masse f. ‖ Battoir (in laundering). ‖ TECHN. Hie f. (for paving) ; mouton m. (for pile-driving). ‖ CULIN. Pilon m. ‖ **Beetle-brain**, n. Tête (f.) de bois.
— v. tr. Enfoncer, marteler au maillet. ‖ FIG. Ecraser.

beetle n. ZOOL. Scarabée, escarbot m. ; *black beetle*, cafard ; *Colorado beetle*, doryphore. ‖ **Beetle-crusher**, n. FAM. Godasse f. ; bateau m. (boots).

beetle adj. Proéminent. ‖ **Beetle-browed**, adj. Aux sourcils broussailleux ; FAM. Sourcilleux, peu plaisant.
— v. intr. Etre proéminent (to project). ‖ Surplomber (to overhang). ‖ FIG. Menacer (crag).

beetroot [bi:tru:t] n. BOT. Betterave f.

beeves [bi:vz]. See BEEF.

befall [bi'fɔ:l] v. intr. (12). Arriver, advenir, survenir. (See HAPPEN.)
— v. tr. Arriver à, échoir à.

befit [bi'fit] v. tr. (1). Convenir à ; être digne de.

befitting [-iŋ] adj. Convenable, séant.

befog [bi'fɔg] v. tr. (1). Envelopper de brouillard. ‖ FIG. Embrumer.

befool [bi'fu:l] v. tr. Duper.

before [bi'fɔ:*] adv. En avant, en tête, devant, par-devant (in front of) ; *from befcre*, de devant. ‖ Avant, auparavant, précédemment (previously) ; *the day before*, le jour précédent, la veille ; *she had never seen him before*, elle ne l'avait encore jamais vu ; *you should have told me so before*, vous auriez dû me le dire plus tôt. ‖ Déjà (earlier) ; *a film he had seen before*, un film qu'il avait déjà vu.
— prep. Devant (the church). ‖ Devant, en présence de (s.o.) ; *to have before one*, avoir sous les yeux. ‖ Devant ; *the work I have before me*, le travail qui m'attend. ‖ En avance sur ; *two hours before the time*, deux heures d'avance. ‖ Avant ; *before long*, avant peu ; *the day before yesterday*, avant-hier. ‖ Avant de ; *before speaking*, avant de parler. ‖ De préférence à ; *to take a book before another*, prendre un livre plutôt qu'un autre. ‖ JUR. Par-devant (a judge, a notary).
— conj. Avant que ; *it was not long before he came*, il ne tarda pas à venir. ‖ Plutôt que de ; *he would die before he yielded*, il aimerait mieux mourir que céder.

beforehand [-hænd] adv. D'avance ; au préalable ; *to be beforehand with*, devancer, prévenir ; *to pay beforehand*, payer d'avance.

befoul [bi'faul] v. tr. Souiller, polluer. ‖ FIG. Salir.

befriend [bi'frend] v. tr. Traiter en ami, agir en ami avec ; aider.

befuddle [bi'fʌdl] v. tr. Embrouiller, emberlificoter (to confuse) ; émécher (to make drunk).

beg [beg] v. tr. (1). Mendier (of, à, auprès de) ; *to beg one's way to Rome*, mendier pour aller à Rome, aller à Rome en mendiant. ‖ Solliciter (of, de) [favour, help] ; demander (leave, pardon) ; *I beg to differ*, permettez-moi d'être d'un autre avis. ‖ Prier, supplier (to, de) [to entreat]. ‖ PHILOS. *Begging the question*, pétition de principe ; *to beg the question*, faire une pétition de principe. ‖ *To beg off*, solliciter la grâce de (s.o.).
— v. intr. Mendier, demander l'aumône (of, à). ‖ *To beg for*, demander, solliciter (sth.). ‖ *To beg of*, prier, supplier (to, de) [s.o.]. ‖ *To beg off*, demander à être dispensé (for, de). ‖ *To beg to*, avoir l'honneur de. ‖ FIG. *To go begging*, rester pour compte.

begad! [bi'gæd] interj. Parbleu !, sacrebleu !

began [bi'gæn]. See BEGIN.

beget [bi'get] v. tr. (13). MED. Engendrer, procréer. ‖ ECCLES. *The Only Begotten of the Father*, le Fils Unique du Père. ‖ FIG. Engendrer, susciter, produire, faire naître.

begetter [-ə*] n. Père ; auteur m. (fam.). ‖ FIG. Cause originelle f.

beggar ['begə*] n. Mendiant m. (lit. and fig.). ‖ Indigent, pauvre m. (poor). ‖ FAM. Coquin, fripon, gueux m. ; *beggar on horseback*, va-nu-pieds enrichi ; *beggar's opera*, opéra de quatre sous ; *beggars can't be choosers*, ne choisit pas qui emprunte. ‖ **Beggar-my-neighbour**, n. Bataille f. (game).
— v. tr. Réduire à la mendicité. ‖ Appauvrir. ‖ FIG. Ruiner, dépasser les moyens de, réduire à rien ; *it beggars all description*, cela défie toute description.

beggarly [-li] adj. Indigent, gueux, misérable (poor). ‖ FIG. Piètre, misérable, sordide ; *beggarly wage*, salaire de famine.

beggary [-ri] n. Mendicité, misère f.

begin [bi'gin] v. tr. (14). Commencer, entreprendre (a task) ; *to begin the world* (or) U. S. *life*, débuter dans la vie. ‖ Entamer, amorcer (a conversation). ‖ Se mettre à, entreprendre de ; *to begin eating*, commencer à manger ; *to begin to rain*, se mettre à pleuvoir. ‖ Inaugurer, ouvrir, faire naître (the trouble). — v. intr. Commencer ; *to begin again*, recommencer, reprendre. ‖ MILIT. Se déclencher (attack). **To begin at**, commencer à partir de (or par (the beginning). ‖ **To begin by**, commencer par (doing sth.). ‖ **To begin with**, commencer (or) débuter par (sth.) ; *to begin with*, pour commencer, ·tout d'abord.

beginner [-ə*] n. Commençant, débutant *s*. (novice). ‖ Cause première *f.* ; déterminant *s*. (originator).

beginning [-iŋ] n. Commencement, début *m.* ; *from the beginning*, dès le début, dès les premiers jours ; *in the beginning*, au commencement ; *to make a beginning*, commencer. ‖ Principe *m.* ; origine *f*.

begird [bi'gə:d] v. tr. (70). Ceindre (to gird) ; cerner, environner (to surround).

begone! [bi'gɔn] interj. Hors d'ici, sortez !

begonia [bi'gounjə] n. BOT. Bégonia *m*.

begot [bi'gɔt], **begotten** [-ən]. See BEGET.

begrime [bi'graim] v. tr. Salir, souiller, barbouiller (*with*, de).

begrudge [bi'grʌdʒ] v. tr. Envier ; *to begrudge s.o. his house*, envier sa maison à qqn. ‖ Mesurer, lésiner sur ; *she Legrudges him his food*, elle lui reproche (or) plaint la nourriture (fam.).

beguile [bi'gail] v. tr. Tromper, séduire (to deceive) ; *to beguile s.o. with promises*, endormir qqn avec des promesses. ‖ Dépouiller (*of*, de) ; détourner (*from*, de) ; *to beguile s.o. out of sth.*, soutirer qqch. à qqn. ‖ Charmer (one's leisure) ; faire diversion à (one's sorrow) ; tromper, faire passer (the time).

beguiler [-ə*] n. Trompeur *s*.

beguine [bi'gi:n] n. MUS. Beiguine *f*.

begum ['bi:gəm] n. Bégum *f*.

begun [bi'gʌn] p.p. See BEGIN.

behalf [bi'hɑ:f] n. *On behalf of*, en faveur de, dans l'intérêt de ; pour le compte de, de la part de, au nom de.

behave [bi'heiv] v. intr. Se conduire, se comporter, agir (*towards*, envers, à l'égard de) ; *to behave oneself*, se conduire comme il faut. ‖ Se tenir (children) ; *well-behaved*, sage, posé.

behavio(u)r [-jə*] n. Comportement, maintien *m.* ; tenue *f*. ‖ Conduite, façon (*f*.) d'agir (*towards*, envers). ‖ TECHN., AUTOM., NAUT., AVIAT. Fonctionnement *m.* ; tenue *f*.

behavio(u)rism [-jə,rizm] n. PSYCH. Béhaviorisme *m*.

behavio(u)rist [-jə,rist] adj., n. PSYCH. Béhavioriste *adj., s*.

behead [bi'hed] v. tr. Décapiter.

beheld [bi'held] pret., p.p. See BEHOLD.

behemoth [bi'hi:mɔθ] n. Hippopotame *m*.

behest [bi'hest] n. Ordre *m*. (command).

behind [bi'haind] adv. En arrière ; *to stay behind*, rester en arrière. ‖ Derrière ; *pushed on from behind*, poussé par-derrière. ‖ En retard ; *to be behind with one's studies*, être en retard pour ses études. ‖ Dans ie passé, en arrière ; *my happy days are behind*, les jours heureux pour moi se sont enfuis. ‖ A venir ; *there are greater sorrows behind*, il y a des chagrins plus grands en réserve. — prep. Derrière ; *behind, from behind the wall*, derrière, de derrière le mur ; *to leave children behind one*, laisser des enfants derrière soi. ‖ En arrière de ; en retard sur ; *behind the times*, en retard sur son temps. ‖ Derrière ; *to be behind the scheme*, soutenir le projet. ‖ U. S. FAM. *Behind the eight-ball*, acculé, dans une mauvaise passe. — n. FAM. Derrière, postérieur *m.* ; *to sit on one's behind*, rester le derrière sur sa chaise, ne pas en ficher une ramée.

behindhand [-hænd] adv., adj. En retard (*in*, pour) [doing sth.]. ‖ En reste (*in*, de) [kindness].

behold [bi'hould] v. tr. (15). Voir, apercevoir, contempler, regarder. — interj. Voyez!, tenez!, regardez!, voici !

beholden [-ņ] adj. Obligé, redevable (*to*, à) ; endetté (*to*, envers) ; *he is beholden to you for this good advice*, il vous doit ce bon conseil.

beholder [-ə*] n. Spectateur *m* ; spectatrice *f*.

behoof [bi'hu:f] n. Intérêt *m.* ; *for the* (or) *on behoof of*, dans l'intérêt de, pour le profit de, à l'avantage de. (See BEHALF.)

behove [bi'houv], U. S. **behoove** [-'hu:v] v. impers. Incomber, appartenir ; être utile (*to*, à) ; être du devoir (or) de l'intérêt (*to*, de).

beige [beiʒ] n. Laine écrue *f*. ‖ Beige *m*. (colour). — adj. Beige, écru.

being ['bi:iŋ] n. Existence, vie *f*. (living) ; être *m*. (nature) ; créature *f.*, être *m*. (person). ‖ ECCLES., PHILOS. Etre *m*. — pres. part. Etant. (See BE.) ‖ LOC. *For the time being*, pour le moment.

bejewel [bi'dʒu:əl] v. tr. (1). Endiamanter, couvrir de joyaux.

bel [bɛl] n. PHYS. Bel *m*.

belabo(u)r [bi'leibə*] v. tr. Rouer de coups ; tarauder (fam.). ‖ Invectiver, tomber sur (to abuse).

belated [bi'leitid] adj. Attardé, surpris par la nuit (benighted). ‖ Tardif (information) ; retardé, en retard (person) [see LATE] ; *belated wit*, esprit de l'escalier (or) à retardement.

belaud [bi'lɔ:d] v. tr. Couvrir d'éloges.

belay [bi'lei] v. tr. NAUT. Amarrer. ‖ FAM. Arrêter, stopper. ‖ **Belaying-pin**, n. NAUT. Taquet, cabillot *m*.

belch [beltʃ] v. intr. Eructer, faire un renvoi ; roter (pop.). ‖ U. S. POP. Râler, rouspéter. — v. tr. FIG. *To belch forth* (or) *out*, éructer, cracher, vomir (curses, flame, lava). — n. Renvoi, rot *m.* ; éructation *f*.

beldam ['beldəm] n. Vieille grand-mère *f*. (old woman). ‖ Vieille harpie *f*. (hag).

beleaguer [bi'li:gə*] v. tr. MILIT., FIG. Assiéger.

belfry ['belfri] n. Beffroi *m.* ; tour (*f*.) de guet. ‖ Clocher *m*. ‖ NAUT. Potence de cloche *f*.

Belgian ['beldʒən] adj., n. GEOGR. Belge *s*.

Belgium ['beldʒəm] n. GEOGR. Belgique *f*.

belie [bi'lai] v. tr. (3). Démentir (hopes, fears, promises, words) ; faire mentir (a proverb).

belief [bi'li:f] n. Croyance *f*. (*in*, en, à). ‖ Conviction, opinion *f.* ; *it's my belief that*, je suis persuadé que. ‖ Créance, foi *f.* ; *to obtain belief*, obtenir créance. ‖ Confiance *f*. (*in*, en) [trust]. ‖ ECCLES. Credo *m*. (creed) ; foi *f*. (faith).

believable [bi'li:vəbl] adj. Croyable.

believe [bi'li:v] v. tr. Croire à, être convaincu de, ajouter foi à (sth.) ; croire (s.o.) ; *I don't believe it*, je n'en crois rien ; *if he is to be believed*, à l'en croire ; *to believe one's eyes*, en croire ses yeux. ‖ Croire, penser, juger ; *I believe she is sensible*, je crois qu'elle est de bon conseil. ‖ FAM. *Believe me !*, vous pouvez m'en croire ! — v. intr. Croire (*in*, à). ‖ Penser, croire, estimer (*that*, que). ‖ ECCLES. Croire, avoir la foi.

believer [-ə*] n. Partisan, adepte *s*. (*in*, de) ; *believer in modern theories*, prosélyte des théories modernes. ‖ ECCLES. Croyant *s*.

Belisha [bə'laiʃə] n. *Belisha beacon*, borne lumineuse.

belittle [bilitl] v. tr. Rapetisser. ‖ FIG. Déconsidérer, déprécier, rabaisser ; *to belittle oneself*, se déconsidérer.

Belize [be'li:z] n. GEOGR. Belize *m*.

bell [bel] n. Cloche *f.* ; *the first bell for Mass was ringing*, le premier coup de la messe sonnait ; *with sound of bell*, à son de cloche. ‖ Sonnette *f.* ; timbre *m.* ; *ring at the bell*, coup de sonnette. ‖ Timbre *m*. (of a bicycle) ; grelot *m*. (of a collar) ; clochette, cloche, sonnaille *f*. (of a cow) ; *telephone*

bell, sonnerie du téléphone. ‖ Mus. Pavillon *m.* (of a trumpet). ‖ Naut. Coup (*m.*) de cloche. ‖ Bot. Clochette *f.* ‖ **Bell-buoy,** n. Bouée sonore *f.* ‖ **Bell-flower,** n. Bot. Campanule *f.* ‖ **Bell-founder,** n. Techn. Fondeur (*m.*) de cloches. ‖ **Bell-glass,** n. Agric., Chim. Cloche *f.* ‖ **Bell-mouthed,** adj. Evasé. ‖ **Bell-pull,** n. Cordon (*m.*) [or] poignée (*f.*) de sonnette. ‖ **Bell-push,** n. Bouton (*m.*) de sonnette. ‖ **Bell-ringer,** n. Sonneur *s.* ‖ **Bell-tower,** n. Eccles. Clocher *m.*
— v. tr. Mettre une cloche à. ‖ Fam. *To bell the cat,* attacher le grelot.
— v. intr. *To bell out,* ballonner (skirt).

bell v. intr. Bramer, raire, réer (deer).
— n. Bramement *m.*

belladonna [belə'dɔnə] n. Bot., Med. Belladone *f.*

bellboy ['bel,bɔi], **bellhop** [-,hɔp] n. U. S. Fam. Groom, chasseur *m.*

belle [bel] n. Belle, beauté *f.*

belles lettres [bel'letr] n. Belles-lettres *f. pl.*

belletrist [bel'letrist] n. Homme (or) femme de lettres, essayiste *s.*

bellicose ['belikous] adj. Belliqueux; guerroyeur.

bellicosity [beli'kɔsiti] n. Humeur belliqueuse *f.*

bellied ['belid] adj. *Big-bellied, pot-bellied,* ventru.

belligerency [bi'lidʒərənsi] n. Belligérance *f.*

belligerent [-ənt] adj., n. Belligérant.

bellow ['belou] v. intr. Beugler, mugir (cow, ox). ‖ Mugir (tempest, wind); gronder (thunder). ‖ Fam. Beugler, hurler.
— v. intr. Vociférer.
— v. tr. Clamer; beugler (a song).
— n. Beuglement, mugissement *m.* (of a cow). Mugissement *m.* (of the tempest); grondement, roulement *m.* (of the thunder). ‖ Fam. Hurlement; beuglement *m.*

bellows [-z] n. pl. Soufflet *m.; pair of bellows,* soufflet. ‖ Techn. Soufflet (of a camera); soufflerie *f.* (of a forge). ‖ Mus. Soufflerie *f.* ‖ Fam. Poumons *m. pl.; caisse f.*

belly ['beli] n. Med. Ventre; estomac *m.* (abdomen); sein, ventre *m.; entrailles f. pl.* (womb). ‖ Mus. Table d'harmonie *f.* ‖ Naut. Creux *m.* (of a sail); ventre *m.* (of a ship). ‖ Fig. Panse *f.* (of a pitcher); partie bombée *f.,* renflement *m.* (of a stone). ‖ **Belly-ache,** n. Med. Mal de ventre (or) d'estomac *m.; colique f.; v. intr. Fam. Rouspéter, râler. ‖ **Belly-band,** n. Sous-ventrière *f.* ‖ **Belly-button,** n. Fam. Nombril *m.* ‖ **Belly-land,** v. tr. Aviat. Atterrir sur le ventre. ‖ **Belly-landing,** n. Aviat. Atterrissage (*m.*) sur le ventre. ‖ **Belly-pinched,** adj. Affamé; *to be belly-pinched,* avoir la dent. ‖ **Belly-tank,** n. Aviat. Réservoir de secours *m.*
— v. tr. (2). Gonfler, enfler.
— v. intr. Se gonfler, s'enfler, s'arrondir.

bellyful [-ful] n. Ventrée *f.; to eat a bellyful,* se remplir le jabot (fam.). ‖ Pop. *To have a bellyful,* en avoir plein le dos.

belong [bi'lɔŋ] v. intr. Appartenir (*to,* à); *it belongs to me,* c'est à moi. ‖ Etre originaire (*to,* de) [a place]. ‖ Appartenir (*to,* à); faire partie (*to,* de) [a category]; appartenir, être attaché (*to,* à); être membre (*to,* de) [a party]; *to feel that one doesn't belong,* se sentir étranger. ‖ Relever, dépendre (*to,* de) [s.o.'s duties]. ‖ Aller ensemble; *to belong together,* s'accorder, s'assortir. ‖ U. S. Aller (*with,* avec). ‖ Se classer (*in,* dans, parmi). ‖ Jur. Ressortir (*to,* à); *to belong by right to,* compéter à (s.o.).
— v. impers. Appartenir, être propre (*to,* à); dépendre, être le rôle (*to,* de).

belongings [-iŋz] n. pl. Possessions, affaires *f. pl.; barda m.* (fam.); *personal belongings,* objets personnels. ‖ Fig. Dépendances *f. pl.*

beloved [bi'lʌvd] p. p. Aimé, bien aimé (*by, of,* de).
— [bi'lʌvid] adj., n. Bien-aimé *s.*

below [bi'lou] adv. En bas, plus bas; *from below,* d'en bas. ‖ En dessous (on a lower floor). ‖ En aval (downstream). ‖ Sur terre; *here below,* en ce bas monde, ici-bas. ‖ Ci-dessous; ci-après, plus loin, plus bas (in a lower place). ‖ Au-dessous (in rank). ‖ Mus. Plus bas. ‖ Naut. En bas. ‖ Jur. *Court below,* tribunal inférieur.
— prep. Au-dessous de, plus bas que (in rank); *below the average,* inférieur à la moyenne; *below stairs,* chez les domestiques. ‖ En aval de (a river). ‖ Sports. *Punch below the belt,* coup bas. ‖ Fig. *It is below her to beg,* supplier est indigne d'elle, elle s'abaisserait en suppliant; *that's below you,* vous êtes au-dessus de ça, cela vous diminuerait. ‖ **Below-stage,** n. Theatr. Dessous *m. pl.*

belt [belt] n. Ceinture *f.* ‖ Milit. Ceinturon *m.; machine-gun belt,* bande-chargeur. ‖ Aviat. *Safety belt,* ceinture de fixation. ‖ Naut. Ceinture *f.* (of a ship); *life-belt,* ceinture de sauvetage. ‖ Geogr. Zone *f.* ‖ Agric. Région *f.* ‖ Techn. Courroie *f.* ‖ Med. Ceinture *f.* ‖ Fig. Ceinture *f.* (of hills, trees). ‖ Fam. *To pull one's belt a hole tighter,* se serrer la ceinture d'un cran; *to tighten one's belt,* se mettre la ceinture; U. S. *belt-tightening,* restrictions.
— v. tr. Ceindre; ceinturer. ‖ Donner une raclée à.

belting [-iŋ] n. Techn. Courroies *f. pl.; transmission f.*

belvedere [belvi'diə*] n. Belvédère *m.*

bemire [bi'maiə*] v. tr. Crotter. ‖ Embourber.

bemoan [bi'moun] v. tr. Pleurer (s.o., sth.); déplorer (sth.).

bemuse [bi'mju:z] v. tr. Stupéfier, hébéter.

ben [ben] n. Geogr. Ben *m.* (as part of name); sommet *m.* (peak); montagne *f.,* mont *m.* (mountain).

bench [benʃ] n. Banc *m.* (of stone, wood). ‖ Gradin *m.* (in an amphitheatre); banquette *f.* (in a room). ‖ Banquette (of a road). ‖ Techn. Etabli *m.* (of carpenter); *testing bench,* banc d'essai. ‖ Chim. *Chemical bench,* table de laboratoire. ‖ Jur. Siège (*m.*) de juge (or) de parlementaire; magistrature assise *f.; front bench,* banc des ministres; *opposition benches,* l'opposition (in politics); *to be on the Bench,* siéger au tribunal, être magistrat; *to be raised to the Bench,* être nommé juge. ‖ U. S. *Stand m.* (at a dog show); *bench dog,* chien exposé. ‖ **Bench-mark,** n. Borne (*f.*) de nivellement. ‖ **Bench-stop,** n. Techn. Griffe *f.*
— v. tr. U. S. Sports. Retirer du jeu (a player).

bencher [-ə*] n. Jur. Membre de l'ordre des avocats *m.* (Inns of Court).

bend [bend] v. tr. (16). Courber, ployer, plier (sth.); *on bended knees,* genoux fléchis. ‖ Tendre, bander (a bow). ‖ Incurver, arrondir (a sphere). ‖ Arquer, froncer (one's brows); tourner, diriger (one's eyes); baisser, incliner, pencher (one's head). ‖ Diriger (one's course, way); tourner (one's steps). ‖ Milit. Diriger (*against,* contre; *at,* vers) [cannon, forces]. ‖ Naut. Etalinguer (a cable); enverguer (a sail). ‖ Techn. Cintrer (a beam); fausser (a key). ‖ Fig. Détourner (conversation); plier, faire plier (s.o., the mind, temper, will); incliner, disposer (*to,* à) [s.o.]; *bent upon,* acharné à. ‖ Fig. Tendre, diriger (*on, upon,* vers) [one's energies, mind]. ‖ **To bend back,** réfléchir (light).
— v. intr. Faire un coude, dévier (road). ‖ Fléchir, ployer, se courber (*under,* sous) [a weight]. ‖ Se pencher, se baisser, s'incliner (*forward,* en avant) [to bow]. ‖ Fig. Se courber, s'incliner, plier (*before,* devant); se soumettre, céder (*to,* à).
— n. Courbe, courbure *f.* ‖ Boucle *f.* (of a river); coude, tournant *m.* (of a road). ‖ Salut *m.; inclination f.* ‖ Med. Pli *m.* (of the elbow). ‖ Naut. Pl. Préceintes *f. pl.* ‖ Techn. Coude *m.* (of a pipe).

bend n. Naut. Nœud *m*. ‖ Techn. Moitié de peau tannée *f*. ‖ Fam. Pl. Mal (*m*.) des caissons.
bend n. Blas. Bande *f.; bend sinister*, barre de bâtardise.
bender [-ə*] n. Fam. U. S. Virée, bombe (spree).
beneath [bi'ni:θ] prep. Au-dessous, sous (sth.). ‖ Fig. Sous l'influence de, sous (a grief, a power); au-dessous de (s.o.); *it's beneath you to lie*, ne vous abaissez pas à mentir.
— adv. Au-dessous, dessous (below).
benedicite [,beni'daisiti] n. Eccles. Bénédicité *m*.
Benedictine ['beni'diktin] adj., n. Eccles. Bénédictin *s*.
— [-ti:n] n. Comm. Bénédictine *f*. (liqueur).
benediction ['dik ʃən] n. Bénédiction *f*. (blessing). ‖ Eccles. Bénédiction *f*. (in church); bénédicité *m*. (at table).
benedictory [-'diktəri] adj. De bénédiction.
benefaction [-'fæk ʃən] n. Bienfait; don *m*.
benefactor ['benifæktə*] n. Bienfaiteur *m*.
benefactress [-tris] n. Bienfaitrice *f*.
benefice ['benifis] n. Eccles. Bénéfice *m*.
beneficence [bi'nefisns] n. Bienfaisance *f*.
beneficent [-nt] adj. Bienfaisant.
beneficial [,beni'fiʃəl] adj. Avantageux (to, pour); favorable, salutaire (to, à). ‖ Jur. Relatif à l'usufruit; *beneficial owner*, usufruitier.
beneficially [-əli] adv. Avantageusement.
beneficiary [-əri] adj. Bénéficiaire. ‖ Feudataire.
— n. Bénéficiaire *s.;* bénéficier *m*.
benefit ['benifit] n. Bénéfice, profit, avantage *m*. ‖ Eccles. Privilège *m*. (of clergy); U. S. *Marriage without benefit of clergy*, mariage non béni par l'Eglise. ‖ Jur. Bénéfice *m*. (of the doubt, of inventory); allocation, prestation *f.; family benefit*, allocation familiale; *medical benefit*, secours médical. ‖ Fam. Représentation (or) organisation de charité *f*.
— adj. Jur. *Benefit society*, société de bienfaisance (or) de secours mutuel. ‖ Theatr. *Benefit performance*, représentation donnée au profit d'une œuvre.
— v. tr. Profiter à, être avantageux (or) profitable (or) salutaire pour, faire du bien à; *to love those whom one benefits*, aimer ses obligés.
— v. intr. Profiter, tirer profit (or) avantage (*by*, de).
Benelux ['benilʌks] n. Geogr. Benelux *m*.
benevolence [bi'nevələns] n. Bienveillance *f.; true benevolence*, la véritable bonté. ‖ Bienfaisance *f*. (quality). ‖ Bienfait *m*. (act). ‖ † Emprunt forcé *m*.
benevolent [-ənt] adj. Bienveillant. ‖ Bienfaisant, charitable (to, envers). ‖ Jur. De bienfaisance (society).
Bengal [ben'gɔ:l] n. Geogr. Bengale *m*.
— adj. De Bengale; *Bengal light*, feu de Bengale.
Bengali [beŋ'gɔ:li] adj., n. Geogr., Gramm. Bengali *m*.
benighted [bi'naitid] adj. Attardé, anuité. (See Belated.) ‖ Fig. Obscurci par l'ignorance (mind); à courte vue (policy); *from my benighted point of view*, du point de vue de l'ignorant (or) du profane que je suis.
benign [bi'nain] adj. Affable, bon (kind). ‖ Favorable, profitable, bienfaisant (beneficial). ‖ Med. Bénin.
benignancy [bi'nignənsi] n. Affabilité, bonté; bienveillance *f*. ‖ Condition favorable; bénignité *f*.
benignant [-ənt] adj. Bienveillant, affable. (See Beneficient.) ‖ Profitable, favorable, salutaire.
benignantly [-əntli] adv. Avec bienveillance.
benignity [-iti] n. Bienveillance, affabilité *f*. ‖ Faveur *f.:* bienfait *m*. (act).
Benin [be'ni:n] n. Geogr. Bénin *m*.
benison ['benizn] n. † Bénédiction *f*.
Benjamin ['bendʒəmin] n. Benjamin *s*. (youngest child).

benjamin ['bendʒəmin] n. Bot. Benjoin *m*.
bent [bent] n. Disposition, tournure *f*. (of mind). ‖ Penchant, goût *m*.
— pret., p. p. See Bend.
bentonite ['bentənait] n. Bentonite *f*.
benumb [bi'nʌm] v. tr. Engourdir, endormir (a limb). ‖ Fig. Engourdir (the mind).
Benzedrine ['benzi,dri:n] (nom déposé) n. Med. Benzédrine *f*.
benzene ['benzi:n] n. Chim. Benzène, benzol *m*.
benzine n. Chim., Comm. Benzine *f*.
benzoate ['benzoeit] n. Chim. Benzoate *m*.
benzoic [ben'zouik] adj. Chim. Benzoïque.
benzoin ['benzouin] n. Bot. Benjoin *m*.
benzol ['benzoul] n. Chim. Benzol *m*.
benzoline [-zoli:n] n. Chim. Benzine *f*.
bequeath [bi'kwi:ð] v. tr. Jur., Fig. Léguer.
bequest [bi'kwest] n. Jur. Legs *m*.
berate [bi'reit] v. tr. Réprimander, morigéner.
Berber ['bə:bə*] adj., n. Geogr. Berbère.
berceuse [bɛ'sə:z] n. Berceuse *f*. (lullaby).
bereave [bi'ri:v] v. tr. (17). Priver, dépouiller (*of*, de).
bereaved [-d] adj. Orphelin (child); veuf (husband); endeuillé, solitaire (person); veuve (wife).
bereavement [-mənt] n. Perte *f*. (of a relation). ‖ Deuil *m.;* isolement *m.;* solitude *f*. (after s.o.'s death).
bereft [bi'reft] pret. See Bereave.
beret ['bere] n. Béret *m*.
berg [bə:g] n. Geogr. Iceberg *m*.
bergamot ['bə:gəmɔt] n. Bot. Bergamote *f*. (pear); bergamotier *m*. (tree). ‖ Comm. Bergamote (perfume).
berhyme [bi'raim] v. tr. Mettre en vers. ‖ Chansonner (to satirize).
beriberi ['beri'beri] n. Med. Béribéri *m*.
berkelium [bə'ki:liəm] n. Chim. Berkélium *m*.
Berlin [bə'lin] n. Geogr. Berlin *m*.
— adj. De Prusse (blue).
berlin n. Berline *f*. (carriage).
berm [bə:m] n. Milit. Berme, banquette *f*. ‖ Techn. Risberme *f*.
Bermuda [bə'mju:də] n. Geogr. Bermudes *f*. pl. ‖ Naut. *Bermuda rig*, gréement bermudien, bermudien. ‖ Comm. *Bermuda shorts, bermudas*, bermuda.
Bermudian [-jən] n. Geogr. Habitant (*s*.) des Bermudes.
— adj. Geogr. Des Bermudes. ‖ Naut. *Bermudian mainsail*, voilure Marconi.
Bernardine ['bə:nə:dain] adj., n. Eccles. Bernardin *m*.
berried ['berid] adj. Bot. A baies. ‖ Zool. Œuvé.
berry ['beri] n. Bot. Baie *f*. ‖ Grain *m*. (of coffee, wheat). ‖ Zool. Frai, œuf *m*. (in fish-roe).
— v. intr. (2). Bot. Se garnir de baies.
berserk [bə'zə:k] n. † Berserk *m*. (Norse warrior).
— adj. Fou furieux, fou de rage; *to go berserk*, devenir fou furieux, devenir enragé.
berth [bə:θ] n. Naut. Evitage *m.;* évitée *f.;* mouillage *m*. ‖ Naut. Cabine *f*. ‖ Ch. de f. Couchette *f*. ‖ Fam. Emploi *m.;* place *f.; to find a soft berth*, trouver un bon fromage, arriver à se caser doucetement; *to give s.o. a wide berth*, se tenir à distance respectueuse de.
— v. tr. Naut. Donner un poste à; accoster, amarrer (a ship). ‖ Naut. Donner une cabine à. ‖ Ch. de f. Donner une couchette à.
— v. intr. Naut. Mouiller. ‖ Naut. Avoir une cabine. ‖ Ch. de f. Avoir une couchette.
beryl ['beril] n. Béryl *m*.
beryllium [bə'riliəm] n. Chim. Béryllium *m*.
beseech [bi'si:tʃ] v. tr. (18). Solliciter (leave) [to, de]; implorer (pardon). [See Beg.] ‖ Supplier, prier, implorer (s.o.) [*for*, pour obtenir].
beseeching [-iŋ] adj. Suppliant, pressant.
beseem [bi'si:m] v. tr. Convenir à. (See Suit.)

beseemingly [-iŋli] adv. D'une manière convenable (or) seyante.

beset [bi'set] v. tr. (122). Parsemer (with, de) [to stud]. ‖ Encombrer (a road) [with, de]; gêner (s.o.) [with, par]. ‖ Attaquer, assiéger, serrer de près (s.o.). ‖ FIG. Assaillir, environner.

besetment [-mənt] n. Encerclement, investissement m. (of a town). ‖ FIG. Point faible, péché mignon m.

besetting [-iŋ] adj. Habituel, mignon (sin); harcelant (temptation).

beside [bi'said] prep. A côté de, près de (close to). ‖ En comparaison de, comparé à, à côté de, auprès de (in comparison with). ‖ Hors de, en dehors de, à côté de (aside from). ‖ Hors de (out of); to be beside oneself, être hors de soi (or) de ses gonds, ne plus se posséder.

besides [-z] adv. En outre, de plus, en plus (in addition, moreover). ‖ De plus, d'autre part, d'ailleurs, en outre (as well). ‖ De plus, d'autre (else); nothing besides, rien de plus.
— prep. En plus de, en dehors de, outre (in addition to); besides being a slacker he was a numskull, c'était non seulement un paresseux mais un lourdaud. ‖ Que (than); there are others besides him, il y en a d'autres que lui. ‖ Hormis, sans compter (except).

besiege [bi'si:dʒ] v. tr. MILIT., FIG. Assiéger (with, de).

besieger [-ə*] n. MILIT. Assiégeant m.

beslaver [bi'slævə*] v. tr. Couvrir de bave. ‖ FAM. Flagorner, lécher les bottes de.

beslobber [bi'slɔbə*] v. tr. Baver sur. ‖ FAM. Couvrir de baisers mouillés.

besmear [bi'smiə*] v. tr. Souiller, barbouiller.

besmirch [bi'smə:tʃ] v. tr. Tacher, salir. ‖ FIG. Salir, souiller.

besom ['bi:zəm] n. Balai (m.) en ramilles.

besot [bi'sɔt] v. tr. (1). Abrutir, abêtir, hébéter.

besought [bi'sɔ:t] pret., p. p. See BESEECH.

bespangle [bi'spæŋgl̩] v. tr. Parsemer, clouter (with, de).

bespatter [bi'spætə*] v. tr. Crotter, éclabousser (with, de). ‖ FIG. Eclabousser, salir (s.o.'s reputation); to bespatter s.o. with flattery, accabler qqn de flatteries.

bespeak [bi'spi:k] v. tr. (19). † Parler à. ‖ Commander (a meal); réserver, retenir (a room). ‖ FIG. Faire prévoir, laisser présager (to foreshadow); témoigner de, prouver (to show).

bespectacled [bi'spektəkl̩d] adj. A lunettes.

bespoke [bi'spouk] adj. COMM. Sur commande; bespoke tailor, tailleur à façon.
— pret. See BESPEAK.

besprinkle [bi'spriŋkl̩] v. tr. Asperger, arroser (with, de) [a liquid]. ‖ Saupoudrer (with, de) [a powder]. ‖ Parsemer. (See BESPANGLE.)

best [best] adj. superl. Meilleur; the best thing about him is, ce qu'il y a de mieux chez lui c'est. ‖ Plus beau; best clothes, habits du dimanche, plus beaux atours. ‖ Plus grand; the best part of, la plus grande partie de, la plupart de. ‖ LOC. Best man, garçon d'honneur.
— adv. Mieux, le mieux; as best he could, de son mieux; to know best, être le mieux à même de juger (or) le mieux placé pour savoir; to think it best to, juger plus expédient de; he had best stay, il ferait mieux de rester. ‖ Le plus; the best looking girl, la plus jolie fille.
— n. Mieux m.; at one's best, sous son meilleur jour, à son avantage; en forme; in one's best, dans ses plus beaux atours; the best of it, le plus joli de l'affaire; to the best of my judgment, autant que je puisse en juger; to do one's best, faire de son mieux; to get the best out of s.o., tirer de qqn le maximum (or) ce qu'il a de meilleur; to get (or) have the best of, l'emporter sur; to have the best

of it, avoir la meilleure part, tirer le meilleur numéro; to make the best of, s'arranger de, tirer le meilleur parti de; with the best, aussi bien que les meilleurs (or) qu'un autre. ‖ COMM. Meilleur m.; meilleure qualité f. ‖ U. S. Sunday best, habits du dimanche. ‖ Best-seller, n. COMM. Best-seller, auteur (or) livre à succès, super-succès (m.) de librairie.
— v. tr. FAM. Rouler, refaire avoir.

bestead [bi'sted] v. tr., intr. Etre utile à, aider, servir.

bestead p. p. Entouré, environné (by, with, de); ill bestead, en mauvaise posture.

bestiary ['bestiəri] n. Bestiaire m.

bestial ['bestjəl] adj. ZOOL., FIG. Bestial.

bestiality [,besti'æliti] n. Bestialité f.; acte bestial m.

bestir [bi'stə:*] v. tr. (1). To bestir oneself, s'activer, se remuer, se démener.

bestow [bi'stou] v. tr. Ranger, placer, déposer (to deposit). ‖ Loger, installer; caser (fam.) [to provide with lodging]. ‖ Accorder, conférer (upon, à) [a favour]; to bestow sth. upon s.o., gratifier qqn de qqch. ‖ Appliquer, consacrer, employer, mettre (on, upon, à) [one's energies, goods, labour].

bestowal [-əl] n. Don m. (act).

bestrew [bi'stru:] v. tr. Joncher, couvrir (with, de). ‖ Eparpiller (with, sur).

bestride [bi'straid] v. tr. (164). Enfourcher, chevaucher (a horse). ‖ Etre à cheval (or) à califourchon sur, chevaucher (a chair). ‖ Enjamber (a brook, place).

bet [bet] n. Pari m.
— v. tr. (1). Parier (against, contre; on, sur; with, avec). ‖ FAM. Bet you can't!, chiche!; I'll bet you won't do it, je vous défie de le faire; you can bet your boots that, je vous parie la lune que.
— v. intr. Parier; to bet on a horse, jouer un cheval. ‖ FAM. You bet!, tu parles!

beta ['bi:tə] n. Bêta m. (greek letter); niveau (m.) au-dessus de la moyenne, B m. (in school marks). ‖ PHYS. Beta particles, rays, particules, rayons bêta.

betake [bi'teik] v. tr. (174). To betake oneself, se rendre (to, à). ‖ FIG. Se livrer, se mettre, s'adonner (to, à).

betatron ['beitətrɔn] n. PHYS. Bétatron m.

betel ['bi:təl] n. BOT. Bétel.

bête noire [bet'nwa:r] n. Bête noire f.

bethel ['beθəl] n. ECCLES. Lieu saint m.; temple (m.) de dissidents. ‖ U. S. Chapelle (f.) de marins.

bethink [bi'θiŋk] v. tr. (178). To bethink oneself, réfléchir, se souvenir; s'aviser (to, de).

betide [bi'taid] v. tr., intr. † Advenir, arriver.

betimes [bi'taimz] adv. † Tôt, de bonne heure (early); promptement, vite (quickly). ‖ A temps, assez tôt (in good time).

betoken [bi'toukən] v. tr. Présager (to foreshow). ‖ Révéler, dénoter (see INDICATE).

betook [bi'tuk] pret. See BETAKE.

betray [bi'trei] v. tr. Trahir (s.o.). ‖ Livrer, révéler, dévoiler (plans, secrets); trahir, livrer (s.o.). ‖ MILIT. Trahir. ‖ JUR. Trahir. ‖ Séduire, abuser de (a woman). ‖ FIG. Trahir, révéler (age); trahir, révéler, laisser deviner (or) percer (fear, intentions); trahir, tromper, décevoir (hope, trust).

betrayal [-əl] n. Trahison f.

betrayer [-ə*] n. Traître m.; traîtresse f. (of, envers). ‖ JUR. Séducteur m.

betroth [bi'trouð] v. tr. Fiancer.

betrothal [-əl] n. Fiançailles f. pl.

betrothed [-d] n. Fiancé e.

better ['betə*] adj. Meilleur (than, que); to be better than, valoir mieux que; to be better than one's word, réaliser (or) tenir plus qu'on n'a promis, aller au-delà de ses promesses; to hope for better things, espérer mieux; to make sth. better,

améliorer qqch. ‖ Plus grand, plus important (room). ‖ Plus complet (acquaintance). ‖ SPORTS. Plus fort (than, que). ‖ FAM. That's better!, j'aime mieux ça!
— adv. Mieux (than, que); better and better, de mieux en mieux; better still, et qui mieux est; nobody better, mieux que personne; so much the better, tant mieux; to be the better for, se trouver bien de, se féliciter de; to esteem s.o. the better for it, en estimer qqn d'autant plus; to know better, voir plus loin, en savoir plus long, ne pas se laisser abuser; to think better of it, reviser son opinion, en revenir, se raviser; to think better of, avoir meilleure opinion de (s.o.); you had better speak, vous feriez mieux de parler. ‖ Plus; to like s.o. better and better, aimer qqn de plus en plus. ‖ MED. To be better, aller mieux, se rétablir. ‖ FAM. Better off, plus argenté.
— n. Supérieur m. (person). ‖ Avantage m.; supériorité f.; to get the better of, avoir le dessus (or) l'avantage sur, l'emporter sur (a rival); dominer, surmonter (uneasiness); rouler (fam.). ‖ Amélioration f. (improvement).
— v. tr. Améliorer (see IMPROVE); to better oneself, améliorer sa condition. ‖ Surpasser (to outdo).
— v. intr. S'améliorer.

better, bettor n. Parieur s.

betterment [-mənt] n. Amélioration f. ‖ FIN. Plus-value f.

betting [-iŋ] n. Pari m.; betting house, maison de jeu. ‖ Betting news, n. SPORTS. Résultat (m.) des courses.

between [bi'twi:n] prep. Entre (two persons, two things). ‖ Entre (interval); between Paris and London, entre Paris et Londres; between whiles, de temps en temps. ‖ Entre (connecting); bond between friends, lien entre amis (or) unissant des amis; to ply between Paris and Orleans, faire la navette entre Paris et Orléans. ‖ Entre (separating); the distance between them, la distance qui les sépare. ‖ Entre (sharing); to divide between, partager entre. ‖ Entre, parmi (choice); to choose between a dress and a hat, choisir entre une robe et un chapeau. ‖ Entre (combined action); between them Paul and Peter lifted the weight, à eux deux Pierre et Paul soulevèrent le poids. ‖ Entre (combined effect); between work and study I have no time for reading, entre mon travail et mes études je n'ai plus le temps de lire. ‖ Entre (combined possession); they have ten pounds between them, ils ont dix livres à eux deux (or) tous. ‖ Entre (reciprocity); the friendship between them, l'amitié qu'ils se portent. ‖ Entre (divided between); between crying and laughing, entre le rire et les larmes. ‖ Entre (from one to the other); between twenty and thirty, de vingt à trente. ‖ Entre (confined to); between you and me, entre nous, de vous à moi. ‖ Between-maid, n. Aide-domestique f. (aux ordres de la cuisinière et de la femme de chambre). ‖ Between-season, n. Demi-saison f.
— adv. Entre, au milieu, dans l'intervalle; betwixt and between, entre les deux; far between, très espacés, rares (visits).

betwixt [bi'twikst]. See BETWEEN.

bevatron ['beivətron] n. Bévatron m.

bevel ['bevəl] n. Angle oblique m. ‖ Biseau m. ‖ TECHN. Fausse équerre f. ‖ Bevel-edge, n. Bord en chanfrein m. ‖ Bevel-gear, n. AUTOM. Engrenage conique m.
— v. tr. (1). Biseauter.
— v. intr. Aller en biseau (or) en biais.

beverage ['bevəridʒ] n. Breuvage m.; boisson f.

bevy ['bevi] n. Harde f. (of deer); vol m. (of larks). ‖ FIG. Essaim m.; cohorte, troupe f.; bevy of beauty, essaim de jolies filles.

bewail [bi'weil] v. tr. Déplorer, se lamenter sur.
— v. intr. Se lamenter.

beware [bi'wɛə*] v. intr. Prendre garde, se méfier; beware of pickpockets, attention aux pickpockets.
— v. tr. Prendre garde à, se méfier de.

bewilder [bi'wildə*] v. tr. Egarer (in, dans). ‖ FIG. Désorienter, effarer, ahurir, déconcerter.

bewilderment [-mənt] n. Egarement, effarement m.; confusion f.

bewitch [bi'witʃ] v. tr. Ensorceler. ‖ FIG. Charmer, fasciner.

bey [bei] m. Bey m.

beylic [-lik] adj. Beylical.

beyond [bi'jɔnd] prep. Au-delà de, de l'autre côté de (the Alps, the door); en dehors de (the walls). ‖ Au-delà de, plus de (a week); to be beyond fifty, avoir dépassé la cinquantaine. ‖ En plus de, outre; beyond what he has already done, outre ce qu'il a déjà fait. ‖ Plus que; nothing beyond what I already knew, rien de plus que ce que je savais déjà. ‖ Au-dessus de (s.o.'s abilities); en avance sur (s.o.'s age); hors de (s.o.'s control, reach); beyond bearing, belief, description, hope, intolérable, incroyable, indescriptible, désespéré; it's beyond me, cela me dépasse; to go beyond one's authority, outrepasser ses pouvoirs; to go beyond one's duties, sortir du cadre de ses attributions.
— adv. Là-bas, plus loin.
— n. Au-delà m.

bezant ['beznt] n. † Besant m.

bezel ['bezl] n. Biseau m. (of a chisel). ‖ Chaton m. (holding a gem). ‖ Facette f. (of a diamond).

bezique [bi'zi:k] n. Bésigue m.

Bhutan [bu:'tɑ:n] n. GEOGR. Bhoutan m.

biannual [bai'ænjuəl] adj. Bisannuel.

bias ['baiəs] n. Biais m. (in cloth). ‖ SPORTS. Fort m. (in bowling). ‖ RADIO. Tension f. ‖ FIG. Préjugé, parti pris m.; prévention, idée préconçue f. (prejudice). ‖ FIG. Tendance f.; penchant m. (inclination); vocational bias, déformation professionnelle.
— v. tr. (1). FIG. Influencer. ‖ Prévenir (against, contre).
— N. B. On peut employer indifféremment biassed ou biased aux pret. et p. p.

biaxial [bai'æksəl] adj. PHYS. A deux axes, bi-axé.

bib [bib] v. intr. (1). FAM. Siffler, chopiner, biberonner.
— n. Bavette f., bavoir m. (for child). ‖ Bavette (of an apron). ‖ Bib-cock, n. Robinet coudé m.

bibasic [bai'beisik] adj. CHIM. Bibasique.

bibber ['bibə*] n. FAM. Soiffard m.

bibelot ['bi:blo] n. Bibelot m.

Bible [baibl] n. Bible f. ‖ Bible-thumper, n. FAM. Evangéliste de carrefour m.
— adj. Bible paper, papier bible.

biblical ['biblikəl] adj. Biblique.

bibliographer [,bibli'ɔgrəfə*] n. Bibliographe s.

bibliographic(al) [,bibliɔ'græfik(əl)] adj. Bibliographique.

bibliography [,bibli'ɔgrəfi] n. Bibliographie f.

bibliomania [,biblio'meiniə] n. Bibliomanie f.

bibliophile ['bibliofail] n. Bibliophile s.

bibliophilism [,bibli'ɔfəlizm] n. Bibliophilie f.

bibulous ['bibjuləs] adj. Absorbant, spongieux; bibulous paper, papier qui boit. ‖ FAM. Suceur.

bicameral ['bai'kæmərəl] adj. Bicaméral; bicameral system, bicamérisme.

bicarbonate [bai'kɑ:bənət] n. CHIM. Bicarbonate m.

bice [bais] n. Gris bleu m.

bicentenary [,baisen'ti:nəri] adj. Du bicentenaire (marking a 200th anniversary).
— n. Bicentenaire m. (anniversary).

bicentennial [-'teniəl] adj. Bicentenaire (occurring every 200 years, lasting 200 years).
— n. Bicentenaire m. (anniversary).

bicephalous [bai'sefələs] adj. Bicéphale.

biceps ['baiseps] n. MED. Biceps m.

BICYCLE — BICYCLETTE

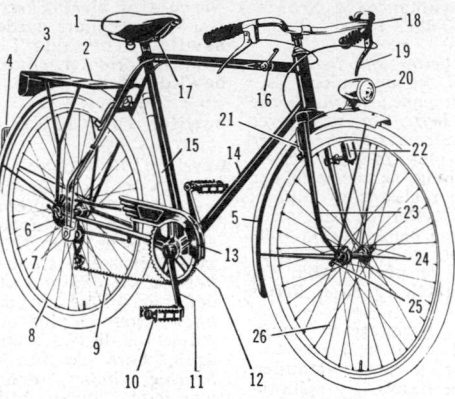

Selle	Saddle	1
Porte-bagages	Carrier	2
Sacoche	Tool-bag	3
Feu arrière	Rearlight	4
Garde-boue	Mudguard	5
Pignon à 3 vitesses Three-speed gear		6
Dérailleur—Derailleur gear-changer (US) gearbox		7
Jante	Rim	8
Chaîne	Chain	9
Pédale	Pedal	10
Manivelle	Pedal-crank	11
Plateau de pédalier Chain-wheel		12
Carter	Chain-guard	13

14	Cadre	Frame
15	Pompe	Pump
16	Manette du dérailleur Gear-change lever;(US)gearshift	
17	Potence	Saddle pillar
18	Guidon	Handle-bar
19	Poignée de frei Brake lever	
20	Phare	Light
21	Frein	Brak
22	Alternateur	Dynam
23	Fourche	For
24	Moyeu	Hu
25	Ecrou papillon	Butterfly-nu
26	Rayon	Spok

bichloride ['bai'klɔːraid] n. CHIM. Bichlorure *m.*

bichromate [-'kroumit] n. CHIM. Bichromate *m.*

bicker ['bikə*] v. intr. Se chamailler (persons). || Trembloter, vaciller (flame); crépiter (hail); vaciller, scintiller (light); murmurer (stream); battre, claquer (rain).
— n. Prise (*f.*) de bec; *local bickering,* querelles (or) rivalités de clocher.

biconcave [bai'kɔnkeiv] adj. Biconcave.

biconvex [-veks] adj. Biconvex.

bicuspid [bai'kʌspid] adj. MED. Bicuspidé.
— n. MED. Prémolaire bicuspidée *f.*

bicycle ['baisikl] n. AUTOM. Bicyclette *f.* || **Bicycle-rickshaw,** n. Vélo-pousse, vélo-taxi *m.*
— v. intr. Aller à bicyclette; faire de la bicyclette.

bicyclist [-klist] n. Cycliste *s.*

bid [bid] v. tr. (20). Inviter, prier; *to bid s.o. to dinner,* inviter qqn à dîner. || Dire (farewell); *to bid defiance to,* porter un défi à. || Commander, ordonner (to order); *she bade him work,* elle lui enjoignit de travailler. || Appeler, demander (in cards). || COMM., FIN. Offrir (a price); miser (a-sum).
— v. intr. (20). Faire une offre, offrir un prix (*for,* pour); enchérir (*over,* sur); contre-offrir; *to bid up,* lever la mise. || FIG. *To bid fair to succeed,* paraître devoir réussir, promettre de réussir, s'annoncer comme devant réussir.
— n. FIN. Offre; mise; enchère *f.; higher bid,* surenchère. || COMM. Contre-offre *f.* || Appel *m.;* demande *f.* (in cards); *to raise the bid,* relancer || U. S. Devis *m.;* soumission *f.* || U. S. FAM. Invitation *f.* (to become a member). || FIG. Tentative *f.; suicide bid,* tentative de suicide; *to make a bid for,* faire son possible pour.

biddable [-əbl] adj. Docile, soumis.

bidden [-n̩] p. p. See BID.

bidder [-ə*] n. FIN. Offrant, enchérisseur *m.; to the highest bidder,* au plus offrant.

bidding [-iŋ] n. Ordre *m.; he needed no second bidding,* il ne se l'est pas fait dire deux fois. || FIN. Enchères *f. pl.* (at auction).

bide [baid] v. tr., intr. † Attendre. || Rester, séjourner. (See ABIDE.) || LOC. *To bide one's time,* se réserver.

bidet ['bidɛ] n. Bidet *m.*

biennial [bai'enjəl] adj. Bisannuel, biennal.
— n. BOT. Plante biennale *f.*

bier [biə*] n. Civière *f.* (for coffin). || U. S. Bière *f.* (coffin).

biff [bif] n. FAM. Gnon *m.* (cuff).
— v. tr. FAM. Cogner; *to biff s.o. in the face,* coller son poing sur la figure de qqn.

biffin ['bifin] n. BOT. Pomme rouge *f.* || CULIN Flan (*m.*) aux pommes.

bifocal [bai'foukl] adj. PHYS. Bifocal.

bifurcate ['baifəːkeit] v. tr., intr. Bifurquer.
— [-kit] adj. Bifurqué.

bifurcation [,baifəːˈkeiʃən] n. Bifurcation *f.*

big [big] adj. Gros (person, thing); *to grow big* (or *bigger,* grossir, engraisser. || Grand (hotel); *the Bi Three,* les Trois Grands; *bigger than life,* plu grand que nature. || Important; *to do big things* faire de grandes choses. || Fastueux; *to live in big way,* mener grand train. || Noble, magnanime grand (heart). || Lourd (*with,* de) [consequences] chargé, gonflé (*with,* de) [news]. || Orgueilleux, far faron (proud). || MED. *Big with child,* enceinte. COMM. *Big business,* grosses affaires. || FAM. *Bi bug* (or *pot,* gros bonnet, grosse légume; U. S. *Bi time,* le gros jeu; *to grow too big for one's boots* péter dans sa peau. || **Big-bellied,** adj. Pansu, ven tripotent. || **Big-boned,** adj. A forte charpente ossu. || **Big-end,** n. TECHN. Tête de bielle *f.* || **Big head,** n. FAM. Gros (*m.*) plein de soupe. || **Big-horn** n. ZOOL. Bighorn, mouflon (*m.*) d'Amérique.
— adv. FAM. *To look big,* déplacer de l'air, faire l monsieur; *to talk big,* battre la grosse caisse, fair le hâbleur; le prendre de haut.

bigamist ['bigəmist] n. Bigame *m.*

bigamous [-əs] adj. Bigame.

bigamy [-i] n. Bigamie *f.*

bigaroon [,bigəˈruːn] n. BOT. Bigarreau *m.*

bight [bait] n. Baie *f.* || NAUT. Double *m.* (in rope).

bigness ['bignis] n. Grosseur *f.*

bigot ['bigət] n. Fanatique *s.* (*for, to,* de); *religiou bigot,* bigot.

bigotry [-ri] n. Fanatisme *m.* || Bigoterie *f.*

bigwig ['bigwig] n. FAM. Gros bonnet *m.;* huile

bike [baik] n. FAM. Vélo *m.;* bécane *f.*

bikini [bi'kiːni] n. Bikini *m.*

bilateral [bai'lætərəl] adj. Bilatéral.

bilberry ['bilbəri] n. BOT. Airelle *f.*

bilbo ['bilbou] n. MILIT. † Rapière *f.*

bile [bail] n. MED., FAM. Bile *f.* || **Bile-stone,** n MED. Calcul biliaire *m.*

bilge [bildʒ] n. Ventre *m.* (of a cask). || Eau sta gnante *f.* || NAUT. Fond (*m.*) de cale; petits fonds || FAM. *To talk bilge,* dire des idioties.
— v. tr. NAUT. Défoncer, crever (a ship).
— v. intr. NAUT. Faire eau.

bilharzia [bil'hɑːtsjə] n. MED. Bilharzie *f.*

bilharziasis [,bilhɑːˈtsaiəsis] n. MED. Bil harziose *f.*

biliary ['biljəri] adj. MED. Biliaire.

bilingual [bai'liŋgwəl] adj. Bilingue.

bilingualism [-izm̩] n. Bilinguisme m.
bilious ['biljəs] adj. MED. Bilieux; de bile; *bilious attack*, embarras gastrique, légère crise de foie. ‖ FAM. Colérique, hypocondriaque.
biliousness [-nis] n. MED. Affection hépatique f.; accès (m.) de bile.
bilk [bilk] v. tr. FAM. Rouler, blouser (to swindle); filer sans payer (a debt). ‖ FAM. Plaquer, laisser choir (to chuck).
bill [bil] n. ZOOL., NAUT. Bec m. ‖ GEOGR. Promontoire m.
— v. intr. Becqueter. ‖ FAM. *To bill and coo*, se bécoter.
bill [bil] n. MILIT. Hallebarde f. ‖ AGRIC. Serpe f.
bill n. Affiche f. (poster). ‖ Menu m.; *bill of fare*, carte, menu. ‖ THEATR. Programme m.; *to head the bill*, être en vedette sur l'affiche; *to fill the bill*, tenir l'affiche. ‖ JUR. Projet (m.) de loi. ‖ JUR. Plainte f.; résumé (m.) des chefs d'accusation. ‖ COMM. Facture, note, addition f.; mémoire m.; *bill of costs*, état des frais; *bill of sale*, acte de vente. ‖ COMM. Billet, effet m.; traite f.; *bill of exchange*, lettre de change. ‖ FIN. Bon m. : *Exchequer bill*, bon du Trésor; *foreign bill*, devise étrangère. ‖ U. S. FIN. Billet (m.) de banque. ‖ NAUT. *Bill of health, lading*, patente, connaissement. ‖ FAM. *To draw up a stiff bill*, saler la note; *to foot the bill*, régler la douloureuse. ‖ **Bill-board**, n. Panneau d'affichage m. ‖ **Bill-book**, n. COMM. Echéancier m. ‖ **Bill-broker**, n. FIN. Agent de change m. ‖ **Bill-file**, n. COMM. Pique-notes m. ‖ **Bill-poster, bill-sticker,** n. Colleur (m.) d'affiches.
— v. tr. Afficher (sth.) ‖ Placarder d'affiches (a wall). ‖ COMM. Facturer. ‖ U. S. Annoncer.
billet ['bilit] n. MILIT. Billet de logement m. (order); logement (m.) chez l'habitant (place); *to allot billets*, répartir le cantonnement. ‖ FIG. Poste m. ‖ FAM. *Cushy billet*, fromage.
— v. tr. MILIT. Loger, cantonner.
billfold ['bil‚fould] n. U. S. Porte-billets, portefeuille m.
billiards ['biljədz] n. pl. SPORTS. Billard m. ‖ **Billiard-marker**, n. Marqueur m. ‖ **Billiard-table,** n. Billard m.
billingsgate ['biliŋzget] n. Halle (f.) au poisson. ‖ FAM. Langage (m.) de poissarde.
billion ['biljən] n. Billion (10¹²) m.; U. S. milliard (10⁹) m.
billow ['bilou] n. Vague, lame f.; flot m. (of water). ‖ FIG. Flot (of people, smoke, sound).
— v. intr. Onduler, ondoyer, rouler.
billowy [-i] adj. Houleux.
billy ['bili] n. Matraque f. ‖ U. S. Bâton m. (of a policeman). ‖ **Billy-can**, n. Gamelle f.
billycock ['bilikɔk] n. FAM. Melon m. (hat).
billy-goat ['biligout] n. ZOOL. Bouc m. ‖ *Billy-goat beard*, bouc.
billy-o(h) ['bili‚ou] n. FAM. *Like billy-o(h)*, rudement, vachement; *it's raining like billy-o(h)*, il pleut des cordes; *to fight like billy-o(h)*, se battre à mort; *to run like billy-o(h)*, courir comme un dératé.
bimanal ['bimən̩l], **bimanous** [-əs] adj. ZOOL. Bimane.
bimane ['baimein] n. ZOOL. Bimane s.
bimetallic ['bai‚me'tælik] adj. Bimétallique.
bimetallism ['bai'metəlizm̩] n. Bimétallisme m.
bimonthly [bai'mʌnθli] adj., n. Bimensuel adj., m.
bimotored [bi'moutə:d] adj. AVIAT. Bimoteur.
bin [bin] n. Huche f. (for bread); coffre m. (for coal, corn); casier m. (for wine).
— v. tr. Mettre dans un coffre; ranger dans un casier.
binary ['bainəri] adj. Binaire.
binate [-et] adj. BOT. Biné.
binaural [bai'nɔ:rəl] adj. Binaural, biaural (hear-

ing, sound transmission and recording). ‖ MED. Biauriculaire (stethoscope).
bind [baind] v. tr. (21). Lier, attacher, ficeler (to tie). ‖ Ligoter, garrotter, enchaîner (to chain up). ‖ Border (to edge); entourer, cercler (*with*, de) [to wreathe]. ‖ Unir, réunir, assembler, attacher (to unite). ‖ JUR. Ratifier (an agreement); consolider (duties); *to bind s.o. over to*, enjoindre à qqn de, obliger qqn à. ‖ MED. Constiper; resserrer (fam.); *to bind up*, bander (a wound). ‖ COMM. Ratifier (a bargain). ‖ TECHN. Mettre en apprentissage (*to*, chez) [to indenture]. ‖ TECHN. Relier (*in*, en) [a book]; *to bind up*, relier en un seul volume. ‖ FIG. Contraindre, forcer, obliger (*to*, à) [to compel]; *bound to*, astreint à, tenu de; *he's bound to be late*, il sera en retard, c'est certain; *to bind s.o. down to*, contraindre qqn à. ‖ FIG. Lier, engager (*by*, par; *to*, à).
— v. intr. Durcir. ‖ TECHN. Se coincer. ‖ MED. Constiper.
— n. MUS. Ligature f. ‖ TECHN. Blocage, coincement m.
binder [-ə*] n. Cahier d'écolier m. ‖ TECHN. Relieur s. ‖ AGRIC. Lieuse f. ‖ ARCHIT. Attache f. ‖ FAM. Crampon m.
bindery [-əri] n. TECHN. Atelier (m.) de reliure.
binding [-iŋ] n. Action (f.) de lier. ‖ Bordure f.; liséré, galon m. ‖ TECHN. Reliure f. ‖ TECHN. Coincement m. ‖ SPORTS. Fixation, attache f. (of skis).
— adj. TECHN. Agglomérant (material). ‖ MED. Astringent, constipant. ‖ FIG. *To be binding on*, être obligatoire pour, lier (or) engager (s.o.).
bindweed [-wi:d] n. BOT. Liseron m.
binge [bindʒ] n. FAM. Noce, virée, bombe f.
bingo ['biŋgou] n. Bingo m.
— interj. Crac!, vlan!
binnacle ['binək̩l] n. NAUT. Habitacle m.
binocular [bai'nɔkjulə*] adj. Binoculaire.
binoculars [-ləz] n. Jumelle f.
binomial [bai'noumiəl] n. MATH. Binôme m.
— adj. MATH. Binomial.
binominal [bai'nɔminl̩] adj. Binomial, binominal; *binominal system*, système binominal (of scientific nomenclature).
bint [bint] n. POP. Gonzesse, nana f.
binuclear [bai'njukliə*] adj. PHYS. Binucléaire.
biochemistry [‚baio'kemistri] n. Biochimie f.
biodegradable [‚baiodi'greidəbl̩] adj. Biodégradable.
biofeedback [‚baio'fi:dbæk] n. PSYCH. Biofeedback m.
biogenesis [-'dʒenisis] n. Biogenèse f.
biographer [bai'ɔgrəfə*] n. Biographe s.
biographical [‚baio'græfikəl] adj. Biographique.
biography [bai'ɔgrəfi] n. Biographie f.
biological [‚baio'lɔdʒikəl] adj. MED. Biologique. ‖ MILIT. Microbien (warfare). ‖ PHYS. *Biological shield*, écran thermique.
biologist [bai'ɔlədʒist] n. Biologiste s.
biology [-dʒi] n. Biologie f.
biomathematics [baio‚mæθə'mætiks] n. Biomathématique f.
biometry [bai'ɔmətri] n. Biométrie f.
bionics [bai'ɔniks] n. Bionique f.
biophysics [‚baio'fiziks] n. Biophysique f.
biopsy [‚bai'ɔpsi] n. MED. Biopsie f.
bioscience [baio'saiəns] n. Sciences (f. pl.) de la vie.
biosphere ['baiə‚sfiə*] n. Biosphère f.
biosynthesis [‚baio'sinθisis] n. Biosynthèse f.
biotherapy [‚baio'θerəpi] n. MED. Biothérapie f.
biotic [bai'ɔtik] adj. Biotique.
biotope ['baio‚toup] n. Biotope m.
bipartisan [‚baipɑ:ti'zæn] adj. Biparti, bipartite.
bipartite [bai'pɑ:tait] adj. Biparti, bipartite.
biped ['baiped] adj., n. ZOOL. Bipède m.

biplane ['baiplein] n. AVIAT. Biplan *m*.
bipolar [bai'poulə] adj. Bipolaire.
biquadratic [,baikwə'drætik] adj. MATH. Bicarré.
— n. MATH. Equation bicarrée *f*.
birch [bə:tʃ] n. BOT. Bouleau *m*. ‖ Verges *f. pl.*
— v. tr. Fouetter.
bird [bə:d] n. ZOOL. Oiseau *m*. (bird); gibier (*m*.) à plumes (game-bird). ‖ SPORTS. Volant *m*. (shuttle-cock). ‖ CULIN. Volaille *f.; veal bird*, paupiette de veau. ‖ THEATR. *To give s.o. the bird*, siffler qqn. ‖ FAM. Oiseau, pierrot, coco *m*. (person); poule *f*. (woman). ‖ LOC. *Birds of a feather*, gens du même acabit (or) tabac (or) tonneau; *bird in the bush and bird in the hand*, l'ombre et la proie; *a little bird told me*, mon petit doigt me l'a dit; *to kill two birds with one stone*, faire coup double (or) d'une pierre deux coups. ‖ **Bird-cage**, n. Cage, volière *f*. ‖ **Bird-fancier**, n. Oiselier *m*. ‖ **Bird's eye**, adj. A vol d'oiseau, d'ensemble, général; n. BOT. Véronique *f.;* COMM. Œil-de-perdrix *m*. (pattern woven into linens). ‖ **Bird's-foot**, n. BOT. Pied (*m*.) d'alouette. ‖ **Bird's-nest**, v. tr. Dénicher les oiseaux. ‖ **Bird's-nester**, n. Dénicheur d'oiseaux.
birdie [-i] n. FAM. Petit oiseau *m*. ‖ SPORTS. Birdie *m*. (at golf).
biretta [bi'retə] n. ECCLES. Barrette *f*.
birth [bə:θ] n. Naissance *f*. (act, result); *from birth*, dès le berceau. ‖ Portée *f*. (of an animal). ‖ Origine, extraction, naissance *f*. (lineage). ‖ MED. Accouchement *m*. ‖ FIG. Origine, genèse; éclosion *f*. ‖ **Birth-control**, n. Limitation des naissances *f*. ‖ **Birth-mark**, n. MED. Nævus *m.;* envie *f*. ‖ **Birth-place**, n. Lieu (*m*.) de naissance, pays natal *m.;* maison natale *f*. ‖ **Birth-rate**, n. Natalité *f*. ‖ **Birth-stone**, n. Pierre (*f*.) du mois.
birthday [-dei] n. Anniversaire *m.; birthday party*, fête d'anniversaire. ‖ FAM. *In one's birthday suit*, dans le plus simple appareil.
birthright [-rait] n. Droit du sang (or) d'aînesse. ‖ Patrimoine *m*.
Biscay ['biskei] n. GEOGR. Biscaye *f.; Bay of Biscay*, golfe de Gascogne.
biscuit ['biskit] n. CULIN. Biscuit *m*. ‖ U. S. CULIN. Petit pain chaud *m*. ‖ COMM. Biscuit (porcelain).
bisect [bai'sekt] v. tr. Couper en deux. ‖ MATH. Bissecter.
— v. intr. Bifurquer. (See FORK.)
bisector [-ə*] n., **bisectrix** [-riks] n. MATH., PHYS. Bissectrice *f*.
bisexual ['bai'seksjuəl] adj. Bisexué.
bishop ['biʃəp] n. ECCLES. Evêque *m*. ‖ Fou *m*. (chessman). ‖ Bichof *m*. (drink).
bishopric [-rik] n. ECCLES. Evêché *m*. (district); épiscopat *m*. (function).
bisk [bisk] n. CULIN. Bisque *f*.
bismuth ['bizməθ] n. Bismuth *m*.
bison ['baisn] n. invar. ZOOL. Bison *m*.
bisque [bisk] n. SPORTS. Bisque *f*.
bisque n. COMM. Biscuit *m*. (porcelain). ‖ Bisque, jaune-rouge (colour).
bisque n. U. S. CULIN. Glace (*f*.) aux noisettes (ice cream); bisque *f*. (soup).
bissextile [bi'sekstail] adj. Bissextile.
— n. Année bissextile *f*. (See LEAP-YEAR.)
bistort ['bistɔ:t] n. BOT. Bistorte *f*.
bistoury ['bisturi] n. MED. Bistouri *m*.
bistre ['bistə*] adj., n. Bistre *m*.
bistro ['bi:strou] n. Bistro(t) *m.;* restaurant (*m*.) de style bistro(t).
bisulphate [bai'sʌlfeit] n. CHIM. Bisulfate, sul-fate acide *m*.
bit [bit] n. Morceau, bout, brin, fragment *m.;* bribe *f*. ‖ Coin *m*. (of landscape); *bit of garden*, bout de jardin. ‖ Petite pièce *f*. (small coin). ‖ Court passage, bout de texte *m*. (in a book). ‖ TECHN. Mèche *f*. (drill). ‖ CULIN. Morceau *m.;* bouchée *f*.

(of food). ‖ THEATR. Bout de rôle *m*. ‖ FAM. Bout de temps *m.; not a bit*, pas du tout, pas un brin; *to be a bit of a musician*, être quelque peu musicien; *to do one's bit*, faire sa part; *to give s.o. a bit of one's mind*, donner à qqn un échantillon de sa pensée; *to go to bits*, s'effondrer; se dégonfler (fam.).
bit n. Mors (on a bridle). ‖ FAM. *To take the bit in one's teeth*, prendre le mors aux dents.
— v. tr. (1). Mettre le mors à (a horse). ‖ FIG. Brider, refréner.
bit n. INFORM. Bit *m*.
bit pret. See BITE.
bitch [bitʃ] n. ZOOL. Chienne; louve, renarde *f*. ‖ FAM. Rosse *f*. (woman).
— v. intr. U. S. FAM. Pester, rouspéter, râler.
bite [bait] v. tr. (22). Mordre (s.o., sth.); *to bite s.o. on the arm*, mordre qqn au bras; *to bite off*, détacher d'un coup de dent. ‖ Ronger; *to bite one's nails*, se ronger les ongles. ‖ Piquer (flea, snake). ‖ Piquer, brûler (cold, frost, wind). ‖ AUTOM. Adhérer à, coller à (wheels). ‖ TECHN. Ronger, manger (acid); mordre (file, screw). ‖ CULIN. Brûler, piquer (pepper). ‖ FIG. Prendre, attraper, rouler (to deceive). ‖ FAM. *To bite off more than one can chew*, avoir les yeux plus gros que le ventre; *to bite one's tongue*, se mordre la langue; *to bite s.o.'s head off*, rembarrer qqn; *what's biting you?*, quelle mouche vous pique?
— v. intr. Mordre (dog). ‖ Piquer, brûler (cold). ‖ TECHN. Mordre (file). ‖ SPORTS. Mordre (fish). ‖ FIG. Mordre à l'hameçon, se laisser prendre.
— n. Morsure *f*. (act, wound); coup (*m*.) de dent (biting). ‖ Bouchée *f*. (mouthful); morceau *m*. (snack). ‖ Piqûre *f*. (of insect). ‖ CULIN. Piquant *m*. (of a sauce). ‖ TECHN. Mordant *m.;* prise *f*. ‖ AUTOM. Adhérence *f*. ‖ SPORTS. Touche *f*. (in fishing); *I've got a bite*, ça a mordu. ‖ FIG. Mordant *m*.
biter [-ə*] n. Animal (*m*.) qui mord. ‖ Trompeur *m.; the biter bit*, le trompeur trompé.
biting [-iŋ] adj. Mordant, piquant, cuisant (cold) mordant, caustique, incisif (style, tone of voice).
bitten ['bitn] p. p. See BITE.
bitter ['bitə*] adj. Amer (acrid). ‖ Glacial (day wind). ‖ FIG. Acerbe (critic); amer (disappointment person); profond (contempt); cruel (enemy, experience, remorse); violent (quarrel); *to the bitter end*, jusqu'au bout. ‖ **Bitter-apple, bitter-gourd** n. BOT. Coloquinte *f*. ‖ **Bitter-ender**, n. Jusqu'au boutiste *s*. ‖ **Bitter-sweet**, adj. Aigre-doux; n. BOT douce-amère *f.;* FIG. amère douceur *f*.
— n. Amertume *f*. ‖ Amer; bitter *m*. (drink). FIG. Amertume, souffrance *f*.
bitterly [-li] adv. Amèrement. ‖ Glacialement; *it' bitterly cold*, il fait un froid de loup. ‖ FIG. Ave amertume, âprement.
bittern ['bitə:n] n. ZOOL. Butor *m*.
bitterness ['bitənis] n. Amertume *f*. ‖ Rigueur *f* (of cold). ‖ FIG. Amertume; âpreté, acrimonie *f*.
bitts [bits] n. pl. NAUT. Bittes *f. pl.*
bitty ['biti] adj. Hétéroclite, disparate, de bric e de broc (which don't match); décousu (discon-nected).
bitumen [bi'tju:min] n. Bitume *m*.
bituminize [-naiz] v. tr. Bituminer.
bivalence ['bai'veiləns] n. Bivalence *f*.
bivalent [-ənt] adj. Bivalent.
bivalve ['baivælv] adj., n. Bivalve.
bivouac ['bivuæk] n. MILIT. Bivouac *m*.
— v. intr. MILIT. Bivouaquer.
bi-weekly [bai'wi:kli] adj. Bihebdomadaire.
bi-yearly [-'jiəli] adj. Bisannuel, bienna (occurring every two years); qui se produit deu fois par an (occurring twice a year).
— adv. Tous les deux ans; deux fois par an.
biz [biz] interj. FAM. *Good biz!*, chic alors!
bizarre [bi'zɑ:*] adj. Bizarre; grotesque; exce trique.

bizone ['baizoun] n. MILIT. Bizone *f*.

blab [blæb] v. tr. (1). Révéler (a secret); *to blab out*, ébruiter.
— v. intr. Jaser, bavarder.
— n. Jaseur, indiscret *s*.

black [blæk] adj. Noir (colour); *black tie*, cravate noire; « smoking »; *black and white*, noir sur blanc (writing). ‖ Noir, nègre (negro). ‖ Vêtu de noir (dark-clothed). ‖ Noir, sombre, couvert (sky). ‖ MED. *Black and blue*, ecchymosé, couvert de bleus; *Black Death*, Peste noire; *black draught*, purgatif; *black eye*, œil poché; œil au beurre noir (fam.). ‖ GEOGR. *Black Country*, Pays noir, région minière; *Black Sea*, mer Noire. ‖ TECHN. *Black letter*, caractère gothique. ‖ CULIN. Noir (coffee); *black pudding*, boudin. ‖ COMM. Noir (market). ‖ JUR. *Black cap*, calotte noire du juge anglais rendant une sentence de mort; *Black Maria*, voiture cellulaire; panier à salade (fam.). ‖ NAUT. *Black flag*, pavillon noir. ‖ ECCLES. *Black friar, monk*, dominicain, bénédictin; *Black Friday*, vendredi saint. ‖ FIG. Noir (book, list); *in s.o.'s black books*, très mal vu, porté sur la liste noire. ‖ FIG. Noir (Hand, mass). ‖ FIG. Bleu, noir (anger); sombre (look); *black in the face*, noir de fureur. ‖ FIG. Sombre (despair, future); noir (ingratitude); *black sheep*, brebis galeuse; *of blackest dye*, de la pire noirceur (crime). ‖ **Black-beetle**, n. ZOOL. Blatte *f*.; cafard *m*. ‖ **Black-box**, n. TECHN. Boîte noire *f*., mouchard *m*. ‖ **Black-currant**, n. BOT. Cassis *m*. ‖ **Black-hole**, n. ASTRON. Trou noir *m*. ‖ **Black-lead**, n. Mine (*f*.) de plomb. ‖ **Black-letter**, adj. FIG. A marquer d'une pierre noire. ‖ **Black-list**, v. tr. Porter sur la liste noire, mettre à l'index. ‖ **Black-out**, n. MILIT., FIG. Black-out *m*.; ELECTR. Panne (or) coupure d'électricité *f*.; MED. Perte de conscience *f*.; THEATRE. Extinction (*f*.) des lumières; v. tr. MILIT. Camoufler les lumières; FIG. Faire le black-out sur, cacher, camoufler; v. intr. MED., FAM. Perdre conscience, tomber dans les pommes. ‖ **Black-shirts**, n. Chemises noires *f*. *pl*.
— n. Noir *m*. (colour). ‖ Noir; deuil *m*. (dark clothing). ‖ Noir, nègre *m*.; négresse *f*. (negro). ‖ Noir (*m*.) de suie (soot). ‖ AGRIC. Charbon *m*.
— v. tr. Noircir (to blacken); noircir, salir (to soil). ‖ Cirer (shoes).

blackamoor [-əmuə*] n. † Nègre; moricaud *s*.

blackball [-bɔːl] n. Vote contraire *m*.
— v. tr. Blackbouler.

blackberry [-bɛri] n. BOT. Mûre *f*.

blackbird [-bəːd] n. ZOOL. Merle *m*.

blackboard [-bɔːd] n. Tableau noir *m*.

blacken [-n] v. tr., intr. Noircir (lit. and fig.).

blackface [-feis] adj. A la peau noire. ‖ TECHN. Gras (in print).
— n. Moricaud *s*. ‖ TECHN. Caractère gras *m*.

blackguard [-gɑːd] n. Grossier *s*. ‖ Vaurien *m*.; fripouille *f*.
— adj. Malembouché, grossier. ‖ Canaille.
— v. tr. Vilipender, invectiver.

blackguardism [-gɑːdizm̩] n. Grossièreté *f*. (in language). ‖ Fripouillerie *f*.

blacking [-iŋ] n. Cirage noir *m*. (for shoes); pâte (*f*.) à noircir (for stoves).

blackish [-iʃ] adj. Noirâtre.

blackleg [-leg] n. Jaune *m*. (strike-breaker). ‖ FAM. Aigrefin *m*.

blackmail [-meil] n. JUR. Chantage *m*.
— v. tr. JUR. Faire chanter; faire du chantage auprès de.

blackmailer [-meilə*] n. JUR. Maître chanteur *m*.

blackness [-nis] n. Couleur noire, noirceur *f*. ‖ Obscurité *f*. (darkness). ‖ FIG. Noirceur *f*.

blacksmith [-smiθ] n. TECHN. Forgeron *m*.

blackthorn [-θɔːn] n. BOT. Prunellier *m*. ‖ Gourdin *m*. (cudgel).

blacky [-i] n. FAM. Négro, moricaud *m*.

bladder ['blædə*] n. MED. *Gall bladder*, vésicule biliaire; *urinary bladder*, vessie. ‖ BOT. Vésicule *f*. ‖ SPORTS. *Football bladder*, vessie de ballon. ‖ FAM. Outre vide *f*.

blade [bleid] n. BOT. Herbe, feuille *f*. (of corn); brin *m*. (of grass); *in the blade*, en herbe. ‖ Lame, épée *f*. (sword). ‖ TECHN. Couperet *m*. (of guillotine); lame *f*. (of knife, saw); aube *f*. (of paddlewheel); lame *f*., plat *m*. (of sword). ‖ AGRIC. Fer *m*. (of spade). ‖ AUTOM. Balai *m*. (of windscreen [or] U. S. windshield wiper). ‖ AVIAT. Pale, ailette *f*. (of propeller). ‖ NAUT. Pale, palette *f*. (of oar). ‖ FAM. *Jolly* (or) *gay old blade*, joyeux drille.

blaeberry ['bleibəri] n. BOT. Airelle *f*.

blah [blɑː] n. U. S. Boniment, bla-bla-bla *m*.

blamable ['bleiməbl] adj. Blâmable.

blame [bleim] n. Blâme *m*. (censure). ‖ Responsabilité de la faute *f*.; *the blame is mine*, c'est ma faute; *to lay the blame upon*, rejeter la responsabilité sur.
— v. t. Blâmer; *to blame s.o. for sth.*, blâmer qqn de qqch., reprocher qqch. à qqn. ‖ FAM. *To blame sth. on s.o.*, mettre qqch. sur le dos de qqn, faire payer les pots cassés à qqn.

blameful [-ful] adj. Blâmable.

blameless [-lis] adj. Irréprochable.

blamelessly [-lisli] adv. Irréprochablement.

blamelessness [-lisnis] n. Irréprochabilité, impeccabilité *f*.

blameworthiness [-,wəːðinis] n. Démérite *m*.; conduite blâmable *f*.

blameworthy [-,wəːði] adj. Blâmable.

blanch [blɑːnʃ] v. tr. AGRIC., CULIN., TECHN. Blanchir. ‖ FIG. Faire blanchir (hair); faire pâlir (or) blêmir (s.o.).
— v. intr. FIG. Blêmir, pâlir.

blancmange [bləˈmɔnʒ] n. CULIN. Blanc-manger *m*.

bland [blænd] adj. Doux, douceureux, suave (manner, person, speech). ‖ Doux (air, drink, food, medicine).

blandish [-iʃ] v. tr. Cajoler, aduler.

blandishment [-iʃmənt] n. Cajolerie, adulation, flatterie *f*.

blandness [-nis] n. Douceur, suavité *f*.

blank [blæŋk] adj. Blanc *m*.; blanche *f*. (colour). ‖ Faux (door, window); nu (wall). ‖ Blanc, vierge (sheet of paper); blanc (space). ‖ FIN., JUR. En blanc (cheque, document). ‖ MILIT. A blanc (ammunition, cartridge, shot). ‖ GEOGR. Muet (map). ‖ GRAMM. Blanc, sans rime (verse). ‖ FIG. Absolu, catégorique (denial); absolu, total (impossibility); morne, vide (look, life); vide (mind); désorienté, abasourdi (person); stérile (year); *to look blank*, avoir l'air ahuri; tomber de la lune (fam.).
— n. Blanc, vide *m*. (empty space). ‖ Billet non gagnant *m*. (lottery ticket). ‖ Noir (*m*.) de la cible; cible *f*. (target). ‖ Tiret *m*. (dash). ‖ *Double blank*, double blanc (in dominoes). ‖ FIN., JUR. *In blank*, en blanc. ‖ U. S. Formule *f*.; formulaire *m*. (form); *application blank*, feuille de demande.
— v. tr. *To blank out*, rayer, effacer (to cross out); masquer, occulter (to obscure).

blanket ['blæŋkət] n. Couverture *f*.; *electric blanket*, couverture chauffante. ‖ FAM. *To throw a wet blanket over*, jeter une douche sur; *wet blanket*, rabat-joie, éteignoir.
— v. tr. Couvrir d'une couverture. ‖ Berner, passer à la couverte. ‖ NAUT. Déventer. ‖ FIG. Couvrir, englober. ‖ U. S. RADIO. Intercepter, couvrir. ‖ FIG. Etouffer (question, scandal).
— adj. FAM. *Blanket statement*, énoncé (or) propos général.

blankly ['blæŋkli] adv. D'un air morne, sans vie, l'esprit vide (vacuously). ‖ Catégoriquement, nettement (flatly).

blanky ['blæŋki] adj. Satané, sacré.
blanquette [blɑ̃'kɛt] n. CULIN. Blanquette *f.*
blare [blɛə*] n. MUS. Sonnerie de trompette *f.* ‖ FAM. Cornage *m.*
— v. intr. MUS. Trompeter, sonner. ‖ FAM. Corner, claironner.
— v. tr. MUS. *To blare out,* sonner. ‖ FAM. *To blare forth,* corner, trompeter (the news).
blarney ['blɑ:ni] n. Boniment *m.;* cajolerie *f.*
— v. tr. Flagorner, embobeliner (s.o.).
— v. intr. Distribuer de l'eau bénite de cour.
blasé ['blɑ:zei] adj. Blasé.
blaspheme [blæs'fi:m] v. tr., intr. Blasphémer.
blasphemer [-ə*] n. Blasphémateur *m.;* blasphématrice *f.*
blasphemous ['blæsfiməs] adj. Blasphématoire *f.*
blasphemy [-i] n. Blasphème *m.*
blast [blɑ:st] n. Rafale *f.;* souffle *m.* (of wind). ‖ Explosion, charge *f.* (of explosive). ‖ TECHN., MILIT. Souffle *m.* ‖ MUS. Sonnerie *f.* (of a trumpet). ‖ FAM. *At full blast,* à toute allure; à plein rendement. ‖ Blast-effect, n. MILIT. Effet du souffle *m.* ‖ Blast-furnace, n. TECHN. Haut fourneau *m.* ‖ Blast-off, n. Mise (*f.*) à feu; départ *m.* ‖ Blast-pipe, n. Tuyère *f.* (in astrophysics).
— v. intr. Miner, faire sauter. ‖ MILIT. *To blast one's way through,* se frayer un chemin à coup de bombes (or) de grenades). ‖ BOT. Flétrir. ‖ FIG. Démolir, ruiner (reputation).
blat [blæt] v. intr., tr. See BLEAT, BLAB, BLURT.
blatancy ['bleitənsi] n. Aspect criard *m.* ‖ Caractère flagrant *m.*
blatant [-ənt] adj. Criard, braillard (noisy). ‖ Criard, voyant (showy). ‖ FIG. Criant; flagrant.
blather ['blæðə*] v. intr. FAM. Parler à tort et à travers; noyer le poisson.
blaze [bleiz] n. Flamme, flambée *f.;* flamboiement, embrasement *m.; in a blaze,* en feu. ‖ Eclat *m.* (of diamonds, searchlights). ‖ FIG. Eclat *m.* (of anger, beauty, fame); *blaze of oratory,* envolée oratoire, sursaut d'éloquence. ‖ FAM. Pl. Enfer *m.; to run like blazes,* courir comme un dératé; *to send to blazes,* envoyer au bain, envoyer balader. ‖ Blaze-up, n. FAM. Eclat *m.*
— v. intr. Flamber, flamboyer. ‖ Briller, étinceler (jewels, metal, sun) [with, de]. ‖ **To blaze away,** tirer sans relâche (to shoot); parler avec chaleur (or) volubilité (to speak); travailler fébrilement (or) sans répit (to work). ‖ **To blaze out,** se mettre à flamber (fire). ‖ **To blaze up,** s'embraser; FIG. s'emporter, prendre la mouche, faire un éclat.
blaze n. Etoile *f.;* chanfrein *m.* (on an animal's face). ‖ Encoche, marque *f.* (on a tree).
— v. tr. Marquer, griffer (a tree). ‖ FIG. *To blaze the trail,* frayer la piste.
blazer [-ə*] n. SPORTS. Blazer *m.* ‖ FAM. Craque *f.;* bobard *m.* ‖ U. S. Casserole *f.*
blazon ['bleizn] n. BLAS. Blason *m.;* science héraldique *f.* ‖ FIG. Parade *f.* (of virtues).
— v. tr. BLAS. Blasonner. ‖ FIG. Publier; *to blazon abroad,* claironner aux quatre vents (fam.).
bleach [bli:tʃ] v. tr. Blanchir (to whiten). ‖ Décolorer; oxygéner (hair).
— v. intr. Blanchir, se décolorer.
bleak [bli:k] n. ZOOL. Ablette *f.*
bleak adj. Battu par le vent, désolé, nu (land). ‖ Glacial (cold). ‖ FIG. Sombre, désolé, froid.
blear [bliə*] adj. Chassieux (eye). ‖ Indistinct, vague, indécis (outline). ‖ FIG. Imprécis (mind). ‖ **Blear-eyed,** adj. Aux yeux chassieux.
bleary [-ri] adj. Chassieux (person).
bleat [bli:t] v. intr. ZOOL. Bégueter (goat); bêler (sheep). ‖ FIG. Bêler; geindre.
— v. tr. *To bleat out,* dire d'une voix bêlante, chevroter.
— n. ZOOL., FIG. Bêlement *m.*

bleater [-ə*] n. FAM. Geignard, bêleur *s.*
bleating [-iŋ] n. Bêlement *m.*
bleb [bleb] n. Bulle *f.* (in glass, water). ‖ MED. Ampoule *f.* (blister).
bled [bled] pret. See BLEED.
bleed [bli:d] v. intr. (23). Saigner; *to bleed at the nose,* saigner du nez. ‖ Répandre son sang (*for,* pour). ‖ Déteindre, couler (colour, dye). ‖ BOT. Pleurer. ‖ TECHN. Fuir (gas, water). ‖ FIG. Saigner, souffrir, se déchirer (heart). ‖ FAM. Cracher, casquer, s'exécuter, se fendre.
— v. tr. Saigner, faire une saignée à. ‖ BOT. Suinter (sap). ‖ FAM. Sucer, pressurer (s.o.); *to bleed oneself white for,* se saigner à blanc (or) aux quatre veines pour.
bleeding [-iŋ] adj. Saignant.
— n. Saignement *m.;* saignée *f.* ‖ BOT. Suintement, pleur *m.* ‖ TECHN. Fuite *f.*
blemish ['blemiʃ] n. Tare; tache *f.*
— v. tr. Entacher; gâter.
blench [blen(t)ʃ] v. intr. Reculer; broncher.
— v. tr. Fermer les yeux sur, s'aveugler sur.
blend [blend] v. tr. Mélanger, mêler (*with,* à, avec). [See MIX.] ‖ Fondre, allier (colours, tastes). ‖ Couper (wine). ‖ FIG. Fusionner, fondre (ideas).
— v. intr. Se mêler, se mélanger (*with,* à). ‖ Se fondre, s'allier.
— N. Mélange *m.* ‖ GRAMM. Amalgame *m.*
— N. B. *Blend,* régulier, peut faire aussi *blent* aux temps passés.
blende n. Blende *f.*
blennorrhagia [blenɔ'reidʒiə] n. MED. Blennorragie *f.*
bless ['bles] v. tr. Bénir (s.o., sth.); *God bless you,* Dieu vous bénisse! ‖ Remercier, bénir, exalter (to glorify). ‖ Favoriser, douer (*with,* de); rendre heureux (*with,* avec); *to be blessed with,* avoir la chance (or) le bonheur d'avoir, être favorisé de, jouir de. ‖ FAM. *God bless me!,* Seigneur!, par exemple!; *blest if I saw him!,* le diable m'emporte si je l'ai vu!
— N. B. *Bless,* régulier, peut faire *blest* aux pret., p. p.
blessed [-id], **blest** [blest] adj. ECCLES. Béni (holy); bienheureux (beatified). ‖ FIG. Béni, heureux (fate, times); gratifié, favorisé, doué (*with,* de). ‖ FAM. *Every blessed day,* tous les jours que le bon Dieu fait; *that blessed boy!;* ce sacré (or) fichu gamin!
— n. ECCLES. Bienheureux *m. pl.* (collectively).
blessedness [-idnis] n. ECCLES. Béatitude *f.* ‖ FIG. Félicité *f.*
blessing [-iŋ] n. Bénédiction *f.* ‖ Bénédiction, chance, faveur; approbation *f.* ‖ ECCLES. Bénédicité *m.* (at meals).
blether ['bleðə*] v. intr. Baliverner.
— n. Baliverne *f.;* bla-bla-bla *m.*
blew [blu:] pret. See BLOW.
blight [blait] n. AGRIC. Nielle *f.* (smut); brouissure *f.* (frost-nip); rouille *f.* (rust). ‖ ZOOL. Puceron *m.* (insect). ‖ FIG. Fléau *m.;* influence pernicieuse *f.*
— v. tr. AGRIC. Nieller; brouir; rouiller. ‖ FIG. Ruiner, détruire.
blighter [-ə*] n. FAM. Zèbre, type *m.*
Blighty ['blaiti] n. MILIT., FAM. Angleterre, mère patrie *f.; a Blighty one,* blessure assurant son rapatriement à celui qui en est victime.
blimey ['blaimi] interj. Bon Dieu!
blimp [blimp] n. AVIAT. Dirigeable éclaireur *m.;* vedette aérienne *f.* ‖ FAM. Cul-de-plomb *m.*
blind [blaind] adj. Aveugle; *a blind man, woman,* un, une aveugle; *blind in one eye,* borgne. ‖ Faux (door, window); aveugle (wall). ‖ Caché (ditch, patch); reculé (valley); *blind alley,* cul-de-sac, impasse; *blind coal,* anthracite; *blind date,* rendezvous avec qqn qu'on ne connaît pas; *blind letter,*

lettre à l'adresse mal mise. ‖ Fɪɢ. Aveugle (anger, force, hazard, obedience, passion) ; *blind side,* point faible. ‖ Fɪɢ. Aveugle *(to,* à) ; *to be blind to,* fermer les yeux sur, refuser de voir, ignorer, s'aveugler sur. ‖ **Blind-alley,** adj. Fɪɢ. Sans issue, sans avenir. ‖ **Blind-man's buff,** n. Colin-maillard *m.* ‖ **Blind-stitch,** n. Point perdu *m. ;* v. intr. Coudre à points perdus. ‖ **Blind-worm,** n. Zooʟ. Orvet *m.*
— adj. A l'aveuglette. ‖ Aᴠɪᴀᴛ. *To fly blind,* voler sans visibilité. ‖ Fᴀᴍ. Complètement ; *blind drunk,* fin saoul, noir.
— v. tr. Aveugler.
— v. intr. Aᴜᴛᴏᴍ. *To blind along,* foncer à l'aveuglette, rouler à tombeau ouvert. ‖ Pᴏᴘ. Jurer.
— n. Aveugles *m. pl.* (collectively). ‖ Store *m. ; shop, Venetian blind,* banne, jalousie. ‖ Œillère *f.* (harness). ‖ Mɪʟɪᴛ. Blinde *f.* ‖ Fɪɢ. Masque *m.*
blindfold [-fould] adj. Aux yeux bandés.
— adv. Les yeux bandés. ‖ Fɪɢ. Aveuglément.
— v. tr. Bander les yeux à. ‖ Fɪɢ. Aveugler.
— n. Bandeau *m.* ‖ Fɪɢ. Obstacle *m.,* écran *(m.)* qui empêche de voir.
blinding [-iŋ] n. Tᴇᴄʜɴ. Ensablement *m.* ‖ Aᴜᴛᴏᴍ. Eblouissement *m.*
— adj. Aveuglant. ‖ Eblouissant (dazzling).
blindly [-li] adv. A l'aveuglette.
blindness [-nis] n. Mᴇᴅ. Cécité *f.* ‖ Fɪɢ. Aveuglement *m. (to,* devant, à l'égard de).
blink [bliŋk] v. intr. Clignoter, cligner des yeux (to wink). ‖ Guigner, regarder les yeux mi-clos. ‖ Vaciller, clignoter (to twinkle). ‖ Fɪɢ. Fermer les yeux *(at,* sur).
— v. tr. Eluder (a question). ‖ Ignorer, refuser de voir (a fact).
— n. Clignotement *m.* ‖ Lueur *f.* (gleam). ‖ Reflet lumineux *m.* ‖ Fɪɢ. Aperçu *m.* (glimpse). ‖ Fᴀᴍ. U. S. *On the blink,* détraqué.
blinker [-ə*] n. Œillère *f.* (harness). ‖ Aᴜᴛᴏᴍ. Clignotant *m.* ‖ Aᴠɪᴀᴛ. Phare *m.* ‖ Fɪɢ. *To wear blinkers,* avoir des œillères.
bliss [blis] n. Joie, félicité *f.* ‖ Eᴄᴄʟᴇs. Béatitude *f.*
blissful [-ful] adj. Bienheureux.
blister ['blistə*] n. Mᴇᴅ. Ampoule *f.* (on skin) ; vésicatoire *m.* (vesicatory). ‖ Tᴇᴄʜɴ. Cloque *f.* (in painting). ‖ Aᴠɪᴀᴛ. Coupole *f. ;* encorbellement *m.*
— v. intr. Mᴇᴅ. Se couvrir d'ampoules. ‖ Tᴇᴄʜɴ. Coquiller (bread).
— v. tr. Mᴇᴅ. Couvrir d'ampoules ; appliquer un vésicatoire. ‖ Fɪɢ. Flétrir. ‖ U. S. Fᴀᴍ. Rosser.
blithe ['blaið], **blithesome** [-səm] adj. Gai, enjoué ; folâtre.
blithely [-li] adv. Gaiement.
blithering ['bliðəriŋ] adj. Fᴀᴍ. Bavard, jacasseur (talkative) ; *blithering idiot,* sale crétin.
blitz [blits] n. Aᴠɪᴀᴛ. Bombardement *m.* ‖ Fɪɢ. Action énergique ; campagne de surprise *f.*
— v. tr. Détruire par bombardement.
blitzkrieg [-kri:g] n. Mɪʟɪᴛ. Guerre-éclair *f.*
blizzard ['blizəd] n. Tempête (or) tourmente de neige *f.*
bloat ['blout] v. tr. Enfler, gonfler, bouffir. ‖ Boursoufler. ‖ Fɪɢ. Bouffir, gonfler *(with,* de).
— v. intr. Enfler ; se gonfler. ‖ Météoriser.
bloat v. tr. Cᴜʟɪɴ. Fumer (herrings).
bloated [-id] adj. Cᴜʟɪɴ. Saur (herring).
bloater [-ə*] n. Cᴜʟɪɴ. Hareng saur *m.*
blob [blɔb] n. Tache *f.* (of colour, paint) ; goutte *f.* (of honey) ; pâté *m.* (of ink). ‖ Fᴀᴍ. Bévue *f.*
— v. intr. (1). Cracher, baver (fountain-pen).
— v. tr. U. S. Eclabousser.
bloc [blɔk] n. Bloc *m.* (in politics).
block n. Bloc *m. ;* masse *f.* (of metal) ; bloc, quartier *m.* (of rock) ; bloc (of stone) ; souche, bille *f.* (of wood). ‖ Ais *m.* (of a butcher) ; tronchet *m.* (of a cooper) ; forme *f.* (of a hatter) ; tête *f.* (of a milliner). ‖ Billot *m.* (of scaffold). ‖ Cube *m.* (toy,

brick). ‖ Obstacle, blocage *m. ;* obstruction *f.* ‖ Aᴜᴛᴏᴍ. Encombrement, embouteillage *m.* ‖ Sᴘᴏʀᴛs. Point de blocage *m. ;* interception *f.* ‖ Mᴇᴅ. Blocage *m.* ‖ Jᴜʀ. Obstruction *f.* ‖ Aʀᴄʜɪᴛ. Grosse brique creuse *f. ;* block, pâté, îlot *m.* (of buildings) ; *block of flats,* immeuble, maison de rapport. ‖ Cʜ. ᴅᴇ ꜰ. Tronçon *m.* (line) ; rame *f.* (train). ‖ Mɪʟɪᴛ. Taquet *m.* ‖ Aᴠɪᴀᴛ. Bloc de bois de remplissage *m.* ‖ Nᴀᴜᴛ. Cale, poulie *f.* ‖ Aʀᴛs. Planche *f. ;* cliché *m.* ‖ Cᴜʟɪɴ. Billot, hachoir *m.* (butcher's) ; motte *f.* (of butter). ‖ Tᴇᴄʜɴ. Poulie, moufle *f. ;* palan *m. ; brake block,* sabot de frein ; *differential block,* mouflette ; *feed block,* bloc d'alimentation. ‖ Fɪɢ. Souche *f. ; chip off the old block,* fils de son père, digne rejeton d'une noble race. ‖ Fᴀᴍ. Bûche *f. ;* soliveau *m.* (blockhead).
— adj. En brique (coal). ‖ *Block letters,* grandes capitales ; *block writing,* écriture en lettres d'imprimerie. ‖ Cʜ. ᴅᴇ ꜰ. *Block system,* bloc-système.
— v. tr. Bloquer, barrer, boucher ; *to block up,* boucler, bloquer, obstruer (to obstruct) ; caler (to wedge). ‖ Sᴘᴏʀᴛs, Fɪɴ. Bloquer. ‖ Tᴇᴄʜɴ. Enformer (a hat) ; bloquer, enrayer (a wheel) ; se bloquer (wheel). ‖ Aʀᴛs. *To block in, out,* esquisser, ébaucher, silhouetter. ‖ Fɪɢ. Entraver (to hinder) ; esquisser (to sketch).
blockade [blɔ'keid] n. Mɪʟɪᴛ. Blocus *m.* ‖ U. S. Blocage *m.* (by snow). ‖ **Blockade-runner,** n. Forceur de blocus *m.*
— v. tr. Mɪʟɪᴛ. Faire le blocus de. ‖ Bloquer, obstruer (door, view).
blockbuster ['blɔk,bʌstə*] n. Mɪʟɪᴛ. Bombe explosive *f.* ‖ Fɪɢ. Bombe, dynamite *f. ; this film will be a blockbuster,* ce film va faire un tabac.
blockhead ['blɔkhed] n. Fᴀᴍ. Souche, bûche, buse, tête *(f.)* de bois.
blockhouse [-haus] n. Mɪʟɪᴛ. Blockaus *m.*
blockish [-iʃ] adj. Fᴀᴍ. Borné, épais.
bloke [blouk] n. Fᴀᴍ. Zèbre *m.* (fellow).
blond [blɔnd] adj., n. Blond *m.*
blonde adj., n. Blonde *f.*
blood [blʌd] n. Mᴇᴅ. Sang *m.* ‖ Sang, meurtre *m.* (murder). ‖ Sang rouge *m.* (blush). ‖ Sang *m. ;* colère (anger) ; indignation ; frayeur *f.* (fear) ; *bad blood,* colère ; haine ; *he's got her in his blood,* il l'a dans la peau ; *in cold blood,* de sang-froid ; *his blood was up,* le sang lui bouillait ; *to make s.o.'s blood boil,* faire bouillir (or) damner qqn ; *to make s.o.'s blood run cold,* glacer le sang de qqn. ‖ Sang *m. ;* famille (family) ; parenté (kinship) ; descendance (lineage) ; race *f. ; blood feud,* vendetta ; *of Irish blood,* de race irlandaise ; *he is not of my blood,* il n'est pas de mon sang ; *to run in the blood,* être dans le sang, être héréditaire. ‖ Dandy *m.* ‖ Fɪɢ. Sang. ‖ **Blood-and-thunder,** adj. A péripéties, à sensation (novel). ‖ **Blood-bank,** n. Mᴇᴅ. Banque (*f.*) du sang. ‖ **Blood-cell,** n. Mᴇᴅ. Globule *m.* ‖ **Blood-count,** n. Mᴇᴅ. Numération globulaire *f.* ‖ **Blood-curdling,** adj. Fᴀᴍ. A vous tourner le sang, à faire frémir. ‖ **Blood-group,** n. Mᴇᴅ. Groupe sanguin *m.* ‖ **Blood-grouping,** n. Mᴇᴅ. Recherche (*f.*) du groupe sanguin. ‖ **Blood-horse,** n. Zooʟ. Pur-sang *m.* ‖ **Blood-letting,** n. Mᴇᴅ. Saignée *f.* ‖ **Blood-money,** n. Fɪɢ. Prix du sang *m.* ‖ **Blood-poisoning,** n. Mᴇᴅ. Empoisonnement du sang *m.* ‖ **Blood-pressure,** n. Mᴇᴅ. Tension artérielle, pression sanguine *f.* ‖ **Blood-red,** adj. Rouge sang. ‖ **Blood-relation,** n. Parent (*s.*) par le sang. ‖ **Blood-stained,** adj. Souillé de sang. ‖ **Blood-sucker,** n. Zooʟ. Sangsue *f.* ‖ **Blood-sugar,** n. Mᴇᴅ. Glycémie *f. ;* dosage du glucose *m.* ‖ **Blood-test,** n. Mᴇᴅ. Examen du sang *m.* ‖ **Blood typing,** n. U. S. Mᴇᴅ. Recherche (*f.*) du groupe sanguin. ‖ **Blood-urea,** n. Mᴇᴅ. Urée sanguine *f.* ‖ **Blood-vessel,** n. Mᴇᴅ. Vaisseau sanguin *m.*

— adj. De sang; *blood bath*, bain de sang. ‖ Sanguin; *blood orange*, sanguine.
— v. tr. MED. Faire une saignée à. (See BLEED.) ‖ SPORTS, FIG. Acharner.

bloodhound [-haund] n. ZOOL. Limier *m.* ‖ FIG. Limier, détective *m.*

bloodily [-ili] adv. D'une manière sanguinaire, sauvagement.

bloodiness [-inis] n. Goût sanguinaire *m.*

bloodless [-lis] adj. Exsangue (without blood). ‖ Sans effusion de sang (without bloodshed). ‖ Anémié, pâle. ‖ Sans vitalité (or) énergie. ‖ Cruel, sans cœur.

bloodlessly [-lisli] adv. Sans effusion de sang.

bloodroot [-rut] n. BOT. Sanguinaire *f.*

bloodshed [-ʃed] n. Effusion (*f.*) de sang; meurtre, carnage *m.*; boucherie *f.*

bloodshot [-ʃɔt] adj. MED. Injecté de sang (eyes).

bloodstone [-stoun] n. Sanguine *f.*

bloodthirstiness [-,θəːstinis] n. Soif (*f.*) de sang; goûts sanguinaires *m. pl.*

bloodthirsty [-,θəːsti] adj. Altéré de sang.

bloody [-i] adj. Couvert de sang, sanglant, ensanglanté. ‖ Rouge sang (blood-red). ‖ FIG. Sanguinaire. ‖ POP. Sacré, damné. ‖ **Bloody-minded,** adj. Hargneux.
— adv. POP. Diablement, bougrement.
— v. tr. (2). Ensanglanter.

bloom [bluːm] n. Fleur, floraison *f.* ‖ BOT. Velouté *m.* (of plums). ‖ FIG. Eclat *m.*; fleur *f.*
— v. intr. Fleurir, s'épanouir, être en fleur. ‖ FIG. S'épanouir, resplendir, être florissant.

bloomer [-ə*] n. Culotte bouffante *f.* (for women). ‖ FAM. Balourdise, boulette, gaffe *f.* (See BONER.)

blooming [-iŋ] adj. Fleuri, en fleur. ‖ FIG. Epanoui, florissant. ‖ FAM. Fichu, fieffé, sacré.

blossom ['blɔsəm] n. BOT., FIG. Fleur *f.* ‖ **Blossom-faced,** adj. Au visage bourgeonnant.
— v. intr. Fleurir, être en fleur. ‖ FIG. S'épanouir.

blot [blɔt] n. Pâté *m.* (of ink). ‖ Rature *f.* (erasure). ‖ FIG. Tache *f.*
— v. tr. (1). Tacher (to stain). ‖ Buvarder, sécher (to dry). ‖ **To blot out,** raturer (FIG. masquer, éclipser, effacer; U. S. liquider (to kill).
— v. intr. Boire (paper); couler, cracher (pen).

blotch [blɔtʃ] n. Tache *f.* (stain). ‖ MED. Pustule *f.* (boil); tache *f.* (on the skin); *blotchy,* couperosé.
— v. tr. MED. Couvrir de taches.

blotter ['blɔtə*] n. Buvard *m.* ‖ COMM. Brouillard *m.* ‖ JUR. U. S. *Police blotter,* registre des arrestations.

blotting [-iŋ] adj. Qui sèche. ‖ **Blotting-pad,** n. Sous-main *m.* ‖ **Blotting-paper,** n. Buvard *m.*

blotto ['blɔtou] adj. POP. Bourré, rond, schlass.

blouse [blauz] n. Blouse *f.* (of peasants). ‖ Blouse; corsage, chemisier *m.* (of women). ‖ MILIT., NAUT. Vareuse *f.*

blow [blou] v. intr. (24). Souffler (wind) [*from,* de; *upon,* sur]. ‖ Venter; *it was blowing,* il faisait du vent. ‖ Souffler, respirer fort, être essoufflé; *to blow short,* être poussif (horse). ‖ S'envoler; *to blow out of the window,* s'envoler par la fenêtre. ‖ MUS. Sonner, retentir, résonner (instrument); jouer, souffler, sonner (*on,* de) [musician]. ‖ FIG. Dire du mal (*on, upon,* de); *to blow upon s.o.'s character,* salir la réputation de qqn. ‖ **To blow about,** être poussé par le vent de-ci de-là (leaves). ‖ **To blow in,** entrer (*at,* par) [wind]. ‖ FAM. Entrer en passant (person). ‖ **To blow off,** s'envoler (hat). ‖ **To blow out,** s'éteindre (fire). ‖ AUTOM. Eclater (tyre); ELECTR. Sauter (fuse). ‖ **To blow over,** se calmer (storm). ‖ AGRIC. Se coucher (crops); FIG. S'apaiser (scandal). ‖ **To blow up,** TECHN. Exploser (boiler); sauter (mine).
— v. tr. Souffler; émettre (a breath); *to blow bubbles,* faire des bulles de savon; *to blow s.o. a kiss,* envoyer un baiser à qqn. ‖ Souffler sur;

ranimer (the fire). ‖ Insuffler (*into,* dans) [air]. ‖ Faire fonctionner (the bellows). ‖ Chasser (or) pousser en soufflant (*against,* contre) [hail]. ‖ Essouffler (an animal, s.o.) [to put out of breath]. ‖ Faire souffler; *to blow one's nose,* se moucher. ‖ Pondre sur (flies). ‖ AUTOM. *To blow the horn,* corner, klaxonner. ‖ MUS. Jouer (songs); jouer de, sonner de (a trumpet); souffler dans (a whistle); *to blow a blast on one's trumpet,* donner un bon coup de trompette. ‖ TECHN. Souffler (glass). ‖ ELECTR. Faire sauter (a fuse). ‖ CULIN. Vider (an egg). ‖ FAM. Cafarder; *to blow hot and cold,* virer à tout vent; *to blow one's own trumpet* (or) U. S. *horn,* entonner ses propres louanges. ‖ **To blow away,** emporter, dissiper, chasser, disperser. ‖ **To blow down** (or) **over,** renverser, abattre (a tree); AGRIC. Coucher (the crops). ‖ **To blow in,** enfoncer (a door); FAM. Manger (one's money). ‖ **To blow off,** emporter (s.o.'s hat); TECHN. Vider (a boiler). ‖ **To blow out,** souffler, éteindre (a candle); gonfler (one's cheeks); *to blow one's brains out,* se brûler la cervelle; faire sauter le caisson; TECHN. Vider, purger (a boiler). ‖ **To blow up,** faire sauter (a bridge, a mine); gonfler (a balloon, a tyre); ranimer (the fire); agrandir (a photograph); FIG. *To be blown up with conceit,* être gonflé d'orgueil, se gober; FAM. *To blow s.o. up,* enguirlander qqn, sonner les cloches à qqn.
— n. Souffle; coup de vent *m.* ‖ Œufs *m. pl.*; chiure *f.* (of flies). ‖ MUS. *Blow at* (or) *on one's trumpet,* coup de trompette. ‖ **Blow-lamp,** n. TECHN. Chalumeau *m.* ‖ **Blow-off,** adj. TECHN. D'extraction, de vidange, d'évent. ‖ **Blow-out,** n. TECHN. Soufflage *m.*; AUTOM. Eclatement *m.,* crevaison *f.* (of tyre); FAM. Gueuleton *m.*; *to have a good blow-out,* se caler les côtes. ‖ **Blow-up,** n. Agrandissement photographique *m.*

blow n. BOT., FIG. Floraison *f.*; épanouissement *m.*
— v. intr. (24). BOT. S'épanouir, s'ouvrir (flower). ‖ FIG. S'épanouir.

blow n. Coup *m.*; *without striking a blow,* sans coup férir. ‖ SPORTS. Coup *m.*; *blows,* encaisse. ‖ FIG. Coup, choc *m.* (*at, on,* à).

blower [-ə*] n. Tablier *m.* (of a fire-place). ‖ TECHN., MUS. Souffleur *m.* ‖ FAM. Téléphone *m.*

blowfly [-flai] n. ZOOL. Mouche à viande *f.*

blowgun [-gʌn] n. Sarbacane *f.* ‖ Pistolet *m.* (for painting).

blowhole [-houl] n. TECHN. Event *m.*

blown [bloun] p. p. See BLOW.

blowpipe [-paip] n. Chalumeau *m.* ‖ Sarbacane *f.* ‖ TECHN. Canne *f.*; (of blower). ‖ MUS. Porte-vent *m.* (of bagpipe).

blowy [-i] n. Venteux.

blowzed ['blauzd], **blowzy** [-i] adj. Haut en couleur, rougeaud, coloré (ruddy). ‖ Mal peigné, échevelé, ébouriffé (unkempt).

blubber ['blʌbə*] v. intr. Pleurnicher; chialer (fam.).
— v. tr. Balbutier en pleurnichant. ‖ Gonfler (or) mouiller de larmes.
— n. Blanc (*m.*) de baleine. ‖ Pleurnicherie *f.* ‖ ZOOL. Méduse *f.*
— adj. Gonflé. ‖ **Blubber-lipped,** adj. Lippu.

blubbery [-ri] adj. Bouffi, gonflé.

bludgeon ['blʌdʒən] n. Trique, matraque *f.*; gourdin *m.*; *bludgeon man,* matraqueur.
— v. tr. Matraquer.

blue [bluː] adj. Bleu (colour); *blue jeans,* bleu. ‖ NAUT. *Blue Peter,* pavillon de partance. ‖ CULIN. *Blue* (or) *Danish cheese,* bleu; *blue mould,* moisissure (of cheese). ‖ MED. *Blue baby,* enfant bleu; *blue pill,* pilule au mercure. ‖ ZOOL. Bleu (fox). ‖ FIG. Bleu (blood); *to be true blue,* être bon teint (ou) orthodoxe. ‖ FAM. Bleu (funk); cafardeux (person, thing); gras, salé (talk); *blue devils,* papillons noirs; *blue ruin,* tord-boyaux; *I've told you*

so till I'm blue in the face, je me tue à vous le dire; U. S. *like a blue streak,* comme une flèche, au triple galop; *to feel blue,* broyer du noir; *once in a blue moon,* tous les trente-six du mois, à la semaine des quatre jeudis. ‖ **Blue-black,** adj. Bleu-noir. ‖ **Blue-book,** n. Livre bleu; U. S. bottin *m.* ‖ **Blue-collar,** adj. *Blue-collar worker,* ouvrier, travailleur manuel *m.* ‖ **Blue-moulded,** adj. CULIN. Persillé (cheese). ‖ **Blue-nose,** n. U. S. Puritain *m.*; bégueule *f.* ‖ **Blue-pencil,** v. tr. (1). Marquer au crayon bleu; couper, censurer. ‖ **Blue-print,** n. Bleu, photocalque *m.*; FAM. Plan *m.*; v. tr. planifier. ‖ **Blue-stone,** n. CHIM. Sulfate de cuivre, vitriol *m.* — n. Bleu *m.* (colour); *dark* (or) *mazarine blue,* bleu foncé; *Prussian blue,* bleu de Prusse. ‖ Mer, grande bleue *f.* (sea); azur, ciel *m.* (sky); *out of the blue,* tombant du ciel. ‖ CHIM. Bleu *m.* (dye, laundry-blue). ‖ SPORTS. Insigne d'athlète *m. pl.*; équipe *f.*; *Dark, Light Blues,* équipe d'Oxford, de Cambridge. ‖ MILIT. Pl. Garde montée *f.* ‖ MUS. Pl. Blues *m. pl.* ‖ FAM. Pl. Cafard *m.*; idées noires *f. pl.*; papillons noirs *m. pl.*; *to have the blues,* broyer du noir.
— v. tr. Bleuir (to dye); passer au bleu (to use laundry-blue [or] U. S. bluing on). ‖ FAM. Lessiver (one's money).

bluebell [-bel] n. BOT. Jacinthe (*f.*) des bois.

bluebottle [-bɔtḷ] n. ZOOL. Mouche bleue *f.* ‖ BOT. Bluet, bleuet *m.*

bluejacket [-,dʒækət] n. NAUT. Marsouin, col-bleu *m.*

bluestocking [-,stɔkiŋ] n. Bas-bleu *m.*

bluey ['blu:i] n. Balluchon *m.*, musette *f.* (bundle) [in Australia]; *to hump bluey,* trimarder. ‖ ZOOL. Chien (*m.*) de berger. ‖ FAM. Procès-verbal, P.-V. *m.* (summons).

bluff [blʌf] adj. A pic, escarpé. ‖ FIG. Bourru, brusque. (See BLUNT.) ‖ **Bluff-bowed,** adj. NAUT. Renflé. ‖ **Bluff-headed,** adj. Camard.
— n. A-pic; escarpement *m.*

bluff n. Défi *m.*; *to call s.o.'s bluff,* relever le défi de qqn. ‖ FAM. Bluff; montage de coup *m.*
— v. tr., intr. FAM. Bluffer.

bluffer [-ə*] n. FAM. Bluffeur, faiseur *s.*

bluffness [-nis] n. Brusquerie, rudesse amicale *f.*

bluing ['blu:iŋ] n. U. S. Bleu *m.* (laundry-blue).
— N. B. On l'orthographie aussi *blueing.*

bluish [-iʃ] adj. Bleuâtre. ‖ **Bluish-green,** adj. Bleu-vert, glauque. ‖ **Bluish-grey,** adj. Gris-bleu.

blunder ['blʌndə*] v. intr. Faire un faux pas; *to blunder along,* avancer à tâtons; *to blunder on,* trouver en tâtonnant; *to blunder upon sth.,* tomber sur qqch. par hasard; *to blunder through,* en sortir en pataugeant. ‖ Commettre une bévue; gaffer, faire une boulette (fam.).
— v. tr. Gâcher (a business); bousiller (fam.). ‖ *To blunder an opportunity away,* laisser passer une occasion par maladresse; *to blunder out a secret,* laisser sottement échapper un secret.
— n. Bévue, balourdise; gaffe, boulette (fam.); *to make bad blunders,* en faire de belles.

blunderbuss [-bʌs] n. MILIT. † Tromblon *m.* ‖ U. S. FAM. Gaffeur *s.*

blunderer [-ə*] n. Gaffeur *s.*

blundering [-iŋ] adj. Maladroit, malavisé.
— n. Maladresse *f.*; cafouillage *m.* (fam.).

blunderingly [-iŋli] adv. Maladroitement.

blunge ['blʌndʒ] v. tr. ARTS. U. S. Mêler d'eau.

blunt [blʌnt] adj. Emoussé (edge, knife, point); épointé (pencil). ‖ MATH. Obtus (angle). ‖ FIG. Brutal (fact); brusque, bourru, qui a son franc parler, d'une franchise rude (person). ‖ FIG. Obtus; bouché (fam.) [mind].
— v. tr. Emousser (a knife); épointer (a pencil). ‖ FIG. Emousser, engourdir, insensibiliser.
— v. intr. S'émousser.

bluntly [-li] adv. FIG. Carrément, sans mettre de gants.

bluntness [-nis] n. Etat (*m.*) de ce qui est émoussé; épointement *m.* ‖ FIG. Brusquerie, rude franchise *f.*

blur [blə:*] v. tr. (1). Barbouiller d'encre (to blot); *blurred letters,* lettres baveuses. ‖ Brouiller, estomper, noyer; *to become blurred,* se brouiller, devenir flou. ‖ MED. Brouiller, troubler (sight). ‖ FIG. Troubler (judgment); ternir, salir (s.o.'s character).
— n. Tache d'encre, bavochure *f.*; barbouillage *m.* ‖ Buée *f.* (of breath). ‖ Brouillard, aspect indistinct, estompage *m.*; vision trouble *f.* ‖ FIG. Ternissure *f.*

blurb [blə:b] n. Exposé (*m.*) flatteur d'un ouvrage sur la jaquette.

blurt [blə:t] v. tr. *To blurt out,* jeter, lancer, lâcher (a word).

blush [blʌʃ] v. intr. Rosir, rougir, s'empourprer (dawn, flower). ‖ Rougir, devenir rouge (or) pourpre (person); *to blush scarlet,* devenir cramoisi. ‖ Rougir, avoir honte (*for, with,* de) [pleasure; shame].
— v. tr. Rougir de.
— n. Rose *m.*; lueur rose *f.* (of dawn); rouge, incarnat *m.* (of flowers). ‖ Rougeur, roseur *f.*; *blush of modesty,* rougeur pudique; *with a blush,* en rougissant. ‖ LOC. *At the first blush,* à première vue, au premier contact.

blushing [-iŋ] adj. Rougissant, empourpré. ‖ Timide (bashful).

blushingly [-iŋli] adv. En rougissant.

bluster ['blʌstə*] v. intr. Mugir (sea); faire rage (storm, wind). ‖ FIG. Tempêter, déblatérer, tonitruer (*at,* contre). ‖ FIG. Déplacer de l'air, faire le fendant (to swagger).
— v. tr. *To bluster out,* déblatérer (insults, threats).
— n. Fracas *m.* ‖ FIG. Eclat *m.* (noisy talk); fanfaronnade, rodomontade *f.* (swagger).

blusterer [-rə*] n. Tapageur *s.* ‖ Fanfaron, bravache *m.*

blustering [-riŋ] adj. Furieux (sea, wind). ‖ FIG. Fanfaron.

blusteringly [-riŋli] adv. Bruyamment. ‖ FIG. Avec violence; avec forfanterie.

blusterous [-rəs] adj. Bruyant, tapageur.

boa ['bouə] n. ZOOL., COMM. Boa *m.*

boar [bɔ:*] n. ZOOL. Verrat (hog); sanglier *m.* (wild boar); *old boar,* solitaire; *young wild boar,* marcassin. ‖ CULIN. *Boar's head,* hure.

board [bɔ:d] n. Planche *f.* (plank); *ironing board,* planche à repasser. ‖ Panneau d'affichage, tableau, écriteau *m.* ‖ Carton *m.*; *Bristol board,* bristol. Cartonnage *m.*; *in boards,* cartonné (book). ‖ Table (*f.*) de jeu; *to sweep the board,* lever les enjeux. ‖ Table (*f.*) de salle à manger; repas *m.*; nourriture, pension *f.*; *board and lodging,* gîte et couvert, logement et nourriture; *full board,* pension complète. ‖ Table (*f.*) de conseil; conseil, comité; office, ministère m.; *board of directors,* conseil d'administration; *board of inquiry,* commission d'enquête; *Board of Trade,* ministère du Commerce, U. S. chambre de commerce; *examination board,* commission d'examen; *National Wheat Board,* Office du blé. ‖ NAUT. Bord *m.*; *on board the « Normandie »,* à bord du *Normandie.* ‖ NAUT. Bordée *f.*; *to make a board,* tirer un bord. ‖ AUTOM. *Caution board,* poteau avertisseur, signal de danger. THEATR. Pl. Planches *f. pl.*; scène *f.*; *to go on the boards,* monter sur les planches; *to tread the boards,* faire du théâtre. ‖ AVIAT. Bord *m.*; *on board,* à bord. ‖ FIG. *To go by the board,* tomber à l'eau. ‖ **Board-money,** n. Indemnité de nourriture *f.* ‖ **Board-room,** n. Salle (*f.*) du conseil. ‖ **Board-school,** n. Ecole primaire *f.* ‖ **Board-walk,** n. U. S. Passage en bois *m.*; promenade planchéiée en bord de mer.

— v. tr. Planchéier (partition); *to board up*, entourer de planches (or) d'une palissade. ‖ Cartonner (a book). ‖ Nourrir, avoir en pension (s.o.). ‖ NAUT. Aborder, accoster, prendre à l'abordage; arraisonner (a ship). ‖ NAUT. Monter à bord de. ‖ CH. DE F., AUTOM. Monter dans (a bus, a train). — v. intr. Etre en pension, prendre pension (*with, chez*). ‖ Etre pensionnaire (at school).

boarder [-ə*] n. pensionnaire *s.; to take in boarders*, prendre des pensionnaires. ‖ Interne *s.* (at school). ‖ NAUT. Abordeur *m.*

boarding [-iŋ] n. Planchéiage *m.* ‖ Cartonnage *m.* (of books). ‖ Pension, nourriture *f.;* couvert *m.* ‖ NAUT. Accostage, abordage; arraisonnement *m.* ‖ **Boarding-house,** n. Pension de famille *f.* ‖ **Boarding-school,** n. Pensionnat *m.;* pension *f.*

boarhound ['bɔ:haund] n. ZOOL. Vautre *m.*

boast [boust] n. Vantardise; hâblerie *f.; to make boast of*, se faire gloire de. ‖ Objet d'orgueil *m.; to be the boast of*, faire l'orgueil de.

— v. intr. Se vanter, s'enorgueillir, se prévaloir, se glorifier (*about, of*, de); *to boast that one has succeeded*, se vanter d'avoir réussi.

— v. tr. Se vanter de. ‖ Se faire gloire de posséder, s'enorgueillir de.

boaster [-ə*] n. Vantard *s.*

boastful [-ful] adj. Vantard, vaniteux. ‖ Prétentieux, arrogant.

boastfully [-fuli] adv. Avec vanité (or) jactance.

boasting [-iŋ] n. Jactance, fanfaronnade, forfanterie *f.*

boat [bout] n. NAUT. Bateau, canot *m.;* embarcation, barque *f.; by boat*, en bateau. ‖ NAUT. Paquebot *m.;* péniche *f.* (on canals). ‖ AVIAT. *Flying boat*, hydravion à coque. ‖ FAM. *Boats*, bateaux (shoes); *in the same boat*, du même convoi, à la même enseigne; *to miss the boat*, manquer le coche. ‖ **Boat-builder,** n. NAUT. Constructeur (*m.*) d'embarcations. ‖ **Boat-hook,** n. NAUT. Gaffe *f.* ‖ **Boat-house,** n. NAUT. Garage pour canots *m.* ‖ **Boat-load,** n. NAUT. Batelée *f.* ‖ **Boat-race,** n. NAUT. Course (*f.*) à l'aviron; régate *f.* ‖ **Boat-shaped,** adj. En forme de bateau; CULIN. *Boat-shaped tart*, barquette. ‖ **Boat-song,** n. MUS. Barcarolle *f.* ‖ **Boat-train,** n. CH. DE F. Train (*m.*) de marée; train (*m.*) correspondant au bateau. ‖ **Boat-yard,** n. NAUT. Chantier maritime *m.*

— v. intr. Aller en bateau, canoter.

— v. tr. Transporter en bateau.

boatful [-ful] n. NAUT. Batelée *f.*

boating [-iŋ] n. NAUT. Canotage *m.* ‖ COMM. Transport par bateau *m.*

boatman [-mən], (pl. **boatmen**) n. NAUT. Batelier *m.* ‖ Loueur de canots *m.*

boatswain ['bousn̩] n. NAUT. Maître d'équipage *m.; boatswain's mate*, maître de manœuvre, second maître.

bob [bɔb] n. Pendeloque *f.;* gland *m.* ‖ Pendant *m.* (of the ear). ‖ Queue *f.* (of a kite). ‖ Boucle ou mèche courte *f.* (short curl); coiffure à la Jeanne d'Arc *f.* (haircut); perruque *f.* (wig); *bob of hair*, chignon. ‖ Queue écourtée *f.* (of a horse). ‖ Coup léger *m.; tape *f.* ‖ Courte révérence *f.* (curtsy). ‖ PHYS. Lentille *f.* (of a pendulum). ‖ TECHN. Balancier *m.* (on a steam-engine); plomb *m.* (of a plumb-line). ‖ SPORTS. Bobsleigh *m.;* bouchon *m.* (on a fishing line). ‖ AGRIC. U. S. Veau (*m.*) à la mamelle. ‖ FAM. Shilling *m.; a bob a nob*, un shilling par tête; *to be without a bob*, n'avoir pas un radis. ‖ **Bob-sled** (or) **-sleigh,** n. SPORTS. Bobsleigh, traîneau *m.*

— v. tr. (1). Taper légèrement. Ecourter (hair, tail); *to wear one's hair bobbed*, être coiffé à la Jeanne d'Arc. ‖ Faire balancer (or) osciller (or) sautiller.

— v. intr. (1). Se balancer, osciller; sautiller; pendiller; *to bob up and down in the water*, danser

sur l'eau. ‖ Faire une courte révérence (*to*, à). ‖ **To bob for,** essayer de saisir avec les dents. ‖ **To bob up,** FIG. Surgir subitement; FAM. *To bob up again*, revenir sur le tapis.

bobbery ['bɔbəri] n. FAM. Boucan, potin, raffut *m.*

bobbin ['bɔbin] n. Bobine *f.;* fuseau *m.* ‖ † Bobinette *f.* ‖ **Bobbin-lace,** n. Dentelle (*f.*) au fuseau.

bobbish ['bɔbiʃ] adj. FAM. Fringant.

bobby [-i] n. FAM. Flic *m.* ‖ **Bobby-pin,** n. Pince (*f.*) à cheveux. ‖ **Bobby-socks,** n. pl. Socquettes *f. pl.* ‖ **Bobby-soxer,** n. FAM. U. S. Bobby-soxer, jeune admiratrice *f.*

bobstay [-stei] n. NAUT. Sous-barbe *f.* (of bowsprit).

bobtail [-teil] n. NAUT. Queue écourtée *f.* (of a horse). ‖ Cheval (or) chien (*m.*) à queue écourtée.

— adj. A queue écourtée.

— v. tr. Ecourter la queue de.

Boche [bɔʃ] n., adj. POP. † Boche *s.*, adj.

bock [bɔk] n. U. S. Bière (*f.*) de Munich.

bod [bɔd] n. FAM. Individu, type, mec *m.*

bode [boud] v. tr. Prédire.

— v. intr. Présager; augurer.

bodeful [-ful] adj. De mauvais présage. (See OMINOUS.)

bodice ['bɔdis] n. Corsage *m.* ‖ Cache-corset *m.* ‖ U. S. Veste-boléro *f.*

bodiless [-ilis] adj. Sans corps. ‖ FIG. Incorporel.

bodily [-ili] adj. Du corps, corporel; physique; matériel; *in bodily fear*, craignant pour sa vie (or) peau (fam.).

— adv. Corporellement. ‖ En personne. ‖ En chœur, en masse.

boding ['boudiŋ] n. Présage *m.*

— adj. De mauvais augure. (See OMINOUS.)

bodkin ['bɔdkin] n. Poinçon *m.* ‖ Passe-lien, passe-lacet n. ‖ Epingle (*f.*) à cheveux (hairpin). ‖ LOC. *To ride bodkin*, monter en fourchette (or) en lapin; *to sit bodkin between*, s'asseoir en sandwich entre.

Bodleian [bɔd'liə:n] adj., n. Bodléienne (library).

body ['bɔdi] n. Corps *m.; dead body*, corps, cadavre, dépouille. ‖ Corsage *m.* (of a dress). ‖ Corpus, recueil, code *m.* (book); corps (of a speech). ‖ Masse *f.* (of people, of water). ‖ Classe, masse *f.;* rang, groupe *m.* ‖ Ensemble *m.; full body of harmony*, harmonieux ensemble. ‖ Corps *m.;* consistance *f.* (of fabric, paper, wine). ‖ JUR. Corps, groupement *m.; corporation *f.; constituent body*, corps (or) collège électoral; *public body*, organisme public; *in a body*, en corps, ensemble, collectivement; *over my dead body*, à mon corps défendant. ‖ AUTOM. Carrosserie *f.* ‖ NAUT. Coque *f.* ‖ AVIAT. Fuselage *m.* ‖ MILIT. Corps *m.; the main body*, le gros des troupes. ‖ ARCHIT. Corps (of a building); nef *f.* (of a church). ‖ CHIM. Corps *m.* ‖ MATH. Solide *m.* ‖ TECHN. Corps *m.* (in printing). ‖ FAM. Type, individu, corps *m.; just enough to keep body and soul together*, juste de quoi ne pas crever de faim. ‖ **Body-building,** n. SPORTS. Culturisme *m.* ‖ **Body-colour,** n. ARTS. Gouache *f.* ‖ **Body-snatcher,** n. Déterreur (*m.*) de cadavres.

— v. tr. (2). Donner un corps à; incorporer; *to body forth*, donner une forme à; représenter, symboliser.

bodyguard [-,gɑ:d] n. Garde du corps *m.*

bodywork [-,wə:k] n. AUTOM. Carrosserie *f.*

boffin ['bɔfin] n. FAM. Chercheur, savant (*m.*) employé aux recherches secrètes.

bog ['bɔg] n. Fondrière *f.;* marais *m.* ‖ POP. Cabinets *m. pl.;* chiottes *f. pl.* (argot).

— v. tr. (1). Embourber, enliser; *to get bogged down*, s'embourber.

bogey ['bougi] n. SPORTS. Normale (*f.*) du parcours (in golf). ‖ FAM. Croquemitaine, épouvantail *m.*

boggle ['bɔgl] v. intr. Tressauter, sursauter. ‖ **To boggle at,** hésiter à, reculer devant (to hesitate);

biaiser (or) équivoquer au sujet de (to shuffle). ‖
To **boggle over**, patauger (or) nager dans.
boggy ['bɔgi] adj. Marécageux; effondré.
bogie ['bougi] n. CH. DE F. Bogie *m*.
bogle ['bougl] n. Lutin *m*. ‖ Epouvantail *m*. (bug-bear).
bogus ['bougəs] adj. Faux, factice; à la gomme, à la noix (fam.); *bogus concern*, attrape-nigaud; *bogus transactions*, transactions véreuses.
bogy ['bougi] n. Croquemitaine *m*.
Bohemia [bou'hi:mjə] n. GEOGR. Bohême *f*. ‖ FIG. Bohème *f*.
Bohemian [-ən] adj., n. GEOGR. Bohémien *s*.
bohemian n. FIG. Bohème *s*.
— adj. FIG. De bohème.
bohemianism [-ənizm̥] n. Mœurs (*f. pl.*) de la bohème; vie de bohème *f*.
boil [bɔil] n. MÉD. Furoncle; clou *m*. (fam.).
boil n. Ebullition *f.; on the boil*, prêt à bouillir. ‖ Remous *m*. (in a stream).
— v. intr. CULIN. Bouillir; *to boil away* (or) *down*, se réduire par ébullition; *to boil over*, se sauver (milk); déborder (water); *to boil up*, monter (milk).
‖ FIG. *To boil down*, se ramener, se réduire (*to*, à).
‖ FAM. Bouillir, bouillonner (*with*, de); *he is always boiling over*, il ne décolère pas; *to keep the pot boiling*, faire bouillir la marmite (to earn a living); maintenir le train (to keep up the rate).
— v. tr. CULIN. Faire cuire à la coque (an egg); faire cuire à l'eau (potatoes); faire bouillir (water).
‖ FIG. *To boil down*, condenser (a book).
boiled [-d] adj. CULIN. Bouilli; à l'eau; au naturel; *boiled beef*, bouilli; *boiled egg*, œuf à la coque.
‖ Empesé (shirt). ‖ FAM. *Boiled shirt*, personnage gourmé (or) pontifiant; plastronneur. ‖ U. S. FAM. Plein, rétamé (drunken).
boiler [-ə*] n. CULIN. Récipient (*m*.) pour faire bouillir; *double boiler*, bain-marie; *range boiler*, bouillotte. ‖ CULIN. Légume (*m*.) à cuire à l'eau.
‖ TECHN. Chaudière *f*. ‖ **Boiler-house**, n. TECHN. Salle (*f*.) des chaudières. ‖ **Boiler-maker**, n. Chaudronnier *m*. ‖ **Boiler-making**, n. Chaudronnerie *f*.
‖ **Boiler-man**, n. TECHN. Chauffeur *m*. ‖ **Boiler-plate**, n. TECHN. Tôle de chaudière *f*. ‖ **Boiler-room**, n. NAUT. Chaufferie *f*. ‖ **Boiler suit**, n. Bleu *m*.; combinaison *f*.
boiling [-iŋ] n. Ebullition *f*. ‖ FAM. Ebullition *f.;* bouillonnement *m*. ‖ POP. *The whole boiling*, tout le tremblement (or) bazar.
boisterous ['bɔistərəs] adj. Houleux, tumultueux, agité (sea); violent (wind). ‖ Turbulent, tapageur, bruyant (boy); exubérant, tapageur (spirits).
boisterously [-li] adv. Tapageusement.
boisterousness [-nis] n. Violence *f.;* déchaînement *m*. ‖ Turbulence, diablerie *f*. (of a boy).
bold [bould] adj. Audacieux, hardi, brave, décidé (audacious); intrépide, impavide (fearless); *to make bold to*, oser, s'enhardir à, se permettre de.
‖ Impudent, hardi, effronté, osé (shameless). ‖ Escarpé, à pic (steep). ‖ TECHN. Gros (characters, letters); *to write a bold hand*, avoir une grosse écriture. ‖ ARTS. Marqué (relief). ‖ FIG. Vigoureux (style). ‖ **Bold-face**, n. TECHN. Gras *m*. (in printing).
‖ **Bold-faced**, adj. TECHN. Gras (character); FIG. Effronté.
boldly [-li] adv. Audacieusement, hardiment. ‖ Avec effronterie. ‖ Abruptement, à pic. ‖ FIG. Vigoureusement, nettement.
boldness [-nis] n. Audace, hardiesse, intrépidité *f*. (courage). ‖ Effronterie, impudence *f*. ‖ Escarpement *m*. (steepness). ‖ FIG. Vigueur, précision *f*.
bole [boul] n. BOT. Tronc *m*. (of a tree). ‖ GEOL. Terre bolaire *f.;* bol *m*.
bolection [bou'lekʃən] n. ARCHIT. Moulure *f*.
bolero [bə'lɛərou] n. MUS. Boléro *m*.

bolero ['bɔlərou] n. COMM. Boléro *m*.
boletus [bɔ'litəs] n. BOT. Bolet *m*.
bolide ['bɔlid] n. ASTRON. Bolide *m*.
Bolivia [bɔ'livjə] n. GEOGR. Bolivie *f*.
Bolivian [-ən] n. GEOGR. Bolivien *s*.
boll [boul] n. BOT. Graine *f*. (of cotton, flax).
bollard ['bɔləd] n. NAUT. Poteau d'amarrage *m*.
bollix ['bɔliks] v. tr. ARG. Bousiller (to wreck); saloper (to botch); semer la merde dans (to muddle).
bollocks ['bɔləks] n. See BALLOCKS.
bolometer [bou'lɔmətə:*] n. PHYS. Bolomètre *m*.
boloney [bə'louni] n. FAM. Foutaise *f*.
Bolshevik ['bɔlʃəvik] adj., n. Bolchevique *adj., s*.
Bolshevization [,bɔlʃəvai'zeiʃən] n. Bolchevisation *f*.
Bolshevize ['bɔlʃevaiz] v. tr. Bolcheviser.
Bolshevism [-izm̥] n. Bolchevisme *m*.
Bolshevist [-ist] adj., n. Bolcheviste *s*.
bolster ['boulstə*] n. Traversin; polochon (fam.) [on a bed]. ‖ TECHN. Coussin *m*. (of an engine); lisoir *m*. (of a vehicle).
— v. tr. Mettre un traversin (or) un coussin sous; rembourrer. ‖ FIG. Appuyer, étayer; *to bolster up*, soutenir (*with*, de).
bolt [boult] n. Carreau; trait *m*. (from a crossbow).
‖ Eclair; coup (*m*.) de foudre. (See THUNDERBOLT.)
‖ Verrou, loquet *m*. (for a door); pêne *m*. (of a lock). ‖ COMM. Coupe, pièce *f*. (of cloth); rouleau *m*. (of paper). ‖ TECHN. Boulon *m.;* cheville *f.;* key bolt, goupille. ‖ MILIT. *Bolt of a rifle*, culasse mobile. ‖ FIG. Départ brusque *m.;* fuite *f*. ‖ FAM. *Bolt from the blue*, coup de tonnerre; tuile imprévue, nouvelle foudroyante; *to shoot one's bolt*, se décarcasser. ‖ **Bolt-head**, n. TECHN. Tête (*f*.) de boulon. ‖ **Bolt-hole**, n. Terrier *m.;* MILIT. Abri *m.;* FAM. Porte de sortie *f*. ‖ **Bolt-position**, n. MILIT. Verrou *m*. ‖ **Bolt-rope**, n. NAUT. Ralingue *f*.
— v. tr. Verrouiller; *to bolt in*, enfermer au verrou; *to bolt out*, mettre le verrou contre. ‖ TECHN. Boulonner, cheviller, goujonner. ‖ FIG. Epauler, soutenir. ‖ FAM. Lâcher, planter là; *to bolt down*, empiffrer, descendre, engloutir (food).
— v. intr. Partir brusquement; s'emballer (horse).
‖ FAM. Décamper, décaniller.
— adv. Comme un dard; *bolt upright*, droit comme un i (or) une flèche.
bolt v. tr. Bluter, tamiser. ‖ FIG. Passer au crible.
bolter [-ə*] n. Cheval (*m*.) qui s'emballe.
bolter n. Blutoir, tamis *m*.
bolus ['boulǝs] n. MÉD. Bol *m.;* boulette *f*.
bomb [bɔm] n. MILIT. Bombe *f.; flash, smoke bomb*, bombe éclairante, fumigène; *hydrogen bomb, H-bomb*, bombe à hydrogène, bombe H; *letter bomb*, lettre piégée; *time bomb*, bombe à retardement. ‖ LOC. *To go like a bomb*, faire un malheur (or) un tabac (to be successful), aller à la vitesse de l'éclair (to be very fast); *to cost a bomb*, valoir une fortune. ‖ **Bomb-aimer**, n. AVIAT. Bombardier *m*. ‖ **Bomb-bay**, n. MILIT., AVIAT. Soute *f*.
‖ **Bomb-crater**, n. MILIT. Entonnoir *m*. ‖ **Bomb-destroy**, v. tr. AVIAT. Détruire par bombardement.
‖ **Bomb-disposal**, n. MILIT., TECHN. Déminage, désamorçage *m.; bomb disposal squad*, équipe de démineurs. ‖ **Bomb-proof**, adj. MILIT. A l'épreuve des bombes. ‖ **Bomb-rack**, n. MILIT. Porte-bombes; berceau (*m*.) à bombes. ‖ **Bomb-release**, n. MILIT. Lancement (*m*.) de bombes. ‖ **Bomb-shell**, n. MILIT. Obus *m.;* FIG. *To come like a bomb-shell*, tomber comme la foudre. ‖ **Bomb-sight**, n. AVIAT. Viseur de bombardement *m*. ‖ **Bomb-site**, n. Zone (*f*.) rasée par les bombardements. ‖ **Bomb-thrower**, n. MILIT. Lance-bombes *m*.
— v. tr. MILIT., AVIAT. Bombarder; arroser de bombes; *bombed out*, sinistré; *to bomb out*, obliger à fuir par les bombardements; *to bomb up*, charger de bombes.

bombard [bɔm'bɑːd] v. tr. NAUT., PHYS., FIG. Bombarder (with, de).

bombardier [ˌbɔmbə'die *] n. MILIT. Caporal (m.) d'artillerie. ‖ AVIAT. U. S. Bombardier m. (man).

bombardement [bɔm'bɑːdmənt] n. MILIT., AVIAT., NAUT. Bombardement, marmitage m. ‖ PHYS. Bombardement of the electrons, bombardement électronique.

bombardon [bɔm'bɑːdən] n. MUS. Bombardon m.

bombasine [ˌbɔmbə'ziːn] n. See BOMBAZINE.

bombast ['bɔmbæst] n. Grandiloquence, emphase f.; pathos, style ampoulé m. (See FUSTIAN.)

bombastic [bɔm'bæstik] adj. Ampoulé, grandiloquent, emphatique.

bombastically [-əli] adv. Avec grandiloquence.

Bombay duck [bɔm'bei'dʌk] n. CULIN. Poisson (m.) cuit dans le sable.

bombazine [ˌbɔmbə'ziːn] n. Bombasin m. (fabric).

bombe [bɔ̃b] n. CULIN. Bombe f.

bomber ['bɔmə*] n. AVIAT. Bombardier m. (person, plane).

bombyx ['bɔmbiks] n. ZOOL. Bombyx m.

bona fide ['bounə'faidi] adj., De bonne foi; sérieux (offer); authentique (traveller).

bona fides [-'faidiːz] n. JUR. Bonne foi f.

bonanza [bo'nænze] n. TECHN. Riche veine (f.) de minerai. ‖ FAM. Mine f. (of profits); filon m.; in bonanza, en veine.
— adj. Prospère.

bonbon ['bɔnbɔn] n. Bonbon m.

bonbonniere [ˌbɔnbɔn'jɛ:r] n. Bonbonnière f.

bond [bɔnd] n. Lien m. (tie). ‖ Pl. Fers m. pl.; chaînes f. pl.; captivité f.; servage m. ‖ FIN. Bon, titre m.; valeur f. ‖ JUR. Obligation; caution f.; engagement; contrat m.; COMM. Entrepôt, entreposage m.; in bond, entreposé. ‖ ARCHIT. Apparei? m. ‖ TECHN. Assemblage; appareil, joint m. ‖ **Bond-note,** n. JUR. Acquit-à-caution m. ‖ **Bond-stone,** n. ARCHIT. Parpaing m. ‖ **Bond-store,** n. Entrepôt m.
— v. tr. Entreposer (goods). ‖ ARCHIT. Maçonner; appareiller. ‖ U. S. Lier par une garantie financière.
— adj. Esclave, en esclavage.

bondage [-idʒ] n. Esclavage, servage m.; servitude, captivité f. ‖ FIG. Esclavage, asservissement m.

bonded [-id] adj. Entreposé, en douane (goods). ‖ D'entreposage; bonded warehouse, entrepôt réel, magasins généraux. ‖ FIN. Garanti par une obligation (debt).

bondholder ['bɔnd,houldə*] n. FIN. Porteur (s.) d'obligation; obligataire s.

bondsman ['bɔndzmən] n. Serf, esclave m.

bone [boun] n. MED. Os m. ‖ Pl. Ossements, restes m. pl. (remains). ‖ ZOOL. Arête f. (fish-bone). ‖ COMM. Baleine f. (of stays). ‖ MUS. Pl. Castagnettes f. pl. ‖ FAM. Pl. Dés m. pl. (dice). ‖ FAM. Bone of contention, pomme de discorde; a bone to pick with, un compte à régler avec, maille à partir avec; I feel it in my bones, qqch. me le dit; not to make old bones, ne pas faire de vieux os; to make no bones about (of), ne pas faire de manières pour, ne pas y aller avec le dos de la cuiller (or) par quatre chemins au sujet de. ‖ **Bone-black,** n. Noir animal m. ‖ **Bone dry,** adj. Archisec. ‖ **Bone idle,** adj. Cossard, flemmard. ‖ **Bone-lace,** n. Dentelle (f.) au fuseau. ‖ **Bone lazy,** adj. Cossard, qui a un poil dans la main. ‖ **Bone-setter,** n. Rebouteux s. ‖ **Bone-shaker,** n. † Vélocipède m.; FAM. Tapecul m.
— v. tr. Désosser (meat). ‖ Enlever les arêtes de (fish). ‖ Baleiner (stays). ‖ POP. Barboter, chauffer, piquer (to steal). ‖ U. S. FAM. To bone up, bûcher, potasser, buriner.

bonehead ['boun'hed] n. U. S. FAM. Philistin m.; tête (f.) de bois.

boner ['bounə*] n. U. S. FAM. Bourde, boulette, gaffe, énormité f. (See BLUNDER.)

bonfire ['bɔnfaiə*] n. Feu (m.) de joie; feu de jardin m.

bongo ['bɔŋgou] n. MUS. Bongo m.

bonhomie ['bɔnɔmi:] n. Bonhomie f.

bonnet ['bɔnit] n. Béguin, bonnet m. (for children); béret m. (for men); capote f.; bavolet m. (for women). ‖ ARCHIT. Capuchon m. (of chimney). ‖ AUTOM. Capot m. ‖ NAUT. Bonnette f.
— v. tr. Coiffer; mettre un béret à. ‖ Enfoncer le chapeau jusqu'aux yeux de. ‖ FAM. Secouer, bousculer, houspiller.

bonny ['bɔni] adj. Joli, beau; plantureux, éclatant de santé.

bonsai ['bɔnsai] n. BOT. Bonsai m.

bonus ['bounəs] n. Boni m.; prime, gratification, guelte f.; sursalaire m. ‖ FIN. Dividende (or) bénéfice exceptionnel m.

bony ['bouni] adj. Osseux. ‖ Anguleux, maigre (thin). ‖ CULIN. Plein d'arêtes (fish); plein d'os (flesh).

bonze [bɔnz] n. Bonze m.

boo [bu:] interj., n. Hou!, peuh!; he wouldn't say boo to a goose, il a peur de son ombre.
— v. tr. Huer, chahuter, conspuer.
— v. intr. Pousser des huées.

boob [bub] n. FAM. Ballot; emplâtre, entraveur m. ‖ POP. Nichon m.

booby ['bu:bi] n. Nigaud s.; bêta, benêt m. ‖ SPORTS. Dernier m. ‖ ZOOL. Fou m. ‖ **Booby-hatch,** n. NAUT. Ecoutillon m.; U. S. FAM. Asile, cabanon m. ‖ **Booby-trap,** n. Attrape-nigaud, traquenard m.; MILIT. Mine-piège.

boodle ['bu:dl] n. FAM. Fric, pèze m. (money). ‖ U. S. FAM. Pot-de-vin, arrosage m. (bribe); caisse noire f. (for political bribery).

boogie-woogie ['bu:gi'wu:gi] n. MUS. Boogie-woogie m.

boohoo [bu:'hu] n. FAM. Braiment m. (weeping).
— v. intr. FAM. Braire (to weep noisily).

book [buk] n. Livre m.; book club, club du livre; class book, livre de classe. ‖ Livre (division of a book); chant m. (in a poem). ‖ Cahier m. (copybook). ‖ ECCLES. Bible f. ‖ COMM., FIN., JUR. Livre, registre m.; on the books, porté sur les registres; to keep the books, tenir la comptabilité (or) les livres (or) les comptes. ‖ SPORTS. Livre de paris m.; to make a book, inscrire les paris. ‖ FIG. Autorité livresque f.; by the book, selon les règles; d'après le texte; without book, de mémoire; sans autorité. ‖ FAM. To be in s.o.'s bad books, être mal vu de qqn; to be in s.o.'s good books, être dans les petits papiers de qqn; to suit s.o.'s book, faire le compte (or) l'affaire de qqn. ‖ **Book-end,** n. Serre-livre m. ‖ **Book-jacket,** n. Jaquette f. ‖ **Book-knowledge,** n. Connaissances livresques f. pl. ‖ **Book-learning,** adj. Erudition f.; savoir théorique (or) livresque m. ‖ **Book-mark,** n. Signet m. ‖ **Book-muslin,** n. Organdi m. ‖ **Book-plate,** n. Ex-libris m. ‖ **Book-rest,** n. Appuie-livre m. ‖ **Book-shop,** n. Librairie f. ‖ **Book-value,** n. FIN. Valeur comptable f. ‖ **Book-wrapper,** n. Liseuse f.
— v. tr. Inscrire, enregistrer, noter; to book in, out, inscrire (or) s'inscrire à l'arrivée, à la sortie. ‖ COMM. Passer écriture de. ‖ THEATR. Louer, retenir, réserver (a seat). ‖ CH. DE F. Louer, retenir (a seat); prendre (a ticket); to book through to, prendre un billet direct pour. ‖ FAM. To be booked, être pris (or) retenu.

bookbinder [-,baində*] n. Relieur m.

bookbinding [-,baindiŋ] n. Reliure f.

bookcase [-keis] n. Bibliothèque f. (cabinet).

bookie [-i] n. FAM., SPORTS. Bookmaker m.

booking [-iŋ] n. Inscription; location, réservation

f. ‖ **Booking-office,** n. CH. DE F. Guichet (*m.*) de distribution des billets.
bookish [-iʃ] adj. Studieux (person); livresque (person, style).
bookkeeper [-,kipə*] n. FIN. Comptable *s.*
bookkeeping [-,kipiŋ] n. FIN. Comptabilité *f.; single entry bookkeeping,* unigraphie; *double entry bookkeeping,* comptabilité en partie double.
booklet [-lit] n. Opuscule, livret *m.*
bookmaker [-,meikə*] n. Bookmaker *m.*
bookmobile [-'moubi:l] n. U. S. Bibliobus *m.;* bibliothèque circulante *f.*
bookrack [-ræk] n. Rayon *m.* (or) étagère (*f.*) de bibliothèque.
bookseller [-selə*] n. Libraire *m.; second-hand bookseller,* bouquiniste.
bookstall [-stɔ:l], U. S. **bookstand** n. Etalage (*m.*) de librairie. ‖ CH. DE F. Bibliothèque de gare *f.*
bookstore [-stɔ:*] n. U. S. Librairie *f.*
bookworm [-wə:m] n. ZOOL. Anobion *m.* ‖ FAM. Rat (*m.*) de bibliothèque.
boom [bu:m] n. NAUT. Tangon *m.; harbour boom,* panne de barrage. ‖ AVIAT. Longeron *m.;* membrure *f.*
boom v. intr. Gronder, tonner, mugir, ronfler. ‖ ZOOL. Mugir (bittern); bourdonner (insect).
— n. Grondement, mugissement, ronflement *m.* ‖ ZOOL. Mugissement *m.* (of the bittern); bourdonnement *m.* (of insects).
boom v. intr. COMM., FIN. Prospérer, faire un boom.
— v. tr. Faire prospérer, faire du battage (or) de la réclame pour, lancer (sth.). [See BOOST.] ‖ Soutenir, faire valoir (s.o.); *to boom s.o. for chairman,* pousser qqn à la présidence.
— n. FIN. Boom, emballement des cours *m.;* prospérité *f.* ‖ COMM. Vogue *f.*
— adj. Relatif à un boom; *boom town,* ville-champignon; ville prospère.
boomerang ['bu:məræŋ] n. Boumerang *m.* ‖ FIG. Choc en retour *m.*
boon [bu:n] n. Faveur *f.; avantage m.* (blessing). ‖ Requête *f.*
boon adj. Joyeux (companion).
boondock(s) ['bu:n,dɔk(s)] n. (or) n. pl. U. S. FAM. Contrée perdue, région inhabitée *f.*
boor [buə*] n. † Manant *m.* ‖ FIG. Rustre, butor *m.*
boorish [-iʃ] adj. Fruste, balourd, rustaud.
boorishness [-iʃnis] n. Rusticité, grossièreté *f.;* manque (*m.*) d'éducation.
boost [bu:st] v. tr. Faire de la réclame (or) du battage (or) du tam-tam pour, prôner. (See BOOM.) ‖ ELECTR. Survolter. ‖ FIG. Renforcer.
booster [-ə*] n. ELECTR. Survolteur *m.* ‖ RADIO. Amplificateur *m.* ‖ MILIT. Batterie (*f.*) de renfort. ‖ FAM. Prôneur, épauleur *m.* ‖ **Booster-rocket,** n. Fusée (*f.*) d'appoint, fusée porteuse *f.* ‖ **Booster-shot,** n. MÉD. Piqûre (*f.*) de rappel.
boosting [-iŋ] n. FAM. Battage *m.*
boot [bu:t] n. Botte *f.* (top-boot); brodequin *m.* (laced boot); botillon *m.;* bottine, chaussure montante *f.* (coming above ankle); *to put on one's boots,* se botter; se chausser. ‖ Brodequin *m.* (of torture). ‖ AUTOM. Coffre *m.* ‖ NAUT., FAM. Apprenti marin *m.* ‖ FAM. *In seven-league boots,* à pas de géant; *the boot is on the other foot,* c'est tout juste le contraire; *too big for his boots,* gonflé, pétant dans sa peau ; *to die with one's boots on,* mourir à la tâche; *to give s.o. the boot,* flanquer qqn dehors; *to lick the boots of,* lécher les bottes de. ‖ **Boot-and-saddle,** n. MILIT. Bouteselle *m.* ‖ **Boot-hook,** n. Tire-botte *m.* ‖ **Bootmaker,** n. Bottier *m.* ‖ **Boot-tree,** n. Embauchoir, tendeur *m.*
— v. tr. FAM. *To boot s.o. into the Ministry,* bombarder qqn ministre; *to boot upstairs,* faire grimper les échelons à (s.o); *to boot out,* flanquer dehors.

boot n. Avantage, profit *m.; to boot,* en (or) de plus, par surcroît.
— v. intr. † Servir à, profiter à.
bootblack [-blæk] n. Cireur, décrotteur (*m.*) de chaussures.
booted [-id] adj. Botté.
bootee [bu:'ti:] n. Chausson d'enfant *m.* ‖ Botillon *m.* (for women).
booth [bu:ð] m. Baraque *f.* (at fairs, markets). ‖ Isoloir *m.* (at elections). ‖ Cabine *f.* (cinema, language centre, telephone).
bootjack ['bu:tdʒæk] n. Tire-botte *m.*
bootlace [-leis] n. Lacet de soulier *m.*
bootleg [-leg] n. Tige de botte *f.*
— adj. U. S. FAM. De contrebande.
— v. intr. U. S. FAM. Faire de la contrebande.
bootlegger [-legə*] n. U. S. Contrebandier d'alcool *m.*
bootless [-lis] adj. Sans bottes.
bootless adj. Sans profit.
bootlick [-lik] v. tr. FAM. Lécher les bottes de.
bootlicker [-likə*] n. FAM. Lécheur (*m.*) de bottes; lèche-cul *m.* (pop.).
boots [-s] n. Cireur, décrotteur, garçon d'étage *m.* (in a hotel).
booty ['bu:ti] n. Butin *m.*
booze [bu:z] n. Ribote, noce *f.* (spree). ‖ FAM. Gnôle *f.* (drink).
— v. intr. FAM. Siroter.
boozer [-ə*] n. POP. Fêtard, soulographe *m.*
boozy [-i] adj. FAM. Soûlard, soûlaud *m.*
bop [bɔp] n. MUS. Be-bop, bop *m.*
bo-peep [bou'pi:p] n. Cache-cache, coucou *m.*
boracic [bo'ræsik] adj. CHIM. Borique.
borage ['bɔridʒ] n. BOT. Bourrache *f.*
borate ['bɔ:reit] n. CHIM. Borate *m.*
borax [-æks] n. CHIM. Borax *m.*
Bordeaux [bɔ:'dou] n. Bordeaux *m.* (city, wine); *Bordeaux mixture,* bouillie bordelaise.
border ['bɔ:də*] n. Bord, côté *m.* (side). ‖ Bordure, lisière, marge *f.* (margin). ‖ Frontière, limite *f.* (limit). ‖ Bordure *f.,* bordé *m.* (on a dress). ‖ AGRIC. Bordure *f.* (of flowers, shrubs). ‖ GEOGR. Marche *f.* ‖ **Border-line,** n. Ligne de démarcation *f.; border-line case,* cas limite.
— v. tr. Border; entourer; encadrer (*with,* de). ‖ Border, toucher, limiter (to bound).
— v. intr. **To border on,** être contigu à, être limitrophe de (country); FIG. Avoisiner; confiner à.
borderer [-rə*] n. GEOGR. Frontalier *m.*
borderland [-lænd] n. GEOGR. Marche *f.;* pays (*m.*) frontière. ‖ FIG. Limite, frontière *f.*
bore [bɔ:*] v. tr. Vriller, percer, perforer. ‖ TECHN. Aléser (a cylinder); creuser (a tunnel); creuser, forer (a well). ‖ FIG. Frayer (one's way).
— v. intr. Faire des sondages (*for,* à la recherche de). ‖ Se percer (wood). ‖ SPORTS. Bourrer.
— n. TECHN. Alésage *m.;* trou de sondage *m.;* calibre *m.* ‖ MILIT. Ame *f.;* calibre *m.*
bore n. FAM. Raseur, assommeur, crampon *m.* (person); bassinoire, barbe, scie *f.* (situation, thing).
— v. tr. FAM. Bassiner, assommer, raser, casser les pieds à; *to be bored to death,* crever d'ennui.
bore n. Mascaret *m.*
bore pret. See BEAR.
boreal ['bɔ:riəl] adj. Boréal.
boredom ['bɔ:dəm] n. Ennui *m.; to cure of boredom,* désennuyer.
borehole ['bɔ:houl] n. TECHN. Puits, trou de sondage *m.*
borer ['bɔ:rə*] n. Vrille; perforatrice *f.;* foret, alésoir *m.* ‖ ZOOL. Insecte térébrant *m.*
boric ['bɔ:rik] adj. CHIM. Borique.
born [bɔ:n] adj. Né (*of,* de); *the town where he was born,* la ville qui l'a vu naître. ‖ FIG. Né; *born musician,* musicien-né. ‖ FAM. *He was not*

born yesterday, il n'est pas né d'hier (or) tombé de la dernière pluie.
borne p. p. See BEAR.
boron ['bɔ:rɔn] n. CHIM. Bore *m.*
borough ['bʌrə*] n. Bourg *m.;* circonscription électorale *f.*
borrow ['bɔrou] v. tr. Emprunter (*from, of,* à); *to borrow upon usury,* emprunter à usure. ‖ MATH. Retenir (in a subtraction). ‖ FIG. Emprunter, adopter; *borrowed plumes,* les plumes du paon.
borrower [-ə*] n. Emprunteur *s.*
borrowing [-iŋ] n. Emprunt *m.*
Borstal ['bɔ:stəl] n. JUR. *Borstal institution,* maison de redressement.
bort [bɔ:t] n. Egrisée *f.*
borzoi ['bɔ:zɔi] n. ZOOL. Barzoï *m.*
boscage ['bɔskidʒ] n. Bocage *m.*
bosh [bɔʃ] n., interj. FAM. Idiotie, stupidité *f.*
bosk [bɔsk], **bosket** [-it] n. Bosquet *m.* (grove); fourré *m.* (thicket).
bosky [-i] adj. Boisé; touffu.
bo's'n ['bousn] n. NAUT. Maître d'équipage *m.* (See BOATSWAIN.)
bosom ['buzəm] n. Sein, giron *m.* (lap). ‖ Sein *m.;* poitrine *f.* (breast). ‖ Devant *m.* (of a dress); plastron *m.* (of a shirt). ‖ Surface *f.* (of a river). ‖ FIG. Sein *m.* (of one's family).
— adj. Du sein. ‖ FIG. Intime (friend).
boson ['bouzɔn] n. PHYS. Boson *m.*
Bosphorus ['bɔsfərəs] n. GEOGR. Bosphore *m.*
boss [bɔs] n. FAM. Patron *m.; to be keener than the boss,* être plus royaliste que le roi. ‖ U. S. *Political boss,* manitou du parti.
— v. tr. FAM. Faire marcher, mener, régenter; contrôler.
boss n. Bosse *f.* (See PROTUBERANCE.) ‖ Bossette *f.* (of the bit). ‖ Bosse *f.* (of a shield). ‖ ARCHIT. Bosse. ‖ TECHN. Bossage *m.* ‖ AVIAT. Moyeu *m.* (of a propeller).
boss-eyed ['bɔs'aid] adj. POP. Borgne (one-eyed); bigleux, qui a un œil qui dit zut à l'autre (cross-eyed). ‖ De traviole, de guingois (crooked).
Boston ['bɔstən] n. Boston *m.* (card game, city, dance).
botanic(al) [bo'tænik(əl)] adj. BOT. Botanique.
botanist ['bɔtənist] n. BOT. Botaniste *s.*
botanize [-naiz] v. intr. BOT. Faire de la botanique, botaniser, herboriser.
botany [-i] n. BOT. Botanique *f.* (science, textbook).
botch [bɔtʃ] v. tr. FAM. Ravauder, rafistoler (to repair). ‖ FAM. Saboter, bousiller, louper, cochonner. (See BUNGLE.)
— n. FAM. Ravaudage, rafistolage *m.* ‖ FAM. Bousillage, sabotage *m.*
botcher [-ə*] n. FAM. Ravaudeur *s.* ‖ FAM. Bousilleur *s.*
botchy [-i] adj. FAM. Rapetassé, rafistolé. ‖ FAM. Bousillé, saboté, cochonné.
both [bouθ] adj. Les deux, l'un et l'autre; *on both sides,* des deux côtés, de part et d'autre.
— pron. Tous les deux; l'un et l'autre; *both will come,* l'un et l'autre viendront; *both of us,* nous deux; *both of them wore blue dresses,* toutes les deux portaient une robe bleue.
— adv. A la fois, aussi bien, également, ensemble; *both his parents were Polish,* son père comme sa mère était Polonais; *to be both plain and stupid,* être à la fois laid et bête.
bother ['bɔðə*] v. tr. Ennuyer, importuner (to bore); raser, embêter (fam.); *he can't be bothered to,* ça l'empoisonne (or) l'agace de. ‖ Inquiéter, tourmenter (to concern); tracasser (fam.); *to bother one's head about,* se mettre martel en tête au sujet de. ‖ U. S. Désorienter, ahurir, mettre mal à l'aise; *a big city bothers him,* la grande ville le trouble, il est tout perdu dans une grande ville.

— v. intr. Se tourmenter, se tracasser; *she doesn't bother about anything,* elle ne se bile pas (fam.).
— interj. Zut!, flûte!; *bother him!,* au diable le raseur!
— n. Ennui *m.;* gêne; rase, scie *f.* (fam.). ‖ Souci, tracas; embêtement *m.* (fam.). [See ANNOY.]
botheration [,bɔðə'reiʃən] n. FAM. Embêtement, empoisonnement *m.*
— interj. Zut!, au diable!, quel poison!
bothersome ['bɔðəsəm] adj. Gênant; raseur (fam.). ‖ Inquiétant, agaçant.
Botswana [bu'tʃwɑ:nə] n. GEOGR. Botswana *m.*
bottle ['bɔtl] n. Bouteille *f.;* flacon *m.* (small); bocal *m.* (wide-mouthed); carafe *f.* (for water); *beer bottle,* canette; *hot-water botte,* bouillotte, boule d'eau chaude. ‖ MED. Biberon *m.; brought up on the bottle,* élevé au biberon. ‖ FAM. Dive bouteille, libation *f.; to hit the bottle,* caresser la bouteille. ‖ **Bottle-brush,** n. Rince-bouteilles *m.* ‖ **Bottle-drainer,** n. Egouttoir (*m.*) à bouteilles. ‖ **Bottle-glass,** n. Verre (*m.*) à bouteilles. ‖ **Bottle-green,** adj. Vert bouteille. ‖ **Bottle-imp,** n. Ludion *m.* ‖ **Bottle-neck,** n. Goulot *m.;* NAUT. Goulet *m.;* AUTOM., FIG. Encombrement, embouteillage *m.* ‖ **Bottle-opener,** n. Ouvre-bouteilles *m. inv.,* décapsuleur *m.* ‖ **Bottle-rack,** n. Casier (*m.*) à bouteilles, porte-bouteilles *m. inv.* ‖ **Bottle-washer,** n. Laveur (*m.*) de bouteilles; factotum *m.*
— v. tr. Mettre en bouteille, embouteiller (wine); *bottled in bond,* vieilli en entrepôt. ‖ CULIN. Mettre en bouteille (or) bocal (preserves). ‖ **To bottle up,** AUTOM. Embouteiller (the traffic); FIG. Ravaler, rentrer, contenir (one's anger).
bottle n. AGRIC. Botte *f.* (of hay).
bottom ['bɔtəm] n. Fond *m.* (of a barrel, box, pile, well); fond, siège *m.* (of a chair); queue *f.* (of a class); bas *m.* (of a dress, page); pied *m.* (of a tree). ‖ NAUT. Fond (of a river, of the sea); carène *f.* (of a ship); bateau, navire *m.* (ship); *in French bottoms,* sous pavillon français. ‖ GEOGR. Creux, contrebas, bas-fond *m.* ‖ SPORTS. Endurance *f.;* fond *m.* (stamina). ‖ FIG. Fond, fondement *m.; at bottom,* au fond. ‖ FIG. Base, source, origine, cause *f.* ‖ FAM. Fondement; derrière, postérieur *m.* (buttocks). ‖ FAM. *Bottoms up!,* videz vos verres!; cul sec! (pop.).
— adj. Inférieur, du bas (lowest); *bottom end,* bas bout; *bottom stair,* marche du bas, première marche de l'escalier. ‖ Dernier (last); *to bet one's bottom dollar,* parier son dernier sou. ‖ Fondamental (basic). ‖ U. S. D'alluvion (land).
— v. tr. Mettre un fond à (a barrel, box); canner (a chair). ‖ NAUT. Sonder. ‖ TECHN. Empierrer (a road). ‖ FIG. Fonder (*upon, sur*) [one's opinion]; aller au fond de, examiner à fond (a subject).
— v. intr. Atteindre (or) toucher le fond.
bottomed [-d] adj. A fond.
bottomless [-lis] adj. Sans fond (box); sans fond (or) siège (chair). ‖ JUR. Sans fondement (accusation). ‖ FIG. Sans fond, insondable.
bottomry [-ri] n. JUR., NAUT. Bomerie *f.; bottomry load,* prêt à la grosse aventure.
botulism ['bɔtju,lizm] n. MED. Botulisme *m.*
bouclé ['bu:klei] adj. Bouclé (wool).
boudoir ['bu:dwɑ:*] n. Boudoir *m.* (room).
bouffant ['bu:fɔ:ŋ] adj. Bouffant (hair, dress).
bougainvillaea [,bu:gən'viliə] n. BOT. Bougainvillée *f.,* bougainvillier *m.*
bough [bau] n. Rameau *m.;* branche *f.*
bought [bɔ:t] pret., p. p. See BUY.
bougie ['bu:ʒi] n. MED. Bougie *f.*
bouillabaisse ['bujəbɛs] n. CULIN. Bouillabaisse *f.*
bouillon ['bu:ljɔn] n. CULIN. Bouillon, consommé *m.; bouillon cube,* bouillon Kub.
boulder ['bouldə*] n. Galet *m.;* grosse pierre roulée *f.* ‖ GEOL. Roche erratique *f.* ‖ **Boulder-clay,**

Geol. Terrain (or) dépôt erratique *m.* ‖ **Boulder-period,** n. Geol. Période glaciaire *f.*

boulevard ['bulvɑ:*] n. Boulevard *m.;* artère *f.*

bounce [bauns] v. intr. Bondir; sauter, se précipiter, se ruer (*into,* dans; *out of,* hors de); *to bounce in,* entrer en trombe. ‖ Bondir, rebondir (to rebound). ‖ Fin. Etre retourné pour non-provision (cheque). ‖ Fam. Plastronner, bluffer.
— v. tr. Faire rebondir (a ball). ‖ Pousser, activer, mettre l'épée dans les reins à (s.o.); *to bounce s.o. into doing sth.,* décider qqn à faire qqch. sans lui laisser le temps de se retourner; *to bounce sth. out of s.o.,* extorquer qqch. à qqn par le bluff. ‖ U. S. Fam. Flanquer dehors, saquer, vider.
— n. Bond, saut *m.* (jump). ‖ Bond, rebondissement *m.* (rebound). ‖ Fam. Bluff *m.;* esbrouffe, vanterie *f.* ‖ Fam. U. S. Renvoi *m.;* *to get the bounce,* recevoir son paquet.
— adv. Tout à trac, en trombe, d'un bond.

bouncer [ə*] n. Fam. Mensonge éhonté *m.;* craque *f.* (lie). ‖ Fam. Mastodonte, éléphant *m.* (big person or thing). ‖ Fam. Hâbleur, faiseur *m.* (braggart). ‖ Fin. Chèque (*m.*) sans provision. ‖ U. S. Expulseur, videur *m.* (chucker-out).

bouncing [-iŋ] adj. Enorme (big); avenant (buxom); robuste, vigoureux, plantureux (strong).

bound [baund] n. Borne *f.* (See LIMIT.) ‖ Sports. *Out of bounds,* hors du jeu. ‖ Fig. Borne, limite *f.* (*to,* à); *within bounds,* dans la juste mesure, avec modération.
— v. tr. Borner, limiter.
— v. intr. Avoir sa frontière (or) ses limites (*on,* sur).

bound n. Bond, saut *m.* (jump); *at a bound,* d'un bond (or) élan. ‖ Rebondissement *m.* (rebound).
— v. intr. Bondir, sauter (to leap); rebondir (to rebound). ‖ Fig. Bondir (*with,* de).

bound adj. Naut. *Bound for,* en partance pour, via, à destination de. ‖ Fam. Prêt à partir pour.

bound p.p. See BIND. ‖ Lié; *bound up in* (or) *with,* entièrement lié (or) dévoué à; se rapportant à. ‖ Forcé, obligé, contraint (*to,* de) [compelled]. ‖ Destiné, promis (*to,* à) [fated]; certain (*to,* de); résolu, déterminé, décidé (*to,* à) [resolved]. ‖ Med. Constipé; resserré (fam.). ‖ Techn. Relié (book).

boundary [-əri] n. Limite, frontière, borne *f.;* *boundary stone,* borne.

bounden [-n̩] adj. Strict, obligatoire; impérieux, sacré (duty).

bounder [-ə*] n. Fam. Bluffeur, m'as-tu-vu, plastronneur, arriviste *m.*

boundless [-lis] adj. Sans borne; infini; illimité.

bounteous ['bauntiəs] adj. Généreux, bienveillant. ‖ Abondant, copieux.

bounteousness [-nis] n. Générosité, largesse *f.* ‖ Abondance *f.*

bountiful ['bauntiful] adj. Généreux, libéral. ‖ Abondant.

bounty [-i] n. Générosité, libéralité *f.* ‖ Don libéral *m.;* libéralité (gift). ‖ Gratification *f.* (bonus). ‖ Comm., Milit. Prime *f.*

bouquet [bu'kei] n. Bouquet *m.* (of flowers, wine).

bourbon ['bə:bn] n. U. S. Bourbon *m.* (whiskey). **Bourbon** ['buəbn] n. † Bourbon *s.* ‖ U.S. Réactionnaire *s.* ‖ Culin. *Bourbon biscuit,* biscuit fourré au chocolat.

bourdon ['buədn] n. Mus. Bourdon *m.*

bourgeois ['buəʒwa] n. Bourgeois *m.* ‖ Techn. Corps neuf *m.* (in printing).

bourgeoisie [,buəʒwa'zi] n. Bourgeoisie *f.*

bourn [buən] n. † Ruisseau *m.*

bourn n. † Limite, borne *f.*

Bourse [buəs] n. Bourse *f.* (stock exchange).

bouse [bu:z] n. Fam. Gnole *f.* (drink); beuverie *f.* (drinking).
— v. tr., intr. Fam. Siroter, boire.

bout [baut] n. Coup, tour *m.;* fois *f.* ‖ Sports.

Assaut *m.* (in boxing); passe *f.* (in fencing). ‖ Med. Attaque *f.* (See FIT.) ‖ Fam. Partie *f.*

boutique [bu:'ti:k] n. Boutique (*f.*) de frivolités d'une maison de couture.

boutonnière [,bu:t'njɛə*] n. U. S. Boutonnière *f.* (flower).

bovid ['bouvid] adj. Zool. Bovidé.

bovine [-ain] adj. Zool., Fam. Bovin.

bow [bou] n. Arc *m.;* *to draw the bow,* tirer à l'arc. ‖ Arçon *m.* (of a saddle). ‖ Courbe, anse *f.* (curve). ‖ Nœud plat *m.* (bowknot). ‖ Mus. Archet *m.* ‖ Fig. *To bend the bow of Ulysses,* entreprendre un travail d'Hercule; *to have two strings to one's bow,* avoir deux cordes à son arc. ‖ Fam. Galéjade *f.;* *to draw the long bow,* exagérer, galéjer. ‖ **Bow-cal(l)ipers,** n. Math. Compas sphérique *m.* ‖ **Bow-compass,** n. Math. Compas-balustre *m.* ‖ **Bow-legged,** adj. Bancal. ‖ **Bow-saw,** n. Techn. Scie (*f.*) à chantourner. ‖ **Bow-shot,** n. Portée (*f.*) d'arc. ‖ **Bow-spring,** n. Bow-spring *m.* ‖ **Bow-string,** n. Corde (*f.*) d'acier; Fig. lacet d'étrangleur *m.* ‖ **Bow-tie,** n. Nœud papillon *m.* ‖ **Bow-window,** n. Bow-window, fenêtre en saillie *f.*
— v. intr. Mus. Tirer l'archet.

bow [bau] n. Salut *m.;* courbette; inclination de tête *f.* ‖ Fig. *To make one's bow,* se présenter (entrance); faire ses adieux (leaving).
— v. intr. S'incliner, saluer; *she bowed back to me,* elle me rendit mon salut; *to bow down,* se baisser; *to bow and scrape,* faire des courbettes, se répandre en salutations. ‖ Ployer, plier, fléchir, s'incliner, se courber (*before, to,* devant; *under,* sous); *to bow to the storm,* laisser passer l'orage, courber le dos.
— v. tr. Courber (one's back); incliner, courber (one's head); fléchir (the knee). ‖ Exprimer par un salut; *to bow one's admiration,* témoigner son admiration par des courbettes. ‖ **To bow down,** courber, accabler, écraser, faire ployer (*under,* sous) [s.o.]. ‖ **To bow in,** faire entrer en saluant; *he bowed her in,* d'un salut il l'invita à entrer. ‖ **To bow out,** quitter (or) congédier en saluant; *to bow oneself out,* se retirer en s'inclinant, saluer et prendre congé.

bow n. Naut. Avant *m.;* proue, étrave *f.;* *on the bow,* par le bossoir. ‖ Naut. Têtier, rameur d'avant *m.* (rower). ‖ Aviat. Proue de la coque *f.;* nez *m.* ‖ **Bow-cap,** n. Aviat. Chapeau (*m.*) de proue. ‖ **Bow-chaser,** n. Naut. Canon (*m.*) de chasse. ‖ **Bow-side,** n. Naut. Tribord *m.* ‖ **Bow-stiffener,** n. Aviat. Raidisseur (*m.*) de la proue. ‖ **Bow-timbers,** n. Naut. Bossoirs *m. pl.*
— adj. Naut. De la proue; de l'avant.

bowdlerize ['baudləraiz] v. tr. Expurger (a book); *bowdlerized version,* version *ad usum delphini.*

bowel ['bauəl] n. Med. Intestin, boyau *m.* ‖ Fig. Pl. Entrailles *f. pl.* (of the earth); *bowels of compassion,* pitié.
— v. tr. (1). Eventrer.

bower ['bauə*] n. Berceau (*m.*) de verdure; tonnelle *f.* ‖ Boudoir *m.* ‖ Demeure, maisonnette *f.*

bower n. Naut. Ancre (*f.*) de bossoir.

bowie-knife ['boui,naif] n. Couteau-poignard *m.*

bowl [boul] n. Bol *m.* ‖ Coupe (cup); jatte (platter); écuelle *f.* (porringer). ‖ Cuvette *f.;* bassin *m.;* vasque *f.* (basin). ‖ Sébile *f.* (of a beggar). ‖ Culot (of a lamp); fourneau (of a pipe); cuilleron, creux *m.* (of a spoon). ‖ Electr. *Bowl type electric fire,* radiateur parabolique. ‖ Fam. Bouteille; beuverie *f.* ‖ U. S. Fam. Amphithéâtre *m.*

bowl n. Sports. Boule *f.;* U. S. quille *f.*
— v. tr. Rouler, faire rouler (to roll). ‖ Sports. Lancer, rouler, bôler (in cricket). ‖ **To bowl out,** Sports. Mettre hors jeu; Fam. renverser. ‖ **To bowl over,** Sports., Fam. Renverser.
— v. intr. Jouer aux boules; U. S. jouer aux quilles.

‖ **To bowl along**, rouler, avancer en roulant. ‖
SPORTS. Servir (*to*, à).
bowler [-ə*] n. Melon *m.; cape f.* (hat). ‖ MILIT.,
FAM. *Battle bowler*, casque. ‖ **Bowler-hat**, v. tr.
FAM. Limoger. ‖ **Bowler-hatting**, n. FAM. Limogeage *m.*
bowler ['boulə*] n. SPORTS. Lanceur *m.* (in cricket); joueur (*m.*) de boules (or) de quilles.
bowline ['boulain] n. NAUT. Bouline *f.; on a
bowline*, près du vent. ‖ **Bowline-knot**, n. Nœud
de cabestan *m.*
bowling ['bouliŋ] n. Jeu (*m.*) de boules (or) de
quilles. ‖ SPORTS. Service *m.* ‖ **Bowling-alley**, n.
Boulodrome *m.* ‖ **Bowling-green**, n. Boulingrin *m.*
bowman ['boumən] (pl. **bowmen**) n. Archer *m.*
bowman ['baumən] (pl. **bowmen**) n. SPORTS.
Têtier, rameur d'avant *m.*
bowsprit ['bousprit] n. NAUT. Beaupré *m.*
bow-wow ['bau'wau] n. Aboi, aboiement; oua-
oua *m.* (fam.). ‖ FAM. Toutou *m.*
box [bɔks] n. BOT. Buis *m.*
box n. *Box on the ear*, claque, gifle *f;* soufflet *m.*
— v. tr. Boxer avec, boxer. ‖ *To box s.o.'s ears*,
gifler, claquer, souffleter qqn.
— v. intr. SPORTS. Boxer, être boxeur.
box [ˌbɔks] (pl. **boxes** [-iz]) n. Boîte *f.;* carton *m.*
(carton); caisse *f.* (case); coffret *m.* (casket);
coffre *m.* (chest); malle *f.* (trunk); *Post Office box,*
casier postal. ‖ Siège du conducteur *m.* (driver's
seat). ‖ Box, compartiment, cabinet *m.* (at a restaurant). ‖ Pavillon *m.* (country house). ‖ Cadeau
m.; Christmas box, étrennes; cadeaux de Noël. ‖
Article encadré *m.* (newspaper article). ‖ MILIT.
Guérite *f.* ‖ CH. DE F. Poste *m.;* cabine *f.* ‖ THEATR.
Loge, baignoire *f.* ‖ SPORTS. Box *m.* (for horses).
‖ JUR. Banc *m.* (for the jury, the press); barre *f.*
(for the witnesses); *to be in the box*, paraître à la
barre. ‖ COMM. Caisse *f.* (money-box). ‖ ECCLES.
Tronc *m.* ‖ AUTOM. Boîte *f.* (of brakes); carter *m.*
(of gear). ‖ TECHN. Corps *m.* (of a pump); moyeu
m. (of a wheel); cassetin *m.* (in printing); *rocker
box*, boîtier de culbuteur. ‖ ELECTR. Bac *m.* ‖ **Box-
bed**, n. Lit clos; lit-cage *m.* ‖ **Box-calf**, n. Box-calf,
box *m.* ‖ **Box-camera**, n. Détective *m.* (photogr.).
‖ **Box-car**, n. CH. DE F. Fourgon, wagon, tombereau *m.* ‖ **Box-coat**, n. Pardessus vague *m.* ‖
Box girder, n. TECHN. Poutre (*f.*) à caissons. ‖ **Box
number**, n. Numéro (*m.*) de boîte postale (in a post
office); numéro de référence (in a newspaper advertisement). ‖ **Box-office**, n. THEATR. Bureau (*m.*) de
location, guichet *m.; a box-office success*, pièce qui
fait recette, qui a du succès. ‖ **Box-pleat**, n. Pli
creux *m.* ‖ **Box-spanner** (or) **-wrench**, n. TECHN.
Clef (*f.*) à tube. ‖ **Box-tail**, n. AVIAT. Gouvernail
tubulaire *m.* ‖ **Box-tricycle**, n. Triporteur *m.*
— v. tr. Mettre en boîte (or) en caisse (or) en box.
‖ NAUT. *To box the compass*, réciter la rose des
vents. ‖ JUR. Déposer; verser aux débats (a document). ‖ **To box in**, encaisser. ‖ **To box off**, compartimenter. ‖ **To box up**, empiler, tasser. ‖ FAM.
To box the compass, boucler la boucle, revenir à
ses premières amours.
boxer [-ə*] n. SPORTS. Boxeur *m.*
Boxer [-ə*] n. GEOGR., ZOOL. Boxer *m.*
boxful [-ful] n. Pleine boîte (or) caisse *f.;* contenu
(*m.*) d'une boîte.
boxing [-iŋ] n. SPORTS. Boxe *f.* ‖ **Boxing-glove**,
n. SPORTS. Gant (*m.*) de boxe. ‖ **Boxing-match**, n.
SPORTS. Match (or) combat (*m.*) de boxe.
Boxing Day [-iŋdei] n. Jour (*m.*) des étrennes.
boy [bɔi] n. Garçon *m.* (lad, youth); fils *m.* (son).
‖ Boy *m.* (servant). ‖ Ecolier, élève *m.* (pupil); *old
boys' day*, le jour des anciens élèves. ‖ *Boy scout,*
boy-scout, scout. ‖ NAUT. Mousse *m.* ‖ FAM. Gars
m.; old boy, mon vieux; *wide boy*, chevalier d'industrie; U. S. *oh boy!*, chouette alors! ‖ **Boy-
friend**, n. Amoureux, flirt *m.*

boycott ['bɔikɔt] v. tr. Boycotter.
— n. Boycottage *m.*
boyhood ['bɔihud] n. Enfance, adolescence *f.*
boyish [-iʃ] adj. Enfantin, puéril (childish). ‖ D'enfant, de garçonnet. ‖ Garçonnier.
boyishness [-iʃnis] n. Puérilité, gaminerie *f.*
Boyle ['bɔil] n. PHYS. *Boyle's Law*, loi de Mariotte.
bra [brɑ:] n. FAM. Soutien-gorge *m.*
brace [breis] n. Couple; paire *f.* (of animals, persons). [See PAIR.] ‖ Agrafe, attache *f.* (fastener). ‖
Pl. Bretelles *f. pl.* ‖ ARCHIT. Entretoise *f.;* étrésillon *m.* ‖ AUTOM. Croisillon *m.; trunk brace,*
amarreur pour bagages. ‖ NAUT. Bras *m.* (of a yard).
‖ MED. Armature orthopédique *f.* (splints); rectificateur dentaire *m.* (dental device). ‖ TECHN. Accolade *f.* (in printing); *brace and bit*, vilebrequin.
— N. B. *Brace*, au sens de couple, est invariable.
— v. tr. Attacher, lier (to tie). ‖ Soutenir, consolider, étayer (to prop up). ‖ ARCHIT. Entretoiser,
étrésillonner. ‖ NAUT. Brasser. ‖ TECHN. Accolader.
‖ MED. Tonifier, fortifier; *to brace up*, revigorer.
‖ FIG. Bander, tendre (one's energies); *to brace
oneself up*, bander ses forces.
bracelet ['breislit] n. Bracelet *m.* ‖ FAM. Pl. Bracelets; menottes *f. pl.* (handcuffs).
bracer ['breisə*] n. SPORTS. Bracelet d'archer *m.*
(in fencing). ‖ FAM. Tonique, stimulant *m.*
brach [brætʃ] n. ZOOL. Braque *m.; lice f.*
brachial ['breikiəl] adj. MED. Brachial.
brachiate ['breikiət] adj. BOT. Décussé.
brachiopod ['brækiɔpɔd] n. ZOOL. Brachiopode *m.*
brachycephalic ['brækike'fælik] adj. MED. Brachycéphale.
brachygraphy [brə'kigrəfi] n. Brachygraphie *f.*
bracken ['brækən] n. BOT. Fougère arborescente
f. (fern); fougeraie *f.* (mass).
bracket ['brækit] n. Console, potence *f.;* bras,
tasseau *m.* (support). ‖ Rayon *m.;* étagère *f.* (shelf).
‖ Crochet *m.* (in printing). ‖ ELECTR. Applique *f.*
‖ MILIT. Fourchette *f.* (in ranging). ‖ JUR. Tranche
f.; bracket progression, progressivité par tranches.
‖ **Bracket-seat**, n. Strapontin *m.*
— v. tr. Mettre entre crochets (in printing). ‖ MILIT.
Encadrer. ‖ FIG. Grouper (or) classer ex aequo.
brackish [-iʃ] adj. Saumâtre (lit. and fig.).
brad [bræd] n. Semence *f.*, clou de tapissier *m.*
bradawl ['brædɔ:l] n. TECHN. Poinçon *m.*
Bradshaw ['bradʃɔ:] n. CH. DE F. Chaix, indicateur *m.* (time-table).
brae [brei] n. GEOGR. Flanc (*m.*) de coteau (or) de
colline, coteau *m.* (hillside); versant *m.* (bank) [in
Scotland].
brag [bræg] n. Hâblerie, vanterie *f.*
— v. intr. (1). Se vanter (*of*, de).
— v. tr. Se vanter de. (See BOAST.)
braggadocio [ˌbrægə'doutʃiou] n. Fier-à-bras *m.*
(boaster); forfanterie *f.* (boasting).
braggart ['brægət] adj., n. Hâbleur, fanfaron, fendant; tranche-montagne *m.* (fam.).
Brahman ['brɑ:mən] n. Brahmane *m.*
Brahmanism [-izm] n. Brahmanisme *m.*
Brahmin ['brɑ:min] n. Bramine *m.*
brahminee [ˌbrɑ:mi'ni:] n. Femme brahmane *f.*
— ['brɑ:mini] adj. Brahmanique.
braid [breid] v. tr. Tresser, natter (hair, straw).
‖ Entrelacer (*with*, avec) [flowers, hair]. ‖ Couronner d'un bandeau. ‖ Soutacher, galonner. ‖
ELECTR. Guiper; mettre sous tresse.
— n. Tresse, natte *f.* ‖ Ruban pour cheveux *m.* ‖
Soutache, passementerie, ganse, tresse *f.;* galon *m.*
‖ MILIT. Galon *m.*
brail [breil] n. NAUT. Cargue *f.*
— v. tr. **To brail up**, carguer.
Braille [breil] n. Braille *m.*
— v. tr. Imprimer (or) transcrire en braille.
brain [brein] n. MED. Cerveau *m.* ‖ FAM. Pl.

Cervelle *f.*; méninges *f. pl.* ‖ FAM. Tête, idée *f.*; *to have got it on the brain*, n'avoir que ça dans le ciboulot. ‖ **Brain-child**, n. FAM. Enfant de l'esprit *m.*; conception personnelle *f.* ‖ **Brain drain**, n. Exode (*m.*) des cerveaux. ‖ **Brain-fag**, n. MED. Anémie (or) fatigue cérébrale *f.* ‖ **Brain-fever**, n. MED. Fièvre cérébrale *f.* ‖ **Brain-pan**, n. MED. Boîte crânienne *f.*; FAM. Ciboulot *m.* ‖ **Brainpower**, n. Capacités intellectuelles *f. pl.*, intelligence *f.* ‖ **Brainstorm**, n. MED. Transport au cerveau *m.*; FAM. Idée (*f.*) de génie. ‖ **Brains-trust**, U. S. **brain trust**, n. Brain-trust, groupe d'experts *m.* ‖ **Brainteaser** (or) **-twister**, n. Casse-tête *m. inv.* ‖ **Brainwash**, v. tr. Faire un lavage de cerveau à; FIG. Bourrer le crâne à. ‖ **Brain-washing**, n. Lavage de cerveau *m.*; FIG. Bourrage de crâne *m.* ‖ **Brainwave**, n. MED. Onde cérébrale *f.*; FAM. Inspiration géniale, trouvaille, idée lumineuse *f.* ‖ **Brain-work**, n. Travail intellectuel *m.*
— v. tr. Défoncer le crâne à, faire jaillir la cervelle de.
brainless [-lis] adj. Sans cervelle, stupide.
brainy [-i] adj. Intelligent, à l'esprit vif.
braise [breiz] v. tr. CULIN. Braiser.
brake [breik] n. Fourré, hallier *m.*
brake n. Break *m.* (wagonnet).
brake n. BOT. Fougère *f.* (fern).
brake n. Brisoir *m.* (for hemp). ‖ AGRIC. Brise-mottes *m.*
— v. tr. Briser, broyer (flax, hemp).
brake n. AUTOM. Frein *m.* ‖ **Brake-band**, n. AUTOM. Bandage de frein *m.* ‖ **Brake-block** (or) **-shoe**, n. AUTOM. Sabot de frein *m.* ‖ **Brake-drum**, n. AUTOM. Tambour de frein *m.* ‖ **Brake fluid**, n. AUTOM. Liquide de frein, Lockheed *m.* (nom déposé). ‖ **Brake horsepower**, n. AUTOM. Puissance (*f.*) au frein. ‖ **Brake light**, n. AUTOM. Stop *m.* (on vehicle). ‖ **Brake-lining**, n. AUTOM. Garniture (*f.*) de frein.
— v. tr., intr. Freiner.
brakesman [-smən] n. CH. DE F. Serre- (or) garde-frein *m.*
bramble ['bræmbl] n. BOT. Ronce *f.* ‖ **Brambleberry**, n. BOT. Mûre *f.* ‖ **Bramble-rose**, n. BOT. Eglantine *f.*
brambly [-i] adj. Plein de ronces; épineux.
bran [bræn] n. Son *m.* (of wheat).
branch [brɑ:ntʃ] n. BOT. Branche *f.* (See BOUGH.) CH. DE F., TECHN. Embranchement *m.* ‖ FIN. Succursale *f.* ‖ GEOGR. Bras *m.* (of a river). ‖ MILIT. Arme *f.*; service *m.* ‖ FIG. Branche (of a family, science). ‖ **Branch-depot**, n. Dépôt auxiliaire *m.* ‖ **Branch-office**, n. Bureau auxiliaire *m.* ‖ **Branch-pilot**, n. NAUT. Lamaneur *m.*
— v. intr. BOT. *To branch forth* (or) *out*, pousser des branches. ‖ *To branch away* (or) *off*, se bifurquer, se ramifier (river, road). ‖ FIG. *To branch off*, se séparer, diverger; *to branch out*, se ramifier, étendre ses ramifications.
— v. tr. ELECTR. Brancher.
branchiae ['bræŋkii:] n. Pl. ZOOL. Branchies *f. pl.*
branchial [-əl] adj. ZOOL. Branchial.
branchy ['brɑ:ntʃi] adj. Branchu.
brand [brænd] n. Brandon, tison *m.* ‖ Glaive *m.* (sword). ‖ Marque infamante, flétrissure *f.* (stigma). ‖ Fer (*m.*) à marquer (iron); marque *f.* (on cattle). ‖ COMM. Marque *f.* ‖ AGRIC. Brouissure *f.* (blight). ‖ **Brand-iron**, n. Fer (*m.*) à marquer. ‖ **Brand-new**, adj. Tout neuf, flambant neuf.
— v. tr. Marquer au fer rouge (a criminal). ‖ Marquer (cattle). ‖ COMM. Marquer (goods). ‖ MED. Cautériser. ‖ FIG. Flétrir. ‖ FAM. *To brand sth. on s.o.'s memory*, inscrire qqch. en lettres de feu dans la mémoire de qqn.
brandied [-id] adj. Alcoolisé; à l'eau-de-vie.
brandish ['brændiʃ] v. tr. Brandir.
brandy ['brændi] n. Eau-de-vie *f.*; brandy *m.*

— v. tr. (2). Corser d'eau-de-vie. ‖ Conserver à l'eau-de-vie.
brash [bræʃ] adj. Irréfléchi, impulsif (rash); impudent, effronté (cheeky); arrogant, cavalier (self-assertive); criard, tapageur (flashy).
brashly [-li] adv. Impulsivement; impudemment, effrontément; arrogamment, cavalièrement; tapageusement.
brashness [-nis] n. Irréflexion, impulsivité *f.*; impudence, effronterie *f.*; arrogance *f.*; aspect (*m.*) criard (or) tapageur.
brass [brɑːs] n. † Bronze, airain *m.* ‖ Cuivre jaune, laiton *m.* ‖ MUS. Cuivres *m. pl.* ‖ TECHN. Coussinet *m.* ‖ MILIT., FAM. U. S. Galonnard *m.* ‖ FAM. Culot, toupet *m.* (See CHEEK.) ‖ POP. Pognon, pèze *m.* (money). ‖ **Brass-gutted**, adj. FAM. Increvable, bâti à chaux et à sable.
— adj. De bronze, d'airain; de (or) en cuivre; en laiton. ‖ MUS. *Brass winds*, cuivres. ‖ MILIT. *Brass hat*, galonnard. ‖ FAM. *Brass tacks*, les faits, le fond de l'affaire, les questions essentielles.
— v. intr. FAM. *To be brassed off*, avoir le cafard. ‖ FAM. *To brass up*, casquer.
brassard [bræ'sɑːd] n. Brassard *m.*
brasserie ['bræsəri:] n. Brasserie *f.* (room in a restaurant).
brassiere ['bræsiɛə*] n. Soutien-gorge *m.*; strapless brassiere, bustier.
brassiness ['brɑːsinis] n. Toupet *m.*; effronterie *f.*
brassy [-i] adj. De bronze, de cuivre. ‖ FAM. Culotté. (See CHEEKY.)
— n. SPORTS. Brassie *m.*
brat [bræt] n. FAM. Gosse, moutard, gamin *m.*
bravado [brə'vɑːdou] n. Bravade *f.*
brave [breiv] adj. Brave, valeureux (courageous). ‖ Elégant (fashionable).
— v. tr. Braver, défier (to defy); braver, affronter (to brave); *to brave it out*, payer d'audace.
bravery [əri] n. Bravoure, valeur *f.* ‖ Elégance *f.* (appearance); parure *f.* (dress).
bravo ['brɑː'vou] n. Spadassin, bravo *m.*
bravo [brɑː'vou] interj., n. Bravo *m.*
bravura [brə'vjuərə] n. Panache *m.*, bravade *f.* ‖ MUS. Morceau (*m.*) de bravoure.
brawl [brɔːl] v. intr. Brailler, beugler; gueuler (pop.). ‖ Se bagarrer (to quarrel). ‖ Bruire (river).
— n. Braillerie; gueulerie *f.* (pop.). ‖ Bagarre, dispute *f.* (quarrel). ‖ Bruissement, murmure *m.* (of a river).
brawler [-ə*] n. Braillard, gueulard *m.* (fam.). ‖ Bagarreur *m.*
brawn [brɔːn] n. MED. Muscle *m.* ‖ CULIN. Fromage (*m.*) de tête.
brawniness [-inis] n. Musculature *f.*
brawny [-i] adj. Musclé; costaud (fam.).
bray [brei] n. Braiment *m.*
— v. intr. Braire.
— v. tr. *To bray out*, brailler.
bray v. tr. Broyer.
braze [breiz] v. tr. Braser.
braze v. tr. Cuivrer.
brazen [-ŋ] adj. D'airain, de bronze; de cuivre, de laiton. ‖ Cuivré (sound). ‖ FIG. Effronté, impudent. ‖ **Brazen-faced**, adj. Impudent.
— v. tr. *To brazen it out*, crâner.
brazier ['breiziə*] n. Brasero *m.*
brazier n. Chaudronnier *m.* ‖ **Brazier-wares**, n. Chaudronnerie *f.*
Brazil [brə'zil] n. GEOGR. Brésil *m.* ‖ COMM. Noix (*f.*) du Brésil (nut); bois (*m.*) du Brésil (wood).
Brazilian [brə'ziljən] adj., n. GEOGR. Brésilien *s.*
breach [briːtʃ] n. Brisure, rupture, cassure *f.* (breaking). ‖ Vide, trou *m.* (See GAP.) ‖ MILIT. Brèche, trouée *f.* ‖ NAUT. Rupture de vagues *f.*; paquet (*m.*) de mer. ‖ JUR. Infraction, violation; inexécution *f.*; non-accomplissement *m.*; *breach of close*, effraction; *breach of confidence*, manque-

ment au secret professionnel ; *breach of contract*, rupture de contrat ; *breach of discipline*, manquement à la discipline ; *breach of the peace*, attentat contre l'ordre public ; *breach of trust*, abus de confiance. ‖ Fig. Rupture, brouille, cessation des relations, *f.* (falling out) ; *the breach between us*, le fossé creusé entre nous.
— v. tr. Faire une trouée dans, ouvrir une brèche dans.
— v. intr. Zool. Bondir hors de l'eau (whale).

bread [bred] n. Pain *m.; slice of bread and butter*, tartine de beurre. ‖ Culin. *Bread and milk*, soupe au lait. ‖ Eccles. *Altar bread*, hostie, pain d'autel. ‖ Fig. Pain *m.* (of affliction, tears). ‖ Fam. *His bread is buttered on both sides*, il a du foin dans les bottes, il nage dans l'opulence ; *to know which side one's bread is buttered*, savoir de quel côté se trouve la manne ; *to take the bread out of s.o.'s mouth*, tirer le pain de la bouche à qqn. ‖ **Bread-and-butter**, adj. Fam. De remerciement (letter) ; d'enfance, de jeunesse (period) ; jeune (person) ; de digestion (visit) ; n. Fam. Croûte *f.* (livelihood). ‖ **Bread-basket**, n. Corbeille (*f.*) [or] panier (*m.*) à pain ; Fam. Gésier, jabot, coco *m.* ‖ **Bread-crumb**, n. Culin. Chapelure *f.; v.* tr. Paner. ‖ **Bread-flour**, n. Farine panifiable *f.* ‖ **Bread-winner**, n. Soutien (*m.*) de famille (person) ; gagne-pain *m.* (work).

breadline ['bred,lain] n. U. S. File (*f.*) d'attente devant une soupe populaire. ‖ Niveau (*m.*) de subsistance ; *to live on the breadline*, gagner tout juste le minimum vital.

breadth [bredθ] n. Largeur *f.; in breadth*, de large, en largeur. ‖ Lé *m.* (of cloth). ‖ Arts, Mus. Largeur, ampleur *f.* ‖ Fig. Largeur *f.* (of mind, understanding, view). ‖ Fam. *By a hair's breadth*, de l'épaisseur d'un cheveu, d'un rien, d'un comma, d'un iota.

break [breik] v. tr. (25).

---

1. Casser. — 2. Disperser. — 3. Amortir. — 4. Arrêter. — 5. Agric. — 6. Milit. — 7. Sports. — 8. Fin. — 9. Jur. — 10. Med. — 11. Fig. — 12. To break away. — 13. To break down. — 14. To break in. — 15. To break off. — 16. To break through. — 17. To break up.

---

1. Casser, rompre, briser (sth.) ; *to break open a safe*, fracturer un coffre-fort. ‖ 2. Disperser, dissiper, ouvrir (the clouds) ; ouvrir, frayer (a way). ‖ 3. Amortir, adoucir (a blow). ‖ 4. Arrêter, interrompre, suspendre (a journey). ‖ 5. Agric. Briser, écraser (clods) ; défoncer (ground). ‖ 6. Milit. Casser (a non-commissioned officer) ; rompre (the ranks). ‖ 7. Sports. Dresser (a horse) ; *to break its knees*, se couronner (horse). ‖ 8. Fin. Faire sauter (a bank, s.o.). ‖ 9. Jur. Violer, enfreindre (law) ; briser (strike) ; *to break gaol*, s'évader de prison ; *to break the peace*, troubler l'ordre public. ‖ 10. Med. Briser, ruiner (s.o.'s health). ‖ 11. Fig. Briser, anéantir (s.o.'s courage, a rebellion, s.o.'s will) ; briser, crever (s.o.'s heart) ; annoncer (news) ; manquer à, violer (one's promise) ; *to break faith with*, manquer de parole à ; *to break s.o. of a habit*, guérir (or) corriger qqn d'une habitude. ‖ 12. To break away, détacher (*de*, from) [sth.]. ‖ 13. To break down, abattre, renverser (a wall) ; Fin. Détailler (accounts) ; Fig. Briser, renverser (the opposition). ‖ 14. To break in, défoncer (a cask) ; enfoncer (a door) ; Fig. Mater, dompter (an animal, s.o.) ; *to break oneself into*, se rompre (or) se plier à. ‖ 15. To break off, casser, briser (sth.) ; Fig. Rompre (an engagement) ; faire cesser (a habit) ; interrompre, cesser (a task). ‖ 16. To break through, enfoncer, faire une trouée dans, percer ; Aviat. Franchir (the sound barrier) ; Fig. Rompre, enfreindre. ‖ 17. To break up, Archit. Démolir

(a house) ; Agric. Ameublir (the ground) ; Jur. Dissoudre (an assembly) ; rompre (a coalition) ; démembrer (an empire) ; disperser (a crowd) ; Milit. Lever (a camp) ; fractionner (a column).
— v. intr. (25).

---

1. Se casser. — 2. Se disperser. — 3. Rompre. — 4. Se libérer. — 5. Poindre. — 6. Commencer. — 7. Devenir notoire. — 8. Sports. — 9. Naut. — 10. Milit. — 11. Fin. — 12. Med. — 13. Gramm. — 14. To break away. — 15. To break down. — 16. To break forth. — 17. To break in. — 18. To break off. — 19. To break out. — 20. To break up.

---

1. Se casser, se briser, se rompre, casser. ‖ 2. Se disperser, se séparer (to scatter). ‖ 3. Rompre, cesser les relations (*with*, avec) [*to fall out*] ; se départir (*with*, de) (one's habits). ‖ 4. Se libérer (*from*, de) ; *to break loose*, se détacher. ‖ 5. Poindre, se lever (day) ; changer, s'altérer (weather) ; *the heat-wave was breaking*, la vague de chaleur touchait à sa fin. ‖ 6. Commencer, se mettre (*into*, à) ; éclater (*into*, en) ; *she broke into song*, elle entonna soudain une chanson, elle se mit brusquement à chanter ; *she broke into sobs*, elle éclata en sanglots. ‖ 7. Devenir notoire, commencer à circuler (news, story). ‖ 8. Sports. Dévier (ball) ; rompre (in fencing). ‖ 9. Naut. Apparaître hors de l'eau (périscope) ; dériver (ship) ; *to break a flag*, déferler un signal. ‖ 10. Milit. Faire une percée (*through*, dans) ; se débander (troops). ‖ 11. Fin. Faire faillite ; sauter (fam.). ‖ 12. Med. Percer (abscess) ; s'altérer (health) ; muer (voice). ‖ 13. Gramm. Fracturer (vowels). ‖ 14. To break away, se détacher ; se dégager, s'échapper (*from*, de) ; Sports. Se détacher (cyclist, runner). ‖ 15. To break down, s'interrompre, s'arrêter court (speaker) ; Med. S'altérer (health) ; s'ébranler (mind) ; avoir une dépression nerveuse, tomber malade (person) ; Autom. Avoir une panne ; Fin. Diviser, compartimenter (expenditure) ; Fig. S'effondrer (argument) ; échouer (plan) ; s'écrouler (résistance). ‖ 16. To break forth, jaillir (light) ; éclater (storm) ; Fig. Se répandre, s'extérioriser (*into*, en). ‖ 17. To break in, surgir (idea, person) ; s'interposer, s'entremettre (between two persons) ; *to break in on* (or) *upon*, interrompre brusquement ; Jur. Entrer par effraction. ‖ 18. To break off, s'interrompre (to stop) ; se dégager (*from*, de) ; rompre (*with*, avec) ; *to break off from work*, prendre un moment de répit. ‖ 19. To break out, éclater (fire, storm) ; s'exclamer ; se laisser répandre (*into*, en) ; Milit. Eclater (war) ; Med. Se déclarer (disease) ; se rouvrir (wound) ; *to break out into*, se couvrir de (pimples). ‖ 20. To break up, se disperser (clouds, crowd) ; débâcler (ice) ; entrer en vacances (pupils) ; se séparer (people) ; se défoncer (road) ; se gâter (weather) ; se répartir (work) ; Naut. Etre en perdition (ship) ; Jur. Se désunir, se disjoindre (group) ; se disloquer, se séparer (meeting) ; Med. S'altérer ; *he is breaking up*, sa santé se délabre ; Fig. Se dénouer (friendship) ; Fam. Baisser, se casser (old person).
— n. Brisure, cassure, rupture *f.* ‖ Trouée, brèche *f.* (breach). ‖ Trou *m.; lacune f.* (gap) ; repos, répit *m.; interruption, cesse, pause f.* (interval) ; *break in continuity*, solution de continuité ; *without a break*, sans discontinuer. ‖ Point, lever *m.* (of day) ; éclaircie *f.* (in cloudy sky) ; changement *m.* (of weather). ‖ Break *m.* (wagonnet). ‖ Archit. Brisis ; coude *m.* (in a wall). ‖ Milit. Percée, trouée *f.* ‖ Ch. de f. Arrêt *m.* ‖ Sports. Effet *m.* (on the ball) ; série *f.* (in billiards). ‖ Fin. Effondrement *m.* (in prices). ‖ Med., Mus. Altération *f.* ‖ Mus. Transition mélodique *f.* (jazz) ; changement de registre *m.* (singing). ‖ Gramm. Points (*m. pl.*)

de suspension. ‖ GEOL. Faille *f.* ‖ RADIO. *Break in transmission,* incident technique. ‖ FIG. Rupture, brouille *f.* (falling out). ‖ FAM. Bourde, gaffe *f.* (blunder). ‖ FAM. Chance *f.; he got a break,* il a eu de la veine. ‖ **Break-through,** n. MILIT. Percée *f.;* GEOL. Affleurement *m.* ‖ **Break-up,** n. Débâcle *f.* (of the ice); changement *m.* (in the weather); MED. Affaiblissement *m.* (of health); NAUT. Bris *m.* (of a ship); FIG. Désagrégation, dispersion, ruine; fin *f.*

breakable [-əbl] adj. Cassable, fragile.

breakage [-idʒ] n. Casse *f.;* bris *m.* (breaking). ‖ Objets cassés *m. pl.;* cassure *f.* ‖ JUR. Réfection pour casse *f.*

breakdown [-daun] n. Arrêt subit *m.* ‖ FIN. Effondrement *m.;* déconfiture *f.* ‖ MED. Défaillance, dépression nerveuse *f.* ‖ AUTOM., TECHN. Panne *f.; breakdown service,* service de dépannage. ‖ FAM. Fiasco, four *m.* (failure); *to have a breakdown,* rester en carafe.

breaker [-ə*] n. Dresseur *m.* ‖ NAUT. Brisant *m.* (wave). ‖ ELECTR. Interrupteur *m.*

breaker n. NAUT. Baril (*m.*) d'eau (keg).

breakfast ['brekfəst] n. Petit déjeuner *m.; continental breakfast,* petit déjeuner à la française.
— v. intr. Déjeuner, prendre son petit déjeuner.

breaking ['breikiŋ] n. Bris, cassage *m.; breaking and entering,* vol avec effraction. ‖ **Breaking-point,** n. TECHN., FIG. Point (*m.*) de rupture. ‖ **Breaking-strength,** n. TECHN. Energie (*f.*) de rupture.

breakneck ['breiknek] adj. A se casser le cou, de casse-cou; *to run at breakneck speed,* rouler à tombeau ouvert.

breakwater [ˌwɔ:tə*] n. NAUT. Brise-lames *m.;* jetée *f.;* môle *m.*

bream [bri:m] v. tr. NAUT. Brusquer.

bream n. ZOOL. Brème *f.*

breast [brest] n. MED. Poitrine *f.* (of a person); sein *m.* (of a woman). ‖ ZOOL. Poitrail *m.* (of an animal). ‖ ECCLES. *To beat one's breast,* battre sa coulpe. ‖ FIG. Cœur *m.;* conscience *f.* (of a person); sein *m.* (of the sea). ‖ FAM. *To make a clean breast of it,* dire ce qu'on a sur la conscience, se déboutonner. ‖ **Breast-deep,** adv. Enfonçant jusqu'à la poitrine. ‖ **Breast-drill,** n. TECHN. Chignole *f.* ‖ **Breast-feed,** v. tr. MED. Nourrir au sein. ‖ **Breast-pocket,** n. Poche intérieure *f.* ‖ **Breast-stroke,** n. SPORTS. Brasse *f.* ‖ **Breast-pump,** n. MED. Tire-lait *m.* ‖ **Breast-wall,** n. ARCHIT. Mur de soutènement *m.*
— v. tr. Faire face à, affronter (to face). ‖ SPORTS. Fendre (the waves); *to breast the bar,* faire un rétablissement à la barre fixe.

breastbone [-boun] n. MED. Sternum *m.* ‖ ZOOL. Bréchet *m.*

breastplate [-pleit] n. Pectoral *m.* ‖ MILIT., TECHN. Plastron *m.*

breastsummer [-sʌmə*] n. ARCHIT. Sommier *m.*

breastwork [-wə:k] n. TECHN. Abattage *m.* ‖ MILIT. Parapet; épaulement *m.* ‖ NAUT. Rambarde *f.*

breath [breθ] n. Haleine *f.;* souffle *m.; out of breath,* hors d'haleine, à bout de souffle; *short of breath,* essoufflé. ‖ Respiration *f.; last breath,* dernier soupir; *to draw breath,* respirer. ‖ Souffle, murmure *m.; below* (or) *under one's breath,* à voix très basse, en un souffle, dans un murmure. ‖ Souffle de vent *m.;* brise *f.; to go out for a breath of air,* sortir prendre l'air. ‖ Parfum, arôme *m.* (of flowers). ‖ GRAMM. *In one breath,* d'une seule émission de voix. ‖ FAM. *In the same breath,* sans souffler, d'une haleine; *it's a waste of breath,* c'est gaspiller sa salive (or) perdre son vent; *not to be named in the same breath with,* ne pas monter à la cheville de; *to take s.o.'s breath away,* estomaquer qqn, en boucher un coin à qqn. ‖ **Breath-taking,** adj. FAM. Soufflant, ahurissant, à couper le souffle. ‖ **Breath test,** n. Alcootest *m.,* test (*m.*) d'alcoolémie.

breathalyse ['breθəˌlaiz] v. tr. Soumettre à l'alcootest.

breathalyser [-ə*] n. Alcootest *m.* (instrument).

breathe [bri:ð] v. intr. Respirer; *to breathe heavily,* panteler, ahaner. ‖ Respirer, reprendre haleine; souffler (*upon,* sur). ‖ Respirer, vivre, être vivant (to live). ‖ Exhaler un parfum (flowers). ‖ Soupirer, exhaler un souffle (person, wind). ‖ Parler, émettre un son (to speak); *not to breathe a word about,* ne pas dire un traître mot de. ‖ FIG. *To breathe upon,* ternir; *to breathe away,* respirer, être libéré.
— v. tr. Respirer (air). ‖ Laisser souffler (or) respirer (a horse). ‖ Faire sortir, faire prendre l'air à (s.o.). ‖ Exhaler, émettre (an odour, a sigh); *to breathe one's last,* rendre le dernier soupir. ‖ Murmurer (words). ‖ GRAMM. Aspirer (the h); *breathed consonants,* consonnes sourdes. ‖ FIG. Respirer, manifester, exhaler (to betoken); *to breathe gentleness,* respirer la douceur. ‖ FIG. Insuffler, inspirer (*into,* à); transfuser (*into,* dans).

breather [-ə*] n. Moment de répit *m.* (rest). ‖ Bol d'air *m.;* courte promenade *f.* ‖ MED. *Mouth breather,* personne qui respire par la bouche. ‖ FAM. Exercice (*m.*) qui dilate les poumons; moment (*m.*) pour souffler.

breathing [-iŋ] n. MED. Respiration *f.;* souffle *m.* ‖ GRAMM. Aspiration *f.;* esprit *m.* (in Greek). ‖ FAM. Répit *m.;* détente *f.* ‖ **Breathing-hole,** n. Soupirail *m.* ‖ **Breathing-space,** n. Moment de répit; temps de souffler *m.*
— adj. Respiratoire (apparatus, exercises).

breathless ['breθlis] adj. Inanimé, sans vie (lifeless); hors d'haleine, oppressé, essoufflé (panting). ‖ Etouffant, sans un souffle d'air (stifling). ‖ FIG. Haletant, en haleine.

breathlessness [-lisnis] n. Essoufflement *m.*

breathy [-i] adj. Sur le souffle (speech, voice).

bred [bred] pret., p.p. See BREED.

breech [bri:tʃ] n. MILIT. Culasse *f.* (of gun); *revolving breech,* barillet. ‖ Pl. Culotte *f.;* pantalon *m.* ‖ THEATR. *Breeches part,* rôle d'hommes joué en travesti. ‖ **Breech-block,** n. MILIT. Bloc (*m.*) de culasse. ‖ **Breech-birth** (or) **-delivery,** n. MED. Accouchement par le siège *m.* ‖ **Breech-loader,** n. MILIT. Arme (*f.*) qui se charge par la culasse. ‖ **Breech-mechanism,** n. MILIT. Mécanisme (*m.*) de répétition. ‖ **Breeches-buoy,** n. NAUT. Bouée-culotte *f.*

breed [bri:d] v. tr. (26). MED. Engendrer, procréer. ZOOL. Produire, porter (to bring forth); couver (to hatch). ‖ AGRIC. Faire l'élevage de. ‖ FIG. Elever, éduquer (to train up); *he was bred to the medical profession,* il était destiné à la médecine. ‖ FIG. Faire naître, engendrer. ‖ FAM. *It is bred in the bone,* c'est dans le sang.
— v. intr. MED. Avoir des enfants. ‖ ZOOL. Faire des petits; se reproduire. ‖ AGRIC. Faire de l'élevage. ‖ FIG. Naître (to originate); se propager (to spread). ‖ FIG. Faire naître, engendrer.
— n. ZOOL. Race, espèce *f.* ‖ FIG. Race, sorte, espèce *f.;* type *m.; men of the same breed,* des gens du même acabit.

breeder [-ə*] n. ZOOL. Reproducteur *m.* ‖ AGRIC. Eleveur *s.* ‖ FIG. Auteur *m.* (originator) ‖ **Breeder reactor,** n. PHYS. Surrégénérateur, surgénérateur *m.*

breeding [-iŋ] n. AGRIC. Elevàge *m.* ‖ FIG. Education *f.;* savoir-vivre *m.*

breeze [bri:z] n. Brise *f.* (wind). ‖ FAM. Grabuge *m.* ‖ U. S. FAM. Vent *m.* (speed, words).
— v. intr. Survoler; parcourir.

breeze n. ZOOL. Taon *m.*

breeze n. Charbonnaille *f.* ‖ **Breeze-block,** n. ARCHIT. Carreau *m.*

breezy [-i] adj. Eventé, aéré. ‖ FIG. Désinvolte, enjoué, jovial.

bremsstrahlung ['brem,ʃtrɑ:ləŋ] n. Phys. Bremsstrahlung *f.*, rayonnement *(m.)* de freinage.

Bren–gun ['brengʌn] n. Fusil mitrailleur *m.*

brethren ['breðrin] n. pl. Eccles. Frères *m. pl.* ‖ Jur. Confrères *m. pl.*

breve [bri:v] n. Eccles. Bref *m.* ‖ Gramm. Brève *f.* ‖ Mus. Carrée *f.*

brevet ['brevit] n. Milit. *Brevet rank,* grade honorifique. ‖ Jur. Brevet *m.*
— v. tr. Milit. Promouvoir à un grade honorifique.

breviary ['bri:viəri] n. Eccles. Bréviaire *m.*

brevity ['breviti] n. Brièveté *f.* (shortness); concision *f.* (terseness).

brew [bru:] v. tr. Brasser (ale, beer). ‖ Préparer (punch); faire infuser (tea). ‖ Fig. Comploter, tramer; mijoter (fam.) [to plot].
— v. intr. Faire de la bière. ‖ Fig. Se tramer, se préparer. ‖ Fam. Se mijoter; *there's trouble brewing,* ça va barder, il y a de l'eau dans le gaz. ‖ Fam. Milit. *To brew up,* faire du thé.
— n. Brassin (amount brewed); brassage *m.* (brewing). ‖ Confection *f.* (of tea).

brewage [-idʒ] n. Liqueur *(f.)* de malt *m.* ‖ Brassage *m.*

brewer [-ə*] n. Brasseur *m.*

brewery [-əri] n. Brasserie *f.*

briar ['braiə*] n. Ronces *f. pl.* ‖ Bot. Eglantier *m.* ‖ Fam. *To fall out of the briars into the thorns,* tomber de Charybde en Scylla; *to leave s.o. in the briars,* laisser qqn dans le pétrin.

bribe [braib] n. Présent corrupteur; pot-de-vin *m.*; *bribe given under the counter,* dessous de table. ‖ Fig. Appât *m.*
— v. tr. Corrompre, suborner, soudoyer, acheter.
— v. intr. Donner des pots-de-vin.

briber [-ə*] n. Corrupteur *m.*; corruptrice *f.*

bribery [-əri] n. Corruption, subornation *f.*

bric-à-brac ['brikə,bræk] n. Bric-à-brac *m.*

brick [brik] n. Brique *f.* ‖ Pain *m.* (of soap). ‖ Pl. Jeu *(m.)* de construction. ‖ Fam. Brave type *m.*; *to dance about like a cat on hot bricks,* se démener comme un diable dans un bénitier; *to drop a brick,* faire une gaffe; *to make bricks without straw,* faire une omelette sans œufs. ‖ Brick-bat, n. Briqueton *m.*; Fam. Brocard *m.* ‖ Brick-kiln, n. Techn. Four à briques. ‖ Brick-red, adj. Brique (colour). ‖ Brick-yard, n. Briqueterie *f.*
— v. tr. Briqueter; *to brick up,* murer de briques.

bricklayer [-,leiə*] n. Archit. Briqueteur *m.*

brickle ['brikl] adj. Fragile.

brickwork [-wə:k] n. Archit. Briquetage *m.*

bricky [-i] adj. En brique. ‖ Brique (colour).

bridal ['braidl] n. † Noce *f.*
— adj. Conjugal (bed); nuptial (chamber, procession); de mariée (veil).

bride [braid] n. Bride *f.* (in needlework).

bride n. Fiancée, promise *f.* (about to be married); jeune mariée *f.* (just married). ‖ Eccles. Epouse *f.* (of Christ). ‖ Bride-cake, n. Culin. Gâteau *(m.)* de noces.

bridegroom [-grum] n. Fiancé, futur, promis (about to be married); jeune marié *m.* (just married).

bridesmaid [-zmeid] n. Demoiselle *(f.)* d'honneur.

bridesman [-zmən] n. Garçon *(m.)* d'honneur.

bridewell ['braidwel] n. † Maison de correction *f.*

bridge [bridʒ] n. Archit., Milit. Pont *m.* ‖ Naut. Passerelle *f.* ‖ Milit. Charnière *f.* (between two allied armies). ‖ Med. Dos *m.*, arête *f.* (of the nose); bridge *m.* (in dentistry). ‖ Mus. Chevalet *m.* (of a violon). ‖ Arts. Pont *m.* (in dancing). ‖ Ch. de f. *Railway bridge,* pont-rail. ‖ Bridge *m.* (in cards). ‖ Fig. *To burn one's bridges,* couper les ponts. ‖ Bridge-building, n. Milit. Pontage *m.* ‖ Bridge-head, n. Milit. Point d'appui *m.* (on, sur).

Bridge-platoon, n. Milit. Peloton de pontage *m.* ‖ **Bridge-work,** n. Med. Bridge *m.* (in dentistry).
— v. tr. Construire un pont sur. ‖ Fin. *To bridge the gap,* faire la soudure. ‖ Fig. *To bridge over,* faire le pont entre, enjamber.

bridle ['braidl] n. Bride *f.* (harness); *to give one's horse the bridle,* lâcher la bride à son cheval. ‖ Naut. Branche *f.* ‖ Aviat. Corde en forme de fourche *f.* ‖ Fig. Frein *m.* ‖ Bridle-bridge, n. Pont léger *m.* ‖ Bridle-path, n. Piste cavalière *f.* ‖ Bridle-way, n. Chemin muletier *m.*
— v. tr. Brider. ‖ Fig. *To bridle in,* brider, freiner, refréner. (See curb.) ‖ Fam. *To bridle the horse by the tail,* mettre la charrue avant les bœufs.
— v. intr. Se rebiffer (angrily); se rengorger (proudly); se raidir, redresser la tête (scornfully).

bridoon [bri'du:n] n. Bridon *m.*

brief [bri:f] n. Résumé *m.*; *in brief,* en bref. ‖ Jur. Dossier *m.*; cause, affaire *f.*; *to hold a brief for,* plaider pour, défendre. ‖ Eccles. Bref *m.* ‖ Brief-case, n. Serviette *f.*; porte-documents *m.*
— v. tr. Jur. Confier une cause à (a barrister); établir le dossier de (a case). ‖ Aviat., Milit. Exposer succinctement un plan à; donner des instructions à. ‖ Fig. Documenter (on, sur) [s.o.].
— adj. Bref, prompt (quick); bref, court (short); concis (terse).

briefing [-iŋ] n. Milit., Aviat. Instructions *f. pl.*; renseignements tactiques *m. pl.*; briefing *m.*

briefless [-lis] adj. Jur. Sans cause (barrister).

briefly [-li] adv. Brièvement.

briefness [-nis] n. Brièveté *f.*

briefs [-s] n. pl. Cache-sexe, slip *m.*

brier ['braiə*] n. See briar.

brier n. Bot. Bruyère *f.* ‖ Comm. Pipe en racine de bruyère *f.*

brig [brig] n. Naut. Brick *m.*

brigade [bri'geid] n. Milit. Brigade *f.* ‖ Fam. *One of the old brigade,* un vieux de la vieille.
— v. tr. Milit. Embrigader; former en brigade.

brigadier [brigə'diə*] n. Milit. Général *(m.)* de brigade.

brigand ['brigənd] n. Brigand *m.*

brigandage [-idʒ] n. Brigandage *m.*

brigantine ['brigənti:n] n. Naut. Brigantin *m.*

bright [brait] adj. Brillant; vif (colour, eye, fire, light); clair (day, room, weather); étincelant (gem, star); poli (metal, steel); brillanté (silk thread). ‖ Eclatant (beauty); radieux, lumineux (look, smile). ‖ Brillant (future); brillant, lumineux (idea); brillant, glorieux (period). ‖ Brillant, bien doué, étincelant; gai, vif, enjoué (person).
— adv. Brillamment, avec luminosité (or) éclat.

brighten [-n] v. tr. Faire briller, rendre brillant. ‖ Rendre lumineux (a room). ‖ Polir (a metal). ‖ Fig. Ranimer, raviver; illuminer; égayer.
— v. intr. *To brighten up,* s'éclaircir (weather). ‖ Fig. S'éclairer, s'animer, s'illuminer (person).

brightly [-li] adv. Brillamment.

brightness [-nis] n. Brillant, éclat *m.*; splendeur *f.* ‖ Fig. Vivacité *f.* (of mind); coloris *m.*; couleur *f.* (of style).

brill [bril] n. Zool. Barbue *f.*

brilliance ['briljəns], **brilliancy** [-i] n. Eclat, lustre, brillant *m.*

brilliant [-ənt] adj., n. Brillant *m.*

brilliantine [,briljən'ti:n] n. Brillantine *f.*

brilliantly ['briljəntli] adv. Brillamment, avec brio.

brim [brim] n. Bord *m.* (of a glass, hat, water). ‖ Brim-full, adj. Plein à déborder, rempli jusqu'au bord.
— v. tr. (1). Remplir jusqu'au bord.
— v. intr. Etre plein à déborder. ‖ Fig. *To brim over,* déborder (with, de).

brimmer [-ə*] n. Verre arasé *m.* ‖ Rasade *f.*

brimstone ['brimstən] n. Chim. Soufre *m.*

brindle(d) ['brindl(d)] adj. Tavelé, moucheté.

brine [brain] n. Onde amère, mer f. (ocean); pleurs m. pl. (tears). || CULIN. Saumure f. || Brine-pit, n. Saline f.
— v. tr. CULIN. Plonger dans la saumure; saler.

bring [briŋ] v. tr. (27). Amener, mener, conduire, accompagner (s.o.); apporter (sth.). || Faire monter (into, à) [blush, tears]; faire venir (s.o., sth.). || Ramener, mettre, porter; to bring to light, mettre à jour; to bring to memory, rappeler à la mémoire; to bring to reason, mettre (or) ramener à la raison; to bring to perfection, porter à la perfection. || Engendrer (disaster); attirer (division, reproach, ruin); procurer (glory); causer, amener, apporter (result); to bring to pass, faire arriver, occasionner. || Amener, conduire, persuader, pousser (s.o.) [to, à]; that brought him on to his feet, cela le fit se lever. || Réduire, amener, conduire (to, à); to bring s.o.'s plans to nought, déjouer les plans de qqn. || AGRIC. Produire (crops). || FIN., COMM. Rapporter, produire (interests); s'élever à, rapporter (price). || JUR. Intenter (an action); soumettre (a case); porter (a charge); déférer (a dispute); avancer, fournir (evidence); to bring to justice, traduire en justice. || MED. To bring into the world, mettre au monde. || To bring about, amener, occasionner, provoquer, causer, faire arriver (to cause); opérer, effectuer, réaliser, accomplir (to effect). || To bring back, ramener (s.o.); rappeler (a recollection); rapporter (sth.); to bring back to earth, récupérer (a satellite). || To bring down, abattre (s.o., sth.); faire crouler (the house); faire descendre (sth.); FIN. Faire baisser (prices); MATH. Abaisser (a figure); FIG. Abattre, abaisser (pride). || To bring forth, MED. Enfanter, mettre au monde; ZOOL. Mettre bas; BOT. Produire; FIG. Causer, soulever, occasionner (to cause); manifester, mettre à jour (to disclose). || To bring forward, avancer (a chair, meeting); JUR. Avancer, alléguer (evidence, a proof); produire (a plea, witness); COMM. Reporter (an amount). || To bring in, introduire (s.o.); rentrer, apporter (sth.); FIN. Rapporter (interest); JUR. Déposer (a Parliamentary bill); rendre (a verdict); déclarer (guilty); FIG. Lancer (a fashion). || To bring off, sauver (people on board ship); faire aboutir, réussir (sth.); to bring it off, réussir son coup. || To bring on, MED. Produire, provoquer, causer; AGRIC. Faire pousser; THEATR. Amener, apporter sur la scène; JUR. Faire venir; FIG. Introduire. || To bring out, faire sortir (s.o.); sortir, mettre dehors (sth.); faire paraître (a book); faire faire ses débuts dans le monde à (a young lady); laisser échapper, proférer (a word); FIN. Introduire (stocks); THEATR. Faire débuter, lancer (an actor, a play); AGRIC. Faire s'ouvrir (flowers); FIG. Mettre en lumière (or) en vedette, faire ressortir (colour, meaning, quality). || To bring over, amener, importer, transporter (from, de); FIG. Gagner, convertir (to, à). || To bring round, faire venir (s.o., sth.); apporter (sth.); MED. Ranimer; FIG. Ramener, rallier; convaincre, persuader; FAM. Ravigoter. || To bring to, NAUT. Mettre en panne; MED. Ranimer; FAM. Bloquer, stopper. || To bring together, rassembler, réunir; faire rencontrer, mettre en présence (or) contact. || To bring under, assujettir, soumettre. || To bring up, élever (animals, children); faire monter (or) avancer (s.o., sth.); MED. Vomir; JUR. Traduire, citer; NAUT. Mouiller; FIG. Evoquer, soulever, mettre sur le tapis (a question).

bringing-up ['briŋiŋʌp] n. Education f.

brinjal ['brindʒəl] n. BOT. Aubergine.

brink [briŋk] n. Bord m.; brink of the crater, lèvres de l'entonnoir. || FIG. Bord m. (see VERGE); on the brink, à deux doigts de, à la veille de, sur le point (or) bord de.

briny ['braini] adj. Très salé, saumâtre. || Amer (tears).
— n. FAM. Mer f.

brio ['bri:o] n. MUS. Brio m.

brioche ['bri:ɔʃ] n. CULIN. Brioche f.; pain brioché m.

briquette [bri'ket] n. Briquette f. (fuel)

brisance [bri:'zɑ̃:s] n. PHYS. Brisance f.

brisk [brisk] adj. Vif (air); mousseux (ale); pétillant (champagne); vif, alerte (movement); actif, animé, vif, alerte (person); émerillonné (fam.). || COMM. Actif (trade). || FIN. Animé (market). || MILIT. Nourri (fire).
— v. tr. Activer, animer.
— v. intr. To brisk up, s'animer; s'activer.

brisket ['briskit] n. CULIN. Poitrine f.

brisling ['brisliŋ] n. CULIN. Sprat m.

bristle ['brisl] n. Poil m. (of a brush). || ZOOL. Poil raide m.; soie f. (of boar, hog). || BOT. Soie f.; poil m. || FAM. To set up one's bristles, se hérisser, se rebiffer, montrer les dents.
— v. tr. Hérisser.
— v. intr. Se hérisser; être hérissé (with, de). || FAM. Se hérisser, se mettre en boule.

bristly [-il] adj. A poil raide. Hérissé (beard, hair).

Bristol ['bristl] n. GEOGR. Bristol. || COMM. Bristol board, bristol.

Brit [brit] n. FAM. Angliche, rosbif s.

Britain ['britən] n. GEOGR. Grande-Bretagne f.

Britannia [bri'tænjə] n. Albion, Britannia f.
— adj. Anglais (metal).

Britannic [bri'tænik] adj. Britannique.

Briticism ['britisizm] n. Anglicisme m.

British ['britiʃ] adj. Britannique, de Grande-Bretagne, d'Angleterre.
— n. Britanniques m. pl. (collect.).

Britisher [-ə*] n. Sujet britannique m.

Briton ['britən] n. † Breton s. || Sujet britannique m.

Brittany ['britəni] n. GEOGR. Bretagne f.

brittle ['britl] adj. Cassant, fragile. || CULIN. Friable, croustillant. (See CRISP, CRUMBLY.)

brittleness [-nis] n. Fragilité f.

broach [broutʃ] n. ARCHIT. Flèche d'église f. || CULIN. Broche f. (See SPIT.) || TECHN. Perçoir, foret m.
— v. tr. Entamer, ouvrir (a box); mettre en perce (a cask). || CULIN. Embrocher. || TECHN. Percer, forer, aléser. || FIG. Entamer, aborder.

broad [brɔ:d] adj. Large (river, room, shoulders); vaste, spacieux (room); vaste, étendu, immense (world). || Eclatant (fire, light); in broad daylight, en plein jour. || Fort, prononcé (accent); gras, gros (laughter). || ECCLES. Libéral (church). || ARTS, MUS. Large. || FIG. Ample (evidence); clair, évident, visible, manifeste (fact, hint); grossier, salé (joke, story); truculent (language); tolérant, libéral, large (mind, view); répandu (use, sense). || Broad-bean, n. BOT. Grosse fève f. || Broad-gauge, adj. CH. DE F. A voie large; FAM. U. S. Large, libéral. || Broad-minded, adj. A l'esprit large, libéral. || Broad-pawed, adj. Pataud (dog).
— n. Largeur, partie large f. || Pl. Marais m. pl. || U. S. FAM. Poupée f. (girl).
— adv. Largement, complètement; généralement.

broadcast [-kɑ:st] adj. AGRIC. Semé à la volée. || RADIO. Diffusé. || FIG. Répandu, diffusé.
— adv. AGRIC. A la volée. || FIG. A profusion.
— v. tr. AGRIC. Semer à la volée. || RADIO. Diffuser, radiodiffuser. || FIG. Répandre, diffuser.
— N. B. Le pret. est broadcasted; le p. p. broadcast ou broadcasted.
— n. RADIO. Diffusion, radiodiffusion, émission f.

broadcaster [-kɑ:stə*] n. RADIO. Personnalité de la radio f. (person); émetteur m. (transmitter).

broadcasting [-kɑ:stiŋ] n. RADIO. Radiophonie,

radiodiffusion *f.; broadcasting station*, station de radio, poste émetteur.

broadcloth [-klɔθ] n. Tissu (*m.*) pour hommes. ‖ U. S. Popeline *f.*

broaden [-ŋ] v. tr. Elargir. (See WIDEN.) — v. intr. S'élargir.

broadly [-li] adv. Largement. ‖ D'une façon générale; dans les grandes lignes; *broadly speaking*, en gros; généralement parlant.

broadness [-nis] n. Grossièreté *f.*

broadsheet [-ʃiːt] n. Placard *m.* (advertising; political massage).

broadside [-said] n. NAUT. Bordée *f.* (of guns); flanc *m.* (of a ship). ‖ FAM. Escarmouche *f.* — adv. NAUT. *Broadside on*, par le travers.

broadsword [-sɔːd] n. Sabre *m.*

broadtail [-teil] n. ZOOL. Caracul *m.* ‖ COMM. Breitschwanz *m.* (lamb); caracul *m.* (sheep).

broadways [-weiz] adv. En largeur.

brocade [bro'keid] n. Brocart; broché *m.* — v. tr. Brocher (cloth).

broccoli ['brɔkəli] n. AGRIC., CULIN. Brocoli *m.*

broché [bro'ʃei] adj. n. Broché *m.*

brochette [bro'ʃet] n. Brochette *f.* (of medals). ‖ CULIN. Brochette *f.* (skewer).

brochure [bro'ʃjuə*] n. Brochure *f.*

brock [brɔk] n. ZOOL. Blaireau *m.* (See BADGER.) ‖ FAM. Type puant *m.*

brocket ['brɔkit] n. ZOOL. Daguet *m.*

brogue [broug] n. Accent irlandais (or) dialectal *m.*

brogue n. Soulier (*m.*) de fatigue, mocassin *m.*

broil [brɔil] n. Bagarre, rixe, querelle *f.*

broil n. CULIN. Grillade *f.* — v. tr. CULIN. Griller, faire cuire sur le gril. — v. intr. CULIN. Griller. ‖ FAM. Cuire, rôtir; *it's broiling hot here*, on cuit ici.

broiler [-ə*] n. CULIN. Gril *m.; ρ*ôtisserie *f.* ‖ CULIN. Poulet (*m.*) à rôtir. ‖ U. S. Journée torride *f.* ‖ **Broiler house**, n. AGRIC. Local (*m.*) pour l'élevage industriel des poulets.

broke [brouk] adj. FAM. Fauché, ratissé, raclé. — pret. See BREAK.

broken [-ən] adj. Brisé, cassé, fracturé. (See BREAK.) ‖ Entrecoupé (sleep, tones, words); brisé, cassé, altéré (voice); Tourmenté, dentelé (coast); accidenté (ground); incertain (weather); ‖ Maté, brisé (person); rompu, violé (promise); abattu, découragé (spirit). ‖ FIN. Failli (bankrupt); ruiné (ruined). ‖ MED. Délabré (health). ‖ MATH. *Broken members*, fractions. ‖ GRAMM. Défectueux, mauvais (English). ‖ **Broken-down**, adj. TECHN. Détraqué; AUTOM. En panne. ‖ **Broken-hearted**, adj. Au cœur brisé. ‖ **Broken-toothed**, adj. Edenté, aux dents cassées. ‖ **Broken-winded**, adj. Poussif.

brokenly [-ənli] adv. D'une manière entrecoupée, par à-coups, irrégulièrement.

broker ['broukə*] n. FIN. Courtier *m.* ‖ Brocanteur *m.* (second-hand dealer).

brokerage [-ridʒ] n. FIN. Courtage *m.* (fee).

broking ['broukiŋ] n. FIN. Courtage *m.* (trade).

brolly ['brɔli] n. FAM. Pépin, pébroc *m.* (umbrella). ‖ MILIT., FAM. Pépin, pébroc *m.* (parachute).

bromic ['broumik] adj. CHIM. Bromique.

bromide [-aid] n. CHIM. Bromure *m.* ‖ FAM. Raseur *m.* (person); platitude *f.* (remark). — adj. Au gélatinobromure (paper).

bromidic [brou'midik] adj. FAM. Plat, terne, conventionnel.

bromine ['broumain] n. CHIM. Brome *m.*

bronchia ['brɔŋkiə] n. pl. MED. Bronches *f. pl.*

bronchial [-əl] adj. MED. Bronchique, bronchial; *bronchial tube*, bronche.

bronchiole [brɔn'kioul] n. MED. Bronchiole *f.*

bronchitis [-'kaitis] n. MED. Bronchite *f.*

bronchocele ['brɔŋko,siːl] n. MED. Goitre *m.*

broncho-pneumonia [,brɔŋkounju:'mounjə] n MED. Broncho-pneumonie *f.*

bronco ['brɔŋkou] n. ZOOL. Cheval (*m.*) sauvage de l'Ouest américain. ‖ **Bronco-buster**, n. U. S FAM. Cow-boy (*m.*) qui débourre les chevaux.

brontosaurus [brɔntə'sɔːrəs] n. ZOOL. Bronto saure *m.*

bronze [brɔnz] n. Bronze (colour, metal, work). — adj. En bronze; couleur de bronze. — v. tr. Bronzer, brunir, basaner. — v. intr. Se bronzer, se brunir, se tanner.

brooch [broutʃ] n. Broche *f.* (jewel).

brood [bruːd] n. Couvée *f.* ‖ FAM. Nichée *f.* (o children); foule *f.* (of ideas); flopée *f.* (of persons) ‖ FAM. Engeance *f.* — v. intr. Couver. (See HATCH.) ‖ FIG. Couver menacer (danger, storm); ruminer, broyer du noi (person). ‖ **To brood over**, méditer sur, rumine (an idea); planer sur (the scene). — v. tr. Couver (eggs, fire).

brooder [-ə*] n. Couveuse *f.* (hen). ‖ U. S. Couveuse artificielle *f.*

broody [-i] adj. Prêt à couver (hen). ‖ FAM. Rêveur

brook [bruk] v. tr. Supporter, souffrir, tolérer

brook n. Ruisseau *m.*

brooklet [-lit] n. Ruisselet *m.*

broom [bruːm] n. BOT. Genêt *m.* ‖ COMM. Balai *m. small broom*, balayette. ‖ **Broom-stick**, n. Manche à balai *m.;* U. S. FAM. Mollet de coq *m.* (leg).

broth [brɔθ] n. CULIN. Bouillon; potage *m.* ‖ FAM *A broth of a boy*, un vrai numéro; un bon type.

brothel ['brɔθəl] n. Bordel *m.*

brother ['brʌðə*] n. Frère *m.* ‖ Compagnon, ami collègue, confrère *m.* ‖ COMM. *Johnson Bros. and Co.* Johnson frères et Cⁱᵉ. ‖ JUR. Maître, mon che confrère *m.* ‖ ECCLES. Frère *m.* ‖ **Brothers-in-arms**, n. pl. MILIT. Frères d'armes. ‖ **Brother-in-law**, n. Beau-frère *m.* — N. B. *Brethren* est le pl. aux sens jur. et ecclés.

brotherhood [-hud] n. Fraternité *f.* (between brothers); confraternité *f.* (between colleagues). ‖ Confrérie *f.* (association).

brotherly [-li] adj. Fraternel.

brougham [bruːm] n. Coupé *m.*

brought [brɔːt] pret., p.p. See BRING.

brouhaha [bru:'hɑːhɑː] n. Tumulte, scandale *m.* (commotion); brouhaha, tintamarre *m.* (hubbub, uproar).

brow [brau] n. NAUT. Passerelle.

brow n. Sourcil *m.* (eyebrow); front *m.* (forehead); *heavy brow*, front soucieux; *to knit one's brows*, froncer le sourcil. ‖ Bord *m.* (of a cliff); sommet *m.* (of a hill).

browbeat [-biːt] v. tr. Rabrouer, brusquer, malmener, rudoyer.

brown [braun] adj. Brun (bear, colour, shirt); jaune, gold (boots); écru (holland); marron (leather); gris-brun (paper); hâlé, bronzé (person). ‖ CULIN. Bis (bread); roux (butter); non glacé (rice); doré (roast); *brown sugar*, cassonade; U. S. *brown betty*, gâteau de pain aux pommes. ‖ FAM. *In a brown study*, rêveur, méditatif; plongé dans de sombres pensées; *to do s.o. brown*, refaire (or) roustir qqn; *to do sth. up brown*, fignoler qqch. ‖ **Brown-out**, n. MILIT. U. S. Camouflage partiel (*m.*) des lumières. — n. Brun *m.* ‖ CULIN. Doré, rissolé *m.* ‖ FAM. Rond *m.* (halfpenny). — v. tr., intr. Brunir. ‖ Bronzer, hâler. ‖ CULIN. Rissoler, dorer. ‖ FAM. **To brown off**, inquiéter, déprimer; *browned-off*, cafardeux, qui broie du noir

brownie [-i] n. Farfadet *m.* (goblin). ‖ Jeannette *f.* (girl scout). ‖ *Brownie*, Kodak brownie *m.* ‖ U. S. Gâteau (*m.*) au chocolat et aux noix.

browning [-iŋ] n. Browning *m.* (pistol). ‖ CULIN. Roux *m.*

brownish [-iʃ] n. Brunâtre.

brownstone ['braun,stoun] n. U. S. Grès brunrouge m. (sandstone); maison (f.) à la façade en grès brun-rouge.

browse [brauz] n. Brout m.; pousses f. pl. ‖ Action (f.) de brouter.
— v. tr., intr. Brouter. ‖ Bouquiner.

brucellosis [,bru:si'lousis] n. MED. Brucellose f.

bruise [bru:z] n. MED. Contusion; ecchymose f.; bleu m. (fam.). ‖ TECHN. Mâchure f.; bosselage m.
— v. tr. MED. Contusionner, meurtrir. (See CONTUSE.) ‖ TECHN. Bosseler (metal); mâchurer (wood); écraser, piler (to crush). ‖ FIG. Meurtrir, choquer.
— v. intr. Etre meurtri; se meurtrir facilement.

bruiser [-ə*] n. FAM. Cogneur m.

bruit [bru:t] n. Rumeur f.
— v. tr. Ebruiter, faire courir le bruit que; to be bruited about, se répandre.

brumous ['bruməs] adj. Brumeux (foggy); hivernal (wintry).

brunch ['brʌnʃ] n. U. S. FAM. Petit déjeuner et déjeuner combinés m.

Brunei [bru:'nai] n. GEOGR. Brunei m.

brunette [bru'net] n. Brunette f.

brunt [brʌnt] n. Poids m. (of an argument); choc, fort m. (of an attack).

brush [brʌʃ] n. Brosse f. ‖ Brossage m.; coup (m.) de brosse (act). ‖ Effleurement m.; éraflure f. (light touch). ‖ Queue f. (of a fox). ‖ ARTS. Pinceau m. ‖ PHYS. Faisceau, pinceau m. (of rays). ‖ AGRIC. Broussailles f. pl. ‖ ELECTR. Balai m. ‖ MILIT. Escarmouche f. ‖ FAM. Abord, contact, m. ‖ FAM. Brossée f. (quarrel). ‖ **Brush-maker**, n. Brossier m. ‖ **Brush-off**, n. FAM. Coup de balai m. (dismissal). ‖ **Brush-up**, n. Coup (m.) de brosse. ‖ **Brushwork**, n. ARTS. Facture f.
— v. tr. Brosser (clothes, dust). ‖ Erafler (to graze); effleurer, frôler (to touch). ‖ ARTS. Brosser (a canvas). ‖ **To brush away**, écarter, balayer. ‖ **To brush off**, enlever à la brosse; FAM. Bazarder, liquider (to dismiss). ‖ **To brush up**, faire reluire à la brosse; FIG. Repolir; FAM. Dérouiller, dégourdir (s.o.); rafraîchir (one's English).
— v. intr. Passer en frôlant.

brushwood [-wud] n. Broussailles f. pl. (brush); brindilles f. pl.; bois mort m.

brushy [-i] adj. Broussailleux.

brusque [brusk] adj. Brusque, bourru. (See BLUNT.)

brusqueness [-nis] n. Brusquerie f.

Brussels ['brʌslz] n. GEOGR. Bruxelles f.
— adj. De Bruxelles (carpet, lace). ‖ CULIN. Brussels sprouts, choux de Bruxelles.

brutal ['bru:tl] adj. Brutal. (See BESTIAL.)

brutality [bru'tæliti] n. Brutalité f. (act, quality).

brutalize ['bru:təlaiz] v. tr. Abrutir.

brute [bru:t] n. Brute f. (animal, person). ‖ FAM. A brute of a job, un métier de chien.
— adj. Brutal; bestial; by brute force, de vive force.

brutify [-ifai] v. tr. (2). Abrutir.
— v. intr. S'abrutir.

brutish [-iʃ] adj. Bestial, de brute. (See BESTIAL.) ‖ Stupide, grossier.

brutishness [-iʃnis] n. Bestialité; brutalité f.

Brythonic [bri'θɔnik] n. Brittonique m.

B. Sc. [bi:es'si] abbr. Bachelor of Science, licencié ès sciences.

B.S.T. [bi:es'ti] abbr. British Summer Time, heure d'été en Grande-Bretagne.

bub [bʌb] n. FAM. Nichon m.

bubble ['bʌbl] n. Bulle f. ‖ CULIN. Bouillon, bouillonnement m.; bubble and squeak, restes de choux et de pommes de terre sautés. ‖ TECHN. Soufflure f. ‖ FAM. Chimère; bulle (f.) de savon; to prick the bubble, dégonfler qqn, crever le ballon.
— adj. MED. Bubble bath, bain gazeux (bath);

produit pour bain (solution). ‖ FAM. Chimérique.
— v. intr. Faire des bulles. ‖ CULIN. Bouillonner. ‖ FIG. To bubble over with high spirits, déborder de gaieté. ‖ **Bubble-gum**, n. U. S. Chewing-gum à bulles.
— v. tr. Faire des bulles dans.

bubbly [-i] adj. Plein de bulles. ‖ FAM. Gazeux, pétillant; champagnisé.
— n. FAM. Mousseux, vin champagnisé m.

bubo ['bju:bou] (pl. **buboes**) n. MED. Bubon m.

bubonic [bju:'bɔnik] adj. MED. Bubonique.

bubonocele [bju:'bɔnəsi:] n. MED. Hernie inguinale f.

buccal ['bʌkəl] adj. MED. Buccal.

buccaneer [,bʌkə'niə*] n. Boucanier, flibustier m.

buck [bʌk] n. ZOOL. Daim; chevreuil m.; mâle du chamois, du lapin, du lièvre m. ‖ FAM. Jeune fat, dandy m.; old buck, vieux marcheur, vieux dégoûtant. ‖ U. S. POP. Dollar m. ‖ **Buck-bean**, n. BOT. Trèfle (m.) d'eau. ‖ **Buck fever**, n. FAM. U. S. Excitation (f.) des chasseurs novices. ‖ **Buck-shot**, n. MILIT. Chevrotine f. ‖ **Buck-tooth**, n. MED. Dent (f.) en avant.
— v. tr. To buck up, remonter, ravigoter, remettre debout (s.o.).
— v. intr. SPORTS. Faire un saut de mouton (horse). ‖ To buck up, se ressaisir; FAM. Se remonter; se requinquer, se ravigoter (fam.).

buck n. Lessive f. (clothes, lye).
— v. tr. Faire tremper, lessiver.

buck n. U. S. Couteau de poker m. ‖ FAM. To pass the buck to, renvoyer la balle à.

bucket ['bʌkit] n. Seau m. ‖ TECHN. Auget; godet; porte-fouet m. ‖ MILIT. Lance bucket, botte de lance. ‖ FAM. To give kick the bucket, passer l'arme à gauche. ‖ **Bucket-seat**, n. AUTOM., AVIAT. Siège-baquet m. ‖ **Bucket-shop**, n. U. S. Officine (f.) de courtier marron.
— v. tr. FAM. Fatiguer, surmener (a horse).
— v. intr. SPORTS. Presser le retour sur l'avant.

bucketful [-ful] n. Seau, plein seau m.

buckle ['bʌkl] n. Boucle f. ‖ TECHN. Voile m. (of a wheel).
— v. tr. Boucler. ‖ TECHN. Voiler, fausser. ‖ To buckle on, revêtir (one's armour); ceindre (one's sword).
— v. intr. Se boucler. ‖ TECHN. Se voiler, se fausser. ‖ To buckle to, U. S. to buckle down, FAM. S'y atteler; se coller au boulot. ‖ To buckle up, FAM. Flancher.

buckler [-ə*] n. MILIT., FIG. Bouclier m.
— v. tr. Protéger, défendre.

buckram ['bʌkrəm] n. Bougran m.; toile gommée f. ‖ FIG. Attitude gourmée f.
— adj. Raide. ‖ FIG. Gourmé (attitude, style).

bucksaw ['bʌksɔ:] n. Scie (f.) à refendre.

buckshee [bʌk'ʃi:] adj. FAM. Aux frais de la princesse; à l'œil.

buckskin [-skin] n. COMM. Daim m. ‖ Pl. Culotte (f.) en daim.

buckthorn ['bʌkθɔ:n] n. BOT. Bourdaine f., aune noir m., nerprun m.

buckwheat ['bʌkwi:t] n. BOT. Sarrasin, blé noir m. ‖ CULIN. Buckwheat cake, galette de sarrasin.

bucolic [bju:'kɔlik] adj., n. Bucolique f.

bud [bʌd] n. BOT. Bourgeon, bouton m. ‖ AGRIC. Ecusson m. ‖ FIG. To nip in the bud, tuer dans l'œuf, étouffer dans le germe.
— v. intr. BOT. Bourgeonner. ‖ FIG. Pointer.
— v. tr. AGRIC. Ecussonner.

bud n. U.S. FAM. Pote m.

Buddha ['budə] n. Bouddha m.

Buddhism [-izm] n. Bouddhisme m.

Buddhist [-ist] adj., n. Bouddhiste s.

budding ['bʌdiŋ] n. BOT. Bourgeonnement m. ‖

AGRIC. Ecussonnage *m.* ‖ **Budding-knife,** n. AGRIC. Ecussonnoir *m.*
— adj. BOT. Bourgeonnant. ‖ FIG. En herbe.
buddleia ['bʌdliə] n. BOT. Buddleia *m.*
buddy ['bʌdi] n. U. S. FAM. Copain *m.*
budge [bʌdʒ] v. intr. Bouger ; faire bouger.
budgerigar ['bʌdʒəri,gɑ:*] n. ZOOL. Perruche *f.*
budget ['bʌdʒit] n. † Sac *m.* ‖ FIN. Budget *m.*
— v. tr. FIN. Comptabiliser, inscrire au budget.
budgetary [-əri] adj. Budgétaire.
budgie ['bʌdʒi] n. ZOOL., FAM. Perruche *f.*
buff [bʌf] n. COMM. Buffle *m.* (leather). ‖ Chamois *m.* (colour). ‖ FAM. Cuir *m.* (skin) ; *stripped to the buff,* nu comme un ver. ‖ U. S. FAM. Fanatique, enthousiaste *m.*
— adj. Chamois.
buff n. † Coup ; *blind man's buff,* colin-maillard.
buffalo ['bʌfələu] n. ZOOL. Buffle ; bison *m.*
— v. tr. FAM. U. S. Blouser.
buffer ['bʌfə*] n. CH. DE F. Tampon *m.* ‖ U. S. Pare-chocs *m.* ‖ FAM. *Old buffer,* vieux bonze. ‖ **Buffer-state,** n. Etat-tampon *m.* ‖ **Buffer-stop,** n. Butoir *m.*
buffet ['bʌfit] n. Buffet *m.* (piece of furniture).
— ['bufei] n. Buffet *m.* (counter, restaurant). ‖ **Buffet car,** n. CH. DE F. U. S. Voiture-restaurant *m.* ‖ **Buffet-lunch** (or) **-supper,** n. Lunch, lunch debout *m.*
buffet ['bʌfit]. n. Coup de poing *m. ;* bourrade *f.* ‖ Soufflet *m.* ‖ FIG. *Buffets of fortune,* coup du sort.
— v. tr. Souffleter, battre ; cahoter. ‖ Se débattre (*with,* contre).
buffoon [bʌ'fu:n] n. Bouffon ; bateleur *m.*
— v. intr. Bouffonner.
buffoonery [-ri] n. Bouffonneries *f. pl.*
bug [bʌg] m. ZOOL. Punaise *f.* ‖ ZOOL., FAM. Bestiole *f.* (insect). ‖ FAM. Microbe *m.* (germ). ‖ FAM. *Big bug,* gros bonnet, ponte. ‖ FAM. Fana *s. ; fire-bug* pyromane. ‖ FAM. Virus *m.,* marotte *f.* (obsession). ‖ FAM. Micro caché *m.* ‖ FAM. Défaut *m.,* imperfection *f.* ‖ † Génie, lutin *m.* ‖ **Bug-eyed,** adj. FAM. Aux yeux en boules de loto. ‖ **Bug-house,** n. FAM. Cabanon, asile *m.*
— v. tr. (1). FAM. Casser les pieds à (to bother). ‖ FAM. Cacher des micros dans ; *this room's bugged,* il y a des micros dans cette pièce.
bugaboo [bʌgə'bu:] n. Croquemitaine *m.; bugaboo tale,* conte de revenants.
bugbear ['bʌgbɛə*] n. Epouvantail, croquemitaine, cauchemar *m.;* bête noire *f.*
bugger ['bʌgə*] n. JUR. Sodomite *m.* ‖ FAM. Bougre *m.*
buggy [bʌgi] n. Boghei *m.*
bugle ['bju:gl] n. MUS. Clairon *m.* ‖ **Bugle-call,** n. MUS. Sonnerie (*f.*) de clairon.
bugle n. Longue perle (*f.*) de verre noir.
bugler [-glə*] n. MUS. Clairon *m.* (musician).
bugloss ['bju:glɔs] n. BOT. Buglosse *f.*
Buhl [bu:l] n., adj. Boulle *m.*
build [bild] v. tr. (28). ARCHIT. Bâtir, construire, élever ; faire bâtir (see CONSTRUCT) ; *the house is being built,* la maison se bâtit ; *to build in,* entourer de constructions (a garden) ; murer (a window). ‖ FIG. Bâtir édifier, établir. ‖ **To build up,** construire, bâtir, édifier (a plan, theory) ; *to build up connections,* se créer une clientèle (or) des relations ; *to build up speed,* prendre de la vitesse, accélérer.
— n. ARCHIT. Construction, structure *f.* ‖ FAM. Charpente, carrure, taille *f. ;* châssis *m.* (fam.).
builder [-ə*] n. ARCHIT. Entrepreneur *m.* ‖ NAUT. Constructeur *m.*
building [-iŋ] n. ARCHIT. Construction *f.* (act.) ‖ ARCHIT. Edifice ; bâtiment, immeuble *m.; bâtisse,* construction *f.* ‖ **Building - association** (or) **-society,** n. JUR. Coopérative immobilière *f.; building and loan association,* société de prêt à la

construction. ‖ **Building-plot,** n. Lotissement *m* ‖ **Building-trade,** n. Industrie (*f.*) du bâtiment. **Building-up,** n. MED. Consolidation *f.;* raffermis sement *m.* (of health) ; FIG. Echafaudage *m.* (o plans).
— adj. A bâtir ; *building land,* terrain à bâtir.
built [bilt] pret., p.p. See BUILD.
bulb [bʌlb] n. BOT. Bulbe, oignon *m.* ‖ CULIN Tête *f.* (of garlic). ‖ MED. Bulbe *m.* ‖ CHIM. Ballo *m.* ‖ PHYS. Boule, ampoule *f.* (of a thermometer) ‖ ELECTR. Ampoule, lampe *f.* ‖ TECHN. Poire *f. wet bulb,* psychromètre *m.* ‖ Foyer *m.* (of a pipe)
bulbous [-əs] adj. Bulbeux.
Bulgaria [bʌl'gɛəriə] n. GEOGR. Bulgarie *f.*
Bulgarian [-n] adj., n. GEOGR. Bulgare *s.*
bulge [bʌldʒ] n. Bosse *f.* ‖ Augmentation tempo raire *f.* (in number). ‖ MILIT. Saillant *m.*
— v. intr. Faire une bosse ; bomber, se renfler.
— v. tr. Bourrer, gonfler.
bulger [-ə*] n. SPORTS. Crosse à face convexe *f*
bulimia [bju:'laimiə] n. MED. Boulimie *f.*
bulk [bʌlk] n. Masse *f.* (of humanity, of a nation) corpulence *f.* (of a person) ; masse *f.;* volume *m* (of a thing). ‖ COMM. *Bulk buying,* achat massif *in bulk,* en gros, par grosses quantités. ‖ NAUT Chargement *m.; bulk cargo,* marchandises en vrac *in bulk,* en vrac. ‖ FAM. Majeure partie *f.*
— v. intr. Tenir de la place, occuper du volume ‖ **To bulk up,** s'entasser, grossir ; *to bulk up to* arriver à un total de.
— v. tr. Entasser (or) évaluer en vrac.
bulkhead [-hed] n. NAUT. Cloison *f.* ‖ AVIAT Travée (*f.*) de fuselage.
bulkiness [-inis] n. Corpulence *f.* (of a person) volume *m.* (of a thing).
bulky [-i] adj. Corpulent, massif (person) ; volu mineux (thing).
bull [bul] n. ZOOL., ASTRON. Taureau *m.* ‖ ZOOL Mâle *m.* (of the elephant, elk, moose, rhinoceros walrus, whale). ‖ ZOOL. FAM. Bouledogue *m.* (dog) ‖ FIN. Haussier *m.* ‖ FAM. MILIT. Astiquage (*m.*) à outrance. ‖ FAM. *A bull in a china-shop,* un éléphan dans un magasin de porcelaine, un chien dans ur jeu de quilles ; *to take the bull by the horns,* prendre le taureau par les cornes. ‖ POP. U. S. Vache *f* (cop). ‖ **Bull-baiting,** n. Combat (*m.*) de chiens e de taureaux. ‖ **Bull-calf,** n. ZOOL. Jeune tau reau *m. ;* FAM. Blanc-bec *m.* ‖ **Bull-headed,** adj Entêté, borné, obstiné. ‖ **Bull's-eye,** n. Œil-de bœuf *m.* (window) ; lanterne sourde *f.* (lantern) blanc, centre *m.* (of a target) ; NAUT. Moque *f.* verre de hublot *m.*
— v. tr. ZOOL. Saillir, couvrir (a cow). ‖ FIN. Ten ter de faire hausser les. cours.
— v. intr. FIN. Spéculer à la hausse.
bull n. ECCLES. Bulle *f.*
bull n. FAM. Boulette, bévue *f.* (blunder) ; calino tade *f.* (expression).
bulldog ['buldɔg] n. ZOOL. Bouledogue *m.* ‖ MILIT Revolver bouledogue *m.* ‖ FAM. Cerbère *m.* (usher) ‖ **Bulldog clip,** n. Pince (*f.*) à papier.
bulldoze ['buldouz] v. tr. Passer au bulldozer. ‖ FAM. U. S. Blouser ; malmener.
bulldozer [-ə*] n. Bulldozer, chasse-terre, boutoir *m.*
bullet ['bulit] n. MILIT. Balle *f.* ‖ **Bullet-headed,** adj. A la tête ronde. ‖ **Bullet-proof,** adj. A l'épreuve des balles ; v. tr. blinder. ‖ **Bullet-splash,** n. Ecra sement (*m.*) de la balle.
bulletin ['bulitin] n. Bulletin, communiqué *m.* (publication, statement) ; U. S. *Bulletin board,* tableau d'affichage.
— v. tr. U. S. Publier, communiquer, annoncer.
bullfight ['bulfait] n. Course (*f.*) de taureaux.
bullfighter [-ə*] n. SPORTS. Matador, torero *m.*
bullfighting [-iŋ] n. SPORTS. Tauromachie *f.*

bullfinch ['bulfintʃ] n. Zool. Bouvreuil *m.* ‖ Sports. Bull-finch *m.*

bullfrog [-frɔg] n. Zool. Grenouille d'Amérique *f.*

bullhead [-hed] n. Zool. Chabot *m.* ‖ Fam. Cabochard *m.*

bullion ['buljən] n. Fin. Lingot *m.; stock in bullion,* encaisse métallique.

bullion n. Frange, cannetille *f.*

bullock ['bulək] n. Zool. Bœuf *m.* (See ox.)

bullring ['bul'riŋ] n. Sports. Arène *f.*

bully ['buli] n. Bravache, fanfaron *m.* (See braggart.) ‖ Souteneur *m.* (pimp). ‖ Tyranneau, persécuteur *m.*
— v. tr. (2). Faire le fendant. ‖ Tyranniser, brimer, persécuter. ‖ Houspiller, malmener; intimider.

bully adj. U. S. Fam. Epatant, bœuf.
— interj. Bravo!

bully n. Sports. Coup d'envoi *m.* (in hockey).
— v. intr. (2). Sports. *To bully off,* engager (in hockey).

bully, U. S. bully beef n. Culin. Bœuf (*m.*) en conserve; singe *m.* (fam.).

bullying [-iŋ] n. Brimade; persécution, tyrannie *f.*

bullyrag ['buliræg] v. intr. Fam. Intimider, secouer.

bulrush ['bulrʌʃ] n. Bot. Jonc *m.*

bulwark ['bulwə:k] n. Brise-lame *m.* ‖ Archit. Rempart *m.* ‖ Naut. Pl. Pavois, bastingage *m.* ‖ Fig. Rempart, bouclier *m.*

bum [bʌm] n. Fam. Flemmard, cossard *m.; on the bum,* détraqué. ‖ U. S. Noce, bringue *f.* (spree). ‖ U. S. Clochard *m.*
— adj. Fam. U. S. Moche; de camelote; *bum steer,* faux renseignement.
— v. intr. Fam. U. S. Vivre aux crochets des autres (to sponge). ‖ Fam. Pinter (to drink).
— v. tr. Fam. U. S. Ecornifler; *to bum a dinner off,* se faire payer à dîner par.

bum n. Fam. Derrière *m.* (See buttocks.) ‖ **Bum-boat,** n. Naut. Canot d'approvisionnement *m.* ‖ **Bum-freezer,** n. Pet-en-l'air *m.* (jacket). ‖ **Bum-wad,** n. Pop. U. S. Torche-cul *m.*

bumbershoot ['bʌmbə'ʃut] n. U. S. En-cas *m.*

bumble ['bʌmbl̩] n. Fam. Rond-de-cuir prétentieux *m.; M.* Lebureau.

bumble-bee ['bʌmbl̩bi:] n. Zool. Bourdon *m.*

bumbo ['bʌmbou] n. Culin. Punch froid *m.*

bumf [bʌmf] n. Milit., Fam. Paperasses *f. pl.* ‖ Pop. Torche-cul *m.*

bump [bʌmp] v. tr. Cogner. (See knock.) ‖ Naut. Tamponner, buter contre. ‖ Autom. Cahoter. ‖ Fam. Cirer. ‖ **To bump off,** U. S. Fam. Démolir, descendre (s.o.).
— v. intr. Autom. Etre cahoté. ‖ **To bump against,** buter contre, heurter. ‖ **To bump into,** rencontrer par hasard, tomber sur.
— n. Choc, coup *m.* ‖ Bosse *f.* (bump). ‖ Aviat. Rafale ascendante *f.*
— adv. Tête baissée, brutalement, d'un choc.

bumper ['bʌmpə*] n. Plein verre *m.* ‖ Autom. Pare-chocs *m.*
— adj. Fam. Exceptionnel.

bumpkin ['bʌmpkin] n. Péquenot *m.*

bumptious ['bʌmpʃəs] adj. Suffisant, outrecuidant, arrogant.

bumpy ['bʌmpi] adj. Bosselé, cahoteux, défoncé.

bun [bʌn] n. Culin. Brioche (*f.*) aux raisins; petit pain au lait *m.* ‖ Chignon *m.* ‖ U. S. Fam. Cuite *f.; to have a bun on,* être éméché.

buna ['bjunə] n. Caoutchouc synthétique *m.*

bunch [bʌnʃ] n. Régime *m.* (of bananas); bouquet *m.* (of flowers); grappe *f.* (of grapes); touffe *f.* (of grass); poignée *f.,* paquet *m.* (of twigs). ‖ Trousseau *m.* (of keys); flot, nœud *m.* (of ribbons). ‖ Groupe, noyau *m.* (of people); *the pick of the bunch,* le dessus du panier.

— v. tr. Botteler; grouper; nouer. ‖ **To bunch up,** retrousser, trousser (one's dress).
— v. intr. Se grouper, se tasser, se serrer.

bundle ['bʌndl̩] n. Ballot, balluchon *m.* (of clothes); paquet *m.* (of linen, letters); liasse *f.* (of papers). ‖ Botte *f.* (of carrots, hay); fagot *m.* (of firewood); faisceau, paquet *m.* (of sticks). ‖ Fig. Paquet *m.* (of nerves).
— v. tr. **To bundle in,** entasser, fourrer. ‖ **To bundle up,** empaqueter, emballer, botteler; mettre en liasse. ‖ Fam. **To bundle away** (or) **off,** expédier, renvoyer.
— v. intr. **To bundle in,** s'entasser vivement. ‖ **To bundle up,** s'emmitoufler. ‖ **To bundle off,** Fam. Décamper, décaniller.

bung [bʌŋ] n. Bonde *f.* (cork). ‖ **Bung-hole,** n. Bonde *f.* (hole).
— v. tr. Mettre une bonde à (a cask). ‖ Fam. **To bung up,** pocher (s.o.'s eyes); resserrer, constiper (s.o.).

bungalow ['bʌŋgəlou] n. Bungalow *m.*

bungle ['bʌŋgl̩] v. intr. Faire du mauvais travail; bâcler, saboter. (See botch.)
— v. tr. Cochonner, bousiller, saboter, louper.
— n. Sabotage, gâchis, bousillage *m.*

bungler [-ə*] n. Saboteur, bousilleur *m.*

bunion ['bʌnjən] n. Med. Oignon *m.* (on the foot).

bunk [bʌŋk] n. Ch. de f., Naut. Couchette *f.*
— v. intr. Dormir en couchette. ‖ U. S. Fam. Se coucher.

bunk v. intr. Fam. Filer, décaniller.
— n. Fam. Cavalage *m.; to do a bunk,* se donner de l'air, se débiner, se tirer des flûtes. ‖ Fam. Sornettes *f. pl.* (bunkum).

bunker [-ə*] n. Naut. Soute *f.* ‖ Milit. Casemate blindée *f.; bunker,* blockhaus *m.* ‖ Sports. Banquette *f.* (in golf).

bunkmate [-'meit] n. U. S. Compagnon (*m.*) de couchette.

bunkum ['bʌŋkəm] n. Fam. Sornettes *f. pl.;* bla-bla-bla *m.;* frime, fumisterie, foutaise, ineptie *f.*

bunny ['bʌni] n. Fam. Jeannot lapin *m.*

Bunsen burner ['bʌnsn̩'bə:nə*] n. Bec (*m.*) Bunsen.

bunt [bʌnt] n. Agric. Carie *f.* (of wheat).

bunt n. Naut. Fond *m.* (of a sail). ‖ Aviat. Ressource *f.*

bunt v. tr. U. S. Sports, Fig. Frapper doucement.

bunting [-iŋ] n. Etamine *f.* (cloth). ‖ Pavoisement *m.;* drapeaux *m. pl.* ‖ U. S. Burnous *m.* (baby's garment). ‖ Zool. Bruant *m.*

buoy [bɔi] n. Naut. Bouée; balise flottante *f.; light buoy,* photo-phare. ‖ Fig. Bouée de sauvetage; appui *m.* ‖ **Buoy-rope,** n. Orin *m.*
— v. tr. **To buoy out,** baliser. ‖ **To buoy up,** faire flotter; Fig. Epauler, appuyer, remonter, soutenir, mettre à flot.

buoyage [-idʒ] n. Aviat., Naut. Balisage *m.*

buoyancy [-ənsi] n. Naut. Flottabilité *f.* ‖ Aviat. Force ascensionnelle, portance *f.* ‖ Fin. Fermeté *f.* (of prices). ‖ Fig. Alacrité, gaieté *f.* (cheerfulness); souplesse *f.* (elasticity); ressort *m.* (energy).

buoyant [-ənt] adj. Naut. Qui peut flotter; qui permet de flotter. ‖ Fin. Ferme, soutenu (market). ‖ Fig. Plein d'allant, allègre, gai (cheerful); plein de ressort, prompt à réagir (energetic).

bur(r) [bə:*] n. Bot. Teigne *f.* (of burdock). ‖ U. S. Fam. Crampon *m.* (person).

bur(r) n. Grasseyement *m.*

burble ['bə:rbl̩] adj. Aviat. *Burble point,* point de fissure.
— v. intr. Bafouiller; *to burble with laughter,* glousser de rire.

burbot ['bə:bət] n. Zool. Lotte *f.;* barbot *m.*

burden ['bə:dn̩] n. Fardeau, faix *m.; beast of burden,* bête de somme. ‖ Naut. Tonnage *m.* ‖ Fin. Charge pécuniaire *f.;* frais (*m. pl.*) à charge. ‖ Jur.

Burden of proof, obligation de faire la preuve. ‖ Fɪɢ. Fardeau, poids *m.;* charge *f.*
— v. tr. Charger, peser sur.
burden n. Thème *m.* (of a speech). ‖ Mᴜs. Refrain *m.*
burdensome [-səm] adj. Lourd, pesant.
burdock ['bə:dɔk] n. Bᴏᴛ. Bardane *f.*
bureau [bjuə'rou] (pl. **bureaux** [-rouz]) n. Bureau *m.* (writing-desk). ‖ U. S. Commode *f.* (chest of drawers). ‖ Bureau, service *m.* (department, office); U. S. *Publicity bureau,* agence de publicité.
bureaucracy [bjuə'rɔkrəsi] n. Bureaucratie *f.*
bureaucrat ['bjuərokræt] n. Bureaucrate *s.*
bureaucratic [bjuərɔ'krætik] adj. Bureaucratique.
burette [bjuə'ret] n. Cʜɪᴍ. Eprouvette graduée *f.*
burgee [bə:'dʒi:] n. Nᴀᴜᴛ. Guidon *m.*
burgeon ['bə:dʒən] n. Bᴏᴛ. Bourgeon *m.*
— v. intr. Bᴏᴛ. Bourgeonner.
burgess [̣'bə:dʒis] n. † Bourgeois *m.* ‖ U. S. † Conseiller municipal *m.*
burgh ['bʌrə] n. Bourg *m.*
burgher ['bə:gə*] n. Bourgeois *m.*
burglar ['bə:glə*] n. Cambrioleur, voleur *m.* ‖ **Burglar-proof,** adj. Incrochetable.
burglarious [bə:'glɛəriəs] adj. De cambriolage (attempt).
burglary [-ri] n. Jᴜʀ. Cambriolage *m.*
burgle ['bə:gl] v. tr. intr. Jᴜʀ. Cambrioler.
burgomaster ['bə:go,mɑ:stə*] n. Bourgmestre *m.* ‖ Zᴏᴏʟ. Goéland des glaciers *m.*
Burgundy ['bə:gəndi] n. Gᴇᴏɢʀ. Bourgogne *f.* ‖ Cᴏᴍᴍ. Bourgogne *m.* (wine).
burial ['beriəl] n. Enterrement *m.;* obsèques, funérailles *f. pl.* ‖ **Burial-ground,** n. Cimetière *m.* ‖ **Burial-service,** n. Eᴄᴄʟᴇs. Office des morts, service funèbre *m.*
— adj. Des morts, mortuaire.
burin ['bjuərin] n. Aʀᴛs. Burin *m.* (for engraving).
burke [bə:k] v. tr. Fɪɢ. Enterrer, escamoter (a question); étouffer (a scandal).
burl [bə:l] n. Bourron, époutri *m.* (in cloth, wool). ‖ Ronce, veine *f.* (in wood); *walnut burl,* ronce de noyer.
— v. tr. Tᴇᴄʜɴ. Enouer, époutier.
burlap ['bə:læp] n. Toile (*f.*) à sac (or) d'emballage.
burlesque [bə:'lesk] adj. Burlesque (comic); caricatural (parodying).
— n. Parodie *f.* ‖ Tʜᴇᴀᴛʀ. Burlesque *m.*
— v. tr. Parodier. (See PARODY.)
burliness ['bə:linis] n. Corpulence, carrure *f.*
burly [-i] adj. Corpulent, solidement charpenté, d'une belle carrure.
Burma ['bə:mə] n. Gᴇᴏɢʀ. Birmanie *f.*
Burmese [bə:'mi:z] adj., n. Gᴇᴏɢʀ. Birman *s.*
burn [bə:n] n. Ruisseau *m.* (in Scotland).
burn v. tr. (29). Brûler, consumer; calciner; *to burn to a cinder,* carboniser. ‖ Incendier, enflammer, mettre le feu à (a town). ‖ Brûler, brûler vif; faire mourir sur le bûcher (s.o.). ‖ Brûler (coal); *to burn oil,* chauffer au mazout. ‖ Brûler, faire brûler, allumer (candles, heaters, lights); *to burn daylight,* brûler la chandelle à midi. ‖ Faire en brûlant; *to burn a hole in one's coat,* faire un trou de cigarette à son veston. ‖ Brûler, se brûler; *to burn one's fingers,* se brûler les doigts. ‖ Brûler, corroder, ronger (the metal, the skin). ‖ Brûler, bronzer, basaner (the skin). ‖ Marquer au fer rouge (to brand). ‖ Cᴜʟɪɴ. Laisser attacher (milk, sauce); brûler (a roast). ‖ Mᴇᴅ. Brûler, cautériser. ‖ Tᴇᴄʜɴ. Cuire (bricks, pottery); vulcaniser (rubber). ‖ Fɪɢ. Brûler, enflammer *(with,* de) [anger, desire]. ‖ Fᴀᴍ. *Money to burn,* argent à gogo; *to burn one's finger over,* se faire échauder. ‖ **To burn away,** consumer. ‖ **To burn down,** incendier; consumer, dévorer. ‖ **To burn off,** enlever au feu. ‖ **To burn out,** brûler jusqu'au bout (a candle); griller (a lamp);

burned out of one's house, chassé de chez soi pa[r] le feu, sinistré par incendie; Fɪɢ. *to burn onesel*[f] *out,* s'user, se consumer, brûler la chandelle pa[r] les deux bouts. ‖ **To burn up,** brûler totalement[,] consumer; Fᴀᴍ. incendier (to scold); *to burn u*[p] *the road,* brûler la route.
— v. intr. Brûler, flamber, être en flammes; *to burn blue,* brûler avec une flamme bleue. ‖ Brûler, flam[-]ber (mouth, throat). ‖ Cᴜʟɪɴ. Brûler. ‖ Fɪɢ. Brûler[,] flamber *(with,* de) [anger, desire]. ‖ Fᴀᴍ. Brûler (i[n] games). ‖ Fᴀᴍ. Corner, tinter (ears). ‖ **To burr**[n] **away,** se consumer. ‖ **To burn down,** baisse[r] (fire). ‖ **To burn into,** ronger (a metal); Fɪɢ[.] Impressionner, se graver dans (memory). ‖ **To burr**[n] **out,** s'éteindre (fire); griller (lamp). ‖ **To burn u**[p] flamber, monter (fire); *to burn up in the atmosphere* se volatiliser (or) se désintégrer dans l'atmosphère[.]
— n. Brûlure *f.* ‖ **Burn-up,** n. Volatilisation *f.*
burner [-ə*] n. Brûleur *m.* ‖ Tᴇᴄʜɴ. Cuiseur *m.*
burnet ['bə:nit] n. Bᴏᴛ. Pimprenelle *f.*
burning ['bəniŋ] adj. Brûlant, enflammé, en feu[.] ‖ Fɪɢ. Ardent (desire, faith, thirst); violent (indigna[-] tion); brûlant (question); cuisant (sensation); véhé[-] ment (words). ‖ **Burning-bush,** n. Bᴏᴛ. Buisso[n] ardent *m.*
— n. Brûlure *f.* ‖ Incendie *m.* ‖ Cᴜʟɪɴ. Brûlé roussi *m.* ‖ Tᴇᴄʜɴ. Cuite *f.* ‖ Fɪɢ. Ardeur, flamme *f*
burnish ['bə:niʃ] v. tr. Brunir, polir, roder (a metal); satiner (a photographic print).
— v. intr. Se polir.
burnisher [-ə*] n. Brunisseur *m.* (person); brunis[-] soir *m.* (tool).
burnt [bə:nt] pret., p. p. See BURN.
burnoose, burnous [bə:'nu:z] n. Burnous *m.*
burp [bə:p] v. intr. Roter. (See BELCH.)
— n. Rot *m.*
burr [bə:*] n. Asᴛʀᴏɴ. Halo *m.* ‖ Tᴇᴄʜɴ. Barbe *f.* (of metal); ébarboir *m.* (tool). ‖ Gʀᴀᴍᴍ. Grasseye[-] ment *m.* ‖ Fᴀᴍ. Crampon *m.* (See BUR.)
— v. tr. Gʀᴀᴍᴍ. Grasseyer. ‖ Parler indistinc[-] tement. ‖ Bourdonner, vrombir (to whirr).
burrow ['bʌrou] n. Terrier *m.* (of rabbits, foxes)[.] ‖ Fᴀᴍ. Gîte *m.*
— v. tr. Creuser. ‖ Fɪɢ. **To burrow into,** fouiller[,] creuser.
bursa ['bə:sə] n. Mᴇᴅ., Zᴏᴏʟ. Bourse séreuse *f.*
bursar ['bə:sə*] n. Boursier *m.* (student); éco[-] nome *m.* (treasurer).
bursary [-ri] n. Economat *m.*
bursitis [bə:'saitis] n. Mᴇᴅ. Bursite *f.*
burst [bə:st] v. intr. (30). Sauter (boiler); éclater, exploser (bomb, powder); crever (bubble, cloud); *to burst in pieces,* voler en éclats. ‖ Crever, éclater déborder, regorger *(with,* de) [to overflow]. ‖ S'ou[-] vrir; *to burst open,* s'ouvrir violemment. ‖ S'échap[-] per *(from,* de); se précipiter *(into,* dans); *to burst into a gallop,* prendre le galop. ‖ Eclater; *to burst into laughter,* éclater de rire; *to burst into tears* fondre en larmes. ‖ Mᴇᴅ. Crever, percer (abscess) ‖ Bᴏᴛ. S'ouvrir, percer (bud); *to burst into bloom* s'épanouir. ‖ Fɪɢ. Eclater *(upon,* à) [s.o.'s ears view]; se briser, éclater *(with,* de) [emotion]; débor[-] der *(with,* de) [joy]; crever, éclater *(with,* de[)] [pride]. ‖ **To burst forth,** jaillir (blood); éclate[r] (storm); surgir (sun); Fɪɢ. Eclater *(into,* en). ‖ T[o] **burst in,** faire irruption, entrer en trombe; Fɪɢ S'immiscer brusquement *(into,* dans); *the truth burst in upon me,* la vérité éclata à mes yeux. ‖ **To burst out,** s'exclamer (person); se répandre éclater *(into,* en); Mᴇᴅ. Se déclarer (disease).
— v. tr. Crever (a balloon); rompre (banks); écla[-] ter (a bomb, shell); faire sauter (a boiler); one's buttons); éborder, remplir à crever (a gran[-] ary). ‖ Fᴀᴍ. *To burst one's sides with laughing,* crever de rire, rire à se faire péter la sous-ventrière[.] ‖ **To burst in,** enfoncer (a door). ‖ **To burst out,** faire sauter.

— n. Eclatement *m.;* explosion *f.* ‖ Jaillissement *m.* (of flames). ‖ Mouvement brusque *m.; with a burst,* dans un sursaut. ‖ Sports. Galop *m.;* course *f.; burst of speed,* temps de vitesse; emballage. ‖ Milit. Rafale *f.* (of fire); éclatement *m.* (of shell). ‖ Fig. Explosion *f.* (of anger, indignation); tonnerre *m.* (of applause); crise *f.* (of crying); élan, transport *m.* (of eloquence, love); accès *m.* (of enthusiasm); débordement *m.* (of joy). ‖ Fam. *To burst a blood vessel,* en prendre un coup de sang.

burthen ['bəːðən] n. Thème *m.* (of a speech). ‖ Mus. Refrain *m.*

burton ['bəːtn] n. Bière *f.* ‖ Naut. Palan *m.* ‖ Aviat. Fam. *To go for a burton,* être descendu et boire le bouillon.

Burundi [bəˈrundi] n. Geogr. Burundi *m.*

bury [ˈberi] v. tr. (2). Enterrer, inhumer (s.o.); enterrer, enfouir (sth.). ‖ Enfoncer, plonger (one's hands, a knife) [*into,* dans]. ‖ Fig. Enterrer, dissimuler, celer (to hide). ‖ **To bury oneself,** s'enterrer (*in,* dans); Fig. Se plonger (*in,* dans).

bus [bʌs] (pl. **bus(s)es** [-iz]) n. Autobus *m.* ‖ Autom. Fam. Bagnole *f.* ‖ U. S. Autom. Car *m.* (between localities). ‖ Aviat. Fam. Coucou *m.* ‖ ‖ Loc. *To miss the bus,* louper le coche. ‖ **Bus-conductor,** n. Receveur *m.;* Electr. Barre (*f.*) omnibus. ‖ **Bus lane,** n. Couloir d'autobus *m.* ‖ **Bus-shelter,** n. Abribus *m.* (nom déposé). ‖ **Bus-station,** n. Gare routière *f.* ‖ **Bus-stop,** n. Arrêt d'autobus *m.*
— v. intr. (1). Fam. Aller en autobus.
— v. tr. (1). U. S. Transporter, dans les cars scolaires, les enfants des quartiers riches vers les écoles des quartiers pauvres, et inversement, pour favoriser la déségrégation.

busboy ['bʌsbɔi] n. U. S. Aide-serveur *m.*

busby ['bʌsbi] n. Colback *m.*

bush [buʃ] n. Broussailles *f. pl.* (brushwood); buisson *m.* (shrub); fourré *m.* (thicket). ‖ Brousse *f.* (woodland); *to take to the bush,* prendre le maquis. ‖ Broussailles (of hair, whisker). ‖ Enseigne *f.;* bouchon *m.* (of vintner). ‖ **Bush-fighter,** U. S. **bush-whacker,** n. Franc-tireur *m.* ‖ **Bush-fighting,** U. S. **bush-whacking,** n. Milit. Guérilla *f.* ‖ ‖ **Bush-jacket,** n. Saharienne *f.* ‖ **Bush-ranger,** n. Broussard *m.*
— v. tr. Décorer (or) planter de buissons.
— v. intr. Pousser en broussaille. ‖ Avoir la forme d'un buisson. ‖ Fam. U. S. *To be bushed,* être claqué (or) éreinté.

bush n. Techn. Bague *f.,* collier *m.* (lining a circular orifice); coussinet *m.* (supporting a shaft); fourreau *m.,* manchon *m.,* gaine *f.* (insulating electric wire).
— v. tr. Techn. Baguer.

bushel ['buʃl] n. Boisseau *m.*

bushing ['buʃiŋ] n. See bush (techn.).

bushman ['buʃmən] (pl. **bushmen**) n. Colon *m.* ‖ Broussard *m.* (backwoodsman). ‖ Boschiman *m.*

bushy ['buʃi] adj. Buissonneux, broussailleux; touffu. ‖ Fig. Epais (beard); en broussailles (hair).

busily ['bizili] adv. Activement, avec affairement.

business ['biznis] n. Affaire *f.;* rôle *m.; it was his business to see to it,* c'était à lui d'y veiller; *mind your own business,* occupez-vous de vos affaires, mêlez-vous de ce qui vous regarde; *to make it one's business to do sth.,* se charger de faire qqch.; *to send s.o. about his business,* renvoyer qqn à ses chères études, envoyer bouler qqn. ‖ Métier *m.;* affaire, occupation *f.; my line of business,* ma partie; *to follow a business,* exercer une profession; *to know one's business,* connaître son affaire. ‖ Travail *m.; the business of the day,* l'ordre du jour. ‖ Affaire *f.;* objet, sujet *m.; the business of the book,* l'objet du livre; *to come* (or) U. S. *to get down to business,* en venir au sujet. ‖ Affaire *f.;* objet (*m.*) d'une démarche; *that's my business here,* voilà la raison de ma venue; *to have business*

with, avoir affaire à. ‖ Affaire, question sérieuse *f.; to make a business of it,* en faire une affaire d'Etat. ‖ Theatr. Jeux (*m. pl.*) de scène. ‖ Comm. Affaires *f. pl.; on business,* pour affaires; *piece of business,* affaire, opération; *to be in, out of business,* être dans les affaires, retiré des affaires; *to do business with,* faire des affaires avec; *to go into business,* entrer dans les affaires; *to set up in business,* s'établir. ‖ Comm. Fonds de commerce *m.;* maison *f.; building business,* entreprise de construction; *to manage an important business,* diriger une grosse affaire. ‖ Fam. Bizness *m.; a miserable business,* une lamentable histoire, une triste affaire, une piètre politique; *to mean business,* parler sérieusement. ‖ **Business-girl,** n. Jeune employée *f.;* U. S. Fam. Respectueuse *f.* ‖ **Business-like,** adj. Pratique, méthodique, efficient (person); net, prosaïque (style); sérieux (transaction). ‖ **Business-suit,** n. U. S. Complet veston *m.*
— adj. Ouvrable (day); de travail, d'ouverture (hours); de travail (suit). ‖ Comm. De commerce (house); d'affaires (matters); des affaires, commerçant (quarter); commercial (term); de commerce, de gestion des affaires (studies); *big business man,* brasseur d'affaires; *business man, woman,* homme, femme d'affaires.

busk [bʌsk] n. Busk *m.* (for corsets).

busker ['bʌskə*] n. Musicien (*s.*) de la rue (or) du métro, musicien qui fait la manche; bateleur *m.*

buskin ['bʌskin] n. Cothurne *m.* ‖ Fig. Tragédie.

busman ['bʌsmən] (pl. **busmen**) n. Conducteur (or) receveur d'autobus *m.* ‖ Fam. *To take a busman's holiday,* passer ses vacances à travailler.

bussing ['bʌsiŋ] n. U. S. Ramassage scolaire *m.* (See to bus.)

bust [bʌst] n. Med., Arts. Buste *m.* ‖ Fam. Poitrine, gorge *f.* (of a woman). ‖ **Bust-bodice** (or) **-supporter,** n. Soutien-gorge *m.*

bust [bʌst] v. tr. Fam. Péter, esquinter (to break). ‖ Réduire à la faillite, ruiner (to ruin). ‖ Dégrader (to demote). ‖ Donner un marron à (to thump). ‖ Faire une descente dans (to raid).
— v. intr. Fam. Péter, casser (to break). ‖ Faire faillite.
— n. Fam. Bide, four, fiasco *m.* (failure). ‖ Déconfiture *f.* (ruin). ‖ Gnon, marron *m.* (thump). ‖ Descente *f.,* raid *m.* (raid). ‖ Beuverie *f.* (drinking bout); *to go on the bust,* se pinter.
— adj. Fam. Pété, esquinté (broken). ‖ Fauché (bankrupt); *to go bust,* faire faillite, se casser la figure.

bustard ['bʌstəd] n. Zool. Outarde *f.*

busted ['bʌstid] adj. See bust (adj.).

buster ['bʌstə*] n. Fam. U. S. Enormité *f.* ‖ Fam. U. S. Bringue *f.* ‖ U. S. Bousilleur *m.*
— v. intr. U. S. Aviat. Voler à une vitesse normale.

bustle ['bʌsl] n. Tournure *f.* (of a skirt).

bustle v. tr. Presser, bousculer, mener tambour battant; activer (fam.).
— v. intr. Se presser, s'affairer, se démener, s'agiter, s'empresser.
— n. Affairement, remue-ménage *m.; in a bustle,* en plein branle-bas.

bustling [-iŋ] adj. Affairé, empressé; *bustling with life,* plein de vie et d'animation, trépidant.

busy ['bizi] adj. Occupé (person) [*at, in, over, with,* à, de]; *busy reading,* occupé à lire. ‖ Actif; *to keep oneself busy,* s'activer. ‖ Chargé (day); affairé (person); affairant (task); *busy time,* période de presse. ‖ Passant (street); grouillant d'activité (town). ‖ Occupé (telephone line). ‖ Comm. Commerçant (quarter, street); *at one's busiest,* en plein coup de feu. ‖ Ch. de f. D'affluence, de pointe (hours).
— n. Pop. Cogne *m.* (policeman).

— v. tr. (2). *To busy oneself with,* s'activer à, s'occuper de; se mêler de.

busybody [-bɔdi] n. Mouche (*f.*) du coche; ardélion, officieux, important *m.*

busyness [-nis] n. Fait (*m.*) d'être très occupé; affairement, surmenage *m.*

but [bʌt] adv., conj., prep., pron. Excepté, sauf, hormis (except); *all but a few of his books were bound,* presque tous ses livres étaient reliés. ‖ Que, seulement que; *none other but him,* nul autre que lui; *she seemed anything but proud,* elle semblait rien moins qu'orgueilleuse; *who else but my sister?,* qui d'autre que ma sœur? ‖ Si seulement; *could we but rid ourselves of him!,* si seulement nous pouvions nous débarrasser de lui! ‖ Si ce n'est, si... ne; *who knows but he might succeed?,* qui sait s'il ne pourrait réussir? ‖ Sans que; *I could not look at him but I found him looking at me,* je ne pouvais le regarder sans le surprendre en train de me regarder. ‖ Que (after a comparative); *he no sooner saw him but he went out,* il ne l'eut pas plus tôt vu qu'il sortit. ‖ Que... ne; *I don't doubt but he will answer,* je ne doute pas qu'il ne réponde; *not a paper but contains an allusion to the strike,* pas un journal qui ne contienne une allusion à la grève. ‖ Mais; *he is very kind but too shy,* il est très aimable mais trop timide; ‖ Cependant, pourtant; *one can but try,* on peut toujours essayer. ‖ **But for,** sans; *but for me,* sans moi; n'eût été moi, si je n'avais été là. ‖ **But that,** que... ne; *she was not so sound asleep but that she couldn't hear me,* elle n'était pas si profondément endormie qu'elle ne pût m'entendre. ‖ **But what,** si... ne; que... ne; *I don't know but what it is worse,* je ne sais si ce n'est pas pire. ‖ **Not but that,** ce n'est pas que; *not but that I was unhappy,* je ne veux pas dire que j'étais malheureux, ce n'était pas que je fusse malheureux.

— n. Mais *m.; there are no buts about,* il n'y a pas de mais!; pas d'objection!

— v. tr. Objecter; *but me no buts,* il n'y a pas de mais.

butadiene [‚bjutə'di:n] n. CHIM. Butadiène *m.*

butane ['bjutein] n. CHIM. Butane *m.*

butch [butʃ] adj. POP. Costaud (man), hommasse (woman); *butch haircut,* coupe de cheveux en brosse.

— n. POP. Dur, costaud *m.* (man); gouine *f.* (lesbian).

butcher ['butʃə*] n. Boucher *m.; butcher's boy,* garçon boucher, livreur; *butcher's meat,* viande de boucherie; *butcher's wife,* bouchère; *butcher's shop,* boucherie. ‖ U. S. THEATR., CH. DE F. Vendeur (*m.*) de bonbons et de revues. ‖ FAM., MED. Charcutier *m.* (surgeon). ‖ FAM. Boucher *m.*

— v. tr. Massacrer. ‖ MED., FAM. Charcuter. ‖ FAM. Massacrer (to botch).

butcherly [-li] adj. Cruel, sanguinaire.

— adv. Sauvagement, comme un boucher.

butchery [-ri] n. Métier de boucher *m.* ‖ U. S. Boucherie *f.* (shop); abattoir *m.* (slaughterhouse). ‖ MILIT., NAUT. Boucherie *f.* ‖ FIG. Boucherie *f.;* carnage *m.*

butler ['bʌtlə*] n. Maître d'hôtel; intendant *m.; butler's pantry,* office.

butt [bʌt] n. Barrique, *f.* (barrel).

butt n. Gros bout, bout *m.* (thick end). ‖ Bout, chicot, reste *m.* (stump). ‖ Mégot *m.* (of cigarette). ‖ Croupon *m.* (leather). ‖ MILIT. Crosse *f.* (of rifle). ‖ BOT. Base *f.* (of leaf-stalk); souche *f.* (of tree). ‖ ZOOL. Poisson plat *m.* ‖ FAM. U. S. Postérieur, derrière *m.* ‖ **Butt-end,** n. Gros bout *m.* ‖ **Butt-joint,** n. TECHN. Joint abouté *m.; v.* tr. abouter. ‖ **Butt-strap,** n. TECHN. Eclisse *f.* ‖ **Butt-weld,** n. TECHN. Soudure (*f.*) en bout; v. tr. Souder à bout.

butt n. MILIT. Cible *f.* (target); pl. champ de tir,

polygone *m.* (range). ‖ FIG. Victime *f.;* bouc émissaire; objet (*m.*) de risée; tête (*f.*) de Turc; *to be a butt for ridicule,* se trouver en butte au ridicule.

butt v. intr. Frapper à coups de tête (*against,* contre); donner un coup de corne (*at,* à). ‖ Foncer, buter, tomber (*against, upon,* à) [to bump into]. ‖ TECHN. S'abouter (*against, upon,* à). ‖ FIG. Intervenir, s'immiscer (*into,* dans); *to butt in,* se mêler à tout, dire son mot; mettre son grain de sel (fam.); s'immiscer dans les affaires des autres.

— v. tr. Donner un coup de corne à. ‖ Buter contre. ‖ TECHN. Abouter.

— n. Coup (*m.*) de corne (or) de tête; *to go full butt at,* donner tête baissée dans.

butter ['bʌtə*] n. CULIN. Beurre *m.; brown butter sauce,* beurre noir. ‖ FAM. *To look as if butter would not melt in one's mouth,* faire la sainte nitouche, n'avoir pas l'air d'y toucher. ‖ **Butter bean,** n. AGRIC. Haricot beurre *m.* ‖ **Butter-biscuit,** n. CULIN. Petit-beurre *m.* ‖ **Butter-colour** adj. Beurre. ‖ **Butter-cooler,** n. Beurrier rafraî chisseur *m.* ‖ **Butter-dish,** n. Beurrier *m.* ‖ **Butter factory,** n. Beurrerie *f.* ‖ **Butter-fingered,** adj FAM. Maladroit, aux mains de beurre. ‖ **Butter-fingers,** n. pl. FAM. Brise-fer *m.* ‖ **Butter-industry** n. Industrie beurrière *f.* ‖ **Butter-muslin,** n. Etamine *f.* ‖ **Butter-paper,** n. Papier beurre (or) sulfurisé *m.* ‖ **Butter-pat,** n. Bain (*m.*) de beurre coquilles (*f. pl.*) de beurre. ‖ **Butter-pear,** n. BOT Beurré *m.* ‖ **Butter-scotch,** n. Caramel (*m.*) au beurre.

— v. tr. CULIN. Beurrer. ‖ FAM. *To butter s.o. up* passer la main dans le dos à qqn.

buttercup ['bʌtəkʌp] n. BOT. Bouton-d'or *m.*

butterfat [-fæt] n. U. S. Crème *f.*

butterfly ['bʌtəflai] n. ZOOL., FIG. Papillon *m.*

— adj. Papillonnant.

— v. intr. Papillonner.

butterine ['bʌtəri:n] n. CULIN. Margarine *f.*

buttermilk [-milk] n. Babeurre *m.*

buttery [-ri] adj. Butyreux, de beurre.

buttery [-ri] n. Dépense *f.* (store-room). ‖ Crémerie *f.* (restaurant).

buttock ['bʌtək] n. Fesse *f.* ‖ Pl. Croupe *f.* (of an animal); derrière *m.* (of a person). ‖ NAUT. Fesse ‖ CULIN. Culotte *f.*

button ['bʌtn] n. Bouton *m.* (on a garment). Bouton *m.* (of door, doorbell, electric lamp). ‖ BOT Bouton *m.* (of flowers, mushrooms). ‖ SPORTS. Bouton *m.* (of foil). ‖ CULIN. *Chocolate buttons,* pastilles de chocolat. ‖ FAM. Pl. Groom, chasseur *m* ‖ FAM. *Not to be worth a button,* ne pas valoir les quatre fers d'un chien; *to touch the button,* presser sur le bouton, déclencher les événements; *to take by the button,* tenir par le revers de la veste. ‖ **Button-hook,** n. Tire-bouton, crochet (*m.*) à bottine. ‖ **Button-link,** n. Bouton (*m.*) de manchette ‖ **Button-stick,** n. MILIT. Patience *f.* ‖ **Button-over,** adj. Croisé (coat). ‖ **Button-on,** adj. Qu boutonne par-dessus.

— v. tr. Boutonner (s.o.). ‖ SPORTS. Moucheter (foil). ‖ *To button up,* boutonner entièrement FAM. *Buttoned up mouth,* bouche cousue.

— v. intr. Boutonner, se boutonner (garment). BOT. Bourgeonner.

buttonhole [-houl] n. Boutonnière *f.* (in a garment); *buttonhole stitch,* point de boutonnière. Boutonnière *f.* (flower). ‖ MED. Boutonnière *f.*

— v. tr. Faire une boutonnière à. ‖ MED. Inciser ‖ FAM. Retenir par la veste; accrocher, cramponner.

buttonholer [-houlə*] n. FAM. Crampon *m.*

buttress ['butris] n. ARCHIT. Contrefort, pilier d'arc-boutant *m.* ‖ FIG. Pilier, soutien *m.*

— v. tr. ARCHIT. Arc-bouter, soutenir. ‖ FIG Etayer.

butyl ['bjutil] n. Chim. Butyle *m*.
butylene [-i:n] n. Chim. Butylène *m*.
butyric [bju'tirik] adj. Chim. *Butyric acid*, acide butyrique.
butyrin ['bjutirin] n. Butyrine *f*.
butyrous [-əs] adj. Butyreux.
buxom ['bʌksəm] adj. Dodu, grassouillet, potelé (plump). ‖ † Avenant, gracieux (comely).
buxomness [-nis] n. Beauté potelée *f*. ‖ † Grâce, mine avenante *f*.
buy [bai] v. tr. (31). Acheter, acquérir. (See Purchase.) ‖ Jur. Acheter, corrompre (to bribe). ‖ Comm. *Bought of*, doit à; *bought note*, bordereau d'achat. ‖ Fig. Acheter, payer. ‖ Fam. U. S. Adopter (s.o.'s point of view) ‖ **To buy back**, racheter. ‖ **To buy in**, acquérir, acheter, racheter. ‖ **To buy off**, acheter, se débarrasser à prix d'argent de. ‖ **To buy out**, désintéresser (a partner); acheter les droits de (s.o.). ‖ **To buy over**, corrompre. ‖ **To buy up**, acheter en bloc, rafler.
— n. Achat *m*.; acquisition *f*.
buyer [-ə*] n. Comm. Acheteur *s*.; acquéreur *m*. (consumer); acheteur *m*. (employee).
buzz [bʌz] v. tr. Chuchoter (gossip); répandre (rumours). ‖ Lancer (stones). ‖ Techn. Transmettre par vibrateur. ‖ Aviat. Frôler en volant (a building, plane). ‖ Fam. Téléphoner à.
— v. intr. Bourdonner (insects). ‖ Méd. Tinter, bourdonner (ears). ‖ Techn. Vrombir (motor). ‖ Fam. Bavarder avec un bourdonnement de voix. ‖ **To buzz off**, Fam. Se barrer, se tailler, filer.
— n. Bourdonnement *m*. (of insects). ‖ Zool. Bourdon *m*. ‖ Fam. Bourdonnement *m*. (of conversation); *buzz of approval*, murmure d'approbation. ‖ **Buzz-bomb**, n. Milit. V1. ‖ **Buzz saw**, n. U. S. Techn. scie mécanique, scie circulaire *f*.
buzz v. tr. Jeter, lancer. ‖ Fam. Liquider (a bottle).
buzzard ['bʌzəd] n. Zool. Buse *f*.; busard *m*.; U. S. urubu *m*. ‖ Fam. Buse *f*.; U. S. vautour *m*.
buzzer ['bʌzə*] n. Electr. Vibreur, vibrateur, trembleur, couineur *m*. ‖ Pl. Fam. Téléphonistes *m. pl*. ‖ **Buzzer-call**, n. Appel vibré *m*.
buzzerphone [-foun] n. U. S. Téléphone à vibreur *m*.
by [bai] prep. Par, de (agency); *knocked down by a car*, renversé par une auto; *a book by Charles Morgan*, un livre de Charles Morgan. ‖ Par, à (means); *by chance*, par hasard; *by heaven's help*, avec l'aide du ciel; *by sound of trumpet*, à son de trompe. ‖ Près, près de, à côté de (space); *close*

by the church, tout près de l'église; *sit down by me*, asseyez-vous près de moi. ‖ A, de, sur (measure); *by far*, de beaucoup; *by the pound*, à la livre; *taller by a head*, plus grand d'une tête; *twenty feet by forty*, vingt pieds sur quarante. ‖ A, pendant, vers (time); *by day*, pendant le jour; *by next Monday*, avant lundi prochain; *by the time when*, au moment où; *by then*, avant ce moment-là; *to work by the hour*, travailler à l'heure. ‖ A, par, selon, d'après (manner); *by mistake*, par erreur; *by rule*, selon les règles; *by your watch*, d'après votre montre. ‖ Par (conséquence); *by nature*, par nature; *by right of birth*, par droit de naissance.
— adv. Près, auprès; *near by*, tout près; *the train flew by*, le train passa en trombe. ‖ De côté; *put some money by*, mettez quelque argent de côté. ‖ En passant; *much time has gone by since*, beaucoup de temps s'est écoulé depuis. ‖ U. S. *By and large*, généralement parlant. ‖ **By-and-by**, adv. Plus tard, bientôt; à l'avenir. ‖ **By-election**, n. Election partielle *f*. ‖ **By-lane**, n. Ruelle *f*. ‖ **By-law**, n. Jur. Ordonnance *f*.; arrêté, règlement administratif *m*. ‖ **By-pass**, n. Techn. Conduit (*m*.) de dérivation; Autom. Voie (*f*.) d'évitement, déviation, *f*.; Electr. Dérivation *f*.; v. tr. Dériver, dévier; contourner. ‖ **By-play**, n. Théatr. Jeu (*m*.) de scène en aparté; Fig. Evénements secondaires *m. pl*. ‖ **By-product**, n. Sous-produit, dérivé *m*. ‖ **By-road**, n. Route vicinale (ou) écartée *f*. ‖ **By-way**, n. Route écartée; voie privée *f*.; Fig. A-côté *m*.
bye adj. Secondaire. See by.
bye n. Chose secondaire *f*.; *by the bye*, à propos, au fait. ‖ Sports. Balle passée *f*. (in cricket).
bye interj. Fam. Salut!, ciao! (goodbye).
bye-bye ['bai'bai] n. Fam. Dodo *m*.; *to go byebyes*, aller faire dodo.
— interj. Fam. Salut!, ciao! (goodbye).
bygone ['baigɔn] adj. Passé, d'autrefois.
— n. pl. Passé *m*.
bypath [-pɑ:θ] n. Chemin détourné (or) écarté *m*.
byre [-baiə*] n. Agric. Etable *f*.
Byronic [bai'rɔnik] adj. Byronien.
byssinosis [,bisi'nousis] n. Méd. Byssinose *f*.
bystander ['bai,stændə*] n. Spectateur *m*.; spectatrice *f*.; assistant *s*.
bystreet [-stri:t] n. Rue écartée *f*.
byte [bait] n. Inform. Byte *m*.
byword [-wə:d] n. Dicton *m*.; *to become a byword*, passer en proverbe. ‖ Objet (*m*.) de dérision.
Byzantine [bai'zæntain] adj., n. Geogr. Byzantin *s*.

C

c [si:] n. C, c *m*. ‖ Cent *m*. (Roman numeral). ‖ Mus. Do, ut *m*. ‖ Chim. Carbone *m*. ‖ Phys. C., coulomb *m*.; ^0C, degré Celsius, degré centigrade *m*.
— adj. En C. ‖ Troisième (in a sequence).
cab [kæb] n. Fiacre *m*. ‖ Autom. Taxi *m*. ‖ Ch. de f. Cabine de locomotive *f*. ‖ **Cab-rank**, n. Station (*f*.) de taxis.

cabal [kə'bæl] n. Cabale, intrigue *f*. ‖ Coterie *f*.
— v. intr. (1). Intriguer, comploter.
cabala ['kæbələ] n. Cabale *f*. (doctrine).
cabalist [-ist] n. Cabaliste *m*.
cabalistic ['kæbə'listik] adj. Cabalistique.
cabaret ['kæbərei] n. Cabaret, café-concert *m*. ‖ Attractions (*f. pl*.) au cabaret; *cabaret song*, chanson réaliste.

cabbage ['kæbidʒ] n. AGRIC., CULIN. Chou *m.; Savoy cabbage*, chou frisé. ‖ **Cabbage-butterfly**, n. ZOOL. Papillon blanc *m*. ‖ **Cabbage-leaf**, n. Feuille (*f.*) de chou. ‖ **Cabbage-lettuce**, n. AGRIC. Laitue pommée *f*. ‖ **Cabbage-tree**, n. BOT. Palmiste *m*. **cabbage** n. Retaille *f*.
— v. tr., intr. Retailler.

cabby ['kæbi] n. FAM. Cocher de fiacre; chauffeur (*m.*) de taxi.

caber ['keibə*] n. Tronc (*m.*) d'arbre émondé. ‖ SPORTS. *Tossing the caber*, lancer de troncs d'arbres (Scottish game).

cabin ['kæbin] n. Cabane, case *f*. ‖ NAUT. Cabine *f*. ‖ AVIAT. Habitacle *m.; carlingue *f*. ‖ **Cabin-boy**, n. NAUT. Mousse, petit commissaire *m*. ‖ **Cabin-class**, n. NAUT. Deuxième classe *f*. ‖ *Cabin cruiser*, n. NAUT. Cabin-cruiser *m*.
— v. tr. Enfermer à l'étroit.

cabinet [-it] n. Cabinet, bonheur-du-jour *m*. (piece of furniture); cabinet, bureau *m*. (room). ‖ JUR. Cabinet *m*. (meeting, room); *to form a cabinet*, former le ministère; *Cabinet Minister*, ministre, membre du gouvernement; *Shadow-Cabinet*, cabinet fantôme. ‖ **Cabinet-maker**, n. Ebéniste *m*. ‖ **Cabinet-work**, n. Ebénisterie *f*.
— adj. *Cabinet size*, format album. ‖ JUR. De cabinet (council). ‖ FIG. Confidentiel.

cable ['keibl] n. Câble *m*. (rope); *cable's length*, encablure. ‖ Câble, câblogramme *m*. (cablegram). ‖ ELECTR. Câble *m*. ‖ NAUT. Encablure *f*. ‖ ARCHIT. Rudenture *f*. ‖ FAM. *To slip one's cable*, se laisser glisser. ‖ **Cable-car**, n. TECHN. Téléphérique *m.; télécabine, télébenne *f*. ‖ **Cable-railway**, n. CH. DE F. Funiculaire *m*.
— v. tr. Attacher (or) remorquer avec un câble. ‖ Câbler, télégraphier. ‖ ARCHIT. Rudenter.
— v. intr. Câbler.

cablegram [-græm] n. Câblogramme *m*.
cablet [-it] n. NAUT. Câbleau *m*.
cableway [-wei] n. Blondin *m*.
cabman ['kæbmən] (pl. **cabmen**) n. Cocher de fiacre; chauffeur de taxi *m*. (See CABBY.)
cabochon ['kæbəʃən] n. Cabochon *m*.
caboodle [kə'bu:dl] n. FAM. *The whole caboodle*, tout le tremblement.
caboose [kə'bu:s] n. NAUT. Cambuse *f*. ‖ CH. DE F. Fourgon *m*.
cabotage ['kæbətidʒ] n. NAUT. Cabotage *m*.
cabriolet [kæbrio'lei] n. Cabriolet *m*.
ca'canny [kə'kæni] adj. See CANNY.
cacao [kə'keiou] n. Cacao *m*. ‖ BOT. Cacaoyer *m*.
cachalot ['kæʃələt] n. ZOOL. Cachalot *m*.
cache [kæʃ] n. Cache, cachette *f*. (place); objet caché *m*. (thing).
— v. tr. Cacher. (See HIDE.)
cachet [kaʃe] n. MED. Cachet *m.; capsule *f*. ‖ FIG. Cachet *m.; marque *f*.
cachectic [kə'kektik] adj. MED. Cachectic.
cachexia [-siə] n. MED. Cachexie *f*.
cachinnate ['kækineit] v. intr. Rire bruyamment.
cachinnation [kæki'neiʃən] n. Rire bruyant *m*.
cachou ['kæʃu:] n. Cachou *m*.
cacique [kæ'ʃi:k] n. Cacique *m*.
cack [kæk] n. FAM. Caca *m*.
cackle ['kækl] v. tr., intr. Cacarder (goose); caqueter (hen). ‖ FAM. Glousser (to chuckle); caqueter, jaser (to prattle). ‖ Se pavaner (to boast).
— n. Caquet *m*. ‖ FAM. Gloussement (laughter) *m.; caquetage *m*. (talk).
cackler [-ə*] n. Caqueteur s.
cacodylate [kæko'dileit] n. CHIM. Cacodylate *m*.
cacophony [kæ'kɔfəni] n. Cacophonie *f*.
cactus ['kæktəs] n. BOT. Cactus *m*.
cad [kæd] n. FAM. Malotru *m*. (boor); canaille, fripouille *f*. (scoundrel).
cadastral [kə'dæstrəl] n. Cadastral.

cadaver [kə'dævə*] n. MED. Cadavre, corps *m*.
cadaveric [kə'dævərik] adj. MED. Cadavérique, de cadavre.
cadaverous [-əs] adj. Cadavéreux, livide, blême; *cadaverous face*, mine de déterré.
caddie ['kædi] n. SPORTS. Caddie, cadet *m*.
— v. intr. SPORTS. Servir de caddie.
caddish ['kædiʃ] adj. De goujat, grossier.
caddishness [-nis] n. Goujaterie; canaillerie *f*.
caddy ['kædi] n. Boîte (*f.*) à thé.
cade [keid] n. BOT. Cade *m*. ‖ **Cade-oil**, n. Huile (*f.*) de cade.
cade n. Caque *f*. (keg).
cadence ['keidəns] n. Cadence *f*.
cadency ['keidənsi] n. Branche cadette *f*.
cadenza [kə'denzə] n. MUS. Cadence *f*. (solo passage).
cadet [kə'det] n. Cadet *m*. ‖ MILIT. Cadet, élève officier *m*.
cadge [kædʒ] v. intr. Colporter, faire le colporteur. (See PEDDLE.) ‖ FAM. Ecornifler.
— v. tr. FAM. Quémander; *to cadge sth. from s.o.*, taper qqn de qqch.
cadger [-ə*] n. Colporteur *m*. (see PEDLAR); coquetier ambulant *m*. (dealer in eggs); camelot *m*. (street hawker). ‖ FAM. Ecornifleur, tapeur s.
Cadiz ['keidiz] n. GEOGR. Cadix *f*.
Cadmean [kad'mi:ən] adj. A la Pyrrhus (victory).
cadmium ['kædmiəm] n. CHIM. Cadmium *m*.
cadre ['kɑ:də*] n. MILIT., FIG. Cadre *m*.
caduceus [kə'dju:siəs] n. MED. Caducée *m*.
caducity [-siti] n. Caducité *f*.
caducous [-kəs] adj. Caduc *m.*, caduque *f*.
caecal ['si:kəl] adj. MED. Cæcal.
caecum [-əm] n. MED. Cæcum *m*.
Caesarean [si:'zɛəriən] adj. MED. Césarien. ‖ FIG. Impérial.
caesium ['si:ziəm] n. CHIM. Cæsium *f*.
caesura [si:'zjuərə] n. Césure *f*.
café ['kæfei] n. Café, café-restaurant *m*.
— adj. Café au lait (colour). ‖ **Café-owner**, n. Cafetier *m*. ‖ *Café society*, n. U. S. Habitués (*m. pl.*) des cafés et boîtes de nuit.
cafeteria [kæfə'ti:əriə] n. Cafeteria, restaurant de libre service *m*.
caffeine ['kæfii:n] n. CHIM. Caféine *f*. ‖ **Caffeine-free**, adj. Décaféiné.
caftan ['kæftən] n. Cafetan *m*.
cage [keidʒ] n. Cage *f*. ‖ Cabine *f*. (of a lift).
— v. tr. Encager, mettre en cage.
cagey [-i] adj. FAM. Madré, finaud, retors.
cahoots [kə'hu:ts] n. FAM. Complicité *f.; in cahoots*, de mèche.
caiman ['keimən] n. ZOOL. Caïman *m*.
Cain [kein] n. Caïn *m*. ‖ FAM. *To raise Cain*, faire un chahut monstre.
cairn [kɛən] n. Cairn *m*.
cairngorm ['kɛən,gɔ:m] n. GEOL. Quartz enfumé *m*.
Cairo ['kaiərou] n. GEOGR. Le Caire *m*.
caisson ['keisən] n. MILIT., TECHN. Caisson *m*. ‖ NAUT. Bateau-porte *m*.
caitiff ['keitif] adj., n. † Couard, lâche *m*.
cajole [kə'dʒoul] v. tr. Cajoler. (See COAX.)
cajoler [-ə*] n. Cajoleur s.
cajolery [-əri] n. Cajolerie *f*.
cake [keik] n. †, CULIN. Galette *f*. ‖ CULIN. Gâteau *m*. ‖ COMM. Tablette *f*. (of chocolate); tourteau *m*. (of fruit); bloc *m*. (of ice); pain *m*. (of soap); pavé *m*. (of tobacco). ‖ FAM. *To sell like hot cakes*, se vendre comme des petits pains; *a piece of cake*, du nanan, du gâteau; *that takes the cake*, c'est champion!; U. S. *cakes and ale*, les bons côtés de la vie.
— v. tr. Durcir, coaguler; transformer en bloc compact. ‖ Couvrir d'une croûte (*with*, de).
— v. intr. S'agglutiner, se coaguler; faire croûte.

calabash ['kæləbæʃ] n. Calebasse *f*. ‖ **Calabash-tree**, n. Bot. Calebassier, *m*.
calaber ['kæləbə*] n. Zool., Comm. Petit-gris *m*.
calaboose [kælə'bus] n. U. S. Taule *f*. (prison).
calamary ['kæləməri] n. Zool. Seiche *f*.
calamine ['kæləmein] n. Chim. Calamine *f*.
calamitous [kə'læmitəs] adj. Calamiteux (event); catastrophique (person).
calamity [-ti] n. Calamité *f*. (disaster). ‖ Adversité *f*.; malheur *m*.; *calamity prophet*, prophète de malheur; *Calamity Jane*, Cassandre.
calash [kə'læʃ] n. Cabriolet *m*. (bonnet); calèche *f*. (carriage).
calcareous [kæl'kɛəriəs] adj. Calcaire.
calcification [kælsifi'keiʃən] n. Calcification *f*.
calcify ['kælsifai] v. tr., intr. (2). Calcifier; se calcifier.
calcimine [-main] n. Badigeon *m*.
calcination [kælsi'neiʃən] n. Calcination *f*.
calcine ['kælsain] v. tr. Chim., Fam. Calciner.
— v. intr. Se calciner.
calcite ['kælsait] n. Chim. Calcite.
calcium [-siəm] n. Calcium *m*.
calculable ['kælkjuləb‖] adj. Calculable.
calculate [-leit] v. tr. Math. Calculer. ‖ Fig. Calculer, combiner; arranger, régler, organiser.
— v. intr. Math. Calculer, faire des calculs. ‖ Fig. Calculer, combiner (to plan); compter, s'appuyer (*on*, *upon*, sur) [to rely].
calculating [-leitiŋ] adj. Prudent (cautious); combinard (scheming). ‖ **Calculating-machine**, n. Machine (*f*.) à calculer.
calculation [kælkju'leiʃən] n. Math., Fig. Calcul *m*.
— N.B. En math., on emploie aussi le pl. *calculuses*.
calculator ['kælkjuleitə*] n. Math. Calculateur *m*.; calculatrice *f*. ‖ Techn. Machine (*f*.) à calculer (machine); barème *m*. (table).
calculous [-əs] adj. Méd. Calculeux.
calculus [-əs] (pl. **calculi** [-ai]) n. Méd., Math. Calcul *m*.
— N. B. En math., on emploie aussi le pl. *calculuses*.
caldron ['kɔːldrən] n. Culin. Chaudron *m*. ‖ Techn. Chaudière *f*.
calefacient [kæli'feiʃənt] adj., n. Méd. Réchauffant *m*.
calefactory [-'fæktəri] adj. Calorifique.
— n. Archit. Chauffoir *m*. (in a monastery).
calendar ['kælində*] n. Calendrier *m*. ‖ Annuaire *m*. (directory). ‖ Jur. Rôle *m*. ‖ U. S. Ordre du jour *m*. ‖ *Calendar day*, jour ouvrable.
calender n. Calandre *f*.
— v. tr. Calandrer.
calends ['kælendz] n. pl. Calendes *f*. pl.
calf [kɑːf] (pl. **calves** [kɑːvz]) n. Zool. Veau *m*. ‖ Zool. Petit *m*. (of elephant, hippopotamus, seal, whale). ‖ Comm. Veau; box, box-calf *m*. ‖ Naut. Glaçon flottant *m*. ‖ Fig. *Golden calf*, veau d'or. ‖ **Calf-love**, n. Amour juvénile *m*.
calf (pl. **calves**) n. Méd. Mollet *m*. ‖ **Calf-length trousers**, n. Corsaire, pantalon corsaire *m*.
calfskin [-skin] n. Comm. Veau, cuir de veau *m*.
Caliban ['kœlibæn] n. Caliban *m*. ‖ Fig. Brute *f*.
calibrate ['kælibreit] v. tr. Calibrer. ‖ Graduer (a thermometer). ‖ Radio. Etalonner.
calibration [,kæli'breiʃən] n. Calibrage, étalonnage *m*.; *calibration number*, nombre-étalon.
calibre, U. S. caliber ['kælibə*] n. Techn., Fig. Calibre *m*.
calico ['kælikou] n. Calicot *m*.; U. S. indienne *f*., imprimé *m*. ‖ **Calico-bush**, n. Bot. Kalmie *f*.
California [kæli'fɔːnjə] n. Geogr. Californie *f*.
Californian [-iən] adj., n. Geogr. Californien *s*.
californium [-iəm] n. Chim. Californium.
caliginous [kə'lidʒinəs] adj. Obscur, ténébreux. (See dark.)

caliper ['kælipə*] n. See calliper.
caliph ['kælif] n. Calife *m*.
caliphate [-eit] n. Califat *m*.
calisthenics [,kælis'θeniks] n. See callisthenics.
calix ['keiliks] (pl. **calices** [-isi:z]) n. Méd. Calice *m*.
calk [kɔːk] v. tr. Ferrer à glace.
— n. Crampon (*m*.) à glace.
calk v. tr. Décalquer, calquer.
calk v. tr. U. S. See caulk.
calkin ['kɔːkin] n. Grappe *f*. (of horseshoe); crampon *m*. (of shoe).
calking [-iŋ] n. Décalquage *m*.
call [kɔːl] v. tr. (1). Appeler, héler, faire venir (s.o.). ‖ Crier (to shout). ‖ Annoncer (one's game). ‖ Appeler, éveiller, réveiller (to awaken). ‖ Appeler, nommer (s.o., sth.); *properly so called*, proprement dit; *to call s.o. by a name*, donner à qqn une appellation; *to call s.o. names*, traiter qqn de tous les noms; *to be called John*, s'appeler Jean. ‖ Appeler, diriger, attirer (s.o.'s attention) [*to*, sur]; évoquer, rappeler (sth.) [*to*, à]; *to call to mind*, remettre à l'esprit, remémorer; se rappeler. ‖ Mettre (sth.) [*in*, *into*, en]; *to call into existence*, faire naître; *to call in question*, mettre en doute. ‖ Appeler, juger, estimer, trouver, considérer comme, qualifier de; *to call s.o. a fool*, traiter qqn d'imbécile. ‖ Theatr. Rappeler (an actor). ‖ Milit. Appeler (the annual contingent); *to call the roll*, faire l'appel. ‖ Sports. Appeler (birds). ‖ Jur. Appeler, faire venir (a case); réunir (a council); tirer au sort (the jury); fixer, réunir (a meeting); convoquer (Parliament); *to call to the Bar*, inscrire au barreau; *to call a division*, passer un vote. ‖ **To call aside**, prendre à part. ‖ **To call away**, distraire (attention); faire sortir, obliger à partir (s.o.). ‖ **To call back**, rappeler. ‖ **To call down**, faire descendre, appeler; U. S. Fam. Enguirlander. ‖ **To call forth**, exciter, développer (admiration); faire appel à, rappeler (one's courage); évoquer (memory, spirit); faire naître, soulever (protestations). ‖ **To call in**, faire entrer (s.o.); Méd. Faire appel à, faire venir (a doctor); Fin. Faire rentrer (one's money). ‖ **To call off**, annuler, décommander (an appointment); rompre, résilier (a deal); rappeler (a dog); détourner (s.o.) [*from*, de]. ‖ **To call out**, faire sortir (s.o.); provoquer en duel (s.o.); faire mettre en grève (worker); Milit. Faire intervenir (the military). ‖ **To call over**, faire appel. ‖ **To call up**, faire monter (s.o.); téléphoner à, appeler (or) demander au téléphone (s.o.); évoquer (idea, memory, spirit); Milit. Mobiliser, appeler.
— v. intr. Appeler, crier. ‖ Crier (bird); carcailler (quail). ‖ S'arrêter (*at*, à, devant); entrer en passant (*at*, dans); *to call at*, passer chez, aller voir, rendre visite à (s.o.). ‖ Naut. Faire escale, toucher (*at*, à). ‖ **To call for**, appeler (s.o.); commander (sth.); faire prendre, aller chercher (s.o., sth.); demander, exiger, réclamer, nécessiter (attention, measures, solution, volunteers). ‖ **To call off**, se dédire. ‖ **To call on**, aller voir, rendre visite à, passer chez (s.o.). ‖ **To call out**, appeler, crier; *to call out for*, demander à grands cris. ‖ **To call upon**, invoquer (God's name); fréquenter, rendre visite à (a friend); faire appel à (s.o.'s generosity); donner la parole à (an orator); *to call upon s.o. for sth*, demander qqch. à qqn, faire appel à qqn pour obtenir qqch.; *to call upon s.o. to do sth*, inviter qqn à faire qqch.; exiger de qqn qu'il fasse qqch.; mettre qqn en demeure de faire qqch.
— n. Cri, appel *m*.; *within call*, à portée de voix. ‖ Appel *m*. (*from*, de); *telephone call*, appel téléphonique, coup de fil (or) de téléphone. ‖ Appel nominal *m*. (roll-call). ‖ Cri *m*. (of a bird). ‖ Besoin, utilité, nécessité *f*.; *there is no call for laughter*, il n'y a pas lieu de rire. ‖ Courte visite *f*. (*at*, chez;

on, a). ‖ COMM. Demande *f.* (*for*, de). ‖ FIN. Appel de fonds *m.; money on call*, argent payable (or) remboursable à vue. ‖ JUR. Convocation, sommation *f.* ‖ MILIT. Appel *m.* (of an annual contingent); sonnerie *f.* (music). ‖ NAUT. Escale *f.* ‖ SPORTS. Appeau *m.* (in shooting). ‖ ECCLES. Vocation *f.* (*to, pour*). ‖ THEATR. Rappel *m.* ‖ FIG. Voix *f.* (of conscience); appel *m.* (of duty); sollicitations *f. pl.* (of hunger, sleep). ‖ Call-bell, n. Sonnette *f.;* timbre (*m.*) de table. ‖ Call-bird, n. SPORTS. Appelant *m.* ‖ Call-box, call-station, n. Cabine téléphonique *f.* ‖ Call-boy, n. THEATR. Avertisseur *m.* ‖ Call-girl, n. Prostituée (*f.*) retenue par téléphone. ‖ Call-money, n. FIN. Emprunt (*m.*) remboursable sur demande. ‖ Call-number, n. Numéro de téléphone *m.* ‖ Call-over, n. Appel nominal *m.* ‖ Call-sign, n. RADIO., AVIAT. Indicatif *m.* ‖ Call-slip, n. Fiche de bibliothèque *f.* ‖ Call-up, n. MILIT., NAUT. Appel *m.*

caller [-ə*] n. Personne (*f.*) qui appelle. ‖ Visiteur *s.* ‖ Caller-up, n. Demandeur au téléphone *m.*

calligraph ['kæligrɑ:f] v. tr. Calligraphier.

calligraphy [kə'ligrəfi] n. Calligraphie *f.*

calling ['kɔ:liŋ] n. Appel *m.* ‖ Vocation *f.* ‖ Métier *m.;* profession *f.* ‖ Visite *f.* (*on*, à); *calling card, hours*, carte, heures de visite. ‖ Calling-forth (or) up, n. Evocation *f.* ‖ Calling-in, n. FIN. Retrait *m.* ‖ Calling out, n. Appel désespéré, cri *m.;* provocation *f.* ‖ Calling together, n. Convocation *f.*

calliper ['kælipə*] n. MATH. Compas *m.*
— v. tr. Calibrer; mesurer au compas.

callisthenics [,kælis'θeniks] n. SPORTS. Gymnastique suédoise *f.*

callosity [kæ'lɔsiti] n. MED. Callosité *f.* ‖ FIG. Dureté *f.;* endurcissement *m.* (of heart).

callous ['kæləs] adj. Calleux. ‖ FIG. Dur, endurci.

callow ['kælou] adj. ZOOL. Sans plumes. ‖ FAM. Novice; *callow youth*, blanc-bec.

callus ['kæləs] n. MED. Cal, durillon *m.*

calm [kɑ:m] adj. Calme (answer, day, mind, sea). ‖ FAM. Fort, corsé.
— n. NAUT. Calme *m.;* bonace *f.; dead calm*, calme plat. ‖ FIG. Calme *m.*
— v. tr. Calmer. (See APPEASE.)
— v. intr. *To calm down*, se calmer; s'apaiser. ‖ NAUT. Calmir.

calmative ['kælmətiv] adj., n. MED. Calmant *m.*

calmly ['kɑ:mli] adv. Avec calme, calmement.

calmness [-nis] n. Calme, sang-froid *m.*

calomel ['kæləmel] n. MED. Calomel *m.*

Calor gas ['kælə*'gæs] n. (nom déposé). Gaz butane, butane *m.*

caloric [kə'lɔrik] n. Calorique *m.*

caloricity [kælɔ'risiti] n. Caloricité *f.*

calorie ['kæləri] n. PHYS. Calorie *f.*

calorific [kælə'rifik] adj. Calorifique.

calorimeter [-'rimitə*] n. Calorimètre *m.*

calorimetry [-'rimitri] n. Calorimétrie *f.*

calorization [kæləri'zei∫ən] n. Calorisation *f.*

calotte [kə'lɔt] n. ECCLES. Calotte *f.*

calque [kælk] n. GRAMM. Calque *m.*

caltrop ['kæltrəp] n. MILIT. † Chausse-trape *f.* ‖ BOT. Chardon *m.*

calumet ['kælju:met] n. Calumet *m.*

calumniate [kə'lʌmnieit] v. tr. Calomnier.

calumniation [kə,lʌmni'ei∫ən] n. Calomnie *f.* (act).

calumniator [kə'lʌmnieitə*] n. Calomniateur *m.*, calomniatrice *f.*

calumniatory [kə,lʌmni'eitəri], calumnious [kə'lʌmniəs] adj. Calomnieux.

calumny ['kælʌmni] n. Calomnie *f.*

Calvary ['kælvəri] n. ECCLES., ARCHIT. Calvaire *m.*

calve [kɑ:v] v. intr. ZOOL., NAUT. Vêler (cow, iceberg).
— v. tr. ZOOL. Mettre bas. ‖ NAUT. Vêler.

Calvinism ['kælvinizm] n. ECCLES. Calvinisme *m.*

Calvinist [-ist] n. ECCLES. Calviniste *s.*

Calvinistic [kælvi'nistik] adj. Calviniste.

calyx ['keiliks] (pl. calyxes, calyces [-isi:z]) n. BOT. Calice *m.*

cam [kæm] n. TECHN. Came *f.* ‖ Cam-shaft, n. TECHN. Arbre (*m.*) à cames.

camber ['kæmbə*] n. Bombement *m.* (of a road). ‖ ARCHIT., AVIAT. Cambrure *f.* ‖ NAUT. Tonture *f.*
— v. tr. Cambrer (a beam); bomber (a road). ‖ NAUT. Tonturer.
— v. intr. Se cambrer (beam); bomber (road).

cambist ['kæmbist] n. FIN. Cambiste *m.*

Cambodia [kæm'boudiə] n. GEOGR. Cambodge *m.*

Cambrian ['kæmbriən] adj., n. GEOGR. Gallois *s.* ‖ GEOL. Cambrien *m.*

cambric ['keimbrik] n. Batiste *f.* (cloth). ‖ Mouchoirs *m. pl.* ‖ U. S. *Cambric tea*, thé au lait.

came [keim] pret. See COME.

came n. Plomb *m.* (for stained-glass windows).

camel ['kæməl] n. ZOOL. Chameau *m.; she-camel*, chamelle. ‖ NAUT. Chameau *m.* ‖ Camel-corps, n. MILIT. Méharistes *m. pl.*

cameleer [kæmi'liə*] n. Chamelier *m.*

camellia [kə'mi:liə] n. BOT. Camélia *m.*

cameo ['kæmiou] n. Camée *m.*

camera ['kæmərə] n. Appareil photographique *m.; camera obscura*, chambre noire. ‖ JUR. Chambre *f.; in camera*, à huis clos; *in camera*, en délibéré. ‖ CINEM. *Motion-picture camera*, caméra.

cameraman [-,mən] n. CINEM. Caméraman *m.*

camerlingo [,kæmə:'liŋgou] n. Camerlingue *m.*

cami-knickers [kæmi'nikə:z] n. Chemise-culotte *f.*

camisole ['kæmisoul] n. † Camisole *f.* ‖ Cache-corset *m.*

camomile ['kæmomail] n. BOT. Camomille *f.* ‖ MED. *Camomile tea*, camomille.

camouflage ['kæmufla:ʒ] n. MILIT., FIG. Camouflage *m.*
— v. tr. MILIT., FIG. Camoufler.

camp [kæmp] n. Camp, campement *m.* (of nomads, travellers). ‖ Camp *m.* (persons); *holiday camp*, colonie de vacances. ‖ Camping *m.* ‖ MILIT. Camp *m.* ‖ FIG. Camp, parti *m.; in the same camp*, du même bord. ‖ Camp-bed, n. Lit de camp *m.* ‖ Camp-chair, n. Chaise pliante (*f.*) de jardin. ‖ Camp-craft, n. SPORTS. Art du camping *m.* ‖ Camp-equipment, n. Matériel de campement *m.* ‖ Camp-fire, n. Feu de camp *m.* ‖ Camp-follower, n. Racaille (*f.*) qui suit une armée; cantinier *s.* ‖ Camp-meeting, n. U. S. Réunion religieuse (*f.*) en plein air. ‖ Camp-stool, n. Pliant *m.*
— v. intr. Camper. ‖ To camp out, faire du camping, camper.
— v. tr. MILIT. Faire camper.

camp adj. FAM. Maniéré (affected); efféminé (effeminate); homosexuel (homosexual); m'as-tu-vu, voyant (showy); kitsch, rétro (kitsch).
— n. FAM. Affectation, pose *f.* (behaviour).
— v. tr. FAM. Rendre affecté (or) efféminé; *to camp it up*, en rajouter, poser pour la galerie.

campaign [kæm'pein] n. MILIT., FIG. Campagne *f.*
— v. intr. Faire campagne.

campaigner [-ə*] n. MILIT. Vétéran.

campanile [kæmpə'ni:li] n. ARCHIT. Campanile *m.*

campanology [-'nɔlədʒi] n. Art du sonneur *m.*

campanula [kəm'pænjulə] n. BOT. Campanule *f.*

campeachy [kæm'pi:t∫i] m. Campêche *m.*

camper ['kæmpə*] n. SPORTS. Campeur *s.*

camphor ['kæmfə*] n. CHIM. Camphre *m.* ‖ Camphor-tree, n. BOT. Camphrier *m.*

camphorate [-fɔreit] v. tr. Camphrer.

camping ['kæmpiŋ] n. SPORTS. Camping *m.; to go camping*, faire du camping. ‖ MILIT. Campement *m.*

campion ['kæmpiən] n. BOT. Lychnis, silène *m.*

campsite ['kæmpsait] n. Terrain de camping, camping m.

campus [-əs] n. U. S. Terrain (m.) de collège ou d'école, campus m.

camwood ['kæmwud] n. Bois de campêche m.

can [kæn] v. Pouvoir, être capable de ; *she cannot speak in public,* elle ne peut parler en public. ‖ Pouvoir, avoir envie de ; *I could have wept,* j'en aurais pleuré. ‖ Pouvoir, avoir la possibilité de ; *it cannot be realized,* c'est impossible à réaliser ; *that can be taken to pieces,* démontable ; *ugly as could be,* laid autant que faire se peut. ‖ Savoir, être en mesure de ; *she can speak English,* elle sait parler anglais. ‖ Pouvoir, avoir la permission de (may) ; *you can go,* vous pouvez disposer.

can n. Canette f. (of beer) ; bidon m. (of milk). ‖ Boîte (f.) en fer blanc (or) à conserve (tin). ‖ FAM. *To let s.o. carry the can,* faire payer à qqn les pots cassés. ‖ **Can-opener,** n. Ouvre-boîte m.
— v. tr. (1). CULIN. Mettre en conserve, conserver.

Canada ['kænədə] n. GEOGR. Canada m.
— adj. Du Canada.

Canadian [kə'neidjən] adj., n. GEOGR. Canadian s.

canal [kə'næl] n. MED., GEOGR. Canal m.
— v. tr. (1). Canaliser (a country).

canalize ['kænəlaiz] v. tr. Canaliser (a country, a river).

canapé ['kænəpi] n. CULIN. Canapé m.

canard [kæ'nɑ:d] n. FAM. Canard m. (false news).

Canary [kə'nɛəri] adj. GEOGR. Canaries (Islands).

canary n. ZOOL. Canari, serin m. ‖ Serin m. (colour). ‖ U. S. Mouchard m. ‖ **Canary-seed,** n. BOT. Millet m. ‖ **Canary-yellow,** adj. Jaune serin.

canasta [kə'næstə] n. Canasta f.

cancan ['kænkæn] n. Cancan m. (dance).

cancel ['kænsəl] v. tr. (1). Biffer, rayer, barrer (a word). ‖ Annuler (a journey, an order) ; *to cancel an invitation,* décommander les invités, annuler une invitation. ‖ JUR. Résilier (a contract) ; révoquer (a decree, a will) ; radier (a mortgage). ‖ FIN., COMM. Annuler (a cheque, an order). ‖ MATH. Diviser par (a common factor).
— n. Annulation f. ‖ Deleatur m. (in printing). ‖ CH. DE F. Pl. Poinçonneuse f. (tool).

cancellated [-leitid] adj. BOT. Réticulé. ‖ MED. Poreux.

cancellation [,kænsə'leiʃən] n. Fait (m.) d'effacer. ‖ Annulation f. ; contre-ordre m.

cancer ['kænsə*] n. ASTRON., MED. Cancer m. ‖ **Cancer-producing,** adj. MED. Cancérigène.

cancerous [-əs] adj. MED. Cancéreux.

cancroid ['kæŋkrɔid] adj. MED. Cancériforme.
— n. MED., ZOOL. Cancroïde m.

candela [kæn'di:lə] n. PHYS. Candela f.

candelabrum [,kændi'lɑ:brəm] (pl. **candelabra** [-brə]) n. Candélabre m.
— N. B. L'usage moderne tend à employer *candelabra* au sing., *candelabras* au pl.

candescent [kæn'desnt] adj. Incandescent.

candid ['kændid] adj. Franc, sincère, loyal ; *candid friend,* ami qui se pique de franchise (or) qui vous dit vos quatre vérités. ‖ Impartial ; libre de toute prévention (mind). ‖ FAM. *Candid camera,* petit appareil pour photographie impromptue.

candidacy [-əsi] n. U. S. Candidature f.

candidate [-it] n. Candidat s. (for, à).

candidature [-itʃə*] n. Candidature f.

candidly [-kændidli] adv. Franchement. ‖ Impartialement.

candidness [-nis] n. Franchise f. ‖ Impartialité f.

candied ['kændid] adj. CULIN. Candi, confit, glacé.
— † Doucereux.

candle [kændl] n. *Tallow candle,* chandelle ; *wax candle,* bougie. ‖ ECCLES. Cierge m. ‖ ELECTR. Bougie f. ‖ FIG. *Not to be fit to hold a candle to,* ne pas venir à la cheville de ; *to burn the candle*

at both ends, brûler la chandelle par les deux bouts ; *to hold a candle to the devil,* tenir la chandelle. ‖ **Candle-end,** n. Bout (m.) de chandelle. ‖ **Candle-grease,** n. Suif m. ‖ **Candle-power,** n. ELECTR. Bougie f. ‖ **Candle-snuffer,** n. Moucheur (m.) de chandelles ; mouchette f.

candlelight [-lait] n. Lumière d'une chandelle f. ; *by candlelight,* à la chandelle.

Candlemas [-məs] n. ECCLES. Chandeleur f.

candlestick ['kændl,stik] n. Bougeoir, chandelier m.

cando(u)r ['kændə*] n. Franchise, spontanéité f. ‖ Impartialité f.

candy ['kændi] n. Sucre candi m. ‖ U. S. Bonbon m. ; *candy store,* confiserie.
— v. tr. (2). Confire, glacer (fruit) ; faire cristalliser (or) candir (sugar).
— v. intr. Se candir (sugar).

cane [kein] n. Canne f. (walking stick). ‖ Férule, canne f (stick). ‖ BOT. Canne f. (of bamboo, rattan, reed). ‖ COMM. Bâton m. ; baguette f. (of sulphur, wax). ‖ **Cane-sugar,** n. Sucre (m.) de canne.
— v. tr. Fouetter. ‖ Canner (a chair).

canescent [kə'nesnt] adj. Blanchissant.

cangue [kæŋg] n. Cangue f.

canicular [kə'nikjulə*] adj. Caniculaire.

canine ['kænain] adj. ZOOL. Canin, de chien. ‖ MED. *Canine tooth,* canine.
— n. MED. Canine f. (See CUSPID, EYE-TOOTH.)

canister ['kænistə*] n. Boîte métallique f. ‖ MILIT. Boîte à mitraille f. ; *ammonia canister,* cartouche d'ammoniaque. ‖ ECCLES. Boîte à hosties f.

canker ['kæŋkə*] n. MED. Ulcère, chancre m. ‖ BOT., FIG. Chancre m. ‖ **Canker-worm,** n. BOT. Ver rongeur m.
— v. tr. MED., FIG. Ronger, ulcérer.
— v. intr. MED. S'ulcérer, se gangrener.

cankered [-əd] adj. MED. Ulcéré. ‖ FIG. Ulcéré, aigri.

cankerous [-rəs] adj. Dévorant, rongeur.

cannabis ['kænəbis] n. Cannabis, chanvre indien m. ; *cannabis resin,* cannabine, hachisch.

canned [kænd] adj. CULIN. En boîte, en conserve ; *canned goods,* conserves. ‖ FAM. Enregistré (music, speech). ‖ U. S. Rétamé (drunk) ; figé (hackneyed).

cannel ['kænl] n. Houille grasse f. (coal).

canner ['kænə*] n. Conserveur m.

cannery [-ri] n. Conserverie f.

cannibal ['kænibəl] n., adj. Cannibale m. (See ANTHROPOPHAGOUS.)

cannibalism [-lizm] n. Cannibalisme m.

cannibalize [-laiz] v. tr. TECHN. Démonter et réutiliser (an engine).

cannikin ['kænikin] n. Petit bidon m.

cannon ['kænən] n. MILIT. Pièce d'artillerie f. ; canon m. ‖ TECHN. Canon m. (of bit, key). ‖ SPORTS. Carambolage m. (in billiards). ‖ **Cannon-ball,** n. MILIT. Boulet de canon m. ‖ **Cannon-bit,** n. Canon de mors m. ‖ **Cannon-bone,** n. ZOOL. Canon m. ‖ **Cannon-fodder,** n. FAM. Chair (f.) à canon. ‖ **Cannon-shot,** n. Portée (f.) de canon (range) ; coup de canon m. (shot).
— v. intr. Caramboler (in billiards). ‖ Se jeter, se précipiter (against, sur) ; se heurter (against, contre).
— v. tr. U. S. Canonner.

cannonade [,kænə'neid] n. MILIT. Canonnade f.
— v. tr., intr. MILIT. Canonner.

cannoneer, cannonier [,kænə'niə*] n. MILIT. Canonnier-servant m.

cannot ['kænɔt]. See CAN.

cannula ['kænjulə] n. MED. Canule f.

canny ['kæni] adj. Prudent, circonspect (cautious) ; malin, rusé, finaud (shrewd) ; *canny Scot's answer,* réponse de Normand. ‖ **Ca'canny,** adj. FAM. Tout

doux; hésitant; *ca'canny strike,* grève perlée;
v. intr. FAM. Se la couler douce.

canoe [kə'nu:] n. NAUT. Canoë *m.; pirogue f.*
‖ FIG. *To paddle one's own canoe,* diriger sa barque.
— v. intr. NAUT. Faire du canoë.

canoeist [-ist] n. NAUT. Canoéiste, canotier *m.*

cañon ['kænjən] n. GEOGR. Cañon, canyon *m.*

canon ['kænən] n. Canon *m.;* règle *f.* (law). ‖
MUS., TECHN. Canon *m.* ‖ ECCLES. Canon *m.* (body
of laws; part of mass); chanoine *m.* (priest).

canoness [-is] n. Chanoinesse *f.*

canonical [kə'nɔnikəl] adj. ECCLES. Canonial, canonique (hours); de chanoine, du chapitre. ‖ MUS.
En forme de canon. ‖ FIG. Autorisé, qui fait foi
(or) autorité.
— n. pl. ECCLES. Vêtements sacerdotaux *m. pl.*

canonicate [kə'nɔnikeit] n. ECCLES. Canonicat *m.*

canonist ['kænənist] n. ECCLES. Canoniste *m.*

canonization [,kænənai'zeiʃən] n. ECCLES. Canonisation *f.*

canonize ['kænənaiz] v. tr. ECCLES. Canoniser.

canonry [-ri] n. ECCLES. Canonicat *m.*

canopy ['kænəpi] n. Baldaquin, ciel *m.* (of a bed);
dais *m.* (of a throne). ‖ ARCHIT. Baldaquin. ‖
ECCLES. Conopée *m.* ‖ AVIAT. *Ejectable canopy,*
verrière largable. ‖ FIG. Voûte *f.* (of the sky).
— v. tr. Surmonter d'un baldaquin (or) d'un dais
(or) d'un dôme.

canorous [kə'nɔ:rəs] adj. Mélodieux, musical, harmonieux.

cant [kænt] n. Pan coupé *m.* (bevelled edge); inclinaison *f.* (slope). ‖ Poussée déviatrice *f.* ‖ **Cant-
hook,** n. Grappin *m.*
— v. intr. ARCHIT. Pencher, s'incliner. ‖ NAUT.
Eviter.
— v. tr. Pencher, incliner (to tilt). ‖ Mettre en
biais; retourner (to overturn); pousser, repousser
(to toss). ‖ Couper les coins, biseauter (to bevel).
‖ NAUT. Mettre à la bande.

cant n. Argot de métier, jargon *m.* ‖ Langage
conventionnel *m.;* lieux communs *m. pl.* ‖ Phraséologie *f.;* boniment *m.* ‖ Tartuferie *f.;* puritanisme hypocrite *m.*
— adj. Conventionnel, banal, stéréotypé (language).
— v. intr. Parler avec hypocrisie; papelarder.

cant n. Encan *m.;* enchère *f.*
— v. tr. Vendre à l'encan.

cantaloup(e) ['kæntəlu:p] n. BOT. Cantaloup *m.*

cantankerous [kæn'tæŋkərəs] adj. Acariâtre,
revêche, hargneux.

cantankerousness [-nis] n. Irascibilité, hargne,
mauvaise humeur *f.*

cantata [kæn'tɑ:tə] n. MUS. Cantate *f.*

cantatrice [kɑ̃tæ'tri:s] n. MUS. Cantatrice *f.*

canteen [kæn'ti:n] n. Cantine *f.* (restaurant). ‖
MILIT. Bidon *m.* (flask); cantine *f.* (mess-tin). ‖
NAUT. Cambuse *f.* ‖ SPORTS. Ustensiles de campe-
ment *m.* ‖ CULIN. Ménagère *f.* ‖ **Canteen-cup,** n.
MILIT. Quart *m.* ‖ **Canteen-keeper,** n. MILIT. Can-
tinier *m.;* NAUT. Cambusier *m.*

canter ['kæntə*] n. Petit galop *m.* ‖ FAM. *To win
in a canter,* arriver dans un fauteuil.
— v. intr. Aller au petit galop.
— v. tr. Mener au petit galop.

canter n. Tartufe; puritain hypocrite *m.*

Canterbury ['kæntəbəri] n. GEOGR. Canterbury,
Cantorbéry (†). ‖ BOT. *Canterbury bell,* campanule
carillon. ‖ MUS. Casier (*m.*) à musique.

cantharis ['kænθəris] (pl. **cantharides** [kæn'θæ-
ridi:z]) n. ZOOL. Cantharide *f.*

canticle ['kæntikl] n. ECCLES. Cantique, hymne
m. ‖ Pl. Cantique (*m.*) des Cantiques.

cantilever ['kæntili:və*] n. ARCHIT. Encorbellement *m.* ‖ TECHN. Cantilever *m.* ‖ **Cantilever-
bridge,** n. Pont à encorbellement *m.*

cantle ['kæntl] n. Tranche *f.* (slice). ‖ Troussequin *m.* (of a saddle).

canto ['kæntou] n. Chant *m.* (of a poem).

canton ['kæntɔn] n. Canton *m.* (district). ‖ BLAS.
Canton.
— [kæn'tən] v. tr. Diviser en cantons.
— [kæn'tu:n] v. tr. MILIT. Cantonner.

cantonal ['kæntənl] adj. Cantonal.

cantonment [kæn'tu:nmənt] n. MILIT. Cantonnement *m.; close cantonment,* cantonnement-bivouac.

cantor ['kæntɔ:*] n. MUS., ECCLES. Maître (*m.*) de
chapelle, premier chantre *m.* (in church); cantor *m.*
(in German churches); hazan *m.* (in synagogue).

canvas ['kænvəs] n. Grosse toile *f.; tailor's canvas*
toile tailleur. ‖ Toile de tente *f.; under canvas,* sous
la tente. ‖ Canevas *m.* ‖ NAUT. Voile à voile *f.* ‖
ARTS. Toile; peinture *f.* ‖ **Canvas-stretcher,** n.
Châssis *m.*
— adj. En toile; *canvas chair,* chaise pliante; *canvas shoes,* espadrilles. ‖ De toile, de tente; *canvas
town,* village de toile.

canvass n. Campagne électorale *f.*
— v. tr. Discuter (to discuss); scruter, examiner
soigneusement (to examine). ‖ Faire une tournée
électorale dans (a district); solliciter la voix de (a
voter). ‖ COMM. Démarcher, visiter (the customers),
prospecter (a town).
— v. intr. Faire une campagne électorale (*for,* en
faveur de). ‖ COMM. Prospecter la clientèle, faire
la place (or) le démarcheur.

canvasser [-ə*] n. Agent (or) courtier électoral *m.*
‖ COMM. Placier, démarcheur, représentant, prospecteur *m.*

canyon ['kænjən] n. GEOGR. Cañon *m.*

canzonet [,kænzo'net] n. MUS. Chansonnette *f.*

caoutchouc ['kautʃu:k] n. Caoutchouc *m.*

cap [kæp] n. Bonnet *m.* (of a baby); toque *f.* (of a
judge, professor, woman); casquette *f.* (visored
cap); *cap of liberty,* bonnet phrygien. ‖ Capsule *f.*
(of a bottle); capuchon *m.* (of a fountain-pen);
coiffe *f.* (of a fuse); chape *f.* (of a magnetic needle)
chapeau *m.* (of a valve); cuvette *f.* (of a watch). ‖
MILIT. Képi *m.,* casquette *f.* (of an officer); coiffe
calotte *f.* (of a shell); bonnet (*m.*) de police (of a
soldier). ‖ NAUT. Chouquet *m.* (of a mast); béret *m.*
(of a sailor). ‖ AUTOM. Bouchon *m.* (of a radiator)
‖ ARCHIT. Chapiteau *m.* ‖ SPORTS. Casquette *f.*
(headgear); équipier *m.* (player). ‖ ECCLES. Calotte
f. ‖ BOT. Chapeau *m.* (of a mushroom). ‖ ZOOL.
Capuchon *m.* ‖ FAM. *The cap fits,* l'allusion porte
to set one's cap at, jeter le grappin (or) son dévolu
sur; *to throw one's cap over the windmill,* jeter son
bonnet par-dessus les moulins. ‖ **Cap-a-pie,** adv
De pied en cap. ‖ **Cap-paper,** n. Papier d'emballage
m. ‖ **Cap-stone,** n. ARCHIT. Pierre (*f.*) de faîte.
— v. tr. (1). Coiffer (s.o.). ‖ Capsuler (a bottle).
Couvrir, couronner (*with,* de) ‖ SPORTS. Choisir
pour l'équipe nationale (a player). ‖ MILIT. Amorcer (shell). ‖ FAM. Surpasser, renchérir sur; *to
cap the climax,* atteindre le comble; *that caps
everything!,* c'est le bouquet!

capability [,keipə'biliti] n. Possibilité *f.* (*to,* de)
‖ Pl. Capacités, possibilités *f. pl.;* moyens *m. pl*

capable ['keipəbl] adj. Capable, susceptible (of
de). ‖ Capable, compétent, qualifié, apte (able).

capably [-i] adv. Avec compétence (or) capacité.

capacious [kə'peiʃəs] adj. De grande capacité
spacieux, vaste.

capaciousness [-nis] n. Grande capacité *f.;* vastes
proportions *f. pl.*

capacitance [kə'pæsitəns] n. ELECTR. Capacité
électrostatique *f.*

capacitate [-eit] v. tr. Rendre capable (*for,* de). ‖
JUR. Habiliter (*for, to,* à); donner qualité (or) pou
voir (*for, to,* pour).

capacitor [-ə*] n. ELECTR. Condensateur *m.*

capacity [-i] n. Capacité, contenance *f.*; *filled to capacity*, rempli au maximum, comble. ‖ Faculté, possibilité (*for*, de); aptitude, capacité *f.*; talent *m.* (*for*, pour). ‖ Qualité *f.*; titre *m.*; *in his capacity as*, en sa qualité de. ‖ JUR. Qualité, capacité *f.*; pouvoir, caractère *m.*; *in one's official capacity*, dans l'exercice de ses fonctions.

caparison [kə'pærisn] n. Caparaçon *m.*

cape [keip] n. Cape *f.* ‖ Mante *f.* (mantle); collet *m.*, pèlerine *f.* (tippet).

cape n. GEOGR. Cap *m.* (headland); promontoire *m.* (promontory); *Cape Horn*, le cap Horn; *Cape of Good Hope*, le cap de Bonne-Espérance; *Cape Town*, Le Cap; *Cape Verde islands*, îles du Cap-Vert.

caper ['keipə*] n. BOT. Câprier *m.* ‖ CULIN. Câpre *f.* ‖ *Caper-sauce*, n. CULIN. Sauce (*f.*) aux câpres.

caper n. Cabriole *f.*; entrechat *m.*; *to cut a caper*, faire des gambades. ‖ FAM. Entourloupette *f.*
— v. intr. GEOGR. Cabrioler, gambader; faire des entrechats. (See GAMBOL.)

capercailzie [ˌkæpə'keilzi], **capercaillie** [-keilji] n. ZOOL. Coq (*m.*) de bruyère.

capful ['kæpful] n. Pleine casquette *f.* ‖ NAUT. Bouffée *f.* (of wind). ‖ FAM. Poignée *f.*

capias ['keipiæs] n. JUR. Mandat d'amener.

capillarity [ˌkæpi'læriti] n. Capillarité *f.*

capillary [kə'piləri] adj., n. Capillaire, *m.*

capital ['kæpitl] adj. Capital, principal; *capital city*, capitale. ‖ Capital, primordial, dominant, essentiel. ‖ Majuscule, capitale (letter). ‖ NAUT. *Capital ship*, bâtiment de ligne. ‖ COMM. *Capital goods*, biens de production. ‖ FIN. Du capital; *capital levy*, impôt sur le capital. ‖ JUR. Capital (crime); *capital punishment*, peine capitale; *capital sentence*, condamnation à mort. ‖ FAM. Fameux, épatant, chic, formidable.
— interj. Parfait!, chic!
— n. Capitale *f.* (city). ‖ Capitale, majuscule *f.* (letter). ‖ ARCHIT. Chapiteau *m.* ‖ FIN. Capital *m.*; capitaux *m. pl.*; *capital invested*, mise de fonds. ‖ FIG. Profit *m.*; *to make capital out of*, tirer parti (or) profit de.

capitalism [-əlizm] n. Capitalisme *m.*

capitalist [-əlist] n. Capitaliste *s.*

capitalistic [ˌkæpitə'listik] adj. Capitaliste.

capitalization [ˌkæpitəlai'zeiʃən] n. FIN. Capitalisation *f.*

capitalize ['kæpitəlaiz] v. tr. FIN. Capitaliser. ‖ FIG. Tourner à son profit.

capitally [-əli] adv. Principalement, surtout. ‖ JUR. Par la peine de mort. ‖ FAM. Fameusement, formidablement, merveilleusement.

capitation [ˌkæpi'teiʃən] n. JUR. Capitation; taxe par tête *f.*

Capitol [ˌkæpitl] n. Capitole; monument public *m.*

capitular [kæ'pitjulə*] adj. ECCLES. Capitulaire.

capitulary [-əri] n. JUR. Capitulaire *m.*

capitulate [-eit] v. intr. MILIT., FIG. Capituler.

capitulation [kəˌpitju'leiʃən] n. Résumé énumératif (*m.*) des points principaux; récapitulation *f.* ‖ JUR., MILIT. Capitulation *f.* (See SURRENDER.)

capon ['keipən] n. ZOOL. Chapon *m.*

caponize [-aiz] v. tr. Chaponner.

caporal [ˌkæpə'rɑ:l] n. Caporal *m.* (tobacco).

capote [kæ'pɔt] n. Capote *f.* (bonnet, cloak, hood).

caprice [kə'pri:s] n. Caprice *m.*

capricious [kə'priʃəs] adj. Capricieux.

capriciously [-li] adv. Capricieusement.

capriciousness [-nis] n. Caprice *m.*; inconstance *f.*

Capricorn ['kæprikɔ:n] n. ASTRO. Capricorne *f.*

caprine ['kæprain] adj. ZOOL. Caprin.

capriole ['kæprioul] adj. Cabriole *f.*
— v. intr. Cabrioler. (See CAPER.)

capsicum ['kæpsikəm] n. BOT. Piment; poivron *m.*

capsize [kæp'saiz] v. intr. NAUT. Chavirer. ‖ AUTOM. Capoter.

— v. tr. NAUT. Faire chavirer. ‖ AUTOM. Faire capoter. (See UPSET.)
— n. NAUT. Chavirement *m.* ‖ AUTOM. Capotage *m.*

capstan ['kæpstən] n. NAUT. Cabestan *m.*

capsular ['kæpsjulə*] adj. Capsulaire.

capsule [-sju:l] n. Capsule *f.* (of a bottle). ‖ BOT., CHIM. Capsule. ‖ MED. Capsule, gélule *f.* ‖ RADIO. *Transmitter capsule*, pastille microphonique.
— v. tr. Capsuler. ‖ U. S. Condenser.

captain ['kæptin] n. MILIT., SPORTS. Capitaine *m.* ‖ NAUT. Capitaine de vaisseau. *m.* ‖ ZOOL. Grondin *m.* ‖ FIG. Capitaine, chef *m.* (in industry); *captain of a school*, major.
— v. tr. MILIT. Commander. ‖ SPORTS. Etre le capitaine de. ‖ FIG. Diriger.

captaincy [-si] n. MILIT. Grade de capitaine *m.*; *to obtain one's captaincy*, passer capitaine.

captainship [-ʃip] n. MILIT. Fonctions (*f. pl.*) de capitaine. ‖ FIG. Direction *f.*

caption ['kæpʃən] n. Intitulé, en-tête; sous-titre *m.*, légende *f.*; chapeau *m.* (heading). ‖ JUR. Prise (*f.*) de corps, arrestation *f.* (arrest).

captious [-ʃəs] adj. Captieux, insidieux. (See SPECIOUS.) ‖ Vétilleux, pointilleux, chicaneur (quibbling).

captiousness [-nis] n. Esprit chicaneur *m.*

captivate ['kæptiveit] v. tr. Captiver (to absorb); captiver, fasciner, séduire (to bewitch).

captivating [-iŋ] adj. Captivant.

captive ['kæptiv] adj. Captif, prisonnier. ‖ De captif, de captivité (state).
— n. Captif *s.* (See PRISONER.)

captivity [kæp'tiviti] n. Captivité *f.*

captor ['kæptə*] n. JUR. Ravisseur *m.* ‖ NAUT. Vaisseau capteur *m.*

capture ['kæptʃə*] n. Prise *f.* (booty); capture (seizure).
— v. tr. Capturer.

capuche [kə'pu:ʃ] n. ECCLES. Capuce *m.*

capuchin [kæpu'ʃi:n] n. Cape (*f.*) à capuchon. ‖ ECCLES. Capucin *m.* ‖ ZOOL. Sapajou *m.*

car [kɑ:*] n. † Char *m.* (of the sun). ‖ AUTOM. Voiture *f.*; automobile *f.* ‖ CH. DE F. U. S. Wagon *m.*; voiture *f.* ‖ AVIAT. Nacelle *f.* ‖ U. S. Cabine (*f.*) d'ascenseur. ‖ *Car-fare*, n. Prix du trajet en tramway *m.* ‖ **Car-licence**, n. AUTOM. Carte grise *f.* ‖ **Carload**, n. Voiturée *f.* ‖ **Car-park**, n. AUTOM. Parking, parc de stationnement *m.* ‖ **Car-sickness**, n. Mal des transports *m.*

carabineer [ˌkærəbi'niə*] n. MILIT. Carabinier *m.*

caracole ['kærəkoul] n. Caracole *f.*
— v. intr. Caracoler.

caracul ['kærəkʌl] n. COMM. Caracul *m.*

carafe [kə'rɑ:f] n. Carafe *f.* (decanter); carafon *m.* (small carafe).

caramel ['kærəmel] n. CULIN. Caramel *m.*; *caramel custard*, crème caramélisée.

caramelize [-aiz] v. tr. CULIN. Caraméliser.

carapace ['kærəpeis] n. Carapace *f.*

carat ['kærət] n. Carat *m.*

caravan [kærə'væn] n. Caravane *f.* ‖ Roulotte *f.* (vehicle). ‖ AUTOM. Roulotte-remorque, caravane *f.*
— v. tr. AUTOM. Circuler en roulotte-remorque.

caravaneer [-iə*] n. Caravanier *m.*

caravanserai [-sərai] n. Caravansérail *m.*

caravel ['kærəvel] n. NAUT. Caravelle *f.*

caraway ['kærəwei] n. BOT., CULIN. Cumin, carvi *m.*

carbide ['kɑ:baid] n. CHIM. Carbure *m.*

carbine ['kɑ:bain] n. MILIT. Carabine *f.*

carbohydrate [ˌkɑ:bo'haidreit] n. CHIM. Hydrate de carbone, glucide *m.*

carbolic [kɑ:'bɔlik] adj. CHIM. Phénique; *carbolic acid*, carbol, phénol.

carbon ['kɑ:bən] n. CHIM. Carbone *m.* ‖ ELECTR., ARTS. Charbon *m.* ‖ Carbone *m.* (copy, paper). ‖ **Carbon-copy**, n. Double (*m.*) au carbone. ‖ Car-

bon dating, n. Datation *(f.)* au carbone 14 (or) au radiocarbone. ‖ **Carbon dioxide,** n. CHIM. Dioxyde de carbone, gaz carbonique *m.; carbon dioxide snow,* neige carbonique. ‖ **Carbon monoxide,** n. CHIM. Monoxyde de carbone *m.* ‖ **Carbon paper,** m. Papier carbone *m.*

carbonaceous [kɑ:bəˈneiʃəs] adj. Charbonneux. ‖ CHIM. Carboné.

carbonate [ˈkɑ:bənit] n. CHIM. Carbonate *m.*
— [-eit] v. tr. CHIM. Carbonater.

carbonic [ka:ˈbɔnik] adj. CHIM. Carbonique.

carboniferous [kɑ:bəˈnifərəs] adj. Carbonifère.

carbonize [ˈkɑ:bənaiz] v. tr. CHIM. Carboniser. ‖ TECHN. Calaminer (an engine); passer au carbone (paper); charbonner (wood).

carbonyl [ˈkɑ:bɔnil] n. CHIM. Carbonyle *m.*

carborundum [kærbəˈrʌndəm] n. CHIM. Carborundum *m.*

carboxyl [ka:ˈbɔksail] n. CHIM. Carboxyle *m.*

carboxylic [kɑ:bɔkˈsilik] adj. CHIM. *Carboxylic acid,* acide carboxylique.

carboy [ˈkɑ:bɔi] n. Bonbonne *f.*

carbuncle [ˈkɑ:bʌŋkl̩] n. Escarboucle *f.* ‖ MED. Anthrax *m.* ‖ FAM. Bouton *m.*

carbuncular [-kjulə*] adj. MED. Charbonneux.

carburet [kɑ:bjuˈret] v. tr. CHIM. Carburer.

carburettor [-ə*] n. AUTOM. Carburateur *m.*

carburize [ˈkɑ:bjuraiz] v. tr. TECHN. Carburer.

carcass, carcase [ˈkɑ:kəs] n. Carcasse *f.* (of animal); cadavre *m.* (of animal, man). ‖ NAUT., TECHN. Charpente, carcasse *f.* ‖ FAM. Carcasse, peau *f.*

carcinogen [kɑ:ˈsinədʒən] n. MED. Substance cancérigène *f.*

carcinogenic [ˌkɑ:sinəˈdʒənik] adj. MED. Cancérigène.

carcinoma [kærsiˈnoumə] n. MED. Carcinome *m.*

card [kɑ:d] n. Carte *f.* (playing card); *to play one's cards well,* bien mener son jeu. ‖ Carte de visite *f.* (visiting-card). ‖ Carte *f.* (postcard, written invitation); *wedding card,* faire-part de mariage. ‖ Carte *f.* (printed programme); *admission card,* carte d'entrée; *race card,* programme des courses. ‖ Fiche *f.; school record card,* fiche scolaire. ‖ COMM. Carte *f.* (of wool). ‖ NAUT. Rose *(f.)* des vents. ‖ FAM. Original, numéro *m.* (person); *on the cards,* écrit, probable; *to ask for one's card,* rendre son tablier; *to speak by the card,* parler comme un augure; *to throw up the cards,* abandonner la partie. ‖ **Card-case,** n. Porte-cartes *m.* ‖ **Card-catalogue** (or) **-file** (or) **-index,** n. Fichier *m.* ‖ **Card-sharper,** n. Tricheur, bonneteur *m.* ‖ **Card-table,** n. Table *(f.)* de jeu.

card n. TECHN. Carde *f.*
— v. tr. Carder.

cardan [ˈkɑ:dən] adj. TECHN. *Cardan joint,* cardan, joint de cardan, joint universel; *cardan shaft,* arbre à cardan.

cardboard [-bɔ:d] n. Carton *m.*

carder [-ə*] n. Cardeuse *f.* (machine); cardeur *s.* (person).

cardia [ˈkɑ:diə] n. MED. Cardia *m.*

cardiac [ˈkɑ:diæk] adj. MED. Du cœur; cardiaque.
— n. MED. Remède cardiaque *m.*

cardigan [ˈkɑ:digən] n. Cardigan *m.*

cardinal [ˈkɑ:dinl̩] adj. Cardinal (number, point, virtue). ‖ Rouge vif (colour).
— n. ECCLES., ZOOL. Cardinal *m.* ‖ Rouge cardinal *m.* (colour).

cardinalate [-it], **cardinalship** [-ʃip] n. ECCLES. Cardinalat *m.*
— adj. ECCLES. Cardinalice (purple).

cardiogram [ˈkɑ:diougræm] n. MED. Cardiogramme *m.*

cardiograph [-grɑf] n. MED. Cardiographe *m.*

cardiologist [kɑ:diˈɔlɔdʒist] n. Cardiologue *m.*

cardiology [-dʒi] n. MED. Cardiologie *f.*

cardio-vascular [ˌkɑ:diouˈvæskjulə*] adj. MED. Cardio-vasculaire.

cardoon [kɑ:ˈdu:n] n. BOT. Cardon *m.*

care [kɛə*] n. Attention *f.; to take care,* faire attention, prendre garde. ‖ Soin *m.;* précaution *f.; to take care of,* prendre soin de. ‖ Soin *m.,* garde *f.; care of,* aux bons soins de (on a letter); *to put sth. in s.o.'s care,* confier à qqn la garde (or) le soin de qqch. ‖ Charge *f.; cares of State,* responsabilités d'Etat. ‖ Attentions *f. pl.;* ménagements *m. pl.; tender care,* sollicitude. ‖ Souci *m.;* inquiétude, préoccupation *f.; to have a care for,* être soucieux de, se préoccuper de. ‖ **Care-free,** adj Sans souci, insouciant. ‖ **Care-laden,** adj. Soucieux, chargé de soucis. ‖ **Care-taker,** n. Gardien concierge *s.;* U. S. Intérimaire *s.* ‖ **Care-worn,** adj Rongé par le souci.
— v. intr. Se soucier; *I don't care,* ça m'est égal. je m'en moque, je m'en soucie peu, peu me chaut ; *if you care to,* si vous en avez envie; si cela vous chante (fam.). ‖ *To care about* (or) *for,* se soucier de, s'intéresser à; *to care for nothing,* se désintéresser (or) se moquer de tout. ‖ *To care for,* avoir de la sympathie pour (s.o.); trouver plaisir à (sth.) *I don't care for him,* il ne me plaît pas; *I don't care for such a life,* une vie pareille ne me dit rien, je n'aimerais pas une vie pareille, vivre de la sorte ne me plairait pas. ‖ *To care for,* s'occuper de (children); soigner (an invalid). ‖ FAM. *I don't care a bean* (or) *a hang* (or) *two hoots,* je m'en fiche je m'en bats l'œil.

careen [kəˈri:n] v. tr. NAUT. Caréner.
— v. intr. NAUT. Donner de la bande.

careenage [-idʒ] n. NAUT. Carénage *m.*

career [kəˈriə*] n. Course *f.; in full career,* à tout vitesse. ‖ Carrière, profession *f.* ‖ FIG. Carrière vie *f.*
— v. intr. Aller à toute vitesse.

careerist [kəˈri:rist] n. Arriviste, ambitieux *s.*

careful [ˈkɛəful] adj. Attentif, approfondi, soigné (work); soigneux (workman). ‖ Prudent, circonspect (person); *to be careful that,* faire attention que, prendre garde que, avoir soin que. ‖ Soigneux (of, de); précautionneux (of, à l'égard de). ‖ Attentif (for, à); plein d'égards (for, pour).

carefully [-i] adv. Avec soin (attentively); avec prudence (cautiously).

carefulness [-nis] n. Soin *m.* ‖ Attention, précaution *f.* ‖ Sollicitude *f.*

careless [ˈkɛəlis] adj. Insouciant, sans souci (of de). [See CARE-FREE.] ‖ Négligent, insouciant (of de); inattentif, indifférent (of, à); sans précaution (of, pour). ‖ Sans artifice, naturel, spontané (grace) ‖ Inconsidéré, irréfléchi, étourdi (word).

carelessly [-li] adv. Avec insouciance (or) négligence; négligemment.

carelessness [-nis] n. Insouciance *f.* ‖ Négligence *f.;* laisser-aller, manque de soin *m.* ‖ Etourderie *f.*

caress [kəˈres] n. Caresse *f.*
— v. tr. Caresser. ‖ Cajoler, câliner.

caressingly [-iŋli] adv. D'une manière caressante avec câlinerie.

caret [ˈkærət] n. TECHN. Signe (*m.*) d'omission (in printing).

cargo [ˈkɑ:gou] n. NAUT. Cargaison *f.* ‖ **Cargo boat** (or) **-steamer,** n. NAUT. Cargo *m.*

Carib [ˈkærib] adj., n. GEOGR. Caraïbe *s.*

Caribbean [kæriˈbiːən] adj. GEOGR. Caraïbe *Caribbean sea,* mer des Antilles.

Caribbees [kæribiːz] n. pl. GEOGR. Petites Antille *f. pl.*

caribou [ˈkæribuː] n. ZOOL. Caribou *m.*

caricatural [ˌkærikəˈtjuərəl] adj. Caricatural.

caricature [-ˈtjuə*] n. Caricature *f.* ‖ Charge parodie *f.* (in literature).
— v. tr. Caricaturer. ‖ Tourner en ridicule.

caricaturist [-tjʋərist] n. Caricaturiste m.
caries ['kɛərii:z] (pl. caries) n. invar. MED. Carie f.
carillon [kə'riljən] n. Carillon m.
— v. intr. Carillonner.
carious ['kɛəriəs] adj. MED. Carié, gâté.
carking ['kɑ:kiŋ] adj. Rongeur, lourd (care);
dévorant (grief).
carling ['kɑ:liŋ] n. NAUT. Elongis m.
Carlovingian [kɑ:lo'vindʒiən] adj., n. Carolingien s.
carmagnole ['kæmənjoul] n. Carmagnole f.
carman ['kɑ:mən] (pl. carmen) n. Charretier, voiturier m. ‖ AUTOM. Camionneur m. ‖ COMM.
Livreur m. ‖ U. S. Conducteur de tramway m.
carmelite ['kɑ:milait] n. ECCLES. Carme m.
(monk); carmélite f. (nun).
carmine ['kɑ:main] adj., n. Carmin m.
carnage ['kɑ:nidʒ] n. Carnage m. (See SLAUGHTER.)
carnal ['kɑ:nl] adj. Charnel, de la chair (fleshly).
‖ Sexuel; to have carnal knowledge of, avoir
des relations sexuelles avec. ‖ Mondain, matériel
(worldly).
carnality [kɑ:'næliti] n. Sensualité f.
carnation [kɑ:'neiʃən] n. Incarnat m.
— adj. Incarnadin.
carnation n. BOT. Œillet m.
carnet ['kɑ:nei] n. AUTOM. Triptyque m.
carnival ['kɑ:nivəl] n. Carnaval m.; jours gras
m. pl. ‖ Fête, réjouissance f. (festivity). ‖ U. S. Fête
foraine f. ‖ FIG. Débauche, orgie f.
carnivora [kɑ:'nivərə] n. pl. ZOOL. Carnivores
m. pl.
carnivorous [-əs] adj ZOOL. Carnivore, carnassier.
carny ['kɑ:ni] v. tr. FAM. Cajoler, amadouer.
carob ['kærəb] n. BOT. Caroube f. ‖ Carob-tree,
n. BOT. Caroubier m.
carol ['kærəl] n. Ramage m. (of birds); chant m.
(of the lark). ‖ MUS. Chant joyeux m.; Christmas
carol, noël.
— v. tr. (1). Chanter (to celebrate).
— v. intr. Chanter (bird); tire-lirer (lark). ‖ MUS.
Chanter gaiement.
Caroline ['kærəlain] adj. Du temps de Charlemagne (or) des rois Charles d'Angleterre.
Carolingian [kærə'lindʒjən] adj., n. Carolingien s.
carom ['kærəm] n. SPORTS. U. S. Carambolage m.
— v. intr. U. S. Caramboler.
carotene ['kærəti:n] n. CHIM. Carotène m.
carotid [kə'rɔtid] adj., n. MED. Carotide f.
carousal [kə'rauzəl] n. Beuverie, bamboche, bombe,
noce, bringue f.
carouse [kə'rauz] v. intr. Nocer, bambocher.
— n. Beuverie f. (See CAROUSAL.)
carousel [kærə'sel] n. † Carrousel m. ‖ TECHN.
Tapis roulant, convoyeur m. ‖ U. S. Manège m.
carouser [-ə*] n. Noceur, fêtard m.
carp [kɑ:p] n. ZOOL. Carpe f.; young carp, carpeau.
carp v. intr. To carp at, critiquer, débiner, déblatérer sur (s.o.); trouver à redire à (sth.).
carpenter ['kɑ:pəntə*] n. ARCHIT. Charpentier,
menuisier m. (See JOINER.) ‖ Carpenter-scene, n.
THEATR. Scène (f.) jouée devant les toiles pendant
un changement de décor.
— v. intr. Menuiser.
carpentry [-ri] n. ARCHIT. Charpenterie, grosse
menuiserie f. (trade, work); charpente f. (of building).
carper ['kɑ:pə*] n. Censeur, zoïle; débineur m.
(fam.) ‖ FAM. Rouspéteur, ronchon m.
carpet ['kɑ:pit] n. Tapis m. ‖ FIG. On the carpet,
sur la sellette (person); sur le tapis (subject). ‖
Carpet-beater, n. Tapette f. ‖ Carpet-bed, n.
AGRIC. Parterre m. ‖ Carpet-rod, n. Tringle (f.) de
tapis. ‖ Carpet-sweeper, n. Balai mécanique m.
— v. tr. Recouvrir d'un tapis. ‖ FIG. Mettre sur la
sellette.

carpetbagger [-bægə*] n. FAM. U. S. Candidat (m.)
à la députation hors de son département.
carping ['kɑ:piŋ] adj. Pointilleux, vétilleux, malveillant, chicaneur. (See CAPTIOUS.)
— n. Critique malveillante, chicane f.; débinage
m. (fam.).
carpingly [-li] adv. Avec chicanerie (or) malveillance; de façon pointilleuse.
carpus ['kɑ:pəs] n. MED. Carpe m.
Carrara [kə'rɑ:rə] n. Carrara marble, carrare.
carriage ['kæridʒ] n. Transport, charriage, port m.
(conveyance). ‖ Frais (m. pl.) de port; factage m.
(cost); carriage to pay, port dû. ‖ Conduite, gestion, direction f. (of affairs). ‖ Maintien m.; attitude, posture, pose f. (bearing); comportement m.
(behaviour). ‖ Voiture f. (vehicle); carriage and
pair, voiture (or) équipage à deux chevaux. ‖
TECHN. Chariot m. (of a typewriter); châssis m. (of
a vehicle). ‖ MILIT. Affût m. (of a gun). ‖ JUR.
Vote m. ‖ PHYS. Chariot m. (of the rocket). ‖
Carriage-builder, n. Carrossier m. ‖ Carriage-
clock, n. Pendulette (f.) de voyage. ‖ Carriage-
dog, n. ZOOL. Danois m. ‖ Carriage-drive, n.
Allée (f.) pour voitures. ‖ Carriage-folk, n. Gens
(m. pl.) possédant un équipage. ‖ Carriage-for-
ward, adj. En port dû. ‖ Carriage-free, adj.
Franco. ‖ Carriage-paid, adj. En port payé. ‖
Carriage-way, n. Route carrossable f. ‖ Carriage-
window, n. Glace de portière f.
carriageable [-əbl] adj. Carrossable, charretier.
carrier ['kæriə*] n. Voiturier, camionneur, roulier,
transporteur m. ‖ MILIT. Transport m.; voiturette f.;
ammunition carrier, ravitailleur en munitions; full-
track cargo carrier, Bren carrier, chenillette; troop
carrier, transport de troupes. ‖ NAUT. Porte-avions
m.; landing-craft carrier, bateau-gigogne. ‖ AUTOM.
Porte-bagages m. ‖ U. S. MED. Germ carrier, porteur de bacilles. ‖ U. S. Rural carrier, facteur rural.
‖ Carrier-bag, n. Sac (m.) en papier (or) en plastique
(for shopping). ‖ Carrier-borne, adj. NAUT., AVIAT.
Embarqué. ‖ Carrier-pigeon, n. ZOOL. Pigeon voyageur m. ‖ Carrier-wave, n. RADIO. Onde électromagnétique continue, onde porteuse f.
carrion ['kæriən] n. Charogne f.
— adj. De charogne. ‖ Pourri, répugnant.
carrot ['kærət] n. BOT. Carotte f.
— n. pl. FAM. Poil (m.) de carotte.
carroty [-i] adj. Carotte, roux, rouge.
carrousel [kærə'sel] n. See CAROUSEL.
carry ['kæri] v. tr. (2.)

┌───┐
│ 1. Porter. — 2. Porter sur soi. — 3. Tenir. —│
│ 4. Comporter. — 5. Entraîner. — 6. Emporter. │
│ — 7. Pousser. — 8. Remporter. — 9. MILIT. — │
│ 10. ARCHIT. — 11. TECHN. — 12. MATH. —   │
│ 13. AGRIC. — 14. MED. — 15. JUR. — 16. COMM. │
│ — 17. To carry about. — 18. To carry along. │
│ — 19. To carry away. — 20. To carry back. — │
│ 21. To carry down. — 22. To carry forward.   │
│ — 23. To carry off. — 24. To carry on. —   │
│ 25. To carry out. — 26. To carry over. —   │
│ 27. To carry through.   │
└───┘

1. Porter (a basket, a package, s.o.); charrier
(goods); transporter (a load, s.o.); to carry twenty
persons, contenir vingt personnes (motor-coach);
to have as much as one can carry, en avoir sa
charge. ‖ 2. Porter sur soi, emporter avec soi;
porter (a sword, a watch). ‖ 3. Porter, tenir (one's
head). ‖ 4. Comporter, présenter; revêtir (a meaning); to carry authority, faire autorité; to carry
oneself proudly, se comporter orgueilleusement. ‖
5. Entraîner; inspirer; apporter; to carry consequences, entraîner des conséquences; to carry
death, porter (or) apporter la mort. ‖ 6. Entraîner,
emporter, transporter, soulever; to carry conviction,

emporter la conviction. ‖ **7.** Porter, pousser, conduire, mener (*to*, à); *to carry for*, amener loin; *to carry s.o. to*, porter (or) pousser (or) entraîner qqn à; *to carry to success*, mener à bonne fin. ‖ **8.** Remporter, gagner sur; *to carry all before one*, marcher en vainqueur, l'emporter sur tous les tableaux. ‖ **9.** MILIT. Emporter, enlever (a position); porter (a war). ‖ **10.** ARCHIT. Porter, soutenir, supporter (a beam, a vault). ‖ **11.** TECHN. Amener (pipes, water); conduire (sound). ‖ **12.** MATH. Reporter, retenir (a figure). ‖ **13.** AGRIC. Porter, produire (a crop). ‖ **14.** MED. *To carry a child*, porter un enfant, être enceinte. ‖ **15.** JUR. Faire passer, voter (a bill); être grevé de (a mortgage). ‖ **16.** COMM. Etre chargé de (goods, stocks). ‖ **17.** *To carry about*, porter sur soi, transporter. ‖ **18.** *To carry along*, entraîner, emporter. ‖ **19.** *To carry away*, entraîner, emporter (*by*, par) [s.o., sth.]; MED. Enlever, emporter; FIG. Transporter, soulever, ravir. ‖ **20.** *To carry back*, ramener (s.o.); rapporter (sth.); FIG. Ramener en arrière, reporter, faire remonter. **21.** *To carry down*, descendre, faire descendre; FIG. Faire accepter (or) passer; faire avaler (fam.). **22.** *To carry forward.* MATH. Reporter. ‖ **23.** *To carry off*, remporter (a prize); emmener, enlever (s.o.); emporter (sth.); MED. Enlever, emporter (sth.); FIG. Faire accepter (or) passer. ‖ **24.** *To carry on*, diriger (business); continuer, poursuivre, soutenir, reprendre (a conversation); entretenir (a correspondence); poursuivre, continuer (a tradition); exercer (a profession, a trade). ‖ **25.** *To carry out*, emporter, porter dehors (s.o., sth.); COMM. Exécuter (an order); FIG. Accomplir, mettre à exécution (a decision, an idea); effectuer (an experiment); satisfaire à (an obligation); exécuter (a plan); opérer (a reform); mettre en pratique (a theory); mener à bonne fin (an undertaking). ‖ **26.** *To carry over*, faire passer du côté opposé; FIN. Reporter. ‖ **27.** *To carry through*, tirer d'une difficulté, aider (s.o.); exécuter, réaliser, mener à terme (sth.).
— v. intr. Effectuer des transports, faire le voiturier. ‖ Porter (sound, voice). ‖ MILIT. Porter (*to*, jusqu'à). ‖ *To carry on*, continuer, persister, aller jusqu'au bout (to continue); se comporter (or) se conduire sottement (or) violemment (to behave); *to carry on with*, flirter (or) marcher avec (fam.).
— n. MILIT. Port (*m.*) d'armes (position); portée *f.* (of gun). ‖ SPORTS. Trajet *m.* (of a golf ball). ‖ NAUT. Portage *m.* ‖ **Carry-all**, n. U. S. Carriole *f.*; fourre-tout *m. inv.* (bag). ‖ **Carry-cot**, n. Porte-bébé *m.* ‖ **Carry-over**, n. FIN. Report *m.*

carrying(s)-on [͵kæriiŋ(z)'ɔn] n. (or) n. pl. FAM. Manières *f. pl.* (questionable behaviour); histoires, intrigues *f. pl.* (flirtation).

cart [kɑːt] n. Charrette *f.*; *tip cart*, tombereau. ‖ Voiturette *f.*; *apple cart*, voiture des quatre-saisons. ‖ MILIT. Fourgon *m.* ‖ FAM. *To put the cart before the horse*, mettre la charrue avant les bœufs; *to put s.o. in the cart*, mettre qqn dans le pétrin. ‖ **Cart-horse**, n. ZOOL. Cheval de trait *m.* ‖ **Cart-ladder**, n. Ridelle *f.* ‖ **Cart-load**, n. Charretée *f.* ‖ **Cart-wheel**, n. Roue de charrette *f.*; SPORTS. Roue *f.*
— v. tr. Charrier, camionner, voiturer, transporter. ‖ MILIT., FAM. Charrier, mettre en boîte (s.o.).

cartage [-idʒ] n. Camionnage, transport *m.*

carte [kɑːt] n. SPORTS. Quarte *f.* (in fencing).

carte n. Carte (*f.*) de restaurant; *à la carte*, à la carte. ‖ FIG. *Carte blanche*, carte blanche.

cartel [kɑːtəl] n. Cartel *m.*

cartelize [-aiz] v. intr. COMM. Former un cartel.

carter ['kɑːtə*] n. Charretier *m.* ‖ AUTOM. Camionneur *m.*

Cartesian [kɑːˈtiːziən] adj., n. Cartésien *m.*

cartful ['kɑːtful] n. Charretée *f.*

Carthage ['kɑːθidʒ] n. GEOGR. Carthage *f.*

Carthaginian [kɑːθəˈdʒinjən] adj., n. GEOGR. Carthaginois *s.*

Carthusian [kɑːˈθjuːziən] n. ECCLES. Chartreux *m.* ‖ FAM. Elève (*m.*) au collège de Charterhouse.
— adj. ECCLES. De Chartreux. ‖ FAM. De Charterhouse.

cartilage ['kɑːtilidʒ] n. MED. Cartilage *m.*

cartilaginous [͵kɑːtiˈlædʒinəs] adj. MED. Cartilagineux.

cartographer [kɑːˈtɔgrəfə*] n. Cartographe *s.*

cartographic [-ik] adj. Cartographique.

cartography [-i] n. Cartographie *f.*

cartomancy ['kɑːtəmænsi] n. Cartomancie *f.*

carton ['kɑːtən] n. Carton *m.* (box). ‖ SPORTS. Blanc (*m.*) de cible; mouche *f.*

cartoon [kɑːˈtuːn] n. Dessin satirique (or) humoristique *m.*; caricature *f.* ‖ ARTS. Carton *m.* (sketch). ‖ CINEM. Dessin animé.
— v. tr., intr. Caricaturer.

cartoonist [-ist] n. Caricaturiste, dessinateur humoriste *m.* ‖ Dessinateur (*m.*) de dessins animés.

cartouche [kɑːˈtuːʃ] n. ARCHIT. Cartouche *m.* ‖ MILIT. Gargousse *f.*

cartridge ['kɑːtridʒ] n. MILIT. Gargousse *f.* (of gun); cartouche *f.* (of rifle). ‖ **Cartridge-bag**, n. MILIT. Gargousse *f.* ‖ **Cartridge-belt**, n. MILIT. Cartouchière *f.* (belt); bande-chargeur *f.* (strip). ‖ **Cartridge-clip**, n. MILIT. Chargeur *m.* ‖ **Cartridge-paper**, n. Papier à cartouche *m.*

cartulary ['kɑːtjuləri] n. ECCLES. Cartulaire *m.*

cartwright ['kɑːtrait] n. Charron *m.*

carve [kɑːv] v. tr. ARTS. Sculpter, tailler, ciseler (*in, out of*, dans; *on*, sur). ‖ CULIN. Découper. ‖ FIG. Tailler; *to carve one's way*, s'ouvrir un chemin. ‖ FAM. Dépecer. ‖ **To carve out**, tailler; *to carve out a career for oneself*, se tailler une carrière. ‖ **To carve up**, diviser, dénombrer, dépecer.
— v. intr. ARTS. Sculpter. ‖ CULIN. Découper.

carvel ['kɑːvəl] n. NAUT. Caravelle *f.*

carver ['kɑːvə*] n. ARTS. Sculpteur, ciseleur *s.* ‖ CULIN. Couteau (*m.*) à découper (knife); personne (*f.*) qui découpe (person). ‖ † Ecuyer tranchant *m.*

carving [-iŋ] n. ARTS. Sculpture *f.* ‖ CULIN. Découpage *m.* ‖ **Carving-fork**, n. CULIN. Fourchette (*f.*) à découper. ‖ **Carving-knife**, n. CULIN. Couteau (*m.*) à découper. ‖ **Carving-up**, n. Dépeçage *m.*

caryatid [kæriˈætid] n. ARCHIT. Cariatide *f.*
— N. B. Deux pluriels : *caryatids*, *caryatides*.

cascade [kæsˈkeid] n. Cascade *f.* (See WATERFALL). ‖ FIG. Chute *f.* (of drapery); flot *m.* (of lace); pluie *f.* (of sparks).
— v. intr. Cascader, tomber en cascade.

cascara [kæsˈkɑːrə] n. BOT., MED. *Cascara sagrada*, cascara sagrada *f.*

case [keis] n. Cas, fait, événement *m.*; circonstance *f.*; *as the case may be*, selon le cas; *in any case*, en tout cas, dans tous les cas; *should such be the case*, le cas échéant; *to state the case*, exposer les faits. ‖ Cas, état *m.*; position, situation *f.*; *a bad case*, dans une mauvaise posture. ‖ Affaire *f.* *it's a case for the electrician*, ça regarde l'électricien; *the case is not pressing*, il n'y a pas péril en la demeure. ‖ Cas, exemple *m.* (instance); *it's the case with you*, c'est votre cas. ‖ Cas, problème *m.* *difficult case*, cas difficile. ‖ MED. Cas *m.* ‖ JUR. Affaire, cause, instance; matière (*f.*) à poursuites procès *m.*; considérants *m. pl.*; *concrete* (or) *individual case*, cas d'espèce; *in this particular case* en l'espèce; *there is no case against*, il n'y a pas lieu à poursuites contre; *to get up the case against* instruire contre; *to win one's case*, gagner son procès. ‖ GRAMM. Cas *m.* ‖ FAM. Type, caractère *m.* *hard case*, mauvais sujet. ‖ **Case-book**, n. JUR. Recueil (*m.*) de jurisprudence. ‖ **Case-history**, n. MED. Dossier médical *m.* ‖ **Case-law**, n. JUR.

Jurisprudence *f. ;* précédents *m. pl.* ‖ **Case-study,** n. Etude (*f.*) de cas, monographie *f.*

case n. Caisse *f.* (for packing). ‖ Boîte *f.* (box); écrin *m.* (casket); coffre *m.* (chest); cageot *m.* (crate). ‖ Caisse *f.* (quantity). ‖ Enveloppe *f.* (covering); couverture *f.* (of book); étui *m.* (for cigarettes, glasses); gaine *f.* (for a knife); fourreau *m.* (for an umbrella); boîtier *m.* (for a watch). ‖ TECHN. Chemise, boîte *f.* ‖ AUTOM. Carter *m.* ‖ COMM. Vitrine *f.* (display case). ‖ MED. Trousse *f.* ‖ MUS. Buffet *m.* (organ-case); boîte *f.* (violin-case). ‖ TECHN. Casse *f. ; upper, lower case,* haut, bas de casse (in printing). ‖ CULIN. Peau *f.* (of sausage). ‖ **Case-bottle,** n. Bouteille carrée *f.* ‖ **Case-harden,** v. tr. TECHN. Aciérer, cémenter; FIG. Endurcir. ‖ **Case-knife,** n. Couteau (*m.*) à gaine. ‖ **Case-shot,** n. MILIT., † Mitraille *f.*
— v. tr. Mettre en caisse (or) sous enveloppe. ‖ Envelopper; barder (*with,* de).

casein ['keisiin] n. Caséine *f. ; to produce casein,* caséifier.

casemate ['keismeit] n. MILIT. Casemate *f.*

casement ['keismənt] n. Battant (*m.*) de fenêtre (frame); croisée *f.* (window). ‖ **Casement-cloth,** n. Tissu de rideaux *m.* ‖ **Casement-window,** n. Croisée, fenêtre *f.*

caseous ['keiziəs] adj. Caséeux.

cash [kæʃ] n. Argent liquide, numéraire *m. ;* espèces *f. pl. ; out of cash,* démuni d'argent. ‖ FIN. Caisse, encaisse *f. ; cash in* (or) U. S. *on hand,* disponibilités, fonds en caisse, *shortness of cash,* gêne de trésorerie ; *to make up one's cash,* faire la caisse. ‖ COMM. *Cash offer,* offre réelle ; *cash on delivery,* livraison contre remboursement ; *to pay cash down,* payer comptant (or) cash. ‖ **Cash-and-carry,** adj. COMM. Au comptant et à emporter. ‖ **Cash-balance,** n. FIN. Solde (*m.*) de caisse. ‖ **Cash-book,** n. FIN. Livre (*m.*) de caisse. ‖ **Cash-clerk,** n. COMM. Caissier *f.* ‖ **Cash-desk,** n. Caisse *f.* ‖ **Cash-discount,** n. COMM. Escompte (*m.*) au comptant. ‖ **Cash-register,** n. COMM. Caisse enregistreuse *f.*
— v. tr. Changer (a banknote); encaisser, toucher (a cheque). ‖ **To cash in,** FIN. Déposer en banque ; U. S. FAM. Clamser (to die). ‖ **To cash in on,** U. S. Tirer profit de.

cashew [kə'ʃu:] n. BOT. Anacarde *m.* (nut); anacardier *m.* (tree).

cashier [kæˈʃiə*] n. FIN. Caissier *s.*

cashier [kəˈʃiə*] v. tr. Renvoyer. ‖ MILIT. Casser.

cashmere ['kæʃmiə*] n. GEOGR., COMM. Cachemire *m.*

casing ['keisiŋ] n. Enveloppe *f.* ‖ TECHN. Revêtement *m. ;* chemise *f.* ‖ AUTOM. Carter *m.* ‖ NAUT. Manchon *m.* (of rudder).

casino [kə'si:nou] n. Casino *m.*

cask [kɑ:sk] n. Tonneau *m. ;* barrique *f.*

casket ['kɑ:skit] n. Ecrin, coffret *m.* (for jewels); cassette *f.* (for money). ‖ U. S. Cercueil *m.* (coffin).

Caspian ['kæspjən] adj. GEOGR. Caspienne (sea).

casque [kæsk] n. Casque *m.* (of a suit of armour).

Cassandra [kə'sændrə] n. Cassandre *f.*

cassation [kæ'seiʃən] n. JUR. Cassation *f.*

cassava [kə'sɑ:və] n. Manioc *m.*

casserole ['kæsəroul] n. CULIN. Daubière *f.* (saucepan); cassoulet, ragoût (*m.*) en daube (stew). ‖ CHIM. Casserole *f.*

cassette [kæ'set] n. Cassette *f.* (sound recording); *cassette recorder,* magnétophone à cassettes. ‖ Chargeur *m.* (photo).

cassock ['kæsək] n. ECCLES. Soutane *f.*

cassowary ['kæsəwəri] n. ZOOL. Casoar *m.*

cast [kɑ:st] v. tr. (32). Lancer, jeter (*at,* à) [See THROW]. ‖ Jeter, couler (*at,* à) [a glance]. ‖ Jeter, projeter (*on,* sur) [a light, a shadow]. ‖ Se dépouiller de (a garment, the slough); perdre (leaves) ; *to cast feathers,* muer (bird) ; *to cast a shoe,* se déferrer (horse). ‖ Tirer, dresser (a horoscope) ; *to cast lots,*

tirer au sort. ‖ Classer, disposer, ordonner (to distribute). ‖ Pondre, déposer (eggs); mettre bas prématurément (young). ‖ MILIT. Réformer (a horse, soldier). ‖ NAUT. Jeter (anchor). ‖ SPORTS. Terrasser (a wrestler). ‖ FIG. *Cast in the same mould,* décollé, décalqué. ‖ **To cast aside,** rejeter, mettre de côté. ‖ **To cast away,** rejeter ; repousser ; NAUT. *To be cast away,* faire naufrage. ‖ **To cast down,** baisser (one's eyes) ; MILIT. Jeter bas (one's weapons) ; FIG. Abattre, accabler (s.o.). ‖ **To cast in,** partager ; *to cast in one's lot with,* partager le sort de. ‖ **To cast off,** rejeter ; mettre au rebut ; NAUT. Larguer, décapeler ; FIG. S'affranchir de, se détacher de. ‖ **To cast out,** expulser, chasser. ‖ **To cast up,** lever au ciel (one's eyes) ; reprocher (sth.) ; MATH. Calculer ; MED., FIG. Vomir, rejeter.
— v. intr. Jeter les dés. ‖ SPORTS. Jeter la ligne. ‖ MATH. Calculer. ‖ TECHN. Gauchir. ‖ MED. Vomir. ‖ FIG. Conjecturer, délibérer. ‖ **To cast about,** se mettre en quête (*for,* de); chercher le moyen (*how to,* de). ‖ **To cast back,** retourner en arrière ; FIG. Revenir. ‖ **To cast off,** arrêter les mailles (in knitting) ; NAUT. Abattre.
— n. Lancement, jet *m.* (of stones). ‖ Coup *m.* (of the dice, of net). ‖ Chute, disposition *f.* (of a drapery). ‖ Expression *f.* (of the face) ; forme *f.* (of features). ‖ Nuance, touche *f.* (of a colour). ‖ Genre, ton *m.* (in literature). ‖ MATH. Addition *f.* (of figures). ‖ ZOOL. Couple *m.* (of hawks) ; régurgitation *f.* (vomit). ‖ SPORTS. Mouche *f.* (bait) ; bonne place *f. ;* lancer *m.* (throw) [in fishing]. ‖ THEATR. Distribution, interprétation ; troupe *f.* ‖ TECHN. Fonte *f. ;* cliché *m* (in printing). ‖ ARTS. Coulage *m.* (act) ; moule *m.* (mould) ; moulage, plâtre, bronze *m.* (statue). ‖ MED. Plâtre *m.* (plaster form) ; léger strabisme *m.* (squint) ; calcul *m.* (calculus). ‖ FIG. Nature, caractéristique, trempe *f.* (kind) ; tournure *f.* (of fancy) ; disposition *f.* (of temper) ; tour *m.* (of thought) ; *cast of mind,* mentalité.
— adj. Fondu. ‖ **Cast-iron,** n. Fonte *f. ;* adj. En fonte ; FIG. D'acier, de fer.

castanet [kæstə'net] n. MUS. Castagnette *f.*

castaway ['kɑ:stə,wei] adj., n. NAUT. Naufragé *s.* ‖ FIG. Réprouvé *s.*

caste [kɑ:st] n. Caste *f.* ‖ FIG. Rang *m. ; to lose caste,* déroger.

castellan ['kæstələn] n. Gouverneur de château *m.*

castellated [-leitid] adj. ARCHIT. Parsemé de châteaux forts (district) ; de style féodal (mansion) ; crénelé (wall). ‖ TECHN. Crénelé (nut).

caster ['kɑːstə*] n. TECHN. Fondeur *m.* ‖ Roulette *f.* (for furniture). ‖ See CASTOR.

castigate ['kæstigeit] v. tr. Châtier, corriger (s.o.). ‖ Critiquer sévèrement (a book, a play).

castigation [kæsti'geiʃən] n. Châtiment *m.* ‖ Rude critique *f. ;* éreintement *m.* (fam.).

castigator ['kæstigeitə*] n. Personne (*f.*) qui châtie. ‖ Critique *m.*

Castile [kæs'ti:l] n. GEOGR. Castille *f.*

Castilian [-jən] adj., n. GEOGR. Castillan *s.*

casting ['kɑːstiŋ] adj. Qu'on lance. ‖ JUR. Prépondérant (voice).
— n. Jet, lancer, lancement *m.* (act). ‖ TECHN. Fonte *f.* (act) ; pièce fondue *f.* ‖ ARTS. Moulage *m.* ‖ THEATR. Distribution *f.*

castle ['kɑ:sl] n. ARCHIT. Château fort, castel *m.* ‖ Tour *f.* (in chess). ‖ FIG. *Castles in the air,* châteaux en Espagne. ‖ **Castle-builder,** n. FAM. Bâtisseur (*s.*) de châteaux en Espagne ; faiseur (*s.*) de projets chimériques.
— v. tr., intr. Roquer (in chess).

castor ['kɑːstə*] n. MED. Castoréum *m.* ‖ COMM. Castor *m.* (hat).

castor n. CULIN. Saupoudroir *m.* (for salt, sugar) ; burette *f.* (for vinegar) ; *castors,* huilier.

castor-oil ['kɑːstə'rɔil] n. MED. Huile de ricin. ‖ BOT. *Castor-oil plant,* ricin.

CASTLE — CHÂTEAU FORT

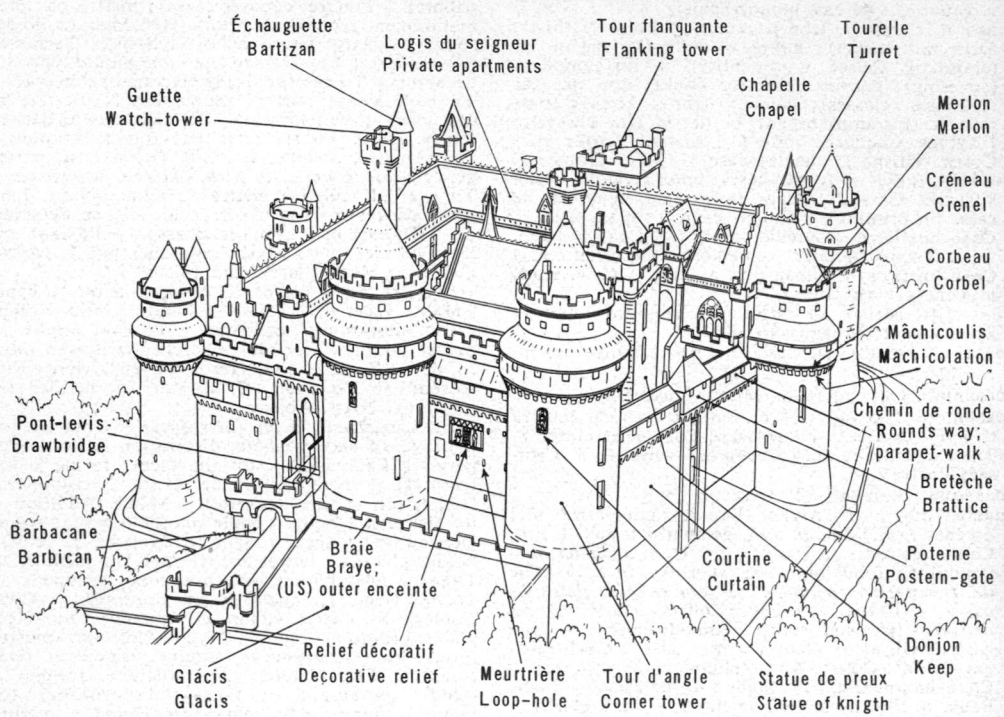

Échauguette
Bartizan

Logis du seigneur
Private apartments

Tour flanquante
Flanking tower

Tourelle
Turret

Guette
Watch-tower

Chapelle
Chapel

Merlon
Merlon

Créneau
Crenel

Corbeau
Corbel

Mâchicoulis
Machicolation

Pont-levis
Drawbridge

Chemin de ronde
Rounds way;
parapet-walk

Bretèche
Brattice

Barbacane
Barbican

Braie
Braye;
(US) outer enceinte

Courtine
Curtain

Poterne
Postern-gate

Donjon
Keep

Glacis
Glacis

Relief décoratif
Decorative relief

Meurtrière
Loop-hole

Tour d'angle
Corner tower

Statue de preux
Statue of knigth

---

castrametation [,kæstrəmi'teiʃən] n. MILIT. Castramétation f.

castrate [kæs'treit] v. tr. Châtrer, castrer (an animal); émasculer (a man). [See GELD.] ‖ FAM. Châtrer, expurger (a text).

castration [-'treiʃən] n. Castration f.

castrato [-'trɑːtou] n. MUS. Castrat m.

casual ['kæʒjuəl] adj. Fortuit, accidentel, casuel; de hasard, de rencontre, de fortune. ‖ A bâtons rompus (conversation). ‖ Temporaire (labourer); irrégulier, intermittent, temporaire (work). ‖ Cavalier, désinvolte (answer, manners, person). ‖ **Casual-ward**, n. Asile (m.) de nuit temporaire.
— n. Travailleur temporaire m. (labourer); indigent temporaire m. (poor).

casually [-i] adv. Fortuitement, accidentellement, par hasard. ‖ Irrégulièrement, par à-coups, temporairement. ‖ Avec désinvolture (or) sans gêne.

casualness [-nis] n. Insouciance, désinvolture f.; sans-gêne m.

casualty [-ti] n. Accident m. ‖ MED. Accidenté s. ‖ MILIT. Victime f.; casualties, pertes, morts et blessés; casualty list, état de pertes.

casuist ['kæzjuist] n. ECCLES., FAM. Casuiste m.

casuistic [kæzju'istik] adj. Casuiste, propre à la casuistique.

casuistry [-ri] n. ECCLES., FAM. Casuistique f.

casus belli ['kɑːsus'beliː] n. Casus belli m. inv.

cat ['kæt] n. ZOOL. Chat m., chatte f. (domesticated); félin m. (wild). ‖ Chat (m.) à neuf queues (whip). ‖ Bistoquet m. (in game). ‖ NAUT. Capon m. ‖ FAM. Chipie, rosse f. (woman). ‖ FAM. It's raining cats and dogs, il tombe une pluie diluvienne, il pleut à seaux; there is not enough room to swing a cat, il n'y a pas la place de se retourner; the cat is out of the bag, voilà le grand mot lâché; to lead a cat-and-dog life, s'entendre comme chien et chat,

faire mauvais ménage; to wait for the cat to jump attendre de voir où souffle le vent (or) comment tournent les événements. ‖ **Cat-burglar**, n. Monte-en-l'air m. ‖ **Cat-eyed**, adj. Qui voit la nuit, aux yeux de chat. ‖ **Cat-fish**, n. ZOOL. Chat marin; poisson-chat m. ‖ **Cat-head**, n. NAUT. Bossoir (m.) de capon. ‖ **Cat-house** n. POP. Maison de passe f. ‖ **Cat-lap**, n. FAM. Lavasse, tisane f.; jus (m.) de chaussette. ‖ **Cat-lick**, n. FAM. Bout (m.) de toilette; v. intr. FAM. Se laver le bout du nez. ‖ **Cat-nap**, v. intr. FAM. Ne dormir que d'un œil; n. Sommeil léger m. ‖ **Cat-o'-nine-tails**, n. JUR., NAUT. Chat (m.) à neuf queues; garcette f. ‖ **Cat's cradle** n. Berceau m.; scie f. (game). ‖ **Cat's-eye**, n. Œil-de-chat m. (gem); AUTOM. Feu arrière m. (or a bicycle); cataphote m. (highway reflector). ‖ **Cat's-paw**, n. NAUT. Risée f.; FAM. Dupe (f.) qui tire les marrons du feu. ‖ **Cat's-whisker**, n. RADIO Chercheur m. ‖ **Cat-that-has-just-eaten-the-canary**, adj. FAM. Innocent (air). ‖ **Cat-trap**, n. Chatière f. ‖ **Cat-walk**, n. AVIAT. Coursive f.
— v. tr. (1). NAUT. Caponner. ‖ POP. Dégobiller

catabolism [kə'tæbə,lizm̩] n. MED. Catabolisme m.

catachresis [kætə'kriːsis] n. GRAMM. Catachrèse f

cataclasm ['kætə,klæzm] n. Rupture f., éclatement m.

cataclysm ['kætəklizm] n. Cataclysme m.

cataclysmic [kætə'klizmik] adj. De cataclysme.

catacomb ['kætəkoum] n. Catacombe f.

catafalque [-fælk] n. Catafalque m.

Catalan ['kætələn] adj., n. GEOGR. Catalan s.

catalepsis ['kætələpsis], **catalepsy** [-si] n. MED Catalepsie f.

cataleptic [kætə'leptik] adj. MED. Cataleptique.

catalog(ue) ['kætələg] n. Catalogue m.
— v. tr. Cataloguer, faire le catalogue de.

Catalonia [kætə'louniə] n. GEOGR. Catalogne *f.*
catalpa [kə'tælpə] n. BOT. Catalpa *m.*
catalyse ['kætəlaiz] v. tr. CHIM. Catalyser.
catalysis [kə'tælisis] n. CHIM. Catalyse *f.*
catalyst ['kætəlist] n. CHIM., FIG. Catalyseur *m.*
catalytic [kætə'litik] adj. CHIM. Catalytique.
catamaran [,kætəmə'ræn] n. NAUT. Catamaran *m.* ‖ FAM. Harpie, mégère *f.*
catamite ['kætəmait] n. Jeune inverti *m.*
catamountain ['kætə'mauntin] n. ZOOL. Chattigre *m.* ‖ FAM. Tigre *m.*
cataplasm ['kætəplæzm̩] n. MED. Cataplasme *m.* (See POULTICE.)
cataplectic ['kætə,plektik] adj. MED. Cataplectique.
cataplexy [-ksi] n. MED. Cataplexie *f.*
catapult [-pʌlt] n. Lance-pierres *m.;* fronde *f.* (sling-shot). ‖ MILIT., AVIAT. Catapulte *f.* ‖ **Catapult-launched**, adj. AVIAT. Catapultable. ‖ **Catapult-launching** (or) **-start**, n. AVIAT. Catapultage *m.*
— v. tr. MILIT., AVIAT. Catapulter.
cataract ['kætərækt] n. GEOGR., MED. Cataracte *f.* ‖ FIG. Déluge *m.*
catarrh [kə'tɑ:*] n. MED. Catarrhe *m.*
catarrhal [-rəl] adj. MED. Catarrhal.
catarrhous [-rəs] adj. MED. Catarrheux.
catastrophe [kə'tæstrəfi] n. Catastrophe *f.*
catastrophic [kætə'strɔfik] adj. Catastrophique.
catatonia [,kætə'touniə] n. MED. Catatonie *f.*
catatonic [-'tɔnik] adj., n. Catatonique *adj., s.*
catcall ['kætkɔ:l] n. THEATR. Coup de sifflet *m.*
— v. tr., intr. THEATR. Siffler.
catch [kætʃ] v. tr. (33). Attraper, saisir, prendre (to seize); attraper, prendre, capturer (to trap). ‖ Attraper, rattraper, retenir, soutenir (to prevent from falling). ‖ Prendre, accrocher; *to catch one's foot in,* se prendre le pied dans. ‖ Prendre (fire). ‖ Attraper, rattraper, atteindre (s.o.); prendre (the train). ‖ Administrer, porter (a blow); atteindre, frapper (s.o.). ‖ Prendre, attraper, surprendre *(at,* à) [s.o.]; *if I catch him!,* s'il me tombe sous la patte! ‖ Attirer (s.o.'s attention, eyes); retenir, garder (one's breath); frapper (s.o.'s ear); lancer (a glance); *to catch sight of,* prendre un bref aperçu de, apercevoir, entrevoir. ‖ Percevoir (a taste); attraper (a tone); attraper, saisir, comprendre (a word). ‖ SPORTS. Attraper (the ball); mettre hors jeu (the batsman). ‖ MED. Attraper, prendre (a disease). ‖ ARTS. Attraper, saisir (a likeness). ‖ JUR. Attraper, prendre (a thief). ‖ FAM. Attraper (to entrap); *catch me,* penses-tu qu'on m'y reprenne!; *he didn't half catch it!,* U. S. *he really did catch it,* qu'est-ce qu'il a pris!; *to catch it,* écoper, ramasser; *to catch it hot,* en prendre pour son grade. ‖ **To catch on**, FIG. Prendre pied. ‖ **To catch out,** SPORTS. Mettre hors jeu. ‖ **To catch up**, adopter, prendre (to acquire); interrompre, couper la parole à (to interrupt); se rattraper (to make up); rattraper, atteindre (to overtake).
— v. intr. Prendre (ice, fire, wood). ‖ S'accrocher, se raccrocher, se retenir *(at,* à); se prendre, s'accrocher, s'enchevêtrer *(in,* dans). ‖ TECHN. Accrocher (key, lock); mordre, prendre (nut). ‖ CULIN. Attacher. ‖ FIG. Sauter *(at,* sur) [an opportunity]. ‖ **To catch on,** U. S. Saisir, piger (to understand); FAM. Prendre (to become popular). ‖ **To catch over,** prendre (to congeal).
— n. Prise, capture *f.* (act, thing); prise, proie *f.* (person). ‖ Bribe *f.* (of a conversation). ‖ Soubresaut *m.; with a catch in one's voice,* d'une voix entrecoupée. ‖ TECHN. Ardillon *m.* (of buckle); loquet *m.* (on door); mentonnet *m.* (of latch); cliquet *m.* (of wheel); loqueteau *m.* (of window). ‖ SPORTS. Prise de la balle *f.* (catching); pêche,

prise *f.* (in fishing). ‖ MUS. Chanson à reprises *f.* ‖ FAM. Attrape *f.; catch question,* colle *f.* ‖ FAM. Hic *m.;* difficulté *f.* ‖ **Catch-as-catch-can,** n. SPORTS. Catch *m.* ‖ **Catch-basin,** n. GEOL. Bassin collecteur *m.* ‖ **Catch crop,** n. AGRIC. Culture dérobée *f.* ‖ **Catch-phrase,** n. Rengaine, scie *f.;* slogan *m.*
catchall [-,ɔ:l] n. U. S. Débarras, fourre-tout *m.*
catcher [-ə*] n. Preneur *m.* ‖ SPORTS. Rattrapeur *m.* (in baseball).
catching [-iŋ] adj. MED., FAM. Contagieux.
catchment [-mənt] n. Captage *m.* ‖ **Catchment area,** bassin hydrographique, aire de drainage (of a river), secteur géographique (of a hospital, of a school).
catchpenny [-peni] n. FAM. Camelote *f.;* attrapenigaud *m.*
catchpole [-poul] n. JUR. Huissier servant *m.*
catchup ['kætʃəp] n. CULIN. Ketchup *m.*
catchword [-wə:d] n. TECHN. Mot-souche *m.* (of dictionary article); réclame *f.* (at the foot of a page); mot-vedette *m.* (at the top of a page). ‖ THEATR. Réplique *f.* ‖ FAM. Rengaine *f.,* slogan *m.*
catchy [-i] adj. Facile à retenir (poem, tune). ‖ Insidieux, à traquenard (question).
catechesis [kæte'ki:sis] n. ECCLES. Catéchèse *f.*
catechetic [-'ketik] adj. ECCLES. Catéchétique. ‖ FAM. Par demandes et réponses.
catechism ['kætikizm̩] n. ECCLES. Catéchisme *m.*
catechist [-kist] n. ECCLES. Catéchiste *s.*
catechize [-kaiz] v. tr. ECCLES. Catéchiser. ‖ FIG. Interroger.
catechizer [-kaizə*] n. ECCLES. Catéchiste *m.* ‖ FIG. Interrogateur, questionneur *m.*
catechu ['kætiʃu:] n. Cachou *m.*
catechumen [kæti'kju:mən] n. ECCLES. Catéchumène *s.*
categorical [kæti'gɔrikəl] adj. Catégorique.
categorize ['kætigəraiz] v. tr. Ranger par catégories.
category [-i] n. Catégorie *f.*
catenarian [kæti'nɛəriən], **catenary** [kə'ti:nəri] n., adj. TECHN. Caténaire *f.*
catenate ['kætineit] v. tr. FIG. Enchaîner. (See LINK.)
catenation [kæti'neiʃən] n. FIG. Enchaînement *m.*
cater ['keitə*] v. intr. Pourvoir *(for,* aux besoins [or] plaisirs de). ‖ Approvisionner.
cater ['keitə*] n. † Quatre *m.* ‖ **Cater-cornered,** adj. Diagonal. ‖ **Cater-cousin,** n. Cousin au quatrième degré *m.;* FIG. Intime *m.*
caterer [-rə*] n. Pourvoyeur *m.* ‖ COMM. Traiteur *m.* (of food); fournisseur *m.* (of goods).
cateress [-ris] n. Pourvoyeuse *f.*
caterpillar ['kætəpilə*] n. ZOOL., TECHN. Chenille *f.* ‖ FAM. Profiteur *m.,* sangsue *f.* ‖ **Caterpillar-chain,** n. TECHN. Chenille, chaîne sans fin *f.* ‖ **Caterpillar-tractor,** n. AUTOM. Autochenille *f.;* caterpillar *m.* ‖ **Caterpillar-wheel,** n. TECHN. Roue à chenille *f.*
caterwaul ['kætəwɔ:l] v. intr. Miauler (cat). ‖ FAM. Faire du chahut.
caterwauling [-iŋ] n. Miaulement *m.* ‖ FAM. Sabbat *m.*
catgut ['kætgʌt] n. MUS. Corde *(f.)* à violon. ‖ SPORTS. Corde de raquette *f.* ‖ MED. Catgut *m.*
catharsis [kə'θɑ:sis] n. MED. Purgation *f.* ‖ PHILOS. Catharsis *f.*
cathartic [-tik] adj., n. MED. Cathartique *m.*
cathedral [kə'θi:drəl] n. ARCHIT. Cathédrale *f.*
— adj. Cathédral.
catherine-wheel ['kæθərinwi:l] n. Soleil *m.* (fireworks). ‖ SPORTS. Roue *f.* (somersault). ‖ ARCHIT. Rosace *f.* (window).
catheter ['kæθitə] n. MED. Cathéter *m.*
catheterize [-,raiz] v. tr. MED. Cathétériser.

cathetometer [kæθi'tɔmitə*] n. Phys. Cathéto-mètre m.

cathode ['kæθoud] n. Electr. Cathode f.
— adj. Cathodique (rays). ‖ Cathode-ray tube, n. Tube cathodique m.

cathodic [kə'θɔdik] adj. Electr. Cathodique.

Catholic [ˈkæθəlik] adj. Eccles. Catholique. ‖ Fig. Universel; éclectique, libéral.
— n. Eccles. Catholique s.

Catholicism [kɑˈθɔlisizm̩] n. Eccles. Catholicisme m.

catholicity [kæθəˈlisiti] n. Eccles. Catholicité f. ‖ Fig. Universalité, libéralité f. (of ideas); éclectisme m. (in taste).

catholicon [kəˈθɔlikən] n. Med. Panacée f. (See panacea.)

cation ['kætiən] n. Electr. Cation m.

catkin ['kætkin] n. Bot. Chaton m.

catlike [-laik] adj. Félin, souple et silencieux.

catling [-liŋ] n. Zool. Chaton, petit chat m. ‖ Med. Scalpel m.

catmint [-mint], U. S. catnip [-nip] n. Bot. Herbe (f.) aux chats.

catoptric [kəˈtɔptrik] adj. Phys. Catoptrique.

catoptrics [-s] n. sg. Phys. Catoptrique f.

catsuit [ˈkætsjuːt] n. Combinaison f. (one-piece trouser-suit).

catsup ['kætsəp] n. Culin. Ketchup m.

cattish [ˈkætiʃ], catty [-i] adj. Fam. Rosse.

cattle [ˈkætl] n. Agric. Bétail m.; bestiaux m. pl.; bêtes f. pl. ‖ Fam. Chevaux m. pl. (horses); troupeau m. (persons). ‖ Cattle-cake, n. Agric. Aliment concentré du bétail, tourteau m. ‖ Cattle-grid, U. S. cattle-guard, n. Sur une route, tranchée (f.) recouverte de barres pour empêcher le bétail de vagabonder. ‖ Cattle-lifter, U. S. cattle-thief, n. Jur. Voleur de bétail m. ‖ Cattle-lifting, U.S. cattle-theft, n. Jur. Abigéat, vol de bétail m. ‖ Cattle-pen, n. Agric. Parc à bestiaux m. ‖ Cattle-plague, n. Peste bovine f. ‖ Cattle-show, n. Agric. Concours (or) comice agricole m. ‖ Cattle-truck, n. Ch. de F. Wagon (m.) à bestiaux.

Caucasian [kɔːˈkeizjən] adj., n. Geogr. Caucasien s.

Caucasus [ˈkɔːkəsəs] n. Geogr. Caucase m.

caucus [ˈkɔːkəs] n. Comité électoral m.
— v. intr. Se grouper en comité électoral.

caudal [ˈkɔːdl̩] adj. Zool. Caudal.

caudate [-deit] adj. Bot. A queue.

caught [kɔːt] n. See catch.

caul [kɔːl] n. Résille f. (hairnet). ‖ Fond (m.) de coiffe (cap). ‖ Culin. Toilette f. ‖ Med. Amnios m.; coiffe f. (fam.). ‖ Fam. Born with a caul, né coiffé.

cauldron [ˈkɔːldrən] n. Culin. Chaudron m.

caulescent [kɔːˈlesn̩t] adj. Bot. Caulescent.

cauliflower [ˈkɔliflauə*] n. Agric., Culin. Chou-fleur m.

caulk [kɔːk] v. tr. Calfeutrer. ‖ Naut. Calfater. ‖ Techn. Mater. ‖ U. S. Etanchéifier.

caulker [-ə*] n. Naut. Calfat m. ‖ Techn. Matoir m.

causal [ˈkɔːzəl] adj. Gramm., Fig. Causal.

causality [kɔːˈzæliti] n. Philos. Causalité f.

causation [kɔːˈzeiʃən] n. Causalité f.

causative [ˈkɔːzətiv] adj. Qui est la cause (of, de). ‖ Gramm. Causatif.

cause [kɔːz] n. Cause, raison f.; sujet, motif m. (See motive.) ‖ Cause f.; parti m. (side); to make common cause with, faire cause commune avec. ‖ Jur. Cause f.; procès m. ‖ Philos. Cause, origine f.; principe m. ‖ Cause-list, n. Jur. Rôle (m.) d'audience.
— v. tr. Causer, produire, déterminer, provoquer. (See occasion.) ‖ Faire; to cause s.o. to do sth., faire faire qqch. à qqn; to cause sth. to be done, faire faire qqch.

causeless [-lis] adj. Sans cause (or) raison (or)

motif. ‖ Inexplicable. ‖ Sans fondement (groundless).

causeway [ˈkɔːzwei] n. Chaussée, levée f. (raised road). ‖ † Voie pavée f. (paved road).

caustic [ˈkɔːstik] adj., n. Chim., Fig. Caustique m.

caustically [-li] adv. Caustiquement.

causticity [kɔːsˈtisiti] n. Chim., Fig. Causticité f.

cauterization [ˌkɔːtəraiˈzeiʃən] n. Med. Cautérisation f.

cauterize [ˈkɔːtəraiz] v. tr. Med. Cautériser. ‖ Fig. Blinder, endurcir.

cautery [-i] n. Med. Cautère m.

caution [ˈkɔːʃən] n. Prudence, précaution, circonspection f. (wariness). ‖ Mise en garde f.; avertissement m. (admonition). ‖ Jur. Caution f.; répondant, garant m.; caution money, cautionnement. ‖ Fam. Numéro; drôle de pistolet m.
— v. tr. Mettre en garde, avertir.

cautionary [-əri] adj. Avertisseur. ‖ Jur. Donné en garantie; cautionary judgment, ordonnance de saisie conservatoire.

cautious [ˈkɔːʃəs] adj. Prudent, circonspect, avisé.

cautiously [-li] adv. Prudemment, avec circonspection. (See carefully.)

cavalcade [kævəlˈkeid] n. Calvacade f. ‖ Theatr., Cinem. Spectacle historique m.

cavalier [kævəˈliə*] n. Cavalier m. (escort). ‖ Milit. Cavalier m. ‖ † Royaliste (m.) partisan de Charles Ier.
— adj. Cavalier. ‖ Royaliste.

cavalierly [-li] adv. Cavalièrement.

cavalry [ˈkævəlri] n. Milit. Cavalerie f.; cavalry officer, officier de cavalerie.

cavalryman [-mən] (pl. cavalrymen) n. Milit. Cavalier m.

cavatina [kævəˈtiːnə] n. Mus. Cavatine f.

cave [keiv] n. Caverne f. ‖ Cave-art, n. Arts. Art rupestre m. ‖ Cave-bear, n. Zool. Ours (m.) des cavernes. ‖ Cave-hunting, n. Sports. Spéléologie f. ‖ Cave-man, n. Homme (m.) des cavernes.
— v. tr. Creuser. (See hollow.) ‖ To cave in, enfoncer, aplatir.
— v. intr. To cave in, fléchir (beam); s'ébouler, s'affaisser, céder (ground). ‖ Fam. Caner (person).

cave [ˈkeivi] interj. Fam. Vingt-deux!; to keep cave, faire le guet.

caveat [ˈkeiviæt] n. Avertissement m. ‖ Comm. Caveat emptor, mise en garde de l'acheteur contre tout risque possible. ‖ Jur. Notification d'opposition f.; to enter a caveat, mettre opposition.

cavern [ˈkævəːn] n. Caverne f. (See cave.)

cavernous [-əs] adj. Caverneux (rock, sound). ‖ Cave (eyes).

cavesson [ˈkævəsən] n. Caveçon m.

caviar(e) [kæviˈɑː*] n. Culin. Caviar m. ‖ Fig. Caviar to the general, de la confiture aux chiens.

caviare [kæviˈɑː*] v. tr. Caviarder.

cavil [ˈkævil] v. intr. (1) Ergoter, discutailler, chicaner (about, at, sur).
— n. Ergotage m.; ergoterie, argutie f.

caviller [-ə*] n. Ergoteur, chicaneur m.

cavitation [kæviˈteiʃən] n. Aviat., Naut. Cavitation f.

cavity [ˈkæviti] n. Cavité, excavation f.; creux m. ‖ Med. Cavité f. ‖ Techn. Cavity wall, mur à double cloison.

cavort [kəˈvɔːt] v. intr. U. S. Fam. Cabrioler.

cavy [ˈkeivi] n. Zool. Cobaye, caviidé m.

caw [kɔː] v. intr. Croasser.
— n. Croassement m.

cay [kei] n. Geogr. Cordon littoral m.

Cayenne [keiˈen] n. Geogr. Cayenne f. ‖ Culin. Poivre (m.) de Cayenne.

cayman [ˈkeimən] n. Zool. Caïman m. ‖ Geogr. Cayman Islands, îles Caïmans.

C.B.I. [siːbiːˈai] abbr. Confederation of British

Industry, Confédération de l'industrie britannique, équivalent britannique du C. N. P. F.

cease [si:s] n. Cesse *f.*
— v. tr. Cesser, arrêter. (See STOP.) ‖ **Cease-fire,** n. MILIT. Cessez-le-feu *m.*
— v. intr. To cease from, cesser, s'interrompre de, arrêter de.

ceaseless [-lis] adj. Incessant, sempiternel.

ceaselessly [-li] adv. Sans cesse (or) arrêt (or) fin ; continuellement. (See CONTINUALLY.)

cecity ['si:siti] n. MED. Cécité *f.* ‖ FIG. Aveuglement *m.*

cecum ['si:kəm] n. U. S., MED. Cæcum *m.* (See CAECUM.)

cedar ['si:də*] n. BOT., COMM. Cèdre *m.* ‖ **Cedarwood,** n. Cèdre, bois de cèdre *m.*

cede ['si:d] v. tr. Céder, concéder.

cedilla [si'dilə] n. Cédille *f.*

ceil [si:l] v. tr., intr. TECHN., AVIAT. Plafonner.

ceiling ['si:liŋ] n. ARCHIT., AVIAT., FIN. Plafond *m.* ‖ NAUT. Vaigre *f.; vaigrage m.* ‖ FAM. U. S. *To hit the ceiling,* sortir de ses gonds. ‖ **Ceilingbeam,** n. ARCHIT. Doubleau *m.*

celadon ['selədən] n. Céladon *m.*

celandine ['selən,dain] n. BOT. Grande chélidoine *f.* (greater celandine) ; ficaire *f.* (lesser celandine).

celebrant ['selibrənt] n. ECCLES. Célébrant *m.*

celebrate [-breit] v. tr. Célébrer, solemniser (an event). ‖ Célébrer, glorifier (s.o.). ‖ ECCLES. Célébrer (the mass).
— v. intr. ECCLES. Célébrer.

celebrated [-breitid] adj. Célèbre.

celebration [seli'brei/ən] n. Célébration *f.* ‖ Commémoration *f.* (of an event).

celebrity [sə'lebriti] n. Célébrité *f.* (fame, person).

celeriac [sə'leriæk] n. BOT. Céleri-rave *m.*

celerity [sə'leriti] n. Célérité *f.*

celery ['seləri] n. BOT. Céleri *m.* ‖ CULIN. *Celery salad,* céleri rémoulade.

celesta [si'lestə] n. MUS. Célesta *m.*

celeste [si'lest] adj., n. Bleu ciel *m.*

celestial [-jəl] adj. ASTRON., GEOGR., ECCLES. Céleste.

celibacy ['selibəsi] n. Célibat *m.*

celibate [-bit] adj., n. Célibataire *s.*

cell [sel] n. ZOOL., MED., BOT., MILIT. Cellule *f.* ‖ JUR. Cellule *f.; to set up a cell,* noyau *m.;* noyauter (political activity). ‖ ELECTR. Elément (*m.*) de pile ; *photo-electric cell,* cellule photoélectrique.

cellar ['selə*] n. Cellier *m.* (for provisions) ; cave *f.* (for wines). ‖ **Cellar-plate,** n. Glissière *f.* (See CHUTE, COAL-FLAP.)
— v. tr. Encaver, garder à la cave.

cellarage [-rid3] n. Caves *f. pl.* ‖ Encavement *m.*

cellarer [-rə*] n. ECCLES. Cellérier *m.*

cellaret [selə'ret] n. Cave à liqueurs *f.* (cabinet).

cellist ['t∫elist] n. MUS. Violoncelliste *m.*

cello ['t∫elou] n. MUS. Violoncelle *m.*

celloidin [se'lɔidin] n. Celloïdine *f.*

Cellophane ['selofein] n. Cellophane *f.*

cellular ['seljulə*] adj. Cellulaire.
— n. Cellular *m.* (linen).

cellule ['selju:l] n. MED. Cellule *f.*

cellulitis [,selju'laitis] n. MED. Cellulite *f.*

Celluloid ['seljulɔid] n. Celluloïd *m.*

cellulose [-lous] adj. Celluleux.
— n. CHIM. Cellulose *f.*

celt [selt] n. Eolithe *m.*

Celt [kelt, selt] n. GEOGR. Celte *s.*

Celtic [-ik] adj. GEOGR. Celtique, celte.
— n. Celtique *m.* (language).

celtium ['sɛltjəm] n. CHIM. Celtium *m.*

Celtologist [kel'tɔlədʒist] n. Celtisant *s.*

celtuce ['seltəs] n. CULIN. Laitue-céleri.

cement [si'ment] n. ARCHIT., FIG. Ciment *m.* ‖ TECHN., MED. Cément *m.*

— v. tr. ARCHIT., FIG. Cimenter. ‖ TECHN. Cémenter. ‖ MED. Obturer.

cementation [,si:men'tei/ən] n. ARCHIT. Cimentage *m.* ‖ TECHN. Cémentation *f.*

cemetery ['semitri] n. Cimetière *m.*

cenobite ['si:nobait] n. U. S. Cénobite *m.*

cenotaph ['senotæf] n. Cénotaphe *m.*

cense [sens] v. tr. ECCLES. Encenser.

censer [-ə*] n. Encensoir *m.* (See THURIBLE.)

censor [-ə*] n. Censeur *m.*
— v. tr. Censurer (letters, news, plays).

censorial [sen'sɔ:riəl] adj. Censorial.

censorious [-iəs] adj. Pointilleux, dénigreur, tatillon, malveillant, hypercritique (person) ; désapprobateur (word).

censorship ['sensə/ip] n. Censure *f.*

censurable ['sen/ərəbl] adj. Censurable, blâmable.

censure ['sen/ə*] n. Censure, critique *f.;* blâme *m.*
— v. tr. Censurer, critiquer, blâmer.

census ['sensəs] n. JUR. Recensement, cens *m.*

cent [sent] n. FIN. Cent *m.* (percentage) ; *per cent,* pour cent. ‖ U. S. Cent *m.* (coin).

centaur ['sentɔ:*] n. Centaure *m.*

centaury [-ri] n. BOT. Centaurée *f.*

centenarian [senti'nɛəriən] adj., n. Centenaire *s.*

centenary ['sentinəri] adj. Centenaire ; *centenary celebrations,* fêtes du centenaire.
— n. Centenaire *m.* (anniversary). ‖ † Période (*f.*) de cent ans.

centennial [sen'tenjəl] adj. Centenaire, centennal.
— n. Centenaire *m.* (anniversary).

center ['sentə*] n. U. S. See CENTRE.

centesimal [sen'tesiməl] adj. MATH. Centésimal.

centigrade ['sentigreid] adj. Centigrade.

centigram(me) [-græm] n. Centigramme *m.*

centilitre [-li:tə*] n. Centilitre *m.*

centimetre [-mi:tə*] n. Centimètre *m.*

centiped(e) [-pi:d] n. ZOOL. Myriapode ; millepattes *m.* (fam.).

central ['sentrəl] adj. Central. ‖ GEOGR. *Central African Republic,* République centrafricaine ; *Central America,* Amérique centrale.
— n. U. S. Central téléphonique *m.* (exchange) ; téléphoniste (*s.*) du central (operator).

centralism [-lizm] n. Centralisme *m.*

centralist [-list] n. Centraliste *s.*

centrality [sen'træliti] n. Position centrale *f.*

centralization [,sentrəlai'zei/ən] n. Centralisation *f.*

centralize [,sentrəlaiz] v. tr. Centraliser.
— v. intr Se centraliser.

centre ['sentə*] n. MATH., MILIT., AVIAT., COMM., PHYS., MED., JUR. Centre *m.* ‖ TECHN. Pointe *f.;* point, centre *m.; dead centre,* point mort ; *off centre,* décentré. ‖ SPORTS. Cercles *m. pl.* (of a target). ‖ Centre *m.; rest centre,* centre d'accueil ; *travel centre,* office de tourisme. ‖ **Centre-board,** n. NAUT. Dérive *f.* ‖ **Centre-fold,** n. Double page centrale *f.* (in magazine, newspaper). ‖ **Centre-forward,** n. SPORTS. Avant-centre *m.* ‖ **Centre-half,** n. SPORTS. Demi-centre *m.* ‖ **Centre-punch,** n. TECHN. Pointeau *m.* ‖ **Centre spread,** n. See CENTRE-FOLD.
— v. tr. Centrer ; marquer le centre de. ‖ SPORTS. Centrer. ‖ FIG. Centrer, concentrer, axer (*in, on, round, upon*).
— v. intr. Frapper au centre (of a target). ‖ Se concentrer (*in, dans ; on,* sur) ; converger (*on,* vers) ; se circonscrire (*on, autour de*). ‖ FAM. Se rassembler (*round, autour de*) [s.o.].

centric ['sentrik] adj. Du centre, central.

centrifugal [sen'trifjugəl] adj. Centrifuge.
— n. Centrifugeur *m.*

centrifuge ['sentri,fju:dʒ] n. Centrifugeur *m.*, centrifugeuse *f.* (machine).
— v. tr. Centrifuger.

centripetal [sen'tripitl] adj. Centripète.
centrism ['sentrizm] n. Centrisme m.
centrist [-ist] adj., n. Centriste adj., s.
centuple ['sentjupl] adj., n. Centuple m. (See HUNDREDFOLD.)
— v. tr. Centupler.
centuplicate [sen'tju:plikeit] v. tr. Centupler.
— [-kit] n. Centuple m.
centurion [sen'tjuəriən] n. † Centurion m.
century ['sentʃuri] n. Siècle m. ‖ † MILIT. Centurie f. ‖ SPORTS. Cent points m. pl. ‖ U. S. POP. Century note, billet de cent dollars.
cephalalgy ['sefəlældʒi] n. MED. Céphalalgie f.
cephalic [sə'fælik] adj. MED. Céphalique.
cephalopod ['sefələpɔd] n. ZOOL. Céphalopode m.
cepheid ['si:fiid] n. ASTRON. Céphéide f.
ceramic [si'ræmik] adj. ARTS. Céramique.
ceramics [-iks] n. sg. ARTS. Céramique f.
cerate ['serit] n. MED. Cérat m.
Cerberus ['sə:bərəs] n. † FAM. Cerbère m.
cereal ['siəriəl] adj., n. AGRIC. Céréale f. ‖ CULIN. Pl. Flocons (m. pl.) d'avoine; farine (f.) à potage.
cerebellum [seri'beləm] n. MED. Cervelet m.
cerebral ['seribrəl] adj. MED. Cérébral. ‖ GRAMM. Cacuminal.
cerebrate [-breit] v. intr. U. S. Penser, cogiter.
cerebration [,seri'breiʃən] n. PSYCH. Travail mental m. ‖ FAM. Cogitation f.
cerebro-spinal ['serebrɔ'spainl] adj. MED. Cérébro-spinal.
cerebro-vascular [-'væskjulə*] adj. MED. Cérébral vasculaire, cérébral.
cerebrum ['seribrəm] n. MED. Cerveau m.
cerecloth ['siəklɔ:θ], **cerement** ['siəmənt] n. Suaire m.
ceremonial [seri'mounjəl] adj. De cérémonie.
— n. Cérémonial m.; étiquette f. ‖ ECCLES. Rituel m.
ceremonious [-əs] adj. Cérémonieux. (See FORMAL.)
ceremoniously [-əsli] adv. Cérémonieusement.
ceremoniousness [-əsnis] n. Manières cérémonieuses f. pl.
ceremony ['seriməni] n. Cérémonie f. (function). ‖ Cérémonies f. pl.; to stand on ceremony, faire des façons. ‖ † Rite m.
cerise [sə'ri:z] adj., n. Cerise m. (colour).
cerium ['siəriəm] n. CHIM. Cérium m.
cert [sə:t] n. FAM. Certitude; it's a dead cert, c'est tout cuit.
certain ['sə:tn] adj. Certain, sûr, assuré; for certain, certainement, pour sûr. ‖ Sûr, certain, indiscutable, indéniable (unquestionable). ‖ Certain, sûr, persuadé, convaincu (convinced). ‖ Certain, appréciable, notable. ‖ Certain, quelconque (undetermined). ‖ Certain, particulier (some).
certainly [-li] adv. Certainement, assurément, sans doute, bien sûr. (See SURELY.) ‖ Indiscutablement, indéniablement.
certainty [-ti] n. Certitude f. (fact, quality, state); for a certainty, à coup sûr, positivement. ‖ Certitude, conviction f. ‖ Fait (or) événement certain m.
certifiable [,sə:ti'faiəbl] adj. Certifiable.
certificate [sə'tifikit] n. Certificat, diplôme m. ‖ MED. Certificat m. ‖ JUR. Certificate of good character, certificat de bonne vie et mœurs; bankrupt's certificate, concordat.
— [-eit] v. tr. Diplômer; donner un certificat à. ‖ JUR. Accorder le concordat à.
certificated [-eitid] adj. Diplômé. ‖ JUR. Concordataire.
certification [,sə:tifi'keiʃən] n. Certification f. ‖ Certificat m.
certificatory [sə'tifikətəri] adj. Certificatif.
certified ['sə:tifaid] adj. Certifié, diplômé (person). ‖ JUR. Certifié conforme (copy). ‖ FIN. Certifié, visé (cheque). ‖ COMM. Garanti (milk).

certify [-fai] v. tr. (2). Certifier, assurer. ‖ FIN. Certifier; ordonnancer. ‖ COMM. Garantir. ‖ PSYCH. Interner.
certitude ['sə:titju:d] n. Certitude f.
cerulean [si'ru:liən] adj. Céruléen.
cerumen [si'ru:men] n. MED. Cérumen m.
ceruse ['siəru:s] n. Céruse f.
cervical [sə:'vaikəl] adj. MED. Cervical.
cervidae ['sə:vidi:] n. pl. ZOOL. Cervidés m. pl.
cervine [-vain] adj. ZOOL. Cervin.
cervix ['sə:viks] (pl. **cervices** [sə'vaisi:z]) n. MED. Col m.; cervix uteri, col de l'utérus.
cess [ses] n. FIN. Impôt m.; assiette (f.) de l'impôt.
— v. tr. Imposer.
cessation [se'seiʃən] n. Cessation, suspension, interruption f.; arrêt m. ‖ MILIT. Cessation of hostilities, armistice.
cession ['seʃən] n. Cession f.
cessionary [-ri] n. Cessionnaire; ayant cause m.
cesspit ['sespit] n. AGRIC. Fosse (f.) à purin.
cesspool [-pu:l] n. Fosse d'aisance f. ‖ FIG. Cloaque m.
cetacean [si'teiʃiən] adj., n. ZOOL. Cétacé m.
cetaceous [-ʃiəs] adj. ZOOL. Cétacé.
cetane ['si:tein] n. CHIM. Cétane m.; cetane number, indice de cétane.
Ceylon [si'lɔn] n. GEOGR. Ceylan.
cf. [si:ef] abbr. confer, cf.
Chad [tʃæd] n. GEOGR. Tchad m.
chafe [tʃeif] v. tr. Frotter, frictionner. ‖ User (or) érafler en frottant (to wear away). ‖ Se frotter, (against, contre). ‖ FIG. Irriter, échauffer, exaspérer.
— v. intr. S'user, s'écorcher, s'érafler. ‖ Se frotter (against, contre). ‖ FIG. S'irriter, s'échauffer.
— m. Usure par friction; écorchure, éraflure f. ‖ FIG. Irritation f.
chafer [-ə*] n. ZOOL. Coléoptère, hanneton m.
chaff [tʃɑ:f] n. AGRIC. Bale, balle f. (of wheat). ‖ Paille hachée f. ‖ FIG. Vétille, broutille f. ‖ FAM. Chinage m., taquinerie f.
— v. tr. AGRIC. Hacher (straw). ‖ FAM. Chiner, blaguer, charrier.
chaffer [-ə*] n. FAM. Railleur, chineur, blagueur m.
chaffer ['tʃæfə*] v. intr. Marchander. (See HAGGLE.)
— v. tr. Marchander (sth.). ‖ To chaffer away, liquider, bazarder (fam.); FAM. Gâcher, gaspiller (one's time).
chafferer [-rə*] n. Marchandeur s.
chaffinch ['tʃæfinʃ] n. ZOOL. Pinson m.
chaffingly ['tʃɑ:fiŋli] adv. En badinant.
chaffy ['tʃɑ:fi] adj. AGRIC. De balle; plein de balle. ‖ Léger comme de la balle. ‖ FIG. De pacotille, piètre.
chafing-dish ['tʃeifiŋdiʃ] n. CULIN. Chauffeplat, m.; réchaud (m.) de table bain-marie.
chagrin ['ʃægri:n] n. Contrariété, mortification f.; désappointement m.
— v. tr. Contrarier, chagriner.
chain [tʃein] n. Chaîne f. (for a dog). ‖ Chaîne f.; (surveyor's, usher's). ‖ Pl. Chaînes, entraves f. pl.; fers m. pl. (fetters). ‖ TECHN. Chaîne f.; to form a chain, travailler à la chaîne. ‖ GEOGR. Chaîne f. (of mountains). ‖ CHIM. Chaîne f. (of atoms, reactions). ‖ FIG. Chaîne, série f.; enchaînement m. ‖ **Chain-armour**, n. † Cotte de mailles f. ‖ **Chain-bridge**, n. Pont suspendu m. ‖ **Chain-coupling**, n. CH. DE F. Chaîne (f.) d'attelage. ‖ **Chain-drive**, n. TECHN. Commande par chaîne f. ‖ **Chain-gang**, n. Forçats (m. pl.) à la chaîne. ‖ **Chain-letter**, n. Chaîne f. (to be circulated). ‖ **Chain-lock**, n. AUTOM. Chaîne (f.) antivol. ‖ **Chain-plate**, n. NAUT. Cadène f. ‖ **Chain-pump**, n. TECHN. Pompe hydraulique f. ‖ **Chain-reaction**, n. CHIM., PHYS. Réaction en chaîne f. ‖ **Chain-saw**, n. TECHN. Tronçonneuse f. ‖ **Chain-smoker**, n. Personne (f.) qui fume

cigarette sur cigarette, fumeur (m.) à la chaîne. ‖
Chain-stitch, n. Point (m.) de chaînette; v. tr.
Coudre au point de chaînette. ‖ **Chain-store,** n.
COMM. Magasin (m.) à succursales multiples. ‖
Chain-wale, n. NAUT. Porte-hauban m.
— v. tr. Enchaîner (lit. and fig.). ‖ Barrer à l'aide
d'une chaîne (a street). ‖ TECHN. Chaîner.
chainlet [-lit] n. Chaînette f.
chair [tʃɛə*] n. Siège m. (see SEAT); to take a
chair, prendre un siège, s'asseoir. ‖ Chaise f.;
folding-chair, chaise pliante. ‖ Chaire f. (professorship). ‖ Fauteuil présidentiel m.; présidence f.;
to be voted into the chair, être appelé à la présidence. ‖ Président m.; Chair! chair!, à l'ordre!;
to address the chair, en appeler au président. ‖
Fonctions (f. pl.) de maire (mayoralty). ‖ U. S.
Electric chair, chaise (ou) fauteuil électrique. ‖
Chair-attendant (or) **-keeper,** n. Chaisière f.
‖ **Chair car,** n. CH. DE F. U. S. Voiture-salon m. ‖
Chair-lift, n. TECHN. Télésiège m. ‖ **Chair-maker,**
n. Chaisier m. ‖ **Chair-mender,** n. Rempailleur s.
— v. tr. Elire président. ‖ Porter en triomphe. ‖
U. S. Présider.
chairman [-mən] (pl. **chairmen**) n. Président m. ‖
Chaisier; porteur m. ‖ U. S. Chairman of a department, directeur d'études d'une section en Faculté.
chairmanship [-mənʃip] n. Présidence f.
chairperson [-'pə:sn̩] n. Président m. (man); présidente f. (woman).
chairwoman [-'wumən] (pl. **chairwomen** [-'wi-
min]) n. Présidente f.
chaise [ʃeiz] n. Cabriolet m. ‖ **Chaise-longue,** n.
Chaise longue f.
chalcanthite [kæl'kænθait] n. CHIM. Cyanose f.
chalcedony [-'sedəni] m. Calcédoine f.
chalcographer [kæl'kɔɡrəfə*] n. ARTS. Chalcographe m.
chalcography [-fi] n. ARTS. Chalcographie f.
chalcopyrite [‚kælkə'pairait] n. Chalcopyrite f.
Chaldean [-'di:ən] adj., n. GEOGR. Chaldéen s.
chaldron [tʃɔ:ldrən] n. Mesure (f.) à charbon.
chalet ['ʃælei] n. Chalet m.
chalice [tʃælis] n. ECCLES., BOT. Calice m. ‖
Coupe f. (cup).
chalk [tʃɔ:k] n. Craie f.; by a long chalk, de
beaucoup, de loin. ‖ MED. French chalk, talc. ‖
COMM. Ardoise f. (fam.). ‖ FAM. Not to know chalk
from cheese, ne savoir ni A ni B. ‖ Chalk-line, n.
Trait (m.) à la craie; ligne (f.) au cordeau; v. tr.
Ligner au cordeau. ‖ **Chalk-pit,** n. Crayère f.
— v. tr. Marquer (or) écrire à la craie. ‖ Blanchir
(or) frotter de craie. ‖ MED. Talquer. ‖ To chalk
out, FIG. Tracer, déterminer. ‖ To chalk up,
COMM. Porter sur l'ardoise.
chalky [-i] adj. Crayeux, marneux (soil); calcaire
(water). ‖ FIG. Crayeux, terreux (complexion).
challenge ['tʃælindʒ] n. Défi m.; to issue a challenge, lancer un défi; to take up the challenge,
relever le défi. ‖ MILIT. Qui-vive m.; sommation
f. ‖ JUR. Récusation f.
— v. tr. Défier; provoquer en duel (to defy). ‖
Mettre en question, contester, objecter à (to question). ‖ Demander, réclamer, exiger (to call for).
‖ NAUT. Héler. ‖ MILIT. Crier qui-vive à; faire une
sommation à. ‖ JUR. Récuser. ‖ FIG. Sommer.
— v. intr. Provoquer. ‖ Donner de la voix (hounds).
challengeable [-əbl] adj. Revendi-
quable, exigible. ‖ MILIT. Qui peut être arrêté par
sommation. ‖ JUR. Récusable.
challenger [-ə*] n. Provocateur m. ‖ Revendicateur m. ‖ MILIT. Sentinelle (f.) au qui-vive. ‖
JUR. Récusateur m. ‖ SPORTS. Challenger m.
chalybeate [kə'libiit] adj. MED. Ferrugineux
(water).
chamade [ʃə'mɑ:d] n. MILIT. Chamade f.
chamber ['tʃeimbə*] n. Chambre f. (bedroom);
salle f. (room). ‖ Pl. Logement m. ‖ JUR. Chambre

f. (of Commerce). ‖ Pl. JUR. Cabinet d'avocat (or)
de magistrat m.; étude (f.) d'avoué; judge in chambers, juge des référés. ‖ MED. Chambre, cavité f.
(of the eye). ‖ MILIT. Chambre f. (of a revolver).
‖ FAM. Pot (m.) de chambre, vase (m.) de nuit.
(See JERRY.) ‖ **Chamber-concert,** n. MUS. Concert
(m.) de musique de chambre. ‖ **Chamber-counsel,**
n. JUR. Avocat-conseil m. ‖ **Chamber-music,** n.
MUS. Musique de chambre f. ‖ **Chamber-pot,** n.
Pot (m.) de chambre.
— v. tr. MILIT. Chambrer. ‖ TECHN. Evider.
chambered [-əd] adj. A compartiments, chambré.
chamberlain [-əlin] n. Chambellan m. ‖ ECCLES.
Camérier m.
chambermaid [-meid] n. Femme de chambre f.
(in hotels; U. S. in private houses).
chambray ['ʃæmbrei] n. Batiste f.
chameleon [kə'mi:ljən] n. ZOOL., FIG. Caméléon m.
chameleonic [‚kəmi:lj'ɔnik] adj. FIG. Changeant,
ondoyant et divers.
chamfer ['tʃæmfə*] n. Chanfrein m. (bevel); cannelure f. (groove).
— v. tr. Chanfreiner; canneler.
chamois ['ʃæmwɑ:] n. ZOOL., COMM. Chamois m.
— adj. Chamois (fawn-coloured).
— v. tr. Chamoiser.
chamomile ['kæmomail] n. BOT. Camomille f.
champ [tʃæmp] n. Mâchonnement m.; mastication f.
— v. tr., intr. Mâchonner; mâcher. (See MUNCH.)
‖ FIG. To champ at the bit, ronger son frein.
champ n. FAM. Champion s.
champagne [ʃæm'pein] n. Champagne m. (colour,
wine).
— n. GEOGR. Champagne f.
— adj. Champagne (colour). ‖ De Champagne.
champaign n. Plaine, campagne f.
champion ['tʃæmpjən] n. SPORTS. Champion s. ‖
FIG. Champion, défenseur, supporter m. ‖ FAM.
Crack m.
— adj. Maître; sans rival; de première classe. ‖
FAM. That's champion!, c'est de première !
— v. tr. Se faire le champion de, prendre fait et
cause pour, défendre. (See SUPPORT.)
championship [-ʃip] n. SPORTS. Championnat m.
‖ FIG. Défense f.
chance ['tʃɑ:ns] n. Hasard m.; by chance, par
hasard. ‖ Chance f.; risque m.; to take one's
chances, courir sa chance. ‖ Chance, possibilité f.;
give youth a chance!, place aux jeunes!; an off
chance of, une vague chance de; the chances are
that, il y a de grandes chances que. ‖ Chance, occasion f.; to have an eye to the main chance, savoir
saisir la balle au bond. ‖ **Chance-comer,** n. Survenant m. ‖ **Chance-medley,** n. JUR. Homicide involontaire m.; FIG. Inadvertance f.
— adj. De hasard, fortuit, accidentel, inattendu,
aléatoire.
— v. impers. Arriver, advenir. (See HAPPEN.)
— v. tr. Courir la chance de, risquer.
— v. intr. Avoir la bonne fortune (or) l'occasion
(to, de); venir (to, à). ‖ To chance upon, rencontrer par hasard.
chancel ['tʃɑ:nsəl] n. ARCHIT. Chœur m. (in a
church).
chancellery [-ləri] n. Chancellerie f.
chancellor [-lə*] n. Chancelier m. (in courts,
dioceses, embassies, universities). ‖ Ministre m. ‖
JUR., ECCLES. Chancelier m.
chancellorship [-ləʃip] n. Chancelariat m.
chancery ['tʃɑ:nsəri] n. JUR. Cour de la chancellerie f. ‖ SPORTS. Cour d'équité f. ‖ Cravate f.; to get s.o.'s head in chancery, cravater qqn.
‖ FAM. In chancery, dans la gueule du loup, dans
de beaux draps.

chancre ['ʃæŋkə*] n. Med. Chancre m.
chancroid [-krɔid] n. Med. Chancroïde m.
chancrous [-krəs] adj. Med. Chancreux.
chancy ['tʃɑːnsi] adj. Fam. Chanceux, hasardeux, risqué. (See RISKY.)
chandelier [ʃændə'liə*] n. Lustre m.
chandler ['tʃɑːndlə*] n. † Fabricant (or) marchand (m.) de chandelles. ‖ Comm. Marchand (m.) de couleurs, droguiste m.
chandlery [-dləri] n. Droguerie, épicerie-bazar f.
change [tʃeindʒ] n. Changement m. (from, de ; to, en, pour) ; change for the better, changement en mieux ; change in the weather, changement de temps ; it makes a change, cela vous change les idées ; just for a change, pour changer (or) varier un peu. ‖ Distraction, innovation, variété f.; to like change, aimer la nouveauté. ‖ Rechange m.; change of horses, relais ; change of linen, linge de rechange. ‖ Echange m.; to be a gainer by the change, gagner au change. ‖ Pl. Carillon m.; to ring the changes, carillonner. ‖ Pl. Jur. Changes in the cabinet, remaniement ministériel. ‖ Med. Change of life, retour d'âge, âge critique. ‖ Phys. At change, au variable (barometer). ‖ Fin. Monnaie f.; no change given, on est tenu de faire l'appoint ; to give change for, rendre la monnaie de. ‖ Fin. Bourse f. ‖ Fig. Pl. Vicissitudes f. pl.; hauts et bas m. pl. (of life). ‖ Fam. To take the change out of s.o., rendre à qqn la monnaie de sa pièce. ‖ Change-ringing, n. Carillon m.
— v. tr. .Changer de ; to change one's clothes, se changer ; to change one's mind, changer d'avis. ‖ Transformer, changer, modifier (into, en). ‖ Echanger, troquer, changer de ; to change hands, changer de mains ; to change one thing for another, échanger une chose contre une autre. ‖ Ch. de f. All change !, tout le monde descend ! ; to change trains, changer de train. ‖ Autom. To change buses, changer d'autobus. ‖ Fin. Changer, faire la monnaie de (a bank note). ‖ Fam. To change front, tourner casaque (or) la veste.
— v. intr. Changer, se modifier, se transformer (into, to, en) [to alter]. ‖ Se changer, changer d'habits (to put on other clothes). ‖ Faire un échange (to barter). ‖ Astron. Changer de quartier (moon). ‖ Ch. de f. Changer, changer de train. ‖ To change about, faire volte-face. ‖ To change down, Autom. Passer à une vitesse inférieure. ‖ To change over, passer (from, de ; to, à) ; Electr. Commuter. ‖ To change up, Autom. Passer à une vitesse supérieure.
changeable [-əbl] adj. Changeant, variable, versatile, inconstant. ‖ Changeant (silk).
changeful [-ful] adj. Changeant, inconstant.
changeless [-lis] adj. Immuable, constant.
changeling [-liŋ] n. Enfant (m.) changé en nourrice ; enfant substitué m.
changer [-ə*] n. Fin., Electr. Changeur m.
channel ['tʃænl] n. Conduit, canal m. (for liquids) ; rigole f. (on a street) ; lit m. (of a river). ‖ Chenal m. (of a harbour). ‖ Archit. Cannelure f. ‖ Geogr. Canal m.; English Channel, Manche f.; Channel Islands, îles Anglo-Normandes. ‖ Comm. To open up a new channel for, créer un nouveau débouché pour. ‖ Fig. Canal, intermédiaire m.; through official (or) the usual channels, par la voie hiérarchique. ‖ Fig. Voie f. (of communication).
— v. tr. (1). Creuser des rigoles (or) des canaux dans. ‖ Archit. Canneler.
channels [-z] n. pl. Naut. Porte-haubans m.
chant [tʃɑːnt] n. Mus. Mélodie lente ; mélopée f. ‖ Mus., Eccles. Psalmodie f.; plain chant m.
— v. tr. Eccles. Psalmodier. ‖ Fig. Chanter (s.o.'s praises). ‖ Fam. Maquignonner (a horse).
chanter [-ə*] n. Eccles. Chantre m. ‖ Mus. Chalumeau m. (in a bagpipe). ‖ Fam. Maquignon m.
chanterelle [tʃɑːntə'rel] n. Bot. Chanterelle f.

chanticleer [,tʃænti'kliə*] n. Chanteclair m.
chantress ['tʃɑːntris] n. Mus. Chanteuse f.
chantry [-tri] n. Archit. Chantrerie f. ‖ Eccles. Fondation de messes f.
chanty ['ʃænti] n. Mus. Chansons (f.) de marins.
chaos ['keiɔs] n. Chaos m. (lit. and fig.).
chaotic [kei'ɔtik] adj. Chaotique.
chaotically [-li] adv. Dans le désordre.
chap ['tʃæp] n. Gerçure, crevasse f.
— v. tr. (1). Gercer, crevasser.
— v. intr. Se gercer, se crevasser.
chap n. pl. Babines f. pl. (of an animal). ‖ Pl. Joues, bajoues f. pl. (cheeks). ‖ Culin. Joue (of pig). ‖ Techn. Mâchoires f. pl. (of a vice). ‖ Chap-fallen, adj. L'oreille basse, penaud.
chap n. Fam. Type, bonhomme m.
chaparejos [,ʃæpə'reious], chaps [tʃæps, ʃæps] n. pl. U. S. Jambières (f. pl.) en cuir.
chap-book [-'buk] n. Livre populaire m.
chape [tʃeip] n. Bout m. (of a scabbard) ; bouterolle f. (of a sword). ‖ Attache f. (of a buckle). ‖ Coulant m. (on a belt).
chapel ['tʃæpəl] n. Archit. Chapelle f. (church oratory) ; oratoire m. (in a house) ; temple m. (for non-conformists) ; chapel of ease, chapelle de secours. ‖ Eccles. Office m.; to keep a chapel, assister à l'office. ‖ Techn. Atelier m.; association f.
chaperon ['ʃæpəroun] n. Chaperon m. (person).
— v. tr. Chaperonner.
chaperonage [-idʒ] n. Surveillance f.
chaplain ['tʃæplin] n. Eccles. Chapelain m. ‖ Milit. Aumônier m.
chaplaincy [-si], chaplainship [-ʃip] n. Eccles. Chapellerie f. ‖ Milit. Aumônerie f.
chaplet ['tʃæplit] n. Guirlande f. ‖ Eccles. Archit. Chapelet m.
chapman ['tʃæpmən] (pl. chapmen) n. Colporteur m. (See PEDLAR.)
chappie ['tʃæpi] n. Fam. Type, bonhomme m.
chappy adj. Craquelé, gercé, crevassé.
chaps [tʃæps, ʃæps] n. U. S. See CHAPAREJOS.
chapter ['tʃæptə*] n. Chapitre m. (of a book). ‖ Eccles. Chapitre (of canons). ‖ Fig. Chapitre épisode m. (of life). ‖ Fam. Kyrielle f. (of accidents) ; to give chapter and verse, citer ses références. ‖ Chapter-house, n. Eccles. Salle (f.) du chapitre ; maison canoniale f.
— v. tr. Diviser en chapitres.
char [tʃɑː*] v. tr. (1). Charbonner, carboniser.
— v. intr. Charbonner, se carboniser. (See BURN.)
— n. Noir animal m.
char v. intr. (1). Faire des ménages.
— n. Fam. Femme de ménage f. (See CHARWOMAN.)
char n. Zool. Ombre, omble m.
charabanc ['ʃærəbæŋ] n. † Char à bancs m. ‖ Autom. Car, autocar m.
character ['kæriktə*] n. Caractère m.; lettre f (letter). ‖ Caractère, genre m.; caractéristique particularité f. ‖ Caractère m.; force morale, fermeté, énergie, volonté f. (fortitude). ‖ Caractère cachet m. (style). ‖ Réputation f. (for, de) ; of bad character, de mauvais renom, de fâcheuse réputation. ‖ Personnalité, individualité, originalité f. Personnage m. (in a novel) ; personnage m., personnalité f. (in society). ‖ Renseignements m. pl. (of sur) [character sheets]. ‖ Certificat m.; attestation f.; evidence of character, témoignage de moralité. Theatr. Personnage, rôle m.; character actor acteur de genre ; character part, rôle de composition ; comedy of character, comédie de caractère in character, dans son rôle. ‖ Fig. Harmonie f. accord m.; to be out of character with, ne pas s'accorder avec, manquer de consistance avec (sth.). ‖ Fam. Type ; numéro, phénomène m.
— v. tr. Ecrire, imprimer.

characteristic [ˌkærɪktə'rɪstɪk] adj. Caractéristique. ‖ MED. Diacritique.
— m. Caractéristique, note (or) marque dominante *f.; propre m.; leading characteristic,* dominante. ‖ MATH. Caractéristique *f.*

characteristically [-li] adv. D'une façon caractéristique, typiquement.

characterization [ˌkærɪktərai'zei ʃən] n. Caractérisation *f.* ‖ THEAT. Personnification *f.*

characterize ['kærɪktəraiz] v. tr. Caractériser, qualifier, dépeindre. ‖ Caractériser, être caractéristique de.

characterless ['kærɪktəlis] adj. Sans caractère; fade. ‖ Sans références (or) certificat.

charade [ʃə'rɑːd] n. Charade *f.*

charcoal ['tʃɑːkoul] n. Charbon de bois *m.* ‖ **Charcoal-burner,** n. Charbonnier *m.* ‖ **Charcoalpan,** n. Brasero *m.* ‖ **Charcoal-grey,** adj. Gris foncé.

charge [tʃɑːdʒ] n. Charge *f.;* faix, fardeau *m.* *(on,* pour) [load]. ‖ Charge, responsabilité *f.; to take charge of,* se charger de. ‖ Charge, garde *f.;* soin *m.; in charge of,* confié à la garde (or) aux soins de. ‖ Chose (or) personne en charge *f.; to be a charge on,* être à la charge de. ‖ Recommandation, instruction *f.; to have strict charge to,* avoir reçu le conseil formel de. ‖ Charge, fonction *f.;* emploi *m.* ‖ Chargé, gestionnaire *m. (of,* de); préposé *m. (of,* à). ‖ Charge, attaque *f.; to return to the charge,* revenir à la charge. ‖ MILIT. Charge (of explosive); charge *f.* (attack, signal); motif *(m.)* de punition. ‖ FIN. Coût, prix *m.;* frais *m. pl.; at my own charge,* à mes frais; *to make a charge for,* compter, facturer. ‖ JUR. Charge; inculpation; plainte *f.;* chef *(m.)* d'accusation; *to lay a charge against,* porter une accusation (or) plainte contre; *to take s.o. in charge,* arrêter qqn. ‖ ELECTR. Charge *f.* ‖ ECCLES. Mandement *m.* (of a bishop); charge *f.;* ouailles *f. pl.* (of a priest). ‖ **Charge-hand,** n. Responsable *(s.)* d'une équipe (or) d'une tâche, adjoint *(s.)* du contremaître. ‖ **Charge-nurse,** n. Surveillante *f.* (in a hospital). ‖ **Charge-sheet,** n. Cahier *(m.)* des délits et écrous.
— v. tr. Charger, emplir, remplir *(with,* de) [to fill]. ‖ Charger *(with,* de) [to entrust]. ‖ Enjoindre à, ordonner à, sommer; donner pour instructions à *(to,* de) [to order]. ‖ ELECTR., MILIT. Charger. ‖ FIN. Mettre à la charge, passer au débit, porter au compte *(on,* de); prélever (a commission); imputer, passer *(to,* à) [a sum]; faire payer, demander, prendre *(for,* pour) [a price]; payer *(to,* à) [the cost]; *to charge s.o. too much for sth.,* compter qqch. trop cher à qqn. ‖ JUR. Accuser, charger; inculper, prévenir *(with,* de) [s.o.]. ‖ FIG. Imputer *(upon,* à) [a fault]; charger, accuser *(with,* de) [s.o.]. ‖ FIG. Charger, garnir, bourrer, saturer *(with,* de) [memory].
— v. intr. MILIT. Charger. ‖ *To charge down upon,* foncer sur; *to charge into,* donner dans. ‖ JUR., FIG. Alléguer *(that,* que).

chargé [ʃɑː'ʒe] n. JUR. Chargé *(m.)* d'affaires.

chargeable ['tʃɑːdʒəbl] adj. A la charge *(to,* de) [person, thing]. ‖ FIN. Imposable (land); imputable *(to,* à) [loss, sum]; à la charge, aux frais *(to,* de) [sum]. ‖ JUR. Accusable, inculpable *(with,* de) [person].

charger [-ə*] n. TECHN. Chargeur *m.* ‖ MILIT. Cheval *(m.)* de guerre (horse); chargeur *m.* (of a rifle).

charily ['tʃɛərili] adv. Avec économie. ‖ Avec prudence.

chariness [-nis] n. Economie *f.* ‖ Prudence *f.*

charing ['tʃɑːriŋ] n. Ménages *m. pl.;* action *(f.)* de faire des ménages.

chariot ['tʃæriət] n. † Char, carrosse *m.* ‖ MILIT. † Chariot *m.*
— v. tr. Conduire en char (or) en carrosse.
— v. intr. Rouler carrosse.

charisma [kə'rizmə] (pl. **charismata** [-əte] n. Charisme *m.*

charismatic [ˌkæriz'mætik] adj. Charismatique.

charitable ['tʃæritəbl] adj. Charitable, de charité (deed); charitable (person); de bienfaisance *(to,* envers) [society]. ‖ Indulgent, libéral.

charitably [-bli] adv. Charitablement.

charity ['tʃæriti] n. Charité *f.; for charity's sake, out of mere charity,* par charité pure. ‖ Charité, bienveillance, indulgence *f.; to be out of charity with,* ne pas être bien avec, n'avoir pas de tendresse pour. ‖ Charité, action charitable *f.;* acte *(m.)* de charité (kindness). ‖ Charité, générosité, aumône *f.* (alms); *to live on charity,* vivre de charités. ‖ Société philanthropique, œuvre de bienfaisance, institution charitable *f.* (society). ‖ **Charity-bazaar,** n. Vente de charité *f.* ‖ **Charity-boy,** n. Orphelin, pupille *m.* ‖ **Charity-girl,** n. Orpheline, pupille *f.* ‖ **Charity-school,** n. Orphelinat *m.*

charivari ['ʃɑːri'vɑːri] n. Charivari *m.*

charlady ['tʃɑː,leidi] n. Femme *(f.)* de ménage.

charlatan ['ʃɑːlətən] n. Charlatan *m.*

charlatanical [ˌʃɑːlə'tænikəl] adj. Charlatanesque. (See QUACKISH.)

charlatanism ['ʃɑːlətənizm] n. Charlatanisme *m.*

charlatanry [-ri] n. Charlatanerie *f.*

Charles [tʃɑːlz] n. Charles *m.* ‖ ASTRON. *Charles's Wain,* Chariot, Grande Ourse.

Charley horse ['tʃɑːli,hɔːs] n. U.S. FAM. Crampe *f.*

Charlie ['tʃɑːli] n. FAM. Charlot *m.,* cloche *f.* (fool); type, gars *m.* (chap). ‖ MILIT., POP. Viet *m.* (Vietnamese). ‖ Pl. FAM. Flotteurs, roberts, nichons *m. pl.* (breasts).

charlotte ['ʃɑːlət] n. CULIN. Charlotte *f.*

charm [tʃɑːm] n. ZOOL. Vol *m.;* bande *f.* (of finches).

charm n. Charme, enchantement *m.* (See SPELL.) ‖ Charme *m.;* fascination, séduction, attraction *f.; to fall a victim to the charms of,* tomber sous le charme de. ‖ Pl. Charmes, appas *m. pl.* (of a woman). ‖ Amulette *f.;* fétiche, talisman, porte-bonheur *m.* ‖ Pendeloque, breloque *f.* (trinket).
— v. tr. Charmer (snakes). ‖ Charmer, enchanter, ensorceler (to bewitch); *to charm away s.o.'s cares,* distraire qqn de ses soucis. ‖ Charmer, enchanter *(by, with,* par) [s.o.]. ‖ Protéger magiquement; *to bear a charmed life,* être béni des dieux; être verni (fam.).

charmer [-ə*] n. Charmeur *s.* (of snakes). ‖ FIG. Charmeur *s.;* enchanteresse *f.*

charming [-iŋ] adj. Charmant.

charmingly [-iŋli] adv. De manière charmante, avec charme.

charnel ['tʃɑːnl] adj. D'ossements. ‖ **Charnel-house,** n. Charnier, ossuaire *m.*
— n. Charnier, ossuaire *m.*

Charon ['kɛərən] n. Caron *m.* ‖ FAM. Nautonier *m.*

charry ['tʃɑːri] adj. U. S. Charbonneux.

chart [tʃɑːt] n. TECHN. Graphique, diagramme; tableau *m.* ‖ MED. Courbe *f.* ‖ NAUT. Carte marine *f.*
— v. tr. TECHN. Inscrire sur un graphique (or) tableau. ‖ NAUT. Porter sur la carte.

charter [-ə*] n. Charte *f.; Atlantic Charter,* charte de l'Atlantique. ‖ JUR. Statuts *m. pl.* (of a society). ‖ FIN. Privilège *m.* ‖ AVIAT., NAUT. Affrètement *m.; charter flight,* vol en charter. ‖ **Charter member,** n. JUR. Membre fondateur *m.* ‖ **Charter-party,** n. NAUT. Charte-partie *f.*
— v. tr. Accorder une charte (or) un privilège à. ‖ JUR. Accorder un contrat à; *chartered accountant,* expert comptable. ‖ NAUT., AVIAT. Affréter, fréter; *chartered plane,* charter. ‖ FAM. Fréter. (See HIRE.)

charterer [-ərə*] n. NAUT. Affréteur m.

chartist [-ist] n. † Chartiste s.

Chartreuse [ʃα:'trə:z] n. Chartreuse f. (liqueur). — adj. Chartreuse, vert jaune (colour).

charwoman ['tʃα:wumən] (pl. **charwomen** [-wimin]) n. Femme (f.) de journée (or) de ménage.

chary ['tʃɛəri] adj. Econome, avare, chiche (of, de) [stingy]. ‖ Prudent, circonspect, avisé (of, à l'égard de) [cautious]; timide, emprunté (of, devant) [shy].

Charybdis [kə'ribdis] n. Charybde m.

chase [tʃeis] n. Chasse, poursuite f. ‖ SPORTS. Chasse f. (hunters, hunting); gibier chassé m. (game); droit (m.) de chasse (licence); chasse réservée f. (preserve); butterfly chase, chasse aux papillons. ‖ NAUT. Navire (m.) pris en chasse (pursued ship); chasse f. (pursuit). ‖ FAM. To go on a wild goose chase, courir après le vent. ‖ **Chase-gun**, n. NAUT. Canon (m.) de chasse.
— v. tr. Chasser, pourchasser, donner la chasse à; poursuivre, courir après. ‖ FAM. Chase yourself!, va te faire pendre ailleurs!

chase n. ARCHIT. Rainure f. (for drain pipes). ‖ MILIT. Volée f. (of a gun).

chase n. TECHN. Châssis m. (for printing).

chase v. tr. Enchâsser (in, dans) [a diamond]; ciseler (gold); repousser (metal); fileter (a screw).

chaser [-ə*] n. SPORTS. Chasseur m. ‖ NAUT. Pièce de chasse f. (gun); navire (m.) qui donne la chasse (ship). ‖ FAM. Pousse-café; rince-gueule m. (pop.).

chaser n. ARTS. Ciseleur s. ‖ TECHN. Peigne m.

chasm ['kæzm̩] n. GEOGR. Crevasse, gorge f.; gouffre m. ‖ Lacune f.; hiatus m. (gap). ‖ FIG. Abîme m. (between, entre).

chassé ['ʃæsei] n. Chassé m. (dance).
— v. intr. Danser le chassé.

chassis ['ʃæsi:] n. AUTOM., MILIT., RADIO. Châssis m. ‖ AVIAT. Train (m) chariot d'atterrissage m. ‖FAM. U. S. Châssis (body).

chaste [tʃeist] adj. Chaste, pur (virtuous). ‖ Pudique, modeste (modest). ‖ Simple, net, pur, dépouillé (style).

chasten ['tʃeisn̩] v. tr. Châtier, éprouver. ‖ Corriger, amender; assagir, modérer. ‖ FIG. Châtier (one's style).

chastise [tʃæs'taiz] v. tr. Châtier, punir (to punish). ‖ Corriger, battre (to beat). [See BEAT, CASTIGATE, THRASH.]

chastisement ['tʃæstizmənt] n. Châtiment m.; correction f.

chastity ['tʃæstiti] n. Chasteté, continence f. ‖ Modestie, pudeur f. ‖ Simplicité, pureté f. ‖ **Chastity-belt**, n. Ceinture de chasteté f.

chasuble ['tʃæzubl̩] n. ECCLES. Chasuble f.

chat [tʃæt] v. intr. (1). Bavarder, causer; jaser, papoter. (See CHATTER.)
— m. Bavardage m.; causette f.; occasion (f.) de bavarder.

château ['ʃα:tou] n. Château m.

chattels ['tʃætls] n. pl. JUR. Biens meubles m. pl.

chatter ['tʃætə*] v. intr. Babiller (apes); jaser, jacasser, caqueter (birds). ‖ Bavarder, causer, papoter (persons). ‖ Claquer (teeth). ‖ TECHN. Cogner (engine); brouter (tool).
— n. Babil m. (of apes); jacasserie f.; caquetage m. (of birds). ‖ Bavardage, papotage m. (of persons). ‖ Claquement m. (of teeth). ‖ TECHN. Claquement m. (of engine); broutage m. (of tool).

chatterbox [-bɔks] n. FAM. Moulin (m.) à paroles; mitrailleuse, jacasse f.; salivard m. (pop.).

chatterer [-rə*] n. Bavard s.

chattering [-riŋ] n. See CHATTER n.

chatty ['tʃæti] adj. Causeur, bavard (person). ‖ Familier, causant; du style de la conversation.

chauffer ['tʃɔ:fə*] n. Réchaud portatif m.

chauffeur [ʃou'fə*] n. AUTOM. Chauffeur m.

chauffeuse [-'føz] n. AUTOM. Femme chauffeur f.

chauvinism ['ʃouvinizm̩] n. Chauvinisme m. ‖ FAM. Male chauvinism, phallocratie.

chauvinist [-ist] n. Chauvin s. ‖ FAM. Male chauvinist, phallocrate.

chaw [tʃɔ:] n. Chique f.
— v. tr. Chiquer. ‖ POP. Mâcher, mastiquer.

cheap [tʃi:p] adj. Bon marché, pas cher (dealer, price, thing); dirt cheap, pour rien, d'un prix dérisoire, très avantageux; to come cheaper, revenir moins cher, coûter meilleur marché. ‖ Réduit, à prix réduit; on the cheap, au rabais. ‖ Sans grande valeur, de piètre qualité; cheap and nasty, en toc. ‖ THEATR., CH. DE F. A prix réduit. ‖ FIN. Déprécié (money). ‖ FIG. Sans valeur; sans profondeur, piètre; facile (success); to feel cheap, se sentir petit garçon; to hold life cheap, faire bon marché de sa vie; to make oneself cheap, se déprécier. ‖ FAM. Mal fichu; to feel cheap, ne pas être dans son assiette; ne pas savoir où se mettre. ‖ POP. U. S. Cheap skate, rat (miser). ‖ **Cheap-jack**, n. Camelot m.

cheapen [-ən] v. tr. Baisser le prix de (sth.). ‖ FIG. To cheapen oneself, se déprécier.
— v. intr. Baisser, être moins cher.

cheaply [-li] adv. A bon marché (or) compte, pas cher, à bas prix.

cheapness [-nis] n. Bon marché m. ‖ FIG. Médiocrité f.; faux éclat (of style).

cheat [tʃi:t] n. Trompeur (deceiver); filou, escroc m. (swindler). ‖ Tricheur s.; tricherie f. (at games) ‖ Tromperie f. (deceit); escroquerie f. (swindle).
— v. tr. Tromper, duper, rouler (to deceive). ‖ Frauder (to defraud); filouter, escroquer (to swindle); to cheat s.o. out of sth., extorquer qqch. à qqn. ‖ FIG. Tromper (fatigue, time).
— v. intr. Frauder (to defraud). ‖ Tricher (at games).

cheater [-ə*] n. Trompeur; tricheur s.; U. S. FAM. Pl. Besicles m. pl.

cheating [-iŋ] adj. Trompeur. ‖ Frauduleux.
— n. Tromperie f. ‖ Escroquerie f. ‖ Fraude f. ‖ Tricherie f.

check [tʃek] n. Echec m. (to, à) [in chess]. ‖ Arrêt m. (stop); interruption, pause f. ‖ Contrôle pointage m.; vérification f.; to keep a check on avoir droit de regard sur. ‖ Vu m.; marque (f.) de contrôle. ‖ Carreau, damier m.; tissu à carreaux m. broken check, pied-de-poule. ‖ MILIT. Revers m. ‖ SPORTS. Perte (f.) du pied (in hunting). ‖ CH. DE F Bulletin (m.) de consigne. ‖ THEATR. Contre marque f. ‖ FIN. U. S. Chèque m. ‖ FIG. Obstacle échec, frein m.; restriction; contrainte f.; to hold (or) keep in check, tenir en échec, faire échec à to put a check on, mettre un frein à. ‖ FAM. T hand (or) pass in one's checks, passer l'arme gauche. ‖ **Check-analysis**, n. Contre-analyse f. **Check-inspection**, n. MED. Contre-visite f. **Check-list**, n. Liste (f.) de contrôle. ‖ **Check-nut** n. TECHN. Contre-écrou m. ‖ **Check-patterned**, adj. A damiers, à carreaux. ‖ **Check-point**, n. MILIT Poste de contrôle m. ‖ **Check-up**, n. Examen de contrôle m.; MED. Check-up, bilan (m.) de santé ‖ **Check-valve**, n. TECHN. Soupape de retenue f.
— v. tr. Faire échec à (in chess). ‖ Arrêter, enraye (to stop). ‖ Vérifier, contrôler (to control); pointer cocher (to mark). ‖ U. S. Mettre au vestiair (a wrap). ‖ FIN. Apurer, vérifier (an account). ‖ CH. DE F. Faire enregistrer (one's luggage); contrô ler (the tickets). ‖ FIG. Refréner, contenir, réprimer ‖ **To check off**, pointer, cocher. ‖ **To check out** U. S. CH. DE F. Retirer (one's luggage). ‖ **To check up**, contrôler; faire le point de.
— v. intr. S'arrêter, broncher, hésiter, marquer le pas (at, devant). ‖ SPORTS. Perdre le pied (in hunt ing). ‖ **To check in**, s'inscrire (at an hotel). **To check out**, régler sa note (at an hotel); FAM

Plier bagage (to die). ‖ **To check up on**, examiner, étudier.

checker [-ə*] n. See CHEQUER. ‖ U. S. Contrôleur *m.* ‖ Pl. U. S. Jeu (*m.*) de dames.

checking [-iŋ] pr. p. See CHECK. ‖ **Checking-account**, n. U.S., FIN. Compte courant *m.*

checkmate [-'meit] n. Echec et mat *m.* (in chess). ‖ FIG. Echec *m.*

— v. tr. Mater (in chess). ‖ FIG. Damer le pion à.

checkroom [-'rum] n. U. S. Vestiaire *m.* ‖ CH. DE F. U. S. Consigne *f.*

cheek [tʃi:k] n. MED. Joue *f.* ‖ ARCHIT. Chambranle *m.* (of door). ‖ TECHN. Mâchoire *f.* (of a vice). ‖ NAUT. *Rudder cheek*, safran du gouvernail. ‖ FAM. Aplomb, front, toupet *m.; impudence*, nargue, effronterie *f.; it's a piece of damned cheek*, c'est se ficher du monde ; *to have the cheek of the devil*, avoir un culot monstre (or) infernal. ‖ FAM. *Cheek by jowl*, joue contre joue ; cul et chemise (pop.) ; *with one's tongue in one's cheek*, hypocritement ; ironiquement.

— v. tr. Narguer, se montrer insolent avec.

cheekbone [-boun] n. MED. Pommette *f.*

cheekiness [-inis] n. FAM. Toupet, aplomb, front ; culot *m.*

cheeky [-i] n. FAM. Effronté, hardi ; culotté (fam.). [See SAUCY.]

cheep [tʃi:p] v. intr. Gazouiller (bird) ; piauler (young bird).

— n. Gazouillis ; piaulement *m.*

cheer [tʃiə*] n. † Mine *f.* ‖ Chère, nourriture *f.* (food). ‖ Disposition *f.; état d'esprit m.;* gaieté, joie *f.* ‖ Pl. Acclamations *f. pl.;* applaudissements, hourras, bravos *m. pl.* ‖ FAM. *Cheers!*, à la vôtre !

— v. tr. Réconforter, encourager, remonter (to comfort) ; égayer, dérider (to gladden). ‖ Applaudir, acclamer (to acclaim). ‖ **To cheer on**, encourager, pousser (*to*, à). ‖ **To cheer up**, égayer ; réconforter ; ragaillardir.

— v. intr. Réconforter, remonter le moral ; égayer. ‖ Applaudir ; pousser des vivats. ‖ FAM. *Cheer!*, à la vôtre !, à votre santé ! ‖ **To cheer up**, se réjouir, prendre courage (or) espoir.

cheerful [-ful] adj. Plaisant, attrayant, gai, riant (face, room, thing) ; gai, allègre, plein d'entrain, d'humeur joyeuse, d'un cœur joyeux (person).

cheerfully [-fuli] adv. Gaiement ; avec bonne grâce.

cheerfulness [-fulnis] n. Entrain, enjouement *m.;* bonne humeur, gaieté *f.* (of persons). ‖ Gaieté *f.* (of a landscape, room).

cheerily [-rili] adv. Gaiement ; de bon cœur.

cheeriness [-rinis] n. Gaieté ; bonne humeur *f.*

cheering [-riŋ] adj. Réconfortant ; réjouissant.

— m. Acclamations *f. pl.;* hourras, vivats, *m. pl.*

cheerio ['tʃiːəri'ou] interj. FAM. A la vôtre ! (in drinking) ; au revoir, bon courage ! (at parting).

cheerless ['tʃiəlis] adj. Morne, sombre, triste, maussade, peu engageant (person, thing). ‖ Sans entrain ; sans bonne volonté.

cheerlessly [-lisli] adv. Avec tristesse (or) maussaderie. ‖ Sans ardeur.

cheery [-i] adj. Gai ; égayant ; plein de vie.

cheese [tʃiːz] n. CULIN. Fromage *m.; cottage cheese*, fromage blanc ; *cream cheese*, petit suisse, demi-sel ; *goat's-milk cheese*, fromage de chèvre ; *green cheese*, fromage frais. ‖ CULIN. Gelée *f.* ‖ U. S. FAM. *Big cheese*, gros bonnet. ‖ FAM. *Hard cheese!*, pas de veine !, manque de pot ! ‖ **Cheese-cake**, n. CULIN. Talmouse *f.* ‖ **Cheese-cover**, n. Cloche (*f.*) à fromage. ‖ **Cheese-dairy**, n. Fromagerie *f.* ‖ **Cheese-drainer**, n. Cagerotte *f.* ‖ **Cheese-finger**, n. CULIN. Baguette (*f.*) au fromage. ‖ **Cheese-hopper**, n. ZOOL. Asticot *m.* ‖ **Cheese-maker**, n. Fromager *s.* ‖ **Cheese-muslin**, n. Etamine *f.* ‖ **Cheese-paring**, n. Croûte (*f.*) de fromage ; FAM. Economie (*f.*) de bouts de chandelle. ‖

Cheese-rennet, n. Présure *f.* ‖ **Cheese-straws**, n. CULIN. Allumettes (*f. pl.*) au fromage. ‖ **Cheese-taster**, n. Sonde (*f.*) à fromage.

cheese v. tr. POP. Laisser tomber ; *cheese it! the cops!*, vingt-deux ! les flics ! ; *to be cheesed off*, se barber, en avoir marre.

cheesecloth [-klɔθ] n. U. S. Etamine *f.*

cheesemonger [-mʌŋgə*] n. COMM. Marchand (*s.*) de fromage.

cheesy [-i] adj. Caséeux ; à odeur (ou) aspect de fromage.

cheesy adj. FAM. U. S. Miteux, minable.

cheetah ['tʃiːtə] n. ZOOL. Guépard *m.*

chef [ʃef] n. Chef *m.* (in a restaurant).

chef-d'œuvre [ʃeˈdœːvr] n. Chef-d'œuvre *m.*

cheiropteran [kaiəˈrɔptərən] n. ZOOL. See CHIROPTERAN.

chelate ['kiːleit] adj. CHIM. Chélaté.

chemical ['kemikəl] adj. CHIM. Chimique ; *chemical engineer*, ingénieur chimiste ; *chemical engineering*, génie chimique. ‖ MILIT. *Chemical warfare*, guerre chimique.

— n. CHIM. Produit chimique *m.*

chemically ['kemikli] adv. Chimiquement.

chemico-physical ['kemikouˈfizikəl] adj. Physico-chimique.

chemise [ʃəˈmiːz] n. Robe-chemisier, chasuble *f.*

chemisette [ʃemiˈzet] n. Chemisette *f.; plastron m.*

chemist ['kemist] n. CHIM. Chimiste *s.* ‖ MED. Pharmacien *s.*

chemistry [-ri] n. CHIM. Chimie *f.*

chemosynthesis [ˌkemouˈsinθisis] n. MED. Chimiosynthèse *f.*

chemotherapy [kemoˈθerəpi] n. MED. Chimiothérapie *f.*

chenille [ʃəˈniːl] n. Chenille *f.* (fabric).

cheque [tʃek] n. FIN. Chèque *m.* (*for*, de) ; *travellers' cheque*, traveller's cheque, chèque de voyage ; *cheque card*, carte de garantie. ‖ **Cheque-book**, n. FIN. Carnet de chèques, chéquier *m.*

chequer ['tʃekə*] n. Damier, carreau *m.; étoffe* (*f.*) à carreaux.

— v. tr. Quadriller ; orner de damiers (or) de carreaux. ‖ Diaprer, bigarrer.

chequered [-əːd] adj. A carreau, à damier. ‖ FAM. Varié ; *chequered career*, vie mouvementée, vie pleine de traverses.

cherish ['tʃeriʃ] v. tr. Chérir, dorloter, couver, veiller sur. ‖ FIG. Entretenir (feelings, hatred, memory) ; nourrir, chérir (hope, illusions).

cheroot [ʃəˈruːt] n. Cigare (*m.*) de Manille.

cherry ['tʃeri] n. BOT. Cerise *f.; wild cherry*, merise *f.* ‖ **Cherry-bob**, n. Grappe (*f.*) de cerises en pendant d'oreille. ‖ **Cherry-brandy**, n. Cherry *m.;* eau-de-vie (*f.*) de cerises. ‖ **Cherry-laurel**, n. BOT. Laurier-cerise *m.* ‖ **Cherry-liqueur**, n. Guignolet *m.* ‖ **Cherry-orchard**, n. Cerisaie *f.* ‖ **Cherry-pie**, n. CULIN. Tourte (*f.*) aux cerises ; BOT. Héliotrope *m.* ‖ U. S. ZOOL. Palourde *f.* ‖ **Cherry-stone**, n. Noyau (*m.*) de cerise ; U. S. ZOOL. Palourde *f.* ‖ **Cherry-tree**, n. BOT. Cerisier *m.* ‖ **Cherry-wood**, n. COMM. Cerisier, merisier *m.*

— adj. Cerise (cherry-red).

cherub ['tʃerəb] (pl. **cherubs** [-z], **cherubim** [-im]) n. ECCLES. Chérubin *m.*

cherubic [tʃeˈruːbik] adj. De chérubin.

chervil ['tʃəːvil] n. BOT., CULIN. Cerfeuil *m.*

Cheshire ['tʃeʃə*] adj. CULIN. *Cheshire cheese*, chester.

— m. GEOGR. Cheshire *m.*

chess [tʃes] n. Echecs *m. pl.* ‖ **Chess-board**, n. Echiquier *m.* ‖ **Chess-man**, n. Pièce *f.* (or) pion (*m.*) du jeu d'échecs.

chest [tʃest] n. Caisse, boîte *f.; coffre m.; chest of drawers*, commode *f.* ‖ Coffret *m.* (for opium, tea). ‖ FIN. Fonds (*m. pl.*) en caisse (fund) ; caisse *f.; coffre m.* ‖ MED. Poitrine *f.* ‖ FAM. *To get it* *off one's chest*, déballer (or) déverser ce qu'on a sur le cœur ; *to throw out one's chest*, cambrer la taille, faire des effets de torse. ‖ **Chest-protector**, n. Plastron *m.* ‖ **Chest-voice**, n. Mus. Voix de poitrine *f.*

chesterfield ['tʃestə,fiːld] n. Chesterfield *m.* (sofa). ‖ Pardessus *(m.)* droit à col de velours (overcoat).

chestnut ['tʃesnʌt] n. Bot. Châtaigne *f.* ‖ Culin. Châtaigne *f.; marron m.* ‖ Zool. Alezan *m.* (horse). ‖ Fig. *To pull s.o.'s chestnuts out of the fire*, tirer les marrons du feu pour qqn. ‖ Fam. Blague éventée ; vieille histoire *f.*
— adj. Châtain (colour). ‖ Zool. Alezan (horse).

chesty ['tʃesti] adj. Fam. Qui a du coffre, à la poitrine large. ‖ Plastronneur (boasting). ‖ Fam. Fragile des bronches.

cheval-glass [ʃə'vælglɑːs] n. Psyché *f.* (mirror).

chevalier [ʃevə'liəːr] n. Chevalier *m.* ‖ † Prétendant *m.*

chevaux-de-frise [ʃə'voudə'friːz] n. pl. Milit. Chevaux de frise *m. pl.*

cheviot ['tʃeviət] n. Cheviotte *f.*

chevron [ʃevrən] n. Archit., Milit., Blas. Chevron *m.*

chevy ['tʃevi] n. Chasse *f.* ‖ Barres *f. pl.* (game).
— v. tr. (2). Pourchasser.

chew [tʃuː] v. tr. Mâchonner, mâcher, mastiquer ; chiquer. ‖ Zool. *To chew the cud*, ruminer.
— v. intr. Chiquer. ‖ Fam. Ruminer ; *to chew at it*, ruminer l'affaire ; *to chew over* (or) *upon*, ruminer, remâcher, ressasser.
— n. Mâchonnement *m.; mastication f.* ‖ Chique *f.*

chewer [-əˣ] n. Chiqueur *s.*

chewing [-iŋ] n. Mâchonnement *m.* ‖ **Chewing-gum**, n. Chewing-gum *m.*

chiaroscuro [ki,ɑːrɔs'kjuərou] n. Arts. Clair-obscur *m.*

chibouk [ʃi'buːk] n. Chibouque *f.*

chic [ʃik] adj. Fam. Chic.

chicane [ʃi'kein] n. Chicane *f.*
— v. tr., intr. Chicaner.

chicanery [-ri] n. Jur. Chicane ; chicanerie *f.*

chick [tʃik] n. Zool. Oiseau nouvellement éclos *m.* (bird) ; poussin *m.* (chicken). ‖ Fam. Poulet *s.* (child). ‖ Pop. U. S. Pépée *f.* (girl).

chickabiddy ['tʃikəbidi] n. Fam. Cocotte *f.* (term of endearment).

chicken ['tʃikin] n. Zool. Poulet *s.; poussin m.* ‖ Culin. Volaille *f.* ‖ U. S. Pop. Froussard *m.* ‖ Fam. Tendron *m.; I am no spring chicken*, je ne suis pas né de ce matin ; *he was no chicken*, ce n'était plus un gosse. ‖ **Chicken-breasted**, adj. Med. Rachitique. ‖ **Chicken-hearted**, adj. Fam. Froussard ; poule mouillée. ‖ **Chicken-livered**, adj. Fam. U. S. Trouillard, qui a les foies. ‖ **Chicken-pox**, n. Med. Varicelle *f.*
— v. intr. Fam. U. S. *To chicken out*, caner.

chickling ['tʃikliŋ] n. Bot. Gesse *f.*

chick-pea ['tʃik'piː] n. Bot.. Culin. Pois chiche *m.*

chickweed [-wid] n. Bot. Mouron *m.*

chicle ['tʃikl] n. Chicle *m.*

chicory ['tʃikəri] n. Bot., Culin. Chicorée *f.* (in coffee) ; endive *f.* (in salads).

chide [tʃaid] v. tr. (34). Gronder.
— v. intr. Gronder, ronchonner. ‖ Murmurer *(against*, contre).

chief [tʃiːf] n. Chef *m.* ‖ Blas. Chef. ‖ Fam. Patron *m.*
— adj. Principal ; en chef. ‖ Jur. *Lord Chief Justice of England*, président du tribunal du Banc de la Reine ; *Chief Justice of the United States*, Président de la Cour suprême des Etats-Unis.
— adv. Avant tout, surtout.

chiefly [-li] adv. Principalement.

chieftain [-tən] n. Chef *m.* (of a clan, group).

chieftainship [-tənʃip] n. Fonction *f.* (or) rang *(m.)* de chef.

chiffon ['ʃifɔn] n. Mousseline de soie *f.* ‖ Pl. Chiffons *m. pl.*
— adj. En mousseline. ‖ Culin. Mousseux, gonflé ; meringué.

chiffonier [ʃifɔ'niːəˣ] n. Chiffonnier *m.* (chest of drawers).

chignon ['ʃiːnjɔn] n. Chignon *m.*

chigoe ['tʃigou] n. Zool. Chique *f.*

chilblain ['tʃilblein] n. Med. Engelure *f.*

chilblained [-d] adj. Med. Couvert d'engelures.

child [tʃaild] (pl. **children** ['tʃildrən]) n. Enfant *m.; to become a child again*, retomber en enfance. ‖ Med. *With child*, enceinte. ‖ Fig. Conséquence, suite *f.; child of my imagination*, produit de mon imagination. ‖ Loc. *Child's play*, jeu d'enfant, enfance de l'art. ‖ **Child-bearing**, n. Med. Gestation, grossesse *f.* ‖ **Child-bed**, n. Med. Couches *f. pl.* ‖ **Child-birth**, n. Med. Accouchement *m.* ‖ **Child-proof**, adj. A l'épreuve des enfants.
— adj. Infantile ; *child labour*, travail des enfants ; *child welfare centre*, centre de protection infantile ; *child welfare*, protection de l'enfance.

childe n. † Chevalier *m.*

Childermas ['tʃildəməs] n. Eccles. Innocents, Saints Innocents *m. pl.*

childhood ['tʃaildhud] n. Enfance *f.; verging on a state of second childhood*, prêt à retomber en enfance.

childish [-iʃ] adj. Enfantin ; puéril.

childishness [-iʃnis] n. Enfantillage *m.; puérilité f.*

childless [-lis] adj. Sans enfants.

childlike [-laik] adj. Enfant, innocent, pur ; d'enfant ; candide.

Chile ['tʃili] n. Geogr. Chili *m.; Chile nitre, saltpetre*, nitrate, salpêtre du Chili. ‖ Bot. *Chile pine*, araucaria.

Chilean [-ən] adj., n. Geogr. Chilien *adj., s.*

chili ['tʃili] n. See chilli.

chill [tʃil] n. Fraîcheur *f.; to take the chill off*, amortir, dégourdir (water) ; chambrer (wine). ‖ Med. Refroidissement, coup de froid *m.* (cold) ; frisson *m.* (shiver). ‖ Techn. Coquille *f.* ‖ Fig. Froid *m.; to cast a chill over*, jeter un froid sur, glacer.
— adj. Glacé (cool) ; frissonnant, transi, gelé (shivering). ‖ Froid, glacial.
— v. tr. Refroidir, transir, glacer, geler (s.o.). ‖ Bot. Geler (plant). ‖ Techn. Couler en coquille. ‖ Culin. Congeler, frigorifier (meat).
— v. intr. Se refroidir.

chil(l)i ['tʃili] n. Bot., Culin. Piment *m.*

chilliness [-'tʃilinis] n. Froid *m.; fraîcheur, froidure f.* ‖ Med. Frissonnement *m.* ‖ Fig. Froideur *f.*

chilling [-iŋ] adj. Froid, glacial, réfrigérant ; qui fait frissonner.

chilly [-i] adj. Frileux (person) ; frais, frisquet, froid (weather). ‖ Med. Frissonnant. ‖ Fig. Froid, réfrigérant.

chime [tʃaim] n. Carillon *m.; to ring the chimes*, carillonner. ‖ Fig. Harmonie *f.*
— v. tr. Carillonner (the bells) ; sonner (the hour). ‖ Fig. S'accorder, s'entendre, être à l'unisson (*with*, avec). ‖ Fam. Ressasser.
— v. intr. Carillonner. ‖ Fig. **To chime in**, faire chorus, surenchérir ; *to chime in with*, s'associer (or) applaudir à ; s'harmoniser (or) se concilier avec ; s'accorder avec.

chime n. Jable *m.* (of a barrel).

chimera [kai'miərə] n. Chimère *f.*

chimere [tʃi'miəˣ] n. Eccles. Simarre *f.*

chimerical [kai'merikəl] adj. Chimérique.

chimney ['tʃimni] n. Archit., Geogr., Naut., Sports. Cheminée *f.* ‖ Verre *m.* (of a lamp). ‖ **Chimney-corner**, n. Coin du feu *m* ‖ **Chimney-**

flue, n. ARCHIT. Tuyau (*m.*) de la cheminée. ‖ **Chimney-jack,** n. Mitre *f.* ‖ **Chimney-piece,** n. Cheminée *f.;* manteau (*m.*) de la cheminée. ‖ **Chimney-pot,** n. Cheminée *f.;* pot (*m.*) de cheminée; FAM. *Chimney-pot hat,* tuyau de poêle. ‖ **Chimney-stalk,** n. Cheminée d'usine *f.* ‖ **Chimney-sweep,** n. Ramoneur *m.* ‖ **Chimney-sweeper,** n. Ramoneuse *f.* (brush); ramoneur *m.* (person).

chimpanzee [ˌtʃimpənˈzi:] n. ZOOL. Chimpanzé *m.*

chin [tʃin] n. MED. Menton *m.; double chin,* double menton. ‖ FAM. *To keep one's chin up,* relever la tête, tenir bon (or) le coup. ‖ **Chin-deep,** adj. Enfoncé jusqu'au menton.

China [ˈtʃainə] n. GEOGR. Chine *f.* ‖ COMM. Porcelaine *f.* (dishes, porcelain). ‖ **China-clay** n. Kaolin *m.* ‖ **China-closet,** n. Vitrine *f.*
— adj. De Chine; *China crape, Sea,* crêpe, mer de Chine. ‖ De porcelaine; *china dealer,* marchand de porcelaine; *china industry,* industrie porcelainière. ‖ BOT. *China aster,* reine-marguerite.

Chinaman [-mən] (pl. **chinamen**) n. GEOGR. Chinois *m.* ‖ NAUT. Navire (*m.*) commerçant avec la Chine. ‖ FAM. U. S. *Not to have a Chinaman's chance,* ne pas avoir l'ombre d'une chance.

chinaware [-wɛə*] n. Porcelaine *f.* (crockery, dishes).

chinch [tʃintʃ] n. ZOOL. U. S. Punaise *f.*

chinchilla [tʃinˈtʃilə] n. ZOOL., COMM.; Chinchilla *m.*

chin-chin [ˈtʃinˈtʃin] interj. FAM. Au revoir! ‖ A la vôtre!
— v. tr. Dire au revoir. ‖ Trinquer. ‖ U. S. Jaser.

chincough [ˈtʃinkɔf] n. MED. Coqueluche *f.*

chine [tʃain] n. MED., CULIN. Echine *f.* ‖ GEOGR. Arête *f.*

chine n. Ravin *m.*

Chinese [tʃaiˈni:z] adj. GEOGR. Chinois. ‖ LOC. Vénitien (lantern); indéchiffrable (puzzle); de Chine (white).
— n. GEOGR., GRAMM. Chinois *s.*

Chink [tʃiŋk] n. FAM. Chinetoque *s.* (Chinese).

chink n. Fissure, fente, lézarde *f.* (in a wall). ‖ Jour, interstice *m.* ‖ FIG. *Chink in the armour,* défaut de la cuirasse, point faible.

chink n. Tintement *m.* (of coins, glasses).
— v. tr. Faire tinter; *to chink glasses,* trinquer.
— v. intr. Tinter.

chinoiserie [ʃinˈwɑːzəri] n. ARTS. Chinoiserie *f.*

chinse, chintz [tʃins] v. tr. NAUT. Etouper.

chintz [tʃints] n. Indienne, perse *f.* (cloth).

chip [tʃip] n. Brèche *f.* (on the blade of a knife); ébréchure, écornure *f.* (on the edge of a plate). ‖ Simili-paille *m.* (for hats). ‖ Fragment, éclat, copeau *m.* (of metal, wood). ‖ Déchet, débris *m.* ‖ Jeton *m.* (used in games). ‖ ELECTR. Pastille, tranche, puce *f.* (fam.) [of silicon]; microcircuit *m.* (microchip). ‖ Pl. CULIN. Frites, pommes frites *f. pl.* ‖ SPORTS. Coup (*m.*) en dessous (in golf). ‖ FIG. *Chip off the old block,* rejeton de la vieille souche, digne héritier de la famille. ‖ FAM. *He's had his chips,* il est cuit (or) fichu; U.S. *in the chips,* plein aux as ; *to have a chip on one's shoulder,* être bagarreur.
— v. tr. (1). Ebrécher, écailler, écorner. ‖ Faire voler en éclats (the glass); *to chip wood,* faire des copeaux. ‖ Casser (the shell of an egg). ‖ CULIN. Tailler en lamelles. ‖ ARTS. Tailler, sculpter, buriner. ‖ SPORTS. Prendre en dessous (golf ball); faire un croc-en-jambe (wrestling).
— v. intr. S'ébrécher, s'écailler, s'écorner. ‖ Briser la coquille (chicken). ‖ **To chip at,** faire voler des éclats de (a block of stone); FAM. Se ficher de. ‖ **To chip in,** FAM. Mettre son grain de sel.

chipmunk [ˈtʃipˌmʌŋk] n. ZOOL. Chipmunk, écureuil terrestre américain *m.*

chipper [-ə*] v. intr. Gazouiller.
— adj. U. S. FAM. En forme, guilleret, vif.

chippie [-i] n. U. S. FAM. Pierreuse *f.* (streetwalker).

chippy [-i] adj. CULIN. Grumeleux. ‖ FAM. Hargneux, mal luné, quinteux. ‖ POP. *To feel chippy,* être vaseux.

chiromancer [ˈkaiərəmænsə*] n. Chiromancien *s.*

chiromancy [-si] n. Chiromancie *f.*

chiropodist [kaiəˈrɔpədist] n. Pédicure *m.*

chiropody [-di] n. Art *m.* (or) soins du pédicure.

chiropractic [ˌkaiərəˈpræktik] n. MED. Chiropraxie *f.*

chiropractor [-tə*] n. MED. Chiropractor *m.*

chiropteran [kaiˈrɔptərən] n. ZOOL. Chiroptère *m.*

chirp [tʃə:p] n. Gazouillis, pépiement *m.* (of birds); chant *m.* (of crickets).
— v. intr. Gazouiller, pépier (birds); chanter (crickets). ‖ Gazouiller (baby, person).

chirpy [-i] adj. Gai, chantonnant; de bonne humeur.

chirr [tʃə:*] n. Stridulation *f.*
— v. intr. Striduler.

chirrup [ˈtʃirəp] v. intr. Gazouiller, pépier. ‖ SPORTS. Exciter.

chisel [ˈtʃizl] n. TECHN. Ciseau *m.; hollow chisel,* gouge; *mortise chisel,* bédane; *roughing-out chisel,* ébauchoir. ‖ ARTS. Burin *m.* ‖ FAM. Filouterie *f.*
— v. tr. (1). ARTS. Sculpter, buriner, ciseler. ‖ FAM. Resquiller; extorquer, griveler; *to chisel s.o. out of sth.,* soutirer (or) carotter qqch. à qqn.

chiseller [-ə*] n. ARTS. Ciseleur, sculpteur *m.* ‖ FAM. Carotteur, escroc, griveleur *m.*

chit [tʃit] n. FAM. Gamin, gosse *s.*

chit n. Note *f.* ‖ Ticket *m.*

chit-chat [ˈtʃitˌtʃæt] n. FAM. Bavardage, potin *m.*

chitterlings [ˈtʃitəliŋz] n. CULIN. Andouille *f.*

chivalrous [ˈʃivələrəs] adj. Chevaleresque.

chivalry [-ri] n. Chevalerie *f.* (knighthood, knights). ‖ Courtoisie *f.;* qualités chevaleresques *f. pl.*

chive [tʃaiv] n. BOT., CULIN. Ciboulette, civette *f.*

chiv(v)y [ˈtʃivi] v. tr. (2). Tarabuster, houspiller (to nag).

chlamys [ˈklæmis] n. † Chlamyde *f.*

chloral [ˈklɔ:rəl] n. CHIM. Chloral *m.*

chlorate [-it] n. CHIM. Chlorate *m.*

chloric [-ik] adj. CHIM. Chlorique.

chloride [-aid] n. CHIM. Chlorure *m.*

chlorinate [ˈklɔ:rineit] v. tr. Javelliser (water).

chlorination [klɔ:riˈneiʃən] n. CHIM. Chloruration *f.* ‖ Javellisation *f.*

chlorine [ˈklɔ:ri:n] n. CHIM. Chlore *m.*

chlorodyne [ˈklɔ:rədain] n. MED. Chlorodyne *f.*

chloroform [-fɔ:m] n. MED. Chloroforme *m.*
— v. intr. MED. Chloroformer.

chloromycetin [ˌklɔrəmaiˈsi:tin] n. MED. Chloromycétine *f.*

chlorophyll [ˈklɔrəfil] n. BOT. Chlorophylle *f.*

chloropicrin [ˌklɔrəˈpikrin] n. CHIM. Chloropicrine *f.*

chloroplast [ˈklɔrəˌplæst] n. BOT. Chloroplaste *m.*

chlorosis [klɔ:ˈrousis] n. MED. Chlorose *f.*

chlorotic [-tik] adj. MED. Chlorotique.

choc [tʃɔk] n. FAM. Chocolat *m.* ‖ **Choc-ice,** n. Glace (*f.*) enrobée de chocolat, esquimau *m.*

chock [tʃɔk] n. Cale *f.* (See WEDGE.) ‖ NAUT. Chantier *m.*
— v. tr. Caler (a wheel). ‖ NAUT. Mettre sur chantier. ‖ TECHN. Coincer. ‖ FAM. Embarrasser, encombrer, bourrer.
— adv. A force, à bloc. ‖ **Chock-a-block,** adj. NAUT. A bloc, à plein; FIG. Bondé. ‖ **Chock-full,** adj. Bondé, plein à craquer, archiplein, comble.

chocker [ˈtʃɔkə*] adj. FAM. Cafardeux.

chocolate [ˈtʃɔkəlit] n. Chocolat *m.*
— adj. Au chocolat; U. S. *chocolate candy,* chocolat, crotte au chocolat. ‖ Chocolat (colour).

choice [tʃɔis] n. Choix *m.; for choice,* de préférence; *to be s.o.'s choice for,* être choisi par qqn pour; *to fix one's choice on,* jeter son dévolu sur.

‖ COMM. Choix, assortiment *m.* ‖ FAM. Elite, crème, fine fleur *f.*
— adj. Choisi, de choix, d'élite, raffiné. ‖ COMM. *Choicest,* de premier choix, grand choix, de grande marque.
choicely [-li] adv. Avec goût, d'une façon choisie.
choiceness [-nis] n. Qualité, excellence ; minutie *(f.)* du choix.
choir ['kwaiə*] n. MUS. Chœur *m.;* chorale *f.* ‖ MUS., ECCLES. Maîtrise *f.; to sing in the choir,* chanter au lutrin. ‖ ARCHIT., ECCLES. Chœur *m.* ‖ **Choir-boy,** n. MUS., ECCLES. Jeune choriste *m.* ‖ **Choir-master,** n. MUS. Chef de chœur *m.;* ECCLES. Maître de chapelle *m.* ‖ **Choir-school,** n. ECCLES., MUS. Maîtrise, manécanterie *f.*
— v. tr., intr. MUS. Chanter en chœur.
choke [tʃouk] n. TECHN. Obstruction *f.;* blocage *m.* (act) ; étranglement *m.* (constriction) ; étrangleur (valve). ‖ MED. Etranglement, étouffement *m.* ‖ AUTOM. Starter *m.* ‖ MILIT. Etranglement, choke-bore *m.* (of a rifle). ‖ **Choke-coil,** n. ELECTR. Bobine *(f.)* d'étouffement. ‖ **Choke-damp,** n. Molette *f.;* gaz irrespirable *m.* ‖ **Choke-pear,** n. Poire d'angoisse *f.*
— v. tr. Etouffer, suffoquer, étrangler (s.o., s.o.'s voice). ‖ Etouffer (the fire). ‖ Boucher, obstruer, engorger (a pipe). ‖ FIG. Etouffer, contenir. ‖ **To choke back,** comprimer, contenir, étouffer (feelings). ‖ **To choke down,** étouffer, ravaler (sobs). ‖ **To choke off,** étrangler, étouffer, écraser (an enterprise, s.o.) ; envoyer promener (a bore). ‖ **To choke up,** engorger, obstruer.
— v. intr. Etouffer, s'étrangler. ‖ TECHN. S'engorger, se boucher. ‖ **To choke up,** étouffer.
choke n. BOT. Foin *m.* (of artichokes).
chokecherry [-'tʃeri] n. U. S. BOT. Merise de Virginie *f.*
choker [-ə*] n. Collet *m.* (fur tippet) ; foulard *m.* (necktie). ‖ FAM. Carcan *m.* (collar) ; collier *m.* (necklace). ‖ FAM. Argument-massue *m.; that's a choker,* ça vous la boucle, ça vous en bouche un coin.
choking [-iŋ] adj. Suffocant (gas). ‖ FIG. Etouffé ; étranglé (voice).
choky [-i] adj. Suffocant, étouffant.
choledoch ['kɔlidɔk] adj., n. MED. Cholédoque *m.*
choler ['kɔlə*] n. MED. † Bile *f.* ‖ FIG. † Colère *f.*
cholera ['kɔlərə] n. MED. Choléra *m.; bilious* (or) *summer cholera,* cholérine.
choleric [-ik] adj. Colérique, coléreux.
cholesterol [kə'lɛstəroul] n. MED. Cholestérol *m.*
choline ['koulin] n. MED. Choline *f.*
choose [tʃuːz] v. tr. (35). Choisir, faire choix de (to select). ‖ Choisir, opter pour *(between, from,* entre) ; *there is nothing to choose between them,* ils ne valent pas mieux l'un que l'autre. ‖ Choisir, élire (a chairman, a president).
— v. intr. Choisir, faire un choix. ‖ Décider, vouloir ; *as you choose,* comme vous l'entendrez, à votre gré ; *if you choose,* si cela vous dit (or) convient ; *I cannot choose but,* je ne peux faire autrement que de.
chooser [-ə*] n. Personne *(m.)* qui choisit.
choosing [-iŋ] n. Choix *m.*
choosy [-i] adj. FAM. Difficile, chipoteur.
chop [tʃɔp] n. CULIN. Coup *(m.)* de hache. ‖ CULIN. Côtelette *f.* ‖ AGRIC. Paille hachée *f.; foin haché m.*
— v. tr. (1). Couper à la hache, trancher. ‖ CULIN. Hacher. ‖ MED. Gercer. ‖ FIG. Hacher, entrecouper (one's words). ‖ **To chop down,** abattre. ‖ **To chop off,** trancher, couper. ‖ **To chop up,** hacher, couper en morceaux.
— v. intr. (1). Donner un coup de hache ; donner un coup *(at,* à). ‖ **To chop back,** retourner brusquement, faire volte-face. ‖ **To chop in,** FAM. Dire son mot, mettre son grain de sel.

chop n. NAUT. Clapotis *m.* (of waves) ; saute *f.* (of wind). ‖ FIG. Changement *m.;* évolution *f.*
— v. tr. (1). Echanger ; *to chop logic,* discutailler, ergoter.
— v. intr. (1). NAUT. Clapoter (waves) ; varier, sauter (wind). ‖ FAM. Varier, girouetter ; *to chop and change,* tourner à tout vent, changer d'idée comme de chemise, fluctuer.
chop n. JUR. Licence *f.;* permis *m.* (in China, India). ‖ COMM. Marque *f.* (in China). ‖ FAM. *First chop,* premier choix, *nec plus ultra.*
chop n. Babine f. (See CHAP) ; *to lick one's chops,* se pourlécher les babines.
chop-chop [tʃɔp'tʃɔp] interj. FAM. Et que ça saute !
— adv. FAM. Rapido, fissa.
chopper [-ə*] n. Couperet *m.* ‖ CULIN. Hachoir *m.* ‖ AGRIC. Coupe-racines *m.*
chopping [-ŋ] n. Coupe *f.* ‖ CULIN. Hachage *m.* ‖ **Chopping-block,** n. Billot *m.;* CULIN. Hachoir *m.* ‖ **Chopping-knife,** m. CULIN. Hachoir *m.*
chopping n. FAM. *Chopping and changing,* fluctuations, changements multiples.
choppy ['tʃɔpi] adj. NAUT. Agité (sea) ; clapoteux (waves) ; variable (wind).
choppy adj. † MED. Crevassé, gercé.
chopstick ['tʃɔpstik] n. Baguette *f.* (eating utensil).
chop-suey [tʃɔp'suːi] n. Chop-suey *m.,* fricassée *(f.)* de viande et de légumes.
choral ['kɔːrəl] adj. MUS., ECCLES. Choral *m.; choral society,* chorale *f.*
choral(e) [kɔ'rɑːl] n. MUS., ECCLES. Choral *m.* (hymn, tune) ; chorale *f.* (choral society).
chord [kɔːd] n. MUS., MATH. Corde *f.* ‖ MED. *Vocal chord,* corde vocale ; *spinal chord,* moelle épinière. ‖ FIG. Corde *f.; to strike a sympathetic chord,* faire vibrer la corde sensible.
chord n. MUS. Accord *m.; broken* (or) *spread chord,* arpège.
— v. tr., intr. MUS. Harmoniser.
chore [tʃɔː*] n. Travail *(m.)* de routine ; boulot *m.* (fam.).
chorea [kɔ'riə] n. MED. Chorée *f.*
choreographic [kɔriɔ'græfik] adj. Chorégraphique.
choreography [kɔre'ɔgrəfi] n. Chorégraphie *f.*
chorist ['kɔrist] n. THEATR. Choriste *s.*
chorister [-ə*] n. ECCLES. Choriste *s.*
choroid ['kɔːrɔid] adj., n. MED. Choroïde *f.*
chortle ['tʃɔːtl̩] v. intr. FAM. Pouffer, glousser (see CHUCKLE) ; s'esclaffer *(over,* au sujet de).
chorus ['kɔːrəs] n. Chœur *m.* (in literature). ‖ MUS. Chœur *m.* (singers, song) ; refrain *m.* (of a song) ; *to join in the chorus,* chanter au refrain, reprendre en chœur. ‖ FIG. Concert *m.* (of protest). ‖ **Chorus-girl,** n. THEATR. Girl *f.*
— v. intr., tr. Chanter (or) réciter en chœur.
chose [tʃouz], **chosen** [-n̩]. See CHOOSE.
chough [tʃʌf] n. ZOOL. Choucas *m.*
chouse [tʃaus] n. FAM. Escroquerie, filouterie *f.*
— v. tr. FAM. Extorquer ; *to chouse sth. out of s.o.,* carotter qqch. à qqn.
chow [tʃau] n. ZOOL. Chow-chow *m.*
chow n. U. S. MILIT. Boustifaille, mangeaille *f.*
chowder ['tʃaudə*] n. CULIN. Cotriade *f.*
chrestomathy [kres'tɔməθi] n. Chrestomathie *f.*
chrism ['krizm̩] n. ECCLES. Chrême *m.*
chrismal [-məl] n. ECCLES. Chrémeau *m.*
Christ [kraist] n. ECCLES. Christ ; Jésus-Christ *m.*
christen ['krisn̩] v. tr. ECCLES. Baptiser. ‖ Appeler ; *to christen s.o. after,* donner à qqn le nom de
Christendom [-dəm] n. ECCLES. Chrétienté *f.*
christening ['krisniŋ] n. ECCLES. Baptême *m.*
Christhood ['kraisthud] n. ECCLES. Qualité messianique *f.*
Christian ['kristjən] n. ECCLES., FAM. Chrétien *s.*
— adj. ECCLES. Chrétien ; des chrétiens (doctrine, era, teachings, virtues) ; *Christian name,* nom de

CHRISTIAN NAMES AND FAMILIAR FORMS
PRÉNOMS ANGLAIS ET LEURS DIMINUTIFS

Andrew	Andy	André
Ann, Anne, Anna	Nan, Nancy, Annie	Anne
Anthony	Tony	Antoine
Augustus	Gus	Auguste
Benjamin	Ben, Bennie	Benjamin
Catherine, Kathleen	Kate, Kitty, Cathy	Catherine
Charles	Charley, Charlie	Charles
Daniel	Dan, Danny	Daniel
David	Davy, Dave	David
Dorothy	Dolly, Dot	Dorothée
Edward	Eddie, Ted, Teddy, U. S. Ed	Edouard
Eleanor	Nora, Nell, Nelly	Eléonore
Elizabeth, Elisabeth	Bess, Betty, Betsy, Lizzy, Liz	Elisabeth
Florence	Flossie, Florry, Flo	Florence
Francis	Frank, Franky	François
Frederick	Fred, Freddy	Frédéric
George	Georgie	Georges
Henry	Harry, Hank	Henri
Isabel, Isabella	Bella	Isabelle
James	Jim, Jimmie	Jacques
John	Johnny, Jack, Jacky	Jean
Jane, Joan, Jean	Janie, Jeanie, Jenny	Jeanne
Joseph	Joe	Joseph
Lawrence	Larry	Laurent
Magdalen, Madeleine	Maud	Madeleine
Mary	May, Mae, Moll, Molly, Polly	Marie
Michael	Micky, Mike	Michel
Nicholas	Nick	Nicolas
Patrick	Pat	Patrick
Peter	Pete	Pierre
Philip	Phil	Philippe
Richard	Dick, Dicky	Richard
Robert	Bob, Bobby	Robert
Samuel	Sam, Sammy	Samuel
Stephen	Steve	Etienne
Thomas	Tom, Tommy	Thomas
William	Will, Willy, Bill, Billy	William [ou Guillaume]

baptême, prénom. ‖ Fig. Charitable, chrétien. ‖ Fam. Chrétien, civilisé.

Christianity [,kristi'æniti] n. Eccles. Christianisme *m.*; caractère du chrétien *m.*; pratiques chrétiennes *f. pl.*

Christianize ['kristjənaiz] v. tr. Christianiser.

Christianly [-li] adv. Eccles. Chrétiennement.

Christlike ['kraistlaik] adj. Eccles. Semblable au Christ ; évangélique.

Christliness [-linis] n. Eccles. Esprit chrétien *m.*

Christmas ['krisməs] n. Eccles. Noël, jour de Noël *m.; Father Christmas,* le Père Noël. ‖ **Christmas-box** (or) **-present,** n. Petit noël, cadeau de Noël *m.;* étrennes *f. pl.* ‖ **Christmas-card,** n. Carte (*f.*) de Noël. ‖ **Christmas-rose,** n. Bot. Rose (*f.*) de Noël. ‖ **Christmas-stocking,** n. Soulier (or) sabot de Noël *m.* ‖ **Christmas-tide,** n. Temps de Noël *m.* ‖ **Christmas-tide,** n. Temps de Noël *m.* ‖ **Christmas-tree,** n. Arbre de Noël *m.*

christology [kris'tɔlədʒi] n. Eccles. Christologie *f.*

chromate ['kroumət] n. Chim. Chromate *m.*

chromatic [kro'mætik] adj. Arts. Chromatique ; polychrome. ‖ Mus. Chromatique.

chromatics [-tiks] n. Arts. Chromatique *f.*

chromatin ['kroumətin] n. Med. Chromatine *f.*

chromatography [,kroumə'tɔgrəfi] n. Chim. Chromatographie *f.*

chrome [kroum] n. Comm. Chrome *m.*
— adj. Chromé (steel, leather). ‖ Jaune chrome (colour). ‖ **Chrome-nickel,** adj. Techn. Au chrome-nickel (steel).
— v. tr. Chromer.

chromic [-ik] adj. Chim. Chromique.

chromium [-iəm] n. Chim. Chrome *m.*

chromo ['kroumo] n. Fam. Chromo *m.*

chromolithograph [,kroumo'liθəgrɑ:f] n. Arts. Chromolithographie *f.* (colour print).

chromophotograph(y) [-fət'ɔgrəf(i)] n. Chromophotographie *f.*

chromosome ['krouməsoum] n. Med. Chromosome *m.*

chronic ['krɔnik] adj. Med. Chronique. ‖ Fam. Habituel, invétéré (constant); insupportable, affreux (unbearable).

chronicity [krɔ'nisiti] n. Med. Chronicité *f.*

chronicle ['krɔnikl] n. Chronique *f.*
— v. tr. Enregistrer, faire la chronique de.

chronicler [-iklə*] n. Chroniqueur *m.* (historian).

chronograph [-ogrɑ:f] n. Chronographe *m.*

chronological [krɔnə'lɔdʒikl] adj. Chronologique.

chronologically [-li] adv. Chronologiquement.

chronology [krə'nɔlədʒi] n. Chronologie *f.*

chronometer [-mitə*] n. Chronomètre *m.*

chronometric [krɔnə'metrik] adj. Chronométrique.

chronometry [krə'nɔmitri] n. Chronométrie *f.*

chronoscope ['krɔnə,skoup] n. Chronoscope *m.*

chrysalis ['krisəlis] (pl. **chrysalises** [-iz]) n. Zool. Chrysalide *f.*

chrysanthemum [kri'sænθəməm] n. Bot. Chrysanthème *m.*

chrysolite ['krisolait] n. Chrysolithe *f.*

chrysoprase [-preiz] n. Chrysoprase *f.*

chub [tʃʌb] (pl. **chub**) n. Zool. Chevaine *m.*

chubby ['tʃʌbi] adj. Joufflu. (See PLUMP.) ‖ *Chubby umbrella,* tom-pouce, en-cas. ‖ **Chubby-faced,** adj. Joufflu.

chuck [tʃʌk] n. Culin. Paleron de bœuf *m.* ‖ Fam. U. S. Boustifaille *f.* (See CHOW.) ‖ **Chuck wagon,** n. U. S. Cantine tractée *f.*

chuck n. FAM. Poulet s. (term of endearment). || Chuck-chuck, n. FAM. Cocotte f.

chuck n. ZOOL. Gloussement. || FAM. Claquement (m.) de la langue.
— v. intr. ZOOL. Glousser. || FAM. Claquer de la langue.

chuck n. TECHN. Mandrin m.
— v. tr. TECHN. Mandriner.

chuck v. tr. Tapoter, pincer; to chuck s.o. under the chin, prendre le menton à qqn. || Lancer, envoyer, jeter. || FAM. Chuck it !, assez ! || To chuck away, jeter, galvauder, gaspiller. || To chuck out, FAM. Sortir, vider. || To chuck up, FAM. Envoyer dinguer (ou) balader, balancer, lâcher.
— m. Tapotement m.; petite tape f. || Action (f.) de lancer. || FAM. Lâchage; renvoi m.; to give s.o. the chuck, balancer qqn.

chucker-out ['tʃʌkəraut] n. FAM. Expulseur m. (See BOUNCER.)

chuckle ['tʃʌkl̩] n. FAM. Gloussement m. (See CHORTLE.)
— v. intr. ZOOL. Glousser. || FAM. Pouffer, glousser; rire sous cape. || To chuckle over, se moquer de, se gausser de.

chucklehead [-hed] n. FAM. Balourd m.

chuffed [tʃʌft] adj. FAM. Drôlement content, aux anges (happy). || FAM. En rogne, contrarié (unhappy).

chug [tʃʌg] n. TECHN. Souffle m. || AUTOM. Toux f.; raté m.
— v. intr. TECHN. Souffler. || AUTOM. Cogner, tousser, pétarader.

chum [tʃʌm] n. FAM. Copain m.
— v. intr. To chum up, FAM. Fraterniser (with, avec).

chummy [-i] adj. FAM. Bon copain.

chump [tʃʌmp] n. Bloc de bois m.; souche f. || Gros bout m. || FAM. Boule, cabèche f.; off one's chump, déboussolé, toqué. || FAM. Ballot m. || Chump-chop, n. CULIN. Côte (f.) de mouton.

chunk [tʃʌŋk] n. Quignon m. (of bread); gros morceau m. (of cheese). || Bloc m. (of wood).

church [tʃəːtʃ] n. ECCLES. Eglise f. (all Christians, sect); clergé m.; ordres m. pl. (clerical profession); office m. (religious service). || ARCHIT. Eglise f.; temple m. || Church-goer, n. ECCLES. Pratiquant s. || Church-going, adj. ECCLES. Pratiquant. || Church-rate, n. ECCLES. Dîme f. || Church-service, n. ECCLES. Office m. || Church-text, n. Caractères gothiques m. pl. || Church-time, n. ECCLES. Heure (f.) de l'office.
— adj. D'église.
— v. tr. Conduire à l'église pour fêter les relevailles. || POP. To be churched, avoir passé par l'église, être marié devant le curé.

churching [-iŋ] n. Relevailles f. pl.

churchman [-mən] n. (pl. churchmen) n. ECCLES. Anglican m. (layman); ecclésiastique m. (priest).

churchwarden [-'wɔːdn̩] n. ECCLES. Marguillier m. || FAM. Churchwarden's pipe, longue pipe en terre.

churchwoman [-wumən] (pl. churchwomen [-wimin]) n. ECCLES. Anglicane f.

churchy [-i] adj. Bigot, cagot; bondieusard, calotin (fam).

churchyard [-'jɑːd] n. Cimetière m.
— adj. FAM. Qui sent la tombe, sépulcral.

churl [tʃəːl] n. † Manant m. || Rustre, malotru m. (boor). || FAM. Ronchon, crin m. (grouser); rat, grigou m. (niggard).

churlish [-iʃ] adj. Fruste, grossier, mal dégrossi (boorish). || FAM. Grincheux, ronchon (grumpy); serré, regardant (miserly).

churlishness [-iʃnis] n. Manque (m.) d'éducation; grossièreté f. || FAM. Hargne f.; mauvais caractère m. (peevishness); ladrerie, pingrerie f. (stinginess).

churn [tʃəːn] n. CULIN. Baratte f. (machine); bidon m. (milk-can). || TECHN. Malaxeur m.

— v. tr. CULIN. Baratter (butter, cream). || Battre, fouetter (water). || AUTOM. Faire tourner (the engine). || FIG. Brasser, agiter.
— v. intr. CULIN. Faire du beurre. || NAUT. Bouillonner (sea).

chute [ʃuːt] n. Glissière f. (See SHOOT.) || Manche à charbon m. (coal chute); refuse chute, vide-ordures. || GEOGR. Rapide m. (of a river). || U. S. Parachute m.

chutney ['tʃʌtni] n. CULIN. Chutney m., condiment (m.) à base de vinaigre, de pommes, de gingembre, de piments, etc.

chyle [kail] n. MED. Chyle m.

chyme [kaim] n. MED. Chyme m.

C.I.A. [siːaiˈei] abbr. Central Intelligence Agency, C. I. A., service de renseignements américain.

ciborium [siˈbɔːriəm] n. ECCLES. Ciboire m. (See PYX.) || ARCHIT. Ciborium m.

cicada [siˈkeidə] n. ZOOL. Cigale f.

cicatrice ['sikətris], cicatrix [siˈkeitriks] (pl. cicatrices ['sikəˈtraisiːz]) n. MED. Cicatrice f.

cicatricial [sikəˈtriʃəl] adj. MED. Cicatriciel.

cicatricle [siˈkætrikl̩] n. Germe d'œuf m. || BOT. Cicatricule f.

cicatrization [ˌsikətriˈzeiʃən] n. Cicatrisation f.

cicatrize ['sikətraiz] v. tr. MED. Cicatriser. || Marquer de cicatrices.
— v. intr. MED. Se cicatriser.

cicely ['sisili] n. BOT. Cerfeuil musqué m.

Cicero ['sisərou] n. Cicéron m.

cicerone [ˌtʃitʃəˈrouni] n. Cicerone m.

cicisbeo [ˌtʃitʃizˈbeiou] n. Sigisbée m.

C.I.D. [siːaiˈdiː] abbr. Criminal Investigation Department, service de police judiciaire britannique.

cider ['saidə*] n. Cidre m.; hard, sweet cider, cidre fermenté, doux. || Cider-cup, n. Boisson (f.) au cidre. || Cider-house, n. Cidrerie f. || Cider-press, n. Pressoir à cidre m.

cigar [siˈgɑː*] n. Cigare m. || Cigar-case, n. Etui à cigares m. || Cigar-cutter, n. Coupe-cigare m. || Cigar-holder, n. Fume-cigare m. || Cigar-maker, n. Cigarière f. || Cigar store, n. U. S. Bureau de tabac m.

cigarette [sigəˈret] n. Cigarette f. || Cigarette-card, n. Vignette-réclame f. || Cigarette-case, n. Etui (m.) à cigarettes. || Cigarette-holder, n. Fume-cigarette m. || Cigarette-paper, n. Papier (m.) à cigarettes.

ciliary ['siliəri] adj. MED. Ciliaire.

cilice ['silis] n. Cilice m.

cilium ['siliəm] (pl. cilia [-ə]) n. MED., BOT. Cil m.

cinch [sintʃ] n. U. S. Sangle f. (pack, girth). || FAM. Prise f. (grip). || FAM. That's a cinch, c'est l'enfance de l'art (easy); c'est du tout cuit (sure).

cinchonine ['sinkonain] n. CHIM. Cinchonine f.

cincture ['siŋktʃə*] n. Ceinture (belt). || ARCHIT. Filet m.
— v. tr. Ceinturer (with, de).

cinder ['sində*] n. Escarbilles f. pl. (of burnt coal). || Scories f. pl. (of a furnace, volcano). || Pl. Cendres f. pl. || Cinder-guard, n. Pare-feu m. || Cinder-path (or) -track, n. SPORTS. Piste cendrée f.

Cinderella [sindəˈrelə] n. Cendrillon f.

ciné ['sini]. See CINEMA. || Ciné-camera, n. Caméra f. || Ciné-club, n. Ciné-club m. || Ciné-film, n. Ciné-film m.

cinema ['sinimə] n. FAM. Cinéma m.

Cinemascope [-ˌskoup] n. Cinémascope m.

cinematic [sinəˈmætik] adj. Relatif au cinéma (or) au film.

cinematics [-iks] n. Cinématique f.

cinematograph [siniˈmætəgrɑːf] n. CINEM. Cinématographe m.
— v. tr. Cinématographier.

cinematographer [-ə*] n. Cinéaste m.

cinematographic [ˌsinimætəˈgræfik] adj. Cinématographique.

cinematography [,sinimə'tɔɡrəfi] n. Cinématographie *f.*

Cinerama [,sinə'rɑ:mə] n. Cinérama *m.*

cineraria [sinə'rɛəriə] n. Bot. Cinéraire *f.*

cinerary ['sinərəri] adj. Cinéraire (urn).

cineration [sinə'reiʃən] n. Incinération *f.*

cinereous [si'ni:əriəs] adj. Gris cendré.

Cingalese [,siŋɡə'li:z] adj., n. Geogr. Cingalais *s.*

cinnabar ['sinəbɑ:*] n. Cinabre *m.*

cinnamic [si'næmik] adj. Chim. Cinnamique.

cinnamon ['sinəmən] n. Bot. Cinname, cannelle *f.*

cinque [siŋk] n. Cinq *m.* (on cards or dice).

cinquecento [tʃiŋkwi'tʃentou] n. Arts. Art, style *m.* (or) littérature (*f.*) du XVIᵉ siècle italien.

cinquefoil ['siŋkəfɔil] n. Archit., Bot. Quintefeuille *f.*

Cinque-Ports ['siŋk'pɔ:ts] n. pl. Geogr. Les Cinq Ports *m. pl.*, ports de la côte sud-est de l'Angleterre dotés de privilèges par les rois anglo-saxons.

cipher ['saifə*] n. Math. Chiffre arabe *m.* (arabic numeral); zéro *m.* (zero). ‖ Milit. Chiffre, code secret *m.; Cipher officer,* officier du chiffre. ‖ Chiffre, monogramme *m.* ‖ Mus. Cornement *m.* (of organ-note). ‖ Fam. *Mere cipher,* zéro en chiffre, nullité.
— v. tr. Math., Milit. Chiffrer.
— v. intr. Math. Calculer. ‖ Mus. Corner.

circa ['sə:kə] prép. Vers (with dates).

circadian [sə:'keidiən] adj. Circadien, nycthéméral.

circle ['sə:kl] n. Cercle *m.; to stand in a circle,* faire cercle. ‖ Math. Cercle *m.;* circonférence *f.* ‖ Astron. Orbite *f.* (of a planet); révolution *f.;* cours *m.* ‖ Geogr. Cercle *m.* ‖ Med. Cerne *m.* (round the eyes). ‖ Aviat. Diamètre *m.* (of the propeller). ‖ Autom. *Turning circle,* rayon de braquage. ‖ Ch. de F. Ceinture (*f.*) du métro; *inner, outer circle,* petite, grande ceinture (in Paris). ‖ Sports. Soleil *m.* (in gymnastics). ‖ Theatr. Balcon *m.; galerie f.; upper circle,* deuxième balcon. ‖ Philos. *Vicious circle,* cercle vicieux. ‖ Fig. Cercle *m.;* sphère *f.* (of knowledge); cercle, groupe, milieu *m.* (of persons).
— v. tr. Encercler, environner, entourer. ‖ Faire le tour de.
— v. intr. Tourner (*about, round,* autour de); décrire un cercle. ‖ *To circle round,* circuler (news, object). ‖ Milit. Se rabattre (*upon,* sur).

circlet ['sə:klit] n. Petit cercle *m.* ‖ Bandeau *m.* (on the arm); anneau *m.* (ring).

circuit ['sə:kit] n. Pourtour *m.;* circonférence *f.* ‖ Circuit, détour, tour *m.* ‖ Astron. Révolution *f.* ‖ Theatr. Tournée *f.* ‖ Electr. Circuit *m.* ‖ Jur. Tournée (*f.*) des juges d'assises; ressort du tribunal itinérant *m.* ‖ Sports. Circuit, parcours *m.* ‖ Fig. Suite, série, succession *f.;* circuit, enchaînement *m.* (of acts, changes). ‖ *Circuit-breaker,* n. Electr. Disjoncteur *m.*

circuitous [sə:'kjuitəs] adj. Indirect, qui fait un détour (road). ‖ Fig. Détourné (course, means).

circuitously [-li] adv. En se détournant, en faisant un détour. ‖ Fig. De façon détournée (or) indirecte; indirectement.

circular ['sə:kjulə*] adj. Circulaire, en cercle (round). ‖ Circulaire (moving in a circle); *circular letter,* circulaire. ‖ Math. Circulaire, du cercle. ‖ Ch. de F. De ceinture (railway); circulaire (tour).
— n. Circulaire *f.*

circularize [-raiz] v. tr. Envoyer des circulaires à.

circularly [-li] adv. Circulairement, en rond.

circulate ['sə:kjuleit] v. intr. Med., Fin., Fig. Circuler. ‖ Math. Se répéter.
— v. tr. Faire circuler.

circulating [-iŋ] adj. Qui circule; circulant (library). ‖ Math. *Circulating decimals,* fraction périodique. ‖ Comm. *Circulating contract,* filière.

circulation [,sə:ku'leiʃən] n. Med., Bot., Fin. Circulation *f.* ‖ Comm. Tirage *m.* (of a newspaper); *circulation manager,* directeur du service expédition; *for private circulation,* hors commerce (book). ‖ Fig. Mise en circulation, diffusion *f.* (of news).

circulative ['sə:kjulətiv] adj. Tendant à circuler. ‖ Qui favorise la circulation.

circulatory [-əri] adj. Med., Bot. Circulatoire.

circumambiency [,sə:kəm'æmbiənsi] n. Ambiance *f.*

circumambient [-ənt] adj. Ambiant.

circumambulate [,sə:kəm'æmbjuleit] v. intr. Aller de-ci de-là. ‖ Fig. Tergiverser; tourner autour du pot (fam.).
— v. tr. Faire le tour de.

circumbendibus [-'bendibəs] n. Fam. Circonlocutions, périphrases *f. pl.;* moyens détournés *m. pl.*

circumcise ['sə:kəmsaiz] v. tr. Circoncire. ‖ Fig. Purifier.

circumcision [sə:kəm'siʒən] n. Circoncision *f.* (festival, rite).

circumference [sə'kʌmfərəns] n. Circonférence *f.*

circumflex ['sə:kəmfleks] adj. Gramm., Med. Circonflexe.
— m. Gramm. Accent circonflexe *m.*
— v. tr. Gramm. Mettre un accent circonflexe sur.

circumfluent [sə'kʌmfluənt] adj. Qui arrose (or) baigne (or) entoure.

circumfuse [sə:kəm'fju:z] v. tr. Baigner (*in,* dans, *with,* de). ‖ Répandre.

circumjacent [-'dʒeisənt] adj. Circonjacent, voisin.

circumlocution [-lə'kju:ʃən] n. Circonlocution, périphrase *f.;* détour *m.* ‖ Fam. *Circumlocution Office,* MM. les Ronds-de-Cuir.

circumlunar [-'lu:nə] adj. Astron., Astronaut. Circumlunaire.

circumnavigate [-'nævigeit] v. tr. Naut. Faire le tour de.

circumnavigation [-nævi'geiʃən] n. Naut. Circumnavigation *f.*

circumpolar [-'poulə*] adj. Astron. Circumpolaire.

circumrotation [-,ro'teiʃən] n. Circumgiration *f.*

circumscribe ['sə:kəmskraib] v. tr. Encercler. ‖ Math., Fig. Circonscrire.

circumscription [,sə:kəm'skripʃən] n. Inscription (*f.*) en courbe (round a medal). ‖ Circonscription, délimitation *f.* (act); circonscription, région délimitée *f.* (space). ‖ Limite *f.;* contour *m.* (outline). ‖ Math. Circonscription *f.* (*about, by,* à).

circumsolar [,sə:kəm'soulə*] adj. Astron. Circumsolaire.

circumspect ['sə:kəmspekt] adj. Circonspect.

circumspection [,sə:kəm'spekʃən] n. Circonspection *f.*

circumstance ['sə:kəmstəns] n. Circonstance *f.;* événement, fait *m.* (event); *to take circumstances into account,* faire la part des circonstances; *to struggle against circumstances,* nager contre le courant.‖ Circonstance, condition, situation *f.;* état de fait *m.; under no circumstances,* en aucun cas. ‖ Circonstance *f.;* détail *m.; with great circumstance,* en grande pompe. ‖ Situation de fortune *f.;* moyens pécuniaires *m. pl.; in bad, easy circumstances,* gêné, à l'aise; *narrow circumstances,* mauvaise passe.

circumstanced [-t] adj. Placé dans une situation donnée; *well circumstanced,* dans une bonne situation; aisé.

circumstantial [,sə:kəm'stænʃəl] adj. Circonstancié, détaillé (full of details). ‖ Accessoire, subsidiaire (incidental). ‖ Jur. Indirect, par déduction (evidence). ‖ Gramm. Explicatif (clause).

circumstantiality [ˈsə:kəm,stænʃi'æliti] n. Ensemble (*m.*) des détails; accumulation (*f.*) de détails.

circumstantially [,sə:kəm'stænʃəli] adv. En détail. ‖ Accessoirement, subsidiairement.
circumstantiate [-ieit] v. tr. Donner des détails circonstanciés sur.
circumterrestrial [,sə:kəmtə'restriəl] adj. Circumterrestre.
circumvallate [,sə:kəm'væleit] v. tr. MILIT. Entourer de retranchements.
circumvallation [sə:kəm,və'leiʃən] n. MILIT. Circonvallation f.; retranchements m. pl.
circumvent [sə:kəm'vent] v. tr. Circonvenir. ‖ MILIT., JUR. Tourner.
circumvention [-'venʃən] n. Tromperie, duperie f. ‖ JUR. Circonvention f.
circumvolution [-,və'ljuːʃən] n. Circonvolution, sinuosité f.; détour, méandre m. ‖ MED. Circonvolution f. (of the brain).
circus ['sə:kəs] (pl. circuses [-iz]) n. THEATR., GEOGR. Cirque m. ‖ Rond-point m. (place).
cirque [sə:k] n. GEOGR. Cirque m. (amphitheatre); entonnoir (excavation).
cirrhosis [si'rousis] n. MED. Cirrhose f.
cirrus ['sirəs] (pl. cirri [-ai]) n. Cirrus m. (cloud). ‖ BOT. Vrille f.
cisalpine [sis'ælpain] adj. GEOGR. Cisalpin.
cissy ['sisi] n. See SISSY.
Cistercian [sis'tə:ʃiən] adj., n. ECCLES. Cistercien m.
cistern ['sistən] n. Réservoir m. (in the roof); chasse d'eau f. (of a w.c.); underground cistern, citerne. ‖ PHYS. Cuvette f. (of a barometer). ‖ TECHN. Cuve f.
cit [sit] n. FAM. Bourgeois m.
citadel ['sitədl] n. Citadelle f. ‖ NAUT. Réduit m.
citation [sai'teiʃən] n. Citation f. ‖ JUR., MILIT. Citation f.
cite [sait] v. tr. Citer. (See QUOTE.) ‖ Citer en exemple. ‖ MILIT., JUR. Citer.
cithara ['siθərə] n. MUS. Cithare f.
cithern ['siθən] n. MUS. Cistre m.
citied ['sitid] adj. Couvert de villes (earth). ‖ Urbanisé (like a city).
citified ['sitifaid] adj. Urbanisé, citadin.
citizen ['sitizn] n. † Bourgeois m. ‖ Citoyen s. (of a nation). ‖ Civil m. (civilian); citadin m. (townsman). ‖ JUR. Ressortissant, sujet m.
citizenship [-ʃip] n. JUR. Nationalité f.; droit (m.) de cité.
citrate ['sitreit] n. CHIM. Citrate m.
citric [-rik] adj. CHIM. Citrique.
citrine [-rin] adj. Citrin, jaune citron.
citron [-rən] n. BOT. Cédrat m. (fruit); cédratier m. (tree); citronnier m. (wood).
citronella [sitrə'nelə] n. BOT. Citronnelle f.
citr(o)us ['sitrəs] adj. BOT. Du genre citrus; citr(o)us fruits, agrumes. (See CITRUS.)
citrus ['sitrəs] n. BOT. Agrumes m. pl.
city ['siti] n. Ville, cité f. (town). ‖ COMM. Cité f.; centre (m.) des affaires. ‖ City-bred, adj. Elevé en ville. ‖ City-hall, n. ARCHIT. Hôtel (m.) de ville; JUR. Municipalité f. ‖ City-state, n. Etat-cité m.
— adj. De la ville. ‖ COMM., FIN. Du commerce; des finances.
civet ['sivit] n. Civette f. (cat, extract).
civic ['sivik] adj. Civique (centre, guard, rights, virtues); communautaire (restaurant). ‖ Civil (affairs, rights).
civil ['sivil] adj. JUR. Civil (affairs, death, institutions, law, list, marriage, rights, year); civil servant, fonctionnaire; civil service, fonction publique. ‖ MILIT. Passif (defence); civil (war). ‖ TECHN. Civil (engineer). ‖ FIG. Civil, poli.
civilian [si'viljən] n. Civil m.
— adj. De civil.
civilist ['sivilist] n. JUR. Civiliste m.
civility [si'viliti] n. Civilité f.

civilizable ['sivilaizəbl] adj. Civilisable.
civilization [,sivilai'zeiʃən] n. Civilisation f.
civilize ['sivilaiz] v. tr. Civiliser; to become civilized, se civiliser.
civilizer [-ə*] n. Civilisateur m.
civilizing [-iŋ] adj. Civilisateur m.; civilisatrice f.
civilly ['sivili] adv. Avec civilité, poliment. ‖ JUR. Civilement.
civism [-izm] n. Civisme m.
civvies [-iz] n. pl. FAM. Vêtements civils m. pl.; in civvies, en pékin. (See MUFTI.)
clack [klæk] n. Claquement m. ‖ TECHN. Clapet m. ‖ FAM. Jacasserie f.; caquet m.; cut your clack!, la ferme!
— v. intr. Claquer. ‖ FAM. Jacasser.
clad [klæd] p.p. Revêtu, habillé (in, with, de). [See CLOTHE.]
cladding [-iŋ] n. TECHN. Revêtement m.
claim [kleim] n. Prétention, revendication f.; to lay claim to, prétendre à. ‖ Demande, réclamation f.; refusal to allow a claim, fin de non-recevoir; to set up a claim, faire une réclamation. ‖ Droit, titre m.; to put in a claim, faire valoir ses droits. ‖ FIN. Dette f.; to collect a claim, toucher une créance.
—v. tr. Revendiquer, exiger, réclamer (a right, title). ‖ Exiger, mériter, demander (attention). ‖ Prétendre à, émettre des prétentions à; to claim acquaintance with, prétendre connaître; to claim to be, se dire, se prétendre. ‖ Affirmer, assurer, prétendre (to assert).
claimant [-ənt] n. Prétendant m. (for, to, à). ‖ JUR. Requérant s.; rightful claimant, ayant droit.
claimless [-lis] adj. JUR. Sans droit (or) titre.
clairaudience [klɛər'ɔ:diəns] n. Clairaudience f.
clairvoyance [-'vɔiəns] n. Voyance, seconde vue f. ‖ FIG. Clairvoyance f.
clairvoyant [-'vɔiənt] adj., n. Voyant m. ‖ FIG. Clairvoyant.
clairvoyante [-'vɔiənt] n. Voyante, dormeuse f.
clam [klæm] n. ZOOL. Palourde f. ‖ Clam-chowder, n. CULIN. Soupe (f.) aux palourdes. ‖ Clam-diggers, n. pl. U. S. Corsaire m. (trousers).
clam n. Agrafe f. (See CLAMP.)
clam v. intr. FAM. U. S. To clam up, la boucler, la fermer.
— n. FAM. To be a clam, être muet comme la tombe; he's a clam, c'est un tombeau.
clamant ['klæmɑnt] adj. FIG. Criant, urgent, pressant.
clambake [-beik] n. U. S. Pique-nique (m.) aux palourdes. ‖ U. S. FAM. Four, fiasco m.
clamber ['klæmbə*] n. Grimper en s'aidant des mains (or) en rampant.
— n. Escalade f.
clamminess ['klæminis] n. Moiteur froide et gluante f. ‖ Consistance pâteuse f. (of bread).
clammy [-i] adj. Humide et froid (hands); suintant (wall). ‖ Pâteux (bread).
clamorous ['klæmərəs] adj. Criard, braillard, vociférant. ‖ Bruyant (noisy). ‖ Revendicateur m., revendicatrice f. (for, de). ‖ FIG. Criant. (See CLAMANT.)
clamorously [-li] adv. A grands cris.
clamo(u)r ['klæmə*] n. Clameur, vocifération f.; cri m. ‖ Revendication, réclamation f.
— v. intr. Vociférer, pousser des cris, clamer (against, contre); to clamour for, réclamer à cor et à cri.
— v. tr. Forcer par des cris; to clamour s.o. down, faire taire qqn par des clameurs.
clamp [klæmp] n. Crampon; valet; serre-joint m.; presse; main de fer; agrafe; mordache; pince f. ‖ ELECTR. Serre-fil m. ‖ NAUT. Blin m. ‖ MED. Clamp m.
— v. tr. Cramponner, serrer; presser; pincer.
— v. intr. FAM. To clamp down on s.o., visser qqn.
clamp n. Pas pesant m.
— v. intr. Marcher d'un pas pesant.

clamp n. TECHN. Haie *f.* (of bricks for burning). ‖ AGRIC. Silo *m.* (of potatoes).

clan [klæn] n. Clan *m.*

clandestine [klæn'destin] adj. Clandestin.

clang [klæ ŋ] n. Bruit métallique, son vibrant *m.* — v. intr. Retentir, résonner ; émettre un son métallique. — v. tr. Faire retentir (or) résonner.

clangorous ['klæŋgərəs] adj. Retentissant, résonnant, sonore.

clango(u)r [-ə*] n. Bruit métallique, son éclatant *m.* — v. intr. Retentir, résonner.

clank [klæ ŋk] n. Cliquetis *m. ;* son fêlé *m.* — v. intr. Cliqueter ; rendre un son fêlé. — v. tr. Faire cliqueter (or) rendre un son mat.

clannish ['klæniʃ] adj. Qui a l'esprit de clan ; partisan.

clannishness [-niʃnis] n. Esprit (*m.*) de clan (or) de coterie.

clanship [-ʃip] n. Système du clan *m.* ‖ Esprit de corps *m.*

clansman [-zmən] (pl. **clansmen**) n. Membre du clan *m.*

clap [klæp] v. tr. (1). Battre, claquer ; *to clap one's hands,* battre des mains. ‖ FAM. Flanquer, fourrer. ‖ **To clap on,** mettre vivement (the brakes). ‖ **To clap to,** fermer vivement. ‖ **To clap up,** FAM. Boucler (a bargain, s.o.). — v. intr. Claquer, se fermer en claquant. ‖ Battre (wings). ‖ Applaudir ; battre des mains. — n. Claquement *m.* ‖ Coup *m.* (of thunder). ‖ Applaudissements, battements (*m. pl.*) de mains. ‖ Tape *f.* (*on,* sur).

clap n. MED., ARGOT. Chaude-pisse *f.*

clapboard ['klæpbɔ:d] n. ARCHIT. U. S. Bardeau *m.*

clapper ['klæpə*] n. Battant *m.* (of a bell). ‖ Claquet *m.* (of a mill) ; clapet *m.* (of a pump). ‖ Claquette *f.*

claptrap ['klæptræp] n. Bobard, boniment, bla-bla-bla *m.* — adj. Creux, vide, à effets.

claque [klæk] n. THEATR. Claque *f.*

claret ['klærit] n. Bordeaux *m.* (colour, wine). ‖ SPORTS., FAM. Sang *m.* — adj. Bordeaux (colour).

clarification [,klærifi'keiʃən] n. Clarification *f.* ‖ Collage *m.* (of wine).

clarifier ['klærifaiə*] n. Clarificateur *m.* ‖ Colle *f.* (for wine).

clarify [-fai] v. tr. (2). Clarifier. ‖ FIG. Eclaircir. — v. intr. Se clarifier. ‖ FIG. S'éclaircir.

clarinet [klæri'net] n. MUS. Clarinette *f.*

clarion ['klæriən] n. MUS. Clairon *m.* — v. tr. *To clarion forth,* proclamer à son de trompe, claironner.

clarity ['klæriti] n. Clarté *f.*

claro ['klɑrou] adj. Blond et doux (cigar).

clash [klæʃ] v. intr. Cliqueter, résonner. ‖ Se heurter, s'entrechoquer (to collide) ; se heurter, se jeter (*against, into,* contre) ; se jeter (*into,* dans). ‖ FIG. Jurer, détonner (*with,* avec) [colours]. ‖ FIG. Etre en désaccord, se heurter, ne pas s'entendre (*with,* avec) ; être en contradiction (or) en opposition (*with,* avec). — v. tr. Heurter, choquer, entrechoquer. ‖ Sonner (bells) ; faire résonner (cymbals). ‖ AUTOM. Faire grincer (the gears). — n. Fracas, bruit métallique ; heurt sonore *m.* ‖ MILIT. Choc *m.* (of armies) ; cliquetis *m.* (of weapons). ‖ FIG. Disparate *m.* (of colours) ; conflit *m.* (of interests, opinions) ; désaccord *m.*

clasp [klɑ:sp] n. Agrafe *f.,* fermoir *m.* ‖ Etreinte *f.* (with arms, hands). ‖ MILIT. Agrafe. ‖ MED. Griffe *f.* ‖ **Clasp-knife,** n. Couteau pliant *m.*

— v. tr. Agrafer, attacher, fermer. ‖ Etreindre ; serrer (s.o.'s hand) ; embrasser, enlacer (s.o.) ; *to clasp one's hands,* joindre les mains. — v. intr. S'agrafer, se fermer, s'accrocher.

class [klɑ:s] n. Classe, catégorie, caste, position *f. ;* rang *m. ; governing class,* classe dirigeante ; *lower classes,* basses classes ; *upper classes,* classes élevées. ‖ Classe *f. ;* cours *m.* (at school) ; *to take a class,* faire la classe. ‖ Classement (*m.*) par mentions aux examens. ‖ U. S. Promotion scolaire *f.* ‖ MILIT. Classe *f.* (in foreign armies). ‖ NAUT. Cote *f.* ‖ BOT., ZOOL. Classe *f.* ‖ COMM. Qualité *f.* ‖ CH. DE F. Classe *f. ; to travel first class,* voyager en première. ‖ FIG. Qualité *f. ;* ordre *m. ; in a class by itself,* hors concours, unique. ‖ **Class-book,** n. Livre (*m.*) de classe. ‖ **Class-consciousness,** n. Sens (*m.*) de la solidarité de classe. ‖ **Class-mate,** n. Camarade (*m.*) de classe, condisciple *m.* ‖ **Class-room,** n. Salle de classe *f.* ‖ **Class-struggle,** n. Lutte (*f.*) des classes. — v. tr. Classer, coter, classifier. — v. intr. Etre classé (or) coté (or) classifié.

classic ['klæsik] adj., n. Classique *m.*

classical [-əl] adj. Classique.

classically [-əli] adv. Classiquement.

classicism ['klæsisizm] n. Classicisme *m.* ‖ Humanisme *m.* ‖ Style classique *m.*

classicist [-ist] n. Classique *m.* ‖ Humaniste *m.*

classifiable ['klæsifaiəbl] adj. Classifiable.

classification ['klæsifi'keiʃən] n. Classification *f.*

classifier ['klæsifaiə*] n. Classificateur *m.*

classify [-ifai] v. tr. (2). Classer, classifier ; *classified ads,* petites annonces classées. ‖ FIG. Classer « secret ».

classy [-i] adj. FAM. Ultra-chic, sensass.

clatter ['klætə*] n. Fracas, bruit claquant, claquement *m.* ‖ Bruit (*m.*) de couverts (or) de vaisselle. ‖ Caquetage *m.* (chatter) ; brouhaha *m.* (of conversation). ‖ ZOOL. Craquètement *m.* (of the stork). — v. tr. Choquer, entrechoquer. — v. intr. Cliqueter, résonner. ‖ ZOOL. Craqueter (cicada, stork). ‖ FAM. Caqueter, jacasser. — adj. Cliquetant, retentissant, résonnant.

clause [klɔ:z] n. GRAMM. Proposition *f. ;* membre (*m.*) de phrase. ‖ JUR. Disposition *f.* (of a law) ; avenant *m.* (of an insurance policy) ; clause *f.* (of a treaty).

claustral ['klɔ:strəl] adj. Claustral.

claustrophobia [,klɔ:strə'foubiə] n. PSYCH. Claustrophobie *f.*

claustrophobic [-ic] adj. PSYCH. Claustrophobe.

clavichord ['klævikɔ:d] n. MUS. Clavecin *m.*

clavicle ['klævikl] n. MED. Clavicule *f.*

claviform ['klævifɔ:m] adj. En forme de massue.

claw [klɔ:] n. ZOOL. Serre *f.* (of a bird of prey) ; ongle *m.* (of a little bird) ; pince *f.* (of a lobster) ; griffe *f.* (of a tiger) ; *to sharpen its claws,* faire ses griffes (cat). ‖ TECHN. Valet *m.* (of a bench) ; pied-de-biche *m.* (of a hammer). ‖ FAM. Griffe, patte *f.* ‖ **Claw-hammer,** n. TECHN. Marteau fendu *m. ;* FAM. Queue-de-pie *f.* — v. tr. Agripper, serrer (to clutch). ‖ Egratigner, griffer (to scratch) ; déchirer avec les griffes (or) les serres (to tear). ‖ NAUT. Déhaler. ‖ FAM. Gratter. — v. intr. S'accrocher, s'agripper (*at,* à). ‖ NAUT. *To claw off,* se déhaler.

clay [klei] n. Argile, glaise *f.* ‖ FIG. Argile *f. ;* limon *m.* ‖ **Clay-pigeon,** n. SPORTS. Pigeon artificiel *m.* ‖ **Clay-pit,** n. Argilière *f.* ‖ **Clay-slate,** n. Schiste argileux *m.*

clayey [-i] adj. Glaiseux, argileux.

claymore ['kleimɔ:*] n. Claymore *f.*

clean [kli:n] adj. Propre, nettoyé, lavé. ‖ Propre, net ; *clean copy,* texte au net ; *clean paper,* papier blanc ; *to leave a clean plate,* faire plat net. ‖ Propre, ami de la propreté. ‖ Egal, régulier, uni ;

clean timber, bois net. ‖ Fin (ankle). ‖ Arts. Dégagé (outline). ‖ Jur. *Clean sheet*, casier judiciaire vierge. ‖ Fin. Libre (bill). ‖ Sports. Franc, adroit (jump) ; impeccable (player). ‖ Fig. Propre, net (hands) ; pur (mind). ‖ Fam. *To make a clean breast of it*, vider son sac, tout déballer ; *to make a clean sweep*, donner un grand coup de balai. ‖ **Clean-bred**, adj. Pur sang. ‖ **Clean-cut**, adj. Bien délimité, net, clair ; Fam. Bien découplé (athlete). ‖ **Clean-handed**, adj. Fig. Intègre, propre. ‖ **Clean-limbed**, adj. Bien découplé. ‖ **Clean-out**, n. Curage *m.* ; Fam. Coup de balai *m.* ‖ **Clean-tongued**, adj. Bien élevé, au langage correct. ‖ **Clean-up**, n. Nettoyage *m.* ; Fam. Rafle *f.*
— adv. Proprement. ‖ Net, nettement. ‖ Fam. Entièrement, proprement.
— v. tr. Nettoyer, laver ; *to clean oneself up*, se débarbouiller. ‖ Culin. Éplucher (the vegetables). ‖ Agric. Nettoyer, désherber. ‖ **To clean out**, nettoyer ; Fam. Plumer, nettoyer, faucher, mettre à sec. ‖ **To clean up**, nettoyer, arranger, mettre en ordre.
cleaner [-ə*] n. Dégraisseur *m.* (device, person, preparation) ; *dry cleaners*, nettoyeur à sec. ‖ Appareil de nettoyage *m.* ; *vacuum cleaner*, aspirateur.
cleaning [-iŋ] n. Nettoyage *m.* ‖ **Cleaning woman**, n. U. S. Femme (*f.*) de ménage.
cleanliness ['klenlinis] n. Propreté *f.* (habit, state).
cleanly ['klenli] adj. Propre, net. ‖ De propreté (habits).
— ['kli:nli] adv. Proprement.
cleanness ['kli:nnis] n. Propreté *f.* (condition, quality).
cleanse [klenz] v. tr. Nettoyer, curer. ‖ Med. Dépurer (blood) ; nettoyer (a wound). ‖ Eccles. Guérir (a leper). ‖ Fig. Purifier (soul).
cleansing [-iŋ] n. Nettoiement, curage *m.* ‖ Nettoyage *m.* ; *cleansing cream*, crème de démaquillage. ‖ Med. Dépuration *f.* ‖ Fig. Purification *f.*
— adj. Détersif.
clear [kliə*] adj. Clair, brillant, lumineux (bright) ; clair, dégagé, sans nuages (cloudless). ‖ Clair, net, propre (clean). ‖ Clair, transparent, translucide (pellucid). ‖ Clair, perceptible (audible). ‖ Clair, sonore, cristallin (resonant). ‖ Clair, distinct, net (distinct). ‖ Libre, dégagé, ouvert (open). ‖ Clair, compréhensible, facile à saisir (easily understood) ; *to be clear on the matter*, saisir pleinement la question ; *to get sth. clear*, en avoir le cœur net ; *to make clear*, expliciter (an affirmation) ; *to make it clear to s.o. that*, faire comprendre à qqn que ; amener qqn à se rendre compte que ; *to make oneself clear*, se faire comprendre. ‖ Clair, évident, patent, manifeste (obvious) ; *to become clear*, se définir. ‖ Éclairé, assuré, persuadé, convaincu (certain) ; *it is clear to you that*, il vous paraît hors de doute que. ‖ Entier, complet, plein, absolu (complete) ; *a clear hour*, une heure de battement ; *four clear days*, quatre jours entiers. ‖ Clair, lucide (perceptive) ; clair, pur, innocent (pure). ‖ Débarrassé, délivré, libéré, libre (*of*, de) [free]. ‖ Jur. Absolu, net (majority). ‖ Fin. *Clear loss*, perte sèche ; *clear profit*, bénéfice net. ‖ Ch. de f. *Clear road*, voie libre. ‖ Milit. *All clear!*, fin d'alerte. ‖ Fam. *Clear as mud*, clair comme du jus de boudin. ‖ **Clear-cut**, adj. Net, précis. ‖ **Clear-eyed**, adj. Aux yeux clairs ; Fig. Clairvoyant. ‖ **Clear-headed**, adj. A l'esprit clair. ‖ **Clear-sighted**, adj. Fig. Clairvoyant, à la vue juste. ‖ **Clear-toned**, adj. Au timbre clair.
— adv. Clair, net ; clairement, distinctement ; *to speak out loud and clear*, parler à haute et intelligible voix. ‖ Totalement, entièrement (completely). ‖ A l'écart, loin (*of*, de) ; *to keep clear of s.o.*, éviter qqn ; *to stand clear*, s'écarter, se tenir à distance. ‖ Naut. Au large (*of*, de).
— v. tr. Éclairer, éclaircir (to make clear). ‖ Débar-

rasser, dégager, déblayer, désencombrer ; *to clear the letter-box*, lever la boîte aux lettres ; *to clear the table*, enlever le couvert ; *to clear the way for*, libérer le passage pour, faire place à ; *to clear sth. out of the way*, enlever qqch. qui embarrasse ; tirer qqch. de là (fam.). ‖ Sauter, franchir d'un bond, passer par-dessus (to leap over) ; *to clear an obstacle*, franchir un obstacle. ‖ Sports. Dégager (the ball). ‖ Milit. Nettoyer (the trenches) ; *to clear a field of mines*, déminer un champ. ‖ Naut. Dédouaner (goods) ; quitter (the harbour) ; parer (the rocks) ; décharger (*of*, de) [a ship] ; expédier (a ship) ; *to clear the deck*, faire le branle-bas. ‖ Agric. Défricher (a field) ; coller (wine). ‖ Techn. Déboucher (a pipe). ‖ Med. Dépurer (blood) ; dégager, libérer (the bowels) ; *to clear one's throat*, s'éclaircir la voix. ‖ Culin. Clarifier (a liquid). ‖ Jur. Innocenter, disculper (*of*, de) ; *to clear the court*, faire évacuer la salle. ‖ Comm. *To clear goods*, enlever (or) rafler les marchandises (customers) ; solder (or) liquider les marchandises (dealers). ‖ Fin. Solder, arrêter (an account) ; gagner net, faire un bénéfice net de (*ou of*, sur) [an amount] ; virer (a cheque) ; acquitter, se libérer de (a debt) ; purger (a mortgage). ‖ Fig. Décharger, libérer (one's conscience) ; éclairer (s.o.'s mind) ; débroussailler (a question). ‖ Fam. *To clear the ground*, déblayer le terrain. ‖ **To clear away**, enlever, ôter ; Fig. Dissiper. ‖ **To clear off**, Comm. Solder (goods) ; Fin. Payer (debts) ; purger (a mortgage) ; Fam. *To clear off arrears*, rattraper l'arriéré. ‖ **To clear out**, nettoyer, déblayer, désencombrer ; Comm. Liquider (a stock) ; Fam. *To clear s.o. out*, vider (or) faire déloger qqn. ‖ **To clear up**, ranger, mettre en ordre ; Fig. Éclaircir, dissiper (a doubt) ; tirer au clair (a matter).
— v. intr. Se dégager, se découvrir (sky) ; s'éclaircir (weather). ‖ Culin. Se clarifier (liquid). ‖ Naut. Prendre la mer (ship). ‖ Fig. S'éclairer, s'éclaircir. ‖ **To clear off** (or) **out**, Fam. Filer, décamper.
clearance [-rəns] n. Débarras *m.* ‖ Techn. Jeu, dégagement, espace libre *m.* ‖ Naut. Dédouanement *m.* ; *clearance outwards*, congé. ‖ Milit. Libération *f.* (of an officer) ; *mine clearance*, déminage. ‖ Comm. Soldes *m. pl.* ; *clearance sale*, liquidation réalisation du stock. ‖ Fin. Compensation *f.* ; présentation (*f.*) à l'encaissement (of a cheque). ‖ Sports. Dégagement *m.* ‖ U. S. Certificat de loyalisme *m.*
clearing [-riŋ] n. Éclaircie, embellie *f.* (of the weather). ‖ Dégagement, désencombrement, déblaiement *m.* (in general) ; levée *f.* (of the letter-box) ; évacuation *f.* (of the room). ‖ Culin. Clarification *f.* (of a liquid). ‖ Agric. Défrichement *m.* (of a field) ; éclaircissement *m.* (of a forest) ; clairière *f.* (in a forest). ‖ Med. Libération, décharge *f.* (of the bowels). ‖ Jur. Justification *f.* (*of*, de). ‖ Naut. Dédouanement *m.* ; *clearing declaration*, déclaration d'embarquement. ‖ Comm. Solde *m.* ; liquidation *f.* ‖ Fin. Liquidation *f.* (of an account) ; compensation *f.* (of a cheque) ; *under the clearing procedure*, par clearing, par voie de compensation. ‖ **Clearing-bank**, n. Fin. Banque (*f.*) de virement. ‖ **Clearing-house**, n. Fin. Chambre de compensation *f.*
clearly [-li] adv. Clairement. ‖ Évidemment.
clearness [-nis] n. Clarté, luminosité *f.* (brightness). ‖ Clarté, transparence, limpidité *f.* ‖ Clarté, netteté *f.*
cleat [kli:t] n. Techn. Tasseau *m.* ‖ Electr. Serrefil *m.* ‖ Naut. Taquet *m.*
cleavage ['kli:vidʒ] n. Geol. Clivage, délit *m.* ‖ Med. Division *f.* (of a cell). ‖ Fig. Scission, division *f.* ‖ Fam. Décolleté *m.*
cleave [kli:v] v. tr. (36). Fendre. ‖ Geol. Cliver. ‖ Fig. Séparer, désunir.
— v. intr. Se fendre. ‖ Geol. Se cliver. ‖ Fig. Se frayer un chemin (*through*, à travers).

cleave v. intr. (36). Coller, adhérer (*to*, à). [See STICK.] ‖ FIG. S'attacher (*to*, à).

cleaver ['kli:və*] n. Couperet *m*. (chopper).

cleek [kli:k] n. SPORTS. Cleek *m*. (in golf).

clef [klef] n. MUS. Clef, clé *f*.

cleft [kleft] n. Fente *f*.

cleft adj. Fourchu (stick). ‖ MED. Fendu (palate). ‖ FAM. *In a cleft stick*, dans une impasse, mal pris.

cleg [kleg] n. ZOOL. Taon *m*.

clem [klem] v. intr. (1). FAM. Claquer du bec; la crever.

clematis ['klemətis] n. BOT. Clématite *f*.

clemency ['klemənsi] n. Clémence *f*. (*to*, envers) [of a person]. ‖ Douceur, clémence *f*. (of the weather).

clement [-ənt] adj. Clément (*to*, envers) [person]. ‖ Doux, clément (weather).

clementine ['klemən,ti:n] n. AGRIC. Clémentine *f*.

clench [klenʃ] v. tr. Serrer, crisper (one's fists); serrer (teeth). ‖ Serrer, empoigner (*in*, dans) [sth.]. ‖ TECHN. Rabattre (a nail); river (a rivet). ‖ NAUT. Étalinguer (a rope). ‖ COMM. Conclure (a bargain). ‖ FIG. Asseoir (an agreement).
— v. intr. Se rabattre (nail); se river (rivet). ‖ Se serrer, se crisper (fists); se serrer (teeth).
— n. Rivetage *m*. ‖ Crispation, étreinte *f*. ‖ NAUT. Etalingure *f*.

clencher [-ə*] n. FAM. Argument définitif *m*. (See CLINCHER.)

clepsydra ['klepsidrə] n. † Clepsydre *f*.

clerestory ['kliəstɔ:ri] n. ARCHIT. Claire-voie *f*.

clergy ['klə:dʒi] n. ECCLES. Clergé *m*. ‖ † Clergie *f*.

clergyman [-mən] (pl. **clergymen**) n. ECCLES. Ecclésiastique *m*.

cleric ['klerik], **clerical** [-əl] adj. ECCLES. Ecclésiastique, du clergé, de clerc. ‖ Clérical. ‖ De copiste; *clerical error*, faute de copiste, erreur matérielle. ‖ COMM., FIN., JUR. De commis, d'employé, de clerc; de bureau; *clerical duties*, fonctions de bureaucrate; *clerical work*, travail de bureau.
— n. Clérical *m*.

clericalism [-əlizm] n. Cléricalisme *m*.

clerihew ['kleri,hju:] n. Quatrain humoristique *m*.

clerk [klɑ:k] n. ECCLES. Clerc *m*. ‖ † Clerc, savant *m*. (scholar). ‖ JUR. Clerc *m*. (of an attorney); *Clerk of the Court*, greffier; *head* (or) *managing clerk*, principal; *town clerk*, secrétaire de mairie. ‖ COMM., FIN. Commis, employé *m*. ‖ CH. DE F. *Mail clerk*, convoyeur des postes. ‖ ARCHIT. Conducteur *m*. (of works). ‖ SPORTS. *Clerk of the course*, commissaire. ‖ U. S. COMM. Vendeur *s*.

clerkly [-li] adj. De clerc; *clerkly hand*, écriture moulée. ‖ † Docte.

clerkship [-ʃip] n. JUR. Cléricature *f*.

clever ['klevə*] adj. Adroit, habile (*at*, dans; *with*, de); agile (*at*, à). ‖ Habile, ingénieux (action, device); intelligent, éveillé, prompt, à l'esprit vif (person); intelligent, prompt (reply). ‖ Savant, capable; fort (*at*, en). [See LEARNED.] ‖ FAM. Malin, astucieux. (See CUNNING.) ‖ **Clever-clever**, adj. Trop futé (or) malin.

cleverly [-li] adv. Habilement, adroitement, intelligemment.

cleverness [-nis] n. Habileté, adresse *f*. (*at*, à). ‖ Finesse, habileté *f*. ‖ Ingéniosité *f*. ‖ Intelligence, science, promptitude (*f*.) d'esprit.

clew [klu:] n. Pelote *f*. (of thread). ‖ NAUT. Araignée *f*. (of a hammock); point (*m*.) d'écoute (of a sail). ‖ FIG. Fil directeur *m*. (See CLUE.) ‖ **Clew-line**, n. NAUT. Cargue-point *m*.
— v. tr. Peloter, pelotonner (thread). ‖ FIG. Mettre sur la piste. ‖ **To clew up**, NAUT. Carguer.

cliché ['kliʃe] n. TECHN. Cliché *m*. (in printing).

‖ FIG. Cliché, poncif *m*.; expression consacrée *f*. (See PLATITUDE.)

click [klik] n. Bruit de déclic *m*. ‖ TECHN. Cliquet *m*. ‖ GRAMM. Claquement *m*. (of the tongue).
— v. intr. Faire un bruit sec; cliqueter. ‖ SPORTS. Forger (horse). ‖ **To click with**, FAM. Taper dans l'œil à; *I've clicked*, j'ai fait une touche.
— v. tr. MILIT. *To click one's heels*, claquer les talons. ‖ GRAMM. *To click one's tongue*, clapper de la langue.

client ['klaiənt] n. Client *s*.

clientele [kli:ɑ:n'teil] n. JUR., COMM., MED. Clientèle *f*. ‖ THEATR. Habitués *m*. *pl*.

cliff [klif] n. Falaise *f*.; rocher à pic *m*. (on seashore). ‖ SPORTS. Varappe *f*. (in mountaineering). ‖ **Cliff-dweller**, n. U. S. Troglodyte *m*.; U. S. FAM. Locataire (*m*.) d'une maison de rapport.

cliffsman [-smən] (pl. **cliffsmen**) n. SPORTS. Varappeur *m*.

cliffy [-i] adj. Escarpé, à pic, abrupt.

climacteric [klaimæk'terik] adj. MED. De la ménopause. ‖ FIG. Critique, crucial.
— n. MED. Climatérique *f*.

climactic [klai'mæktik] adj. A l'apogée, au zénith.

climate ['klaimit] n. Climat *m*. (weather condition). ‖ Pays *m*. (region). ‖ FIG. Climat *m*.

climatic [klai'mætik] adj. Climatique. ‖ MED. Climatologique.

climatize ['klaimətaiz] v. tr. Acclimater.

climatological ['klaimətɔ'lɔdʒikəl] adj. Climatologique.

climatology [,klaimə'tɔlɔdʒi] n. Climatologie *f*.

climatotherapy [,klaimətɔ'θerəpi] n. MED. Climatothérapie *f*.

climax ['klaimæks] n. GRAMM. Gradation *f*. ‖ FIG. Comble, sommet, summum, apogée *m*.; *as a climax to*, comme clou à.
— v. tr. Amener au point culminant.
— v. intr. Atteindre le point. culminant.

climb [klaim] v. tr. Monter (a hill, stairs); monter sur (a ladder); grimper à (a tree); escalader (a wall). ‖ SPORTS. Escalader (a cliff); gravir, faire l'ascension de (a mountain). ‖ FIG. Gravir, monter. ‖ **To climb down**, descendre de (a tree). ‖ **To climb over**, escalader. ‖ **To climb up**, gravir, escalader, grimper sur.
— v. intr. Monter (road). ‖ Grimper, monter (person). ‖ SPORTS. Faire une ascension, varapper. ‖ BOT. Grimper (plants). ‖ AVIAT. Prendre de la hauteur, monter. ‖ ASTRON. Monter (sun). ‖ FIG. S'élever, monter. ‖ **To climb down**, descendre; SPORTS. Effectuer une descente; FAM. Se dégonfler, en rabattre, baisser pavillon.
— n. Montée, côte *f*. (hill). ‖ SPORTS. Montée, ascension *f*. ‖ AVIAT. Montée *f*. ‖ FIG. Ascension, élévation *f*. ‖ **Climb-down**, n. Descente *f*.; FAM. Reculade *f*., lâchage *m*. ‖ **Climb-indicator**, n. AVIAT. Indicateur (*m*.) de montée.

climber [-ə*] n. Grimpeur *s*. ‖ BOT. Plante grimpante *f*. ‖ ZOOL. Grimpeur *m*. (bird). ‖ SPORTS. Ascensionniste, alpiniste *s*. ‖ FIG. Arriviste *s*.

climbing [-iŋ] adj. Grimpeur. ‖ BOT. Grimpant. ‖ AVIAT. Ascendant; ascensionnel. ‖ AUTOM. De montée, en côte.
— n. Montée, escalade *f*. ‖ FIG. Arrivisme *m*. ‖ **Climbing-irons**, n. pl. Crampons *m*. *pl*.; grimpettes *f*. *pl*.

clime [klaim] n. Région *f*.; ciel *m*. (See CLIMATE.)

clinch [klinʃ] v. tr. TECHN. Rabattre (a nail); river (a rivet). ‖ NAUT. Etalinguer. ‖ COMM. Conclure (a bargain). ‖ FAM. Consolider, boucler; *that clinches it*, ça coupe court à tout.
— v. intr. TECHN. Se rabattre (nail); se river (rivet). ‖ SPORTS. S'accrocher, lutter corps à corps (in boxing). ‖ FAM. U. S. Etre rivé.
— n. TECHN. Rivetage *m*. ‖ NAUT. Etalingure *f*. ‖ SPORTS. Corps à corps, clinch *m*.

clincher [-ə*] n. Techn. Crampon m. ‖ Naut. Etalingure f. ‖ Autom. Gouttière f. ‖ Fam. Argument définitif m. (See choker.)

cling [kliŋ] v. intr. (37). Se cramponner, s'accrocher (to, à) [to hold fast]. ‖ Se coller, s'attacher, coller, adhérer (to, à) [to stick]. ‖ Autom. Coller (to, à) [the road]. ‖ Fig. Rester attaché (to, à); tenir bon (to, pour); to cling tightly to, être à cheval sur, ne pas démordre de (one's principles).

clinger [-ə*] n. Fam. Crampon, pot (m.) de colle.

clinging [-iŋ] adj. Collant, qui moule (garment). ‖ Tenace (odour). ‖ Bot. Clinging root, crampon. ‖ Fam. Clinging vine, crampon (woman).

clingstone [-stoun] n. Bot. Alberge f.

clinic ['klinik] n. Med. Clinique f.

clinical [-l] adj. Med. Clinique (lecture); médical (thermometer). ‖ Eccles. Des malades. ‖ Fig. Purement scientifique.

clinician [kli'niʃən] n. Med. Clinicien m.

clink [kliŋk] n. Cliquetis; tintement m.
— v. tr. Faire tinter (or) cliqueter; to clink glasses with, trinquer avec.
— v. intr. Tinter; cliqueter.

clink [kliŋk] n. Fam. Taule f.; bloc m. (prison).

clinker [-ə*] n. Brique vitrifiée f.; clinker m. (brick). ‖ Mâchefer m.

clinker n. Fam. Type (m.) [or] chose (f.) formidable. ‖ U.S., Fam. Couac m. (wrong note in music); boulette f., couac m. (blunder); bide m. (flop).

clinker-built ['kliŋkə,bilt] adj. Techn., Naut. Construit (or) assemblé à clin.

clinking [-iŋ] adj. Fam. Epatant, formidable.

clinkstone [-stoun] n. Phonolithe f.

clinometer [klai'nɔmitə*] n. Clinomètre, indicateur (m.) de pente.

clip [klip] n. Pince, attache, griffe, agrafe f.; wire paper-clip, trombone. ‖ Clip m. (jewel). ‖ Techn. Collier m. (of a pipe). ‖ Milit. Chargeur m. ‖ Sports. Croc-en-jambe m. (in football).
— v. intr., tr. (1). Serrer, pincer. ‖ Agrafer (papers). ‖ Ecourter, abréger (one's words).

clip n. Coupe f. (of hair). ‖ Tonte f. (shearing, wool). ‖ Fam. Gnon m., taloche f. (blow). ‖ Fam. U.S. Pas rapide m. (pace).
— v. tr. (1). Couper (s.o.'s hair). ‖ Tondre (a sheep). ‖ Ebarber (a coin); couper, rogner (wings). ‖ Ch. de f. Poinçonner (tickets). ‖ Fam. Manger, avaler (one's words); clipped form, forme tronquée, abréviation.

clipboard [-bɔ:d] n. Planchette (f.) avec une pince.

clipper [-ə*] n. Tondeur s. (person). ‖ Pl. Tondeuse f. (tool). ‖ Ebarbeur m. (person). ‖ Aviat., Naut. Clipper m. ‖ Sports. Cheval très rapide m. (horse).

clippie [-i] n. Fam. Receveuse f. (in the bus).

clipping [-iŋ] n. Coupe f. (of hair). ‖ Tonte f. ‖ Pl. Rognures f. pl. ‖ U.S. Coupure de presse f.; clipping bureau, argus de la presse.
— adj. Coupant. ‖ Rapide (swift). ‖ Fam. Epatant, formidable.

clique [kli:k] n. Clique, coterie, chapelle f. (See coterie.)

clitoral ['klitərəl] adj. Med. Clitoridien m.

clitoris ['klitəris] n. Med. Clitoris m.

cloak [klouk] n. Manteau m.; cloak and dagger, cape et épée. ‖ Fig. Masque, couvert m.; apparence f.; under the cloak of anonymity, dans l'ombre de l'anonymat. ‖ Fam. To have a cloak for the rain, avoir une couverture en cas de besoin; cloak and dagger boys, Intelligence Service. ‖ ‖ Cloak-room, n. Ch. de f. Consigne f.; U.S. Theatr. Vestiaire m.
— v. tr. Couvrir d'un manteau. ‖ Fig. Déguiser, masquer.
— v. intr. Mettre un manteau.

clobber ['klɔbə*] n. Pop. Barda m. (equipment, belongings); fringues f. pl. (clothes).

clobber v. tr. Pop. Frapper, frapper sec (to hit); flanquer une rouste (or) une raclée à (to thrash); écraser, battre à plate couture (to defeat); éreinter, descendre en flammes (to criticize).

cloche [klɔʃ] n. Comm., Agric. Cloche f. (hat, glass cover).

clock [klɔk] n. Baguette, grisotte f. (on a stocking).

clock n. Horloge f. (large); pendule f. (smaller); Dutch clock, coucou; grandfather clock, comtoise, vieille horloge; twenty-four hours by the clock, vingt-quatre heures d'horloge (or) durant. ‖ Bot. Aigrette f. ‖ Aviat. Deviation clock, plate-forme de régulation. ‖ Fam. Montre f. (watch). ‖ Fam. To fix s.o.'s clock, abîmer le portrait de qqn. ‖ Clockmaker, n. Horloger m. ‖ O'clock, n. Heure f.; three o'clock, trois heures; Fam. Like one o'clock, comme sur des roulettes.
— v. intr. Pointer; to clock in, out, pointer à l'arrivée, au départ. ‖ Fam. Chronométrer.
— v. tr. Sports. Fam. Chronométrer (a runner).

clocklike [-laik] adj. Régulier comme une horloge.

clockwise [-waiz] adv., adj. Dans le sens des aiguilles d'une montre.

clockwork [-wə:k] n. Mouvement (m.) d'horlogerie (of a clock). ‖ Rouages m. pl.; mécanisme m. (of a toy). ‖ Fam. Regular as clockwork, réglé comme du papier à musique.
— adj. Mécanique; clockwork engine, locomotive mécanique (toy). ‖ Régulier, précis; d'horloge.

clod [klɔd] n. Agric. Motte f. (of clay, earth); terre f. (soil). ‖ Culin. Talon de collier m. (of beef). ‖ Fam. Cul-de-plomb m.; borne f. (dolt). ‖ Clodbreaker, n. Agric. Brise-mottes m. ‖ Clod-hopper, n. Fam. Cul-terreux, rustre m. (boor); godillot m. (shoe).
— v. tr. (1). Bombarder de mottes de terre.

cloddish [-iʃ] adj. Fam. Balourd.

cloddy [-i] adj. Agric. Rempli de mottes.

clog [klɔg] n. Billot m. (for a cow); entrave f. (for a horse). ‖ Galoche f.; sabot m. (shoe). ‖ Fig. Entrave f. (See hindrance.)
— v. tr. (1). Entraver (an animal). ‖ Obstruer (a passage); boucher, encrasser (a pipe). ‖ Fig. Entraver. (See hinder.)
— v. intr. S'agglomérer (earth). ‖ S'obstruer, s'encrasser (pipe).

cloggy [-i] adj. Aggloméré (lumpy); collant (sticky). ‖ Fig. Gênant.

cloisonne [klwæ'zɔni] adj., n. Arts. Cloisonné.

cloister ['klɔistə*] n. Archit., Eccles. Cloître m.
— v. tr. Archit. Entourer d'un cloître. ‖ Eccles. Cloîtrer.

cloistral [-trəl] adj. Claustral.

clone [kloun] n. Bot., Med. Clone m.

close [klous] adj. Clos, fermé (shut). ‖ Renfermé, confiné (atmosphere); renfermé, mal aéré (place); de renfermé (smell); lourd, étouffant (weather). ‖ Bien fermé, ajusté, collant (coat). ‖ Serré, dense (grain, rain, weave, writing). ‖ Fin. Fermé (credit). ‖ Comm. Sans marge, juste (price). ‖ Jur. Scellé (writ); close corporation, société exclusive; close imprisonment, secret. ‖ Sports. Serré (contest, game, match); close season, temps où la chasse est fermée. ‖ Milit. Rapproché (combat); serré (order); immédiat (support); couvert (terrain). ‖ Gramm. Fermé (sound, vowel). ‖ Fig. Fermé, peu accessible (club, society). ‖ Fig. Intime (friend); voisin, proche, rapproché (interval); étroit, suivi (relationship); exact, fidèle (resemblance); at close quarters, de près; à l'étroit. ‖ Fig. Concis, précis (argument); étroit (attention); direct (contact); minutieux, attentif, strict, soigneux (examination, study); attentif (observer, watch); serré (reasoning, translation). ‖ Fig. Renfermé, secret (person); dissimulé, bien caché (secret); impénétrable (silence). ‖ Fam. Serré, grippe-sou (stingy). ‖ Fam. To have a close shave, y échapper de justesse (mort); it was a close thing,

il était moins une. ‖ **Close-fisted,** adj. FAM. Dur
à la détente, grippe-sou, pas donneur, aux doigts
crochus. ‖ **Close-fitting,** adj. Ajusté, collant. ‖
Close-grained, adj. Au grain serré. ‖ **Close-hauled,** adj. NAUT. Au plus près. ‖ **Close-mouthed,**
adj. FAM. Taciturne, peu bavard. ‖ **Close-set,** adj.
Serré, rapproché. ‖ **Close-shaven,** adj. Rasé de
près. ‖ **Close-stool,** n. Chaise percée *f*. ‖ **Close-tongued,** adj. FAM. Cadenassé, à la bouche cousue.
‖ **Close-up,** n. THEATR. Premier (or) gros plan *m*. ;
FIG. Détail grossi *m*.
— adv. Etroitement (tightly) ; *close shut,* hermétiquement clos ; *to fit close,* bien ajuster. ‖ Près ;
close by, tout près, tout contre ; *close to,* à proximité de, tout près de, à deux pas de. ‖ A l'écart,
au secret ; *to keep close,* rester caché. ‖ A ras ; *to
cut hair close,* couper les cheveux ras. ‖ NAUT.
Close to the wind, au plus près. ‖ FAM. *Close to
the wind,* en frisant l'illégalité.
— n. Enclos, clos *m*. ‖ ARCHIT. Enceinte *f*.
close [klouz] v. tr. Fermer, clore (the door) ; boucher (an opening). ‖ Serrer (the ranks). ‖ ELECTR.
Fermer (a circuit). ‖ FIG. Achever, terminer, conclure, clore, clôturer. ‖ **To close in,** clôturer,
enclore. ‖ **To close up,** boucher, bloquer, fermer
à bloc.
— v. intr. Fermer, clore ; se fermer, se clore. ‖
Etreindre ; se fermer, se refermer (*round,* sur). ‖
S'aborder de front, se prendre corps à corps (*with,*
avec) [to grapple]. ‖ S'accorder, s'entendre (*with,*
avec) [s.o.] ; s'entendre (*with,* sur) [sth.] (to agree).
‖ FIG. Terminer, achever, clore, conclure, clôturer.
‖ **To close down,** COMM. Fermer boutique. ‖
Achever l'émission. ‖ **To close in,** se raccourcir
(days) ; tomber (night) ; MILIT. Se rapprocher ; *to
close in on,* envelopper, cerner. ‖ **To close up,**
s'obstruer, se boucher (aperture) ; se serrer (persons) ; MED. Se refermer (wound) ; MILIT. *To close
up to the right,* serrer à droite ; COMM. Fermer
(shop).
— n. Tombée, chute (of day). ‖ MILIT., SPORTS.
Corps à corps *m*. ‖ MUS. Pause *f*. ‖ FIG. Conclusion, fin, clôture *f*.
closed [klouzd] adj. Fermé (door) ; barré (road) ;
to find the door closed, trouver porte close. ‖ JUR.
Closed session, huis clos ; *closed shop,* organisation industrielle qui n'admet que des travailleurs
syndiqués. ‖ PHYS., SPORTS, GRAMM. Fermé. ‖
THEATR. « *Closed* », « relâche ». ‖ FAM. *Closed book,*
qqch. d'hermétique ; affaire classée. ‖ **Closed-circuit,** adj. En circuit fermé.
closely ['klousli] adv. † Secrètement. ‖ Etroite-
ment ; de près. ‖ FIG. De près, minutieusement
(attentively). ‖ FIG. Intimement, de près.
closeness [-nis] n. Lourdeur *f*. (of the atmosphere,
weather) ; odeur (*f*.) de renfermé, manque d'air *m*.
(in a room). ‖ Trame serrée *f*. (of a texture). ‖ Compacité, lourdeur *f*. (of a substance). ‖ Proximité *f*.
(of relationship ; *closeness of friendship,* intimité.
‖ Exactitude *f*. (of a resemblance) ; fidélité *f*. (of a
translation). ‖ Minutie, rigueur *f*. (of an examination, a study). ‖ Caractère taciturne (or) renfermé
m. (of s.o.). ‖ FAM. Pingrerie *f*. (stinginess).
closet ['klozit] n. Penderie *f*. (clothes-closet). ‖
Cabinet, petit bureau *m*. (private room). ‖ Cabinets
m. pl. (water-closet). ‖ THEATR. *Closet play,* pièce
pour la lecture et non pour la scène. ‖ FAM. *Closet
strategist,* stratège en chambre.
— v. tr. Prendre à part, recevoir dans son bureau ;
chambrer (fam.) ; *to closet oneself with,* s'enfermer
avec, se claquemurer avec (fam.).
closing ['klouziŋ] adj. Terminal, final, ultime, dernier. ‖ FIN. De clôture (prices).
— n. Fermeture *f*. ‖ FIN. Clôture *f*.
closure ['klouʒə*] n. Clôture *f*. ‖ JUR. Clôture *f*.
‖ FIG. Conclusion, fin *f*.
— v. tr. JUR. Appliquer la clôture à (a bill) ; clôturer (a debate).

clot [klɔt] n. CULIN. Grumeau *m*. (of flour) ; caillot
m. (of milk). ‖ MED. Caillot *m*. (of blood). ‖ FAM.
Cul-de-plomb *m*. (See CLOD.)
— v. tr. (1). CULIN. Cailler, coaguler. ‖ MED. Coaguler.
— v. intr. (1). CULIN. Se cailler. ‖ MED. Se coaguler.
cloth [klɔθ] (pl. **cloths**) n. Tissu, drap *m*. ; étoffe *f*.
(fabric). ‖ *American cloth,* toile cirée. ‖
Nappe *f*. (table-cloth). ‖ Linge, chiffon, torchon *m*.
(for cleaning). ‖ THEATR. Toile *f*. ‖ NAUT. Toile,
voile *f*. ‖ AVIAT. Bâche *f*. ‖ ECCLES. Soutane *f*. ;
the cloth, le clergé. ‖ **Cloth-binding,** n. Reliure-
toile *f*. ‖ **Cloth-maker,** n. Drapier *m*.
clothe [klouð] v. tr. (38). Habiller, vêtir (*in, with,*
de). ‖ FIG. Revêtir, couvrir (*in, with,* de).
clothes [klouðz] n. pl. Habits, vêtements *m. pl.* ;
in plain clothes, en civil ; *in one's best clothes,* en
toilette ; *suit of clothes,* complet ; *to put on, to take
off one's clothes,* s'habiller, se déshabiller. ‖ Literie *f*. (bedclothes). ‖ Linge (*m*.) à blanchir. ‖ FAM.
Don't put off your clothes until you go to bed, ne
vous dépouillez pas avant votre mort. ‖ **Clothes-basket,** n. Panier à linge *m*. ‖ **Clothes-brush,** n.
Brosse (*f*.) à habits. ‖ **Clothes-horse,** n. Séchoir-
chevalet *m*. ; U. S. FAM. Mannequin *m*. (elegant
person). ‖ **Clothes-line,** n. Etendoir *m*. ; corde
f. ‖ **Clothes-peg,** n. Patère *f*. ‖ **Clothes-pin,** n.
Pince (*f*.) à linge. ‖ **Clothes-press,** n. Armoire
lingère *f*. ‖ **Clothes prop** (or) U. S. **pole,** n.
Perche (*f*.) d'étendoir. ‖ **Clothes-rack,** n. Porte-
habits *m*. ‖ **Clothes tree,** n. U. S. Portemanteau *m*.
clothier ['klouðiə*] n. Drapier *m*. (dealer, maker).
‖ Marchand (*m*.) de vêtements de confection.
clothing [-iŋ] n. Habillement *m*. (covering). ‖ Vêtements *m. pl.* (clothes). ‖ ECCLES. Prise (*f*.) d'habit.
‖ **Clothing-coupon-book,** n. Carte (*f*.) de textile.
clou [klu] n. FAM. Clou *m*. (chief attraction).
cloud [klaud] n. Nuage *m*., nue, nuée *f*. (in the
sky). ‖ Nuage *m*. (in a liquid) ; tache noire *f*. (in
marble) ; voile *m*. ; buée *f*. (on a mirror). ‖ Nuage,
tourbillon *m*. (of dust, smoke, steam) ; nappe *f*. (of
gas). ‖ FIG. Nuée *f*. (of arrows, locusts) ; ombre *f*.
(on s.o.'s face) ; *under a cloud,* en proie à la tristesse (depressed) ; en butte aux soupçons (under
suspicion). ‖ FAM. *In the clouds,* dans les nuages. ‖
LOC. *Every cloud has its silver lining,* toute médaille
a son revers, toute nuit a son aube. ‖ **Cloud-burst,**
n. Averse *f*. ‖ **Cloud-castle, cloud-cuckoo-town,**
n. BRIT. Lieu chimérique, château (*m*.) en Espagne.
‖ **Cloud-capped,** adj. Couronné de nuages. ‖
Cloud-chamber, n. PHYS. Chambre d'ionisation
f. ‖ **Cloud-land,** n. Royaume (*m*.) des fées ; pays
des rêves *m*. ‖ **Cloud-travel,** n. Route (*f*.) que
suivent les nuages.
— v. tr. Couvrir de nuages (the sky). ‖ Troubler
(a liquid) ; ternir, embuer (a mirror). ‖ Chiner, moirer (a fabric) ; marbrer (leather) ; veiner (wood). ‖
FIG. Assombrir (s.o.'s face) ; obscurcir, obnubiler
(s.o.'s mind) ; ternir (s.o.'s reputation) ; *to cloud the
issue,* brouiller les cartes.
— v. intr. Se couvrir de nuages, s'obscurcir (sky). ‖
FIG. Se voiler, se rembrunir, s'assombrir (face) ;
s'obscurcir, s'obnubiler (mind) ; se ternir (reputation).
cloudily [-ili] adv. D'une manière nuageuse.
cloudiness [-inis] n. Aspect (or) état nuageux *m*.
(of the sky). ‖ Aspect trouble *m*. (of a liquid). ‖
FIG. Air sombre *m*. (of s.o.'s face) ; obscurité *f*. (of
style).
cloudless [-lis] adj. Sans nuages, serein.
cloudy [-i] adj. Nuageux, sombre, moutonneux, couvert (sky). ‖ Chiné, moiré (fabric) ; taché, nuageux
(gem) ; marbré (leather) ; trouble (liquid). ‖ FIG.
Nébuleux (idea) ; sombre (person) ; nuageux (style).
clough [klʌf] n. Ravin *m*.
clout [klaut] n. Pièce *f*. (for patching). ‖ † Bout

(m.) d'étoffe; *cast ne'er a clout till May is out*, en avril ne quitte pas un fil. ‖ Sports. Flèche (*f.*) au but (shot); cible *f.* (target). ‖ Fam. Torgnole *f.* (blow). ‖ Fam. Poids *m.*, influence *f.* (influence). — v. tr. Rapiécer. ‖ Fam. Gifler.

clove [klouv] n. Bot. Clou (*m.*) de girofle. ‖ **Clove-pink,** n. Bot. Œillet-giroflée *m.* ‖ **Clove-tree,** n. Bot. Giroflier *m.*

clove n. Culin. Gousse *f.* (of garlic).

clove. See CLEAVE.

clove hitch [-hitʃ] n. Demi-clé (*f.*) à capeler (knot).

cloven ['klouvn̩] adj. *Cloven hoof,* sabot fendu (of a cow); pied fourchu (of the devil).

clover ['klouvə*] n. Bot. Trèfle *m.* ‖ Fam. *In clover,* comme un coq en pâte.

clown [klaun] n. Manant, vilain *m.* (peasant). ‖ Rustre, lourdaud *m.* (boor). ‖ Theatr. Paillasse, clown *m.*

clownery [-əri] n. Theatr. Bouffonnerie, clownerie, pitrerie *f.*

clownish [-iʃ] adj. Frustre, rustre, grossier (boorish); gauche, balourd (clumsy).

cloy [kloi] v. tr. Rassasier (with, de). ‖ Fig. Rassasier, dégoûter, lasser, blaser. (See GLUT.)

club [klʌb] n. Trique, massue, matraque *f.*; gourdin *m.* (bludgeon). ‖ Catogan *m.* (of hair). ‖ Trèfle *m.* (card). ‖ Club, cercle *m.*; association, société *f.* ‖ Cotisation *f.* (subscription). ‖ Sports. Club *m.*; crosse *f.* (in golf, hockey, polo). ‖ Fam. *To cut a club to knock one's own brain out,* chercher le bâton pour se faire battre. ‖ **Club-foot,** n. Med. Pied-bot *m.* ‖ **Club-footed,** adj. Med. Pied-bot. ‖ **Club-law,** n. Droit du plus fort *m.* ‖ **Club-man,** n. Clubman, membre d'un club; cercleux *m.* (fam.). ‖ **Club-room,** n. Salle (*f.*) de club (or) de réunion. ‖ **Club-sandwich,** n. Culin. Gros sandwich panaché *m.* ‖ **Club-steak,** n. Bifteck dans l'aloyau *m.* — v. tr. (1). Matraquer. ‖ Se servir comme d'une massue de (a rifle). ‖ Réunir (persons); mettre en commun, rassembler (resources). ‖ Milit. Jeter en désordre dans. — v. intr. (1). Se réunir, se grouper, s'associer (*with,* avec) [to unite]; *to club together,* se cotiser (*to,* pour). ‖ Naut. Dériver sur son ancre.

clubbable [-əbl̩] adj. Sociable, à l'esprit d'équipe.

cluck [klʌk] n. Gloussement *m.* — v. intr. Glousser. — v. tr. Fam. *To cluck one's disapproval,* exprimer sa désapprobation par un gloussement de mépris.

clue [klu:] n. Fil directeur, indice *m.*; *to have a clue,* être au courant, en avoir une idée; *to have the clue,* avoir trouvé le joint. ‖ Définition *f.* (of a crossword).

clump [klʌmp] n. Massif *m.*, touffe *f.* (of flowers); massif *m.* (of shrubs); bouquet *m.* (of trees). ‖ Bruit de pas lourd *m.* (tramp). ‖ **Clump-sole,** n. Double semelle *f.* — v. tr. Grouper en massif (flowers, shrubs, trees). ‖ Mettre une double semelle à (shoes). — v. intr. Se grouper en massif. ‖ Marcher d'un pas lourd. (See TRAMP.)

clumpish [-iʃ] adj. Lourd et gauche.

clumsily ['klʌmzili] adv. Avec gaucherie (or) maladresse. ‖ Fig. Sans délicatesse (or) tact.

clumsiness [-inis] n. Gaucherie, maladresse *f.* ‖ Incommodité *f.*; manque (*m.*) de maniabilité (of an object); lourdeur *f.* (of shape). ‖ Fig. Manque de tact *m.*; gaucherie *f.*

clumsy [-i] adj. Gauche, inhabile, maladroit. (See AWKWARD.) ‖ Mal construit, peu maniable, incommode (object); lourd, disgracieux (shape). ‖ Fig. Sans tact, gauche (person); gauche, lourd, inélégant (style).

clung [klʌŋ]. See CLING.

cluster ['klʌstə*] n. Régime *m.* (of bananas); bouquet *m.* (of flowers); grappe *f.* (of fruit, trees);

massif *m.* (of shrubs). ‖ Pâté *m.* (of houses); groupe, rassemblement *m.* (of people). ‖ Zool. Essaim *m.* (of bees). ‖ Astron. *Cluster of stars,* amas stellaire. ‖ Milit. *Cluster bomb,* bombe cluster (or) en paquetage. — v. intr. Se rassembler, se grouper, se ramasser. ‖ S'attrouper. — v. tr. Rassembler, grouper, ramasser.

clutch [klʌtʃ] n. Griffe *f.* (of an animal); serre *f.* (of a bird of prey). ‖ Etreinte, prise *f.* (action, grasp); *to make a clutch at,* tenter d'agripper. ‖ Sports. Prise *f.* (in wrestling). ‖ Autom. Embrayage *m.*; *clutch pedal, foot clutch,* pédale d'embrayage; *to disengage, to let in the clutch,* débrayer, embrayer. ‖ Techn. Griffe, mâchoire *f.* (of a crane). ‖ Fam. Poigne, griffe *f.*; *to fall into s.o.'s clutches,* tomber sous la patte de qqn. ‖ U. S. Crise *f.* ‖ **Clutch-disc,** n. Autom. Disque d'embrayage *m.* ‖ **Clutch-fork,** n. Autom. Embrayeur *m.* — v. tr. Empoigner, agripper, saisir, étreindre. — v. intr. Se cramponner, s'accrocher, s'agripper (*at,* à); se saisir (*at,* de).

clutch n. Couvée *f.* (chicks, eggs).

clutter ['klʌtə*] n. Désordre, remue-ménage *m.*; pagaïe *f.* — v. tr. Jeter en désordre. (See JUMBLE.) — v. intr. Faire du désordre. ‖ S'agiter, s'affairer, se démener. (See BUSTLE.)

clyster ['klistə*] n. Med. Clystère *m.*

co [kou] pref. ‖ **Co-administrator,** n. Comm. Cogérant *m.* ‖ **Co-ally,** n. Allié *m.* ‖ **Co-author,** n. Co-auteur *m.* ‖ **Co-belligerent,** n. Milit. Cobelligérant *m.* ‖ **Co-defendant,** n. Jur. Coaccusé *m.* ‖ **Co-director,** n. Codirecteur, coadministrateur *m.* ‖ **Co-directress,** n. Codirectrice *f.* ‖ **Co-driver,** n. Autom. Coéquipier *m.* ‖ **Co-education,** n. See COEDUCATION. ‖ **Co-heir,** n. Jur. Cohéritier *m.* ‖ **Co-heiress,** n. Jur. Cohéritière *f.* ‖ **Co-latitude,** n. Astron. Colatitude *f.* ‖ **Co-op,** n. Coopérative *f.* (shop); U. S. appartement (*m.*) en copropriété (or) en colocation. ‖ **Co-operate,** v. intr. See COOPERATE. ‖ **Co-opt,** v. tr. Jur. Coopter. ‖ **Co-optation,** n. Jur. Cooptation *f.* ‖ **Co-ordinate,** v. tr., n., adj. See COORDINATE. ‖ **Co-partnership,** n. Comm. Coassociation *f.* ‖ **Co-pilot,** n. Aviat. Copilote *m.* ‖ **Co-proprietor,** n. Copropriétaire *m.* ‖ **Co-respondent,** n. Jur. Complice *s.*, tiers *m.* (in divorce suit). ‖ **Co-signatory,** adj., n. Cosignataire *adj., s.* ‖ **Co-star,** n. Cinem. Partenaire *s.*; v. intr. (1) partager la vedette; v. tr. (1) avoir pour vedettes principales. ‖ **Co-surety,** n. Jur. Cofidéjusseur *m.* ‖ **Co-trustee,** n. Jur. Coadministrateur *m.* ‖ **Co-vendor,** n. Jur. Colicitant *m.* ‖ **Co-walker,** n. Double *m.* (in spiritualism). ‖ **Co-worker,** n. Collaborateur *s.* (associate), collègue *s.* (fellow worker).

Co. [kou] Jur. Abbr. *Company,* société, Sté; *and Co.* (fam.), et compagnie, et tutti quanti. ‖ Geogr. Abbr. *County,* comté.

c/o [si:ou] abbr. *care of,* aux bons soins de, chez, c/o.

coach [koutʃ] n. † Carrosse *m.*; *coach and four,* carrosse à quatre chevaux. ‖ Coche *m.*; diligence *f.* (stage-coach). ‖ Autom. Voiture *f.*; car *m.* ‖ Ch. de F. Voiture *f.*; wagon *m.* ‖ Sports. Entraîneur *m.* ‖ Fam. Répétiteur, préparateur *m.* (tutor). ‖ **Coach-box,** n. Siège *m.* (coachman's). ‖ **Coach-builder,** n. Autom. Carrossier *m.* ‖ **Coach-house,** n. Remise *f.* ‖ **Coach-office,** n. † Bureau (*m.*) de diligence. ‖ **Coach-work,** Autom. Carrosserie *f.* — v. tr. *To coach it,* aller (or) s'y rendre en diligence. ‖ Préparer à un examen (a pupil); chauffer (fam.). ‖ Sports. Entraîner. ‖ Fam. *To coach up,* catéchiser, endoctriner. — v. intr. Voyager en diligence.

coachman [-mən] (pl. **coachmen**) n. Cocher *m.*

coaction [kou'ækʃən] n. Contrainte *f.* (See COERCION.)

coadjutant [kou'ædʒutənt] adj. Coadjuvant.
— n. Assistant, aide m.
coadjutor [-ə*] n. ECCLES. Coadjuteur m.
coagulable [ko'ægjuləbl̩] adj. Coagulable.
coagulant [-lənt] adj., n. Coagulant.
coagulate [-leit] v. tr. Coaguler.
— v. intr. Se coaguler.
coagulation [ko,ægju'leiʃən] n. Coagulation f.
coal [koul] n. Houille f.; charbon m.; diamant noir m.; hard coal, anthracite. ‖ Charbon, tison m. (ember). ‖ FAM. To blow the coals, jeter de l'huile sur le feu; to carry coals to Newcastle, apporter de l'eau à la mer; to haul s.o. over the coals, jeter feu et flamme contre qqn, mettre qqn sur le gril, passer un abattage à qqn. ‖ **Coal-bed**, n. Banc (m.) de houille. ‖ **Coal-bin**, n. Coffre à charbon m. ‖ **Coal-bucket**, n. Seau à charbon m.; MILIT., FAM. Casque allemand m. ‖ **Coal-bunker**, n. NAUT. Soute (f.) à charbon. ‖ **Coal-cellar**, n. Cave (f.) à charbon. ‖ **Coal-dust**, n. Poussier m. ‖ **Coal-face**, n. Front (m.) de taille. ‖ **Coal-field**, n. Bassin houiller m. ‖ **Coal-fired**, adj. A charbon (boiler); au charbon (heating). ‖ **Coal-flap**, n. Glissière f., tampon m. (See CELLAR-PLATE.) ‖ **Coal-gas**, n. Gaz (m.) de houille. ‖ **Coal-heaver**, n. Transporteur (or) déchargeur de charbon m. ‖ **Coal-hod**, n. Seau à charbon m. ‖ **Coal-measure**, n. Formation houillère f. ‖ **Coal-merchant**, n. Charbonnier, marchand de charbon m. ‖ **Coal-mine**, n. Houillère f. ‖ **Coal-miner**, n. Mineur m. ‖ **Coal-mining**, n. Charbonnage m. ‖ **Coal-oil**, n. CHIM. Huile minérale f. ‖ **Coal-pit**, n. Mine f. ‖ **Coal-scuttle**, n. Seau à charbon m. ‖ **Coal-tar**, n. Coltar, coaltar, goudron (m.) de houille.
— v. tr. Charbonner, réduire en charbon (a substance). ‖ NAUT. Fournir en charbon.
— v. intr. NAUT. S'approvisionner en charbon. ‖ FAM. To coal up, se caler les côtes, faire son plein.
coaler [-ə*] n. NAUT. Charbonnier m. (See COLLIER.)
coalesce [,koə'les] v. intr. MED. Se souder. ‖ COMM. Se combiner. ‖ FIN. Fusionner. ‖ FIG. S'unir, se grouper.
coalescence [-n̩s] n. MED. Soudure f. ‖ FIG. Fusion, combinaison, union f.; groupement m.
coalition [,koə'liʃən] n. Coalition f.
coalitionist [-nist] n. Ligueur m.
coalmouse ['koulmaus] (pl. **coalmice** [-mais]) n. ZOOL. Mésange charbonnière f.
coaly ['kouli] adj. Houilleux m. ‖ Noir (black). ‖ Riche en charbon.
coarse [kɔːs] adj. Commun, ordinaire, vulgaire (commun). ‖ Gros, rude, grossier, rêche (rough); coarse red wine, gros rouge. ‖ Grossier, vulgaire (crude); grossier, cru, indécent (obscene). ‖ **Coarse-grained**, adj. A gros grain. ‖ **Coarse-featured**, adj. Aux traits grossiers. ‖ **Coarse-minded**, adj. Sans finesse, à l'esprit vulgaire.
coarsely [-li] adv. Grossièrement. ‖ FIG. Avec vulgarité.
coarsen [-ən] v. tr. Rendre vulgaire (or) grossier; action is but coarsened thought, l'action n'est que la pensée épaissie (or) matérialisée.
coarseness [-nis] n. Vulgarité, grossièreté, crudité f. ‖ Rudesse f.; manque (m.) de finesse.
coast [koust] n. Côte f.; littoral, rivage m. (seashore). ‖ SPORTS. Descente en roue libre f. (on bicycle). ‖ U. S. Piste inclinée f. (incline); descente (f.) en toboggan (slide). ‖ FAM. The coast is clear, la route est libre. ‖ **Coast-defence**, n. Défense côtière f. ‖ **Coast-guard**, n. NAUT. Garde-côte m.; coast-guardpath, sentier douanier. ‖ **Coast-guardsman**, n. NAUT. Garde-côte m.
— adj. Côtier.
— v. intr. NAUT. Caboter. ‖ SPORTS. Descendre en roue libre. ‖ U. S. Descendre en toboggan.
coaster [-ə*] n. NAUT. Caboteur m. ‖ U. S. Sous-verre m.
— adj. SPORTS. A contre-pédalage (brake).

coasting [-iŋ] adj. NAUT. De cabotage; coasting trade, cabotage.
coastline [-lain] n. Littoral m.
coastwise [-waiz] adv. Le long de la côte.
coat [kout] n. † Cotte f.; coat of mail, cotte de maille. ‖ Habit, objet d'habillement m.; house coat, robe de chambre (or) d'intérieur. ‖ Habit m. (dress-coat); veste f.; veston m. (lounge-coat); manteau, pardessus m. (overcoat). ‖ Couche f. (of dust, moss, paint, snow). ‖ MILIT. Capote f. ‖ BOT. Pelure f. (of an onion); écorce f. (of an orange); peau f. (of a peach). ‖ ZOOL. Pelage m. (of an animal); robe f. (of a horse). ‖ MED. Membrane, tunique, enveloppe f. ‖ BLAS. Coat of arms, blason, armoiries. ‖ FAM. To lace s.o.'s coat, caresser l'échine à qqn; to turn one's coat, tourner la veste (or) casaque. ‖ **Coat-frock**, n. Robe-manteau f. ‖ **Coat-rack**, n. Portemanteau m.
— v. tr. Couvrir d'un manteau. ‖ Enduire, couvrir (with, de). ‖ ELECTR. Armer. ‖ MED. Enrober, dragéifier (a pill). ‖ CULIN. Enrober (with chocolate); dorer (with egg yolk).
coated [-id] adj. MED. Chargé, saburral (tongue). ‖ TECHN. Couché (paper).
coatee [kou'tiː] n. Jaquette (f.) à courtes basques. ‖ MILIT. Tunique f.
coating ['koutiŋ] n. Enduit, revêtement m. ‖ Tissu pour pardessus m.
coax [kouks] v. tr. Cajoler, câliner, amadouer, entortiller; to coax s.o. into doing sth., amener qqn par la flatterie à faire qqch. ‖ Obtenir par la flatterie; to coax sth. out of s.o., soutirer qqch. à qqn en l'amadouant.
— v. intr. Cajoler, câliner, flatter, enjoler.
coaxer [-ɔ*] n. Cajoleur, câlineur, flatteur s.
coaxial [kou'æksiəl] adj. MATH. Coaxial.
coaxing ['kouksiŋ] adj. Cajoleur, câlineur; coaxing girl, petite chatte; coaxing manners, manières félines, câlineries.
coaxingly [-li] adv. Avec cajolerie, d'un air calin.
cob [kɔb] n. Tête (f.) de moineau (coal). ‖ ZOOL. Cob, bidet m. (horse); cygne mâle m. (swan). ‖ BOT. Epi de maïs m. (maize, U. S. corn); grosse noisette f. (nut). ‖ CULIN. Boule f. (bread).
cob n. ARCHIT. Torchis m.; to work in cob, torcher.
cobalt ['koubɔːlt] n. Cobalt m.
cobber ['kɔbə*] n. FAM. Copain, pote m. (in Australia).
cobble ['kɔbl̩] n. Pavé rond m. ‖ Gaillette f. (coal). ‖ **Cobble-stone**, n. Pavé rond m.
— v. tr. Paver.
cobble v. tr. Rapetasser, rafistoler.
cobbler [-ə*] n. Cordonnier, savetier m. ‖ FAM. Rafistoleur m.
cobbler n. CULIN. U. S. Tourte (f.) aux fruits (cake); boisson glacée f. (drink).
cobby ['kɔbi] adj. Trapu.
coble ['koubl̩] n. NAUT. Barque plate f.
Cobol ['kou,bɔl] n. INFORM. Cobol m.
cobra ['koubrə] n. ZOOL. Cobra m.; Indian cobra, serpent à lunettes.
cobweb ['kɔbweb] n. Toile d'araignée f. ‖ FIG. Rets m. pl.
coca ['koukə] n. Coca f. ‖ **Coca-cola**, n. Coca-Cola s.
cocaine [ko'kein] n. Cocaïne f.; coco f. (fam.). ‖ **Cocaine-addict**, n. Cocaïnomane s.
cocainize [-aiz] v. tr. MED. Anesthésier à la cocaïne.
cocainomaniac [ko,keinə'meiniæk] n. MED. Cocaïnomane s.
coccus ['kɔkəs] (pl. **cocci** ['kɔkai]) n. MED. Microcoque m.
coccyx ['kɔksiks] n. MED. Coccyx m.
Cochin-China ['koutʃin'tʃainə] n. GEOGR. Cochinchine f.
Cochin-Chinese [-iz] n. GEOGR. Cochinchinois s.

cochineal ['kɔtʃini:l] n. Chim. Cochenille f.

cochlea ['kɔklia] n. Med. Limaçon m. (of the ear).

cock [kɔk] n. Zool. Coq m. (rooster); oiseau mâle m. (cock-bird); mâle m. (male). ‖ Coq de clocher m.; girouette f. (weather-cock). ‖ Aiguille f. (of balance); style m. (of sundial). ‖ Robinet m. (tap); *fuel cock,* robinet d'essence. ‖ Relevé m. (of hat); retroussis m. (of nose). ‖ Coup d'œil de coin m. (glance). ‖ Agric. Meulon m. ‖ Milit. Chien m. (of rifle); *arm at half, full cock,* arme en repos, armée. ‖ Fam. Coq m.; *cock of the walk,* coq du village; *old cock,* vieux frère; *that cock won't fight,* ça ne prend pas! ‖ Argot. Queue f. (penis); *to talk cock,* déconner. ‖ **Cock-a-doodle-do,** n. Cocorico m. ‖ **Cock-a-hoop,** adj. Jubilant; fier comme Artaban. ‖ **Cock-and-bull,** adj. A dormir debout; du coq à l'âne. ‖ **Cock-crow,** n. Chant du coq m.; aurore, aube f. ‖ **Cock-eyed,** adj. Med. Louche, bigle; Fam. De travers; de traviole (pop.). ‖ **Cock-fight,** n. Combat de coqs m.; Fam. *Cock-fighting chair,* voyeuse; *that beats cock-fighting,* c'est plus fort que de jouer au bouchon. ‖ **Cock-horse,** n. Fam. Dada m.; adv. A califourchon. ‖ **Cock-loft,** n. Mansarde f. (garret). ‖ **Cock-metal,** n. Bronze pour robinets m. ‖ **Cock-shy,** n. Jeu de massacre m. ‖ **Cock-sparrow,** n. Fam. Petit coq rageur m. (person). ‖ **Cock-sure,** adj. Tranchant, plein d'assurance, outrecuidant (cocky); convaincu, assuré (certain). ‖ **Cock-up,** n. Techn. Lettrine f. (in printing). — v. tr. Dresser, redresser (ears). ‖ Mettre sur l'oreille (one's hat). ‖ Cligner (to wink); *to cock one's eyes,* lancer une œillade (or) un coup d'œil de côté. ‖ Agric. Mettre en meule. ‖ Milit. Armer (a rifle). ‖ Techn. Armer (photogr.).

cockade [kɔ'keid] n. Cocarde f.

cockaigne [kɔ'kein] n. Pays (m.) de cocagne.

cockatoo [,kɔkə'tu:] n. Zool. Cacatoès m.

cockatrice ['kɔkətrais] n. Zool. Basilic m.

cockbill ['kɔkbil] v. tr. (1). Naut. Mettre en veille (the anchor); apiquer (a yard).

cockboat [-bout] n. Naut. Coquet m.

cockchafer ['kɔk,tʃeifə*] n. Zool. Hanneton m.

cocked [kɔkt] adj. *Cocked hat,* chapeau à cornes; bicorne (two-pointed); tricorne (three-pointed); *cocked over one ear,* sur l'oreille. ‖ Fam. *To knock into a cocked hat,* aplatir (to handle roughly); abasourdir (to leave speechless).

cocker ['kɔkə*] n. Zool. Cocker m. (dog).

cocker v. tr. Dorloter. (See coddle.)

cockerel ['kɔkrəl] n. Zool. Cochet m. ‖ Fam. Petit coq rageur m.

cocket ['kɔkit] n. Jur. Acquit (m.) de la douane.

cockish ['kɔkiʃ] adj. Fam. Sûr de soi. (See cooky.)

cockle ['kɔkl] n. Bot. Nielle f.

cockle n. Zool. Clovisse f. (See winkle.) ‖ *Hot cockles,* main chaude (game). ‖ *Cockles of the heart,* tréfonds du cœur. ‖ **Cockle-boat,** n. Naut. Coquet m.; coquille de noix f. (fam.).

cockle n. Poêle m. (stove).

cockle v. intr. Se recoquiller, se froisser (paper). ‖ Goder, se chiffonner (cloth).
— v. tr. Froisser (paper). ‖ Chiffonner (cloth).
— n. Froissure f. (of paper). ‖ Faux pli m. (of cloth).

cockney ['kɔkni] n. Cockney m. (dialect, person).

cockneyese [,kɔkni'i:z] n. Parler cockney m.

cockneyfy ['kɔknifai] v. tr. (2). Donner l'allure cockney à.

cockneyism ['kɔkniizm] n. Locution (or) prononciation (f.) cockney.

cockpit ['kɔkpit] n. Sports. Arène f. (for cockfighting). ‖ Naut. † Cockpit m. (for the steersman); poste (m.) des blessés (on a warship). ‖ Aviat. Cockpit, habitacle, poste de pilotage m.; carlingue f. ‖ Fig. Arènes f. pl. ‖ **Cockpit-starter,** n. Démarreur de bord m.

cockroach ['kɔkroutʃ] n. Zool. Blatte f.; cafard, cancrelat, ravet m.

cockscomb [-skoum] n. Zool. Crête f. (of the rooster). ‖ Bot. Crête-de-coq f. ‖ Fam. Fat, freluquet m.

cockshut [-ʃʌt] n. Crépuscule m.

cockspur [-spə:*] n. Ergot m.

cocktail [-teil] n. Cocktail m. ‖ Zool. Cheval anglaisé m.
— adj. De cocktail (dress); *cocktail party,* cocktail; *cocktail snacks,* amuse-gueules.

cocky ['kɔki] adj. Sûr de soi, suffisant, arrogant, tranchant.

coco(a) ['koukou] n. Bot. Noix (f.) de coco (nut); cocotier m. (tree). ‖ Fam. Caboche f. ‖ **Coco-** (or) **cocoa-nut,** n. Bot. Noix (f.) de coco; *coco-nut oil,* huile de coco; *coco-nut-tree,* cocotier.

cocoa n. Cacao m. (drink, powder). ‖ Chocolat m. (colour).
— adj. De cacao (butter).

cocoon [kə'ku:n] n. Cocon m.
— v. intr. Coconner.

Cocose [kə'kous] n. Culin. Cocose f.

cocotte [kə'kɔt] n. Fam. Cocotte f. (tart).

cod [kɔd] n. Zool., Culin. Morue f.; *dried, fresh, salt cod,* merluche, cabillaud, morue salée. ‖ **Cod-fish,** n. Zool. Morue f. ‖ **Cod-fisher,** n. Naut. Morutier m. ‖ **Cod-liver,** n. Foie (m.) de morue; Med. *Cod-liver oil,* huile de foie de morue.

C.O.D. [si:ou'di:] Comm. Abbr. *Cash* (or U. S.) *collect on delivery,* envoi contre remboursement (by mail); paiement à la livraison.

coda ['koudə] n. Mus. Coda f. ‖ Fig. Appendice m.

coddle ['kɔdl] v. tr. Choyer, dorloter, mignoter, chouchouter, couver (see cocker); *to coddle oneself,* se dorloter. ‖ Culin. U. S. Faire bouillir doucement, cement, faire mijoter. (See simmer.)

code [koud] n. Code m. (of honour, of behaviour). ‖ Jur., Inform., Med. Code m. ‖ Milit. Chiffre m. ‖ **Code-book,** n. Code m. ‖ **Code-name,** n. Nom de code m. ‖ **Code-number,** n. Numéro de code, chiffre codé m.
— v. tr. Coder. ‖ Milit. Chiffrer.

codein ['koudi:n] n. Chim., Med. Codéine f.

codex ['koudeks] (pl. **codices** [-isi:z]) n. Med. Codex m.

codger ['kɔdʒə*] n. Fam. Drôle de coco m.

codicil ['kɔdisil] n. Jur. Codicille m.

codification [,koudifi'keiʃən] n. Jur. Codification f.

codify ['koudifai] v. tr. (2). Codifier.

codling ['kɔdliŋ] n. Zool. Jeune morue f.

codling n. Bot. Pomme f.

cods(wallop) ['kɔdz(,wɔləp)] n. Fam. Foutaise f.

coed [,kou'ed] n. Etudiante (f.) d'un établissement mixte.
— adj. Mixte (education, school).

coeducation [,kouedju'keiʃən] n. Enseignement mixte m., mixité (f.) de l'enseignement.

coeducational [-əl] adj. Mixte (education, school).

coefficient [,koi'fiʃənt] n. Math., Phys., Fig. Coefficient m.

coelacanth ['si:lə,kænθ] n. Zool. Cœlacanthe m.

coelanterata [,si:lentə'reitə] n. pl. Zool. Cœlentérés m. pl.

coeliac ['si:liæk] adj. Med. Cœliaque.

coemption [ko'empʃən] n. Accaparement m.

coenobite ['si:nobait] n. Eccles. Cénobite m.

coequal [ko'i:kwəl] adj., n. Egal s.

coerce [ko'ə:s] v. tr. Contraindre (*into,* à). [See force.]

coercible [-ibl] adj. Coercible; contraignable.

coercion [ko'ə:ʃən] n. Contrainte, coercition f.

coercive [ko'ə:siv] adj. Coercitif.

coercively [-li] adj. De force.

coeternal [,koui'tə:nl] adj. Coéternel.

coeval [kou'i:vəl] adj. Du même âge (*with*, que); contemporain (*with*, de).
— n. Contemporain *s*.
coexecutor [,koueg'zekjutə*] n. JUR. Coexécuteur *m*.
coexecutrix [-triks] n. JUR. Coexécutrice *f*.
coexist ['kouig'zist] v. intr. Coexister.
coexistence [-əns] n. Coexistence *f*.
coexistent [-ənt] adj. Coexistant.
coextensive [kouiks'tensiv] adj. Coétendu. (See COMMENSURATE, COTERMINOUS.)
coffee ['kɔfi] n. BOT., CULIN. Café *m.; cup of coffee*, café-crème. ‖ **Coffee-bean**, n. Grain de café *m*. ‖ **Coffee-break**, n. Pause café *f*. ‖ **Coffee-cream**, n. CULIN. Crème (*f*.) au café. ‖ **Coffee-cup**, n. Tasse (*f*.) à café. ‖ **Coffee-grounds**, n. Marc de café *m*. ‖ **Coffee-house**, n. Café *m*. (pub); *coffee-house keeper*, cafetier. ‖ **Coffee-mill**, n. Moulin à café *m*. ‖ **Coffee-percolator**, n. Percolateur *m*. ‖ **Coffee-pot**, n. Cafetière, verseuse *f.;* filtre *m*. ‖ **Coffee-room**, n. Café *m.;* salle (*f*.) de café. ‖ **Coffee-roaster**, n. Brûloir, diable *m*. ‖ **Coffee-spoon**, n. Cuiller (*f*.) à café. ‖ **Coffee-stall**, n. Cantine roulante (*f*.) de plein air. ‖ **Coffee-table**, n. Table basse *f.; coffee-table book*, édition (*f*.) de luxe qu'on laisse en évidence. ‖ **Coffee-tree**, n. BOT. Caféier *m*.
coffer ['kɔfə*] n. Coffre *m.;* caisse *f*. (for money). ‖ ARCHIT. Caisson *m*. ‖ Pl. FIN. Trésor public *m*.
— v. tr. Mettre au coffre. ‖ ARCHIT. Diviser en caissons.
cofferdam ['kɔfə:dæm] n. NAUT. Cofferdam *m*.
coffin ['kɔfin] n. Cercueil *m.;* bière *f*. ‖ ZOOL. Cavité (*f*.) du sabot (of a horse). ‖ **Coffin-maker**, n. Fabricant (*m*.) de cercueils. ‖ **Coffin-nail**, n. FAM. Cibiche *f*. (cigarette). ‖ **Coffin-plate**, n. Plaque (*f*.) de cercueil.
— v. tr. Mettre en bière. ‖ FAM. Enterrer.
cog [kɔg] n. TECHN. Dent *f*. (of a gear). ‖ FAM. Simple rouage *m*. (person); *to slip a cog*, faire une gaffe; avoir un moment d'absence. ‖ **Cog-rail**, n. CH. DE F. Crémaillère *f*. ‖ **Cog-wheel**, n. TECHN. Roue dentée *f*.
— v. tr. TECHN. Denter, endenter.
— v. intr. TECHN. S'engrener.
cog v. tr. (1). Manipuler en trichant (dice).
cogency ['koudʒənsi] n. Force convaincante, puissance *f*. (of an argument). ‖ JUR. Bien-fondé *m*.
cogent [-ənt] adj. Puissant, concluant, déterminant, convaincant. (See CONCLUSIVE.) ‖ Irrésistible, péremptoire (compelling).
cogently [-əntli] adv. D'une façon concluante, avec puissance.
cogged ['kɔgd] adj. TECHN. Denté (wheel).
cogged adj. Pipé (dice).
cogitable ['kɔdʒitəbl] adj. Concevable.
cogitate [-teit] v. intr. Méditer; cogiter (fam.).
— v. tr. Méditer, réfléchir à, projeter. ‖ PHILOS. Concevoir.
cogitation [,kɔdʒi'teiʃən] n. Réflexion *f*. ‖ PHILOS. Cogitation *f*.
cogitative ['kɔdʒiteitiv] adj. Méditatif, absorbé, pensif. (See THOUGHTFUL.)
cognac ['kounjæk] n. Cognac *m*. (brandy).
cognate ['kɔgneit] adj. JUR. Parent. ‖ GRAMM. Allié, apparenté; *cognate accusative*, objet interne.
— n. Congénère *s*. ‖ JUR. Cognat, parent *s*. ‖ GRAMM. Mot apparenté *m*.
cognation [kɔg'neiʃən] n. JUR. Cognation *f*. ‖ GRAMM. Parenté *f*.
cognition [kɔg'niʃən] n. Perception, sensation, notion, intuition *f*. ‖ PHILOS. Cognition *f*.
cognizable ['kɔgnizəbl] adj. Perceptible, sensible. ‖ JUR. Tombant sous le coup de la loi, de la compétence du tribunal.
cognizance [-zəns] n. Connaissance *f.; to take cognizance of*, prendre connaissance de. ‖ Compé-

tence *f.; within my cognizance*, de mon rayon. ‖ JUR. Ressort *m.;* compétence *f*. (of the court). ‖ BLAS. Emblème *m.;* armes *f. pl.*
cognizant [-zənt] adj. Informé, instruit, ayant connaissance (*of*, de). ‖ JUR. Compétent (*of*, pour).
cognize [kəg'naiz] v. tr. Avoir conscience de.
cognomen [kɔg'noumen] n. Surnom *m*. (nickname); nom (*m*.) de famille (surname).
cognoscible [-'nɔsibl] adj. Connaissable.
cohabit [kou'hæbit] v. intr. Cohabiter.
cohabitant [-ənt] n. Cohabitant *s*.
cohabitation [,kouhæbi'teiʃən] n. Cohabitation *f*.
cohere [kou'hiə*] v. intr. Adhérer, s'agglomérer. (See STICK.) ‖ FIG. Tenir, se tenir (arguments); être cohésif (style); être en accord (or) en cohésion (or) consistent (*with*, avec).
coherence [-rəns], **coherency** [-ənsi] n. Adhérence *f*. ‖ FIG. Cohérence *f*.
coherent [-rənt] adj. Adhérent; aggloméré. ‖ FIG. Cohérent, logique, consistant.
coherently [-rəntli] adv. Avec cohésion. ‖ FIG. Avec cohérence.
coherer [-rə*] n. ELECTR. Cohéreur *m*.
cohesion [kou'hi:ʒən], **cohesiveness** [-sivnis] n. Cohésion *f*.
cohesive [-siv] adj. Cohésif.
cohort ['kouhɔ:t] n. Cohorte *f*.
coif [kɔif] n. † Coiffe; calotte *f*.
coiffure [kwɑ:'fjuə] n. Coiffure *f*. (hair-style).
coign [kɔin] n. Coin *m.; coign of vantage*, position favorable.
coil [kɔil] v. tr. Enrouler, lover (a rope); enrouler, torsader (one's hair); *to coil oneself*, se pelotonner. ‖ ELECTR. Bobiner. ‖ NAUT. Gléner.
— v. intr. Onduler, serpenter (river). ‖ **To coil up**, se lover (snake).
— n. Rouleau *m*. (of cord, wire); tour *m*. (turn). ‖ Rouleau, chignon *m*. (of hair); macaron *m*. (over the ears). ‖ Anneau *m*. (of snake). ‖ Cercle, tourbillon *m*. (of smoke). ‖ ELECTR. Bobine; spire *f*. ‖ CHIM. Serpentin *m*. ‖ Coil-winding, n ELECTR. Solénoïde *m*.
coil n. † Branle-bas, bruit *m*. (See TURMOIL.)
coin [kɔin] n. FIN. Monnaie *f*. (money); pièce de monnaie *f*. (piece). ‖ FIG. *To pay s.o. in his own coin*, rendre à qqn la monnaie de sa pièce. ‖ **Coin-box**, n. Cabine téléphonique *f*. ‖ **Coin-op**, n. Laverie automatique *f*.
— v. tr. Frapper (coins, medals). ‖ Forger, fabriquer, inventer (tales, words). ‖ FAM. *To coin money*, remplir son escarcelle, faire des affaires d'or.
coinage [-idʒ] n. FIN. Frappe *f*. (act, process); monnaie *f*. (coins); système monétaire *m*. (system). ‖ FIG. Invention, fabrication *f*. (of a tale); création *f*. (of a word).
coincide ['kouin'said] v. intr. Coïncider.
coincidence [kou'insidəns] n. Coïncidence *f*.
coincident [-dənt] adj. Coïncident.
coincidental [kou,insi'dentl] adj. De coïncidence.
coiner ['kɔinə*] n. FIN. Contrefacteur, faux-monnayeur *m*. (counterfeiter); monnayeur *m*. (minter). ‖ FIG. Inventeur, créateur *m*.
coinstantaneity [,kouinstəntə'neiiti] n. Synchronisme *m.;* simultanéité *f*.
coir ['kɔiə*] n. Coir *m.;* fibre (*f*.) de coco. ‖ **Coir-mat**, n. Paillasson, tapis-brosse *m*.
coition [kou'iʃən], **coitus** ['kouitəs] n. MED. Coït *m*.
coke [kouk] n. Coke *m*. (fuel). ‖ **Coke-iron**, n. Fonte (*f*.) au coke. ‖ **Coke-oven**, n. Four à coke *m*.
— v. tr. Cokéfier.
— v. intr. Se cokéfier.
coke n. FAM. Melon *m.;* cape *f*. (hat).
coke n. FAM. Cocaïne *f*. ‖ FAM. Coca-Cola *f*.
col [kɔl] n. GEOGR. Col *m*. (pass).
cola ['koulə] n. BOT. Cola *m*.
colander ['kʌləndə*] n. Passoire *f*.

colchicum ['kɔlkikəm] n. Bот. Colchique m.
cold [kould] adj. Froid; *cold front*, masse d'air froid; *cold snap*, courte offensive du froid; *it is cold*, il fait froid; *to be cold*, avoir froid; *to get cold*, se refroidir. ‖ Frigorifique (room, store). ‖ Sports. Froid (scent). ‖ Arts. Froid (colour, light). ‖ Med. Froid (abscess); *cold sore*, herpès. ‖ Milit. *Cold steel*, arme blanche; *cold war*, guerre froide. ‖ Fig. Froid, inamical, sans cordialité (or) chaleur (without affection); froid, indifférent, sans enthousiasme (without ardour); froid, calme, objectif, détaché (without passion); *in cold blood*, de sangfroid. ‖ Fig. Froid, déprimant, réfrigérant; *cold comfort*, maigre consolation; *to throw cold water on*, refroidir, doucher. ‖ Fam. Froid (dead); *to have cold feet*, avoir froid aux yeux; *to knock cold*, étendre raide. ‖ **Cold-blooded**, adj. Zool. A sang froid; Fig. Insensible, dur, flegmatique. ‖ **Cold-chisel**, n. Techn. Burin m. ‖ **Cold-cream**, n. Crème de beauté f.; *cold-cream m.* ‖ **Cold-draw**, v. tr. Techn. Ecrouir. ‖ **Cold-hearted**, adj. Au cœur dur, impitoyable. ‖ **Cold-heartedness**, n. Insensibilité, froideur f. ‖ **Cold-short**, adj. Cassant, aigre (iron). ‖ **Cold-shoulder**, v. tr. Fam. Faire grise mine à, battre froid à. ‖ **Cold-storage**, n. Techn. Conservation (f.) frigorifique (or) par le froid; Fig. *to put into cold-storage*, laisser en suspens, remettre à plus tard.
— n. Froid m.; froidure f. ‖ Med. Rhume m.; *cold in the head, on the chest*, rhume de cerveau, de poitrine; *to have a cold*, être enrhumé; *to catch* (ou) *take cold*, s'enrhumer, prendre froid. ‖ Fam. *To be left out in the cold*, rester en plan, être mis à l'écart.
coldish [-iʃ] adj. Frisquet. ‖ Fig. Frais.
coldly [-li] adv. Froidement.
coldness [-nis] n. Froideur f.
cole [koul] n. Bот. Chou m.
coleslaw [-,slɔ:] n. U. S. Culin. Salade (f.) de chou cru.
coleoptera [,kɔli'ɔptərə] n. Zool. Coléoptères m. pl.
colewort ['koulwə:t] n. Bот. Chou vert m.
colic ['kɔlik] n. Med. Colique f.
— adj. Med. Du côlon. ‖ De colique.
colicky [-i] adj. Med. Coliqueux.
Coliseum [,kɔli'siəm] n. Colisée m.
colitis [kɔ'laitis] n. Med. Colite f.
collaborate [kɔ'læbəreit] n. Collaborer.
collaboration [,kɔlæbə'reiʃən] n. Collaboration f. ‖ Collaboration f.; collaborationnisme m. (with the enemy).
collaborator [kɔ'læbəreitə*] n. Collaborateur m., collaboratrice f.
collage [kɔ'lɑ:ʒ] n. Arts. Collage m.
collagen ['kɔlədʒən] n. Med. Collagène m.
collapse [kə'læps] v. intr. S'écrouler, s'effondrer (person). ‖ Se dégonfler (balloon). ‖ Tomber, faire la culbute (government). ‖ Fin. S'effondrer (prices). ‖ Techn. Gauchir (wheel). ‖ Archit. Fléchir (beam); s'écrouler (building). ‖ Fig. S'effondrer (defence); s'écrouler (institution).
— n. Chute f. (of the government). ‖ Fin. Effondrement m. (of prices). ‖ Med. Collapsus m. ‖ Archit. Fléchissement m. (of a beam); effondrement, écroulement m. (of a building). ‖ Fig. Effondrement, écroulement m.
collapsible [-ibl̩] adj. Pliant.
collar ['kɔlə*] n. Col m. (of coat, shirt); collet m. (of overcoat). ‖ Faux-col, m. (for men); collerette f., col m. (for women); *Byron collar*, col Danton. ‖ Collier m. (for dogs, horses). ‖ Collier m.; chaîne f. (around the neck). ‖ Zool. Collier m. (of an animal). ‖ Bот. Collet m. (of a root). ‖ Techn. Anneau, collier, collet m.; bague f. ‖ Culin. Roulade f. (of meat). ‖ Fam. *To be once more in collar*, reprendre le collier. ‖ **Collar-beam**, n. Archit.

Entrait m. ‖ **Collar-bone**, n. Med. Clavicule f. ‖ **Collar-button** (or) stud, n. Bouton de col m. ‖ **Collar-work**, n. Travail de cheval m.
— v. tr. Prendre au collet, colleter. ‖ Culin. Rouler. ‖ Techn. Baguer. ‖ Sports. Arrêter (in football); *to collar round the waist*, ceinturer (in wrestling). ‖ Fam. Cramponner (to buttonhole); rafler, choper (to pinch).
collaret(te) [,kɔlə'ret] n. Collerette f.
collate [kɔ'leit] v. tr. Collationner (with, avec); comparer (with, à). ‖ Eccles. Nommer (to, à).
collateral [kɔ'lætərəl] adj. Parallèle (street). ‖ Concomitant (fact); correspondant (phenomenon). ‖ Secondaire, accessoire (cause). ‖ Jur., Med. Collatéral. ‖ Fin. Subsidiaire.
— n. Jur. Collatéral m. ‖ Fin. Nantissement m.
collation [kɔ'leiʃən] n. Collation, comparaison f. (with, avec). ‖ Eccles., Culin. Collation f.
collator [kɔ'leitə*] n. Collationneur s. ‖ Eccles. Collateur m.
colleague ['kɔli:g] n. Collègue s.; confrère m.; consœur f. (See FELLOW-WORKER.)
collect ['kɔlekt] n. Eccles. Collecte f. (prayer).
collect [kɔ'lekt] v. tr. Rassembler, grouper, réunir (to gather). ‖ Collectionner, faire collection de (books, pictures, stamps). ‖ Ramasser, collecter (eggs, examination papers). ‖ Fin. Toucher (a bill); encaisser (a cheque); percevoir (rent, taxes); amasser (wealth); *to collect a debt*, opérer une rentrée. ‖ Сн. de f. Prendre à domicile (the luggage); ramasser (the tickets). ‖ Fig. Recueillir (documents, news); rassembler (one's thoughts, wits); *to collect oneself*, se reprendre.
— v. intr. Se rassembler, se grouper, se réunir (persons); s'amasser, s'entasser (things).
collect adj., adv. U.S. En P.C.V.; *to call s.o. collect*, appeler qqn en P.C.V.
collectable [-əbl̩] adj. Fam. Percevable, encaissable recouvrable.
collectanea [,kɔlek'teiniə] n. Anthologie f.
collected [kɔ'lektid] adj. Fig. Calme, froid, maître de soi; plein de sang-froid. ‖ Fig. Recueilli.
collectedly [-li] adv. Avec sang-froid.
collection [kɔ'lekʃən] n. Rassemblement; groupement m.; réunion f. (gathering). ‖ Collection, accumulation f.; amas m. (mass). ‖ Collection f. (o. pictures, stamps). ‖ Collection (in dressing); *summer collection*, collection d'été. ‖ Ramassage m (of eggs); levée f. (of mail). ‖ Collecte f. (money) ‖ Eccles. Quête f.; *to take up the collection*, faire la quête. ‖ Fin. Encaissement m.; perception f. *for collection*, aux fins de recouvrement. ‖ **Collection-taker**, n. Eccles. Quêteur s.
collective [kɔ'lektiv] adj. Gramm. Collectif. ‖ Сн de f. Collectif (ticket). ‖ Jur. Indivis (ownership) *collective bargaining*, négociations en vue d'ur contrat collectif. ‖ Milit. Collectif (security). Bот. Composé (fruit).
— n. Gramm. Collectif, nom collectif m.
collectively [-li] adv. Collectivement.
collectivism [-izm̩] n. Collectivisme m.
collectivist [-ist] n. Collectiviste m.
collectivity [,kɔlek'tiviti] n. Collectivité f.
collector [kɔ'lektə*] n. Collectionneur s. ‖ Fin Encaisseur m. (of bills, debts); percepteur, receveur m. (of revenue, taxes). ‖ Eccles. Quêteur s ‖ Сн. de f. Contrôleur m. ‖ Techn. Collecteur m.
colleen [kɔ'li:n] n. Fille f. (girl) [in Ireland].
college ['kɔlidʒ] n. Collège m. ‖ Ecole supérieur f.; *technical college*, école d'arts et métiers. Milit., Naut. *Military, Naval College*, Ecole militaire, navale. ‖ Mus. Conservatoire m. ‖ Agric *Agricultural college*, institut agronomique. ‖ U. S Université f. (without graduate division). ‖ Eccles *Sacred College*, sacré collège. ‖ Jur. Collège, corp constitué m.: académie f.; *College of Physicians*

Académie de Médecine. ‖ Archit. Collège *m*. (building).

collegial [kɔ'li:dʒiəl] adj. De collège, collégial.

collegian [-iən] n. Etudiant *s*.

collegiate [-iət] adj. De collège, collégial. ‖ Supérieur (school). ‖ Eccles. Collégial (church); *collegiate church*, collégiale.

collet ['kɔlit] n. Chaton *m*. (holding gem).

collide [kə'laid] v. intr. Se heurter, se tamponner; *to collide with*, heurter, tamponner, emboutir, entrer en collision avec. ‖ Naut. Aborder. ‖ Fig. Se heurter (*with*, contre); s'opposer (*with*, à); entrer en conflit (*with*, avec).

collie ['kɔli] n. Zool. Colley *m*.

collier ['kɔliə*] n. Mineur *m*. ‖ Naut. Charbonnier *m*. (See coaler.)

colliery [-jəri] n. Houillère, mine (*f*.) de charbon.

colligate ['kɔligeit] v. tr. Philos. Colliger, rapprocher (facts).

collimate ['kɔlimeit] v. tr. Phys. Collimater.

collision [kɔ'liʒən] n. Collision, percussion *f*.; choc, heurt *m*. ‖ Autom. Collision *f*. ‖ Ch. de f. Tamponnement *m*. ‖ Naut. Abordage *m*. ‖ Fig. Conflit *m*.; opposition *f*. (See clash.)

collocate ['kɔlɔkeit] v. tr. Arranger, disposer. ‖ Jur. Colloquer.

collocation [,kɔlo'keiʃən] n. Arrangement *m*.; disposition *f*. ‖ Jur. Collocation *f*.

collocutor ['kɔlokju:tə*] n. Interlocuteur *m*.; interlocutrice *f*. (See colloquist.)

collodion [kə'loudiən] n. Chim. Collodion *m*.

collogue [kə'loug] v. intr. Conférer en particulier, tenir un colloque secret.

colloid ['kɔlɔid] n. Chim. Colloïde *m*.

colloidal [kə'lɔidəl] adj. Chim. Colloïdal.

collop ['kɔlɔp] n. † Bourrelet *m*. (of flesh). ‖ Culin. Tranche *f*. (of meat).

colloquial [kɔ'loukwiəl] adj. Familier, parlé, de la conversation.

colloquialism [-izm] n. Tournure (or) expression familière *f*.

colloquially [-li] adv. Familièrement, dans le langage de la conversation.

colloquist ['kɔlɔkwist] n. Interlocuteur *m*.; interlocutrice *f*.

colloquium [kə'loukwiəm] (pl. **colloquia** [-kwiə]) n. Colloque *m*.

colloquy [-i] n. Colloque, entretien *m*.; conversation, conférence *f*. ‖ Dialogue *m*. (literary work).

collotype ['kɔloutaip] n. Techn. Phototypie *f*.

collude [kɔ'lju:d] v. intr. Agir de connivence; comploter (*with*, avec).

collusion [-ʒən] n. Collusion *f*.

collusive [-siv] adj. Collusoire.

collyrium [kɔ'li:əriəm] n. Med. Collyre *m*.

collywobbles ['kɔliwɔblz] n. pl. Med., Fam. Borborygmes *m*. pl.; coliques *f*. pl.

colocynth ['kɔlosinθ] n. Bot. Coloquinte *f*.

cologne [kə'loun] n. Eau (*f*.) de Cologne.

Colombia [kə'lɔmbiə] n. Geogr. Colombie *f*.

colon ['koulən] n. Med. Côlon *m*.

colon n. Gramm. Deux-points *m*. pl.

colonel ['kə:nl] n. Milit. Colonel *m*.; *colonel's lady*, colonelle.

colonelcy [-si] n. Milit. Grade de colonel *m*.

colonial [kɔ'lounjəl] adj. Colonial; *Colonial Office*, ministère des Colonies. ‖ Milit. *Colonial troops*, coloniale.
— n. Colonial *m*.

colonialism [kɔ'louniə,lizm] n. Colonialisme *m*.

colonialist [-,list] adj., n. Colonialiste *adj.*, *s*.

colonist ['kɔlənist] n. Colon *m*. (settler).

colonization [,kɔlənai'zeiʃən] n. Colonisation *f*.

colonize ['kɔlənaiz] v. tr. Coloniser (to settle).
— v. intr. S'établir aux colonies.

colonizer [-ə*] n. Colonisateur *m*.; colonisatrice *f*.

colonnade [,kɔlə'neid] n. Archit. Colonnade *f*.

colonnaded [-id] adj. Archit. A colonnade.

colony ['kɔləni] n. Colonie *f*.

colophon ['kɔləfən] n. Colophon *m*.

colophony [kə'lɔfəni] n. Mus.. Colophane *f*. (See rosin.)

Colorado [,kɔlə'rɑ:dou] n. Geogr. Colorado *m*. ‖ Zool. *Colorado beetle*, doryphore.

coloration [,kʌlə'reiʃən] n. Coloration *f*.; coloris, ton *m*. ‖ Milit. *Protective coloration*, maquillage protecteur.

colorific [-'rifik] adj. Colorant. ‖ Très coloré.

colorimeter [-'rimitə*] n. Colorimètre *m*.

colossal [kə'lɔsl] adj. Colossal. (See enormous.)

colossally [-i] adv. Colossalement.

Colosseum [,kɔlə'siəm] n. Archit. Colisée *m*.

colossus [kə'lɔsəs] n. Colosse *m*.
— N. B. Deux pluriels : *colossuses, colossi*.

colostomy [kə'lɔstəmi] n. Med. Colostomie *f*.

colo(u)r ['kʌlə*] n. Couleur, teinte *f*.; ton, coloris *m*. (hue); *primary colour*, couleur génératrice (or) fondamentale. ‖ Couleur, teinture *f*. (dye); couleur, peinture *f*. (paint); *fast colour*, grand teint. ‖ Couleur *f*.; teint *m*. (complexion); *a man of colour*, un homme de couleur; *to lose colour*, pâlir. ‖ Pl. Couleurs *f*. pl. (of a club, a party). ‖ Arts. Couleur *f*. ‖ Milit. Pl. Couleurs *f*. pl.; drapeau *m*. (flag); *with the colours*, sous les drapeaux. ‖ Naut. Pavillon *m*. ‖ Fig. Couleur *f*.; aspect *m*.; *local colour*, couleur locale; *in its true colours*, sous son vrai jour. ‖ Fig. Couleur *f*.; prétexte *m*.; *under colour of*, sous prétexte (or) couleur de. ‖ Fam. *To come through with flying colours*, gagner flamberge au vent, remporter un trophée; *to nail one's colours to the mast*, tenir envers et contre tout; *to see the colour of s.o.'s money*, voir la couleur de l'argent de qqn. ‖ **Colour bar**, n. Discrimination raciale *f*. ‖ **Colour-bearer**, n. Milit. Porte-drapeau *m*. ‖ **Colour-blind**, adj. Med. Daltonien. ‖ **Colour-blindness**, n. Med. Daltonisme *m*. ‖ **Colour-box**, n. Boîte (*f*.) de couleurs. ‖ **Colour code**, n. Code (*m*.) des couleurs. ‖ **Colour-fast**, adj. Garanti grand teint. ‖ **Colour line**, n. U. S. Barrière (*f*.) entre les Blancs et les Noirs. ‖ **Colour print**, n. Arts. Chromo *m*. ‖ **Colour photography**, n. Photographie (*f*.) en couleurs. ‖ **Colour scheme**, n. Mélange (or) choix de couleurs *m*. ‖ **Colour supplement**, n. Supplément (*m*.) en couleurs (or) illustré.
— v. tr. Colorer, donner de la couleur à. ‖ Teindre, teinter (to dye); colorier, peindre (to paint). ‖ Fig. Colorer (a description, one's style). ‖ Fig. Dénaturer, masquer (feelings, opinions, views). ‖ Fam. Culotter (a pipe).
— v. intr. Se colorer. ‖ Changer de couleur. ‖ Rougir (to blush).

colourable [-rəbl] adj. Spécieux, trompeur. ‖ Jur. *Colourable imitation*, contrefaçon

coloured [-d] adj. Coloré; de couleur.
— n. Personne (*f*.) de couleur. ‖ Coloured, métis *s*. (in South Africa).

colourful [-ful] adj. Eclatant, vif, brillant (landscape). ‖ Pittoresque, original (character); intéressant, suggestif (incident).

colouring [-riŋ] n. Coloration *f*. ‖ Coloriage *m*. (act). ‖ Coloris *m*. (hue). ‖ Teint coloré *m*. (complexion). ‖ Fig. Faux-semblant *m*.; fausse apparence *f*.; travestissement *m*. (of facts).

colourist [-rist] n. Coloriste *m*.

colourless [-lis] adj. Incolore, terne, fade, sans couleur.

coloury [-ri] adj. Comm. De bonne couleur.

colt [koult] n. Milit. Colt, pistolet *m*.

colt n. Zool. Poulain m. ‖ Naut. Garcette f. ‖ Fam. Béjaune, bleu, apprenti, gamin m. ‖ **Colt's tail**, n. Cirrus m. (cloud).
coltish [-iʃ] adj. Fig. Folâtre, fringant (frisky); jeunet, inexpérimenté (novice).
colubrine ['kɔljubrain] adj. Zool. De serpent. ‖ Fig. Sournois.
columbarium [kɔlʌm'bæriəm] n. Colombaire m. ‖ Colombier m. (dove-cot).
columbine ['kɔləmbain] n. Colombine f. ‖ Bot. Ancolie f.
Columbus [kə'lʌmbəs] n. Colomb m.
column ['kɔləm] n. Archit., Milit., Naut., Phys., Autom. Colonne f.
columnar [kə'lʌmnə*] adj. En colonne. ‖ Comme une colonne.
columnist ['kɔləmnist] n. U. S. Journaliste, collaborateur régulier d'un journal m.
colza ['kɔlzə] n. Bot. Colza m. ‖ **Colza-oil**, n. Huile (f.) de colza.
coma ['koumə] (pl. **comae** [-iː]) n. Astron. Chevelure f. (of a comet). ‖ Bot. Barbe f. (of a plant). ‖ Phys. Aigrette f.
coma n. Med. Coma m.; in a coma, dans le coma.
comatose [-ətous] adj. Med. Comateux.
comb [koum] n. Peigne, démêloir m.; to run the comb through one's hair, se donner un coup de peigne. ‖ Etrille f. (curry-comb). ‖ Rayon de miel m. (honeycomb). ‖ Techn. Peigne m.; carde f. (for wool). ‖ Zool. Crête f. (of a cock). ‖ Milit. Cimier m. (of a helmet). ‖ Naut. Crête (of a wave). ‖ Geogr. Crête (of a mountain). ‖ Electr. Balai m. ‖ Fam. To cut s.o.'s comb, faire baisser le caquet à qqn. ‖ **Comb-out**, n. Fam. Rafle f.; ratissage m.
— v. tr. Peigner; to comb one's hair, se peigner. ‖ Techn. Peigner, carder (wool). ‖ Milit. Battre (the country). ‖ **To comb down**, étriller (a horse). ‖ **To comb out**, démêler (hair); Fam. Rafler, ratisser; to comb the house for sth., fouiller toute la maison pour trouver qqch.
— v. intr. Naut. Déferler (wave).
combat ['kʌmbət] n. Combat m. ‖ **Combat-car**, n. Autom., Milit. Automitrailleuse f. ‖ **Combat-mission**, n. Milit. Mission (f.) de combat m. ‖ **Combat-outpost**, n. Milit. Avant-poste de combat m. ‖ **Combat-post**, n. Milit. Poste de combat m. ‖ **Combat-practice**, n. Milit. Exercice de tir de combat m. ‖ **Combat-zone**, n. Milit. Zone (f.) de combat.
— v. tr. Combattre. (See battle.)
— v. intr. Se battre (for, pour; with, contre).
combatant [-ənt] n. Milit. Combattant m.
— adj. Milit. Combattant. ‖ Fig. Combatif.
combative [-iv] adj. Combatif.
combativeness [-ivnis] n. Combativité f.
combe [kuːm] n. Combe f.
comber ['koumə*] n. Techn. Peigneuse f. (machine); peigneur s. (person). ‖ Naut. Vague déferlante f.
combination [ˌkɔmbi'neiʃən] n. Combinaison f. ‖ Association f. (of persons). ‖ Chemise-culotte f. (undergarment). ‖ Jur. Syndicat m. (of workmen). ‖ Math., Chim. Combinaison f. ‖ Fig. Concours m. (of circumstances); coalition f. (of interests). ‖ **Combination-lock**, n. Serrure à combinaison f. ‖ **Combination-room**, n. Salle de réunion f.
combine [kəm'bain] v. tr. Combiner, unir, joindre, conjuguer. ‖ Chim. Combiner.
— v. intr. S'unir, s'associer, se fusionner. ‖ Jur. Se syndiquer (workmen). ‖ Chim. Se combiner. ‖ Fig. Se liguer (against, contre).
— ['kɔmbain] n. Jur. Corporation f. ‖ Comm. Trust m. ‖ Fin. Horizontal combine, consortium m. ‖ **Combine-harvester**, n. Agric. Moissonneuse-batteuse f.
combined [kəm'baind] adj. Combiné (operation); combined set, combiné (telephone). ‖ Joint (with, à).

combing ['koumiŋ] n. Coup de peigne m. (action). ‖ Pl. Démêlures f. pl. (hair). ‖ Techn. Peignage, cardage m. (process).
combustibility [kəm,bʌsti'biliti] n. Combustibilité f.
combustible [kəm'bʌstibl] adj. Combustible. ‖ Fam. Emporté, bouillant, ardent.
— n. Combustible m. ‖ Matière inflammable f.
combustion [-'bʌstʃən] n. Combustion f. ‖ Autom. Internal combustion engine, moteur à combustion interne. ‖ **Combustion-chamber**, n. Techn. Chambre de combustion (or) d'explosion f.

---

1. Venir. — 2. Arriver. — 3. Parcourir. — 4. Aboutir. — 5. Se situer. — 6. Advenir. — 7. Se produire. — 8. Devenir. — 9. *To come at.* — 10. *To come by.* — 11. *To come for.* — 12. *To come from.* — 13. *To come in.* — 14. *To come into.* — 15. *To come of.* — 16. *To come on.* — 17. *To come over.* — 18. *To come through.* — 19. *To come to.* — 20. *To come together.* — 21. *To come under.* — 22. *To come on, upon.* — 23. *To come within.* — 24. Math. — 25. Fin. — 26. Jur. — 27. Comm. — 28. Med. — 29. Culin. — 30. Fam. — 31. *To come about.* — 32. *To come across.* — 33. *To come along.* — 34. *To come away.* — 35. *To come back.* — 36. *To come by.* — 37. *To come down.* — 38. *To come in.* — 39. *To come near.* — 40. *To come off.* — 41. *To come on.* — 42. *To come out.* — 43. *To come over.* — 44. *To come round.* — 45. *To come through.* — 46. *To come to.* — 47. *To come up.* — 48. Mots composés.

---

come [kʌm] v. intr. (39).
1. Venir; are you coming?, venez-vous?; time to come, temps futur, avenir. ‖ 2. Venir, arriver (to arrive); he has come, il est venu; he is come, il est arrivé. ‖ 3. Parcourir, faire, suivre (to go over); to come a little way, faire un bout de chemin. ‖ 4. Aboutir, arriver (to reach); the bus route comes near the station, la ligne d'autobus aboutit près de la gare. ‖ 5. Venir, se situer, se placer (to exist); after two comes three, après deux vient trois. ‖ 6. Advenir, arriver, survenir (to happen); how come you to have written this letter?, comment se fait-il que vous ayez écrit cette lettre?; whatever may come, quoi qu'il arrive (or) advienne. ‖ 7. Se produire, arriver, surgir (to occur); a misunderstanding came between us, une mésentente s'éleva entre nous; a knock came at the door, on frappa à la porte. ‖ 8. Se révéler, être, devenir (to become); to come loose, se relâcher; to come right, s'arranger; to come all right again, bien tourner; to come straight again, se redresser; to come true, se révéler exact, ‖ 9. Arriver, accéder (at, à, jusqu'à) [to reach]. ‖ 10. Mettre la main (by, sur); entrer en possession (by, de); to come by, se procurer (a book); se faire (an opinion). ‖ 11. Venir (for, à la recherche de); to come for, venir chercher, venir prendre (a book); what do you come here for?, qu'est-ce que vous venez faire ici? ‖ 12. Venir (from, de; de la part de); provenir (from, de); an answer came from him, une réponse vint de sa part; he comes from Dublin, il est originaire de Dublin (native); to come from Paris, venir de Paris. ‖ 13. Entrer (in, into, dans); to come into collision, entrer en collision; to come in sight, apparaître. ‖ 14. Venir (into, à); to come into arriver à (knowledge); entrer dans (its present form, a party, a room); venir à (s.o.'s mind); entrer en possession de (one's own); adhérer à (a scheme); entrer à (s.o.'s service). ‖ Résulter, venir, provenir découler (of, de); tenir (of, à); nothing came of it il n'en est rien advenu. ‖ 15. Descendre, être issu venir (of, de); appartenir (of, à) [a family]. ‖

16. Retomber, se retrouver (*on*, sur). ‖ 17. Passer (*over*, de l'autre côté de); s'emparer, se saisir (*over*, de); s'appesantir (*over*, sur); *a change has come over her life*, un changement s'est opéré dans sa vie; *to come over a bridge*, traverser un pont; *what has come over him?*, qu'est-ce qui lui a pris? ‖ 18. Venir à bout (*through*, de) [difficulties]; passer (*through*, par) [the wood]. ‖ 19. Venir (*to*, à); *to come to*, conclure (an agreement); approcher de (a crisis); prendre (a decision); arriver à, venir à, atteindre (one's destination); accomplir (one's fate); aboutir à, en arriver à (a quarrel); aborder (a question); venir trouver, se rendre auprès de (s.o.); arriver à, advenir à (s.o.); venir à, venir à l'esprit de (s.o.); venir à (s.o.'s knowledge); aboutir à, se ramener à, revenir à (an argument); aboutir à, parvenir à (success); monter sur (the throne); en venir ·à, en arriver à (one's turn); *if any hurt should come to you*, s'il vous arrivait quelque accident; *to come to light*, venir au jour, se faire jour, se révéler; *to come to pass*, se réaliser, se faire. ‖ 20. Venir (*together*, ensemble); *to come together*, se rassembler; *to come together again*, se réconcilier. ‖ 21. Venir (*under*, à) [s.o.'s notice]. ‖ 22. Tomber (*on*, *upon*, sur); s'emparer (*upon*, de); *a new light had come upon me*, une lumière nouvelle s'était faite en moi; *it came upon me that*, l'idée me vint que; *to come upon s.o.*, tomber sur qqn. ‖ 23. Entrer (*within*, dans); faire partie (*within*, de). ‖ 24. MATH. *To come right*, tomber juste. ‖ 25. FIN. Revenir, s'élever, se monter (*to*, à); *to come cheap*, revenir bon marché; *to come up to*, se monter à. ‖ 26. JUR. *To come before the judge*, venir (case); *to come to* (or) *into*, entrer en possession de; *to come upon s.o. for damages*, réclamer une indemnité à qqn; *to come within the law*, tomber sous le coup de la loi. ‖ 27. COMM. Exister; se faire. ‖ 28. MED. *To come to one's senses*, reprendre connaissance (or) ses sens. ‖ 29. CULIN. Prendre (sauce). ‖ 30. FAM. *How come?*, comment ça se fait-il?; d'où ça vient-il?; *to come it too strong*, y aller fort, attiger. ‖ 31. **To come about**, arriver, advenir, survenir, se produire (to happen); NAUT. Tourner, virer (wind). ‖ 32. **To come across**, rencontrer; FAM. *If I come across him!*, s'il me tombe sous la patte!; *you don't come across it every day*, on n'en trouve pas à la douzaine, ça ne se trouve pas dans le pas d'une mule. ‖ 33. **To come along**, avancer, marcher. ‖ 34. **To come away**, s'en aller, partir (person); se détacher, tomber (thing). ‖ 35. **To come back**, revenir, retourner. ‖ 36. **To come by**, passer. ‖ 37. **To come down**, descendre; ARCHIT. S'écrouler, tomber; SPORTS. *To come down on a double rope*, faire une descente en rappel; FIG. Se transmettre; déchoir; *to come down in the world*, se déclasser; *to come down to*, se ramener à, se borner à, se réduire à (argument); FAM. *I haven't come down to that*, je n'en suis pas là; *to come down upon*, s'en prendre à, tomber sur le paletot de; *to come down with*, fournir l'argent à, décaisser. ‖ 38. **To come in**, apparaître (fashion); entrer, rentrer, pénétrer (person); commencer (season); devenir, se révéler (useful); *to come in upon s.o.*, interrompre qqn; SPORTS. Arriver (horse, runner); NAUT. Monter (tide); BOT. Donner (wheat); JUR. Arriver au pouvoir (party); FIN. Etre présenté (invoice); *to come in for*, recevoir pour sa part, hériter de; FAM. Intervenir; *where do I come in?*, quand est-ce que j'entre en jeu?; qu'est-ce que je deviens? ‖ 39. **To come near**, approcher de (s.o.); FIG. Manquer de, faillir, être près de, être à deux doigts de; *I came near fainting*, pour un peu je me serais évanoui. ‖ 40. **To come off**, se détacher, s'enlever (page, wheel); s'en aller, partir (stain); SPORTS. Se jouer (match); FIG. Avoir lieu, se produire (event); se réaliser, réussir (project); FAM. S'en tirer, s'en sortir, se tirer

d'affaire. ‖ 41. **To come on**, avancer, s'avancer, s'approcher (person); survenir, arriver, éclater (storm); *it came on to rain*, il se mit à pleuvoir; JUR. Venir en discussion (bill); venir (case); THEATR. Paraître, entrer en scène, faire son entrée (actor); être représenté (or) joué (play); FIG. Continuer, poursuivre; avancer, progresser. ‖ 42. **To come out**, sortir, paraître, être publié (book); sortir, se montrer, paraître, apparaître (moon, person); SPORTS. Terminer; BOT. Pousser, sortir, germer; MED. Sortir; PHYS. Se développer (photo); THEATR. Débuter; FIG. Se manifester, se montrer, se révéler, se divulguer; se faire jour (secret, truth); *to come out of*, sortir de, échapper à; FAM. *To come out with*, cracher, accoucher de, sortir (words). ‖ 43. **To come over**, venir d'un autre côté (or) de loin; FIG. Venir d'un autre parti; passer à l'autre camp; *to come over s.o.*, saisir (or) affecter (or) changer qqn. ‖ 44. **To come round**, revenir par période (feast); MED. Se ranimer, revenir à soi; se rétablir, entrer en convalescence; NAUT. Venir au vent; FIG. Retrouver son calme; FAM. Faire une apparition. ‖ 45. **To come through**, CH. DE F. Passer sans s'arrêter. ‖ 46. **To come to**, Céder, y venir; NAUT. Venir sur bâbord (or) tribord; MED. Reprendre ses sens. ‖ 47. **To come up**, apparaître, naître (fashion); monter, gravir (person); BOT. Pousser, germer, pointer (plant); NAUT. Se lever (wind); JUR. Comparaître; COMM. Etre mis en vente; FIG. Revenir, devenir à la mode (idea); se poser, venir sur le tapis, être soulevé (question); *to come up to*, atteindre (a degree); réaliser (expectations); répondre à (hope); égaler (s.o.); être à la hauteur de (a task); se mettre à (work); *to come up with*, atteindre, rejoindre; proposer, suggérer. ‖ 48. **Come-and-go**, n. Va-et-vient m. ‖ **Come-at-able**, adj. Accessible. ‖ **Come-back**, n. Retour m.; U. S. FAM. réplique f.; *to make a come-back*, faire une rentrée. ‖ **Come-down**, n. Déchéance, chute; dégringolade f. (fam.). ‖ **Come-on**, n. Geste d'appel; U.S. appât m. ‖ **Come-uppance**, n. FAM. *To get one's come-uppance*, récolter ce qu'on mérite.
— interj. *Come!*, allons, voyons!; *come on!*, venez!; venez-y!; *come up*, hop, hardi!

comedian [kə'mi:diən] n. Auteur comique m. (writer). ‖ THEATR. Comédien s. (in the legitimate theatre); comique s. (in variety). ‖ FIG. Comédien s.

comedienne [kəmi:'djen] n. THEATR. Comédienne (in variety). ‖ CINEM. Actrice (f.) de cinéma.

comedist [ˈkɔmidist] n. Auteur comique m.

comedo [ˈkɔmidɔ] (pl. **comedones** [kɔmiˈdouniz]) n. MED. Comédon; point noir m. (fam.).

comedy [ˈkɔmidi] n. THEATR. Comédie f. (art, play). ‖ MUS. *Musical comedy*, opérette. ‖ FIG. Comédie f.; *to cut the comedy*, mettre fin à la comédie.

comeliness [ˈkʌmlinis] n. Grâce, joliesse f.; charme m. ‖ † Bienséance f.

comely [-i] adj. Beau, charmant, attirant, avenant. (See BEAUTIFUL.) ‖ † Bienséant.

comer [ˈkʌmə*] n. Arrivant, survenant, venant m.; *first comer*, premier arrivé (or) arrivant; *to all comers*, à tout venant. ‖ FAM. U. S. Jeune espoir m.

comestible [kəˈmestibl] adj., n. CULIN. Comestible m.

comet [ˈkɔmit] n. ASTRON. Comète f.

comfit [ˈkʌmfit] n. Dragée f. ‖ **Comfit-box**, n. Drageoir m.; bonbonnière f. ‖ **Comfit-maker**, n. Confiseur m.

comfort [ˈkʌmfət] n. Confort m.; aises f. pl. ‖ Pl. Bien-être m.; aisance f. ‖ FIG. Réconfort, encouragement m.; satisfaction f. ‖ FIG. Soulagement m.; consolation f. ‖ **Comfort station**, n. U. S. Toilette f.; lavatory m.
— v. tr. Réconforter, encourager (to hearten); consoler, soulager (to solace).

comfortable [-əbl̩] adj. Confortable, commode;

very comfortable hotel, hôtel de grand confort. ‖ A l'aise ; *I'm quite comfortable here*, je me trouve (or) sens bien ici ; *to make oneself comfortable*, se mettre à son aise, faire comme chez soi. ‖ Rassurant, tranquillisant. ‖ Rassuré, sans inquiétude (*about*, sur) ; *a comfortable sense of accomplishment*, la douce sensation d'avoir accompli sa tâche. ‖ FIN. Aisé, large, suffisant (income).

comfortably [-əbli] adv. Confortablement, commodément, agréablement, à l'aise. ‖ FIN. A l'aise, dans l'aisance.

comforter [-ə*] n. Consolateur *m.* ; consolatrice *f.* ‖ Cache-nez *m.* (scarf). ‖ Sucette *f.* (dummy teat). ‖ U. S. Edredon *m.* ‖ ECCLES. Esprit consolateur *m.*

comforting [-iŋ] adj. Réconfortant, encourageant ; consolant.

comfortless [-lis] adj. Sans confort, incommode. ‖ Délaissé, sans consolation.

comfy ['kʌmfi] adj. FAM. Confortable (thing) ; bien (person).

comic ['kɔmik] adj. Comique, amusant. ‖ Humoristique. ‖ THEATR. Comique.
— n. THEATR. Comique, acteur comique *m.* ‖ Pl. Dessins humoristiques *m. pl.* ; bandes dessinées *f. pl.*

comical [-l] adj. Comique, drôle, amusant, cocasse.

comicality [kɔmi'kæliti], **comicalness** ['kɔmikəlnis] n. Comique *m.* (of an event). ‖ Drôlerie *f.*

comically ['kɔmikəli] adv. Comiquement.

Cominform ['kɔminfɔ:m] n. Kominform *m.*

coming ['kɔmiŋ] adj. A venir, futur (age) ; prochain (year). ‖ FIG. Qui promet, d'avenir ; *coming man*, jeune espoir ; *the coming thing*, le succès dans l'air.
— n. Arrivée, venue *f.* ; *coming away, back, between*, départ, retour, interposition ; *coming in*, entrée, introduction ; *coming on*, début, commencement ; *coming out*, sortie, apparition ; début ; *coming up*, ascension, approche. ‖ ECCLES. Avènement *m.*

Comintern ['kɔmintə:n] n. Komintern *m.*

comitia [kɔ'miʃiə] n. pl. † Comices *m. pl.*

comity ['kɔmiti] n. Courtoisie *f.* ‖ JUR. *Comity of nations*, application courtoise des lois d'un pays dans un autre pays.

comma ['kɔmə] n. Virgule *f.* ; *inverted commas*, guillemets ; *to begin, to close the inverted commas*, ouvrir, fermer les guillemets. ‖ MUS. Comma *m.* ‖ MED. Virgule *f.* (bacillus).

command [kɔ'mɑ:nd] v. tr. Ordonner, requérir, exiger, enjoindre ; *to command s.o. to do sth.*, ordonner (or) intimer l'ordre à qqn de faire qqch. ; *to command sth. to be done*, donner l'ordre de faire qqch. ‖ Contrôler, exercer une autorité (or) juridiction sur (to control). ‖ Commander, dominer (to dominate). ‖ Avoir vue sur, donner sur (to overlook). ‖ MILIT., NAUT. Commander (an army, a position, a ship). ‖ FIG. Disposer de (money, skill, vocabulary) ; dominer, commander à (one's passions) ; commander, inspirer, susciter (respect).
— v. intr. Donner un ordre, ordonner, commander. ‖ MILIT., NAUT. Avoir le commandement. ‖ FIG. Agir en chef.
— n. Ordre *m.* ; *Royal command*, invitation du roi ; *by s.o.'s command*, sur l'ordre (or) les injonctions de qqn. ‖ MILIT. Commandement *m.* ; *holding a command*, titulaire d'un commandement ; *to be in command of*, être à la tête de, avoir sous les ordres. ‖ MILIT. Hommes *m. pl.* ; troupes *f. pl.* ; *defence command*, troupes de défense. ‖ MILIT. Région militaire *f.* ; *coastal-defence command*, zone fortifiée de défense côtière. ‖ AVIAT. *Air command*, brigade aérienne. ‖ NAUT. Maîtrise *f.* (of the sea). ‖ FIN. Disposition *f.* ; *money at one's command*, argent dont on peut disposer. ‖ INFORM. Commande *f.*, ordre *m.* ‖ FIG. Maîtrise *f.* (of a language, over oneself). ‖ **Command module,**

n. ASTRONAUT. Module (*m.*) de commande. ‖ **Command post,** n. MILIT. Poste de commandement *m.*

commandant [,kɔmən'dænt] n. MILIT. Commandant *m.*

commandeer [-'diə*] v. tr. Réquisitionner.

commander [kə'mɑ:ndə*] n. Chef *m.* (chief). ‖ Commandeur *m.* (of an order). ‖ NAUT. Capitaine (*m.*) de frégate. ‖ AVIAT. Chef de bord *m.* ‖ MILIT. Commandant *m.* ; *tank commander*, chef de char. ‖ **Commander-in-chief,** n. MILIT. Commandant en chef *m.*

commandership [-əʃip] n. Commandement *m.*

commanding [-iŋ] adj. Imposant (air) ; de commandement (tone). ‖ Dominant, éminent, élevé (position).

commandment [-mənt] n. ECCLES. Commandement *m.*

commando [-ou] n. MILIT. Corps franc *m.*

commeasurable [kə'meʒərəbl] adj. Proportionné, de même mesure (or) taille. (See COMMENSURATE.)

comme il faut [kɔmil'fo] adj., adv. Comme il faut.

commemorate [kə'memɔreit] v. tr. Commémorer.

commemoration [kə,memɔ'reiʃən] n. Commémoration *f.* ‖ ECCLES. Commémoraison *f.*

commemorative [kə'memərətiv] adj. Commémoratif.

commence [kə'mens] v. tr. JUR., ECCLES., MILIT. Commencer. (See BEGIN.)

commencement [-mənt] n. Commencement *m.* (See BEGINNING.) ‖ JUR. Date d'entrée en vigueur, prise (*f.*) d'effet. ‖ U. S. *Commencement exercises*, cérémonie de remise des diplômes universitaires.

commend [kə'mend] v. tr. Remettre, confier, livrer (*to*, à) [to entrust]. ‖ Recommander, louer, approuver, faire l'éloge de (to praise) ; *to commend oneself to*, se recommander à, être du goût de, être approuvé par. ‖ † *Commend me to your father*, rappelez-moi au souvenir de Monsieur votre père. ‖ FAM. *Commend me to a good cake*, parlez-moi d'un bon gâteau !

commendable [-əbl] adj. Louable ; recommandable. (See PRAISE-WORTHY.)

commendably [-əbli] adv. D'une façon louable.

commendam [kə'mendəm] n. ECCLES. Commende *f.*

commendation [,kɔmen'deiʃən] n. Action (*f.*) de confier (entrusting). ‖ Recommandation *f.* ‖ Louange, approbation *f.* (praise).

commendatory [kɔ'mendətəri] adj. Laudatif, élogieux, approbatif. ‖ De recommandation. ‖ ECCLES. Commendataire (abbey, priest) ; des agonisants (prayer).

commensal [kə'mensəl] adj. Qui mange à la même table. ‖ ZOOL. Commensal.
— n. Commensal *s.*

commensalism [-izm] n. ZOOL. Commensalisme *m.*

commensurability [kə,menʃərə'biliti] n. Commensurabilité *f.*

commensurable [kə'menʃərəbl] adj. Commensurable, ayant une commune mesure (*to, with*, avec) ; proportionné (*to*, à).

commensurate [-it] adj. De même mesure (*with*, que) ; coétendu (*with*, à). ‖ Proportionné (*to, with*, à).

comment ['kɔment] n. Commentaire *m.* ; annotation, observation *f.* ‖ Remarque, critique *f.*
— v. intr. *To comment upon*, commenter ; faire des remarques sur ; critiquer.
— v. tr. Commenter.

commentary [-əri] n. Commentaire *m.* ‖ RADIO. *Running commentary*, reportage en direct.

commentate ['kɔmən,teit] v. intr. RADIO. Commenter ; faire le commentaire (*on*, de).

commentation [,kɔmən'teiʃən] n. Commentaire *m.* (act).

commentator ['kɔmənteitə*] n. Commentateur m.; commentatrice f.

commerce ['kɔmə:s] n. COMM. Commerce international (or) en gros m.; affaires commerciales extérieures f. pl.; in commerce, dans les affaires. ‖ JUR. Commerce sexuel (or) amoureux m.

commercial [kə'mə:ʃəl] adj. COMM. Commercial (product); commerçant (quarter, street); de commerce (school, traveller); vénal, marchand, commercial (value); du commerce (world). ‖ FIN. Commercial, de commerce (bank); commercial instrument, effet négociable. ‖ JUR. Commercial (law); Commercial Court, tribunal consulaire. ‖ TECHN. Utile (efficiency). ‖ AUTOM. Utilitaire (vehicle).
— n. RADIO. Annonce publicitaire f.

commercialese [,kɔmə:ʃə'li:z] n. FAM. Style commercial m.

commercialism [kə'mə:ʃəlizm̩] n. COMM. Esprit commerçant; mercantilisme m. ‖ Pratique (or) expression (f.) du commerce.

commercialization [kəmə:,ʃəli'zeiʃən] n. COMM. Commercialisation f.

commercialize [kə'mə:ʃəlaiz] v. tr. COMM. Commercialiser.

commercially [-əli] adv. COMM. Commercialement.

Commie ['kɔmi] n. FAM. Communiste, coco s.

comminate ['kɔmineit] v. tr., intr. Anathématiser.

commination [,kɔmi'neiʃən] n. ECCLES. Commination f. ‖ FIG. Menace f.

comminatory ['kɔminətəri] adj. Comminatoire. (See THREATENING.)

commingle [kɔmiŋgl] v. tr. Mélanger.
— v. intr. Se mélanger, se mêler (with, avec).

comminute ['kɔminju:t] v. tr. Fragmenter. ‖ JUR. Morceler (a property).

commiserable [kɔ'mizərəbl̩] adj. Pitoyable, digne de commisération.

commiserate [-reit] v. tr. Avoir de la pitié (or) commisération pour.
— v. intr. S'apitoyer (with, sur); compatir aux malheurs (with, de).

commiseration [kɔ,mizə'reiʃən] n. Commisération, compassion, pitié f.

commiserative [kɔ'mizərətiv] adj. Pitoyable, compatissant.

commissar [kɔmi'sɑ:r] n. Commissaire du peuple m.

commissarial [,kɔmi'sɛəriəl] adj. Du commissaire. ‖ ECCLES. Du vicaire général. ‖ MILIT. De l'intendance.

commissariat [-riit] n. MILIT. Intendance f. ‖ Commissariat, ministère m. (in U.S.S.R.).

commissary ['kɔmisəri] n. Commissaire, délégué m. ‖ MILIT. Officier (m.) d'intendance. ‖ U. S. COMM. Magasin coopératif m. ‖ ECCLES. Vicaire général m.

commission [kə'miʃən] n. Commission f.; comité m. (see COMMITTEE); commission of enquiry, commission d'enquête. ‖ ARTS. Commande f.; done on commission, fait sur commande. ‖ TECHN. Usage, service m. ‖ ECCLES. Action f. ‖ JUR. Consommation, perpétration f. (of a crime). ‖ JUR. Délégation (f.) de pouvoir, mandat m. ‖ JUR. Fonctions f. pl.; commission of the peace, charge de juge de paix; on the commission, en exercice. ‖ MILIT. Brevet m.; date of commission, date de promotion; to throw up one's commission, démissionner. ‖ NAUT. Armement m.; to put a ship in, out of commission, armer, désarmer un navire. ‖ COMM. Commission, guelte f.; courtage m. (see FACTORAGE); on a commission basis, à la commission. ‖ **Commission-agent**, n. COMM. Courtier m. ‖ **Commission-day**, n. JUR. Jour (m.) de l'ouverture des assises.
— v. tr. Passer une commande à (an artist); work commissioned by the publisher, ouvrage exécuté sur commande de l'éditeur. ‖ Donner pouvoir (or) mission à, déléguer (s.o.). ‖ MILIT. Promouvoir au grade de, nommer à un commandement (an officer). ‖ NAUT. Mettre en service (a ship).

commissionaire [kə,miʃə'nɛə*] n. Commissionnaire, coursier s.

commissioned [kə'miʃənd] adj. JUR. Commissionné, délégué. ‖ MILIT. Breveté (officer). ‖ NAUT. Mis en service (ship).

commissioner [-ŋə*] n. Membre (m.) d'un comité (or) d'une commission, commissaire m. ‖ Préfet m. (of police).

commissure ['kɔmisjuə*] n. MED. Commissure f.

commit [kə'mit] v. tr. (1). Confier, livrer, commettre (to, à) [see CONFIDE, ENTRUST]; to commit oneself to, se confier à, s'en remettre à; to commit sth. to paper, coucher qqch. par écrit. ‖ Commettre (a crime, an offence). [See PERPETRATE.] ‖ Risquer, compromettre (one's honour); not to commit oneself, ne pas se compromettre; to commit oneself with, se commettre avec. ‖ Engager; committed literature, littérature engagée; to commit oneself, s'engager, prendre un engagement. ‖ JUR. Ecrouer, emprisonner (a criminal, thief); faire interner (a madman); to commit for trial, mettre en accusation. ‖ JUR. Renvoyer devant une commission (a bill).

commitment [-mənt], **committal** [kə'mitl̩] n. Action (f.) de confier, mandat m. ‖ Engagement m. (pledge). ‖ JUR. Mandat de dépôt m.; incarcération f. (of an accused); perpétration f. (of a crime); procédure (f.) d'internement (of a madman). ‖ JUR. Renvoi (m.) à une commission (of a bill). ‖ FIN. Engagement financier m. ‖ LOC. Committal to the earth, to the deep, enterrement, immersion.

committed [kə'mitid] adj. Convaincu (devoted); engagé (politically aligned).

committee [kə'miti] n. Comité m.; Joint Production Committee, comité d'entreprise. ‖ Commission f.; Committee of Ways and Means, commission du Budget; judicial committee of employers and workmen, commission paritaire. ‖ Bureau m.; executive committee of an association, bureau d'une société. ‖ Comité électoral m. ‖ JUR. Curateur m. ‖ **Committee-man** (or) **-woman**, n. Membre (m.) d'un comité. ‖ **Committee-room**, n. Permanence f.

commode [kə'moud] n. Commode f. (piece of furniture). ‖ Chaise percée f. ‖ FAM. Commodités f. pl.

commodious [-iəs] adj. Spacieux.

commodity [kə'mɔditi] n. COMM. Denrée f.; produit m.; tax on commodities, taxe à la consommation. ‖ **Commodity-money**, n. FIN. Système monétaire (m.) indexé sur le prix des produits de consommation.

commodore [kɔmədɔ:*] n. NAUT. Commodore m. ‖ SPORTS. Président d'un Yacht-Club m.

common ['kɔmən] adj. Commun (to everyone) [interests room]. ‖ Commun, public; common crier, crieur public; common prostitute, fille publique. ‖ Commun, général; common kitchen utensil, faitout; common sense, bon sens, sens commun. ‖ Familier, usuel, habituel. ‖ Commun, ordinaire (method); fréquent (occurrence); courant (opinion); the common run of humanity, le commun des mortels. ‖ Commun, ordinaire, vulgaire (manners); common or garden, ordinaire; common man, homme du commun (or) peuple; common people, peuple, commun, masse. ‖ GRAMM. Commun (noun); of common gender, des deux genres. ‖ MATH. Commun (denominator, divisor, multiple). ‖ MILIT. Simple (soldier). ‖ ECCLES. Book of Common Prayer, liturgie anglicane. ‖ JUR. Municipal (council); coutumier (law); common property, biens collectifs. ‖ FIN. Ordinaire (stock). ‖ MUS. Parfait (chord); à deux (or) quatre temps (measure). ‖ **Common-lawyer**, n. JUR. Civiliste m.
— n. Terrain communal m. ‖ JUR. Common of

pasturage, droit de pacage. ‖ LOC. *In common*, en commun; *in common with*, en accord avec; *out of the common*, inhabituel, peu ordinaire, hors du commun. ‖ See COMMONS.

commonage [-idʒ] n. Commun *m*. (commonalty). ‖ Communauté *f*. (of rights). ‖ JUR. Vaine pâture *f*. (land); droit de pacage *m*. (right).

commonalty [-əlti] n. Commun *m.; gens* (*m. pl.*) du peuple. ‖ Communauté humaine *f*. ‖ JUR. Corporation *f.;* corps constitué *m*.

commoner [-ə*] n. Roturier *s*. ‖ Parlementaire (*m*.) de la Chambre des communes. ‖ Étudiant non boursier *m*. ‖ JUR. Personne (*f*.) qui a droit de pacage.

commonly [-li] adv. Communément, généralement, ordinairement, à l'ordinaire, d'habitude. ‖ D'une façon banale (or) commune (or) ordinaire (or) vulgaire; vulgairement.

commonness [-nis] n. Fréquence *f*. (of an event). ‖ Banalité, vulgarité *f*.

commonplace [-pleis] adj. Banal, commun, ordinaire, quelconque. (See TRITE.)
— n. Banalité, platitude *f.;* lieu commun, truisme *m*. ‖ **Commonplace-book**, n. Mémorandum *m*.
— v. intr. Dire des platitudes; s'exprimer en lieux communs. ‖ Prendre note de, noter.

Commons ['kɔmənz] n. pl. Peuple; tiers état *m*. ‖ Chambre (*f*.) des communes.

commons n. pl. † Réfectoire *m*. (dining-room). ‖ Pl. Chère *f*. (food); *on short commons*, réduit à la portion congrue.

commonweal ['kɔmənwi:l] n. Bien public; Etat *m*.

commonwealth [-welθ] n. République, démocratie *f*. ‖ Commonwealth, empire *m.;* confédération *f*. ‖ U. S. Chacun (*m*.) des Etats des Etats-Unis. ‖ † Bien public *m*.

commotion [kɔ'mouʃən] n. Agitation, secousse, commotion *f.;* ébranlement *m*. ‖ Branle-bas, tumulte, remue-ménage, brouhaha *m*. (confusion). ‖ Emoi, trouble *m.; in a state of commotion*, bouleversé, vivement ému. ‖ Trouble, remous *m.;* insurrection *f*.

communal ['kɔmjunl] adj. Communal (council); banal (mill). ‖ Public; *communal kitchen*, soupe populaire. ‖ Commun; collectif (life). ‖ JUR. *Communal estate*, communauté conjugale. ‖ † De la commune.

communalism [-əlizm] n. JUR. Théorie *f*. (or) système (*m*.) de la décentralisation des pouvoirs.

communalist [-əlist] s. JUR. Communaliste *s*.

commune [kə'mju:n] v. intr. Converser; être en relations intimes, communier (*with*, avec); *to commune with oneself*, se recueillir, méditer. ‖ ECCLES. U. S. Communier.
— ['kɔmju:n] n. Commune *f*. (administrative unit). ‖ Communauté *f*. (group).

communicable [kə'mju:nikəbl] adj. Communicable. ‖ MED. Transmissible.

communicant [-ənt] n. Informateur *m*., informatrice *f*. ‖ ECCLES. Fidèle, pratiquant *s*. (belonging to a Church); communiant *s*. (receiving Holy Communion).

communicate [-eit] v. tr. Communiquer, faire connaître (or) parvenir, transmettre (*to*, à) [information, messages]. ‖ Partager (*with*, avec) [to share]. ‖ ECCLES. Donner la communion à, communier (s.o.). ‖ FIG. Communiquer, insuffler, faire partager (emotion, feelings).
— v. intr. Communiquer, se mettre en rapport, entrer en contact (or) relations (*with*, avec). ‖ Communiquer (*with*, avec); *to communicate with one another*, communiquer, se commander (rooms). ‖ ECCLES. Communier, recevoir la communion.

communication [kə,mju:ni'keiʃən] n. Communication *f*. (*by*, par). ‖ Communication *f.;* contact, commerce, rapport *m*. (*with*, avec). ‖ Compagnie *f.; evil communications corrupt good manners*, les

mauvaises compagnies corrompent les bonnes mœurs. ‖ Communication, information *f.;* message, renseignement *m*. ‖ Communication, transmission *f.;* moyen (*m*.) de communication (or) d'accès (way). ‖ MILIT. Liaison, communication *f.; communications zone*, zone d'étapes; *technical communication*, moyens techniques de liaison. ‖ CH. DE F. *Communication cord*, sonnette d'alarme.

communicative [kə'mju:nikətiv] adj. Communicatif, expansif.

communicativeness [-kətivnis] n. Nature expansive *f*.

communicator [-keitə*] n. Transmetteur, communicateur *m*.

communion [kə'mju:njən] n. Communion, participation, possession communautaire *f.;* partage *m*. ‖ Communion (*f*.) d'idées; relations intimes *f. pl.;* rapports *m. pl.* (*with*, avec). ‖ ECCLES. Communion *f.; to make one's Easter Communion*, faire ses pâques. ‖ **Communion-rail** (or) **-table**, n. ECCLES. Sainte table, table de communion *f*.

communiqué [kɔ'mju:nikei] n. Communiqué *m*.

communism ['kɔmjunizm] n. Communisme *m*.

communist [-ist] adj., n. Communiste *s*.

communistic [,kɔmju'nistik] adj. Communisant.

communistically [-əli] adv. A la façon communiste; *communistically inclined*, à tendances communistes.

community [kə'mju:niti] n. Communauté *f.;* groupement *m*. ‖ Communauté; collectivité, société *f*. ‖ ECCLES. Communauté *f*. (monastery); ordre *m*. (order). ‖ FIG. Communauté, identité *f*. (of interests, spirit); solidarité *f*. (of social life). ‖ **Community centre**, n. Foyer socioculturel *m*. ‖ **Community-chest** (or) **-fund**, n. FIN. Fonds commun *m*. ‖ **Community centre**, n. Foyer socioculturel *m*.

communize ['kɔmju,naiz] v. tr. Collectiviser (land). [See COLLECTIVIZE.] ‖ Faire passer au communisme, communiser (a country, a people).

commutability [kə,mju:tə'biliti] n. Permutabilité, interchangeabilité *f*. ‖ JUR. Commutabilité *f*.

commutable [kə'mju:təbl] adj. Interchangeable. ‖ JUR. Commuable.

commutate ['kɔmjuteit] v. tr. ELECTR. Commuter.

commutation [,kɔmju'teiʃən] n. Echange *m.;* substitution *f*. ‖ FIN. Indemnité en espèces *f*. ‖ JUR. *Commutation of punishment*, commutation de peine. ‖ ELECTR. Commutation *f*. ‖ CH. DE F. U. S. Abonnement *m.;* trajet journalier *m.; commutation ticket*, carte d'abonnement.

commutative [kə'mju:tətiv] adv. Commutatif.

commutator ['kɔmjuteitə*] n. ELECTR. Commutateur *m*. (See SWITCH.) ‖ ELECTR., TECHN. Collecteur *m*. ‖ **Commutator-bar**, n. TECHN. Lame (*f*.) de collecteur.

commute [kə'mju:t] v. tr. Echanger, interchanger, substituer. ‖ Echanger, faire l'échange (*for*, pro, contre, avec). ‖ JUR. Commuer (*into*, en). ‖ ELECTR. Commuter.
— v. intr. Parcourir quotidiennement un long trajet entre le lieu de résidence et le lieu de travail.

commuter [-ə*] n. Banlieusard, habitant (*s*.) de la grande banlieue.

Comoro ['kɔmə,rou] n. GEOGR. *Comoro islands*, Comores *f. pl*.

compact ['kɔmpækt] n. Contrat, pacte *m.;* convention *f*. (See COVENANT.)

compact ['kɔmpækt] n. Poudrier *m*.
— [kəm'pækt] adj. Compact, dense, tassé; peu embarrassant. ‖ Concis, condensé, bref (terse). ‖ FIG. Bourré, pétri, rempli, plein (*of*, de).
— v. tr. Rendre compact, tasser, resserrer, ramasser. ‖ Condenser. ‖ FIG. Bourrer, former, composer (*of*, de).

compactly [-li] adv. D'une façon compacte. ‖ Avec un faible encombrement, sous un volume réduit.

compactness [-nis] n. Densité, compacité *f.* ‖ Concision *f.*

companion [kəm'pænjən] n. Compagnon *m.*; compagne *f.*; *companion in misfortune*, compagnon d'infortune. ‖ Personne de compagnie *f.*; *lady companion*, dame de compagnie. ‖ Pendant *m.* (of a pair). ‖ Compagnon *m.* (of an Order of Knighthood). ‖ **Companion-in-arms**, n. Compagnon (*m.*) d'armes.
— v. tr. Accompagner.
— v. intr. Tenir compagnie (*with*, à) [s.o.]; aller de pair (*with*, avec) [sth.].

COMPANIES — SOCIÉTÉS

deed of partnership	acte de société
Board of Directors	conseil d'administration
general meeting	assemblée générale
director	administrateur
managing director	administrateur délégué
partner	associé
sleeping partner, U. S. silent partner	commanditaire
outlay	mise de fonds
employer, employee	employeur, employé
go-slow strike, U. S. slow-down strike	grève perlée
work-to-rules action	grève du zèle
Conciliation Board	conseil des prud'hommes
resumption of work	reprise du travail
boom	mouvement d'affaires
depression, recession	crise
slump	effondrement [prix]
bankruptcy, failure	faillite
to go bankrupt	faire faillite
balance-sheet	bilan
to file one's petition	déposer son bilan
auditor	commissaire aux comptes
turnover	chiffre d'affaires
competition	concurrence
supply and demand	l'offre et la demande
liquidator, trustee	liquidateur
to float a concern	lancer une affaire
to carry on business	faire des affaires
founder's shares	part de fondateur
power of attorney	pouvoir, procuration
style	raison sociale
branch	filiale, succursale
head office	maison mère, siège social
joint stock company	société par actions
limited company	société à responsabilité limitée

companion n. NAUT. Capot; dôme *m.* ‖ **Companion-ladder**, n. NAUT. Echelle (*f.*) des cabines (or) de commandement. ‖ **Companion-way**, n. NAUT. Capot *m.*

companionable [-əbl̩] adj. Sociable.

companionship [-ʃip] n. Camaraderie *f.* (fellowship); *for the sake of companionship*, par désir de compagnie. ‖ Equipe *f.* (group).

company ['kʌmpəni] n. Compagnie *f.*; *in company with*, en compagnie de; *to bear* (or) *keep s.o. company*, tenir compagnie à qqn; *to keep company together*, aller de compagnie; *to part company with*, se séparer de. ‖ Compagnie, réunion, société, assemblée *f.*; *large company*, nombreuse société. ‖ Compagnie, fréquentation *f.*; *bad company*, mauvaises fréquentations; *he is no fit company for you*, ce n'est pas une compagnie pour vous. ‖ COMM. Société *f.*; *trade company*, corps de métier. ‖ THEATR. Compagnie, troupe *f.* ‖ MILIT. Compagnie *f.* ‖ NAUT. Equipage *m.*
— v. intr. Se trouver en compagnie (*with*, de).

comparable ['kɔmpərəbl̩] adj. Comparable (*to, with*, à).

comparative [kəm'pærətiv] adj. Relatif, comparatif. ‖ MED. Comparé (anatomy). ‖ GRAMM. Comparatif (adjectif); comparé (linguistics, literature).

— n. GRAMM. Comparatif *m.*; *in the comparative*, au comparatif.

comparatively [-li] adv. Comparativement. ‖ Relativement (*to, with*, à).

compare [kəm'pɛə*] v. tr. Comparer, assimiler, égaler (*to*, à); mettre en parallèle (*to*, avec) [to liken]. ‖ Comparer, mettre en comparaison (or) balance (*with*, avec). ‖ GRAMM. Former les degrés de comparaison de. ‖ FAM. *To compare notes*, échanger des vues.
— v. intr. Se comparer, être comparable (*with*, à); rivaliser (*with*, avec).
— n. Comparaison *f.*; *beyond compare*, incomparablement.

comparison [kəm'pærisn̩] n. Comparaison *f.*; *in comparison with*, en comparaison de; *to bear* (or) *stand comparison with*, soutenir la comparaison avec. ‖ GRAMM. Comparaison *f.*

compart [kəm'pɑːt], U. S. **compartmentalize** [kəm,pɑːt'mentə,laiz], v. tr. Compartimenter, subdiviser.

compartment [-mənt] n. Compartiment *m.*; subdivision *f.* ‖ CH. DE F., NAUT. Compartiment *m.*

compartmentation [kəm,pɑːtmən'teiʃən] n. Compartimentage, cloisonnement *m.*

compass ['kʌmpəs] n. Etendue *f.* (extent); limites, bornes *f. pl.* (limits); portée *f.* (reach); espace, champ, rayon *m.* (scope). ‖ MUS. Portée *f.* (of instrument, voice). ‖ NAUT. Boussole *f.*; *point of the compass*, quart de compas. ‖ MATH. Compas *m.* (See COMPASSES.) ‖ AVIAT. *Radio compass*, radio-compas. ‖ **Compass-card**, n. Rose (*f.*) des vents. ‖ **Compass-course**, n. NAUT. Route magnétique *f.* ‖ **Compass-saw**, n. TECHN. Egoïne *f.*
— v. tr. Faire le tour de. ‖ Encercler, entourer (to surround). ‖ Comprendre, saisir, percevoir, embrasser. (See UNDERSTAND.) ‖ Arriver (or) parvenir à bien (to achieve); accomplir, réaliser, en venir à (to perform). ‖ Projeter (to plan); comploter, machiner, préméditer (to plot).

compasses ['kʌmpəsiz] n. pl. MATH. Compas *m.*; *wing compasses*, compas à quart de cercle. (See DIVIDERS.)

compassion [kəm'pæʃən] n. Compassion *f.* (*on, de, pour*). [See PITY.]

compassionate [-it] adj. Compatissant; *compassionate leave*, congé spécial accordé à l'occasion d'un deuil.

compassionately [-itli] adv. Avec compassion.

compassionateness [-itnis] n. Humanité *f.*

compatibility [kəm,pæti'biliti] n. Compatibilité *f.* (*with*, avec).

compatible [kəm'pætibl̩] adj. Compatible (*with*, avec).

compatriot [kəm'pætriət] n. Compatriote s. (See FELLOW-COUNTRYMAN.)
— adj. Du même pays.

compeer [kɔm'piə*] n. Pair *m.* (equal). ‖ FAM. Compagnon, compère *m.*

compel [kəm'pel] v. tr. (1). Contraindre, astreindre, forcer, obliger, pousser (*to*, à). [See FORCE.] ‖ Imposer, forcer, commander (*from*, de) [admiration, respect].

compellation [,kɔmpə'leiʃən] n. Appellation *f.*; titre *m.*

compelling [kəm'peliŋ] adj. Astreignant, forcé. ‖ Irrésistible.

compendious [kəm'pendiəs] adj. Compendieux, succinct. (See CONCISE.)

compendium [-əm] n. Abrégé, condensé, compendium *m.*

compensate ['kɔmpenseit] v. tr. Compenser, faire compensation, contrebalancer (in force, weight). ‖ Rémunérer (*for*, de, pour) [to pay]. ‖ Indemniser, dédommager (*for*, de; *with*, par) [to recompense]. ‖ TECHN. Compenser, neutraliser.
— v. intr. Donner une indemnité (or) un dédom-

magement (*for*, pour). ‖ **To compensate for**, faire compensation.
compensating [-iŋ] adj. Compensateur *m*., compensatrice *f*.
compensation [,kɔmpen'seiʃən] n. Compensation *f*.; dédommagement *m*. (*for*, de); indemnité *f*. (*for*, pour). ‖ Indemnisation *f*.; *War Damage Compensation*, dommages de guerre; *Workmen's Compensation Act*, loi sur les accidents du travail. ‖ TECHN., PHYS. Compensation *f*. ‖ U. S. Rémunération *f*. ‖ **Compensation-arm**, n. TECHN. Bras de rappel *m*. ‖ **Compensation-pendulum**, n. Balancier compensateur *m*.
compensative [kəm'pensətiv] adj. Compensatif, compensatoire.
compensator ['kɔmpenseitə*] n. PHYS., ELECTR. Compensateur *m*.
compensatory [-əri] adj. Compensatoire.
compete [kəm'piːt] v. intr. Concourir, entrer en compétition, se mettre sur les rangs (*for*, pour); participer (*in*, à). ‖ Faire concurrence (*with*, à); rivaliser (*in*, de; *with*, avec); *competed for*, couru, disputé.
competence ['kɔmpitəns], **competency** [-i] n. Compétence, capacité f. (*for*, pour; *in*, en); aptitude *f*. (*for*, à; *in*, en). ‖ FIN. Aisance *f*.; revenus suffisants *m*. *pl*. ‖ JUR. Compétence (of the Court).
competent [-ənt] adj. Compétent, capable, qualifié (efficient). ‖ Qualifié, compétent (*for*, pour). ‖ Suffisant, honnête (sufficient). ‖ Loisible, possible (*to*, à) [permissible]. ‖ JUR. Compétent (court); admissible, recevable (evidence); habile (person).
competition [,kɔmpi'tiʃən] n. Compétition, concurrence, rivalité *f*. (*for*, pour). ‖ Concours *m*. (*for*, pour); *not for competition*, hors concours. ‖ COMM. Concurrence *f*. ‖ SPORTS. Compétition. ‖ AUTOM. Course *f*.
competitive [kəm'petitiv] adj. De concours; déterminé par concours; *competitive examination*, concours.
competitor [-ə*] n. Compétiteur *m*.; compétitrice *f*.; concurrent *s*.
compilation [,kɔmpi'leiʃən] n. Compilation *f*. (act, text).
compile [kəm'pail] v. tr. Compiler, recueillir (materials). ‖ Composer par compilation, compiler (a book).
compiler [-ə*] n. Compilateur *m*.; compilatrice *f*.
complacence [kəm'pleisns], **complacency** [-i] n. Contentement, satisfaction *f*. ‖ Contentement de soi *m*.; vaine complaisance, vanité *f*. (smugness).
complacent [-nt] adj. Content (or) satisfait de soi, suffisant (self-satisfied). ‖ Complaisant, obligeant (obliging).
complacently [-ntli] adv. Complaisamment.
complain [kəm'plein] v. intr. Se plaindre (*against*, contre; *of*, de; *to*, à). ‖ Formuler une plainte (or) réclamation. " Se lamenter, gémir.
complainant [-ənt] n. JUR. Plaignant *s*.
complaint [kəm'pleint] n. Elégie *f*. (in literature). ‖ Plainte, lamentation *f*.; gémissement *m*.; doléances *f*. *pl*.; *to make complaints*, se lamenter. ‖ Grief, sujet (*m*.) de plainte. ‖ Réclamation *f*. (claim). ‖ JUR. Plainte *f*. ‖ MED. Maladie, affection *f*.; *what's her complaint?*, de quoi se plaint-elle (or) souffre-t-elle?
complaisance [kəm'pleizəns] n. Complaisance, obligeance *f*.; *out of complaisance*, par complaisance. ‖ Courtoisie, déférence *f*.
complaisant [-ənt] adj. Complaisant, obligeant, serviable. ‖ Déférent, courtois (polite). ‖ FAM. Complaisant, coulant.
complement ['kɔmplimənt] n. Complément *m*. ‖ Personnel *m*.; *full complement*, grand complet. ‖ MILIT., NAUT. Effectif *m*. ‖ TECHN. Charge *f*. ‖ MATH., MED., MUS. Complément *m*. ‖ GRAMM. Complément; attribut *m*.
— v. tr. Compléter; servir de complément à.

complementary [,kɔmpli'mentəri] adj. Complémentaire.
complete [kəm'pliːt] adj. Complet, entier, total (whole). ‖ Achevé, fini, terminé, conclu (finished). ‖ Parfait, accompli, consommé (perfect).
— v. tr. Accomplir, finir, achever, terminer, mettre fin à (to finish). ‖ Parfaire, parachever (to make perfect). ‖ Compléter (to make whole); *to complete a set of china*, rappareiller un service de porcelaine.
completely [-li] adv. Complètement, entièrement, parfaitement.
completeness [-nis] n. Plénitude *f*.
completion [kəm'pliːʃən] n. Achèvement *m*. (act). ‖ Accomplissement *m*.; réalisation *f*. ‖ Parachèvement *m*.; plénitude, perfection *f*. ‖ JUR. Exécution *f*. (of a contract).
completive [-tiv] adj. Complétif.
complex ['kɔmpleks] adj. Complexe.
— n. Complexe, tout complexe *m*. ‖ PHILOS., MED. Complexe *m*.
complexion [kəm'plekʃən] n. Teint *m*. (of the skin). ‖ MED. Complexion, constitution *f*.; tempérament *m*. ‖ FIG. Caractère, aspect *m*.; nature *f*.
complexity [-siti] n. Complexité *f*. ‖ Complication *f*.
compliance [kəm'plaiəns] n. Conformité *f*. (*with*, avec); acquiescement *m*. (*with*, à); *in compliance with*, en accord avec, conformément à. ‖ Basse complaisance, servilité *f*.
compliant [-ənt] adj. Accommodant, souple, docile. (See YIELDING.) ‖ Servile.
compliantly [-əntli] adv. Avec docilité; complaisamment; dans un esprit d'accommodement.
complicacy ['kɔmplikəsi] n. Complexité *f*. (condition, quality); complication *f*. (thing).
complicate [-keit] v. tr. Compliquer (*with*, de).
complication [,kɔmpli'keiʃən] n. MED., FIG. Complication *f*.
complicity [kəm'plisiti] n. Complicité *f*. (*in*, dans).
compliment ['kɔmplimənt] n. Compliment, éloge *m*.; louange *f*. (praise); *to pay a compliment to*, adresser un compliment à. ‖ Pl. Compliments, hommages *m*. *pl*.; civilités *f*. *pl*.; *to wish s.o. the compliments of the season*, offrir à qqn les souhaits de saison. ‖ † Cadeau *m*. (gift).
— [-ment] v. tr. Complimenter, féliciter (*on*, de); adresser des compliments à (*on*, pour). ‖ Faire don (or) hommage (*with*, de); *out of compliment*, à titre de cadeau.
complimentary [,kɔmpli'mentəri] adj. Elogieux, flatteur. ‖ En l'honneur de. ‖ Gracieux, à titre gracieux; *complimentary copy*, livre offert en hommage; *complimentary ticket*, billet de faveur.
complin(e) ['kɔmplin] n. ECCLES. Complies *f*. *pl*.
comply [kəm'plai] v. intr. (2). Obéir; céder, se plier, se soumettre (*with*, à). ‖ **To comply with**, observer, respecter (a clause); remplir, accomplir (a formality); faire droit à, prêter attention à (a request); se conformer à (s.o.'s wishes).
component [kəm'pounənt] adj. Composant, constituant.
— n. CHIM. Composant *m*. ‖ TECHN., PHYS. Composante *f*.
comport [kəm'pɔːt] v. intr. S'harmoniser, s'accorder, se marier (*with*, avec); convenir (*with*, à).
— v. tr. *To comport oneself*, se comporter, se conduire. (See BEHAVE.)
comportment [-mənt] n. Comportement *m*.; conduite, manière (*f*.) d'être. (See BEHAVIOUR.)
compose [kəm'pouz] v. tr. Composer, constituer, former (*of*, de); *to be composed of*, se composer de, consister en. ‖ Disposer, organiser, agencer; *to compose oneself*, s'installer, s'organiser. ‖ Composer, écrire (a book); construire (a work). ‖ ARTS., TECHN., Composer. ‖ MUS. Composer (music);

mettre en musique (words). ‖ Fig. Apaiser, calmer, pacifier (s.o.'s anger, mind); arranger, régler, apaiser (a quarrel); *compose yourself!*, reprenez-vous!, calmez-vous!; *to compose one's countenance*, composer son visage.

composed [-d] adj. Tranquille, calme; maître de soi, posé. (See COOL).

composedly [-idli] adv. Avec calme; froidement.

composer [-ə*] n. Mus. Compositeur *m.*; compositrice *f.*

composing [-iŋ] adj. De composition. ‖ Med. Calmant.
— n. Techn. Composition *f.* (in printing). ‖ **Composing-stick,** n. Composteur *m.*

composite ['kɔmpəzit] adj. Archit. Composite. ‖ Bot. Des composacées. ‖ Naut. Composite, mixte. ‖ Ch. de F. Mixte, à trois classes. ‖ Geol. Mixte (cone). ‖ Cinem. *Composite shot,* impression combinée. ‖ Math. Composé (number).
— n. Chim. Composé *m.* ‖ Archit. Ordre composite *m.* ‖ Bot. Composée *f.*

composition [,kɔmpə'ziʃən] n. Composition, constitution *f.* (*of,* de). ‖ Mélange *m.*; composition *f.* (mixture). ‖ Composition, rédaction, création *f.* (of a literary work); composition, œuvre *f.*; ouvrage *m.* (work). ‖ Rédaction, narration, dissertation, composition *f.* (schoolwork); thème *m.* (translation). ‖ Mus., Chim., Techn. Composition *f.* ‖ Gramm. Construction *f.* (of a sentence); composition *f.* (of a word). ‖ Archit. Stuc *m.* ‖ Med. Constitution, nature *f.* ‖ Jur. Accommodement, arrangement, compromis *m.*; *to come to a composition,* venir à composition. ‖ Fin. Transaction *f.*; *composition tax,* impôt forfaitaire. ‖ Milit. Capitulation *f.* ‖ Fig. Composé, assemblage *m.* (of, de); imitation, composition *f.*

compositor [kəm'pɔzitə*] n. Techn. Compositeur *m.* (See TYPE-SETTER.)

compos mentis ['kɔmpɔs'mentis] adj. Jur. Sain d'esprit.

compost ['kɔmpɔst] n. Agric. Compost *m.*
— v. tr. Agric. Composter.

composure [kəm'pouʒə*] n. Calme, flegme, sang-froid *m.*; maîtrise (*f.*) de soi.

compotation [,kɔmpə'teiʃən] n. Beuverie *f.*

compotator [-tə*] n. Compagnon (*m.*) de beuverie.

compote ['kɔmpout] n. Culin. Compote, marmelade *f.* ‖ Compotier *m.* (fruit-dish).

compound [kɔm'paund] v. tr. Chim. Composer (*of,* de); mêler, mélanger. ‖ Jur. Régler à l'amiable (a difference); pactiser avec (a felony).
— v. intr. Composer; transiger (*for,* au sujet de, pour; *with,* avec); s'arranger à l'amiable (*with,* avec). ‖ Fin. *To compound for a tax,* payer un impôt à forfait.
— ['kɔmpaund] adj. Chim. Composé, combiné. ‖ Math. Composé (interest); complexe (number). ‖ Med. Compliqué (fracture). ‖ Techn. Compound (engine). ‖ Mus. Composé (time). ‖ Gramm. Complexe (sentence); composé (tense, word).
— n. Chim. Composé *m.* ‖ Gramm. Mot composé *m.* ‖ Techn. Compound *m.*

compound n. Enclos, terrain *m.* (of house, factory); camp (*m.*) d'habitation attaché à une mine (in South Africa); camp (of P. O. W.s).

compoundable [-əbl] adj. Réglable à l'amiable.

comprehend [,kɔmpri'hend] v. tr. Comprendre, renfermer, inclure, englober (to include). ‖ Fig. Comprendre, contenir, impliquer (to imply); comprendre, saisir, percevoir (to understand).

comprehensibility ['kɔmpri,hensi'biliti], **comprehensibleness** [,kɔmpri'hensiblnis] n. Compréhensibilité *f.*

comprehensible [,kɔmpri'hensibl] adj. Qui peut être renfermé (or) inclus (or) embrassé. ‖ Fig. Compréhensible, intelligible.

comprehensibly [-bli] adv. Intelligiblement.

comprehension [,kəmpri'henʃən] n. Portée, étendue, amplitude *f.*; *word of wide comprehension,* mot d'une acception très étendue. ‖ Compréhension, intelligence *f.*

comprehensive [-siv] adj. Compréhensif, étendu, de grande portée, de large acception, vaste, plein (inclusive); *comprehensive measure,* mesure d'ensemble. ‖ Compréhensif, intelligent, apte à saisir.

comprehensively [-sivli] adv. Avec amplitude; dans un sens très large,

compress [kɔm'pres] v. tr. Comprimer. ‖ Fig. Condenser.
— v. intr. Se comprimer.
— ['kɔmpres] n. Med. Compresse *f.* ‖ Techn. Compresseur *m.*

compressibility [kəm,presi'biliti] n. Compressibilité *f.*

compressible [kəm'presibl] adj. Compressible.

compression [kəm'preʃən] n. Compression *f.* ‖ Fig. Concentration, réduction *f.*

compressive [-siv] adj. Compressif, de compression.

compressor [-sə*] n. Compresseur *m.*

comprise [kəm'praiz] v. tr. Comprendre, renfermer, inclure, englober, comporter, contenir, embrasser. (See INCLUDE.)

compromise ['kɔmprəmaiz] n. Compromis *m.*; transaction *f.* ‖ Accord amiable, arrangement *m.*
— v. intr. Transiger, aboutir à un compromis.
— v. tr. Régler par un compromis. ‖ Compromettre, mettre en péril, risquer; *to compromise oneself with,* se compromettre avec.

comptometer [kɔmp'tɔmitə*] n. Techn. Machine (*f.*) à calculer. (See ARITHMOMETER.)

comptroller [kən'troulə*] n. Econome, intendant, administrateur *m.* ‖ Fin. Contrôleur *m.* ‖ U. S. Auditeur (*m.*) à la Cour des comptes.

compulsion [kəm'pʌlʃən] n. Contrainte, coercition *f.*; *under compulsion,* de force. ‖ Psych. Compulsion *f.*

compulsive [-siv] adj. Forcé, coercitif. ‖ Psych. Compulsif; *compulsive neurosis,* névrose obsessionnelle. ‖ Fig. Acharné, forcené.

compulsively [-sivli], **compulsorily** [-sərili] adv. Par contrainte, de force, d'office.

compulsory [-səri] adj. Forcé, obligatoire; astreignant, requis, exigé. ‖ Coercitif, de contrainte. (See COMPELLING.)

compunction [kəm'pʌŋkʃən] n. Remords, scrupule *m.* ‖ Eccles. Componction *f.*

compunctious [-ʃəs] adj. Plein de componction. ‖ Engendrant le remords.

compurgation ['kɔmpə:'geiʃən] n. Jur. Témoignage justificatif *m.*

compurgator [-tə*] n. Jur. Témoin justificateur, compurgateur *m.*

computable [kəm'pju:təbl] adj. Calculable, estimable; supputable.

computation [,kɔmpju'teiʃən] n. Math. Calcul *m.*; estimation, évaluation *f.* ‖ Eccles. Comput *m.*

compute [kɔm'pju:t] v. tr. Math. Calculer, évaluer, estimer (at, à).

computer [-ə*] n. Machine (*f.*) à calculer, calculatrice *f.* ‖ Inform. Ordinateur *m.* (digital), calculateur *m.* (analog, hybrid); *computer science,* informatique.

computerize [-ə,raiz] v. tr. Informatiser. ‖ Mettre sur ordinateur.

comrade ['kɔmrid] n. Camarade *s.*; *to make a comrade of,* lier camaraderie avec, devenir le camarade de.

comradeship [-ʃip] n. Camaraderie, fraternité *f.*

con [kɔn] adv., n. Contre *m.*; *pro and con,* pour et contre.

con v. tr. (1). Apprendre, étudier.

con v. tr. (1). Naut. Commander, gouverner.

con n. FAM. Escroquerie *f.*
— adj. FAM. *Con man,* escroc ; *con trick,* attrape-couillons, escroquerie.
— v. tr. (1). FAM. Escroquer, rouler, entuber.
conation [kou'nei∫ən] n. PHILOS. Volition *f.*
concatenate [kən'kætineit] v. tr. FIG. Enchaîner.
— [-it] adj. Lié, enchaîné.
concatenation [kən,kæti'nei∫ən] n. Enchaînement, concours *m.* (of circumstances). ‖ Série, chaîne *f.* (series).
concave ['kɔnkeiv] adj. Concave.
— n. Ligne (or) surface concave *f.; objet concave *m.*
— v. tr. U. S. Rendre concave.
concavity [kən'kæviti] n. Concavité *f.*
conceal [kən'si:l] v. tr. Celer, cacher, dissimuler. ‖ Garder secret, ne pas révéler (information).
concealment [-mənt] n. Action (*f.*) de cacher ; *to keep in concealment,* demeurer caché. ‖ Cachette, retraite *f.* (place). ‖ JUR. Recel *m.;* non-révélation ; non-présentation *f.* ‖ FIG. Dissimulation *f. ; secret *m.*
concede [kən'si:d] v. tr. Concéder, reconnaître, admettre (to acknowledge) ; accorder, concéder (to grant).
conceit [kən'si:t] n. Vanité, prétention, suffisance *f.; contentement de soi *m.; out of sheer conceit,* par pure gloriole. ‖ Imagination *f. ; in my own conceit,* selon ma propre appréciation. ‖ Expression brillante *f. ; trait d'esprit *m.* ‖ Pl. Concetti *m. pl.* (in literature).
— v. tr. † Penser, imaginer.
conceited [-id] adj. Vaniteux, prétentieux, suffisant, content de soi.
conceitedly [-idli] adv. Avec vanité ; d'un air avantageux.
conceivable [kən'si:vəbḷ] adj. Concevable, imaginable, croyable.
conceive [-'si:v] v. tr. Concevoir, imaginer, penser, croire (to imagine). ‖ Comprendre, saisir, concevoir (to understand). ‖ Concevoir, éprouver, ressentir (to feel). ‖ Exprimer, formuler, rédiger, élaborer (to express). ‖ MED. Concevoir (a child).
— v. intr. Penser ; se faire une idée (*of,* de). ‖ MED. Concevoir.
concenter [kən'sentə*] U. S. see CONCENTRE.
concentrate ['kɔnsentreit] v. tr. CHIM., FIG., MILIT. Concentrer.
— v. intr. Se concentrer, converger. ‖ Fixer son attention, se concentrer (*upon,* sur) ; s'appliquer (*upon,* à).
concentrated [-id] adj. CHIM. Concentré. ‖ MILIT. Convergent (fire). ‖ FIG. Rapidement mené (action) ; concentré (efforts, mind).
concentration [,kɔnsen'trei∫ən] n. CHIM., MILIT., FIG. Concentration f. ‖ **Concentration camp,** n. MILIT. Camp (*m.*) de concentration ; *prisoner in a concentration camp,* concentrationnaire.
concentrative ['kɔnsentreitiv] adj. De concentration.
concentrator [-tə*] n. CHIM., TECHN. Concentrateur *m.*
concentre [kən'sentə*] v. tr. Concentrer, centrer, faire converger.
— v. intr. Se concentrer, converger, se grouper, se centrer.
concentric [-trik] adj. Concentrique.
concept ['kɔnsept] n. Concept *m.* (See IDEA.)
conception [kən'sep∫ən] n. MED., FIG. Conception *f.*
conceptive [-tiv] adj. PHILOS. Conceptif.
conceptual [-tjuəl] adj. PHILOS. Conceptuel.
concern [kən'sə:n] v. tr. Concerner, regarder, toucher à ; *as concerns,* en ce qui concerne (or) touche, quant à, à propos de. ‖ Impliquer, mettre en jeu ; *to be concerned in,* être impliqué (or) en jeu dans, entrer dans. ‖ Concerner, intéresser, regarder, être l'affaire de ; *the persons concerned,* les intéressés ;

I am not concerned to, ce n'est pas mon affaire de ; *to concern oneself in* (or) *with,* s'occuper de, s'intéresser à ; *to be concerned in,* s'intéresser à, s'attacher à, avoir pour but (or) tâche de ; *to be concerned with,* avoir pour objet de, traiter de ; *to whom it may concern,* à qui de droit. ‖ Affliger, inquiéter, peiner ; *to be concerned about* (or) *at* (or) *for* (or) *to,* être affecté (or) soucieux de ; *to concern oneself about,* s'inquiéter de.
— n. Rapport *m. ; relation *f.* (*with,* avec) ; *to have no concern with,* être sans rapport avec, n'avoir rien à voir avec. ‖ Affaire *f. ; it's no concern oj mine,* ce n'est pas mon affaire, cela ne me concerne (or) regarde pas, je n'ai pas à me mêler de cela. ‖ Intérêt *m.* (*in,* dans) ; *to have a concern in,* avoir quelque intérêt dans. ‖ Souci *m. ; inquiétude *f.* (see CARE) ; *to show great concern about,* se montrer fort affecté (or) soucieux de. ‖ COMM. Entreprise, firme, affaire, maison *f. ; établissement *m.* ‖ FAM. Truc, fourbi *m.*
concerned [-d] adj. Intéressé ; impliqué (*in,* dans). ‖ Affecté, soucieux, inquiet (*about, at, for,* de).
concerning [-iɳ] prep. Concernant, regardant, touchant à, à propos de, au sujet de, relativement à.
concernment [-mənt] n. Part, participation *f.* (*in,* à) ; intérêt *m.* (*in,* dans) ; implication *f.* (*in,* dans). ‖ Importance, conséquence *f.* ‖ Anxiété, inquiétude *f. ; souci *m. ; sollicitude *f.* ‖ † Affaire, occupation *f.*
concert ['kɔnsət] n. MUS. Concert *m. ; in concert,* à l'unisson. ‖ FIG. Concorde, harmonie *f. ; ensemble *m. ; in concert with,* de conserve avec, d'accord avec. ‖ **Concert-grand,** n. MUS. Piano de concert *m.* ‖ **Concert-hall,** n. MUS. Salle (*f.*) de concert. ‖ **Concert-master,** n. MUS. Premier violon soliste *m. ; Concert-pitch,** n. MUS. Diapason de concert *m. ; FAM. Pleine forme *f. ; to keep up to concert-pitch,* se maintenir au plus haut diapason.
— adj. MUS. De concert ; *concert performer,* concertiste.
— [kən'sə:t] v. tr. Concerter, combiner, arranger, organiser.
— v. intr. Se concerter (*with,* avec).
concertante [,kɔntʃə:'tænti] adj. MUS. Concertant (part).
concerted [kən'sə:tid] adj. MUS. Concertant, orchestré (symphony). ‖ MILIT. D'ensemble (action). ‖ FIG. Concerté, combiné.
concertina [,kɔnsə'ti:nə] n. MUS. Concertina *m.* ‖ MILIT. Réseau à boudin *m.*
concertina'd [-d] adj. FAM. En accordéon.
concerto [kən'tʃɛətou] n. MUS. Concerto *m.*
concession [kən'seʃən] n. JUR., FIG. Concession *f.* ‖ COMM. Réduction *f.* ‖ U. S. COMM. Licence *f.*
concessionaire [kən,seʃə'nɛə*] n. Concessionnaire *s.*
concessionary [kən'seʃnəri] adj. Concédé (land, privilege) ; concessionnaire (society).
— n. Concessionnaire *m.*
concessive [-'sesiv] adj. Impliquant une concession. ‖ GRAMM. Concessif.
conch [kɔɳk] n. ZOOL. Coquille *f.* ‖ † Conque *f.*
concha ['kɔɳkə] n. MED. Conque *f.* (of the ear) ; oreille externe *f.* ‖ ARCHIT. Voûte d'abside *f.*
conchoid ['kɔɳkɔid] adj., n. MATH. Conchoïde *f.*
conchology [kɔɳ'kɔlədʒi] n. ZOOL. Conchyliologie *f.*
conchy ['kɔntʃi] n. FAM. Objecteur (*m.*) de conscience.
concierge [,kɔnsi'ɛəʒ] n. Concierge *s.*
conciliar [kɔn'siliə*] adj. Conciliaire.
conciliate [-lieit] v. tr. Concilier, accorder (to reconcile). ‖ Gagner, amener, attirer (*to,* à). ‖ Gagner, obtenir, se concilier (esteem, favour, goodwill). ‖ Réconcilier, apaiser (to placate).
conciliation [kən,sili'eiʃən] n. Conciliation *f.; conciliation board,* conseil d'arbitrage. ‖ Réconciliation *f.*

conciliative [kən'silieitiv] adj. Conciliant, accommodant, arrangeant, coulant.

conciliator [-ieitə*] n. Conciliateur *m.*; conciliatrice *f.*

conciliatory [-iətəri] adj. Conciliatoire, conciliateur; *conciliatory spirit*, esprit de conciliation.

concinnity [kən'siniti] n. Harmonie, élégance *f.* (of style).

concise [kən'sais] adj. Concis.

concisely [-li] adv. Avec concision, succinctement.

conciseness [-nis], **concision** [kən'siʒən] n. Concision *f.*

conclave ['kɔnkleiv] n. ECCLES. Conclave *m.* ‖ FIG. Assemblée *f.*; conseil *m.*

conclude [kən'klu:d] v. tr. Conclure, régler (one's affairs); effectuer, conclure, aboutir à (an agreement). ‖ Conclure, achever, terminer, finir (to end). ‖ Conclure, déduire, inférer (to infer).
— v. intr. Conclure, achever (*by, with*, par, sur). ‖ Se terminer, s'achever (*with*, par, sur). ‖ Conclure (*in favour of*, à). ‖ Décider, déterminer (*to*, de).

conclusion [-ʒən] n. Conclusion *f.*; aboutissement, arrangement, établissement *m.* (settlement). ‖ Conclusion, fin, issue *f.* (close). ‖ Conclusion, déduction *f.* (inference). ‖ Conclusion, décision *f.*; *to try conclusions with*, engager la discussion avec, rompre une lance avec, entrer en contestation avec.

conclusive [-siv] adj. Conclusif, concluant.

conclusively [-sivli] adv. D'une manière concluante.

concoct [kən'kɔkt] v. tr. CULIN. Confectionner, composer. ‖ FIG. Combiner; fabriquer, monter, inventer; machiner.

concoction [-'kɔkʃən] n. CULIN. Mélange *m.*; préparation, confection *f.* ‖ FIG. Combinaison, élaboration *f.* (of a plot); machination *f.*; montage *m.* (fam.).

concomitance [kən'kɔmitəns], **concomitancy** [-i] n. Concomitance *f.*

concomitant [-ənt] adj. Concomitant.
— n. Cortège, accompagnement *m.*; suite *f.*; circonstances concomitantes *f. pl.*

concord ['kɔŋkɔ:d] n. Concorde, harmonie, union, paix, entente *f.*; accord *m.* (*with*, avec). ‖ GRAMM. Accord *m.*; *to be in concord with*, s'accorder avec. ‖ MUS. Accord *m.* ‖ † Accord, traité *m.*

concordance [kən'kɔ:dəns] n. Concordance, correspondance *f.* (*between*, entre; *with*, avec). ‖ Index *m.*; *real, verbal concordance*, index par matières, alphabétique. ‖ ECCLES. Concordance *f.* (of the Bible).

concordant [-ənt] adj. Concordant, s'accordant (*with*, avec). ‖ MUS. Harmonieux.

concordantly [-əntli] adv. En harmonie, en accord.

concordat [-it] n. ECCLES. Concordat *m.*

concourse ['kɔŋkɔ:s] n. Concours *m.*; affluence *f.* (of people). ‖ Foule *f.* (crowd). ‖ Lieu de rassemblement *m.* (place). ‖ U. S. Carrefour *m.* (in a park); salle (*f.*) des pas perdus (hall); cours, boulevard *m.* (thoroughfare). ‖ PHYS. Rencontre (of atoms). ‖ FIG. Concours *m.* (of circumstances).

concrescence [kən'kresns] n. MED. Concrétion *f.*

concrete ['kɔnkri:t] adj. Concret (real). ‖ GRAMM., MATH. Concret. ‖ JUR. D'espèce (case). ‖ TECHN. En béton; *concrete mixer*, bétonnière; *concrete work*, bétonnage. ‖ FAM. *To be concrete from the neck up*, en avoir une couche.
— n. Objet concret *m.* ‖ PHILOS. Concret *m.* ‖ ARCHIT. Béton, ciment *m.*; *in concrete*, en dur.
— v. tr. ARCHIT. Bétonner, cimenter.
— [kən'kri:t] v. tr. Concréter, solidifier.
— v. intr. Se concréter, se solidifier.

concretely ['kɔnkri:tli] adv. D'une manière concrète.

concreting [kən'kri:tiŋ] n. ARCHIT. Bétonnage *m.*

concretion [-ʃən] n. Concrétion *f.*

concretize ['kɔnkritaiz] v. tr. U. S. Concrétiser.

concubinage [kən'kju:binidʒ] n. Concubinage *m.*

concubinary [-nəri] adj. Concubin.
— n. Concubinaire *s.*

concubine ['kɔnkjubain] n. Concubine *f.* ‖ Seconde femme *f.* (among polygamous peoples).

concupiscence [kən kju:pisns] n. Concupiscence *f.*

concupiscent [-ņt] adj. Concupiscent.

concur [kən'kə:*] v. intr. (1). Concourir, coïncider, arriver en même temps (to coincide). ‖ Concourir, coopérer, contribuer (*in, to*, à). ‖ Etre d'accord, s'entendre, se rencontrer (*with*, avec); être de l'avis (*with*, de).

concurrence [kən'kʌrəns] n. Coïncidence, rencontre, conjonction *f.*; *in concurrence with*, concurremment avec. ‖ Concours *m.* (of circumstances). [See CONCATENATION.] ‖ Coopération, contribution *f.* (of persons). ‖ Assentiment, accord *m.* (*in*, à) [agreement]. ‖ MATH. Point de concours *m.* ‖ JUR. Conflit *m.* (of rights).

concurrent [-ənt] adj. Coexistant, coïncidant, simultané. ‖ Coopérant, concourant, contribuant. ‖ Convergent, concourant, parallèle. ‖ Harmonieux, concordant, d'accord (in agreement). ‖ MATH., TECHN. Concourant. ‖ JUR. Identique (interests); concomitant (lease); commun (powers); opposé, en conflit (rights).
— n. Circonstance concomitante *f.*

concurrently [-əntli] adv. Concurremment; conjointement.

concuss [kən'kʌs] v. tr. Secouer. ‖ MED. Commotionner. ‖ FIG. Intimider.

concussion [-'kʌʃən] n. Secousse *f.*; choc *m.* ‖ MED. Commotion cérébrale *f.*

condemn [kən'dem] v. tr. Condamner, blâmer. (See CENSURE.) ‖ Condamner, convaincre de culpabilité (to convict). ‖ JUR. Condamner (*to*, à). ‖ JUR., FIN. Confisquer (goods). ‖ MED. Condamner (a sick person). ‖ TECHN. Réformer, déclarer inutilisable. ‖ FIG. Condamner, obliger, contraindre (*to*, à) [s.o.]. ‖ U. S. Exproprier.

condemnable [-nəbl] adj. Condamnable.

condemnation [,kɔndem'neiʃən] n. Condamnation *f.* ‖ U. S. Expropriation *f.*

condemnatory [kən'demnətəri] adj. Condamnatoire.

condemned [-d] adj. JUR. Condamné; *condemned person*, condamné. ‖ TECHN. Réformé, mis au rebut.

condensable [kən'densəbl] adj. Condensable.

condensation [,kɔnden'seiʃən] n. Condensation *f.* (act, liquid, product).

condense [kən'dens] v. tr. PHYS. Condenser (gas, vapour); concentrer (rays). ‖ FIG. Condenser, résumer.
— v. intr. Se condenser.

condenser [-ə*] n. ELECTR., TECHN. Condensateur *m.* ‖ PHYS. Condenseur *m.* (for gas, vapour); condensateur *m.* (for light).

condescend [,kɔndi'send] v. intr. Condescendre, daigner. ‖ S'abaisser (*to*, à); descendre (*to*, jusqu'à). [See STOOP.] ‖ Se montrer condescendant (*to*, envers, à l'égard de).

condescending [-iŋ] adj. Condescendant. (See PATRONIZING.)

condescendingly [-iŋli] adv. Avec condescendance.

condescension [,kɔndi'senʃən] n. Condescendance *f.*; air supérieur *m.*

condign [kɔn'dain] adj. Mérité, juste (adequate). ‖ FAM. Exemplaire.

condignly [-li] adv. Justement.

condiment ['kɔndimənt] n. CULIN. Condiment *m.*

condisciple [kɔn,di'saipl] n. Condisciple *s.*

condition [kən'diʃən] n. Condition, clause, stipulation *f.* (see PREREQUISITE); *on condition that*, à condition que. ‖ Condition, base essentielle *f.* ‖ Condition, circonstance *f.*; *working conditions*, conditions du travail. ‖ Condition *f.*; état *m.* (state); *in a condition to*, en état de. ‖ Condition,

position, situation *f.*; rang *m.* (rank). ‖ Comm. Condition (of sale). ‖ Jur. Condition *f.*; *terms and conditions*, modalités. ‖ Sports. Forme, condition *f.* ‖ Aviat. *Overspeed condition*, puissance de décollage. ‖ Fam. *In an interesting condition*, dans une situation intéressante.
— v. tr. Stipuler, indiquer. ‖ Déterminer, conditionner; *to be conditioned by*, dépendre de, découler de. ‖ Etre solidaire de (or) essentiel à; *the two things condition each other*, les deux choses se conditionnent (or) sont interdépendantes. ‖ Comm. Conditionner. ‖ Sports. Mettre en forme.

conditional [kən'diʃnl̩] adj. Conditionnel. ‖ Conditionné (*on*, par); dépendant (*on*, de). ‖ Gramm. Conditionnel.
— n. Gramm. Conditionnel *m.*

conditioned [kən'diʃənd] adj. Dans certaines conditions. ‖ En un certain état. ‖ Conditionné, déterminé (*by*, par). ‖ Conditionné, climatisé (air). ‖ Comm., Philos., Med. Conditionné. ‖ Sports. Dans une certaine forme.

conditioner [-ə*] n. Conditionneur *m.*

condolatory [kɔn'doulətəri] adj. De condoléance.

condole [kən'doul] v. intr. Prendre part à la douleur (*with*, de); exprimer sa sympathie, offrir ses condoléances (*with*, à). [See commiserate.]

condolence [-əns] n. Condoléance *f.*

condom ['kɔndəm] n. Med. Préservatif *m.*

condominium [,kɔndə'miniəm] n. Condominium *m.*

condone [kən'doun] v. tr. Réparer (to atone for); pardonner (to forgive).

condor ['kɔndɔ:*] n. Zool. Condor *m.*

condottiere [,kɔndə'tjɛəre] (pl. **condottieri** [-ri]) n. Condottiere *m.*

conduce [kən'dju:s] v. intr. Conduire, amener, faire aboutir (*to*, à).

conducive [-iv] adj. Tendant; contribuant (*to*, à); efficace (*to*, pour); favorable (*to*, à).

conduct ['kɔndəkt] n. Conduite *f.*; fait (*m.*) de conduire (leading). ‖ Conduite, attitude *f.*; comportement *m.* (behaviour); *disorderly conduct*, inconduite. ‖ Conduite, direction *f.* (of a firm). ‖ Conduite *f.* (of negotiations, of a work). ‖ Milit. *Conduct sheet*, feuille de punitions.
— [kən'dʌkt] v. tr. Conduire, mener (to lead). ‖ Diriger, être à la tête de, avoir la haute main sur (to manage). ‖ *To conduct oneself*, se conduire, se comporter, agir. ‖ Mus. Conduire (an orchestra). ‖ Electr. Etre conducteur de, conduire. ‖ Jur. Conduire, procéder à (an enquiry); *to conduct s.o.'s case*, assurer la défense de qqn.

conductance [kən'dʌktəns] n. Electr. Conductance *f.*

conductibility [kən,dʌkti'biliti] n. Phys. Conductibilité *f.*

conductible [kən'dʌktibl̩] adj. Conductible.

conduction [-ʃən] n. Phys. Conduction *f.*

conductive [-tiv] adj. Phys. De conduction. ‖ Electr. Conducteur *m.*; conductrice *f.*

conductivity [,kɔndʌk'tiviti] n. Phys. Conductivité, conductibilité *f.*

conductor [kən'dʌktə*] n. Conducteur, cicerone, guide *m.* ‖ Directeur, chef *m.* (manager). ‖ Mus. Chef d'orchestre *m.* ‖ Electr. Conducteur *m.* ‖ Autom., Ch. de f. Receveur *m.*; U. S. Chef de train *m.*

conductress [-ris] n. Conductrice *f.* ‖ Autom. Receveuse *f.*

conduit ['kɔndit] n. Conduit, tuyau *m.*; canalisation *f.* ‖ ['kɔndjuit]. Electr. Tube *m.*

condyle ['kɔndil] n. Med. Condyle *m.*

cone [koun] n. Math., Techn., Geol., Astron. Cône *m.* ‖ Naut., Milit. *Cone of dispersion*, cône d'éclatement. ‖ Radio. Cône *m.* (of silence). ‖ Culin. Cornet *m.* ‖ Bot. Pomme (*f.*) de pin, cône *m.* ‖ **Cone-clutch**, n. Techn. Embrayage à cône *m.* ‖

Cone-pulley, n. Techn. Cône-poulie *m.* ‖ **Cone-shaped**, adj. Conique.
— v. tr. Donner une forme conique à. ‖ Aviat. Etre pris par un cône de projecteurs.
— v. intr. Bot. Porter des cônes.

coney ['kouni] n. Zool., Comm. Lapin *m.* (animal, fur).

confab [kən'fæb] n. Fam. Causette *f.*
— v. intr. Fam. Tailler une bavette.

confabulate [-juleit] v. intr. Converser, bavarder, causer.

confabulation [kən,fæbju'leiʃən] n. Conciliabule *m.*; causette *f.*

confect [kən'fekt] v. tr. U. S. Confectionner, mélanger, combiner.

confection [kən'fekʃən] n. Confection (*f.*) par mélange. ‖ Culin. Confit; bonbon *m.*; sucrerie, friandise *f.* ‖ Comm. Confection; vêtement (*m.*) de confection. ‖ Med. Electuaire *m.*
— v. tr. Comm. Confectionner. ‖ Culin. Faire (bonbons, ice-cream); confire (fruit).

confectioner [-ə*] n. Culin. Confiseur *m.*; U. S. *confectioner's sugar*, sucre glace.

confectionery [-əri] n. Confiserie *f.* (business, confections, shop, trade).

confederacy [kən'fedərəsi] n. Confédération *f.* (group). ‖ Fédération, ligue *f.* (league). ‖ Conspiration *f.* (conspiracy). ‖ U. S. Etats confédérés *m. pl.*

confederate [-it] adj. Confédéré.
— n. Confédéré *m.* ‖ Complice *s.*; membre (*m.*) d'une conspiration.
— [-eit] v. tr. Confédérer.
— v. intr. Se confédérer (*with*, avec).

confederation [kən,fedə'reiʃən] n. Confédération *f.* (act, group).

confederative [kən'fedərətiv] adj. Confédératif; fédératif.

confer [kən'fə:*] v. tr. (1). Conférer, attribuer, accorder, adjuger (*on*, à).
— v. intr. Conférer, s'entretenir, échanger des vues (*with*, avec).

conference ['kɔnfərəns] n. Conférence, consultation *f.* ‖ Conférence, réunion, assemblée *f.*; *press conference*, conférence de presse. ‖ Eccles. Congrès annuel *m.* (Methodist).

conferment [kən'fə:mənt] n. Action (*f.*) de conférer. (See bestowal.) ‖ Milit. Collation *f.* (of a rank). ‖ Fig. Octroi *m.* (of a favour, honour, title).

confess [kən'fes] v. tr. Confesser, avouer, reconnaître, admettre (a fault, a crime); *to stand confessed as*, se révéler comme. ‖ Confesser, manifester (an opinion). ‖ Eccles. Confesser (a penitent); confesser, se confesser de (one's sins).
— v. intr. Passer aux aveux; *to confess to*, reconnaître, avouer, se confesser de, se reconnaître (or) s'avouer coupable de. ‖ Eccles. Confesser; se confesser.

confessant [-nt] n. Eccles. Pénitent *s.*

confessedly [-idli] adv. De l'aveu général (unanimously). ‖ De son propre aveu (avowedly).

confession [kən'feʃən] n. Aveu *m.*; reconnaissance, confession *f.* (admission). ‖ Jur. Aveux *m. pl.*; *to make a full confession*, faire des aveux complets. ‖ Eccles. Confession *f.* (of faith, sins); pl. Confessions (sects).

confessional [-ənl] adj. Eccles. Confessionnel.
— n. Eccles. Confessionnal *m.*; *under the seal of the confessional*, sous le secret de la confession.

confessor [-ə*] n. Eccles. Confesseur *m.* (martyr, priest). ‖ Jur. Coupable (*s.*) qui avoue.

confetti [kən'feti] n. Confettis *m. pl.*

confidant [,kɔnfi'dænt] n. Confident *m.*

confidante n. Confidente *f.*

confide [kən'faid] v. tr. Confier (*to*, à) [difficulties, duty, object, person, secret]; *to confide secrets to*, faire des confidences à.

— v. intr. Se fier (*in*, à); avoir confiance (*in*, en); compter, se reposer (*in*, sur). ‖ S'ouvrir, se livrer, se confier (*in*, à); *to confide in s.o. about sth.*, confier qqch. à qqn.

confidence ['kɔnfidəns] n. Confiance *f.* (*in*, en); *to take s.o. into one's confidence*, se confier à qqn. ‖ Confiance *f.*; espoir *m.* (in the future). ‖ Confiance en soi, assurance *f.*; *to gather confidence*, prendre de l'assurance. ‖ Suffisance. prétention *f.* (conceit). ‖ Confidence *f.* (*to*, à); *told in strict confidence*, strictement confidentiel. ‖ Jur. *Motion of no confidence*, motion de défiance; *to ask for a vote of confidence*, poser la question de confiance. ‖ **Confidence-game** (or) **-trick**, n. U. S. Vol (*m.*) à l'américaine. ‖ **Confidence-man**, n. U. S. Escroc *m.* (See CON.)

confident [-dənt] adj. Persuadé, sûr, convaincu (*of*, de); confiant, plein de confiance (*of*, en). ‖ Assuré, plein d'assurance, sûr de soi (self-confident). ‖ Suffisant (conceited); effronté (impudent).

confidential [,kɔnfi'denʃəl] adj. Libre, en confiance (*with*, avec) [person]; *to be confidential with*, faire des confidences à. ‖ Confidentiel, dit en confidence (talk). ‖ Intime (friend); particulier (secretary). ‖ De confiance; *confidential agent* (or) *clerk*, homme de confiance.

confiding [kən'faidiŋ] adj. Confiant.

configuration [kən,figju'reiʃən] n. Configuration *f.*

configure [kən'figə*] v. tr. Configurer.

confine ['kɔnfain] n. Confin *m.*; borne, limite *f.* — [kən'fain] v. tr. Confiner, enfermer, détenir (*in*, *within*, dans) [to shut up]. ‖ Emprisonner, enfermer. ‖ Confiner, retenir; clouer (fam.) [*to*, à]; *to be confined to the house*, rester confiné chez soi, ne pas pouvoir mettre le nez dehors. ‖ Limiter; *to confine oneself to*, se cantonner (or) confiner dans, se borner à, s'en tenir à. — v. intr. Confiner (*on, to, with*, à); être à la limite (*on, to, with*, de).

confined [kən'faind] adj. Confiné (air); resserré (space). ‖ Med. Alité (person); en couches (woman).

confinement [-mənt] n. Jur. Emprisonnement *m.*; réclusion, détention *f.*; *in close confinement*, au secret. ‖ Med. Alitement *m.*; obligation (*f.*) de garder la chambre (for sick people); couches *f. pl.* (for women). ‖ Fig. Restriction, limitation *f.*

confirm [kən'fə:m] v. tr. Affirmer, renforcer, fortifier (to strengthen). ‖ Confirmer, corroborer (see CORROBORATE); ratifier, entériner, sanctionner (to ratify). ‖ Confirmer, authentifier, prouver la vérité de (to authenticate). ‖ Confirmer, ancrer, pousser, rendre invétéré (to incite); *to be confirmed in*, se confirmer (or) s'ancrer dans (one's opinion). ‖ Jur. Homologuer, entériner (a decision, a deed); valider (an election). ‖ Eccles. Confirmer.

confirmand [kɔn,fə:'mænd] n. Eccles. Confirmand *m.*

confirmation [-'meiʃən] n. Confirmation, ratification *f.* ‖ Eccles. Confirmation *f.*

confirmative [kən'fə:mətiv] adj. Confirmatif. ‖ Gramm. *Confirmative question*, demande d'assentiment.

confirmatory [-təri] adj. Confirmatoire. ‖ Eccles. De la confirmation.

confirmed [kən'fə:md] adj. Confirmé, prouvé. ‖ Invétéré, endurci. ‖ Eccles. Confirmé.

confiscable [kən'fiskəbl] adj. Confiscable.

confiscate ['kɔnfiskeit] v. tr. Confisquer (*from*, à). — adj. U. S. Aux biens confisqués (person); confisqué (thing).

confiscation [,kɔnfis'keiʃən] n. Confiscation *f.*

conflagrant [kən'fleigrənt] adj. En feu. (See ABLAZE.)

conflagration [,kɔnflə'greiʃən] n. Conflagration *f.* (burning). ‖ Incendie *m.* (fire).

conflict ['kɔnflikt] n. Conflit, désaccord *m.*; dispute *f.*; *to come into conflict with*, entrer en lutte avec. ‖ Milit. Conflit, combat *m.*; bataille *f.* ‖ Jur., Philos. Conflit *m.* ‖ Fig. Conflit, choc, heurt *m.* — [kən'flikt] v. intr. Etre (or) entrer en conflit (*with*, avec). ‖ S'opposer, se heurter (*with*, à).

conflicting [kən'fliktiŋ] adj. En conflit (or) contradiction (*with*, avec); opposé (*with*, à).

confliction [-ʃən] n. Antagonisme *m.*

confluence ['kɔnfluəns], **conflux** ['kɔnflʌks] n. Confluent *m.* (of rivers); croisée *f.* (of road). ‖ Med. Confluence *f.*

confluent [-ənt] adj. Qui se rejoignent (rivers, roads). ‖ Med. Confluent. — n. Confluent *m.* (of two rivers). ‖ Jonction *f.*

conform [kən'fɔ:m] v. tr. Conformer, adapter (*to*, à); modeler (*to*, sur); *to conform oneself to*, se conformer à. — v. intr. Prendre la forme (*to*, de). ‖ Etre en conformité (*to*, *with*, avec). ‖ Se conformer, se plier, s'adapter (*to*, à). ‖ Eccles. Etre conformiste.

conformability [kən,fɔ:mə'biliti] n. Conformité *f.*

conformable [kən'fɔ:məbl] adj. Conforme (*to*, à). ‖ Adapté, correspondant (*to*, à); en accord, compatible (*to*, avec). ‖ Modelable, accommodant; docile. (See COMPLIANT.) ‖ Geol. Conforme.

conformably [-li] adv. Conformément (*to*, à).

conformation [,kɔnfə:'meiʃən] n. Conformation, configuration, forme, structure *f.* ‖ Adaptation *f.*; fait de se conformer (*to*, à).

conformism [kən'fɔ:mizm] n. Conformisme *m.*

conformist [-ist] n. Eccles. Conformiste *s.*

conformity [-iti] n. Conformité, ressemblance, correspondance *f.* (*to, with*, avec); *in conformity with*, à l'avenant de. ‖ Adaptation, conformité, soumission *f.* (*to, with*, à); *in conformity with*, conformément à.

confound [kən'faund] v. tr. Détruire, anéantir, ruiner (to destroy). ‖ Confondre, brouiller, mêler, mettre en désordre (to mingle). ‖ Confondre (*with*, avec); ne pas distinguer (*with*, de); prendre (*with*, pour) [to confuse]. ‖ Confondre, rendre confus, remplir de confusion (to abash). ‖ Fam. Sacrer contre; *confound him!*, le diable l'emporte !

confounded [-id] adj. Fam. Sacré, satané, fichu, fieffé; *it's a confounded nuisance*, c'est empoisonnant.

confoundedly [-didli] adv. Fam. Bigrement, diantrement, diablement.

confraternity [,kɔnfrə'tə:niti] n. Confraternité *f.* (brotherhood). ‖ Confrérie *f.* (group).

confrère ['kɔnfrɛə*] n. Confrère *m.*

confront [kən'frʌnt] v. tr. Affronter, faire face à (to face). ‖ Affronter, braver, défier (to defy). ‖ Se trouver en face de, s'opposer à, se heurter à (to meet). ‖ Comparer, collationner, confronter (to collate). ‖ Confronter (*with*, avec); mettre en présence (*with*, de).

confrontation [,kɔnfrʌn'teiʃən] n. Confrontation *f.*

Confucianism [kən'fju:ʃjənizm] n. Confucianisme *m.*

confuse [kən'fju:z] v. intr. Brouiller, mêler, mettre le désordre dans, bouleverser (to mingle). ‖ Confondre (*with*, avec); ne pas distinguer (*with*, de); prendre (*with*, pour) [to confound]. ‖ Rendre confus, brouiller, embrouiller (to puzzle); *to get confused*, se brouiller (memory); s'embrouiller (person). ‖ Confondre, embarrasser, troubler (to disconcert).

confusedly [-idli] adv. Confusément (vaguely). ‖ Avec confusion, d'un air confus (with confusion).

confusion [kən'fju:ʒən] n. Confusion, agitation *f.*; désordre, bouleversement *m.* (disorder); mélange, pêle-mêle *m.* (mingling); *to fall into confusion*, se désorganiser. ‖ Confusion *f.*; manque (*m.*) de netteté (indistinctness). ‖ Confusion (*of*, de ; *with*, avec) ; méprise *f.* (mistake). ‖ Confusion, honte *f.* ; embarras, désarroi *m.* (abashment) ; *to make confusion more confounded*, accroître la confusion. ‖ † Confusion, ruine *f.*

confutation [͵kɔnfjuˈteiʃən] n. Réfutation *f.*

confute [kənˈfjuːt] v. tr. Réfuter (an argument) ; convaincre d'erreur, réfuter les arguments de (s.o.).

congé [ˈkɔːʒei] n. Congé, renvoi *m.* (dismissal). ‖ Congé *m.* (leave-taking) ; *to take congé*, prendre congé. ‖ † Salut *m.* (bow).

congeal [kənˈdʒiːl] v. tr. Congeler, geler (to freeze). ‖ Coaguler, cailler (blood) ; figer (oil).
— v. intr. Se congeler, se geler. ‖ Se coaguler, se cailler (blood) ; se figer (oil).

congealable [-əbl] adj. Congelable. (See FREEZABLE.)

congealment [-mənt], **congelation** [͵kɔndʒiˈleiʃən] n. Congélation *f.*

congener [ˈkɔndʒinə*] n. Congénère (*to*, de).
— n. Congénère *s.* (*of*, de).

congeneric [͵kɔndʒiˈnerik] adj. BOT. Congénère.

congenerous [kənˈdʒenərəs] adj. MED. Congénère.

congenial [kənˈdʒiːniəl] adj. Approprié, convenable. propre (*to*, à) ; fait (*to*, pour) [proper]. ‖ Sympathique, aimable, agréable (agreeable). ‖ Apparenté (*to*, *with*, à) ; en accord, en sympathie (*to*, *with*, avec) ; conforme au tempérament (*to*, *with*, de).

congeniality [kən͵dʒiːniˈæliti] n. Appropriation *f.* ‖ Affinité, attirance, sympathie ; concordance, conformité *f.* (of tastes).

congenital [kənˈdʒenitl] adj. Congénital.

conger [ˈkɔŋgə*] n. ZOOL. Congre *m.*

congeries [kɔnˈdʒiəriːz] n. invar. Amas, entassement, ramassis *m.* ; accumulation *f.* (See HEAP.)

congest [kənˈdʒest] v. tr. MED. Congestionner. ‖ FIG. Surpeupler (a country) ; embouteiller ; engorger, congestionner (fam.) [a street].
— v. intr. MED. Se congestionner. ‖ FIG. Etre surpeuplé (nation) ; être embouteillé (street) ; *congested state of the railways*, encombrement des transports ferroviaires.

congestion [-ʃən] n. MED. Congestion *f.* ‖ FIG. Surpeuplement *m.* (of a country) ; embouteillage *m.* (of traffic).

congestive [-tiv] adj. MED. Congestif.

conglomerate [kənˈglɔməreit] v. tr. Conglomérer.
— v. intr. Se conglomérer.
— [-it] adj. Congloméré.
— n. Conglomérat *m.*

conglomeration [kən͵glɔməˈreiʃən] n. GEOL. Agrégation *f.*

conglutinate [kənˈgluːtineit] v. tr. Conglutiner.
— v. intr. Se conglutiner.

Congo [ˈkɔŋgou] n. GEOGR. Congo *m.* (state, river).

Congolese [͵kɔŋgəˈliːz] adj., n. GEOGR. Congolais *adj.*, *s.*

congou [ˈkɔŋgou] n. CULIN. Thé noir (*m.*) de Chine.

congratulate [kənˈgrætjuleit] v. tr. Congratuler. ‖ Féliciter, complimenter, louanger (*on*, de) ; *to congratulate each other*, se congratuler, échanger des félicitations ; *to congratulate oneself on*, se féliciter (or) louer de.

congratulation [kən͵grætjuˈleiʃən] n. Congratulation *f.* ‖ Pl. Félicitations *f. pl.* ; compliments *m. pl.*

congratulator [kənˈgrætjuleitə*] n. Congratulateur *m.* ; congratulatrice *f.*

congratulatory [-lətəri] adj. Congratulateur ; congratulatoire.

congregate [ˈkɔŋgrigeit] v. tr. Rassembler, réunir, assembler.
— v. intr. Se rassembler, s'assembler, se réunir.
— [-git] adj. Rassemblé, réuni.

congregation [͵kɔŋgriˈgeiʃən] n. Assemblée, réu-

nion *f.* (meeting). ‖ Rassemblement, assemblage *m.* ‖ ECCLES. Congrégation *f.* (of cardinals, monks, nuns) ; assemblée, assistance *f.* (of people).

congregational [-l] adj. ECCLES. De l'assemblée des fidèles ; en assemblée. ‖ Congrégationaliste (church).

congregationalism [-əlizm] n. ECCLES. Congrégationalisme *m.*

congregationalist [-əlist] n. ECCLES. Congrégationaliste *s.*

congress [ˈkɔŋgres] n. Congrès *m.* ; *member of a Congress*, congressiste ; *Trade Union Congress*, Confédération générale du travail. ‖ U. S. Congrès *m.* (body, legislature) ; session (*f.*) du Congrès (session).

congressional [kɔŋˈgreʃənl] adj. Du Congrès.

congressman [ˈkɔŋgresmən] (pl. **congressmen**) n. U. S. Membre (*m.*) du Congrès.

congresswoman [-wumən] (pl. **congresswomen**) n. U. S. Femme (*f.*) membre du Congrès.

congruence [ˈkɔŋgruəns], **congruity** [kɔŋˈgruiti] n. Correspondance, conformité, harmonie *f.* ; accord *m.* (agreement). ‖ Convenance, appropriation, congruité *f.* (*with*, à) [appropriateness]. ‖ MATH. Congruence *f.*

congruent [-ənt] adj. En conformité, en harmonie, d'accord (*with*, avec) ; conforme (*with*, à). ‖ Convenable (*with*, à). ‖ MATH. Congru, congruent (*with*, à).

congruous [ˈkɔŋgruəs] adj. Convenable, congru, approprié (*with*, à). ‖ ECCLES. Congru (grace).

congruously [-li] adv. Convenablement, congrûment (appropriately). ‖ Conformément (*with*, à) ; en conformité, en harmonie (*with*, avec).

conic [ˈkɔnik] adj. MATH. Conique.
— n. pl. Coniques *m. pl.*

conical [-l] adj. Conique, de forme conique.

conicalness [-əlnis], **conicity** [koˈnisiti] n. MATH. Conicité *f.*

conifer [ˈkounifə*] n. BOT. Conifère *m.*

coniferous [kouˈnifərəs] adj. BOT. Résineux (forest) ; conifère (tree).

coniform [ˈkounifɔːm] adj. Conique.

coni(i)ne [ˈkounain] n. CHIM. Conine *f.*

coniroster [kouniˈrɔstə*] n. ZOOL. Conirostre *m.*

conirostral [-trəl] adj. ZOOL. Conirostre.

conjecturable [kənˈdʒɛktʃərəbl] adj. Conjecturable, qu'on peut conjecturer ; présupposable (fam.).

conjectural [-tʃərəl] adj. Conjectural.

conjecturally [-tʃərəli] adv. Par conjecture.

conjecture [-tʃə*] n. Conjecture, supposition *f.*
— v. tr. Conjecturer, supposer.
— v. intr. Faire des conjectures.

conjoin [kənˈdʒɔin] v. tr. Adjoindre, conjoindre, associer.
— v. intr. S'unir.

conjoint [-t] adj. Uni, combiné, associé, joint.

conjointly [-tli] adv. Conjointement.

conjugal [ˈkɔndʒugəl] adj. Conjugal (rights).

conjugality [͵kɔndʒuˈgæliti] n. Etat conjugal, conjungo *m.*

conjugally [ˈkɔndʒugəli] adv. Conjugalement.

conjugate [ˈkɔndʒugit] adj. BOT., PHYS., MED., MATH., GRAMM. Conjugué.
— n. Conjugué *m.* ·
— [-geit] v. tr. MED., GRAMM. Conjuguer.
— v. intr. MED. Se conjuguer ; s'accoupler.

conjugation [͵kɔndʒuˈgeiʃən] n. GRAMM., MED. Conjugaison *f.*

conjunct [kənˈdʒʌŋkt] adj., n. Conjoint *s.*

conjunction [-ʃən] n. Conjonction, connexion, union, jonction *f.* ; *in conjunction with*, conjointement avec, par combinaison avec. ‖ Rencontre, coïncidence *f.* (of events). ‖ ASTRON., GRAMM. Conjonction *f.*

conjunctiva [͵kɔndʒʌŋkˈtaivə] n. MED. Conjonctive *f.*

conjunctive [kən'dʒʌŋktiv] adj. MED., GRAMM. Conjonctif.
— n. GRAMM. Mode conjonctif m. (mood); conjonction f. (word).
conjunctively [-tivli], **conjunctly** [-li] adv. Conjointement.
conjunctivitis [kəndʒʌŋkti'vaitis] n. MED. Conjonctivite f.
conjuncture [kən'dʒʌŋktʃə*] n. Conjoncture, circonstance f. ‖ Situation critique f.
conjuration [,kɔndʒu'reiʃən] n. Conjuration, incantation f. (spell). ‖ Conjuration, évocation f. (of devils). ‖ Conjuration, supplication f. (entreaty).
conjure ⌊kən'dʒuə*] v. tr. Conjurer, prier, supplier.
— ['kʌndʒə*] v. tr. To conjure down, conjurer, exorciser; to conjure up, évoquer, faire apparaître. ‖ FIG. To conjure away, faire disparaître, escamoter (to juggle away); to conjure into, changer en (to turn into); to conjure up, faire apparaître, évoquer (to evoke).
conjurer ['kʌndʒərə*] n. † Sorcier s. ‖ Prestidigitateur, escamoteur, illusionniste m. (juggler). ‖ FAM. Sorcier m.
conjuring [-iŋ] n. † Sorcellerie, magie f. ‖ Prestidigitation f.; illusionnisme, escamotage m.
— adj. De magie (book). ‖ De passe-passe (trick).
conk [kɔŋk] n. FAM. Gnon sur le crâne m. (blow); caboche f. (head); pif, blair m. (nose).
— v. intr. AUTOM., FAM. To conk out, caler, rester en panne (motor).
— v. tr. FAM. Cogner, tabasser.
conker ['kɔŋkə*] n. Marron (m.) d'Inde. ‖ Pl. Jeu (m.) d'enfants qui consiste à briser le marron suspendu à une ficelle tenue par l'adversaire.
connate ['kɔneit] adj. Inné (innate). ‖ Né (with, au même moment que). ‖ MED. Congénital.
connatural [kɔ'nætʃrəl] adj. Naturel, spontané, inné (to, chez, en); inhérent (to, à). ‖ Congénère, de même nature (cognate).
connect [kə'nekt] v. tr. Allier, apparenter (families, persons); to be connected with, être parent de. ‖ Mettre en relations (or) rapport (with, avec). ‖ Mettre en communication (with, avec) [by telephone]. ‖ ELECTR. Connecter; mettre en contact (with, avec); brancher (with, sur). ‖ TECHN. Raccorder (pipes); embrayer (shafts); engrener (wheels). ‖ CH. DE F. Relier (with, à); assurer la correspondance de (with, avec). ‖ FIG. Mettre du lien (or) de la cohésion dans, faire découler logiquement, enchaîner (arguments); rattacher, relier, associer (to, with, à) [ideas].
— v. intr. Se relier, se raccorder, se réunir, se rejoindre. ‖ Se joindre, s'unir (with, à). ‖ CH. DE F. Correspondre (with, avec).
connected [-id] adj. Apparenté; en relations; en rapport (with, avec). ‖ JUR., BOT. Connexe. ‖ FIG. Lié, cohérent (ideas).
connectedly [-idli] adv. Logiquement, de manière cohérente, avec suite.
connecting [-iŋ] adj. D'union, de jonction, de liaison (between, entre). ‖ ELECTR. De connexion (wire). ‖ AUTOM. Connecting gear, embrayage; connecting rod, bielle. ‖ TECHN. De raccord (pipe). ‖ MILIT. De liaison (group); de correspondance (post).
connection, connexion [kə'nekʃən] n. Union, liaison, connexion f. ‖ Communication f.; telephone connection, communication téléphonique; wrong connection, faux numéro, fausse communication. ‖ Famille f. (family); parenté f. (relationship); parent, allié s. (relative); to form a connection with, s'allier (or) s'apparenter à. ‖ Relations f. pl.; rapports m. pl. (intercourse); to break off all connection with, cesser tout contact avec; to have powerful connections, avoir de puissantes relations. ‖ TECHN. Raccord, raccordement m. (of pipes). ‖

AUTOM. Embrayage m. ‖ ELECTR. Prise, connexion f. ‖ CH. DE F. Correspondance f. (with, avec). ‖ JUR. Affin m. (relative); criminal connection, liaison adultérine; sexual connection, rapports sexuels. ‖ COMM. Relations d'affaires f. pl. (business connection); clientèle f. (goodwill). ‖ AVIAT. Air connection, liaison aérienne. ‖ ECCLES. Secte f. ‖ FIG. Connexité, relation, liaison f.; rapport, lien m. (with, avec); in this connection, à ce sujet; à ce point de vue; dans cet ordre d'idées. ‖ FIG. Liaison, suite, cohérence f.; enchaînement m. (of ideas, words).
connective [-tiv] adj. MED. Connectif.
connexity [kɔ'neksiti] n. Connexité f.
conning ['kɔniŋ] adj. NAUT. De commandement. ‖ **Conning-tower**, n. NAUT. Tourelle (f.) de commandement (of a battleship); kiosque m. (of a submarine).
conniption [kə'nipʃən] n. U. S., FAM. Accès (m.) de fureur (or) de rage.
connivance [kə'naivəns] n. Connivence, complicité f.; in connivance with s.o., with s.o.'s connivance, de connivence avec qqn, avec la complicité de qqn.
connive [-naiv] v. intr. Etre de connivence (at, dans; with, avec); être complice (at, de); tremper (at, dans). ‖ Fermer les yeux (at, sur); simuler l'ignorance (at, de).
connoisseur [,kɔnə'sə:*] n. Connaisseur s. (of, in, en). [See EXPERT.]
connotation [,kɔno'teiʃən] n. Sens total m. ‖ Sens-suggéré m.; implication f. ‖ PHILOS. Compréhension, connotation f.
connote [kə'nout] v. tr. Impliquer (to imply); suggérer, faire venir à l'esprit (to suggest). ‖ FAM. Signifier (to mean).
connubial [kə'nju:biəl] adj. Conjugal (contracts, rites, state).
connubially [-li] adv. Conjugalement.
conoidal [kou'nɔidl] adj. Conoïdal.
conquer ['kɔŋkə*] v. tr. MILIT. Vaincre, battre (an enemy, s.o.); conquérir, subjuguer (a nation); obtenir (victory). ‖ FIG. Surmonter, vaincre (difficulties, fear, passions); conquérir (freedom, s.o.'s heart); subjuguer. (heart).
— v. intr. Vaincre.
conquerable [-rəbl] adj. MILIT. Qu'on peut vaincre (army); prenable (fortified town); qu'on peut conquérir (nation). ‖ FIG. Maîtrisable (difficulties, fear); domptable (passions).
conqueror [-rə*] n. Vainqueur m. (victor). ‖ Conquérant m.; William the Conqueror, Guillaume le Conquérant.
conquest ['kɔŋkwest] n. Conquête f. (act, territory). ‖ FAM. Conquête f. (act, person); to make a conquest of, faire la conquête de (s.o.).
conquistador [kən'kwistədɔr] n. Conquistador m.
consanguine [kɔn'sæŋgwin], **consanguineous** [,kɔnsæŋ'gwiniəs] adj. Consanguin.
consanguinity [-'gwiniti] n. Consanguinité f. (See AGNATION.)
conscience ['kɔnʃəns] n. Conscience f.; for conscience's sake, par acquit de conscience; in all conscience, en conscience; to have an uneasy conscience, n'avoir pas la conscience tranquille; upon my conscience, la main sur la conscience. ‖ JUR. Conscience clause, article sauvegardant la liberté de conscience. ‖ **Conscience-money**, n. Argent (m.) restitué au Trésor par scrupule de conscience. ‖ **Conscience-stricken**, adj. Pris de remords.
conscienceless [-lis] adj. Sans conscience; dénué de scrupule.
conscientious [,kɔnʃi'enʃəs] adj. Consciencieux. ‖ De conscience (objector).
conscientiously [-li] adv. Consciencieusement.
conscientiousness [-nis] n. Conscience, honnêteté f., droiture f.

conscious ['kɔnʃəs] adj. Conscient, ayant conscience (of, de); to become conscious of, prendre conscience de, s'apercevoir de, avoir le sentiment de. ‖ Conscient, perçu (or) ressenti clairement; conscious guilt, culpabilité dont on a conscience. ‖ Conscient, intentionnel; conscious humour, humour voulu. ‖ Embarrassé, emprunté, gêné (self-conscious). ‖ PHILOS. Conscient. ‖ MED. Conscient, qui a sa connaissance; to become conscious, revenir à soi, reprendre ses sens.
— n. PHILOS. Conscient m.

consciously [-li] adv. Consciemment, sciemment.

consciousness [-nis] n. Conscience, perception, connaissance, impression f.; sentiment m.; to awake to the consciousness of, prendre conscience de. ‖ PHILOS. Conscience f. ‖ MED. Connaissance f.

conscribe [kən'skraib], **conscript** [-'skript] v. tr. MILIT. Enrôler par conscription.

conscript ['kɔnskript] adj., m. MILIT. Conscrit m. ‖ JUR. Labour conscript, requis du travail. ‖ NAUT. Naval conscript, inscrit maritime.
— v. tr. [kən'skript] MILIT. Enrôler, appeler (into, dans); conscripted into the army, appelé sous les drapeaux.

conscription [kən'skripʃən] n. MILIT. Conscription f.

consecrate ['kɔnsikreit] adj. ECCLES. Consacré.
— v. tr. ECCLES. Sacrer (a bishop); consacrer (the Host, a church). ‖ FIG. Consacrer, vouer (to, à). [See DEVOTE.]

consecration [,kɔnsi'kreiʃən] n. ECCLES. Sacre m. (of a bishop); consécration f. (of the Host, a church). ‖ FIG. Consécration, ratification f. (of a custom, an idea); consécration f., dévouement m. (to, à) [of a person].

consectary [kən'sektəri] n. Corollaire m.

consecution [,kɔnsi'kju:ʃən] n. Suite logique f.; enchaînement m. ‖ GRAMM. Concordance f. (of tenses). ‖ MUS. Suite f.

consecutive [-tiv] adj. Consécutif, successif, de suite. ‖ Consécutif, dû (to, à); résultant (to, de). ‖ GRAMM., MUS. Consécutif.

consecutively [-tivli] adv. Consécutivement, successivement, de suite; d'affilée (fam.).

consenescence [,kɔnsi'nesn̩s] n. MED. Sénescence f.: vieillissement m.

consensus [-əs] n. Unanimité f. (of opinions). ‖ MED. Consensus m.

consent [kən'sent] v. intr. Consentir, donner son accord, acquiescer, souscrire (to, à).
— n. Consentement, assentiment, acquiescement, accord m.; by common consent, de l'aveu général, d'un commun accord. ‖ Approbation, permission f. (See LEAVE.)

consentaneity [kən,sentə'ni:iti] n. Conformité, unanimité f.

consentaneous [,kɔnsen'teiniəs] adj. Conforme (to, with, à); consistant, d'accord (to, with, avec). ‖ Unanime.

consentient [kən'senʃənt] adj. D'accord, unanime, du même avis (in, sur, à propos de). ‖ Consentant (to, à). ‖ Concourant (forces).

consequence ['kɔnsikwəns] n. Conséquence, conclusion f. (inference). ‖ Conséquence, répercussion f.; résultat, effet m.; in consequence of, par suite de. ‖ Conséquence, importance f.; man of consequence, personnage important, personnalité marquante; to be of no consequence, être sans importance, ne pas tirer à conséquence.

consequent [-ənt] adj. Conséquent, logique (logical). ‖ Découlant, dérivant, résultant, étant la conséquence (on, de); dû (on, à). ‖ PHILOS. Conséquent.
— n. Conséquence, suite f.; résultat m. ‖ PHILOS., MATH. Conséquent m.

consequential [,kɔnsi'kwenʃəl] adj. Résultant,

dérivé (to, de); consécutif (to, à); consequential effects, répercussions f. ‖ JUR. Indirect (damages). ‖ FAM. Suffisant, prétentieux, important (conceited).

consequentiality ['kɔnsi,kwenʃi'æliti] n. PHILOS. Enchaînement m.; logique f. (of ideas). ‖ FAM. Importance, prétention f. (conceit).

consequently ['kɔnsikwəntli] adv. En conséquence, par conséquent.

conservable [kən'sə:vəbl̩] adj. Conservable.

conservancy [-ənsi] n. JUR. Conservation f.; conservancy measures, mesures conservatoires.

conservation [,kɔnʃə'veiʃən] n. Conservation, préservation f. ‖ PHYS. Conservation of energy, conservation de l'énergie (lit.), économie d'énergie (fig.).

conservatism [kən'sə:vətizm] n. Conservatisme m.

conservative [-tiv] adj. Préservatif; conservateur. ‖ Prudent (cautious); modéré, raisonnable (moderate). ‖ Conservateur (art, party); des conservateurs (views).
— n. Conservateur m.: conservatrice f. (in politics).

conservatoire [-,twɑ:*] n. MUS., ARTS. Conservatoire m.

conservator [-tə*] n. Conservateur m.; conservatrice f. (of forests, museum); conservator of rivers, commissaire fluvial. ‖ U. S. Curateur m.

conservatory [-tri] n. Jardin d'hiver m. (in a private home). ‖ AGRIC. Serre f. ‖ MUS., ARTS. Conservatoire m.

conserve [kən'sə:v] n. CULIN. Confiture (or) conserve (f.) de fruits.
— v. tr. CULIN. Mettre en conserve. ‖ FIG. Conserver, préserver, économiser.

conshie, conchie ['kɔnʃi] n. FAM. Objecteur (m.) de conscience.

consider [kən'sidə*] v. tr. Considérer, examiner, observer, scruter; réfléchir à, peser (to ponder); all things considered, tout bien considéré. ‖ Considérer, regarder, contempler (to look at). ‖ Considérer, estimer, tenir (or) compter pour (to esteem); to consider oneself bound by an oath, se considérer comme lié par un serment; to consider s.o. to be, considérer qqn comme étant; to be considered happy, passer pour heureux. ‖ Considérer, prendre en considération, tenir compte de, avoir des égards pour (to take into account).
— v. intr. Réfléchir, méditer, peser le pour et le contre.

considerable [-rəbl̩] adj. Considérable, important, notable (difference, man, number, pleasure, success); considérable (sum). ‖ Digne de considération, remarquable (noteworthy). ‖ Digne d'attentions (or) d'égards.

considerably [-rəbli] adv. Considérablement.

considerate [-rit] adj. Prévenant, attentionné, obligeant (to, towards, pour, envers). ‖ Réfléchi, avisé (thoughtful).

considerately [-ritli] adv. Avec prévenance. ‖ D'une manière prudente.

considerateness [-ritnis] n. Attentions, prévenances f. pl.; égards m. pl. (for, to, envers).

consideration [kən,sidə'reiʃən] n. Considération, réflexion f.; after due consideration, après mûre réflexion; to leave out of consideration, ne pas envisager, laisser de côté. ‖ Etude, délibération f.; examen m.; for your kind consideration, à votre aimable attention; under consideration, à l'étude, à l'examen. ‖ Considération, raison f.; in consideration of, en considération (or) raison de, étant donné que, eu égard à. ‖ Considération f.; aspect m.; material considerations, considérations (or) questions matérielles. ‖ Considération, estime, déférence f.; out of consideration for, par égard pour. ‖ Importance f.; to be taken into consideration, entrer en ligne de compte; to take into consideration, prendre en considération (or) ligne de compte.

attacher de l'importance à. ‖ Compensation, contre-partie *f.*; dédommagement *m.*; *for a consideration*, moyennant compensation; *in consideration of*, moyennant, en échange de. ‖ FIN. Rétribution *f.*; *for a good, valuable consideration*, à titre gracieux, onéreux. ‖ FIN. Provision *f.*; *to give consideration for*, provisionner. ‖ FIN. Contre-valeur *f.*

considering [kən'sidəriŋ] prep. Vu, eu égard à, en raison de, étant donné.
— adv. Malgré tout, toutefois, tout bien considéré.
— conj. pr. *Considering that*, attendu que, considérant que.

consign [kən'sain] v. tr. COMM. Consigner, expédier en consignation (*to*, à) [goods]. ‖ FIN. Consigner, déposer a sum). ‖ FIG. Confier, remettre (to entrust); livrer (*to*, à) [to give up].

consignation [,kɔnsig'neiʃən] n. COMM. Expédition *f.*; *to the consignation of*, envoyé en consignation à. ‖ FIN. Consignation *f.*; dépôt *m.*

consignee [,kɔnsai'ni:] n. COMM. Destinataire, consignataire *s.*

consigner, consignor [kən'sainə*] n. COMM. Expéditeur, consignateur *m.*; expéditrice, consignatrice *f.*

consignment [-mənt] n. COMM. Envoi *m.*; expédition *f.* (of goods); expédition *f.*; arrivage *m.* (goods sent); *consignment note*, lettre de voiture, bordereau d'expédition. ‖ FIN. Consignation *f.*; dépôt *m.*; *Deposit and Consignment Office*, Caisse des dépôts et consignations.

consilient [kən'siliənt] adj. Concordant. (See ACCORDANT.)

consist [kən'sist] v. intr. To consist of, consister en, être composé (or) fait de, se composer de. ‖ To consist in, consister en (or) à, résider en. ‖ † To consist with, s'accorder avec, être consistant avec.

consistence [-əns] n. Consistance *f.* ‖ PHILOS. Conséquence *f.*

consistency [-ənsi] n. Consistance *f.* (of a liquid, substance). ‖ FIG. Consistance, stabilité, solidité, fermeté, assise *f.* (firmness); consistance, uniformité, suite logique *f.* (logical connection).

consistent [-ənt] adj. Compatible (*with*, avec). ‖ En accord, en harmonie (*with*, avec). ‖ Logique, stable, consistant. ‖ PHILOS. Conséquent.

consistently [-əntli] adv. En accord (or) conformité (*with*, avec); conformément (*with*, à). ‖ Avec logique (or) consistance, avec de la suite dans les idées, conséquemment.

consistorial [,kɔnsis'tɔ:riəl] adj. Consistorial.
consistory [kən'sistəri] n. ECCLES. Consistoire *m.*
consociate [kən'souʃiit] adj., n. Associé *s.*
— [-eit] v. tr. Associer.
— v. intr. S'associer.
consociation [kən,souʃi'eiʃən] n. Association *f.*
consolable [kən'souləbl] adj. Consolable.
consolation [,kɔnsə'leiʃən] n. Consolation *f.* (see COMFORT); *to turn for consolation to*, chercher une consolation dans.
consolatory [kən'sɔlətəri] adj. Consolateur *m.*; consolatrice *f.* (See COMFORTING.)
console [kən'soul] v. tr. Consoler.
console ['kɔnsoul] n. ARCHIT., MUS., RADIO. Console *f.*; *control console*, bureau électronique (in a language laboratory). ‖ Console-table, n. Console *f.*
consolidate [kən'sɔlideit] v. tr. Consolider, solidifier. ‖ FIN. Consolider (debts, funds). ‖ COMM. Fusionner (companies). ‖ JUR. Joindre (actions, suits). ‖ MILIT. Consolider, fortifier (positions). ‖ FIG. Sceller (an alliance); consolider, raffermir (union).
— v. intr. Se consolider, se fortifier, se raffermir.
consolidation [kən,sɔli'deiʃən] n. Consolidation *f.*; raffermissement *m.* ‖ FIN. Consolidation *f.* ‖ COMM. Fusion *f.*

consols ['kɔnsəls] n. pl. FIN. Consolidés *m. pl.*; rentes consolidées *f. pl.*
consommé [,kɔnsə'mei] n. CULIN. Consommé *m.*
consonance ['kɔnsənəns] n. GRAMM. Assonance *f.* ‖ MUS. Consonance *f.* ‖ PHYS. Résonance *f.* ‖ FIG. Harmonie *f.*; accord *m.*
consonant [-ənt] adj. GRAMM. Assonant. ‖ MUS. Consonant. ‖ FIG. En harmonie, d'accord (*with*, avec).
consonant [-ənt] n. GRAMM. Consonne *f.*
consonantal [kɔnsə'næntəl] adj. GRAMM. Consonantique, de consonne.
consonantly ['kɔnsənəntli] adv. Conformément (*to*, à); en accord (*to*, avec).
consort ['kɔnsɔ:t] adj. Consort (prince).
— n. Conjoint *s.* (husband, wife). ‖ NAUT. Conserve *f.*; *in consort*, de conserve.
— [kən'sɔ:t] v. intr. S'accorder, s'harmoniser (to harmonize). ‖ S'unir, s'associer (*with*, à) [to keep company]; se lier (*with*, avec) [to make friends].
— v. tr. Fréquenter, fraterniser avec.
consortium [kən'sɔ:ʃjəm] n. Consortium *m.*
conspecific [kɔnspi'sifik] adj. ZOOL., BOT. De (or) appartenant à la même espèce, conspécifique.
conspectus [kən'spektəs] n. Vue générale *f.* ‖ Sommaire, tableau synoptique *m.*
conspicuous [kən'spikjuəs] adj. Evident, en évidence, en vue, visible. (See NOTICEABLE.) ‖ Remarquable, frappant, marquant (*by*, *for*, par) [striking]. ‖ Eminent, remarquable, insigne, exceptionnel (outstanding). ‖ Voyant (showy); *to make oneself conspicuous by* (or) *through*, se faire remarquer par, se singulariser par. ‖ FAM. *To be conspicuous by one's absence*, briller par son absence.
conspicuously [-li] adv. Visiblement, en évidence. ‖ Remarquablement, supérieurement, exceptionnellement.
conspicuousness [-nis] n. Evidence *f.*; aspect visible *m.* ‖ FIG. Eminence, supériorité *f.*; caractère exceptionnel *m.*
conspiracy [kən'spirəsi] n. Conspiration *f.* (See PLOT.)
conspirator [-ə*] n. Conspirateur *m.*; conjuré *m.* (See PLOTTER.)
conspiratress [-tris] n. Conspiratrice *f.*
conspire [kən'spaiə*] v. intr. Conspirer, comploter (*against*, contre); *to conspire together*, se conjurer. ‖ Conspirer, concourir (*to*, à).
— v. tr. Comploter, machiner, combiner (s.o.'s ruin). [See PLOT.]
conspiring [-riŋ] adj. Conspirateur *m.*, conspiratrice *f.*
conspue [kən'spju:] v. tr. Conspuer.
constable ['kʌnstəbl] n. Constable *m.* (in England); agent (*m.*) de police (in France); *rural constable*, garde champêtre. ‖ Gouverneur *m.* (of the Tower of London). ‖ † MILIT. Connétable *m.*
constabulary [kən'stæbjuləri] adj. De police.
— n. Police *f.*; agents (*m. pl.*) de police; *county constabulary*, gendarmerie, police rurale.
constancy ['kɔnstənsi] n. Constance, fermeté *f.* (steadfastness). ‖ Constance, fidélité *f.* (truth). ‖ Constance, persévérance *f.* ‖ Constance, invariabilité, stabilité *f.* ‖ ELECTR. Constance.
constant [-ənt] adj. Constant, incessant, continuel. (See CONTINUAL.) ‖ Constant, ferme, inébranlé (steadfast). ‖ Constant, invariable, stable (unchanging). ‖ Constant, fidèle (*to*, à).
— n. PHYS., MATH. Constante *f.*
constantly [-əntli] adv. Constamment. (See CONTINUALLY.)
constellate ['kɔnstəleit] v. tr. Consteller (*with*, de). [See SPANGLE.]
— v. intr. Se grouper en constellation.
constellation [,kɔnstə'leiʃən] n. ASTRON. Constellation *f.*

consternate ['kɔnstəneit] v. tr. Atterrer. (See DISMAY.)

consternation [,kɔnstə'neiʃən] n. Atterrement m. (dismay).

constipate ['kɔnstipeit] v. tr. MED. Constiper. ‖ CHIM. † Condenser (vapour).

constipation [,kɔnsti'peiʃən] n. MED. Constipation f. (See COSTIVENESS.)

constituency [kən'stitjuənsi] n. Circonscription électorale f. (district); électeurs m. pl. (voters). ‖ FAM. Clientèle f.

constituent [-ənt] adj. Constituant (assembly, element); commettant, électeur (person).
— n. Elément, composant m. ‖ Commettant, mandant m. ‖ Electeur m.; électrice f. (voter).

constitute ['kɔnstitjuːt] v. tr. Constituer, former (to form); composer (to make up). ‖ Constituer, instituer, établir (to establish). ‖ Instituer, désigner, nommer (to appoint); to constitute oneself, se constituer, s'instituer. ‖ JUR. Constituer (a gouvernment); établir (an institution); instituer (a law). ‖ MED. Constituer.

constitution [,kɔnsti'tjuːʃən] n. Constitution, formation f. ‖ Constitution, composition f. (of, de). ‖ Constitution, institution f.; établissement m. ‖ JUR. Statuts m. pl. (of a corporation, a society); constitution (of a government, a State). ‖ MED. Constitution f.; tempérament m. (physical); mental constitution, caractère, disposition mentale.

constitutional [-ʃn̩] adj. JUR., MED. Constitutionnel. ‖ U. S. Fédéral (law).
— n. FAM. Promenade hygiénique f.; to take one's constitutional, faire son petit tour quotidien.

constitutionalist [-ʃnəlist] n. Constitutionnel m. ‖ JUR. Spécialiste du droit constitutionnel m.

constitutionalize [-ʃnəlaiz] v. tr. Légitimer, rendre constitutionnel.

constitutionally [-ʃnəli] adv. MED. Constitutionnellement. ‖ JUR. Selon la constitution.

constitutive ['kɔnstitjutiv] adj. Constitutif, de base, fondamental, essentiel (basic). ‖ Constituant (component).

constrain [kən'strein] v. tr. Réprimer, contraindre, contenir (to restrain); to constrain oneself to, faire un effort sur soi pour, se contenir pour. ‖ Emprisonner, enfermer (to confine). ‖ Contraindre, forcer, obliger (to, à). [See FORCE.] ‖ Obtenir par la force; to constrain s.o.'s consent, extorquer le consentement de qqn. ‖ Produire de force; to constrain a laugh, se contraindre à rire.

constrained [-d] adj. Obligé, contraint, forcé (compelled); contraint, forcé, peu naturel (unnatural).

constrainedly [-idli] adv. Par force, sous la contrainte. ‖ D'un air contraint.

constraint [kən'streint] n. Contrainte, pression f. (compulsion); contrainte, entrave f. (fetters). ‖ Contrainte, retenue f. (restraint); contrainte, gêne f.; embarras m. (uneasiness). ‖ JUR. Contrainte (f.) par corps.

constrict [kən'strikt] v. tr. Contracter, resserrer, rétracter, rétrécir (to contract). ‖ Serrer, pincer, étrangler, gêner, comprimer (to cramp). ‖ MED. Resserrer (tissues).

constriction [-ʃən] n. Constriction f.

constrictive [-tiv] adj. Constrictif.

constrictor [-tə*] n. MED. Compresseur m. (instrument); constricteur m. (muscle). ‖ ZOOL. Boa constricteur m. (snake).

constringe [kən'strindʒ] v. tr. See CONSTRICT.
— v. intr. MED. Se resserrer.

constringent [-ənt] adj. MED. Constringent.

construct [kən'strʌkt] v. tr. ARCHIT. Construire, édifier. (See BUILD.) ‖ TECHN. Construire (an engine). ‖ MATH. Construire, dessiner (a triangle). ‖ GRAMM. Construire (a sentence); to be constructed with, se construire avec, gouverner. ‖ FIG. Edifier, bâtir (a theory).

— [-'kɔnstrʌkt] n. U. S. FIG. Construction (f.) de l'esprit.

construction [-ʃən] n. ARCHIT. Construction f. (act); construction, bâtisse f.; édifice, bâtiment m. (building). ‖ GRAMM. Construction f. ‖ FIG. Construction, édification f. (of a theory). ‖ FIG. Interprétation f.; to put a bad construction on, mal interpréter, prendre dans le mauvais sens.

constructional [-ʃən] adj. De construction (defect); constructional set, jeu de construction.

constructionist [-ʃənist] n. U. S. Interprétateur m.

constructive [-tiv] adj. De la construction. ‖ Constructif, créateur (formative). ‖ Déduit, inféré, établi par déduction (deduced). ‖ Implicite, virtuel, sous-entendu (implied).

constructively [-tivli] adv. Par déduction.

constructivism [-ti,vizm̩] n. ARTS. Constructivisme m.

constructor [-tə*] n. Constructeur m. (of cars, engines). ‖ NAUT. Ingénieur (m.) de constructions navales.

construe [kən'struː] v. tr. GRAMM. Construire, faire la construction (or) le mot-à-mot (or) l'analyse grammaticale. ‖ FIG. Interpréter, expliquer, motiver (actions).
— v. intr. GRAMM. Avoir une construction grammaticale; not to construe, avoir une construction contraire à la grammaire.

consubstantial [,kɔnsəb'stænʃəl] adj. ECCLES. Consubstantiel.

consubstantiality ['kɔnsəb,stænʃi'æliti] n. ECCLES. Consubstantialité f.

consubstantiate [,kɔnsəb'stænʃieit] v. tr. ECCLES. Unir consubstantiellement.
— v. intr. ECCLES. S'unir consubstantiellement.

consubstantiation ['kɔnsəb,stænʃi'eiʃən] n. ECCLES. Consubstantiation f.

consuetude ['kɔnswitjuːd] n. JUR. Coutume f. ‖ Relations sociales f. pl.

consuetudinary [,kɔnswi'tjuːdinəri] adj., n. JUR. Coutumier.

consul ['kɔnsəl] n. Consul m.; Consul général consul général.

consular [-ə*] adj. Consulaire.

consulate [-it] n. Consulat m. (functions, office, position).

consulship [-ʃip] n. Consulat m. (functions).

consult [kən'sʌlt] v. tr. Consulter, se référer à (a book); consulter, demander l'avis de (a person). ‖ FIG. Consulter, considérer (one's interests, wishes) ménager, avoir égard à (s.o.'s feelings).
— v. intr. Converser, conférer, s'entretenir, être en conférence (with, avec) [to converse]. ‖ Prendre conseil (with, de); to consult together, se consulter.

consultant [-ənt] n. MED. Médecin consultant m ‖ JUR. Expert-conseil m. ‖ TECHN. Ingénieur-conseil m.

consultation [,kɔnsəl'teiʃən] n. Consultation f (act, advice). ‖ MED. Consultation f. ‖ JUR. Conférence f.; colloque m.; to hold a consultation conférer.

consultative [kən'sʌltətiv] adj. Consultatif. (See ADVISORY.)

consulting [-iŋ] adj. MED. Consultant. ‖ TECHN Conseil (engineer). ‖ MED. Consulting room, cabinet de consultation; salle d'examen.

consumable [kən'sjuːməbl̩] adj. COMM. Consommable.

consume [kən'sjuːm] v. tr. Consumer, brûler (to burn up); consumer, détruire (to destroy). ‖ Consommer (to use up); to be consumed, se consommer (articles of food). ‖ FIG. User, gaspiller (one's energy); gaspiller, jeter (one's money); perdre (one's time) [see SQUANDER]; to be consumed, se consumer (energy). ‖ FIG. Consumer, dévorer, brû

ler (with, de) [curiosity]; to be consumed with grief, se consumer de chagrin.
— v. intr. Se consumer.

onsumedly [-idli] adv. Extrêmement, excessivement.

onsumer [-ə*] n. COMM. Consommateur m.; consommatrice f.; consumer goods, denrées de consommation; consumer resistance, résistance du consommateur à la vente.

onsummate [kən'sʌmit] adj. Achevé, fieffé (arrant); consommé, accompli, parfait (perfect).
— ['kʌnsʌmeit] v. tr. Consommer (a crime, marriage); to be consummated, se consommer (marriage). ‖ Achever, parfaire (to finish).

onsummately [kən'sʌmitli] adv. A la perfection, totalement.

onsummation [,kɔnsə'meiʃən] n. Consommation f. (of a crime, marriage). ‖ Consommation, fin f.; achèvement m. ‖ Perfection f. (of an art). ‖ Accomplissement parfait, couronnement m. (of a life). ‖ Fin f., résultat souhaité m. (end).

onsumption [kən'sʌmpʃən]. COMM. Consommation f. (of commodities). ‖ TECHN. Consommation, dépense f. (of fuel, gas, petrol). ‖ MED. Tuberculose f.; galloping consumption, phtisie galopante.

onsumptive [-tiv] adj. Dévastateur, destructeur, destructif (destructive); dilapidateur, ruineux (wasteful). ‖ COMM. De consommation (power). ‖ MED. Tuberculeux, de tuberculeux.
— n. MED. Tuberculeux, poitrinaire, phtisique s.; tubar (fam.).

onsumptiveness [-tivnis] n. MED. Terrain tuberculeux m.

ontact ['kɔntækt] n. Contact m. (touch); to lose contact with, perdre contact avec. ‖ Relation f.; one of our contacts, un de nos correspondants. ‖ ELECTR. Contact m.; bulb contact, plot de lampe; to break, to make contact, couper, mettre le contact (or) courant. ‖ MATH. Contact, point de contact m. ‖ PHYS. Contact potential, potentiel de contact. ‖ MED. Contact lens, verres de contact. ‖ MILIT. Contact m.; to establish contact with, entrer en contact avec. ‖ AVIAT. Contact flying, vol de contact; vol d'accompagnement d'infanterie. ‖ FIG. Contact, rapport m.; preliminary contacts, prise de contact.
— [kən'tækt] v. tr. FAM. Prendre contact avec; contacter (fam.).
— v. intr. FAM. Prendre contact.
— adj. Qui établit le contact; contact book, livre pour grand public; contact man, employé chargé de liaison.

ontagion [kən'teidʒən] n. MED., FIG. Contagion f.

ontagious [-əs] adj. MED., FIG. Contagieux m. (See INFECTIOUS.)

ontagiously [-əsli] adv. Par contagion.

ontagiousness [-əsnis] n. MED. Contagiosité f.

ontain [kən'tein] v. tr. Contenir (in capacity). [See HOLD.] ‖ Contenir, renfermer, comporter (to comprise); information contained in the newspaper, information fournie par le journal. ‖ MATH. Etre divisible par. ‖ MILIT. Contenir, arrêter (the enemy). ‖ FIG. Contenir, refréner, réprimer; not to contain oneself for, ne pas se tenir de; to contain oneself, se contenir.

ontainable [-əbḷ] adj. Maîtrisable, réprimable.

ontainer [-ə*] n. Récipient m. ‖ TECHN. Container, conteneur m.

ontaminate [kən'tæmineit] v. tr. MED. Contaminer. (See INFECT.)

ontamination [kən,tæmi'neiʃən] n. MED. Contamination f.

ontango [kən'tæŋgou] m. FIN. Report m. ‖ Contango-day, n. Jour (m.) des reports.

ontemn [kən'tem] v. tr. Mépriser. (See DESPISE.)

ontemner [-nə*] n. Contempteur m.; contemp-

trice f. ‖ JUR. Personne coupable (f.) d'outrages à magistrats.

contemplate ['kɔntempleit] v. tr. Contempler, regarder intensément (to gaze at). ‖ Méditer, réfléchir sur (to think about). ‖ Etudier, envisager, considérer (to study). ‖ Prévoir, avoir en vue (to expect); projeter, avoir l'intention de (to intend).
— v. intr. Méditer, réfléchir, être en contemplation.

contemplation [,kɔntem'pleiʃən] n. Contemplation, observation f.; examen m. (gazing). ‖ Contemplation, méditation f. ‖ Prévision f.; in contemplation of, en prévision de, dans l'attente de. ‖ Projet m.; to have sth. in contemplation, avoir quelque projet en tête.

contemplative ['kɔntəmpleitiv] adj. Méditatif, pensif, songeur. ‖ ECCLES. Contemplatif.

contemplator [-ə*] n. Contemplateur m.; contemplatrice f.

contemporaneity [kən,tempɔrə'neiti] n. Contemporanéité f.

contemporaneous [kən,tempə'reinjəs] adj. Contemporain (with, de).

contemporaneously [-li] adv. A la même période (or) époque (with, que).

contemporary [kən'tempərəri] adj. Contemporain (with, de).
— n. Contemporain s. ‖ Confrère m. (journalese).

contemporize [-raiz] v. tr. Rendre contemporain; faire coïncider dans le temps; synchroniser.

contempt [kən'tempt] n. Mépris m. (for, pour) [s.o.]; beneath contempt, plus que méprisable; in contempt of, au mépris de. ‖ Dédain m.; to treat with contempt, traiter dédaigneusement. ‖ JUR. Défaut m.; non-comparution f. (non-appearance); contempt of Court, outrage à magistrat; direct contempt, délit d'audience.

contemptibility [kən,tempti'biliti] n. Nature méprisable, ignominie, bassesse f.

contemptible [kən'temptibḷ] adj. Méprisable, indigne (despicable).

contemptibly [-bli] adv. De manière méprisable.

contemptuous [kən'temptjuəs] adj. Méprisant (of, pour); dédaigneux (of, de). ‖ Méprisant, de mépris, de dédain (disdainful).

contemptuously [-li] adv. Avec mépris, dédaigneusement.

contemptuousness [-nis] n. Caractère méprisant, air de mépris m.

contend [kən'tend] v. intr. Lutter, entrer en lutte, combattre (for, pour; with, contre). ‖ Entrer en compétition (to contest); to contend with s.o. for the prize, disputer le prix à qqn. ‖ Disputer, discuter, contester (with, avec) [to argue].
— v. tr. Affirmer, assurer, soutenir, prétendre (to assert).

contending [-iŋ] adj. JUR. Contestant.

content ['kɔntent] n. Surface, superficie f. (area); capacité, contenance f. (capacity); volume m.; teneur f.; octane content, indice d'octane. ‖ Pl. See CONTENTS. ‖ GRAMM. Content clause, proposition de développement.

content [kən'tent] n. Contentement m.; to one's heart's content, à cœur joie; tout son saoul. ‖ JUR. Vote favorable, oui m. (in the House of Lords).
— adj. Content, satisfait (with, de); she is content with little, elle se contente de peu. ‖ Disposé, consentant (to, à); he is content to do it, il ne demande pas mieux que de le faire. ‖ JUR. Qui émet un vote favorable.
— v. tr. Contenter, satisfaire; to content oneself with, se contenter de.

contented [-id] adj. Content, satisfait.

contentedly [-idli] adv. Avec satisfaction (or) contentement; en se contentant de son sort.

contention [kən'tenʃən] n. Contention, controverse f.; démêlé, différend m. (See DISCORD.) ‖ Point discuté, objet (m.) de discussion. ‖ Emulation, rivalité, compétition *f.* || Prétention, affirmation *f.; my contention is that*, je prétends (or) soutiens que.

contentious [-ʃəs] adj. Querelleur, ergoteur, chicanier. || JUR. Litigieux (case); contentieux (jurisdiction); *contentious matters*, le contentieux.

contentment [kən'tentmənt] n. Contentement *m.*

contents ['kɔntents] n. pl. Contenu *m.* (of a book, cask, letter). || Matières *f. pl.; table of contents*, table des matières.

conterminal [kən'tə:minl] adj. Contigu.

conterminous [-əs] adj. Contigu, attenant (*with*, à); limitrophe (*with*, de). [See ADJACENT.] || Se rejoignant par les extrémités, bout à bout (abutting). || De même durée (or) étendue (*with*, que). [See COEXTENSIVE.]

contest ['kɔntest] n. Contestation, discussion, controverse *f.* (dispute). || Conflit *m.* (*with*, avec). [See CONFLICT.] || SPORTS. Epreuve, compétition *f.; athletic contest*, concours athlétique.
— [kən'test] v. tr. Contester, mettre en question, discuter (to dispute). || MILIT. Disputer (field, victory). || JUR. Contester (a debt); disputer (a seat in Parliament); attaquer (a will); *contested case*, matière contentieuse. || SPORTS. Entrer en compétition pour (a race).
— v. intr. Entrer en contestation (or) en conflit (*against, with*, avec). || SPORTS. Se mettre sur les rangs (*for*, pour).

contestable [kən'testəbl] adj. Contestable.

contestant [-ənt] n. JUR. Contestant.

contestation [,kɔntes'teiʃən] n. Contestation, discussion *f.; litige m.*

context ['kɔntekst] n. Contexte *m.* || FAM. *In this context*, à propos, à ce sujet.

contextual [kən'tekstjuəl] adj. Relatif au contexte.

contexture [-ʃə*] n. Texture *f.* (of a fabric); tissu *m.* (fabric). || Contexture, structure *f.* (of a literary composition). || MED. Contexture (of bones).

contiguity [,kɔnti'gjuiti] n. Contiguïté *f.*

contiguous [kən'tigjuəs] adj. Contigu, adjacent, attenant (*to*, à). [See ADJACENT.] || Suivant, immédiatement proche. || MATH. Adjacent.

contiguously [-əsli] adv. En contiguïté (*with*, to).

continence ['kɔntinəns] n. Continence *f.* || Modération, retenue *f.*

continent [-ənt] adj. Continent (chaste). || Modéré, retenu, sobre (temperate).

continent n. GEOGR. Continent *m.* || † Contenant *m.*

continental [,kɔnti'nentl] adj. Continental; *continental tour*, voyage circulaire sur le continent; *continental breakfast*, petit déjeuner à la française. || GEOL. *Continental drift*, dérive des continents; *continental shelf*, plateau continental.
— n. Habitant (*s.*) du continent européen. || U. S. FAM. Papier-monnaie (*m.*) sans valeur; *not worth a continental*, qui ne vaut pas une guigne.

continently ['kɔntinəntli] adv. Avec continence.

contingency [kən'tindʒənsi] n. Eventualité *f.; in case of a contingency*, en cas d'imprévu. || FIN., COMM. Pl. Frais imprévus *m. pl.; contingency appropriation*, allocation de crédits extraordinaires. PHILOS. Contingence *f.*

contingent [-ənt] adj. Eventuel, imprévu, aléatoire, problématique (accidental). || Dépendant (*on, upon*, de); *to be contingent upon*, dépendre de, être soumis à la condition que. || PHILOS. Contingent. || JUR. Casuel, éventuel (condition); conditionnel (right).
— n. Contingent *m.* || † Evénement imprévu *m.*

contingently [-əntli] adv. Eventuellement, problématiquement, d'une manière aléatoire, par hasard. || Sous la dépendance (*on, upon*, de); à la condition (*on, upon*, que).

continual [kən'tinjuəl] adj. Continuel.

continually [-əli] adj. Continuellement, tout le temps, sans interruption (or) cesse (ceaselessly).

continuance [-əns] n. Continuation, poursuite (of an action); prolongation *f.* (of a situation, state). || Long séjour *m.* (in a place); persistance (in a state). || Durée *f.* (duration).

continuant [-ənt] n. GRAMM. Continue *f.*

continuation [kən,tinju'eiʃən] n. Continuation, suite *f.* (of a book); *continuation classes* (or) *schoo* cours du soir. || Extension, continuation *f.; prolon* gement *m.* || FIN. Report *m.* || Pl. Guêtres *f. pl.*

continuative [kən'tinjuətiv] adj. Qui sert a cont nuer. || GRAMM. Duratif.

continuator [-eitə*] n. Continuateur *m.; continua* trice *f.*

continue [kən'tinju:] v. tr. Continuer, poursuivr (to pursue). || Reprendre, continuer, poursuivre (t resume); *to be continued*, à suivre. || Continuer, n pas cesser (*to*, de); persister (*to*, à). || Continue prolonger (to extend). || Conserver, maintenir (i à, dans, en) [to keep]. || FIN. Reporter. || JUF Ajourner, remettre.
— v. intr. Continuer, poursuivre (to go on). Continuer, reprendre (to resume). || Continue durer (to last). || Persister, persévérer (*in*, dans). Rester, demeurer; *to continue in one's offic* conserver ses fonctions; *to continue obstinat* demeurer opiniâtre. || Continuer à; *to continu* playing, continuer à jouer. || Continuer à séjourne (*at, in*, à); *to continue in Lyons for two year* rester encore deux ans à Lyon.

continued [-d] adj. MATH. Continu.

continuity [,kɔnti'njuiti] n. Continuité *f.* || CINEI Continuité littéraire *f.; continuity girl*, script-gir continuity man, découpeur.

continuous [kən'tinjuəs] adj. MATH., CH. DE F ELECTR., FIG. Continu. || THEATR. *Continuous pe formance*, spectacle permanent. || NAUT. *Continuou voyage*, continuité du voyage. || ARCHIT. Flam boyant (style).

continuously [-əsli] adv. Continuellement, sar arrêt.

continuum [-əm] n. PHILOS. Continu *m.*

contort [kən'tɔ:t] v. tr. Contorsionner, contourne

contortion [kən'tɔ:ʃən] n. Contorsion *f.*

contortionist [-ʃnist] n. Contorsionniste, disl qué *m.*

contortive [-tiv] adj. De contorsion.

contour ['kɔntuə*] n. Contour *m.* (of a figur land, object); profil *m.* (of ground). || Courbe (*f* de niveau. || **Contour-interval**, n. Equidistance || **Contour-line**, n. Ligne (*f.*) de contour; courb (*f.*) de niveau; *master contour line*, courbe ma tresse. || **Contour-map**, n. Carte hypsométrique
— v. tr. Dessiner le contour de. || Contourner (hill). || Construire en contournant (a road).

contra ['kɔntrə] prep., n. Contre *m.* || FIN. Contr partie *f.; per contra*, en compensation. || **Contra entry**, n. FIN. Contre-écriture *f.* || **Contra-indicat** v. tr. MED. Contre-indiquer. || **Contra-indicatio** n. MED. Contre-indication *f.*

contraband ['kɔntrəbænd] n. JUR., MILIT. Contr bande *f.*
— adj. De contrebande (goods).

contrabandist [-ist] n. Contrebandier *s.* (Se SMUGGLER.)

contrabass ['kɔntrə'beis] n. MUS. Contrebasse (instrument).

contrabassist [-ist] n. MUS. Contrebasse *f.* (mus cian).

contraception [,kɔntrə'sepʃən] n. MED. Contr ception *f.*

contraceptive [-tiv] n. MED. Contraceptif *m.*
— adj. MED. Contraceptif, anticonceptionnel.

contract ['kɔntrækt] n. Pacte, accord, traité *m.* convention *f.* (agreement); *as per contract*, selon le conventions; *by private contract*, à l'amiable, d gré à gré; *underwriting contract*, convention synd cale. || Contrat *m.; contract of benevolence*, contr nilatéral ; *marriage contract*, contrat de mariage ; ⊃ *enter into a contract with*, passer un contrat vec. ‖ Contrat d'entreprise ; *to have a contract for*, voir l'entreprise de. ‖ Adjudication *f.; on contract*, forfait ; *supply contract*, marché de fournitures. JUR. *Conditions of contract*, cahier des charges ; ⊅w *of contract*, droit des obligations; *rights granted y contract*, droits contractuels. ‖ MED. *Contract urse*, infirmière auxiliaire (or) contractuelle.

- [kən'trækt] v. tr. Contracter (bodies); froncer ⊃yebrows); contracter, crisper (features); *to be ⊃ntracted*, se contracter. ‖ GRAMM., MED., JUR., 'IG. Contracter.

- v. intr. Se contracter (bodies); se froncer (eye-⊃rows); se crisper (features). ‖ GRAMM. Se contrac-⊃r (word). ‖ JUR. Passer un contrat (*for*, pour).

⊃ntracted [kən'træktid] adj. GRAMM. Contracte, ⊃ntracté.

⊃ntractible [-tibḷ], contractile [-tail] adj. Con-⊃actile.

⊃ntraction [-ʃən] n. Contraction *f.* (of bodies); ⊃ispation *f.* (of features). ‖ GRAMM. Contraction *f.* MED., FIG. Fait (*m.*) de contracter.

⊃ntractor [-tə*] n. Contractant, adjudicataire *m.* Entrepreneur *m.* ‖ MILIT. Fournisseur *m.* ‖ MED. ⊅uscle contracteur *m.*

⊃ntractual [-tjuəl] adj. JUR. Contractuel ; conven-⊃onnel.

⊃ntracture [-tʃə*] n. MED. Contracture *f.*

⊃ntradict [ˌkɔntrə'dikt] v. tr. Contredire (s.o.); ⊃ *contradict each other*, se contredire (recipr.); ⊃ *contradict oneself*, se contredire (reflex.).

⊃ntradiction [-ʃən] n. Contradiction *f.* (*to*, avec). Contredit *m.; to give a contradiction to*, donner ⊃ démenti à. ‖ PHILOS. Antinomie *f.*

⊃ntradictious [-ʃəs] adj. Contrariant, ergoteur, ⊅isonneur.

⊃ntradictiousness [-ʃəsnis] n. Esprit (*m.*) de ⊃ntradiction.

⊃ntradictor [-tə*] n. Contradicteur *m.*

⊃ntradictorily [-tərili] adv. Contradictoirement.

⊃ntradictory [-təri] adj. Contradictoire. ‖ Contre-⊅sant, qui contredit.

⊃ntradistinction [ˌkɔntrədis'tiŋkʃən] n. Con-⊅aste *m.* (*to*, avec).

⊃ntradistinctive [-tiv] adj. De contraste, contrasté.

⊃ntradistinguish [ˌkɔntrədis'tiŋgwiʃ] v. tr. Dis-⊅nguer par contraste (*from*, de); mettre en contraste *rom*, avec).

⊃ntralto [kən'træltou] n. MUS. Contralto *m.*

⊃ntraposition [ˌkɔntrəpə'ziʃən] n. Opposition, ⊅ntithèse *f.*

⊃ntraprop ['kɔntrəprɔp] n. AVIAT., FAM. Contre-⊅élice *f.*

⊃ntraption [kən'træpʃən] n. FAM. Machin, sys-⊅me, truc *m.* (device); truc *m.* (makeshift).

⊃ntrapuntal [ˌkɔntrə'pʌntḷ] adj. MUS. Du contre-⊃oint.

⊃ntrapuntist ['kɔntrəpʌntist] n. MUS. Contra-⊃ontiste *s.*

⊃ntrariant [kən'trɛəriənt] adj. Contraire, hostile ⊃o, à).

⊃ntrariety [ˌkɔntrə'raiəti] n. Opposition *f.; dés-⊃ccord *m.* (of interests, opinions).

⊃ntrarily ['kɔntrərili] adv. Contrairement (*to*, à).

⊃ntrariness [-nis] n. Esprit (*m.*) de contradiction.

⊃ntrarious [kɔn'trɛəriəs] adj. Contrariant (event, ⊅rson); hostile, revêche, acariâtre (person); con-⊅aire (weather).

⊃ntrariwise ['kɔntrəriwaiz] adj. En sens contraire ⊅n the opposite direction). ‖ D'autre part, de l'autre ⊃ôté (on the other hand). ‖ D'une manière contra-⊅ante (or) désobligeante (perversely).

⊃ntrary ['kɔntrəri] adj. Contraire, opposé (*to*, à); ⊃ntrary to nature*, contre nature. ‖ Hostile, défa-⊃orable, contraire (*to*, à). ‖ NAUT. Contraire (winds).

- [kən'trɛəri] adi. FAM. Contrariant (contra-

rious); obstiné, volontaire; cabochard (fam.). [See WILLED.]

— ['kɔntrəri] adv. Contrairement (*to*, à); au contraire (*to*, de); en opposition (*to*, avec); *contrary to reason*, en dépit du bon sens ; *to act contrary to*, contrevenir.

— n. Contraire, opposé *m.* (*of*, de); *by contraries*, à rebours, en sens inverse ; *on the contrary*, au contraire ; *to the contrary*, à l'encontre ; *to have nothing to say to the contrary*, ne rien trouver à objecter (or) redire ; *unless you hear to the contrary*, à moins d'avis contraire, sauf contrordre.

contrast ['kɔntrɑːst] n. Contraste *m.; opposition *f.* (*between*, entre); *in contrast with*, par contraste avec; *to form a contrast to*, contraster avec, faire contraste avec.

— [kən'trɑːst] v. tr. Faire contraster, mettre en contraste (*with*, avec); opposer (*with*, à). ‖ Contraster, contrarier (colours).

— v. intr. Faire contraste, contraster (*with*, avec); trancher (*with*, sur). ‖ Se contrarier (colours).

contrasty [kən'trɑːsti] adj. TECHN. Heurté (nega-tive); contraste (paper); contrasté (print).

contravallation [ˌkɔntrəvə'leiʃən] n. MILIT. Con-trevallation *f.*

contravene [ˌkɔntrə'viːn] v. tr. S'opposer à, aller à l'encontre de, agir contrairement à, contrarier (s.o.'s plans). ‖ Opposer un démenti à, contredire (a statement). ‖ JUR. Contrevenir à.

contravener [-ə*] n. JUR. Contrevenant *s.*

contravention [ˌkɔntrə'venʃən] n. Contravention, transgression, infraction *f.; in contravention of*, en violation de, en contravention avec.

contretemps ['kɔntrətɑ̃] n. Contretemps *m.;* mésaventure *f.*

contribute [kən'tribjuːt] v. intr. Contribuer, coo-pérer, aider, concourir (*to*, à). [See CONDUCE.] ‖ Collaborer, apporter sa collaboration (*to*, à) [a magazine]. ‖ FIN. Contribuer, souscrire, payer sa contribution ; *to contribute to assets*, fournir des capitaux.

— v. tr. Ecrire, rédiger (articles). ‖ FIN. Payer (one's share) ; contribuer pour, souscrire (a sum).

contribution [-ʃən] n. Contribution, participa-tion *f.; to lay under contribution*, mettre à contri-bution. ‖ Article *m.* (*to*, dans) Ḻa newspaper]. ‖ FIN. Cotisation, contribution *f.; contribution pro rata*, quote-part. ‖ MILIT. Contribution, réquisi-tion *f.* ‖ JUR. Apport *m.*

contributor [-tə*] n. Collaborateur, auteur *m.* (*to*, de). ‖ FIN. Souscripteur *m.*

contributory [-təri] adj. Contribuant, contribu-taire. ‖ JUR. Entrant en ligne de compte ; *contribu-tory cause*, cause accessoire ; *contributory insurance scheme*, sécurité sociale.

— n. FIN. Contributaire *m.*

contrite ['kɔntrait] adj. ECCLES. De contrition (act) ; contrit (person).

contritely [-li] adv. Avec contrition (or) repentir.

contrition Ḻkən'triʃən] n. ECCLES. Contrition *f.*

contrivance [kən'traivəns] n. Invention, combi-naison *f.* (act); ingéniosité *f.*, artifice, esprit (*m.*) d'invention (capacity); combinaison *f.*, plan *m.* (project); procédé *m.*, invention *f.* (practice). ‖ Combine, manigance, machination *f.* (pejorative). ‖ Dispositif, système, engin, machin, truc *m.* (See CONTRAPTION.)

contrive [kən'traiv] v. tr. Inventer, imaginer, concevoir (*to*, de, pour) [a means]. ‖ Arranger, organiser, ménager (an effect). ‖ Machiner, com-biner (pejorative). ‖ TECHN. Inventer (a device).

— v. intr. S'ingénier (*to*, à) [to exercise one's wits]. ‖ Réussir, arriver, parvenir (*to*, à) [to succeed]. ‖ Trouver moyen (*to*, de); s'arranger (*to*, pour) [to manage]. ‖ FAM. S'en tirer, s'en sortir, s'arranger ; se débrouiller (fam.) ; se dépatouiller (pop.).

contriver [-ə*] n. Inventeur *m.*; inventrice *f.* ‖ Combinard, machinateur *m.* (pejorative). ‖ FAM. Débrouillard *s.*

control [kən'troul] n. Domination, autorité, haute main *f.*; pouvoir *m.* (over, sur); *the fire was under control,* l'incendie était circonscrit; *under Russian control,* sous la domination russe, sous la coupe des Russes; *these circumstances are beyond our control,* ces circonstances ne dépendent pas de nous. ‖ Maîtrise *f.*; ascendant, empire *m.*; *his control of the French language,* sa maîtrise de la langue française; *to regain control of oneself,* retrouver la maîtrise de soi (or) le contrôle de ses nerfs, se ressaisir. ‖ Restriction, limitation, contrainte *f.*; *to get rid of controls,* se débarrasser de toutes les restrictions. ‖ Contrôle *m.*; vérification, surveillance *f.*; *administrative control,* contrôle administratif. ‖ FIN. Dirigisme *m.*; *exchange control,* contrôle des changes. ‖ JUR. Réglementation *f.*; *birth control,* limitation des naissances. ‖ TECHN. Commande *f.*; controller *m.* ‖ AVIAT. *Control column,* manche à balai; *control desk, room,* table, cabine des commandes; *control surface,* gouvernail; *control tower,* tour de contrôle; *control wire,* câble de commande; *remote control,* télécommande; *out of control,* désemparé. ‖ MILIT. Contrôle *m.* ‖ RADIO. *Volume control,* réglage de l'intensité sonore; modérateur du son; bouton de puissance. ‖ SPORTS. Contrôle, pointage *m.* ‖ MED. *Control case,* cas témoin. ‖ PHILOS. Esprit contrôleur *m.* (in spiritualism).
— v. tr. (1). Commander, diriger, avoir la haute main sur (to direct). ‖ Contrôler, vérifier (to verify). ‖ FIN. Régler, régir (financial affairs). ‖ FIG. Maîtriser, gouverner, contenir, réprimer.

controllable [-əbl̩] adj. Contrôlable, vérifiable. ‖ Domptable.

controlled [-d] adj. COMM. Dirigé (economy). ‖ FIN. Taxé (price); *sold at controlled price,* vendu à la taxe; *to fix a controlled price for,* taxer.

controller |-ə] n. Contrôleur *m.* (device, person).

controlment [-mənt] n. Contrôle *m.*

controversial [,kɔntrə'və:ʃəl] adj. Controversable.

controversialist [-ʃəlist] n. Controversiste *s.*

controversy [kɔntrəvə:si] n. Controverse, discussion *f.* (see ARGUMENT); *without controversy,* sans contestation, incontestablement. ‖ Dispute, querelle *f.*

controvert [-və:t] v. tr. Controverser, débattre (to discuss). ‖ Contredire, contester, mettre en question (to deny).

controvertible [-və:tibl̩] adj. Controversable, discutable, contestable.

controvertist [-və:tist] n. Controversiste *s.*

contumacious [,kɔntju'meiʃəs] adj. Insubordonné, rebelle, réfractaire. ‖ JUR. Contumace.

contumaciously [-li] adv. Avec opiniâtreté, obstinément.

contumacy ['kɔntjuməsi] n. Insubordination, rébellion *f.* ‖ Opiniâtreté *f.*; entêtement *m.* ‖ JUR. Contumace *f.*

contumelious [,kɔntju'mi:liəs] adj. Injurieux, insultant, outrageant (offensive). ‖ Méprisant, insolemment dédaigneux (contemptuous).

contumeliously [-li] adv. D'une manière outrageante (offensively). ‖ Avec un insolent dédain (contemptuously).

contumely ['kɔntjumili] n. Injure, insolence *f.*; outrage *m.* (offense). ‖ Mépris, dédain insolent *m.* (contemptuousness).

contuse [kən'tju:z] v. tr. MED. Contusionner.

contused [-d] adj. MED. Contus.

contusion [kən'tju:ʒən] n. MED. Contusion, meurtrissure *f.* (See BRUISE).

conular ['kɔnjulə:*] adj. En forme de cône.

conundrum |kə'nʌndrəm] n. Devinette *f.*

conurbation [,kɔnə:'beiʃən] n. GEOGR. Conurbation *f.*

convalesce |,kɔnvə'les] v. intr. MED. Etre ‹ convalescence; *to finish convalescing,* achever de rétablir.

convalescence [-ns] n. MED. Convalescence *f.*

convalescent [-nt] adj. MED. De convalescen (hospital); convalescent (person).
— n. MED. Convalescent *s.*

convection [kən'vekʃən] n. PHYS. Convection
— adj. ELECTR. De convection (current).

convector [-tə*] n. TECHN. Appareil de chauffa (*m.*) par convection.

convene [kən'vi:n] v. tr. Convoquer (an asse bly); assembler (persons). ‖ JUR. Citer (befor devant).
— v. intr. Se rassembler, se réunir, tenir séance.

convener [-ə*] n. Secrétaire convocateur *m.*

convenience [-jəns] n. Convenance, opportuni *f.*; *matter of convenience,* affaire d'à-propos, que tion d'opportunité. ‖ Convenance, utilité *f.*; acco raisonnable *m.*; *marriage of convenience,* maria de convenance. ‖ Convenance, commodité *f.*; *your convenience,* quand vous le pourrez, à lois quand cela vous dérangera le moins; *to meet s.o. convenience,* faire l'affaire de qqn, convenir à qq ‖ Confort, objet pratique (or) de confort *m.*; cor modité *f.*; *a lift* (or) U. S. *an elevator is a gre convenience,* l'ascenseur est une grande commodit *to have every modern convenience,* avoir tout confort moderne. ‖ Commodités *f. pl.* (water-closet *public convenience,* chalet de nécessité, édicule. Pl. Aises *f. pl.*; *to like one's conveniences,* aim son confort. ‖ COMM. *At your earliest convenienc* avec toute la rapidité possible. ‖ CULIN. *Convenien food,* aliment prêt à l'emploi.

convenient [-jənt] adj. Loisible, possible; *if it convenient to you,* si cela ne vous dérange p trop, si cela vous est possible. ‖ Acceptable; *if is convenient to you,* si vous n'y voyez pas d'ob tacle (or) d'inconvénient, si cela vous convient (qq agrée. ‖ Commode (access, hour); pratique (gadge *convenient to hand,* sous la main.

conveniently [-jəntli] adv. Commodément; sa inconvénient.

convent ['kɔnvənt] n. ECCLES. Couvent *m.*

conventicle [-ikl̩] n. Conventicule *m.*

convention [kən'venʃən] n. Convention *f.*; co trat, accord *m.* (contract). ‖ Convention, règle (standard). ‖ Assemblée *f.* (assembly); réunion (meeting). ‖ Convenances *f. pl.*; usages *m.* (decency).

conventional [-ʃnl̩] adj. De convention, conve tionnel. ‖ Classique (weapons).

conventionalism [-ʃnəlizm̩] n. Conformisme, fc malisme *m.*

conventionalist [-ʃnəlist] n. Conformiste, form liste *s.* ‖ Conventionnel *m.* (historically).

conventionality |kən,venʃə'næliti] n. Conve tion, bienséance *f.*; usage *m.* ‖ Caractère (or) cor portement conventionnel *m.* ‖ Banalité, phrase ‹ convention *f.*

conventionalize [kən'venʃnəlaiz] v. tr. Rend conventionnel. ‖ ARTS. Traiter avec banalité (c selon le mode standard.

conventionally [-li] adv. Conventionnellement.

conventionary [-ri] adj. Par convention.
— n. JUR. Locataire (*s.*) de bonne foi.

conventual [kən'ventjuəl] adj., n. ECCLES. Co ventuel *s.*

converge [kən'və:dʒ] v. intr. Converger.
— v. intr. Faire converger.

convergence [-əns], **convergency** [-ənsi] n. Co vergence *f.*

convergent [-ənt], **converging** [-iŋ] adj. Conve gent.

onversable [kən'və:səbl̩] adj. Causeur, sociable, le relation agréable.

onversance ['kɔnvəsn̩s] n. Familiarité f. (with, avec); habitude f. (with, de).

onversant [-nt] adj. Familier, intime (with, avec). ‖ En relations (or) rapports (in, with, avec). ‖ Versé (with, dans); expérimenté, entendu, émérite (with, en); au courant (with, de); compétent (with, en matière de).

onversation [,kɔnvə'seiʃən] n. Conversation f. (talk); to engage s.o. in conversation, to enter into conversation with s.o., engager la conversation avec qqn; to provide a topic of conversation, défrayer a conversation. ‖ Entretien m.; to have a conversation with, s'entretenir avec. ‖ ARTS. Conversation piece, scène d'intérieur. ‖ JUR. Criminal conversation, commerce adultère.

onversational [-əl] adj. De conversation. ‖ Causeur (person). ‖ INFORM. Conversationnel.

onversation(al)ist [-(ə)list] n. Causeur s.

onversazione ['kɔnvə,sætsi'ouni] n. Réunion artistique (or) littéraire f.

onverse [kən'və:s] v. intr. Converser, s'entretenir, causer (about, de; with, avec); parler (about, de; with, à). [See SPEAK].
— ['kɔnvə:s] n. Conversation f. (talk). ‖ Commerce m.; rapports m. pl. (with, avec).

onverse ['kɔnvə:s] adj., n. MATH. Réciproque f. ‖ PHILOS. Converse f.

onversely [-li] adv. En contrepartie; réciproquement, vice versa.

onversion [kən'və:ʃən] n. Conversion, mutation, transformation f. (into, en). ‖ ECCLES., MATH., PHILOS. Conversion f. ‖ FIN. Conversion f.; fraudulent conversion of stocks, lavage des titres.

onvert [kən'və:t] v. tr. Convertir, transformer, changer (into, en). ‖ FIN., MATH., TECHN., CHIM., ECCLES., PHILOS. Convertir (to, à).
— ['kɔnvə:t] n. ECCLES. Converti s.

onverted [-id] adj., n. ECCLES. Converti s. ‖ FIG. To preach to the converted, prêcher un converti.

onverter [-ə*] n. TECHN. Convertisseur m. ‖ RADIO. Commutatrice f.; adaptateur m. ‖ ELECTR. Transformateur m.

onvertibility [kən,və:ti'biliti] n. Convertibilité f.

onvertible [kən'və:tibl] adj. Convertissable (into, en; to, à). ‖ FIN. Convertible. ‖ AUTOM. Décapotable. ‖ GRAMM. Interchangeable (terms).
— n. AUTOM. Voiture décapotable f.

onvertiplane [kən'və:ti,plein] n. AVIAT. Convertible m.

onvex [kən'veks] adj. Convexe.

onvexity [-iti] n. Convexité f.

onvey [kən'vei] v. tr. Transporter, apporter, porter (to carry). ‖ Amener, accompagner, conduire (to lead). ‖ Transmettre, faire connaître, communiquer (to transmit). ‖ Exprimer, rendre, traduire (to express); to convey one's meaning, faire comprendre son idée. ‖ MILIT. Convoyer, escorter. ‖ PHYS. Transmettre. ‖ JUR. Aliéner, céder, transférer (to, à).

onveyance [-əns] n. Transport, convoyage m. (act). ‖ Moyen de transport, véhicule m.; voiture f. (vehicle); public means of conveyance, transports en commun. ‖ Transmission, communication f. (of, de). ‖ Expression, traduction f. (of ideas). ‖ JUR. Cession f.; transfert m.

onveyancer [-ənsə*] n. JUR. Homme (m.) de loi spécialisé dans les affaires de transfert.

onveyancing [-ənsiŋ] n. JUR. Cession (f.) de biens; procédure translative f.

onveyor [-ə*] n. Porteur s. ‖ Voiturier, transporteur, convoyeur m. (carrier). ‖ ELECTR. Conducteur m. ‖ AVIAT. Chariot (m.) de queue. ‖ **Conveyor-belt,** n. TECHN. Bande transporteuse f.; conveyor-belt work, travail à la chaîne.

onvict ['kɔnvikt] n. JUR. Condamné, forçat,

---

convict m.; convict colony, colonie pénitentiaire; convict establishment, bagne; convict prison, maison centrale; former convict, repris de justice.
— [kən'vikt] v. tr. JUR. Déclarer coupable, convaincre (of, de); condamner. ‖ FIG. Convaincre (of, de) [error].

conviction [kən'vikʃən] n. JUR. Condamnation f. ‖ ECCLES. Pl. Convictions, croyances. ‖ FIG. Conviction f.; to carry conviction, emporter la conviction.

convictive [-tiv] adj. Convaincant.

convince [kən'vins] v. tr. Convaincre, persuader (of, de).

convinced [-d] adj. Convaincu, persuadé; to be firmly convinced that, avoir l'intime persuasion (or) la ferme conviction que; to allow oneself to be convinced, se laisser convaincre.

convincement [-mənt] n. Conviction f.

convincible [-ibl] adj. Qu'on peut convaincre.

convincing [-iŋ] adj. Convaincant. (See VALID.) ‖ Prenant, d'une vérité frappante.

convincingly [-iŋli] adv. D'une manière convaincante. ‖ D'une façon prenante (or) saisissante.

convivial [kən'viviəl] adj. De festin, de banquet; convivial evening, soirée passée à banqueter. ‖ Jovial et ami de la table; he is a man of convivial habits, il aime la bonne chère, c'est une bonne fourchette (or) un joyeux vivant. ‖ PHILOS. Convivial.

conviviality [kən,vivi'æliti] n. Jovialité, gaieté à table f.; fait (m.) d'être bon convive. ‖ Pl. Festins et banquets m. pl. ‖ PHILOS. Convivialité f.

convocation [,kɔnvə'keiʃən] n. Convocation f. ‖ Collante f. (fam.) [for an examination]. ‖ Assemblée universitaire f. ‖ ECCLES. Synode m.

convoke [kən'vouk] v. tr. Convoquer.

convolute ['kɔnvəlju:t] adj. BOT. Convoluté.
— n. BOT. Enroulement m.
— v. tr. BOT. S'enrouler autour de.
— v. intr. BOT. S'enrouler.

convoluted [-id] adj. BOT. Convoluté. ‖ MED. Qui décrit des circonvolutions; convoluted tubule, tubule (or) tube contourné. ‖ FIG. Complexe, intriqué.

convolution [,kɔnvə'lju:ʃən] n. Enroulement m. (coiling); tour m., spire f. (coil). ‖ MED. Circonvolution f. (of the brain).

convolve [kən'vɔlv] v. tr. Enrouler.
— v. intr. S'enrouler.

convolvulus [-vjuləs] (pl. **convolvuluses** [-vjuləsiz]) n. BOT. Volubilis, liseron m.

convoy [kən'vɔi] v. tr. MILIT. Escorter. ‖ NAUT. Convoyer.
— ['kɔnvɔi] n. MILIT. Escorte f.; convoi m. ‖ NAUT. Convoi m.

convoyer ['kɔnvɔiə*] n. NAUT. Escorteur, convoyeur m.

convulse [kən'vʌls] v. tr. MED. Convulser. ‖ FIG. Convulsionner, bouleverser. ‖ FAM. Désopiler; to be convulsed with laughter, se tordre de rire.

convulsion [-ʃən] n. MED. Convulsion f. ‖ FIG. Convulsion, agitation, secousse f.; bouleversement m. ‖ FAM. Convulsions of laughter, rire convulsif.

convulsionary [-ʃənəri] n. Convulsionnaire s.

convulsive [-siv] adj. Convulsif.

convulsively [-sivli] adv. Convulsivement.

cony ['kouni] n. ZOOL., COMM. Lapin m.

coo [ku:] v. intr., tr. ZOOL., FAM. Roucouler.
— n. Roucoulement m.

cook [kuk] n. CULIN. Cuisinier s.; first-rate cook, cordon bleu; she is a good cook, elle cuisine bien. ‖ NAUT. Coq m. ‖ FAM. Cuistot m. ‖ **Cook-general,** n. Cuisinière, bonne (f.) à tout faire. ‖ **Cook-house,** n. NAUT. Coquerie f.; MILIT. Cuisine f.; to be on cook-house fatigue, être de soupe. ‖ **Cook-shop,** n. FAM. Gargote f. ‖ **Cook-stove,** n. U. S. CULIN. Cuisinière f. (stove).
— v. tr. CULIN. Faire cuire, cuire, faire préparer.

‖ FAM. Ereinter; *to cook s.o.'s goose*, préparer à qqn un plat de sa façon, régler son compte à qqn. ‖ FAM. Fricoter, cuisiner (accounts). ‖ **To cook up,** FAM. Goupiller, combiner, fricoter.
— v. intr. CULIN. Cuisiner, faire la cuisine (cook); cuire (food). ‖ FAM. *He is cooked,* il est cuit (or) flambé; *his goose is cooked,* il a son compte.

cookbook [-,buk] n. U. S. Livre (m.) de cuisine.

cooker [-ə*] n. CULIN. Cuisinière f. (stove); cuiseur m. (vessel); *pressure cooker,* cocotte-minute. ‖ CULIN. Légume (m.) qui cuit facilement; fruit (m.) à cuire.

cookery [-əri] n. CULIN. Cuisine f. (art, practice). ‖ **Cookery-book,** n. Livre (m.) de cuisine.

cookie [-i] n. CULIN. Pain brioché m. (bun); U. S. gâteau sec m. ‖ U. S. FAM. Gars m. (boy); fille f. (girl).

cooking [iŋ] n. CULIN. Cuisson f. (act); cuisine f. (preparation); *cooking utensils,* batterie de cuisine; *good plain cooking,* U. S. *home cooking,* cuisine bourgeoise; *to do the cooking,* faire la cuisine. ‖ FAM. Cuisine f.; fricotage, tripotage, tripatouillage m. ‖ **Cooking-range** (or) **-stove,** n. Cuisinière f.

cooky [-i] n. FAM. Cuisinière f. (person).

cool [ku:l] adj. Frais m.; fraîche f.; *to go* (or) *get cool,* se rafraîchir, fraîchir; *to leave to get cool,* laisser refroidir. ‖ COMM. « *Keep in a cool place* », « tenir au frais, craint la chaleur ». ‖ SPORTS. *Cool scent,* voie faible. ‖ FIG. Calme, impassible, froid (composed); froid, indifférent, sans cordialité (irresponsive); tiède, sans ardeur (lacking zeal); *keep cool,* ne vous énervez pas; *to be cool with,* battre froid à. ‖ FAM. Culotté, sans gêne; *to be a cool hand* (or) *one,* avoir du culot; n'avoir pas froid aux yeux; ne pas se biler. ‖ FAM. Sans exagération, au bas mot; *she lost a cool thousand pounds,* elle a perdu mille livres tout sec.
— n. Frais m.; fraîcheur f.; *in the cool,* au frais, à la fraîcheur.
— v. tr. Rafraîchir, refroidir. ‖ FIG. Refroidir, doucher.
— v. intr. Se rafraîchir, se refroidir. ‖ FIG. Tomber (anger); se refroidir (friendship). ‖ **To cool down,** FIG. S'apaiser, tomber (anger); se défâcher, se calmer (person). ‖ **To cool off,** FIG. Se refroidir (enthusiasm).

cooler [-ə*] n. Refroidisseur m. (air cooler). ‖ Garde-manger (m.) pour tenir au frais. ‖ FAM. Boisson rafraîchissante f. (drink). ‖ FAM. Douche f. ‖ FAM. U. S. Violon m.; taule f.

coolie ['ku:li] n. Coolie m.

cooling ['ku:liŋ] n. Refroidissement, rafraîchissement m. ‖ TECHN. Réfrigération f.
— adj. Rafraîchissant (drink).

coolish [-iʃ] adj. Frisquet.

coolly [-li] adv. Fraîchement. ‖ FIG. Froidement; avec sang-froid; avec froideur.

coolness [-nis] n. Frais m.; fraîcheur f. ‖ FIG. Froideur f. (chilliness); sang-froid, flegme m. (composure).

coomb [ku:m] n. GEOGR. Combe f.

coon [ku:n] n. ZOOL. Raton laveur m. ‖ FAM. Nègre, moricaud s. ‖ FAM. Type m.

coop [ku:p] n. AGRIC. Mue f. ‖ U. S. FAM. *To fly the coop,* décamper.
— v. tr. **To coop up,** mettre en cage (hens); enfermer, claustrer (persons).

cooper ['ku:pə*] n. Tonnelier m.; *cooper's wood,* merrain. ‖ Marchand de vin m.
— v. tr. Réparer (cask). ‖ **To cooper up,** FAM. Rafistoler, rapetasser.

cooperage [-rid3] n. Tonnellerie f.

cooperate [kou'ɔpə,reit] v. intr. Coopérer (with, avec); contribuer (in, à).

cooperation [kou,ɔpə'reiʃən] n. Coopération f.

cooperative [kou'ɔpərətiv] adj. Coopératif. ‖

U. S. *Cooperative apartment,* appartement en copr▮ priété (or) en colocation.
— n. Coopérative f.

coordinate [kou'ɔ:dinit] adj. Coordonné.
— n. MATH. Coordonnée f. ‖ Pl. COMM. Coordonn▮ m. pl.
— v. tr. [-eit] Coordonner.

coordination [kou,ɔ:di'neiʃən] n. Coord▮ nation f.

coot [ku:t] n. ZOOL. Foulque f. ‖ FAM. *Bald as coot,* chauve comme un genou. ‖ FAM. U. S. *O▮ coot,* vieux bonze.

cop [kɔp] n. TECHN. Cannette f.

cop n. FAM. Flic, sergot m.; *courtesy cop,* motar▮
— v. tr. FAM. Coincer, pincer, choper (s.o.). ‖ FA▮ Ecoper de; *to cop it,* écoper, trinquer; *to g▮ copped,* se faire coincer.

copal ['koupəl] n. Copal m.

coparcenary ['kou'pɑ:sinəri] n. JUR. Indivision

coparcener [-ə*] n. JUR. Cohéritier, indivisaire

copartner ['kou'pɑ:tnə*] n. Coassocié s.

copartnership [-ʃip] n. Coassociation f.

cope [koup] n. ECCLES., TECHN. Chape f. ‖ ARCHI▮ Chaperon m. ‖ FIG. Voûte f. (of heaven); voile ▮ (of night).
— v. tr. ECCLES. Couvrir d'une chape. ‖ ARCHI▮ Chaperonner. ‖ FIG. Envelopper d'un manteau; su▮ monter d'une voûte.

cope v. intr. FAM. Se débrouiller, s'en tirer. ‖ FA▮ Venir à bout (with, de); se mesurer (with, avec▮

copeck ['koupek] n. Kopeck m.

coper ['koupə*] n. Maquignon m. (horse-deale▮

coper n. NAUT. Bateau-bar m.

copernik [ko'pə:nik] n. CHIM. Copernic m.

copier ['kɔpiə*] n. Copiste m. (copyist, imitator▮

copilot ['kou,pailət] n. AVIAT. Copilote m.

coping ['koupiŋ] n. ARCHIT. Larmier m. (of bridge); faîte m. (of a building); chaperon m. (▮ a wall). ‖ **Coping-stone,** n. ARCHIT., FIG. Couro▮ nement m.

copious ['koupjəs] adj. Copieux. (See PLENTIFUL▮ ‖ FIG. Riche, abondant.

copiously [-li] adv. Copieusement.

copiousness [-nis] n. Abondance, profusion f. ‖ FIG. Richesse, ampleur f.

copolymer [kou'pɔlimə*] n. CHIM., TECHN▮ Copolymère m.

copper ['kɔpə*] n. Cuivre rouge m. (metal). ‖ Piè▮ (f.) de billon; sou m. ‖ Couleur cuivre (colour) ‖ TECHN. Chaudron f. ‖ FAM. Gosier m.; *to ha▮ hot coppers,* avoir mal aux cheveux (or) la gueu▮ de bois. ‖ **Copper-coloured,** adj. Cuivré. ‖ **Coppe▮ glance,** n. CHIM. Sulfure cuivreux m. ‖ **Coppe▮ pyrites,** n. CHIM. Chalcopyrite f.
— adj. De cuivre; en cuivre. ‖ Cuivré.
— v. tr. Cuivrer (a metal).

copper ['kɔpə*] n. POP. Flic. (See COP.)

copperas ['kɔpərəs] n. CHIM. Vitriol m.; coupe▮ rose f.

copperhead ['kɔpəhed] n. ZOOL. Trigonocéphal▮ m. (snake).

copperplate ['kɔpəpleit] n. Plaque (f.) de cuivre▮ ‖ ARTS. Gravure en taille-douce f.; *copperpla▮ handwriting,* écriture calligraphiée.

coppersmith [-smiθ] n. Chaudronnier m.

coppery ['kɔpəri] adj. Cuivreux (containing cop▮ per); cuivré (copper-coloured); *to turn copper▮* se cuivrer.

coppice ['kɔpis] n. Taillis, breuil m. (See COPSE▮

copra ['kɔprə] n. Copra m.

coprology [kə'prɔlədʒi] n. Scatologie f.

copse [kɔps] n. Taillis m. (See COPPICE.)
— v. tr. Planter en taillis.

copsy [-i] adj. En taillis.

Copt [kɔpt] n. GEOGR. Copte s. (person).

Coptic [-ik] adj., n. Copte m. (language).

copula ['kɔpjulə] n. GRAMM. Copule f.

opulate [-eit] v. intr. S'accoupler.
opulation [,kɔpju'lei∫ən] n. Copulation ƒ.;
accouplement m.
opulative ['kɔpjulətiv] adj. GRAMM. Copulatif.
opy ['kɔpi] n. Copie, imitation ƒ. ‖ Reproduction,
transcription ƒ. ‖ Copie ƒ.; manuscrit m.; fair copy,
copie au net; rough copy, brouillon. ‖ Double m.;
carbon copy, copie carbone, double; top copy,
fort, original (typed); copy letter book, copie-lettres.
‖ Copie ƒ.; sujet d'article m. (in journalism). ‖
Modèle m. (pattern). ‖ Exemplaire m. (of a book);
livraison ƒ. (of a magazine); numéro m. (of a newspaper). ‖ JUR. Copie ƒ.; certified copy, ampliation;
first authentic copy, grosse exécutoire; to make a
copy of a deed, expédier un acte. ‖ ARTS. Copie.
‖ Copy-book, n. Cahier (m.) d'écriture; FAM. To
blot one's copy-book, entacher sa réputation. ‖
Copy-holder, n. Porte-copie m. ‖ Copy-reader,
n. Lecteur (m.) d'imprimerie. ‖ Copy-writer, n.
Rédacteur publicitaire, rédacteur-concepteur s.
— v. tr. (2). Copier, imiter, reproduire. ‖ Copier,
transcrire.
— v. intr. Copier, faire une copie.
opycat [-kæt] n. FAM. Singe m. (imitateur).
opyist [-ist] n. Copiste s.
opyright [-rait] n. JUR. Copyright m.; propriété
littéraire ƒ.; droit (m.) de reproduction; copyright
reserved, tous droits réservés; out of copyright,
dans le domaine public.
— adj. JUR. Aux droits réservés; placé sous la propriété littéraire.
— v. tr. JUR. Réserver les droits de publication de.
oquelicot ['koukli,kou] n. BOT. Coquelicot m. ‖
Coquelicot m. (colour).
oquet [kɔ'ket] adj. Coquet, flirteur.
— v. intr. (1). Flirter (with, avec) [s.o.]. ‖ Jouer
(with, avec) [an idea].
oquetry ['kɔkitri] n. Coquetterie ƒ.
oquette [kou'ket] n. Coquette ƒ.
oquettish [-i∫] adj. Aguichant, provocant, flirteur, coquet.
oquettishly [-i∫li] adv. Coquettement.
or! [kɔ:*] interj. FAM. Ça alors!, dis donc!
oracle ['kɔrəkḷ] n. NAUT. Coracle m.
oral ['kɔrəl] n. Corail m. ‖ Hochet m. (toy). ‖
ZOOL. Œufs (m. pl.) de homard.
— adj. En corail; de corail (necklace, shoal). ‖
Corail, couleur de corail; corallin (lips). ‖ Coralligène (limestone). ‖ GEOGR. Coral Sea, mer de
Corail.
oralline [-ain] adj. Corallin, corail (red). ‖ Corallien.
— n. Coralline ƒ.
or anglais ['kɔ:r'ɑ:ɳglei] n. MUS. Cor anglais m.
orbel ['kɔ:bəl] n. ARCHIT. Console ƒ.; corbeau
m. ‖ Corbel-table, n. Encorbellement m.
— v. tr. (1). ARCHIT. Soutenir par une console.
— v. intr. ARCHIT. Former un encorbellement.
orbie ['kɔ:bi] n. ZOOL. Corbeau m. ‖ Corbie-
gable, n. ARCHIT. Pignon à redans m.
ord [kɔ:d] n. Corde ƒ. (rope). ‖ Côte ƒ. (on a
fabric). ‖ Velours côtelé m. (corduroy). ‖ Pl. Pantalon de velours m. (trousers). ‖ Corde ƒ. (measure
of wood). ‖ ELECTR. Fil m. ‖ MED. Spinal cord,
moelle épinière; umbilical cord, cordon ombilical;
vocal cord, corde vocale.
— v. tr. Encorder, ligoter, lier. ‖ Corder (wood).
ordage [-idʒ] n. NAUT. Cordages m. pl.
orded [-id] adj. Ligoté, encordé (person). ‖ Perlé
(cotton); côtelé (velvet).
ordelier [,kɔ:di'liə*] n. Cordelier m.
ordial ['kɔ:diəl] adj., n. Cordial m.
ordiality [,kɔ:di'æliti] n. Cordialité ƒ.
ordially ['kɔ:diəli] adv. Cordialement.
ordillera [kɔ:di'ljɛərə] n. GEOGR. Cordillère ƒ.
ordite ['kɔ:dait] n. MILIT. Cordite ƒ.
ordon ['kɔ:dən] n. Cordon m.; cordelière ƒ. ‖

Cordon m. (decoration). ‖ ARCHIT., MILIT. Cordon.
‖ MED. Sanitary cordon, cordon sanitaire. ‖ Cordon-bleu, n. CULIN. Cordon-bleu m.
— v. tr. To cordon off, établir un cordon autour.
Cordova ['kɔ:dəvə] n. GEOGR. Cordoue ƒ.
Cordovan [-ən] n. Cuir (m.) de Cordoue.
— adj. De Cordoue.
corduroy ['kɔ:djuroi] n. Velours côtelé m. ‖ Pl.
Pantalon en velours côtelé m.
— adj. En velours côtelé. ‖ U. S. En rondins,
fasciné (road).
— v. tr. U. S. Bâtir en rondins (a road).
core [kɔ:] n. Cœur m. (of a mass). ‖ Trognon,
cœur m. (of an apple). ‖ ELECTR. Noyau m. ‖ NAUT.
Mèche ƒ. (of rope). ‖ MED. Bourbillon m. (of a
boil). ‖ TECHN. Centre,. noyau m. (of a mould).
‖ FIG. Cœur, fond, tréfonds m.; rotten to the core,
pourri jusqu'à la moelle; to get to the core of,
approfondir, creuser. ‖ Core-maker, n. TECHN.
Noyauteur m.
— v. tr. CULIN. Enlever le cœur de, vider, évider
(a fruit). ‖ To core out, évider, noyauter.
coreligionist ['kouri'lidʒənist] n. ECCLES. Coreligionnaire s.
corf [kɔ:f] n. Benne ƒ. (in mines). ‖ Banneton m.
(in fishing).
corgi ['kɔ:gi] n. ZOOL. (Welsh) corgi, welsh corgi.
coriaceous [,kɔri'ei∫əs] adj. Coriace.
coriander [,kɔri'ændə*] n. Coriandre ƒ.
Corinthian [-iən] adj., s. GEOGR. Corinthien s.
— n. Sportif amateur m.
corium ['kɔ:riəm] n. MED. Corion m.
cork [kɔ:k] n. Liège m. ‖ Bouchon m.; to draw
the cork of a bottle, déboucher une bouteille. ‖
Cork-cutter, n. Bouchonnier m. ‖ Cork-drawer,
n. Tire-bouchon m. ‖ Cork-leg, n. MED. Jambe
artificielle ƒ. ‖ Cork-oak, n. BOT. Chêne-liège m.
‖ Cork-penny, n. Bouchon m. (game) ‖ Cork-
tipped, adj. A bout de liège (cigarette).
— v. tr. Boucher (a bottle). ‖ Noircir au bouchon
(one's face).
corkage ['kɔ:kidʒ] n. Droit (m.) de bouchon.
corked [-t] adj. Bouché (bottle); qui a goût de
bouchon (wine). ‖ Noirci au bouchon (face). ‖
U. S. POP. Flapi, moulu.
corker [-ə*] n. FAM. Craque ƒ. (lie). ‖ FAM. Argument (m.) massue. (See CHOKER.) ‖ FAM. Numéro,
type formidable m.; he's a corker, il est impayable.
corkscrew [-skru:] n. Tire-bouchon m.
— adj. En tire-bouchon (curl); en colimaçon (staircase). ‖ AVIAT. Corkscrew spin, descente en tire-
bouchon.
— v. intr. Tire-bouchonner (curl); tourner en colimaçon (staircase); vriller (wire).
oorky [-i] adj. De liège.
corm [kɔ:m] n. BOT. Bulbe m.
cormorant ['kɔ:mərənt] n. ZOOL. Cormoran m.
corn [kɔ:n] n. BOT. Grain m. (of pepper, wheat);
blé m. (wheat); avoine ƒ. (oats); céréale ƒ.; indian
corn, maïs; feed of corn, picotin. ‖ U. S. Maïs m.
(maize). ‖ FAM. U. S. Eau-de-vie (ƒ.) de grain (corn
whisky). ‖ FAM. U. S. Salade ƒ., baratin m. ‖ Corn
bread (or) pone, n. U. S. Pain de maïs m. ‖ Corn-
chandler, n. Grainetier m. ‖ Corn-cob, n. Epi de
maïs m. ‖ Corn-colour, n. Couleur paille (or) maïs ƒ.
‖ Corn-factor, n. Minotier m. ‖ Corn-fed, adj. De
grain (pullet); FAM. Dodu, replet. ‖ Corn-flour, n.
Farine (ƒ.) de céréales (or) de blé; U. S. farine de
maïs. ‖ Corn-flower, n. BOT. Bluet m. ‖ Cornmeal, n. CULIN. U. S. Farine (ƒ.) de maïs. ‖ Corn-
salad, n. AGRIC., CULIN. Mâche, doucette ƒ. ‖
Corn silk, n. U. S. Barbe (ƒ.) de maïs. ‖ Corn
stalk, n. U. S. Tige (ƒ.) de maïs. ‖ Corn-trade,
n. COMM. Commerce (m.) des céréales. ‖ Corn
whisky, n. Eau-de-vie (ƒ.) de grain.
— v. tr. Granuler, réduire en grains. ‖ AGRIC.
Nourrir de grain. ‖ CULIN. Saler (meat).

corn n. MED. Cor *m*. (on the toes); *soft corn*, œil-de-perdrix. ‖ FAM. *To tread on s.o.'s corns*, marcher sur les pieds de qqn. ‖ **Corn-killer** (or) **-plaster**, n. MED. Coricide *m*. ‖

cornea ['kɔ:niə] n. MED. Cornée *f*.

corned [kɔ:nd] adj. CULIN. Salé, en conserve, en boîte (beef).

cornel ['kɔ:n̩] n. BOT. Cornouiller *m*. (tree). ‖ **Cornel-berry**, n. BOT. Cornouille *f*. (dogberry).

cornelian [kɔ:'ni:ljən] n. Cornaline *f*.

corneous ['kɔ:niəs] adj. Corné. (See HORNY.)

corner ['kɔ:nə*] n. Coin *m*. (of an angle, a book); angle, coin *m*. (of a house, street); *chimney corner*, coin du feu; *the corner house*, la maison du coin; *to cut a corner*, prendre un raccourci; *to put a child in the corner*, mettre un enfant au coin. ‖ Coin *m*.; cachette *f*.; *done in a corner*, fait en sous-main. ‖ Encoignure *f*.; cabinet *m*. (piece of furniture); *corner piece*, meuble de coin. ‖ MED. Coin *m*. (of the eye, mouth). ‖ CH. DE F. Coin *m*.; *corner seat*, place de coin. ‖ AUTOM. *To cut a corner close*, prendre un virage à la corde. ‖ FIN. Accaparement *m*.; *to make a corner in*, mettre la main sur. ‖ FIG. Mauvais pas *m*.; *driven into a corner*, poussé dans ses retranchements; *to turn the corner*, sortir d'une impasse, dépasser le cap critique. ‖ FAM. U. S. *To cut corners*, rogner les dépenses; bâcler un travail. ‖ **Corner-stone**, n. ARCHIT., FIG. Pierre angulaire *f*.; U. S. première pierre *f*. (laid at a formal ceremony). ‖ **Corner-tile**, n. ARCHIT. Tuile cornière *f*.
— v. tr. Mettre des coins à. ‖ Mettre dans un coin. ‖ FIN., COMM. Accaparer. ‖ FIG. Mettre au pied du mur, pousser dans ses retranchements; coincer.
— v. intr. Former un coin. ‖ Etre placé de coin. ‖ FIN., COMM. Se livrer à l'accaparement (*in*, de).

cornered [-d] adj. A coins. ‖ A angles. ‖ FIG. Acculé.

cornet ['kɔ:nit] n. MUS. Cornet à pistons *m*. ‖ TECHN. Cornet *m*. ‖ ECCLES. Cornette *f*. ‖ MILIT. Cornette *m*.

cornetist [-ist] n. MUS. Cornettiste *m*.

cornflakes ['kɔ:nfleiks] n. pl. CULIN. Paillettes (*f. pl.*) de maïs.

cornice ['kɔ:nis] n. ARCHIT. Corniche *f*.

Cornish ['kɔ:niʃ] adj. GEOGR. De Cornouailles.
— n. Cornique *m*. (language).

cornstarch ['kɔ:n,stɑ:tʃ] n. U. S. Farine (*f*.) de maïs.

cornucopia [,kɔ:nju'koupjə] n. Corne d'abondance *f*. ‖ FIG. Surabondance *f*.

cornuted [kɔ:'nju:tid] adj. Cornu. ‖ FAM. Cornard (cuckolded).

Cornwall ['kɔ:nwəl] n. GEOGR. Cornouaille *f*.

corny ['kɔ:ni] adj. AGRIC. Producteur de blé (or) U. S. de maïs. ‖ FAM. Racorni. ‖ U. S. Rebattu.

corny adj. MED. De cor; ayant des cors (on the feet).

corolla [kə'rɔlə] n. BOT. Corolle *f*.

corollary [kə'rɔləri] n. Corollaire *m*.

corona [kə'rounə] (pl. **coronae** [-i:]) n. Corona *m*. (cigar). ‖ ECCLES. Lustre rond *m*. (chandelier). ‖ MED. Sommet *m*. (of a skull); couronne *f*. (of a tooth). ‖ ARCHIT. Larmier *m*. (of a cornice). ‖ ASTRON. Couronne *f*. (during an eclipse); halo *m*. (of moon, sun). ‖ BOT. Couronne *f*. ‖ ELECTR. Couronne lumineuse *f*.

coronal ['kɔrən̩] n. Diadème *m*. (crown). ‖ Guirlande *f*. (wreath).

coronal [kə'roun̩] adj. MED., ASTRON. Coronal.

coronary ['kɔrənəri] adj., n. MED. Coronaire *f*.

coronation [,kɔrə'neiʃən] n. Couronnement, sacre *m*. (of a sovereign); *coronation day*, jour du couronnement (or) *coronation oath*, serment du sacre.

coroner ['kɔrənə*] n. JUR. Coroner *m*., officier (*m*.) de justice chargé d'enquêter sur les cas de mort suspecte.

coronet ['kɔrənit] n. Diadème *m*. (for women). Tortil *m*. (of a baron); couronne *f*. (of an earl, duke, a marquis).

coroneted [-id] adj. Portant la couronne de pair

corporal ['kɔ:pərəl] n. ECCLES. Corporal *m*.

corporal n. MILIT. Caporal, brigadier *m*.; *mess corporal*, caporal d'ordinaire. ‖ NAUT. *Ship's cor poral*, caporal d'armes. ‖ AVIAT. Caporal-chef *m* ‖ COMM. Caporal *m*. (tobacco).

corporal adj. Corporel. (See BODILY.) ‖ JUR. Person nel, individuel.

corporality [,kɔ:pə'ræliti] n. Corporéité *f*. ‖ P Besoins physiques (or) matériels *m. pl*.

corporally ['kɔ:pərəli] adv. Corporellement.

corporate [-it] adj. JUR. Constitué (body); constitu en société (business); municipal (land, office); *cor porate name*, raison sociale; *corporate town*, mun cipalité; *status of body corporate*, personnalit civile (or) morale.

corporately [-itli] adv. En corps, en groupe.

corporation [,kɔ:pə'reiʃən] n. Corporation, sociét *f*.; groupement corporatif *m*.; *municipal corpora tion*, municipalité, conseil municipal; *public cor poration*, régie. ‖ U. S. Organisme *m*. ‖ FAM Bedaine, panse, rotondité *f*. (abdomen).

corporatism ['kɔ:pərətizm] n. Corporatisme *m*.

corporative [-tiv] adj. De corporation, corporati

corporator [-tə*] n. Membre (*m*.) d'une corpora tion. ‖ Conseiller municipal *m*.

corporeal [kɔ:'pɔ:riəl] adj. Corporel. (See COR PORAL.) ‖ Matériel; physique; tangible. ‖ JUR *Corporeal property*, biens réels et tangibles.

corporeality [kɔ:,pɔ:ri'æliti] n. Matérialité *f*.

corporeity [,kɔ:pɔ:'ri:iti] n. Corporéité *f*. ‖ Person nalité physique *f*.

corposant ['kɔ:pəznt] n. NAUT. Feu Saint-Elme *m*

corps [kɔ:] (pl. **corps** [kɔ:z]) n. MILIT. Corps *m* (formation); *officer reserve corps*, cadre des off ciers de réserve; *Veterinary Corps*, service vétéri naire; *volunteer corps*, commando; *corps d'élite* corps d'élite. ‖ THEATR. *Corps de ballet*, corps d ballet.

corpse ['kɔ:ps] n. Cadavre, corps *m*. ‖ SPORTS Toquard *m*.

corpsman ['kɔ:mən] (pl. **corpsmen**) n. MED MILIT. U. S. Ambulancier *m*.

corpulence ['kɔ:pjuləns], **corpulency** [-i] n. Co pulence *f*.

corpulent [-ənt] adj. Corpulent, puissant.

corpus ['kɔ:pəs] n. Corpus, recueil *m*. ‖ JUR. *Cor pus delicti*, corps du délit. ‖ FIN. Capital *m*. ECCLES. *Corpus Christi*, Fête-Dieu.

corpuscle ['kɔ:pʌs̩], **corpuscule** [kɔ:'pʌskju:l n. Corpuscule *m*. ‖ PHYS. Molécule *f*. ‖ MED. Glo bule *m*. ‖ ELECTR. Electron *m*.

corpuscular [kɔ:'pʌskjulə*] adj. PHYS. Molécu laire. ‖ MED. Corpusculaire.

corral [kə'ræl] n. Corral *m*.
— v. tr. Enfermer dans un corral. ‖ Clôturer.

correct [kə'rekt] v. tr. Corriger, améliorer (t amend). ‖ Corriger, redresser, rectifier (to rectify) ‖ Corriger, guérir (*of*, de) [to wean]. ‖ Corriger châtier, battre (to beat). ‖ PHYS., CHIM., ASTRON Corriger.
— adj. Correct (behaviour, person); exact (state ment); bon (taste); juste (weight).

corrected [-id] adj. Corrigé. ‖ PHYS. *Corrected fo temperature*, ramené aux conditions normales d température.

correction [kə'rekʃən] n. Correction, rectificatio *f*.; *under correction*, sauf erreur. ‖ Correction émendation *f*. ‖ Correction *f*.; châtiment corpore *m*. (chastisement). ‖ PHYS., MATH. Correction *f*. JUR. *House of correction*, maison de redressemen (or) de correction.

correctional [-̩] adj. Correctionnel.

corrective [kə'rektiv] adj., n. Correctif *m.* (*of*, à, de).

correctly [-li] adv. Correctement ; avec correction.

correctness [-nis] n. Correction, convenance *f.* (of behaviour) ; rectitude *f.* (of judgment) ; exactitude, correction, justesse *f.* (of a report) ; correction (of style). ‖ Mus. Justesse *f.* (of ear).

corrector [-ə*] n. Correcteur *m.; correctrice *f.* ‖ Corrigeur *m.*

correlate ['kɔrileit] n. Corrélatif *m.*
— v. tr. Mettre en corrélation (*with*, avec).
— v. intr. Se trouver en corrélation (*with*, avec).

correlation [kɔri'leiʃən] n. Corrélation *f.*

correlative [kə'relətiv] adj., n. Corrélatif *m.*

correlatively [-li] adv. Corrélativement.

correspond [,kɔris'pɔnd] v. intr. Correspondre, communiquer (*with*, avec) ; écrire (*with*, à). ‖ Correspondre, répondre ; être conforme (*to*, à). ‖ S'accorder, être d'accord (*with*, avec).

correspondence [-əns] n. Correspondance *f.; *courrier *m.* (mail). ‖ Correspondance, corrélation *f.; *accord *m.* (*between*, entre ; *to, with*, avec). ‖ Milit. Intelligence *f.* (with the enemy). ‖ **Correspondence-clerk**, n. Comm. Correspondancier *s.* ‖ **Correspondence-course**, n. Cours (*m.*) par correspondance.

correspondent [-ənt] n. Correspondant *m.; *military correspondent*, correspondant de guerre, rédacteur militaire.
— adj. Correspondant (*to, with*, à).

corresponding [-iŋ] adj. Correspondant.

corridor ['kɔridɔ:*] n. Corridor, passage, couloir *m.* ‖ Ch. de f., Geogr. Couloir *m.*

corrie ['kɔri] n. Geogr. Cirque *m.* (in Scotland).

corrigendum [kɔri'dʒendəm] (pl. **corrigenda** [-ə]) n. Erratum *m.* (pl. errata).

corrigible ['kɔridʒibl] adj. Corrigible.

corroborant [kə'rɔbərənt] adj. Corroborant. ‖ Med. Tonique, fortifiant. (See invigorating.)
— n. Fait corroborant *m.* ‖ Med. Tonique *m.*

corroborate [-eit] v. tr. Corroborer.

corroboration [kə,rɔbə'reiʃən] n. Corroboration *f.; in corroboration of*, à l'appui de.

corroborative [kə'rɔbərətiv], **corroboratory** [-əri] adj. Corroboratif, corroborant.

corroborator [kə'rɔbəréitə*] n. Jur. Témoin à l'appui *m.*

corrode [kə'roud] v. tr. Corroder.
— v. intr. Se corroder.

corrosion [kə'rouʒən] n. Corrosion *f.*

corrosive [-siv] adj., n. Corrosif *m.*

corrosiveness [-sivnis] n. Corrosivité *f.*

corrugate ['kɔrugeit] v. tr. Onduler (cardboard, iron) ; canneler, strier (glass) ; gaufrer (paper) ; plisser, rider (a surface).
— v. intr. Se plisser, se rider ; onduler.

corrugated [-id] adj. Cannelé (mirror) ; gaufré (paper) ; *corrugated iron*, tôle ondulée.

corrugation [,kɔru'geiʃən] n. Plissement *m.; *ondulation *f.*

corrupt [kə'rʌpt] adj. Corrompu (language, morals, person, text) ; *corrupt practices*, corruptions électorales, tractations louches ; trafic d'influence.
— v. tr. Corrompre (language, morals, persons). ‖ Jur. Corrompre, acheter, suborner, soudoyer. (See bribe.)
— v. intr. Se corrompre.

corrupter [-ə*] n. Corrupteur *m.; corruptrice *f.*

corruptibility [kə,rʌpti'biliti] n. Corruptibilité *f.*

corruptible [kə'rʌptibl] adj. Corruptible.

corrupting [-iŋ] adj. Corrupteur *m.; corruptrice *f.*

corruption [kə'rʌpʃən] n. Corruption, putréfaction *f.* (of meat). ‖ Corruption, altération *f.* (of a language, text) ; corruption, dépravation *f.* (of morals, persons). ‖ Jur. Corruption *f.; corruption of blood*, perte des droits civils.

corruptly [kə'rʌptli] adv. Par corruption.

corruptness [-nis] n. Vénalité *f.*

corsage [kɔ:'sɑ:ʒ] ['kɔ:sədʒ] n. Corsage *m.* (bodice). ‖ U. S. Garniture (or) fleur (*f.*) de corsage.

corsair ['kɔ:sɛə*] n. Naut. Corsaire *m.*

corselet ['kɔ:slit] n. Gaine *f.* (undergarment). ‖ † Corselet *m.* (armour). ‖ Zool. Corselet *m.*

corset ['kɔ:sit] n. Corset *m.* (See stays.)

Corsica ['kɔ:sikə] n. Geogr. Corse *f.*

Corsican [-ən] n. Geogr. Corse *s.*

cortège [kɔ:'teiʒ] n. Cortège ; cortège funéraire *m.*

cortex ['kɔ:teks] (pl. **cortices** ['kɔ:tisi:z]) n. Bot. Ecorce *f.* (of a tree). ‖ Med. Substance corticale *f.*

cortical ['kɔ:tikəl] adj. Bot., Med. Cortical.

cortin(e) ['kɔ:tin] n. Med. Cortine *f.*

cortisone ['kɔ:tisoun] n. Med. Cortisone *f.*

corundum [kə'rʌndəm] n. Corindon *m.*

coruscant [kə'rʌskənt] adj. Scintillant.

coruscate ['kɔrəskeit] v. intr. Scintiller. (See sparkle.)

coruscation [,kɔrəs'keiʃən] n. Scintillement *m.* ‖ Astron. Coruscation *f.* ‖ Fig. Facettes *f. pl.; *brillant *m.* (of wit).

corvette [kɔ:'vet] n. Naut. Corvette *f.* (See sloop.)

corvine ['kɔ:vain] adj. De corbeau.

coryphaeus ['kɔri'fi:əs] n. † Coryphée *m.*

coryphee [,kɔri'fi:] n. Theatr. Coryphée *m.*

coryza [kə'raizə] n. Med. Coryza *m.*

cos [kɔs] n. Agric. Romaine *f.* (lettuce).

cosecant ['kou'si:kənt] n. Math. Cosécante *f.*

cosh [kɔʃ] n. Gourdin *m.; trique *f.*
— v. tr. Matraquer.

cosher [-ə*] v. tr. Choyer, dorloter.

cosily ['kouzili] adv. Douillettement ; confortablement ; à l'aise.

cosine ['kousain] n. Math. Cosinus *m.*

cosmetic [kɔz'metik] n. Cosmétique *m.* ‖ Pl. Produits (*m. pl.*) de beauté.

cosmetician [,kɔzmə'tiʃən] n. Vendeur (*m.*) de produits de beauté ; esthéticien *s.*

cosmic ['kɔzmik] adj. Cosmique.

cosmogonic [,kɔzmo'gɔnik] adj. Cosmogonique.

cosmogony [kɔz'mɔgəni] n. Philos. Cosmogonie *f.*

cosmographer [kɔz'mɔgrəfə*] n. Cosmographe *s.*

cosmographic [,kɔzmə'græfik] adj. Cosmographique.

cosmography [kɔz'mɔgrəfi] n. Cosmographie *f.*

cosmological [,kɔzmo'lɔdʒikəl] adj. Cosmologique.

cosmology [kɔz'mɔlədʒi] n. Cosmologie *f.*

cosmonaut ['kɔzmano:t] s. Cosmonaute *s.*

cosmopolitan [,kɔzmo'pɔlitən] adj., n. Cosmopolite *s.*

cosmopolitanism [-izm] n. Cosmopolitisme *m.*

cosmos ['kɔzmɔs] n. Cosmos *m.*

Cossack ['kɔsæk] n. Cosaque *m.* ‖ Pl. Pantalon bouffant *m.*

cosset ['kɔsit] n. Zool. Agneau favori élevé au biberon *m.* ‖ U. S. Favori ; chouchou *m.*
— v. tr. Fam. Chouchouter, choyer, dorloter. (See cosher.)

cost [kɔst] n. Prix, coût *m.; cost price*, prix coûtant. ‖ Frais *m. pl.; cost free*, sans frais, gratuit. ‖ Jur. Dépens *m. pl.* ‖ Fig. Prix ; *at all costs, at any cost*, à tout prix ; *at small cost*, à bon compte ; *to count the cost*, évaluer les risques. ‖ Fig. Dépens *m. pl.; to s.o.'s cost*, aux dépens de qqn. ‖ **Cost-book**, n. Fin. Livre (*m.*) des charges. ‖ **Cost-effective**, adj. Rentable. ‖ **Cost-plus**, n. Comm. Evaluation (*f.*) au prix coûtant augmenté d'un bénéfice raisonnable.
— v. intr. (40). Coûter ; *it costs the earth*, cela coûte les yeux de la tête. ‖ Fig. Coûter ; *it costs me an effort*, cela me coûte ; *to cost s.o. time and effort*, coûter (or) demander à qqn du temps et des efforts.
— v. tr. Comm. Evaluer le prix de.

costal ['kɔstl] adj. MED. Costal.

costard ['kɔstəd] n. AGRIC. Pomme f. ‖ FAM. Caboche f. (head).

Costa Rica ['kɔstə'riːkə] n. GEOGR. Costa Rica m.

Costa Rican [-ən] adj., s. GEOGR. Costaricain adj., s.

costate ['kɔsteit] adj. A côtes.

coster ['kɔstə*], **costermonger** [-,mʌŋgə*] n. COMM. Marchand (s.) des quatre-saisons (see BARROW-BOY); coster's cart, petite voiture.

costive ['kɔstiv] adj. MED. Constipé. ‖ ARTS. Au travail difficile. ‖ FAM. Serré (niggardly).

costiveness [-nis] n. MED. Constipation f. ‖ ARTS. Lenteur (f.) au travail. ‖ FAM. Lésinerie f.

costliness ['kɔstlinis] n. Cherté f.; prix élevé m. ‖ Somptuosité f.

costly [-li] adj. Coûteux, onéreux. ‖ Somptueux, riche, précieux.

costume ['kɔstjum] n. Costume m.; riding costume, costume de cheval. ‖ THEATR. Costume m.; costume jewellery, bijoux en toc.
— [kɔs'tjuːm] v. tr. Costumer.

costumier [kɔs'tjuːmiə*] n. Costumier m.

cosy ['kouzi] adj. Confortable, douillet (see COMFORTABLE); cosy little house, nid; it's cosy here, on se sent bien ici. ‖ A son aise, confortablement installé (person).
— n. Causeuse f. (piece of furniture). ‖ Couvre-théière m. (tea-cosy).

cot [kɔt] n. Lit d'enfant; petit lit; lit de camp (ou) de camping m.; couchette f. ‖ NAUT. Cadre m. ‖ **cot-case**, n. Malade alité s. ‖ **Cot-death**, n. Décès (m.) brutal de nourrisson.

cot n. Abri m. (shelter). ‖ Cahute, cabane, chaumière f. (cottage). ‖ MED. Doigt protecteur m. (for hurt finger).

cotangent ['kou'tændʒənt] n. MATH. Cotangente f.

cote [kout] n. AGRIC. Abri m.

coterie ['koutəri] n. Coterie f.; club des partisans m.

cothurnus [kə'θəːnəs] (pl. **cothurni** [-ai]) n. Cothurne m. (buskin).

cotillion [ko'tiljən], **cotillon** [kɔti'jõ] n. MUS. Cotillon m.

cottage ['kɔtidʒ] n. Chaumière f.; cottage industry, artisanat; travail à domicile. ‖ Villa f.; cottage m. ‖ MUS. Droit (piano). ‖ CULIN. De maison, blanc (cheese); cottage loaf, pain de ménage. ‖ AGRIC. Cottage farming, petite culture. ‖ MED. Cottage hospital, petit hôpital rural.

cottager [-ə*] n. AGRIC. Agriculteur m.

cottar, cotter ['kɔtə*] n. † Tenancier m.

cotter ['kɔtə*] n. TECHN. Clavette f. ‖ **Cotter-pin**, n. TECHN. Goupille f.

cotton ['kɔtn] n. Coton m. (material, thread). ‖ Cotonnade f. (fabric); printed cotton, percale imprimée, indienne. ‖ BOT. Cotonnier m. ‖ MED. Absorbent cotton, coton hydrophile. ‖ **Cotton-batting**, n. U. S. Nappe (f.) de coton. ‖ **Cotton-cake**, n. AGRIC. Tourteau m. ‖ **Cotton-flannel**, n. Flanelle coton f. ‖ **Cotton-gin**, n. TECHN. Egreneuse f. (machine). ‖ **Cotton-mill**, n. Cotonnerie, filature (f.) de coton. ‖ **Cotton-plant**, n. BOT. Cotonnier m. ‖ **Cotton-seed**, n. BOT. Graine (f.) de coton; cottonseed oil, huile de coton. ‖ **Cotton-velvet**, n. Velours de coton m. ‖ **Cotton-wool**, n. Ouate f.; MED. Absorbent cotton-wool, coton hydrophile; FAM. To bring up in cotton-wool, élever dans du coton (a child). ‖ **Cotton-worker**, n. Cotonnier m.
— adj. De coton; cotonnier.
— v. intr. FAM. Sympathiser (with, avec). ‖ To **cotton on** (or) U. S. **up to**, FAM. Etre attiré par; I don't cotton on to your plan, votre projet ne me

dit pas grand-chose; we cotton on to each other, entre nous ça colle.

cottony [-i] adj. Cotonneux.

cotyledon [,kɔti'liːdən] n. BOT. Cotylédon m.

cotyledonous [-əs] adj. BOT. Cotylédoné.

couch [kautʃ] n. Couche f.; lit m. (bed). ‖ Divan, sofa m. ‖ Lit (m.) d'orge (in brewing). ‖ **Couch-grass**, n. BOT. Chiendent m.
— v. tr. Coucher (on, sur). ‖ SPORTS. Coucher, mettre en arrêt (a lance). ‖ MED. Abaisser (a cataract). ‖ FIG. Rédiger; coucher (in writing). ‖ FIG. Dissimuler.
— v. intr. Se coucher, gîter (animals). ‖ Se tapir, s'aplatir (dog; person). ‖ S'entasser (leaves). ‖ S'embusquer (look-out).

couchant ['kautʃænt] adj. BLAS. Couchant.

couchette [kuːˈʃet] n. CH. DE F. Couchette f.

cougar ['kuːgə*] n. ZOOL. Puma m.

cough [kɔf] n. MED. Toux f. ‖ TECHN. Hoquet m.; the engine gave a few sputtering coughs, le moteur hoqueta à plusieurs reprises. ‖ **Cough-drop** (or) **-lozenge**, n. MED. Pastille de pâte pectorale f. ‖ **Cough mixture**, n. MED. Sirop (m.) contre la toux.
— v. intr. MED. Tousser.
— v. tr. To **cough out**, cracher en toussant. ‖ To **cough up**, MED. Cracher (blood); expectorer (phlegm); FAM. Cracher au bassinet, casquer; cough it up!, alors siffle-le !

could [kud]. See CAN.

coulomb ['kuləm] n. ELECTR. Coulomb m.

coulter ['koultə*] n. AGRIC. Coutre m.

council ['kaunsil] n. Conseil m.; assemblée f.; Council of State, Conseil d'Etat; County Council, conseil général. ‖ MILIT. Air, Army Council, Conseil supérieur de l'Air, de la Guerre; Allied War Council, Conseil supérieur interallié. ‖ ECCLES. Concile m.; parish council, conseil de fabrique. ‖ **Council-board**, n. Table (f.) du conseil; Conseil m. ‖ **Council-chamber**, n. Chambre (f.) du conseil. ‖ **Council flat**, n. H. L. M. m. (or) f. ‖ **Council house**, n. Pavillon (m.) loué par la mairie.

councillor [-ə*] n. Conseiller s.; membre (m.) d'un conseil.

councilman [-mən] (pl. **councilmen**) n. U. S. Conseiller municipal m.

counsel ['kaunsəl] n. Conseil, avis m.; to take counsel with, demander conseil à, prendre conseil de, consulter; to take counsel together, se consulter. ‖ Projet m.; to keep one's own counsel, garder ses idées pour soi, ne pas dévoiler ses intentions. ‖ JUR. Avocat-conseil, avocat, défenseur m.; to be counsel for, plaider pour.
— v. tr. Conseiller, donner un avis (or) un conseil à (s.o.); conseiller, préconiser (sth.).

counsellor [-ə*] n. Conseiller m. (adviser). ‖ JUR. Conseiller d'ambassade. ‖ **Counsellor-at-law**, n. JUR. Avocat-conseil m. (in Ireland).

count [kaunt] n. Compte, calcul m. (reckoning). ‖ Montant, compte, total m. (sum). ‖ JUR. Chef (m.) d'accusation. ‖ **Count-down**, n. Décompte à rebours m. ‖ **Count-out**, n. JUR. Ajournement m. (in politics); SPORTS. Compte m. (in boxing).
— v. tr. Compter, calculer, dénombrer (to reckon); mistakes don't count, erreur n'est pas compte. ‖ Compter, inclure dans un compte (to include). ‖ FIG. Compter (or) tenir pour, considérer comme; to count oneself happy, se juger (or) s'estimer heureux. ‖ To **count in**, inclure dans un compte, comprendre, englober. ‖ To **count off**, séparer en comptant. ‖ To **count out**, compter un à un; JUR. ajourner (the House); SPORTS. Eliminer (a player); to be counted out, aller à terre pour le compte (in boxing). ‖ To **count up**, totaliser, additionner, compter.
— v. intr. Compter (to name numbers) [up to, jusqu'à]. ‖ Compter, entrer en ligne de compte.

être compris (or) inclus, figurer (*among*, au nombre de) [to be included]. ‖ Compter, dater ; *counting from tomorrow*, à dater de demain. ‖ Compter, avoir de la valeur (or) de l'importance ; *that doesn't count*, ça ne compte pas ; *to count as three*, compter pour trois. ‖ Compter, faire fond (*on*, sur) ; se fier (*on*, à). [See RELY.]

count [kaunt] n. Comte *m.* (foreign title).

countenance ['kautinəns] n. Air *m.* ; expression, mine, figure *f.* ; *sad countenance*, triste mine ; *to change countenance*, changer de visage ; *to keep one's countenance*, garder son sérieux. ‖ Contenance *f.* (bearing) ; *to keep oneself in countenance*, se donner une contenance ; *to put s.o. out of countenance*, faire perdre contenance à qqn, déconcertancer qqn. ‖ Appui *m.* ; *to give countenance to*, appuyer.
— v. tr. Soutenir, appuyer (*in*, dans) [s.o.] ; approuver (sth.).

counter ['kauntə*] n. Compteur *m.* (checker). ‖ Jeton *m.* ‖ Comm. Comptoir *m.* ; *over the counter*, au comptant ; *under the counter*, en dessous de table. ‖ Fin. Caisse *f.* (in a bank) ; *over the counter*, aux guichets ; U. S. au marché officieux. ‖ **Counter-jumper**, n. Fam. Calicot *m.*

counter n. Contrefort *m.* (of a shoe).

counter n. Poitrail *m.* (of a horse). ‖ Naut. Voûte *f.*

counter adv. A l'opposé, à contresens, en direction inverse. ‖ A l'encontre, à l'opposé (*to*, de) ; contrairement (*to*, à).
— adj. Opposé, contraire (*to*, à). ‖ Faisant pendant, apparié (*to*, à).
— n. Sports. Contre *m.* (in boxing, fencing).
— v. tr. Aller à l'encontre de, contrarier. ‖ Sports. Contrer (in boxing) ; parer (in fencing). ‖ Fig. Déjouer, contrer.
— v. intr. Sports. Contrer.

counter pref. Contre. ‖ **Counter-approaches**, n. pl. Milit. Contre-approches *f. pl.* ‖ **Counter-attack**, n. Milit. Contre-attaque *f.* ; v. tr. Contre-attaquer. ‖ **Counter-batter**, v. tr. Milit. Contrebattre. ‖ **Counter-battery**, n. Milit. Contrebatterie *f.* ‖ **Counter-brace**, v. tr. Archit. Entretoiser. ‖ **Counter-check**, n. Techn. Force contraire *f.* ‖ **Counter-claim**, n. Jur. Défense (*f.*) au contraire ; conclusions reconventionnelles *f. pl.* ‖ **Counter-clockwise**, adv. En sens inverse des aiguilles d'une montre. ‖ **Counter-current**, n. Contre-courant *m.* ‖ **Counter-declaration**, n. Contre-déclaration *f.* ‖ **Counter-demonstration**, n. Contre-manifestation *f.* ‖ **Counter-demonstrator**, n. Contre-manifestant *s.* ‖ **Counter-disengagement**, n. Sports. Contre-dégagement *m.* ‖ **Counter-espionage**, n. Milit. Contre-espionnage *m.* ‖ **Counter-fugue**, n. Mus. Contre-fugue *f.* ‖ **Counter-inquiry**, n. Jur. Contre-enquête *f.* ‖ **Counter-intelligence**, n. Milit. Contre-espionnage *m.* ‖ **Counter-irritant**, n. Med. Révulsif *m.* ‖ **Counter-irritation**, n. Med. Révulsion *f.* ‖ **Counter-manœuvre**, n. Contre-manœuvre *f.* ‖ **Counter-melody**, n. Mus. Contre-chant *m.* ‖ **Counter-nut**, n. Techn. Contre-écrou *m.* ‖ **Counter-offensive**, n. Milit. Contre-offensive *f.* ‖ **Counter-operation**, n. Milit. Contre-opération *f.* ‖ **Counter-order**, n. Contrordre *m.* ‖ **Counter-plea**, n. Jur. Réplique *f.* ‖ **Counter-poison**, n. Med. Contrepoison, antidote *m.* ‖ **Counter-preparation**, n. Milit. Contre-préparation *f.* ‖ **Counter-project**, n. Contreprojet *m.* ‖ **Counter-proof**, n. Arts. Contre-épreuve *f.* ‖ **Counter-propaganda**, n. Contrepropagande *f.* ‖ **Counter-proposition**, n. Contreproposition *f.* ‖ **Counter-reconnaissance**, n. Milit. Contre-reconnaissance *f.* ‖ **Counter-revolution**, n. Contre-révolution *f.* ‖ **Counter-signature**, n. Jur. Contreseing *m.* ‖ **Counter-sortie**, n. Milit. Contre-sortie *f.* ‖ **Counter-statement**, n. Jur. Contre-mémoire *m.* ‖ **Counter-stroke**, n. Milit. Retour offensif *m.* ; Fig. Contrecoup *m.* ‖ **Counter-**

tenor, n. Mus. Haute-contre *f.* ‖ **Counter-term**, n. Gramm. Antonyme *m.* ‖ **Counter-valuation**, n. Contre-expertise *f.*

counteract [,kauntə'rækt] v. tr. Contrecarrer (to cross) ; neutraliser (to neutralize).

counteraction [-'ræk,ʃən] n. Contre-mesure *f.* ‖ Opposition *f.* ; antagonisme *m.* ‖ Neutralisation *f.*

counterattraction ['kauntərə'træk,ʃən] n. Concurrence, attraction rivale *f.*

counterbalance ['kauntə,bæləns] n. Contrepoids *m.* ‖ Balancier *m.* (of a clock).

counterbalance [,kauntə'bæləns] v. tr. Contrebalancer.

counterblast ['kauntə,blɑ:st] n. Riposte *f.* (*to*, à) ; contre-attaque *f.*

counterchange ['kauntə't,ʃeindʒ] v. tr. Echanger, interchanger. ‖ Diversifier, bigarrer (to variegate).

countercharge ['kauntət,ʃɑ:dʒ] n. Jur. Contre-accusation, contre-plainte *f.*

countercheck [-t,ʃek] n. Obstacle, empêchement *m.* ‖ Réplique, riposte *f.*

counterculture [-,kʌltʃə*] n. Contre-culture *f.*

counterfeit [-fi:t] adj. Faux, contrefait (document, money). ‖ Fig. Faux, feint, simulé.
— n. Contrefaçon *f.* (forging) ; faux *m.* (product).
— v. tr. Feindre, simuler (to fake).

counterfeiter [-fi:tə*] n. Contrefacteur *m.* (See FORGER.)

counterfeiting [-fi:tiŋ] n. Contrefaçon ; contrefaction *f.*

counterfoil [-fɔil] n. Talon *m.* (of a cheque, receipt).

counterfort [-fɔ:t] n. Archit., Geogr. Contre-fort *m.*

counterman [-mən] (pl. **countermen**) n. U. S. Serveur *m.* (at a soda fountain or bar).

countermand [,kauntə'mɑ:nd] v. tr. Contremander, décommander (an invitation). ‖ Révoquer, annuler (an order) ; donner contrordre à (s.o.).
— ['kauntə'mɑ:nd] n. Contrordre, contremandement *m.*

countermarch ['kauntəmɑ:ʃ] n. Milit. Contre-marche *f.*

countermark [-mɑ:k] n. Comm. Contremarque *f.*

countermeasure [-meʒə*] n. Contre-mesure *f.*

countermine [-main] n. Milit. Contre-mine *f.* ‖ Fig. Contre-ruse, contre-intrigue *f.*
— v. tr. Milit., Fig. Contre-miner.

countermove [-,mu:v] n. Riposte *f.*

counterpane [-pein] n. Couvre-pieds ; couvre-lit *m.* ‖ † Courtepointe *f.*

counterpart [-pɑ:t] n. Duplicata, double *m.* (copy). ‖ Pendant *m.* (of ornament, picture). ‖ Comm. Contrepartie *f.* ‖ Fig. Complément, pendant *m.* ; *woman is the counterpart of man*, la femme est complémentaire de l'homme.

counterplot [-plɔt] n. Contre-intrigue *f.*
— v. tr. Contre-miner.

counterpoint [-pɔint] n. Mus. Contrepoint *m.*

counterpoise [-pɔiz] n. Contrepoids *m.* (See COUNTERWEIGHT.) ‖ Equilibre *m.* ; balance *f.*
— v. tr. Faire contrepoids à. ‖ Contrebalancer, compenser. ‖ Conserver en équilibre.

counterproductive [-prə'dʌktiv] adj. Inefficace, qui a des effets contraires à ceux qui sont désirés.

counterscarp [-,skɑ:p] n. Milit. Contrescarpe *f.*

countersign [-sain] n. Contreseing *m.* ‖ Milit. Mot (*m.*) d'ordre (or) de passe ; consigne *f.*
— v. tr. Contresigner.

countersink [-'siŋk] v. tr. (135). Techn. Fraiser ; noyer.

countervail [-veil] v. tr. Contrebalancer, compenser. ‖ Neutraliser, contrecarrer.
— v. intr. Prévaloir (*against*, contre).

counterweight [-weit] n. Contrepoids *m.*

-- v. tr. Faire contrepoids à, contrebalancer, équilibrer. || Mettre un contrepoids à.

counterwork ['wə:k] n. MILIT. Contre-fortification f.; contre-attaques f. pl.

— v. tr. FIG. Contrecarrer.

— v. intr. Opérer une contre-action.

countess ['kauntis] n. Comtesse f.

counting ['kauntiŋ] n. Compte, dénombrement m. || **Counting-house**, U. S. **countingroom**, n. FIN., COMM. Bureau (m.) de la comptabilité.

countless [-lis] adj. Incalculable, innombrable.

countrified ['kʌntri:faid] adj. Provincial, campagnard; she is very countrified, elle est très province.

country ['kʌntri] n. Pays m.; région, contrée f. (district). || Pays m.; nation f. (land). || Patrie f. (mother-land); pays natal m. (native country). || Campagne f. (rural region); in the open country, en pleine (or) rase campagne. || Province f. (provinces); fresh from the country, frais débarqué de sa province. || JUR. Corps électoral m.; to appeal (or) go to the country, en appeler au pays. || **Country-house**, n. Maison de campagne f. || **Country-seat**, n. Résidence de campagne f. || **Countryside**, n. Campagne f.; pays m. (people, region). || **Country-wide**, adj. S'étendant à l'ensemble du pays.

— adj. Campagnard (accent, gentleman). || De la campagne; country folk (or) people, gens de la campagne, campagnards. || A la campagne (life). || De province (cousin); his country ways have stuck to him, il est bien resté de sa province. || JUR. Paysan (party).

country-dance [-dɑ:ns] n. MUS. Contredanse f.

countryman [-mən] (pl. **countrymen**) n. Campagnard, paysan, homme (m.) de la campagne. || Compatriote m. || Ressortissant, sujet m. (of a specified country).

countrywoman [-,wumən] (pl. **countrywomen**) [-,wimin] n. Campagnarde, paysanne, femme de la campagne f. || Compatriote f.

county ['kaunti] n. Comté m. || JUR. County court, tribunal d'instance; county corporate, ville-arrondissement; county town, chef-lieu de comté.

coup [ku:] n. Coup m. (stratagem); coup de grâce, de main, d'Etat, de théâtre, coup de grâce, de main, d'Etat, de théâtre. || SPORTS. Coup parfait m. (in billiards).

coupé ['ku:pe] n. Coupé m.

couple ['kʌpl] n. Couple, laisse f. (leash). || Couple, paire f. (of eggs); couple m. (of persons). || TECHN. Couple m. || ELECTR. Couplage m. || ARCHIT. Moise f. || FAM. He has a couple of things to do, il a une chose ou deux à faire.

— v. tr. Coupler (dogs). || Accoupler (two animals); marier (two persons). || ELECTR. Coupler (two currents); in the current. || CH. DE F. Accrocher (two carriages). || FIG. Associer, relier (with, à).

— v. intr. S'accoupler (animals); s'unir (persons).

coupler ['kʌplə*] n. CH. DE F. Attelage m. || MUS. Pédale (f.) d'accouplement (in an organ).

couplet [-it] n. Distique m.

coupling [-iŋ] n. Accouplement m. (of animals); union f. (of persons). || ELECTR. Couplage m. || **Coupling-box**, n. TECHN. Manchon d'accouplement m. || **Coupling-chain**, n. CH. DE F. Chaîne (f.) d'attelage. || **Coupling-rod**, n. CH. DE F. Bielle (f.) d'accouplement.

coupon ['ku:pɔn] n. Coupon, ticket m.; bread coupon, ticket de pain; clothing coupons, points de textile. || FIN. Coupon m. || **Coupon-book**, n. Carte f.; clothing coupon-book, carte de textile.

courage ['kʌridʒ] n. Courage m.; bravoure, vaillance, valeur f.; to screw one's courage to the sticking point, rassembler tout son courage.

courageous [kə'reidʒəs] adj. Courageux, brave.

courageously [-li] adv. Courageusement.

courgette [kuə'ʒet] n. BOT., CULIN. Courgette f.

courier ['kuriə*] n. Courrier m.

course [kɔ:s] n. Cours, courant m.; in course of time, avec le temps, à la longue; in course of, en cours de; in due course, en temps voulu (or) opportun; in the course of, au cours de, dans le courant de; pendant. || Route, voie, direction f.; to change one's course, changer de direction f.; to hold one's course, suivre son chemin. || Programme m. (of education); série f. (of lectures); cycle m. (of studies); U. S. Programme universitaire semestriel; holiday course, cours de vacances. || ASTRON. Cours m. (of the moon, sun); course, carrière f. (of the sun). || GEOGR. Direction f. (of a lode); cours m. (of a river). || AGRIC. Assolement m. || ARCHIT. Assise f. || COMM. Courant m. (of affairs). || JUR. By course of law, selon la loi. || FIN. Cote f. (of exchange). || MED. Cours m. (of a disease); série f. (of injections); règles f. pl. (periods); to put s.o. on a course of medicine, prescrire un traitement à qqn. || MILIT. Trajet m. (of a bullet). || NAUT. Voile basse f. (sail); route f. (way); to change one's course, changer le cap. || SPORTS. Piste f.; champ (m.) de course (race-course); parcours, terrain m. (in golf); close course, circuit fermé. || TECHN. Galerie f. (in a mine); course f. (of a piston). || CULIN. Service, plat m.; first course, entrée; main course, plat de résistance. || FIG. Cours m., marche f. (of events, time); cours m. (of life, things); as a matter of course, comme de bien entendu, comme de juste, comme il est naturel; of course, naturellement, bien entendu, bien sûr; that's a matter of course, cela va sans dire, c'est évident. || FIG. Voie, direction f.; course of action, ligne de conduite; to take one's own course, agir à son idée, en faire à sa tête.

— v. tr. Faire courir. || SPORTS. Courir, courre (in hunting).

— v. intr. Couler, courir (blood, liquid).

courser [-ə*] n. ZOOL. Coursier m. (steed).

coursing [-iŋ] n. SPORTS. Chasse (f.) au lièvre; coursing m.

court [kɔ:t] n. Cour f. (courtyard). || Cul-de-sac m.; impasse f. (blind alley). || Cour f. (of a sovereign); at court, à la cour. || ARCHIT. Manoir m.; Hampton Court, le château de Hampton. || ECCLES. Parvis m. || SPORTS. Terrain m. (for basketball, handball); court m. (for tennis). || JUR. Cour f., tribunal m.; court ruling, décision de justice; court of petty sessions, tribunal correctionnel; open court, audience publique; police, special court, tribunal de simple police, d'exception; to hold (or) sit in court, tenir audience; to rule out of court, débouter. || JUR. Commission f. (of inquiry). || FIG. Cour, faveur f.; to fall out of court with, tomber en défaveur auprès de. || FIG. Cour f. (wooing); to pay court to, faire la cour à. || **Court-card**, n. Figure f. (in cards). || **Court-day**, n. JUR. Jour (m.) d'audience. || **Court-guide**, n. Bottin mondain m. || **Court-hand**, n. JUR. Grosse f. (handwriting). || **Court-house**, n. ARCHIT. Palais (m.) de justice; tribunal m. || **Court-martial** (pl. courts-martial), n. MILIT. Tribunal militaire, conseil (m.) de guerre; v. tr. (1). MILIT. Traduire en conseil de guerre; to be court-martialled, passer en conseil de guerre. || **Court-record**, n. JUR. Procès-verbal (m.) d'audience. || **Court-room**, n. JUR. Salle d'audience f. || **Court-plaster**, n. MED. Taffetas (m.) d'Angleterre.

— v. tr. Courtiser, faire la cour à (to woo). || Rechercher, chercher (an opportunity). || Prier, demander à (s.o.); to court s.o. into doing sth., solliciter qqn de faire qqch. || Courir à, aller au-devant de (disappointment, failure). || Inviter à, provoquer; to court inquiry, demander une enquête.

courteous ['kə:tiəs] adj. Courtois (to, envers).

courteously [-li] adv. Courtoisement.

courteousness [-nis] n. Courtoisie f. (to, envers).

courtesan [,kɔ:ti'zæn] n. Courtisane f. (prostitute).

courtesy ['kə:tisi] n. Courtoisie *f.*; *courtesy of the road*, politesse de la route. ‖ Gracieuseté *f.*; *by courtesy*, à titre gracieux; *by courtesy of*, avec la gracieuse permission de, avec l'aimable concours de. ‖ Pl. Procédés courtois *m. pl.*; politesses *f. pl.* — ['kə:tsi] n. Révérence *f.* (See CURTSY.)

courtier ['kɔ:tjə*] n. Courtisan *m.* (at a royal court).

courtliness ['kɔ:tlinis] n. Courtoisie, distinction *f.*

courtly [-li] adj. Courtois, distingué, élégant.

courtship [-ʃip] n. Cour *f.* (woo).

courtshoe [-ʃu] n. Escarpin *m.*

courtyard [kɔ:t'jɑ:d] n. Cour *f.* (of a house).

couscous ['ku:sku:s] n. CULIN. Couscous *m.*

cousin ['kʌzn] n. Cousin *s.*; *cousin german, first cousin*, cousin germain; *cousin once removeu*, *second cousin*, cousin issu de germain (or) au second degré; *female cousin*, cousine. ‖ FAM. *To call cousins with*, fraterniser avec, être cousin avec, cousiner.

cousinship [-ʃip], **cousinhood** [-hud] n. Cousinage *m.*

couture ['kutyr] n. Couture *f.*; *good couture house*, bonne maison de couture; *haute couture look*, cachet haute couture.

couturier [ku:'ty:riei] n. Couturier *m.*

couturière [ku:tur'jɛə*] n. Couturière *f.*

covalence [kou'veiləns], **covalency** [-si] n. CHIM. Covalence *f.*

covalent [kou'veilənt] adj. CHIM. Covalent, de covalence; *covalent bond*, liaison covalente (or) de covalence.

cove [kouv] n. GEOGR. Anse, crique, baie *f.* ‖ ARCHIT. Cintre *m.*; voûte *f.*
— v. tr. ARCHIT. Cintrer.

cove n. POP. Mec, type *m.* (guy).

coven ['kʌvn] n. Assemblée (*f.*) de sorcières.

covenant ['kʌvinənt] n. JUR. Pacte, traité *m.*; convention *f.* ‖ ECCLES. Alliance *f.*

covenanted [-id] adj. Contractuel.

covenanter [-ə*] n. JUR. Partie contractante *f.*

coventrize ['kʌvəntraiz] v. tr. MILIT. Détruire par bombardement.

Coventry [-tri] n. GEOGR. Coventry. ‖ FAM. *To send to Coventry*, mettre en quarantaine, reléguer.

cover ['kʌvə*] v. tr. Couvrir (*with*, de) [mud]. ‖ Recouvrir (the roofs). ‖ Couvrir, vêtir (to clothe); *to cover oneself up*, se couvrir, s'habiller chaudement. ‖ ZOOL. Couver (eggs); couvrir, saïllir (a female). ‖ SPORTS. Couvrir (an area, a bet, a player); *distance covered*, parcours. ‖ COMM. *Covering letter*, lettre avec pièce jointe. ‖ FIN. Couvrir (expenses, losses); *to be covered*, être à couvert. ‖ JUR. Viser (a case). ‖ MILIT. Couvrir, protéger (the rear of the army); *to cover a target*, battre un objectif; *to cover s.o. with a firearm*, mettre qqn en joue. ‖ FIG. Couvrir, parcourir (a distance); couvrir (a noise); couvrir, comprendre, englober, embrasser (a subject); *to cover the ground*, couvrir l'étendue du sujet; *to cover with honours*, couvrir d'honneurs; *to cover oneself with glory*, se couvrir de gloire. ‖ FIG. Couvrir, cacher, dissimuler (to hide). ‖ **To cover in**, recouvrir; remplir. ‖ **To cover up**, recouvrir, cacher, dissimuler.
— n. Couverture *f.* (of bed, book); couvercle *m.* (of box, saucepan); housse *f.* (of chair); tapis *m.* (of a table); fourreau *m.* (of umbrella). ‖ Enveloppe *f.* (of letter); bande *f.* (of newspaper); *under registered cover*, en recommandé; *under separate cover*, sous pli séparé. ‖ Couvert, abri *m.*; *to give s.o. cover*, abriter qqn, fournir un abri à qqn; *to seek cover*, se mettre à l'abri; *to take cover*, se mettre à couvert; *under cover of*, à l'abri de. ‖ Couvert, fourré *m.* (thicket). ‖ SPORTS. Gîte, terrier *m.* (of game); remise *f.* (of winged game); *to break cover*, débûcher; *to drive to cover*, embûcher. ‖

MILIT. Couvert *m.*; *accidental* (or) *improvised cover*, abri de fortune; *to take cover*, s'embusquer; se planquer (fam.). ‖ AVIAT. Outer cover, couverture de protection. ‖ NAUT. Etui *m.* (of boat, sails). ‖ AUTOM. Enveloppe *f.* (of tyre). ‖ JUR., COMM. Nantissement *m.* ‖ FIN. Couverture *f.*; *without cover*, à découvert. ‖ CULIN. Couvert *m.* ‖ FIG. Couvert, prétexte *m.*; apparence *f.*; *under cover of*, sous couvert (or) prétexte de; sous le masque de. ‖ **Cover-charge**, n. Couvert *m.* ‖ **Covercrop**, n. AGRIC. U. S. Culture intercalaire *f.* ‖ **Cover-girl**, n. Cover-girl *f.* ‖ **Cover note**, n. AUTOM. Attestation d'assurance *f.* ‖ **Cover-point**, n. Couvreur *m.* (in cricket).

coverage [-ridʒ] n. U. S. FIN. Montant couvert *m.*; risques couverts *m. pl.* (in insurance). ‖ Couverture *f.* (in a newspaper).

coverlet [-lit] n. Couvre-lit *m.* (bedspread); couvre-pieds *m.* (counterpane).

covert ['kʌvət] adj. Couvert, abrité (sheltered). ‖ JUR. *Feme covert*, femme en puissance de mari. ‖ FIG. Voilé, caché, déguisé, indirect.
— n. Couvert, fourré *m.* (thicket). ‖ SPORTS. Gîte, terrier *m.* (of game). ‖ **Covertcloth**, n. U. S. Tissu pour manteau *m.*

covertly [-li] adv. A mots couverts; d'une manière voilée; en secret.

coverture ['kʌvətjuə*] n. Abri, refuge *m.* ‖ JUR. Condition de la femme mariée *f.*

covet ['kʌvit] v. tr. Convoiter; guigner (fam.).

covetous [-əs] adj. Avide (*of*, de); *covetous look*, regard de convoitise; *covetous desires*, convoitises. ‖ Avaricieux, cupide. (See GREEDY.)

covetously [-əsli] adv. Avec convoitise, avidement. ‖ Avec cupidité.

covetousness [-əsnis] n. Convoitise, avidité, insatiabilité *f.* ‖ Cupidité *f.* (See GREEDINESS.)

covey ['kʌvi] n. ZOOL. Compagnie *f.* (of grouse, partridges); vol *m.* (of partridges).

coving ['kouviŋ] n. ARCHIT. Voussure *f.*

cow [kau] (pl. **cows** [-z], **kine** [kain]) n. ZOOL. Vache *f.*; *milk cow*, laitière. ‖ ZOOL. Femelle *f.* (of the buffalo, elephant, whale); *cow seal*, phoque femelle. ‖ LOC. *The time of the lean cows*, la période des vaches maigres. ‖ **Cow-bell**, n. AGRIC. Sonnaille *f.* ‖ **Cow-catcher**, n. CH. DE F. Chasse-pierres; ramasse-piétons *m. pl.*; fender *m.* ‖ **Cow-fish**, n. ZOOL. Lamantin *m.* ‖ **Cow-hide**, n. Cuir (*m.*) de vache, vache *f.* (leather); fouet *m.* (whip); v. tr. fouetter. ‖ **Cow-house**, n. AGRIC. Etable *f.* ‖ **Cow-lick**, n. Epi *m.* (in the hair). ‖ **Cow-parsley**, n. BOT. Persil sauvage *m.* ‖ **Cow-patch**, n. Bouse de vache *f.* ‖ **Cow-shed**, n. Etable *f.*

cow v. tr. Intimider, effaroucher.

coward ['kauəd] adj., n. Couard, poltron, lâche *s.*

cowardice [-is], **cowardliness** [-linis] n. Couardise, poltronnerie, lâcheté *f.*

cowardly [-li] adj. Poltron, lâche.
— adv. Lâchement.

cowbird [-bə:d] n. ZOOL. U. S. Bergeronnette *f.*

cowboy ['kauboi] n. Vacher, bouvier *m.* ‖ U. S. Cowboy *m.*

cower ['kauə*] v. intr. Se blottir, s'accroupir, s'accroupetonner. ‖ FIG. Rentrer la tête dans les épaules, plier l'échine (*before*, devant).

cowgirl ['kaugə:l] n. Vachère *f.*

cowhand [-hænd] n. U. S. Cowboy *m.*

cowherd [-hə:d] n. Vacher, bouvier *m.*

cowl [kaul] n. ECCLES. Capuchon *m.*; coule *f.*, capuce *m.*; *penitent's cowl*, cagoule. ‖ ARCHIT. Mitre *f.* (of chimney). ‖ AVIAT., NAUT., AUTOM. Capot *m.*
— v. tr. ARCHIT. Mettre une mitre à. ‖ AVIAT., NAUT., AUTOM. Mettre un capot à.

cowl n. AGRIC. Comporte, baste *f.* (tub). ‖ **Cowl-staff**, n. Perche (*f.*) pour porter la baste.

cowman ['kaumən] (pl. **cowmen**) n. Vacher; U. S. Eleveur, propriétaire d'un ranch *m*.
cowpox [-poks] n. MED. Vaccine *f*.
cowpuncher [-,pʌnʃə*] n. U. S. FAM. Cowboy *m*.
cowrie, cowry ['kauri] n. ZOOL. Porcelaine *f*., cyprée *f*.
cowslip ['kauslip] n. BOT. Coucou *m*.
cox [koks] n. NAUT. Barreur *m*.
— v. tr., intr. NAUT. Barrer.
coxa ['koksə] n. MED. Hanche *f*. (hip).
coxal [-əl] adj. MED. Coxal.
coxalgia [koks'æ ldʒiə] n. MED. Coxalgie *f*.
coxcomb ['kokskoum] n. Petit-maître, fat, dandy *m*. (See COCKSCOMB.) ‖ BOT. Crête-de-coq *f*.
coxcombical [koks'koumikəl] adj. Affecté, fat, vain, avantageux.
coxcombry ['kokskəmri] n. Fatuité *f*.
coxswain ['koksn] n. NAUT. Patron (*m*.) de barque. ‖ NAUT., SPORTS. Barreur *m*. (steersman).
coy [koi] adj. Timide (shy); *coy of speech*, peu causant. ‖ Qui joue à l'effarouchée, coquette et mijaurée (demure).
coyly [-li] adv. Avec timidité.
coyness [-nis] n. Timidité, réserve *f*.
coyote [koi'out] [kə'jouti] n. ZOOL. Coyote *m*.
coypu ['koipu] n. ZOOL. Castor du Chili *m*.
cozen ['kʌzn] v. tr. Filouter, empiler (s.o.); extorquer (*out of*, à) [sth.].
crab [kræb] n. ZOOL. Crabe *m*. ‖ ASTRON. Cancer *m*.; Ecrevisse *f*. ‖ TECHN. Treuil *m*. ‖ NAUT. Dérivation *f*. ‖ NAUT. *To catch a crab*, engager un aviron. ‖ MED. Morpion *m*. ‖ **Crab-capstan**, n. NAUT. Cabestan volant. ‖ **Crab-louse**, n. MED. Morpion *m*.
— v. intr. Pêcher le crabe. ‖ AVIAT. Dériver, voler en crabe.
— v. tr. AVIAT. Faire voler en crabe.
crab n. BOT. Pomme sauvage *f*. ‖ FAM. Crin *m*. (crabbed person). ‖ **Crab-apple**, n. BOT. Pomme sauvage *f*. ‖ **Crab-tree**, n. BOT. Pommier sauvage *m*.
— v. intr. FAM. Rouspéter, récriminer.
— v. tr. FAM. Débiner, déblatérer contre.
crabbed [-id] adj. Acariâtre, grincheux, grognon, renfrogné (peevish). ‖ Revêche, de mauvaise humeur (cross-grained). ‖ Difficile; *crabbed author*, auteur hermétique; *crabbed handwriting*, écriture de chat, pattes de mouche; *crabbed style*, style entortillé.
crabbedly [-idli] adv. Avec mauvaise humeur, en grognant; d'un air bourru. ‖ Illisiblement.
crack [kræk] v. tr. Faire craquer avec un bruit sec. Faire claquer (a whip). ‖ Casser (a nut). ‖ Fendre, fendiller (earth); fendre, fêler (glass, stone); lézarder (wall). ‖ MED. Fracturer (bone); crevasser (skin); casser (voice). ‖ FIG. Démolir, ruiner (s.o.'s credit). ‖ FIG. Débiter, lancer (jokes); ‖ FAM. Trouver la solution de, résoudre; *a hard nut to crack*, un fichu problème à résoudre, du fil à retordre (difficulty); un type pas commode (person). ‖ FAM. *To crack a bottle*, boire une bouteille; *to crack a crib*, faire un fric-frac, cambrioler. ‖ **To crack down**, FAM. Tomber sur le dos de; *to crack down on s.o.*, enguirlander qqn. ‖ **To crack on**, NAUT. Déployer; *to crack on sail*, mettre toutes les voiles. ‖ **To crack up**, FAM. Vanter, faire mousser. ‖ **Crack-jaw**, adj. FAM. A démantibuler la mâchoire.
— v. intr. Craquer, claquer, émettre un bruit sec. ‖ Se fendiller (earth); se fendre, se fêler (glass, stone); se casser (nut); se lézarder (wall); claquer (whip). ‖ MED. Se fracturer (bone); se crevasser, se gercer (skin); muer (boy's voice); se casser (old man's voice). ‖ FIG. S'effondrer, craquer. ‖ FAM. Flancher (to break down); jaser, jaboter (to chatter); plaisanter (to joke); *get cracking!*, grouillez! au boulot!; U. S. *to crack wise*, dire des bons mots. ‖ **To crack up**, AVIAT. S'écraser; FIN. Faire un krach; FAM. Se vanter (to boast); s'effondrer, flancher (to break down).

— n. Craquement, bruit sec *m*. ‖ Détonation *f*. (of a firearm); claquement *m*. (of a whip). ‖ Coup sec *m*. (blow). ‖ Fêlure, fissure, fente *f*. (See CRANNY.) ‖ Causette *f*.; bavardage *m*. (gossip). ‖ SPORTS. Crack *m*. ‖ FAM. Bon mot *m*. (joke); instant, clin d'œil *m*. (trice). ‖ POP. Fricfrac *m*. (burglary). ‖ POP. U. S. Brocard *m*. (gibe); tentative *f*. (try). ‖ **Crack-brained**, adj. FAM. Au cerveau fêlé, toqué. — adj. FAM. De première, terrible, sensationnel; *crack shot, regiment*, tireur, régiment d'élite.
cracked [-t] adj. FAM. Fêlé, toqué, cinglé, détraqué.
cracker [-ə*] n. Pétard *m*. (firework). ‖ CULIN. Diablotin *m*.; U. S. petit-beurre, biscuit sec, craquelin *m*. ‖ Pl. Papillotes *f. pl*. (hair-curlers). ‖ **Crackerbarrel**, U. S. FAM. En chambre, au petit pied; *cracker-barrel philosophers*, philosophes du café du commerce. ‖ **Cracker jack**, n. U. S. FAM. Crack *m*.
crackers [-ə:z] adj. FAM. Toqué.
cracking [-iŋ] n. CHIM. Cracking, craquage *m*.
crackle [krækḷ] n. Crépitement *m*. (of fire, wood); grésillement *m*. (of snow). ‖ Craquelure *f*. (on china); craquelé *m*. (china). ‖ Friture *f*. (on the telephone).
— v. intr. Crépiter, pétiller (fire, wood); grésiller (sth. frying, snow).
crackleware [-wεə*] n. ARTS. Craquelé *m*.
crackling ['kræklin] n. Crépitement; grésillement *m*. ‖ CULIN. Couenne rissolée *f.*; pl. fritons, grattons *m. pl*.
cracknel ['kræknḷ] n. CULIN. Croquignole *f*.
crackpot ['krækpot] n. FAM. Dingo *m*.
cracksman ['kræksmən] (pl. **cracksmen**) n. FAM. Cambrioleur *m*.
cracky ['kræki] adj. Craquelé, fendillé. ‖ FAM. Cinglé. (See CRACKED.)
Cracovian ['krə'kouviən] adj., n. GEOGR. Cracovien *s*.
Cracow ['krækou] n. GEOGR. Cracovie *f*.
cradle ['kreidḷ] n. Berceau *m*. ‖ NAUT. Ber, berceau *m*. ‖ AGRIC. Râteau *m*. (for scythe). ‖ ARTS, MILIT., TECHN. Berceau *m*. ‖ MED. Arceau, cerceau *m*. (over a bed); gouttière *f*. (splint). ‖ FIG. Berceau *m*. ‖ **Cradle-scythe**, n. AGRIC. Faux (*f*.) à râteau. ‖ **Cradle-song**, n. Berceuse *f*. ‖ **Cradle-telephone**, n. Téléphone automatique, poste de téléphone moderne *m*.
— v. tr. Coucher dans un berceau. ‖ Bercer. ‖ AGRIC. Faucher avec une faux à râteau. ‖ FIG. *Cradled in luxury*, élevé dans le luxe.
craft [krɑːft] n. Adresse, habileté, dextérité *f*. (See ART.) ‖ Ruse, astuce *f.*; artifice *m*. (guile). ‖ Art manuel; métier *m*. (trade). ‖ Corps de métier *m*. (corporation). ‖ NAUT. Bâtiment *m*.; embarcation *f*. ‖ AVIAT. Appareil *m*. ‖ **Craft union**, n. U. S. Association professionnelle *f*.
craftily [-ili] adv. Habilement, avec adresse (skilfully). ‖ Avec ruse (or) astuce (cunningly).
craftsman [-smən] (pl. **craftsmen**) n. Artisan ouvrier *m*. ‖ FIG. Réalisateur *m*.
craftsmanship [-smənʃip] n. Habileté, adresse *f*. art *m*. ‖ Métier *m*. (in writer).
crafty [-i] adj. Rusé, astucieux, malin. (See SLY.)
crag [kræg] n. Rocher escarpé *m*. ‖ SPORTS. Varappe *f*.
craggedness [-idnis], **cragginess** [-inis] n. Nature rocailleuse *f*. (of the ground).
craggy [-i] adj. Escarpé, à pic; rocailleux.
cragsman [-zmən] (pl. **cragsmen**) n. SPORTS. Varappeur *m*.
crake [kreik] n. ZOOL. Râle *m*.
cram [kræm] v. tr. (1). Bourrer, bonder, garnir, combler (*with*, de) [to pack full]. ‖ Empiler entasser, pousser de force (*into*, dans) [to force] ‖ Bourrer, gaver, gorger (*with*, de) [to stuff]; *to cram oneself with food*, s'empiffrer. ‖ AGRIC. Engraisser (fowl); gaver (goose). ‖ FAM. Farcir

(one's memory); chauffer, bourrer (a student); potasser (a subject). ‖ **Cram-shop**, n. FAM. Boîte (*f.*) à bachot.
— v. intr. Se bourrer, se gaver, se gorger (*with*, de). ‖ FAM. Bachoter, buriner. ‖ FAM. Blaguer.
— n. Cohue, presse, ruée, foule *f.* (crowd). ‖ FAM. Chauffage, bachotage, bourrage *m.* ‖ FAM. Craque, blague *f.*

crambo ['kræmbou] n. Corbillon *m.;* bouts-rimés *m. pl.* ‖ FAM. Rimaillerie *f.*

crammer ['kræmə*] n. FAM. Chauffeur, répétiteur, bachoteur *m.; crammer's*, boîte à bachot. ‖ FAM. Craque, sornette *f.* (fib); blagueur, bourreur de crâne *m.* (person).

cramming [-iŋ] n. Entassement *m.* ‖ AGRIC. Gavage *m.* ‖ FAM. Bachotage, bourrage *m.*

cramp [kræmp] n. MED. Crampe *f.;* pl. Coliques *f. pl.* ‖ **Cramp-fish**, n. ZOOL. Poisson-torpille *m.*
— v. tr. MED. Saisir de crampes, donner des crampes à.

cramp n. TECHN. Crampon; étau; serre-joint *m.; small cramp*, cramponnet. ‖ FIG. Crispation, contrainte *f.* ‖ FAM. Tenailles *f. pl.; under the cramp of fear*, tenaillé par la peur. ‖ **Cramp-iron** n. ARCHIT. Crampon *m.;* ancrure *f.*
— v. tr. TECHN. Cramponner. ‖ FAM. *To cramp s.o.'s style*, ôter ses moyens à qqn. ‖ **To cramp up**, comprimer.

cramped [kræmt] adj. Comprimé, resserré. ‖ Illisible, indéchiffrable (writing).

crampon ['kræmpən] n. TECHN. Crampon *m.*

cranberry ['krænbəri] n. BOT. Airelle *f.*

crane [krein] n. ZOOL. Grue *f.* ‖ TECHN. Grue *f.; overhead travelling crane*, pont-grue, pont roulant. ‖ CH. DE F. Prise d'eau *f.* ‖ CULIN. Siphon *m.;* crémaillère *f.* (of chimney). ‖ **Crane-fly**, n. ZOOL. Tipule *f.*
— v. tr. TECHN. Elever à la grue. ‖ FAM. *To crane one's neck*, tendre le cou.
— v. intr. *To crane at*, SPORTS. Refuser (horse). ‖ FAM. Caner devant.

craneman [-mən] (pl. **cranemen**) n. TECHN. Grutier *m.*

cranial ['kreiniəl] adj. MED. Crânien; *cranial index*, indice céphalique.

cranium [-əm] (pl. **crania** [-ə]) n. MED. Crâne *m.* (See SKULL.)

crank [kræŋk] n. TECHN., AUTOM. Manivelle *f.* ‖ **Crank-case**, n. AUTOM. Carter *m.* ‖ **Crank-gear**, n. Pédalier *m.* ‖ **Crank-pin**, n. TECHN. Tourillon *m.* ‖ **Crank-shaft**, n. TECHN. Arbre *m.;* AUTOM. Vilebrequin *m.* ‖ **Crank-starter**, n. AUTOM. Démarreur (*m.*) à manivelle.
— v. tr. TECHN. Couder. ‖ TECHN. Mettre une manivelle à. ‖ AUTOM., TECHN. Faire partir à la manivelle.
— v. intr. TECHN. Tourner la manivelle.

crank n. Bizarrerie (*f.*) de langage, originalité *f.* ‖ Caprice *m.*, lubie *f.* (whim). ‖ Extravagance *f.* (action, idea). ‖ FAM. Excentrique *m.*

cranky [-i] adj. Détraqué (out of order); branlant, disjoint (shaky). ‖ Excentrique, original (odd). ‖ Revêche; à cran (fam.) [cross]. ‖ NAUT. Rouleux.

cranny ['kræni] n. Fissure, lézarde *f.*

crap [kræp] n. ARG. Merde *f.; to have a crap*, chier. ‖ FIG. Foutaise *f.*, conneries *f. pl.* (nonsense); foutoir, merdier *m.* (junk).
— v. intr. (1). ARG. Chier. ‖ U. S., ARG. *To crap out*, se planter.

crape [kreip] n. Crêpe *m.* (See CRÊPE.)

crapehanger [-,hæŋə*] n. U. S. FAM. Chevalier (*m.*) à la triste figure, porteur (*m.*) de diable en terre, rabat-joie *m.*
— v. tr. Orner de crêpe.

craped [-t] adj. Crêpé.

crappy ['kræpi] adj. ARG. Merdique.

craps [kræps] n. pl. U. S. Dés *m. pl.* (dice).

crapulence ['kræpjuləns] n. Crapule, débauche *f.*

crapulent [-lənt], **crapulous** [-ləs] adj. Crapuleux, arsouille, ivrogne.

crash [kræʃ] v. intr. Retentir avec fracas; faire un bruit fracassant; *to crash into*, enfoncer avec fracas. ‖ AVIAT. S'écraser; casser du bois (fam.); *to crash into a hill*, percuter contre une colline. ‖ FIN. S'effondrer, faire un krach. ‖ AUTOM. *To crash into*, emboutir, tamponner.
— v. tr. Fracasser; jeter avec fracas; *to crash one's way through*, se frayer un chemin en écrasant tout sur son passage. ‖ AVIAT. Fracasser au sol.
— n. Fracas, bruit fracassant *m.* ‖ FIN. Krach *m.* ‖ **Crash-dive**, n. NAUT. Brusque plongée *f.* (of a submarine); v. intr. AVIAT. S'écraser en piqué. ‖ **Crash-helmet**, n. SPORTS. Casque *m.* ‖ **Crash-land**, v. intr. AVIAT. Atterrir en catastrophe. ‖ **Crash-proof**, adj. Résistant au choc.
— adj. Accéléré (course, programme); *to do a crash job*, mettre le paquet. ‖ Brutal (stop, tackle).

crash n. Toile (*f.*) à torchon.

crass [kræs] adj. Epais. ‖ FIG. Crasse (ignorance); grossier (mind); stupide, obtus (person).

crassitude [-itju:d] n. Stupidité, grossièreté; ignorance crasse *f.*

cratch [krætʃ] n. AGRIC. Râtelier *m.*

crate [kreit] n. Cageot *m.;* charasse *f.* ‖ AVIAT., FAM. Coucou, zinc *m.* ‖ AUTOM., FAM. Bagnole *f.*

crater ['kreitə*] n. GEOL., ELECTR. Cratère *m.* ‖ MILIT. Entonnoir *m.*

cravat [krə'væt] n. † Cravate *f.* ‖ Foulard *m.* (scarf).

crave [kreiv] v. tr. Solliciter, implorer (*of, from*, de). ‖ Souhaiter, désirer intensément (to long for).
— v. intr. *To crave after* (or) for, languir de, soupirer après, souhaiter, désirer. (See DESIRE.)

craven [-ņ] adj., n. Poltron *s.* (See COWARDLY.)

cravenette [,krævə'net] v. tr. U. S. Imperméabiliser.
— n. U. S. Imperméabilisation *f.* (action); tissu imperméabilisé *m.* (fabric).

craving ['kreiviŋ] n. Désir intense; besoin tyrannique *m.;* soif *f.* (*for*, de); passion *f.* (*for*, pour).
— adj. Dévorant (appetite). ‖ FIG. Passionné, intense (desire); tyrannique (need).

craw [krɔ:] n. ZOOL. Jabot *m.* (of a bird). ‖ FAM. *It sticks in my craw*, je ne peux pas avaler ça.

craw n. ZOOL. Langouste *f.*

crawfish ['krɔ:fiʃ] n. ZOOL. U. S. See CRAYFISH.

crawl [krɔ:l] v. intr. Ramper; *to crawl out*, sortir en rampant. ‖ Ramper, se traîner (to creep); *to crawl on one's hands and knees*, se traîner à quatre pattes. ‖ Avancer à pas lents, se traîner (to move slowly). ‖ Grouiller, fourmiller, foisonner (*with*, de) [to swarm]. ‖ AUTOM. Marauder (taxi). ‖ U. S. FIG. Ramper, s'aplatir (to fawn). ‖ FAM. Avoir des fourmillements, avoir la chair de poule. ‖ FAM. *To crawl up the wall*, en devenir fou, patauger dans les difficultés. ‖ **To crawl along**, v. intr. AUTOM. Marauder.
— n. Reptation *f.*, rampement *m.* (of a snake). ‖ Marche lente *f.* ‖ AUTOM. Maraude *f.* (of a taxi). ‖ SPORTS. Crawl *m.* ‖ **Crawl-stroke**, n. SPORTS. Crawl *m.* ‖ **Crawl-swimmer**, n. SPORTS. Crawleur *s.*

crawl n. Vivier *m.* (for fish); parc *m.* (for turtles).

crawler [-ə*] n. Barboteuse *f.* (baby's garment). ‖ AUTOM. Taxi (*m.*) en maraude. ‖ CH. DE F., FAM. Tortillard *m.* ‖ ZOOL., FAM. Pou *m.* (louse).

crayfish ['kreifiʃ] n. ZOOL. Ecrevisse *f.* (freshwater crustacean); langouste *f.* (spiny lobster).

crayon ['kreiən] n. ARTS. Fusain; pastel *m.* (drawing, medium). ‖ ELECTR. Crayon *m.* ‖ FIG. Esquisse, ébauche *f.* (sketch).
— v. tr. ARTS. Dessiner au fusain (or) au pastel; crayonner. ‖ FIG. *To crayon out*, ébaucher.

craze [kreiz] v. tr. ARTS. Craqueler (pottery). ‖ FAM. Fêler, rendre timbré, détraquer.
— v. intr. ARTS. Se craqueler. ‖ FAM. Devenir cinglé.
— n. FAM. Fêlure *f.*; cinglage, toquage m. ‖ FAM. Manie, marotte, mode *f.* (fad); toquade, foucade, passade *f.* (whim); *he has a craze for building*, il a la maladie de la pierre, c'est un bâtisseur à tous crins.
craziness [-inis] n. Délabrement m. (of building). ‖ FAM. Détraquage, dérangement, toquage m.
crazy [-i] adj. Délabré (building); branlant; déglingué (fam.) [furniture]. ‖ TECHN. A dalles irrégulières (paving); à morceaux bigarrés (quilt). ‖ FAM. Toqué, maboul (see CRACKED); *crazy about*, fou de, passionné de, toqué de.
creak [kri:k] n. Grincement m. (of a hinge); craquement m. (of new boots).
— v. intr. Grincer (hinge); craquer (shoes).
cream [kri:m] n. Crème *f.* (of milk). ‖ CULIN. Crème *f.*; *cream cheese, puff, sauce*, fromage, chou, sauce à la crème; *cream of tomato soup*, purée de tomates. ‖ Crème de beauté *f.*; cold cream m. ‖ Crème à chaussure *f.*; cirage m. (shoe cream). ‖ CHIM. Crème *f.*; *cream of tartar*, bitartrate de potasse. ‖ FIG. Crème, fleur, élite *f.*; *the cream of the crop*, le dessus du panier; *the cream of the joke*, le sel de l'histoire. ‖ **Cream-coloured**, adj. Crème. ‖ **Cream-laid**, adj. Vergé blanc (paper). ‖ **Cream-wove**, adj. Vélin blanc (paper).
— v. intr. Se couvrir de crème. ‖ Mousser (to foam).
— v. intr. Mettre de la crème dans (coffee). ‖ Ecrémer (milk). ‖ Battre en crème (butter). ‖ FIG. Ecrémer.
creamer [-ə*] n. Ecrémeuse *f.* (machine); écrémoir m. (pitcher). ‖ U. S. Pot (m.) à crème.
creamery [-əri] n. Crémerie *f.*
creamy [-i] adj. Crémeux.
crease [kri:s] n. Faux pli m.; *full of creases*, grimaçant (garment). ‖ Pli du pantalon m. ‖ SPORTS. Ligne de limite *f.* (in cricket).
— v. tr. Froisser, plisser, chiffonner, marquer de faux plis.
— v. intr. Se froisser, se plisser, se chiffonner.
creaseless [-lis] adj. Infroissable (cloth).
creasy [-i] adj. Froissé, chiffonné.
create [kri'eit] v. tr. ECCLES., THEATR., FIG. Créer. ‖ POP. Rouspéter; faire une scène.
creatine ['kriə,ti:n] n. MED. Créatine *f.*
creation [-'eiʃən] n. Création *f.*
creative [kri'eitiv] adj. Créateur m.; créatrice *f.*
creativeness [-nis] n. Pouvoir créateur m.
creator [kri'eitə*] n. ECCLES. Créateur m. ‖ THEATR., FIG. Créateur m.; créatrice *f.*
creature ['kri:tʃə*] n. Créature *f.*; animal m. ‖ Créature, personne *f.*, être m.; *what poor creatures we are!*, ce que c'est que de nous! ‖ FIG. Créature, âme damnée *f.*; instrument m. (of, de) [tool]; jouet m. (of circumstances). ‖ LOC. *Creature comforts*, le confort matériel.
crèche [kreiʃ] n. Crèche, pouponnière *f.* (public nursery). ‖ ECCLES. U. S. Crèche *f.* (crib).
credence ['kri:dəns] n. Créance *f.* (see CREDIT); *to give credence to*, accorder créance (or foi à. ‖ Crédit m.; *to gain credence*, prendre crédit. ‖ ECCLES. Crédence *f.*
credential [kri'denʃəl] n. Pl. Lettre de créance *f.* ‖ Pl. Certificat m. (of a servant); ‖ Pl. Pièces (*f. pl.*) d'identité. ‖ Pl. U. S. Copie certifiée (*f.*) des diplômes.
credenza [kre'dentsə] n. Crédence *f.* (piece of furniture).
credibility [,kredi'biliti] n. Crédibilité *f.*
credible ['kredibl] adj. Croyable, admissible. (See PLAUSIBLE.)
credibly [-li] adv. Plausiblement.

credit ['kredit] n. Créance *f.* (credence); crédit m. (confidence); *to give credit*, donner créance, faire crédit; *to lend credit to*, accréditer. ‖ Crédit, prestige m.; réputation *f.* (good name). ‖ Crédit m.; influence *f.* (with, auprès de). ‖ Honneur m.; *to be a credit to*, faire honneur à; *to take credit for*, s'attribuer le mérite de; *to one's credit*, à son honneur; *with credit*, fort honorablement. ‖ Mention *f.* (in education). ‖ COMM. Credit; *on credit*, à crédit; *to give s.o. credit*, faire crédit à qqn. ‖ FIN. Crédit m.; *credit balance*, solde créditeur; *credit circulation*, circulation fiduciaire; *letter of credit*, accréditif; *on credit*, à terme; *tax credits*, déductions fiscales; *to give s.o. credit for*, créditer qqn de. ‖ Pl. CINEM. Générique m. ‖ **Credit card**, n. FIN. Carte (*f.*) de crédit. ‖ **Credit rating**, n. FIN. Degré (*m.*) de solvabilité.
— v. tr. FIN. Créditer (with, de) [an account, s.o.]; porter au compte (a sum). ‖ FIG. Imputer; *to credit s.o. with a talent*, prêter (or) attribuer un talent à qqn. ‖ Croire, ajouter foi à.
creditable [-əb] adj. Louable (praiseworthy). ‖ Estimable, honorable.
creditably [-əbli] adv. Avec honneur.
creditor [-ə*] n. Créancier s. (person). ‖ FIN. Crédit, avoir m.
credo ['kri:dou] n. ECCLES. Credo m.
credulity [kri'dju:liti] n. Crédulité *f.*
credulous ['kredjuləs] adj. Crédule.
credulously [-li] adv. Avec crédulité.
creed [kri:d] n. ECCLES. Credo m.; *Apostles' Creed*, Symbole des apôtres. ‖ FIG. Profession de foi, croyance *f.*; *the dust of creeds outworn*, le linceul de pourpre où dorment les dieux morts.
creek [kri:k] n. GEOGR. Crique, anse *f.* (bay); cluse *f.* (vale). ‖ U. S. Cours (*m.*) d'eau (stream).
creel [kri:l] n. Manne, glène *f.* (angler's). ‖ TECHN. Porte-bobines m. (in spinning).
creep [kri:p] v. intr. (41). Ramper (to crawl). ‖ Glisser, avancer furtivement (or) sans bruit. ‖ Se faufiler, se couler, se glisser (into, dans). ‖ Se hérisser; *to make s.o.'s flesh creep*, donner la chair de poule à. ‖ BOT., CHIM. Grimper. ‖ CH. DE F. Cheminer. ‖ NAUT. *To creep for*, draguer. ‖ PHYS. Fluer. ‖ FIG. S'insinuer (into, dans; over, en). ‖ FIG. Ramper (to fawn).
— n. Fait (*m.*) de ramper. ‖ Pl. Chair de poule *f.* (fam.). ‖ U. S. FAM. Chien couchant, cafard m. (toady). ‖ **Creep-hole**, n. Trou m.
creeper [-ə*] n. BOT. Plante grimpante *f.* ‖ ZOOL. Grimpereau m. ‖ NAUT. Grappin m. ‖ U. S. Barboteuse *f.* (baby's garment). ‖ Pl. U. S. Crampons m. pl. (for boots).
creeping [-iŋ] n. Reptation *f.* (crawling). ‖ FAM. Chair de poule *f.*
— adj. Rampant.
creepy [-i] adj. Rampant. ‖ FIG. Horrifié, qui a la chair de poule (afraid); horrifiant, qui donne la chair de poule (terrifying).
cremate [kri'meit] v. tr. Crémer. (See INCINERATE.)
cremation [kri'meiʃən] n. Crémation *f.*
crematorium [,kremə'tɔ:riəm], **crematory** ['kremətəri] n. Four crématoire m.
crematory ['kremətəri] adj. Crématoire.
crenel ['krenəl] n. ARCHIT. Créneau m.
— v. tr. (1). ARCHIT. Créneler.
crenellate [-eit] v. tr. ARCHIT. Créneler.
Creole ['kri:oul] adj., n. Créole s.
creosol ['kri:osɔl] n. CHIM. Créosote *f.*
creosote ['kriəsout] n. CHIM. Créosote *f.*
crêpe [kreip] n. Crêpe m. (cloth, rubber); *crêpe de Chine*, crêpe de Chine; *satin crêpe*, crêpe satin. ‖ CULIN. *Crêpe Suzette*, crêpe Suzette. ‖ **Crêpe-rubber**, n. Crêpe m.
— adj. Gaufré (paper); de crêpe (sole).
crépinette ['kreip'net] n. CULIN. Crépinette *f.*
crepitate ['krepiteit] v. intr. MED. Crépiter.

crepitation [krɛpi'teiʃən] n. MED. Crépitation f.
crept [krɛpt] pret., p.p. See CREEP.
crepuscular [kri'pʌskjulə*] adj. Crépusculaire.
crescendo [kri'ʃendou] adv. MUS. Crescendo;
crescendo passage, passage exécuté crescendo.
— n. FIG. Comble, point culminant m.
crescent l'krɛsn̩t] n. ASTRON., GEOGR. Croissant m.
|| MUS. Turkish Crescent, pavillon chinois. ||
ARCHIT. Rue en demi-lune f.
— adj. Croissant, augmentant (increasing). || En
croissant, en demi-lune (crescent-shaped). || Cres-
cent-type wrench, n. TECHN. Clef anglaise f.
cresol ['krɛsɔl] n. CHIM. Crésol m.
cress [krɛs] n. BOT. Cresson m.
crest [krɛst] n. Crête f. (comb); huppe f. (tuft). ||
MILIT. † Heaume m. (helmet); cimier, panache m.
(plume). || GEOGR. Crête f. (of a mountain). || NAUT.
Crête f. (of a wave). || ARCHIT. Faîte m. || MED.
Arête f. (of a bone). || ZOOL. Crinière f. (mane). ||
BLAS. Ecusson m. || Crest-fallen, adj. FAM. La
crête (or) l'oreille basse, défrisé.
— v. tr. Orner d'un panache (or) d'une aigrette. ||
FIG. Monter jusqu'au sommet.
— v. intr. NAUT. Moutonner (wave).

CRICKET

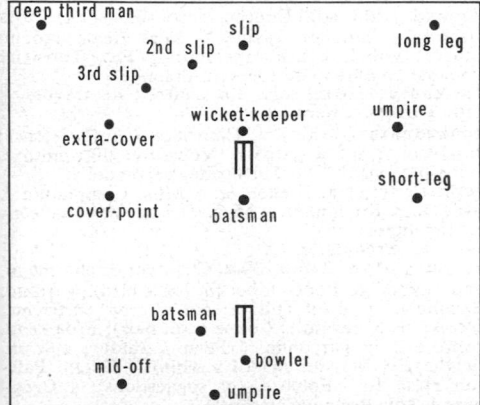

deep third man
slip
2nd slip   long leg
3rd slip
wicket-keeper   umpire
extra-cover
short-leg
cover-point   batsman

batsman
mid-off   bowler
umpire

cretaceous [kri'teiʃəs] adj. GEOL. Crétacé.
cretin ['krɛtin] n. MED. Crétin m.
cretinism [-izm̩] n. MED. Crétinisme m.
cretonne ['krɛtɔn] n. Cretonne f.
crevasse [krə'væs] n. Crevasse f. (in a glacier). ||
U. S. Fissure f. (in a dyke).
— v. tr. U. S. Crevasser.
crevice ['krɛvis] n. Fente, fissure f. (in a rock);
crevasse, lézarde f. (in a wall). [See CRANNY.]
crew [kru:] n. NAUT. Equipage m. || MILIT. Gun
crew, servants de pièce; tank crew, équipage de
char. || AVIAT. Equipe f.; équipage m.; ground
crew, équipe au sol. || CH. DE F., SPORTS. Equipe f.
|| FIG. Bande f. (gang). || Crew-space, n. NAUT.
Poste d'équipage m.
— v. tr. NAUT. Manœuvrer.
— v. intr. NAUT. Servir d'équipier (for, à); être
sous les ordres (for, de).
crew pret. See CROW.
crewcut ['kru:'kʌt] n. U. S. Coupe (f.) de cheveux
en brosse; to have a crewcut, être coiffé en brosse.
crewel ['kruəl] n. Laine à tapisserie (or) broderie f.
crib [krib] n. Mangeoire f. (manger); râtelier m.
(rack); stalle f. (stall). || Cahute, bicoque f. (hovel).

|| Berceau m. (cradle). || Manne, nasse f. (creel). ||
Boisage m. (in a mine). || ECCLES. Crèche f. (repro-
duction miniature). || U. S. Coffre m. (for grain,
salt). FAM. Traduction juxtalinéaire f.; corrigé de
texte m. (school-work). || FAM. Plagiat m. || POP.
to crack a crib, faire un fric-frac.
— v. tr. (1). Confiner, claquemurer. || FAM. Copier,
plagier. || FAM. Barboter, chauffer, piquer (to
steal) [from, à].
crick [krik] n. MED. Lumbago m. (in the back);
torticolis m. (in the neck).
— v. tr. Donner le lumbago (or) le torticolis à.
cricket ['krikit] n. ZOOL. Grillon m.
cricket n. SPORTS. Cricket m. || FAM. Fair play m.;
that's not cricket, ce n'est pas de jeu. || Cricket-
ground (or) -field, n. SPORTS. Terrain de cricket m.
— v. intr. SPORTS. Jouer au cricket.
cricketer [-ə*] n. SPORTS. Joueur (s.) de cricket.
crier ['kraiə*] n. Crieur s.; town crier, tambour de
ville. || JUR. Huissier audiencier m.
crikey l'kraiki] interj. FAM. Fichtre!
crime [kraim] n. JUR., FAM. Crime; crime wave,
recrudescence de la criminalité. || Crime-writer, n.
Auteur (m.) de romans policiers.
Crimea [krai'miə] n. GEOGR. Crimée f.
Crimean [-ən] adj. GEOGR. De Crimée.
criminal ['krimin̩l] adj. JUR. Criminel (action);
adultérin (conversation); Criminal Investigation
Department, Police judiciaire. || JUR. Au criminel
(lawyer); to take criminal proceedings against,
poursuivre au criminel.
— n. JUR. Criminel s.
criminalist [-əlist] n. Criminaliste s.
criminality [,krimi'næliti] n. Criminalité f.
criminally ['kriminəli] adv. Criminellement.
criminate [-neit] v. tr. Incriminer. || Condamner.
crimination [,krimi'neiʃən] n. Incrimination f.
criminologist [,krimi'nɔlədʒist] n. Criminologiste s.
criminology [-dʒi] n. Criminologie f.
criminy ['krimini] interj. FAM. Saprelotte!
crimp [krimp] v. tr. NAUT., MILIT. Racoler.
— n. NAUT., MILIT. Racoleur m.
crimp [krimp] v. tr. Gaufrer, crêper (cloth); tuyau-
ter (linen). || Friser, crépeler (hair). || TECHN.
Mouler (leather); onduler (sheet-iron); emboutir
(shoe-upper). || CULIN. Taillader (a fish).
crimson ['krimzn̩] adj. Pourpre (with, de).
— n. Cramoisi, pourpre m.
— v. tr. Teindre en pourpre.
— v. intr. S'empourprer.
cringe [krindʒ] v. intr. S'accroupir. (See COWER.) ||
FIG. Faire des platitudes; s'aplatir (before, to,
devant).
— n. Courbette f.
cringle ['kriŋgl] n. NAUT. Patte de bouline f.
crinite ['krainait] adj. ZOOL., BOT. Chevelu, velu.
crinkle ['kriŋkl] v. intr. Onduler (to ripple). || Se
froncer, se plisser, se froisser, se chiffonner (to
wrinkle). || Bruire, froufrouter, crisser (to rustle).
— v. tr. Onduler. || Froisser, plisser, chiffonner.
— n. Ondulation, ride f. || France f.
crinkly [-li] adj. Ondulé, ridé (ripply); onduleux
(wavy); froissé, chiffonné (wrinkled).
crinoline ['krinəli:n] n. Crinoline f.
cripple ['kripl] n. MED. Boiteux, estropié, infirme
s.; éclopé, bancroche, béquillard s. (fam.). || MILIT.
Mutilé m. || ARCHIT. Echafaud m.
— v. tr. MED. Estropier. || NAUT. Désemparer. ||
MILIT. Immobiliser. || FIG. Paralyser.
crisis ['kraisis] (pl. crises [-i:z]) n. Crise f.;
cabinet crisis, crise ministérielle. || Point crucial m.;
to draw to a crisis, arriver au moment crucial.
crisp [krisp] adj. Crépu (hair); raide, cassant
(paper). || Sec, frisquet, vivifiant, vif (air); cra-
quant (snow). || CULIN. Croustillant, croquant

(bacon, pie); friable, cassant (biscuit); *crisp almond,* praline. ‖ FIG. Net, précis (analysis); animé (dialogue); vif, guilleret (manner); alerte (style).
— n. CULIN. *Potato crisps,* pommes chips.
— v. tr. Crêper, crépeler (cloth, hair). ‖ CULIN. Rendre croustillant.
— v. intr. Se crêper, se crépeler. ‖ CULIN. Devenir croustillant.

crispate ['krispeit] adj. ZOOL., BOT. Crépu.

crispation [kris'peiʃən] n. Frisure ʃ. (curling). ‖ MED. Crispation ʃ. (of the muscles); chair de poule ʃ. (of the skin).

crispbread ['krisp,bred] n. Biscuit (*m.*) de seigle.

crisper [krispə*] n. Fer (*m.*) à friser.

crispness [-nis] n. Crépure ʃ. (of hair). ‖ Froid piquant *m.* (of air); dureté craquante ʃ. (of snow). ‖ CULIN. Qualité croustillante ʃ. ‖ FIG. Vivacité ʃ.

crispy [-i] adj. Frisé, crépu (hair). ‖ CULIN. Croustillant. ‖ FIG. Vif.

criss-cross ['kriskrɔːs] n. Croix ʃ. (signature). Entrecroisement, croisillon *m.* ‖ FIG. Interférence ʃ. ‖ **Criss-cross-row,** n. † Alphabet *m.*
— adj. En croix, croisé, entrecroisé. ‖ FAM. Crispé, de mauvais poil.
— adv. Avec des croisillons, en s'entrecroisant. ‖ FAM. De travers, de guingois.
— v. tr. Entrecroiser.
— v. intr. S'entrecroiser.

cristate ['kristeit] adj. ZOOL. Crêté.

cristobalite [kris'toubə,lait] n. Cristobalite ʃ.

criterion [krai'tiəriən] (pl. **criteria** [-e]) n. Critérium, critère *m.* (See TEST.)

critic ['kritik] n. Critique, censeur *m.; slashing critic,* éreinteur (fam.).

critical [-əl] adj. Critique (dissertation, study); critique, exigeant, tatillon (person); *critical faculty,* sens critique. ‖ Critique, dangereux, délicat, crucial (situation). ‖ MED. Critique (age, state). ‖ PHYS. Limite (angle); critique (temperature); *critical point,* point de transformation.

critically [-əli] adv. D'une manière critique. ‖ Au moment décisif. ‖ MED. Dangereusement.

criticism ['kritisizm] n. Critique ʃ. (act, review). ‖ Critique ʃ.; blâme *m.* (censure); *open to criticism,* critiquable.

criticizable [-saizəb!] adj. Critiquable.

criticize [-saiz] v. tr. Critiquer (to blame, to review).
— v. intr. Critiquer.

criticizer [-saizə*] n. Critiqueur s. (faultfinder).

critique [kri'tiːk] n. Critique ʃ. (art, review).

croak [krouk] n. ZOOL. Coassement *m.* (of frogs); croassement *m.* (of ravens).
— v. intr. Coasser (frog); croasser (raven). ‖ Faire le prophète de malheur, voir tout en noir. ‖ Grommeler, grogner (to grumble). ‖ FAM. Crever, claquer, défunter (to die).
— v. tr. Dire d'une voix lugubre. ‖ FAM. Descendre, démolir (to kill).

croaker [-ə*] n. Prophète de malheur, rabat-joie, pessimiste *m.*

Croat ['krouət] n. GEOGR. Croate s.

Croatian [krou'eiʃən] adj., n. GEOGR. Croate s.

crochet ['krouʃəi] n. Crochet *m.* (knitting). ‖ **Crochet-needle,** n. Crochet *m.* ‖ **Crochet-wool,** n. Coton perlé *m.* ‖ **Crochet-work,** n. Ouvrage (or) travail (*m.*) au crochet.
— v. tr. Faire au crochet.
— v. intr. Faire du crochet.

crocheted [-ʃeid] adj. Au crochet.

crock [krɔk] n. Cruche ʃ. (jar); pot (*m.*) de terre (pot); tesson *m.* (in flowerpots).

crock n. ZOOL., FAM. Rosse, carne ʃ. (horse). ‖ AUTOM., FAM. Bagnole, guimbarde, casserole ʃ. (car). ‖ FAM. *An old crock,* un vieux décati (or) débris; une vieille rombière.

— v. tr. SPORTS. Claquer (a horse); fouler (one's leg). ‖ FAM. *To be crocked,* rester sur le carreau.
— v. intr. **To crock up,** SPORTS. Se claquer.

crockery ['krɔkəri] n. Poterie; faïence ʃ. (earthenware).

crocket ['krɔkit] n. ARCHIT. Crochet *m.*

crocky ['krɔki] adj. FAM. Claqué, décati, fichu.

crocodile ['krɔkədail] n. ZOOL. Crocodile *m.* ‖ FAM. Défilé (*m.*) par deux.
— adj. De crocodile (tears). ‖ TECHN. Crocodile (spanner). ‖ **Crocodile bird,** n. ZOOL. Pluvian *m.*

crocodilian [krɔkə'diliən] adj. ZOOL. Crocodilien.

crocus ['kroukəs] (pl. **crocuses** [-iz]) n. BOT. Crocus *m.* ‖ Safran *m.* ‖ CHIM. Tripoli *m.*

Croesus ['kriːsəs] n. Crésus *m.*

croft [krɔft] n. AGRIC. Clos *m.; petite* ferme ʃ.

crofter [-ə*] n. AGRIC. Affermataire, fermier *m.*

cromlech ['krɔmlek] n. Cromlech *m.*

crone [kroun] n. FAM. Vieille ratatinée ʃ.

crony ['krouni] n. FAM. Copain *m.* (See CHUM.)

crook [kruk] n. Houlette ʃ. (of a shepherd). ‖ Croc, crochet *m.* (hook). ‖ Courbe, courbure ʃ.; coude *m.* (curve). ECCLES. Crosse ʃ. (of a bishop). ‖ FAM. Escroc, voleur *m.* (swindler).
— adj. Tordu. ‖ **Crook-backed,** adj. Bossu, voûté. ‖ **Crook-kneed,** adj. Cagneux.
— v. tr. Recourber ‖ FAM. *To crook the elbow,* lever le coude.
— v. intr. Se recourber.

crooked [-id] adj. Courbe, recourbé (stick); tors (wood). ‖ Sinueux (path). ‖ Tors (leg); crochu (nose); voûté, courbé (person). ‖ FIG. Tortueux (means); malhonnête (person, practice).

crookedly [-idli] adv. En courbe; de travers. ‖ FIG. Tortueusement.

crookedness [-idnis] n. Courbure ʃ. (of a stick); sinuosité ʃ. (of a path). ‖ Voussure, difformité ʃ. (of a person). ‖ FIG. Tortuosité, perversité ʃ.

croon [kruːn] n. Fredon *m.* ‖ MUS. Complainte ʃ.
— v. intr. Fredonner. ‖ MUS. Chanter des chansons sentimentales.
— v. tr. Fredonner.

crooner [-ə*] n. RADIO., FAM. Chanteur de charme *m.*

crop [krɔp] n. ZOOL. Jabot *m.* (of a bird). ‖ AGRIC. Récolte ʃ.; *in crop,* cultivé; *out of crop,* en friche; *second crop,* regain. ‖ Coupe ʃ. (of hair); *Eton crop,* coiffure à la garçonne. ‖ Peau ʃ. (hide); cuir *m.* (leather). ‖ Manche *m.* (of a whip). ‖ CULIN. Paleron *m.* ‖ FIG. Foule ʃ. (of suggestions). ‖ **Crop-eared,** adj. Bretaudé, essorillé.
— v. tr. (1). Brouter, tondre (the grass). ‖ Couper, écourter (ears, tail); couper court, tondre (hair); bretauder (a horse). ‖ AGRIC. Récolter; *to crop with,* semer de.
— v. intr. (1). AGRIC. Porter une récolte, produire, ‖ **To crop forth** (or) **out,** percer, poindre, pointer. ‖ **To crop out** (or) **up,** GEOL. Affleurer; FIG. Surgir, survenir.

cropper [-ə*] n. Tondeuse; ébarbeuse ʃ. (machine); tondeur, ébarbeur s. (person). ‖ AGRIC. Plante productrice ʃ. (plant); affermataire, agriculteur *m.* (person). ‖ FAM. Dégringolade ʃ.; *to come a cropper,* prendre un billet de parterre, ramasser une pelle (or) bûche (lit.); tomber sur un bec (fig.).

croquet ['kroukei] n. SPORTS. Croquet *m.* (game). ‖ coup roqué *m.*
— v. tr. SPORTS. Croquer.

croqueted [-d] adj. SPORTS. Croqué.

croquette [krou'ket] n. CULIN. Croquette ʃ.

crosier ['krouʒə*] n. ECCLES. Crosse ʃ.

cross [krɔs] n. Croix ʃ.; *to take the Cross,* se croiser, partir pour la croisade. ‖ Croix (of an order); *Military Cross,* croix de guerre. ‖ Croix ʃ. (emblem); *cross of Lorraine,* croix de Lorraine; *small cross,* croisette. ‖ Biais *m.* (in a fabric); *on the cross,* en biais. ‖ ASTRON. *The Southern Cross,* la Croix du Sud. ‖ MED. *Red Cross*, la Croix-Rouge. ‖ MED. Croisement *m.* (of races); métis *s.* (person). ‖ FIG. Mélange *m.* (mixing); croix, épreuve *f.* (trial). ‖ FAM. Escroquerie *f.* (See CROOK.)

— v. tr. Croiser (one's legs); *to cross one's fingers*, faire la croix avec deux doigts. ‖ Croiser, couper (to intersect). ‖ Croiser, rencontrer (to meet). ‖ Croiser, faire des croisements de (animals, plants). ‖ Traverser, passer (the ocean, a river, a road); traverser (s.o.'s mind). ‖ Barrer (one's t's); écrire en travers de (a letter). ‖ Chevaucher, être à califourchon sur (a horse, saddle); *a bridge crossing the river Don*, un pont sur le Don. ‖ † Signer; faire une croix sur. ‖ ECCLES. *To cross oneself*, se signer, fire le signe de la croix. ‖ FIN. Barrer (a cheque). ‖ FIG. Contrecarrer, contrarier, déranger; se mettre en travers de, aller à l'encontre de (to thwart). ‖ FAM. *To cross one's heart*, jurer ses grands dieux; *to cross s.o.'s palm*, graisser la patte à qqn. ‖ **To cross off** (or) **out**, barrer, biffer, rayer. ‖ **To cross over**, traverser.

— v. intr. Se croiser (letters, roads, persons). ‖ Traverser, passer de l'autre côté. ‖ NAUT. Faire une traversée. ‖ SPORTS. Couper (in polo).

— adj. Transversal, en travers, en croisement (transverse). ‖ En renvoi, en rappel. ‖ Croisé, métisse (breed). ‖ FIG. Contraire, opposé, hostile (*to*, à). ‖ FAM. Fâché, irrité; *as cross as two sticks*, à cran, d'une humeur de dogue. ‖ **Cross-action,** n. JUR. Action reconventionnelle *f.* ‖ **Cross-arrow,** n. MILIT. † Carreau (*m.*) d'arbalète. ‖ **Cross-bar,** n. ARCHIT. Croisillon *m.* ‖ **Cross-beam,** n. ARCHIT. Traverse *f.* ‖ **Cross-bench,** n. JUR. Siège (*m.*) de député indépendant; adj. FAM. Impartial, modéré. ‖ **Cross-bones,** *m. pl.* Os (*m. pl.*) en croix. ‖ **Cross-bow,** n. MILIT. † Arbalète *f.* ‖ **Cross-breed,** n. Produit de croisement *m.* (animal); métis *s.* (person); v. tr. (26). Croiser. ‖ **Cross-channel,** n. JUR. Passerelle *f.* ‖ **Cross-check,** v. intr. Recouper; FIG. Se recouper. ‖ **Cross-country,** adv. A travers champs; SPORTS. *Cross-country running*, cross, cross-country. ‖ **Cross-current,** n. NAUT. Courant latéral (or) de côté *m.*; FIG. Tendance conflictuelle *f.* ‖ **Cross-cut,** n. Coupe (*f.*) en travers (cut); chemin (*m.*) de traverse (path); scie (*f.*) à deux mains (saw). ‖ **Cross-examination,** n. JUR. Contre-interrogatoire *m.* ‖ **Cross-examine,** v. tr. JUR. Contre-interroger, contre-examiner. ‖ **Cross-eyed,** adj. MED. Qui louche, bigleux. ‖ **Cross-fertilize,** v. tr. BOT., ZOOL. Croiser avec une espèce différente; FIG. apporter un sang neuf à. ‖ **Cross-fire,** n. MILIT. Feu croisé *m.* ‖ **Cross-grain,** n. Fibre torse *f.* ‖ **Cross-grained,** adj. A fibre torse (wood); FAM. Hargneux, hérissé. ‖ **Cross-guard,** n. Quillon *m.* (of a sword). ‖ **Cross-hatch,** v. tr. ARTS. Contre-hachurer. ‖ **Cross-hatching,** n. ARTS. Contre-hachure *f.* ‖ **Cross-legged,** adj. Les jambes croisées. ‖ **Cross-light,** n. ARTS. Faux jour *m.*; FIG. Jour nouveau *m.* ‖ **Cross-over,** n. CH. DE F. Bretelle *f.*; MED. *Crossing-over*, enjambement *m.* ‖ **Cross-patch,** n. FAM. Chameau, grincheux *m.* (man); chipie *f.* (woman). ‖ **Cross-piece,** n. ARCHIT. Entretoise, moise *f.* ‖ **Cross-ply,** adj. AUTOM. A carcasse croisée (or) diagonale (tyre). ‖ **Cross-purposes,** n. pl. Propos interrompus *m. pl.* (game); FIG. Buts opposés, points (*m. pl.*) de vue contraires; *at cross-purposes*, en désaccord. ‖ **Cross-question,** n. JUR. Contre-interrogatoire *m.*; v. tr. Contre-interroger. ‖ **Cross-refer,** v. tr. (1). Renvoyer à (s.o.); v. intr. (1). Faire un renvoi (*to*, à). ‖ **Cross-reference,** n. Renvoi *m.* ‖ **Cross-rolls,** n. pl. SPORTS. Pas croisés *m. pl.* (in skating). ‖ **Cross-sect,** v. tr. Partager par le travers. ‖ **Cross-section,** n. Coupe transversale *f.*; FIG. Tranche *f.* (of life); catégorie *f.* (of people). ‖ **Cross-staff,** n. TECHN. Goniomètre *m.* ‖ **Cross-stitch,** n. Point de croix *m.* ‖ **Cross-trees,** n. pl. NAUT. Barres traversières *f. pl.* ‖ **Cross-wind,** n. Vent latéral (or) de côté *m.*

crosse [krɔs] n. SPORTS. Crosse *f.* (for lacrosse).

crosshead [-hed] n. TECHN. Crossette *f.* ‖ Sous-titre *m.* (in an article).

crossing [-iŋ] n. Croisement *m.* (of races, roads). ‖ NAUT. Traversée *f.*

crossjack [-dʒæk] n. NAUT. Voile barrée *f.*

crosslet [-lit] n. BLAS. Croisette *f.*

crossleted [-litid] adj. BLAS. Croisetté.

crossly [-li] adv. D'une manière bourrue (or) acariâtre, avec humeur.

crossness [-nis] n. Humeur, irritabilité *f.*

crossroad(s) ['krɔs,roud(z)] n. Carrefour, croisement *m.* ‖ FIG. Carrefour *m.*, croisée (*f.*) des chemins.

crossways [-weiz], **crosswise** [-waiz] adv. En croix, en travers.

crossword ['krɔs,wə:d] n. Mots croisés *m. pl.*; *to do a crossword puzzle*, faire des mots croisés.

crotch [krɔtʃ] n. Fourche *f.* (of a branch). ‖ Aine *f.* (of body); entrejambe *m.* (of trousers).

crotchet ['krɔtʃit] n. Crochet *m.* (porter's). ‖ MUS. Noire *f.* ‖ FAM. Toquade *f.* (See CAPRICE.)

crotcheteer [,krɔtʃi'tiə*] n. Fantasque, original.

crotchety ['krɔtʃiti] adj. Fantasque, capricieux, excentrique. ‖ Quinteux, acariâtre.

crouch [krautʃ] v. intr. S'accroupir. (See COWER.) ‖ Se ramasser (before springing). ‖ FAM. Ramper, s'aplatir (to fawn).

— n. Accroupissement *m.* ‖ Prise (*f.*) d'élan.

croup [kru:p] n. MED. Croup *m.*

croup n. Croupe *f.* (of a horse).

croupier ['kru:piə*] n. Croupier *m.*

crow [krou] n. ZOOL. Corneille *f.* ‖ FIG. *White crow*, merle blanc. ‖ FAM. *As the crow flies*, à vol d'oiseau, en ligne droite. ‖ FAM. U. S. *To eat crow*, avaler des couleuvres. ‖ **Crow-bar,** n. TECHN. Bec-de-corbin *m.* ‖ **Crow-bill,** n. MED. Tire-balle *m.* ‖ **Crow-foot,** n. MED. Patte-d'oie *f.*; MILIT. Chausse-trape *f.*; NAUT. Araignée *f.*; BOT. Renoncule *f.* ‖ **Crow's-nest,** n. NAUT. Nid (*m.*) de pie.

crow v. intr. (42). Chanter, coqueriquer (rooster). ‖ Gazouiller (baby). ‖ FIG. Exulter, triompher; *to crow over one's victory*, chanter victoire; *to crow over s.o.*, triompher bruyamment de qqn.

— n. Cocorico, chant du coq *m.* ‖ Gazouillis, gazouillement *m.* (of a baby).

crowd ['kraud] n. Foule, multitude *f.* (concourse). ‖ Foule, cohue, presse *f.* (throng). ‖ Foule, nuée, armée *f.* (swarm). ‖ Foule, masse *f.*; peuple *m.* (mob). ‖ Tas *m.*; masse *f.* (heap). ‖ FAM. Bande, clique *f.*

— v. intr. S'assembler, s'attrouper, se presser. ‖ Se frayer un passage (*into*, dans; *through*, à travers). ‖ **To crowd in** (or) **out** (or) **up**, entrer, sortir, monter en foule.

— v. tr. Assembler, rassembler, attrouper. ‖ Bourrer, entasser, empiler (to cram); presser, tasser, pousser (*into*, dans) [to press]. ‖ Bonder, bourrer, encombrer (*with*, de). ‖ SPORTS. Gêner, entraver. ‖ FAM. U. S. Relancer (a debtor); pressurer (s.o.). ‖ NAUT. *To crowd on sail*, faire force de voiles. ‖ **To crowd out**, repousser faute de place.

crown [kraun] n. Couronne, guirlande *f.*; diadème *m.* (of roses). ‖ Couronne *f.* (of a king). ‖ Couronne, monarchie *f.*; pouvoir royal *m.* ‖ Calotte *f.*; fond *m.* (of a hat). ‖ Sommet *m.* (of a hill); faîte *m.* (of a roof); cime *f.* (of a tree). ‖ TECHN. Table *f.* (of an anvil). ‖ AUTOM. Axe *m.* (of a road). ‖ NAUT. Collet *m.* (of an anchor). ‖ MED. Couronne *f.* (of a tooth). ‖ FIN. Couronne *f.* (coin). ‖ FIG. Couronnement *m.* ‖ **Crown cap,** n. U. S. Capsule *f.* ‖ **Crown-cork,** n. Capsule *f.*; *to remove the crown-cork from a bottle*, décapsuler une bouteille. ‖ **Crown-crane,** n. ZOOL. Demoiselle de Numidie *f.*

‖ **Crown-glass,** n. Crown-glass m. ‖ **Crown-lens,** n. PHYS. Lentille (f.) en crown-glass.
— adj. De la Couronne; *Crown debts*, créances de la Couronne; *Crown lands*, terres domaniales; *Crown Prince*, kronprinz. ‖ JUR. *Crown law*, droit criminel.
— v. tr. Couronner (*with*, de) [s.o., sth.] ‖ Couronner, récompenser (to reward). ‖ Couronner, combler; *to crown s.o.'s misfortunes*, pour comble de malheur. ‖ Damer (in draughts [or] U. S. checkers). ‖ MED. Couronner, mettre une couronne à (a tooth). ‖ TECHN. Bomber (a road). ‖ U. S. FAM. Flanquer un coup sur la tête à.

croze [kro:uz] n. TECHN. Jable m.

crozier ['krouʒə*] n. ECCLES. Crosse f.

crucial ['kru:ʃəl] adj. Décisif, critique. ‖ PHILOS., MED. Crucial.

cruciate ['kru:ʃeit] adj. BOT., ZOOL. Cruciforme.

crucible ['kru:sibl̩] n. CHIM., FIG. Creuset m.

cruciferous [kru:'sifərəs] adj. BOT., ARCHIT. Crucifère.

crucifers ['kru:sifə:z] n. BOT. Crucifères f. pl.

crucifix [-fiks] n. ECCLES. Crucifix, christ m.

crucifixion [,kru:si'fik∫ən] n. ECCLES. Crucifiement m.; crucifixion f.

cruciform ['kru:si,fɔ:m] adj. Cruciforme.

crucify [-fai] v. tr. (2). Crucifier, mettre en croix. ‖ FIG. Mortifier (to mortify); maîtriser (to subdue); torturer, crucifier (to torment).

crude [kru:d] adj. TECHN. Brut (material). ‖ BOT. Non mûr, vert (fruit). ‖ MED. Latent (disease); non assimilé (food). ‖ GRAMM. Sans désinence (word). ‖ FIG. Cru, grossier (expression); cru, vif (light); fruste, grossier, mal dégrossi (manners); brutal (reality, statement); rudimentaire, sommaire, ébauché (work).

crudely [-li] adv. Imparfaitement; crûment; brutalement; grossièrement.

crudeness [-nis], **crudity** [-iti] n. Crudité f. ‖ FIG. Forme ébauchée f.; état rudimentaire m.

cruel ['kruəl] adj. Cruel (act, person).

cruelly [-i] adv. Cruellement.

cruelty ['kruəlti] n. Cruauté f.

cruet ['kruit] n. CULIN. Huilier, vinaigrier m.; burette f. ‖ **Cruet-stand,** n. CULIN. Ménagère f.

cruise [kru:z] v. intr. NAUT. Croiser. ‖ AUTOM. Marauder (taxi). ‖ AVIAT. Voler. ‖ FIG. Excursionner. ‖ POP. Draguer.
— n. NAUT. Croisière f. ‖ MILIT. *Cruise missile*, missile de croisière.

cruiser ['kru:zə*] n. NAUT. Croiseur m.; *battle cruiser*, croiseur de bataille.

cruising [-iŋ] adj. En croisière. ‖ De croisière; économique (speed). ‖ AUTOM. En maraude.
— n. NAUT. Croisière f. ‖ AUTOM. Maraude f.

cruller ['krʌlə*] n. U. S. CULIN. Beignet m.

crumb [krʌm] n. Miette f. (fragment); mie f. (soft part). ‖ FIG. Miette f.; brin m. (bit). ‖ **Crumb-scoop,** n. Ramasse-miettes m.
— v. tr. Emietter. ‖ CULIN. Paner. ‖ FAM. Passer le ramasse-miettes sur.

crumble ['krʌmbl̩] v. tr. Emietter, effriter. ‖ FIG. Morceler.
— v. intr. S'émietter (bread); s'effriter (stone). ‖ FIG. Se pulvériser; se désagréger.

crumbly [-i] adj. Friable. (See BRITTLE.)

crumbs! [krʌmz] interj. FAM. Flûte!, crotte!, zut!

crummy ['krʌmi] adj. FAM. Accorte. ‖ FAM. Argenté, rupin.

crump [krʌmp] n. Coup violent m. ‖ **Crump-hole,** n. MILIT. Entonnoir m.

crumpet ['krʌmpit] n. CULIN. Crêpe beurrée f. ‖ FAM. Caboche f.; citron m. (head). ‖ POP. *A bit of crumpet*, une poule.

crumple ['krʌmpl̩] v. tr. Froisser, chiffonner, friper. ‖ FAM. U. S. Flancher.
— v. intr. Se froisser, se chiffonner, se friper.

crunch [krʌnʃ] v. tr. Croquer, écraser, broyer (with the teeth). ‖ Ecraser, piétiner, faire craquer en marchant.
— v. intr. **To crunch over,** avancer en écrasant (or) faisant craquer qqch.
— n. Bruit de broiement m.; craquement m. ‖ Ecrasement m.

cruor ['kru:ɔ*] n. MED. Sang caillé m.

crupper ['krʌpə*] n. Croupe f. (of a horse); *on the crupper*, en croupe. ‖ Croupière f. (harness).

crural ['kruərəl] adj. MED. Crural.

crusade [kru:'seid] n. MILIT., FIG. Croisade f.
— v. intr. Partir à la croisade.

crusader [-ə*] n. Croisé m.

crush [krʌʃ] v. tr. Ecraser, broyer (to pound); *to crush the clods of*, émotter. ‖ Ecraser, aplatir (to bash in). ‖ Ecraser, comprimer, tasser (to cram). ‖ Froisser, chiffonner (to crumple). ‖ TECHN. Bocarder; concasser. ‖ FIG. Ecraser, accabler (to overwhelm); écraser, opprimer, dominer (to subdue). **To crush out,** exprimer, extraire (juice); FIG. Réprimer (a revolt).
— v. intr. S'écraser, se presser, se tasser, s'empiler; *to crush in*, s'écraser pour entrer; *to crush up*, se serrer.
— n. Ecrasement m. ‖ Presse, foule, bousculade f. (crowd). ‖ FAM. Béguin m. (on, pour) [infatuation]. ‖ **Crush-barrier,** n. Barrière métallique de protection f. ‖ **Crush-hat,** n. Chapeau claque m.

crusher [-ə*] n. TECHN. Broyeur m. ‖ FAM. Coup (m.) de massue (floorer). ‖ U. S. POP. Tombeur m.

crushing [-iŋ] n. Ecrasement m.; broyage m. ‖ TECHN. Bocardage, concassage m.

crust [krʌst] n. Croûte f. (of bread, pie). ‖ Croûte f.; croûton m. (of bread). ‖ Dépôt, tanin m (of wine). ‖ Couche f. (of rust, snow). ‖ GEOL. *Crust of the earth*, écorce terrestre. ‖ BOT. Ecorce f. ‖ ZOOL. Carapace f. ‖ MED. Croûte f. ‖ FAM. *The upper crust*, le gratin. ‖ FAM. U. S. Culot m. (cheek).
— v. tr. Former croûte sur.
— v. intr. Former croûte.

crustacea [krʌs'teiʃiə] n. pl. ZOOL. Crustacés m. pl.

crustacean [-ʃiən] adj. ZOOL. Crustacéen.
— n. ZOOL. Crustacé m.

crusted ['krʌstid] adj. Couvert d'une croûte, qui a formé croûte. ‖ Dépouillé, décanté (wine). ‖ FIG. Antique, démodé, vétuste. ‖ FAM. Encroûté.

crustily [-ili] adv. Avec rudesse.

crustiness [-inis] n. FIG. Rudesse, brusquerie humeur revêche f.; rude écorce f. ‖ Dureté f.; insensibilité f.

crusty [-i] adj. Couvert d'une grosse croûte. ‖ FIG. Rude, brusque, bourru; qui a une rude écorce.

crutch [krʌtʃ] n. MED. Béquille f. ‖ TECHN. Support m. ‖ ARCHIT. Etançon m. ‖ AUTOM. Béquille f (of a motorcycle).

crux [krʌks] n. Hic m. (difficulty). ‖ Point crucial m. ‖ Nœud m. (of a matter).

cry [krai] (pl. **cries** [-z]) n. Cri m. (shout); *to give* (or) *to utter a cry*, pousser un cri. ‖ Cri, appel m (call); supplication f. (entreaty). ‖ Larmes f. pl.; pleurs m. pl.; *to have a good cry*, pleurer tout son saoul, avoir une bonne crise de larmes. ‖ Rumeur publique f.; *there is a general cry against her*, ce n'est qu'un cri contre elle. ‖ SPORTS. Voix f.; clabaudage m. (of dogs). ‖ FAM. *A far cry*, une bonne distance; *in full cry after*, acharné contre; *it is a far cry to*, il y a loin d'ici à. ‖ **Cry-baby,** n. FAM. Pleurnicheur; chialeur s. (fam.).
— v. tr. (2). Crier; *to cry shame upon*, crier hard sur. ‖ Implorer; *to cry mercy*, crier grâce, implorer merci. ‖ Pleurer, verser (tears); *to cry one's eyes out*, s'user les yeux à pleurer. ‖ Proclamer, annoncer, publier (to proclaim). ‖ COMM. Crier. ‖ **To cry down,** rabaisser (to belittle); dénigrer, décrier (to

disparage). ‖ **To cry up**, exalter, vanter, glorifier (to praise).

— v. intr. Crier, pousser des cris. ‖ S'écrier. ‖ Pleurer (*with*, de). [See WEEP.] ‖ SPORTS. Donner de la voix, clabauder (hounds). ‖ **To cry for**, solliciter, implorer, avoir grand besoin de (sth.). ‖ **To cry off**, se retirer, ne plus se mêler de qqch. ‖ **To cry out**, crier ; *to cry out for*, demander à grands cris ; *to cry out with pain*, pousser des cris de douleur. ‖ **To cry to**, implorer, solliciter (s.o.).

crying [-iŋ] adj. FIG. Criant, patent.

cryogen ['kraiədʒən] n. Liquide (or) mélange cryogène m.

cryogenic [,kraiə'dʒenik] adj. Cryogénique, cryogène.

cryogenics [-s] n. sg. Cryogénie, cryologie f.

cryolite ['kraiə,lait] n. Cryolithe f.

crypt [kript] n. ARCHIT. Crypte f.

cryptanalysis [-ə'nælisis] n. Cryptanalyse f.

cryptic [-ik] adj. Cryptique, abscons, abstrus. ‖ Occulte.

cryptogam ['kriptogæm] n. BOT. Cryptogame m.

cryptogram ['kriptogræm], **cryptograph** [-grɑ:f] n. Cryptogramme m.

cryptographer [krip'tɔgrəfə*] n. Cryptographe s.

cryptography [-i] n. Cryptographie f.

cryptology [krip'tɔlədʒi] n. Cryptologie f.; code m.

crystal ['kristl] n. Cristal m. ‖ RADIO. Cristal m. ‖ U. S. Verre m. (over a watch).

— adj. De cristal, cristallin.

crystalline ['kristəlain] adj. Cristallin. ‖ MED. *Crystalline lens*, cristallin (of the eye).

crystallization [,kristəlai'zəiʃən] n. Cristallisation f.

crystallize ['kristəlaiz] v. tr. Cristalliser.

— v. intr. Se cristalliser.

crystallizing [-iŋ] adj. A cristalliser ; *cristallizing vessel*, cristallisoir.

crystallography [,kristə'lɔgrəfi] n. Cristallographie f.

CS [si:'es] n. *CS gas*, gaz C. S., gaz lacrymogène m.

C. S. E. [si:es'i:] abbr. *Certificate of Secondary Education*, en Grande-Bretagne, diplôme décerné à la fin de la troisième.

cub [kʌb] n. ZOOL. Ourson m. (young bear) ; renardeau m. (young fox) ; lionceau m. (young lion). ‖ Louveteau m. (boy-scout). ‖ FAM. Gosse m.; *cub reporter*, reporteur novice.

— v. tr., intr. (2). ZOOL. Mettre bas.

Cuba ['kju:bə] n. GEOGR. Cuba.

cubage ['kju:bidʒ] n. Cubage m.

Cuban [-ən] adj., n. GEOGR. Cubain s.

cube [kju:b] n. MATH. Cube m. ‖ CULIN. Bouillon cube, cube m.

— v. tr. MATH. Cuber. ‖ TECHN. Paver en cubes. ‖ CULIN. Couper en cubes.

— adj. MATH. *Cube root*, racine cubique.

cubic [-ik] adj. MATH. Cubique (content, power, shape) ; du troisième degré (equation) ; cube (foot).

cubical [-ikl] adj. MATH. Cubique ; *to have a cubical content of*, cuber.

cubicle [-ikl] n. Box m.; cabine f. (compartment). ‖ Alcôve, cellule f. (in a dormitory).

cubism ['kju:bizm] n. ARTS. Cubisme m.

cubist [-ist] n. ARTS. Cubiste s.

cubit ['kju:bit] n. Coudée f.

cubital [-l] adj. MED. Cubital.

cubitus [-əs] n. MED. Cubitus m.

cuboid ['kju:bɔid] adj. Cuboïde. ‖ MED. *Cuboid bone*, os cuboïde.

cuckold ['kʌkəld] adj., n. FAM. Cocu, cornard m.

— v. tr. FAM. Cocufier.

cuckoldom [-əm] n. FAM. Cocuage m.

cuckoldry [-dri] n. FAM. Cocufiage m.

cuckoo ['kuku] n. ZOOL. Coucou m.

— adj. *Cuckoo clock*, coucou. ‖ FAM. Sonné

(crazy) ; bêta (silly). ‖ **Cuckoo-flower**, n. BOT. Cardamine (m.) des prés.

— v. intr. FAM. U. S. Imiter le coucou.

cucumber ['kju:kʌmbə*] n. BOT. Concombre m. ‖ FAM. *Cool as a cucumber*, la tête froide, maître de soi. ‖ U. S. *Cucumber tree*, magnolia.

cucurbit [kju:'kə:bit] n. CHIM. Cucurbite f. ‖ BOT. Courge f.

cucurbitaceae [,kjukə:bi'teisii:] n. BOT. Cucurbitacécs f. pl.

cucurbitaceous [-ʃəs] adj. Cucurbitacé.

cud [kʌd] n. ZOOL. Bol alimentaire (m.) des ruminants ; *to chew the cud*, ruminer. ‖ FAM. Chique f.

cudbear ['kʌdbɛə*] n. BOT., CHIM. Orseille f.

cuddle ['kʌdl] v. tr. Caresser, câliner (see CARESS) ; peloter (pop.).

— v. intr. S'enlacer ; se peloter (pop.). ‖ **To cuddle up**, se pelotonner.

— n. Enlacement m.; étreinte f.

cuddling [-iŋ] n. Pelotage m. (pop.).

cuddy ['kʌdi] n. Placard m. (closet) ; armoire f. (cupboard). ‖ NAUT. Tille f.

cuddy n. ZOOL., FAM. Bourricot, bourin m.

cudgel ['kʌdʒəl] n. Trique f.; gourdin ; assommoir m. (See CLUB.) ‖ FAM. *To take up the cudgels on behalf of*, entrer en lice pour, prendre fait et cause pour.

— v. tr. (1). Bâtonner, donner une volée de coups de bâton à. ‖ FAM. *To cudgel one's brains*, se creuser la cervelle.

cudgelling [-iŋ] n. Volée (f.) de coups de bâton ; bastonnade f.

cue [kju:] n. † THEATR. Rôle m. (part). ‖ THEATR. Fin de tirade, réplique f.; *to give s.o. his cue*, donner la réplique à qqn. ‖ FIG. Indication, directive f.; mot d'ordre m.; *to take one's cue from*, prendre les consignes de, se mettre à la remorque de.

— v. tr. THEATR. Donner la réplique à. ‖ FIG. Alerter (to inform) ; *to cue in*, donner le top à, faire signe à.

cue n. SPORTS. Queue (f.) de billard. ‖ † Queue f. (of wig). ‖ **Cue-ball**, n. SPORTS. Boule (f.) de billard.

cueist [-ist] n. SPORTS. Joueur de billard m.

cuff [kʌf] n. Poignet m.; manchette f. (of a shirt) ; *cuff button* (or) *link*, bouton de manchette. ‖ Parement m. (of coat sleeve) ; *cuff protector*, gardemanche ; *double cuff*, manchette mousquetaire. ‖ U. S. Revers de pantalon m. ‖ FAM. *Off the cuff*, à l'improviste.

cuff v. tr. Calotter, gifler. (See SLAP.)

— n. Calotte, gifle f.

cuirass [kwi'ræs] n. MILIT., ZOOL. Cuirasse f.

— v. tr. MILIT. Cuirasser (a soldier).

cuirassier [kwirə'si:ə*] n. MILIT. Cuirassier m.

cuish [kwiʃ], **cuisse** [kwis] n. MILIT. † Cuissart m.

cuisine [kwi'zi:n] n. CULIN. Cuisine f. (cooking).

cul-de-lampe ['kydlæmp] n. ARCHIT. Cul-de-lampe m.

cul-de-sac ['kʌldəsæk] n. Cul-de-sac m. (blind alley).

culinary ['kju:linəri] adj. CULIN. Culinaire.

cull [kʌl] v. tr. Cueillir (flowers). ‖ FIG. Choisir, sélectionner.

— n. AGRIC. Animal (m.) choisi pour l'engrais. ‖ U. S. Pl. Déchets m. pl.

cullet ['kʌlit] n. TECHN. Calcin m.

cully ['kʌli] n. FAM. † Gobeur s. (dupe). ‖ POP. Copain (pal).

culm [kʌlm] n. Poussier m.

culm n. BOT. Chaume m. (of grasses).

culminant ['kʌlminənt] adj. ASTRON. Culminant.

culminate [-eit] v. intr. Culminer.

culmination [,kʌlmi'neiʃən] n. ASTRON. Culmination f. ‖ FIG. Zénith, pinacle m. (See ACME.)

culotte(s) [kju:'lɔt(s)] n. (or) n. pl. Jupe-culotte f.

culpability [ˌkʌlpə'biliti] n. Culpabilité f.
culpable ['kʌlpəbl̩] adj. Coupable. (See GUILTY.)
culpably [-bli] adv. Coupablement.
culprit ['kʌlprit] n. Coupable s. ‖ JUR. Prévenu s.
cult [kʌlt] n. ECCLES., FIG. Culte m.
cultivable ['kʌltivəbl̩] adj. Cultivable.
cultivate [-eit] v. tr. AGRIC. Cultiver (plants, soil); travailler au cultivateur (soil). ‖ FIG. Cultiver (an art, a friend, one's mind). ·
cultivation [ˌkʌlti'veiʃən] n. AGRIC., FIG. Culture f. (act, state).
cultivator ['kʌltiveitə*] n. AGRIC. Cultivateur m. (machine, person); cultivatrice f. (person).
cultual ['kʌltjuəl] adj. ECCLES. Cultuel.
cultural ['kʌltʃərəl] adj. AGRIC. Cultural. ‖ FIG. Culturel.
culture ['kʌltʃə*] n. AGRIC. Culture f. (of plants, soil). ‖ AGRIC. Elevage m.; culture of bees, fish, oysters, silk, apiculture, pisciculture, ostréiculture, sériciculture. ‖ MED. Culture f.; culture fluid (or) medium, bouillon de culture; culture tube, tube à culture. ‖ FIG. Culture f. (general, physical).
— v. tr. AGRIC., MED., FIG. Cultiver.
culver ['kʌlvə*] n. ZOOL. Ramier m.
culverin ['kʌlvərin] n. MILIT. † Couleuvrine f.
culvert ['kʌlvə:t] n. ARCHIT. Aqueduc m. ‖ ELECTR. Conduit souterrain m.
cum [kʌm] pref. Avec. ‖ **Cum-coupon,** n. FIN. Coupon attaché m.
cumber ['kʌmbə*] v. tr. Encombrer (with, de) [to hinder]. ‖ Surcharger (to burden).
— n. Encombrement m.
cumbersome ['bəsəm], **cumbrous** [-brəs] adj. Encombrant, embarrassant. ‖ Lourd, pesant (heavy).
cumin ['kʌmin] n. BOT. Cumin m.
cummerbund ['kʌmə,bʌnd] n. Large ceinture f.
cumulate ['kju:mjulit] adj. Accumulé.
— [-eit] v. tr. Accumuler. ‖ JUR. Cumuler.
— v. intr. S'accumuler.
cumulation [ˌku:mju'leiʃən] n. Accumulation f. ‖ JUR. Cumul m.; cumulation f. (of sentences).
cumulative ['kju:mjulətiv] adj. JUR. Plural (voting); cumulative evidence, preuve par accumulation de témoignages. ‖ FIN. Composé (interests).
cumulus [-əs], (pl. **cumuli** [-ai]) n. Cumulus m.
cuneal ['kju:niəl] adj. En forme de coin.
cuneiform [-ifɔ:m] adj. GRAMM. Cunéiforme.
— n. Ecriture cunéiforme f.
cunning ['kʌniŋ] n. Finesse, pénétration, acuité f. (keenness); habileté, adresse f. (skill); ruse, astuce, fourberie f. (slyness).
— adj. Fin, habile, adroit. (See CLEVER.) ‖ Malin, futé, pénétrant. (See SHREWD.) ‖ Rusé, astucieux, sournois, fourbe. (See SLY.) ‖ FAM. U. S. Gentil.
cunningly [-li] adv. Finement, habilement. ‖ Avec pénétration. ‖ Avec ruse (or) fourberie. ‖ U. S. Gentiment.
cunt [kʌnt] n. ARG. Con m. (vagina). ‖ ARG. Con s. (insult).
cup [kʌp] n. Tasse f.; tea-cup, tasse à thé. ‖ Gobelet m.; timbale f. (metal cup). ‖ Tasse, pleine tasse f. (cupful); cup of tea, tasse de thé. ‖ Boisson f.; claret cup, bordeaux glacé au citron. ‖ Bonnet m. (of brassiere). ‖ SPORTS. Coupe f. (prize); trou m. (in golf). ‖ BOT. Calice m. (of a flower). ‖ TECHN. Godet m. ‖ MILIT. Coupelle f. ‖ GEOGR. Cuvette f. ‖ MED. Emboîture f. (of a bone); ventouse f. (glass bowl). ‖ ECCLES. Calice m. ‖ FIG. Coupe f. (of pleasures); calice m. (of sorrow). ‖ FAM. Just my cup of tea, mon dada, ma marotte (fad); mes oignons, mon rayon (line); to be in one's cups, avoir un verre de trop (or) dans le nez.
— v. tr. (1). Mettre en forme de coupe (hand). Mettre des ventouses à. ‖ SPORTS. Trouer (in golf).
cupboard ['kʌbəd] n. Buffet m. (cuddy); placard m. (in wall). ‖ FAM. Cupboard love, amour intéressé, reconnaissance du ventre.

cupcake ['kʌpkeik] n. CULIN. Petit four m.
cupel ['kju:pəl] n. CHIM. Coupelle f.
— v. tr. (1). CHIM. Coupeller.
Cupid ['kju:pid] n. Cupidon, Eros m. ‖ ARTS. Amour m.
cupidity [kju'piditi] n. Cupidité f. (See AVARICE.)
cupola ['kju:pələ] n. ARCHIT. Dôme m.; coupole f. ‖ MILIT., NAUT. Coupole f. ‖ TECHN. Cubilot m.
cuppa ['kʌpə] n. FAM. Tasse (f.) de thé.
cupped [kʌpt] adj. En forme de coupe; with one's hands cupped around one's mouth, les mains en porte-voix.
cupper ['kʌpə*] n. MED. Ventouseur s.
cuprammonium [ˌkjuprə'moujnəm] n. CHIM. Liqueur cupro-ammoniacale f.
cupreous ['kju:priəs] adj. Cuivreux.
cupric ['kju:prik] adj. CHIM. Cuprique.
cupriferous [kju'prifərəs] adj. CHIM. Cuprifère.
cupro-nickel [ˌkju:prou'nikl̩] n. Cupronickel m.
cupule ['kju:pjul] n. BOT. Cupule f.
cur [kə:*] n. ZOOL. Corniaud, cabot, chien bâtard m. ‖ FAM. Chien m. (person).
curable [ˌkjuərəbl̩] adj. MED. Curable.
curacoa [ˌkjuərə'sou] n. Curaçao m.
curacy ['kjuərəsi] n. ECCLES. Vicariat m.
curare [kjuə'rɑːri] n. Curare m.
curate ['kjuərit] n. ECCLES. Vicaire m.
curative ['kjuərətiv] adj., n. MED. Curatif.
curator [kjuə'reitə*] n. Conservateur m. (of a library, museum). ‖ JUR. Curateur m.
curatrix [-triks] n. JUR. Curatrice f.
curb [kə:b] n. Gourmette f. (harness). ‖ Bord du trottoir m. (kerb); margelle f. (of well). ‖ Courbe f (disease of horses). ‖ FIG. Frein m. ‖ **Curb-bit,** n. Mors (m.) à gourmette. ‖ **Curb-roof,** n. ARCHIT. Comble brisé m.
— v. tr. Gourmer (a horse). ‖ Border (a pavement) ‖ FIG. Contraindre (constrain); refréner, brider. (See RESTRAIN.) ‖ U. S. FAM. Curb your dog, faites faire votre chien dans le ruisseau.
curd [kə:d] n. CULIN. Lait caillé m.; caillebotte f
curdle [kə:dl̩] v. tr. Cailler, coaguler. (See CLOT.) ‖ FAM. To curdle s.o.'s blood, glacer le sang dans les veines de qqn.
— v. intr. Se cailler, se coaguler. ‖ FAM. Se figer, se glacer.
cure [kjuə*] n. MED. Remède m. (remedy). ‖ MED. Cure f.; fruit cure, cure de fruits; to take the cure at, faire une cure à. ‖ ECCLES. Charge f. (of souls) cure f. (vicarship). ‖ CULIN. Salaison f. (of fish meat). ‖ **Cure-all,** n. FAM. Panacée f.
— v. tr. MED. Guérir (of, de). ‖ CULIN. Saler fumer. ‖ TECHN. Vulcaniser (rubber). ‖ FIG. Porter remède à; remédier à.
curé ['kju:rei] n. ECCLES. Curé m.
cureless ['kuəlis] adj. MED. Incurable.
curfew ['kə:fju] n. Couvre-feu m.
curia ['kjuəri] n. Curie f.
curial [-əl] adj. Curial.
curio ['kjuəriou] n. ARTS. Bibelot, objet curieux m.; curiosité f.
curiosity [ˌkjuəri'ɔsiti] n. Curiosité f. (inquisitiveness). ‖ Curiosité, étrangeté, bizarrerie f. (strangeness). ‖ Curiosité, rareté, f.; objet curieux m. **Curiosity-shop,** n. Magasin (m.) d'antiquités.
curious ['kjuəriəs] adj. Curieux, avide de savoir to be curious of, avoir la curiosité de. ‖ Curieux indiscret (inquisitive). ‖ Méticuleux, précis, détaill (accurate). ‖ Curieux, étrange, inusité, singulie (strange). ‖ Curieux, extraordinaire (eccentric).
curiously [-li] adv. Curieusement. ‖ Avec soin (or précision (accurately). ‖ Curieusement, singulière ment.
curium ['kjuəriəm] n. CHIM., PHYS. Curium m.
curl ['kə:l] n. Boucle f. (of hair); false, side cur chichi, guiche; in curl, bouclé; out of curl, défrisé

‖ Spirale, volute *f.* (of smoke); ondulation *f.* (of waves); ronce *f.* (in grain of wood). ‖ AGRIC. Maladie *(f.)* des pommes de terre. ‖ FIG. Pli *m.;* *with a curl of the lip,* la lèvre dédaigneuse. ‖ **Curl-paper,** n. Papillote *f.*
— v. tr. Boucler, faire boucler (hair). ‖ Retrousser (one's lip); *to curl oneself up,* se mettre en boule (cat); se pelotonner (person).
— v. intr. Boucler. ‖ **To curl up,** se mettre en boule (cat, hedgehog); se coucher en rond (dog); s'enrouler (paper, rope); se coucher en chien de fusil (person).

curlew ['kə:lju:] n. ZOOL. Courlis *m.*

curler ['kə:lə*] n. Bigoudi, U. S. rouleau *m.* ‖ NAUT. Vague déferlante *f.* ‖ SPORTS. Curler *m.*

curlicue ['kə:likju:] n. Fioriture *f.* (in handwriting). ‖ SPORTS. Figure *(f.)* de patinage.

curling ['kə:liŋ] n. Frisure, ondulation *f.* (of hair). ‖ Ondulation (of waves). ‖ SPORTS. Jeu de palet *(m.)* sur glace. ‖ **Curling-iron,** n. Fer *(m.)* à friser. ‖ **Curling-pin,** n. Epingle *(f.)* à friser; bigoudi *m.*

curly [-i] adv. Bouclé (hair). ‖ A grain ondulé (wood). ‖ AGRIC. Frisé (lettuce).

curmudgeon [kə:'mʌdʒən] n. FAM. Mauvais coucheur, sale bougre *m.* (cross-patch); rat, ladre (miser).

currant ['kʌrənt] n. BOT. Groseille *f.; black currant,* cassis *m.* ‖ CULIN. Raisin *(m.)* de Corinthe. ‖ **Currant-bush,** n. BOT. Groseillier.

currency ['kʌrənsi] n. FIN. Circulation *f.* (of money); *paper currency,* circulation fiduciaire; *export of currency,* exportation de capitaux. ‖ FIN. Monnaie *(f.)* ayant cours; devise *f.* ‖ FIG. Cours m.; *to gain currency,* s'accréditer; *to give currency to,* répandre, diffuser (a rumour).

current [-ənt] adj. Courant, commun, habituel (usual). ‖ Admis, reçu, accepté (accepted). ‖ Courant, en cours; *current affairs,* questions d'actualité; *current events,* événements du jour, actualités; *current issue,* dernier numéro; *current year,* année en cours. ‖ FIN. Courant (expenses); consenti (loan); en cours (money); *current market prices,* le courant du marché; *current rate of exchange,* cours du jour.
— n. Courant *m.* (of air, water). ‖ Cours *(m.)* d'eau (stream). ‖ ELECTR. Courant *m.* ‖ FIG. Cours, courant *m.*

curricle ['kʌrikl] n. Voiture *(f.)* à deux chevaux.

curriculum [kə'rikjuləm] n. Programme scolaire *m.*

currier ['kʌriə*] n. TECHN. Corroyeur *s.*

currish ['kə:riʃ] adj. Bon à jeter aux chiens; *this currish boy,* ce chien de garçon! ‖ Hargneux, qui montre les dents, d'une humeur de dogue (snarling).

currishly [-li] adv. Hargneusement.

currishness [-nis] n. Hargne *f.*

curry ['kʌri] v. tr. (2). Etriller (a horse); corroyer (leather). ‖ FIG. *To curry favour with,* chercher à amadouer, se mettre bien avec. ‖ **Curry-comb,** n. Etrille *f.; v.* tr. U. S. Etriller (a horse).

curry n. CULIN. Curry, cari *m.*
— v. tr. (2). CULIN. Epicer au curry.

curse [kə:s] n. Malédiction *f.; under a curse,* sous le coup d'une malédiction. ‖ Juron *m.;* imprécation *f.* ‖ ECCLES. Excommunication *f.* ‖ FIG. Calamité *f.*
— v. tr. Maudire; *curse him!,* au diable soit-il! ‖ ECCLES. Excommunier. ‖ FAM. *To be cursed with,* être affligé de, souffrir de.
— v. intr. Jurer, blasphémer.

cursed ['kə:sid], **curst** [kə:st] adj. Maudit, odieux, abominable. ‖ FAM. Sacré.

cursive ['kə:siv] adj. Cursif.
— n. Cursive *f.*

cursor [-ə*] n. TECHN. Curseur *m.*

cursorily [-ərili] adv. En courant, hâtivement; superficiellement; à la va-vite (fam.).

cursoriness [-ərinis] n. Hâte, rapidité *f.*

cursory [-əri] adj. Hâtif, superficiel; *cursory reading,* lecture rapide; lecture en diagonale (fam.).

curt [kə:t] adj. Sec, bref, brusque. (See BLUNT.) ‖ Concis, condensé (terse).

curtly [-li] adv. D'un ton cassant (or) sec.

curtail [kə:'teil] v. tr. Ecourter, raccourcir, diminuer (a text). ‖ FIN. Réduire, restreindre (expenses). ‖ FIG. Priver *(of,* de) [s.o.]; *to curtail s.o. of sth.,* rogner qqch. à qqn.

curtailment [-mənt] n. Diminution *f.;* raccourcissement *m.* ‖ FIN. Réduction *f.*

curtain ['kə:tn] n. Rideau *m.; blind curtain,* store; *iron curtain,* rideau de fer. ‖ THEATR. Rideau *m.* ‖ MILIT. Courtine *f.* ‖ FIG. Rideau, voile *m.; to raise the curtain on,* dévoiler. ‖ FAM. Dernière heure *f.;* baisser de rideau *m.* (death). ‖ **Curtain-call,** n. THEATR. Rappel *m.* ‖ **Curtain-lecture,** n. FAM. Chicane *(f.)* sur l'oreiller. ‖ **Curtain-raiser,** n. THEATR. Lever de rideau *m.* (play); FIG. Préambule *m.* ‖ **Curtain-speech,** n. THEATR. Allocution (or) annonce *(f.)* au baisser de rideau.
— v. tr. Garnir de rideaux. ‖ Cacher sous des rideaux.

curtly ['kə:tli] adv. D'un ton cassant, sèchement. ‖ D'une manière concise.

curtness [-nis] n. Brusquerie *f.* ‖ Concision *f.*

curtsy ['kə:tsi] n. Révérence *f.*
— v. intr. Faire la révérence *(to,* à).

curule ['kjuərju:l] adj. Curule.

curvaceous [kə:'veiʃəs] adj. FAM. Bien roulée, bien balancée (woman); galbée (leg).

curvature ['kə:vətʃə*] n. Courbure *f.* ‖ MED. Déviation *f.; to cause curvature of the spine,* dévier la colonne vertébrale.

curve [kə:v] n. Courbe *f.* ‖ Courbe *f.;* graphique *m.; consumption curve,* courbe de consommation. ‖ MATH. Courbe *f.* ‖ MILIT. *Accuracy curve,* courbe de justesse. ‖ ARCHIT. Voussure *f.* (of an arch); cambrure *f.* (of a beam). ‖ AUTOM. Tournant, virage *m.* ‖ ARTS. Pistolet *m.* (of draftsman). ‖ FAM. Pl. Rondeurs *f. pl.* (plumpness). ‖ **Curve-tracer,** n. MATH. Curvigraphe *m.*
— v. tr. Courber. (See BEND.) ‖ ARCHIT. Cintrer.
— v. intr. Se courber. ‖ MATH. Décrire une courbe.

curvet ['kə:vit] n. SPORTS. Courbette *f.*
— v. intr. (1). SPORTS. Faire des courbettes (in equitation).

curvilinear [,kə:vi'liniə*] adj. MATH. Curviligne.

cushat ['kʌʃət] n. ZOOL. Ramier *m.*

cushion ['kuʃən] n. Coussin *m.* ‖ Carreau *m.* (in lacemaking); rond de cuir *m.* (on office-chair); pelote *f.* (for pins). ‖ Tournure *f.* (beneath skirt). ‖ Fourchette *f.* (or horse's hoof). ‖ TECHN. Matelas *m.* ‖ SPORTS. Bande *f.* (in billiards); *stroke off the cushion,* doublé. ‖ CULIN. Culotte *f.* (of pork); noix *f.* (of veal). ‖ FAM. Bourrelet, matelas *m.* (of fat).
— v. tr. Orner de coussins. ‖ Rembourrer (a seat). ‖ Faire asseoir sur des coussins. ‖ TECHN. Matelasser. ‖ SPORTS. Acculer à la bande (in billiards). ‖ FIG. Etouffer (a matter); amortir (a shock). ‖ FAM. Chouchouter (to cosset).

cushy ['kuʃi] adj. FAM. Pépère; *cushy job,* assiette au beurre, fromage, filon; *a cushy life,* une vie ouatée (or) douillette; *to have a cushy time,* se chouchouter, se mignoter.

cusp [kʌsp] n. Pointe *f.* ‖ MATH. Sommet *m.* (of a curve). ‖ ARCH. Lobe *m.* ‖ ASTRON. Corne *f.* (of the moon). ‖ BOT., MED. Cuspide *f.*

cuspidate ['kʌspidit] adj. BOT. Cuspidé. ‖ MED. Canine (tooth).

cuspidor [-ə*] n. Crachoir *m.* (See SPITTOON.)

cuss [kʌs] n. FAM. Type *m.* (guy). ‖ FAM. Juron *m.* (curse); *a tinker's cuss,* un pet de lapin.
— v. intr. Jurer, sacrer.
— v. tr. Maudire, pester après.

cussed [-id] adj. FAM. Entêté, contrariant; *a cussed fellow,* un enquiquineur.

cussedness [-idnis] n. Esprit (*m.*) de contradiction; *general cussedness of things,* continuelle ironie des choses, perpétuels bâtons dans les roues.

custard ['kʌstəd] n. CULIN. Crème renversée *f.;* flan *m.; custard powder,* entremets (or) crème en poudre; *custard tart,* dariole.

custodial [kʌs'toudiəl] adj. De gardien.
— m. ECCLES. Custode *f.*

custodian [-ən] n. Gardien *s.* ‖ Concierge *s.* (of a building). ‖ Conservateur *m.*, conservatrice *f.* (of a museum).

custody ['kʌstədi] n. Garde *f.* (see CARE); *in safe custody,* sous bonne garde. ‖ Emprisonnement *m.;* détention *f.; in custody,* en état d'arrestation; *to give into custody,* remettre entre les mains de la police.

custom ['kʌstəm] n. Coutume, pratique courante *f.;* usage *m.* (established usage); *as the custom is,* selon la coutume. ‖ Coutume, habitude *f.* (habit); *ill custom,* mauvaise habitude. ‖ JUR. Droit coutumier *m.* ‖ COMM. Clientèle *f.* ‖ Pl. Droits (*m. pl.*) de douane. ‖ **Custom-house,** n. Douane *f.; custom-house officer,* douanier. ‖ **Customs-union,** n. Union douanière *f.*
— adj. U. S. Fait sur commande. ‖ **Custom-built,** adj. U. S. Hors série. ‖ **Custom-made,** adj. U. S. Sur mesure (clothes). ‖ **Custom tailor,** n. U. S. Tailleur (*m.*) à façon.

customary [-əri] adj. Coutumier, habituel (*with,* à). ‖ JUR. Coutumier (law); d'usage (right); selon la coutume locale (tenant).
— n. JUR. Coutumier *m.*

customer [-ə*] n. COMM. Client *s.; to attract customers,* attirer le chaland. ‖ FAM. Client, citoyen, type *m.; he is a tough customer,* il n'est pas commode; *nasty customer,* mauvais coucheur.

customize ['kʌstə‚maiz] v. tr. Fabriquer sur commande (to make to order). ‖ AUTOM. Personnaliser.

cut [kʌt] n. Coupe, coupure *f.* (cutting). ‖ Coupure, entaille *f.* (notch); *saw cut,* trait de scie. ‖ Coupure; estafilade *f.* (slash); *Coup tranchant *m.;* taillade *f.; sword cut,* coup d'épée. ‖ Coup cinglant *m.* (with, de); *to give the horse a cut with one's whip,* cingler le cheval d'un coup de fouet. ‖ Raccourci *m.* (way); *to take a short cut,* couper (or) prendre au plus court. ‖ Coupure *f.* (in an article, a play). ‖ Coupon *m.* (of cloth). ‖ Coupe *f.* (of a pack of cards); *to draw cuts,* tirer à la courte paille. ‖ Coupe (of a coat); taille *f.* (of a diamond). ‖ Silhouette, ligne *f.* (of the body); coupe (of the face). ‖ Illustration, planche *f.* (in a book). ‖ ARTS. Gravure (*f.*) sur bois (woodcut). ‖ ELECTR. *Power cut,* coupure de courant. ‖ TECHN. Taille *f.* (of a file); passe *f.* (of a machine-tool). ‖ CH. DE F. Tranchée *f.* ‖ AGRIC. Enture *f.* (graft). ‖ MED. Incision *f.* ‖ SPORTS. Coupé *m.* ‖ FIN. Réduction *f.* (in prices, wages). ‖ CULIN. Morceau *m.* (piece); tranche *f.* (slice). ‖ FAM. Remarque mordante *f.* (sarcasm); affront *m.* (snub). ‖ FAM. Séchage *m.* (absence from school). ‖ FAM. Cran *m.; that's a cut above me,* je ne suis pas tout à fait à la hauteur. ‖ POP. Part *f.* (of profits). ‖ **Cut-away,** n. Jaquette *f.* (coat). ‖ **Cut - and‚-come-again,** n. FAM. Revenez-y; du réchauffé *m.* ‖ **Cut-back,** n. CINEM. Retour (*m.*) en arrière; FIN. Réduction, économie *f.* ‖ **Cut-in,** n. CINEM. Sous-titre, encart *m.;* ELECTR. Conjoncteur *m.* ‖ **Cut-off,** n. TECHN. Obturateur *m.* (of a cylinder); détente *f.* (of a valve); U. S. Bras mort *m.* (of a river); raccourci *m.* (short cut); *cut-off period,*

place d'escamotage. ‖ **Cut-out,** n. CINEM. Décor découpé *m.;* ELECTR. Coupe-circuit; interrupteur *m.;* AUTOM. Echappement libre *m.* ‖ **Cut-price,** adj. COMM. A prix réduit, au rabais; *cut-price shop,* magasin qui vend à bas prix. ‖ **Cut-throat,** adj. Coupe-jarret *m.; cut-throat den,* coupe-gorge; adj. Acharné, sans merci (competition); à trois (bridge). ‖ **Cut-up,** n. Ereintement *m.* (criticism); U. S. Farceur *m.* (joker).
— v. tr. (43). Couper, trancher, tailler; *to cut one's nails,* se couper les ongles. ‖ Couper, entailler, encocher (to notch). ‖ Couper, faire une estafilade à (to slash); *to cut one's finger,* se couper le (or) au doigt. ‖ Couper, croiser, traverser (to intersect); *to cut one another,* se couper, se croiser (roads). ‖ Couper, faire des coupures à (a text); réduire, rogner (fam.); *to cut a long story short,* bref, pour en finir; *to cut sth. short,* abréger (or) écourter qqch., couper court à qqch. ‖ Creuser, percer (a channel, an opening); *to cut one's way through,* s'ouvrir un chemin à travers. ‖ Couper (a card, a pack of cards). ‖ Tailler (a diamond); fileter (a screw). ‖ Couper (a coat); ciseler (velvet). ‖ Couper (alcohol, wine); dissoudre (grease). ‖ Interrompre; *to cut s.o. short,* couper la parole à qqn. ‖ Faire (a caper, a joke); *to cut a figure,* faire bonne figure. ‖ Rompre; *to cut a connection with,* cesser les relations avec. ‖ Couper; *the north wind cut his face,* la bise lui coupait le visage. ‖ CULIN. Découper (meat). ‖ AGRIC. Couper, abattre (to hew); couper, faucher (to mow); couper, moissonner (to reap). ‖ MILIT. *To cut to pieces,* tailler en pièces. ‖ NAUT. Filer (one's moorings). ‖ AUTOM. *To cut a corner close,* prendre un tournant à la corde. ‖ SPORTS. Couper (a ball); battre (a record). ‖ MED. Inciser (an abscess); couper, châtrer (an animal); percer (a tooth). ‖ COMM. *To cut prices,* vendre à bas prix. ‖ FIN. Diminuer, réduire (wages). ‖ CINEM. Faire le découpage de (a film). ‖ ARTS. Graver, sculpter. ‖ FAM. Couper à, sécher (a class); *cut your clack!,* bouclez-la; la ferme!; *to cut it fine,* compter juste; *to cut one's wisdom teeth,* prendre de l'expérience; *to cut one's teeth on,* se faire les dents sur; *to cut oneself to pieces,* se décarcasser, se mettre en petits morceaux; *to cut s.o. to pieces,* mettre qqn en charpie; *to cut s.o. dead,* passer raide près de qqn. ‖ **To cut away,** élaguer; dégager. ‖ **To cut down,** raccourcir (a dress); AGRIC. Faucher (corn); abattre (trees); FIN. Comprimer, réduire (expenses); FIG. Couper, tronquer (a speech). ‖ **To cut off,** découper, détacher, prélever (a part, piece); MED. Amputer, couper (a limb); enlever, emporter (s.o.) MILIT. Couper la retraite à (the enemy); TECHN. Couper la communication téléphonique de; ELECTR. Couper (the current); AUTOM. Couper (the motor); FIG. Rompre (the negotiations); isoler (s.o.); *to cut oneself off from,* se séparer de. ‖ **To cut out,** couper, éliminer, retrancher, émonder (*from,* de); couper, tailler (a garment); ARTS. Sculpter, tailler (*out of,* dans); MED. Supprimer, renoncer à (drinking, smoking); FIG. *To be cut out for,* être taillé pour (or) de taille à, avoir l'étoffe de; FAM. *Cut it out!,* suffit!, cessez!; *to cut a rival out,* couper l'herbe sous le pied à un rival, évincer (or) supplanter un rival; *work cut out for s.o.,* travail tout tracé. ‖ **To cut up,** défoncer, raviner (road); couper (wood); CULIN. Découper (meat); MILIT. Tailler en pièces, anéantir; FIG. Affecter, démoraliser, désoler (s.o.); FAM. Ereinter (a book).
— v. intr. Couper, tailler, trancher (*into,* dans). ‖ Couper (across, à travers); passer (through, à travers); *to cut through the air,* fendre l'air; *to cut through s.o.'s coat,* transpercer le manteau de qqn. ‖ Couper (at cards). ‖ Se couper; *wood cuts easily,* le bois se coupe facilement. ‖ SPORTS, AUTOM. Couper. ‖ FIG. Empiéter (*into,* sur); *to cut both ways,* être à deux tranchants. ‖ FAM. *Cut and dried*

tout fait ; *to cut and come again*, remettre ça, y reve-nir ; *to cut and run*, mettre les bouts, détaler ; U. S. *to cut loose*, s'en donner librement. ‖ **To cut away**, FAM. Détaler. ‖ **To cut back**, revenir en arrière. ‖ **To cut in**, enlever la danseuse d'un autre (in dancing) ; remplacer un joueur (in playing) ; s'immiscer dans une conversation, intervenir ; SPORTS. Couper le passage ; AUTOM. Se faufiler ; *to cut in on s.o.*, faire une queue de poisson. ‖ **To cut up**, U. S. Faire le pitre ; FAM. *To cut up trough*, réagir avec violence.

cutaneous [kju'teiniəs] adj. Cutané.

outch [kʌtʃ] n. Cachou *m.*

cute [kju:t] adj. FAM. Futé. ‖ Malin, finassier (cunning) ; avisé (sagacious) ; dégourdi, déluré (sharp). ‖ Gentil, attirant, attrayant (nice).

cuteness [-nis] n. FAM. Pénétration, finesse *f.* (See CUNNING.) ‖ U. S. Gentillesse, gracieuseté *f.*

cuticle ['kju:tikl] n. BOT. Cuticule *f.* ‖ MED. Cuticule ; envie f. (of a finger-nail) ; épiderme *m.* (epidermis) ; *cuticle scissors*, ciseaux de manucure.

cutis ['kju:tis] n. MED. Derme *m.*

cutlass [ˈkʌtləs] n. NAUT. Sabre d'abordage *m.* ‖ U. S. Coutelas *m.*

cutler [-ə*] n. Coutelier *m.*

cutlery [-əri] n. Coutellerie *f.* (business, work). ‖ Coutellerie (instruments) ; *canteen of cutlery*. ménagère ; *to buy cutlery*, acheter des couverts.

cutlet ['kʌtlit] n. CULIN. Côtelette *f.* (mutton, veal, from the ribs) ; escalope *f.* (veal, from the leg) ; croquette *f.* (chopped fish or meat).

cutpurse ['kʌtpəːs] n. Coupe-gousset *m.*

cutter [-ə*] n. Coupeur *s.* (of garments). ‖ Tailleur *m.* ; *stone-cutter*, tailleur de pierre. ‖ CINEM. Découpeur *s.* (of films). ‖ TECHN. Coupoir *m.* ‖ ARCHIT. Brique taillable *f.* ‖ NAUT. Cutter, cotre *m.* (British cutter) ; patrouilleur *m.* (coast-guard cutter) ; patache *f.* (revenue cutter) ; canot *m.* (of warships). ‖ MED. Incisive *f.* (tooth). ‖ U. S. Traîneau *m.* (sledge, U. S. sleigh).

cutting [-iŋ] n. Action *(f.)* de couper, coupe *f.* ; coupage *m.* ‖ Coupe *f.* ; abattage *f.* (of trees). ‖ Taille *f.* (of a diamond, a garment). ‖ Percement *m.* (of a channel) ; percée *f.* (in a wood). ‖ Objet coupé *m.* (piece cut off) ; coupon *m.* (of cloth) ; coupure *f.* (from a newspaper). ‖ AUTOM., CH. DE F. Route (or) voie encaissée *f.* ‖ SPORTS. Taille *f.* (in mountaineering). ‖ AGRIC. Taille (of rose-trees) ; bouture *f.* (slip). ‖ FIN. Réduction *f.* (of prices, wages). ‖ CULIN., TECHN., CINEM. Découpage *m.* — adj. Coupant, tranchant (knife, tool). ‖ Cinglant (rain) ; piquant, glacial, qui coupe le visage (wind). ‖ FIG. Blessant, mordant. (See INCISIVE.) ‖ **Cutting-nippers**, n. pl. TECHN. Pinces coupantes *f. pl.*

outtingly [-iŋli] adv. D'une manière mordante, à l'emporte-pièce.

cuttle ['kʌtl], **cuttlefish** [-fiʃ] n. ZOOL. Seiche *f.* ‖ **Cuttle-bone**, *n.* ‖ Os *(m.)* de seiche.

cutty ['kʌti] adj. Court. (See SHORT.) ‖ **Cutty-stool**, n. ECCLES. Sellette *f.* — n. FAM. Brûle-gueule *m.* (pipe).

cutwater [-wɔ:tə*] n. NAUT. Etrave *f.* ‖ ARCHIT. Bec *m.*

outwork [-wə:k] n. Broderie *(f.)* à jour.

cuvage [ky'vα:3] n. Cuvage *m.* (of wine).

cyanamide [sai'ænə,maid] n. CHIM. Cyanamide *f.* (or) *m.*

cyanic [sai'ænik] adj. CHIM. Cyané ; *cyanic acid*, acide cyanique.

cyanide ['saiənaid] n. CHIM. Cyanure *m.*

cyanhydric [saiən'haidrik] adj. CHIM. Cyanhydrique. (See HYDROCYANIC.)

cyanogen [sai'ænədʒin] n. CHIM. Cyanogène *m.*

cyanosis [saiə'nousis] n. MED. Cyanose *f.*

cybernetic [ˌsaibə'netik] adj. Cybernétique.

cybernetics [-s] n. sg. Cybernétique *f.*

cyclamen ['sikləmən] n. BOT. Cyclamen *m.*

cycle ['saikl] n. Cycle *m.* ; *business cycle*, cycle des affaires ; *Charlemagne cycle*, cycle de Charlemagne. ‖ Bicyclette ; bécane *f.* ; vélo *m.* (See BIKE.) ‖ **Cycle-car**, n. AUTOM. Cyclecar *m.* ‖ **Cycle-path**, n. Piste cyclable *f.* — v. intr. Faire de la bicyclette. ‖ Revenir par cycle.

cyclic(al) ['siklik(əl)] adj. Cyclique.

cycling ['saikliŋ] n. Cyclisme *m.* — adj. De bicyclette ; cycliste (suit) ; à bicyclette (tour). ‖ **Cycling-race**, n. Course cycliste *f.* ‖ **Cycling-tourist** n. Cyclotouriste *s.*

cyclist [-ist] n. Cycliste *s.*

cyclo-cross ['saiklokrɔs] n. SPORTS. Cyclo-cross *m.*

cycloid [-id] n. MATH. Cycloïde *m.*

cycloidal [-idl] adj. MATH. Cycloïdal.

cyclometer [sai'klɔmitə*] n. Compteur *(m.)* de bicyclette.

cyclone ['saikloun] n. Cyclone. ‖ **Cyclone-cellar**, n. U. S. Abri anti-cyclone *m.*

cyclonic ['saiklɔnik] adj. Cyclonal.

cyclopaedia [ˌsaiklo'pi:diə] n. Encyclopédie *f.*

cyclopean [-'pi:ən] adj. Cyclopéen.

Cyclops ['saiklɔps] n. Cyclope *m.*

cyclorama [ˌsaiklo'rα:mə] n. CINEM. Cyclorama *m.*

cyclostyle ['saiklə,stail] n. Machine *(f.)* à polycopier. — v. tr. Polycopier.

cyclothymic [-'θaimik] adj., n. MED. Cyclothymique *s.*

cyclotron ['saiklotrɔn] n. ELECTR. Cyclotron *m.*

cyesis [sai'i:sis] n. MED. Gestation *f.*

cygnet ['signit] n. ZOOL. Jeune cygne *m.*

cylinder ['silində*] n. TECHN., MATH., AUTOM. Cylindre *m.* ; *cylinder capacity* (or), *charge*, cylindrée ; *a six-cylinder car*, une six-cylindres.

cylindric(al) [si'lindrik(əl)] adj. Cylindrique.

cylindroid ['silindrɔid] adj., n. Cylindroïde.

cyma ['saimə] n. ARCHIT. Cimaise *f.* (See DADO.)

cymar [si'mα:*] n. Simarre *f.*

cymbal ['simbəl] n. MUS. Cymbale *f.*

cymbalist [-ist] n. MUS. Cymbalier *m.*

cymoscope ['saimoskoup] n. Détecteur *(m.)* d'ondes.

cynegetic [ˌsaini'dʒetik] adj. Cynégétique.

cynegetics [-s] n. Cynégétique *f.*

cynic ['sinik] adj., n. MED., PHILOS. Cynique. ‖ See CYNICAL.

cynical [-l] adj. Sceptique, revenu de tout, désabusé (disillusioned). ‖ Sarcastique, caustique (sarcastic) ; railleur, persifleur (sneering).

cynically [-əli] adv. Avec scepticisme. ‖ D'un ton railleur.

cynicism ['sinisizm] n. Scepticisme, esprit désabusé *m.* ‖ Causticité *f.* ; goût *(m.)* de la raillerie. ‖ Pl. Railleries, rosseries *f. pl.*

cynocephalus [ˌsaino'sefələs] n. ZOOL. Cynocéphale *m.*

cynosure ['sinəˌʃuə*] n. ASTRON. Petite ourse *f.* ‖ FAM. Centre *(m.)* d'attraction, point *(m.)* de mire.

cypher ['saifə*] n. See CIPHER.

cyphosis [sai'fousis] n. MED. Cyphose *f.*

cypress ['saipris] n. BOT. Cyprès *m.*

Cyprian ['sipriən] adj., n. GEOGR. Cypriote *s.* ‖ Cyprien (Christian name). ‖ FIG. Débauché.

Cypriot(e) ['sipriət] adj., n. GEOGR. Cypriote *s.*

Cyprus ['saiprəs] n. GEOGR. Chypre *f.*

cyst [sist] n. MED. Vésicule *f.* (bladder) ; kyste *m.* (growth).

cystitis [sis'taitis] n. MED. Cystite ƒ.
cystotomy [sis'tɔtəmi] n. MED. Cystotomie ƒ.
cytisus ['sitisəs] n. BOT. Cytise m.
cytology [sai'tɔlədʒi] n. MED. Cytologie ƒ.
cytoplasm ['saitou,plæzm̩] n. MED. Cyto-plasme m.
czar [zɑ:*] n. Czar, tsar m. ‖ U. S. FAM. Roi m.

czarevitch ['zɑ:rəvitʃ] n. Czarevitch m.
czarina [zɑ:'ri:nə] n. Czarine, tsarine ƒ.
Czech [tʃek] adj., n. GEOGR. Tchèque.
Czechoslovak [tʃeko'slouvæk] n. GEOGR. Tchéco-slovaque s.
Czechoslovakia [tʃekoslo'vækiə] n. GEOGR. Tché-coslovaquie ƒ.

D

d [di:] n. D, d m. ‖ TECHN. En D. ‖ MUS. Ré m. ‖ FIN. Penny m. ‖ PHYS. Densité ƒ. ‖ Cinq cents (Roman numeral). ‖ CHIM. Deutérium m. ‖ D-day, n. Jour J m.
D. A. [di:'ei] U. S. Abbr. District Attorney, procu-reur du gouvernement.
dab [dæb] v. tr. (1). Tapoter (to pat). ‖ Tamponner (with, avec); to dab with a sponge, éponger. ‖ Appliquer par touches légères (paint).
— n. Tape ƒ. (pat). ‖ Touche ƒ.; soupçon m. (bit). ‖ Tache ƒ. (of ink, mud). ‖ Pl. Empreintes digitales ƒ. pl. (thumb-print).
— adv. FAM. U. S. Exactement; right dab in the middle, en plein dans le milieu.
dab n. ZOOL. Limande ƒ.
dab adj. FAM. Calé, fort.
— n. FAM. Expert s.
dabber ['dæbə*] n. Tampon m.
dabble ['dæbl̩] v. tr. Eclabousser (to splash); asperger (to sprinkle); humecter (to wet).
— v. intr. Barboter (in water). ‖ FAM. Donner (in, dans); se mêler (in, de); to dabble in poetry, politics, rimailler, politicailler.
dabbler [-ə*] n. Barboteur s. ‖ FAM. Piètre ama-teur m.; dabbler in literary work, écrivailleur, écrivassier.
dabster ['dæbstə*] n. FAM. Expert m. (dab). ‖ ARTS, FAM. Barbouilleur m.
dace [deis] n. ZOOL. Vandoise ƒ.
dachshund ['dakshund] n. ZOOL. Dachshund m.
dacron ['dækrən] n. Dacron m. (fabric).
dactyl ['dæktil] n. Dactyle m.
dactylic [dæk'tilik] adj. Dactylique.
— n. Dactyle m.
dad [dæd], daddy [-i] n. FAM. Papa m. ‖ Daddy-long-legs, n. ZOOL. Tipule ƒ. (cranefly); U. S. Fau-cheux m. (arachnid).
dadaist ['dɑ:dəist] n. ARTS. Dadaïste s.
dado ['deidou] n. ARCHIT. Dé m. (of a pedestal); lambris m. (of a room); cimaise ƒ. (See CYMA.)
daedal ['di:dəl], daedalian [di:'deiliən] adj. Habile, expert, ingénieux (skilful). ‖ Compliqué, en labyrinthe, inextricable (intricate).
daemon ['di:mən] n. Démon m.
daffingly ['dæfiŋli] adv. En badinant, en folâ-trant.
daffodil ['dæfədil] n. BOT. Jonquille ƒ.; coucou m.
— adj. Jonquille (colour).
daffy ['dæfi] adj. FAM. U. S. Toqué. (See CRACKED.)
daft [dɑ:ft] adj. FAM. Cinglé (see CRACKED); to go daft over, s'enticher (or) se toquer de.
daftness [-nis] n. FAM. Loufoquerie ƒ.

dag [dæg] n. ZOOL. Dague ƒ. (of a stag).
dagger ['dægə*] n. Dague ƒ.; poignard m. ‖ TECHN. Obèle m.; double dagger, diésis. ‖ FIG. At daggers drawn with, à couteaux tirés avec; to look daggers at, foudroyer qqn du regard.
dago ['deigou] n. POP. Métèque m.
daguerreotype [də'gerotaip] n. Daguerréotype m.
dahlia ['deiljə] n. BOT. Dahlia m. ‖ FAM. Blue dahlia, merle blanc, oiseau bleu.
daily ['deili] adj. Journalier, quotidien. ‖ Daily-dozen, n. FAM. Gymnastique quotidienne ƒ. ‖ Daily-help, n. Femme de journée, aide journalière ƒ.
— adv. Tous les jours, quotidiennement.
— n. Quotidien m. (newspaper).
daintily ['deintili] adv. Délicatement, gracieuse-ment; avec raffinement.
daintiness [-nis] n. Délicatesse ƒ.; raffinement m. (of taste). ‖ Elégance ƒ. (of garments); finesse ƒ. (of shape).
dainty ['deinti] adj. Délicat, choisi, raffiné (taste). ‖ Délicat, difficile (appetite, person). ‖ Elégant, fin (shape). ‖ Elégant, soigné (well-dressed). ‖ Gentil à croquer (nice).
— n. CULIN. Friandise ƒ.
daiquiri ['daikiri] n. Punch, daiquiri m.
dairy ['dɛəri] n. Laiterie ƒ. (farm, place, store). ‖ Dairy cattle, n. ZOOL. Vaches laitières ƒ. pl. ‖ Dairy products, n. pl. Produits laitiers m. pl.
dairymaid [-meid] n. Laitière ƒ. (woman).
dairyman [-mən] (pl. dairymen) n. Laitier m.
dais ['deiis] n. Estrade ƒ.
daisy ['deizi] n. BOT. Pâquerette, marguerite ƒ. ‖ FAM. Perle ƒ. (person); merveille ƒ. (thing); to push up the daisies, manger les pissenlits par la racine. ‖ Daisyham, n. CULIN. U. S. Jambon fumé m.
dakota [də'koutə] n. AVIAT. Dakota m.
dale [deil] n. Vallée ƒ.; val m.
dalesman [-zmən] (pl. dalesmen) n. Habitant (m.) des vallées du nord de l'Angleterre.
dalliance ['dæliəns] n. Flirtage m. (flirting); badi-nage m. (trifling). ‖ Cajoleries ƒ. pl. ‖ † Lambine-rie ƒ.
dally ['dæli] v. intr. (2). Flirter, badiner (with, avec). ‖ Folâtrer, jouer (to play). ‖ FIG. Badiner (with, avec); se jouer (with, de). ‖ FAM. Lambiner, lanterner, traînasser. (See LOITER.)
— v. tr. To dally away, perdre (one's time).
dalmatic [dæl'mætik] n. ECCLES. Dalmatique ƒ.
Dalsyham, n. CULIN. Dalmatique ƒ.
daltonian [dɔl'touniən] adj., n. MED. Daltonien s.
daltonism [-izm̩] n. MED. Daltonisme m.
dam [dæm] n. Digue ƒ. (of channel); barrage m. (of lake). ‖ FAM. Réservoir m. (water). ‖ Dam-

175

buster, n. AVIAT. Torpille aérienne lourde *f.* (bomb); aviateur (*m.*) chargé de détruire des barrages (person). ‖ **Dam-stone,** n. TECHN. Dame *f.* — v. tr. (1). Endiguer (a river). ‖ Construire un barrage sur. ‖ FIG. Endiguer.

dam [dæm] n. ZOOL., FAM. Femelle, mère *f.*

damage ['dæmidӡ] n. Dommage, dégât *m.,* déprédation *f.; to make good the damage,* réparer les dégâts. ‖ JUR. Pl. Dommages-intérêts *m. pl.* ‖ MILIT. *War damage compensation,* dommages de guerre. ‖ NAUT. *Damage for detention,* contrestaries. ‖ FIG. Dommage, détriment, préjudice *m.* ‖ FAM. *what's the damage?,* cela fait combien? (bill).
— v. tr. Endommager. (See INJURE.) ‖ FIG. Léser, porter tort à.

damageable [-əbl] adj. Dommageable.

damascene [dæmə'si:n] v. tr. Damasquiner.

Damascus [də'mæskəs] n. GEOGR. Damas. ‖ ECCLES. *Road to Damascus,* chemin de Damas.

damask ['dæməsk] n. Damas *m.* (linen, silk, steel). ‖ Incarnat *m.* (colour).
— adj. Damasquiné (blade, steel); damassé (fabric, steel). ‖ Incarnat, rose pourpre (deep pink).
— v. tr. Damasquiner (a blade); damasser (a fabric). ‖ Empourprer.

dame [deim] n. Dame *f.; Dame Fortune,* Dame Fortune. ‖ Vieille douairière *f.* (old woman). ‖ JUR. Dame *f.* ‖ U.S. POP. Typesse *f.*

damfool ['dæmfu:l] adj. FAM. Idiot, crétin.
— n. FAM. Sale crétin *s.;* vieille cloche *f.;* triple buse *f.*

dammit ['dæmit] interj. POP. Bon Dieu!

damn ['dæm] v. tr. † Condamner. ‖ Maudire, pester contre (See CURSE.) ‖ ECCLES. Damner. ‖ FIG. Faire échouer, condamner, causer la perte de.
— v. intr. Pester, sacrer, jurer (to swear).
— n. Juron *m.* ‖ FAM. *Not to care a damn,* s'en ficher totalement.
— adj. ARG. Sacré, damné.
— interj. ARG. Bon Dieu!

damnable ['dæmnəbl] adj. Damnable. ‖ FAM. Exécrable.

damnably [-i] adv. D'une manière damnable (or) condamnable. ‖ FAM. Diantrement, bigrement.

damnation [dæm'neiʃən] n. ECCLES. Damnation *f.,* dam *m.* ‖ FIG. Ereintement *m.*
— interj. Damnation!

damnatory ['dæmnətəri] adj. ECCLES. Du dam. ‖ FAM. Condamnant, accablant.

damned [dæmd] adj. ECCLES. Damné. ‖ FAM. Sacré; *damned nuisance,* enquiquineur (person); empoisonnement (thing).
— n. ECCLES. Damnés *m. pl.* ‖ FAM. *To suffer the tortures of the damned,* souffrir comme un damné.
— adv. FAM. Bigrement, bougrement.

damnedest ['dæmdist] n. FAM. *To do one's damnedest,* faire son maximum (or) tout son possible.

damnify ['dæmnifai] v. tr. (2) JUR. Léser.

damning [-iŋ] adj. Condamnant, accablant, écrasant.

damp [dæmp] n. Humidité *f.* (moisture). ‖ Mofette *f.* (choke-damp); grisou *m.* (fire-damp). ‖ FIG. Tristesse *f.;* froid *m.* ‖ **Damp-proof,** adj. Hydrofuge; *damp-proof course,* couche isolante.
— adj. Humide, moite. (See WET.)
— v. tr. Humecter (to moisten). ‖ Etouffer (a fire). ‖ PHYS. Amortir, étouffer (a sound). ‖ ELECTR. Amortir (oscillations). ‖ FIG. Couper (the appetite); diminuer (ardour, zeal); *to damp s.o.'s. spirits,* refroidir (or) déprimer qqn.
— v. intr. **To damp off,** AGRIC. pourrir par excès d'humidité.

dampen [-ən] v. tr. U.S. See DAMP.
— v. intr. S'humidifier. ‖ FIG. Se refroidir.

damper [-ə*] n. Mouilleur *m.* (for stamps). ‖ TECHN. Registre *m.* ‖ AUTOM. Amortisseur de vilebrequin *m.* ‖ MUS. Etouffoir *m.* ‖ CULIN., FAM. Plat bourra-

tif *m.* ‖ FAM. Douche *f.* (event); rabat-joie *m.* (persons); *to put the damper on,* refroidir, défriser.

damping [-iŋ] n. Humectation *f.* ‖ TECHN., PHYS. Amortissement *m.*

dampish [-iʃ] adj. Moite, à peine humide.

dampness [-nis] n. Humidité *f.*

damsel ['dæmzəl] n. Damoiselle †; demoiselle *f.* ‖ **Damsel-fly,** n. ZOOL. Demoiselle, libellule *f.*

damson ['dæmzən] n. BOT. Prune (*f.*) de Damas (fruit); prunier *m.* (tree).
— adj. Prune (colour).

Danaides [dæ'neiidi:z] n. pl. Danaïdes *f. pl.*

dance [dɑ:ns] n. Danse *f.* (art, movement, music); *Dance of Death,* danse macabre. ‖ Bal *m.,* soirée dansante *f.* (ball). ‖ MED. *Saint Vitus's dance,* danse de Saint-Guy. ‖ FAM. *To lead s.o. a dance,* faire valser qqn. ‖ **Dance-frock,** n. Robe (*f.*) de bal. ‖ **Dance-hall,** n. Dancing *m.* ‖ **Dance-hostess,** n. Entraîneuse *f.* ‖ **Dance-music,** n. MUS. Musique de danse *f.* ‖ **Dance-programme,** n. Carnet de bal *m.*
— v. intr. Danser; *to dance with,* danser avec (a man); faire danser (a woman). ‖ Danser, gambader (*with,* de) [to skip]. ‖ FAM. *To dance to another tune,* chanter sur un autre ton; *to dance to every fiddle,* tourner à tous les vents.
— v. tr. Danser (a tango); *to be danced,* se danser. ‖ Faire danser (a bear, child). ‖ FAM. See ATTENDANCE.

dancer [-ə*] n. Danseur *s.*

dancing [-iŋ] adj. Dansant. ‖ FAM. *My dancing days are over,* mes beaux jours sont finis.
— n. Danse *f.* (act). ‖ **Dancing-girl,** n. Almée, bayadère *f.* ‖ **Dancing-master,** n. Maître (*m.*) à danser. ‖ **Dancing-partner,** n. Danseur *m.* ‖ **Dancing-party,** n. Soirée dansante, sauterie *f.* ‖ **Dancing-school,** n. Cours (*m.*) de danse. ‖ **Dancing-shoes,** n. Souliers (*m. pl.*) de bal.

dandelion ['dændilaiən] n. BOT. Pissenlit *m.*

dander ['dændə*] n. FAM. U.S. Colère *f.; to get s.o.'s dander up,* échauffer la bile de qqn.

dandify ['dændifai] v. tr. (2). Tirer à quatre épingles, pomponner.

dandle ['dændl] v. tr. Faire sauter (or) danser (a child). ‖ Dorloter, câliner. (See CARESS.)

dandruff ['dændrəf] n. MED. Pellicules *f. pl.*

dandy ['dændi] n. Dandy *m.* ‖ Voiture (*f.*) de laitier (dandy-cart). ‖ NAUT. Dinguet *m.*
— adj. FAM. *Fine and dandy,* en forme, en train. ‖ FAM. U.S. Chic.

dandyish [-iʃ] adj. De gandin.

Dane [dein] n. GEOGR., ZOOL. Danois *m.*

danger ['deinӡə*] n. Danger *m.* (*to,* pour); *to realize one's danger,* se rendre compte du danger qu'on court. ‖ CH. DE F. Arrêt *m.* (signal). ‖ **Danger list,** n. MED. *To be on the danger list,* être dans un état critique. ‖ **Danger money,** n. Prime (*f.*) de risque. ‖ **Danger zone,** n. MILIT. Zone dangereuse *f.*

dangerous [-rəs] adj. Dangereux (*to,* pour).

dangerously [-rəsli] adv. Dangereusement.

dangle ['dæŋgl] v. intr. Pendiller (to hang); brimbaler (to swing); *with one's arms dangling,* les bras ballants. ‖ FAM. *To dangle after,* être sans cesse aux trousses de.
— v. tr. Balancer, laisser pendiller. ‖ FIG. Faire miroiter.

dangler [-ə*] n. FAM. Amoureux *m.*

Danish ['deiniʃ] adj., n. Danois *m.* (language).

dank [dæŋk] adj. Humide. (See WET.)

dannert ['dænə:t] adj. Barbelé (wire).

danseuse [dæn'su:z] n. Danseuse *f.; premiere danseuse,* danseuse étoile.

Dantean [dæn'ti:ən], **Dantesque** [-'tesk] adj. Dantesque.

Danube ['dænju:b] n. GEOGR. Danube *m.* ‖ MUS. *The Blue Danube Waltz,* le Beau Danube Bleu.
dap [dæp] n. Rebondissement *m.* (See BOUNCE.)
— v. tr. Faire rebondir (a ball).
— v. intr. Rebondir (ball, stone). ‖ Plonger (bird). ‖ SPORTS. Pêcher à la trembleuse.
dapper ['dæpə*] adj. Pimpant (spruce). ‖ Actif dégourdi, vif (active).
dapple ['dæpl] v. tr. Tacheter.
— v. intr. Se tacheter (skin); se pommeler (sky).
— n. Tacheture *f.;* aspect pommelé *m.*
— adj. Tacheté, moucheté, bigarré, pommelé. ‖ **Dapple-grey,** adj. Gris pommelé.
darbies ['dɑ:biz] n. pl. FAM. Bracelets *m. pl.* (handcuffs).
dare [dεə*] v. tr. (44). Oser; *she dared not* (or) *didn't dare* (or) *durst not ask him,* elle n'osait pas le questionner. ‖ Défier, braver (to defy). ‖ Défier, affronter (to face). ‖ LOC. *I dare say,* à mon sens, il me semble que. ‖ **Dare-devil,** n. FAM. Risque-tout, casse-cou, trompe-la-mort *m.*
— n. Défi *m.; to take a dare,* relever un défi.
daring [-iŋ] adj. Audacieux (audacious); osé (bold).
— n. Audace *f.*
daringly [-iŋli] adv. Audacieusement.
dark [dɑ:k] adj. Sombre; obscur, noir; *dark night,* nuit ténébreuse; *to grow dark,* s'assombrir. ‖ Foncé (colour); bruni, bronzé (complexion); brun (hair); noir, nègre (race). ‖ Sourd (lantern); *dark room,* chambre noire. ‖ SPORTS, FAM. *Dark horse,* outsider. ‖ FIG. Ténébreux, obscur (ages, designs); sombre (future, threat); noir (ignorance, oblivion); mystérieux, obscur (word); *keep it dark,* motus!
— n. Obscurité *f.;* ténèbres *f. pl.* (absence of light). ‖ Nuit *f.; after dark,* à la nuit close. ‖ ARTS. Ombre *f.* ‖ FIG. Ignorance *f.;* noir *m.; in the dark about,* ignorant de, non instruit de; *leap in the dark,* saut dans l'inconnu.
darken [-ən] v. tr. Obscurcir, assombrir (the sky); obscurcir, voiler (the sun). ‖ Foncer (a colour); bronzer, brunir (the complexion). ‖ FIG. Rembrunir (s.o.'s brow); assombrir (the future); obscurcir (s.o.'s mind). ‖ FAM. *Not to darken s.o.'s door,* ne pas mettre les pieds chez (or) embarrasser qqn.
— v. intr. S'obscurcir, s'assombrir, se voiler (sky, sun). ‖ Se foncer (colour); se brunir (complexion). ‖ FIG. Se rembrunir (brow); s'assombrir (future); s'obscurcir (mind).
darkie [-i] n. See DARKY.
darkish [-iʃ] adj. Plutôt sombre.
darkle [-l] v. intr. S'obscurcir (to darken). ‖ Se dissimuler (to hide).
darkly [-li] adv. D'un air sombre (gloomily); d'un air sinistre (luridly); mystérieusement (mysteriously); obscurément (obscurely).
darkness [-nis] n. Obscurité *f.;* ténèbres *f. pl.* (dark). ‖ FIG. Noirceur *f.* (evil); ignorance *f.;* secret *m.*
darksome [-səm] adj. Obscur.
darky [-i] n. FAM. Négro, moricaud *m.*
darling ['dɑ:liŋ] adj., n. Chéri *s.; spoilt darling,* enfant gâté.
darn [dɑ:n] n. Reprise *f.*
— v. tr. Repriser.
darn interj. Flûte! (See DAMN.)
darned [dɑ:nd] adj. FAM. Sacré; *he's a darned fool,* il en tient une sacrée couche.
— adv. Drôlement, sacrément.
darnel ['dɑ:nl] n. BOT. Ivraie *f.,* ray-grass *m.*
darner ['dɑ:nə*] n. Œuf (*m.*) à repriser (ball); aiguille (*f.*) à repriser (needle); ravaudeur *s.* (person).
dart [dɑ:t] n. MILIT. Dard, javelot *m.* ‖ ZOOL. Dard *m.* ‖ SPORTS. Jet *m.* (of missile). ‖ Pl. Fléchettes *f. pl.* (game). ‖ FIG. Brusque élan *m.;* départ (*m.*) en flèche; *to make a dart at,* bondir sur, s'élancer sur. ‖ FIG. Trait *m.*

— v. tr. Lancer (a look, a missile); darder (rays).
— v. intr. Foncer, se précipiter (*at, upon,* sur). ‖ **To dart away,** partir comme une flèche (or) un bolide.
dartboard [-,bɔ:d] n. Cible (*f.*) du jeu de fléchettes.
dartre ['dɑ:tə*] n. MED. Dartre *f.* (tetter).
dartrous [-rəs] adj. MED. Dartreux.
dash [dæʃ] v. tr. Cogner, heurter (to knock); lancer, jeter, précipiter (to throw); flanquer (fam.); *to dash to pieces,* écraser, fracasser, réduire en miettes. ‖ Eclabousser (*with,* de) [to splash]; *dashed with colour,* rehaussé de touches de couleur. ‖ CULIN. Relever (*with,* de) [spice]; couper, mêler (*with,* de) [water]. ‖ FIG. Décontenancer, désorienter; démonter (fam.) [to abash]; anéantir, briser (to destroy); décourager, abattre (to dishearten). ‖ **To dash at,** se précipiter sur. ‖ **To dash away,** écarter (or) enlever vivement. ‖ **To dash down,** jeter à terre; flanquer par terre (fam.). ‖ **To dash off,** exécuter à la va-vite, enlever; bâcler, torcher (fam.).
— v. intr. Se précipiter, s'élancer (to rush); *to dash in,* entrer en coup de vent, se ruer à l'intérieur. ‖ Se briser, s'écraser (*against,* sur, contre). ‖ AUTOM. S'emboutir (*into,* contre).
— n. Fracassement *m.* (smash). ‖ Choc (*m.*) sur l'eau, clapotement *m.* (plash). ‖ Eclaboussement, jet *m.* (splash). ‖ Ruée *f.;* élan *m.* (*at,* sur) [rush]. ‖ Touche *f.* (of colour). ‖ Trait *m.* (in Morse code); tiret *m.* (in printing). ‖ CULIN. Goutte, larme *f.;* doigt *m.* (of brandy); pointe *f.* (of garlic, vanilla); filet *m.* (of vinegar). ‖ AUTOM., AVIAT. See DASH-BOARD. ‖ FIG. Allant, entrain, dynamisme *m.* (go); allure *f.* (style); *to cut a dash,* faire de l'effet (or) de l'épate. ‖ **Dash-board,** n. TECHN. Tableau (*m.*) de commande; AVIAT. Tableau de bord *m.;* AUTOM. Garde-boue *m.* (splash-board); tableau de bord *m.; dash-board light,* éclaireur de tablier; *dash-board mirror,* rétroviseur. ‖ **Dash-pot,** n. AUTOM. Amortisseur *m.*
dasher [-ə*] n. TECHN. Baratton *m.,* palette *f.* (in a churn). ‖ FAM. Epateur *s.* ‖ U. S. AUTOM. Garde-boue *m.*
dashing [-iŋ] adj. Fougueux, fringant (horse). ‖ Brillant, fringant (elegant); dynamique, plein d'allant (spirited). ‖ Tapageur, faiseur d'épate (showy).
dashingly [-iŋli] adv. Avec brio (or) fougue (or) élégance.
dastard ['dæstəd] n. Poltron, lâche *m.*
dastardliness [-linis] n. Lâcheté *f.*
dastardly [-li] adj. Couard, lâche (see COWARDLY); infâme (crime).
data ['deitə, 'dɑ:tə] (pl. **data**) n. INFORM. Donnée *f.; data bank,* banque de données; *data processing,* informatique, traitement des données.
— n. pl. See DATUM.
datable [-əbl] adj. Datable.
date [deit] n. Date *f.; to fix a date for,* prendre date pour. ‖ Date, époque *f.; to make a date,* faire date. ‖ Mode *f.; out of date,* hors d'usage, périmé (no longer in use); démodé (old-fashioned); *up to date,* usité, en usage (in use); moderne, actuel, à la page, dans le train, au goût du jour (modern); à jour, au point, au courant (posted up). ‖ JUR. *One year after date,* à un an de date. ‖ COMM. *To date,* à ce jour; FIN., COMM. Echéance *f.* ‖ FAM. Rendez-vous *m.; to make a date with,* donner rendez-vous à. ‖ FAM. Flirt (*m.*) avec qui l'on a rendez-vous. ‖ **Date-cancel,** v. tr. (1). Oblitérer. ‖ **Date-line,** n. Date (*f.*) et lieu (*m.*) [at head of article]; GEOGR. Ligne (*f.*) de changement de date. ‖ **Date-stamp,** n. Timbre, tampon, cachet *m.* (instrument); cachet *m.* (mark).
— v. tr. Dater (a letter); *to date back,* antidater. ‖ Dater, assigner une date à (an event). ‖ FAM. U. S. Donner rendez-vous à, prendre date avec.

— v. intr. Dater (from, de); to date back to, remonter à; to date from the distant past, remonter très haut; to date from years before, dater de loin. ‖ Compter (from, à partir de). ‖ Etre démodé, dater (to be old-fashioned).

date n. Bot. Datte f. (fruit); dattier m. (tree). ‖ **Date-palm**, n. Bot. Dattier m.

dated [-id] adj. En date, daté (from, de) [a place]; dated April 5th, en date (or) daté du 5 avril. ‖ Démodé (old-fashioned).

dateless [-lis] adj. Sans date, non daté. ‖ Sans âge, immémorial, de toute antiquité.

dative ['deitiv] adj., n. Gramm. Datif m.

datum ['deitəm] (pl. **data** [-ə]) n. Donnée, indication f.; élément (m.) d'information. ‖ Techn. Repère m. ‖ **Datum-line**, n. Ligne (f.) de repère (or) de niveau. ‖ **Datum-plan**, n. Plan (m.) de comparaison. ‖ **Datum-point**, n. Point de repère m.; cote f.

datura [də'tjuərə] n. Bot. Datura m.

daub [dɔ:b] v. tr. Enduire, badigeonner, barbouiller (with, de) [to smear]. ‖ Etaler (on, sur). ‖ Archit. Torcher, plâtrer. ‖ Arts. Barbouiller.
— v. intr. Arts. Barbouiller, peinturlurer.
— n. Badigeonnage, barbouillage m. ‖ Enduit m.; couche f. (coating). ‖ Archit. Torchis m. ‖ Arts. Navet m.; croûte f.

dauber [-ə*], **daubster** [-stə*] n. Arts. Barbouilleur m.

dauby [-i] adj. Gluant, poisseux. ‖ Arts. Barbouillé.

daughter ['dɔ:tə*] n. Fille f. ‖ **Daughter-in-law**, n. Belle-fille, bru f.

daughterly [-li] adj. Filial, de fille.

daunt [dɔ:nt] v. tr. Abattre, décourager (to dishearten); intimider, effrayer (to intimidate).

dauntless [-lis] adj. Intrépide, indomptable.

dauntlessly [-lisli] adv. Intrépidement.

dauntlessness [-lisnis] n. Intrépidité f.

dauphin ['dɔ:fin] n. Dauphin m.

dauphiness [-nis] n. Dauphine f.

davenport ['dævənpɔ:t] n. Secrétaire, bureau m. ‖ U. S. Canapé-lit m.

davit ['dævit] n. Naut. Bossoir m.

davy ['deivi] n. Fam. To take one's davy that, ficher son billet que.

Davy Jones ['deivi' dʒounz] n. Fam. Neptune m.; to go to Davy Jones's locker, boire le grand bouillon.

davy-lamp ['deivi'læmp] n. Lampe (f.) davy (or) de mineur.

daw [dɔ:] n. Zool. Choucas m.

dawdle ['dɔ:dl] v. intr. Flâner. (See LOITER.)
— v. tr. To dawdle away, perdre en flânant.
— n. Flâneur s.

dawdler [-ə*] n. Flâneur s.

dawn [dɔ:n] n. Aurore, aube f.; lever du jour m. (daybreak); dawn chorus, concert matinal des oiseaux. ‖ Fig. Aube f.; premiers rayons m. pl.; éveil m.
— v. intr. Poindre, naître, se lever (day). ‖ Commencer à se dessiner (landscape). ‖ Fig. Pointer (hope); naître (idea); se faire jour (truth); it dawned on her that, l'idée naquit en elle que, elle se prit à songer que.

dawning [-iŋ] n. Aube f. (See DAWN.) ‖ Orient, est m.

day [dei] n. Jour m. (of the week); D-day, jour J; day by day, de jour en jour; day in, day out, un jour après l'autre, tous les jours que le Bon Dieu fait; every day, tous les jours; from day to day, d'un jour à l'autre; one day, un jour; the day before, la veille; the next day, le lendemain; the next day but one, le surlendemain; this day, aujourd'hui. ‖ Jour m., journée f. (day-time); by the day, à la journée; eight-hour day, journée de huit heures. ‖ Jour m. (daylight); it was broad day, il faisait grand

jour. ‖ Jour, jour (m.) de réception (at-home day). ‖ Jour, temps m.; époque f.; at this time of day, à l'heure actuelle; in these days, de nos jours, à notre époque; the best painter of his day, le meilleur peintre de son temps; those were happy days, c'était le bon temps. ‖ Temps m.; vie f.; to have had one's day, avoir fait son temps; to spend one's days in, passer sa vie (or) ses jours à. ‖ Jur. Days of grace, délai de grâce. ‖ Milit., Fig. Victoire f.; to lose the day, perdre la victoire (or) la partie. ‖ Fam. To call it a day, débrayer pour la journée; to know the time of day, connaître les ficelles. ‖ **Day-bed**, n. Lit de repos m. ‖ **Day-boarder**, n. Demi-pensionnaire s. ‖ **Day-book**, n. Comm., Fin. Journal, brouillard m. ‖ **Day-dream**, n. Rêverie, rêvasserie f.; v. tr. rêver, rêvasser. ‖ **Day-dress**, n. Robe (f.) d'après-midi. ‖ **Day-fly**, n. Zool. Ephémère m. ‖ **Day-labourer**, n. Journalier, ouvrier (s.) à la journée. ‖ **Day-nursery**, n. Crèche, garderie f. ‖ **Day-pupil**, n. Externe; U. S. demi-pensionnaire s. ‖ **Day release course**, n. Cours (m. pl.) dispensés aux jeunes pendant leur apprentissage. ‖ **Day-return**, n. Ch. de f. Billet (m.) aller et retour à prix réduit valable un jour. ‖ **Day-school**, n. Externat m. ‖ **Day-shift**, n. Equipe (f.) de jour. ‖ **Day-star**, n. Astre (m.) du jour (sun); étoile (f.) du matin (star). ‖ **Day-temperature**, n. Température (f.) diurne. ‖ **Day-work**, n. Travail (m.) à la journée.

daybreak [-breik] n. Point du jour, petit matin m.

daylight [-lait] n. Jour m.; lumière (f.) du jour; by daylight, de jour. ‖ Jour, interstice m. (open space). ‖ Fig. Grand jour m.; to let daylight into, mettre au grand jour. ‖ Fam. Solution f. (of a problem); achèvement, fin m. (of a task). ‖ U. S. To burn daylight, perdre son temps, gaspiller les bonnes heures. ‖ Fam. Organes vitaux essentiels m. pl.; to shoot the daylights out of s.o., to let daylight into s.o., descendre qqn d'un coup de fusil. ‖ **Daylight-saving time**, n. Heure (f.) d'été.

daylong [-lɔŋ] adj. De toute la journée.
— adv. Tout le long de la journée.

daytime ['dei,taim] n. Jour m.; journée f.; in the daytime, pendant la journée.

daze [deiz] v. tr. Etourdir (to stun); hébéter, abrutir (to stupefy). ‖ Eblouir (to dazzle). ‖ Fam. Abasourdir, ahurir (to bewilder).
— n. Etourdissement m. ‖ Abrutissement m. ‖ Eblouissement m. ‖ Fam. Ahurissement m.

dazedly [-idli] adv. D'un air ahuri.

dazzle ['dæzl] v. tr. Eblouir, aveugler (by light). ‖ Fig. Eblouir; to dazzle people with words, en mettre plein la vue.
— n. Eblouissement m. (lit. and fig.).

dazzling [-iŋ] adj. Eblouissant (lit. and fig.).

dazzlingly [-iŋli] adv. De façon éblouissante.

D.C., d.c. [di:'si:] abbr. Direct current, courant continu.

deacon ['di:kən] n. Eccles. Diacre m.

deaconess [-nis] n. Diaconesse f.

deaconship [-ʃip] n. Eccles. Diaconat m.

deactivate [di:'ækti,veit] v. tr. Chim. Désactiver.

dead [ded] adj. Mort (animal, person, plant); a dead woman, une morte. ‖ Crevé, sans élasticité (ball); détendu (spring). ‖ Eteint (coal, fire). ‖ Terne, mat (colour); mat (gold); plat, terne (picture); sourd, assourdi (sound). ‖ Plat (calm); invariable, parfait (level); mort (waters). ‖ Creux (hours); mort (season). ‖ De rebut (letters). ‖ Agric. Improductif (soil). ‖ Archit. Faux, aveugle (arch, window). ‖ Electr. A plat (cell). ‖ Comm. Stagnant (business). ‖ Fin. Fictif (account); irrécouvrable (loan); sec (loss); improductif (money). ‖ Jur. En désuétude (law); mort (hand, letter). ‖ Med. Sourd (ache); mort, engourdi (limb). ‖ Mus. Funèbre (march). ‖ Gramm. Mort (language). ‖ Fig. Absolu (certainty); sourd (to, à) [person]; absolu, total,

profond (secret). ‖ Fam. *Dead loss*, bon à rien (person); perte sèche (transaction); *dead men*, cadavres de bouteilles; *dead shot*, tireur hors ligne, fameux fusil; *dead spit*, portrait craché. ‖ **Dead-beat**, adj. Electr. Apériodique; Fam. Claqué, rompu, éreinté; n. Techn. Galvanomètre *m.*; Fam. U. S. Profiteur, écornifleur *s.* (sponge); chevalier (*m.*) d'industrie. ‖ **Dead-centre**, n. Techn. Point mort *m.* ‖ **Dead-end**, n. Cul-de-sac *m.*; impasse *f.* Electr., Radio. Bout mort *m.*; adj. Sans avenir (job); qui ne mène nulle part (policy); *dead-end kid*, blouson noir, voyou, zonard; en cul-de-sac (street). ‖ **Dead-eye**, n. Naut. Moque *f.* ‖ **Dead-fall**, n. Assommoir *m.* (trap). ‖ **Dead-fire**, n. Feu (*m.*) Saint-Elme. ‖ **Dead-head**, n. Contre-pointe *f.* (of lathe); Ch. de f., Theatr. Personne (*f.*) munie d'un billet gratuit. ‖ **Dead heat**, n. Sports. Dead-heat *m.* (in horse racing); *it was a dead heat*, ils sont arrivés ex æquo. ‖ **Dead-leaf**, adj. Feuille-morte (colour); Aviat. En feuille morte (descent). ‖ **Dead-light**, n. Fausse fenêtre *f.*; Naut. Contre-sabord, faux hublot *m.* ‖ **Dead-line**, n. Délimitation, ligne de repère; Fig. Dernière limite *f.*; Fam. Date limite *f.* ‖ **Dead-lock**, n. Serrure (*f.*) à pêne dormant; Fig. Impasse *f.* ‖ **Dead-nettle**, n. Bot. Ortie blanche *f.* ‖ **Dead-pan**, adj. Sans expression (face); pince sans rire (humour). ‖ **Dead-reckoning**, n. Naut. Estime *f.* ‖ **Dead-weight**, n. Naut. Chargement (*m.*) en lourd; Fig. Poids lourd *m.*
— n. Morts *m. pl.*; *the dead ride fast*, les morts vont vite. ‖ Fig. Cœur *m.* (of night, winter).
— adv. Juste, en plein; *dead in the centre*, en plein milieu; *dead on time*, juste à l'heure. ‖ Totalement; *dead drunk*, ivre mort; *dead set*, farouchement déterminé; *dead tired*, claqué, tué. ‖ Net; *to stop dead*, s'arrêter pile.

deaden [-ṇ] v. tr. Amortir (a blow); assourdir (a sound). ‖ Amatir (gold). ‖ Eventer (wine). ‖ Fig. Emousser (feeling); diminuer (vitality).
— v. intr. S'amortir (blow); s'assourdir (sound). ‖ S'éventer (wine). ‖ Fig. S'émousser (sensibility); diminuer (vitality).

deadly [-li] adj. Mortel, fatal (blow); à mort (combat); meurtrier (weapon). ‖ Mortel (dullness); de mort, mortel (gloom, paleness); intense (haste). ‖ Jur. Ecrasant (evidence). ‖ Eccles. Mortel, capital (sin). ‖ Fig. Mortel (enemy, insult).
— adv. Mortellement.

deadness [-nis] n. Matité *f.* (of colour, gold). ‖ Comm. Stagnation *f.* ‖ Med. Engourdissement *m.* ‖ Culin. Event *m.* ‖ Fig. Apathie; insensibilité *f.* (to, envers).

deaf [def] adj. Med. Sourd. ‖ Bot. Vide (nut). ‖ Fig. Sourd, insensible (to, à). ‖ **Deaf-and-dumb**, adj. Des sourds-muets (alphabet, language); sourd-muet (person); n. pl. Sourds-muets *s. pl.* ‖ **Deaf-mute**, n. Sourd-muet *s.*

deafen [-ṇ] v. tr. Assourdir (to make deaf). ‖ Assourdir, casser les oreilles (*with*, noise). ‖ Etouffer, noyer (a sound). ‖ Archit. Insonoriser, hourder (a wall).

deafly [-li] adv. Sourdement.

deafness [-nis] n. Med. Surdité *f.*

deal [di:l] n. Bois blanc, sapin *m.* ‖ Madrier *m.*
— adj. En bois blanc.

deal n. Quantité *f.*; *a good* (or) *great deal*, beaucoup (*of*, de). ‖ Donne *f.* (in cards); *your deal!*, à vous de donner! ‖ Fam. Affaire, tractation *f.*
— v. tr. (45). Distribuer, partager, répartir (*to, entre*). ‖ Allonger, assener, décocher, flanquer (a blow). ‖ Donner (cards). ‖ **To deal out**, administrer, dispenser.
— v. intr. Donner, faire (in cards). ‖ **To deal by** (or) **with**, se conduire à l'égard de, agir envers, traiter (*as*, comme) [s.o.]; *to deal well by*, en user bien avec. ‖ **To deal in**, Comm. Faire le commerce de. ‖ **To deal with**, Comm. Régler (an order); conclure (a piece of business); commercer avec

(another firm); se servir (or) se fournir chez (one's regular tradesman); Fig. Maîtriser, résoudre (a difficulty); avoir affaire à, traiter avec (s.o.); traiter de, toucher à, s'occuper de, se mêler de (a subject); *pleasant to deal with*, d'un commerce agréable.

dealer [-ə*] n. Joueur (*s.*) qui donne les cartes. ‖ Comm. Marchand, négociant *s.* (in, en).

dealing [-iŋ] n. Donne *f.* (of cards); distribution *f.* (of gifts). ‖ Pl. Relations *f. pl.*; rapports, contacts *m. pl.* (with, avec); menées, tractations *f. pl.*, trafics *m. pl.* (manœuvres). ‖ Comm. Commerce *m.* (in, de, en); pl. négociations *f. pl.*; Fig. Comportement *m.*; manière (*f.*) d'agir (with, envers).

dealt [delt] pret., p. p. See deal.

deambulation [di,æmbju'leiʃən] n. Promenade *f.*

dean [di:n] n. Eccles. Doyen *m.* ‖ Doyen *m.* (of college, faculty). ‖ U. S. Doyen *s.* (senior).

deanery [-əri] n. Eccles. Doyenné *m.*

deanship [-ʃip] n. Décanat (in a faculty). ‖ Eccles. Doyenné *m.*

dear [diə*] adj. Cher (to, à); chéri, aimé (beloved). ‖ Cher (in letters). ‖ Précieux; *for dear life*, comme s'il allait de la vie. ‖ Comm., Fin. Cher, coûteux (see costly); *to get dearer*, renchérir, augmenter. ‖ Fam. Gentil, charmant (nice).
— n. Chéri *s.* (child, person); cher *s.* (friend). ‖ Fam. Trésor, amour *m.*
— adv. Tendrement; *to hold dear*, chérir (s.o.); tenir à (sth). ‖ Comm. Cher. ‖ Fig. Chèrement.
— interj. Dieu!, mon Dieu!

dearie [-ri] n. Fam. Mon petit *m.*, chéri *s.*; *dearie me!*, Oh! mon Dieu!

dearly [-li] adv. See dear adv.

dearness [-nis] n. Affection *f.*; attachement *m.* ‖ Comm. Cherté *f.*

dearth [də:θ] n. Disette *f.*

deary ['diəri] n. See dearie.

death [deθ] n. Mort *f.*, trépas *m.*; *it is death to*, il est interdit sous peine de mort de; *to do to death*, faire mourir; *to put to death*, mettre à mort. ‖ Mort *f.* (personification); *the jaws of Death*, les griffes de la mort. ‖ Mort, cause de mort *f.*; *to be death to*, causer la mort de. ‖ Sports. Hallali *m.*; curée *f.* ‖ Med. *Black Death*, Peste noire. ‖ Jur. Décès *m.*; *civil death*, mort civile; *proof of death*, constatation de décès. ‖ Pl. Nécrologie *f.* ‖ Fig. Fin, mort *f.* (ending). ‖ Fam. *She will be the death of him*, elle le fera mourir, elle le conduira au tombeau; *to be in at the death*, arriver à l'hallali, assister à la fin des fins; *to catch one's death*, attraper la crève; *to work oneself to death over sth.*, s'échiner à faire qqch. ‖ **Death-bed**, n. Lit (*m.*) de mort; Fam. *death-bed repentance*, conversion in extremis. ‖ **Death-bell**, n. Glas *m.* ‖ **Death-blow**, n. Coup mortel *m.* ‖ **Death certificate**, n. Certificat de décès *m.* ‖ **Death-chamber**, n. Chambre mortuaire *f.*; U. S. salle d'exécution *f.* (in a prison). ‖ **Death-duties**, n. pl. Jur. Droits (*m. pl.*) de succession. ‖ **Death-feud**, n. Guerre à mort *f.* ‖ **Death-house**, n. Jur. U. S. Quartier (*m.*) de la mort (in a prison). ‖ **Death-mask**, n. Masque mortuaire *m.* ‖ **Death penalty**, n. Peine (*f.*) de mort. ‖ **Death-rate**, n. Mortalité *f.* ‖ **Death-rattle**, n. Med. Râle *m.* ‖ **Death-roll**, n. Eccles. Nécrologe *m.* ‖ **Death's-head**, n. Tête de mort *f.*; Zool. *death's-head moth*, sphinx à tête de mort. ‖ **Death-ray**, n. Rayon (*m.*) qui tue (or) de la mort. ‖ **Death-trance**, n. Med. Léthargie, catalepsie *f.* ‖ **Death-trap**, n. Endroit (or) véhicule dangereux *m.*; Autom. Croisement dangereux *m.* ‖ **Death-warrant**, n. Arrêt (*m.*) de mort. ‖ **Death-watch beetle**, n. Zool. Horloge de la mort, vrillette *f.* ‖ **Death-wish**, n. Psych. Instinct (*m.*) de mort.

deathless [-lis] adj. Immortel.

deathlessly [-lisli] adv. Immortellement.

deathlessness [-lisnis] n. Immortalité *f.*

deathlike [-laik] adj. De mort, cadavéreux (paleness); de mort, sépulcral (silence); *to look death-like,* avoir une mine de déterré.

deathly [-li] adj. Mortel; de mort.
— adv. Mortellement; *deathly pale,* pâle comme la mort, d'une pâleur mortelle.

deathsman [-smən] n. Bourreau *m.*

deatomization [di,ætɔmai'zeiʃən] n. PHYS. Désatomisation *f.*

deb [dɛb] n. FAM. Deb *f.* (See DEBUTANTE).

debacle [dei'bɑ:kl] n. Débâcle *f.*

debag [di:'bæg] v. tr. (1). FAM. Enlever le falzar à, déculotter.

debar [di'bɑ:*] v. tr. (1). Exclure (*from,* de). ‖ Interdire à (*from,* de) [s.o.]; *to debar s.o. sth.,* refuser qqch. à qqn, priver qqn de qqch.

debark [di'bɑ:k] v. tr., intr. NAUT. Débarquer.

debarkation [,di:bɑ:'keiʃən] n. NAUT. Débarquement *m.*

debase [di'beis] v. tr. FIN. Déprécier. ‖ FIG. Avilir.

debasement [-mənt] n. FIN. Dépréciation *f.* ‖ FIG. Avilissement *m.*

debatable [di'beitəbl] adj. Discutable; débattable.

debate [di'beit] v. tr. Débattre, discuter, argumenter sur (a question); contester, controverser (a statement). ‖ Examiner, réfléchir sur; *to debate with oneself,* délibérer en son for intérieur. ‖ † Disputer.
— v. intr. Discuter (*with,* avec); être en discussion. ‖ Délibérer (*on,* sur).
— n. Controverse, discussion *f.* (controversy); *matter in debate,* objet de discussion. ‖ Débat *m.* (in public); conférence contradictoire *f.* (with two teams); parlote *f.* (fam.); *full dress debate,* grand débat.

debater [-ə*] n. Argumentateur *m.;* argumentatrice *f.;* *to be a good debater,* avoir l'art de la discussion; être un bon controversiste.

debating [-iŋ] adj. De discussion; *debating point,* matière à controverse; *debating society,* société de conférences contradictoires (or) de parlote (fam.).

debauch [di'bɔːtʃ] n. Débauche *f.*
— v. tr. Débaucher (a person); séduire, détourner (a woman). ‖ FIG. Corrompre. (See PERVERT.)

debauchee [,debɔ:'tʃi:] n. Débauché *s.*

debaucher [ˈdebɔ:tʃə*] n. Corrupteur *m.;* corruptrice *f.* (See CORRUPTER.)

debauchery [di'bɔ:tʃəri] n. Débauche *f.;* *to turn to debauchery,* se débaucher. ‖ Corruption *f.;* *debauchery of youth,* détournement de mineurs.

debenture [di'bentʃə*] n. FIN. Obligation *f.* ‖ COMM. Certificat de drawback *m.*

debilitant [di'bilitənt] n. MED. Débilitant *m.*

debilitate [-teit] v. tr. Débiliter. (See WEAKEN.)

debility [-ti] n. MED. Débilité *f.*

debit ['debit] n. FIN. Débit *m.*
— adj. FIN. Débiteur (account).
— v. tr. FIN. Débiter (*with,* de) [an account, s.o., a sum); *debited,* porté au débit.

debonair [,debə'nɛə*] adj. Jovial (gay); courtois, affable (polite). ‖ † Bonhomme, débonnaire (mild).

debonairness [-nis] n. Jovialité. ‖ Courtoisie *f.* ‖ † Bonhomie *f.*

debouch [di'bu:ʃ] v. intr. MILIT. Déboucher.

debouchment [-mənt] n. MILIT., GEOGR. Débouché *m.*

debrief [di:'bri:f] v. tr. Interroger au retour d'une mission. ‖ MILIT. *To be debriefed,* faire un rapport.

debris ['debris] n. Décombres *m. pl.*

debt [det] n. Dette *f.;* *to be out of debt,* ne plus avoir de dettes; *to run into debt,* faire des dettes, s'endetter. ‖ FIN. *National debt,* dette publique; *outstanding debts,* créances à recouvrer. ‖ FIG. Dettes *f.;* *to be in s.o.'s debt,* demeurer en reste avec qqn (or) l'obligé de qqn. ‖ **Debt-collector,** n. FIN. Agent de recouvrement *m.*

debtor [-ə*] n. FIN. Débiteur *m.,* débitrice *f.* ‖ FIN. Doit *m.*

debug [di:'bʌg] v. tr. (1). FAM. Débarrasser des micros. ‖ FAM. Corriger les défauts (or) les imperfections de (machine, system). ‖ FAM. Déparasiter, désinsectiser.

debunk [di:'bʌŋk] v. tr. FAM. Déboulonner, dégringoler, descendre, dégonfler, détrôner.

debut ['debju:] n. Début *m.; to make one's debut,* faire ses débuts dans le monde (girl); faire ses premières armes (person). ‖ THEATR. Début *m.*

debutant [deby'tænt] n. THEATR. Débutant *m.*

debutante n. Jeune fille (*f.*) qui fait ses débuts (or) son entrée dans la vie mondaine. ‖ THEATR. Débutante *f.*

decade ['dekeid] n. Décade *f.* (ten days); décennie *f.* (ten years).

decadence ['dekədəns] n. Décadence *f.*

decadent [-ənt] adj., n. Décadent *m.*

decaffeinate [di'kæfi,neit] v. tr. CULIN. Décaféiner.

decagon ['dekə,gɔn] n. GEOM. Décagone *m.*

decagram(me) ['dekəgræm] n. MATH. Décagramme *m.*

decal ['di:kæl] n. U. S. Décalcomanie *f.*

decalage [,deikæ'lɑ:ʒ] n. AVIAT. Décalage *m.* (of wings).

decalcification [di:,kælsifi'keiʃən] n. MED. Décalcification *f.*

decalcify [di:'kælsifai] v. tr. (2). MED. Décalcifier; *to become decalcified,* se décalcifier.

decalcomania [,dikælko'meiniə] n. Décalcomanie *f.*

decalitre ['dekæli:tə*] n. MATH. Décalitre *m.*

decalogue [-lɔg] n. ECCLES. Décalogue *m.*

decametre [-mi:tə*] n. MATH. Décamètre *m.*

decamp [di'kæmp] v. intr. MILIT. Lever le camp. ‖ FAM. Décamper.

decanal [di'keinl] adj. Décanal.

decant [di'kænt] v. tr. Décanter.

decantation [,di:kæn'teiʃən] n. Décantage *m.*

decanter [di'kæntə*] n. Carafe *f.;* carafon *m.*

decapitate [di'kæpiteit] v. tr. Décapiter. (See BEHEAD.)

decapitation [di,kæpi'teiʃən] n. Décapitation *f.*

decapod ['dekəpɔd] n. ZOOL. Décapode *m.*

decarbonize [di:'kɑ:bənaiz] v. tr. Décalaminer, décarburer.

decasyllable [dekə'siləbl] n. GRAMM. Décasyllabe *m.*

decathlon [di'kæθlɔn] n. SPORTS. Décathlon *m.*

decay [di'kei] v. intr. ARCHIT. Se délabrer (building). [See MOULDER.] ‖ COMM. Péricliter. ‖ BOT. Se flétrir (flower); dépérir (plant). ‖ CULIN. Se gâter, pourrir. (See SPOIL.) ‖ MED. Se faner (beauty); décliner (eyesight, health); s'affaiblir (race); se carier, se gâter (teeth). ‖ FIG. S'envoler (friendship); s'enfuir (hope).
— v. tr. ARCHIT. Délabrer, détériorer. ‖ BOT., CULIN. Faire pourrir. ‖ MED. Carier.
— n. ARCHIT. Délabrement *m.;* décrépitude *f.* ‖ BOT. Dépérissement *m.* ‖ CULIN. Corruption *f.;* pourrissement *m.* ‖ MED. Déclin *m.* (of health, sight); affaiblissement *m.* (of race); carie *f.* (of teeth). ‖ PHYS. Désintégration graduelle *f.* ‖ FIG. Déclin *m.;* décadence, déchéance *f.*

decease [di'si:s] n. Décès *m.*
— v. intr. JUR. Décéder.

deceased [-t] adj. Décédé, défunt, feu.
— n. Défunt *s.*

decedent [di'si:dənt] n. JUR. De cujus *m.*

deceit [di'si:t] n. Tromperie *f.* (cheating, fraud); fourberie *f.* (double-dealing); supercherie *f.* (trick). ‖ Apparence trompeuse *f.* (illusion).

deceitful [-ful] adj. Trompeur, menteur (cheating); trompeur, illusoire (illusive); fourbe (two-faced).

deceitfully [-fuli] adv. Faussement; mensongèrement; par fourberie.

deceive [di'si:v] v. tr. Tromper, duper; *to deceive*

oneself, s'abuser (*in*, sur); se leurrer (*with*, de). ‖ Tromper (one's husband, wife). ‖ Fig. Tromper (hope).
— v. intr. Tromper.
deceiver [-ə*] n. Trompeur, dupeur *s*. (cheat); fourbe *s*. (double-dealer).
decelerate [di:'seləreit] v. tr., intr. Ralentir.
december [di'sembə*] n. Décembre *m*.
decency ['di:snsi] n. Décence, modestie, pudeur *f*. (respectability). ‖ Convenance, bienséance *f*. (propriety).
decennary [di'senəri] adj. Décennal.
— n. Décennie f.
decennial [-jəl] adj. Decennal.
decent ['di:snt] adj. Décent, modeste, pudique (chaste). ‖ Décent, bienséant (decorous). ‖ Convenable, acceptable, passable (satisfactory). ‖ Bien, comme il faut (respectable). ‖ Fam. Gentil, aimable (*of*, à; *to*, pour). ‖ Pop. Habillé (clothed).
decently [-li] adv. Décemment. ‖ Convenablement.
decentralization [di:,sentrəlai'zeiʃən] n. Décentralisation *f*.
decentralize [di:'sentrəlaiz] v. tr. Décentraliser.
decentre [di:'sentə*] v. tr. Phys. Décentrer.
deception [di'sepʃən] n. Tromperie, duperie (act); erreur *f*., mécompte *m*. (result); supercherie *f*. (trick).
deceptive [-tiv] adj. Trompeur, décevant, menteur (delusive). [See fallacious.]
deceptively [-tivli] adv. Mensongèrement.
deceptiveness [-tivnis] n. Apparence trompeuse *f*.
dechristianize [di:'kristjənaiz] v. tr. Déchristianiser.
decibel ['desibel] n. Phys. Décibel *m*.
decide [di'said] v. tr. Décider, déterminer (s.o.). ‖ Dédider de, résoudre (an affair); régler (a conflict).
— v. intr. Décider, statuer; *to decide in favour of*, donner gain de cause à. ‖ Se décider (*on*, pour) [s.o.]; se déterminer, se décider, se résoudre (*on*, à) [sth.].
decided [-id] adj. Net, marqué (difference); décidé, résolu (manner, person, tone); déterminé, précis (opinion); catégorique, net (refusal).
decidedly [-idli] adv. Nettement; catégoriquement. ‖ Incontestablement.
decidedness [-idnis] n. Esprit (*m*.) de décision.
decider [-ə*] n. Arbitre, juge *m*. ‖ Sports. Epreuve subsidiaire *f*. (after a draw); belle *f*. (third game); but, essai, panier décisif *m*.
deciduous [di'sidjuəs] adj. Bot., Zool. Caduc. ‖ Fig. Transitoire, éphémère.
decigram(me) ['desigræm] n. Math. Décigramme *m*.
decilitre ['desili:tə*] n. Math. Décilitre *m*.
decimal [-məl] adj. Math. Décimal.
— n. Math. Décimale *f*.; *five decimal two*, cinq virgule deux.
decimalize [-mə,laiz] v. tr. Décimaliser.
decimate [-meit] v. tr. Décimer.
decimation ['desi'meiʃən] n. Décimation *f*.
decimetre ['desimi:tə*] n. Math. Décimètre *m*.
decipher [di'saifə*] v. tr. Déchiffrer.
— n. Déchiffrage *m*.
decipherable [-rəbl] adj. Déchiffrable.
decision [di'siʒən] n. Décision, détermination *f*.; parti *m*.; *what decision has she come to?*, qu'a-t-elle décidé? ‖ Décision, résolution, fermeté *f*. ‖ Jur. Décision *f*.; décret *m*.
decisive [di'saisiv] adj. Décisif, concluant, définitif, probant. (See conclusive.) ‖ Décisif, critique (critical). ‖ Décidé, résolu, catégorique (firm).
decisively [-li] adv. Catégoriquement.
deck [dek] n. Naut. Pont *m*.; *freeboard deck*, plage d'un cuirassé; *lower deck*, premier pont; *main* (or) *upper deck*, pont supérieur; *to clear the decks*, faire le branle-bas. ‖ Autom. Impériale *f*.

(of bus). ‖ Aviat., Fam. Sol *m*. ‖ U. S. Jeu *m*. (of cards). [See pack.] ‖ Fam. *On deck*, prêt à l'action. ‖ **Deck-cargo**, n. Naut. Pontée *f*. ‖ **Deck-chair**, n. Transat, transatlantique *m*. ‖ **Deck-erection** n. Naut. Super-structure *f*. ‖ **Deck-hand**, Naut. Homme de pont *m*. ‖ **Deck-house**, n. Naut. Rouf *m*. ‖ **Deck-land**, v. intr. Aviat. Apponter. ‖ **Deck-tennis**, n. Sports. Tennis de bord *m*.
— v. tr. Orner, parer (to trim); *decked out*, endimanché, en grande tenue, sur son trente et un. ‖ Naut. Ponter.
deckle ['dekl] n. Techn. Cadre (*m*.) de la forme (in paper manufacturing). ‖ **Deckle-edge**, n. Barbes (*f. pl.*).
declaim [di'kleim] v. tr., intr. Déclamer.
declamer [-ə*] n. Déclamateur *m*.; déclamatrice *f*.
declamation [deklə'meiʃən] n. Déclamation *f*.
declamatory [di'klæmətəri] adj. Déclamatoire.
declarant [di'klɛərənt] n. Jur. Déclarant *s*.
declaration [deklə'reiʃən] n. Déclaration *f*. ‖ Fin. Déclaration (of income); réponse *f*. (of options). ‖ Jur. *Declaration of the poll*, proclamation des résultats du scrutin. ‖ Milit. Déclaration (of war).
declarative [di'klærətiv] adj. Déclaratif.
declaratory [-təri] adj. Jur. Déclaratoire.
declare [di'klɛə*] v. tr. Déclarer, assurer (to assert); déclarer, faire connaître (to disclose); déclarer, proclamer, annoncer (to make public); déclarer, professer (to profess); *to declare one's love*, déclarer son amour, se déclarer; *to declare oneself*, se déclarer, s'avouer, se reconnaître. ‖ Annoncer (in cards). ‖ Jur. Déclarer à la douane. ‖ Milit. Déclarer (*upon*, à) [war]. ‖ **To declare off**, rompre, ne pas donner suite à.
— v. intr. Se déclarer (*against, for*, contre, pour).
declaredly [-ridli] adv. Ouvertement, d'une manière déclarée.
declasse [,deiklɑ:'sei] adj., n. Déclassé, déchu *s*.
declassify [di:'klæsi,fai] v. tr. (2). Considérer comme n'étant plus secret, autoriser la divulgation de.
declension [di'klenʃən] n. Pente, descente *f*. (slope). ‖ Déviation *f*. (*from*, de). ‖ Déclin *m*. ‖ Gramm. Déclinaison *f*.
declinable [di'klainəbl] adj. Gramm. Déclinable.
declination [dekli'neiʃən] n. Inclination, pente *f*. (slope). ‖ Non-acceptation *f*.; refus *m*. (refusal). ‖ Phys., Astron. Déclinaison *f*.
decline [di'klain] v. intr. Pencher, être en pente, s'incliner (ground). ‖ Baisser, décliner (day). ‖ Med. Décliner (health). ‖ Fin. Baisser (prices). ‖ Fig. Décliner (influence).
— v. tr. Pencher. ‖ Décliner (an invitation, a responsibility). [See refuse.] ‖ Gramm. Décliner.
— n. Déclin *m*., baisse *f*. (of the day). ‖ Med. Maladie de langueur *f*. ‖ Fin. Baisse *f*. (of prices). ‖ Fig. Déclin *m*.; décadence, régression *f*.
declining [-iŋ] adj. Déclinant, du déclin; *in one's declining years*, au déclin de sa vie.
declinometer [dekli'nɔmitə*] n. Phys. Déclinomètre *m*.
declivity [di'kliviti] n. Déclivité *f*.
declivous [di'klaivəs] adj. Déclive.
declutch [di:'klatʃ] v. intr. Autom. Débrayer.
decoct [di'kɔkt] v. tr. U. S. Extraire par décoction.
decoction [-ʃən] n. Décoction *f*.
decode [di:'koud] v. tr. Déchiffrer, décrypter. (See decypher.)
decoder [-ə*] n. Milit. Officier du chiffre, décrypteur *m*.
decoke [di:'kouk] v. tr. Techn. Décalaminer.
— n. Techn. Décalaminage *m*.
decollate [di:'kɔleit] v. tr. Décoller. (See behead.)
decollation [,di:ko'leiʃən] n. Décollation *f*.
décolletage [dei'kɔltɑ:ʒ] n. Décolletage *m*.
décolleté [dei'kɔltei] adj. Décolleté (dress, person).

decolonization [diː‚kɔlənaiz'eiʃən] n. Décolonisation *f.*

decolo(u)rization [diː‚kʌlɔrai'zeiʃən] n. Décoloration *f.*

decolo(u)rize [diː'kʌləraiz] v. tr. Décolorer.

decolo(u)rizer [-ə*] n. Décolorant *m.*

decompensation [‚diːkɔmpən'seiʃən] n. MED. Décompression *f.*

decomplex [di'kɔmpleks] adj. Complexe.

decomposable [‚diːkɔm'pouzəbl̩] adj. Décomposable.

decompose [-'pouz] v. tr. Décomposer, faire pourrir. ‖ CHIM. Décomposer. (See PUTREFY.) ‖ FIG. Analyser, décomposer.
— v. intr. Se décomposer (to rot).

decomposition [‚diːkɔmpə'ziʃən] n. Décomposition *f.*

decompress [‚diːkɔm'pres] v. tr. PHYS., MATH. Décomprimer.

decompression [-'preʃən] n. PHYS., MATH., MED. Décompression *f.*

decongestant [‚diːkən'dʒestənt] adj., n. MED. Décongestionnant *adj., m.*

deconsecrate [di'kɔnsikreit] v. tr. ECCLES. Désaffecter (a church).

decontaminate [‚diːkən'tæmineit] v. tr. Désinfecter.

decontrol [‚diːkən'troul] v. tr. FIN. Détaxer.

decor [di'kɔ:*] n. Décor *m.*

decorate ['dekəreit] v. tr. Décorer (a room, s.o.).

decoration [‚dekə'reiʃən] n. Décoration *f.*

decorative ['dekərətiv] adj. Décoratif; *decorative artist*, décorateur, ensemblier.

decorator [-tə*] n. Décorateur *m.; décoratrice f.*

decorous ['dekərəs] adj. Bienséant, comme il faut.

decorum [di'kɔːrəm] n. Décorum *m.* (etiquette). ‖ Tenue *f.* (dignity).

decoy [di'kɔi] n. SPORTS. Canardière *f.* (pond); appeau, leurre, appelant *m.* (See LURE.) ‖ FAM. Compère *m.* (of a swindler); *police decoy*, amorce de la police.
— v. tr. SPORTS. Leurrer, piper (birds). ‖ JUR. Séduire (woman). ‖ FIG. Attirer dans un piège.

decrease [di'kriːs] v. intr. Décroître, diminuer.
— v. tr. Diminuer, amoindrir. ‖ Diminuer (knitting).
— ['diːkriːs] n. Décroissance, diminution *f.*

decree [di'kriː] n. † Edit *m.* ‖ JUR. Arrêt *m.;* ordonnance *f.* (of court); décret *m.* (of the Parliament); *decree absolute*, ordonnance de divorce. ‖ ECCLES. Décret *m.* (of God); décrétale *f.* (of the Pope).
— v. tr. Décréter, prononcer (penalty).

decrement ['dekrimənt] n. Diminution *f.* ‖ MATH. Décrément *m.* ‖ BLAS. *Moon in decrement*, croissant contourné.

decrepit [di'krepit] adj. Décrépit, décati.

decrepitude [-tjuːd] n. Décrépitude *f.*

decrescent [di'kresənt] adj. Décroissant.

decretal [di'kriːtl̩] n. ECCLES. Décrétale *f.*

decretist [-tist] n. ECCLES., JUR. Canoniste *m.*

decry [di'krai] v. tr. (2). Décrier (s.o.). [See DISPARAGE.] ‖ FIN. Décrier (money).

decryptograph [di'kriptɔgrɑ:f] v. tr. Décrypter.

decuman ['dekjuːmən] adj. Enorme (wave).

decubitus [diː'kjuːbitəs] n. MED. Décubitus *m.*

decumbent [di'kʌmbənt] adj. BOT., ZOOL. Couché.

decuple ['dekjupl̩] adj., n. Décuple *m.*
— v. tr. Décupler.
— v. intr. Se décupler.

dedicate ['dedikeit] v. tr. ECCLES. Dédier, consacrer. ‖ U. S. Ouvrir, inaugurer. ‖ FIG. Dédier (a book); dédier, vouer (one's life). [See DEVOTE.]

dedicated [-id] adj. Dévoué (devoted); *dedicated teacher*, enseignant qui aime son métier; acharné, passionné, enragé (keen); convaincu (convinced).

dedication [dedi'keiʃən] n. Dédicace *f.* (of a book). ‖ ECCLES. Dédicace *f.*

dedicatory ['dedikətəri] adj. Dédicatoire.

deduce [di'djuːs] v. tr. Faire découler (*from*, de). ‖ PHILOS. Déduire (*from*, de). [See INFER.]

deducible [-ibl̩] adj. PHILOS. Déductible.

deduct [di'dʌkt] v. tr. COMM. Déduire, défalquer (to abate); *to be deducted from*, entrer en déduction de.

deductible [-ibl̩] adj. Déductible.

deduction [-ʃən] n. PHILOS. Déduction *f.* ‖ COMM. Déduction, défalcation *f.;* abattement *m.; after deduction of*, déduction faite de.

deductive [-tiv] adj. PHILOS. Déductif.

deductively [-tivli] adv. PHILOS. Par déduction.

deed [diːd] n. Action *f.; a good deed is never lost*, un bienfait n'est jamais perdu. ‖ Exploit *m.; heroic deeds*, exploits héroïques. ‖ Fait *m.; in deed, if not in name*, en fait, sinon de nom. ‖ JUR. Contrat *m.* (see COVENANT); acte notarié *m.* (document); *deed of partnership*, contrat de société. ‖ **Deed-poll**, n. JUR. Acte unilatéral *m.*
— v. tr. JUR. U. S. Transférer par un acte, faire donation de.

deejay ['diː‚dʒei] n. FAM. Disc-jockey *m.*

deem [diːm] v. tr. Juger, estimer.
— v. intr. Avoir une opinion (*of, de*, sur).

deep [diːp] adj. Profond; *five feet deep*, profond de cinq pieds, ayant cinq pieds de profondeur. ‖ Foncé (colour). ‖ Large (hem); profond (fold). ‖ Enfoncé (*in*, dans); *deep in mud*, bien embourbé. ‖ MED. Enfoncé (eye); profond (sleep, wound, wrinkle). ‖ MUS. Grave (sound, voice). ‖ FIG. Profond, intense (despair); extrême, total (disgrace); profond, vif (interest); profond (dissimulation, feelings, learning, thinker); pénétrant, profond (influence, mind); profond, total (mystery, silence); profond, noir (night); peu clair, obscur (scheme); profond, épais (shadow); profond (sigh); grave (sin); *deep drinker*, grand buveur. ‖ FIG. *Deep in*, absorbé par (study); plongé (or) abîmé dans (thought); *deep in the human heart*, connaissant parfaitement le cœur humain; *deep in love*, profondément amoureux. ‖ FAM. Malin; *a deep one*, une vieille ficelle. ‖ FAM. *It's too deep for me*, c'est trop fort pour moi; *to go off the deep end*, s'emballer (to flare up).
— adv. Profondément; *to sleep deep*, dormir profondément. ‖ Dans les bas-fonds; *to run deep*, couler à une grande profondeur, stagner (water). ‖ Profondément, en pénétrant; *deep into the night*, très avant dans la nuit. ‖ Copieusement; *to play deep*, jouer gros. ‖ **Deep-dyed**, adj. U. S. Entièrement teint; FAM. Fieffé, pur sang (arrant). ‖ **Deep-freeze**, n. Congélateur *m.; congélation f.;* v. tr. congeler. ‖ **Deep-fry**, v. tr. CULIN. Faire cuire en pleine friture. ‖ **Deep-laid**, adj. FIG. Ténébreux. ‖ **Deep-mouthed**, adj. Qui aboie fort (hound); FAM. Fort en gueule (person). ‖ **Deep-read**, adj. Versé (in, dans). ‖ **Deep-rooted**, adj. Profondément ancré (or) enraciné. ‖ **Deep-sea**, adj. Des grandes profondeurs. ‖ **Deep-seated**, adj. MED. Bronchial (cough); FIG. Bien établi. ‖ **Deep-set**, adj. Enfoncé (eye); FIG. Fermement établi.
— n. Océan *m.; mer f.* (sea). ‖ Abîme, gouffre *m.* (abyss). ‖ Pl. Profondeurs *f. pl.* ‖ Milieu *m.* (of night); cœur *m.* (of winter).

deepen [-ən] v. tr. Creuser (a well). ‖ Foncer (a colour). ‖ MUS. Rendre plus grave (a sound). ‖ FIG. Accroître, augmenter.
— v. intr. Se creuser, prendre de la profondeur, s'approfondir. ‖ Se foncer (colour). ‖ MUS. Devenir plus grave. ‖ FIG. S'accroître, augmenter; s'intensifier.

deeply [-li] adv. Profondément. ‖ Extrêmement.

deepness [-nis] n. Profondeur *f.*

deer [diə*] n. † Bête sauvage f. ‖ Zool. Cervidé m.; cerf m.; *fallow deer*, daim. ‖ **Deer-hound**, n. Zool. Chien courant, lévrier (m.) d'Ecosse.

deerskin [-skin] n. Daim m. (leather).

deerstalker [-'stɔ:kə*] n. Sports. Chasseur (m.) à l'affût. ‖ Comm. Chapeau (m.) de chasse (hat).

de-escalation [di:,eskə'leiʃən] n. Désescalade f.

deface [di'feis] v. tr. Défigurer (sth.); lacérer (a poster); mutiler (a statue); dégrader (a wall). ‖ Oblitérer (a stamp). ‖ Rendre illisible, effacer (an inscription). [See DISFEATURE.]

defacement [-mənt] n. Détérioration, dégradation f. ‖ Lacération f. ‖ Mutilation f. ‖ Oblitération f. ‖ Effacement m.

de facto [dei'fæktou] adj., adv. De facto, de fait.

defalcate [di'fælkeit] v. intr. Jur. Détourner des fonds (to embezzle).

defalcation [,di:fæl'keiʃən] n. Jur. Détournement (m.) de fonds.

defamation [defə'meiʃən] n. Diffamation f.

defamatory [di'fæmətəri] adj. Diffamatoire.

defame [di'feim] v. tr. Diffamer.

default [di'fɔ:lt] n. Défaut m. (want); *in default of*, à défaut de, faute de. ‖ Jur. Défaut m.; non-comparution f. (civil law); contumace f. (criminal law); *default of heirs*, déshérence f. ‖ Sports. Forfait m.
— v. intr. Jur. Faire défaut. ‖ Fin. Ne pas tenir ses engagements. ‖ Sports. Déclarer forfait.
— v. tr. Jur. Condamner par défaut.

defaulter [-ə*] n. Auteur (m.) de détournements; concussionnaire m. (embezzler). ‖ Jur. Défaillant s.; contumace s. (absentee); délinquant s. (offender). ‖ Milit. Réfractaire, insoumis m. (absentee); puni m. (offender).

defeasance [di'fi:zəns] n. Jur. Abrogation f.; *defeasance clause*, clause résolutoire.

defeasible [-ib] adj. Jur. Annulable.

defeat [di'fi:t] v. tr. Défaire, vaincre. ‖ Mettre en minorité (the Government). ‖ Jur. Annuler. ‖ Fig. Faire échec à; *to defeat s.o. in his plans*, déjouer les projets de qqn.
— n. Insuccès, échec m. ‖ Milit. Défaite f. ‖ Jur. Annulation f.

defeatism [di'fi:tizm̩] n. Défaitisme m.

defeatist [-ist] adj., n. Défaitiste s.

defeature [di'fi:tʃə*] v. tr. Défigurer, rendre méconnaissable.

defecate ['di:fikeit] v. intr. Med. Déféquer.
— v. tr. Clarifier, purifier.

defecation [,di:fi'keiʃən] n. Med. Défécation f.

defect [di'fekt] n. Défaut, manque m.; déficience f. (lack). ‖ Défectuosité f.; défaut m. (flaw); *constructional defect*, vice de construction; *defect in pronunciation*, défaut de prononciation. ‖ Fig. Défaut m. (fault).
— v. intr. Faire défection; *to defect to the East, to the West*, passer à l'Est, à l'Ouest.

defection [di'fekʃən] n. Défection f. ‖ Eccles. Apostasie f.

defective [-tiv] adj. Défectueux. ‖ Gramm. Défectif. ‖ Med., Fig. Déficient (in, en).

defectively [-tivli] adv. Défectueusement.

defectiveness [-tivnis] n. Défectuosité f.; état défectueux m.

defector [di'fektə*] n. Transfuge s.

defence [di'fens] n. Milit. Défenses f. pl.; ouvrages défensifs f; défenseurs m. pl. ‖ Jur., Fig. Défense f. ‖ Med., Psych. *Defence mechanism*, mécanisme de défense.

defenceless [-lis] adj. Sans défense.

defend [di'fend] v. tr. Défendre, protéger (contre, against); *to defend oneself*, se défendre. ‖ Défendre, soutenir, prendre le parti de (to support). ‖ Jur. Défendre.

defendant [-ənt] n. Jur. Défendeur m.; défenderesse f.; *called by the defendant*, cité par la défense.

defender [-ə*] n. Défenseur m.

defenestration [di:,feni'streiʃən] n. Défenestration f.

defense [di'fens] U. S. See DEFENCE.

defensible [di'fensib] adj. Défendable.

defensive [-siv] adj. Défensif, de défense (attitude, operation); *United States defensive waters*, eaux intéressant la défense des Etats-Unis.
— n. Défensive f.; *to assume the defensive*, se mettre sur la défensive.

defensively [-sivli] adv. Défensivement, sur la défensive.

defer [di'fə*] v. tr. (1). Différer, reculer, remettre. (See DELAY.) ‖ Jur. Suspendre (a judgment). ‖ Milit. Mettre en sursis.
— v. intr. Différer.

defer v. intr. (1). Déférer, accéder (to, à). ‖ Se rendre, s'en rapporter (to, à).

deference ['defərəns] n. Déférence f. (to, pour); respect m.; *out of deference to public opinion*, par respect humain; *with all due deference to you*, sauf votre respect.

deferent [-ənt] adj. Math., Med. Déférent.

deferential [defə'renʃəl] adj. Déférent, plein d'égards (to, envers).

deferentially [-ʃəli] adv. Avec déférence (or) respect.

deferred [di'fəd] adj. Jur., Milit. Ajourné. ‖ Fin. Différé.

defiance [di'faiəns] n. Défi m.; bravade f.; *to set at defiance*, braver. ‖ Mépris m.; *in defiance of*, au mépris de.

defiant [-ənt] adj. De défi (challenging). ‖ Défiant (suspicious).

defiantly [-əntli] adv. D'un air de défi.

deficiency [di'fiʃənsi] n. Déficience f. ‖ Med. *Deficiency disease*, avitaminose; *mental deficiency*, débilité mentale. ‖ Fin. Déficit budgétaire m. ‖ Comm. Découvert m.

deficient [-ənt] adj. Déficient (in, en).
— n. Med. Déficient, débile mental s.

deficiently [-əntli] adv. D'une manière déficiente; insuffisamment.

deficit ['defisit] n. Fin. Déficit m. ‖ Comm. Découvert m.

defier [di'faiə*] n. Provocateur m.; provocatrice f.

defilade [defi'leid] n. Milit. Défilement m.
— v. tr. Milit. Défiler.

defile [di'fail] v. intr. Milit. Défiler.
— ['di:fail] n. Geogr. Défilé m.

defile v. tr. Souiller, polluer (to dirty). ‖ Déflorer, violer (a woman).

defilement [-mənt] n. Souillure f.

definable [di'fainəb] adj. Définissable.

define [di'fain] v. tr. Délimiter (the boundaries). ‖ Définir (a situation, a word).

definite ['definit] adj. Délimité (powers). ‖ Défini, explicite; net, précis (answer). ‖ Assuré, positif; *it's definite that*, il est certain que. ‖ Gramm. Défini.

definitely [-li] adv. Explicitement, définitivement, avec précision. ‖ Fam. Assurément, certainement.

definiteness [-nis] n. Caractère défini m. ‖ Précision f.

definition [defi'niʃən] n. Délimitation f. (of powers). ‖ Netteté f. (in photography); *bad definition*, flou. ‖ Gramm., Eccles., Radio. Définition f.

definitive [di'finitiv] adj. Définitif.

definitively [-li] adv. Définitivement.

deflagrable ['defləgreib] adj. Déflagrant.

deflagrate [-greit] v. tr. Enflammer, embraser.
— v. intr. Déflagrer, prendre feu.

deflagration [deflə'greiʃən] n. Déflagration f.

deflagrator ['deflægreitə*] n. Déflagrateur *m*.
deflate [di'fleit] v. tr. Dégonfler. ‖ Fin. Amener la déflation de.
deflation [di'fleiʃən] n. Dégonflement *m*. ‖ Fin. Déflation *f*.
deflationary [-əri] adj. Fin. Déflationniste.
deflect [di'flekt] v. tr. Dériver, détourner (a stream). ‖ Phys. Faire dévier, dévier. ‖ Autom. Braquer (whccls).
— v. intr. Se détourner. ‖ Phys. Dévier.
deflection, deflexion [-ʃən] n. Déviation *f*. ‖ Phys. Déflexion *f*. (of light); déviation *f*. (of compass). ‖ Techn. Fléchissement *m*. ‖ Milit. Dérive *f*. ‖ Autom. Braquage *m*.
deflector [-tə*] n. Techn. Déflecteur *m*.
defloration [,di:flɔ:'reiʃən] n. Bot. Défloraison *f*. ‖ Jur. Défloration *f*.
deflower [di'flauə] v. tr. Déflorer.
defoliant [di:'fouliənt] adj., n. Défoliant *adj., m*.
defoliate [di:'fouli,eit] v. tr. Défolier.
defoliation [,di:fouli'eiʃən] n. Bot. Défoliation *f*.
deforest [di:'fɔrist] v. tr. Déboiser.
deforestation [,di:fɔrəs'teiʃən] n. Déboisement *m*.
deform [di'fɔ:m] v. tr. Med. Déformer, contrefaire (a body); enlaidir (s.o.). ‖ Phys. Déformer (a wave). ‖ Techn. Fausser.
deformation [,di:fɔ:'meiʃən] n. Déformation, altération *f*.
deformity [di'fɔ:miti] n. Med. Difformité *f*. ‖ † Laideur *f*.
defraud [di'frɔ:d] v. tr. Jur. Frauder. ‖ Fig. Léser; faire tort à (*of*, de) [s.o.].
defray [di'frei] v. tr. Fin. Couvrir (the cost); payer (the expenses); *to defray s.o.'s expenses*, défrayer qqn, rembourser les frais à qqn.
defrayal [-əl], **defrayment** [-mənt] n. Fin. Défrai *m*.
defrock [di:'frɔk] v. tr. Eccles. Défroquer.
defrost [di:'frɔst] v. tr. Autom., Aviat., Techn. Dégivrer. ‖ Culin. Décongeler.
defroster [-ə*] n. Autom., Aviat., Techn. Dégivreur *m*.
deft [deft] adj. Adroit. (See dexterous.)
deftly [-li] adv. Avec adresse.
deftness [-nis] n. Adresse, dextérité *f*.
defunct [di'fʌŋkt] adj., n. Défunt *s*. (See dead.)
defuse [di:'fju:z] v. tr. Désamorcer (explosive). ‖ Fig. Désamorcer, dédramatiser (event, crisis).
defy [di'fai] v. tr. (2). Défier, mettre au défi (*to*, de) [to dare]. ‖ Défier, braver (to face). ‖ Défier, ne pas craindre, être à l'épreuve de (to resist).
dégagé [,deigæ'ʒei] adj. Fig. Dégagé (manner).
degarnish [di:'gɑ:niʃ] v. tr. Dégarnir.
degas [di:'gæs] v. tr. (1). Phys., Chim. Dégazer.
degauss [di:'gaus] v. tr. Naut. Désaimanter.
degeneracy [di'dʒenərəsi] n. Dégénérescencc *f*.
degenerate [-it] adj., n. Dégénéré *s*.
— [-eit] v. intr. Dégénérer (*into*, en).
degeneration [di,dʒenə'reiʃən] n. Dégénération *f*.
deglutition [,di:glu:'tiʃən] n. Med. Déglutition *f*.
degradation [,degrə'deiʃən] n. Milit., Phys., Arts, Geol., Fig. Dégradation *f*.
degrade [di'greid] v. tr. Milit., Phys., Arts, Geol., Fig. Dégrader.
— v. intr. Med. Dégénérer. ‖ Geol. Se dégrader.
degrading [-iŋ] adj. Dégradant.
degrease [di'gri:s] v. tr. Dégraisser.
degree [di'gri:] n. Degré *m*. (step). ‖ Degré, point *m*. (pitch); *by degrees*, graduellement ; *to a degree*, au premier chef, au suprême degré. ‖ Diplôme, grade universitaire *m*. ; *he took his degree in the same year as I*, il était de la même promotion que moi. ‖ Rang *m*.; condition *f*.; *of high degree*, de haut lignage. ‖ Degré *m*. (of relationship). ‖ Eccles. Degré *m*. (of the altar). ‖ Phys. Degré *m*.; *to stand at ten degrees*, marquer dix degrés. ‖ Math., Geogr.

Degré *m*. ‖ Mus. Degré *m*. ; ligne de la portée *f*. ‖ Gramm. Degré *m*. (of comparison). ‖ Jur. *Murder in the first, second degree*, assassinat, meurtre ; *third degree*, troisième degré, passage à tabac.
degression [di'greʃən] n. Fin. U. S. Dégression *f*.
degressive [-siv] adj. Fin. U. S. Dégressif.
degustate [di'gasteit] v. tr. Déguster.
dehisce [di'his] v. intr. Bot., Med. S'ouvrir.
dehorn [di:'hɔ:n] v. tr. Décorner.
dehort [di:'hɔ:t] v. tr. Dissuader.
dehortation [di:hɔ:'teiʃən] n. Dissuasion *f*.
dehortative [di:'hɔ:tətiv] adj. Dissuasif.
dehumanize [di:'hju:mə,naiz] v. tr. Déshumaniser.
dehumidify [di:'hju:midifai] v. tr. (2). Naut. Assécher.
dehydrate [di:'haidreit] v. tr. Chim. Déshydrater.
dehydrated [-id] adj. Culin. En poudre (egg).
dehydrogenate [di:,hai'drɔdʒeneit] v. tr. Chim. Déshydrogéner.
dehydrogenation [di:,haidrɔdʒe'neiʃən] n. Chim. Déshydrogénation *f*.
de-ice [di:'ais] v. tr. Dégivrer (windscreen, plane).
de-icer [di:'aisə*] n. Antigivre, dégivreur *m*.
deicide ['di:isaid] n. Eccles. Déicide *m*.
deictic ['daiktik] adj. Gramm. Démonstratif. ‖ Philos. Directement probant.
deification [,di:ifi'keiʃən] n. Déification *f*.
deify ['di:ifai] v. tr. (2). Déifier. (See divinise.)
deign [dein] v. tr. Daigner.
deionize [di:'aiə,naiz] v. tr. Chim. Désioniser.
deism ['di:izm] n. Déisme *m*.
deist [-ist] n. Déiste *s*.
deistic [di:'istik] adj. Déiste.
deity ['di:iti] n. Divinité, déité *f*.
déjà vu ['deiʒæ 'vu:] n. Déjà vu *m*.
deject [di'dʒekt] v. tr. Fig. Déprimer, abattre.
dejecta [-ə] n. pl. Med., Geogr. Déjections *f. pl*.
dejectedly [-idli] adv. Avec découragement.
dejection [di'dʒekʃən] n. Med. Déjection. ‖ Fig. Abattement *m*.
dejector [-tə*] n. Med. Purgatif *m*.
dejectory [-təri] adj. Med. Purgatif.
de jure [dei'dʒuərei] adj., adv. De droit, de jurc.
dekko ['dekou] n. Pop. Coup d'œil *m*. ; *to have a dekko*, zyeuter.
delacerate [di'læsəreit] v. tr. Déchiqueter.
delaine [di'lein] n. Mousseline de laine *f*.
delate [di'leit] v. tr. Dénoncer.
delation [-ʃən] n. Délation *f*.
delator [-tə*] n. Délateur *m*. ; délatrice *f*.
delay [di'lei] v. tr. Différer (an action); retarder (s.o.). ‖ Techn. Contrarier l'avance de.
— v. intr. Tarder, s'attarder.
— n. Retard, délai *m*. ; *to make no delay in*, ne pas tarder à. ‖ Entrave *f*. ; empêchement *m*.
delaying [-iŋ] adj. Dilatoire (action).
dele ['di:li] n. Deleatur *m*.
— v. tr. Supprimer. (See delete.)
deleble ['deləbl] adj. Effaçable.
delectable [di'lektəbl] adj. Délicieux. ‖ Culin. Délectable.
delectation [,di:lek'teiʃən] n. Délectation *f*.
delectus [di'lektəs] n. Anthologie *f*.
delegacy ['deligəsi] n. Délégation *f*.
delegate [-git] n. Délégué *s*.
— [-geit] v. tr. Déléguer. (See depute.) ‖ Jur. *Delegated legislation*, décrets-lois.
delegatee [deligə'ti:] n. Jur. Délégataire *m*.
delegation [,deli'geiʃən] n. Délégation, députation *f*. (act, persons).
delete [di'li:t] v. tr. Supprimer, biffer, rayer.
deleterious [,deli'tiəriəs] adj. Délétère.
deletion [di:'li:ʃən] n. Rature *f*. (act) ; suppression *f*. (text).
delft [delft] n. Delft *m*. (earthenware).

deliberate [di'librit] adj. Délibéré, voulu, intentionnel (purposive). ‖ Prudent, circonspect, réfléchi (cautious). ‖ Lent, précautionneux; *to take deliberate aim*, prendre son temps pour viser.
— [-eit] v. tr. Délibérer au sujet de, réfléchir sur, peser.
— v. intr. Délibérer (*on*, sur; *with*, avec). ‖ Réfléchir (to ponder).

deliberately [-itli] adv. De propos délibéré, délibérément (voluntarily). ‖ Avec circonspection (circumspectly). ‖ Lentement, à loisir (slowly).

deliberation [di,libə'reiʃən] n. Délibération, réflexion *f.* ‖ Délibération *f.; débat m.* ‖ Circonspection, réflexion *f.* ‖ Lenteur, pondération *f.*

deliberative [di'libərətiv] adj. Délibératif (advice); délibérant (assembly).

delible ['delibl] adj. Effaçable.

delicacy ['delikəsi] (pl. **delicacies** [-kəsiz]) n. Délicatesse, finesse *f.* (of the face); fragilité *f.* (of a petal, a vase). ‖ MED. Fragilité *f.* (of constitution). ‖ TECHN. Sensibilité *f.* (of a compass). ‖ CULIN. Mets délicat *m.; friandise f.* ‖ FIG. Délicatesse, pudeur *f.; tact m.* (of a person); raffinement *m.* (of taste); légèreté, douceur *f.* (of touch).

delicate [-kit] adj. Délicat, fin, doux (air, colour, odour). ‖ Fin (linen, work). ‖ Fragile (petal, vase). ‖ MED. Fragile (health, person, stomach); *in a delicate condition*, dans une position intéressante. ‖ TECHN. Sensible (compass). ‖ CULIN. Fin (food). ‖ FIG. Délicat, pudique (modest); raffiné, quelque peu efféminé (overnice); délicat, plein de tact (tactful). ‖ FIG. Délicat (question); délicat, raffiné (taste); léger (touch).

delicately [-kitli] adv. Délicatement.

delicateness [-kitnis] n. Douceur *f.* (softness). ‖ Nature délicate *f.* (effeminacy).

delicatessen [,delikə'tɛsn] n. pl. CULIN. Plats cuisinés *m. pl.* (meats); charcuterie *f.* (shop).

delicious [di'liʃəs] adj. Délicieux.

deliciously [-li] adv. Délicieusement.

delict ['dilikt] n. JUR. Délit *m.*

deligate [,dilai'geit] v. tr. MED. Ligaturer.

delight [di'lait] v tr. Charmer, ravir.
— v. intr. Se complaire, se délecter, trouver son plaisir (*in*, à); faire ses délices (*in*, de).
— n. Délice *m.* (See PLEASURE.)

delighted [-id] adj. Ravi, enchanté (*with*, de).

delightful [-ful] adj. Ravissant, charmant, délicieux.

delightfully [-fuli] adv. Avec charme, délicieusement; à ravir.

delightfulness [-fulnis] n. Délice, charme, enchantement *m.*

Delilah [di'lailə] n. Dalila *f.*

delimit [di'limit], **delimitate** [-eit] v. tr. Délimiter.

delimitation [di,limi'teiʃən] n. Délimitation *f.*

delimitative [-tiv] adj. Délimitatif.

delineate [di'linieit] v. tr. ARTS. Esquisser, ébaucher. ‖ FIG. Dépeindre, décrire (to describe).

delineation [di,lini'eiʃən] n. ARTS. Dessin *m.* (drawing); esquisse *f.* (sketch). ‖ FIG. Description *f.*

delineator [di'linieitə*] n. ARTS. Dessinateur *m.;* dessinatrice *f.* ‖ FIG. Peintre *s.* (of character).

delinquency [di'liŋkwənsi] n. JUR. Délit *m.* (fault); culpabilité *f.* (guilt). ‖ FIN. U. S. *Delinquency amount*, montant du trop perçu.

delinquent [-ənt] adj. JUR. Délinquant, coupable. ‖ FIN. *Delinquent taxes*, impôts non payés à temps; majoration pour retard de paiement.
— n. JUR. Délinquant *s.; juvenile delinquents*, jeunesse délinquante.

deliquesce [,deli'kwes] v. intr. Fondre. ‖ CHIM. Se liquéfier. ‖ BOT. Se ramifier (leaf veins). ‖ FIG. Tomber en déliquescence.

deliquescence [-ns] n. Déliquescence *f.; in a state of deliquescence*, en déliquescence.

deliquescent [-nt] adj. Déliquescent.

deliration [,deli'reiʃən] n. MED. Délire *m.*

delirious [di'liriəs] adj. MED., FIG. Délirant (*with*, de).

delirium [-əm] n. MED. Délire *m.; delirium tremens*, delirium tremens. ‖ FIG. Délire, transport *m.*

delitescence [,dili'tesns] n. MED. Délitescence *f.*

delitescent [-nt] adj. MED. Délitescent.

deliver [di'livə*] v. tr. Délivrer, libérer (*from*, de) [to free]. ‖ Jeter, lancer (a ball); assener, porter (a blow). ‖ Distribuer (the mail); porter, remettre (a parcel). ‖ Transmettre (a message); formuler, exprimer (an opinion); prononcer (a speech); *to deliver oneself of*, émettre. ‖ MED. Mettre au monde (a child); délivrer (a pregnant woman); *to be delivered of*, accoucher de. ‖ JUR. Signifier, notifier, prononcer. ‖ COMM. Livrer (goods); *to be delivered*, livrable à domicile. ‖ MILIT. Déclencher (an attack); livrer (a battle); envoyer (a missile). ‖ **To deliver over**, remettre; transmettre (*to*, à). ‖ **To deliver up**, remettre, céder (*to*, à); restituer, rendre.

deliverable [di'livərəbl] adj. Livrable.

deliverance [-əns] n. Délivrance, libération *f.* (*from*, de). ‖ JUR. Déclaration *f.;* prononcé *m.*

deliveree [di,livə'ri:] n. U. S. Destinataire *s.*

deliverer [di'livərə*] n. Libérateur *m.;* libératrice *f.* ‖ Orateur *m.;* oratrice *f.* (orator). ‖ COMM. Livreur *s.*

delivery [-i] n. Distribution *f.* (of blows). ‖ Distribution (of the mail); remise *f.* (of a parcel); U. S. *General Delivery*, poste restante. ‖ Prononcé *m.* (of a speech); élocution, diction *f.* (style of speaking). ‖ MED. Délivrance *f.* ‖ COMM. Livraison *f.; delivery free*, rendu franco; *to take delivery*, prendre livraison, réceptionner. ‖ JUR. Transfert *m.* ‖ TECHN. Débit *m.* (of water).

dell [del] n. Vallon *m.*

delocalization [di,loukəlai'zeiʃən] n. Délocalisation *f.*

delocalize [di'loukəlaiz] v. tr. Délocaliser.

delouse [di'laus] v. tr. Epouiller.

delousing [-iŋ] n. Epouillage *m.*

Delphi ['delfai] n. GEOGR. Delphes *m.*

Delphic ['delfik] adj. De Delphes (oracle).

delphin ['delfin] adj. Ad usum Delphini (édition).

delphinium [del'finiəm] n. BOT. Delphinium *m.*

delta ['deltə] n. GRAMM., GEOGR. Delta *m.* ‖ PHYS. *Delta rays*, rayons delta. ‖ AVIAT. *Delta wing*, aile delta (or) en delta.

deltaic [del'teiik] adj. GEOGR. Formant un delta.

deltoid ['deltɔid] adj., n. MED. Deltoïde *m.*

delude [di'lju:d] v. tr. Tromper (see DECEIVE); *to delude oneself regarding*, se bercer d'illusions sur.

deluge ['delju:dʒ] n. Déluge *m.* (lit. and fig.).
— v. tr. Inonder, submerger (lit. and fig.).

delusion [di'lju:ʒən] n. Tromperie *f.* ‖ Illusion *f.* ‖ MED. Hallucination *f.; delusions of grandeur*, folie des grandeurs.

delusive [-siv] adj. Trompeur (deceiving); illusoire (illusory).

delusiveness [-sivnis] n. Nature trompeuse *f.*

de luxe [di'luks] adj. COMM. De luxe, de qualité supérieure.

delve [delv] v. tr. AGRIC. Bêcher.
— v. intr. AGRIC. Bêcher, creuser. ‖ Descendre, être en pente (road). ‖ FIG. Fouiller (*into*, dans); *to delve into books*, se plonger dans les livres.
— n. Creux *m.*

demagnetization [di,mægnitai'zeiʃən] n. Désaimantation, démagnétisation *f.*

demagnetize [di'mægnə,taiz] v. tr. Démagnétiser, désaimanter.

demagogic [,demə'gogik] adj. Démagogique.

demagogism ['deməgogizm] n. Démagogie *f.*

demagogue [-gog] n. Démagogue *m.*

demagoguery ['demə,gogri] n. U. S. Démagogie *f.*

demagogy ['deməgogi] n. Démagogie f.
demand [di'mɑ:nd] v. tr. Exiger, réclamer ; mettre en demeure (from, of, de). ‖ Exiger de savoir, vouloir connaître. ‖ JUR. To demand a penalty against, requérir contre.
— n. Exigence, prétention f. ‖ COMM. Demande f.; débit, débouché m. (for, pour). ‖ FIN. Demand bill, loan, billet, prêt à vue ; on demand, sur demande. ‖ FAM. He is in great demand, on se l'arrache. ‖ Demand feeding, n. U. S. Alimentation (f.) au rythme demandé par l'enfant.
demandable [-əbḷ] adj. Exigible.
demandant [-ənt] n. JUR. Demandeur m.; demanderesse f.
demanding [-iŋ] adj. Revendicatif ; exigeant.
demarcate ['di:mɑ:keit] v. tr. Délimiter.
demarcation [,di:mɑ:'keiʃən] n. Démarcation f.
demarche [də'mɑ:ʃ] n. JUR. Changement (m.) de politique. ‖ FIG. Ligne d'action f.
dematerialization [,dimətiəriəlai'zeiʃən] n. Dématérialisation f.
dematerialize [,di:mə'tiəriəlaiz] v. tr. Dématérialiser.
— v. tr. Se dématérialiser.
demean [di'mi:n] v. réfl. To demean oneself, se conduire, agir (to behave); s'abaisser, s'avilir (to lower oneself).
demeanour [-ə*] n. Comportement m.; conduite f.
dement [di'ment] v. tr. MED. Rendre fou, conduire à la folie.
— n. MED. U. S. Dément s.
demented [-id] adj. MED. Dément ; demented person, dément.
dementedly [-idli] adv. Follement.
dementia [di'menʃiə] n. MED. Démence f.
demerara [,demə'rɛərə] n. Cassonade f.
demerit [di:'merit] n. Démérite m. ‖ U. S. Blâme m.
demesne [di'mein] n. Domaine m. ‖ JUR. Pleine propriété f. ‖ FIG. Domaine, rayon m. (of activity).
demi ['demi] pref. Demi. ‖ Demi-bastion, n. MILIT. Demi-bastion m. ‖ Demi-god, n. Demi-dieu m. ‖ Demi-lune, n. MILIT. Demi-lune f. ‖ Demi-monde, n. Demi-monde m. ‖ Demi-rep, n. FAM. Demi-mondaine f. ‖ Demi-sel, n. CULIN. Demi-sel m. ‖ Demi-vierge, n. Demi-vierge f.
demigrate ['demigreit] v. intr. Emigrer.
demijohn ['demidʒɔn] n. Dame-jeanne f.
demilitarization [di,militəri'zeiʃən] n. Démilitarisation f.
demilitarize [di'militəraiz] v. tr. Démilitariser.
demineralization [di,minərəlai'zeiʃən] n. MED. Déminéralisation f.
demineralize [di'minərəlaiz] v. tr. MED. Déminéraliser.
demisable [di'maizəbḷ] adj. JUR. Légable ; transférable ; cessible.
demise [di'maiz] v. tr. JUR. Léguer (an estate); transmettre (sovereignty).
— n. Décès m. ‖ JUR. Cession (f.) par legs.
demisemiquaver ['demisemi,kweivə*] n. MUS. Triple croche f.
demission [di'miʃən] n. Démission f.
demist [di'mist] v. tr. Enlever la buée de.
demister [-ə*] n. AUTOM. Antibuée m.
demit [di'mit] v. tr. (1). Résigner, se démettre de.
— v. intr. Donner sa démission.
demitasse ['demi,tæs] n. U. S. Moka m. (coffee); tasse (f.) à moka (cup).
demiurge ['di:miə:dʒ] n. Démiurge m.
demob [di'mɔb] v. tr. (1). MILIT., FAM. Démobiliser.
— n. MILIT., FAM. Démobilisé m.
demobilization [di,moubilai'zeiʃən] n. MILIT. Démobilisation f.
demobilize [di:'moubilaiz] v. tr. MILIT. Démobiliser.

democracy [di'mɔkrəsi] n. Démocratie f.
democrat ['demokræt] n. Démocrate s.
democratic [-ik] adj. Démocratique.
democratically [-ikəli] adv. Démocratiquement.
démocratization [di,mokrətai'zeiʃən] n. Démocratisation f.
democratize [di'mɔkrətaiz] v. tr. Démocratiser.
— v. intr. Se démocratiser.
démodé [,deimou'dei] adj. Démodé.
demographer [di'mɔgrəfə*] n. Démographe m.
demographic [demɔ'græfik] adj. Démographique.
demography [-fi] n. Démographie f.
demoiselle [,dəmwa'zɛl] n. Demoiselle f. ‖ ZOOL. Demoiselle de Numidie f. (crane); libellule, demoiselle f. (dragonfly).
demolish [di'mɔliʃ] v. tr. Démolir.
demolisher [-ə*] n. Démolisseur s.
demolishment [-mənt], **demolition** [dimə'liʃən] n. Démolition f.
demon ['di:mən] n. ECCLES., FIG. Démon m.
demonetization [di:,mɔnitai'zeiʃən] n. FIN. Démonétisation f.
demonetize [di:'mɔnitaiz] v. tr. FIN. Démonétiser.
demoniac [di'mouniæk] adj. Démoniaque.
— n. Possédé s.
demoniacal [,di:mə'naiəkəl] adj. Démoniaque.
demoniast [,di:'mouniæst] n. Démonolâtre s.
demonism ['di:mənizm] n. Démonisme m.
demonolatry [di:mə'nɔlətri] n. Démonolâtrie f.
demonology [-lədʒi] n. Démonologie f.
demonstrability [di,mɔnstrə'biliti] n. Démonstrabilité f.
demonstrable [di'mɔnstrəbḷ] adj. Démontrable.
demonstrably [-li] adv. Indiscutablement.
demonstrate ['demənstreit] v. tr. Démontrer. ‖ COMM. Faire la démonstration de. ‖ FIG. Manifester.
— v. intr. Manifester. ‖ MILIT. Faire une démonstration militaire.
demonstration [,deməns'treiʃən] n. Démonstration probante f. ‖ MATH., MED., MILIT. Démonstration. ‖ JUR. Manifestation, démonstration populaire f. ‖ COMM. Démonstration f.; demonstration car, model, voiture, appareil de démonstration. ‖ ECCLES. Manifestation religieuse f. ‖ Demonstration-school, n. Ecole annexe f. (of a training college).
demonstrative [di'mɔnstrətiv] adj. Probant. ‖ GRAMM., FIG. Démonstratif.
— n. GRAMM. Démonstratif m.
demonstratively [-li] adv. D'une façon démonstrative.
demonstrator ['demənstreitə*] n. COMM. Démonstrateur m.; démonstratrice f. ‖ CHIM. Chef (m.) de travaux. ‖ MED. Préparateur m.; préparatrice f. ‖ JUR. Manifestant s.
demoralization [di,mɔrəlai'zeiʃən] n. Démoralisation f.
demoralize [di'mɔrəlaiz] v. tr. Démoraliser (to dishearten). ‖ Dépraver (to deprave).
demoralizer [-ə*] n. Démoralisateur m.; démoralisatrice f. ‖ Corrupteur m.; corruptrice f.
demote [di'mout] v. tr. U. S. Rétrograder.
demotic [di'mɔtik] adj., n. GRAMM. Démotique adj., m.
demount [di'maunt] v. tr. Démonter.
demountable [-əbḷ] adj. Démontable.
demulcent [di'mʌlsənt] adj., n. MED. Emollient m.
demur [di'mə:*] v. intr. (1). Hésiter, avoir des scrupules (at, sur). ‖ Formuler des objections courtoises (at, to, sur). [See OBJECT.] ‖ † Atermoyer. ‖ JUR. Opposer une exception.
— n. Tergiversation f. (delay). ‖ Objection f.
demure [di'mjuə*] adj. Réservé, posé, grave (sober). ‖ Pudique (coy); aux airs de sainte nitouche, qui fait mine de rien (fam.).
demurely [-li] adv. Avec calme, d'un ton posé (soberly). ‖ Avec un air de sainte nitouche (fam.).

demureness [-nis] n. Réserve, gravité *f*. ‖ Air pudibond *m.; mines (f. pl.)* de sainte nitouche.
demurrable [di'mʌrəbl] adj. JUR. Opposable.
demurrage [-idʒ] n. NAUT. Surestaries *f. pl.*
demurrer [-ə*] n. JUR. Exception *f*.
den [den] n. Antre, tanière *f*. (lair). ‖ Fosse *f.; Daniel in the lions' den,* Daniel dans la fosse aux lions. ‖ Repaire, bouge *m*. (haunt). ‖ FAM. Cagibi, antre *m.;* piaule, turne *f*.
denary ['di:nəri] adj. Décimal.
denationalize [di:'næʃnəlaiz] v. tr. Dénationaliser.
denaturalize [di:'nætʃrəlaiz] v. tr. Dénaturer. ‖ JUR. Dénaturaliser.
denaturant [-ənt] n. CHIM. Dénaturant *m*.
denaturation [di:,neitʃə'reiʃən] n. CHIM. Dénaturation *f*.
denature [di:'neitʃə*] v. tr. CHIM. Dénaturer.
denazification [di:,nɑ:tsifi'keiʃən] n. Dénazification *f*.
— adj. De dénazification (court, panel).
denazify [di'nɑ:tsifai] v. tr. (2). Dénazifier.
dendrite ['dendrait] n. Dendrite *f*.
dene [di:n] n. Dune *f*.
dene n. Vallon *m*.
denegation [,di:ni'geiʃən] n. Dénégation *f*.
dengue ['deŋgi] n. MED. Dengue *f*.
deniable [di'naiəbl] adj. Niable.
denial [di'naiəl] n. Refus *m*. (refusal). ‖ Démenti *m*. (to, à); dénégation *f*. (negation). ‖ Reniement, rejet *m*. (rejection). ‖ Oubli (*m*.) de soi; abnégation *f*. (self-denial). ‖ JUR. *Denial of justice,* déni de justice.
denicotinize [di:'nikətinaiz] v. tr. Dénicotiniser.
denier [di'naiə*] n. Dénégateur *m.;* dénégatrice *f*.
denier [di'niə*] n. Denier *m*. (coin).
— ['dɛniə*] n. Denier *m*. (in hosiery).
denigrate ['di:nigreit] v. tr. Dénigrer.
denigration [,di:ni'greiʃən] n. Dénigrement *m*.
denigrator ['di:nigreitə*] n. Dénigreur *s*.
denim ['denim] n. Jean *m*., toile (*f*.) jean; *denim jacket,* veste en jean. ‖ Pl. Blue-jean *m*. (trousers); ensemble en jean *m*. (outfit).
denitrate [di:'naitreit], **denitrify** [-trifai] v. tr. CHIM. Dénitrifier.
denitration [,di:nai'treiʃən] n. CHIM. Dénitrification *f*.
denizen ['denizn] n. Habitant, hôte *m*. ‖ JUR. Etranger (*s*.) ayant droit de cité. ‖ GRAMM. Emprunt étranger *m*. ‖ BOT. Plante acclimatée *f*. ‖ ZOOL. Animal acclimaté *m*.
— v. tr. JUR. Donner droit de cité à.
Denmark ['denmɑ:k] n. GEOGR. Danemark *m*.
denominate [di'nɔmineit] v. tr. Dénommer. (See CALL.)
denomination [di,nɔmi'neiʃən] n. Dénomination *f.;* nom *m*. ‖ Classe, sorte *f*. (kind). ‖ ECCLES. Confession *f*.
denominational [di,nɔmi'neiʃnl] adj. ECCLES. Confessionnel.
denominative [di'nɔminətiv] adj. Dénominatif.
denominator [-neitə*] n. MATH. Dénominateur *m*.
denotation [,di:nou'teiʃən] n. Notation *f.;* signe *m.* ‖ Indication *f*. (of, de). ‖ Signe *m.;* manifestation *f*. ‖ GRAMM. Sens *m*. (of a word). ‖ PHILOS. Extension, dénotation *f*.
denotative [di'noutətiv] adj. Indicatif (of, de).
denote [di'nout] v. tr. Dénoter, marquer (to indicate). ‖ Signifier, vouloir dire (to mean).
denouement [de'nu:mɑ̃] n. THEATR., FIG. Dénouement *m*.
denounce [di'nauns] v. tr. JUR. Dénoncer (a thief, a treaty). ‖ † Annoncer. ‖ FIG. Dénoncer (an abuse); flétrir (s.o.); critiquer violemment (sth.).
denouncer |-ə*] n. Dénonciateur *m.;* dénonciatrice *f*.

dense [dens] adj. Dense, épais, tassé. ‖ PHYS. Opaque (negative). ‖ FAM. Crasse (ignorance); lourd (mind, person).
densely [-li] adv. D'une manière dense. ‖ FAM. Stupidement.
densimeter [den'simetə*] n. CHIM. Densimètre *m*.
densitometer [densi'tɔmetə*] n. PHYS. Densitomètre *m*.
density ['densiti] n. Densité, épaisseur *f*. ‖ PHYS., ELECTR. Densité *f*. ‖ FAM. Lourdeur (*f*.) d'esprit; stupidité *f*.
dent [dent] n. Bossellement *m.;* bosse *f.;* trace (*f*.) de coup. ‖ Brèche *f*. (in blade). ‖ FIG. Brèche; *to put a big dent in,* entamer fortement.
— v. tr. Cabosser, bosseler. ‖ Ecorner, ébrécher.
dental [-l] adj. MED. Dentaire; *dental room,* cabinet dentaire; *dental technician,* mécanicien dentiste. ‖ GRAMM. Dental.
— n. GRAMM. Dentale *f*.
dentate [-eit] adj. ZOOL. Denté. ‖ BOT. Dentelé.
dentation [den'teiʃən] n. Dentelure *f*.
dentele ['dɑtəlei] n. BLAS. Dentelé *m*.
denticulation [,dentikju'leiʃən] n. Dentelure, découpure *f*.
dentifrice ['dentifris] n. Dentifrice *m*.
dentine [-ti:n] n. MED. Ivoire (*m*.) des dents.
dentist [-tist] n. Dentiste *m*.
dentistry [-tistri] n. MED. Art dentaire *m*.
dentition [den'tiʃən] n. MED. Dentition *f*.
denture ['dentʃə*] n. MED. Dentier; râtelier *m*. (fam.). [See PLATE.]
denudate ['denjudeit] v. tr. Dénuder.
denudation [,denju:'deiʃən] n. Dénudation *f*.
denude [di'nju:d] v. tr. Dénuder. (See STRIP.) ‖ FIG. Dépouiller.
denumerable [di'nju:mərəbl] adj. Dénombrable.
denunciation [di,nʌnsi'eiʃən] n. JUR., MILIT. Dénonciation *f*. ‖ † Annonce *f*. ‖ FIG. Dénonciation, condamnation *f*. (of, de); violente critique *f*. (of, contre).
denunciative [di'nʌnsieitiv] adj. Dénonciateur *m*., dénonciatrice *f*. ‖ JUR. Comminatoire (decree).
denunciator [di'nʌnsieitə*] n. Dénonciateur *m.;* dénonciatrice *f*. (See DENOUNCER.)
deny [di'nai] v. tr. Opposer un démenti à, démentir (to repudiate). ‖ Nier, se défendre de (to negate); *I don't deny it,* je n'en disconviens pas. ‖ Refuser (sth.) [*to,* à]; opposer un refus à (s.o.); *to be denied the door,* trouver visage de bois; *to deny the door to s.o.,* refuser de recevoir qqn; *to deny oneself,* se renoncer; *to deny oneself sth.,* se refuser qqch.; *to be denied a request,* voir rejeter sa requête. ‖ Renier (to disown).
deodorant [di:'oudərənt], **deodorizer** [-aizə*] n. Désodorisant *m*.
deodorization [di,oudərai'zeiʃən] n. Désodorisation *f*.
deodorize [di:'oudəraiz] v. tr. Désodoriser. ‖ Défruiter (olive oil).
deontology [,di:ɔn'tɔlədʒi] n. Déontologie *f*.
deoppilate [di:'ɔpileit] v. tr. MED. Désobstruer.
deordinate [di:'ɔ:dnit] adj. Hors de l'ordre.
deoxidate [di:'ɔksideit], **deoxidize** [-daiz] v. tr. CHIM. Désoxyder.
deoxidation [di:ɔksi'deiʃən], **deoxidization** [di:,ɔksidai'zeiʃən] n. CHIM. Désoxydation *f*.
deoxidizer [di:'ɔksidaizə*] n. CHIM. Désoxydant *m*.
deoxygenate [di:,ɔk'sidʒineit] v. tr. CHIM. Désoxygéner.
deoxygenation [di:ɔk,sidʒi'neiʃən] n. CHIM. Désoxygénation *f*.
deoxyribonucleic [di'ɔksi,raibounju:'kleiik] adj. MED. *Deoxyribonucleic acid,* acide désoxyribonucléique.
depart [di'pɑ:t] v. intr. Partir (*from,* de) [to go

away]; se retirer (to leave). ‖ Se départir; s'écarter (*from*, de); faire dérogation (*from*, à) [to diverge]. ‖ Partir, mourir (to die).
— v. tr. Quitter; *to depart this life*, quitter cette terre.
departed [-id] adj. Achevé, passé, révolu (bygone). ‖ Mort, disparu (dead).
— n. Morts, défunts *m. pl.*
department [di'pɑːtmənt] n. Service *m.*; direction *f.* (in the Civil Service). ‖ Ministère *m.* (in a Government). ‖ Département (in a library). ‖ Section *f.* (in a college). ‖ GEOGR. Département *m.* (in France). ‖ COMM. Rayon *m.* (in a store); *department store*, grand magasin. ‖ FIG. Rayon, champ (*m.*) d'activité.
departmental [ˌdiːpɑːt'mentl̩] adj. D'un service; ministériel. ‖ GEOGR. Départemental.
departure [di'pɑːtʃə*] n. Départ *m.; to take one's departure*, partir. ‖ Déviation *f.* (*from*, à); abandon *m.* (*from*, de). ‖ NAUT. Chemin est et ouest *m.* ‖ FIG. Orientation, tendance *f.*; départ *m.*
depasture [di'pɑːstʃə*] v. intr. Paître. (See GRAZE.)
— v. tr. Paître dans (a meadow). ‖ Faire paître (the cattle).
depauperate [diː'pɔːpəreit] v. tr. Appauvrir.
depauperation [diːˌpɔːpə'reiʃən] n. Appauvrissement *m.*
depauperize [diː'pɔːpəraiz] v. tr. Tirer de l'indigence.
depend [di'pend] v. intr. Dépendre (*upon*, de); *it does not depend upon our will*, cela ne se commande pas. ‖ Dépendre, être à la charge (*on, upon*, de); *to depend on oneself*, se suffire. ‖ Compter, faire fond (*upon*, sur); se fier (*upon*, à). ‖ JUR. Etre pendant (suit). ‖ † Pendre.
dependable [-əbl̩] adj. De confiance, sur qui l'on peut compter.
dependant [-ənt] n. Protégé; pensionnaire *s.* ‖ Pl. Domesticité *f.*
dependence [-əns] n. Dépendance, subordination *f.* (*upon*, à); connexité *f.* (*upon*, avec). ‖ Dépendance *f.* (*upon, on*, envers, à l'égard de); fait (*m.*) d'être à la charge. ‖ Confiance *f.* (*on, upon*, en).
dependency [-ənsi] n. ARCHIT., GEOGR. Dépendance *f.*
dependent [-ənt] adj. Dépendant (*on*, de); subordonné (*on*, à); *dependent statement*, énonciation indirecte. ‖ Dépendant, tributaire; à charge (*on*, de). ‖ Confiant (*on*, en). ‖ GRAMM. Indirect (question).
— n. Personne à charge *f.* ‖ Protégé *s.*
depeople [di'piːpl̩] v. tr. Dépeupler.
depersonalize [di'pəːsnəlaiz] v. tr. Dépersonnaliser.
dephase [diː'feiːz] v. tr. ELECTR. Déphaser.
dephasing [diː'feiziŋ] n. ELECTR. Déphasage *m.*
dephosphorization [diːˌfɔsfərai'zeiʃən] n. CHIM. Déphosphoration *f.*
dephosphorize [diː'fɔsfəraiz] v. tr. CHIM. Déphosphorer.
depict [di'pikt] v. tr. ARTS. Peindre. ‖ FIG. Dépeindre.
depiction [-ʃən] n. ARTS., FIG. Peinture *f.*
depilate [depileit] v. tr. Epiler.
depilation [ˌdepi'leiʃən] n. Epilation *f.*
depilator ['depileitə*] n. Epileur *s.*
depilatory [di'pilətəri] adj., n. Dépilatoire *m.*
deplane [di'plein] v. intr. U. S. Descendre d'avion.
deplenish [di'pleniʃ] v. tr. Vider. ‖ COMM. Dégarnir, démunir (*of*, de).
deplete [di'pliːt] v. tr. Epuiser (to exhaust). ‖ Vider, dégarnir (to deplenish). ‖ MILIT. Décimer. ‖ MED. Décongestionner.
depletion [-ʃən] n. Epuisement *m.* ‖ MED. Déplétion *f.*

deplorable [di'plɔːrəbl̩] adj. Déplorable, regrettable; lamentable.
deplorably [-bli] adv. Déplorablement.
deplore [di'plɔː*] v. tr. Déplorer; se lamenter sur (or) de. (See LAMENT.)
deploy [di'plɔi] v. tr. MILIT. Déployer.
— v. intr. MILIT. Se déployer.
deployment [-mənt] n. MILIT. Déploiement *m.*
deplumation [diːplu'meiʃən] n. ZOOL. Mue *f.*
deplume [di'pluːm] v. tr. Déplumer.
depoetize [diː'pouetaiz] v. tr. Dépoétiser.
depolarization [diːˌpoulerai'zeiʃən] n. ELECTR. Dépolarisation *f.*
depolarize [diː'pouləraiz] v. tr. ELECTR. Dépolariser.
depolarizer [-ə*] n. ELECTR. Dépolarisant *m.*
depoliticize [ˌdiːpə'litiˌsaiz] v. tr. Dépolitiser.
depolymerize [diː'pɔliməˌraiz] v. tr. CHIM. Dépolymériser.
depone [di'poun] v. intr. JUR. Déposer.
deponent [-ənt] adj. GRAMM. Déponent.
— n. GRAMM. Déponent, verbe déponent *m.* ‖ JUR. Déposant *m.*
depopulate [di'pɔpjuleit] v. tr. Dépeupler.
— v. intr. Se dépeupler.
depopulation [dipɔpju'leiʃən] n. Dépopulation *f.*
depopulator [di'pɔpjuleitə*] n. Facteur (*m.*) de dépopulation.
deport [di'pɔːt] v. tr. JUR. Expulser (an alien); déporter (a convict). ‖ FIG. *To deport oneself*, se comporter.
deportation [ˌdiːpɔː'teiʃən] n. JUR. Expulsion *f.*; déportation *f.*
deportee [diːpɔː'tiː] n. JUR. Déporté *s.*
deportment [di'pɔːtmənt] n. Maintien *m.* ‖ FIG. Comportement *m.*
deposal [di'pouzl̩] n. Déposition *f.* (of a king).
depose [di'pouz] v. tr. Déposer, détrôner (a king). ‖ JUR. Attester par déposition.
— v. intr. JUR. Déposer.
deposit [di'pɔzit] n. Dépôt *m.* (sediment). ‖ GEOL. Gisement *m.* ‖ FIN. Dépôt, cautionnement *m.*; consignation *f.* (act, sum).
— v. tr. Déposer, poser. ‖ FIN. Déposer, mettre en dépôt, faire un dépôt de.
depositary [-əri] n. Dépositaire, consignataire *m.* ‖ JUR. Séquestre *m.* ‖ U. S. Entrepôt *m.*
deposition [ˌdipɔ'ziʃən] n. Dépôt *m.* (of a sediment). ‖ Déposition *f.* (of a king). ‖ JUR. Déposition *f.* ‖ ECCLES. Descente de croix *f.*
depositor [di'pozitə*] n. FIN. Déposant *m.*; *depositor's book*, livret de dépôt.
depository [-əri] n. Lieu de dépôt, entrepôt *m.* (storehouse). ‖ Dépositaire *s.* (trustee).
depot ['depou] n. COMM. Dépôt, entrepôt *m.* ‖ MILIT., AUTOM. Dépôt. ‖ **Depot-ship**, n. NAUT. Navire ravitailleur *m.*
— ['diːpou] n. CH. DE F. U. S. Gare *f.*
depravation [ˌdeprə'veiʃən] n. Dépravation *f.* (act, fact).
deprave [di'preiv] v. tr. Dépraver. (See DEBASE.)
depravity [di'præviti] n. Dépravation *f.* (state). ‖ ECCLES. Corruption originelle *f.*
deprecable ['deprikəbl̩] adj. Désapprouvable.
deprecate [-keit] v. tr. Désapprouver (sth.). ‖ † Tenter de détourner par la prière.
deprecation [ˌdepri'keiʃən] n. Désapprobation *f.* ‖ Supplication *f.*
deprecative ['deprikətiv], **deprecatory** ['deprikeitri] adj. ECCLES. Déprécatif. ‖ Qui essaie de fléchir.
depreciable [di'priːʃiəbl̩] adj. Dépréciable.
depreciate [-eit] v. tr. FIN. Déprécier, dévaloriser (sth.). ‖ COMM. Amortir. ‖ FIG. Déprécier. (See DISPARAGE.)
— v. intr. FIN., FIG. Se déprécier. ‖ FIN. Baisser (prices).

depreciation [di‚pri:ʃi'eiʃən] n. Fɪɴ. Dépréciation, dévalorisation; baisse, moins-value ƒ. ‖ Fɪɢ. Dénigrement m.

depreciative [di'pri:ʃieitiv], **depreciatory** [-əri] adj. Dépréciateur m.; dépréciatrice ƒ. ‖ Péjoratif.

depreciator [-ə*] n. Fɪɴ. Dépréciateur m.; dépréciatrice ƒ.

depredation [‚depri'deiʃən] n. Déprédation ƒ.

depredator ['depardeitə*] n. Déprédateur m.; déprédatrice ƒ.

depredatory [di'predatri] adj. De déprédation.

depress [di'pres] v. tr. Abaisser, baisser. ‖ Aᴜᴛᴏᴍ. Appuyer sur (the pedal). ‖ Mᴀᴛʜ. Abaisser (an equation). ‖ Jᴜʀ. Depressed classes, classes hors caste. ‖ Fɪɴ. Faire baisser (prices). ‖ Cᴏᴍᴍ. Provoquer une crise de. ‖ Fɪɢ. Déprimer, décourager (to dishearten); abattre, affaiblir (to weaken).

depressant [-ənt] adj., n. Mᴇᴅ. Sédatif m.

depression [di'preʃən] n. Abaissement m.; baisse ƒ. ‖ Gᴇᴏɢʀ., Asᴛʀᴏɴ., Mᴇᴅ. Dépression ƒ. ‖ Fɪɴ. Baisse ƒ. ‖ Cᴏᴍᴍ. Trade depression, crise économique. ‖ Fɪɢ. Découragement, accablement m. (See ᴅᴇᴊᴇᴄᴛɪᴏɴ.)

depressive [di'presiv] adj. Dépressif.

depressor [-ə*] n. Mᴇᴅ. Abaisseur m. ‖ Eʟᴇᴄᴛʀ. Survolteur m.

depressurize [di'preʃə‚raiz] v. tr. Dépressuriser.

deprivable [di'praivəbl] adj. Privable.

deprival [di'praivəl] n. Privation ƒ.

deprivation [‚depri'veiʃən] n. Privation ƒ. ‖ Perte ƒ. (loss). ‖ Jᴜʀ. Deprivation of office, retrait d'emploi.

deprive [di'praiv] v. tr. Priver (of, de). ‖ Jᴜʀ. Destituer (of, de) [an office]; déposséder (of, de) [property]. ‖ Fɪɢ. Déposséder.

deprived [-d] adj. Dépossédé, privé; the deprived ones of this world, les déshérités de ce monde.

Dept. Written abbr. for department, département, service, section.

depth [depθ] n. Profondeur ƒ.; in depth, en profondeur, de profondeur. ‖ Hauteur ƒ. (of water); out of one's depth, ayant perdu pied. ‖ Nᴀᴜᴛ. Fond m. (of the sea); creux m. (of a ship). ‖ Tᴇᴄʜɴ. Profondeur; hauteur ƒ. ‖ Mᴜs. Gravité ƒ. ‖ Aʀᴛs. Intensité ƒ. ‖ Pl. Profondeurs; in the depths of, au fin fond de, au comble de. ‖ Fɪɢ. Profondeur ƒ. (of emotion, feelings, silence, thoughts); cœur m. (of night, winter). ‖ Fᴀᴍ. To be out of one's depth, avoir perdu pied; être hors de son élément. ‖ Depth-charge, n. Nᴀᴜᴛ. Grenade sous-marine ƒ. ‖ Depth-gauge, n. Nᴀᴜᴛ. Sondeur m.

depurate ['depjureit] v. tr. Dépurer. (See ᴘᴜʀɪғʏ.) — v. intr. Se dépurer.

depuration [di‚pjuə'reiʃən] n. Dépuration ƒ.

depurative [di'pjuərativ] adj., n. Dépuratif.

deputation [‚depju:'teiʃən] n. Députation ƒ. (act, persons).

depute [di'pju:t] v. tr. Déléguer (authority, functions, s.o.); députer (s.o.).

deputize ['depju:taiz] v. intr. Assurer l'intérim, faire fonction (for, de); to deputize for, être délégué par intérim à la place de. ‖ Tʜᴇᴀᴛʀ. Servir de doublure (for, à). — v. tr. U. S. Déléguer, députer.

deputy ['depjuti] n. Délégué s. ‖ Suppléant s. ‖ Député m.; Chamber of Deputies, Chambre des députés. ‖ Deputy-chairman, n. Vice-président s. ‖ Deputy-judge, n. Jᴜʀ. Juge suppléant m. ‖ Deputy-mayor, n. Jᴜʀ. Maire adjoint m.

deracinate [di'ræsineit] v. tr. Déraciner. (See ᴜᴘʀᴏᴏᴛ.)

derail [di'reil] v. intr. Cʜ. ᴅᴇ ғ. Dérailler.

derailleur [-ə*] adj. Derailleur gear, dérailleur.

derailment [-mənt] n. Cʜ. ᴅᴇ ғ. Déraillement m.

derange [di'reindʒ] v. tr. Déranger, bouleverser (to disorder). ‖ Déranger, incommoder (to disturb). ‖ Tᴇᴄʜɴ., Mᴇᴅ. Déranger, détraquer.

derangement [-ment] n. Tᴇᴄʜɴ., Mᴇᴅ. Dérangement m.

deration [di:'ræʃən] v. tr. Cᴏᴍᴍ. Ne plus rationner, mettre en vente libre.

deratization [di:‚rætai'zeiʃən] n. Dératisation ƒ.

derby (['dɑ:bi], U.S. ['də:bi]) n. Gᴇᴏɢʀ. Derby m. ‖ Sᴘᴏʀᴛs. Grand prix (m.) de Derby. ‖ U. S. Melon m. (bowler); course ƒ. (race); pl. menottes ƒ. pl. (handcuffs).

derelict ['derilikt] adj. Abandonné, délaissé (forsaken). ‖ Négligent. (See ʀᴇᴍɪss.) — n. Nᴀᴜᴛ. Épave ƒ.; navire abandonné m.; derelict land, relais de mer. ‖ Jᴜʀ. Bien sans maître m. ‖ Fɪɢ. Épave humaine ƒ.

dereliction [‚deri'likʃən] n. Abandon m. (act, state). ‖ Négligence ƒ.; dereliction of duty, manquement au devoir, négligence dans le service. ‖ Nᴀᴜᴛ. Retrait, recul m. (of the sea).

derequisition [di:‚rekwi'ziʃən] v. tr. Déréquisitionner.

derestrict [‚di:ri'strikt] v. tr. Mettre fin à la limitation de, libérer. ‖ Aᴜᴛᴏᴍ. Supprimer (or) lever la limitation de vitesse sur; derestricted road, route sans limitation de vitesse.

deride [di'raid] v. tr. Tourner en dérision. (See ʀɪᴅɪᴄᴜʟᴇ.)

de rigueur [dəri'gə:*] adj. De rigueur.

derision [di'riʒən] n. Dérision ƒ.; to be held in derision by, être la risée de (or) tourné en dérision par. ‖ Objet (m.) de dérision (laughing-stock).

derisive [di'raisiv], **derisory** [-səri] adj. Moqueur, railleur (mocking). ‖ Dérisoire (ridiculous).

derisively [-sivli] adv. D'un ton moqueur.

derivable [di'raivəbl] adj. Gʀᴀᴍᴍ. Dérivable (from, de). ‖ Fɪɴ. Qu'on peut tirer (from, de).

derivation [‚deri'veiʃən] n. Pʜɪʟᴏs., Gʀᴀᴍᴍ., Mᴀᴛʜ. Dérivation ƒ.

derivative [di'rivətiv] adj., n. Mᴀᴛʜ., Cʜɪᴍ., Gʀᴀᴍᴍ. Dérivé m.

derivatively [-li] adv. Par dérivation.

derive [di'raiv] v. tr. Retirer, tirer (from, de). ‖ Faire provenir (or) découler (from, de). [See ᴏʀɪɢɪɴᴀᴛᴇ.] ‖ Cʜɪᴍ., Gʀᴀᴍᴍ. Dériver. — v. intr. Découler, provenir, émaner (from, de).

derm [də:m], **derma** [-ə], **dermis** [-is] n. Mᴇᴅ. Derme m. (See ᴄᴜᴛɪs.)

dermal [-əl] adj. Mᴇᴅ. Dermique.

dermatitis [‚də:mə'taitis] n. Mᴇᴅ. Dermatite, dermite ƒ.

dermatologist [-'tɔlədʒist] n. Mᴇᴅ. Dermatologiste m.

dermatology [-'tɔlədʒi] n. Mᴇᴅ. Dermatologie ƒ.

dermatosis [-'tousis] n. Mᴇᴅ. Dermatose ƒ.

dermic ['də:mik] adj. Mᴇᴅ. Dermique.

derogate ['derogeit] v. intr. Porter atteinte (from, à); to derogate from s.o.'s authority, diminuer l'autorité de qqn. ‖ Déroger (from, à)

derogation [dero'geiʃən] n. Atteinte ƒ. (from, à); to the derogation of, aux dépens de. ‖ Jᴜʀ. Dérogation ƒ. (from, à). ‖ Fɪɢ. Amoindrissement m.; without derogation, sans déroger.

derogatory [di'rɔgətəri] adj. Attentatoire (from, à). ‖ Jᴜʀ. Dérogatoire (from, à). ‖ Fɪɢ. Dérogeant (to, à) [s.o.'s dignity]; indigne (to, de) [s.o.'s rank]; derogatory to s.o., qui abaisse qqn.

derrick ['derik] n. Tᴇᴄʜɴ. Derrick, chevalement m. ‖ Nᴀᴜᴛ. Mât (m.) de charge.

derring-do ['deriŋ'du:] n. Vaillance ƒ.; courage indomptable m.; deeds of derring-do, hauts faits, grands exploits.

derringer ['derindʒə*] n. U. S. Derringer m.

derv [də:v] n. Aᴜᴛᴏᴍ. Gasoil m.

dervish ['də:viʃ] n. Derviche m.

desalinate [di:'sæli,neit], **desalt** [di:'sɔlt] v. tr. Dessaler.

descant ['deskænt] n. Mus. Déchant *m.* (counterpoint); mélodie *f.* (melody); dessus *m.* (voice). — [dis'kænt] v. tr. Mus. Accompagner en déchant. ‖ Fig. Disserter (*on*, sur); phraser (fam.).

descend [di'send] v. tr. Descendre. — v. intr. Descendre (*from*, de). ‖ Milit. Faire une descente. ‖ Jur. Descendre, être issu (*from*, de); descendre, se transmettre, passer (*to*, à). ‖ Fig. Descendre, dégénérer (to degenerate); descendre, tomber, s'abattre, se jeter (*on*, *upon*, sur); descendre, s'abaisser (*to*, à).

descendant [-ənt] n. Descendant *s.*

descended [-id] adj. Apparenté; *well descended*, de bonne famille.

descendent [-ənt] adj. Descendant.

descendible [-iəl] adj. Jur. Transmissible.

descent [di'sent] n. Descente *f.* (action, motion). ‖ Descente, pente, inclinaison *f.* (slope). ‖ Descendance *f.* (lineage); génération *f.* ‖ Jur. Transmission *f.* ‖ Sports, Aviat. Descente *f.* ‖ Fig. Déchéance, chute *f.*

describable [dis'kraibəbl] adj. Descriptible.

describe [-'kraib] v. tr. Décrire, relater, faire une description de (to tell about). ‖ Décrire, tracer (to trace). ‖ Présenter (*as*, comme); qualifier (*as*, de). ‖ Math. Décrire.

description [dis'krip ʃən] n. Description *f.* ‖ Sorte, variété *f.*; genre *m.* (kind). ‖ Math. Tracé *m.* ‖ Jur. Signalement *m.*; fiche signalétique *f.*

descriptive [-tiv] adj. Descriptif. ‖ Jur. Signalétique. ‖ Math. Descriptif.

descriptively [-tivli] adv. D'une manière descriptive.

descry [dis'krai] v. tr. (2). Discerner, apercevoir, distinguer (to see). ‖ Détecter, découvrir (to discover).

desecrate ['desikreit] v. tr. Profaner. ‖ Consacrer (*to*, à) [evil].

desecration [,desi'krei ʃən] n. Profanation *f.*

desecrator [-tə*] n. Profanateur *m.*; profanatrice *f.*

desegregate [di:'segri,geit] v. tr. Mettre fin à (or) abolir la ségrégation dans.

desensitize [di:'sensi,taiz] v. tr. Désensibiliser.

desensitizer [di:'sensitaizə*] n. Désensibilisateur *m.*

desert [di'zə:t] n. Mérite *m.* ‖ Pl. Dû *m.*; *to get one's deserts*, avoir ce qu'on mérite.

desert ['dezət] adj. Désertique (desolate); inculte (uncultivated); désert (wild). ‖ Fig. Aride. — n. Désert *m.* (wilderness). ‖ Région désolée *f.* — [di'zə:t] v. tr. Abandonner, quitter. ‖ Milit. Déserter. ‖ Jur. Quitter, délaisser. — v. intr. Milit., Fig. Déserter.

deserter [di'zə:tə*] n. Milit. Déserteur *m.*

desertful [di'zə:tful] adj. Méritoire.

desertion [di'zə: ʃən] n. Abandon *m.*; défection *f.* ‖ Milit. Désertion *f.*

deserve [di'zə:v] v. tr. Mériter. (See merit.) — v. intr. Mériter (*of*, de); *to deal with s.o. as he deserves*, en user avec qqn comme il le mérite.

deservedly [-idli] adj. A juste titre, à bon droit.

deserving [-iŋ] adj. Méritoire (action); méritant (person). ‖ Digne, susceptible (*of*, de).

deshabille [,deizæ'bi:ei] n. *In déshabillé,* en déshabillé.

desiccant ['desikənt] adj., n. Dessiccatif, siccatif *m.*

desiccate [-keit] v. tr. Dessécher.

desiccation [,desi'kei ʃən] n. Dessiccation *f.*

desiccative ['desikətiv] adj. Dessiccatif, siccatif.

desiderate [di'zidəreit] v. tr. Souhaiter, éprouver le besoin de, aspirer à.

desiderative [-ətiv] adj. Gramm. Désidératif. — n. Gramm. Verbe désidératif *m.*

desideratum [di,zidə'rɑ:təm] (pl. **desiderata** [-tə]) n. Condition *f.*, nécessité *f.*, besoin *m.* (necessity); aspiration *f.*, but souhaité *m.* (aspiration).

design [di'zain] n. Dessein, projet *m.* (purpose). ‖ Intention, vue, idée *f.* (*on*, sur) [intent]; *by design*, à dessein. ‖ Plan *m.* (scheme); action (*f.*) selon un plan. ‖ Comm. Modèle *m.* ‖ Archit. Plan *m.* ‖ Arts. Dessin, motif *m.* (of a fabric); esquisse *f.* (in painting); ébauche *f.* (in sculpture). — v. tr. Avoir le dessein (or) l'intention de, projeter, former le projet de (to intend). ‖ Combiner, concevoir, imaginer (to contrive). ‖ Destiner, réserver (*for*, à). ‖ Comm. Dessiner un modèle de. ‖ Techn., Archit. Faire le plan de. ‖ Arts. Esquisser, ébaucher. — v. intr. Comm. Créer des modèles. ‖ Techn. Faire des plans (or) une étude.

designate ['dezignit] adj. Désigné. — [-neit] v. tr. Désigner (*for*, *to*, pour).

designation [,dezig'nei ʃən] n. Désignation *f.*

designedly [di'zainidli] adv. A dessein.

designer [-ə*] n. Comm. Dessinateur *m.*; dessinatrice *f.* ‖ Theatr. Décorateur *m.*; décoratrice *f.* ‖ Fig. Comploteur *m.*

designing [-iŋ] adj. Comploteur, intrigant. — n. Comm. Dessin *m.*; création *f.* ‖ Techn. Etude *f.*

desilverize [di:'silvəraiz] v. tr. Désargenter.

desinence ['desinəns] n. Gramm. Désinence *f.* (See ending.)

desinential [-ʃəl] adj. Gramm. Désinentiel.

desipience [di'sipiəns] n. Puérilité, sottise *f.*

desirability [di,zaiərə'biliti] n. Caractère désirable *m.*

desirable [di'zaiərəbl] adj. Désirable.

desire [di'zaiə*] n. Désir *m.* (*for*, de). — v. tr. Désirer, souhaiter (to wish). ‖ Demander (*to*, à) [sth.]; prier (*to*, de) [s.o.].

desirous [-rəs] adj. Désireux (*of*, de).

desist [di'zist] v. intr. Cesser, s'arrêter (*from*, de) [to stop]. ‖ Renoncer (*from*, à) [to give up]. ‖ Se désister (*from*, de) [a candidacy].

desistance [-əns] n. Désistement *m.* (*from*, de).

desk [desk] n. Bureau *m.* (with flat top); pupitre *m.* (with sloping top). ‖ Chaire *f.* (of a professor). ‖ Bureau *m.* (post in an office). ‖ Comm. Caisse *f.* ‖ Mus. Place (*f.*) à l'orchestre. ‖ U. S. Eccles. Lutrin *m.* ‖ U. S. Rédaction *f.* (editorial department of a newspaper). ‖ **Desk-pad,** n. Sous-main *m.*

desolate ['desəlit] adj. Désolé, ruiné, ravagé (waste); désolé, désert (wild). ‖ Désolé, abandonné (forlorn); seul, solitaire (lonely). ‖ Désolé, affligé, malheureux (disconsolate). — [-leit] v. tr. Désoler, ruiner, ravager (to devastate). ‖ Désoler, dépeupler, rendre désert (to depopulate). ‖ Abandonner, délaisser (to forsake). ‖ Désoler, livrer à la désolation (to cause to despair).

desolately [-litli] adv. D'un air désolé. ‖ Dans la désolation.

desolation [,desə'lei ʃən] n. Désolation, ruine, dévastation *f.* ‖ Abandon *m.*; solitude *f.* (loneliness). ‖ Désolation *f.* (despair).

despair [dis'pɛə*] n. Désespoir *m.* (act, person, thing). — v. intr. Désespérer (*of*, de).

despairing [-riŋ] adj. Désespéré. (See hopeless.)

despairingly [-riŋli] adv. Désespérément, avec désespoir (sorrowfully).

despatch [dis'pætʃ] v. tr. See dispatch.

desperado [,despə'reidou] n. Risque-tout, casse-cou *m.*; tête brûlée *f.*

desperate ['despərit] adj. Réduit au désespoir, poussé à bout, aux abois (hard pressed). ‖ Capable de tout, ne reculant devant rien (ruthless). ‖ Acharné, éperdu; presque désespéré (hopeless). ‖ Med. Mortel (disease); héroïque (remedy).

desperately [-itli] adv. Désespérément, à corps perdu, avec acharnement (violently).

desperation [‚despə'reiʃən] n. Désespoir m.; in sheer desperation, aux cent coups. ‖ Excitation (or) témérité désespérée f.; in desperation, poussé à bout; en désespoir de cause.

despicable ['despikəbl] adj. Dédaignable; méprisable. (See CONTEMPTIBLE.)

despicably [-bli] adv. D'une manière méprisable.

despise [dis'paiz] v. tr. Dédaigner, mépriser.

despite [dis'pait] n. Dépit m.; despite of, in despite of, en dépit de. ‖ Haine f. (hatred); rancune f. (malice). ‖ Dépit m. (offended pride). ‖ † Outrage m. — prep. En dépit de, malgré.

despiteful [-ful] adj. Rancunier (malicious); malveillant, haineux, méchant (spiteful).

despoil [dis'pɔil] v. tr. Dépouiller, spolier (of, de) [s.o.]; piller (sth.).

despoiler [-ə*] n. Spoliateur m.; spoliatrice f.

despoilment [-mənt], **despoliation** [dis‚pouli'eiʃən] n. Spoliation f.

despond [dis'pɔnd] v. intr. Perdre courage, se laisser abattre. — n. † Découragement, désespoir m.

despondency [-ənsi] n. Découragement m.

despondent [-ənt], **desponding** [-iŋ] adj. Découragé.

despondently [-əntli], **despondingly** [-iŋli] adv. Avec découragement, sans courage.

despot ['despɔt] n. Despote m.

despotic [des'pɔtik] adj. Despotique.

despotically [-əli] adv. Despotiquement.

despotism ['despɔtizm] n. Despotisme m.; reign of despotism, régime du bon plaisir.

despumate ['dəspjumeit] v. tr. Ecumer.

despumation [‚dispju'meiʃən] n. Ecumage m.

desquamate ['deskwəmeit] v. tr. MED. Desquamer. — v. intr. MED. Se desquamer.

desquamation [‚diskwə'meiʃən] n. MED. Desquamation f.

dessert [di'zə:t] n. CULIN. Dessert m.; fruits m. pl. ‖ CULIN. U. S. Entremets, plat sucré m. ‖ **Dessert-plate**, n. Assiette (f.) à dessert. ‖ **Dessert-service**, n. Service à dessert m. ‖ **Dessert-spoon**, n. Cuiller (f.) à dessert.

destination [‚desti'neiʃən] n. Destination f.

destine ['destin] v. tr. Destiner, vouer (for, to, à). ‖ Fixer, déterminer; it was destined that, le sort a voulu que, il était écrit que. ‖ NAUT. Destined for, en partance pour.

destiny [-i] n. Destinée f.; destin m. (See FATE.) ‖ Pl. Parques f. pl.

destitute ['destitju:t] adj. Dépourvu, dénué (of, de). [See DEVOID.] ‖ Dénué de ressources, indigent (see POOR); absolutely destitute, dans un complet dénuement. — n. Indigents m. pl.

destitution [‚desti'tju:ʃən] n. Dénuement m. (lack). ‖ Indigence f. (poverty). ‖ JUR. Destitution f. (of rights).

destroy [dis'trɔi] v. tr. Détruire, démolir (to demolish). ‖ Détruire, annihiler (to annihilate). ‖ Tuer (to kill); to destroy oneself, se suicider.

destroyable [-əbl] adj. Destructible.

destroyer [-ə*] n. Destructeur m.; destructrice f. ‖ NAUT. Destroyer, contre-torpilleur m.

destruct [di'strʌkt] v. tr. Détruire volontairement, désintégrer (missile). — n. Destruction volontaire, désintégration f.

destructible [dis'trʌktibl] adj. Destructible.

destruction [-ʃən] n. Destruction, perte; ruine f.; to rush to one's destruction, courir à sa perte. ‖ Destruction f.; ravage m. (demolition).

destructionist [-ʃənist] n. Destructeur m.; destructrice f.

destructive [-tiv] adj. Destructif (criticism); destructive critic, éreinteur. ‖ Destructeur m., destructrice f. (effect). — n. Destructeur m., destructrice f.

destructively [-tivli] adv. D'une manière funeste.

destructiveness [-tivnis] n. Pouvoir destructeur m. (power); manie destructrice, destructivité f. (tendency).

destructor [-tə*] n. Incinérateur m.

desuetude [di'switju:d] n. Désuétude f.

desulfur, desulphur [di:'sʌlfə*], **desulfurize, desulphurize** [-əraiz] v. tr. CHIM. Désulfurer.

desultorily ['desəltərili] adv. A bâtons rompus; sans suite; sans méthode.

desultoriness [-ərinis] n. Décousu, manque (m.) de suite (or) de méthode.

desultory [-əri] adj. A bâtons rompus (conversation); fait au hasard (reading); décousu, sans suite (thought); sans méthode (work).

detach [di'tætʃ] v. tr. Détacher, séparer (from, de). ‖ MILIT. Détacher.

detachable [-əbl] adj. Détachable, séparable, amovible; detachable collar, faux col.

detached [-d] adj. Détaché, séparé; semi-detached, jumelle (house). ‖ MILIT. Détaché; detached-service warrant, lettre de mission. ‖ FIG. Détaché. (See INDIFFERENT.)

detachment [-mənt] n. Détachement m. (act). ‖ MILIT., JUR. Détachement m.; on detachment, détaché. ‖ MED. Décollement m. (of the retina). ‖ CH. DE F. Dételage m. ‖ FIG. Détachement (from, de); indifférence f. (from, à l'égard de).

detail [di'teil] n. Détail m.; précision f. ‖ ARTS. Détail m. ‖ MILIT. Détachement m. (of troops); extrait de l'ordre du jour m. — [di'teil] v. tr. Détailler. ‖ MILIT. Détacher (for, pour).

detain [di'tein] v. tr. Détenir, conserver (to keep). ‖ Retenir, retarder (to delay). ‖ JUR. Détenir.

detainee [ditei'ni:] n. JUR. Détenu s.

detainer [di'teinə*] n. JUR. Détention f.; writ of detainer, mandat de dépôt. ‖ JUR. Détenteur m., détentrice f. (withholder).

detainment [-mənt] n. JUR. Détention (f.) de fonds. ‖ NAUT. Détention (f.) de navire.

detartarizer [di:'tɑ:təraizə*] n. TECHN. Détartreur m.

detect [di'tekt] v. tr. Déceler, découvrir; détecter (fam.) [to find]. ‖ Discerner, entrevoir, apercevoir (to see). ‖ RADIO. Détecter.

detectable [-əbl], **detectible** [-ibl] adj. Discernable. ‖ Trouvable.

detectaphone [di'tektəfoun] n. FAM. Mouchard m.

detecting [-tiŋ] adj. Détecteur m.; détectrice f. ‖ **Detecting-valve**, n. ELECTR. Détectrice f.

detection [-ʃən] n. Découverte f. ‖ RADIO. Détection f.; repérage m. ‖ JUR. Dépistage m.

detective [-tiv] adj. Révélateur m., révélatrice f. ‖ Policier (novel). ‖ Détective (camera). — n. JUR. Détective; agent (m.) de la sûreté.

detector [-tə*] n. Avertisseur m. (fire alarm). ‖ TECHN., RADIO. Détecteur m.

detent [di'tent] n. TECHN. Détente f.

detente [dei'tãnt] n. FIG. Détente f.

detention [di'tenʃən] n. Détention, conservation f. (withholding). ‖ Retenue f. (at school). ‖ Retard involontaire m. (delay). ‖ JUR. Détention f. ‖ MILIT. Detention centre, prison militaire.

deter [di'tə:*] v. tr. (1). Détourner, décourager (from, de).

detergent [di'dʒənt] adj., n. Détersif, détergent m.

deteriorate [di'tiəriəreit] v. tr. Détériorer. ‖ FIG. Déprécier, rabaisser. — v. intr. Se détériorer (to spoil). ‖ FIG. Baisser (person); dégénérer (race); empirer (situation).

deterioration [di‚tiəriə'reiʃən] n. Détérioration f. ‖ FIG. Avilissement, amoindrissement m.; déchéance f. ‖ FIG. Aggravation f. (of the situation).

determent [di'tə:mənt] n. Détournement *m.* ; *for the determent of,* pour détourner. ‖ Dissuasion *f.*

determinable [di'tə:minəbl̩] adj. Déterminable. ‖ CHIM. Dosable. ‖ JUR. Soumis à une condition résolutoire.

determinant [-ənt] adj., n. MATH. Déterminant *m.*

determinate [-it] adj. Déterminé, défini. ‖ Etabli, déterminé, décidé. ‖ Définitif, fixé.

determinately [-itli] adv. D'une manière bien déterminée. ‖ Définitivement.

determination [di,tə:mi'neiʃən] n. Détermination, fixation, délimitation *f.* (settling). ‖ Détermination, résolution, intention, décision *f.* (resolve). ‖ Détermination, fermeté, résolution *f.* (resoluteness) ; *with an air of determination,* d'un air délibéré. ‖ MED. Afflux *m.* (of blood). ‖ JUR. Résiliation *f.* (of contract) ; fixation *f.* (of penalty) ; arrêt *m.* (decision).

determinative [di'tə:minətiv] adj. Déterminant. ‖ GRAMM. Déterminatif.
— n. Facteur déterminant *m.* ‖ GRAMM. Déterminatif *m.*

determine [di'tə:min] v. tr. Déterminer (the causes, dimensions, distance, hour, sum, value). ‖ Déterminer, causer (an accident, a disease). ‖ Déterminer, décider, pousser (s.o.). ‖ Régler, résoudre (a contest, a quarrel). ‖ JUR. Résilier (an agreement) ; résoudre (a contract).
— v. intr. Se déterminer, se résoudre (on, à) ; décider (on, de). ‖ JUR. Expirer, prendre fin.

determined [-d] adj. Déterminé, établi, fixé (settled). ‖ Déterminé, décidé, fermement résolu (resolute).

determinism [-izm̩] n. PHILOS. Déterminisme *m.*

determinist [-ist] n. PHILOS. Déterministe *s.*

deterrent [di'terənt] adj. Décourageant. ‖ Préventif, inhibitoire. ‖ FAM. Détournant, dissuadant (to, de) [influence].
— n. Préventif *m.* ‖ Elément dissuasif *m.* ; force de dissuasion ; arme d'intimidation *f.*

detersion [di'tə:ʃən] n. MED. Détersion *f.*

detersive [-siv] adj., n. Détersif *m.*

detest [di'test] v. tr. Détester. (See HATE.)

detestability [di,testə'biliti] n. Caractère détestable *m.*

detestable [di'testəbl̩] adj. Détestable (hateful).

detestableness [-nis] n. Caractère détestable *m.*

detestably [-bli] adv. Détestablement.

detestation [,di:tes'teiʃən] n. Horreur, détestation *f.* ‖ Objet (*m.*) d'horreur.

dethrone [di'θroun] v. tr. Détrôner.

dethronement [-mənt] n. Détrônement *m.*

detinue ['detinju:] n. JUR. Détention illégale *f.*

detonate ['detoneit] v. intr. Détoner, éclater.
— v. tr. Faire détoner, faire éclater.

detonation [,deto'neiʃən] n. Détonation, explosion *f.*

detonative ['detoneitiv] adj. Détonant, explosif.

detonator [-ə*] n. Détonateur *m.* ; amorce *f.* ‖ CH. DE F. Pétard *m.*

detour ['di:tuə*] n. Détour, circuit *m.* ; déviation *f.*

detoxicate [di:'tɔksikeit] v. tr. MED. Désintoxiquer.

detoxication [di:,tɔksi'keiʃən] n. MED. Désintoxication *f.*

detract [di'trækt] v. tr. Diminuer (*from*, de) [sth.] ; ôter (*from*, à). ‖ Agir en détracteur de, dénigrer (to disparage).
— v. intr. **To detract from,** amoindrir, nuire à.

detraction [-ʃən] n. Détraction *f.* ; dénigrement *m.*

detractive [-tiv], **detractory** [-təri] adj. Dénigreur ; de dénigrement.

detractor [-tə*] n. Détracteur *m.* ; détractrice *f.*

detrain [di'trein] v. tr., intr. CH. DE F., MILIT. Débarquer.

detriment ['detrimənt] n. Détriment *m.* (see PREJUDICE) ; *to the detriment of,* aux dépens de.

detrimental [,detri'mentəl] adj. Préjudiciable, dommageable, nuisible (to, à) ; désavantageux (to,

pour) ; *to prove detrimental to,* tourner au détriment de.

detrimentally [-li] adv. D'une manière dommageable.

detrition [di'triʃən] n. Détrition *f.*

detritus [di'traitəs] n. Détritus *m. pl.*

detrude [di'tru:d] v. tr. Renverser, jeter à bas.

detruncate [di:'trʌŋkeit] v. tr. Tronquer.

deuce [dju:s] n. Deux *m.* (on a card, die). ‖ SPORTS A deux de jeu, quarante A (in tennis).

deuce n. FAM. Diable *m.* ; *the deuce to pay,* le diable à confesser ; *to play the deuce with,* jouer un tour infernal à ; *what the deuce do you want?,* que diantre voulez-vous ?

deuced [-id] adj. FAM. Du diable.
— adv. FAM. Diablement, diantrement.

deuterium [dju:'tiəriəm] n. CHIM. Deutérium *m*

Deuteronomy [,dju:tə'rɔnəmi] n. ECCLES. Deutéronome *m.*

devaluate [di:'væljueit], **devalue** [di:'vælju] v. tr. FIN., FIG. Dévaluer.

devaluation [,di:vælju'eiʃən] n. FIN. Dévaluation *f.*

devastate ['devəsteit] v. tr. Dévaster.

devastating [-iŋ] adj. Dévastateur *m.* ; dévastatrice *f.*

devastation [,devəs'teiʃən] n. Dévastation *f.*

devastator ['devəsteitə*] n. Dévastateur *m.* ; dévastatrice *f.*

develop [di'veləp] v. tr. (1). Développer, amplifier (to enlarge upon). ‖ Mettre à jour, faire connaître (to disclose) ; développer, exposer (to set forth). ‖ Développer, fortifier (to strengthen). ‖ Exploiter, faire valoir, mettre en valeur, développer les ressources de (to expand). ‖ MATH., MUS., MILIT., COMM. Développer. ‖ CHIM., ELECTR. Engendrer, développer. ‖ MED. Contracter. ‖ TECHN. Développer (in photography). ‖ FIG. Contracter, prendre (a habit) ; faire preuve de, manifester (a talent).
— v. intr. Se développer, s'amplifier ; augmenter (to grow). ‖ Se développer, se fortifier (to become stronger) ; se développer, évoluer (to evolve) ; se développer, progresser (to expand). ‖ Se révéler, se manifester, se déceler (to become apparent).

developable [-əbl̩] adj. MATH. Développable.

developer [-ə*] n. Promoteur *s.* (of property). ‖ TECHN. Révélateur *m.* (in photography).

development [-mənt] n. Développement *m.* ; amplification *f.* ‖ Développement, exposé *m.* ‖ Evénement *m.* : *new development,* fait (or) facteur nouveau. ‖ MED., MUS., MATH., TECHN. Développement *m.* ‖ COMM. Extension *f.* ; développement *m.* ‖ BOT., ZOOL. Evolution *f.* ‖ FIG. Progrès, développement *m.* ; évolution *f.* (of events, ideas). ‖ **Development area,** n. Région (*f.*) à mettre en valeur.

developmental [,diveləp'mentl̩] adj. Du développement. ‖ MED. De croissance. ‖ FIG. De l'évolution.

deverbative [di'və:bətiv] adj. GRAMM. Déverbatif.

deviant ['di:viənt] adj., n. PSYCH. Déviant *adj., s.*

deviate ['di:vieit] v. intr. Dévier, s'éloigner, s'écarter, se détourner (*from,* de).
— n. ['di:viit] PSYCH. Déviant *s.*

deviation [,di:vi'eiʃən] n. Déviation *f.* (*from,* de). ‖ NAUT. Déroutement *m.* ‖ PHILOS. Déviation *f.* ‖ FIG. Ecart *m.*

deviationism [di:vi'eiʃənizm̩] n. Déviationnisme *m.*

deviationist [-ist] n. Déviationniste *s.*

device [di'vais] n. Expédient, moyen, truc *m.* ‖ Stratagème *m.* ; combine *f.* (fam.). [trick]. ‖ Dispositif, système, appareil *m.* ; invention *f.* (contrivance). ‖ BLAS. Devise *f.* ‖ ARTS. Dessin ornemental *m.* ‖ Pl. FAM. Plans *m. pl.* ; activités *f. pl.* ; *to leave s.o. to his own devices,* livrer qqn à lui-même ; laisser qqn se dépatouiller (fam.).

devil ['devl̩] n. ECCLES. Démon, diable *m.* ‖ Secré-

taire *m*. (lawyer's); apprenti *m*. (printer's); nègre *m*. (writer's). ‖ CULIN. Diable *m*. (machine); grillade épicée *f*. (meat). ‖ FAM. Diable *m*.; *be a devil*, laissez-vous tenter; *between the devil and the deep blue sea*, entre Charybde et Scylla, entre l'enclume et le marteau; *devil's dam*, diablesse; *a devil of a noise*, un potin d'enfer (or) de tous les diables; *poor devil*, pauvre diable (or) hère; *talk of the devil and he'll appear*, parlez du loup, on en voit la queue; *to send to the devil*, envoyer au diable. ‖ POP. *Devil's bones, books*, dés, cartes à jouer; *devil's dancing-hour*, minuit. ‖ **Devil-dodger**, n. POP. Cureton *m*. ‖ **Devil-drawer**, m. FAM. Artiste (*s*.) qui tire le diable par la queue. ‖ **Devil-fish**, n. ZOOL. Poulpe *m*. (octopus); U. S. raie *f*. ‖ **Devil-may-care**, adj., n. FAM. Casse-cou *m*.; tête folle *f*. ‖ **Devil-worship**, n. Démonolâtrie *f*.
— v. tr. (1). CULIN. Epicer fortement.
— v. intr. FAM. Faire le nègre.
devilet [-it] n. FAM. Diablotin *m*.
devilish [-iʃ] adj. Diabolique, démoniaque.
— adv. Diablement.
devilishly [-iʃli] adv. ECCLES. Diaboliquement. ‖ FAM. Diantrement, bigrement; *it's devilishly hard to bring it off*, c'est le diable à réussir.
devilishness [-iʃnis] n. Caractère diabolique *m*.
devilism [-izm̩] n. Satanisme *m*.
devilment [-mənt] n. Diablerie *f*.; *to be full of devilment*, avoir le diable au corps.
devilry [-ri] n. Magie noire *f*. (magic). ‖ Satanisme *m*.; conduite diabolique *f*. (behaviour); méchanceté démoniaque *f*. (wickedness). ‖ Diablerie, nature endiablée *f*. ‖ ECCLES. Démonologie *f*.
devious ['diːviəs] adj. Tortueux (path). ‖ FIG. Instable, vagabond (mind); détourné, tortueux (ways).
deviously [-li] adj. De manière détournée (or) tortueuse.
deviousness [-nis] n. Détours *m*. *pl*.
devisable [di'vaizəbl̩] adj. Concevable, imaginable. ‖ JUR. Disponible par testament.
devise [di'vaiz] v. tr. Concevoir, inventer (to invent); projeter (to plan). ‖ Combiner, manigancer, machiner (to plot). ‖ JUR. Léguer par testament.
— n. JUR. Dispositions testamentaires *f*. *pl*. (clause); legs *m*. (gift).
devisee [‚divai'ziː] n. JUR. Légataire *m*.
deviser [-ə*] n. Inventeur *m*.; inventrice *f*.
devisor [-ə*] n. JUR. Testateur *m*.; testatrice *f*.
devitalize [diː'vaitəlaiz] v. tr. Dévitaliser.
devitrification [diː‚vitrifi'keiʃən] n. Dévitrification *f*.
devitrify [diː'vitrifai] v. tr. (2). Dévitrifier.
devoid [di'vɔid] adj. Dépourvu, exempt, dénué (of, de).
devolution [‚diːvə'luʃən] n. Transmission, délégation *f*. (of, de). ‖ MED. Dégénérescence *f*. ‖ JUR. Dévolution *f*.
devolve [di'vɔlv] v. tr. Déléguer, transmettre. ‖ † Dérouler.
— v. intr. Incomber, échoir (*upon*, à). ‖ JUR. Etre dévolu (*on, to, upon*, à).
devote [di'vout] v. tr. Consacrer, vouer (*to*, à); *to devote oneself to*, s'adonner à, se livrer à.
devoted [-id] adj. Voué, consacré (dedicated). ‖ Fidèle, dévoué, attaché (*to*, à). ‖ Dévot, fervent (zealous). ‖ † Voué au malheur (doomed).
devotedly [-idli] adv. Avec attachement (or) dévouement.
devotedness [-idnis] n. Dévouement *m*.
devotee [‚devo'tiː] n. ECCLES. Dévot *s*. ‖ FIG. Dévot, fervent *s*.
devotion [di'vouʃən] n. ECCLES. Dévotion, piété *f*.; pl. Dévotions *f*. *pl*. ‖ FIG. Dévouement, attachement *m*.; consécration *f*. (*to*, à).
devotional [-ʃn̩l] adj. ECCLES. De piété (articles); dévot (attitude); pieux (soul).

devotionalist [-ʃnəlist] n. Bigot, cagot *s*.
devour [di'vauə*] v. tr. Dévorer (lit. and fig.).
devouringly [-riŋli] adv. Avec avidité.
devout [di'vaut] adj. ECCLES. Dévot. (See PIOUS.) ‖ FIG. Fervent; zélé.
devoutly [-li] adv. ECCLES. Dévotement, avec dévotion. ‖ FIG. Avec ferveur.
devoutness [-nis] n. ECCLES. Dévotion *f*. ‖ FIG. Ferveur *f*.
dew [djuː] n. Rosée *f*. (lit. and fig.). ‖ **Dew-berry**, n. BOT. Mûre *f*. ‖ **Dew-claw**, n. ZOOL. Ergot *m*. (of the dog). ‖ **Dew-fall**, n. Serein *m*. ‖ **Dew-point**, n. Point (*m*.) de condensation. ‖ **Dew-worm**, n. ZOOL. Ver (*m*.) de terre.
— v. impers. Tomber (dew).
— v. tr. Mouiller, emperler (*with*, de).
dewlap [-læp] n. ZOOL. Fanon *m*. ‖ FAM. Double menton *m*.
dewy [-i] adj. De rosée. ‖ Humide de rosée (wet).
dexter ['dekstə*] adj. Dextre.
dexterity [deks'teriti] n. Dextérité *f*. (adroitness); habileté *f*. (cleverness). ‖ Droiterie *f*. (right-handedness).
dext(e)rous ['dekstərəs] adj. Habile et précis, plein de dextérité. ‖ Droitier (right-handed).
dexterously [-li] adv. Avec dextérité.
dextran ['dekstrən], **dextrone** [-stroun] n. MED. Dextran *m*.
dextrin [-strin] n. CHIM. Dextrine *f*.
dextrose [-strous] n. CHIM. Dextrose *f*.
dey [dei] n. Dey *m*.
dhoti ['douti] n. Dhooty, dhoti *m*.
diabetes [‚daiə'biːtiːz] n. MED. Diabète *m*.
diabetic [-'betik] adj., n. MED. Diabétique *s*.
diabolic(al) [‚daiə'bɔlik(əl)] adj. Diabolique. (See DEVILISH.)
diabolically [-əli] adv. Diaboliquement.
diabolism [dai'æbɔlizm̩] n. Satanisme *m*. ‖ Diablerie, sorcellerie *f*. ‖ Nature (or) action diabolique *f*.
diabolo [di'æbɔlɔ] n. Diabolo *m*.
diachronic [‚daiə'krɔnik] adj. Diachronique.
diacid [dai'æsid] adj. CHIM. Biacide.
diaconal [dai'ækɔnl̩] adj. ECCLES. Diaconal.
diaconate [-nit] n. ECCLES. Diaconat *m*.
diacritic(al) [‚daiə'kritik(əl)] adj. GRAMM. Diacritique. ‖ FIG. Pénétrant, fin, nuancé (mind).
diadem ['daiədem] n. Diadème *m*.
diademed [-d] adj. Couronné d'un diadème.
diaeresis [dai'iərəsis] (pl. **diaereses** [-iːz]) n. GRAMM. Tréma m. ‖ Diérèse *f*. (in prosody).
diagnose ['daiəgnouz], **diagnosticate** [daiəg'nɔstikeit] v. tr. MED. Diagnostiquer.
diagnosis [‚daiəg'nousis] (pl. **diagnoses** [-iːz]) n. MED. Diagnostic *m*.; diagnose *f*.
diagnostic [-'nɔstik] adj. MED. Diagnostic.
— n. MED. Symptôme *m*. ‖ Pl. Diagnose *f*.
diagonal [dai'ægɔnl̩] adj. Diagonal, oblique.
— n. MATH., COMM. Diagonale *f*.
diagonally [-əli] adv. En diagonale, obliquement.
diagram ['daiəgræm] n. TECHN. Diagramme, graphique, schéma *m*. ‖ PHYS. Courbe *f*. ‖ MATH. Figure *f*. ‖ ELECTR. Schéma *m*.
— v. tr. (1). TECHN. Représenter par un diagramme.
diagrammatic [‚daiəgrə'mætik] adj. Schématique.
diagrammatically [-əli] adv. Schématiquement.
diagraph ['daiəgrɑ:f] n. Diagraphe *m*.
dial ['daiəl] n. Cadran solaire *m*. (sun dial). ‖ Cadran *m*. (on a clock, radio, telephone). ‖ TECHN. Boussole *f*. (of a miner). ‖ FAM. Balle, bille, bobine, bouille, gueule *f*. (face). ‖ **Dial-sight**, n. MILIT. Goniomètre *m*. ‖ **Dial-telephone**, n. Automatique *m*.
— v. intr. (1). Faire (or) composer un numéro au téléphone.
— v. tr. RADIO. Syntoniser, chercher.

dialect ['daiǝlekt] n. Dialecte m.; dialect atlas, atlas linguistique. ‖ Patois, jargon m.
dialectal [‚ḍaiǝ'lektḷ] adj. GRAMM. Dialectal.
dialectic [-ik] adj., n. PHILOS. Dialectique f.
dialectically [-ǝli] adv. PHILOS. Dialectiquement.
dialectician [‚daiǝlek'tiʃǝn] n. PHILOS. Dialecticien s.
dialectology [-'tɔlǝdʒi] n. GRAMM. Dialectologie f.
dialling ['daiǝliŋ] pr. p. See DIAL. ‖ Dialling tone, n. Tonalité f. (of telephone).
dialogist [dai'ælǝdʒist] n. Dialoguiste m.
dialogize [-dʒaiz] v. intr. Dialoguer.
dialogue ['daiǝlɔg] n. Dialogue m.; dialogue writer, dialoguiste.
dialyse ['daiǝlaiz] v. tr. CHIM. Dialyser.
dialysis [dai'ælisis] n. CHIM. Dialyse f.
diamagnetism [‚daiǝ'mægnǝtizm] n. PHYS. Diamagnétisme m.
diamanté [‚daiǝ'mænti] adj. Pailleté.
— n. Tissu pailleté.
diamantiferous [‚daiǝmǝn'tifǝrǝs] adj. Diamantifère.
diameter [dai'æmitǝ*] n. Diamètre m.
diametrical [‚daiǝ'metrikǝl] adj. Diamétral. ‖ FIG. Absolu, total (opposition); aux antipodes.
diametrically [-ǝli] adv. Diamétralement.
diamond ['daiǝmǝnd] n. Diamant m.; flawed diamond, macle; synthetic diamond, brillant synthétique; set with diamonds, diamanté. ‖ Pl. Carreau m. (playing cards). ‖ TECHN. Diamant m. (glazier's; in printing). ‖ MATH., COMM. Losange m. ‖ SPORTS. U. S. Terrain de baseball m. ‖ FIG. A rough diamond, une rude écorce, un diamant dans sa gangue. ‖ Diamond-bearing (or) -yielding, adj. Diamantifère, diamantin. ‖ Diamond-dust, n. Egrisée f. ‖ Diamond-merchant, n. Diamantaire m. ‖ Diamond-shaped, adj. En losange. ‖ Diamond wedding, n. Noces (f. pl.) de diamant. — adj. De diamant, en diamant. ‖ MATH., COMM. En losange.
— v. tr. Diamanter, parer de diamants.
diapason [‚daiǝ'peizn] n. MUS. Diapason, registre m. (pitch); diapason m. (tuning fork). ‖ MUS. Flots (m. pl.) d'harmonie (harmony); prestant m. (of an organ).
diaper ['daiǝpǝ*] n. Couche f. (for babies). ‖ Linge (f.) nid d'abeilles (linen). ‖ Serviette hygiénique f. (sanitary towel). ‖ ARCHIT. Décoration (f.) en losanges.
— v. tr. Mettre une couche à (a baby). ‖ Diaprer (to variegate). ‖ ARCHIT. Losanger.
diaphanous [dai'æfǝnǝs] adj. Diaphane.
diaphoresis [‚daiǝfǝ'ri:sis] n. MED. Diaphorèse f.
diaphragm ['daiǝfræm] n. MED., BOT., PHYS. Diaphragme m.
diaphragmatic [‚daiǝfræg'mætik] adj. Diaphragmatique.
diarist ['daiǝrist] n. Personne (f.) qui tient un journal.
diarize [-aiz] v. intr. Tenir son journal.
— v. tr. Consigner dans son journal.
diarrhoea [‚daiǝ'riǝ] n. MED. Diarrhée f.
diarrhoeic [-:ik] adj. MED. Diarrhéique.
diary ['daiǝri] n. Journal m.; diary of social events, carnet de la vie mondaine.
diascopy [dai'æskǝpi] n. PHYS. Diascopie f.
Diaspora [dai'æspǝrǝ] n. Diaspora f.
diastase ['daiǝsteis] n. MED. Diastase f.
diastole [dai'æstǝli] n. MED. Diastole f.
diathermic [‚daiǝ'θǝ:mik] adj. Diathermique.
diathermize [-maiz] v. tr. MED. Traiter à la diathermie.
diathermy ['daiǝθǝ:mi] n. MED. Diathermie f.
diatom ['daiǝtǝm] n. BOT. Diatomée f.
diatomic [‚daiǝ'tɔmik] adj. CHIM. Diatomique (with two atoms); divalent (bivalent).

diatonic [‚daiǝ'tɔnik] adj. MUS. Diatonique.
diatribe ['daiǝtraib] n. Diatribe f.
diazo [dai'eizou] n. CHIM. Diazo compound, diazoïque. ‖ TECHN. Diazocopie f.
dibasic [dai'beisik] adj. CHIM. Dibasique.
dibber ['dibǝ*] n. AGRIC. Plantoir m.
dibble ['dibḷ] v. tr. AGRIC. Planter (or) trouer au plantoir.
— v. intr. AGRIC. Utiliser un plantoir.
— n. AGRIC. Plantoir m.
dibs [dibs] n. pl. Osselets m. pl. (game). ‖ POP. Fric m. (money).
dice [dais] n. pl. Dés m. pl. (See DIE.)
— v. intr. Jouer aux dés.
— v. tr. To dice away, perdre aux dés. ‖ CULIN. Couper en dés. ‖ TECHN. Quadriller.
dicey ['daisi] adj. FAM. Risqué, hasardeux (risky); dangereux, mauvais (dangerous); peu sûr, douteux, incertain (unreasonable).
dichotomy [di'kɔtǝmi] n. ASTRON., BOT., PHILOS. Dichotomie f.
dichromatic [‚daikrou'mætik] adj. Dichromatique.
Dick [dik] n. Richard m. (diminutive). ‖ POP. U. S. Limier, détective m.
dickens ['dikinz] n. FAM. Diable m. (See DEUCE.)
dicker ['dikǝ*] n. COMM. Dizaine f.
dicker v. tr. U. S. Marchander.
dickey, dicky ['diki] n. Plastron-chemisette m. (for women). ‖ Bavoir m. (bib); tablier m. (pinafore). ‖ AUTOM. Spider m. ‖ ZOOL. Anon, baudet m. (ass); petit oiseau m. (bird).
— adj. FAM. Flanchard (weak).
dicotyledon ['dai‚kɔti'li:dǝn] n. BOT. Dicotylédone f.
dicotyledonous [-ǝs] adj. BOT. Dicotylédone.
Dictaphone ['diktǝfoun] n. Dictaphone m.
dictate ['dikteit] n. Diktat, ordre m.
— [dik'teit] v. tr. Dicter (to, à). ‖ FIG. Dicter, suggérer.
— v. intr. Donner des ordres (to, à); I won't be dictated to, je n'aime pas à être régenté.
dictation [dik'teiʃǝn] n. Dictée f. ‖ FIG. Manifestations (f. pl.) d'autorité; dictat m.
dictator [dik'teitǝ*] n. Dictateur m.
dictatorial [‚diktǝ'tɔ:riǝl] adj. Dictatorial.
dictatorship [dik'teitǝʃip] n. Dictature f.
diction ['dikʃǝn] n. Style parlé m. ‖ Diction, élocution f.
dictionary [-ri] n. Dictionnaire m. ‖ GRAMM. Dictionary spelling, orthographe d'usage. ‖ FAM. Walking dictionary, encyclopédie vivante, dictionnaire ambulant.
dictum ['diktǝm] (pl. dicta [-ǝ]) n. Affirmation f. ‖ Maxime f. ‖ JUR. Remarque superfétatoire f.
did [did] pret. See DO.
didactic [dai'dæktik] adj. Didactique.
didactics [-tiks] n. pl. Didactique f.
diddle ['didḷ] v. tr. FAM. Carotter, entôler, empiler (see CHOUSE); to be diddled, être chocolat. ‖ U. S. Baguenauder (to potter).
diddler [-ǝ*] n. FAM. Carotteur s.
dido ['daidou] n. FAM. U. S. Frasque f. (prank).
die [dai] (pl. dice [-z]) n. Dé m. (game). ‖ CULIN. Dé.
— (pl. dies [-s]) n. TECHN. Filière f. (for drawing wire); coin m. (for stamping money). ‖ ARCHIT. Dé m. (dado). ‖ Die-cast, v. tr. TECHN. Couler sous pression. ‖ Die-sinker, n. Médailleur m.
die [dai] v. intr. (3). Mourir (by, par; of, de); to die hard, avoir la vie dure. ‖ Défaillir, se serrer (heart); his heart died within him, le cœur lui manqua. ‖ FIG. Mourir, disparaître, s'éteindre (things). ‖ FAM. To be dying to, mourir d'envie de; to die with laughter, mourir de rire. ‖ LOC. Never say die, il ne faut jamais désespérer, ne jetez pas le manche après la cognée. ‖ To die away, FIG. Mourir, s'éva-

nouir, se dissiper, s'éteindre. ‖ **To die down**, FIG. Baisser, tomber, s'apaiser. ‖ **To die out**, s'éteindre, expirer, mourir. ‖ **Die-hard**, adj. A tout crin ; n. Jusqu'au-boutiste *s. ;* conservateur intransigeant *m.* — v. tr. Mourir ; *to die a dog's death*, mourir comme un chien.

dielectric [,daii'lektrik] adj., n. ELECTR. Diélectrique *m.*

dieresis [dai'erisis] n. U.S. See DIAERESIS.

diesel ['di:zḷ] n. TECHN. Diesel *m. ; diesel engine*, moteur diesel ; *diesel oil*, gasoil. ‖ **Diesel-electric**, adj., n. CH. DE F. Diesel-électrique *adj., m.*

diesis ['daiəsis] n. Diésis *m.* ‖ MUS. Dièse *m.*

diet ['daiət] n. Alimentation *f.* (daily fare). ‖ MED. Régime *m. ; short diet*, diète. ‖ FIG. Régime *m.* — v. tr. MED. Mettre au régime. — v. intr. MED. Se mettre au régime.

diet n. JUR. Diète *f.* (assembly). — n. Régime alimentaire *m.* (of a hospital, prison).

dietetic [,daiə'tetik] adj. MED. Diététique.

dietetician [,daiəte'tiʃən], **dietician** [,daiə'tiʃən] n. MED. Diététicien *s.*

dietetics [,daii'tetiks] n. sg. MED. Diététique *f.*

differ ['difə*] v. intr. Différer, se différencier, être différent (*from*, de) [to be unlike]. ‖ Différer d'opinion, être en désaccord, ne pas s'entendre (*on*, sur ; *with*, avec) [to disagree].

difference ['difrəns] n. Différence, dissemblance, divergence *f.* (*between*, entre ; *from*, avec ; *in*, *of*, de) ; *what's the difference?*, qu'est-ce que ça fait ? ‖ Différence, disparité *f.* ; écart *m.* (*in*, de) ; *to split the difference*, couper la poire en deux. ‖ Différence, discrimination, distinction *f.* ‖ Différend *m. ;* contestation, querelle *f.* (quarrel). ‖ MATH., FIN. Différence *f.* — v. tr. Différencier.

different [-ənt] adj. Différent, distinct, dissemblable (*from*, *to*, de). ‖ FAM. Différent, varié, divers.

differential [,difə'renʃəl] adj. MATH., TECHN., MED., FIN. Différentiel. — n. TECHN. Différentiel *m.* ‖ MATH. Différentielle *f.*

differentiate [-ʃieit] v. tr. Différencier. — v. intr. Se différencier.

differentiation [,difərenʃi'eiʃən] n. Différenciation *f.*

differently ['difrəntli] adv. Différemment.

difficult ['difikəlt] adj. Difficile, peu aisé (*to*, à) ; difficultueux, dur (see HARD). ‖ FIG. Difficile, peu commode (person, temper).

difficulty [-i] n. Difficulté *f. ; with difficulty*, difficilement. ‖ Obstacle *m. ;* difficulté *f. ; to remove a difficulty*, aplanir une difficulté. ‖ Ennui *m. ; in difficulties*, en difficultés. ‖ Pl. Difficultés, objections *f. pl. ; to make difficulties*, faire des difficultés.

diffidence ['difidəns] n. Manque (*m.*) d'assurance.

diffident [-ənt] adj. Qui manque de confiance en soi, dépourvu d'assurance (person) ; embarrassé (smile) ; *to be diffident*, se défier de soi-même.

diffidently [-əntli] adv. Avec hésitation, sans assurance, timidement.

diffract [di'frækt] v. tr. PHYS. Diffracter.

diffraction [-ʃən] n. PHYS. Diffraction *f.*

diffuse [di'fju:s] adj. PHYS., MED., FIG. Diffus. — [di'fju:z] v. tr. PHYS., FIG. Diffuser. — v. intr. PHYS., FIG. Se diffuser.

diffusely [-li] adv. D'une façon diffuse.

diffuser [-ə*] n. TECHN. Diffuseur *m.*

diffusion [di'fju:ʒən] n. PHYS., FIG. Diffusion *f.*

diffusive [-siv] adj. Diffusif.

dig [dig] v. tr. (46). Creuser (a hole, a well). ‖ Enfoncer (*in*, *into*, dans) [one's nails, spurs] ; *to dig s.o. in the ribs*, bourrer les côtes à qqn. ‖ AGRIC. Piocher (with a pick) ; bêcher (with a spade) ; *to dig potatoes*, arracher les pommes de terre. ‖ FAM. Ra-

foler de. ‖ **To dig in**, enterrer ; *to dig oneself in*, MILIT. Se creuser un abri, se retrancher ; FIG. S'incruster, s'accrocher, s'ancrer ; *to dig one's heels in*, tenir bon ; FAM. Se buter, s'entêter. ‖ **To dig out**, déterrer, extraire (lit. and fig.). ‖ **To dig up**, AGRIC. Retourner (the ground) ; FIG. Déterrer, exhumer. — v. intr. Creuser, faire un trou (*into*, dans). ‖ Faire des fouilles (*for*, pour trouver ; *into*, dans). ‖ FAM. Loger en garni. ‖ FAM. U. S. *To dig at* (or) *into*, piocher (to swot up). — n. Bourrade *f.* (poke). ‖ AGRIC. Bêchage *m.* ‖ FAM. Coup (*m.*) de patte ; *to have a dig at*, lancer une pierre dans le jardin de. ‖ FAM. U. S. Bûcheur *m.* (at school). ‖ FAM. Pl. Meublé *m. ; in digs*, en pension ; en meublé.

digest ['daidʒest] n. Condensé, digeste *m.* ‖ JUR. Digeste. — [di'dʒest] v. tr. Condenser, abréger, résumer (to summarize). ‖ Classer, ordonner, organiser (to arrange). ‖ MED. Digérer ; faire digérer. ‖ FIG. Digérer, assimiler (to assimilate). ‖ FAM. Digérer, avaler, encaisser (to stomach). — v. intr. MED. Se digérer.

digestible [di'dʒestibḷ] adj. MED. Digestible.

digestion [di'dʒestʃən] n. MED., FIG. Digestion *f.*

digestive [-tiv] adj., n. Digestif *m.*

digger ['digə*] n. AGRIC. Plantoir *m.* (dibble) ; arrachoir *m.* (grubber) ; bêcheur *m.* (person). ‖ TECHN. Chercheur d'or *m.* (gold-digger) ; terrassier *m.* (navvy). ‖ FAM. Digger-up, dénicheur.

digging [-iŋ] n. AGRIC. Bêchage *m.* ‖ TECHN. Terrassement *m. ;* fouilles *f. pl.* ‖ Pl. Minière *f.* ‖ FAM. Pl. Meublé, garni *m.* (furnished apartment).

dight [dait] adj. † Orné.

digit ['didʒit] n. MATH. Chiffre *m.* ‖ MED., ASTRON., FIG. Doigt *m.*

digital [-ḷ] adj. MED. Digital. ‖ INFORM. Digital ; *digital readout*, affichage digital ; *digital watch*, montre à affichage digital ; *digital computer*, calculateur numérique, ordinateur. — n. MUS. Touche *f.* (on the piano or organ).

digitalin [-əlin] n. MED. Digitaline *f.*

digitalis [,didʒi'teilis] n. BOT. Digitale *f.* (See FOXGLOVE.) ‖ MED. Digitaline *f.*

digitate ['didʒitit] adj. BOT. Digité.

digitigrade ['didʒiti,greid] adj., n. ZOOL. Digitigrade *adj., m.*

diglot ['daiglot] adj. U.S. Bilingue. (See BILINGUAL.) — n. U. S. Edition bilingue *f.*

dignified ['dignifaid] adj. Solennel, digne, imposant.

dignify [-fai] v. tr. (2). Donner de la dignité à. ‖ FAM. Décorer (*with*, de).

dignitary [-təri] n. Dignitaire *s.*

dignity [-ti] n. Dignité, gravité *f.* (seriousness). ‖ Dignité *f.* (self-respect). ‖ Dignité *f. ;* rang *m.* (position). ‖ FAM. *It doesn't go with his dignity*, c'est contraire à sa dignité.

digraph ['daigrɑ:f] n. GRAMM. Digramme *m.*

digress [dai'gres] v. intr. Dévier, s'écarter (*from*, de). [See DEVIATE.] ‖ Faire une digression (to divagate).

digression [-'greʃən] n. Digression *f. ; to ramble off into digression*, se lancer dans des digressions.

digressive [-'gresiv] adj. Digressif.

dihedral [dai'hi:drəl] adj. MATH. Dièdre *m.*

dihedron [-drən] n. MATH. Dièdre *m.*

dike, dyke [daik] n. Digue *f.* (dam) ; fossé *m.* (ditch) ; remblai *m.* (ridge) ; muraillon *m.* (wall). ‖ GEOL. Filon, dyke *m.* — v. tr. Endiguer.

diktat ['diktɑ:t] n. Diktat *m.*

dilacerate [di'læsəreit] v. tr. Lacérer.

dilapidate [di'læpideit] v. tr. Dégrader, délabrer (a building) ; abîmer, gâcher (one's clothes). Dilapider (one's fortune).

— v. intr. Se délabrer (building) ; tomber en loques (clothes).

dilapidated [-id] adj. Délabré.

dilapidation [di,læpi'deiʃən] n. Délabrement *m.* (of a building) ; usure *f. ;* état loqueteux *m.* (of clothes). ‖ Dilapidation *f.* (of one's fortune). ‖ Jur. Dégradations *f. pl.* (See DISREPAIR.)

dilatability [dai,leitə'biliti] n. Dilatabilité *f.*

dilatable [dai'leitəbl] adj. Dilatable.

dilatant [-ənt] n. MED. Dilatant *m.*

dilatation [,dailə'teiʃən] n. Dilatation *f.*

dilate [dai'leit] v. tr. Dilater.
— v. intr. Se dilater. ‖ Fig. S'étendre (*upon,* sur).

dilating [-iŋ] adj. Dilatateur *m. ;* dilatatrice *f.*

dilator [-ə*] n. MED. Dilatateur *m.*

dilatorily ['dilətərili] adv. D'une manière dilatoire.

dilatoriness [-rinis] n. Lenteur *f.* (*in,* à).

dilatory [-ri] adj. Lent. ‖ Jur. Dilatoire.

dildo ['dildou] (pl. **dildos** [-z]) n. Pop. Godemiché, gode *m.*

dilemma [di'lemə] n. Philos. Dilemme *m. ; on the horns of a dilemma,* enfermé dans un dilemme.

dilettante [,dile'tænti] n. Dilettante *s.*
— adj. De dilettante.

dilettantism [-izm] n. Dilettantisme *m.*

diligence ['dilidʒəns] n. Diligence, application *f. ;* soin *m.* (care). ‖ Persévérance, constance *f.*

diligent [-ənt] adj. Diligent (effort) ; diligent, travailleur (person).

diligently [-əntli] adv. Diligemment.

dill [dil] n. Bot. Fenouil *m.*

dilly-dally ['dili'dæli] v. intr. Fam. Barguiner, hésitailler (to hesitate) ; lanterner, lambiner (to loiter) ; baguenauder (to trifle).

diluent ['diljuənt] adj., n. Diluant *m.*

dilute [dai'lju:t] adj. Dédoublé (alcohol) ; délavé (colour) ; dilué (liquid) ; délayé (paste). ‖ Fig. Edulcoré, atténué, adouci.
— v. tr. Dédoubler (alcohol) ; délaver (colour) ; diluer (liquid) ; délayer (paste). ‖ Fig. Edulcorer.
— v. intr. Se délaver (colour) ; se diluer (liquid) ; se délayer (paste). ‖ Fig. S'édulcorer.

dilution [-ʃən] n. Dédoublage *m.* (of alcohol) ; délavage *m.* (of a colour) ; dilution *f.* (of a liquid). ‖ Jur. *Dilution of labour,* adjonction de travailleurs non qualifiés. ‖ Fig. Edulcoration *f.*

diluvial [dai'lju:viəl], **diluvian** [-ən] adj. Diluvial ; diluvien.

dim [dim] adj. Terne (colour) ; faible, vague, pâle (light) ; indistinct, estompé (outline) ; sombre, obscur (room) ; brouillé, voilé, trouble (sight) ; sourd, mat (sound). ‖ Fig. Confus, incertain, imprécis ; *dim view,* noir pronostic, vue sombre ; *to take a dim view of,* envisager sans enthousiasme. ‖ **Dim-sighted,** adj. MED. A la vue trouble. ‖ **Dim-out,** n. U. S. Camouflage partiel (*m.*) des lumières. ‖ **Dim-wit,** n. U. S. Fam. Bêta *m.*
— v. tr. (1). Ternir (a colour) ; obscurcir (light, room) ; estomper (outlines) ; brouiller, voiler, troubler (sight) ; assourdir (sound). ‖ Autom. Baisser, mettre en code (the headlights). ‖ Fig. Rendre confus (memory) ; obscurcir, éclipser (s.o.'s glory).
— v. intr. Se ternir (colour) ; s'obscurcir (light) ; s'estomper (outlines) ; se voiler, se troubler (sight). ‖ Fig. S'effacer (memory).

dime [daim] n. Fin. U. S. Dîme *f.* ‖ **Dime novel,** n. Fam. U. S. Roman (*m.*) à treize sous. ‖ **Dime store,** n. Comm. U. S. Uniprix, monoprix, prix unique *m.*

dimension [di'menʃən] n. Dimension *f.* (size).

dimensioned [-d] adj. Dimensionné. ‖ Techn. Coté (sketch).

diminish [di'miniʃ] v. tr. Diminuer, réduire (to reduce) ; diminuer, raccourcir (to shorten).
— v. tr. Diminuer, décliner.

diminished [-t] adj. Diminué. ‖ Jur. *Diminished responsability,* responsabilité atténuée.

diminuendo [di,minju'endou] adv., adj., n. Diminuendo, decrescendo *adj., m. inv. ; diminuendo passage,* morceau exécuté diminuendo (or) decrescendo.

diminution [,dimi'nju:ʃən] n. Diminution *f.*

diminutive [di'minjutiv] adj. Tout petit, minuscule. (See SMALL.) ‖ Gramm. Diminutif.
— n. Gramm. Diminutif *m.*

diminutively [-li] adv. En miniature. ‖ Gramm. Comme diminutif.

dimity ['dimiti] n. Brillanté *m.*

dimly ['dimli] adv. D'une manière terne. ‖ Obscurément, vaguement, confusément.

dimmer [-ə*] n. Autom. Réducteur code *m.* ‖ Electr. Régulateur d'éclairage *m.*

dimness [-nis] n. Matité *f. ;* aspect terne *m.* (of colour, metal). ‖ Faiblesse *f.* (of light, sight). ‖ Vague *m.,* imprécision *f.* (of memory).

dimorphic [dai'mɔ:fik], **dimorphous** [-əs] adj. Chim., Bot. Dimorphe.

dimple ['dimpl] n. Fossette *f.* (on cheek). ‖ Ride *f.* (on water).
— v. tr. Creuser des fossettes dans (the cheeks). ‖ Rider (water).
— v. intr. Se creuser de fossettes. ‖ Se rider.

din [din] n. Tapage, vacarme, fracas *m.* (See NOISE.) ‖ Fam. *To kick up a din,* faire un boucan du tonnerre ; faire du foin.
— v. tr. (1). Assourdir (the ears). ‖ Rabâcher ; *to din sth. into s.o.'s ears,* corner qqch. dans les oreilles de qqn, casser les oreilles de qqn avec qqch.
— v. intr. Faire du tapage.

dine [dain] v. intr. Dîner ; *to dine off,* faire son repas de ; *to dine out,* dîner en ville.
— v. tr. Traiter, recevoir à dîner (s.o.). ‖ Contenir (diners).

diner [-ə*] n. Dîneur *s.* ‖ Convive *s.* (guest). ‖ CH. DE F. U. S. Voiture-restaurant *m.* ‖ U. S. Petit restaurant bon marché *m.*

dinette [di'net] n. U. S. Coin-repas.

ding [diŋ] v. intr. Résonner (to ring).
— v. tr. See DIN.

ding-dong [,diŋ'dɔŋ] adj. Où chacun prend tour à tour la tête, au coude à coude (race) ; où chacun prend tour à tour le dessus, acharné (battle).
— n. Tintement *m. ;* ding dong *m. inv.* (sound of bells). ‖ Fam. Prise (*f.*) de bec, engueulade *f.* (argument). ‖ Fam. Fiesta *f.* (party).
— adv. A tour de bras (violently).

dinghy ['diŋgi] n. Naut. Canot, youyou ; doris *m.*

dinginess ['dindʒinis] n. Aspect minable *m. ;* saleté *f.*

dingle ['diŋgl] n. Geogr. Vallon *m.*

dingo ['diŋgou] (pl. **dingoes** [-z]) n. Zool. Dingo *m.* ‖ Pop. Ordure *f.,* salaud *m.*

dingy ['dindʒi] adj. Mal tenu, d'aspect minable.

dining ['dainiŋ] n. Dîner *m.* ‖ **Dining-car,** n. CH. DE F. Voiture-restaurant *m.* ‖ **Dining-room,** n. Salle (*f.*) à manger (room) ; *dining-room suite,* salle à manger (furniture).

dinky ['diŋki] adj. Fam. Mignon.

dinner ['dinə*] n. Dîner *m. ; public dinner,* banquet. ‖ CH. DE F. Service *m.* ‖ **Dinner-call,** n. Visite de digestion *f.* ‖ **Dinner-dress,** n. Robe (*f.*) de dîner. ‖ **Dinner-jacket,** n. Smoking *m.* ‖ **Dinner-mat,** n. Dessous (*m.*) d'assiette. ‖ **Dinner-party,** n. Dîner *m.* (meal) ; convives *m. pl.* (guests) ; *to have a doll's dinner-party,* faire la dinette. ‖ **Dinner-set,** n. Service (*m.*) de table. ‖ **Dinner-waggon,** n. Table roulante *f.*

dinosaur ['dainə,sɔ:*] n. Zool. Dinosaure *m.*

dint [dint] n. Trace (*f.*) de coup ; bosselure *f.* (See DENT.) ‖ Force *f. ; by dint of,* à force de. ‖ Fig. Atteinte *f.* (in a reputation).
— v. tr. Bosseler, bossuer.

diocesan [dai'ɔsizn] adj., n. Eccles. Diocésain *s.*

diocese ['daiəsis] n. ECCLES. Diocèse m.
diode ['daioud] n. ELECTR. Diode f.
dioptre [dai'ɔptə*] n. PHYS. Dioptrie f.
dioptric [dai'ɔptrik] adj. PHYS. Dioptrique.
— f. PHYS. Dioptrie f.
dioptrics [-s] n. PHYS. Dioptrique f.
diorama [daio'rɑ:mə] n. Diorama m.
dioxide [dai'ɔksaid] n. CHIM. Bioxyde m.
dip [dip] v. tr. (1). Tremper, plonger (to immerse).
‖ Baisser, faire baisser ; faire pencher (the scale).
‖ AUTOM. Baisser, mettre en code (the headlights).
‖ NAUT. Faire marquer (a flag).
— v. intr. Plonger, se plonger. ‖ Descendre, plonger (ground, road) ; pencher (scale) ; baisser (sun).
‖ AUTOM. Se mettre en code (driver) ; basculer (headlights). ‖ AVIAT. Piquer. ‖ FIG. To dip into, feuilleter, parcourir (a book) ; pénétrer (the future) ; to dip pretty deep into one's capital, entamer joliment sa fortune.
— n. Plongeon m.; plongée f. (plunge). ‖ Baignade f. (bathe); to have a dip in, faire trempette dans. ‖ Quantité puisée f. (quantity). ‖ Chandelle f. (candle). ‖ Déclivité, pente f. (of a road). ‖ PHYS., GEOL. Inclinaison f. ‖ ASTRON. Dépression (f.) de l'horizon. ‖ **Dip-needle**, n. Boussole d'inclinaison f. ‖ **Dip-net**, n. Epuisette f. ‖ **Dip-pipe**, n. TECHN. Coupe-air m. ‖ **Dip-stick**, n. AUTOM. Jauge f. ‖ **Dip-switch**, n. AUTOM. Manette (f.) des phares.
diphase ['daifeiz] adj. ELECTR. Diphasé.
diphtheria [dif'θiəriə] n. MED. Diphtérie f.
diphtheric [-θerik] adj. MED. Diphtérique.
diphthong ['difθɔŋ] n. GRAMM. Diphtongue f.
diphthongization [,difθɔŋgai'zeiʃən] n. GRAMM. Diphtongaison f.
diphthongize ['difθɔŋgaiz] v. tr. Diphtonguer.
diplodocus [di'plɔdəkəs] n. ZOOL. Diplodocus m.
diploid ['diplɔid] adj. MED. Diploïde.
— n. MED. Noyau diploïde m.
diploma [di'ploumə] n. Diplôme m.; to grant a diploma to, diplômer.
diplomacy [di'plouməsi] n. JUR., FIG. Diplomatie f.
diplomat ['diplǝmæt], **diplomatist** [di'ploumətist] n. JUR., FIG. Diplomate m.
diplomatic [,diplo'mætik] adj. Diplomatique ; diplomatic bag (or) U. S. pouch, valise diplomatique.
diplomatics [-s] n. JUR. Diplomatique f.
diplomatize [di'ploumətaiz] v. intr. Etre diplomate ; agir avec diplomatie.
diplopia [di'ploupiə] n. MED. Diplopie f.
dipole ['daipoul] n. RADIO. Petite antenne f.
dipper ['dipə*] n. Plongeur s. ‖ CULIN. Louche f. ‖ ZOOL. Martin-pêcheur m. ‖ ASTRON. U. S. Big Dipper, Grande Ourse f. ‖ ECCLES., FAM. Baptiste m. ‖ AUTOM. Basculeur m. ‖ **Dipper-switch**, n. AUTOM. Basculeur (m.) de phares.
dippy ['dipi] adj. FAM. Toqué.
dipso ['dipsou] (pl. dipsos [-z]) n. FAM. Soûlographe, poivrot, picoleur s.
dipsomania [,dipso'meiniə] n. MED. Dipsomanie f.
dipsomaniac [-æk] n. MED. Dipsomane s.
diptera ['diptərə] n. pl. ZOOL. Diptères m. pl.
dipteral [-əl] adj. ARCHIT. Diptère.
dipterous [-əs] adj. ZOOL. Diptère.
diptych ['diptik] n. Diptyque m.
dire ['daiə*] adj. Affreux, horrible ; sinistre.
direct [di'rekt], [dai'rekt] adj. Direct, droit (straight). ‖ Direct, net, catégorique (straightforward). ‖ Direct, immédiat. ‖ Direct, absolu, complet. ‖ JUR. Direct, descendant (lineage, proof). ‖ FIN. Direct (tax). ‖ MILIT. Direct fire, tir de plein fouet. ‖ ELECTR. Continu (current). ‖ GRAMM. Direct (complement, object, speech). ‖ **Direct-actionist**, n. Partisan (m.) de l'action directe. ‖ **Direct-coupled**, adj. RADIO. Monté en direct.

— adv. Directement, tout droit, en ligne droite. ‖ Directement, sans intermédiaire. ‖ JUR. En ligne directe.
— v. tr. Mettre l'adresse sur (an envelope) ; adresser (a letter). ‖ Diriger, braquer, pointer (toward, sur) [an instrument]. ‖ Diriger, orienter (to, vers) [one's steps]. ‖ Diriger, conduire, indiquer la direction à (s.o.). ‖ COMM. Diriger, mener, administrer. ‖ THEATR. Mettre en scène. ‖ FIG. Diriger, appliquer (one's attention) ; adresser (a remark) [to, à] ; diriger, guider (s.o.). ‖ FIG. Ordonner à, donner des instructions à.
— v. intr. Ordonner (that, que) ; to be directed by, être chargé par. ‖ Diriger (to manage).
direction [di'rekʃən] n. Direction, orientation f.; sens m. (way). ‖ Adresse f. (on a letter). ‖ Direction, conduite f. (management). ‖ Direction f.; directeurs m. pl. (staff). ‖ Pl. Directions, instructions f. pl.; directions for use, mode d'emploi. ‖ THEATR. Mise en scène f. ‖ AUTOM. U. S. Direction light, clignotant. ‖ FIG. Cours m. (of the opinion) ; direction (of work). ‖ **Direction-board**, n. Panneau indicateur (m.) de direction. ‖ **Direction-finder**, n. RADIO. Radiogoniomètre m. ‖ **Direction-indicator**, n. AUTOM. Clignotant ; bras m.
directional [-ʃənl] adj. RADIO. Directionnel (aerial) ; radiogoniométrique (loop). ‖ COMM. Directeur (committee).
directive [-tiv] adj. Directeur m.; directrice f.
— n. Directive, instruction f.
directly [di'rektli] adv. Directement. ‖ Immédiatement. ‖ U. S. Sans retard, bientôt.
— conj. FAM. Dès que.
directness [-nis] n. Droite ligne f. ‖ FIG. Netteté f. (of an answer).
director [-ə*] n. Ordonnateur m. (of a ceremony). ‖ COMM. Directeur, administrateur m. ‖ ECCLES. Directeur (m.) de conscience. ‖ THEATR. Directeur (m.) de production ; U. S. metteur (m.) en scène.
directorate [-ərət] n. Directorat m. ‖ U. S. Conseil (m.) d'administration.
directorial [,dairek'tɔ:riəl] adj. Directorial.
directorship [di'rektəʃip] n. Directorat m.; direction f.
directory [-təri] adj. Directeur m.; directrice f.
— n. Annuaire m. ‖ † Directoire m.
directress [-tris] n. Directrice f.
directrix [-triks] (pl. directrices [-trisi:z]) n. Directrice f. (woman). ‖ MATH. Directrice f.
direful ['daiəful] adj. Affreux, terrible, sinistre.
dirge ['də:dʒ] n. Thrène, hymne funèbre m. ‖ Lamentation, élégie f.
dirigible ['diridʒibl] adj., n. AVIAT. Dirigeable m.
diriment ['dirimənt] adj. JUR. Dirimant.
dirk [də:k] n. Poignard m.
— v. tr. Poignarder.
dirt [də:t] n. Boue, fange f. (See MUD.) ‖ Saleté f. (dirtiness) ; crasse f. (filth). ‖ Propos orduriers m. pl.; to talk dirt, dire des cochonneries. ‖ TECHN. Terrain aurifère m. ‖ U. S. Terre battue f. ‖ FIG. Boue f.; to throw dirt at s.o., traîner qqn dans la boue ; to treat s.o. like dirt, traiter qqn plus bas que terre. ‖ FAM. Sale coup m.; saleté, crasse f.; to eat dirt, avaler des couleuvres. ‖ **Dirt-cheap** adj. Pour rien, à vil prix. ‖ **Dirt farmer**, n. FAM. U. S. Fermier exploitant m. ‖ **Dirt-track**, n. SPORTS Cendrée f.; dirt-track racing, courses motocyclistes sur cendrée.
dirtily [-ili] adv. Salement. ‖ Grossièrement.
dirtiness [-inis] n. Saleté f. ‖ Grossièreté f. (obscenity). ‖ FIG. Bassesse f.
dirty [-i] adj. Boueux, fangeux, crotté (muddy). ‖ Sale, malpropre (unclean). ‖ Sale, peu net ; dirty grey, gris sale. ‖ Sale, grossier, ordurier (obscene). ‖ Vilain ; dirty weather, sale temps. ‖ FIG. Sale a dirty old man, un vieux dégoûtant ; dirty trick sale tour ; saloperie (pop.).

— adv. FAM. *Dirty big (or) great,* maous, maousse.
— v. tr. (2). Salir (lit. and fig.).
— v. intr. Se salir.
disability [ˌdisəˈbiliti] n. Incapacité *f.* ‖ MED. Invalidité *f.*
disable [disˈeibl̩] v. tr. Rendre incapable, mettre hors d'état *(from,* de). ‖ Rendre inapte *(for,* à). ‖ MED. Estropier, rendre impotent. ‖ NAUT. Désemparer. ‖ TECHN. Mettre hors d'usage, détraquer, mettre en panne. ‖ JUR. Frapper d'incapacité *(from,* à).
disabuse [ˌdisəˈbjuːz] v. tr. Désabuser, dessiller les yeux de.
disaccord [ˌdisəˈkɔːd] n. Désaccord *m.*
— v. intr. Etre en désaccord, ne pas s'entendre.
disaccustom [ˌdisəˈkʌstəm] v. tr. Déshabituer.
disadvantage [ˌdisədˈvɑːntidʒ] n. Désavantage *m.; at a disadvantage,* dans un mauvais moment ; sous un jour désavantageux ; handicapé, désavantagé.
disadvantaged [-d] adj. Défavorisé (class, group).
disadvantageous [ˌdisædvənˈteidʒəs] adj. Désavantageux.
disaffect [ˌdisəˈfekt] v. tr. Se détacher de (s.o.). ‖ Aliéner (a tribe).
disaffected [-id] adj. Mal disposé *(to,* envers). ‖ Dissident (tribe).
disaffection [ˌdisəˈfekʃən] n. Désaffection *f. (to,* envers). ‖ Tendance à la dissidence *f.*
disaffirm [ˌdisəˈfəːm] v. tr. Revenir sur (a decision). ‖ JUR. Dénoncer (an agreement, a contract) ; casser (a sentence).
disagree [ˌdisəˈgriː] v. intr. Etre en désaccord, ne pas s'accorder *(or)* s'entendre *(with,* avec) [persons] ; différer, ne pas concorder (things). ‖ Se disputer, se quereller (to dissent). ‖ Ne pas convenir, être contraire *(with,* à) [to prove unsuitable].
disagreeable [-əbl̩] adj. Désagréable *(to,* à).
— n. pl. Désagréments *m. pl.*
disagreeableness [-əbl̩nis] n. Nature désagréable *f.* ‖ Désagrément *m.*
disagreeably [-əbli] adv. Désagréablement.
disagreement [-mənt] n. Désaccord *m.; discordance f. (between,* entre). ‖ Querelle, brouille *f.*
disallow [ˌdisəˈlau] v. tr. Rejeter, repousser, ne pas admettre. ‖ Ne pas permettre (to prohibit).
disannul [ˌdisəˈnʌl] v. tr. Annuler.
disapparel [ˌdisəˈpærəl] v. tr. Dévêtir.
disappear [ˌdisəˈpiə*] v. intr. Disparaître.
disappearance [-rəns] n. Disparition *f.*
disappoint [ˌdisəˈpɔint] v. tr. Tromper (expectation) ; décevoir (hope) ; décevoir, désappointer (s.o.). ‖ Manquer de parole à, faire faux bond à (after promising). ‖ Faire échouer, contrecarrer, (s.o.'s plans).
disappointed [-id] adj. Déçu (ambition, hope) ; déçu, désappointé *(in,* par) [person] ; U. S. *to be a disappointed dancer,* être un danseur manqué. ‖ Contrecarré *(of,* par).
disappointment [-mənt] n. Déception *f.; désappointement m.* ‖ Déboire, contretemps *m.*
disapprobation [ˌdisæproˈbeiʃən], **disapproval** [ˌdisəˈpruːvəl] n. Désapprobation *f.*
disapprobatory [ˌdisəproˈbeitəri] adj. Désapprobateur *m.; désapprobatrice f.*
disapprove [ˌdisəˈpruːv] v. tr. Désapprouver.
— v. intr. Exprimer sa désapprobation *(of,* de) ; trouver à redire *(of,* à).
disapprovingly [-iŋli] adv. Avec désapprobation.
disarm [disˈɑːm] v. tr., intr. MILIT., FIG. Désarmer.
disarmament [-əmənt] n. MILIT. Désarmement *m.*
disarming [-iŋ] adj. FIG. Désarmant.
disarrange [ˌdisəˈreindʒ] v. tr. Déranger.
disarrangement [-mənt] n. Dérangement, désordre *m.*

disarray [ˌdisəˈrei] n. Désordre *m.* (See CONFUSION.) ‖ Négligé *m.; in disarray,* à demi habillé.
— v. tr. Mettre en désordre ; dévêtir. ‖ MILIT. Mettre en déroute.
disarticulate [ˌdisɑːˈtikjuleit] v. tr. Désarticuler (see DISJOINT) ; désosser (fam.).
disarticulation [ˌdisɑːtikjuˈleiʃən] n. Désarticulation *f.*
disassemble [ˌdisəˈsembl̩] v. tr. TECHN. Démonter.
disassociate [ˌdisəˈsouʃieit] v. tr. Dissocier.
disassociation [ˌdisəsousiˈeiʃən] n. Dissociation *f.*
disaster [diˈzɑːstə*] n. Désastre *m.* (calamity). ‖ Catastrophe *f.; air disaster,* catastrophe aérienne. ‖ FAM. Mésaventure *f.*
disastrous [-trəs] adj. Désastreux. (See CALAMITOUS.)
disastrously [-trəsli] adv. Désastreusement.
disavow [ˌdisəˈvau] v. tr. Désavouer.
disavowal [-əl] n. Désaveu *m.*
disband [disˈbænd] v. tr. MILIT. Licencier (troops).
— v. intr. MILIT. Se débander (to break into a rout) ; se séparer (to disperse).
disbandment [-mənt] n. MILIT. Licenciement *m.*
disbar [disˈbɑː*] v. tr. (1). JUR. Exclure du barreau.
disbelief [ˌdisbiˈliːf] n. Incrédulité *f.*
disbelieve [-ˈliːv] v. tr. Ne pas croire.
— v. intr. Refuser de croire *(in,* à).
disbeliever [-ˈliːvə*] n. Incrédule *s.*
disbranch [disˈbrɑːnʃ] v. tr. AGRIC. Ebrancher.
disbud [disˈbʌd] v. tr. AGRIC. Ebourgeonner.
disburden [disˈbəːdən] v. tr. Décharger *(of,* de). ‖ Se décharger de *(upon,* sur).
disburse [disˈbəːs] v. tr., intr. Débourser, décaisser.
disbursement [-mənt] n. Déboursement *m.* (act) ; débours *m. pl.* (expenditure).
disc [disk] n. Disque *m.* ‖ MED. Disque *m.; slipped disc,* hernie discale. ‖ AUTOM. Disque *m.* (parking disk) ; *disc zone,* zone bleue *(or)* à stationnement réglementé. ‖ MUS. Disque *m.; disc jockey,* disc jockey. ‖ **Disc brake,** n. AUTOM. Frein à disque *m.* ‖ **Disc harrow,** n. AGRIC. Pulvériseur *m.* ‖ **Disc-shaped,** adj. Discoïde.
discalceate [disˈkalsieit], **discalced** [-ˈkalst] adj. ECCLES. Déchaussé, déchaux.
discard [disˈkɑːd] v. tr. Ecarter (a playing card) ; se défausser de (a suit). ‖ Renvoyer, congédier (a servant). ‖ Mettre de côté *(or)* au rancart (sth.). ‖ PHYS. *To discard in flight,* larguer (part of a rocket). ‖ FIG. Renoncer à.
— v. intr. Ecarter ; se défausser.
— n. Ecart *m.; défausse f.* ‖ U. S. Déchet *m.*
discern [diˈsəːn] v. tr., intr. Discerner, percevoir. ‖ Distinguer, dissocier (to separate).
discernible [-ibl̩] adj. Discernable, perceptible.
discerning [-iŋ] adj. Judicieux, pénétrant, fin.
— n. Discernement *m.; pénétration f.*
discernment [-mənt] n. Discernement *m.*
discharge [disˈtʃɑːdʒ] v. tr. Congédier, renvoyer (a servant). ‖ Décharger (colour, dye). ‖ Libérer, exempter *(from,* de) (s.o.). ‖ NAUT. Décharger (the cargo, a ship) ; débarquer (a crew). ‖ MILIT. Décocher (an arrow) ; décharger (a gun) ; lancer (a projectile) ; réformer (a soldier for unfitness) ; libérer (a soldier from service) ; licencier (troops). ‖ AUTOM. Décharger (passengers). ‖ ELECTR. Décharger (battery). ‖ CHIM. Emettre (gas, steam) ; TECHN. Débiter (water) ; *to discharge its waters into,* se déverser dans. ‖ JUR. Réhabiliter (a bankrupt) ; acquitter (a defendant) ; congédier (the jury) ; annuler (an order of the court) ; élargir (a prisoner). ‖ FIN. Apurer (an account) ; payer, acquitter (a bill) ; régler (a debt) ; solder (one's liabilities). ‖ MED. Renvoyer guéri (a patient) ; jeter (pus). ‖ FIG. Accomplir (a duty) ; remplir (a function).

— v. intr. Déteindre (colour, stuff). ‖ Se déverser, se jeter (into, dans) [water]. ‖ MED. Suppurer (abscess). ‖ NAUT., MILIT., ELECTR. Se décharger. — n. Congédiement, renvoi m. (of a servant). ‖ Décoloration f. (of a material); décolorant m. (bleaching agent). ‖ NAUT. Déchargement; débarquement m. ‖ MILIT. Décochement m. (of arrows); décharge f. (of a gun); libération, démobilisation f. (of a soldier); réforme f. (of a disabled soldier); licenciement m. (of troops); full discharge, congé libérable. ‖ ELECTR. Décharge f. ‖ CHIM. Emission f. ‖ TECHN. Débit m. (of a pump, stream). ‖ JUR. Réhabilitation f. (of a bankrupt); acquittement m. (of a defendant); congédiement m. (of the jury); annulation f. (of an order); élargissement m., libération f. (of a prisoner). ‖ FIN. Apurement m. (of an account); paiement (of a bill); règlement m. (of a debt); final discharge, quitus. ‖ MED. Suppuration f. (of an abcess); exeat m. (of a patient). ‖ FIG. Exercice m. (of duties); accomplissement m. (of a vow).

discharger [-ə*] n. ELECTR. Excitateur m.

disciple [di'saipḷ] n. Disciple s.

disciplinable ['disiplinəbḷ] adj. Disciplinable.

disciplinarian [,disipli'nɛəriən] n. Disciplinaire s.

disciplinary ['disiplinəri] adj. MILIT. De discipline (companies); disciplinaire (punishment). ‖ FIG. De discipline.

discipline [-plin] n. Discipline f. ‖ Châtiment m. ‖ ECCLES., MILIT. Discipline f.
— v. tr. Discipliner. ‖ Punir. (See PUNISH.)

disclaim [dis'kleim] v. tr. Rejeter (an authority, a responsibility); to disclaim any participation to, se défendre d'avoir pris part à. ‖ JUR. Renoncer à (one's rights).

disclaimer [-ə*] n. Déni, rejet, désaveu m.; dénégation f. ‖ JUR. Désistement m.; renonciation f.

disclose [dis'klouz] v. tr. Découvrir, dévoiler (to uncover). ‖ Faire connaître, révéler, divulguer. (See REVEAL.)

disclosure [-'klouʒə*] n. Révélation f. (act, thing).

disco ['diskou] (pl. **discos** [-z]) n. FAM. Discothèque f. (dance-hall); soirée dansante (f.) avec disques et animateur (dance); disco music, disco, musique disco.

discobolus [dis'kɔbələs] n. SPORTS. Discobole m.

discography [dis'kɔɡrəfi] n. Discographie f.

discoid ['diskɔid] adj. Discoïde.

discolour [dis'kʌlə*] v. tr. Décolorer.
— v. intr. Se décolorer.

discolouration [dis,kʌlə'reiʃən] n. Décoloration f.

discomfit [dis'kʌmfit] v. tr. MILIT. Déconfire (†); battre. ‖ FAM. Déconcerter, décontenancer.

discomfiture [-ʃə*] n. MILIT. Déconfiture f. ‖ FIG. Déconvenue f.; échec m.

discomfort [dis'kʌmfət] n. Inconfort m.; incommodité f. ‖ MED. Malaise m. ‖ FIG. Inquiétude, gêne f.; souci m.
— v. tr. Incommoder. ‖ FIG. Inquiéter, tourmenter; incommoder, gêner.

discommend [dis,kə'mend] v. tr. Désapprouver. ‖ Dénigrer, parler contre.

discommode [,diskə'moud] v. tr. Incommoder, déranger. ‖ Importuner.

discompose [,diskəm'pouz] v. tr. Défaire, altérer (s.o.'s countenance); troubler, bouleverser (s.o.).

discomposure [-'pouʒə*] n. Décomposition, altération f. (of the face); trouble m. (of a person).

disconcert [,diskən'sə:t] v. tr. Déconcerter, décontenancer, dérouter (s.o.). ‖ Déranger, bouleverser, gêner (plans).

disconcerting [-iŋ] adj. Déconcertant.

disconcertment [-mənt] n. Trouble, embarras m. ‖ Fait (m.) de déconcerter.

disconformity [,diskən'fɔ:miti] n. Manque (m.) de conformité.

disconnect [,diskə'nekt] v. tr. Disjoindre, détacher, séparer (from, de). ‖ Couper (a telephone line). ‖ TECHN. Désembrayer; découpler. ‖ ELECTR. Débrancher (a battery); rompre (a circuit); déconnecter (lead).

disconnected [-id] adj. Décousu, incohérent (speech, writing).

disconnection [,diskə'nekʃən] n. TECHN. Débrayage; découplage m. ‖ ELECTR. Disjonction f. ‖ FIG. Incohérence f.; aspect décousu m.

disconsolate [dis'kɔnsəlit] adj. Triste, sans joie, morose (landscape); inconsolable, plein de désolation (person).

discontent [,diskən'tent] n. Mécontentement m.
— adj. Mécontent (with, de).
— v. tr. Mécontenter.

discontented [-id] adj. Mécontent, insatisfait (with, de). [See DISSATISFIED].

discontentedly [-idli] adv. Avec mécontentement.

discontinuance [,diskən'tinjuəns] n. Discontinuation, interruption f.

discontinue [-'tinju] v. tr. Discontinuer, interrompre. ‖ Mettre fin à; cesser d'utiliser. ‖ Suspendre (a newspaper subscription). ‖ JUR. Interrompre, abandonner (a case).
— v. intr. Prendre fin.

discontinuity [dis,kɔnti'nju:iti] n. Discontinuité, interruption f. ‖ Manque (m.) de suite.

discontinuous [,diskən'tinjuəs] adj. Discontinu.

discord ['diskɔ:d] n. Discorde, division f. (dissension). ‖ Discordance f.; bruit discordant m. (clash). ‖ MUS. Dissonance f.
— [dis'kɔ:d] v. intr. Etre en désaccord, ne pas s'entendre (with, avec). ‖ Discorder, dissoner. ‖ MUS. Former une dissonance.

discordance [dis'kɔ:dəns] n. Désaccord m.; discorde f. ‖ MUS. Discordance f. (of sounds).

discordant [-ənt] adj. En désaccord, opposé. ‖ Discordant (sound). ‖ MUS. Dissonant.

discotheque ['diskə,tek] n. Discothèque f. (dance-hall).

discount ['diskaunt] n. COMM. Rabais m.; réduction, remise f. ‖ FIN. Escompte m. ‖ FIG. At a discount, peu apprécié, mal coté. ‖ **Discount-bank,** n. FIN. Comptoir (m.) d'escompte.
— [dis'kaunt] v. tr. COMM. Rabattre, décompter, faire un rabais de. ‖ FIN. Escompter. ‖ FIG. Escompter, envisager d'avance (to anticipate); faire peu de cas de (an opinion); en rabattre sur, ne pas prendre argent comptant (a statement).

discountable [-əbḷ] adj. FIN. Escomptable. ‖ FIG. Assez exagéré.

discountenance [dis'kauntinəns] v. tr. Se montrer peu favorable à, décourager. ‖ U. S. Décontenancer.

discourage [dis'kʌridʒ] v. tr. Décourager, rebuter (by, par). [See DISHEARTEN]. ‖ Décourager, dissuader (from, de). [See DISSUADE].

discouragement [-mənt] n. Découragement m.

discouraging [-iŋ] adj. Décourageant.

discourse ['diskɔ:s] n. Conversation f.; to hold discourse with s.o. on sth., s'entretenir de qqch. avec qqn. ‖ Discours m.; communication f. (in speech); étude, dissertation f. (in writing).
— [dis'kɔ:s] v. intr. S'entretenir, converser, conférer (to talk). ‖ Discourir, disserter (on, upon, sur).

discourteous [dis'kə:tiəs] adj. Discourtois, impoli.

discourtesy [-si] n. Discourtoisie f. (act); impolitesse f. (remark).

discover [dis'kʌvə*] v. tr. Découvrir, trouver, faire la découverte de (to find out). ‖ Découvrir, se rendre compte de (to realize). ‖ † Révéler, dévoiler (to disclose).

discovery [-əri] n. Découverte f. (act, thing). ‖ JUR. Communication f. (of documents). ‖ THEATR. Dénouement m.

discredit [dis'kredit] n. Discrédit *m*. (see DISRE-PUTE); *to be a discredit to*, déshonorer; *to bring discredit on oneself, to fall into discredit*, se discréditer. ‖ Doute *m.; to throw discredit upon*, mettre en doute. ‖ COMM. Perte (*f.*) de crédit.
— v. tr. Discréditer (*with*, auprès de); jeter le discrédit sur; démonétiser (fam.). ‖ Douter, mettre en doute, élever des doutes sur.

discreditable [-əbl] adj. Peu honorable (*to*, pour).

discreet [dis'kri:t] adj. Discret, réservé, peu bavard (secret). ‖ Plein de discernement, avisé, circonspect. (See CAREFUL.)

discreetly [-li] adv. Discrètement; avec réserve (or) circonspection.

discrepancy [di'krepənsi] n. Désaccord *m.*; discordance, contradiction *f*. (*between*, entre). [See INCONSISTENCY.]

discrepant [-ənt] adj. En opposition (or) contradiction (*from, with*, avec).

discrete [dis'kri:t] adj. Distinct. ‖ MATH., MED. Discret. ‖ PHILOS. Abstrait.

discretion [dis'kreʃən] n. Discrétion, latitude, liberté de décision *f.; it lies within your own discretion*, il dépend de vous de, vous avez toute discrétion pour. ‖ Raison *f.; discernement m.; age of discretion*, âge de raison; *air of discretion*, air entendu. ‖ Discrétion, réserve, circonspection *f*.

discretionary [-əri] adj. JUR. Discrétionnaire.

discriminant [dis'kriminənt] adj., n. MATH. Discriminant *m*.

discriminate [-eit] v. intr. Discriminer, faire le départ, établir une discrimination (*between*, entre).
— v. tr. Distinguer (*from*, de). [See DISTINGUISH.]
— [-it] adj. Distinct. ‖ Averti, avisé.

discriminating [-eitiŋ] adj. Avisé, judicieux (person); distinctif (sign). ‖ JUR. Différentiel (tariff).

discrimination [,diskrimi'neiʃən] n. Discrimination *f.; without any racial discrimination*, sans distinction de race. ‖ Discernement, sens perceptif *m*.

discriminative [dis'kriminətiv] adj. Avisé (person); distinctif (sign).

discriminatory [dis'kriminətəri] adj. Discriminatoire (measure, law).

discrown [dis'kraun] v. tr. Découronner.

discursive [dis'kə:siv] adj. Décousu, incohérent. ‖ PHILOS. Discursif.

discus ['diskəs] n. SPORTS. Disque *m*. ‖ Discus-thrower, n. SPORTS. Discobole, lanceur de disque *m*.

discuss [dis'kʌs] v. tr. Discuter, s'entretenir de, échanger des vues sur. ‖ FAM. S'enfiler, se taper (to drink, to eat).

discussible [-ibl] adj. Discutable.

discussion [dis'kʌʃən] n. Discussion *f.; under discussion*, en discussion, non décidé; *subject for discussion*, objet du débat. ‖ FAM. Dégustation *f*.

discutient [dis'kju:ʃiənt] adj. MED. Résolutif.

disdain [dis'dein] n. Dédain n. (See CONTEMPT).
— v. tr. Dédaigner (See DESPISE.)

disdainful [-ful] adj. Dédaigneux. (See SCORNFUL.)

disdainfully [-fuli] adv. Dédaigneusement.

disease [di'zi:z] n. MED. Maladie *f.; mal m*. ‖ FIG. Mal *m*.
— v. tr. Rendre malade.

diseased [-d] adj. MED. Malade. ‖ FIG. Morbide, malsain.

disembark [,disim'bɑ:k] v. tr., intr. NAUT. Débarquer.

disembarkation [,disimbɑ:'keiʃən] n. NAUT. Débarquement *m*.

disembarrass [,disim'bærəs] v. tr. Débarrasser (*of*, de). ‖ Démêler (*from*, de).

disembodiment [,disim'bɔdimənt] n. MILIT. Libération *f*. ‖ FIG. Désincarnation *f*.

disembody ['bɔdi] v. tr. (2). MILIT. Libérer. ‖ FIG. Désincarner.

disembogue [,disim'boug] v. intr. NAUT. Déboucher (river); débouquer (ship). ‖ FAM. Se déverser (*into*, dans).
— v. tr. NAUT., FAM. Déverser.

disembosom [,disim'buzəm] v. tr. *To disembosom oneself*, épancher son cœur, se livrer; se déboutonner (fam.).

disembowel [,disim'bauəl] v. tr. Vider, déboyauter; éviscérer.

disembroil [-'brɔil] v. tr. Débrouiller.

disenchant [,disin'tʃɑ:nt] v. tr. Désenchanter.

disenchantment [-mənt] n. Désenchantement *m*.

disencumber [,disin'kʌmbə*] v. tr. Désencombrer. ‖ JUR. Déshypothéquer.

disendow [,disin'dau] v. tr. Spolier.

disendowment [-mənt] n. ECCLES. Sécularisation (*f.*) des biens ecclésiastiques.

disenfranchise [,disin'fræntʃaiz] v. tr. See DISFRANCHISE.

disengage [,disin'geidʒ] v. tr. CHIM., SPORTS, FIG. Dégager. ‖ MILIT *To disengage one's troops*, effectuer un décrochage; *disengaging action*, décrochage.
— v. intr. CHIM., FIG. Se dégager. ‖ SPORTS. Dégager.
— n. SPORTS. Dégagement *m*.

disengaged [-d] adj. Libre (person, seat). ‖ TECHN. Débrayé.

disengagement [-mənt] n. CHIM., SPORTS. Dégagement *m*. ‖ JUR. Rupture (*f.*) de fiançailles. ‖ PHYS. *Nuclear disengagement*, dénucléarisation. ‖ ‖ FIG. Détachement *m*. (*from*, de).

disentangle [,disin'tæŋgl] v. tr. Dépêtrer (*from*, de) [s.o.]. ‖ Démêler, débrouiller, désentortiller, désenchevêtrer (sth.). ‖ FIG. Dénouer (a plot); débrouiller (a puzzle).
— v. intr. Se dépêtrer. ‖ Se débrouiller, se désenchevêtrer. ‖ FIG. Se dénouer.

disentanglement [-mənt] n. Démêlage *m*. (of string). ‖ Dégagement *m*. (of s.o.). ‖ FIG. Dénouement *m*. (of a situation).

disenthral [,disin'θrɔ:l] v. tr. (1). Affranchir.

disentomb [,disin'tu:m] v. tr. Exhumer. (See DISINTER.)

disestablish [,disis'tæbliʃ] v. tr. JUR., ECCLES. Séparer de l'Etat (the Church).

disestablishment [-mənt] n. JUR., ECCLES. Séparation (*f.*) de l'Eglise et de l'Etat.

disesteem [,disis'ti:m] v. tr. Mésestimer, sousestimer.
— n. Mésestime *f*.

disfavour [dis'feivə*] n. Défaveur *f*. (See DISGRACE.) ‖ Désapprobation f. (disapproval). ‖ Déconsidération *f*. (See DISCREDIT.)
— v. tr. Se montrer défavorable à.

disfeature [dis'fi:tʃə*] v. tr. Défigurer.

disfiguration [dis,figjuə'reiʃən] n. Enlaidissement *m*.

disfigure [dis'figə*] v. tr. Défigurer. (See DISFEATURE.) ‖ Enlaidir (s.o.). ‖ FIG. Gâter.

disforest [dis'fɔrist] v. tr. Déboiser.

disfranchise [dis'fræntʃaiz] v. tr. JUR. Priver des droits civiques (citizen); priver des droits de représentation (voter, place).

disfrock [dis'frɔk] v. tr. Défroquer.

disgorge [dis'gɔ:dʒ] v. tr. Dégorger, vomir, rendre (to vomit). ‖ Décharger, déverser (waters). ‖ FAM. Cracher (to give up).
— v. intr. Vomir. ‖ Se déverser. ‖ FAM. Rendre gorge.

disgrace [dis'greis] v. tr. Disgracier. (See DISFAVOUR.) ‖ Déshonorer. (See DISHONOUR.)
— n. Disgrâce *f.; in disgrace*, en pénitence (child); en disgrâce (person). ‖ Déshonneur *m.;* turpitude *f*. (dishonour). ‖ Honte *f.; there is no disgrace in being failed*, il n'y a pas de déshonneur à être refusé à un examen.

disgraceful [-ful] adj. Déshonorant. (See SHAME-FUL.)

disgracefully [-fuli] adv. Honteusement.

disgracefulness [fulnis] n. Déshonneur *m.*; ignominie *f.*

disgruntled [dis'grʌntl̩d] adj. Mécontent, insatisfait.

disguise [dis'gaiz] v. tr. Déguiser, travestir (s.o., one's voice, writing). ‖ FIG. Déguiser, farder (the facts); dissimuler, déguiser (one's intentions). — n. Déguisement, travesti *m.* (clothes); *in the disguise of*, déguisé en. ‖ FIG. Déguisement, travestissement *m.* (of facts). ‖ FIG. Faux-semblant *m.*; *to throw off all disguise*, jeter le masque.

disgust [dis'gʌst] n. Dégoût *m.* (at, for, towards, pour). ‖ FIG. Ecœurement *m.* — v. tr. Dégoûter, écœurer (lit. and fig.).

disgusting [-iŋ] adj. Dégoûtant, écœurant.

disgustingly [-iŋli] adv. D'une manière dégoûtante.

dish [diʃ] n. CULIN. Plat *m.* (container, dishful, food); *to wash the dishes*, faire la vaisselle. ‖ CHIM. Capsule *f.* ‖ TECHN. Cuvette *f.* ‖ U. S. FAM. Beau brin (*m.*) de femme (woman). ‖ **Dish-cloth**, n. Torchon *m.* ‖ **Dish-drainer**, n. Egouttoir *m.* ‖ **Dish-mop**, n. Lavette *f.* ‖ **Dish-pan**, n. Bassine à vaisselle *f.* ‖ **Dish-warmer**, n. Chauffe-plat *m.* ‖ **Dish-washer**, n. Lave-vaisselle *m.* (machine); laveur (*m.*) de vaisselle, plongeur *s.* (person). ‖ **Dish-water**, n. Eau de vaisselle *f.*; FAM. Eau (*f.*) de boudin. — v. tr. CULIN. Apprêter, accommoder. ‖ TECHN. Bomber. ‖ FAM. Arranger, trousser, servir (arguments, facts); couler, enfoncer (opponents).

dishabille [‚disə'bi:l] n. Déshabillé *m.* (garment, state).

dishabituate [‚disə'bitjueit] v. tr. Déshabituer, désaccoutumer.

disharmonious [‚dishɑ:'mouniəs] adj. Inharmonieux.

disharmonize [dis'hɑ:mənaiz] v. tr. Rendre inharmonique.

disharmony [-ni] n. MUS., FIG. Inharmonie *f.*

dishearten [dis'hɑ:tn̩] v. tr. Décourager, démoraliser, déprimer. (See DISCOURAGE.)

disheartenment [-mənt] n. Découragement *m.*

dished [diʃt] adj. CULIN. Apprêté, cuisiné. ‖ FAM. Cuit, fichu, coulé.

dishevelled [di'ʃevəld] adj. Echevelé, les cheveux en bataille (person); ébouriffé (hair, person). ‖ Mal tenu, négligé, débraillé (person).

dishful ['diʃful] n. Plat *m.*; platée *f.*

dishonest [dis'ɔnist] adj. Malhonnête.

dishonestly [-li] adv. Malhonnêtement.

dishonesty [-i] n. Malhonnêteté *f.*

dishonour [dis'ɔnə*] n. Déshonneur *m.* ‖ COMM. Non-paiement *m.* — v. tr. Déshonorer (one's family, a woman); *to dishonour oneself*, se déshonorer. ‖ Traiter irrespectueusement. ‖ COMM. Laisser protester (a bill); ne pas payer (a cheque).

dishonourable [-rəbl] adj. Déshonorant (action); sans honneur (person); *to hold it dishonourable to*, trouver déshonorant de.

dishonourably [-rəbli] adv. De manière déshonorante, à son déshonneur.

dishorn [dis'hɔ:n] v. tr. Ecorner.

dishouse [dis'hauz] v. tr. Déloger, expulser.

dishy ['diʃi] adj. POP. Girond, sexy, bath.

disillusion [‚disi'lju:ʒən] n. Désillusion *f.* — v. tr. Désillusionner, décevoir, désabuser.

desillusionment [-mənt] n. Désillusionnement *m.* ‖ Dégrisement *m.* (from passion).

disincarnate ['disin‚kɑ:nit] adj. Désincarné.

disincentive [‚disin'sentiv] n. FAM. Préventif *m.*

disinclination [‚disinkli'neiʃən] n. Manque d'em-

pressement *m.* (for, pour); répugnance, mauvaise volonté *f.* (to, à).

disincline [-'klain] v. tr. Inspirer peu d'empressement, mal disposer (for, to, pour); détourner (for, to, de).

disincorporate [‚disin'kɔ:pəreit] v. tr. JUR. Dissoudre (partnership).

disinfect [‚disin'fekt] v. tr. Désinfecter.

disinfectant [-tənt] adj., n. Désinfectant *m.*

disinfection [-ʃən] n. Désinfection *f.*

disinfest [‚disin'fest] v. tr. Déparasiter, désinsectiser (person, place); dératiser (place).

disinfestation [‚disinfes'teiʃən] n. *Rat desinfestation*, dératisation.

disinflation [‚disin'fleiʃən] n. FIN. Désinflation *f.*

disingenuous [‚disin'dʒenjuəs] adj. Faussement candide; retors; *disingenuous tricks*, finasseries.

disingenuousness [-nis] n. Finasserie *f.*

disinherit [‚disin'herit] v. tr. Déshériter.

disinheritance [-əns] n. Déshéritement *m.* ‖ JUR. Exhérédation *f.*

desintegrate [dis'intigreit] v. tr. Désintégrer. ‖ FIG. Désagréger. — v. intr. Se désagréger (lit. and fig.).

disintegration [‚disinti'greiʃən] n. Effritement *m.* ‖ Désintégration *f.* ‖ FIG. Désagrégation *f.*

disinter [‚disin'tə:*] v. tr. (1). Déterrer. (See DISENTOMB.)

disinterested [dis'intrəstid] adj. Désintéressé (unselfish). ‖ Impartial (unbiased). ‖ Indifférent (in, à) [uninterested].

disinterestedly [-li] adv. Avec désintéressement.

disinterestedness [-nis] n. Désintéressement *m.* ‖ Manque d'intérêt *m.*; indifférence *f.*

disinterment [‚disin'tə:mənt] n. Déterrement *m.* (See EXHUMATION.)

disinvestment [‚disin'vestmənt] n. FIN. Désinvestissement *m.*

disjoin [dis'dʒɔin] v. tr. Disjoindre (to sunder).

disjoint [dis'dʒɔint] v. tr. Disloquer. ‖ MED. Désarticuler (a bone); déboîter (the shoulder). ‖ CULIN. Découper (fowl). ‖ TECHN. Démonter. — v. intr. Se disloquer. ‖ MED. Se désarticuler.

disjointed [-dʒɔintid] adj. Disloqué. ‖ MED. Désarticulé. ‖ FIG. Décousu, incohérent. (See DISCURSIVE.)

disjunction [dis'dʒʌŋkʃən] n. Séparation *f.* (from, de). ‖ GRAMM., PHILOS. Disjonction *f.*

disjunctive [-tiv] adj. Disjonctif. — n. GRAMM. Disjonctive *f.*

disk [disk] n. See DISC.

dislike [dis'laik] v. tr. Ne pas aimer. ‖ Détester, avoir de l'aversion pour (s.o., sth.); éprouver de l'antipathie pour, trouver déplaisant (s.o.). — n. Antipathie *f.* (for, of, pour) [s.o.]; *to have a strong dislike for*, avoir qqn dans le nez, ne pas pouvoir sentir qqn. ‖ Aversion *f.*; dégoût *m.* (for of, pour) [sth.].

dislocate ['dislokeit] v. tr. Disloquer; démancher, déglinguer (fam.). ‖ Déranger, déplacer (to dislodge). ‖ MED. Désarticuler.

dislocation [‚dislo'keiʃən] n. Dislocation *f.* ‖ Déplacement, dérangement *m.* ‖ MED. Luxation *f.*

dislodge [dis'lɔdʒ] v. tr. Déloger (to oust); dénicher (fam.). ‖ Détacher, faire se détacher. ‖ SPORTS. Débucher, dégîter.

dislodgement [-mənt] n. Délogement *m.*

disloyal [dis'lɔiəl] adj. Déloyal (to, envers). ‖ Infidèle, traître (to, à).

disloyalty [-ti] n. Déloyauté *f.*

dismal ['dizməl] adj. Sombre (gloomy). ‖ Triste, morne, pessimiste, lugubre (dreary); *a dismal Jimmy*, un broyeur de noir, un cafardeux. — n. pl. FAM. Cafard *m.*

dismantle [dis'mæntl̩] v. tr. MILIT. Démanteler.

‖ Naut. Dégréer. ‖ Techn. Démonter. ‖ Fig. Dépouiller (of, de). [See STRIP.]

dismantling [-iŋ] n. Milit. Démantèlement m. ‖ Naut. Dégréement m. ‖ Techn. Démontage m.

dismast [dis'mɑ:st] v. tr. Naut. Démâter.

dismay [dis'mei] v. tr. Atterrer, consterner. (See CONSTERNATE.) ‖ Effrayer, démonter, abattre. (See DAUNT.) ‖ Terrifier, épouvanter (to appall).
— n. Atterrement m.; consternation f. ‖ Découragement m. ‖ Effroi m. ‖ U. S. Gêne, consternation f.

dismember [dis'membə*] v. tr. Milit., Med., Fig. Démembrer.

dismemberment [-mənt] n. Démembrement m.

dismiss [dis'mis] v. tr. Congédier, renvoyer, remercier, mettre à la porte (a servant). ‖ Jur. Acquitter (an accused); rejeter (an appeal); dissoudre (an assembly); classer (a case); révoquer (an official). ‖ Milit. Rayer des rôles; dismiss!, rompez! ‖ Sports. Mettre hors jeu. ‖ Fig. Bannir, écarter, chasser (from, de) [a thought]; écarter (a topic of conversation).

dismissal [-əl] n. Renvoi, congédiement m. (of a servant). ‖ Congé m. (of a visitor). ‖ Jur. Acquittement m. (of the accused); rejet m. (of an appeal); révocation f. (of an official). ‖ Milit. Dégradation f.

dismount [dis'maunt] v. intr. Mettre pied à terre; descendre (from, de).
— v. tr. Descendre de (one's horse); désarçonner, démonter (a rider); faire descendre (s.o. from a horse). ‖ Techn. Démonter.

disnature [dis'neitʃə*] v. tr. Dénaturer.

disobedience [,disə'bi:djəns] n. Désobéissance f.

disobedient [-ənt] adj. Désobéissant.

disobey [,disə'bei] v. tr. Désobéir à (an order, s.o.). ‖ Jur. Enfreindre (the law).
— v. intr. Désobéir.

disoblige [,disə'blaidʒ] v. tr. Désobliger. ‖ Refuser de rendre service à.

disobliging [-iŋ] adj. Désobligeant. ‖ Peu complaisant.

disobligingness [-iŋnis] n. Désobligeance f. ‖ Défaut (m.) de complaisance.

disorder [dis'ɔ:də*] n. Désordre m. (See CONFUSION.) ‖ Tumulte, tapage m. (din). ‖ Troubles, désordres m. pl. (public disturbances). ‖ Med. Trouble m.
— v. tr. Mettre en désordre (or) sens dessus dessous, bouleverser, déranger (a room). ‖ Mettre le désordre dans (the ranks). ‖ Med. Déranger; détraquer (fam.). ‖ Fig. Jeter le trouble dans (s.o.'s mind).

disorderliness [-linis] n. Désordre m.; nature désordonnée f. ‖ Esprit de désordre m. (or) d'émeute. ‖ Fig. Dérèglement. m.

disorderly [-li] adj. En désordre, désordonné (untidy). ‖ Tapageur, tumultueux, turbulent (mob); révolutionnaire (spirit). ‖ Jur. Disorderly house, maison de prostitution; maison de jeu. ‖ Fig. Dévergondé (imagination); déréglé (life).

disorganization [dis,ɔ:gənai'zeiʃən] n. Désorganisation f.

disorganize [dis'ɔ:gənaiz] v. tr. Désorganiser.

disorient [dis'ɔ:riənt], **disorientate** [-eit] v. tr. Mal orienter. ‖ Fig. Désorienter.

disown [dis'oun] v. tr. Nier (a fact); renier (one's signature). ‖ Désavouer (an agent, one's offspring).

disparage [dis'pæridʒ] v. tr. Discréditer, dénigrer.

disparagement [-mənt] n. Dépréciation, dévalorisation f. ‖ Dénigrement m. (See DETRACTION.)

disparaging [-iŋ] adj. Dépréciateur m.; dépréciatrice f. ‖ Peu flatteur, humiliant (to, pour).

disparate [,dispərit] adj. Disparate.
— n. pl. Disparates f. pl.

disparity [dis'pæriti] n. Disparité f.

dispart [dis'pɑ:t] v. tr. Départir (to distribute); séparer (to divide).
— v. intr. Se séparer. ‖ Se répartir.
— n. Milit. Ecart m.

dispassionate [dis'pæʃnit] adj. Sans passion, calme, placide. ‖ Froid, impartial, objectif.

dispatch [dis'pætʃ] v. tr. Dépêcher, envoyer (a messenger). [See SEND.] ‖ Expédier (a letter, a parcel). ‖ Comm. Expédier, acheminer (goods). ‖ Fam. Expédier (business, dinner); envoyer ad patres, achever (s.o.).
— n. Expédition f. (of a letter); envoi m. (of a messenger). ‖ Dépêche f. (message). ‖ Rapidité, diligence, promptitude f. (haste). ‖ Exécution f. (of s.o.). ‖ Comm. Entreprise de messagerie f.; dispatch note, bulletin d'expédition. ‖ Milit. Mention in dispatches, citation à l'ordre du jour. ‖ Fam. Expédition f. (of business, dinner). ‖ Dispatch-boat, n. Naut. Aviso m. ‖ Dispatch-box, n. Valise diplomatique f. ‖ Dispatch-rider, n. Milit. Estafette f.

dispatcher [-ə*] n. Expéditeur m.; expéditrice f. ‖ Ch. de f. Dispatcher m.

dispel [dis'pel] v. tr. (1). Dissiper. (See SCATTER.)

dispensable [dis'pensəbl] adj. Dont on peut se passer, peu important. ‖ Dispensable, administrable. ‖ Eccles. Pardonnable (sin); dispensable (vow).

dispensary [-əri] n. Med. Dispensaire m. (hospital); officine, pharmacie f. (laboratory); milk dispensary, œuvre de la goutte de lait.

dispensation [,dispen'seiʃən] n. Dispensation f. (See DISTRIBUTION.) ‖ Administration f. ‖ Fait (m.) d'être dispensé. ‖ Jur. Exemption f. ‖ Eccles. Dispense f. (exemption); loi religieuse f. (system); dispensation of Providence, disposition providentielle, décret providentiel.

dispense [dis'pens] v. tr. Dispenser. (See DISTRIBUTE.) ‖ Administrer. ‖ Dispenser, exempter (from, de). ‖ Med. Préparer (medicine).
— v. intr. Se dispenser, se passer (with, de). ‖ Jur. Ne pas insister (with, sur).

dispeople [dis'pi:pl] v. tr. Dépeupler. (See DEPOPULATE.)

dispersal [dis'pə:səl] n. Dispersion f.

disperse [dis'pə:s] v. tr. Disperser, éparpiller, disséminer (to scatter). ‖ Disperser, chasser, dissiper (to dispel). ‖ Répandre, faire courir (to propagate). ‖ Med. Résoudre (a tumour). ‖ Phys. Décomposer (light).
— v. intr. Se disperser.

dispersedly [-idli] adv. De-ci de-là.

dispersion [dis'pə:ʃən] n. Dispersion f. ‖ Feux m. pl. (of a diamond).

dispirit [dis'pirit] v. tr. Déprimer (to depress); décourager (to dishearten).

dispiritedness [-idnis] n. Dépression f.; découragement m.

dispiteous [dis'pitjəs] adj. Sans pitié.

displace [dis'pleis] v. tr. Déplacer (from, de). ‖ Remplacer (by, par); évincer, supplanter (in, dans). ‖ Jur. Destituer. ‖ Electr. Décaler. ‖ Fin. Déclasser (shares).

displaced [-d] adj. Déplacé (person, thing).

displacement [-mənt] n. Déplacement m. ‖ Remplacement m. (by, par). ‖ Jur. Destitution f. ‖ Electr. Décalage m. ‖ Fin. Déclassement m. ‖ Phys. Déplacement m.

display [dis'plei] v. tr. Déployer, étaler, exposer (to spread out). ‖ Manifester, montrer, révéler, déployer (to give proof of). ‖ Etaler, exhiber, faire parade (or) étalage de (to show off). ‖ Comm. Mettre à l'étalage (or) en montre. ‖ Techn. Mettre en vedette (in printing).
— n. Déploiement, étalement m. ‖ Manifestation, révélation f. ‖ Etalage m.; parade, ostentation f.; to make a great display of affection, faire beaucoup

de démonstrations. ‖ TECHN. Vedette *f.* ‖ COMM. Etalage *m.;* exposition, montre *f.; window display,* art de l'étalage. ‖ **Display-window,** n. COMM. Vitrine *f.*

displease [dis'pli:z] v. tr. Déplaire à. ‖ Contrarier, mécontenter; *displeased at,* mécontent de.

displeasing [-iŋ] adj. Déplaisant.

displeasure [dis'pleʒə*] n. Déplaisir, ennui *m.; to s.o.'· great displeasure,* au grand dam de qqn. ‖ Colère *f.* (anger).

displume [dis'plu:m] v. tr. Déplumer.

disport [dis'pɔ:t] v. tr. *To disport oneself,* s'ébattre, folâtrer (to frolic); s'amuser (to play).
— n. Divertissement, jeu *m.*

disposable [dis'pouzəbḷ] adj. Disponible. ‖ JUR. *Disposable portion of estate,* quotité disponible. ‖ U. S. COMM. *Disposable handkerchiefs,* mouchoirs en papier; *disposable wrapping,* emballage perdu.

disposal [-'pouzḷ] n. Résolution *f.* (of a question). ‖ JUR. *Disposal of property,* dispositions testamentaires. ‖ COMM. Cession, vente *f.;* placement *m.* ‖ U. S. Rejet *m.*

dispose [-'pouz] v. tr. Disposer, placer, organiser (to place). ‖ Disposer, arranger, régler (to settle). ‖ Disposer, décider; *to dispose oneself to,* se disposer à. ‖ Disposer, incliner, porter (to, à); *well disposed towards,* bien disposé envers.
— v. intr. Disposer (to decide). ‖ **To dispose of,** se débarrasser de (a bore); disposer de, avoir la disposition de (one's capital); river son clou à (an interlocutor); expédier (a meal); lever (an objection); trancher (a question); disposer de, régler le sort de (s.o.); disposer de, employer (one's time); COMM. Céder (one's business); vendre, écouler, placer (goods); FAM. Envoyer *ad patres* (s.o.).

disposition [,dispə'ziʃən] n. Disposition, humeur, inclination *f.;* penchant *m.* (tendency); *in a disposition to,* disposé à. ‖ Caractère, tempérament *m.;* nature *f.* (temper). ‖ Disposition, organisation *f.;* agencement *m.* (order). ‖ Disposition, mesure *f.;* arrangement, préparatif *m.* ‖ JUR. Disposition testamentaire *f.* (disposal); droit (*m.*) de disposer (rights); *disposition inter vivos,* donation entre vifs. ‖ ECCLES. Décret providentiel *m.*

dispossess [,dispə'zes] v. tr. Déposséder (of, de). ‖ JUR. Exproprier, dessaisir de.

dispossession [,dispə'zeʃən] n. Dépossession *f.* ‖ JUR. Expropriation *f.*

dispraise [dis'preiz] v. tr. Blâmer. (See CENSURE.)
— n. Blâme *m.*

disproof [dis'pru:f] n. Réfutation *f.*

disproportion [,disprə'pɔ:ʃən] n. Disproportion *f.*
— v. tr. Disproportionner.

disproportional [-ḷ], **disproportionate** [-it] adj. Disproportionné.

disproportionately [-itli] adv. D'une manière disproportionnée (to, avec).

disprove [dis'pru:v] v. tr. Réfuter.

disputable ['dispjutəbḷ] adj. Discutable, douteux.

disputably [-i] adv. Douteusement, de façon contestable.

disputant ['dispjutənt] n. Partenaire (*s.*) dans la discussion. ‖ Contradicteur *m.;* controversiste *s.*
— adj. Qui discute.

disputation [,dispju'teiʃən] n. Discussion *f.;* débat *m.* ‖ Discussion, contestation *f.*

disputatious [-əs] adj. Raisonneur; discutailleur (fam.).

dispute [dis'pju:t] n. Discussion *f.;* débat *m.* (debate); *in dispute,* en discussion. ‖ Discussion, contestation *f.; beyond dispute,* hors de question, incontestable. ‖ Discussion, dispute *f.* (quarrel). ‖ JUR. Litige *m.; industrial, trade dispute,* conflit industriel, du travail; *under dispute,* en litige.
— v. intr. Discuter, disputer (to argue). ‖ Se disputer (to quarrel).

— v. tr. Discuter (an order). ‖ Discuter, disputer, débattre (a question). [See DISCUSS.] ‖ Mettre en doute, contester (a fact, a statement). ‖ Disputer (a game, possession, prize, pre-eminence, victory). ‖ MILIT. Résister à (the advance).

disqualification [dis,kwɔlifi'keiʃən] n. Incapacité, inaptitude *f.* (for, à). ‖ SPORTS. Disqualification *f.* ‖ JUR. Inhabileté *f.*

disqualify [dis'kwɔlifai] v. tr. (2). Rendre inapte (for, à); mettre dans l'incapacité (for, de). [See INCAPACITATE.] ‖ SPORTS. Disqualifier. ‖ JUR. Rendre inhabile (for, à).

disquiet [dis'kwaiət] adj. Inquiet, troublé.
— n. Inquiétude *f.*
— v. intr. Inquiéter, troubler, mettre mal à l'aise.

disquieting [-iŋ] adj. Inquiétant, troublant.

disquietude [-ju:d] n. Inquiétude *f.;* trouble *m.*

disquisition [,diskwi'ziʃən] n. Traité *m.;* longue étude *f.* (on, sur). ‖ † Enquête *f.*

disrate [dis'reit] v. tr. NAUT. Rétrograder.

disregard [disri'gɑ:d] v. tr. Ne pas attacher d'importance à, ne pas tenir compte de, ne pas se soucier de. ‖ Manquer d'égards envers.
— n. Négligence, insouciance *f.* (of, for, à l'égard de). ‖ Irrespect, manque (*m.*) d'égards (for, envers). ‖ JUR. Violation *f.* (of the law).

disregardful [-ful] adj. Négligent, peu soucieux (of, de); indifférent (of, à). ‖ Peu respectueux (of, envers).

disrelish [dis'reliʃ] n. Répugnance *f.;* dégoût *m.*
— v. tr. Avoir de la répugnance pour.

disrepair [,disri'pɛə*] n. Délabrement *m.*

disreputable [dis'repjutəbḷ] adj. Déshonorant (action); mal famé (house, place); perdu de réputation, peu honorable, de mauvaise vie (person). ‖ **Disreputable-looking,** adj. D'aspect louche.

disreputably [-i] adv. De manière peu honorable.

disrepute [,disri'pju:t] n. Discrédit *m.*

disrespect [,disris'pekt] n. Irrespect *m.*
— v. tr. Manquer de respect à.

disrespectful [-ful] adj. Irrespectueux.

disrespectfully [-fuli] adv. Irrespectueusement.

disrobe [dis'roub] v. tr. Dévêtir. (See UNDRESS.)
— v. intr. Se dévêtir.

disroot [dis'ru:t] v. tr. AGRIC., FAM. Déraciner. (See UPROOT.)

disrupt [dis'rʌpt] v. tr. Faire éclater (or) crouler. ‖ FIG. Disloquer.

disruption [-ʃən] n. Eclatement brutal *m.* ‖ FIG. Rupture, scission, dislocation *f.*

disruptive [-tiv] adj. TECHN. Disruptif.

disruptor [-tə*] n. ELECTR. Disrupteur *m.* ‖ FAM. Chambardeur *m.*

dissatisfaction [dis,sætis'fækʃən] n. Insatisfaction *f.;* mécontentement *m.* (at, with, de).

dissatisfactory [-təri] adj. Peu satisfaisant.

dissatisfied [dis'sætisfaid] adj. Peu satisfait.

dissatisfy [-fai] v. tr. (2). Mécontenter.

disseat [dis'si:t] v. tr. Déloger de son siège.

dissect [di'sekt] v. tr. Découper. ‖ MED. Disséquer. ‖ FIG. Dépouiller (a book); dépecer, dépiauter (fam.).

dissection [di'sekʃən] n. Découpage *m.* ‖ MED. Dissection *f.* ‖ FIG. Dépouillement *m.*

dissector [-tə*] n. MED. Dissecteur *m.* (person); scalpel *m.* (tool).

disseize [dis'si:z] v. tr. JUR. Déposséder (of, de).

disseizin [dis'si:zin] n. JUR. Eviction *f.*

dissemble [di'sembḷ] v. tr. Dissimuler (a fact, feeling). ‖ Simuler, feindre (virtue). ‖ Feindre l'ignorance de.
— v. intr. Dissimuler; feindre.

dissembler [-ə*] n. Dissimulateur *m.;* dissimulatrice *f.*

dissembling [-iŋ] adj. Dissimulé, sournois.
— n. Dissimulation *f.*

disseminate [di'semineit] v. tr. Disséminer. ‖ Fig. Propager.

dissemination [di,semi'nei∫ən] n. Dissémination f.

disseminator [di'semineitə*] n. Propagateur m.; propagatrice f.

dissension [di'sen∫ən] n. Dissension, division f.

dissent [di'sent] v. intr. Etre en dissentiment (or) désaccord, diverger d'opinion (about, sur; from, avec); être d'un avis contraire (from, à). ‖ Eccles. Etre dissident.
— n. Désaccord, dissentiment m.; divergence f. ‖ Eccles. Dissidence f.

dissenter [-ə*] n. Dissident s.

dissentient [di'sen∫iənt] adj. Opposé (from, à).
— n. Dissident s.

dissepiment [di'sepimənt] n. Bot., Med. Cloison f.

dissert [di'sə:t], **dissertate** ['disə:teit] v. intr. Disserter (on, sur).

dissertation [,disə:'tei∫ən] n. Discours m. (speech); mémoire m., dissertation f. (thesis).

disserve [dis'sə:v] v. tr. Desservir (with, auprès de) [s.o.].

disservice [-is] n. Mauvais service m.

dissever [dis'sevə*] v. tr. Séparer.
— v. intr. Se séparer.

disseverable [-ərəbl] adj. Séparable, divisible.

dissidence ['disidəns] n. Dissentiment, désaccord m. (See DISSENT.) ‖ Dissidence f.

dissident [-ənt] adj., n. Dissident s.

dissimilar [di'similə*] adj. Dissemblable (from, to, de). [See DIFFERENT.]

dissimilarity [,disimi'læriti] n. Dissemblance f.

dissimilation [-'lei∫ən] n. Gramm. Dissimilation f.

dissimilitude [,disi'militju:d] n. Dissimilitude f.

dissimulate [di'simjuleit] v. tr., intr. Dissimuler. (See DISSEMBLE.)

dissimulation [di,simju'lei∫ən] n. Dissimulation f.

dissimulator [-tə*] n. Dissimulateur m.; dissimulatrice f.

dissipate ['disipeit] v. tr. Dissiper, chasser, disperser (clouds, mist). ‖ Fig. Disperser, éparpiller (one's efforts); dissiper, gaspiller (one's resources); dissiper, déranger (s.o.).
— v. intr. Se dissiper (lit. and fig.).

dissipated [-id] adj. Dissolu, débauché (dissolute).

dissipation [,disi'pei∫ən] n. Dispersion f. (of clouds). ‖ Fig. Dispersion f. (of one's energies); dissipation (of resources, a person).

dissociable [di'sou∫iəbl] adj. Dissociable.

dissocial [-∫əl] adj. Insociable.

dissociate [-∫ieit] v. tr. Désunir, séparer (see SEPARATE); to dissociate oneself from, se désolidariser de. ‖ Chim. Dissocier.
— v. intr. Comm. Rompre une association.

dissociation [di,sou∫i'ei∫ən] n. Séparation, dissociation f. ‖ Chim., Philos. Dissociation f.

dissolubility [di,sɔlju'biliti] n. Dissolubilité f.

dissoluble [di'sɔljubl] adj. Dissoluble.

dissolute ['disəlju:t] adj. Dissolu.

dissolutely [-li] adv. D'une manière dissolue.

dissoluteness [-nis] n. Débauche f.

dissolution [,disə'lu:∫ən] n. Dissolution, fonte f. ‖ Jur. Résiliation f. (of a contract); dissolution f. (of a marriage, meeting, society). ‖ Fin. Liquidation f.

dissolvable [di'zɔlvəbl] adj. Soluble (in, dans). ‖ Jur. Dissoluble.

dissolve [di'zɔlv] v. tr. Dissoudre, faire fondre (to liquefy). ‖ Désagréger, décomposer (to disintegrate). ‖ Jur. Résilier (a contract); dissoudre (a society). ‖ Fig. Dissiper, disperser (clouds); disperser (crowd); dissiper (illusions).
— v. intr. Se dissoudre, fondre. ‖ Cinem. Enchaîner (into, sur). ‖ Fig. Fondre (into tears).
— n. Cinem. Enchaînement m.

dissolvent [-ənt] adj., n. Dissolvant m.

dissonance ['disənəns] n. Mus. Dissonance f. ‖ Fig. Dissentiment m.

dissonant [-ənt] adj. Mus. Dissonant. ‖ Fig. En désaccord (from, to, avec).

dissuade [di'sweid] v. tr. Dissuader, détourner (from, de). ‖ Désapprouver, déconseiller (an action).

dissuasion [-ʒən] n. Dissuasion f.

dissuasive [-siv] adj. Dissuasif.

dissyllabic [,disi'læbik] adj. Gramm. Dissyllabique.

dissyllable [di'siləbl] n. Gramm. Dissyllabe m.

dissymmetrical [,disi'metrikəl] adj. Dissymétrique.

dissymmetry [di'simetri] n. Dissymétrie f.

distaff ['distɑ:f] n. Quenouille f. ‖ Fig. Côté féminin f.; on the distaff side, du côté maternel.

distance ['distəns] n. Distance f. (from, de) [in space]; at a distance, à distance, de loin; at a distance of two kilometres, à deux kilomètres de distance. ‖ Distance (in time); at a distance of two centuries, à deux cents ans d'écart. ‖ Eloignement m.; the senses are deceived by distance, l'éloignement trompe les sens. ‖ Lointain m.; in the distance, au loin. ‖ Mus. Intervalle m. ‖ Arts. Lointain m. ‖ Sports. Distance éliminatoire f. ‖ Fig. Distance f.; to keep one's distance, tenir ses distances; distance of manner, allure distante.
— v. tr. Distancer (to outrun). ‖ Eloigner, situer à distance. ‖ Arts. Reculer, donner de la profondeur à.

distant [-ənt] adj. Distant (period, sound); éloigné (place); ten miles distant, à dix milles de là. ‖ Jur. Eloigné (cousin). ‖ Fig. Distant. (See ALOOF.)

distantly [-əntli] adv. De loin. ‖ Fig. Avec réserve (or) hauteur.

distaste [dis'teist] n. Dégoût m. (for, pour). [See AVERSION.]

distasteful [-ful] adj. Culin. Peu alléchant, de goût déplaisant (food). ‖ Fig. Déplaisant (to, à).

distemper [dis'tempə*] n. Med. Maladie f. (of dogs); dérangement, malaise m. (of persons). ‖ Jur. Désordre m.
— v. tr. Med. Déranger; détraquer (fam.).

distemper n. Arts. Détrempe f.; badigeon m.
— v. tr. Arts. Peindre en détrempe.

distend [dis'tend] v. tr. Distendre. ‖ Med. Dilater, ballonner.
— v. intr. Se distendre. ‖ Med. Se ballonner.

distensible [dis'tensibl] adj. Extensible. ‖ Med. Dilatable.

distension, U. S. **distention** [-∫ən] n. Distension f. ‖ Med. Dilatation f.; ballonnement m.

distich ['distik] n. Distique m.

distil [dis'til] v. intr. (1). Couler goutte à goutte. ‖ Chim. Se distiller.
— v. tr. Faire couler goutte à goutte. ‖ Chim., Fig. Distiller.

distilland ['distilənd] n. Chim. Produit (m.) à distiller.

distillate ['distilit], **distilment** [dis'tilmənt] n. Chim. Produit (m.) de la distillation.

distiller [dis'tilə*] n. Chim. Distillateur m.

distillery [-əri] n. Chim. Distillerie f.

distinct [dis'tiŋkt] adj. Distinct, séparé, différent (from, de). ‖ Distinct, net (memory, outline, voice). ‖ Net, précis, bien défini (tendency).

distinction [-'tiŋk∫ən] n. Distinction, discrimination f. (between, entre). ‖ Distinction, décoration f. ‖ Qualité distinctive f. ‖ Distinction f.; raffinement m. ‖ Distinction, valeur f.; writer of distinction, écrivain de marque; to gain distinction, se distinguer.

distinctive [-'tiŋktiv] adj. Distinctif. (See CHARACTERISTIC.)

distinctly [-'tiŋktli] adv. Distinctement. ‖ Nettement; incontestablement.

distinctness [-'tiŋktnis] n. Netteté *f.* ‖ Différenciation *f.* (*from*, de).

distingué [di:s'taŋei] adj. Distingué.

distinguish [dis'tiŋgwiʃ] v. tr. Distinguer, discerner, apercevoir (to discern); *to be distinguished*, se distinguer. ‖ Distinguer, caractériser, définir (to define). ‖ Classer, classifier, ranger (*into*, en) [to classify]. ‖ Distinguer, différencier (*from*, de); faire la différence (*from*, avec). [See DISCRIMINATE.] ‖ Distinguer, remarquer, mettre en relief (to notice); *to distinguish oneself*, se distinguer.
— v. intr. Distinguer, établir la distinction (*between*, entre).

distinguishable [-əbl] adj. Distinguable, reconnaissable. ‖ Qu'on peut distinguer (*from*, de).

distinguished [-t] adj. Distingué, raffiné. ‖ Distingué, éminent.

distort [dis'tɔ:t] v. tr. Déformer, décomposer (face). ‖ FIG. Défigurer, déformer, dénaturer; *to become distorted*, se déformer.

distortion [dis'tɔ:ʃən] n. Déformation *f.* (of an image). ‖ Décomposition *f.* (of features); contorsion *f.* (of lines). ‖ FIG. Déformation, dénaturation, déviation *f.*

distortionist [-nist] n. SPORTS. Contortionniste *s.* ‖ ARTS. Caricaturiste *s.*

distract [dis'trækt] v. tr. Distraire (*from*, de). ‖ Désaxer (life); rendre fou, affoler (s.o.).

distractedly [-idli] adv. Follement. ‖ Eperdument.

distraction [dis'trækʃən] n. Distraction, inattention; inadvertance *f.* ‖ Distraction, diversion, récréation *f.*; amusement *m.* ‖ Trouble, affolement *m.*; agitation *f.* ‖ Déraison *f.* (madness); *to drive to distraction*, rendre fou, conduire à la folie.

distrain [dis'trein] v. intr. JUR. Saisir.

distrainee [,distrei'ni:] n. JUR. Saisi *m.*

distrainer [dis'treinə*] n. JUR. Saisissant *m.*

distraint [-'treint] n. JUR. Saisie *f.*

distraught [dis'trɔ:t] adj. Egaré.

distress [dis'tres] n. Détresse, désolation, angoisse *f.*; désarroi *m.* (anguish). ‖ Détresse, misère *f.* (poverty). ‖ Détresse *f.*; péril *m.* (danger). ‖ MED. Epuisement *m.* ‖ NAUT. *In distress*, en perdition. ‖ JUR. Saisie-gagerie *f.* ‖ **Distress-sale**, n. JUR. Vente (*f.*) de biens saisis. ‖ **Distress-warrant**, n. JUR. Mandat (*m.*) de saisie.
— v. tr. Désoler, affliger (to afflict); angoisser, rendre anxieux (to anguish). ‖ MED. Epuiser.

distressed [-t] adj. Attristé, peiné (upset). ‖ Appauvri, dans le besoin, indigent (impoverished); *distressed area*, région en plein marasme économique. ‖ Patiné à l'ancienne (made to look old).

distressing [-iŋ] adj. Désolant, angoissant (grievous). ‖ Désolé, angoissé (afflicted). ‖ Dans la détresse, misérable (poor). ‖ MED. Epuisé.

distributable [dis'tribju:təbl] adj. Distribuable.

distributary [-jutəri] n. GEOGR. Défluent *m.*

distribute [-ju:t] v. tr. Distribuer, répartir (to allot); distribuer, classer (to classify); distribuer, dispenser (to dispense); distribuer, disperser (to disperse); distribuer, diviser (to divide).

distribution [,distri'bju:ʃən] n. Distribution, répartition; classification; dispensation; dispersion; division *f.*

distributive [dis'tribjutiv] adj., n. GRAMM. Distributif.

distributor [-ə*] n. Distributeur *m.*; distributrice *f.* ‖ COMM. Concessionnaire *m.* ‖ AUTOM. Delco *m.*; *distributor arm*, retors du Delco.

district ['distrikt] n. District *m.*; région *f.* (country). ‖ Circonscription *f.* (constituency); canton *m.* (within a department); arrondissement *m.* (in Paris); quartier *m.* (in a town); secteur *m.* (served by public utility). ‖ JUR. U. S. *District attorney*, procureur du gouvernement; *district court*, Cour fédérale. ‖ COMM. *District manager*, directeur régional.

distrust [dis'trʌst] n. Défiance *f.* ‖ Soupçons *m. pl.*
— v. tr. Se défier (or) méfier de.

distrustful [-ful] adj. Défiant (*of*, à l'égard de). ‖ Qui n'a pas confiance en soi. (See DIFFIDENT.)

distrustfully [-fuli] adv. Avec méfiance.

disturb [dis'tə:b] v. tr. Troubler, agiter (to agitate); troubler, inquiéter (to disquiet); déranger (to trouble). ‖ PHYS. Perturber. ‖ JUR. Troubler dans la jouissance d'un droit.

disturbance [-əns] n. Trouble *m.*; agitation *f.*; *disturbance in the night*, tapage nocturne. ‖ Trouble, soulèvement *m.*; émeute *f.* (riot). ‖ Trouble *m.*; anxiété, inquiétude *f.* (anguish). ‖ Dérangement *m.* (trouble). ‖ PHYS. Perturbation *f.* ‖ JUR. Trouble (*m.*) de jouissance.

disunion [dis'ju:njən] n. Désunion *f.*

disunite [,disju'nait] v. tr. Désunir.
— v. intr. Se désunir.

disuse [dis'ju:z] v. tr. Ne plus utiliser, cesser d'employer.
— [dis'ju:s] n. Abandon *m.*; mise (*f.*) de côté (discarding). ‖ Désuétude *f.* (of a custom, word); *to fall into disuse*, se perdre (practice). ‖ JUR. Abrogation *f.* (of a law).

disyllabic [,disi'læbik] adj. GRAMM. Disyllabique.

disyllable [di'siləbl] n. GRAMM. Disyllabe *m.*

ditch [ditʃ] n. Fossé *m.* (trench). ‖ Caniveau *m.* (beside a road); rigole *f.* (in a field); douve *f.* (surrounding a castle). ‖ SPORTS. Douve *f.* ‖ FAM. Grande tasse *f.* (sea); *to die in the last ditch*, tenir jusqu'à la dernière limite.
— v. tr. Creuser un fossé dans. ‖ AUTOM. Faire verser (a car). ‖ FAM. Laisser tomber (s.o.).
— v. intr. Creuser un fossé. ‖ AUTOM. Verser dans le fossé. ‖ AVIAT. Faire un amerrissage forcé.

ditcher [-ə*] n. Cantonnier *m.*

dither ['diðə*] v. intr. FAM. Trembler, s'agiter.
— n. FAM. Tremblotement *m.*; *in a dither*, dans tous ses états.

dithery [-ri] adj. FAM. Tremblotant, nerveux.

dithyramb ['diθiræm] n. Dithyrambe *m.*

dithyrambic [diθi'ræmbik] adj. Dithyrambique.

dittany ['ditəni] n. BOT. Dictame *m.*

ditto ['ditou] n. Idem. ‖ COMM. Dito *m.* ‖ **Ditto-machine**, n. Duplicateur *m.*

ditty ['diti] n. MUS. Chansonnette *f.*

ditty-bag ['ditibæg] n. NAUT. Trousse *f.*

diuresis [,daiju'ri:sis] n. MED. Diurèse *f.*

diuretic [-'retik] adj., n. MED. Diurétique *m.*

diurnal [dai'ə:nl] adj. Diurne. ‖ † Journalier.
— n. † Journal *m.* (diary). ‖ ECCLES. Diurnal *m.*

diva ['di:və] n. THEATR. Diva *f.*

divagate [,daivəgeit] v. tr. Errer. (See WANDER.) ‖ FIG. Divaguer.

divagation [,daivə'geiʃən] n. Errance *f.* ‖ FIG. Divagation *f.*

divalent [dai'veilənt] adj. CHIM. Bivalent.

divan [di'væn] n. Divan *m.* (council, room, sofa). ‖ Fumoir *m.* (smoking room). ‖ **Divan-bed**, n. Divan-lit *m.* ‖ **Divan-cover**, n. Jeté de lit *m.*

divaricate [dai'værikeit] adj. ZOOL., BOT. Divariqué.
— v. intr. Bifurquer. (See FORK.)

dive [daiv] v. intr. Enfoncer, plonger (*into*, dans) [one's hand]. ‖ SPORTS. Plonger, faire un plongeon (*into*, dans). ‖ NAUT. Plonger, faire une plongée. ‖ AVIAT. Piquer. ‖ FIG. Se plonger (*into*, dans). ‖ FAM. S'engouffrer, se précipiter, piquer du nez (*into*, dans).
— n. Action (*f.*) de plonger; *to make a dive into*, fouiller (or) fourrager dans. ‖ SPORTS. Plongeon *m.* ‖ NAUT. Plongée *f.* ‖ AVIAT. Piqué *m.* ‖ U. S. Assommoir, bistrot *m.*; boîte *f.* ‖ **Dive-bomb**, v. tr. AVIAT. Bombarder en piqué. ‖ **Dive-bombing**, n. AVIAT. Bombardement en piqué *m.*

diver [-ə*] n. SPORTS. Plongeur *s.* ‖ NAUT. Scaphandrier *m.* ‖ ZOOL. Plongeon *m.*

diverge [dai'və:dʒ] v. intr. S'écarter, dévier, bifurquer. (See DEVIATE.) ‖ PHYS., MATH. Diverger, différer.
— v. tr. Faire diverger.

divergence [-əns] n. PHYS., MATH., FIG. Divergence f.

divergent [-ənt] adj. PHYS., MATH., FIG. Divergent.

divers ['daivə:z] adj. Divers, plusieurs (several).

diverse [dai'və:s] adj. Divers, différent. (See DIFFERENT.) ‖ Varié, diversifié.

diversely [-li] adv. Diversement.

diversification [dai,və:sifi'keiʃən] n. Variation f.

diversify [dai'və:sifai] v. tr. (2). Diversifier. (See VARY.)

diversion [dai'və:ʃən] n. Déviation f. (of a river). ‖ Diversion f.; dérivatif m. (from, à). ‖ Divertissement m., distraction f. (pastime). ‖ AUTOM. Déviation f. ‖ MILIT. Diversion f.

diversionary [-ri] adj. MILIT. De diversion.

diversity [dai'və:siti] n. Diversité f.

divert [dai'və:t] v. tr. Détourner, dévier (from, de); faire dévier (the conversation). ‖ Distraire (from, de) [the attention]; to divert s.o. from his grief, faire diversion à la douleur de qqn. ‖ Divertir (see AMUSE); to divert oneself, se distraire, se divertir. ‖ MILIT. Distraire (from, de) [troops].

diverting [-iŋ] adj. Divertissant.

dives ['daivi:z] n. Mauvais riche m.

divest [dai'vest] v. tr. Dépouiller (of, de) [clothing]. ‖ FIG. Déposséder (of, de) [one's rank]; priver (of, de) [one's rights]; to divest oneself of, se dépouiller de. (See STRIP.)

divestiture [-itʃə*] n. JUR. Dépossession f.

divestment [-mənt] n. Dépouillement m. ‖ JUR. Dépossession f.

dividable [di'vaidəbl] adj. Divisible.

divide [di'vaid] v. tr. Diviser, séparer (see SEPARATE); partager (in, into, en). ‖ Répartir, distribuer (see DISTRIBUTE); se partager (among, entre); to be divided into, se répartir en. ‖ MATH. Diviser (by, par). ‖ JUR. Faire voter. ‖ FIG. Diviser, désunir.
— v. intr. Se diviser, se séparer; se partager. ‖ MATH. Etre divisible (by, par). ‖ JUR. Voter, procéder au scrutin.
— n. U. S. Ligne (f.) de partage des eaux.

divided [-id] adj. Divise. ‖ **Divided-skirt,** n. Jupe-culotte f.

dividend ['dividend] n. MATH., FIN. Dividende m. ‖ FAM. Pl. Profits m. pl. ‖ **Dividend-warrant,** n. Coupon (m.) d'arrérages.

divider [di'vaidə*] n. ELECTR. Diviseur m. ‖ Pl. MATH. Compas (m.) à pointes sèches.

dividual [di'vidjuəl] adj. Divisible (separable); divisé (separate); partagé (shared).

divination [,divi'neiʃən] n. Divination f.

divinatory [di'vinətəri] adj. Divinatoire (art).

divine [di'vain] adj. ECCLES., FIG., FAM. Divin.
— n. ECCLES. Théologien; ecclésiastique m.

divine v. tr., intr. Deviner.

divinely [-li] adv. ECCLES., FIG. Divinement.

diviner [-ə*] n. Devin m., devineresse f.

diving ['daiviŋ] n. SPORTS. Plongeon m. ‖ AVIAT. Piqué m. ‖ **Diving-bell,** n. NAUT. Cloche (f.) à plongeur. ‖ **Diving-board,** n. SPORTS. Plongeoir m. ‖ **Diving-suit,** n. NAUT. Scaphandre m.

divining [di'vainiŋ] adj. Divinatoire (rod).

divinity [di'viniti] n. Divinité f. (deity); dieu m. (god). ‖ ECCLES. Divinité f. (divine being or nature); théologie f. (study). ‖ CULIN. U. S. Divinity fudge, sorte de nougat.

divinize ['divinaiz] v. tr. Diviniser. (See DEIFY.)

divisibility [di,vizi'biliti] n. Divisibilité f.

divisible [di'vizibl] adj. Divisible.

division [di'viʒən] n. Division, séparation f. ‖ Partage m.; répartition, distribution f. ‖ Séparation, cloison f. (partition). ‖ Division, subdivision f.; compartiment m. (section). ‖ Degré m. (of a scale). ‖

MATH., MILIT. Division f. ‖ JUR. Vote, scrutin m.; to insist on a division, exiger la mise aux voix. ‖ FIG. Division, désunion, dissension f. (discord).

divisional [-l] adj. MILIT. Divisionnaire.

divisive [di'vaiziv] adj. Qui entraîne la division.

divisor [-ə*] n. MATH. Diviseur m.

divorce [di'vɔ:s] n. JUR. Divorce m. (from, d'avec); to sue for a divorce, demander le divorce. ‖ FIG. Divorce.
— v. tr. JUR. Prononcer le divorce de (a couple); divorcer d'avec (one's husband, wife); to have been divorced, avoir (or) être divorcé.

divorcee [,divɔ:'si:] n. Divorcé s.

divorcement [di'vɔ:smənt] n. JUR. Divorce m.; bill of divorcement, ordonnance de divorce. ‖ FIG. Divorce.

divot ['divət] n. SPORTS. Motte (f.) de gazon (in golf).

divulgation [,daivʌl'geiʃən], **divulgence** [di'vʌlʒəns] n. Divulgation f.

divulge [di'vʌldʒ] v. tr. Divulguer. (See REVEAL.)

divvy ['divi] n. FAM. Quote-part f. ‖ FIN. FAM. Dividende m.
— v. tr. (2). To divvy up, FAM. Partager, se partager.

dixie ['diksi] n. MILIT. Gamelle; marmite f.

D.I.Y. [di:ai'wai] abbr. do-it-yourself, bricolage m.

dizzily ['dizili] adv. Avec une impression de vertige. ‖ Vertigineusement.

dizziness [-nis] n. MED. Vertige, étourdissement m.

dizzy [-i] adj. MED. Vertigineux (heights). ‖ MED. Etourdi, pris de vertige (person). ‖ U. S. FAM. Sot.
— v. tr. (2). MED. Donner le vertige à, faire tourner la tête à.

D.N.A. [di:en'ei] n. MED. Abbr. deoxyribonucleic acid, acide désoxyribonucléique, A. D. N.

do [du:] v. tr. (47).

---

1. Accomplir. — 2. Travailler à. — 3. Terminer. — 4. Occasionner. — 5. Arranger. — 6. Traduire. — 7. Parcourir. — 8. Visiter. — 9. Rendre. — 10. Mettre. — 11. Contrefaire. — 12. Convenir. — 13. THEATR. — 14. AUTOM. — 15. COMM. — 16. CULIN. — 17, 18. FAM. — 19. To do again. — 20. To do away with. — 21. To do down. — 22. To do in. — 23. To do out. — 24. To do over. — 25. To do up.

---

1. Faire, accomplir, effectuer (to perform); if do it I can, si faire se peut; never do things by halves, ne faites jamais rien à moitié; to do one's duty, work, faire son devoir, son travail; to have nothing to do with, n'avoir rien à faire (or) à voir avec; do what she would, she couldn't, elle a eu beau faire, elle n'a pas pu; he has nothing to do with it, il n'entre pas là-dedans; what can I do about it?, que voulez-vous que j'y fasse?; what else can be done?, qu'y faire?; what have you done with my umbrella?, qu'avez-vous fait de mon parapluie? ‖ 2. Faire, travailler à, s'occuper à; to do nothing, ne rien faire; to do too much, en faire trop. ‖ 3. Terminer, achever, finir (to end); has she done weeping?, a-t-elle fini de pleurer? ‖ 4. Faire, causer, occasionner (to cause); to do harm, faire du tort; who did this to you?, qui vous a fait cela? ‖ 5. Arranger, mettre au net; nettoyer (to clean); to do one's hair, se coiffer; to do one's nails, se faire les ongles; to do one's shoes, faire ses chaussures. ‖ 6. Traduire (to translate); to do Shakespeare into French, mettre Shakespeare en français. ‖ 7. Faire, parcourir, couvrir (to cover) [distance]. ‖ 8. Visiter (to tour); to do France in three months, visiter la France en trois mois; to do the valley of the Loire, faire la vallée de la Loire. ‖ 9. Rendre (to give); to do the honours of, faire les honneurs de; to do justice, a service, rendre justice, un service. ‖

10. Mettre ; *to do to death,* mettre à mort. ‖
11. Faire, contrefaire (to feign) ; *to do the great lady,* faire la grande dame. ‖ 12. Convenir (to suit) ; *that will do me very well,* ça m'ira très bien. ‖
13. THEATR., FAM. Jouer (a part) ; monter (a play). ‖ 14. AUTOM. *To do sixty miles an hour,* faire du cent à l'heure. ‖ 15. COMM. *To do only wholesale dealing,* ne faire que le gros ; *to do the suburbs,* faire (or) prospecter la banlieue. ‖ 16. CULIN. Cuire (food) ; traiter (guests) ; *to do oneself well,* ne se priver de rien, bien se nourrir ; *well done,* bien cuit. ‖ 17. FAM. Ereinter, esquinter ; *to be done,* n'en plus pouvoir, être à bout. ‖ 18. FAM. Refaire (to sheat) ; *to do s.o. out of sth.,* carotter qqch. à qqn ; *you've been done,* on vous a eu. ‖ 19. To do again, refaire. ‖ 20. To do away with, abolir (a custom) ; supprimer (s.o., sth.). ‖ 21. To do down, FAM. Rouler, refaire (s.o.). ‖ 22. To do in, FAM. Ereinter, esquinter (to exhaust) ; POP. Buter, zigouiller, refroidir (to kill). ‖ 23. To do out, nettoyer, faire (to clean). ‖ 24. To do over, enduire (*with,* de) ; refaire. ‖ 25. To do up, emmailloter (a baby) ; boutonner (a dress) ; emballer (goods) ; cacheter (a letter) ; envelopper (a parcel) ; retaper (an old hat) ; refaire, remettre à neuf (a room) ; CULIN. Préparer, accommoder (food) ; FAM. Ereinter (s.o.) ; *done up,* fourbu, brisé, mort, à bout ; *to do up one's face,* se maquiller ; faire le ravalement (fam.).
— v. intr.

> 1. Agir. — 2. Travailler. — 3. Finir. — 4. Procéder. — 5. Convenir. — 6. Suffire. — 7. Se porter. — 8. Fonctionner. — 9. To do for. — 10. To do with. — 11. To do without.

1. Agir, faire (to behave) ; *he did right,* il a bien fait ; *to do better to,* faire mieux de ; *to do well by,* bien agir envers ; *he will do well,* il réussira. ‖ 2. Agir, travailler (to work) ; *in doing we learn,* on apprend en travaillant. ‖ 3. Faire, finir (to finish) ; *have you done?,* terminé? ‖ 4. Agir, procéder (to proceed) ; *how shall I do?,* comment faire (or) m'y prendre? ‖ 5. Convenir (to be suitable) ; *the blue hat will do,* le chapeau bleu ira bien (or) fera l'affaire. ‖ 6. Suffire (to be sufficient) ; *that will do!,* ça suffit, assez! ‖ 7. Aller, se porter (to fare) ; *he is doing well,* il se porte bien ; *how do you do?,* comment allez-vous? ; enchanté de faire votre connaissance. ‖ 8. Aller, fonctionner (to go on) ; *nothing going,* rien ne va, rien à faire, ça ne marche pas. ‖ 9. To do for, FAM. Tenir le ménage de ; FAM. Faire son affaire à (to kill) ; *to be done for,* avoir son compte ; *to do for oneself,* se couler. ‖ 10. To do with, se contenter de (to be content with) ; avoir du rapport avec, regarder (to concern) ; avoir affaire à (to deal with) ; en avoir fini avec (to finish). ‖ 11. To do without, se passer de ; *I can do without your remarks,* je vous dispense de vos observations. — v. substitute. Faire ; *I'll warn him.* — *Don't,* je vais l'avertir. — N'en faites rien ; *may I look at your book?* — *Please do,* puis-je regarder votre livre? — Faites ; *she wrote this letter much better than he could have done,* elle a écrit cette lettre beaucoup mieux qu'il n'aurait pu le faire. ‖ *Don't act as they do,* n'agissez pas comme eux ; *do you like wine?* — *I do, I don't,* aimez-vous le vin? — Oui, non ; *he sings well.* — *Does he?,* il chante bien. — Vraiment? ; *he sings well, so does she,* il chante bien, elle aussi ; *you eat too much.* — *I certainly do,* vous mangez trop. — C'est bien vrai ; *you hate me!* — *I don't,* vous me détestez. — Pas du tout.
— v. auxil. *Did her mother help her?,* sa mère l'aidait-elle? ; *didn't your brother deliver a lecture?,* votre frère n'a-t-il pas fait une conférence? ; *do not lie,* ne mentez pas ; *he does not do what he is told,* il ne fait pas ce qu'on lui dit. ‖ (Inversion.) *Never*

did I say anything of the sort, jamais je n'ai rien dit de tel. ‖ (Emphasis.) *Do give my best wishes to your father,* veuillez transmettre mes meilleurs vœux à Monsieur votre père ; *do stay to dinner with us,* restez dîner avec nous ; *do come and see me,* venez me voir, je vous prie ; *she did transmit your request to him,* elle lui a certainement transmis votre demande.
— n. FAM. Escroquerie *f.*

do [dou] n. MUS. Do, ut *m. invar.*

do. Written abbr. for *ditto,* idem, id.

doable ['du:əbl] adj. Faisable.

dobbin ['dɔbin] n. ZOOL. Percheron, cheval de trait (or) de labour *m.* ‖ U. S. FAM. Canasson *m.*

Doberman(n) ['doubəmən] n. ZOOL. *Doberman (pinscher),* doberman.

doc [dɔk] n. FAM. Toubib *m.*

docile ['dousail] adj. Docile.

docility [do'siliti] n. Docilité *f.*

dock [dɔk] n. BOT. Patience *f.*

dock n. Tronçon *m.* (of the tail). ‖ Trousse-queue *m.* — v. tr. Couper la queue à, écouer (an animal). ‖ † Couper les cheveux à (s.o.). ‖ Retrancher, rogner, (*off,* sur). ‖ **Dock-tailed,** adj. Courtaud (horse).

dock n. JUR. Banc (*m.*) des accusés.

dock n. NAUT. Bassin, dock *m.* (see DRY-DOCK) ; *floating dock,* dock flottant ; *wet dock,* bassin à flot. ‖ NAUT. Quai *m.* (wharf) ; *loading dock,* embarcadère. ‖ CH. DE F. Quai de garage *m.* ‖ AUTOM. *In dock,* en réparation. — v. tr. NAUT. Faire entrer en dock. ‖ CH. DE F. Garer. — v. intr. NAUT. Entrer en dock.

dockage [-idʒ] n. NAUT., JUR. Droits (*m. pl.*) de bassin.

docker [-ə*] n. Docker *m.*

docket [-it] n. Fiche *f.* (of a document). ‖ JUR. Registre (*m.*) des jugements ; U. S. Rôle *m.* (causelist) ; bordereau, dossier *m.* (list) ; récépissé (*m.*) de douane. — v. tr. Faire une fiche pour, étiqueter. ‖ JUR. Consigner.

dockland [-,lænd] n. Quartier (*m.*) des docks.

dockyard [-jɑ:d] n. NAUT. Arsenal, port maritime *m.* ; chantier (*m.*) de constructions navales.

doctor ['dɔktə*] n. Docteur *m.* ; *Doctor of Laws, of Science,* docteur en droit, ès sciences. ‖ MED. Docteur, médecin *m.* (see PHYSICIAN) ; *Doctor X,* le docteur X ; *to be under the doctor's care,* être entre les mains du médecin, suivre un traitement. ‖ ECCLES. Docteur *m.* (of the church). — v. tr. Donner le grade de docteur à. ‖ MED. Soigner ; *to doctor oneself,* se droguer. ‖ FAM. Rafistoler, retaper (to do up) ; tripatouiller (to tamper with). — v. intr. U. S. MED. Pratiquer la médecine (doctor) ; être en traitement (patient).

doctoral [-rəl] adj. Doctoral ; *doctoral dissertation,* thèse de doctorat.

doctorate [-rət] n. Doctorat *m.* ; *to take one's doctorate,* passer son doctorat (or) sa thèse.

doctrinaire [,dɔktri'nɛə *], **doctrinarian** [-riən] n. Doctrinaire *m.* — adj. De doctrinaire.

doctrinal [dɔk'trainl] adj. Doctrinal.

doctrine ['dɔktrin] n. Doctrine *f.* ; *it is a matter of doctrine that,* il est de doctrine courante que.

document ['dɔkjumənt] n. Document *m.* ; *to collect documents,* se documenter. ‖ COMM. *Draft with documents attached,* traité documentaire. ‖ JUR. Pièce à conviction *f.* ‖ **Document-case,** n. Porte-documents *m.* — [-ment] v. tr. Documenter. ‖ Prouver à l'aide de documents.

documentary [,dɔkju'mentəri] adj. Documentaire.

‖ Cinem. *Documentary director,* documentariste; *documentary film,* documentaire.
— n. Cinem. Documentaire *m.*

documentation [,dɔkjumen'teiʃən] n. Documentation *f.*

dodder ['dɔdə*] n. Bot. Cuscute *f.*

dodder v. intr. Branler (or) dodeliner du chef (to nod); chanceler, avancer en tremblotant; traîner la patte (fam.) [to walk]. ‖ Autom. **To dodder along,** aller son petit train; rouler pépère (fam.).

dodderer [-ə*] n. Fam. Décati, croulant, gâteux *m.*

doddle ['dɔdl] n. Fam. *It's a doddle,* c'est de la tarte (or) du gâteau.

dodecagon [dou'dekəgɔn] n. Math. Dodécagone *m.*

dodecahedron [,doudekə'hi:drən] n. Math. Dodécaèdre *m.*

dodge [dɔdʒ] v. intr. Se jeter de côté; *to dodge about,* faire des tours et des détours. ‖ Sports. Esquiver. ‖ Fig. Biaiser, tergiverser, user de détours.
— v. tr. Esquiver (a blow). ‖ Éluder (a difficulty, question); échapper à (a pursuer); éviter (s.o.); *to dodge the column,* tirer au flanc, se défiler. ‖ Déplacer, promener çà et là (to move). ‖ Dérouter, amener par des petits chemins, faire marcher, lanterner (to baffle).
— n. Saut (or) mouvement de côté *m.* ‖ Fig. Détour, subterfuge *m.; to be up to all the dodges,* connaître tous les trucs (or) tous les joints (or) toutes les ficelles. ‖ Fam. Système, truc *m.; invention f.* (contraption).

Dodgem ['dɔdʒəm] n. (nom déposé). Auto tamponneuse *f.*

dodger [-ə*] n. Milit. Embusqué *m.* ‖ Fam. Roublard *m.*

dodgy [-i] adj. Malin.

dodo ['doudou] n. Zool. Dodo, dronte *m.* ‖ Fig. Fam. Fossile *m.; as dead as a, the dodo,* complètement mort.
— N.B. Deux pluriels : *dodos, dodoes.*

doe [dou] n. Zool. Daine *f.* (female deer); hase *f.* (female hare); lapine *f.* (female rabbit). ‖ **Doe-skin,** n. Daim *m.*

doer ['duə*] n. Personne agissante (or) active *f.* ‖ Faiseur; auteur *m.* (*of,* de).

does [dʌz]. See DO.

doff [dɔf] v. tr. Enlever, ôter. (See TAKE OFF.)

dog [dɔg] n. Zool. Chien *m.* ‖ Zool. Mâle *m.* (of fox, jackal, wolf). ‖ Techn. Clameau *m.* (clamp); chien, cliquet *m.* (pawl). ‖ Fam. Type *m.; dirty dog,* salaud, sale bougre. ‖ Fam. *A dog's life,* une vie de chien; *every dog has his day,* à chacun vient sa chance; *to be top dog,* avoir le dessus, tenir le bon bout; *to go to the dogs,* aller de travers (or) à la ruine, ne pas tourner rond (business concerns); mal tourner (persons); U. S. *to put on the dog,* faire de l'épate; faire le joli cœur; U. S. *to work like a dog,* travailler comme un forcené. ‖ **Dog-biscuit,** n. Biscuit de chien *m.* ‖ **Dog-collar,** n. Collier *m.;* Fam. Col romain *m.* (clerical). ‖ **Dog-days,** n. Canicule *f.* ‖ **Dog-ear,** n. Corne *f.;* v. tr. Corner (a page). ‖ **Dog-fight,** n. Combat (*m.*) de chiens; Aviat. Duel aérien, combat tournoyant *m.;* Fam. Bagarre *f.* ‖ **Dog-fish,** n. Zool. Chien de mer *m.* ‖ **Dog-headed,** adj. Cynocéphale. ‖ **Dog-iron,** n. Techn. Crochet d'assemblage *m.* ‖ **Dog-kennel,** n. Chenil *m.* ‖ **Dog-latin,** n. Latin (*m.*) de cuisine. ‖ **Dog-rose,** n. Bot. Eglantine *f.* ‖ **Dog-show,** n. Exposition canine *f.* ‖ **Dog-star,** n. Astron. Sirius *m.* ‖ **Dog-tired,** adj. Fam. Fourbu, éreinté, vanné. ‖ **Dog-watch,** n. Naut. Petit quart *m.*
— v. tr. Suivre, filer (s.o.); *to dog s.o.'s footsteps,* emboîter le pas à qqn. ‖ Techn. Serrer avec un clameau. ‖ Fig. Cramponner.

dogberry ['dɔgberi] n. Bot. Cornouille *f.* ‖ **Dog-berry-tree,** n. Bot. Cornouiller *m.*

doge [doudʒ] n. Doge *m.*

dogged ['dɔgid] adj. Obstiné. (See STUBBORN.)

doggedly [-li] adv. Avec opiniâtreté.

doggedness [-nis] n. Ténacité, opiniâtreté *f.*

dogger ['dɔgə*] n. Naut. Dogre *m.*

doggerel ['dɔgərəl] adj. De mirliton (verse).
— n. Rimaillerie *f.*

doggie ['dɔgi] n. Fam. Toutou *m.*

doggish [-iʃ] adj. Hargneux, grincheux. (See SNAPPISH.) ‖ U. S. Fam. Plastronneur.

doggo ['dɔgou] adj. Fam. *To lie doggo,* se tenir peinard.

doggone ['dɔgɔn] adj. Pop. Sacré, satané.
— adv. Pop. Vachement, sacrément, fichtrement.
— v. tr. Pop. *Doggone it,* la vache!; *doggone him,* quel salaud!

doggy ['dɔgi] n. Fam. Toutou *m.*
— adj. De chien; à chiens, qui aime les chiens.

doghouse ['dɔghaus] n. Niche (*f.*) à chien; chenil *m.* ‖ U. S. Fam. Trente-sixième dessous *m.*

dogma ['dɔgmə] n. Eccles., Fig. Dogme *m.*

dogmatic [dɔg'mætik] adj. Eccles., Philos., Fig. Dogmatique.

dogmatically [-əli] adv. Dogmatiquement.

dogmatics [-s] n. Eccles. Dogmatique *f.*

dogmatism ['dɔgmətizm] n. Dogmatisme *m.*

dogmatist [-tist] n. Dogmatiste *m.*

dogmatize [-taiz] v. tr. Dogmatiser.

do-gooder [du:'gudə*] n. Redresseur (*m.*) de torts.

dogwood ['dɔgwud] n. Bot. Cornouiller *m.*

doh [dou] n. Mus. See DO.

doily ['dɔili] m. Garde-nappe, napperon *m.*

doing ['duiŋ] n. Œuvre *f.; it is not of my doing,* je n'y suis pour rien. ‖ Action *f.* ‖ Agissement *m.;* conduite *f.;* pl. façons (*f. pl.*) d'agir; faits et gestes *m. pl.* ‖ Pl. Fam. Gala *m.;* réjouissances *f. pl.*

doings ['du:iŋz] n. sg. Fam. Machin, truc, bidule *m.*

doit [dɔit] n. Fin. Liard *m.* ‖ Fam. Rien *m.*

doldrums ['dɔldrəmz] n. pl. Naut. Calme plat *m.* (calm); zone (*f.*) des calmes (region). ‖ Fam. Cafard *m.* (blues); marasme *m.* (stagnation).

dole [doul] n. Distribution *f.* (of money). ‖ Charités *f. pl.;* secours *m. pl.* (alms). ‖ Jur. Allocation (*f.*) de chômage. ‖ † Destinée *f.*
— v. tr. **To dole out,** distribuer parcimonieusement (or) au compte-gouttes (fam.).

dole n. † Douleur *f.*

doleful [-ful] adj. Morne, lugubre (appearance); plaintif (cry); triste (news); triste, dolent, lamentable (person).

dolefully [-fuli] adv. Tristement.

dolefulness [-fulnis] n. Tristesse, mélancolie, allure dolente *f.*

dolichocephalic [,dɔlikouse'fælik] adj. Dolichocéphale.

doll [dɔl] n. Poupée *f.* (girl, toy).
— v. tr. **To doll up,** orner.
— v. intr. Fam. **To doll up,** se parer; se bichonner.

dollar ['dɔlə*] n. Fin. Dollar *m.* ‖ U. S. *Dollar diplomacy,* diplomatie par allocation de crédits.

dollop ['dɔləp] n. Fam. Tas *m.*

dolly ['dɔli] n. Poupée *f.* (doll). ‖ Agitateur *m.* (in laundering). ‖ Med., Fam. Poupée *f.* (bandaged finger). ‖ Techn. Chariot *m.* ‖ Cinem. Chariot, travelling *m.* ‖ Fam. Poupée, minette *f.* ‖ **Dolly-bird,** n. Fam. Minette, poupée *f.* ‖ **Dolly-mixture,** n. Bonbons assortis *m. pl.*
— adj. Fam. Mignon, chouette.
— v. tr. (2). Fam. **To dolly up,** bichonner, pomponner (person); briquer (place).
— v. intr. (2). Cinem. *To dolly in, up,* faire un travelling avant, avancer la caméra; *to dolly out,* faire un travelling arrière, reculer la caméra.

dolman ['dɔlmən] n. Doliman *m.* ‖ MILIT. Dolman *m.* ‖ **Dolman-sleeve,** n. Manche-kimono *f.*

dolmen ['dɔlmən] n. Dolmen *m.*

Dolomite ['dɔləmait] n. GEOL. Dolomite *f.* ‖ Pl. GEOGR. Dolomites *f. pl.*

dolomitic [,dɔlə'mitik] adj. Dolomitique.

dolorous ['dɔlərəs] adj. Douloureux.

dolose [do'lous] adj. JUR. Dolosif.

dolour ['doulə*] n. Douleur *f.*

dolphin ['dɔlfin] n. ZOOL. Daurade *f.* (fish); dauphin *m.* (mammal). ‖ NAUT. Bouée (*f.*) de corps mort.

dolt [doult] n. FAM. Cruche, gourde *f.*

doltish [-iʃ] adj. FAM. Lourdaud.

domain [do'mein] n. Domaine *m.* (lit. and fig.).

domanial [do'meiniəl] adj. Domanial.

dome [doum] n. ARCHIT. Coupole *f.;* dôme *m.* ‖ FIG. Dôme *m.;* voûte *f.* ‖ FAM. U. S. Caillou *m.* (head).
— v. tr. Couvrir d'un dôme. ‖ Donner la forme d'un dôme à.

Domesday Book ['du:mzdei'buk] n. † JUR. Cadastre national anglais (*m.*) en 1086.

domestic [də'mestik] adj. Domestique, de la maison (in general); ménager (arts); *domestic strife,* querelles de ménage; *domestic workers,* employés de maison. ‖ National; intérieur (market). ‖ ZOOL. Domestique (animal). ‖ FAM. Casanier, pantouflard, popote (person).
— n. Domestique *s.* (See SERVANT.) ‖ Pl. U. S. Rayon ménager *m.*

domestically [-əli] adv. Domestiquement.

domesticate [-eit] v. tr. ZOOL. Domestiquer, apprivoiser (animal). ‖ BOT. Acclimater. ‖ FIG. Civiliser. ‖ FAM. Rendre pot au feu (or) casanier.

domestication [do,mesti'keiʃən] n. ZOOL. Domestication *f.* ‖ BOT. Acclimatation *f.* ‖ FIG. Civilisation *f.* ‖ FAM. Esprit casanier *m.*

domesticity [,doumes'tisiti] n. Vie de famille *f.* ‖ Pl. Affaires domestiques *f. pl.* ‖ ZOOL. Domesticité *f.* ‖ FAM. Amour du foyer *m.*

domicile ['dɔmisail] n. Domicile *m.* ‖ COMM. Lieu de paiement *m.* (of a bill).
— v. tr. Installer (s.o.). ‖ COMM. Domicilier (a bill).
— v. intr. S'installer, se domicilier.

domiciliary [,dɔmi'siljəri] adj. Domiciliaire.

domiciliate [-ieit] v. tr. Domicilier, installer (*to*, à).
— v. intr. Se domicilier, s'installer.

domiciliation [,dɔmisili'eiʃən] n. Installation *f.* ‖ COMM. Domiciliation *f.*

dominance ['dɔminəns] n. Prédominance *f.* ‖ U.S. Autorité *f.*

dominant [-nənt] adj. Qui domine (height). ‖ MUS., FIG. Dominant.
— n. MUS. Dominante *f.*

dominate [-neit] v. tr., intr. Dominer (lit. and fig.).

dominating [-neitiŋ] adj. Dominateur *m.;* dominatrice *f.* (nation).

domination [,dɔmi'neiʃən] n. ECCLES., FIG. Domination *f.*

dominative ['dɔmi,neitiv] adj. Dominatif.

domineer [,dɔmi'niə*] v. intr. *To domineer over,* dominer tyranniquement, tyranniser, opprimer.

dominical [do'minikəl] adj. Dominical.

Dominican [-kən] adj. ECCLES., GEOGR. Dominicain.
— n. ECCLES. Dominicain *s.*

dominion [də'minjən] n. Domination *f.;* empire *m.* (over, sur); *under dominion of,* sous la férule de. ‖ GEOGR. Dominion *m.* ‖ JUR. Possession *f.*

domino ['dɔminou] (pl. **dominoes** [-z]) n. Domino *m.* (game); *to play dominoes,* jouer aux dominos. ‖ Domino (cloak, mask).

don [dɔn] n. Hidalgo *m.* (nobleman); don *m.* (title). ‖ Professeur *m.* (in a university). ‖ FAM. As, crack *m.* (at, en).

don v. tr. (1). Mettre, enfiler, revêtir (a garment). [See PUT ON.] ‖ S'habiller de (a certain colour or material).

donate [do'neit] v. tr. Donner (sth.); faire don à (s.o.) [*with*, de]. ‖ MED. Donner (blood).

donation [do'neiʃən] n. JUR. Donation *f.*

donative ['dounətiv] adj. Relatif à une donation.
— n. Largesse *f.:* don *m.* (See PRESENT.)

donatory [-təri], **donee** [do'ni:] n. JUR. Donataire *s.*

donatrix [do'neitriks] n. JUR. Donatrice *f.*

done [dʌn] p. p. See DO.
— adj. Correct, convenable; *it isn't done,* ça ne se fait pas; *the done thing,* ce qui se fait, l'usage consacré. ‖ CULIN. Cuit. ‖ FAM. Epuisé, éreinté (exhausted); *done in, up,* fourbu, crevé. ‖ FAM. *Done for,* cuit, fichu (ruined); fichu (dead); subclaquant (almost dead). ‖ LOC. *To be, have done with,* ne plus vouloir entendre parler de.
— interj. D'accord! marché conclu!

donjon ['dɔndʒən] n. Cachot *m.*

donkey ['dɔŋki] n. ZOOL., FAM. Ane, baudet, bourricot *m.* ‖ LOC. *To talk the hind leg(s) off a donkey,* être bavard comme une pie, être un moulin à paroles. ‖ **Donkey-boy,** n. Anier *m.* ‖ **Donkey-jacket,** n. Grosse veste *f.*

donnee [do'nei] n. Donnée *f.;* thème, sujet *m.*

donnish ['dɔniʃ] adj. Professoral. ‖ FAM. Pédant.

donor ['dounə*] n. JUR. Donateur *m.* ‖ MED. Donneur *m.*

don't [dount]. See DO.
— n. Interdiction *f.* (prohibition); chose (*f.*) à ne pas faire (recommendation). ‖ **Don't know,** n. Personne (*f.*) sans opinions.

donzel ['dɔnzl] n. † Damoiseau, page *m.*

doodah ['du:dɑ:], U. S. **doodad** ['du:dæd] n. FAM. Truc, bidule, fourbi *m.;* *all of a doodah,* dans tous ses états.

doodle [du:dl] n. Griffonnage, petit dessin *m.* ‖ FAM. Benêt, nigaud *m.*
— v. intr. Griffonner des petits dessins.

doodlebug ['du:dlbʌg] n. ZOOL. Bourdon *m.* ‖ MILIT., FAM. V 1. ‖ U. S. Baguette (*f.*) de sourcier.

doom [du:m] n. † Décret *m.* ‖ JUR., ECCLES. Jugement *m.* ‖ FIG. Mort *f.* (death); destin tragique *m.*
— v. tr. † Décréter (as a penalty). ‖ JUR., ECCLES. Condamner, vouer (*to*, à). ‖ FIG. Destiner à un sort tragique *s.*

doomsday [-zdei] n. ECCLES. Jour du Jugement dernier *m.* ‖ FAM. *Till doomsday,* in vitam aeternam, jusqu'à la fin des temps. ‖ LOC. *Doomsday Book,* cadastre national anglais du XIᵉ siècle.

door [dɔ:*] n. Porte *f.* (of a closet, cupboard, house, room); *revolving door,* tambour. ‖ Pièce *f.* (room); *three doors away,* trois portes plus loin. ‖ Domicile *m.; out of doors,* au-dehors; *within doors,* dedans, chez soi; *to be always knocking at s.o.'s door,* être toujours pendu à la sonnette de qqn; *there's the door,* prenez la porte! ‖ CH. DE F., AUTOM. Portière *f.* ‖ FIG. Porte *f.; the open door to negotiations,* la porte ouverte aux négociations. ‖ FAM. *To lay at the door of,* mettre sur le dos de; *to lie at s.o.'s door,* retomber sur le dos de qqn. ‖ **Door-bell,** n. Sonnette *f.;* COMM., FAM. *Door-bell-pusher,* démarcheur, placier. ‖ **Door-curtain,** n. Portière *f.* ‖ **Door-frame,** U. S. **Door trim,** n. Chambranle *m.* ‖ **Door-hinge,** n. TECHN. Paumelle *f.* ‖ **Door-keeper,** n. Portier, concierge; pipelet *m.* (fam.). ‖ **Door-knob,** n. Bouton (*m.*) de porte. ‖ **Door-mat,** n. Paillasson *m.* ‖ **Door-nail,** n. Clou (*m.*) de porte; FAM. *Dead as a door-nail,* mort et bien mort. ‖ **Door-plate,** n. Plaque de porte *f.* ‖ **Door-post,** n. Montant (*m.*) de porte. ‖ **Door-spring,** n. Blount, ferme-porte *m.* ‖ **Door-step,** n. Seuil *m.; he is always on my door-step,* il ne sort pas de chez moi. ‖ **Door-stop,** n. Butoir, entrebâilleur *m.* ‖ **Door-strap,** n. AUTOM., CH. DE F. Courroie de portière *f.* ‖ **Door-to-door transport,** n. COMM. Porte-à-porte *m.*

doorman ['dɔ:mən] (pl. **doormen**) n. Portier, ouvreur (*m.*) de porte.

doorway [-wei] n. Portail *m.* ‖ Fig. Porte *f. ;* moyen d'accès *m.* (to, à).

dope [doup] n. Aviat. Enduit *m.* ‖ Med. Anesthésique *m.* ‖ Sports. Doping *m.* ‖ Fam. Stupéfiant *m. ;* drogue *f.* ‖ Fam. Tuyau *m.; to give s.o. all the dope,* donner tous les détails à qqn. ‖ Fam. Crétin *m.,* nouille *f.* (simpleton). ‖ **Dope-fiend,** n. Morphinomane *s.* ‖ **Dope peddler,** n. U. S. Trafiquant (*m.*) de stupéfiants.
— v. tr. Aviat. Enduire. ‖ Med. Ancsthésicr. ‖ Sports. Doper. ‖ Fam. Droguer. ‖ Fam. U. S. *To dope out,* avoir des tuyaux sur, combiner.
— v. intr. Fam. Se droguer.

dop(e)y [-i] adj. Fam. Drogué ; abruti.

doppelgänger ['dɔpl,geŋə*] n. Double *m.* (in spiritualism).

dor ['dɔ:*] n. Zool. Bourdon *m.*

Dora ['dɔ:rə] n. Fam. Anastasie, la censure *f.*

dorado [do'rɑ:dou] n. Zool., Astron. Dorade *f.*

Dorcas ['dɔ:kəs] n. Dame de charité *f.; Dorcas society,* ouvroir *m.*

Dorian ['dɔ:riən] adj. Mus., Geogr. Dorien.

Doric ['dɔrik] adj. Archit. Dorique.
— n. Archit. Dorique *m.* ‖ Geogr. Dorien *s.* ‖ Fam. Accent du terroir *m.*

dorm [dɔ:m] n. Fam. Dortoir *m.*

dormancy ['dɔ:mənsi] n. Sommeil *m.*

dormant [-mənt] adj. Bot., Techn., Blas. Dormant. ‖ Jur. En sommeil ; non appliqué ; en désuétude ; *to lie dormant,* rester en souffrance. ‖ Fig. Assoupi.

dormer [-ə*] n. Archit. Lucarne *f.*

dormition [dɔ:'miʃən] n. Eccles. Dormition *f.*

dormitory [-itəri] n. Dortoir *m.* ‖ U. S. Pavillon (*m.*) des étudiants.
— adj. *Dormitory suburb,* cité-dortoir.

dormouse ['dɔ:maus] n. Zool. Loir *m.*

Dorothy bag ['dɔrəθibæg] n. Sac-aumônière *m.*

dorsal ['dɔ:səl] adj. Med. Dorsal.

dory ['dɔ:ri] n. Zool. Dorée *f.*

dory n. Naut. Doris *m.*

dosage ['dousidʒ] n. Med. Dosage *m.* (amount); posologie *f.* (determination); administration (*f.*) des remèdes (giving).

dose [dous] n. Med. Dose *f.; dose of aspirin,* comprimé (or) cachet d'aspirine. ‖ Fig. Dose *f.*
— v. tr. Med. Donner en doses (a medicine); donner un médicament à, médicamenter (s.o.); *to dose oneself with,* se soigner (or) traiter à. ‖ Techn. Alcooliser (wine).

doss [dɔs] n. Pop. Pieu *m.* (bed); *to do a doss,* aller au plumard. ‖ **Doss-house,** n. Fam. Asile (*m.*) de nuit.
— v. intr. Pop. Pioncer (to sleep).

dosser ['dɔsə*] n. Hotte *f.*

dosser n. Pop. Habitué (*m.*) des asiles de nuit.

dossier ['dɔsiei] n. Dossier *m.* (documents).

dot [dɔt] n. Point *m.* (above an i ; in Morse code); *on the dot,* pile, recta. ‖ Fam. Gosse *m.*
— v. tr. (1). Mettre un point sur (an i). ‖ Pointiller (a line); *dotted Swiss,* plumetis (cloth). ‖ Mus. Pointer (a note). ‖ Fig. Eparpiller, parsemer, piqueter (with, de). ‖ Fam. *I dotted him one,* je lui ai flanqué un gnon ; *to dot one's i's,* mettre les points sur les i.
— v. intr. Faire des points. ‖ Math. *To dot and carry one,* poser et retenir un. ‖ Fam. Clopiner, claudiquer.

dotage ['doutidʒ] n. Radotage *m.* ‖ Fam. Raffolement *m.*

dotal ['doutəl] adj. Jur. Dotal.

dotard ['doutəd] n. Radoteur, gâteux *s.*

dotation [dou'teiʃən] n. Jur. Dotation *f.*

dote [dout] v. tr. Radoter. ‖ Fam. Raffoler (upon, de).

dotterel ['dɔtrəl] n. Zool. Guignard *m.*

dotty ['dɔti] adj. Pointillé ; moucheté. ‖ Fam. Cinglé, bouffé aux mites. (See batty.)

double ['dʌbl] adj. Double (of, de) [dimension, quantity]. ‖ Double (first rate); *double elephant,* grand aigle (paper). ‖ Double, en deux exemplaires (in duplicate). ‖ Double, plié en deux (folded). ‖ Double, redoublé (repeated). ‖ A deux, pour deux ; *double bed,* lit à deux places, grand lit. ‖ Astron., Bot., Ch. de f., Geogr., Math., Med., Phys., Sports. Double. ‖ Fin. Double (tax); *double entry,* en partie double (book-keeping). ‖ Milit. *Double time,* pas gymnastique. ‖ Fig. Double (game, life); à deux faces, plein de duplicité, fourbe (person). ‖ Fam. *Double talk,* paroles creuses (or) ambiguës ; *to perform the double act,* se mettre la corde au cou (to get married). ‖ **Double-acting,** adj. A double effet. ‖ **Double-barrelled,** adj. Milit. A deux coups (gun); Fig. A deux tranchants; Fam. A rallonge (name). ‖ **Double-bass,** n. Mus. Contrebasse *f.* ‖ **Double-bedded,** adj. A deux lits. ‖ **Double-blank,** n. Double-blanc *m.* ‖ **Double-boiler,** n. Culin. Bain-marie *m.* ‖ **Double-bottomed,** adj. A double fond. ‖ **Double-breasted,** adj. Croisé (coat). ‖ **Double-check,** v. tr. Revérifier, recontrôler. ‖ **Double-cross,** v. tr. U. S. Fam. Rouler, doubler (to cheat). ‖ **Double-crosser,** n. Fam. Faux jeton *m.* ‖ **Double-dealing,** n. Duplicité *f.;* adj. Fourbe. ‖ **Double-decker,** n. Naut. Deux-ponts *m.; Autom.* Autobus (*m.*) à deux étages; Fam. Double sandwich *m.* ‖ **Double-(de)clutch,** v. intr. Autom. Faire un double débrayage. ‖ **Double-Dutch,** n. Fam. Charabia, jargon *m.* ‖ **Double-edged,** adj. A double tranchant. ‖ **Double-entendre,** n. Expression à double entente *f.* ‖ **Double-faced,** adj. Double-face (cloth); Fig. A double face. ‖ **Double-feature,** adj. Theatr. Double (programme). ‖ **Double-ganger,** n. Double *m.* (in spiritualism). ‖ **Double glazing,** n. Survitrage *m.* ‖ **Double-handed,** adj. A double usage. ‖ **Double-headed,** adj. Bicéphale, à deux têtes ; Ch. de f. A deux locomotives. ‖ **Double-jointed,** adj. Désarticulé, souple comme du caoutchouc. ‖ **Double-lock,** v. tr. Fermer à double tour. ‖ **Double-park,** v. tr. Autom. Parquer en double file. ‖ **Double-quick,** adj. Milit. Gymnastique (pas); adv. Au pas gymnastique. ‖ **Double-scull,** n. Naut. Aviron à couple *m.* ‖ **Double-six,** n. Double-six *m.* ‖ **Double-standard,** n. Code (*m.*) de morale à deux aspects. ‖ **Double-stopping,** n. Mus. Double corde *f.* ‖ **Double take,** n. Mouvement (*m.*) de surprise. ‖ **Double-think,** n. Malhonnêteté intellectuelle *f.* ‖ **Double-time,** n. Salaire double *m. ;* Milit. Pas (*m.*) de gymnastique.
— adv. Double ; *double or nothing,* quitte ou double ; *to see double,* voir double. ‖ A deux ; *to ride double,* monter à deux.
— n. Double *m.* (of, de). ‖ Double (of a person); pendant *m.* (of a thing). ‖ Contre *m.* (at bridge). ‖ Techn. Doublon *m.* (in printing). ‖ Fin., Sports. Double *m.* ‖ Milit. Pas gymnastique *m.* ‖ Fam. *At* (or) *on the double,* au pas de course.
— v. tr. Doubler (in quantity, size, weight). ‖ Doubler, replier (to fold). ‖ Serrer. ‖ Milit. Redoubler (one's pace). ‖ Naut., Theatr., Sports. Doubler. ‖ Fig. Redoubler (anxiety). ‖ *To double up,* loger dans la même pièce (passengers). ‖ Fam. *To double up,* faire se plier en deux.
— v. intr. Doubler, se doubler (to become double). ‖ Se doubler, se replier (to fold up). ‖ Faire un crochet, revenir sur ses pas (to turn backward). ‖ Milit. Prendre le pas gymnastique. ‖ Sports. *On a doubled rope,* en rappel (in mountaineering). ‖ *To double up,* se plier en deux (to coil up) ; partager une chambre (with, avec); *to double up with laughter,* se tordre de rire.

doublet ['dʌblit] n. Pourpoint *m.* (jacket). ‖ Gramm. Doublet *m.* ‖ Phys. Objectif double *m.*

doubleton ['dʌbltən] n. Doubleton *m.,* deux cartes (*f. pl.*) d'une même couleur.

doubloon [dʌb'lu:n] n. Fin. Doublon *m.*

doubly ['dʌbli] adv. Doublement; *doubly so as*, d'autant plus que.

doubt [daut] n. Doute *m.* (*about*, sur; *as, to*, au sujet de); *no doubt*, sans doute, probablement; *there is no doubt about it*, c'est indubitable, il n'y a pas à dire; *to be no longer a matter of doubt*, cesser d'être douteux; *without doubt*, sans aucun doute, indubitablement, à coup sûr. ‖ Point délicat *m.; incertitude f.* (See UNCERTAINTY.) ‖ † Crainte *f.*
— v. tr. Douter de, mettre en doute (to question). ‖ † Avoir peur de.
— v. intr. Douter, être incertain. ‖ Douter, ne pas être sûr (*about, of*, de). ‖ Se demander (*whether*, si).

doubtful [-ful] adj. Douteux, incertain, problématique, non assuré (problematical). ‖ Douteux, peu clair, ambigu, vague (not definite). ‖ Douteux, équivoque, suspect, trouble, louche (questionable). ‖ Dubitatif, indécis (dubious). ‖ Plein de doutes, hésitant (*as to, of*, au sujet de, sur).

doubtfully [-fuli] adv. D'un air dubitatif, avec doute. ‖ D'une manière indécise. ‖ Avec ambiguïté.

doubtless [-lis] adv. Indubitablement.
— SYN. : INDUBITABLY, UNDOUBTEDLY.

douceur [du:'sə:*] n. Pourboire *m.* (gratuity). ‖ Pot-de-vin *m.* (bribe). ‖ U. S. Amabilité *f.*

douche [du:ʃ] n. MED. Douche *f.* (externally); injection *f.* (internally); bock *m.* (device).
— v. tr. MED. Doucher; donner une injection à.
— v. intr. MED. Se doucher; prendre une injection.

dough [dou] n. CULIN. Pâte *f.* ‖ FAM. Fric *m.*, oseille, galette *f.* (money).

doughboy [-,bɔi] n. U. S. FAM. Soldat américain *m.*

doughnut [-nʌt] n. CULIN. Beignet; pet-de-nonne *m.*

doughtily ['dautili] adv. Avec vaillance.

doughty [-i] adj. † Vaillant.

doughy ['doui] adj. CULIN. Pâteux.

dour ['duə*] adj. Buté (obstinate); austère (stern).

douse, dowse [daus] v. tr. Tremper, arroser, doucher (to drench). ‖ Eteindre, souffler (to put out). ‖ NAUT. Amener (sails).

dove [dʌv] n. ZOOL. Colombe *f.* (See CULVER.) ‖ FAM. *My dove*, mon pigeon. ‖ **Dove-colour**, adj. Gorge-de-pigeon. ‖ **Dove-cot(e)**, n. Colombier *m.; FAM. To flutter the dovecots*, jeter une pierre dans la mare aux grenouilles.

Dover ['douvə*] n. GEOGR. Douvres; *Straits of Dover*, pas de Calais.

dovetail ['dʌvteil] n. TECHN. Queue d'aronde *f.*
— v. tr. TECHN. Assembler à queue d'aronde, adenter. ‖ FIG. Raccorder (facts).
— v. intr. Se raccorder, s'engrener.

dowager ['dauədʒə*] n. Douairière *f.*

dowdiness ['daudinis] n. Habillement négligé; fagotage *m.* (fam.).

dowdy [-i] adj. Mal habillé; mal torché (or) ficelé, fagoté (fam.).
— n. Femme mal habillée (or) moche *f.;* épouvantail *m.* (fam.).

dowel ['dauəl] n. ARCHIT. Goujon *m.*
— v. tr. (1). ARCHIT. Goujonner.

dower ['dauə*] n. JUR. Douaire *m.* (of a widow); dot *f.* (of a girl). ‖ FIG. Don inné *m.*
— v. tr. JUR. Doter (a girl); assigner un douaire à (a widow). ‖ FIG. Douer (*with*, de).

down [daun] n. ZOOL., BOT. Duvet *m.* ‖ FAM. Duvet, poil follet *m.*

down n. Colline *f.* (hill); dune *f.* (sand-dune).

down adv. En bas, vers le bas; *head down*, la tête en bas; *to ski down*, descendre à skis; *she fell down in a faint*, elle tomba évanouie. ‖ En bas; *don't kick a man when he is down*, ne frappez pas un homme à terre; *the curtains were down*, les rideaux étaient baissés; *the wind is down*, le vent s'est calmé. ‖ En bas, en descendant; *down to the present time*, jusqu'à nos jours. ‖ En bas, diminué; *to bring down s.o.'s pride*, rabattre l'orgueil de qqn; *to calm down*, se calmer. ‖ En écrivant, sur

le papier; *to take down s.o.'s name*, prendre le nom de qqn; *write down what I shall dictate*, écrivez ce que je dicterai. ‖ En attaquant; *the dogs ran down the stag*, les chiens ont forcé le cerf. ‖ COMM. Comptant, cash. ‖ MED. Alité, au lit (*with*, avec). ‖ AUTOM. A plat (tyre). ‖ FAM.. *Down at heels*, désargenté (person); éculé (shoes); *down it came!*, et patatras!; *down in the mouth*, la mine longue. ‖ **Down-and-outer**, n. U. S. FAM. Pouilleux, miséreux *m.* ‖ **Down-hearted**, adj. Découragé. ‖ **Down-stream**, adv. En aval. ‖ **Down-stroke**, n. Plein *m.* (in writing); TECHN. Course descendante *f.*
— interj. A bas; *down with X!*, à bas X, conspuez X! ‖ Couchez! (to a dog).
— prep. Au bas de; *down the hill*, au pied de la colline; *to go down the hill*, descendre la côte. ‖ En descendant; *up and down the room*, de long en large dans la pièce. ‖ Le long de; *to slide down the wall*, glisser le long du mur. ‖ En suivant; *down stream*, en suivant le courant, au fil de l'eau.
— adj. Qui descend. ‖ CH. DE F. Montant, d'aller (train). ‖ MUS. Fort (beat). ‖ FIN. Diminué (price). ‖ COMM. Comptant. ‖ FAM. Mal en point; *down and out*, dans le trente-sixième dessous.
— n. Infortune *f.; the ups and downs of life*, les hauts et les bas de la vie. ‖ FAM. Rancune *f.; to have a down on*, avoir une dent contre, être très monté contre.
— v. tr. FAM. Descendre (a plane, s.o.); *to down a drink*, s'envoyer un verre. ‖ FAM. Mettre bas, déposer; *to down tools*, se mettre en grève.

downbeat [-,bi:t] adj. Morose, sombre, pessimiste (gloomy). ‖ Détendu, décontracté (relaxed).

downcast [-,kɑ:st] adj. Baissé (look). ‖ FIG. Abattu (disheartened).
— n. TECHN. Puits d'appel d'air *m.* (shaft).

downer [-ə*] n. FAM. Tranquillisant, sédatif *m.* (drug); cause de déprime *f.* (experience).

downfall [-fɔ:l] n. Chute *f.* (of rain, snow). ‖ SPORTS. Assommoir *m.* (trap). ‖ JUR. Chute (of the ministry). ‖ FIG. Effondrement *m.* (of hopes, persons); déchéance *f.* (of persons); dégringolade *f.*

downgrade [-greid] n. CH. DE F. Descente *f.* ‖ FIG. Déclin *m.; déchéance, décadence f.*
— v. tr. U. S. Réduire en importance.

downhearted ['daun'hɑ:tid] adj. Découragé. (See DESPONDENT.)

downhill [-'hil] adv. En pente; *to go downhill*, descendre. ‖ FIG. Sur le déclin; sur le retour (fam.); *to go downhill*, décliner.
— n. Descente, pente *f.* ‖ FIG. Déclin *m.*
— ['daunhil] adj. En pente. ‖ SPORTS. *Downhill race*, descente (in ski-ing). ‖ FAM. Aisé.

downpipe [-paip] n. Tuyau (*m.*) de descente, gouttière *f.*

downpour ['daunpɔ:*] n. Grosse averse, pluie battante *f.*

downright [-rait] adj. Sans détour, direct, franc (person, language). ‖ Fieffé, véritable, parfait (out-and-out).
— adv. Nettement, carrément, tout à fait absolument.

downrightness [-raitnis] n. Droiture *f.; tempérament direct m.*

downstairs [daun'stɛəz] adv. En bas de l'escalier; *to go* (or) *come downstairs*, descendre l'escalier. En bas (on a lower floor).
— ['daunstɛəz] adj. Du bas.
— n. U. S. Rez-de-chaussée *m.*

downtown [-taun] n. Centre ville *m.*, quartier (*m.* des affaires.
— adj. Du centre ville, du quartier des affaires.
— adv. Dans le centre, dans le quartier des affaires.

downtrodden ['daun'trɔdṇ] adj. Piétiné. ‖ FIG. Opprimé.

downward ['daunwəd] adj. Descendant (move

ment, road); postérieur (time). ‖ Fin. A la baisse (tendency).

downward(s) [-z] adv. En bas, vers le bas, en descendant. ‖ Vers l'époque actuelle, jusqu'à l'heure présente.

downwash ['daunwɔʃ] n. Aviat. Air déplacé m.

downwind [-wind] adj., adv. Sous le vent.

downy ['dauni] adj. Duveteux. ‖ Semblable au duvet.

dowry ['dauri] n. Jur. Dot f. (of girl); douaire m. (of a widow); *to espouse a wife for the sake of her dowry*, épouser une dot. ‖ Fig. Don inné m.

dowse [daus] v. tr. See douse.

dowse [dauz] v. intr. Faire de la radiesthésie; *dowsing rod*, baguette de sourcier.

dowser [-ə*] n. Radiesthésiste s.

doxology [dɔk'sɔlədʒi] n. Eccles. Doxologie f.

doxy ['dɔksi] n. Grue f. (whore).

doyen ['dɔiən] n. Doyen s. (of a group, profession, society).

doze [douz] v. intr. Sommeiller; somnoler.
— n. Somnolence f.; demi-sommeil, assoupissement m. (drowsiness); petit somme m. (nap); *in a doze*, assoupi.

dozen ['dʌzn̩] n. Douzaine f.; *a baker's dozen*, treize à la douzaine; *dozens of times*, des douzaines de fois; *two dozen eggs*, deux douzaines d'œufs.

dozy ['douzi] adj. Endormi (drowsy). ‖ Fam. Demeuré, fada (stupid); feignant, flemmard (lazy).

Dr. Written abbr. for *Doctor*, docteur, Dr.

drab [dræb] n. Teinte terne f. (colour); bure f. (fabric). ‖ Fig. Grisaille f.
— adj. Terne, gris (lit. and fig.).

drab n. Souillon f. (slut). ‖ Catin f. (prostitute).
— v. intr. Courir le jupon (or) le cotillon (man); faire la putain (woman).

drabble ['dræbl̩] v. tr. Crotter, salir de boue.
— v. intr. Se crotter, patauger dans la boue.

drachm [dræm] n. Drachme f. (coin, weight).

drachma ['drækmə] n. Fin. Drachme f. (coin).

draconian [dræ'kouniən] adj. Draconien.

draff [dræf] n. Dépôt m.; lie f. (dregs). ‖ Eaux sales f. pl. (See slops.) ‖ Fig. Lie.

draft [drɑːft] n. Brouillon m. (of a letter). [See draught.] ‖ Arts. Esquisse f. ‖ Jur. Minute f. (of an act); projet m. (of an agreement). ‖ Fin. Retrait m. (of money); traite f. (bill). ‖ Milit. Contingent m. (of recruits); détachement m. (of troops).
— v. tr. Faire un brouillon de. ‖ Arts. Esquisser. ‖ Jur. Faire la minute (or) le projet de. ‖ Milit. Affecter, désigner (troops).

draftee [dræ:f'tiː] n. Milit. U. S. Conscrit m.; recrue f.

draftsman ['drɑːftsmən] (pl. draftsmen) n. Arts. Dessinateur m. ‖ Jur. Rédacteur (m.) de projets de loi.

drafty ['drɑːfti] adj. See draughty.

drag [dræg] v. tr. (1). Traîner, entraîner, tirer (see pull); *to drag one's feet*, traînasser, traîner les pieds. ‖ Techn. Draguer (a river). ‖ Naut. Chasser sur (the anchor). ‖ Autom. Enrayer (a wheel). ‖ Agric. Herser (a field). ‖ Fig. Arracher (*from*, à); *to drag s.o. away from his work*, distraire qqn de son travail. ‖ **To drag along**, traîner; traînailler (fam.). ‖ **To drag in**, introduire de force (lit. and fig.). ‖ **To drag on**, traîner (one's life); faire traîner (a speech). ‖ **To drag out**, faire sortir de force; Fig. Traîner, faire traîner. ‖ **To drag up**, tirer en haut, extraire; Fam. Elever à la va-comme-je-te-pousse (a child); remettre sur le tapis, déterrer, ressortir (an old story).
— v. intr. Traîner à terre. ‖ Se traîner (affair, conversation, person, time). ‖ Naut. Chasser (anchor). ‖ Techn. Draguer.
— n. Marche ralentie f.; ralentissement m. ‖ Patin, frein m. (brake). ‖ Drag m. (coach). ‖ Techn.

Drague f. ‖ Naut. Gaffe f. (hook); drège f. (net). ‖ Fig. Entrave f.; *to be a drag on*, être un boulet pour. ‖ Pop. Raseur s. (person); enquiquinement m. (chose); *what a drag*, c'est la barbe, c'est casse-pieds. ‖ Pop. Vêtement (m.) de travesti; *in drag*, en travesti; *drag queen*, travelo. ‖ **Drag-bar**, n. Barre (f.) d'attelage. ‖ **Drag-line**, n. Techn. Drag-line m. ‖ **Drag-link**, n. Barre (f.) de rappel. ‖ **Drag-net**, n. Drège f.; U. S. Rafle f.

dragee [dræ'ʒei] n. Med. Dragée f.

draggle ['drægl̩] v. tr. Crotter, souiller de boue, laisser traîner dans la boue. ‖ **Draggle-tail**, n. Fam. Souillon f.
— v. intr. Se crotter. ‖ Traîner, traînailler (fam.).

dragoman ['drægoumən] n. Drogman m.
— N. B. Deux pluriels : *dragomans, dragomen*.

dragon ['drægən] n. Dragon m. (lit. and fig.). ‖ **Dragon-fly**, n. Zool. Libellule f. ‖ **Dragon's blood**, n. Sang-dragon m. ‖ **Dragon-tree**, n. Bot. Dragon-nier m.

dragoon [drə'guːn] n. Milit., Zool., Fig. Dragon m.
— v. tr. Mener à la trique, gendarmer. ‖ Contraindre (*into*, à).

drain [drein] v. tr. Vider entièrement (cup, glass). ‖ Essorer (linen); assécher (a marsh, mine); drainer (a piece of ground, water). ‖ Techn. Purger (a cylinder); vidanger (engine sump); désamorcer (a pump). ‖ Med. Drainer (an abscess). ‖ Fig. Epuiser (ressources, strength). ‖ Fam. Mettre à sec (s.o.'s purse); *to drain s.o. dry*, saigner qqn à blanc.
— v. intr. Egoutter, s'égoutter (linen); s'écouler (water).
— n. Fossé d'écoulement m.; caniveau m. (channel); canalisation f.; conduit d'écoulement, tuyau (m.) de vidange (pipe); *drain pipe*, tuyau d'égout. ‖ Med. Drain m. ‖ Fin. *Drain of money*, drainage de capitaux. ‖ Fig. Perte f. (of strength). ‖ Fam. Saignée f. (on, à).

drainage [-idʒ] n. Drainage m. ‖ **Drainage-basin**, n. Bassin hydrographique m. ‖ **Drainage-tube**, n. Med. Drain m.

drainer [-ə*] n. Egouttoir m. (device). ‖ Draineur m. (person).

draining [-iŋ] pr. p. See drain. ‖ **Draining board**, n. Egouttoir m. (of a sink).

drake [dreik] n. Zool. Canard m.; *wild drake*, malard.

dram [dræm] n. Drachme f. (weight). ‖ Fam. Goutte f., petit verre m. (of alcoholic, drink). ‖ **Dram-shop**, n. Fam. Assommoir, estaminet.

drama ['drɑːmə] n. Theatr. Théâtre, art dramatique m. (art); drame m. (play). ‖ Fig. Drame m.

dramatic [drə'mætik] adj. Dramatique (effect, irony, style, work); *the dramatic element in a novel*, le dramatique d'un roman. ‖ Théâtral (critic). ‖ Mus. Fort (tenor). ‖ Fig. Spectaculaire, frappant.

dramatically [-əli] adv. Dramatiquement. ‖ Fig. De façon spectaculaire, frappante.

dramatics [-s] n. sg. (or) pl. Theatr. Art dramatique, théâtre m. ‖ Fig. Comédie f.; théâtre, cinéma m. (histrionics).

dramatis personae ['drɑːmətis pə'sounai] n. Liste (f.) des personnages (of a play). ‖ Fig. Protagonistes s. pl.

dramatist ['dræmətist] n. Theatr. Auteur dramatique m. (See dramaturge.)

dramatize [-taiz] v. tr. Theatr. Adapter pour la scène. ‖ Fig. Dramatiser.
— v. intr. Theatr. S'adapter pour la scène.

dramaturge [-təːdʒ], **dramaturgist** [-təːdʒist] n. Theatr. Dramaturge m.

drank [dræŋk] pret. See drink.

drape [dreip] v. tr. Draper. ‖ Fam. *To drape one-self in one's dignity*, se draper dans sa dignité.
— n. Draperie f. ‖ Rideau m. (curtain).

draped [-t] adj. Drapé.
draper [-ə*] n. † Drapier *m.* ‖ Comm. Marchand (*m.*) de nouveautés.
drapery [-əri] n. Draperie *f.* ‖ Comm. Nouveautés *f. pl.* (cloth, trade). ‖ Arts. Drapé *m.*
drastic ['dræstik] adj. Med. Drastique. ‖ Fig. Energique (measures) ; massif (reduction).
drastically [-əli] adv. Energiquement.
drat! [dræt] interj. Au diable !
draught [drɑːft] n. Traction *f.; draught horse,* cheval de trait. ‖ Tirage *m.* (of a chimney). ‖ Action (*f.*) de tirer ; *beer on draught,* bière à la pression. ‖ Trait *m.; gorgée f.; at a draught,* d'un trait. ‖ Courant d'air, vent coulis *m.* (wind). ‖ Pl. Dames *f. pl.* (game). ‖ Sports. Coup de filet *m.;* pêche *f.* ‖ Med. Potion *f.* ‖ Naut. Tirant (*m.*) d'eau. ‖ See Draft. ‖ **Draught-board,** n. Damier *m.* ‖ **Draught-tube,** n. Bourrelet *m.* (on a door).
— v. tr. See Draft.
draughtsman [-smən] (pl. **draughtsmen**) n. Pion *m.* (in draughts). ‖ Arts. Dessinateur industriel *m.*
draughty [-i] adj. Plein de courants d'air.
draw [drɔː] v. tr. (48). Tirer, traîner (a coach, a vehicle). ‖ Tirer (a bolt, a curtain) ; baisser (the blinds) ; lever (a drawbridge). ‖ Puiser (water) ; tirer (*from,* de) [wine]. ‖ Aspirer (air, liquid). ‖ Tirer, retirer, ôter (*from, out of,* de) ; arracher (a nail). ‖ Passer, glisser (*over,* sur ; *through,* à travers, sous) [one's arm, hand]. ‖ Tirer au sort ; *to draw the first prize at,* décrocher le gros lot à ; *to draw lots for sth.,* tirer qqch. au sort ; *to draw straws,* tirer à la courte paille. ‖ Tirer (a card) ; faire tomber (the trumps). ‖ Arts. Dessiner. ‖ Geogr. Dresser (a map). ‖ Math. Tracer (a circle) ; tirer (a line). ‖ Med. Faire mûrir (an abscess) ; arracher (a tooth). ‖ Culin. Vider (a fowl) ; faire infuser (tea). ‖ Techn. Démouler (a casting) ; extraire (coal) ; étirer, tréfiler (wire). ‖ Naut. Jauger. ‖ Autom. Remorquer (a car). ‖ Milit. Toucher (rations) ; *to draw the swords,* dégainer, tirer sabre au clair. ‖ Jur. Rédiger (a contract). ‖ Fin. Tirer (a cheque) ; toucher (money). ‖ Comm. Attirer (customers). ‖ Sports. Tirer (the ball) ; bander, tendre (a bow) ; *to draw a game with,* faire match nul avec. ‖ † Ecarteler ; éviscérer. ‖ Fig. Contracter (features) ; *his face was drawn,* il avait les traits tirés. ‖ Fig. Attirer (crowd, look, love, vengeance) ; détourner (*from,* de) [s.o.] ; engager (*into,* dans) [s.o.] ; *to feel drawn to,* se sentir porté vers. ‖ Fig. Etablir (comparisons) ; tirer (*from,* de) [conclusions] ; puiser (information, strength) ; faire traîner en longueur (a speech) ; *to draw a blank,* faire chou blanc. ‖ **To draw away,** entraîner ; Fig. Détourner (*from,* de). ‖ **To draw in,** faire entrer (s.o., sth.) ; rentrer (its claws) ; tirer, serrer (the reins) ; Fig. Entraîner (or) engager dans. ‖ **To draw off,** tirer, retirer (one's shoes) ; soutirer (wine) ; Milit. Retirer (troops) ; Med. Tirer, prendre (blood) ; Fig. Détourner (attention). ‖ **To draw on,** mettre (one's gloves) ; Fig. Entraîner, pousser (*to,* à) [s.o.]. ‖ **To draw out,** sortir, retirer (sth.) ; arracher (a nail) ; Techn. Etirer (wire) ; Arts. Tracer (pattern, plan) ; Fin. Retirer (money) ; Fig. Faire traîner (an affair) ; Fam. Faire parler, délier la langue à, tirer de sa coquille (s.o.). ‖ **To draw up,** remonter, faire remonter, relever (a blind, one's sleeves) ; *to draw oneself up,* se redresser ; Techn. Serrer (a nut) ; Naut. Tirer à sec (a boat) ; Milit. Aligner (troops) ; Jur. Rédiger (a document) ; Fin. Etablir (an account) ; Fig. Dresser, établir (a plan).
— v. intr. Tirer (horse). ‖ Tirer (chimney) ; tirer (*on,* sur) [a cigarette] ; marcher (pump). ‖ Tirer (*to,* à) ; se diriger (*towards,* vers) ; *to draw near,* s'approcher (or) se rapprocher de. ‖ Naut. Porter (sails) ; haler (wind). ‖ Sports. Tirer (in fencing) ; *to draw ahead,* se détacher (runner) ; *to draw from the stock,* piocher (at dominoes) ; *to draw level,*

égaliser (at football) ; *to draw with,* faire match nul (avec). ‖ Med. Tirer (plaster). ‖ Culin. Infuser (tea). ‖ Theatr. Prendre, marcher, attirer le public (play). ‖ Fin. Tirer, prélever (*on,* sur) ; *to be drawn,* sortir au tirage. ‖ Fig. Faire appel (*on,* à).
— n. Traction *f.* (of a horse, a vehicle). ‖ Tirage *m.* (of a chimney). ‖ Tirage au sort *m.* (act) ; loterie, tombola *f.* (lottery) ; lot *m.* ‖ Culin. Infusion *f.* ‖ Comm. Réclame *f.* ‖ Theatr. Pièce (*f.*) à succès. ‖ Sports. Tiré *m.* (in fencing) ; match nul *m.* ‖ Techn. Etirage *m.* ‖ Fig. Effort *m.* ‖ Fam. Attraction *f.; to be a draw,* faire florès. ‖ Fam. Astuce (*f.*) pour attirer les confidences.
drawback [-bæk] n. Fin. Remise, réduction *f.* (*from,* sur). ‖ Jur., Fin. Drawback *m.* ‖ Fig. Inconvénient *m.* (*to,* à).
drawbridge [-bridʒ] n. Archit. Pont-levis *m.* (of a castle) ; pont basculant *m.* (modern).
drawee [drɔː'iː] n. Fin., Comm. Accepteur *m.*
drawer ['drɔːə*] n. Puiseur *m.* (of water) ; tireur *m.* (of wine). ‖ Techn. Extracteur *m.* ‖ Comm., Fin. Tireur, souscripteur *m.* ‖ Med. Arracheur *m.* (of teeth). ‖ Arts. Dessinateur *m.*
— ['drɔːə*] n. Tiroir *m.*
drawers ['drɔːəz] n. pl. Caleçon *m.* (for men) ; pantalon *m.* (for women). ‖ Sports. Culotte *f.*
drawing ['drɔːiŋ] n. Puisage *m.* (of water) ; tirage *m.* (of wine). ‖ Tirage *m.;* action (*f.*) de tirer. ‖ Techn. Démoulage *m.* (of casting) ; extraction *f.* (of coal) ; étirage *m.* (of wire). ‖ Fin. Traite *f.;* tirage *m.* ‖ Arts. Dessin *m.; out of drawing,* mal dessiné ; *rough, working drawing,* ébauche, épure. ‖ **Drawing-account,** n. Fin. Compte personnel *m.* ‖ **Drawing-board,** n. Arts. Planche (*f.*) à dessin. ‖ **Drawing-book,** n. Arts. Cahier (or) album à dessin *m.* ‖ **Drawing-card,** n. Fam. Attraction *f.* ‖ **Drawing-knife,** n. Techn. Plane *f.* ‖ **Drawing-mill,** n. Techn. Tréfilerie *f.* ‖ **Drawing-pen,** n. Arts. Tire-ligne *m.* ‖ **Drawing-pin,** n. Punaise *f.* ‖ **Drawing-room,** n. Salon *m.*
drawl [drɔːl] n. Voix traînante *f.*
— v. intr. Parler d'un ton traînant.
— v. tr. Dire d'un ton traînant.
drawn [drɔːn] p. p. See Draw. ‖ **Drawn-butter,** n. Culin. Beurre fondu *m.* ‖ **Drawn-work,** n. Broderie (*f.*) à fils tirés ; jours *m. pl.*
dray [drei] n. Haquet *m.* ‖ **Dray-horse,** n. Zool. Cheval de trait *m.*
drayman [-mən] (pl. **draymen**) n. Voiturier, camionneur *m.*
dread [dred] v. tr. Craindre, redouter, être terrifié par. (See Fear.)
— adj. Redoutable, terrifiant (dreadful). ‖ Redouté, craint, inspirant une crainte respectueuse (awesome).
— n. Terreur, épouvante *f.;* effroi *m.* (fear). ‖ Crainte religieuse (or) respectueuse *f.* (awe).
dreadful [-ful] adj. Redoutable, terrible, terrifiant, effroyable (fearful). ‖ Fam. Terrible, épouvantable ; *to make dreadful statements,* dire des énormités.
dreadfully [-fuli] adv. D'une manière terrifiante (or) terrible. ‖ Fam. Epouvantablement ; *dreadfully ugly,* laid à faire peur.
dreadnought [-nɔːt] n. Gros drap *m.* (cloth) ; paletot-pilote *m.* (coat). ‖ Naut. Dreadnought *m.*
dream [driːm] n. Rêve, songe *m.* (when sleeping). ‖ Rêve *m.;* rêverie, songerie *f.* (when awake). ‖ Fig. Rêve *m.* (aspiration). ‖ Fam. Rêve, idéal *m.;* merveille, splendeur *f.* ‖ **Dream-book,** n. Clef (*f.*) des songes. ‖ **Dream-reader,** n. Interprète (*m.*) des songes.
— v. intr. (49). Rêver (*of,* de, à) ; faire un rêve (*of,* sur). ‖ Rêver ; rêvasser, se perdre en rêveries. ‖ Fig. Songer (*of,* à) ; s'aviser, avoir l'idée (*of,* de).
— v. tr. Rêver (sth.). ‖ Fig. Songer, se figurer, imaginer (to fancy). ‖ **To dream away,** gaspiller en rêveries (one's time). ‖ **To dream up,** inventer sous l'inspiration, concevoir sous l'effet de l'imagination.

dreamer [-ə*] n. Rêveur s. ‖ Fig. Rêveur s. (muser); songe-creux m. (wool-gatherer).
dreamily [-ili] adv. Comme en rêve.
dreaminess [-inis] n. Rêverie, songerie f. (state).
dreamland [-lænd] n. Pays (m.) des songes.
dreamless [-lis] adj. Sans rêve.
dreamy [-i] adj. Plein de rêves (sleep). ‖ Vague (idea, scene); berceur (melody); visionnaire, rêveur, illuminé (idealist); rêveur, songeur (look, person).
drearily ['driərili] adv. Lugubrement.
dreariness [-inis] n. Tristesse f.; aspect lugubre m.
dreary [-i] adj. Lugubre, d'une morne tristesse, sinistre. (See DISMAL.)
dredge [dredʒ] n. Naut. Drague f.
— v. tr., intr. Draguer.
dredge v. tr. Saupoudrer (over, sur; with, de).
dredger [-ə*] n. Naut. Dragueur m. (boat, person); drague f. (machine).
dredger n. Saupoudroir m.
dreg [dreg] n. Reste, brin m.
dreggy [-i] adj. Trouble (drink); plein de lie (wine).
dregs [-z] n. pl. Lie f. (lit. and fig.).
drench [drenʃ] n. Breuvage purgatif (for animals). ‖ Averse violente; saucée f. (fam.).
— v. tr. Purger (a sick animal). ‖ Abreuver largement. ‖ Tremper, inonder, arroser (with, de). [See SOAK.] ‖ Techn. Tremper (skins).
drencher [-ə*] n. Violente averse; saucée f. (fam.).
dress [dres] v. tr. Habiller, vêtir (in, de, en) [s.o.]; dressed to kill, sur son tra-la-la. ‖ Orner, parer, arranger (with, de) [sth.]; to dress one's hair, se coiffer. ‖ Techn. Apprêter (cloth); préparer (cotton, wool); mégir, préparer (skins); équarrir (stone); dégrossir (timber); corroyer (wood). ‖ Naut. Pavoiser (a ship). ‖ Milit. Rectifier (the ranks); aligner (troops). ‖ Sports. Panser (a horse). ‖ Agric. Façonner (a field); cultiver (a garden); tailler (a fruit-tree). ‖ Comm. To dress the window, faire la vitrine. ‖ Med. Panser (a wound, a wounded person). ‖ Culin. Accommoder, apprêter (food); habiller (fowl); assaisonner (a salad). ‖ To dress down, Fam. Dresser, arranger, sabouler (to scold); dresser, donner une frottée à (to thrash). ‖ To dress out, parer, empanacher. ‖ To dress up, parer; attifer, nipper (fam.); to dress oneself up, se mettre en grande toilette, s'endimancher.
— v. intr. S'habiller; to dress with taste, s'habiller avec goût. ‖ S'habiller; se mettre en tenue de soirée (on a ceremonial occasion). ‖ Milit. S'aligner. ‖ To dress up, s'habiller avec soin; se bichonner (fam.); Milit. Avancer à l'alignement.
— n. Habillement m.; articles of dress, objets d'habillement. ‖ Habits, vêtements m. pl.; costume m.; court dress, habit de cour. ‖ Tenue, mise f.; in full dress, en grande tenue (men); en grande toilette (women). ‖ Toilette, parure f.; to be fond of dress, être coquette, aimer la toilette; to talk dress, parler chiffons. ‖ Robe f. (for women); evening dress, robe du soir. ‖ Dress-circle, n. Theatr. Corbeille f.; premier balcon m. ‖ Dress-coat, n. Habit, frac m. (men's formal dress). ‖ Dress-hanger, n. Cintre m. ‖ Dress-preserver (or) -shield, n. Dessous de bras m. ‖ Dress-rehearsal, n. Theatr. Couturières f. pl.; générale. f. ‖ Dress-suit, n. Tenue de soirée f.
dressage ['dresɑ:ʒ] n. Sports. Dressage m. (of horses); épreuve (f.) de dressage (competition).
dresser [-ə*] n. Buffet (m.) de cuisine; panetière (cupboard). ‖ Vaisselier, dressoir m. (with open shelves). ‖ U. S. Coiffeuse f. (dressing-table).
dresser n. Techn. Apprêteur m. (of skins); équarrisseur m. (of stones) [persons]; batte, pointerolle f. (tools). ‖ Med. Assistant (m.) en chirurgie. ‖ Theatr. Habilleuse f. ‖ Fam. Dandy m.
dressing [-iŋ] n. Toilette f. (act). ‖ Vêtements, habits m. pl.; toilette f. (clothes). ‖ Techn. Apprêt m. (for cloth); préparation f. (of cotton, wool);

graisse f. (for leather); mégissage m. (of skins); équarrissage m. (of stones); corroyage m. (of wood). ‖ Milit. Alignement m. ‖ Naut. Pavoisement; pavois m. ‖ Agric. Façon f.; fumage; engrais m. ‖ Med. Pansement m. ‖ Culin. Assaisonnement m. ‖ Fam. Savon m. (talking-to); tournée f. (thrashing). ‖ Dressing-case, n. Nécessaire (m.) de toilette. ‖ Dressing-down, n. Fam. Savon m. (talking-to); tournée f. (thrashing). ‖ Dressing-gown, n. Robe de chambre f. ‖ Dressing-room, n. Cabinet (m.) de toilette; Theatr. Loge f. ‖ Dressing-station, n. Milit. Poste de secours m. ‖ Dressing-table, n. Coiffeuse f.
dressmaker [-‚meikə*] n. Couturière f. (woman); dressmaker's hand (or) help, midinette, cousette. ‖ Couturier m. (man).
dressmaking [-‚meikiŋ] n. Couture f.
dressy [-i] adj. Fam. Elégant, chic (clothes, person).
drew [dru:]. See DRAW.
drib [drib] n. Fam. In dribs and drabs, petit à petit, par petits paquets, au compte-gouttes.
dribble ['dribl] v. intr. Goutter, dégoutter, couler goutte à goutte (to trickle). ‖ Baver (to slaver). ‖ Sports. Dribbler.
— v. tr. Faire couler goutte à goutte. ‖ Sports. Dribbler.
— n. Dégouttement m. (of water). ‖ Sports. Dribble m.
driblet [-lit] n. Petite quantité f.; in driblets, au compte-gouttes.
dried [draid] p. p. See DRY. ‖ Culin. Sec (fruit); séché (meat, fish); en poudre (egg, milk).
drier ['draiə*] n. Séchoir m. (device); siccatif m. (substance).
drift [drift] n. Poussée f. (by a current of air or water). ‖ Traînée f. (of clouds); nuage m. (of dust); rafale f. (of rain, snow). ‖ Amoncellement, tas m. (of sand, of falling snow). ‖ Naut., Aviat. Derive f. (of plane, ship). ‖ Naut. Sens m. (course); vitesse f. (speed) [of currents]. ‖ Milit. Dérivation f. (of projectiles). ‖ Comm. Cours (of affairs). ‖ Geol. Apports m. pl.; glacial drift, moraine. ‖ Techn. Alésoir m. (broach); mandrin m. (drift-pin); chasse-rivet m. (drift-punch). ‖ Fig. Marche f. (of events); intention, tendance f. (of a person); portée f., sens m. (of questions). ‖ Fam. Laisser-aller (m.) à vau-l'eau. ‖ Drift-anchor, n. Naut. Ancre flottante f. ‖ Drift-angle, n. Angle (m.) de dérive. ‖ Drift-indicator, n. Techn. Dérivomètre m. ‖ Drift-net, n. Naut. Traînée f. ‖ Drift-sand, n. Sable mouvant m. ‖ Drift-wood, n. Bois flotté m.
— v. intr. Aller à la dérive (on the water); être poussé (or) chassé (by the wind); s'entasser, s'amonceler (sand, snow). ‖ Naut., Aviat. Dériver. ‖ Fig. Se laisser aller (into, à); to let things drift, laisser courir les événements. ‖ Fig. Tendre (events, questions). ‖ To drift along, Fam. Flâner. ‖ To drift in, Fam. Entrer en passant.
— v. tr. Charrier, entraîner (down-stream); faire flotter (wood). ‖ Pousser, chasser (clouds). ‖ Amonceler, entasser (sand, snow). ‖ Recouvrir (with, de). ‖ Techn. Mandriner.
drifter [-ə*] n. Voyageur sans but, nomade s., trimardeur m. ‖ Naut. Drifter, chalutier m.
driftpin [-pin] n. Techn. Mandrin m.
drill [dril] n. Techn. Foret m. (auger); mèche f. (bit); vilebrequin m. (brace); foreuse, perforatrice f. (machinery); perceuse f. (hand tool). ‖ Med. Roulette f. ‖ Milit. Exercice m. ‖ Gramm. Exercice pratique m. ‖ Fig. Entraînement m. ‖ Drill-book, n. Milit. Théorie f. ‖ Drill-ground, n. Milit. Champ (m.) de manœuvres. ‖ Drill-master, n. Milit. Instructeur m. ‖ Drill-press, n. Techn. Foreuse (f.) à colonnes. ‖ Drill-sergeant, n. Milit. Instructeur m.
— v. tr. Percer (a hole). ‖ Techn. Forer. ‖ Milit.

Faire faire l'exercice à. ‖ Ch. de F. Tirer. ‖ Fig. Entraîner, exercer; chauffer (fam.). — v. intr. Faire un trou. ‖ Techn. Forer. ‖ Milit. Faire l'exercice. ‖ Fig. S'exercer, s'entraîner.

drill n. Agric. Sillon *m.* (furrow); semoir *m.* (machine). — v. tr. Agric. Semer en rayons, rayonner.

drill n. Coutil, treillis *m.* (fabric).

drily ['draili]. See DRYLY.

drink [driŋk] v. tr. (50). Boire (beer, water); manger (one's soup). ‖ Boire, vider (cup, glass). ‖ Boire à, porter un toast à; *to drink s.o.'s success,* lever son verre au succès de qqn. ‖ Obtenir en buvant; *to drink success to s.o.,* boire au succès de qqn; *to drink oneself into debt,* s'endetter par ivrognerie. ‖ Fig. Boire, absorber (ink). ‖ Fam. Boire (one's wages). ‖ **To drink away,** boire (one's fortune); noyer (one's sorrows). ‖ **To drink down,** Fam. Avaler, boire d'un trait. ‖ **To drink in,** Fig. Boire des yeux (a sight, s.o.); boire (s.o.'s words); Fam. Gober, avaler (a joke). ‖ **To drink off,** boire d'un trait. ‖ **To drink up,** vider; boire. — v. intr. Boire (excessively, moderately); consommer (in a bar). ‖ Boire, porter un toast (*to,* à). — n. Boisson *f.; after-dinner drink,* digestif; *strong drinks,* spiritueux, alcools; *to have a drink,* consommer, prendre quelque chose (in a pub or U. S. bar). ‖ Verre *m.; to stand s.o. a drink,* offrir un verre (or) un glass (or) à boire à qqn. ‖ Fig. Ivresse *f.; in drink,* dans les vignes du Seigneur; *under the influence of drink,* en état d'ébriété; *to take to drink,* se livrer à la boisson. ‖ Fam. Tasse *f.* (sea).

drinkable [-əbl] adj. Buvable (good); potable (suitable); *this wine is quite drinkable,* ce vin se laisse boire. — n. pl. Fam. Boisson *f.*

drinker [-ə*] n. Buveur *s.*

drinking [-iŋ] n. Boire *m.* (act). ‖ Fig. Boisson, ivrognerie *f.* ‖ **Drinking-bout,** n. Beuverie *f.* ‖ **Drinking-fountain,** n. Fontaine Wallace *f.* ‖ **Drinking-song,** n. Chanson (*f.*) à boire. ‖ **Drinking-water,** n. Eau potable *f.*

drip [drip] v. intr. (1). Dégoutter; couler goutte à goutte. (See DRIBBLE.) ‖ S'égoutter. ‖ Dégoutter (*with,* de). — v. tr. Faire couler goutte à goutte; faire égoutter. — n. Goutte *f.* (drop). ‖ Dégouttement *m.* ‖ Archit. Larmier *m.* ‖ Fam. Nouille *f.* (simpleton). ‖ **Drip-cock,** n. Techn. Purgeur *m.* ‖ **Drip-feed,** n. Techn. Compte-gouttes *m.* ‖ **Drip-coffee,** n. Café filtre *m.* ‖ **Drip-moulding,** n. Archit. Larmier *m.* ‖ **Drip-dry,** adj. A repassage superflu, qui ne se repasse pas.

dripping [-iŋ] n. Ruissellement, dégouttement *m.* (act); gouttes *f. pl.; égouttture f.* (drops). ‖ Culin. Graisse *f.* (from roast meat). ‖ **Dripping-pan,** n. Culin. Lèchefrite *f.* ‖ **Dripping-tube,** n. Med. Compte-gouttes *m.*

drive [draiv] v. tr. (51). Pousser devant soi (to push forward). ‖ Chasser (*from, out of,* de); refouler (*into,* dans); *to drive s.o. back,* faire rebrousser chemin à qqn. ‖ Décocher (a blow); lancer (*at,* à) [a projectile]. ‖ Techn. Faire marcher, actionner (a machine); enfoncer (a nail); serrer (a nut); percer (a tunnel); forer (a well). ‖ Ch. de F. Conduire (a locomotive). ‖ Autom. Conduire (a car); conduire, transporter (s.o.). ‖ Sports. Renvoyer, chasser (the ball); rabattre (game). ‖ Comm. Passer, conclure (a bargain); traiter (business); exercer (a trade). ‖ Fig. Pousser, amener, conduire (*to,* à) [to induce]; pousser, obliger (to force); *I was driven to it,* on m'y a contraint. ‖ Fig. Surmener, faire travailler excessivement (to overwork). ‖ Fig. Remettre, faire traîner (to postpone). ‖ Fam. *To drive a quill,* gratter du papier; *to drive sth. into s.o.'s head,* enfoncer qqch. dans la tête de qqn. — v. intr. Etre poussé, avancer sous la poussée. ‖

Se jeter (to rush); *the rain was driving against the windows,* la pluie battait (or) fouettait les fenêtres. ‖ Autom. Conduire (driver); aller en voiture, rouler (*to,* à) [passengers]; *to drive away,* partir en voiture; *to drive on the horn,* klaxonner abusivement; *to drive over,* écraser. ‖ Sports. Driver (in tennis). ‖ Techn. S'enfoncer (nail). ‖ Fig. Tendre, en venir (*at,* à) [to intend]; s'acharner, s'atteler, travailler à force (*at,* à) [to work hard]. — n. Train de bois flotté *m.* (floating logs). ‖ Voie carrossable *f.* (road). ‖ Autom. Promenade *f.* (or) trajet (*m.*) en voiture (trip). ‖ Autom. Propulsion *f.;* conduite *f.; left hand drive,* conduite à gauche; *with front wheel drive,* à traction avant. ‖ Techn. Commande, transmission *f.* ‖ Sports. Battue *f.* (in hunting); coup droit, drive *m.* (in tennis). ‖ U. S. Campagne de propagande *f.* ‖ Fig. Tendance *f.* (of events); effort *m.* (of a person). ‖ Fig. Dynamisme *m.; to lack drive,* manquer d'allant. ‖ **Drive-in,** adj. U. S. Accordant accès aux voitures; n. U. S. Restaurant, « restauvolant »; cinéma (*m.*) de route.

drivel ['drivl] v. intr. (1). Baver (to slaver). ‖ Radoter (to talk twaddle). — n. Bave *f.* ‖ Radotage *m.*

driveller [-lə*] n. Baveur *s.* ‖ Radoteur *s.*

driven ['drivn] p. p. See DRIVE.

driver ['draivə*] n. Cocher *m.* (coachman); conducteur *m.* (of cart, tram-car). ‖ Autom. Conducteur *m.* (of car); chauffeur *m.* (of taxi). ‖ Ch. de F. Mécanicien *m.* ‖ Agric. Conducteur, toucheur *m.* (of cattle). ‖ Techn. Roue motrice *f.* (driving-wheel). ‖ Sports. Driver *m.* (in golf).

driving [-iŋ] n. Autom. Conduite *f.* ‖ Techn. Commande *f.* ‖ **Driving-belt,** n. Techn. Courroie de transmission *f.* ‖ **Driving-licence,** n. Autom. Permis (*m.*) de conduire. ‖ **Driving-school,** n. Autom. Auto-école *f.* ‖ **Driving-test,** n. Autom. Examen (*m.*) du permis de conduire. ‖ **Driving-wheel,** n. Techn. Roue de transmission *f.*

drizzle ['drizl] v. intr. Bruiner, pleuvoter. — n. Bruine *f.;* crachin *m.*

drizzly [-li] adj. De bruine, bruineux.

drogue [droug] n. Naut. Ancre flottante *f.* ‖ Aviat. Cône-ancre *m.* (sea anchor); manche (*f.*) à air (wind-sock).

droll [droul] adj. Drôle. (See COMIC.) ‖ Drôle, bizarre. (See QUAINT.) — n. † Bouffon *m.* — v. intr. † Faire des drôleries.

drollery [-ri] n. Drôlerie *f.* (act, quality, remark).

drollness [-nis] n. Drôlerie *f.* (quality).

drolly [-li] adv. Drôlement (comically, quaintly).

dromedary ['drɔmədəri] n. Zool. Dromadaire *m.*

drone [droun] n. Bourdonnement *m.* ‖ Zool. Faux bourdon *m.* (male bee). ‖ Mus. Bourdon *m.* (of a bagpipe). ‖ Aviat. Avion téléguidé *m.* (plane); vrombissement *m.* (of the plane). ‖ Fam. Bourdonnement, ronronnement *m.* (of a speaker, voice). ‖ Fam. Parasite, oisif *m.* — v. intr. Zool. Bourdonner (bees). ‖ Fam. Bourdonner, parler dans un ronron. ‖ Fam. Vivre en parasite. — v. tr. Fam. Ronronner, dire sur un ton monotone. ‖ Fam. *To drone away one's life,* mener une vie de parasite (or) d'oisif.

drool [dru:l]. See DRIVEL.

droop [dru:p] v. intr. Se baisser (head, eyes); se voûter, se casser (person). ‖ Bot. Languir, s'affaisser (flowers). ‖ Fig. Décliner, s'affaiblir, s'alanguir. — v. tr. Pencher (head); baisser (eyes). — n. Inclinaison *f.* (of head); abaissement *m.* (of eyelids); courbe *f.* (of shoulders). ‖ Fig. Abattement *m.; langueur f.*

drooping [-iŋ] adj. Baissé (head, eyes); tombant, voûté (shoulders). ‖ Bot. Languissant (flower). ‖ Fig. Languissant; abattu.

drop [drɔp] n. Goutte *f.* (of blood, rain, sweat.

water). ‖ Pendeloque *f.* (of chandelier) ; pendant *m.* (ear-ring) ; pendentif *f.* (necklace). ‖ Bonbon *m.* ; *peppermint drops,* pastilles de menthe. ‖ Fondrière *f.* ; précipice *m.* (abyss) ; hauteur de chute *f.*, saut *m.* (depth). ‖ Dénivellation *f.* (in the ground) ; *sheer drop,* descente à pic. ‖ Techn. Cache-entrée *m.* (of a lock) ; chute *f.* (of a pile-driver). ‖ Phys. Baisse *f.* (in temperature). ‖ Electr. *Drop in voltage,* chute de potentiel. ‖ Fin. Baisse *f.* (in prices). ‖ Med. Goutte *f.* (medicine). ‖ U. S. Fente (*f.*) de boîte aux lettres (slot). ‖ Fig. Goutte *f.* ; *a drop in the bucket,* une goutte d'eau dans la mer. ‖ Fam. Doigt *m.* ; goutte *f.* (of rum) ; *to take a drop,* boire la goutte ; *to have a drop too much,* tenir une cuite. ‖ Fam. Trappe *f.* (on the gallows). ‖ Fam. *At the drop of a hat,* au signal donné, sans hésiter ; *to get the drop on,* gagner de vitesse. ‖ **Drop-bottle,** n. Med. Flacon (*m.*) compte-gouttes. ‖ **Drop-curtain,** n. Theatr. Rideau d'entracte *m.* ‖ **Drop-forge,** v. tr. Techn. Etamper ; emboutir. ‖ **Drop-hammer,** n. Techn. Marteau-pilon *m.* ‖ **Drop-head,** adj. Autom. Décapotable. ‖ **Drop-kick,** n. Sports. Coup tombé *m.* ‖ **Drop-leaf,** n. Volet (*m.*) de table. ‖ **Drop-light,** n. Electr. Baladeuse *f.* ‖ **Drop-out,** n. Lycéen (or) étudiant (*s.*) qui abandonne ses études ; marginal *s.* ‖ **Drop-scene,** n. Theatr. Toile (*f.*) de fond ; Fig. Dernier acte *m.* ‖ **Drop-shot,** n. Sports. Amorti *m.* (in tennis). ‖ **Drop-stitch,** n. Maille sautée *f.*
— v. intr. (1). Goutter, couler goutte à goutte (*from,* de) [to dribble] ; s'égoutter. ‖ Tomber, choir, s'écrouler (*into,* dans ; *on,* sur ; *with,* de) [to fall] ; *to be ready to drop,* ne plus tenir debout. ‖ Baisser (voice) ; tomber, se calmer (wind). ‖ Se placer ; *to drop to the rear,* se laisser dépasser, rester en arrière. ‖ Fin. Baisser (prices). ‖ Fig. Tomber, cesser, prendre fin (conversation) ; tomber (sentence, words). ‖ Fam. Tomber ; *to drop on s.o.,* tomber sur le dos de qqn (to scold) ; *to drop upon s.o.,* tomber sur qqn (to meet). ‖ **To drop away,** s'en aller peu à peu, s'égayer. ‖ **To drop behind,** rester en arrière, se laisser devancer. ‖ **To drop in,** entrer en passant. ‖ **To drop off,** tomber (leaves) ; Fam. Défunter (to die) ; piquer un somme (to fall asleep). ‖ **To drop out,** tomber ; Fig. abandonner ses études (student) ; vivre en marge de la société ; Sports. Abandonner, renoncer.
— v. tr. Faire tomber goutte à goutte (water). ‖ Laisser tomber, perdre (a stitch). ‖ Laisser tomber (or) choir (a burden) ; lâcher (sth.). ‖ Griffonner, écrire à la hâte (a letter). ‖ Baisser (eyes, voice) ; verser (tears). ‖ Autom. Surbaisser (the chassis) ; déposer (s.o., sth.). ‖ Naut. Mouiller (anchor). ‖ Aviat. Lâcher, parachuter (a parachutist). ‖ Sports. *To drop a goal,* marquer un but au coup tombé. ‖ Zool. Mettre bas (sheep). ‖ Math. Abaisser (a perpendicular). ‖ Fig. Cesser, interrompre (a conversation, negotiations) ; renoncer à (an idea, a habit) ; glisser (a remark) ; lâcher (one's work) ; *to drop s.o.'s acquaintance,* cesser les relations avec qqn. ‖ Fam. Laisser tomber (a friend) ; manger (money) ; descendre (s.o.) ; U. S. *To drop a brick,* faire une gaffe. ‖ Loc. *To drop a curtsey,* faire une révérence.
droplet [-lit] n. Gouttelette *f.*
dropper [-ə*] n. Med. Compte-gouttes *m.*
dropping [-iŋ] n. Chute *f.* (act, thing). ‖ Med. Descente *f.* (of womb). ‖ Zool. Mise bas *f.* ‖ Autom. Surbaissement *m.* ‖ Aviat. Dépôt par parachute *m.* ‖ Pl. Fiente, crotte *f.* (of animals) ; gouttes *f. pl.* (of water).
— adj. Dégouttelant, tombant goutte à goutte. ‖ **Dropping-tube,** n. Med. Compte-gouttes *m.*
dropsical ['drɒpsikəl] adj. Med. Hydropique.
dropsy [-si] n. Med. Hydropisie *f.*
drosophila [drɔ'sɔfilə] n. Zool. Drosophile *f.*
dross [drɔs] n. Techn. Scories *f. pl.* ‖ Fig. Lie *f.*

drossy [-i] adj. Contenant des impuretés. ‖ Fig. De rebut.
drought [draut], **drouth** [drauθ] n. Sécheresse *f.* (See dryness.) ‖ † Soif *f.*
droughty ['drauti] adj. De sécheresse ; sec, aride. ‖ † Altéré.
drove [drouv] pret. See drive.
drove n. Zool. Troupeau (*m.*) en marche. ‖ Techn. Ciseau *m.* (in stone-cutting). ‖ Fig. Foule (*f.*) en mouvement ; bande *f.*
— v. tr. Agric. Conduire (cattle).
drover [-ə*] n. Agric. Toucheur *s.* ‖ Comm. Marchand (*m.*) de bestiaux.
drown [draun] v. intr. Se noyer.
— v. tr. Noyer ; *to drown oneself,* se noyer. ‖ Inonder, submerger, noyer (to flood). ‖ Couvrir, étouffer, assourdir (a sound). ‖ Fam. Noyer (one's sorrows).
drowse [drauz] v. intr. Somnoler ; *to drowse off,* s'assoupir, plonger dans un demi-sommeil. ‖ Fig. Sommeiller.
— v. tr. Assoupir ; *to drowse away one's time,* passer son temps à sommeiller.
— n. Somnolence *f.*
drowsily [-ili] adv. En somnolant. ‖ D'un air apathique.
drowsiness [-inis] n. Somnolence *f.* ; demi-sommeil *m.* (See doze.) ‖ Fig. Apathie *f.*
drowsy [-i] adj. Somnolent, sommeillant, assoupi. (See sleep.) ‖ Endormant, soporifique (lethargic). ‖ Fig. Apathique, nonchalant, endormi.
drub [drʌb] v. tr. (1). Bâtonner (to cudgel) ; rosser (to thrash). ‖ Fig. Battre.
drubbing [-iŋ] n. Fam. Raclée, dégelée, volée, frottée, tournée, trempe, tripotée *f.* (thrashing). ‖ Fam. Pile *f.* (defeat).
drudge [drʌdʒ] n. Fam. Trimeur, forçat *m.* ; *to lead the life of a drudge,* mener une vie d'esclave.
— v. intr. Fam. Trimer, turbiner.
drudgery [-əri] n. Fam. Travail fastidieux ; métier d'esclave ; turbin (fam.) *m.* ; corvée *f.*
drug [drʌg] n. Med. Produit pharmaceutique *m.* ; drogue *f.* (fam.) [remedy] ; drogue *f.*, stupéfiant *m.* (stupefacient). ‖ Comm. *Drug on the market,* article invendable *m.* ‖ **Drug-addict** (or) **-fiend,** n. Med. Toxicomane *s.* ‖ **Drug-traffic** n. Trafic (*m.*) des stupéfiants.
— v. tr. (1). Droguer (s.o.) ; *to drug oneself,* se droguer. ‖ Droguer, mettre un narcotique dans (a drink). ‖ Fig. Rassasier, écœurer.
drugget ['drʌgit] n. Droguet *m.* (fabric).
druggist ['drʌgist] n. Med. U. S. Pharmacien-droguiste *m.*
drugstore ['drʌgstɔ:*] n. Med. U. S. Pharmacie *f.* ; drugstore *m.*
druid ['druːid] n. Druide *m.*
druidess [-is] n. Druidesse *f.*
druidic(al) [druː'idik(əl)] adj. Druidique.
drum [drʌm] n. Baril, bidon *m.* ; gonne *f.* (container). ‖ Mus. Tambour *m.* (instrument, musician) ; *big drum,* grosse caisse. ‖ Med. Tympan *m.* ‖ Archit. Tambour *m.* ‖ Techn. Tambour, cylindre *m.* ‖ Electr. Bobine *f.* ; dévidoir *m.* ‖ Zool. Mugissement *m.* (of the bittern). ‖ Fam. Tambourinage *m.* (sound). ‖ **Drum-barrel,** n. Mus. Caisse *f.* (of a drum). ‖ **Drum-beat,** n. Coup de tambour *m.* ‖ **Drum brake,** n. Autom. Frein à tambour *m.* ‖ **Drum-call,** n. Mus. Batterie (*f.*) de tambour. ‖ **Drum major,** n. Milit. Tambour-major *m.*
— v. intr. (1). Mus. Battre du tambour. ‖ Zool. Mugir (bittern). ‖ Fam. Tambouriner, pianoter (*with,* avec). ‖ Fam. Faire du battage (*for,* pour) [to boost].
— v. tr. Mus. Tambouriner, tapoter (a tune). ‖ Fam. Tambouriner (or) pianoter avec (one's fingers). ‖ Fam. Seriner (*into,* à) [sth.]. ‖ **To drum up,** Fam.

Battre le rappel de. ‖ **To drum out**, MILIT. Dégrader.

drumfire [-faiə*] n. MILIT. Tir de barrage, feu roulant m.

drumhead [-hed] n. MUS. Peau (f.) de tambour. ‖ MED. Membrane (f.) du tympan. ‖ NAUT. Chapeau de cabestan m. ‖ MILIT. *Drumhead service,* service religieux en plein air.

drummer [-ə*] n. MUS. Tambour m. (musician). ‖ COMM. U. S. Commis voyageur m.

drumming [-iŋ] n. Tambourinage m.

drumstick [-stik] n. MUS. Baguette (f.) de tambour. ‖ CULIN. Pilon m., cuisse f. (of fowl). ‖ POP. Guibolle, flûte f. (leg).

drunk [drʌŋk] adj. Ivre, saoul. ‖ FIG. Enivré, ivre. — n. POP. Saoulard, pochard, poivrot m. (drunkard); soulographie f. (intoxication).
— p. p. See DRINK.

drunkard [-əd] n. Ivrogne m.; ivrognesse f.

drunken [-ən] adj. Saoul. (See DRUNK.) ‖ Alcoolique, ivrogne (addicted to drink). ‖ D'ivrogne (caused by intoxication). ‖ En zigzag.

drunkenly [-ənli] adv. Comme un ivrogne.

drunkenness [-ənnis] n. Ivrognerie f. (habitual); ivresse f. (temporary).

drupe [dru:p] n. BOT. Drupe f.

druse [dru:z] n. GEOL. Druse f.

dry [drai] adj. Sec m., sèche f. (land, summer). ‖ Sec, desséché (flower, leaf, wood). ‖ Sec, asséché, à sec (spring, well); *to run dry,* tarir, s'assécher, se tarir. ‖ ZOOL. Tari (cow). ‖ CULIN. Sec (bread); sec, non sucré (wine); *extra dry,* brut (champagne). ‖ MED. Sec (cough). ‖ ELECTR. Sec (battery, cell). ‖ CHIM. **Dry ice,** neige carbonique. ‖ FIN. Liquide (money). ‖ NAUT. A sec, échoué (ship). ‖ AUTOM. *To run dry,* avoir une panne d'essence. ‖ U. S. FAM. Sec, adepte du régime sec. ‖ COMM. *Dry measure,* mesure de capacité pour matières sèches. ‖ COMM. U. S. *Dry goods,* nouveautés; *dry-goods store,* magasin de nouveautés. ‖ FIG. Sec, froid (answer, reception); sec, sans fioritures (facts, style); caustique, froid (humour); insipide, sans intérêt (lecture); aride (question, subject). ‖ FAM. *Not to be dry behind the ears yet,* têter encore sa mère, n'être pas sevré. ‖ **Dry-clean,** v. tr. Nettoyer à sec. ‖ **Dry-cleaning,** n. Nettoyage (m.) à sec. ‖ **Dry-dock,** n. NAUT. Cale sèche f.; v. tr. NAUT. Mettre en cale sèche; FAM. *in dry-dock,* en rade. ‖ **Dry-eyed,** adj. Sans larmes, l'œil sec. ‖ **Dry-nurse,** n. Nourrice sèche f.; v. tr. Elever au biberon. ‖ **Dry-point,** n. ARTS. Pointe sèche f.; v. tr. Faire de la pointe sèche. ‖ **Dry-rot,** n. BOT. Pourriture sèche f.; FAM. Corruption lente f. (social decay). ‖ **Dry-salt,** v. tr. CULIN. Saler (meat). ‖ **Dry-salter,** n. CULIN. Marchand (m.) de salaisons; COMM. Marchand (m.) de couleurs, droguiste m. (chandler). ‖ **Dry-shod,** adj. A pied sec. ‖ **Dry-stone,** adj. ARCHIT. En pierres sèches. ‖ **Dry-wash,** n. Blanchissage sans repassage m.
— v. tr. Faire sécher (linen). ‖ Essuyer (with, avec) [dishes]. ‖ Assécher, sécher (a marsh); tarir (a well). ‖ MED. Dessécher (skin). ‖ CULIN. Délaiter (butter); faire sécher (fruit). ‖ AGRIC. Tarir (cow). ‖ **To dry up,** sécher entièrement; FAM. Sécher.
— v. intr. Sécher, se sécher (to become dry); sécher, se tarir, s'assécher (to go dry); sécher, se dessécher (to parch). ‖ **To dry up,** se sécher entièrement; se tarir complètement; FAM. La boucler.

dryad ['draiəd] n. Dryade f.

dryer ['draiə*] n. See DRIER.

dryly ['draili] adv. Sèchement. ‖ Ironiquement, d'un air mi-figue mi-raisin.

dryness [-nis] n. Sécheresse f. (See DROUGHT.) ‖ Siccité f. ‖ FIG. Causticité f. (of humour); aridité f. (of a subject); sécheresse f. (of tone).

D. S. O. [di:es'ou] abbr. *Distinguished Service Order,* Ordre du service distingué, décoration militaire britannique.

dual ['djuəl] adj. A deux, double. ‖ TECHN. Double (ignition). ‖ RADIO. Accouplé (loudspeakers). ‖ AUTOM. Jumelé (tyres); *dual carriageway,* route à chaussées séparées. ‖ AVIAT. Double (control). ‖ PSYCH. *Dual personality,* dédoublement de la personnalité. ‖ **Dual-purpose,** adj. A double usage.
— n. GRAMM. Duel m.

dualism [-izm] n. Dualisme m.

dualiste [-ist] n. Dualiste m.

dualistic [djuə'listik] adj. Dualiste.

duality [dju'æliti] n. Dualité f.

dub [dʌb] v. tr. (1). † Adouber, armer (a knight). ‖ Conférer le grade (or) titre de chevalier à. ‖ TECHN. Graisser (leather). ‖ FAM. Qualifier de (to call).
— n. U. S. Battement de tambour m. ‖ FAM. U. S. Balourd m.

dub v. tr. MUS. U. S. Enregistrer par doublage (a record). ‖ CINEM. Doubler par synchronisation (a dialogue, a film).

dubbin ['dʌbin] n. Dégras m.; graisse (f.) de phoque.
— v. tr. Graisser, passer de la graisse sur.

dubbing [-iŋ] n. † Adoubement m. ‖ TECHN. Dégras m.

dubbing [-iŋ] n. CINEM. Doublage m.; synchronisation f.

dubiety [dju'baiəti] n. Etat dubitatif, doute m. (See UNCERTAINTY.)

dubious ['dju:biəs] adj. Douteux, vague, ambigu (not clear). ‖ Hésitant, incertain (irresolute); sceptique (about, sur). ‖ Incertain, indécis, douteux, non assuré (doubtful). ‖ Douteux, discutable (questionable). ‖ Douteux, suspect, louche, équivoque, peu intéressant (shady).

dubiously [-li] adv. Avec doute; d'une façon douteuse.

dubiousness [-nis] n. Doute m.; incertitude f. (See UNCERTAINTY.) ‖ Nature suspecte (or) douteuse f.

dubitation [,dju:bi'teiʃən] n. Doute m.; indécision f.

dubitative ['dju:bitətiv] adj. Dubitatif.

ducal ['dju:kəl] adj. Ducal.

ducat ['dʌkət] n. Ducat m.

duchess ['dʌtʃis] n. Duchesse f. ‖ POP. Bourgeoise f.

duchy [-i] n. Duché m.

duck [dʌk] n. ZOOL. Cane f. (female duck); canard m. (drake); *wild duck,* canard sauvage. ‖ CULIN. Canard m. ‖ SPORTS. Zéro m. (in cricket). ‖ AUTOM. Camion amphibie m. ‖ FIN. *Lame duck,* failli, décavé. ‖ FAM. Chou, trésor m. (darling). ‖ FAM. *Lame duck,* canard boiteux, pauvre type; *it's like water off a duck's back,* ça glisse sans entrer, autant cracher en l'air; *to play* (at) *ducks and drakes,* faire des ricochets sur l'eau; *to play* (at) *ducks and drakes with one's money,* gaspiller son argent; *to turn up one's eyes like a duck in thunder,* tourner des yeux de merlan frit. ‖ **Duck-bill,** n. ZOOL. Ornithorynque m. ‖ **Duck-board,** n. Caillebotis m. ‖ **Duck-footed,** adj. ZOOL. Palmé. ‖ **Duck-shooting,** n. SPORTS. Chasse (f.) au canard sauvage.

duck n. Toile f. ‖ FAM. Pl. Pantalon blanc m.

duck v. intr. Plonger rapidement (to dive). ‖ Esquiver en se courbant. ‖ Baisser vivement la tête. ‖ FAM. Se plonger.
— v. tr. Baisser vivement (the head). ‖ Faire faire un plongeon à (s.o.). ‖ FAM. Esquiver (a blow).
— n. Brusque plongeon m. ‖ Rapide inclinaison de la tête f. ‖ SPORTS. Esquive f.

ducker [-ə*] n. ZOOL. Plongeon m. ‖ SPORTS. U. S. Plongeur s. ‖ U. S. Eleveur (or) chasseur (m.) de canards.

ducking [-iŋ] n. Bain forcé m. ‖ **Ducking-stool,** n. Sellette (f.) à plongeon.

duckling [-liŋ] n. ZOOL. Caneton *m.* ‖ FAM. *Ugly duckling*, laideron.

duckweed [-wi:d] n. BOT. Lentille d'eau *f.*

ducky [-i] adj. FAM. Chou, délicieux.
— n. FAM. Chou, trésor, poulet *m.* (darling).

duct [dʌkt] n. TECHN. Conduite, cheminée *f.* (for gas). ‖ ELECTR. Tube *m.* ‖ MED. Canal, conduit *m.*

ductile ['dʌktail] adj. Souple, flexible. ‖ TECHN. Ductile. ‖ FIG. Malléable, souple.

ductility [dʌk'tiliti] n. Souplesse, plasticité *f.* ‖ TECHN. Ductilité *f.* ‖ FIG. Souplesse *f.*

ductless ['dʌktlis] adj. MED. A sécrétion interne (glands).

dud [dʌd] adj. Incapable (person). ‖ FIN. Sans provision (chèque); faux (note). ‖ COMM. *Dud stock*, rossignols. ‖ FAM. Moche; à la manque.
— n. MILIT. Obus non éclaté *m.* ‖ COMM. Rossignol *m.* ‖ FAM. Raté *m.; a dud at mathematics*, nul (or) un cancre en maths; *a dud at football*, un zéro au football. ‖ Pl. Défroque *f.;* frusques *f. pl.*

dude [dju:d] n. FAM. U. S. Poseur *s.*

dudgeon ['dʌdʒən] n. Colère *f.*

due [dju:] adj. Dû, convenable, adéquat (suitable). ‖ Opportun, voulu, favorable (seasonable). ‖ Dû, qu'on doit, qui revient (*to*, à) [merited]. ‖ Dû, imputable (*to*, à); occasionné (*to*, par) [caused]. ‖ FIN. Dû (*to*, à); échu (bill); U. S. *due bill*, reconnaissance de dette; *due date*, échéance. ‖ CH. DE F., AVIAT. Attendu, prévu, qui doit arriver (*at*, à). ‖ U. S. *Due to*, à cause de, par suite de (because of).
— adv. Carrément, en plein.
— n. Dû *m.; to give s. o. his due*, rendre justice à qqn. ‖ FIN. Dû *m.; to pay one's dues*, payer ses dettes. ‖ JUR. Pl. Droits *m. pl.* ‖ NAUT. *Harbour dues*, droits de mouillage. ‖ U. S. Pl. Souscription *f.;* abonnement *m.* (to a club).

duel ['djuəl] n. Duel *m.; duel with swords*, duel à l'épée.
— v. intr. (1). Se battre en duel.

duellist [-ist] n. Duelliste *m.*

duenna [dju:'enə] n. Duègne *f.*

duet [dju:'et] n. MUS. Duo *m.* ‖ FIG. Couple *m.*

duettist [-ist] n. MUS. Duettiste *s.*

duff [dʌf] n. CULIN. Pudding *m.* ‖ U. S. Humus *m.*
duff v. tr. FAM. U. S. Maquiller. (See FAKE.)
— adj. FAM. Sans valeur; de la petite bière, de la gnognotte.

duffel ['dʌfl] n. Molleton *m.* (cloth). ‖ U. S. FAM. Equipement de camping *m.* ‖ **Duffel-bag**, n. Sac de paquetage *m.* ‖ **Duffel-coat**, n. Duffel-coat *m.*

duffer ['dʌfə*] n. COMM. Colporteur *m.* ‖ FIG. Faux *m.* (article); faussaire, maquilleur, falsificateur (faker). ‖ FAM. Cruche, gourde *f.* (person); cancre *m.* (schoolboy).

duffle ['dʌfl] n. See DUFFEL.

dug [dʌg] pret., p. p. See DIG.

dug n. ZOOL. Tétine *f.* (of animal); pis *m.* (of cow).

dug-out ['dʌgaut] n. MILIT. Abri *m.* ‖ NAUT. Pirogue *f.* ‖ FAM., MILIT. Vieille culotte de peau *f.*

duke [dju:k] n. Duc *m.*

dukedom [-dəm] n. Duché *m.* (territory); titre de duc *m.* (title).

dulcet ['dʌlsit] adj. Mélodieux. ‖ † Suave.

dulcify ['dʌlsifai] v. tr. (2). Edulcorer; adoucir.

dulcimer ['dʌlsimə*] n. MUS. Tympanon *m.*

dulcin ['dʌlsin] n. CHIM. Dulcine *f.*

Dulcinea [,dʌlsi'niə] n. Dulcinée *f.*

dulcitone ['dʌlsitoun] n. MUS. Typhophone *m.*

dull [dʌl] adj. Lourd, lent, borné, peu dégourdi, peu brillant (obtuse). ‖ Morne, triste, sans joie (cheerless); déprimé, abattu (dejected); terne, monotone (drab); insipide, plat (flat); sans éclat (lack-lustre); sans vie (or) entrain (lifeless); morne; morose, maussade (sullen); ennuyeux, assommant, abrutissant (tedious); atone, vide (vacant); *I find life dull*, le temps me pèse (or) dure. ‖ Terne, mat (colour); sourd, mat (noise); gris, maussade, triste (weather). ‖ MED. Sourd (pain); peu aiguisé (sense); *dull hearing*, ouïe dure. ‖ FIN. Inactif, languissant (market). ‖ TECHN. Emoussé (tool).
— v. tr. Alourdir (mind); hébéter (s.o.). ‖ Ternir (a colour); assourdir (a sound). ‖ MED. Amortir (pain); émousser (senses). ‖ TECHN. Emousser. ‖ FIG. Affaiblir, émousser (attention); attrister (life, person).
— v. intr. S'alourdir (mind). ‖ Se ternir (colour, metal); s'assourdir (sound). ‖ MED. S'amortir (pain); s'émousser (sense). ‖ FIG. S'attrister.

dullard [-əd] n. FAM. Non-valeur, nullité *f.;* crétin, balourd *m.* (fam.).

dullish [-iʃ] adj. Borné (mind, person). ‖ Embêtant (tedious).

dullness [-nis] n. Lourdeur (*f.*) d'esprit. ‖ Tristesse, maussaderie *f.;* aspect morne, manque (*m.*) de vie (or) d'éclat (cheerlessness). ‖ Caractère ennuyeux *m.* (tediousness). ‖ Matité *f.* (of colour, sound). ‖ MED. *Dullness of hearing*, dureté d'oreille. ‖ FIN. Marasme *m.* (of business); inactivité *f.* (of market). ‖ TECHN. Manque de tranchant *m.*

dully [-li] adv. Lourdement. ‖ D'une manière terne (or) ennuyeuse.

dulotic ['dju'lotik] adj. ZOOL. Esclavagiste (ant).

duly ['dju:li] adv. Dûment, convenablement (properly). ‖ A point, à temps (on time).

dumb [dʌm] adj. MED. Muet. ‖ FIG. Muet (*with*, de). ‖ FAM. Gourde, bécasse, borné (stupid). ‖ FAM. *Dumb blonde*, blonde évaporée. ‖ **Dumbbell**, n. SPORTS. Haltère *f.;* U. S. FAM. Gourde *f.* (blockhead). ‖ **Dumb-show**, n. THEATR. Pantomime *f.* ‖ **Dumb-waiter**, n. Desserte, table roulante *f.;* U. S. Monte-plats *m.*

dumbfound [dʌm'faund] v. tr. Désarçonner, ébahir; *to be dumbfounded*, être sidéré, en avoir perdu la parole.

dumbly ['dʌmli] adv. En silence.

dumbness [-nis] n. MED., FIG. Mutisme *m.*

dumdum ['dʌmdʌm] adj. MILIT. Dumdum (bullet).

dummy ['dʌmi] n. Simulacre; objet factice *m.* ‖ Mort *m.* (at bridge). ‖ COMM. Mannequin *m.* (in dressmaking, in a shop-window). ‖ TECHN. Maquette *f.* (in printing). ‖ FIN. Prête-nom, homme de paille *m.* ‖ MED. Sucette *f.* (for babies). ‖ FAM. Bêta, ballot *m.* ‖ FAM. SPORTS. Feinte *f.*
— adj. A trois, avec un mort (bridge). ‖ Faux, factice; *dummy work*, trucage. ‖ FIN. Agissant comme prête-nom (or) couverture.
— v. tr. (2). SPORTS. Feinter.
— v. tr. (2). U. S. FAM. *To dummy up*, la boucler, la fermer.

dump [dʌmp] v. tr. Décharger, déverser. ‖ FIN., COMM. Vendre en faisant du dumping.
— v. intr. Se décharger, se déverser. ‖ Jeter au rebut. ‖ FIN. Faire du dumping.
— n. Bruit (*m.*) de chute. ‖ Amas, tas *m.* (of rubbish). ‖ Dépotoir *m.* (place). ‖ MILIT. Dépôt *m.* ‖ TECHN. Basculeur *m.* ‖ FAM. *A dull dump*, un trou à moitié mort. ‖ **Dump-lorry, dump-truck**, n. Tombereau, camion (*m.*) à bascule.

dump n. Palet *m.* (game). ‖ FAM. Poussah, gros père *m.* (man); dondon *f.* (woman).

dumpish [-iʃ] adj. FAM. Cafardeux, déprimé.

dumpling ['dʌmpliŋ] n. CULIN. Dumpling *m.;* boulette pour garniture *f.; apple dumpling*, pomme enrobée de pâte, bourdelot.

dumps [dʌmps] n. FAM. Cafard *m.; in the dumps*, broyant du noir.

dumpy ['dʌmpi] adj. Courtaud, boulot; rondouillard (fam.); *dumpy umbrella*, tom-pouce.

dun [dʌn] n. FIN. Gris foncé.

dun n. FIN. Demande (*f.*) de remboursement (demand); créancier impatient *m.* (person).
— v. tr. (1). FIN. Relancer (a debtor).

dunce [dʌns] n. FAM. Ane *m.;* bourrique *f.* ‖ FAM. Cancre *m.* (schoolboy); *dunce's cap*, bonnet d'âne.

dunderhead ['dʌndəhed] n. Crétin, idiot *m.*

dune [dju:n] n. Dune *f.*

dung [dʌŋ] n. Crotte, fiente *f.* (of animals); bouse *f.* (of cow); crottin *m.* (of horse). ‖ AGRIC. Fumier *m.* ‖ **Dung-beetle,** n. ZOOL. Boursier *m.*
— v. tr. AGRIC. Fumer (a field).

dungaree [dʌŋgə'ri:] n. Treillis *m.* (fabric). ‖ Pl. Bleu *m.;* combinaison, salopette *f.*

dungeon ['dʌnʒən] n. Cul-de-basse-fosse *m.;* oubliette *f.* ‖ ARCHIT. Donjon *m.*

dunghill ['dʌŋhil] n. Tas de fumier *m.*

dunk [dʌŋk] v. tr. Tremper (*into,* dans) [bread].
— v. intr. Faire trempette, tremper des mouillettes.

Dunkirk [dʌn'kə:k] n. GEOGR. Dunkerque *f.* ‖ FAM. Retraite forcée, défaite retentissante *f.*

dunlin ['dʌnlin] n. ZOOL. Alouette (*f.*) de mer.

dunnage ['dʌnidʒ] n. NAUT. Fardage *m.*

dunno [dʌ'nou] contraction of *I do not know,* FAM. J'sais pas!

dunnock ['dʌnək] n. ZOOL. Accenteur mouchet *m.*

duo [dju'ou] n. MUS. Duo *m.*

duodecimal [,dju:o'desiməl] adj. MATH. Duodécimal *m.*
— n. pl. MATH. Calcul duodécimal *m.*

duodecimo [-mou] n. In-douze *m.* (book, size).

duodenal [,dju:o'di:nəl] adj. MED. Duodénal.

duodenitis [,dju:odə'naitis] n. MED. Duodénite *f.*

duodenum [,dju:o'di:nəm] n. MED. Duodénum *m.*

duologue ['djuələg] n. Dialogue *m.* ‖ THEATR. Duodrame *m.*

dupe [dju:p] n. Dupe *f.;* dindon (*m.*) de la farce.
— v. tr. Duper. (See CHEAT.)

duper [-ə*] n. Dupeur *s.*

dupery [-əri] n. Duperie *f.*

duple ['dju:pl̩] adj. Double. ‖ MUS. Binaire.

duplex ['dju:pleks] adj. Double. ‖ ELECTR., RADIO. Duplex; *duplex process,* duplex. ‖ U. S. *Duplex apartment,* appartement à deux étages; *duplex house,* maison double.
— v. tr. ELECTR., RADIO. Duplexer.

duplicate ['dju:plikit] adj. Double, en double, en duplicata. ‖ Double (doubled). ‖ De rechange; identique.
— n. Double, duplicata *m.;* copie exacte *f.; in duplicate,* en deux exemplaires, en double expédition; par duplicata. ‖ JUR. Ampliation *f.* ‖ TECHN. Contretype *m.* ‖ COMM. Contrepartie *f.*
— [-keit] v. tr. Faire en double exemplaire. ‖ Doubler. ‖ Copier, reproduire. ‖ Tirer au duplicateur. ‖ ECCLES. *To duplicate masses,* biner.

duplicating ['dju:plikeitiŋ] n. Duplication *f.* ‖ Tirage au duplicateur *m.* ‖ **Duplicating-machine,** n. Duplicateur *m.*

duplication [-ʃən] n. Duplication *f.*

duplicator ['dju:plikeitə*] n. Duplicateur *m.*

duplicity [dju:'plisiti] n. Duplicité *f.* (See DOUBLE-DEALING.)

durability [,djuərə'biliti] n. Durée *f.*

durable ['djuərəbl̩] adj. Durable.
— n. pl. Biens durables *m. pl.*

durably [-bli] adv. Durablement.

Dural ['djuərəl], **Duralumin** [djuə'rælju:min] n. CHIM. Duralumin *m.*

dura mater ['djuərə'meitə*] n. MED. Dure-mère *f.*

durance ['djuərəns] n. JUR. Emprisonnement *m.;* détention *f.*

duration [djuə'reiʃən] n. Durée *f.*

duress [djuə'res] n. JUR. Contrainte, coercition *f.* (compulsion); captivité *f.* (imprisonment).

durian ['djuəriən] n. BOT. Durione *f.* (fruit); durion *m.* (tree).

during ['djuəriŋ] prep. Durant, pendant.

durst [də:st] pret. See DARE.

dusk [dʌsk] n. Crépuscule *m.;* tombée de la nuit, demi-obscurité *f.* (twilight). ‖ Obscurité *f.* (gloom).
— adj. Sombre.
— v. tr. Assombrir.
— v. intr. S'assombrir.

duskiness [-inis] n. Semi-obscurité *f.* ‖ Hâle *m.* (of complexion).

dusky [-i] adj. Obscur, sombre (gloomy). ‖ Hâlé, bistré, brun (swarthy).

dust [dʌst] n. Poussière *f.; to cover with dust,* empoussiérer. ‖ Poudre *f.; to throw dust in s.o.'s eyes,* jeter de la poudre aux yeux de qqn. ‖ Pl. Cendres *m. pl.* (of a dead person). ‖ BOT. Pollen *m.* ‖ FIG. Poussière *f.; to bite the dust,* mordre la poussière; *to lick the dust,* ramper servilement; U. S. *to take no one's dust,* ne pas se laisser dépasser. ‖ LOC. *Small rain lays great dust,* petite pluie abat grand vent. ‖ **Dust bowl,** n. U. S. Région dénudée *f.* ‖ **Dust-cart,** n. AUTOM. Voiture (*f.*) des boueux. ‖ **Dust-cloth,** n. Housse *f.;* U. S. chiffon (*m.*) à épousseter. ‖ **Dust-coat,** n. Cache-poussière *m.* ‖ **Dust-coloured,** adj. Cendré. ‖ **Dust-cover,** (or) **-jacket,** n. Couvre-livre *m.;* liseuse *f.* ‖ **Dust-disease,** n. MED. Chalicose *f.* ‖ **Dust-hole,** n. Vide-ordures *m.* ‖ **Dust-pan,** n. Pelle (*f.*) à ordures. ‖ **Dust-shot,** n. MILIT. Cendrée *f.*
— v. tr. Epousseter (to rid of dust). ‖ Saupoudrer (*with,* de) [powder]. ‖ FAM. *To dust s.o.'s jacket,* tanner le cuir à qqn.
— v. intr. Epousseter, faire le ménage. ‖ Faire poudrette, s'ébrouer dans la poussière (bird). ‖ **To dust out,** U. S. FAM. Décamper. ‖ **Dust-up,** n. FAM. Coup de chien (or) de torchon *m.;* prise (*f.*) de bec.

dustbin [-bin] n. Poubelle, boîte à ordures *f.; dustbin raker,* chiffonnier.

duster [-ə*] n. Essuie-meubles. ‖ U. S. Cache-poussière *m.*

dustiness [-inis] n. Etat poussiéreux *m.*

dusting [-iŋ] n. Epoussetage *m.* ‖ Saupoudrage *m.* ‖ FAM. Tournée, raclée *f.*

dustman [-mən] (pl. **dustmen**) n. Boueux, boueur *m.* ‖ FAM. Marchand de sable *m.* (in folklore).

dusty [-i] adj. Poussiéreux (covered with dust); poudreux (powdery). ‖ Cendré (dust-coloured). ‖ FAM. *Not so dusty,* pas si moche.

Dutch [dʌtʃ] adj. GEOGR. Hollandais. ‖ † Allemand. ‖ CULIN. *Dutch cheese,* Hollande, tête-de-mort; *Dutch oven,* rôtissoire. ‖ AGRIC. *Dutch barn,* hangar. ‖ BOT. *Dutch elm disease,* maladie (or) galle de l'orme. ‖ FAM. *Dutch courage,* courage puisé dans le vin.
— n. GEOGR. Hollandais *m. pl.* ‖ GRAMM. Hollandais, néerlandais *m.* (language). ‖ † Allemand *m.* ‖ FAM. *It's Dutch to me,* c'est du chinois pour moi; *to go Dutch,* partager les frais, payer son écot. ‖ U. S. FAM. *To be in Dutch,* être mal vu.

Dutchman [-mən] (pl. **Dutchmen**) n. GEOGR. Hollandais *m.* ‖ MUS. *Flying Dutchman,* Vaisseau fantôme.

Dutchwoman [-wumən] (pl. **Dutchwomen** [-wimin]) n. GEOGR. Hollandaise *f.*

duteous ['dju:tiəs] adj. Déférent. (See DUTIFUL.) ‖ Obéissant.

dutiable [-əbl̩] adj. JUR. Soumis aux droits de douane.

dutiful [-ful] adj. Plein d'égards (considerate); soumis (obedient); déférent (respectful).

dutifully [-fuli] adv. Avec déférence (or) soumission.

dutifulness [-fulnis] n. Déférence; soumission *f.; dutifulness of children,* piété filiale.

duty ['dju:ti] n. Déférence *f.; in duty to,* par respect pour, en conformité avec. ‖ Devoir *m.; as in duty bound,* comme de bien entendu; *for duty's sake,* par devoir; *to be s.o.'s duty to,* être du devoir de qqn de. ‖ Office *m.; to do duty for,* faire office (or) fonction de, remplacer. ‖ Garde *f.; to be on duty for the day,* être de jour; *to do dinner duty,* surveiller le réfectoire (at school). ‖ Pl. Attributions, fonctions *f. pl.;* charge *f.; public duties,* fonctions publiques; *to take up one's duties,* entrer

en fonctions. ‖ Pl. Devoirs *m. pl.;* civilités *f. pl.*
(regards). ‖ Milit. Service *m.; off duty,* libre;
on duty, de service; *on special duty,* en service
commandé. ‖ Fin. Pl. Droits *m. pl.* ‖ Techn. Rendement *m.* (of a machine). ‖ **Duty-free,** adj. Fin.
Exempt de droits, en franchise.

duumvir [dju'ʌmvə*] n̩. Duumvir.

duvet ['du:vei] n. Couette *f.*

duvetin [djuvə'ti:n] n. Duvetine *f.*

dwarf [dwɔ:f] n. Nain *s.;* nabot *m.* (fam.). [See
Midget.]
— adj. Nain; rabougri.
— v. tr. Empêcher la croissance de. ‖ Rapetisser.

dwarfish [-iʃ] adj. De nain; nabot (person); rabougri (thing). ‖ Minuscule; riquiqui (fam.).

dwarfishness [-iʃnis] n. Nanisme *m.;* extrême
petitesse *f.*

dwarfism [-izm̩] n. Nanisme *m.*

dwell [dwel] v. intr. (52). Habiter, demeurer, résider (*in,* à, dans). [See Live.] ‖ Rester, s'appuyer,
se fixer (*on,* sur). ‖ S'étendre; s'appesantir, insister
(*on,* sur) [to expatiate]. ‖ Sports. Hésiter (horse).
— n. Techn. Pause *f.*

dweller [-ə*] n. Habitant, *s.* (*in, on* de). ‖ Sports.
Sauteur hésitant *m.* (horse).

dwelling [-iŋ] n. Habitation, demeure *f.* (See
Domicile.) ‖ Fig. Insistance *f.* ‖ **Dwelling-house,**
n. Maison d'habitation *f.* ‖ **Dwelling-place,** n.
Demeure *f.*

dwelt [-t] pret., p. p. See Dwell.

dwindle ['dwindl] v. intr. Diminuer. (See Decrease.) ‖ **To dwindle away,** s'affaiblir, dépérir.

dwindling [-dliŋ] adj. En diminution, qui se raréfie. ‖ Dépérissant.

dyad ['daiəd] n. Dyade *f.* ‖ Chim. Radical divalent *m.*

dye [dai] n. Teinte, couleur *f.;* ton *m.* (colour).
‖ Teinture *f.* (colouring matter). ‖ Fig. *Of the
deepest dye,* de la pire noirceur. ‖ **Dye-house, dyeworks,** n. Teinturerie *f.* ‖ **Dye-stuff,** n. Matière
colorante *f.*
— v. tr. Teindre; *to have a dress dyed blue,*
faire teindre une robe en bleu.
— v. intr. Se teindre.

dyed [-d] adj. Teint. ‖ **Dyed-in-the-wool,** adj.
Teint avant tissage; Fam. Convaincu, pur sang,
bon teint; vrai de vrai, dur à cuire.

dyer [-ə*] n. Teinturier *s.*

dying [-iŋ] adj. Mourant (person); *dying words,*
dernières paroles.

dyke [daik]. See Dike.

dynamic [dai'næmik] adj. Phys. Dynamique. ‖
Med. Fonctionnel. ‖ Fig. Dynamique, énergique
(personality); *dynamic force,* dynamisme.
— n. Phys. Force motrice *f.* ‖ Pl. Phys. Dynamique *f.*

dynamism ['dainəmizm̩] n. Dynamisme *m.*

dynamite ['dainəmait] n. Dynamite *f.*
— v. tr. Faire sauter à la dynamite, dynamiter.

dynamo ['dainəmou] n. Electr. Dynamo *f.; high-tension dynamo,* dynamo-tension; *low-tension
dynamo,* dynamo-quantité. ‖ **Dynamo-electric,** adj.
Electr. Dynamo-électrique.

dynamometer [,dainə'mɔmitə*] n. Electr. Dynamomètre *m.*

dynamometric [,dainəmo'metrik] adj. Electr.
Dynamométrique.

dynamometry [,dainə'mɔmetri] n. Electr. Dynamométrie *f.*

dynamotor [,dainə'moutə*] n. Electr. Dynamoteur *m.*

dynast ['dinəst] n. Dynaste *m.*

dynastic [di'næstik] adj. Dynastique.

dynasty ['dinəsti] n. Dynastie *f.*

dynatron ['dainətrɔn] n. Electr. Dynatron *m.*

dyne [dain] n. Phys. Dyne *f.*

dysenteric ['disn̩'terik] adj. Med. Dysentérique.

dysentery ['disn̩tri] n. Med. Dysenterie *f.*

dysfunction [dis'fʌŋkʃən] n. Dysfonctionnement *m.*

dyslexia [dis'leksiə] n. Dyslexie, alexie *f.*

dyslexic [dis'leksik] adj., n. Dyslexique, alexique
adj., s.

dyslogistic [,dislo'dʒistik] adj. Péjoratif.

dysmenorrhoea [,dismənə'ri:ə] n. Med. Dysménorrhée *f.*

dyspepsia [dis'pepsiə] n. Med. Dyspepsie *f.*

dyspeptic [-tik] adj. n. Med. Dyspeptique.

dyspnoea [dis'pni:] n. Med. Dyspnée *f.*

dysprosium [dis'prousiəm] n. Chim. Dysprosium *m.*

dystrophy ['distrəfi] n. Med. Dystrophie *f.;
muscular dystrophy,* dystrophie musculaire progressive.

E

e [i:] n. E, e *m.* ‖ Mus. Mi *m.* ‖ Geogr. E., est *m.*
(east); de l'est (or) oriental (eastern).

each [i:tʃ] adj. Chaque.
— pron. Chacun. ‖ Comm. Pièce, chacun. ‖ **Each
other,** l'un l'autre; réciproquement.

eager ['i:gə*] adj. Impatient, pressé, anxieux (person); *eager to begin,* brûlant de commencer; *to be
eager for,* rechercher avidement, désirer trouver. ‖
‖ Ardent, impétueux, violent (desire). ‖ † Mordant,
aigre (wind).

eagerly [-li] adv. Avec impatience (or) zèle, ardemment, passionnément.

eagerness [-nis] n. Impatience, anxiété *f.;* zèle,
enthousiasme, *m.* ‖ Désir ardent *m.;* avidité *f.*

eagle ['i:gl] n. Zool. Aigle *m.* ‖ Milit., Blas.
Aigle *f.* ‖ U. S. Aigle *m.* (10 dollars). ‖ **Eagle-owl,**
n. Zool. Grand duc *m.*

eaglet ['i:glit] n. Zool. Aiglon *m.*

eagre ['i:gə*] n. Naut. Mascaret *m.* (See Bore.)

ear [iə*] n. Med. Oreille *f.* (organ); ouïe *f.* (sense).
‖ Mus. Oreille *f.; to have no ear for music,* n'avoir
pas d'oreille. ‖ Culin. Anse, oreille *f.* (of porringer). ‖ Loc. *To be all ears,* être tout oreilles;
to go in at one ear and go out at the other, entrer

par une oreille et sortir par l'autre ; *to give every-body one's ear*, prêter l'oreille à chacun ; *to have an ear to the ground*, guetter les réactions extérieures ; *to have the ear of*, avoir l'oreille de ; *to listen with half an ear*, écouter d'une oreille distraite ; *to turn a deaf ear to*, faire la sourde oreille à ; *up to the ears*, jusqu'au cou. ‖ **Ear-ache**, n. MED. Mal (*m.*) d'oreilles ; otalgie *f.* ‖ **Ear-drop**, n. Pendant (*m.*) d'oreille ; pl. MED. Gouttes auriculaires *f. pl.* ‖ **Ear-drum**, n. MED. Tympan *m.* ‖ **Ear-flap**, n. Oreillette *f.* (of a cap). ‖ **Ear-plug**, n. Boule (*f.*) Quiès (nom dép.). ‖ **Ear-ring**, n. Boucle d'oreille *f.* ‖ **Ear-shot**, n. Portée d'ouïe *f. ; within ear-shot*, à portée de voix. ‖ **Ear-splitting**, adj. Assourdissant. ‖ **Ear-training**, n. MUS. Solfège *m.* ‖ **Ear-trumpet**, n. MED. Cornet acoustique *m.* ‖ **Ear-wax**, n. MED. Cérumen *m.*

ear n. BOT. Epi *m.*
— v. intr. BOT. Epier.

earl [ə:l] n. Comte *m.*

earldom [-dəm] n. Comté *m.*

early ['ə:li] adj. Matinal, de bonne heure, tôt. ‖ Anticipé ; *to come to an early grave*, avoir une fin prématurée. ‖ Proche, prochain (in the near future). ‖ Passé, d'autrefois (in ancient times). ‖ BOT. Précoce, de primeur ; hâtif.
— adv. Tôt, de bonne heure ; *the earliest he can come*, le plus tôt qu'il puisse venir. ‖ Au début (in, de). ‖ Avant ; *he let me off five minutes early*, il m'a laissé partir cinq minutes plus tôt.

earmark ['iəmɑ:k] n. AGRIC. Marque *f.* ‖ FIG. Signe distinctif *m. ;* caractéristique *f.*
— v. tr. AGRIC. Marquer à l'oreille. ‖ FIN. Réserver, cantonner (a sum) ; affecter (for, à). ‖ FIG. Marquer ; identifier.

earn [ə:n] v. tr. Gagner (salary). ‖ FIN. Rapporter (interest). ‖ FIG. Mériter (praise).

earnest ['ə:nist] adj. Ardent, intense, empressé (eager) ; sérieux (serious) ; convaincu, zélé (zealous).
— n. Sérieux *m. ; in earnest*, sérieusement, sans rire, pour de bon.

earnest ['ə:nist] n. FIN. Arrhes *f. pl. ; earnest money*, avance sur paiement. ‖ FIG. Gage *m.*

earnestly [-li] adv. Avec ardeur (or) empressement. ‖ Avec sérieux (or) conviction.

earnestness [-nis] n. Ardeur *f. ;* zèle *m.* ‖ Conviction, décision *f.* ‖ Sérieux *m.*

earnings ['ə:niŋz] n. pl. Gain, salaire *m. ;* appointements, honoraires *m. pl.* ‖ FIN. Bénéfices *m. pl.*

earphone ['iə:foun], **earpiece** [-pi:s] n. Ecouteur *m.*

earth [ə:θ] n. Terre *f. ;* monde *m.* (world). ‖ Terre *f.* (land) ; terre *f.*, sol *m.* (ground). ‖ AGRIC., ELECTR., CHIM. Terre *f.* ‖ SPORTS. Terrier *m.* ‖ FAM. *Down to earth*, réaliste, pratique, les pieds sur terre ; *why on earth ?*, pourquoi diable ? ‖ **Earth-moving**, n. Nivellement du sol *m.* ‖ **Earth-shaking**, adj. FIG. Stupéfiant, prodigieux.
— v. tr. AGRIC. Butter (plants) ; couvrir de terre (seeds). ‖ ELECTR. Mettre à la terre. ‖ SPORTS. Acculer au terrier (an animal).
— v. intr. SPORTS. Se terrer (fox).

earthen [-ən] adj. En terre ; de terre.

earthenware [-ənwɛə*] n. Faïence *f.*

earthliness ['ə:θlinis] n. Amour (*m.*) des biens terrestres. ‖ Mondanité *f. ;* esprit du siècle *m.*

earthling [-liŋ] n. Créature humaine *f.* ‖ Mondain *s.* (worldling).

earthly [-li] adj. Terrestre (terrestrial). ‖ Mondain ; profane (worldly). ‖ FAM. Possible, au monde. ‖ **Earthly-minded**, adj. Terre à terre ; mondain.

earthquake [-kweik] n. Tremblement (*m.*) de terre. ‖ FIG. Bouleversement *m.*

earthwork [-wə:k] n. MILIT. Ouvrage (*m.*) de terre. ‖ TECHN. Terrassement *m.*

earthworm [-wə:m] n. ZOOL. Ver (*m.*) de terre.

earthy [-i] adj. Terreux. ‖ FIG. Grossier, fruste, matériel ; truculent.

earwig ['iəwig] n. ZOOL. Perce-oreille *m.*

ease [i:z] n. Aise *f. ; at ease*, à l'aise. ‖ Aises *f. pl. ;* confort *m. ; to take one's ease*, prendre ses aises. ‖ Secours *m. ; chapel of ease*, chapelle de secours. ‖ Aisance *f. ; with the greatest of ease*, avec la plus grande aisance. ‖ FIN. Aise *f.* ‖ MILIT. Repos *m.*
— v. tr. Apaiser, alléger, calmer (anxiety, pain). ‖ Rassurer, réconforter (mind). ‖ Donner de l'aisance à, desserrer, relâcher (a rope) ; *to ease the cupboard into place*, placer le buffet en douceur. ‖ NAUT. Mollir (sail).
— v. intr. Se détendre ; *the situation has eased*, une détente s'est produite. ‖ **To ease down**, ralentir. ‖ **To ease off**, se reposer (person) ; dételer (fam.) ; se détendre (situation).

easeful [-ful] adj. Apaisant. ‖ Paisible, sans souci (careless). ‖ Sans ardeur, indolent.

easel ['i:zl] n. ARTS. Chevalet *m.*

easement ['i:zmənt] n. ARCHIT. Annexe *f. ;* dégagement ; bâtiment de secours *m.* ‖ † Apaisement *m.* ‖ JUR. Droit (*m.*) de servitude.

easily [-ili] adv. Aisément, sans difficulté ; *more easily said than done*, plus facile à dire qu'à faire. ‖ Avec calme ; en prenant son temps. ‖ Sans heurt. ‖ FAM. Très probablement, assurément.

easiness [-inis] n. Aisance *f.* ‖ Confort, sentiment (*m.*) d'aise. ‖ Nonchalance, indolence, *f.*

east [i:st] n. Est, levant *m.* ‖ GEOGR. Orient *m. ; Far East*, Extrême-Orient.
— adj. A l'est ; de l'est.
— adv. A l'est (of, de).

eastbound ['i:st,baund] adj. En direction de l'est.

Easter ['i:stə*] n. Pâques *m.* ‖ **Easter-day**, n. Jour de Pâques *m.* ‖ **Easter-egg**, n. Œuf (*m.*) de Pâques.

easterly [-li] adj. D'est.
— adv. De (or) vers l'est.
— n. Vent d'est *m.*

eastern ['i:stən] adj. Tourné vers l'est, face à l'est. ‖ GEOGR. D'Orient, oriental.
— n. GEOGR. Oriental *s.* ‖ ECCLES. Membre (*m.*) de l'Eglise d'Orient.

eastward [-wəd] adj., adv. En direction de l'est.

easy ['i:zi] adj. Aisé, facile, simple (not difficult) ; *just too easy*, enfantin. ‖ Sans souci, tranquille (quiet). ‖ Confortable ; *easy chair*, fauteuil. ‖ Ami du confort, indolent, nonchalant (idle). ‖ Plein d'aisance, simple, sans embarras (not awkward). ‖ Souple, docile (compliant) ; tolérant, accommodant, facile (tractable). ‖ Modéré, tranquille, prenant son temps (unhurried). ‖ FIN. Peu demandé (commodity) ; calme (market). ‖ FAM. *On easy street*, à l'aise, la poche bien garnie ; *an easy mark*, un gogo ; *easier situation*, détente ; *easy money*, argent vite gagné ; *easy slope*, pente douce.
— adv. Aisément, facilement. ‖ Sans souci ; *to take it easy*, en prendre à son aise ; se la couler douce, rester peinard (fam.). ‖ Doucement ; *go easy on the champagne !*, tout doux sur le champagne ! ‖ **Easy-going**, adj. SPORTS. Facile (horse) ; FIG. Nonchalant, qui prend son temps ; pépère (fam.).
— n. FAM. Moment de repos *m. ; have an easy*, soufflez un peu !

eat [i:t] v. tr. (53). Manger (food). ‖ FIG. Manger, ronger. (See CORRODE.) ‖ FAM. *To make s.o. eat his words*, faire rentrer à qqn les paroles dans la gorge. ‖ **To eat away**, manger jusqu'au bout, dévorer ; corroder. ‖ **To eat off**, dévorer ; *to eat s.o.'s head off*, manger (or) avaler qqn (fam.). ‖ **To eat out**, ronger ; *to eat one's heart out*, se consumer de chagrin. ‖ **To eat up**, dévorer (lit. and fig.) ; AUTOM. *To eat up the miles*, dévorer la route.
— v. intr. Manger (person). ‖ Se manger (food). ‖ **To eat into**, FIG. Ronger, pénétrer dans, corroder, attaquer.

eatable [-əbl] adj. Mangeable ; comestible.
— n. pl. Victuailles *f. pl.*

eaten [-n̩] p. p. See EAT.

eater [-ə*] n. Mangeur *s*. ‖ CULIN. Fruit au couteau *m*.

eating [-iŋ] n. Fait de manger *m*. ‖ Chère, nourriture *f*. ‖ **Eating-house**, n. Restaurant *m*.

eats [i:ts] n. pl. FAM. Mangeaille *f*.

eau-de-Cologne [‚ou də kə'loun] n. Eau (*f*.) de Cologne.

eau-de-vie [‚ou də 'vi:] n. Eau-de-vie *f*.

eaves [i:vz] n. pl. Larmier *m*.

eavesdrop [-drop] v. intr. (1). Ecouter aux portes, prêter une oreille indiscrète ; *to be always eavesdropping*, être toujours aux écoutes.

eavesdropper [-drɔpə*] n. Ecouteur (*m*.) aux portes.

ebb [eb] n. Reflux *m*. ‖ FIG. Chute *f. ;* déclin *m*. ‖ **Ebb-tide**, n. NAUT. Jusant *m*.
— v. intr. Refluer (*from*, de) [flood, tide]. ‖ FIG. Décliner, décroître. (See WANE.)

ebon ['ebən] adj. D'ébène.

ebonite [-ait] n. Ebonite *f*.

ebonize [-aiz] v. tr. Noircir comme l'ébène.

ebony ['ebəni] n. Ebène *f*. ‖ **Ebony-tree**, n. BOT. Ebénier *m*.
— adj. D'ébène.

ebullience [i'bʌljəns] n. Ebullition *f*. ‖ FIG. Exubérance *f*.

ebullient [-ənt] adj. Bouillonnant ; effervescent. ‖ FIG. Exubérant.

ebullition [ebʌ'liʃən] n. Ebullition *f*. ‖ FIG. Explosion *f.;* débordement *m*.

eccentric [ek'sentrik] adj., n. TECHN. Excentrique. ‖ FIG. Original *s*.

eccentricity [‚eksen'trisiti] n. TECHN., MATH., FIG. Excentricité *f*.

ecchymosis [eki'mousis] n. MED. Ecchymose *f*.

ecclesiastic [i‚kli:zi'æstik] adj., n. ECCLES. Ecclésiastique *m*.

ecclesiastical [-tikəl] adj. ECCLES. Ecclésiastique.

ecclesiasticism [-tisizm̩] n. Cléricalisme *m*.

Ecclesiasticus [-tikəs] n. ECCLES. Ecclésiastique *m*. (book).

ecdysis ['ekdisis] (pl. **ecdyses** [-si:z]) n. ZOOL. Ecdysis *f*.

echelon ['eʃələn] n. MILIT., AVIAT. Echelon *m*.
— v. tr. MILIT., AVIAT. Former en échelons, échelonner.

echinoderm [i'kainou‚də:m] n. ZOOL. Echinoderme *m*.

echinus [e'kainəs] n. ZOOL. Ourson (*m*.) de mer. ‖ ARCHIT. Echine *f*.

echo ['ekou] (pl. **echoes** [-z]) n. Echo *m*. (lit. and fig.). ‖ **Echo-sounder**, n. NAUT. Echosondeur, sondeur à écho, *m*.
— v. intr. Faire écho (room, voice).
— v. tr. Répéter, se faire l'écho de (ideas, words) ; *to echo back*, faire écho à.

echoic [-ik] adj. D'écho. ‖ GRAMM. D'harmonie imitative.

echolocation [‚ekoulou'keiʃən] n. Echolocation *f*.

eclair [ei'klɛə*] n. CULIN. Eclair *m*.

eclampsia [ek'læmpsiə] n. MED. Eclampsie *f*.

eclat [ei'klɑ:] n. Eclat *m*. (effect); ostentation *f*. (ostentation) ; réussite éclatante *f*. (success).

eclectic [ek'lektik] adj., n. Eclectique *m*.

eclecticism [-sizm̩] n. PHILOS. Eclectisme *m*.

eclipse [i'klips] n. ASTRON., FIG. Eclipse *f*.
— v. tr. ASTRON., FIG. Eclipser ; *to become eclipsed*, s'éclipser.

ecliptic [i'kliptik] adj., n. ASTRON. Ecliptique *m*.

eclogue ['eklɔg] n. Eglogue *f*.

eclosion [i'klouʒən] n. ZOOL. Eclosion *f*. (of larva, of pupa).

ecological [‚i:kɔ'lɔdʒikl̩] adj. Ecologique.

ecologist [i:'kɔlɔdʒist] n. Ecologiste *s*.

ecology [i:'kɔlədʒi] n. Ecologie *f*.

econometrics [i‚kɔnə'metriks] n. sg. Econométrie *f*.

economic [i:kə'nɔmik] adj. JUR., FIN., MED., GEOGR. Economique.

economical [-əl] adj. Economique (apparatus, method, speed, store). ‖ Econome. (See THRIFTY.)

economically [-əli] adv. Economiquement. ‖ JUR. Au point de vue économique.

economics [-iks] n. sg. FIN. Situation économique *f*. ‖ JUR. Economie, économie politique *f*.

economist [i'kɔnəmist] n. JUR. Economiste *m*. ‖ FAM. Personne économe *f*.

economize [-maiz] v. tr. Economiser. (See SPARE.)
— v. intr. Faire des économies, économiser (*on*, sur).

economizer [-maizə*] n. Economiseur *m*.

economy [-mi] n. JUR. Economie *f.;* système économique *m*. ‖ FIN. Economie, épargne *f.; for economy's sake*, par économie. ‖ MED. Economie *f*. ‖ **Economy-size**, adj. COMM. Economique, géant (tube, packet) ; FIG. Enorme, gigantesque.

ecosystem ['i:kou‚sistəm] n. Ecosystème *m*.

ecru ['eikru:] adj. Ecru.

ecstasize ['ekstəsaiz] v. tr. Plonger dans l'extase, ravir, transporter.
— v. intr. S'extasier.

ecstasy [-si] n. ECCLES., MED. Extase *f*. ‖ FIG. Extase, joie délirante *f.;* transport *m*. (see RAPTURE) ; *to go into ecstasies over*, s'extasier devant.

ecstatic [eks'tætik] adj. MED., ECCLES., FIG. Extatique.

ecstatically [-əli] adv. MED., ECCLES., FIG. Avec extase (or) transport.

ectoplasm ['ektoplæzm̩] n. Ectoplasme *m*.

ecumenical [i:kju'menikəl] adj. ECCLES. Œcuménique.

eczema ['ekzimə] n. MED. Eczéma *m*.

eczematous [ek'zemətəs] adj. MED. Eczémateux.

edacious [i'deiʃəs] adj. Vorace, dévorant. (See VORACIOUS.)

edacity [i'dæsiti] n. Voracité *f*.

Edam ['i:dəm] n. CULIN. Hollande *m*. (cheese).

eddy ['edi] n. Remous *m*. (of air, water) ; tourbillon *m*. (of wind).
— v. intr. (2). Tourbillonner. (See WHIRL.)

edelweiss ['eidlvais] n. BOT. Edelweiss *m*.

edema [i'di:mə] n. U. S. MED. Œdème *m*.

Eden ['i:dn̩] n. ECCLES., FIG. Eden, paradis terrestre *m*.

edentate [i'denteit] adj. ZOOL. Edenté.

edge [edʒ] n. Tranchant, fil *m*. (of a blade) ; *to set an edge to*, affûter, aiguiser. ‖ Bord *m*. (border) ; marge *f*. (margin) ; lisière *f*. (skirt). ‖ Tranche *f*. (of book, coin, plank). ‖ TECHN. Arête *f*. (of beam). ‖ GEOGR. Arête, saillie *f*. ‖ SPORTS. Carre *f*. (of skate). ‖ FIG. Mordant *m.; to take the edge off*, émousser. ‖ FAM. *To have the edge on s.o.*, enfoncer qqn ; *to be on edge*, être crispé (or) à cran (or) exaspéré, avoir les nerfs à vif (or) à fleur de peau ; *not to put too fine an edge on it*, ne pas mâcher les mots. ‖ **Edge-tool**, n. TECHN. Instrument tranchant *m*.
— v. tr. Aiguiser, affûter, affiler (to sharpen). ‖ Border, ourler (*with*, de). ‖ Glisser ; *to edge into*, s'insinuer dans ; *to edge one's way through*, se faufiler à travers.
— v. intr. Se glisser, s'avancer de biais (or) avec précaution ; *to edge away from*, s'éloigner peu à peu (or) furtivement de.

edged [-d] adj. Tranchant (blade). ‖ Bordé (*with*, de). ‖ A tranches (book).

edgeless [-lis] adj. Emoussé.

edgeways [-weiz], **edgewise** [-waiz] adv. De côté, de biais, de chant. ‖ Bord à bord. ‖ FAM. *I couldn't* *get a word in edgeways*, impossible de placer un mot!

edging [-iŋ] n. Bordure f.

edgy [-i] adj. Tranchant. ‖ ARTS. Aux contours accusés. ‖ FAM. Nerveux, crispé, à cran.

edible ['edibl] adj. Comestible; mangeable. (See EATABLE.) ‖ Alimentaire (fats).
— n. pl. Victuailles f. pl.

edict ['i:dikt] n. Edit, décret m.

edification [,edifi'keiʃən] n. FIG. Edification f.

edificatory [-təri] adj. Edifiant.

edifice ['edifis] n. ARCHIT. Edifice m. (See BUILDING.)

edify ['edifai] v. tr. FIG. Edifier, faire l'édification de. ‖ † Edifier, bâtir.

edifying [-iŋ] adj. Edifiant.

edit ['edit] v. tr. Editer (an author's work, a text). ‖ Préparer pour la publication, surveiller la publication de (a manuscript). ‖ Diriger, être le rédacteur en chef de (a newspaper).

edition [id'iʃən] n. Edition f.; tirage m.; *first edition*, édition princeps; *smaller edition*, réduction; *to be in its second edition*, en être à sa seconde édition.

editor ['editə*] n. Editeur m. (of text). ‖ Rédacteur en chef (of a newspaper); *news editor*, rédacteur aux informations (or) actualités.

editorial [,edi'tɔ:riəl] adj., n. Editorial m. ‖ **Editorial writer**, n. U. S. Editorialiste s.

editorship ['editəʃip] n. Rédaction f. (in a publishing house). ‖ Fonctions (f. pl.) de rédacteur en chef (of a newspaper). ‖ Profession (f.) d'éditeur; édition f.; direction de publication f.

educable ['edju:kəb] adj. Educable.

educate [-keit] v. tr. Eduquer, instruire, faire l'éducation de, former (a child); *to be well educated*, avoir fait de bonnes études, avoir reçu une bonne éducation. ‖ Dresser (an animal).

education [,edju'keiʃən] n. Education, formation f. (bringing up). ‖ Enseignement m. (schooling); *adult education*, enseignement post-scolaire. ‖ Instruction f.; *general education*, instruction de base. ‖ Dressage m. (of animals).

educational [-l] adj. Instructif, éducateur (works). ‖ D'enseignement. ‖ CINEM. Educatif, documentaire.

educative ['edjukeitiv] adj. Educatif, instructif. ‖ Educateur (methods).

educator [-ə*] n. Educateur m.; éducatrice f. ‖ Spécialiste (s.) de pédagogie.

educe [i'dju:s] v. tr. Extraire, tirer. ‖ FIG. Déduire, inférer, induire.

educt [i'dʌkt] n. CHIM. Corps extrait m. ‖ FIG. Déduction f.

eduction [-ʃən] n. TECHN. Echappement m.

edulcorate [i'dʌlkəreit] v. tr. MED., CHIM. Edulcorer.

E. E. C. [i:i:'ci:] abbr. *European Economic Community*, Communauté Economique Européenne, C. E. E.

eel [i:l] n. ZOOL., CULIN., FIG. Anguille f. ‖ **Eel-pie**, n. CULIN. Pâté (m.) d'anguilles.

e'en [i:n] adv. Même. (See EVEN.)

e'en n. Soir m. (See EVEN.)

e'er [ɛə*] adv. Toujours. (See EVER.)

eerie ['iəri] adj. Craintif par superstition; timoré. ‖ Etrange, inquiétant, mystérieux. (See WEIRD.)

eeriness [-nis] n. Surnaturel, mystère m.

eff [ef] v. intr. POP. *Eff off*, fous le camp; *to eff and blind*, dire des grossièretés.

efface [i'feis] v. tr. Effacer (*from*, de). [See ERASE.] ‖ FIG. Effacer; *to efface oneself*, s'effacer.

effacement [-mənt] n. FIG. Effacement m.

effect [i'fekt] n. Effet, résultat m. (result); *of no effect*, sans effet. ‖ Efficacité f.; *to take effect*, avoir (or) faire son effet. ‖ Effet m.; action, influence f. (*on*, sur). ‖ Effet, propos m., intention f. (purpose); *to speak to that effect*, parler dans ce sens (or)

à cet effet. ‖ Accomplissement m.; exécution f.; *to carry into effect*, réaliser, exécuter. ‖ Fait m.; *in effect*, en fait, en pratique. ‖ Effet m.; impression f.; *meant for effect*, à effet (words). ‖ Pl. Effets m. pl. (belongings). ‖ JUR. *To take effect*, prendre effet (law). ‖ ARTS. Pl. Effets m. pl. ‖ CINEM. Pl. Trucage m.; *sound effects*, bruitage.
— v. tr. Effectuer, accomplir; exécuter (to accomplish); *to be effected*, s'effectuer, se réaliser. ‖ FIN. Effectuer (a payment); souscrire (an insurance policy).

effective [i'fektiv] adj. Efficace (efficacious); *to be effective*, produire (or) faire son effet. ‖ Effectif, réel (actual). ‖ Qui fait de l'effet, frappant, impressionnant (impressive). ‖ MILIT. Effectif.
— n. MILIT. Pl. Effectif m.

effectively [-li] adv. Efficacement. ‖ Effectivement. ‖ De manière impressionnante.

effectiveness [-nis] n. Efficacité f. ‖ Effet m.; sensation f.

effectual [i'fektjuəl] adj. Efficace (*in*, pour) [action, reply]. ‖ Valable, probant, sérieux (valid).

effectually [-əli] adv. Efficacement; selon l'effet souhaité.

effectuate [-eit] v. tr. Effectuer. (See EFFECT.)

effeminacy [i'feminəsi] n. Caractère efféminé m.

effeminate [-nit] adj. Efféminé (person); *to become effeminate*, s'efféminer. ‖ ARTS. Décadent.
— v. tr. Efféminer.
— v. intr. S'efféminer.

efferent ['efərənt] adj. MED. Efférent.

effervesce [efə'ves] v. intr. Etre en effervescence. ‖ FIG. Etre surexcité; bouillir (fam.).

effervescence [-ns] n. Effervescence f.(lit. and fig.).

effervescent [-nt] adj. Effervescent. ‖ FIG. Exubérant, en effervescence, surexcité.

effete [e'fi:t] adj. A bout de forces, épuisé (exhausted). ‖ Devenu inefficace, stérile, vain.

efficacious [efi'keiʃəs] adj. Efficace.

efficaciously [-li] adv. Efficacement.

efficaciousness [-nis], **efficacy** ['efikəsi] n. Efficacité f.

efficacity [,efi'kæsiti] n. ECCLES. Efficacité f.

efficiency [i'fiʃənsi] n. Efficacité, efficience f. (of work). ‖ Compétence, efficience, valeur f. (of a person). ‖ COMM. *Efficiency expert*, expert en rendement (or) en organisation; *Business Efficiency Exhibition*, Salon de l'équipement de bureau.

efficient [-ənt] adj. Efficient (cause); efficace, efficient (work). ‖ Compétent, capable, expérimenté; de bon rendement, à la hauteur (person).

efficiently [-əntli] adv. Efficacement. ‖ Avec compétence.

effigy ['efidʒi] n. Effigie f.

effloresce [,eflɔ:'res] v. intr. BOT. Etre en fleur. ‖ CHIM. Effleurir.

efflorescence [-ns] n. BOT. Floraison, efflorescence f. ‖ CHIM. Efflorescence, délitescence f.

efflorescent [-nt] adj. BOT. En fleur. ‖ CHIM. Efflorescent, délitescent.

effluence ['efluəns] n. Emanation f.

effluent [-ənt] adj., n. Effluent m.

effluvium [e'flu:viəm] (pl. **effluvia** [-iə]) n. Effluve m.

efflux ['eflʌks] n. Ecoulement m. (outflow).

effort ['efət] n. Effort m.

effortless [-lis] adj. Facile, aisé.

effrontery [e'frʌntəri] n. Effronterie f. (See IMPUDENCE.)

effulgence [e'fʌldʒəns] n. Eclat m.

effulgent [-ənt] adj. Eclatant, rayonnant, resplendissant. (See RADIANT.)

effuse [e'fju:s] adj. BOT. Diffus.
— [e'fju:z] v. tr. Déverser (to pour out); diffuser (to spread).
— v. intr. Se déverser; se répandre.

effusion [e'fju:ʒən] n. Effusion *f.*; déversement *m.* (outpouring). ‖ ECCLES. Effusion *f.* ‖ MED. Epanchement *m.* ‖ FIG. Flot *m.* (of words).

effusive [-siv] adj. Débordant. ‖ FIG. Exubérant, démonstratif, expansif.

effusively [-sivli] adv. Avec effusion; *to receive s.o. effusively*, faire un accueil empressé à qqn.

effusiveness [-sivnis] n. Effusion, exubérance *f.* ‖ Caractère expansif *m.* ‖ Epanchement *m.*

eft [eft] n. ZOOL. Triton *m.*

e. g. [i:'dʒi:] abbr. *exempli gratia*, par exemple, par ex.

egalitarian [i,gæli'tɛəriən] adj., n. Egalitaire *adj., s.*

egalitarianism [-izm̩] n. Egalitarisme *m.*

egg [eg] n. CULIN. Œuf *m.* ‖ FAM. AVIAT. Bombe *f.* ‖ FAM. *A good egg*, un bon zigue. ‖ **Egg-beater** (or) **-whisk**, n. CULIN. Fouet *m.*; batteuse *f.* ‖ **Egg-boiler**, n. CULIN. Coquetière *f.* ‖ **Egg-cell**, n. MED. Ovule *m.* ‖ **Egg-cup**, n. CULIN. Coquetier *m.* ‖ **Egg-merchant**, n. COMM. Coquetier *m.* ‖ **Egg-flip** (or) **-nog**, n. CULIN. Lait (*m.*) de poule. ‖ **Egg-head**, n. FAM. U. S. Intellectuel *m.* ‖ **Egg-plant**, n. BOT. Aubergine *f.* ‖ **Egg-poacher**, n. CULIN. Pocheuse *f.* ‖ **Egg-shaped**, adj. Ovoïde; *egg-shaped ornament*, ove. ‖ **Egg-shell**, n. Coquille (*f.*) d'œuf; adj. Très fragile et mince (fragile); coquille d'œuf (yellowish).
— v. tr. CULIN. Dorer.

egg v. tr. *To egg on*, pousser, inciter. (See URGE.)

eglantine ['eglantain] n. BOT. Eglantine *f.*

ego ['egou] n. MED., PHILOS. Ego, moi *m.*

egocentric [,egou'sentrik] adj. Egocentriste.

egocentricity [,egousen'trisəti] n. Egocentrisme *m.*

egoism ['egouizm̩] n. Egoïsme *m.* (See SELFISH-NESS.) ‖ Egocentrisme *m.*: suffisance *f.* (conceit).

egoist [-ist] n. Egoïste *s.* ‖ Egotiste *s.*

egoistically [egou'istikəli] adv. Avec égoïsme, égoïstement.

egomania [,egou'meiniə] n. Manie égocentrique *f.*

egotism ['egotizm̩] n. Egotisme *m.*

egotist [-tist] n. Egotiste *s.*

egotize [-taiz] v. intr. Egoïser.

egregious [i'gri:dʒiəs] adj. Insigne, remarquable, notoire, signalé, énorme (fam.).

egregiously [-li] adv. D'une façon éclatante.

egregiousness [-nis] n. Caractère insigne *m.*; énormité *f.* (fam.).

egress ['i:gres] n. Sortie, issue *f.* (lit. and fig.). ‖ ASTRON. Emersion *f.*

egression [i'greʃən] n. Sortie *f.*

egret ['i:grət] n. BOT., ZOOL. Aigrette *f.*

Egypt ['i:dʒipt] n. GEOGR. Egypte *f.*

Egyptian [-ʃən] adj., n. GEOGR. Egyptien *s.*

Egyptologist [,i:dʒip'tɔlədʒist] n. Egyptologue *s.*

Egyptology [-dʒi] n. Egyptologie *f.*

eh [ei] interj. Hé!, Hein?

eider ['aidə*] n. ZOOL. Eider *m.* ‖ **Eider-down**, n. Duvet *m.* (down); édredon *m.* (quilt).

eidetic [ai'detik] adj., n. PSYCH. Eidétique *adj., s.*

eight [eit] adj. Huit; *to be eight*, avoir huit ans.
— n. Huit *m.* ‖ SPORTS. Equipe (*f.*) de huit (in rowing); huit *m.* (in skating). ‖ FAM. *To have one over the eight*, prendre une biture. ‖ U. S. FAM. *Behind the eight ball*, dans le pétrin.

eighteen [ei'ti:n] adj., n. Dix-huit *s.*

eighteenth [-θ] adj., n. Dix-huitième *s.* (in a series). ‖ Dix-huit (chapter, date, king).

eighth [eitθ] adj. Huitième. ‖ Huit.
— n. Huitième *s.* ‖ MUS. Octave *f.*

eighthly [-li] adv. Huitièmement.

eightieth ['eitiiθ] adj., n. Quatre-vingtième *s.*

eighty ['eiti] adj., n. Quatre-vingts *s.*

eikon ['aikən] n. Icône *f.* (See IKON.)

einsteinium [ain'stainiəm] n. CHIM. Einsteinium *m.*

eisteddfod [ai'stedfəd] n. Eisteddfod *m.*, concours (*m.*) annuel de musique et de chant au pays de Galles.

either ['aiðə*], ['i:ðə*] adj., pron. L'un ou l'autre, n'importe lequel (one or the other). ‖ L'un et l'autre, les deux (each of two).
— conj. **Either... or**, ou... ou, soit... soit, ou bien... ou bien.
— adv. Non plus, pas davantage.

ejaculate [i'dʒækjuleit] v. tr. Ejaculer (fluids). ‖ Pousser (a cry).
— v. intr. S'exclamer.

ejaculation [i.dʒækju'leiʃən] n. MED., ECCLES. Ejaculation *f.* ‖ ECCLES. Oraison jaculatoire *f.*

ejaculatory [i'dʒækjulətəri] adj. MED. Ejaculatoire.

eject [i'dʒekt] v. tr. Emettre, lancer (smoke); éjecter (steam, water). ‖ Chasser, expulser (*from*, de); sortir (fam.).
— n. COMM. Article de rebut *m.*

ejection [i'dʒekʃən] n. Ejection *f.* (of steam, water). ‖ Expulsion *f.* (of a person).

ejector [-tə*] n. Ejecteur *m.* ‖ AVIAT. *Ejector seat*, siège éjectable; *ejector canopy*, verrière largable.

eke [i:k] v. tr. *To eke out*, augmenter, accroître; faire durer, économiser (supplies).

el [el] n. U. S. FAM. Métro aérien *m.*

elaborate [i'læbərət] adj. Soigné. ‖ Compliqué, détaillé.
— [-reit] v. tr. MED., FIG. Elaborer.
— v. intr. Donner des détails (*on*, sur).

elaborately [i'læbəritli] adv. Avec soin. ‖ En détail.

elaborateness [-nis] n. Soin, fini; minutie *f.* ‖ Complication *f.* (of a mechanism).

elaboration [i,læbə'reiʃən] n. Elaboration *f.* ‖ Production *f.*

elan [ei'lɑ:n] n. Elan *m.*, ardeur *f.* ‖ PHILOS. *Elan vital*, élan vital.

eland ['i:lənd] n. ZOOL. Éland de Derby *m.*

elapse [i'læps] v. intr. S'écouler (time).

elastic [i'læstik] adj. Elastique (fabric). ‖ FIG. Elastique (conscience); souple (regulations); plein de ressort, qui a de la ressource (temper).
— n. Elastique *m.* (rubber band).

elastically [-əli] adv. Avec élasticité.

elasticated [-eitid] adj. Elastique.

elasticity [,elæs'tisiti] n. Elasticité *f.* (of body). ‖ FIG. Elasticité *f.* (of conscience); souplesse *f.* (of regulations, temper).

elastomer [i'læstəmə] n. Elastomère *m.*

elate [i'leit] v. tr. Ravir, enivrer, enthousiasmer. ‖ Enivrer, enorgueillir.

elation [i'leiʃən] n. Ravissement, transport *m.* (rapture). ‖ Enivrement *m.* (of success). ‖ Orgueil exultant *m.* (pride).

elbow ['elbou] n. MED. Coude *m.*; *to lean one's elbows on*, s'accouder sur. ‖ FIG. Coude *m.* (of bar, river, road). ‖ FAM. *At one's elbow*, à portée de la main; *to be out at elbows*, être déguenillé; *to rub elbows with famous people*, coudoyer les gens célèbres; *up to one's elbows*, jusqu'au cou. ‖ **Elbow-grease**, n. FAM. Huile (*f.*) de coude. ‖ **Elbow-room**, n. Espace *m.*; *to have elbow-room*, avoir ses coudées franches, avoir du champ.
— v. tr. Coudoyer, pousser du coude; *to elbow s.o. aside*, écarter qqn du coude. ‖ Frayer à coups de coude; *to elbow one's way through the crowd*, passer à travers la foule en jouant des coudes.
— v. intr. Jouer des coudes.

elder ['eldə*] adj. Plus âgé, aîné (older). ‖ Plus ancien (senior); *elder statesman*, vétéran de la politique. ‖ Supérieur.

— n. Aîné *m.* ‖ Doyen *m.* (senior). ‖ Supérieur *m.* ‖ Eccles. Ancien *m.* (in the Presbyterian Church).
elder n. Bot. Sureau *m.*
elderly [-li] adj. Mûr, d'un certain âge; *elderly people,* vieilles gens.
eldest [-ist] adj. Aîné, plus âgé.
elecampane [,elikəm'pein] n. Bot. Aulnée *f.*
elect [i'lekt] adj., n. Elu *s.*
— v. tr. Elire (*to,* à).
election [i'lekʃən] n. Election *f.* ‖ **Election-time,** n. Période électorale *f.*
electioneer [i,lekʃə'niə*] v. intr. Faire la campagne électorale.
elective [i'lektiv] adj. Electif (office); électoral (propagande). ‖ Chim. Electif (affinity). ‖ U. S. A option, facultatif.
— n. U. S. Matière à option *f.*
elector [-ə*] n. Electeur *m.*
electoral [-rəl] adj. Electoral.
electorate [-rit] n. Corps électoral *m.* (body); circonscription électorale *f.* (district). ‖ Electorat *m.* (in the Holy Roman Empire).
electress [i'lektris] n. Electrice *f.*
electret [i'lektrət] n. Electr. Electret *m.*
electric [i'lektrik] adj. Electr. Electrique (chair, fence, wire); *electric eye,* cellule photoélectrique; *electric shock,* décharge; *to get an electric shock,* recevoir du jus (fam.); *electric wielding,* électrosoudure.
— n. pl. Electricité *f.,* circuits électriques *m. pl.*
electrical [-əl] adj. Electr. Concernant l'électricité (in general); électricien (engineer); électrique (machine).
electrically [-əli] adv. Electr. Electriquement, à l'électricité.
electrician [,elek'triʃən] n. Electr. Electricien *m.*
electricity [-siti] n. Electr., Fig. Electricité *f.*
electrification [i,lektrifi'keiʃən] n. Electr. Electrification *f.* (of railway); électrisation *f.* (of substance).
electrify [i'lektrifai] v. tr. (2). Electr. Electrifier; électriser. ‖ Fig. Electriser, galvaniser.
electrize [-traiz] v. tr. Electr., Fig. Electriser.
electrobiology [i'lektrobai'ɔlədʒi] n. Electrobiologie *f.*
electrocardiogram [i'lektro'kɑ:dio,græm] n. Med. Electrocardiogramme *m.*
electrochemical [-'kemikḷ] adj. Electr. Electrochimique.
electrochemistry [-'kemistri] n. Electr. Electrochimie *f.*
electroconvulsive [-kən'vʌlsiv] adj. Med. *Electroconvulsive therapy,* convulsivothérapie électrique, électrochocs.
electrocute [i'lektrokju:t] v. tr. Electrocuter.
electrocution [i,lektro'kju:ʃən] n. Electr. Electrocution *f.*
electrode [i'lektroud] n. Electr. Electrode *f.*
electrodynamic [i'lektrodai'næmik] adj. Electr. Electrodynamique.
— n. Electr. Electrodynamique *f.*
electrodynamometer [i'lektro,dainə'mɔmitə*] n. Electr. Electrodynamomètre *m.*
electroencephalogram [-en'sefələ,græm] n. Med. Electroencéphalogramme *m.*
electroencephalography [-en,sefə'lɔgrəfi] n. Med. Electroencéphalographie *f.*
electrolier [i,lektro'liə*] n. Suspension électrique *f.;* lustre *m.*
electrolyse [i'lektrɔlaiz] v. tr. Electr. Electrolyser.
electrolysis [ilek'trɔlisis] n. Chim., Med. Electrolyse *f.*
electrolyte [i'lektrolait] n. Electr. Electrolyte *m.*
electrolytic [i,lektro'litik] adj. Electr. Electrolytique.

electromagnet [i'lektro'mægnit] n. Electr. Electro-aimant *m.*
electromagnetic [i'lektromæg'netik] adj. Electr. Electromagnétique.
electromagnetism [-'mægni,tizm̩] n. Electr. Electromagnétisme *m.*
electromechanical [-mi'kænikḷ] adj. Electromécanique.
electrometallurgy [i'lektrome'tælədʒi] n. Electrométallurgie *f.*
electrometer [ilek'trɔmitə*] n. Electr. Electromètre *m.*
electrometry [-tri] n. Electr. Electrométrie *f.*
electromotive [i,lektro'moutiv] adj. Electr. Electromoteur *m.;* électromotrice *f.*
electron [i'lektrɔn] n. Electr. Electron *m.; electron gun,* canon à électrons; *electron lens, microscope,* lentille, microscope électronique.
electronic [ilek'trɔnik] adj. Electr. Electronique.
electronics [-iks] n. sg. Electr. Electronique *f.*
electrophoresis [i,lektrofə'ri:sis] n. Electr., Chim. Electrophorèse *f.*
electroplate [i'lektro,pleit] v. tr. Electr., Techn. Plaquer par galvanoplastie.
— n. Articles (*m. pl.*) plaqués par galvanoplastie.
electropositive [-'pozitiv] adj. Electr. Electropositif.
electropuncture [-'pʌŋktʃə*] n. Med. Electroponcture *f.*
electroscope [i'lektroskoup] n. Electr. Electroscope *m.*
electroshock [i'lektro'ʃɔk] n. Med. Electrochoc *m.*
electrostatic [-'stætik] adj. Electr. Electrostatique.
electrostatics [-'stætiks] n. pl. Electr. Electrostatique *f.*
electrotechnology [-tek'nɔlədʒi] n. Electrotechnique *f.*
electrotherapeutics [i,lektro,θerə'pju:tiks] n. Med. Electrothérapeutique, électrothérapie *f.*
electrotherapy [i,lektro'θerəpi] n. Med. Electrothérapie *f.*
electrotype [i'lektrotaip] n. Techn. Electrotype; galvano *m.* (fam.).
— v. tr. Electrotyper.
electrotypy [-i] n. Techn. Electrotypie *f.*
electrovalency [i,lektro'veilənsi] n. Phys., Chim. Electrovalence *f.*
electrum [i'lektrəm] n. Electrum *m.*
electuary [i'lektjuəri] n. Med. Electuaire *m.*
eleemosynary [,elii:'mɔsinəri] adj. D'aumône; donné par charité; qui vit d'aumônes.
elegance ['eligəns] n. Elégance *f.* (See SMARTNESS.)
elegant [-ənt] adj. Elégant. ‖ Choisi; distingué.
elegantly [-əntli] adv. Elégamment.
elegiac [,eli'dʒaiək] adj. Elégiaque.
— n. Couplet élégiaque *m.* ‖ Pl. Elégie *f.*
elegize ['elidʒaiz] v. tr. Célébrer dans une élégie.
elegy [-dʒi] n. Elégie *f.*
element ['elimənt] n. Chim., Phys., Med., Electr., Gramm. Elément *m.* ‖ Eccles. Pl. Espèces *f. pl.* ‖ Fig. Elément *m.*
elemental [-ḷ] adj. Des éléments. ‖ Primordial, fondamental (primal). ‖ Essentiel, constitutif. ‖ Chim. Elémentaire (body, part).
— n. Esprit élémental *m.,* élémental *m.*
elementary [-əri] adj. Elémentaire, fondamental (basic). ‖ Elémentaire, rudimentaire (rudimentary); *elementary teacher,* professeur des classes élémentaires. ‖ Chim. Simple.
elemi ['elimi] n. Med., Bot., Chim. Elémi *m.*
elephant ['elifənt] n. Zool. Eléphant *m.; young elephant,* éléphanteau.
elephantiasis [,elifən'taiəsis] n. Med. Eléphantiasis *m.*
elephantine [,eli'fæntain] adj. Zool. Eléphantin. ‖ Fig. Eléphantesque, d'éléphant.

elevate ['eliveit] v. tr. Elever, lever, soulever. (See LIFT.) ‖ Lever (the eyes); élever, hausser (the voice). ‖ Elever, promouvoir (*to*, à) [a person]. ‖ FIG. Elever, exalter (one's mind). ‖ FAM. Exciter, émoustiller.

elevated [-id] adj. Elevé. ‖ CH. DE F. Aérien (railway). ‖ FAM. Gai, émoustillé.
— n. FAM. U. S. Métro aérien *m.*

elevation [eli'vei ʃən] n. Elévation, érection *f.* ‖ ARCHIT., ECCLES. Elévation *f.* ‖ MATH. Elévation *f.*; *sectional elevation*, coupe transversale. ‖ GEOGR. Altitude *f.* ‖ FIG. Noblesse, élévation *f.* (loftiness); élévation, promotion; dignité, position élevée *f.* (rank).

elevator [-tə*] n. Monte-charge *m.* ‖ TECHN., AGRIC., MED. Elévateur *m.* ‖ AVIAT. Gouvernail (*m.*) d'altitude (or) de profondeur. ‖ U. S. Ascenseur *m.*

eleven [i'levn̩] adj., n. Onze *m.* ‖ SPORTS. Equipe *f.* (in cricket).

eleventh [-θ] adj., n. Onzième *s.* ‖ Onze *m.* (date, rank).

elevon ['eli,vɔn] n. AVIAT. Elevon *m.*

elf [elf] (pl. **elves** [elvz]) n. Elfe, génie *m.* ‖ FIG. Diablotin, lutin *m.*

elfin [-in] adj. Féerique.
— n. FAM. Petit diable *m.*

elfish [-iʃ] adj. Féerique, diabolique. ‖ Malicieux, espiègle (impish). ‖ Tout petit (small).

elicit [i'lisit] v. tr. Provoquer, faire naître, susciter (smile). ‖ Mettre à jour, dévoiler (truth). ‖ Obtenir (*from*, de); arracher (*from*, à).

elide [i'laid] v. tr. GRAMM. Elider.

eligibility [,elidʒi'biliti] n. Eligibilité *f.* ‖ Pl. Qualités attrayantes *f. pl.*

eligible ['elidʒibl] adj. Eligible (*for*, à). ‖ Désirable, attirant; *eligible young man*, bon parti, épouseur possible.
— n. Eligible *s.*

Elijah [i'laidʒə] n. ECCLES. Elie *m.*

eliminate [i'limineit] v. tr. MED., MATH., FIG. Eliminer.

elimination [i,limi'neiʃən] n. MED., MATH., FIG. Elimination *f.*; *by a process of elimination*, en procédant par élimination.

eliminatory [i'limi,nətori] adj. Eliminatoire (method, examination).

Elisha [i'laiʃə] n. ECCLES. Elisée *m.*

elision [i'liʒən] n. Elision *f.*

elite [ei'li:t] n. Elite *f.*

elixir [i'liksə*] n. Elixir *m.*

Elizabethan [i,lizə'bi:θən] adj., n. Elisabéthain *s.*

elk [elk] n. ZOOL. Elan *m.*

ell [el] n. Aune *f.* ‖ U. S. Aile *f.* (of house).

ellipse [i'lips] n. MATH. Ellipse *f.*

ellipsis [-sis] (pl. **ellipses** [-si:z]) n. GRAMM. Ellipse *f.*

ellipsoid [-sɔid] n. MATH. Ellipsoïde *m.*

ellipsoidal [-sɔidl] adj. MATH. Ellipsoïdal.

elliptic(al) [-tik(əl)] adj. MATH., GRAMM. Elliptique.

elm [elm] n. BOT. Orme *m.* (tree, wood); *young elm*, ormeau.

elocution [,elə'kju:ʃən] n. Diction, déclamation *f.* (art); élocution *f.* (manner).

elocutionary [-əri] adj. De l'élocution. ‖ Déclamatoire.

elocutionist [-ist] n. Professeur (*m.*) de diction. ‖ Diseur *s.*; récitateur *m.*

elongate ['i:lɔŋgeit] v. tr. Allonger.
— v. intr. S'allonger.
— adj. Allongé; allant en s'amincissant.

elongation [,i:lɔŋ'geiʃən] n. Elongation *f.* ‖ Allongement *m.*

elope [i'loup] v. intr. JUR. Quitter avec un amant le domicile paternel (or) conjugal; se faire (or) se laisser enlever pour se marier; lever le pied (fam.).

elopement [-mənt] n. Fugue amoureuse *f.*; enlèvement consenti *m.*

eloquence ['eləkwəns] n. Eloquence *f.*

eloquent [-ənt] adj. Eloquent, disert.

eloquently [-əntli] adv. Eloquemment.

else [els] adj. Autre; *somebody else*, qqn d'autre. ‖ De plus; *is there anything else?*, y a-t-il qqch. de plus (or) encore autre chose?
— adv. Ailleurs; *nowhere else*, nulle part ailleurs; *where else?*, à quel autre endroit? ‖ Sinon, autrement, dans l'autre cas, ou bien (if not).

elsewhere [-'wɛə*] adv. Ailleurs, autre part; *elsewhere in Russia*, dans les autres parties de la Russie.

elucidate [i'lju:sideit] v. tr. Elucider. (See EXPLAIN.)

elucidation [i,lju:si'deiʃən] n. Elucidation *f.*

elude [i'lju:d] v. tr. Eviter, esquiver (a blow); éluder (a difficulty, question, responsibility); dépasser (s.o.).

elusion [i'lju:ʒən] n. Echappatoire, dérobade, esquive *f.*

elusive [-siv] adj. Fuyant, évasif. ‖ Déconcertant, difficile à saisir.

elusiveness [-sivnis] n. Caractère fuyant (or) évasif *m.*; nature insaisissable *f.*

elusory [-səri] adj. Fuyant.

elution [i:'lu:ʃən] n. CHIM. Elution *f.*

Elysian [i'liziən] adj. Elyséen.

Elysium [-əm] n. Elysée *m.*

elytron ['elitrɔn] (pl. **elytra** [-ə]) n. ZOOL. Elytre *m.*

Elzevir ['elziva*] n. Elzévir *m.*

em [em] n. TECHN. Cadratin *m.*

'em [əm] representation of *them*, FAM. Les, eux, elles, leur.

emaciate [i'meiʃieit] v. tr. MED. Emacier (face); amaigrir (person); *to become emaciated*, se décharner, s'émacier. ‖ AGRIC. Appauvrir (soil). ‖ BOT. Etioler (plant); *to become emaciated*, s'étioler.

emaciation [i,meiʃi'eiʃən] n. MED. Emaciation *f.* (of face); gros amaigrissement *m.* (of a person).

emanate ['eməneit] v. intr. CHIM., FIG. Emaner (*from*, de).

emanation [,emə'neiʃən] n. CHIM., FIG. Emanation *f.*

emanative [-tiv] adj. Emanant, d'émanation.

emancipate [i'mænsipeit] v. tr. Affranchir (a slave). ‖ JUR. Emanciper. ‖ FIG. Libérer, dégager.

emancipation [i,mænsi'peiʃən] n. Affranchissement *m.* (of a slave). ‖ Emancipation *f.*

emasculate [i'mæskjuleit] v. tr. Emasculer (lit. and fig.).
— [-lit] adj. Emasculé.

emasculation [i,mæskju'leiʃən] n. Emasculation *f.* (lit. and fig.).

embalm [im'bɑ:m] v. tr. Embaumer (a corpse). ‖ Embaumer, parfumer (to perfume). ‖ FIG. Conserver pieusement; mettre sous globe (fam.).

embalmment [-mənt] n. Embaumement *m.*

embank [im'bæŋk] v. tr. Endiguer, encaisser (a river); remblayer (a roadway).

embankment [-mənt] n. Digue *f.* (of a river); remblai *m.* (of a road).

embar [im'bɑ:*] v. tr. JUR. Arrêter.

embargo [im'bɑ:gou] (pl. **embargoes** [-z]) n. NAUT., FIG. Embargo *m.* (*on*, sur).
— v. tr. NAUT. Mettre l'embargo sur.

embark [im'bɑ:k] v. tr. NAUT. Embarquer.
— v. intr. NAUT., FIG. S'embarquer (*in*, dans; *on*, sur).

embarkation [,embɑ:'keiʃən] n. NAUT. Embarquement *m.*

embarrass [im'bærəs] v. tr. Embarrasser, gêner, entraver (to impede). ‖ Embarrasser, troubler, décontenancer (to abash). ‖ Compliquer, embrouiller (to complicate). ‖ FIN. Gêner, mettre en difficulté.

embarrassment [-mənt] n. Embarras *m.*
embassy ['embəsi] n. Ambassade *f.*
embattle [im'bætl] v. tr. ARCHIT., BLAS. Bastiller. ‖ MILIT. Ranger en bataille.
embay [im'bei] v. tr. NAUT. Encaper.
embed [im'bed] v. tr. (1). AGRIC. Disposer en parterre. ‖ TECHN. Encastrer. ‖ FIG. Fixer (in mind).
embellish [im'beliʃ] v. tr. Embellir. (See BEAUTIFY.) ‖ Décorer, orner. (See ADORN.) ‖ FIG. Embellir, enjoliver, agrémenter, broder.
embellishment [-mənt] n. Embellissement *m.* (lit. and fig.)
ember ['embə*] n. Tison *m.;* braise, cendre rouge *f.*
Ember adj. ECCLES. Des Quatre-Temps. ‖ **Ember-days,** n. ECCLES. Quatre-Temps *m. pl.*
embezzle [im'bezl] v. intr. JUR. Commettre des détournements. (See DEFALCATE.)
— v. tr. JUR. Détourner (money).
embezzlement [-mənt] n. JUR. Détournement (*m.*) de fonds.
embitter [im'bitə*] v. tr. Envenimer (a quarrel); aigrir, rendre amer (s.o.).
emblaze [im'bleiz] v. tr. Illuminer (to light up); embraser (to set on fire).
emblazon [im'bleizən] v. tr. BLAS. Blasonner (with, de). ‖ FIG. Célébrer, vanter, exalter.
emblem ['embləm] n. Emblème *f.* ‖ BLAS. Devise *f.*
emblematic [,embli'mætik] adj. Emblématique.
emblematize [-taiz] v. tr. Etre l'emblème de, symboliser.
emblements ['emblmənts] n. pl. AGRIC. Récoltes (*f. pl.*) sur pied.
embodiment [im'bodimənt] n. Incorporation *f.* ‖ FIG. Incarnation *f.*
embody [im'bodi] v. tr. (2). Incorporer, incarner (to incarnate). ‖ Incorporer, inclure, englober (to include). ‖ Matérialiser, concrétiser, donner corps à. ‖ FIG. Incarner.
embog [im'bog] v. tr. (1). Embourber.
embolden [im'bouldən] v. tr. Enhardir.
embolism ['embəlizm] n. MED. Embolie *f.* ‖ Embolisme *m.*
embosom [im'buzəm] v. tr. Embrasser, presser sur son sein (to embrace). ‖ Englober; enclore (to enclose).
emboss [im'bos] v. tr. Gaufrer (paper); frapper (velvet). ‖ ARTS. Travailler en bosse, bosseler.
embossment [-mənt] n. Gaufrage *m.* (of paper); frappe *f.* (of velvet). ‖ ARTS. Bosselage *m.*
embowel [im'bauəl] v. tr. Eviscérer, étriper, éventrer.
embower [im'bauə*] v. tr. Cacher (or) abriter dans la verdure.
embrace [im'breis] v. tr. Embrasser, enlacer, étreindre, serrer dans ses bras (to hug). ‖ Embrasser, couvrir, englober, enclore, comprendre (to encompass). ‖ Embrasser, enfermer, contenir (to contain). ‖ Embrasser, saisir (to perceive). ‖ Embrasser, adopter (a career, a cause, an opinion); répondre à (an offer); sauter sur, saisir (an opportunity).
— v. intr. S'embrasser, s'enlacer.
— n. Embrassement *m.* (hug).
embracement [-mənt] n. Embrassement, enlacement *m.*
embranchment [im'brɑ:ntʃmənt] n. Embranchement *m.* (See RAMIFICATION.)
embrasure [im'breiʒə*] n. ARCHIT., MILIT. Embrasure *f.*
embrocate ['embrokeit] v. tr. MED. Oindre, faire une embrocation à.
embrocation [,embro'keiʃən] n. MED. Embrocation *f.* (act); lotion *f.;* liniment *m.* (liquid).
embroider [im'broidə*] v. tr. Broder, enjoliver.
— v. intr. Broder (lit. and fig.).

embroidery [-ri] n. Broderie *f.* ‖ FIG. Broderie *f.;* enjolivement *m.*
embroil [im'broil] v. tr. Embrouiller (affairs); brouiller (persons).
embroilment [-mənt] n. Imbroglio *m.*
embrown [im'braun] v. tr. Brunir, embrunir.
embryo ['embriou] n. MED., FIG. Embryon *m.*
— adj. MED., BOT., FIG. Embryonnaire.
embryology [,embri'olədʒi] n. MED. Embryologie *f.*
embryonic ['onik] adj. MED., FIG. Embryonnaire.
embus [im'bʌs] v. tr. Transporter en autobus.
— v. intr. Monter en autobus.
emcee [em'si:] n. FAM. Animateur, présentateur *s.* (of a show).
emend [i'mend], **emendate** ['i:mendeit] v. tr. Emender (a passage, a text).
emendation [,i:men'deiʃən] n. Emendation *f.*
emendator ['i:mendeitə*] n. Emendateur *m.*
emerald ['emərəld] n. Emeraude *f.* (colour, stone). ‖ TECHN. Corps six *m.* (in printing).
— adj. Emeraude (green). ‖ En émeraude. ‖ GEOGR. *Emerald Isle,* la Verte Erin.
emerge [i'mə:dʒ] v. intr. Emerger (*from,* de) [a hole]. ‖ JUR. Ressortir, découler. ‖ FIG. Se faire jour, apparaître, se dégager; *emerging peoples,* pays en voie de développement.
emergence [-əns] n. Emergence *f.* ‖ GEOL. Exondation *f.*
emergency [-ənsi] n. Etat (*m.*) d'urgence; situation critique, crise *f.* (see EXIGENCE); *case of emergency,* cas d'urgence, circonstance imprévue; *to provide for emergencies,* parer à toute éventualité; *to rise to the emergency,* se montrer à la hauteur des circonstances. ‖ MED. Urgence *f.* ‖ U. S. *To call « emergency »,* appeler police-secours.
— adj. De fortune (bridge); provisoire (dwelling) *emergency exit,* sortie de secours.
emergent [-ənt] adj. Emergent.
emeritus [i:'meritəs] adj. Honoraire, émérite.
emersion [i'mə:ʃən] n. Emersion *f.*
emery ['eməri] n. Emeri *m.* ‖ **Emery-board,** n. Lime émeri, lime (*f.*) en carton. ‖ **Emery-cloth,** n. Toile émeri *f.* ‖ **Emery-paper,** n. Papier émeri (or) de verre *m.*
emetic [i'metik] adj., n. MED. Emétique *m.*
emigrant ['emigrant] n., adj. Emigrant *s.*
emigrate [-greit] v. intr. Emigrer.
emigration [,emi'greiʃən] n. Emigration *f.* (act); émigrants *m. pl.* (persons).
émigré ['emigrei] n. Emigrant *s.; the émigré world,* le monde des émigrants. ‖ Emigré *m.* (during the French Revolution).
eminence ['eminəns] n. GEOGR., MED., ECCLES. Eminence *f.* ‖ Distinction, prééminence *f.; to achieve eminence as,* se distinguer comme. ‖ LOC. *Eminence grise,* éminence grise.
eminent [-ənt] adj. Eminent.
eminently [-əntli] adv. Eminemment.
emir [e'miə*] n. Emir *m.*
emirate [e'miərit] n. Emirat *m.*
emissary ['emisəri] n. Emissaire *s.*
emission [i'miʃən] n. PHYS., CHIM., MED., FIN. Emission *f.*
emissive [-siv] adj. Emissif (power).
emit [i'mit] v. tr. (1). Emettre, dégager (fumes, heat); exhaler, émettre (an odour); émettre (a sound); déverser, débiter (water). ‖ FIN. Emettre (paper money).
emitter [i'mitə*] n. RADIO. Emetteur *m.*
emmet ['emit] n. † ZOOL. Fourmi *f.*
emollient [i'moliənt] adj., n. MED. Emollient *m.*
emolument [i'moljumənt] n. Emoluments *m. pl.*
emote [i'mout] v. intr. Manifester de l'émoi.
emotion [i'mouʃən] n. Emotion *f.;* émoi *m.*

emotional [-l] adj. Emotif (disturbance); émotif, émotionnable (person).
emotionalism [-lizm] n. Emotivité f.
emotionalist [-list] n. Emotif s.
emotive [i'moutiv] adj. Emouvant; émotif.
emotiveness [-nis] n Emotivité f.
emove [i'mu:v] v. tr. Emouvoir, émotionner.
empale [im'peil] v. tr. Empaler.
empanel [im'pænl] v. tr. (1). JUR. Porter (or) choisir parmi les membres du jury.
empathy ['empəθi] n. Pénétration par sympathie f.
empennage [im'penidʒ] n. AVIAT. Empennage m.
emperor ['empərə*] n. Empereur m. ‖ ZOOL. Papillon m.; Emperor moth, paon de nuit.
emphasis ['emfəsis] n. GRAMM. Accent m.; accentuation f. (stress). ‖ FIG. Force, intensité f. ‖ FIG. Importance f.; poids m.; to place emphasis on, porter une attention spéciale à, mettre l'accent sur.
emphasize [-saiz] v. tr. GRAMM. Accentuer, mettre l'accent sur. ‖ FIG. Donner de la force à. ‖ FIG. Faire valoir, mettre en relief, détacher, appuyer sur.
emphatic [im'fætik] adj. GRAMM. Accentué, appuyé, emphatique. ‖ FIG. Catégorique, énergique, formel (act, person, word); magistral (defeat).
emphatically [-əli] adv. Catégoriquement, énergiquement, formellement. ‖ Décidément, vraiment, à coup sûr (absolutely).
emphysema [,emfi'si:mə] n. MED. Emphysème m.
emphysematous [,emfi'semətəs] adj. MED. Emphysémateux.
empire ['empaiə*] n. Empire (lit. and fig.); Empire style, style Empire.
empiric [em'pirik] n. Empirique m. ‖ Charlatan m.
empiric(al) [em'pirik(l)] adj. Empirique.
empiricism [em'pirisizm] n. Empirisme m.
empiricist [-sist] n. Empiriste m.
emplacement [em'pleismənt] n. MILIT. Emplacement m.
employ [im'plɔi] v. tr. Employer, utiliser, se servir de (sth.). ‖ Employer, faire travailler (as, comme; to, à) [s.o.].
— n. Service m.; he is in my employ, je l'emploie.
employee [,emplɔi'i:], **employé** [-'ei] n. Employé s.
employer [im'plɔiə*] n. Employeur m.; employers' union, syndicat patronal.
employment [-mənt] n. Emploi m.; full employment, plein emploi; employment agency, bureau de placement; employment exchange, agence nationale pour l'emploi.
empoison [im'pɔizn] v. tr. Empoisonner. ‖ FIG. Empoisonner (s.o.'s life); envenimer (a quarrel); aigrir (s.o.'s temper). [See EMBITTER.]
emporium [em'pɔ:riəm] n. COMM. Centre commercial, grand marché m. (market); grand magasin m. (store).
empower [im'pauə*] v. tr. JUR. Donner les pouvoirs à, nantir d'un pouvoir, habiliter (to, à). ‖ FIG. Rendre capable (to, de). [See ENABLE.]
empress ['empris] n. Impératrice f. ‖ FIG. Reine f.
emptiness ['emptinis] n. Vide m. ‖ FIG. Vide, néant m; vanité f.
empty ['empti] adj. Vide; empty of, sans, dépourvu de. ‖ Vide, sans chargement (truck). ‖ FAM. To feel empty, avoir un petit creux; on an empty stomach, à jeun. ‖ FAM. Vidé (drained of energy). ‖ FIG. Vide (look); creux (words, talk); en l'air (promises). ‖ **Empty-handed**, adj. Les mains vides; to come back empty-handed, revenir bredouille. ‖ **Empty-headed**, adj. A la tête creuse, sans cervelle.
— n. COMM. Emballage vide m.
— v. tr. (2) Vider (into, dans).
— v. intr. Se vider. ‖ Confluer (into, avec); se jeter, s'évacuer (into, dans) [river].
empurple [im'pə:pl] v. tr. Empourprer.

empyema [,empai'i:mə] n. MED. Empyème m.
Empyrean [,empai'ri:ən] adj., n. Empyrée.
emu ['i:mju:] n. ZOOL. Emeu m.
emulate ['emjuleit] v. tr. Tenter d'égaler, rivaliser d'émulation avec; she has emulated your generosity, elle s'est faite votre émule en générosité.
emulation [,emju'leiʃən] n. Emulation f.; in emulation of each other, à qui mieux mieux.
emulative ['emjulətiv] adj. Résultant de l'émulation. ‖ Plein d'émulation.
emulator [-ə*] n. Emule s.
emulous ['emjuləs] adj. Plein d'émulation. ‖ Emule (of, de); rivalisant (of, avec). ‖ Ambitieux (of, de). ‖ † Jaloux, envieux.
emulously [-li] adv. Avec émulation, à qui mieux mieux.
emulsify [i'mʌlsifai] v. tr. Emulsionner.
emulsion [i'mʌlʃən] n. Emulsion f.
emunctory [i'mʌŋktəri] adj., n. MED. Emonctoire m.
en [en] n. TECHN. Demi-cadratin m.
enable [i'neibl] v. tr. Rendre capable, mettre à même, permettre à (to, de). ‖ JUR. Donner pouvoir à, habiliter. (See EMPOWER.)
enact [i'nækt] v. tr. Décréter (to decree). ‖ Accomplir; to be enacted, se dérouler. ‖ JUR. Donner force de loi à (a bill); promulguer, voter (a law). ‖ THEATR. Représenter (a play).
enactment [-mənt] n. JUR. Décret m.; ordonnance f. (decree); promulgation f. (of a law).
enamel [i'næməl] n. ARTS, MED. Email m.
— v. tr. (1). Emailler (metal); émailler, vernisser (pottery).
enamelling [-iŋ] n. Emaillage m. (act); émaillure f. (work).
enamo(u)r [i'næmə*] v. tr. Enamourer; to be enamoured of, s'éprendre de. ‖ FIG. Captiver, séduire.
encage [in'keidʒ] v. tr. Encager, mettre en cage.
encamp [in'kæmp] v. intr. Camper.
— v. tr. Mettre dans un camp. ‖ Faire camper.
encampment [-mənt] n. Campement m.
encapsulate [in'kæpsju,leit] v. tr. TECHN. Enfermer dans une capsule. ‖ FIG. Résumer, condenser, abréger (to summarize); comporter, englober (to include).
encase [in'keis] v. tr. Mettre en caisse (or) en étui, encaisser. ‖ Envelopper, enfermer, couvrir.
encash [in'kæʃ] v. tr. FIN. Encaisser.
encashment [-mənt] n. FIN. Encaissement m.
encaustic [en'kɔ:stik] adj., n. ARTS. Encaustique f.
encephalic [,ense'fælik] adj. MED. Encéphalique.
encephalitis [en,sefə'laitis] n. MED. Encéphalite f.
encephalogram [en'sefələ,græm] n. MED. Electroencéphalogramme, encéphalogramme m.
encephalograph [-,grɑ:f] n. MED. Appareil (m.) d'enregistrement électroencéphalographique.
encephalon [en'sifələn] n. MED. Encéphale m.
enchain [in't,rein] v. tr. Enchaîner.
enchainment [-mənt] n. Enchaînement m.
enchant [in't,rɑ:nt] v. tr. Enchanter (lit. and fig.).
enchanter [-ə*] n. Enchanteur m.
enchanting [-iŋ] adj. Enchanteur m.; enchanteresse f.; ravissant.
enchantment [-mənt] n. Enchantement m.
enchantress [-ris] n. Enchanteresse f.
enchase [in't,reis] v. tr. Enchâsser.
encipher [in'saifə*] v. tr. Chiffrer, coder (message).
encircle [in'sə:kl] v. tr. Encercler.
encircling [-iŋ] adj. Encerclant. ‖ MILIT. Enveloppant (movement).
enclasp [in'klɑ:sp] v. tr. Serrer, embrasser.
enclave [en'kleiv] n. Enclave f.
enclitic [in'klitik] adj., n. GRAMM. Enclitique m.
enclose [in'klouz] v. tr. Enclore, enfermer (to shut

in). ‖ Enclore, entourer (to encircle). ‖ Renfermer, inclure, contenir (to contain). ‖ Inclure, joindre, insérer (to insert); *enclosed herewith*, sous ce pli.
enclosure [-ʒəˈ] n. Clôture *f.* (act, fence). ‖ Enclos *m.* (close); enceinte *f.* (precinct). ‖ Pièce jointe *f.* (document).
encode [inˈkoud] v. tr. Coder (message).
encomiast [enˈkoumiəst] n. Panégyriste *m.* (See EULOGIST.)
encomiastic [en,koumiˈæstik] adj. Louangeur.
encomium [enˈkoumiəm] n. Panégyrique *m.*
encompass [inˈkʌmpəs] v. tr. Encercler, entourer, cerner (to surround). ‖ Contenir, inclure (to contain) [*with, within, dans*].
encompassment [-mənt] n. Encerclement *m.*
encore [ɔŋˈkɔ:ˈ] n. THEATR. Rappel *m.* (for another appearance); bis *m.* (for repetition).
— interj. THEATR. Bis.
— v. tr. THEATR. Bisser.
encounter [inˈkauntəˈ] v. tr. MILIT. Rencontrer, affronter. ‖ FIG. Rencontrer, faire face à (difficulties); rencontrer par hasard, tomber sur (s.o.).
— n. MILIT. Rencontre *f.*; combat *m.* ‖ FIG. Rencontre *f.*
encourage [inˈkʌridʒ] v. tr. Enhardir (to embolden); encourager, donner du cœur à, remonter (to hearten); aider, soutenir, appuyer, encourager (to support). ‖ Encourager, pousser (*to,* à) [to incite]; encourager, stimuler (to spur on).
encouragement [-mənt] n. Encouragement *m.* (*from,* de la part de; *to,* à) [act, thing].
encouraging [-iŋ] adj. Encourageant.
encroach [inˈkroutʃ] v. intr. Empiéter (*on, upon,* sur) [s.o.'s property, rights]. ‖ S'ingérer (*on, upon,* dans) [s.o.'s preserves]. ‖ Abuser (*on, upon,* de) [s.o.'s time].
encroachment [-mənt] n. Empiétement *m.*
encrust [inˈkrʌst] v. tr. Encroûter (to cover with a crust). ‖ Incruster (*with,* de).
— v. intr. S'encroûter.
encumber [inˈkʌmbəˈ] v. tr. Encombrer, gêner, entraver (to hinder); encombrer, obstruer, embarrasser (to obstruct). ‖ JUR. Grever. ‖ FIN. Surcharger (the market). ‖ FIG. Accabler (*with,* de) [claims].
encumbrance [-brəns] n. Encombrement, embarras *m.* ‖ Gêne, entrave *f.* ‖ JUR. Charge *f.*
encyclic [enˈsaiklik] adj., n. ECCLES. Encyclique *f.*
encyclop(a)edia [en,saikloˈpidiə] n. Encyclopédie *f.* (lit. and fig.).
encyclop(a)edic(al) [en,saikloˈpi:dik(əl)] adj. Encyclopédique.
encyclop(a)edism [en,saikloˈpi:dizm] n. Connaissances encyclopédiques *f. pl.*
encyclop(a)edist [-dist] n. Encyclopédiste *m.*
end [end] n. Limite, borne, fin *f.* (boundary). ‖ Bout *m.*; extrémité *f.*; *end on,* de front; *end to end,* bout à bout; *on end,* debout (egg); dressé (hair); *to make ends* (or) U. S. *both ends meet,* joindre les deux bouts. ‖ Bout, morceau, fragment, reste *m.* (remnant). ‖ Fin *f.*; terme, point final, achèvement *m.* (finish); *there is an end to everything,* tout n'a qu'un temps; *to argue without end,* discuter à perte de vue; *to bring to an end,* achever, terminer; *to come to an end,* s'achever, se terminer, finir. ‖ Fin, mort *f.* (death); *to be near one's end,* n'en avoir plus pour longtemps. ‖ Fin *f.*; but *m.* (aim). ‖ Fin, intention *f.*; objet, propos, dessein *m.* (purpose); *to this end,* dans ce dessein. ‖ Fin, conséquence *f.*; résultat *m.* (outcome). ‖ PHILOS. Fin, cause finale *f.* ‖ FAM. *At a loose end,* désœuvré; *dead end,* situation sans issue; *it did me no end of good,* ça m'a fait un bien énorme; *he is no end of a fellow,* il n'y a pas plus chic type; *to keep one's end up,* tenir son bout; *to go in off the deep end,* perdre patience; *to make an end of s.o.,* envoyer qqn ad

patres. ‖ **End-all,** n. Fin (*f.*) de tout. ‖ **End-leaf, end-paper,** n. Feuille de garde *f.*
— v. tr. Finir, terminer, achever (to finish). ‖ JUR. Dénouer (crisis). ‖ † Achever (to kill). ‖ FAM. *To end it all,* en finir avec la vie.
— v. intr. Finir, se terminer, s'achever, prendre fin (to terminate). ‖ Finir, mourir (to die). ‖ Finir (*by,* par; *in,* en); s'achever (*in,* par). ‖ Avoir pour effet (*in,* de).
endamage [inˈdæmidʒ] v. tr. Endommager. ‖ FIG. Etre préjudiciable à.
endanger [inˈdeinʒəˈ] v. tr. Exposer au danger, mettre en péril (to imperil). ‖ Risquer (to risk). ‖ ZOOL., BOT. *Endangered species,* espèce en voie de disparition.
endear [inˈdiəˈ] v. tr. Rendre cher; *to endear oneself to,* se faire aimer de.
endearing [-riŋ] adj. Attirant, attachant (attractive). ‖ Cajoleur, caressant, câlin (winning).
endearment [-mənt] n. Affection *f.* ‖ Caresse, câlinerie *f.*
endeavo(u)r [inˈdevəˈ] n. Effort *m.*; tentative *f.* [*after,* en vue de]. (See EFFORT.)
— v. intr. Faire tous ses efforts.
— v. tr. Tenter de, essayer de, s'efforcer de.
endemic [enˈdemik] adj. MED. Endémique.
— n. MED. Endémie *f.*
ending [ˈendiŋ] n. Fin *f.* (See END.) ‖ GRAMM. Désinence, terminaison *f.*
endive [ˈendiv] n. BOT. Chicorée frisée, escarole *f.* (chicory); endive *f.*
endless [ˈendlis] adj. Sans fin, infini, éternel. ‖ Incessant, continuel, perpétuel (unceasing). ‖ Sans fin, interminable. ‖ TECHN. Sans fin (chain).
endlessly [-li] adv. Sans fin, éternellement. ‖ Incessamment, perpétuellement, continuellement. ‖ Interminablement; *to argue endlessly,* discuter à perte de vue.
endlessness [-nis] n. Perpétuité *f.*
endocarditis [,endo,kɑˈdaitis] n. MED. Endocardite *f.*
endocardium [-ˈkɑːdiəm] n. MED. Endocarde *m.*
endocarp [ˈendokɑːp] n. BOT. Endocarpe.
endocrine [ˈendokrain] adj. MED. Endocrine.
— n. MED. Glande endocrine *f.*
endocrinology [,endokraiˈnɔlɔdʒi] n. MED. Endocrinologie *f.*
endogamous [enˈdɔɡəməs] adj. Endogame (person); endogamique (marriage).
endogamy [enˈdɔɡəmi] n. Endogamie *f.*
endogeneous [enˈdɔdʒənəs] adj. Endogène.
endorse [inˈdɔːs] v. tr. JUR. Viser (a passport). ‖ FIN. Endosser (a cheque); avaliser (a money order). ‖ FIG. Se ranger à (a decision); approuver, soutenir, sanctionner (a project).
endorsee [,endoˈsiː] n. FIN. Endossataire *m.*
endorsement [inˈdɔːsmənt] n. FIN. Endos, aval *m.* (*on,* de). ‖ FIG. Appui *m.*; adhésion *f.*; *favorable endorsement,* avis favorable.
endorser [-əˈ] n. FIN. Endosseur *m.*
endoscope [ˈendoskoup] n. MED. Endoscope *m.*
endosmosis [,endɔzˈmousis] n. MED., PHYS. Endosmose *f.*
endow [inˈdau] v. tr. FIN. Faire une dotation à (a hospital). ‖ FIG. Douer, doter, pourvoir (*with,* de) [a quality].
endowment [-mənt] n. Dot *f.* (dower); dotation *f.* (foundation). ‖ FIG. Don *m.* (talent).
endue [inˈdjuː] v. tr. Habiller. ‖ FIG. Investir (*with,* de) [an office]; douer (*with,* de) [virtues].
endurable [inˈdjuərəbl] adj. Endurable, tolérable, supportable. (See BEARABLE.)
endurance [-əns] n. Résistance *f.* (to fatigue); endurance *f.* (to pain). ‖ Epreuves *f. pl.* (hardship). ‖ Durée *f.* (duration).
endure [inˈdjuəˈ] v. tr. Endurer, souffrir, supporter, tolérer. (See BEAR.)

— v. intr. Durer (to continue). ‖ Endurer, résister tenir (to hold out).

enduring [-riŋ] adj. Endurant. ‖ Durable (lasting).

endways ['endweiz], **endwise** [-waiz] adv. Debout (on end). ‖ Bout à bout (end to end); de côté, de chant (edgewise); en long (lengthwise).

enema ['enəmə] n. MED. Lavement, clystère m.

enemy ['enəmi] adj., n. Ennemi s. (to, de). ‖ **Enemy-occupied**, adj. MILIT. Occupé par l'ennemi.

energetic [ˌenə'dʒetik] adj. Energique, agissant (see ACTIVE); énergique, vigoureux, fort (forceful).

energetically [-əli] adv. Energiquement.

energetics [ˌenə'dʒetiks] n. sg. PHYS. Energétique f.

energism ['enədʒizm] n. PHILOS. Energisme m.

energize [-dʒaiz] v. tr. Donner de l'énergie à; activer, stimuler.
— v. intr. Déployer de l'énergie; s'activer.

energizing [-dʒaiziŋ] adj. MED. Energétique.

energumen [ˌenə'gju:mən] n. Energumène m. ‖ Fanatique s.

energy ['enədʒi] n. Energie, force f. (strength); énergie, fermeté f. (vigour). ‖ Potentiel actif m.; capacité énergique f. ‖ Pl. Activités f. pl. ‖ PHYS. Energie f.; energy demand, bilan énergétique.

enervate [e'nə:vit] adj. Enervé, sans nerf (or) force, mou, abattu (flabby). ‖ Faible, affaibli, débilité, dévitalisé (weakened).
— [-veit] v. tr. Enerver, abattre, amollir. ‖ Affaiblir, débiliter.

enervation [ˌenə'veiʃən] n. Amollissement m. ‖ Affaiblissement m.

enfant terrible [ãfã tɛ'ribl] n. Enfant terrible s. (lit. and fig.).

enfeeble [in'fi:bl] v. tr. Affaiblir. (See WEAKEN.)

enfeeblement [-mənt] n. Affaiblissement m.

enfeoff [in'fef] v. tr. JUR. † Inféoder.

enfeoffment [-mənt] n. JUR. † Inféodation f.

enfetter [in'fetə*] v. tr. Mettre dans les fers. ‖ FIG. Enchaîner. (See ENCHAIN.)

enfilade [ˌenfi'leid] n. MILIT. Enfilade f.
— v. tr. MILIT. Prendre en enfilade.

enfold [in'fould] v. tr. Enrouler, envelopper, plier (to wrap up). ‖ Embrasser, enlacer (to clasp). ‖ Plisser (to pleat).

enforce [in'fɔ:s] v. tr. Renforcer, soutenir, faire valoir (by, par). ‖ Forcer, obliger, contraindre (to compel). ‖ Imposer par la force (on, à). ‖ JUR. Faire respecter (the law).

enforcedly [-idli] adv. Par la force, de force.

enforcement [-mənt] n. Contrainte, coercition f. ‖ JUR. Application f. (of the law).

enframe [in'freim] v. tr. Encadrer.

enfranchise [in'fræntʃaiz] v. tr. Affranchir (a slave). ‖ JUR. Donner le droit dc vote à (s.o.); octroyer la franchise à (a town). ‖ FIG. Libérer, affranchir. (See FREE.)

enfranchisement [-tʃizmənt] n. Affranchissement m. (of a slave). ‖ JUR. Octroi (m.) du droit de vote (or) de franchise.

engage [in'geidʒ] v. tr. Engager (to plight); to engage oneself to, s'engager à, promettre de. ‖ Fiancer (to betroth); to become engaged to, se fiancer à. ‖ Louer, retenir, réserver (to reserve) [a room]. ‖ Engager, embaucher, s'assurer les services de (to employ); I'll engage you, je vous prends à mon service. ‖ Engager, entraîner (to involve); to engage s.o. in conversation, engager la conversation avec qqn. ‖ Engager, séduire, attirer (to attract); retenir (s.o.'s attention). ‖ Occuper (to keep busy); to be engaged, être pris. ‖ MILIT. Engager le combat contre (the enemy); troops were engaged, les troupes ont donné. ‖ TECHN. Engager (machinery); to engage the gears, embrayer. ‖ FIN. Engager, mettre en gage (to pledge). ‖ SPORTS. Engager (swords).
— v. intr. S'engager (to, à); promettre (to, de) [to

guarantee]. ‖ S'engager; s'embarquer (fam.) [in, dans]; to engage in conversation with, engager la conversation avec. ‖ MILIT. Engager le combat. ‖ TECHN. S'engager, s'embrayer. ‖ SPORTS. Engager (in fencing).

engaged [-d] adj. Fiancé (betrothed). ‖ Occupé (busy); engaged signal, sonnerie « occupé ».

engagement [-mənt] n. Engagement m. (indenture, promise); to enter into an engagement, prendre un engagement. ‖ Fiançailles f. pl. (betrothal). ‖ Engagement m. (of an employee). ‖ Engagement, rendez-vous m.; I have a previous engagement, je me suis déjà engagé, j'ai déjà pris un engagement. ‖ MILIT., SPORTS. Engagement m. ‖ TECHN. Embrayage, engrenage m.

engaging [-iŋ] adj. Engageant, attirant, séduisant.

engarland [in'gɑ:lənd] v. tr. Orner de guirlandes, enguirlander. (See ENWREATHE.)

engender [in'dʒendə*] v. tr. FIG. Engendrer, produire, créer.

engine ['endʒin] n. TECHN. Machine f. ‖ AUTOM. Moteur m. ‖ CH. DE F. Machine, locomotive f. ‖ MILIT. Engin m. (of warfare). ‖ FIG. Engin, agent, instrument m. ‖ **Engine-driver**, n. TECHN. Mécanicien m. ‖ **Engine-nacelle**, n. AVIAT. Fuseau moteur m. ‖ **Engine-room**, n. Chambre (f.) des machines. ‖ n. CH. DE F. Hangar (m.) des locomotives. ‖ **Engine-trouble**, n. AUTOM. Panne (f.) de moteur.

engineer [ˌendʒi'niə*] n. TECHN. Ingénieur m. (technician); mécanicien, métallo m. (workman). ‖ RADIO. Radio, sound engineer, ingénieur radio, du son. ‖ MILIT. Soldat (or) officier du génie m.; pl. génie m. ‖ CH. DE F. U. S. Mécanicien m.
— v. tr. TECHN. Construire, faire les plans de. ‖ FAM. Manigancer, machiner.

engineering [-riŋ] n. TECHN. Génie civil m.; logistique industrielle f.; human engineering, ergonomie. ‖ NAUT. Mécaniciens m. pl. ‖ FAM. Manigance, machination f.

enginery ['endʒinəri] n. TECHN. Machinerie f.; machines f. pl. ‖ FIG. Manigance f.

engird [in'gə:d] v. tr. Entourer.

England ['inglənd] n. GEOGR. Angleterre f.

Englander [-ə*] n. GEOGR. Anglais s.

English ['ingliʃ] adj. GEOGR. D'Angleterre, anglais.
— n. Anglais m. (language). ‖ Anglais m. pl. (Englishmen). ‖ Corps douze m. (in printing).
— v. tr. Traduire en anglais (to translate). ‖ Angliciser (to Anglicize).

Englishism [-izm] n. U. S. Caractéristique (f.) du peuple anglais. ‖ U. S. Anglicisme m. (in speech).

Englishman [-mən] (pl. **Englishmen**) n. GEOGR. Anglais m.

Englishwoman [-ˌwumən] (pl. **Englishwomen** [-ˌwimin]) n. GEOGR. Anglaise f.

englut [in'glʌt] v. tr. Engloutir.

engorge [in'gɔ:dʒ] v. tr. Dévorer, engloutir (to devour); engloutir, ingurgiter, avaler (to gobble). ‖ MED. Engorger.
— v. intr. Engloutir, bâfrer.

engorgement [-mənt] n. Gorgement m. ‖ MED. Engorgement m.

engraft [in'grɑ:ft] v. tr. AGRIC. Greffer. ‖ FIG. Implanter.

engrail [in'greil] v. tr. Denteler, endenter. ‖ BLAS. Engrêler.

engrain [in'grein] v. tr. Teindre.

engram ['engræm] n. PSYCH. Engramme m.

engrave [in'greiv] v. tr. ARTS, FIG. Graver.

engraver [-ə*] n. ARTS. Graveur s.

engraving [-iŋ] n. ARTS. Gravure f.

engross [in'grous] v. tr. JUR. Grossoyer (a document). ‖ FIG. Monopoliser, accaparer (conversation); absorber (s.o.'s attention, s.o.).

engrossment [-mənt] n. JUR. Grosse f. ‖ FIG. Monopolisation f.; accaparement m.

engulf [in'gʌlf] v. tr. Engouffrer; *to be engulfed,* s'engouffrer.
enhance [in'hɑ:ns] v. tr. Intensifier, rehausser.
enhancement [-mənt] n. Rehaussement *m.*
enharmonic ['enhɑ:'mɔnik] adj. Mus. Enharmonique.
enigma [i'nigmə] n. Enigme *f.*
enigmatic(al) [,enig'mætik(əl)] adj. Enigmatique.
enigmatically [-əli] adv. Enigmatiquement.
enisle [i'nail] v. tr. Changer en île. ‖ Mettre dans une île. ‖ Fig. Isoler.
enjambment [en'dʒæmbmənt] n. Gramm. Enjambement *m.*
enjoin [in'dʒɔin] v. tr. Enjoindre à, ordonner à (s.o.); ordonner, exiger (sth.) [to command]. ‖ Imposer à, prescrire à (to prescribe). ‖ Interdire à (*from,* de) [to prohibit].
enjoy [in'dʒɔi] v. tr. Jouir de, profiter de, prendre plaisir à (to relish); *to enjoy life,* se donner du bon temps. ‖ Jouir de, avoir l'usage de, posséder (a privilege). ‖ **To enjoy oneself,** se divertir, s'amuser, prendre du plaisir, passer du bon temps.
enjoyable [-əbḷ] adj. Dont on tire du plaisir, agréable. (See PLEASANT.) ‖ Dont on peut jouir, profitable.
enjoyment [-mənt] n. Jouissance *f.;* plaisir *m.* (pleasure); possession *f.*
enkindle [in'kindḷ] v. tr. Allumer. ‖ Fig. Attiser (passions); enflammer (s.o.).
enlace [in'leis] v. tr. Enlacer.
enlarge [in'lɑ:dʒ] v. tr. Agrandir, développer. ‖ Agrandir (in photography). ‖ Fig. Développer, accroître. ‖ U. S. Elargir, libérer.
— v. intr. S'agrandir. ‖ **To enlarge on,** développer, discourir longuement sur, s'étendre sur.
enlargement [-mənt] n. Agrandissement, développement *m.* ‖ Appendice *m.* (to a book). ‖ Agrandissement *m.* (in photo). ‖ Med. Hypertrophie *f.* ‖ Fig. Accroissement *m.* (of s.o.'s fortune); long développement *m.* (on, upon, sur) [a subject].
enlarger [-ə*] n. Agrandisseur *m.* (in photography).
enlighten [in'laitṇ] v. tr. † Illuminer. ‖ Fig. Eclairer, fournir des lumières, édifier (on, sur).
enlightenment [-mənt] n. Eclaircissements *m. pl.;* lumières *f. pl.* (on, sur); édification *f.* (fam.).
enlist [in'list] v. tr. Milit. Enrôler. (See ENROLL.) ‖ Fig. Obtenir, gagner (s.o.'s help, support); enrôler, recruter, gagner (s.o.).
— v. intr. Milit. S'enrôler (in, dans); *to enlist before the usual age,* devancer l'appel. ‖ Fig. S'enrôler.
enlistment [-mənt] n. Milit. Enrôlement *m.* (act); durée (*f.*) du service (period). ‖ Fig. Enrôlement.
enliven [in'laivṇ] v. tr. Animer (a conversation); corser (a story). ‖ Stimuler (business).
en masse [ɑ̃'mas] adv. En masse, en bloc.
enmesh [in'meʃ] v. tr. Prendre dans les rets.
enmity ['enmiti] n. Inimitié *f.*
ennoble [i'noubḷ] v. tr. Anoblir. ‖ Fig. Ennoblir, élever, grandir.
ennoblement [-mənt] n. Anoblissement *m.* ‖ Fig. Ennoblissement *m.*
ennui [ɑ̃:nwi] n. Ennui *m.* (boredom).
enology [i:'nɔlədʒi] n. U. S. Œnologie *f.*
enormity [i'nɔ:miti] n. Monstruosité, abomination, atrocité *f.* (of a crime). ‖ Enormité, immodération *f.* (of a demand).
enormous [-məs] adj. † Monstrueux, abominable. ‖ Enorme (in amount, degree, size).
— Syn. : HUGE, IMMENSE, TREMENDOUS.
enormously [-məsli] adv. Enormément.
enough [i'nʌf] adj. Suffisant, assez de; *to be enough to,* suffire pour (or) à; *to have influence enough to,* avoir assez d'influence (or) une influence suffisante pour.
— adv. Assez, suffisamment, en suffisance; *it's*

good enough, c'est assez bon, ça suffira bien; bon, ça va. ‖ Fam. U. S. Bien, très, tout à fait; *he was happy enough to meet you,* il était tout plein content de vous rencontrer.
— interj. Assez!, il suffit!, ça va!
— n. Suffisance *f.*
enounce [i'nouns] v. tr. Proclamer, déclarer, énoncer (to proclaim). ‖ Prononcer, mentionner (to utter).
enouncement [-mənt] n. Proclamation, déclaration, énonciation *f.* ‖ Mention *f.*
en passant [ɔn pæ'sɑ:nt] adv. En passant, à propos, incidemment; *to take en passant,* prendre en passant (in chess).
enplane [in'plein] v. intr. Aviat. Monter en avion.
enquire [in'kwaiə*]. See INQUIRE.
enrage [in'reidʒ] v. tr. Enrager, exciter, mettre en fureur, rendre furieux.
enrapture [in'ræptʃə*] v. tr. Enchanter, transporter, ravir.
enrich [in'ritʃ] v. tr. Enrichir (*with,* de) [lit. and fig.]; *to enrich oneself,* s'enrichir. ‖ Agric. Fertiliser. ‖ Med. Vitaminiser (bread).
enrichment [-mənt] n. Enrichissement *m.* (lit. and fig.).
enrobe [in'roub] v. tr. Vêtir d'une robe (or) d'un costume officiel.
enrol(l) [in'roul] v. tr. (1). Porter sur une liste. ‖ Milit., Fig. Enrôler.
— v. intr. Etre inscrit sur une liste. ‖ Milit., Fig. S'enrôler. (See ENLIST.)
enrol(l)ment [-mənt] n. Inscription sur une liste *f.* ‖ Milit., Fig. Enrôlement *m.*
enroot [in'ru:t] v. tr. Enraciner, implanter.
ensanguine [in'sæŋgwin] v. tr. Ensanglanter.
ensconce [in'skɔns] v. tr. Cacher, dissimuler (to conceal). ‖ Blottir; *to ensconce oneself,* se rencogner; *to ensconce oneself in an armchair,* se pelotonner dans un fauteuil.
ensemble [ɑ̃:sɑ̃bl] n. Comm., Mus. Ensemble *m.* ‖ Theatr. Troupe (*f.*) au complet.
enshrine [in'ʃrain] v. tr. Eccles. Enchâsser. ‖ Fig. Conserver religieusement; mettre sous globe (fam.).
enshroud [in'ʃraud] v. tr. Envelopper, dissimuler, voiler (in, de).
ensign ['ensain] n. Insigne *m.* (badge). ‖ Naut. Pavillon; enseigne *m.* (flag); porte-drapeau *m.* (standard-bearer). ‖ Naut. U. S. Enseigne de vaisseau *m.*
ensilage ['ensilidʒ] n. Agric. Ensilotage *m.*
— v. tr. Agric. Ensiloter, mettre en silo.
ensile ['ensail] v. tr. Agric. Ensiloter.
enslave [in'sleiv] v. tr. Réduire en esclavage.
enslavement [-mənt] n. Asservissement *m.*
enslaver [in'sleivə*] n. Esclavagiste *m.* ‖ Fig. Envoûteur *m.* (man); enchanteresse *f.* (woman).
ensnare [in'snɛə*] v. tr. Prendre au piège.
ensphere [in'sfiə*] v. tr. Englober.
ensue [in'sju:] v. intr. Résulter, découler, s'ensuivre (*from,* de).
en suite [ɑ̃'sɥit] adv. En enfilade; *bathroom en suite,* salle de bains attenante.
ensure [in'ʃuə*] v. tr. Assurer (*against,* contre).
enswathe [in'sweið] v. tr. Emmailloter.
entablature [en'tæblətʃə*] n. Archit. Entablement *m.*
entail [in'teil] v. tr. Jur. Substituer (property). ‖ Fig. Entraîner, occasionner (expenditure); nécessiter (work).
— n. Jur. Substitution *f.* ‖ Fig. Suite, succession *f.*
entangle [in'tæŋgl] v. tr. Embrouiller, entortiller, enchevêtrer; empêtrer (fam.). ‖ Compliquer, embrouiller; emberlificoter (fam.).
entanglement [-mənt] n. Embrouillement, enche-

vêtrement, empêtrement *m.* ‖ Complication *f.;* embrouillamini *m.*

entente [ɔːn'tɔːnt] n. Entente *f.* (in politics).

enter ['entə*] v. intr. Entrer, pénétrer (*into,* dans) [a room]. ‖ To enter for, prendre rang pour, s'inscrire pour. ‖ **To enter into,** entrer dans (composition, explanation, projects); prendre part à (conversation); entrer en (correspondence); comprendre (a joke); entamer (negotiations). ‖ To enter on (or) upon, commencer, entreprendre (to begin); prendre possession de, entrer en jouissance de.
— v. tr. Entrer dans, pénétrer dans (a room). ‖ Devenir membre de (a club); inscrire, porter sur la liste (a name); s'inscrire à (a school); *to enter one's name for the summer school,* se faire inscrire aux cours d'été. ‖ Commencer, se mettre à (to start upon). ‖ JUR. Intenter (an action); interjeter (an appeal); déposer, inscrire au dépôt légal (a book); déclarer (a cargo); élever, formuler (a protest).

enteric [in'terik] adj. MED. Intestinal (disorder); typhoïde (fever).

enteritis [ˌentə'raitis] n. MED. Entérite *f.*

enterocolitis [ˌentəˈroˌkəˈlaitis] n. MED. Entérocolite *f.*

enterprise ['entəpraiz] n. Esprit (*m.*) d'entreprise; caractère entreprenant *m.; spirit of enterprise,* esprit d'initiative. ‖ Entreprise aventureuse, aventure *f.* ‖ COMM. *Private enterprise,* secteur privé (in economics).

enterprising [-iŋ] adj. Entreprenant; plein d'initiative. ‖ Aventureux, hardi (bold).

entertain [ˌentə'tein] v. tr. Divertir, amuser, distraire. (See AMUSE.) ‖ Recevoir (guests). ‖ Poursuivre, entretenir (conversation, relations). ‖ Nourrir (doubts); entretenir (hope); élever (objections).
— v. intr. Donner une réception, recevoir.

entertainer [-ə*] n. Amuseur *s.*

entertaining [-iŋ] adj. Divertissant. (See AMUSING.)

entertainment [-mənt] n. Divertissement, amusement *m.;* distraction *f.* ‖ Réception; hospitalité *f.* ‖ THEATR. Spectacle *m.*

enthalpy ['enθəlpi] n. PHYS. Enthalpie *f.*

enthrall [in'θrɔːl] v. tr. Asservir. ‖ FIG. Captiver.

enthrone [in'θroun] v. tr. Placer sur le trône, introniser (a king). ‖ ECCLES. Introniser (a bishop). ‖ FIG. Placer sur un piédestal.

enthronization [in,θrouni'zeiʃən] n. Intronisation *f.*

enthuse [in'θjuːz] v. tr. FAM. Enthousiasmer.
— v. intr. FAM. S'enthousiasmer, montrer de l'enthousiasme (*over, upon,* pour).

enthusiasm [-ziæzm̩] n. Enthousiasme *m.*

enthusiast [-ziæst] n. Enthousiaste, passionné, fervent *s.* (*for,* de).

enthusiastic [in,θjuːzi'æstik] adj. Enthousiaste, fervent, passionné (*about,* de); *to become enthusiastic over,* s'enthousiasmer pour, prendre feu et flammes pour.

enthusiastically [-əli] adv. Avec enthousiasme.

entice [in'tais] v. tr. Attirer, tenter.

enticement [-mənt] n. Attrait *m.;* tentation, séduction *f.*

entire [in'taiə*] adj. Entier, complet, total. (See COMPLETE.) ‖ MED. Entier (animal).
— n. COMM. Porter *m.* (ale). ‖ ZOOL. Etalon *m.* (horse). ‖ FIG. Entier *m.;* totalité, entièreté *f.*

entirely [-li] adv. Entièrement.

entirety [-ti] n. Totalité, entièreté *f.;* entier *m.*

entitle [in'tait] v. tr. Intituler, donner un nom (or) un titre à. ‖ Donner droit (*to,* à); donner qualité (*to,* pour) [to empower].

entity ['entiti] n. PHILOS. Entité *f.*

entomb [in'tuːm] v. tr. Enterrer, mettre au tombeau. ‖ FIG. Ensevelir.

entomological [ˌentəmə'lɔdʒikəl] adj. ZOOL. Entomologique.

entomologist [ˌentə'mɔlədʒist] n. ZOOL. Entomologiste *s.*

entomology [-dʒi] n. ZOOL. Entomologie *f.*

entourage [ˌɔntu'rɑː:ʒ] n. FIG. Entourage (persons).

entr'acte ['ɔntrækt] n. THEATR. Entracte *m.* (interval); interlude *m.* (performance).

entrails ['entreilz] n. pl. MED. Intestins *m. pl.* ‖ FIG. Entrailles *f. pl.*

entrain [in'trein] v. tr. CH. DE F. Faire prendre le train; mettre dans le train.
— v. intr. CH. DE F. Prendre le train, s'embarquer.

entrance ['entrəns] n. Entrée *f.* (*into,* dans) [of s.o.]. ‖ Entrée *f.* (to building); *entrance hall,* hall, vestibule; *tradesmen's entrance,* entrée de service. ‖ Entrée *f.* (fee); *to pay one's entrance fee,* acquitter les droits d'entrée. ‖ Admission *f.*

entrance [in'trɑːns] v. tr. Jeter en transe. ‖ FIG. Transporter (*with,* de). [See ENRAPTURE.]

entrancement [-mənt] n. Ravissement *m.*

entrant ['entrənt] n. Arrivant *s.* ‖ SPORTS. Participant *s.*

entrap [in'træp] v. tr. Attraper, prendre au piège.

entreat [in'triːt] v. tr. Supplier, conjurer, implorer.

entreatingly [-iŋli] adv. Instamment.

entreaty [-i] n. Supplication *f.* (prayer); demande instante *f.* (request).

entrée ['ɔntrei] n. Droit (*m.*) d'entrée (fee). ‖ CULIN. Entrée *f.*

entrench [in'trentʃ] v. tr. MILIT., FIG. Retrancher, se retrancher.
— v. intr. Empiéter. (See ENCROACH.)

entrenchment [-mənt] n. MILIT., FIG. Retranchement *m.*

entre nous [ɑ̃trə'nu] adv. Entre nous, en confidence.

entrepôt [ɑ̃trə'po] n. Entrepôt *m.*

entrepreneur [ˌɔntrəprəˈnə:*] n. Entrepreneur *m.*

entropy ['entrəpi] n. PHYS., MATH. Entropie *f.*

entrust [in'trʌst]~v. tr. Charger (*with,* de) [s.o.]. ‖ Confier (*to,* à) [sth.]. (See COMMIT.)

entry ['entri] n. Entrée *f.* (entering); *to make an entry,* faire une entrée. ‖ Entrée, inscription *f.; author, subject entry,* fiche auteur, sujet. ‖ Mot-souche *m.;* entrée *f.* (in a dictionary). ‖ Entrée (way in); *no entry,* entrée interdite, passage interdit. ‖ FIN. Ecritures *f. pl.* (in book-keeping); *by double, single entry,* en partie double, simple. ‖ JUR. Entrée en possession (or) jouissance *f.; forcible entry,* violation de domicile. ‖ JUR. Entrée *f.* (at a customhouse). ‖ SPORTS. Participant *s.* (entrant); liste (*f.*) des concurrents (list). ‖ U.S. Entrée *f.* (hall).

entryway [-wei] n. U. S. Entrée *f.*

entwine [in'twain] v. tr. Entrelacer.
— v. intr. S'entrelacer.

entwist [in'twist] v. tr. Entrelacer (to entwine); entortiller (*with,* de) [to twist].

enucleate [iː'njuːkliːeit] v. tr. MED. Enucléer. ‖ FIG. Expliquer, éclaircir, élucider.

enucleation [iː,njuːkliː'eiʃən] n. MED. Enucléation *f.* ‖ FIG. Eclaircissement *m.*

enumerate [i'njuːməreit] v. tr. Enumérer.

enumeration [i,njuːmə'reiʃən] n. Enumération *f.* (act, list).

enumerative [i'njuːmərətiv] adj. Enumératif.

enumerator [-reitə*] n. Enumérateur *m.;* énumératrice *f.*

enunciable [i'nʌnʃieibl̩] adj. Enonçable.

enunciate [-eit] v. tr. Annoncer, proclamer (to proclaim); définir, énoncer, émettre, exprimer, formuler (to state). ‖ Prononcer, articuler (to utter).

enunciation [i,nʌnʃi'eiʃən] n. Proclamation, déclaration *f.* ‖ Enonciation, définition *f.* ‖ Prononciation, articulation *f.*

enuresis [enju'riːsis] n. MED. Enurésie *f.*

enuretic [-'retik] adj., n. MED. Enurétique *adj., s.*

envelop [in'veləp] v. tr. Envelopper.

envelope ['envəloup] n. Enveloppe *f.* (of letter); *to put in an envelope,* mettre sous enveloppe. ‖ MATH., AVIAT., MED. Enveloppe *f.*

envelopment [in'veləpmənt] n. Enveloppement *m.* (wrapping up); enveloppe *f.* (wrapper).

envenom [in'venəm] v. tr. Empoisonner. ‖ MED., FIG. Envenimer. (See EMBITTER.)

enviable ['enviəbl] adj. Enviable.

envious ['enviəs] adj. Envieux, jaloux (*of,* de). ‖ † Jaloux d'égaler (emulous); malveillant (spiteful).

enviously [-li] adv. Envieusement.

environ [in'vaiərən] v. tr. Environner, entourer (*with,* de). ‖ Encercler, cerner.

— ['environz] n. pl. Environs, alentours *m. pl.*

environment [-mənt] n. Environnement, entourage *m.* ‖ MED., PHILOS. Milieu *m.*

envisage [in'vizidʒ] v. tr. Envisager, faire face à (to face); envisager, considérer (to look at).

envoi ['envɔi] n. Envoi *m.* (in poetry).

envoy n. Emissaire *m.* (messenger). ‖ Plénipotentiaire *m.* (ambassador).

envy ['envi] n. Envie *f.* (*at, of,* à l'égard de, au sujet de); *to be the envy of,* être un objet d'envie pour, être envié de, faire envie à; *to be green with envy,* en faire une jaunisse (fam.).

— v. tr. (2). Envier, être envieux de; considérer avec envie. (See COVET.)

enwrap [in'ræp] v. tr. Envelopper. (See WRAP.)

enwreathe [in'ri:ð] v. tr. Enguirlander. (See ENGARLAND.)

enzyme ['enzaim] n. CHIM., MED. Enzyme *m.* or *f.*

eocene ['i:osi:n] adj. GEOL. Eocène.

eolith ['i:oliθ] n. Eolithe *m.*

eolithic [,i:o'liθik] adj. Eolithique.

eon ['i:ən] n. Eon *m,*

eosine ['i:əsin] n. CHIM. Eosine *f.*

epact ['i:pækt] n. Epacte *f.*

epaulet(te) ['epɔ:let] n. MILIT. Epaulette *f.*

epeirogenesis [i,pairou'dʒenisis] n. GEOL. Ep(e)irogenèse *f.*

epergne [i'pə:n] n. CULIN. Surtout *m.*

ephebe [i'fi:b] n. Ephèbe *m.*

ephedrine ['efidrin] n. MED. Ephédrine *f.*

ephemera [i'femərə] n. ZOOL. Ephémère *m.*

— N. B. Le pluriel : *ephemeras* est préférable à *ephemerae.*

ephemeral [-əl] adj. Ephémère. (See TRANSIENT.)

ephemeris [-is] (pl. **ephemerides** [,efi'meridi:z]) n. Ephéméride *f.*

epic ['epik] adj. Epique.

— n. Epopée *f.;* poème épique *m.*

epicarp ['epi,kɑ:p] n. BOT. Epicarpe *m.*

epicene ['episi:n] adj. GRAMM. Epicène.

epicentre, U. S. **epicenter** ['epi,sentə*] n. GEOL., FIG. Epicentre *m.*

epicure ['epikjuə*] n. Gourmet *m.* (connoisseur); épicurien *m.* (pleasure-seeker).

epicurean [,epikjuə'ri:ən] adj., n. Epicurien *s.*

epicureanism [-izm̩] n. PHILOS. Epicurisme *m.*

epicurism ['epikjuərizm̩] n. FAM. Epicurisme *m.*

epicycle ['episaik̩l] n. MATH. Epicycle *m.*

epidemic [,epi'demik] n. MED. Epidémie *f.*

epidemic(al) [-ik(əl)] adj. MED. Epidémique.

epidemiology [,epi,di:mi'ɔlədʒi] n. MED. Epidémiologie *f.*

epidermal [,epi'də:məl] adj. MED. Epidermique.

epidermis [-mis] n. MED. Epiderme *m.*

epidiascope [,epidaiə'skoup] n. Lanterne magique *f.,* projecteur *m.*

epigastrium [,epi'gæstriəm] n. MED. Epigastre *m.*

epiglottis [-'glotis] n. MED. Epiglotte *f.*

epigone ['epigoun] n. BOT. Epigone *m.* ‖ ARTS. Décadent *m.*

epigram ['epigræm] n. Epigramme *f.*

epigrammatist [,epi'græmətist] n. Compositeur (*m.*) d'épigrammes.

epigrammatize [-taiz] v. intr. Composer des épigrammes.

epigraph ['epigrɑ:f] n. Epigraphe *f.*

epigraphy [e'pigrəfi] n. Epigraphie *f.*

epilepsy ['epilepsi] n. MED. Epilepsie *f.*

epileptic [,epi'leptik] adj., n. MED. Epileptique *s.*

epilogue ['epilog] n. Epilogue *m.*

epinephrine [,epi'nefrin] n. U. S. MED. Adrénaline *f.*

Epiphany [i'pifəni] n. ECCLES. Epiphanie *f.*

epiphenomenon [,epifi'nɔmə,nɔn] n. Epiphénomène *m.*

epiphysis [i'pifəsis] n. MED. Epiphyse *f.*

episcopacy [i'piskəpəsi] n. ECCLES. Episcopat *m.* (episcopate); épiscopalisme *m.* (system).

episcopal [-əl] adj. ECCLES. Episcopal.

episcopalian [i,piskə'peiliən] adj., n. ECCLES. Episcopalien *m.,* épiscopalienne *f.*

episcopate [i'piskəpit] n. ECCLES. Episcopat *m.*

episode ['episoud] n. Episode *m.*

episodic [,epi'sɔdik] adj. Episodique.

episodically [-əli] adv. Episodiquement.

epistemology [i,pisti'mɔlədʒi] n. Epistémologie *f.*

epistle [i'pisl̩] n. ECCLES., FAM. Epître *f.*

epistolarian [,epistə'lɛəriən] n. Epistolier *m.*

epistolary [i'pistɔləri] adj. Epistolaire.

epistyle ['epistail] n. ARCHIT. Architrave *f.*

epitaph ['epitɑ:f] n. Epitaphe *f.*

epitaxial [,epi'tæksiəl] adj. ELECTR. Epitaxial.

epithalamium [,epiθə'leimiəm] n. Epithalame *m.*

epithelium [,epi'θi:ljəm] n. Epithélium *m.*

epithet ['epiθet] n. GRAMM. Epithète *f.*

epitome [i'pitəmi] n. Abrégé *m.*

epitomize [-maiz] v. tr. Abréger.

epizooty [ipi'dzɔəti] n. MED. Epizootie *f.*

epoch ['i:pɔk] n. Epoque *f.; to mark an epoch,* faire époque. ‖ **Epoch-making,** adj. Qui fait époque, inoubliable.

eponym [i'pɔnim] n. Eponyme *m.*

eponymous [-əs] adj. Eponyme.

epopee [e'opi:], **epopoeia** [eo'pi:jə] n. Epopée *f.* (poem, poetry).

epos ['epɔs] n. Epopée *f.* (events, poem, poetry).

epoxide [i'pɔksaid] n. CHIM. Epoxyde *m.*

epoxy [i'pɔksi] adj. CHIM. Epoxyde, époxydique.

— n. CHIM. Résine époxyde *f.*

Epsom ['epsəm] n. GEOGR. Epsom. ‖ CHIM. *Epsom salts,* sulfate de magnésium.

equability [,ekwə'biliti] n. Egalité, uniformité *f.* (See EVENNESS.)

equable ['ekwəbl̩] adj. Egal, uniforme, équilibré.

equably [-bli] adv. Avec égalité (or) uniformité.

equal ['i:kwəl] adj. Egal (*to,* à); *she is equal to you,* elle est votre égale; *other things being equal,* toutes choses égales. ‖ Egal, sur le même plan; *on equal terms,* à armes égales, sur un pied d'égalité. ‖ A la hauteur, au niveau (*to,* de); de force (*to,* à). ‖ SPORTS. *Equal on points,* à égalité.

— n. Egal *s.* (*of,* de). ‖ MATH. Pl. Nombres égaux *m. pl.*

— v. tr. (1). Egaler, être l'égal de (s.o.); égaler, équivaloir à (sth.).

equality [i:'kwɔliti] n. Egalité *f.; where there is equality of,* à égalité de.

equalization [,i:kwəlai'zeiʃən] n. Egalisation *f.*

equalize ['i:kwəlaiz] v. tr. Egaliser.

equally [-li] adv. Egalement; *equally matched,* de force égale.

equanimity [,i:kwə'nimiti] n. Egalité d'âme, équanimité *f.*

equate ['ikweit] v. tr. MATH. Mettre en équation. ‖ FIG. Déclarer (ou) rendre équivalent (*to,* à).

equation [i'kweiʃən] n. MATH., CHIM., ASTRON., PHILOS. Equation *f.* ‖ FIN. *Equation of payments,* échéance commune. ‖ FIG. Egalisation *f.*

equator [i'kweitə*] n. GEOGR. Equateur *m.*

equatorial [,ekwə'tɔ:riəl] adj. GEOGR. Equatorial.

— n. ASTRON. Equatorial *m.*

equerry ['ekwəri] n. Ecuyer *m.*
equestrian [i'kwestriən] adj. Equestre (order, statue); d'équitation (performances).
— n. Cavalier *s.*
equiangular ['i:kwi'æŋgju:lə*] adj. MATH. Equiangle.
equidistant [-'distənt] adj. MATH. Equidistant.
equilateral [-'lætərəl] adj. MATH. Equilatéral.
equilibrate [-'laibreit] v. tr. Equilibrer.
— v. intr. S'équilibrer.
equilibration [i:,kwilai'breiʃən] n. Equilibrage *m.*
equilibrist [i:'kwilibrist] n. Equilibriste *s.*
equilibrium [,i:kwi'libriəm] n. Equilibre, aplomb *m.* (lit. and fig.); *to be in equilibrium,* se tenir en équilibre.
— N. B. Deux pluriels : *equilibriums, equilibria.*
equimultiple [,i:kwi'mʌltipl] adj. Equimultiple.
equine ['i:kwain] adj. ZOOL. Du cheval, équin.
equinoctial [,i:kwi'nɔkʃəl] adj. D'équinoxe. ‖ GEOGR. Equinoxial (line); équatorial (region).
— n. Tempête (*f.*) d'équinoxe. ‖ GEOGR. Ligne équinoxiale *f.*
equinox ['i:kwinɔks] n. ASTRON. Equinoxe *m.*
equip [i'kwip] v. tr. (1). MILIT., NAUT., FIG. Equiper; *to equip oneself,* s'équiper. ‖ FAM. Outiller.
equipage ['ekwipidʒ] n. Equipage *m.* (carriage, retinue); équipement *m.* (equipment).
equipment [i'kwipmənt] n. MILIT., NAUT. Equipement *m.* (*of,* de). ‖ TECHN. Outillage *m.* ‖ AUTOM. Matériel roulant *m.* ‖ FIN. *Capital equipment,* capitaux d'investissement.
equipoise ['i:kwipɔiz] n. Equilibre *m.* (balance); contrepoids *m.* (counterpoise).
equipollence [,i:kwi'pɔləns] n. Equivalence, équipollence *f.*
equipollent [-ənt] adj. Equivalent, équipollent (*with,* à).
equiponderant [,i:kwi'pɔndərənt] adj. De même poids (*to,* que).
equipotential [,i:kwipo'tenʃəl] adj. PHYS. Equipotentiel.
equitable ['ekwitəbl] adj. Equitable. (See JUST.)
equitably [-bli] adv. Equitablement, avec équité.
equitation [,ekwi'teiʃən] n. SPORTS. Equitation *f.*
equity ['ekwiti] n. Equité *f.* (See JUSTICE.) ‖ JUR. *Equity of a statute,* esprit d'une loi. ‖ FIN. Part résiduaire *f.*
equivalence [i'kwivələns] n. Equivalence *f.*
equivalent [-ənt] adj., n. Equivalent *m.; to be equivalent to,* équivaloir à.
equivocal [i'kwivəkəl] adj. Equivoque, douteux; louche, trouble (conduct, reputation); incertain, douteux (outcome); équivoque, à double sens, ambigu (words).
equivocally [-əli] adv. De façon équivoque.
equivocate [-eit] v. intr. Equivoquer, biaiser, faire une réponse de Normand; se défiler (fam.). [See QUIBBLE.]
equivocation [i,kwivə'keiʃən] n. Ambiguïté *f.;* faux-fuyant, détour *m.* ‖ Equivocation *f.*
equivocator [i'kwivəkeitə*] n. Matois, finassier *m.;* Normand *s.* (fam.).
equivoque ['ekwivouk] n. Equivoque *f.;* fauxfuyant *m.* (quibble). ‖ Jeu de mots *m.* (pun).
er [ə] interj. Euh!
era ['iərə] n. Ere *f.* (See PERIOD.)
eradiation [i,reidi'eiʃən] n. Irradiation *f.*
eradicable [i'rædikəbl] adj. Déracinable.
eradicate [-eit] v. tr. Déraciner (lit. and fig.).
eradication [i,rædi'keiʃən] n. AGRIC. Eradication *f.* ‖ FIG. Extirpation *f.*
eradicator [i'rædikeitə*] n. Extirpateur *m.* ‖ Corector *m.* (ink remover).
erasable [i'reizəbl] adj. Effaçable.
erase [i'reiz] v. tr. Effacer; raturer, gratter. ‖ FIG. Effacer.

eraser [-ə*] n. Grattoir *m.* (knife); gomme *f.* (rubber); chiffon *m.* (for the blackboard).
erasure [i'reiʒə*] n. Grattage *m.;* rature *f.*
erbium ['ə:biəm] n. CHIM. Erbium *m.*
ere [εə*] prep. † Avant.
— conj. † Avant que.
Erebus ['eribəs] n. Erèbe *m.*
erect [i'rekt] adj. Droit, debout (upright). ‖ Hérissé, dressé (bristling).
— v. tr. Dresser, mettre debout. ‖ ARCHIT. Elever, ériger. ‖ TECHN. Assembler. ‖ MATH. Elever (a perpendicular). ‖ MED. Faire gonfler. ‖ FIG. Elever (barriers); ériger (a principe).
erectile [-tail] adj. Erectile.
erection [-ʃən] n. ARCHIT., MED. Erection *f.* ‖ TECHN. Assemblage, montage *m.*
erectness [i'rektnis] n. Position droite *f.*
erector [-ə*] n. TECHN. Ajusteur-monteur *m.* ‖ MED. Erecteur *m.*
eremite ['erimait] n. Ermite *m.*
eremitic(al) [,eri'mitik(əl)] adj. Erémitique.
erethism ['eriθizm] n. MED. Eréthisme *m.*
erg [ə:g], **ergon** ['ə:gɔn] n. PHYS. Erg *m.*
ergonomics [,ə:gə'nɔmiks] n. sg. Ergonomie *f.*
ergot ['ə:gət] n. BOT. Ergot *m.*
ergotism [-izm] n. MED. Ergotisme *m.*
Erin ['erin] n. GEOGR. Erin *f.*
Erinyes [i'rini:z] n. pl. Erinnyes *f. pl.*
ermine ['ə:min] n. ZOOL., COMM., BLAS. Hermine *f.* (animal, fur).
ermined ['ə:mind] adj. Garni d'hermine (garment); vêtu d'hermine (person). ‖ BLAS. Herminé.
erne [ə:n] n. ZOOL. Aigle (*m.*) de mer.
erode [i'roud] v. tr. Eroder (rocks). ‖ Corroder (metal).
— v. intr. S'éroder. ‖ Se corroder.
erogenous [i'rɔdʒinəs] adj. Erogène.
erosion [i'rouʒən] n. Erosion *f.*
erosive [-siv] adj. Erosif.
erotic [i'rɔtik] adj. Erotique.
— n. Poème érotique *m.* ‖ U. S. Libertin *m.*
eroticism [-isizm] n. MED. Erotisme *m.*
err [-ə*] v. intr. Errer, se tromper, se fourvoyer (to be mistaken). ‖ Dévier du droit chemin, tomber dans l'errement; pécher (*on the side of,* par).
errancy ['ərənsi] n. Errance *f.*
errand ['erənd] n. Course, commission *f.; to go* (*or) to run errands,* faire des courses; *to go on an errand,* faire une course. ‖ Message, objet (*m.*) d'une course. ‖ **Errand-boy,** n. COMM. Coursier, garçon (*m.*) de courses. ‖ **Errand-girl,** n. COMM. Coursière *f.*
errant ['erənt] adj. Errant.
errantry [-ri] n. Chevalerie *f.*
erratic [i'rætik] adj. Errant, vagabond. (See DEVIOUS.) ‖ MED., GEOL. Erratique. ‖ FIG. Excentrique, original.
erratum [i'reitəm] (pl. **errata** [-ə]) n. Erratum *m.*
erroneous [i'rounjəs] adj. Erroné.
error ['erə*] n. Erreur, confusion, méprise *f.* (mistake); erreur, opinion fausse *f.* (wrong belief). ‖ Erreur *f.;* errement *m.* (transgression); *to see the error of one's ways,* revenir de ses erreurs. ‖ Faute *f.; printer's error,* coquille.
ersatz [ə:'zæts] n. Ersatz. (See SUBSTITUTE.)
Erse [ə:s] n. GRAMM. Gaélique, erse *m.*
erst [ə:st] adv. † Autrefois.
erstwhile ['ə:st,wail] adj. Ancien, d'autrefois.
erubescent [,eru'besnt] adj. Erubescent.
eructate [i'rʌkteit] v. tr., intr. Eructer.
eructation [,i:rʌk'teiʃən] n. Eructation *f.*
erudite ['eru:dait] adj. Erudit, savant, docte.
— n. pl. Erudits *m. pl.*
erudition [,eru:'diʃən] n. Erudition *f.*
erupt [i'rʌpt] v. intr. Jaillir (geyser, lava); faire éruption (volcano). ‖ MED. Percer (teeth). ‖ FIG. Se déchaîner, exploser.

eruption [-ʃən] n. Jaillissement m. (of a geyser); éruption f. (of a volcano). ‖ MED. Eruption f. (on the skin); percée f. (of teeth). ‖ FIG. Explosion f.
eruptive [-tiv] adj. MED., GEOL. Eruptif.
erysipelas [,eri'sipiləs] n. MED. Erysipèle m.
erythema [,eri'θi:mə] n. MED. Erythème m.
erythrocyte [i'riθrou,sait] n. MED. Erythrocyte m., hématie f.
escalade [,eskə'leid] n. Escalade f.
— v. tr. Escalader.
escalate ['eskə,leit] v. intr. Monter, grimper (prices); s'intensifier, s'amplifier (war).
— v. tr. Intensifier.
escalation [,eskə'leiʃən] n. Escalade, montée, intensification, amplification f.
escalator ['eskəleitə*] n. Escalier roulant, élévator m. ‖ U. S. *Cost-of-living escalator,* échelle mobile des salaires.
escapade [,eskə'peid] n. Escapade f.
escape [is'keip] n. Action (f.) de s'échapper, fuite f. (flight). ‖ Manière (f.) de s'échapper; *to have a narrow escape,* l'échapper belle; *we had a narrow escape,* nous avons eu chaud (fam.). ‖ TECHN. Echappement m. (of gas); fuite f. (of steam). ‖ JUR. *Escape clause,* clause évasive, échappatoire. ‖ ASTRONAUT. *Escape velocity,* vitesse de libération. ‖ FIG. Evasion f. ‖ **Escape-hatch,** n. AVIAT., NAUT. Trappe (f.) de secours. ‖ **Escape-pipe,** n. TECHN. Tuyau d'échappement m. ‖ **Escape-shaft,** n. TECHN. Puits de secours m. (in a mine).
— v. intr. S'échapper, s'enfuir (to get away); s'évader (from a prison). ‖ Echapper à (s.o.). ‖ En réchapper, s'en tirer. ‖ TECHN. Fuir (gas, water); s'échapper (steam). ‖ FIG. Echapper (*from,* à).
— v. tr. Echapper à, éviter, esquiver (to avoid). ‖ FIG. Echapper à, fuir (s.o., s.o.'s memory); *a moan escaped her lips,* une plainte lui échappa.
escapee [,iskei'pi:] n. Echappé, évadé, fugitif s.
escapement [i'skeipmənt] n. TECHN. Echappement m. (of clock, of piano).
escapism [i'skeipizm] n. FIG. Evasion f.
escapist [-ist] adj. FIG. D'évasion (literature).
escapologist [,eskə'pɔlədʒist] n. Illusionniste (s.) spécialisé dans les numéros d'« évasion ».
escarp [is'kɑ:p] n. MILIT. Escarpe f.
escarpment [-mənt] n. Escarpement m.
eschatology [,eskə'tɔlədʒi] n. ECCLES. Eschatologie f.
escheat [is'tʃi:t] n. JUR. Déshérence f. (default); bien (m.) tombé en déshérence (property).
— v. intr. JUR. Tomber en déshérence; *to escheat into,* échoir par déshérence à.
— v. tr. JUR. Confisquer (*to,* pour); *to escheat an estate,* faire échoir une succession.
eschew [is'tʃu:] v. tr. Se détourner de, éviter.
escort ['eskɔ:t] n. MILIT., NAUT. Escorte f. ‖ Cavalier m. (of a woman).
— [is'kɔ:t] v. tr. MILIT., NAUT. Escorter, faire escorte à. ‖ Accompagner, escorter (accompany).
escribed [i'skraibd] adj. MATH. Exinscrit.
escritoire [eskri'twɑ:*] n. Secrétaire m.
esculent ['eskjulənt] adj., n. Comestible m. (See EATABLE.)
escutcheon [is'kʌtʃən] n. BLAS. Ecu, écusson m. ‖ TECHN., NAUT. Ecusson m. ‖ FIG. *A blot on one's escutcheon,* une tache sur son nom.
esker ['eskə*], **eskar** ['eskɑ:*] n. GEOL. Ôs, esker m.
Eskimo ['eskimou] adj., n. GEOGR. Esquimau m.; esquimaude f. ‖ *Eskimo pie,* esquimau.
esophagus [i:'sofəgəs] n. MED. Œsophage m.
esoteric [,eso'terik] adj. Esotérique (doctrine, literature). ‖ Confidentiel (plan).
esoterism [i'sɔtərizm] n. Esotérisme m.
espadrille [,espə'dril] n. Espadrille f.
espalier [es'pæliə*] n. AGRIC. Espalier m.
— v. tr. AGRIC. Mettre en espalier.
esparto [es'pɑ:tou] n. Spart m.

especial [es'peʃəl] adj. Spécial.
especially [-əli] adv. Spécialement, surtout.
espial [is'paiəl] n. Espionnage m.; observation f. ‖ Découverte, révélation f.
espionage [,espiə'nɑ:ʒ] n. MILIT. Espionnage m.
esplanade [,esplə'neid] n. Esplanade f.
espousal [is'pauzəl] n. Epousailles f. pl. ‖ FIG. Ralliement m. (of, à); adoption f. (of, de).
espouse [is'pauz] v. tr. Marier (to give in marriage); épouser (to marry). ‖ FIG. Se rallier à (a cause); adopter, épouser (an idea).
espresso [e'spresou] (pl. **espressos** [-z]) n. Express m. (coffee); café m. (coffee bar).
espy [is'pai] v. tr. (2). Discerner, apercevoir. (See DESCRY.)
Esq. Written abbr. for *Esquire,* Monsieur (titre de courtoisie qui se place à la suite du prénom et du nom sur les adresses des correspondances).
Esquimau ['eskimou] adj., n. GEOGR. Esquimau m.; esquimaude f. (See ESKIMO.)
esquire [is'kwaiə*] n. † Ecuyer m. ‖ Monsieur (courtesy title). ‖ Cavalier m. (with a lady).
essay ['esei] n. Essai m.; tentative f. (See ATTEMPT.) ‖ Essai m.; rédaction, composition f. (in schools); dissertation f. (at the university).
— [e'sei] v. tr. Essayer, éprouver, mettre à l'essai (to test). ‖ Essayer, tenter (to attempt).
— v. intr. Essayer, faire un essai.
essayist [-ist] n. Essayiste m.
essence ['esns] n. PHILOS., CHIM. Essence f.
essential [i'senʃəl] adj. PHILOS., CHIM. Essentiel.
— n. Essentiel m.
essentiality [i,senʃi'æləti] n. Qualité essentielle f.; fait essentiel m.
essentially [i'senʃəli] adv. Essentiellement; par essence.
establish [is'tæbliʃ] v. tr. Etablir, fonder, instituer (a business house, government, nation). ‖ Etablir, installer, asseoir; *to establish oneself as a butcher,* s'établir boucher. ‖ ECCLES. Reconnaître comme institution d'Etat. ‖ JUR. Etablir (a charge). ‖ MILIT. S'établir sur (positions). ‖ FIG. Etablir, asseoir, affirmer (one's credit); établir, prouver, démontrer (a fact, one's innocence); établir, faire reconnaître (a precedent, theory).
establishment [-mənt] n. Etablissement m.; fondation, institution f. (act); établissement m.; institution f. (house). ‖ Etablissement m. (of one's children). ‖ Train (m.) de vie (style of living); moyens m. pl. ‖ ECCLES. Eglise établie f. ‖ MILIT. *War establishment,* effectifs de guerre. ‖ JUR. Etablissement m. (of a charge). ‖ FIG. Etablissement m.; démonstration f.
estate [is'teit] n. Etat m.; *to come to man's estate,* arriver à l'âge d'homme. ‖ Etat m.; *third estate,* tiers état. ‖ FIN. Biens m. pl.; possessions f. pl. (fortune); propriété f.; domaine m. (land, property). ‖ JUR. Bilan m. (of a bankrupt); état (m.) de la succession (of a dead person). ‖ FAM. *The fourth estate,* les journalistes, la presse. ‖ **Estate-agency,** n. COMM. Agence immobilière f. ‖ **Estate-agent,** n. COMM. Agent immobilier m. ‖ **Estate-car,** n. AUTOM. Break m. ‖ **Estates-General,** n. Etats généraux m. pl.
esteem [is'ti:m] v. tr. Estimer, priser, apprécier. (See APPRECIATE.) ‖ Estimer, considérer, juger (to regard).
— n. Estime f. (See REGARD.)
ester ['estə*] n. CHIM. Ester m.
esthete ['i:sθi:t] n. U. S. Esthète m.
estimable ['estiməbl] adj. Estimable, évaluable. ‖ Estimable, respectable.
estimate [-eit] v. tr. Estimer, évaluer, apprécier. ‖ FIG. Estimer, juger, évaluer, jauger (to gauge).
— [-it] n. Estimation, évaluation f. (appraisal); *at a rough estimate,* à vue de nez, grosso modo.

approximativement. ‖ TECHN., COMM. Devis *m.; estimate of quantities and costs,* devis estimatif. ‖ FIN. Pl. Crédits budgétaires *m. pl.*

estimation [,esti'meiʃən] n. Estimation *f.* (action). ‖ FIG. Opinion *f.;* avis *m.* (judgment); estime *f.* (regard).

estimative ['estimətiv] adj. Estimatif.

estimator ['estimeitə*] n. Estimateur *m.*

estival ['estivəl] adj. Estival.

Est(h)onia [e'stouniə] n. GEOGR. Estonic *f.*

Est(h)onian [-niən] adj., n. Estonien *adj., s.*

estop [es'tɔp] v. tr. (1). JUR. Opposer une fin de non-recevoir à.

estrange [is'treindʒ] v. tr. Eloigner, séparer, dépayser. ‖ Désaffectionner, détacher, détourner *(from,* de); aliéner l'affection de *(from,* pour).

estrangement [-mənt] n. Eloignement, détachement *m.;* désaffection *f.*

estreat [is'tri:t] n. JUR. Copie authentique *f.;* extrait *m.*

estrogen ['estrədʒən] n. U. S. MED. Œstrogène *m.*

estrogenic [,estrə'dʒenik] adj. U. S. MED. Œstrogène.

estuary ['estjuəri] n. Estuaire *m.*

esurience [i'sjuəriəns] n. Voracité *f.*

esurient [-ənt] adj. Vorace, goulu (edacious*)*, affamé (hungry).

et al. Written abbr. for *et alii* (= and others), et autres, et coll. (= collaborateurs).

et cetera, etc. [et'setrə] loc. Et cætera.
— n. Addendum; extra *m.*

etch [etʃ] v. tr., intr. ARTS. Graver à l'eau-forte. ‖ TECHN. Décaper.

etcher [-ə*] n. ARTS. Aquafortiste *s.*

etching [-iŋ] n. ARTS. Eau-forte *f.*

eternal [i'tə:nl] adj. Eternel, sans fin (everlasting). ‖ Eternel, immuable, inchangeable (unchangeable). ‖ Perpétuel, incessant, sempiternel (endless).
— n. ECCLES. Eternel *m.*

eternally [-əli] adv. Eternellement. ‖ Perpétuellement, sans arrêt.

eternity [-iti] n. Eternité *f.*

eternize [-aiz] v. tr. Eterniser.

ethane ['eθein] n. CHIM. Ethane *m.*

ethanol ['eθənoul] n. CHIM. Alcool éthylique, éthanol *m.*

ether ['i:θə*] n. Ether *m.* (air); ciel *m.;* régions éthérées *f. pl.* (sky). ‖ CHIM., PHYS. Ether *m.* ‖ MED. *Ether addict,* éthéromane.

ethereal [i:'θiəriəl] adj. Ethéré, céleste (regions). ‖ Ethéré, léger (grace). ‖ CHIM. Ethéré.

etherify [-fai] v. tr. (2). CHIM. Ethérifier.

etherization [,i:θərai'zeiʃən] n. Ethérisation *f.*

etherize ['i:θəraiz] v. tr. MED. Ethériser, anesthésier à l'éther.

ethic ['eθik] n. Morale *f.*

ethic(al) ['eθik(əl)] adj. PHILOS. Moral (act); éthique (problem). ‖ JUR. Conforme au code d'une profession.

ethically [-əli] adv. Moralement, sur le plan de la morale (or) de l'éthique.

ethics ['eθiks] n. sg. PHILOS. Morale, éthique *f.* ‖ Pl. FAM. Moralité *f.*

Ethiopia [,i:θi'oupjə] n. GEOGR. Ethiopie *f.*

Ethiopian [-ən] adj., n. GEOGR. Ethiopien *s.*

ethnic ['eθnik] n. U. S. FAM. Membre (*m.*) d'une minorité raciale.

ethnic(al) ['eθnik(əl)] adj. Ethnique.

ethnically [-əli] adv. Sous l'angle ethnique.

ethnographer [eθ'nɔgrəfə*] n. Ethnographe *m.*

ethnographic [,eθnə'græfik] adj. Ethnographique.

ethnography [eθ'nɔgrəfi] n. Ethnographie *f.*

ethnologic(al) [,eθnə'lɔdʒik(əl)] adj. Ethnologique.

ethnologist [eθ'nɔlədʒist] n. Ethnologue *m.*

ethnology [-dʒi] n. Ethnologie *f.*

ethology [i'θɔlədʒi] n. Ethologie *f.*

ethos ['i:θɔs] n. Génie *m.* (of a race, of a literary work).

ethyl ['eθil] n. CHIM. Ethyle *m.*
— adj. CHIM. Ethylique (alcohol); *ethyl hydride,* éthane.

ethylene ['eθili:n] n. CHIM. Ethylène *m.*

etiolate ['i:tioleit] v. tr. BOT. Etioler.
— v. intr. BOT. S'étioler.

etiolation [,i:tio'leiʃən] n. BOT., MED., FIG. Etiolement *m.*

etiology [,i:ti'ɔlədʒi] n. Etiologie *f.*

etiquette [,eti'ket] n. Etiquette *f.;* cérémonial, protocole *m.* ‖ Bonnes manières *f. pl.* (decorum).

Etna ['etnə] n. GEOGR. Etna *m.* ‖ CHIM. Réchaud à alcool *m.*

Eton ['i:tn] n. GEOGR. Eton. ‖ *Eton College,* Eton; *Eton crop,* coiffure à la garçonne; *Eton jacket,* Eton (coat).

Etruscan [i'trʌskən] adj., n. GEOGR. Etrusque *s.*

et seq(q). Written abbr. for *et sequentes* (= and following), et suiv. (= suivant, suivante, suivantes).

etymological [,etimə'lɔdʒikəl] adj. GRAMM. Etymologique.

etymologically [-i] adv. Etymologiquement.

etymologize [,eti'mɔlədʒaiz] v. tr. Chercher l'étymologie de.
— v. intr. Travailler l'étymologie.

etymology [-dʒi] n. Etymologie *f.*

etymon ['etimɔn] n. GRAMM. Mot-base (*m.*) des dérivés.

eucalyptus [,ju:kə'liptəs] n. BOT., CHIM., MED. Eucalyptus *m.; eucalyptus oil,* essence d'eucalyptus.

Eucharist ['ju:kərist] n. ECCLES. Eucharistie *f.*

Eucharistic [-ik] adj. ECCLES. Eucharistique.

eudiometer [,ju:di'ɔmitə*] n. PHYS., CHIM. Eudiomètre *m.*

eugenic [ju:'dʒenik] adj. Eugénique.

eugenics [-iks] n. sg. Eugénisme *m.;* eugénique *f.*

eulogia [ju:'loudʒiə] n. ECCLES. Eulogie *f.*

eulogist ['ju:lədʒist] n. Panégyriste *m.*

eulogistic [,ju:lə'dʒistik] adj. Laudatif, louangeur. (See LAUDATORY.)

eulogize ['ju:lədʒaiz] v. tr. Composer le panégyrique de. ‖ FIG. Louer hautement, exalter.

eulogy [-dʒi] n. Panégyrique *m.* (See ENCOMIUM.)

eunuch ['ju:nək] n. Eunuque *m.*

euonymus [ju:'ɔniməs] n. BOT. Fusain *m.*

euphemism ['ju:fimizm] n. GRAMM. Euphémisme *m.*

euphemistic [,ju:fi'mistik] adj. GRAMM. Euphémique.

euphemistically [-əli] adv. Par euphémisme.

euphemize ['ju:fimaiz] v. intr. S'exprimer par euphémisme.
— v. tr. Exprimer par un euphémisme.

euphonic [ju:'fɔnik], **euphonious** [-'founiəs] adj. Euphonique.

euphonium ['founiəm] n. MUS. Tuba *m.*

euphony ['ju:fəni] n. Euphonie *f.*

euphorbia [ju:'fɔ:biə] n. BOT. Euphorbe *f.* (See SPURGE.)

euphoria [ju:'fouriə] n. U. S. Euphorie *f.*

euphoriant [-riənt] adj., n. Euphorisant *adj., m.*

euphoric [-ik] adj. U. S. Euphorique.

euphuism [ju:fjuizm] n. Euphuisme *m.*

euphuist [-ist] n. Euphuiste *m.*

euphuistic [,ju:fju'istik] adj. Euphuistique. ‖ Ampoulé. (See BOMBASTIC.)

Eurasia [ju:'reiʒə] n. GEOGR. Eurasie *f.*

Eurasian [-ən] adj., n. GEOGR. Eurasien *s.*

Euratom [juə'rætəm] n. Euratom *m.*

eureka [ju'ri:kə] interj. Eurêka!

eurhythmic [ju:'riθmik] adj. Rythmique, eurythmique.
— n. pl. Gymnastique rythmique *f.*

Eurocrat ['juərə,kræt] n. Eurocrate s.
Eurodollar ['juərɔ,dɔlə*] n. FIN. Eurodollar m.
Europa [juə'roupə] n. Europe f. (in mythology).
Europe ['juərəp] n. GEOGR. Europe f.
European [,juərə'pi:ən] adj., n. GEOGR. Européen s.
Europeanize [-aiz] v. tr. Européaniser.
europium [ju'roupiəm] n. CHIM. Europium m.
Eustachian [ju:'steikiən] adj. MED. Eustachian tube, trompe d'Eustache.
eutectic [ju:'tektik] adj. PHYS. Eutectique; eutectic point, temperature, température, point d'eutexie.
— n. PHYS. Eutectique m.
euthanasia [,ju:θə'neiziə] n. Euthanasie f.
evacuant [i'vækjuənt] adj., n. MED. Evacuant m.
evacuate [-eit] v. tr. MED., MILIT., FIG. Evacuer.
— v. intr. S'évacuer.
evacuation [i,vækju'ei ʃən] n. Evacuation f.
evacuee [-'i:] n. Evacué s.
evade [i'veid] v. tr. FIG. Echapper à, éviter, éluder, esquiver. (See ESCAPE.)
evaluate [i'væljueit] v. tr. Evaluer. (See ESTIMATE.)
evaluation [i,vælju'ei ʃən] n. Evaluation f.
evanesce [,i:və'nes] v. intr. S'évanouir, s'évaporer, disparaître. (See VANISH.)
evanescent [-nt] adj. Evanescent, fugace, fugitif.
evangelical [,i:væn'dʒelikl̩] adj. Evangélique.
evangelicalism [-əlizm̩] n. Evangélisme m.
evangelism [i'vændʒi,lizm̩] n. Prédication (f.) de l'Evangile. ‖ Evangélisme m. (evangelicalism).
evangelist [-list] n. Evangéliste m. (writer of the gospels); évangélisateur s. (preacher).
evangelize [-,laiz] v. tr. Evangéliser, christianiser.
evaporable [i'væpərəbl̩] adj. Evaporable.
evaporate [-reit] v. tr. Evaporer; faire évaporer; to evaporate down, réduire par évaporation. ‖ CHIM. Déshydrater.
— v. intr. S'évaporer.
evaporation [i,væpə'rei ʃən] n. Evaporation f. ‖ CHIM. Déshydratation par évaporation f.
evaporator [i'væpəreitə*] n. CHIM. Evaporateur m.
evasion [i'veiʒən] n. Fait (m.) d'éluder; évasion f.; dérobade f. (of, à) [a rule]. ‖ Echappatoire f. (See ELUSION.) ‖ Faux-fuyant, détour m.
evasive [-siv] adj. Evasif.
evasively [-sivli] adv. Evasivement.
eve [i:v] n. Veille f. ‖ ECCLES. Vigile f.
evection [i'vek ʃən] n. ASTRON. Evection f.
even ['ivən] adv. Même; even if, même si. ‖ Exactement, juste; even now, même maintenant; à l'instant même; even so, tout juste, précisément.
— adj. Plat, uni (flat); even with, de niveau avec, à ras (or) à fleur de; to become even, s'égaliser; to make even, unifier, aplanir. ‖ Uniforme, égal, constant, régulier (not varying). ‖ Calme, tranquille, serein, égal (placid). ‖ Egal, équilibré (equable). ‖ Egal, semblable, identique (equal). ‖ Juste, équitable, satisfaisant (fair). ‖ MATH. Pair (number). ‖ FIN. Rond, juste (sum). ‖ **Even-handed**, adj. Impartial. ‖ **Even-minded**, adj. Au caractère égal.
— v. tr. Unifier, aplanir, égaliser (ground).
even n. Soir m.
evening [-iŋ] n. Soir m.; evening star, étoile du soir; I shall see you again in the evening, à ce soir! je vous reverrai ce soir; the evening before, la veille au soir; tomorrow evening, demain soir. ‖ Soirée f.; during the evening, pendant la soirée. ‖ Soirée f. (party); evening dress, wear, tenue, vêtements de soirée; evening gown, robe du soir. ‖ THEATR. Evening performance, soirée. ‖ FIG. Soir, déclin m. (of a career, life).
evenly [-li] adv. Uniformément, d'une manière égale.
evenness [-nis] n. Egalité f. (lit. and fig.)

evensong [-sɔŋ] n. ECCLES. Prière (f.) du soir (prayer); vêpres f. pl. (vespers).
event [i'vent] n. Evénement m.; the course of events, le cours des événements. ‖ Cas m. (occurrence); at all events, en tout état de cause, en tout cas, de toute manière; in the event of, au cas où, dans l'éventualité de, s'il arrivait que, si éventuellement. ‖ Conséquence f.; résultat m. (outcome). ‖ SPORTS. Epreuve f.; event m.
eventful [-ful] adj. Important (conversation); mémorable, marquant (day). ‖ Mouvementé, épique, fertile en événements (life, travel).
eventide ['i:vəntaid] n. Soir m.
eventual [i'ventjuəl] adj. Eventuel, possible (contingent). ‖ Final, définitif (ultimate).
eventuality [i,ventju'æliti] n. Eventualité f.; in all eventualities, en toute hypothèse.
eventually [i'ventjuəli] adv. Eventuellement. ‖ Finalement, en définitive, en fin de compte.
eventuate [-eit] v. intr. Arriver finalement, finir par arriver. ‖ Finir, se conclure (in, par); aboutir (in, à); avoir pour résultat (in, de).
ever [ّ'evə*] adv. Toujours (always); for ever and a day, pour toujours; for ever and ever, à tout jamais, à perpétuité; I have been here ever since lunch, je suis là depuis le déjeuner; to live for ever, ne jamais périr; yours ever, bien cordialement vôtre. ‖ A plusieurs reprises; ever and anon, de temps en temps. ‖ Jamais, une fois (at any time); if he ever came back, si jamais il revenait, s'il lui arrivait de revenir; no one ever told me, personne ne me l'a jamais dit. ‖ FAM. Ever so, extrêmement, énormément; ever so little, fort peu, presque pas de; who ever can have seen you?, qui donc (or) qui diable a pu vous voir?; worst ever, sans précédent. ‖ **Ever-changing**, adj. Instable, papillotant, fluctuant, oscillant (person).
evergreen [-,gri:n] adj. BOT. Sempervirent, toujours vert. ‖ FIG. Toujours vert (old person).
— n. BOT. Semper virens m. invar.
everlasting [,evə'lɑːstiŋ] adj. Eternel, sans fin. (See ETERNAL.) ‖ Perpétuel, incessant, sempiternel (never-ceasing).
— n. Eternité f. ‖ Lasting m. (fabric). ‖ BOT. Immortelle f. ‖ ECCLES. Eternel m.
evermore [-'mɔ:*] adv. Toujours.
eversion [i'və: ʃən] n. MED. Eversion f. (in surgery); ectropion m. (of eyelids).
evert [i'və:t] v. tr. MED. Retourner, pratiquer l'éversion de.
every ['evri] adj. Chaque, chacun de, tout; every day of the week, chaque jour (or) tous les jours de la semaine. ‖ Tout; she was given every chance to, on lui a donné toutes les chances possibles de. ‖ LOC. Every now and then, every so often, de temps en temps; every other (or) third day, tous les deux (or) trois jours.
everybody [-bɔdi] pron. Tout le monde, tous, chacun.
everyday [-'dei] adj. De tous les jours, ordinaire (clothes, work). ‖ Courant, usuel (English); courant (life); habituel (occurrence); journalier (routine). ‖ COMM. Ordinaire, quelconque (person).
everyone [-wʌn] pron. Tout le monde, tous, chacun (everybody).
everything [-θiŋ] pron. Tout.
everywhere [-hwɛə*] adv. Partout, de toutes parts, de tous côtés, en tous lieux; everywhere he goes, partout où il va.
evict [i'vikt] v. tr. JUR. Expulser.
eviction [i'vik ʃən] n. JUR. Eviction f.
evidence ['evidəns] n. Evidence, notoriété f. (conspicuousness). ‖ évidence f.; caractère manifeste m. (obviousness). ‖ Indication; preuve certaine f. (proof); marque évidente f. (sign). ‖ JUR. Déposition f. (of a witness); témoin m. (witness); circumstantial evidence, preuves indirectes;

discovery of new evidence, découverte de faits nouveaux ; *to give evidence*, déposer, témoigner ; *to turn Queen's evidence*, témoigner contre un complice. ‖ Fin. Titre *m.* (of indebtedness).
— v. tr. Mettre en évidence, révéler, montrer (to show up). ‖ Jur. Attester, témoigner de, porter témoignage de.

evident [-ənt] adj. Evident.

evidential [‚evi'denʃəl] adj. Evident, probant (cogent) ; évident, manifeste (obvious). ‖ Jur. Fondé sur des preuves.

evidently ['evidəntli] adv. Evidemment, d'une façon évidente, manifestement.

evil ['i:vəl] adj. Mauvais, dépravé (immoral) ; mauvais, méchant (wicked). ‖ Mauvais, funeste, néfaste (baleful) ; mauvais, nuisible (harmful).
— N. B. Les comp. et superl. de *evil* sont *worse* et *worst ;* on trouve cependant *more* (ou) *most evil.*
— n. Mal *m.* (depravity) ; mal *m.; méchanceté f.* (wickedness). ‖ Mal, malheur, désastre *m.* (misfortune). ‖ Med. Mal *m., maladie f.* ‖ **Evil-doer,** n. Méchant, mauvais, malfaisant *s.* ‖ **Evil-doing,** n. Malfaisance *f.* ‖ **Evil-eye,** n. Mauvais œil *m.*
— adv. Mal. ‖ **Evil-minded,** adj. Méchant (malicious) ; malintentionné, malveillant (malevolent) ; qui a mauvais esprit (salacious).

evince [i'vins] v. tr. Montrer, manifester (a desire) ; faire preuve de (a quality).

eviscerate [i'visəreit] v. tr. Eviscérer, éventrer. (See disembowel.) ‖ Fig. Affaiblir, énerver ; anéantir ; enlever sa force à ; vider de sa substance.

evocable ['evəkəbl̩] adj. Evocable.

evocation [‚evo'keiʃən] n. Evocation *f.*

evocative [i'vɔkətiv] adj. Evocateur *m.; évocatrice f.*

evoke [i'vouk] v. tr. Evoquer, rappeler (the past) ; évoquer (spirits). ‖ Jur. Evoquer (a cause).

evolute ['i:vəlju:t] n. Math. Développée *f.*

evolution [‚i:və'lju:ʃən] n. Med., Milit., Naut., Sports. Evolution *f.* ‖ Phys. Dégagement *m.* ‖ Math. Extraction de racine *f.* ‖ Fig. Développement *m.; évolution, marche f.*

evolutionism [-izm̩] n. Evolutionnisme *m.*

evolutionist [-ist] n. Evolutionniste *m.*

evolutionistic [-istik] adj. Evolutionniste.

evolve [i'vɔlv] v. tr. Faire évoluer. ‖ Phys. Dégager (gas) ; émettre (heat). ‖ Fig. Développer (an argument) ; dégager, tirer (a conclusion).
— v. intr. Med., Fig. Evoluer (*into*, vers) ; se développer (*into*, en).

evulsion [i'vʌlʃən] n. Evulsion *f.*

ewe [ju:] n. Zool. Brebis *f.* ‖ **Ewe-lamb,** n. Zool. Agnelle *f.;* Fig. trésor *m.* ‖ **Ewe-necked,** adj. Zool. A encolure de cerf (horse).

ewer ['juə*] n. Pot (*m.*) à eau (pitcher). ‖ † Aiguière *f.*

ex [eks] prep. Fin. Sans ; *ex dividend*, coupon détaché. ‖ Comm. Dégagé de, hors de ; *ex ship*, transbordé ; *ex store*, en magasin ; *price ex works*, prix à l'usine (ou) départ usine.
— pref. Ex, ancien.

exacerbate [eks'æsə:beit] v. tr. Exaspérer, exacerber (a pain, s.o.).

exacerbation [eks‚æsə'beiʃən] n. Exacerbation *f.* (of pain, person).

exact [ig'zækt] adj. Exact, précis, juste (accurate) ; exact, strict (rigorous).

exact v. tr. Extorquer (*of, from*, de) [money]. ‖ Fig. Imposer (*of, from*, à).

exacting [-iŋ] adj. Exigeant, difficile (person) ; ardu, dur, épuisant (work).

exaction [eg'zækʃən] n. Exaction *f.*

exactitude [ig'zækti̩tju:d] n. Exactitude, précision, justesse *f.* (accuracy) ; exactitude, ponctualité *f.* (punctuality).

exactly [-li] adv. Exactement ; *to reveal exactly what one is thinking*, révéler le fond de sa pensée.

exactness [-nis] n. Exactitude, précision *f.*

exactor [-ə*] n. Exacteur *m.*

exaggerate [ig'zædʒəreit] v. tr., intr. Exagérer.

exaggeratedly [-idli] adv. Exagérément.

exaggeration [ig‚zædʒə'reiʃən] n. Exagération *f.*

exaggerator [ig'zædʒəreitə*] n. Exagérateur *m.; exagératrice f.*

exalt [eg'zɔ:lt] v. tr. Intensifier, soutenir (colours). ‖ Exalter, enivrer, transporter (to elate). ‖ Exalter, porter aux nues, glorifier, vanter hautement (to extol).

exaltation [‚egzɔ:l'teiʃən] n. Exaltation, excitation *f.;* transport *m.* (rapture). ‖ Exaltation, augmentation *f.;* accroissement, renforcement *m.* (strengthening). ‖ Exaltation, glorification *f.* ‖ Eccles. Exaltation *f.* (of the Cross, of a Pope).

exam [ig'zæm] n. Fam. Examen *m.*

examinant [-inənt] n. Examinateur *m.; examinatrice f.*

examination [ig‚zæmi'neiʃən] n. Examen *m.* (of candidates) ; *to sit for* (*or*) *to take an examination*, passer un examen. ‖ Examen *m.* (of a matter) ; inspection, investigation *f.; under examination*, à l'examen, à l'étude. ‖ Jur. Instruction *f.* (of a case) ; interrogatoire *m.* (of a defendant) ; *customs examination*, visite douanière. ‖ Med. Examen *m.*

examine [ig'zæmin] v. tr. Examiner (sth.). ‖ Examiner, interroger, faire passer un examen à (a student). ‖ Jur. Instruire (a case) ; interroger (a defendant) ; faire déposer (a witness). ‖ Eccles. *To examine one's conscience*, s'examiner. ‖ Med. Examiner (a patient) ; *to have oneself examined, to get examined*, se faire examiner.
— v. intr. Se livrer à l'examen (*into*, de) ; se faire une opinion (*into*, sur).

examinee [ig‚zæmi'ni:] n. Candidat *s.*

examiner [ig'zæminə*] n. Examinateur *m.; examinatrice f.*

examining [-iŋ] adj. Jur. *Examining magistrate*, juge d'instruction.

example [ig'zɑ:mpl̩] n. Exemple *m.; after* (*or*) *following the example of*, à l'exemple de ; *for example*, par exemple ; *for example's sake*, pour l'exemple ; *to hold s.o. up as an example*, citer qqn en exemple ; *to set an example*, donner l'exemple ; *without example*, sans exemple, sans précédent.
— v. tr. Donner un exemple de, appuyer par un exemple.

exanimate [ig'zænimit] adj. Med. Inanimé. ‖ Fig. Sans vie, sans animation.

exasperate [ig'zɑ:spəreit] v. tr. Exaspérer, exacerber (a pain, s.o.).

exasperating [-iŋ] adj. Exaspérant.

exasperation [ig‚zæ:spə'reiʃən] n. Exaspération *f.* (of a pain, of s.o.).

ex cathedra [eksə'θi:drə] adv., adj. Eccles., Fig. Ex cathedra.

excavate ['ekskəveit] v. tr. Creuser (to dig) ; excaver, former une cavité dans (to hollow out). ‖ Déterrer en creusant (to unearth) ; faire des fouilles dans (a site).

excavation [‚ekskə'veiʃən] n. Excavation *f.* (act, hole). ‖ Fouille *f.; timbered excavation*, fouille blindée.

excavator ['ekskəveitə*] n. Techn. Excavateur *m.; fouilleuse f.*

exceed [ik'si:d] v. tr. Dépasser, outrepasser (a limit) ; excéder (a quantity). ‖ Fig. Dépasser (expectations) ; surpasser (hopes) ; excéder, outrepasser (powers).
— v. intr. Dépasser les bornes. ‖ Commettre des excès.

exceedingly [-iŋli] adv. Extrêmement.

excel [ik'sel] v. tr. (1). Dépasser, surpasser, dominer.
— v. intr. Exceller (*in*, à, en) ; se montrer supérieur (*in*, en).

excellence ['eksələns] n. Excellence, prééminence *f.* ‖ Mérite supérieur *m.;* qualité par excellence *f.*

excellency [-ənsi] n. Excellence *f.* (title).

excellent [-ənt] adj. Excellent, supérieur, prééminent.

except [ik'sept] v. intr. Soulever des objections (*against,* contre).
— v. tr. Excepter (*from,* de). ‖ JUR. Récuser (a witness).
— prep. Excepté, à l'exception de, exception faite de, en dehors de, hormis, sauf; *except that,* sauf que, excepté que.
— conj. † Sauf que. (See UNLESS.)

excepting [-iŋ] prep. A l'exception de, sauf, hormis.

exception [ik'sepʃən] n. Exception *f.* (*to,* à); *by way of an exception,* à titre d'exception, par exception; *to be an exception to,* faire exception à; *to make an exception to,* faire une exception à; *with certain exceptions,* sauf exception; *with that exception,* à cela près; ceci excepté. ‖ Objection *f.* (*to,* à); *to take exception to,* élever des objections contre, trouver à redire à (to object); se froisser de, se formaliser de, se sentir blessé par (to resent). ‖ JUR. Exception *f.* (of defence); récusation *f.* (of a witness).

exceptionable [-əbl̩] adj. Qui prête à objection.

exceptionably [-əbli] adv. D'une manière qui appelle des réserves.

exceptional [-əl] adj. Exceptionnel.

exceptionally [-əli] adv. Exceptionnellement, par exception. ‖ Extraordinairement.

exceptive [ek'septiv] adj. PHILOS. Exceptionnel. ‖ FAM. Chicaneur, vétilleux, contrariant.

excerpt [ek'sə:pt] v. tr. Prendre des extraits de (a book); extraire, choisir (*from,* de) [a passage].
— ['eksə:pt] n. Extrait, fragment, passage, morceau choisi *m.*

excerption [ek'sə:pʃən] n. Choix (*m.*) d'extraits (choice); extrait *m.* (extract).

excess [ek'ses] n. Excès *m.* (*of,* de; *over,* sur); *to excess,* à l'excès, jusqu'à l'excès. ‖ Excédent *m.; in excess of,* en plus de, au surplus de. ‖ Pl. Excès *m. pl.*
— adj. Excédentaire (profits, weight). ‖ CH. DE F. *Excess fare,* supplément; *excess luggage* (or) U. S. *baggage,* excédent de bagages.

excessive [-iv] adj. Excessif.

excessively [-ivli] adv. Excessivement, à l'excès, avec excès.

exchange [iks'tʃeindʒ] v. tr. Echanger, troquer (*for,* contre). ‖ Interchanger, échanger, faire un échange de (*with,* avec); *to exchange posts with,* permuter avec.
— v. intr. Faire un échange, troquer. ‖ S'échanger (*for,* contre).
— n. Echange, troc *m.* (*for,* contre; *of,* de); *exchange of posts,* permutation. ‖ Echange *m.;* substitution *f.* ‖ Objet d'échange *m.* (thing). ‖ Central *m.; « Exchange, please! »,* la ville, s'il vous plaît! (telephone centre). ‖ FIN. Bourse *f.* (place); *Labour Exchange,* Bourse du travail, office de la main-d'œuvre; *Stock Exchange,* Bourse des valeurs. ‖ FIN. Change *m.; at the current rate of exchange,* au cours du jour; *bill of exchange,* lettre de change; *operations in foreign exchange,* opérations de change.
— adj. D'échange (value); *exchange student,* étudiant qui pratique un échange. ‖ FIN. *Exchange broker,* cambiste; *exchange premium,* agio.

exchangeable [-əbl̩] adj. Echangeable (*for,* contre). ‖ FIN. Changeable.

exchequer [iks'tʃekə*] n. FIN. Trésor public *m.; Chancellor of the Exchequer,* chancelier de l'Echiquier. ‖ JUR. Echiquier *m.* (court). ‖ FAM. Fonds *m. pl.;* cassette *f.*

excipient [ik'sipiənt] n. MED. Excipient *m.*

excisable [ek'saizəbl̩] adj. FIN. Imposable.

excise [ek'saiz] n. FIN. Administration (*f.*) des contributions indirectes (office); impôt indirect *m.;* excise *f.* (tax).
— v. tr. FIN. Imposer, appliquer un impôt indirect sur. ‖ FAM. Pressurer.

excise v. tr. BOT. Faire une incision dans. ‖ MED. Exciser, pratiquer l'excision de. ‖ FAM. Découper.

exciseman [-mən] (pl. **excisemen**) n. FIN. Employé (*m.*) des contributions indirectes (or) de la régie.

excision [ek'siʒən] n. BOT. Incision *f.* ‖ MED. Excision *f.* ‖ FIG. Rejet *m.;* excommunication *f.* ‖ FAM. Coupure *f.*

excitability [ik,saitə'biliti] n. Excitabilité *f.*

excitable [ik'saitəbl̩] adj. Excitable.

excitant ['eksitənt] n. MED. Excitant *m.*

excitation [,eksi'teiʃən] n. PHYS., ELECTR., FIG. Excitation *f.*

excitative [ek'saitətiv] adj. Excitant.

excitatory [-əri] adj. Excitateur *m.;* excitatrice *f.*

excite [ik'sait] v. tr. Inciter, pousser à (to urge); exciter, stimuler, activer (to stimulate). ‖ Exciter, agiter (to agitate); exciter, énerver, irriter (to irritate); impressionner, émouvoir (to move); exciter, susciter, soulever, éveiller (to provoke); surexciter, exalter, transporter (to transport); *to get excited,* s'exciter, s'échauffer. ‖ ELECTR., MED. Exciter.

excited [-id] adj. Excité, agité, énervé; échauffé, fiévreux. ‖ Emu, impressionné, bouleversé. ‖ ELECTR., MED. Excité.

excitedly [-idli] adv. En état d'excitation, avec fièvre (or) agitation.

excitement [-mənt] n. Excitation, agitation, fièvre *f.;* énervement *m.* ‖ Emoi, bouleversement *m.;* émotion violente *f.* ‖ Agitation, animation *f.;* mouvement *m.*

exciter [ik'saitə*] n. ELECTR., FIG. Excitateur *m.;* excitatrice *f.*

exciting [-iŋ] adj. Excitant, énervant (irritating). ‖ Emouvant, bouleversant, impressionnant (moving). ‖ Passionnant, palpitant (interesting); *exciting game,* jeu mouvementé; *exciting woman,* femme désirable. ‖ ELECTR. D'excitation (battery).

exclaim [iks'kleim] v. intr. S'exclamer. ‖ Protester (*against,* contre).

exclamation [,iksklə'meiʃən] n. Exclamation *f.* ‖ GRAMM. *Exclamation mark,* point d'exclamation.

exclamatory [eks'klæmətəri] adj. Exclamatif.

exclude [iks'klu:d] v. tr. Exclure, refuser d'admettre (to leave out); exclure, rejeter, éliminer, expulser (*from,* de). ‖ Exclure, empêcher (to prevent).

exclusion [iks'klu:ʒən] n. Exclusion *f.* (*from,* de); *to the exclusion of,* à l'exclusion de, hormis. ‖ Exclusion, expulsion *f.;* renvoi *m.*

exclusive [-siv] adj. Exclusif (consideration, person, right). ‖ Incompatible; *to be mutually exclusive,* s'exclure. ‖ Fermé (club). ‖ COMM. Exclusif (article); *exclusive of,* non compris, en excluant. ‖ CINEM. En exclusivité; *exclusive rights,* exclusivité. ‖ U. S. Choisi, select, chic.

exclusively [-sivli] adv. Exclusivement.

exclusiveness [-sivnis] n. Exclusivité *f.*

exclusivism [-sivizm] n. Exclusivisme *m.*

excogitate [eks'kɔdʒiteit] v. tr. Inventer, imaginer, combiner (to contrive); manigancer, machiner (to plot).

excogitation [eks,kɔdʒi'teiʃən] n. Excogitation *f.* (of a problem). ‖ Invention, combinaison *f.*

excommunicate [,ekskə'mju:nikeit] v. tr. ECCLES. Excommunier.
— [-kit] adj., n. ECCLES. Excommunié *s.*

excommunication [ekskə,mju:ni'keiʃən] n. ECCLES. Excommunication *f.*

excoriate [eks'kɔ:rieit] v. tr. MED. Excorier; *to be excoriated,* s'excorier.

excrement ['ekskrimənt] n. MED. Excrément *m.*
excremental [,ekskri'mentļ] adj. Excrémentiel, excrémenteux.
excrescence [iks'kresn̞s] n. MED. Excroissance *f.*
excrescent [-n̞t] adj. MED. Constituant une excroissance. ‖ GRAMM. Excrescent.
excreta [iks'kri:tə] n. pl. MED. Excrétions *f. pl.*
excrete [-'kri:t] v. tr. MED. Excréter.
excretion [-ʃən] n. MED. Excrétion *f.*
excruciate [iks'kru:ʃieit] v. tr. Torturer.
excruciating [-iŋ] adj. Déchirant, torturant, suppliant, crucifiant.
excruciation [iks,kru:ʃi'eiʃən] n. Supplice *m. ;* torture *f.* (lit. and fig.).
exculpate ['ekskʌlpeit] v. tr. Disculper ; *to exculpate oneself from,* se disculper de.
exculpation [,ekskʌl'peiʃən] n. Disculpation *f.*
exculpatory [eks'kʌlpətəri] adj. Disculpant ; justificatif. (See VINDICATORY.)
excurrent [eks'kʌrənt] adj. BOT. Excurrent. ‖ MED. Artériel (blood).
excursion [eks'kə:ʃən] n. Excursion *f.* (trip) ; *to make an excursion,* excursionner. ‖ CH. DE F. *Excursion train,* train de plaisir. ‖ MILIT. Sortie *f. ;* raid *m.* ‖ ASTRON. Ecart *m.* ‖ FIG. Digression *f.* (in speech).
excursionist [-ʃənist] n. Excursionniste *s.*
excursive [-siv] adj. D'excursion (trip). ‖ FIG. Vagabond (imagination) ; fait au hasard, en diagonale, sans méthode (reading) ; décousu, digressif, sans suite (speech).
excursus [-səs] n. Appendice *m.* (in a book) ; digression *f.* (in a literary work).
— N. B. Deux pluriels : *excursuses, excursus* (mais non *excursi*).
excusable [eks'kju:zəbļ] adj. Excusable (*for,* de).
excusatory [-ətəri] adj. Justificatif, justifiant, qui peut excuser.
excuse [eks'kju:s] n. Excuse *f.* (*for,* à) ; *to admit of no excuse,* n'avoir pas d'excuse (behaviour) ; *to have no excuse,* n'avoir pas d'excuse (person) ; *to make excuses,* s'excuser ; *to make excuses for s.o.,* excuser qqn ; *to make sth. one's excuse,* faire valoir (or) invoquer qqch. pour (or) comme excuse ; *to offer a valid excuse,* alléguer une excuse valable. ‖ FAM. Semblant *m. ; a sad excuse for a garden,* un triste spécimen de jardin, un misérable ersatz de jardin.
— [-'kju:z] v. tr. Excuser ; *to excuse oneself for,* s'excuser de ; *to excuse s.o. sth.,* pardonner qqch. à qqn. ‖ Dispenser, exempter (*from,* de) [a duty].
ex-directory [eksdi'rektəri] adj. Qui n'est pas dans l'annuaire (number, subscriber).
execrable ['eksikrəbļ] adj. Exécrable, abominable, détestable.
execrably [-əbli] adv. Exécrablement.
execrate [-eit] v. tr. Exécrer, détester. (See ABHOR.) ‖ Maudire. (See CURSE.)
execration [,eksi'kreiʃən] n. Exécration, détestation, horreur *f.* ‖ Malédiction, exécration *f.* (curse).
executable [eg'zekju:təbļ] adj. Exécutable.
executant [-tənt] n. MUS. Exécutant *s.*
execute ['eksikju:t] v. tr. Exécuter, accomplir (an order). ‖ Exercer, remplir (duties). ‖ FIN. Effectuer. ‖ JUR. Valider, passer (a contract) ; exécuter (a criminal, a judgment) ; appliquer, exécuter (the law) ; signer (a treaty). ‖ THEATR., MUS., ARTS. Exécuter.
execution [,eksi'kju:ʃən] n. Exécution *f. ;* accomplissement *m.* (of an idea) ; *to be put into execution* entrer en voie d'exécution. ‖ Exercice *m.* (of duties). ‖ JUR. Validation *f.* (of a contract) ; exécution *f.* (of a criminal) ; application, exécution *f.* (of a judgment) ; exécutoire *m. ;* saisie-exécution *f.* (writ). ‖ THEATR., MUS., ARTS. Exécution. ‖ FIG. Ravage *m. ;* destruction *f.*

executioner [-ə*] n. Exécuteur (*m.*) des hautes œuvres ; bourreau *m.*
executive [eg'zekjutiv] adj. Exécutif (government, power). ‖ D'exécution (ability) ; U. S. *executive position,* poste administratif ; *executive secretary,* secrétaire de direction ; *executive staff,* cadres subalternes. ‖ U. S. *Executive Mansion,* la Maison-Blanche (in Washington) ; le palais du gouverneur d'un Etat (in a State capital).
— n. Exécutif *m.* (branch, group). ‖ Agent (*m.*) d'exécution (man). ‖ Administrateur *m.*
executor ['eksikju:tə*] n. Exécuteur *m.*
— [eg'zekjutə*] n. Exécuteur testamentaire *m.*
executory [eg'zekjutəri] adj. JUR. Exécutoire.
executrix [-triks] n. Exécutrice testamentaire *f.*
exegesis [,eksi'dʒi:sis] n. ECCLES. Exégèse *f.*
exegete ['eksidʒi:t] n. ECCLES. Exégète *m.*
exegetic(al) [,eksi'dʒetik(əl)] adj. ECCLES. Exégétique.
exegetics [-iks] n. sg. ECCLES. Théologie exégétique *f.*
exemplar [eg'zemplə*] n. Modèle *m.* (of virtue). ‖ Exemplaire, spécimen *m.* (of work).
exemplarity [,egzem'plæriti] n. Exemplarité *f.*
exemplary [eg'zempləri] adj. Exemplaire (behaviour, life, punishment). ‖ Typique. ‖ JUR. *Exemplary damages,* pénalité en sus des dommages-intérêts.
exemplification [eg,zemplifi'keiʃən] n. Démonstration (*f.*) par l'exemple. ‖ Exemple *m. ;* illustration *f.* ‖ JUR. Ampliation *f.*
exemplify [eg'zemplifai] v. tr. (2). Démontrer par des exemples ; illustrer. ‖ Servir d'exemple de. ‖ JUR. Faire une ampliation de.
exempt [eg'zempt] adj. Exempt (*from,* de) [obligation, tax] ; exempté (*from,* de) [service].
— n. Exempté *s.*
— v. tr. Exempter ; *to exempt oneself from,* s'exempter de, se dispenser de.
exemption [eg'zempʃən] n. Exemption *f.* (*from,* de). ‖ JUR. *Personal exemptions,* déductions pour charges de famille.
exequies ['eksikwiz] n. pl. Obsèques *f. pl. ; to attend the exequies,* suivre le convoi.
exercisable ['eksəsaizəbļ] adj. Exerçable.
exercise [-saiz] n. Exercice, devoir *m.* (at school) ; *Greek exercise,* thème grec ; *practical exercises,* travaux pratiques. ‖ MILIT. Exercice *m.* ‖ SPORTS. Exercice *m. ; breathing exercises,* gymnastique respiratoire. ‖ MUS. Exercice *m. ; to practise exercises,* faire des exercices. ‖ ECCLES. Exercice *m.* (office) ; pratique *f.* (of religion). ‖ U. S. Pl. Cérémonie *f.* ‖ FIG. Exercice *m.* (of duties, imagination, rights) ; pratique *f.* (of virtue).
— v. tr. Exercer (one's body) ; *to exercise oneself,* s'exercer. ‖ MILIT. Faire faire l'exercice à, exercer (troops). ‖ FIG. Exercer (authority, influence) ; exercer, remplir (duties, profession) ; exercer, user de (one's rights). ‖ FIG. Embarrasser, rendre perplexe ; exercer la sagacité de.
— v. intr. S'exercer. ‖ SPORTS. Faire de l'exercice. ‖ MILIT. Faire l'exercice.
exercitation [eg,zə:si'teiʃən] n. Essai, exercice *m.* (at school). ‖ Exercice *m.* (training).
exergue [ek'zə:g] n. Exergue *m.*
exert [ig'zə:t] v. tr. Déployer (influence, power, talent). ‖ *To exert oneself,* se dépenser, se donner du mal, mettre tout en œuvre (*for,* pour).
exertion [ig'zə:ʃən] n. Effort *m. ;* exertion *f.* ‖ Exercice *m.* (of power).
exeunt ['eksiʌnt] v. intr. THEATR. Sortent.
exfoliate [eks'foulieit] v. intr. BOT., MED. S'exfolier.
exfoliation [eks,fouli'eiʃən] n. BOT., MED. Exfoliation *f.*
ex gratia [eks'greiʃə] adv., adj. Sans obligation légale (payment).

exhalation [‚eksə'lei∫ən] n. Exhalaison, évaporation *f.* (act); exhalaison, émanation *f.;* effluve *m.* (result). ‖ FIG. Extériorisation *f.*

exhale Leks'heil] v. tr. Exhaler, émettre (gas, smell, smoke, vapour). ‖ Exhaler, expirer (air). ‖ FIG. Exhaler, donner cours à (one's anger).
— v. intr. S'exhaler.

exhaust Lig'zɔ:st] v. tr. Tirer, soutirer (*from,* de) [air, gas]. ‖ Vider; mettre à sec (a cask, a well). ‖ Epuiser, exténuer (s.o.); crever, éreinter, esquinter, mettre sur le flanc (fam.). ‖ FIG. Epuiser (a subject).
— n. TECHN. Echappement *m.* ‖ **Exhaust-pipe,** n. TECHN. Tuyau d'échappement *m.*

exhaustible [-ibḷ] adj. Epuisable.

exhaustion [-∫ən] n. Epuisement *m.;* to talk oneself into a state of exhaustion, parler à n'en plus pouvoir. ‖ TECHN., MATH. Exhaustion *f.*

exhaustive L-tiv] adj. Complet, exhaustif.

exhaustless [-lis] adj. Inépuisable.

exhibit [ig'zibit] v. tr. JUR. Exhiber, présenter, produire (documents, passport, ticket). ‖ THEATR., SPORTS. Exhiber. ‖ ARTS. Exposer. ‖ FIG. Déployer, faire montre de (impatience).
— v. intr. ARTS. Faire une exposition.
— n. JUR. Document *m.;* exhibition, présentation *f.* (of documents). ‖ ARTS. Envoi, objet exposé *m.* ‖ U. S. ARTS. Exposition *f.*

exhibition [‚eksi'bi∫ən] n. JUR. Exhibition, production *f.* (of documents). ‖ ARTS. Exposition *f.;* Ideal Home Exhibition, Salon des Arts ménagers. ‖ Bourse (*f.*) d'études (at school). ‖ FIG. Exhibition *f.;* étalage *m.*

exhibitioner [-ə*] n. Boursier *s.* (student).

exhibitionism [-izm̩] n. MED. Exhibitionnisme *m.*

exhibitionist [-ist] n. MED. Exhibitionniste *s.*

exhibitor [eg'zibitə*] n. Exposant *s.* ‖ CINEM. Directeur de cinéma *m.*

exhilarant [eg'zilərənt] adj., n. MED. Exhilarant *m.*

exhilarate [eg'ziləreit] v. tr. Egayer, animer.

exhilaration [eg‚zilə'rei∫ən] n. Egaiement *m.* (act); gaieté, animation *f.* (result).

exhort Lig'zɔ:t] v. tr. Exhorter, pousser, inciter (*to,* à) [s.o.]. ‖ Recommander (action, measures).

exhortation [‚egzɔ:'tei∫ən] n. Exhortation *f.* (*to,* à). [See ADMONISHMENT.]

exhumation [‚ekshju:'mei∫ən] n. Exhumation *f.*

exhume [eks'hju:m] v. tr. Exhumer, déterrer (lit. and fig.).

exigence ['eksidʒəns], **exigency** [-i] n. Besoin *m.;* nécessité *f.* (need); exigence, urgence *f.* ‖ Etat (*m.*) d'urgence; situation (or) circonstance critique *f.* (See EMERGENCY.)

exigent [-ənt] adj. Urgent, pressant. ‖ Exigeant (exacting).

exigible ['eksidʒibḷ] adj. Exigible (*against, from,* de).

exiguity [‚eksi'gjuiti] n. Exiguïté *f.*

exiguous [eg'zigjuəs] adj. Exigu.

exile ['eksail] n. Exil *m.* ‖ Exilé *s.* (person). ‖ ECCLES. Captivité *f.*
— v. tr. Exiler (*from,* de). [See BANISH.]

exility [eg'ziliti] n. Minceur *m.* ‖ FIG. Fragilité *f.*

exist [eg'zist] v. intr. Exister, être (to be). ‖ Exister, se trouver (*in,* dans) [to occur]. ‖ Exister, vivre (to live).

existence [-əns] n. Existence *f.* (fact, manifestation, state); to have been in existence for ten years, exister depuis dix ans. ‖ PHILOS. Etre *m.;* entité *f.*

existent [-ənt] adj. Existant.

existential [‚egzis'ten∫əl] adj. PHILOS. Existentiel.

existentialism [-izm̩] n. PHILOS. Existentialisme *m.*

existentialist [-ist] n. PHILOS. Existentialiste *s.*

exit ['eksit] n. Sortie *f.* (way out). ‖ THEATR. Sortie *f.* ‖ FAM. Fin *f.* (death).
— loc. THEATR. Exit (stage direction).
— v. intr. Partir, sortir (to leave). ‖ Rendre la main (at cards). ‖ FAM. Mourir, rendre l'âme (to die).

ex libris [eks'li:bris] n. Ex-libris *m. invar.*

exocrine ['eksou‚krain] adj. MED. Exocrine.

Exodus ['eksədəs] n. ECCLES., FIG. Exode *m.*

ex officio ['eksə'fi∫iou] adj., adv. D'office.

exogamous [ek'sɔgəməs] adj. Exogame (person); exogamique (marriage).

exogamy [-mi] n. Exogamie *f.*

exogenous [ek'sɔdʒinəs] adj. Exogène.

exonerate [ig'zɔnəreit] v. tr. Dispenser de, exempter, décharger de (a burden, an obligation). ‖ JUR. Disculper (s.o.).

exoneration [eg‚zɔnə'rei∫ən] n. Exonération, exemption *f.* (*from,* de).

exophthalmus [‚eksɔf'θælməs] n. MED. Exophtalmie *f.*

exorbitance [eg'zɔ:bitəns] n. Exorbitance, outrance, énormité *f.*

exorbitant [-ənt] adj. Exorbitant, extravagant (demand); exorbitant, prohibitif (price).

exorbitantly [-əntli] adv. De façon exorbitante.

exorcism ['eksɔ:sizm̩] n. ECCLES. Exorcisme *m.*

exorcist [-ist] n. ECCLES. Exorciste *m.*

exorcize [-aiz] v. tr. ECCLES. Exorciser.

exordial [ek'zɔ:diəl] adj. D'exorde, d'introduction.

exordium [-əm] n. Exorde *m.*

exosmosis [‚eksɔs'mousis] n. MED., PHYS. Exosmose *f.*

exoteric [‚ekso'terik] adj. Exotérique (doctrine); populaire (opinion).

exothermic [-θə:mik] adj. CHIM. Exothermique.

exotic [ek'sɔtik] adj. Exotique. ‖ **Exotic-sounding,** adj. A consonance exotique.
— n. Exotique *s.* ‖ BOT. Plante exotique *f.*

exoticism [-tisizm̩] n. Exotisme *m.*

expand [eks'pænd] v. tr. Déployer, étendre (to spread out). ‖ Elargir (to enlarge). ‖ MED., CHIM. Dilater. ‖ MATH. Développer (an equation). ‖ FIG. Développer (an idea, a topic).
— v. intr. Se déployer, s'étendre. ‖ S'élargir. ‖ MED., CHIM. Se dilater. ‖ MATH. Se développer. ‖ FIG. Se développer (idea); se livrer (person).

expandable [-əbḷ] adj. Extensible; dilatable.

expanse [eks'pæns] n. Etendue *f.* (extent). ‖ Expansion *f.*

expansibility [eks‚pænsi'biliti] n. PHYS. Expansibilité *f.*

expansible [eks'pænsibḷ] adj. Extensible. ‖ PHYS. Expansible.

expansion [-∫ən] n. Expansion, extension *f.;* élargissement *m.* ‖ Etendue *f.* ‖ MATH. Développement *m.* ‖ PHYS. Dilatation *f.;* expansion *f.* ‖ TECHN. Détente *f.* (of steam).

expansionism [-∫ənizm̩] n. Expansionnisme *m.*

expansionist [-∫ənist] n. Expansionniste *s.*

expansive [eks'pænsiv] adj. Etendu, large (extended). ‖ CHIM. Dilatable. ‖ PHYS. Expansif. ‖ FIG. Expansif, démonstratif, communicatif.

expansiveness [-nis] n. Etendue, possibilité d'étendue *f.* ‖ CHIM. Dilatation *f.* ‖ FIG. Expansibilité *f.* ‖ FAM. Convivial expansiveness, chaleur communicative des banquets.

expatiate [eks'pei∫ieit] v. intr. Disserter, discourir, s'étendre (*on,* sur). [See DILATE.] ‖ Errer çà et là, aller à l'aventure (to roam).

expatiation [eks‚pei∫i'ei∫ən] n. Dissertation *f.;* long discours (or) développement *m.* ‖ Prolixité *f.*

expatriate [eks'peitrieit] v. tr. Exiler (s.o.); to expatriate oneself, s'expatrier.
— adj., n. Expatrié *s.*

expatriation [eks‚peitri'ei∫ən] n. Expatriation *f.*

expect [eks'pekt] v. tr. Attendre (s.o.) [to await]. ‖ Compter sur (s.o.) [to rely]. ‖ Compter sur.

s'attendre à; *I expected as much*, je m'y attendais; *I don't expect you to answer me*, je ne compte pas sur une réponse de votre part; *I expect to see you tomorrow*, je compte vous voir demain; *I should not have expected that of you*, je n'attendais (or) ne croyais pas ça de vous. ‖ Attendre, exiger; *you expect too much from me*, vous me demandez trop. ‖ FAM. Supposer, espérer, présumer. ‖ FAM. *To be expecting*, attendre un heureux événement.

expectancy [-ənsi] n. Attente, expectative *f.* (expectation). ‖ Espérance *f.* (of birth, inheritance).

expectant [-ənt] adj. D'expectative, d'attente. ‖ MED. Expectant, d'expectation (medicine, treatment); *expectant mother*, femme enceinte, future maman.

expectation [,ekspek'teiʃən] n. Expectative *f.; to live in expectation*, vivre dans l'expectative. ‖ Prévision *f.; in expectation of*, en prévision de. ‖ ‖ Perspective *f.; happiness in expectation*, le bonheur en perspective. ‖ Probabilité *f.; expectation of life*, espérance de vie. ‖ Pl. Espérances *f. pl.* (of a birth, a legacy). ‖ MED. Expectation *f.*

expectorant [eks'pektərənt] adj., n. MED. Expectorant *m.*

expectorate [-reit] v. tr., intr. MED. Expectorer.

expectoration [eks,pektə'reiʃən] n. MED. Expectoration *f.* (act, sputum).

expediency [iks'pi:diənsi] n. Convenance *f.; on grounds of expediency*, pour des raisons de convenance. ‖ Opportunisme *m.; expedient f.*) de l'intérêt personnel. ‖ Opportunité *f.* (advisability).

expedient [-ənt] adj. Avantageux, utile (useful). ‖ Expédient, politique (*to*, de) [advisable]; *it's not expedient to say all that you think*, tout ce qu'on pense n'est pas bon à dire.
— n. Expédient *m.* (see RESOURCE); *to resort to expedients*, user d'expédients.

expedite ['ekspidait] v. tr. Expédier (business, task).
— adj. Expéditif.

expedition [,ekspi'diʃən] n. Expédition *f.* (exploration, journey, march). ‖ Expédition *f.* (of business); promptitude, manière expéditive (*f.*) (speed). ‖ MILIT. Expédition *f.*

expeditionary [-əri] adj. MILIT. Expéditionnaire (force).

expeditious ['ekspi'diʃəs] adj. Expéditif.

expel [eks'pel] v. tr. (1). Expulser, exclure, refouler (*from*, de). [See EJECT.]

expellable [-əbl] adj. Expulsable.

expellent [-ənt] adj. MED., FIG. Expulsif.

expend [eks'pend] v. tr. Dépenser (one's money); épuiser (one's resources). ‖ FIG. Dépenser (efforts).

expendable [-əbl] adj. MILIT. Sacrifié.

expenditure [eks'pendit ʃə*] n. FIN. Dépense *f.; capital expenditure*, augmentation de capital. ‖ FIG. Dépense *f.* (of time).

expense [eks'pens] n. FIN. Dépense *f.; to go to the expense of*, faire la dépense de. ‖ FIN. Pl. Frais, débours *m. pl.; general expenses*, frais généraux; *expense account*, indemnité pour frais professionnels; *to have all expenses paid*, être entièrement défrayé. ‖ JUR. *Legal expenses*, frais de justice. ‖ FIG. Dépens *m. pl.; at the expense of*, aux dépens (or) au prix de.

expensive [-iv] adj. Coûteux, onéreux, cher. (See COSTLY.)

expensively [-ivli] adv. Au prix d'une grosse dépense, d'une manière onéreuse.

expensiveness [-ivnis] n. Cherté *f.*

experience [eks'piəriəns] n. Expérience *f.* (in, of, de); *to know from experience*, avoir fait l'expérience de, connaître par expérience. ‖ Expérience *f.; incident vécu m.; it hasn't happened in my experience*, je n'en ai pas fait l'expérience, cela ne m'est jamais arrivé.

— v. tr. Faire l'expérience de (to gain experience of); ressentir (to feel); rencontrer (to meet with).

experienced [-t] adj. Expérimenté (*in*, en). ‖ Plein d'expérience, sage.

experiential [eks,piəri'enʃəl] adj. Appuyé sur l'expérience; empirique.

experiment [eks'periment] v. intr. Faire une expérience, expérimenter (*on*, *upon*, sur).
— [-ənt] n. CHIM., PHYS., FIG. Expérience *f.; as an experiment*, à titre d'expérience.

experimental [eks,peri'mentl] adj. Expérimental. ‖ Fait à titre d'expérience (tentative).

experimentalist [-əlist] n. Expérimentateur *m.;* expérimentatrice *f.*

experimentally [-əli] adv. Expérimentalement.

experimentation [eks,perimen'teiʃən] n. Expérimentation *f.*

expert ['ekspə:t] n. Expert, spécialiste *m.; with the eye of an expert*, d'un œil expérimenté. ‖ MED. *Medical expert*, médecin expert.
— [eks'pə:t] adj. Expert (*in*, en, dans). ‖ D'expert, de spécialiste; *according to expert opinion*, à dire d'expert; *expert advice*, les avis autorisés.

expertise [,ekspə:'ti:z] n. Expertise *f.* ‖ Compétence *f.*

expertly [eks'pə:tli] adv. De façon experte.

expertness [-nis] n. Maîtrise *f.*

expiable ['ekspiəbl] adj. Expiable.

expiate [-eit] v. tr. Expier.

expiation [,ekspi'eiʃən] n. Expiation *f.*

expiatory ['ekspiətəri] adj. Expiatoire.

expilation [,ekspi'leiʃən] n. JUR. Détournement (*m.*) de succession; spoliation *f.*

expiration [,ekspi'reiʃən] n. MED., JUR., FIG. Expiration *f.*

expire [eks'paiə *] v. tr., intr. JUR., MED., FIG. Expirer.

expiry [-ri] n. JUR. Expiration *f.*

explain [eks'plein] v. tr. Expliquer, donner l'explication de; *to explain away*, élucider (or) justifier tant bien que mal par ses explications; *to explain oneself*, s'expliquer.
— v. intr. Donner des explications, expliquer.

explainable [-əbl] adj. Explicable.

explanation [,eksplə'neiʃən] n. Explication *f.* (exposition, reason).

explanatory [eks'plænətəri] adj. Explicatif.

expletive [eks'pli:tiv] adj., n. GRAMM. Explétif *m.*

explicable ['eksplikəbl] adj. Explicable.

explicate [-keit] v. tr. Expliquer, faire l'explication de, commenter (a text). ‖ Élucider, expliciter (an obscure point).

explication [,ekspli'keiʃən] n. Exposé *m.* (detailed account). ‖ Explication, interprétation *f.*

explicative ['eksplikətiv], **explicatory** [-təri] adj. Explicatif.

explicit [eks'plisit] adj. Explicite, défini, clair. (See DEFINITE.) ‖ Exact, précis, net, carré (outspoken); *to be explicit about*, s'expliquer (ou) donner des précisions au sujet de.

explicitly [-li] adv. Explicitement, en termes explicites, clairement.

explicitness [-nis] n. Netteté, précision *f.;* caractère explicite *m.*

explode [eks'ploud] v. tr. PHYS., CHIM. Faire exploser (or) détoner. ‖ FIG. Discréditer, réduire à néant; crever (fam.).
— v. intr. PHYS., CHIM. Exploser, sauter.

exploit ['eksploit] n. Exploit, haut fait *m.*

exploit [eks'ploit] v. tr. Exploiter (lit. and fig.).

exploitable [-əbl] adj. TECHN. Exploitable.

exploitation [,eksploi'teiʃən] n. Exploitation *f.* (lit. and fig.).

exploiter [eks'ploitə*] n. AGRIC. Exploitant *m.* ‖ FIG. Exploiteur *m.*

exploration [,eksplɔ:'reiʃən] n. Exploration *f.* ‖

MED. Sondage *m.;* exploration *f.* ‖ FIG. Recherche attentive *f.* (See SCRUTINY.)

exploratory [eks'plɔːrətəri] adj. Exploratif.

explore [eks'plɔː*] v. tr. Explorer. ‖ MED. Sonder. ‖ FIG. Scruter.

explorer [-rə*] n. Explorateur *m.;* exploratrice *f.* ‖ MED. Explorateur *m.* (See PROBE.)

explosion [eks'plouʒən] n. Explosion *f.* (lit. and fig.)

explosive [-siv] adj. Explosif. ‖ GRAMM. *Explosive consonant,* explosive.
— n. Explosif *m.* ‖ GRAMM. Explosive *f.* (See STOP.)

exponent [eks'pounənt] adj. Qui expose (or) interprète.
— n. Exposeur *s.* (of methods, principles). ‖ Représentant *s.; the leading exponent of this art,* le chef de file et principal représentant de cet art. ‖ MATH. Exposant *m.* ‖ MUS. Exécutant *s.*

exponential [-ʃəl] adj. MATH. Exponentiel.

export ['ekspɔːt] n. COMM. Exportation *f.* (act); article (*m.*) d'exportation (goods); *to do an export trade,* faire de l'exportation. ‖ FIN. *Export of money,* exportation de capitaux.
— [eks'pɔːt] v. tr. COMM. Exporter.

exportable [eks'pɔːtəbl] adj. COMM. Exportable.

exportation [,ekspɔː'teiʃən] n. COMM. Exportation *f.* (*from,* en provenance de; *of,* de).

exporter [eks'pɔːtə*] n. COMM. Exportateur *m.;* exportatrice *f.*

exporting [-iŋ] adj. COMM. Exportateur.

expose [eks'pouz] v. tr. Exposer, placer (*to,* à); *to expose to the sun,* exposer au soleil. ‖ Exposer (new-born infants). ‖ Dévoiler (a crime); démasquer (s.o.). ‖ Exposer, faire poser (in photography). ‖ COMM. Mettre en montre (goods). ‖ U. S. Exposer, faire une exposition de (pictures).

exposé [.ekspou'zei] n. Mise en lumière, mise (*f.*) à jour; dévoilement *m.;* révélation *f.* (of a discreditable thing). ‖ Exposé *m.;* relation *f.* (account).

exposition [,ekspo'ziʃən] n. Exposition *f.* (*to,* à) [a danger]. ‖ Exposition (*of,* de) [an infant]. ‖ Exposition, introduction *f.* (of a literary work); exposé *m.,* exposition *f.* (of facts, ideas). ‖ COMM. Exposition, montre *f.* ‖ MUS. Exposition *f.* ‖ U. S. Exposition (of works of art).

expositive [eks'pozitiv], **expository** [-əri] adj. Descriptif, expositif.

expositor [-ə*] n. Exposeur *s.*

ex post facto ['ekspoust'fæktou] adj. JUR. A effet rétroactif (law).

expostulate [eks'pɔstjuleit] v. intr. *To expostulate with,* gourmander, raisonner, en remontrer à.

expostulation [eks,pɔstju'leiʃən] n. Remontrance *f.*

exposure [eks'pouʒə*] n. Exposition *f.* (*to,* à) [cold, danger]. ‖ Exposition (of a child). ‖ Pose, exposition *f.* (in photography); *to make an exposure,* prendre un cliché; *double exposure,* surimpression; *exposure meter,* posemètre, cellule photoélectrique. ‖ Révélation, dénonciation *f.* (of imposture). ‖ COMM. Exposition *f.* ‖ JUR. *Indecent exposure,* exhibitionnisme, attentat à la pudeur.

expound [eks'pound] v. tr. Expliquer, analyser (a text); exposer point par point (a theory).

express [eks'pres] v. tr. Exprimer, extraire (juice). ‖ Exprimer, dénoter (energy); exprimer, émettre (an opinion); formuler (a thought, a wish); *to express oneself,* s'exprimer. ‖ ARTS. Exprimer, représenter, symboliser. ‖ MATH. Exprimer.

express adj. Exprès *m.;* expresse *f.* (intention, order, reason). ‖ Exact (image). ‖ Rapide; *express letter,* lettre par exprès. ‖ CH. DE F. Express (train). ‖ SPORTS. Ultra-rapide (bullet, rifle). ‖ AUTOM. U. S. *Express way,* autoroute.
— adv. Par exprès. ‖ Très rapidement.
— n. Exprès *m.* (courier); message par exprès *m.*

(message). ‖ CH. DE F. Express *m.* ‖ SPORTS. Fusil ultra-rapide *m.* ‖ COMM. Transport rapide *m.*

expressage [-idʒ] n. Transport rapide *m.* (act, charge).

expressible [eks'presibl̩] adj. Exprimable.

expression [eks'preʃən] n. Expression *f.* (of juice). ‖ Expression *f.* (of joy, on the face); *beyond expression,* au-delà de toute expression. ‖ ARTS, MATH., GRAMM. Expression.

expressionism [-izm] n. ARTS. Expressionnisme *m.*

expressionist [-ist] adj., n. ARTS. Expressionniste *adj., s.*

expressionless [-lis] adj. Dénué d'expression, inexpressif. ‖ Sans signification.

expressive [əks'presiv] adj. Expressif, significatif; *expressive of,* exprimant, dénotant.

expressiveness [-nis] n. Expressivité *f.*

expressly [eks'presli] adv. Expressément, explicitement (definitely). ‖ Exprès, volontairement (on purpose).

expressman [-mən] (pl. **expressmen**) n. COMM. Employé (*m.*) des transports rapides.

expropriate [eks'prouprieit] v. tr. JUR. Exproprier (a proprietor, property). ‖ FIG. Déposséder (s.o.).

expropriation [eks,proupri'eiʃən] n. JUR. Expropriation *f.*

expulsion [eks'pʌlʃən] n. Expulsion *f.* ‖ Renvoi *m.* (*from,* de) [a school].
— SYN. : EJECTION, EVICTION.

expulsive [-siv] adj. Expulsif.

expunge [eks'pundʒ] v. tr. Effacer. (See ERASE.) ‖ Supprimer. (See DELETE.)

expurgate ['ekspəːgeit] v. tr. Expurger. (See BOWDLERIZE.)

expurgation [,ekspəː'geiʃən] n. Expurgation *f.*

exquisite ['ekskwizit] adj. Parfait, fait à la perfection, soigné (elaborate). ‖ Délicat, exquis, raffiné, fin (delicate). ‖ MED., CULIN. Exquis.
— n. Muscadin *m.* (See BEAU.)

exquisitely [-li] adv. Parfaitement, avec soin. ‖ Délicatement, avec raffinement; *exquisitely polite,* d'une politesse exquise. ‖ MED. Intensément, violemment. ‖ CULIN. Exquisement.

exquisiteness [-nis] n. Perfection *f.* ‖ Délicatesse *f.;* raffinement *m.* ‖ MED. Intensité, acuité *f.*

exsanguinate [ek'sæŋgwineit] v. tr. Saigner à blanc.

exsanguine [-gwin] adj. Exsangue, anémique. (See BLOODLESS.)

exscind [ek'sind] v. tr. Exciser.

exsiccate ['eksikeit] v. tr. CHIM. Dessécher.

exsiccator [-ə*] n. CHIM. Siccatif *m.*

extant [eks'tænt] adj. JUR. Encore existant, subsistant, non éteint, extant.

extemporaneous [eks,tempə'reinjəs], **extemporary** [iks'tempərəri] adj. Improvisé (fireplace). ‖ Impromptu (speech).

extemporaneously [-li] adv. Impromptu.

extempore [eks'tempəri] adj., adv. Impromptu.

extemporization [eks,tempərai'zeiʃən] n. Improvisation *f.*

extemporize [eks'temperaiz] v. tr., intr. Improviser.

extend [eks'tend] v. tr. Donner de l'extension à. ‖ Etendre, allonger (one's arm); prolonger (a street, a wall). ‖ FIN., COMM. Accorder des délais de paiement pour (a debt); porter, reporter (a sum) [in book-keeping]; proroger (time-limit). ‖ JUR. Saisir (a property). ‖ SPORTS. Pousser, forcer, faire donner son maximum à. ‖ CH. DE F. Prolonger (a ticket). ‖ FIG. Apporter (help); étendre (one's influence, knowledge); manifester (sympathy).
— v. intr. S'étendre (lit. and fig.); se dérouler (landscape); *to extend beyond the wall,* dépasser le mur.

extended [-id] adj. Etendu, prolongé (lit. and fig.). ‖ GRAMM. *Extended meaning,* extension (of word).

extendible [-ibl], **extensible** [iks'tensibl] adj. Extensible.

extensibility [eks,tensi'biliti] n. Extensibilité *f.*

extensile [eks'tensail] adj. Extensible.

extension [-ʃən] n. Extension, étendue *f.* (extent). ‖ Extension *f.;* prolongement *m.* (in space). ‖ Extension *f.;* prolongation *f.* (in time); *extension of term,* prolongation de durée. ‖ Cours libres *m. pl.* (in a university). ‖ Poste *m.* (telephone); *extension 22,* poste 22. ‖ MED., JUR. Extension *f.* ‖ COMM. Prorogation *f.* ‖ TECHN. Rallonge *f.* ‖ **Extension-ladder,** n. TECHN. Echelle à coulisse *f.* ‖ **Extension-table,** n. Table à rallonge *f.*

extensive [-siv] adj. Etendu, vaste (spacious). ‖ AGRIC. Extensif. ‖ FIG. Etendu, vaste, large (knowledge); considérable (part, use).

extensively [-sivli] adv. D'une manière étendue. ‖ FIG. Largement, considérablement, en grand.

extensiveness [-sivnis] n. Etendue, ampleur *f.*

extensometer [,eksten'sɔmitə*] n. TECHN. Extensomètre *m.*

extensor [eks'tensə*] adj., n. MED. Extenseur *m.*

extent [eks'tent] n. Etendue *f.* (in space); *in its full extent,* dans toute son extension. ‖ JUR. Saisie *f.* ‖ COMM. *Extent of trade,* éventail des affaires. ‖ FIG. Portée *f.; to the full extent of,* dans toute la mesure de; *to a certain extent,* dans une certaine mesure, jusqu'à un certain point (or) degré.

extenuate [eks'tenjueit] v. tr. Diminuer, affaiblir (to weaken). ‖ Edulcorer, atténuer, minimiser, pallier (a fault); excuser (s.o.).

extenuating [-iŋ] adj. JUR. Atténuant (circumstances).

extenuation [eks'tenju'eiʃən] n. Edulcoration, atténuation *f.*

extenuative [eks'tenjuətiv], **extenuatory** [-təri] adj. Atténuant.

exterior [eks'tiəriə*] adj. Extérieur, du dehors. (See OUTER.) ‖ Extérieur, étranger (foreign). ‖ MATH. Externe (angle).
— n. Extérieur *m.* (of building, person); *a pleasant exterior,* des dehors plaisants. ‖ CINEM. Extérieur.

exteriority [eks,tiəri'ɔriti] n. PHILOS. Extériorité *f.*

exteriorization [eks,tiəriərai'zeiʃən] n. PHILOS. Extériorisation *f.*

exteriorize [eks'tiəriəraiz] v. tr. PHILOS. Extérioriser. (See EXTERNALIZE.)

exterminate [eks'tə:mineit] v. tr. Exterminer.

exterminating [-iŋ] adj. Exterminateur *m.;* exterminatrice *f.*

extermination [eks,tə:mi'neiʃən] n. Extermination *f.*

exterminator [eks'tə:mineitə*] n. Exterminateur *m.;* exterminatrice *f.*

exterminatory [-təri] adj. Exterminateur *m.;* exterminatrice *f.*

extern [eks'tə:n] n. U. S. Externe *s.*

external [eks'tə:nl] adj. Extérieur, du dehors (exterior). ‖ Extérieur, étranger (foreign); *external events,* affaires extérieures. ‖ Extérieur, superficiel. ‖ PHILOS. Extérieur. ‖ MED. Externe (use).
— n. Extérieur *m.* ‖ Pl. Apparences *f. pl.*

externalization [eks,tə:nəlai'zeiʃən] n. Extériorisation *f.*

externalize [eks'tə:nəlaiz] v. tr. Extérioriser.

externally [-li] adv. Extérieurement.

exterritorial [eks,teri'tɔ:riəl] adj. JUR. Possédant l'exterritorialité.

exterritoriality [eks,teritɔ:ri'æliti] n. JUR. Exterritorialité *f.*

extinct [eks'tiŋkt] adj. Eteint (fire). ‖ FIG. Eteint, disparu (race).

extinction [-ʃən] n. Extinction *f.* (lit. and fig.).

extinctive [-tiv] adj. Extinctif.

extinguish [eks'tiŋgwiʃ] v. tr. Eteindre (fire, light).

‖ JUR. Eteindre (a debt). ‖ FIG. Eteindre, tuer, anéantir (hope); éteindre (family, race).

extinguisher [-ə*] n. Eteignoir *m.* (for candles); extincteur *m.* (for fire).

extinguishment [-mənt] n. Extinction *f.*

extirpate ['ekstə:peit] v. tr. Extirper, déraciner. (See ERADICATE.)

extirpation [,ekstə:'peiʃən] n. Extirpation *f.;* déracinement *m.* (lit. and fig.).

extirpator [,ekstə:'peitə*] n. AGRIC. Extirpateur *m.*

extol [eks'toul] v. tr. Exalter, porter aux nues.

extort [eks'tɔ:t] v. tr. Extorquer, soutirer (from, à) [money, ransom]. ‖ Arracher (from, à) [confession, promise]. ‖ Solliciter (a text); faire dévier (or) détourner de son sens (a word).

extortion [-ʃən] n. Extorsion *f.* (from, envers; of, de).

extortionate [-ʃənit] adj. Extorsionnaire (person); exorbitant, excessif (price).

extortioner [-ʃənə*], **extortionist** [-ʃənist] n. Extorqueur *s.*

extra ['ekstrə] adj. En plus, en supplément, supplémentaire (additional); non compris, en plus (not included in charge); *extra charge,* supplément.
— adv. En supplément; très, ultra, extrêmement (extremely).
— n. Supplément, extra *m.; to pay for the extras,* régler les suppléments. ‖ Edition spéciale *f.* (of newspaper). ‖ Extra *m. invar.* (temporary servant). ‖ CINEM. Figurant *s.*
— pref. Extra-. ‖ **Extra-curricular,** adj. Hors programme. ‖ **Extra-sensory,** adj. Extra-sensoriel. ‖ **Extra-uterine,** adj. MED. Extra-utérin.

extract ['ekstrækt] n. Extrait *m.* (of a book); *to make extracts from,* tirer des extraits de. ‖ CULIN. Extrait, concentré *m.; meat extract,* extrait de viande. ‖ MED. Extrait. ‖ JUR. *Extract from police records,* extrait du casier judiciaire.
— [eks'trækt] v. tr. Extraire (from, de). ‖ MATH., MED. Extraire. ‖ FIG. Extorquer, soutirer (money); arracher (from, à) [a promise]; tirer (from, de) [pleasure].

extraction [-ʃən] n. TECHN., MATH., MED., FIG. Extraction *f.* ‖ AGRIC. *Extraction rate,* taux de blutage (of flour).

extractor [eks'træktə*] n. TECHN., MILIT. Extracteur *m.* ‖ MED. Davier *m.*

extraditable ['ekstrədaitəbl] adj. JUR. Justifiant l'extradition (act); susceptible d'extradition (person).

extradite ['ekstrədait] v. tr. JUR. Extrader.

extradition ['ekstrə'diʃən] n. JUR. Extradition *f.*

extrados [eks'treidəs] n. ARCHIT. Extrados *m.*

extragalactic [,ekstrəgə'læktik] adj. ASTRON. Extragalactique.

extramarital [,ekstrə'mæritl] adj. Extra-conjugal.

extramural [,ekstrə'mjuərəl] adj. Extra-muros (district). ‖ Hors Faculté (in a university).

extraneous [eks'treinjəs] adj. Etranger (to, à).

extraordinarily [eks'trɔ:dinrili] adv. Extraordinairement.

extraordinariness [-rinis] n. Extraordinaire *m.*

extraordinary [-ri] adj. Extraordinaire, hors du commun, rare. ‖ Exceptionnel, remarquable. ‖ JUR. *Envoy extraordinary,* délégué (or) ambassadeur extraordinaire.
— n. MILIT. Rations supplémentaires *f. pl.*

extrapolate [eks'træpəleit] v. tr. Extrapoler.

extrapolation [,ekstræpə'leiʃən] n. Extrapolation *f.*

extraterritorial [,ekstrə,teri'tɔ:riəl] adj. JUR. Qui jouit de l'exterritorialité (ambassador); d'exterritorialité (right).

extraterritoriality [-,tɔ:ri'æliti] n. JUR. Exterritorialité *f.*

extravagance [eks'trævəgəns] n. Extravagance *f.* (in behaviour, conduct, speech). ‖ Dévergondage *m.* (of imagination). ‖ Prodigalité *f.*; gaspillage *m.* (in spending).

extravagant [-ənt] adj. Extravagant (behaviour, conduct, idea, person, speech). ‖ Dévergondé (imagination). ‖ Prodigue, gaspilleur (person); extravagant, exorbitant, excessif, outrancier, prohibitif (price).

extravagantly [-əntli] adv. D'une manière extravagante, avec extravagance.

extravaganza [eks,trævə'gænzə] n. Extravagance *f.* (in behaviour, speech). ‖ Histoire extravagante *f.* ‖ THEATR., MUS. Fantaisie *f.*

extravagate [eks'trævəgeit] v. tr. Extravaguer.

extravasate [eks'trævəseit] v. tr. MED. Extravaser. — v. intr. S'extravaser.

extravasation [eks,trævə'seiʃən] n. MED. Extravasation *f.*

extreme [iks'tri:m] adj. Extrême, dernier, le plus (or) très éloigné (farthest). ‖ Extrême, le plus (or) très grand (utmost). ‖ Extrême, intense (deep). ‖ Extrême, excessif, abusif, outré (exaggerated); *extreme in one's views*, d'opinions extrêmes. ‖ Extrême, rigoureux, très sévère (drastic). ‖ Extrémiste (opinions). ‖ ECCLES. *Extreme unction*, extrême-onction *f.*
— n. Extrême *m.*; *in the extreme*, à l'extrême, au plus haut degré; *to carry to extremes*, pousser à l'extrême; *to go to extremes*, se porter aux extrêmes. ‖ Extrémité *f.*; dernier degré; fond *m.* (of distress). ‖ MATH. Extrême *m.*

extremely [-li] adv. Extrêmement.

extremism [iks'tri:mizm̩] n. Extrémisme *m.*

extremist [-ist] n., adj. Extrémiste *s.*

extremity [iks'tremiti] n. Extrémité, fin *f.*; bout *m.* (end). ‖ Extrémité *f.*; extrême degré, summum *m.* (last degree). ‖ Extrémité, urgence *f.*; besoin extrême *m.* (necessity). ‖ Extrémité, mort *f.*; *to be at the last extremity*, être à l'extrémité (or) aux portes du tombeau. ‖ Pl. Extrémités; mesures extrêmes *f. pl.* ‖ MED. Pl. Extrémités *f. pl.*

extricable ['ekstrikəbl̩] adj. Qu'on peut démêler.

extricate ['ekstrikeit] v. tr. CHIM. Libérer (a gas, heat). ‖ FIG. Dégager; dépêtrer [fam.] (*from*, de) [a difficulty, an embarrassment].

extrication [,ekstri'keiʃən] n. Libération *f.*

extrinsic [eks'trinsik] adj. Extrinsèque.

extroversion [,ekstrə'və:ʃən] n. PHILOS., MED. Extroversion *f.*

extrude [eks'tru:d] v. tr. Rejeter, expulser. ‖ TECHN. Projeter.
— v. intr. Faire saillie, dépasser.

extrusion [-ʒən] n. Expulsion *f.* ‖ TECHN. Extrusion *f.*; filage, profilé *m.*

exuberance [eg'zju:bərəns] n. Exubérance *f.* (See EBULLIENCE.)

exuberant [eg'zju:bərənt] adj. Exubérant, luxuriant (vegetation). ‖ Exubérant, démonstratif (person).

exuberantly [-li] adv. Avec exubérance.

exudation [,eksju:'deiʃən] n. Exsudation *f.* (act); exsudat *m.* (matter).

exude [eg'zju:d] v. tr., intr. Exsuder.

exult [ig'zʌlt] v. intr. Exulter, jubiler. ‖ *To exult over*, chanter victoire.

exultancy [-ənsi], **exultation** [,egzʌl'teiʃən] n. Exultation, jubilation *f.* ‖ Triomphe *m.*

exultant [ig'zʌltənt] adj. Exultant, jubilant. ‖ Triomphant.

exultantly [-li] adv. Avec exultation.

exutory [eg'zju:təri] n. MED. Exutoire *m.*

exuviae [eg'zju:vii:] n. pl. ZOOL. Dépouilles *f. pl.* (of crabs, snakes).

exuviate [-eit] v. tr. ZOOL. Se dépouiller de.

eyas ['aiəs] n. ZOOL. Faucon niais *m.*

eye [ai] n. MED. Œil *m.* ‖ TECHN. Œillet *m.* (of a boot); porte *f.* (of a hook); œil, trou *m.* (in the handle of a tool); boucle *f.* (of metal or thread); chas, trou *m.* (of a needle). ‖ BOT. Œil *m.* (of potato). ‖ ZOOL. Œil *m.* (on a peacock's tail feather). ‖ MILIT. Mouche *f.* (on a target); *eyes right!*, tête à droite! ‖ NAUT. *In the eye of the wind*, contre le vent. ‖ FIG. Vue, vision *f.*; regard *m.*; *to see with half an eye*, voir du premier coup d'œil. ‖ Expression *f.*; *to view with a jaundiced eye*, regarder d'un œil envieux. ‖ Estimation *f.*; *to have an accurate eye*, avoir le compas dans l'œil; *to have a good eye for*, avoir le coup d'œil pour. ‖ Attention *f.*; *to catch s.o.'s eye*, tirer l'œil à; *to have a keen eye*, être très observateur; *to have an eye to*, avoir l'œil à; *to keep an eye on*, tenir l'œil à. ‖ Observation, vigilance *f.*; *to have one's eye on*, avoir l'œil sur; *to keep one's eyes open*, ouvrir l'œil; *to keep one's weather eye open*, se tenir à carreau. ‖ Clairvoyance *f.*; *to open one's eyes*, ouvrir les yeux, y voir enfin clair; *to shut one's eyes to*, fermer les yeux sur, s'aveugler sur. ‖ Opinion *f.*; *in the eyes of*, aux yeux de, au regard de; *to bring s.o. into the public eye*, mettre qqn en vue, faire connaître qqn; *to see eye to eye*, voir du même œil. ‖ FAM. *My eye!*, mince alors! (astonishment); mon œil! (contradiction); *to feast one's eyes on*, se repaître la vue de, se rincer l'œil de; *to give s.o. the glad eye, to make sheep's eyes at s.o.*, faire les yeux doux à qqn, lancer une œillade à qqn; faire de l'œil à qqn. ‖ **Eye-bank**, n. Banque (*f.*) des yeux. ‖ **Eye-bath**, n. MED. Œillère *f.* ‖ **Eye-glass**, n. Monocle *m.*; *eye-glasses*, lorgnon, pince-nez *m.*; U. S. lunettes *f. pl.* ‖ **Eye-liner**, n. Eye-liner *m.* ‖ **Eye-opener**, n. FAM. Nouvelle sensationnelle, surprise, révélation *f.* (news); U. S. FAM. Rince-gosier matinal *m.* ‖ **Eye-patch**, n. MED. Couvre-œil *m.* ‖ **Eye-shade**, n. Visière *f.* ‖ **Eye-shadow**, n. Ombre (*f.*) [or] fard (*m.*) à paupières. ‖ **Eye-tooth**, n. MED. Canine *f.* ‖ **Eye-wash**, n. Collyre *m.*; FAM. Tape-à-l'œil *m.*, frime *f.* (pretension), foutaise, ineptie *f.* (nonsense).
— v. tr. Mesurer du regard; dévisager d'un air soupçonneux; *to eye from head to foot*, toiser de haut en bas.

eyeball [-bɔ:l] n. MED. Globe oculaire *m.*

eyebeam [-bi:m] n. Regard vif (or) perçant, coup d'œil *m.*

eyebrow [-brau] n. MED. Sourcil *m.* ‖ FAM. *That made him raise his eyebrows*, ça l'a fait tiquer.

eyeful [-ful] n. MED. Pleine œillère *f.* ‖ FAM. Ce qu'on peut voir d'un coup d'œil; *to get an eyeful*, se rincer l'œil, s'en mettre plein la vue.

eyehole [-houl] n. MED. Orbite *f.* ‖ ARCHIT. Judas *m.* (See PEEP-HOLE.)

eyelash [-læʃ] n. MED. Cil *m.* ‖ FAM. *To hang on by one's eyelashes*, tenir à un fil.

eyelet [-lit] n. Œillet *m.* (of boot, for a cord, in embroidered work). ‖ **Eyelet-embroidery**, n. U. S. Broderie anglaise *f.*

eyelid [-lid] n. MED. Paupière *f.*

eyepiece [-pi:s] n. PHYS. Oculaire *m.*

eyeshot [-ʃɔt] n. Portée (*f.*) du regard.

eyesight [-sait] n. MED. Vue *f.*

eyesore [-sɔ:*] n. Objet déplaisant *m.*; vilain tableau *m.* (fam.).

Eyetie ['aitai] n. POP. Rital *m.* (Italian).

eyewater [-,wɔ:tə*] n. MED. Humeur aqueuse *f.* (moisture); collyre *m.* (lotion).

eyewitness [-,witnis] n. JUR. Témoin oculaire *m.*

eyot [eit] n. MED. Ilot *m.*

eyrie ['ɛəri] n. ZOOL. Aire *f.* (nest); nichée *f.* (young). ‖ ARCHIT. Nid d'aigle *m.* (house).

Ezekiel [i'zi:kjəl] n. Ezéchiel *m.*

F

f [ef] n. F, f m. ‖ Mus. Fa m. ‖ Chim. Fluor m. ‖ Phys. Farad m. ‖ Math. Fonction f. ‖ U. S. Fam. Zéro pointé m. (mark).

F. Abbr. *Fahrenheit*, Fahrenheit.

fa [fɑ:] n. Mus. Fa m. *invar.*

F.A. [ef'ei] abbr. *Football Association*, appellation des fédérations britanniques de football ; *F. A. Cup*, coupe d'Angleterre.

fab [fæb] adj. Pop. Sensass, formidable, du tonnerre.

Fabian ['feibiən] adj. Temporisateur (person) ; de temporisation (policy) ; *Fabian Society*, association de socialistes modérés.

fable ['feibl] n. Fable f. (in literature). ‖ Mythe m. ; légende, f. (in fiction). ‖ † Intrigue f. (of a literary work). ‖ Fig. Fable, invention (falsehood). — v. intr. Ecrire des fables. ‖ Fig. Raconter des histoires.

fabled [-d] adj. Mythique, fabuleux, légendaire. ‖ Imaginaire, inventé.

fabler [-ə*] n. Affabulateur m.

fabric ['fæbrik] n. Contexture, structure, charpente f. (texture). ‖ Tissu m. ; étoffe f. (cloth). ‖ Eccles. Fabrique f. ‖ Archit., Fig. Edifice m.

fabricant [-kənt] n. U. S. Fabricant m.

fabricate [-keit] v. tr. Construire, fabriquer (to build). ‖ Jur. Forger, fabriquer (a document). ‖ Fig. Faire (a lie) ; inventer (reasons) ; monter (a story) ; controuver (a text).

fabrication [,fæbri'keiʃən] n. Construction, fabrication f. ‖ Jur. Fabrication, contrefaçon f. ‖ Fig. Invention f. ; montage m.

fabricator ['fæbrikeitə*] n. Jur. Fabricateur, contrefacteur, faussaire m. ‖ Fig. Menteur, affabulateur m.

fabulist ['fæbjulist] n. Fabuliste m. (in literature). ‖ Fam. Affabulateur m. ; affabulatrice f.

fabulous [-ləs] adj. Fabuleux, légendaire, mythique. ‖ Fabuleux, imaginaire. (See fictitious.) ‖ Incroyable, peu sûr (incredible). ‖ Fam. Fabuleux, prodigieux, stupéfiant (astounding).

fabulously [-ləsli] adv. Fabuleusement, prodigieusement.

façade [fæ'sɑ:d] n. Archit., Fig. Façade f.

face [feis] n. Figure, face f. ; visage m. (of s.o.) ; *face to face*, nez à nez, face à face ; *in the face of parental opposition*, en dépit de l'opposition des parents ; *in the face of*, en face de ; au nez de (s.o.) ; *I said it in his face*, je le lui ai dit en face, je ne le lui ai pas envoyé dire ; *to look square in the face*, regarder dans le blanc des yeux ; *to set one's face against*, se buter au sujet de ; *to show one's face*, faire une apparition. ‖ Mine, contenance f. ; *to pull (or) wear a long face*, faire triste mine, faire un nez ; *to put a bold face on*, envisager avec hardiesse ; *to put a good face on*, faire bon visage à. ‖ Grimace f. ; *to make faces*, faire des grimaces (at, à). ‖ Endroit m. (of a card, fabric) ; cadran m. (of a clock) ; face f. (of sth.). ‖ Topographie f. (of an area) ; surface f. (of the earth). ‖ Milit. *Face to*, face à (the enemy). ‖ Archit. Façade f. ‖ Techn. Plat m. (of a tool). ‖ Fin. *Face value*, valeur nominale. ‖ Fig. Face, tournure f. (of things). ‖ Fig. Face, apparence f. ; *to take sth. at face value*, prendre qqch. argent comptant. ‖ Fig. Prestige m. ; *to lose face*, perdre la face ; *to save one's face*, sauver la face. ‖ **Face-ache**, n. Méd. Névralgie faciale f. ; Fam. Mocheté f. (ugly

person), face (f.) de carême (mournful person). ‖ **Face-cloth** (or) **-flannel**, n. Gant (m.) de toilette. ‖ **Face-lift** (or) **-lifting**, n. Lifting, lissage m. ‖ **Face-paint**, n. Fam. Peinture f., badigeon m. (make-up). ‖ **Face-saving**, adj. Qui sauve la face. — v. tr. Faire face à (s.o.) ; faire face à, regarder, être orienté vers (sth.). ‖ Tourner de face (a card). ‖ Revêtir (with, de) [a surface]. ‖ Mettre un revers à (a coat) ; mettre un parement à (a cuff, uniform). ‖ Culin. Glacer (with, de) [caramel]. ‖ Archit. Mettre un revêtement à. ‖ Techn. Aplanir (a stone). ‖ Fig. Affronter, faire front (or) face à (danger, enemy), rencontrer (difficulties) ; se présenter à, se trouver devant (s.o.). ‖ Fam. *To face the music*, faire front, tenir tête à l'orage. — v. intr. Etre orienté (or) exposé (or) tourné (towards, vers). ‖ Milit. *To face about*, faire demi-tour ; U. S. *left face!*, demi-tour à gauche. ‖ *To face up to*, faire face à.

faceless [-lis] adj. Sans visage ; anonyme.

facer [-ə*] n. Fam. Gifle f. ; coup sur le nez m. (lit. and fig.). ‖ Fam. Tuile f. ; pépin m.

facet ['fæsit] n. Facette f.

faceted [-id] adj. A facettes.

facetiae [fə'siʃii:] n. pl. Facéties f. pl.

facetious [-ʃəs] adj. Facétieux.

facetiously [-ʃəsli] adv. Facétieusement.

facetiousness [-ʃəsnis] n. Humeur facétieuse, bouffonnerie f.

facia ['feiʃiə] n. Enseigne f. (of a shop). ‖ Autom. Tableau de bord m. ‖ Archit. See fascia.

facial ['feiʃəl] adj. Facial ; du visage. — n. Fam. Traitement esthétique pour le visage m.

facies ['feiʃi,i:z] (pl. facies) n. Méd., Géol. Faciès m.

facile ['fæsail] adj. Facile, commode, aisé. (See easy.) ‖ Fig. Facile, accommodant (affable) ; influençable.

facilitate [fə'siliteit] v. tr. Faciliter (sth.) ; *to facilitate s.o. in sth.*, faciliter qqch. à qqn.

facility [-ti] n. Facilité, simplicité f. (easiness). ‖ Facilité, aisance f. (ease). ‖ Facilité, possibilité f. (for, de). ‖ Habileté, facilité, dextérité f. (skill). ‖ Facilité, aptitude f. ; talent m. ‖ Souplesse, docilité, complaisance f. (yieldingness). ‖ Comm., Fin. Pl. Facilités (for, de) ; aménagements ; *storage facilities*, dispositifs spéciaux d'entreposage, magasinages.

facing ['feisiŋ] n. Revers m. (of coat) ; parement m. (of cuff, uniform). ‖ Archit. Revêtement m. — prep. Face à, en face de ; *facing east*, exposition à l'est.

facsimile [fæk'simili] n. Fac-similé m. — v. tr. Faire un fac-similé de.

fact [fækt] n. Fait, état de fait m. ; *accomplished fact*, fait accompli, situation de fait. ‖ Fait m. ; réalité f. ; *as a matter of fact, in fact*, de fait, en fait, en réalité, à dire vrai ; *facts of life*, mystères de la vie ; *in point of fact*, par le fait, en fait ; *it's a matter of fact*, c'est un fait. ‖ Jur. Fait m.

faction ['fækʃən] n. Faction f.

factious ['fækʃəs] adj. Factieux, séditieux.

factiousness [-nis] n. Esprit (m.) de faction.

factitious [fæk'tiʃəs] adj. Factice.

factitiously [-li] adv. D'une manière factice.

factitive ['fæktitiv] adj. Gramm. Factitif.

factor [-tə*] n. Agric. Régisseur m. (in Scotland). ‖ Comm. Agent (m.) de vente ; courtier m. ‖ Jur.

Séquestre m. ‖ MATH. Facteur m.; *highest common factor*, plus grand commun diviseur. ‖ MED. Facteur m. ‖ TECHN. Facteur, coefficient m. ‖ FIG. Facteur, élément m.; *personal factor*, facteur humain.

factorage [-təridʒ] n. COMM. Courtage m. (business); commission f. (charges).

factorial [fæk'tɔːriəl] adj. MATH. Factoriel.
— n. MATH. Factorielle f.

factory ['fæktəri] n. TECHN. Fabrique, usine, manufacture f. (works). ‖ COMM. Comptoir m.; factorerie f. (foreign depot). ‖ AGRIC. *Factory farming*, élevage industriel. ‖ NAUT. *Factory ship*, navire-usine.

factotum [fæk'toutəm] n. Factotum m.

factual ['fæktjuəl] adj. Positif. (See ACTUAL.)

facula ['fækjulə] (pl. **faculae** [-iː]) n. ASTRON. Facule f.

facultative ['fækəltətiv] adj. Facultatif; à option. ‖ Incertain, conditionnel (contingent). ‖ D'une faculté. ‖ Constituant une faculté (or) possibilité (permissive). ‖ ZOOL. Occasionnel (parasite).

faculty [-ti] n. Faculté, option f. ‖ Faculté, possibilité f. (authorization, power) [of, de]. ‖ Faculté f.; don m. (talent) [for, de]. ‖ Faculté f. (of arts, law, science). ‖ U. S. Corps professoral m.; *faculty and students*, les professeurs et les étudiants. ‖ PHILOS., MED. Faculté f.; *to be in possession of all one's faculties*, jouir de toutes ses facultés. ‖ ECCLES. Dispense f.

fad [fæd] n. Marotte, manie f. (See HOBBY.) ‖ Lubie, f. (crotchet); Snobisme m.; folie f. (for a passing fashion); *latest fad*, dernier cri.

faddish [-iʃ] adj. Lunatique.

faddist [-ist] n. Lunatique; maniaque s.

faddy [-i] adj. Exigeant, difficile. ‖ Lunatique.

fade [feid] v. intr. Passer, pâlir, se faner, déteindre (colour); *it will soon fade*, c'est un déjeuner de soleil. ‖ BOT. Se faner, se flétrir (plant). ‖ THEATR., RADIO. *To fade in, out*, apparaître, disparaître progressivement; s'ouvrir, se fermer. ‖ FIG. S'évanouir, mourir, disparaître (see VANISH); *to fade away*, s'éteindre (smile); *to fade into*, se fondre dans. ‖ **Fade-in**, n. THEATR., RADIO. Fading. ‖ **Fade-out**, n. THEATR., RADIO. Fading m.; FAM. *To do a fade-out*, s'éclipser à l'anglaise.
— v. tr. Déteindre. ‖ BOT. Faner (a plant).

fadeless [-lis] adj. Qui ne se fane pas.

fading [-iŋ] n. RADIO. Fading, évanouissement m.

faecal ['fiːkəl] adj. MED. Fécal.

faeces ['fiːsiːz] n. pl. MED., CHIM. Fèces f. pl.

faery ['fɛəri] adj. Féerique.
— n. Pays (m.) des fées.

fag [fæg] n. Corvée f.; travail ingrat m. (drudgery); fatigue f. (weariness) ‖ Nègre m. (at school). ‖ FAM. Cibiche f., clope m. ‖ POP. Pédé m., fiotte f., pédale f. ‖ **Fag-end**, n. Bout m.; FAM. Mégot m.
— v. tr. FAM. Ereinter, esquinter, crever (to exhaust).
— v. intr. FAM. Se crever, s'éreinter, s'esquinter. ‖ Servir de nègre à (a schoolboy).

faggot ['fægət] n. Fagot m. (of branches, twigs). ‖ TECHN. Faisceau m. ‖ MILIT. Fascine f. ‖ POP. Pédé m.
— v. tr. Fagoter, mettre en fagots (firewood). ‖ Orner d'un point de chausson (in sewing).

Fahrenheit ['fɑːrənhait] adj. n. PHYS. Fahrenheit m.

faience [fai'ɔːns] n. Faïence f.

fail [feil] v. int. Manquer, se montrer insuffisant, faire défaut (to be missing). ‖ Manquer, avoir insuffisamment, être à court (in, de) [to lack]. ‖ Manquer, faillir (in, à) [to fall short]. ‖ Manquer, négliger, omettre (to, de) [to omit]. ‖ Manquer, ne pas s'accomplir (not to come true). ‖ Manquer, rater; échouer, ne pas réussir (in, à) [to miscarry]. ‖ Ne pas parvenir, ne pas réussir (to, à) [not to succeed]. ‖ Ne pas aboutir (of, à) [not to achieve]. ‖ Baisser, décliner, diminuer, s'affaiblir (to weaken).

‖ COMM. Faire faillite; *to fail for ten millions*, faire une faillite de 10 millions. ‖ TECHN. Tomber en panne, avoir des ratés; faire long feu.
— v. tr. Manquer à, faire défaut à (to be lacking); *his memory is failing him*, sa mémoire baisse; *to fail to answer an invitation*, se dérober à une invitation. ‖ Manquer à, laisser choir, abandonner (to leave). ‖ Echouer à (an exam); ajourner (a pupil).
— n. Faute f.; *without fail*, sans faute, assurément.

failing [-iŋ] n. Défaut, manquement m. (act). ‖ Echec, insuccès m. (failure). ‖ Défaut, point faible m.; imperfection, faiblesse f. (See FAULT.) ‖ COMM. Faillite, f. (act).
— prep. Faute de, à défaut de.

failure ['feiljə*] n. Défaut, manquement m. (fact, state). ‖ Echec, insuccès m. (unsuccess); *to be a failure*, tomber à plat, finir en queue de poisson, faire fiasco (fam.). ‖ Raté, fruit sec, pauvre type m. (person). ‖ TECHN. Panne f.; *failure of engine through shortage of petrol*, U. S. *engine failure because of lack of gasoline*, panne sèche. ‖ COMM. Faillite f.

fain [fein] adj. Tout disposé (to, à) [eager]; heureux (to, de) [glad]; prêt (to, à) [ready]. ‖ Forcé, contraint, poussé (compelled).
— adv. Bien, avec joie, volontiers.

faint [feint] adj. Faible, sans vigueur (or) force (weak). ‖ Faible, sans courage, craintif (timid). ‖ Faible; défaillant, prêt à s'évanouir (with, de) [about to collapse]. ‖ Faible, peu clair, confus, imprécis, indistinct (dim). ‖ **Faint-hearted**, adj. Pusillanime.
— n. MED. Evanouissement m. (see SWOON); pâmoison f.
— v. intr. MED. S'évanouir, se trouver mal; se pâmer (†). ‖ † Languir, faiblir.

faintly [-li] adv. Faiblement. ‖ Craintivement, timidement. ‖ Confusément, vaguement.

faintness [-nis] n. Faiblesse f.

faints [-s] n. CHIM. Alcools (m. pl.) de tête (or) de queue.

fair [fɛə*] adj. Beau m.; belle f. (person). [See BEAUTIFUL.] ‖ Clair, blanc (complexion); blond (hair). ‖ Bon, beau (road); beau clair (weather). ‖ Net, propre; *fair copy*, copie au net. ‖ Moyen, passable (average); suffisant, satisfaisant (sufficient). ‖ Aimable, plaisant; *fair words*, de belles paroles. ‖ Franc, loyal (honest); juste, impartial, sans parti pris (unprejudiced). ‖ Avantageux, prometteur; *to be in a fair way to*, être en bon chemin pour. ‖ SPORTS. *Fair defeat*, juste défaite; *fair play*, franc jeu. ‖ FAM. *Fair enough!*, bon, ça va! ‖ **Fair-haired**, adj. Blond; FAM. Favori, chéri. ‖ **Fair-weather**, adj. FIG. Des beaux jours (friend).
— n. † Beauté f. (woman).
— adv. Avec amabilité (or) courtoisie (courteously). ‖ Bien, convenablement, d'une manière satisfaisante; *to bid fair to*, avoir des chances de. ‖ Au propre, au net (after corrections). ‖ Droit, en plein (straight). ‖ Carrément, loyalement, franchement (squarely).
— v. tr. TECHN. Aplanir (timbers).
— v. intr. † S'éclairer, tourner au beau (weather).

fair n. Foire f.; *fun fair*, parc des attractions, fête foraine. ‖ Vente de charité f. (bazaar). ‖ **Fairground**, n. Champ (m.) de foire.

fairing ['fɛəriŋ] n. AVIAT. Profilage, carénage m.

fairly ['fɛəli] adv. Bien. ‖ Equitablement, honnêtement, loyalement. ‖ Modérément, passablement, assez. ‖ Clairement, distinctement. ‖ En vérité, réellement, bel et bien; *his hands fairly talk*, c'est tout juste si ses mains ne parlent pas.

fairness [-nis] n. Beauté f. ‖ Clarté, blancheur f. (of complexion); blondeur f. (of hair). ‖ Clarté, beauté f., ensoleillement m. (of weather). ‖ Netteté *f.* (of a copy). ‖ Franchise, loyauté. ‖ Justice, impartialité, droiture *f.*

fairway [-wei] n. NAUT. Chenal navigable *m.* ‖ SPORTS. Chemin normal *m.* (in golf).

fairy ['fεəri] n. Fée *f.* ‖ FAM. Tante, tapette *f.* (homosexual). ‖ **Fairy-story** (or) **-tale,** n. Conte (*m.*) de fées.
— adj. Féerique (castle); magique (ring); féerique, enchanteur (sight); de fée (tale).

fairyland [-lænd] n. Pays (*m.*) des fées.

fait accompli [fetakɔ'pliː] n. Fait accompli *m.*

faith [feiθ] n. Foi, loyauté *f.; bad faith,* mauvaise foi. ‖ Foi, fidélité *f.* ‖ Foi *f.;* honneur *m.; to plight one's faith,* engager sa foi. ‖ Foi, parole *f.; in faith,* en vérité, ma parole; *to break faith,* manquer de parole. ‖ Foi, confiance *f.* (in, en) [trust]. ‖ Foi, croyance *f.* (in, en) [belief]. ‖ Foi, force, autorité *f.; on the faith of,* sur la foi de. ‖ ECCLES. Foi *f.* ‖ **Faith-cure, faith-healing,** n. Guérison par la foi *f.* ‖ **Faith-healer,** n. Guérisseur *s.*

faithful [-ful] adj. Fidèle, constant. ‖ Fidèle, fidèlement attaché (*to, à*). ‖ Fidèle, sûr, sur qui on peut compter (reliable). ‖ Loyal, honnête (fair). ‖ Digne de foi (credible); digne de confiance (trustworthy). ‖ Fidèle, exact, juste (accurate). ‖ ECCLES. *The faithful,* les fidèles.

faithfully [-fuli] adv. Fidèlement. ‖ Loyalement.

faithfulness [-fulnis] n. Fidélité, constance *f.* ‖ Loyauté, honnêteté, probité *f.*

faithless [-lis] adj. Infidèle (*to, à*); inconstant. ‖ Déloyal (*to,* envers); traître, perfide (treacherous). ‖ Peu sûr, à qui on ne peut se fier (unreliable). ‖ Infidèle, inexact (inaccurate). ‖ ECCLES. Infidèle, incroyant.

faithlessly [-lisli] adv. Infidèlement. ‖ Avec déloyauté.

faithlessness [-lisnis] n. Infidélité *f.* (*to, à*). ‖ Déloyauté *f.* ‖ ECCLES. Incroyance *f.*

fake [feik] n. NAUT. Glène *f.*
— v. tr. NAUT. Lover (a cable).

fake n. Maquillage, trucage *m.;* falsification *f.* ‖ Objet truqué; faux *m.;* bidon *m.* (fam.).
— adj. Maquillé, truqué, falsifié (bogus). ‖ Faux, prétendu (doctor); feint (emotion).
— v. tr. Maquiller, truquer, falsifier. ‖ MUS. Improviser (a passage). ‖ FIG. Feindre.

faker [-ə*] n. FAM. Falsificateur, truqueur, camoufleur *s.*

faking [-iŋ] n. Falsification *f.*

fakir ['fɑ:kiə*], [fə'kiə*] n. Fakir *m.*

fa la, fa la [fɑ:'lɑ:] n. Tralala *m.* (refrain).

Falange ['fælændʒ] n. Phalange *f.* (in Spain).

Falangist [-ist] n. Phalangiste *s.*

falchion ['fɔːltʃən] n. Cimeterre *m.*

falcon ['fɔː(l)kən] n. ZOOL., SPORTS. Faucon *m.*

falconer [-ə*] n. Fauconnier *m.*

falconet [-it] n. ZOOL. Falconelle *f.* ‖ MILIT. Fauconneau *m.*

falconry [-ri] n. Fauconnerie *f.*

falderal [fældə'ræl] n. Brimborion *m.;* bagatelle *f.* (trifle). ‖ Bêtise, sottise *f.* (nonsense).

faldstool ['fɔːldstuːl] n. Prie-Dieu *m.* (prayer stool). ‖ Lutrin *m.* (singing-desk). ‖ ECCLES. Faldistorium *m.* (bishop's chair).

Falkland Islands ['fɔːklənd'ailəndz] n. pl. GEOGR. Iles (*f. pl.*) Falkland.

fall [fɔːl] v. intr. (54). Tomber, choir (*from,* de); *to fall again,* retomber; *to fall out of the window,* tomber par la fenêtre; *to let fall,* laisser tomber. ‖ Tomber en ruine, crouler, s'écrouler, s'effondrer (building); tomber, s'abattre (tree). ‖ Tomber, avoir du tombant (coat, dress). ‖ Descendre, s'incliner, être en pente (ground); se jeter, déboucher (*into,* dans) [river]. ‖ Baisser, tomber (flames). ‖ S'allonger (face); tomber, se poser, se fixer (*on,* sur)

[look]; baisser, tomber, s'assourdir (voice); *his glance fell,* il baissa les yeux; *the remark fell from him,* la remarque tomba de ses lèvres. ‖ Tomber (date); tomber, arriver, survenir, avoir lieu (event). ‖ Tomber, approcher (night). ‖ Tomber, se jeter, se précipiter, se ruer, fondre (*on,* sur) [to rush]. ‖ Tomber, rencontrer (to meet); *to fall upon s. o.,* tomber sur qqn. ‖ Se diviser, se classer, se ranger, entrer (*into,* dans) [classes]. ‖ Commencer, se mettre (*to, à*); *to fall into conversation with,* entrer en conversation avec; *to fall into a habit,* prendre (or) contracter une habitude; *to fall to work,* se mettre au travail. ‖ Devenir, tomber; *to fall in love,* tomber amoureux; *to fall a prey to,* devenir la proie de; *to fall under suspicion,* devenir suspect. ‖ Echoir, incomber, revenir (*to, à*); *it has fallen to me to,* il m'a échu en partage de. ‖ GRAMM. Tomber, porter (*on,* sur) [stress]. ‖ ZOOL. Naître (animals). ‖ MED. Baisser, tomber (fever); *to fall ill,* tomber malade. ‖ ASTRON. Filer (star). ‖ NAUT. Calmer (sea); baisser (tide); tomber, s'apaiser, se calmer (wind). ‖ MILIT. Tomber (soldier); tomber, capituler (*to,* aux mains de) [town]; *to fall by the sword,* périr par l'épée. ‖ THEATR. Tomber (curtain); *to let fall the curtain,* baisser le rideau. ‖ JUR. Tomber, être renversé (government). ‖ FIN. Baisser, diminuer, être en baisse (price); s'avilir (value); *to fall due,* venir à échéance. ‖ FIG. Retomber (*on,* sur) [blame, responsibility, suspicion]; tomber, déchoir, se dégrader, s'avilir (person); tomber, succomber (woman); tomber, décliner, baisser, décroître (zeal). ‖ **To fall about,** tomber de-ci de-là. ‖ **To fall away,** s'affaisser (ground); ECCLES. Apostasier; MED. S'émacier (body); FIG. Disparaître, tomber (prejudices); *to fall away from s. o., sth.,* abandonner (ou) lâcher qqn, qqch. ‖ **To fall back,** tomber à la renverse; MILIT. Se replier; FIG. Se rabattre (*on,* sur). ‖ **To fall behind,** rester en arrière; SPORTS. Se laisser distancer. ‖ **To fall down,** tomber à terre, choir; se prosterner (*before,* devant); s'écrouler (building); échouer (plan, person; *to fall down a precipice,* tomber dans un précipice. ‖ **To fall for,** donner dans, se laisser prendre (*to fall for a blonde,* s'amouracher d'une blonde; *to fall for it,* gober le morceau. ‖ **To fall in,** s'effondrer (building); se creuser (cheeks); MILIT. Former les rangs; FIN. Echoir, arriver à échéance (debt); JUR. Expirer (lease); FIG. *To fall in with,* consentir à (un arrangement); se conformer à (an opinion); accéder à (a request); rencontrer, tomber sur (s. o.); coïncider avec (sth.). ‖ **To fall off,** tomber (in general); passer, déteindre (colour); décliner, baisser (popularity, talent, zeal); baisser, ralentir (speed); abandonner, lâcher (supporters); FIN. Diminuer (profits); NAUT. Abattre sous le vent. ‖ **To fall out,** tomber; MILIT. Rompre les rangs; FIG. Advenir, arriver, se passer (things); *to fall out with,* se brouiller avec (s. o.). ‖ **To fall over oneself,** FAM. U. S. Se mettre en quatre (*to,* pour). ‖ **To fall through,** FIG. S'échouer, tomber à l'eau. ‖ **To fall to,** se mettre à, s'attaquer à.
— n. Chute *f.; to have a fall,* faire une chute. ‖ Chute *f.* (of leaves, rain, snow); chute d'eau, cascade, cataracte, *f.* (waterfall). ‖ Baisse *f.;* reflux *m.* (of tide); baisse (of waters). ‖ Eboulement (of earth); dénivellation *f.* (of ground); pente *f.* (of a road). ‖ Abattis *m.* (of trees). ‖ Tombant *m.* (of a dress). ‖ Baisse *f.* (of temperature, weight); chute *f.* (of voice). ‖ Chute, tombée *f.* (of day); déclin *m.* (of year); U. S. automne *m.* ‖ ECCLES. Chute *f.* (of man). ‖ MILIT. Chute, reddition *f.* (of a town). ‖ JUR. Chute *f.;* renversement *m.* (of a government). ‖ THEATR. Baisser *m.;* chute *f.* (of the curtain). ‖ ZOOL. Mise bas *f.* (dropping of young); portée *f.* (litter). ‖ FIN. Dépréciation *f.* (of currency); baisse (in prices). ‖ SPORTS. Point (*m.*) de chute (of the ball); chute *f.* (of a player). ‖

Fig. Chute, défaite, déchéance *f.; to ride for a fall,* courir à sa perte; *to try a fall with,* s'essayer à la lutte avec. ‖ U. S. Fam. *Fall guy,* bouc émissaire. ‖ **Fall-in,** n. Milit. Rassemblement *m.* ‖ **Fall-out,** n. Phys. Poussière (or) retombée radioactive *f.*

fallacious [fə'leiʃəs] adj. Fallacieux.

fallacy ['fæləsi] n. Caractère fallacieux *m.; nature trompeuse f.* (delusive quality). ‖ Opinion erronée; idée fallacieuse *f.* (error). ‖ Raisonnement faux; argument fallacieux *m.* ‖ Sophisme *m.*

fal-lal [fæ'læl] n. Colifichet *m.* ‖ Pl. Falbalas.

fallen ['fɔ:ln] adj. Tombé. ‖ Milit. Pris. ‖ Eccles. Déchu (angel). ‖ Fig. Déchu, tombé, perdu.

fallibility [fæli'biliti] n. Faillibilité *f.*

fallible ['fælibl] adj. Faillible.

falling ['fɔ:liŋ] adj. Med. *Falling sickness,* épilepsie, haut mal. ‖ Astron. *Falling star,* météore, étoile filante. ‖ Aviat. *Falling-leaf roll,* descente en feuille morte.
— n. Chute *f.* ‖ **Falling away,** n. Fin. Glissement (*m.*) en bourse; Med. Amaigrissement *m.;* Eccles. Apostasie *f.;* Geol. Affaissement *m.* (of ground); Fig. Défection *f.,* lâchage *m.* (of supporters). **Falling back,** n. Milit. Repli *m.;* retraite *f.* ‖ **Falling in,** n. Ecroulement *m.* (of a building); Milit. Rassemblement *m.;* Jur. Expiration *f.;* Fin. Echéance *f.;* Fig. Acceptation *f.* (*with,* de) [sth.]; accord *m.* (*with,* avec) [s. o.]. ‖ **Falling off,** n. Comm. Ralentissement *m.;* Fin. Fléchissement *m.;* Fig. Défection *f.* ‖ **Falling out,** n. Chute *f.* (of hair); Fig. Brouille *f.*

fallow ['fælou] adj. Agric. En jachère (or) friche. ‖ Fig. Inculte (mind).
— n. Agric. Jachère *f.;* terrain délaissé *m.*
— v. tr. Agric. Laisser en jachère.

fallow adj. Fauve (colour). ‖ Zool. *Fallow deer,* daim.

false [fɔ:ls] adj. Faux, erroné (erroneous); faux, inexact (inaccurate). ‖ Faux (mistaken); *false step,* faux pas. ‖ Faux, menteur (lying); faux, trompeur (misleading); faux, contraire à la vérité (untrue). ‖ Faux, fourbe (double-dealing); faux, traître, déloyal (treacherous) [*to,* envers]. ‖ Faux, peu net (uncertain). ‖ Faux, factice; contrefait, imité, en imitation (counterfeit); *false hair,* postiche. ‖ Faux, non authentique (not genuine). ‖ Faux, artificiel, dénaturé (artificial). ‖ Jur. Illegal (imprisonment). ‖ Mus. Faux (note). ‖ Techn. Double (bottom); faux (key). ‖ Sports. Faux (start). ‖ Theatr. *False face,* masque. ‖ **False alarm,** n. Fausse alerte *f.* ‖ **False-hearted,** adj. Faux; traître. ‖ **False pretences,** n. pl. Jur. *Under false pretences,* par des moyens frauduleux.
— adv. Avec fausseté, faussement; *to play s. o. false,* tromper (or) trahir qqn, agir faussement à l'égard de qqn.

falsehood [-hud] n. Fausseté *f.* (falseness); conception fausse *f.* (false belief, idea); mensonge *m.* (lie).

falsely [-li] adv. Faussement.

falseness [-nis] n. Fausseté, inexactitude *f.* (falsity). ‖ Fausseté, fourberie *f.* (duplicity).

falsetto [fɔl'setou] n. Mus. Fausset *m.*
— adv. Mus. D'une voix de fausset.
— adj. Mus. De fausset.

falsies ['fɔlsiz] n. Fam. Faux seins *m.* pl.

falsification [ˌfɔlsifi'keiʃən] n. Falsification *f.*

falsify ['fɔ:lsifai] v. tr. (2). Falsifier (to fake). ‖ Déformer, dénaturer (to distort). ‖ Rendre faux; *to falsify a hope,* anéantir un espoir, tromper une espérance. ‖ Réfuter, prouver la fausseté de (to confute); *the prophecy is falsified by the event,* la réalisation dément la prophétie.

falsity [-ti] n. Fausseté, inexactitude *f.* (of, de).

falstaffian [fɔls'tɑ:fiən] adj. Obèse.

falter ['fɔltə*] v. intr. Vaciller, chanceler (to totter). ‖ Balbutier, bégayer, bredouiller (to stam-

mer); *to falter through one's lesson,* ânonner sa leçon. ‖ Fig. Flotter, balancer, chanceler (to waver); broncher (fam.); *his resolution faltered,* sa résolution s'ébranla.
— v. tr. Bredouiller, balbutier.

falteringly [-riŋli] adv. En balbutiant (or) bredouillant. ‖ En vacillant (or) chancelant.

fame [feim] n. Réputation *f.* (repute). ‖ Renom *m.;* célébrité, renommée *f.* (glory). ‖ Rumeur publique, voix populaire *f.;* bruit (*m.*) qui court; on-dit *m.* (rumour).

famed [-d] adj. Fameux, réputé (*for,* pour); célèbre (*for,* par); *ill-famed,* malfamé.

familiar [fə'miljə*] adj. † Domestique, familier. ‖ Familier, favori (pet). ‖ Familier, amical (friendly); familier, intime (intimate). ‖ Familier, libre (with, avec) [bold]. ‖ Familier, commun, courant, ordinaire (common). ‖ Familier (*to,* à); bien connu (*to,* de) [well known]; *among familiar faces,* en pays de connaissance.
— n. Familier, ami, intime *m.* ‖ Esprit familier *m.* (spirit). ‖ Eccles. Familier *m.*

familiarity [fəˌmili'æriti] n. Familiarité *f.* (with, avec). ‖ Pl. Familiarités *f. pl.* (liberties).

familiarize [fə'miljəraiz] v. tr. Familiariser (*with,* avec).

familiarly [-əli] adv. Familièrement.

family ['fæmili] n. Famille *f.; as a family party,* en famille; *family circle, name,* cercle, nom de famille; *family man,* père de famille, homme marié; homme d'intérieur. ‖ Jur. *Family allowance,* allocation familiale. ‖ Zool., Bot., Gramm. Famille *f.* ‖ Blas. *Family tree,* arbre généalogique. ‖ Fam. *In the family way,* dans une position intéressante. ‖ **Family planning,** n. Planning familial *m.,* contrôle (*m.*) des naissances.

famine ['fæmin] n. Famine *f.* (starvation). ‖ Disette, pénurie *f.* (scarcity).

famish [-iʃ] v. tr. Affamer, faire mourir de faim. (See **starve.**)
— v. intr. Etre réduit à la famine. ‖ Fam. Mourir de faim.

famous ['feiməs] adj. Fameux.

famously [-li] adv. Fameusement.

fan [fæn] n. Eventail *m.* ‖ Techn. Ventilateur rotatif *m.* ‖ Agric. Van *m.* ‖ **Fan-belt,** n. Autom. Courroie (*f.*) de ventilateur. ‖ **Fan-blade,** n. Techn. Aile (*f.*) de ventilateur. ‖ **Fan-jet,** n. Aviat. Turbo-réacteur à double flux *m.* ‖ **Fan-light,** n. Archit. Eventail *m.;* imposte *f.* ‖ **Fan-maker,** n. Eventailliste *m.* ‖ **Fan-shaped,** adj. En éventail. ‖ **Fan-tail,** n. Zool. Pigeon-paon *m.;* Techn. Queue-d'aronde *f.*
— v. tr. (1). Eventer (s.o.); *to fan oneself with,* s'éventer avec. ‖ Souffler sur, attiser (fire). ‖ Agiter avec un éventail (air); chasser avec un éventail (flies). ‖ Disposer en éventail. ‖ Agric. Vanner (grain). ‖ U. S. Fouiller. ‖ Fig. Exciter. ‖ Fam. *To fan the air,* battre l'air.
— v. intr. Se déployer en éventail.

fan n. Fam. Fanatique, passionné, fervent *s.* (of, de); emballé, fana, mordu (fam.). ‖ Admirateur passionné, adorateur *m.;* admiratrice *f.* (devotee). ‖ **Fan-club,** n. Club (*m.*) de fans. ‖ **Fan-mail,** n. Courrier (*m.*) des admirateurs.

fanatic [fə'nætik] adj., n. Fanatique *s.*

fanatical [-əl] adj. Fanatique.

fanatically [-əli] adv. Fanatiquement.

fanaticism [fə'nætisizm] n. Fanatisme *m.*

fanaticize [-saiz] v. tr. Fanatiser; rendre fanatique de.
— v. intr. Devenir fanatique de.

fancier ['fænsiə*] n. Amateur *s.* ‖ Comm. Marchand spécialiste *s.*

fanciful [-ful] adj. Imaginatif, rêveur, d'imagination dévergondée. ‖ Fantaisiste, de fantaisie (fantastic). ‖ Capricieux, lunatique (whimsical). ‖ Imaginaire, chimérique (unreal). ‖ Fantastique, étrange (odd).

fancifully [-fuli] adv. Avec fantaisie (or) caprice. ‖ D'une manière chimérique (or) fantastique.

fancy ['fænsi] n. Imagination *f.* (in general). ‖ Fantaisie, nature fantaisiste *f.* ‖ Fantaisie, lubie *f.;* désir, caprice *m.* (whim); passade, toquade *f.* (fam.). ‖ Fantaisie, inclination; toquade *f.* (fam.); goût *m.* (liking); *to take a fancy to,* se sentir attiré par; s'amouracher de (fam.) [s.o.]; sc mcttrc à aimer, se sentir du goût pour (sth.). ‖ Imagination, idée, chimère *f.* (idea). ‖ Fantaisie amoureuse *f.* ‖ SPORTS. *The fancy,* les amateurs de boxe. ‖ COMM. Fantaisie *f.* ‖ **Fancy-free,** adj. Sans amour, libre. — adj. Fantaisiste, de fantaisie (fanciful). ‖ D'imagination, d'invention. ‖ D'agrément, de divertissement. ‖ Costumé; *fancy dress,* déguisement, domino, travesti. ‖ COMM. De fantaisie; *fancy bread,* pain de fantaisie; *fancy goods,* nouveautés, articles de Paris; *fancy work,* ouvrages de dames; *fancy waistcoat,* gilet fantaisie. ‖ COMM. De luxe; *fancy shop,* magasin de luxe; *graded fancy,* marqué de qualité supérieure. ‖ ZOOL. De luxe (animals). ‖ SPORTS. Difficile. ‖ FIN. Extravagant, exorbitant, excessif, fantaisiste (price). ‖ FAM. *Fancy man,* amant de cœur, gigolo (fam.); *fancy woman,* maîtresse.
— v. tr. (2). Imaginer, s'imaginer (to imagine). ‖ S'imaginer, supposer, se figurer (to suppose); *fancy meeting you there!,* je ne m'attendais pas à vous trouver là. ‖ Etre attiré par, avoir du goût pour; *a thing he fancies,* une chose qui lui fait envie. ‖ Trouver plaisant; aimer, se prendre de fantaisie pour (to be fond of); *to fancy oneself,* être content de soi, se prendre pour quelqu'un. ‖ Elever, faire l'élevage de (to breed).

fandango [fæn'dæŋgou] n. Fandango *m.*

fanfare ['fænfɛə*] n. MUS. Fanfare *f.*

fanfaronade [fænfærə'nɑːd] n. Fanfaronnade *f.*

fang [fæŋ] n. ZOOL. Croc *m.* (of dogs); crochet à venin *m.* (of snakes). ‖ MED. Racine *f.* (of teeth). ‖ TECHN. Soie *f.* (of file, knife).

fanner ['fænə*] n. AGRIC. Van *m.*

fanny ['fæni] n. ARG. Con *m.* (female genitals). ‖ U. S. POP. Cùl *m.,* miches *f. pl.* (bottom).

fanon ['fænən] n. ECCLES. Manipule *m.*

fantasia [fæn'teiziə] n. MUS. Fantaisie *f.* (composition); pot-pourri *m.* (medley).

fantasize ['fæntə,saiz] v. intr. Fantasmer.
— v. tr. S'imaginer.

fantast ['fæntæst] n. Rêveur, songe-creux *m.*

fantastic [fæn'tæstik] adj. Imaginaire, irréel, chimérique (unreal). ‖ Excentrique, extravagant, fantasque, fantaisiste. ‖ Fantastique, bizarre, grotesque, étrange (quaint).

fantastically [-əli] adv. D'une manière chimérique, par pure imagination. ‖ Par fantaisie, de façon excentrique. ‖ Fantastiquement, bizarrement.

fantasy ['fæntəsi] n. Imagination débridée *f.* ‖ Illusion *f.;* fantasme *m.* ‖ Caprice *m.;* lubie, fantaisie *f.* (whim). ‖ Fioriture, ornementation *f.* ‖ MUS. Fantaisie *f.*

F. A. O. [efei'ou] abbr. *Food and Agriculture Organization,* organisation des Nations unies pour l'alimentation et l'agriculture, F. A. O.

far [fɑ:*] adv. Loin (in space, time); *as far as,* aussi loin que; autant que; *as far as I can,* dans la mesure de mes possibilités; *as far as the eye can see,* à perte de vue; *as far back as,* d'aussi loin que, dès (in time); *by far,* de loin, de beaucoup; *far and near,* partout, en tous lieux; *far and wide,* partout, de tous côtés (everywhere); largement (widely); *far away,* au loin; *far be it from me to,* loin de moi l'idéc dc; *far from,* loin dc; *far from it,* loin de là, tant s'en faut; *far into,* très avant dans, profondément dans; *far off,* au loin, dans le lointain; *how far is it from X to Y?,* combien

y a-t-il de X à Y?; *how far have you got with?,* où en êtes-vous de?; *in so far as,* dans la mesure où, pour autant que; *so far,* jusqu'ici (or) là; *so far as,* autant que, dans la mesure où; *so far so good,* jusque-là c'est bon; *thus far,* jusqu'ici; *to carry far,* mener loin; *to go far,* aller loin (lit. and fig.); *to go far to,* contribuer à; *to go so far as to,* aller jusqu'à; *to go too far,* aller trop loin, dépasser les bornes; ‖ Beaucoup; *far and away,* de beaucoup, grandement; *far better,* beaucoup mieux. ‖ **Far-away,** adj. Rêveur, lointain, perdu (look); éloigné, lointain (place, time); éteint (voice). ‖ **Far-between,** adj. Espacé, rare (houses, vjsits). ‖ **Far-famed,** adj. Très célèbre. ‖ **Far-fetched,** adj. FIG. Forcé; recherché; tiré par les cheveux (fam.). ‖ **Far-flung,** adj. Dispersé, éloigné. ‖ **Far-gone,** adj. FIG. Avancé, bien parti. ‖ **Far-off,** adj. Lointain, éloigné. ‖ **Far-out,** adj. FAM. Extra, super. ‖ **Far-reaching,** adj. A longue portée. ‖ **Far-seeing,** adj. Prévoyant, qui voit loin. ‖ **Far-sighted,** adj. MED. Presbyte, hypermétrope; FIG. Prévoyant, qui voit loin. ‖ **Far-sightedness,** n. MED. Presbytie *f.;* FIG. Prévoyance *f.*
— adj. Lointain, éloigné; *in the far future,* dans un lointain avenir. ‖ Long (distance, journey). ‖ Autre, plus éloigné; *the far side of,* l'autre côté de.

farad ['færəd] n. ELECTR. Farad *m.*

faradaic [-eiik] adj. ELECTR. Faradique.

faraday ['færədei] n. ELECTR. Faraday *m.; Faraday effect,* phénomène (or) effet de Faraday.

farandole [færæn'dɔl] n. MUS. Farandole *f.*

farce [fɑ:s] n. THEATR., CULIN. Farce *f.* ‖ FIG. Comédie grossière *f.;* grotesque *m.*
— v. tr. CULIN. Farcir (with, de). ‖ FIG. Farcir, truffer.

farcical [-ikəl] adj. Bouffon, risible; rigolo, marrant (fam.). ‖ Grotesque, ridicule.

farcy [-i] n. MED. Farcin *m.*

fare [fɛə*] n. Prix (*m.*) de la place (in a bus, train); course *f.;* prix (*m.*) de la course (in a taxi) [charge]; *fares please!,* tout le monde est servi? (in a bus). ‖ Voyageur *s.* (in a bus, train); client *s.* (in a taxi) [passenger]. ‖ CULIN. Nourriture, chère *f.;* ordinaire *m.*
— v. intr. Voyager (to travel). ‖ Advenir, arriver, résulter (with, de) [to happen]. ‖ Aller, être, se trouver (to get on); *he is faring well in his business,* ses affaires vont bien, il réussit dans ses affaires; *to fare alike,* être dans le même état. ‖ CULIN. Se nourrir, manger; *to fare badly,* faire maigre chère, avoir une piètre table.

farewell [-'wel] n. Adieu *m.; to bid s.o. farewell,* dire adieu (or) faire ses adieux à qqn.
— adj. D'adieu (gesture, speech).
— interj. Adieu!

farina [fə'rainə] n. CULIN. Farine *f.* (of corn, nuts); fécule (of potatoes). ‖ CHIM. Amidon *m.*

farinaceous [færi'neiʃəs] adj. CULIN. Farineux.

farinose ['færinous] adj. BOT. Farinacé.

farm [fɑ:m] n. AGRIC. Ferme (house); ferme, métairie, exploitation agricole *f.* (land). ‖ Entreprise (*f.*) d'élevage (for raising fish). ‖ FIN. Fermage *m.* ‖ **Farm-hand,** n. AGRIC. Valet de ferme. ‖ **Farm-house,** n. AGRIC. Ferme, maison de ferme, *f.* ‖ **Farm-labourer,** n. AGRIC. Ouvrier agricole *m.* ‖ **Farm-stead,** n. AGRIC. Ferme *f.;* domaine *m.* ‖ **Farm-yard,** n. AGRIC. Cour de ferme *f.*
— v. tr. AGRIC. Cultiver, exploiter (to cultivate); affermer, louer (to rent). ‖ FIN. Affermer. ‖ Prendre en nourrice (children); prendre en charge (paupers). ‖ **To farm out,** affermer (land); donner en exploitation à l'extérieur (work).
— v. intr. AGRIC. Etre fermier, cultiver la terre.

farmer [-ə*] n. AGRIC. Fermier, cultivateur, exploitant agricole *m.; farmer's wife,* fermière. ‖ Eleveur *s.* ‖ FIN. Fermier; *farmer general,* fermier général.

farmerette [-əret] n. U. S. FAM. Fille de ferme *f.*

farming [-ing] n. AGRIC. Culture *f.* (of lands);
mixed farming, polyculture. ‖ AGRIC., FIN. Affermage *m.* ‖ Elevage *m.; fur farming,* élevage des animaux à fourrure. ‖ Fait (*m.*) de prendre en nourrice (babies).

farrago [fə'reigou] n. Fouillis, méli-mélo; salmigondis *m.* (See JUMBLE.)

farrier ['færiə*] n. Maréchal-ferrant *m.* ‖ † Vétérinaire *m.*

farriery [-ri] n. Maréchalerie *f.* ‖ Art vétérinaire *m.*

farrow ['færou] n. ZOOL. Portée (*f.*) de petits cochons.
— v. intr. ZOOL. Cochonner.
— v. tr. ZOOL. Mettre bas (pigs).

fart [fɑːt] n. POP. Pet *m.*
— v. intr. POP. Péter.

farther ['fɑːðə*] adj. compar. Plus éloigné (in space or time); *to get farther and farther away from,* s'éloigner de plus en plus de. ‖ Plus ample, additionnel, complémentaire. (See FURTHER.) ‖ GEOGR. *Farther India,* Indochine.
— adv. Plus loin (*than,* que) [in space or time]. ‖ Davantage (to a greater degree). ‖ De plus (moreover).

farthermost [-moust] adj. Le plus distant.

farthest ['fɑːðist] adj. Le plus éloigné.
— adv. Le plus loin.

farthing ['fɑːðiŋ] n. FIN. Farthing *m.* ‖ FAM. Liard *m.; it's not worth a brass farthing,* ça ne vaut pas tripette (fam.).

farthingale ['fɑːðiŋgeil] n. Vertugadin *m.*

fasces ['fæsiːz] n. pl. Faisceaux *m. pl.* (of lictors).

fascia ['fæʃiə] n. Bandeau *m.* (fillet). ‖ MED. Fascia *m.* (in anatomy); bandage, pansement *m.* (in surgery). ‖ ARCHIT. Cordon *m.*

fasciate [-ʃieit] adj. BOT. Fascié. ‖ ZOOL. Rayé.

fascicle ['fæsikl] n. Petit faisceau *m.* ‖ Fascicule *m.* (booklet). ‖ BOT. Bouquet *m.* (of flowers, leaves).

fasciculus [-juləs] n. MED. Faisceau *m.* (of nerve fibres).

fascinate ['fæsineit] v. tr. Fasciner (by look or terror). ‖ FIG. Charmer, ensorceler, éblouir.

fascinating [-iŋ] adj. Fascinant; fascinateur *m.;* fascinatrice *f.* ‖ FIG. Enchanteur, ensorcelant, attirant, captivant.

fascination [fæsi'neiʃən] n. Fascination *f.* ‖ FIG. Enchantement, ensorcellement *m.;* attirance *f.*

fascine [fæ'siːn] n. MILIT. Fascine *f.; fascine work,* fascinage.

Fascism ['fæʃizm] n. Fascisme *m.*

Fascist [-ist] n. Fasciste *s.*

fashion ['fæʃən] n. Forme *f.* (shape). ‖ Façon, coupe *f.* (of a dress); mode *f.* (in dress); *in fashion,* à la mode; *out of fashion,* démodé. ‖ Bon ton *m.;* bonnes manières (or) façons *f. pl.* (in conduct, speech); *man of fashion,* homme distingué; *woman of fashion,* élégante. ‖ Habitude, coutume, manière (*f.*) d'être (way of acting). ‖ Façon, manière *f.; after the fashion of,* à la manière (or) façon de. ‖ Sorte *f.; after* (or) *in a fashion,* en quelque sorte (in a manner); n'importe comment, plutôt mal que bien (somehow); jusqu'à un certain point (to some extent). ‖ **Fashion-plate**, n. Gravure de mode *f.* (person, picture). ‖ **Fashion-show**, n. Présentation de collection *f.* ‖ **Fashion-writer**, n. Chroniqueur (*m.*) de mode.
— v. tr. Former (to shape). ‖ Façonner, mouler (to mould). ‖ Accommoder (*to,* à) [to fit].

fashionable [-əbl] adj. A la mode, chic, élégant; *furs are fashionable,* la fourrure se porte beaucoup.
— n. Elégant, dandy *m.*

fashionably [-əbli] adv. A la mode, élégamment.

fashioned [-d] adj. Selon une mode.

fast [fɑːst] n. Jeûne *m.; to break one's fast,* rompre le jeûne (after fasting); déjeuner (in the

morning). ‖ **Fast-day**, n. ECCLES. Jour de jeûne *m.*
— v. intr. Jeûner. ‖ ECCLES. Faire abstinence (or) maigre (to abstain from meat); jeûner (to refrain from eating).

fast adj. Ferme, solide, stable (firm). ‖ Solidement, attaché (fastened). ‖ Résistant; *fast colour,* couleur solide (or) indélébile. ‖ Rapide, prompt; *fast typist,* dactylo rapide. ‖ Permettant la vitesse; *fast highway,* autoroute, autodrome. ‖ En avance; *fast clock,* pendule qui avance. ‖ FIG. Fidèle, loyal, dévoué (faithful); sûr, de confiance (trustworthy). ‖ FIG. Dévergondé, menant une vie de dissipation (dissipated); libre, émancipé (uninhibited); *a fast one,* une roublardise.
— adv. Fermement, solidement, d'une manière stable (firmly). ‖ Fixement, solidement, fortement (fixedly). ‖ Profondément, bien, complètement (thoroughly). ‖ Rapidement, vivement, vite, en vitesse (quickly). ‖ † Près (near). ‖ FIG. D'une manière dévergondée, à grandes guides. ‖ LOC. *To play fast and loose,* jouer double jeu.

fasten ['fɑːsn] v. tr. Attacher, fixer (to fix). ‖ Lier (to bind); agrafer (to buckle); boutonner (to button); fermer (to lock). ‖ Attribuer, imposer (*on,* à) [to attribute]; imputer (*on,* à); rejeter (*on,* sur) [to impute]. ‖ FIG. Fixer, arrêter, attacher (*on,* sur) [one's attention, gaze].
— v. intr. S'attacher, se fixer; se lier; s'agrafer, se boutonner; se fermer. ‖ Se cramponner, s'accrocher (*on,* à). ‖ FIG. Se concentrer (*on,* sur).

fastener [-ə*] n. Agrafe *f.* (hook); *paper fastener,* trombone.

fastening [-iŋ] n. Attache *f.* (act, way). ‖ Attache *f.* (in general); verrou *m.* (bolt); crochet *m.* (clasp); agrafe *f.* (hook).

fastidious [fəs'tidiəs] adj. Difficile, délicat; chipoteur. (See DAINTY.)

fastidiousness [-nis] n. Excès (*m.*) de délicatesse; chipotage *m.* (about one's food). ‖ Fait (*m.*) d'être difficile à satisfaire.

fastigiate [fæ'stidʒeit] adj. BOT. Fastigié.

fastness ['fɑːstnis] n. Fermeté, solidité, stabilité *f.* (firmness). ‖ Rapidité, promptitude *f.* (quickness). ‖ Forteresse *f.* (stronghold). ‖ FIG. Dissipation, licence *f.* (laxity); liberté excessive *f.* (free manners).

fat [fæt] adj. Gras (greasy). ‖ Gros (fleshy); gras (too plump). ‖ Profitable, lucratif (paying). ‖ Gras, riche, fertile (productive). ‖ Bien rempli; *a fat book,* un livre épais; *a fat purse,* une bourse bien pleine. ‖ Stupide, lourd (dull). ‖ FAM. *A fat lot I care!,* je m'en fiche pas mal!; *he's a fat chance,* la chance lui glisse entre les doigts, il ne tient pas le bout du gras (pop.).
— n. Graisse *f.* (fleshiness). ‖ Pl. Corps gras *m.* ‖ CULIN. Graisse *f.* (cooking fat); gras *m.* (of meat); pl. matières grasses. ‖ CHIM. Glycérides *m. pl.* ‖ FAM. *The fat is in the fire,* le sort en est jeté, l'affaire est faite; *to chew the fat,* tailler une bavette.
— v. tr., intr. (1). Engraisser.

fatal ['feitl] adj. Fatal, fatidique, inévitable (bound to happen). ‖ Fatal, funeste, désastreux (*to,* à) [ruinous]. ‖ Déplorable, pernicieux (*to,* pour) [baneful]. ‖ Fatal, mortel (mortal). ‖ Fatal, du destin; *Fatal Sisters,* Parques.

fatalism [-təlizm] n. Fatalisme *m.*

fatalist [-təlist] n. Fataliste *s.*

fatalistic [feitə'listik] adj. Fataliste.

fatality [fə'tæliti] n. Fatalité *f.* (destiny). ‖ Calamité *f.;* désastre *m.* (disaster). ‖ Effet fatal (or) mortel *m.* (deadliness). ‖ Mort accidentelle *f.* (death).

fatally ['feitəli] adv. Fatalement, inévitablement. ‖ Mortellement.

fate [feit] n. Destin, sort *m.* (fatality). ‖ Destinée *f.;* sort, lot *m.* (lot). ‖ Mort, fin *f.* (death). ‖ Pl. Parques *f. pl.*

fated [-id] adj. Décrété par le destin. ‖ Voué, destiné (*to*, à). ‖ Voué à la mort (or) à l'anéantissement, condamné (doomed).

fateful [-ful] adj. † Prophétique, divinatoire. ‖ ‖ Important, de grande portée, décisif (significant). ‖ Fatal, voulu par le destin. ‖ Fatal, mortel, de mauvais augure (ominous).

father [fɑːðə*] n. Père *m.* (parent); *from father to son*, de père en fils. ‖ Père *m.* (protector); *to be a father to*, agir comme un père envers. ‖ Père, inventeur, créateur, fondateur *m.* (founder). ‖ Doyen *m.* (Senior). ‖ † Père conscrit *m.* (senator). ‖ Pl. Pères, ancêtres, aïeux *m. pl.* (forefathers). ‖ Eccles. *Father confessor*, père spirituel; *Father X*, le père X, le révérend père X (monk); *l'abbé X*, Monsieur l'abbé X (priest); *God the Father*, Dieu le Père; *the Holy Father*, le Saint-Père; *the Fathers of the Church*, les Pères de l'Eglise. ‖ Theatr. *Heavy father*, père noble. ‖ Fam. *Father Christmas*, le Père Noël. ‖ **Father-in-law**, n. Beau-père *m.*
— v. tr. Etre le père de, engendrer. ‖ Agir en père à l'égard de. ‖ Etre l'auteur de, créer, inventer, enfanter, donner naissance à. ‖ Assumer la paternité de; prendre la responsabilité de.

fatherhood [-hud] n. Paternité *f.*

fatherland [-lænd] n. Pays natal *m.* (native land); patrie *f.* (mother-country).

fatherless [-lis] adj. Orphelin de père, sans père.

fatherliness [-linis] n. Attitude paternelle *f.*

fatherly [-li] adj. Paternel.
— adv. Paternellement.

fathom [ˈfæðəm] n. † Toise *f.* (measure). ‖ Naut. Brasse *f.*
— v. tr. Naut. Sonder. ‖ † Englober, embrasser. ‖ Fig. Aller au fond de, pénétrer.

fathomless [-lis] adj. Insondable.

fatidical [fəˈtidikəl] adj. Fatidique (number); prophétique (utterance).

fatigue [fəˈtiːɡ] n. Fatigue *f.; dropping with fatigue*, tombant de fatigue. ‖ Travail harassant *m.* (toil). ‖ Milit. Corvée *f.; fatigue dress* (or) U. S. *clothes*, tenue de corvée; *fatigue duty*, corvée. ‖ Techn. Fatigue *f.* (in metal, wood).
— v. tr. Fatiguer. ‖ Techn. Fatiguer, user.

fatling [ˈfætliŋ] n. Agric. Jeune bête (*f.*) à l'engrais.

fatness [-nis] n. Embonpoint *m.; grosseur f.; rotondité f.* (fam.). ‖ Graisse *f.* ‖ Fig. Fertilité *f.*

fatten [-n] v. tr. Engraisser. ‖ Fig. Grossir (one's purse).
— v. intr. Engraisser.

fattish [-iʃ] adj. Grassouillet.

fatty [-i] adj. Graisseux.
— n. Fam. Bouboule, bon gros *s.*

fatuity [fəˈtjuiti] n. Sottise *f.*

fatuous [ˈfætjuəs] adj. Sot. (See SILLY.)

faucal [ˈfɔːkəl] adj. Med. Guttural.

fauces [ˈfɔːsiːz] n. pl. Med. Gorge *f.; gosier m.*

faucet [ˈfɔːsət] n. Techn. Robinet à fausset *m.*

faugh [fɔː] interj. Pouh! pouah! (disgust); fi! (scorn).

fault [fɔːlt] n. † Manque, défaut *m.;* faute *f.* (lack). ‖ Défaut *m.;* imperfection *f.* (failing). ‖ Faute, erreur *f.* (mistake). ‖ Faute *f.;* méfait *m.* (misdeed). ‖ Faute *f.* (blame); *to a fault*, excessivement, avec abus; *to find fault*, critiquer; *to find fault with*, trouver à redire à; critiquer. ‖ Geol. Faille *f.* ‖ Comm. *With all faults*, tel quel. ‖ Sports. Défaut *m.* (in hunting); faute *f.* (in tennis). ‖ **Fault-finder**, n. Critiqueur, criticailleur *s.* ‖ **Fault-finding**, adj. Critique, hypercritique.
— v. tr. Geol. Provoquer une faille dans.
— v. intr. Geol. Présenter une faille.

faultily [-ili] adv. Fautivement.

faultiness [-inis] n. Imperfection *f.*

faultless [-lis] adj. Sans défaut, parfait.

faultlessly [-lisli] adv. Sans défaut, parfaitement.

faulty [-i] adj. Imparfait, défectueux. ‖ † En faute.

faun [fɔːn] n. Faune *m.;* faunesse *f.* (deity).

fauna [ˈfɔːnə] n. Zool. Faune *f.*

faunist [-ist] n. Zool. Zoologiste *m.*

faute de mieux [ˈfoʊtdəˈmjəː] adv. Faute de mieux.

faux pas [foʊˈpɑː] n. Faux pas *m.*, impair *m.*, bévue *f.*

favo(u)r [ˈfeivə*] n. Faveur *f.* (liking); *in high favour with*, en grande faveur (or) bien en cour auprès de; *to find favour*, rencontrer les bonnes grâces de, trouver grâce devant. ‖ Faveur, permission, autorisation *f.* (leave). ‖ Faveur *f.* (indulgence); favoritisme *m.* (partiality); *with favour*, favorablement. ‖ Faveur, aide *f.* (help); *under favour of night*, à la faveur (or) sous le couvert de la nuit. ‖ Faveur *f.;* service *m.* (kindness); *for favour of publication in your columns*, avec prière d'insérer. ‖ Faveur, considération *f.;* bénéfice, intérêt *m.* (behalf); *to decide in s.o.'s favour*, donner gain de cause à. ‖ Faveur *f.;* ruban *m.* (ribbon). ‖ Souvenir *m.* (gift). ‖ Pl. Faveurs *f. pl.* (of a woman). ‖ Comm. *Your favour*, votre honorée. ‖ † Charme, attrait *m.* (charm); traits *m. pl.;* visage *m.* (features).
— v. tr. Considérer avec faveur, apprécier (to like). ‖ Favoriser, considérer avec favoritisme, accorder des faveurs à (to be partial to). ‖ Favoriser, aider (to help); soutenir (to support). ‖ Faire une amabilité (or) une grâce (or) un plaisir à, accorder une faveur à; *to favour s.o. with*, gratifier qqn de; faire à qqn le plaisir de. ‖ Ressembler à (to look like). ‖ Sports. Ménager.

favourable [-rəbl] adj. Favorable, propice (*to*, à). ‖ Favorable, bien disposé (*to*, envers).

favourableness [-rəblnis] n. Dispositions favorables *f. pl.*

favourably [-rəbli] adv. Favorablement.

favoured [ˈfeivəd] adj. Favorisé; privilégié. ‖ De visage, d'aspect.

favourite [ˈfeivərit] adj. Favori, préféré. (See PREFERRED.)
— n. Favori *m.;* favorite *f.;* préféré *s.*

favouritism [-izm] n. Favoritisme *m.;* cote (*f.*) d'amour (fam.).

fawn [fɔːn] n. Zool. Fauve *m.* (See FALLOW.) ‖ Zool. Faon *m.*
— adj. Fauve.
— v. intr. Zool. Faonner.

fawn v. intr. Ramper, se coucher, flatter (dog). ‖ Fig. Faire le chien couchant, ramper (see CRINGE); courber l'échine; s'aplatir (fam.) [*on*, devant].

fawning [-iŋ] n. Flatterie, caresse *f.* ‖ Fig. Servilité, bassesse; flagornerie *f.*
— adj. Servile; rampant. ‖ Flagorneur, patelin.

fay [fei] adj., n. Fée *f.* (See FAIRY.)

faze [feiz] v. tr. U. S. Fam. Affecter, troubler.

F.B.I. [ˈefbiːˈai] abbr. U.S. *Federal Bureau of Investigation*, service de sécurité américain, F. B. I.

F.C. [ˈefˈsiː] abbr. *Football Club*, club de football.

fealty [ˈfiːəlti] n. Loyalisme *m.;* féauté *f.*

fear [fiə*] n. Peur *f.* (fright); *to stand in great fear of*, avoir grand peur de. ‖ Peur, crainte *f.* (apprehension); *for fear of falling*, de peur de tomber; *for fear you should fall*, de peur (or) crainte que vous ne tombiez; *I have a fear that*, j'ai peur que, je crains que. ‖ Motif (*m.*) de crainte; *there is no fear of failure*, il n'y a aucune crainte d'échec. ‖ Fam. *No fear!*, pas de danger!; soyez tranquille (or) sans crainte!
— v. tr. Avoir peur de, craindre. ‖ Craindre, redouter, appréhender (*from*, de, de la part de) [sth.]. ‖ Fam. *I fear I am late*, je suis désolé, je crois bien être en retard; *I fear he is not here*, je regrette, mais je crois qu'il n'y est pas.

— v. intr. Avoir peur, craindre (to be afraid [or] anxious). ‖ Douter (to be doubtful); *I didn't fear but that she would come*, je ne doutais pas qu'elle ne vînt, j'étais persuadé qu'elle viendrait.

fearful [-ful] adj. Effrayant, terrifiant (causing fear). ‖ Effrayé, craintif, peureux, timoré (see AFRAID); *to be fearful of*, avoir peur de, craindre; *to be fearful to do sth.*, hésiter (or) avoir peur de faire qqch. ‖ FAM. Terrible, formidable, effroyable; *a fearful fright*, une belle peur; *it's a fearful nuisance*, c'est diablement embêtant.

fearfully [-fuli] adv. Terriblement, d'une manière terrifiante. ‖ Craintivement, peureusement, avec crainte. ‖ FAM. Terriblement, effroyablement.

fearfulness [-fulnis] n. Nature effrayante f. (*of*, de) [sth.]. ‖ Nature timorée, pusillanimité f.

fearless [-lis] adj. Sans peur, brave, intrépide; *fearless of*, sans crainte de.

fearlessly [-lisli] adv. Sans crainte.

fearlessness [-lisnis] n. Intrépidité f.

fearnought [-nɔːt] n. Frise f. (cloth). ‖ U.S. Risque-tout s. (person).

fearsome [-səm] adj. Effrayant (frightful). ‖ Effrayé (frightened); timoré (timid).

feasibility [fiːziˈbiliti] n. Possibilité, praticabilité f.

feasible [ˈfiːzib] adj. Faisable, praticable, possible, réalisable. ‖ Admissible, croyable, probable, vraisemblable. ‖ Approprié, adapté.

feasor [-ə*] n. JUR. Auteur m.

feast [ˈfiːst] n. ECCLES. Fête f. ‖ CULIN. Festin m. (See BANQUET.) ‖ FIG. Fête f.; régal m. ‖ Feast-day, n. Jour (m.) de fête.
— v. tr. CULIN. Fêter, donner un festin pour, traiter royalement; régaler. ‖ FIG. Enchanter; *to feast one's eyes on*, enchanter ses regards de; se gorger la vue de; boire (or) manger des yeux.
— v. intr. CULIN. Banqueter, festoyer, bambocher (see REVEL); se régaler (*on*, de). ‖ FIG. Se délecter, faire ses délices (*on*, de).

feaster [-ə*] n. Hôte m.

feat [fiːt] n. Haut fait m. (See EXPLOIT.) ‖ Tour m.; *feat of acrobatics, strength*, tour d'adresse, de force.

feather [ˈfeðə*] n. Plume f. (of bird). ‖ Penne f. (of an arrow). ‖ Plumet m.; *a feather in one's cap*, une plume au chapeau, une nouvelle cocarde. ‖ Humeur, veine f.; *in fine feather*, en pleine forme. ‖ Plumage m.; *birds of a feather*, gens du même bord (or) acabit. ‖ Toilette f.; *in full feather*, toutes voiles dehors, en grande tenue. ‖ Bagatelle f.; brimborion m.; paille f. (fam.). ‖ TECHN. Paille f. (in a gem). ‖ FAM. *In high feather*, jubilant; *to show the white feather*, avoir la frousse. ‖ **Feather-bed**, n. Lit (m.) de plume; duvet m. ‖ FAM. Traitement (m.) de faveur. — v. tr. FAM. Favoriser, mignoter, gâter. ‖ **Feather-brain**, n. Tête de linotte f. ‖ **Feather-brained**, adj. Sans cervelle. ‖ **Feather-broom** (or) -duster, n. Plumeau m. ‖ **Feather-dealer**, n. Plumassier s. ‖ **Feather-edge**, n. TECHN. Biseau m. ‖ **Feather-stitch**, n. Point (m.) d'épine. ‖ **Feather-weight**, adj., n. SPORTS. Poids plume m.
— v. tr. Emplumer, couvrir de plume. ‖ Empenner (an arrow). ‖ SPORTS. Plumer. ‖ AVIAT. Mettre en drapeau (a propeller). ‖ NAUT. Coucher, mettre à plat (oars). ‖ FAM. *To feather one's nest*, se remplir les poches, faire sa pelote.
— v. intr. Mettre les plumes, se couvrir de plumes. ‖ Ressembler à une plume; se mouvoir comme une plume. ‖ NAUT. Plumer.

feathered [-d] adj. Emplumé, couvert de plumes; *feathered game*, gibier à plumes. ‖ Empenné (arrow). ‖ AVIAT. *Feathered propeller*, hélice en drapeau. ‖ FIG. Rapide (swift); ailé (winged).

feathering [-riŋ] n. Plumage m. (of birds). ‖ Empennage m. (of arrows). ‖ ARCHIT. Lobes m. pl.

feathery [-əri] adj. Couvert de plumes (feathered). ‖ Duveteux, léger (light); doux (soft).

feature [ˈfiːtʃə*] n. Trait m. (of the face). ‖ Pl. Visage m.; physionomie, tête f.; *play of the features*, jeux de physionomie. ‖ Gros titre m., article (m.) à sensation (in a newspaper). ‖ THEATR. Clou m. (chief attraction). ‖ CINEM. Grand film m. ‖ FIG. Trait saillant m.; caractéristique, marque dominante f.; élément caractéristique m.
— v. tr. Décrire, représenter, dépeindre (to portray); *picture featured on our cover*, image reproduite sur notre couverture. ‖ Dominer, être caractéristique de. ‖ Rendre dominant (or) caractéristique. ‖ Mettre en vedette. ‖ FAM. Imaginer.

featured [-d] adj. Aux traits, de visage. ‖ Mis en avant. ‖ THEATR. En vedette.

featureless [-lis] adj. Sans rien de marquant, terne, peu caractéristique, uniforme.

featuring [-riŋ] adj. THEATR. Ayant au programme.

febrifugal [febˈrifjugəl] adj. MED. Fébrifuge.

febrifuge [ˈfebrifjuːdʒ] n. MED. Fébrifuge m.

febrile [ˈfiːbrail] adj. MED. Fiévreux (person); fébrile (pulse).

February [ˈfebruəri] n. Février m.

feckless [ˈfeklis] adj. Incapable (ineffective); mou, sans énergie (or) caractère (spiritless). ‖ Insouciant (careless); indifférent (unconcerned). ‖ Etourdi, irréfléchi (thoughtless).

feculence [ˈfekjuləns] n. Aspect trouble; dépôt m.

feculent [-ənt] adj. Plein de dépôt, trouble, bourbeux (turbid). ‖ Sale, vicié, souillé (foul).

fecund [ˈfekənd] adj. MED. Fécond, prolifique (race, woman). ‖ BOT. Fécond, productif, fertile (earth).

fecundate [ˈfekəndeit] v. tr. MED., BOT. Féconder.

fecundation [ˌfekʌnˈdeiʃən] n. MED., BOT. Fécondation f.

fecundity [fiˈkʌnditi] n. MED., BOT. Fécondité f.

fed [fed] pret., p. p. See FEED. ‖ FAM. *To be fed up*, en avoir marre (or) soupé (or) plein le dos (or) pardessus la tête.

fedayeen [fəˈdɑːjiːn] n. pl. Fedayin (or) feddayin m. invar.

federal [ˈfedərəl] adj., n. Fédéral.

federalism [-izm] n. Fédéralisme m.

federalist [-list] n. Fédéraliste s.

federalize [-aiz] v. tr. Fédérer.

federate [ˈfedərit] adj. Fédéré.
— [-reit] v. tr. Fédérer, unir en fédération. ‖ Unir, grouper.
— v. intr. Se fédérer. ‖ Se grouper.

federation [fedəˈreiʃən] n. Fédération f.

federative [ˈfedərətiv] adj. Fédératif.

fee [fiː] n. † Fief m. (See FEUD.) ‖ Emoluments m. pl. (for professional services); honoraires m. pl. (of a doctor, lawyer). ‖ Pourboire m.; gratification f. (tip). ‖ Droits m. pl.; *entrance, registration fee*, droits d'entrée, d'inscription. ‖ JUR. Biens successoraux m. pl. ‖ **Fee-simple**, n. JUR. Pleine propriété f.
— v. tr. Rétribuer, verser des honoraires à. ‖ Acheter. (See BRIBE.)
— N. B. Le pret. et le p. p. sont feed.

feeble [ˈfiːbl] adj. Faible, chancelant, débile, invalide (infirm). ‖ Fragile, sans résistance (frail). ‖ Faible, timide, peu efficace (ineffective). ‖ Faible, influençable, sans caractère (or) énergie (spiritless). ‖ **Feeble-minded**, adj. A l'esprit faible; MED. Mentalement déficient; FIG. Faible, irrésolu; n. MED. *The feeble-minded*, les déficients mentaux.

feebleness [-nis] n. Faiblesse, débilité f. ‖ Timidité, faiblesse f.; manque (m.) d'énergie (or) de caractère.

feebly [ˈfiːbli] adv. Faiblement.

feed [fiːd] v. tr. (55). Nourrir (animals, babies, persons). ‖ Donner à manger (fodder, food) [*to*, à]. ‖ Alimenter (a river, stove); *to feed coal into the*

stove, mettre du charbon dans le poêle, alimenter le poêle en charbon ; *to feed the fire with coal*, alimenter le feu en charbon. ‖ AGRIC. Nourrir, engraisser (animals); faire paître (cattle); faire paître l'herbe de (a meadow). ‖ MED. Nourrir (the tissue). ‖ TECHN. Contrôler l'avance de (a tool). ‖ SPORTS. Alimenter (a player). ‖ THEATR. Donner la réplique à (an actor). ‖ FIG. Alimenter (s.o.'s anger); nourrir (hope); assouvir, contenter, satisfaire (one's vanity); entretenir, nourrir (*with*, de) [s.o.]. ‖ **To feed up**, engraisser (to fatten); rassasier (to satiate).
— v. intr. Se nourrir, faire sa nourriture (*on*, de). ‖ AGRIC. Paître. ‖ FIG. Profiter (*on*, de); *to feed on s.o.*, sucer qqn (fam.).
— n. Action (*f.*) de nourrir. ‖ AGRIC. Fourrage *m.* (fodder); pâturage, pacage *m.* (pasture); ration *f.* (for cattle, horses); pâtée *f.* (for fowls). "‖ TECHN. Alimentation *f.* (of boiler); avance *f.* (of tool). ‖ FAM. Gueuleton *m.* (blow out). ‖ **Feed-bag**, n. Musette-mangeoire *f.*; FAM. U.S. *To put on the feedbag*, casser la croûte. ‖ **Feed-pipe**, n. TECHN. Tuyau (*m.*) d'alimentation. ‖ **Feed-wire**, n. ELECTR. Fil (*m.*) d'amenée.

feedback [-bæk] n. ELECTR. Réaction *f.* ‖ CYBERN. Rétroaction *f.*, feed-back *m.; information feedback*, retour d'information; *feed-back loop*, boucle d'asservissement. ‖ MED. Feed-back, rétrocontrôle *m.* ‖ FIG. Réaction *f.*, feed-back *m.*

feeder [-ə*] n. Mangeur *s.* (eater). ‖ Bavoir *m.*; petite serviette *f.* ‖ Biberon *m.* (feeding-bottle). ‖ Affluent *m.* (tributary). ‖ AGRIC. Eleveur *s.* (of cattle). ‖ TECHN. Canal (*m.*) d'amenée (head-race); alimenteur *m.* (of machine); artère, conduite *f.* ‖ ELECTR. Feeder, câble (*m.*) d'alimentation. ‖ CH. DE F. Ligne secondaire, voie d'amenée *f.* ‖ FIG Fournisseur, pourvoyeur *s.*

fee-fi-fo-fum ['fiːˈfaiˈfouˈfʌm] interj. Hum, quel fumet !

feel [fiːl] v. tr. (56). Palper, tâter (to touch); *to feel one's way*, avancer à tâtons. ‖ Sentir, avoir la sensation de ; *to feel one's legs*, se sentir solide (or) d'aplomb sur ses jambes; *to feel s.o. moving*, sentir remuer qqn. ‖ Ressentir, éprouver (emotion, joy, pain, sympathy). ‖ Ressentir, être affecté par ; *to feel the cold*, être sensible au froid. ‖ Ressentir, subir, supporter ; *to feel it severely*, en souffrir durement ; le sentir passer (fam.); *to feel s.o's vengeance*, subir la vengeance de qqn. ‖ Avoir l'impression (or) le sentiment de, sentir, pressentir ; *I feel it in my bones that I shall succeed*, qqch. me dit (or) je pressens que je réussirai ; *I feel that you are wrong*, j'ai l'impression que vous vous trompez. ‖ MILIT. Tâter (the enemy); reconnaître (the ground). ‖ MED. Tâter (the pulse).
— v. intr. Tâtonner ; *to feel about in*, tâtonner dans, aller à tâtons dans ; *to feel for sth.*, chercher qqch. à tâtons ; *to feel in*, fouiller sans y voir dans. ‖ Donner la sensation de ; *it feels like swimming*, cela fait l'effet de nager, on dirait qu'on nage ; *to feel heavy*, paraître lourd ; *to feel soft*, être doux au toucher. ‖ Trouver, penser, avoir le sentiment ; *if that's the way you feel about it*, si tel est votre point de vue (or) votre sentiment. ‖ Sentir, être ému ; *if that's the way you feel about it !*, si c'est tout l'effet que ça te fait ! ; *to feel for s.o.*, éprouver de la pitié pour qqn ; *to feel for* (or) *with s.o. in his sorrow*, prendre part à la douleur de qqn. ‖ Se sentir, se trouver ; *how do you feel?*, comment vous sentez-vous ? ; que ressentez-vous ? ; *to feel all the better for it*, s'en trouver mieux ; *to feel certain that*, avoir la certitude que, être certain que ; *to feel in high spirits*, se sentir plein d'enthousiasme ; *to feel like a cake*, avoir envie d'un gâteau ; *to feel like doing sth.*, se sentir porté à faire qqch.; *when he feels like it, he can he charming*, il est charmant quand il veut ; *to feel up*

to, se sentir le courage de ; *to feel up to doing it*, se sentir à la hauteur de l'entreprise. ‖ FAM. *To feel cheap*, se sentir dans ses petits souliers.
— n. Toucher *m.; to know by the feel of it*, reconnaître au toucher. ‖ Sensation *f.* (perceived through touch). ‖ MED. Tact *m.*

feeler [-ə*] n. Tâteur *m.* (person). ‖ ZOOL. Antenne *f.* (of an insect); tentacule *m.* (of an octopus); corne *f.* (of a snail). ‖ FIG. Ballon d'essai *m.*

feeling [-iŋ] n. Toucher, tact *m.* (sense of touch). ‖ Tâtage, palpage *m.* (touching). ‖ Sensation *f.* (physically); sentiment *m.* (towards, envers); *no ill feelings!*, sans rancune ! ; *to have kind feelings for*, porter amitié à. ‖ Goût, sens *m.; he has a feeling for music*, il a le sens de la musique ; *the feeling for nature*, le sentiment de la nature. ‖ Sentiment *m.;* opinion *f.* ‖ Susceptibilité, sensibilité *f.; to hurt s.o.'s feelings*, froisser qqn. ‖ Sentiment *m.;* prémonition *f.; I have a feeling that I shall succeed*, je pressens que je réussirai. ‖ Sentiment *m.;* réaction sentimentale *f.; I can't trust my own feelings*, je ne peux me fier à mes impressions. ‖ Atmosphère, impression *f.; the house has a feeling of sadness about it*, la maison donne une impression de tristesse. ‖ MUS., ARTS. Ame *f.;* sentiment *m.*

feelingly [-iŋli] adv. Avec sentiment.

feet [fiːt]. See FOOT.

feign [fein] v. tr. Inventer (an excuse); monter (a story). ‖ Contrefaire, imiter. (See SHAM.) ‖ Feindre, simuler (see ASSUME); *to feign to be dead*, faire le mort.
— v. intr. Feindre.

feint [feint] n. Feinte *f.* (see SHAM); *to make a feint of*, feindre de. ‖ SPORTS, MILIT. Feinte *f.*
— v. intr. Faire semblant. ‖ SPORTS, MILIT. Faire une feinte.

feint adj. Réglé (paper).

feldspar ['feldspɑː] n. Feldspath *m.*

felicitate [fiˈlisiteit] v. tr. † Rendre heureux. ‖ Féliciter (*on*, de). [See CONGRATULATE.]

felicitation [ˌfilisiˈteiʃən] n. Félicitation *f.*

felicitous [fiˈlisitəs] adj. Heureux (expression, style, writer); *to have a felicitous style*, écrire avec bonheur.

felicity [-ti] n. Félicité *f.* (See BLISS.) ‖ Bonheur *m.;* bonne fortune *f.* ‖ Bonheur (*m.*) d'expression ; art (*m.*) de la trouvaille heureuse (in speaking, writing).

felid ['fiːlid] n. ZOOL. Félidé *m.*

feline ['fiːlain] adj., n. ZOOL., FIG. Félin *m.*

fell [fel] pret. See FALL.

fell v. tr. Faire tomber, jeter à terre, renverser (s.o.). ‖ Abattre (a tree). ‖ Rabattre (a seam).
— n. Abattis *m.* (of trees). ‖ Couture rabattue *f.* (seam).

fell adj. Féroce. (See FIERCE.) ‖ † Meurtrier (deadly).

fell n. Peau *f.* (of animals). ‖ **Fell-monger**, n. COMM. Peaussier *m.* ‖ **Fell-mongering**, n. Délainage *m.*

fell n. Colline rocheuse *f.* (hill); lande *f.* (moor).

fellah ['felə] n. Fellah *m.*
— N. B. Noter les pluriels : *fellaheen, fellahin, fellahs.*

feller ['felə*] n. Renverseur, tombeur *s.* ‖ Rabatteur *m.* (in sewing). ‖ U.S. FAM. Type *m.* (fellow).

felloe ['felou] n. Jante *f.* (See RIM.)

fellow n. Camarade *m.; good fellow*, bon copain (fam.). ‖ Compagnon *m.;* compagne *f.* ‖ Egal, pareil, semblable *m.* (peer). ‖ Pendant *m.* (mate); *to find the fellow of a glove*, réassortir un gant. ‖ Professeur *m.* (of a college); membre *m.* (of a learned society); U.S. *teaching fellow*, assistant. ‖ Homme *m.;* personne *f.; a fellow can't work all day long*, on ne peut pas travailler toute la journée. ‖ Individu, particulier, citoyen, quidam *m.* (contemptuously). ‖ FAM. Type *m.; a jolly old fellow*, un joyeux drille ; *an old fellow*, un vieux bonhomme ; *poor fellow*, pauvre garçon. ‖ **Fellow-author**, n. Co-auteur *s.;* collaborateur *m.*, collaboratrice *f.* ‖

Fellow-boarder, n. Commensal, compagnon (m.) de table. ‖ **Fellow-candidate**, n. Colistier m. (in politics). ‖ **Fellow-citizen**, n. Concitoyen s. ‖ **Fellow-countryman**, n. Compatriote m. ‖ **Fellow-creature**, n. Semblable m. ‖ **Fellow-feeling**, n. Sentiment (m.) de camaraderie; sympathie, compréhension mutuelle f. ‖ **Fellow-my-leader**, adj. FAM. A la remorque. ‖ **Fellow-passenger**, n. Compagnon de voyage m. ‖ **Fellow-prisoner**, n. JUR. Codétenu s. ‖ **Fellow-soldier**, n. MILIT. Camarade de régiment, frère (m.) d'armes. ‖ **Fellow-student**, n. Condisciple s. ‖ **Fellow-sufferer**, n. Compagnon (m.) de misère. ‖ **Fellow traveller**, n. Compagnon de voyage m.; FAM. Communisant, sympathisant communiste s. ‖ **Fellow-worker**, n. Collègue s. (of a clerk); compagnon de travail m. (of a workman); collaborateur m. (fellow-author).

fellowship [-ʃip] n. Camaraderie f. (See COMRADESHIP.) ‖ Fraternité, solidarité f. (of men). ‖ Communauté f. (of activity, experience, interest). ‖ Compagnie, société, association f. (group). ‖ Titre de membre m. (of a learned society). ‖ Poste de professeur m.; bourse (f.) de recherches (in a university).

felly ['feli] n. Jante f.

felo-de-se ['feloudi'si] n. JUR. Suicide m. (act); auteur (m.) d'une tentative de suicide; suicidé s. (person).

felon ['felən] n. MED. Panaris m.

felon n. JUR. Criminel s.
— adj. Vil (base); criminel.

felonious [fi'lounjəs] adj. Vil (base). ‖ JUR. Criminel, délictueux.

felonry ['felənri] n. JUR. Pègre f.

felony ['feləni] n. JUR. Délit majeur, crime m.

felspar ['felspɑ*] n. Feldspath m.

felt [felt] pret., p. p. See FEEL.

felt n. Feutre m. ‖ **Felt-maker**, n. Feutrier m.
— adj. En (or) de feutre; felt hat, feutre.
— v. tr. Feutrer.
— v. intr. Se feutrer.

felting [-iŋ] n. Feutrage m.

felucca [fi'lʌkə] n. NAUT. Felouque f.

female ['fi:meil] adj. ZOOL., BOT., TECHN. Femelle. ‖ MED. Féminin. ‖ FIG. Des femmes, féminin.
— n. Jeune fille f. (girl); femme f. (woman). ‖ BOT., ZOOL., POP. Femelle f.

feme [fem] n. JUR. Femme f.; feme covert, sole, femme en puissance de mari, seule (or) célibataire.

feminality [femi'næliti] n. Féminité f. ‖ Parure féminine f.; bijou, colifichet m. (trinket).

feminelty [-'ni:iti] n. Féminité f.

feminine ['feminin] adj. Féminin, de femme. (See WOMANLY.) ‖ Efféminé. (See WOMANISH.) ‖ GRAMM. Féminin.
— n. GRAMM. Féminin m.

femininity [femi'niniti] n. Féminité f. ‖ Gent féminine f.; femmes f. pl. (womankind).

feminism ['feminizm] n. Féminisme m.

feminist [-nist] adj., n. Féministe s.

feminity [-niti] n. See FEMININITY.

feminize [-naiz] v. tr. Féminiser.
— v. intr. Se féminiser.

femoral ['femərəl] adj. MED. Fémoral.

femur ['fi:mə*] (pl. **femora** [-mərə]) n. MED. Fémur m.

fen [fen] n. Marécage m. (bog); marais m. (marshland). ‖ **Fen-fire**, n. Feu follet m.

fence [fens] n. Clôture f. (enclosure); palissade f. (paling). ‖ SPORTS. Escrime f. ‖ JUR. Receleur s. (person); lieu de recel m. (place). ‖ FIG. Barrière, protection f. ‖ FIG. Joute oratoire f. (debate). ‖ FAM. On the fence, en balance, n'ayant pas encore pris parti, oscillant. ‖ **Fence-season**, n. SPORTS. Période de fermeture f. (in hunting). ‖ **Fence-wall**, n. Mur (m.) de clôture.

— v. tr. Clôturer, enclore; to fence in, palissader. ‖ FIG. Protéger, garder, défendre.
— v. intr. SPORTS. Faire de l'escrime (or) des armes (in fencing); sauter la haie (in steeplechasing). ‖ JUR. Faire du recel. ‖ FIG. To fence with, esquiver (a question); jouter avec, argumenter avec (s.o.).

fenceless [-lis] adj. Sans clôture. ‖ FIG. Sans protection.

fencer [-ə*] n. SPORTS. Escrimeur s. (in fencing); sauteur m. (in steeplechasing).

fencing [-iŋ] n. Clôture f. (act, material). ‖ JUR. Recel m. ‖ SPORTS. Escrime f. ‖ **Fencing-master**, n. SPORTS. Maître (m.) d'armes. ‖ **Fencing-school**, n. SPORTS. Salle (f.) d'armes.

fend [fend] v. tr. Défendre. ‖ Résister; parer; to fend off, repousser, rejeter, détourner.
— v. intr. Lutter (for, pour); to fend for oneself, s'arranger seul; se dépatouiller tout seul (fam.).

fender [-ə*] n. Garde-feu m. (fire-screen). ‖ AUTOM. Pare-chocs m. (bumper-bar); U. S. Garde-boue m. (wing). ‖ NAUT. Défense f. ‖ U. S. CH. DE F. Chasse-pierre m. (cow-catcher).

fenestra [fi'nestrə] n. MED. Fenêtre f. (of the tympanum).

fenestrate [fi'nestreit] adj. ZOOL. Fenestré.

fenestration [feni'streiʃən] n. ARCHIT. Fenêtrage (or) fenestrage m. ‖ MED. Fenestration f. ‖ ZOOL., BOT. Etat fenestré m.

Fenian ['fi:niən] adj., n. Fénian s.

fennel ['fenl] n. BOT. Fenouil m.

fenny ['feni] adj. Marécageux.

fenugreek ['fenjugri:k] n. BOT. Fenugrec m.

feoff [fef] n. Fief m.
— v. tr. Donner à fief à. ‖ JUR. Donner en toute propriété à.

feoffee [fe'fi:] n. JUR. † Feudataire m.

feoffment [-mənt] n. JUR. Inféodation, saisine f.

feral ['fiərəl] adj. Mortel, fatal. ‖ Funèbre, sombre (gloomy).

feral adj. Féroce, brutal. ‖ Sauvage (wild).

feria ['fiəriə] n. ECCLES. Férie f.

ferial [-əl] adj. ECCLES. Férial.

ferine ['fiərain] adj. Sauvage.

ferity ['feriti] n. Sauvagerie f.

ferment ['fə:mənt] n. Ferment m. (substance). ‖ Fermentation f. ‖ FIG. Excitation, fermentation, effervescence f.
— v. intr. Fermenter (lit. and fig.).
— v. tr. Faire fermenter. ‖ FIG. Exciter, agiter, mettre en effervescence.

fermentation [fə:men'teiʃən] n. Fermentation f. (lit. and fig.).

fermentative [fə'mentətiv] adj. Fermentatif.

fermion ['fə:miən] n. PHYS. Fermion m.

fermium ['fə:miəm] n. CHIM. Fermium m.

fern [fə:n] n. BOT. Fougère f.

fernery [-əri] n. BOT. Fougeraie f.

ferny ['fə:ni] adj. Plein de fougères.

ferocious [fə'rouʃəs] adj. Féroce.

ferociousness [-nis] n. Férocité, cruauté, sauvagerie f.

ferocity [fə'rɔsiti] n. Férocité f.

ferrate ['fereit] n. CHIM. Ferrate m.

ferreous ['feriəs] adj. CHIM. Ferreux.

ferret ['ferit] n. ZOOL. Furet m. ‖ FAM. Sbire m.
— v. tr. SPORTS. Prendre au furet (in hunting). ‖ FAM. To ferret out, détecter, dégoter, dénicher, déterrer.
— v. intr. SPORTS. Chasser au furet. ‖ FAM. To ferret about, fureter, fouiner.

ferrety [-i] adj. De furet. ‖ FAM. Fureteur.

ferriage ['feriidʒ] n. NAUT. Transport par bac m. (transportation); frais (m. pl.) de transport (charge).

ferric ['ferik] adj. CHIM. Ferrique.

ferriferous [fe'rifərəs] adj. CHIM. Ferrifère.

ferrite ['ferait] n. TECHN. Ferrite m.

ferrochromium ['ferou'kroumiəm] n. CHIM. Ferrochrome *m*.
ferroconcrete [-'kɔnkri:t] n. ARCHIT. Béton (or) ciment armé *m*.
ferrocyanide [-'saiənaid]n. CHIM. Ferrocyanure *m*.
ferromagnetic [-mæg'netik] adj. Ferromagnétique.
ferrotype [-taip] n. Ferrotype *m*. (in photography).
ferrous ['ferəs] adj. CHIM. Ferreux.
ferruginous [fə'ru:dʒinəs] adj. CHIM. Ferrugineux.
ferrule ['ferəl] n. Bout ferré *m*. (cap); virole *f*. (ring). ‖ TECHN. Manchon *m*. (tube).
— v. tr. Viroler.
ferry ['feri] n. NAUT. Bac *m*. (boat); lieu de passage en bac *m*. (place); transport en bac *m*. (transportation). ‖ AVIAT. Livraison (*f*.) par air. ‖ **Ferry-boat**, n. NAUT. Bac transbordeur *m*. ‖ **Ferry-pilot**, n. NAUT. Convoyeur *m*.
— v. tr. (2). NAUT. Traverser en bac (a river); faire traverser en bac (passengers); *to be ferried across a stream*, passer un cours d'eau en bac. ‖ AVIAT. Livrer par air.
— v. intr. NAUT. Passer en bac.
ferryman [-mən] n. NAUT. Passeur *m*. ‖ † Nautonier *m*.
fertile ['fə:tail] adj. Fertile. (See FECUND.) ‖ Fertilisant (warmth). ‖ Fécondé (egg).
fertility [fə:'tiliti] n. Fertilité *f*.
fertilizable ['fə:tilaizəbl] adj. Fertilisable.
fertilization [,fə:tilai'zeiʃən] n. Fertilisation *f*.
fertilize ['fə:tilaiz] v. tr. AGRIC. Fertiliser. ‖ MED., BOT. Féconder.
fertilizer [-ə*] n. AGRIC. Engrais *m*. ‖ BOT. Fertiliseur, fécondateur *m*.
ferula ['feru:lə] n. BOT. Férule *f*. ‖ † Sceptre *m*.
ferule ['feru:l] n. Férule *f*.
— v. tr. Donner de la férule à.
fervency ['fə:vənsi] n. Ferveur *f*.
fervent [-vənt] adj. Brûlant, incandescent. ‖ FIG. Fervent, ardent.
fervently [-vəntli] adv. Ardemment, avec ferveur.
fervid ['fə:vid] adj. Bouillant, ardent, fervent.
fervidly [-li] adv. Avec ardeur (or) passion.
fervo(u)r ['fə:və*] n. Chaleur intense *f*. ‖ FIG. Ardeur, ferveur, chaleur *f*. (in, à); *to work up to a fervour*, passionner.
fescue ['feskju] n. Baguette *f*. (teacher's pointer). ‖ BOT. Fétuque *f*.
fess(e) [fes] n. BLAS. Fasce *f*.
festal ['festl] adj. Gai, de fête.
fester ['festə*] v. intr. MED. S'envenimer, amasser. ‖ FIG. Se gâter (to decay); s'envenimer, s'aigrir (to embitter).
— v. tr. MED. Envenimer, rendre purulent. ‖ FIG. Gâter; envenimer.
— n. MED. Pustule *f*.
festival ['festivəl] n. ECCLES. Fête *f*. ‖ MUS. Festival *m*. ‖ FIG. Allégresse, gaieté *f*.
— adj. Gai, de fête.
festive [-tiv] adj. Gai, de fête (festal). ‖ Gai, jovial, fêtard.
festivity [fes'tiviti] n. Gaieté, joie *f*. (mirth). ‖ Fête *f*. (festival). ‖ Pl. Festivités *f*. *pl*.
festoon [fes'tu:n] n. Feston *m.;* guirlande *f*.
— v. tr. Festonner; orner de guirlandes.
festoonery [-əri] n. Décoration (*f*.) en festons.
fetal ['fi:tl]. See FOETAL.
fetch [fetʃ] v. tr. Amener, aller chercher (s.o.); *come and fetch him*, venez le chercher. ‖ Aller, ramener, chercher, apporter (sth.); *to fetch back*, ramener; *to fetch in*, faire entrer (a child). ‖ Tirer (blood, tears, water); asséner, porter (a blow); pousser (a groan, a sigh); faire (a leap); *to fetch one's breath*, reprendre haleine. ‖ TECHN. Amorcer (a pump). ‖ FIN. Atteindre (a price). ‖ NAUT. Aborder (a vessel). ‖ FAM. Faire

de l'effet sur, séduire; emballer (fam.). ‖ **To fetch up**, MED. Vomir; U. S. Atteindre, arriver à.
— v. intr. Aller et venir; *to fetch and carry*, faire les commissions (or) les menus travaux. ‖ NAUT. *To fetch about*, tirer des bordées; *to fetch up at a port*, parvenir au port. ‖ **To fetch up**, FAM. Finir, échouer.
— n. Ruse *f.;* stratagème, tour *m*. (See DODGE.)
fetching [-iŋ] adj. FAM. Chic (hat); tire-l'œil (headline); intéressant (paleness); emballant (story).
fête [feit] n. Fête (*f*.) de village. ‖ ECCLES. Fête *f*. (of a saint).
— adj. De fête (day).
— v. tr. Fêter.
fetid ['fi:tid] adj. Fétide, puant. (See NOISOME.)
fetidness [-nis] n. Fétidité, puanteur *f*.
fetish ['fetiʃ] n. Fétiche *m.; to make a fetish of*, avoir le culte de (sth.).
fetishism [-izm] n. Fétichisme *m*.
fetishist [-ist] n. Fétichiste *s*.
fetlock ['fetlɔk] n. Fanon *m*. (hair); boulet *m*. (joint) [of horse].
fetor ['fi:tə*] n. Puanteur *f*.
fetter ['fetə*] n. pl. Fers *m*. *pl*. ‖ Entrave *f*. (lit. and fig.).
— v. tr. Mettre aux fers, enchaîner (s.o.). ‖ Entraver (lit. and fig.)
fettle ['fetl] n. Forme, condition *f*.
fetus ['fi:təs] n. U.S. MED. Fœtus *m*.
feud [fju:d] n. JUR. Fief *m*.
feud n. Haine héréditaire *f.; at feud with*, brouillé à mort avec; *blood feud*, vendetta.
— v. intr. S'entre-déchirer, perpétuer une vendetta.
feudal [-l] adj. Féodal.
feudalism [-lizm] n. Féodalité *f*. (system).
feudality [fju'dæliti] n. Féodalité *f*. (state). ‖ Fief *m*. (feud).
feudalize ['fju:dəlaiz] v. tr. Inféoder.
feudatory [-ətəri] adj., n. Feudataire *m*. (*to*, de).
fever ['fi:və*] n. MED., FIG. Fièvre *f*.
— v. tr. MED. Donner la fièvre à. ‖ FIG. Enfiévrer.
feverish ['fi:vəriʃ] adj. MED. Fiévreux (climate, person); fébrile (person). ‖ FIG. Fébrile.
feverishly [-li] adv. Fiévreusement.
feverishness [-nis] n. MED. Fébrilité *f*.
feverous ['fi:vrəs] adj. MED. Fiévreux.
few [fju:] adj. Peu de; *few enemies*, peu (or) un petit nombre d'ennemis. ‖ Rares, peu nombreux; *they are few*, ils ne sont pas nombreux. ‖ Quelques; *every few days*, à quelques jours d'intervalle; *with few exceptions*, à quelques exceptions près.
— pron. Peu; *few of them*, un petit nombre d'entre eux. ‖ *A few*, quelques-uns, un certain nombre. ‖ FAM. *Quite a few*, pas mal.
— n. *The few*, la minorité. ‖ AVIAT. *The Few*, le glorieux petit groupe.
fewness [-nis] n. Petit nombre *m.;* rareté *f*.
fey [fei] adj. Voué à la mort (fated). ‖ Lunatique, de l'autre monde.
fez [fez] n. Fez *m*.
ff. Written abbr. for *following pages*, et suivantes; *see pages 19 ff.*, voir p. 19 et suiv.
fiancé [fi'ɔnsei] n. Fiancé *m*.
fiancée n. Fiancée *f*.
fiasco [fi'æskou] n. Fiasco *m*.
fiat ['faiæt] n. JUR. Ordonnance (or) autorisation judiciaire *f*.
— adj. FIN. Fiduciaire (currency).
— v. tr. JUR. Autoriser.
fib [fib] n. Petit mensonge *m*. (lie). ‖ FAM. Craque, blague *f*. (See CRAMMER.)
— v. intr. (1). FAM. Dire des craques.
fibber [-ə*] n. FAM. Blagueur *s*.
fibre ['faibə*] n. MED. Fibre *f*. ‖ COMM. Fibre *f.; staple fibre*, fibranne; *vegetable fibre*, crin végétal; *man-made fibre*, fibre synthétique. ‖ FIG. Fibre, trempe *f*. ‖ **Fibre-cell**, n. MED. Fibrocellule *f*.

fibreglass [-,glɑ:s] n. Fibre (f.) de verre ; laine (f.) de verre (for insulation).

fibril ['faibril] n. BOT., MED. Fibrille f.

fibrillary [fai'briləri] adj. Fibrillaire.

fibrillation [,faibri'leiʃən] n. MED. Fibrillation f.

fibrin ['faibrin] n. Fibrine f.

fibro-cement ['faibro,si'ment] n. Fibrociment m.

fibroid ['faibrɔid] adj. MED. Fibreux, fibroïde.
— n. MED. Fibrome m.

fibroma [fai'broumə] (pl. **fibromata** [-mətə]) n. MED. Fibrome m.

fibrosis [fai'brousis] (pl. **fibroses** [-i:z]) n. MED. Fibrose f.

fibrositis ['faibro'saitis] n. MED. Rhumatisme musculaire m.; cellulite f.

fibrous ['faibrəs] adj. Fibreux.

fibula ['fibjulə] (pl. **fibulae** [-i:]) n. MED. Péroné m.

fiche [fi:ʃ] n. Microfiche f.

fichu ['fi:ʃju] n. Fichu m.

fickle ['fikḷ] adj. Inconstant. ‖ **Fickle-hearted**, adj. Inconstant ; au cœur d'artichaut m. (fam.).

fickleness [-nis] n. Inconstance f.

fictile ['fiktail] adj. ARTS. D'argile, de céramique.

fiction ['fikʃən] n. Fiction f. ‖ Ouvrage (m.) d'imagination. ‖ Fiction, invention f. (figment).

fictional [-l] adj. D'imagination.

fictionize [-aiz] v. tr. Romancer.

fictitious [fik'tiʃəs] adj. Fictif, imaginaire (character) ; fictif (name). ‖ Fictif, simulé (fight, quarrel).

fictitiously [-li] adv. Fictivement.

fictitiousness [-nis] n. Caractère fictif m.

fictive ['fiktiv] adj. Fictif.

fid [fid] n. Cale f.; coin m. (wedge). ‖ NAUT. Clef f. (of mast) ; splicing fid, épissoir.

fiddle ['fidḷ] n. MUS., FAM., NAUT. Violon m. ‖ FAM. Combine f.; face as long as a fiddle, figure longue d'une aune ; fit as a fiddle, en pleine forme ; to play second fiddle, jouer en sous-fifre. ‖ **Fiddle-faddle**, n. Baliverne f.; adj. Baguenaudier ; v. intr. Baguenauder. ‖ **Fiddle-maker**, n. MUS. Luthier m.
— v. intr. MUS., FAM. Jouer du violon. ‖ FAM. Se démener, se trémousser. (See FIDGET.) ‖ **To fiddle with**, FAM. Trifouiller, bricoler.
— v. tr. MUS., FAM. Jouer du violon. ‖ FAM. To fiddle away one's time, passer son temps à musarder. ‖ FAM. Maquiller (the accounts).

fiddlededee [-di'di:] interj. Baliverne !

fiddler [-ə*] n. MUS. Violoneux m.

fiddlestick [-stik] n. MUS. Archet m. ‖ FAM. Pl. Sornettes, balivernes f. pl.

fiddling [-iŋ] adj. FAM. Musard, bricoleur (person) ; insignifiant, sans valeur (thing).
— n. FAM. Combine f.

fiddly [-i] adj. Enquiquinant, agaçant, pas commode.

fidelity [fi'deliti] n. Fidélité f. (accuracy, loyalty).

fidget ['fidʒit] n. Agitation f.; mouvement nerveux, tressaut m.; to have the fidgets, avoir la bougeotte. ‖ Agité s.; frétillon m. (person).
— v. intr. Se démener, se trémousser ; to fidget about, ne pas tenir en place ; to fidget with, tripoter nerveusement. ‖ S'impatienter ; piaffer (fam.).
— v. tr. Agacer, énerver ; asticoter (fam.).

fidgety [-i] adj. Agité, remuant (restless). ‖ Impatient, nerveux, fébrile (nervous).

fiducial [fi'dju:ʃiəl] adj. PHYS., MATH., ASTRON. Fiduciel.

fiduciary [-əri] adj., n. JUR., COMM. Fiduciaire adj., m.

fie [fai] interj. Fi ! ‖ **Fie-fie**, adj. FAM. Vilain.

fief [fi:f] n. Fief m.

field [fi:ld] n. Terrain m.; oil field, gisement pétrolifère. ‖ Etendue f. (of ice, snow, water). ‖ AGRIC. Champ m. ‖ MILIT. Aire (f.) des opérations (area) ;

campagne, bataille f. (battle) ; champ (m.) de bataille (battlefield) ; in the field, en campagne ; to take the field, entrer en campagne. ‖ SPORTS. Champ m. (in baseball) ; terrain (in cricket, football) ; lot (m.) des concurrents (entrants) ; joueurs m. pl. (players) ; équipe (f.) en jeu (team). ‖ ELECTR., PHYS., BLAS. Champ m. ‖ TECHN. Champ m. (of a coin, flag). ‖ FIG. Champ, cercle m. (of activity) ; to take the field, se mettre en campagne. ‖ **Field-artillery**, n. MILIT. Artillerie de campagne f. ‖ **Field-day**, n. MILIT. Jour (m.) de grandes manœuvres ; U. S. Manifestation sportive f.; FAM. Grand jour m. ‖ **Field-glasses**, n. pl. MILIT. Jumelles (f. pl.) de campagne. ‖ **Field-hospital**, n. MILIT., MED. Hôpital (m.) de campagne. ‖ **Field-kitchen**, n. MILIT. Roulante f. (fam.). ‖ **Field-marshal**, n. MILIT. Feld-maréchal m. ‖ **Field-mouse**, n. ZOOL. Mulot m. ‖ **Field-sports**, n. pl. Sports (m. pl.) de plein air ; chasse et pêche f. ‖ **Field-vole**, n. ZOOL. Campagnol m. ‖ **Field-winding**, n. ELECTR. Bobinage inducteur m. ‖ **Field-work**, n. Travail (m.) [or] enquête (f.) sur le terrain ; MILIT. Ouvrage (m.) de campagne.
— v. intr. SPORTS. Tenir le champ (in cricket).
— v. tr. SPORTS. Arrêter et relancer (a ball) ; réunir (a team).

fielder ['fi:ldə*] n. SPORTS. Fielder, homme de champ m.

fieldfare [-feə*] n. ZOOL. Litorne f.

fiend [fi:nd] n. ECCLES., FIG. Démon m. ‖ U. S. FAM. Emballé, mordu m.; cigarette fiend, fumeur enragé.

fiendish [-iʃ] adj. Diabolique.

fiendishness [-iʃnis] n. Diablerie, férocité diabolique f.

fierce [fiə:s] adj. Féroce (animal) ; ardent, brûlant (desire) ; farouche, féroce (envy, hatred) ; acharné (labour) ; féroce, cruel, sauvage, violent (person) ; violent, furieux (storm, wind) ; affreux (weather). ‖ AUTOM. Brusque, brutal (brake, clutch).

fiercely [-li] adv. Férocement, furieusement.

fierceness [-nis] n. Férocité f. (of an animal, a person) ; violence f. (of a desire, a storm).

fierily ['faiərili] adv. Avec flamme (or) passion.

fieriness [-nis] n. Flamme, ardeur f.; feu m.

fiery ['faiəri] adj. Embrasé (atmosphere) ; ardent, feu (colour) ; flamboyant (eyes) ; ardent, enflammé (glance) ; ardent, fougueux (horse, person) ; enflammé (imagination, speech) ; violent (passion) ; cuisant (taste) ; de feu, bouillant (temper). ‖ Inflammable (gas) ; grisouteux (mine). ‖ SPORTS. Dur (cricket-pitch).

fiesta [fi'estə] n. Fête f. (religious). ‖ Carnaval m., fête, fiesta f.

fife [faif] n. MUS. Fifre m. (instrument).
— v. intr. MUS. Jouer du fifre.

fifer [-ə*] n. MUS. Fifre m. (musician).

fifteen ['fif'ti:n] adj., n. Quinze m.; about fifteen, une quinzaine.

fifteenth [-θ] adj. Quinzième (fractional, numeral) ; quinze (after dates, names).
— n. Quinzième s.

fifth [fifθ] adj. Cinquième (fractional, numeral) ; fifth column, cinquième colonne. ‖ Cinq ; Charles the Fifth, Charles Quint ; Charles V ; Henry the Fifth, Henri V ; April 5th, le 5 avril.
— n. Cinquième s. ‖ MUS. Quinte f.

fifthly [-li] adv. Cinquièmement.

fiftieth ['fiftiəθ] adj., n. Cinquantième s.

fifty ['fifti] adj., n. Cinquante m.; about fifty people, une cinquantaine de personnes. ‖ **Fifty-fifty**, adv. FAM. De compte (m.) à demi, moitié-moitié.

fig [fig] n. BOT. Figue f. (fruit) ; figuier m. (tree). ‖ FAM. A fig for, la barbe pour. ‖ **Fig-eater**, n. ZOOL. Becfigue m. ‖ **Fig-leaf**, n. BOT. Feuille (f.)

de figuier; ARTS. Feuille de vigne *f.* ‖ **Fig-wort,** n. BOT. Ficaire *f.*

fig. Written abbr. for *figure*, figure, schéma.

fight [fait] n. Lutte, bataille *f.; to have a fight,* se battre. ‖ Combativité *f.; to show fight,* témoigner d'une humeur belliqueuse, montrer de la résistance; *to take all the fight out of,* enlever tout ressort à (s.o.). ‖ MILIT. Bataille *f.;* combat *m.* ‖ SPORTS. Combat *m.* (in boxing); *to put up a good fight,* se défendre honorablement. ‖ FIG. Lutte *f.* — v. intr. (57). Se battre, combattre, lutter (for pour). ‖ MILIT. Livrer bataille, se battre. ‖ SPORTS. Combattre. ‖ FIG. Lutter. ‖ FAM. Se quereller. — v. tr. Se battre contre, combattre (s.o., sth.). ‖ Livrer; *to fight a battle,* livrer bataille; *to fight a duel,* se battre en duel; *to fight the good fight,* combattre pour la bonne cause. ‖ Lutter pour; *to fight one's way out,* se frayer une sortie de haute lutte. ‖ SPORTS. Faire combattre (cocks). ‖ FIG. Discuter (a point). ‖ **To fight down,** vaincre, écraser. ‖ **To fight it out,** lutter jusqu'au bout. ‖ **To fight off,** MILIT. Repousser.

fighter [-ə*] n. Batailleur *s.* (person). ‖ MILIT. Combattant *m.* ‖ AVIAT. Chasseur *m.* ‖ **Fighter-bomber,** n. AVIAT. Chasseur-bombardier *m.*

fighting [-iŋ] adj. Qui se bat. ‖ MILIT. Sous les armes, combattant; de combat. ‖ FIG. Enflammé (speech). ‖ U. S. FAM. Maigre (chance). ‖ **Fighting-cock,** n. Coq de combat *m.;* U. S. FAM. Vrai coq *m.* (person). ‖ **Fighting fund,** n. Fonds de soutien *m.* — n. Rixe, lutte *f.* ‖ MILIT., SPORTS. Combats *m.*

figment ['figmənt] n. Invention *f.* (See FICTION.)

figuration [,figju'reiʃən] n. Figuration *f.* (act). ‖ Configuration, forme *f.* (shape). ‖ Figuration, ornementation *f.*

figurative ['figjurətiv] adj. Figuratif, représentatif, symbolique. ‖ GRAMM., FIG. Figuré, imagé.

figuratively [-li] adv. GRAMM. Au figuré.

figure ['figə*] n. Forme, silhouette *f.;* corps *m.; a figure of fun,* une caricature; *to have a good figure,* être bien tourné. ‖ Ligne *f.; to keep one's figure,* garder la ligne. ‖ Figure, personnalité *f.* (person). ‖ Figure, apparence *f.; to cut a brilliant figure,* faire belle figure; *to cut a sorry figure,* se montrer lamentable. ‖ ARTS. Personnage *m.;* figure *f.* (in painting); motif, dessin *m.* (drawing); figure, illustration *f.* ‖ SPORTS. Figure *f.* (in dancing, skating). ‖ MATH. Chiffre *m.* (number); *figures for August,* les statistiques du mois d'août; *to be quick at figures,* calculer vite; *to have no head for figures,* n'être pas doué pour le calcul, ne rien comprendre aux chiffres; *to reach a high figure,* atteindre un chiffre (or) prix élevé. ‖ GRAMM., MATH., MUS. Figure *f.* — v. tr. Figurer, représenter. ‖ Figurer, symboliser. ‖ Décorer, orner de motifs; *to figure a cloth,* imprimer un tissu. ‖ MATH. Marquer en chiffres, chiffrer. ‖ GRAMM. Représenter par une image. ‖ FAM. Se figurer, s'imaginer (s.o.); compter, penser, s'imaginer (sth.). ‖ **To figure out,** calculer, supputer; FAM. comprendre; *I can't figure it out,* ça me dépasse. — v. intr. Figurer (as, comme; on, sur). ‖ MATH. Faire des chiffres, calculer. ‖ **To figure on,** compter sur, escompter. ‖ **To figure out,** se chiffrer, se montrer.

figured ['figə:d] adj. A dessins; imprimé (fabric); broché (silk).

figurehead [-hed] n. NAUT. Figure de proue *f.* ‖ FIG. Personnage représentatif *m.;* figure de proue *f.*

figurine [figju'ri:n] n. Figurine *f.*

Fiji ['fi:dʒi] n. GEOGR. Iles (*f. pl.*) Fidji (or) Fiji.

filagree ['filə,gri:] n. See FILIGREE.

filament ['filəmənt] n. Filament *m.* ‖ PHYS., BOT. Filet *m.* ‖ ELECTR. Filament *m.*

filamentous [filə'mentəs] adj. Filamenteux.

filariasis [filə'raiəsis] n. MED. Filariose *f.*

filature ['filətʃə*] n. Filature *f.* (act, place); dévidoir *m.* (reel); dévidage *m.* (reeling).

filbert ['filbə:t] n. BOT. Noisette, aveline *f.* (fruit); avelinier *m.* (tree).

filch [filtʃ] v. tr. FAM. Chaparder, barboter, chiper.

filcher [-ə*] n. FAM. Chapardeur *s.*

filching [-iŋ] n. FAM. Chapardage, barbotage *m.*

file [fail] n. TECHN. Lime *f.* — v. tr. TECHN. Limer.

file n. File, queue *f.* (of carriages, persons); *to take one's place in the file,* se mettre à la queue. ‖ Collection *f.* (of a newspaper); archives *f. pl.* (of papers). ‖ Classeur, casier *m.; card-index file,* fichier; *on file,* en fiches, classé. ‖ MILIT. File, colonne (*f.*) par deux; *rank and file,* gradés et soldats. ‖ JUR. Dossier *m.* ‖ FAM. *Rank and file,* le commun, le tout venant (people). ‖ **File-clerk,** n. Employé (*s.*) au fichier. — v. intr. Marcher à la file; *to file in,* entrer à la queue leu leu. ‖ MILIT. *To file off,* défiler. — v. tr. Classer (documents). ‖ MILIT. *To file off,* faire défiler. ‖ JUR. Déposer, verser au dossier; *to file one's petition,* déposer son bilan.

filemot ['filimɔt] adj., n. Feuille-morte, roux *m.* (colour).

filer ['failə*] n. Limeur *m.*

filet ['fi:lei] n. Filet *m.* (net). ‖ CULIN. Filet *m.* (of fish, meat).

filial ['filjəl] adj. Filial.

filiation [fili'eiʃən] n. Filiation *f.*

filibuster ['filibʌstə*] n. Flibustier *m.* ‖ FAM. Manœuvrier, obstructionniste *m.* (in politics). — v. intr. Flibuster. ‖ FAM. Faire de l'obstruction.

filiform ['filifɔ:m] adj. Filiforme.

filigree [-gri:] n. Filigrane *m.* — v. tr. Filigraner.

filing ['failiŋ] n. Limage *m.* ‖ Pl. Limaille (*f.*) de fer.

filing n. Classement *m.* ‖ JUR. Dépôt au dossier *m.*

fill [fil] v. tr. Emplir, remplir (with, de); *to fill one's pipe,* garnir (or) bourrer sa pipe. ‖ Boucher, obturer (holes); combler, remblayer (low land). ‖ Apprêter (a fabric). ‖ Occuper (an office, a position); *to fill the chair,* présider. ‖ Placer à (a post); combler, pourvoir à (a vacancy). ‖ CULIN. Remplir, bourrer (the stomach); rassasier (s.o.). ‖ MED. Plomber (a tooth); *to fill a prescription,* exécuter une ordonnance; *to fill a tooth with gold,* aurifier une dent. ‖ THEATR. Remplir (a part). ‖ AUTOM. Faire le plein de (a radiator); *filled to capacity,* complet (bus). ‖ NAUT. Faire porter (sails). ‖ FIG. Assouvir, satisfaire (one's desires); remplir, occuper (one's free time). ‖ FAM. Combler (the measure); *to fill the bill,* être à la hauteur. ‖ **To fill in,** combler (a ditch, a hole); remplir (a form); FIN. Libeller (a cheque). ‖ **To fill out,** gonfler (a balloon); FIG. Bourrer, étoffer (a text); U. S. Remplir (a form). ‖ **To fill up,** remplir jusqu'au bord (a glass); remplir (a form); boucher, combler (a hole); FAM. *To fill s.o. up with a story,* bourrer le mou à qqn. — v. intr. Se remplir, s'emplir. ‖ NAUT. Porter. ‖ **To fill out,** se gonfler; se remplir (cheeks); profiter, grossir (person); se remplumer (fam.). ‖ **To fill up,** s'emplir, se combler; AUTOM., NAUT. Faire le plein (with, de). — n. Content, saoul *m.* (fam.); *to eat one's fill,* manger tout son content; *to drink one's fill,* boire jusqu'à plus soif. ‖ Quantité (*f.*) pour remplir; *a fill of tobacco,* une pipe de tabac. ‖ AUTOM. Plein *m.* ‖ **Fill-in,** n. Suppléant, intérim *m.* ‖ **Fill-up,** n. Remplissage *m.*

filler [-ə*] n. Compte-gouttes *m.* (for fountain-pen); entonnoir *m.* (for paraffin). ‖ Mastic *m.* (before painting); Remplisseur *s.* (person). ‖ Pesée *f.* (in a newspaper). ‖ Rechange *m.* (for a note-book).

fillet ['filit] n. Bandeau *m.* (around the head). ‖

Bande *f.;* filet *m.* ‖ ARCHIT. Moulure, baguette *f.* ‖ TECHN. Filet *m.* (of screw). ‖ CULIN. Filet *m.* (of beef); rouelle *f.* (of veal). ‖ BLAS. Filet *m.*
— v. tr. Entourer d'un bandeau. ‖ Garnir d'un filet (or) d'une baguette. ‖ CULIN. Lever les filets de.

filling ['filiŋ] n. Remplissage *m.* ‖ Remblayage *m.* (of ditch). ‖ MED. Obturation *f.* (of a tooth). ‖ **Filling-station**, n. Poste d'essence *m.; filling station attendant,* pompiste.
— adj. FAM. Bourratif (food).

fillip ['filip] n. Chiquenaude *f.* ‖ Tonique, stimulant *m.* ‖ FAM. Broutille *f.* (See FLIP.)
— v. tr. Donner une chiquenaude à. ‖ Tonifier, stimuler.
— v. intr. Donner une chiquenaude.

fillister ['filistə*] n. ARCHIT. Feuillure *f.* (groove); feuilleret *m.* (plane).

filly ['fili] n. ZOOL. Pouliche *f.* ‖ FAM. Fringante jouvencelle *f.*

film [film] n. Pellicule, membrane *f.* (skin). ‖ Voile *m.* (of mist, smoke). ‖ Fil *m.* (of a cobweb). ‖ MED. Taie *f.* (over the eyes). ‖ TECHN. Pellicule *f.* (for photographs). ‖ CINEM. Film *m.; to act for the films,* faire du cinéma; *to make a film,* tourner un film. ‖ **Film-cutter**, n. CINEM. Monteur *m.* ‖ **Film-goer**, n. Cinéphile *s.* ‖ **Film-producer**, n. CINEM. Producteur *s.* ‖ **Film-script**, n. CINEM. Script *m.* ‖ **Film-star**, n. Star, vedette (*f.*) de cinéma. ‖ **Film-store**, n. CINEM. Cinémathèque *f.* ‖ **Film-story**, n. Ciné-roman *m.* ‖ **Film-strip**, n. CINEM. Film fixe d'enseignement *m.*
— v. tr. Couvrir d'une pellicule. ‖ Voiler. ‖ MED. Couvrir d'une taie. ‖ CINEM. Filmer.
— v. intr. Se couvrir d'une pellicule. ‖ Se voiler.

filminess ['filminis] n. Transparence, légèreté *f.* ‖ Flou, vague *m.*

filmy [-mi] adj. Mince et fragile, transparent, diaphane (gauzy). ‖ Flou, voilé, embrumé (hazy). ‖ MED. Membraneux.

filter ['filtə*] n. Filtre *m.* ‖ **Filter-paper**, n. Papier-filtre *m.* ‖ **Filter-tip**, n. Bout filtrant *m.*
— v. tr., intr. Filtrer (lit. and fig.).

filtering [-riŋ] n. Filtrage *m.* (of impurities). ‖ Dépoussiérage *m.* (of air). ‖ FIG. Infiltration *f.*

filth [filθ] n. Ordure *f.* ‖ FIG. Obscénité *f.*

filthily [-ili] adv. D'une façon ordurière.

filthiness [-inis] n. Saleté *f.* ‖ FIG. Obscénité *f.*

filthy [-i] adj. Sale. ‖ FIG. Ordurier, obscène.

filtrate ['filtreit] v. tr., intr. Filtrer.
— [-trit] n. Filtrat *m.*

filtration [fil'treiʃən] n. Filtration *f.*

fin [fin] n. ZOOL. Nageoire *f.* (of fish); aileron *m.* (of shark). ‖ AVIAT. Ailette *f.;* plan (*m.*) de dérive. ‖ TECHN. Bavure *f.* ‖ FAM. Aile *f.* (arm); pince, cuillère *f.* (hand).

finable ['fainəbl] adj. JUR. Passible d'amende.

finagle [fi'neigl] v. tr. U. S. FAM. Manigancer, bricoler, se débrouiller pour avoir. (See WANGLE.)
— v. intr. U. S. FAM. Tripoter.

final ['fainl] adj. Final, ultime (last). ‖ Définitif (answer); *to take it as final,* se le tenir pour dit. ‖ JUR. Concluant, décisif (evidence); exécutoire, sans appel (judgment). ‖ PHILOS. Final (cause). ‖ FIN. Final *instalment,* versement libératoire. ‖ MILIT. Final *action,* combat décisif.
— n. Belle *f.* (at cards). ‖ SPORTS. Finale *f.* ‖ U. S. Pl. Examens trimestriels (or) semestriels *m. pl.*

finale [fi'nɑːli] n. Conclusion *f.* ‖ MUS. Finale *m.*

finalist ['fainəlist] n. SPORTS. Finaliste *s.*

finality [fai'næliti] n. Caractère décisif *m.* ‖ JUR. Irrévocabilité *f.* ‖ PHILOS. Finalité *f.*

finalize ['fainə,laiz] v. tr. Mettre au point, donner une tournure définitive à (plan); conclure (deal).

finally ['fainəli] adv. Finalement. ‖ Définitivement.

finance [fi'næns] n. FIN. Finance *f.*
— v. tr. FIN. Financer. ‖ COMM. Commanditer.

financer [-sə*] n. COMM. Commanditaire *m.*

financial [-ʃəl] adj. Financier (editor, news, state); pécuniaire (loss); fiscal (resources, year); de la finance (world); *financial statement,* bilan.

financier [-siə*] n. FIN. Financier *m.*

finch [fintʃ] n. ZOOL. Pinson *m.*

find [faind] v. tr. (58). Trouver (by accident, by searching). ‖ Trouver, rencontrer (to meet with); *to find s.o. out,* ne pas trouver qqn chez lui. ‖ Trouver, se procurer (to get); *not to be found,* introuvable. ‖ Trouver, découvrir (to discover); *find oneself,* se trouver, trouver sa voie. ‖ Trouver, recevoir (to receive); *to find a hearty welcome,* trouver un accueil cordial. ‖ Trouver, inventer (to invent). ‖ Trouver, voir, déterminer; *to find no sense in,* ne trouver aucun sens à. ‖ Trouver, constater, s'apercevoir (to perceive); *you'll find that he is right,* vous verrez qu'il a raison. ‖ Trouver, établir, constater (to establish); *it has been found that,* on a constaté (or) déterminé que. ‖ Trouver, retrouver; *to find one's way back,* ne pas se perdre en rentrant; *to find one's way into,* se faufiler dans. ‖ Trouver, considérer, estimer, juger (to deem); *to find it impossible to,* se trouver dans l'impossibilité de. ‖ Trouver, sentir (to feel); *I found my attention wandering,* je sentais fuir mon attention; *to find oneself obliged to,* se trouver obligé de. ‖ Apprendre, découvrir, venir à savoir; *that's a mistake, I find,* c'est une erreur, à ce que j'apprends. ‖ Atteindre (to reach); *the punch found my nose,* le coup m'atteignit au nez. ‖ Fournir, pourvoir (in, en) [to supply]; *all found,* tout fourni. ‖ JUR. Déclarer (guilty); *to find a sum in damages,* accorder une somme à titre de dommages-intérêts; *to find a true bill against,* prononcer la mise en accusation de. ‖ **To find out,** trouver, découvrir (to discover); apprendre, venir à savoir (to learn); résoudre (to resolve); apprécier à sa valeur réelle (s.o., sth.); *she has been found out,* maintenant on sait ce qu'elle vaut, elle a été démasquée; *to find out about,* se renseigner sur, obtenir des éclaircissements sur.
— v. intr. SPORTS. Lever le gibier. ‖ JUR. Rendre un verdict (against, contre; for, en faveur de).
— n. Trouvaille *f.* ‖ SPORTS. Vue *f.*

finder [-ə*] n. Trouveur *s.* ‖ PHYS. Viseur *m.* (of camera); chercheur *m.* (of telescope).

finding [-iŋ] n. Découverte *f.* (discovery); trouvaille *f.* (find). ‖ JUR. Décision *f.; pl.* conclusions *f. pl.; case finding,* dépistage. ‖ U. S. Pl. Fournitures *f. pl.* (supplies); accessoires *m. pl.* (tools).

fine [fain] adj. Fin, aigu (edge); fin, pur (gold); fin, délicat (lace); fin (linen); fin, mince, ténu (thread). ‖ Beau, superbe (athlete, baby, flower); beau (day, weather); choisi, beau (language); distingué (scholar); parfait (state); excellent (teacher). ‖ Fin, subtil (distinction); fin, raffiné, délicat (feelings); fin, pénétrant (understanding). ‖ MUS., ARTS. Beau. ‖ FAM. Joli; *a fine fellow,* un joli monsieur; *it would be a fine thing if,* il ferait beau voir que; *that's all very fine,* tout ça c'est bien joli.
— adv. Bien. ‖ Fin, finement. ‖ SPORTS. Fin. ‖ FAM. *To cut it fine,* y arriver tout juste. ‖ **Fine-grained**, adj. Au grain serré (wood). ‖ **Fine-looking**, adj. Beau *m.;* belle *f.*
— n. Beau temps *m.* ‖ TECHN. Pl. Fines *f. pl.*
— v. tr. Affiner (gold); clarifier (liquid); *to fine away* (or) *down* (or) *off,* affiler, amincir. ‖ FIG. Affiner.
— v. intr. Se clarifier (liquid); *to fine away,* s'amincir. ‖ FIG. S'affiner.

fine n. JUR. Amende *f.* (penalty); pas (*m.*) de porte (paid by a tenant). ‖ LOC. *In fine,* enfin.
— v. tr. JUR. Infliger une amende à.
— v. intr. JUR. Verser une indemnité compensatrice.

finedraw ['fain'drɔ:] v. tr. (48). Stopper, rentraire.

finedrawn [-'drɔːn] adj. Perdu (mend); ténu (thread); étiré (wire). ‖ SPORTS. Amené au poids minimum. ‖ FIG. Subtil.

finely [-li] adv. Finement. ‖ Magnifiquement. ‖ FAM. Joliment.

fineness [-nis] n. Finesse ƒ. ‖ Beauté ƒ. ‖ Titre *m.* (of gold).

finery [-əri] n. Atours *m. pl.* ‖ TECHN. Affinerie ƒ. ‖ FIG. Subtilité ƒ.

finespun [-'spʌn] adj. Ténu (thread).

finesse [fi'nes] n. Finesse, ruse ƒ. (craft); finesse, habileté ƒ. (skill). ‖ Impasse ƒ. (in bridge, whist).
— v. intr. Finasser. ‖ Faire une impasse.
— v. tr. Traiter avec ruse. ‖ Faire l'impasse de.

finger ['fiŋgə*] n. Doigt *m.; first, middle, ring finger,* index, médius, annulaire. ‖ FAM. *Not to stir a finger to,* ne pas lever le petit doigt pour; *to have a finger in the pie,* avoir part au gâteau; y avoir mis son nez; *to have put one's finger on it,* y avoir mis le doigt. ‖ U. S. POP. Mouchard, indicateur *m.* ‖ **Finger-alphabet,** n. Alphabet (*m.*) des sourds-muets. ‖ **Finger-biscuit,** n. CULIN. Langue-de-chat ƒ. ‖ **Finger-bowl,** n. Rince-doigts *m.* ‖ **Finger-breadth,** n. Doigt *m.* (dimension). ‖ **Finger-plate,** n. Plaque de propreté ƒ. (on a door). ‖ **Finger-post,** n. Poteau indicateur *m.* ‖ **Finger-print,** n. JUR. Empreinte digitale ƒ. ‖ **Finger-stall,** n. MED. Doigtier *m.* ‖ **Finger-touch** (or) **-work,** n. TECHN. Doigté *m.*
— v. tr. Manier, toucher du doigt. ‖ MUS. Toucher de (an instrument); indiquer le doigté de (a passage). ‖ FAM. Toucher, palper (money).

fingering [-riŋ] n. Maniement *m.* ‖ MUS. Doigté *m.* ‖ FAM. Palpage *m.*

fingering n. Laine fine à tricoter ƒ. (wool).

fingerling [-liŋ] n. ZOOL. Saumoneau *m.* ‖ U. S. Petit poisson *m.*

fingertip [-tip] n. Bout du doigt *m.; to the, one's fingertips,* jusqu'au bout des doigts; *to have at one's fingertips,* connaître sur le bout des doigts.

finial ['fainiəl] n. ARCHIT. Finial *m.*

finical ['finikəl], **finicky** [-i] adj. Précieux (affected); difficile (fastidious); vétilleux (particular).

finicality [fini'kæliti] n. Préciosité ƒ. ‖ Exigence ƒ.

finicky ['finiki] adj. FAM. Pointilleux, méticuleux (person); soigné, fignolé (work).

finis ['fainis] n. Fin ƒ. (See END.)

finish ['finiʃ] v. tr. Finir, achever, terminer. (See END.) ‖ Parachever, parfaire (to polish); *to finish off,* mener à bonne fin. ‖ TECHN. Usiner. ‖ FAM. *To finish off,* achever, finir (to kill).
— v. intr. Se finir, s'achever, se terminer (to be finished). ‖ Finir, achever; *have you finished?,* terminé? (on the phone).
— n. Fin ƒ. (end). ‖ Fini *m.* (polish). ‖ SPORTS. Mise à mort ƒ. (in hunting); arrivée ƒ. (of a race). ‖ FIG. Raffinement *m.* (in manners). ‖ FAM. *To be in at the finish,* être là pour la finale.

finisher [-ə*] n. Coup (*m.*) de grâce. ‖ TECHN. Finisseur *m.*

finishing [-iŋ] adj. Qui finit; *finishing touch,* coup de fion; *finishing stroke,* coup de grâce.
— n. Finissage *m.*

finite ['fainait] adj. PHILOS., MATH., GRAMM. Fini.

fink [fiŋk] n. U. S. POP. Jaune *s.* (strikebreaker). ‖ Ordure ƒ., fumier, salaud *m.* (bastard). ‖ Indic *m.,* mouchard *s.* (informer). ‖ Détective *m.*

Finland ['finlənd] n. GEOGR. Finlande ƒ.

Finn [fin] n. GEOGR. Finlandais, Finnois *s.*

finnan-haddock ['finnən-'hædək] n. CULIN. Haddock fumé *m.*

finned [find] adj. ZOOL. A nageoires.

Finnic ['finik] adj. Finnois (language).

Finnish [-iʃ] adj., n. Finnois *s.*

finny ['fini] adj. En forme de nageoire (fin-like). Poissonneux (ocean). ‖ ZOOL. A nageoires.

fiord [fjɔːd] n. See FJORD.

fir [fə:*] n. BOT. Sapin *m.; Scotch fir,* pin sylvestre. ‖ **Fir-cone,** n. BOT. Pomme (ƒ.) de pin. ‖ **Fir-wood,** n. BOT. Sapinière ƒ.

fire ['faiə*] n. Feu *m.; to catch fire,* prendre feu; *to set fire to,* mettre le feu à. ‖ Incendie *m.; victim of a fire,* sinistré. ‖ Lueur fulgurante ƒ.; flamboiement *m.* (of lightning). ‖ Coup de feu *m.; to hang fire,* faire long feu; *to miss fire,* rater. ‖ MILIT. Feu *m.; rapid fire,* tir rapide; *to open fire,* ouvrir le feu. ‖ AUTOM. Allumage *m.* ‖ FIG. Feu roulant *m.* (of criticism); flamme ƒ. (of patriotism, zeal); *with fire,* avec feu. ‖ LOC. *He won't set the Thames on fire,* il n'a pas inventé le fil à couper le beurre (or) la poudre; *to go through fire and water for,* se jeter au feu pour; *to set the world on fire,* faire parler de soi. ‖ **Fire-alarm,** n. Avertisseur d'incendie *m.* ‖ **Fire-arm,** n. Arme (ƒ.) à feu. ‖ **Fire-ball,** n. Globe de feu *m.;* MILIT. Grenade incendiaire ƒ.; U. S. Champignon *m.* (nuclear). ‖ **Fire-box,** n. CH. DE F. Foyer *m.* ‖ **Fire-brand,** n. Tison *m.;* FAM. Brandon (*m.*) de discorde. ‖ **Fire-brick,** n. Brique réfractaire ƒ. ‖ **Fire-brigade,** U. S. **Fire-department,** n. Sapeurs-pompiers *m. pl.* ‖ **Fire-clay,** n. Terre réfractaire ƒ. ‖ **Fire-damp,** n. Grisou *m.* ‖ **Fire-dog,** n. Chenet, landier *m.* ‖ **Fire-eater,** n. Avaleur de feu *m.;* FAM. Matamore *m.* ‖ **Fire-engine,** n. Pompe (ƒ.) à incendie. ‖ **Fire-escape,** n. Echelle (ƒ.) de sauvetage; escalier de secours *m.* ‖ **Fire-extinguisher,** n. Extincteur *m.* ‖ **Fire-fly,** n. ZOOL. Luciole ƒ. ‖ **Fire-guard,** n. Pare-feu, pare-étincelles *m.* ‖ **Fire-insurance,** n. Assurance (ƒ.) contre l'incendie. ‖ **Fire-irons,** n. pl. Garniture (ƒ.) de foyer. ‖ **Fire-lighter,** n. Allume-feu *m.* ‖ **Fire-plug,** n. Bouche (ƒ.) d'incendie. ‖ **Fire-policy,** n. Police d'assurance (ƒ.) contre l'incendie. ‖ **Fire-power,** n. MILIT. Puissance (ƒ.) de feu. ‖ **Fire-raiser,** n. Incendiaire *s.* ‖ **Fire-raising,** n. Incendie volontaire *m.* ‖ **Fire-station,** n. Caserne (ƒ.) de pompiers. ‖ **Fire-trap,** n. Piège (*m.*) en cas d'incendie. ‖ **Firewater,** n. U. S. FAM. Gnôle ƒ.
— v. tr. Mettre le feu à (a house); faire exploser (a mine). ‖ Sécher au feu (to dry). ‖ Chauffer (an oven). ‖ ARTS. Cuire (pottery). ‖ MED. Cautériser. ‖ MILIT. Tirer (a bullet); tirer un coup de, décharger (a gun); envoyer, lancer (a rocket); *to be fired on,* essuyer des coups de feu; *to fire one's shot,* faire le coup de feu. ‖ FIG. Enflammer. ‖ FAM. Lancer (a remark); balancer, expédier, saquer (s.o.). ‖ **To fire off,** MILIT. Tirer; FAM. Décocher.
— v. intr. Prendre feu. ‖ Exploser. ‖ AUTOM., TECHN. Tourner, marcher. ‖ MILIT. Partir (shot). ‖ ARTS. Réagir à la cuisson (pottery). ‖ FIG. S'enflammer. ‖ **To fire up,** FAM. S'emporter, s'emballer, monter.

firebug [-bʌg] n. U. S. FAM. Boute-feu, incendiaire, pyromane *s.*

firecracker [-krækə*] n. FAM. Pétard *m.*

firelock [-lɔk] n. Fusil (*m.*) à pierre.

fireman [-mən] n. (pl. **firemen**) n. Pompier *m.* ‖ CH. DE F. Chauffeur *m.*

fireplace [-pleis] n. Âtre *m.;* cheminée ƒ.

fireproof [-pruːf] adj. Calorifuge, ignifuge, incombustible, ininflammable. ‖ CULIN. Allant au four.
— v. tr. Ignifuger.

fireside [-said] n. Coin du feu *m.;* cheminée ƒ.; *fireside chair,* chauffeuse.

firewood [-wud] n. Bois de chauffage *m.*

firework [-wə:k] n. Pièce (ƒ.) d'artifice. ‖ Pl. Feu d'artifice *m.* ‖ FAM. Coups (*m. pl.*) de feu; rixe ƒ.

firing ['faiəriŋ] n. Chauffe ƒ. (of an oven); cuisson ƒ. (of pottery). ‖ Combustible *m.* (fuel). ‖ MILIT. Feu, tir *m.; firing squad,* peloton d'exécution. ‖ **Firing-line,** n. MILIT., FIG. Première ligne ƒ., front *m.*

firkin ['fə:kin] n. Tonnelet *m.* (for butter); caque ƒ. (for fish). ‖ Quartaut *m.* (40 litres).

firm [fə:m] n. Comm. Firme, maison *f.*
firm adj. Ferme, solide, dur. ‖ Ferme, fixe, stable. ‖ Ferme, résolu, déterminé. ‖ Fin. Ferme.
— adv. Fermement, ferme ; *to stand firm,* tenir bon.
— v. tr. Affermir.
— v. intr. S'affermir.
firmament ['fə:məmənt] n. Firmament *m.*
firmly ['fə:mli] adv. Fermement.
firmness [-nis] n. Fermeté, dureté *f.* ‖ Fermeté, détermination *f.* ‖ Fin. Fermeté *f.*
first [fə:st] adj. Premier (in rank, in a series) ; *first floor,* premier étage, U. S. rez-de-chaussée. ‖ Unième ; *twenty-first,* vingt et unième. ‖ Theatr. *First night,* première. ‖ Med. *First aid,* soins d'urgence. ‖ Loc. *First name,* prénom ; *in the first place,* en premier lieu ; *of the first water,* de la plus belle eau. ‖ **First-born,** adj. Premier-né. ‖ **First-class,** adj. Ch. de f. De première classe ; Fam. De premier ordre. ‖ **First-fruits,** n. pl. Agric. Primeurs *f. pl.;* Fig. Prémices *f. pl.* ‖ **First-hand,** adj. De première main. ‖ **First-nighter,** n. Theatr. Habitué (*s.*) des premières. ‖ **First-rate,** adj. De premier ordre.
— adv. Premièrement, d'abord, en premier lieu, pour commencer ; *first of all, first and foremost,* avant tout ; *first and last,* en tout et pour tout ; U. S. *first off,* de prime abord. ‖ Pour la première fois ; *when I saw you first,* quand je vous ai vu pour la première fois. ‖ Ch. de f. En première. ‖ Fam. Plutôt (preferably) ; *he'd die first,* il aimerait mieux mourir.
— n. Premier *s.* (person, thing). ‖ Commencement, début *m.; at first,* d'abord ; *from the very first,* dès le début. ‖ Mention (*f.*) très bien (in an exam). ‖ Comm. Pl. Marchandises (*f. pl.*) de tout premier choix. ‖ U. S. Début *m.* (of the month, year).
firstly [-li] adv. Premièrement.
firth [fə:θ] n. Geogr. Estuaire *m.*
fiscal ['fiskəl] adj. Fin. Fiscal (charge) ; budgétaire (year). ‖ Jur. *Procurator fiscal,* procureur général (in Scotland).
fish [fiʃ] n. Zool., Astron. Poisson *m.* ‖ Culin. *Fish ball,* boulette de poisson. ‖ Fam. Type *m.; poor fish,* gringalet ; *queer fish,* drôle de paroissien (or) de pierrot. ‖ Loc. *To have other fish to fry,* avoir d'autres chiens à fouetter. ‖ **Fish-bone,** n. Arête *f.* ‖ **Fish-bowl,** n. Bocal (*m.*) à poissons rouges. ‖ **Fish-breeding,** n. Pisciculture *f.* ‖ **Fish-cake,** n. Culin. Croquette (*f.*) de poisson. ‖ **Fish-eye,** n. Fish-eye *m.* (lens). ‖ Fam. Poissarde *f.* ‖ **Fish-farm,** n. Etang piscicole *m.* ‖ **Fish-farming,** n. Pisciculture *f.* ‖ **Fish-finger,** n. Culin. Bâtonnet de poisson *m.* ‖ **Fish-glue,** n. Colle (*f.*) de poisson. ‖ **Fish-hold,** n. Naut. Parc à poisson *m.* ‖ **Fish-hook,** n. Hameçon *m.;* Naut. Traversière *f.* ‖ **Fish-joint,** n. Ch. de f. Eclissage *m.* ‖ **Fish-kettle,** n. Culin. Poissonnière *f.* ‖ **Fish-plate,** n. Ch. de f. Eclisse *f.* ‖ **Fish-pond,** n. Vivier *m.* ‖ **Fish-slice,** n. Culin. Spatule *f.* ‖ **Fish story,** n. U.S. Fam. Histoire (*f.*) à dormir debout. ‖ **Fish-worm,** n. Asticot *m.*
— N. B. Deux pluriels : *fish, fishes.*
— v. intr. Pêcher ; *to fish for,* pêcher (a fish). ‖ Fam. *To fish for compliments,* quêter les compliments.
— v. tr. Pêcher (fish, pearls, a river) ; *to fish out* (or) *up,* repêcher. ‖ Fam. *To fish secrets out of s.o.,* tirer les vers du nez à qqn.
fish v. tr. Naut. Jumeler. ‖ Ch. de f. Eclisser.
fisherman [-əmən] (pl. **fishermen**) n. Pêcheur *m.*
fisherwoman [-əwumən] (pl. **fisherwomen**) n. Pêcheuse *f.*
fishery [-əri] n. Pêcherie *f.*
fishing [-iŋ] n. Pêche *f.* ‖ **Fishing-boat,** n. Naut. Bateau-pêcheur *m.* ‖ **Fishing-gear,** n. Attirail (*m.*) de pêche. ‖ **Fishing-rod,** n. Canne à pêche *f.*

fishmonger [-mʌngə*] n. Comm. Marchand (*m.*) de poisson.
fishnet [-net] adj. A résilles (stocking).
fishwife [-waif] (pl. **fishwives** [-waivz]) n. Comm. Marchande (*f.*) de poisson. ‖ Fam. Poissarde, harengère *f.*
fishy [-i] adj. De poisson (odour, taste) ; poissonneux (river). ‖ Vitreux (eye, stare). ‖ Fam. Louche ; *it looks fishy to me,* ça ne me dit rien qui vaille, il y a du tripotage là-dedans.
fissile ['fisail] adj. Fissile.
fission ['fiʃən] n. Phys. Fission, désintégration *f.*
— v. tr. Phys. Fissionner.
— v. intr. Phys. Se fissionner.
fissionable [-əbḷ] adj. Phys. Fissible, fissile.
fissure ['fiʃə*] n. Fissure *f.* (See cranny.)
— v. tr. Fissurer.
— v. intr. Se fissurer.
fist [fist] n. Med. Poing *m.* ‖ Fam. Cuillère, pince *f.* (hand) ; écriture *f.* (handwriting).
— v. tr. Cogner du poing. ‖ Naut. Empoigner (an oar).
fistic ['fistik] adj. Sports, Fam. De la boxe.
fisticuffs ['fistikʌfs] n. pl. Empoignade *f.; * rixe (*f.*) à coups de poing.
fistula ['fistjulə] n. Med. Fistule *f.*
fistular [-ə*] adj. Med. Fistulaire.
fistulous [-əs] adj. Med. Fistuleux.
fit [fit] n. Med., Fig. Accès *m.;* attaque, crise *f.* ‖ Loc. *By fits and starts,* par à-coups.
fit adj. Adéquat, approprié, convenable ; *a dinner fit for a king,* un dîner de roi. ‖ Convenable, à propos, juste ; *he thinks fit to,* il juge bon de. ‖ Convenable, acceptable ; *fit to eat,* mangeable ; *fit for company,* présentable. ‖ Apte, propre (*for,* à) ; capable, à même (*for,* de) ; *he is not fit for his job,* il n'est pas digne de sa tâche. ‖ Disposé, prêt ; *fit to drop,* prêt à tomber de fatigue. ‖ Med. Dispos. ‖ Sports. En forme.
— v. tr. S'ajuster à ; *the coat fits him like a glove,* le manteau lui va comme un gant (or) le moule ; *fitted carpet,* tapis cloué ; *to fit too tight,* être trop juste. ‖ Ajuster, adapter (*into,* dans). ‖ Préparer, disposer (*for,* à) [s.o.] ; arranger, disposer (*for,* pour) [sth.]. ‖ Equiper, garnir, munir (*with,* de). ‖ Fig. S'adapter, s'accorder (*with,* avec). ‖ **To fit in,** emboîter ; Fig. Faire concorder (*with,* avec). ‖ **To fit on,** essayer (clothes). ‖ **To fit out,** aménager (a house) ; Techn. Equiper ; Naut. Armer. ‖ **To fit up,** aménager (a house) ; Techn. Monter, appareiller ; Autom. Habiller.
— v. intr. S'emboîter, s'encastrer (*in,* dans) ; s'ajuster, s'adapter (*on,* sur). ‖ Aller bien (clothes). ‖ Ch. de f. Correspondre. ‖ **To fit in,** Techn. S'ajuster, s'emboîter ; Fig. S'accorder, concorder (*with,* avec).
— n. Ajustement *m.* ‖ Façon *f.* (of clothes). ‖ **Fit-out,** n. Equipement *m.*
fitch [fitʃ] n. U. S. Sconse *m.* (fur).
fitchet ['fitʃit], **fitchew** ['fitʃu:] n. Zool. Putois *m.*
fitful ['fitful] adj. Changeant, capricieux (humour, light, person). ‖ Med. Quinteux (cough).
fitfully [-i] adv. Par à-coups (or) accès.
fitly [fitli] adv. Convenablement (suitably). ‖ A propos (at the right time).
fitness [-nis] n. Convenance, justesse *f.;* à-propos *m.* ‖ Aptitude *f.* ‖ Med., Sports. Bonne forme *f.*
fitter [-ə*] n. Essayeur *s.* (in tailoring). ‖ Techn. Monteur, ajusteur *s.*
fitting [-iŋ] n. Ajustage *m.* ‖ Equipement *m.* (of a house) ; pl. aménagements *m. pl.* ‖ Techn. Montage *m.* ‖ **Fitting-out,** n. Equipement *m.* ‖ **Fitting-shop,** n. Techn. Atelier d'ajustage *m.* ‖ **Fitting-up,** n. Installation *f.*
— adj. Ajusté (garment). ‖ Approprié, fait à propos, convenable, juste.

five [faiv] adj., n. Cinq *adj., m. invar.* ‖ **Five-year plan,** n. Plan quinquennal *m.*

fivefold [-fould] adj. Quintuple; *to increase fivefold,* quintupler.

fiver [-ə*] n. FAM. Billet (*m.*) de cinq livres (or) U. S. de cinq dollars.

fives [-z] n. Balle (*f.*) au mur (game).

fix [fiks] v. tr. Fixer (lit. and fig.). ‖ FAM. Pincer; *he'll fix him!,* il le pincera au demi-cercle! ‖ U. S. FAM. Graisser la patte à. ‖ U. S. FAM. Réparer; *to fix up,* arranger, mettre en règle; *to fix up one's face,* se maquiller.
— v. intr. Se fixer. ‖ Fixer son choix (on, sur). ‖ U. S. FAM. *Breakfast is fixed,* le petit déjeuner est prêt; *everyone is well fixed,* tout le monde a ce qu'il lui faut.
— n. FAM. Mauvaise passe *f.; in a fix,* dans le pétrin. ‖ U. S. FAM. Pot-de-vin *m.*

fixation [fik'seiʃən] n. Fixation *f.*

fixative ['fiksətiv] adj., n. Fixatif.

fixature [-tʃə*] n. Fixatif *m.*

fixed [fikst] adj. Fixe. ‖ FIN. Immobilisé (capital); à terme (deposit); *fixed charges,* frais généraux. ‖ U. S. FAM. *Well fixed,* comme un coq en pâte. ‖ **Fixed-head,** adj. AUTOM. Non décapotable.

fixedly [-idli] adv. Fixement.

fixedness [-nis] n. Fixité *f.*

fixer [-ə*] n. Fixateur *m.* (in photography). ‖ U. S. FAM. Graisseur (*m.*) de patte. ‖ U. S. FAM. Réparateur *m.* (trouble-shooter).

fixing [-iŋ] n. Fixation *f.* ‖ Fixage *m.* (in photography). ‖ U. S. Pl. CULIN., FAM. Garniture *f.* ‖ TECHN. Pl. Accessoires *m. pl.*

fixity [-iti] n. Fixité *f.*

fixture [-tʃə*] n. Objet fixe *m.* ‖ JUR. Meuble fixe *m.; inventory of fixtures,* état des lieux; *landlord's fixtures,* immeubles par destination. ‖ SPORTS. Epreuve prévue *f.* ‖ FAM. *She is a fixture,* elle fait partie des meubles.

fizz [fiz] n. Pétillement; pschitt *m.* (fam.). ‖ FAM. Boisson gazeuse *f.;* champagne *m.* ‖ **Fizz-water,** n. Eau gazeuse *f.*
— v. intr. Pétiller, fuser.

fizzle [-l] v. intr. Fuser, pétiller. ‖ **To fizzle out,** faire fiasco, finir en queue de poisson; foirer (fam.).
— n. Pétillement *m.* (fizz). ‖ FAM. Fiasco *m.*

fizzy [-i] adj. Pétillant, gazeux.

fjord [fjɔːd] n. Fjord *m.*

flab [flæb] n. FAM. Graisse *f.,* embonpoint *m.*

flabbergasted ['flæbəgɑːstid] adj. Eberlué, ébahi, ébaubi; épaté, époustouflé, baba (fam.).

flabbiness ['flæbinis] n. Avachissement *m.;* mollesse *f.*

flabby [-i] adj. Avachi, flasque; désossé (fam.).

flabellate [flæ'beileit] adj. BOT. Flabellé.

flaccid ['flæksid] adj. Flasque.

flaccidity [flæk'siditi] n. Flaccidité *f.*

flag [flæg] n. MILIT. Drapeau *m.; flag of truce,* drapeau parlementaire; *white flag bearer,* parlementaire. ‖ NAUT. Pavillon *m.* ‖ ZOOL. Queue *f.* (of a setter). ‖ **Flag-captain,** n. NAUT. Capitaine de pavillon *m.* ‖ **Flag-lieutenant,** n. NAUT. Aide de camp de l'amiral *m.* ‖ **Flag-pole,** n. Mât *m.* ‖ **Flag station** (or) **stop,** n. U.S. CH. DE F. Arrêt facultatif *m.* ‖ **Flag-waving,** adj. FAM. Cocardier; n. MILIT. Signalisation *f.;* FAM. Chauvinisme *m.*
— v. tr. (1). Pavoiser (a house). ‖ NAUT. Pavoiser (a boat); transmettre par signaux (a message). ‖ CH. DE F. Arrêter. ‖ U. S. Arrêter, héler (a taxi); accoster (a woman).

flag v. intr. (1). Pendre mollement. ‖ S'affaisser, devenir flasque. ‖ FIG. Faiblir (attention, courage, interest); défaillir (strength); fléchir (zeal).

flag n. Dalle *f.;* pl. dallage *m.*

flag n. BOT. Iris *m.*

flag n. ZOOL. Rémige *f.* (feather).

flagellate ['flædʒeleit] v. tr. Flageller.
— n., adj. BOT., ZOOL. Flagellé *m., adj.*

flagellation [ˌflædʒe'leiʃən] n. Flagellation *f.*

flageolet [flædʒo'let] n. MUS., BOT. Flageolet *m.*

flagitious [flæ'dʒiʃəs] adj. Abject, infâme.

flagitiousness [-nis] n. Abjection *f.*

flagon ['flægən] n. Buire *f.* (for wine). ‖ COMM. Magnum *m.* (bottle). ‖ ECCLES. Burette *f.*

flagrant ['fleigrənt] adj. Flagrant. (See GLARING.) ‖ Enorme. (See OUTRAGEOUS.)

flagrantly [-li] adv. D'une manière flagrante.

flagship ['flægʃip] n. NAUT. Vaisseau amiral *m.*

flagstaff [-stɑːf] n. MILIT. Hampe (*f.*) de drapeau. ‖ NAUT. Mât de pavillon *m.*

flagstone [-stoun] n. Dalle *f.*

flail [fleil] n. AGRIC. Fléau *m.*
— v. tr. AGRIC. Battre au fléau.

flair [flɛə*] n. Flair *m.; to have a flair for a bargain,* avoir le nez creux, flairer l'occasion.

flak [flæk] n. MILIT. Tir (*m.*) de D.C.A. ‖ FIG. Tir (*m.*) nourri de critiques, attaque virulente *f.*

flake [fleik] n. Flocon *m.* (de neige); duvet *m.* (of tree). ‖ Flammèche *f.* (of fire); écaille *f.;* éclat *m.* (of mica, soap). ‖ CULIN. Coquille *f.* (of butter); flocon *m.* (of cereals); feuilleté *f.* (of pastry). ‖ BOT. Œillet panaché *m.*
— v. tr. Ecailler (painting). ‖ Couvrir de flocons.
— v. intr. **To flake away** (or) **off,** s'écailler (painting); tomber en flocons (snow).

flake n. Claie *f.* (for fish); *fruit flake,* fruitier. ‖ NAUT. Plate-forme *f.*

flaky [-i] adj. Floconneux. ‖ Ecailleux. ‖ CULIN. Feuilleté.

flamboyant [flæm'bɔiənt] adj. Flamboyant.

flame [fleim] n. Flamme *f.; to commit to the flames,* condamner au feu. ‖ Eclat *m.* (of a colour); feu *m.* (of a diamond). ‖ FAM. Passion *f.* (love); flamme, ardeur *f.* (zeal); *an old flame of his,* une de ses anciennes. ‖ **Flame-proof,** adj. Ininflammable, ignifugé, incombustible. ‖ **Flame-thrower,** n. MILIT. Lance-flammes *m. invar.*
— v. tr. Signaler par des feux. ‖ MED. Flamber. ‖
— v. intr. Flamber (fire, house). ‖ Briller, étinceler (diamond). ‖ FIG. S'enflammer. ‖ **To flame up,** s'enflammer, prendre feu (lit. and fig.).

flamen ['fleimen] n. † Flamine *m.*

flamenco [flə'meŋkou] (pl. **flamencos** [-z]) n. Flamenco *m.*

flaming ['fleimiŋ] adj. Flambant, en feu, en flammes (burning). ‖ Flamboyant, rutilant (red). ‖ FIG. Ardent, enflammé. ‖ FAM. Délirant (enthusiasm).

flamingo [flə'miŋgou] n. ZOOL. Flamant *m.*

flammable ['flæməbl] adj. Inflammable.

flan [flæn] n. CULIN. Tarte *f.* ‖ TECHN. Flan *m.*

Flanders ['flɑːndəz] n. GEOGR. Flandre *f.*

flange [flændʒ] n. ARCHIT. Aile *f.* (of beam). ‖ TECHN. Embase *f.* (of a cylinder); collet *m.* (of a pipe); mâchoire *f.* (of a pulley); boudin *m.* (of a wheel); *flange-cooled engine,* moteur à ailettes. ‖ CH. DE F. Patin *m.* (of a rail). ‖ AUTOM. Joue *f.* (of wing).
— v. tr. Border.

flank [flæŋk] n. MED., GEOGR. Flanc *m.* ‖ MILIT. Flanc *m.* ‖ **Flank-guard,** n. MILIT. Flanc-garde *m.*
— v. tr. Flanquer. ‖ MILIT. Prendre de flanc.

flanker [-ə*] n. MILIT. Flanqueur *m.* (man); flanc *m.* (work).

flanking [-iŋ] adj. MILIT. De flanc, tournant (movement).

flannel ['flænl] n. Gant (*m.*) de toilette (facecloth). ‖ Flanelle *f.* (cloth). ‖ Pl. Pantalon (*m.*) de flanelle (trousers). ‖ FAM. Baratin *m.* (bunkum); lèche, pommade *f.* (flattery); vantardise *f.* (bragging).
— v. tr. (1) Laver, essuyer, frotter. ‖ FAM. Faire de la lèche à, passer de la pommade à (to flatter).

flannelette [flænl'et] n. Pilou *m.*; flanelle (*f.*) de coton.

flap [flæp] n. Tape *f.* (slap). ‖ Claquement *m.* (of a flag); coup *m.* (of wing). ‖ Couvre-nuque *m.* (of cap). ‖ Pan *m.* (of coat); bord *m.* (of hat); patte *f.* (of pocket). ‖ Trappe *f.* (of cellar); battant *m.* (of a table). ‖ Rabat *m.* (of an envelope); rebras *m.* (of a book-jacket). ‖ AVIAT. Volet, aileron *m.* ‖ MED. Lobe *m.* (of ear); lambeau *m.* (of flesh). ‖ FAM. Affolement *m.; to get in a flap*, s'affoler, prendre les choses au tragique. ‖ **Flap-eared**, adj. ZOOL. Aux oreilles pendantes. ‖ **Flap-seat**, n. AUTOM. Strapontin *m.* ‖ **Flap-valve**, n. TECHN. Clapet *m.*
— v. tr. (1). Taper, frapper (to slap). ‖ Battre; *to flap one's arms about*, battre des bras.
— v. intr. Claquer (flag, sails); battre (shutter, wings). ‖ Pendre (to hang down).

flapdoodle [-'du:dl] n. Baliverne *f.*, boniment *m.*

flapjack ['flæpdʒæk] n. U. S. CULIN. Grande crêpe *f.*

flapper [-ə*] n. Tapette *f.* (fly-swatter). ‖ ZOOL. Halbran *m.* (bird); large nageoire *f.* (fin); queue (*f.*) de crustacé (tail). ‖ FAM. Gamine *f.* (girl); battoir *m.* (hand).

flare [flɛə*] v. intr. Briller d'une lumière vive mais irrégulière, jeter de brusques éclats. ‖ S'évaser, s'élargir (skirt). ‖ FIG. Flamboyer. ‖ **To flare up**, flamboyer ; MILIT. Se rallumer (fighting) ; FIG. S'emporter, jeter feu et flamme.
— v. tr. Evaser, élargir.
— n. Eclat vif, mais irrégulier *m.; flamme vacillante *f.* ‖ Pavillon *m.* (of a funnel); évasement *m.* (of a skirt). ‖ AVIAT. *Landing flare*, feu d'atterrissage. ‖ MILIT. Feu signalisateur, artifice éclairant *m.* ‖ **Flare-path**, n. AVIAT. Piste balisée *f.* ‖ **Flare-up**, n. Flambée *f.* (lit. and fig.).

flaring [-riŋ] adj. Vacillant, brillant d'un éclat irrégulier. ‖ Evasé (skirt). ‖ FIG. Eclatant.

flash [flæʃ] n. Eclat brusque, éclair *m.; flash of lightning*, éclair. ‖ Instant *m.; in a flash*, dans un éclair, en une seconde. ‖ NAUT. Chasse d'eau *f.* ‖ CINEM. Plan éclair *m.* ‖ FIG. Eclair *m.* (of genius, pity); lueur *f.* (of hope); trait *m.* (of wit). ‖ FAM. Tape-à-l'œil *m.* (ostentation); langue verte *f.* (slang). ‖ U. S. FAM. Nouvelle éclair *f.* ‖ LOC. *Flash in the pan*, feu de paille. ‖ **Flash-back**, n. Retour (*m.*) de flamme ; CINEM. retour en arrière *m.; scène rétrospective *f.; flash-back technique*, technique de la rétrospective. ‖ **Flash bulb**, n. Flash *m.*, ampoule (*f.*) de flash. ‖ **Flash-lamp**, n. ELECTR. Lampe de poche *f.* ‖ **Flash-light**, n. Flash, éclair de magnésium *m.*; NAUT., AVIAT. Feu (*m.*) à éclats ; U. S. Torche électrique. ‖ **Flash-point**, n. CHIM. Point (*m.*) de flamme (or) d'éclair ; FIG. Point critique *m.*
— v. intr. Jeter des éclairs, jeter un éclat vif et bref. ‖ Luire comme un éclair ; *to flash with anger*, étinceler de colère (eyes). ‖ Aller comme un éclair ; *to flash by*, passer en trombe ; *to flash through s.o.'s mind*, fulgurer dans l'esprit de qqn. ‖ NAUT. Se précipiter (waves). ‖ **To flash up**, FAM. S'emballer, jeter son feu. (See FLARE.)
— v. tr. Faire étinceler (a diamond) ; brandir (a sword). ‖ Projeter, darder ; *to flash fire*, lancer des éclairs. ‖ Lancer (messages, news). ‖ TECHN. Plaquer (in glass-making). ‖ TECHN. Donner une chasse à (a river). ‖ CINEM. Projeter. ‖ FAM. Faire miroiter (money) ; décocher (a smile).
— adj. Voyant, tapageur (clothes) ; épateur (person). ‖ FIN. Faux (money). ‖ FAM. *Flash lingo*, langue verte.

flasher [-ə*] n. Clignotant *m.* ‖ POP. Exhibitionniste *m.*

flashy [-i] adj. Voyant, tapageur (clothes) ; vêtu d'une manière voyante (person) ; clinquant (style).

flask [flɑ:sk] n. Flacon *m.; fiasque *f.* (bottle) ; *drinking flask*, gourde. ‖ CHIM. Ballon *m.*

flasket [-it] n. Fiole *f.* (bottle). ‖ Corbeille *f.* (basket).

flat [flæt] adj. Plat (land, roof, surface). ‖ Aplati (curve) ; épaté (nose) ; rabattu (seam). ‖ Etalé, à plat (body, person) ; *to fall flat on one's face*, tomber à plat ventre ; *to lay s.o. flat*, aplatir qqn. ‖ CULIN. Plat, fade, insipide (drink). ‖ FIN. Plat, inactif (market) ; uniforme (rate). ‖ ARTS. *Flat patch*, embu. ‖ MUS. Bémol (note) ; sourd (sound) ; *to sing flat*, chanter faux (or) au-dessous du ton. ‖ GRAMM. Sans désinence (or) déterminatif. ‖ SPORTS. Plat (race). ‖ AUTOM. A plat, crevé, dégonflé (tyre). ‖ NAUT. Plat (calm). ‖ FIG. Net, catégorique, formel (denial, refusal) ; plat, monotone, sans intérêt (existence, speech, style). ‖ U. S. FAM. Décavé (penniless). ‖ **Flat-boat**, n. NAUT. Plate *f.* ‖ **Flat-car**, n. U. S. CH. DE F. Plate-forme *f.* ‖ **Flat-coated**, adj. ZOOL. A poils ras (dog). ‖ **Flat-fish**, n. ZOOL. Poisson plat, pleuronecte *m.* ‖ **Flat-footed**, adj. Aux pieds plats. ‖ **Flat-iron**, n. Fer (*m.*) à repasser. ‖ **Flat-nosed**, adj. Camard. ‖ **Flat-tire**, n. U. S. FAM. Rabat-joie *m.* ‖ **Flat-top**, n. U. S. FAM. Porte-avions *m.*
— adv. A plat ; *to fall flat*, tomber à plat. ‖ MUS. Faux. ‖ FIG. Catégoriquement. ‖ **Flat-broke**, adj. U. S. FAM. A la côte, fauché.
— n. Surface plane *f.* ‖ Plat *m.* (of hand, sword). ‖ Plaine *f.; plateau *m.* (land) ; marais *m.* (marsh). ‖ Appartement *m.* (in a house). ‖ NAUT. Plate *f.* (boat) ; bas-fonds *m.* (shallow). ‖ THEATR. Ferme *f.* ‖ MUS. Bémol *m.* ‖ AUTOM. Crevaison *f.*
— v. tr. (1). Aplatir.

flatfoot [-fut] n. U. S. FAM. Flic *m.*

flatlet [-lit] n. Studio (*m.*) avec cuisine et salle d'eau ; petit logement *m.*

flatly [-li] adv. A plat. ‖ FIG. Catégoriquement ; platement.

flatness [-nis] n. Aplatissement *m.; platitude *f.* ‖ MUS. Baisse (*f.*) de ton. ‖ ARTS. Embu *m.* ‖ CULIN. Fadeur *f.* ‖ FIG. Platitude, monotonie *f.*

flatten [-n] v. tr. Aplatir. ‖ Etaler. ‖ MUS. Bémoliser. ‖ CULIN., FIG. Affadir. ‖ ARCHIT. *Flattened arch*, arc surbaissé. ‖ FAM. Mettre à plat, dégonfler.
— v. intr. S'aplatir ; s'étaler. ‖ CULIN., FIG. S'affadir. ‖ FAM. Se dégonfler, perdre pied. ‖ **To flatten out**, AVIAT. Redresser ; *flattening-out*, arrondi.

flatter ['flætə*] v. tr. Flatter, flagorner, encenser (to overpraise). ‖ Flatter de vains espoirs ; endormir (fam.). ‖ Flatter (the ear, eye, a portrait). ‖ *To flatter oneself*, se flatter, se vanter (on, de) [cleverness] ; se flatter, se bercer (with, de) [hopes].

flatterer [-rə*] n. Flatteur *s.*

flattering [-riŋ] adj. Flatteur.

flatteringly [-riŋli] adv. Flatteusement.

flattery [-ri] n. Flatterie *f.*

flattish ['flætiʃ] adj. Un peu aplati.

flatulence ['flætjuləns] n. MED. Flatulence *f.* ‖ FIG. Prétention *f.* (of s.o.); boursouflure *f.* (of style).

flatulent [-ənt] adj. MED. Flatulent. ‖ FIG. Gonflé (person) ; ampoulé (style).

flatus ['fleitəs] n. MED. Flatuosité *f.* ‖ FIG. Souffle *m.*
— N. B. Deux pluriels : *flatuses, flatus* ; jamais *flati*.

flatways ['flætweiz] adv. A plat.

flaunt [flɔ:nt] v. intr. Flotter, se balancer (flag) ; s'ériger (plume). ‖ FIG. Se pavaner, se rengorger, parader.
— v. tr. Faire flotter. ‖ FIG. Afficher (one's opinions) ; étaler, faire parade de (one's wealth).
— n. FIG. Etalage *m.; ostentation *f.*

flaunting [-iŋ] adj. Flottant (flag). ‖ FIG. Prétentieux, tapageur, insolent.

flautist ['flɔ:tist] n. MUS. Flûtiste *s.*

flavescent [flə'vesnt] adj. BOT. Flavescent.

flavo(u)r [-və*] n. CULIN. Saveur *f.* (taste) ; fumet

m. (of meat); bouquet, arôme *m.* (of wine). ‖ FIG.
Parfum *m.* (of adventure).
— v. tr. CULIN. Assaisonner, relever (*with*, de)
[garlic, vinegar]; parfumer (*with*, de) [rhum]. ‖
FIG. Assaisonner.
flavorous ['fleivərəs] adj. CULIN. Savoureux
(meat); parfumé (wine).
flavouring [-vəriŋ] n. CULIN. Parfum *n.* (lemon,
rhum); assaisonnement, condiment *m.* (vinegar).
flavourless [-vəlis] adj. CULIN. Sans saveur.
flaw [flɔ:] n. Défaut *m.* (in article); fêlure *f.* (in
china, glass); crapaud *m.* (in diamond); paille *f.*
(in metal); fissure, fente *f.* (in wood). ‖ JUR. Vice
(*m.*) de forme. ‖ FIG. Défaut *m.*
— v. tr. Abîmer, endommager.
— v. intr. S'abîmer, s'endommager.
flawless [-lis] adj. Sans défaut.
flax [flæks] n. BOT., COMM. Lin *m.*
flaxen [-ən] adj. COMM. De lin. ‖ FAM. Blond,
filasse.
flay [flei] v. tr. Ecorcher. ‖ FIG. S'acharner sur.
flea [fli:] n. ZOOL.- Puce *f.* ‖ AVIAT. *Flying flea*,
pou du ciel. ‖ FAM. *A flea in one's ear*, une rebuffade. ‖ **Flea-bite**, n. ZOOL. Piqûre de puce *f.;*
FAM. Broutille, bêtise *f.* ‖ **Flea-bitten**, adj. Mordu
par les puces; FIG. Moucheté. ‖ **Flea market**, n.
Marché (*m.*) aux puces, puces (*f. pl.*). ‖ **Flea-pit**, n.
FAM. Nid (*m.*) à puces (cinema).
fleck [flek] n. Particule *f.* (of dust); petite tache *f.*
(of sunlight). ‖ MED. Tache de rousseur *f.*
— v. tr. Tacheter, moucheter. ‖ Emailler (*with*, de).
flection ['flekʃən] n. See FLEXION.
fled [fled] pret., p. p. See FLEE.
fledge [fledʒ] v. tr. Empenner (an arrow); emplumer (a bird).
fledgling [-liŋ] n. ZOOL. Oiseau à peine emplumé
m. ‖ FAM. Béjaune *m.*
— adj. FAM. Débutant, en herbe.
flee [fli:] v. intr. (59). Fuir, s'enfuir. ‖ Se réfugier
(*to*, auprès de). ‖ FIG. Fuir, disparaître.
— v. tr. Fuir, s'enfuir de, (a place). ‖ FIG. Fuir
(a danger).
fleece [fli:s] n. Toison *f.* ‖ Moutonnement *m.* (of
clouds). ‖ Ouatine *f.* (lining-cloth);
— v. tr. Tondre (sheep). ‖ Couvrir d'une toison
(or) d'un moutonnement. ‖ FIG. Dépouiller, mettre
en coupe réglée; déplumer (fam.).
fleecer [-ə*] n. FAM. Ecorcheur, estampeur *s.*
fleecy [-i] adj. Laineux, crépu (hair); moutonneux
(sea, sky); floconneux (snow, wool).
fleet [fli:t] n. NAUT., AVIAT. Flotte *f.* ‖ CH. DE F.
Train *m.*
fleet n. GEOGR. Crique *f.* ‖ † Prison pour dettes *f.*
fleet adj. Rapide. ‖ **Fleet-footed**, adj. Au pied
léger.
fleet adj., adv. A fleur de terre.
fleeting ['fli:tiŋ] adj. Ephémère, fugitif.
Fleming ['flemiŋ] n. GEOGR. Flamand *s.*
Flemish [-iʃ] adj., n. Flamand *s.*
flench [flentʃ], **flense** [flenz] v. tr. Dépecer, écorcher, dépouiller.
flesh [fleʃ] n. Chair *f.* (of animal, fruit, man). ‖
Embonpoint *m.;* graisse *f.; in flesh*, bien en chair;
to lose flesh, perdre du poids; *to put on flesh*,
grossir. ‖ Etre vivant *m.;* créature *f.; flesh and
blood*, nature humaine; *his own flesh and blood*,
sa famille. ‖ ECCLES. *To eat flesh*, faire gras. ‖
CULIN. Viande *f.; flesh diet*, alimentation carnée.
‖ FIG. Chair *f.;* désir charnel *m.; flesh and spirit*,
la chair et l'esprit. ‖ FAM. *In the flesh*, en chair et
en os; *to make s.o.'s flesh creep*, donner la chair
de poule à qqn. ‖ **Flesh-coloured**, adj. Couleur
chair. ‖ **Flesh-eating**, adj. Carnivore. ‖ **Flesh-fly**,
n. ZOOL. Mouche à viande *f.* ‖ **Flesh-glove**, n,
Gant de crin *m.* ‖ **Flesh-pot**, n. FAM. Bonne chère
f. ‖ **Flesh-tints**, n. pl. ARTS. Chairs, carnations

f. pl. ‖ **Flesh-wound**, n. MED. Blessure superficielle *f.*
— v. tr. Acharner (dogs). ‖ Engraisser (to fatten).
‖ TECHN. Echarner (hide). ‖ FIG. Etrenner (one's
pen); assouvir (one's passions).
fleshiness [-inis] n. Embonpoint *m.*
fleshings [-iŋz] n. pl. SPORTS. Maillot chair *m.*
fleshless [-lis] adj. Décharné.
fleshliness [-linis] n. Désirs charnels *m. pl.*
fleshly [-li] adj. Charnel.
fleshy [-i] adj. Charnu.
fleur-de-lis ['flə:də'li:] n. Fleur (*f.*) de lis.
fleuret ['flu:rit] n. ARCHIT. Fleurette *f.*
flew [flu:] pret. See FLY.
flex [fleks] v. tr. MED., GEOL. Fléchir.
flex n. ELECTR. Fil souple *m.*
flexibility [fleksi'biliti] n. Flexibilité *f.* ‖ AUTOM.
Souplesse *f.* ‖ FIG. Souplesse, docilité *f.*
flexible ['fleksibl] adj. Flexible. ‖ AUTOM., ELECTR.,
FIG. Souple.
flexile [-sil] adj. Flexible.
flexion [-ʃən] n. MATH., GRAMM. Flexion *f.*
flexional [-ʃənl] adj. MATH., GRAMM. Flexionnel.
flexor [-sə*] n. MED. Fléchisseur *m.*
flexuosity [,fleksju'ɔsiti] n. Flexuosité *f.*
flexuous ['fleksjuəs] adj. Fluxueux.
flexure [-ʃə*] n. Fléchissement *m.* ‖ GEOL.
Flexure *f.*
flibbertigibbet ['flibəti'dʒibit] n. FAM. Braque,
hurluberlu *m.*
flick [flik] n. Chiquenaude *f.* (with finger). ‖ Petit
coup *m.* (snap). ‖ Claquement *m.* (sound). ‖ Sursaut
m. (movement). ‖ U.S. Pl. FAM. Ciné *m.* ‖ **Flick-
knife**, n. Couteau (*m.*) à ouverture automatique (or)
à cran d'arrêt.
— v. intr. *To flick out of sight*, s'éclipser.
— v. tr. Donner une chiquenaude (or) un petit
coup à (see FLIP); *to flick off*, faire tomber d'une
chiquenaude. ‖ Faire claquer (a whip).
flicker [-ə*] v. intr. Battre des ailes (bird); voltiger (flag); vaciller (flame); frémir (leaves); clignoter, papilloter (light); osciller (needle); danser
(shadow); souffler par bouffées (wind). ‖ FIG. Vaciller (hope); *his life is flickering out*, il s'éteint;
a smile flickered on his lips, un sourire hésita sur
ses lèvres.
— n. Vacillement, tremblotement *m.* ‖ Lueur vacillante *f.* (light). ‖ FIG. Frisson *m.* (of fear). ‖ U.S.
Pl. FAM. Ciné *m.* ‖ ELECTR. Papillotement *m.*
flight [flait] n. Fuite *f.; to put to flight*, mettre
en fuite; *to take to flight*, prendre la fuite.
flight [flait] n. Vol *m.* (act); envol, essor *m.*
(soaring); *to take one's flight*, s'envoler, prendre
sa volée (or) son vol. ‖ Migration *f.* (act); volée *f.*
(distance); vol *m.* (flock). ‖ MILIT. Vol *m.;* volée
f. (of arrows); course, trajectoire, portée *f.* (of a
projectile). ‖ AVIAT. Vol *m.* (of a plane); *blind
flight*, pilotage sans visibilité; *first flight*, baptême
de l'air; *non-stop flight*, vol sans escale. ‖ AVIAT.
Escadrille *f.* (formation); U. S. Unité (*f.*) composée
de trois avions; *flight formation*, formation de vol.
‖ ARCHIT. Volée *f.* (of stairs); *flight of stairs*,
étage d'escalier; *flight of steps*, perron. ‖ BOT.
Balle *f.* (of oat). ‖ FIG. Elan, essor *m.* (of fancy);
envolée *f.* (of oratory); trait *m.* (of wit). ‖ **Flight
control**, n. AVIAT. Commande (*f.*) de vol. ‖ **Flight-
deck**, n. NAUT. Pont d'envol *m.* (of aircraft-carrier);
AVIAT. Poste de pilotage *m.* ‖ **Flight-officer**, n.
AVIAT. Officier aviateur *m.* ‖ **Flight-path**, n. AVIAT.
Trajectoire (*f.*) de vol. ‖ **Flight-recorder**, n. AVIAT.
Enregistreur de vol *m.* ‖ **Flight-time**, n. ZOOL.
Période (*f.*) d'essaimage (of bees).
— v. tr. Tirer au vol.
— v. intr. Voler en groupe, émigrer (birds).
flightiness [-inis] n. FIG. Légèreté *f.*
flightless [-lis] adj. Incapable de voler, inapte au
vol.

flighty [-i] adj. Léger, frivole. ‖ Volage, inconstant. ‖ FAM. Timbré (crazy).

flim-flam ['flimflæm] n. FAM. Baliverne *f.* (See CRAMMER.) ‖ U. S. Escroquerie *f.*

flimsiness ['flimzinis] n. Fragilité *f.* (of cloth, paper). ‖ FIG. Fragilité *f.* (of evidence); pauvreté *f.* (of an excuse); frivolité *f.* (of a person).

flimsy [-zi] adj. Fragile (cloth, paper). ‖ FIG. Fragile, maigre (evidence); pauvre (excuse, style).
— n. Papier pelure *m.* (paper). ‖ FAM. Fafiot *m.* (banknote); papier *m.* (reporter's copy).

flinch [flinʃ] v. intr. Reculer (to draw back). ‖ Broncher, sourciller (to wince).

flinders ['flindəz] n. pl. Eclats *m. pl.*

fling [fliŋ] v. tr. (60). Jeter, lancer; *to fling the door wide open,* ouvrir brusquement la porte; *to fling oneself into,* se jeter dans. ‖ Rejeter; *to fling aside all restraint,* se départir de toute contrainte. ‖ Décocher (abuse, epigrams). ‖ **To fling out,** ouvrir brusquement, jeter (one's arms); jeter dehors (s.o.). ‖ **To fling up,** jeter en l'air; *to fling up its heels,* ruer; *to fling up one's job,* flanquer là son travail.
— v. intr. Se précipiter (to dash). ‖ **To fling out,** ruer (horse); *to fling out at s.o.,* décocher des injures à qqn.
— n. Action (*f.*) de lancer (throw). ‖ Ruade *f.* (of horse). ‖ FAM. Coup (*m.*) de patte; *a fling at you,* une pierre dans votre jardin. ‖ FAM. Tentative *f.*; *to have a fling at sth.,* essayer de faire qqch. pour voir. ‖ FAM. Bon temps *m.*; *youth must have its fling,* il faut que jeunesse se passe.

flint [flint] n. Silex *m.* (quartz). ‖ Pierre (*f.*) à briquet (for cigarette-lighter); pierre (*f.*) à fusil (gunflint). ‖ FIG. Roc *m.*; pierre *f.*; *heart of flint,* cœur de pierre. ‖ FAM. To skin a flint, tondre un œuf. ‖ **Flint-lock,** n. Fusil (*m.*) à pierre.

flinty [-i] adj. De silex, siliceux. ‖ FIG. De pierre, d'airain.

flip [flip] v. tr. (1). Donner une chiquenaude à; *to flip off,* ôter d'une chiquenaude. ‖ Secouer, agiter (a fan); faire claquer (a whip).
— v. intr. Donner une chiquenaude. ‖ Donner un léger coup (at, à).
— n. Chiquenaude *f.* ‖ AVIAT. Petit tour de vol *m.* ‖ **Flip-flop,** n. Flic flac *m.* (noise); SPORTS. Flipflap, saut périlleux *m.*; ELECTR. Flip-flop *m.*, bascule (*f.*) monostable (or) bistable; Pl. COMM. Tongs *f. pl.* (sandals) [nom déposé].

flippancy ['flipənsi] n. Désinvolture *f.*

flippant [-ənt] adj. Cavalier.

flippantly [-əntli] adv. D'un air dégagé, cavalièrement.

flipper [-ə*] n. ZOOL. Aile *f.* (of penguin); nageoire *f.* (of seal); aileron *m.* (of shark). ‖ FAM. Aile *f.* (arm); pince, cuillère *f.* (hand).

flirt [flə:t] v. tr. Donner une chiquenaude à. (See FLIP.) ‖ Agiter, secouer (a fan).
— v. intr. Flirter.
— n. Secousse, saccade *f.* (movement). ‖ Flirteur *s.* (person).

flirtation [flə:'teiʃən] n. Flirt *m.* (act).

flit [flit] v. intr. (1). Se mouvoir vivement; *to flit about,* aller et venir sans bruit. ‖ Voleter, voltiger (bird). ‖ FIG. Voltiger; *a smile flitted across his face,* un sourire erra sur son visage. ‖ FAM. Filer, mettre la clé sous le paillasson.
— n. Déménagement *m.*; *to do a moonlight flit,* déménager à la cloche de bois.

flitch [flitʃ] n. CULIN. Flèche *f.* (of bacon).

flitter ['flitə*] v. intr. Voleter, voltiger. ‖ **Flittermouse,** n. ZOOL. Chauve-souris *f.*

flivver ['flivə*] n. AUTOM., FAM. Tacot *m.* ‖ AVIAT., FAM. Zinc *m.* ‖ FAM. Fichaise, brouille *f.*

flix [fliks] n. COMM. Castor *m.* (fur).

float [flout] v. intr. Flotter. ‖ NAUT. Etre à flot, se renflouer. ‖ SPORTS. Faire la planche. ‖ FIN. Etre en circulation. ‖ FIG. Circuler, courir (rumour); planer (vision). ‖ FAM. *To float along with the stream,* aller à la va-comme-je-te-pousse; *to float on air,* nager dans l'euphorie.
— v. tr. Faire flotter. ‖ Entraîner, pousser (clouds, leaves); flotter (wood). ‖ NAUT. Renflouer (a ship). ‖ COMM. Lancer, créer (a company). ‖ FIN. Lancer, émettre (a loan). ‖ FIG. Lancer, mettre en circulation (a rumour).
— n. Masse flottante *f.* (of ice); flotte *f.* (of net); train *m.* (of wood). ‖ Char de cortège *m.* ‖ NAUT. Radeau *m.* ‖ AVIAT. Flotteur, ballonnet *m.* ‖ AUTOM. Flotteur *m.* (of carburettor). ‖ TECHN. Lime à taille simple *f.* (file); aplanisseuse *f.* (smoother). ‖ SPORTS. Flotteur, bouchon *m.* (of a fishing-line); galet *m.* (of a fishing-net). ‖ THEATR. Rampe *f.* ‖ **Floatfeed,** adj. AUTOM. A réglage par flotteur (carburettor). ‖ **Float-plane,** n. AVIAT. Hydravion à flotteurs *m.* ‖ **Float-valve,** n. TECHN. Soupape (*f.*) à flotteur.

floatable [-əbl] adj. Flottable.

floatage [-idʒ] n. Flottage *m.* (of wood). ‖ NAUT. Flottabilité *f.* (buoyancy); œuvres mortes *f. pl.* (part above water-line); tonnage à flot *m.* (ships).

floatation [flou'teiʃən] n. NAUT. Flottaison *f.* ‖ COMM. Lancement *m.* (of a firm). ‖ FIN. Emission *f.* (of a loan).

floating ['floutiŋ] adj. NAUT. Flottant; de navigation. ‖ FIN. Flottant (debt); *floating capital,* fonds de roulement. ‖ MED. Flottant (kidney). ‖ *Floating voter,* électeur flottant.
— n. Flottement *m.* ‖ Flottage *m.* (of wood). ‖ NAUT. Mise (*f.*) à flot. ‖ COMM. Lancement *m.*

floccule ['flɔkjul] n. CHIM. Flocon, précipité *m.*

flocculent [-ənt] adj. Floconneux.

flock [flɔk] n. Flocon *m.* (of cotton, wool); tontisse *f.* (for paper); bourre *f.* (of wool-refuse). ‖ CHIM. Flocon *m.* ‖ **Flock-paper,** n. Papier velouté *m.*

flock n. Vol *m.*, bande *f.* (of birds); troupeau *m.* (of geese, goats, sheep). ‖ Foule *f.* (crowd). ‖ ECCLES. Ouailles *f. pl.*
— v. intr. Former un vol (birds); s'assembler en troupeau (geese). ‖ S'attrouper (persons); *to flock in,* entrer en masse; *to flock to,* affluer vers.

floe [flou] n. Glace flottante, banquise *f.*

flog [flɔg] v. tr. (1). Fouetter, fustiger, donner le fouet à; *to flog learning into s.o.,* faire entrer la science en qqn. à coups de verge. ‖ FAM. *To flog a dead horse,* enfoncer une porte ouverte; soutenir une théorie périmée.

flogging [-giŋ] n. Fouet *m.* ‖ Flagellation *f.*

flood [flʌd] n. Flot, flux *m.* (of tide). ‖ Onde, eau *f.* (water). ‖ Inondation, crue *f.* (rise in water-level). ‖ Flot *m.* (of light). ‖ ECCLES. Déluge *m.* ‖ FIG. Flot, déluge *m.* ‖ **Flood-gate,** n. Ecluse *f.* ‖ **Floodlight,** v. tr. Illuminer par projecteurs (a building).
— n. Eclairage direct (or) par projecteurs.
— v. tr. Faire déborder (a river). ‖ Submerger, inonder (lit. and fig.).
— v. intr. Déborder (river). ‖ Jaillir à flots (light).

floor [flɔ:*] n. Plancher, parquet *m.* (of a room); *laying of floors,* parquetage. ‖ Carrelage *m.* (of a kitchen). ‖ Etage *m.* (storey); *the neighbour on the floor above,* le voisin du dessus. ‖ Fond *m.* (of the sea). ‖ ARCHIT., AGRIC. Aire *f.* ‖ JUR. Prétoire *m.* (of the court); hémicycle *m.* (of the Chamber of Deputies). ‖ FIN. Plancher *m.* (of prices); parquet *m.* (of the Stock Exchange). ‖ NAUT. Varangue *f.* ‖ U. S. Droit (*m.*) à la parole; *to take the floor,* prendre la parole. ‖ **Floor-cloth,** n. Linoléum *m.* ‖ **Floor-lamp,** n. Torchère *f.* ‖ **Floor-leader,** n. Chef de parti *m.* ‖ **Floor-maker,** n. Parqueteur *m.* ‖ **Floor-plank,** n. Lame (*f.*) de parquet. ‖ **Floorwaiter,** n. Garçon d'étage *m.* ‖ **Floor-walker,** n. U. S. COMM. Inspecteur de magasin *m.*
— v. tr. Parqueter, planchéier (a room). ‖ Carreler

(a kitchen). ‖ SPORTS, FAM. Terrasser. ‖ FIG. Désarçonner; suffoquer; souffler (fam.).

floorer [-rə*] n. TECHN. Parqueteur *m.* ‖ FAM. Coup (*m.*) de massue.

floozy ['flu:zi] n. U.S. FAM. Poule, cocotte *f.*

flop [flɔp] adv. En faisant floc (or) plouf (into water); mollement (to the ground). ‖ FIG. *To go flop,* s'écrouler, se casser la figure (fam.).
— n. Floc, bruit mat *m.* (sound). ‖ FAM. Four, bide *m.* (failure). ‖ U.S. POP. Plumard, pieu *m.* ‖ U.S. POP. **Flop-house,** n. Asile (*m.*) de nuit.
— v. intr. (1). Tomber avec un bruit mat, faire floc; tomber mollement. ‖ FAM. Faire un bide (to fail). ‖ POP. Pioncer, roupiller (to sleep). ‖ **To flop along,** marcher à pas pesants. ‖ **To flop down,** s'affaler, s'effondrer.

floppy [-i] adj. Mou, flasque (cloth, hat); lâche (garment); mollasse (person).

flora ['flɔ:rə] n. BOT. Flore *f.*
— N. B. Deux pluriels : *floras, florae.*

floral [-əl] adj. A fleurs (cloth). ‖ BOT. Floral.

florescence [flɔ:'resns] n. BOT. Floraison *f.*

florescent [-nt] adj. BOT. En fleur.

floriated ['flɔ:rieitid] adj. A fleurs.

floriculture [-kʌltʃə*] n. AGRIC. Horticulture, floriculture *f.*

floriculturist [flɔ:ri'kʌltjurist] n. AGRIC. Horticulteur *m.*

florid ['flɔrid] adj. Coloré (complexion). ‖ FIG. Coloré (narrative); fleuri (style).

floridity [flɔ'riditi] n. Coloration *f.* (of complexion). ‖ FIG. Couleur *f.,* coloris *m.*

floriferous [-fərəs] adj. BOT. Florifère.

florin ['flɔrin] n. FIN. Florin *m.*

florist ['flɔrist] n. COMM. Fleuriste *s.*

floss [flɔs] n. Bourre de soie *f.,* floss *m.* ‖ **Floss-silk,** n. Filoselle *f.*

flossy [-i] adj. Soyeux. ‖ U.S. FAM. Pimpant (elegant); tapageur (showy).
— n. U.S. FAM. Belle *f.*

flotage ['floutidʒ] n. U.S. See FLOATAGE.

flotation [flou'teiʃən] n. U.S. See FLOATATION.

flotilla [flɔ'tilə] n. NAUT. Flottille *f.* (of boats); escadrille *f.* (of destroyers).

flotsam ['flɔtsəm] n. JUR. Epave flottante *f.; flotsam and jetsam,* choses de flot et de mer.

flounce [flauns] n. Mouvement brusque, soubresaut *m.*
— v. intr. Avoir des mouvements brusques; *to flounce in,* entrer brusquement. ‖ Sursauter, se démener.

flounce n. Volant *m.* (of a dress).
— v. tr. Garnir de volants.

flounder ['floundə*] n. ZOOL. Carrelet *m.*

flounder ['flaundə*] v. intr. Patauger; *to flounder about in the water,* se débattre dans l'eau; *to flounder in an explanation,* s'embarrasser dans ses explications; s'enferrer, s'enfoncer, se noyer (fam.).
— n. Pataugeage; cafouillage *m.* (fam.).

flour ['flauə*] n. Farine *f.* (of mustard, wheat). ‖ Fécule *f.* (potato-flour). ‖ **Flour-milling,** n. Minoterie *f.*
— v. tr. Réduire en farine (grain). ‖ CULIN. Fariner. ‖ FAM. Enfariner (s.o.'s face).

flourish ['flʌriʃ] v. intr. Fleurir, être florissant, prospérer (to thrive). ‖ S'épanouir, être en pleine prospérité (to be in one's prime). ‖ Faire de grands gestes (to gesticulate). ‖ User d'un style fleuri (in writing). ‖ MUS. Faire des fioritures (in a passage); jouer une fanfare (trumpets). ‖ BOT. Prendre, devenir vivace.
— v. tr. Faire des moulinets avec (a stick); brandir (a sword); *to flourish one's arms,* faire de grands gestes. ‖ Orner de fioritures.
— n. Eclat, épanouissement *m.* (prosperity). ‖ Geste large *m.* (of arms); moulinet *m.* (of stick); brandissement *m.* (of sword). ‖ Parafe *m.* (after signature);

fioriture *f.* (of style). ‖ MUS. Fanfare *f.* (of trumpets); fioriture *f.* (in a passage).

flourishing [-iŋ] adj. Florissant.

floury ['flauəri] adj. CULIN., BOT. Farineux. ‖ FIG. Enfariné (face).

flout [flaut] v. tr. Défier (danger).
— v. intr. Se moquer (at, de). [See SCOFF.]
— n. Moquerie *f.*

flow [flou] v. intr. Couler, s'écouler (stream); *to flow back,* refluer; *to flow down, in,* tomber, entrer à flots; *to flow past, out,* s'écouler. ‖ Flotter (flag, hair). ‖ S'écouler (crowd); couler (tears). ‖ NAUT. Monter (tide). ‖ MED. Circuler, courir, couler (blood). ‖ FIG. Couler avec aisance (lines, style); dériver, provenir (*from,* de) [result].
— n. Ecoulement, flot *m.* (of a liquid); cours *m.* (of a river); flux *m.* (of tide). ‖ Drapé *m.* (of a dress). ‖ TECHN. Coulée *f.* (of metal); débit *m.* (of a pump). ‖ MED. Flot, flux *m.* (of blood). ‖ FIG. Effusion *f.* (of feelings); affluence *f.* (of goods); flot *m.* (of words).

flower ['flauə*] n. BOT. Floraison *f.* (blossom); fleur *f.* (plant); *in flower,* en fleur, épanoui; *to lay flowers on a grave,* fleurir une tombe; *out of flower,* défleuri. ‖ CHIM. Fleur *f.* (of sulfur, wine). ‖ GRAMM. *Flowers of speech,* fleurs de rhétorique. ‖ Pl. Fioritures *f. pl.* ‖ FIG. Fleur, crème, élite *f.* (of society). ‖ **Flower-bed,** n. AGRIC. Parterre *m.;* plate-bande, corbeille *f.* ‖ **Flower-de-luce,** n. BLAS. Fleur (*f.*) de lis. ‖ **Flower-girl,** n. Bouquetière *f.* ‖ **Flower-holder,** n. Porte-bouquet *m.* ‖ **Flower-pot,** n. Pot (*m.*) de fleurs. ‖ **Flower-stand,** n. Jardinière *f.;* U.S. Kiosque (*m.*) de fleuriste.
— v. intr. AGRIC., FIG. Fleurir, s'épanouir.
— v. tr. AGRIC. Faire fleurir; FIG. Fleurir, orner de fleurs.

floweret [-ret] n. BOT. Fleurette *f.*

flowering [-riŋ] adj. AGRIC., FIG. Fleuri, en fleur. ‖ COMM. A fleurs (cloth).
— n. Floraison *f.*

flowery [-ri] adj. Fleuri (cloth, meadow, style).

flowing ['flouiŋ] adj. Coulant (stream, style); montant (tide). ‖ Long (beard); flottant (drapery).

flown [floun] p. p. See FLY.

flown adj. † Gonflé. ‖ TECHN. A ramages (porcelain).

flu [flu:] n. MED., FAM. Grippe *f.*

fluctuate ['flʌktjueit] v. intr. Ondoyer (waves). ‖ FIG. Flotter, fluctuer. (See VACILLATE.)

fluctuation [,flʌktju'eiʃən] n. Fluctuation *f.*

flue [flu:] n. Tuyau, conduit (*m.*) de fumée.

flue n. Peluches *f. pl.*

flue v. tr. Evaser.
— v. intr. S'évaser.

fluency ['flu:ənsi] n. Facilité d'élocution *f.* (in speaking); facilité *f.* (in writing).

fluent [-ənt] adj. Facile, coulant (speech, style); *to be a fluent speaker,* avoir un débit facile.

fluently [-əntli] adv. Facilement, couramment, d'abondance.

fluff [flʌf] n. Peluche *f.* (of cloth); duvet *m.* (of dust, fur); laine *f.* (of hair). ‖ Mouton *m.* (dust). ‖ THEATR. Loup *m.* ‖ FAM. Cuir *m.* (blunder); jeunesse *f.* (woman).
— v. tr. Rendre pelucheux. ‖ THEATR. Louper (one's entrance); bouler (one's lines). ‖ **To fluff out** (or) **up,** faire bouffer.
— v. intr. Pelucher.

fluffy ['flʌfi] adj. Duveteux, pelucheux (cloth); flou (outline). ‖ Ebouriffé (bird); gonflé (feathers).

fluid ['flu:id] adj. Fluide, liquide. ‖ MILIT. Mouvant (battle, front). ‖ FIG. Fluide, coulant; incertain, mouvant (situation).
— n. Liquide *m.* ‖ CHIM., PHYS., ELECTR. Fluide *m.*

fluidic [-'idik] adj. Fluidique.

fluidics [-iks] n. sg. TECHN. Fluidique *f.*

fluidify [flu:'idifai] v. tr. (2). Fluidifier.

fluidity [flu:'iditi] n. Fluidité f.
fluidize ['flu:i,daiz] v. tr. Fluidiser.
fluke [flu:k] n. Fer m. (of an arrow, lance). ‖ Lobe m. (of a whale's tail). ‖ NAUT. Patte d'ancre f.
fluke n. ZOOL. Carrelet m. ‖ MED. Douve f.
fluke n. SPORTS. Raccroc m. (in billiards). ‖ FAM. Coup (m.) de chance.
— v. tr. Avoir par un coup de chance.
— v. intr. Avoir un coup de chance.
fluky [-i] adj. Dû à la chance. ‖ Incertain, changeant (breeze).
flume [flu:m] n. Canalisation f. (of water). ‖ Buse, abée f. (of mill). ‖ U. S. Ravin où coule un torrent.
— v. tr. Canaliser.
flummery ['flʌməri] n. CULIN. Flan m. ‖ FAM. Boniment m. (claptrap); flagornerie f. (flattery).
flummoxed ['flʌməksd] adj. FAM. Démonté, désorienté, déferré; to be flummoxed, ne pas savoir sur quel pied danser.
flump [flʌmp] n. Floc, plouf, bruit (m.) de chute lourde. (See FLOP.)
— v. intr. Tomber avec un bruit lourd.
— v. tr. Laisser tomber avec un bruit sourd.
flunk [flʌnk] v. tr. U. S. FAM. Rater, se faire coller à (to fail in); faire échouer (to cause to fail); coller, recaler (to pluck).
— n. FAM. Recalé, collé s. (student). ‖ Recalage, collage m. (failing).
flunkey [-i] n. Larbin, laquais m. (servant).
flunkeyism [-iizm] n. Flagornerie f.
fluor ['flu:ə*] n. Fluorine f.
fluorescence [fluə'resns] n. Fluorescence f.
fluorescent [-nt] adj. Fluorescent. ‖ ELECTR. A incandescence.
fluoridate ['fluəri,deit] v. tr. Fluoriser.
fluoridation [,fluəri'deiʃən] n. Fluorisation f.
fluoride ['fluə,raid] n. CHIM. Fluorure m.
fluorine [-ri:n] n. CHIM. Fluor m.
fluoroscope [-rə,skoup] n. TECHN. Fluoroscope m.
fluorspar ['fluə,spɑ:*] n. GEOL. Spath-fluor m., flusspath m., fluorine f.
flurry ['flʌri] n. Rafale f. (See GUST.) ‖ Convulsion f. (spasm). ‖ Agitation f.; émoi m.
— v. tr. (2). Agiter, émouvoir.
flush [flʌʃ] n. Chasse d'eau f. (in a W. C.) ‖ Nettoyage (m.) à grande eau (cleansing). ‖ Eclat m. (of colour, light). ‖ Rougeur f.; afflux de sang m. (blush). ‖ Flush m. (in poker). ‖ MED. Hot flush, bouffée de chaleur. ‖ SPORTS. Envolée f. (of birds). ‖ FIG. Avalanche, pluie f.; débordement m. (shower). ‖ FIG. Eclat m. (of beauty, health, youth); élan m. (of joy); ivresse f. (of success); not to be in the first flush of youth, ne pas être de la première jeunesse.
— adj. Plein à déborder, débordant, en crue (stream). ‖ Abondant, prospère; flush with money, bien pourvu d'argent; plein aux as (pop.). ‖ A ras, affleurant; flush screw, écrou noyé; flush with, au ras (or) niveau de, à fleur de, aligné (or) nivelé sur.
— adv. De niveau, à ras. ‖ Droit; flush in the face, droit dans le nez.
— v. intr. Jaillir à flots (stream); to flush over, déborder. ‖ Monter (blood); rougir, s'empourprer (face, person). ‖ Eclater, rutiler (colour, light); s'empourprer (sky). ‖ BOT. Eclater en pousses nouvelles. ‖ SPORTS. Se lever (birds).
— v. tr. Nettoyer à grande eau, rincer largement (to clean); to flush the W. C., tirer la chasse d'eau. ‖ Inonder (a meadow). ‖ Faire rougir, empourprer (to make blush or glow). ‖ Mettre à ras (or) au niveau (to make level). ‖ BOT. Faire pousser (plants). ‖ SPORTS. Faire se lever (birds). ‖ FIG. Exciter, exalter (with, par).
fluster ['flʌstə*] v. tr. † Griser (to make tipsy). ‖ Troubler, déconcerter, rendre nerveux; as flustered

as an old hen with one chick, empêtré comme une poule qui a trouvé un couteau.
— v. intr. S'énerver, se troubler.
— n. Enervement, trouble m.
flute [flu:t] n. MUS. Flûte f. (instrument, musician, organ-stop). ‖ ARCHIT. Cannelure f. ‖ Tuyau m. (in cloth).
— v. intr. MUS. Jouer de la flûte. ‖ FIG. Prendre un ton flûté.
— v. tr. MUS. Jouer sur la flûte. ‖ Tuyauter (a cloth). ‖ ARCHIT. Canneler.
fluting [-iŋ] n. Tuyautage m. ‖ ARCHIT. Cannelure f. ‖ **Fluting-iron**, n. (fer m.) à tuyauter.
flutist [-ist] n. Flûtiste s.
flutter ['flʌtə*] n. Balancement m., oscillation f. (of fan); battement m. (of wings). ‖ MED. Pulsations rapides f. pl. ‖ FIG. Agitation f.; émoi, bouleversement m.; to cause a flutter in the dovecotes, lancer une pierre dans la mare aux grenouilles. ‖ FAM. Spéculation f. (or) pari (m.) sans importance.
— v. intr. Voleter (in short flight); battre des ailes (without flying). ‖ Palpiter, battre, claquer (in the wind). ‖ MED. Palpiter (heart); battre fébrilement (pulse). ‖ FIG. S'agiter, se démener, s'affairer (to bustle); papillonner (to flit about); to flutter with joy, frémir de joie.
— v. tr. Agiter, secouer (flag, ribbon); to flutter its wings, battre des ailes. ‖ FIG. Agiter, troubler, causer l'émoi de.
fluty ['flu:ti] adj. Flûté.
fluvial ['flu:viəl] adj. Fluvial.
flux [flʌks] (pl. **fluxes** [-iz]) n. Flot, flux m. (of water). ‖ TECHN., NAUT., PHYS., MATH. Flux m. ‖ FIG. Flot m. (of ideas); flot, afflux, flux m.; affluence f. (of people); flot, torrent m. (of words). ‖ FIG. Vicissitudes f.; in a state of flux, dans l'instabilité, en période de changements continuels.
— v. intr. Couler à flots, ruisseler.
— v. tr. TECHN. Fondre (metal).
fluxion [-ʃən] n. † Flux m. ‖ MATH. Fluxion f.
fly [flai] adj. FAM. A la coule, malin, roublard, affranchi.
fly n. ZOOL., SPORTS. Mouche f. ‖ FIG. Fly in the ointment, ombre au tableau; fly on the wheel, mouche du coche, ardélion; to take the fly, mordre à l'appât. ‖ FAM. There aren't any flies on him, il n'est pas tombé de la dernière pluie; il a du vice. ‖ **Fly-blow**, n. Chiures (f. pl.) de mouche. ‖ **Fly-catcher**, n. Attrape-mouches m. ‖ **Fly-fishing**, n. SPORTS. Pêche à la mouche f. ‖ **Fly-net**, n. Emouchoir m. ‖ **Fly-paper**, n. Papier attrape-mouches m. ‖ **Fly-spray**, n. Bombe insecticide f. ‖ **Fly-weight**, n. SPORTS. Poids mouche m. ‖ **Fly-whisk**, U. S. **fly-swatter**, n. Chasse-mouches m.
fly [flai] v. intr. (61). Voler (bird); to fly about, voltiger; to fly away, s'envoler. ‖ Voler (projectile); to let fly an arrow, lancer (or) décocher une flèche; to send sth. flying, faire voler qqch., lancer qqch. à la volée. ‖ Voler, sauter (cork, screw); flotter (hair, flag); voler, jaillir (sparks); sauter, tourner (wind); to fly open, s'ouvrir brusquement (door). ‖ Voler, s'élancer, se précipiter; courir (to, à). ‖ S'enfuir, fuir (from, de). [See FLEE.] ‖ ARCHIT. Monter, s'élancer (flèche, stair). ‖ AVIAT. Voler; to fly over, past, survoler, défiler; to fly to, aller en avion à. ‖ FIG. Fuir, s'envoler (time); to fly by, passer comme un éclair. ‖ FIG. S'exalter; to fly high, viser haut; to fly in the face of, porter un défi à (s.o.); aller contre (sth.); to fly into a passion, s'emporter; to fly off the handle, sortir de ses gonds. ‖ FAM. My watch has flown, ma montre s'est envolée; to let fly at, s'en prendre à (s.o.). ‖ **To fly off**, s'envoler (bird); sauter (button); filer (person); to fly off at a tangent, prendre la tangente. ‖ **To fly out**, s'envoler (bird); sortir vivement (person).

— v. tr. Faire voler (a bird, a kite). ‖ Fuir, s'enfuir de (to flee from). ‖ Fuir, éviter (to avoid). ‖ NAUT. *To fly à flag*, battre pavillon. ‖ AVIAT. Piloter (aircraft); survoler (the Atlantic); transporter en avion (passengers).

— n. Vol *m.; on the fly*, en vol, au vol. ‖ Battant *m.* (of a flag); patte *f.* (of a garment); braguette *f.* (of trousers); auvent *m.* (of a tent). ‖ Fiacre *m.* (carriage). ‖ TECHN. Régulateur; receveur mécanique *m.* ‖ THEATR. Cintre *m.* ‖ **Fly-bill**, n. Prospectus *m.* (handbill); feuille volante *f.* (leaf); papillon *m.* (poster). ‖ **Fly-by-night**, adj. Mal financé; n. Noctambule *s.* (night-prowler); U. S. FAM. financier (*m.*) qui lève le pied. ‖ **Fly-half**, n. SPORTS. Demi (*m.*) d'ouverture. ‖ **Fly-leaf**, n. Feuille de garde *f.* ‖ **Fly-over**, n. ARCHIT. Pontbretelle, pont routier *m.* ‖ **Fly-past**, n. AVIAT. Défilé aérien *m.* ‖ **Flywheel**, n. TECHN. Volant *m.*

flyer [-ə*] n. ZOOL. Etre ailé *m.* ‖ AVIAT. Aviateur *m.;* aviatrice *f.* ‖ SPORTS. Coureur véloce *m.* (horse). ‖ TECHN. Aile *f.* (of windmill). ‖ U. S. CH. DE F. Express *m.* ‖ U. S. FAM. Prospectus *m.*

flying [-iŋ] adj. ZOOL. Volant (fish); *flying adder*, libellule. ‖ AVIAT. *Flying boat*, hydravion monocoque; *flying centre*, centre d'aviation; *flying man*, aviateur. ‖ MILIT. Volant (bomb, bridge); mobile (column); *with flying colours*, drapeau déployé (or) au vent. ‖ JUR. *Flying squad*, équipe volante de police. ‖ SPORTS. Avec élan (jump); en voltige (leap); lancé (start). ‖ ARCHIT. *Flying buttress*, arcboutant. ‖ FIG. Court, hâtif; *flying visit*, visite éclair; *with flying colours*, brillamment.

— n. ZOOL., AVIAT. Vol *m.*

F.M. [ef'em] abbr. *Frequency modulation*, modulation de fréquence.

F.O. [ef'ou] abbr. *Foreign Office*, en Grande-Bretagne, ministère des Affaires étrangères, Foreign Office.

foal [foul] n. ZOOL. Poulain *m.* (colt); ânon *m.* (donkey); pouliche *f.* (filly).

— v. tr. Mettre bas.

— v. intr. Pouliner.

foam [foum] n. Ecume *f.* (on horses, of waves). ‖ Ecume, bave *f.* (slaver). ‖ Mousse *f.* (on beer).

— v. intr. Ecumer, bouillonner (waves). ‖ Ecumer, baver (to slaver). ‖ Mousser (beer). ‖ FAM. *To foam at the mouth*, écumer de rage. ‖ **Foam-rubber**, n. Caoutchouc mousse *m.*

foamy [-i] adj. Ecumeux.

f.o.b. [efou'bi:] abbr. *free on board*, fob.

fob [fɔb] v. tr. (1). FAM. Rouler (s.o.); *to fob off*, refiler (with, à).

fob n. Gousset *m.*

— v. tr. (1). Empocher.

focal ['foukəl] adj. PHYS., MATH. Focal.

focalization [foukəlai'zeiʃən] n. Mise (*f.*) au point, focalisation *f.*

focalize ['foukəlaiz] v. tr. Mettre au point.

fo'c's'le ['fouksl] n. NAUT. See FORECASTLE.

focus [-əs] n. PHYS., MATH., MED. Foyer *m.; in focus*, au point.

— N. B. Deux pluriels : *foci, focuses.*

— v. tr. PHYS. Faire converger (rays); mettre au point (a telescope). ‖ FIG. Concentrer (one's attention).

— v. intr. PHYS., FIG. Converger.

fodder ['fɔdə*] n. AGRIC. Fourrage *m.*

— v. tr. AGRIC. Affourrager, affener.

foe [fou] n. Ennemi *s.*

foetal ['fl:tl] adj. MED. Fœtal.

foetid ['fetid] adj. See FETID.

foetus ['fi:təs] n. MED. Fœtus *m.*

fog [fɔg] n. Brouillard *m.* (see MIST); buée *f.* (on windows). ‖ Voile *m.* (on a film, photograph.). ‖ NAUT. Brume *f.; fog bank*, banc de brume. ‖ FAM. *In a fog*, dans le brouillard, perdu. ‖ **Fog-bound**, adj. Immobilisé par le brouillard (traveller,

plane), paralysé par le brouillard (airport). ‖ **Fog-dispersing**, adj. Antibrouillard. ‖ **Fog-horn**, n. NAUT. Corne de brume *f.* ‖ **Fog-lamp** (or) **-light**, n. AUTOM. Phare antibrouillard *m.* ‖ **Fog-signal**, n. CH. DE F. Pétard *m.*

— v. tr. (1). Embrumer (a landscape); embuer (windows). ‖ Voiler (a photograph). ‖ FIG. Embrumer, obscurcir.

— v. intr. S'embrumer. ‖ Se voiler (film). ‖ CH. DE F. Poser des pétards. ‖ FAM. *To be a little fogged*, être quelque peu dans le brouillard, ne plus y piger grand-chose.

foggy ['fɔgi] adj. Brumeux (misty). ‖ FIG. Vague (idea); embrumé, brumeux (mind).

fog(e)y ['fougi] n. FAM. Vieille baderne *f.*

foible ['fɔibl] n. Point faible *m.* ‖ SPORTS. Faible *m.* (in a sword).

foil [fɔil] n. Feuille *f.* (of metal); tain *m.* (in a mirror). ‖ Paillon *m.* (in jewelry). ‖ ARCHIT. Lobe *m.* ‖ FIG. Repoussoir, contraste *m.*

— v. tr. Décorer de feuilles de métal. ‖ Monter sur paillon. ‖ FIG. Servir de repoussoir à.

foil n. SPORTS. Fleuret *m.*

foil v. tr. SPORTS. *To foil the scent*, dépister la meute. ‖ FIG. Faire échouer, déjouer.

— n. SPORTS. Foulée, voie *f.* (scent, track).

foist [fɔist] v. tr. Insérer (*into*, dans). ‖ Attribuer (to ascribe); refiler (*on*, à) [to fob off with]. ‖ Introniser, introduire (*upon*, parmi); *to foist oneself on*, s'installer chez.

fold [fould] n. AGRIC. Bergerie *f.;* parc (*m.*) à moutons. ‖ FIG. Bercail *m.*

— v. tr. AGRIC. Mettre en pâture (a meadow); parquer (sheep).

fold v. tr. Plier, replier; *to fold a blanket in two*, redoubler une couverture; *to fold sth. about* (or) *around s.o.*, plier (or) enrouler qqch. autour de qqn. ‖ Envelopper, entourer (*in*, de). ‖ Serrer, enlacer, presser (*in*, dans); *to fold s.o. to one's heart*, serrer qqn sur son cœur. ‖ Croiser; *to fold one's arms*, se croiser les bras.

— v. intr. Se replier; *to fold back*, se rabattre. ‖ THEATR. Faire un four. ‖ U. S. *To fold up*, plier boutique, liquider; s'effondrer.

— n. Pli *m.* (of cloth, garment). ‖ Pli, repli *m.* (of ground).

folder [-ə*] n. Plioir *m.* (instrument); plieur *s.* (person). ‖ Dépliant *m.* (circular). ‖ Chemise *f.* (for papers); cahier *m.* (student's). ‖ Pl. Binocle *m.*

folding [-iŋ] adj. Pliant (bed, chair); à battant (door, table); *folding screen*, paravent.

foliage ['fouliidʒ] n. BOT. Feuillage *m.*

foliate [-it] adj. BOT. Folié.

— [-eit] v. tr. Folioter (a book). ‖ Etamer (a mirror). ‖ ARCHIT. Orner de lobes.

— v. intr. Se feuilleter.

foliation [fouli'eiʃən] n. Foliotage *m.* (of a book). ‖ BOT. Foliation *f.* ‖ TECHN. Etamage *m.* (of mirrors). ‖ GEOL. Schistosité *f.* ‖ ARCHIT. Rinceaux *m. pl.*

folic ['foulik] adj. *Folic acid*, acide folique.

folio ['fouliou] n. In-folio *m.* (book); folio *m.* (sheet); *first folio*, édition princeps.

— v. tr. Paginer, folioter.

foliole [-oul] n. BOT. Foliole *f.*

folk [fouk] n. † Peuple *m.; folk etymology*, étymologie populaire. ‖ Gens *m. pl.* (people). ‖ Pl. FAM. Parents *m. pl.*, famille *f.* ‖ **Folk-lore**, n. Folklore *m.* ‖ **Folk-music**, n. Musique folklorique *f.* ‖ **Folk-song**, n. Chanson folklorique *f.* (traditional), chanson folk *f.* (contemporary).

folksy ['fouksi] adj. U. S. FAM. Sociable, populaire.

follicle ['fɔlikl] n. MED., BOT. Follicule *m.*

follow ['folou] v. tr. Suivre, marcher derrière (to go after); suivre, marcher le long de (to go along). ‖ Suivre, venir après, succéder à (to come after).

‖ Suivre, poursuivre, s'attacher à (to pursue). ‖ S'ensuivre de, résulter de, découler de (to result from). ‖ Suivre, poursuivre, exercer (to practise). ‖ Suivre, s'intéresser à, écouter attentivement (to be attentive to); suivre, comprendre (to understand); suivre, étudier, observer (to watch over). ‖ Suivre, se ranger à, adopter (to act upon); suivre, se conformer à (to conform to); suivre, se laisser conduire par, obéir à (to obey); suivre, soutenir, appuyer (to support); *to follow suit*, emboîter le pas. ‖ Suivre, prendre pour modèle (to imitate). ‖ SPORTS. *To follow the hounds*, suivre la chasse. ‖ **To follow up**, suivre de près (s.o.); FIG. Donner suite (a letter); exploiter (a success); *to follow up with*, renforcer par, faire suivre de.
— v. intr. Suivre (person, thing, words); *as follows*, comme suit. ‖ S'ensuivre, découler (*from*, de) [result]. ‖ **To follow on**, continuer.
— n. Seconde portion *f.* (in restaurant). ‖ SPORTS. Coulé *m.* (in billiards).

follower [-ə*] n. Suivant *s.*; pl. suite *f.* ‖ Partisan, adepte *m.* ‖ TECHN. Plateau *m.* ‖ FAM. Galant, amoureux *m.*

following [-iŋ] adj. Suivant.
— n. Poursuite *f.* ‖ Suite *f.* (of a king); *she has a large following*, elle est très entourée. ‖ Partisans, adeptes *m. pl.*
— prép. A la suite de, après.

folly ['fɔli] n. Sottise, bêtise *f.*; *it would be an act of folly*, ce serait de la démence (or) de la folie douce. ‖ Folie *f.* (expensive undertaking).

foment [fo'ment] v. tr. MED., FIG. Fomenter.

fomentation [foumən'teiʃən] n. MED., FIG. Fomentation *f.*

fond [fɔnd] adj. † Naïf (belief, person). ‖ Tendre, affectueux (loving). ‖ Trop indulgent, faible (doting). ‖ Doux, caressé, chéri (hope). ‖ *Fond of*, friand, (or) gourmand (or) fou de (chocolate); amateur de (music); attaché à (s.o.); *to be fond of s.o.*, aimer qqn, avoir un penchant pour qqn, porter de l'amitié à qqn; *to be fond of doing sth.*, aimer à (or) avoir plaisir à faire qqch.

fondle ['fɔndl] v. tr. Caresser, cajoler; *to fondle the girls*, lutiner les filles.

fondness ['fɔndnis] n. Tendresse, affection *f.* (*for*, pour). ‖ Excès (*m.*) d'indulgence; faiblesse *f.*

fondue ['fɔndjuː] n. CULIN. Fondue *f.*

font [fɔnt] n. ECCLES. Fonts baptismaux *m. pl.* (for baptismal water); bénitier *m.* (for holy water). ‖ Réservoir *m.* (of lamp).

font n. U.S. TECHN. See FOUNT.

fontanel(le) [,fɔntə'nel] n. MED. Fontanelle *f.*

food [fuːd] n. Nourriture *f.*; aliments *m. pl.*; *food value*, valeur nutritive; *complete food*, aliment complet. ‖ AGRIC. Pâture *f.* (for cattle); pâtée *f.* (for dog, poultry). ‖ JUR. Ravitaillement *m.*; vivres *m. pl.*; *Ministry of Food*, ministère du Ravitaillement. ‖ FIG. Nourriture, pâture *f.*; *food for thought*, matière à réflexion. ‖ FAM. *To be food for the worms*, engraisser les vers. ‖ **Food-chain**, n. Chaîne alimentaire *f.* ‖ **Food-poisoning**, n. MED. Intoxication alimentaire *f.* ‖ **Food-processing**, adj. Agro-alimentaire. ‖ **Food-stuff**, n. Denrée alimentaire *f.*

fool [fuːl] n. Sot, imbécile *s.*; *fool's cap*, bonnet d'âne; *he is no fool*, il n'est vraiment pas bête; *to play the fool*, faire le Jacques (or) l'idiot; *to make a fool of oneself*, se conduire comme un imbécile. ‖ Dupe *f.*; *to go on a fool's errand*, aller décrocher la lune; *to make a fool of s.o.*, se payer la tête de qqn. ‖ Bouffon, fou *m.* (jester). ‖ **Fool-proof**, adj. Indétraquable, indéréglable (mechanism); à toute épreuve (plan).
— v. tr. Berner, duper; *they fooled you*, on vous a fait marcher. ‖ **To fool away**, gaspiller sottement.
— v. intr. Bêtifier, faire le fou (or) l'idiot; *to fool around*, baguenauder, traîner.

fool n. CULIN. Compote (*f.*) de fruits à la crème.

foolery [-əri] n. Sottise, ânerie *f.*

foolhardiness ['fuːl,hɑːdinis] n. Témérité, folle audace *f.*

foolhardy [-di] adj. Téméraire; *foolhardy person*, casse-cou, risque-tout.

foolish ['fuːliʃ] adj. Sot (silly); stupide, insensé, absurde. ‖ Penaud, pantois; décontenancé; *to feel foolish*, rester tout bête.

foolishly [-li] adv. Sottement; *to act foolishly*, faire des extravagances.

foolishness [-nis] n. Sottise, bêtise, stupidité *f.*

foolscap ['fuːlskæp] n. Papier ministre (or) écolier *m.*

foot [fut] (pl. **feet** [fiːt]) n. Pied *m.*; *on foot*, à pied; *on one's feet*, debout, sur ses jambes; *under foot*, sous les pieds, aux pieds, au sol; *to be sure of foot*, avoir le pied sûr. ‖ Pas *m.*; démarche *f.*; *light foot*, démarche légère. ‖ Bas, pied *m.* (of a bed); pied *m.* (of a boot, column, glass, mountain, stocking, tree, wall); bas *m.* (of a page); bout *m.* (of a table). ‖ ZOOL. Patte *f.* (of animals). ‖ CULIN. Pied *m.* (of calf, pig, sheep). ‖ MATH. Pied *m.* (measure). ‖ GRAMM. Pied *m.* (in verse). ‖ NAUT. Fond *m.* (of sail). ‖ MILIT. Infanterie *f.*; fantassins *m. pl.* ‖ FIG. Aplomb, équilibre *m.*; *carried off one's feet*, transporté; emballé (fam.); *on one's feet*, sur pied; *to find one's feet*, trouver son aplomb (or) le joint; *to keep one's feet*, tenir pied. ‖ FIG. Position *f.*; pied *m.*; *to put one's best foot forward*, donner un bon coup de collier; *to put one's foot down*, prendre position; se cabrer, regimber (*upon*, contre); opposer son veto (*upon*, à); *to put one's foot in it*, mettre les pieds dans le plat. ‖ FAM. *To get cold feet*, se refroidir, caner; *to stand on one's own feet*, voler de ses propres ailes. ‖ **Foot-and-mouth disease**, n. MED. Fièvre aphteuse *f.* ‖ **Foot-bath**, n. Bain (*m.*) de pieds. ‖ **Foot-brake**, n. AUTOM. Frein (*m.*) à pédale. ‖ **Foot-bridge**, n. Passerelle *f.* ‖ **Foot-muff**, n. Chancelière *f.* ‖ **Foot-note**, n. Note (*f.*) en bas de page. ‖ **Foot-page**, n. Chasseur, groom *m.* ‖ **Foot-pan**, n. Bain (*m.*) de pieds (utensil). ‖ **Foot-passenger**, n. Piéton *m.* ‖ **Foot-plate**, n. CH. DE F. Plate-forme de locomotive *f.* ‖ **Foot-race**, n. SPORTS. Course (*f.*) à pied. ‖ **Foot-slogger**, n. MILIT., FAM. Pousse-cailloux, biffin *m.* ‖ **Foot-soldier**, n. MILIT. Fantassin *m.* ‖ **Foot-stone**, n. ARCHIT. Première pierre *f.*
— v. tr. *To foot it*, danser (to dance); y aller à pied (to walk). ‖ Rempiéter (a stocking). ‖ *To foot up*, additionner, totaliser (a column of figures). ‖ FAM. *To foot the bill*, régler la note; casquer (fam.).
— v. intr. *To foot up to*, se monter à (sum).

footage [-idʒ] n. CINEM. Métrage *m.* (of a film).

football [-bɔːl] n. SPORTS. Ballon *m.* (ball); football *m.* (game).

footballer [-bɔːlə*] n. SPORTS. Joueur de football, footballer *m.*

footboard [-bɔːd] Marchepied *m.*

footboy [-bɔi] n. Chasseur, groom *m.*

footfall [-fɔːl] n. Bruit de pas, pas *m.*

footguards [-gɑːdz] n. pl. MILIT. Gardes (*m. pl.*) à pied.

foothills [-hil] n. pl. Contreforts *m. pl.* (of a mountain range).

foothold [-hould] n. Point d'appui *m.* ‖ FIG. Pied *m.*; *to lose one's foothold*, perdre pied.

footing [-iŋ] n. Point d'appui *m.* (foothold). ‖ MATH. *Footing up*, addition. ‖ FIG. Pied *m.*; position *f.*; *on an equal footing with*, sur un pied d'égalité avec.

footle ['fuːtl] v. intr. FAM. Faire l'âne; *to footle about*, baguenauder.

footlights ['futlaits] n. pl. THEATR. Rampe *f.*

footloose [-luːs] adj. FAM. Libre comme l'air.

footman [-mən] (pl. **footmen**) n. Valet de pied *m.*

footpace [-peis] n. Pas *m.* (speed).

footpath [-pɑ:θ] n. Piste (f.) pour piétons. ‖ Trottoir m. (pavement).

footprint [-print] n. Empreinte (f.) de pas.

footsie [-si] n. FAM. *Play footsie with s.o.*, faire du pied à qqn.

footsore [-sɔ:ˑ] adj. MED. Aux pieds endoloris.

footstalk [-stɔ:k] n. BOT. Pétiole m.

footstep [-step] n. Pas m. (noise, print); *to follow in s.o.'s footsteps*, emboîter le pas à qqn; suivre les traces de qqn.

footstool [-stu:l] n. Tabouret m.

footwarmer [-ˌwɔ:mə*] n. Chaufferette f. ‖ CH. DE F. Bouillotte f.

footwear [-wɛə*] n. Chaussures f. pl.; *footwear specialist*, chausseur.

footwork [-wə:k] n. SPORTS. Jeu (m.) de jambes.

foozle [ˈfu:zl̩] v. tr. FAM. Louper, cochonner, saboter. (See BUNGLE.)

fop [fɔp] n. Fat m. ‖ Dandy m.

foppery [-əri] n. Fatuité f. ‖ Elégance prétentieuse f.

foppish [-iʃ] adj. Fat (vain). ‖ D'une élégance prétentieuse.

foppishness [-iʃnis] n. Fatuité f.

for [fɔ:*] prep. Pour, au profit de; *to work for mankind*, travailler pour l'humanité. ‖ En raison de, à cause de; *but for me*, sans moi; *famous for*, célèbre par; *useful for its medicinal properties*, utile en raison de ses propriétés médicinales; *for want of*, faute de; *matter for pride*, sujet d'orgueil; *to cry for joy*, pleurer de joie. ‖ Pour, en ce qui regarde; *easy for you*, facile pour vous; *it is not for me to*, ce n'est pas à moi de. ‖ Pour, pour le compte de; *I answer for him*, je réponds pour lui. ‖ Pour, à la place de; *to sign for s.o.*, signer pour qqn. ‖ En qualité de, comme; *for instance*, par exemple; *he was given up for dead*, on le laissa pour mort; *what do you think of that for a hat?*, que pensez-vous de ça comme chapeau? ‖ Pour, eu égard à, en considération de; *for all I know*, pour autant que je sache; *thoughtful for his age*, réfléchi pour son âge. ‖ Pour, en vue de; *field for inquiry*, champ de recherche; *request for money*, demande d'argent; *to do sth. for pleasure*, faire qqch. par plaisir; *it's a case for him to decide*, voilà un cas où c'est à lui de décider; *he handed me the letter for me to read*, il m'a passé la lettre pour que je la lise. ‖ Pour, à destination de; *to go for the doctor*, aller chercher le médecin; *now for it!*, et maintenant en avant!; *to leave for the U. S. A.*, partir pour les Etats-Unis. ‖ Pour, en échange de; *a cheque for ten pounds*, un chèque de dix livres; *indebted, grateful, for*, redevable, reconnaissant de; *sold for a high price*, vendu à un prix élevé; *word for word*, mot à mot. ‖ Pendant, pour; *for ever*, pour toujours; *for five weeks*, pendant cinq semaines. ‖ Depuis, il y a; *he has been at school for three years*, il y a trois ans qu'il est à l'école; *I had not seen him for twenty years*, je ne l'avais pas vu de vingt ans, il y avait (or) voilà vingt ans que je ne l'avais vu. ‖ A, vers, sur une étendue de; *you can see for twelve miles around*, on peut voir à douze milles à la ronde. ‖ Malgré; *for all that*, en dépit de tout. ‖ LOC. *Oh! for a day of rest!*, Oh! un jour de repos!

— conj. Car, parce que.

forage [ˈfɔridʒ] n. AGRIC. Fourrage m. (see FODDER); affourragement m. (act). ‖ **Forage-cap**, n. MILIT. Bonnet (m.) de police.

— v. tr. AGRIC. Donner du fourrage à (an animal); fourrager (a country). ‖ FIG. Ravager, saccager (to plunder).

— v. intr. AGRIC. Fourrager. ‖ FAM. *To forage for*, chercher en fouillant; *to forage in*, fourrager dans.

forager [-ə*] n. Fourrageur s.

forasmuch [fərəzˈmʌtʃ] conj. Vu, étant donné, attendu (as, que).

foray [ˈfɔrei] n. Razzia f.

— v. intr. Faire une razzia. (See PLUNDER.)

forbade [fəˈbæd] pret. See FORBID.

forbear [ˈfɔ:bɛə*] n. Ancêtre m. (See ANCESTOR.)

forbear [fɔ:ˈbɛə*] v. tr. (62). S'abstenir de.

— v. intr. S'abstenir (from, de). ‖ Se montrer patient; *to forbear with*, montrer de l'indulgence pour (s.o.); supporter patiemment (sth.).

forbearance [-rəns] n. Abstention f. (from, of, de). ‖ Patience, longanimité f.

forbearing [-riŋ] adj. Patient, indulgent, tolérant.

forbid [fɔ:ˈbid] v. tr. (63). Défendre, interdire (to prohibit). ‖ Interdire l'accès de; *to forbid s.o. the house*, défendre sa porte à qqn. ‖ Empêcher, interdire (to prevent); *heaven forbid that!*, le ciel me (or) nous en préserve!

forbidden [-n̩] p. p. See FORBID.

forbidding [-iŋ] adj. Désagréable, rébarbatif, rebutant. ‖ Sombre, menaçant (weather).

forbiddingly [-diŋli] adv. D'une manière rebutante, d'un air rébarbatif.

forbore [fɔ:ˈbɔ:*] pret. See FORBEAR.

forborne [fɔ:ˈbɔ:n] p. p. See FORBEAR.

force [fɔ:s] n. Force f. (strength); *spent force*, force épuisée. ‖ Force, violence f.; *by main force*, de vive force; *by sheer force of*, à force de. ‖ Force f., nombre m.; *in force*, en force. ‖ Force, efficacité f. (effectiveness); *there is force in this statement*, voici une affirmation qui a sa valeur. ‖ Force, influence f.; *spent force*, autorité ruinée. ‖ JUR. *Into force*, en vigueur; *the Force*, la force publique, la police. ‖ MILIT. Corps m.; pl. effectifs, m. pl.; forces, troupes f. pl.; *armoured force*, engins blindés; *covering force*, troupes de couverture; *expeditionary force*, corps expéditionnaire; *field force*, armée en campagne; *home forces*, troupes métropolitaines. ‖ PHYS. Force f. ‖ **Force-feed**, adj. TECHN. Sous pression; v. tr. gaver (a goose). ‖ **Force-pump**, n. Pompe foulante f.

— v. tr. Forcer, obliger, contraindre (to compel). ‖ Mouvoir par la force; *to force back*, repousser de force; *to force in* (or) *into*, faire entrer de force; *to force out of*, arracher de force à; *to force upon*, imposer à. ‖ Forcer (the pace, one's voice); *to force a laugh*, rire d'un rire forcé, se contraindre à rire. ‖ Forcer, enfoncer (a door); forcer, fausser (a key). ‖ GRAMM. Forcer (the meaning of a word). ‖ AGRIC. Forcer (plants). ‖ MILIT. Forcer (a blockade); prendre d'assaut (a town). ‖ FAM. Pousser, chauffer (a student).

forced [-t] adj. Forcé (labour, march, sale, smile, landing).

forceful [-ful] adj. Puissant, vigoureux.

forcemeat [-mi:t] n. CULIN. Farce f.

forceps [-eps] n. invar. MED. Davier m. (in dentistry); forceps m. (in obstetrics); *artery forceps*, pince hémostatique.

forcible [-ibl̩] adj. Forcé, imposé (enforced). ‖ Vigoureux, plein de force (forceful).

forcibly [-ibli] adv. De force (under compulsion). ‖ Avec force (forcefully).

ford [fɔ:d] n. Gué m.

— v. tr., intr. Passer à gué.

fordable [-əbl̩] adj. Guéable.

fore [fɔ:*] adj. De devant (legs); antérieur, de devant (side). ‖ NAUT. D'avant. ‖ **Fore-cabin**, n. NAUT. Cabine (f.) d'avant.

— adv. A l'avant. ‖ **Fore-and-aft**, adj. NAUT. Aurique. ‖ **Fore-named**, adj. Susnommé, susdit, précité, déjà nommé.

— prep. Devant.

— interj. Attention devant!

— n. NAUT. Avant m. ‖ FIG. *To come to the fore*, se faire connaître.

forearm [ˈfɔ:rɑ:m] n. MED. Avant-bras m.

forearm [fɔ:ˈrɑ:m] v. tr. Prémunir.

forebear [ˈfɔ:bɛə*] n. U. S. Ancêtre m.

forebode [fɔ:'boud] v. tr. Présager, augurer, laisser prévoir, faire pressentir (to portend). ‖ Pressentir, avoir le pressentiment de (to anticipate).

foreboding [-iŋ] n. Mauvais présage (or) augure m. ‖ Sombre pressentiment m.

forebrain ['fɔ:brein] n. MED. Cerveau antérieur m.

forecast ['fɔ:kɑ:st] n. Pronostic m., prévision f. — [fɔ:'kɑ:st] v. tr. (32). Pronostiquer; augurer, prédire, prévoir (the future); prévoir (the weather).

forecastle ['fouksḷ] n. NAUT. Gaillard d'avant m.; plage (f.) avant.

foreclose [fɔ:'klouz] v. tr. Exclure, interdire (from, de). ‖ JUR. Forclore; to foreclose a mortgage, saisir un immeuble hypothéqué. ‖ FIG. Aller au-devant de.

foreclosure [fɔ:'klouʒə*] n. JUR. Forclusion f.

foreconscious [fɔ:'kɔnʃəs] adj. Préconscient.

forecourt ['fɔ:,kɔ:t] n. Avant-cour f.

foredone [-'dʌn] adj. FAM. Ereinté, fourbu.

foredoomed [-'du:md] adj. Condamné d'avance; foredoomed to failure, voué à l'échec.

forefather [-,fɑ:ðə*] n. Ancêtre m. (See ANCESTOR.)

forefinger [,-fiŋgə*] n. MED. Index m.

forefoot [-fut] (pl. **forefeet**) [-fi:t] n. ZOOL. Patte (f.) de devant. ‖ NAUT. Etrave f.

forefront [-frʌnt] n. Premier rang m. ‖ MILIT. Première ligne f. ‖ FIG. Premier plan m.

foregather [-'gæðə] v. tr. See FORGATHER.

forego [-'gou] v. tr., intr. (72). Précéder.

foregoer [-ə*] n. Prédécesseur m.

foregoing [-iŋ] adj. Précédent, ci-dessus. (See PREVIOUS.) — n. Ce qui précède.

foregone [fɔ:'gɔn] adj. D'autrefois, passé (past). ‖ Réglé d'avance, inévitable (determined). ‖ Prévu, escompté, pressenti (anticipated).

foreground ['fɔ:graund] n. ARTS, FIG. Premier plan m.

forehand [-hænd] adj. SPORTS. Droit (stroke). — n. SPORTS. Avant-main f. (of a horse); coup droit m. (in tennis).

forehead ['fɔrid] n. MED. Front m.

foreign ['fɔrin] adj. Etranger (to, à) [person]. ‖ De l'étranger; Foreign Office, ministère des Affaires étrangères; foreign aid, aide étrangère. ‖ COMM. Extérieur (trade). ‖ FIN. Foreign bill, lettre de change sur l'étranger; foreign exchange, change. ‖ MED., MILIT., ECCLES., FIG. Etranger. ‖ **Foreign-going**, adj. NAUT. Long-courrier, au long cours.

foreigner [-ə*] n. Etranger s. (See ALIEN.)

foreignism [-izṃ] n. Expression (or) coutume étrangère f.

forejudge [fɔ:'dʒʌdʒ] v. tr. Préjuger.

foreknow [-'nou] v. tr. (87). Savoir d'avance, préconnaître.

foreknowledge [-'nɔlidʒ] n. Préconnaissance, prescience f. (See PRECOGNITION.)

foreland ['fɔ:lənd] n. GEOGR. Pointe de terre f.; cap, promontoire m. (See HEADLAND.) ‖ MILIT. Berme f.

foreleg [-leg] n. ZOOL. Patte (f.) de devant (of a dog); jambe (f.) de devant (of a horse).

forelock [-lɔk] n. Mèche (f.) sur le front; toupet m. ‖ FAM. By the forelock, par les cheveux.

forelock [-lɔk] n. TECHN. Clavette f. — v. tr. Claveter.

foreman [-mən] (pl. **foremen**) n. TECHN. Contremaître m.; chef (m.) de fabrication. ‖ JUR. Premier juré m.

foremast [-mɑ:st] n. NAUT. Mât (m.) de misaine.

foremost [-moust] adj. Premier, le premier. — adv. En premier, en avant, au premier rang.

forename [-neim] n. Prénom m.

forenoon [fɔ:'nu:n] n. Matinée f.

forensic [fɔ'rensik] adj. JUR. Legal (argument, medicine); du barreau (eloquence); de pratique, juridique (term).

foreordain ['fɔ:rɔ:'dein] v. tr. Préordonner, prédéterminer.

forepeak ['fɔ:pi:k] n. NAUT. Avant-bec m.

foreplane [-plein] n. TECHN. Riflard m.

foreplay [-plei] n. Préliminaires m. pl., caresses f. pl. (before sexual intercourse).

forerun [-'rʌn] v. tr. (114). Devancer.

forerunner ['fɔ:,rʌnə *] n. Précurseur m. (person). ‖ Signe avant-coureur m. (foretoken).

foresail ['fɔ:seil] n. NAUT. Misaine f.

foresee [fɔ:'si:] v. tr. (117). Prévoir.

foreseeing [-iŋ] adj. Prévoyant.

foreshadow [fɔ:'ʃædou] v. tr. Laisser pressentir, faire prévoir, présager. (See PORTEND.)

foreshore ['fɔ:ʃɔ:*] n. NAUT. Plage découverte à marée basse f. ‖ JUR. Laisse de mer f.

foreshorten [fɔ:'ʃɔ:tṇ] v. tr. ARTS. Dessiner en raccourci.

foreshortening [-iŋ] n. ARTS. Raccourci m.; vue en perspective f.

foreshow [fɔ:'ʃou] v. tr. (129). Préfigurer, prédire, indiquer à l'avance. (See FORETELL.)

foresight ['fɔ:sait] n. Prévision f. (forecast); prévoyance f. (forethought). ‖ MILIT. Guidon m. (of fire-arm).

foreskin [-skin] n. MED. Prépuce m.

forest ['fɔrist] n. BOT., FIG. Forêt f. ‖ **Forest-tree**, n. BOT. Arbre (m.) de haute futaie.
— v. tr. Boiser.

forestall [fɔ:'stɔ:l] v. tr. COMM. Accaparer. ‖ FIG. Prévenir, devancer. (See ANTICIPATE.)

forester ['fɔristə*] n. Forestier m. ‖ BOT. Arbre (m.) de haute futaie. ‖ ZOOL. Animal (m.) des forêts.

forestry [-ri] n. Forêts f. pl. (land). ‖ Sylviculture f. (science).

foretaste ['fɔ:teist] n. Avant-goût m. — [fɔ:'teist] v. tr. Avoir un avant-goût de.

foretell [fɔ:'tel] v. tr. (177). Prédire, pronostiquer (to predict). ‖ Présager, annoncer, augurer, faire prévoir (to portend).

forethought ['fɔ:θɔ:t] n. Prévoyance f. (foresight). ‖ JUR. Préméditation f.

foretoken [-toukṇ] n. Présage, signe avant-coureur. — [fɔ:'toukṇ] v. tr. Présager, annoncer, augurer, faire prévoir. (See PORTEND.)

foretooth ['fɔ:tu:θ] (pl. **foreteeth** [-ti:θ]) n. MED. Dent (f.) de devant.

foretop [-tɔp] n. NAUT. Hune de misaine f. ‖ **Foretop-sail**, n. NAUT. Petit hunier m.

forewarn [fɔ:'wɔ:n] v. tr. Prévenir, avertir (to warn). ‖ Prémunir, mettre en garde contre (to forearm).

forewoman ['fɔ:wumən] (pl. **forewomen**) n. COMM. Première f.

foreword [-wə:d] n. Avant-propos m. (by, de).

foreyard [-jɑ:d] n. NAUT. Vergue de misaine f.

forfeit ['fɔ:fit] n. Gage m. (in games). ‖ JUR. Dédit m. (for breach of contract); amende f. (fine); confiscation f. (of property). — adj. Confisqué, perdu. — v. tr. Etre dépossédé de, perdre; having forfeited one's rights, déchu de ses droits; to forfeit one's driving licence, se voir retirer son permis de conduire.

forfeiture [-tʃə*] n. JUR. Retrait m. (of a licence); confiscation f. (of a property); déchéance f. (of rights); forfaiture f. (of a title).

forgather [fɔ:'gæðə*] v. intr. S'assembler (to gather); se rencontrer (with, avec).

forgave [-geiv] pret. See FORGIVE.

forge [fɔ:dʒ] n. TECHN. Forge f. ‖ **Forge-hammer**, n. TECHN. Marteau-pilon m. — v. tr. TECHN. Forger. ‖ JUR. Faire un faux en; contrefaire. ‖ FIG. Forger, inventer, fabriquer. — v. intr. TECHN. Etre forgé, se forger. ‖ JUR. Faire un faux.

forge v. intr. Avancer avec difficulté ; *to forge ahead*, passer devant ; en mettre un coup (fam.).

forger [-ə*] n. TECHN. Forgeur *m.* ∥ JUR. Faussaire *s.* (See COUNTERFEITER.) ∥ FIG. Forgeur, inventeur *s.*

forgery [-əri] n. JUR. Falsification *f.* (of documents) ; contrefaçon *f.* (of money) ; faux *m.* (document).

forget [fə'get] v. tr. (64). Oublier ; *best forgotten*, qu'il vaut mieux ne pas rappeler ; *to forget oneself*, s'oublier. ∥ **Forget-me-not**, n. BOT. Myosotis *m.*
— v. intr. Oublier, faire un oubli.

forgetful [-ful] adj. Oublieux (memory) ; oublieux, négligent (person) ; de l'oubli (sleep).

forgetfulness [-fulnis] n. Oubli chronique, manque (*m.*) de mémoire. ∥ Négligence *f.*

forgettable [-əbḷ] adj. Oubliable.

forgivable [fə'givəbḷ] adj. Pardonnable.

forgive [fə:giv] v. tr. (65). Pardonner (offence) ; pardonner à (offender) [see PARDON] ; *forgive me that I didn't come, forgive me for not coming, forgive my not coming*, pardonnez-moi de n'être pas venu. ∥ Remettre (a debt) ; faire grâce de (a punishment). [See ABSOLVE.]

forgiven [-n̩] p. p. See FORGIVE.

forgiveness [-nis] n. Pardon *m. ; to ask s.o.'s forgiveness*, demander pardon à qqn. ∥ Remise *f.* (of a debt). ∥ Indulgence, clémence *f.*

forgiving [-iŋ] adj. Indulgent, clément, miséricordieux.

forgo [fɔ:'gou] v. tr. (72). S'abstenir de, renoncer à. (See RELINQUISH.)

forgot [fə'gɔt], **forgotten** [-'gɔtn̩] pret., p. p. See FORGET.

fork [fɔ:k] n. Bifurcation, fourche *f.* (of roads). [See BRANCH.] ∥ Zigzag *m.* (of lightning). ∥ Fourche *f.* (of trousers). ∥ AGRIC. Fourche *f.* ∥ CULIN. Fourchette *f.* ∥ MUS. Diapason *m.* ∥ AUTOM. Fourche *f.* (of cycle) ; fourchette *f.* (of gear-change). ∥ **Fork-lift truck**, n. TECHN. Chariot élévateur *m.*, gerbeuse *f.*
— v. tr. AGRIC. Remuer à la fourche, fourcher. ∥ TECHN. Assécher (a mine). ∥ Fourcher (in chess). ∥ FAM. *To fork out*, abouler, allonger (money).
— v. intr. Bifurquer, fourcher (river, road). ∥ Etre en forme de fourche. ∥ FAM. *To fork out*, casquer.

forked [-t] adj. Fourchu (branch, tongue) ; bifurqué (road). ∥ A dents (fork). ∥ En zigzag (lightning).

forlorn [fɔ'lɔ:n] adj. Abandonné (deserted). ∥ Malheureux, misérable (wretched). ∥ Désespéré, sans espoir (desperate). ∥ MILIT. *Forlorn hope*, troupe sacrifiée. ∥ FIG. *Forlorn hope*, tentative désespérée.

form [fɔ:m] n. Forme *f.* (appearance, shape) ; *in the form of*, sous forme de. ∥ Forme *f. ;* corps *m.* ∥ Forme *f. ;* moule *m.* (mould). ∥ Banc *m.* (bench) ; classe *f.* (in school). ∥ Formule *f. ;* formulaire, imprimé, bulletin *m. ; to fill up a form*, remplir une formule (or) fiche. ∥ Formalité *f. ; a matter of form*, simple question de formalité. ∥ Forme *f. ;* rite *m. ; for form's sake*, pour la forme. ∥ Forme, étiquette *f. ; good form*, bon ton, savoir-vivre ; *it's not good form*, cela ne se fait pas, c'est de mauvais genre. ∥ Forme, règle *f. ; in due form*, en bonne et due forme, dans les règles. ∥ Forme, sorte *f. ;* type *m. ; two forms of government*, deux formes de gouvernement. ∥ Gîte *m.* (of a hare). ∥ GRAMM., PHILOS., MUS., TECHN. Forme *f.* ∥ MED., SPORTS. Forme, condition *f. ;* état *m. ; below one's usual form*, inférieur à soi-même ; *to be out of form*, n'être pas en forme. ∥ **Form-fitting**, adj. Moulant, collant (dress).
— v. tr. Former, façonner, faire (*after*, sur, d'après ; *from, out of*, de) [to shape]. ∥ Former, dessiner, tracer (curves). ∥ Former, mouler (to mould). ∥ Former, disposer, organiser ; *to form lines*, se mettre en rangs. ∥ JUR. Former (a cabinet, ministry) ; constituer (a company) ; *they formed themselves into a company*, ils se constituèrent en société. ∥ GRAMM. Construire (sentences) ; former (words). ∥ MILIT. *Form fours !*, colonne par quatre !
∥ FIG. Former, contracter (an alliance) ; concevoir (a doubt, hope) ; former (faculty, mind) ; contracter, prendre (habits) ; se faire (an idea, opinion) ; former, donner une formation à (s.o.) ; formuler, prononcer (a word).
— v. intr. Prendre forme, se former, se dessiner (to take shape). ∥ Se constituer, se former (to take form). ∥ MILIT. Se former (*into*, en).

formal ['fɔ:məl] adj. De pure forme (invitation). ∥ Cérémonieux (bow) ; de cérémonie (dinner). ∥ Formaliste, à cheval sur les convenances (person). ∥ Traditionnel (use) ; conventionnel (style) ; *formal afternoon dress*, robe classique d'après-midi. ∥ Formel, catégorique, explicite (consent, denial). ∥ JUR. En bonne forme, dans les règles ; *formal defect*, vice de forme. ∥ PHILOS. Formel. ∥ ARTS. Stylisé (flower). ∥ COMM. *Formal order*, bon de commande.

formaldehyde [fɔ:'mældihaid] n. CHIM. Formaldéhyde *m.*

formalin ['fɔ:məlin] n. CHIM. Formol *m.*

formalism ['fɔ:məlizm̩] n. Formalisme *m.*

formalist [-ist] n. Formaliste ; conformiste *m.* (See CONVENTIONALIST.)

formality [fɔ:'mæliti] n. Formalité *f. ; to comply with a formality*, remplir une formalité. ∥ Cérémonie, étiquette *f. ; cérémonial m. ;* formes *f. pl.* ∥ Raideur, froideur compassée *f.* (rigidity of manner).

formalize ['fɔ:məlaiz] v. tr. Régler le cérémonial (or) les formalités de. ∥ Donner une forme à (to shape). ∥ Guinder, rendre compassé (to make stiff).

formally [-li] adv. De pure forme, pour la forme. ∥ Selon les règles, en bonne et due forme. ∥ Cérémonieusement, d'un air compassé.

format ['fɔ:mæt] n. Format *m.*

formation [fɔ:'meiʃən] n. AVIAT., MILIT. Formation *f. ; attack formation*, dispositif d'attaque. ∥ FIG. Formation *f.*

formative ['fɔ:mətiv] adj. De formation (years). ∥ GRAMM., MED. Formatif. ∥ ART. Plastique.
— n. GRAMM. Elément formatif *m.*

former ['fɔ:mə*] adj. Antérieur, précédent (earlier). ∥ Ancien, ex-. ∥ Passé, d'autrefois (past).
— pron. Le premier, celui-là.

formerly [-li] adv. Autrefois, jadis, dans le temps ; précédemment.

formic ['fɔ:mik] adj. CHIM. Formique.

formidable ['fɔmidəbḷ] adj. Terrifiant, redoutable (dreadful). ∥ FAM. Formidable, énorme.

formidably [-bli] adv. Redoutablement. ∥ FAM. Formidablement.

formless ['fɔ:mlis] adj. Informe.

formula ['fɔ:mjulə] (pl. **formulae** [-li:], **formulas** [-ləs]) n. MED., MATH., FIG. Formule *f.*

formulary [-ləri] n. Formulaire *m.*
— adj. De formule, de commande.

formulate [-leit] v. tr. Formuler.

fornicate ['fɔ:nikeit] v. intr. Forniquer.

fornication [fɔ:ni'keiʃən] n. Fornication *f.*

fornicator ['fɔ:nikeitə*] n. Fornicateur *m.*

fornicatress [-tris] n. Fornicatrice *f.*

forsake [fə'seik] v. tr. (66). Abandonner, délaisser (s.o.) ; renoncer à, s'abstenir de, abandonner (sth.).

forsaken [-n̩] p. p. ; **forsook** [fɔ'su:k] pret. See FORSAKE.

forsooth [fɔ'su:θ] adv. Vraiment, en vérité.

forspent [-'spent] adj. Epuisé. (See EXHAUSTED.)

forswear [-swɛə*] v. tr. (168). Abjurer, renier solennellement (to deny) ; renoncer par serment à (to renounce) ; *to forswear oneself*, se parjurer.

forsythia [fɔ:'saiθiə] n. BOT. Forsythia *m.*

fort [fɔ:t] n. MILIT. Fortification *f. ;* fort *m.*

fortalice ['fɔ:təlis] n. MILIT. Fortin *m.*

forte [fɔ:t] n. Fort *m. ;* supériorité *f.*

forte ['fɔ:ti] n., adv. Mus. Forte m. inv., adv. — adj. Forte passage, morceau joué forte.

forth [fɔ:θ] adv. En avant (onward); and so forth, et ainsi de suite, etc. || En dehors (out); to call s.o. forth to the rescue, appeler qqn à la rescousse.

forthcoming [fɔ:θ'kʌmiŋ] adj. Prochain, futur, à venir (events). || Prêt à paraître, en cours de publication (book).

forthright [-'rait] adv. Immédiatement, tout de suite (at once). || Nettement, carrément (frankly). — ['fɔ:θrait] adj. Net, carré, brutal (truth).

forthwith ['fɔ:θ'wiδ] adv. Sur-le-champ.

fortieth ['fɔ:tiiθ] adj., n. Quarantième s.

fortification [,fɔ:tifi'keiʃən] n. Milit. Fortification f. || Fig. Renforcement m.

fortify ['fɔ:tifai] v. tr. (2). Milit., Fig. Fortifier, renforcer.

fortitude ['fɔ:titju:d] n. Force morale, endurance, énergie f. (See GRIT.)

fortnight ['fɔ:tnait] n. Quinzaine f.; quinze jours m. pl; deux semaines f. pl.

fortnightly [-li] adv. Tous les quinze jours. — adj. Bimensuel. — n. Bimensuel m. (magazine).

Fortran ['fɔ:træn] n. Inform. Fortran m.

fortress ['fɔ:tris] n. Forteresse f.; Fortress Europe, la forteresse européenne.

fortuitous [fɔ:'tju:itəs] adj. Fortuit. (See ACCIDENTAL.)

fortuitously [-li] adv. Fortuitement.

fortunate ['fɔ:tjunit] adj. Fortuné, chanceux (person); to be fortunate in, avoir à se louer de. || Favorable, heureux (occasion).

fortunately [-li] adv. Par chance; par bonheur, heureusement.

fortune ['fɔ:tjun] n. Fortune f.; destin, sort m. (fate). || Fortune, chance f. (luck). || Fortune f.; hasard m. (hazard). || Fortune, richesse f. (wealth); to make a fortune, faire fortune; to marry a fortune, épouser une dot. || Bonne aventure f.; to tell s.o.'s fortune, dire la bonne aventure à qqn. || **Fortune-hunter**, n. Coureur (m.) de dot. || **Fortune-teller**, n. Diseur (s.) de bonne aventure; cartomancien s. (by cards).

forty ['fɔ:ti] adj., n. Quarante m.; the forties, les années quarante; to be in the late forties, friser la cinquantaine.

forum ['fɔ:rəm] n. Archit. Forum m. || Jur. Tribunal compétent m.

forward ['fɔ:wəd] adj. En tête (ahead); en avant (onward). || Précoce, avancé, en avance (precocious). || Avancé, progressiste (progressive). || Audacieux, présomptueux, téméraire (bold); entreprenant, trop hardi, ambitieux (pushing). || Effronté (impertinent); prompt (to, à); empressé, impatient (to, de). || Comm. A terme (buying). — n. Sports. Avant m. || Fin. Report m. (in book-keeping). — adv. En avant, vers l'avant (onward); to take a step forward, faire un pas en avant; to put forward, mettre en avant, avancer. || En avance; to get forward with one's work, avancer son travail, s'avancer. || En vue; to push oneself forward, se mettre en avant; se pousser (fam.). || Naut. A l'avant. || Fin. To carry forward, reporter. || **Forward-looking**, adj. Progressiste, entreprenant, plein d'initiative. — interj. En avant! — v. tr. Faire suivre (see TRANSMIT); please forward, prière de faire suivre. || Comm. Expédier; acheminer (goods). || Bot. Forcer, pousser (plants). || Fig. Favoriser, soutenir.

forwarder [-ə*] n. Expéditeur m.; expéditrice f. (of a parcel). || Comm. Transitaire m. || Fig. Promoteur m.; promotrice f.

forwarding [-iŋ] n. Avancement m. (development). || Expédition f.; envoi m. (of a letter, parcel). ||

Comm. Forwarding agent, transitaire, expéditionnaire. || Bot. Forçage m.

forwardness [-nis] n. Avancement m. (development). || Précocité f. (precociousness). || Modernisme, progressisme m. (progressiveness). || Témérité, présomption, hardiesse f. (boldness). || Esprit (m.) d'entreprise, empressement m. (readiness). || Ardeur f. (eagerness). || Effronterie f. (pertness).

forwards [-z] adv. See FORWARD.

fossa ['fɔsə] n. Med. Fosse f.

fosse [fɔs] n. Fossé m. (See DITCH.)

fossick ['fɔsik] v. intr. Fam. Fourgonner, farfouiller.

fossil ['fɔsl] adj., n. Zool., Bot., Fam. Fossile m.

fossiliferous ['fɔsi'lifərəs] n. Fossilifère.

fossilize ['fɔsilaiz] v. tr. Zool., Bot. Fossiliser. || Fam. Encroûter. — v. intr. Zool., Bot. Se fossiliser. || Fam. S'encroûter.

foster ['fɔstə*] n. † Alimentation f. || **Foster-brother**, n. Frère de lait m.; frère adoptif m. || **Foster-child**, n. Enfant (s.) placé en nourrice; enfant adoptif s. || **Foster-father**, n. Père nourricier m.; père adoptif m. || **Foster-mother**, n. Mère nourricière f.; mère adoptive f. — v. tr. Nourrir, élever. || Fig. Protéger (arts); être favorable à (development); engendrer (disease); développer, nourrir (friendship); nourrir (hope); encourager (opinions); fomenter (sedition).

fosterage [-ridʒ] n. Mise en nourrice f. (act); fait (m.) d'élever (rearing); fait (m.) d'être élevé (state). || Fig. Encouragement m.; incitation f.

fostering [-liŋ] n. Nourrisson m. (baby); enfant adopté s. (child).

fought [fɔ:t] pret., p. p. See FIGHT.

foul [faul] adj. Vicié (air); sale (linen); nauséabond, fétide, infect, puant (odour); encrassé (pen); engorgé (pump); dégoûtant, répugnant (sight); bourbeux (water). || Naut. Engagé (anchor, rope); to run foul of, aborder, entrer en collision avec. || Autom. To run foul of, tamponner; entrer dedans (fam.). || Sports Bas (blow); déloyal (play); foul play, tricherie. || Jur. Foul play, meurtre. || Fig. Infâme, odieux (deed); grossier, obscène (talk); impur (thought); foul play, perfidie. || Fam. Infect, dégoûtant, sale (weather); to fall foul of s.o., entrer dans le chou à qqn. || **Foul-mouthed**, adj. Mal embouché. — adv. Déloyalement; to play s.o. foul, faire une crasse à qqn. — n. Naut. Abordage m. || Autom. Collision f.; tamponnage, accrochage m. || Sports. Infraction, faute f.; coup interdit m. || Fig. Foul and fair, le meilleur et le pire. — v. tr. Salir (to dirty); souiller (to soil). || Encrasser, engorger (to choke). || Naut. Engager (anchor); aborder, entrer en collision avec (a ship). || Autom. Tamponner, heurter, accrocher, entrer dans. || Sports. Gêner, couper, se mettre en travers de. || Fig. Salir. — v. intr. Se salir, se souiller (to become dirty). || S'encrasser, s'engorger (to become clogged). || Naut. S'engager (anchor); se heurter (ships). || Autom. Se tamponner. || Sports. Manquer aux règles.

foulard ['fu:lɑ:(d)] n. Foulard m.

foulness ['faulnis] n. Saleté, malpropreté f. (dirtiness); encrassement m. (clogging); fétidité, puanteur f. (stink). || Fig. Infamie, noirceur f. (of a deed); grossièreté, obscénité f. (of talk).

foumart ['fu:mɑ:t] n. Zool. Putois m.

found [faund] pret., p. p. See FIND.

found v. tr. Techn. Fondre.

found v. tr. Archit. Poser les fondations de. || Fig. Fonder, créer (a chair, an empire); édifier (a fortune); fonder, appuyer, établir (an opinion, a statement); to found oneself on, se fonder sur. — v. intr. Se fonder (on, upon, sur).

foundation [faun'deiʃən] n. ARCHIT. Fondation *f.* ‖ Fond *m.* (of dress, hat); rang (*m.*) de base (in knitting). ‖ FIG. Fondation, création *f.* (act, institution); fondement *m.* (of fortune, opinion, suspicion); *entirely without foundation*, dénué de tout fondement. ‖ **Foundation-garment**, n. Gaine *f.* ‖ **Foundation-net**, n. Sparterie *f.* ‖ **Foundation-scholar**, n. Boursier *s.* ‖ **Foundation-stone**, n. ARCHIT. Première pierre *f.*

founder [-ə*] n. COMM., FIG. Fondateur *m.*

founder n. TECHN. Fondeur *s.*

founder v. intr. S'effondrer (building, ground). ‖ S'effondrer (to collapse); boiter bas (to fall lame) [horse]. ‖ NAUT. Sombrer. ‖ FIG. S'effondrer.
— v. tr. Faire s'effondrer. ‖ NAUT. Couler.
— n. Fourbure *f.* (of horse).

foundering ['faundəriŋ] n. Effondrement *m.* ‖ NAUT. Submersion *f.*

foundling ['faundliŋ] n. Enfant trouvé *s.*

foundress [-ris] n. Fondatrice *f.*

foundry [-ri] n. TECHN. Fonderie *f.*

fount [faunt] n. Réservoir *m.* (of fountain-pen) ‖ FIG. Source *f.* ‖ FAM. Puits *m.* (of knowledge).

fount [faunt] n. TECHN. Fonte *f.*

fountain ['fauntin] n. Source *f.* (of a river). ‖ Fontaine *f.*; *drinking fountain*, borne-fontaine, fontaine Wallace. ‖ Jet (*m.*) d'eau, fontaine *f.* (in a garden). ‖ Réservoir *m.* (for ink, oil). ‖ FIG. Source *f.* ‖ **Fountain-pen**, n. Stylo *m.*

four [fɔ:*] adj., n. Quatre *m.* ‖ LOC. *A carriage and four*, un attelage à quatre chevaux; *the four hundred*, les deux cents familles; *to go on all fours*, marcher à quatre pattes; *to go on all four with*, marcher de pair avec. ‖ **Four-bank**, adj. TECHN. A quatre rangs. ‖ **Four-course**, adj. AGRIC. Quadriennal. ‖ **Four-dimensional**, adj. A quatre dimensions. ‖ **Four-engined**, adj. AVIAT. Quadrimoteur. ‖ **Four-footed**, adj. ZOOL. Quadrupède. ‖ **Four-handed**, adj. ZOOL. Quadrumane; MUS. à quatre mains. ‖ **Four-in-hand**, n. Attelage (*m.*) à quatre; U. S. FAM. *Four-in-hand tie*, cravate-plastron. ‖ **Four-leaf**, adj. BOT. A quatre feuilles. ‖ **Four-letter word**, n. Gros mot *m.* ‖ **Four-part**, adj. MUS. A quatre voix. ‖ **Four-poster**, n. Lit (*m.*) à colonnes. ‖ **Four-stroke**, adj. AUTOM. A quatre temps.

fourflusher [-ˌflʌʃə*] n. U. S. FAM. Bluffeur *m.*

fourfold ['fɔ:fould] adj. Quadruple.
— adv. Au quadruple, multiplié par quatre.

fourpence [-pəns] n. pl. Quatre pence *m. pl.*

fourpenny [-pni] adj. De quatre pence.

fourscore ['skɔ:*] adj. Quatre-vingts.

foursome [-səm] n. SPORTS. Partie (*f.*) de double.

fourteen [-'ti:n] adj., n. Quatorze *adj.*, *m. invar.*

fourteenth [-'ti:nθ] adj., n. Quatorzième *m.* (in general); quatorze *m.* (with a title).

fourth [fɔ:θ] adj. Quatrième. ‖ Quatre (with a date, a title). ‖ U. S. FAM. *Fourth estate*, la presse souveraine.
— n. Quart *m.* ‖ MUS. Quarte *f.*

fourthly [-li] adv. Quatrièmement.

fowl [faul] n. ZOOL. CULIN. Volaille *f.* ‖ ZOOL. † Volatile *m.*; *wild fowl*, gibier d'eau. ‖ **Fowl-run**, n. Elevage (*m.*) de volaille; basse-cour (*f.*) d'élevage.
— v. intr. SPORTS. Oiseler (with a net); chasser (with a gun).

fowler ['faulə*] n. SPORTS. Oiseleur *m.* (with a net); chasseur *m.* (with a gun).

fox [fɔks] n. ZOOL., FIG. Renard *m.* ‖ **Fox-brush**, n. Queue (*f.*) de renard. ‖ **Fox-hole**, n. Renardière *f.*; MILIT. Gourbi; trou de tirailleur *m.* ‖ **Fox-hunt**, n. SPORTS. Chasse (*f.*) au renard; v. intr. Chasser au renard. ‖ **Fox-terrier**, n. ZOOL. Fox-terrier *m.* ‖ **Fox-trot**, n. MUS. Slow *m.*
— v. tr. Réparer (boots). ‖ Piquer, salir (books). ‖ FAM. Rouler (s.o.).
— v. intr. Se piquer (beer, book). ‖ FAM. Renarder,

jouer au plus fin; *to fox about*, fouiner partout.

foxglove [-glʌv] n. BOT. Digitale *f.*

foxhound [-haund] n. ZOOL. Foxhound n.

foxiness [-inis] n. Ruse *f.*; roublardise *f.* (fam.).

foxy [-i] adj. Rusé; renard (fam.) [wily]. ‖ Roux, brique (reddish-brown). ‖ Piqué, tacheté (paper).

foyer ['fɔiei], ['fwaje] n. THEATR. Foyer *m.*

fracas ['frækɑ:] n. Altercation, querelle *f.* (quarrel); rixe, bagarre *f.* (brawl).

fraction ['frækʃən] n. CHIM., MATH., ECCLES., FIG. Fraction *f.*

fractional [-l] adj. CHIM. Fractionné (distillation). ‖ MATH. Fractionnaire. ‖ FIN. Divisionnaire (currency).

fractionary [-əri] adj. Fractionnaire, fragmentaire.

fractionate [-neit] v. tr. CHIM. Dissocier.

fractious ['frækʃəs] adj. Rétif (animal); maussade, revêche (person).

fracture ['fræktʃə*] n. MED. Fracture *f.* ‖ GEOL. Cassure *f.*
— v. tr. MED. Fracturer.
— v. intr. MED. Se fracturer.

fragile ['frædʒail] adj. Fragile.

fragility [fræ'dʒiliti] n. Fragilité *f.*

fragment ['frægmənt] n. Fragment *m.*
— [fræg'ment] v. tr. Fragmenter.
— v. intr. Se fragmenter.

fragmentary [-əri] adj. Fragmentaire.

fragmentation [ˌfrægmen'teiʃən] n. Fragmentation *f.*; *fragmentation bomb*, bombe à fragmentation.

fragrance ['freigrəns] n. Odeur agréable *f.*; parfum *m.* (See SCENT.)

fragrant [-ənt] adj. Parfumé, embaumé.

frail [freil] n. COMM. Couffin *m.*; couffe *f.*

frail adj. Fragile (brittle). ‖ MED. Faible, délicat, frêle (health, person). ‖ FAM. De petite vertu (woman).
— n. U. S. Poule *f.* (tart).

frailty [-ti] n. Fragilité *f.* ‖ MED. Faiblesse, délicatesse, fragilité *f.* ‖ FIG. Faiblesse *f.*

fraise [freiz] n. Fraise *f.* (collar). ‖ MILIT., TECHN. Fraise *f.*

frame [freim] v. tr. Former, façonner, modeler (to shape). ‖ ARTS. Encadrer (a picture, s.o.). ‖ JUR. Formuler, articuler (a law); ourdir (a plot). ‖ FIG. Formuler (an answer); émettre (a theory); concevoir (a thought); articuler, prononcer (a word). ‖ FAM. Monter un coup contre (s.o.); manigancer (sth.).
— n. Bois *m.* (of a bed); métier (for tapestry); carcasse *f.* (of umbrella); monture *f.* (of a pair of spectacles). ‖ TECHN. Bâti *m.* (of an engine); table dormante *f.* (for ore dressing). ‖ AUTOM. Cadre *m.* (of bicycle); châssis *m.* (of car). ‖ MILIT. Affût *m.* (of gun). ‖ NAUT. Membrure *f.* (of ship); couple *m.* (timber). ‖ ARCHIT. Charpente *f.* (of building); chambranle *m.*; (of door); châssis *m.* (of window). ‖ ARTS. Cadre *m.* (of picture). ‖ AGRIC. Châssis *m.* ‖ MED. Stature, taille *f.* (build); ossature *f.* (skeleton). ‖ RADIO. Trame *f.* (in television). ‖ FIG. Système *m.* (of government); disposition *f.*; état *m.* (of mind); *in a bad frame of mind*, mal disposé, de mauvaise humeur. ‖ U. S. FAM. Châssis *m.* (body). ‖ **Frame-aerial**, n. RADIO. Cadre (*m.*) de T. S. F. ‖ **Frame-house**, n. ARCHIT. Maison (*f.*) en bois. ‖ **Frame-up**, n. U. S. FAM. Coup monté *m.*

framer [-ə*] n. ARTS. Encadreur *m.* ‖ FIG. Auteur *m.*

framework [-wə:k] n. ARCHIT. Charpente *f.* ‖ TECHN. Revêtement *m.* (of pit-shaft); travail au métier *m.* (in tapestry). ‖ THEATR. Portant *m.* ‖ FIG. Charpente, ossature, structure *f.*

framing [-iŋ] n. Construction *f.*; façonnement *m.* (shaping). ‖ ARTS. Encadrement *m.* ‖ JUR. Rédaction *f.* (of a law); organisation *f.* (of a plot). ‖

FIG. Conception *f.* (of an idea); élaboration *f.* (of a novel). ‖ **Framing-chisel,** n. TECHN. Bédane *m.*

franc [fræ ŋk] n. FIN. Franc *m.*

France [frɑ:ns] n. GEOGR. France *f.*

franchise [ˈfræntʃaiz] n. † Franchise, immunité *f.* ‖ JUR. Droit *(m.)* de cité (or) de vote. ‖ U. S. Concession *f.*; privilège *m.*
— v. tr. U. S. COMM. Accorder une concession à.

Franciscan [frænˈsiskən] adj., n. ECCLES. Franciscain *adj., s.*

francium [ˈfrænsiəm] n. CHIM. Francium *m.*

francophone [ˈfræ ŋkouˌfoun] adj., n. Francophone *adj., s.*

frangibility [frændʒiˈbiliti] n. Fragilité *f.*

frangible [ˈfrændʒibḷ] adj. Fragile.

frangipane [ˈfrændʒipein] n. BOT., CULIN. Frangipane *f.*

franglais [frɑˈgle] n. Franglais *m.*

Frank [fræ ŋk] n. GEOGR. Franc *m.*; Franque *f.*

frank adj. Franc, direct (action); franc, sincère (person).

frank v. tr. Affranchir; *franking-machine,* machine à affranchir.

frankfurter [ˈfræ ŋkfə:tə *] n. CULIN. Saucisse *(f.)* de Francfort.

frankincense [ˈfræ ŋkin,sens] n. Encens *m.*

Frankish [ˈfræ ŋkiʃ] adj. GEOGR. Franc *m.;* franque *f.*

franklin [-lin] n. † Franc-tenancier *m.*

frankly [-li] adv. Franchement.

frankness [-nis] n. Franchise *f.*

frantic [ˈfræntik] adj. Frénétique, forcené; *frantic with,* fou de.

frantically [-əli] adv. Frénétiquement, avec frénésie. ‖ FAM. Terriblement.

frap [fræp] v. tr. (1). NAUT. Brider (a rope); ceintrer (a ship).

fraternal [frəˈtə:nḷ] adj. Fraternel.

fraternally [-əli] adv. Fraternellement.

fraternity [-iti] n. Fraternité *f.* (brotherliness). ‖ Confrérie *f.; writing fraternity,* association des écrivains. ‖ U. S. Club *(m.)* d'étudiants.

fraternization [,frætə:naiˈzeiʃən] n. Fraternisation *f.*

fraternize [ˈfrætə:naiz] v. intr. Fraterniser (with, avec).

fratricidal [frætriˈsaidḷ] adj. Fratricide.

fratricide [ˈfrætrisaid] n. Fratricide *m.* (crime, criminal).

fraud [frɔ:d] n. Tromperie, supercherie *f.* (deceit); fraude, duperie *f.* (deception). ‖ Imposteur, fumiste, monteur de coup *m.* (fam.) [person]; objet *(m.)* de déception, attrape-nigaud; montage de coup *m.* (thing); *the match was a fraud,* le match n'était que du chiqué. ‖ JUR. Dol *m.*

fraudulence [ˈfrɔ:djuləns] n. Acte frauduleux *m.* (act); improbité *f.* (quality).

fraudulent [-ənt] adj. Frauduleux (bankrupt); dolosif (clause); déloyal (competition); entaché de fraude (transaction).

fraudulently [-əntli] adv. Frauduleusement.

fraught [frɔ:t] adj. Chargé, pourvu (with, de). ‖ FIG. Gros, lourd (with, de); fertile (with, en).

fray v. tr. n. Bagarre *f.; to enter the fray,* descendre dans l'arène.

fray v. tr. Effranger, effiler (a cloth). ‖ ZOOL. Frayer.
— v. intr. S'effiler, s'effranger.
— n. Effilochure *f.*

frazzle [ˈfræzḷ] n. FAM. *To a frazzle,* complètement, absolument; *to beat to a frazzle,* battre à plate couture; *worn to a frazzle,* crevé, éreinté.

freak [fri:k] n. Lubie, toquade *f.;* caprice *m.* (whim). ‖ Frasque, fredaine *f.* (prank). ‖ Monstre *m.* (monstrosity). ‖ FAM. Fana *s.; film freak,* dingue de cinéma. ‖ POP. Freak *m.,* marginal *s.* ‖ **Freak-out,** n. POP. Défonce *f.*
— v. intr. POP. *To freak out,* flipper (to go wild);

se défoncer (to get high); devenir marginal (to drop out).
— v. tr. POP. *To freak out,* faire flipper.

freaked [-t] adj. Bigarré.

freakish [-iʃ] adj. Capricieux, lunatique (whimsical). ‖ Monstrueux, phénoménal (abnormal).

freakishness [-iʃnis] n. Nature fantasque (or) capricieuse *f.*

freckle [ˈfrekḷ] n. MED. Tache de rousseur, éphélide *f.*
— v. tr. MED. Couvrir de taches de rousseur.
— v. intr. MED. Se couvrir de taches de rousseur.

freckly [ˈfrekli] adj. Couvert de taches de rousseur.

free [fri:] adj. Libre, en liberté (bird); *to set a slave free,* affranchir un esclave; *to set free a prisoner,* libérer un prisonnier. ‖ Libre, indépendant (city, people, state). ‖ Libre, non occupé (person, table, time); *free day,* jour de liberté. ‖ Libre, sans entraves (love); *to be free of,* avoir la libre disposition de; *to give s.o. a free hand,* donner carte blanche à qqn, laisser à qqn les coudées franches. ‖ Libre, dégagé (road); *free pass,* carte de circulation; *to be free of s.o.'s house,* avoir ses entrées libres chez qqn. ‖ Libre, détaché, non attaché (rope). ‖ Libre (choice); spontané (offer). ‖ Souple, aisé, dégagé (gait); franc, direct, ouvert (manner, person, speech). ‖ Libre, désinvolte, sans façons (manner, person); *free and easy,* libre (life); cavalier (manner); *to make free with,* prendre des libertés avec (s.o.); user sans façons de (sth.). ‖ Libre, sans contraintes (life); *free fight, free for all,* bagarre, mêlée. ‖ Libre, licencieux, grivois (language); *free of speech,* peu gêné dans ses propos. ‖ Libéral, généreux, large (with, de) [person]; abondant, copieux (supply); *free with one's money,* dépensier, qui ne compte pas; *to be free with one's hands,* avoir la main leste. ‖ Libéré, affranchi, dégagé, débarrassé *(from,* de) [work]; *to shake oneself free from,* se libérer de, s'affranchir de. ‖ Enclin, porté *(in, to,* à) [criticism]. ‖ GRAMM. Franc, aisé, net (style); libre, non littéral (translation); libre (verse); *free adjunct,* complément juxtaposé. ‖ PHILOS. *Free will,* libre arbitre. ‖ FIN. Libre (market); *free of duty,* exempt de droits; *free of tax,* net d'impôts. ‖ COMM. Gratuit (admission, sample); libre, sans restriction (sale); *free trade,* libre-échange; *free on rail,* franco gare; *post free,* franco de port. ‖ PHYS. Libre (energy). ‖ CHIM. Libre (gas); brut (gold). ‖ TECHN. Libre (wheel); *free motion,* jeu. ‖ NAUT. Franc (port); favorable (wind); *running free,* largue. ‖ SPORTS. Franc du collier (horse); *free kick,* coup franc placé. ‖ AUTOM. Libre (wheel). ‖ THEATR. De faveur (ticket). ‖ **Free-and-easiness,** n. Sans-gêne *m.* ‖ **Free-and-easy,** n. FAM. Beuverie *f.* ‖ **Free-board,** n. NAUT. Accastillage, franc-bord *m.; freeboard deck,* place. ‖ **Free-hand,** adj., adv. ARTS. A main levée. ‖ **Free-handed,** adj. Au cœur sur la main, généreux. ‖ **Free-house,** n. Bar *(m.)* en gérance libre. ‖ **Free-lance,** n. Franc-tireur *(m.)* de la politique (or) du journalisme; adj. Indépendant; v. intr. Faire du journalisme indépendant. ‖ **Free-liver,** n. Viveur *m.* ‖ **Free-loader,** n. FAM. Parasite, écornifleur *m.* ‖ **Free-mindedness,** n. Insouciance *f.* ‖ **Free-range,** adj. *Free-range hen, egg,* poulet, œuf fermier *m.* ‖ **Free-spoken,** adj. Qui a son franc-parler. ‖ **Free-style,** n. SPORTS. Nage libre *f.* ‖ **Free-thinker,** n. Libre-penseur *s.* ‖ **Free-trader,** n. COMM. Libre-échangiste *s.* ‖ **Free-wheel,** v. intr. AUTOM. Marcher en roue libre. ‖ **Free-will,** adj. Volontaire, de plein gré.
— adv. Librement, sans contrainte. ‖ COMM. Franco, gratis; *sent free on request,* envoyé franco (or) gratuitement sur demande. ‖ NAUT. *To sail free,* avoir du largue.
— v. tr. Libérer, délivrer (people, prisoners); affranchir (slaves). ‖ Dégager (to clear), débarrasser *(from,* de) [to rid]; *to free oneself from,* se

dégager de. ‖ Exempter, dispenser, libérer (from, de). ‖ Fin. Détaxer. ‖ Comm. Mettre en vente libre.
freebooter [-ˌbuːtə*] n. † Flibustier m. ‖ Fam. Maraudeur s.
freedman ['friːdmən] (pl. **freedmen**) n. Affranchi m.
freedom ['friːdəm] n. Liberté, indépendance f. (of nations, people). ‖ Liberté f. (of action, movement) ; freedom of speech, franc-parler. ‖ Aisance f. (of manner, style). ‖ Libre usage m. (of sth.) ; to have the freedom of s.o.'s house, avoir des petites entrées chez qqn. ‖ Sans-gêne m. ‖ Absence f. (from, de) [care] ; exemption f. (from, de) [work]. ‖ Jur. Freedom from arrest, immunité parlementaire (or) diplomatique ; freedom of a city, droit de cité, titre de citoyen d'honneur. ‖ Comm. Entrée libre f.; libre accès m. ‖ Fin. Exemption (from tax). ‖ Eccles. Freedom of worship, libre pratique.
freehold [-hould] n. † Franc-alleu m. ‖ Jur. Propriété foncière perpétuelle f.
freeholder [-ə*] n. † Franc-tenancier m. ‖ Jur. Propriétaire foncier (m.) à perpétuité.
freely [-li] adv. Librement. ‖ Franchement, à cœur ouvert (frankly) ; sans façons, sans gêne (without ceremony). ‖ Avec générosité, largement (generously) ; abondamment (profusely). ‖ De plein gré, volontairement (willingly). ‖ Gratuitement (gratis).
freeman [-mən] (pl. **freemen**) n. Homme libre m.; freeman of a city, citoyen d'honneur.
freemason [-meisn] n. Franc-maçon m.
freemasonry [-meisnri] n. Franc-maçonnerie f.
freesia ['friːziə] n. Bot. Freesia m.
freestone [-stoun] n. Archit. Pierre de taille f.
freeway [-wei] n. U. S. Autoroute f.
freeze [friːz] v. intr. (67). Geler ; se geler ; to freeze up, geler, se prendre ; to freeze together, se congeler en formant bloc. ‖ Fig. Se glacer (blood) ; frozen with terror, glacé d'épouvante ; to freeze up, prendre un air glacial. ‖ Fam. Till hell freezes, jusqu'à la Saint-Glinglin ; to freeze on to, se cramponner à.
— v. tr. Geler, glacer. ‖ Culin. Congeler (meat). ‖ Fin. Geler, bloquer (accounts). ‖ Fig. To freeze s.o. with a look, glacer qqn du regard. ‖ Fam. To freeze out, boycotter.
— n. Gel m.; gelée f.
freeze-dry [-drai] v. tr. Lyophiliser.
freezer [-ə*] n. Culin. Sorbetière f. ‖ Glacière f.
freezing [-iŋ] adj. Glacial. ‖ Phys. De congélation (point). ‖ Fig. Réfrigérant, glacial.
freight [freit] n. Naut. Affrètement, nolisement m. (act) ; fret, nolis m.; cargaison f. (cargo) ; transport m. ‖ U. S. Ch. de f. Chargement m.; transport m.; freight train, train de marchandises ; freight elevator, monte-charge. ‖ **Freight-plane**, n. Aviat. Avion de transport m.
— v. tr. Naut. Affréter (to take on hire) ; charger (to load) ; to freight out, fréter. ‖ U. S. Transporter.
freightage [-idʒ] n. Fret m. (cost, cargo) ; affrètement m. (hiring of ship), transport (m.) des marchandises (transportation).
freighter [-ə*] n. Naut. Affréteur m. (charterer) ; cargo m. (ship). ‖ Comm. Exportateur m. (abroad) ; transporteur, convoyeur m. (inland).
French [frentʃ] adj. Français (character) ; des Français (emperor) ; de France (king) ; de français (lesson). ‖ Culin. French beans, haricots verts ; French dressing, assaisonnement pour salade ; French roll, petit pain. ‖ Archit. French window, porte-fenêtre. ‖ Mus. French horn, cor d'harmonie. ‖ Pop. French letter, capote anglaise.
— n. Français m. (language). ‖ Pl. Les Français m. pl. (people).
Frenchify [-ifai] v. tr. (2). Franciser.
Frenchman [-mən] (pl. **Frenchmen**) n. Geogr. Français m. ‖ Naut. Navire français m.
Frenchwoman [-wumən] (pl. **Frenchwomen** [-wimin]) n. Française f.

frenetic [fri'netik] adj. Frénétique, déchaîné.
frenzy ['frenzi] n. Med. Délire m. ‖ Fig. Frénésie f. (of anger) ; fureur f. (of despair) ; transport m. (of joy).
— v. tr. Rendre fou.
Freon ['friːɔn] n. Chim. Fréon m.
frequency ['friːkwənsi] n. Med., Electr., Fig. Fréquence f.; frequency modulation, modulation de fréquence.
frequent [-kwənt] adj. Fréquent, répandu (customs). ‖ Fréquent, nombreux (visits) ; familier, habituel (visitor). ‖ Med. Rapide (pulse).
— [fri'kwent] v. tr. Fréquenter.
frequentation [friːkwən'teiʃən] n. Fréquentation f.
frequentative [fri'kwentətiv] adj., n. Gramm. Fréquentatif m.
frequenter [-ə*] n. Familier m. (of a house) ; pilier m. (of a pub).
frequently [-li] adv. Fréquemment.
fresco ['freskou] n. Arts. Fresque f.; fresco painter, fresquiste.
— v. tr. Arts. Peindre à fresque.
fresh [freʃ] adj. Frais m.; fraîche f. (air, odour, weather, wind). ‖ Med. Frais (complexion) ; frais et dispos (person). ‖ Culin. Frais (butter, fish, meat) ; doux (water). ‖ Milit. Frais (troops). ‖ Fig. Spontané, vif (conversation) ; frais, récent (date, information, memory, news) ; nouveau (start) ; fresh from, frais émoulu de. ‖ Fam. Impertinent, effronté.
— adv. De frais, fraîchement. ‖ Naut. To blow fresh, fraîchir. ‖ **Fresh-comer**, n. Nouveau venu s. ‖ **Fresh-cut**, adj. Frais coupé. ‖ **Fresh-painted**, adj. Fraîchement peint.
— n. Fraîcheur f.; frais m.
freshen [-n] v. tr. Rafraîchir (lit. and fig.). ‖ Fam. Ragaillardir.
— v. intr. Se rafraîchir (temperature) ; fraîchir (weather).
freshening [-niŋ] n. Rafraîchissement m.
fresher [-ə*] n. Fam. Etudiant (s.) de 1re année ; nouveau m., nouvelle f.
freshet [-it] n. Avalaison, crue f. (overflowing). ‖ Courant (m.) d'eau douce (flowing into the sea).
freshly [-li] adv. Fraîchement. ‖ Récemment. ‖ Avec fraîcheur.
freshman [-mən] (pl. **freshmen**) n. Etudiant (s.) de première année.
freshness [-nis] n. Fraîcheur f. (of air, flower). ‖ Med. Fraîcheur (of complexion) ; vigueur f. (of a person) ; éclat m. (of youth). ‖ Fig. Fraîcheur f. (of impression) ; nouveauté f. (of news).
freshwater [-wɔːtə*] adj. Culin., Naut. D'eau douce. ‖ U. S. Fam. Sans renom, obscur (college) ; de province (town).
fret [fret] v. tr. (1). Ronger (to corrode, to gnaw). ‖ User, creuser en frottant (to rub). ‖ Med. Ecorcher (skin). ‖ Naut. Rider, troubler, agiter (water). ‖ Fig. Enerver, agacer (to irritate) ; tracasser, tourmenter, inquiéter (to worry).
— v. intr. Se ronger, être rongé. ‖ S'user, se creuser. ‖ Med. S'écorcher. ‖ Naut. Se rider. ‖ Fig. Pleurnicher (child) ; se ronger, se tourmenter (person).
— n. Agacement m.; irritation f. ‖ Inquiétude f.; tourment m.; to be in a fret, se tracasser.
fret n. Mus. Touchette f.
fret n. Archit. Grecque f. ‖ Blas. Frette f. ‖ **Fretsaw**, n. Techn. Scie (f.) à découper.
— v. tr. Archit. Orner.
fretful [-ful] adj. Grognon, maussade (baby) ; agacé, irritable (person).
fretfulness [-fulnis] n. Irritabilité, maussaderie f.
fretwork [-wəːk] n. Découpage, travail ajouré m. (openwork) ; ornementation f. (of ceilings).
Freudian ['frɔidiən] adj. Philos. Freudien.
friability [fraiə'biliti] n. Friabilité f.
friable ['fraiəbl] adj. Friable.

friar [fraiə*] n. ECCLES. Moine, religieux *m.; Black, Grey, White Friars*, dominicains, franciscains, carmes. ‖ MED. *Friar's balsam*, teinture de benjoin.

friary [-ri] n. ECCLES. Monastère *m.*

fribble ['fribl] v. intr. Baguenauder.

fricassee [frikə'si:] n. CULIN. Fricassée *f.*
— v. tr. CULIN. Fricasser.

fricative ['frikətiv] adj. GRAMM. Fricatif.
— n. GRAMM. Fricative *f.*

friction ['frikʃən] n. TECHN., AVIAT. Frottement *m.* ‖ MED. Friction *f.; friction glove*, gant de crin. ‖ FAM. Tirage, tiraillement *m.; friction f.* ‖ **Friction-cone**, n. TECHN. Cône (*m.*) à friction. ‖ **Friction-proof**, adj. Antifriction. ‖ **Friction-tape**, r. ELECTR. Chatterton *m.*

Friday ['fraidi] n. Vendredi *m.* ‖ ECCLES. *Good Friday*, Vendredi saint.

fridge [fridʒ] n. FAM. Frigo *m.*

friend [frend] n. Ami *m.; amie f.; to be friends with*, être lié d'amitié avec; *to make friends with*, faire amitié avec, se lier avec. ‖ Ami, soutien, protecteur *m.* (supporter); ami, partisan *m.* (sympathizer); *friend at court*, ami influent. ‖ ECCLES. Quaker *m.*

friendless [-lis] adj. Sans ami, délaissé, isolé.

friendliness [-linis] n. Disposition amicale (or) bienveillante; amitié *f.* (*between*, entre).

friendly [-li] adj. Amical, d'ami. ‖ Bienveillant, sympathique. ‖ Favorable, propice. ‖ JUR. De secours mutuel (society).
— adv. Amicalement, avec amitié.
— n. SPORTS. Match amical *m.*

friendship [-ʃip] n. Amitié *f.*

Friesian ['fri:ziən] adj. GEOGR., ZOOL. Frison *s.*

Friesland ['fri:zlənd] n. GEOGR. Frise *f.*

frieze [fri:z] n. Ratine *f.* (cloth).

frieze n. ARCHIT. Frise *f.*

frig [frig] v. intr., tr. (1). POP. Baiser (to copulate).

frigate ['frigit] n. NAUT., ZOOL. Frégate *f.*

frigging ['frigiŋ] adj. POP. *That frigging car*, cette saloperie de voiture.
— adv. Vachement.

fright [frait] n. Frayeur, peur *f.; effroi m.* (see FEAR); *in a fright*, effrayé; *to get off with a bad fright*, en être quitte pour la peur; *to take fright*, prendre peur, s'effrayer. ‖ FAM. Caricature, guenon, horreur *f.* (person).

frighten [-ən] v. tr. Effrayer, faire peur à : *to frighten away*, faire fuir en effrayant, effaroucher; *to frighten s.o. into doing sth.*, faire faire qqch. à qqn par intimidation.

frightful [-ful] adj. Effroyable, terrible, affreux.

frightfully [-fuli] adv. Effroyablement, terriblement, affreusement.

frightfulness [-fulnis] n. Horreur, abomination *f.* ‖ Terrorisme *m.*

frigid ['fridʒid] adj. Froid, glacial (zone). ‖ MED. Frigide. ‖ FIG. Glacé (politeness); glacial (person).

frigidity [fri'dʒiditi] n. MED. Frigidité *f.* ‖ FIG. Froideur *f.*

frill [fril] n. † Fraise *f.* ‖ Ruche *f.* (of lace); jabot *m.* (of shirt). ‖ CULIN. Papillote *f.* (on ham-knuckle); fraise *f.* (of veal). ‖ ZOOL. Collerette *f.* (of bird). ‖ TECHN. Plissement *m.* (in photography). ‖ Pl. FAM. Embarras, chichi *m.* (affectation); fioritures *f.* (flourishes).
— v. tr. Rucher.

frillies [-iz] n. pl. FAM. Dessous (*m. pl.*) à fanfreluches.

frilling [-iŋ] n. Ruché *m.*

frilly [-i] adj. A volants, à fanfreluches. ‖ FIG. Fleuri.

fringe [frindʒ] n. Frange *f.; effilé m.* (trimming). ‖ Frange (of hair). ‖ Lisière *f.* (of forest); bordure *f.* (of trees). ‖ FIG. Marge *f.* (of society).
— v. tr. Franger.
— v. intr. S'effranger, s'effilocher.

frippery ['fripəri] n. Camelote, pacotille *f.* (in

dress). ‖ Falbalas *m. pl.; fanfreluches f. pl.* (finery). ‖ Clinquant *m.* (in style).

frisbee ['frizbi:] n. SPORTS. Frisbee *m.* (nom déposé).

frisk [frisk] n. Cabriole, gambade *f.*
— v. intr. Cabrioler, gambader, folâtrer. ‖ Frétiller (dog); caracoler (horse).
— v. tr. *To frisk its tail*, remuer la queue. ‖ U. S. FAM. Fouiller (to search); chauffer (to steal).

friskily [-ili] adv. En folâtrant (or) frétillant.

frisky [-i] adj. Frétillant (dog); fringant (horse); folâtre, sémillant (person).

frit [frit] n. TECHN. Fritte *f.*
— v. tr. TECHN. Fritter.

fritillary [fri'tiləri] n. BOT. Fritillaire *f.*

fritter [-ə*] n. CULIN. Beignet *m.*

fritter v. tr. Effriter. ‖ FIG. *To fritter away*, gaspiller, éparpiller.

frivol ['frivəl] v. intr. Vivre frivolement, baguenauder.
— v. tr. *To frivol away one's time*, passer son temps en frivolités (or) à flirter.

frivolity [fri'vɔliti] n. Frivolité *f.*

frivolous ['frivələs] adj. Frivole. ‖ Injustifié (complaint); futile (reason).

frizz [friz], **frizzle** ['frizl] n. Frisure, crêpelure *f.*
— v. tr. Friser, frisotter, crêper. (See CRIMP.)

frizz, **frizzle** v. intr. CULIN. Grésiller, crépiter.
— v. tr. CULIN. Faire frire, griller.

frizzy ['frizi] adj. Frisé, crépu.

fro [frou] adv. *To and fro*, de long en large; *to go to and fro*, aller et venir.

frock [frɔk] n. Robe *f.* (dress). ‖ AGRIC. Blouse *f.* ‖ NAUT. Maillot *m.* ‖ ECCLES. Froc *m.; to give up the frock*, se défroquer. ‖ **Frock-coat**, n. Redingote *f.*

frog [frɔg] n. ZOOL. Grenouille *f.* ‖ U. S. FAM. Français *s.* ‖ FAM. *Frog in the throat*, chat dans la gorge. ‖ **Frog-eater**, n. Mangeur (*s.*) de grenouilles; FAM. Français *s.* ‖ **Frog-fish**, n. ZOOL. Baudroie *f.* ‖ **Frog-march**, v. tr. Traîner de force (prisoner).

frog n. Brandebourg *m.* (on jacket). ‖ MILIT. Bélière *f.* ‖ CH. DE F. Croisement *m.*

frog n. ZOOL. Fourchette *f.* (of horse's foot).

froggy [-i] adj. De grenouille. ‖ Plein de grenouilles.

frogman [-mən] (pl. **frogmen**) n. Homme-grenouille *m.*

frolic ['frɔlik] v. tr. Folâtrer, gambader, cabrioler (to frisk). ‖ Batifoler, s'amuser (to play).
— n. Folâtrerie, gambade *f.; ébat m.* ‖ Fredaine, gaminerie *f.* (prank).

frolicker [-ə*] n. Batifoleur *m.*

frolicsome [-səm] adj. Folâtre, fringant (frisky); espiègle, gamin, gai (merry).

from [frɔm] prep. De; *far from*, loin de; *from among*, d'entre; *from the bottom of my heart*, du fond de mon cœur; *from Shakespeare*, tiré de Shakespeare; *from under*, de dessous; *ill from cold*, malade de froid; *passengers from London*, voyageurs venant de Londres; *to date from*, dater de; *to distinguish from*, distinguer de (or) d'avec; *to get from*, obtenir de; *to translate from*, traduire de. ‖ A; *to escape from*, échapper à (danger); *to tear from*, arracher à. ‖ Avec, de; *made from milk*, fait avec du lait. ‖ Contre, de; *shelter from danger*, abri contre le danger; *to shelter from sun*, abriter du soleil. ‖ Dans; *to learn from books*, apprendre dans les livres. ‖ Depuis; *from the beginning*, depuis le commencement; *from the Middle Ages*, depuis le Moyen Age. ‖ Devant; *to shrink from danger*, reculer devant le danger. ‖ D'après; *don't judge from appearances*, ne jugez pas d'après les apparences; *from nature*, d'après nature; *from what I know*, d'après ce que je sais. ‖ Par, à cause de; *death from want*, la mort par suite de privations; *from curiosity*, par curiosité. ‖ Pour; *from good motives*, pour de bons motifs.

frond [frɔnd] n. Bot. Fronde *f.*

frondescence [frɔn'desn̩s] n. Frondaison *f.*

front [frʌnt] n. Front *m.;* face *f.; in front of,* devant, en face de. ‖ Avant, devant *m.; in front,* en avant, devant; *in front of,* devant, en avant (or) en tête de; *in the front,* au premier rang. ‖ Frange *f.* (of false hair); ‖ Chemisette *f.* (dicky); plastron *m.* (of man's shirt); passe *f.* (of woman's hat). ‖ Autom. Avant *m.* ‖ Archit. Façade *f.* (of a house). ‖ Comm. Devanture *f.* (of a shop); ‖ Milit. Front *m.; at the front,* au front, sur le front. ‖ Naut. Promenade *f.* (at seaside); *sea front,* front de mer. ‖ Jur. *United* (or) *Common, Popular Front,* Front commun, populaire. ‖ U. S. Prête-nom *m.* (figure-head); chasseur *m.* (bell-hop). ‖ Fig. Contenance *f.; to put on a bold front,* faire bonne contenance. ‖ Fig. Front, toupet *m.;* effronterie *f.* (cheek). ‖ Fig. Première place *f.; to come to the front,* prendre la vedette, percer (person); passer au premier plan (subject). ‖ Fig. Façade *f.*
— adj. De face; *front view,* vue de face. ‖ D'avant, de devant (row). ‖ Archit. De devant (door); de façade (wall). ‖ Ch. de f. De tête (carriage). ‖ Autom. *Front wheel,* roue avant; *front wheel drive,* traction avant. ‖ Jur. Ministériel, des ministres (bench). ‖ Gramm. D'avant, palatal (vowel). ‖ Fig. Premier (rank); *to have a front seat,* être aux premières loges. ‖ **Front-page,** adj. U. S. Sensationnel, donné à la une (news).
— adv. Par-devant. ‖ Milit. *Eyes front!,* fixe!
— v. tr. Archit. Ravaler (a building); donner sur (a street); revêtir la façade (*with,* de). ‖ Milit. Etablir le front de. ‖ Fig. Affronter, faire front à, tenir tête à; *to front with,* confronter avec.
— v. intr. Archit. Faire face (*to, towards, upon,* à). ‖ Milit. Faire front.

frontage [-idʒ] n. Terrain (*m.*) en bordure (on the sea-front). ‖ Archit. Exposition *f.* (exposure); façade *f.* (front); terrain (*m.*) de façade (land); alignement *m.* (line).

frontal [-əl] n. Fronteau *m.* (band). ‖ Med. Frontal *m.* ‖ Archit. Façade *f.* ‖ Eccles. Devant d'autel *m.*
— adj. Med. Frontal. ‖ Milit. De front; *to make a frontal attack against,* attaquer de front.

frontier ['frʌntiə*] n. Frontière *f.*
— adj. Frontalier.

frontiersman [frʌn'tiəzmən] n. Frontalier *s.* ‖ U. S. Broussard *m.*

frontispiece ['frʌntispi:s] n. Frontispice *m.* ‖ Fam. Devanture *f.* (face).

frontlet ['frʌntlit] n. Fronteau, phylactère *m.* (band). ‖ Zool. Front *m.* ‖ Eccles. Devant d'autel *m.*

fronton [-ən] n. Archit. Fronton *m.*

frost [frɔst] n. Gelée *f.; glazed frost,* verglas; *twenty degrees of frost,* vingt degrés au-dessous de zéro. ‖ Fig. Neige *f.* (of hair). ‖ Fam. Four, fiasco *m.* ‖ **Frost-bite** n. Med. Gelure *f.* ‖ **Frost-bitten,** adj. Gelé; Bot. Broui. ‖ **Frost-hardy,** adj. Résistant au gel. ‖ **Frost-shoe,** n. Fer (*m.*) à glace; v. tr. (127). Ferrer à glace. ‖ **Frost-work,** n. Fleurs (*f. pl.*) de givre.
— v. tr. Geler (to freeze); givrer (to rime). ‖ Diamanter (flowers); givrer, dépolir (glass). ‖ Culin. Glacer (cake); U. S. congeler (vegetables). ‖ Fig. Enneiger (hair).

frostiness [-inis] n. Froid glacial *m.* ‖ Fig. Froideur glaciale *f.*

frosty [-i] adj. Glacial (cold); glacé (frozen); givré (rimy). ‖ Fig. Glacial.

froth [frɔθ] n. Mousse *f.* (on beer, soap). ‖ Culin., Naut., Med. Ecume *f.* ‖ Fig. Bulle (*f.*) de savon.
— v. intr. Mousser; écumer.
— v. tr. Faire mousser.

frothy [-i] adj. Mousseux (beer, soap). ‖ Culin.

Ecumeux. ‖ Med. Ecumant. ‖ Naut. Ecumant, moutonneux. ‖ Fig. Creux, fumeux.

froward ['frouəd] adj. Obstiné.

frowardness [-nis] n. Obstination *f.*

frown [fraun] v. intr. Froncer les sourcils (in attention, disapprobation, sternness); se renfrogner (in displeasure); *to frown upon,* regarder d'un œil sévère, tourner un regard mécontent vers (s.o.); désapprouver; faire le nez sur (fam.) [sth.]. ‖ Fig. Se faire menaçant, avoir l'air hostile (things).
— v. tr. *To frown away* (or) *down s.o.,* faire sortir (or) taire qqn d'un froncement de sourcils.
— n. Froncement (*m.*) de sourcils; regard sévère *m.* ‖ Fig. Aspect menaçant *m.;* hostilité *f.*

frowning [-iŋ] adj. Sourcilleux (brow); renfrogné (face); menaçant (look).

frowst [fraust] n. Odeur (*f.*) de renfermé; renfermé *m.* (See fug.)
— v. intr. S'acagnarder.

frowsty ['frausti] adj. Qui sent le renfermé (room); confiné (air).

frowzy ['frauzi] adj. Qui sent le renfermé (fuggy). ‖ Mal tenu, peu soigné (dowdy).

froze [frouz] pret., **frozen** ['frouzən] p.p. See freeze.

fructiferous [frʌk'tifərəs] adj. Bot. Fructifère.

fructification [ˌfrʌktifi'keiʃən] n. Bot., Fig. Fructification *f.*

fructify ['frʌktifai] v. tr. (2). Féconder; faire fructifier.
— v. intr. Fructifier.

fructose ['frʌktous] n. Chim. Lévulose *m.;* sucre de fruit *m.*

frugal ['fru:gəl] adj. Frugal (meal, person). ‖ Econome. (See thrifty.)

frugality [fru'gæliti] n. Frugalité *f.* (at table). ‖ Economie *f.* (thrift).

frugally ['fru:gəli] adv. Frugalement.

fruit [fru:t] n. Bot. Fruit, produit *m.* (of earth); fruit *m.* (of tree). ‖ Fig. Fruit, résultat *m.; to bear fruit,* porter fruit. ‖ **Fruit-cake,** n. Culin. Cake *m.* ‖ **Fruit-cup,** n. Culin. Coupe (*f.*) de fruits. ‖ **Fruit-loft,** n. Fruitier *m.* (room). ‖ **Fruit-machine,** n. Machine (*f.*) à sous. ‖ **Fruit-salad,** n. Salade (*f.*) de fruits; Milit. Fam. Rangée (*f.*) de médailles, batterie de cuisine *f.* ‖ **Fruit-shop,** n. Comm. Fruiterie *f.* ‖ **Fruit-stand,** n. Culin. Compotier *m.;* U.S. Comm. Etalage (*m.*) de fruits. ‖ **Fruit-tree,** n. Agric. Arbre fruitier *m.* ‖ **Fruit-wall,** n. Agric. Espalier *m.*
— v. intr. Bot. Porter des fruits.

fruitage [-idʒ] n. Fruits *m. pl.*

fruiter [-ə*] n. Agric. Bon arbre fruitier *m.* ‖ Naut. Navire (*m.*) pour le transport des fruits.

fruiterer [-ərə*] n. Comm. Fruitier *s.*

fruitful [-ful] adj. Agric. Fécondant (rain); fertile (soil); productif (tree). ‖ Med. Fécond (person). ‖ Fig. Fructueux (work); *fruitful in,* fertile en.

fruitfulness [-fulnis] n. Agric. Fertilité *f.* (of soil); productivité *f.* (of a tree). ‖ Med., Fig. Fécondité *f.*

fruition [fru:'iʃən] n. Réalisation *f.* (of hopes); jouissance *f.* (of things desired).

fruitless ['fru:tlis] adj. Bot. Stérile. ‖ Fig. Infructueux, stérile, vain.

fruity [-i] adj. De fruit (taste); fruité (wine). ‖ Fam. Pimenté, épicé (story).

frumenty ['fru:mənti] n. Culin. Bouillie (*f.*) de froment.

frump [frʌmp] n. Fam. *Old frump,* vieille toupie.

frumpish [-iʃ] adj. Fam. Fagoté (dowdy); revêche, acariâtre (vixenish).

frustrate [frʌs'treit] v. tr. Contrecarrer (efforts, s.o.); faire échouer (a plan); déjouer (a plot). ‖ Frustrer (hopes); décevoir (s.o.).

frustration [frʌs'treiʃən] n. Anéantissement *m.*

(of a plan, plot). ‖ Déception, déconvenue *f*. ‖ Frustration *f*. (of hopes). ‖ MED. Frustration *f*.

frustum ['frʌstəm] n. MATH. Tronc *m*. (of a cone).
— N. B. Deux pluriels : *frusta, frustums*.

fry [frai] n. ZOOL. Alevin, frai, fretin *m*. ‖ FAM. *Small fry*, menu fretin.

fry v. tr. (2). CULIN. Frire, faire frire. ‖ POP. U. S. Griller (to electrocute).
— v. intr. CULIN. Frire.
— n. CULIN. Friture *f.; lamb's fry*, fressure d'agneau.

fryer [-ə*] n. CULIN. Volaille (*f*.) à frire (fowl); poêle (*f*.) à frire (pan); friturier *s*. (person).

frying [-iŋ] n. CULIN. Friture *f*. ‖ FAM. Friture *f*. (on the phone). ‖ **Frying-basket**, n. CULIN. Friteuse *f*. ‖ **Frying-pan**, n. CULIN. Poêle (*f*.) à frire; FAM. *Out of the frying pan into the fire*, de Charybde en Scylla.

ft. Written abbr. for *foot* (or) *feet*, pied, pieds (measure).

fuchsia ['fju:ʃə] n. BOT. Fuchsia *m*.

fuchsin(e) ['fu:ksin] n. Fuchsine *f*.

fuck [fʌk] v. tr. ARG. Baiser; *fuck you*, va te faire foutre; *fuck me*, putain, merde alors. ‖ **To fuck up**, ARG. Merder, bousiller.
— v. intr. ARG. Baiser. ‖ **To fuck about**, ARG. Déconner. ‖ **To fuck off**, ARG. Foutre le camp.
— n. ARG. Baise *f*. (act); baiseur *s*. (person). ‖ LOC. ARG. *Not to give, care a fuck*, s'en foutre, s'en contrefoutre; *why, how the fuck*, Bon Dieu pourquoi, comment. ‖ **Fuck-all**, n. ARG. Rien *m.; to do fuck-all*, ne rien foutre. ‖ **Fuck-up**, n. ARG. Merdier *m*.
— interj. ARG. Bordel !, Putain !

fucking ['fʌkiŋ] adj. ARG. *That fucking car*, cette putain de voiture.
— adv. ARG. Vachement.

fucus ['fju:kəs] n. BOT. Fucus, varech *m*.

fuddle ['fʌdl] v. intr. Emécher, griser (with, de) [to intoxicate]. ‖ Obscurcir les idées de (to confuse).
— v. intr. Se griser; *to be slightly fuddled*, être un peu parti.
— n. Griserie *f*. (intoxication). ‖ Nuage *m*., brume *f*. (confusion).

fuddy-duddy ['fʌdi'dʌdi] n. FAM. Tatillon *m*. (fussy); vieux rococo *m*. (old-fashioned).

fudge [fʌdʒ] n. Baliverne, sornette *f*. (humbug). ‖ Blague, craque *f*. (fib). ‖ CULIN. Fondant *m*. ‖ TECHN. Blanc (*m*.) pour insertion tardive.

fudge v. tr. Bâcler (to scamp). ‖ Truquer, cuisiner (to fake). ‖ TECHN. Insérer en dernière heure.

fuel ['fjuəl] n. Combustible *m*. ‖ Propergol *m*. ‖ AUTOM. Carburant *m*. ‖ FIG. Aliment *m.; to add fuel to the fire*, jeter de l'huile sur le feu. ‖ **Fuel cell**, n. ELECTR. Pile (*f*.) à combustible. ‖ **Fuel injection**, n. TECHN. Injection *f*. ‖ **Fuel-oil**, n. Gas-oil, mazout *m*. ‖ **Fuel-pump**, n. Distributeur (*m*.) d'essence. ‖ **Fuel-saving**, adj. Economique.
— v. tr. Pourvoir en combustible (or) carburant.
— v. intr. S'approvisionner en combustible (or) carburant.

fug [fʌg] n. Renfermé *m*. (See FROWST.) ‖ Mouton, duvet *m*. (fluff). ‖ FAM. *To have a good fug*, se calfeutrer douillettement.

fugacious [fju:'geiʃəs] adj. Fugace. ‖ ZOOL. Ephémère.

fugacity [fju:'gæsiti] n. Fugacité *f*.

fugal ['fju:gl] adj. MUS. Fugué.

fuggy ['fʌgi] adj. A odeur de renfermé.

fugitive ['fju:dʒitiv] adj. Fugitif, en fuite (prisoner). ‖ FIG. Fugitif, éphémère.
— n. Fugitif *s*. ‖ Réfugié *s*.

fugleman ['fju:glmən] (pl. **fuglemen**) n. MILIT., FIG. Chef (*m*.) de file.

fugue [fju:g] n. MUS., MED. Fugue *f*.

fugued [-d] adj. MUS. Fugué.

fulcrum ['fulkrəm] (pl. **fulcra** [-ə] ; U. S. **fulcrums** [-krəmz]) n. TECHN. Pivot *m*. ‖ FIG. Point d'appui *m*.
— v. intr. Pivoter (on, sur).

fulfil [ful'fil] v. tr. (1). Accomplir, remplir, s'acquitter de (a duty, promise, task); obéir à (law); exécuter (an order). ‖ Remplir (conditions); exaucer (a prayer, a wish). ‖ Accomplir (a prophecy); répondre à (a purpose). ‖ Achever (a period, a task).

fulfilment [-mənt] n. Accomplissement *m*. (of a duty, prophecy, wish); exécution *f*. (of an order).

fulgent ['fʌldʒənt] adj. Eclatant.

full [ful] adj. Plein, rempli (filled). ‖ Plein, rempli, comble, bondé (*of*, de) [crowded]. ‖ Plein, entier, complet, total (see COMPLETE); *at full length*, tout du (or) au long; *full hour*, heure entière; *full powers*, pleins pouvoirs; *full text*, texte intégral; *full view*, vue totale; *full weight*, poids juste. ‖ Extrême, absolu; *at full speed*, à toute vitesse; *full dress*, grande tenue. ‖ Abondant, riche, large; *full account*, compte rendu détaillé; *for fuller information*, pour plus ample informé; *full particulars*, détails complets. ‖ Ample, large, bouffant, étoffé (skirt). ‖ Titulaire (professeur). ‖ MED. Plein, rond (face); fort (lip). ‖ ASTRON. Plein (moon). ‖ JUR. Légal (age); *full session*, assemblée plénière. ‖ FIN. Fort (price); *full fare*, plein tarif. ‖ MUS. Plein (sound, voice). ‖ NAUT. Plein (sail). ‖ AUTOM. *Full up!*, complet ! (bus). ‖ GRAMM. *Full stop*, point. ‖ FIG. Chargé (day); *full of*, plein de (gratitude, ideas); plein de, pénétré de (one's importance, subject); comblé de (honours, money); plein de, rempli de (hope, terror); absorbé par (one's thoughts); chargé de (years). ‖ **Full-back**, n. SPORTS. Arrière *m*. ‖ **Full-blooded**, adj. ZOOL. Pur sang; MED. Sanguin; FIG. Vigoureux. ‖ **Full-bodied**, adj. CULIN. Corsé (wine). ‖ **Full-cream**, adj. CULIN. Non écrémé (milk). ‖ **Full-dress**, adj. De cérémonie; THEATR. *Full-dress rehearsal*, répétition générale, couturières. ‖ **Full-fashioned**, U. S. Diminué (stocking). ‖ **Full-fashioning**, n. Diminution *f*. ‖ **Full-length**, adj. En pied (portrait). ‖ **Full-mouthed**, adj. ZOOL. A denture complète; FAM. A voix forte. ‖ **Full-page**, adj. Hors texte. ‖ **Full-size**, n. Grandeur nature *f*. ‖ **Full-time**, adj. A temps plein. ‖ **Full-up**, adj. FAM. Rassasié, bien calé.
— adv. Pleinement, totalement; *to know full well*, savoir très bien. ‖ Au moins, largement; *full three miles*, au moins trois milles. ‖ Juste, en plein; *full in the face*, en plein dans le nez, en pleine figure. ‖ **Full-grown**, adj. MED. Adulte; BOT. De haute futaie (tree).
— n. Plein *m*. ‖ Ensemble, entier *m.; in full*, tout au long, intégralement; *to the full*, complètement, à plein. ‖ ASTRON. *At the full*, dans son plein (moon).
— v. tr. Faire bouffer, donner de l'ampleur à (a sleeve, skirt).

full v. tr. Fouler (cloth).

fuller [-ə*] n. Foulon *m.; fuller's earth*, terre à foulon.

fuller n. TECHN. Déforgeoir *m*.
— v. tr. TECHN. Déforger.

fullness [-nis]. See FULNESS.

fully [-i] adv. Entièrement, pleinement, totalement, complètement. ‖ Au moins, largement, pour le moins. ‖ **Fully-fashioned**, adj. Entièrement diminué (stocking).

fulminant ['fʌlminənt] adj. Fulminant. ‖ MED. Foudroyant.

fulminate [-neit] v. intr. Exploser, détoner. ‖ ECCLES., FAM. Fulminer.
— v. tr. ECCLES., FAM. Fulminer.
— n. CHIM. Fulminate *m*.

fulminatory [-ətouri] adj. Fulminatoire.

fulminic [fʌl'minik] adj. CHIM. Fulminique.
fulness ['fulnis] n. Plénitude *f.* ‖ Ampleur *f.* (of skirt, voice). ‖ Abondance, ampleur *f.* (of details); richesse *f.* (of style). ‖ ECCLES. Consommation *f.* (of time).
fulsome ['fʌlsəm] adj. Répugnant, bas (flattery).
fulsomeness [-nis] n. Bassesse écœurante *f.* (of flattery).
fulvous ['fʌlvəs] adj. Fauve (colour).
fumarole ['fju:məroul] n. Fumerolle *f.*
fumble ['fʌmbl] v. intr. Tâtonner ; *to fumble for*, chercher à tâtons ; *to fumble in*, farfouiller dans ; *to fumble with*, manipuler maladroitement. ‖ Hésiter ; *to fumble for words*, tâtonner en parlant, chercher ses mots.
— n. Tâtonnement *m.*
fumbler [-blə*] n. Maladroit *s.*
fume [fju:m] n. Fumée, vapeur, émanation *f.* ‖ CULIN. Pl. Fumées *f. pl.* (of wine). ‖ FIG. Fumée (of glory) ; bouffée *f.* (of enthusiasm). ‖ FAM. Rage *f.*
— v. intr. Fumer, émettre des vapeurs. ‖ S'exhaler (gas) ; monter (smoke). ‖ FAM. Fumer, rager.
— v. tr. Exposer à la fumée. ‖ ECCLES. Encenser.
fumigate ['fju:migeit] v. tr. Désinfecter par fumigations ; *to fumigate with*, faire des fumigations de.
fumigation [fju:mi'geiʃən] n. Fumigation *f.*
fumy ['fju:mi] adj. Fumeux.
fun [fʌn] n. Amusement *m. ; to have great fun*, s'amuser beaucoup ; *to spoil the fun*, faire le rabatjoie. ‖ Plaisanterie *f. ; bit of fun*, badinerie ; *for* (or) *in fun*, pour rire ; *he is great fun*, il est très drôle ; c'est un rigolo (pop.) ; *to make fun of*, se moquer de ; se payer la tête de (fam.). ‖ Drôlerie *f. ; I don't see the fun of it*, je ne trouve pas cela drôle ; *like fun*, comme en se jouant ; à la rigolade (fam.).
— adj. FAM. Drôle, amusant, rigolo.
funambulist [fju:'næmbjulist] n. Funambule *s.*
function ['fʌnkʃən] n. Cérémonie, solennité *f. ; society function*, réunion mondaine. ‖ MATH., MED., JUR., FIG. Fonction *f.*
— v. intr. Fonctionner.
functional [-l] adj. MED., MATH. Fonctionnel.
functionarism [-ərizm̩] n. Fonctionnarisme *m.*
functionary [-əri] n. Fonctionnaire *s.*
— adj. Fonctionnel.
functionate [-eit] v. intr. Fonctionner.
fund [fʌnd] n. FIN. Fonds *m. ;* pl. fonds *m. pl. ; public funds*, deniers publics ; *in funds*, en fonds ; *to be pressed for funds*, manquer de disponibilités. ‖ FIN. Pl. Rentes (*f.*) sur l'Etat ; *to buy funds*, acheter de la rente. ‖ FIG. Fonds *m.* ‖ **Fund-holder**, n. FIN. Rentier *m.*
— v. tr. FIN. Consolider (a debt) ; *to fund money*, acheter de la rente.
fundament ['fʌndəmənt] n. MED. Anus ; fondement *m.* ‖ U. S. Fondement *m. ;* base *f.*
fundamental [fʌndə'mentl] adj. Fondamental.
— n. Principe fondamental *m.* ‖ MUS. Fondamentale *f.*
fundamentalism [-izm̩] n. ECCLES. Fondamentalisme *m.*
fundamentally [-əli] adv. Fondamentalement, à la base, foncièrement.
funeral ['fju:nərəl] adj. Funèbre (ceremony, march); funéraire (urne); *funeral procession*, convoi *m.*
— n. Funérailles *f. pl. ;* obsèques *f. pl. ;* enterrement *m.* (ceremonies); convoi *m.* (procession). ‖ FAM. *It's not my funeral*, ce n'est pas mes oignons.
funereal [fju:'niəriəl] adj. Funèbre, lugubre.
fungible ['fʌndʒibl] adj. JUR. Fongible.
fungicide ['fʌndʒi,said] n. Fongicide *m.*
fungoid ['fʌŋgɔid] adj. BOT. Fongoïde, fongique. ‖ MED. Fongueux.
fungous ['fʌŋgəs] adj. MED., BOT. Fongueux.
fungus (pl. **fungi** [-dʒai]) n. BOT. Champignon vénéneux ; mycète *m.* ‖ MED. Fongus *m.*

funicular [fju'nikjulə *] adj., n. TECHN., CH. DE F. Funiculaire *m.*
funk [fʌŋk] n. FAM. Frousse *f.* (fear); froussard *s.* (person). ‖ **Funk-hole**, n. MILIT. Gourbi *m. ;* guitoune *f. ;* FAM. Planque *f.*
— v. tr. FAM. Avoir la frousse (or) trouille de (to fear); se dégonfler devant (to shirk).
— v. intr. FAM. Avoir la frousse ; se dégonfler.
funky ['fʌŋki] adj. FAM. Froussard, trouillard (cowardly). ‖ FAM. Puant, qui cocotte (evil-smelling). ‖ FAM. Qui parle aux tripes (soulful). ‖ FAM. In, dans le vent (fashionable).
funnel ['fʌnl] n. Entonnoir *m.* ‖ CH. DE F., NAUT., TECHN. Cheminée *f.*
— v. tr. (1). Faire passer dans un entonnoir (liquid); mettre en entonnoir (hands). ‖ FIG. Canaliser.
— v. intr. (1). S'engouffrer (*into*, dans).
funnelled [-d] adj. En entonnoir.
funny ['fʌni] adj. Drôle, comique (see COMIC); *the funny part of it*, le plaisant de l'affaire. ‖ Bizarre, étrange (queer). ‖ **Funny-bone**, n. MED., FAM. Petit juif *m.* (in the elbow). ‖ **Funny-looking**, adj. FAM. Drôlement bâti. ‖ **Funny-man**, n. Pitre *m.* ‖ **Funny papers**, n. pl. U. S. Pages comiques *f. pl.*
— n. pl. U. S. FAM. Pages comiques *f. pl.*
funny n. NAUT. Skiff *m.*
fur [fə:*] n. Fourrure *f. ; fur coat*, manteau de fourrure. ‖ COMM. Pl. Pelleteries *f. pl.* ‖ ZOOL. Pelage *m.* (of animals). ‖ SPORTS. Gibier à poil *m.* (game). ‖ MED. Empâtement *m.* (of tongue). ‖ TECHN. Tartre, entartrage *m.* (in boiler). ‖ CULIN. Dépôt *m.* (in bottle). ‖ **Fur-lined**, adj. Doublé de fourrure ; *fur-lined coat*, pelisse.
— v. tr. (1). Fourrer (garment), vêtir d'une fourrure (person). ‖ Empâter (tongue). ‖ Entartrer (kettle, boiler).
— v. intr. (1). *To fur up*, s'entartrer (boiler, kettle).
furbelow ['fə:bilou] n. Falbala *m.*
furbish ['fə:biʃ] v. tr. Fourbir, briquer (to polish). ‖ Remettre à neuf ; retaper (fam.) [to renovate].
furcate ['fə:keit] adj. Fourchu.
— v. intr. Bifurquer. (See BRANCH.)
furious ['fjuəriəs] adj. Furieux ; *to grow furious*, entrer en fureur. ‖ AUTOM. *Furious driving*, excès de vitesse.
furiously [-li] adv. Furieusement. ‖ AUTOM. A une vitesse excessive.
furl [fə:l] v. tr. Fermer, replier (a fan); rouler (an umbrella); serrer (a tent). ‖ NAUT. Ferler (a sail). ‖ MILIT. Mettre en berne (a flag).
— v. intr. Se replier, s'enrouler.
furlong ['fə:lɔŋ] n. Furlong *m.* (201 metres).
furlough ['fə:lou] n. Congé *m.* ‖ MILIT. Permission *f. ; men on furlough*, permissionnaires.
— v. tr. Donner un congé à. ‖ MILIT. Donner une permission à.
furnace ['fə:nis] n. Fournaise *f.* (hot place). ‖ Calorifère *m.* (for domestic heating). ‖ TECHN., CHIM. Fourneau *m.* ‖ TECHN., CH. DE F. Foyer *m.* ‖ CULIN. Four, fourneau *m.* ‖ PHYS. *Atomic furnace*, bouilleur atomique. ‖ FIG. Creuset (*m.*) de l'adversité.
— v. tr. Chauffer dans un fourneau.
furnish ['fə:niʃ] v. tr. Fournir, pourvoir, munir (with, de) [to supply]. ‖ Fournir, procurer (to give). ‖ Meubler ; *a furnished apartment*, un garni. ‖ FIG. Meubler (one's memory).
furnishing [-iŋ] n. Fourniture *f.* (act, article). ‖ Action (*f.*) de meubler ; *house-furnishing firm*, maison d'ameublement. ‖ Pl. Ameublement *m.* (furniture). ‖ U. S. Pl. Equipements (*m. pl.*) [or] installations diverses (*f. pl.*) d'un immeuble (fixtures); articles (*m. pl.*) d'habillement (clothes).
furniture ['fə:nitʃə*] n. Ameublement *m. ;* meubles *m. pl. ; piece of furniture*, meuble ; *set of furniture*, mobilier. ‖ Garniture, ferrure *f.* (on a door). ‖ Harnachement *m.* (harness). ‖ U. S. Equi-

pement *m.* (of machine, ship). ‖ Fɪɢ. Ornement, meuble *m.* (of mind); contenu *m.* (of pocket). ‖
Furniture-remover (or) U. S. **mover,** n. Déménageur *m.* ‖ **Furniture-van,** n. Aᴜᴛᴏᴍ. Voiture (*f.*) de déménagement. ‖ **Furniture-warehouse,** n. Garde-meuble *m.*
furore [fju'rɔːre] n. Fᴀᴍ. Fureur, folie, rage *f.*
furred [fəːd] adj. Fourré (lined); garni de fourrure (trimmed). ‖ Habillé de fourrure (dressed). ‖ Tᴇᴄʜɴ. Entartré. ‖ Mᴇᴅ. Chargé (tongue).
furrier ['fʌriə*] n. Cᴏᴍᴍ. Fourreur *s.*
furring ['fəːriŋ] n. Garniture (or) doublure de fourrure *f.* ‖ Tᴇᴄʜɴ. Détartrage *m.* (cleaning); entartrage *m.* (coating). ‖ Nᴀᴜᴛ. Soufflage *m.* ‖ Aʀᴄʜɪᴛ. Fourrure *f.*
furrow ['fʌrou] n. Aɢʀɪᴄ., Fɪɢ. Sillon *m.* ‖ Aʀᴄʜɪᴛ. Rainure *f.* (See ɢʀᴏᴏᴠᴇ.) ‖ Nᴀᴜᴛ. Sillage *m.* ‖ Aᴜᴛᴏᴍ. Cassis *m.* (across the road). ‖ Mᴇᴅ. Ride *f.* (on the face).
— v. tr. Aɢʀɪᴄ., Fɪɢ. Labourer. ‖ Aʀᴄʜɪᴛ. Canneler. ‖ Nᴀᴜᴛ., Fɪɢ. Sillonner. ‖ Aᴜᴛᴏᴍ. Défoncer (road). ‖ Mᴇᴅ. Rider.
furry ['fəːri] adj. See ғᴜʀʀᴇᴅ. ‖ Semblable à de la fourrure (fur-like).
further ['fəːðə*] adv. Plus loin, plus avant; *to go further,* avancer, aller plus loin. ‖ Davantage; *not to know any further,* ne pas en savoir davantage; *to draw further back,* se reculer davantage. ‖ De plus, en outre, au surplus (moreover). ‖ Fᴀᴍ. Au diable.
— adj. Plus éloigné; *on the further side,* de l'autre côté. ‖ Plus ample, plus grand; *to go into further details,* entrer plus avant dans les détails. ‖ Additionnel, supplémentaire, en plus; *one further question,* encore une question; *without further ado,* sans plus de cérémonie. ‖ *Further education,* formation continue.
— v. tr. Favoriser, servir.
furtherance [-rəns] n. Avancement, progrès *m.* ‖ Aide (*f.*) en vue du progrès (help).
furthermore [-mɔː*] adv. En outre, de plus.
furthermost [-moust] adj. Le plus éloigné.
furthest ['fəːðist]. See ғᴀʀᴛʜᴇsᴛ.
furtive ['fəːtiv] adj. Furtif, subreptice. ‖ Fripon, de voleur (thievish).
furtively [-li] adv. Furtivement.
furuncle ['fjuərʌŋkḷ] n. Mᴇᴅ. Furoncle *m.*
fury ['fjuəri] n. Furie *f.* (goddess, virago). ‖ Furie, fureur *f.; in a fury,* en rage, en fureur, hors de soi. ‖ Fᴀᴍ. Acharnement *m.*
furze [fəːz] n. Bᴏᴛ. Ajonc *m.*
furzy [-i] adj. Couvert d'ajoncs.
fuscous ['fʌskəs] adj. Sombre.
fuse [fjuːz] v. tr. Fondre (a metal). ‖ Fɪɢ. Fusionner.
— v. intr. Se fondre. ‖ Eʟᴇᴄᴛʀ. Sauter (light). ‖ Mᴇᴅ. Se souder (bones). ‖ Fɪɢ. S'amalgamer.
— n. Eʟᴇᴄᴛʀ. Fusible, plomb *m.*
fuse n. Fusée *f.* (in pyrotechnics). ‖ Mɪʟɪᴛ. Fusée,

amorce *f.* ‖ Tᴇᴄʜɴ. Etoupille, mèche *f.* (in mining).
— v. tr. Tᴇᴄʜɴ. Etoupiller.
fusee [fjuːˈziː] n. Allumette-tison *f.* (match). ‖ Tᴇᴄʜɴ. Fusée *f.* (in a watch). ‖ Mᴇᴅ. Suros *m.*
fusel ['fjuːzḷ] n. Fusel oil, huile de Fusel.
fuselage ['fjuːzilɑːʒ] n. Aᴠɪᴀᴛ. Fuselage *m.*
fusibility [ˌfjuːziˈbiliti] n. Fusibilité *f.*
fusible ['fjuːzibḷ] adj. Fusible.
fusiform ['fjuːzifɔːm] adj. Fusiforme.
fusilier [fjuːziˈliə*] n. Mɪʟɪᴛ. Fusilier *m.*
fusillade [fjuːziˈleid] n. Mɪʟɪᴛ. Fusillade *f.*
— v. tr. Mɪʟɪᴛ. Fusiller (persons); soumettre à une fusillade (a place).
fusion ['fjuːʒən] n. Tᴇᴄʜɴ. Fusion, fonte *f.* ‖ Fɪɢ. Fusion. ‖ U. S. Coalition *f.* (of political parties).
fuss [fʌs] n. Fᴀᴍ. Histoires, cérémonies *f. pl.;* embarras, chichis *m. pl.; to make a fuss about it,* en faire tout un plat. ‖ **Fuss-pot,** U. S. **fuss-budget,** n. Fᴀᴍ. Faiseur d'embarras, chichiteur *s.*
— v. intr. Faire des embarras (or) des histoires.
— v. tr. Tracasser.
fussily [-ili] adv. En faisant des embarras, en se donnant de l'importance.
fussiness [-inis] n. Affairement *m.* ‖ Embarras *m. pl.;* air important *m.*
fussy ['fʌsi] adj. Affairé, empressé, qui déplace de l'air, qui fait l'important (bustling). ‖ Chichiteux, qui fait des cérémonies (fuss-pot). ‖ Voyant, tarabiscoté (showy).
fustian ['fʌstiən] n. Futaine *f.* ‖ Fɪɢ. Grandiloquence *f.* (bombast).
— adj. De futaine. ‖ Fɪɢ. Grandiloquent.
fustigate ['fʌstigeit] v. tr. Fustiger.
fustigation [fʌstiˈgeiʃən] n. Fustigation *f.*
fusty ['fʌsti] adj. Sentant le renfermé. (See ғᴜɢɢʏ.) ‖ Fᴀᴍ. Vieux jeu.
futile ['fjuːtail] adj. Futile, infructueux (vain). ‖ Puéril (childish). ‖ Futile, frivole (frivolous).
futility [fjuːˈtiliti] n. Futilité *f.*
futtock ['fʌtək] n. Nᴀᴜᴛ. Allonge *f.*
future ['fjuːtʃə*] adj. Futur, à venir, d'avenir. ‖ Gʀᴀᴍᴍ. Futur. ‖ Fɪɴ. A terme.
— n. Avenir, futur *m.; in future,* à l'avenir. ‖ Gʀᴀᴍᴍ. Futur *m.* ‖ Fɪɴ. Opérations (*f. pl.*). ‖ Fɪɢ. Avenir (situation). ‖ Fᴀᴍ. Futur *s.* (fiancé).
futurism [-rizm] n. Aʀᴛs. Futurisme *m.*
futurist [-rist] adj., n. Aʀᴛs. Futuriste *s.*
futuristic [-ˈristik] adj. Futuriste.
futurity [fjuːˈtjuəriti] n. Avenir *m.* ‖ Eᴄᴄʟᴇs. Vie future *f.*
futurology [-ˈrɔlədʒi] n. Futurologie *f.*
fuze [fjuːz]. See ғᴜsᴇ.
fuzz [fʌz] n. Duvet *m.;* peluche *f.* (fluff). ‖ Cheveux bouffants *m. pl.* (hair). ‖ Flou *m.* (in photography). ‖ *Unwanted fuzz,* poils superflus.
fuzzy ['fʌzi] adj. Duveteux, pelucheux (fluffy). ‖ Flou, bouffant, frisotté (frizzed). ‖ Flou, vague (blurred).
fy [fai] interj. Fi !
fylfot ['filfɔt] n. Svastika *m.;* croix gammée *f.*

G

g [dʒiː] n. G, g *m.* ‖ Mᴜs. Sol *m. invar.* ‖ **G-man,** n. U. S. Fᴀᴍ. Agent du F.B.I. *m.* ‖ **G-string,** n. Mᴜs. Corde (*f.*) de sol; Fɪɢ. Cache-sexe *m. invar.* ‖

G-suit, n. Aᴠɪᴀᴛ., Asᴛʀᴏɴᴀᴜᴛ. Vêtement (*m.*) anti-accélération (or) anti-g.
gab [gæb] n. Fᴀᴍ. Bagou(t) *m.* (glibness); tapette *f.*

(talkativeness); *to have the gift of the gab,* savoir vendre sa salade; avoir la langue bien pendue.

gabardine [,gæbə'di:n] n. Gabardine *f.*

gabble ['gæbḷ] n. Caquetage *m.;* jacasserie *f.* || Bredouillage *m.*
— v. intr. Jacasser (to chatter); bredouiller (to jabber).
— v. tr. Bredouiller, bafouiller.

gabbro ['gæbrou] (pl. **gabbros** [-z]) n. GEOL. Gabbro *m.*

gabby ['gæbi] adj. FAM. Disert, jacasseur (chattering); bredouilleur (jabbering).

gabion ['geibiən] n. MILIT. Gabion *m.*

gable ['geibḷ] n. ARCHIT. Pignon *m.* || **Gable-end,** n. ARCHIT. Pignon *m.*

gabled [-d] adj. ARCHIT. En pignon.

Gabon [gə'bɔn] n. GEOGR. Gabon *m.*

gaby ['geibi] n. Bêta *m.*

gad [gæd] n. AGRIC. Aiguillon *m.* || TECHN. Coin *m.;* pince *f.*

gad! interj. Sapristi!, bon sang!

gad n. Flânerie *f.*
— v. intr. (1). *To gad about,* galoper de-ci de-là, vadrouiller, courailler, courir la pretantaine.

gadabout [-əbaut] n. FAM. Personne (*f.*) qui a toujours le pied levé; vadrouilleur, coureur *s.*

gadfly ['gædflai] n. ZOOL. Taon *m.*

gadget ['gædʒit] n. FAM. Bidule, truc *m.* (See CONTRAPTION.)

gadroon [gə'dru:n] n. Godron *m.*

Gael [geil] n. GEOGR. Gaël *m.*

Gaelic [-ik] adj., n. Gaélique *m.*

gaff [gæf] n. Gaffe *f.;* harpon *m.* || NAUT. Corne *f.* || FAM. *To blow the gaff,* manger le morceau, vendre la mèche. || FAM. U. S. *To stand the gaff,* encaisser, payer les pots cassés. || **Gaff-hook,** n. NAUT. Gaffeau *m.*
— v. tr. Gaffer (a fish). || U. S. Truquer.

gaff n. FAM. Beuglant *m.*

gaffe [gæf] n. Bévue, maladresse *f.,* impair *m.*

gaffer [-ə*] n. FAM. Contremaître *m.* || FAM. Vieux *m.; Gaffer Smith,* le père Smith.

gag [gæg] n. Bâillon *m.* || MED. Ouvre-bouche *m.* || THEATR. Gag *m.* || JUR. Clôture *f.* (in Parliament). || FAM. Blague *f.*
— v. tr. (1). Bâillonner. || JUR. Clôturer. || FIG. Museler, bâillonner. || FAM. Monter le coup à.
— v. intr. Avoir des haut-le-cœur (to retch). || THEATR. Cascader. || FAM. Blaguer (to joke).

gaga ['gægə] adj. FAM. Gaga, gâteux. || FAM. Cinglé; *to go gaga over,* s'enticher bêtement de (s. o.).

gage [geidʒ] n. Gage *m.* || JUR. Nantissement *m.* || FAM. Défi *m.*
— v. tr. Donner en gage (to pledge). || FIG. Engager.

gage n. NAUT. Position (*f.*) sous le vent.

gage U. S. See GAUGE.

gaggle ['gægḷ] n. ZOOL. Troupeau *m.* (of geese, swans).
— v. intr. ZOOL. Cacarder (geese).

gaiety ['geiəti] n. Gaieté *f.* || Couleur *f.; éclat m.* (in dress). || Pl. Réjouissances *f. pl.*

gaily ['geili] adv. Gaiement. || Avec éclat.

gain [gein] n. Accroissement *m.; gain in weight,* augmentation de poids. || FIN. Gain, bénéfice *m.* || TECHN. Avance *f.* (of a watch). || FIG. Avantage *m.*
— v. tr. FIN. Gagner (money, one's living). || TECHN. Avancer de (ten minutes). || MILIT. Gagner (a battle); *to gain the day,* remporter la victoire. || FIG. Atteindre (one's destination); acquérir (s.o.'s esteem); gagner, s'attirer (friends, partisans); obtenir (information); conquérir (one's liberty); atteindre (a place); se concilier (s.o.'s sympathy); *to gain ground, time,* gagner du terrain, du temps; *to gain s.o.'s goodwill,* se concilier qqn.
— v. intr. Gagner; *to gain by the change,* gagner au change. || Gagner, trouver avantage (by, à). || Augmenter (in, de); *to gain in prestige,* voir s'accroître son prestige, gagner en prestige; *to gain in weight,* prendre du poids. || Gagner, empiéter (on, sur). || SPORTS. Gagner de vitesse, prendre de l'avance (on, sur). || TECHN. Avancer (watch).

gainer [-ə*] n. FIN. Gagneur *s.* || SPORTS., FIG. Gagnant *s.; to be the gainer by,* gagner à.

gainful [-ful] adj. Rémunérateur, lucratif, rentable. || Apre au gain (grasping).

gainsay [gein'sei] v. tr. Contredire; *I don't gainsay it,* je n'en disconviens pas.

gait [geit] n. Démarche *f.; with unsteady gait,* d'un pas mal assuré. || Allure *f.; awkward gait,* dégaine, touche. || Cadence *f.; fast gait,* cadence rapide.

gaiter ['geitə*] n. Guêtre *f.*

gaitered [-d] adj. Guêtré.

gal [gæl] n. FAM. Fille, copine *f.*

gal. Written abbr. for *gallon(s),* gallon(s) (measure).

gala ['geilə] [,gɑ:lə] n. Gala *m.; gala dress,* tenue de gala.

galactic [gə'læktik] adj. ASTRON. Galactique.

galalith ['gæləliθ] n. Galalithe *f.*

galantine [gælən'ti:n] n. CULIN. Galantine *f.*

galanty show [gə'læntiʃou] n. THEATR. Ombres chinoises *f. pl.*

galaxy ['gæləksi] n. ASTRON. Galaxie *f.* || FIG. Constellation *f.*

gale [geil] n. Coup de vent *m.; to blow a gale,* souffler violemment.

gale n. JUR. Terme de loyer *m.*

galena [gə'li:nə] n. Galène *f.*

galenic [gə'lenik] adj. Galénique.

Galilean [gælə'li:ən] adj., n. GEOGR. Galiléen *s.*

Galilee ['gælili:] n. GEOGR. Galilée *f.* || ARCHIT. Porche (*m.*) d'église.

gall [gɔ:l] n. MED. Bile *f.* || ZOOL. Fiel *m.* || FIG. Amertume *f.* || U. S. FAM. Culot *m.* (cheek). || **Gall-bladder,** n. MED. Vésicule biliaire *f.* || **Gallstone,** n. MED. Calcul biliaire *m.*

gall n. MED. Ecorchure, excoriation *f.* || FIG. Egratignure, blessure *f.*
— v. tr. MED. Ecorcher, excorier. || FIG. Irriter, agacer (to annoy); égratigner, blesser (to offend).

gall n. BOT. Galle *f.*

gallant ['gælənt] adj. Elégant, beau, superbe (attire); splendide, noble (steed). || Vaillant, brave (man); *gallant deed,* action d'éclat.
— [gə'lænt] adj. Galant (person); d'amour (poem).
— n. Elégant *m.* (man of fashion). || Galant, galantin *m.* (ladies' man).
— v. intr. Faire le galantin. || Faire la cour (with, à).

gallantly ['gæləntli] adv. Vaillamment.
— [gə'læntli] adv. Galamment.

gallantry ['gæləntri] n. Bravoure, vaillance f. (courage). || Elégance *f.* || Galanterie *f.* (act, conduct, speech). || Intrigue amoureuse *f.*

galleon ['gæliən] n. NAUT. Galion *m.*

gallery ['gæləri] n. ARCHIT. Galerie, tribune *f.* || THEATR. Paradis *m.* || ECCLES. Tribune *f.* || ARTS. Galerie *f.* (for works of art); musée *m.* (museum). || TECHN. Galerie (in mining). || FAM. Galerie; *to play to the gallery,* cabotiner; tenir un rôle pour la galerie.
— v. tr. (2). Orner d'une galerie.

galley ['gæli] n. NAUT. Coquerie *f.* (kitchen); yole *f.* (rowboat); galère *f.* (slave-ship). || AVIAT. Office *m.* || TECHN. Galée *f.* (in printing). || **Galley-proof,** n. Placard *m.* || **Galley-slave,** n. NAUT. Galérien *m.*

Gallic ['gælik] adj. GEOGR. Gaulois. || CHIM. Gallique.

Gallican ['gælikən] adj., n. ECCLES. Gallican *s.*

Gallicanism [-izm] n. ECCLES. Gallicanisme *m.*

Gallicism ['gælisizm] n. GRAMM. Gallicisme *m.*

galligaskins [,gæli'gæskinz] n. pl. † Grègues *f. pl.* || FAM. Falzard *m.*

gallimaufry [‚gæli'mɔːfri] n. Salmigondis *m*.
gallinaceous [‚gæli'neiʃəs] adj. Zool. Gallinacé.
galling ['gɔːliŋ] adj. Med., Fig. Irritant.
— n. Med. Ecorchure *f*. ‖ Fig. Blessure *f*.
gallinule ['gæli‚njuːl] n. Zool. Porphyrion *m*. (porphyrio); poule d'eau *f*. (moorhen).
gallipot ['gælipɔt] n. Med. Petit pot *m*.
gallivant [‚gæli'vænt] v. intr. Courailler, courir le guilledou.
gallon ['gælən] n. Gallon *m*.
galloon [gə'luːn] n. Galon *m*. (See BRAID.)
gallop ['gæləp] n. Galop *m*.; *full, hand gallop*, grand, petit galop. ‖ Fam. Galopade *f*. (ride).
— v. intr. (1). Galoper. ‖ Fam. *To gallop through a book*, lire un livre à la va-vite.
— v. tr. Faire galoper.
gallopade [‚gælə'peid] n. Mus. Galop *n*. (dance).
galloping ['gæləpiŋ] adj. Galopant.
— n. Galop *m*.
gallows ['gælouz] n. invar. Gibet *m*.; potence *f*. ‖ **Gallows-bird**, n. Fam. Gibier (*m*.) de potence.
galluses ['gæləsiz] n. pl. Fam. Bretelles *f. pl*.
galop ['gæləp] n. Mus. Galop *m*. (dance).
— v. intr. Mus. Danser un galop.
galore [gə'lɔː*] adv. A foison, en masse; à gogo, à la pelle (fam.).
galosh [gə'lɔʃ] n. † Galoche *f*. ‖ Pl. Caoutchoucs *m. pl*. (overshoes).
galumph [gə'lʌmf] v. intr. Fam. Caracoler, se pavaner.
galvanic [gæl'vænik] adj. Electr. Galvanique. ‖ Fam. Crispé (smile).
galvanism ['gælvənizm] n. Galvanisme *m*.
galvanization [‚gælvənai'zeiʃən] n. Galvanisation *f*.
galvanize ['gælvənaiz] v. tr. Galvaniser. ‖ Fig. Galvaniser, électriser.
galvanometer [‚gælvə'nɔmitə*] n. Electr. Galvanomètre *m*.
galvanoplastics [‚gælvəno'plæstiks] n. pl. Galvanoplastie *f*.
galvanoscope [gæl'vænoskoup] n. Galvanoscope *m*.
galyak ['gæliæk] n. Comm. Breitschwanz *m*. (fur).
gam [gæm] n. Fam. Guibolle *f*. (leg).
gambado [gæm'beidou] n. Gambade *f*. ‖ Fig. Frasque *f*.
— v. intr. Gambader. ‖ Fig. Faire des frasques.
Gambia ['gæmbiə] n. Geogr. Gambie *f*.
gambit ['gæmbit] n. Gambit *m*. (in chess).
gamble ['gæmbl] v. intr. Jouer. ‖ Fig. Prendre des risques.
— v. tr. Jouer; *to gamble away*, perdre au jeu (one's fortune). ‖ Fig. Risquer.
— n. Jeu *m*. ‖ Fig. Entreprise risquée *f*.
gambler [-ə*] n. Joueur *s*.
gambling [-iŋ] n. Jeu *m*. (act). ‖ **Gambling-house**, U. S. **Gambling spot**, n. Tripot *m*.
gamboge [gæm'buːʒ] n. Bot. Gomme-gutte *f*.
gambol ['gæmbəl] n. Gambade *f*.
— v. intr. (1). Gambader.
game [geim] n. Objet d'amusement *m*.; *to make game of*, tourner en dérision, se jouer de; *what a game!* que c'est drôle! ‖ Sports. Jeu *m*.; *card game*, jeu de cartes; *to play a good game*, bien jouer. ‖ Sports. Partie *f*. (at cards); match *m*. (at football); *odd game*, belle; *to be game*, avoir gagné; *to be game all*, être à égalité; *to have (or) play a game of billiards*, faire une partie de billard. ‖ Sports. Gibier *m*. (in hunting); *big game*, grands fauves. ‖ Culin. Gibier *m*. ‖ Zool. Troupeau *m*. (of swans). ‖ Comm. Pl. Equipement (*m*.) de joueur (apparatus). ‖ Fig. Jeu (of life); *paying game*, entreprise lucrative; *the game is in his hands*, il tient le jeu en main, il a beau jeu (or) la partie belle; *the game is up with him*, il a perdu la partie; *to play*

s.o.'s game, faire le jeu de qqn; *to play the game*, jouer le jeu. ‖ Fig. Jeu, manège *m*.; manœuvre, manigance *f*.; *he saw through your game*, il a deviné votre jeu; *to spoil s.o.'s game*, déjouer les combinaisons de qqn. ‖ Fam. *Fair game for*, proie idéale pour. ‖ **Game-bag**, n. Gibecière, carnassière *f*.; carnier *m*. ‖ **Game-ball**, n. Sports. Balle décisive *f*. ‖ **Game-cock**, n. Coq de combat *m*. ‖ **Game-licence**, n. Permis (*m*.) de chasse. ‖ **Game-preserve**, n. Chasse réservée, réserve *f*.
— v. tr., intr. Jouer.
— adj. Fam. Crâne; *to be game*, avoir du cœur au ventre; *to be game for anything*, n'avoir peur de rien; *to die game*, mourir fièrement.
game adj. Fam. Estropié; *to have a game leg*, être boiteux.
gamekeeper ['geim‚kiːpə*] n. Garde-chasse *m*.
gameness ['geimnis] n. Crânerie *f*.
gamesmanship [-zmən‚ʃip] n. Art (*m*.) de gagner par des moyens psychologiques, art (*m*.) et manière (*f*.) de gagner.
gamesome [-səm] adj. Folâtre. (See FROLICSOME.)
gamester [-stə*] n. Joueur *s*.
gamete ['gæmiːt] n. Med. Gamète *m*.
gamin ['gæmin] n. Gamin *m*.
gamine [gə'miːn] n. Gamine *f*.
gamma ['gæmə] n. Gamma *m*. (letter). ‖ Phys. *Gamma radiations, rays*, radiations, rayons gamma.
gammer ['gæmə*] n. Fam. Vieille *f*.; *gammer Smith*, la mère Smith.
gammon ['gæmən] n. Culin. Quartier de lard fumé *m*. (bacon); jambon fumé *m*. (ham).
— v. tr. Culin. Fumer.
gammon n. Fam. Blague, baliverne *f*.
— v. intr. Fam. Blaguer.
— v. tr. Fam. Mettre en boîte, emmener en bateau.
gammon n. Naut. Liure *f*.
gammy ['gæmi] adj. Fam. Estropié, fou (leg).
gamp [gæmp] n. Fam. Riflard, pépin *m*.
gamut ['gæmət] n. Mus., Fig. Gamme *f*.
gamy ['geimi] adj. Sports. Giboyeux (wood). Culin. Faisandé (meat).
gander ['gændə*] n. Zool. Jars *m*. ‖ Fam. Oie *f*. U. S. Pop. *To take a gander*, jeter un coup d'œil.
gang [gæŋ] n. Bande, clique *f*. (of persons). ‖ Jur. Bande *f*., gang *m*. (of criminals); convoi *m*. (of prisoners). ‖ Techn. Equipe *f*. (of workmen); jeu *m*. (of tools). ‖ **Gang-board, gang-plank**, n. Naut. Planche (*f*.) de débarquement. ‖ **Gangland**, n. La pègre *f*., le milieu; *gangland killing*, règlement de comptes dans le milieu. ‖ **Gang plough**, n. Agric. Charrue polysoc *f*. ‖ **Gang saw**, n. Techn. Scie multiple *f*.
— v. intr. U. S. Former un gang. ‖ S'associer (with, à). ‖ Fam. *To gang up on*, attaquer en bande, se liguer contre.
gang v. intr. Fam. Aller.
ganger ['gæŋgə*] n. Techn. Chef (*m*.) d'équipe.
gangling ['gæŋgliŋ] adj. Dégingandé, qui a grandi trop vite, trop grand pour son âge.
ganglion ['gæŋgliən] (pl. **ganglia** [-ə]) n. Med. Ganglion *m*. ‖ Fig. Centre *m*. (of activity); foyer *m*. (of energy).
ganglionic [‚gæŋgli'ɔnik] adj. Med. Ganglionnaire.
gangrene ['gæŋgriːn] n. Med. Gangrène *f*.
— v. tr. Med. Gangrener.
— v. intr. Med. Se gangrener.
gangrenous [-əs] adj. Med. Gangreneux.
gangster ['gæŋstə*] n. Gangster, bandit *m*.
gangsterism [-rizm] n. Gangstérisme *m*.
gangue [gæŋ] n. Gangue *f*.
gangway ['gæŋwei] n. Passage *m*. ‖ Naut. Passerelle *f*. (bridge); passavant *m*. (fore and aft); coupée *f*. (opening). ‖ Autom. Couloir *m*. (in a bus). Theatr. Allée *f*. ‖ Jur. Allée (*f*.) partageant

Chambre des communes ; *members below the gang-way,* les indépendants.
— interj. Dégagez !, libérez le passage !

gannet ['gænit] n. Zool. Fou, fou de Bassan *m.* ‖ Fam. Goinfre *s.,* bâfreur *s.*

gantry ['gæntri] n. Chantier *m.* (for barrels). ‖ Techn. Portique *m.* (for crane).

gaol [dʒeil] n. Jur. Prison ; geôle † *f.* ‖ **Gaol-bird,** n. Gibier (*m.*) de potence. ‖ **Gaol-book,** n. Jur. Livre d'écrou *m.* ‖ **Gaol-break,** n. Evasion *f.* ‖ **Gaol-delivery,** n. Jur. Levée (*f.*) d'écrou.
— v. tr. Emprisonner.

gaoler [-ə*] n. Jur. Geôlier *m.*

gaoleress [-əris] n. Jur. Geôlière *f.*

gap [gæp] n. Brèche *f.* (in hedge, wall). ‖ Trou, vide *m.* (hole). ‖ Solution de continuité *f.* ; jour, interstice *m.* (*between,* entre). ‖ Fin. *To bridge the gap,* faire la soudure ; *to close the gap,* supprimer l'écart (in the balance of payment). ‖ Fig. Lacune *f.* (in education) ; vide *m.* (in life) ; trou *m.* (in memory) ; hiatus *m.* (in narrative) ; abîme *m.* (between ideas, natures).

gape [geip] v. intr. Bâiller (person, seam). ‖ Être béant, s'ouvrir (chasm). ‖ Bayer aux corneilles, béer, badauder, rester bouche bée (*at,* devant). ‖ Baver d'envie, tirer la langue (*after,* devant) [sth.] ‖ Se pâmer (*with,* de) [admiration]. ‖ Zool. Ouvrir le bec tout grand (bird).
— n. Bâillement *m.* (yawn). ‖ Badauderie *f.* (stare). ‖ Ouverture béante *f.* (chasm). ‖ Zool. Large ouverture (*f.*) du bec. ‖ **Gape-seed,** n. Fam. Appât (*m.*) pour les badauds ; miroir (*m.*) aux alouettes.

gaper [-ə*] n. Fam. Badaud, gobe-mouche *m.*

gaping [-iŋ] n. Bouche bée (person) ; béant (thing).

garage ['gærɑ:ʒ] n. Autom. Garage *m.* ; *garage proprietor,* garagiste.
— v. tr. Autom. Garer, mettre au garage.

garb [gɑ:b] n. Costume *m.* ‖ Fig. Apparence *f.* ; extérieur *m.*
— v. tr. Vêtir (*in,* de).

garbage [-idʒ] n. Ordures *f. pl.* ; détritus *m. pl.* ; U. S. *garbage can,* boîte à ordures, poubelle ; U. S. *garbage collector, garbage man,* boueux, éboueur. ‖ Culin. Déchets *m. pl.* ‖ Fig. Rebut *m.* ; *literary garbage,* écrits orduriers (obscene) ; littérature bonne à mettre au cabinet (worthless).

garble ['gɑ:bḷ] v. tr. Fausser (an account) ; dénaturer (facts) ; tronquer (a quotation) ; mutiler (a text) ; tripatouiller (fam.).

garden ['gɑ:dṇ] n. Jardin *m.* ; *flower, kitchen, market garden,* jardin d'agrément, potager, maraîcher. ‖ Pl. Jardin public, parc *m.* ‖ Pl. Rue (*f.*) avec jardins (street). ‖ **Garden-city,** n. Cité-jardin *f.* ‖ **Garden-engine,** n. Pompe (*f.*) d'arrosage. ‖ **Garden-frame,** n. Agric. Châssis *m.* ‖ **Garden-party,** n. Garden-party *f.* ‖ **Garden-stuff,** n. Agric. Produits maraîchers *m. pl.* ‖ **Garden-seat,** n. Banc de jardin *m.*
— adj. De jardin (plants) ; de jardinage (tools).
— v. intr. Jardiner.

gardener [-ə*] n. Jardinier *m.* ; *landscape gardener,* jardinier paysagiste.

gardenia [gɑ'di:niə] n. Bot. Gardénia *m.*

gardening ['gɑ:dniŋ] n. Jardinage *m.*

garfish ['gɑ:fiʃ] n. Zool. Aiguille de mer *f.*

gargantuan [gɑ:'gæntjuən] adj. Gargantuesque.

gargle ['gɑ:gḷ] v. tr. Méd. *To gargle one's throat,* se gargariser.
— v. intr. Méd. Se gargariser.
— n. Méd. Gargarisme *m.*

gargoyle ['gɑ:goil] n. Archit. Gargouille *f.*

garish ['gɛəriʃ] adj. Cru, éblouissant (glaring). ‖ Voyant, criard (gaudy).

garishness [-nis] n. Crudité *f.* (of light). ‖ Aspect criard *m.* ; couleurs voyantes, fioritures excessives *f. pl.* (showiness).

garland ['gɑ:lənd] n. Guirlande *f.* (See wreath.)

‖ Anthologie *f.* ‖ Naut. Elingue *f.* ‖ Fig. Palme *f.*
— v. tr. Enguirlander, parer de guirlandes. ‖ Fig. Couronner.

garlic ['gɑ:lik] n. Bot. Ail *m.*

garment ['gɑ:mənt] n. Vêtement *m.*
— v. tr. Vêtir, habiller.

garner ['gɑ:nə*] n. Agric. Grenier à grain *m.*
— v. tr. Agric. Engranger. ‖ Fig. Accumuler.

garnet ['gɑ:nit] n. Grenat *m.*

garnish ['gɑ:niʃ] v. tr. Garnir, orner, parer. ‖ Culin. Garnir (*with,* de). ‖ Jur. Saisir-arrêter.
— n. Culin. Garniture *f.*

garnishee [,gɑ:ni'ʃi:] n. Jur. Tiers saisi *m.*

garnisher ['gɑ:niʃə*] n. Garnisseur *s.* ‖ Jur. Saisissant *m.*

garnishment [-mənt] n. Garniture *f.* ‖ Jur. Saisie-arrêt *f.* ; appel (*m.*) d'un tiers en justice.

garniture [gɑ:nitʃə*] n. Garniture *f.*

garret ['gærit] n. Galetas *m.* (apartment) ; grenier *m.* (attic) ; mansarde *f.* (room).

garreteer [,gæri'tiə*] n. Bohème, locataire (*m.*) de mansarde.

garrison ['gærisṇ] n. Milit. Garnison *f.*
— adj. Milit. De place (artillery) ; de garnison (life).
— v. tr. Milit. Placer une garnison dans (a town) ; mettre en garnison (troops).

garrot [-ət] n. Zool., Méd. Garrot *m.*

garrotte [gə'rɔt] n. Garrot *m.* (instrument) ; garrotte *f.* (torture). ‖ Fam. Coup du lapin *m.*
— v. tr. Etrangler. ‖ Fam. Serrer le kiki à.

garrulity [gæ'ru:liti] n. Loquacité *f.*

garrulous ['gæruləs] adj. Loquace, disert (person) ; bavard, babillard (stream) ; verbeux (style).

garrulousness [-nis] n. Loquacité, verbosité *f.*

garter ['gɑ:tə*] n. Jarretière *f.* ‖ U. S. Fixe-chaussette *m.*
— v. tr. Mettre une jarretière à (an undergarment) ; attacher avec une jarretière (one's stockings). ‖ **Garter belt,** n. U. S. Porte-jarretière *m.*

gas [gæs] n. Phys., Chim. Gaz *m.* ‖ Culin. Gaz *m.* ; *by gas,* au gaz. ‖ Méd. Gaz anesthésiant *m.* ‖ Milit. Gaz asphyxiant *m.* ‖ Techn. Grisou *m.* (in mining). ‖ Autom. U. S. Fam. Essence *f.* ; *to step on the gas,* appuyer sur le champignon, mettre plein gaz. ‖ Fam. Baratin, bla-bla-bla, verbiage, vent *m.* ‖ **Gas-bacillus,** n. Méd. Vibrion septique *m.* ‖ **Gas-bag,** n. Enveloppe (*f.*) de ballon à gaz ; Aviat. Ballonnet *m.* ; Fam. Phraseur, baratineur *m.* ‖ **Gas-burner,** n. Bec de gaz *m.* ‖ **Gas-chamber,** n. Chambre à gaz. ‖ **Gas-cooker,** n. Culin. Réchaud à gaz *m.* ‖ **Gas-cooled,** adj. Phys. *Gas-cooled reactor,* réacteur graphite-gaz. ‖ **Gas-detector,** n. Techn. Détecteur de grisou *m.* ‖ **Gas-engine,** n. Techn. Moteur à gaz *m.* ‖ **Gas-fire,** n. Radiateur à gaz *m.* ‖ **Gas-fired,** adj. A gaz (boiler) ; au gaz (central heating). ‖ **Gas-fitter,** n. Gazier *m.* ‖ **Gas-fixture,** n. Appareil à gaz *m.* ‖ **Gas-gangrene,** n. Méd. Gangrène gazeuse *f.* ‖ **Gas-generator,** n. Gazogène *m.* ‖ **Gasholder,** n. Gazomètre, réservoir à gaz *m.* ‖ **Gas-main,** n. Techn. Conduite (*f.*) de gaz. ‖ **Gas-mantle,** n. Techn. Manchon (*m.*) à incandescence. ‖ **Gas-mask,** n. Milit. Masque à gaz *m.* (See respirator.) ‖ **Gas-meter,** n. Compteur à gaz. ‖ **Gas-propelled,** adj. Autom. A gazogène (car). ‖ **Gas-range,** n. Culin. Fourneau à gaz *m.* ‖ **Gas-ring,** n. Brûleur *m.* ; réchaud à gaz *m.* ‖ **Gas-saver,** n. Culin. Economiseur de gaz. ‖ **Gas-shelter,** n. Milit. Abri (*m.*) contre les gaz. ‖ **Gas station,** n. U. S. Poste (*m.*) d'essence. ‖ **Gas turbine,** n. Turbine (*f.*) à gaz. ‖ **Gas-works,** n. Usine (*f.*) à gaz.
— adj. Du gaz, gazier (industry). ‖ Au gaz (range).
— v. tr. (1). Passer au gaz. ‖ Méd. Asphyxier ; *to gas oneself,* s'asphyxier. ‖ Milit. Gazer.
— v. intr. Dégager des gaz. ‖ Fam. Baratiner, laïusser, pérorer.

gasconade [ˌgæskəˈneid] n. Gasconnade *f.*
— v. intr. Gasconner.
Gascony [ˈgæskəni] n. GEOGR. Gascogne *f.*
gaselier [ˌgæsəˈliə*] n. Suspension (*f.*) à gaz.
gaseous [ˈgeisiəs] adj. Gazeux.
gash [gæʃ] n. Balafre *f.* (scar) ; entaille, estafilade *f.* (slash). ‖ Décousure *f.* (by horns, tusks).
— v. tr. Balafrer (face) ; entailler, entamer (flesh).
gasiform [ˈgæsifɔːm] adj. Gazéiforme.
gasify [-fai] v. tr. (2). Gazéifier.
gasket [ˈgæskit] n. NAUT. Raban *m.* ‖ AUTOM. Joint (*m.*) de culasse.
gasogene [ˈgæsodʒiːn] n. Seltzogène.
gasoline [ˈgæsoliːn] n. U. S. Essence *f.*
gasometer [gæˈsɔmitə*] n. Gazomètre *m.*
gasp [gɑːsp] v. intr. Haleter ; *to gasp for air*, suffoquer ; *to make s.o. gasp*, couper le souffle à qqn.
— v. tr. **To gasp out**, exhaler (a breath) ; dire dans un souffle (a word).
— n. Souffle, soupir *m.* ; *at one's last gasp*, à l'agonie.
gasper [-ə*] n. FAM. Cibiche *f.*
gasping [-iŋ] n. Halètement *m.* ; suffocation *f.*
gaspingly [-iŋli] adv. En haletant, hors de souffle.
gasteropod [ˈgæstərɔpɔd] n. ZOOL. Gastéropode *m.*
gastralgia [gæsˈtrældʒiə] n. MED. Gastralgie *f.*
gastric [ˈgæstrik] adj. MED. Gastrique.
gastritis [gæsˈtraitis] n. MED. Gastrite *f.*
gastro-enteritis [ˈgæstrouˌentəˈraitis] n. MED. Gastro-entérite *f.*
gastro-intestinal [-ˌinˈtestinəl] adj. MED. Gastro-intestinal.
gastronome [ˈgæstrəˌnoum] n. Gastronome *s.*
gastronomy [-ˈtrɔnəmi] n. Gastronomie *f.*
gastropod [ˈgæstrəpɔd] n. ZOOL. Gastropode, gastéropode *m.*
gat [gæt] n. POP. Pétard, rigolo, flingue *m.*
gate [geit] n. Porte *f.* (of castle, town) ; porte cochère *f.* (of house) ; grille *f.* (of public garden). ‖ ECCLES. Portail *m.* ‖ CH. DE F. Barrière *f.* (of level-crossing). ‖ NAUT. Vanne, écluse *f.* ‖ CINEM. Fenêtre *f.* (for projector). ‖ SPORTS. Entrée *f.* ‖ GEOGR. Défilé *m.* ‖ FAM. U. S. *To give s.o. the gate*, montrer la porte à qqn. ‖ **Gate-crash**, v. intr. FAM. Resquiller ; v. tr. Resquiller pour prendre part à (a party). ‖ **Gate-crasher**, n. FAM. Passe-volant, resquilleur *m.* ‖ **Gate-keeper**, n. CH. DE F. Garde-barrière *s.* ‖ **Gate-money**, n. SPORTS. Entrée *f.* (price). ‖ **Gate-post**, n. Montant *m.*
— v. tr. Consigner (a student).
— v. intr. AVIAT. Voler à la vitesse maximum.
gateau [ˈgætou] n. CULIN. Gâteau *m.*
gatehouse [ˈgeitˌhous] n. ARCHIT. Corps (*m.*) de garde (in a castle) ; loge *f.* (in a public garden).
gateway [ˈgeitwei] n. Portail *m.* ; grande porte *f.* ‖ FIG. Porte *f.*
gather [ˈgæðə*] v. tr. Assembler, réunir, grouper (to reunite). ‖ Amasser, accumuler, recueillir, rassembler (to collect). ‖ Prendre, reprendre, retrouver, acquérir (to gain) ; *to gather breath*, reprendre haleine ; *to gather dirt*, s'encrasser. ‖ Ramasser, rassembler ; *to gather oneself*, se ramasser ; *to gather one's energies*, rassembler ses forces. ‖ Froncer (one's eyebrows, a skirt). ‖ SPORTS. Cueillir (the ball). ‖ AGRIC. Cueillir (flowers) ; rentrer (the harvest) ; récolter (wheat). ‖ ZOOL. *To gather honey*, butiner. ‖ **To gather up**, recueillir (to collect), ramasser (to pick up) ; rassembler (to sum up, to summon up) ; *to gather up one's limbs*, ramener ses membres ; *to gather oneself up*, se pelotonner, se recroqueviller.
— v. intr. S'assembler, se réunir, se grouper, se rassembler (persons) ; s'accumuler, s'entasser (things). ‖ Augmenter, croître, grandir (to increase). ‖ Conclure, déduire (to infer) ; *to gather from*,

penser d'après. ‖ MED. Mûrir, amasser (abscess) ; se former (pus).
— n. Fronce *f.* (See PUCKER.)
gathering [-riŋ] n. Assemblage, rassemblement *m.* (act) ; assemblée, réunion *f.* (group). ‖ Fronces *f. pl.* ; froncis *m.* ‖ AGRIC. Cueillette *f.* (of fruit) ; récolte *f.* (of wheat).
gauche [gouʃ] adj. Emprunté, maladroit, gauche (awkward) ; qui manque de tact (tactless).
gaucherie [ˈgouʃəri] n. Gaucherie *f.*
gaucho [ˈgautʃou] n. Gaucho *m.*
gaud [gɔːd] n. Clinquant *m.* ; parure voyante *f.* ‖ Colifichet *m.* (bauble). ‖ Pl. Cérémonies fastueuses *f. pl.*
gaudily [-ili] adv. Avec un faste de mauvais goût. ‖ Somptueusement.
gaudiness [-inis] n. Eclat de mauvais goût ; clinquant, tape-à-l'œil *m.* (fam.). ‖ Faste *m.*
gaudy [-i] adj. Voyant, clinquant, de mauvais goût. ‖ Fastueux, somptueux.
— n. Agapes *f. pl.*
gauge [geidʒ] n. Jauge *f.* (of cask). ‖ Calibre *m.* ; *calliper gauge*, calibre de précision. ‖ Indicateur *m.* ; *angle gauge*, goniomètre ; *oil gauge*, indicateur de niveau d'huile. ‖ Troussequin *m.* (in carpentry). ‖ CH. DE F. *Loading gauge*, gabarit de chargement ; *narrow gauge*, voie étroite ; *standard gauge*, écartement normal. ‖ AUTOM. Ecartement *m.* (of wheels) ; *petrol* (or) U. S. *gasoline gauge*, jauge d'essence. ‖ AVIAT. *Height gauge*, altimètre. ‖ NAUT. (See GAGE.) ‖ CINEM. Pas *m.* ‖ FIG. Capacité *f.* ; *to take s.o.'s gauge*, jauger qqn. ‖ **Gauge-glass**, n. TECHN. Indicateur de niveau *m.*
— v. tr. Froncer, bouillonner (a skirt). ‖ TECHN. Jauger (a cask) ; gabarier (a metal plate) ; calibrer (a nut) ; cuber (a tank) ; standardiser (tools). ‖ ARCHIT. Doser (plaster) ; trusquiner (wood). ‖ FIG. Jauger (s.o.'s capacities) ; peser, prévoir (events).
gauger [-ə*] n. Jaugeur *m.*
Gaul [gɔːl] n. GEOGR. Gaule *f.* (country) ; Gaulois *s.* (person).
Gaulish [-iʃ] adj., n. Gaulois *s.*
Gaullist [ˈgɔːlist] n. Gaulliste *s.*
gaunt [gɔːnt] adj. Creux (cheek) ; émacié, décharné étique (face, person). ‖ FIG. Lugubre (desolate) ; féroce (grim).
gauntlet [ˈgɔːntlit] n. Gantelet *m.* (in armour) ‖ AUTOM., SPORTS. Gant à crispin *m.* (glove) ; crispin *m.* (part). ‖ FIG. *To take up, to throw down the gauntlet*, relever, jeter le gant.
gauntlet n. *To run the gauntlet*, MILIT. Passer par les baguettes ; NAUT. Courir la bouline. ‖ FIG. Passer sous les Fourches Caudines, subir un assaut.
gauntness [ˈgɔːntnis] n. Extrême maigreur *f.*
gauss [gaus] (pl. **gauss** [or] **gausses** [-iz]) n. PHYS. Gauss *m.* (unit).
gauze [gɔːz] n. Gaze *f.* (of cotton, silk) ; *wire gauze*, toile métallique. ‖ Vapeur, brume *f.* (haze).
gauzy [-i] adj. Léger, diaphane.
gavage [ˈgævɑːʒ] n. Gavage *m.*
gave [geiv]. See GIVE.
gavel [ˈgævl] n. Marteau *m.* (of auctioneer, o chairman).
— v. intr. (1). Ramener l'ordre en frappant d marteau.
gavotte [gəˈvɔt] n. MUS. Gavotte *f.*
gawk [gɔːk] n. FAM. Godiche *s.* ; *gawk of a man* escogriffe ; *gawk of a woman*, cavale, carcan d femme.
— v. intr. FAM. Regarder d'un air stupide (o godiche, regarder avec des yeux ronds.
gawky [-i] adj. FAM. Godiche (awkward) ; dégin gandé (gangling).
gawp [gɔːp] v. intr. See GAWK.
gay [gei] adj. Gai, joyeux (person) ; *gay dog*, joyeu drille. ‖ Gai, éclatant (colour) ; riche, somptueu

(dress). ‖ Débauché; *to lead a gay life,* courir le guilledou. ‖ Pop. Homosexuel; d'homosexuel.

gaze [geiz] v. intr. *To gaze at,* fixer, contempler fixement.
— n. Contemplation *f.* (act); regard fixe (or) admiratif *m.* (stare). ‖ Point (*m.*) de mire.

gazebo [gə'zi:bou] n. Belvédère *m.* ‖ U. S. Pop. Andouille *f.*

gazelle [gə'zel] n. Zool. Gazelle *f.*

gazer ['geizə*] n. Curieux *s.;* contemplateur *m.,* contemplatrice *f.*

gazette [gə'zet] n. Gazette *f.* (magazine); Journal officiel *m.* (official publication).
— v. tr. Publier à l'Officiel; *he was gazetted today,* sa nomination a paru aujourd'hui à l'Officiel.

gazetteer [ˌgæzi'tiə*] n. † Gazetier *m.* ‖ Dictionnaire géographique *m.*

gazing [-iŋ] adj. Curieux (crowd).

gazpacho [gəz'pɑ:tʃou] (pl. **gazpachos** [-z]) n. Culin. Gaspacho *m.*

gazump [gə'zʌmp] v. tr. Fam. Truander; pigeonner en vendant plus cher que le prix convenu.

G.B. [dʒi:'bi:] abbr. *Great Britain,* Grande-Bretagne.

G.C.E. [dʒi:si:'i:] abbr. *General Certificate of Education,* examen de fin d'études secondaires.

gear [giə*] n. Habillement *m.* (clothing); harnachement *m.* (harness). ‖ Ustensiles, appareils, outils *m. pl.* (appliances). ‖ Sports. Attirail, équipement *m.* ‖ Techn. Mécanisme, dispositif *m.* ‖ Techn. Engrenage *m.; in gear,* engrené, enclenché; *out of gear,* désengrené, détraqué, hors de marche. ‖ Autom. Embrayage *m.; to throw into, out of gear,* embrayer, débrayer. ‖ Autom. Développement *m.* (for a bicycle); vitesse *f.* (for a car); *in low, top gear,* en première, quatrième vitesse; *neutral gear,* point mort; *reversing gear,* marche arrière. ‖ Naut. Appareaux *m. pl.* ‖ **Gear-box,** n. Autom. Boîte (*f.*) de changement de vitesse. ‖ **Gear case,** n. Autom. Carter *m.* ‖ **Gear lever,** U. S. **Gear shift,** n. Autom. Levier (*m.*) des vitesses. ‖ **Gear-wheel,** n. Pignon *m.* (of bicycle); Techn. Roue (*f.*) d'engrenage.
— v. tr. Harnacher (a horse). ‖ Techn. Donner un développement à (a bicycle); engrener (a wheel). ‖ Fig. Adapter, ajuster (*to,* à). ‖ **To gear up,** préparer, mettre sur le pied de guerre; *geared up,* fin prêt. ‖ **To gear down,** Autom. Rétrograder; Techn. Démultiplier.
— v. intr. Techn. S'engrener, engrener.

gearing [-riŋ] n. Techn. Engrenage *m.*

gecko ['gekou] n. Zool. Gecko *m.*
— N. B. Deux pluriels: *geckos, geckoes.*

gee [dʒi:] interj. U. S. Sapristi!
— interj. *Gee up!,* Hue!

gee-gee [dʒi:'dʒi:] n. Fam. Dada *m.* (horse).

geezer ['gi:zə*] n. Pop. Mec, type, zèbre *m.; old geezer,* vieux schnock (or) bonze.

Gehenna [gi'henə] n. Géhenne *f.*

Geiger counter ['gaigə'kauntə*] n. Phys. Compteur (de) Geiger *m.*

geisha ['geiʃə] n. Geisha *f.*
— N. B. Deux pluriels: *geisha, geishas.*

gel [dʒel] n. Chim. Colloïde *m.*
— v. intr. Se coaguler.

gelatine ['dʒelәti:n] n. Gélatine *f.* ‖ Milit. *Explosive gelatine,* plastic.

gelatinous [dʒi'lætinəs] adj. Gélatineux.

gelation [dʒi'leiʃən] n. Congélation *f.*

gelation n. Gélification *f.* (formation of a gel).

geld [geld] v. tr. Châtrer. (See castrate.)

gelder [-ə*] n. Hongreur *m.*

gelding [-iŋ] n. Castration *f.* (act); animal châtré; hongre *m.* (horse).

gelignite ['dʒeligˌnait] n. Techn. Gélignite, dynamite gélatinée *f.*

gem [dʒem] n. Gemme, pierre précieuse *f.* ‖ U. S. Culin. Petit tourteau *m.* (muffin). ‖ Fig. Bijou, joyau *m.; perle f.*

— v. tr. (1). Orner de pierres précieuses.

geminate ['dʒeminit] adj. Géminé.
— [-neit] v. tr. Géminer.

Gemini [-nai] n. pr. Astron. Gémeaux *m. pl.*

gemma ['dʒemə] (pl. **gemmae** [-i:]) n. Bot., Zool. Gemme *f.*

gemmate [dʒe'meit] v. intr. Bot. Gemmer; bourgeonner.

gemmology [dʒe'mɔlədʒi] n. Gemmologie *f.*

gen [dʒen] n. Fam. Tuyaux, rancards *m. pl.*
— v. tr. (1). *To gen up,* Fam. Mettre au parfum, rancarder.
— v. intr. (1). *To gen up,* Fam. Se rancarder.

gendarme ['ʒɔndɑ:m] n. Milit., Geol. Gendarme.

gender ['dʒendə*] n. Gramm. Genre *m.*
— v. tr. Engendrer.

gene [dʒi:n] n. Med. Gène *m.*

genealogical [ˌdʒi:niə'lɔdʒikəl] adj. Blas. Généalogique (tree).

genealogist [ˌdʒi:ni'ælədʒist] n. Généalogiste *m.*

genealogy [-dʒi] n. Généalogie *f.*

general ['dʒenərəl] adj. Général (characteristic, classification, election, enquiry, term, welfare). ‖ Non spécialisé; *general reader,* lecteur moyen, grand public; *general servant,* bonne à tout faire. ‖ Général, en chef; *agent general,* agent général. ‖ Comm. En tous genres (dealer); *general shop* (or) U. S. *store,* bazar. ‖ Naut. En cueillette (cargo). ‖ Milit. Général (headquarters).
— n. Ensemble *m.* (*of,* de); *in general,* en général, d'une façon générale. ‖ Eccles. Général *m.* ‖ Milit. Général *m.; brigadier-, major-general,* général de brigade, de division. ‖ Mus., Milit. Générale *f.* ‖ Fam. Bonne (*f.*) à tout faire (servant).

generalissimo [ˌdʒenərə'lisimou] n. Milit. Généralissime *m.*

generality [ˌdʒenə'ræliti] n. Caractère général *m.* ‖ Généralité *f.; the generality of,* la plupart de.

generalization [ˌdʒenərəlai'zeiʃən] n. Généralisation *f.*

generalize ['dʒenərəlaiz] v. tr., intr. Généraliser.

generalizer [-ə*] n. Généralisateur *m.*

generally ['dʒenərəli] adv. Généralement; en général, dans l'ensemble.

generalship ['dʒenərəlʃip] n. Milit. Généralat *m.* (authority, rank); stratégie, tactique *f.* (skill).

generate ['dʒenəreit] v. tr. Engendrer.

generation [ˌdʒenə'reiʃən] n. Génération *f.* (act, degree, period, people); *the rising generation,* la nouvelle géné* (fam.).

generative ['dʒenərətiv] adj. Générateur *m.; génératrice f.* ‖ Producteur *m.; productrice f.; productif.*

generator [-ə*] n. Med., Techn. Générateur *m.* ‖ Electr. Génératrice *f.* ‖ Chim. Gazogène *m.* ‖ *Generator-gas,* n. Gaz pauvre *m.*

generic [dʒi'nerik] adj. Générique.

generically [-əli] adv. Génériquement.

generosity [ˌdʒenə'rɔsiti] n. Générosité *f.*

generous ['dʒenərəs] adj. Généreux, libéral; *generous to a fault,* généreux jusqu'à la faiblesse. ‖ Généreux, large, copieux, abondant. ‖ Agric. Riche, fertile (soil). ‖ Culin. Généreux (wine).

generously [-li] adv. Généreusement.

Genesis ['dʒenisis] n. Eccles., Fig. Genèse *f.*

genetic [dʒi'netik] adj. Philos., Med. Génétique.

genetics [-s] n. pl. Med., Philos. Génétique *f.*

geneva [dʒi'ni:və] n. Genièvre, gin *m.*

Geneva n. Geogr. Genève *f.; Geneva Convention,* convention de Genève.

Genevan [-ən], **Genevese** [dʒeni'vi:z] adj., n. Geogr. Genevois *m.*

genial ['dʒi:njəl] adj. Med. Génien.

genial adj. † Nuptial (bed); génésique (instinct). ‖ Doux et calme, clément, favorable (climate); réconfortant, vivifiant (warmth). ‖ Bienveillant, cordial, affable, ouvert (person); génial (talent).

geniality [,dʒi:ni'æliti] n. Douceur f. (of climate); cordialité f. (of person).
genially ['dʒi:njəli] adv. Cordialement.
genic ['dʒenik] adj. MED. Génique.
geniculate [dʒi'nikjulit] adj. BOT., MED. Géniculé.
genie ['dʒi:ni] (pl. genii [-ai]) n. Djinn, génie m.
genii ['dʒi:n,iai] n. pl. See GENIE, GENIUS.
genista [dʒi'nistə] n. BOT. Genêt m.
genital ['dʒənitḷ] adj. MED. Génital.
genitals [-s] n. pl. MED. Organes génitaux m. pl.
genitive ['dʒənitiv] adj., n. GRAMM. Génitif m.
genito-urinary ['dʒenitou'juərinəri] adj. MED. Génito-urinaire, uro-génital.
genius ['dʒi:njəs] (pl. genii [-ai]) n. Génie, lutin, démon m.
genius (pl. geniuses [-iz]) n. Génie m.; caractéristique dominante f. (of an age, a language, a nation). ‖ Génie m.; personne géniale f. (person). ‖ (No plural.) Génie m. (mental capacity).
Genoa ['dʒenoə] n. GEOGR. Gênes f. ‖ CULIN. Genoa cake, pain de Gênes.
genocide ['dʒenə,said] n. Génocide m.
genotype [-,taip] n. MED. Génotype, génome m.
genre ['ʒɑ:nrə] n. ARTS. Genre m.; genre-painting, tableau de genre.
gent [dʒent] n. COMM., FAM. Homme m.
genteel [dʒen'ti:l] adj. Distingué, de bon ton; bien élevé, d'un bon milieu (ironically).
gentian ['dʒenʃiən] n. BOT. Gentiane f.
gentile ['dʒentail] n. ECCLES. Gentil m.
— adj. ECCLES. Des Gentils.
gentility [dʒen'tiliti] n. Bonne famille (or) naissance; bourgeoisie f. ‖ Distinction. f.
gentle ['dʒentḷ] adj. Noble, bien né, de bonne famille. ‖ Doux, modéré; to use gentle methods, employer la douceur. ‖ Aimable (disposition, reader); gentil (rebuke); faible (sex); léger (tap).
— n. pl. † Nobles, gentilshommes m. pl. ‖ ZOOL. Asticot m.
gentlefolk [-fouk] n. Gens (m. pl.) comme il faut; personnes (f. pl.) de bonne extraction; distressed gentlefolk, les pauvres honteux; les économiquement faibles.
gentlehood [-hud] n. Distinction, race f. ‖ Bonne bourgeoisie f.
gentleman [-mən] (pl. gentlemen) n. † Gentilhomme m. ‖ Gentleman, galant homme, homme du monde, homme distingué m. ‖ Monsieur m.; ladies and gentlemen, mesdames et messieurs. ‖ Cavalier m. (of a lady in dancing). ‖ JUR. Rentier m. ‖ SPORTS. Amateur m. ‖ COMM. Homme m. ‖ FAM. The old gentleman, le Diable, le Malin. ‖ Gentleman-at-arms, n. Gentilhomme (m.) de la garde. ‖ Gentleman-commoner, n. Etudiant privilégié m. (at Oxford and Cambridge). ‖ Gentleman-farmer, n. AGRIC. Gentleman-farmer m.
gentlemanlike [-mənlaik], gentlemanly [-mənli] adv. De bon ton (manner); bien élevé, distingué, courtois; de bonne extraction (person).
gentleness [-nis] n. Douceur f.
gentlewoman [-,wumən] (pl. gentlewomen [-,wimin]) n. Dame, demoiselle; femme distinguée f.
gently [-i] adv. † Noblement. ‖ Avec douceur, doucement. ‖ Doucement, graduellement.
gentry ['dʒentri] n. Petite noblesse, haute bourgeoisie, gentry f. ‖ Gent f. (ironically).
genual ['dʒenjuəl] adj. MED. Du genou.
genuflect ['dʒenjuflekt] v. intr. Faire la génuflexion.
genuflexion [,dʒenju'flekʃən] n. Génuflexion f.
genuine ['dʒenjuin] adj. ZOOL. De pure race (animal). ‖ FIN. De bon aloi, vrai (coin). ‖ COMM. Pur, naturel, authentique (article); véritable (pearl); sérieux (purchases). ‖ FIG. Sincère (belief, person); vrai, authentique (document, nobility).
genuinely [-li] adv. Véritablement; authentiquement. ‖ Sincèrement.
genus ['dʒi:nəs] (pl. genera ['dʒenərə]) n. PHILOS., MED., ZOOL. Genre m.
geocentric [,dʒi:o'sentrik] adj. ASTRON. Géocentrique.
geochemical [,dʒi:ou'kemikḷ] adj. Géochimique.
geochemistry [-'kemistri] n. Géochimie f.
geodesic [-'desik] adj. Géodésique.
geodesist [dʒi:'ɔdisist] n. Géodésien m.
geodesy [-si] n. Géodésie f.
geographer [dʒi'ɔgrəfə*] n. Géographe s.
geographic(al) [dʒio'græfik(əl)] adj. Géographique.
geography [dʒi'ɔg-əfi] n. Géographie f. (book science). ‖ FAM. To show s.o. the geography of the house, montrer le petit coin à qqn.
geologic(al) [dʒio'lɔdʒik(əl)] adj. Géologique.
geologist [dʒi'ɔlɔdʒist] n. Géologue s.
geologize [-dʒaiz] v. intr. Faire de la géologie.
— v. tr. Etudier la géologie de.

GEOGRAPHY — GÉOGRAPHIE

affluent	tributary	indigène, aborigène	native, aboriginal
archipel	archipelago	insulaire	insular (adj.), islander (n.)
banquise	icefield; ice-pack	marais, marécage	marsh, swamp
bras de mer	inlet	marée haute, basse	high, low tide
cardinaux (points)	cardinal (points)	mer agitée	choppy sea
carte	map	mer belle	smooth sea
carte marine	chart	méridien	meridian
chaîne de montagne	mountain range	mont, montagne	mount, mountain
chute, cascade	fall, waterfall	moutons [de la mer]	white horses [waves]
col [de montagne]	(mountain) pass	muette (carte)	skeleton [map]
confluent	confluence	occidental	Western
continent	mainland; continent	oriental	Eastern
cours d'eau; fleuve	stream; river	orienter (s')	to take bearings
crue	spate	plateau	plateau
détroit	strait	portulan	portolano; portulan
dune	sandhill; dune	presqu'île	peninsula
échelle	scale	ressortissant	national
échelle (à l')	to scale	rivage	shore, beach, strand
estuaire	estuary; firth (Ecosse)	rive	bank, side
état-major (carte d')	Ordnance Survey map	rose des vents	mariner's card
fleuve	river	routière (carte)	road (map)
flux et reflux	ebb and flow	ruisseau	brook, rivulet
île	island	tempéré (climat)	temperate (climate)
îlot	islet	vallée	valley
		volcan	volcano

geology [-dʒi] n. Géologie f.
geomagnetism [-'mægni,tizm̩] n. Géomagnétisme m.
geomancy ['dʒiomænsi] n. Géomancie f.
geometer [dʒi'ɔmitə*] n. MATH. Géomètre m. ‖ ZOOL. Chenille arpenteuse f.
geometric(al) [dʒio'metrik(əl)] adj. MATH. Géométrique.
geometrically [-əli] adv. MATH. Géométriquement.
geometrician [,dʒiome'triʃən] n. MATH. Géomètre s.
geometry [dʒi'ɔmitri] n. Géométrie f.
geomorphology [-mɔ:'fɔlədʒi] n. Géomorphologie f.
geophysics [,dʒio'fiziks] n. Géophysique f.
geopolitics [-'pɔlitiks] n. pl. Géopolitique f.
George [dʒɔ:dʒ] n. Georges m. (name). ‖ Saint-Georges m. (insignia). ‖ AVIAT., FAM. Pilote automatique m.
georgette [dʒɔ:'dʒet] n. Crêpe Georgette m.
Georgian ['dʒɔ:dʒiən] adj. Du temps des rois George.
Georgian adj., n. GEOGR. Géorgien s.
georgic ['dʒɔ:dʒik] n. Géorgique f.
geostatics [,dʒio'stætiks] n. pl. Géostatique f.
geostationary [-'steiʃənəri] adj. ASTRONAUT. Géostationnaire.
geothermal [-'θə:məl] adj. Géothermique.
geotropism [dʒi'ɔtrəpizm̩] n. Géotropisme m.
geranium [dʒi'reinjəm] n. BOT. Geranium m.
gerfalcon ['dʒə:,fɔ:kən] n. ZOOL. Gerfaut m.
geriatric [,dʒeri'ætrik] adj. MED. Gériatrique.
geriatrics [-ks] n. sg. MED. Gériatrie f.
germ [dʒə:m] n. BOT., FIG. Germe m. ‖ MED. Bacille m. (bacillus); microbe, germe m. (of a disease). ‖ **Germ-carrier,** n. MED. Porteur (m.) de bacilles. ‖ **Germ-killer,** n. MED. Microbicide m. ‖ **Germ-warfare,** n. MILIT. Guerre bactériologique f.
— v. intr. FIG. Germer.
German ['dʒə:mən] adj. † Germain, germanique. ‖ GEOGR. Allemand; *German Democratic Republic,* République démocratique allemande.
— n. † Germain m. ‖ GEOGR. Allemand s.
german adj. Germain (cousin). ‖ FIG. Apparenté (to, à).
germane [dʒə:'mein] adj. FIG. Allié, apparenté, se rapportant (to, à).
Germanic [dʒə:'mænik] adj., n. Germanique m.
Germanist ['dʒə:mənist] n. Germaniste s.
Germanity [dʒə:'mæniti] n. Germanisme m.
germanium [dʒə:'meiniəm] n. CHIM. Germanium m.
Germanize ['dʒə:mənaiz] v. tr. Germaniser.
— v. intr. Se germaniser.
Germanophobia [,dʒə:mænə'foubiə] n. Germanophobie f.
Germany [-ni] n. GEOGR. Allemagne f.; *Federal Republic of Germany,* République fédérale d'Allemagne.
germen ['dʒə:men] n. BOT. Germe m.
germicide ['dʒə:misaid] adj., n. MED. Bactéricide, microbicide m.
germinal [-n̩] adj. MED. Germinal. ‖ FIG. En germe, embryonnaire.
germinate [-neit] v. intr. Germer.
— v. tr. Faire germer.
germination [,dʒə:mi'neiʃən] n. BOT. Germination f.
gerontocracy [,dʒerɔn'tɔkrəsi] n. Gérontocratie f.
gerontologist [-lədʒist] n. MED. Gérontologue s.
gerontology [-lədʒi] n. MED. Gérontologie f.
gerrymander ['gerimændə*] v. tr. FAM. Cuisiner, truquer (an election).
— n. FAM. Cuisine électorale f.

gerund ['dʒerənd] n. GRAMM. Gérondif m. (in Anglo-Saxon, Latin); substantif verbal m. (in English).
gerundive [dʒi'rʌndiv] n. GRAMM. Gérondif, adjectif verbal m. (in Latin).
— adj. GRAMM. Du gérondif.
gesso ['dʒesou] (pl. **gessoes** [-z]) n. Plâtre de Paris, gesso m.
Gestalt [gə'ʃtælt] n. PSYCH. Gestalt f.; *gestalt psychology,* gestaltisme, théorie de la forme.
Gestapo [gə'stɑ:pou] n. Gestapo f.
gestate ['dʒesteit] v. tr. MED., FIG. Porter en gestation.
gestation [dʒes'teiʃən] n. MED., FIG. Gestation f.
gesticulate [dʒes'tikjuleit] v. tr. Gesticuler, faire des gestes.
— v. tr. Mimer, traduire par gestes.
gesticulation [dʒes,tikju'leiʃən] n. Gesticulation f.
gesticulator [dʒes'tikjuleitə*] n. Gesticulateur m.; gesticulatrice f.
gesture ['dʒestʃə*] n. Geste m.
— v. intr. Gesticuler, faire des gestes.
— v. tr. Exprimer par gestes.

get [get] v. tr. (68).

1, 2. Se procurer, procurer. — 3. Acquérir. — 4. Obtenir. — 5. Atteindre. — 6. Prendre. — 7. Chercher. — 8. Recevoir. — 9. Faire parvenir. — 10. Mettre. — 11. Avoir, se faire. — 12. Préparer. — 13. Faire. — 14. Rendre. — 15. FIN. — 16. COMM. — 17. MED., ZOOL. — 18. MED. — 19. MATH. — 20. ECCLES. — 21. RADIO. — 22, 23, 24, 25, 26. FAM. — 27, 28, 29. FAM. U. S. — 30. To get along. — 31. To get away. — 32. To get back. — 33. To get down. — 34. To get in. — 35. To get into. — 36. To get off. — 37. To get on. — 38. To get out. — 39. To get through. — 40. To get under. — 41. To get up.

1. Se procurer; dégoter (fam.); *where did you get those shoes?,* où avez-vous trouvé (or) où vous êtes-vous procuré ces souliers? ‖ 2. Procurer; *I'll get it for you,* je vais vous chercher ça; *to get sth. for s.o.,* faire avoir (or) procurer qqch. à qqn. ‖ 3. Acquérir; *to get a bad name,* se faire une mauvaise réputation; *to get sth. by heart,* apprendre qqch. par cœur. ‖ 4. Obtenir (leave, mercy, result); *can you get the door to shut?* pouvez-vous réussir à fermer la porte?; *get him to leave,* persuadez-le de partir; *to get s.o. to do sth.,* obtenir de qqn qu'il fasse qqch., décider (or) amener qqn à faire qqch.; *to get stripes,* décrocher des galons. ‖ 5. Atteindre; *I've got him, je le tiens; to get s.o. in the eye,* atteindre qqn à l'œil. ‖ 6. Prendre; *to get hold of,* se saisir de; *to get a wife,* prendre femme; *to get s.o. by the throat,* prendre qqn à la gorge; *what's got him?,* qu'est-ce qui lui a pris? ‖ 7. Chercher; *get me my books,* apportez-moi mes livres; *go and get your books,* allez chercher vos livres. ‖ 8. Recevoir (a blow, a letter). ‖ 9. Faire parvenir; *to get an article to the editor,* remettre un article au rédacteur en chef; *to get sth. home,* faire parvenir qqch. chez soi. ‖ 10. Mettre; *to get s.o. into trouble,* mettre qqn dans l'embarras; *to get s.o. on to a subject,* mettre qqn sur un sujet. ‖ 11. Avoir, se faire (an idea); *to get sth. on the brain,* être obsédé par qqch.; *to get wind of,* avoir vent de. ‖ 12. Faire, préparer; *to get dinner for s.o.,* faire le dîner pour qqn. ‖ 13. Faire (with a past participle); *to get sth. done by s.o.,* faire faire qqch. par qqn; *to get one's clothes brushed,* faire brosser ses habits. ‖ 14. Rendre (with an adjective); *to get one's hands dirty,* se salir les mains. ‖ 15. FIN. Obtenir (a profit); gagner (a sum of

money); *to get nothing by it*, n'y rien gagner; *to get sth. out of it*, y trouver son profit. ‖ **16.** Comm. Se fournir; *to get one's things at X's*, se servir chez X. ‖ **17.** Med., Zool. Engendrer; *to get with child*, engrosser (pop.). ‖ **18.** Med. Attraper (a disease); *the pain gets him in the head*, le mal le tient dans la tête. ‖ **19.** Math. Obtenir (a total). ‖ **20.** Eccles. U. S. *To get religion*, se convertir. ‖ **21.** Radio. Avoir, prendre, accrocher (a station); avoir (s.o. on the phone). ‖ **22.** Fam. Avoir, posséder (with *have*); *have you got any?*, en avez-vous?; *she has got red hair*, elle est rouquine. ‖ **23.** Fam. Attraper, ramasser; *to get it hot*, en prendre pour son grade; *to get ten years*, attraper dix ans. ‖ **24.** Fam. Avoir; *I'll get him*, j'aurai sa peau. ‖ **25.** Fam. Devoir (with *have*); *you have got to leave*, il faut que vous partiez. ‖ **26.** Fam. Comprendre; *you have got it*, vous avez saisi. ‖ **27.** Fam. U. S. Observer, remarquer; *did you get his look?*, avez-vous visé son air? ‖ **28.** Fam. U. S. Embarrasser; *the problem gets me*, c'est trop fort pour moi. ‖ **29.** Fam. U. S. Enthousiasmer; *that really gets me*, ça m'a vraiment emballé. ‖ **30. To get along**, faire avancer, amener. ‖ **31. To get away**, arracher, entraîner (s.o.). ‖ **32. To get back**, faire rentrer, replacer (*into*, dans); faire revenir, recouvrer; Fam. *To get one's own back*, prendre sa revanche. ‖ **33. To get down**, descendre (a book); décrocher (one's hat); Aviat., Sports. Descendre; Fig. Noter (on paper); Fam. Avaler, faire descendre (food); agacer, décourager (s.o.); *don't let it get you down*, ne vous en faites pas; *he gets me down*, il me tape sur le système. ‖ **34. To get in**, rentrer; faire entrer, introduire; Agric. Engranger; Fin., Comm. Recouvrer, faire rentrer; Fam. Flanquer (a blow); *to get one's hand in*, se faire la main. ‖ **35. To get into**, faire entrer, introduire; *to get s.o. into a habit*, faire prendre une habitude à qqn. ‖ **36. To get off**, ôter, enlever (one's clothes, a stain); expédier (a letter); Jur. Faire acquitter; Naut. Renflouer; Fam. Tirer d'affaire, tirer de là. ‖ **37. To get on**, mettre, enfiler (one's clothes); faire progresser (a pupil, a work). ‖ **38. To get out**, enlever, tirer, sortir, extraire (*of*, de); tirer (a cork); arracher (a nail); enlever (a stain); *to get out a book*, sortir un livre; Autom. Sortir (a car); Naut. Mettre à la mer (a boat); Fin. Dresser (an account); Fig. Etablir (a list); dresser (plans); résoudre (a problem); *to get a secret, money out of s.o.*, arracher un secret, soutirer de l'argent à qqn; *to get s.o. out of a habit*, débarrasser qqn d'une habitude; Fam. *To get out of a mess*, tirer du pétrin. ‖ **39. To get through**, faire recevoir (a pupil); Jur. Faire adopter (a bill); *to get through the customs*, faire passer à la douane. ‖ **40. To get under**, maîtriser (a fire). ‖ **41. To get up**, faire lever (or) monter (s.o.); monter (sth.); Theatr. Monter (a play); Comm. Présenter, parer, habiller (an article); Fig. Préparer (a lecture); monter (a plot); forger (a story); Fam. *To get one's back up*, ne rien vouloir entendre, se monter; *to get oneself up*, se pomponner, se mettre sur son trente et un (to dress); se maquiller (to make up); se déguiser, s'attifer (*as*, en).
— v. intr.

---

1. Arriver. — 2. Devenir. — 3. Se mettre à. — 4. To get about. — 5. To get along. — 6. To get at. — 7. To get away. — 8. To get back. — 9. To get by. — 10. To get down. — 11. To get in. — 12. To get into. — 13. To get off. — 14. To get on. — 15. To get out. — 16. To get over. — 17. To get round. — 18. To get through. — 19. To get to. — 20. To get together. — 21. To get under. — 22. To get up.

---

1. Arriver (*from*, de; *to*, à); *they were both out to get there first*, c'était à qui des deux arriverait le premier. ‖ **2.** Devenir; *to get angry*, se fâcher; *to get beaten*, se faire battre; *to get caught in the rain*, être pris par la pluie; *to get old*, vieillir. ‖ **3.** Se mettre à; *to get cracking*, s'y mettre, se remuer; *to get doing sth.*, se mettre à faire qqch. ‖ **4. To get about**, circuler, s'ébruiter (news); circuler, se déplacer (persons); Med. Etre de nouveau sur pied. ‖ **5. To get along**, s'en aller; Fig. Progresser, avancer; *to get along with s.o.*, s'accorder avec qqn.; *to get along without sth.*, se passer de qqch. ‖ **6. To get at**, atteindre, parvenir à (a place); atteindre, toucher, accéder jusqu'à (s.o.); Fig. Découvrir, parvenir à (truth); Fam. Entortiller, avoir (to bamboozle); travailler, acheter (to bribe); *what is he getting at?*, où veut-il en venir? ‖ **7. To get away**, partir, s'en aller (person); se sauver, filer (*with*, avec) [prisoner]; *to get away from*, se soustraire à, se débarrasser de; Autom. Démarrer; Fam. *You won't get away with it*, tu ne t'en tireras pas comme ça, tu ne l'emporteras pas en paradis. ‖ **8. To get back**, revenir, retourner, reculer. ‖ **9. To get by**, passer près; Fam. S'en tirer sans peine; *I'll get by*, je m'en tirerai bien sans me fouler; *his father doesn't let him get by with anything*, son père ne lui passe rien. ‖ **10. To get down**, descendre, (*from*, *off*, de); Fig. S'attaquer à, s'atteler à (a task). ‖ **11. To get in**, entrer, rentrer (*through*, par); Jur. Etre élu; Fam. *To get in with s.o.*, se mettre dans les petits papiers de qqn. ‖ **12. To get into**, mettre (one's clothes); pénétrer dans (a place); Autom., Ch. de f. Monter dans; Fig. Contracter (a habit); *to get into a rage*, se mettre en fureur; *to get into the way of*, se faire à, prendre l'habitude de. ‖ **13. To get off**, descendre (passenger, rider); se sauver, partir (to go away); *to get off one's chair*, se lever de sa chaise; Autom. Démarrer (car); descendre (person); *to get off the road*, déboîter; Ch. de f. Partir (train); *to get off at the next station*, descendre à la prochaine; Aviat. Décoller; Fig. Se faire dispenser de, se dégager de (a duty); Fam. S'en tirer; *to get off cheap* (or) U. S. *easy*, en être quitte à bon compte; Fam. Faire une touche; *to get off with a boy*, accrocher avec un garçon. ‖ **14. To get on**, continuer, poursuivre (to go on); avancer, s'avancer (to proceed); Ch. de f. Monter dans (the train); Fig. S'entendre, s'accorder (to agree); vieillir, monter en graine (to grow old); avancer, progresser (to make progress); réussir, parvenir, faire son chemin (to succeed); *to be getting on for*, approcher de (an age, a date); Fam. *How are you getting on?*, comment ça va?; *to get on one's legs*, prendre la parole en public; *to get on s.o.'s nerves*, porter sur les nerfs à qqn. ‖ **15. To get out**, sortir (*of*, de); Autom., Ch. de f. Descendre (*of*, de); Fig. S'ébruiter (news); Fig. Se tirer de (a difficulty); se soustraire à (a duty); se défaire de (a habit); échapper à (an obligation); Fam. *Get out!*, fichez-moi le camp! ‖ **16. To get over**, franchir (a wall); Med. *To get over a disease*, se remettre d'une maladie; *to get over it*, se rétablir, se remettre; Fig. En finir avec, triompher de (difficulties, habits); passer sur (a fault); Fam. Envoûter (s.o.); *to get over it*, s'y faire, en prendre son parti. ‖ **17. To get round**, tourner, faire le tour de; Med. Ranimer; Fig. Tourner (a difficulty); contourner (the law); Fam. Entortiller, embobeliner (s.o.). ‖ **18. To get through**, traverser, se frayer un chemin dans (a crowd); passer à travers (a hedge); passer par (the window); Jur. Passer, être reçu (candidate); arriver au bout de (one's money, task); s'en tirer (person); *to get through to*, obtenir la communication avec. ‖ **19. To get to**, arriver, parvenir (*to*, à); finir (*to*, par); *to get to work*, se mettre au travail. ‖ **20. To get together**, s'assembler, se réunir (to assemble); Fam. Arriver à s'en-

tendre (to agree). ‖ **21. To get under,** passer par-dessous; NAUT. *To get under sail,* appareiller. ‖ **22. To get up,** monter à (a ladder); monter sur (a rock); se lever *(from,* de) [person]; NAUT. Grossir (sea); s'élever (wind); SPORTS. Rebondir (ball); FIG. Arriver, en être *(to,* à).
— n. ZOOL. Produit *m.* (of a stallion). ‖ **Get-at-able,** adj. Accessible. ‖ **Get-away,** n. AUTOM. Démarrage *m.;* SPORTS. Départ *m.* (of a runner); échappée *f.* (spurt); FAM. Fuite *f.* ‖ **Get-out,** n. Echappatoire *f.* ‖ **Get-up,** n. Habillement *m.;* accoutrement *m.* (pejor.) [costume]; déguisement *m.* (fancy dress); maquillage *m.* (make-up); COMM. Habillage *m.,* présentation *f.;* U. S. allant *m.* ‖ **Get-rich-quick,** adj. Véreux, vite enrichi (person); qui promet la lune (plan).
getter [-ə*] n. Acquéreur *m.* ‖ ZOOL. Reproducteur *m.* ‖ **Getter-up,** n. FAM. Organisateur *m.;* organisatrice *f.*
getting [-iŋ] n. Fait *(m.)* d'atteindre (or) d'obtenir; acquisition *f.* ‖ **Getting across,** n. Traversée *f.* ‖ **Getting away,** n. Départ *m.* ‖ **Getting back,** n. Retour *m.;* FIN. Recouvrement *m.;* FIG. Reprise *f.* ‖ **Getting in,** n. AGRIC. Engrangement *m.;* FIN. Rentrée *f.* ‖ **Getting into,** n. Entrée *(f.)* dans [house]; FIG Admission *(f.)* à [a club]; acquisition *(f.)* de [habits]. ‖ **Getting off,** n. Expédition *f.* (of a letter); AVIAT. Décollage *m.;* NAUT. Renflouage *m.;* JUR. Acquittement *m.* ‖ **Getting out,** n. Publication *f.* (of a book); arrachage *m.* (of a nail); NAUT. Mise *(f.)* à flot. ‖ **Getting over,** n. Franchissement *m.;* escalade *f.;* MED. Guérison *f.* ‖ **Getting through,** n. Passage *(m.)* par; FIG. Succès *m.* ‖ **Getting together,** n. Rassemblement *m.* ‖ **Getting up,** n. Lever *m.;* COMM. Présentation *f.;* THEATR. Montage *m.;* NAUT. Gréage *m.;* FIG. Préparation *f.* (of a lecture); organisation *f.* (of a show).
geum ['dʒi:əm] n. BOT. Geum *m.,* benoîte *f.*
gew-gaw ['gju:gɔ] n. Colifichet *m.*
geyser ['geizə*] n. GEOL. Geyser *m.* ‖ TECHN. Chauffe-bain *m.* ‖ FAM. Soupe *(f.)* au lait.
Ghana ['gɑ:nə] n. GEOGR. Ghana *m.*
ghastliness ['gɑ:stlinis] n. Aspect sinistre *m.* ‖ Pâleur mortelle *f.*
ghastly [-li] adj. Horrible, effrayant. ‖ Blême, blafard (light); blême, livide, mortellement pâle (person).
— adv. Horriblement.
Ghent [gent] n. GEOGR. Gand *m.*
cherkin ['gə:kin] n. BOT., CULIN. Cornichon *m.*
ghetto ['getou] (pl. **ghettos** [-z]) n. Ghetto *m.*
ghost [goust] n. Ame *f.;* esprit, souffle *m.* (spirit). ‖ Esprit, spectre, fantôme, revenant *m.* (apparition). ‖ PHYS. Image secondaire *f.* ‖ ECCLES. *Holy Ghost,* Saint-Esprit. ‖ FIG. Ombre *f.;* soupçon *m.* (hint). ‖ FAM. Nègre *m.* (writer's). ‖ **Ghost-write,** v. intr. U. S. FAM. Faire le nègre. ‖ **Ghost writer,** n. Nègre *m.* ‖ **Ghost town,** n. U. S. Ville morte *f.*
— v. tr. Récrire (rewrite). ‖ Hanter (haunt).
— v. intr. Servir de nègre *(for,* à).
ghostly [-li] adj. Macabre, sépulcral, spectral. ‖ ECCLES. Spirituel.
ghoul [gu:l] n. Goule *f.* ‖ FIG. Déterreur de cadavres *m.*
G.H.Q. [dʒi:eitʃ'kju:] abbr. *General Headquarters,* Grand Quartier général, G. Q. G.
G.I. [dʒi:'ai] n. U. S. MILIT. Soldat, G. I. *m.*
— adj. U. S. MILIT. De l'armée (abbr. for *government issue*).
giant ['dʒaiənt] n. Géant *m.*
— adj. De géant (stride); géant (tree).
giantess [-is] n. Géante *f.*
gib [dʒib] n. TECHN. Contre-clavette.
gib [gib] n. ZOOL. Matou *m.* (a cat).
gibber ['dʒibə*] v. tr., intr. Baragouiner. ‖ Pousser des cris rauques (or) inarticulés.
— n. Baragouinage *m.*

gibberish ['gibəriʃ] n. Baragouin, charabia *m.*
gibbet ['dʒibit] n. Gibet *m.;* potence *f.* (See GALLOWS.)
— v. tr. Pendre. ‖ FIG. Clouer au pilori.
gibbon ['gibən] n. ZOOL. Gibbon *m.*
gibbosity [gi'bɔsiti] n. Gibbosité, bosse *f.*
gibbous ['gibəs] adj. Gibbeux. ‖ Bossu (hump-backed).
gibe [dʒaib] n. Raillerie *f.;* sarcasme *m.*
— v. tr., intr. Railler. (See SCOFF.)
giber [-ə*] n. Railleur *s.*
giblets ['dʒiblits] n. pl. CULIN. Abattis *m. pl.*
Gibraltar [dʒi'brɔ:ltə*] n. GEOGR. Gibraltar *f.; Strait of Gibraltar,* détroit de Gibraltar.
giddily ['gidili] adv. Vertigineusement. ‖ A la légère, avec insouciance.
giddiness [-nis] n. Vertige, éblouissement *m.* ‖ FIG. Frivolité, légèreté *f.* (fickleness); étourderie *f.* (heedlessness).
giddy ['gidi] adj. Etourdi. pris de vertige; *I feel giddy,* la tête me tourne. ‖ Vertigineux, qui donne le vertige (height). ‖ Giratoire, tournoyant (whirling). ‖ FIG. Frivole, léger (fickle); étourdi, écervelé (heedless). ‖ **Giddy-head,** n. FAM. Papillon *m.;* tête de linotte *f.* ‖ **Giddy-pated,** adj. FAM. Au cerveau d'oiseau.
— v. tr. (2). Donner le vertige à.
gift [gift] n. Don *m.; to make a gift of,* faire don de. ‖ Cadeau, présent *m.; gift for gift,* donnant donnant. ‖ COMM. Prime *f.* ‖ JUR. *As a gift,* à titre d'avantage; *deed of gifts,* donation entre vifs; *in the gift of,* à la discrétion de. ‖ FIG. Don, talent *m.;* bosse *f.* (fam.). ‖ **Gift-shop,** n. Boutique *(f.)* de cadeaux. ‖ **Gift token** (or) **voucher,** n. Chèque-cadeau *m.* ‖ **Gift-wrap,** v. tr. (1). Faire un paquet-cadeau pour.
— v. tr. Donner. ‖ FIG. Douer.
gifted [-id] adj. Doué.
gig [gig] n. Cabriolet *m.* ‖ NAUT. Youyou *m.* (rowboat); baleinière *f.* (whale-boat).
gig n. MUS. Engagement *(m.)* de courte durée, gig *m.*
— v. intr. Donner un concert, jouer dans un gig.
gigantic [dʒai'gæntik] adj. Gigantesque; de géant.
gigantism ['dʒaigæn,tizm] n. Gigantisme *m.*
giggle ['gigl] n. Gloussement *m.* (laughter).
— v. intr. Glousser, risoter.
gigolo ['ʒigəlou] n. Gigolo *m.* ‖ POP. Maquereau *m.* (pimp).
gild [gild] v. tr. (69). Dorer. ‖ **Gilt-edged,** adj. Doré sur tranches (book); FIN. De père de famille (securities).
gilder [-ə*] n. Doreur *s.*
gilding [-iŋ] n. Dorure *f.*
gill [gil] n. Ruisseau encaissé *m.* (brook); gorge boisée *f.* (wooden ravine).
gill n. ZOOL. Fanon *m.* (of bird); pl. ouïes, branchies *f. pl.* (of fish). ‖ BOT. Pl. Feuillets *m. pl.* (of mushrooms). ‖ TECHN. Ailette *f.* ‖ FAM. Bajoue *f.*
— v. tr. Prendre par les ouïes (a fish). ‖ CULIN. Vider (a fish); éplucher (a mushroom).
gill [dʒil] n. Gill *m.*
gillie ['gili] n. SPORTS. Gillie, guide *(m.)* de chasse (or) de pêche.
gillyflower ['dʒili,flauə*] n. BOT. Giroflée *f.*
gilt [gilt] adj. Doré. (See GILD.)
— n. Dorure *f.*
gilthead ['gilthed] n. ZOOL. Daurade *f.*
gimbals ['dʒimblz] n. pl. NAUT. Cardan *m.*
gimcrack ['dʒimkræk] n. Babiole, broutille *f.* (See KNICK-KNACK.)
— adj. De camelote (furniture); en toc (jewels).
gimlet ['gimlit] n. TECHN. Vrille *f.* ‖ CULIN. Tire-bouchon *(m.)* à main. ‖ **Gimlet-eyed,** adj. FAM. A l'œil en vrille.
— v. tr. Vriller.

gimme ['gimi:] v. tr. (representation of *give me*) POP. Donne-moi, passe-moi, file-moi.

gimmick ['gimik] n. U. S. Machin, truc *m.* (gadget); tour *m.* (trick). ‖ Astuce (or) caractéristique personnelle *f.; to cultivate a gimmick*, se donner un petit genre.

gimp [gimp] n. Passement *m.* (braid); guipure, ganse *f.* (lace).

gin [dʒin] n. SPORTS. Trébuchet *m.* (snare). ‖ TECHN. Chèvre *f.;* treuil *m.* (for hoisting); égreneuse *f.* (for separating cotton).
— v. tr. (1). SPORTS. Prendre au piège. ‖ TECHN. Egrener (cotton).

gin [dʒin] n. Gin *m.* (liquor). ‖ **Gin-shop,** U. S. **gin-mill,** n. SPORTS. Bistrot, caboulot *m.*

ginger ['dʒindʒə*] n. BOT. Gingembre *m.* ‖ FIG. Entrain, allant *m.* ‖ FAM. Rouquin *s.* ‖ **Ginger-ale** (or) **-beer,** n. Boisson gazeuse (*f.*) au gingembre. ‖ **Ginger-nut,** U. S. **ginger-snap,** II. CULIN. Gâteau sec au gingembre *m.*
— adj. Roux.
— v. tr. CULIN. Parfumer au gingembre. ‖ FAM. Dégourdir, secouer.

gingerbread [-bred] n. CULIN. Pain (*m.*) d'épice.
— adj. CULIN. En pain d'épice. ‖ FAM. En nougat, tarabiscoté.

gingerly [-li] adv. Tout doux.

gingham ['giŋəm] n. Vichy *m.* (material). ‖ FAM. Pépin *m.* (umbrella).

gingival [dʒin'dʒaivəl] adj. MED. Gingival.

gink [giŋk] n. POP. Oiseau, drôle d'oiseau, zèbre, loustic *m.*

gipsy ['dʒipsi] n. Bohémien, romanichel, gitan *s.* ‖ FAM. Fripon, coquin *s.* ‖ **Gipsy-rose,** n. BOT. Scabieuse *f.* ‖ **Gipsy-table,** n. Guéridon pliant *m.*

giraffe [dʒi'rɑːf] n. ZOOL. Girafe *f.*

girandole ['dʒirəndoul] n. Lustre *m.* (chandelier); girandole *f.* (ear-pendant); ‖ TECHN. Girandole *f.;* soleil *m.* (firework).

girasole ['dʒirəsoul] n. Girasol *m.*

gird [gəːd] v. tr. (70). Ceindre; *to gird one's loins*, se ceindre les reins; *to gird on one's sword*, ceindre son épée. ‖ ECCLES. Revêtir (*with*, de). ‖ FIG. Entourer, ceinturer, environner. ‖ FAM. *To gird up one's loins*, retrousser ses manches, cracher dans ses mains.

gird v. tr., intr. Railler.
— n. Raillerie *f.*

girder [-ə*] n. ARCHIT. Poutre *f.; small girder*, poutrelle.

girdle ['gəːdl] n. CULIN. Tourtière *f.*

girdle n. Ceinture *f.* ‖ AGRIC. Incision circulaire *f.* ‖ COMM. Ceinture, gaine *f.* ‖ FIG. Ceinture *f.*

girl [gəːl] n. Fille, jeune fille *f.; little girl*, fillette, petite fille. ‖ Bonne *f.* (servant). ‖ FAM. *Best girl*, petite amie; *the Jones girls*, les petites Jones; *old girl!*, ma vieille!; *girl Friday*, secrétaire. ‖ **Girlfriend,** n. Amie, petite amie *f.* ‖ **Girl guide,** n. Guide, éclaireuse *f.*

girlhood [-hud] n. Enfance, jeunesse *f.* (of a woman).

girlie [-i] n. Fillette, petite chérie *f.*
— adj. *Girlie magazine*, magazine de femmes nues.

girlish [-iʃ] adj. De petite (or) de jeune fille.

girlishness [-iʃnis] n. Enfance, jeunesse *f.*

giro ['dʒairou] n. FIN. Virement *m.* (transfer). ‖ FIN. Chèques postaux *m. pl.* (post-office banking system); *giro account*, C. C. P., compte courant postal.

Girondist [dʒi'rɔndist] adj., n. Girondin *m.*

giroplane ['dʒairoplein] n. AVIAT. Giravion *m.*

girt [gəːt] v. tr. See GIRD.

girt [gəːt], **girth** [gəːθ] n. Sangle *f.* (harness). ‖ Circonférence *f.* (of tree). ‖ Tour (*m.*) de taille; *of ample girth*, corpulent.
— v. tr. Sangler (a horse). ‖ Avoir une circonférence (or) un tour de. ‖ Mesurer.

gist [dʒist] n. JUR. Fondement essentiel, fort *m.* ‖ FIG. Fond, point principal *m.;* essence *f.*

gittern ['gitəːn] n. MUS. Cithare *f.*

give [giv] v. tr. (71).

---

1. Offrir. — 2. Remettre. — 3. Conférer. — 4. Infliger. — 5. Occasionner. — 6. Adonner. — 7. Faire, donner. — 8. Faire, formuler. — 9. Faire, exécuter. — 10. Adresser. — 11. Emettre. — 12. Présenter. — 13. Accorder. — 14. Concéder. — 15. FIN. — 16. JUR. — 17. ZOOL., BOT., AGRIC. — 18. MATH. — 19. THEATR. — 20. MUS. — 21. FAM. — 22. To give away. — 23. To give back. — 24. To give for. — 25. To give forth. — 26. To give in. — 27. To give off. — 28. To give out. — 29. To give over. — 30. To give up.

---

1. Donner, offrir, faire don (or) cadeau de; *I had it given to me*, je me le suis fait donner; *to be given sth.*, recevoir qqch. en cadeau; *to give s.o., sth., to give sth. to s.o.*, donner qqch. à qqn. ‖ 2. Donner, remettre (a message); *to give sth. into s.o.'s hands*, remettre qqch. entre les mains de qqn. ‖ 3. Donner, conférer (a title). ‖ 4. Donner, infliger (a punishment). ‖ 5. Donner, occasionner; *to give pleasure*, faire plaisir, causer du plaisir. ‖ 6. Donner, adonner; *to give one's life for*, donner sa vie pour; *to give oneself to*, se consacrer à, s'adonner à. ‖ 7. Faire, donner; *to give alms*, faire l'aumône; *to give an account of*, faire un compte rendu de; *to give to understand*, donner à entendre. ‖ 8. Formuler, faire (a promise). ‖ 9. Exécuter; faire (a gesture, a jump). ‖ 10. Adresser (a smile); *to give s.o. a cold glance*, jeter à qqn un regard glacial. ‖ 11. Pousser (a cry, sigh); faire (a lecture); émettre (words); *to give a recitation*, dire des vers; *to give a reply*, riposter. ‖ 12. Présenter (a suggestion); porter (a toast); *to give s.o. one's compliments*, présenter à qqn ses compliments. ‖ 13. Accorder, prêter; *to give attention to*, faire attention à; *to give ear, help to*, prêter l'oreille, secours à. ‖ 14. Concéder; *to give ground*, céder du terrain; *to give s.o. a point*, céder à qqn sur un point; *to give way*, céder. ‖ 15. FIN. Donner, payer; *to give five pounds for sth.*, payer qqch. cinq livres. ‖ 16. JUR. Rendre (a decision, a sentence); *to give evidence*, déposer. ‖ 17. ZOOL., BOT., AGRIC. Donner, produire. ‖ 18. MATH. *Given*, étant donné. ‖ 19. THEATR. Donner, représenter. ‖ 20. MUS. Donner (a concert); *to give s.o. a song*, chanter qqch. pour qqn. ‖ 21. FAM. *Give me a good cake*, parlez-moi d'un bon gâteau; *I would give a lot to know*, je donnerais gros pour savoir. ‖ 22. To give away, conduire à l'autel (the bride); distribuer (prizes); donner faire cadeau de (sth.). FAM. Dénoncer; donner (s.o.); *to give oneself away*, se trahir. ‖ 23. To give back, rendre, restituer. ‖ 24. To give for, donner pour, faire passer pour, considérer comme. ‖ 25. To give forth, publier (news); émettre, faire entendre (a sound). ‖ 26. To give in, remettre (a document, a parcel); donner (one's name). ‖ 27. To give off, émettre, dégager (heat); émettre, exhaler (odour); CHIM. Dégager; BOT. Faire (shoots). ‖ 28. To give out, distribuer (to distribute); émettre (to emit); faire connaître, divulguer (to make public); annoncer, proclamer (to proclaim); *to give oneself out for*, s'intituler, se dire, se faire passer pour; *to give s.o. out for*, faire passer (or) donner qqn pour. ‖ 29. To give over, abandonner, remettre (to hand over); cesser, finir (to stop); *given over to*, adonné à, en proie à. ‖ 30. To give up, résigner (one's appointment); se retirer de (business); abandonner, délaisser (one's friends, work); se dessaisir de (one's property); rendre (the ghost); renoncer à (a habit, an idea); cesser son abonnement à (a newspaper); céder

(ones' seat); s'adonner à, se livrer à (study, vice); abandonner (the struggle); MED. Condamner; JUR. Faire arrêter; *to give oneself up*, se rendre, se constituer prisonnier; FAM. *To give it up*, abandonner la partie, donner sa langue au chat.
— v. intr. Donner, avoir ,l'habitude de donner (to make gifts). ‖ Céder (*under*, sous); *the door has given*, la porte a cédé. ‖ Donner, ouvrir (*into*, dans; *on*, sur). ‖ LOC. *To give and take*, faire des concessions mutuelles. ‖ **To give in**, renoncer, abandonner (to relinquish); céder (*to*, à) [to yield]. ‖ **To give out**, faire défaut, manquer (patience, strength); s'épuiser (stores); FAM. Etre à bout. ‖ **To give over**, renoncer. ‖ **To give up**, renoncer, abandonner; donner sa langue au chat (fam.).
— n. Elasticité *f*. ‖ **Give-and-take**, n. Echange (*m*.) de bons procédés; adj. de concessions mutuelles. ‖ **Give-away**, adj. Vil (price); n. FAM. Dénonciation *f*.
given [-ṇ] adj. Donné, déterminé; *given my strength*, étant donné ma force. ‖ Adonné, enclin (*to*, à). ‖ U. S. *Given name*, prénom. ‖ FAM. *She is given that way!*, elle est comme ça.
giver [-ə*] n. Donateur *m*.; donatrice *f*.
giving [-iŋ] n. Don *m*.; donateur *f*.; fait (*m*.) de donner. ‖ JUR. Adjudication *f*. (of damages); prononcé *m*. (of a sentence). ‖ FIG. Engagement *m*. (of one's word). ‖ **Giving away**, n. Distribution *f*. (of prizes); dénonciation *f*. (of s.o.). ‖ **Giving back**, n. Restitution *f*. ‖ **Giving forth**, n. Publication *f*. (of news); émission *f*. (of sound). ‖ **Giving in**, n. Remise *f*. (*de*, of). ‖ **Giving off**, n. Exhalaison *f*. ‖ **Giving out**, n. Distribution *f*.; proclamation *f*.; épuisement *m*. ‖ **Giving up**, n. Abandon *m*.
gizmo ['gizmou] (pl. **gizmos** [-z]) n. U. S. FAM. Bidule, machin *m*.; gadget *m*.
gizzard ['gizəd] n. ZOOL. Gésier *m*. ‖ FAM. *It sticks in his gizzard*, il ne digère pas ça, il a ça sur le cœur.
glabrous ['gleibrəs] adj. Glabre.
glacé ['glæsei] adj. Glacé (fruit, leather).
glacial ['gleisiəl] adj. Glacial (wind). ‖ CHIM. En cristaux. ‖ GEOL. Glaciaire.
glaciated [-sieitid] adj. GEOL. Qui a été soumis à l'action glaciaire; couvert de glaciers; *glaciated terrain*, relief glaciaire.
glaciation [-si'eiʃən] n. GEOL. Glaciation *f*.
glacier ['glæsjə*] n. GEOL. Glacier *m*.
glaciology [ˌglæsi'ɔlədʒi] n. GEOL. Glaciologie *f*.
glacis ['glæsis] n. MILIT. Glacis *m*.
glad [glæd] adj. Content, joyeux, heureux (*of*, de) [happy]. ‖ Agréable, heureux (giving pleasure). U. S. FAM. *Glad hand*, accueil cordial. ‖ FAM. *To give s.o. the glad eye*, faire les yeux doux à qqn; *glad rags*, habits du dimanche, beaux atours.
gladden [-ṇ] v. tr. Réjouir, égayer.
glade [gleid] n. Clairière *f*.
gladiator ['glædieitə*] n. Gladiateur *m*.
gladiatorial [ˌglædiə'tɔːriəl] adj. De gladiateur.
gladiolus [ˌglædi'ouləs] (pl. **gladioli** [-ai]) n. BOT. Glaïeul *m*.
gladly ['glædli] adv. Avec joie (joyfully); avec plaisir, volontiers (willingly).
gladness [-nis] n. Joie *f*.
gladsome [-səm] adj. Joyeux, réjoui (cheerful); réjouissant (cheering).
Gladstone-bag ['glædstən*bæg] n. Sac américain *m*.
glair [glɛə*] n. CULIN. Blanc d'œuf *m*. ‖ MED. Glaire *f*.
— v. tr. Glairer.
glaireous [-riəs], **glairy** [-ri] adj. MED. Glaireux.
glamorize ['glæməˌraiz] v. tr. Enjoliver, idéaliser.
glamo(u)r ['glæmə*] n. Enchantement, ensorcellement *m*. ‖ Charme *m*.; magie; fascination *f*. ‖

Prestige, éclat *m*. ‖ **Glamour-girl**, n. FAM. Ensorceleuse *f*.
— v. tr. Enchanter, ensorceler, fasciner.
glamorous ['glæmərəs] adj. Enchanteur, fascinateur, prestigieux (spectacle). ‖ Excitant (flirtation); romantique (night, scene); enchanteur (way of life). ‖ Séduisante, fascinatrice, enchanteresse; croustillante (fam.) [woman].
glance [glɑːns] v. intr. Regarder rapidement; *to glance aside*, détourner le regard; *to glance at*, jeter un coup d'œil à; *to glance over*, parcourir des yeux. ‖ FIG. Glisser une allusion (*at*, à) [to hint]; *to glance off*, effleurer, glisser sur (a subject). MILIT. Etinceler (weapons); *to glance aside* (or) *off*, ricocher (projectile); dévier (sword).
— v. tr. Jeter; *to glance one's eye over*, jeter un œil sur.
— n. Coup d'œil *m*.; *amorous glance*, œillade. ‖ Eclair, éclat *m*. (of steel). ‖ MILIT. Ricochet *m*. SPORTS. Coup de biais *m*. ‖ FIG. Aperçu *m*. ‖ **Glance-coal**, n. Anthracite *m*.
glancing [-iŋ] adj. Oblique (blow).
gland [glænd] n. MED. Glande *f*.
glanders ['glændəz] n. pl. Morve *f*.
glandiferous [glæn'difərəs] adj. BOT. Glandifère.
glandiform ['glændifɔːm] adj. Glandiforme.
glandular [-djulə*] adj. MED. Glandulaire.
glandulous [-djuləs] adj. Glanduleux.
glans [glænz] (pl. **glandes** ['glændiːz]) n. MED. Gland *m*.
glare [glɛə*] v. intr. Etinceler, briller. ‖ Jeter un regard furieux (*at*, à).
— v. tr. Trahir par le regard; *to glare anger at*, lancer un regard de colère à.
— n. Eclat éblouissant *m*.; lumière crue *f*. ‖ AUTOM. Eblouissement *m*. ‖ FIG. Regard flamboyant *m*.
glaring [-riŋ] adj. Eblouissant, aveuglant (light, sun). ‖ Eclatant (colour). ‖ FIG. Flamboyant (eye); flagrant, qui crève les yeux (fact, injustice).
glass [glɑːs] n. Verre *m*. (substance); *cut glass*, cristal taillé; *pane of glass*, carreau, vitre. ‖ Verrerie *f*.; cristaux *m*. *pl*.; *glass industry*, industrie du verre; *hollow glass*, gobeleterie. ‖ Verre *m*.; *champagne glass*, coupe à champagne; *wine glass*, verre à vin. ‖ Verre *m*. (of a picture, watch). ‖ Sablier *m*. (hour-glass); baromètre *m*. (weatherglass). ‖ Monocle *m*.; pl. lunettes *f*. *pl*.; lorgnon *m*. ‖ Glace *f*.; miroir *m*. (looking-glass). ‖ AUTOM. Glace *f*. ‖ COMM. Vitrine *f*. ‖ AGRIC. Serre *f*.; châssis *m*. ‖ MED. *Cupping glass*, verre à ventouse. ‖ PHYS. Lentille, loupe *f*.; verre grossissant *m*. (magnifying glass); lorgnette *f*.; jumelles *f*. *pl*. (opera-glasses); longue-vue *f*. (telescope). ‖ **Glassblower**, n. Verrier-souffleur *m*. ‖ **Glass-case**, n. COMM. Vitrine *f*. ‖ **Glass-cloth**, n. Toile (*f*.) émeri (emery cloth); essuie-verres *m*. (tea-towel). ‖ **Glasscutter**, n. Vitrier *m*. (man); diamant *m*. (tool). ‖ **Glass-eye**, n. MED. Œil de verre *m*. ‖ **Glass-fiber**, n. Fibre (*f*.) de verre. ‖ **Glass-frame**, n. AGRIC. Châssis *m*. ‖ **Glass-house**, n. AGRIC. Serre *f*.; FAM. Taule *f*. ‖ **Glass-paper**, n. Papier de verre *m*. ‖ **Glass-partition**, n. Vitrage *m*. ‖ **Glass-roof**, n. Verrière *f*. ‖ **Glass-ware**, n. Verrerie *f*. ‖ **Glasswool**, n. Laine (*f*.) de verre. ‖ **Glass-works**, n. Verrerie *f*. (factory).
— adj. De verre, en verre (bottle); vitré (door); *glass shade*, globe (of a clock).
— v. tr. Mirer, refléter. ‖ Vitrer (a door); mettre sous verre (a picture).
glassful [-ful] n. Verre, plein verre *m*.
glassy [-i] adj. Semblable au verre; transparent. ‖ Uni, lisse (smooth). ‖ Vitreux (eye).
Glauber's salt ['glaubəz'sɔlt] n. MED. Sulfate (*m*.) de soude.
glaucoma [glɔ'koumə] m. MED. Glaucome *m*.
glaucous ['glɔːkəs] adj. Glauque.
glaze [gleiz] v. tr. Vitrer (a door); mettre sous

verre (a picture). ‖ Vernir (leather); satiner, lustrer (material); surglacer (paper); vitrifier (tiles). ‖ ARTS. Glacer (a photograph); vernisser (pottery). ‖ CULIN. Glacer (cakes). ‖ MED. Rendre vitreux (eye). ‖ FIG. *To glaze over,* voiler.
— v. intr. MED. Devenir vitreux (eye). ‖ **To glaze over,** se glacer.
— n. Vernis *m.* (of leather, pottery); lustre, cati *m.* (of material); brillant *m.* (of paper). ‖ CULIN. Glace *f.* ‖ MED. Aspect vitreux *m.*

glazer [-ə*] n. Vernisseur *s.*
glazier ['gleiziə*] n. Vitrier *m.*
glazing [-iŋ] n. Vitrerie; pose (*f.*) des vitres. ‖ Vernissage *m.* (act); vernis *m.* (product). ‖ ARTS. Glacis *m.*
gleam [gli:m] n. Lueur *m.*
— v. intr. Luire.
gleamy [-i] adj. Luisant, miroitant.
glean [gli:n] v. tr., intr. AGRIC., FIG. Glaner.
gleaner [-ə*] n. AGRIC. Glaneur *s.*
gleaning [-iŋ] n. AGRIC., FIG. Glanage *m.* (act); glanure *f.* (result).
glebe [gli:b] n. AGRIC. Glèbe *f.* ‖ ECCLES. Manse *f.*
glee [gli:] n. MUS. Chant choral (*m.*) à plusieurs parties; U. S. *glee club,* chorale. ‖ FIG. Allégresse *f.*
gleeful [-ful], **gleesome** [-səm] adj. Allègre, joyeux.
gleep [gli:p] n. PHYS. Pile atomique *f.*
gleet [gli:t] n. MED. Ecoulement purulent *m.*
glen [glen] n. Vallée encaissée, gorge *f.*
glengarry [glen'gæri] n. Calot écossais *m.*
glenoid(al) ['gli:nɔid(əl)] adj. MED. Glénoïdal, glénoïde.
glib [glib] adj. Lisse, glissant (surface). ‖ Coulant (speech); délié (tongue); *glib talker,* beau parleur. ‖ Patelin (answer); éhonté (lie).
glibly [-li] adv. Aisément. ‖ D'un ton patelin. ‖ Avec volubilité; avec bagou.
glibness [-nis] n. Faconde *f.;* bagou *m.* ‖ Volubilité *f.*
glide [glaid] v. intr. Avancer en glissant, glisser. ‖ Avancer à pas de loup (person); *to glide out,* se glisser en dehors. ‖ S'écouler (time). [See ELAPSE.] ‖ AVIAT. Faire du vol plané; vélivoler; *to glide down to land,* atterrir en vol plané.
— v. tr. Faire glisser; mouvoir sans heurts.
— n. Glissement *m.* ‖ ARTS. Glissade *f.;* glissé *m.* (in dancing). ‖ MUS. Port (*m.*) de voix. ‖ GRAMM. Voyelle furtive *f.*
glider [-ə*] n. AVIAT. Planeur *m.* ‖ NAUT. Hydroglisseur *m.* ‖ U. S. Siège (*m.*) à glissière. ‖ **Gliderpilot,** n. AVIAT. Vélivole *m.*
gliding [-iŋ] n. Glissement *m.* ‖ AVIAT. Vol plané *m.*
glim [glim] n. FAM. Lumignon *m.;* camoufle *f.* ‖ U. S. POP. Feu *m.;* allumettes *f. pl.*
glimmer [-ə*] v. intr. Briller faiblement, entreluire (light); miroiter (water).
— n. Lueur tremblante *f.* ‖ Miroitement *m.* (of water). ‖ FIG. Lueur *f.*
glimpse [glimps] n. Brève apparition *f.* (of the moon). ‖ Aperçu *m.* (lit. and fig.).
— v. tr. Entrevoir.
— v. intr. Poindre.
glint [glint] v. intr. Luire. ‖ FIG. Etinceler.
— n. Reflet *m.;* lueur *f.*
glissade [gli'sɑ:d] n. SPORTS. Glissade *f.*
— v. intr. Glisser.
glisten ['glisn], **glister** ['glistə*] v. intr. Scintiller, briller, chatoyer (gold, light); miroiter (water).
— n. Scintillement; miroitement *m.*
glitter ['glitə*] v. intr. Scintiller, chatoyer, briller (gold, light); brasiller (water). ‖ FIG. Rutiler, resplendir.
— n. Scintillement *m.* ‖ FIG. Eclat, brillant *m.*
glittering [-riŋ] adj. Scintillant, étincelant; rutilant, resplendissant.

gloaming ['gloumiŋ] n. Crépuscule *m.*
gloat [glout] v. intr. *To gloat on* (or) *over* (or) *upon,* couver du regard, dévorer des yeux, se repaître la vue de, jeter des regards avides sur. ‖ FAM. Jubiler; faire les gorges chaudes (*over,* de).
global ['gloubəl] adj. Global. ‖ En forme de globe, sphérique. ‖ Universel, mondial.
globe [gloub] n. Globe *m.;* sphère *f.* ‖ Bocal rond *m.* (for goldfish). ‖ GEOGR. Globe *m.;* terre *f.* ‖ MED. Globe. ‖ ELECTR. U. S. Ampoule *f.* ‖ TECHN. Sphère, rotule *f.* ‖ **Globe-trotter,** n. Globe-trotter *m.*
— v. tr. Rendre sphérique.
— v. intr. Devenir sphérique.
globose [-ous], **globous** [-əs] adj. Sphérique.
globular ['glɔbjulə*] adj. Sphérique, en boule. ‖ Globuleux.
globule [-ju:l] n. Gouttelette *f.* ‖ MED. Globule *m.*
globulin [-julin] n. MED. Globuline *f.*
glomerate ['glɔməreit] adj. MED., BOT. Congloméré.
glonoin ['glɔnouin] n. MED. Glonoïne, nitroglycérine *f.*
gloom [glu:m] n. Obscurité *f.;* ténèbres *f. pl.* ‖ FIG. Tristesse, mélancolie, humeur sombre, allure ténébreuse *f.;* vague (*m.*) à l'âme.
— v. intr. S'assombrir, se couvrir (sky). ‖ FIG. S'attrister, s'assombrir, se rembrunir.
— v. tr. Assombrir, obscurcir (sky). ‖ FIG. Assombrir.
gloomily [-ili] adv. D'un air sombre.
gloomy [-i] adj. Obscur, sombre, ténébreux. ‖ FIG. Sombre, mélancolique, ténébreux; *to feel gloomy,* avoir des idées noires.
glorification [,glɔ:rifi'keiʃən] n. Glorification *f.* ‖ FAM. Réjouissance *f.*
glorify ['glɔ:rifai] v. tr. (2). ECCLES. Glorifier. ‖ FIG. Glorifier, magnifier, célébrer (s.o.). ‖ FAM. Embellir, auréoler (sth.).
gloriole [-oul] n. ECCLES. Auréole *f.*
glorious [-iəs] adj. Glorieux, d'éclat (deed); glorieux, illustre (person). ‖ Radieux (day); resplendissant (sky). ‖ FIG. Eclatant, resplendissant, splendide. ‖ FAM. Fameux, exquis, épatant (enjoyable); brindezingue, parti (tipsy).
gloriously [-əsli] adv. Glorieusement. ‖ Avec splendeur, magnifiquement.
glory ['glɔ:ri] n. Gloire *f.;* titre (*m.*) de gloire. ‖ Gloire, renommée, célébrité *f.* (fame). ‖ Gloire, louange *f.;* honneur *m.* ‖ Gloire, splendeur, magnificence *f.;* rayonnement *m.* ‖ ECCLES. Gloire, vie bienheureuse *f.* (bliss); gloire, auréole *f.* (halo). ‖ FAM. *To be in one's glory,* être aux anges; *to be in all one's glory,* avoir revêtu ses plus beaux atours; *to go to glory,* aller dans le sein d'Abraham; *to send to glory,* envoyer « ad patres ». ‖ **Glory-hole,** n. MILIT. Abri *m.;* FAM. Capharnaüm *m.*
— v. intr. Se glorifier, se faire gloire, s'enorgueillir (*in,* de).
gloss [glɔs] n. Lustre, brillant, éclat *m.;* *to lose its gloss,* se délustrer. ‖ Cati *m.* (of material); *to take the gloss off,* décatir. ‖ FAM. Vernis *m.*
— v. tr. Lustrer. ‖ FIG. *To gloss over,* édulcorer, atténuer.
gloss n. Glose *f.* (between the lines); commentaire *m.* (note). ‖ Glossaire *m.* ‖ Paraphrase, interprétation erronée *f.*
— v. tr. Gloser; commenter. ‖ FIG. Paraphraser, interpréter faussement.
— v. intr. Gloser.
glossarist [-ərist] n. Auteur de glossaire.
glossary [-əri] n. Glossaire *m.*
glossator [glɔ'seitə*] n. Glossateur *f.*
glossiness ['glɔsinis] n. Lustre, brillant *m.*
glossy [-i] adj. Lustré, luisant, brillant, vernissé.

‖ Glacé (photograph); sur papier couché. ‖ Fɪɢ. Doucereux, onctueux; spécieux.
— n. Revue (f.) de mode de luxe (magazine). ‖ Photo (f.) sur papier glacé.

glottal [ˈglɔtəl] adj. Mᴇᴅ. Glottique; *glottal stop*, coup de glotte.

glottis [-is] n. Mᴇᴅ. Glotte f.
— N. B. Noter les pl. *glottises, glottides.*

Gloucester [ˈglɔstə*] n. Gᴇᴏɢʀ. Gloucester m. ‖ Cᴜʟɪɴ. *Double Gloucester*, sorte de chester.

glove [glʌv] n. Gant m.; *excuse my glove*, excusez-moi de garder mon gant; *rubber gloves*, gants de caoutchouc; *to take off one's gloves*, se déganter. ‖ Fᴀᴍ. *To be hand in glove*, s'entendre comme larrons en foire, être comme les deux doigts de la main (*with*, avec); *to fit like a glove*, aller comme un gant; *to handle with kid gloves*, manier doucement; *to take up the glove*, relever le gant. ‖ **Glove-box, glove compartment**, n. Aᴜᴛᴏᴍ. Boîte (f.) à gants; vide-poches m. *invar*. ‖ **Glove-factory**, n. Ganterie f. ‖ **Glove-maker**, n. Gantier s. ‖ **Glove-stretcher**, n. Ouvre-gants m., quille f.
— v. tr. Ganter.

glover [ˈglauə*] n. Gantier m.

glow [glou] v. intr. Rougeoyer, être embrasé (or) incandescent (or) rouge (coals, metal). ‖ Rutiler (colour); être en feu; rougir, s'empourprer (complexion); flamboyer (eyes); briller, rayonner (face). ‖ Fɪɢ. S'enflammer, s'embraser.
— n. Rougeoiement m.; incandescence f. (of coal). ‖ Embrasement m. (of sun). ‖ Rougeur f.; éclat vermeil m. (of complexion). ‖ Mᴇᴅ. Réaction de chaleur, chaude euphorie f. ‖ Fɪɢ. Chaleur f. (of enthusiasm); embrasement, feu m. (of passion); ardeur f. (of youth). ‖ Fᴀᴍ. U. S. *To have a glow on*, être éméché. ‖ **Glow-discharge**, n. Décharge luminescente f. ‖ **Glow-lamp**, n. Eʟᴇᴄᴛʀ. Lampe à incandescence f.; Tʜᴇᴀᴛʀ. Lampe à lueur f. ‖ **Glow-worm**, n. Zᴏᴏʟ. Ver luisant m.

glower [ˈglauə*] v. intr. Faire grise mine (*at*, à).

glowing [ˈglouiŋ] adj. Incandescent, rougeoyant, embrasé (coal). ‖ En feu, rouge, vermeil (complexion). ‖ Fɪɢ. Enthousiaste (person); chaleureux (style, terms).

gloxinia [glɔkˈsiniə] n. Bᴏᴛ. Gloxinia m.

gloze [glouz] v. intr. † Gloser. ‖ Flagorner. ‖ Fɪɢ. Glisser (*over*, sur).

glucinium [ˌgluˈʃinjəm] n. Cʜɪᴍ. Glucine f.; glucinium m.

glucose [ˈgluːkous] n. Cʜɪᴍ. Glucose m.

glue [gluː] n. Glu f. ‖ Colle forte f.
— v. tr. Coller.
— N . B. Noter le part. prés. *gluing.*

gluey [-i] adj. Gluant.

glug-glug [ˈglʌgˈglʌg] n. Glouglou m.

gluing [-iŋ] n. Collage m.

glum [glʌm] adj. Renfrogné, morose. (See ꜱᴜʟʟᴇɴ.)

glume [gluːm] n. Bᴏᴛ. Glume f.

glumness [ˈglʌmnis] n. Maussaderie f.

glut [glʌt] v. tr. (1). † Engloutir. ‖ Gaver, gorger. ‖ Cᴏᴍᴍ. Engorger (the market).
— n. Rassasiement m. (of appetite). ‖ Satiété f. (disgust). ‖ Cᴏᴍᴍ. Surabondance f. (of goods); engorgement m. (of the market).

glutamate [ˈgluːtə,meit] n. Cʜɪᴍ. Glutamate m.

glutamic [gluːˈtæmik] adj. Cʜɪᴍ. *Glutamic acid*, acide glutamique.

gluten [ˈgluːtən] n. Gluten m.

glutinous [-tinəs] adj. Glutineux.

glutton [ˈglʌtn] n. Glouton m. ‖ Fᴀᴍ. Dévoreur m.; *glutton for work*, bourreau de travail.

gluttonous [-əs] adj. Glouton, goulu, goinfre.

gluttonously [-əsli] adv. Gloutonnement.

gluttony [-i] n. Gloutonnerie f.

glycerin(e) [-iːn] n. Mᴇᴅ., Cʜɪᴍ. Glycérine f.

glycerinate [ˈglisərineit] v. tr. Glycériner.

glycerol [-əl] n. Cʜɪᴍ. Glycérine f.

glycine [ˈglaisiːn] n. Cʜɪᴍ. Glycine f., glycocolle m.

glycogen [ˈglaikodʒən] n. Cʜɪᴍ. Glycogène m.

glycogenic [ˈglaikoˈdʒenik] adj. Mᴇᴅ. Glycogénique.

glycol [ˈglaikɔl] n. Cʜɪᴍ. Glycol m.

glycolysis [glaiˈkɔlisis] (pl. **glycolyses** [-iːz]) n. Mᴇᴅ. Glycolyse f.

G. M. T. [dʒiːemˈtiː] abbr. *Greenwich Mean Time*, G. M. T.

gnarl [nɑːl] n. Bᴏᴛ. Nœud m.

gnarled [-d] adj. Bᴏᴛ., Mᴇᴅ. Noueux. ‖ Fᴀᴍ. Ronchon.

gnash [næʃ] v. tr. Grincer; *to gnash one's teeth*, grincer des dents.
— v. intr. Grincer des dents (person); grincer (teeth).

gnashing [-iŋ] n. Grincement m.

gnat [næt] n. Zᴏᴏʟ. Moustique m.

gnaw [nɔː] v. tr. Ronger (lit. and fig.).
— v. intr. To gnaw at, ronger.
— N. B. Au p. p. on trouve *gnawed* ou *gnawn*.

gnawing [-iŋ] n. Rongement m. ‖ Mᴇᴅ. Tiraillement m. (of hunger, stomach). ‖ Fɪɢ. Morsure f. (of remorse).
— adj. Rongeur.

gneiss [nais] n. Gᴇᴏʟ. Gneiss m.

gnome [noum] n. Gnome m.

gnome n. Sentence f.

gnomic [-ik] adj. Gnomique.

gnosis [ˈnousis] n. Gnose f.

gnostic [ˈnɔstik] adj., n. Gnostique s.

gnosticism [-sizm̩] n. Gnosticisme m.

G. N. P. [dʒiːenˈpiː] abbr. *gross national product*, Fɪɴ. Produit national brut, P. N. B.

gnu [njuː] n. Zᴏᴏʟ. Gnou m.

go [gou] v. intr. (72).

---

1. Aller. — 2. Aller, se mouvoir. — 3. Aller, marcher. — 4. Aller pour. — 5. Aller faire. — 6. Aller, conduire. — 7. Porter. — 8. Se placer. — 9. Atteindre. — 10. Se présenter. — 11. Casser. — 12. Faire. — 13. Tᴇᴄʜɴ. — 14. Aᴜᴛᴏᴍ. — 15. Mɪʟɪᴛ. — 16. Nᴀᴜᴛ. — 17. Mᴀᴛʜ. — 18. Sᴘᴏʀᴛs. — 19. Cᴏᴍᴍ. — 20. Fɪɴ. — 21. Jᴜʀ. — 22. Mᴇᴅ. — 23. Fɪɢ. Se présenter. — 24. Fɪɢ. Tourner. — 25. Fɪɢ. Devenir. — 26. Fɪɢ. Demeurer. — 27. Fɪɢ. S'avancer. — 28. Fɪɢ. Suivre. — 29. Fɪɢ. Etre aboli. — 30. Fɪɢ. Etre sacrifié. — 31. Fᴀᴍ. — 32. To be going. — 33. To go about. — 34. To go after. — 35. To go against. — 36. To go along. — 37. To go at. — 38. To go away. — 39. To go back. — 40. To go beyond. — 41. To go by. — 42. To go down. — 43. To go for. — 44. To go forward. — 45. To go in. — 46. To go into. — 47. To go off. — 48. To go on. — 49. To go out. — 50. To go over. — 51. To go round. — 52. To go through. — 53. To go to. — 54. To go together. — 55. To go towards. — 56. To go under. — 57. To go up. — 58. To go with. — 59. To go without. — 60. To let go.

---

1. Aller (*from*, de; *to*, à, en); *to go to England, to London*, aller en Angleterre, à Londres. ‖ 2. Aller, se mouvoir; *to come and go*, aller et venir. ‖ 3. Aller, marcher; *to go the pace*, aller bon pas. ‖ 4. Aller; *to go and fetch, and see*, aller chercher, voir. ‖ 5. Aller faire; *to go on an errand*, faire une course. ‖ 6. Aller, conduire; *that road, that train goes to Paris*, cette route, ce train va (or) mène à Paris. ‖ 7. Partir, s'en aller; *it's time to go*, il est l'heure de partir; *let me go*, laissez-moi m'en aller; *you may go*, vous pouvez disposer. ‖ 8. Aller, se

placer, se ranger; *the handkerchiefs go in the first drawer,* les mouchoirs vont dans le premier tiroir. ‖ **9.** Aller, atteindre; *the belt won't go around your waist,* la ceinture ne fera pas le tour de votre taille. ‖ **10.** Aller, marcher, se présenter; *to go in rags, naked,* aller en haillons, tout nu. ‖ **11.** Céder, casser, se briser, se rompre; *the mast went in the storm,* le mât céda pendant la tempête; *to go to pieces,* partir en morceaux. ‖ **12.** Faire: *to go bang,* faire pan. ‖ **13.** TECHN. Marcher, fonctionner (clock, motor). ‖ **14.** AUTOM. *To go strong,* carburer; *to go at 50 miles an hour,* faire du 80 à l'heure. ‖ **15.** MILIT. *Who goes there?,* qui va là? ‖ **16.** NAUT. *All gone!,* tout est largué! ‖ **17.** MATH. *4 into 22 goes 5 times, and 2 over,* en 22 il va 5 fois 4, et il reste 2. ‖ **18.** SPORTS. Annoncer (at cards); miser (to stake). ‖ **19.** COMM. Marcher; *to keep, to set an affair going,* maintenir, mettre une affaire en train. ‖ **20.** FIN. Avoir cours (currency). ‖ **21.** JUR. *Going, going, gone!,* une fois, deux fois, adjugé!; *to go bail for,* se porter caution pour. ‖ **22.** MED. Partir, s'en aller, disparaître (pain, person); baisser (sight); *how goes it?,* comment ça va?; *to keep a patient going,* soutenir un malade. ‖ **23.** FIG. Se présenter, se développer; *as far as that goes,* pour ce qui concerne ce point; *as the saying goes,* selon le dicton; *as things go,* dans l'état actuel des choses; *how does the story go?,* comment se déroule l'histoire? ‖ **24.** FIG. Tourner, se présenter; *to go badly,* tourner mal; *to go well,* bien marcher, réussir. ‖ **25.** FIG. Devenir; *to go mad,* devenir fou. ‖ **26.** FIG. Demeurer; *to go unrewarded,* rester sans récompense. ‖ **27.** FIG. Aller, s'avancer; *to go too far,* exagérer; attiger (fam.). ‖ **28.** FIG. Aller, suivre; *to go one's way,* agir à sa guise, suivre son idée. ‖ **29.** FIG. Etre aboli, disparaître (abuse); s'écouler, passer (time). ‖ **30.** FIG. Etre sacrifié (or) abandonné; *the country house must go,* il faut renoncer à la maison de campagne. ‖ **31.** FAM. *Go on!,* allez-y!; *they have gone and done it!,* ils ont fait un joli coup!; *to go halves,* faire les parts égales; *to go west,* passer l'arme à gauche. ‖ **32. To be going,** approcher de; *to be going forty,* avoir près de quarante ans; *to be going to,* aller, être sur le point de (to be about to); avoir l'intention de, projeter de, compter (to intend to). ‖ **33. To go about,** se mettre à, vaquer à (to be busy at); s'occuper de (to be occupied with); aller de-ci de-là (to circulate). NAUT. *To go about,* virer de bord. ‖ **34. To go after,** FAM. Courir après, poursuivre. ‖ **35.** FIG. Aller contre, démentir (one's word); tourner contre, être contraire à (s.o.). ‖ **36. To go along,** s'accorder (to agree); continuer (to continue); avancer (to proceed); *to go along with,* accompagner. ‖ **37. To go at,** attaquer, se jeter sur (to attack); se mettre, se donner, s'atteler (to work at); *to go at it,* y aller. ‖ **38. To go away,** s'en aller, partir. ‖ **39. To go back,** remonter (memory); revenir en arrière (person); *to go back on,* manquer à (a promise); faire faux bond à (s.o.). ‖ **40. To go beyond,** dépasser. ‖ **41. To go by,** passer (person); s'écouler, passer (time); *to go by s.o.,* passer près de qqn; *to go by the name of,* être connu sous le nom de; *to go by what s.o. says,* se fier à ce que qqn dit, agir d'après l'avis de qqn. ‖ **42. To go down,** descendre (person); partir en vacances, en avoir fini avec les études (student); baisser (temperature, tide); tomber (wind). NAUT. Sombrer. AUTOM. Se dégonfler (tyre). MED. Se digérer (food); descendre (fam.). FIG. Déchoir (person); être perpétué (in history); être noté (on paper). ‖ **43. To go for,** aller chercher (s.o., sth.). FIN. Etre vendu pour, partir pour (a sum); FIG. Compter pour (little, much); FAM. Tomber sur, prendre à partie (an enemy); marcher pour, être entiché de (a friend, a woman);

affectionner (sth.); *I don't go for it,* ça ne m'emballe pas beaucoup; *that goes for nothing,* ça ne compte pas; *to go for each other,* se prendre aux cheveux. ‖ **44. To go forward,** avancer (person, work); *what is going forward?,* qu'est-ce qui se passe? ‖ **45. To go in,** entrer (person); se cacher (sun); *to go in for,* poser sa candidature à (an appointment); se présenter à, affronter (a competition, an examination); suivre (a course of lectures); adopter (a doctrine); s'offrir (a jewel); faire de, se mêler de (politics); s'adonner à, pratiquer (sports); se livrer à (a vice); *to go in with,* se joindre à (s.o.); *what shall I go in?,* qu'est-ce que je vais mettre? ‖ **46. To go into,** entrer en (action); entrer dans (a career, a room); se lancer dans (a discussion); prendre (mourning); approfondir, pénétrer (a question); MED. Etre pris de (a disease). ‖ **47. To go off,** s'en aller, partir (to depart); se passer, arriver (to happen); s'abîmer, se gâter (to spoil); MILIT. Partir (rifle); MED. S'évanouir; *to go off one's head,* perdre la raison. ‖ **48. To go on,** continuer, poursuivre (to continue); arriver, se passer, se dérouler (to happen); avancer (to proceed); y aller, prendre son tour (to take place); *to be gone on s.o.,* tomber amoureux de qqn; *to go on sth.,* s'appuyer sur qqch.; *to go on at,* s'en prendre à, en avoir après (s.o.); THEATR. *To go on,* faire son entrée; COMM. *To go on with,* suivre (a line). ‖ **49. To go out,** sortir (to, pour); aller sur le terrain (duellist); être renversé (government); quitter le pouvoir (minister); quitter le pays (traveller); passer de mode, s'éteindre (use); se mettre en grève, débrayer (workmen); *to go out of,* quitter (a place); *to go out to,* être attiré vers, sympathiser avec. ‖ **50. To go over,** verser, basculer (load); changer de clan, passer à un autre parti (person); vérifier, revoir, examiner (an account); retoucher (a drawing); repasser (a lesson). NAUT. Traverser, faire la traversée vers; THEATR. Passer la rampe, réussir. ‖ **51. To go round,** faire le tour; *to go a long way round,* faire un grand détour; *to go round to s.o.,* aller faire un tour chez qqn. ‖ **52. To go through,** traverser (the fire, a room); réciter (a lesson); ECCLES. Célébrer; MUS. Exécuter; FIG. Dépouiller (a book); remplir (a mission, a part); étudier à fond (a subject); subir, traverser (trials); *he is going through it,* il souffre beaucoup; *to go through with,* achever, mener à bien. ‖ **53. To go to,** aller à, se rendre à (a place); aller à, revenir à, passer aux mains de (a person); s'adresser à, aller trouver (s.o.); JUR. *To go to the country,* en appeler au pays; MILIT. *To go to war,* entrer en guerre; CH DE F. *To go to and fro,* faire la navette; † *Go to!,* allons!, voyons!, FIG. *To go to the head,* monter à la tête; *to go to prove,* servir à prouver; *to go to the trouble of doing sth.,* se mettre en peine de (or) se donner du mal pour faire qqch. ‖ **54. To go together,** aller ensemble, s'harmoniser, s'assortir; FAM. S'accorder, marcher ensemble (lovers). ‖ **55. To go towards,** aller vers (a place, s.o.); contribuer à (a result). ‖ **56. To go under,** se coucher (sun); couler (swimmer); FIG. Sombrer, succomber, être vaincu. ‖ **57. To go up,** monter (person); FIN. Monter (prices); TECHN. Sauter (mine); *to go up for,* se présenter à (an examination); *to go up from,* s'élever de; *to go up in,* monter dans (or) en; *to go up to,* aller à (London); marcher vers (s.o.); entrer à (the university). ‖ **58. To go with,** aller avec, se marier (or) s'assortir avec (a colour, a dress); suivre (the crowd, the times); accompagner (s.o.); MED. *To go with child,* être enceinte; FAM. Marcher avec (a lover); *to go hard with s.o.,* aller mal pour qqn. ‖ **59. To go without,** se passer de (sth); *to go without saying,* aller de soi (or) sans dire. ‖ **60. To let go,** lâcher prise; *to let go sth.,* laisser échapper (or) lâcher qqch.; *to*

let it go at that, s'en tenir là, passer ; *to let oneself go,* se laiser aller, s'abandonner ; *to let oneself go on,* s'étendre sur.
— (pl. **goes** [gouz]). n. Action (*f.*) d'aller ; allée *f.* ; aller *m.* (act). ‖ Mouvement *m. ; to be always on the go,* être toujours sur la brèche, ne pas avoir une minute à soi ; *to keep s.o. on the go,* faire pivoter qqn. ‖ Fig. Tentative *f. ;* effort, essai *m. ; at one go,* d'un seul coup ; *to have a go at sth.,* tenter le coup ; *to have another go,* remettre ça ; reprendre du poil de la bête. ‖ Fig. Allant *m. ; to have plenty of go,* avoir beaucoup de dynamisme. ‖ Fam. *Is it a go?,* alors c'est fait ? ; *it's all the go,* ça fait fureur ; *no go!,* rien à faire ; *a pretty go,* un joli gâchis ; *to make a go of it,* en faire un succès. ‖ **Go-ahead,** adj. Entreprenant, plein d'allant, qui va de l'avant. ‖ **Go-between,** n. Intermédiaire *s. ;* entremetteur *s.* (pej.). ‖ **Go-by,** n. Fait (*m.*) de passer près de qqn ; *to give s.o. the go-by,* brûler la politesse à qqn. ‖ **Go-cart,** n. Poussette, charrette *f.* (baby-carriage) ; chariot, « Bébétrott » *m.* (for learning to walk) ; charrette (*f.*) à bras (handcart). ‖ **Go-getter,** n. Débrouillard, ambitieux, arriviste *s.* ‖ **Go-off,** n. Départ *m.* ‖ **Go-slow,** adj. Attentiste ; *go-slow strike,* grève perlée. ‖ **Go-to-meeting,** adj. Fam. Du dimanche (clothes). ‖ **Go-to-sleep,** adj. Endormi, nonchalant.
— adj. Fam. En bon ordre, O.K. ; *all conditions are go,* tout est O.K. ‖ Fam. Dans le vent, à la mode, in (fashionable).

goad [goud] n. Agric., Fig. Aiguillon *m.*
— v. intr. Agric. Aiguillonner. ‖ Fig. Stimuler, aiguillonner, piquer. (See SPUR.)

goal [goul] n. Sports., Fig. But *m.* ‖ **Goal-keeper,** n. Sports. Goal, gardien (*m.*) de buts. ‖ **Goal-kick,** n. Sports. Coup (*m.*) de pied de but, dégagement (*m.*) aux six mètres, six mètres *m.* ‖ **Goal-line,** Sports. Ligne (*f.*) de but. ‖ **Goal-mouth,** n. Sports. *In the goal-mouth,* devant les buts.

goat [gout] n. Zool. Bouc *m.* (he-goat) ; chèvre *f.* (she-goat). ‖ Comm. Mongolie *f.* ‖ Astron. Capricorne *m.* ‖ Culin. *Goat's-milk cheese,* fromage de chèvre. ‖ Fig. Satyre *m.* ‖ U. S. Fam. Dindon *m.* ‖ Fam. Idiot. ‖ **Goat-foot,** n. Satyre, faune *m.*

goatee [gou'ti:] n. Bouc *m.* (beard).

goatherd ['gouthə:d] n. Chevrier *m.*

goatish [-iʃ] adj. Zool. De bouc (odour). ‖ Fig. Libidineux.

goatling [-liŋ] n. Zool. Chevreau, cabri *m. ;* chevrette *f.*

goatskin [-skin] n. Outre *f.* (bottle) ; peau de chèvre *f.* (skin).

goatsucker [-,sʌkə*] n. Zool. Engoulevent *m.*

gob [gɔb] n. Pop. Four *m.* (mouth). ‖ U. S. Pop. Marsouin *m.* ‖ **Gob-fire,** n. Combustion spontanée *f.* (in mining).
— v. intr. (1) Pop. Cracher.

gobbet ['gɔbit] n. † Morceau *m.* (of flesh). ‖ Fig. Extrait (*m.*) à commenter.

gobble ['gɔbl] v. tr. Fam. Engloutir, enfourner, ingurgiter (food). ‖ **Gobble-stitch,** n. Gros point *m.*
— v.intr. Fam. Bâfrer, mettre les bouchées doubles.

gobble v. intr. Zool. Glouglouter (male turkey).

gobbledygook [,gɔbḷdi'guk] n. U. S. Fam. Palabre, charabia *m.*

gobbler ['gɔblə*] n. Goinfre *m.*

gobbler n. Zool. Dindon *m.*

goblet ['gɔblit] n. † Gobelet *m.* ‖ Verre à pied *m.*

goblin ['gɔblin] n. Lutin, elfe, farfadet *m.*

goby ['goubi] n. Zool. Gobie *m.*

god [gɔd] n. Divinité *f. ;* dieu *m.* (deity). ‖ Idole *f.*

God [gɔd] n. Eccles. Dieu *m.* ‖ Fam. *God's own country,* paradis terrestre, pays de cocagne ; U. S. les Etats-Unis. ‖ **God-botherer,** n. Fam. Calotin, bigot *m.* ‖ **God-fearing,** adj. Religieux, craignant Dieu. ‖ **God-forsaken,** adj. Misérable ; *God-forsaken place,* trou perdu.

godchild [-tʃaild] (pl. **godchildren** [-ʃildrən]). n. Filleul *s.*

goddaughter [-,dɔ:tə*] n. Filleule *f.*

goddess ['gɔdis] n. Déesse *f.* ‖ Fig. Idole *f.*

godfather ['gɔd,fɑ:ðə*] n. Parrain *m.*
— v. tr. Eccles. Etre le parrain de. ‖ Fig. Parrainer.

godhead ['gɔdhed] n. Divinité *f.*

godless [-lis] adj. Irréligieux, athée, impie.

godlike [-laik] adj. Divin.

godliness [-linis] n. Dévotion, piété *f.*

godly [-li] adj. Dévot, pieux, religieux.

godmother [-,mʌðə*] n. Marraine *f.*

godparent ['gɔd,pɛərənt] n. Parrain *m. ;* marraine *f.*

godsend ['gɔdsend] n. Aubaine *f. ;* chopin *m.* (fam.) [see WINDFALL] ; *to come as a godsend,* tomber du ciel.

godship [-ʃip] n. Divinité *f.*

godson [-sʌn] n. Filleul *m.*

godspeed [-'spi:d] n. Bonne chance *f.*

godwit [-gɔdwit] n. Zool. Barge *f.*

goer [-gouə*] n. Allant, passant *m. ;* personne (*f.*) qui va. ‖ Sports. Marcheur *s.*

gofer ['goufə*] n. Culin. Gaufre *f.*

goffer ['goufə*] v. tr. Tuyauter (laundry) ; gaufrer (paper).
— n. Fer (*m.*) à tuyauter (instrument). ‖ Tuyauté *m.* (flutes).

goffering [-riŋ] n. Tuyautage *m.*

goggle ['gɔgl] v. intr. Sortir de la tête, être saillant (eyes) ; rouler de gros yeux (person).
— v. tr. *To goggle one's eyes,* rouler les yeux.
— adj. En boules de loto (eyes). ‖ **Goggle-eyed,** adj. Aux yeux saillants.
— n. pl. Lunettes protectrices (*f. pl.*) [or] de motocycliste. ‖ Med. Tournis *m.*

goglet ['gɔglit] n. Alcarazas *m. ;* gargoulette *f.*

going ['gouiŋ] adj. Qui va, allant. ‖ En action, en marche, qui va bien (running). ‖ Existant, qui soit (in existence).
— n. Action (*f.*) d'aller (act). ‖ Allure, marche *f. ;* train, pas *m.* ‖ Etat du terrain (*m.*) pour la marche ; *rough going,* route mauvaise. ‖ Fig. Progrès *m. ;* avance *f.* ‖ **Going away,** n. Départ *m.* ‖ **Going-back,** n. Retour *m. ;* Fig. Recul *m.* ‖ **Going-down,** n. Descente *f.* (of a person) ; coucher *m.* (of sun) ; baisse *f.* (of temperature) ; Autom. Dégonflement *m.* (of a tyre). ‖ **Going in,** n. Entrée *f. ;* Fig. Inscription, admission *f.* ‖ **Going off,** n. Départ *m.* (of a person, a rifle). ‖ **Going-on-strike,** n. Débrayage *m. ;* grève *f.* ‖ **Goings-on,** n. Conduite, attitude *f. ;* manigances *f. pl.* ‖ **Going out,** n. Sortie *f.* ‖ **Going through,** n. Dépouillement *m. ;* lecture attentive *f.* ‖ **Going up,** n. Fin. Hausse *f.*

goitre ['gɔitə*] n. Med. Goitre *m.*

goitrous [-trəs] adj. Med. Goitreux.

gold [gould] n. Or *m.* ‖ **Gold-bearing,** adj. Aurifère. ‖ **Gold-beater,** n. Techn. Batteur d'or *m. ; gold-beater's skin,* baudruche. ‖ **Gold-bug,** n. Zool. Scarabée d'or *m.* ‖ **Gold-digger,** n. Chercheur d'or *s. ;* U. S. Fam. Maîtresse coûteuse, sangsue *f.* ‖ **Gold-field,** n. Terrain aurifère *m.* ‖ **Gold-fish,** n. Zool. Cyprin, poisson rouge *m.* ‖ **Gold-leaf,** n. Feuille (*f.*) d'or en or en feuille. ‖ **Gold-mine,** n. Mine (*f.*) d'or (lit. and fig.). ‖ **Gold plate,** n. Vaisselle (*f.*) d'or (vessels) ; Techn. Placage or *m.* (metal). ‖ **Gold-plated,** adj. Plaqué or. ‖ **Gold-rush,** n. Ruée (*f.*) vers l'or. ‖ **Gold-washer,** n. Orpailleur *m.*
— adj. D'or, en or (necklace). ‖ Or (colour). ‖ Fin. Or (standard, value).

goldbrick ['gouldbrik] v. intr. U. S. Milit. Tirer au flanc. ‖ Fam. Se défiler.

goldbricker [-ə*] n. U. S. Tireur au flanc, embusqué *m.*

golden ['gouldən] adj. D'or (calf, fleece); en or (necklace). ‖ Doré; d'or (colour, hair). ‖ ZOOL. *Golden eagle*, aigle fauve (or) royal *m.* ‖ FIG. D'or (age, number, rule, wedding); doré (legend); *golden mean*, juste milieu.

goldfinch [-finʃ] n. ZOOL. Chardonneret *m.*

goldilocks [-ilɔks] n. Boucle (*f.*) d'or (in fairy tale); blondinet *s.* ‖ BOT. Renoncule (*f.*) tête d'or; linosyris vulgaire *m.*

goldsmith [-smiθ] n. Orfèvre *m.*

golf [gɔlf] n. SPORTS. Golf *m.* (game). ‖ **Golf-ball,** n. SPORTS. Balle (*f.*) de golf; TECHN. Sphère *f.* (in typewriter). ‖ **Golf-club,** n. SPORTS. Club *m.*, crosse *f.* (stick); club de golf (association). ‖ **Golf-course** (or) **-links,** n. SPORTS. Golf, terrain de golf, links *m.* — v. intr. SPORTS. Faire du golf.

golfer [-ə*] n. SPORTS. Joueur (*s.*) de golf.

golliwog ['gɔliwɔg] n. Poupée (*f.*) de chiffon grotesque.

golly ['gɔli] interj. Ciel!

golosh [gə'lɔʃ] n. See GALOSH.

gonad ['gɔnæd] n. MED. Gonade *f.*

gondola ['gɔndələ] n. NAUT. Gondole *f.* ‖ AVIAT. Nacelle *f.* ‖ U. S. NAUT. Plate *f.* ‖ U. S. CH. DE F. Wagon-plate-forme (or) -tombereau *m.*

gondolier [,gɔndə'liə*] n. NAUT. Gondolier *m.*

gone [gɔn] p.p. See GO. — adj. Parti, absent (person). ‖ Sonné (hour), écoulé, passé (time). ‖ MED. *Gone with child,* enceinte. ‖ JUR. Adjugé. ‖ FAM. Entiché, toqué (*on,* de) [in love with]; *far gone,* parti, paff, pompette, éméché (tipsy); *gone with the wind,* irrémédiablement disparu; « autant en emporte le vent ».

goner [-ə*] n. FAM. Type fini; homme perdu *m.*

gonfalon ['gɔnfələn] n. Gonfalon *m.*

gong [gɔŋ] n. Gong *m.*

goniometer [,gouni'ɔmitə*] n. Goniomètre *m.*

gonna ['gɔnə] v. intr. (representation of *going to*). POP. *I'm, he's gonna,* j'vais, i'va.

gonococcus [,gɔnə'kɔkəs] n. MED. Gonocoque *m.*

gonorrhoea [-'riə:] n. MED. Blennorragie *f.*

goo [gu:] n. FAM. Machin poisseux (or) gluant *m.* (sticky stuff); guimauve, eau de rose *f.* (sentimentality).

goober ['gubə*] n. U. S. FAM. Cacahuète *f.*

good [gud] adj. Bon *m.*; bonne *f.* (advice, family, person, story); sage (child); *as good as gold,* sage comme une image. ‖ Bon, brave (man, people). ‖ Bon, bienveillant; *good turn,* service; *good word,* bonne parole, parole de recommandation. ‖ Bon, favorable (luck); bon, agréable, aimable (fellow); bon, joyeux (humour); bon, agréable (life, time); *good afternoon, evening,* bonsoir; *good morning,* bonjour. ‖ Bon, salutaire (*for,* pour) [custom, diet]. ‖ Bon, favorable (*for,* pour); *in good time,* en temps opportun. ‖ Beau, joli, bien (face); *good looks,* belle apparence, bonne mine. ‖ Bon, large, grand (distance); *a good while,* un bon moment. ‖ Bon, convenable, satisfaisant; *good manners,* savoir-vivre. ‖ Bon, compétent, expert; *good swimmer,* bon nageur. ‖ Honorable, digne; *good name,* bonne réputation. ‖ MED. Bon (health, sight). ‖ CULIN. Frais (egg); bon, satisfaisant (meal). ‖ ECCLES. *Good Friday,* vendredi saint. ‖ FIN. Bon (*for,* pour). ‖ FAM. *A good sort,* une bonne bête; *a good thrashing,* une bonne raclée; *not so good!,* pas très brillant! ‖ **As good as,** virtuellement, pratiquement, pour ainsi dire (nearly), aussi bon (or) bien que (sth. else). ‖ **To make good,** prospérer; FIN. Combler (a deficit); compenser (expenses, a loss); *to make good a loss to s.o.,* indemniser (or) dédommager qqn d'une perte; JUR. Etablir le bien fondé de (one's claim); réparer (damages); faire valoir (one's rights); FIG. Réparer (an injustice); tenir, remplir (one's promise); accomplir (one's

purpose); démontrer (a statement). ‖ **Good-bye,** n. Au revoir, adieu *m.* ‖ **Good-fellowship,** n. Camaraderie *f.* ‖ **Good-for-nothing,** adj. Bon à rien. ‖ **Good-hearted,** adj. Au cœur généreux, qui a bon cœur. ‖ **Good-humoured,** adj. De joyeuse (or) bonne humeur, gai. ‖ **Good-looking,** adj. Bien, beau, plaisant. ‖ **Good-natured,** adj. Aimable, cordial, affable, bon. ‖ **Good-tempered,** adj. Qui a bon caractère, de caractère égal. ‖ **Good-time Charlie,** n. FAM. Jouisseur, joyeux vivant *m.* — N. B. Le comp. est *better;* le superl. *best.*

— n. Bons, gens (*m. pl.*) de bien (persons). ‖ Bien *m.*; *to do good,* faire le bien. ‖ Avantage *m.*; *for s.o.'s good,* pour le bien de qqn; *so much to the good,* autant de gagné; *what's the good of running?,* à quoi bon courir? ‖ Résultat souhaitable *m.*; *no good,* inutile (useless); sans valeur (worthless); *to be up to no good,* préparer un mauvais coup. ‖ Résultat décisif *m.*; *for good,* pour de bon; *for good and all,* pour tout de bon. ‖ JUR. Pl. Biens meubles *m. pl.* ‖ COMM. Pl. Marchandises *f. pl.* ‖ CH. DE F. *Goods train,* train de marchandises; *by goods,* par train de marchandises. ‖ FAM. *A lot of good that will do you!,* la belle avance!, ça vous fera une belle jambe!; *a piece of goods,* une bonne pièce (person); *that's the goods!;* à la bonne heure!; *to deliver the goods,* prouver ses capacités, faire le turbin promis; U.S. *to have the goods on s.o.,* tenir le bon bout contre qqn.

goodies ['gudiz] See GOODY.

goodish [-iʃ] adj. Assez bon.

goodliness [-linis] n. Bel aspect *m.*; beauté *f.*

goodly [-li'] adj. Beau, gracieux, plaisant. ‖ Grand, considérable, important.

goodman [-mən] n. † Maître (*m.*) de maison; *goodman Smith,* le père Smith.

goodness [-nis] n. Bonté *f.* (of s.o.); qualité *f.* (of sth.). — interj. Ciel!; *for goodness' sake,* pour l'amour de Dieu; *my goodness!,* bonté divine!

goodwife ['gud,waif] n. † Maîtresse de maison *f.*; *goodwife Smith,* la mère Smith.

goodwill [-'wil] n. Bonne volonté *f.*; bon vouloir *m.* ‖ Bienveillance, bonne disposition *f.* ‖ COMM. Clientèle *f.*

goody ['gudi], **goody-goody,** adj. FAM. Edifiant, respectable; *the goody-goodies,* les gens respectables, les bien-pensants. ‖ FAM. U. S. Pl. Friandises *f. pl.* — interj. Chouette!, chic!

gooey ['gui] adj. FAM. A l'eau de rose (sentimental). ‖ U. S. FAM. Gluant (sticky).

goof [guf] n. U. S. FAM. Toqué *m.* — v. intr. U. S. FAM. *To goof off,* tirer au flanc.

goofy [gufi] adj. U. S. FAM. Maboul. (See BATTY.)

goo-goo ['gu'gu] adj. U. S. FAM. *To make goo-goo eyes at,* faire les yeux doux à.

gook [guk, gu:k] n. U. S. POP. Jaune, Asiatique *s.*

goon [gu:n] n. POP. Cloche, enflure *f.*, cornichon *m.* (stupid person). ‖ POP. Homme (*m.*) de main, nervi *m.* (thug).

goosander [gu:'sændə*] n. ZOOL. Harle *m.*

goose [gu:s] (pl. **geese** [gi:s]) n. ZOOL., CULIN. Oie *f.* ‖ FAM. Oie, dinde, bécassine, pécore *f.*; *simple little goose,* oie blanche. ‖ POP. *To cook s.o.'s goose,* régler son compte à qqn. ‖ **Gooseflesh,** n. MED. Chair de poule *f.* ‖ **Goose-quill,** n. Plume d'oie *f.* ‖ **Goose-step,** n. MILIT. Pas (*m.*) de l'oie.

goose [gu:s] (pl. **gooses** [-iz]) n. TECHN. Carreau *m.* (pressing iron).

gooseberry ['guzbəri] n. BOT. Groseille (*f.*) à maquereau. ‖ FAM. Chaperon *m.* ‖ U.S. FAM. Bobard *m.*

gopher ['goufə*] n. ZOOL. Geomys, gauphre *m.* (rodent); spermophile, écureuil terrestre *m.* (ground squirrel).

Gordian ['gɔːdiən] adj. Gordien (knot).
gore [gɔ:*] n. Sang m.
gore v. tr. Corner, blesser d'un coup de corne.
gore n. Godet, soufflet m. (in a garment). ‖ NAUT. Pointe f. ‖ AVIAT. Fuseau m.
— v. tr. Tailler à godet (or) en pointe.
gored [gɔ:d] adj. A godet, en forme (skirt).
gorge [gɔ:dʒ] n. MED., GEOGR., MILIT. Gorge f. ‖ FIG. Cœur, estomac m. ‖ FAM. Ripaille f.; gavage m.
— v. tr. Gorger, rassasier (s.o.); engloutir, enfourner (sth.).
— v. intr. S'empiffrer, se bourrer, se gorger (on, de).
gorgeous [-əs] adj. Somptueux, splendide, fastueux. ‖ Flambant, étincelant, reluisant. ‖ U. S. Ravissant (woman).
gorgeousness [-əsnis] n. Somptuosité, splendeur f.; faste, éclat m.
gorget [-it] n. † Gorgerin, hausse-col m. (in armour); gorgerette f. (for women). ‖ MED. Gorgeret m. ‖ MILIT. Ecusson m.
gorgonize ['gɔ:gənaiz] v. tr. Méduser, pétrifier; to gorgonize s.o. with a stony stare, regarder qqn en chien de faïence.
gorilla [gɔ'rilə] n. ZOOL. Gorille m.
gormandize ['gɔ:məndaiz] n. Gourmandise f.
— v. intr. Se gorger, s'empiffrer.
— v. tr. Dévorer, avaler. (See GUZZLE.)
gormandizer [-ə*] n. Goinfre m.
gormless ['gɔ:mlis] adj. FAM. Bouché, gourde.
gorse [gɔ:s] n. BOT. Ajonc m.
gorsy [-i] adj. Couvert d'ajoncs.
gory ['gɔ:ri] adj. Sanglant (fight); ensanglanté (person).
gosh [gɔʃ] interj. Nom d'un chien!
goshawk ['gɔshɔ:k] n. ZOOL. Autour m.
gosling ['gɔzliŋ] n. ZOOL. Oison m.
gospel ['gɔspəl] n. ECCLES. Evangile m. ‖ FAM. Gospel truth, parole d'Evangile.
gospeller [-ə*] n. ECCLES. Diacre m.; hot gospeller, évangéliste zélé.
gossamer ['gɔsəmə*] n. Fils (m. pl.) de la Vierge. ‖ Etoffe translucide, gaze f. (cloth).
— adj. Arachnéen.
gossip ['gɔsip] n. † Compère m.; commère f. ‖ Bavard s. (person). ‖ Bavardage m. (chatter); commérage m.; cancans m. pl. (tittle-tattle); scandalous gossip, chronique scandaleuse. ‖ **Gossip-shop**, n. FAM. Potinière f.
— v. intr. Bavarder (to chatter); cancaner (to talk scandal).
gossiper [-ə*] n. Bavard s. (chatterer); cancanier, potinier s. (scandalmonger).
gossipy [-i] adj. De potins, de commérages (conversation); bavard, potinier (person); anecdotique (style).
got [gɔt]. See GET.
Goth [gɔθ] n. GEOGR. Goth m. ‖ FIG. Vandale m.
gotha ['goutə] n. Gotha m.
Gotham ['gɔθəm] n. U. S. FAM. New York m.
Gothic ['gɔθik] adj. GEOGR., ARCHIT. Gothique. ‖ GRAMM. Gotique. ‖ FIG. Barbare.
— n. ARCHIT. Gothique m.
Gothicism [-θisizm] n. ARCHIT. Gothique m. ‖ FIG. Vandalisme m.; barbarie f.
gotta ['gɔtə] v. aux. (representation of got to, have got to). POP. I, we gotta go, faut que j'y aille, qu'on y aille.
gotten ['gɔtn] p. p. See GET.
gouache [gu'a:ʃ] n. ARTS. Gouache f.
gouge [gaudʒ] n. TECHN. Gouge f.
— v. tr. TECHN. Gouger. ‖ U. S. Empiler (s.o.). ‖ FAM. To gouge out s.o.'s eyes, faire sauter les yeux à qqn.
goulash ['gu:læʃ] n. CULIN. Goulache, goulasch m.
gourd [guəd] n. BOT. Courge f. ‖ Gourde f. (bottle). ‖ **Gourd-family,** n. BOT. Cucurbitacées f. pl.

gourmand ['guəmənd] adj., n. Glouton, goinfre (glutton); gourmand (fond of eating) adj., s.
gourmandise [,gɔ:mən'di:z] n. Gloutonnerie, goinfrerie f.; gourmandise f.
gourmet ['guəmei] n. Gourmet; bon vivant m.
gout [gaut] n.† Goutte f. (drop). ‖ MED., AGRIC. Goutte f.
gouty [-i] adj. MED. Goutteux, podagre.
govern ['gʌvən] v. tr. Diriger, administrer (affairs); être le gouverneur de (a city); gouverner (a country); diriger (a household). ‖ GRAMM. Gouverner (a case, mood). ‖ AUTOM. Régler (speed). ‖ FIG. Régir, déterminer (events); guider (opinion, person); dominer, maîtriser (one's temper).
— v. intr. Gouverner.
governance [-əns] n. Gouvernement m. (of a state). ‖ Organisation f. (of a match). ‖ FIG. Empire m.; autorité, domination f.
governess [-is] n. Gouvernante f. (of children).
governing [-iŋ] adj. Gouvernant; governing body, conseil d'administration (or) de gestion. ‖ Dominant; governing idea, idée maîtresse, dominante.
government [-mənt] n. ‖ Direction, gestion, administration f. (of a society). ‖ Gouvernement m. (of a State); system of government, régime. ‖ Cabinet, ministère m. ‖ Gouvernement m. (territory). ‖ COMM. Gouverne f. ‖ FIG. Empire m.; maîtrise f.
— adj. De l'Etat, public (gen.); gouvernemental (newspaper, party); administratif (department). ‖ Du gouverneur (house). ‖ FIN. Government bond, obligation d'Etat, bon du Trésor; government securities, fonds d'Etat; government stock, fonds d'Etat (or) publics. ‖ **Government issue,** adj. U. S. Distribué par le gouvernement (equipment). ‖ **Government surplus,** n. Surplus m. pl.
governmental [,gʌvən'mentl] adj. Gouvernemental; du gouvernement.
governor ['gʌvənə*] n. Gouverneur m. (of a bank, province, town); administrateur m. (of institution); directeur m. (of a prison). ‖ TECHN. Régulateur m. ‖ FAM. Patron m. (boss); paternel (father). ‖ **Governor-general,** n. Gouverneur général m.
governorship [-ʃip] n. Fonctions (f. pl.) de gouverneur.
gowk [gauk] n. ZOOL. Coucou m. ‖ FAM. Niais m.
gown [gaun] n. Robe f. (for dons, officials, students, women). ‖ † Toge f.
gowned [-d] adj. En robe.
gownsman [-zmən] (pl. **gownsmen**) n. Etudiant m.
goy [gɔi] n. Goy s.
— N. B. Deux pluriels : goys, goyim.
G. P. [dʒi:'pi:] abbr. General practitioner, MED. Médecin généraliste, généraliste.
grab [græb] n. Mouvement (m.) pour saisir. ‖ Emprise, étreinte f. ‖ TECHN. Benne preneuse, pelle automatique f.; grappin m. ‖ FIG. Rapacité f. ‖ **Grab bag,** n. FAM. U. S. Sac à surprise.
— v. tr. Agripper, empoigner, étreindre. (See SNATCH.) ‖ Capturer (to arrest). ‖ FIG. Accaparer, mettre la main sur. ‖ FAM. To grab a bite, manger un morceau sur le pouce.
— v. intr. To grab at, s'agripper à, se raccrocher à (s.o.); tenter de saisir; tendre les griffes vers (fam.) [sth].
grabber [-ə*] n. Accapareur s.
grabble ['græbl] v. intr. To grabble for, chercher à tâtons.
graben ['grɑ:bn] n. GEOL. Graben, fossé tectonique (or) d'effondrement m.
— N. B. Deux pluriels : graben, grabens.
grace [greis] n. Grâce, distinction f. (beauty). ‖ Grâce, faveur f. (favour); in the bad graces of, mal vu de. ‖ Grâce f.; pardon m. (forgiveness). ‖ Grâce, merci, clémence f. (clemency). ‖ Grâce, bonne volonté f.; with a bad, good grace, de mauvaise, bonne grâce. ‖ Pudeur, décence, convenance

f. (decency). ‖ Grâce *f.;* répit *m.* (temporary exemption). ‖ Grâce (title). ‖ Pl. Grâces, minauderies *f. pl.* ‖ Grâce (deity). ‖ ECCLES. Grâce (of God); grâces *f. pl.* (after meal); bénédicité (before meal); *in this year of grace,* en l'an de grâce. ‖ JUR. Amnistie *f.* ‖ MUS. Agréments *m. pl.* ‖ FAM. *He has the saving grace of,* sa planche de salut, c'est. ‖ **Grace-cup,** n. Dernier verre *m.* ‖ **Grace-note,** n. MUS. Agrément *m.*
— v. tr. Honorer (with, de). ‖ Orner (with, de). ‖ MUS. Agrémenter.

graceful [-ful] adj. Gracieux.
gracefully [-fuli] adv. Gracieusement.
gracefulness [-fulnis] n. Grâce, gracieuseté *f.*
graceless [-lis] adj. † Sans grâce, balourd. ‖ ECCLES. Perdu, hors de l'état de grâce. ‖ FAM. Impudent, hardi, cynique.
gracious ['greiʃəs] adj. † Gracieux, attirant, aimable. ‖ Courtois, plein de bonne grâce (to, envers). ‖ Bon, bienveillant, compatissant (to, envers). ‖ ECCLES. Miséricordieux.
— Interj. Miséricorde!, Ciel!
graciously [-li] adv. Gracieusement, avec bonne grâce. ‖ Avec bonté, généreusement.
graciousness [-nis] n. Grâce *f.* ‖ Bienveillance, aménité *f.* ‖ ECCLES. Miséricorde *f.*
grad [græd] n. FAM. Licencié, diplômé *s.* (of a school, a university).
gradate [grə'deit] v. tr. Dégrader.
— v. intr. Se dégrader (colours).
gradation [-'deiʃən] n. Gradation *f.*
grade [greid] n. Degré *m.;* qualité *f.* ‖ Catégorie, classe *f.* (for things). ‖ Grade, rang *m.* (for persons). ‖ COMM. *Up to grade,* de qualité standard. ‖ GRAMM. Degré apophonique *m.* ‖ U. S. Classe élémentaire *f.* (form); note *f.* (mark); *grade school,* école primaire. ‖ U. S. CH. DE F. Rampe, pente *f.* ‖ U. S. Niveau *m.* ‖ FIG. *To make the grade,* se montrer à la hauteur. ‖ **Grade crossing,** n. U. S. CH. DE F. Passage à niveau *m.*
— v. tr. Dégrader (colours). ‖ Calibrer (a photograph). ‖ AGRIC. Croiser (animals). ‖ COMM. Classer, trier (goods). ‖ U. S. Noter (compositions). ‖ U. S. CH. DE F. Régulariser la pente. ‖ FIG. Graduer (difficulties); *to grade up,* améliorer; classer dans une catégorie supérieure.
gradient [-iənt] n. Pente *f.* (See DECLIVITY.)
gradin [-in] n. Gradin *m.*
gradual ['grædjuəl] adj. Graduel, progressif.
— n. ECCLES. Graduel *m.*
gradually ['grædjuəli] adv. Graduellement, par gradation.
graduate [-eit] v. tr. Graduer. ‖ Dégrader (colours). ‖ Conférer un diplôme à (a student). ‖ CHIM. Concentrer.
— v. intr. Se changer graduellement (into, en). ‖ Passer sa licence.
— [-it] adj. Du troisième cycle (studies).
— [-it] n. Licencié, diplômé *s.* ‖ MED. Verre gradué *m.*
graduated [-eitid] adj. Gradué; *in graduated stages,* par paliers. ‖ Diplômé (student). ‖ FIN. Progressif (surtax).
graduation [,grædju'eiʃən] n. Graduation, progression *f.* ‖ Remise (*f.*) des diplômes (by the University); réception (*f.*) d'un grade (by students). ‖ CHIM., MED. Graduation *f.*
Graeco-Roman ['gri:kou'roumən] adj. Gréco-romain.
graffito [græ'fi:tou] (pl. **graffiti** [-ail]) n. Graffiti *m.* pl. ‖ ARTS. Sgraffite *m.*
graft [grɑːft] n. AGRIC., MED. Greffe *f.* ‖ U. S. Pot-de-vin *m.;* *graft system,* corruption.
— v. tr. AGRIC., MED., FIG. Greffer (in, upon, sur). ‖ U. S. Escroquer (of, de).
— v. intr. U. S. Tripoter.
graftage [-idʒ]n. AGRIC., MED. Greffage *m.*

grafter [-ə*] n. AGRIC. Greffeur *s.* (person); greffoir, écussonneur *m.* (tool). ‖ U. S. Tripoteur *m.*
grafting [-iŋ] n. AGRIC., MED. Greffage *m.;* Greffe *f.* ‖ **Grafting-knife,** n. AGRIC. Greffoir *m.*
grail [greil] n. Graal *m.*
grain [grein] n. Grain *m.* (of corn, salt, sand). ‖ Grain (of leather); poil *m.* (of material); fil *m.* (of stone); veines *f. pl.;* fibres *m. pl.* (of wood). ‖ Teinture *f.; in grain,* bon teint. ‖ Grain *m.* (weight). ‖ Pl. Drêche *f.* (of barley). ‖ U. S. AGRIC. Blé *m.* ‖ FIG. Grain, brin *m.; once f.; that's a grain of comfort,* c'est déjà une consolation. ‖ FAM. *Against the grain,* à rebrousse-poil, à rebours. ‖ **Grain-elevator,** n. U. S. AGRIC. Silo *m.*
— adj. De grain (alcohol).
— v. tr. AGRIC. Grener, réduire en grains, égrener, granuler (leather); grener (paper); dépoiler (skin); marbrer (wood).
— v. intr. Se granuler.
grained [-d] adj. Grenu, grenelé, granulé.
grainer ['greinə*] n. TECHN. Peigne *m.*
grains [greinz] n. Foëne *f.* (harpoon).
gram [græm] n. Gramme *m.*
gram n. BOT. Pois chiche *m.*
gramarye ['græməri] n. † Magie *f.*
graminaceous [,græmi'neiʃəs] adj. BOT. Des graminées.
grammar ['græmə*] n. Grammaire *f.* ‖ **Grammar-school,** n. Collège, lycée *m.;* U. S. Ecole primaire *f.*
grammarian [grə'mɛəriən] n. Grammairien *s.*
grammatical [grə'mætikəl] adj. Grammatical.
grammatically [-əli] adv. Grammaticalement.
gram(me) [græm] n. Gramme *m.* ‖ **Gramme-atom,** n. CHIM. Atome-gramme *m.* ‖ **Gramme-calory,** n. PHYS. Petite calorie *f.* ‖ **Gramme-molecule,** n. CHIM. Molécule-gramme *f.*
gramophone ['græməfoun] n. Gramophone, phonographe *m.*
grampus ['græmpəs] n. ZOOL. Epaulard *m.* ‖ FAM. Vieux poussif *m.*
gran [græn] n. FAM. Grand-mère, mémé *f.*
granary ['grænəri] n. Grenier *m.*
grand [grænd] adj. Grand (duke, hotel, master). ‖ Grand, important (ballroom, banquet, staircase). ‖ Grand, noble (manner, person, work). ‖ Grandiose, magnifique (scenery). ‖ Complet, général (total). ‖ MUS. Grand (chorus); à queue (piano). ‖ FAM. Epatant, formidable, grandiose. ‖ **Grand-aunt,** n. Grand-tante *f.* ‖ **Grand-dad,** n. Bon-papa *m.* ‖ **Grand-daughter,** n. Petite-fille *f.* ‖ **Grand-nephew,** n. Petit-neveu *m.* ‖ **Grand-niece,** n. Petite-nièce *f.* ‖ **Grand-uncle,** n. Grand-oncle *m.*
— n. MUS. Piano (*m.*) à queue. ‖ FAM. Mille livres ; U. S. Mille dollars ; brique *f.*
grandam [-əm] n. † Grand-mère *f.*
grandchild [-tʃaild] (pl. **grandchildren** [-tʃildrən]) n. Petit-fils *m.;* petite-fille *f.* ‖ Pl. Petits-enfants *m. pl.*
grandee [græn'di:] n. Grand *m.* (Spanish). ‖ FAM. Manitou *m.*
grandeur ['grændʒə*] n. Grandeur *f.* ‖ Splendeur, magnificence *f.*
grandfather ['grændfɑ:ðə*] n. Grand-père *m.* ‖ *Grandfather clock,* horloge comtoise.
grandiloquence [græn'diləkwəns] n. Grandiloquence, emphase *f.*
grandiloquent [-ənt] adj. Grandiloquent. (See BOMBASTIC.)
grandiose ['grændious] adj. Grandiose.
grandiosity [,grændi'ositi] n. Grandiose *m.*
grandly ['grændli] adv. Avec grandeur. ‖ Grandiosement.
grandma ['grænmɑ:] n. Grand-maman, bonnemaman, mémé *f.*
grand mal ['grɔn'mæl] n. MED. Grand mal *m.* (form of epilepsy).

grandmother ['grændmʌðə*] n. Grand-mère f.
grandmotherly [-li] adj. Trop indulgent (kindly).
‖ FAM. Affairé, important, trop zélé (fussy).
grandparent [-,pɛərənt] n. Grand-père m.; grand-
mère f. ‖ Pl. Grands-parents m. pl.
grandsire [-,saiə*] n. Aïeul m.
grandstand [-stænd] n. SPORTS. Tribune f. ‖ FAM.
U. S. Grandstand play, déploiement pour la galerie.
— v. intr. U. S. FAM. Jouer pour la galerie.
grange [greinʒ] n. † Grange f. ‖ U. S. Fédération
agricole f. ‖ Manoir m.
grangerize ['greinʒəraiz] v. tr. Illustrer, truffer
(a book).
granite ['grænit] n. Granit m.
granitic [grə'nitik] adj. Granitique.
granny ['græni] n. Grand-maman f. ‖ Nœud d'ajut
m. (knot). ‖ FAM. Vieille commère f.
grant [grɑ:nt] v. tr. Accorder, octroyer (a favour);
concéder (a permission); exaucer (a prayer); faire
droit à, accéder à (request). ‖ Admettre, accorder,
concéder; to take it for granted, considérer comme
quantité négligeable (person); considérer comme
admis (or) convenu (thing). ‖ LOC. I beg your
pardon! — Granted!, je vous demande pardon —
Je vous en prie.
— n. Octroi m. (of a favour); concession f. (of
permission). ‖ U. S. Concession (f.) de terrain. ‖
JUR. Cession f. (of a property); acte (m.) de donation. ‖ JUR. Subvention, allocation f. ‖ Grant-
aided, adj. JUR. Subventionné par l'Etat.
grantee [grɑ:n'ti:] n. Donataire m.
grantor [-'tɔ:*] n. JUR. Donateur m.
granular ['grænjulə*] adj. Granuleux.
granulate [-leit] v. tr. Granuler.
— v. intr. Se granuler.
granulation [,grænju'leiʃən] n. Granulation f.
granule ['grænju:l] n. Granule m.
granulous [-əs] adj. Granuleux.
grape [greip] n. BOT. Grain de raisin m. ‖ Pl.
Raisin m.; raisins m. pl. ‖ Grape-brandy, n. Eau-
de-vie (f.) de marc. ‖ Grape-fruit, n. Pamplemousse m. ‖ Grape-juice, n. Jus de raisin m. ‖
Grape-shot, n. Mitraille f. ‖ Grape-stone, n.
Pépin de raisin m. ‖ Grape-vine, n. Vigne, treille
f.; FAM. Potins m. pl.; moyens (m. pl.) de réception
ou de diffusion d'informations.
grapery [-əri] n. Serre (f.) à raisins.
graph [grɑ:f] n. Graphique m. ‖ MATH. Graphe m.
‖ Graph paper, n. COMM. Papier millimétré (or)
millimétrique m.
graphic ['græfik] adj. MATH., ARTS., GEOL., Graphique. ‖ FIG. Pittoresque.
graphically [-əli] adv. Graphiquement. ‖ Avec
pittoresque.
graphics [-ks] n. sg. Représentation graphique f.;
graphiques m. pl. ‖ Pl. Illustrations f. pl. (in a book).
graphite ['græfait] n. Graphite m.
graphologist [græ'fɔlədʒist] s. Graphologue s.
graphology [-dʒi] n. Graphologie f.
grapnel ['græpnəl] n. Grappin m.
grapple ['græpl] v. tr. Saisir au grappin. ‖ Agripper. (See GRIP.) ‖ Empoigner à bras le corps.
— v. intr. Lutter à bras le corps; se colleter (with,
avec). ‖ NAUT. Jeter le grappin (with, sur).
— n. Grappin m. (tool). ‖ Corps à corps m. (fight).
grappling [-iŋ] n. Grappin m. ‖ Colletage m. ‖
NAUT. Abordage m. ‖ Grappling-iron, n. NAUT.
Grappin m.
grasp [grɑ:sp] v. tr. Saisir, empoigner, étreindre.
‖ FIG. Saisir, pénétrer.
— v. intr. Se saisir, tenter de s'emparer (at, de).
— n. Poigne f. ‖ Etreinte f.; to lose one's grasp,
lâcher prise; within one's grasp, entre ses mains,
en son pouvoir. ‖ FIG. Compréhension f.
grasping [-iŋ] adj. FIG. Avare, cupide, avide. (See
GREEDY.)

graspingly [-iŋli] adv. Avidement, avec cupidité.
grass [grɑ:s] n. Herbe f.; blade of grass, brin
d'herbe. ‖ Gazon m.; pelouse f. (lawn). ‖ Pâture
f.; herbage m. (pasture); at grass, au vert. ‖ Pl.
BOT. Graminées f. pl. ‖ TECHN. Surface f. (in
mining). ‖ FAM. As green as grass, bien de son
village; to let the grass grow under one's feet,
traînailler, perdre son temps. ‖ Grass-cutter, n.
Tondeuse (f.) à gazon. ‖ Grass-green, adj. Vert
pré. ‖ Grass-grown, adj. Herbu. ‖ Grass-land,
n. AGRIC. Prairie f. ‖ Grass-plot, n. Pelouse f. ‖
Grass-roots, adj. U. S. FAM. Populaire. ‖ Grass-
snake, n. ZOOL. Couleuvre f. ‖ Grass-widow, n.
Veuve occasionnelle (or) temporaire f.; U. S.
Divorcée, séparée f. ‖ Grass-work, n. TECHN. Travail (m.) à la surface.
— v. tr. Enherber, gazonner, couvrir d'herbe
(ground). ‖ Blanchir sur l'herbe (linen). ‖ Remonter
à la surface (mineral). ‖ FAM. Descendre.
grassnopper [-hɔpə*] n. ZOOL. Sauterelle f. ‖
AVIAT., FAM. Avion (m.) de liaison.
grassy [-i] adj. Herbeux. ‖ Vert pré, verdoyant
(green).
grate [greit] n. Grille f.; grillage m. ‖ FAM. Foyer
m. (fireplace).
— v. tr. Griller.
grate v. tr. CULIN. Râper (cheese). ‖ Frotter avec
un grincement (an object); to grate one's teeth,
grincer des dents.
— v. intr. Grincer. ‖ To grate on, écorcher (the
ear); agacer (the nerves).
grateful ['greitful] adj. Réconfortant, rasserénant,
agréable, plaisant (thing). ‖ Reconnaissant (to,
envers) [person].
gratefully [-i] adv. Agréablement. ‖ Avec gratitude (or) reconnaissance.
gratefulness [-nis] n. Agrément, réconfort m. ‖
Gratitude, reconnaissance f.
grater ['greitə*] n. Râpe f.
graticule ['græti,kju:l] n. ARTS. Graticule f. ‖
TECHN. Réticule m. (in optics).
gratification [,grætifi'keiʃən] n. FIN. Gratification f. ‖ FIG. Contentement m.; cause de satisfaction f.
gratified ['grætifaid] adj. Satisfait, comblé (person); satisfait (tone of voice).
gratify ['grætifai] v. tr. (2). FIN. Gratifier, donner
une gratification à. ‖ FIG. Satisfaire (a whim); se
laisser aller à (an impulse); faire plaisir à, être
agréable à (s.o.).
gratifying [-iŋ] adj. Agréable, satisfaisant.
gratin [gra'tɛ̃] n. CULIN. Gratin m.; au gratin, au
gratin.
grating ['greitiŋ] n. Grille f.; grillage m.
grating adj. Grinçant. ‖ De crécelle (voice). ‖ FIG.
Irritant.
— n. Grincement m. ‖ Pl. Râpures f. pl. ‖ FIG.
Effet énervant m.
gratingly [-li] adv. En grinçant. ‖ FIG. D'une
manière irritante.
gratis ['greitis] adv. Gratis.
gratitude ['grætitju:d] n. Gratitude, reconnaissance f. (envers, to; pour, for).
gratuitous [grə'tju:itəs] adj. FIN., FIG. Gratuit.
gratuitously [-təsli] adv. Gratuitement.
gratuity [-ti] n. Pourboire m. (See TIP.) ‖ JUR.
Pécule m. ‖ NAUT., MILIT. Prime de démobilisation f.
gratulate ['grætjuleit] v. tr. † Congratuler.
gratulatory [-lətəri] adj. De félicitation f.
gravamen [grə'veimen] n. JUR. Grief m.; gravamen of a charge, matière d'un crime.
grave [greiv] n. Tombe f.; tombeau m.; pauper's
grave, fosse commune. ‖ Grave-clothes, n. Linceul
m. ‖ Grave-digger, n. Fossoyeur m. ‖ Grave-yard,
n. Cimetière m.
— v. tr. Mettre au tombeau.

grave adj. Grave, sérieux, important, de poids (weighty). ‖ Grave, sérieux (ominous). ‖ Grave, solennel (sedate). ‖ Sombre, sévère (dull). ‖ Mus. Grave, bas. ‖ Gramm. Grave (accent).
— n. Gramm. Accent grave *m.*
grave v. tr. † Sculpter. ‖ Arts., Fig. Graver.
grave v. tr. Naut. Radouber.
gravel ['grævəl] n. Gravier *m.* ‖ Med. Gravelle *f.* ‖ **Gravel-pit,** n. Gravière *f.*
— v. tr. (1). Caillouter, gravillonner, sabler. ‖ Fig. Embarrasser ; coller (fam.).
gravelly [-i] adj. Cailouteux. ‖ Med. Graveleux.
graven ['greivən] adj. † Taillé, sculpté ; *graven image,* idole. ‖ Arts. Gravé.
graver [-ə*] n. Arts. Burin *m.*
gravestone ['greivstoun] n. Pierre tombale *f.*
gravid ['grævid] adj. Zool., Med. Gravide.
gravimetry [grə'vimitri] n. Phys., Chim. Gravimétrie *f.*
graving ['greiviŋ] n. † Taille *f.* ‖ Arts. Gravure *f.* ‖ **Graving-tool,** n. Burin *m.*
graving n. Naut. Radoub *m.* ‖ **Graving-beach,** n. Naut. Cale (*f.*) d'échouage.
gravitate ['græviteit] v. intr. Graviter (*round,* autour de); être attiré (*towards,* vers).
gravitation [ˌgrævi'teiʃən] n. Gravitation *f.*
gravity ['græviti] n. Phys., Fig. Gravité *f.*
gravy ['greivi] n. Culin. Sauce *f.;* jus *m.* ‖ U. S. Pop. Gratte *f.;* grappillage, profit facile *m.* ‖ **Gravy-boat,** n. Culin. Saucière *f.* ‖ **Gravy-train,** n. U. S. Fam. Assiette (*f.*) au beurre.
gray [grei] adj., v. See GREY.
grayling ['greiliŋ] n. Zool. Ombre *m.*
graze [greiz] v. tr. Frôler, raser (to touch). ‖ Érafler, égratigner (to scratch).
— v. intr. Passer en rasant.
— n. Frôlement, effleurement *m.* ‖ Éraflure, égratignure *f.*
graze v. intr. Paître, brouter. ‖ Faire de l'élevage.
— v. tr. Paître, brouter (grass) ; pâturer dans (a meadow). ‖ Faire paître, paître (cattle). [See DEPASTURE.]
grazier [-iə*] n. Agric. Éleveur *s.*
grazing [-iŋ] n. Agric. Élevage *m.*
grease [gri:s] n. Graisse *f.; wool grease,* suint. ‖ Techn. Lubrifiant *m.;* graisse *f.; cart grease,* cambouis. ‖ Med. Crapaudine *f.* ‖ Fam. Pommade *f.* ‖ **Grease-box** (or) **cup,** n. Techn. Graisseur *m.;* boîte à graisse *f.* ‖ **Grease-monkey,** n. U. S. Fam. Mécano *m.* ‖ **Grease-paint,** n. Theatr. Fard gras *m.* ‖ **Grease-pan,** n. Culin. Lèchefrite *f.* ‖ **Grease-proof,** adj. Comm. *Grease-proof paper,* papier sulfurisé. ‖ **Grease-trap,** n. Boîte à graisse *f.*
— [gri:z], [gri:s] v. tr. Graisser. ‖ Techn. Lubrifier, graisser. ‖ Fig. *To grease the wheels,* huiler les rouages ; *to grease s.o.'s palm,* graisser la patte à qqn.
greaser ['gri:zə*] n. Techn. Graisseur *m.*
greasiness ['gri:zinis] n. Graisse, nature graisseuse *f.* ‖ Fig. Onction *f.*
greasy ['grisi] adj. Graisseux.
— ['grizi] adj. Gras ; glissant ; *greasy pole,* mât de cocagne. ‖ Med. Malandreux (horse). ‖ Naut. Gras (weather). ‖ Fig. Onctueux. ‖ U. S. Fam. *Greasy spoon,* gargote (cook-shop).
great [greit] adj. Grand, haut de taille (in size). ‖ Grand, nombreux (in number). ‖ Grand, intense (in degree). ‖ Grand, éminent, illustre, supérieur. ‖ Grand, grandiose, imposant (impressive). ‖ Grand, noble. ‖ Grand, notable, important. ‖ Grand, principal (main). ‖ Arrière (designating a relationship). ‖ Fam. Splendide, fameux, épatant ; *great at,* fort (or) calé en. ‖ Fam. U. S. *A great hand,* un as. ‖ **Great-aunt,** n. Grand-tante *f.* ‖ **Gread-grandchild** (pl. *great-grand-children*), n. Arrière-petit-fils *m.;* arrière-petite-fille *f.;* pl. arrière-petits-enfants *m. pl.* ‖ **Great-grand-daughter,** n. Arrière-petite-fille *f.* ‖ **Great-grand-father,** n. Arrière-grand-père *m.* ‖ **Great-grand-mother,** n. Arrière-grand-mère *f.* ‖ **Great-grand-parent,** n. Arrière-grand-parent *m.* ‖ **Great-grand-son,** n. Arrière-petit-fils *m.* ‖ **Great-hearted,** adj. Au grand cœur. ‖ **Great-nephew,** n. Petit-neveu *m.* ‖ **Great-niece,** n. Petite-nièce *f.* ‖ **Great-uncle,** n. Grand-oncle *m.*
— n. Grands *m. pl.* ‖ Pl. Dernier examen pour le grade de « Bachelor of Arts » (at Oxford).
greatcoat [-kout] n. Pardessus, paletot *m.* (for men). ‖ Milit. Capote *f.*
greaten [-n] v. tr. Grandir.
— v. intr. Se grandir.
greatly [-li] adv. Grandement, très, fort, beaucoup (much) ; *greatly annoyed,* vivement contrarié. ‖ Avec grandeur (or) noblesse.
greatness [-nis] n. Grandeur *f.*
greave [gri:v] n. † Grève, jambière *f.* (armour).
greaves [gri:vz] n. pl. Culin. Fritons, cretons, rillons *m. pl.*
grebe [gri:b] n. Zool. Grèbe *m.*
Grecian ['gri:ʃən] adj. Grec *m.;* grecque *f.*
— n. Helléniste *s.* (scholar).
grecism [-sizm] n. Hellénisme *m.*
grecize [-saiz] v. tr., intr. Helléniser.
gree [gri:] n. Jur. Réparation, satisfaction *f.*
Greece [gri:s] n. Geogr. Grèce *f.*
greed [gri:d] n. Avidité *f.* (See COVETOUSNESS.)
greedily [-ili] adv. Avidement.
greediness [-inis] n. Voracité, avidité, gloutonnerie, cupidité *f.*
greedy [-i] adj. Vorace, avide, glouton, goulu. ‖ Fig. Cupide, avide, rapace, âpre au gain.
Greek [gri:k] n. Geogr., Eccles. Grec *m.;* Grecque *f.* ‖ Gramm. Grec *m.* (language). ‖ Fam. Grec, escroc *m.* ‖ Fam. *Greek to me,* de l'hébreu pour moi.
— adj. Geogr. Grec *m.;* grecque *f.* ‖ Gramm. De grec (book). ‖ Eccles. Grec ; orthodoxe (Catholic, church, rite). ‖ Techn. Grégeois (fire). ‖ U. S. *Greek letter fraternity,* association (or) club d'étudiants.
green [gri:n] adj. Vert (colour). ‖ Agric. Vert, verdoyant ; *green December,* mois de décembre doux ; *green food,* fourrage vert. ‖ Culin. Salé (bacon) ; vert, pas mûr (fruit) ; cru (meat) ; *green goods,* fruits et légumes. ‖ Med. Vert, blême, livide (complexion) ; frais (wound) ; *to turn green,* verdir. ‖ Techn. Vert (leather). ‖ Autom. *Green light,* feu vert. ‖ Fig. Vivace (memory) ; vert, frais, neuf (new) ; jeune, inexpérimenté, naïf (person) ; *not to be so green as to believe,* n'avoir pas la naïveté de croire. ‖ Fig. Vert, plein de vie, vigoureux (full of vitality). ‖ U. S. Fam. *Green stuff,* fafiots. ‖ **Green belt,** n. Ceinture verte *f.* (around a town). ‖ **Green card,** n. Autom. Carte verte *f.* ‖ **Green-eyed,** adj. Aux yeux verts ; Fig. Jaloux. ‖ **Green-fly,** n. Zool. Puceron *m.* ‖ **Green-peak,** n. Zool. Pivert *m.* ‖ **Green-room,** n. Theatr. Foyer (*m.*) des acteurs. ‖ **Green-stuff,** n. Agric. Verdure *f.* ; Culin. Légumes verts *m. pl.* ‖ **Green-table,** n. Table (*f.*) de jeu ; tapis vert *m.*
— n. Vert *m.* (colour). ‖ Agric. Verdure *f.* ‖ Culin. Pl. Légumes verts *m. pl.* ‖ Sports. Terrain ; turf *m.* ‖ Fig. Verdeur *f.*
— v. intr. Verdir, verdoyer.
— v. tr. Verdir. ‖ Fam. Monter le coup à.
greenback [-bæk] n. U. S. Fam. Fafiot *m.*
greenery [-əri] n. Verdure *f.; feuillage m.* ‖ Agric. Serre *f.*
greenfinch [-finʃ] n. Zool. Verdier *m.*
greengage [-geidʒ] n. Agric. Reine-claude *f.*
greengrocer [-ˌgrousə*] n. Comm. Marchand (*m.*) de légumes, fruitier *m.*
greengrocery [-ˌgrousəri] n. Comm. Fruiterie *f.* (shop). ‖ Pl. Légumes et fruits *m. pl.* (goods).

greenhorn [-hɔ:n] n. Coquebin, blanc-bec, béjaune *m.*; serin *m.* (fam.).
greenhouse [-haus] n. AGRIC. Serre *f.*
greening [-iŋ] n. AGRIC. Pomme verte *f.*
greenish [-iʃ] adj. Verdâtre.
Greenland [-lənd] n. GEOGR. Groenland *m.*
greenness [-nis] n. Verdeur *f.* (colour). ‖ AGRIC. Verdure *f.* ‖ FIG. Verdeur, vitalité *f.* ‖ FIG. Manque (*m.*) de maturité; inexpérience, naïveté *f.*
greenshank [-ʃænk] n. ZOOL. Aboyeur *m.*
greensickness [-siknis] n. MED. Chlorose *f.*
greenstone [-stoun] n. Pierre verte, diorite *f.*
greensward [-swɔ:d] n. Tapis (*m.*) de verdure, pelouse *f.*
Greenwich ['grinidʒ] n. GEOGR. Greenwich *m.* ‖ *Greenwich time,* heure de Greenwich.
greenwood ['gri:nwud] n. Forêt verte *f.*
greet [gri:t] v. tr. Saluer, accueillir (*with,* avec, par). ‖ Parvenir à; *to greet the eyes,* s'offrir aux regards.
greet v. intr. Pleurer, gémir, se lamenter (in Scotland).
greeting [-iŋ] n. Salut *m.* (salutation). ‖ Accueil *m.* (welcome). ‖ Pl. Compliments, souhaits *m. pl.*
gregarious [gri'gɛəriəs] adj. ZOOL. Grégaire. ‖ FIG. Sociable.
gregariously [-li] adv. En bandes.
gregariousness [-nis] n. ZOOL., FIG. Grégarisme *m.*
grege [gri:dʒ] adj. Grège.
Gregorian [gri'gɔ:riən] adj. Grégorien.
— n. MUS. Grégorien, chant grégorien *m.*
gremlin ['grɛmlin] n. FAM. AVIAT. Mauvais génie *m.*
grenade [gri'neid] n. MILIT. Grenade *f.*
grenadier [,grenə'diə*] n. MILIT. Grenadier *m.*
grenadine [,grenə'di:n] n. Grenadine *f.*
grew [gru:]. See GROW.
grey [grei] adj. Gris (colour); *to turn grey,* grisonner, blanchir (hair). ‖ ECCLES. *Grey friar,* franciscain. ‖ MED. Blême (complexion); gris (matter). ‖ FIG. Sombre (outlook). ‖ **Grey-headed,** adj. Aux cheveux gris, grisonnant, poivre et sel.
— n. Gris *m.* (colour). ‖ Ecru *m.* (for fabrics). ‖ ZOOL. Cheval gris *m.*
— v. tr., intr. Grisailler (colour); grisonner (hair).
greybeard [-biəd] n. Grison, barbon *m.*
greyhound [-haund] n. ZOOL. Levrette *f.* (bitch); lévrier *m.* (dog). ‖ NAUT. *Ocean greyhound,* paquebot rapide *m.*
greyish [-iʃ] adj. Grisâtre. ‖ ZOOL. Louvet.
greylag [-læg] n. ZOOL. Bernacle *f.* (goose).
greyness [-nis] n. Teinte grise, grisaille *f.*
grid [grid] n. Grille *f.* ‖ CULIN. Gril *m.* ‖ RADIO., TECHN. Grille *f.*
griddle ['gridl̩] n. TECHN. Crible *m.* ‖ CULIN. Tourtière *f.*
— v. tr. TECHN. Cribler. ‖ CULIN. Cuire à la tourtière.
griddlecake [-,keik] n. CULIN. U. S. Crêpe *f.*
gride [graid] v. intr. Grincer.
— n. Grincement *m.*
gridiron ['grid,aiən] n. NAUT., THEATR., CULIN. Gril *m.* ‖ U. S. SPORTS. Terrain de football *m.*
grief [gri:f] n. Affliction, désolation *f.*; chagrin *m.*; *to come to grief,* avoir un accident; tourner mal, se trouver en mauvaise posture. ‖ **Grief-stricken,** adj. Désolé, navré.
grievance ['gri:vəns] n. JUR. Doléance *f.* (complaint); injustice *f.*; tort *m.* (detriment); grief *m.* (ground for complaint); *to have a grievance against,* avoir à se plaindre de (or) un grief contre.
grieve [gri:v] v. tr. Affliger, désoler, peiner; chagriner; *it grieves me to,* il me coûte de, cela me peine (or) chagrine de.
— v. intr. S'affliger, se désoler (*at,* de).
grievous [-əs] adj. Douloureux (cry); cruel (loss); affreux, pénible (news, pain). ‖ Atroce, odieux (crime); grave (error, fault).

grievously [-əsli] adv. Douloureusement, cruellement. ‖ Atrocement; grièvement.
griffin ['grifin] n. Nouveau venu *m.*
griffin n. Griffon *m.*
griffon ['grifən] n. ZOOL. Griffon *m.* (dog).
grift [grift] v. intr. U. S. FAM. Magouiller, trafiquer, tripoter.
— n. U. S. FAM. Magouille *f.*; trafic, tripotage *m.*
grig [grig] n. † ZOOL. Grillon *m.* (cricket); anguille *f.* (eel). ‖ FAM. U. S. Vif-argent *m.* (person).
grill [gril] v. tr. CULIN. Griller, faire griller. ‖ JUR. Cuisiner. ‖ FIG. Mettre sur le gril (or) sur des charbons ardents.
— v. intr. CULIN. Griller. ‖ FIG. Etre sur le gril.
— n. CULIN. Gril *m.* (gridiron); grillade *f.* (food). ‖ **Grill-room,** n. Grill-room *m.*; rôtisserie *f.*
grill(e) [gril] n. Grille *f.* (of convent parlour); judas *m.* (of a door).
grilse [grils] n. ZOOL. Saumoneau *m.*
grim [grim] adj. Macabre, sinistre, lugubre (ghastly). ‖ Menaçant, sévère, redoutable (threatening). ‖ Résolu, intrépide (relentless). ‖ Impitoyable, inexorable, inflexible (pitiless).
grimace [gri'meis] n. Grimace *f.*
— v. intr. Grimacer. ‖ FIG. Faire des grimaces.
grimalkin [gri'mælkin] n. Raminagrobis, mistigri *m.* (cat). ‖ Vieille chouette (or) toupie *f.* (woman).
grime [graim] n. Saleté *f.*; noir *m.* (sooty dirt).
— v. tr. Salir, noircir.
griminess [-inis] n. Saleté, noirceur *f.*
grimly ['grimli] adv. D'un air sinistre (or) menaçant. ‖ Inflexiblement, inexorablement. ‖ Avec acharnement.
grimness [-nis] n. Air sinistre (or) menaçant *m.*; aspect macabre *m.* ‖ Implacabilité, inflexibilité *f.* ‖ Acharnement *m.*
grimy [-i] adj. Sale, noir, barbouillé de noir.
grin [grin] v. intr. (1). Rire à belles dents (in joy); grimacer un sourire (in pain); ricaner (in scorn).
— v. tr. Exprimer par un sourire (or) une grimace.
— n. Large sourire *m.* (smile); ricanement *m.* (sneer); grimace *f.* (wry face).
grind [graind] v. tr. (73). Ecraser, broyer, piler (to crush). ‖ Moudre, concasser (to pulverize). ‖ Grincer; racler; *to grind one's teeth,* grincer des dents. ‖ MUS., FAM. Moudre. ‖ TECHN. Meuler (chisel, lens); égriser (diamonds). ‖ FAM. Rabâcher, ressasser, seriner; *to grind a lesson into a boy's head,* enfoncer une leçon dans la tête d'un enfant en la lui serinant.
— v. intr. S'écraser, se broyer, se piler. ‖ Se moudre, se concasser. ‖ Grincer; racler. ‖ TECHN. S'aiguiser, s'affûter. ‖ FAM. Potasser, bûcher, piocher, buriner.
— n. Broyage *m.* ‖ Moulure *f.* ‖ Grincement, raclement *m.* ‖ TECHN. Affûtage *m.* ‖ SPORTS. Steeplechase *m.*; marche pénible *f.* (walk). ‖ FAM. Turbinage, boulot *m.* (drudgery). ‖ U. S. FAM. Bûcheur *m.*
grinder [-ə*] n. Broyeur *m.* ‖ TECHN. Rémouleur *m.* (person); affûteuse *f.* (tool). ‖ MED. Molaire *f.* (tooth).
grindstone [-stoun] n. TECHN. Meule *f.* ‖ FAM. *To have one's nose to the grindstone,* buriner sans dételer, ne pas lever le nez de sur le boulot.
gringo ['griŋgou] (pl. gringos [-z]) n. Gringo, Ricain *m.*
grip [grip] n. Etreinte *f.* (See GRASP.) ‖ Poignée *f.* (handle). ‖ Prise *f.*; *to get to grips,* en venir aux prises. ‖ TECHN. Serrage *m.* ‖ FIG. Compréhension, pénétration *f.* (mental grasp); emprise *f.* (mastery); *to lose one's grip on the situation,* perdre pied. ‖ FAM. U. S. Trousse, petite valise *f.*
— v. tr. Etreindre, empoigner. ‖ Serrer; *to grip hold of,* s'agripper à. ‖ FIG. Saisir, étreindre, empoigner.
gripe [graip] v. tr. Etreindre, empoigner. (See GRASP.) ‖ MED. Donner des coliques à. ‖ TECHN.

Gripper. ‖ NAUT. Amarrer. ‖ FIG. Etreindre, tordre. — v. intr. MED. Avoir des coliques. ‖ NAUT. Venir au vent. ‖ U. S. FAM. Maugréer, ronchonner, rouspéter (*at*. contre). — n. Etreinte, prise *f.* ‖ Poignée *f.* (handle). ‖ MED. Pl. Coliques, tranchées, épreintes *f. pl.* ‖ NAUT. Saisine *f.* ‖ FAM. U. S. Rouspétance *f.*

griper [-ə*] n. FAM. U. S. Ronchon, grognon, grogneur, bougon *m.*

gripsack ['gripsæk] n. U. S. Valise *f.*

griskin ['griskin] n. CULIN. Echine (*f.*) de porc.

grisly ['grizli] adj. Horrible, effroyable (terrifying). ‖ Macabre, sinistre, lugubre (ghastly).

grist [grist] n. AGRIC. Blé (*m.*) à moudre (grain). ‖ Brai *m.* (in brewing). ‖ FIG. Profit *m.; all is grist that comes to his mill,* il fait flèche de tout bois. ‖ FAM. U. S. Quantité *f.*

gristle ['grisl] n. Cartilage *m.*

gristly ['grisli] adj. Cartilagineux.

grit [grit] n. Gravier *m.* (gravel); sable *m.* (sand). ‖ Grès *m.* (gritstone). ‖ Grain *m.* (of a stone). ‖ FAM. Cran *m.* — v. intr. Crisser, craquer. — v. tr. Sabler. ‖ FIG. *To grit one's teeth,* grincer des dents (in anger); serrer les dents, tenir bon (in determination).

grits [-s] n. pl. CULIN. Gruau (*m.*) d'avoine; U. S. gruau de maïs *m.*

gritty [-i] adj. Graveleux; sablonneux. ‖ BOT. Grumeleux (pear). ‖ FIG. Rocailleux. ‖ U. S. Plein de cran.

grizzle ['grizl] v. intr. FAM. Pleurnicher.

grizzled [-d] adj. Gris, grisonnant, poivre et sel (hair).

grizzly [-li] adj. Gris, grisonnant (hair, person). ‖ ZOOL. Gris, grizzlé (bear). — n. ZOOL. Ours gris *m.*

groan [groun] v. intr. Gémir, se plaindre (*beneath, under, with,* de, à cause de). ‖ Grogner (in disapproval). ‖ FIG. Soupirer (*for,* après); languir (*for,* de). — v. tr. **To groan down,** faire taire en grognant. ‖ **To groan out,** raconter en gémissant. — n. Gémissement *m.;* plainte *f.* ‖ Grognement, murmure *m.*

groat [grout] n. Sou *m.*

groats [grouts] n. pl. CULIN. Gruau (*m.*) d'avoine (or) de froment.

grocer ['grousə*] n. COMM. Epicier *s.; at the grocer's,* à l'épicerie.

grocery [-ri] n. COMM. Epicerie f. (business, supplies). ‖ U. S. Epicerie *f.* (shop).

grog [grɔg] n. Grog *m.* ‖ **Grog-blossom,** n. FAM. Bourgeon *m.* (on the nose). ‖ **Grog-blossomed,** adj. FAM. Bourgeonné. ‖ **Grog-shop,** n. FAM. Bistrot, caboulot *m.* — v. intr. (1). Boire. — v. tr. Ebouillanter (a cask).

groggy [-i] adj. Gris, éméché, parti (tipsy). ‖ Habitué à boire (bibulous). ‖ Chancelant, titubant, vacillant; sonné (fam.) [shaky]. ‖ ZOOL. Faible des jambes de cheval (horse).

grogram ['grɔgrəm] n. Gros-grain *m.*

groin [grɔin] n. MED. Aine *f.* ‖ ARCHIT. Nervure *f.* (fillet); arête *f.* (rib).

groin n. U. S. See GROYNE.

groined [-d] adj. ARCHIT. A arêtes, en arcsdoubleaux (vault).

grommet ['grɔmit] n. See GRUMMET.

groom [grum] n. Valet (*m.*) d'écurie, palefrenier *m.* ‖ Gentilhomme (*m.*) de la chambre du roi. ‖ FAM. Marié *m.* (bridegroom). — v. tr. Panser (a horse). ‖ FAM. Soigner, astiquer, bichonner. ‖ FAM. *To groom s.o. for stardom,* préparer qqn à devenir vedette.

groomsman [-zmən] n. Garçon d'honneur *m.*

groove [gru:v] n. Rainure *f.* (See FURROW.) ‖

TECHN. Gorge *f.* (of a piston, pulley). ‖ ARCHIT. Cannelure *f.* (of a column). ‖ MUS. Sillon *m.* (of a record). ‖ FAM. Routine *f.* ‖ POP. U. S. *In the groove,* comme sur des roulettes. — v. tr. Canneler, rayer.

grooving [-iŋ] n. Rainurage *m.* ‖ Cannelure *f.* ‖ **Grooving-plane,** TECHN. Bouvet (*m.*).

groovy [-vi] adj. POP. Sensas, chouette, bath (excellent); dans le vent (fashionable).

grope [group] v. intr. Tâtonner; *to grope for,* chercher à tâtons; *to grope one's way,* chercher son chemin (or) avancer à tâtons.

gros-grain ['grougrein] n. Gros-grain *m.* (ribbon).

gross [grous] n. Grosse *f.* (twelve dozen).

gross adj. Gros, gras, obèse, très fort (too fat). ‖ Dense, épais (thick). ‖ Brut; en gros, total. ‖ CULIN. Grossier. ‖ FIG. Grossier, flagrant, aveuglant (glaring); grossier, grivois, cru, indécent (obscene); grossier, fruste, sans délicatesse, lourd (unrefined). ‖ **Gross national product,** n. FIN. Produit national brut, P. N. B. *m.* — n. *In the gross,* en gros, en bloc. ‖ U. S. Recette brute *f.* — v. tr. U. S. Produire en recette brute.

grossly [-li] adv. Grossièrement.

grossness [-nis] n. Enormité *f.* (of a crime). ‖ Grossièreté *f.* (of language).

grotesque [gro'tesk] adj. ARCHIT., FIG. Grotesque. — n. Grotesque *m.*

grotto ['grɔtou] (pl. **grottoes, grottos** [-z]) n. Grotte *f.*

grotty ['grɔti] adj. POP. Dégueulasse, cradingue (dirty); moche, tocard (ugly).

grouch [grautʃ] n. FAM. U. S. Rouspéteur *s.* — v. intr. FAM. U. S. Rouspéter, ronchonner.

grouchy [-i] adj. Ronchon.

ground [graund] adj. Dépoli (glass); à l'émeri (stopper). ‖ CULIN. Moulu (coffee). ‖ See GRIND.

ground n. Terre *f.* (earth); sol *m.*, terre *f.* (soil). ‖ Terrain *m.* (piece of land). ‖ Pl. Parc *m.* (attached to house). ‖ GEOGR. Territoire, sol *m.* ‖ SPORTS. Terrain. ‖ ARTS. Fond *m.* (background). ‖ NAUT. Fond (of the sea). ‖ ELECTR. Terre *f.* ‖ CULIN. Pl. Marc *m.* (of coffee). [See DREGS.] ‖ JUR. Pl. Considérants *m. pl.* ‖ FIG. Terrain, sujet, champ (*m.*) d'étude; *forbidden ground,* terrain interdit ; *to break up new ground,* donner le premier coup de pioche ; *to lose ground,* perdre du terrain. ‖ FIG. Position *f.; he stood his ground well,* il s'est bien défendu ; il a bien tenu son bout (fam.). ‖ FIG. Fondement *m.;* base, assise *f.* (basis) ; raison *f.;* motif *m.* (motive) ; *from the ground up,* de bout en bout ; *on the ground that,* sous prétexte que ; *to touch ground,* toucher terre, trouver une assiette solide. ‖ FAM. *Above ground,* en vie ; *to go over the same ground,* chanter toujours la même antienne ; *to suit s.o. down to the ground,* faire l'affaire de qqn. ‖ **Ground-bait,** n. SPORTS. Amorce (*f.*) de fond ; v. tr. Amorcer. ‖ **Ground-bass,** n. MUS. Basse contrainte *f.* ‖ **Ground-beacon,** n. AVIAT. Balise *f.* ‖ **Ground-clearance,** n. AVIAT. Distance (*f.*) au sol. ‖ **Ground-colour,** n. Première couche *f.* (in painting) ; ARTS. Teinte (*f.*) de fond. ‖ **Ground-crew, ground-staff,** n. AVIAT. Personnel rampant *m.* ‖ **Ground-floor,** n. Rez-(*m.*)-de-chaussée ; COMM. *Ground-floor price,* dernier prix ; FIG. *To get in on the ground-floor,* se mettre à pied d'œuvre dès le début. ‖ **Ground-game,** n. SPORTS. Gibier à poil *m.* ‖ **Ground-hog,** n. ZOOL. U. S. Marmotte d'Amérique *f.;* FAM. *Ground-hog day,* la Chandeleur. ‖ **Ground-landlord,** n. Propriétaire foncier *m.* ‖ **Ground-line,** n. ELECTR. Ligne de terre *f.;* ARTS. Ligne (*f.*) de fond. ‖ **Ground-note,** n. MUS. Tonique *f.* ‖ **Ground-nut,** n. Arachide *f.* ‖ **Ground-organization,** n. AVIAT. Infrastructure. *f.* ‖ **Ground-pine,** n. BOT. Ivette *f.* ‖ **Ground-plan,** n. ARCHIT. Plan horizontal *m.;* FIG. Plan (*m.*) de

base. ‖ **Ground-plate**, n. ELECTR. Prise de terre
f. ‖ **Ground-rent**, n. JUR. Redevance foncière f. ‖
Ground-sea, n. NAUT. Mer grosse (f.) sur les côtes.
‖ **Ground-speed**, n. AVIAT. Vitesse (f.) au sol. ‖
Ground-swell, n. NAUT. Lame (f.) de fond. ‖
Ground-wire, n. ELECTR. Fil (m.) de terre.
— v. tr. ARTS. Faire un fond à. ‖ MILIT. Reposer
(arms). ‖ NAUT. Echouer (a ship). ‖ ELECTR. Mettre
à la terre. ‖ U. S. AVIAT. Empêcher de voler. ‖
FIG. Fonder, asseoir, appuyer (on, sur).
— v. intr. NAUT. S'échouer. ‖ AVIAT. Se poser,
atterrir. ‖ FIG. Well grounded in, ayant des connaissances solides en.
groundage [-idʒ] n. NAUT. Droits (m. pl.) de
mouillage.
grounding [-iŋ] n. NAUT. Echouage m. ‖ FIG.
Assise f. (of an argument); base, connaissance fondamentale f. (in, en).
groundless [-lis] adj. Dénué de fondement, mal
fondé, sans motif, gratuit.
groundlessness [-lisnis] n. Absence (f.) de fondement (or) de raison.
groundling [-liŋ] n. ZOOL. Loche f.; poisson de
fond m. ‖ BOT. Plante rampante f. ‖ THEATR.
† Spectateur (s.) du parterre. ‖ AVIAT. Rampant m.
‖ FAM. Menu fretin m.
groundsel ['graunsəl] n. BOT. Séneçon m.
groundsheet ['graund,ʃiːt] n. Tapis de sol m.
(in a tent).
groundwork ['graundwəːk] n. ARTS. Fond m. ‖
FIG. Plan, canevas m. (of a novel); fondement m.;
base, assise f. (of a society).
group [gruːp] n. Groupe m.; to form a group, se
grouper. ‖ ARTS. Ensemble m. (of colours). ‖
MATH. Tranche f. (of figures). ‖ GEOGR. Massif m.
(of mountains). ‖ CH. DE F. Faisceau m. (of sidings).
‖ MED. Blood group, groupe sanguin. ‖ PSYCH. Group
therapy, thérapie de groupe.
— v. tr. Grouper.
— v. intr. Se grouper.
groupage [-idʒ], **grouping** [-iŋ] n. Groupement m.
groupie ['gruːpi] n. POP. Groupie f., fervente (f.)
de groupes pop.
grouse [graus] n. invar. ZOOL. Grouse, tétras, coq
(m.) de bruyère.
grouse v. intr. FAM. Rouspéter, récriminer.
— n. Raison (f.) de se plaindre; grief m. ‖ FAM.
Rogne f.
grout [graut] n. Mortier liquide m.
— v. tr. ARCHIT. Couler, sceller au ciment.
grout v. tr., intr. Fouir.
grove [grouv] n. Bocage, bosquet m.
grovel ['grɔvl] v. intr. (1). Se vautrer, se traîner
(in, dans). ‖ FIG. Ramper, s'aplatir, courber l'échine
(before, to, devant).
groveller [-ə*] n. FIG. Chien couchant m.
grovelling [-iŋ] adj. FIG. Rampant.
— n. FIG. Aplatissement m.
grow [grou] v. intr. (74). BOT. Pousser, croître. ‖
MED. Grandir, se développer (body, person). ‖ FIG.
Augmenter, croître, grandir, se développer. ‖ FIG.
Devenir; to grow better, s'améliorer; to grow dark,
s'obscurcir; to grow old, vieillir; to grow weary,
se fatiguer. ‖ FAM. They don't grow on every tree,
ça ne se trouve pas à la douzaine (or) dans le pas
d'une mule. ‖ **To grow down**, pousser à l'envers;
FIG. Décroître. ‖ **To grow in**, pousser en dedans;
FIG. S'incruster. ‖ **To grow into**, devenir (a man).
‖ **To grow on**, s'imposer à; agir peu à peu sur;
plaire de plus en plus à. ‖ **To grow out of**, devenir
trop grand pour (one's clothes); perdre en grandissant (a habit). ‖ **To grow to**, parvenir à, arriver à (manhood). ‖ **To grow up**, devenir adulte;
atteindre la maturité; FIG. Se répandre, se développer.
— v. tr. AGRIC. Faire pousser (or) venir, cultiver,
faire. ‖ Laisser pousser (one's beard).

grower [-ə*] n. AGRIC. Cultivateur, producteur m.;
direct from the grower, de provenance directe, du
producteur au consommateur. ‖ BOT. Plante d'une
certaine croissance f.
growing [-iŋ] n. MED., BOT. Croissance f. ‖ AGRIC.
Culture f.
growl [graul] v. intr. Grogner, gronder (at, contre)
[dog]. ‖ FIG. Grogner, ronchonner.
— v. tr. Grogner, grommeler.
— n. Grognement m.
growler [-ə*] n. FAM. Grognon, ronchon m. (See
GRUMBLER.) ‖ FAM. Fiacre m. ‖ U. S. Tonnelet (m.)
de bière, grosse cannette f.
grown [groun]. See GROW. ‖ Grown over with,
couvert de. ‖ **Grown-up**, n. Adulte m.; grande personne f.
growth [grouθ] n. BOT. Pousse, croissance f. (act);
récolte f. (of corn); cuvée f., cru m. (of wine); végétation f.; second growth, regain. ‖ MED. Croissance f. (of a person); excroissance, tumeur, grosseur f. (tumour); new growth, néoplasme. ‖ COMM.
Développement m.; extension f. ‖ FIG. Accroissement m.
groyne [grɔin] n. TECHN. Epi m. (along a shore).
grub [grʌb] n. ZOOL. Larve f.; asticot m. (fam.).
‖ FAM. Trimardeur m. (drudge); gratte-papier m.
(literary hack). ‖ POP. Boustifaille f. (food). ‖ U. S.
Bûcheur s. (at school). ‖ **Grub-screw**, n. Vis sans
tête f. ‖ **Grub-street**, n. Monde du bas journalisme m.
— v. tr. (1). Fouir, bêcher; to grub up, défricher
(the soil); déterrer (sth.). ‖ FAM. Donner à manger à (to feed).
— v. intr. Fouir, fouiller (among, dans). ‖ FAM.
To grub along, trimer, peiner. ‖ POP. Bouffer, boulotter (to eat).
grubber [-ə*] n. AGRIC. Défricheur s. (person);
extirpateur m. (tool). ‖ FAM. Bûcheur s. (at school).
‖ POP. Dévorant, bouffeur s.
grubbing [-iŋ] n. AGRIC. Défrichement, essouche-
ment m. ‖ **Grubbing-hoe**, n. AGRIC. Hoyau m.
grubby [-i] adj. AGRIC. Véreux. ‖ FIG. Sale, malpropre, crasseux.
grubstake [-steik] n. U. S. FAM. Commandite f.
— v. tr. U. S. FAM. Commanditer.
grudge [grʌdʒ] v. tr. Donner à contrecœur (or) en
rechignant; plaindre (fam.); to grudge s.o. sth.,
lésiner sur qqch. à l'égard de qqn. ‖ Voir d'un
mauvais œil; to grudge s.o. a privilege, reprocher
un privilège à qqn.
— n. Rancune f.; to bear grudges, garder rancune,
nourrir une rancune; to bear s.o. a grudge, en vouloir à qqn.
grudging [-iŋ] adj. Accordé à regret (gift); lésineur, chiche (person).
grudgingly [-iŋli] adv. A contrecœur, à regret, en
rechignant.
gruel [gruəl] n. CULIN. Gruau m. ‖ FAM. Trempe f.
— v. tr. (1). FAM. Ereinter.
gruelling [-iŋ] adj. Ereintant (race).
— n. FAM. Raclée f.
gruesome ['gruːsəm] adj. Horrible, terrifiant, horrifiant (grisly). ‖ Macabre, lugubre (ghastly).
gruff [grʌf] adj. Rude, brusque, bourru, revêche.
gruffness [-nis] n. Brusquerie f.
grumble ['grʌmbl] v. intr. Grogner, grommeler,
ronchonner, bougonner, marmonner; maugréer (at,
contre). ‖ Se plaindre (about, de).
— v. tr. To grumble sth. out, grommeler (or) marmonner qqch.
— n. Grognement m.; bougonnerie f.; murmure m.
‖ FAM. Pl. To have the grumbles, être de mauvais poil.
grumbler [-ə*] n. Ronchon, bougon, grognard m.
grumbling [-iŋ] adj. Ronchon.
grumblingly [-iŋli] adv. En ronchonnant.

grume [gru:m] n. MED. Caillot *m*. (of blood); liquide visqueux *m*.

grummet ['grʌmit] n. NAUT. Erse *f*. ‖ TECHN. Œillet, passe-fil *m*. ‖ MILIT. Bourdalou *m*. (in cap).

grumous [-əs] adj. MED. Coagulé (blood). ‖ CULIN. Grumeleux.

grumpish ['grʌmpiʃ], **grumpy** [-i] adj. Grincheux, maussade, renfrogné, grognon.

Grundy ['grʌndi] n. *Mrs. Grundy*, l'esprit bégueule, le genre collet monté.

grundyism [-izm] n. Inquiétude (*f.*) du qu'en-dira-t-on *m.*; pudibonderie *f*.

grunt [grʌnt] n. ZOOL., FIG. Grognement *m*.
— v. intr., tr. ZOOL., FIG. Grogner. ‖ FAM. Râler.

grunter [-ə*] n. ZOOL., FAM. Cochon *m*. ‖ FIG. Grognard, grogneur *s*. ‖ U. S. FAM. Lutteur *m*.

grunting [-iŋ] adj. Grogneur, grognon.

gruntingly [-iŋli] adv. En grognant.

gryphon ['grifn] n. Griffon *m*.

guana ['gwɑ:nə] n. ZOOL. Iguane *m*.

guano ['gwɑ:nou] (pl. **guanos** [-z]) n. ZOOL., AGRIC. Guano *m*.
— v. tr. AGRIC. Fertiliser avec du guano.

guarantee [ˌgærən'ti:] n. JUR. Cautionné *m*. (person); garant, répondant *m.*; caution *f*. (pledge); garantie *f.*; aval *m*. (security); *guarantee funds*, fonds de garantie.
— v. tr. JUR. Garantir, cautionner (s.o.); avaliser (sth.). ‖ COMM. *Guaranteed vintage*, appellation contrôlée. ‖ FIG. Répondre de (one's conduct); garantir, assurer (*that*, que).

guarantor [ˌgærən'tɔ:*] n. JUR. Garant *m*.

guaranty ['gærənti] n. JUR. Garantie de paiement *f*.

guard [gɑ:d] n. Garde, surveillance *f*. (act); garde *m*. (person); garde, protection *f*. (safeguard). ‖ MILIT. Garde *m*. (soldier); garde *f*. (troop); *on guard at*, de garde à; *to mount guard*, monter la garde. ‖ CH. DE F. Chef de train *m*. ‖ SPORTS. Garde *f*. (in boxing, fencing). ‖ TECHN. Dispositif (*m.*) de sûreté (in machinery); garde *f*. (of a sword). ‖ FIG. Gardes *f. pl.; off one's guard*, au dépourvu; *on one's guard*, sur ses gardes; *to put s.o. on his guard against*, mettre qqn en garde contre. ‖ **Guard-boat**, n. NAUT. Patrouilleur *m*. ‖ **Guard-chain**, n. Chaîne de montre *f*. (for men); sautoir *m*. (for women). ‖ **Guard-house** (or) **-room**, n. MILIT. Corps (*m.*) de garde (for military guard); salle de police *f*. (for prisoners). ‖ **Guard-iron**, n. CH. DE F. Chasse-pierres *m*. ‖ **Guard-net**, n. ELECTR. Filet protecteur *m*. ‖ **Guard-rail**, n. Garde-fou *m.;* CH. DE F. Contre-rail *m*. ‖ **Guard-ship**, n. NAUT. Stationnaire *m*.
— v. tr. Garder, protéger (*against, from*, contre). [See PROTECT.] ‖ Garder, escorter, mettre sous bonne garde (a prisoner). ‖ TECH. Protéger. ‖ FIG. Surveiller (one's words); mettre en garde (*against, from*, contre) [s.o.]; *to guard oneself*, se tenir sur ses gardes.
— v. intr. Se garder, se méfier (*against*, de); se prémunir (*against*, contre).

guarded [-id] adj. Prudent, circonspect (answer, speech). ‖ TECHN. Protégé. ‖ JUR. Gardé à vue (prisoner).

guardedly [-idli] adv. Sans se découvrir, avec circonspection (or) réserve.

guardian ['gɑ:djən] n. Gardien, protecteur *m*. ‖ JUR. Tuteur *m.;* tutrice *f*. (of a minor); conservateur *m.;* conservatrice *f*. (of a museum).
— adj. ECCLES. Gardien (angel). ‖ FIG. Tutélaire.

guardianship [-ʃip] n. JUR. Tutelle, curatelle *f*. (of a minor); conservation *f*. (of a museum). ‖ FIG. Protection *f*.

guardsman ['gɑ:dzmən] (pl. **guardsmen**) n. MILIT. Soldat (*m.*) de la Garde.

Guatemala ['gwɑtəmɑ:lə] n. GEOGR. Guatemala *m*.

guava ['gwɑ:və] n. BOT. Goyave *f*. (fruit); goyavier *m*. (tree).

gubernatorial [ˌgju:bənə'tɔ:riəl] adj. De gouverneur. ‖ U. S. Gouvernemental. ‖ FAM. Paternel.

gudgeon ['gʌdʒən] n. ZOOL. Goujon *m*. ‖ FAM. Jobard *m*.

gudgeon n. TECHN. Tourillon *m*. ‖ ARCHIT. Goujon *m*.

guelder rose ['geldə'rouz] n. BOT. Boule-de-neige *f*.

guerdon ['gə:dən] n. Récompense *f*.

Guernsey ['gə:nzi] n. GEOGR. Guernesey. ‖ NAUT. Jersey *m.;* vareuse *f*. ‖ ZOOL. Guernesey (cattle).

gue(r)rilla [gə'rilə] n. MILIT. Guérillero *m.; guerilla warfare*, war, guérilla.

guess [ges] n. Supposition, conjecture *f.; I give you a thousand guesses*, je vous le donne en mille; *to make a guess at*, se livrer à des suppositions au sujet de. ‖ Trouvaille *f.; easy guess*, devinette facile; *lucky guess*, hypothèse heureuse. ‖ U. S. Avis *m.;* opinion *f.; my guess is that*, je pense que. ‖ **Guess-work**, n. Empirisme *m.;* simple conjecture *f.; by guess-work*, au jugé.
— v. tr., intr. Supposer, conjecturer. (See SURMISE.) ‖ Deviner, trouver; *to guess right*, deviner juste. ‖ Estimer, évaluer (to estimate). ‖ U. S. Penser, croire; *I guess so!*, peut-être bien!; c'est mon avis!

guess-rope ['ges,roup], **guest-rope** ['gest,roup] n. NAUT. Câble (*m.*) de remorque, faux bras *m*.

gues(s)timate ['gestimit] n. FAM. Estimation, conjecture, supposition *f.; at a guesstimate*, à vue de nez.

guest [gest] n. Invité, convive, hôte *m*. (at s.o.'s table). ‖ Pensionnaire *s*. (in a boarding-house); client *m*. (in a hotel). ‖ Membre invité *m*. (in a club). ‖ **Guest-house**, n. Pension de famille *f*. ‖ **Guest-room**, n. Chambre (*f.*) d'ami.

guff [gʌf] n. POP. Foutaises, bêtises *f. pl*.

guffaw [gʌ'fɔ:] n. Gros rire *m*.
— v. intr. Rire bruyamment.
— v. tr. Dire avec un gros rire.

guggle ['gʌgl] v. intr. Glousser. (See GURGLE.)

Guiana [gi'ɑ:nə] n. GEOGR. Guyane *f*.

guidable ['gaidəbl] adj. Guidable.

guidance [-əns] n. Conduite, direction, dictée *f*. ‖ Gouverne *f*. ‖ Guidage *m*. (of a rocket).

guide [gaid] n. Guide *m*. (book, person, scout); *writing guide*, transparent. ‖ TECHN. Glissière *f*. ‖ MILIT. Guide *m*. ‖ FIG. Indication *f*. ‖ **Guide-dog**, n. Chien (*s.*) d'aveugle. ‖ **Guide-line**, n. Principe, principe directeur *m*. ‖ **Guide-post**, n. Poteau indicateur *m*. ‖ **Guide-rope**, n. AVIAT. Guiderope *m*.
— v. tr. Guider, diriger. ‖ AVIAT. Piloter.

guided [-id] adj. Guidé. ‖ AVIAT. *Guided missile*, engin téléguidé.

guidon ['gaidən] n. MILIT. Guidon *m*.

guild [gild] n. Guilde *f*.

guildhall ['gild'hɔ:l] n. Hôtel (*m.*) de ville.

guile [gail] n. Ruse, astuce *f*. (cunning). ‖ Fourberie, tromperie *f*. (deceit).

guileful [-ful] adj. Rusé, astucieux (cunning). ‖ Fourbe, trompeur (deceitful).

guilefully [-fuli] adv. Avec ruse (or) fourberie.

guileless [-lis] adj. Sans astuce, candide, naïf. ‖ Franc, loyal.

guilelessness [-lisnis] n. Candeur, innocence, naïveté *f*. ‖ Franchise *f*.

guillemot ['gilimɔt] n. ZOOL. Guillemot *m*.

guillotine ['giloti:n] n. Guillotine *f*. (lit. and fig.).
— v. tr. Guillotiner. ‖ FIG. Passer à la guillotine.

guilt [gilt] n. Culpabilité *f*. ‖ † Crime *m*.

guiltily [-ili] adv. Coupablement; d'un air coupable.

guiltiness [-inis] n. Culpabilité *f*.

guiltless [-lis] adj. Innocent. ‖ FAM. N'ayant aucune expérience, ignorant (*of*, de); *guiltless of moustache*, vierge de toute moustache.

guiltlessness [-lisnis] n. Innocence *f*.

guilty [-i] adj. Coupable (*of*, de) [see CULPABLE];

found guilty, reconnu coupable. ‖ Coupable (act) ; chargé, lourd, peu tranquille (conscience) ; de coupable (look).

guimp [gimp]. See GIMP.

Guinea ['gini] n. GEOGR., FIN. Guinée *f.* ‖ **Guinea-Bissau**, n. GEOGR. Guinée-Bissau *f.* ‖ **Guinea-fowl** (or) **-hen**, n. ZOOL. Pintade *f.* ‖ **Guinea-pig**, n. ZOOL., MED. Cobaye *m.* ; FAM. Administrateur (*m.*) de société tout juste bon à toucher ses jetons de présence.

guise ⌊gaiz] n. † Coutume, guise *f.* ‖ † Costume, vêtement *m.* (dress). ‖ Apparence *f.* ; aspect *m.* ‖ FIG. Masque, couvert, semblant *m.* (pretence).

guitar [gi'tɑ:*] n. MUS. Guitare *f.*

guitarist [-rist] n. MUS. Guitariste *s.*

gulch [gʌltʃ] n. U. S. Ravin *m.*

gules [gju:lz] n. BLAS. Gueules *m. pl.*
— adj. BLAS. De gueules.

gulf [gʌlf] n. GEOGR. Golfe *m.* ‖ FIG. Gouffre, abîme *m.*
— v. tr. Engouffrer, abîmer, engloutir.

gull [gʌl] n. ZOOL. Goéland *m.* ; mouette *f.*

gull n. FAM. Jobard, gobeur, dindon, gogo *m.* ; poire *f.*
— v. tr. Duper, refaire, rouler.

gullet ['gʌlit] n. MED. Œsophage *m.* ‖ GEOGR. Ravin, goulet *m.* ‖ NAUT. Goulet *m.* ‖ FAM. Gosier, kiki *m.* (throat).

gullibility ⌊,gʌli'biliti] n. FAM. Jobardise *f.*

gullible ['gʌlibl̩] adj. Crédule, jobard, gobeur ; *gullible man*, gobe-mouches.

gully ['gʌli] n. Rigole *f.* ; ruisseau *m.* ‖ GEOL. Couloir *m.* ‖ **Gully-hole**, n. Bouche (*f.*) d'égout.
— v. tr. Raviner.

gully n. Couteau de boucher *m.*

gulp [gʌlp] v. tr. Avaler, engloutir, enfourner, gober ; *to gulp down a drink*, lamper (or) s'envoyer un verre. ‖ FIG. *To gulp back* (or) *down*, ravaler, dévorer (one's tears).
— v. intr. Avoir la gorge serrée.
— n. Lampée, gorgée *f.* (drink) ; goulée, bouchée *f.* (food). ‖ Serrement (*m.*) de gorge.

gum ⌊gʌm] n. Gomme *f.* ; *gum arabic, dragon, gum benjamin*, ben-join. ‖ Gomme, résine *f.* (resin). ‖ Gomme, colle *f.* (glue). ‖ BOT. Gommier, eucalyptus (*m.*) (tree). ‖ COMM. U. S. Caoutchouc (rubber). ‖ U. S. Chewing-gum *m.* ‖ **Gum-tree**, n. BOT. Gommier *m.*
— v. tr. Gommer, coller. ‖ TECHN. *To gum up*, encrasser. ‖ U. S. *To gum up*, bousiller.
— v. intr. Sécréter de la gomme. ‖ TECHN. *To gum up*, s'encrasser.

gum n. MED. Gencive *f.*

gum n. FAM. *By gum!*, Sacrédié!, crénom!

gumbo ['gʌmbou] (pl. **gumbos** [-z]) n. BOT. Okra, gombo *m.* ‖ CULIN. Soupe (*f.*) au gombo. ‖ GRAMM. Créole (*m.*) de Louisiane.

gumboil ['gʌmbɔil] n. MED. Fluxion *f.* ; abcès (*m.*) aux gencives.

gumboot ['gʌm,bu:t] n. Botte (*f.*) en caoutchouc.

gumdrop [-drɔp] n. U. S. Boule de gomme *f.*

gumma ['gʌmə] n. MED. Gomme syphilitique *f.*

gummy ['gʌmi] adj. Gommeux ; collant. ‖ MED. Enflé (ankle) ; chassieux (eyes).

gumption ['gʌmpʃən] n. FAM. Jugeote *f.* ; bon sens *m.* (common sense) ; entregent, esprit (*m.*) de débrouillardise (enterprise).

gumshoe ['gʌmʃu:] n. U. S. FAM. Caoutchouc *m.* (overshoe). ‖ U. S. POP. Détective *m.*
— v. intr. U. S. POP. Espionner, marcher sans bruit.

gun ⌊gʌn] n. MILIT. Canon *m.* ; *multiple-barrel gun*, pièce à canons multiples. ‖ MILIT. Coup de canon *m.* (discharge). ‖ MILIT. Fusil *m.* (rifle) ; *automatic gun*, fusil mitrailleur automatique ; *air gun*, carabine à air comprimé. ‖ Pistolet *m.* (for painting). ‖ SPORTS. Chasseur, fusil *m.* (person). ‖ FAM. *Big gun*, gros bonnet, huile ; *to go great guns*, marcher

tambour battant ; *to stick to one's guns*, s'accrocher à ses positions. ‖ **Gun-barrel**, n. Canon de fusil *m.* ‖ **Gun-carriage**, n. Affût de canon *m.* ‖ **Gun-cotton**, n. Fulmicoton *m.* ‖ **Gun-crew**, n. MILIT. Peloton (*m.*) de pièce. ‖ **Gun-deck**, n. NAUT. Batterie *f.* ‖ **Gun-dog**, n. Chien (*m.*) de chasse. ‖ **Gun-fire**, n. MILIT. Tir (*m.*) d'artillerie. ‖ **Gun-layer**, n. MILIT. Pointeur *m.* ‖ **Gun-lock**, n. Platine (*f.*) de fusil. ‖ **Gun-metal**, n. Bronze (*m.*) à canon ; gris métallisé *m.* ‖ **Gun-port**, n. NAUT. Sabord *m.* ‖ **Gun-running**, n. Contrebande (*f.*) d'armes. ‖ **Gun-shy**, adj. Qui a peur des coups de feu. ‖ **Gun-sponge**, n. MILIT. Ecouvillon *m.* ‖ **Gun-stick**, n. Baguette (*f.*) de fusil. ‖ **Gun-vessel**, n. NAUT. Canonnière-aviso *f.*
— v. intr. U. S. SPORTS. *To gun after* (or) *for*, chasser au fusil. ‖ FAM. *To gun for s.o.*, pourchasser qqn.
— v. tr. U. S. *To gun* (to shoot). ‖ FAM. U. S. *To gun it*, appuyer sur le champignon.

gunboat [-bout] n. NAUT. Canonnière *f.* ‖ U. S. FAM. Pl. Bateaux *m. pl.* ; godasses *f. pl.* (shoes).

gunman [-mən] (pl. **gunmen**) n. U. S. Bandit, gangster *m.*

gunner [-ə*] n. MILIT. Canonnier, artilleur *m.* ‖ NAUT. Canonnier *m.* ‖ SPORTS. Chasseur, fusil *m.*

gunnery [-əri] n. MILIT. Canonnage, tir (*m.*) d'artillerie ; balistique *f.* ‖ TECH. Fabrication (*f.*) des canons.

gunny ['gʌni] n. Toile (*f.*) de jute ; *gunny sack*, sac en toile de jute.

gunpoint ['gʌn,pɔint] n. *At gunpoint*, sous la menace d'une arme à feu.

gunpowder ['gʌn,paudə*] n. MILIT. Poudre *f.* ‖ CULIN. Thé vert *m.* ‖ FAM. *He didn't invent gunpowder*, il n'a pas inventé le fil à couper le beurre.

gunshot [-ʃɔt] n. MILIT. Coup de feu *m.* (shot). ‖ Portée (*f.*) de canon (or) de fusil (range).

gunsmith [-smiθ] n. Armurier *m.*

gunwale ['gʌnl̩] n. NAUT. Plat-bord *m.*

guppy ['gʌpi] n. ZOOL. Guppy *m.*

gurgitation [,gə:dʒi'teiʃən] n. Bouillonnement *m.*

gurgle ['gə:gl] v. intr. Gargouiller (rain) ; murmurer, gazouiller (stream) ; glouglouter (water). ‖ Roucouler (person) ; *to gurgle with laughter*, rire gras ; glousser.
— n. Gargouillement *m.* (of rain) ; murmure *m.* (of stream) ; glouglou *m.* (of water). ‖ Roucoulement *m.* (of person).

gurnet ['gə:nit] n. ZOOL. Grondin *m.*

guru ['guru:] n. Gourou *m.*

gush [gʌʃ] v. intr. Bouillonner (blood, torrent) ; jaillir (spring) ; jaillir, ruisseler (tears). ‖ FAM. S'attendrir, faire des démonstrations.
— v. tr. Déverser, lancer des jets (water).
— n. Bouillonnement ; jaillissement *m.* ‖ FIG. Flot *m.* ‖ FAM. Effusion, exubérance, sensiblerie *f.*

gushing [-iŋ] adj. Jaillissant. ‖ FAM. Exubérant, démonstratif ; *gushing person*, embrasseur, faiseur de démonstrations.

gushingly [-iŋli] adj. En jaillissant. ‖ FAM. Avec effusion, chaleureusement.

gushy [-i] adj. Démonstratif.

gusset ['gʌsit] n. Soufflet *m.* (in a garment). ‖ ARCHIT. Cornière *f.* ‖ BLAS. Gousset *m.*

gust [gʌst] n. Jet *m.* (of flames) ; bouffée *f.* (of smoke) ; *gust of rain*, ondée *f.* ; *gust of wind*, coup de vent, grain, bourrasque. ‖ FIG. Accès *m.* (of laughter, rage).
— v. intr. Souffler par rafales.

gustation [gʌs'teiʃən] n. Gustation *f.*

gusto ['gʌstou] n. Goût, plaisir *m.* ; *with gusto*, avec délectation.

gusty [-i] adj. Venteux, orageux (weather). ‖ FIG. Emballé, vif (temper).

gut [gʌt] n. ZOOL. Boyaux, intestin *m.* ‖ MUS. Corde *f.* ‖ GEOGR. Boyau, goulet *m.* ‖ FAM. Pl. Panse, bedaine *f.* ; *to knife s.o. in the guts*, crever la pail-

lasse à qqn. ‖ Fam. Pl. Cran, estomac *m.* (pluck);
to have no guts, n'avoir rien dans le ventre.
— adj. Fondamental, vital (issue); viscéral (reaction).
— v. tr. (1). Zool. Déboyauter, éviscérer, étriper
(an animal); vider (fish). ‖ Fig. Extraire la substance de (a book); ne laisser que les quatre murs de
(a house).
gutsy ['gʌtsi] adj. Fam. Goinfre, glouton (greedy);
courageux, qui a du cran (brave); passionné, qui
parle aux tripes (soulful).
gutta-percha ['gʌtə'pə:tʃə] n. Gutta-percha *f.*
gutter ['gʌtə*] n. Gouttière *f.* (under a roof). ‖
Caniveau *m.* (along a road); ruisseau *m.* (in a
street). ‖ Rigole *f.* (drain). ‖ Rainure *f.* (groove). ‖
Fam. Ruisseau *m.;* boue *f. to pick a living in the
gutter,* chercher sa vie dans les poubelles. ‖ **Gutter-
snipe,** n. Voyou *m.* (adult); gamin (*m.*) des rues,
poulbot, gavroche, titi *m.* (child). ‖ **Gutter-press,** n.
Presse (*f.*) de bas étage.
— v. intr. Couler (candle); s'écouler en ruisseaux
(water).
— v. tr. Mettre des gouttières à (a house). ‖ Raviner, sillonner (the soil).
guttural ['gʌtərəl] adj. Gramm. Guttural.
— n. Gramm. Gutturale *f.*
guv [gʌv], **guv'nor** ['gʌvnə] n. Fam. Patron,
chef *m.* (boss); paternel, vieux *m.* (father).
guy [gai] n. Naut. Hauban, gui, étai *m.*
— v. tr. Naut. Haubaner.
guy n. Fam. Epouvantail *m.;* personne mal ficelée *f.*
‖ Fam. *To do a guy,* filer; *to give s.o. the guy,* planter là qqn. ‖ Fam. U. S. Type, citoyen, zèbre *m.;
great guy,* type épatant; *a regular guy,* un gars
comme il faut.
— v. tr. Faire une effigie de. ‖ Theatr. Charger
(a part). ‖ Fig. Tourner en ridicule (to josh); faire
marcher (to tease).
— v. intr. Fam. Décamper, filer.
Guyana [gai'ænə] n. Geogr. Guyana *f.*
guzzle ['gʌzḷ] v. tr. Fam. Lamper, siffler (drink);
bâfrer, bouffer (food).
— v. intr. Fam. Pomper (to drink); goinfrer (to eat).
guzzler [-ə*] n. Fam. Soiffard, pochard *s.* (drunkard); goinfre *m.* (gormandizer).
gybe [dʒaib] n. Naut. Empannage *m.*
— v. tr. Naut. Gambéyer (a sail).
— v. intr. Naut. Gambéyer (sail); empanner (ship).

gyle [gail] n. Brassin *m.*
gym [dʒim] n. Sports, Fam. Gymnastique *f.* (exercises); gymnase *m.* (hall); *gym shoes,* chaussures de
tennis.
gymkhana [dʒim'ka:nə] n. Sports. Concours hippique *m.* ‖ Autom. Gymkhana *m.*
gymnasium [dʒim'neizjəm] n. Sports. Gymnase
m. ‖ Lycée allemand *m.*
— N. B. Deux pluriels : *gymnasiums, gymnasia.*
gymnast ['dʒimnæst] n. Sports. Gymnaste *s.*
gymnastic [dʒim'næstik] adj. Sports. Gymnastique.
gymnastics [-s] n. pl. Sports, Fig. Gymnastique *f.*
gynaeceum [,dʒaini'siəm] n. Gynécée *m.*
gyn(a)ecological [,dʒainikə'lɔdʒikəl] adj. Med.
Gynécologique.
gyn(a)ecologist [-dʒist] n. Med. Gynécologue *s.*
gyn(a)ecology [-dʒi] n. Med. Gynécologie *f.*
gyp [dʒip] n. Domestique (*m.*) à l'université.
gyp v. tr. U. S. Fam. Refaire, entôler, échauder;
to gyp s.o. out of sth., escroquer qqch. à qqn.
— n. U. S. Fam. Carottier, escroc *m.*
gyps [dʒips] n. Gypse *m.*
gypseous [-iəs] adj. Gypseux.
gypsophila [dʒip'sɔfilə] n. Bot. Gypsophile *f.*
gypsum [-əm] n. Gypse *m.* ‖ **Gypsum-quarry,** n.
Plâtrière *f.*
gypsy ['dʒipsi] n. Romanichel *m.;* gipsy *f.;* gitan *s.*
gyrate [,dʒaiə'reit] v. intr. Tournoyer, décrire des
girations.
gyration [-'reiʃən] n. Giration *f.*
gyratory ['dʒaiərətəri] adj. Giratoire.
gyre ['dʒaiə*] n. Mouvement giratoire *m.*
— v. intr. Tournoyer, tourner.
gyrocompass [-ro,kʌmpəs], **gyro** ['dʒaiərə] n.
Gyrocompas *m.*
— N. B. Les pluriels sont *gyrocompasses* et *gyros.*
gyrometer [,dʒaiə'rɔmitə*] n. Gyromètre *m.*
gyropilot ['dʒaiəro'pailət] n. Appareil gyroscopique de pilotage, pilote automatique *m.*
gyroplane ['dʒaiərə,plein] n. Aviat. Giravion
m.
gyroscope ['dʒaiəro,skoup], **gyro** ['dʒaiərə]
n. Gyroscope *m.*
gyroscopic [,dʒaiəro'skɔpik] adj. Gyroscopique.
gyrostabilizer [-'stæbilaizə*] n. Aviat. Gyrostabilisateur *m.*
gyve [dʒaiv] n. † Pl. Fers *m. pl.*
— v. tr. † Enchaîner.

h [eitʃ] (pl. **hs, h's** [-iz]) n. H, h *m.* ‖ Chim.
Hydrogène *m.* ‖ Phys. Henry *m.* ‖ **H-bomb,** n.
Milit. Bombe H *f.* ‖ **H-iron,** n. Techn. Fer à double
T *m.*
ha [hɑ:] interj. Ha!
— v. tr. Faire ha; *to hum and ha,* ânonner.
habeas corpus ['heibiəs'kɔ:pəs] n. Jur. Habeas
corpus *m.*
haberdasher ['hæbədæʃə*] n. Comm. Mercier *s.* ‖
U. S. Comm. Chemisier *m.*
haberdashery [-ri] n. Comm. Mercerie *f.* (goods,
shop). ‖ U. S. Chemiserie; confection (*f.*) pour
hommes (men's outfitting).

habergeon [-hæbədʒən] n. † Haubergeon *m.*
habit ['hæbit] n. Costume *m.* ‖ Eccles. Costume
religieux *m.* ‖ Med. Constitution *f.;* tempérament
m.; a man of healthy habit, un homme de bonne
santé. ‖ Zool., Bot. Habitus *m.* ‖ Fig. Tendance *f.;
habit of mind,* tournure d'esprit. ‖ Fig. Habitude *f.;
from* (or) *out of habit,* par habitude; *to be in the
habit of,* avoir coutume (or) l'habitude de; *when
a habit has been acquired,* quand le pli est pris.
— v. tr. Habiller, vêtir. ‖ † Habiter.
habitable ['hæbitəbl] adj. Habitable.
habitableness [-nis], **habitability** [,hæbitə'biliti]
n. Habitabilité *f.*

habitant ['hæbitənt] n. Habitant s.
— [abi'tɑ̃] n. Canadien français m.
habitat ['hæbitæt] n. Habitat m.
habitation [ˌhæbi'teiʃən] n. Habitation f. (act, place).
habitual [hə'bitjuəl] adj. Habituel.
habitually [-i] adv. Habituellement. ‖ Par habitude.
habituate [hə'bitjueit] v. tr. Habituer (to, à). ‖ U. S. FAM. Fréquenter.
habitué [-ei] n. Habitué m.
hachure [hæ'ʃjuə*] n. ARTS. Hachure f.
— v. tr. ARTS. Hachurer.
hacienda [ˌhæsi'endə] n. Hacienda f.
hack [hæk] n. Entaille, coupure, taillade f. ‖ TECHN. Pioche f.; pic m. ‖ SPORTS. Coup de pied m. (on the shins). ‖ MED. U. S. Toux sèche f. ‖ **Hack-saw**, n. TECHN. Scie (f.) à métaux.
— v. tr. Entailler, taillader. ‖ Tailler à la hache. ‖ SPORTS. Donner un coup de pied à. ‖ FAM. Charcuter, massacrer (to mangle).
— v. intr. **To hack at**, tailler, sabrer, écharper. ‖ MED. Toussoter.

hack n. ZOOL. Cheval de louage m. (horse); cheval (m.) de selle (saddle-horse); rosse f. (worn-out horse). ‖ U. S. Voiture (f.) de louage (carriage) voiturier m. (man). ‖ FAM. Trimardeur m. (drudge), écrivain à gages, nègre m. (writer).
— adj. Mercenaire (writer); de mercenaire (work).
— v. tr. Louer (a horse). ‖ FIG. User, banaliser.
— v. intr. Aller au petit trot. ‖ FAM. Servir de nègre (for, à).

hack n. Claie f. (for drying cheese). ‖ † Mangeoire (f.) de faucon.
— v. tr. U. S. Faire sécher sur la claie.

hacking [-iŋ] adj. MED. Sec (cough).
hackle ['hækl] n. TECHN. Drège f.; échanvroir m. ‖ ZOOL. Pl. Camail m. ‖ SPORTS. Mouche artificielle f. (in fishing). ‖ FAM. *With one's hackles up*, hérissé, dressé sur ses ergots.
— v. tr. TECHN. Peigner, échanvrer.
hackle v. tr. Taillader. (See HACK.) ‖ FAM. Massacrer, mutiler.
hackly [-li] adj. Hachuré (fracture); déchiqueté (rock); rugueux (surface).
hackney ['hækni] n. ZOOL. Cheval de louage, bidet m. (hack); cheval (m.) de selle (saddle-horse). ‖ FAM. Trimardeur m. (drudge). ‖ **Hackney-coach**, n. Voiture (f.) de louage (or) de place.
— v. tr. Banaliser; rebattre, ressasser, rabâcher.
had [hæd] pret., p.p. See HAVE.
haddock [ˈhædək] n. ZOOL. Haddock, aiglefin m.
Hades ['heidi:z] n. Hadès m. (deity); Enfers m. pl. (Underworld).
hadron ['hædrɔn] n. PHYS. Hadron m.
haematin ['hi:mətin] n. CHIM. Hématine f.
haematite ['hemətait] n. GEOL. Hématite f.
haematocele ['hemətouˌsi:l] n. MED. Hématocèle f.
haematocrit [-krit] n. MED. Hématocrite m.
haematology [hi:məˈtɔlədʒi] n. MED. Hématologie f.
haematoma [ˌhi:məˈtoumə] n. MED. Hématome m.
— N.B. Deux pluriels : *haematomas, haematomata.*
haematuria [-ˈtjuəriə] n. MED. Hématurie f.
haemoglobin [ˌhi:moˈgloubin] n. MED. Hémoglobine f.
haemolysin [-ˈlaisin] n. MED. Hémolysine f.
haemolysis [-ˈlaisis] n. MED. Hémolyse f.
haemolytic [-ˈlitik] adj. MED. Hémolytique f.
haemophilia [-ˈfiljə] n. MED. Hémophilie f.
haemophiliac [-ˈfiljək] n. MED. Hémophile s.
haemoptysis [hi:ˈmɔptisis] n. MED. Hémoptysie f.; crachement de sang m.
haemorrhage ['heməridʒ] n. MED. Hémorragie f.
haemorrhagic [heməˈrædʒik] adj. MED. Hémorragique.

haemorrhoids ['hemərɔidz] n. pl. MED. Hémorroïdes f. pl. (See PILES.)
haemostat ['hi:məstæt] n. MED. Hémostatique m.; pince hémostatique f.
hafnium ['hæfniəm] n. CHIM. Hafnium m.
haft [hɑ:ft] n. Manche m. (of a knife); poignée f. (of a sword).
— v. tr. Emmancher.
hag [hæg] n. Sorcière f. ‖ FAM. Vieille bique (or) guenon (or) taupe f. ‖ **Hag-ridden**, adj. Hanté par les cauchemars.
hag n. Fondrière f.
haggard ['hægəd] adj. Hagard, égaré (wild-eyed). ‖ Hâve, défait, altéré, décomposé (drawn). ‖ † Hagard (hawk).
— n. † Hagard m.
haggis ['hægis] n. CULIN. Haggis m., panse de brebis farcie f.
haggish ['hægiʃ] adj. De sorcière.
haggle ['hægl] v. intr. Marchander; *to haggle over,* débattre (a price).
hagiographer [hægiˈɔgrəfə*] n. ECCLES. Hagiographe m.
hagiography [-i] n. ECCLES. Hagiographie f.
Hague [heig] n. GEOGR. *The Hague,* La Haye f.
ha-ha ['hɑ:ˌhɑ:] n. Saut-de-loup m., ha-ha m. (sunk fence).
hail [heil] n. Grêle f. ‖ **Hail-storm**, n. Averse de grêle f. ‖ **Hail-stone**, n. Grêlon m.
— v. impers. Grêler. ‖ FIG. *To hail down on,* faire pleuvoir sur.
hail interj. Salut !
— n. Salut m. (salutation). ‖ Appel m. (call); *within hail,* à portée de voix.
— v. tr. Saluer (as, du titre de) [to salute]. ‖ Héler, appeler (to call). ‖ NAUT. Arraisonner (a ship).
— v. intr. NAUT. Venir (from, de).
hair [hɛə*] (pl. **hairs** [-z]) n. Poil m. (of animals); crin m. (of horse); soie f. (of pigs); *against the hair,* à rebrousse-poil. ‖ Poil m. (on human body); cheveu m. (on human head). ‖ FIG. *To miss by a hair,* manquer de l'épaisseur d'un cheveu. ‖ FAM. *Not to turn a hair,* ne pas tiquer (or) broncher, ne pas remuer un cil ; *to split hairs,* couper les cheveux en quatre, discuter sur des pointes d'aiguille.
— n. invar. Cheveux m. pl.; chevelure f.; *to do one's hair,* se coiffer. ‖ FIG. *To make s.o.'s hair stand on end,* faire dresser les cheveux sur la tête de qqn. ‖ FAM. U. S. *To get in s.o.'s hair,* porter sur les nerfs à qqn; *to let one's hair down,* en prendre à son aise. ‖ FAM. *Keep your hair on!,* ne vous frappez pas ! ‖ **Hair-cut**, n. Coupe (f.) de cheveux; *to have a hair-cut,* se faire couper les cheveux. ‖ **Hair-do**, n. Coiffure f. ‖ **Hair-line**, n. Naissance (f.) des cheveux (on the head); délié m. (in handwriting). ‖ **Hair-net**, n. Résille f. ‖ **Hair-piece**, n. Postiche m., perruque f. ‖ **Hair-raiser**, n. FAM. Histoire terrifiante f. ‖ **Hair-raising**, adj. FAM. Horrifique, à faire dresser les cheveux. ‖ **Hair-setting**, n. Mise (f.) en plis. ‖ **Hair-shirt**, n. Haire f.; cilice m. ‖ **Hair-slide**, n. Barrette (f.) à cheveux. ‖ **Hair-splitting**, n. Ergotage m.; adj. Trop subtil. ‖ **Hair-stroke**, n. Délié m. ‖ **Hair-style**, n. Coiffure f. ‖ **Hair-wash**, n. Shampooing m.
hairbreadth [-bredθ] n. Epaisseur (f.) d'un cheveu.
— adj. De l'épaisseur d'un cheveu.
hairbrush [-brʌʃ] n. Brosse (f.) à cheveux.
haircloth [-klɔθ] n. Thibaude f. (for carpets); tissu-crin m. (for furniture). ‖ ECCLES. Haire f.
hairdresser [-dresə*] n. Coiffeur s.
hairiness ['hɛərinis] n. Aspect velu (or) poilu m.
hairless ['hɛəlis] adj. Sans poil (animal); glabre (face); chauve (head).
hairpin [-pin] n. Epingle (f.) à cheveux. ‖ FAM. *Hairpin bend,* lacet (on a road).

hairspring ['hɛə,spriŋ] n. TECHN. Ressort spiral, spiral *m*.
hairy ['hɛəri] adj. Poilu, velu (on body); chevelu (on head).
Haiti ['heiti] n. GEOGR. Haïti *f*.
Haitian ['heiʃiən] n., adj. GEOGR. Haïtien *s., adj*.
hake [heik] n. ZOOL. Merluche *f*.; colin *m*.
halberd ['hælbə:d] n. Hallebarde *f*.
halberdier [,hælbə'diːə*] n. Hallebardier *m*.
halcyon ['hælsiən] n. ZOOL. Alcyon *m*.
— adj. Alcyonien, serein (day).
hale [heil] adj. Vigoureux, solide ; *to be hale and hearty*, se porter comme un charme.
hale v. tr. † Haler.
half [hɑːf] (pl. halves [hɑːvz]) n. Moitié *f*. (*of, de*); *to cut in halves*, couper en deux; *to go halves with*, être de moitié avec; *too long by half*, trop long de moitié. ‖ Demie *f*.; *half a cup*, une demi-tasse; *half past two*, deux heures et demie; *two and a half*, deux et demi. ‖ Semestre *m*. (at school). ‖ SPORTS. Mi-temps *f*. (of the match); demi *m*. (player). ‖ FAM. *His better half*, sa moitié; *to listen with half an ear*, écouter d'une oreille distraite; *you are too talkative by half*, vous êtes rudement trop bavard. ‖ **Half-back**, n. SPORTS. Demi-arrière *m*. ‖ **Half-blood**, n. Métis, sang-mêlé *m*. ‖ **Half-boarder**, n. Demi-pensionnaire *s*. ‖ **Half-boot**, n. Demi-botte *f*. ‖ **Half-bottle**, n. Demi-bouteille *f*. ‖ **Half-breed**, n. MED. Métis *m*.; ZOOL. Demi-sang *m*. ‖ **Half-brother**, n. Demi-frère *m*. ‖ **Half-cock**, n. Cran (*m*.) de sûreté; FAM. *To go off at half-cock*, mal démarrer. ‖ **Half-cup**, n. Demi-tasse *f*. ‖ **Half-dozen**, n. Demi-douzaine *f*. ‖ **Half-fare**, adj. CH. DE F. A demi-tarif; n. Demi-place *f*. ‖ **Half-hitch**, n. NAUT. Demi-clef *f*. ‖ **Half-hogshead**, n. Demi-pièce *f*. ‖ **Half-holiday**, n. Demi-congé, congé de l'après-midi *m*. ‖ **Half-length**, n. SPORTS. Demi-longueur *f*.; adj. ARTS. En buste (portrait). ‖ **Half-life**, n. PHYS. Demi-vie *f*. ‖ **Half-light**, n. Demi-jour *m*. ‖ **Half-mast**, v. tr. Mettre en berne; adj. *At half mast*, en berne. ‖ **Half-mourning**, n. Demi-deuil *m*. ‖ **Half-pay**, n. MILIT. Demi-solde *f*. ‖ **Half-pint**, n. FAM. Demi-portion *f*. (person). ‖ **Half-price**, adj., adv. A demi-tarif, à moitié prix. ‖ **Half-ration**, n. Demi-ration *f*. ‖ **Half-roll**, n. AVIAT. Demi-tonneau *m*. ‖ **Half-section**, n. MILIT. Demi-groupe *m*. ‖ **Half-time**, adj. A demi-journée; *half-time work*, mi-temps; n. SPORTS. Mi-temps *f*. ‖ **Half-tone**, n. ARTS. Demi-teinte *f*.; MUS. Demi-ton. ‖ **Half-track**, n. MILIT. Half-track *m*. ‖ **Half-turn**, n. Demi-tour *m*. ‖ **Half-volley**, n. SPORTS. Demi-volée *f*.; v. intr. Prendre une balle entre bond et volée. ‖ **Half-wave**, n. PHYS. Demi-onde *f*. ‖ **Half-wit**, n. FAM. U. S. Idiot *m*. ‖ **Half-year**, n. Semestre scolaire *m*.
halfpenny ['heipəni] (pl. halfpence [-pəns]) n. Demi-penny, sou *m*. ‖ (Pl. halfpennies [-pəniz]) n. Pièce (*f*.) d'un demi-penny.
halibut ['hælibət] n. ZOOL. Flétan *m*.
halieutic [hæli'ju:tik] adj., n. Halieutique *f*.
halitosis [,hæli'tousis] (pl. halitoses [-iːz]) n. Mauvaise haleine *f*.
hall [hɔːl] n. Salle, grande salle *f*. (in a castle, a public building). ‖ Réfectoire *m*. (in a college); *servants' hall*, office, salle commune des domestiques. ‖ Hall *m*. (in a hotel); vestibule *m*. (in a house). ‖ Château *m*. (mansion); pavillon universitaire *m*. (for students). ‖ ECCLES. *Parish hall*, salle des œuvres. ‖ MUS. *Concert hall*, salle de concert. ‖ JUR. Palais (*m*.) de justice; hôtel (*m*.) de ville. ‖ U. S. Couloir, corridor *m*. ‖ **Hall-mark**, n. Poinçon (*m*.) de garantie (for gold or silver); FIG. Sceau *m*.; v. tr. Poinçonner.
hallelujah [hæli'luːjə] n. Alléluia *m*.
— N.B. Orthographes : *alleluia, alleluiah, halleluiah*.
halliard ['hɔːljəd] n. NAUT. Drisse *f*.
hallo [hə'lou] interj. Holà! Ohé! ‖ Allô!
— v. intr. Lancer un appel.
— n. Ohé, appel *m*.

halloo [hə'luː] interj. Ohé! ‖ SPORTS. Taïaut!
— v. intr., tr. Appeler. ‖ SPORTS. Huer.
hallow ['hælou] n. † ECCLES. Saint *m*.
hallowed [-id] p. p. ECCLES. Sanctifié.
— [-d] adj. ECCLES. Saint, bénit (ground).
Hallowe'en [,hælou'iːn] n. Veille de la Toussaint *f*., Halloween *f*.
hallucinate [hə'ljuːsineit] v. tr. Halluciner.
hallucination [hə,ljuːsi'neiʃən] n. Hallucination *f*.
hallucinatory [hə'ljuːsineitəri] adj. Hallucinatoire.
hallucinogen [-sinə,dʒen] n. Hallucinogène *m*.
hallucinogenic [-'dʒenik] adj. Hallucinogène.
hallway ['hɔːlwei] n. U. S. Couloir, vestibule *m*.
halo ['heilou] (pl.haloes, halos [-z]) n. Cerne *m*. ‖ ASTRON., FIG. Halo *m*. ‖ ECCLES., FIG. Auréole *f*.
— v. tr. (4). ASTRON. Entourer d'un halo. ‖ ECCLES., FIG. Auréoler, nimber.
halogen ['hælodʒən] n. CHIM. Halogène *m*.
halogenous [hə'lodʒinəs] adj. CHIM. Halogène.
haloid ['hæloid] adj., n. CHIM. Haloïde *m*.
halt [hɔlt] n., interj. Halte *f*.
— v. intr. Faire halte.
— v. tr. Faire arrêter.
halt adj. † Boiteux, clopinant.
— n. Estropiés *m. pl*.
— n. † Boiterie *f*.
— v. intr. Boiter, boitiller, clopiner (in walking). ‖ Hésiter (in speaking). ‖ FIG. Boiter, clocher.
halter [-ə*] n. † Pendaison *f*. (hanging); hart *f*. (rope). ‖ Licou, licol *m*. (harness). ‖ U. S. Corsage bain de soleil *m*.
— v. tr. † Pendre. ‖ Mettre un licou à. ‖ FAM. Mettre la corde au cou à.
halting [-iŋ] adj. Boiteux, clopinant (person). ‖ FIG. Anonnant (speaker); hésitant (speech); heurté (style); boiteux (verse).
haltingly [-iŋli] adv. Cahin-caha, en clopinant (or) boitillant, clopin-clopant (in walking). ‖ FIG. Avec hésitation, en ânonnant (in speaking).
halve [hɑːv] v. tr. Partager (or) diviser en deux. ‖ FIN. Diminuer de moitié. ‖ TECHN. Emboîter.
halyard ['hɔːljəd] n. NAUT. Drisse *f*.
ham [hæm] n. † Jarret *m*. ‖ CULIN. Jambon *m*. ‖ FAM. Pl. Fesses *f. pl*. ‖ FAM. Cabotin *m*. ‖ Ham-fisted, adj. Avec des mains comme des battoirs; FIG. Maladroit, empoté.
— adj. CULIN. Au jambon (sandwich). ‖ FAM. *Ham actor*, cabotin.
— v. tr. FAM. THEATR. Massacrer (a part).
hamadryad [hæmə'draiæd] n. Hamadryade *f*.
hamburger ['hæmbə:gə*] n. CULIN. Hamburger, bifteck haché *m*.
hames [heimz] n. pl. Attelles *f. pl*.
Hamite ['hæmait] n. Chamite *s*.
Hamitic [hæ'mitik] adj. Chamitique.
hamlet ['hæmlit] n. Hameau *m*.
hammer ['hæmə*] n. TECHN., MUS., MED. Marteau *m*. ‖ MILIT. Percuteur, chien de fusil *m*. ‖ JUR. Marteau *m*.; *to come under the hammer*, être vendu aux enchères. ‖ FAM. *To go at it hammer and tongs*, y aller à bras raccourcis. ‖ **Hammer-cloth**, n. Housse (*f*.) de siège. ‖ **Hammer-drill**, n. TECHN. Perforatrice à percussion *f*. ‖ **Hammer-harden**, v. tr. TECHN. Ecrouir. ‖ **Hammer-head**, n. TECHN. Tête (*f*.) de marteau, pilon *m*.; ZOOL. Marteau *m*. ‖ **Hammer-lock**, n. SPORTS. Torsion (*f*.) du bras.
— v. tr. TECHN. Marteler. ‖ AGRIC. Battre (a scythe). ‖ FIN. Exécuter (a defaulter); faire baisser (prices). ‖ FAM. Enfoncer, faire entrer (*into*, dans); *to hammer it home*, appuyer sur la chanterelle, enfoncer le clou. ‖ U. S. FAM. Ereinter. ‖ **To hammer down**, TECHN. Aplatir au marteau. ‖ **To hammer in**, enfoncer à coups de marteau. ‖ **To hammer out**, TECHN. Etendre au marteau; FIG. Inventer, forger

(an excuse); marteler (verse); U. S. résoudre (a difficulty).
— v. intr. *To hammer at*, AVIAT., MILIT. Pilonner; FIG. S'acharner sur; FAM. Tarabuster (s.o.); bûcher (sth.).

hammering [-riŋ] n. Martelage *m.* (act); martèlement *m.* (noise). ‖ MILIT., AVIAT. Pilonnage *m.* ‖ FAM. Rossée, dégelée *f.*

hammerless [-lis] adj. Hammerless (shotgun).

hammock ['hæmək] n. Hamac *m.* ‖ **Hammockchair**, n. Transatlantique, transat *m.*

hammy ['hæmi] adj. FAM. Pompier.

hamper ['hæmpə*] n. Manne (basket); bourriche *f.* (for oysters).

hamper v. tr. Gêner, entraver; empêtrer (fam.). [s.o.]. ‖ Brouiller (a lock).

hamshackle ['hæmʃækl] v. tr. Entraver (cattle).

hamster ['hæmstə] n. ZOOL. Hamster *m.*

hamstring ['hæmstriŋ] n. MED. Tendon du jarret *m.*
— v. tr. (166). Couper le jarret à.

hanap ['hænəp] n. Hanap.

hand [hænd] n. MED. Main *f.; hand in hand*, la main dans la main; *to lay one's hand on*, mettre la main sur; *to take s.o.'s hand*, donner la main à qqn. ‖ TECHN. Travail manuel *m.; done by hand*, fait à la main. ‖ TECHN. Palme *f.* (measure); indicateur *m.* (on a signpost); index *m.* (in typography); aiguille *f.* (of a watch). ‖ TECHN. Travailleur, ouvrier *m.;* pl. main-d'œuvre *f.;* factory hand, ouvrier d'usine; *no hands wanted*, pas d'embauche; *to need hands*, manquer de bras (or) de personnel. ‖ AGRIC. Farm hand, valet de ferme. ‖ NAUT. Marin *m.; lost with all hands*, perdu corps et biens. ‖ JUR. *Hands up!*, haut les mains! ‖ COMM. *In hand*, en magasin. ‖ FIN. *Cash in hand*, encaisse; *from hand to hand*, de la main à la main. ‖ SPORTS. Jeu *m.;* partie *f.* (at cards); *to win hands down*, gagner dans un fauteuil. ‖ FIG. Maniement *m.; to rule s.o. with a high hand*, tenir la dragée haute à qqn; *with a heavy hand*, avec poigne, à la cravache. ‖ FIG. Main, écriture *f.; by the same hand*, de la même main; *to write a good hand*, avoir une bonne écriture. ‖ FIG. Main *f.;* côté *m.; on all hands*, de tous côtés; *on the left hand*, à gauche; *on the one hand... on the other hand*, d'une part... d'autre part. ‖ FIG. Main, proximité *f.; at hand*, à portée de la main, tout proche (near); prêt (ready); *to hand*, sous la main. ‖ FIG. Main, habileté *f.; to keep one's hand in*, s'entretenir la main. ‖ FIG. Personne habile *f.*, a new hand at, novice dans; *to be a good hand at*, avoir la main à, être calé en. ‖ FIG. Main *f.;* jeu *m.; to show one's hand*, dévoiler son jeu, démasquer ses batteries. ‖ FIG. Main, possession *f.; in hand*, en main; *in one's own hands*, par-devers soi; *to change hands*, changer de mains; *to put into the hands of*, remettre aux mains de. ‖ FIG. Main, emprise *f.; to eat out of s.o.'s hand*, dépendre entièrement de qqn; *to fall into the hands of*, tomber aux mains de; *to force s.o.'s hand*, forcer la main à qqn; *to get the upper hand of*, prendre l'avantage (or) la haute main sur; *to have the upper hand*, tenir le haut du pavé; *to get out of hand*, s'émanciper, ruer dans les brancards. ‖ FIG. Bras *m.;* charge *f.; to have on one's hands*, avoir sur les bras; *to have one's hands full*, en avoir sa charge (or) son content (or) plein les bras. ‖ FIG. Main, aide *f.; to give a hand*, donner un coup de main; *to join hands*, s'associer. ‖ FIG. Main, participation *f.; to have a hand in it*, avoir un doigt dans l'affaire; *without my having any hand in it*, absolument en dehors de moi. ‖ FIG. Main, origine, source *f.; at first hand*, de première main. ‖ FIG. Etude *f.; in* (or) *on hand*, en discussion (or) délibération, en chantier; *off hand*, impromptu; *out of hand*, incontinent, sans préparation. ‖ FIG. Main,

promesse (*f.*) de mariage. ‖ FAM. *A cool hand*, un type qui n'a pas froid aux yeux; *from hand to mouth*, au jour le jour; *not to do a hand's turn*, ne rien faire de ses dix doigts; *off hand*, par-dessus la jambe; *to put one's hand down*, mettre la main au gousset, débourser, décaisser, casquer; *to throw up one's hands*, lever les bras au ciel; *well in hand*, bien emmanché (affair); *you couldn't see your hand in front of you*, on n'y voyait pas le poing dans l'air. ‖ **Hand-bag**, n. Sac (*m.*) à main. ‖ **Handball**, n. SPORTS. Hand-ball *m.* ‖ **Hand-barrow**, n. Civière *f.;* brancard *m.* ‖ **Hand-brake**, n. AUTOM. Frein (*m.*) à main. ‖ **Hand cream**, n. Crème (*f.*) pour les mains. ‖ **Hand-gallop**, n. Petit galop *m.* ‖ **Hand-glass**, n. Miroir (*m.*) [or] loupe (*f.*) à main. ‖ **Hand-grenade**, n. MILIT. Grenade à main *f.* ‖ **Hand-gun**, n. Arme (*f.*) à feu de poing, revolver *m.* ‖ **Hand-list**, n. Catalogue, inventaire *m.* (of books). ‖ **Hand luggage**, n. Bagage (*m.*) à main. ‖ **Hand-made**, adj. Fait à la main. ‖ **Hand-mill**, n. CULIN. Moulin *m.* ‖ **Hand-picked**, adj. FIG. Soigneusement choisi, trié sur le volet. ‖ **Hand-picking**, n. Ramassage (*m.*) à la main. ‖ **Hand-rail**, n. Main courante *f.* ‖ **Hand-saw**, n. TECHN. Scie à main *f.* ‖ **Hand-set**, n. Combiné téléphonique *m.* ‖ **Hand-sewn**, adj. Cousu main. ‖ **Hand-to-hand**, adj. MILIT. Corps à corps (fight). ‖ **Hand-written**, adj. Manuscrit, autographe.
— v. tr. Donner la main, tenir par la main. ‖ Passer; *to hand about*, faire circuler. ‖ NAUT. Serrer (a sail). ‖ U. S. Concéder, accorder. ‖ FIG. Transmettre. ‖ FAM. *You've got to hand it to him!*, devant lui, chapeau!; *to hand out soft soap*, passer la main dans le dos. ‖ **Hand-me-down**, adj. U. S. FAM. Décrochez-moi-ça; d'occasion.

handbell [-bel] n. Sonnette, clochette *f.*

handbill [-bill] n. Prospectus *m.*

handbook [-buk] n. Manuel *m.* (at school); guide *m.* (for journey).

handcar [-kɑ:*] n. CH. DE F. Draisine *f.*

handcart [-kɑ:t] n. COMM. Petite voiture, voiture (*f.*) des quatre-saisons. (See APPLE-CART.)

handcuff [-kʌf] n. Pl. Menottes *f. pl.*
— v. tr. Mettre les menottes à.

handcuffed [-kʌfd] adj. Menottes au poignet.

handful [-ful] n. Poignée *f.* ‖ FAM. Teigne *f.*

handgrip [-grip] n. Prise; empoignade *f.* (fam.). ‖ Poignée (*f.*) de mains (handshake).

handhold [-hould] n. Prise *f.* (gripping, support).

handicap ['hændikæp] n. Handicap *m.*
— v. tr. (1). Handicaper.

handicraft ['hændikrɑ:ft] n. Métier manuel *m.* (trade); habileté manuelle *f.* (skill); travail manuel *m.* (work).

handicraftsman [-ʃmən] (pl. **handicraftsmen**) n. Artisan *m.* ‖ Bricoleur *m.* (handyman).

handily ['hændili] adv. Adroitement. (See DEFTLY.) ‖ A portée de la main, sous la main, commodément (conveniely).

handiness [-nis] n. Adresse, habileté manuelle, dextérité *f.* ‖ Commodité, maniabilité *f.*

handiwork [-wə:k] n. Travail manuel, ouvrage *m.* ‖ FIG. Œuvre *f.;* ouvrage *m.*

handkerchief ['hæŋkətʃif] n. Mouchoir *m.; fancy handkerchief*, pochette; foulard (for the neck).

handle ['hændl] n. Anse *f.* (of a basket); manche *m.* (of a broom); poignée *f.* (of a door); brancard *m.* (of a handcart); queue *f.* (of a pan); brimbale *f.* (of a pump); bras *m.* (of a wheelbarrow); *to remove the handle of*, démancher. ‖ ELECTR. Manette *f.* ‖ AUTOM. Manivelle *f.* ‖ FIG. Arme *f.;* prétexte *m.; to give a handle to*, donner prise à. ‖ FAM. *To fly off the handle*, sortir de ses gonds; *to have a handle to one's name*, avoir un nom à rallonge.
— v. tr. Manipuler, manier, tenir en mains (sth.).

‖ TECHN. Manœuvrer. ‖ COMM. Tenir (articles); brasser (business). ‖ FIG. Contrôler, avoir la haute main sur (to control); traiter de, s'occuper de (to deal with); mener, diriger, gouverner (to direct); manier, traiter (to treat).

handlebars [-bɑ:z*] n. pl. Guidon m. (of a bicycle).

handout ['hænd,aut] n. U. S. FAM. Aumône, distribution gratuite f. (gift); prospectus (folder); bulletin (m.) de presse (release).

handsel ['hænsəl] n. Etrenne f. (New Year's gift). ‖ COMM. Etrenne f. (first sale). ‖ FIN. Arrhes f. pl. ‖ FIG. Spécimen, acompte m.
— v. tr. Etrenner (for the first time). ‖ Inaugurer. ‖ Donner des étrennes à (s.o.).

handshake ['hændʃeik] n. Poignée de main f.; shake-hand m.

handsome ['hænsəm] adj. Beau m.; belle f. (lit. and fig.). [See BEAUTIFUL.] ‖ LOC. Handsome apology, réparation d'honneur; to do the handsome thing, faire un beau geste.

handsomely [-li] adv. Avec beauté (or) élégance (elegantly). ‖ Avec générosité, généreusement, largement (generously). ‖ NAUT. En douceur.

handsomeness [-nis] n. Beauté f. ‖ FIG. Générosité f.

handspike ['hændspaik] n. NAUT. Anspect. ‖ MILIT. Levier (m.) de manœuvre.

handstand [-stænd] n. SPORTS. Arbre droit m., équilibre (m.) sur les mains.

handwriting ['hænd,raitiŋ] n. Ecriture f.

handy ['hændi] adj. Prêt, sous la main, accessible (close at hand). ‖ Maniable, commode, pratique (convenient). ‖ Utile; it may come in handy, cela peut servir. ‖ Adroit, habile, plein de dextérité. (See DEXTEROUS.) ‖ NAUT. Maniable (ship). ‖ **Handy-dandy,** n. Jeu (m.) de « dans quelle main est-ce ? ».

handyman [-mən] n. Factotum m. (servant). ‖ Bricoleur m. (potterer).

hang [hæŋ] v. tr. Pendre (s.o.); to hang oneself, se pendre.
— v. intr. Etre pendu (person); let him go hang!, qu'il aille se faire pendre ailleurs!
— v. tr. (75). Suspendre, accrocher, pendre (on, à) [one's clothes]. ‖ Tapisser, tendre; garnir, orner (with, de) [a wall]. ‖ Poser (wall-papers). ‖ Exposer (pictures). ‖ Laisser pendre; to hang one's head, baisser la tête. ‖ **To hang out,** suspendre au-dehors (in general); étendre (the washing); MILIT. Arborer (a flag); U. S. FAM. To hang out one's shingle, s'établir, ouvrir un magasin (or) un cabinet. ‖ **To hang up,** suspendre (one's hat, a picture); raccrocher (the receiver). ‖ FIG. Ajourner (a plan); retarder (s.o.).
— v. intr. Etre accroché (or) suspendu, pendre (clothes, pictures); pendre, tomber, retomber (curtains). ‖ Pendre, pencher, être en pente, s'incliner (to bend, to lean). ‖ Balancer, osciller (to swing). ‖ **To hang about,** flânocher; rôdailler; to hang about s.o., coller à qqn. ‖ **To hang back,** rester en arrière; FIG. Hésiter à aller de l'avant. ‖ **To hang down,** pendre (hair); pencher (tower). ‖ **To hang on,** tenir bon; se suspendre, s'accrocher (to, à); to hang on circumstances, dépendre des circonstances; to hang on (or) upon s.o.'s lips, être suspendu aux lèvres de qqn. ‖ **To hang out,** pendre dehors; FAM. Percher (to dwell); to hang out over, surplomber. ‖ **To hang over,** surplomber; U. S. FIG. Survivre. ‖ **To hang together,** se tenir (argument); se tenir les coudes (persons); tenir debout (story); se tenir d'aplomb, tenir (thing).
— n. Tombant m. (of a curtain, a dress). ‖ Pente, inclinaison f. (slope). ‖ FIG. Tendance, inclination f. ‖ FAM. Coup (m.) de main; to get the hang of sth., attraper le chic (or) prendre le truc pour faire qqch. ‖ FAM. Brin m.; it's not worth a hang, ça ne vaut pas

un radis (or) pas tripette. ‖ **Hang-glider,** n. SPORTS. Delta-plane m. ‖ **Hang-out,** n. FAM. Point de chute m. ‖ **Hang-up,** n. FAM. Complexe m.

hangar ['hæŋə*] n. AVIAT. Hangar m.

hanger n. Crochet m. (in general); portemanteau, cintre m. (coat-hanger); patère f. (curtain-hook, hat-peg); crémaillère f. (pot-hanger). ‖ Coteau boisé m. (wood). ‖ Jambage m. (in handwriting). ‖ Poignard, coutelas m.; dague f. (dagger). ‖ JUR. Bourreau m. (hangman). ‖ TECHN. Poseur m. (person); suspenseur m. (thing). ‖ U. S. Pancarte f. (placard); soustitre m. (on newspaper). ‖ **Hanger-back,** n. FAM. Traînard, renâcleur s. ‖ **Hanger-on,** n. FAM. Parasite; crampon m.

hanging [-iŋ] n. Accrochage m.; hanging closet, penderie (of clothes, pictures). ‖ Pose f. (of bells, wall-papers). ‖ Pendaison f. (of a person); to deserve hanging, être bon à pendre. ‖ Pl. Tentures, draperies f. pl. (curtains).
— adj. Suspendu (bridge, garden); battant (door); pendant (chandelier); tombant (sleeve); en encorbellement (stair). ‖ Féroce (judge); patibulaire (look); pendable (matter).

hangman [-mən] (pl. **hangmen**) n. Bourreau m.

hangnail [-neil] n. MED. Envie f.

hangover [-ouvə*] n. U. S. FAM. Gueule (f.) de bois; to have a hangover, avoir mal aux cheveux.

hank [hæŋk] n. Echeveau m. ‖ NAUT. Anneau m.

hanker ['hæŋkə*] v. intr. Languir, brûler (after, de); soupirer (after, après).

hankering [-riŋ] n. Soif, envie violente, nostalgie f. (after, for, de).

hanky ['hæŋki] n. FAM. Mouchoir m.

hanky-panky ['hæŋki'pæŋki] n. Tour (m.) de passe-passe. ‖ FAM. Montage de coup m.

Hansard ['hænsɑ:d] n. Compte rendu officiel (m.) des débats parlementaires.

hansom ['hænsəm] n. Cab m.

Hants [hænts] n. GEOGR. Hampshire m. (abbrev.).

hap [hæp] n. Hasard m.; chance f. (luck). ‖ Destinée f. (fortune). ‖ Pl. Evénements m. pl.
— v. intr. Survenir par hasard.

ha'penny ['heipni] n. FAM. See HALFPENNY.

haphazard ['hæp'hæzəd] n. Hasard m.
— adj. Au hasard, au petit bonheur.
— adv. Au hasard, à l'aventure.

hapless ['hæplis] adj. Infortuné, malchanceux.

haploid ['hæplɔid] adj. MED. Haploïde.

ha'p'orth ['heipəθ] n. Valeur (f.) d'un sou; not to have a ha'p'orth of heart, n'avoir pas pour deux sous de cœur.

happen ['hæpən] v. intr. Arriver, advenir, survenir, se produire (to occur); it might happen that, il pourrait se faire que. ‖ Arriver; what has happened to him?, qu'est-ce qu'il lui est arrivé ? ‖ Se trouver par hasard (to chance); if he happened to die, s'il venait à mourir. ‖ FAM. Tomber (on, sur) [s.o.].

happening [-iŋ] n. Evénement m.

happenstance [-,stæns] n. U. S. Hasard m., coïncidence f., concours (m.) de circonstances.

happily ['hæpili] adv. Heureusement (in general); avec bonheur (felicitously); dans le bonheur (joyfully); par bonheur (luckily).

happiness [-nis] n. Bonheur m. ‖ GRAMM. Bonheur m.; justesse f. (in style).

happy ['hæpi] adj. Heureux (day, event, person); heureux, réussi (marriage). ‖ GRAMM. Heureux (phrase). ‖ **Happy-go-lucky,** adj. A la va-comme-je-te-pousse (fashion); insouciant (person).

harakiri ['hɑ:rə'ki:ri] n. Harakiri m.; to commit harakiri, faire harakiri.

harangue [hə'ræŋ] n. Harangue f.
— v. tr. Haranguer.
— v. intr. Prononcer une harangue.

harass ['hærəs] v. tr. Tourmenter, tracasser, harasser (to worry). ‖ Harceler; asticoter (fam.) [to harry].

harassment [-mənt] n. Tracas, tourment m. (worry). ‖ Harcèlement ; asticotage m. (fam.).

harbinger ['hɑ:bindʒə*] n. MILIT. † Fourrier m. ‖ FIG. Messager s. ; avant-coureur m. ; avant-courrière f. ; annonciateur m. ; annonciatrice f.
— v. tr. Annoncer.

harbo(u)r ['hɑ:bə*] n. NAUT. Port m. ‖ FIG. Port, havre, asile m. ‖ **Harbour-dues**, n. pl. NAUT. Droits (m. pl.) de mouillage. ‖ **Harbour-master**, n. NAUT. Capitaine de port m.ꞏ‖ **Harbour-works**, n. NAUT. Installation portuaire f.
— v. tr. Héberger, abriter (s.o.). ‖ JUR. Receler (a criminal). ‖ FIG. Nourrir (hopes, suspicions) ; *to harbour a grudge,* garder rancune.
— v. intr. Se réfugier, se mettre à l'abri.

harbourage [-ridʒ] n. Asile, abri m. ‖ NAUT. Mouillage m.

hard [hɑ:d] adj. Dur (rock, substance) ; *on the cold hard ground,* sur la dure ; *to become hard,* durcir. ‖ Dur, froid, inclément, rigoureux (winter). ‖ MED. Ferme, vigoureux (muscles) ; sclérosé, scléreux (tissues) ; *hard of hearing,* dur d'oreille. ¶ MILIT. Dur, acharné (fight). ‖ SPORTS. Sévère, chaudement disputé (match). ‖ FIN. Ferme, soutenu (market) ; *hard cash,* espèces sonnantes et trébuchantes ; *hard currency,* devises fortes. ‖ CHIM. Fort, alcoolisé, riche en alcool (drink) ; calcaire (water) ; vert (wine). ‖ AGRIC., ARTS, GRAMM. Dur. ‖ FIG. Dur, difficile (problem, task) ; dur, ardu (question) ; *hard to accomplish,* d'exécution difficile. ‖ FIG. Brutal (fact) ; rigoureux (fate) ; dur, pénible (life) ; rude, dur (times) ; dur, fatigant, ingrat (work) ; dur, endurant, énergique (worker) ; *hard luck,* malchance ; *it's hard work for him to,* il a beaucoup de mal à ; *to have a hard time of it,* en voir de dures. ‖ FIG. Dur (heart, person, voice) ; dur, sévère, sans pitié (on, to, towards, envers, pour) [master, words] ; *hard and fast,* strict, inflexible (rule) ; *to grow hard,* s'endurcir. ‖ FIG. Difficile, exigeant, peu commode (person) ; *hard to get on with,* difficile à vivre.
— adv. Ferme (firmly) ; *to hold on hard,* tenir solidement. ‖ Fort, dur (strenuously) ; *to be freezing hard,* geler ferme ; *to be raining hard,* pleuvoir dru, ‖ Difficilement, avec difficulté ; *to be hard put to it,* se débattre dans les difficultés, être dans de beaux draps ; avoir beaucoup de mal (to, à) ; *to die hard,* avoir la vie dure ; *to go hard with s.o.,* aller mal pour qqn. ‖ Dur, durement, avec acharnement (energetically) ; *to be hard at it,* en mettre un coup, s'y atteler dur. ‖ Durement, avec dureté (or) rudesse (severely). ‖ Tout près ; *hard by,* tout contre, tout à côté ; *to follow hard after,* suivre de près. ‖ NAUT. Tout. ‖ FAM. *To be hard up,* tirer le diable par la queue, être dans la purée (or) la dèche ; *to be hard up for,* être à court de. ‖ **Hard-bitten,** adj. FAM. Dur à cuire. ‖ **Hard-boil,** v. tr. CULIN. Durcir, faire cuire dur (an egg). ‖ **Hard-boiled,** adj. CULIN. Dur (egg) ; U. S. FAM. Consommé, expérimenté. ‖ **Hard-drawn,** adj. De haute résistance. ‖ **Hard-featured,** adj. Aux traits durs. ‖ **Hard-fisted,** adj. FAM. Dur à la détente. ‖ **Hard-headed,** adj. FIG. Positif, réaliste, à la tête froide. ‖ **Hard-hearted,** adj. Au cœur dur. ‖ **Hard-heartedness,** n. Dureté (f.) de cœur. ‖ **Hard-line,** adj. Intransigeant. ‖ **Hard-mouthed,** adj. Dur de bouche (horse). ‖ **Hard-nosed,** adj. FAM. Obstiné, coriace. ‖ **Hard-set,** adj. Durci (cement) ; couvé (egg). ‖ **Hard-tack,** n. NAUT. Biscuit (m.) de mer. ‖ **Hard-top,** n. AUTOM. Voiture non décapotable f. ‖ **Hard-won,** adj. Chèrement disputé, conquis de haute lutte. ‖ **Hard-working,** adj. Travailleur, bûcheur (student).

hardback ['hɑ:d,bæk] adj. Relié.
— n. Livre relié ; *in hardback,* en édition reliée.

hardboard [-,bɔ:d] n. TECHN. Isorel m. (nom déposé).

harden ['hɑ:dn] v. tr. Durcir, rendre dur. ‖ MED. Endurcir, aguerrir (persons) ; indurer, scléroser (tis-

sues) ; *to harden oneself to,* s'aguerrir à. ‖ TECHN. Tremper (steel). ‖ FIG. Endurcir (heart).
— v. intr. Durcir, se durcir. ‖ MED. S'aguerrir (person) ; s'indurer, se scléroser (tissues). ‖ TECHN. Se tremper. ‖ FIG. S'endurcir.

hardening [-iŋ] n. Durcissement m. ‖ MED. Aguerrissement m. (of persons) ; induration, sclérose f. (of tissues). ‖ TECHN. Trempe f. ‖ FIG. Endurcissement m.

hardihood ['hɑ:dihud] n. Hardiesse f.

hardily [-li] adv. Vigoureusement. ‖ FIG. Hardiment, audacieusement.

hardiness [-nis] n. Vigueur, robustesse f. ‖ FIG. Hardiesse, intrépidité f.

hardly ['hɑ:dli] adv. Durement, avec dureté, rudement, sévèrement (harshly). ‖ Durement, difficilement, avec peine, péniblement (not easily). ‖ A peine, presque pas (scarcely) ; *hardly anyone,* presque personne ; *it can hardly be doubted that,* il n'est guère douteux que ; *you need hardly say,* il est à peine besoin de dire, il va sans dire. ‖ A peine, tout juste (than, que) [only just]. ‖ Certainement pas, sûrement pas (not likely).

hardness [-nis] n. Dureté (of a substance). ‖ Rigueur f. (of winter). ‖ CHIM. Dureté f. (of water). ‖ FIN. Raffermissement m. (of the market). ‖ FIG. Difficulté f. (of a problem, a question). ‖ FIG. Rigueur, dureté f. (of fate, life, times). ‖ FIG. Dureté, sécheresse f. (of heart) ; dureté, sévérité f. (of a person). ‖ FAM. Parcimonie f.

hardshell [-,ʃel] adj. A la carapace dure. ‖ FAM. Rigoriste, conservateur.

hardship [-,ʃip] n. Rigueur f. ‖ Epreuve, tribulation f.

hardware [-wɛə*] n. COMM. Quincaillerie f. (articles) ; *hardware dealer,* quincaillier ; *hardware shop* (or) *store,* quincaillerie. (See IRONMONGERY.) ‖ INFORM. Hardware, matériel m.

hardwareman [-wɛəmən] (pl. **hardwaremen**) n. COMM. Quincaillier m.

hardy ['hɑ:di] adj. Vigoureux, robuste (person). ‖ BOT. Vivace, résistant (plant). ‖ FIG. Hardi, audacieux, intrépide.

hare ['hɛə*] n. ZOOL. Lièvre m. ; *doe-hare,* hase. ‖ SPORTS. *Hare and hounds,* rallye-paper. ‖ FAM. *To run with the hare and hunt with the hounds,* ménager la chèvre et le chou, nager entre deux eaux. ‖ **Hare-brained,** adj. A cervelle d'oiseau, à tête de linotte, écervelé. ‖ **Hare-lip,** n. MED. Bec-de-lièvre m.
— v. intr. Courir comme un lièvre ; filer, se précipiter.

harebell [-bel] n. BOT. Campanule, clochette f.

harehound [-haund] n. ZOOL. Chien courant m.

harem ['hɛərəm] n. Harem m.

haricot ['hærikou] n. CULIN. Haricot de mouton, navarin m. ‖ **Haricot-bean,** n. BOT. Haricot blanc m. ‖ **Haricot-mutton,** n. CULIN. Navarin m.

hark [hɑ:k] v. intr. *To hark to,* écouter, prêter une oreille attentive à. ‖ SPORTS. *To hark back,* prendre le contre-pied. ‖ FIG. *To hark back to,* revenir sur (sth.).
— v. tr. SPORTS. Rappeler (dogs).

harken [-n] v. intr. *To harken to,* écouter.

harl(e) [hɑ:l] n. Barbe f. (of feather) ; filament m. (of flax, hemp).

harlequin ['hɑ:likwin] n. THEATR., ZOOL. Arlequin m.
— adj. Bigarré, d'arlequin. ‖ Oblique (lenses).

harlequinade [,hɑ:likwi'neid] n. Arlequinade f.

harlot ['hɑ:lət] n. Prostituée f.
— v. intr. Se prostituer.

harlotry [-ri] n. Prostitution f.

harm [hɑ:m] n. Mal, tort, préjudice, dommage m. (hurt) ; *to come to harm,* traverser une mauvaise période ; *to do harm to,* nuire à, faire du tort à ; *to keep out of harm's way,* se tirer des pieds. ‖

Méchanceté *f.*; mauvais desseins *m. pl.; there is no harm in her,* ce n'est pas une méchante femme.
— v. tr. Faire du mal (or) du tort à, nuire à. ‖ JUR. Porter préjudice à, léser; causer un dommage à.

harmful [-ful] adj. Malfaisant, nuisible (person); nocif, nuisible (thing). ‖ JUR. Dommageable, préjudiciable.

harmfulness [-fulnis] n. Malfaisance *f.* (of a person); nocivité *f.* (of a thing).

harmless [-lis] adj. Inoffensif (animal); sans méchanceté (person); anodin, sans nocivité (thing). ‖ † Intact, sain et sauf.

harmlessly [-lisli] adv. Sans malice, innocemment. ‖ Sans mal.

harmlessness [-lisnis] n. Douceur *f.* (of an animal); innocence, absence de méchanceté *f.* (of a person); innocuité *f.; caractère inoffensif *m.* (of a thing).

harmonic [hɑːˈmɔnik] adj., n. MUS., MATH., ELECTR. Harmonique *m.*

harmonica [-ə] n. MUS. Harmonica *m.*

harmonically [-əli] adv. Harmoniquement.

harmonious [hɑːˈmounjəs] adj. Harmonieux, plaisant (arrangement); en harmonie, en accord (feelings, ideas). ‖ MUS. Harmonieux, mélodieux.

harmonist [ˈhɑːmənist] n. MUS. Harmoniste *s.*

harmonium [hɑːˈmounjəm] n. MUS. Harmonium *m.*

harmonize [ˈhɑːmənaiz] v. tr. Harmoniser, mettre en harmonie (*with*, avec). ‖ MUS. Harmoniser.
— v. intr. S'harmoniser (*with*, avec).

harmony [-ni] n. MUS., FIG. Harmonie *f.*

harness [ˈhɑːnis] n. † Harnois *m.* ‖ Harnais, harnachement *m.; a set of harness,* un harnais. ‖ AVIAT. Ceinture *f.* (for a parachute). ‖ TECHN. Harnais *m.* (of loom); équipement *m.* (in general). ‖ FAM. *In double harness,* dans les liens du conjungo; *to be back in harness,* avoir repris le collier; *to live in harness,* être attelé à la besogne. ‖ **Harness-maker,** n. Bourrelier, sellier *m.* ‖ **Harness-room,** n. Sellerie *f.*
— v. tr. Harnacher (a horse). ‖ TECHN. Aménager (a river, waterfall).

harp [hɑːp] n. MUS. Harpe *f.*
— v. intr. MUS. Jouer de la harpe. ‖ **To harp on,** FAM. Ressasser, rabâcher; *he's always harping on that,* c'est sa turlutaine; *to be always harping on the same string,* chanter la même antienne, cirer le même bouton.

harper [-ə*] n. † Ménestrel *m.* ‖ MUS. Harpiste *s.*

harpist [-ist] n. MUS. Harpiste *s.*

harpoon [hɑːˈpuːn] n. Harpon *m.*
— v. tr. Harponner.

harpooner [-ə*] n. Harponneur *m.*

harpsichord [ˈhɑːpsikɔːd] n. MUS. Clavecin *m.*

harpy [ˈhɑːpi] n. Harpie *f.*

harquebus [ˈhɑːkwibəs] n. † Arquebuse *f.*

harridan [ˈhæridən] n. FAM. Vieille sorcière *f.*

harrier [ˈhæriə*] n. ZOOL. Busard *m.* (bird); braque *m.* (dog); ‖ SPORTS. Pl. Meute *f.* (dogs); chasseurs *m. pl.* (hunters); crossmen *m. pl.* (runners).

harrow [ˈhærou] v. tr. Dévaster.

harrow n. AGRIC. Herse *f.* ‖ FIG. Epreuve, adversité, tribulation *f.*
— v. tr. AGRIC. Herser. ‖ FIG. Déchirer, labourer (s.o.'s heart); torturer (s.o.).

harrowing [-iŋ] adj. Déchirant, poignant, navrant.
— n. AGRIC. Hersage *m.* ‖ FIG. Déchirement *m.*

harry [ˈhæri] v. tr. (2). Ravager, dévaster, piller (a country); dépouiller (s.o.). ‖ FIG. Harceler.

Harry n. Henri, Riri (name). ‖ FAM. *Old Harry,* Lucifer; *to play Old Harry with,* en faire voir de dures à.

harsh [hɑːʃ] adj. Discordant, criard, rauque, éraillé (to the ear); dur, heurté, déplaisant (to the eye); âpre, râpeux (to the taste); rêche, râpeux, rugueux (to the touch). ‖ FIG. Rude, bourru (person); rude, dur (words).

harshly [-li] adv. Rudement, désagréablement.

harshness [-nis] n. Discordance *f.* (to the ear); heurt, aspect déplaisant *m.* (to the eye); âpreté (to the taste); rudesse, rugosité *f.* (to the touch). ‖ FIG. Rudesse, dureté *f.*

hart [hɑːt] n. ZOOL. Cerf *m.* (See STAG.) ‖ **Hart's-tongue,** n. BOT. Scolopendre *f.*

hartshorn [-ʃɔːn] n. ZOOL. Corne (*f.*) de cerf. ‖ CHIM. *Salt of hartshorn,* sels; *spirit of hartshorn,* ammoniaque.

harum-scarum [ˈhɛərəmˈskɛərəm] adj. Ecervelé.
— n. FAM. Tête (*f.*) en l'air (or) de linotte.

harvest [ˈhɑːvist] n. AGRIC. Moisson, récolte *f.* (crop); moisson (season). ‖ FIG. Moisson *f.* ‖ **Harvest-bug,** n. ZOOL. Aoûtat *m.*
— v. tr. AGRIC., FIG. Moissonner, récolter.
— v. intr. AGRIC. Faire la moisson.

harvester [-ə*] n. AGRIC. Moissonneuse *f.* (machine); moissonneur *s.* (person).

harvestman [-mən] (pl. **harvestmen**) n. U. S. AGRIC. Moissonneur *s.* ‖ U. S. ZOOL. Faucheux *m.* (See DADDY-LONG-LEGS.)

has [hæz]. See HAVE. ‖ **Has-been,** n. FAM. Vieux ramollot, décati *m.; he's a has-been,* il a beaucoup baissé, il a fait son temps, il survit à sa gloire.

hash [hæʃ] v. tr. CULIN. Hacher. ‖ FAM. U. S. *To hash it over,* discuter le coup.
— n. CULIN. Hachis, émincé *m.; U. S. POP. *hash house,* gargote, *f.* ‖ FAM. Gâchis *m.* (mess); *to settle s.o.'s hash,* régler son compte à qqn.

hash n. POP. Hasch *m.* (hashish).

hashish [ˈhæʃiʃ] n. Haschisch *m.*

haslet [ˈhæzlit] n. CULIN. Fressure *f.*

hasp [hɑːsp] n. Moraillon *m.* (in general); fermoir (for book covers); loquet *m.* (for a door). ‖ Echeveau *m.* (of thread).
— v. tr. Fermer au loquet, cadenasser.

hassle [ˈhæsl] n. FAM. Prise (*f.*) de bec, engueulade *f.*, accrochage *m.* (argument); enquiquinement *m.* (trouble).
— v. tr. FAM. Enquiquiner, casser les pieds à.
— v. intr. FAM. Avoir une prise de bec, s'engueuler (*with*, avec).

hassock [ˈhæsək] n. Coussin-agenouilloir *m.* (cushion). ‖ Touffe d'herbe *f.* (tussock).

hastate [ˈhæsteit] adj. BOT. Hasté.

haste [heist] n. Hâte, célérité, promptitude *f.* (speed); *to make haste,* se hâter. ‖ Hâte, précipitation. (See HURRY.)
— v. intr. † Se hâter.

hasten [ˈheisn] v. tr. Hâter, presser, accélérer, activer.
— v. intr. Se hâter, se presser, se dépêcher.

hastily [ˈheistili] adv. Hâtivement, à la hâte, précipitamment. ‖ A la légère, hâtivement. ‖ Vivement, avec vivacité.

hastiness [-nis] n. Hâte, rapidité *f.* ‖ Hâte, précipitation *f.* ‖ Vivacité, brusquerie *f.*

hasty [ˈheisti] adj. Hâtif, précipité (done with haste). ‖ Rapide, prompt (quick). ‖ Irréfléchi, inconsidéré, précipité (rash). ‖ Vif, emporté, violent (impetuous).

hat [hæt] n. Chapeau *m.; hats off!,* chapeaux bas!; *to keep one's hat on,* rester couvert (man); garder son chapeau (woman). ‖ FAM. *To take off one's hat to,* tirer son chapeau à; *to talk out of (or) U. S. through one's hat,* déraisonner; *under one's hat,* strictement pour soi. ‖ **Hat-block,** n. Forme (*f.*) à chapeaux. ‖ **Hat-box,** n. Carton (*m.*) à chapeaux. ‖ **Hat-lining,** n. Coiffe *f.* ‖ **Hat-maker,** n. Chapelier *s.* ‖ **Hat-peg,** n. Patère *f.* ‖ **Hat-pin,** n. Epingle (*f.*) à chapeaux. ‖ **Hat-rack,** U. S. **Hat tree,** n. Porte-chapeaux *m.* ‖ **Hat-shop,** n. Chapellerie *f.* (for men); boutique de modiste *f.* (for

women). ‖ **Hat-trick,** n. SPORTS. Trois victoires consécutives *f. pl.*; *to score a hat-trick*, marquer trois buts dans le même match.
— v. tr. Chapeauter, coiffer d'un chapeau.

hatband [-bænd] n. Ruban de chapeau *m.*

hatch [hætʃ] n. Demi-porte *f.* ‖ NAUT. Vanne d'écluse *f.* (floodgate); écoutille *f.* (hatchway); *under hatches*, dans la cale. ‖ FAM. *Down the hatch!*, à la vôtre!

hatch v. tr. Faire éclore (birds); faire couver (eggs). ‖ FIG. Couver, nourrir (an idea); tramer, ourdir (a plot).
— v. intr. Eclore (bird, egg).
— n. Eclosion *f.* (act); couvée *f.* (brood).

hatch v. tr. ARTS. Hachurer.
— n. ARTS. Hachure *f.*

hatchback [-bæk] n. AUTOM. Hayon *m.* (door); voiture (*f.*) à hayon (car).

hatchery ['hætʃəri] n. AGRIC. Couveuse *f.*, incubateur *m.*

hatchet ['hætʃit] n. Hachette *f.* ‖ FIG. *To bury the hatchet*, enterrer la hache de guerre. ‖ **Hatchet-face,** n. Figure (*f.*) en lame de couteau.

hatchment ['hætʃmənt] n. Ecusson funéraire *m.*

hatchway ['hætʃwei] n. NAUT. Ecoutille *f.*

hate [heit] v. tr. Haïr, exécrer, avoir en horreur (to abhor). ‖ En vouloir à, être fâché contre (for, à cause de, de) [to bear a grudge against]. ‖ FAM. Détester, ne pas pouvoir supporter (or) souffrir (to dislike). ‖ FAM. Etre désolé (or) navré de.
— n. Haine *f.* ‖ FAM. Bête noire *f.*

hateful [-ful] adj. Haïssable. ‖ FAM. Odieux, détestable.

hatefully [-fuli] adv. Odieusement.

hatefulness [-fulnis] n. Odieux; caractère odieux *m.*

hatred ['heitrid] n. Haine *f.* (de, of).

hatter ['hætə*] n. Chapelier *m.*

hauberk ['hɔːbəːk] n. Haubert *m.*

haughtily ['hɔːtili] adv. Avec hauteur, hautainement; d'un air altier.

haughtiness [-nis] n. Hauteur, morgue *f.* (See ARROGANCE.)

haughty ['hɔːti] adj. Hautain, plein de morgue. (See ARROGANT.) ‖ Altier, superbe (lofty).

haul [hɔːl] v. tr. Traîner, tirer, haler. ‖ NAUT. Haler. ‖ AUTOM. Remorquer (a car); camionner (goods).
— v. intr. Traîner, tirer, haler. ‖ NAUT. Haler (sailor); vénir (ship); tourner, haler (wind).
— n. Traction; action (*f.*) de haler. ‖ Trajet, parcours *m.* ‖ Prise *f.*; coup de filet *m.*

haulage [-idʒ] n. Halage *m.* ‖ AUTOM. Camionnage *m.*

hauler [-ə*] n. Haleur *m.*

haulier ['hɔːljə*] n. TECHN. Hercheur *m.* ‖ AUTOM. Camionneur *m.*

haulm [hɔːm] n. BOT. Fane *f.*

haunch [hɔːnʃ] n. MED. Hanche *f.* ‖ CULIN. Cuissot *m.* (of venison). ‖ ARCHIT. Rein *m.* (of a vault). ‖ FAM. Pl. Derrière, arrière-train *m.* ‖ **Haunch-bone,** n. MED. Os iliaque *m.*

haunt [hɔːnt] v. tr. Hanter (a place); fréquenter (s.o.). ‖ FIG. Hanter, obséder (memory); assiéger (person).
— v. intr. Fréquenter, hanter.
— n. Lieu fréquenté *m.* (of, par). ‖ Repaire *m.* (of criminals). ‖ Tanière *f.* (of wild beasts).

haunter [-ə*] n. Habitué *s.*; *haunter of theatres*, coureur de théâtres.

hautboy ['(h)ɔubɔi] n. MUS. Hautbois *m.* (See OBOE.) ‖ BOT. Capron *m.* (fruit); capronier *m.* (tree).

hauteur [ou'təː] n. Condescendance, arrogance, hauteur, morgue *f.*

Havana [hə'vænə] n. GEOGR. La Havane *f.* ‖ FAM. Havane *f.* (cigar).

---

have [hæv] v. tr. (76).

> 1. Avoir, posséder. — 2. Tenir, saisir. — 3. Prendre, absorber. — 4. Prendre, utiliser. — 5. Jouir de. — 6. Avoir, concevoir. — 7. Avoir, entretenir. — 8. Tolérer, supporter. — 9. Savoir. — 10. Dire. — 11. Voir. — 12. Faire. — 13. FAM. — 14. To have better. — 15. To have in. — 16. To have it. — 17. To have just. — 18. To have... left. — 19. To have on. — 20. To have to. — 21. To have up.

1. Avoir, posséder; *have you a watch?*, avez-vous une montre?; *I must have a dictionary*, il me faut un dictionnaire; *to have blue eyes*, avoir les yeux bleus; *to have credit*, avoir du crédit. ‖ **2.** Tenir, saisir violemment; *to have s.o. by the hair*, tenir qqn par les cheveux. ‖ **3.** Prendre, absorber; *to have a cigar*, fumer un cigare; *to have dinner, lunch*, dîner, déjeuner; *to have a drink*, prendre (ou) boire un verre; *will you have one?*, une petite goutte? ‖ **4.** Prendre, utiliser; *to have a taxi*, prendre un taxi. ‖ **5.** Jouir de; *to have a good time*, passer un bon moment; *to have a talk*, avoir un entretien; *to have a walk*, faire une promenade. ‖ **6.** Avoir, concevoir; *to have a grudge against*, en avoir contre. ‖ **7.** Avoir, entretenir; *to have dealings with*, avoir des relations avec. ‖ **8.** Tolérer, supporter; *I won't have this nonsense*, je ne laisserai pas passer cette sottise. ‖ **9.** Savoir, posséder; *he had Shakespeare by heart*, il savait Shakespeare par cœur. ‖ **10.** Dire; *as gossip has it*, selon les racontars, comme dit la rumeur publique. ‖ **11.** Voir; *he wouldn't have his wife do so*, il ne voudrait pas voir sa femme agir ainsi. ‖ **12.** Faire; *we are having our wireless set repaired*, nous faisons réparer notre poste de T.S.F. ‖ **13.** FAM. Avoir, rouler, mettre dedans, refaire; *you've been had*, on vous a eu. ‖ **14. To have better,** faire mieux; *you had better not lie*, vous feriez mieux de ne pas mentir. ‖ **15. To have in,** faire entrer; recevoir (guests). ‖ **16. To have it;** *he's had it*, il est fait (or) cuit (or) flambé (or) frit (or) fichu (fam.); *if you will have it that he is honest*, si vous soutenez (ou) prétendez qu'il est honnête; *I'm not having it*, je n'encaisse pas ça, je la trouve mauvaise (fam.); *to have it in for*, garder une dent contre (fam.); *to have it out*, en avoir le cœur net, tirer ça au clair; s'expliquer (*with*, avec). ‖ **17. To have just,** venir de; *I have just finished*, je viens de finir. ‖ **18. To have... left,** rester; *I have only two pounds left*, il ne me reste que deux livres. ‖ **19. To have on,** porter, être habillé de; *to have nothing on*, être nu, n'avoir rien sur soi. ‖ **20. To have to,** avoir à, devoir; *he had to come back*, il a dû revenir; *he had to pay twenty francs*, il en a eu pour vingt francs; *I have to go on an errand*, il faut que j'aille en commission; *to have nothing to do but, to have only to*, n'avoir qu'à; *to have to do with*, avoir à faire à, se rapporter à. ‖ **21. To have up,** faire monter; JUR. Assigner; arrêter.
— v. intr. † **To have at,** foncer sur; *have at you!*, défends-toi!
— v. aux. Avoir; *I have eaten*, j'ai mangé; *I would give you some money, but I haven't got any*, je voudrais vous donner de l'argent, mais je n'en ai pas; *I have lived here for two years*, j'habite ici depuis deux ans; *since I was operated on, I have been in good health*, depuis que j'ai été opéré, je me porte bien. ‖ Etre; *I had gone too far*, je m'étais avancé (or) j'étais allé trop loin; *I have helped myself*, je me suis servi; *they have complained to his father*, ils se sont plaints à son père; *we have noticed it*, nous nous en sommes aperçus.
— n. FAM. Pl. Possédants *m. pl.*; *the haves and have-nots*, les riches et les pauvres. ‖ **Have-on,** m. FAM. Bateau, montage de coup *m.*

haven ['heivn] n. NAUT. Port *m*. ‖ FIG. Havre, refuge, asile *m*. (See HARBOUR.)

haver ['heivə] v. intr. Radoter, parler pour ne rien dire (to babble). ‖ Hésiter, vaciller (to hesitate).

haversack ['hævəsæk] n. SPORTS. Sac de camping *m*. ‖ MILIT. Musette *f*.

having ['hæviŋ] n. Avoir *m*.; possession *f*.

havoc ['hævək] n. Ravages *m. pl.*; grabuge *m*. (fam.); *to make havoc of, to play havoc with*, causer des dégâts à.
— v. tr. Ravager, dévaster.

haw [hɔ:] interj. Dia! (to horse); heu! (See HUM.) ‖ Haw-haw, n. Rire bête *m*.; v. intr. Rire bêtement.
— v. intr. Tourner à gauche (horse). ‖ Anonner.
— v. tr. Diriger à gauche (a horse).

haw n. BOT. Aubépine *f*. (tree); baie de l'aubépine, cenelle *f*. (berry).

hawk [hɔ:k] n. ZOOL. Faucon *m*. (See FALCON.) ‖ FAM. Vautour, rapace *m*. (grasping person); *he doesn't know a hawk from a handsaw*, il n'y connaît rien de rien. ‖ Hawk-eyed, adj. Au regard d'aigle. ‖ Hawk-moth, n. ZOOL. Sphinx *m*. ‖ Hawk-nose, n. Nez aquilin (or) en bec d'aigle *m*.
— v. intr. SPORTS. Chasser au faucon. ‖ To hawk at, fondre sur (a prey).
— v. tr. Fondre sur.

hawk v. intr. MED. Graillonner.
— v. tr. To hawk up, MED. Expectorer.

hawk n. TECHN. Taloche *f*. (plasterer's).

hawk v. tr. COMM. Colporter.

hawker [-ə*] n. COMM. Colporteur *m*.; *street hawker*, camelot *m*.

hawker [-ə*] n. SPORTS. Fauconnier *m*. (See FALCONER.)

hawking [-iŋ] n. SPORTS. Chasse (*f*.) au faucon.

hawking n. MED. Graillonnement *m*.

hawking n. COMM. Colportage *m*.

hawse [hɔ:z] n. NAUT. Evitage *m*.; *clear hawse*, chaînes claires; *to anchor in a ship's hawse*, mouiller dans les ancres d'un navire. ‖ Hawse-hole, n. NAUT. Ecubier *m*.; FAM. Petite porte *f*.

hawser ['hɔ:zə*] n NAUT. Haussière *f*.

hawthorn ['hɔ:θɔ:n] n. BOT. Aubépine *f*.

hay [hei] n. AGRIC. Foin *m*.; *to make hay*, faner, faire les foins. ‖ FAM. Méli-mélo *m*.; *to make hay of*, embrouiller. ‖ U. S. FAM. Pieu, plumard *m*. (bed); *to hit the hay*, se pieuter. ‖ Hay-fever, n. MED. Rhume (*m*.) des foins.
— v. tr. AGRIC. Faner (grass); mettre en prairie (land).

haycock ['heikɔk] n. AGRIC. Meulon de foin *m*.

hayloft ['heilɔft] n. AGRIC. Fenil, grenier à foin *m*.

haymaker ['hei,meikə*] n. AGRIC. Faneur *s*. ‖ U. S. FAM. Coup de poing en assommoir *m*.

haymaking [-iŋ] n. AGRIC. Fenaison *f*.

hayseed ['heisi:d] n. U. S. FAM. Cul-terreux *m*.

haystack ['heistæk] n. AGRIC. Meule (*f*.) de foin.

haywire ['heiwaiə*] adj. FAM. *To go haywire*, tourner la tête (person); tourner mal (plans).

hazard ['hæzəd] n. Hasard *m*.; fortune *f*. ‖ Hasard *m*.; chance *f*.; *at all hazards*, à tout hasard. ‖ Risque, péril, aléa *m*. (see DANGER); *to run the hazard*, courir le risque. ‖ SPORTS. Obstacle *m*. (in golf); trou gagnant *m*. (in real tennis).
— v. tr. Hasarder, risquer. (See VENTURE.)

hazardous [-əs] adj. Hasardeux, incertain, aléatoire. ‖ Hasardeux, risqué, périlleux (risky).

haze ['heiz] n. Brume *f*.; brouillard (*m*.) de chaleur. ‖ FIG. Incertitude *f*.; brouillard *m*. (fam.).
— v. tr. Embrumer.

haze v. tr. NAUT. Accabler de corvées. ‖ U. S. Brimer (in school).

hazel ['heizl] n. BOT. Noisetier, coudrier *m*. ‖ Couleur noisette *f*. ‖ Hazel-nut, n. Noisette *f*.
— adj. Couleur noisette.

hazily ['heizili] adv. Indistinctement, brumeusement, nébuleusement.

haziness [-nis] n. Etat brumeux *m*. ‖ FIG. Vague *m*.; nébulosité *f*.

hazy ['heizi] adj. Brumeux. ‖ FIG. Vague, flou, nébuleux. ‖ FAM. Parti, éméché (tipsy).

he [hi:] pron. Il; *he called them*, il les a appelés. ‖ Lui *m*.; *he, a writer!*, lui, un écrivain!; *he being gone*, lui parti. ‖ Ce *m*.; *he is my father-in-law*, c'est mon beau-père. ‖ Celui *m*.; *he who told you so is a fool*, celui qui vous a dit cela est un sot.
— n. (pl. hes, he's). Mâle *m*. (animal); homme *m*. (man).
— adj. Mâle. ‖ He-goat, n. ZOOL. Bouc *m*.

head [hed] n. MED. Tête *f*.; *head of hair*, chevelure. ‖ TECHN. Pointe *f*. (of arrow); tête *f*., chevet *m*. (of bed); fond *m*. (of cask); musoir *m*. (of dam); fer *m*. (of hammer, spear); bief *m*. (of mill); tête *f*. (of nail, pin); pression *m*. (of steam); pommeau *m*. (of stick); chapiteau *m*. (of still); bout *m*. (of table); *head of water*, hauteur de chute (or) piézométrique. ‖ En-tête *m*. (of a chapter); haut *m*. (of a column, page); titre *m*. (on a newspaper); U. S. *scare head*, grosse manchette. ‖ MATH. *To reckon in one's head*, calculer de tête. ‖ BOT. Pomme, tête *f*. (of a cabbage); bouquet *m*. (of flowers, leaves); tête (of a tree); *head of celery*, pied de céleri; *head of lettuce*, laitue; *to form a head*, pommer. ‖ ZOOL. Hure *f*. (of boar). ‖ CULIN. Mousse *f*.; faux col *m*. (fam.) [on beer]; crème *f*. (on milk); *potted head*, fromage de tête. ‖ MED. Tête *f*. (of an abscess); *to come to a head*, aboutir, mûrir. ‖ MUS. Peau *f*. (of a drum). ‖ FIN. Face *f*. (of a coin). ‖ GEOGR. Promontoire, cap *m*. ‖ NAUT. Pomme *f*. (of a mast); nez *m*. (of a ship); *head wind*, vent debout; *how is her head?*, où est le cap? ‖ SPORTS. *To win by a short head*, gagner (or) coiffer d'une courte tête. ‖ AUTOM. Toit *m*. ‖ FIG. Tête, unité *f*.; *a* (or) *per head*, par tête (cattle, persons); la pièce (goods). ‖ FIG. Tête *f*.; premier rang *m*.; *at the head of*, à la tête de, en tête de. ‖ FIG. Chef *m*. (of the family); directeur *m*. (of a school); *head of the French department*, directeur des études de français. ‖ FIG. Partie *f*.; point *m*. (of a speech); *classified under several main heads*, rangés sous plusieurs chefs; *on that head*, sur ce chapitre, à cet égard; *under the same head*, sous la même rubrique. ‖ FIG. Point décisif, aboutissement *m*.; *to come to a head*, aborder la phase critique. ‖ FIG. Importance *f*., *to gather head*, prendre des proportions. ‖ FIG. Tête, intelligence *f*.; *to put their heads together*, se consulter; *to speak over the head of*, ne pas se mettre à la portée de; *use your head*, faites travailler vos méninges. ‖ FIG. Tête, aptitude *f*.; *he has a head for mathematics*, il a des dispositions pour les mathématiques (or) la bosse des mathématiques. ‖ FIG. Tête, raison *f*.; *to be off one's head*, avoir perdu la boule (or) la carte (or) le nord; *to go to s.o.'s head*, porter à la tête de qqn; *to lose one's head*, perdre la tête, s'affoler; *to take sth. into one's head*, se mettre qqch. en tête; *to turn s.o.'s head*, tourner la tête à qqn. ‖ FIG. Tête, idée *f*.; *give him his head*, laissez-le faire à sa tête. ‖ FAM. *Head and shoulders above*, d'une coudée au-dessus; *I can't make head or tail of it*, je n'y comprends rien, je m'y perds; *to keep one's head above water*, surnager, se tenir à flot; *to talk s.o.'s head off*, casser la tête (or) les oreilles à qqn. ‖ Head-dress, n. Coiffure *f*. ‖ Head-hunter, n. Chasseur (*m*.) de têtes. ‖ Head-money, n. FIN. Capitation *f*. ‖ Head-on, adj., adv. De front. ‖ Head-rest, n. Appui-tête *m*., repose-tête *m*. invar. ‖ Head-shrinker, n. Réducteur (*m*.) de têtes; FAM. psychanalyste *s*. ‖ Head-voice, n. MUS. Voix de tête *f*., fausset *m*. ‖ Head-word, n. Mot-souche *m*.
— v. tr. Contourner (to go round); diriger, tourner (*for*, vers) [to turn]. ‖ Intituler, mettre en tête de

(a chapter). ‖ TECHN. Mettre un fond à (a cask) ; mettre une tête à (a nail). ‖ NAUT. *To head the ship for,* mettre le cap sur. ‖ SPORTS. *To head the ball,* jouer de la tête, faire un crâne. ‖ AGRIC. Etêter (a tree). ‖ FIG. Etre à la tête de (to command) ; venir en tête de (to precede). ‖ **To head back,** rabattre, faire refluer. ‖ **To head off,** barrer la route à, faire rebrousser chemin à (s.o.) ; FIG. Faire dévier (a question) ; détourner (s.o.).
— v. intr. Se diriger (*for,* vers). ‖ BOT. Pommer (cabbage) ; épier (grain). ‖ MED. Mûrir (abscess). ‖ NAUT. Mettre le cap, gouverner (*for,* sur). ‖ FIG. *To head for ruin,* courir à sa perte.

headache [-eik] n. MED. Mal (*m.*) de tête ; *sick headache,* migraine. ‖ FIG. Casse-tête *m.* ‖ FAM. *Dutchman's headache,* gueule de bois.

headachy [-eiki] adj. MED. Sujet aux maux de tête, migraineux. ‖ FAM. Qui casse la tête, qui donne la migraine.

headed [-id] adj. A tête. ‖ A chevelure. ‖ A en-tête (paper). ‖ A pommeau (cane). ‖ BOT. Pommé, cabus (cabbage).

header [-ə*] n. TECHN. Tonnelier fonceur *m.* ‖ ARCHIT. Boutisse *f.* ‖ SPORTS. Tête *f.* (in football) ; plongeon *m.* (in swimming). ‖ U. S. FAM. Dégringolade *f.*

heading [-iŋ] n. Intitulé, exergue *m.,* tête *f.* (of a chapter) ; en-tête *m.* (of document, letter) ; chapeau *m.* (introductory paragraph). ‖ TECHN. Galerie (*f.*) d'avancement (in mining). ‖ SPORTS. Tête *f.* (in football).

headland [-lənd] n. GEOGR. Promontoire, cap *m.* (See FORELAND.) ‖ AGRIC. Tournière *f.*

headless [-lis] adj. Sans tête (body, nail). ‖ ZOOL. Acéphale. ‖ FIG. Sans chef.

headlight [-lait] n. AUTOM. Phare *m.* ‖ CH. DE F. Fanal *m.* ‖ U. S. FAM. Bouchon (*m.*) de carafe.

headline [-lain] n. En-tête *m.* ; titre, "sous-titre *m.* ‖ Pl. Gros titres *m. pl. ; to hit (or) make the headlines,* faire la une.

headlong [-lɔŋ] adv. La tête la première. ‖ FIG. Tête baissée.
— adj. Escarpé (cliff). ‖ La tête la première (fall). ‖ FIG. Impétueux, précipité, fougueux.

headman [-mən] m. Chef *m.*

headmaster [-'mɑ:stə*] n. Principal, directeur *m.*

headmistress [-'mistris] n. Directrice *f.*

headmost [-moust] adj. Premier, de tête.

headphone [-foun] n. RADIO. Ecouteur *m. ;* pl. casque *m.*

headquarters ['hed'kwɔ:təz] n. pl. MILIT. Quartier général *m.*

headroom [-,ru:m] n. Hauteur *f.* (under a bridge) ; hauteur sous plafond (in a building). ‖ FIG. Liberté (*f.*) de mouvement.

headsman ['hedzmən] n. Bourreau *m.* (See EXECUTIONER.)

headspring [-spriŋ] n. Source *f.*

headstock [-stɔk] n. TECHN. Poupée *f.*

headstone [-stoun] n. Pierre tombale de tête *f.* ‖ ARCHIT. Pierre angulaire *f.* (See CORNERSTONE.)

headstrong [-strɔŋ] adj. Entêté, têtu ; cabochard (fam.).

headway [-wei] n. Progrès *m.* ‖ Intervalle *m.* (in time). ‖ NAUT. Erre *f.* ‖ ARCHIT. Hauteur libre *f.*

heady [-i] adj. Entêtant (scent) ; capiteux (wine). ‖ FIG. Emporté, violent (person). ‖ POP. Intelligent.

heal [hi:l] v. tr. MED. Guérir (a disease, a patient) ; guérir, cicatriser (a wound). ‖ FIG. Régler (differences) ; apaiser, remédier à (grief, troubles). ‖ Heal-all, n. FAM. Panacée *f.*
— v. intr. MED. Se guérir, se cicatriser. ‖ FIG. S'apaiser.

healer [-ə*] n. Guérisseur *s.* ‖ U. S. Remède *m.*

healing [-iŋ] adj. MED. Cicatrisant (ointment) ; curatif (remedy) ; en voie de cicatrisation (sore). ‖ FIG. Apaisant.

— n. MED. Guérison *f.* (of a disease) ; cicatrisation *f.* (of a sore).

health [helθ] n. MED. Santé *f.* ‖ JUR. Hygiène *f.* ‖ FAM. Toast *m. ; to drink s.o.'s health,* boire à la santé de qqn, porter un toast en l'honneur de qqn. ‖ **Health-centre,** n. Centre (*m.*) d'hygiène. ‖ **Health-officer,** n. MILIT. Officier (*m.*) de santé ; inspecteur (*m.*) d'hygiène. ‖ **Health-resort,** n. MED. Station climatique *f.* ‖ **Health service,** n. Organisation de la santé publique et de la Sécurité sociale *f.*

healthful [-ful] adj. Salubre (air) ; salutaire (effect).

healthfulness [-fulnis] n. Salubrité *f.*

healthily [-ili] adv. Sainement.

healthiness [-inis] n. Salubrité *f.* (of a climate) ; santé *f.* (of a person).

healthy [-i] adj. Sain, salubre (air, climate) ; robuste (appetite) ; florissant (look) ; sain, en bonne santé, bien portant (person) ; sain (skin) ; *to make healthier,* assainir. ‖ FIG. Vigoureux.

heap [hi:p] n. Tas, amoncellement, amas *m.* (mass). ‖ FAM. Tas *m. ;* foule *f. ;* flopée *f.* (fam.) ; *to be left all of a heap,* rester pantois.
— v. tr. Charger, remplir (*with,* de). ‖ FIG. Combler (*with,* de). ‖ **To heap up,** entasser, empiler, amonceler.

heaping [-iŋ] n. Entassement *m.*

hear [hiə*] v. tr. (77). Entendre ; *people can't hear one another,* on ne s'entend plus ; *to hear s.o. say sth.,* entendre dire qqch. à (or) par qqn ; *to hear s.o. crying,* entendre pleurer qqn. ‖ Ecouter, entendre ; *he refused to hear me,* il a refusé de m'entendre. ‖ Entendre, recevoir ; *I cannot hear you now,* je ne puis vous recevoir maintenant. ‖ Assister à (lectures) ; faire réciter (lessons). ‖ Apprendre (a piece of news). ‖ Entendre dire ; *I have heard he is ill,* j'ai entendu dire qu'il est malade. ‖ MUS., RADIO. Ecouter. ‖ JUR. Connaître de (a dispute) ; entendre (a witness). ‖ ECCLES. Assister à (mass). ‖ U. S. LOC. *I hear you talking,* j'approuve entièrement vos paroles. ‖ **To hear out,** écouter jusqu'au bout.
— v. intr. Entendre, avoir bonne ouïe. ‖ Recevoir des nouvelles (*from,* de) ; *let me hear from you,* donnez-moi de vos nouvelles, écrivez-moi. ‖ **To hear about** (or) **of,** entendre parler, avoir connaissance de ; *this is the first I have heard of it,* c'est ma première nouvelle ; *you'll hear more of this!,* vous entendrez parler de moi, vous aurez de mes nouvelles, il vous en cuira (threat). ‖ **To hear of,** entendre parler de ; prêter une oreille complaisante à ; *he won't hear of it,* il ne veut rien savoir, il ne l'entend pas de cette oreille.
— interj. *Hear! hear!,* très bien, bravo !

heard [hə:d] pret., p. p. See HEAR.

hearer ['hiərə*] n. Auditeur *m. ;* auditrice *f. ;* pl. auditoire *m.*

hearing [-riŋ] n. MED. Ouïe *f.* ‖ Portée d'ouïe *f. ; in s.o.'s hearing,* en la présence de qqn ; *to come to s.o.'s hearing,* venir aux oreilles de qqn ; *within hearing,* à portée de voix. ‖ Possibilité (*f.*) d'être entendu ; audience *f. ; she was refused a hearing,* on refusa de l'entendre. ‖ MUS. Audition *f.* ‖ JUR. Audition (of a witness) ; *to put down for hearing,* audiencer (a case).

hearken ['hɑ:kən] v. intr. Prêter l'oreille (*to,* à).

hearsay ['hiəsei] n. Ouï-dire *m.* ‖ JUR. *Hearsay evidence,* déposition faite sous la foi d'un tiers, preuve par simple ouï-dire.

hearse [hə:s] n. Corbillard *m.* ‖ ECCLES. Hersé *f.* ‖ **Hearse-cloth,** n. Drap mortuaire *m.*

heart [hɑ:t] n. MED. Cœur *m.* ‖ Cœur, centre *m.* (of the town) ; plein, fort, cœur *m.* (of winter). ‖ BOT. Fond *m.* (of artichoke) ; cœur (of cabbage). ‖ AGRIC. Etat *m.* (of the land) ; *in good heart,* en bon rendement. ‖ Pl. Cœur *m.* (at cards). ‖ FIG. Cœur, sentiment *m. ; after my own heart,* selon mon cœur ; *from one's heart,* du fond du cœur ;

heart and soul, corps et âme ; *to have at* (or) *to lay to heart*, prendre à cœur ; *to set one's heart on doing*, prendre à cœur de faire ; *to wear one's heart on one's sleeve*, avoir le cœur sur les lèvres ; *with a heavy heart*, le cœur gros. ‖ Cœur *m.* ; sensibilité *f.* ; *to eat one's heart out*, se ronger. ‖ Cœur *m.* ; émotion *f.* ; *to have one's heart in one's mouth*, être plein d'appréhension. ‖ Cœur *m.* ; humeur *f.* ; *to be in no heart for laughing*, n'avoir pas le cœur (or) n'être pas d'humeur à rire. ‖ Cœur, courage *m.* ; *out of heart*, découragé ; *to have one's heart in the right place*, *in one's work*, avoir le cœur bien placé, à l'ouvrage; *to lose, to take heart*, perdre, prendre courage. ‖ Cœur, entrain *m.* ; *to one's heart's delight* (or) *content*, à cœur joie ; *with half a heart*, sans enthousiasme ; *with a light heart*, de gaieté de cœur. ‖ Cœur, attachement, amour *m.* ; *to lose one's heart to*, tomber amoureux de. ‖ Cœur, for intérieur *m.* ; *at heart*, au fond de soi (or) du cœur ; *in one's heart of hearts*, par-devers soi, au plus profond du cœur. ‖ Cœur *m.* ; mémoire *f.* ; *by heart*, par cœur. ‖ FAM. *Dear heart*, mon cœur, mon amour. ‖ **Heart-attack**, n. MED. Crise cardiaque *f.* ‖ **Heart-break**, n. Chagrin déchirant, déchirement *m.* ‖ **Heart-breaking** (or) **-rending**, adj. Déchirant, qui fend le cœur. ‖ **Heart-broken**, adj. Au cœur brisé, navré. ‖ **Heart-burning**, n. Animosité *f.* ‖ **Heart-case**, n. MED. Cardiaque *s.* ‖ **Heart-disease**, n. MED. Maladie (*f.*) de cœur. ‖ **Heart-searching**, adj. Scrutateur, pénétrant ; n. scrupule *m.* ‖ **Heart-sick**, adj. Découragé, navré, désolé. ‖ **Heart-strings**, n. pl. Fibres sensibles *f. pl.* ‖ **Heart-whole**, adj. Libre (heart-free) ; sincère (genuine) ; sans découragement, plein de courage (undismayed).

heartache [-eik] n. Peine (*f.*) de cœur ; chagrin angoissant *m.*

heartbeat [-bi:t] n. MED. Pulsation *f.* ; battement du cœur *m.*

heartburn [-bə:n] n. MED. Pyrosis *m.* ; brûlures (*f. pl.*) d'estomac.

hearten [-ən] v. tr. Encourager.
— v. intr. **To hearten up**, reprendre courage.

heartfelt [-felt] adj. Senti, sincère, venant du fond du cœur.

hearth [hɑ:θ] n. Foyer, âtre *m.* ‖ **Hearth-rug**, n. Devant de foyer *m.*

hearthstone [-stoun] n. Pierre (*f.*) d'âtre. ‖ Poudre (or) pierre (*f.*) à récurer. ‖ U. S. Foyer *m.* (home).

heartily [ˈhɑːtili] adv. Cordialement, chaleureusement, de grand (or) bon (or) tout cœur. ‖ Sincèrement, franchement. ‖ Profondément, totalement. ‖ Avec appétit.

heartiness [-inis] n. Cordialité *f.* ‖ Sincérité *f.* ‖ Empressement, zèle *m.* ‖ Vigueur *f.* (of appetite).

heartless [-lis] adj. Sans cœur.

heartlessly [-lisli] adv. Sans cœur ; impitoyablement ; avec dureté.

heartlessness [-lisnis] n. Manque de cœur *m.* ; dureté, inhumanité *f.*

hearty [-i] adj. Cordial, chaleureux. ‖ Sincère, franc. ‖ Empressé, zélé. ‖ Gros (appetite, eater); copieux, plantureux (meal) ; vigoureux, solide (person). ‖ AGRIC. Fertile (land).
— n. NAUT. Gars *m.*

heat [hi:t] n. Chaleur *f.* ; *red heat*, rouge. ‖ PHYS. Calorique *m.* ; *heat constant*, constante calorifique. ‖ MED. Rougeur *f.* ‖ ZOOL. Rut *m.* ; chaleur *f.* ‖ TECHN. Chaude *f.* ‖ AGRIC. *To sow in heat*, semer sur couche. ‖ SPORTS. Série, manche *f.* ‖ FIG. Fièvre *f.* (of composition) ; feu *m.* (of discussion) ; chaleur *f.* (of the moment) ; ardeur, fougue *f.* (of youth). ‖ FIG. Surexcitation, vivacité *f.* ; *to get into a heat*, s'échauffer, s'enflammer. ‖ **Heat-absorbing**, adj. Qui absorbe la chaleur. ‖ **Heat-energy**, n. PHYS. Énergie thermique *f.* ‖ **Heat-insulating**, adj. Calorifuge. ‖ **Heat-insulation**, n.

Calorifugeage *m.* ‖ **Heat-proof**, adj. Résistant à la chaleur. ‖ **Heat-stroke**, n. MED. Coup (*m.*) de chaleur. ‖ **Heat-wave**, n. Vague de chaleur *f.*
— v. tr. Chauffer. ‖ MED. Échauffer. ‖ FIG. Échauffer, enflammer.
— v. intr. S'échauffer.

heated [-id] adj. Chaud (air) ; chauffant (mat) ; chauffé (room). ‖ FIG. Chaud, animé (argument) ; échauffé, excité (person) ; vif (word).

heater [-ə*] n. Chauffeur *s.* (person). ‖ Appareil de chauffage *m.* ; *car heater*, chaufferette pour auto ; *electric heater*, radiateur électrique ; *gas heater*, chauffe-eau à gaz. ‖ ELECTR. Filament de chauffage *m.* ‖ U. S. POP. Rigolo *m.* (pistol).

heath [hi:θ] n. Lande *f.* ‖ BOT. Bruyère *f.* ‖ **Heath-bell**, n. BOT. Clochette *f.* ‖ **Heath-cock**, n. ZOOL. Tétras *m.*

heathen [ˈhi:ðən] adj., n. Païen *s.*

heathendom [-dəm] n. Paganisme *m.* (belief); païens *m. pl.* (people).

heathenish [-iʃ] adj. Païen, de païen. ‖ FAM. Inculte, barbare.

heathenism [-izm] n. Paganisme *m.* ‖ Barbarie *f.*

heathenize [-aiz] v. tr. Paganiser.
— v. intr. Devenir païen.

heather [ˈheðə*] n. BOT. Bruyère *f.* ‖ FAM. Maquis *m.*

heathery [-ri] adj. Couvert de bruyère.

heathy [ˈhi:θi] adj. Couvert de landes.

heating [ˈhi:tiŋ] n. Chauffage *m.* ; *district heating*, chauffage urbain. ‖ **Heating-apparatus**, n. Calorifère *m.* (for building). ‖ **Heating-pipe**, n. Conduit (*m.*) de chaleur. ‖ **Heating-power**, n. Pouvoir calorifique *m.*

heave [hi:v] v. tr. (78). Lever, soulever (a weight). ‖ Pousser (a groan, sigh). ‖ Lancer, jeter (stones). ‖ NAUT. Lever (the anchor) ; haler (the ship). ‖ **To heave back**, NAUT. Dériver. ‖ **To heave down**, NAUT. Caréner. ‖ **To heave off**, NAUT. Déhaler, renflouer.
— v. intr. Se soulever. ‖ Se soulever, palpiter, se gonfler (breast). ‖ MED. Haleter (to pant) ; avoir des nausées (person) ; se soulever (stomach). ‖ NAUT. Virer (ship) ; *to heave in sight*, poindre. ‖ **To heave to**, NAUT. Se mettre en panne.
— N.B. Au sens nautique, *to heave* fait *hove* aux prét. et p. p.
— n. Soulèvement, gonflement *m.* (act) ; effort (*m.*) pour soulever. ‖ MED. Palpitation *f.* (of the breast) ; soulèvement *m.* ; nausée *f.* (of stomach). ‖ GÉOL. Déplacement latéral *m.*

heaven [ˈhevn] n. Ciel, paradis *m.* ; béatitude céleste *f.* ‖ Ciel, Dieu *m.* ; Providence *f.* ; *good heavens!*, bonté divine ! ‖ Pl. Ciel, firmament *m.* (sky). ‖ FAM. *To move heaven and earth to*, remuer ciel et terre pour, se mettre en quatre (or) se démancher pour. ‖ **Heaven-sent**, adj. Providentiel, inespéré.

heavenliness [-linis] n. Caractère céleste *m.*

heavenly [-li] adj. Céleste, du ciel. ‖ FAM. Divin.

heaver [ˈhi:və*] n. Déchargeur, débardeur *s.*

heavily [ˈhevili] adv. Lourdement. ‖ Pesamment, laborieusement. ‖ Fortement ; *to lose heavily*, perdre gros ; *to rain heavily*, pleuvoir dru.

heaviness [-nis] n. Pesanteur, lourdeur *f.* ; poids *m.* ‖ Appesantissement, alourdissement, abattement *m.* (of body, mind). ‖ Mauvais état *m.* (of a road).

heavy [ˈhevi] adj. Lourd, pesant (see WEIGHTY) ; *to make heavier*, alourdir. ‖ Gros (rain, sea, weather) ; couvert, bas (sky). ‖ Violent (blow) ; lourd, pesant (sleep, tread). ‖ TECHN. *Heavy type*, caractères gras ; *heavy worker*, travailleur de force. ‖ PHYS. Lourd (water). ‖ CH. DE F. Gros (baggage). ‖ SPORTS. Lourd (weight). ‖ FIN. Gros, fort (loss) ; lourd (market) ; garni (purse). ‖ MILIT. Nourri, violent (fire) ; lourd (gun) ; de campagne (outfit). ‖

AGRIC. Gros (crop); gras (soil). ‖ AUTOM. Malaisé (road). ‖ MED. Gros (cold); grossier, gros (features). ‖ ZOOL. *Heavy with young*, gravide. ‖ CULIN. Grand (drinker); gros (eater); lourd (food). ‖ THEATR. Noble (father); tragique (part). ‖ FIG. Indigeste (book); lourd, pesant (mind, person, style). ‖ FIG. Chargé (day); lourd (odour, silence, task). ‖ FIG. Triste, pénible (fate, news); gros (heart). ‖ **Heavy-duty,** adj. TECHN. Spécial pour gros travaux, résistant. ‖ **Heavy-handed,** adj. Maladroit, à la main lourde (clumsy); sévère, oppressif (harsh). ‖ **Heavy-hearted,** adj. Au cœur lourd, accablé.
— adv. Lourd, lourdement; *to lie heavy on,* peser sur, charger.
— n. pl. MILIT. Dragons *m. pl.*; artillerie lourde *f.*
heavyweight [-,weit] n. SPORTS. Poids lourd *m.* ‖ FIG. Gros bonnet *m.*
hebdomad ['hebdomæd] n. Semaine *f.*
hebdomadal [heb'dɔmədəl] adj. Hebdomadaire.
hebetate ['hebiteit] v. tr. Hébéter.
— v. intr. S'abrutir.
Hebraic [hi:'breiik] adj. Hébraïque.
Hebraism ['hi:breiizm] n. Hébraïsme *m.*
Hebraist [-ist] n. Hébraïsant *s.*
Hebrew ['hi:bru:] n., adj. Hébreu *m.*
hecatomb ['hekətu:m] n. Hécatombe *f.*
heck [hek] interj. FAM. Flûte!; *what, how the heck,* que, comment diable!; *a heck of a good player,* un sacré bon joueur.
heckle ['hekl] v. tr. Harceler de questions.
heckler [-ə*] n. Questionneur *s.* ‖ Interrupteur *m.* (in politics).
hectare [hektɑ:] n. Hectare *m.*
hectic ['hektik] adj. MED. De tuberculeux (cough); hectique (fever); fiévreux, empourpré (person). ‖ FAM. Trépidant, excitant, enivrant (wild).
— n. MED. Fièvre (or) rougeur hectique *f.*
hectogram(me) ['hektɔgræm] n. Hectogramme *m.*
hectograph ['hektɔgrɑ:f] n. Autocopiste *m.* (instrument); autocopie *f.* (process).
hectolitre [-li:tə*] n. Hectolitre *m.*
hectometre [-mi:tə*] n. Hectomètre *m.*
hector ['hektə*] n. Matamore *m.*
— v. tr. Malmener.
— v. intr. Faire le matamore.
hectowatt ['hektowɔt] n. ELECTR. Hectowatt *m.*
heddle ['hedl] n. TECHN. Lice *f.* (of a loom).
hedge [hedʒ] n. Haie *f.* ‖ FIG. Barrière *f.* ‖ FAM. *To sit on the hedge,* se tenir à carreau. ‖ **Hedge-hop,** v. intr. AVIAT. Voler en rase-mottes. ‖ **Hedge-hopping,** n. AVIAT. Rase-mottes *m.* ‖ **Hedge-sparrow,** n. ZOOL. Accenteur mouchet *m.*
— adj. Interlope (press); de bas étage (tavern). ‖ JUR. Marron (lawyer).
— v. tr. Enclore, entourer d'une haie. ‖ FIN. Compenser, faire la contre-partie de. ‖ FIG. Entourer. ‖ **To hedge in,** entourer (*with,* de). ‖ **To hedge off,** séparer (*from,* de).
— v. intr. AGRIC. Tailler les haies. ‖ FIN. Faire la contrepartie. ‖ FIG. S'abriter, se couvrir; *to hedge behind the rules,* se retrancher derrière les règlements. ‖ FIG. Chercher des échappatoires, user de faux-fuyants.
hedgehog ['hedʒhɔg] n. ZOOL., MILIT., FIG. Hérisson *m.*
— adj. MILIT. En hérisson (defence).
hedgehoggy [-i] adj. FIG. Epineux; hérissé; *to get hedgehoggy,* se mettre en boule.
hedger ['hedʒə*] n. Tailleur (*m.*) de haies.
hedgerow ['hedʒrou] n. Bordure (*f.*) de haies.
hedonic [hi:'dɔnik] adj. Hédonique.
— n. pl. Hédonisme *m.*
hedonism ['hi:dənizm] n. Hédonisme *m.*
hedonist [-ist] n. Hédoniste *s.*
heebie-jeebies ['hi:bi'dʒi:biz] n. pl. FAM.

Déprime *f.* (depression); trac *m.*, trouille *f.* (nervousness); chair de poule *f.* (revulsion).
heed [hi:d] v. tr. Faire attention à, prendre garde à.
— v. intr. Faire attention, prendre garde.
— n. Attention *f.; to take heed,* prendre garde.
heedful [-ful] adj. Vigilant; attentif (*of,* à). ‖ Circonspect, prudent.
heedfully [-fuli] adv. Attentivement; soigneusement; avec circonspection.
heedfulness [-fulnis] n. Attention, vigilance *f.* ‖ Circonspection, prudence *f.*
heedless [-lis] adj. Etourdi, insouciant. ‖ Inattentif (*of,* à); peu soucieux (*of,* de).
heedlessly [-lisli] adv. A l'étourdie, étourdiment; avec insouciance.
heedlessness [-lisnis] n. Etourderie; insouciance *f.* (*of,* de). ‖ Négligence, inattention *f.*
hee-haw ['hi:'hɔ:] n. Hi-han *m.* (see BRAY); ho-ho *m.* (laugh).
— v. intr. Braire.
heel [hi:l] n. Talon *m.* (of foot, shoe, stocking). ‖ NAUT., CH. DE F., MUS. Talon. ‖ FIG. *The heel of Achilles,* le défaut de la cuirasse, le talon d'Achille. ‖ U. S. POP. Canaille *f.* ‖ LOC. *To cool one's heels,* croquer le marmot, faire le pied de grue; *to lay by the heels,* fourrer au bloc; *to show a clean pair of heels, to take to one's heels,* prendre ses jambes à son cou; *to tread on s.o.'s heels,* talonner qqn, marcher sur les talons de qqn; *to turn on one's heels,* tourner les talons. ‖ **Heel-cap,** n. Contrefort *m.* (of shoes). ‖ **Heel-tap,** n. Rondelle de hausse *f.* (on shoes); FAM. Fond de verre *m.*
— v. tr. Mettre (ou) refaire un talon à (shoes, stockings). ‖ Marcher sur les talons de (s.o.). ‖ SPORTS. Talonner. ‖ U. S. POP. Pourvoir (with money).
— v. intr. NAUT. Mettre à la talon.
heel n. NAUT. Bande, gîte *f.*
— v. intr. NAUT. Donner de la bande, gîter.
— v. tr. NAUT. Mettre à la bande.
heft [heft] n. U. S. FAM. Poids *m.* (weight). ‖ U. S. FIG. Majeure partie *f.; gros *m.* (bulk).
— v. tr. Soulever (pour lift); soupeser (to poise).
hefty [-i] adj. U.S. FAM. Costaud. (See STALWART.)
hegemonic [hi:gi'mɔnik] adj. Possédant l'hégémonie.
hegemony [hi:'gemɔni] n. Hégémonie *f.*
Hegira ['hedʒirə] n. Hégire *f.*
heifer ['hefə*] n. ZOOL. Génisse *f.*
heigh [hei] interj. Eh!; oh!
height [hait] n. Hauteur, taille *f.* (see STATURE); *ten feet in height,* dix pieds de haut. ‖ Hauteur, altitude *f.* ‖ GEOGR. Hauteur, éminence, montagne *f.; height sickness,* mal des montagnes. ‖ FIG. Hauteur, élévation *f.* ‖ FIG. Apogée *f.;* sommet, faîte, comble *m.; at the height of the season,* en pleine saison; *in the height of fashion,* à la toute dernière mode; *to be at its height,* battre son plein.
heighten [-n] v. tr. Relever, rehausser. ‖ MED. Aggraver. ‖ FIN., FIG. Augmenter.
— v. intr. S'élever; se rehausser. ‖ Augmenter.
heinous ['heinəs] adj. Odieux (crime).
heinously [-li] adv. Odieusement.
heinousness [-nis] n. Odieux *m.* (*of,* de); énormité, atrocité *f.*
heir ['ɛə*] n. Héritier *m.* (*to,* de). ‖ **Heir-at-law,** n. JUR. Héritier naturel *m.*
heirdom [-dəm] n. JUR. Héritage *m.* (inheritance). ‖ Qualité (*f.*) d'héritier (heirship).
heiress [-ris] n. Héritière *f.* ‖ **Heiress-hunter,** n. Coureur (*m.*) de dot.
heirloom [-lu:m] n. Bijou (or) meuble (or) souvenir (*m.*) de famille.
heirship [-ʃip] n. JUR. Qualité (*f.*) d'héritier.
heist [haist] n. U.S. POP. Braquage *m.* (hold-up); casse, fric-frac *m.* (burglary).
— v. tr. Cambrioler, braquer.

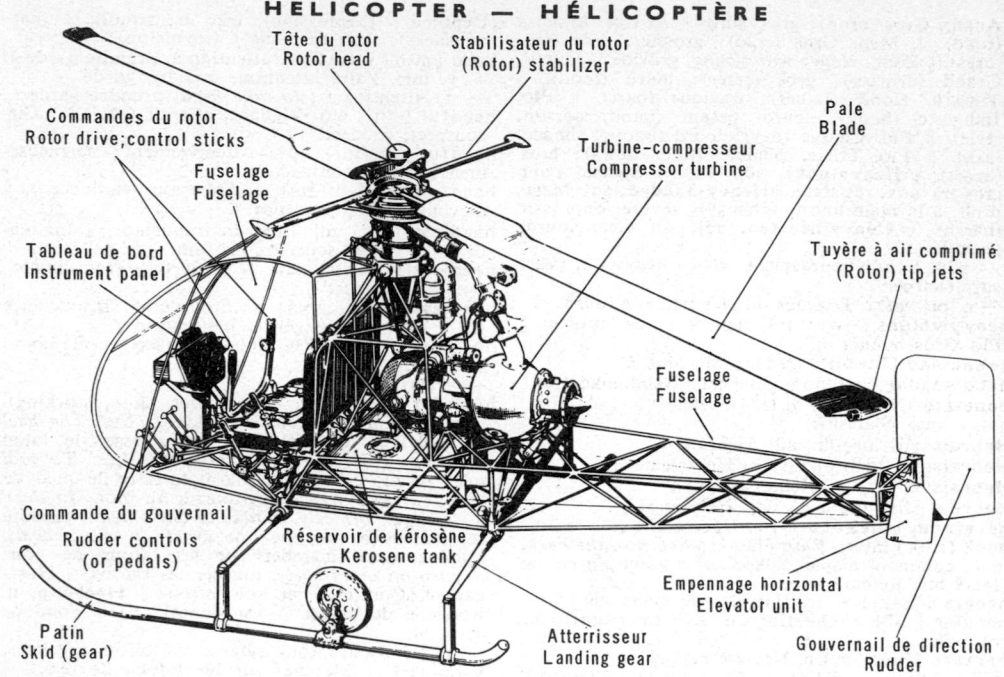

Tête du rotor
Rotor head

Stabilisateur du rotor
(Rotor) stabilizer

Commandes du rotor
Rotor drive;control sticks

Pale
Blade

Turbine–compresseur
Compressor turbine

Fuselage
Fuselage

Tableau de bord
Instrument panel

Tuyère à air comprimé
(Rotor) tip jets

Fuselage
Fuselage

Commande du gouvernail
Rudder controls
(or pedals)

Réservoir de kérosène
Kerosene tank

Empennage horizontal
Elevator unit

Patin
Skid (gear)

Atterrisseur
Landing gear

Gouvernail de direction
Rudder

held [held] pret., p. p. See HOLD.
heliborne ['helibɔ:n] adj. Héliporté.
helical ['helikəl], **helicoid** ['helikɔid], **helicoidal** [,heli'kɔidəl] adj. Hélicoïde, hélicoïdal.
helicon ['helikən] n. MUS. Hélicon m.
helicopter ['heli,kɔptə*] n. AVIAT. Hélicoptère m. ‖ **Helicopter-borne**, adj. AVIAT. Héliporté.
heliocentric [,hi:lio'sentrik] adj. Héliocentrique.
heliochrome ['hi:liokroum] n. Photographie en couleur, héliochromie f.
heliograph [-grɑ:f] n. Héliographe m. ‖ Héliogravure f.
— v. tr. Communiquer par héliographe. ‖ Reproduire par héliogravure.
heliogravure [,hi:liogrə'vjuə*] n. Héliogravure f.
helioscope ['hi:lioskoup] n. Hélioscope m.
heliostat [-stæt] n. Héliostat m.
heliotherapy [,hi:lio'θerəpi] n. Héliothérapie f.
heliotrope ['heljotroup] n. BOT. Héliotrope f.
heliotypy [-taipi] n. Héliotypie f.
heliport ['heli,pɔ:t] n. AVIAT. Héliport m.
helium ['hi:ljəm] n. CHIM. Hélium m.
helix ['hi:liks] (pl. **helices** ['hi:lisi:z]) n. MED. Hélix m. ‖ MATH. Hélice f. ‖ ARCHIT. Spirale f. ‖ ZOOL. Colimaçon m.
hell [hel] n. Enfer m. ‖ FAM. A hell of a noise, un boucan infernal ; till hell freezes over, jusqu'à la saint-glinglin ; to get (or) U. S. to catch hell, prendre qqch. pour son grade ; to give s.o. hell, faire passer un mauvais quart d'heure à qqn ; to hell with him !, qu'il aille au diable ! ‖ **Hell-bent**, adj. U. S. FAM. Acharné en diable (for, on, à). ‖ **Hell-cat**, n. Harpie f. ‖ **Hell-fire**, n. Feu de l'enfer m. ‖ **Hell-hound**, n. Suppôt d'enfer m.
hellbender [-bendə*] n. U. S. Fêtard m. (person) ; bringue, noce f. (spree).
helebore ['helibɔ:*] n. BOT. Ellébore f.
Hellenic ['heli:nik] adj. Hellénique.
hellenism ['helinizm] n. Hellénisme m.
hellenist [-ist] n. Helléniste s.

hellenize [-aiz] v. tr., intr. Helléniser.
hellish ['heliʃ] adj. Infernal.
— adv. FAM. Sacrément, vachement.
hellishly [-li] adv. Diaboliquement, d'une manière infernale.
hellishness [-nis] n. Méchanceté infernale (or) démoniaque ; diablerie f.
hello [he'lou] interj., v. intr. See HALLO.
helm [helm] n. NAUT. Barre f. ; gouvernail m. ; to be at the helm, tenir la barre. ‖ FIG. Direction f. ; to be at the helm, tenir le gouvernail (or) les rênes.
— v. tr. FIG. Gouverner, diriger.
helm n. † Heaume m.
helmet [-it] n. Casque m. ; pith (or) sun helmet, casque colonial. ‖ MILIT. Steel helmet, casque m. ‖ PHYS. Chapiteau m. (of retort).
helmeted [-itid] adj. Casqué.
helminth ['helminθ] n. MED. Helminthe m.
helminthic [hel'minθik] adj. MED. Vermifuge.
helmsman ['helmzmən] n. NAUT. Timonier, homme (m.) de barre.
helot ['helət] n. Ilote m.
helotism [-izm̩] n. Ilotisme m.
help [help] v. tr. Aider, prêter assistance (or) secours à, venir en aide à ; you can't help it, vous n'y pouvez rien ; it can't be helped, il n'y a rien à faire ; to help in, out, over, aider à entrer, à sortir, à surmonter. ‖ Aider, faciliter ; that doesn't help much, ça n'arrange pas grand-chose. ‖ Servir (at table) ; to help oneself to, se servir de. ‖ Empêcher, éviter ; I can't help it, je n'y peux rien. ‖ S'empêcher de, se garder de, se retenir de ; one cannot help wondering whether, on ne peut s'empêcher de se demander si. ‖ FAM. Not to do more than one can help, ne pas en faire plus que de raison ; to help a lame dog over the stile, dépanner un canard boiteux. ‖ **Help-yourself**, adj. COMM. De libre service (counter, store).
— n. Aide, assistance f. ; secours, appui m. ; mutual

help, entraide; *to cry for help*, appeler à l'aide; *to go to s.o.'s help*, prêter secours à. ‖ Remède *m.*; *there's no help for it*, c'est irréparable (or) irrémédiable (or) sans recours. ‖ Aide *m.* (person); *home help*, aide ménagère; *mother's help* (or) U. S. *helper*, aide familiale. ‖ U. S. Domestique, employé *m.*; « *help wanted* », offres d'emplois.

helper [-ə*] .n. Aide, assistant, auxiliaire *m.*

helpful [-ful] adj. Secourable, serviable (person); utile (thing). ‖ MED. Salutaire (remedy).

helping [-iŋ] n. Aide *f.* ‖ Portion *f.* (at table).
— adj. Secourable; *to give a helping hand to*, donner un coup de main à.

helpless [-lis] adj. Sans recours (or) appui (or) protection. ‖ Réduit à l'impuissance, incapable de s'en sortir; désemparé.

helplessly [-lisli] adv. Sans secours. ‖ Sans ressort (or) initiative. ‖ Irrémédiablement, sans espoir.

helplessness [-lisnis] n. Manque d'appui *m.*; isolement, délaissement *m.* ‖ Impuissance *f.*; manque de ressort *m.*; incapacité (*f.*) de s'en sortir.

helpmate [-meit] n. † Moitié *f.* (spouse). ‖ Collaborateur *m.*; collaboratrice *f.*

helter-skelter ['heltə'skəltə*] adv. Pêle-mêle, à la débandade, à la six-quatre-deux (fam.).
— adj. Désordonné.
— n. Débandade, bousculade *f.* ‖ Fouillis, tohubohu *m.*

helve [helv] n. TECHN. Manche *m.* ‖ FAM. *To throw the helve after the hatchet*, risquer le tout pour le tout.

Helvetian [hel'vi:ʃiən] adj. GEOGR. Helvétien, helvétique.
— n. Helvète *s.*

hem [hem] n. Bord *m.* (border). ‖ Ourlet *m.*; *false hem*, faux ourlet. ‖ **Hem binding**, n. U.S. Extrafort *m.* ‖ **Hem-line**, n. Bas (*m.*) d'une jupe; *hemlines are getting lower* (or) *higher*, les jupes rallongent (or) raccourcissent; *knee-length hem-lines*, ourlets aux genoux.
— v. tr. (1). Border. ‖ Ourler. ‖ **To hem in**, encercler, cerner, entourer.

hem interj. Hem!
— v. intr. Faire hum; *to hem and haw*, ânonner.

hema- ['hemə-]. See HAEMA-.

hemeralopic [,hemərə'loupik] adj. Nyctalope.

hemicycle ['hemisaikḷ] n. Hémicycle *m.*

hemiplegia [,hemi'pli:dʒiə] n. MED. Hémiplégie *f.*

hemiplegic [-ik] adj., n. MED. Hémiplégique *s.*

hemipter [he'miptə*] n. ZOOL. Hémiptère *m.*

hemisphere ['hemisfiə*] n. Hémisphère *m.*

hemispherical [,hemi'sferikəl] adj. Hémisphérique.

hemistich ['hemistik] n. Hémistiche *m.*

hemlock ['hemlɔk] n. BOT. Ciguë *f.*

hemo-. See HAEMO-.

hemp [hemp] n. Chanvre *m.* (fibre, plant, rope). ‖ Eupatoire *f.* ‖ **Hemp-field**, n. Chènevière *f.* ‖ **Hemp-seed**, n. Chènevis *m.*

hempen [-ən] adj. De chanvre.

hemstitch ['hemstitʃ] n. Ourlet à jour *m.*
— v. tr. Ourler à jour.

hen [hen] n. ZOOL. Poule *f.* (fowl); femelle *f.* (of birds, lobsters). ‖ FAM. *Old church hen*, vieille grenouille de bénitier; *old hen*, vieille dinde. ‖ **Hen-bird**, n. ZOOL. Oiseau femelle *m.* ‖ **Hen-coop**, n. Cage (*f.*) à poules. ‖ **Hen-house**, n. Poulailler *m.* ‖ **Hen-roost**, n. Juchoir, perchoir; poulailler *m.*

henbane ['henbein] n. BOT. Jusquiame *f.*

hence [hens] adv. D'ici (from here). ‖ D'où, pour cela, à cause de cela (therefore). ‖ D'ici, à partir d'aujourd'hui (from now). ‖ D'ici-bas, de ce bas monde (from this life).
— interj. † Hors d'ici!

henceforth [-'fɔ:θ] adv. Dorénavant, à l'avenir, désormais.

henchman ['hentʃmən] (pl. **henchmen**) n. † Page, suivant *m.* ‖ Partisan, séide *m.*

hendecagon [hen'dekəgən] n. MATH. Hendécagone *m.*

hendecasyllabic ['hen,dekəsi'læbik] adj., n. Hendécasyllabe *m.*

hendiadys [hen'daiədis] n. GRAMM. Hendyadis *m.*

henna ['henə] n. Henné *m.*
— v. tr. Teindre au henné.

hennery ['henəri] n. Basse-cour *f.* ‖ AGRIC. Elevage (*m.*) de volailles.

henpeck ['henpek] v. tr. Dominer, mener par le bout du nez (one's husband).

henpecked [-t] adj. Enjuponné, dominé par sa femme.

hep [hep] adj. U. S. FAM. Affranchi, averti; au courant, à la page, dans le train; *to get hep*, se dégourdir, se dessaler, se mettre à la coule. ‖ **Hep-cat**, n. FAM. Fanatique (*s.*) du swing (or) du rock'n roll.

hepatic [hi'pætik] adj. MED. Hépatique.

hepatitis [hepe'taitis] n. MED. Hépatite *f.*

heptagon ['heptəgən] n. MATH. Heptagone *m.*

heptane ['heptein] n. CHIM. Heptane *m.*

heptarchy ['heptɑ:ki] n. Heptarchie *f.*

Heptateuch ['heptətju:k] n. ECCLES. Heptateuque *m.*

heptavalent [hep'tævələnt] adj. CHIM. Heptavalent, septivalent.

her ⌊hə*⌋ pron. pers. (objective case). Elle; *I remember her*, je me souviens d'elle; *with her*, avec elle. ‖ La; *I saw her*, je la vis, je l'ai vue. ‖ Lui; *take this letter to her*, apportez lui cette lettre. ‖ Celle; *to her who told you so*, à celle qui vous l'a dit.
— adj. poss. Son, sa, ses (denoting a feminine possessor); *it's her book*, c'est son livre.

herald ['herəld] n. Héraut *m.* ‖ Messager *m.*
— v. tr. Annoncer, proclamer. ‖ Introduire, faire entrer (to usher in).

heraldic [he'rældik] adj. BLAS. Héraldique.

heraldry ['herəldri] n. BLAS. Science héraldique *f.*; blason *m.*; *book of heraldry*, armorial.

herb [hə:b] n. BOT. Herbe potagère *f.*; *sweet herbs*, fines herbes. ‖ MED. Herbe médicinale (or) officinale *f.* ‖ **Herb-shop**, n. Herboristerie *f.*

herbaceous [hə:'beiʃəs] adj. Herbacé.

herbage ['hə:bidʒ] n. AGRIC. Herbages *m. pl.* ‖ JUR. Droit (*m.*) de pâture.

herbal ['hə:bəl] adj. D'herbes.
— n. Herbier *m.* (book).

herbalist [-ist] n. BOT. Botaniste *m.* ‖ MED. Herboriste *s.*

herbarium [hə:'bɛəriəm] n. BOT. Herbier *m.*

herbivora [hə:'bəvərə] n. pl. Herbivores *m. pl.*

herbivorous [-əs] adj. ZOOL. Herbivore.

herborist ['hə:bərist] n. BOT. Herboriseur *m.* ‖ MED. Herboriste *s.*

herborization [,hə:bərai'zeiʃən] n. Herborisation *f.*

herborize ['hə:bəraiz] v. intr. Herboriser.

herby ['hə:bi] adj. Herbeux. (See GRASSY.) ‖ BOT. Herbacé.

Herculean [,hə:kju'li:ən] adj. Herculéen.

Hercules ['hə:kjuli:z] n. Hercule *m.*

herd [hə:d] n. ZOOL. Troupeau *m.* ‖ FIG. Populace *f.*; troupeau, peuple *m.*; *the common herd*, le vulgum pecus. ‖ **Herd-book**, n. Herd-book.
— v. intr. ZOOL. *To herd together*, s'attrouper. ‖ FIG. S'accoler, s'acoquiner (with, à).
— v. tr. ZOOL. Rassembler en troupeau. ‖ FIG. Attrouper.

herd [hə:d] n. Berger, pâtre *m.*
— v. tr. Garder (cattle).

herdsman [-zmən] n. (pl. **herdsmen**) n. Berger; bouvier, pâtre *m.*

here [hiə*] adv. Ici, en ce lieu ; *from here*, d'ici ; *here and there*, çà et là. ‖ En ce monde, sur la terre ; *here below*, ici-bas. ‖ Ici, maintenant, à ce moment (now). ‖ Ci, voici ; *here is Mr. Smith*, voici M. Smith ; *here we are*, nous voici ; *the man here says*, cet homme-ci dit. ‖ FIG. *Neither here nor there*, hors de propos.
— interj. Présent ! (answering a roll call). ‖ Ecoutez !, tenez ! (to call attention) ; *look here !*, dites donc !, regardez voir ! (fam.). ‖ FAM. *Here goes !*, allons-y donc !

hereabout(s) ['hiərə,baut(s)] adv. Non loin d'ici, dans les parages (or) environs, aux alentours.

hereafter [hiə'rɑ:ftə*] adv. Plus tard, après (in the future). ‖ Ci-après (following this). ‖ Dans l'autre monde (or) vie (after death).
— n. Temps futur, avenir *m.* (future). ‖ Vie future *f.*, au-delà *m.* (after death).

hereby [-'bai] adv. Par ceci, par là, par ces moyens. ‖ JUR. Par le présent acte (ou) les présentes.

hereditable [hi'reditəbl] adj. JUR. Héritable, transmissible (property).

hereditament [,heri'ditəmənt] n. JUR. Bien transmissible par héritage *m.*

hereditarily [hi'reditərili] adv. Héréditairement.

hereditary [-əri] adj. MED., FIG. Héréditaire.

heredity [-i] n. MED. Hérédité *f.* (See GENETICS.)

herein ['hiə'rin] adv. Sur ce point, en ceci (in this matter) ; dans ce lieu, ici (in this place) ; ci-inclus (in this writing).

hereinafter [-'ɑ:ftə*] adv. Ci-après.

hereof ['hiə'rɔv] adv. De ceci, à ce sujet.

heresiarch [hi'reziɑ:k] n. ECCLES. Hérésiarque *m.*

heresy ['herisi] n. ECCLES. Hérésie *f.*

heretic ['herətik] n. ECCLES. Hérétique *s.*

heretical [hi'retikəl] adj. ECCLES. Hérétique.

hereto [hiə'tu:] adv. En plus de ceci, en outre. ‖ Ci-joint.

heretofore ['hiətu'fɔ:*] adv. Autrefois, jusqu'ici, ci-devant.

hereunder ['hiə'rʌndə*] adv. Ci-dessous.

hereupon ['hiərə'pɔn] adv. Là-dessus, sur ce point (upon this). ‖ Sur ce, là-dessus (at once).

herewith ['hiə'wið] adv. Avec ceci, ci-joint.

heritable ['heritəbl] adj. JUR. Héréditaire (bonds) ; apte à hériter (person) ; héritable (property).

heritage [-idʒ] n. JUR., FIG. Héritage *m.* ‖ ECCLES. Eglise *f.* (church) ; peuple élu *m.* (the Jews).

heritor ['heritə*] n. JUR. Héritier *s.* (See HEIR.)

herl [hə:l] n. SPORTS. Mouche artificielle *f.*

hermaphrodism [hə:'mæfrədizm] n. Hermaphrodisme *m.*

hermaphrodite [-dait] adj. MED., ZOOL. Hermaphrodite. ‖ NAUT. *Hermaphrodite brig*, brickgoélette.
— n. MED., ZOOL. Hermaphrodite *s.*

hermeneutic(al) [,hə:mi'nju:tik(əl)] adj. Herméneutique.

hermeneutics [-iks] n. sg. Herméneutique *f.*

hermetic [hə:'metik] adj. † Alchimique. ‖ Hermétique.

hermetically [-əli] adv. Hermétiquement.

hermit ['hə:mit] n. Ermite, solitaire *m.* ‖ *Hermitcrab*, n. ZOOL. Bernard-l'ermite *m.*

hermitage [-idʒ] n. Ermitage *m.*

hern [hə:n] n. ZOOL. Héron *m.*

hernia ['hə:njə] n. MED. Hernie *f.*

hernial [-əl] adj. MED. Herniaire.

herniated [-eitid] adj. MED. Hernié.

hero ['hiərou] (pl. **heroes** [-z]) n. Héros *m.* (chief character, superman, warrior). ‖ *Hero-worship*, n. Culte (*m.*) des héros.

heroic [hi'rouik] adj. Héroïque (age, person, remedy, poem, verse). ‖ MUS. Fort (tenor).
— n. Vers héroïque, décasyllabe *m.* ‖ Pl. Grandiloquence *f.*

heroically [-əli] adv. Héroïquement, avec héroïsme.

heroi-comic [hə,roui'kɔmik] adj. Héroï-comique.

heroin [hi'rouin] n. CHIM. Héroïne *f.*

heroine ['herouin] n. Héroïne *f.*

heroism [-izm] n. Héroïsme *m.*

heroize [-aiz] v. tr. Transformer en héros.
— v. intr. Jouer au héros.

heron ['herən] n. ZOOL. Héron *m.*

herpes ['hə:pi:z] n. MED. Herpès *m.*

herpetic [hə:'petik] adj. MED. Herpétique.

herring ['heriŋ] n. ZOOL. Hareng *m.* ‖ CULIN. *Red herring*, hareng saur. ‖ FAM. *Red herring*, procédé (or) objet (*m.*) servant à détourner l'attention. ‖ *Herring-bone*, adj. Au point de chausson (stitch) ; ARCHIT. En épi (work) ; ARTS. A chevrons (pattern) ; n. ZOOL. Arête (*f.*) de hareng.

hers [hə:z] pron. poss. A elle, le sien, la sienne, les siens, les siennes.

herself [hə:'self] pron. Elle-même (intensive) ; *she came herself*, elle vint elle-même (or) en personne. ‖ Se (reflexive) ; *she has tired herself out*, elle s'est épuisée de fatigue. ‖ LOC. *By herself*, toute seule ; *she is not herself*, ce n'est plus elle, elle a perdu la maîtrise de soi ; elle ne se connaît plus (fam.).

hertz [hə:ts] n. PHYS. Hertz *m.* (unit).

Hertzian ['hə:tsiən] adj. PHYS. Hertzien.

hesitancy ['hezitənsi] n. Hésitation, incertitude *f.*

hesitant [-ənt] adj. Hésitant, indécis. (See RELUCTANT.)

hesitate ['heziteit] v. intr. Hésiter (about, as to, au sujet de, sur) ; *to hesitate for a word*, hésiter pour trouver un mot. ‖ Hésiter, balancer, osciller (to waver). ‖ Hésiter, reculer (to be reluctant) [*to*, à]. ‖ Hésiter, ânonner, bafouiller (to stammer).

hesitating [-iŋ] adj. Hésitant.

hesitatingly [-iŋli] adv. Avec hésitation.

hesitation [,hezi'teiʃən] n. Hésitation, indécision, irrésolution *f.* ‖ Hésitation, incertitude *f.* ; doute *m.*

Hesperian [hes'piəriən] adj. Occidental.

Hesperus ['hespərəs] n. ASTRON. Vénus, étoile (*f.*) du berger.

hest [hest] n. † Ordre *m.*

het [het] adj. FAM. *Het up*, agité, excité, énervé (excited) ; en rogne (angry).

hetaera [hi'tiərə], **hetaira** [hi'tairə] n. Hétaïre *f.*

heteroclite ['hetəroklait] adj. GRAMM. Irrégulier. ‖ FIG. Hétéroclite.

heterodox ['hetərədɔks] adj. Hétérodoxe.

heterodoxy [-i] n. Hétérodoxie *f.*

heterodyne ['hetərodain] adj., n. RADIO. Hétérodyne *m.*

heterogamy [,hetə'rɔgəmi] n. Hétérogamie *f.*

heterogeneity [,hetərodʒi'ni:iti] n. Hétérogénéité *f.*

heterogeneous [,hetəro'dʒi:niəs] adj. Hétérogène.

heterogenesis [-'dʒenisis] n. Hétérogénie *f.*

heteromorphic [-'mɔ:fik] adj. Hétéromorphe.

heteroplasty ['hetərəplæsti] n. MED. Hétéroplastie *f.*

heterosexual [-'seksjuəl] adj., n. Hétérosexuel *adj., s.*

heterosexuality [-,seksju'æliti] n. Hétérosexualité *f.*

heuristic [hjuə'ristik] adj. PHILOS. Heuristique.

heuristics [-ks] n. sg. PHILOS. Heuristique *f.*

hew [hju:] v. tr. (79). Tailler, équarrir (a stone) ; couper (a tree).
— v. intr. Tailladder, frapper d'estoc et de taille, donner des coups de hache.
— N.B. Le p. p. peut être *hewed* ou *hewn.*

hewing [-iŋ] n. Taille *f.* (of stones) ; abattage *m.* (of trees).

hex [heks] n. U. S. Porte-guigne *m.*
— v. intr. Porter la guigne.

hexad ['heksæd] adj., s. CHIM. Hexavalent *m.*

hexagon ['heksəgən] n. MATH. Hexagone m.
hexagonal [hek'sægən] adj. MATH. Hexagonal.
hexahedral [,heksə'hi:drəl] adj. MATH. Hexaèdre.
hexahedron [-ən] n. MATH. Hexaèdre m.
hexameter [hek'sæmitə*] n. Hexamètre m.
hexametric [,heksə'metrik] adj. Hexamètre.
hexane ['heksein] n. CHIM. Hexane m.
hexavalent [hek'sævələnt] adj. CHIM. Hexavalent.
hey [hei] interj. Hein? (question); hé! (surprise).
heyday ['heidei] n. Eclat m. (of glory); printemps m. (of life); faîte m. (of prosperity); fleur f. (of youth).
H. G. V. [eitʃdʒi:'vi:] abbr. Heavy goods vehicle, AUTOM. Poids lourd m.
hi [hai] interj. Hé! ohé! ‖ U. S. FAM. Salut!
hiatus [hai'eitəs] (pl. **hiatuses** [-iz]) n. Lacune f.; trou, blanc m. (gap). ‖ GRAMM. Hiatus m.
hibernant ['haibənənt] n. Hivernant m. ‖ ZOOL. Hibernant m.
hibernate [-neit] v. intr. Hiverner. ‖ ZOOL. Hiberner. ‖ FIG. Somnoler, paresser.
hibernation [,haibə'neiʃən] n. Hivernation f. ‖ ZOOL. Hibernation f.
Hibernian [hai'bə:niən] adj., n. GEOGR. Irlandais s.
Hibernicism [-nisizm] n. GRAMM. Idiotisme irlandais m.
hibiscus [hai'biskəs] n. BOT. Hibiscus m.
hiccough, hiccup ['hikʌp] n. MED. Hoquet m.
— v. intr. MED. Avoir le hoquet, hoqueter.
— v. tr. Dire en hoquetant.
hick [hik] n. U. S. FAM. Bouseux, péquenot, culterreux m.; hick town, bled.
hickory ['hikəri] n. BOT. Hickory, noyer (m.) d'Amérique.
hid [hid] pret., **hidden** [-n] p. p. See HIDE.
hide [haid] v. tr. (80). Cacher; to hide one's face, se cacher le visage; to hide sth. from sight, dérober qqch. à la vue. ·‖ FIG. Cacher, tenir secret, dissimuler (an event). [See CONCEAL.]
— v. intr. Se cacher. ‖ FIG. To hide behind s.o., se servir de qqn comme d'un paravent. ‖ Hideand-seek, n. Cache-cache m. ‖ Hide-out, n. FAM. Planque f.
hide n. ZOOL., FAM. Cuir m.; peau f. ‖ BOT. Ecorce f.
— v. tr. FAM. Rosser.
hideous ['hidiəs] adj. Atroce, abominable (crime); hideux, horrible, affreux (person).
hideously [-li] adv. Atrocement; hideusement, horriblement.
hideousness [-nis] n. Atrocité, horreur f. (of a crime); hideur f. (of a person).
hiding ['haidiŋ] n. Retraite f. (condition); cachette f. (place). ‖ Hiding-place, n. Cachette f.
hiding n. FAM. Dégelée, tripotée, trempe, pile f.
hie [hai] v. intr. Faire hâte, se hâter.
— v. tr. Hâter.
hierarchic(al) [,haiə'rɑ:kik(əl)] adj. Hiérarchique.
hierarchy ['haiərɑ:ki] n. Hiérarchie f.
hieratic [,haiə'rætik] adj. Hiératique.
hieroglyph ['haiərəglif] n. Hiéroglyphe m.
hieroglyphic [,haiərə'glifik] adj. Hiéroglyphique.
— n. pl. Hiéroglyphes m. pl.
Hieronymus [haiə'rɔniməs] n. ECCLES. Jérôme m.
hi-fi ['hai'fai] n. TECHN., MUS. Chaîne f. (apparatus); hi-fi f. (hobby).
— adj. TECHN., MUS. De haute fidélité.
higgle ['higl] v. intr. Marchander.
higgledy-piggledy ['higldi'pigldi] adj., adv. Pêle-mêle.
high [hai] adj. Haut, grand (in general). ‖ Grand, de haute taille (tall). ‖ Montant (collar, dress). ‖

GEOGR. Haut, élevé, grand (altitude); High Egypt, haute Egypte; high ground, hauteur. ‖ NAUT. Grand (Admiral); haut (tide, waters); fort (wind); high and dry, échoué (ship); on the high seas, en haute mer. ‖ AVIAT. A grande hauteur (flight). ‖ MILIT. De haute puissance (explosive). ‖ SPORTS. D'une grande hauteur (dive, jump). ‖ ELECTR. Haut (frequency). ‖ PHYS. Haut (pression, température). ‖ TECHN. High gears, grande multiplication. ‖ MATH. Higher mathematics, mathématiques supérieures. ‖ AUTOM. Grand (road, speed, street). ‖ FIN. Elevé (price, rate); haut coté (stocks); gros, élevé (wages). ‖ JUR. Grand (Chancellor); haut, suprême (court); haut (treason). ‖ MED. Elevé (fever, pression). ‖ ARTS. Vif (colour). ‖ MUS. Haut (note); aigu, haut (voice). ‖ GRAMM. Haut (German). ‖ CULIN. Avancé (meat); relevé, épicé (sauce); faisandé (venison); high living, bonne chère (or) table; high tea, goûter dinatoire. ‖ ECCLES. Haut (church); grand (priest); high altar, maître-autel; high mass, grand-messe; the Most High, le Très-Haut. ‖ FIG. Haut, reculé, éloigné (antiquity); grand, plein (day); plein (light, noon). ‖ FIG. Mondain, luxueux (life). ‖ FIG. Elevé, noble, supérieur (language, mind, thought); élevé, haut (position); high school, collège; high table, table des professeurs. ‖ FIG. Haut (opinion); élogieux, flatteur (term). ‖ FIG. Hautain (look); altier, arrogant (person); violent (words); high hand, autoritarisme. ‖ FIG. Réjoui, exultant; in high spirits, tout joyeux. ‖ FAM. Parti, gai, paf, éméché (tipsy); défoncé (drugged). ‖ LOC. On one's high horse, sur ses grands chevaux (angry); du haut de sa taille (lofty). ‖ **High-born,** adj. De haute naissance. ‖ **High-Church,** adj. ECCLES. De la haute Eglise. ‖ **High-class,** adj. De grande classe, chic (things); de la bonne société (people). ‖ **High-crowned,** adj. A la calotte haute (hat); en dos d'âne (road). ‖ **High-falutin',** adj. Déclamatoire, ronflant (fam.); n. Ton déclamatoire m. ‖ **High-fidelity,** n. TECHN., MUS. Haute-fidélité f.; adj. De haute fidélité. ‖ **High-flyer,** n. FAM. Ambitieux s. ‖ **High-frequency,** adj. ELECTR. A haute fréquence. ‖ **High-grade,** adj. COMM. De qualité supérieure (fuel); high-grade petrol, supercarburant. ‖ **High-handed,** adj. Autoritaire; to be high-handed with, tenir la dragée haute à. ‖ **High-handedly,** adv. Avec autoritarisme, tyranniquement. ‖ **High-hat,** n. U. S. Snob, poseur s. ‖ **High-key,** adj. CINEM. Lumineux. ‖ **High-level,** adj. A un haut niveau, à un niveau élevé (talks). ‖ **High-minded,** adj. D'âme noble, aux sentiments élevés. ‖ **High-muck-a-muck,** n. U. S. POP. Gros bonnet m. ‖ **High-octane,** adj. CHIM. A indice d'octane élevé. ‖ **High-pitched,** adj. MUS. Aigu; ARCHIT. Surhaussé (arch); pointu (roof); FIG. Noble. ‖ **High-powered,** adj. TECHN. Puissant; FIG. Entrepreneur, dynamique. ‖ **High-pressure,** adj. TECHN. A haute pression; FAM. Energique et persuasif; v. tr. U. S. FAM. Gonfler à bloc. ‖ **High-priced,** adj. Coûteux, onéreux. ‖ **High-proof,** adj. CHIM. A forte teneur en alcool. ‖ **High-rise,** adj. A high-rise block (or) building, une tour. ‖ **High-sounding,** adj. Grandiloquent; ronflant (fam.). ‖ **High-speed,** adj. A grande vitesse, rapide, ultra-rapide; high-speed steel, acier rapide (or) à coupe rapide. ‖ **High-spirited,** adj. Intrépide (courageous); fougueux, plein d'entrain (lively). ‖ **High-strung,** adj. FIG. U. S. Tendu, nerveux; sous pression (fam.). ‖ **High-tension,** adj. ELECTR. A haute tension; high-tension dynamo, dynamo-tension. ‖ **High-toned,** adj. MUS. Aigu; FIG. De haute moralité; U. S. FAM. De premier chic.
— adv. Haut, en haut; to aim high, viser haut. ‖ De haut; twenty feet high, vingt pieds de haut. ‖ Loin, haut (in the past). ‖ FIN. Gros; as high as, jusqu'à (a price). ‖ NAUT. Avec rage (or) violence. ‖ MUS. Haut. ‖ FIG. Fortement, avec intensité; to run high, s'attiser (animosity); words ran high, le ton de la discussion monta. ‖ U. S. Mexico City

is 7,350 feet high, Mexico est à 7 350 pieds d'altitude.
— n. Haut *m.* (high level); *from on high*, d'en haut; *on high*, là-haut, au ciel. ‖ U. S. Fam. Record, niveau *m.* ‖ U. S. Autom. *In high*, en quatrième vitesse.
highball [-bɔːl] n. U. S. Fam. Whisky et soda *m.*
highboy [-bɔi] n. U. S. Chiffonnier *m.* (tallboy).
highbrow [-brau] n. Fam. Intellectuel, cérébral *s.*
— adj. D'intellectuel.
higher [haiə] adj. Supérieur (see HIGH); *higher education*, enseignement supérieur; *higher mathematics*, mathématiques supérieures. ‖ **Higher-ups**, n. pl. Fam. Supérieur(e)s *s. pl.*
highland [-lənd] n. Pays (*m.*) de montagne; hautes terres *f. pl.* ‖ Geogr. *The Highlands*, les Highlands.
— adj. De montagne.
highlander [-ləndə*] n. Montagnard *s.*
highlight [-lait] n. Arts. Rehaut *m.* ‖ Fig. Trait marquant *m.* (of the system). ‖ Fam. Clou *m.* (of a spectacle).
— v. tr. U. S. Mettre en vedette (or) en pleine lumière.
highly [-li] adv. Hautement, extrêmement, à un haut degré; *highly coloured*, haut en couleur. ‖ Hautement, favorablement, flatteusement.
highness [-nis] n. Altesse *f.* (prince, princess); Hautesse *f.* (Sultan). ‖ Fin. Élévation *f.* (in prices). ‖ Naut. Violence *f.* (of the wind). ‖ Fig. Élévation, noblesse *f.* (of mind); fougue *f.* (of passion).
hight [hait] p.p. † Appelé.
highway ['haiwei] n. Route principale, grande route *f.*; grand chemin *m.* ‖ Jur. Voie publique *f.*; *Highways department*, voirie.
highwayman [-mən] (pl. **highwaymen**) n. Voleur de grand chemin, détrousseur *m.*
hijack ['hai,dʒæk] v. tr. S'emparer de, saisir de force (a lorry, goods). ‖ Aviat. Détourner.
— n. Vol, détournement *m'.* ‖ Aviat. Détournement d'avion *m.*, acte (*m.*) de piraterie aérienne.
hijacker [-kə] n. Aviat. Pirate de l'air *m.*
hijacking [-kiη] n. Aviat. Piraterie aérienne *f.*
hike [haik] v. intr. Excursionner, faire des randonnées (or) du tourisme à pied. ‖ Vagabonder.
— v. tr. Fam. Traîner (sth.). ‖ U. S. Faire monter (prices); augmenter (production). ‖ **To hike up**, remonter (one's trousers).
— n. Randonnée, excursion *f.* ‖ U. S. Hausse, augmentation *f.*
hiker [-ə*] n. Excursionniste *s.*
hilarious [hi'lɛəriəs] adj. Hilare, très gai (merry); désopilant, tordant (funny).
hilariousness [-nis] n. Hilarité, gaieté *f.*
hilarity [hi'lærəti] n. Hilarité *f.*
hill [hil] n. Colline *f.*; coteau, vallonnement *m.*; *rounded hill*, mamelon; *up hill and down dale*, par monts et par vaux. ‖ Côte, montée, rampe *f.* (on road); descente *f.* (slope). ‖ Monticule *m.*; butte, élévation (mound). ‖ Milit., Techn. Cote; *hill 648*, cote 648. ‖ Autom. *Speed up-hill*, vitesse en côte. ‖ U. S. Fam. Capitole *m.* ‖ **Hill-folk**, n. Montagnards *m. pl.* ‖ **Hill-side**, n. Flanc de coteau *m.* **Hill-top**, n. Sommet (*m.*) d'une colline.
— v. tr. Agric. Butter, chausser (a plant).
hillbilly [-,bili] n. U. S. Fam. Montagnard *s.*
hillock [-ək] n. Monticule, mamelon, tertre *m.*; butte *f.*
hilly [-i] adj. Montueux, vallonné, accidenté; montagneux; à fortes côtes.
hilt [hilt] n. Poignée *f.* ‖ Fig. *Up to the hilt*, jusqu'à la garde.
— v. tr. Mettre une poignée à.
hilum ['hailəm] n. Bot. Hile *m.*
him [him] pron. pers. (objective case). Le, l'; *she loves him*, elle l'aime. ‖ Lui; *I was thinking of him*, je pensais à lui. ‖ Celui; *to him who*, à celui qui.

himself [him'self] pron. Lui-même (intensive); *he came himself*, il vint lui-même. ‖ Se (reflexive); *he avenged himself*, il s'est vengé.
hind [haind] n. Zool. Biche *f.*
hind n. Valet (*m.*) de ferme.
hind adj. Postérieur; de derrière; *hind quarters*, train de derrière, arrière-train. (See CROUP.) ‖ Autom. *Hind wheel*, roue arrière.
hindbrain [-brein] n. Med. Cerveau postérieur *m.*
hinder ['hində*] v. tr. Gêner, entraver, embarrasser (to impede). ‖ Retarder, arrêter (to delay). ‖ Empêcher, arrêter, retenir (*from*, de) [to prevent].
hinder ['haində*] adj. Postérieur, de derrière.
hindermost ['haindəmoust], **hindmost** ['haindmoust] adj. Dernier, ultime.
Hindi ['hindi] n. Hindî *m.* (language).
Hindoo [hin'duː]. See Hindu.
hindrance ['hindrəns] n. Gêne, entrave *f.*; obstacle *m.* ‖ Empêchement *m.*
hindsight ['haindsait] n. Milit. Hausse *f.* (of a rifle). ‖ Fig. Rétrospective; leçon de l'expérience *f.*
Hindu ['hin'duː] adj., s. Geogr., Eccles. Hindou *s.*
Hinduism ['hinduːizm] n. Eccles. Hindouisme *m.*
Hindustan [,hinduː'stɑːn] n. Geogr. Hindoustan *m.*
Hindustani [,hinduː'stɑːni] adj. Hindou (language).
— n. Hindoustani *m.* (language).
hinge [hindʒ] n. Techn. Gond *m.* (of door); charnière *f.* (stamp-hinge). ‖ Fig. Pivot *m.*; charnière, plaque tournante *f.* ‖ Fam. *Off one's hinges*, déboussolé.
— v. tr. Techn. Mettre un gond (or) une charnière à.
— v. intr. Techn. Pivoter (on, sur). ‖ Fig. Etre axé (on, sur).
hinny ['hini] n. Zool. Bardeau, bardot *m.*
hinny v. intr. U. S. Hennir.
hint [hint] n. Allusion, insinuation *f.*; *to take the hint*, comprendre à demi-mot; *to throw out a hint that*, donner à entendre que. ‖ Comm. Conseil, mode d'emploi *m.* ‖ Fig. Aperçu *m.*; idée *f.* ‖ Fig. Nuance *f.*; soupçon *m.*; *a vague hint of melancholy*, un je ne sais quoi de mélancolique.
— v. tr. Insinuer, laisser entendre.
— v. intr. Faire allusion (*at*, à).
hinterland ['hintə,lænd] n. Geogr. Hinterland *m.*, arrière-pays *m. inv.*
hip [hip] n. Med. Hanche *f.* ‖ Archit. Arête *f.* ‖ Fam. *On the hip*, acculé, en mauvaise posture; *to smite hip and thigh*, battre à plate couture. ‖ **Hip-bath**, n. Bain de siège *m.* ‖ **Hip-bone**, n. Med. Os iliaque (or) coxal *m.* ‖ **Hip-flask**, n. Flasque (*f.*) de poche. ‖ **Hip-joint**, n. Med. Articulation iliaque (or) coxale (or) de la hanche *f.* ‖ **Hip-pocket**, n. Poche (*f.*) revolver. ‖ **Hip-roof**, n. Archit. Toit (*m.*) en croupe. ‖ **Hip-swaying**, adj. Fam. Déhanché (walk).
hip n. Bot. Cynorrhodon; gratte-cul *m.* (fam.).
hip n. Fam. Cafard *m.*
— v. tr. (1). Fam. Rendre cafardeux, turlupiner.
hip interj. *Hip, hip hooray!*, hip, hip, hip hourra!
hip adj. See HEP.
hippie, hippy ['hipi] adj., s. Hippie (or) hippy *adj., s.*
hippo ['hipou] (pl. **hippos** [-z]) n. Fam. Hippopotame *m.*
hippocampus [,hipo'kæmpəs] n. Zool. Hippocampe *m.*
hippodrome ['hipədroum] n. Hippodrome *m.*
hippogriff, hippogryph ['hipəgrif] n. Hippogriffe *m.*
hippophagous [hi'pɔfəgəs] adj. Hippophage.
hippopotamus [,hipə'pɔtəməs] (pl. **hippopotamuses** [-məsiz], **hippopotami** [-mai]) n. Zool. Hippopotame *m.*

hippy ['hipi] adj., s. See HIPPIE.
hippy adj. Aux hanches rebondies.
hipster ['hipstə*] adj. Taille basse.
— n. pl. Pantalon (m.) taille basse.
hipster ['hipstə*] n. U. S. POP. Zazou m.
hire ['haiə*] n. Gages m. pl.; salaire m. (wages).
‖ Location f.; louage m.; for hire, à louer; on hire,
en location. ‖ FIN. Loyer m. (of capital). ‖ U. S.
Embauchage m. (of persons). ‖ **Hire-purchase,** n.
Vente (f.) à tempérament, location-vente f.
— v. tr. Louer (sth.); to hire out, loucr. ‖ U. S.
Engager, embaucher (s.o.).
hired [-əd] adj. Loué; de louage (carriage). ‖ MILIT.
Mercenaire (troops). ‖ JUR. A gages, soudoyé
(assassin). ‖ U. S. Hired girl, bonne.
hireling [haiəliŋ] n. Mercenaire s.
hirsute ['hə:sju:t] adj. Hirsute.
his [hiz] adj. poss. Son, sa, ses (denoting a masculine possessor). ‖ Le, la, les; he broke his leg,
il s'est cassé la jambe; with his hands in his
pockets, les mains dans les poches.
— pron. pers. A lui, le sien, la sienne, les siens,
les siennes; my glove and his, mon gant et le sien;
a friend of his, un de ses amis, un ami à lui.
hispanic [hi'spænik] adj. Hispanique.
— n. U. S. Américain (s.) de langue espagnole.
hiss [his] v. intr. Siffler.
— v. tr. Siffler (s.o.). ‖ Siffler, émettre d'une voix
sifflante (words). ‖ To hiss off, THEATR. Chasser
sous les sifflets.
— n. Sifflement m. ‖ THEATR. Sifflet m. ‖ GRAMM.
Sifflante f.
histamine ['histəmi:n] n. MED. Histamine f.
histology ['histɔlədʒi] n. MED. Histologie f.
historian [his'tɔ:riən] n. Historien m.
historiated [-eitid] adj. Historié.
historic [his'tɔrik] adj. Historique (castle).
historical [-əl] adj. Historique (document, method,
novel); d'histoire (painter). ‖ FAM. Mémorable
(meeting).
historicity [,histə'risiti] n. Historicité f.
historiographer [,histɔ:ri'ɔgrəfə*] n. Historiographe s.
historiography [-i] n. Historiographie f.
history ['histəri] n. Histoire f. (of persons, people,
plants, things); to make history, bâtir de l'histoire.
‖ THEATR. Drame historique m.
histrion ['histriən] n. Histrion m.; to play the
histrion, jouer la comédie.
histrionic [,histri'ɔnik] adj. THEATR., FIG. Théâtral.
— n. pl. THEATR. Art du théâtre m. ‖ FIG. Comédie f.
hit [hit] v. tr. (81). Frapper, heurter, atteindre, toucher (on, sur) [s.o.]; to hit one's head against,
se cogner la tête contre. ‖ Toucher, atteindre (the
mark). ‖ Porter, lancer, envoyer (a blow). ‖ FIG.
Toucher, blesser, piquer (to affect); to hit home,
porter; FIG. Rencontrer, trouver, tomber sur; to hit
it, to hit the nail on the head, mettre le doigt dessus,
taper dans le mille. ‖ FIG. Convenir (to suit); to hit
s.o.'s fancy, plaire à qqn. ‖ To hit back, riposter,
renvoyer la balle. ‖ To hit off, saisir, attraper (a
likeness); imiter, charger (s.o.); to hit it off, être
bons amis; accrocher (fam.) [with, avec]. ‖ To hit
up, U. S. POP. To hit it up, mettre les gaz.
— v. intr. Se heurter, se cogner (against, on, à).
‖ Donner des coups (at, à); cogner (at, sur). ‖
FIG. Tomber (on, sur). ‖ FAM. Cadrer, coller (with,
avec). ‖ To hit out, cogner (at, sur); riposter par
des coups.
— n. Coup m. (blow). ‖ SPORTS. Touche f. ‖
THEATR., MUS. Succès m. ‖ FIG. Réussite f. (success); trouvaille f. (in guessing). ‖ FIG. Trait (m.)
qui porte; coup (m.) de patte (fam.); a hit at you,
une pierre dans votre jardin. ‖ **Hit-and-run,** adj.
MILIT. Eclair (raid); AUTOM. hit-and-run driver,

chauffard. ‖ **Hit-the-baby,** n. U. S. Jeu de massacre m.
hitch [hitʃ] v. tr. Faire mouvoir d'une secousse.
‖ Accrocher, attacher, fixer (to tie). ‖ NAUT. Amarrer. ‖ FIG. Raccrocher, rattacher (into, à). ‖ FAM.
Faire en auto-stop; to hitch a ride to, voyager en
auto-stop jusqu'à. ‖ **To hitch up,** remonter (one's
trousers); atteler (to harness).
— v. intr. Clocher, boitiller, sautiller (to hobble);
se mouvoir par saccades. ‖ S'accrocher. ‖ U. S.
FAM. S'accrocher, cadrer, coller (with, avec) [to
agree]; to get hitched, se marier.
— n. Secousse, saccade f. ‖ NAUT. Clef f. ‖ MILIT.
U. S. Hitch of duty, période militaire. ‖ RADIO.
Technical hitch, incident technique. ‖ FAM. Anicroche f.; contretemps m.; without a hitch, sans
accroc. ‖ U. S. FAM. Trajet à l'œil (or) en auto-
stop m. ‖ **Hitch-hike,** v. intr. FAM. Faire de l'auto-
stop. ‖ **Hitch-hiker,** n. FAM. Auto-stoppeur s. ‖
Hitch-hiking, n. FAM. Auto-stop m.
hither ['hiðə*] adv. Ici.
— adj. De ce côté-ci.
hitherto ['hiðə'tu] adv. Jusqu'ici.
hitherward [-wəd] adv. Par ici.
Hitlerism ['hitlərizm] n. Hitlérisme m.
Hitlerite ['hitlərait] adj. Hitlérien.
Hittite ['hitait] adj., n. GEOGR. Hittite s.
hive [haiv] n. Ruche f. (bees, container). ‖ FIG.
Ruche f. (busy crowd); essaim m. (swarm).
— v. tr. Mettre dans une ruche (bees); recueillir
(a swarm). ‖ FIG. Entasser, stocker (goods).
— v. intr. ZOOL. Entrer dans une ruche (swarm).
‖ FIG. Vivre en communauté. ‖ **To hive off,** essaimer.
hives ['haivz] n. pl. MED. Urticaire f.
H. M. [eitʃʃ'em] abbr. His (or) Her Majesty, Sa
Majesté, S. M.
H.M.S [eitʃʃem'es] abbr. His (or) Her Majesty's
Ship, H. M. S., abréviation précédant le nom des
bateaux de la marine de guerre britannique.
ho [hou] interj. Ho!
hoar [hɔ:*] adj. Blanchi (hair); chenu (person).
‖ Blanc (frost). ‖ **Hoar-frost,** gelée blanche f.
— n. Givre m.; gelée blanche f. ‖ FIG. Frimas
m. pl.
hoard [hɔ:d] n. Amas, entassement m.; accumulation f. (heap). ‖ Trésor m. (treasure).
— v. tr. Amasser, entasser, accumuler. ‖ FIG. To
hoard up, garder précieusement.
— v. intr. Entasser; thésauriser.
hoarding [-iŋ] n. Entassement m.; accumulation f.
‖ Thésaurisation f. (of money).
hoarding [-iŋ] n. Panneau d'affichage m. (bill-
board). ‖ ARCHIT. Clôture de chantier f.
hoarse [hɔ:s] adj. MED. Enroué (person); rauque,
enroué (voice); to be hoarse, avoir la voix prise.
hoarsen [-n] v. tr. MED. Enrouer.
— v. intr. MED. S'enrouer.
hoarseness [-nis] n. MED. Enrouement m.
hoary ['hɔ:ri] adj. Blanc neigeux (hair); chenu
(person). ‖ BOT., ZOOL. Duveteux et blanc. ‖
FIG. Vénérable.
hoax [houks] n. Attrape f.; canulard m. (fam.).
— v. tr. Attraper, berner; monter un canulard à,
faire marcher (fam.).
hob [hɔb] n. Plaque chauffante latérale f. (of a
fireplace). ‖ TECHN. Vis f. ‖ SPORTS. Patin m. (of
a sledge).
hobble [-hɔbl] v. intr. Clocher, clopiner.
— v. tr. Faire clopiner (s.o.). ‖ Entraver (a horse).
— n. Boitillement m. ‖ Entrave f. (for horses). ‖
Hobble-skirt, n. Jupe entravée f.
hobbledehoy ['hɔbldi'hɔi] n. Dadais m.
hobby ['hɔbi] n. Dada m.; manie, marotte f. (See
FAD.) ‖ Violon (m.) d'Ingres; passe-temps favori m.
‖ **Hobby-horse,** n. Cheval de bois m.; † draisienne f.

hobgoblin ['hɔb'gɔblin] n. Lutin *m.* ‖ FIG. Epouvantail *m.*

hobnail ['hɔbneil] n. Caboche *f.* (nail).
— v. tr. Ferrer (shoes).

hobnob [-ɔb] v. intr. (1). Boire (*with*, avec). ‖ FIG. S'acoquiner (*with*, avec).

hobo ['houbou] n. Saisonnier *m.* (worker); vagabond, clochard *m.* (tramp).
— v. intr. U. S. *To hobo it*, vivre en clochard.

hock [hɔk] n. Jarret *m.* (horse's).
— v. tr. Couper le jarret à.

hock n. Flûte (*f.*) à champagne, verre (*m.*) à vin du Rhin (glass); vin du Rhin *m.* (wine).

hock n. U. S. FAM. Gage *m.* (pawn); *in hock*, chez ma tante. ‖ **Hock-shop**, n. FAM. Mont-de-piété *m.*
— v. tr. U. S. FAM. Mettre au clou.

hockey ['hɔki] n. SPORTS. Hockey *m.*

hocus ['houkəs] v. tr. (1). Mystifier; rouler (fam.). [See HOAX.] ‖ Droguer (a drink, s.o.).

hocus-pocus [-'poukəs] n. Tour (*m.*) de passe-passe (by conjurers). ‖ Attrape *f.* (trickery).
— v. intr. (1). Faire des tours de passe-passe.
— v. tr. Tromper; rouler (fam.).

hod [hɔd] n. ARCHIT. Oiseau *m.*

hodge-podge ['hɔdʒpɔdʒ] n. Salmigondis *m.*

hodman ['hɔdmən] (pl. **hodmen**) n. ARCHIT. Aide-maçon *m.* ‖ FIG. Manœuvre *m.*

hodograph ['hɔdəgræf] n. PHYS. Hodographe *m.*

hoe [hou] n. AGRIC. Houe, binette *f.; Dutch* (or) U. S. *garden hoe*, sarcloir; *grub hoe*, hoyau.
— v. tr., intr. AGRIC. Houer, biner, sarcler.

hog [hɔg] n. ZOOL. Porc, pourceau, cochon *m.* (See PIG.) ‖ NAUT. Goret *m.* ‖ FAM. Cochon *m.; to go the whole hog*, y aller à fond, risquer le paquet. ‖ **Hog-back**, n. Dos d'âne *m.* ‖ **Hog-raiser**, n. U. S. AGRIC. Eleveur (*m.*) de porcs. ‖ **Hog-tie**, v. tr. U. S. FAM. Ligoter. ‖ **Hog-wash**, n. Eaux (*f. pl.*) de vaisselle; FAM. Lavasse *f.;* U. S. FAM. Foutaise *f.* ‖ **Hog-wild**, adj. U. S. POP. En rogne, hors de soi.
— v. tr. Arquer. ‖ Anglaiser (a horse's mane). ‖ NAUT. Goreter. ‖ FAM. Accaparer.
— v. intr. S'arquer, faire un dos d'âne.

hogbacked [-bækt] adj. En dos d'âne.

hoggish [-iʃ] adj. De cochon.

hoggishness [-iʃnis] n. Saleté et goinfrerie *f.*

hogmanay [ˌhɔgməˈnei] n. Saint-Sylvestre *f.* (in Scotland).

hogpen [-pen] n. U. S. Porcherie *f.* (See PIGSTY.)

hogshead ['hɔgzhed] n. Barrique *f.*

hoick [hɔik] n. Saccade *f.*
— v. tr., intr. AVIAT. Cabrer, redresser.

hoi polloi ['hɔipəˈlɔi] n. Plèbe, populace *f.*

hoist [hɔist] v. tr. Hisser. (See LIFT.) ‖ NAUT. Hisser (a flag); *to hoist the boats out*, mettre les canots à la mer. ‖ MILIT. *Hoisting the colours*, lever des couleurs. ‖ TECHN., FAM. Remonter.
— n. Action (*f.*) de hisser; *to give s.o. a hoist*, aider qqn à se hisser. ‖ NAUT. Guindant *m.* (of mast); ralingue *f.* (of sail). ‖ TECHN. Grue *f.* (crane); monte-charge *m.* (for goods); corde, cordée *f.;* palan *m.* (rope).

hoist p.p. † *To be hoist with one's own petard*, se prendre à son propre piège.

hoity-toity [ˌhɔitiˈtɔiti] adj. FAM. Bêcheur.
— interj. Turlututu!

hokey-pokey [houki'pouki] n. CULIN. Glace *f.* ‖ FAM. Salmigondis *m.*

hokum ['houkəm] n. U. S. FAM. Boniments (*m. pl.*) à la noix; fumisterie *f.* (eyewash); bla-bla-bla sentimental *m.* (mawkishness).

holarctic [houˈlɑːktik] adj. ZOOL., BOT. Holarctique.

hold [hould] v. tr. (82). Tenir, saisir, maintenir (to grasp); *to hold in one's hand*, tenir dans la main. ‖ Tenir, retenir, immobiliser (to hold back); *to hold the train*, empêcher le train de partir. ‖

Tenir, placer (to keep in place). ‖ Tenir, soutenir (to keep from falling); *to hold the roof*, soutenir le toit. ‖ Tenir, contenir; *to hold a quart*, contenir un litre. ‖ Tenir, porter; *to hold oneself upright*, se tenir droit. ‖ Tenir, conserver; *hold the line*, ne quittez pas (on the phone). ‖ ECCLES. Jouir de (a living); célébrer (a service). ‖ MUS. Tenir, prolonger (a note). ‖ AUTOM. Tenir (the road). ‖ FIN. Détenir (funds, stocks). ‖ JUR. Remplir (a function, service); tenir, occuper (an office, a position); tenir (a meeting, session). ‖ JUR. Etre nanti de (a contract); présider (a court); détenir, garder (prisoners). ‖ SPORTS. Détenir (a record). ‖ FIG. Tenir, avoir (a conversation). ‖ FIG. Retenir, arrêter (s.o.'s attention, s.o.); tenir (one's tongue); *there's no holding him*, il n'y a pas moyen de le tenir; *to hold one's peace*, se retenir, se contenir; *to hold s.o. to his word*, contraindre qqn à tenir sa promesse; *to hold sth. in mind*, garder qqch. en mémoire. ‖ FIG. Soutenir, maintenir; défendre (one's opinion). ‖ FIG. Considérer, estimer, juger, tenir; *to hold a statement to be true*, considérer une déclaration comme vraie; *to hold s.o. responsible*, tenir qqn pour responsable. ‖ FAM. *Hold your horses!*, arrêtez!, minute!; *that doesn't hold water*, ça ne tient pas debout; *to hold the baby* (or) U. S. *the bag*, payer les pots cassés, écoper; *to hold one's own*, tenir son bout. ‖ **To hold back**, retenir; FIG. Contenir, garder secret. ‖ **To hold down**, baisser; maintenir à terre. ‖ **To hold forth**, exposer. ‖ **To hold in**, retenir; FIG. Maîtriser; *to hold oneself in*, se contenir. ‖ **To hold off**, tenir éloigné. ‖ **To hold on**, maintenir; FIG. Se maintenir, durer; **To hold out**, tendre (one's hand); tenir (sth.); FIG. Présenter, offrir. ‖ **To hold over**, ajourner, différer. ‖ **To hold together**, maintenir unis; FIG. Assurer l'union de. ‖ **To hold up**, lever, relever (one's head); soutenir (sth.); JUR. Arrêter (a train); dévaliser (s.o.); FIN. Retenir, différer (a payment); AUTOM. Embarrasser (the traffic); FIG. Citer, présenter (*as*, comme) [s.o.].
— v. intr. Tenir, être solide (nail, rope). ‖ FIG. Tenir bon, résister. ‖ FIG. Se maintenir, durer, demeurer; *to hold good*, demeurer valable. ‖ FIG. Continuer, persister (*on*, dans). ‖ Rester attaché, s'en tenir (*to*, à) [a belief, an opinion]; être partisan, être du parti (*with*, de). ‖ **To hold back**, rester en arrière; FIG. Se réserver (*for*, pour); se retenir (*from*, de). ‖ **To hold forth**, pérorer, faire des discours; tenir un topo (fam.) [*on*, sur]. ‖ **To hold in**, ne pas lâcher les rênes; FIG. Tenir le manche. ‖ **To hold off**, se tenir éloigné (*from*, de); se montrer peu empressé (*from*, à); NAUT. Tenir le large. ‖ **To hold on**, se maintenir, se cramponner (*to*, à); FIG. Tenir bon; tenir le coup (fam.). ‖ FAM. *Hold on!*, minute! ‖ **To hold out**, tenir, résister (*against*, contre). ‖ **To hold together**, se tenir; rester unis, faire bloc. ‖ **To hold up**, se tenir (horse); se maintenir (person, weather).
— n. Prise, étreinte *f.* (grasp); *to get hold of*, saisir de; *to keep hold of*, tenir fermement; *to take hold of*, se saisir de, prendre prise sur. ‖ Prise *f.* (thing to hold by); *to afford a hold to*, offrir une prise à. ‖ SPORTS. Prise *f.* ‖ JUR. Tenure *f.* (*upon*, sur); prise *f.* (*on*, sur). ‖ **Hold-all**, n. Fourre-tout *m.* ‖ **Hold-up**, n. JUR. Hold-up *m.*, attaque à main armée (attack); entrave *f.* (difficulty).

hold n. NAUT. Cale *f.*

holder [-ə*] n. JUR. Titulaire *m.* (of an office). ‖ FIN. Porteur, détenteur *m.* (of stocks); *holder on trust*, dépositaire *m.* ‖ AGRIC. Tenancier *m.* (of a farm); *small holder*, petit fermier. ‖ TECHN. Support *m.; bicycle holder*, suspenseur; *curtain holder*, embrasse; *flat-iron holder*, poignée de fer à repasser. ‖ SPORTS. Détenteur *m.* (of a record).

holdfast [-fɑːst] n. TECHN. Serre-joint, crampon *m.* ‖ BOT. Crampon. ‖ FIG. Soutien *m.*

holding [-iŋ] n. Tenue *f.* ‖ TECHN. Fixation *f.* ‖ AGRIC. Possession, tenure *f.* (of lands); propriété, ferme *f.* ‖ FIN. Possession *f.* (of stocks); pl. avoir, dossier, portefeuille *m.; fonds, capitaux m. pl.* (stocks). ‖ JUR. Tenue *f.* (of a session); *holding of the court,* jurisprudence (on a question).
— adj. Détenteur *m.;* détentrice *f.* ‖ FIN. *Holding company,* trust de valeurs, holding.

holdover [-,ouvə*] n. U. S. Survivance *f.* ‖ U. S. Bénéficiaire (*m.*) d'une reconduction de poste.

hole [houl] n. Trou, creux *m.; to dig a hole,* creuser un trou. ‖ Trou, orifice *m.; to cut a hole in,* pratiquer une ouverture dans. ‖ Trou *m.;* déchirure *f.; to wear a hole in,* trouer; *to wear into holes,* se trouer (garment). ‖ Trou *m.;* brèche *f.; to make holes in,* ébrécher, entamer, faire un trou dans. ‖ ZOOL. Trou *m.* (made by mice); terrier *m.* (made by rabbits). ‖ SPORTS. Trou *m.* (in golf). ‖ FIN. Trou *m.; to be thirty pounds in the hole,* avoir un trou de trente livres. ‖ FIG. Défaut *m.; to pick holes in,* relever les points faibles de. ‖ FAM. Boîte *f.* (house); pétrin (mess); trou *m.* (place); *your hole!,* à vous le pompon! ‖ **Hole-and-corner,** adj. FAM. Fait en sous-main (or) sous la table. ‖ **Hole-proof,** adj. Indéchirable (stockings).
— v. tr. Faire un trou dans, percer (a wall). ‖ Percer (a tunnel). ‖ Trouer (one's garments). ‖ SPORTS. Bloquer (in billiards); poter (in golf).
— v. intr. Se trouer (stockings). ‖ ZOOL. Se terrer. ‖ **To hole out,** SPORTS. Poter. ‖ **To hole up,** U. S. Se terrer, se cacher.

holiday ['hɔlidei] n. Jour de congé, congé *m.; Bank Holiday,* jour férié; *on holiday,* en congé. ‖ Pl. Vacances *f. pl.; holidays with pay,* congés payés; *holiday task,* devoir de vacances. ‖ ECCLES. Jour (*m.*) de fête. ‖ **Holiday camp,** n. Camp (*m.*) de vacances. ‖ **Holiday-maker,** n. Vacancier, villégiaturiste, estivant *s.*
— v. intr. Passer ses vacances.

holily ['houlili] adv. Saintement.

holiness [-nis] n. Sainteté *f.* (title, virtue).

holism ['houlizm] n. PHILOS. Holisme *m.*

Holland ['hɔlənd] n. GEOGR. Hollande *f.* ‖ TECHN. Toile de Hollande *f.*

Hollander [-ə*] n. GEOGR. Hollandais *s.*

Hollands ['hɔləndz] n. Schiedam *m.*

holler ['hɔlə*] v. tr., intr. FAM. Brailler, beugler.
— n. FAM. Braillement, beuglement *m.*

hollo(a) ['hɔlou] interj., n. Holà! *m.*
— v. tr., intr. Crier.

hollow adj. Creux (place, road). ‖ Sourd (sound); caverneux (voice). ‖ MED. Creux (cheek, cough); cave (eye); vide (stomach); *to feel hollow,* avoir le ventre creux. ‖ FIG. Faux (friendship); creux, vide (promise). ‖ **Hollow-glass-ware,** n. Gobeleterie *f.*
— adv. Creux (to sound). ‖ Totalement; *to beat hollow,* battre à plates coutures.
— n. Creux *m.* (of the hand, in a tree). ‖ MED. Cavité *f.* (of a tooth). ‖ GEOGR. Dénivelation *f.* (of the ground); bas-fond *m.;* cuvette *f.* (valley).
— v. tr. **To hollow out,** creuser (in general); raviner (the ground); échancrer (the neck of a dress).
— v. intr. Se creuser.

hollowness [-nis] n. Creux *m.;* cavité *f.* (hole). ‖ FIG. Fausseté *f.* (of friendship); vide *m.* (of a promise).

holly ['hɔli] n. BOT. Houx *m.*

hollyhock ['hɔlihɔk] n. BOT. Rose trémière *f.*

holm(e) [houm] n. Ilot *m.*

holm n. BOT. Yeuse *f.* ‖ **Holm-oak,** n. Yeuse *f.*

holocaust ['hɔləkɔ:st] n. Holocauste *m.*

holograph ['hɔlogrɑ:f] adj. JUR. Olographe.
— n. JUR. Document olographe *m.*

holograph v. tr. PHYS. Holographier.

holographic [,hɔlə'græfik] adj. PHYS. Holographique.

holography [hɔ'lɔgrəfi] n. PHYS. Holographie *f.*

holster ['houlstə*] n. Etui de revolver *m.* ‖ Fonte *f.* (on a saddle).

holt [hoult] n. † Bois *m.* (copse); colline boisée *f.* (hill).

holus-bolus ['houləs'bouləs] adv. FAM. D'un coup (or) d'un trait.

holy ['houli] adj. ECCLES. Saint (Alliance, City, person, Land, Sepulcher, Trinity, Week); bénit (bread, water); sacré (ground, orders); *the Holy Child,* le divin Enfant. ‖ FAM. Sacré (fear).
— n. ECCLES., FIG. *The Holy of Holies,* le Saint des Saints.

holystone ['houlistoun] n. NAUT. Brique *f.*
— v. tr. NAUT. Briquer.

homage ['hɔmidʒ] n. Hommage *m.; to pay homage to,* rendre hommage à.

home [houm] n. Maison, demeure *f.;* domicile *m.; at home,* chez soi; *last home,* dernière demeure. ‖ Foyer, intérieur *m.; a home of one's own,* un chez-soi. ‖ Asile *m.* (for the aged); hospice *m.* (for the blind); foyer *m.* (for sailors, students). ‖ Pays natal *m.;* patrie *f.* (motherland). ‖ ZOOL., BOT. Habitat *m.* ‖ U. S. Pavillon *m.;* maison *f.; the Smith home,* chez les Smith. ‖ FIG. Elément *m.; as if they were at home,* comme en pays conquis; *to feel at home,* se sentir à l'aise; *to make oneself at home,* faire comme chez soi.
— adj. De famille (circle, life); à domicile (care, task); familial (training); domestique (use). ‖ Du pays, national (customs, news). ‖ CH. DE F. De retour (journey); terminus (station). ‖ COMM. Intérieur (trade). ‖ FIN. Du pays (currency); intérieur (market). ‖ JUR. Intérieur (politics); *Home Office,* ministère de l'Intérieur. ‖ MILIT. Métropolitain (army); *Home Guard,* Garde nationale. ‖ FIG. Qui porte, direct.
— adv. Chez soi, à la maison; *to go home,* rentrer chez soi; *to see s.o. home,* accompagner qqn jusque chez lui. ‖ Au pays, dans sa patrie; *to send home,* rapatrier. ‖ TECHN., MILIT. A fond, à bloc. ‖ FIG. A l'idée; *it's the first time that it has come home to me,* c'est la première fois que j'en prends nettement conscience. ‖ FIG. Au but, en plein; *to come home to,* faire impression sur, porter sur; *to go home,* porter, frapper au point sensible. ‖ **Homebody,** n. U. S. FAM. Casanier *s.* ‖ **Home-bred,** adj. Du pays, indigène; FIG. Inné, naturel. ‖ **Homecoming,** adj. Rapatrié; n. Retour au pays *m.* ‖ **Homemade,** adj. Fait à la maison, de ménage; fabrication maison (fam.). ‖ **Home-sick,** adj. Nostalgique. ‖ **Home-sickness,** n. Mal du pays *m.* (See NOSTALGIA.) ‖ **Home-thrust,** n. SPORTS. Botte *f.;* FIG. Coup droit *m.* ‖ **Home-worker,** n. Façonnier *m.*
— v. tr. Abriter, loger, héberger (s.o.).
— v. intr. Revenir chez soi. ‖ ZOOL. Revenir au colombier (pigeon).

homeless [-lis] adj. Sans foyer; sans abri.

homelike [-laik] adj. Familial, intime, comme chez soi.

homeliness [-linis] n. Simplicité *f.* ‖ U. S. Disgrâce physique *f.;* manque (*m.*) de beauté.

homely [-li] adj. Simple, sans façons. ‖ CULIN. *Homely fare,* cuisine bourgeoise. ‖ U. S. Sans beauté, laid. ‖ FIG. Terne, inélégant.

homer [-ə*] n. ZOOL. Pigeon voyageur *m.*

homespun ['houmspʌn] adj. Filé à la maison, de ménage (wool). ‖ FIG. Rustique, grossier.
— n. Homespun *m.* (fabric).

homestead [-sted] n. AGRIC. Exploitation, ferme *f.* ‖ U. S. Bien (*m.*) de famille.

homeward [-wed] adv. Vers la maison (or) la patrie. ‖ Sur le chemin du retour.
— adj. De retour (journey); du retour (way). ‖ NAUT. En route pour son port d'attache (ship).

homework [-wə:k] n. Devoirs (*m. pl.*) à la maison.

homey ['houmi] adj. See HOMY.

homicidal [,hɔmi'saidl] adj. Homicide.

homicide ['hɔmisaid] n. Homicide m. (act, person).
homiletic [,hɔmi'letik] adj. ECCLES. Des homélies.
homiletics [-s] n. sg. ECCLES. Homilétique f.
homily [hɔmili] n. ECCLES. Homélie f. ‖ FAM. Sermon m.
homing ['houmiŋ] adj. Voyageur (pigeon).
hominy ['hɔmini] n. U. S. CULIN. Bouillie (f.) de farine de maïs ; farine de maïs f.
homo ['houmou] (pl. **homos** [-z]) adj., n. POP. Homo, pédé (homosexual) adj., m.
homocentric [,houmo'sentrik] adj. Homocentrique.
hom(o)eopath ['houmiopæθ] n. MED. Homéopathe m.
hom(o)eopathic [,houmio'pæθik] adj. MED. Homéopathique.
hom(o)eopathy [,houmi'ɔpæθi] n. MED. Homéopathie f.
homogeneity [,hɔmodʒi'ni:iti] n. Homogénéité f.
homogeneous [,hɔmo'dʒenias] adj. Homogène.
homogenize [hə'mɔdʒənaiz] v. tr. Rendre homogène, homogénéiser.
homologate [hə'mɔləgeit] v. tr. Homologuer.
homologation [,hɔmolə'geiʃən] n. Homologation f.
homologize [hə'mɔlədʒaiz] v. intr. Correspondre (with, à) ; être homologue (with, à).
— v. tr. Rendre homologue (with, à).
homologous [-gəs] adj. Homologue.
homology [-dʒi] n. Homologie f.
homonym ['hɔmənim] n. Homonyme m.
homonymous [hə'mɔniməs] adj. Homonyme.
homophone ['hɔmə,foun] n. GRAMM. Homophone m.
homosexual [,houmou'seksjuəl] adj., s. Homosexuel adj., s.
homosexuality [,houmou,seksju'æliti] n. Homosexualité f.
homuncule [hə'mʌŋkju:l] n. Homoncule m.
homy ['houmi] adj. FAM. Familial, intime, où l'on se sent chez soi.
Honduras [hɔn'djuərəs] n. GEOGR. Honduras m.
hone [houn] n. Pierre (f.) à aiguiser.
— v. tr. Affûter, affiler.
honest ['ɔnist] adj. Franc, ouvert (face) ; honnête, probe, intègre (person) ; honnête (woman). ‖ Honnêtement acquis (living, money). ‖ Sincère, loyal, franc (effort) ; exact, absolu (truth). ‖ COMM. Loyal et marchand (goods). ‖ FAM. Brave. ‖ **Honest-to-God**, adj. POP. Vrai de vrai.
honestly [-li] adv. Honnêtement. ‖ FAM. Franchement (really).
honesty [-i] n. Honnêteté, probité, intégrité f. (of a person) ; honnêteté, vertu f. (of a woman). ‖ Sincérité, loyauté, franchise f. ‖ Exactitude, véracité f. ‖ BOT. Monnaie-du-pape f.
honey ['hʌni] n. CULIN. Miel m. ‖ FAM. Chéri s. (dear). ‖ **Honey-bee**, n. ZOOL. Abeille, mouche (f.) à miel. ‖ **Honey-dew**, n. Miellée f. ‖ **Honey-mouthed**, adj. FIG. Mielleux, aux paroles mielleuses.
— adj. De miel.
— v. tr. Adoucir, édulcorer (to sweeten). ‖ Flatter, cajoler (to coax).
honeycomb [-koum] n. Rayon de miel m. ‖ TECHN. Nid d'abeille (in a fabric) ; soufflure f. (in metal) ; alvéole m. (in a radiator).
— adj. TECHN. En nid d'abeille (fabric) ; alvéolaire (radiator).
— v. tr. Cribler de trous. ‖ TECHN. Disposer en nid d'abeille. ‖ FIG. Miner. ‖ FAM. Cribler (with, de).
— v. intr. TECHN. S'affouiller (metal).
honeyed [-d] adj. Couvert de miel. ‖ FIG. De miel, mielleux, doucereux, douceâtre (words).
honeymoon [-mu:n] n. Lune (f.) de miel. ‖ Voyage (m.) de noces (trip).
— v. intr. Passer sa lune de miel.

honeymooner [-mu:nə*] n. Nouveau marié s.
honeysuckle [-,sʌkl] n. BOT. Chèvrefeuille m.
Hong Kong ['hɔŋ'kɔŋ] n. GEOGR. Hong Kong f.
honk [hɔŋk] n. AUTOM. Coup de Klaxon m. ; honk-honk !, coin-coin !
— v. intr. AUTOM. Klaxonner.
honky ['hɔŋki] n. POP. Blanc s. (negro slang).
honkytonk ['hɔŋki'tɔŋk] n. U. S. Beuglant m. ; honkytonk joint, bastringue, boui-boui.
honorarium [,ɔnə'rɛəriəm] n. (pl. **honoraria** [-riə]) n. JUR. Honoraires m. pl. (See REMUNERATION.)
honorary ['ɔnərəri] adj. Honorifique (duties) ; honoraire (member) ; d'honneur (president).
honorific [,ɔnə'rifik] adj. Honorifique (expression).
— n. Formule courtoise f.
hono(u)r ['ɔnə*] n. Honneur m. (good name) ; for honour's sake, pour l'honneur ; honour bright !, parole d'honneur ! ; to be on one's honour, être engagé d'honneur ; to lose one's honour, se déshonorer ; word of honour, parole d'honneur. ‖ Honneur, réputation, vertu f. (of a woman). ‖ Honneur m. ; gloire f. (to, pour) ; to be an honour to, faire honneur à. ‖ Honneur, titre honorifique m. ; distinction f. ; honours list, palmarès ; to carry off the honours, remporter la palme. ‖ Honneur m. ; manifestation (f.) de respect ; to pay the last honours to, rendre les derniers honneurs (or) devoirs à. ‖ Examen supérieur m. ; to take honours in, se spécialiser en. ‖ Honneurs m. pl. (at bridge). ‖ JUR., ECCLES. Your Honour, Votre Honneur (title). ‖ COMM. Intervention f.
— v. tr. COMM., FIG. Honorer, faire honneur à.
honourable [-rəb] adj. Honorable.
honourably [-rəbli] adv. Honorablement.
hooch [hutʃ] n. U. S. POP. Gnôle de contrebande f.
hood [hud] n. Capuchon m. ; coule f. (of monk) ; cagoule f. (of penitent) ; épitoge f. (of University graduate) ; capeline f. (of woman). ‖ AUTOM. Capote f. ; U. S. Capot m. (bonnet). ‖ ARCHIT. Hotte f. (of chimney) ; auvent m. (of door). ‖ NAUT. Capot m. ‖ ZOOL. Capuchon m. (of cobra, falcon). ‖ U. S. POP. Bandit m.
hooded ['hudid] adj. Encapuchonné (person) ; à capuche (or) capuchon (garment). ‖ ZOOL. Hooded crow, corneille mantelée. ‖ FIG. Voilé, masqué ; mi-clos (eyes).
hoodlum ['hu:dləm] n. Voyou m.
hoodoo ['hu:du:] n. U. S. FAM. Guigne f., guignon m. (bad luck) ; porte-guigne m. (person).
— v. tr. U. S. FAM. Porter la guigne à. (See HEX.)
hoodwink ['hudwink] v. tr. Bander les yeux à. ‖ FAM. Aveugler, fermer les yeux à ; empaumer, en mettre plein la vue à (fam.).
hooey ['hu:i] n. POP. Idioties, bêtises, foutaises, salades f. pl.
— interj. Foutaises !
hoof [hu:f] (pl. **hoofs, hooves**) n. ZOOL. Sabot m. ; cloven hoof, pied fourchu ; on the hoof, sur pied. ‖ FAM. Paturon m. (foot).
— v. tr. FAM. Donner un coup de pied à. ‖ **To hoof it**, FAM. Danser (to dance) ; prendre le train onze (to walk).
hoofed [-t] adj. ZOOL. A sabot, ongulé.
hoo-ha ['hu:,hɑ:] n. FAM. Raffut, boucan, barouf, tintamarre m. (din, row) ; histoires f. pl. (fuss).
hook [huk] n. Croc, crochet m. ‖ Gond m. (of door). ‖ Agrafe f. (on a dress). ‖ Pointe f. (headland) ; coude m. (in a stream). ‖ SPORTS. Crochet m. (in boxing) ; hameçon m. (in fishing) ; coup tiré m. (in golf). ‖ AGRIC. Faucille f. ‖ FIG. Leurre, appât, piège m. ; to take the hook, gober le morceau. ‖ FAM. By hook or by crook, par tous les biais, de bric et de broc ; hook, line and sinker, et tout le bataclan ; to get one's hooks on to, mettre le grappin sur ; to sling one's hook, mettre les bouts. ‖ **Hook-nose**, n. Nez crochu (or) aquilin m.

— v. tr. Accrocher (to, à). || Agrafer (a dress). || NAUT. Gaffer. || SPORTS. Donner un crochet à (a boxer); prendre (a fish). || FIG. Happer; agripper. || FAM. To hook it, décamper. || To hook in, atteler (a horse); mettre le grappin sur (s.o.); TECHN. Crocheter (a word). || To hook up, agrafer.
— v. intr. S'accrocher. || To hook up, s'agrafer.

hookah ['hukə] n. Narguilé m.

hooked ['hukt] adj. Crochu (nose). || TECHN. A crochet. || U. S. A points noués (rug).

hooker ['hukə*] n. NAUT. Hourque f.

hooker n. SPORTS. Talonneur m. (in rugby).

hook(e)y ['huki] n. U. S. To play hookey, faire l'école buissonnière.

hookup [-,ʌp] n. U. S. FAM. Relais radiophonique m.

hookworm ['hukwə:m] n. MED. Ankylostome m.

hooligan ['hu:ligən] n. Apache, voyou m.

hooliganism [-izm̩] n. Pillage, vandalisme m.

hoop [hu:p] n. Cerceau m.; to trundle a hoop, jouer au cerceau. || Cerceau m. (in a dress). || SPORTS. Arceau m. (in croquet). || TECHN. Cercle m. (of a cask); jante f. (of a wheel). || NAUT. Fretter (a mast). || **Hoop-net**, n. Pantenne, nasse f. || **Hoopskirt**, n. Crinoline f.
— v. tr. TECHN. Cercler. || NAUT. Fretter.

hoop v. intr. See WHOOP.

hoopla ['-'lɑ:] h. U. S. FAM. Battage m.

hoopoe ['hu:pu:] n. ZOOL. Huppe f.

hoosegow ['hu:sgau] n. U. S. POP. Violon, bloc m.; taule f. (prison).

hoot [hu:t] v. intr. Pousser des huées. || ZOOL. Ululer (owl). || AUTOM. Corner, klaxonner. || NAUT. Mugir (siren). || CH. DE F. Siffler.
— v. tr. Huer, conspuer (s.o.); to hoot away (or) out, chasser sous les huées.
— n. Huée f. || ZOOL. Ululement m. || AUTOM. Coup de klaxon m. || NAUT. Mugissement m. || CH. DE F. Sifflet m.

hooter [-ə*] n. AUTOM. Klaxon m. || NAUT. Sirène f. CH. DE F. Sifflet m.

hoove [hu:v] n. MED. Météorisation f.; météorisme m.

hooves [hu:vz]. See HOOF.

hop [hɔp] n. BOT. Houblon m. || **Hop-picker**, n. Cueilleur (s.) de houblon. || **Hop-pole**, n. Echalas m.
— v. tr. (1). Houblonner.
— v. intr. Cueillir le houblon.

hop v. intr. (1). Sauter (animals); sautiller (birds); sauter à cloche-pied (person). || To hop over to, faire un saut à. || To hop off, FAM. Décamper.
— v. tr. Sauter. || FAM. Hop it!, fiche le camp!; to hop the twig, sauter le pas, casser sa pipe, se laisser glisser. || U. S. FAM. To hop a train, sauter dans le train. || To hop up, U. S. POP. Doper.
— n. Saut m. (of animals, persons); sautillement m. (of birds, persons). || FAM. Sauterie f. (dance). || **Hop-off**, n. U. S. AVIAT. FAM. Décollage m.; v. intr. Décoller. ||**Hop-o'-my-Thumb**, n. Petit Poucet m.; FAM. Petit bout d'homme m.

hope [houp] n. Espoir m.; espérance f. (feeling, object, person). || Hope chest, n. U. S. FAM. Trousseau m.
— v. intr. Espérer, avoir de l'espoir. || To hope for, espérer, espérer en (sth.). || To hope in, espérer en, mettre son espoir en.
— v. tr. Espérer; I hope I will see him (or) to see him, I hope I see him, j'espère le voir (or) que je le verrai.

hopeful [-ful] adj. Plein d'espoir; optimiste; to be hopeful that, avoir bon espoir que. || Prometteur, encourageant (future, situation); qui promet, d'avenir (youth).
— n. Espoir m. || FAM. Young hopeful, illustre rejeton, jeune espoir.

hopefully [-fuli] adv. Avec espoir. || D'une façon encourageante (or) prometteuse.

hopefulness [-fulnis] n. Bon espoir; optimisme m. || Indices prometteurs m. pl.

hopeless [-lis] adj. Désespéré (person, situation); désespérant (weather, work). || FAM. Incorrigible (drunkard).

hopelessly [-lisli] adv. Sans espoir, avec désespoir, désespérément. || Irrémédiablement.

hopelessness [-lisnis] n. Désespoir m.; désespérance f. || Vanité f. (of an effort); état désespéré m. (of a situation).

hophead ['hɔp,hed] n. U. S. POP. Drogué s.

hopped up ['hɔptʌp] adj. U. S. POP. Dopé, gonflé à bloc.

hopper ['hɔpə*] n. Sauteur s. (animal, insect, person). || Trémie f. || NAUT. Allège; marie-salope f. || FAM. Puce f. (flea). || **Hopper-car**, CH. DE F. Wagon sans toit à fond ouvrant m.

hopple ['hɔpl] n. Entrave f. (See HOBBLE.)
— v. tr. Entraver (a horse).

hopscotch ['hɔpskɔtʃ] n. Marelle f.

horary ['hɔrəri] adj. Horaire.

Horatian [hɔ'reiʃiən] adj. D'Horace.

horde [hɔ:d] n. Horde f.

horizon [hə'raizn̩] n. Horizon m. (lit. and. fig.).

horizontal [,hɔri'zɔntl̩] adj. ASTRON. De l'horizon. || MATH. Horizontal.
— n. MATH. Horizontale f.

horizontally [-əli] adv. Horizontalement.

hormonal [hɔ:'mounəl] adj. MED. Hormonal.

hormone ['hɔ:moun] n. MED. Hormone f.

horn [hɔ:n] n. ZOOL. Corne f. (of cattle, snail); bois m. (of deer); antenne f. (of insects); aigrette f. (of owl). || Corne f. (substance); horn comb, peigne en corne. || Corne f. (container); horn of plenty, corne d'abondance. || Corne f.; chausse-pied m. (shoe-horn). || Pavillon m. (of gramophone, loudspeaker). || Bras m. (of river). || TECHN. Bigorne f. (of anvil). || AUTOM., NAUT. Corne f. || MUS. Cor, buccin m.; trompe f. || CULIN. Pastry horn, cornet de pâtisserie. || PHILOS. Alternative f. (of a dilemma); on the horns of a dilemma, enfermé dans un dilemme. || FAM. To draw in one's horns, mettre de l'eau dans son vin, rentrer les cornes. || **Horn-owl**, U. S. horned owl, n. ZOOL. Duc m. || **Horn-player**, n. MUS. Corniste, cor m. || **Horn-rimmed**, adj. A monture de corne (glasses).
— v. tr. Mettre des cornes à (to furnish). || Corner, encorner (to gore).
. — v. intr. To horn in, intervenir, s'insinuer.

hornbeam [-bi:m] n. BOT. Charme m.

hornbill [-bil] n. ZOOL. Buceros m.

hornblende [-blend] n. Hornblende f.

horned [-id] adj. ZOOL., PHILOS., FIG. Cornu.

horner [-ə*] n. TECHN. Cornetier m. || MUS. Corniste m.

hornet [-it] n. ZOOL. Frelon m. || FAM. To bring a hornet's nest about one's ears, tomber dans un guêpier.

hornpipe [-paip] n. MUS. Matelote f.

horny [-i] adj. Corné (corneous). || En corne. Cornu (horned). || Calleux (callous). || POP. Paillard. || **Horny-handed**, adj. Aux mains calleuses.

horologe ['hɔrəlɔdʒ] n. Horloge f.

horologer [hɔ'rɔlədʒə*] n. Horloger m.

horology [-dʒi] n. Horlogerie f. || Horométrie f.

horoscope ['hɔrəskoup] n. Horoscope m.

horrendous [hɔ'rendəs] adj. Affreux, épouvantable, effroyable, horrible.

horrent ['hɔrənt] adj. Hérissé.

horrible ['hɔribl̩] adj. Horrible, affreux, hideux (ugly). || Horrible, horrifiant, effrayant, terrifiant (dreadful). || FAM. Affreux.

horribly [-i] adv. Horriblement.

horrid ['hɔrid] adj. † Hirsute. || Horrible, révol-

tant, horrifiant (horrific). ‖ Déplaisant, antipathique (person) ; intolérable, horripilant (thing).
horridly [-li] adv. Affreusement.
horrific [hə'rifik] adj. Horrible, terrifiant.
horrify ['hɔrifai] v. tr. (2). Horrifier.
horror ['hɔrə*] n. Horreur, épouvante f. (fright). ‖ Horreur, atrocité f. ‖ Horreur, répugnance f.; dégoût m. (of, de) [loathing]. ‖ MED. Frisson m.; pl. affres f. pl. (of death) ; hallucinations f. pl. (in delirium tremens). ‖ FAM. It gives me the horrors, ça me donne la chair de poule.
— adj. D'épouvante (film).
hors-d'œuvre [ɔː'dəːvr] n. Hors-d'œuvre m. invar.
— N. B. En anglais, pluriel hors-d'oeuvre ou hors-d'oeuvres.
horse [hɔːs] n. ZOOL. Cheval ; étalon m. (male); change of horse, relais. ‖ SPORTS. Cheval (m.) d'arçons. ‖ MILIT. Cavalerie f. ‖ NAUT. Marchepied m. (foot-rope) ; white horses, moutons. ‖ TECHN. Chevalet m.; chèvre f. (jack) ; cochon m. (in metal); towel-horse, porte-serviettes. ‖ FAM. To back the wrong horse, miser sur le mauvais cheval ; to eat like a horse, manger comme un loup; to ride the high horse, monter sur ses grands chevaux. ‖ **Horse-bean**, n. BOT. Féverole f. ‖ **Horse-block**, n. Montoir m. ‖ **Horse-breaker**, n. Dresseur (m.) de chevaux. ‖ **Horse-butchery**, n. COMM. Boucherie chevaline f. ‖ **Horse-chestnut**, n. BOT. Marron (m.) d'Inde ; horse-chestnut-tree, marronnier. ‖ **Horse-cloth**, n. Couverture (f.) de cheval. ‖ **Horse-dealer**, n. Maquignon m. ‖ **Horse-drawn**, adj. Hippomobile. ‖ **Horse-fly**, n. ZOOL. Taon m. ‖ **Horse-jobbing**, U. S. horse-trade, n. Maquignonnage m. ‖ **Horse-laugh**, n. Rire bruyant m. ‖ **Horse opera**, n. U. S. Western m. ‖ **Horse-path**, n. Piste cavalière f. ‖ **Horse-power**, n. AUTOM., TECHN. Cheval-vapeur m.; puissance (f.) en chevaux ; a four horse-power car, une quatre-chevaux. ‖ **Horse-race**, n. SPORTS. Course (f.) de chevaux. ‖ **Horse-racing**, n. SPORTS. Hippisme m. ‖ **Horse-radish**, n. BOT., CULIN. Raifort m. ‖ **Horse-sense**, n. FAM. Gros bon sens m. ‖ **Horse-show**, n. Concours hippique m. ‖ Horse-tail, n. BOT. Prêle f.
— adj. De cheval (race). ‖ Monté (artillery, Guards).
— v. tr. Fournir un cheval à (s.o.) ; well horsed, bien monté. ‖ Atteler un cheval à (a carriage). ‖ Transporter à dos.
— v. intr. Chevaucher ; monter ; aller à cheval ; faire du cheval.
horseback [-bæk] n. Dos de cheval m.; on horse-back, à cheval.
horseflesh [-fleʃ] n. Viande (f.) de cheval. ‖ Chevaux m. pl.
horsehair [-hɛə*] n. Crin de cheval m.
horseman [-mən] (pl. horsemen) n. Cavalier m.
horsemanship [-mənʃip] n. Equitation f. (art); talent d'écuyer m. (skill).
horseplay [-plei] n. Jeu (m.) de mains.
horseshoe [-ʃuː] n. Fer à cheval m.
— adj. En fer à cheval.
horsewhip [-wip] n. Cravache f.
— v. tr. (1). Cravacher.
horsewoman [-ˌwumən] (pl. horsewomen [-wimin]) n. Amazone f. ‖ Ecuyère f.
horsey ['hɔːsi] adj. See HORSY.
horsiness [-inis] n. Snobisme de jockey m.
horsy [-i] adj. De cheval (smell) ; chevalin (face). ‖ Passionné de chevaux.
hortative ['hɔːtətiv], **hortatory** [-təri] adj. Exhortatif.
horticultural [ˌhɔːti'kʌltʃərəl] adj. Horticole, d'horticulture.
horticulture ['hɔːtikʌltʃə*] n. AGRIC. Horticulture, culture jardinière f.
horticulturist [ˌhɔːti'kʌltʃərist] n. AGRIC. Horticulteur m.
hosanna [hou'zænə] n. ECCLES. Hosanna m.

hose [houz] n. invar. † Haut-de-chausses m. ‖ COMM. Bas m. (stocking).
— (pl. hoses [-iz]) n. TECHN. Tuyau m. (pipe). ‖ NAUT. Manche f.
— v. tr. Arroser au tuyau.
hosier ['houʒə*] n. Bonnetier s.
hosiery [-əri] n. COMM. Bonneterie f. ‖ U. S. Bas m. pl.
hospice ['hɔspis] n. Hospice, asile m.
hospitable ['hɔspitəbl] adj. Hospitalier.
hospitably [-bli] adv. Hospitalièrement.
hospital ['hɔspitl] n. JUR. Hospice, asile m. ‖ MED. Hôpital m. ‖ **Hospital-ship**, n. NAUT. Navire-hôpital m. ‖ **Hospital-train**, n. CH. DE F. Train sanitaire m.
hospitality [ˌhɔspi'tæliti] n. Hospitalité f.
hospitalization [ˌhɔspitəli'zeiʃən] n. MED. Hospitalisation f.
hospitalize ['hɔspitəlaiz] v. tr. MED. Hospitaliser.
hospitaller ['hɔspitlə*] n. † Hospitalier m. ‖ ECCLES. Aumônier d'hôpital m.
host [houst] n. ECCLES. Hostie f.
host n. ECCLES. † Armée. ‖ FAM. Foule f.
host n. Hôte m. ‖ Présentateur s. (on television). ‖ COMM. Hôtelier, aubergiste s. ‖ MED., BOT. Hôte m.
— v. tr. Recevoir (a person) ; présider (an event) ; présenter (a show).
hostage ['hɔstidʒ] n. MILIT. Otage m. ‖ FIG. Gage m.
hostel ['hɔstəl] n. † Hôtel m. ‖ Maison universitaire f.; youth hostel, auberge de la jeunesse.
hostelry [-ri] n. Hôtellerie f.
hostess ['houstis] n. Hôtesse f. ‖ COMM. Hôtelière f. ‖ AVIAT. Air hostess, hôtesse de l'air.
hostile ['hɔstail] adj. Hostile.
hostilely [-li] adv. Hostilement.
hostility [hɔs'tiliti] n. MILIT., FIG. Hostilité f.
hot [hɔt] adj. Brûlant, très chaud ; white hot, chauffé à blanc. ‖ CULIN. Piquant, cuisant (spice) ; U. S. FAM. hot dog, saucisse chaude. ‖ ELECTR. De haute tension. ‖ PHYS. U. S. Radio-actif : hot laboratory, laboratoire de recherches radio-actives. ‖ TECHN. Hot well, condenseur. ‖ SPORTS. Favori (competitor) ; hot tip, tuyau increvable. ‖ MUS. Hot music, swing. ‖ FIN. Fraîchement émis (banknotes). ‖ FIG. Chaud (dispute, pursuit) ; ardent, fougueux, enflammé, impétueux (person, words) ; bouillant, emporté (temper) ; chaud, passionné, qui a du tempérament (woman) ; to get hot, s'échauffer. ‖ FAM. Hot air, foutaise, bla-bla-bla ; hot spot, boîte de nuit ; hot stuff, de première force (person) ; épicé (story) ; in hot water, dans le pétrin ; to give it s.o. hot, sonner les cloches à qqn ; to make the place too hot for, rendre la position intenable à. ‖ FAM. Frais, récent (news) ; hot from London, tout frais arrivé de Londres. ‖ POP. Epatant (excellent) ; chauffé, fauché (stolen). ‖ **Hot-blooded**, adj. Au sang chaud. ‖ **Hot-headed**, adj. A la tête chaude, exalté. ‖ **Hot-foot**, adv. FAM. A toute vitesse. ‖ **Hot-press**, v. tr. TECHN. Catir, satiner. ‖ **Hot rock**, n. U. S. POP. Epateur m. ‖ **Hot-rod**, n. AUTOM. Bolide (m.) de course (car) ; casse-cou m. (person).
— adv. Chaudement, avec chaleur. ‖ Avec violence, coléreusement.
— v. tr. FAM. Chauffer, pousser.
hotbed [-bed] n. AGRIC. Couche f. ‖ FIG. Foyer m.
hotchpotch ['hɔtʃpɔtʃ] n. CULIN., FIG. Salmigondis m.
hotel [hou'tel] n. Hôtel m. (see INN) ; at (or) in a (or) an hotel, à l'hôtel.
hotelier [hə'teljei] n. Hôtelier m.
hothead ['hɔthed] n. FAM. Tête chaude f.
hothouse ['-haus] n. AGRIC. Serre chaude f.
hotly [-li] adv. Chaudement, chaleureusement. ‖ Violemment ; passionnément.
hotness [-nis] n. CULIN. Force f. (of spice). ‖ FIG. Chaleur, ardeur, flamme, fougue f.

hotplate ['hɔt,pleit] n. Plaque chauffante ƒ. (of an electric cooker). ‖ Chauffe-plats m. inv. (plate-warmer).
hotspur [-spə*] n. FAM. Tête brûlée ƒ.
hough [hɔk]. See HOCK.
hound [haund] n. ZOOL. Chien courant m.; pl. meute ƒ. ‖ SPORTS. Poursuivant s. (in « hare and hounds »). ‖ FIG. Chien m. ‖ **Hound's-tooth check**, n. U. S. Pied-de-poule m. (fabric).
— v. tr. SPORTS. Chasser au chien courant. ‖ FIG. Exciter (at, on, contre) [a dog]; to hound s.oℓ down, s'acharner sur qqn.
hour ['auə*] n. Heure ƒ.; an hour and a half, une heure et demie; half an hour, a half-hour, une demi-heure; a quarter of an hour, un quart d'heure; hour by hour, d'une heure à l'autre. ‖ Heure ƒ.; moment m.; at the hour stated, à l'heure dite; the hour has come, c'est le moment; to keep good, late hours, se coucher tôt, tard. ‖ Pl. Heures (ƒ. pl.) de travail; an (or) per hour, à l'heure; eight-hour day, journée de huit heures; out of hours, en dehors des heures ouvrables. ‖ ECCLES. Pl. Heures. ‖ FIG. Heure actuelle ƒ.; the question of the hour, l'événement du jour; to improve the hour, profiter des circonstances. ‖ **Hour-glass**, n. Sablier m. ‖ **Hour-hand**, n. Aiguille (ƒ.) des heures.
houri ['huəri] n. Houri ƒ.
hourly ['auəli] adj. A chaque heure, de toutes les heures. ‖ FIG. De tout instant, incessant.
— adv. D'heure en heure; half-hourly, toutes les demi-heures. ‖ FIG. Continuellement, sans discontinuer.
house [haus] (pl. **houses** ['hauziz]) n. Maison, demeure, habitation ƒ. (dwelling place); at my house, chez moi; out of house and home, à la rue, sans feu ni lieu. ‖ Maison, famille ƒ. (family); maison, maisonnée ƒ. (members of the household). ‖ Ménage m.; to keep house for, tenir le ménage (or) la maison de; to keep open house, tenir table ouverte. ‖ Hôtel m.; public house, café, débit de boissons. ‖ Maison ƒ. (in astrology). ‖ JUR. Chambre ƒ.; House of Commons, Lords, U. S. Representatives, Chambre des Communes, des Lords, U. S. des Représentants; to make a house, réunir le quorum. ‖ THEATR. Salle ƒ. ‖ ECCLES. Maison religieuse ƒ. ‖ COMM. Maison (ƒ.) de commerce; house-to-house canvassing, porte-à-porte. ‖ FIG. Edifice m.; house of cards, château de cartes. ‖ FAM. On the house, aux frais de la princesse. ‖ **House-agent**, n. Agent (m.) de location. ‖ **House-arrest**, n. JUR. Assignation à résidence ƒ.; to be under house arrest, être assigné à résidence. ‖ **House-bound**, adj. Qui ne peut pas sortir de chez soi, cloué à la maison. ‖ **House-cleaning**, n. Grand nettoyage m. ‖ **House-coat**, n. Robe (ƒ.) d'intérieur. ‖ **House-dog**, n. ZOOL. Chien (m.) de garde. ‖ **House-hunting**, n. Chasse (ƒ.) aux appartements. ‖ **House-physician**, n. MED. Interne s. (in a hospital); médecin (m.) attaché à un établissement (in a hotel). ‖ **House-porter**, n. Concierge m. ‖ **House-room**, n. Place (ƒ.) chez soi, logement m. ‖ **House-shoe**, m. Chaussure (ƒ.) d'intérieur. ‖ **House-top**, n. Toit m. ‖ **House-trained**, adj. Propre (pet, infant); FIG. Docile, sage. ‖ **House-warming**, n. Pendaison de crémaillère ƒ.
— [hauz] v. tr. Héberger, abriter, loger, recevoir (s.o.); loger, caser (sth.). ‖ NAUT. Caler (a mast); amener (a sail). ‖ AGRIC. Engranger (crop). ‖ AUTOM. Garer (a car).
— v. intr. Loger, habiter (with, avec). ‖ Se loger.
houseboat ['haus,bout] n. Bateau (m.) [or] péniche (ƒ.) d'habitation.
housebreak ['haus,breik] v. tr. Dresser à la propreté (cat, dog).
— v. intr. Cambrioler (burglar).
housebreaker [-ə*] n. JUR. Cambrioleur s. (burglar). ‖ ARCHIT. Démolisseur m.
housecraft [-krɑ:ft] n. Art ménager m. (domestic science).

houseful [-ful] n. Maisonnée, pleine maison ƒ.
household [-hould] n. Maisonnée, maison, famille ƒ. ‖ Maisonnée, domesticité ƒ.; gens (m. pl.) de maison; the Royal Household, la Maison du Roi. ‖ COMM. Pl. Farine inférieure ƒ.
— adj. De ménage (bread); du ménage (expenses); household gods, dieux lares; household soap, savon de Marseille.
householder [-houldə*] n. Chef (m.) de famille; maître (m.) de maison. ‖ JUR. Logeur m. (owner); locataire m. (lessee).
housekeeper [-,ki:pə*] n. Ménagère, femme (ƒ.) d'intérieur (housewife). ‖ Femme de charge, gouvernante ƒ. (in a private house); intendante ƒ. (in a public institution).
housekeeping [-,ki:piŋ] n. Economie domestique ƒ. (science); affaires (ƒ. pl.) du ménage (work). ‖ **Housekeeping-book**, n. Carnet (m.) de dépenses.
houseleek [-li:k] n. BOT. Joubarbe ƒ.
houseless [-lis] adj. Sans abri.
housemaid [-meid] n. Femme de chambre. ‖ MED. Housemaid's knee, épanchement de synovie.
housewife [-waif] n. Ménagère, maîtresse de maison ƒ. (woman).
— ['hʌzif] n. Ménagère, trousse ƒ.; nécessaire à ouvrage m. (sewing kit).
housewifery ['hʌzifri] n. Tenue (ƒ.) de ménage.
housework ['haus,wə:k] n. Travaux ménagers m. pl.; to do the housework, faire le ménage.
housing ['hauziŋ] n. Logement m.; housing problem, shortage, problème, crise du logement.
housing n. Caparaçon m. (for a horse).
hove [houv] pret., p. p. NAUT. See HEAVE.
hovel ['hɔvəl] n. Appentis m. (shed). ‖ FAM. Baraque, cahute, bicoque ƒ.
hover ['hɔvə*] v. intr. Voltiger (about, autour de) [bird]; planer (over, sur) [eagle]. ‖ Rôder, tourner (about, autour de) [person]; to hover around the ladies, papillonner auprès des dames. ‖ FIG. Rôder (danger); errer (smile).
hovercraft ['hɔvə,krɑ:ft] n. TECHN. Aéroglisseur, hovercraft m.
hoverplane ['hɔvə:plein] n. AVIAT. Piper-cub m.
hovertrain ['hɔvə,trein] n. CH. DE F. Aérotrain m.
how [hau] adv. Comment, de quelle façon; how is it that you don't know about it?, comment se fait-il que vous n'en sachiez rien? ‖ Combien; how far, à quelle distance (place); jusqu'où (time); how long, de quelle longueur (length); how long, combien de temps (duration); how much (or) many, combien, combien de (number); how old is he?, quel âge a-t-il? ‖ Comme, que, combien; how kind of you!, vous êtes bien aimable!; how sorry I am!, combien je suis désolé! ‖ Que; to tell s.o. how, raconter à qqn que. ‖ U. S. How about the captain?, alors, et le capitaine? ‖ U. S. FAM. How come?, comment cela?, pourquoi? ‖ LOC. How so?, comment cela?; how then?, et alors? ‖ **How-d'ye-do**, n. FAM. Pétrin m.
— n. Manière ƒ.
howbeit ['hau'bi:it] adv. † Quoi qu'il en soit.
howdy ['haudi] interj. U. S. Salut!
however [hau'evə*] adv. De quelque manière (or) façon que; however that may be, quoi qu'il en soit. ‖ Quelque (or) si... que; however clever he may be, quelque ingénieux qu'il soit; however little, si peu que ce soit (quantity); si petit que (size).
— conj. Cependant, toutefois, pourtant.
howitzer ['hauitsə*] n. MILIT. Obusier m.
howl [haul] v. intr. Hurler (animal, person); mugir (wind).
— v. tr. Hurler, clamer.
— n. Hurlement m. (of animals, persons). ‖ Huée ƒ. (hoot).
howler [-ə*] n. Hurleur m. (animal, person). ‖ FAM. Enormité, monstruosité, grosse bourde (or) boulette, perle ƒ.; calamity howler, prophète de malheur.

howlet ['haulit] n. Zool. Hulotte *f.*
howling ['hauliŋ] n. Hurlement *m.*
— adj. Hurlant. ‖ Fam. Enorme (mistake) ; criant (injustice) ; fou (success) ; glacé, lugubre (wilderness).
howsoever [,hausou'evə*] adv. De quelque façon que. ‖ Quelque (or) si... que.
hoy [hɔi] interj. Ohé !
hoyden ['hɔidn̩] n. Garçon manqué *m.* (See TOM-BOY.)
hoydenish [-iʃ] adj. Garçonnier.
h. p. Written abbr. for *hire-purchase,* location-vente, achat à tempérament. ‖ Written abbr. for *horse-power,* cheval-vapeur.
H. Q. [eitʃ'kju:] abbr. *headquarters,* quartier géné-ral, Q. G.
H. T. [eitʃ'ti:] abbr. *high tension,* haute tension, H. T.
hub [hʌb] n. Moyeu *m.* (of wheel). ‖ Fig. Pivot, centre *m.* ‖ **Hub-cap, hub-cover, -plate,** n. Autom. Enjoliveur *m.*
hub(by) ['hʌbi] n. Fam. Epoux *m.*
hubble-bubble ['hʌbl̩,bʌbl̩] n. Narguilé *m.* (pipe). ‖ Glouglou, gargouillis *m.* (gurgling). ‖ Brouhaha *m.* (of voices).
hubbub ['hʌbʌb] n. Vacarme, tintamarre, tumulte *m.* ‖ Brouhaha *m.* (of voices).
huckle ['hʌkl̩] n. Med. Hanche *f.* (See HIP.) ‖ **Huckle-bone,** n. Med. Os iliaque *m.* (hip-bone) ; U. S. Astragale *m.* (talus) ; Fam. Osselet *m.*
huckleberry ['hʌklberi] n. Bot. Airelle *f.*
huckster ['hʌkstə*] n. Comm. Colporteur, reven-deur *m.* (See HAWKER.) ‖ U. S. Comm. Vendeur (*m.*) des quatre-saisons ; *huckster's handcart,* petite voi-ture. ‖ Fam. Mercanti, trafiquant *m.* ‖ U. S. Fam. Agent (*m.*) de publicité.
— v. tr. Comm. Colporter, revendre. ‖ Fam. Tra-fiquer de.
— v. intr. Marchander. (See HAGGLE.)
huddle ['hʌdl̩] v. tr. Empiler, entasser (persons, things) ; jeter pêle-mêle (things). ‖ **To huddle on,** enfiler vivement (one's clothes). ‖ **To huddle over,** bâcler (a piece of work). ‖ **To huddle up,** entasser à la va-vite.
— v. intr. S'entasser, s'empiler, se presser (animals, persons). ‖ Se recroqueviller.
— n. Foule *f.* (crowd). ‖ Fouillis *m.* (muddle). ‖ Fam. *To go into a huddle,* tenir une conférence secrète.
hue [hju] n. Huée *f. ; to raise a hue and cry against,* crier haro sur. ‖ Jur. *Hue and cry,* proclamation à cor et à cri.
hue n. Teinte *f.* (See COLOUR.)
hued [-d] adj. Coloré.
huff [hʌf] v. tr. Malmener, secouer (to bully). ‖ Offenser, froisser, irriter (to offend). ‖ Souffler (at draughts).
— v. intr. Se froisser, se formaliser, s'offusquer (to take offence). ‖ S'irriter, s'emporter, se hérisser (to become angry). ‖ Souffler (at draughts).
— n. Irritation, poussée de colère *f. ; to take the huff,* prendre la mouche. ‖ Soufflage *m.* (at draughts).
huffily [-ili] adv. Avec irritation.
huffiness [-inis] n. Susceptibilité *f.* ‖ Humeur peu endurante *f.*
huffish [-iʃ], **huffy** [-i] adj. Susceptible. ‖ Irritable, désagréable (peevish) ; *he got huffy,* la moutarde lui est montée au nez.
hug [hʌg] v. tr. (1). Embrasser, étreindre, serrer dans ses bras. ‖ Zool. Serrer entre ses pattes. ‖ Naut. Serrer (the coast). ‖ Autom. Raser, serrer (the kerb, U. S. the curb). ‖ Fig. Ne pas démordre de, tenir mordicus à (an opinion) ; chérir (a preju-dice) ; *to hug oneself on,* se féliciter de. ‖ **Hug-me-tight,** n. Collant *m.*
— n. Embrassement *m. ;* étreinte *f.* ‖ Sports. Prise, ceinture *f.*

huge [hju:dʒ] adj. Enorme, immense, colossal.
hugely [-li] adv. Enormément.
hugeness [-nis] n. Enormité, immensité, dimension formidable *f.*
hugger-mugger ['hʌgə,mʌgə*] n. Fouillis, fatras *m. ;* pagaille *f.* (muddle). † Secret *m.*
— adj. Désordonné. ‖ † Secret, dissimulé.
— adv. En désordre (or) pagaille. ‖ † En secret.
— v. tr. † Etouffer, cacher.
— v. intr. Mettre la pagaille.
Huguenot ['hju:gənou] n. Eccles. Huguenot *s.*
huh [hʌ] interj. Eh ! (surprise) ; hein ? (interroga-tion) ; peuh ! (contempt, etc.).
hulk [hʌlk] n. Naut. Ponton *m. ;* pl. galères *f. pl.* ‖ Fam. Naut. Vieux rafiot *m.* ‖ Fam. Mastodonte, éléphant *m.*
hulking [-iŋ] adj. Pesant, énorme (bulky). ‖ Balourd, lourdaud (clumsy).
hull [hʌl] n. Bot. Coque *f.* (of nuts) ; cosse, gousse *f.* (of peas). ‖ Naut., Aviat. Coque.
— v. tr. Bot. Monder (barley) ; décortiquer (oats) ; écosser (peas). ‖ Naut. Percer la coque de.
hullabaloo [,hʌləbə'lu:] n. Fam. Boucan, potin *m.*
hulling ['hʌliŋ] n. Bot. Décorticage *m.*
hullo ['hʌ'lou] interj. Hello ! (greeting). ‖ Allô ! (at the phone). ‖ Holà ! (call).
hum [hʌm] v. intr. (1). Zool. Bourdonner (bee). ‖ Mus. Fredonner ; chanter à bouche fermée. ‖ Techn. Vrombir (electric fan) ; ronfler (top). ‖ Aviat. Vrombir. ‖ Fig. Anonner (person) ; bourdonner (voices) ; *to hum and haw,* bafouiller, hésitailler. ‖ Fam. Barder, ronfler, gazer (to bustle).
— v. tr. Mus. Fredonner.
— n. Zool. Bourdonnement *m.* ‖ Mus. Fredon, chantonnement *m.* ‖ Techn., Aviat. Vrombisse-ment *m.* ‖ Fig. Bredouillement *m.* (of a speaker) ; bourdonnement *m.* (of voices).
— interj. Hem !, hum !
hum v. intr. Fam. Puer. (See STINK.)
human ['hju:mən] adj. Humain (being). ‖ Fam. *He is very human,* il a ses petites faiblesses, c'est un homme (imperfect).
— n. Humain, être humain *m.*
humane [hju'mein] adj. Humain, plein d'humanité (kind). ‖ Humaniste ; *humane studies,* humanités.
humanely [-li] adv. Humainement, avec humanité.
humaneness [-nis] n. Humanité *f. ;* sentiments humains *m. pl.*
humanism [-izm] n. Humanisme *m. ;* humanités *f. pl.* (studies). ‖ Humanitarisme *m.* (quality).
humanist [-ist] n. Humaniste *s.*
humanitarian [hju,mæni'tɛəriən] adj., n. Huma-nitaire *s.*
humanitarianism [-izm] n. Humanitarisme *m.*
humanity [hju'mæniti] n. Humanité *f. ;* genre humain *m.* (mankind). ‖ Humanité, nature humaine *f. ;* humanitarisme *m.* (quality). ‖ Pl. Actes (*m. pl.*) d'humanité (actions) ; humanités *f. pl.* (studies).
humanization [,hju:mənai'zeiʃən] n. Humanisa-tion *f.*
humanize ['hju:mənaiz] v. tr. Humaniser.
humankind [,hju:mən'kaind] n. Humanité *f. ;* genre humain *m.*
humanly ['hju:mənli] adv. Humainement, en homme ; au point de vue humain. ‖ Humainement, avec humanité (humanely).
humanness [-nis] n. Qualité (*f.*) propre à l'homme ; expression humaine *f.*
humble ['hʌmbl̩] adj. Humble, modeste. ‖ Fam. *To eat humble pie,* faire amende honorable, filer doux, aller à Canossa.
— v. tr. Humilier, abaisser, mortifier ; *to humble oneself,* s'humilier.
humble-bee [-bi:] n. Zool. Bourdon *m.*
humbleness [-nis] n. Humilité *f.*
humbly ['hʌmbli] adv. Humblement, modestement.
humbug ['hʌmbʌg] n. Blague, sornette *f.* (hoax).

‖ Charlatanisme, montage de coup *m*. (deception).
‖ Blagueur, farceur, monteur de coup *m*. (joker);
entortilleur *m*. (wheedler). ‖ CULIN. Bonbon (*m*.) à
la menthe.
— interj. Balivernes!
— v. tr. (1). FAM. Entortiller, embobeliner, en
conter à, monter le coup à.
— v. intr. FAM. Blaguer.
humdinger ['hʌm,diŋə*] n. FAM. Qqn (or) qqch.
de terrible (or) de génial.
humdrum ['hʌmdrʌm] adj. Monotone, endormant; encroûtant (fam.).
— n. Monotonie, banalité f.
— v. intr. (1). Faire son train-train.
humeral ['hju:mərəl] adj. MED. Huméral.
humerus [-əs] n. MED. Humérus *m*.
humid ['hju:mid] adj. Humide. (See WET.)
humidification [,hju:midifi'keiʃən] n. Humidification f.
humidify [hju:'midifai] v. tr. (2). Humidifier.
humidity [-ti] n. Humidité f. (See DAMPNESS.) ‖
Humidity-proof, adj. Résistant à l'humidité.
humidor ['hju:midə:*] n. Humidificateur *m*.
humiliate [hju:'milieit] v. tr. Humilier.
humiliating [-iŋ] adj. Humiliant.
humiliation [,hjumili'eiʃən] n. Humiliation f.
humility [hju:'militi] n. Humilité f.
hummer ['hʌmə*] n. U. S. POP. Bourreau de travail *m*. (person); élément (*m*.) d'activité (thing).
humming ['hʌmiŋ] adj. ZOOL. Bourdonnant (bee).
‖ MUS. Fredonnant. ‖ TECHN. Vrombissant (electric
fan); ronflant (top). ‖ AVIAT. Vrombissant. ‖ FAM.
En plein essor, qui gaze (affair); à voir trente-six
chandelles (blow). ‖ **Humming-bird**, n. ZOOL.
Oiseau-mouche, colibri *m*.
hummock ['hʌmək] n. Mamelon, monticule *m*.
(See HILLOCK.) ‖ Hummock *m*. (in an ice-field).
humoral ['hju:mərəl] adj. MED. Humoral.
humorist ['hju:mərist] n. Humoriste *m*.
humoristic [hju:mə'ristik] adj. Humoristique.
humorous ['hju:mərəs] adj. Humoristique, plein
d'humour, spirituel (witty). ‖ Humoristique, amusant, comique (droll).
humorously [-li] adv. Avec humour.
humorousness [-nis] n. Drôlerie f.; caractère
humoristique *m*.
humo(u)r ['hju:mə*] n. † MED. Humeur f. ‖
Humeur, disposition (f.) d'esprit; *out of humour*,
d'humeur noire, de mauvaise humeur. ‖ Drôlerie f.;
comique, caractère humoristique *m*. (comicality). ‖
Humour, sens de l'humour *m*. (sense, talent).
— v. tr. Se prêter à, se plier à, passer (s.o.'s fancy);
satisfaire (s.o.'s tastes). ‖ Satisfaire, ne pas contrarier, se soumettre aux exigences de, ménager (s.o.).
humourless [-lis] adj. Dépourvu d'humour.
humoursome [-səm] adj. Capricieux, fantasque,
d'humeur changeante (whimsical). ‖ De mauvaise
humeur, hargneux, grincheux (peevish).
hump [hʌmp] n. Bosse f. (on the back). ‖ Mamelon *m*.; bosse f. (hillock). ‖ FAM. Cafard *m*.
— v. tr. Bossuer, incurver, arrondir; voûter; *to
hump one's back*, voûter le gros dos. ‖ Mettre sur
l'épaule. ‖ FAM. Donner le cafard à.
— v. intr. U. S. FAM. S'évertuer.
humpbacked [-bækt] n. adj. Bossu (person).
humped [-t] adj. Bossu (back, person).
humph [hʌmf] interj. Hum! (doubt).
humpless ['hʌmplis] adj. Sans bosse.
humpty-dumpty ['hʌmpti'dʌmpti] n. FAM. Per
sonne boulotte f.; patapouf *m*.
humpy ['hʌmpi] adj. Bossu; bossué.
humus ['hju:məs] n. Humus *m*.
Hun [hʌn] n. GEOGR. Hun *m*. ‖ FAM. Boche *m*.
hunch [hʌntʃ] n. FAM. Intuition, idée f.; pressentiment *m*.
hunch n. Bosse f. (See HUMP.) ‖ Quignon *m*. (of

bread); gros morceau *m*. (of cheese). [See HUNK.]
— v. tr. Arrondir, voûter; *to hunch one's back*,
se voûter; *with hunched shoulders*, les épaules
remontées. ‖ **To hunch out**, former une bosse.
— v. intr. U. S. Pousser du coude.
hunchback [-bæk] n. Bossu *m*. (See HUMPBACK.)
hunchbacked [-bækt] adj. Bossu.
hunchy [-i] adj. Bossu.
hundred ['hʌndrəd] adj. Cent; *a hundred times*,
cent fois; *two hundred*, deux cents; *two hundred
and thirty*, deux cent trente; *two in a hundred*,
deux sur cent.
— n. Centaine f.; *hundreds of times*, des centaines
de fois. ‖ COMM. *To sell by the hundred*, vendre au
cent. ‖ † Canton *m*.
hundredfold [-fould] n. Centuple *m*.; *a hundredfold*, au centuple.
hundredth [-θ] adj., n. Centième.
hundredweight [-weit] n. Quintal *m*.
hung [hʌŋ] pret., p. p. See HANG.
Hungarian [hʌŋ'gɛəriən] adj., n. GEOGR. Hongrois s.
Hungary ['hʌŋgəri] n. GEOGR. Hongrie f.
hunger ['hʌŋgə*] n. Faim f. ‖ FIG. Soif f. ‖ U. S.
FAM. *Strictly from hunger*, sans intérêt, déplorable.
‖ **Hunger-strike**, n. Grève de la faim f.
— v. intr. Avoir faim. ‖ FIG. Avoir soif de, désirer
ardemment.
— v. tr. Affamer, réduire à la famine; *to hunger
into submission*, soumettre par la famine.
hungrily ['hʌŋgrili] adv. Avidement, voracement.
hungry [-gri] adj. Affamé; *to be hungry*, avoir
faim; *to go hungry*, souffrir de la faim. ‖ Famélique; *to look hungry*, avoir l'air de crever de faim.
‖ AGRIC. Maigre (soil). ‖ FIG. Avide (*for*, de).
hunk [hʌŋk] n. Quignon *m*. (of bread); gros morceau *m*. (of cheese).
hunkers ['hʌŋkə:z] n. pl. FAM. *Sitting on one's
hunkers*, à croupetons.
hunks [hʌŋks] n. Harpagon *m*. (miser).
hunky ['hʌŋki] n. U. S. POP. Immigrant (*m*.) d'Europe centrale. ‖ **Hunky-dory**, adj. U. S. FAM. D'ac.
Hunnish ['hʌniʃ] adj. GEOGR. De Hun. ‖ FAM. De
Boche.
hunt [hʌnt] v. intr. SPORTS. Chasser. ‖ FIG. Faire
la chasse (*after*, *for*, à); être à la recherche (*after*,
for, de).
— v. tr. SPORTS. Chasser (game, wild animals);
monter (a horse); chasser avec (hounds). ‖ Battre,
courir, parcourir (a district). ‖ FIG. Pourchasser,
poursuivre (s.o.). ‖ **To hunt away**, chasser. ‖ **To
hunt down**, forcer (an animal); FIG. Traquer (s.o.).
‖ **To hunt out**, chasser, exclure (s.o.); dénicher,
déterrer, découvrir (sth.). ‖ **To hunt up**, rechercher
(to hunt for); découvrir (to hunt out).
— n. SPORTS. Chasse f. (district, game, hunters).
‖ FIG. Chasse, recherche f. ‖ **Hunt-the-slipper**, n.
Furet *m*. (game).
hunted [-id] adj. Chassé, pourchassé; *a hunted
look*, un regard de bête traquée.
hunter [-ə*] n. SPORTS. Cheval (*m*.) de chasse
(horse). ‖ U. S. Chasseur *m*. (person). ‖ TECHN.
Savonnette f. (watch). ‖ FIG. Pourchasseur *m*.
hunting [-iŋ] n. SPORTS. Chasse (f.) à courre (act,
game). ‖ FIG. Chasse, poursuite f. ‖ **Hunting-box**,
U. S. hunting lodge, n. Pavillon (*m*.) de chasse.
‖ **Hunting-ground**, n. Terrain (*m*.) de chasse. ‖
Hunting-horn, n. MUS. Cor (*m*.) de chasse. ‖
Hunting-knife, n. Couteau (*m*.) de chasse.
huntress [-ris] n. Chasseresse f.
huntsman [-smən] (pl. **huntsmen**) n. Chasseur *m*.
(hunter); veneur, piqueur *m*. (whipper-in).
hurdle ['hə:dl] n. Claie f. ‖ SPORTS. Haie f.;
hundred metres hurdles (or) U. S. *with hurdles*,
100 mètres haies. ‖ FIG. Obstacle *m*.

— v. tr. Entourer de claies. ‖ Sports. Sauter. ‖ Fig. Surmonter (an obstacle).

hurdler [-ə*] n. Fabricant (m.) de claies. ‖ Sports. Coureur (m.) en course d'obstacles.

hurdy-gurdy ['hə:di,gə:di] n. Mus. † Vielle f. ‖ Mus. Orgue de barbarie m. (barrel-organ).

hurl [hə:l] v. tr. Jeter, lancer, précipiter (from, de; on, sur) ; catapulter (fam.).
— n. Lancée f.; jet m.

hurly-burly ['hə:li,bə:li] n. Tintamarre, brouhaha m. (hubbub) ; tohu-bohu m. (medley).

hurrah [hu'rɑ:] interj., n. Hourra m.
— v. intr. Crier hourra.

hurricane ['hʌrikən] n. Ouragan, cyclone m.; tornade f. ‖ **Hurricane-bird,** n. Zool. Frégate f. ‖ **Hurricane-deck,** n. Naut. Pont-promenade m. (on liners) ; pont-abri m. (on warships). ‖ **Hurricane-house,** n. Naut. Nid-de-corbeau m. ‖ **Hurricane-lamp,** n. Lampe-tempête f.

hurried ['hurid] adj. Précipité (departure) ; expédié (meal), pressé, bousculé ; talonné (person) ; fait à la va-vite (work).

hurriedly [-li] adv. Précipitamment, à la hâte.

hurriedness [-nis] n. Précipitation, bousculade f.

hurry ['hʌri] n. Hâte, précipitation, presse f.; affairement m. (see HASTE) ; in a hurry, à la hâte ; there's no hurry, rien ne presse ; what's your hurry?, qu'est-ce qui vous presse? ‖ Hâte, impatience f.; empressement m. (eagerness). ‖ Fam. He won't do it again in a hurry, il ne recommencera pas de sitôt, il n'est pas près de recommencer. ‖ **Hurry-scurry,** adv. En désordre, à la débandade ; à la va-vite ; adj. Désordonné, brouillon ; n. Bousculade, débandade f.; v. intr. Agir fébrilement ; courir à la débandade.
— v. tr. (2). Presser, bousculer, activer (s.o.) ; presser, hâter, activer, accélérer, précipiter (sth.) ; to hurry along (or) away, back, down, out, up, entraîner, faire revenir, faire descendre, faire sortir, faire avancer précipitamment. ‖ **To hurry on,** faire presser, activer, précipiter.
— v. intr. Se presser, se dépêcher (see HUSTLE) ; to hurry over, expédier, faire à la va-vite ; to hurry after, to, courir après, à. ‖ **To hurry up,** se hâter, se dépêcher.

hurst [hə:st] n. Tertre m. (hillock) ; colline boisée f. (holt) ; boqueteau m. (wood). ‖ Banc de sable m. (sandbank).

hurt [hə:t] n. Med. Blessure f.; mal m. ‖ Jur., Fig. Tort, dommage, préjudice m.
— v. tr. (83). Med. Blesser, faire du mal à ; to hurt one's leg, se blesser à la jambe. ‖ Jur. Faire du tort à, causer un dommage (or) préjudice à, nuire à, léser (s.o.) ; détériorer, endommager, porter atteinte à (sth.). ‖ Fig. Froisser, blesser ; if I may say so without hurting your feelings, soit dit sans vous offenser. ‖ U. S. Hurt books, livres défraîchis.
— v. intr. Med. Faire mal, faire souffrir. ‖ Fam. Se détériorer.

hurtful [-ful] adj. Med. Nocif, préjudiciable (to, à). ‖ Fig. Blessant, offensant.

hurtfully [-fuli] adv. D'une manière dommageable (or) blessante.

hurtfulness [-fulnis] n. Nocivité f.

hurtle ['hə:tl] v. tr. Heurter (to strike). ‖ Lancer, jeter, projeter (to hurl).
— v. intr. Retentir (to clatter). ‖ Se heurter, entrer en collision (to collide). ‖ S'élancer avec fracas, arriver en trombe ; se jeter (into, dans). ‖ Tomber comme grêle, pleuvoir dru (rain, projectiles).
— n. Fracas m. (clash) ; collision f.

hurtless [-lis] adj. Inoffensif (harmless). ‖ Sans mal (unharmed).

husband ['hʌzbənd] n. Mari m. ‖ † Cultivateur m. ‖ † Administrateur, dispensateur m.
— v. tr. Ménager (one's money) ; économiser (one's strength). ‖ † Cultiver. ‖ Fam. Marier.

husbandlike [-laik] adj. De mari.

husbandman [-mən] (pl. **husbandmen**) n. Agric. Fermier m.

husbandry [-ri] n. Agric. Culture f. ‖ Jur. Gestion, administration, économie f.

hush [hʌʃ] interj. Chut !
— n. Calme qui précède l'orage m. ‖ Silence m. ‖ **Hush-hush,** adj. Fam. Secret ; v. tr. Etouffer, réduire au silence. ‖ **Hush-money,** n. Pot-de-vin (m.) pour acheter le silence.
— v. intr. Se taire.
— v. tr. Faire taire, calmer. ‖ **To hush up,** Fig. Etouffer.

hushaby ['hʌʃəbai] interj. Dodo !

husk [hʌsk] n. Bot. Bogue f. (of chestnut) ; balle f. (of corn) ; enveloppe f. (of maize, rice) ; écale f. (of nut) ; pelure f. (of onion) ; cosse, gousse f. (of peas). ‖ Fig. Enveloppe grossière f.
— v. tr. Bot. Décortiquer, éplucher (maize) ; écaler (nut) ; monder (oats) ; peler (onions) ; écosser (peas) ; décortiquer (rice).

huskily ['hʌskili] adv. D'une voix rauque.

huskiness [-nis] n. Med. Enrouement m. ‖ U. S. Fam. Santé florissante f.

husky ['hʌski] adj. Bot. Cossu, plein de gousses (peas). ‖ Med. Enroué (person, voice). ‖ U. S. Fam. Costaud.

husky n. Zool. Esquimau m ; esquimaude f.

hussar [hu'ʒɑ:*] n. Milit. Hussard m.

hussy ['hʌzi] n. Garce, traînée f. (trollop). ‖ Fam. Coquine, mâtine, petite futée f. (minx).

hustings ['hʌstiŋs] n. Jur. Cour de justice f. (court) ; tribune électorale f. (platform) ; élections f. pl. (proceedings).

hustle ['hʌsl] v. tr. Pousser, bousculer ; to hustle one another, se bousculer. ‖ Fig. Pousser, forcer (s.o.) ; pousser, faire avancer (sth.) ; to hustle things on, faire marcher les choses.
— v. intr. Avancer en poussant des coudes ; to hustle through the crowd, se frayer un passage dans la foule en jouant des coudes. ‖ Se dépêcher, se hâter, se presser. (See HURRY.) ‖ U. S. Se démener, se remuer, s'activer (to bustle).
— n. Bousculade, presse f. ‖ Fam. U. S. Allant m.; esprit (m.) d'entreprise (or) d'initiative (push).

hustler [-ə*] n. U. S. Fam. Débrouillard, arriviste m. (go-getter) ; bûcheur m. (hard worker) ; type dynamique m. (live wire) ; putain f. (whore).

hut [hʌt] n. Hutte, cabane f. ‖ Milit. Baraquement m.
— v. tr., intr. Milit. Baraquer.

hutch [hʌtʃ] n. Clapier m. (coop). ‖ Huche f. (baker's). ‖ Techn. Wagonnet m. ‖ Fam. Cahute f.

hutment [hʌtmənt] n. Milit. Baraquement m.

huzza [hu'zɑ:] interj., n. Hourra m.
— v. intr. Crier hourra.
— v. tr. Saluer par des hourras.

hyacinth ['haiəsinθ] n. Hyacinthe f. (stone). ‖ Bot. Jacinthe f. (colour, flower).

hyacinthine [,haiə'sinθain] adj. Bleu jacinthe.

hyaena [hai'i:nə] n. See HYENA.

hyaline ['haiəlin] adj. Hyalin, diaphane, translucide.
— n. Mer transparente f. (sea) ; ciel diaphane m. (sky).

hyaloid ['haiələid] adj. Med. Hyaloïde.

hybrid ['haibrid] adj., n. Zool., Bot., Gramm., Fig. Hybride m. ‖ Med. Métis m.

hybridity [hai'briditi] n. Hybridité f.

hybridization [haibridai'zeiʃən] n. Hybridation f.

hybridize ['haibridaiz] v. tr. Hybrider.
— v. intr. S'hybrider.

hydra ['haidrə] n. Hydre m. ‖ Fig. Serpent, monstre, hydre m.

hydracid [hai'dræsid] n. Chim. Hydracide m.

hydrangea [hai'drendʒjə] n. Bot. Hortensia *m.*
hydrant ['haidrənt] n. Prise d'eau; bouche (*f.*) d'incendie.
hydrate [-eit] n. Chim. Hydrate *m.*
— v. tr. Chim. Hydrater.
hydration [hai'dreiʃən] n. Chim. Hydratation *f.*
hydraulic [hai'drɔ:lik] adj. Hydraulique.
hydraulically [-əli] adv. Hydrauliquement.
hydraulician [hai'drɔ:liʃən] n. Hydraulicien *m.*
hydraulics [hai'drɔ:liks] n. sg. Hydraulique *f.*
hydrazine ['haidrə,zi:n] n. Chim. Hydrazine *f.*
hydric ['haidrik] adj. Chim. Hydrogéné; hydrique.
hydride ['haidraid] n. Chim. Hydrure *m.*
hydriodic [,haidri'ɔdik] adj. Chim. *Hydriodic acid,* acide iodhydrique.
hydro ['haidrou] n. Fam. Etablissement thermal *m.*
‖ **Hydro-hotel,** n. Hôtel (*m.*) avec thermes.
hydrobromic [haidro'broumik] adj. Chim. Bromhydrique.
hydrocarbon [-'kɑ:bən] n. Chim. Hydrocarbure *m.*
hydrocele ['haidrosi:l] n. Med. Hydrocèle *f.*
hydrocephalous [,haidro'sefələs] adj. Med. Hydrocéphale.
hydrocephalus [,haidro'sefələs] n. Med. Hydrocéphalie *f.*
hydrochloric [,haidro'klɔ:rik] adj. Chim. Chlorhydrique.
hydrochloride [-aid] n. Chim. Chlorhydrate *m.*
hydrocyanic [,haidrosai'ænik] adj. Chim. Cianhydrique.
hydrodynamic [,haidrodai'næmik] adj. Techn. Hydrodynamique.
hydrodynamics [-ks] n. sg. Hydrodynamique *f.*
hydroelectric [,haidroi'lektrik] adj. Hydroélectrique.
hydroelectricity [,haidroi,lek'trisiti] n. Hydroélectricité *f.*
hydrofluoric [-flu:'ɔrik] adj. Chim. *Hydrofluoric acid,* acide fluorhydrique *m.*
hydrofoil ['haidrə,fɔil] n. Naut. Hydroptère (or) hydrofoil *m.* (boat); aile (*f.*) [or] patin (*m.*) d'hydroptère.
hydrogen ['haidrədʒen] n. Chim. Hydrogène *m.*
— adj. A l'hydrogène (bomb); hydrogène (gas).
hydrogenate [hai'drɔdʒineit], **hydrogenize** [-aiz] v. tr. Chim. Hydrogéner.
hydrographer [hai'drɔgrəfə*] n. Hydrographe *m.*
hydrographic(al) [,haidro'græfik(əl)] adj. Hydrographique.
hydrography [hai'drɔgrəfi] n. Hydrographie *f.*
hydrological [,haidro'lɔdʒikəl] adj. Hydrologique.
hydrology [hai'drɔlədʒi] n. Hydrologie *f.*
hydrolysis [-lisis] (pl. **hydrolyses** [-i:z]) n. Hydrolyse *f.*
hydromagnetic [,haidromæg'netik] adj. Phys. Magnéto-hydrodynamique.
hydromechanics [-mi'kæniks] n. sg. Hydromécanique *f.*
hydromel ['haidrəmel] n. Hydromel *m.* (See MEAD.)
hydrometer [hai'drɔmitə*] n. Hydromètre *m.*
hydrometric [,haidro'metrik] adj. Hydrométrique.
hydrometry [hai'drɔmitri] n. Hydrométrie *f.*
hydropathic [haidro'pæθik] adj. Med. Hydropathe (physician); hydrothérapique (treatment).
— n. Med. Etablissement (*m.*) d'hydrothérapie.
hydropathist [hai'drɔpəθist] n. Med. Hydrothérapeute *m.*
hydropathy [-i] n. Med. Hydrothérapie *f.*
hydrophobia [,haidro'foubiə] n. Med., Fam. Hydrophobie *f.*
hydrophobic [,haidro'foubik] adj. Med., Fam. Hydrophobe.
hydropic [hai'drɔpik] adj. Med. Hydropique.
hydroplane ['haidrɔplein] n. Naut. Hydroplane, hydroglisseur *m.* (motor-boat); barre de plongée *f.* (on a submarine). ‖ Aviat. Hydravion *m.*
— v. intr. Aviat. Hydroplaner.

hydropneumatic [,haidronju'mætik] adj. Hydropneumatique.
hydroponics [-pɔniks] n. sg. Culture hydroponique *f.*
hydropsy [,haidrɔpsi] n. Med. Hydropisie *f.*
hydroscope ['haidroskoup] n. Hydroscope *m.*
hydrosol [-sɔl] n. Chim. Hydrosol *m.*
hydrostat [-stæt] n. Hydrostat *m.*
hydrostatic [,haidro'stætik] adj. Hydrostatique.
hydrostatics [-ks] n. sg. Hydrostatique *f.*
hydrosulphide [-'sʌlfaid] n. Chim. Hydrosulfate *m.*
hydrotherapeutic [-,θerə'pju:tik] adj. Med. Hydrothérapique.
— n. pl. Med. Hydrothérapie *f.*
hydrotherapy [,haidro'θerəpi] n. Med. Hydrothérapie *f.*
hydrothermal [-'θə:məl] adj. Med. Hydrothermal.
hydrous ['haidrəs] adj. Aqueux. ‖ Chim. Hydraté.
hydroxide [hai'drɔksaid] n. Chim. Hydrate *m.*
hydroxy-acid [hai'drɔksi'æsid] n. Chim. Oxacide *m.*
hydroxyl [hai'drɔksil] n. Chim. Hydroxyle *m.*
hyena [hai'i:nə] n. Zool., Fig. Hyène *f.*
hygiene ['haidʒi:n] n. Hygiène *f.* (system).
hygienic(al) [ha'dʒi:nik(el)] adj. Hygiénique.
hygienically [-əli] adv. Hygiéniquement.
hygienics [hai'dʒi:niks] n. sg. Hygiène *f.* (science).
hygienist [-ist] n. Hygiéniste *m.; dental hygienist,* aide-dentiste.
hygrology [hai'grɔlədʒi] n. Hygrologie *f.*
hygrometer [-mitə*] n. Hygromètre *m.*
hygrometric [,haigro'metrik] adj. Hygrométrique.
hygrometry [hai'grɔmitri] n. Hygrométrie *f.*
hygroscope ['haigrəskoup] n. Hygroscope *m.*
hygroscopic [,haigro'skɔpik] adj. Hygroscopique.
hymen ['haimən] n. Med. Hymen *m.* ‖ Jur. Hymen; hyménée *m.*
hymenoptera [,haimə'nɔptərə] n. Zool. Hyménoptères *m. pl.*
hymn [him] n. Eccles. Hymne *f.; cantique m.* ‖ Mus. Hymne *m.* ‖ **Hymn-book,** n. Hymnaire *m.*
— v. tr. Chanter, célébrer, louer, glorifier.
— v. intr. Chanter des hymnes.
hymnal [-nəl] adj. Hymnique.
— n. Eccles. Hymnaire *m.*
hymnist [-nist], **hymnodist** [-nədist], **hymnographer** [him'nɔgrəfə*] n. Hymnographe *m.*
hymnody ['himnədi], **hymnology** [him'nɔlədʒi] n. Hymnologie *f.* (hymns, singing, study); hymnographie *f.* (writing).
hyoid ['haiɔid] adj. Med. Hyoïde.
— n. Med. Os hyoïde *m.*
hypallage [hai'pælədʒi] n. Gramm. Hypallage *f.*
hyperacid [,haipər'æsid] adj. Chim. Hyperacide.
hyperacidity [,haipəræ'siditi] n. Chim. Hyperacidité *f.*
hyperaemia [,haipər'i:miə] n. Med. Hyperémie *f.*
hyperaesthesia ['haipəri:s'θi:siə] n. Med. Hyperesthésie *f.*
hyperbola [hai'pə:bələ] n. Math. Hyperbole *f.*
hyperbole [-i] n. Gramm. Hyperbole *f.*
hyperbolic [,haipə'bɔlik] adj. Math. Hyperbolique.
hyperbolical [-əl] adj. Gramm. Hyperbolique.
hyperbolically [-əli] adv. Gramm. Hyperboliquement.
hyperbolism [hai'pə:bɔlizm] n. Hyperbolisme *m.*
hyperborean [,haipə'bɔ:riən] adj. Hyperboréen. ‖ Fam. Du nord.
— n. Hyperboréen *m.*
hypercritical [-'kritikəl] adj. Hypercritique.
hypercriticize [-saiz] v. tr. Critiquer avec trop de rigueur.

— v. intr. Se montrer trop rigoriste dans ses critiques.

hyperemotional [-i'mouʃənļ] adj. PSYCH. Hyperémotif.

hypermarket [-,mɑ:kit] n. Hypermarché *m.*

hypermetropia [,hàipəmi'troupiə]n. MED. Hypermétropie *f.*

hypermetropic [-'trɔpik] adj. MED. Hypermétrope.

hypersensitive [-'sensitiv] adj. Hypersensible. ‖ Trop susceptible.

hypersonic [-'sɔnik] adj. PHYS., AVIAT. Hypersonique.

hypertension [-'tenʃən] n. MED. Hypertension *f.*

hypertensive [-'tensiv] adj., n. MED. Hypertendu *s.*

hyperthermia [-'θə:miə] n. MED. Hyperthermie *f.*

hyperthyroidism [-'θairɔidizm] n. MED. Hyperthyroïdie *f.*

hypertonic [-'tɔnik] adj. Hypertonique.

hypertrophic [-'trɔfik] adj. Hypertrophique.

hypertrophied [hai'pə:trəfid] adj. Hypertrophié.

hypertrophy [-i] n. MED. Hypertrophie *f.*

hyphen ['haifən] n. Trait (*m.*) d'union.
— v. tr. Mettre un trait d'union à.

hyphenate [-eit] v. tr. Mettre un trait d'union à.

hypnogenetic [,hipnodʒi'netik] adj. Hypnogène.

hypnology [hip'nɔlədʒi] n. Hypnologie *f.*

hypnosis [-'nousis] (pl. **hypnoses** [-iz]) n. Hypnose *f.; induced hypnosis,* hypnose provoquée.

hypnotherapy [,hipnou'θerəpi] n. MED. Hypnothérapie *f.*

hypnotic [-'nɔtik] adj. Hypnotique.
— n. MED. Hypnotique (drug); personne (*f.*) en état d'hypnose (person).

hypnotism ['hipnətizm] n. Hypnotisme *m.*

hypnotist [-tist] n. Hypnotiseur *m.*

hypnotize [-taiz] v. tr. Hypnotiser.

hypo ['haipou] n. CHIM. Hyposulfite (*m.*) de sodium; fixateur *m.* (in photography).

hypo n. U. S. FAM. Piqûre *f.* (injection); seringue *f.* (syringe).

hypochondria [,haipo'kɔndriə] n. Hypocondrie *f.*

hypochondriac [-æk] adj., n. Hypocondriaque *s.*

hypocondrium [-əm] n. MED. Hypocondre *m.*

hypocoristic [-kɔ:'ristik] adj. GRAMM. Hypocoristique.

hypocrisy [hi'pɔkrisi] n. Hypocrisie *f.*

hypocrite ['hipəkrit] n. Hypocrite *s.*

hypocritical [,hipə'kritikəl] adj. Hypocrite; papelard (fam.). [See SANCTIMONIOUS.]

hypocritically [-i] adv. Hypocritement.

hypocycloid [,haipo'saiklɔid] n. MATH. Hypocycloïde *f.*

hypodermic [-'də:mik] adj. MED. Hypodermique, sous-cutané (injection); hypodermique (needle).

hypogastric [-'gæstrik] adj. MED. Hypogastrique.

hypogastrium [-'gæstriəm] n. MED. Hypogastre *m.*

hypogeal [,haipo'dʒi:əl] adj. BOT. Hypogé.

hypogeum [-'dʒiəm] (pl. **hypogea** [-'dʒiə]) n. Hypogée *m.*

hypoglossal [haipo'glɔsəl] adj. MED. Hypoglosse.

hypophosphate [-'fɔsfət] n. CHIM. Hypophosphate *m.*

hypophosphite [-'fɔsfait] n. CHIM. Hypophosphite *m.*

hypophysis [hai'pɔfisis] n. MED. Hypophyse *f.*

hypostatic [,haipo'stætik] adj. Hypostatique.

hyposulphite [-'sʌlfait] n. CHIM. Hyposulfite *m.*

hypotenuse [hai'pɔtinju:s] n. MATH. Hypoténuse *f.*

hypothalamus [,haipo'θæləməs] n. Hypothalamus *m.*

hypothecate [hai'pɔθikeit]v.tr. JUR. Hypothéquer.

hypothermia [-'θə:miə] n. MED. Hypothermie *f.*

hypothesis [hai'pɔθisis] (pl. **hypotheses** [-i:z]) n. Hypothèse *f.*

hypothesize [-aiz] v. intr. Emettre une hypothèse.
— v. tr. Supposer.

hypothetic(al) [,haipə'θetik(əl)] adj. Hypothétique.

hypothyroidism [,haipo'θairɔidizm] n. MED. Hypothyroïdie *f.*

hypsography [hip'sɔgrəfl] n. Hypsographie *f.*

hypsometry [-tri] n. Hypsométrie *f.*

hyssop ['hisəp] n. BOT. Hysope *f.*

hysterectomy [,histə'rektəmi] n. MED. Hystérectomie *f.*

hysteresis [histə'ri:sis] n. PHYS. Hystérésis *f.*

hysteria [his'tiəriə] n. MED. Hystérie *f.* ‖ FAM. Crise (*f.*) de nerfs.

hysteric(al) [his'terik(əl)] adj. MED. Hystérique. ‖ FAM. Nerveux (laugh, person); très excité, hors de soi, frénétique (person); convulsif (sobs); *to become hysterical,* avoir une crise de nerfs. ‖ U. S. FAM. Inénarrable, désopilant (amusing).

hysterically [-əli] adv. MED. Hystériquement. ‖ FAM. Nerveusement; *to cry hysterically,* avoir une violente crise de larmes.

hysterics [his'teriks] n. sg. MED. Crise d'hystérie *f.* ‖ FAM. Crise (*f.*) de nerfs; intense énervement *m.; to go into hysterics over a trifle,* se monter pour des riens.

hysterogenic [,histərə'dʒenik] adj. MED. Hystérogène.

hysterotomy [,histə'rɔtəmi] n. MED. Hystérotomie *f.*

I [ai] n. I, i *m.* ‖ Un *m.* (Roman numeral). ‖ CHIM. Iode *m.* ‖ TECHN. En I.

I [ai] pron. pers. Je, j'; moi; *as tall as I,* aussi grand que moi; *it is I,* c'est moi; *I am cold,* j'ai froid.

iamb ['aiæmb], **iambus** [ai'æmbəs] n. Ïambe *m.*

iambic [ai'æmbik] adj. Ïambique.
— n. Vers ïambique *m.*

ibex ['aibeks] n. ZOOL. Bouquetin *m.*

ibidem ['ibidem] adv. Ibidem.

ibis ['aibis] (pl. **ibises** [-iz]) n. ZOOL. Ibis *m.*

ice [ais] n. Glace *f.* ‖ CHIM. *Dry ice,* neige carbonique. ‖ LOC. *To break the ice,* rompre la glace; *to walk on thin ice,* s'aventurer sur un terrain épineux. ‖ FAM. *To cut no ice,* ne rien casser. ‖ Ice-

age, n. GEOL. Epoque glaciaire *f.* ‖ Ice-axe, n. SPORTS. Piolet *m.* ‖ Ice-bound, adj. NAUT. Pris dans les glaces. ‖ Ice-bucket, n. Seau à champagne *m.* ‖ Ice-cream, n. CULIN. Glace *f.; sorbet, parfait *m.* ‖ Ice-fender, n. NAUT. Paraglace *m.* ‖ Ice-field, n. Champ (*m.*) de glace. ‖ Ice-floe, n. Banc (*m.*) de glace, banquise *f.* ‖ Ice-house, n. Glacière *f.* ‖ Ice-hockey, n. SPORTS. Hockey (*m.*) sur glace. ‖ Ice-jam, n. Embâcle *m.* ‖ Ice-pack, n. NAUT. Banquise *f.* (ice-floe); embâcle *m.* (ice-jam); MED. Vessie de glace *f.* ‖ Ice-pail, n. Seau (*m.*) à glace. ‖ Ice-pudding, n. CULIN. Bombe glacée *f.* Ice-sailing, n. SPORTS. Patinage (*m.*) à la voile. ‖ Ice-skate, n. SPORTS. Patin (*m.*) à glace. ‖ Ice water, n. U. S. Eau glacée *f.*
— v. tr. Glacer, congeler, geler. ‖ CULIN. Glacer (cake, coffee); frapper (champagne); rafraîchir (melon); U. S. *iced fruits*, fruits confits.
iceberg [-bə:g] n. Iceberg *m.*
iceblink [-blink] n. Eclat (*m.*) des glaciers.
icebox [-bɔks] n. U. S. Glacière *f.; réfrigérateur *m.*
icebreaker [-breikə*] n. NAUT. Brise-glace *m.*
Iceland ['aislənd] n. GEOGR. Islande *f.*
Icelander [-ə*] n. GEOGR. Islandais *s.*
Icelandic [ais'lændik] adj., n. Islandais *m.*
iceman ['aismən] (pl. **icemen**) n. COMM. Glacier, marchand (*m.*) de glaces. ‖ SPORTS. Explorateur (*m.*) des glaces.
ichneumon [ik'nju:mən] n. ZOOL. Ichneumon *m.*
ichnography [ik'nɔgrəfi] n. Ichnographie *f.*
ichthyol ['ikθiɔl] n. CHIM. Ichtyol *m.*
ichthyology [,ikθi'ɔlədʒi] n. ZOOL. Ichtyologie *f.*
ichthyosaurus [,ikθiə'sɔ:rəs] n. ZOOL. Ichtyosaure *m.*
icicle ['aisikl̩] n. Glaçon *m.* (from dripping water); stalactite, chandelle *f.* (from falling water).
icing ['aisiŋ] n. Congélation *f.* ‖ CULIN. Glaçage *m.* (of a cake); glace *f.,* glacé *m.* (on a cake); frappage *m.* (of champagne); *icing sugar*, sucre glace. ‖ AVIAT. Givrage *m.* ‖ MED. *Icing liver*, cirrhose du foie.
icon ['aikən] n. ECCLES. Icône *f.*
iconoclasm [ai'kɔnəklæzm̩] n. Iconoclasme *m.*
iconoclast [-klæst] n. Iconoclaste *s.*
iconoclastic [ai,kɔnə'klæstik] adj. Iconoclaste.
iconographer [,aikə'nɔgrəfə*] n. Iconographe *s.*
iconographic [-fik] adj. Iconographique.
iconography [-fi] n. Iconographie *f.*
iconology [,aikɔ'nɔlədʒi] n. Iconologie *f.*
iconometer [-'nɔmi:tə*] n. TECHN. Iconomètre *m.*
iconoscope [-skoup] n. RADIO. Iconoscope *m.*
icosahedron [,aikosə'hi:drən] n. MATH. Icosaèdre *m.*
icteric(al) [ik'terik(əl)] adj. MED. Ictérique.
icterus [i'ktərəs] n. MED. Ictère *m.* (See JAUNDICE.)
ictus ['iktəs] n. GRAMM. Accent *m.* ‖ MED. Ictus *m.; contusion *f.*
icy ['aisi] adj. Glacé (hand, foot); glacé, couvert de glace (mountain); glacial (room, wind). ‖ FIG. Glacial (look, welcome).
id [id] n. PSYCH. Ça *m.*
ID card [,ai'di: kɑ:d] n. U. S. Carte d'identité *f.*
idea [ai'diə] n. Idée *f.* ‖ LOC. *At the bare* (or) *very idea of it*, rien que d'y penser; *to have an idea that*, avoir l'impression que. ‖ Idea-monger, n. Remueur (*m.*) d'idées.
ideal [ai'di:əl] adj., n. Idéal *m.*
idealism [-izm̩] n. Idéalisme *f.*
idealist [-ist] n. Idéaliste *s.*
idealistic [ai,di:ə'listik] adj. Idéaliste.
ideality [,aidi'æliti] n. Idéalité *f.*
idealization [ai,di:əlai'zeiʃən] n. Idéalisation *f.*
idealize [ai'di:əlaiz] v. tr., intr. Idéaliser.
ideally [-li] adv. Idéalement.
ideate [ai'di:eit] v. tr., intr. Imaginer.
ideation [,aidi:'eiʃən] n. PHILOS. Idéation *f.*

idée fixe [ide 'fiks] n. Idée fixe *f.,* dada *m.* (fam.).
idée reçue [ide rə'sy] n. Idée reçue *f.*
idem ['aidem] adv. Idem.
identical [ai'dentikəl] adj. Identique (*with*, à). ‖ Même; *he was the identical man*, c'était cet homme même.
identically [-əli] adv. Identiquement.
identification [ai,dentifi'keiʃən] n. Identification *f.* ‖ AVIAT. *Identification light*, feu d'identification.
identify [ai'dentifai] v. tr. (2). Identifier (s.o.); *to identify oneself with*, s'identifier à.
identikit [-,kit] n. Portrait-robot *m.; photo-robot *f.*
identity [-ti] n. Identité, similitude *f.* (sameness). ‖ Identité, personnalité *f.; identity disc*, plaque d'identité. ‖ THEATR. *Mistaken identity*, quiproquo.
ideogram ['aidiogræm], **ideograph** [ai'diogrɑ:f] n. Idéogramme *m.*
ideologic(al) [,aidio'lɔdʒik(əl)] adj. Idéologique.
ideologist [,aidi'ɔlədʒist], **ideologue** ['aidiə,lɔg] n. Idéologue *s.*
ideology [-dʒi] n. Idéologie f.
ides [aidz] n. pl. Ides *f. pl.*
id est [id est] adv. C'est-à-dire, c.-à-d.; autrement dit.
idiocy ['idiəsi] n. Idiotie *f.*
idiolect ['idiə,lekt] n. GRAMM. Idiolecte *m.*
idiom ['idiəm] n. Idiome *m.* (language); idiotisme *m.* (phrase); style, genre *m.* (style).
idiomatic [,idiə'mætik] adj. Idiomatique. ‖ Familier, courant (colloquial).
idiomatically [-əli] adv. D'une manière idiomatique. ‖ Couramment.
idiosyncrasy [,idio'siŋkrəsi] n. MED. Idiosyncrasie *f.* ‖ FAM. Particularité individuelle, marque distinctive *f.; professional idiosyncrasy*, déformation professionnelle.
idiot ['idiət] n. Idiot *m.; to play the idiot*, faire l'innocent.
idiotic [,idi'ɔtik] adj. Idiot, d'idiot.
idiotically [-əli] adv. Idiotement, stupidement.
idiotism ['idiətizm̩] n. U. S. Idiotie *f.* (act).
idle ['aidl̩] adj. Vain, stérile (act, thought); vain, inutile (fear, tears); vain, futile (pretext, wish); sans fondement (rumours); vain, oiseux (talk). ‖ De loisir, de repos, d'oisiveté (moment); désœuvré, oisif, inoccupé, inactif (person). ‖ Paresseux, nonchalant, indolent. (See SLUGGISH.) ‖ TECHN. En chômage (factory, workman); au repos, arrêté (machine); *idle wheel*, roue intermédiaire; *to run idle*, fonctionner à vide. ‖ FIN. Infructueux; *to lie idle*, dormir (capital).
— v. intr. Demeurer oisif (or) désœuvré; fainéanter. ‖ TECHN. Fonctionner (or) marcher à vide.
— v. tr. *To idle one's time away*, passer son temps à ne rien faire.
idleness [-nis] n. Vanité, inutilité, stérilité, futilité *f.* (of acts, talk, thoughts, wishes). ‖ Oisiveté *f.; désœuvrement *m.* (inaction). ‖ Paresse, indolence, nonchalance *f.* (sluggishness).
idler [-ə*] n. Oisif, désœuvré *s.* ‖ TECHN. Poulie-guide *f.* (pulley); roue intermédiaire *f.* (wheel).
idly [-i] adv. Vainement, futilement, inutilement (uselessly). ‖ Sans rien faire, dans l'oisiveté (inactively). ‖ Paresseusement, avec indolence (sluggishly).
idol ['aidl̩] n. Idole *f.* ‖ PHILOS. Sophisme *m.*
idolater [ai'dɔlətə*] n. Idolâtre *s.* ‖ FIG. Adorateur, admirateur, fanatique *m.*
idolatress [-tris] n. FIG. Adoratrice, admiratrice, fanatique *f.*
idolatrous [-trəs] adj. Idolâtre.
idolatry [-tri] n. Idolâtrie *f.*
idolize ['aidəlaiz] v. tr. FIG. Idolâtrer.
— v. intr. Pratiquer l'idolâtrie.
idyl(l) ['aidil] n. Idylle *f.*
idyllic [ai'dilik] adj. Idyllique.
idyllist ['aidilist] n. Idylliste *m.*

i.e. ['ai'i:] abbrev. C'est-à-dire.

If [if] conj. Si (concession, condition, doubt, hypothesis, wish); *if only*, si seulement. ‖ Fam. *Well, if he hasn't put my hat on!*, allons bon, voilà qu'il a mis mon chapeau! ‖ U. S. Fam. Puisque; *if your wife can sew*, puisque votre femme sait coudre.
— n. Si *m. invar.*

igloo ['iglu:] n. Igloo *m.*

igneous ['igniəs] adj. Igné. (See FIERY.)

ignescent [ig'nesn̩t] adj. Ignescent.

ignis fatuus ['ignis'fætjuəs] n. Feu follet *m.*

ignite [ig'nait] v. tr. Mettre le feu à, enflammer.
— v. intr. S'enflammer, prendre feu.

ignition [ig'niʃən] n. Ignition *f.* ‖ Autom. Allumage *m.; ignition key*, clé de contact.

ignoble [ig'noubl] adj. † Roturier (plebeian). ‖ Fig. Ignoble, vil. (See BASE.)

ignobleness [-nis] n. † Roture, basse naissance *f.* ‖ Fig. Ignominie, bassesse *f.*

ignobly [-i] adv. † De basse naissance. ‖ Fig. Ignoblement.

ignominious [,ignə'miniəs] adj. Ignominieux (degrading); méprisable (despicable).

ignominy ['ignɔmini] n. Ignominie, infamie *f.* (act); ignominie *f.*, déshonneur *m.* (disgrace).

ignoramus [,ignə'rɑ:məs] n. Ignare *m.*
— N. B. Le pluriel est *ignoramuses*, jamais *ignorami.*

ignorance ['ignərəns] n. Ignorance *f.*

ignorant [-ənt] adj. Ignorant.

ignorantly [-əntli] adv. Avec (or) par ignorance.

ignore [ig'nɔ:*] v. tr. Affecter d'ignorer, ne pas prêter attention à, négliger. (See DISREGARD.) ‖ Jur. *To ignore a bill*, prononcer un non-lieu.

iguana [i'gwɑ:nə] n. Zool. Iguane *m.*

ike [aik] n. Radio. U. S. Pop. Iconoscope *m.*

ikon ['aikən] n. See ICON.

ileum ['iliəm] n. Med. Iléon *m.*

ilex ['aileks] (pl. **ilexes** [-iz]) n. Bot. Yeuse *f.;* chêne vert *m.* (holm oak); ilicacée *f.* (holly family).

iliac ['iliæk] adj. Med. Iliaque.

Iliad ['iliæd] n. Iliade *f.*

ilium ['iliəm] n. Med. Os iliaque *m.*

ilk [ilk] adj. † Même. ‖ *Of that ilk*, de cette sorte; de cet acabit (fam.).

ill [il] adj. Mauvais; *ill blood*, malice, animosité. ‖ Med. Malade (*with*, de) [see SICK]; *to be taken ill*, tomber malade.
— N. B. Le comparatif est *worse*, le superlatif *worst.*
— adv. Mal, en mauvaise part; *to take sth. ill*, prendre mal qqch. ‖ Mal, fâcheusement; *to go ill with*, mal tourner pour, aller mal pour. ‖ Guère; *he can ill afford to refuse*, il ne peut guère se permettre de refuser. ‖ Mauvais; *it is ill striving against the stream*, il fait mauvais lutter contre le courant. ‖ **Ill-advised**, adj. Peu judicieux (action); malavisé (person). ‖ **Ill-affected**, adj. Mal disposé. ‖ **Ill-bred**, adj. Mal élevé. ‖ **Ill-conditioned**, adj. Méchant, de mauvaise nature (person); en mauvais état (thing). ‖ **Ill-considered**, adj. Peu réfléchi. ‖ **Ill-defined**, adj. Mal défini. ‖ **Ill-disposed**, adj. Mal disposé (or) intentionné. ‖ **Ill-fated**, adj. Fatal (day); infortuné, malheureux (person). ‖ **Ill-favoured**, adj. Déshérité, disgracié, laid (ugly); déplaisant, répugnant (unpleasant). ‖ **Ill-founded**, adj. Mal fondé. ‖ **Ill-gotten**, adj. Mal acquis. ‖ **Ill-humoured**, adj. De mauvaise humeur. ‖ **Ill-mannered**, adj. Malappris, mal élevé. ‖ **Ill-natured**, adj. Désagréable, méchant. ‖ **Ill-omened**, adj. De mauvais augure. ‖ **Ill-starred**, adj. Néfaste (day); né sous une mauvaise étoile (person). ‖ **Ill-tempered**, adj. Désagréable, de mauvais caractère. ‖ **Ill-timed**, adj. Intempestif, inopportun, malencontreux. ‖ **Ill-treat** (or) **-use**, v. tr. Maltraiter, rudoyer. ‖ **Ill-will**, n. Rancune *f.* (grudge); malveillance *f.* (malice); mauvaise volonté *f.* (unwillingness).

— n. Mal *m.* (evil). ‖ Mal, tort *m.* (harm). ‖ Mal *m.;* mauvaises paroles *f. pl.* (scandal). ‖ Pl. Maux, malheurs *m. pl.;* calamités *f. pl.*

illation [i'leiʃən] n. Déduction *f.*

illative [-tiv] adj. Philos. Déductif. ‖ Gramm. De conséquence.

illegal [i'li:gəl] adj. Jur. Illégal.

illegality [,ili'gæliti] n. Illégalité *f.*

illegally [i'li:gəli] adv. Illégalement.

illegibility [i,ledʒi'biliti] n. Illisibilité *f.*

illegible [i'ledʒibl] adj. Illisible.

illegibly [-bli] adv. Illisiblement.

illegitimacy [,ili'dʒitiməsi] n. Illégitimité *f.*

illegitimate [-mit] adj. Jur. Illégitime (child, request); Philos. Illogique (conclusion). ‖ Gramm. Impropre (word).
— [-meit] v. tr. Déclarer illégitime.

illegitimately [-mitli] adv. Illégitimement.

illiberal [i'libərəl] adj. Sans éducation (or) culture (ill-mannered). ‖ Intolérant, d'esprit étroit (narrow-minded). ‖ Peu généreux, ladre (stingy).

illiberality [i,libə'ræliti] n. Manque (*m.*) d'éducation. ‖ Etroitesse (*f.*) d'esprit. ‖ Manque (*m.*) de libéralité, ladrerie *f.*

illiberally [i'libərəli] adv. Sans distinction (boorishly); sans libéralisme (narrowly); sans libéralité (stingily).

illicit [i'lisit] adj. Illicite.

illicitly [-li] adv. Illicitement.

illimitable [i'limitəbl] adj. Illimité.

illimitableness [-nis] n. Illimitation *f.*

illinium [i'liniəm] n. Chim. Illinium *m.*

illiteracy [i'litərəsi] n. Analphabétisme *m.*

illiterate [-it] adj., n. Illettré, analphabète *s.*

illness ['ilnis] n. Med. Maladie *f.*

illogical [i'lɔdʒikəl] adj. Illogique.

illogicality [i,lɔdʒi'kæliti] n. Illogisme *m.*

illogically [i'lɔdʒikəli] adv. Illogiquement.

illume [i'lju:m] v. tr. Illuminer.

illuminable [i'lju:minəbl] adj. Illuminable.

illuminant [-ənt] adj., n. Eclairant *m.*

illuminate [-eit] v. tr. Illuminer (buildings); éclairer (rooms). ‖ Arts. Enluminer. ‖ Fig. Eclairer, élucider (a subject).

illuminati [i,lju:mi'nɑ:ti] n. pl. Illuminés *m. pl.*

illuminating [i'lju:mineitiŋ] n. Illumination *f.* (of buildings); éclairage *m.* (of rooms). ‖ Arts. Enluminement *m.* ‖ Fig. Elucidation *f.*

illumination [i,lju:mi'neiʃən] n. Illumination *f.* (of buildings); éclairage *m.* (of rooms). ‖ Arts. Enluminure *f.* ‖ Fig. Lumière *f.* (see ENLIGHTENMENT); illumination *f.* (inspiration).

illuminative [i'lju:minətiv] adj. Illuminant, éclairant. ‖ Arts. D'enluminure. ‖ Fig. Elucidant, qui éclaire (or) éclaircit.

illuminator [-eitə*] n. Illuminateur *m.;* illuminatrice *f.* (person). ‖ Eclairage *m.* (apparatus). ‖ Arts. Enlumineur *m.*

illumine [i'lju:min] v. tr. Eclairer (lit. and fig.).

illuminism [-izm̩] n. Illuminisme *m.*

illusion [i'lju:ʒən] n. Tulle illusion *m.* (cloth). ‖ Fig. Illusion *f.*

illusionism [-izm̩] n. Illusionnisme *m.*

illusionist [-ist] n. Visionnaire, illuminé *s.* ‖ Adepte de l'illusionnisme *m.* ‖ Illusionniste *m.* (See CONJURER.)

illusive [i'lju:siv] adj. Trompeur (deceptive); illusoire (unreal).

illusively [-li] adv. Illusoirement.

illusory [i'lju:səri] adj. Illusoire.

illustrate ['iləstreit] v. tr. Illustrer (a book). ‖ Fig. Illustrer, mettre en lumière, faire valoir.

illustration [,iləs'treiʃən] n. Illustration *f.* (of a book). ‖ Fig. Eclaircissement *m.;* élucidation *f.* (clearing up); illustration *f.*, exemple *m.* (instance).

illustrative ['iləstreitiv] adj. Explicatif, qui illustre.

illustratively [-ivli] adv. Pour servir d'exemple, pour illustrer.

illustrator [-ə*] n. ARTS. Illustrateur *m*. ‖ FIG. Exemple *m*.

illustrious [i'lʌstriəs] adj. Illustre.

I. L. O. [ˌaiel'ou] abbr. *International Labour Organization,* Organisation internationale du travail, O. I. T.

image ['imidʒ] n. Image *f*. ‖ ARTS. Statue, image *f*. ‖ GRAMM. Image, ‖ LOC. *The living image of,* le portrait de.
— v. tr. Représenter, dessiner l'image de; *to image sth. to oneself,* se figurer (or) se représenter qqch. ‖ Refléter, reproduire (to mirror). ‖ Décrire, dépeindre (to describe). ‖ Symboliser, figurer, représenter (to typify).

imagery [əri] n. ARTS. Images; statues *f*. *pl.* (images); statuaire *f*. (statuary). ‖ PHILOS. Images mentales *f*. *pl.* ‖ GRAMM. Images *f*. *pl.*

imaginable [i'mædʒinəbl] adj. Imaginable.

imaginably [-inəbli] adv. Autant qu'on puisse l'imaginer.

imaginary [-inəri] adj. Imaginaire.

imagination [iˌmædʒi'neiʃən] n. Imagination *f*.

imaginative [i'mædʒinətiv] adj. D'imagination (literature); imaginatif (person).

imagine [-in] v. tr. Imaginer, se représenter, se figurer. ‖ Concevoir, imaginer; *you can't imagine how much,* vous ne sauriez croire combien. ‖ Imaginer, deviner (to guess). ‖ Imaginer, supposer (to suppose).
— v. intr. Imaginer.

imago [i'meigou] (pl. **imagos** [-z], **imagines** [i'meidʒini:z]) n. ZOOL. Imago *f*.; insecte parfait *m*. ‖ PHILOS. Image *f*.

imam [i'mɑ:m] n. Iman, imam *m*.

imbalance [im'bæləns] n. Déséquilibre *m*.; inadéquation *f*. (of supply and demand).

imbecile ['imbisail] adj. MED. Débile (mentally, physically). ‖ FAM. Imbécile.
— n. MED., FAM. Imbécile *s*.

imbecility [ˌimbi'siliti] n. MED. Débilité *f*. ‖ FAM. Imbécillité *f*.

imbibe [im'baib] v. tr. Aspirer (air); absorber (a drink). ‖ S'imprégner, s'imbiber de (water). ‖ FIG. S'imprégner de, assimiler (ideas).

imbibing [-iŋ] n. Absorption *f*.

imbricate ['imbrikeit] v. tr. Imbriquer.
— [-kit] adj. Imbriqué.

imbrication [ˌimbri'keiʃən] n. Imbrication *f*.

imbroglio [im'brouliou] n. Imbroglio *m*.

imbrue [im'bru:] v. tr. Tremper (in, dans); souiller (with, de) [blood].

imbrute [im'bru:t] v. tr. Abrutir.
— v. intr. S'abrutir.

imbue [im'bju:] v. tr. † Imbiber, imprégner. ‖ FIG. Imprégner, pénétrer; *imbued with,* imbu de.

I. M. F. [ˌaiem'ef] abbr. *International Monetary Fund,* Fonds monétaire international, F. M. I.

imitable ['imitəbl] adj. Imitable.

imitate [-teit] v. tr. Imiter.

imitation [ˌimi'teiʃən] n. Imitation *f*. (act, result). ‖ JUR., COMM. Contrefaçon *f*. ‖ MUS. Imitation *f*. ‖ GRAMM. Pastiche *m*.
— adj. Factice; *imitation jewelry,* bijoux en toc; *imitation leather,* imitation (or) façon cuir, similicuir.

imitative ['imiteitiv] adj. Imitatif.

imitator [-ə*] n. Imitateur *m*.; imitatrice *f*. ‖ JUR., COMM. Contrefacteur *m*.

immaculate [i'mækjulit] adj. ECCLES., FIG. Immaculé. ‖ FAM. Parfait, sans défaut, impeccable (dress).

immanence ['imənəns], **immanency** [-ənsi] n. Immanence *f*.

immanent [-ənt] adj. Immanent. ‖ ECCLES. Omniprésent.

immaterial [ˌimə'tiəriəl] adj. Immatériel (incorporeal). ‖ Négligeable, insignifiant, peu important (unimportant).

immaterialism [-izm] n. Immatérialisme *m*.

immaterialist [-ist] n. Immatérialiste *m*.

immateriality ['iməˌtiəri'æliti] n. Immatérialité *f*. (incorporeality). ‖ Insignifiance *f*. (unimportance).

immaterialize [ˌimə'tiəriəlaiz] v. tr. Immatérialiser.

immature [ˌimə'tjuə*] adj. BOT. Non encore mûr, vert. ‖ † Prématuré. ‖ FIG. Non mûri.

immaturity [-riti] n. BOT., FIG. Immaturité *f*.

immeasurability [iˌmeʒərə'biliti], **immeasurableness** [i'meʒərəblnis] n. Incommensurabilité *f*.

immeasurable [i'meʒərəbl] adj. Incommensurable, immesurable. ‖ FAM. Infini.

immeasurably [-bli] adv. Incommensurablement.

immediacy [i'mi:djəsi] n. Imminence *f*.; caractère immédiat *m*.

immediate [-it] adj. Immédiat (in line, order, relation, space, time). ‖ Immédiat, urgent (danger, delivery, need); *immediate urgency,* première urgence.

immediately [-itli] adv. Immédiatement, tout de suite (at once). ‖ Directement, sans intermédiaire (directly). ‖ JUR. Sans déport.

immedicable [i'medikəbl] adj. MED. Incurable.

immemorial [ˌimi'mɔ:riəl] adj. Immémorial.

immemorially [-əli] adv. De temps immémorial.

immense [i'mens] adj. Immense. ‖ FAM. Epatant, formidable.

immensely [-li] adv. Immensément. ‖ FAM. Formidablement.

immensity [-iti] n. Immensité *f*.

immerge [i'mə:dʒ], **immerse** [i'mə:s] v. tr. Immerger, plonger (to dip). ‖ ECCLES. Baptiser par immersion. ‖ FIG. Plonger (in, dans).

immersion ['imə:ʃən] n. Immersion *f*. ‖ ECCLES. Baptême (*m*.) par immersion. ‖ ASTRON. Immersion *f*. ‖ FIG. Absorption *f*.

immigrant ['imigrənt] n. Immigrant; immigré *m*.

immigrate [-greit] v. intr. Immigrer.
— v. tr. Introduire, faire pénétrer (into, dans).

immigration [ˌimi'greiʃən] n. Immigration *f*.

imminence [i'minəns] n. Imminence *f*. (See IMMEDIACY.)

imminent [-ənt] adj. Imminent.

imminently [-əntli] adv. De façon imminente.

immiscible [i'misibl] adj. Immiscible.

immitigable [i'mitigəbl] adj. Inatténuable, inapaisable. ‖ Inflexible, inexorable, implacable.

immix [i'miks] v. tr. Mêler.

immixture [-tˌrə*] n. Mélange *m*. ‖ FIG. Immixtion *f*.

immobile [i'moubil] adj. Immobile (motionless); fixe, immuable (stable).

immobility [ˌimo'biliti] n. Immobilité *f*.; fixité, immuabilité *f*.

immobilization [iˌmɔbilai'zeiʃən] n. Immobilisation *f*.

immobilize [iˌmɔbilaiz] v. tr. Immobiliser.

immoderate [i'mɔdərit] adj. Immodéré, démesuré (appetite); déréglé (desire).

immoderately [-li] adv. Immodérément.

immoderation [iˌmɔdə'reiʃən] n. Immodération *f*.

immodest [i'mɔdist] adj. Immodeste, impudique (indecent). ‖ † Impudent (bold).

immodesty [-i] n. Immodestie, impudeur *f*. ‖ † Impudence *f*.

immolate ['iməleit] v. tr. Immoler.

immolation [ˌimo'leiʃən] n. Immolation *f*.

immolator ['imoleitə*] n. Immolateur *m*.

immoral [i'mɔrəl] adj. Immoral. ‖ FAM. Libertin, débauché.

immorality [ˌimo'ræliti] n. Immoralité *f*.

immorally [i'mɔrəli] adv. Immoralement.

immortal [i'mɔ:tl] adj. Immortel. ‖ FIG. Impérissable (memory); céleste (vision).
— n. Immortel *s*.

immortality [,imɔ:'tæliti] n. Immortalité *f*.
immortalize [i'mɔ:tǝlaiz] v. tr. Immortaliser.
immortally [-tǝli] adv. Immortellement.
immortelle [,imɔ:'tel] n. Bot. Immortelle *f*.
immovability [i,mu:vǝ'biliti] n. Immuabilité *f*. ‖ Immobilité *f*. ‖ Inflexibilité *f*. ‖ Insensibilité *f*.
immovable [i'mu:vǝbl̩] adj. Immuable (that cannot be moved). ‖ Immobile (motionless). ‖ Jur. Immeuble. ‖ Fig. Inflexible, inébranlable (steadfast); impassible, insensible (unemotional).
— n. pl. Jur. Immeubles *m. pl.*
immovably [-bli] adv. Immuablement. ‖ Fig. Impassiblement.
immune [i'mju:n] adj. Med. Immunisé; vacciné (*from*, contre); *immune body*, anticorps. ‖ Fig. Immunisé.
— n. Med., Fig. Personne immunisée *f*.
immunity [-iti] n. Med., Fig. Immunité *f*. (*from*, contre). ‖ Jur., Milit. Exemption *f*.
immunization [i,mju:nai'zeiʃǝn] n. Immunisation *f*. (*against*, contre).
immunize ['imju:naiz] v. tr. Immuniser (*against*, contre).
immunologic(al) [,imjunǝ'lɔdʒik(l̩)] adj. Med. Immunologique.
immunology [,imju'nɔlǝdʒi] n. Med. Immunologie *f*.
immure [i'mjuǝ*] v. tr. Emmurer. ‖ Eccles., Fig. Cloîtrer.
immurement [i'mjuǝmǝnt] n. Emmurement *m*. ‖ Eccles., Fig. Claustration *f*.
immutability [i,mju:tǝ'biliti] n. Immutabilité, immuabilité *f*.
immutable [i'mju:tǝbl̩] adj. Immuable.
imp [imp] n. Lutin, diablotin *m*. ‖ Fam. Petit diable, polisson *m*.
impact ['impækt] n. Choc, impact *m*.
— [im'pækt] v. tr. Enfoncer, loger (*into*, dans).
— v. intr. Se heurter (*against*, with, contre).
impair [im'pɛǝ*] v. tr. Détériorer, endommager; abîmer (fam.). ‖ Fig. Diminuer, altérer, ébranler.
impairment [-mǝnt] n. Détérioration *f*. ‖ Fig. Altération *f*.
impala [im'pɑ:lǝ] n. Zool. Impala *f*.
impale [im'peil] v. tr. Empaler; *to impale oneself*, s'empaler. ‖ † Palissader. ‖ Blas. Accoler.
impalement [-mǝnt] n. Empalement *m*. ‖ Blas. Réunion *f*.
impalpability [im,pælpǝ'biliti] n. Impalpabilité *f*.
impalpable [im'pælpǝbl̩] adj. Impalpable. ‖ Fig. Imperceptible.
impaludism [im'pælju:dizm̩] n. Med. Paludisme *m*.
impanel [im'pænl̩] v. tr. (1). See EMPANEL.
imparadise [im'pærǝdais] v. tr. Transporter de joie, ravir (s.o.). ‖ Transformer en paradis (a place).
impark [im'pɑ:k] v. tr. Parquer (animals). ‖ Transformer en parc (land).
impart [im'pɑ:t] v. tr. Accorder, attribuer (to grant). ‖ Impartir, donner, communiquer (to give). ‖ Communiquer, faire connaître, faire part de (to make known). ‖ † Avoir part à.
impartial [im'pɑ:ʃǝl] adj. Impartial.
impartiality [,impɑ:ʃi'æliti] n. Impartialité *f*.
impartially [im'pɑ:ʃǝli] adv. Impartialement.
impartible [im'pɑ:tibl̩] adj. Jur. Indivisible.
impartment [im'pɑ:tmǝnt] m. Communication, transmission *f*. (of news).
impassable [im'pɑ:sǝbl̩] adj. Infranchissable, impassable (river); impraticable (road).
impasse [im'pɑ:s] n. Impasse *f*. (lit. and fig.).
impassibility [,impɑ:si'biliti], **impassibleness** [im'pɑ:sibl̩nis] n. Impassibilité *f*.
impassible [im'pɑsibl̩] adj. Impassible.
impassibly [-bli] adv. Impassiblement.
impassion [im'pæʃǝn] v. tr. Passionner.
impassive [im'pæsiv] adj. Insensible. ‖ Invulnérable. ‖ Fig. Impassible, inébranlé.

impassively [-li] adv. Impassiblement.
impassiveness [-nis], **impassivity** [,impæ'siviti] n. Insensibilité *f*. ‖ Fig. Impassibilité *f*.
impaste [im'peist] v. tr. Réduire en pâte, écraser. ‖ Arts. Empâter. ‖ Culin. Couvrir (or) enrober de pâte.
impasto [im'pæstou] n. Arts. Empâtement *m*.
impatience [im'peiʃǝns] n. Impatience *f*. ‖ Intolérance *f*. (*of*, à l'égard de) [sth.]; fait (*m*.) de ne pas pouvoir supporter.
impatient [-ǝnt] adj. Impatient (*for*, de) [sth.]. ‖ Intolérant (*of*, de); *impatient of advice*, incapable de supporter les conseils.
impatiently [-ǝntli] adv. Impatiemment.
impavid [im'pævid] adj. Impavide. (See FEARLESS.)
impawn [im'pɔ:n] v. tr. Fin. Engager, mettre en gage. (See IMPLEDGE.) ‖ Fig. Risquer, engager.
impeach [im'pi:tʃ] v. tr. Attaquer (s.o.'s honour); mettre en doute (s.o.'s probity, veracity). ‖ Blâmer, critiquer (s.o.'s conduct); accuser (s.o.) [*of*, de]. ‖ Jur. Récuser (evidence, a witness); mettre en accusation (an official).
impeachable [-ǝbl̩] adj. Attaquable, critiquable, blâmable (conduct); accusable, incriminable (person); attaquable, contestable (probity, veracity). ‖ Jur. Récusable (evidence, witness); susceptible d'être mis en accusation (official).
impeachment [-mǝnt] n. Dénigrement *m*. (of s.o.'s conduct); accusation *f*. (of s.o.); contestation *f*. (of s.o.'s veracity). ‖ Jur. Récusation *f*. (of evidence, a witness); mise en accusation *f*. (of an official).
impeccability [im,pekǝ'biliti] n. Impeccabilité *f*.
impeccable [im'pekǝbl̩] adj. Eccles., Fam. Impeccable.
impeccably [-bli] adv. Impeccablement.
impecuniosity ['impi,kju:ni'ɔsiti] n. Impécuniosité *f*.
impecunious [,impi'kju:niǝs] adj. Impécunieux.
impedance [im'pi:dǝns] n. Electr. Impédance, force contre-électromotrice *f*.
impede [im'pi:d] v. tr. Entraver, gêner (to hinder). ‖ Retarder, arrêter (to delay).
impediment [im'pedimǝnt] n. Entrave, gêne *f*. (hindrance). ‖ Empêchement, obstacle *m*. ‖ Med. *Impediment in speech*, difficulté de parole.
impedimenta [im,pedi'mentǝ] n. pl. Impedimenta *m. pl*. ‖ Fam. Bagages *m. pl*.
impel [im'pel] v. tr. (1). ‖ Pousser, faire marcher (or) avancer. ‖ Fig. Obliger, forcer (to compel); pousser, inciter (to urge).
impellent [-ǝnt] adj. Déterminant; moteur *m*.; motrice *f*.
— n. Moteur *m*.
impeller [-ǝ*] n. Techn. Roue motrice *f*. ‖ Aviat. Surcompresseur *m*. ‖ Fig. Animateur, instigateur *m*.; animatrice, instigatrice *f*.
impend [im'pend] v. intr. Etre suspendu (*over*, sur). ‖ Fig. Planer.
impendent [-ǝnt] adj. Imminent, prochain, menaçant.
impenetrability [im,penitrǝ'biliti] n. Impénétrabilité *f*.
impenetrable [im'penitrǝbl̩] adj. Impénétrable (*to*, à) [lit. and fig.].
impenetrate [-treit] v. tr. Compénétrer.
impenitence [im'penitǝns] n. Impénitence *f*.
impenitent [-ǝnt] adj., n. Impénitent *s*.
impenitently [-ǝntli] adv. Dans l'impénitence.
imperative [-tiv] adj., n. Gramm. Impératif *m*. ‖ Fig. Impérieux (need); impératif (order).
imperatively [-tivli] adv. Impérativement.
imperativeness [-tivnis] n. Brusquerie f. ‖ Urgence *f*. (See IMPERIOUSNESS.)
imperceptibility ['impǝ,septi'biliti] n. Imperceptibilité *f*.
imperceptible [,impǝ'septibl̩] adj. Imperceptible.

imperceptibly [-bli] adv. Imperceptiblement.
imperfect [im'pə:fikt] adj. Imparfait, inachevé (not complete). ‖ Imparfait, défectueux (faulty). ‖ GRAMM. Imparfait.
— n. GRAMM. Imparfait *m.*
imperfection [,impə'fekʃən] n. Inachèvement, état incomplet *m.* ‖ Imperfection *f.*
imperfectly [im'pə:fiktli] adv. Imparfaitement.
imperforate [im'pə:fərit] adj. Non perforé (stamp). ‖ MED. Imperforé.
imperial [im'piəriəl] adj. Impérial (crown, government). ‖ De l'Empire britannique (federation, trade). ‖ FIG. Impérial, majestueux, auguste, souverain.
— n. Impériale *f.* (beard). ‖ Coffre (*m.*) d'impériale (on a coach).
imperialism [-izm̩] n. Impérialisme, colonialisme *m.*
imperialist [-ist] n. Impérialiste, colonialiste *s.*
imperialistic [im,piəriə'listik] adj. Impérialiste, colonialiste.
imperially [im'piəriəli] adv. Impérialement. ‖ FIG. Majestueusement.
imperil [im'peril] v. tr. Mettre en péril, exposer, risquer.
imperious [im'piəriəs] adj. Impérieux, dominateur (dictatorial). ‖ Impérieux, urgent (imperative).
imperiously [-li] adv. Impérieusement.
imperiousness [-nis] n. Nature impérieuse, arrogance *f.* ‖ Urgence *f.;* caractère impérieux *m.* (See IMPERATIVENESS.)
imperishability [im,periʃə'biliti] n. Caractère impérissable *m.*
imperishable [im'periʃəbl̩] adj. Impérissable.
imperishably [-bli] adv. Impérissablement.
imperium [im'periəm] n. Empire absolu *m.*
impermanence [im'pə:mənəns] n. Caractère éphémère *m.,* précarité *f.* (of feelings); caractère temporaire (or) transitoire *m.* (of arrangement).
impermanent [-t] adj. Ephémère, précaire, fugitif (feeling); temporaire, transitoire (arrangement).
impermeability [,impə:miə'biliti] n. Imperméabilité *f.*
impermeable [im'pə:miəbl̩] adj. Imperméable.
impermissible [,impə'misibl̩] adj. Non admissible, intolérable.
imperscriptible [,impə'skriptibl̩] adj. JUR. Non inscrit (or) enregistré.
impersonal [im'pə:sənl̩] adj. GRAMM., FIG. Impersonnel.
impersonality [im,pə:sə'næliti] n. Impersonnalité *f.*
impersonally [im'pə:sənəli] adv. Impersonnellement.
impersonate [-eit] v. tr. Personnifier. (See EMBODY.) ‖ THEATR. Jouer le rôle de, jouer. ‖ JUR. Usurper l'identité de, se faire passer pour.
impersonation [im,pə:sə'neiʃən] n. Personnification *f.* ‖ THEATR. Imitation *f.* (of an actor); création, interprétation *f.* (of a part). ‖ JUR. Usurpation d'identité *f.*
impersonator [im'pə:səneitə*] n. Personnificateur *m.;* personnificatrice *f.* ‖ THEATR. Imitateur *m.,* imitatrice *f.* (of an actor); interprète *m.* (of a part). ‖ JUR. Usurpateur (*m.*) d'identité.
impersonify [,impə'sɔnifai] v. tr. Personnifier.
impertinence [im'pə:tinəns] n. Manque (*m.*) de pertinence. (See IRRELEVANCE.) ‖ Manque (*m.*) d'à-propos (or) de rapport avec la question (inappropriateness). ‖ Indiscrétion *f.* (intrusiveness). ‖ Impertinence *f.* (impudence).
impertinent [-ənt] adj. Non pertinent (irrelevant). ‖ Hors de propos (inappropriate). ‖ Déplacé, indiscret (intrusive). ‖ Impertinent (*to,* envers) [impudent].
impertinently [-əntli] adv. Sans pertinence; hors de propos. ‖ Indiscrètement. ‖ Avec impertinence,
imperturbability ['impə,tə:bə'biliti] n. Imperturbabilité *f.*

imperturbable [,impə'tə:bəbl̩] adj. Imperturbable.
imperturbably [-bli] adv. Imperturbablement.
impervious [im'pə:viəs] adj. Imperméable (*to,* à). ‖ FIG. Fermé, sourd, inaccessible (*to,* à); vacciné (*to,* contre) [fam.]; *to be impervious to joking,* ne pas comprendre la plaisanterie.
imperviously [-li] adv. Impénétrablement.
imperviousness [-nis] n. Imperméabilité *f.* ‖ FIG. Impénétrabilité *f.*
impetiginous [,impə'tidʒinəs] adj. MED. Impétigineux.
impetigo [,impə'taigou] n. MED. Impétigo *m.*
impetrate ['impitreit] v. tr. Implorer; obtenir par imploration. ‖ ECCLES., JUR. Impétrer.
impetuosity [im,petju'ɔsiti], **impetuousness** [im'petjuəsnis] n. Impétuosité *f.*
impetuous [im'petjuəs] adj. Impétueux.
impetuously [-li] adv. Impétueusement.
impetus ['impitəs] n. Vitesse acquise *f.;* élan *m.* ‖ FIG. Impulsion *f.;* élan, branle *m.*
impiety [im'paiəti] n. Impiété *f.*
impinge [im'pinʒ] v. intr. Entrer en collision (*on, upon,* avec); se heurter (*on, upon,* à). ‖ JUR. Empiéter (*on, upon,* sur).
impingement [-mənt] n. Choc, heurt *m.* ‖ JUR. Empiétement *m.*
impious ['impiəs] adj. Impie.
impiously [-li] adv. Avec impiété.
impish ['impiʃ] adj. Espiègle.
implacability [im,plækə'biliti] n. Implacabilité *f.*
implacable [im'plækəbl̩] adj. Implacable. (See INEXORABLE.)
implacably [-bli] adv. Implacablement.
implant [im'plɑ:nt] v. tr. MED. Implanter. ‖ FIG. Implanter, inculquer, inspirer.
— n. MED. Implant *m.*
implantation [,implɑ:n'teiʃən] n. Implantation *f.*
implausible [im'plɔ:zibl̩] adj. Peu plausible.
impledge [im'pledʒ] v. tr. Engager.
implement ['implimənt] n. AGRIC. Instrument *m.* ‖ TECHN. Outil *m.* ‖ CULIN. Ustensile *m.* ‖ SPORTS, MILIT. Attirail, équipement *m.* ‖ COMM. Article d'habillement (dress) [or] d'ameublement *m.* (furniture). ‖ JUR. Exécution *f.*
— v. tr. Exécuter (a contrat); accomplir (a promise); mettre en œuvre (a decision).
— v. intr. JUR. Instrumenter.
impletion [im'pli:ʃən] n. Remplissage *m.* (act); plénitude *f.* (result).
implicate ['implikeit] v. tr. Impliquer, sous-entendre, supposer, entraîner (to imply). ‖ Impliquer, engager, entraîner (*in,* dans); mêler (*in,* à) [to involve]. ‖ † Entrelacer (to entwine).
implication [,impli'keiʃən] n. Implication *f.*
implicit [im'plisit] adj. Implicite (implied). ‖ Absolu, sans réserve (unquestioning).
implicitly [-li], **impliedly** [im'plaiidli] adv. Implicitement.
implied [im'plaid] adj. Implicite, sous-entendu.
implode [im'ploud] v. intr. TECHN. Imploser.
— v. tr. TECHN. Faire imploser.
implore [im'plɔ:*] v. tr. Implorer.
imploring [-riŋ] adj. Implorant, suppliant.
imploringly [-riŋli] adv. Avec supplication, d'un ton implorant.
implosion [im'plouʒən] n. TECHN. Implosion *f.*
imply [im'plai] v. tr. (2). Impliquer, sous-entendre, supposer (to implicate). ‖ Sous-entendre, insinuer, suggérer (to hint).
impolicy [im'pɔlisi] n. Mauvaise politique *f.* ‖ FAM. Inhabileté *f.*
impolite [,impə'lait] adj. Impoli. (See RUDE.)
impolitely [-li] adv. Impoliment.
impoliteness [-nis] n. Impolitesse *f.*
impolitic [im'pɔlitik] adj. Peu politique, impolitique.

impoliticly [-li] adv. Impolitiquement.
imponderability [im,pɔndərə'biliti] n. Impondérabilité *f.*
imponderable [im'pɔndərəbl̩] adj., n. Impondérable *m.*
import [im'pɔːt] v. tr. Signifier, impliquer, entraîner (to imply). ‖ Exprimer, faire savoir (to express). ‖ Laisser entrevoir, sous-entendre, présager (to suggest). ‖ Importer (*to,* à); être d'importance (*to,* pour) [to concern]. ‖ Comm. Importer (*into,* dans). — v. intr. Importer, avoir de l'importance (to matter).
— ['impɔːt] n. Signification, portée *f.* (meaning). ‖ Importance *f.* (*of,* de). ‖ Comm. Importation *f.* (act, goods).
importable [-əbl̩] adj. Comm. Importable.
importance [im'pɔːtəns] n. Importance *f.; it is of the highest importance that,* il importe au premier chef (or) il est de la plus haute importance que. ‖ Importance, influence, dignité *f.; man of importance,* personnage important. ‖ Fam. Importance *f.; to set up as a person of importance,* faire l'important.
important [-ənt] adj. Important (*for,* pour). ‖ Fam. Important; *to look important,* prendre un air important.
importantly [-əntli] adv. Avec importance.
importation [,impɔː'teiʃən] n. Comm. Importation *f.*
importer [im'pɔːtə*] n. Comm. Importateur *m.;* importatrice *f.*
importunate [im'pɔːtjunit] adj. Insistant, pressant, harcelant (urgent); excédant, importun (troublesome).
importunately [-li] adv. Importunément.
importune [im'pɔːtjuːn] v. tr. Harceler, presser, pousser (to harass). ‖ Importuner, assaillir, assiéger (to besiege). ‖ Fam. Faire des propositions malhonnêtes à (a woman).
importunity [,impɔː'tjuːniti] n. Importunité *f.*
impose [im'pouz] v. tr. Imposer (conditions, a doctrine, one's presence) [*upon,* à]; *to impose oneself,* s'imposer. ‖ Fin. *To impose a tax on,* imposer (s.o.); imposer, mettre un impôt (sur) [sth.]. ‖ Techn. Imposer (pages of type). ‖ Eccles. Imposer (the hands).
— v. intr. En imposer (*upon,* à). ‖ Fam. En faire accroire (*upon,* à); *to be imposed upon,* se laisser monter le coup.
imposing [-iŋ] adj. Imposant.
imposingly [-iŋli] adv. D'une façon imposante.
imposition [,impə'ziʃən] n. Imposition *f.* (act). ‖ Pensum *m.* (at school). ‖ Fait (*m.*) de s'imposer; abus *m.* (on, de); *it is an imposition to ask him to help,* c'est abuser que de lui demander son aide. ‖ Techn. Mise (*f.*) en page. ‖ Fin. Imposition *f.;* impôt *m.* ‖ Eccles. Imposition *f.* (of hands). ‖ Fam. Imposture *f.*
impossibility [im,pɔsi'biliti] n. Impossibilité *f.* (fact, thing).
impossible [im'pɔsibl̩] adj. Impossible. ‖ Fam. Impayable, ridicule (dress, hat); impossible, insupportable (person).
impossibly [-bli] adv. De façon impossible; *not impossibly,* peut-être.
impost ['impoust] n. Fin. Droit d'octroi *m.* ‖ Sports. Handicap *m.*
impost n. Archit. Imposte *f.*
impostor [im'pɔstə*] n. Imposteur *m.*
impostume [im'pɔstjuːm] n. Med. Apostume *m.*
imposture [im'pɔstʃə*] n. Imposture *f.*
impotence ['impətəns], impotency [-i] n. Med. Impotence *f.* (of invalids); impuissance *f.* (of males). ‖ Fig. Impuissance.
impotent [-ənt] adj. Med. Impotent (invalid); impuissant (male). ‖ Fig. Impuissant.
impotently [-əntli] adv. Faiblement, sans force.

impound [im'paund] v. tr. Mettre à la fourrière (animals, cars); enfermer (persons). ‖ Endiguer (water). ‖ Jur. Confisquer, saisir (goods).
impoverish [im'pɔvəriʃ] v. tr. Appauvrir.
impoverishment [-mənt] n. Appauvrissement *m.*
impracticability [im'præktikə'biliti] n. Impraticabilité *f.* ‖ Fig. Nature intraitable *f.*
impracticable [im'præktikəbl̩] adj. Irréalisable (plan); impraticable (road). ‖ Fam. Impossible, intraitable, insociable (person).
impracticably [-bli] adv. Impratiquablement. ‖ Fig. Intraitablement.
impractical [im'præktikl̩] adj. Manquant de sens pratique, irréaliste (person); inapplicable (plan); peu pratique, malcommode (device).
imprecate ['imprikeit] v. tr. Prononcer (curses) [*upon,* contre]; appeler (evil) [*upon,* sur].
imprecation [,impri'keiʃən] n. Imprécation *f.*
imprecatory ['imprikeitəri] adj. Imprécatoire.
imprecise [,impri'sais] adj. Imprécis.
imprecision [,impri'siʒən] n. Imprécision *f.*
impregnability [im,pregnə'biliti] n. Milit. Inexpugnabilité *f.*
impregnable [im'pregnəbl̩] adj. Milit. Imprenable, inexpugnable. ‖ Fig. Inébranlable, indéracinable.
impregnate [im'pregneit] v. tr. Imprégner (*with,* de). ‖ Med. Féconder. ‖ U. S. Agric. Fertiliser. ‖ Fig. Imprégner. (See IMBUE.)
— [im'pregnit] adj. Med. Fécondé (female); enceinte (woman). ‖ Fig. Imprégné, pénétré, imbu, saturé (*with,* de).
impregnation [,impreg'neiʃən] n. Imprégnation *f.* (lit. and fig.). ‖ Med. Fécondation *f.*
impresario [impre'zɑːriou] n. Imprésario *m.*
imprescriptible [,impri'skriptibl̩] adj. Imprescriptible, inaliénable.
impress [im'pres] v. tr. Milit. Enrôler d'office, réquisitionner. ‖ Fig. Faire appel à.
impress ['impres] n. Empreinte *f.* (of fingers, seal). ‖ Estampille *f.* (stamping). ‖ Fig. Marque *f.;* sceau, coin *m.*
— [im'pres] v. tr. Imprimer, marquer (*on,* sur); marquer, sceller (*with,* de). ‖ Techn. Imprimer (*on,* dans) [an idea]; inculquer (*on,* à). ‖ Fig. Pénétrer (*with,* de) [s.o.]. ‖ Fig. Faire impression sur, impressionner (to affect); faire une impression à (to strike); *to impress an idea on s.o.,* inculquer une idée à qqn; *to impress s.o. with an idea,* impressionner qqn par une idée.
impressible [-ibl̩] adj. Qu'on peut marquer d'une empreinte. ‖ Fig. Impressionnable.
impression [im'preʃən] n. Empreinte *f.* (mark). ‖ Techn. Edition *f.* (book); exemplaire imprimé *m.* (copy); impression *f.* (printing). ‖ Med. Empreinte *f.* (in dentistry). ‖ Fig. Impression, idée *f.;* sentiment *m.* (notion); *to create an impression of,* donner l'impression de. ‖ Fig. Impression *f.; to make an impression on* (or) *upon,* faire impression sur. ‖ Fam. Effet *m.; to make no impression on,* ne faire aucun effet sur.
impressionability [im,preʃnə'biliti] n. Impressionnabilité *f.*
impressionable [im'preʃnəbl̩] adj. Impressionnable; sensible (*to,* à).
impressionism [im'preʃnizm̩] n. Arts. Impressionnisme *m.*
impressionist [-ist] n. Arts. Impressionniste *s.*
impressionistic [im,preʃə'nistik] adj. Arts. Impressionniste.
impressive [im'presiv] adj. Impressionnant.
impressively [-li] adv. De façon impressionnante.
impressment [im'presmənt] n. Milit. Enrôlement forcé *m.;* réquisition *f.*
imprint ['imprint] n. Empreinte *f.* ‖ Techn. Indication (*f.*) de l'éditeur (or) de l'imprimeur.
— [im'print] v. tr. Imprimer, marquer (*on,* sur).

‖ TECHN. Imprimer. ‖ FIG. Imprimer, graver, implanter (on, dans); empreindre (with, de); impressionner (with, par).

imprison [im'prizṇ] v. tr. Emprisonner (lit. and fig.).

imprisonment [-mənt] n. Emprisonnement m. (act, result).

improbability [im,prɔbə'biliti] n. Improbabilité f. ‖ Invraisemblance f.

improbable [im'prɔbəbḷ] adj. Improbable (not likely to happen). ‖ Invraisemblable (lacking in verisimilitude).

improbably [-bli] adv. Improbablement. ‖ Invraisemblablement.

improbity [im'prɔbiti] n. Improbité f.

impromptu [im'prɔmptju:] adj., adv., n. Impromptu m. (See EXTEMPORANEOUS.)

improper [im'prɔpə*] adj. Déplacé, impropre, inadapté, inexact (unfit). ‖ Malséant, incorrect (incongruous). ‖ Inconvenant, indécent, de mauvais goût (indecorous). ‖ MATH. Improper fraction, expression fractionnaire. ‖ AUTOM. Improper signalling, avertissement intempestif.

improperly [-li] adv. Improprement, inexactement. ‖ Incorrectement, d'une façon déplacée. ‖ D'une manière inconvenante.

impropriate [im'prouprieit] v. tr. ECCLES. Séculariser.

impropriation [,improupri'eiʃən] n. ECCLES. Sécularisation f.

impropriety [,impro'praiəti] n. Impropriété, inexactitude f. ‖ Incorrection, inconvenance f.

improvable [im'pru:vəbḷ] adj. AGRIC. Amendable. ‖ FIG. Améliorable.

improve [im'pru:v] v. tr. AGRIC. Amender (land). ‖ CULIN. Bonifier (wine). ‖ FIG. Améliorer (in general); développer (gifts); avantager, embellir (s.o.'s looks); cultiver (one's mind); augmenter (one's store of knowledge). ‖ Tirer parti de, profiter de (one's leisure, the occasion).
— v. intr. AGRIC. S'amender (land). ‖ CULIN. Se bonifier (wine). ‖ FIN. Monter (prices). ‖ FIG. S'améliorer (in general); se développer; reprendre. ‖ FIG. Gagner; to improve on acquaintance, gagner à être connu. ‖ To improve upon, COMM. Enchérir sur (an offer); FIG. Surpasser (s.o.); ajouter à, enjoliver (a tale).

improvement [-mənt] n. Amélioration f. (in general); to be an improvement on, valoir mieux que, surpasser. ‖ AGRIC. Amendement m. ‖ MED. Amélioration f.; mieux m. ‖ TECHN. Perfectionnement m. ‖ Pl. Embellissements m. pl.; améliorations f. pl. ‖ FIG. Développement m. (of mind); progrès m. (in studies); mise (f.) à profit (of the occasion).

improver [-ə*] n. Rénovateur m.; rénovatrice f. ‖ JUR. Stagiaire m. ‖ TECHN. Apprenti s.

improvidence [im'prɔvidəns] n. Imprévoyance f.

improvident [-ənt] adj. Imprévoyant (heedless); dépensier (thriftless).

improvidently [-əntli] adv. Sans prévoyance.

improving [im'pru:viŋ] adj. Améliorant (in general). ‖ MED. Amélioré. ‖ FIG. Edifiant (conversation); instructif (book).

improvisation [,imprəvai'zeiʃən] n. Improvisation f.

improvisator [-tə*] n. Improvisateur m.; improvisatrice f.

improvise ['imprəvaiz] v. tr., intr. Improviser.

imprudence [im'pru:dəns] n. Imprudence f.

imprudent [-ənt] adj. Imprudent.

imprudently [-əntli] adv. Imprudemment.

impudence ['impjudəns] n. Impudence f. ‖ Insolence f. (See EFFONTERY.)

impudent [-ənt] adj. Impudent. ‖ Insolent, effronté.

impudently [-əntli] adv. Impudemment. ‖ Insolemment, effrontément.

impudicity [,impju:'disiti] n. Impudicité, impudeur f.

impugn [im'pju:n] v. tr. Critiquer, attaquer (s.o.'s character); mettre en doute (s.o.'s veracity).

impugnable [-əbḷ] adj. Contestable.

impugnment [-mənt] n. Critique f. ‖ Contestation f.

impulse ['impʌls] n. Impulsion, poussée f. ‖ FIG. Impulsion f.; élan m.; a man of impulse, un impulsif; rash impulse, coup de tête.

impulsion [im'pʌlʃən] n. Impulsion, poussée f. ‖ FIG. Instigation f.

impulsive [im'pʌlsiv] adj. Impulsif (force). ‖ FIG. Impulsif (person); irréfléchi (remark).

impulsively [-li] adv. Impulsivement.

impunity [im'pju:niti] n. Impunité f.

impure [im'pjuə*] adj. Non pur, mélangé (mixed). ‖ FIG. Impur.

impurely [-li] adv. D'une manière impure.

impurity [-riti] n. Impureté f. (element, state).

imputability [,impju:tə'biliti] n. Imputabilité f.

imputable [im'pju:təbḷ] adj. Imputable (to, à).

imputation [,impju:'teiʃən] n. Imputation f.

imputative [im'pju:tətiv] adj. Imputatif.

impute [im'pju:t] v. tr. Imputer.

in [in] prep. Dans; in my garden, dans mon jardin; in a week's time, dans l'espace d'une semaine; in terror, dans la terreur. ‖ En; in good health, en bonne santé; in itself, en soi; in proof of, en guise de preuve de; in theory, en théorie; in a white apron, en tablier blanc. ‖ A; each in his way, chacun à sa manière; in support of, à l'appui de; in time, à temps; landscapes in oil, paysages à l'huile; sitting in the light of a lamp, in a window, assis à la lumière de la lampe, à une fenêtre; slow in, lent à. ‖ Chez; in animals, in human beings, chez les animaux, chez les êtres humains. ‖ De; ten feet in height, dix pieds de haut; the best pupil in the class, le meilleur élève de la classe. ‖ Entre, parmi; a day in a thousand, un jour entre mille. ‖ Par; in a high wind, in all weathers, par grand vent, par tous les temps; in self-defence, par instinct de conservation. ‖ Pendant; in the daytime, pendant la journée. ‖ Pour; backward in doing, en retard pour faire. ‖ Selon; in all probability, selon toute probabilité. ‖ Sous; in the rain, sous la pluie. ‖ Sur; one man in ten, un homme sur dix. ‖ U. S. Depuis; I haven't heard from him in years, je n'ai plus de ses nouvelles depuis des années.
— adv. Dedans, à l'intérieur; woolly side in, la laine à l'intérieur; to be in, être à la maison (or) chez soi; we were asked in, on nous demanda d'entrer. ‖ Enfermé, délimité; fenced in, entouré d'une clôture. ‖ Arrivé; apples are now in, c'est la saison des pommes; summer is in, l'été est là; the train is in, le train est arrivé. ‖ A la mode; blue handbags are in, les sacs bleus sont en vogue. ‖ Engagé; we are in for a storm, il va faire de l'orage, nous allons avoir de l'orage. ‖ D'accord; to fall in with, être d'accord avec. ‖ NAUT. Amené (sail); arrivé (ship). ‖ JUR. Au pouvoir; to put s.o. in, porter qqn au pouvoir. ‖ COMM. All in, tout compris. ‖ TECHN., SPORTS. En action; to be in for a race, être inscrit pour une course. ‖ FAM. He's in for it!, il va écoper!; to be all in, être éreinté.
— adj. D'entrée; the in door, la porte d'entrée. ‖ En cours; the « in » tray, la corbeille des affaires à examiner. ‖ **In-built**, adj. Inné, constitutionnel (feeling); TECHN. Incorporé (device). ‖ **In-fighting**, n. SPORTS. Infighting, combat rapproché m.; FIG. Corps à corps m., lutte acharnée f. ‖ **In-laws**, n. Belle-famille f., parents (m. pl.) par alliance; beaux-parents m. pl. ‖ **In-patient**, n. MED. Malade hospitalisé s.
— n. Ins and outs, coins et recoins, êtres m. pl. (in a house); tenants et aboutissants (details). ‖

U. S. FAM. *To have an in with*, avoir l'oreille de, avoir ses entrées chez; *the in's*, les gens en place.
inability [,inə'biliti] n. Incapacité *f*.
in absentia [in æb'sentiə] adv. En son absence. ‖ JUR. Par contumace.
inaccessibility [inək,sesi'biliti] n. Inaccessibilité *f*.
inaccessible [,inək'sesibl] adj. Inaccessible.
inaccuracy [i'nækjurəsi] n. Inexactitude *f*.
inaccurate [-it] adj. Inexact.
inaccurately [-itli] adv. Inexactement, avec inexactitude.
inaction [i'nækʃən] n. Inaction *f*.
inactive [i'næktiv] adj. Inactif.
inactivity [,inæk'tiviti] n. Inactivité *f*.
inadaptability ['inə,dæptə'biliti] n. Inadaptabilité *f*. (*to*, à).
inadequacy [i'nædikwəsi] n. Imperfection, insuffisance *f*.
inadequate [-kwit] adj. Imparfait, insuffisant (insufficent). ‖ Inadéquat, inapproprié (*to*, à).
inadmissibility ['inəd,misi'biliti] n. Inadmissibilité *f*. ‖ JUR. Non-recevabilité *f*.
inadmissible [,inəd'misibl] adj. Inadmissible.
inadvertence [,inəd'və:təns], **inadvertency** [-i] n. Inadvertance *f*. (act, quality).
inadvertent [-ənt] adj. Etourdi, inattentif (not attentive). ‖ Négligent, insouciant (*to*, de) [heedless]. ‖ Commis par inadvertance, non intentionnel (unintentional).
inadvertently [-əntli] adv. Par inadvertance.
inadvisable [,inəd'vaizəbl] adj. Peu recommandé; déconseillé.
inalienability [i,neiliənə'biliti] n. Inaliénabilité *f*.
inalienable [i'neiliənəbl] adj. Inaliénable.
inalterability [i,nɔ:ltərə'biliti] n. Inaltérabilité *f*.
inalterable [i'nɔ:ltərəbl] adj. Inaltérable.
inamorata [in,æmə'rɑ:tə] n. Amante, amoureuse *f*.
inamorato [-tou] n. Amant, amoureux *m*.
inane [i'nein] adj. Vide (space). ‖ FIG. Vain (hope); inepte, sot (person, remark).
— n. Vide *m*.
inanimate [i'nænimit] adj. Inanimé.
inanition [,inə'niʃən] n. Inanition *f*.
inanity [i'næniti] n. Inanité *f*. ‖ Ineptie *f*.
inappeasable [,inə'piə:zəbl] adj. Inapaisable.
inappellable [,inə'peləbl] adj. JUR. Sans appel.
inappetence [i'næpitəns] n. Inappétence *f*.
inapplicability [i,næplikə'biliti] n. Inapplicabilité *f*. (*to*, à).
inapplicable [i'næplikəbl] adj. Inapplicable.
inapposite [i'næpɔzit] adj. Inapproprié. ‖ Hors de propos, sans rapport (*to*, avec).
inappreciable [,inə'pri:ʃiəbl] adj. Inappréciable.
inappreciation ['inə,pri:ʃi'eiʃən] n. Défaut (*m*.) d'appréciation.
inappreciative [,inə'pri:ʃiətiv] adj. Non appréciateur.
inapprehensible [i,nəpri'hensibl] adj. Insaisissable; imperceptible.
inapprehension [-ʃən] n. Incompréhension *f*.
inapproachable [,inə'proutʃəbl] adj. Inapprochable; inabordable.
inappropriate [,inə'prouprit] adj. Non indiqué; non approprié (*to*, à). ‖ Impropre (word).
inapt [i'næpt] adj. Inapte. ‖ Inapproprié.
inaptitude [-itju:d] n. Inaptitude *f*.
inarm [i'nɑ:m] v. tr. Enlacer. (See EMBRACE.)
inarticulate [,inɑ:'tikjulit] adj. Inarticulé (cry). ‖ Incapable d'articuler, bafouillant (person). ‖ ZOOL. Inarticulé. ‖ FIG. Muet, inexprimé.
inartificial [i,nɑ:ti'fiʃəl] adj. Naturel, non artificiel. ‖ Non artistique. ‖ Sans artifice, simple (unaffected).
inartistic [,inɑ:'tistik] adj. Peu artiste (person); peu artistique (thing).

inartistically [-əli] adv. Sans art.
inasmuch [,inəz'mʌtʃ] adv. D'autant plus (*as*, que).
inattention [,inə'tenʃən] n. Inattention *f*. (act, quality). ‖ Manque (*m*.) d'attention (*to*, envers).
inattentive [-tiv] adj. Inattentif (absent-minded). ‖ Sans attentions, peu attentionné.
inaudible [i'nɔ:dibl] adj. Inaudible.
inaudibly [-i] adv. De manière inaudible.
inaugural [i'nɔ:gjurəl] adj. Inaugural, d'ouverture (meeting).
inaugurate [-reit] v. tr. Installer (an official). ‖ Inaugurer (a building). ‖ Inaugurer, mettre en vigueur (a policy).
inauguration [i,nɔ:gju'reiʃən] n. Installation *f*. (of an official). ‖ Inauguration *f*. (of a building, policy).
inaugurator [i'nɔ:gjurətə*] n. Inaugurateur *m*.; inauguratrice *f*.
inauspicious [,inɔ:s'piʃəs] adj. Peu propice, défavorable.
inbeing ['inbi:iŋ] n. Essence *f*.
inboard ['inbɔ:d] adj. NAUT. Intérieur.
— adv. NAUT. A l'intérieur, à bord.
— prep. NAUT. En abord de.
inborn ['in'bɔ:n] adj. Inné. (See INNATE.) ‖ MED. Congénital (weakness).
inbreathe ['in'bri:ð] v. tr. MED., FIG. Insuffler (*into*, à).
inbred ['in'bred] adj. Inné. (See INNATE.) ‖ Consanguin (animal).
inbreeding ['in'bri:diŋ] n. Consanguinité *f*.; mariage consanguin *m*. (of persons). ‖ Croisement consanguin *m*. (of animals).
Inc. [iŋk] U. S. Abbr. *Incorporated*, société, Sté.
Inca ['iŋkə] n. GEOGR. Inca *m*.
incalculable [in'kælkjuləbl] adj. MATH. Incalculable. (See COUNTLESS.) ‖ FIG. Imprévisible (event, importance).
incalculably [-bli] adv. Incalculablement.
incalescence [,inkə'lesns] n. Incalescence *f*.
incandesce [,inkæn'des] v. intr. Devenir incandescent, entrer en incandescence.
incandescence [-ns] n. Incandescence *f*.
incandescent [-nt] adj. Incandescent.
incantation [,inkæn'teiʃən] n. Incantation *f*.
incantatory [in'kæntətəri] adj. Incantatoire. (See SPELL-BINDING.)
incapability [in,keipə'biliti] n. JUR., FIG. Incapacité *f*.
incapable [in'keipəbl] adj. Incapable, non susceptible (*of*, de). ‖ JUR. Incompétent (court); incapable, inhabile (person).
incapacious [,inkə'peiʃəs] adj. MED. Incapable, déficient.
incapacitate [,inkə'pæsiteit] v. tr. Rendre incapable, mettre hors d'état (*from*, de). ‖ JUR. Frapper d'incapacité; interdire. ‖ SPORTS. Disqualifier.
incapacitation [inkə,pæsi'teiʃən] n. Interdit *m*. ‖ FIG. Incapacité *f*.
incapacity [,inkə'pæsiti] n. JUR., FIN. Incapacité *f*.
incarcerate [in'kɑ:səreit] v. tr. Incarcérer. (See IMPRISON.)
incarceration [in,kɑ:sə'reiʃən] n. Incarcération *f*.
incarnadine [in'kɑ:nədain] adj. Incarnadin.
— n. Incarnat *m*.
— v. tr. Teindre en rouge vif.
incarnate [-nit] adj. Incarné.
— [-neit] v. tr. Incarner (lit. and fig.). [See EMBODY.]
incarnation [,inkɑ:'neiʃən] n. ECCLES., FIG. Incarnation *f*.
incase [in'keis]. See ENCASE.
incautious [in'kɔ:ʃəs] adj. Imprudent, irréfléchi.
incendiarism [in'sendjərizm] n. JUR. Tendance (*f*.) à provoquer des incendies volontaires. ‖ FIG. Caractère incendiaire *m*. (of a theory).

incendiary [-i] adj. JUR., FIG. Incendiaire.
— n. Incendiaire *m.* (person). ‖ MILIT. FAM. Bombe incendiaire *f.* ‖ FIG. Brandon (*m.*) de discorde.
incense [in'sens] v. tr. Pousser à bout, exaspérer.
incense ['insens] n. ECCLES., FIG. Encens *m.* ‖ **Incense-bearer**, n. ECCLES. Thuriféraire *m.* ‖ **Incense-boat**, n. ECCLES. Navette *f.* ‖ **Incense-burner**, n. Cassolette *f.;* brûle-parfums *m.* (device); FIG. Encenseur *m.* (person).
— v. tr. Parfumer. ‖ ECCLES., FIG. Encenser.
incensory [-əri] n. ECCLES. Encensoir *m.*
incentive [in'sentiv] adj. Encourageant, stimulant.
— n. Stimulant, aiguillon *m.*
incept [in'sept] v. tr. MED. Ingérer. ‖ FIG. Commencer.
inception [-ʃən] n. Début *m.* ‖ MED. Absorption *f.*
inceptive [-tiv] adj. Initial. ‖ GRAMM. Inchoatif.
— n. GRAMM. Inchoatif *m.*
incertitude [in'sə:titju:d] n. Incertitude *f.*
incessancy [in'sesṇsi] n. Continuité *f.*
incessant [-ṇt] adj. Incessant. (See CONTINUAL.)
incessantly [-ṇtli] adv. Sans cesse.
incest ['insest] n. Inceste *m.*
incestuous [in'sestjuəs] adj. Incestueux.
inch [inʃ] n. Pouce *m.* (measure). ‖ FIG. *Inch by inch,* peu à peu, graduellement, par degrés; *to kill by inches,* faire mourir à petit feu; *within an inch of,* à deux doigts de, à un cheveu de.
— v. tr. Faire avancer peu à peu.
— v. intr. Avancer peu à peu.
inchoate ['inkouit] adj. Naissant, débutant. (See INCIPIENT.) ‖ Rudimentaire. ‖ JUR. Non consommé (crime).
— [-eit] v. tr. † Débuter.
inchoation [,inkou'eiʃən] n. Inchoation *f.*
inchoative [-tiv] adj. GRAMM. Inchoative. (See INCEPTIVE.)
incidence ['insidəns] n. PHYS., JUR. Incidence *f.* ‖ FIG. Portée *f.*
incident [-ənt] n. Incident *m.* (event). ‖ Épisode *m.;* péripétie *f.* (in a novel, play). ‖ JUR. Privilège *m.* (or) servitude (*f.*) de biens.
— adj. Résultant, découlant (*to,* de); tenant (*to,* à). ‖ PHYS. Incident; en incidence (*upon,* sur). ‖ JUR. Attaché, afférent (*to,* à).
incidental [,insi'dentəl] adj. Accidentel, fortuit. ‖ JUR. *Incidental plea of defence,* exception. ‖ MUS. De fond, d'accompagnement (music). ‖ FIN. Accessoire. ‖ GRAMM. *Incidental clause,* incise.
— n. pl. FIN. Faux frais *m. pl.*
incidentally [-əli] adv. Soit dit en passant (or) entre parenthèses; incidemment.
incinerate [in'sinəreit] v. tr. Carboniser. ‖ Incinérer (body). [See CREMATE.]
incineration [,insinə'reiʃən] n. Incinération *f.*
incinerator [in'sinəreitə*] n. Four crématoire *m.* (for the dead). ‖ Incinérateur *m.* (for rubbish).
incipience [in'sipiəns] n. FIG. Naissance; début *m.*
incipient [-ənt] adj. Naissant, débutant, commençant, à ses débuts. (See INCHOATE.)
incise [in'saiz] v. tr. Inciser (to cut). ‖ Graver (to carve).
incision [-'siʒən] n. Incision *f.*
incisive [-'saisiv] adj. Incisif.
incisor [-'saizə*] n. MED. Incisive *f.* (tooth).
incitable [in'saitəbl] adj. Incitable.
incitation [,insi'teiʃən] n. Incitation *f.*
incite [in'sait] v. tr. Inciter (*to,* à). ‖ FAM. Exciter, monter.
incitement [-mənt] n. Incitation, instigation *f.* (*to,* à). ‖ Mobile, motif *m.* (*of,* de). ‖ Stimulant, aiguillon *m.* (incentive).
incivility [,insi'viliti] n. Incivilité *f.* (act, quality).
incivism ['insivizṃ] n. Incivisme *m.*
inclemency [in'klemənsi] n. Inclémence *f.*

inclement [-ənt] n. Inclément.
inclinable [in'klainəbl] adj. Enclin (prone); favorable (*to,* à) [well disposed]. ‖ Inclinable (tilting).
inclination [,inkli'neiʃən] n. Inclinaison *f.* ‖ FIG. Inclination *f.;* penchant *m.* (*for,* pour).
incline [in'klain] v. tr. Incliner. ‖ FIG. Incliner, disposer (s.o.'s mind); diriger (one's steps); *well inclined towards,* dans de bonnes dispositions envers.
— v. intr. S'incliner (person); pencher (thing). ‖ MED. Avoir une propension (*to,* à). ‖ FIG. Tirer (*to,* sur) [colour]; incliner, être enclin (*to,* à) [person]; *to incline to s.o.'s point of view,* pencher vers le point de vue de qqn.
— n. Inclinaison, pente *f.* (slope). ‖ Plan incliné *m.* (sloping plane).
inclinometer [,inkli'nɔmitə*] n. Clinomètre *m.*
inclose [in'klouz]. See ENCLOSE.
inclosure [-ə*]. See ENCLOSURE.
include [in'klu:d] v. tr. Inclure, enclore, renfermer, comprendre, englober.
inclusion [-ʒən] n. Inclusion *f.*
inclusive [-siv] adj. Inclus; *from the first to the fourth day inclusive,* du premier au quatrième jour inclusivement. ‖ Inclusif; *to be inclusive of,* inclure, comprendre. ‖ Global; *inclusive terms,* prix tout compris.
inclusively [-li] adv. Inclusivement.
incognito [in'kɔgnitou] adj., adv. Incognito.
— n. Voyageur incognito *m.* (person). ‖ Incognito *m.* (state).
— N. B. Au sens de « *personne* », *incognito* prend le fém. *incognita* et le pl. *incognitos.*
incognizable [in'kɔ(g)nizəbl] adj. Inconnaissable.
incognizant [-ənt] adj. Ignorant, non informé (*of,* de).
incoherence [,inko'hiərəns] n. Incohérence *f.*
incoherent [-ənt] adj. Incohérent; *incoherent speech,* divagations.
incoherently [-əntli] adv. Sans cohérence, d'une façon incohérente.
incohesive [,inko'hi:siv] adj. Sans cohésion, incohésif.
incombustibility ['inkəm,bʌsti'biliti] n. Incombustibilité *f.*
incombustible [,inkəm'bʌstibl] adj., n. Incombustible *m.* (See FIREPROOF.)
income ['inkʌm] n. FIN. Revenu *m.; income return,* déclaration d'impôt; *income tax,* impôt sur le revenu; *the lowest income-group,* les économiquement faibles.
incomer ['in,kʌmə*] n. Arrivant *m.* ‖ Immigrant *s.* ‖ Intrus *s.* (intruder). ‖ Successeur *m.*
incoming [-iŋ] n. Arrivée *f.* (arrival); entrée *f.* (entrance). ‖ Pl. FIN. Rentrées *f. pl.*
— adj. Arrivant, entrant (coming in). ‖ Commençant (beginning). ‖ Succédant (succeeding). ‖ Immigrant. ‖ FIN. Accru. ‖ NAUT. Montant (tide).
incommensurability ['inkə,menʃərə'biliti] n. Incommensurabilité *f.*
incommensurable [,inkə'menʃərəbl] adj. Incommensurable (immeasurable). ‖ Sans commune mesure, sans point de comparaison (*with,* avec). ‖ MATH. Irrationnel (number).
incommensurate [-it] adj. Incommensurable. ‖ Sans rapport (or) proportion (*to, with,* avec).
incommode [,inkə'moud] v. tr. Incommoder (s.o.); gêner, entraver (walking).
incommodious [-iəs] adj. Incommode. ‖ Trop étroit (narrow).
incommodity [,inkə'mɔditi] n. Incommodité *f.*
incommunicability [,inkə'mju:nikə'biliti] n. Incommunicabilité *f.*
incommunicable [-əbl] adj. Incommunicable.
incommunicado [,inkə,mju:ni'kɑ:dou] adj. JUR. Tenu au secret. ‖ FIG. Coupé du monde extérieur.

incommunicative [-ətiv] adj. Peu expansif, réservé.
incommutable [,inkə'mju:təbḷ] adj. Immuable (immutable). ‖ Non interchangeable. ‖ Jur. Incommutable.
incomparability [in,kɔmpərə'biliti] n. Incomparabilité f.
incomparable [in'kɔmpərəbḷ] adj. Incomparable (to, with, à).
incompatibility ['inkəm,pæti'biliti] n. Incompatibilité f. (with, avec); incompatibility of temperament, incompatibilité d'humeur.
incompatible [,inkəm'pætibḷ] adj. Incompatible.
incompetence [in'kɔmpitəns], incompetency [-i] n. Incompétence f. ‖ Maladresse, incapacité f.
incompetent [-ənt] adj. Incompétent. ‖ Non au niveau (to, de).
— n. Incompétent m. ‖ Incapable s.
incomplete [,inkəm'pli:t] adj. Incomplet. ‖ Dépareillé (collection).
incompletely [-li] adv. Incomplètement.
incompletion [,inkəm'pli:ʃən] n. Inachèvement m.
incompliance [,inkəm'plaiəns] n. Intransigeance, inflexibilité f.
incompliant [-ənt] adj. Intransigeant; non accommodant.
incomprehensibility [in,kɔmprihensi'biliti] n. Incompréhensibilité.
incomprehensible [in,kɔpri'hensibḷ] adj. Incompréhensible.
incomprehension [-ʃən] n. Incompréhension f.
incomprehensive [-siv] adj. Non inclusif. ‖ Fig. Incompréhensif.
incompressibility ['inkəm,presi'biliti] n. Incompressibilité f.
incompressible [,inkəm'presibḷ] adj. Incompressible.
incomputable [-'pju:təbḷ] adj. Incalculable.
inconceivability ['inkən,si:və'biliti] n. Inconcevabilité f.
inconceivable [,inkən'si:vəbḷ] adj. Inconcevable.
inconclusive [-'klu:siv] adj. Peu concluant; non décisif.
incondensable [-'densəbḷ] adj. Non condensable.
incondite [in'kɔndit] adj. Mal construit (literary work). ‖ Peu raffiné, grossier (crude).
incongruent [,inkɔŋ'gruənt] adj. En désaccord (to, avec). ‖ Qui ne convient pas (to, à).
incongruity [-iti] n. Manque (m.) d'harmonie (or) d'appropriation (with, avec). ‖ Incongruité, inconvenance f. (act).
incongruous [in'kɔŋgruəs] adj. Disparate, dissocié, inharmonieux, incompatible. ‖ En désaccord, sans harmonie (or) rapport (with, avec); inapproprié (with, à). ‖ Incongru, inconvenant.
inconsequence [in'kɔnsikwəns] n. Inconséquence f.
inconsequent [-ənt] adj. Sans suite (ideas); inconséquent (mind); illogique (reasoning).
inconsequential [in,kɔnsə'kwenʃəl] adj. Sans importance (or) conséquence (unimportant). ‖ Inconséquent, illogique.
inconsiderable [,inkən'sidərəbḷ] adj. Peu considérable, insignifiant.
inconsiderate [-it] adj. Inconsidéré (thoughtless). ‖ Sans égards (inattentive).
inconsideration [in,kən'sidə'reiʃən] n. Irréflexion f. ‖ Manque (m.) d'égards.
inconsistency [,inkən'sistənsi] n. Inconséquence f. (act); illogisme m. (quality); contradiction, inconsistance f.; désaccord m. (state). [See DISCREPANCY.]
inconsistent [-ənt] adj. Inconséquent. ‖ Inconsistant. ‖ En contradiction (with, avec).
inconsolable [,inkən'souləbḷ] adj. Inconsolable.
inconsonance [in'kɔnsənəns] n. Désaccord m.
inconsonant [-ənt] adj. En désaccord, non en harmonie (with, avec). ‖ Discordant.

inconspicuous [,inkən'spikjuəs] adj. Peu apparent (or) frappant; discret.
inconstancy [in'kɔnstənsi] n. Inconstance f. (in affections). ‖ Instabilité f. (in nature).
inconstant [-ənt] adj. Inconstant (fickle). ‖ Instable (unstable).
inconsumable [,inkən'sju:məbḷ] adj. Non susceptible de se consumer, incombustible (by fire). ‖ Comm. Non consommable (goods).
incontestable [,inkən'testəbḷ] adj. Incontestable. (See INDISPUTABLE.)
incontestably [-bli] adv. Incontestablement.
incontinence [in'kɔntinəns] n. Med., Fig. Incontinence f.
incontinent [-ənt] adj. Incontinent (unchaste). ‖ Med. Incontinent. ‖ Fig. Incontinent of information, incapable de taire une information.
incontinently [-əntli] adv. Incontinent, immédiatement, sur-le-champ.
incontrovertible [in'kɔntrəvə:tibḷ] adj. Incontestable, indiscutable, indéniable, irréfutable. (See INDISPUTABLE.)
inconvenience [,inkən'vi:njəns] n. Inconvénient, désagrément, ennui m. ‖ Gêne f.; embarras; dérangement; tintouin m. (fam.).
— v. tr. Causer du désagrément (or) des inconvénients. ‖ Déranger.
inconvenient [-ənt] adj. Incommode, malcommode (house); gênant, importun (person); inopportun, mal choisi (time); if it is not inconvenient to you, si cela ne vous dérange pas.
inconveniently [-əntli] adv. Incommodément. ‖ D'une manière gênante. ‖ Inopportunément.
inconvertible [,inkən'və:tibḷ] adj. Fin. Inconvertible.
inconvincible [-'vinsibḷ] adj. Impossible à convaincre.
incoordinate [,inkou'ɔ:dinit] adj. Non coordonné.
incoordination ['inkou,ɔ:di'neiʃən] n. Manque (m.) de coordination.
incorporable [in'kɔ:pərəbḷ] adj. Incorporable.
incorporate [-it] adj. Jur. Constitué en société.
— [-eit] v. tr. Incorporer (with, à). ‖ Jur. Constituer en société.
— v. intr. S'incorporer (with, à).
incorporation [in,kɔ:pə'reiʃən] n. Incorporation f. ‖ Jur. Constitution en société f. (of a company); érection en municipalité f. (of a town).
incorporeal [,inkɔ:'pɔ:riəl] adj. Incorporel.
incorporeity [-əti] n. Incorporalité f. (quality). ‖ Entité f. (entity).
incorrect [,inkə'rekt] adj. Incorrect (behaviour, style). ‖ Inexact (statement, views).
incorrectly [-li] adv. Incorrectement. ‖ Inexactement, fautivement.
incorrectness [-nis] n. Incorrection f. ‖ Inexactitude f.; caractère fautif m.
incorrigibility [in,kɔridʒi'biliti] n. Incorrigibilité f.
incorrigible [in'kɔridʒibḷ] adj. Incorrigible.
incorrigibly [-bli] adv. Incorrigiblement.
incorruptibility ['inkɔ,rʌpti'biliti] n. Incorruptibilité f.
incorruptible [,inkɔ'rʌptibḷ] adj. Incorruptible.
incorruptibly [-bli] adv. Incorruptiblement.
increase [in'kri:s] v. intr. Croître, augmenter, se développer.
— v. tr. Accroître, augmenter, développer.
— ['inkri:s] n. Augmentation, multiplication f. (in number); accroissement, développement m. (of speed). ‖ Fin. Augmentation; increase in value, plus-value. ‖ Fig. Redoublement m. (of joy, zeal); surcroît m. (of work).
increate [,inkri:'eit] adj. Eccles. Incréé.
incredibility [in,kredi'biliti] n. Incrédibilité f.
incredible [in'kredibḷ] adj. Incroyable; à dormir debout (story).

incredibly [-bli] adv. Incroyablement.
incredulity [,inkri'dju:liti] n. Incrédulité *f.*
incredulous [in'kredjuləs] adj. Incrédule.
increment ['inkrimənt] n. Accroissement *m.* (increase). ‖ FIN. Incrément *m.; increment value,* plus-value immobilière. ‖ MATH. Différentielle *f.*
incriminate [in'krimineit] v. tr. Incriminer. ‖ JUR. Inculper ; *incriminating documents,* pièces à conviction.
incrimination [in,krimi'neiʃən] n. Incrimination *f.*
incrust [in'krʌst] v. tr. Encroûter, recouvrir d'une croûte. ‖ Incruster (with gems).
incrustation [,inkrʌs'teiʃən] n. Incrustation *f.* (act, decoration). ‖ TECHN. Tartre *m.* (crust); entartrage *m.* (fact). ‖ FIG. Enracinement *m.* (of a habit).
incubate ['inkjubeit] v. tr. Couver (lit. and fig.). ‖ MED. Incuber.
— v. intr. Etre couvé (eggs). ‖ MED., FIG. Couver.
incubation [,inkju'beiʃən] n. Incubation *f.*
incubator ['inkjubeitə*] n. Couveuse *f.*
incubus ['inkjubəs] n. Incube *m.* (demon). ‖ FAM. Fardeau *m.* (burden) ; hantise *f.* (nightmare).
— N. B. Deux pluriels : *incubuses, incubi.*
inculcate ['inkʌlkeit] v. tr. Inculquer (*in, upon,* à, dans).
inculcation [,inkʌl'keiʃən] n. Inculcation *f.*
inculpate ['inkʌlpeit] v. tr. JUR., FIG. Inculper.
inculpation [,inkʌl'peiʃən] n. JUR., FIG. Inculpation *f.*
inculpatory [in'kʌlpətəri] adj. Accusateur *m.;* accusatrice *f.*
incumbent [in'kʌmbənt] n. ECCLES. Titulaire *m.*
— adj. Etendu (*on,* sur) [lying]. ‖ JUR. Sortant. ‖ FIG. Incombant, appartenant (*upon,* à).
incunabulum [,inkju:'næbjuləm] (pl. **incunabula** [-ə]) n. Incunable *m.* (book).
incur [in'kə*] v. tr. (1). FIN. Contracter (debts) ; engager (expenditure) ; supporter (expenses) ; subir, éprouver (loss). ‖ FIG. S'attirer, encourir (s.o.'s anger, blame) ; courir (a danger) ; contracter (an obligation).
incurability [in,kjuərə'biliti] n. MED., FIG. Incurabilité *f.*
incurable [in'kjuərəbl] adj., n. MED. Incurable, *s.*
incuriosity [in,kjuəri'ositi] n. Manque (*m.*) de curiosité.
incurious [in'kjuəriəs] adj. Sans curiosité, peu curieux, discret. ‖ Indifférent. ‖ Peu attrayant (or) intéressant ; sans intérêt.
incursion [in'kə:ʃən] n. MILIT., FIG. Incursion *f.*
incurvation [,inkə:'veiʃən] n. Incurvation *f.*
incurve [in'kə:v] v. tr. Incurver.
incus ['inkəs] n. MED. Enclume *f.* (in the ear).
indebted [in'detid] adj. FIN. Endetté (*to,* envers). ‖ FIG. Redevable (*to,* à ; *for,* de).
indebtedness [-nis] n. FIN., FIG. Dette *f.*
indecency [in'di:snsi] n. Indécence *f.* (immodesty). ‖ Inconvenance *f.* (unbecoming). ‖ Grossièreté *f.* (act, remark).
indecent [-ņt] adj. Indécent. ‖ Inconvenant, grossier (unseemly). ‖ Déplacé, malséant, incongru (improper).
indecently [-ņtli] adv. Indécemment. ‖ Avec inconvenance.
indeciduous [indi'sidjuəs] adj. BOT. Persistant, vert.
indecipherable [,indi'saifərəbl] adj. Indéchiffrable.
indecision [,indi'siʒən] n. Indécision *f.*
indecisive [,indi'saisiv] adj. Indécis (battle, person) ; peu concluant (discussion).
indecisiveness [-nis] n. Caractère indécis *m.;* indécision *f.*
indeclinable [,indi'klainəbl] adj. GRAMM. Indéclinable.
indecomposable [in,di:kəm'pouzəbl] adj. Indécomposable. ‖ CHIM. Indédoublable.

indecorous [,indi'kɔ:rəs] adj. Peu convenable, incorrect (improper). ‖ Malséant, de mauvais goût (in bad taste).
indecorum [,indi'kɔ:rəm] n. Inconvenance *f.,* incorrection (unbecoming). ‖ Faute (*f.*) de goût ; manque d'usage *m.*
indeed [in'di:d] adv. En effet, en vérité, vraiment, à vrai dire.
— interj. Vraiment ! ; *yes indeed !,* mais certainement !, certes oui !
indefatigability [indi,fætigə'biliti] n. Infatigabilité *f.*
indefeasible [,indi'fi:zibl] adj. Irrévocable.
indefeasibly [-bli] adv. Irrévocablement.
indefeasibility ['indi,fi:zi'biliti] n. Irrévocabilité, imprescriptibilité *f.*
indefeasible [,indi'fi:zibl] adj. Irrévocable.
indefeasibly [-bli] adv. Irrévocablement.
indefectible [,indi'fektibl] adj. Indéfectible (unfailing). ‖ Parfait, sans défaut (faultless).
indefensible [-'fensibl] adj. Indéfendable. ‖ FIG. Insoutenable, injustifiable.
indefinable [-'fainəbl-] adj. Indéfinissable.
indefinite [in'definit] adj. Indistinct (blurred); indéfini, incertain, imprécis (vague). ‖ Illimité, indéterminé (unlimited). ‖ GRAMM. Indéfini.
indefinitely [-li] adv. Vaguement, avec imprécision (vaguely). ‖ Indéfiniment (unlimitedly).
indelibility [in,deli'biliti] n. Indélébilité *f.*
indelible [in'dəlibl] adj. Indélébile.
indelibly [-bli] adv. Indélébilement.
indelicacy [in'delikəsi] n. Indélicatesse *f.* (act, quality). ‖ Grossièreté *f.* (act, quality) ; indecency.
indelicate [-it] adj. Indélicat (unrefined). ‖ Grossier, grivois (indecent). ‖ Sans tact (tactless).
indemnification [in,demnifi'keiʃən] n. FIN. Indemnisation *f.* (*for,* de) [act] ; indemnité *f.* (sum). ‖ JUR. Assurance, garantie *f.* (*against,* contre).
indemnify [in'demnifai] v. tr. (2). FIN. Indemniser (*for,* de). ‖ JUR. Garantir (*against,* contre).
indemnity [-ti] n. FIN. Indemnité *f.* ‖ JUR. Garantie, compensation *f.; deed of indemnity,* cautionnement. ‖ JUR. Amnistie *f.*
indemonstrable [,indi'mɔnstrəbl] adj. Indémontrable.
indent [in'dent] v. tr. Bosseler, bossuer (to batter). ‖ Creuser, empreindre (to impress).
— ['indent] n. Creux *m.* ; bosselure *f.*
indent [in'dent] v. tr. Denteler, découper en dentelant. ‖ JUR. Rédiger en double expédition (a contract). ‖ séparer les deux expéditions de (a written contract). ‖ COMM. Passer une commande (*for,* de ; *on,* à). ‖ ARCHIT. Endenter ; *indented trace,* tracé en crémaillère. ‖ TECHN. Rentrer (a line).
— v. intr. Etre dentelé. ‖ JUR. Passer un contrat ; *to indent on s.o. for sth.,* réquisitionner qqch. chez qqn. ‖ COMM. Passer une commande (*for,* de ; *on,* à). ‖ TECHN. Faire un alinéa.
— n. Dentelure *f.* ‖ JUR. Contrat *m.* (contract) ; réquisition *f.* (*for,* de). ‖ COMM. Commande *f.* ‖ ARCHIT. Adent *m.* ‖ TECHN. Renfoncement *m.* (of a line).
indentation [,inden'teiʃən] n. Découpage *m.* (act); dentelure, déchiqueture dentelée *f.* (result). ‖ ARCHIT. Endentement *m.*
indention [in'denʃən] n. TECHN. Renfoncement *m.* (of a line); alinéa *m.*
indenture [-ʃə*] n. JUR. Acte (or) contrat (or) inventaire en double expédition. ‖ Pl. JUR. Contrat d'apprentissage *m.*
— v. tr. JUR. Lier par contrat ; mettre en apprentissage (*to,* chez).
independence [,indi'pendəns] n. Indépendance *f.* (*on,* de). ‖ U. S. *Independence Day,* le 4 juillet. ‖ FIN. Honnête aisance *f.* (income).
independency [-ənsi] n. Indépendance *f.* ‖ Nation indépendante *f.*

independent [-ənt] adj. Indépendant (*of*, de). ‖ JUR. Sans profession (man); autonome, indépendant (nation). ‖ FIN. Suffisant, honnête, permettant de vivre sans travailler (income); *independent gentleman*, rentier. ‖ ECCLES. Congrégationaliste. ‖ MILIT. Indépendant (army); à volonté (fire). ‖ GRAMM. Principal (clause).
— n. Indépendant *m.* ‖ ECCLES. Congrégationaliste *m.*

independently [,indi'pendəntli] adv. Indépendamment (*of*, de). ‖ Avec indépendance.

indescribable [,indis'kraibəbl] adj. Indescriptible.

indestructibility ['indis,trʌkti'biliti] n. Indestructibilité *f.*

indestructible [,indis'trʌktibl] adj. Indestructible.

indestructibly [-bli] adv. Indestructiblement.

indeterminable [,indi'tə:minəbl] adj. Indéterminable (origin). ‖ Interminable (dispute).

indeterminate [-nit] adj. Indéterminé, vague. ‖ Sans solution précise. ‖ JUR. *Indeterminate sentence*, jugement privatif de liberté sans précision de durée. ‖ MATH. Indéterminé.

indetermination ['indi,tə:mi'neiʃən] n. Indétermination *f.* ‖ Absence de solution *f.*

index ['indeks] (pl. **indexes** [-iz]) n. Index *m.* (list). ‖ MED. Index *m.* (finger). ‖ TECHN. Aiguille *f.* ‖ ECCLES. Index *m.; on the Index*, à l'Index.
— (pl. **indices** ['indisi:z]) n. PHYS. Indice *m.* ‖ MATH. Exposant *m.* ‖ JUR. Indice *m.; cost of living index, consumer's price index*, indice du coût de la vie. ‖ FIG. Indice, signe *m.*; indication *f.* ‖ **Index-card**, n. Fiche *f.* ‖ **Index-linked**, adj. JUR., FIN. Indexé. ‖ **Index-number**, n. JUR. Indice *m.*
— v. tr. Faire un index à (a book); répertorier, indexer (words). ‖ ECCLES. Mettre à l'Index.

India ['indjə] n. GEOGR. Inde *f.; India ink*, encre de Chine; *India paper*, papier du Japon, papier bible. ‖ **India-rubber**, adj. En caoutchouc; n. Caoutchouc *m.*; gomme *f.* (See RUBBER.)

Indiaman [-mən] n. NAUT. Long-courrier (*m.*) des Indes (ship).

Indian ['indjən] adj. GEOGR. Indien, Hindou, des Indes. ‖ U. S. AGRIC. *Indian corn*, maïs; *Indian meal*, farine de maïs. ‖ U. S. ZOOL. *Indian ox*, zébu. ‖ BOT. *Indian hemp*, chanvre indien. ‖ COMM. *Indian ink*, encre de Chine. ‖ LOC. *Indian club*, massue; *Indian summer*, été de la Saint-Martin; *Indian giver*, personne qui reprend ses cadeaux.
— n. GEOGR. Indien, Hindou *s.*

Indianist [-ist] n. Indianiste *s.*

indicate ['indikeit] v. tr. Indiquer, faire observer (or) remarquer, signaler (to point out). ‖ Indiquer, montrer (to show). ‖ Indiquer, signifier, prouver (to betoken). ‖ Indiquer, appeler, rendre nécessaire (to show the need for). ‖ Exprimer, exposer (to express). ‖ MED. Indiquer.

indication [,indi'keiʃən] n. Indication *f.*

indicative [in'dikətiv] adj., n. GRAMM. Indicatif *m.*

indicator ['indikeitə*] n. Indicateur *m.; indicatrice *f.* (person). ‖ TECHN., CHIM., CH. DE F. Indicateur *m.* ‖ AUTOM. *Distance indicator*, compteur kilométrique.

indict [in'dait] v. tr. JUR. Poursuivre (*as*, comme); accuser (*for*, de); *to indict sth. as false*, s'inscrire en faux contre qqch.

indictable [-əbl] adj. JUR. Tombant sous le coup de la loi (act); passible de poursuites (person).

indictment [-mənt] n. JUR. Inculpation *f.* (for, de); mise en accusation *f.* (for, pour); *bill of indictment*, acte d'accusation.

Indies ['indiz] n. pl. GEOGR. Indes *f. pl.; Dutch East Indies*, Indes néerlandaises; *East Indies*, Indes; *West Indies*, Antilles.

Indifference [in'difrəns] n. Indifférence *f.;* manque d'intérêt *m.* (to, pour). ‖ Peu (*m.*) d'importance; *matter of indifference*, fait sans importance, quantité négligeable. ‖ † Neutralité *f.*

Indifferent [-ənt] adj. Indifférent (*to*, à). ‖ Peu important, négligeable (to, pour); *it's indifferent to me*, cela m'importe peu. ‖ Médiocre, moyen, passable (average); *very indifferent*, pas fameux. ‖ † Neutre, impartial. ‖ CHIM. Neutre.
— n. Indifférent *s.*

indifferentism [-əntizm] n. Indifférentisme *m.*

indifferently [-əntli] adv. Avec indifférence, indifféremment. ‖ Passablement, médiocrement.

indigence ['indidʒəns] n. Indigence *f.* (See POVERTY.)

indigene ['indidʒi:n] n. Indigène *s.*

indigenous [in'didʒinəs] adj. Indigène.

indigent ['indidʒənt] adj. Indigent. (See POOR.)

indigested [,indi'dʒestid] adj. MED. Non digéré. ‖ FIG. Mal digéré, non assimilé (knowledge); mal composé, confus (text).

indigestibility ['indi,dʒesti'biliti] n. MED. Indigestibilité *f.*

indigestible [,indi'dʒestibl] adj. MED., FIG. Indigeste.

indigestion [-ʃən] n. MED. Digestion difficile *f.; attack of indigestion*, indigestion. ‖ FIG. Manque (*m.*) d'assimilation.

indign [in'dain] adj. † Indigne.

indignant [in'dignənt] adj. Indigné (*at*, à; *with*, contre).

indignantly [-li] adv. Avec indignation.

indignation [,indig'neiʃən] n. Indignation *f.* (at, à, devant); *indignation meeting*, réunion de protestation.

indignity [in'digniti] n. Affront *m.*; insulte *f.* ‖ † Indignité *f.* (state).

indigo ['indigou] n. Indigo *m.* ‖ **Indigo-plant**, n. BOT. Indigotier *m.*

indirect [,indi'rekt] adj. GRAMM., JUR., MILIT., FIG. Indirect.

indirectly [-li] adv. Indirectement.

indiscernible [,indi'sə:nibl] adj., n. Indiscernable *m.*

indiscipline [in'disiplin] n. Indiscipline *f.*

indiscreet [,indis'kri:t] adj. Peu sage, imprudent. ‖ Indiscret.

indiscreetly [-li] adv. Imprudemment. ‖ Indiscrètement.

indiscretion [,indis'kreʃən] n. Imprudence, inconséquence. *f.* ‖ Manque (*m.*) de retenue; *indiscretion of youth*, péché de jeunesse; *passing indiscretion*, écart de conduite passager. ‖ Indiscrétion *f.; calculated indiscretion*, indiscrétion voulue.

indiscriminate [,indis'kriminit] adj. Sans discrimination, aveugle; fait au hasard.

indiscriminately [-li] adv. Sans discrimination, au hasard, à l'aveuglette.

indiscrimination ['indis,krimi'neiʃən] n. Manque (*m.*) de discrimination (or) de discernement.

indispensable [,indis'pensəbl] adj. Indispensable (essential). ‖ Obligatoire, inéluctable (inevitable).

indispensably [-bli] adv. Indispensablement.

indispose [,indis'pouz] v. tr. Rendre incapable (*for, to*, de). ‖ Indisposer, prévenir (*towards*, contre). ‖ Détourner (*from*, de). ‖ MED. Indisposer.

indisposition [,indispə'ziʃən] n. Indisposition *f.* (*towards, to*, contre, envers); éloignement *m.*; répugnance *f.* (*to, towards*, pour). ‖ MED. Indisposition *f.*

indisputability ['indis,pju:tə'biliti] n. Incontestabilité *f.; caractère indiscutable *m.*

indisputable [indis'pju:təbl] adj. Incontestable, indiscutable. (See UNQUESTIONABLE.)

indisputably [-bli] adv. Incontestablement.

indissolubility ['indi,sɔlju'biliti] n. JUR., FIG. Indissolubilité *f.* ‖ CHIM. Insolubilité *f.*

indissoluble [,indi'sɔljub] adj. JUR., FIG. Indissoluble. ‖ CHIM. Insoluble.

indissolubly [-bli] adv. JUR., FIG. Indissolublement. ‖ CHIM. Insolublement.

indistinct [,indis'tiŋkt] adj. Indistinct.

indistinctive [,indis'tiŋktiv] adj. Non distinctif, peu caractéristique.

indistinctly [-'tiŋktli] adv. Indistinctement.

indistinctness [-nis] n. Indistinction; imprécision *f.*

indistinguishable [,indis'tiŋgwiʃəbl]] adj. Indistinguible, indiscernable, imperceptible.

indite [in'dait] v. tr. Composer (verse). ‖ Rédiger (a letter, a text).

inditement [-mənt] n. Composition, rédaction *f.*

inditer [-ə*] n. Compositeur, rédacteur *m.*

individual [,indi'vidjuəl] adj. Individuel (in general). ‖ Séparé, particulier; *individual sound*, son isolé. ‖ Personnel, original, caractéristique (style). — n. Individu *m.; private individual*, simple particulier. ‖ JUR. Personne physique *f.*

individualism [-izm] n. Individualisme *m.*

individualist [-ist] n. Individualiste *m.*

individualistic [,indi,vidjuə'listik] adj. Individualiste.

individuality [,indi,vidju'æliti] n. Individualité *f.*

individualization [,indi,vidjuəlai'zeiʃən], **individuation** [,indi,vidju'eiʃən] n. Individualisation *f.*

individualize [,indi'vidjuəlaiz], **individuate** [-eit] v. tr. Individualiser.

individually [-əli] adv. Individuellement. ‖ Personnellement; *he is speaking individually*, il parle pour lui.

indivisibility ['indi,vizi'biliti] n. Indivisibilité *f.*

indivisible [,indi'vizibl] adj. Indivisible. — n. MATH., PHILOS. Insécable *m.*

indivisum [-vaizəm] n. JUR. Bien indivis *m.*

Indo-China ['indou'tʃainə] n. GEOGR. Indochine *f.*

Indo-Chinese ['indoutʃai'ni:z] adj., n. GEOGR. Indochinois *s.*

indocile [in'dousail] adj. Indocile.

indocility [,indo'siliti] n. Indocilité *f.*

indoctrinate [in'dɔktrineit] v. tr. Endoctriner.

indoctrination [,indɔktri'neiʃən] n. Endoctrinement *m.*

indoctrinator [in'dɔktrineitə*] n. Endoctrineur *s.*

Indo-European ['indou,juərə'piən] adj., n. Indo-européen *s.*

Indo-Germanic [-,dʒə:'mænik] adj., n. Indo-germanique *s.*

indolence ['indələns] n. Indolence *f.*

indolent [-ənt] adj. Indolent.

indolently [-əntli] adv. Indolemment.

indomitable [in'dɔmitəbl] adj. Indomptable.

indomitably [-bli] adv. Indomptablement.

Indonesia [,indo'ni:ziə] n. GEOGR. Indonésie *f.*

Indonesian [-ən] adj., n. GEOGR. Indonésien *s.*

indoor ['indɔ:*] adj. D'intérieur (dress); de société (game); d'appartement (plant); en appartement (photography, work). ‖ MED. Hospitalisé (person); par hospitalisation (relief).

indoors ['in'dɔ:z] adv. A l'intérieur, à la maison; *indoors and outdoors*, chez soi et au-dehors. ‖ A l'abri (under cover).

indorse [in'dɔ:s] v. tr. JUR. Souscrire à, approuver. ‖ FIN. U. S. Endosser. ‖ See ENDORSE.

indraught, U. S. **indraft** ['indrɑ:ft] n. Appel d'air *m.* ‖ Courant remontant, influx *m.* (flow).

indubitable [in'dju:bitəbl] adj. Indubitable.

indubitably [-bli] adv. Indubitablement. (See DOUBTLESS.)

induce [in'dju:s] v. tr. † Déduire, induire (to infer). ‖ Engager, inciter, amener, pousser, décider (*to*, à). [See PERSUADE.] ‖ Provoquer, causer, occasionner, susciter (to effect). ‖ ELECTR. Induire. ‖ MED. Provoquer (hypnosis).

inducement [-mənt] n. Encouragement *m.; incitation *f.* (*to*, à). ‖ Pl. Attraits *m. pl.; séductions *f. pl.* ‖ JUR. Cause déterminante *f.* (of a contract); mobile *m.* (of a crime).

inducer [-ə*] n. Provocateur *m.; provocatrice *f.*

induct [in'dʌkt] v. tr. Initier (*to*, à). ‖ JUR., ECCLES. Installer. ‖ MILIT. Incorporer.

inductance [-əns] n. ELECTR. Inductance *f.; aerial inductance*, self d'antenne.

inductee [indʌk'ti:] n. NAUT. Marine *inductee*, apprenti marin. ‖ MILIT. Incorporé *m.*

inductile [in'dʌktail] adj. TECHN. Inductile. ‖ FIG. Intraitable.

induction [-ʃən] n. Enumération *m.* (of facts). ‖ JUR., ECCLES. Installation *f.* ‖ MILIT. Incorporation *f.* ‖ TECHN. Admission *f.* ‖ PHILOS., ELECTR. Induction *f.* ‖ **Induction-coil**, n. ELECTR. Bobine (*f.*) de self. ‖ **Induction-pipe**, n. TECHN. Tuyau (*m.*) d'admission.

inductive [-tiv] adj. PHILOS. Inductif. ‖ JUR. Incitateur; qui induit (*to*, à). ‖ ELECTR. Inducteur. ‖ MED. Rénovant.

inductively [-tivli] adv. PHILOS., ELECTR. Par induction.

inductor [-tə*] n. ECCLES., JUR. Installateur *m.* ‖ ELECTR. Rotor, inducteur *m.*

indue [in'dju:] v. tr. See ENDUE.

indulge [in'dʌldʒ] v. tr. S'adonner, se livrer, donner libre cours, céder (*to*, à); *to indulge oneself in*, s'abandonner à. ‖ Se prêter à (see HUMOUR); *to indulge oneself*, se passer tous ses caprices, se mignoter, s'écouter; *to indulge s.o.'s fancy*, passer une fantaisie à qqn. ‖ COMM. Donner des délais de paiement à. — v. intr. Se permettre (*in*, de); *to indulge in a day-dream*, s'oublier à rêver; *to indulge in late rising*, se payer le luxe de faire la grasse matinée. ‖ FAM. *To indulge in drink*, siroter, picoler; *will you indulge?*, une petite goutte?

indulgence [-əns] n. Indulgence, clémence *f.* ‖ Complaisance *f.; esprit (*m.*) de conciliation; *with indulgence*, en douceur. ‖ Faveur *f.; to grant one's son every indulgence*, tout passer à son fils. ‖ Complaisance (*f.*) envers soi-même. ‖ Satisfaction *f.; assouvissement *m.* (*in*, de). ‖ Pl. Douceurs *f. pl.* ‖ ECCLES. Indulgence *m.* ‖ COMM. Délai de paiement *m.* — v. tr. ECCLES. Indulgencier.

indulgent [-ənt] adj. Indulgent, clément. ‖ Complaisant, patient, accommodant, faible.

indulgently [-əntli] adv. Avec indulgence, indulgemment.

induline ['indjulain] n. CHIM. Induline *f.*

indult [in'dʌlt] n. ECCLES. Indult *m.*

indurate ['indjuəreit] v. tr. Durcir. ‖ MED. Indurer. ‖ FIG. Endurcir. — v. intr. Durcir, se durcir. ‖ MED. S'indurer. ‖ FIG. S'endurcir.

induration [,indjuə'reiʃən] n. Durcissement *m.* ‖ MED. Induration *f.* ‖ FIG. Endurcissement *m.*

industrial [in'dʌstriəl] adj. Industriel, de l'industrie; *industrial estate* (or U. S.) *park*, zone industrielle (Z. I.). ‖ Du travail (accident, dispute); *industrial relations*, relations salariat-patronat. ‖ MED. Professionnel (disease). ‖ JUR. *Industrial school*, école professionnelle de rééducation.

industrialism [-izm] n. Industrialisme *m.*

industrialist [-ist] n. Industriel *m.*

industrialization [in,dʌstriəlai'zeiʃən] n. Industrialisation *f.*

industrialize [in'dʌstriəlaiz] v. tr. Industrialiser.

industrially [-əli] adv. Industriellement.

industrious [-əs] adj. Travailleur, laborieux, diligent (hard-working). ‖ Industrieux (clever).

industriously [-əsli] adv. Laborieusement (diligently). ‖ Industrieusement (cleverly).

industry ['indʌstri] n. Travail, labeur, effort constant *m.* (work). ‖ TECHN. Industrie *f.; paper industry*, industrie du papier, papeterie.

indwell [in'dwel] v. tr. intr. (52). Habiter.

indweller [-ə*] n. Habitant *s.*

inearth [in'ə:θ] v. tr. Enterrer.
inebriant [in'i:briənt] adj. Enivrant.
inebriate [-it] adj. Enivré, ivre. (See DRUNK.)
— n. Ivrogne *s.* (See DRUNKARD.)
— [-eit] v. tr. Enivrer.
inebriation [,ini:bri'eiʃən] n. Enivrement *m.* (act); ébriété, ivresse *f.* (result).
inebriety [,ini:'braiəti] n. Ivrognerie *f.* (habit); ébriété *f.* (state).
inedible [i'nedibl̩] adj. Immangeable (not eatable); non comestible (not fit to be eaten).
inedited [i'neditid] adj. Inédit (not edited). ‖ Publié sans retouches ni notes (in facsimile).
ineffability [,inəfə'biliti] n. Ineffabilité *f.*
ineffable [i'nefəbl̩] adj. Ineffable.
ineffably [-bli] adv. Ineffablement.
ineffaceable [,ini'feisəbl̩] adj. Ineffaçable.
ineffective [,ini'fektiv] adj. Inefficace, ineffectif (act); incapable, inefficient (person). ‖ ARTS. Sans effets, plat, terne.
ineffectual [-tjuəl] adj. Ineffectif, inefficace, sans effet (act); incapable (person).
inefficacious [,inefi'keiʃəs] adj. MED. Inefficace.
inefficacy [in'efikəsi] n. Inefficacité *f.*
inefficiency [,ini'fiʃənsi] n. Inefficacité *f.* (of an act); inefficience, incapacité *f.* (of a person).
inefficient [-ənt] adj. Inefficace (act); inefficient, incapable (person).
— n. pl. Incapables *m. pl.*
inefficiently [-əntli] adv. Inefficacement.
inelastic [,ini'læstik] adj. Inélastique. ‖ FIG. Sans élasticité (or) souplesse, rigide.
inelasticity [,inilæs'tisiti] n. Inélasticité *f.* ‖ FIG. Manque (*m.*) d'élasticité (or) de souplesse.
inelegance [-i'neligəns] n. Inélégance *f.*
inelegant [-ənt] adj. Inélégant.
ineligibility [i,nelidʒi'biliti] n. Manque (*m.*) d'attrait (or) de convenance (of a job, a house). ‖ Défaut (*m.*) de qualification; insuffisance *f.* (of a person). ‖ JUR. Non-admissibilité *f.* (of an applicant); inéligibilité *f.* (of a candidate). ‖ MILIT. Incapacité (*f.*) au service militaire.
ineligible [i'nelidʒibl̩] adj. Dépourvu d'attraits, ne convenant pas; inacceptable (job, house). ‖ JUR. Inéligible. ‖ MILIT. Impropre au service militaire.
ineluctability [,inelʌktə'biliti] n. Inéluctabilité *f.*
ineluctable [,ini'lʌktəbl̩] adj. Inéluctable.
ineluctably [-bli] adv. Inéluctablement.
inept [i'nept] adj. Inapproprié, peu à propos (inapt). ‖ Inepte, absurde (stupid). ‖ U. S. Gauche, gaffeur, balourd (awkward). ‖ JUR. Vain, sans effet.
ineptitude [-itju:d] n. Défaut d'à-propos *m.* (unfitness). ‖ Ineptie *f.* (act, quality).
inequality [,ini:'kwɔliti] n. Inégalité *f.*
inequitable [i'nekwitəbl̩] adj. Non équitable, injuste, inéquitable.
inequity [-ti] n. Iniquité *f.*
ineradicable [,ini'rædikəbl̩] adj. Indéracinable. (See INEXTIRPABLE.)
inerrability [,inerə'biliti] n. Infaillibilité *f.*
inerrable [i'nerəbl̩] adj. Infaillible.
inert [i'nə:t] adj. PHYS., CHIM., MED., FIG. Inerte.
inertia [i'nə:ʃiə] n. PHYS., ELECTR., FIG. Inertie *f.*
inertness [i'nə:tnis] n. CHIM., FIG. Inertie.
inescapable [,inəs'keipəbl̩] adj. Inévitable.
inessential [,ini'senʃəl] adj. Non essentiel.
inestimable [i'nestiməbl̩] adj. Inestimable.
inestimably [-bli] adv. Inestimablement.
inevitability [i,nevitə'biliti] n. Inévitabilité *f.*
inevitable [i'nevitəbl̩] n. Inévitable.
inevitably [-bli] adv. Inévitablement.
inexact [,inig'zækt] adj. Inexact.
inexactitude [-itju:d] n. Inexactitude *f.*
inexactly [-li] adv. Inexactement.
inexcusability [,inekju:zə'biliti] n. Caractère inexcusable *m.*

inexcusable [,iniks'kju:zəbl̩] adj. Inexcusable.
inexecutable [,inik'sekjutəbl̩] adj. Inexécutable.
inexecution [,iniksə'kjuʃən] n. Inexécution *f.*
inexhaustibility [,inigzɔ:sti'biliti] n. Caractère inépuisable *m.*
inexhaustible [,inig'zɔ:stibl̩] adj. Inépuisable.
inexorability [,ineksɔrə'biliti] n. Inexorabilité *f.*
inexorable [i'neksɔrəbl̩] adj. Inexorable.
inexpediency [,iniks'pi:diənsi] n. Inopportunité *f.*
inexpedient [-ənt] adj. Inopportun, peu expédient.
inexpensive [,iniks'pensiv] adj. Bon marché, pas cher, peu coûteux (or) onéreux.
inexpensively [-li] adv. A bon marché, pas cher, sans grands frais, à peu de frais.
inexperience [,iniks'piəriəns] n. Inexpérience *f.*
inexperienced [-t] adj. Inexpérimenté.
inexpert [,ineks'pə:t] adj. Inexpert (in, à).
inexpiable [i'nekspiəbl̩] adj. Inexpiable. ‖ † Implacable.
inexpiably [-bli] adv. Inexpiablement.
inexplainable [iniks'pleinəbl̩], **inexplicable** [i'neksplikəbl̩] adj. Inexplicable.
inexplicably [-bli] adv. Inexplicablement.
inexplosive [,iniks'plousiv] adj. Inexplosible.
inexpressibility [,inikspresi'biliti] n. Caractère inexprimable *m.*
inexpressible [,iniks'presibl̩] adj. Inexprimable. (See INEFFABLE.)
— n. pl. FAM. Falzard *m.* (trousers).
inexpressibly [-ibli] adv. Inexprimablement.
inexpressive [-iv] adj. Inexpressif.
inexpugnable [,iniks'pʌgnəbl̩] adj. Inexpugnable.
inextensible [,iniks'tensibl̩] adj. Inextensible.
inextinguishable [,iniks'tiŋgwiʃəbl̩] adj. Inextinguible.
inextirpable [iniks'tə:pəbl̩] adj. Inextirpable. (See INERADICABLE.)
inextricability [in,ekstrikə'biliti] n. Inextricabilité *f.*
inextricable [i'nekstrikəbl̩] adj. Inextricable.
inextricably [-bli] adv. Inextricablement.
infallibility [in,fæli'biliti] n. Infaillibilité *f.*
infallible [in'fælibl̩] adj. Infaillible. (See INERRABLE.)
infallibly [-bli] adv. Infailliblement.
infamous ['infəməs] adj. Mal famé (place); infâme (person). ‖ JUR. Noté d'infamie (person); infamant (punishment).
infamously [-li] adv. Abominablement, de façon infâme.
infamy ['infəmi] n. Infamie *f.*
infancy ['infənsi] n. Petite enfance *f.* (see BABYHOOD); *still in infancy,* encore au berceau. ‖ JUR. Minorité *f.* ‖ FIG. Enfance, aurore *f.*; débuts *m. pl.*
infant [-ənt] n. Bébé, nourrisson *m.* (baby); petit enfant, enfant en bas âge *m.* (before seven); *infant death-rate,* mortalité infantile; *infant school,* école maternelle. ‖ JUR. Mineur *s.*
— adj. FIG. Débutant, naissant, en enfance.
infanta [in'fæntə] n. Infante *f.*
infante [-ti] n. Infant *m.*
infanticide [-tisaid] n. JUR. Infanticide *m.* (act, person).
infantile ['infəntail] adj. D'enfant, enfantin (childish). ‖ MED. Infantile (paralysis, state).
infantilism [in'fæntilizm] n. MED. Infantilisme *m.*
infantine ['infəntin] adj. Enfantin.
infantry ['infəntri] n. MILIT. Infanterie *f.*
infantryman [-mən] (pl. **infantrymen**) n. MILIT. Fantassin *m.*
infarct [in'fɑ:kt] n. MED. Infarctus *m.*
infatuate [in'fætjueit] v. tr. Affoler, rendre fou (to make foolish). ‖ Embéguiner, enticher (with, de); *to become infatuated with,* s'infatuer de, se toquer de.

Infatuation [in,fætju'ei∫ən] n. Folie *f.* || Toquade *f.; béguin m.*

Infeasible [in'fi:zibl] adj. Infaisable.

Infect [in'fekt] v. tr. MED. Contaminer; *to infect with a disease,* communiquer une maladie à. || JUR. Entacher. || FIG. Infecter, corrompre, vicier. || FAM. Imprégner, pénétrer (*with,* de); *to infect s.o. with sth.,* communiquer qqch. à qqn.

Infection [-∫ən] n. MED., FIG. Infection, contagion, contamination *f.*

Infectious [-∫əs] adj. Infect. || MED. Infectieux (disease). || FIG. Contagieux.

Infectiousness [-∫əsnis] n. MED. Nature infectieuse *f.* || FIG. Contagion *f.*

Infective [in'fektiv] adj. MED. Infectieux (germ). || FIG. Contagieux.

Infelicitous [,infi'lisitəs] adj. Malheureux.

Infelicity [-ti] n. Malheur *m.* (misfortune). || Parole malheureuse, gaffe *f.* (blunder).

Infer [in'fə:*] v. tr. (1). † Impliquer, indiquer (to imply). || Inférer, déduire, conclure. (See DEDUCE.)

Inferable [-rəbl] adj. Déductible.

Inference ['infərəns] n. Inférence, déduction, conclusion *f.; corollaire m.; by inference,* implicitement, par induction.

Inferential [,infə'ren∫əl] adj. Obtenu par déduction; déductif (proof).

Inferior [in'fiəriə*] adj. Inférieur (*to,* à). || BOT. Infère.
— n. Inférieur *s.*

Inferiority [in,fiəri'ɔriti] n. Infériorité *f.* || MED. *Inferiority complex,* complexe d'infériorité.

Infernal [in'fə:nl] adj. FIG., TECHN., FAM. Infernal.

Infernally [-əli] adv. Infernalement.

Inferno [-ou] n. Enfer. (See HELL.)

Infertile [in'fə:tail] adj. Clair (egg). || AGRIC. Stérile, infertile. || FIG. Stérile.

Infertility [,infə:'tiliti] n. AGRIC. Infertilité *f.* || FIG. Stérilité *f.*

Infest [in'fest] v. tr. Infester (*with,* de).

Infestation [,infes'tei∫ən] n. Infestation *f.*

Infidel ['infidəl] adj., n. ECCLES. Infidèle *s.*

Infidelity [,infi'deliti] n. ECCLES. Incroyance *f.* || JUR. Infidélité *f.* (of husband, wife). || FIG. Déloyauté *f.*

Infield ['infi:ld] n. AGRIC. Enclos cultivé *m.* || SPORTS. Terrain (*m.*) près des guichets.

Infiltrate [in'filtreit] v. tr. Infiltrer (*into,* dans). || Pénétrer, imprégner, imbiber (*with,* de). || JUR. Noyauter (in politics). || MILIT. Faire pénétrer (troops).
— v. intr. S'infiltrer.

Infiltration [,infil'trei∫ən] n. Infiltration *f.* || JUR. Noyautage *m.*

Infinite ['infinit] adj. MATH., FIG. Infini. || GRAMM. Impersonnel.
— n. Infini *m.*

Infinitely [-li] adv. Infiniment.

Infinitesimal [,infini'tesiməl] adj. MATH., FIG. Infinitésimal.
— n. MATH. Infinitésime *f.*

Infinitive [in'finitiv] adj., n. GRAMM. Infinitif *m.*

Infinitude [-tju:d] n. Infinité *f.*

Infinity [-ti] n. Infinité *f.; to infinity,* à l'infini. || MATH. Infini *m.*

Infirm [in'fə:m] adj. MED. Débile, faible. || JUR. Invalide (document). || FIG. Chancelant; *infirm of purpose,* irrésolu.
— v. tr. JUR. Infirmer.

Infirmary [-əri] n. Infirmerie *f.* (in a school). || MED. Hôpital *m.*

Infirmity [-iti] n. MED. Débilité, faiblesse; pl. infirmités *f. pl.* || FIG. Faiblesse, déficience *f.*

Infix [in'fiks] v. tr. Fixer, insérer (*in,* dans). || GRAMM. Infixer. || FIG. Implanter, inculquer, imprimer (*in,* dans).
— ['infiks] n. GRAMM. Infixe *m.*

Inflame [in'fleim] v. tr. Enflammer, mettre le feu à. || MED. Enflammer. || FIG. Allumer (anger); enflammer (courage); attiser (discord).
— v. intr. S'enflammer, s'embraser, prendre feu. || MED. S'enflammer. || FIG. S'allumer, s'échauffer.

Inflammability [in,flæmə'biliti] n. Inflammabilité *f.*

Inflammable [in'flæməbl] adj. Inflammable.
— n. Matière inflammable *f.*

Inflammation [,inflə'mei∫ən] n. Inflammation *f.;* embrasement *m.* || MED. Inflammation *f.* || FIG. Echauffement, feu *m.*

Inflammatory [in'flæmətəri] adj. MED. Inflammatoire. || FIG. Incendiaire.

Inflatable [in'fleitəbl] adj. Gonflable.

Inflate [in'fleit] v. tr. Gonfler (*with,* de). || FIN. Enfler, grossir (prices); *to inflate the currency,* avoir recours à l'inflation. || AUTOM. Gonfler (a tyre). || FIG. Gonfler (*with,* de).

Inflator [-ə*] n. Pompe à bicyclette *f.* || AUTOM. Gonfleur *m.*

Inflation [in'flei∫ən] n. Gonflement *m.* || FIN. Inflation *f.* || FIG. Bouffissure *f.* (with pride); boursouflure *f.* (of style).

Inflect [in'flekt] v. tr. Infléchir. || MUS. Altérer (a note). || GRAMM. Décliner (or) conjuguer.

Inflection [in'flek∫ən] n. See INFLEXION.

Inflective [-tiv] adj. GRAMM. Flexionnel.

Inflexibility [in,fleksi'biliti] n. Inflexibilité *f.*

Inflexible [in'fleksibl] adj. Inflexible.

Inflexibly [-bli] adv. Inflexiblement.

Inflexion [in'flek∫ən] n. GRAMM., MATH., PHYS., TECHN. Inflexion *f.*

Inflexional [-l] adj. GRAMM. A flexion; flexionnel.

Inflict [in'flikt] v. tr. Infliger (a punishment); occasionner (suffering) [*on,* à]. || FAM. *To inflict oneself on,* imposer (or) infliger sa présence à.

Infliction [-∫ən] n. Infliction *f.* (act); châtiment *m.* (punishment). || FAM. Calamité *f.*

Inflorescence [,inflo'resns] n. BOT. Inflorescence *f.* (act); floraison *f.* (result).

Inflow ['inflou] n. Afflux *m.* (See INFLUX.) || FIG. Courant (*m.*) d'immigration.

Influence ['influəns] n. ELECTR. Induction *f.* || FIG. Influence *f.* (*on,* sur [an action, s.o.]; *with,* sur, auprès de [a person]).
— v. tr. Influencer (s.o.); influer sur (sth.).

Influent [-ənt] adj. Qui afflue.
— n. Affluent *m.*

Influential [,influ'en∫əl] adj. Influent.

Influenza [,influ'enzə] n. MED. Grippe *f.;* influenza *m.*

Influenzal [-əl] adj. MED. Grippal.

Influx ['inflʌks] n. Affluence *f.* (of people); afflux *m.* (of water). || Point (*m.*) d'affluence. (See CONFLUENT.) || FIG. Afflux, fort courant *m.* (of ideas).

Inform [in'fɔ:m] v. tr. † Former, façonner (to shape). || Informer, avertir (*of,* de); renseigner (*on,* sur); *to keep oneself informed,* se tenir au courant. || FIG. Animer (*with,* de).
— v. intr. JUR. *To inform against,* dénoncer.

Informal [-l] adj. Sans formalisme (or) cérémonie (dinner). || Non officiel, officieux, privé (step); *to hold an informal meeting,* se réunir en petit comité. || JUR. Hors des formes légales, irrégulier (document).

Informality [,infɔ:'mæliti] n. Absence (*f.*) de formalisme; caractère intime *m.* || JUR. Vice (*m.*) de forme.

Informally [in'fɔ:məli] adv. Sans formalisme, en toute simplicité. || Officieusement. || JUR. Irrégulièrement.

Informant [-ənt] n. Informateur *m.;* informatrice *f.*

Information [,infə'mei∫ən] n. Information *f.; for your information,* à titre d'information. || Rensei-

gnement *m.; Information bureau,* bureau de renseignements. ‖ Instruction *f.;* connaissances *f. pl.* (knowledge). ‖ Jur. Dénonciation *f.* (charge); plainte *f.* (complaint). ‖ U. S. Employé du bureau de renseignements *m.* (person).
informative [in'fɔ:mətiv] adj. Instructif, formateur.
informed [-d] adj. Sans formation. ‖ Au courant, renseigné.
informer [-ə*] n. Délateur, dénonciateur *m.;* délatrice, dénonciatrice *f.* ‖ Jur. Indicateur (*m.*) de police.
infra ['infrə] pref. Infra; *infra dig,* indigne de soi, déshonorant. ‖ **Infra-red,** adj. Phys. Infrarouge.
infraction [in'frækʃən] n. Infraction *f.*
infrangible [in'frændʒibl̩] adj. Infrangible.
infrasonic [,infrə'sɔnik] adj. Phys. Infrasonore.
infrastructure ['infræ'strʌktʃə*] n. Infrastructure *f.*
infrequency [in'fri:kwənsi] n. Rareté *f.*
infrequent [-ənt] adj. Peu fréquent.
infringe [in'frindʒ] v. tr. Enfreindre (a law); contrefaire (a patent).
— v. intr. Empiéter (*upon,* sur).
infringement [-mənt] n. Infraction *f.* (*of,* à) [a law]; contrefaçon *f.* (of a patent).
infuriate [in'fjuərieit] v. tr. Rendre furieux, mettre en fureur.
infuse [in'fju:z] v. tr. Infuser (*into,* dans). ‖ Culin. Faire infuser (tea). ‖ Fig. Infuser, insuffler (*into,* dans). [See Instill.]
infusible [-ibl̩] adj. Infusible.
infusion [in'fju:ʒən] n. Med., Eccles. Infusion *f.*
infusoria [,infju:'sɔ:riə] n. pl. Infusoires *m. pl.*
ingathering ['in,gæðəriŋ] n. Récolte *f.*
ingeminate [in'dʒemineit] v. tr. Réitérer.
ingenious [in'dʒi:njəs] adj. Ingénieux (clever).
ingeniously [-li] adv. Ingénieusement.
ingenue [,ɛ̃ʒei'nju:] n. Theatr. Ingénue *f.*
ingenuity [,indʒi'nju:iti] n. † Ingénuité *f.* ‖ Ingéniosité *f.* (cleverness).
ingenuous [in'dʒenjuəs] adj. Ingénu, naïf, simple (naive). ‖ Sincère, franc, ouvert (candid).
ingenuousness [-nis] n. Ingénuité, naïveté, simplicité. ‖ Sincérité, franchise, spontanéité *f.*
ingerence [in'dʒerəns] *n.* Ingérence, intrusion *f.*
ingest [in'dʒest] v. tr. Med. Ingérer.
ingestion [-ʃən] n. Med. Ingestion *f.*
ingle ['ingl̩] n. Feu d'âtre *m.* ‖ **Ingle-nook,** n. Coin du feu *m.*
inglorious [in'glɔ:riəs] adj. Obscur, sans gloire (not famous). ‖ Peu glorieux, déshonorant, honteux (disgraceful).
ingoing ['ingouiŋ] adj. Entrant.
— n. Entrée *f.*
ingot ['iŋgət] n. Fin. Lingot *m.*
ingrain [in'grein]. See Engrain.
ingrained [-d] adj. Imprégné (*with,* de). ‖ Fig. Invétéré (habit); incrusté, enraciné (*in,* dans).
ingratiate [in'greiʃieit] v. tr. *To ingratiate oneself with,* se faire bien voir de, se concilier les bonnes grâces de; se mettre dans les petits papiers de (fam.).
ingratiating [-iŋ] adj. Insinuant, patelin.
ingratitude ['ingrætitju:d] n. Ingratitude *f.*
ingravescent [,ingrə'vesn̩t] adj. Med. Qui s'aggrave.
ingredient [in'gri:diənt] n. Ingrédient *m.* (See Element.)
ingress ['ingres] n. Entrée *f.* (ingoing). ‖ Droit d'accès *m.* (entrance).
ingrowing ['in,grouiŋ] adj. Med. Qui pousse en dedans (hair); incarné (nail).
ingrown ['ingroun] adj. Med. Incarné (nail). ‖ Fig. Invétéré (habit).
inguinal ['iŋgwinl̩] adj. Med. Inguinal.

ingurgitate [in'gə:dʒiteit] v. tr. Med., Fam. Ingurgiter.
ingurgitation [in,gə:dʒi'teiʃən] n. Ingurgitation *f.*
inhabit [in'hæbit] v. tr. Habiter. (See Dwell.)
inhabitable [-əbl̩] adj. Habitable.
inhabitancy [-ənsi] n. Jur. Domicile *m.* (dwelling); durée de résidence *f.* (period).
inhabitant [-ənt] n. Habitant *s.*
inhabitation [in,hæbi'teiʃən] n. Habitation *f.*
inhabited [in'hæbitid] adj. Habité.
inhalant [in'heilənt] n. Med. Inhalateur *m.* (apparatus); inhalation *f.* (medicine).
inhalation [,inhə'leiʃən] n. Med. Inhalation *f.* (act, medicine).
inhale [in'heil] v. tr. Med. Inhaler. ‖ Fam. Aspirer, respirer (a perfume); avaler (tobacco smoke).
— v. intr. Fam. Avaler la fumée.
inhaler [-ə*] n. Med. Inhalateur *m.*
inharmonic [,inhɑ:'mɔnik] adj. Inharmonique.
inharmonious [,inhɑ:'mounjəs] adj. Inharmonieux, sans harmonie.
inharmoniousness [-nis] n. Défaut (*m.*) d'harmonie; discordance *f.*
inhere [in'hiə*] v. intr. Etre inhérent (*in,* à). ‖ Jur. Appartenir en propre, revenir (*in,* à).
inherence [in'hiərəns] n. Inhérence *f.*
inherent [-ənt] adj. Inhérent (*in, to,* à). ‖ Jur. Propre.
inherently [-əntli] adv. Par inhérence; fondamentalement. ‖ Jur. En propre.
inherit [in'herit] v. tr. Jur. Hériter de (a fortune, a title); *to inherit a fortune from s.o.,* hériter une fortune de qqn.
— v. intr. Hériter (*from,* de) [s.o.].
inheritability [in,herita'biliti] n. Jur. Aptitude (*f.*) à hériter (of s.o.); transmissibilité *f.* (of a title).
inheritable [in'heritəbl̩] adj. Jur. Transmissible, dont on peut hériter (fortune, title); apte à hériter (person).
inheritance [-əns] n. Jur. Héritage *m.;* hoirie *f.; to come into an inheritance,* faire un héritage. ‖ Jur. Succession *f.* ‖ Med. Séquelle d'hérédité *f.* ‖ Fig. Héritage *m.*
inheritor [-ə*] n. Jur. Héritier *m.* (See Heir.)
inheritress [-tris] n. Jur. Héritière *f.* (See Heiress.)
inhesion [in'hi:ʒən] v. tr. Inhérence *f.*
inhibit [in'hibit] v. tr. Interdire (to prohibit). ‖ Retenir, paralyser (s.o). ‖ Med. Inhiber. ‖ Eccles. Interdire (a priest).
inhibition [-ʃən] n. Interdiction *f.* ‖ Med. Inhibition *f.* ‖ Eccles. Interdit *m.*
inhibitory [-təri] adj. Jur. Inhibitoire. ‖ Med., Philos. Inhibiteur.
inhospitable [in'hɔspitəbl̩] adj. Inhospitalier.
inhospitality [in,hɔspi'tæliti] n. Inhospitalité *f.*
inhuman [in'hju:mən] adj. Inhumain.
inhumane [,inhju:'mein] adj. Inhumain, cruel.
inhumanity [,inhju:'mæniti] n. Inhumanité *f.*
inhumanly [in'hju:mənli] adv. Inhumainement.
inhumation [,inhju:'meiʃən] n. Inhumation *f.*
inhume [in'hju:m] v. tr. Inhumer.
inimical [i'nimikəl] adj. Inamical, hostile (unfriendly). ‖ Défavorable; hostile, contraire (adverse).
inimically [-əli] adv. De manière hostile.
inimitable [i'nimitəbl̩] adj. Inimitable.
inimitably [-bli] adv. Inimitablement.
iniquitous [i'nikwitəs] adj. Inique; *iniquitous deed,* iniquité.
iniquity [-ti] n. Iniquité *f.*
initial [i'niʃəl] adj. Initial, du début. ‖ Fig. D'apport (capital); d'installation (expenses).
— n. Initiale *f.* (letter). ‖ Pl. Monogramme *m.* (on garment).
— v. tr. (1). Marquer d'une initiale (garments). ‖

Jur. Emarger (an account); parafer, viser (a document).

initially [-i] adv. Initialement *m*.

initiate [i'niʃieit] v. tr. Inaugurer, instaurer, introduire, mettre en action, lancer (to introduce). ‖ Initier (*in*, à) [a science]. ‖ Admettre (*into*, dans) [a secret society]. ‖ Electr. Amorcer (an arc).
— [-it] adj., n. Initié *s*.

initiation [i,niʃi'eiʃən] n. Inauguration *f.*; début *m.* (beginning). ‖ Initiation (*into*, à).

initiative [i'niʃiətiv] n. Initiative *f*.
— adj. Préliminaire, préparatoire.

initiator [in'iʃieitə*] n. Initiateur *m.*; initiatrice *f*.

initiatory [-təri] adj. Préliminaire (step). ‖ Initiateur *m.*; initiatrice *f*. (rite).

inject [in'dʒekt] v. tr. Med. Injecter (a liquid); faire une piqûre à (s.o); *to inject a limb with a liquid*, injecter un liquide dans un membre.

injection [-ʃən] n. Med. Injection, piqûre *f.*; *to give oneself an injection*, se piquer.

injector [-tə*] n. Injecteur *m.*; pompe à injection *f*.

injudicious [,indʒu'diʃəs] adj. Peu judicieux.

injunct [in'dʒʌŋkt] v. tr. Fam. Enjoindre.

injunction [-ʃən] n. Injonction, recommandation formelle *f*. ‖ Jur. Mise en demeure *f.*; *to give an injunction*, mettre en demeure.

injure ['indʒə*] v. tr. Faire du tort à, nuire à (s.o.); détériorer, endommager (sth.). ‖ Jur. Léser, porter préjudice à (s.o.). ‖ Comm. Avarier (goods). ‖ Med. Blesser (s.o.).

injured [-d] adj. Détérioré. ‖ Jur. Lésé. ‖ Comm. Avarié. ‖ Med. Blessé, accidenté. ‖ Fig. Offensé (person, tone); trompé (wife).

injurious [in'dʒuəriəs] adj. Nuisible, préjudiciable, dommageable (harmful). ‖ Outrageant, injurieux (offensive).

injuriously [-li] adv. De façon dommageable. ‖ Injurieusement.

injury ['indʒəri] n. Tort, préjudice *m.*; *to the injury of*, au détriment de. ‖ Dommage *m.*; dégâts *m. pl.* ‖ Comm., Naut. Avarie *f*. ‖ Med. Blessure *f.*; *internal injuries*, lésions internes.

injustice [in'dʒʌstis] n. Injustice *f*. (act, quality).

ink [iŋk] n. Encre *f*. ‖ Zool. Sépia *f*. (of cuttlefish). ‖ **Ink-bottle**, n. Bouteille d'encre *f*. ‖ **Ink-horn**, n. Encrier *m.*; *ink-horn terms*, mots savants. ‖ **Ink-pad**, n. Tampon encreur *m*. ‖ **Ink-slinger**, n. Barbouilleur, écrivaillon, gratte-papier *m*. ‖ **Ink-stain**, n. Tache d'encre *f.*; *ink-stain remover*, Corrector, encrivore. ‖ **Ink-well**, n. Encrier de pupitre ou de bureau *m*.
— v. tr. Tacher d'encre; *to ink in*, repasser à l'encre. ‖ Techn. Encrer.

inkiness [-inis] n. Noir (*m*.) d'encre.

inking [-iŋ] n. Encrage *m*. ‖ **Inking-ribbon**, n. Ruban (*m*.) à machine.

inkling ['iŋkliŋ] n. Impression, idée *f.*; soupçon *m*. (notion). ‖ Aperçu *m.*; teinture *f*. (hint).

inkpot ['iŋkpɔt] n. Encrier *m*.

inkstand [-stænd] n. Grand encrier de bureau *m*.

inky [-i] adj. Noir d'encre (black); couvert d'encre (stained).

inlaid [in'leid] p.p. See INLAY.

inland ['inlənd] adj. Comm. Indigène (produce); intérieur (trade). ‖ Fin. *Inland Revenue*, contributions; *Inland Revenue stamp*, timbre fiscal. ‖ Naut. Fluvial (navigation).
— [in'lænd] adv. A l'intérieur.
— n. Intérieur *m*.

inlander ['inləndə*] n. Habitant (*s*.) de l'intérieur.

inlay [in'lei] v. tr. (89). Incruster (*with*, de). ‖ Parqueter, mosaïquer (a floor); marqueter (a table); damasquiner (a sword). ‖ Encarter (a page, a plate).
— n. Incrustation; parqueterie; marqueterie *f*. ‖ Encartage *m*. ‖ Med. Plombage *m*.

inlet ['inlet] n. Incrustation *f*. (on a garment). ‖ Techn. Arrivée *f*. (of air); *inlet pipe*, tuyau d'arri-

vée. ‖ Geogr. Crique *f*. (bay); bras (*m*.) de mer (or) de rivière (strip of water).

inmate ['inmeit] n. Habitant, occupant, locataire (of a house). ‖ Pensionnaire *m*. (of an asylum, an institution, a prison).

in memoriam [in mi'mɔ:riəm] adv. In memoriam, à la mémoire de.
— n. Epitaphe *f*.

inmost ['inmoust] adj. Le plus profond. ‖ Fig. Le plus secret (thoughts).

inn [in] n. Auberge *f*. (along the highway). ‖ Hôtellerie *f.*; hôtel *m*. (in town). ‖ Cabaret *m*. (tavern). ‖ Jur. *Inns of Court*, ordres des avocats londoniens.

innards ['inədz] n. pl. Fam. Entrailles *f. pl.*, boyaux *m. pl.* (of a living being); organes (or) mécanismes internes *m. pl.* (of a mechanism).

innate ['i'neit] adj. Inné.

innavigable [i'nævigəbl̩] adj. Innavigable.

inner ['i:nə*] adj. Intérieur (court, sole); interne (side); *on the inner side*, à l'intérieur. ‖ Med. Interne (ear). ‖ Naut. *Inner dock*, arrière-bassin. ‖ Fin. Latent (reserves). ‖ Autom. *Inner tube*, chambre à air. ‖ Fig. Intime (emotions); intérieur (life); secret, profond (meaning).
— n. Cercle (*m*.) près du centre de la cible.

innermost ['inəmoust] adj. Le plus profond (or) intime; *our innermost being*, le tréfonds de notre âme; les replis les plus secrets de notre âme.

innervate [i'nə:veit] v. tr. Med. Innerver.

innervation [,inə:'veiʃən] n. Med. Innervation *f*.

innings ['iniŋz] n. Jur. Accrue *f*. ‖ Sports. Tour (*m*.) de batte. ‖ Fam. *It's my innings*, c'est à moi (or) à mon tour; *to get one's innings*, avoir son tour.
— N. B. En Angleterre, *innings* s'emploie au sing. et au pl. (*a long innings*). En Amérique, le sing. est *inning*.

innkeeper ['in,ki:pə*] n. Aubergiste *s*. (in the country); hôtelier *s*. (in a town).

innocence ['inosn̩s] n. Innocence *f*. (guiltlessness). ‖ Innocence, candeur, naïveté *f*. (simplicity); *to pretend innocence*, faire l'innocent. ‖ Innocence, sottise *f*. (silliness). ‖ † Innocuité *f*.

innocent [-n̩t] adj. Innocent (guiltless); *to proclaim oneself innocent*, proclamer son innocence. ‖ Innocent, naïf (simple). ‖ Innocent, demeuré (silly). ‖ Inoffensif (harmless). ‖ Comm. Autorisé, permis. ‖ Fam. Dépourvu (*of*, de).
— n. Innocent *s*.

innocently [-n̩tli] adv. Innocemment.

innocuity [,inɔ'kju:iti] n. Innocuité *f*.

innocuous [i'nɔkjuəs] adj. Inoffensif.

innovate ['inoveit] v. intr. Innover.

innovation [,ino'veiʃən] n. Innovation *f*. (*in*, à; en; *upon*, par rapport à).

innovator ['inoveitə*] n. Innovateur, novateur *m*.; innovatrice, novatrice *f*.

innoxious [i'nɔkʃəs] adj. Inoffensif.

innoxiousness [-nis] n. Innocuité *f*.

innuendo [,inju'endou] n. Insinuation malveillante *f*. (See HINT.)
— N. B. Le pluriel est *innuendoes*.
— v. intr. Insinuer méchamment.

innumerable [i'nju:mərəbl̩] adj. Innombrable. (See COUNTLESS.)

innumerate [i'nju:mərit] adj. Mauvais en mathématiques; dépourvu de culture mathématique.

innutrition [,inju'triʃən] n. Med. Défaut de nutrition *m*.

innutritious [-ʃəs] adj. Med. Peu nutritif (or) nourrissant.

inobservance [,inəb'zə:vəns] n. Inattention *f*. ‖ Inobservance *f*. (of a custom); inobservation *f*. (of a promise).

inobservant [-ənt] adj. Inattentif. ‖ Qui néglige d'observer.

inoculability [,inɔkjulə'biliti] n. Med. Inoculabilité *f*.

inoculable [i'nɔkjuləbl̩] adj. Med. Inoculable.

inoculate [-eit] v. tr. MED. Inoculer (*into, on*, à); *to inoculate s.o. with a virus*, inoculer un virus à qqn.

inoculation [i,nɔkju'lei ʃən] n. MED. Inoculation f.

inoculator [i'nɔkjuleitə*] n. Inoculateur m.

inodorous [i'noudərəs] adj. Inodore.

inoffensive [,inə'fensiv] adj. Inoffensif (harmless). ‖ Non offensant. ‖ Acceptable, admissible, sans désagrément.

inofficious [,inə'fiʃəs] adj. JUR. Inofficieux.

inoperable [i'nɔpərəbl̩] adj. MED. Inopérable.

inoperative [-tiv] adj. Inopérant.

inopportune [i'nɔpətjuːn] adj. Inopportun.

inopportunely [-li] adj. Inopportunément.

inopportuneness [-nis] n. Inopportunité f.

inordinacy [i'nɔːdinəsi] n. Excès, désordre m.

inordinate [-it] adj. Désordonné, immodéré. (See EXCESSIVE.) ‖ Désordonné, irrégulier; *inordinate hours*, heures indues.

inordinately [-itli] adv. Sans ordre (or) règle (or) mesure; immodérément.

inorganic [,inɔː'gænik] adj. CHIM., MED., GRAMM. Inorganique.

inorganization [i,nɔːgənai'zei ʃən] n. Inorganisation f.; manque (m.) d'organisation.

inosculate [i'nɔskjuleit] v. tr. MED. Aboucher.

— v. intr. MED. S'anastomoser.

inosculation [i,nɔskju'lei ʃən] n. MED. Anastomose f.

input ['in,put] n. ELECTR. Puissance à l'entrée (or) d'alimentation f. (current applied); borne d'entrée f. (terminal). ‖ INFORM. Entrée f., input m. ‖ FIN. Input, intrant m.

— v. tr. (1, 107). INFORM. Introduire, faire entrer (*into*, dans).

— N. B. Le verbe *input* a deux formes de prét. et de p. p. : *input* et *inputted*.

inquest ['inkwest] n. JUR. Enquête criminelle (or) judiciaire f. (act); jury m. (persons).

inquietude [in'kwaiitjuːd] n. Inquiétude f.

inquire [in'kwaiə*] v. intr. S'enquérir, s'informer (*about*, de [sth.]; *after*, de; *of*, auprès de [s.o.]); *to inquire for*, demander à voir (s.o., sth.). ‖ Faire des recherches, se renseigner (*into*, sur). ‖ JUR. Enquêter, faire une enquête (*into*, sur).

— v. tr. S'informer de, chercher à savoir.

inquiring [-riŋ] adj. Curieux, interrogateur, investigateur.

inquiry [-ri] n. Enquête, investigation f. ‖ Demande (f.) de renseignements; *Inquiries*, les Renseignements (office); *to make inquiries about* (or) *after*, s'informer de, faire des recherches sur.

inquisition [,inkwi'zi ʃən] n. Recherche f. (investigation). ‖ ECCLES. Inquisition f. ‖ JUR. Enquête; perquisition f.

inquisitional [-l̩] adj. ECCLES. Inquisitorial. ‖ FIG. Inquisiteur.

inquisitive [in'kwizitiv] adj. Inquisiteur, indiscret (pej.); curieux, questionneur.

inquisitively [-li] adv. Trop curieusement, indiscrètement.

inquisitiveness [-nis] n. Curiosité indiscrète f.

inquisitor [in'kwizitə*] n. ECCLES. Inquisiteur m. ‖ JUR. Enquêteur s.

inquisitorial [in,kwizi'tɔːriəl] adj. Inquisitorial.

inroad ['inroud] n. MILIT. Incursion f. (See RAID.) ‖ MED. Accroc m. (upon, à) [health]. ‖ FIG. Empiétement m. (upon, sur).

inrush ['inrʌʃ] n. Irruption f.

insalivate [in'sæliveit] v. tr. MED. Insaliver.

insalivation [in,sæli'vei ʃən] n. MED. Insalivation f.

insalubrious [,insə'luːbriəs] adj. Insalubre.

insalubrity [-ti] n. Insalubrité f.

insane [in'sein] adj. MED. Fou, dément, aliéné. ‖ FIG. Fou, insensé.

— n. MED. Fous m. pl.

insanely [-li] adv. Follement.

insanitary [in'sænitəri] adj. Malsain, antihygiénique, insalubre.

insanitation [in,sæni'tei ʃən] n. Insalubrité f.

insanity [in'sæniti] n. MED. Démence, aliénation mentale f. ‖ FIG. Insanité f.

insatiability [in,sei ʃiə'biliti] n. Insatiabilité f.

insatiable [in'sei ʃiəbl̩] adj. Insatiable (of, de).

insatiate [-it] adj. FIG. Insatiable.

inscribable [ins'kraibəbl̩] adj. MATH. Inscriptible (in, dans).

inscribe [ins'kraib] v. tr. Inscrire (on, sur) [words, symbols]; marquer (with, de) [a surface]. ‖ Inscrire, enrôler (s.o.). ‖ Dédier, dédicacer (to, à) [a book]. ‖ ARTS. Graver (in, dans). ‖ MATH. Inscrire (in, dans). ‖ FIG. Inscrire, fixer, graver.

inscribed [-d] adj. Inscrit.

inscription [ins'krip ʃən] n. Inscription f. (on a monument). ‖ Dédicace f. (in a book); légende f. (on a coin). ‖ JUR. Transcription d'hypothèque f. ‖ FIN. Inscription f. (of loan).

inscriptive [ins'kriptiv] adj. D'inscription. ‖ De dédicace.

inscrutability [ins,kruːtə'biliti] n. Inscrutabilité f.

inscrutable [ins'kruːtəbl̩] adj. Inscrutable.

insect ['insekt] n. ZOOL. Insecte m. ‖ **Insect-eater**, n. ZOOL. Insectivore m. ‖ **Insect-powder**, n. Poudre insecticide f.

insecticidal [,insekti'saidl̩] adj. Insecticide.

insecticide [in'sektisaid] n. Insecticide m.

insectivora [,insek'tivərə] n. pl. ZOOL. Insectivores m. pl.

insectivorous [-əs] adj. Insectivore.

insectology [,insek'tɔlədʒi] n. ZOOL. U. S. Entomologie f.

insecure [,insi'kjuə*] adj. Peu sûr, incertain (uncertain). ‖ Anxieux, inquiet (anxious). ‖ Peu sûr, dangereux, hasardeux, exposé (dangerous). ‖ Exposé, en danger (in peril).

insecurely [-li] adv. Sans sécurité.

insecurity [-riti] n. Insécurité f.

inseminate [in'semineit] v. tr. MED. Inséminer.

insemination [,insemi'nei ʃən] n. MED. Insémination f.

insensate [in'sensit] adj. MED. Insensible (insensitive); inanimé (insentient). ‖ FIG. Insensé (senseless); insensible (unfeeling).

insensibility [in,sensi'biliti] n. MED. Insensibilité f. (insensitiveness); inconscience f. (unconsciousness.) ‖ FIG. Insensibilité f. (to, à).

insensible [in'sensibl̩] adj. MED. Inconscient. (See INSENTIENT.) ‖ FIG. Insensible (to, à) [imperceptible, indifferent, unfeeling).

insensibly [-bli] adv. Insensiblement.

insensitive [-tiv] adj. Insensible.

insensitiveness [-tivnis] n. Insensibilité f.

insentient [in'sen ʃiənt] adj. MED. Inconscient, inanimé.

inseparability [in,sepərə'biliti] n. Inséparabilité f.

inseparable [in'sepərəbl̩] adj., n. Inséparable s.

inseparably [-bli] adv. Inséparablement.

insert [in'səːt] v. tr. Insérer (in, into, dans); *to insert in*, placer dans; *to insert into*, introduire dans.

— n. Encart m. (in a book). ‖ THEATR. Scèneraccord f. ‖ TECHN. Pièce insérée f.; ajout m.

insertable [-əbl̩] adj. Insérable.

insertion [in'səː ʃən] n. Insertion f. ‖ Entre-deux m.; incrustation f. (needlework).

inset ['in'set] v. tr. (122). Insérer (to insert). ‖ Encarter (a page). ‖ Faire une incrustation de (a piece of material).

— ['inset] n. Encart m. (extra pages); médaillon m. (map, picture). ‖ Incrustation f. (insertion); dépassant m. (to a waistcoat).

inshore ['in'ʃɔː*] adj. Côtier.

— adv. Près de la côte.

inside ['in'said] n. Intérieur, dedans *m.*; face interne *f.*; *inside of the pavement,* côté du trottoir le plus éloigné de la rue. ‖ Intérieur, saint (*m.*) des saints ; *to be on the inside,* être dans le coup. ‖ Pl. FAM. Estomac, ventre *m.*
— ['in‚said] adj. Intérieur, interne ; *inside information,* renseignement de première main (or) obtenu à la source ; *inside story,* histoire authentique ; *inside job,* crime commis par une personne de l'entourage de la victime. ‖ AUTOM. *Inside lane,* voie (or) file de gauche (in Great Britain), de droite (elsewhere). ‖ SPORTS. *Inside track,* corde. ‖ **Inside left, right** n. SPORTS. Intérieur gauche, droit *m.*
— [‚in'said] adv. A l'intérieur, dedans. ‖ FAM. *Inside of,* en l'espace de, en moins de (a specified time). ‖ POP. A l'ombre, en taule.
— [‚in'said] prép. A l'intérieur de, dans. ‖ En l'espace de, en moins de (a specified time).
— *Inside out* loc. adv. ['insaid 'aut] A l'envers ; FIG. *To know sth. inside out,* connaître qqch. à fond.

insider [in'saidə*] n. Personne (*f.*) au courant ; personne dans le coup (fam.).

insidious [in'sidiəs] adj. Insidieux.

insidiously [-li] adv. Insidieusement.

insidiousness [-nis] n. Nature insidieuse *f.*

insight ['insait] n. Pénétration *f.* (*into,* de) ; *penetrating insight,* perspicacité. ‖ Aperçu *m.* (*into,* de) [glimpse].

insignia [in'signiə] n. pl. Insignes *m. pl.*

insignificance [‚insig'nifikəns] n. Insignifiance *f.*

insignificant [-ənt] adj. Insignifiant (unimportant). ‖ Dépourvu de sens (meaningless).

insincere [‚insin'siə*] adj. Peu sincère, hypocrite, faux.

insincerity [-'seriti] n. Manque (*m.*) de sincérité.

insinuate [in'sinjueit] v. tr. Insinuer ; *to insinuate oneself into,* s'insinuer (or) se glisser dans. ‖ Sous-entendre, laisser entendre, insinuer.

insinuatingly [-i‚ŋli] adv. D'une façon insinuante.

insinuation [in‚sinju'eiʃen] n. Insinuation *f.* (See HINT.)

insinuative [in'sinjueitiv], **insinuating** [-iŋ] adj. Insinuant.

insipid [in'sipid] adj. Insipide (lit. and fig.).

insipidity [‚insi'piditi] n. Insipidité *f.*

insipidly [in'sipidli] adv. Insipidement.

insist [in'sist] v. intr. Insister, mettre l'accent (*on,* sur). ‖ Tenir (*on,* à) ; *he insists upon their keeping quiet,* il exige qu'ils se taisent ; *to insist on sth. being done,* insister pour que qqch. se fasse . ‖ JUR. *To insist on a division,* exiger la mise aux voix ; *to insist on one's rights,* faire valoir ses droits.
— v. tr. Affirmer ; *he insists that he is innocent,* il proteste de son innocence.

insistence [-əns], **insistency** [-ənsi] n. Insistance *f.*

insistent [-ənt] adj. Insistant, persistant. ‖ Obsédant. ‖ Instant, pressant.

insistently [-əntli] adv. Avec insistance ; instamment.

in situ [in 'sitju:] adv. In situ.

insobriety [‚inso'braiəti] n. Intempérance *f.*

insolate [‚inso'leit] v. tr. Exposer au soleil, insoler.

insolation [-'leiʃen] n. Insolation *f.*; ensoleillement *m.* (radiation). ‖ MED. Coup de soleil *m.*; insolation *f.* (sunstroke) ; héliothérapie *f.*; bain de soleil *m.* (treatment).

insole ['in‚soul] n. Semelle intérieure *f.*

insolence ['insələns] n. Insolence *f.*

insolent [-ənt] adj. Insolent.

insolently [-əntli] adv. Insolemment.

insolubility [in‚sɔlju'biliti] n. Insolubilité *f.*

insoluble [in'sɔljubl] adj. Insoluble.

insolubly [-bli] adv. Insolublement.

insolvable [in'sɔlvəbl] adj. Insoluble. ‖ FIN. U. S. Insolvable.

insolvency [-ənsi] n. FIN. Insolvabilité· *f.* ‖ JUR. Faillite *f.*

insolvent [-ənt] adj. FIN. Insolvable. ‖ JUR. En faillite ; *to declare oneself insolvent,* déposer son bilan.
— n. JUR. Débiteur insolvable *m.*

insomnia [in'sɔmniə] n. MED. Insomnie *f.*

insomuch [‚insou'mʌtʃ] adv. Tellement, à tel point, au point (*that,* que).

insouciance [in'su:siəns] n. Insouciance *f.*

insouciant [in'su:siənt] adj. Insouciant.

inspect [in'spekt] v. tr. Examiner avec attention. ‖ Inspecter, visiter (to review).

inspection [in'spekʃən] n. Inspection *f.*

inspector [in'spektə*] n. Inspecteur *m.*

inspectoral [-rəl], **inspectorial** [‚inspek'tɔ:riəl] adj. D'inspecteur.

inspectorate [in'spektərit] n. Inspection *f.* (body) ; inspectorat *m.* (office).

inspectorship [-ə‚ʃip] n. Inspectorat *m.* (position).

inspectress [-ris] n. Inspectrice *f.*

inspiration [‚inspi'reiʃen] n. MED. Aspiration, inspiration *f.* ‖ FIG. Inspiration *f.*

inspirational [-l] adj. Inspiré (inspired) ; inspirateur *m.*; inspiratrice *f.* (inspiring).

inspirative [in'spairətiv] adj. FIG. Inspirateur *m.*; inspiratrice *f.*

inspiratory [-təri] adj. MED. Inspirateur.

inspire [in'spaiə*] v. tr. MED. Aspirer, inspirer. ‖ FIG. Inspirer, suggérer, susciter, insuffler (*in, into,* à) ; *to inspire s.o. with fear,* inspirer de la terreur à qqn, remplir qqn de terreur.
— v. intr. MED. Inspirer.

inspirit [in'spirit] v. tr. Animer, vivifier. ‖ Encourager, stimuler. ‖ Egayer, réjouir (to cheer).

inspiriting [-iŋ] adj. Vivifiant. ‖ Stimulant, encourageant. ‖ Egayant, épanouissant.

inspissate [in'spiseit] v. tr. Epaissir.

inspissation [‚inspi'seiʃen] n. Epaississement *m.*

instability [‚instə'biliti] n. Instabilité *f.*

install [in'stɔ:l] v. tr. Installer ; *to install oneself,* s'installer.

installation [‚instɔ'leiʃen] n. Installation *f.* (act, building) ; *industrial installation,* établissement industriel.

instal(l)ment [in'stɔ:lmənt] n. Fascicule *m.*; livraison *f.* (of a magazine) ; feuilleton *m.* (in a newspaper) ; *instalment selling,* vente par fascicule. ‖ FIN. Tranche *f.*; *instalment on account,* acompte provisionnel. ‖ COMM. Versement échelonné, acompte *m.*; *instalment plan,* système de crédit ; *instalment sale* (or) *selling* (or) U. S. *plan,* vente à tempérament. ‖ FIG. Fraction *f.*
— N. B. La graphie *installment* est américaine.

instance ['instəns] n. Instance, demande, sollicitation *f.*; *at the instance of,* sur la demande de, à la requête de. ‖ Cas *m.*; *isolated instance,* cas isolé ; *in the special instance,* en l'espèce. ‖ Exemple *m.* (in which, où) ; *for instance,* par exemple. ‖ Circonstance, occasion *f.*; *in the first instance,* en premier lieu. ‖ JUR. Instance *f.*
— v. tr. Illustrer, appuyer d'un exemple. (See EXEMPLIFY.) ‖ Donner en exemple (to cite).

instancy [-i] n. Imminence *f.* (of a danger) ; urgence *f.* (of a need) ; instance *f.* (of a request).

instant ['instənt] adj. Imminent (danger) ; urgent, instant (need) ; immédiat (obedience) ; instant, pressant (request).
— n. Instant *m.*; *the instant that he arrives,* aussitôt qu' (or) dès qu'il arrivera ; *on the instant,* à l'instant, immédiatement.

instantaneous [‚instən'teinjəs] adj. Instantané.

instantaneously [-li] adv. Instantanément.

instantly ['instəntli] adv. Instantanément, immédiatement. ‖ † Instamment.
— conj. † Dès que, aussitôt que.

instauration [‚instɔ'reiʃen] n. Restauration *f.*

Instaurator [-tə*] n. Restaurateur m.

instead [ins'ted] adv. A la place; *instead of*, au lieu de.

instep ['instep] n. MED. Cou-de-pied m.

instigate ['instigeit] v. tr. Inciter (*to*, à). || Fomenter (rebellion).

instigation [,insti'gei∫ən] n. Instigation f.

instigator ['instigeitə*] n. Instigateur, fomentateur m.; instigatrice, fomentatrice f.

instil(l) [in'stil] v. tr. (1). Instiller. || FIG. Inculquer (*into*, à).

instillation [,insti'lei∫ən] n. Instillation f. || FIG. Inculcation, imprégnation f.

instinct [ins'tiŋkt] adj. Chargé, lourd, rempli (*with*, de).
— ['instiŋkt] n. Instinct m.

instinctive [ins'tiŋktiv] adj. Instinctif.

instinctively [-li] adv. Instinctivement.

institute ['institju:t] n. Institut m. (building, society). || JUR. Pl. Institutes f. pl.
— v. tr. Instituer (to establish). || Fonder, créer, constituer (to found); *newly instituted*, de fondation récente. || Commencer, engager (to initiate). || ECCLES. Investir. || JUR. Intenter (an action); ordonner (an inquiry); entamer (proceedings).

institution [,insti'tju:∫ən] n. Institution f. (act, result, society); *institution child*, enfant de l'assistance publique. || ECCLES. Investiture f. || JUR. Introduction f. (of proceedings).

institutional [-l] adj. Institué (instituted). || Concernant une institution. || Organisé en institution; comportant des œuvres de bienfaisance (religion). || U. S. D'attraction, en vue du prestige social (advertising).

institutionalize [-laiz] v. tr. Etablir en institution. || FAM. Placer dans un établissement charitable.

instruct [ins'trʌkt] v. tr. Instruire (to teach). || Informer, avertir (to apprise). || Donner des instructions (or) des ordres à (to command); *he had instructed you to write*, il vous avait recommandé (or) chargé d'écrire.

instruction [-∫ən] n. Instruction f. (teaching); *medical instruction*, enseignement de la médecine. || Pl. Instructions, indications, directives f. pl.; *instructions for use*, mode d'emploi; *without sufficient instructions*, sans données suffisantes. || TECHN. *Instruction book*, manuel d'entretien. || AUTOM. *Driving instruction*, leçons de conduite. || MILIT. Consigne f.

instructional [-∫ənl] adj. D'instruction (course).

instructive [-tiv] adj. Instructif.

instructor [-tə*] n. Maître m.; U. S. assistant m. (teacher). || MILIT. Instructeur m. || AUTOM. Professeur m. || SPORTS. Moniteur m.

instructress [-tris] n. Maîtresse f. || Monitrice f.

instrument ['instrumənt] n. MUS., TECHN., MED. Instrument m. || JUR. Document officiel m.; *legal instrument*, texte juridique. || COMM. Agent intermédiaire m. || AVIAT. *Instrument flying*, vol aux instruments. || FIG. Instrument m.
— v. tr. JUR. Instrumenter. || MUS. Orchestrer.

instrumental [,instru'mentl] adj. Contributif, utile; *to be instrumental in* (or) *to*, contribuer à, concourir à, être pour quelque chose dans. || TECHN. D'instrument. || MUS., GRAMM. Instrumental.

instrumentalist [-əlist] n. MUS. Instrumentiste m.

instrumentality [,instrumen'tæliti] n. Intermédiaire, concours m.; *through the instrumentality of*, grâce à l'intervention de.

instrumentally [,instru'mentəli] adv. Au moyen d'instruments. || En qualité d'instrument.

instrumentation [,instrumen'tei∫ən] n. Instrumentation f. || MUS. Orchestration f. || PHYS. Appareillage m.

insubmersible [,insəb'mə:səbl] adj. Insubmersible.

insubordinate [,insə'bɔ:dinit] adj. Insubordonné.

insubordination [insə,bɔ:di'nei∫ən] n. Insubordination f.

insubstantial [,insəbs'tæn∫əl] adj. Insubstantiel, immatériel (not solid). || Imaginaire, chimérique (unreal). || Vide, sans consistance (flimsy).

insubstantiality [,insəbstæn∫i'æliti] n. Manque (m.) de substance. || Irréalité f. || Inconsistance f.

insufferable [in'sʌfərəbl] adj. Insupportable.

insufferably [-bli] adv. Insupportablement.

insufficiency [,insə'fi∫ənsi] n. Insuffisance f.

insufficient [-ənt] adj. Insuffisant.

insufficiently [-əntli] adv. Insuffisamment.

insufflate ['insʌfleit] v. tr. Insuffler.

insufflation [,insʌ'flei∫ən] n. Insufflation f.

insufflator ['insʌfleitə*] n. MED. Insufflateur m.

insular ['insjulə*] adj. GEOGR. Insulaire. || MED. En plaques (sclerosis). || FIG. Isolé (insulated); borné, d'esprit étroit (narrow-minded).

insularity [,insju'læriti] n. GEOGR. Insularité f. || FIG. Etroitesse (f.) d'esprit; préjugé m.

insulate ['insjuleit] v. tr. ELECTR., FIG. Isoler.

insulation [,insju'lei∫ən] n. ELECTR. Isolation f. || FIG. Isolement m.

insulator ['insjuleitə*] n. ELECTR. Isolateur m.

insulin ['insjulin] n. MED. Insuline f.

insult ['insʌlt] n. Insulte, injure f.; affront m. || Outrage m.; *insult to common sense*, défi au bon sens. || U. S. MED. Trauma m.
— [in'sʌlt] v. tr. Insulter, injurier.

insulting [in'sʌltiŋ] adj. Insultant.

insuperability [in,sju:pərə'biliti] n. Caractère insurmontable f.

insuperable [in'sju:pərəbl] adj. Insurmontable.

insupportable [,insə'pɔ:təbl] adj. Insupportable. (See INSUFFERABLE.)

insupportably [-bli] adv. Insupportablement.

insuppressible [,insə'presibl] adj. Irrépressible.

insurable [in'∫uərəbl] adj. Assurable.

insurance [-əns] n. Assurance f.; *comprehensive insurance policy*, assurance tous risques; *contributory insurance scheme*, assurances sociales, sécurité sociale; *employers' liability insurance*, U. S. *workmen's compensation insurance*, assurance contre les accidents du travail; *fire, motor-car, old-age insurance*, assurance-incendie, -automobile, -vieillesse; *life insurance*, assurance sur la vie.

insurant [-ənt] n. Assuré s.

insure [in'suə*] v. tr. Assurer.

insurer [-rə*] n. Assureur m.

insurgence [in'sə:dʒəns] n. Insurrection, insurgence f.

insurgent [-ənt] adj., n. Insurgé s.

insurmountable [,insə'mauntəbl] adj. Insurmontable (difficulty); infranchissable (obstacle).

insurrection [,insə'rek∫ən] n. Insurrection f.

insurrectional [-l], **insurrectionary** [-əri] adj. Insurrectionnel.

insurrectionist [-ist] n. Insurgé s.

insusceptibility [,insəsepti'biliti] n. Insensibilité, inaccessibilité (*to*, à).

insusceptible [,insə'septibl] adj. Non susceptible (*of*, de). || Insensible, inaccessible (*to*, à).

intact [in'tækt] adj. Intact.

intaglio [in'tɑ:liou] n. ARTS. Intaille f.

intake ['inteik] n. Diminution f. (in knitting). || TECHN. Appel m. (of air); prise f. (of water); rétrécissement m. (in a pipe); diamètre m. (of a sewer). || MED. *Food intake*, ration. || MILIT. Recrues f. pl.

intangibility [in,tændʒi'biliti] n. Intangibilité f. || FIG. Abstraction f.

intangible [in'tændʒibl] adj. Intangible, impalpable. || JUR. *Intangible property*, biens incorporels. || FIG. Insaisissable, impondérable, informulable.

integer ['intidʒə*] n. MATH. Nombre entier m. || FIG. Tout m.

integral ['intigrəl] adj. Intégrant, constituant

(part) ; *to be an integral part of*, faire partie intégrante de, s'intégrer dans. ‖ MATH., FIG. Intégral.
— n. MATH. Intégrale *f.*
integrality [,inti'græliti] n. Intégralité *f.*
integrally ['intigrəli] adv. Intégralement.
integrand ['inti,grænd] n. MATH. Fonction (*f.*) à intégrer.
integrant [-grənt] adj. Intégrant.
— n. Partie intégrante *f.;* élément *m.*
integrate [-greit] v. tr. Former un tout avcc, compléter ; unifier. ‖ Totaliser, additionner. ‖ Coordonner (forces). ‖ MATH. Intégrer. ‖ ELECTR. *Integrated circuit*, circuit intégré.
— v. intr. S'intégrer.
— [-grit] adj. Intégral, entier.
integration [,inti'grei∫ən] n. Intégration *f.;* U. S. *racial integration*, intégration raciale. ‖ Coordination *f.*
integrationist [-∫ənist] n. Intégrationniste *s.*, partisan (*s.*) de l'intégration raciale.
integrator ['intigreitə*] n. MATH. Intégrateur *m.*
integrity [in'tegriti] n. Intégrité *f.*
integument [in'tegjumənt] n. BOT., ZOOL. Tégument *m.*
integumentary [in,tegju'mentəri] adj. Tégumentaire.
intellect ['intilekt] n. Intelligence *f.;* esprit *m.* (ability, person). ‖ Elite intellectuelle *f.* (intelligentsia). ‖ PHILOS. Intellect ; entendement *m.*
intellectual [-tjuəl] adj. Intellectuel ; *intellectual refinement*, la politesse de l'esprit.
— n. Intellectuel *s.*
intellectualism [-tjuəlizm] n. Intellectualisme *m.*
intellectuality ['inti,lektju'æliti] n. Intellectualité *f.*
intellectualize [,inti'lektjuəlaiz] v. tr. Intellectualiser.
intellectually [-li] adv. Intellectuellement.
intelligence [in'telidʒəns] n. Intelligence *f.* (ability, understanding). ‖ Renseignements *m. pl.;* informations *f. pl.; intelligence record*, dossier de renseignements. ‖ Rapport *m.; literary intelligence*, chronique littéraire. ‖ MILIT. *Intelligence Corps*, service des renseignements militaires; *Intelligence Service*, service secret, deuxième bureau. ‖ MED. *Intelligence quotient*, quotient intellectuel (Q. I.); *intelligence test*, test d'intelligence.
intelligencer [-ənsə*] n. MILIT. Agent secret *m.*
intelligent [-ənt] adj. Intelligent.
intelligential [in,teli'dʒen∫əl] adj. Intellectuel. ‖ D'informations, de renseignements (channel).
intelligently [in'telidʒəntli] adv. Intelligemment.
intelligentsia [inteli'dʒentsiə] n. Elite intellectuelle *f.*
intelligibility [in,telidʒi'biliti] n. Intelligibilité *f.*
intelligible [in'telidʒibl] adj. Intelligible (speech, words).
intelligibly [-bli] adv. Intelligiblement.
intemperance [in'tempərəns] n. Intempérance *f.* ‖ Ivrognerie *f.*
intemperate [-it] adj. D'intempérance (habits); intempérant (person). ‖ Immodéré, excessif (zeal). ‖ Peu clément (climate); violent (wind).
intemperately [-itli] adv. Immodérément.
intend [in'tend] v. tr. Avoir l'intention de; être dans la disposition de, projeter de; *to intend to become a priest*, se destiner au sacerdoce; *to intend to write*, se proposer d'écrire. ‖ Destiner, désigner (*for*, à); *intended for the general reader*, destiné au (or) à l'usage du grand public (book). ‖ Signifier, vouloir dire (see MEAN); *what do you intend by?*, qu'entendez-vous par ?
intendance [in'tendəns] n. Intendance.
intendant [-ənt] n. Intendant *s.*
intended [-id] adj. Intentionnel (act); projeté (voyage). ‖ Futur (husband).
— n. FAM. Fiancé *s.*

intending [-iŋ] adj. En perspective, probable, éventuel, possible.
intendment [-mənt] n. JUR. Volonté réelle *f.; intendment of law*, esprit de la loi, présomption légale.
intense [in'tens] adj. Intense (light, pain). ‖ Concentré (expression); fervent, profond, vivant avec intensité (person).
intensely [-li] adv. Intensément. ‖ FAM. Extrêmement.
intensification [,intensifi'kei∫ən] n. Intensification *f.* ‖ Renforcement *m.*
intensify [in'tensifai] v. tr. (2). Intensifier. ‖ Renforcer (in photography).
— v. intr. S'intensifier.
intension [in'ten∫ən] n. Tension *f.* (of mind); intensité *f.* (of a quality).
intensity [in'tensiti] n. PHYS., ELECTR., FIG. Intensité *f.*
intensive [-siv] adj. Intensif.
intensively [-sivli] adv. Intensivement.
intent [in'tent] n. Intention *f.* (*to*, de); *to all intents and purposes*, à toutes fins utiles; *with specific intent*, dans une intention arrêtée.
— adj. Attentif (*on*, à); absorbé (*on*, par). ‖ Déterminé, décidé, résolu (*on*, à). ‖ Soutenu (application); intense, ardent (look).
intention [in'ten∫ən] n. Intention *f.;* dessein, but *m.; with the best of intentions*, dans la meilleure intention du monde. ‖ MED. Intention *f.*
intentional [-∫nl] adj. Intentionnel, voulu. (See PURPOSIVE.)
intentionally [-∫nəli] adv. Intentionnellement.
intentioned [-∫nd] adj. Intentionné.
intently [in'tentli] adv. Profondément, attentivement, avec grande attention.
intentness [-nis] n. Attention soutenue *f.*
inter ['intə*] adv. Entre. ‖ **Inter-city**, adj. Interurbain; CH. DE F. Rapide (train). ‖ **Inter-departmental**, adj. Interdisciplinaire (at university); interministériel (in government). ‖ **Inter-governmental**, adj. Intergouvernemental. ‖ **Inter-war**, adj. *Inter-war years* (or) *period*, l'entre-deux-guerres.
inter [in'tə:*] v. tr. (1). Enterrer. (See BURY.)
interact ['intərækt] n. THEATR. Intermède *m.* (interlude); entracte *m.* (interval).
— [,intə'rækt] v. intr. Agir l'un sur l'autre; avoir une action réciproque.
interaction [,intə'ræk∫ən] n. Action réciproque *f.*
inter alia [-'reiliə] adv. Entre autres, entre autres choses; notamment.
interallied [,intər'ælaid] adj. Interallié.
interbreed [,intə'bri:d] v. tr. (26). Croiser (animals).
— v. intr. Se reproduire par croisement.
intercalary [in'tə:kələri] adj. Intercalaire.
intercalate [-leit] v. tr. Intercaler.
intercalation [in,tə:kə'lei∫ən] n. Intercalation *f.*
intercede [,inte'si:d] v. intr. Intercéder (*with*, auprès de).
interceder [-ə*] n. Intercesseur *m.*
intercept [,intə'sept] v. tr. Intercepter, capter (light, message). ‖ Arrêter (or) saisir au passage (s.o.); arrêter, stopper (s.o.'s escape); couper (s.o.'s retreat). ‖ MATH. Comprendre.
interception [-∫ən] n. Interception *f.*
interceptive [-tiv] adj. Interceptif.
interceptor [-tə*] n. Intercepteur *m.*
intercession [,intə'se∫ən] n. Intercession *f.*
intercessor [-sə*] n. Intercesseur *m.*
interchange ['intət∫eindʒ] n. Echange *m.* (of compliments, ideas). ‖ Alternance *f.* (of day and night). ‖ CH. DE F. *Interchange service*, correspondance.
— [,intə't∫eindʒ] v. tr. Echanger (*with*, avec) [ideas]. ‖ Interchanger (parts). ‖ Faire alterner (*with*, avec). ‖ ELECTR. Intervertir.

interchangeability [intə,t∫eindʒə'biliti] n. Interchangeabilité f.
interchangeable [,intə't∫eindʒəbḷ] adj. Echangeable (ideas). ‖ Interchangeable (parts). ‖ Alternable (with, avec).
interclass [,intə'klɑ:s] adj. Entre classes diverses (debate).
intercolonial [,intəkə'lounjəl] adj. Intercolonial.
intercolumnar [,intəkə'lʌmnə*] adj. MED. Intercolumnaire. ‖ ARCHIT. Entre deux colonnes.
intercolumniation ['intəkə,lʌmni'ei∫ən] n. ARCHIT. Entre-colonnement m.
intercom [,intə'kɔm] n. FAM. Téléphone intérieur ; interphone m.
intercommunicate [,intəkə'mju:nikeit] v. intr. Communiquer entre soi.
intercommunication ['intəkə,mju:ni'kei∫ən] n. Intercommunication f.
intercommunion [,intəkə'mju:njən] n. Relations intimes f. pl. (between, entre); compénétration f. ‖ ECCLES. Intercommunion f. (among religious groups).
intercommunity [-niti] n. JUR. Communauté f.
interconnected [,intəkə'nektid] adj. Communicant (room). ‖ AVIAT. Conjugué (rudder). ‖ FIG. Etroitement apparenté, en connexion.
intercontinental [,intəkɔnti'nentḷ] adj. Intercontinental.
interconvertible [,intəkən'və:tibḷ] adj. Inter changeable, permutable.
intercostal [,intəkɔstḷ] adj. MED. Intercostal.
intercourse ['intəkɔ:s] n. Relations f. pl. ‖ MED. Sexual intercourse, rapports sexuels. ‖ MILIT. Commerce m. (with the enemy).
intercrop ['intəkrɔp] n. AGRIC. Assolement m.
— [,intə'krɔp] v. tr. AGRIC. Assoler.
intercurrent [,intə'kʌrənt] adj. Intervenu (or) situé dans l'intervalle. (See INTERVENIENT.) ‖ MED. Intercurrent.
interdenominational [,intədi,nɔmi'nei∫nḷ] adj. ECCLES. Interconfessionnel.
interdental [,intə'dentḷ] adj. MED., GRAMM. Interdental.
interdepend [,intədi'pend] v. intr. Etre interdépendants.
interdependence [-əns] n. Interdépendance f.
interdependent [-ənt] adj. Interdépendant.
interdict [,intə'dikt] v. tr. Interdire (from, de). [See FORBID.] ‖ ECCLES. Interdire.
— ['intədikt] n. Interdiction f. ‖ ECCLES. Interdit m.
interdiction [,intə'dik∫ən] n. JUR., FIG. Interdiction f.
interdictory [-təri] adj. JUR. D'interdiction (law); prohibitif (system).
interdigital [,intə'didʒitḷ] adj. MED. Interdigital.
interdisciplinary [,intə'disiplinəri] adj. Interdisciplinaire.
interest ['intrist] n. JUR. Droit, titre m. ; vested interests, droits acquis. ‖ FIN. Intérêts m. pl. ; commandite, participation f. ; to have an interest in, avoir des intérêts (or) être intéressé dans. ‖ FIN. Groupement intéressé m. ; oil interests, les pétroliers, le monde du pétrole. ‖ FIN. Intérêts m. pl. (money, rate); dividendes m. pl. ; back interest, arrérages. ‖ FIG. Intérêt, avantage, profit m. ; in the interest of, dans l'intérêt de. ‖ FIG. Intérêt, attrait m. ; to take a sympathetic interest in, s'intéresser vivement à, se pencher sur. ‖ FIG. Surabondance f. ; to repay with interest, rendre avec usure.
— v. tr. Intéresser, attirer (s.o.). ‖ Diriger, pousser (in, vers) [a pupil]. ‖ FIN. Intéresser (in, à).
interested [-id] adj. Intéressé, attiré, séduit. ‖ Intéressé, non désintéressé (motive, person). ‖ Intéressé (in, par); versé (in, dans).
interesting [-iŋ] adj. Intéressant.
interestingly [-iŋli] adv. De façon intéressante.

interface ['intə,feis] n. INFORM. Interface f.
interfacial [,intə'fei∫əl] adj MATH. Dièdre.
interfacing [-,feisiŋ] n. Toile f., entoilage m. (of collars, cuffs).
interfere [,intə'fiə*] v. intr. To interfere with, intervenir (or) s'immiscer (or) s'ingérer dans, se mêler de (person) [see MEDDLE] ; gêner, contrecarrer, porter atteinte à, entraver [things]. ‖ PHYS. Interférer. ‖ RADIO. To interfere with, brouiller.
interference [-rəns] n. Intervention, immixion, ingérence f. (of a person); interposition (in, dans) [of a thing]. ‖ PHYS. Interférence f. ‖ RADIO. Parasites m. pl.
interferential [,intəfiə'ren∫əl] adj. PHYS. Interférentiel.
interferometer [,intəfə'rɔmitə*] n. PHYS. Interféromètre m.
interferon [,intə'fiərɔn] n. MED. Interféron m.
interfluent [,intə'fluənt] adj. Fondu, enchaîné, combiné.
interfuse [,intə'fju:z] v. tr. Imprégner, saturer, pénétrer, entremêler (with, de). ‖ Se répandre dans, percer dans (s.o.'s remarks).
— v. intr. Se fondre, se mêler, se combiner. (See .COMMINGLE.)
interim ['intərim] n. Intérim m.
— adj. Provisoire (arrangements); intérimaire, par intérim (council, person). ‖ FIN. Provisoire (dividend).
— adv. Dans l'intérim (or) l'intervalle, entre-temps.
interior [in'tiəriə*] adj. Intérieur. ‖ MATH. Interne (angle). ‖ FIG. Intérieur, intime, secret, profond.
— n. Intérieur m. (inside, inland region, internal affairs, subject for painting). ‖ FIG. For intérieur m. (soul). ‖ **Interior decoration**, n. Décoration (f.) d'intérieur. ‖ **Interior decorator**, n. Décorateur s.
interiorly [-li] adv. Intérieurement.
interjacent [,intə'dʒei∫ənt] n. Intermédiaire, interjacent.
interject [,intə'dʒekt] v. tr. Lancer (questions). ‖ Intervenir pour placer (a remark). [See INTERPOSE.] ‖ GRAMM. Interjecter.
— v. intr. Interrompre une conversation.
interjection [-∫ən] n. GRAMM. Interjection f.
interjectional [-∫ənḷ], **interjectory** [-təri] adj. GRAMM. Interjectiel.
interlace [,intə'leis] v. tr. Entrelacer ; entremêler (with, de).
— v. intr. S'entrelacer, s'entremêler.
interlacing [-iŋ] n. Entrelacement m.
interlard [,intə'lɑ:d] v. tr. CULIN., FIG. Entrelarder (with, de).
interleaf ['intəli:f] (pl. **interleaves** [-li:vz]) n. Page blanche interfoliée f.
interleave [intə'li:v] v. tr. Interfolier.
interline [-'lain] v. tr. Interligner (a document, a translation).
interline v. tr. Doubler, molletonner (a garment).
interlinear [-'liniə*] adj. Interlinéaire.
interlineation ['intə,lini'ei∫ən] n. Interlinéation f.
interlining [,intə'lainiŋ] n. Doublure intermédiaire f.
interlock [,intə'lɔk] v. tr. TECHN. Emboîter ; enclencher ; engrener. ‖ FIG. Imbriquer.
— v. intr. TECHN. S'emboîter, s'enclencher ; s'engrener. ‖ FIG. S'imbriquer.
interlocution [,intələ'kju:∫ən] n. Interlocution f.
interlocutor [,intə'lɔkjutə*] n. Interlocuteur m.
interlocutory [-təri] adj. De conversation. (See CONVERSATIONAL.) ‖ JUR. Interlocutoire.
interlocutress [-tris] n. Interlocutrice f.
interlope [,intə'loup] v. intr. COMM. Faire du commerce interlope. ‖ FIG. S'imposer, être de trop, se mêler des affaires d'autrui. (See INTRUDE.)
interloper [-ə*] n. NAUT. Navire interlope m. ‖ COMM. Trafiquant, mercanti m. ‖ FIG. Intrus s.

Interlude ['intəlju:d] n. THEATR. Intermède *m.* ‖ MUS. Interlude *m.* ‖ FIG. Intervalle *m.*

Intermarriage [,intə'mæridʒ] n. Mariage consanguin, intermariage *m.* ‖ Mariage mixte *m.*

Intermarry [,intə'mæri] v. intr. Se marier entre parents (or) entre races différentes.

Intermeddle [,intə'medl̩] v. intr. Intervenir; s'immiscer (*with,* dans); se mêler (*with,* de). [See INTERFERE.]

Intermeddling [-'medliŋ] n. Intervention, intrusion, ingérence *f.*

Intermediary [,intə'mi:diəri] adj., n. Intermédiaire *s.*

Intermediate [-djit] adj., n. Intermédiaire *s.*
— v. intr. S'entremettre; servir d'intermédiaire (*between,* entre).

Interment [in'tə:mənt] n. Enterrement *m.*

Intermezzo [,intə'metsou] n. MUS. Intermezzo *m.* ‖ THEATR. Intermède, intermezzo *m.*
— N. B. Deux pluriels : *intermezzi, intermezzos.*

Interminable [in'tə:minəbl̩] adj. Interminable.

Interminably [-bli] adv. Interminablement.

Intermingle [,intə'miŋgl̩] v. tr. Entremêler (*with,* de). [See COMMINGLE.]
— v. intr. S'entremêler (*with,* à).

Intermission [,intə'miʃən] n. Interruption, trève, pause *f.; without intermission,* sans relâche, sans désemparer. ‖ MED. Intermission *f.* (of fever); intermittence *f.* (of pulse). ‖ U. S. THEATR. Entracte *m.*

Intermissive [-siv] adj. Intermittent.

Intermit [,intə'mit] v. tr. (1). Interrompre.
— v. intr. MED. Etre intermittent (pain, pulse).

Intermittence [-əns] n. Intermittence *f.*

Intermittent [-ənt] adj. Intermittent.

Intermittently [-əntli] adv. Par intermittence.

Intermix [,intə'miks] v. tr. Entremêler. (See COMMINGLE.)
— v. intr. S'entremêler, se mélanger.

Intermixture [-tʃə*] n. Mélange *m.*

Intermolecular [,intəmo'lekjulə*] adj. PHYS. Intermoléculaire.

Intern [in'tə:n] v. tr. MILIT. Interner (aliens, ships).
— v. intr. U. S. MED. Etre interne.
— n. MED. U. S. Interne *s.* ‖ MILIT. U. S. Interné *m.*

Internal [-l̩] adj. TECHN. Interne (combustion). ‖ MATH. Interné (angle). ‖ MED. Intestinal (chill); interne (ear, injuries). ‖ COMM. Intérieur, de l'intérieur (trade). ‖ JUR. Intrinsèque (evidence). ‖ FIN. Intrinsèque (value); *internal revenue,* recettes fiscales. ‖ FIG. Intime (conviction); interne (evidence) [in literature].
— n. pl. MED. Entrailles *f. pl.* ‖ FIG. Qualités essentielles *f. pl.*

Internally [-əli] adv. Intérieurement. ‖ MED. « *Not to be taken internally* », pour usage externe (medicine).

International [,intə'næʃnl̩] adj. International.
— n. MUS. Internationale *f.* (hymn). ‖ SPORTS. International *m.*

Internationalism [-izm̩] n. Internationalisme *m.*

Internationalist [-ist] n. Internationaliste *s.* ‖ JUR. Juriste (*m.*) spécialisé dans le droit international.

Internationalize [-aiz] v. tr. Internationaliser.

Internecine [,intə'ni:sain] adj. MILIT. D'extermination réciproque (war).

Internee [,intə'ni:] n. MILIT. Interné *s.*

Internist ['intə:nist] n. MED. Spécialiste (*s.*) de la pathologie interne, interniste *s.*

Internment [in'tə:nmənt] n. MILIT. Internement *m.* ‖ JUR. Réclusion *f.*

Internship ['intə:nʃip] n. U. S. MED. Internat *m.*

Interoceanic ['intə,rouʃi'ænik] adj. GEOGR. Interocéanique.

Interosculate [intə'rɔskjuleit] v. intr. Se mêler. (See COMMINGLE.) ‖ BOT. Avoir des caractères communs.

Interosseal [-'rɔsiəl] adj. MED. Interosseux.

Interpellant [-:'pelənt] n. JUR. Interpellateur *m.*

Interpellate [in'tə:peleit] v. tr. JUR. Interpeller.

Interpellation [,intə:pe'leiʃən] n. JUR. Interpellation *f.*

Interpellator [,intə:pə'leitə*] n. Interpellateur *m.*

Interpenetrate [,intə'penitreit] v. tr. Pénétrer dans, interpénétrer.
— v. intr. S'interpénétrer.

Interpenetration ['intə,peni'treiʃən] n. Interpénétration *f.*

Interphone ['intəfoun] n. Téléphone intérieur *m.*

Interplanetary [,intə'plænətəri] adj. ASTRON. Interplanétaire; *interplanetary ship,* astronef, vaisseau spatial.

Interplay [,intə'plei] n. Effets combinés *m. pl.*

Interpolate [in'tə:poleit] v. tr. Altérer par interpolation (a book); interpoler (words). ‖ MATH. Interpoler.

Interpolation [in,tə:po'leiʃən] n. Interpolation *f.*

Interpolator [in'tə:poleitə*] n. Interpolateur *m.*; interpolatrice *f.*

Interposal [,intə'pouzl̩], **Interposition** ['intə,-pou'ziʃən] n. Interposition *f.* ‖ Intervention *f.*

Interpose [,intə'pouz] v. tr. Interposer (an object). ‖ FIG. Faire état de, mettre en avant (one's authority); intervenir pour placer (a remark). [See INTERJECT.]
— v. intr. S'interposer. (See INTERVENE.)

Interpret [in'tə:prit] v. tr. Interpréter.
— v. intr. Interpréter. ‖ Servir d'interprète.

Interpretation [in,tə:pri'teiʃən] n. Interprétation *f.*

Interpretative [in'tə:pritətiv] adj. Interprétatif.

Interpreter [-ə*] n. Interprète *m.*

Interpretress [-ris] n. Interprète *f.*

Interracial [,intə'reiʃəl] adj. Interethnique, interracial.

Interregnum [,intə'regnəm] n. Interrègne *m.*
— N. B. Deux pluriels : *interregnums, interregna.*

Interrelated [,intəri'leitid] adj. En corrélation.

Interrelation [-ʃən] n. Corrélation *f.*

Interrogate [in'terəgeit] v. tr. Interroger.

Interrogation [in,terə'geiʃən] n. Interrogation, question *f.* ‖ GRAMM. *Interrogation mark* (or) *note* (or) *point,* point d'interrogation. ‖ JUR. Interrogatoire *m.*

Interrogative [,intə'rɔgətiv] adj. Interrogateur *m.*; interrogatrice *f.* ‖ GRAMM. Interrogatif.
— n. GRAMM. Interrogatif *m.*

Interrogatively [-li] adj. Interrogativement.

Interrogator [in'terəgeitə*] n. Interrogateur *m.*; interrogatrice *f.*

Interrogatory [,intə'rɔgətəri] adj. Interrogateur *m.*; interrogatrice *f.*
— n. Interrogatoire *m.*

Interrupt [,intə'rʌpt] v. tr. Interrompre (a discussion, a person, a speech). ‖ Interrompre, couper (communication); *to interrupt a private conversation,* rompre un tête-à-tête. ‖ Borner, intercepter, obstruer (view).

Interrupter [-tə*] n. Interrupteur *m.*; interruptrice *f.* ‖ ELECTR. Interrupteur, disjoncteur *m.*

Interruption [-ʃən] n. Interruption *f.*

Intersect [,intə'sekt] v. tr. Entrecouper, entrecroiser. ‖ MATH. Intersecter.
— v. intr. S'entrecouper, s'entrecroiser. ‖ MATH. S'intersecter.

Intersection [-ʃən] n. Intersection *f.* ‖ U. S. Carrefour *m.*

Interspace [,intə'speis] n. Intervalle *m.*
— v. tr. Espacer.

Intersperse [-'spə:s] v. tr. Entremêler, parsemer, émailler (*with,* de). ‖ Répandre (*among, between,* dans, parmi).

interstate [-,steit] adj. Entre Etats. ‖ Entre les différents Etats des Etats-Unis, de l'Australie, etc.
interstellar [-'stelə*] adj. ASTRON. Interstellaire, interastral.
interstice [in'tə:stis] n. Interstice *m*.
interstitial [,intə:'stiʃəl] adj. Interstitiel.
intertwine [,intə'twain], **intertwist** [-'twist] v. tr. Entrelacer.
— v. intr. S'entrelacer.
interurban [-'ə:bən] adj. U. S. De banlieue (train).
interval ['intəvəl] n. Intervalle *m*. (in space, time). ‖ Récréation *f*. (at school). ‖ Mus. Intervalle *m*. ‖ SPORTS. Mi-temps *f*. ‖ THEATR. Entracte *m*. ‖ FIG. Distance *f*.
intervene [,intə'vi:n] v. intr. Survenir, intervenir (event); intervenir, s'interposer (person). ‖ S'étendre (*between*, entre).
intervenient [-jənt] adj. Intermédiaire (distance, period); survenu (event); intervenant, interposé (person).
intervention [,intə'venʃən] n. MED., JUR., COMM., FIG. Intervention *f*.
interventionist [-nist] adj., n. JUR. Interventionniste *m*.
interview ['intəvju:] n. Entrevue *f*. ‖ Interview *f*. (article, meeting).
— v. tr. Avoir une entrevue avec. ‖ Interviewer.
intervolve [,intə'vɔlv] v. tr. Enrouler.
interweave [-'wi:v] v. tr. (187). Tisser ensemble, brocher. (See INWEAVE.) ‖ Entrelacer (to intertwine). ‖ FIG. Entremêler.
intestate [in'testit] adj., n. JUR. Intestat *m*.
intestinal [in'testinl] adj. MED. Intestinal. ‖ FAM. U. S. *Intestinal fortitude*, du cœur au ventre.
intestine [-tin] n. MED. Intestin *m*.
— adj. MILIT. Intestine (war).
intimacy ['intiməsi] n. Intimité *f*. ‖ JUR. Rapports sexuels *m*. *pl*.
intimate [-mit] adj. Intime, essentiel (structure). ‖ Intime, personnel, profond (feelings). ‖ Intime, familier (friend). ‖ Intime, approfondi, total (knowledge).
— n. Intime *s*.
intimate [-meit] v. tr. Annoncer, faire savoir (to make known). ‖ Suggérer, impliquer (to suggest). ‖ Intimer, notifier, signifier (to give notice).
intimately [-mitli] adv. Intimement.
intimation [,inti'meiʃən] n. Annonce *f*. (announcement); suggestion *f*. (hint); signification, notification *f*. (notice). ‖ Indication, prémonition *f*. (sign).
intimidate [in'timideit] v. tr. Intimider.
intimidation [in,timi'deiʃən] n. Intimidation *f*.
intimidator [in'timideitə*] n. Intimidateur *m*.; intimidatrice *f*.
intimity [in'timiti] n. Intimité *f*.
into ['intu] prep. En, dans (movement); *to come into contact with*, entrer en contact avec; *to crumble into dust*, tomber en poussière; *to help s.o. into a car*, aider qqn à monter en voiture; *to step into the hall*, entrer dans le vestibule. ‖ Dans, en (change); *lady into fox*, la dame changée en renard; *to exalt a man into a god*, d'un homme faire un dieu. ‖ Dans, en (penetration); *far into the night*, bien avant dans la nuit; *he talked himself into a fat job*, par son bagou il s'est procuré une bonne place.
— adv. Au-dedans; *his car was run into by a lorry* (or) U. S. *truck*, son auto a été emboutie par un camion; *the house was broken into*, la maison fut cambriolée; *to eat into one's capital*, grignoter sa fortune.
intoed ['in'toud] adj. Aux pieds (or) orteils tournés en dedans.
intolerability [,intɔlərə'biliti], **intolerableness** [in'tɔlərəblnis] n. Intolérabilité *f*.

intolerable [in'tɔlərəbl] adj. Intolérable. (See INSUFFERABLE.)
intolerably [-bli] adv. Intolérablement.
intolerance [in'tɔlərəns] n. Intolérance *f*. ‖ ECCLES. Intolérantisme *m*.
intolerant [-ənt] adj., MED., FIG. Intolérant.
intolerantly [-əntli] adv. Intoléramment.
intonation [,into'neiʃən] n. Intonation *f*. ‖ ECCLES. Psalmodie *f*.
intone [in'toun] v. tr. Entonner. ‖ ECCLES. Psalmodier.
in toto [in'toutou] adv. In extenso, dans sa totalité, dans son intégralité.
intoxicant [in'tɔksikənt] n. Alcool, spiritueux *m*.
— adj. Enivrant.
intoxicate [-keit] v. tr. Enivrer (lit. and fig.).
intoxicating [-keitiŋ] adj. Enivrant.
intoxication [in,tɔksi'keiʃən] n. Ivresse *f*. ‖ MED. Intoxication *f*. ‖ FIG. Enivrement *m*.
intractability [in,træktə'biliti] n. Nature intraitable *f*.
intractable [in'træktəbl] adj. TECHN. Difficile à travailler. ‖ MED. Invétéré. ‖ FIG. Intraitable, indocile (person); insoluble (problem).
intractably [-bli] adv. De façon intraitable.
intrados [in'treidɔs] n. ARCHIT. Intrados *m*.
intramural [intrə'mjuərəl] adj. Intra-muros.
intramuscular [-'mʌsjkulə*] adj. MED. Intramusculaire.
intransigency [in'trænsidʒənsi] n. Intransigeance *f*.
intransigent [-ənt] adj., n. Intransigeant *s*.
intransitive [in'trɑ:nsitiv] adj. Intransitif.
intransitively [-li] adv. GRAMM. Intransitivement.
intrant ['intrənt] n. Nouveau membre *m*. (in a club); débutant *s*. (in a profession); entrant *m*. (at school).
intranuclear [,intrə'nju:kliə*] adj. PHYS. Intranucléaire.
intravenous [-'vi:nəs] adj. MED. Intraveineux.
intreat [in'tri:t]. See ENTREAT.
intrench [in'trenʃ]. See ENTRENCH.
intrepid [in'trepid] adj. Intrépide.
intrepidity [,intri'piditi] n. Intrépidité *f*.
intrepidly [in'trepidli] adv. Intrépidement.
intricacy ['intrikəsi] n. Imbroglio *m*. ‖ Dédale, labyrinthe *m*. (of a town). ‖ JUR. Détours *m*. *pl*.; complications *f*. *pl*. (of the law). ‖ FIG. Complexité *f*. (of a problem).
intricate ['intrikit] adj. Embrouillé, compliqué. ‖ FIG. Complexe (problem); contourné (style); tarabiscoté (fam.).
intrigant ['intrigənt] n. Intrigant *m*.
intrigante n. Intrigante *f*.
intrigue [in'tri:g] n. Intrigue *f*.
— v. intr. Intriguer, comploter (*with*, avec). [See PLOT.] ‖ Avoir une liaison (*with*, avec) [to love].
— v. tr. FAM. Attirer l'attention de, intéresser.
intrinsic [in'trinsik] adj. Intrinsèque.
intrinsically [-əli] adv. Intrinsèquement.
introduce [,intrə'dju:s] v. tr. Introduire (*into*, dans) [s.ɔ., sth.]. ‖ Présenter (*to*, à) [s.o.]. ‖ Aborder, faire venir (a question). ‖ JUR. Déposer (a bill) [before Parliament].
introduction [,intrə'dʌkʃən] n. Introduction *f*. (*into*, dans) [of s.o., sth.]. ‖ Introduction (in a book). ‖ Présentation *f*. (*to*, à) [of s.o.]. ‖ MUS. Prélude *m*.
introductory [-təri] adj. Préliminaire (notion); liminaire (page); d'introduction (words).
introjection [,intrə'dʒekʃən] n. PSYCH. Introjection *f*.
intromission [,intro'miʃən] n. PHYS., BOT. Admission *f*. ‖ JUR. Immixtion *f*.
intromit [-'mit] v. tr. (1). Admettre.
introspect [-'spekt] v. intr. PHILOS. Rentrer en

soi-même, examiner son état d'âme, faire de l'introspection.
introspection [-'spekʃən] n. PHILOS. Introspection *f.* ‖ FAM. Repliement (*m.*) sur soi-même.
introspective [-'spektiv] adj. PHILOS. Introspectif. ‖ FAM. Replié sur soi-même.
introversion [-'vəːʃən] n. PHILOS. Introversion *f.* ‖ MED. Invagination *f.; introversion of the eyelid,* entropion. ‖ FIG. Repliement sur soi-même *m.*
introvert [-'vəːt] v. tr. PHILOS. Introvertir. ‖ MED. Retourner. ‖ FIG. *To introvert one's mind,* méditer sur soi-même, se recueillir.
— n. Caractère introverti *m.*
intrude [in'truːd] v. tr. Introduire de force (*into,* dans); *to intrude oneself into,* s'immiscer dans. ‖ Imposer (one's presence) [*on,* à].
— v. intr. Etre importun, déranger. ‖ S'immiscer, s'introduire (*into,* dans). ‖ S'imposer (*on, upon,* à). ‖ Abuser (*on,* de) [s.o.'s time].
intruder [-ə*] n. Intrus *s.* ‖ AVIAT. Intercepteur *m.; intruder raid,* raid d'interception. ‖ MILIT. *Intruder patrol,* patrouille de guet. ‖ JUR. Occupant illicite *s.*
intrusion [in'truːʒən] n. Intrusion *f.* ‖ Dérangement *m.;* visite importune; présence gênante *f.* ‖ JUR. Empiètement, accaparement *m.;* occupation illicite *f.*
intrusive [-siv] adj. Importun, gênant (person). ‖ GRAMM. Excrescent. ‖ GEOL. Intrusif.
intrusively [-sivli] adv. En intrus, importunément, fâcheusement.
intubate ['intjubeit] v. tr. MED. Intuber.
intubation [,intju'beiʃən] n. MED. Intubation.
intuit ['intjuit] v. tr., intr. Connaître intituitivement.
intuition [,intju'iʃən] n. Intuition *f.*
intuitional [-l], **intuitive** [in'tjuitiv] adj. Intuitif.
intuitively [-li] adv. Intuitivement.
intumesce [,intju'mes] v. intr. MED. Se tuméfier, gonfler, enfler.
intumescence [-ns] n. MED. Intumescence *f.*
intumescent [-nt] adj. MED. Tuméfié.
inulin ['injulin] n. CHIM. Inuline *f.*
inunction [i'nʌŋkʃən] n. Onction *f.* (ointing); liniment *m.* (ointment).
inundate ['inʌndeit] v. tr. Inonder.
inundation [,inʌn'deiʃən] n. Inondation *f.*
inurbane [,inəː'bein] adj. Sans urbanité, incivil.
inurbanity [-bæniti] n. Manque (*m.*) d'urbanité; incivilité *f.* (See IMPOLITENESS.)
inure [i'njuə*] v. tr. Aguerrir (*to,* contre); endurcir, rompre (*to,* à).
— v. intr. JUR. Prendre effet, entrer en vigueur.
inurement [-mənt] n. Endurcissement *m.;* accoutumance *f.* ‖ JUR. Mise en vigueur *f.*
inusable [i'njuːzəbl̩] adj. Non utilisable.
inutility [,inju'tiliti] n. Inutilité *f.* (See USELESSNESS.)
invade [in'veid] v. tr. MILIT. Envahir (s.o.'s house); violer (s.o.'s privacy). ‖ MILIT., MED., FIG. Envahir. ‖ JUR. Empiéter sur.
invader [-ə*] n. MILIT. Envahisseur *m.* ‖ JUR. Usurpateur *m.* ‖ FIG. Intrus, envahisseur *m.*
invaginate [in'vædʒineit] v. tr. Engainer. ‖ MED. Invaginer. (See INTROVERT.)
— v. intr. MED. S'invaginer.
invagination [in,vædʒi'neiʃən] n. MED. Invagination *f.*
invalid ['invəliːd] adj. MED. Invalide (infirm); malade (sick); maladif (valetudinary); *invalid chair,* voiture d'infirme.
— n. MED. Invalide, infirme *s.* (incapacitated person); malade (sick person); malade chronique *m.,* personne de santé délicate *f.* (valetudinarian).
— v. tr. MED. Rendre infirme (or) malade. ‖ MILIT. *To invalid out of the army,* réformer.

— v. intr. MED. Devenir infirme (or) malade. ‖ MILIT. Etre réformé.
invalid [in'vælid] adj. JUR. Non valide, invalide.
invalidate [-eit] v. tr. JUR. Invalider.
invalidation [in,væli'deiʃən] n. JUR. Invalidation *f.*
invalidity [,invə'liditi] n. MED. Invalidité *f.* (infirmity); santé chancelante *f.,* maladie chronique *f.* (sickness). ‖ JUR. Invalidité *f.*
invaluable [in'væljuəbl̩] adj. Inappréciable. (See PRICELESS.)
invariability [in,vɛəriə'biliti] n. Invariabilité *f.*
invariable [in'vɛəriəbl̩] adj. Invariable.
invariably [-bli] adv. Invariablement.
invasion [in'veiʒən] n. MILIT. Invasion *f.; invasion barge,* péniche de débarquement. ‖ MED. Invasion *f.* ‖ JUR. Empiétement *m.* (*of,* sur). ‖ FIG. Invasion *f.;* envahissement *m.;* intrusion *f.*
invasive [-ziv] adj. MILIT. D'invasion. ‖ FIG. Envahissant.
invective [in'vektiv] n. Invective, vitupération *f.*
inveigh [in'vei] v. intr. Invectiver.
inveigle [in'viːgl̩] v. tr. Attirer, entraîner. ‖ Séduire, enjôler.
inveiglement [-mənt] n. Enjôlement *m.;* séduction *f.*
invent [in'vent] v. tr. Inventer.
invention [in'venʃən] n. TECHN., ECCLES., FIG. Invention *f.*
inventive [-tiv] adj. Inventif.
inventiveness [-tivnis] n. Génie inventif, esprit (*m.*) d'invention.
inventor [-tə*] n. Inventeur *m.*
inventory ['invəntəri] n. Inventaire *m.*
— v. tr. Inventorier.
inventress [in'ventris] n. Inventrice *f.*
Inverness [,invə'nes] n. GEOGR. Inverness *m.* ‖ COMM. *Inverness cape* (or) *cloak,* macfarlane.
inverse ['in'vəːs] adj., n. Inverse *m.*
inversely [-li] adv. Inversement.
inversion [in'vəːʃən] n. Interversion, inversion *f.* ‖ GRAMM., MATH. Inversion *f.* ‖ MUS. Renversement *m.* ‖ MED. *Sexual inversion,* homosexualité. ‖ FIG. Renversement *m.* (of values).
inversive [-siv] adj. Inversif.
invert [in'vəːt] v. tr. Renverser, retourner (sth.). ‖ Intervertir, renverser (an order). ‖ TECHN., MUS. Renverser. ‖ GRAMM. *Inverted commas,* guillemets.
— ['invəːt] adj. CHIM. Inverti (sugar).
— n. MED. Inverti *s.* ‖ TECHN. Radier *m.*
invertebrate [in'vəːtibrit] adj., n. ZOOL. Invertébré *m.*
invest [in'vest] v. tr. Vêtir (to clothe). ‖ MILIT. Investir. ‖ FIN. Investir, placer (*in,* dans). ‖ JUR., FIG. Investir (*with,* de) [an authority, a right].
— v. intr. FIN. Investir (or) placer de l'argent (*in,* dans). ‖ FAM. *To invest in,* s'offrir, se payer.
investigate [in'vestigeit] v. tr. Examiner en détail; étudier; scruter; se livrer à des investigations sur. ‖ JUR. Enquêter sur.
investigation [in,vesti'geiʃən] n. Examen *m.;* investigation *f.* ‖ JUR. Enquête *f.*
investigative [in'vestigətiv], **investigatory** [-təri] adj., **investigator** [-tə*] n. Investigateur *m.;* investigatrice *f.*
investiture [in'vestitʃə*] n. Investiture *f.* ‖ Remise (*f.*) de décorations.
investment [in'vestmənt] n. † Vêtement *m.* ‖ FIN. Investissement, placement *m.* (of money); pl. Valeurs investies *f. pl.;* portefeuille *m.* (money). ‖ MILIT. Investissement *m.* ‖ JUR., ECCLES. Investiture *f.* ‖ TECHN. Moulage (*m.*) à la cire perdue.
investor [-ə*] n. FIN. Epargnant, actionnaire, capitaliste *m.;* acheteur, détenteur *m.* (in stocks).
inveteracy [in'vetərəsi] n. MED. Chronicité *f.* ‖ FIG. Enracinement; caractère invétéré *m.;* obstination *f.*

inveterate [-it] adj. Invétéré. (See CONFIRMED.) ‖ Chronique. ‖ Obstiné.

inveterately [-itli] adv. Obstinément.

invidious [in'vidiəs] adj. Désobligeant, blessant (comparison); odieux (conduct); ingrat, déplaisant (task). ‖ Propre à susciter l'envie (wealth).

invigilate [in'vidʒileit] v. intr. Surveiller les candidats.

invigorant [in'vigərənt] n. MED. Fortifiant, tonique *m.* (See CORROBORANT.)

invigorate [-eit] v. tr. MED. Revigorer, vivifier, fortifier; ravigoter (fam.).

invigorative [-eitiv] adj. MED. Vivifiant, fortifiant.

invincibility [in,vinsi'biliti] n. Invincibilité *f.*

invincible [in'vinsibl̩] adj. Invincible.

invincibly [-bli] adv. Invinciblement.

inviolability [in,vaiələ'biliti] n. Inviolabilité *f.*

inviolable [in'vaiələbl̩] adj. Inviolable.

inviolably [-bli] adv. Inviolablement.

inviolate [in'vaiəlit] adj. Inviolé.

invisibility [in,vizi'biliti] n. Invisibilité *f.*

invisible [in'vizibl̩] adj., n. Invisible *m.*

invisibly [-bli] adv. Invisiblement.

invitation [,invi'teiʃən] n. Invitation *f.* (act, message). ‖ **Invitation-card,** n. Carton *m.;* carte d'invitation *f.*

invite [in'vait] v. tr. Inviter (*to,* à) [s.o.]; *to invite oneself to dine with s.o.,* demander à dîner à qqn. ‖ FIG. Solliciter (attention); provoquer (confidences, misfortune); inviter à (discussion); susciter (questions, scandal); inviter, convier, encourager (*to,* à) [s.o.]; *to invite ridicule,* prêter à la plaisanterie.
— ['invait] n. FAM. Invitation *f.*

inviting [-iŋ] adj. Alléchant (dinner). ‖ Encourageant (gesture).

invitingly [-iŋli] adv. D'une manière engageante.

invocation [,invo'keiʃən] n. Invocation *f.* (incantation, prayer); *under the invocation of,* sous le vocable de.

invocatory [in'vɔkətəri] adj. Invocatoire.

invoice ['invɔis] n. COMM. Facture *f.* ‖ **Invoice-clerk,** n. COMM. Facturier *s.; typist invoice-clerk,* dactylo-facturière.
— v. tr. COMM. Facturer.

invoke [in'vouk] v. tr. Evoquer (evil spirits). ‖ ECCLES., FIG. Invoquer. ‖ † Implorer.

involuntarily [in'vɔləntərili] adv. Involontairement.

involuntary [-əri] adj. Involontaire.

involute ['invəlu:t] adj. BOT. Involuté. ‖ MATH. A (or) de développante. ‖ FIG. Entortillé; tortueux. ‖ TECHN. Spiral (spring).
— n. MATH. Développante *f.*

involuted [-id] adj. Involuté. ‖ FIG. Entortillé, tortueux. (See INVOLUTE.)

involution [,invə'lu:ʃən] n. BOT., MED. Involution *f.* ‖ MATH. Elévation à une certaine puissance *f.* ‖ FIG. Tortuosité, complication *f.*

involve [in'vɔlv] v. tr. Enrouler (to coil, to roll up); envelopper (*into,* dans) [to wrap]. ‖ Inclure, englober, renfermer (*in,* dans). [See INCLUDE.] ‖ Embrouiller (to complicate). ‖ Impliquer, engager, entraîner (*in,* dans) [to implicate]; mêler (*in,* à); *the person involved,* l'intéressé. ‖ Impliquer, entraîner, supposer (to entail); impliquer, requérir, demander (to require). ‖ Absorber, occuper (*in,* à) [to engross]. ‖ MATH. Elever à une certaine puissance.

involved [-d] adj. Embrouillé, compliqué (see INTRICATE); *the involved regulations,* les règlements compliqués. ‖ Compromis (*in,* dans). ‖ FIN. A prévoir (expenses). ‖ JUR. Grevé de dettes (estate); *the regulations involved,* les règlements en jeu.

involvement [-mənt] n. Enroulement; enveloppe-

ment *m.* ‖ Complication *f. pl.;* imbroglio *m.* (intricacy). ‖ Implication *f.* (*in,* dans). ‖ Engagement *m.* (in politics). ‖ FIN. Difficultés financières *f. pl.*

invulnerability [in,vʌlnərə'biliti] n. Invulnérabilité *f.*

invulnerable [in'vʌlnərəbl̩] adj. Invulnérable.

inwall [in'wɔ:l] v. tr. U. S. Clore de murs.

inward ['inwəd] adj. Interne. (See INTERNAL.) ‖ Intérieur (inland, interior). ‖ Intime (intimate); profond (secret). ‖ Dirigé vers l'intérieur (ingoing). ‖ **Inward-flow,** adj. TECHN. Centripète (turbine).
— adv. U. S. See INWARDS.

inwardly [-li] adv. Intérieurement, en dedans.

inwardness [-nis] n. Essence *f.* (inner nature). ‖ Sens profond *m.* (meaning). ‖ Spiritualité, profondeur de pensée *s.*

inwards [-z] adv. Intérieurement, en dedans. ‖ Vers l'intérieur.
— ['inə:dz] n. pl. FAM. Boyaux, intérieurs *m. pl.*

inweave [in'wi:v] v. tr. (187). Tisser (*into,* dans); brocher (*with,* de).

inwrap [in'ræp]. See ENWRAP.

inwrought ['in'rɔ:t] adj. Broché (interwoven); incrusté (*in,* dans; *with,* de) [inlaid]. ‖ Ouvragé, orné (*with,* de).

iodate ['aiədeit] n. CHIM. Iodate *m.*
— v. tr. MED. Ioder.

iodic [ai'ɔdik] adj. CHIM. Iodique.

iodide ['aiədaid] n. CHIM. Iodure *f.*

iodinate [ai'ɔdineit] v. tr. CHIM. Ioder.

iodination [aiədi'neiʃən] n. CHIM. Iodation *f.*

iodine [-di:n] n. CHIM. Iode *m.*

iodism [-dizm̩] n. MED. Iodisme *m.*

iodize [-daiz] v. tr. MED. Ioder.

iodoform [ai'oudəfɔ:m] n. CHIM. Iodoforme *m.*

ion [aiən] n. ELECTR. Ion *m.*

Ionian [ai'ounjən] adj., n. GEOGR. Ionien *s.*

Ionic [ai'ɔnik] adj. ARCHIT., ELECTR. Ionique.

Ionium [ai'ouniəm] n. PHYS. Ionium *m.*

ionization [,aiɔnai'zeiʃən] n. MED., ELECTR., PHYS. Ionisation *f.*

ionize ['aiɔnaiz] v. tr. ELECTR., PHYS. Ioniser.

ionosphere [ai'ɔnə,sfiə*] n. Ionosphère *f.*

iota [ai'outə] n. Iota *m.* (letter, quantity).

IOU [,aiou'ju:] n. Reconnaissance de dette *f.,* reçu *m.* (abbr. for *I owe you*).

ipecacuanha [,ipikæk'ju'ænə] n. BOT., MED. Ipécacuana; ipéca *m.*

ipso facto ['ipsou 'fæktou] adv. Ipso facto, de ce fait.

I. Q. [,ai'kju:] abbr. *intelligence quotient,* quotient intellectuel, Q. I.

I. R. A. [,aiɑ:*'ei] abbr. *Irish Republican army,* Armée républicaine irlandaise, I. R. A.

Irak [i:'rɑ:k]. See IRAQ.

Iran [i:'rɑ:n] n. GEOGR. Iran *m.*

Irani [-i] adj. GEOGR. Iranien.

Iranian [,ai'reinjən] adj., n. GEOGR. Iranien *s.*

Iraq [i:'rɑ:k] n. GEOGR. Irak *m.*

Iraqi [-i] adj., n. GEOGR. Irakien *s.*

irascibility [i,ræsi'biliti] n. Irascibilité *f.*

irascible [i'ræsibl̩] adj. Irascible.

irate [,aiə'reit] adj. Furieux, irrité. (See ANGRY.)

ire ['aiə*] n. Ire *f.* (See ANGER.)

ireful [-ful] adj. Courroucé.

Ireland ['aiələnd] n. GEOGR. Irlande *f.*

iridescence [,iri'desns] n. Irisation, iridescence *f.*

iridescent [-nt] adj. Irisé, iridescent.

iridium [,aiə'ridiəm] n. CHIM. Iridium *m.*

iris ['aiəris] (pl. **irises** [-iz]) n. BOT., MED. Iris *m.*

Irish ['aiəriʃ] adj. GEOGR. Irlandais; *Irish Free State,* République d'Irlande. ‖ CULIN. *Irish stew* ragoût irlandais. ‖ AGRIC. U. S. *Irish potato,* pomme de terre blanche.
— n. GRAMM. Irlandais *m.* (language). ‖ GEOGR. Irlandais *m. pl.* (people). ‖ U. S. FAM. *To get one's Irish up,* sortir de ses gonds.

Irishism [-izm̩] n. GRAMM. Idiotisme irlandais *m*.
Irishman [-mən] (pl. **Irishmen**) n. GEOGR. Irlandais *m*.
Irishwoman [-,wumən] (pl. **Irishwomen** [-,wimən]) n. GEOGR. Irlandaise *f*.
irk [əːk] v. tr. En coûter à. (See ANNOY.)
irksome [-səm] adj. Ennuyeux, pénible, lassant.
irksomely [-səmli] adv. Péniblement, fastidieusement.
irksomeness [-səmnis] n. Caractère fastidieux *m*.
iron ['aiən] n. Fer *m*. (métal); *cast iron*, fonte; *corrugated iron*, tôle ondulée; *old iron*, ferraille; *pig iron*, gueuse. ‖ TECHN. Fer *m*. (tool); *curling iron*, fer à friser; *electric iron*, fer électrique; *plane iron*, fer de rabot. ‖ SPORTS. Fer *m*. (in golf). ‖ Pl. Fers *m. pl*. (shackles). ‖ MED. Fer *m*. (medicine); pl. Attelles (*f. pl.*) en fer (surgical appliance). ‖ FIG. *Made of iron*, bâti à chaux et à sable; *the iron has entered into his soul*, le froid de la mort l'a pénétré, il a la mort dans l'âme; *to have many irons in the fire*, avoir un tas d'activités (or) beaucoup de pain sur la planche; *to have too many irons in the fire*, se disperser, éparpiller ses efforts. ‖ **Iron-bound**, adj. TECHN. Cerclé (cask); NAUT. Plein de récifs (coast); FIG. Rigide, inflexible. ‖ **Iron-grey**, adj. Gris fer (in general); poivre et sel (hair). ‖ **Iron-mould**, n. Tache de rouille (or) d'encre *f.*; v. tr. Tacher de rouille (or) d'encre; v. intr. Se tacher de rouille (or) d'encre. ‖ **Iron-stone**, n. Minerai de fer *m*.
— adj. De fer (age, curtain, cross, hand, ore). En fer (bridge). ‖ MILIT. De réserve (rations). ‖ MED. *Iron lung*, poumon d'acier. ‖ FIG. De fer, d'acier.
— v. tr. Ferrer (door, stick). ‖ Repasser (clothes). ‖ Mettre aux fers (a prisoner). ‖ FIG. *To iron out*, aplanir (difficulties).
— v. intr. Repasser (laundress).
ironclad [-klæd] adj., n. NAUT. Cuirassé *m*.
ironic(al) [,aiə'rɔnik(əl)] adj. Ironique.
ironically [-əli] adv. Ironiquement.
ironing ['aiəniŋ] -n. Repassage *m*. ‖ **Ironing-board**, n. Planche (*f.*) à repasser.
ironist ['airənist] n. Ironiste *m*.
ironmaster ['aiən,mɑːstə*] n. Maître (*m.*) de forges.
ironmonger [-,mʌŋgə*] n. Quincaillier *m.*; *ironmonger's shop*, quincaillerie.
ironmongery [-,mʌŋgəri] n. Quincaillerie *f*. (hardware).
ironwork ['aiənwəːk] n. Ferrures *f. pl*. (parts); ferronnerie, serrurerie *f*. (work). ‖ ARCHIT. Dentelle *f*. (of a balustrade); charpente (*f.*) en fer (of a house). ‖ Pl. Forge; usine sidérurgique *f*.
irony ['aiəni] adj. De (or) en fer.
irony ['airəni] n. Ironie *f*. ‖ LOC. *Dramatic, Socratic irony*, ironie dramatique, socratique.
irradiance [i'reidiəns] n. Rayonnement *m*.
irradiant [-ənt], **irradiated** [-eitid] adj. Irradiant. ‖ FIG. Rayonnant.
irradiate [-eit] v. tr. Irradier. ‖ FIG. Illuminer.
— v. intr. Irradier.
irradiation [i,reidi'eiʃən] n. PHYS., MED. Irradiation *f*. ‖ FIG. Illumination *f.; rayonnement *m*.
irradiative [i'reidiətiv] adj. Irradiant. ‖ FIG. Illuminant.
irrational [i'ræʃn̩l] adj. Irraisonnable, dépourvu de raison (animal, person). ‖ MATH. Irrationnel. ‖ FIG. Déraisonnable (belief); irrationnel (conduct). — n. MATH. Nombre irrationnel *m*.
irrationalism [-əlizm] n. PHILOS. Irrationalisme *m*.
irrationality [,iræʃ'næliti] n. Irrationalité, déraison *f*. (quality). ‖ Absurdité *f*. (act).
irrationally [i'ræʃnəli] adv. D'une façon irraisonnable; déraisonnablement. ‖ Irrationnellement.

irreclaimability [iri,kleimə'biliti] n. Incorrigibilité *f*.
irreclaimable [,iri'kleiməbl̩] adj. AGRIC. Inamendable. ‖ FIG. Incorrigible.
irrecognizable [i'rekəgnaizəbl̩] adj. Méconnaissable.
irreconcilability [i,rekənsailə'biliti] n. Inconciliabilité *f*. (of beliefs); irréconciliabilité *f*. (of enemies). ‖ Incompatibilité *f*. (of opinions).
irreconcilable [i,rekən'sailəbl̩] adj. Inconciliable (beliefs); irréconciliable (*with*, avec) [enemies]. ‖ Inconciliable (*with*, avec) [opinions].
irrecoverable [,iri'kʌvərəbl̩] adj. Non récupérable (object). ‖ FIN. Irrecouvrable. ‖ FIG. Irréparable, irrémédiable (loss).
irrecoverably [-bli] adv. Irrémédiablement.
irrecusable [,iri'kjuːzəbl̩] adj. JUR., FIG. Irrécusable.
irrecusably [-bli] adv. De manière irrécusable.
irredeemable [,iri'diːməbl̩] adj. FIN. Non amortissable, non remboursable (bonds). ‖ FIG. Irrémédiable (disaster); irréparable, irrachetable (fault); incorrigible, inamendable (person).
irreducibility ['iri,djuːsi'biliti] n. Irréductibilité *f*.
irreducible [-ibl̩] adj. Irréductible.
irrefragable [i'refrəgəbl̩] adj. Irréfragable, irrétutable, irrécusable.
irrefrangible [,iri'frændʒibl̩] adj. Inviolable (law). ‖ PHYS. Irréfrangible (rays).
irrefutability [i,refjutə'biliti] n. Irréfutabilité *f*.
irrefutable [i'refjutəbl̩] adj. Irréfutable.
irrefutably [-bli] adv. Irréfutablement.
irregular [i'regjulə*] adj. BOT., GRAMM., MILIT., FIG. Irrégulier.
— n. pl. MILIT. Irréguliers *m. pl*.
irregularity [i,regju'læriti] n. Irrégularité *f*.
irregularly [i'regjuləli] adv. Irrégulièrement.
irrelevance [i'relivəns], **irrelevancy** [-i] n. Manque (*m.*) de pertinence. (See IMPERTINENCE.) ‖ Manque de rapport (*m.*) avec une question. (See POINTLESSNESS.) ‖ A côté *m*. (side-issue).
irrelevant [-ənt] adj. Sans pertinence. ‖ Hors de cause (questions); hors de propos (remarks). ‖ Sans rapport (*to*, avec); étranger (*to*, à).
irrelevantly [-əntli] adv. Hors de propos.
irrelievable [i'riːləbl̩] adj. Inapaisable.
irreligion [,iri'lidʒən] n. Irréligion *f*.
irreligious [-dʒəs] adj. Irréligieux.
irreligiously [-dʒəsli] adv. Irréligieusement.
irremediable [,iri'miːdiəbl̩] adj. Irrémédiable.
irremediably [-bli] adv. Irrémédiablement.
irremissible [,iri'misibl̩] adj. Irrémissible (crime); inéluctable (duty).
irremovability ['iri,muːvə'biliti] n. JUR. Inamovibilité *f*.
irremovable [,iri'muːvəbl̩] adj. Immuable. ‖ JUR. Inamovible. ‖ FIG. Invincible (difficulty).
irremovably [-bli] adv. Inébranlablement.
irreparability [i,repərə'biliti] n. Irréparabilité *f*.
irreparable [i,repərəbl̩] adj. Irréparable. (See IRREMEDIABLE.)
irreparably [-bli] adv. Irréparablement.
irrepatriable [iri'pætriəbl̩] adj. Non rapatriable.
irreplaceable [,iri'pleisəbl̩] adj. Irremplaçable.
irrepressible [,iri'presibl̩] adj. Irrésistible (force); irréprimable (laughter); irréprimable (movement); intenable, endiablé (person).
irreproachable [,iri'proutʃəbl̩] adj. Irréprochable.
irreproachably [-bli] adv. Irréprochablement.
irresistibility [,irizisti'biliti] adv. Irrésistibilité *f*.
irresistible [,iri'zistibl̩] adj. Irrésistible.
irresistibly [-bli] adv. Irrésistiblement.
irresolute [i'rezəljuːt] adj. Irrésolu. (See INDECISIVE.)
irresolutely [-li] adv. Irrésolument.
irresoluteness [-nis], **irresolution** [i,rezə'ljuːʃən] n. Irrésolution *f*.

irresolvable [,iri'zɔlvəbl̩] adj. Insoluble.
irrespective [-'pektiv] adj. Indépendant (*of*, de). [See REGARDLESS.]
— adv. Indépendamment, sans se soucier (*of*, de).
irrespirable [i'respirəbl̩] adj. Irrespirable.
irresponsibility ['iris,pɔnsi'biliti] n. Irresponsabilité *f.*
irresponsible [,iris'pɔnsibl̩] adj. Irresponsable. ‖ Irréfléchi (act) ; étourdi, dépourvu du sens des responsabilités (person).
irresponsibly [-bli] adv. Irresponsablement.
irresponsive [,iris'pɔnsiv] adj. Fermé, indifférent, insensible (*to*, à).
irresponsiveness [-nis] n. Froideur, indifférence, insensibilité *f.* (*to*, à).
irretentive [,iri'tentiv] adj. Peu fidèle (memory).
irretrievable [,iri'tri:vəbl̩] adj. Irréparable. (See IRREMEDIABLE.)
irretrievably [-bli] adv. Irréparablement ; *irretrievably lost*, irrévocablement perdu.
irreverence [i'revərəns] n. Irrévérence *f.*
irreverent [-ənt] adj. Irrévérencieux.
irreverently [-əntli] adv. Irrévérencieusement.
irreversibility [i,rivə:si'biliti] n. Irréversibilité *f.*
irreversible [,iri'və:sibl̩] adj. Irréversible. ‖ JUR. Irrévocable.
irrevocability [i,revəkə'biliti], **irrevocableness** [i'revəkəbl̩nis] n. Irrévocabilité *f.*
irrevocable [i'revəkəbl̩] adj. Irrévocable.
irrevocably [-bli] adv. Irrévocablement.
irrigable ['irigəbl̩] adj. Irrigable.
irrigate ['irigeit] v. tr. MED., AGRIC. Irriguer. ‖ FIG. Arroser.
irrigation [,iri'geiʃən] n. MED., AGRIC. Irrigation *f.*
irrigator ['irigeitə*] n. MED. Irrigateur ; bock *m.* ‖ AGRIC. Arroseuse *f.*
irritability [,iritə'biliti] n. Irritabilité *f.*
irritable ['iritəbl̩] adj. Irritable.
irritably [-bli] adv. D'un ton irrité, avec humeur.
irritancy ['iritənsi] n. Irritation *f.*
irritant [-ənt] adj., n. MED. Irritant *m.*
irritate [-eit] v. tr. MED. Irriter (an organ, skin) ; envenimer (a wound). ‖ FIG. Irriter.
irritating [-eitiŋ] adj. Irritant.
irritatingly [-eitiŋli] adv. De manière irritante.
irritation [,iri'teiʃən] n. MED., FIG. Irritation *f.*
irritative ['iriteitiv] adj. MED. Irritatif.
irrupt [i'rʌpt] v. intr. Faire irruption (*into*, dans).
irruption [-ʃən] n. Irruption *f.*
I.R.S. [,aiɑ:*'es] U. S. Abbr. *Internal Revenue Service*, services fiscaux (or) des contributions américains.
Isabel ['izəbel], **Isabella** [izə'belə] adj., n. Isabelle *f.* (colour, name).
Isaiah [ai'zaiə] n. Isaïe *m.*
isatin ['izətin] n. CHIM. Isatine *f.*
ischiatic [iski'ætik] adj. MED. Sciatique.
ischium ['iskiəm] n. MED. Ischion *m.*
isinglass ['aiziŋglæ:s] n. CULIN. Gélatine *f.* ‖ TECHN. Mica *m.*
Islam [iz'lɑ:m] n. Islam *m.*
Islamic [iz'læmik] adj. Islamique.
Islamism ['izləmizm̩] n. Islamisme *m.*
island ['ailənd] n. Ile *f.* (isle) ; *small island*, îlot. ‖ Refuge *m.* (in the middle of a street) ; terre-plein *m.* (dividing strip). ‖ ARCHIT., MED. Ilot *m.* ‖ AVIAT., NAUT. Superstructure *f.*
— v. tr. Isoler. ‖ Parsemer.
islander [-ə*] n. Insulaire *s.*
isle [ail] n. Ile *f.* (See ISLAND.)
islet ['ailit] n. Ilot *m.*
ism [izm̩] n. FAM. Théorie *f.*
isobar ['aisobɑ:*] n. Isobare *f.*
isobaric [,aiso'bærik] adj. Isobarique (card) ; isobare (curve, line).
isochromatic [,aisokro'mætik] adj. Isochromatique.

isochronism [ai'sɔkrənizm̩] n. Isochronisme *m.*
isochronous [-nəs] adj. Isochrone.
isoclinal [,aiso'klainəl] adj., n. Isoclinal *m.*
isogloss ['aisou,glɔs] n. GRAMM. Isoglosse *f.*
isogonic [,aiso'gɔnik] adj. MATH. Isogone.
isolate ['aisoleit] v. tr. CHIM., PHYS., ELECTR., MED., FIG. Isoler.
isolation [,aiso'leiʃən] n. CHIM., PHYS. Isolation *f.* ‖ ELECTR., MED., FIG. Isolement *m.*
isolationism [-izm̩] n. Isolationnisme *m.*
isolationist [-ist] n. Isolationniste *m.*
isolator ['aisoleitə*] n. ELECTR. Isolateur, isolant *m.*
isomer ['aisomə*] n. CHIM. Isomère *m.*
isomeric [,aiso'merik] adj. CHIM. Isomère.
isometric(al) [,aiso'metrik(əl)] adj. MATH. Isométrique.
isomorph ['aisomɔ:f] n. Isomorphe *m.*
isomorphism [,aiso'mɔ:fizm̩] n. Isomorphisme *m.*
isomorphous [-fəs] adj. Isomorphe.
isopod ['aisopɔd] n. ZOOL. Isopode *m.*
isosceles [ai'sɔsili:z] adj. MATH. Isocèle.
isotherm ['aisoðə:m] n. Isotherme *f.*
isothermal [,aiso'θə:məl] adj. Isotherme.
isotonic [-'tɔnik] adj. MED. Isotonique.
isotope ['aisotoup] n. CHIM. Isotope *m.*
isotropic [,aiso'trɔpik] adj. PHYS. Isotrope.
isotype ['aisotaip] n. Isotype *m.*
Israel ['izreil] n. Israël *m.* (name, people, state).
Israeli [iz'reili] adj., n. GEOGR. Israélien *s.*
Israelite ['izreiəlait] n. Israélite *s.*
Israelitish [-iʃ] adj. Israélite.
issue ['isju:] n. Sortie *f.* (outgoing). ‖ Sortie, issue *f.* (place) ; débouché *m.* (of passage). ‖ Distribution *f.* (of goods). ‖ Numéro, fascicule *m. ;* livraison *f.* (of a magazine). ‖ GEOGR. Embouchure *f.* (of a river). ‖ MED. Ecoulement *m.* (discharge) ; exutoire *m.* (exutory). ‖ JUR. Postérité, descendance *f.* (offspring) ; *without issue*, sans enfant. ‖ JUR. Contestation *f. ;* litige *m. ; interest at issue*, intérêts en jeu ; *point at issue*, point controversé, objet du litige ; *to be at issue*, être en question (affair) ; être en discussion (person) ; *to join issue with s.o.*, prendre qqn à partie. ‖ JUR. Question *f.* (of fact, law) ; *side issue*, question secondaire, à-côté ; *to confuse the issue*, brouiller les cartes. ‖ FIN. Délivrance *f.* (of passport). ‖ CH. DE F. Distribution *f.* (of tickets). ‖ FIN. Emission *f.* (of banknotes, stamps) ; lancement *m.* (of loan) ; bénéfices, rapports *m. pl.* (profits). ‖ FIG. Résultat, aboutissement *m. ;* conclusion, issue *f. ; in the issue*, en fin de compte ; *to bring to an issue*, faire aboutir.
— v. intr. Sortir, paraître (book). ‖ **To issue forth** (or) **out**, jaillir, couler, s'écouler (blood, liquid) ; sortir *(from*, de) [person]. ‖ **To issue from**, venir de, dériver de, résulter de, être provoqué par (a cause) ; être issu de, sortir de (a family). ‖ **To issue in**, aboutir à, se terminer par, s'achever en.
— v. tr. Publier (a book, a message). ‖ Communiquer (a book in a library) ; *to be issued with*, recevoir par distribution. ‖ Distribuer ; *to issue children with milk*, distribuer du lait aux enfants. ‖ CH. DE F. Distribuer (tickets). ‖ FIN. Emettre (banknotes, cheques, stamps) ; créer (a bill) ; lancer (credits) ; lancer (a loan). ‖ JUR. Délivrer (an execution, a passport) ; lancer (a summons, a writ) ; rendre (a verdict) ; décerner (warrant). ‖ FIG. Donner (an order) ; faire (a proclamation).
issueless [-lis] adj. Sans postérité.
issuing [-iŋ] adj. Né, issu *(from*, de). ‖ FIN. Emetteur *m. ;* émettrice *f.*
isthmus ['isməs] n. GEOGR. Isthme *m.*
— N. B. Deux pluriels : *isthmuses, isthmi.*
it [it] pron. Il, elle, ce, cela, ça (subject) ; *it is cold*, il fait froid ; *it annoys me to see that*, cela me fâche de voir cela ; *it is still winter*, c'est encore l'hiver ;

the table is old but it is strong, la table est vieille mais elle est solide. ‖ Le, la, l', ça, lui (object); *a thing is impossible only when one thinks it so,* une chose n'est impossible que lorsqu'on croit qu'elle l'est; *do you believe it or not?,* le crois-tu ou non? *give him a sweet,* donne-lui un bonbon; *we love our work because we find it interesting,* nous aimons notre travail parce que nous le trouvons intéressant; *where did you find it?,* où l'as-tu trouvé? ‖ En; *I am afraid of it,* j'en ai peur; *I don't care for it,* je ne m'en soucie pas; *I need it,* j'en ai besoin. ‖ Y; *I'll keep it in mind,* j'y penserai; *I'll see to it,* j'y veillerai; *look at it closely,* regardez-y de près. ‖ (Anticipatory); *he thought it useless to proceed further,* il jugea inutile de poursuivre; *I take it that he gives his consent,* je crois comprendre qu'il donne son consentement; *they made it hard for us to find out the truth,* ils nous ont rendu difficile de découvrir la vérité. ‖ (Expletive); *to brazen it out,* payer d'effronterie; *to have the best of it,* être le mieux partagé; *we made it up,* nous nous sommes réconciliés. ‖ (Not translated); *above it,* au-dessus, dessus; *below it,* au-dessous, dessous; *on it,* dessus.
— n. Fam. Sex-appeal, chien *m.; she's got « it »,* elle a du chien, elle a de ça; U. S. *an it girl,* une vamp.

it n. Fam. *Gin and it,* Martini-gin (nom déposé).
Italian [i'tæljən] adj., n. Geogr. Italien *s.*
Italianism [-izm̩] n. Italianisme *m.*
Italianize [-aiz] v. tr., intr. Italianiser.
italic [i'tælik] adj. Gramm., Techn. Italique.
italicize [-saiz] v. tr. Mettre en italique.
italics [i'tæliks] n. pl. Italique *m.*
Italy ['itəli] n. Geogr. Italie *f.*
itch [itʃ] n. Med. Démangeaison *f.* (pruritus); gale *f.* (scabies). ‖ Fam. Démangeaison *f.* (*for,* de).
— v. intr. Med. Démanger; se démanger. ‖ Fam. *To itch for,* crever d'envie de; *to be itching to,* griller d'impatience de, avoir la démangeaison de.
itching [-iŋ] adj. Med. Démangeant. ‖ Fam. *To have an itching palm,* avoir les dents longues.
— n. See ITCH.

item ['aitəm] n. Article *m.; news items,* échos, faits divers (in a paper). ‖ Question *f.;* point *m.* (in a meeting). ‖ Comm. Article *m.* ‖ Jur. Item, article *m.* (in a contract). ‖ Fin. Poste *m.;* rubrique, écriture *f.* (in book-keeping); *to post an item,* passer une écriture. ‖ Theatr. Numéro *m.* (on the programme).
— adv. Item, de plus.
itemize [-aiz] v. tr. Fin. Détailler; spécifier.
iterate ['itəreit] v. tr. Réitérer; répéter.
iteration [,itə'reiʃən] n. Réitération, répétition *f.*
iterative ['itərətiv] adj. Itératif.
itinera(n)cy [ai'tinərə(n)si] n. Fréquents déplacements *m. pl.;* vie itinérante *f.*
itinerancy n. Jur., Eccles. Fonctions itinérantes *f. pl.;* ambulance *f.* (state).
itinerant [-ənt] adj. Eccles., Theatr. Ambulant, itinérant; Jur. Ambulatoire.
itinerary [-əri] adj., n. Itinéraire *m.*
itinerate [-eit] v. intr. Se déplacer, voyager sans cesse.
itineration [,aitinə'reiʃən] n. Continuels déplacements *m. pl.*
its [its] adj. poss. Son, sa, ses.
itself [it'self] pron. Lui-même, elle-même, soi-même, se, moi; *in the House of Lords itself,* en pleine Chambre des Lords; *he is kindness itself,* il est la bonté même; *pleasant in itself,* plaisant (or) agréable en soi; *the lid shuts itself,* le couvercle se ferme de lui-même (or) seul.
itsy-bitsy [,itsi'bitsi] adj. Fam. Tout petit, riquiqui.
ivied ['aivid] adj. Couvert de lierre.
ivory ['aivəri] n. Ivoire *m.* (colour, substance). ‖ Fam. Pl. Boules (*f. pl.*) de billard (balls); dés *m. pl.* (dice); touches (*f. pl.*) de piano (keys); dents *f. pl.* (teeth).
— adj. Ivoirin (creamy-white). ‖ Geogr. *Ivory Coast,* Côte-d'Ivoire. ‖ Fig. *Ivory tower,* tour d'ivoire.
ivy ['aivi] n. Bot. Lierre *m.*
izard ['izəd] n. Zool. Isard *m.*

J

j [dʒei] n. J, j *m.* (letter).
jab [dʒæb] v. tr. (1). Piquer, perforer (*with,* avec). ‖ Enfoncer (*into,* dans) [a knife]. ‖ Sports. Frapper d'un coup sec (or) droit (in boxing).
— n. Coup (*m.*) de pointe. ‖ Med. Piqûre *f.* ‖ Sports. Coup droit *m.*
jabber [-ə*] v. tr., intr. Bredouiller, baragouiner (to mumble). ‖ Jaboter, jacasser (to chatter).
— n. Baragouinage *m.* ‖ Jabotage *m.;* jacasserie *f.*
jabiru ['dʒæbiru] n. Zool. Jabiru *m.*
jaborandi [dʒæbə'rændi] n. Bot., Med. Jaborandi *m.*
jabot [ʒæ'bou] n. Jabot *m.* (frill).
jacaranda [,dʒækə'rændə] n. Bot. Jacaranda *m.*
jacinth ['dʒæsinθ] n. Zircon *m.;* hyacinthe *f.* (gem). ‖ Orange *m.* (colour).

Jack [ʒæk] n. Jeannot *m.* (name); *Jack Frost,* Bonhomme Hiver; *Jack Ketch,* M. Deibler; *Jack Sprat,* Tom Pouce. ‖ Sports. Cochonnet *m.* (at bowls); valet *m.* (card). ‖ Naut. Pavillon *m.* (flag); matelot *m.* (sailor); *Union Jack,* drapeau anglais. ‖ Techn. Jaquemart *m.* (in a clock); vérin *m.* (for lifting). ‖ Autom. Cric *m.* ‖ Zool. Brocheton *m.* ‖ Electr. Jack *m.* ‖ Fam. Type, zigoto *m.; every Jack had his Jill,* chacun avait sa chacune; *every man Jack,* tout un chacun. ‖ U. S. Pop. Fric *m.* (money). ‖ *Jack-a'-dandy,* n. Dandy *m.* ‖ *Jack-boot,* n. Botte à l'écuyère *f.* ‖ *Jack-in-office,* n. Fam. Monsieur Lebureau. ‖ *Jack-in-the-basket,* n. Naut. Vigie *f.* (buoy). ‖ *Jack-in-the-box,* n. Diable à ressort *m.* ‖ *Jack-knife,* n. Couteau pliant *m.;* Sports. Saut (*m.*) de carpe (dive); v. tr. U. S. suriner. ‖ *Jack-of-all-trades,*

n. Bricoleur (handy-man); Maître Jacques, factotum (servant). ‖ **Jack-o'lantern,** n. Feu follet *m.* ‖ **Jack-plane,** n. TECHN. Rabot *m.* ‖ **Jack-pot,** n. Gros lot *m.* ‖ **Jack-pudding,** n. Pitre, clown *m.* ‖ **Jack-straws,** n. pl. Jonchets *m. pl.* (game). ‖ **Jack-tar,** n. NAUT., FAM. Mathurin, marsouin, loup (*m.*) de mer. ‖ **Jack-towel,** n. Essuie-mains à rouleau *m.*
— adj. ZOOL. Mâle. ‖ **Jack-hare,** n. ZOOL. Bouquin *m.* ‖ **Jack-rabbit,** n. U. S. ZOOL. Gros lièvre (*m.*) d'Amérique. ‖ **Jack-snipe,** n. ZOOL. Bécassin *m.*
— v. tr. TECHN., AUTOM. Soulever au vérin (or) au cric. ‖ FIN. Faire monter (prices, wages). ‖ FAM. Lâcher, plaquer (to abandon). ‖ U. S. FAM. *To jack up,* remonter (to encourage).

jack n. BOT. Jaque *m.* (fruit); jaquier *m.* (tree).
jackal ['dʒækɔ:l] n. ZOOL., FIG. Chacal *m.*
jackanapes ['dʒækəneips] n. ZOOL. Singe *m.* ‖ FAM. Mal mouché *m.* (kid); freluquet *m.* (man).
— N. B. Le pluriel est *jackanapeses.*

jackass ['dʒækæs] n. ZOOL. Ane, baudet, bourricot *m.* ‖ FAM. Bourrique *f.*
jackdaw [-dɔ:] n. ZOOL. Choucas *m.*
jacket ['dʒækit] n. Veste *f.*; veston *m.* (men's); jaquette *f.* (women's); *jacket suit,* complet veston. ‖ Jaquette *f.* (for a book); chemise *f.* (for papers). ‖ ZOOL. Robe *f.* (of an animal). ‖ CULIN. Pelure *f.*; *potatoes in their jackets,* pommes de terre en robe de chambre. ‖ SPORTS. Casaque *f.* (of jockey). ‖ MED. *Strait jacket,* camisole de force.
— v. tr. Habiller (s.o.). ‖ Mettre une jaquette (or) une chemise à. ‖ **Jacketed-saucepan,** n. CULIN. Bain-marie *m.*
Jacobean [,dʒækə'bi:ən] adj. Du temps de Jacques Iᵉʳ.
jacobin ['dʒækəbin] n. Jacobin *s.*
jacobite [-ait] n. Jacobite *s.*
jacquard ['dʒækɑ:d] n. Jacquard *m.* (weave); *jacquard loom,* métier jacquard à tisser.
jade [dʒeid] n. Jade *m.* (colour, stone).
jade n. FAM. Rosse, haridelle *f.* (horse). ‖ FAM. Carcan *m.*; carne *f.* (woman).
— v. tr. FAM. Ereinter, esquinter.
jaded [-id] adj. FAM. Ereinté, esquinté, crevé, rompu (exhausted). ‖ Blasé, dégoûté (satiated).
jag [dʒæg] n. U. S. POP. Bombe, bamboche *f.*; *to have a jag on,* être rétamé (drunk).
jag n. Crevé *m.*; dentelure *f.* (in a cloth). ‖ Dent *f.* (of a rock, saw). ‖ Brèche *f.* (in a knife).
— v. tr. Ebrécher (a knife). ‖ Denteler, déchiqueter (rocks).
jagged [-id] adj. Dentelé, déchiqueté (rocks). ‖ Ebréché (knife).
jaguar ['dʒægjuə*] n. ZOOL. Jaguar *m.*
jail [dʒeil] n. U. S. See GAOL.
jailer [-ə*] n. U. S. See GAOLER.
jainism ['dʒeinizm] n. Djaïnisme *m.*
jakes [dʒeiks] n. pl. POP. Goguenots *m. pl.*; chiottes *f. pl.*
jalopy [dʒə'lɔpi] n. U. S. AUTOM. Carriole, bagnole, chignole *f.*; vieux clou, tapecul *m.* (car); vieux zinc *m.* (airplane).
jalousie ['ʒælu,zi:] n. Jalousie *f.* (shutter).
jam [dʒæm] n. Cohue, presse, foule *f.* (throng). ‖ Embouteillage, embarras *m.* (of traffic). ‖ NAUT. Embâcle *m.* ‖ RADIO. Brouillage *m.* ‖ MUS., FAM. *Jam session,* séance de jazz. ‖ FAM. *To get s.o. out of a jam,* tirer qqn du pétrin; *to get out of a jam,* se dédouaner. ‖ **Jam-full,** adj. Plein à craquer.
— v. tr. (1). Serrer, écraser, compresser, comprimer (to crush). ‖ Empiler, tasser (to cram). ‖ Obstruer, encombrer, embouteiller (a street). ‖ TECHN. Bloquer (brakes, a door); *to get jammed,* se coincer. ‖ RADIO. Brouiller.
— v. intr. Se bousculer, s'entasser, se presser. ‖ TECHN. Se bloquer, se coincer. ‖ MUS., FAM. Improviser (in jazz).

jam n. CULIN. Confiture *f.* ‖ FAM. *Money for jam,* affaire en or, argent facilement gagné; *it's real jam,* c'est du gâteau. ‖ **Jam-pot,** n. Pot (*m.*) à confiture.
— v. tr. CULIN. Confire (fruit).
Jamaica [dʒə'meikə] n. GEOGR. Jamaïque *f.*
jamb [dʒæm] n. ARCHIT. Montant, chambranle *m.*
jamboree [dʒæmbə'ri:] n. Jamboree *m.*
James [dʒeimz] n. Jacques *m.*
jamming ['dʒæmiŋ] n. RADIO. Brouillage *m.*
jammy ['dʒæmi] adj. FAM. En or (easy, pleasant); *that's really jammy,* c'est du gâteau. ‖ FAM. Veinard, chanceux (lucky); *to be jammy,* avoir du bol.
Jane [dʒein] n. Jeanne *f.* ‖ FAM. *A plain Jane,* un laideron.
jangle ['dʒæŋgl] v. intr. Faire un bruit de ferraille, résonner comme une vieille casserole. ‖ Criailler (to quarrel).
— v. tr. Faire retentir avec un bruit de ferraille. ‖ FAM. Mettre en boule (nerves).
— n. Bruit discordant *m.* ‖ Criaillerie, prise (*f.*) de bec (bickering).
janissary ['dʒænisəri] n. Janissaire *m.*
janitor ['dʒænitə*] n. Concierge, portier *m.*
Jansenism ['dʒænsənizm] n. Jansénisme *m.*
Jansenist [-ist] n. Janséniste *s.*
January ['dʒænjuəri] n. Janvier *m.*
Janus-faced ['dʒeinəs-'feist] adj. A deux visages.
Jap [dʒæp] n. FAM. Japonais *s.*
Japan [dʒə'pæn] n. GEOGR. Japon *m.* ‖ TECHN. Laque *f.*
— v. tr. (1). Laquer.
Japanese [,dʒæpə'ni:z] adj., n. invar. GEOGR. Japonais *s.* ‖ ARTS. *Japanese curio,* Japonerie.
jape [dʒeip] n. Plaisanterie *f.* (joke). ‖ Tour *m.* (trick).
japonica [dʒə'pɔnikə] n. BOT. Cognassier (*m.*) du Japon.
Japonist ['dʒæpənist] n. ARTS. Japoniste *s.*
jar [dʒɑ:*] n. Jarre *f.*; pot *m.* (earthenware); bocal *m.* (glass). ‖ ELECTR. Bac *m.*; *Leyden jar,* bouteille de Leyde.
jar n. Son discordant *m.* (sound). ‖ Choc, à-coup, contrecoup *m.*; saccade, secousse *f.* (See JOLT.) ‖ FIG. Choc, conflit *m.* (clash); désaccord *m.*; chamaillerie, friction *f.* (quarrel).
— v. intr. Grincer, détonner, rendre un son discordant. ‖ TECHN. Cogner (*upon,* sur) [machine]; vibrer (window). ‖ MUS. Détonner. ‖ FIG. Etre irritant (*upon,* pour); *to jar on s.o.'s nerves,* taper sur les nerfs de qqn. ‖ FIG. Etre en discordance (or) désaccord (*with,* avec); *colour jarring with,* couleur qui jure avec. ‖ FIG. Se chamailler.
— v. tr. Rendre discordant (a sound). ‖ Faire vibrer (a window). ‖ Choquer (ear); ébranler (nerves).
jargon ['dʒɑ:gən] n. Jargon *m.* ‖ FAM. Cafouillage, charabia, baragouin *m.*
jarring ['dʒɑ:riŋ] adj. Disparate (colours); discordant (sounds).
jarvey ['dʒɑ:vi] n. FAM. Automédon *m.*
jasmin(e) ['dʒæsmin] n. BOT. Jasmin *m.*
jasper ['dʒæspə*] n. Jaspe *m.*
jaundice ['dʒɔ:ndis] n. MED. Jaunisse *f.*; ictère *m.* ‖ FIG. Préjugés haineux *m. pl.*; envie *f.*
— v. tr. MED. Donner la jaunisse à. ‖ FIG. Rendre envieux; *jaundiced eye,* œil envieux.
jaunt [dʒɔ:nt] n. Excursion; balade *f.* (fam.)
— v. intr. Faire une excursion.
jauntily [-ili] adv. Avec désinvolture.
jauntiness [-inis] n. Insouciance, vivacité *f.* (sprightliness). ‖ Allure désinvolte *f.*; air délibéré *m.* (offhand manner). ‖ Suffisance, prétention *f.* (swagger)
jaunty [-i] adj. Vif, insouciant (sprightly). ‖ Désinvolte, cavalier (offhand). ‖ Prétentieux, suffisant (swaggering).
Javanese [dʒɑ:və'ni:z] n. GEOGR. Javanais *s.*

javelin ['dʒævlin] n. MILIT. Javelot *m.*; javeline *f.* ‖ SPORTS. *Throwing the javelin,* lancement du javelot.

jaw [dʒɔ:] n. MED., TECHN. Mâchoire *f.* ‖ FIG. Griffes *f. pl.* (of death); gueule *f.* (mouth); laïus *m.* (speech); *hold your jaw!,* ta gueule! ‖ **Jaw-bone,** n. MED. Maxillaire *m.* ‖ **Jaw-breaker,** n. FAM. Mot (*m.*) difficile à prononcer.
— v. intr. FAM. Laïusser, phraser, jaspiner (to speechify). ‖ FAM. Gueuler.
— v. tr. FAM. Enguirlander; engueuler.

jay [dʒei] n. ZOOL. Geai *m.* ‖ FAM. Pie, jacasse *m.* (chatterbox); jobard *m.* (gull); tête (*f.*) en l'air (scatter-brain). ‖ **Jay-walk,** v. intr. FAM. Marcher le nez en l'air, badauder; U. S. FAM. Traverser en dehors du passage clouté. ‖ **Jay-walker,** n. Badaud *m.*; U. S. FAM. Piéton (*m.*) qui traverse en dehors du passage clouté.

jazz [dʒæ:z] n. MUS. Jazz *m.* ‖ FAM. Entrain *m.* ‖ **Jazz-band,** n. MUS. Orchestre de jazz *m.*; FAM. Tapage *m.*
— v. tr. MUS. Arranger (or) jouer en jazz. ‖ FAM. *To jazz up,* animer, mettre de l'entrain dans.

jealous ['dʒeləs] adj. Jaloux (*of,* de). ‖ Jaloux, envieux (envious). ‖ Jaloux, soupçonneux (suspicious). ‖ Jaloux, anxieux, préoccupé (solicitous).

jealously [-li] adv. Jalousement, avec jalousie.

jealousy [-i] n. Jalousie *f.*; *crime of jealousy,* crime passionnel.

jean [dʒi:n] n. Coutil, treillis *m.* (cloth). ‖ Pl. Bleu *m.* (overalls); blue-jean (trousers).

Jeep [dʒi:p] n. (trade mark). AUTOM. Jeep *f.*
— v. tr. AUTOM. Transporter en Jeep.
— v. intr. AUTOM. Rouler en Jeep.

jeer [dʒiə*] n. Raillerie *f.*; brocard, sarcasme *m.* (scoffing). ‖ Huée *f.* (hoot).
— v. intr. *To jeer at,* railler (to gibe); huer, conspuer (to hoot).

Jehu ['dʒi:hju:] n. Jéhu *m.* (name). ‖ FAM. Automédon *m.*

jejune [dʒi'dʒu:n] adj. AGRIC. Aride, pauvre. ‖ FIG. Plat, maigre.

jejuneness [-nis] n. AGRIC. Aridité *f.* ‖ FIG. Sécheresse, platitude *f.*

jejunum [dʒi'dʒu:nəm] n. MED. Jéjunum *m.*

jell [dʒel] v. intr. CULIN. Se solidifier, prendre. ‖ FAM. Réussir, se cristalliser (plan); coller (fam.).

jellied ['dʒelid] adj. CULIN. En gelée.

jelly [-i] n. CULIN. Gelée *f.* (of fruit, meat). ‖ FAM. Compote *f.*; *beaten to a jelly,* réduit en capilotade. ‖ **Jelly-fish,** n. ZOOL. Méduse *f.*

jemmy ['dʒemi] n. Pince-monseigneur *f.*; rossignol *m.* (burglar's tool). ‖ CULIN. Tête (*f.*) de mouton.
— v. tr. Forcer (a door).

je ne sais quoi [ʒən se 'kwa] n. Je ne sais quoi *m.*

jenny ['dʒeni] n. TECHN. Métier (*m.*) à filer.
— adj. ZOOL. Femelle (owl, wren).

jeopardize ['dʒepədaiz] v. tr. Exposer, mettre en danger, risquer. (See ENDANGER.)

jeopardy [-i] n. Danger, risque *m.*

jerboa [dʒə:'bouə] n. ZOOL. Gerboise *f.*

jeremiad [dʒeri'maiəd] n. Jérémiade *f.*

Jericho ['dʒerikou] n. GEOGR. Jéricho. ‖ FAM. *To send s.o. to Jericho,* envoyer coucher qqn.

jerk [dʒə:k] n. CULIN. Viande desséchée *f.*
— v. tr. CULIN. Faire sécher (meat).

jerk n. Saccade, secousse *f.*; *by jerks,* par à-coups. ‖ Coup sec *m.*; *with a jerk,* avec un brusque mouvement. ‖ Pl. Tics *m. pl.*; *to have the jerks,* avoir la bougeotte. ‖ MED. *Knee jerk,* réflexe rotulien. ‖ FAM. U. S. Déplombé *m.* ‖ FAM. *Put a jerk in it!,* allez et que ça saute!
— v. tr. Secouer d'une manière saccadée, donner des secousses à; *to jerk oneself free,* se libérer d'une secousse. ‖ Agiter d'un mouvement brusque. ‖ Lan-

cer d'un coup sec (a stone). ‖ *To jerk out,* prononcer d'un ton saccadé; *to jerk up,* redresser vivement (the head).
— v. intr. Se mouvoir par saccades (or) brusquement; *to jerk open,* s'ouvrir d'une secousse. ‖ Se contracter, se crisper (face).

jerkily [-ili] adv. Par à-coups.

jerkin ['dʒə:kin] n. Justaucorps *m.*

jerky ['dʒə:ki] adj. Saccadé, sautillant.

jerkwater ['dʒə:k,wɑ:tə*] adj. U. S. FAM. *Jerkwater town,* trou.
— n. U. S. CH. DE F. Tortillard *m.*

Jerry ['dʒeri] n. FAM. Jules *m.* (chamber-pot). ‖ MILIT. FAM. Fritz, Fridolin *m.* (German). ‖ **Jerry-built,** adj. De carton, mal bâti (house).

jerrycan ['dʒeri'kæn] n. Jerrycan *m.*; touque *f.*

jersey ['dʒə:zi] n. Jersey (cloth); chandail, sweater *m.* (garment).

Jerusalem [dʒə'ru:sələm] n. GEOGR. Jérusalem *f.* ‖ BOT. *Jerusalem artichoke,* topinambour.

jessamine ['dʒesəmin] n. BOT. Jasmin *m.*

jest [dʒest] n. Plaisanterie *f.*; *in jest,* pour rire, en plaisantant; à la blague (fam.). ‖ Plaisanterie, facétie *f.*; bon mot *m.* (pun). ‖ Raillerie *f.* (taunt). ‖ Risée *f.*; objet (*m.*) de raillerie (laughing-stock).
— v. intr. Plaisanter, faire des plaisanteries (*about,* sur); badiner. ‖ Railler, se moquer (to gibe).

jester [-ə*] m. Plaisantin, farceur *s.* ‖ Railleur, moqueur *s.* ‖ † Bouffon *m.* (fool).

Jesuit ['dʒezjuit] n. ECCLES., FIG. Jésuite *m.*

Jesuitical [,dʒezju'itikəl] adj. ECCLES., FIG. Jésuitique.

Jesuitism ['dʒezjuitizm] n. Jésuitisme *m.*

Jesus ['dʒi:zəs] n. Jésus *m.*

jet [dʒet] n. Jais *m.* (colour, mineral).
— adj. De jais, noir.

jet [dʒet] n. Jet *m.* (of blood, gas, water). ‖ AUTOM. Gicleur *m.* ‖ AVIAT. Avion (*m.*) à réaction; *outlet jet,* tuyère d'éjection. ‖ **Jet-aircraft,** n. AVIAT. Avion (*m.*) à réaction. ‖ **Jet-deflector,** n. AVIAT. Déviateur (*m.*) de jet. ‖ **Jet-engine,** n. AVIAT. Moteur (*m.*) à réaction; turbo-réacteur *m.* ‖ **Jet-fighter,** n. AVIAT. Chasseur (*m.*) à réaction. ‖ **Jet lag,** n. AVIAT. Malaise dû au décalage horaire *m.* ‖ **Jet plane** n. AVIAT. Avion à réaction, jet *m.* ‖ **Jet-propelled,** adj. AVIAT. A réaction.
— v. tr. (1). Faire gicler. ‖ Faire s'élancer.
— v. intr. Gicler. ‖ S'élancer.

jetsam ['dʒetsəm] n. NAUT. Objets (*m. pl.*) jetés à la mer. ‖ JUR. Epaves *f. pl.*

jettison ['dʒetisn] n. NAUT. Délestage *m.*
— v. tr. NAUT. Jeter à la mer. ‖ AVIAT., FIG. Se délester de.

jetty ['dʒeti] adj. Noir comme du jais.

jetty n. NAUT. Jetée *f.* (breakwater); appontement *m.* (landing pier).

Jew [dʒu:] n. Juif *m.* ‖ **Jew-baiting,** n. Persécution (*f.*) des Juifs. ‖ **Jew's harp,** n. MUS. Guimbarde *f.*
— v. tr. POP. Empiler, rouler.

jewel ['dʒu:əl] n. Joyau, bijou *m.* ‖ Pl. Pierreries *f. pl.*; TECHN. Rubis *m.* (of a watch). ‖ FIG. Perle *f.*; trésor *m.* ‖ **Jewel-case,** n. Coffret (*m.*) à bijoux.

jeweller [-e*] n. Joaillier, bijoutier *m.*

jewelry [-ri] n. Joaillerie, bijouterie *f.* (shop, trade). ‖ Joaillerie *f.*; joyaux, bijoux *m. pl.* (gems).

Jewess ['dʒu:is] n. Juive *f.*

Jewish [-iʃ] adj. Juif.

Jewry [-əri] n. Juiverie *f.*

Jezebel ['dʒezəbl] n. Jézabel *f.* ‖ FIG. Messaline *f.* ‖ FAM. *Painted Jezebel,* vieux tableau.

jib [dʒib] n. NAUT. Foc *m.* ‖ TECHN. Flèche *f.* (of a crane). ‖ **Jib-traveller,** n. NAUT. Rocambeau *m.*

jib v. intr. Se dérober (horse). ‖ FIG. Renâcler, se dérober (*at,* devant). ‖ **Jib-door,** n. Porte dérobée *f.*

jibe [dʒaib] See GIBE, GYBE.

jibe v. intr. U.S. FAM. Cadrer, concorder (*with,* avec).

jiffy ['dʒifi] n. Instant *m.; in a jiffy,* en un clin d'œil.
jig [dʒig] n. Gigue *f.* (dance). ‖ TECHN. Jig *m.* ‖ FAM. *The jig is up,* tout est dans le lac, c'est fichu. ‖ **Jig-saw,** n. Scie (*f.*) à chantourner; *jig-saw puzzle,* puzzle.
— v. tr. Faire sautiller. ‖ TECHN. Passer au jig.
— v. intr. Danser la gigue. ‖ Sautiller, gigoter.
jigger [-ə*] n. TECHN. Cribleur *s.* ‖ NAUT. Cotre *m.* (boat); tapecul *m.* (sail); palan *m.* (tackle). ‖ ELECTR. Jigger *m.* ‖ SPORTS. Appuie-queue *m.* (in billiards); fer (*m.*) à face renversée (in golf). ‖ U. S. Petite mesure; goutte *f.* (nip). ‖ FAM. Machin, truc *m.* (See CONTRAPTION.)
jigger n. ZOOL. Chique *f.,* puce (*f.*) chique (chigoe).
jiggered [-əd] pp. FAM. Confondu (confounded); éreinté (exhausted); *I'm jiggered if,* du diable si.
jiggery-pokery [-əri'poukəri] n. FAM. Tour (*m.*) de passe-passe, entourloupette *f.*
jiggle ['dʒigl] v. tr. Secouer, agiter.
— v. intr. Frétiller, s'agiter.
jilt [dʒilt] n. Coquette; lâcheuse *f.* (fam.).
— v. tr. FAM. Lâcher; planter là (a sweetheart).
Jim [dʒim] n. Jacquot. ‖ **Jim-crow,** n. TECHN. Pied-de-biche *m.;* FAM. U. S. Nègre *m.;* adj. U. S. Des nègres, des Noirs.
jim-jams ['dʒim,dʒæmz] n. pl. POP. Delirium tremens *m.* ‖ POP. Frousse, trouille *f.,* trac *m.* (jitters). ‖ POP. Cafard, coup de bourdon *m.* (depression).
jimmy ['dʒimi] n. U.S. Pince-monseigneur *f.,* rossignol *m.* (See JEMMY.)
jingle ['dʒiŋgl] n. Tintement *m.* (of bells); cliquetis *m.* (of chains); sonorité, musique *f.* (of verses). ‖ Slogan publicitaire chanté *m.* ‖ Cariole *f.* (in Australia).
— v. intr. Tinter, tintinnabuler (bell); cliqueter (chains).
— v. tr. Faire tinter (or) cliqueter.
jingo ['dʒiŋgou] (pl. **jingoes**) adj., n. Chauvin *s.*
— interj. *By jingo!,* nom d'un chien!
jingoism [-izm] n. Chauvinisme *m.*
jingoist [-ist] n. Chauvin *s.*
jink [dʒiŋk] n. SPORTS. Esquive *f.* ‖ FAM. *High jinks,* ébats bruyants *m. pl.*
— v. tr. SPORTS. Esquiver.
— v. intr. AVIAT., SPORTS. Se dérober.
jinx [dʒiŋks] n. FAM. Porte-guigne, oiseau de malheur *m.* (See HOODOO.)
— v. tr. Porter la guigne à.
jitney ['dʒitni] n. U. S. POP. Pièce (*f.*) de cinq cents (nickel). ‖ Bus *m.,* navette *f.* (bus).
— adj. POP. U. S. Ringard.
jitter ['dʒitə*] v. intr. FAM. Avoir la frousse, paniquer (to be nervous); avoir la bougeotte, ne pas tenir en place (to move nervously).
jitters ['dʒitəz] n. pl. FAM. Frousse, trouille *f.; to get the jitters,* avoir la frousse, se laisser impressionner; *to give the jitters to,* flanquer la trouille à.
jitterbug [-bag] n. FAM. Alarmiste, défaitiste, paniquard *s.* ‖ FAM. Fanatique (*s.*) du swing.
— v. tr. FAM. Se déhancher (or) se trémousser en dansant.
jittery [-ri] adj. FAM. Froussard, trouillard.
jiu-jitsu [dʒu:'dʒitsu:] n. SPORTS. Jiu-jitsu *m.*
jive [dʒaiv] n. MUS. Swing *m.* ‖ FAM. U. S. Sornette *f.*
— v. intr. MUS. Danser le swing.
Joan [dʒoun] n. Jeanne *f.*
job [dʒɔb] n. Travail à forfait *m.; to work by the job,* faire du travail à la pièce. ‖ Menu travail *m.; to do odd jobs,* bricoler. ‖ Travail, emploi *m.;* occupation *f.; to look for a job,* chercher de l'embauche. ‖ Place *f.; job m.; to get a cushy job,* avoir une bonne planque, trouver un bon fromage (fam.). ‖ Affaire, *f.; it's a bad job,* c'est une mauvaise histoire; *it's my job,* cela me regarde, j'y veillerai;

just the job, juste ce qu'il faut. ‖ Tripotage *m.;* combine *f.* ‖ **Jobs-for-the-boys,** n. pl. Assiette (*f.*) au beurre. ‖ **Job-holder,** n. Fonctionnaire *s.;* pl. Gens (*m. pl.*) en place. ‖ **Job-printer,** n. Imprimeur (*m.*) à façon. ‖ **Job-work,** n. Travail (*m.*) à la pièce.
— adj. De louage (carriage, horse). ‖ COMM. Soldé; *job lot,* occasions.
— v. intr. (1). Bricoler, faire de menus travaux. ‖ FIN. Agioter. ‖ FAM. Tripoter, tripatouiller.
— v. tr. Faire nommer à un poste (s.o.). ‖ Louer (carriages, horses). ‖ FIN. Spéculer sur. ‖ FAM. Tripoter dans.
jobber [-ə*] n. Tâcheron *m.* ‖ FIN. Agioteur, spéculateur; coulissier *m.* ‖ COMM. Intermédiaire *m.* ‖ FAM. Tripoteur *s.*
jobbery [-ri] n. Tripotage *m.*
jobcentre ['dʒɔbsentə*] n. Centre (*m.*) de l'Agence nationale pour l'emploi.
jobless [-lis] adj. Sans emploi (or) travail.
Jock [dʒɔk] n. FAM. Ecossais *m.* ‖ MILIT. FAM. Soldat écossais *m.*
jockey ['dʒɔki] n. SPORTS. Jockey *m.* ‖ U. S. Conducteur, chauffeur *m.*
— v. tr. SPORTS. Monter (a horse). ‖ FAM. Rouler (s.o.); maquignonner (sth.).
— v. intr. NAUT. Manœuvrer. ‖ FAM. Combiner, manigancer; *to jockey for position,* manœuvrer pour se caser.
jock-strap ['dʒɔk,stræp] n. SPORTS., FAM. Suspensoir *m.*
jocose [dʒə'kous] adj. Jovial, enjoué (gay); facétieux (humorous); gouailleur (mocking).
jocoseness [-nis] n. Jovialité; gouaille *f.*
jocosity [dʒə'kɔsiti] n. Jovialité *f.* ‖ Facétie *f.*
jocular ['dʒɔkjulə*] adj. Plaisant, facétieux.
jocularity [,dʒɔkju'læriti] n. Gaieté, humeur facétieuse *f.*
jocund ['dʒɔkənd] adj. Enjoué; jovial.
jocundity [dʒɔ'kʌnditi] n. Enjouement *m.*
jocundly ['dʒɔkəndli] adv. Avec enjouement.
jodhpurs ['dʒɔdpuəz] n. pl. Pantalon de cheval *m.*
jog [dʒɔg] v. tr. (1). Mouvoir par saccades. (See JERK.) ‖ Secouer, cahoter. ‖ Pousser (s.o.'s elbow); pousser du coude (s.o.). ‖ FIG. Rafraîchir, dérouiller (s.o.'s memory).
— v. intr. SPORTS. Courir à petites foulées, faire du jogging (or) du footing. ‖ Avancer au petit trot (of horse). ‖ **To jog along** (or) **on,** aller son petit train, avancer cahin-caha.
— n. Saccade, secousse *f.* (jerk). ‖ Cahot *m.* (of a carriage). ‖ Coup de coude *m.* ‖ Petit trot *m.* ‖ **Jog-trot,** n. Petit trot, trottinement *m.;* FAM. Traintrain *m.* (routine).
jogger [-ə*] n. SPORTS. Amateur (*s.*) de jogging, jogger *s.*
jogging [-iŋ] n. SPORTS. Jogging, footing *m.*
joggle ['dʒɔgl] n. Secousse légère, petite saccade *f.*
— v. tr. Imprimer une petite secousse à.
— v. intr. Branler. ‖ **To joggle along,** avancer par petites secousses.
joggle n. ARCHIT. Goujon *m.*
— v. tr. Goujonner.
John [dʒɔn] n. Jean *m.* ‖ U. S. *John Doe,* M. Dupont. ‖ FAM. *John Barleycorn,* le whisky.
Johnny [-i] n. Jeannot *m.* (name). ‖ FAM. Type *m.* (guy). ‖ U. S. POP. Cabinets *m. pl.* (w.-c.). ‖ **Johnny-come-lately,** n. U. S. Nouveau venu *m.*
join [dʒɔin] v. tr. Joindre, unir (to unite). ‖ Relier (*to,* à) [to connect]. ‖ Retrouver, rejoindre (s.o.). ‖ Se joindre à (s.o.). ‖ S'adjoindre à (a group, s.o.); adhérer à, prendre rang dans (a party, a society); *you'll join us, won't you?,* vous serez des nôtres, n'est-ce pas? ‖ GEOGR. Se jeter dans (a river, the sea). ‖ ECCLES. Entrer dans (an order). ‖ MILIT. Rallier (the troops); rejoindre (one's unit); *to join the Army,* s'engager. ‖ ARCHIT. Assembler, raccor-

der, ajointer. ‖ **To join up,** joindre, assembler ; TECHN. Abouter ; ELECTR. Connecter, accoupler.
— v. intr. Se joindre, s'unir. ‖ Se retrouver, se rejoindre. ‖ Se joindre, se mêler (in, à) ; se joindre, s'associer (with, à). ‖ ARCHIT. S'assembler, s'abouter, se raccorder. ‖ MILIT. S'enrôler.
— n. Raccord, point (m.) de jonction ; couture f. (seam).

joiner [-ə*] n. Menuisier m. ‖ U. S. Clubiste s.

joinery [-ri] n. Menuiserie f.

joining [-iŋ] n. Jonction, réunion f. ‖ TECHN. Assemblage m.

joint [dʒɔint] n. TECHN. Assemblage, joint (act) ; articulation, jointure f. (piece). ‖ MED. Articulation f.; out of joint, démis, déboîté, luxé. ‖ BOT. Nœud m. ‖ GEOL. Diaclase f. ‖ CULIN. Rôti m.; a cut from the joint, une tranche de rôti. ‖ U. S. POP. Boutique, boîte f. (house) ; bistrot m., gargote f. (cheap restaurant). ‖ POP. Joint m. (cigarette). ‖ FIG. Joint in the harness, défaut de la cuirasse, talon d'Achille, point faible ; out of joint, disloqué, de travers.
— v. tr. TECHN. Jointer, articuler, emboîter. ‖ CULIN. Découper (a fowl).
— adj. Réuni, uni, combiné, joint (combined). ‖ FIN. Indivis (account). ‖ JUR. Joint and several, conjoint et solidaire ; joint committee, commission mixte. ‖ **Joint-author,** n. Coauteur m. ‖ **Joint-donee,** n. JUR. Codonataire s. ‖ **Joint-heir,** n. JUR. Cohéritier s. ‖ **Joint-guardian,** n. JUR. Cotuteur m.; cotutrice f. ‖ **Joint-manager,** n. COMM. Codirecteur, cogérant m. ‖ **Joint-manageress,** n. Codirectrice f. ‖ **Joint-obligation,** n. Coobligation f. ‖ **Joint-ownership,** n. Copropriété f. ‖ **Joint-owner,** n. Copossesseur, copropriétaire m. ‖ **Joint-partner,** n. Coassocié s. ‖ **Joint-purchaser,** n. Coacquéreur m. ‖ **Joint-stock,** adj. FIN. Par actions (company). ‖ **Joint-tenant,** n. Colocataire m.

jointer [-ə*] n. TECHN. Varlope f.

jointly [-li] adv. Conjointement.

jointress [-ris] n. Douairière f.

jointure [-ʃə*] n. JUR. Douaire m. (of a wife).
— v. tr. Pourvoir d'un douaire.

joist [dʒɔist] n. ARCHIT. Solive f.

joke [dʒouk] n. Plaisanterie f.; in joke, en plaisantant, pour rire. ‖ Farce, blague f.; tour m. (trick) ; practical joke, mauvais tour. ‖ Chose drôle, amusette f.; it's no joke living alone, ce n'est pas rigolo de vivre seul (fam.).
— v. tr. † Se moquer de.
— v. intr. Plaisanter, parler en plaisantant ; blaguer (fam.) ; you're joking !, ce n'est pas sérieux !

joker [-ə*] n. Plaisantin, blagueur m. ‖ Farceur s. ‖ Joker m. (card). ‖ U. S. Clause ambiguë f.

jollification [ˌdʒɔlifi'keiʃən] n. FAM. Partie de rigolade f.

jollify [dʒɔlifai] v. intr. (2). FAM. Rigoler, s'en donner à cœur joie.
— v. tr. FAM. Faire rigoler.

jollity [-ti] n. Réjouissance f.

jolly [dʒɔli] adj. Joyeux, gai. ‖ Eméché, parti, gris, gai (tipsy). ‖ FAM. Amusant, plaisant, agréable. ‖ FAM. Formidable, fameux. ‖ **Jolly-boat,** n. NAUT. Canot m.
— adv. FAM. Fameusement ; she is jolly glad, elle est drôlement (or joliment) contente.
— n. NAUT. FAM. Marsouin m.; Jolly Roger, pavillon noir.
— v. tr. U. S. FAM. To jolly along, flatter, cajoler.

jolt [dʒoult] n. Secousse, saccade f.; cahot, soubresaut m. ‖ FAM. Choc, coup m. (surprise).
— v. tr., intr. Cahoter, secouer.

Jonah [dʒouna] n. Jonas m. ‖ FAM. Porte-guigne m.

jonquil [dʒɔŋkwil] n. BOT. Jonquille f. ‖ Jonquille m. (colour).
— adj. Jonquille.

Jordan [dʒɔ:dn] n. GEOGR. Jordanie f. (country) ; Jourdain m. (river).

jorum [dʒɔ:rəm] n. Bol m.

josh [dʒɔʃ] v. tr. FAM. Chiner, blaguer (s.o.).

Joshua [dʒɔʃjuə] n. Josué m.

joss [dʒɔs] n. Divinité chinoise f. ‖ **Joss-house,** n. Temple chinois m. ‖ **Joss-stick,** n. Bâtonnet d'encens m.

jostle [dʒɔsl] v. intr. Se cogner (against, with, à). ‖ Jouer des coudes (to elbow) ; se bousculer ; to jostle like a pea on a drum, se démener comme un diable dans un bénitier. ‖ Faire des pieds et des mains (for, pour obtenir).
— v. tr. Bousculer, repousser du coude. ‖ SPORTS. Coincer, serrer (a competitor).
— n. Bousculade, cohue f.

jot [dʒɔt] v. tr. (1). Noter ; to jot down, prendre en note.
— n. Brin m.; not a jot, pas un iota, pas une ombre ; not to care a jot for it, s'en ficher royalement.

jotter [-ə*] n. Bloc-notes m.

jottings [-iŋz] n. pl. Notes f. pl.

joule [dʒu:l] n. PHYS. Joule m. (unit).

jounce [dʒauns] v. tr. Cahoter. (See JOLT.)
— v. intr. Etre cahoté.
— n. Cahot, soubresaut m.

journal [dʒə:nl] n. Journal intime m. (diary). ‖ Journal m. (newspaper). ‖ FIN. Journal, livre m. (in bookkeeping). ‖ JUR. Compte rendu m. (of a committee, legislature). ‖ NAUT. Livre de bord m. ‖ TECHN. Portage m. (of a crankshaft). ‖ **Journal-box,** n. TECHN. Boîte (f.) d'essieu.

journalese [dʒə:nə'li:z] n. FAM. Langage journalistique m.

journalism [dʒə:nəlizm] n. Journalisme m.

journalist [-ist] n. Journaliste s.

journalistic [ˌdʒə:nə'listik] adj. Journalistique.

journalize [dʒə:nəlaiz] v. tr. Ecrire dans son journal. ‖ FIN. Journaliser, porter en comptabilité.

journey [dʒə:ni] n. Voyage m.; to reach one's journey's end, arriver à destination. ‖ Trajet, parcours m.; étape f.; three hours' car journey, trois heures de trajet en voiture. ‖ FAM. Allée et venue f.; voyage m.
— v. intr. Voyager.

journeyman [-mən] (pl. **journeymen**) n. † Journalier m. ‖ Compagnon m. (qualified worker) ; journeyman baker, garçon boulanger ; mitron.

joust [dʒaust] n. Joute f.
— v. intr. Jouter.

Jove [dʒouv] n. Jupiter m. ‖ FAM. By Jove !, bon sang !

jovial [dʒouvjəl] adj. Jovial.

joviality [ˌdʒouvi'æliti] n. Jovialité f.

Jovian [dʒouvjən] adj. Jupitérien.

jowl [dʒaul] n. Mâchoire f. (jaw). ‖ Bajoue f. (of a person) ; cheek by jowl, joue contre joue. ‖ ZOOL. Jabot m. (of a bird) ; fanon m. (of an ox).

joy [dʒɔi] n. Joie f.; to wish s.o. joy of, féliciter qqn de. ‖ **Joy-killer,** n. Rabat-joie m. ‖ **Joy-ride,** n. FAM. Tour (m.) en voiture. ‖ **Joy-stick,** n. AVIAT. FAM. Manche à balai m.
— v. tr. Faire un tour en auto.
— v. tr. Réjouir.
— v. intr. Se réjouir.

joyful [-ful] adj. Joyeux. (See GLAD.)

joyfully [-fuli] adv. Joyeusement.

joyfulness [-fulnis] n. Plénitude de joie f. ‖ Humeur joyeuse f.

joyhop [-hɔp] n. U. S. POP. Tour en avion m.

joyless [-lis] adj. Sans joie.

joyous [dʒɔiəs] adj. Joyeux. (See GLAD.)

joyousness [-nis] n. Humeur joyeuse f.

J.P. [ˌdʒei'pi:] n. Abbr. Justice of the Peace, juge de paix, magistrat laïque et bénévole jugeant principalement les contraventions de simple police.

jubilant ['dʒu:bilənt] adj. Jubilant, radieux.
jubilate [-leit] v. intr. Jubiler.
jubilation [‚dʒu:bi'leiʃən] n. Jubilation *f.*
jubilee ['dʒu:bili:] n. Jubilé, cinquantenaire *m.;* noces (*f. pl.*) d'or.
Judaic [dʒu:'deiik] adj. Judaïque.
Judaize ['dʒu:diaiz] v. tr., intr. Judaïser.
Judas ['dʒu:dəs] n. Judas *m.* (name). ‖ Judas *m.* (spy-hole). ‖ FIG. Judas, traître *m.*
judder ['dʒʌdə'] v. intr. Trépider, faire des soubresauts.
— n. Trépidation *f.*, soubresauts *m. pl.*, saccades *f. pl.*
judge [dʒʌdʒ] n. ECCLES., JUR., SPORTS, FIG. Juge *m.*
— v. tr. JUR., FIG. Juger.
— v. intr. JUR. Rendre un jugement. ‖ SPORTS. Arbitrer. ‖ FIG. Porter un jugement (*of,* sur); juger (*from,* d'après; *of,* de).
judgeship [-ʃip] n. JUR. Judicature *f.*
judgment ['dʒʌdʒmənt] n. JUR., ECCLES. Jugement *m.* ‖ FIG. Jugement, avis *m.* (opinion); jugement, discernement *m.* (good sense); *by judgment,* au jugé. ‖ FAM. Châtiment du ciel *m.* (misfortune). ‖ **Judgment-day,** n. ECCLES. Jour du Jugement dernier *m.*
judicature ['dʒu:dikətʃə'] n. JUR. Cour de justice *f.* (court); magistrature *f.* (judges); judicature *f.* (functions, position).
judicial [dʒu:'diʃəl] adj. De juge, de critique; *judicial faculty,* sens critique. ‖ JUR. Judiciaire (enquiry, power, record); juridique (murder); *judicial separation,* séparation de corps; *to take judicial notice of,* connaître d'office. ‖ FIG. Impartial (unbiased).
judiciary [-əri] adj., n. JUR. Judiciaire *m.*
judicious [-əs] adj. Judicieux.
judiciously [-əsli] adv. Judicieusement.
judiciousness [-əsnis] n. Sagesse *f.;* jugement sain *m.*
judo ['dʒu:dou] n. SPORTS. Judo *m.*
jug [dʒʌg] n. Pot *m.* (for ale, milk, water). ‖ Cruche *f.* (earthenware container); broc *m.* (metal container). ‖ FAM. Bloc *m.*, taule *f.* (prison).
— v. tr. CULIN. Etuver; *jugged hare,* civet de lièvre. ‖ POP. Boucler, coffrer (to imprison).
jug v. intr. Chanter comme le rossignol.
jugate ['dʒu:geit] adj. BOT. Conjugué.
juggle ['dʒʌgl] v. intr. Faire de la prestidigitation. ‖ FAM. *To juggle with,* mettre dans sa poche (s.o.); jongler avec (sth.).
— v. tr. **To juggle away,** escamoter.
— n. Tour (*m.*) de passe-passe, escamotage *m.* (lit. and fig.).
juggler [ə'] n. Jongleur *m.* ‖ Prestidigitateur, escamoteur *m.* ‖ FAM. Embobelineur *m.*
jugglery [-ri] n. Jonglerie *f.* ‖ Tour (*m.*) de prestidigitation. ‖ FAM. Passe-passe *m.*
jughead ['dʒʌghed] n. U. S. POP. Cabochard *s.*
jugular ['dʒʌgjulə'] adj., n. MED. Jugulaire *f.*
jugulate [-leit] v. tr. Etrangler. ‖ MED. Juguler.
juice [dʒu:s] n. CULIN. Jus *m.* (of fruit, meat). ‖ FIG. Suc, piment, piquant *m.* ‖ FAM. Jus *m.* (electricity, petrol, U. S. gasoline); fric *m.* (money).
juiciness [-nis] n. Succulence *f.* (lit. and fig.).
juicy [-i] adj. Juteux, succulent (fruit, meat); *to be juicy,* juter. ‖ Humide (weather). ‖ FIG. Savoureux.
ju-jitsu [dʒu:'dʒitsu:] n. SPORTS. Jiu-jitsu *m.*
jujube ['dʒu:dʒu:b] n. BOT. Jujube *m.* ‖ **Jujube-tree,** n. BOT. Jujubier *m.*
jukebox ['dʒu:kbɔks] n. Juke-box *m.*
julep ['dʒu:lep] n. MED. Julep *m.* ‖ U. S. *Mint julep,* whisky glacé à la menthe.
julienne [‚dʒu:li'en] n. CULIN. Julienne *f.*
Julius ['dʒuljəs] n. Jules *m.*
July [dʒu:'lai] n. Juillet *m.*
jumble ['dʒʌmbl] n. Fouillis, fatras, méli-mélo *m.*

(of things). ‖ Enchevêtrement *m.;* confusion *f.* (of ideas).
— v. tr. Brouiller, jeter pêle-mêle.
— v. intr. S'embrouiller, s'enchevêtrer.
jumbo ['dʒʌmbou] n. TECHN. Manchon de refroidissement *m.* ‖ FAM. Mastodonte, éléphant *m.*
jump [dʒʌmp] n. Bond *m.; at one jump,* d'un bond. ‖ Sursaut *m.; to give s.o. a jump,* faire sursauter qqn. ‖ SPORTS. Saut *m.; high, long, standing jump,* saut en hauteur, en longueur, à pieds joints; *to take a jump,* faire un saut. ‖ SPORTS. Obstacle *m.* (fence, hurdle). ‖ FIN. Saute *f.;* bond *m.* (in prices). ‖ AVIAT. *Jump suit,* combinaison. ‖ FAM. *To get the jump on,* avoir une longueur d'avance sur; *on the jump,* en plein coup de feu. ‖ **Jump-jet,** n. AVIAT. Avion (*m.*) à décollage et atterrissage verticaux.
— v. intr. Bondir, sauter (*out of,* hors de); *to jump up,* sauter sur ses pieds. ‖ Sursauter, tressauter (to start). ‖ FIN. Faire un bond (prices). ‖ FIG. *To jump at,* sauter sur (an offer); *to jump from one thing to another,* sauter du coq à l'âne; *to jump to a conclusion,* conclure sans réflexion.
— v. tr. Sauter, franchir d'un bond (to leap over). ‖ Faire sauter (a child). ‖ Faire sursauter (to startle). ‖ Prendre, souffler (in draughts). ‖ FIN. Faire monter (prices). ‖ CH. DE F. Sauter de (or) dans (a moving train); *to jump the rails,* dérailler. ‖ SPORTS. Faire lever (game); faire sauter (horse). ‖ TECHN. Refouler (a weld). ‖ NAUT. FAM. *To jump ship,* tirer une bordée. ‖ FAM. Rouler (to cheat); gratter, gagner de vitesse (to outstrip); *to jump the gun,* marcher plus vite que les violons, démarrer avant le signal; *to jump the queue,* passer avant son tour; U. S. *to jump a town,* décamper d'une ville. ‖ **Jump-off,** adj. De départ (position).
jumper [-ə*] n. SPORTS., ZOOL. Sauteur *s.* ‖ ELECTR. Jarretière *f.* ‖ COMM. U. S. Livreur *m.* ‖ TECHN. Barre (*m.*) de mine.
jumper n. Jumper *m.* (pull-over). ‖ U. S. Robe (*f.*) sans manches, portée sur une blouse (dress). ‖ U. S. Pl. Barboteuse *f.* (rompers).
jumpiness ['dʒʌmpinis] n. Nervosité, tendance (*f.*) à sursauter.
jumping [-iŋ] n. SPORTS. Jumping *m.* ‖ **Jumping-off-place,** n. Base avancée *f.;* FIG. Extrême limite (*f.*) des possibilités d'arrangement.
jumpy [-i] adj. Nerveux, tressautant (person); saccadé (style). ‖ FIN. Instable (market).
junction ['dʒʌŋkʃən] n. Jonction *f.* ‖ Confluent *m.* (of rivers); bifurcation *f.* (of roads). ‖ CH. DE F. Embranchement *m.* (branch-line); gare régulatrice *f.* (station). ‖ MILIT. Jonction *f.*
juncture [-tʃə*] n. Point (*m.*) de jonction. ‖ MED., TECHN. Jointure *f.* ‖ FIG. Conjoncture *f.; to have reached a critical juncture,* en être au point critique.
June [dʒu:n] n. Juin *m.* ‖ **June-bug,** n. U. S. ZOOL. Hanneton *m.*
jungle ['dʒʌŋgl] n. Jungle *f.*
junior ['dʒu:njə*] adj. Plus jeune, jeune, cadet, junior (younger). ‖ Subalterne, inférieur (subordinate); *junior clerk,* petit commis.
— n. Cadet *s.* ‖ U. S. Etudiant (*s.*) de troisième année.
juniper ['dʒu:nipə*] n. BOT. Genévrier *m.*
junk [dʒʌŋk] n. Etoupe *f.;* vieux cordages *m. pl.* ‖ COMM. Ferraille, chiffonnerie *f.;* bric-à-brac *m.;* rossignols *m. pl.* ‖ NAUT. Singe *m.* (meat). ‖ FAM. Camelote, gnognote *f.* (trash). ‖ POP. Came *f.* (drug). ‖ **Junk-heap,** n. Dépotoir *m.* ‖ **Junk-market,** n. Marché (*m.*) aux puces. ‖ **Junk-shop,** n. Friperie *f.;* boutique (*f.*) de bric-à-brac.
— v. tr. Couper en gros morceaux. ‖ U. S. Mettre au rancart, jeter au rebut.
junk n. NAUT. Jonque *f.*
junket ['dʒʌŋkit] n. CULIN. Lait caillé *m.* ‖ U. S. Excursion *f.* (trip). ‖ U. S. Voyage officiel (*m.*) aux frais de la princesse. ‖ FAM. Gueuleton *m.*

— v. intr. Fam. Faire ripaille; gueuletonner (pop.).
‖ U. S. Voyager aux frais de la princesse.
junketing [-iŋ] n. Fam. Bombance, ripaille *f*.
junkie ['dʒʌŋki] n. Pop. Drogué, camé *s*.
junkman ['dʒʌŋkmən] n. U. S. Chiffonnier *m*.
Juno ['dʒu:nou] n. Junon *f*.
junta ['dʒʌntə] n. Junte *f*.
junto ['dʒʌntou] n. Cabale, faction *f*.
Jupiter ['dʒu:pitə*] n. Jupiter *m*.
jural ['dʒu:rəl] adj. Juridique, légal. ‖ Moral, relatif aux obligations morales.
Jurassic [dʒuə'ræsik] adj. Geol. Jurassique.
jurat ['dʒuəræt] n. Jur. Officier municipal *m*.
juratory ['dʒuərətəri] adj. Jur. Sous serment (declaration); juratoire (obligation).
juridical [dʒu'ridikəl] adj. Jur. Juridique.
jurisconsult ['dʒuəriskən,sʌlt] n. Jur. Jurisconsulte *s*.
jurisdiction [,dʒuəris'dikʃən] n. Jur. Juridiction *f*.
jurisprudence [-'pru:dəns] n. Jur. Jurisprudence *f*.
jurist ['dʒuərist] n. Jur. Juriste *m*. (expert); étudiant en droit *s*. (student).
juror [-ə*] n. Jur. Juré *m*.
jury ['dʒuəri] adj. Med. De bois (leg). ‖ Naut. De fortune (mast, rudder).
jury n. *m*. (for a competition, a contest). ‖ Jur. Jury *m*.; *to sit on the jury*, faire partie du jury. ‖ **Jury-box**, n. Banc (*m*.) des jurés. ‖ **Jury-panel**, n. Liste (*f*.) des jurés.
juryman [-mən] (pl. **jurymen**) n. Jur. Juré *m*.
jurywoman [-'wumən] (pl. **jurywomen**) n. Jur. Femme juré *f*.
just [dʒʌst] adj. Juste, légitime, bien fondé (anger, cause); juste, exact (calculation, opinion); juste, équitable (person); juste, mérité (punishment).
— adv. Juste, justement, précisément, exactement; *just so!*, parfaitement, tout juste!; *I just don't know what happened*, je ne sais vraiment pas ce qui est arrivé; *that's just what I thought*, c'est tout à fait ce que je pensais; *to be very just so*, être très correct (person). ‖ Juste; *just as*, juste au moment où; *just now*, à l'instant, actuellement. ‖ Récemment; *just out*, qui vient de sortir, récemment paru (book); *I have just seen him*, je viens de le voir. ‖ Justement, à ce moment; *I was just thinking that*, je réfléchissais justement que. ‖ Tout juste; *I just escaped being run over*, j'ai failli être écrasé; *I'll just be back*, je serai tout juste rentré. ‖ Juste, seulement; *just one remark*, juste une observation; *just you*, vous seul; *only just to me*, rien qu'à moi; *we shall just drop in*, nous ne vous dirons qu'un tout petit bonjour. ‖ U. S. *Just the same*, quand même. ‖ Fam. *It's just beautiful*, c'est franchement beau; *just sit and look!*, asseyez-vous un peu et

regardez!; *that's just too bad!*, tant pis!, dommage!
justice ['dʒʌstis] n. Justice *f*. (see EQUITY); *in justice to him*, pour lui rendre justice; *this photograph doesn't do justice to my wife*, cette photographie n'avantage pas ma femme; *to do justice to*, rendre justice à. ‖ Jur. Justice *f*. (administration of law); juge (judge); *Justice of the Peace*, juge de paix.
justiceship [-ʃip] n. Judicature *f*.
justiciable [dʒʌs'tiʃiəbl] adj., n. Justiciable *s*.
justiciary [-əri] n. † Justicier *m*. ‖ Jur. *High Court of Justiciary*, Cour suprême de justice.
— adj. De justice.
justifiability [,dʒʌstifaiə'biliti] n. Caractère justifiable *m*.
justifiable ['dʒʌstifaiəbl] adj. Justifiable.
justification [.dʒʌstifi'keiʃən] n. Techn., Eccles., Fig. Justification *f*. (*of, for*, de, à, pour).
justificative ['dʒʌstifikeitiv] adj. Justificatif.
justificatory [-əri] adj. Justificateur *m*.; justificatrice *f*.
justify ['dʒʌstifai] v. tr. (2). Justifier, légitimer (an action); justifier, prouver le bien-fondé de (a declaration); justifier (s.o.); *to justify oneself*, se justifier. ‖ Jur. *To justify bail*, justifier de sa solvabilité. ‖ Techn. Justifier (lines of type); parangonner (different types). ‖ Eccles. Justifier. ‖ Fig. Autoriser (*in*, à); donner le droit (*in*, de); *to be justified in*, être en droit de, être fondé à, avoir toutes raisons pour.
justly ['dʒʌstli] adv. Justement, équitablement. ‖ Exactement (accurately). ‖ A juste titre, avec justesse, à bon droit (rightly).
justness [-nis] n. Justice *f*. (of a cause); justesse *f*. (of an idea).
jut [dʒʌt] v. intr. (1). Faire saillie, dépasser; *to jut out beyond*, dépasser les limites en surplombant.
— n. Saillie *f*.
jute [dʒu:t] n. Jute *m*.
juvenescence [,dʒu:vi'nesns] n. Passage (*m*.) de l'adolescence à la jeunesse.
juvenescent [-nt] adj. Sortant de l'adolescence, au sortir de l'âge ingrat.
juvenile ['dʒu:vinail] adj. Juvénile. ‖ Pour la jeunesse, pour enfants (books, literature). ‖ Jur. *Juvenile adult*, mineur de seize à vingt et un ans; *juvenile court*, tribunal pour enfants; *juvenile offenders*, enfance délinquante.
— n. Adolescent *s*.; jeune *m*. ‖ Livre (*m*.) pour enfants (book). ‖ Theatr. Spécialiste (*m*.) des rôles d'adolescents.
juvenilia [,dʒu:vi'niliə] n. Œuvres (*f*. *pl*.) de jeunesse.
juvenility [,dʒu:vi'niliti] n. Juvénilité *f*.
juxtalinear [,dʒʌkstə'liniə*] adj. Juxtalinéaire.
juxtapose ['dʒʌkstəpouz] v. tr. Juxtaposer.
juxtaposition [,dʒʌkstəpə'ziʃən] n. Juxtaposition *f*.

K

K [kei] n. K, k (letter). ‖ MATH. Constance *f*. ‖ CHIM. Potassium *m*. ‖ ELECTR. Capacité *f*. ‖ NAUT. Nœud *m*.

kabbala [kə'bɑːlə] n. Kabbale *f*. (doctrine).

kabob [kə'bɔb] n. CULIN. Chiche-kebab *m.*; brochette *f*.

Kabyle [kə'bail] n. Kabyle *m*.

Kaffir ['kæfə*] n. Cafre *m*.

kaftan ['kæftæn] n. Cafetan *m*.

kail [keil] n. See KALE.

kaiser ['kaizə*] n. Kaiser *m*.

kale [keil] n. BOT. Chou frisé *m*. ‖ U. S. POP. Oseille *f.*; pèze *m*. (money).

kaleidoscope [kə'laidəskoup] n. Kaléidoscope *m*.

kaleidoscopic [kə,laidə'skɔpik] adj. Kaléidoscopique.

Kalmuck ['kælmuk] adj., n. Kalmouk *s*.

kamikaze [,kæmi'kɑːzi] n. AVIAT. Kamikaze *m*.

Kampuchea [,kæmpu'tʃiə] n. GEOGR. Kampuchéa *m*.

Kanaka ['kænəkə] n. Canaque *s*.

kangaroo [,kæŋgə'ruː] n. ZOOL. Kangourou *m*. ‖ FIN. FAM. Actions minières australiennes *f. pl.* ‖ U. S. POP. *Kangaroo court*, tribunal irrégulier.

Kantian ['kæntiən] adj. PHILOS. Kantien.

Kantism [-izm] n. PHILOS. Kantisme *m*.

kaolin ['keiɔlin] n. Kaolin *m*.

kapok ['kɑːpɔk] n. BOT. Kapok *m*.

kaput [kæ'put] adj. FAM. Kaputt; grillé, fichu, cramé, pété.

karakul ['kærəkəl] n. ZOOL., COMM. Caracul, karakul *m*.

karat ['kærət] n. U. S. See CARAT.

karate [kə'rɑːti] n. SPORTS. Karaté *m*.

Karelia [kə'reiliə] n. GEOGR. Carélie *f*.

karite ['kariti] n. BOT. Karité, karé *m*.

karma ['kɑːmə] n. Karma *m*. ‖ FIG. Destinée *f*.

kart [kɑːt] n. AUTOM. Kart *m*.

karyoplasm ['kæriou,plæzm] n. MED. Suc nucléaire, nucléoplasme, caryoplasme *m*.

karyotype ['kæriə,taip] n. MED. Caryotype *m*.

katydid ['keiti,did] n. ZOOL. Sauterelle d'Amérique *f*.

kayak ['kaiæk] n. NAUT. Kayak *m*.

kebab [kə'bæb] n. CULIN. Chiche-kebab *m.*; brochette *f*.

keck [kek] v. intr. Avoir mal au cœur, avoir des nausées; avoir envie de dégobiller (pop.). ‖ Etre dégoûté (or) soulevé (at, par).

kedge [kedʒ] n. NAUT. Ancre (*f.*) à jet.
— v. tr. NAUT. Haler.
— v. intr. NAUT. Se haler.

kedgeree [,kedʒə'riː] n. CULIN. Plat de riz (*m.*) avec du poisson fumé et des œufs durs.

keel [kiːl] n. NAUT. Quille *f*. (part); navire *m*. (ship); *on an even keel*, sans tangage. ‖ BOT. Carène *f*. ‖ FIG. *On an even keel*, en équilibre.
— v. tr. NAUT. Mettre en carène (a ship). ‖ **To keel over**, NAUT., FIG. Faire chavirer.
— v. intr. NAUT. Chavirer. ‖ **To keel over**, NAUT. Chavirer; FAM. U. S. Tourner de l'œil, tomber dans les pommes (to faint).

keel n. NAUT. Gabarre, charbonnière *f*.

keelson ['kelsn] n. NAUT. Carlingue *f*.

keen [kiːn] n. MUS. Mélopée funèbre *f*. (See DIRGE.)
— v. intr. MUS. Chanter une mélopée funèbre, lamenter.

keen adj. Aigu, acéré (arrow); aiguisé, affilé, tranchant (knife). ‖ FIG. Piquant, vif (air); dévorant (appetite); mordant (cold); pénétrant (intelligence); vif (pleasure); aigu (sound). ‖ FIG. Ardent, plein de zèle (eager); pénétrant, vif, astucieux, futé (shrewd); *keen on*, engoué (or) passionné de, enthousiasmé par. ‖ **Keen-eyed**, adj. Au regard perçant. ‖ **Keen-set**, adj. Affamé (*for*, de). ‖ **Keen-sighted**, adj. Perspicace.

keenly [-li] adv. Aprement, d'une façon mordante. ‖ Avidement. ‖ Ardemment, avec enthousiasme.

keenness [-nis] n. Acuité *f*. (of edge). ‖ Apreté *f*. (of cold). ‖ MILIT. Mordant *m*. (of troops). ‖ MUS. Finesse *f*. (of hearing); acuité *f*. (of pain, sight). ‖ FIG. Profondeur *f*. (of feeling); pénétration *f*. (of intelligence, person); vivacité, ardeur *f.*, zèle *m*. (of a person).

keep [kiːp] v. tr. (84).

---

1. Garder. — 2. Laisser. — 3. Tenir. — 4. Maintenir. — 5. Entretenir. — 6. Faire. — 7. Retenir. — 8. Retarder. — 9. Empêcher. — 10. Suivre. — 11. Observer. — 12. Ne pas faillir à. — 13. Protéger. — 14. Conserver. — 15. Remplir. — 16. AGRIC. — 17. COMM. — 18. FIN. — 19. JUR. — 20. MED. — 21. FAM. — 22. To keep away. — 23. To keep back. — 24. To keep down. — 25. To keep in. — 26. To keep off. — 27. To keep on. — 28. To keep out. — 29. To keep together. — 30. To keep under. — 31. To keep up.

---

1. Garder; *to keep at hand*, garder sous la main. ‖ 2. Laisser; *to keep the door open*, laisser la porte ouverte. ‖ 3. Tenir (a diary); *to keep one's house clean*, tenir sa maison propre; *to keep open house*, tenir table ouverte. ‖ 4. Tenir, maintenir; *to keep s.o. out of the way*, tenir qqn à l'écart; *to keep running*, maintenir en activité. ‖ 5. Tenir, entretenir, avoir; *to keep servants*, avoir des domestiques. ‖ 6. Faire; *to keep s.o. at work, waiting*, faire travailler, attendre qqn. ‖ 7. Garder; retenir; *to keep s.o. for dinner*, retenir qqn à dîner. ‖ 8. Retarder; *don't let me keep you*, que je ne vous retarde pas! ‖ 9. Empêcher, retenir; *to keep from school*, empêcher d'aller à l'école. ‖ 10. Suivre (a path). ‖ 11. Observer, célébrer; *to keep the Sabbath*, observer le jour du sabbat; *to keep s.o.'s birthday*, fêter l'anniversaire de qqn. ‖ 12. Garder, tenir (a promise, secret); *to keep one's word*, tenir parole. ‖ 13. Garder, protéger, sauver; *to keep s.o. from despondency*, garder qqn du découragement; *to keep s.o. from profligacy*, sauver qqn du dévergondage. ‖ 14. Garder, conserver (one's composure); *to keep one's mind free*, garder l'esprit libre. ‖ 15. Remplir (one's obligations). ‖ 16. AGRIC. Elever, faire l'élevage de. ‖ 17. COMM. Tenir (an article). ‖ 18. FIN. Tenir (an account, books). ‖ 19. JUR. Observer (a law, rule); détenir (a prisoner). ‖ 20. MED. *To keep one's bed*, garder le lit. ‖ 21. FAM. *Keep it under your hat*, gardez ça pour vous. ‖ 22. To keep away, tenir éloigné; FIG. Garder (*from*, de). ‖ 23. To keep back, détenir, retenir (money); contenir, résister à (an opponent); taire (secrets). ‖ 24. To keep down, réprimer (a revolt); maîtriser, faire tenir tranquille (a rebellious person); FIN. Maintenir, empêcher de monter (prices). ‖ 25. To keep in, entretenir (fire);

tenir enfermé (s.o.); garder en retenue (a schoolboy); FIG. Réprimer, cacher (feelings); *to keep one's hand in*, s'entretenir la main. ‖ **26. To keep off**, ne pas mettre (one's hat); éloigner, écarter (one's hands, s.o.). ‖ **27. To keep on**, entretenir (fire); garder, conserver (one's hat, a servant); FAM. *To keep one's hair on*, ne pas perdre la tête. ‖ **28. To keep out**, empêcher d'entrer; *to keep out the cold*, se défendre du froid. ‖ **29. To keep together**, garder ensemble (or) unis. ‖ **30. To keep under**, dominer (one's passions); mater, asservir (subordinates). ‖ **31. To keep up**, soutenir, empêcher de tomber (s.o.); empêcher de se coucher (s.o.); FIN. Maintenir (prices); TECHN. Maintenir en bon état (engine); JUR. Entretenir; assurer la vie de (s.o.); FIG. Sauver (appearances); poursuivre (study); maintenir (traditions); *I don't want to keep you up*, je ne veux pas vous faire coucher tard; *keep it up*, allez-y!, continuez!, tenez bon; *to keep one's chin up*, garder bon moral, tenir le coup.

— v. intr.

---
1. Continuer. — 2. Se tenir. — 3. Rester. — 4. Demeurer. — 5. Se conserver. — 6. Attendre. — 7. To keep at. — 8. To keep away. — 9. To keep back. — 10. To keep down. — 11. To keep from. — 12. To keep in. — 13. To keep off. — 14. To keep on. — 15. To keep to. — 16. To keep together. — 17. To keep up.
---

1. Continuer; *to keep working*, continuer à travailler. ‖ Ne pas cesser de, tenir de; *to keep destroying*, s'acharner à détruire. ‖ 2. Se tenir, rester; *to keep aloof from*, se tenir à l'écart de; *to keep ready*, se tenir prêt; *to keep still*, demeurer en place, rester immobile (or) tranquille, se tenir en repos; *to keep within*, se cantonner dans; *to keep within the limits*, ne pas dépasser les bornes. ‖ 3. Demeurer, rester; *to keep faithful to*, rester fidèle à; *to keep silent*, se taire. ‖ 4. Demeurer, se conserver; *to keep in good health*, rester en bonne santé; *to keep in good shape*, rester en forme. ‖ 5. Se conserver; *apples that keep all winter*, des pommes qui se gardent tout l'hiver. ‖ 6. Attendre; *that can keep*, ça peut attendre. ‖ 7. To keep at, harceler (s.o.); s'acharner à (sth.). ‖ 8. To keep away, se tenir éloigné (or) à l'écart. ‖ 9. To keep back, rester en arrière, ne pas avancer. ‖ 10. To keep down, se tapir. ‖ 11. To keep from, s'empêcher de; éviter de; *he can't keep from smoking*, il ne peut se retenir de fumer. ‖ 12. To keep in, rester chez soi (or) enfermé; *to keep in touch with*, rester en contact avec; *to keep in with*, rester en bons termes avec. ‖ 13. To keep off, rester à distance. ‖ 14. To keep on, avancer (person); tenir (thing); *to keep on reading*, continuer à lire; *to keep on at*, harceler. ‖ 15. To keep to, garder; *to keep to the right*, garder sa droite; *to keep to one's room*, garder la chambre. ‖ 16. To keep together, rester ensemble (or) unis. ‖ 17. To keep up, se coucher tard; FIG. Tenir bon; *to keep up with*, aller de pair avec, être au niveau de; *to keep up with the Joneses*, ne pas se laisser distancer par les voisins.
— n. † ARCHIT. Donjon *m.* ‖ Vie, subsistance *f.* (livelihood). ‖ FAM. *He's not worth his keep*, il ne vaut pas son sel; *this time for keeps*, cette fois c'est pour toujours.

keeper [-ə*] n. Gardien, garde *s.* ‖ Conservateur *m.* (of a library, museum). ‖ Coulant (*m.*) de ceinture. ‖ TECHN. Gâche *f.*; contre-écrou *m.* ‖ COMM. Denrée (*f.*) qui se garde bien. ‖ JUR. Observateur *m.* (of laws). ‖ FIG. Détenteur, dépositaire *m.* (of secrets).

keeping [-iŋ] n. Entretien *m.* (of a garden, house, road). ‖ Garde *f.*; *in my keeping*, à ma garde, à mes soins. ‖ Soin *m.* (of an animal, children). ‖ Célébration *f.* (of a birthday, festival). ‖ JUR. Observation *f.* (of laws). ‖ COMM. Tenue *f.* (of shop). ‖ FIN.

Tenue *f.* (of books). ‖ FIG. Harmonie, correspondance *f.*; rapport *m.* (with, avec).
— adj. Qui garde (or) tient. ‖ COMM. De bonne conserve (fruit).

keepsake [-seik] n. Keepsake *m.* (album); souvenir *m.* (object).

keg [keg] n. Baricaut, barriquaut *m.* (of brandy); caque *f.* (of herrings); tonnelet *m.* (of water).

kelp [kelp] n. Varech *m.* ‖ CHIM. Soude (*f.*) de varech.

kelvin ['kelvin] n. PHYS. Kelvin *m.* (unit).

ken [ken] n. Vue *f.* (sight). ‖ FIG. Connaissance, perception *f.*

ken v. tr. Connaître, savoir (in Scotland). [See KNOW.]
— N. B. Le prét. et le p. p. sont *kent*.

kennel ['kenl] n. Chenil *m.* ‖ FAM. Taudis *m.* (hovel).
— v. intr. (1). Etre au chenil.
— v. tr. Mettre au chenil.

kennel n. Ruisseau *m.* (in a street).

Kentish ['kentiʃ] adj. Du Kent.
— n. GRAMM. Kentique *m.*

Kenya ['kenjə] n. GEOGR. Kenya *m.*

kepi ['keipi] n. MILIT. Képi *m.*

kept [kept] pret., p. p. See KEEP. ‖ JUR. *Kept woman*, femme entretenue.

keratin ['kerətin] n. MED., ZOOL. Kératine *f.*

keratitis [,kerə'taitis] n. MED. Kératite *f.*

kerb [kə:b] n. Bord du trottoir *m.* ‖ Margelle *f.* (of a well). ‖ FIN. *On the kerb*, après la clôture *f.* (on Stock Exchange). ‖ **Kerb-broker**, n. FIN. Coulissier *m.* ‖ **Kerb-market**, n. FIN. Coulisse *f.* ‖ **Kerb-stone**, n. Pierre (*f.*) en bordure du trottoir.

kerchief ['kə:tʃif] n. Fichu; mouchoir (*m.*) de tête.

kerf [kə:f] n. Trait (*m.*) de scie; encoche *f.*

kerfuffle [kə'fʌfl] n. FAM. Tapage, charivari, esclandre *m.*

kermes ['kə:mes], ['kə:miz] n. Kermès *m.*

kermis n. U. S. Kermesse *f.*

kernel ['kə:nəl] n. Amande *f.* (of a fruit-stone, nut). ‖ Grain *m.* (of wheat). ‖ FIG. Noyau, cœur *m.*

kerosene ['kerəsi:n] n. CHIM. Kérosène *m.*; huile minérale *f.* ‖ U. S. Pétrole lampant *m.*

kersey ['kə:zi] n. Carisel *m.* (material).

kerseymere ['kə:zimiə*] n. Casimir *m.* (wollen cloth).

kestrel ['kestrəl] n. ZOOL. Emouchet *m.*

ketch [ketʃ] n. NAUT. Dundee, ketch *m.*

ketchup ['ketʃəp] n. CULIN. Sauce tomate très relevée *f.*; ketchup *m.*

ketone ['ki:təoun] n. CHIM. Cétone *f.*

kettle ['ketl] n. Bouilloire *f.*; coquemar *m.* (tea-kettle). ‖ Cocotte, marmite *f.* (stew-pan). ‖ FAM. Gâchis *m.*; *another kettle of fish*, une autre paire de manches; *a pretty kettle of fish*, un bel embrouillamini, un beau dégât. ‖ **Kettle-drum**, n. MUS. Timbale *f.*; FAM. Thé *m.* (tea-party). ‖ **Kettle-drummer**, n. MUS. Timbalier *m.*

key [ki:] n. GEOGR. Cordon littoral *m.* (See CAY.)

key n. Clef, clé *f.*; *skeleton key*, rossignol. ‖ Traduction juxtalinéaire *f.* (crib); livre du maître, corrigé *m.* (book). ‖ TECHN. Clef *f.* (shaft-key); touche *f.* (in typewriter); *sending key*, manipulateur (in telegraphy). ‖ MUS. Clef *f.*; ton *m.* (tonality); touche *f.* (of a piano). ‖ ECCLES. Clef *f.*; *power of the keys*, pouvoir des clefs. ‖ MILIT. Position clef *f.* ‖ FIG. Ton *m.*; *the right key*, la corde sensible; *to give the key*, donner la note. ‖ FIG. Clef *f.* (to, de); *the key to the puzzle*, le mot de l'énigme. ‖ FAM. *To get the key of the street*, se trouver à la rue, loger à la belle étoile; *to speak in a high key*, avoir le verbe haut. ‖ **Key-bolt**, n. TECHN. Boulon (*m.*) à clavette. ‖ **Key-industry**, n. Industrie clef (or) essentielle *f.* ‖ **Key-joint**, n. TECHN. Assemblage (*m.*) à clef. ‖ **Key-man**, n. Spécialiste, homme indispensable *m.*; cheville ouvrière *f.* ‖ **Key-money**, n.

Pas (m.) de porte. ‖ **Key-note,** n. Mus. Tonique ƒ.; Fig. Dominante ƒ. ‖ **Key-point,** n. Point (m.) de commande. ‖ **Key-position,** n. Position clef ƒ. **Key-ring,** n. Anneau brisé, porte-clefs m. ‖ **Key-signature,** n. Mus. Armature ƒ.; *to put the key-signature to a piece of music,* armer la clef. ‖ **Key-word,** n. Mot d'ordre; mot clef m.
— v. tr. Techn. Claveter. ‖ Mus. Accorder. ‖ Fig. Mettre en harmonie avec. ‖ Fam. *To key up,* tendre, surexciter; *keyed up,* très remonté, tendu.

keyboard [-bɔ:d] n. Mus. Clavier m.

keyhole [-houl] n. Trou (m.) de la serrure. ‖ Techn. *Keyhole saw,* scie à guichet. ‖ Fam. *To be always at keyholes,* être toujours aux écoutes.

keyless [-lis] adj. A remontoir (watch).

keystone [-stoun] n. Archit., Fig. Clef de voûte ƒ.

khaki ['kɑ:ki] adj., n. Kaki m.

khan [kɑ:n] n. Khan m.

khedive ['keidi:v] n. Khédive m.

khol [koul] n. Khol m.

kibble ['kibl] v. tr. Ecraser.

kibbutz [ki'buts] (pl. **kibbutzim** [-i:m]) n. Kibboutz m.

kibe [kaib] n. Med. Crevasse ƒ.

kibitz ['kibits] v. intr. Fam. Regarder et importuner des joueurs, tourner autour de joueurs; être prodigue de conseils.

kibitzer [-ə*] n. Fam. Spectateur (m.) prodigue de conseils, conseilleur m.

kibosh ['kaibɔʃ] n. Pop. Baliverne ƒ.; *to put the kibosh on,* clore le bec à (s.o.); en finir avec (sth.).

kick [kik] n. Culot m. (of a bottle).

kick n. Coup de pied m. ‖ Ruade ƒ. (of a horse). ‖ Milit. Recul m. (of a gun). ‖ Techn. Retour m. (backfire). ‖ Sports. Coup m. (in football). ‖ Fam. Renvoi m. ‖ Fam. Plaisir violent m.; *to do sth. for kicks,* faire qqch. histoire de rire;· *to get a kick out of sth.,* s'en payer une tranche. ‖ Fam. Allant m. (of s.o.); piquant m. (of sth.); *to have no kick left in one,* être vidé. ‖ **Kick-off,** n. Sports. Coup d'envoi m. ‖ **Kick-starter,** n. Autom. Démarreur (m.) à pédale.
— v. intr. Donner des coups de pied (person). ‖ Ruer (horse). ‖ Milit. Reculer (gun). ‖ Fig. Regimber, rouspéter (*against, at,* contre). ‖ **To kick about,** traînailler, traîner. ‖ **To kick back,** Autom. Avoir un retour de manivelle; Fam. Ruer dans les brancards. ‖ **To kick off,** Sports. Donner le coup d'envoi; U. S. Fam. Clamser, claquer (to die). ‖ **To kick out,** lancer des ruades (horse).
— v. tr. Donner des coups de pied à; *to kick downstairs,* faire descendre l'escalier à coups de pied. ‖ Sports. Botter (the ball); marquer (a goal). ‖ Fam. *To kick the bucket,* passer l'arme à gauche; *to kick s.o. upstairs,* donner de l'avancement à qqn pour se débarrasser de lui. ‖ **To kick about,** lancer de-ci de-là à coups de pied. ‖ **To kick back,** rendre; Sports. Relancer; Fam. Ristourner. ‖ **To kick in,** enfoncer (the door); U. S. Pop. Payer (one's share). ‖ **To kick off,** enlever d'un coup de pied. ‖ **To kick out,** chasser à coups de pied; Fam. Flanquer dehors. ‖ **To kick up,** soulever (dust); Fam. *To kick up a hullabaloo* (or) *a shindy,* faire du boucan; *to kick up one's heels,* bondir de joie.

kickback [-bæk] n. U. S. Fam. Ristourne ƒ.

kicker [-ə*] n. Zool. Rueur m. (horse). ‖ Sports. Joueur m. ‖ Fam. Rouspéteur s.

kickshaw ['kikʃɔ:] n. Colifichet, brimborion m. (gewgaw); broutille ƒ. (trifle). ‖ Culin. Friandise ƒ.

kid [kid] n. Zool. Chevreau m.; chevrette ƒ. ‖ Comm. Chevreau m. (leather); *kid gloves,* gants de chevreau. ‖ Fam. *To handle with kid gloves,* manier comme du verre cassé. ‖ Fam. Gosse m. (child); gamin m. (boy); U. S. *A candy kid,* un petit crevé.
‖ **Kid-glove,** adj. Fam. En peau de lapin. ‖ **Kid stuff,** n. Pop. U. S. Enfantillage m.

— v. tr. (1). Zool. Mettre bas (goat). ‖ Fam. Bourrer le crâne à; *to kid oneself,* se monter le coup.
— v. intr. Zool. Chevreter. ‖ Fam. Blaguer.

kidder [-ə*] n. Fam. Blagueur s.

kidding [-iŋ] n. Fam. Blague ƒ.; *no kidding,* sans blague, blague à part.

kiddy [-i] n. Fam. Mioche m.

kidnap ['kidnæp] v. tr. (1). Enlever, kidnapper.

kidnapper [-ə*] n. Kidnappeur, ravisseur s.

kidnapping [-iŋ] n. Rapt m.

kidney ['kidni] n. Med. Rein m.; *kidney stone,* calcul du rein. ‖ Culin. Rognon m.; *kidney bean,* soissons, haricot blanc; fayot (fam.); *kidney potato,* saucisse. ‖ Fam. *Of the same kidney,* du même acabit (or) tabac.

kieselguhr ['ki:zl,guə*] n. Geol., Techn. Kieselguhr m.

kilderkin ['kildə:kin] n. Quartant m.

kill [kil] v. tr. Abattre (animals); tuer (persons). ‖ Naut. Couler (a ship). ‖ Fig. Tuer (a colour, time). ‖ Fam. Faire rire (s.o.). ‖ Fam. U. S. Faire sauter (a paragraph, a word). ‖ Loc. *To kill two birds with one stone,* faire d'une pierre deux coups. ‖ **Kill-joy,** n. Fam. Rabat-joie m. ‖ **Kill-or-cure,** adj. Fam. De cheval (remedy). ‖ **Kill-time,** n. Manière (ƒ.) de passer le temps.
— v. intr. *To kill well,* être bon pour la boucherie (animal). ‖ Sports. Servir la bête. ‖ Fam. Faire des conquêtes.
— n. Sports. Mise à mort ƒ. (act); gibier tué m. (animal).

killer [-ə*] n. Tueur s. ‖ U. S. Assassin m. ‖ Fam. Tombeur (m.) de cœurs.

killing [-iŋ] adj. Meurtrier. ‖ Fig. Mortel (anxiety). ‖ Fam. Tuant, crevant (exhausting); gondolant, crevant, désopilant (funny). ‖ Fam. Conquérant; *killing glance,* œillade assassine.
— n. Tuerie ƒ. ‖ Fam. Bonne affaire ƒ.

killingly [-iŋli] adv. Mortellement. ‖ Fam. *A crever de rire.*

kiln [kiln] n. Four m. (oven). ‖ Etuve ƒ. (drying room). ‖ **Kiln-dry,** v. tr. Sécher.

kilo ['ki:lou] (pl. **kilos** [-z]) n. Kilo m. (kilogram). ‖ Kilomètre m.

kilocalorie ['kilo'kæləri] n. Phys. Kilocalorie ƒ.

kilocycle [-,saikl] n. Radio. Kilocycle m.

kilogram(me) [-græm] n. Kilogramme m.

kilolitre [-,li:tə*] n. Kilolitre m.

kilometre [-,mi:tə*] n. Kilomètre m.

kilometric [-'metrik] adj. Kilométrique.

kiloton(ne) ['kilou,tʌn] n. Kilotonne ƒ.

kilowatt [-wɔt] n. Electr. Kilowatt m. ‖ **Kilowatt-hour,** n. Electr. Kilowatt-heure m.

kilt [kilt] n. Kilt m.
— v. tr. Plisser (to pleat); retrousser (to tuck up).

kilter ['kiltə*] n. U. S. Fam. Bon ordre m.; *out of kilter,* détraqué.

kilting ['kiltiŋ] n. Plissure ƒ.; pli m.

kimono [ki'mounou] n. Kimono m.

kin [kin] n. Parenté ƒ.; parents m. pl.
— adj. Apparenté, allié. ‖ Fig. Apparenté.

kind [kaind] adj. Bon, bienveillant (good-hearted). ‖ Aimable, cordial, amical (friendly). ‖ *Be so kind as to,* voulez-vous être assez aimable pour (or) avoir l'amabilité de. ‖ **Kind-hearted,** adj. Au cœur généreux.
— n. Espèce, race ƒ.; genre m.; *rodent kind,* les rongeurs. ‖ Espèce, catégorie, classe, variété ƒ. (class). ‖ Espèce, sorte ƒ.; genre m. (sort). ‖ Nature, tendance ƒ. (bend). ‖ Fin., Comm. *In kind,* en nature. ‖ Eccles. Espèce ƒ.

kindergarten ['kində,gɑ:tn] n. Jardin (m.) d'enfants.

kindle ['kindl] v. tr. Allumer (a fire); embraser (a forest). ‖ Fig. Allumer (anger, passions); enflam-

mer (courage); éveiller, exciter (interest); aviver (suspicions); *to kindle s.o. to*, exciter qqn à.
— v. intr. S'allumer; s'embraser. ‖ FIG. S'allumer; s'enflammer; s'éveiller; s'exciter.
kindliness ['kaindlinis] n. Bonté, amabilité *f.* (of a person). ‖ Douceur *f.* (of a climate); agrément *m.* (of a place).
kindling ['kindliŋ] n. Allumage *m.* ‖ U. S. Margotin, allume-feu *m.* (wood).
kindly ['kaindli] adv. Avec bienveillance, aimablement; *will you kindly*, voulez-vous avoir la bonté de; voulez-vous, je vous prie. ‖ Bien, favorablement; *to take kindly*, prendre bien; *to take kindly to*, être attiré par.
— adj. Bon, bienveillant, aimable. ‖ Doux (climate); agréable (place); favorable (wind).
kindness [-nis] n. Bonté, bienveillance *f.* ‖ Amabilité *f.* (act, quality); bienfait *m.* (act).
kindred ['kindrid] n. Parenté *f.* (kinship); famille *f.* (kinsfolk). ‖ FIG. Parenté, affinité *f.*
— adj. Apparenté (lit. and fig.).
kine [kain] n. pl. ZOOL. Vaches *f. pl.*
kinematic [,kini'mætik] adj. Cinématique.
kinematics [-s] n. sg. Cinématique *f.*
kinematograph [,kini'mætəgræf] n. Cinématographe *m.*
kinematographic [,kinimæto'græfik] adj. Cinématographique.
Kinescope ['kinəskoup] n. Cinescope *m.*
kinesthesis [,kinis'θi:sis] n. MED. Kinesthésie *f.*
kinetic [ki'netik] adj. Cinétique.
kinetics [-s] n. Cinétique *f.*
king [kiŋ] n. Roi *m.; King Alfred*, le roi Alfred. ‖ Roi *m.;* (in cards, chess); dame *f.* (in draughts). ‖ FAM. Roi *m.; King Baby*, l'enfant roi; *king log*, roi soliveau; *fur king*, le roi de la fourrure; *the King's English*, l'anglais correct. ‖ **King-bolt**, n. TECHN. Cheville maîtresse *f.* ‖ **King-craft**, n. Métier de roi *m.* ‖ **King-cup**, n. BOT. Bouton-d'or *m.* ‖ **King-pin**, n. TECHN. Cheville ouvrière; FAM. Gros bonnet, ponte *m.* ‖ **King-post**, n. ARCHIT. Poinçon *m.;* AVIAT. Pylône *m.* ‖ **King-size**, adj. U. S. FAM. Géant (cigarettes).
— v. tr. Faire roi. ‖ FAM. *To king it*, parader, faire le grand seigneur.
kingdom [-dəm] n. Royaume *m.* (realm). ‖ BOT., ZOOL. Règne *m.* ‖ ECCLES. Règne *m.* (of God); royaume *m.* (of heaven). ‖ FIG. Royaume, domaine *m.* ‖ FAM. *He is gone to kingdom-come*, il est passé dans un monde meilleur; *to prepare for kingdom-come*, cirer ses bottes; *to send to kingdom-come*, envoyer « ad patres ».
kingfisher [-,fiʒə*] n. ZOOL. Martin-pêcheur *m.*
kinglet [-lit] n. ZOOL., FAM. Roitelet *m.*
kinglike [-laik] adj. En roi.
kingly [-li] adj. Royal, de roi.
kingship [-ʃip] n. Royauté *f.*
kink [kiŋk] n. Tortillement, nœud *m.* (in wire). ‖ NAUT. Coque *f.* (in rope). ‖ MED. Torticolis *m.* ‖ FIG. Déviation *f.;* lubie *f.* (crotchet); *vocational kink*, déformation professionnelle.
— v. tr. Faire un nœud à, entortiller.
— v. intr. S'entortiller, se nouer.
kinky [-i] adj. Crépu, bouclé (hair). ‖ FAM. Déformé (biased); fantasque (whimsical); qui a des goûts bizarres, un peu pervers (perverted).
kinless ['kinlis] adj. Sans famille.
kinsfolk ['kinzfouk] n. Parents *m. pl.*
kinship ['kinʃip] n. Parenté *f.*
kinsman ['kinzmən] (pl. **kinsmen**) n. Parent *m.*
kinswoman [-,wumən] (pl. **kinswomen**) n. Parente *f.*
kiosk [ki'ɔsk] n. Kiosque *m.*
kip [kip] n. FAM. Pieu, plumard *m.* (bed).
— v. intr. FAM. Se pieuter.
kipper ['kipə*] n. ZOOL. Saumon mâle *m.* ‖ CULIN. Kipper, craquelot *m.* (herring).
— v. tr. CULIN. Saurer.

kirk [kə:k] n. Eglise *f.*
kirsch [kiəʃ] n. Kirsch *m.*
kismet ['kismet] n. Destinée *f.*
kiss [kiss] n. Baiser *m.* ‖ SPORTS. Contrecoup *m.* (at billiards). ‖ CULIN. Bonbon au sucre *m.* ‖ **Kiss-curl**, n. Accroche-cœur *m.*
— v. tr. Embrasser, donner un baiser à; *to kiss one's hand to*, envoyer un baiser à; *to kiss a lady's hand*, baiser la main d'une dame. ‖ SPORTS. Toucher par contre. ‖ FIG. *To kiss the dust*, mordre la poussière.
kisser [-ə*] n. Embrasseur *s.* (person). ‖ FAM. Bouche *f.* (lips).
kissing [-iŋ] n. Embrassade *f.;* baisers *m. pl.* ‖ Baisement *m.* (of feet); *kissing of hands*, baisemain.
kissproof [-pruf] adj. Indélébile, tenace (lipstick).
kit [kit] n. Tonnelet *m.* (for butter); caque *f.* (for fish). ‖ MILIT. Sac *m.* (bag); équipement léger, paquetage *m.* (pack). ‖ TECHN. Trousse *f.;* nécessaire *m.* (for tools). ‖ FAM. *To pack up one's kit*, ramasser son barda. ‖ U. S. FAM. *The whole kit and caboodle*, tout le saint-frusquin.
— v. intr. (1). MILIT. *To be kitted out*, toucher son paquetage.
kitchen ['kitʃin] n. Cuisine *f.* (room). ‖ **Kitchen-equipment**, n. Batterie de cuisine *f.* ‖ **Kitchen-garden**, n. Jardin potager *m.* ‖ **Kitchen-maid**, n. Fille de cuisine *f.* ‖ **Kitchen-police**, n. MILIT. U. S. Corvée de cuisine *f.* ‖ **Kitchen-unit**, n. Bloc-cuisine *m.* ‖ **Kitchen-stuff**, n. Légumes *m. pl.* ‖ **Kitchen-ware**, n. Ustensiles (*m. pl.*) de cuisine.
kitchener [-ə*] n. Cuisinière *f.* (stove). ‖ ECCLES. Cuisinier *m.* ‖ U. S. CULIN. Cuisinier *m.*
kitchenette [,kitʃi'net] n. Kitchenette, cuisine miniature *f.*
kite [kait] n. Cerf-volant *m.* ‖ ZOOL. Milan *m.* ‖ COMM. Billet (*m.*) de complaisance. ‖ NAUT. Voile haute *f.* ‖ FIG. Vautour *m.* (person); ballon d'essai *m.* (thing). ‖ **Kite-balloon**, n. AVIAT. Ballon captif *m.*
— v. intr. Voler. ‖ FIN. Tirer en blanc.
— v. tr. Faire voler. ‖ FIN. *To kite a cheque*, émettre un chèque insuffisamment provisionné.
kith [kiθ] n. Connaissances, relations *f. pl.; kith and kin*, amis et parents, parentèle.
kitsch [kitʃ] n. Kitsch *m.*
kitschy [-i] adj. Kitsch *adj. inv.*
kitten ['kitn] n. ZOOL. Chaton, petit chat *m.* ‖ FAM. Petite coquette *f.* ‖ U. S. Pl. FAM. Moutons *m. pl.* (fluff under beds).
— v. intr. ZOOL. Faire des chats; chatter.
kittenish [-iʃ] adj. Félin, de chat. ‖ FAM. Maniéré, affecté (affected); joueur, enjoué (playful).
kittiwake ['kiti,weik] n. ZOOL. Mouette tridactyle, risse *f.*
kittle ['kitl] adj. Epineux, délicat (points); chatouilleux (person); *kittle cattle*, gens difficiles à manier.
kitty ['kiti] n. Minet, minou *m.* (See KITTEN.)
kitty n. U. S. FAM. Cagnotte *f.* (in poker game). ‖ **Kitty-cat**, n. Bâtonnet *m.* (game).
kiwi ['ki:wi] n. ZOOL., BOT. Kiwi *m.* ‖ FAM., GEOGR. Néo-Zélandais *s.*
klaxon ['klæksn] n. Klaxon *m.* (motor-horn); corne, trompe *f.* (warning signal).
kleptomania [,klepto'meiniə] n. MED. Kleptomanie *f.*
kleptomaniac [-ək] n. MED. Kleptomane *s.*
klystron ['klistrɔn] n. PHYS. Klystron *m.*
knack [næk] n. Tour de main, art *m.;* truc, chic *m.* (fam.) (*for, of*, pour). ‖ † Babiole *f.* (knick-knack).
knacker ['nækə*] n. Equarrisseur *m.* ‖ ARCHIT. Entrepreneur (*m.*) de démolitions.
knackered ['nækəd] adj. POP. Crevé, éreinté.
knag [næg] n. Nœud *m.* (in wood).
knaggy [-i] adj. Noueux. ‖ FAM. Hargneux.

knall-gas ['næl,gæs] n. Chim. Gaz détonant m.
knap [næp] n. Monticule m.
knap v. tr. (1). Casser (stones).
knapsack ['næpsæk] n. Milit. Havresac, sac m.
knapweed [-wi:d] n. Bot. Centaurée f.
knar [nα:*] n. Nœud m. (on a tree trunk).
knarred ['nα:d] adj. Noueux.
knave [neiv] n. † Valet m. (servant). ‖ Valet m. (at cards). ‖ Fig. Fripon m.
knavery [-əri], **knavishness** [-iʃnis] n. Friponnerie f. (rascality). ‖ † Malice f.
knavish [-iʃ] adj. Fripon. ‖ † Malicieux.
knead [ni:d] v. tr. Pétrir (clay, dough). ‖ Med. Masser.
kneading [-iŋ] n. Pétrissage m. (of dough, muscles). ‖ **Kneading-machine,** n. Pétrin mécanique m. ‖ **Kneading-trough,** n. Pétrin m.
knee [ni:] n. Genou m.; on hands and knees, à quatre pattes; on one's (or) bended knees, à genoux; to break its knees, se couronner (horse). ‖ Techn. Genouillère, console f. ‖ Naut. Courbe f. ‖ **Knee-action,** n. Action géniculée f. ‖ **Knee-breeches,** n. pl. Culotte f. ‖ **Knee-cap,** n. † Genouillère f.; Med. Rotule f. ‖ **Knee-deep,** adj. Jusqu'aux genoux (in, dans). ‖ **Knee-hole,** n. Evidement (m.) pour la place des genoux; knee-hole table (or) U. S. desk, bureau ministre. ‖ **Knee-joint,** n. Med. Articulation (f.) du genou; Techn. Joint articulé m. ‖ **Knee-pad,** n. Genouillère f. ‖ **Knee-pan,** n. Med. Rotule f. ‖ **Knee-pipe,** n. Techn. Coude m. ‖ **Knee-reflex,** n. Med. Réflexe rotulien m. ‖ **Knees-up,** n. Fam. Sauterie f.
— v. tr. Pousser du genou; faire du genou à (fam.). ‖ Faire des poches à (trousers). ‖ Techn. Soutenir par une console.
kneel [ni:l] v. intr. (85). S'agenouiller (to, devant).
kneeling [-iŋ] n. Agenouillement m. ‖ **Kneeling-chair,** n. Prie-Dieu m. ‖ **Kneeling-stool,** n. Agenouilloir m.
— adj. A genoux, agenouillé.
knell [nel] n. Glas m.
— v. tr. Sonner le glas de.
— v. intr. Sonner le glas.
knelt [nelt] pret., p. p. See KNEEL.
knew [nju:] pret. See KNOW.
knickerbockers ['nikəbɔkəz] n. pl. Knickerbockers m. pl.
knickers ['nikə:z] n. pl. Culotte, petite culotte f., slip m. (women's underwear). ‖ U. S. Knickerbockers m. pl. ‖ Fam. To get one's knickers in a twist, se mettre dans tous ses états.
— interj. Pop. Et puis merde!
knick-knack ['niknæk] n. Broutille, babiole f. (trifle); colifichet m. (trinket).
knife [naif] (pl. **knives** [naivz]) n. Couteau m.; knife and fork, couvert; knife and fork breakfast, petit déjeuner à l'anglaise. ‖ Med. Bistouri m. ‖ Fam. Before you could say knife, avant d'avoir pu dire ouf; if I get my knife into him, s'il me tombe sous la patte. ‖ **Knife-board,** n. Planche (f.) à couteaux. ‖ **Knife-bridge,** n. Pont (m.) à lame. ‖ **Knife-edge,** n. Tranchant m.; Géogr. Arête f.; Techn. Couteau m. (fulcrum). ‖ **Knife-grinder,** n. Rémouleur m. (person). ‖ **Knife-rest,** n. Porte-couteau m. ‖ **Knife-switch,** n. Electr. Interrupteur à couteau m.
— v. tr. Poignarder; descendre à coups de couteau (fam.); suriner (pop.).
knifester [-stə*] n. Pop. Surineur, boucher m.
knight [nait] n. Chevalier m.; Knight Templar, templier; Cavalier m. (in chess). ‖ Fam. Knight of the pad, bandit de grands chemins; knight of the road, commis voyageur. ‖ **Knight-errant,** n. Chevalier errant m.; Fam. Paladin, don Quichotte m. ‖ **Knight-errantry,** n. Chevalerie errante f.; Fam. Don Quichottisme m.
— v. tr. † Armer chevalier. ‖ Faire chevalier.

knightage [-idʒ] n. Corps (m.) des chevaliers.
knighthood [-hud] n. Chevalerie f. ‖ Qualité (f.) de chevalier.
knightliness [-linis] n. Courtoisie f.; conduite chevaleresque f.
knightly [-li] adj. Chevaleresque (conduct); de chevalerie (order).
knit [nit] v. tr. (86). Tricoter; to knit up, assembler au tricot (a garment). ‖ Contracter; to knit one's brows, froncer le sourcil. ‖ Med. Faire souder (bones). ‖ Fig. Lier, unir (people).
— v. intr. Tricoter. ‖ Se froncer (brows). ‖ Med. Se souder (bones). ‖ Fig. Se lier (persons).
knitter [-ə*] n. Tricoteuse f.
knitting [-iŋ] n. Tricotage m. (action); tricot m. (work). ‖ Med. Soudure f. ‖ Fig. Union f. ‖ **Knitting-needle,** n. Aiguille (f.) à tricoter.
knittle ['nitl̩] n. Naut. Aiguillette f.
knob [nɔb] n. Bosse f. (hump). ‖ Bouton m. (of door, drawer); pomme f. (of stick); rewinding knob, molette de rebobinage (photogr.). ‖ Bot. Nœud m. (See KNAR.) ‖ Morceau m. (of coal, sugar). ‖ U. S. Géogr. Mamelon m. (knoll). ‖ Fam. Caboche, bille f. (head).
— v. tr. (1). Bosseler. ‖ Mettre un bouton (or) une pomme à.
— v. intr. **To knob out,** faire une bosse, bomber.
knobbed [-d] adj. Bosselé. ‖ A bouton (door); à pommeau (stick). ‖ Noueux (tree).
knobble ['nɔbl̩] n. Petite bosse f.
— v. tr. Techn. Tringler (iron). ‖ Sports. Doper (a horse).
knobby [-i] adj. Bosselé. ‖ Bot. Noueux (tree).
knobstick [-stik] n. Trique, massue f. (cudgel). ‖ Canne (f.) à pommeau (stick).
knock [nɔk] v. tr. Cogner, frapper (on, sur); to knock one's elbow, se cogner le coude; to knock a hole in, faire un trou en cognant dans. ‖ Fam. Renverser; it knocks you sideways, c'est époustouflant; that knocks you, ça vous en bouche un coin; anéantir. ‖ U. S. Fam. Ereinter (to criticize). ‖ **To knock about,** bousculer, malmener; **To knock down,** renverser (s.o., sth.); descendre, démolir; to knock for six, U. S. to knock for a loop, démolir (fam.) [s.o.]; abattre (a wall); Comm. Adjuger (at an auction); Fig. Rabaisser, rabattre (s.o.'s pride); U. S. Fam. Mettre le grappin sur (money). ‖ **To knock in,** enfoncer. ‖ **To knock off,** faire tomber d'un coup (sth.); Comm. Faire une diminution de, rabattre (money); Techn. To knock off work, débrayer; Fam. Expédier, torcher (one's work); déboulonner, démolir (s.o.). ‖ **To knock out,** sortir en cognant; débourrer (a pipe); retrancher, barrer (a word); Sports. Mettre knock-out (in boxing); éliminer (in competition); Fam. Etendre (s.o.). ‖ **To knock together,** assembler rapidement. ‖ **To knock up,** mener rondement (an affair); faire lever en cognant (s.o.); Sports. Chasser en l'air (the ball); Fam. Edifier à la va-vite (a house); éreinter, crever, vanner (s.o.); U. S. Pop. Engrosser (a woman).
— v. intr. Cogner, frapper (at, à). ‖ Se cogner, se heurter (against, à, contre). ‖ Autom. Cogner. ‖ Fam. Tomber (against, sur) [s.o.]. ‖ **To knock about,** Fam. Vagabonder, se balader, vadrouiller. ‖ **To knock off,** Techn. Débrayer (striker); cesser son travail (worker). ‖ **To knock together,** se cogner (reciprocally). ‖ **To knock up,** se heurter (against, à, contre); Fam. Etre crevé (or) éreinté.
— n. Coup, choc, heurt m. (against, contre; at, à; on, sur). ‖ Façon (f.) de frapper à la porte (rap). ‖ Autom. Cognement m. (in an engine). ‖ U. S. Fam. Ereintement m. (criticism). ‖ **Knock-down,** adj. D'assommoir (blow); Comm. Imbattable (price); Techn. Démontable (machinery); n. Coup d'assom-

moir *m.*; U. S. Pop. Mot (*m.*) d'introduction (*to*, pour). ‖ **Knock-kneed**, adj. Med. Cagneux (person). ‖ **Knock-me-down**, n. U. S. Fam. Tord-boyaux *m.* (drink). ‖ **Knock-out**, adj. D'assommoir (blow); Comm. Imbattable (price); U. S. Fam. *Knock-out drops*, narcotique; n. Coup d'assommoir *m.*; Sports. Knock-out *m.*; Comm. Gang (*m.*) de brocanteurs (at an auction); Fam. Type renversant (person); chose sensationnelle *f.* (thing). ‖ **Knock-up**, n. Sports. Balles *f. pl.*; *to have a knock-up*, faire des balles.

knockabout [-ˌəbaut] n. U. S. Rixe *f.* ‖ Naut. Yacht *m.* ‖ Theatr. Clown *m.* — adj. Fam. De travail (clothes); de bâton de chaise (life).

knocker [-ə*] n. Heurtoir, marteau *m.* (at door). ‖ Cogneur *m.* (person). ‖ U. S. Fam. Ereinteur *m.*

knocking [-iŋ] n. Cognement *m.* ‖ **Knocking down**, n. Comm. Adjudication *f.* (at auction).

knoll [noul] n. Mamelon, monticule, tertre *m.*; butte *f.* (See hillock.)

knoll v. tr. Sonner (bell, hours); appeler en sonnant, sonner (persons). — v. intr. Tinter.

knot [nɔt] n. Nœud *m.*; *running knot*, nœud coulant; *to tie, to untie a knot*, faire, défaire un nœud; nouer, dénouer. ‖ Chignon *m.* (of hair). ‖ Naut. Nœud *m.*; *to make five knots*, filer cinq nœuds. ‖ Jur. *Marriage knot*, liens conjugaux. ‖ Geol. Nodule *m.* ‖ Bot. Nœud *m.* ‖ Med. Nodosité *f.* ‖ Fig. Nœud *m.* (of a question). — v. tr. (1). Nouer, faire un nœud à; *knotted rope*, corde à nœuds. ‖ Med. Nouer (fingers). ‖ Fig. Enchevêtrer. ‖ Loc. *To knot one's brow*, froncer le sourcil. — v. intr. Se nouer. ‖ Faire du macramé (in needlework).

knotgrass [-grɑs] n. Bot. Renouée *f.*

knottiness [-inis] n. Nodosité *f.* ‖ Fig. Difficulté *f.*

knotty [-i] adj. Bot., Med. Noueux. ‖ Fig. Epineux.

knotwork [-wə:k] n. Macramé *m.* (needlework). ‖ Archit. Entrelacs *m.*

knout [naut] n. Knout *m.* — v. tr. Knouter.

know [nou] v. tr. (87). Savoir, connaître, être au courant de (sth.); *I know she lies*, je sais qu'elle ment; *she is known to lie*, on sait qu'elle ment; *to let s.o. know sth.*, faire savoir (or) dire qqch. à qqn, faire part de qqch. à qqn. ‖ Savoir, connaître, posséder (knowledge, languages); *he doesn't know the first thing about it*, il n'y connaît rien; *to know all about cars*, s'entendre aux autos. ‖ Connaître (a person, place); *known as*, connu sous la dénomination de. ‖ Connaître, voir, fréquenter (friends); *to be among people one knows*, être en pays de connaissance. ‖ Reconnaître (s.o.); *to be known by*, se reconnaître à. ‖ Distinguer, différencier (*from*, de); *you wouldn't know him from an Eskimo*, on le prendrait pour un Esquimau. ‖ Voir, entendre dire, savoir; *I've never known anybody to lie as he does*, je n'ai jamais vu personne mentir comme lui; *she had never been known to weep*, on ne l'avait jamais vu pleurer. ‖ Fam. *To know the ropes*, connaître les ficelles; être au courant des trucs; *to know one's onions*, connaître son affaire; *to know one's stuff*, être à la coule; *to know what's what*, s'y connaître, être à la hauteur. — v. intr. Savoir; *be it known that*, on fait savoir que; *how do I know?*, est-ce que je sais?; *to know how to*, savoir, connaître le moyen de. ‖ Etre au courant, avoir connaissance (*of*, de); *does he know of it?*, est-il renseigné sur ce point? ‖ Juger; *he knows best*, c'est à lui de juger, il est meilleur juge; *he ought to know better*, il devrait avoir plus de raison. — n. Fam. Savoir *m.*; *to be in the know*, être à la page; être dans le secret des dieux. ‖ **Know-all**

know-it-all, n. Fam. Monsieur Je-sais-tout *m.* ‖ **Know-how**, n. Technique *f.*; tour (*m.*) de main, savoir-faire, chic *m.*; manière *f.* ‖ **Know-nothing**, n. Ignorant *s.*

knowable [-əbl] adj. Connaissable.

knower [-ə*] n. Connaisseur *s.*

knowing [-iŋ] adj. Au courant, renseigné, informé. ‖ Instruit. ‖ Malin, finaud, rusé, entendu (shrewd); délibéré, intentionnel (purposeful). ‖ Fam. Affranchi, déniaisé, dessalé.

knowingly [-iŋli] adv. Sciemment, intentionnellement, en connaissance de cause (on purpose). ‖ Habilement, avec ruse (shrewdly).

knowledge ['nɔlidʒ] n. Connaissance *f.* (*of*, de); *it's common knowledge that*, tout le monde sait que; *not to my knowledge*, pas que je sache. ‖ Savoir *m.*; science *f.*; connaissances, lumières *f. pl.*; *having a thorough knowledge of*, possédant à fond. ‖ Jur. *Carnal knowledge*, relations sexuelles.

known [noun] p. p. See know.

knuckle ['nʌkl] n. Med. Jointure (or) articulation (*f.*) du doigt. ‖ Culin. Jarret *m.* (of veal); *knuckle of ham*, jambonneau. ‖ Osselets *m. pl.* (game). ‖ **Knuckle-bone**, n. Osselet *m.* ‖ **Knuckle-duster**, n. Coup-de-poing américain *m.* ‖ **Knuckle-end**, n. Culin. Souris *f.* (of a leg of mutton). ‖ **Knuckle-joint**, n. Techn. Charnière à genouillère *f.* — v. tr. Toucher (or) frapper du revers de la main. — v. intr. **To knuckle down**, toucher la terre des doigts (at marbles); Fam. Plier le dos. ‖ **To knuckle under**, baisser pavillon, mettre les pouces.

knurl [nə:l] n. Nœud *m.* (See knag.) ‖ Techn. Moletage *m.* — v. tr. Techn. Moleter.

knur(r) [nə:*] n. Nœud *m.* (See knag.) ‖ Sports. Boule *f.* (at hockey).

K.O. [kei'ou] abbr. *knock-out*, K.-O. (See knock out.)

koala [kou'ɑ:lə] n. Zool. Koala *m.*

kohl [koul] n. Khôl, kohol, koheul *m.*

kohlrabi ['koul'rɑ:bi] n. Agric. Chou-rave *m.*

kola ['koulə] n. Cola *m.* (nut, tree). ‖ **Kola-nut**, **kola-tree**, n. Cola *m.*

kolkhoz [koul'khouz] n. Kolkhoze *m.*

kommandatura [kɔ'mændətuərə] n. Kommandantur *f.*

kopeck ['koupek] n. Fin. Kopeck *m.*

Koran [kɔ'rɑ:n] n. Coran *m.*

Korea [kə'riə] n. Geogr. Corée *f.*

Korean [-ən] adj., n. Geogr. Coréen.

kosher ['kouʃə*] adj. Kasher. ‖ U. S. Fam. Convenable.

kowtow ['kau'tau] n. Prosternation *f.* — v. intr. Se prosterner. ‖ Fam. Faire des courbettes.

kraal [krɑ:l] n. Corral *m.*

Kremlin ['kremlin] n. Kremlin *m.*

krimmer ['krimə*] n. Comm. Agneau (*m.*) de Crimée (fur).

krypton ['kriptən] n. Chim. Krypton *m.*

kudos ['kju:dɔs] n. Fam. Gloriole *f.*; panache *m.* ‖ Célébrité *f.*

Ku-Klux-Klan ['kju:klʌks'klæn] n. Ku-Klux-Klan *m.*

Ku-Klux-Klanner [-ə*] n. Membre (*m.*) du Ku-Klux-Klan.

kung fu ['kʌŋ'fu:] n. Sports. Kung-fu *m.*

Kurd [kə:d] n. Geogr. Kurde *s.*

Kurdish [-iʃ] adj., n. Geogr., Gramm. Kurde.

Kurdistan [kə:dis'tɑ:n] n. Geogr. Kurdistan *m.*

Kuwait [ku'weit] n. Geogr. Koweït *m.*

kwashiorkor [ˌkwæʃi'ɔ:kə*] n. Med. Kwashiorkor *m.*

kyphosis [ki'fousis] n. Med. Cyphose *f.*

L

l [el] n. L, l *m.* ‖ Cinquante *m.* (Roman numeral). ‖ FIN. Livre *f.* ‖ AUTOM. *L. plate*, « auto-école ». — adj. En L.

la [lɑ:] n. MUS. La *m.*

lab [læb] n. FAM. Labo *m.* (laboratory).

labarum ['læbərəm] n. Labarum *m.*

labefaction [,læbi'fækʃən] n. Décrépitude *f.*

label ['leibl] n. ARCHIT. Larmier *m.* ‖ BLAS. Lambel *m.* ‖ JUR. Codicille *m.* ‖ COMM., FIG. Etiquette *f.*
— v. tr. COMM., FIG. Etiqueter. ‖ CH. DE F. Enregistrer (luggage).

labial ['leibiəl] adj. MED., GRAMM. Labial.
— n. GRAMM. Labiale *f.*

labialization [,leibiəlai'zeiʃən] n. GRAMM. Labialisation *f.*

labialize ['leibiəlaiz] v. tr. GRAMM. Labialiser.

labiate ['leibiit] adj. BOT. Labié.
— n. BOT. Labiée *f.*

labile ['leibil] adj. CHIM., PSYCH. Labile.

labio- [,leibiou] pref. Labio-. ‖ **Labio-dental,** adj., n. GRAMM. Labiodentale, *adj., f.* ‖ **Labio-velar,** adj., n. GRAMM. Labiovélaire, *adj., f.*

laboratory [lə'bɔrətəri], ['læbərətəri] n. Laboratoire *m.*
— adj. De laboratoire.

laborious [læ'bɔ:riəs] adj. Travailleur, laborieux (hard-working). ‖ Laborieux, pénible (difficult).

laboriously [læ'bɔ:riəsli] adv. Laborieusement.

labo(u)r ['leibə*] n. Travail, labeur (toil); *hard labour*, travaux forcés. ‖ Peine *f.*; mal *m.*; *labour lost*, peine perdue. ‖ Travail *m.*; tâche, besogne *f.* (task); *Herculean labours*, travaux d'Hercule. ‖ Main-d'œuvre *f.*; *labour shortage*, rareté de la main-d'œuvre; *skilled labour*, main-d'œuvre spécialisée. ‖ Monde du travail *m.*; classe ouvrière *f.*; *Labour exchange*, Bourse du travail; *Labour Party*, parti travailliste; U. S. *Labor union*, syndicat. ‖ MED. Travail *m.* ‖ **Labour-saving,** adj. Allégeant le travail.
— v. intr. Travailler, besogner, peiner (to toil); travailler (*at*, à [some work]; *for*, pour [the public good]; *in*, pour [a good cause]). ‖ Se donner du mal, faire des efforts (*to*, pour); s'efforcer (*to*, de) [to strive]. ‖ Peiner, fatiguer; *to labour up the hill*, monter la côte péniblement. ‖ MED. Etre en travail. ‖ FIG. *To labour under*, être la victime de.
— v. tr. Travailler, polir (one's style). ‖ Insister sur (a point); pousser (a question). ‖ AGRIC. Labourer.

labourer [-rə*] n. Travailleur *s.* ‖ Manœuvre, ouvrier *m.*

labouring [-riŋ] adj. Ouvrier (class); ouvrable (day). ‖ MED. Haletant, oppressé (breast). ‖ FIG. Anxieux (soul).
— n. Labeur *m.*

labourite [-rait] n. Travailliste *m.*

laburnum [læ'bə:nəm] n. BOT. Cytise *m.*

labyrinth ['læbirinθ] n. ARCHIT., MED., FIG. Labyrinthe *m.*

lac [læk] n. Laque *f.* (See LAKE.)

lace [leis] n. Lacet *m.* (of boots); cordon, lacet *m.* (of a corset). ‖ Galon *m.*; ganse *f.* (braid). ‖ Dentelle *f.*; *Alençon lace*, point d'Alençon; *bobbin lace*, dentelle aux fuseaux. ‖ FAM. U. S. Goutte *f.* (of alcoholic liquor). ‖ **Lace-factory,** n. Dentellerie *f.* (manufacture). ‖ **Lace-glass,** n. Verre filigrané *m.* ‖ **Lace-maker,** n. Dentellière *f.* ‖ **Lace-making,** n.

Dentellerie *f.* (act). ‖ **Lace-pillow,** n. Coussin *m.* ‖ **Lace-work,** n. Dentelles *f. pl.* (lace); passementerie *f.* (trimmings).
— v. tr. Lacer (boots); serrer, comprimer (the waist). ‖ Galonner, ganser, border (*with*, de) [to trim]. ‖ Passer un lacet (*through*, dans). ‖ Orner de dentelle (a garment). ‖ Entrelacer (*with*, de) [to interlace]. ‖ FAM. Arroser (a beverage); rosser (s.o.).
— v. intr. Se lacer (boots); se serrer, se faire la taille fine (person). ‖ FAM. Taper (*into*, sur).

lacerate ['læsəreit] v. tr. Lacérer. ‖ FIG. Déchirer.
— [-rit] adj. Lacéré.

laceration [,læsə'reiʃən] n. Lacération *f.* ‖ MED. Déchirure *f.*

lachrymal ['lækriməl] adj. Lacrymatoire (vase). ‖ MED. Lacrymal.
— n. pl. MED. Glandes lacrymales *f. pl.*

lachrymator ['lækrə,meitə*] n. Gaz lacrymogène *m.*

lachrymatory ['lækrimətəri] adj., n. Lacrymatoire *m.*

lachrymose ['lækrimous] adj. Pleurnicheur; chialeur (pop.).

lacing ['leisiŋ] n. Laçage *m.* (act); lacet *m.* (lace). ‖ FAM. Raclée *f.* (See THRASHING.)

lack [læk] n. Manque *m.*; pénurie *f.* (*of*, de); *for lack of*, à défaut de, faute de; *to supply the lack*, suppléer à ce qui manque.
— v. intr. Manquer, faire défaut (or) faute. ‖ Manquer, être dénué (or) à court (*in*, de).
— v. tr. Manquer de, être dénué de.

lack interj. † Las, hélas! ‖ **Lack-a-day,** interj. Hélas !

lackadaisical [,lækə'deizikəl] adj. Grimacier, minaudier (affected); langoureux; gnan-gnan (fam.) [languid]; nonchalant, apathique (listless).

lackey ['læki] n. Laquais *m.*

lacklustre ['læk,lʌstə*] adj. Terne. (See DULL.)

laconic [lə'kɔnik] adj. Laconique.

laconically [-əli] adv. Laconiquement.

laconism ['lækənizm] n. Laconisme *m.*

lacquer ['lækə*] n. Laque *f.*; vernis du Japon *m.*
— v. tr. Laquer, vernir.

lacrosse [læ:'krɔs] n. SPORTS. Crosse canadienne *f.*

lactase ['lækteis] n. CHIM. Lactase *f.*

lactate ['lækteit] n. CHIM. Lactate *m.*

lactate v. intr. MED., ZOOL. Etre en période de lactation (ou) de sécrétion lactée.

lactation [læk'teiʃən] n. MED. Lactation *f.* (secretion); allaitement (suckling).

lacteal ['læktiəl] adj. MED. De lait (fever); lacté (vessel).

lacteous [-əs] adj. Laiteux. (See MILKY.)

lactescence [læk'tesns] n. Lactescence *f.*

lactic ['læktik] adj. CHIM. Lactique.

lactiferous [læk'tifərəs] adj. MED. Lactifère.

lactometer [-'tɔmitə*] n. Pèse-lait *m.*

lactose [-'tous] n. CHIM. Lactose *m.*

lacuna [lə'kju:nə] (pl. **lacunae** [-i:]) n. Lacune *f.*

lacunar [lə'kjunə*] n. ARCHIT. Caisson *m.*

lacunary [-əri] adj. Lacunaire.

lacustrine [lə'kʌstri:n] adj. Lacustre.

lacy ['leisi] adj. En dentelle (made of lace); comme de la dentelle (like lace).

lad [læd] n. Jeune homme, garçon *m.* ‖ SPORTS. Lad *m.* ‖ FAM. Joyeux drille *m.*

ladder ['lædə*] n. Echelle *f.* ‖ Fil tiré *m.*, maille

(*f.*) qui file, démaillage *m.* (in a stocking); *to make a ladder in*, démailler. ‖ Fig. Echelle *f.;* échelons *m. pl.* (of success). ‖ **Ladder-mender**, n. Remmailleuse *f.* ‖ **Ladder-proof**, adj. Indémaillable. ‖ **Ladder-stitch**, n. Jour (*m.*) échelle; brides *f. pl.*
— v. intr. Se démailler (stocking).
ladderless [-lis] adj. Indémaillable.
lade [leid] v. tr. (88). NAUT. Charger.
laden [-n] adj. Chargé (*with*, de). ‖ Fig. Ecrasé (*with*, de).
la-di-da [,lɑːdiːˈdɑː] n. Poseur, bêcheur *s.*
— adj. Affecté, maniéré (ways of speaking, manners); poseur, qui se donne de grands airs (person).
ladify [ˈleidifai] v. tr. Transformer en dame. ‖ Donner du « lady » à.
lading [ˈleidiŋ] n. NAUT. Chargement *m.*
ladle [ˈleidl̩] n. CULIN. Louche *f.* ‖ TECHN. Poche *f.;* puisard *m.*
— v. tr. CULIN. Servir à la louche. ‖ TECHN. Couler, pucher.
ladleful [-ful] n. Pleine louche *f.*
lady [ˈleidi] n. Dame *f.* ‖ Lady *f.* (title). ‖ ECCLES. *Lady Altar, Chapel*, autel, chapelle de la Sainte Vierge; *Lady Day*, Annonciation; *Our Lady*, Notre-Dame. ‖ CULIN. *Lady finger*, biscuit à la cuiller. ‖ FAM. *Lady Bountiful*, dame de charité; *ladies' man*, homme à femmes. ‖ **Lady-bird** (or) **-bug**, n. ZOOL. Coccinelle, bête (*f.*) à bon Dieu. ‖ **Lady-chair**, n. Chaise anglaise *f.* ‖ **Lady-killer**, n. FAM. Conquistador, tombeur, bourreau (*m.*) des cœurs. ‖ **Lady-love**, n. FAM. Dulcinée *f.*
— adj. Femme (female); *lady barber*, coiffeuse. ‖ D'un niveau social élevé, distingué; *lady help*, aide-ménagère.
ladylike [-laik] adj. De bon ton, raffiné, distingué. ‖ FAM. Efféminé (man).
ladyship [-ʃip] n. Condition d'une lady *f.;* *Her* (or) *Your Ladyship*, Madame *f.* (title).
laevulose [ˈliːvjulous] n. CHIM. Lévulose *m.*
lag [læg] v. intr. (1). Traîner; rester en arrière; s'attarder.
— n. NAUT., ELECTR., PHYS., FIG. Retard *m.*
lag n. JUR. Forçat *m.;* *old lag*, vieux cheval de retour (fam.).
lag n. TECHN. Latte *f.;* lattis; revêtement *m.*
— v. tr. TECHN. Garnir.
lagan [ˈlægən] n. JUR., NAUT. Epaves (*f. pl.*) au fond.
lager [ˈlɑːgə*] n. Bière blonde *f.*
laggard [ˈlægəd] n. Traînard, lambin, retardataire *m.*
— adj. En retard (backward); lent, lambin (slow).
lagger [ˈlægə*] n. Traînard *m.*
lagging [-iŋ] n. En retard, à la traîne.
— n. Retard *m.*
lagoon [ləˈguːn] n. Lagune *f.* ‖ Lagon *m.* (of atoll).
laic [ˈleiik] adj., n. Laïque *s.*
laical [-l̩] adj. Laïque.
laicize [ˈleiisaiz] v. tr. Laïciser.
laid [leid]. See LAY.
laid [leid] adj. Vergé (paper).
lain [lein]. See LIE.
lair [lɛə*]. Bauge *f.* (of a wild boar); antre *m.*, tanière *f.* (of wild animals). ‖ Fig. Repaire *m.*
— v. intr. Se retirer dans sa tanière.
laird [lɛəd] n. Laird *m.*
laissez-faire [leseiˈfeə*] n. JUR., COMM. « Laissez faire, laissez passer », libéralisme économique *m.*
laissez-passer [-paˈse] n. Laissez-passer, sauf-conduit *m.*
laity [ˈleiiti] n. Laïcs *m. pl.* ‖ FAM. Profanes *m. pl.*
lake [leik] n. Lac *m.;* *ornamental lake*, pièce d'eau.
— adj. Des lacs (district); des cités lacustres (dwellers); lacustre (dwelling); lakiste (poet).
lake n. Laque *f.* (See LAC.)
laked [-id] adj. MED. Laqué (blood).

lakelet [ˈleiklit] n. Petit lac *m.*
lakh [læk] n. FIN. Lack, lakh *m.*
lam [læm] n. U. S. FAM. Détalage *m.;* *to take it on the lam*, prendre la poudre d'escampette.
lam v. tr. Bâtonner; *to lam into*, rosser.
lama [ˈlɑːmə] n. Lama *m.* (priest).
lama n. ZOOL. Lama *m.* (See LLAMA.)
lamaism [-izm̩] n. Lamaïsme *m.*
lamasery [ləˈmɑːzəri] n. Lamaserie *f.*
lamb [læm] n. ZOOL. Agncau *m.;* agnelle *f.* ‖ FIG. Agneau *m.*
— v. tr., intr. ZOOL. Agneler.
lambaste, lambast [læmˈbeist] v. tr. FAM. Fustiger, éreinter, tomber à bras raccourcis sur (with words or blows).
lambent [ˈlæmbənt] adj. Effleurant, vacillant, voltigeant (flame). ‖ Rayonnant d'un doux éclat (eyes, sky). ‖ Chatoyant, brillant (style).
lambkin [ˈlæmkin] n. ZOOL. Agnelet *m.* ‖ FAM. Petit agneau *m.*
lamblike [-laik] adj. Doux comme un agneau.
lambrequin [ˈlæmbrəkin] n. Lambrequin *m.*
lambskin [ˈlæmskin] n. Peau (*f.*) d'agneau (skin). ‖ COMM. Mouton *m.* (fur).
lame [leim] adj. MED. Boiteux; *a lame woman*, boiteuse; *to walk lame*, boiter, traîner la jambe. ‖ MED. Estropié, éclopé (by accident); *lame back*, dos endolori. ‖ FIG. Piètre (excuse); boiteux (story, verse). ‖ FAM. *Lame duck*, canard boiteux, pauvre type; FIN. Spéculateur insolvable; U. S. Député blackboulé; fonctionnaire mis à pied.
— v. tr. Estropier, rendre boiteux.
lamé [ˈlɑːmei] n. Lamé *m.*
lamella [ləˈmelə] (pl. **lamellae** [-iː]) n. BOT., ZOOL. Lamelle *f.*
lamellar [-ə*] n. Lamellaire *f.*
lamellate [ˈlæmələit] adj. Lamellé.
lamely [ˈleimli] adv. En boitant (or) clopinant. ‖ FIG. Piètrement.
lameness [-nis] n. MED. Claudication; boiterie *f.* ‖ FIG. Faiblesse *f.*
lament [ləˈment] n. Lamentation *f.* ‖ MUS. Complainte *f.*
— v. tr. Déplorer.
— v. intr. Se lamenter (*for, over*, sur); gémir, se plaindre (*over*, de).
lamentable [ˈlæməntəbl̩] adj. Lamentable, déplorable. ‖ Qui mérite d'être pleuré, digne de regret (person).
lamentably [-bli] adv. Lamentablement.
lamentation [,læmənˈteiʃən] n. Lamentation *f.*
lamina [ˈlæminə] (pl. **laminae** [-iː]) n. TECHN. Lamelle, feuille *f.* (of metal). ‖ BOT. Limbe *m.* (of a leaf).
laminar [ˈlæminə*] adj. GEOL., PHYS. Laminaire.
laminate [-neit] v. tr. TECHN. Laminer (to beat); feuilleter (to split). ‖ Plaquer (*with*, de) [to overlay].
— v. intr. TECHN. Se laminer; se feuilleter.
— adj., n. Lamifié adj., *m.*
lamination [,læmiˈneiʃən] n. TECHN. Laminage; feuilletage *m.*
Lammas [ˈlæməs] n. *Lammas Day*, Premier août *m.*
lammergeyer [ˈlæməgaiə*] n. ZOOL. Gypaète *m.*
lamp [læmp] n. Lampe *f.;* *ceiling lamp*, plafonnier; *spirit lamp*, lampe à alcool. ‖ Réverbère (lamppost). ‖ ELECTR. Lampe, ampoule *f.* (bulb); U. S. *trouble lamp*, baladeuse. ‖ POP. U. S. Pl. Mirettes *f. pl.* (eyes). ‖ **Lamp-black**, n. Noir (*m.*) de fumée. ‖ **Lamp-cabin**, n. CH. DE F. Lampisterie *f.* ‖ **Lamp-chimney**, n. Verre (*m.*) de lampe. ‖ **Lamp-oil**, n. Pétrole lampant *m.* ‖ **Lamp-post**, n. Réverbère *m.;* FAM. Grand flandrin *m.* ‖ **Lamp-shade**, n. Abat-jour *m.* ‖ **Lamp-standard**, n. Torchère *f.*
— v. tr. Orner de lampes. ‖ Illuminer. ‖ POP. U. S. Lorgner, viser.
lampas [ˈlæmpəs] n. Lampas *m.*

lampion ['læmpiǝn] n. Lampion m.
lamplight ['læmplait] n. Lumière de lampe f.; by lamplight, à la lampe.
lamplighter [-ǝ*] n. Allumeur (m.) de réverbères. ‖ FAM. Like a lamplighter, comme une flèche.
lampoon [læm'pu:n] n. Libelle, brocard m.; satire f.
— v. tr. Brocarder; chansonner.
lampooner [-ǝ*] n. Libelliste, satiriste m.
lamprey ['læmpri] n. ZOOL. Lamproie f.
lance [lɑ:ns] n. MILIT. Lance f. (soldier, weapon). ‖ MÉD. Lancette f. ‖ FIG. Free lance, journaliste indépendant. ‖ Lance-corporal, n. MILIT. Caporal suppléant m. ‖ Lance-head, n. Fer (m.) de lance. ‖ Lance-serjeant, n. MILIT. Sergent suppléant m. — v. tr. Transpercer d'une lance. ‖ MÉD. Ouvrir à la lancette.
lanceolate [-iǝlǝt] adj. BOT., ARCHIT. Lancéolé.
lancer [-ǝ*] n. Lancier m. ‖ Pl. Quadrille (m.) des lanciers.
lancet [-it] n. MÉD. Lancette f. ‖ ARCHIT. Ogive à lancette f.
lancinate [-ineit] v. intr. MÉD. Elancer.
lancinating [-ineitiɳ] adj. MÉD. Lancinant.
lancination [,lɑ:nsi'neiʃǝn] n. MÉD. Elancement m.
land [lænd] n. Terre f. (ground, region, soil). ‖ AGRIC. Terre f.; flight from the land, désertion des campagnes. ‖ GEOGR. Land's End, la pointe de la Cornouaille. ‖ JUR. Bien-fonds m.; propriété foncière f.; land act, loi agraire. ‖ NAUT. To make land, atterrir. ‖ Land-agent, n. Régisseur m.; agent foncier m. ‖ Land-bank, n. FIN. Crédit foncier m. ‖ Land-breeze, n. NAUT. Brise de terre f. ‖ Land-carriage, n. Transport (m.) par terre. ‖ Land-forces, n. pl. MILIT. Armée de terre f. ‖ Land-locked, adj. Entouré de terres. ‖ Land-lubber, n. FAM. Marin (m.) d'eau douce. ‖ Land-Rover, n. AUTOM. Voiture agricole (f.) tout-terrain. ‖ Land-tax, n. FIN. Impôt foncier m. ‖ Land-worker, n. AGRIC. Ouvrier agricole m.
— v. tr. NAUT., CH. DE F., AUTOM. Débarquer, déposer (s.o., sth.). ‖ SPORTS. Détacher, prendre (fish). ‖ AVIAT. Faire atterrir. ‖ FAM. Flanquer, allonger (a blow); to land in prison, fourrer en prison. ‖ FAM. Dégoter, décrocher (a job).
— v. intr. NAUT., CH. DE F., AUTOM. Débarquer, descendre. ‖ SPORTS. Se recevoir (jumper); arriver (runner). ‖ AVIAT. Atterrir; to land on the water, amerrir. ‖ FAM. Atterrir, échouer (in, en).
landau ['lændɔ:] n. Landau m.
landaulet [,lændɔ:'let] n. Landaulet m.
landed ['lændid] adj. JUR. Foncier (property); terrien (proprietor).
landfall [-fɔ:l] n. NAUT. Abordage, atterrissage m. ‖ AVIAT. To make a landfall, arriver en vue de la terre.
landholder [-,houldǝ*] n. Propriétaire terrien m.
landing [-iɳ] n. NAUT. Débarquement m. (act); débarcadère m. (place). ‖ AVIAT. Atterrissage m. (on land); amerrissage m. (on water). ‖ SPORTS. Prise f. (of fish). ‖ ARCHIT. Palier m. (of stairs). ‖ Landing-barge (or) -craft, n. NAUT. Péniche (f.) de débarquement. ‖ Landing-carriage (or) -gear, n. AVIAT. Train d'atterrissage, atterrisseur m. ‖ Landing-deck, n. NAUT. Pont d'atterrissage m. ‖ Landing-field, n. AVIAT. Terrain d'atterrissage m. ‖ Landing-net, n. SPORTS. Epuisette f. ‖ Landing-party, n. NAUT. Détachement de débarquement m. ‖ Landing-stage, n. NAUT. Débarcadère m. ‖ Landing-strip, n. AVIAT. Piste (f.) d'atterrissage.
landlady [-,leidi] n. Propriétaire f. (of a house). ‖ Logeuse f. (of furnished apartments). ‖ Hôtelière f. (innkeeper).
landlord [-lɔ:d] n. Propriétaire m. ‖ Logeur m. ‖ Hôtelier m.

landlordism [-lɔ:dizṃ] n. Féodalisme terrien m.
landmark [-mɑ:k] n. Borne f. (boundary-stone). ‖ Point de repère m. (guide). ‖ FIG. Evénement décisif m.; étape importante f.
landmine [-,main] n. MILIT. Fougasse, mine terrestre f.
landowner [-,ounǝ*] n. Propriétaire terrien m.
landscape ['lændskeip] n. Paysage m. ‖ Landscape-gardener, n. AGRIC. Jardinier paysagiste m. ‖ Landscape painter, n. ARTS. Paysagiste m.
landscapist [-ist] n. ARTS. Paysagiste m.
landslide ['lændslaid] n. Glissement de terrain m. ‖ FAM. U. S. Victoire électorale f.
landslip [-slip] n. Glissement de terrain m.
landward [-wǝd] adj., adv. Vers la terre.
lane [lein] n. Sentier, chemin m. (in country); ruelle f. (in town). ‖ Passage clouté m. (in streets). ‖ NAUT., AVIAT. Route f. ‖ SPORTS. Piste f. ‖ FIG. Haie f. (of people).
lang syne ['læɳ'sain] adv. Jadis.
— n. Auld lang syne, le bon vieux temps.
language ['læɳgwidʒ] n. Langage m. (expression, faculty, vocabulary). ‖ Langue f. (of a particular nation). ‖ Language-teacher, n. Professeur (m.) de langues.
languid ['læɳgwid] adj. Languissant, languide, langoureux, apathique; languid look, air penché.
languidly [-li] adv. Langoureusement m.
languidness [-nis] n. Langueur f.
languish ['læɳgwiʃ] v. intr. Languir, s'alanguir. ‖ Prendre un air penché. ‖ MÉD. Languir, dépérir. ‖ FIG. Languir (for, de). [See PINE.]
languishing [-iɳ] adj. Languissant (interest). ‖ Langoureux, alangui (look). ‖ MÉD. De langueur (illness).
— n. Langueur f.
languishingly [iɳli] adv. Languissamment.
languishment [-mǝnt] n. MÉD., FIG. Langueur f.; abattement m.
languor ['læɳgwǝ*] n. Langueur, fatigue f. (weakness). ‖ Indifférence, apathie, inertie f. (listlessness). ‖ Nonchalance, indolence f. (sluggishness). ‖ FIG. Langueur f.
languorous [-rǝs] adj. Langoureux.
laniferous [lǝ'nifǝrǝs] adj. ZOOL. Lanifère.
lank [læɳk] adj. Maigre, efflanqué (animal); décharné (body); creux (cheek); plat, raide (hair); efflanqué, sec, dégingandé (person).
lankiness [-inis] n. Maigreur étique f.; allure dégingandée f.
lanky [-i] adj. Efflanqué, dégingandé.
lanneret ['lænǝrit] n. ZOOL. Laneret m.
lanolin ['lænǝlin] n. Lanoline f.
lansquenet ['lænskǝnit] n. Lansquenet m. (game, person).
lantern ['læntǝn] n. Lanterne f.; lantern lecture, conférence avec projections; magic lantern, lanterne magique, appareil de projection. ‖ NAUT. Lanterne f. (in a lighthouse); fanal m. (of a ship). ‖ ARCHIT. Lanterne f. ‖ Lantern-jawed, adj. FAM. A la figure longue et maigre. ‖ Lantern-slide, n. Plaque (f.) d'appareil à projection.
lanthanum ['lænθǝnǝm] n. CHIM. Lanthane m.
lanyard ['lænjǝd] n. NAUT. Amarrage m. (of knife); ride f. (of shroud). ‖ MILIT. Tire-feu m.
Laodicean [-leiǝdi'si:ǝn] adj., n. ECCLES., FIG. Tiède m.
Laos [laus] n. GEOGR. Laos m.
lap [læp] n. Pan m. (of a garment). ‖ Giron m. (of an apron). ‖ Pli m. (in a sitting position); to sit in s.o.'s lap, s'asseoir sur les genoux de qqn. ‖ GEOGR. Creux m. (of a valley). ‖ ARCHIT. Recouvrement m. ‖ ELECTR. Isolant m. ‖ SPORTS. Tour m. (in a race). ‖ TECHN. Rodoir; polissoir m. ‖ MÉD. Lobe m. (of ear). ‖ FIG. Sein, giron m. ‖ FAM. To be on the last lap, en être à la dernière étape. ‖ Lap-dissolve, n. CINÉM. Fondu superposé

m. ‖ **Lap-dog,** n. Zool. Bichon, chien de man-chon *m.* ‖ **Lap-joint,** n. Archit. Joint à recouvre-ment *m.; v.* tr. Archit. Assembler. ‖ **Lap-pack,** n. Aviat. Parachute ventral *m.* ‖ **Lap robe,** n. U. S. Plaid *m.;* couverture (*f.*) de voyage.
— *v.* tr. (1). Enrouler (*about, around,* autour de; *in,* dans); envelopper (*in,* de). ‖ Poser (*over,* sur). ‖ Archit. Enchevaucher. ‖ Electr. Guiper. ‖ Techn. Polir (gems, glass); roder (metal). ‖ Sports. Boucler (the course, an opponent). Fig. Baigner, nager (*in,* dans) [luxury].
— *v.* intr. S'enrouler. ‖ Archit. Se chevaucher. ‖ **To lap over,** faire saillie, dépasser. ‖ **To lap under,** être rabattu (or) replié, se rabattre.
lap n. Lapement (act); lapée, gorgée *f.* (quantity). Soupe *f.* (for dogs). ‖ Clapotement, clapotis *m.* (of waves).
— *v.* tr. (1). **To lap up,** laper (animal); boire (person); Fam. Gober, avaler (to take in).
— *v.* intr. Laper (animal). ‖ Clapoter (waves).
laparotomy [ˌlæpəˈrɔtəmi] n. Med. Laparotomie *f.*
lapel [ləˈpel] n. Revers *m.* (of a coat).
lapelled [-d] adj. A revers.
lapidary [ˈlæpidəri] adj., n. Lapidaire *m.*
lapidate [-deit] v. tr. Lapider.
lapidation [ˌlæpiˈdeiʃən] n. Lapidation *f.*
lapidify [ləˈpidifai] v. tr. (2). Lapidifier.
— *v.* intr. Se pétrifier.
lapis lazuli [ˌlæpisˈlæzjulai] n. Lapis-lazuli *m.*
Lapland [ˈlæplænd] n. Geogr. Laporie *f.*
Laplander [-ə*] n. Geogr. Lapon *s.*
lappet [ˈlæpit] n. Oreillette *f.* (of cap); barbe *f.* (of coif); basque *f.* (of garment). ‖ Revers *m.* (lapel). ‖ Zool. Fanon *m.* (of a cow). ‖ Med. Lobe *m.* (of ear). ‖ Techn. Cache-entrée *f.* (of key-hole).
lapse [læps] n. Course, marche, fuite *f.* (of time) [act]; laps *m.* (period). ‖ Défaillance *f.* (of memory); *lapse of the pen, tongue,* lapsus calami, linguæ. ‖ Faute *f.;* manquement, faux pas, écart (*m.*) de conduite (moral slip); dérogation (*from,* à) [one's principles]; chute, dégringolade *f.* (fam.) [fall]. ‖ Jur. Expiration *f.* (of the copyright); déchéance *f.* (of a right). ‖ Eccles. Dévolution *f.*
— *v.* intr. Tomber, choir (*into,* dans). ‖ Déchoir, tomber, faillir (to slip). ‖ S'écouler, passer (to elapse). ‖ Jur. Tomber en déchéance, périmer. ‖ Eccles. Tomber en dévolu.
lapwing [ˈlæpwiŋ] n. Zool. Vanneau *m.*
lar [lɑ:*] (pl. **lares** [ˈlɛəri:z]) n. Lare *m.*
larboard [ˈlɑ:bɔ:d] n. Naut. Bâbord *m.* (See PORT.)
— adj. Naut. De bâbord.
larcener [ˈlɑ:sinə*] n. Jur. Voleur *m.*
larcenous [-əs] adj. Jur. Ayant le caractère d'un vol (action); voleur (person).
larceny [-i] n. Jur. Vol *m.; petty larceny,* larcin.
larch [lɑ:tʃ] n. Bot., Comm. Mélèze *m.*
lard [lɑ:d] n. Culin. Saindoux *m.;* panne *f.* ‖ Med. Axonge *f.*
— *v.* tr. Culin. Larder, barder. ‖ Fam. Larder, entrelarder (*with,* de).
lardaceous [lɑ:ˈdeiʃəs] adj. Med. Graisseux.
larder [ˈlɑ:də*] n. Armoire (*f.*) à provisions; dépense *f.* (See PANTRY.)
larding [-iŋ] n. Culin. Lardage *m.* ‖ **Larding-needle** (or) **-pin,** n. Lardoire *f.*
lardon [-ən], **lardoon** [lɑ:ˈdu:n] n. Culin. Barde *f.;* lardon *m.*
lardy [ˈlɑ:di] adj. Lardeux. ‖ **Lardy-dardy,** adj. Fam. Prétentieux, enflé.
large [lɑ:dʒ] adj. Grand (spacious). ‖ Fort, gros (big). ‖ Arts. Large (treatment). ‖ Fin. Gros, fort, important (fortune, loss, sum). ‖ Agric., Comm. Gros (farmer, manufacturer). ‖ Jur. Nombreux (family, population). ‖ Naut. Largue (wind). ‖ Med. Gros (intestine). ‖ Fig. Large (mind, powers, views);

large, important (proportion, scale). ‖ Fig. A l'es-prit large, libéral, sans étroitesse (person); large, généreux (*of,* de; *with,* avec). ‖ **Large-handed,** adj. Généreux, large (with money). ‖ **Large-hearted,** adj. Généreux (kindly). ‖ **Large-heartedness,** n. Générosité, noblesse (*f.*) de cœur. ‖ **Large-minded,** adj. A l'esprit large. ‖ **Large-mindedness,** n. Lar-geur (*f.*) d'esprit. ‖ **Large-scale,** adj. Sur une grande échelle, de grande envergure. ‖ **Large-sized,** adj. Fam. De grande dimension.
— n. *At large,* en liberté (animal, condemned per-son); de bout en bout (narration); dans son ensem-ble (public, society, country). ‖ Jur. *Ambassador at large,* ambassadeur extraordinaire, chargé de mis-sion.
— adv. *By and large,* see BY.
largely [-li] adv. Considérablement, largement (much). ‖ En grande partie, principalement, pour une grande part (mainly). ‖ Largement, amplement, grandement (amply).
largeness [-nis] n. Grandeur, étendue *f.* (in space). ‖ Grosseur *f.* (in mass). ‖ Fig. Largeur *f.* (of mind).
largesse [ˈlɑ:dʒes] n. Largesse *f.*
largo [ˈlɑ:gou] adv., n. Mus. Largo *adv., m.*
lariat [ˈlæriət] n. Longe f. (for picketing horses). ‖ Lasso *m.*
— *v.* tr. Attacher à la longe. ‖ Prendre au lasso.
lark [lɑ:k] n. Fam. Partie, joyeuse équipée; rigo-lade *f.* (fam.) [frolic]; blague, farce *f.* (trick).
— *v.* intr. Fam. S'amuser, faire une partie; chahu-ter, rigoler (fam.).
lark [lɑ:k] n. Zool., Culin. Alouette *f.* ‖ U. S. Zool. Sturnelle *f.*
larkspur [-spə*] n. Bot. Pied-d'alouette *m.*
larrikin [ˈlærikin] n. Voyou *m.*
larrup [ˈlærəp] v. tr. Tabasser. (See THRASH.)
larva [ˈlɑ:və] (pl. **larvae** [-i:]) n. Zool. Larve *f.*
larval [-əl] adj. Zool. Larvaire. ‖ Med. Larvé.
laryngeal [ləˈrindʒiəl] adj. Med. Laryngien.
laryngitis [ˌlærinˈdʒaitis] n. Med. Laryngite *f.*
laryngology [ˌlæriŋˈgɔlədʒi] n. Med. Laryngolo-gie *f.*
laryngoscope [læˈriŋgəskoup] n. Med. Laryngos-cope *m.*
laryngotomy [ˈlæriŋgɔtəmi] n. Med. Laryngoto-mie *f.*
larynx [ˈlæriŋks] n. Med. Larynx *m.*
lasagne [ləˈzænjə] n. pl. Culin. Lasagne *f.* pl.
lascar [ˈlæskə*] n. Naut. Lascar *m.*
lascivious [ləˈsiviəs] adj. Lascif.
lasciviously [-li] adv. Lascivement.
lasciviousness [-nis] n. Lascivité, lubricité *f.*
laser [ˈleizə*] n. Phys., Milit., Med. Laser *m.*
lash [læʃ] v. tr. Ligoter. ‖ Naut. Amarrer.
lash n. Lanière, mèche *f.* (of whip). ‖ Coup de fouet *m.* (stroke). ‖ Fouet *m.* (flogging). ‖ Med. Cil *m.* ‖ Fig. Aiguillon *m.* (of desire); réflexion cin-glante *f.* (remark). ‖ **Lash-out,** n. Ruade *f.* ‖ **Lash-up,** n. Fam. Gâchis, fouillis; U. S. Fam. Improvisation *f.*
— *v.* tr. Fouetter (to flog). ‖ Cingler, battre, fouet-ter (to dash against). ‖ Agiter en coup de fouet; *to lash its tail,* battre de la queue. ‖ Fig. Fouailler, flageller, cingler. ‖ **To lash on,** faire avancer à coups de fouet.
— *v.* intr. Battre (tail). ‖ Donner des coups de fouet; *to lash at,* fouailler, flageller. ‖ **To lash down,** cingler (rain). ‖ **To lash out,** ruer (horse); Fig. Se livrer (*into,* à); Fam. Lancer une remarque cinglante (*at,* à).
lashing [-iŋ] n. Flagellation *f.* (flogging). ‖ Fouet-tement *m.* (of rain). ‖ Fam. Pl. Flopée *f.; lashings of cream,* de la crème tant qu'on veut (or) à gogo.
— adj. Cinglant.
lashing n. Ligotage *m.* ‖ Naut. Amarrage *m.* (act); amarre *f.* (rope). ‖ **Lashing-rope,** n. Naut. Risse *f.*

lass [læs] n. Jeunesse *f.* (girl). ‖ Bonne amie *f.* (sweetheart).

lassie [-i] n. Gamine *f.*

lassitude ['læsitju:d] n. Lassitude *f.*

lasso ['læsou] n. Lasso *m.*
— v. tr. Prendre au lasso.

last [lɑ:st] n. TECHN. Forme (*f.*) à chaussure.

last adj. Dernier, ultime; *last but one,* avant-dernier. ‖ Dernier, précédent (month); *last night,* hier soir, la nuit dernière; *the last three chapters,* les trois derniers chapitres. ‖ FIN. Dernier, le plus bas (price). ‖ JUR. Ultime (heir); dernier (resort). ‖ **Last-ditcher,** n. FAM. Jusqu'au-boutiste *m.*
— adv. En dernier lieu (at the end). ‖ Finalement, enfin (finally). ‖ La dernière fois; *when he wrote last,* la dernière fois qu'il a écrit.
— n. Dernier *s.; the last of the pears,* la dernière poire. ‖ Fin *f.; at last,* enfin, à la fin; *at long last,* à la fin des fins; U. S. *by the last of the week,* avant la fin de la semaine; *to the last,* jusqu'au bout. ‖ Dernière rencontre (or) mention *f.; to see the last of s.o.,* voir qqn pour la dernière fois. ‖ Dernier *s.; in my last,* dans ma dernière lettre. ‖ MED., FIN. Extrémité *f.; to breathe one's last,* rendre le dernier soupir.

last v. intr. Durer; *to last only a week,* ne pas dépasser la semaine; *too good to last,* trop beau pour durer. ‖ COMM. Durer, faire de l'usage.
— v. tr. *To last out, until,* durer jusqu'à (a date); *to last s.o. out,* survivre à qqn.

lastage [-idʒ] n. NAUT. Chargement *m.*

lastex ['læsteks] n. Lastex *m.*

lasting ['lɑ:stiŋ] adj. Durable. ‖ COMM. Solide, résistant, d'usage.
— n. Lasting *m.* (cloth). ‖ FIG. Endurance *f.*

lastingly [-iŋli] adv. Durablement.

lastly [-li] adv. Pour finir, en dernier lieu, enfin.

latch [lætʃ] n. Loquet *m.* (bar). ‖ Pène dormant *m.* (spring-lock); *on the latch,* fermé à demi-tour. ‖ **Latch-string,** n. Cordon de loquet *m.*
— v. tr. Fermer au loquet (door, window). ‖ Tirer, fermer à demi-tour (door). ‖ FAM. U. S. *To latch onto,* s'accrocher à.

latchet [-it] n. Cordon (*m.*) de chaussure.

late [leit] adj. En retard (*for,* pour). ‖ Retardé delayed). ‖ Tard; *it is too late,* il est trop tard. ‖ Tardif (frost, growth, summer). ‖ Avancé (age, hour, season); *in the late afternoon,* vers la fin de l'après-midi; *a late party,* une réunion qui finit tard. ‖ Récent; dernier (rain, years); *of late,* dernièrement, récemment. ‖ Feu, défunt, décédé (person); *his late uncle,* feu son oncle, son pauvre oncle). ‖ GRAMM. Bas (latin).
— adv. Tard; *very late in the night,* bien avant dans la nuit. ‖ En retard (after the appointed time). ‖ Tardivement; *late in life,* sur le tard, à la fin de sa vie. ‖ Récemment; *as late as yesterday,* pas plus tard qu'hier, hier encore. ‖ Antérieurement; *late of York,* autrefois domicilié à York. ‖ **Late-comer,** n. Retardataire; tard venu *s.*

lateen [lə'ti:n] adj. NAUT. Latine (sail).

lately ['leitli] adv. Récemment, dernièrement, depuis peu.

laten [-ņ] v. intr. S'avancer (hour).
— v. tr. Retarder.

latency ['leitənsi] n. Etat latent *m.* ‖ JUR. Latence *f.*

lateness ['leitnis] n. Arrivée tardive (of s.o.). ‖ Caractère tardif *m.;* tardiveté *f.; lateness of the hour,* l'heure avancée. ‖ Date récente *f.* (of an event).

latent ['leitənt] adj. Latent.

latently [-li] adv. De façon latente.

later ['leitə*] adj. Comp. (See LATE.) ‖ Plus tardif, ultérieur, postérieur (date); *later generations,* la postérité. ‖ Dernier en date, plus récent (event).

— adv. comp. (See LATE.) ‖ Plus tard; *a moment later,* un moment après. ‖ FAM. *See you later,* à tout à l'heure. ‖ **Later on,** FAM. Plus tard; par la suite; plus loin.

lateral ['lætərəl] adj. Latéral. ‖ En rocade (road).

laterally [-li] adv. Latéralement.

Lateran ['lætərən] n. ECCLES. Saint-Jean-de-Latran *m.*
— adj. ECCLES. De Latran (Council).

latest ['leitist] adj. Superl. (See LATE.) ‖ Dernier (arrival, news, novelties); *the latest thing in ties,* cravates dernier cri; *the latest thing out,* le tout dernier cri, la dernière mode. ‖ Le plus reculé (posterity); *at the latest,* au plus tard.

latex ['leiteks] n. BOT., COMM. Latex *m.*

lath [lɑ:θ] n. Latte *f.; lath and plaster,* plâtrage. ‖ FAM. *As thin as a lath,* maigre comme un clou.
— v. tr. Latter.

lathe [leiδ] n. TECHN. Tour *m.*
— v. tr. TECHN. Façonner au tour, tourner.

lather ['lɑːδə*] n. Mousse *f.* (of soap). ‖ Ecume *f.* (on a horse).
— v. tr. Savonner. ‖ FAM. Rosser. (See THRASH.)
— v. intr. Mousser (soap). ‖ Etre couvert d'écume (horse).

lathery [-ri] adj. Couvert de mousse de savon (chin). ‖ Mousseux (liquid). ‖ Ecumant, couvert d'écume (horse).

lathing ['lɑːθiŋ] n. Lattage *m.* (act); lattis *m.* (laths).

lathy [-i] adj. FAM. Sec comme une allumette; dégingandé.

latifundium [,læti'fʌndiəm] (pl. **latifundia**) n. Latifundium *m.*

Latin ['lætin] adj., n. Latin *m.*

Latinism [-izm̦] n. Latinisme *m.*

Latinist [-ist] n. Latiniste *s.*

Latinity [lə'tiniti] n. Latinité *f.*

Latinization [,lætini'zeiʃən] n. Latinisation *f.*

Latinize ['lætinaiz] v. tr. Latiniser. ‖ Traduire en latin.
— v. intr. Latiniser.

latish ['leitiʃ] adj., adv. Un peu en retard. ‖ Un peu tard.

latitude ['lætitju:d] n. GEOGR., ASTRON., NAUT., FIG. Latitude *f.* ‖ FAM. Ampleur *f.*

latitudinal [,læti'tju:dinəl] adj. Latitudinal. ‖ Transversal.

latitudinarian [læti,tjudi'nɛəriən] adj., n. ECCLES. Latitudinaire *n.*

latitudinarianism [-izm̦] n. ECCLES. Tolérance *f.*

latrines [lə'tri:nz] n. pl. Latrines *f. pl.*

latter ['lætə*] adj. Dernier (day, part); *latter end,* fin. ‖ Dernier nommé, second de deux; *the latter,* celui-ci, ce dernier, ceux-ci, ces derniers. ‖ **Latter-day,** adj. Moderne, d'aujourd'hui; ECCLES. *The Latter-day Saints,* les Saints du dernier jour, les Mormons.

latterly [-li] adv. Dans les derniers temps. ‖ Dernièrement, récemment. ‖ Par la suite.

lattice ['lætis] n. Treillage, treillis *m.* ‖ **Lattice-making,** n. Grillagerie *f.* ‖ **Lattice-work,** n. Treillis *m.;* grillage *m.*
— adj. A croisillons (bracing); grillagé (door); treillissé (window).

Latvia ['lætviə] n. GEOGR. Lettonie *f.*

Latvian [-iən] adj., n. GEOGR. Lettonien *s.*

laud [lɔ:d] n. ECCLES. Pl. Laudes *f. pl.* ‖ FIG. Louange *f.*
— v. tr. Louer, louanger. (See PRAISE.)

laudability [,lɔ:də'biliti] n. Caractère louable *m.*

laudable ['lɔ:dəbḷ] adj. Louable.

laudably [-bli] adv. Louablement.

laudanum ['lɔdnəm] n. MED. Laudanum *m.; containing laudanum,* laudanisé.

laudation [lɔ:'deiʃən] n. Louange *f.*
laudative ['lɔ:dətiv] adj. Laudatif.
laudatory [-təri] adj. Louangeur, élogieux. (See EULOGISTIC.)
laugh [lɑ:f] v. intr. (1). Rire; *to laugh loud and long,* rire tout son content. ‖ Rire, se moquer (*at,* de). ‖ Etre riant (landscape).
— v. tr. Exprimer par le rire; *to laugh one's approval,* approuver en riant. ‖ Déterminer par le rire; *to laugh s.o. into a better humour,* améliorer en riant l'humeur de qqn; *to laugh s.o. out of sth.,* faire abandonner qqch. à qqn en se moquant de lui. ‖ Ridiculiser, couvrir de ridicule. ‖ **To laugh away,** chasser en riant (cares); faire passer en s'amusant (time). ‖ **To laugh down,** réduire au silence par la moquerie. ‖ **To laugh off,** éluder en riant, tourner en plaisanterie.
— n. Rire *m.; to give a forced laugh,* rire jaune; *to have the laugh on one's side,* avoir les rieurs de son côté.
laughable [-əbl̩] adj. Risible.
laughably [-əbli] adv. Risiblement.
laugher [-ə*] n. Rieur *s.*
laughing [-iŋ] adj. Riant (face); rieur (person). ‖ Risible, à rire (matter). ‖ CHIM. Hilarant (gas). ‖ **Laughing-stock,** n. Objet (*m.*) de risée.
— n. Rire *m.*
laughingly [-iŋli] adv. En riant.
laughter ['lɑ:ftə*] n. Rire *m.; to raise a storm of laughter,* déchaîner l'hilarité. ‖ **Laughter-provoking,** adj. Exhilarant; désopilant.
launch [lɔ:nʃ] v. tr. NAUT. Lancer (a ship). ‖ MILIT. Déclencher (an attack); lancer (a weapon). ‖ FIG. Lancer (s.o.). ‖ FAM. *To launch into eternity,* dépêcher dans l'autre monde.
— v. intr. Se lancer (*into,* dans). ‖ **To launch out,** NAUT. Mettre à la mer; FIG. Se lancer (*on,* dans) [an affair]; se répandre (*into,* en) [explanations].
— n. NAUT. Lancement *m.* (act); chaloupe *f.* (ship); *motor launch,* bateau automobile; *police launch,* vedette de la police.
launching [-iŋ] n. NAUT., FIG. Lancement *m.* ‖ **Launching-pad** (ou) **-site,** n. ASTRONAUT. Aire (*f.*) de lancement.
launder [lɔ:ndə*] n. TECHN. Auge *f.*
— v. tr. Blanchir (clothes).
— v. intr. Se blanchir (fabric).
laundress [lɔ:ndris] n. Blanchisseuse *f.* ‖ JUR. Gardienne *f.*
laundromat ['lɔ:ndroʹmæt] n. U. S. Blanchisserie automatique *f.*
laundry ['lɔ:ndri] n. Blanchisserie *f.* (place). ‖ Lessive *f.; paquet de blanchissage m.; laundry blue,* bleu.
laundryman [-mən] (pl. **laundrymen**) n. Blanchisseur *m.*
laureate ['lɔ:riit] adj. BLAS. Lauré. ‖ FIG. Lauréat (poet).
— [-eit] n. Lauréat *s.*
laurel ['lɔrəl] n. BOT., FIG. Laurier *m.*
— v. tr. (1). Couronner de lauriers.
laurustinus ['lɔrəstainəs] n. BOT. Laurier-tin *m.*
lav [læv] n. POP. Vécés, gogues *m. pl.* (lavatory).
lava ['lɑ:və] n. Lave *f.*
lavabo [lə'veibou] n. ECCLES. Lavabo *m.* (basin, towel); lavement (*m.*) des mains (washing).
lavation [lə'veiʃən] n. Lavage *m.* (See WASHING.)
lavatory ['lævətəri] n. Cabinet (*m.*) de toilette (room). ‖ Lavabo, water-closet *m.* (in street). ‖ CH. DE F. Toilettes *f. pl.*
lave [leiv] v. tr. Baigner.
lavement ['leivmənt] n. MED. Lavement *m.*
lavender ['lævində*] adj., n. BOT., COMM. Lavande *f.*
lavish ['læviʃ] adj. Immodéré, extravagant, inconsidéré (expenses); prodigue (*of,* de) [person].
— v. tr. Prodiguer.

lavishly [-li] adv. A profusion, avec prodigalité.
lavishness [-nis] n. Prodigalité *f.*
law [lɔ:] n. Loi *f.;* règlement *m.; at law,* selon la loi; *to lay down the law,* faire la loi; faire la pluie et le beau temps (fam.). ‖ JUR. Loi *f.; to come under the law,* tomber sous le coup de la loi. ‖ JUR. Législation *f.; as the law at present stands,* dans l'état actuel de la législation. ‖ JUR. Jurisprudence *f.; law reports,* chronique juridique *f.;* recueil de jurisprudence. ‖ JUR. Contentieux *m.; law department,* service du contentieux. ‖ JUR. Droit *m.; law merchant,* droit commercial; *to read law,* faire son droit. ‖ JUR. Justice *f.; action at law,* action en justice; *to be at law,* être en procès; *to go to law with,* intenter une action contre, citer en justice. ‖ CHIM., PHYS., ECCLES., GRAMM. Loi *f.* ‖ SPORTS. Avance *f.* ‖ **Law-abiding,** adj. Respectueux des lois, ami de l'ordre. ‖ **Law-adviser,** n. JUR. Conseiller juridique *m.* ‖ **Law-breaker,** n. JUR. Contrevenant *m.,* auteur (*m.*) d'infractions. ‖ **Law-costs,** n. JUR. Frais (*m. pl.*) de procédure. ‖ **Law-courts,** n. Palais (*m.*) de justice. ‖ **Law-latin,** n. FAM. Latin (*m.*) de cuisine. ‖ **Law-maker,** n. JUR. Législateur *m.* ‖ **Law-man,** n. U. S. Shérif, représentant (*m.*) de la justice. ‖ **Law-officer,** n. JUR. Magistrat *m.* ‖ **Law-term,** n. Terme de droit *m.* (expression); session *f.* (period).
lawful [-ful] adj. JUR. Autorisé (association); légitime (child); valide (contract); légal (currency); licite (trade). ‖ FIG. Légitime; licite.
lawfully [-fuli] adv. JUR. Légalement. ‖ FIG. Légitimement.
lawfulness [-fulnis] n. JUR. Légalité *f.* ‖ FIG. Légitimité *f.*
lawgiver [-givə*] n. JUR. Législateur *m.*
lawless [-lis] adj. JUR. Sans loi. ‖ FIG. Sans frein, anarchique.
lawlessness [-lisnis] n. Anarchie, licence *f.;* désordre *m.*
lawn [lɔ:n] n. Pelouse *f.;* gazon *m.* ‖ **Lawn-mower,** n. Tondeuse (*f.*) à gazon. ‖ **Lawn-tennis,** n. SPORTS. Tennis sur gazon *m.*
lawn n. Linon *m.* (cloth). ‖ FAM. Episcopat *m.*
lawrencium [lɔ'rensiəm] n. CHIM. Lawrencium *m.*
lawsuit ['lɔ:sju:t] n. JUR. Procès au civil *m.*
lawyer ['lɔ:jə*] n. Juriste, jurisconsulte *m.* (legal expert). ‖ Homme (*m.*) de loi (or) de robe.
lax [læks] adj. Lâche (rope). ‖ MED. Relâché (bowels); flasque (flesh). ‖ FIG. Elastique (conscience); vague, flou (idea); relâché (morals); négligent, de mœurs faciles (person); *to become lax,* se relâcher.
laxative ['læksətiv] adj., n. MED. Laxatif *m.*
laxity [-iti] n. Laxité *f.* (of a rope). ‖ MED. Relâchement *m.* (of bowels); distension, flaccidité *f.* (of flesh). ‖ FIG. Elasticité *f.* (of conscience); relâchement *m.* (of morals).
lay [lei] n. Lai *m.* (poem).
lay adj. Laïque. ‖ ECCLES. Lai, convers (brother); converse (sister). ‖ FIG. Profane (non professional).
lay pret. See LIE.
lay v. tr. (89). Etendre, coucher (s.o.); *to lay a child to sleep,* coucher un enfant. ‖ Abattre, terrasser, renverser (an opponent). ‖ Abattre, faire tomber (dust, wind). ‖ Poser, placer (*on,* sur) [a carpet, an object]. ‖ Recouvrir, couvrir (*with,* de) [a surface]. ‖ Mettre, dresser (the table); *to lay for five,* mettre cinq couverts. ‖ Préparer, faire (a fire). ‖ Mettre (*on,* sur); *to lay aside,* mettre de côté; *to lay hands on,* mettre la main sur; *to lay waste,* dévaster. ‖ MILIT. Tendre (an ambush); pointer (a gun); mettre (*to,* devant) [the siege]. ‖ NAUT. Tracer (the course); mouiller (a mine); commettre (a rope). ‖ JUR. Déposer (a complaint); évaluer (damages); infliger (a fine). ‖ FIN. Mettre (*on,* sur) [a tax]. ‖ SPORTS. Faire (a bet); miser sur (a horse);

parier (a sum). ‖ ARCHIT. Etablir, jeter (foundations). ‖ AGRIC. Coucher (corn). ‖ ZOOL. Pondre (eggs). ‖ THEATR. Situer (a scene). ‖ FIG. Présenter, exposer (facts); chasser, détourner (fears); conjurer (ghosts); attacher (*by*, *upon*, à) [importance]; dresser (a plan); ourdir (a plot); soumettre (*before*, à) [a question]; tendre (a trap). ‖ U. S. POP. Coucher avec. ‖ **To lay away**, mettre de côté, ranger. ‖ **To lay back**, replacer, rabattre. ‖ **To lay by**, mettre de côté (or) en réserve. ‖ **To lay down**, poser, déposer (an object); coucher (a person); couvrir (a surface); encaver (wine). ‖ NAUT. Relever (a coast); mettre sur cale (or) en chantier (a ship); MILIT. Déposer (one's arms); CH. DE F. Asseoir (a railway); GEOGR. Dresser (a map); FIG. Imposer, fixer (conditions); sacrifier (one's life); démissionner (one's office); poser, formuler (a principle); tracer (a programme); établir (a rule). ‖ **To lay in**, faire provision de (goods); faire provision; NAUT. Rentrer (oars). ‖ **To lay off**, enlever (a garment); étaler (paint); mettre à pied (workmen). ‖ **To lay on**, porter (blows); étendre, appliquer (paint); FIN. Imposer (taxes); TECHN. Installer (gas, water); SPORTS. Laisser courre (hounds); ECCLES. Imposer (hands); FAM. *To lay it on*, y aller fort. ‖ **To lay out**, faire la toilette de (a dead body); disposer (objects); CULIN. Servir (meal); COMM. Etaler, mettre en montre (goods); NAUT. Elonger (cable); aménager (mine); MILIT. Dresser (camp); TECHN. Tracer (a road); SPORTS. Envoyer au tapis; mettre knock-out (a boxer); FIN. Sortir, débourser (money); FAM. Etendre, descendre (s.o.); *to lay oneself out*, se démener, se mettre en quatre. ‖ **To lay to**, NAUT. Mettre à la cape. ‖ **To lay up**, mettre de côté (*for*, pour); NAUT. Mettre en rade (boat); désarmer (warship); MED. Rendre malade; *laid up*, alité; FIG. Se préparer (trouble).
— v. intr. ZOOL. Pondre. ‖ SPORTS. Parier. ‖ **To lay down**, U. S. FAM. Flancher. ‖ **To lay off**, U. S. FAM. Cesser; *to lay off smoking*, renoncer au tabac. ‖ **To lay to**, NAUT. Etre à la cape.
— n. Direction, orientation *f.* (of land). ‖ NAUT. Commettage *m.* (of a rope). ‖ U. S. POP. Coucherie *f.* ‖ **Lay-by**, n. AUTOM. Refuge (or) garage (*m.*) en bord de route; CH. DE F. Voie (*f.*) de garage. ‖ FAM. Economies *f. pl.* ‖ **Lay-figure**, n. ARTS. Mannequin *m.;* FIG. Fantoche *m.* ‖ **Lay-out**, n. Tracé *m.* (of a road); TECHN. Etude *f.*

layer [-ə*] n. Couche *f.* (of paint). ‖ GEOL. Strate *f.* ‖ ARCHIT. Assise *f.* ‖ AGRIC. Marcotte *f.* ‖ MILIT. Pointeur *m.* ‖ TECHN. Poseur *m.* ‖ ZOOL. Pondeuse *f.* ‖ **Layer-cake**, n. CULIN. Gâteau sandwich *m.*
— v. tr. AGRIC. Marcotter (a rose-tree).
— v. intr. AGRIC. Se coucher (corn).

layette [lei'et] n. Layette *f.*

laying [-iŋ] n. MILIT. Pointage *m.* ‖ TECHN. Pose *f.* ‖ ZOOL. Ponte *f.* ‖ **Laying-down**, n. NAUT. Mise sur cale *f.;* TECHN. Pose *f.;* FIG. Sacrifice *m.* (of one's life); érection *f.* (of a principle). ‖ **Laying-in**, n. Emmagasinage *m.* ‖ **Laying-off**, n. Débauchage *m.* ‖ **Laying-on**, n. TECHN. Installation *f.;* ECCLES., FIN. Imposition *f.;* ARTS. Application *f.* ‖ **Laying-out**, n. Toilette *f.* (of a dead body); disposition *f.* (of objects); tracé *m.* (of a road); COMM. Etalage *m.* (of goods). ‖ **Laying-up**, n. NAUT. Désarmement *m.;* FIN. Entassement *m.* (of money).

layman ['leimən] (pl. **laymen**) n. Laïque, laïc *m.* ‖ FIG. Profane *m.*

lazar ['læzə*] n. MED. Lépreux *m.* ‖ **Lazar-house**, n. MED. Léproserie *f.*

lazaret [.læzə'ret], **lazaretto** [-ou] n. MED. Léproserie *f.* ‖ NAUT. Lazaret *m.*

laze [leiz] v. intr. Flemmarder.
— v. tr. *To laze away*, passer à ne rien faire.
— n. Flemme *f.* (fam.).

lazily [-ili] adv. Avec paresse (or) nonchalance.

laziness [-inis] n. Paresse, indolence *f.*

lazy ['leizi] adj. Paresseux, indolent (motion, person). ‖ Incitant à la paresse (moment). ‖ **Lazy-bones**, n. FAM. Flemmard, cossard, fainéant *s.*
— v. tr., intr. See LAZE.

lea [li:] n. AGRIC. Grasse pâture *f.*

lea n. Echevette *f.* (of yarn).

leach [li:tʃ] v. tr. Filtrer (liquid); extraire par filtration (a soluble substance). ‖ Lessiver (wood ashes).
— v. intr. Filtrer (*through*, à travers). ‖ Se dissoudre.
— n. Filtration *f.* ‖ Lessivage *m.*

lead [led] n. Plomb *m.; red, white lead*, minium, céruse. ‖ Mine *f.* (of pencil). ‖ ARCHIT. Plombs *m. pl.* ‖ TECHN. Interligne *f.* (in typography). ‖ NAUT. Sonde *f.* ‖ FAM. *To swing the lead*, tirer au flanc. ‖ **Lead-covered**, adj. ELECTR. Sous plomb. ‖ **Lead-poisoning**, n. MED. Saturnisme *m.* ‖ **Lead-work**, n. Plomberie *f.*
— v. tr. Plomber; mettre sous plomb. ‖ TECHN. Interligner; *to lead out*, blanchir.
— v. intr. MILIT. S'encrasser (gun barrel).

lead [li:d] v. tr. (90). Conduire, mener (to conduct); montrer (the way). ‖ Canaliser, conduire (steam, water). ‖ Guider, mener, conduire (to guide). ‖ Amener, conduire, entraîner, pousser (*to*, à) [to induce]; engager (*into, to*, dans); *to lead to believe*, donner à croire. ‖ Conduire, être à la tête de (to be the head of); être en tête de (a class); être le chef de (a party). ‖ Mener (a fast life); faire mener à (s.o) [a dog's life]. ‖ MILIT. Diriger (an expedition, a unit). ‖ MUS. Diriger (a ballet, an orchestra). ‖ SPORTS. Attaquer (at cards); mener (the field). ‖ **To lead about**, promener çà et là. ‖ **To lead astray**, détourner (a minor). ‖ **To lead away**, emmener; FIG. Entraîner. ‖ **To lead back**, ramener. ‖ **To lead forth**, emmener, faire sortir. ‖ **To lead in**, amener, faire entrer. ‖ **To lead off**, entamer (the conversation); ouvrir (the negotiations); emmener (s.o.). ‖ **To lead on**, conduire; FAM. Pousser, inciter; FAM. Entortiller.
— v. intr. Passer devant (person). ‖ Mener, conduire (*to*, à) [road]. ‖ SPORTS. Avoir la main (at cards); mener (in a race). ‖ JUR. Etre l'avocat principal. ‖ FIG. Tenir la tête. ‖ **To lead in**, débuter (*with*, par). ‖ **To lead off**, commencer. ‖ **To lead to**, FIG. Aboutir à, mener à, provoquer, susciter, occasionner, entraîner. ‖ **To lead up**, conduire (*to*, à).
— n. Laisse *f.* (for dog). ‖ THEATR. Premier rôle *m.* ‖ GEOL. Fissure *f.* (in ice-field). ‖ TECHN. Avance *f.* (in electricity, mechanics); canal (*m.*) d'amenée (in hydrography); filon *m.* (in mining). ‖ SPORTS. Main *f.* (at cards); *to return a lead*, rejouer la couleur. ‖ RADIO. Nouvelle majeure *f.* ‖ FIG. Direction *f.; to give s.o. a lead*, mettre qqn sur la voie; *to take the lead*, prendre la tête. ‖ FIG. Exemple *m.; to follow s.o.'s lead*, suivre l'exemple de qqn; emboîter le pas à qqn. ‖ FIG. Avance *f.; to take the lead over*, prendre le pas sur. ‖ FAM. *To give the lead*, donner le ton.

leaden ['ledn] adj. De plomb. ‖ MED. Plombé (complexion); lourd (limb). ‖ FIG. De plomb, écrasant, pesant.

leader ['li:də*] n. Guide *m.* ‖ Conducteur (*m.*) d'hommes; chef *m.* (of a party); dirigeant *m.* (of society). ‖ Premier *s.* (in a file). ‖ Article de fond, leader *m.* (in a newspaper). ‖ SPORTS. Cheval (*m.*) de tête (horse). ‖ TECHN. Conduit *m.* ‖ GEOL. Filon *m.* ‖ COMM. Article réclame *m.*

leadership [-ʃip] n. Direction *f.*

leading ['lediŋ] n. Plombage *m.*

leading ['li:diŋ] n. Direction, conduite *f.* ‖ Exemple, modèle *m.*
— adj. De tête, en tête (car, column). ‖ De fond (article). ‖ TECHN. Conducteur (tube). ‖ NAUT. Portant (wind). ‖ MILIT. Marchant (wing). ‖ AUTOM.

Avant (axle). ‖ COMM. De réclame (goods). ‖ JUR. Faisant jurisprudence (case); principal (counsel). ‖ MUS. Sensible (note). ‖ THEATR. Principal (character, part); *leading man*, jeune premier. ‖ FIG. Dominant (idea); marquant (people); suggérant la réponse; qui tend la perche (fam.) [question]. ‖ POP. U. S. *Leading card*, clou. ‖ **Leading-edge,** n. AVIAT. Bord (*m.*) d'attaque. ‖ **Leading-rein,** n. Longe *f.* ‖ **Leading-strings,** n. pl. Lisière *f.* (lit. and fig.).

leadsman ['ledzmən] (pl. **leadsmen**) n. NAUT. Sondeur *m.*

leaf [li:f] (pl. **leaves** [li:vz]) n. Feuillet *m.*; page (of a book). ‖ Rallonge *f.* (of table). ‖ BOT. Pétale *m.* (of flower); feuille *f.*, feuillage *m.* (of tree). ‖ TECHN. Feuille *f.* (of gold, silver). ‖ ARCHIT. Battant, vantail *m.* (of a door); battant *m.* (of shutter). ‖ FIG. *To shake like an aspen leaf*, trembler comme une feuille; *to turn over a new leaf*, tourner la page, recommencer sa vie, faire un nouveau départ. ‖ **Leaf-mould,** n. AGRIC. Terreau *m.*

leafage [-idʒ] n. Feuillage *m.* (See FOLIAGE.)

leafless [-lis] adj. Sans feuille, nu, dénudé (tree.)

leaflet [-lit] n. Prospectus, dépliant *m.*; *propaganda leaflet*, tract. ‖ BOT. Foliole *f.*

leafy [-i] adj. BOT. Feuillu.

league [li:g] n. Lieue *f.*

league n. Ligue *f.*; *to form a league against*, se liguer contre. ‖ JUR. Société *f.* (of Nations). ‖ SPORTS. Association (or) division sportive *f.*
— v. tr. Liguer (*with*, avec).
— v. intr. *To league together*, se liguer, se coaliser.

leaguer [-ə*] n. Ligueur *s.*

leak [li:k] n. Fuite *f.* (lit. and fig.) ‖ NAUT. Voie d'eau *f.*
— v. intr. Fuir, suinter (container, liquid). ‖ NAUT. Faire eau. ‖ FIG. *To leak out*, transpirer (news); se faire jour (truth).

leakage [-idʒ] n. Fuite *f.* ‖ Déperdition, perte *f.* ‖ ELECTR., *Earth leakage*, perte à la terre. ‖ COMM., FIN. Coulage *m.* ‖ FIG. Fuite *f.* (of official secrets).

leakiness [-inis] n. Défaut (*m.*) d'étanchéité.

leaky [-i] adj. Qui fuit (container); qui prend l'eau (shoes). ‖ NAUT. Qui fait eau (ship). ‖ FIG. Défaillant (memory); indiscret (tongue).

lean [li:n] v. intr. (91). S'appuyer (*on*, sur); *to lean back against*, s'adosser à. ‖ Pencher (thing, wall); se pencher, s'incliner (person); *to lean out of the carriage window*, se pencher à la portière. ‖ FIG. Pencher, incliner (*to*, vers); donner (*to*, dans). ‖ FAM. *To lean over backwards*, mettre tout en œuvre.
— v. tr. Appuyer (*against, on*, contre, à). ‖ Incliner, pencher; *to lean one's head back*, renverser la tête.
— n. Inclinaison *f.*; *on the lean*, penché. ‖ **Lean-to,** n. Appentis *m.*; adj. En appentis.

lean adj. CULIN. Maigre (meat). ‖ MED. Maigre, frugal (diet); maigre (person). ‖ FIG. De disette (day); déficitaire (year).
— n. CULIN. Maigre *m.*

leaning [-iŋ] n. Inclinaison *f.* ‖ FIG. Inclination *f.*; penchant *m.* (*towards*, pour).

leanness [-nis] n. Maigreur *f.*

leap [li:p] v. intr. (92). Sauter (*over*, sur, pardessus). ‖ FIG. Bondir (*for*, de); sauter (*at*, sur) [an offer]. ‖ *To leap up*, jaillir, s'élancer (flame); sursauter, bondir (person).
— v. tr. Sauter, franchir d'un bond (a ditch). ‖ Faire sauter (*over*, par-dessus) [a horse].
— n. Saut *m.* (act, distance). ‖ Obstacle (*m.*) à franchir. ‖ FIG. Saut, bond *m.*; *to take a leap in the dark*, se lancer à l'aveuglette; foncer dans le brouillard (fam.). ‖ **Leap-day,** n. Jour intercalaire, 29 février *m.* ‖ **Leap-frog,** n. Saute-mouton *m.* ‖ **Leap-year,** n. Année bissextile *f.*

leaper [-ə*] n. Sauteur *s.*

leaping [-iŋ] adj. Sauteur.
— n. Saut *m.*

leapt [lept]. See LEAP.

learn [lə:n] v. tr. (93). Apprendre (*from*, de) [sth.].
‖ **To learn up,** FAM. Apprendre.
— v. intr. Apprendre, s'instruire (enseigner). ‖ Apprendre (*that*, que).

learned [-id] adj. Erudit, instruit (person). ‖ Savant, docte (scholar); versé (*in*, dans). ‖ Libéral (profession); savant (society).

learnedly [-idli] adv. Savamment.

learner [-ə*] n. Elève *s.*; *quick learner*, esprit prompt à apprendre.

learning [-niŋ] n. Etude *f.* (act). ‖ Savoir *m.*; science *f.* (result).

learnt [lə:nt]. See LEARN.

lease [li:s] n. JUR. Bail *m.*; *farming lease*, bail à ferme; *on lease*, à bail. ‖ FAM. *A new lease of* (or) U. S. *on life*, un regain de vie, un nouveau bail. ‖ **Lease-lend,** n. JUR. Prêt-bail *m.*
— v. tr. Louer. (See HIRE.)

leasehold [-hould] n. Tenure (*f.*) à bail.

leaseholder [-houldə*] n. Bailleur *m.*

leash [li:ʃ] n. Laisse *f.* (of a dog). ‖ FIG. Rêne *f.*; *to hold in leash*, tenir en lisière; *to strain at the leash*, ruer dans les brancards (fam.).

least [li:st] adj. Le moindre (in importance); le plus petit (in size). ‖ MATH. *Least common multiple*, plus petit commun multiple.
— adv. Le moins; *he least of all*, lui moins que quiconque.
— n. Moins *m.*; *at least four ships*, quatre navires au moins; *at the very least*, tout au moins, pour le moins; *not in the least*, pas le moins du monde, nullement, en aucune façon.

leastwise [-waiz], **leastways** [-weiz] adv. Du moins, au moins; en tout cas.

leat [li:t] n. TECHN. Abée *f.*

leather ['leðə*] n. Cuir *m.* (material). ‖ Objet de cuir *m.* (article). ‖ SPORTS. Balle *f.*
— adj. De cuir, en cuir; *fancy leather goods*, maroquinerie. ‖ **Leather-bottle,** n. Outre *f.* ‖ **Leather-cloth,** n. Toile (*f.*) cuir. ‖ **Leather-dresser,** n. Peaussier *m.*
— v. tr. Couvrir de cuir. ‖ FAM. Rosser. (See THRASH.)

leatherette [ˌleðə'ret] n. Similicuir *m.*

leathering ['leðəriŋ] n. FAM. Tannée *f.*

leathern ['leðə:n] adj. En cuir, de cuir; semblable à du cuir.

leatheroid ['leðərɔid] n. Cuir artificiel *m.*

leathery [-i] adj. Semblable à du cuir. ‖ FAM. Coriace, en semelle de botte (steak).

leave [li:v] n. Permission, autorisation *f.*; *to beg leave*, demander la permission; *with or without leave*, sans même solliciter l'autorisation. ‖ Congé *m.*; *to take leave of*, prendre congé de, dire au revoir à. ‖ MILIT. Permission *f.* (in days); congé *m.* (in months). ‖ JUR. *On ticket of leave*, en liberté conditionnelle. ‖ **Leave-taking,** n. Congé, départ, adieu *m.*

leave (94). v. tr. Laisser, rejeter, ne pas prendre (sth.). ‖ Quitter (a place); laisser, quitter (s.o.). ‖ Laisser, délaisser, abandonner. ‖ Laisser, léguer (a fortune). ‖ Laisser (in a certain condition); *to leave alone*, laisser tranquille. ‖ Confier, livrer, laisser le soin de (sth.) [*to*, à]; *I leave it to your sense of fairness*, je laisse à votre loyauté. ‖ *To be left*, rester; *you have no choice left*, il ne vous reste plus de choix. ‖ MATH. Rester; *ten minus three leaves seven*, dix moins trois font sept (or) reste sept. ‖ CH. DE F. *Left luggage*, bagage en consigne; *to leave the track*, dérailler. ‖ **To leave about,** laisser traîner, ne pas ranger. ‖ **To leave behind,** laisser (an odour); oublier (one's umbrella); SPORTS. Dépasser, laisser derrière (a competitor). ‖

To leave off, ne plus mettre (a coat); renoncer à (a habit); *to leave off doing,* cesser de faire. ‖ **To leave out,** exclure, laisser de côté (s.o.); omettre (sth.). ‖ **To leave over,** remettre, différer; *to be left over,* rester.
— v. intr. Partir, s'en aller, prendre congé. ‖ **To leave off,** cesser.

leaved [li:vd] adj. Bot. Feuillu (tree). ‖ Archit. A vantaux (door); à rabattants (folding-screen); à battants (shutter); à rallonges (table).

leaven ['levn] n. Levain m. (lit. and fig.). [See YEAST.]
— v. tr. Faire lever (dough). ‖ Fig. Pétrir, pénétrer (with, de); adoucir (with, par).

leaves [li:vz]. See LEAF.

leavings ['li:viŋz] n. pl. Restes m. pl.

Lebanon ['lebənən] n. Geogr. Liban m.

lecher ['letʃə*] n. Coureur, paillard, noceur m.

lecherous ['letʃrəs] adj. Débauché, lubrique. ‖ Sensuel.

lechery [-ri] n. Débauche f. (See LEWDNESS.)

lectern ['lektə:n] n. Eccles. Lutrin m.

lection ['lekʃən] n. Eccles. Leçon f.

lectionary [-əri] n. Eccles. Lectionnaire m.

lecture ['lektʃə*] n. Cours m.; conférence f. (talk, text). ‖ Fam. Sermon m. (scolding).
— v. tr. Faire un cours (or) une conférence à. ‖ Fam. Sermonner, faire la leçon à.

lecturer [-rə*] n. Conférencier s. ‖ Maître (m.) de conférences (at a University).

lectureship [-ʃip] n. Maîtrise (f.) de conférences.

led [led]. See LEAD.

ledge [ledʒ] n. Méplat m.; saillie f. (of rock). ‖ Banc (m.) de roches (reef). ‖ Archit. Corniche f. ‖ Techn. Veine f.; filon m.

ledger ['ledʒə*] n. Registre m. ‖ Pierre tombale f. (tombstone). ‖ Fin. Grand livre m. (in book-keeping). ‖ **Ledger-board,** n. Rampe supérieure. ‖ **Ledger-line,** n. Sports. Ligne dormante f.; Mus. Ligne supplémentaire f. ‖ **Ledger-paper,** n. Papier (m.) pour comptabilité.

lee [li:] n. Abri m. (against the wind). ‖ Naut. Côté sous le vent m.; *to bring by the lee,* empanner (a ship). ‖ **Lee-helm,** n. Naut. Barre (f.) dessous. ‖ **Lee-side,** n. Naut. Côté sous le vent; Agric. Côté abrité du vent. ‖ **Lee-way,** n. Naut. Dérive f.; Fig. Champ m. (for action); marge f. (of money, time).

leech [li:tʃ] n. † Mire m. ‖ Med. Sangsue f. ‖ Fam. Pot (m.) de colle, poisse f.; crampon m.

leechcraft [-krɑ:ft] n. † Physique, médecine f.

leek [li:k] n. Agric. Poireau m.

leer [liə*] n. Regard sournois m. ‖ Œillade polissonne f.; regard lubrique m. (ogle).
— v. intr. Lorgner méchamment. ‖ Jeter des œillades, faire de l'œil.

leering [-riŋ] n. Sournois, en dessous (sidelong). ‖ Lascif, polisson (lustful).

leery [-ri] adj. Fam. Malin, astucieux (knowing); prudent, soupçonneux (wary).

lees [li:z] n. pl. Lie f. (lit. and fig.)

leeward ['li:wəd] adj., adv. Sous le vent.
— n. Naut. Côté sous le vent m. (See LEE.)

left [left]. See LEAVE.

left adj. Gauche, de (or) à gauche; *on your left hand,* à votre gauche (direction). ‖ **Left-hand,** adj. De gauche; Techn. A gauche; Sports. Du gauche (punch). ‖ **Left-handed,** adj. Gaucher; Fig. Gauche; Fam. De la main gauche (marriage); adv. A gauche. ‖ **Left-hander,** n. Gaucher s.; Sports. Direct du gauche m. ‖ **Left-wing,** adj. De gauche (in politics). ‖ **Left-winger,** n. Homme (m.) [or] femme (f.) de gauche; Sports. Ailier gauche m.
— adv. A gauche.
— n. Gauche f.; *on the left,* à gauche. ‖ Sports. Gauche m. ‖ Jur., Milit., Autom. Gauche f.

leftism [-izm̩] n. Tendances politiques (f. pl.) de gauche.

leftist [-ist] n. Homme (m.) de gauche (in politics).

leftovers ['left'ouvə:z] n. pl. Culin. Restes m. pl.

leftward ['leftwəd] adj., adv. Vers la gauche.

lefty ['lefti] n. U. S. Fam. Gaucher.

leg [leg] n. Med. Jambe f. ‖ Zool. Patte f. (of a dog, fly); jambe f. (of a horse). ‖ Culin. Jarret m. (of beef); cuisse f. (of chicken, frogs); gigot m. (of mutton); cuisseau m. (of veal); cuissot m. (of venison); *leg of pork,* jambon. ‖ Comm. Jambe f. (of chair, table, trousers). ‖ Naut. Bordée f. ‖ Sports. Terrain de gauche m. ‖ Fam. *On one's last legs,* à fond de course; *to give s.o. a leg up,* dépanner qqn; *to have not a leg to stand on,* être à bout d'arguments valables; *to pull s.o.'s leg,* monter un bateau à qqn; *to set s.o. on one's legs again,* remettre qqn sur pied; *to shake a leg,* gambader, gigoter; *to stand on one's own legs,* voler de ses propres ailes. ‖ **Leg-bone,** n. Med. Tibia m. ‖ **Leg-iron,** n. Med. Attelle f. ‖ **Leg-of-mutton,** adj. A gigot (sleeve); Naut. Triangulaire (sail). ‖ **Leg-pull,** n. Fam. Canulard m. ‖ **Leg-puller,** n. Fam. Farceur s. ‖ **Leg-rest,** n. Appui (m.) pour les pieds; Med. Etrier m. ‖ **Leg-up,** n. Fam. Dépannage, coup (m.) de main.
— v. tr. Fam. *To leg it,* jouer des flûtes, cavaler, tricoter (to run); faire le trajet à pattes (to walk).

legacy ['legəsi] n. Jur. Legs m. ‖ **Legacy hunter,** n. Captateur d'héritage. ‖ **Legacy-securing,** adj. Jur. Captatoire.

legal ['li:gəl] adj. Jur. Authentique (act); juridique (adviser, department, position); judiciaire (assistance, proceedings); legal (rights, separation, tender); civil (year); *legal entity,* personne morale.

legalism [-izm] n. Culte (m.) de la légalité.

legality [li'gæliti] n. Jur. Légalité f.

legalization [,li:gəlai'zeiʃən] n. Jur. Légalisation f.

legalize ['li:gəlaiz] v. tr. Jur. Légaliser.

legally [-i] adv. Jur. Légalement; juridiquement; de plein droit.

legate ['legit] n. Eccles. Légat m.

legate [li'geit] v. tr. Jur. Léguer. (See BEQUEATH.)

legatee [,legə'ti:] n. Jur. Légataire m.

legation [li'geiʃən] n. Légation f.

legend ['ledʒənd] n. Légende f. (inscription, story).

legendary ['ledʒəndəri] adj. Légendaire.
— n. Légende dorée f.; légendaire m.

leger ['ledʒə*] adj. Mus. *Leger line,* ligne supplémentaire. (See LEDGER.)

legerdemain ['ledʒədə'mein] n. Prestidigitation f. ‖ Fam. Tour m.

legging ['legiŋ] n. Guêtre m. (for children). ‖ Pl. Leggings m. pl. ‖ Sports. Jambière f.

leggy [-i] adj. Dégingandé, à longues jambes.

Leghorn [le'gɔ:n] n. Geogr. Livourne f. ‖ Zool. Leghorn s. (fowl). ‖ Comm. Paille d'Italie f. (hat).

legibility [,ledʒi'biliti] n. Lisibilité f.

legible ['ledʒibl] adj. Lisible.

legibly [-bli] adv. Lisiblement.

legion ['li:dʒiən] n. Milit., Fig. Légion f.

legionary [-əri] adj. Légionnaire. ‖ Fig. En troupe, par légions.
— n. Milit. Légionnaire m.

legionnaire [-ɛə*] n. Milit. U. S. Légionnaire m.

legislate ['ledʒisleit] v. intr. Jur. Légiférer.

legislation [,ledʒis'leiʃən] n. Jur. Législation f.

legislative ['ledʒislətiv] adj. Jur. Législatif.

legislator [-leitə*] n. Jur. Législateur m.

legislature [-leitʃə*] n. Jur. Législature f. ‖ U. S. Corps législatif m.

legist ['li:dʒist] n. Jur. Légiste m.

legit [lə'dʒit] adj. Fam. Légal, réglo. ‖ Theatr., Fam. Classique. (See LEGITIMATE.)
— n. Theatr.. Fam. Théâtre classique m.

LEGAL TERMS — VOCABULAIRE JURIDIQUE

droit, loi	law	récidive	second (or) third offence
juridiction	jurisdiction	récidiviste	old offender
palais de justice	law-courts	repris de justice	habitual criminal
tribunal	court, tribunal	vol	theft, larceny
cour	court	larcin	petty larceny
tribunal correctionnel	police-court	vol à main armée	armed robbery
— —	Petty Sessions; U. S. lower criminal court	voleur à la tire	pickpocket
		voleur à l'étalage	shop-lifter
tribunal de première instance	Quarter Sessions; U.S. lower civil court	voler	to steal
cour d'assises	the Assizes; U. S. criminal court	cambriolage	burglary
		Au voleur!	Stop thief!
		recel	receiving
cour d'appel	Court of Appeal	recéleur	receiver
Cour de cassation	Supreme Court of Appeal; U. S. highest appellate court	contrebandier	smuggler
		braconnier	poacher
Cour suprême	High Court of Justice; U. S. Supreme Court	malfaiteur	malefactor
		coquin, gredin	rascal, scoundrel
faire son droit	to read law	apache; truand	hooligan; gangster
avocat	counsel; barrister	escroc	swindler
avoué, notaire	solicitor	demander justice	to seek redress
avocat de la Couronne	Queen's Counsel	abus de confiance	breach of trust
procureur	prosecution	détournement de fonds	embezzlement
procureur général	Attorney General	chantage	blackmail, demanding money with menaces
réquisitoire	speech for the prosecution		
plaidoirie	Counsel's speech	maître chanteur	blackmailer
barreau	Bar	complice	accomplice
barre (des témoins)	witness box	corruption	bribery
témoin à charge	evidence for prosecution	pot-de-vin	bribe
— à décharge	evidence for the defence	faussaire	forger
procès	case, suit, trial	faux-monnayeur	counterfeiter
parties	parties, litigants	incendie volontaire	arson
plaignant	plaintiff	empreintes digitales	finger-prints
partie civile	plaintiff (seeking damages for a criminal offence)	assassiner	to murder
		tuer	to kill
défense	defence	meurtre	manslaughter; murder
défendeur	defendant	meurtrier	murderer
jury	jury	délit criminel	misdemeanour
juré	juror, juryman	crime	felony, crime
dresser la liste du jury	to empanel a jury	attentat	criminal attempt
huissier	usher		outrage
greffier	clerk of the Court	criminel	criminal, felon
greffe	record office	A l'assassin!	Murder!
audience à huis clos	hearing in camera; U. S. closed hearing	condamner à	to sentence
		les dépens	the costs
siéger	to sit in court	condamner à mort	to sentence to death
porter plainte	to lodge a complaint	réclusion	solitary confinement
litige	litigation	amende	fine
poursuivre	to prosecute	travaux forcés	penal servitude; U. S. hard labor
intenter un procès à	to bring before a court		
— —	to sue at law	peine de mort	death penalty
article	clause, provision	peine capitale	capital punishment
assigner en justice	to serve a writ on	bourreau	executioner
assignation	writ of summons	bannir	to banish
accuser	to indict, to charge	exiler	to exile
accusation	indictment, charge	exilé	exile
inculpé	accused	forçat	convict
banc des prévenus	dock	extrader	to extradite
témoin oculaire	eye-witness	déportation	deportation
déposer	to give evidence	saisie	seizure
la déposition	the evidence	maison de correction	Borstal institution; U. S. reformatory
prêter serment	to take the oath		
arrêter	to place under arrest	jeunesse délinquante	juvenile delinquents
mandat d'arrêt	warrant for arrest	purger sa peine	to serve one's term
— de perquisition	search warrant	ajournement	adjournment
enquête	enquiry, inquiry	remis à huitaine	adjourned for a week
faire une enquête	to conduct an enquiry	disjoindre	to sever
juge d'instruction	examining magistrate	sursis; sursoir	reprieve; to reprieve
libérer sous caution	to release on bail	amnistie	amnesty
emprisonner	to emprison	appeler	to appeal
mettre en prison	to remand	commuer	to commute
prison	prison, gaol, U. S. jail	casser	to quash, to annul
« panier à salade »	« Black Maria »	débouter	to non-suit; U. S. to dismiss
commissariat	police station	acquittement	acquittal
contre-interrogatoire	cross-examination	prononcer le verdict	to bring in the verdict
comparaître	to appear before the Court	verdict d'acquittement	verdict of not guilty
faire défaut	to abscond	ordonnance de non-lieu	nonsuit
un contumace	a defaulter	« non-lieu »	« no ground for prosecution »
fournir un alibi	to produce an alibi	« attendu que... »	« whereas... »
circonstances atténuantes	extenuating circumstances	les attendus	the items
être pris sur le fait	to be caught in the act	héritier	heir
— — en flagrant délit	— — redhanded	héritière	heiress
aveu	admission	hériter	to inherit
délit	offence	intestat	intestate
délinquant	offender	tester	to make one's will
		légataire universel	sole legatee

legitimacy [li'dʒitiməsi] n. Légitimité *f.;* bien-fondé *m.*

legitimate [-mit] adj. Jur., Fig. Légitime (child, claim, conclusions, king). ‖ Theatr., Mus. Classique; U. S. Régulier.
— [-meit] v. tr. Jur., Fig. Légitimer.

legitimately [-mitli] adv. Légitimement, à bon droit.

legitimation [li,dʒiti'meiʃən] n. Jur. Légitimation *f.*

legitimism [li'dʒitimizm̩] n. Légitimisme *m.*

legitimist [-mist] n. Légitimiste *s.*

legitimize [-maiz] v. tr. Légitimer.

legless ['leglis] adj. Sans pattes (animal); sans jambes (person); sans pieds (table); *legless cripple,* cul-de-jatte.

legume ['legju:m] n. Bot. Fève *f.;* fruit (*m.*) de légumineux. ‖ Pl. Légumes *m. pl.*

leguminous [le'gju:minəs] adj. Bot. Légumineux.

leisure ['leʒə*] n. Loisir *m.; at leisure,* à loisir, sans se presser, en prenant son temps; *at one's leisure,* à ses moments de liberté.

leisured [-d] adj. Qui a des loisirs (having free time); désœuvré (not occupied).

leisurely [-li] adj., adv. A loisir.

leitmotif ['laitmou,ti:f] n. Leitmotiv *m.*

lemma ['lemə] (pl. **lemmata** [-tə]) n. Philos., Math. Lemme *m.*

lemming ['lemiŋ] n. Zool. Lemming *m.*

lemon ['lemən] n. Citron *m.* (fruit); citronnier *m.* (tree). ‖ Fam. U. S. Gogo *m.* ‖ **Lemon-drop,** n. Bonbon acidulé *m.* ‖ **Lemon-squash,** n. Citron pressé *m.* ‖ **Lemon-squeezer,** n. Presse-citron *m.* ‖ **Lemon-tree,** n. Bot. Citronnier *m.*
— adj. Jaune citron (colour). ‖ De (or) au citron.

lemonade [,lemə'neid] n. Limonade *f.*

lemon sole [,lemən 'soul] n. Zool., Culin. Limande *f.*

lemur ['li:mə*] n. Zool. Lémurien *m.*

lend [lend] v. tr. (95). Fin. Prêter (money). ‖ Fig. Prêter; *to lend oneself to,* se prêter à. ‖ Fig. Donner; *to lend cheer to a room,* égayer une pièce; *to lend a hand,* donner un coup de main (*to,* à).

lender [-ə*] n. Fin. Prêteur *s.*

lending [-iŋ] n. Prêt *m.* (act).

length [leŋθ] n. Longueur *f.* (in size); *three feet in length,* trois pieds de long. ‖ Longueur, distance *f.* (in space). ‖ Durée, étendue *f.* (in time). ‖ Bout, morceau *m.* (piece). ‖ Phys. *Focal length,* distance focale. ‖ Loc. *At length,* tout du long, en détail (in full); enfin, à la longue (finally); *to fall full length,* tomber tout de son long.

lengthen [-ən] v. tr. Allonger.
— v. intr. S'allonger.

lengthily [-ili] adv. Longuement.

lengthiness [-inis] n. Longueurs *f. pl.*

lengthways [-weiz], **lengthwise** [-waiz] adv. En long, en longueur.

lengthy [-i] adj. Traînant en longueur, qui n'en finit pas.

leniency ['li:niənsi] n. Douceur, clémence *f.*

lenient [-ənt] adj. Doux, plein d'indulgence. ‖ † Adoucissant.

leniently [-əntli] adv. Doucement, avec clémence.

lenitive ['lenitiv] adj., n. Lénitif *adj., m.*

lenity ['leniti] n. Douceur, indulgence *f.*

lens [lenz] (pl. **lenses** [-i:zl] n. Phys. Lentille *f.* (in general); verre *m.* (of spectacles); loupe *f.* (magnifying glass). ‖ Med. Cristallin *m.* ‖ Techn. Objectif *m.* (in photography).
— v. tr. U. S. Photographier, filmer.

lent [lent]. See lend.

Lent [lent] n. Eccles. Carême *m.*

Lenten ['lentən] adj. Eccles. De carême.

lenticular [len'tikjulə*] adj. Lenticulaire.

lentil ['lentil] n. Bot., Culin. Lentille *f.*

lentisk ['lentisk] n. Bot. Lentisque *m.*

Leo ['liou] n. Léon *m.* (name). ‖ Astron. Lion *m.*

leonine ['li:ənain] adj. Léonin.

leopard ['lepəd] n. Zool. Léopard *m.*

leotard ['liə,tɑ:d] n. Collant, maillot *m.* (for dancer).

leper ['lepə*] n. Med. Lépreux *s.*

lepidopteran [,lepi'dɔptərən] adj., n. Zool. Lépidoptère *m.*

lepidopterist [,lepi'dɔptərist] n. Lépidoptériste *s.,* collectionneur (*s.*) de papillons.

lepidopterous [-rəs] adj. Zool. De lépidoptère.

leprechaun ['leprə,kɔ:n] n. Gnome, lutin, korrigan *m.* (in Irish legends).

leprosy ['leprəsi] n. Med., Fig. Lèpre *f.*

leprous ['leprəs] adj. Med., Fig. Lépreux.

Lesbian ['lezbiən] adj. Lesbien.
— n. Lesbienne *f.*

lese-majesty ['li:z'mædʒisti] n. Lèse-majesté *f.* (pr., fig.).

lesion ['li:ʒən] n. Med., Jur. Lésion *f.*

Lesotho [li'su:tou] n. Geogr. Lesotho *m.*

less [les] adj. (comp. of little). Moindre, plus petit (smaller); *of less value,* de moindre valeur. ‖ Moins de, pas autant de (not so much); *no less courage than,* pas moins de courage que. ‖ Fam. *No less a person than,* rien moins que.
— adv. (comp. of a little). Moins; *all the less* (or) *the less... as,* d'autant moins que; *less and less,* de moins en moins; *less tired than,* moins fatigué que; *no less affectionate than,* pas moins affectueux que; *none the less,* néanmoins; *nothing less than,* rien moins que; *so much the less,* d'autant moins; *still less,* encore moins.
— prep. Math. Moins.
— n. Moins *m.; in less than two days,* en moins de deux jours.

lessee [le'si:] n. Jur. Locataire *m.; lessee nation,* Etat preneur.

lessen ['lesn̩] v. tr., intr. Diminuer.

lesser ['lesə*] adj. (comp. of less). Moindre, plus petit (see less, least); *the lesser evil,* le moindre mal; *the lesser half,* la petite moitié. ‖ Geogr. *Lesser Antilles,* Petites Antilles.

lesson ['lesn̩] n. Leçon *f.* (exercise). ‖ Pl. Devoirs (*m. pl.*) à faire à la maison. ‖ Leçon, répétition *f.* (teaching). ‖ Eccles., Fig. Leçon *f.*
— v. tr. Donner une leçon à.

lessor [le'sɔ:*] n. Bailleur *m.;* bailleresse *f.*

lest [lest] conj. De peur que; *lest we should lose our way,* de crainte (or) de peur de nous égarer. ‖ Que... ne (after verbs of fearing); *I feared lest he should fall,* je craignais qu'il ne tombât.

let [let] n. Obstacle *m.;* entrave *f.* (See hindrance.) ‖ Sports. Balle (*f.*) au filet (in tennis).

let [let] v. tr. (96). Laisser; *to let alone* (or) *be,* laisser tranquille, laisser faire (s.o.); ne pas s'occuper de (sth.); *to let fall, slip,* laisser tomber, échapper; *to let oneself go,* se laisser aller. ‖ Permettre de, autoriser à, laisser; *to let s.o. do sth.,* permettre à qqn de faire qqch. ‖ Faire; *to let know,* faire savoir; *to let s.o. know,* prévenir qqn, mettre qqn au courant. ‖ Med. *To let blood,* faire une saignée. ‖ Jur. Louer (a flat); *house to let,* maison à louer. ‖ **To let down,** allonger (a dress); dénouer (one's hair); descendre (s.o.) [by rope]; Autom. Dégonfler (a tyre); Ch. de f. Baisser (a carriage window); Techn. Détendre (a spring); Fig. Traiter (s.o.); *to let s.o. down gently,* se montrer indulgent avec qqn; Fam. Laisser tomber (a friend). ‖ **To let in,** percer (a door); laisser entrer, faire entrer (s.o., sth.). ‖ **To let into,** percer dans; incruster dans; laisser entrer dans; Fig. Mettre dans (a secret). ‖ **To let off,** décocher (an arrow); Milit. Faire partir (a gun); Techn. Détendre (a spring); lâcher (steam); Jur. Louer (a flat); Fig. Dispenser (s.o.)

[*from,* de] ; faire grâce à (s.o.) [*with,* de]. ‖ **To let out,** laisser fuir (a bird, water) ; élargir (a garment) ; laisser sortir (s.o.) ; Jur. Louer (chairs) ; relâcher (a prisoner) ; Naut. Larguer (sails) ; Fig. Laisser échapper, lâcher (a cry, secret).
— v. intr. Jur. Se louer (house). ‖ **To let on,** Fam. Moucharder ; *to let on about sth. to s.o.,* rapporter qqch. à qqn. ‖ **To let out,** Fam. Dire sa façon de penser (*at,* à) ; *to let out at s.o. with one's fist,* décocher un coup de poing à qqn.
— v. aux. (1st and 3rd pers. of imperative). *Let me look at it closely,* voyons ça de près, que j'y regarde de près ; *let's see,* voyons ; *let there be light,* que la lumière soit !
— n. Jur. Location *f.* ‖ **Let-down,** n. Med. Sautes (*f. pl.*) d'humeur ; Fam. Déception *f.* ; U. S. Fam. Relâchement *m.* ‖ **Let-off,** n. Fam. Chance (*f.*) de s'en tirer sans mal. ‖ **Let-up,** n. Fam. Ralentissement *m.* (*in,* dans).
lethal ['li:θəl] adj. Mortel (see Fatal) ; *lethal chamber,* chambre à gaz.
lethargic [lə'θɑːdʒik] adj. Léthargique.
lethargically [-əli] adv. Léthargiquement.
lethargize ['leθəːdʒaiz] v. tr. Endormir, mettre en état de léthargie.
lethargy [-dʒi] n. Léthargie *f.*
Lethe ['li:θi:] n. Léthé *m.* ‖ Fig. Oubli *m.*
Lethean [li:'θiən] adj. Du Léthé. ‖ Fig. Qui procure l'oubli.
Lett [let] n. Geogr. Letton *s.* ‖ Gramm. Letton *m.*
letter ['letə*] n. Lettre *f.* (of alphabet). ‖ Lettre *f.* (missive) ; *by letter post,* au tarif des lettres ; *dead letter,* lettre au rebut. ‖ Pl. Lettres *f. pl.* ; *man of letters,* homme de lettres. ‖ Jur. *Letter of attorney,* pouvoir. ‖ Techn. Caractère *m.* (in printing) ; *compound letter,* ligature. ‖ Fig. Lettre *f.* (literal meaning). ‖ **Letter-balance,** n. Pèse-lettres *m.* ‖ **Letter-bomb,** n. Lettre piégée *f.* ‖ **Letter-box,** n. Boîte (*f.*) aux lettres. ‖ **Letter-card,** n. Carte-lettre *f.* ‖ **Letter-carrier,** n. U. S. Facteur *m.* ‖ **Letter-case,** n. Porte-lettres *m.* ; Techn. Casse *f.* ‖ **Letter-paper,** n. Papier (*m.*) à lettres. ‖ **Letter-perfect,** adj. U. S. Correct ; Theatr. Sûr (of one's part). ‖ **Letter-press,** n. Presse (*f.*) à copier. ‖ **Letter-weight,** n. Presse-papiers *m.* ‖ **Letter-writer,** n. Recueil (*m.*) de lettres types (book) ; épistolier *s.* (person).
— v. tr. Ecrire en lettres soignées (or) en caractères d'imprimerie. ‖ Mettre un titre à (a book). ‖ Marquer avec des lettres. ‖ Jur. Coter.
lettered ['letəd] adj. Lettré (person). ‖ Marqué de lettres.
lettering [-riŋ] n. Lettrage *m.* (act) ; inscription *f.,* titre *m.*
lettergram [-græm] n. U. S. Lettre-télégramme (*f.*) à tarif réduit.
letterless [-lis] adj. Illettré.
letterpress [-'pres] n. Techn. Impression *f.* ; texte imprimé *m.*
Lettic ['letik], **Lettish** [-iʃ] adj., n. Geogr. Letton *s.*
lettuce ['letis] n. Bot., Culin. Laitue *f.* ‖ Pop. U. S. Oseille *f.* (greenbacks).
leucite ['lju:sait] n. Leucite *m.*
leucocyte ['lju:kəsait] n. Med. Leucocyte *m.*
leucocytosis [ˌlju:kəsai'tousis] n. Med. Leucocytose *f.*
leucoplast ['lju:kəplæst] n. Med. Leucoplaste *m.*
leucorrhoea [ˌlju:kə'riə] n. Med. Leucorrhée *f.*
leucotomy [lju:'kɔtəmi] n. Med. Leucotomie *f.*
leukemia [lju:'ki:miə] n. Med. Leucémie *f.*
Levant [li'vænt] n. Geogr. Levant *m.*
levanter [-ə*] n. Comm. Levantine *f.* (cloth).
Levantine [-ain] adj., n. Geogr. Levantin *s.*
levator [li'veitə*] n. Med. Elévateur *m.*
levee ['levi] n. † Lever *m.* (of king). ‖ Réception royale (*f.*) pour hommes.
levee n. U. S. Levée, digue *f.*

level ['levl] n. Niveau *m.* (instrument). ‖ Niveau *m.* (line) ; *on a level with,* de niveau avec ; *out of level,* dénivelé. ‖ Plan horizontal *m.* (area). ‖ Techn. Galerie *f.* (in mining). ‖ Geogr. Plaine *f.* ‖ Geol. Etage *m.* ‖ Jur. Echelon *m.* ‖ Fig. Niveau, étiage *m.* ‖ Fam. *On the level,* carré, droit, honnête.
— adj. De niveau (*with,* avec). ‖ Plan, horizontal. ‖ Culin. *Level spoonful,* cuillerée arasée. ‖ Fig. *Level with,* au niveau de, égal à. ‖ Fam. *One's level best,* le maximum de ses efforts. ‖ **Level-crossing,** n. Autom. Passage à niveau *m.* ‖ **Level-headed,** adj. Fig. Rassis, équilibré, d'aplomb.
— v. tr. (1). Niveler (ground) ; *the school was levelled by the hurricane,* l'école fut rasée par l'ouragan. ‖ Milit. Braquer (a pistol) ; détruire (a town). ‖ Fig. Lancer (accusations, blows) ; diriger (*at,* contre) [sarcasm]. ‖ **To level away,** aplanir. ‖ **To level out,** égaliser. ‖ **To level up,** Aviat. Redresser.
leveller [-ə*] n. Niveleur *s.*
levelling [-iŋ] n. Nivellement *m.* ‖ **Levelling-pole,** n. Jalon d'arpentage *m.* ‖ **Levelling-rod,** n. Jalonmire *m.*
levelness [-nis] n. Position (*f.*) de niveau. ‖ Planitude *f.* (of a surface). ‖ Fig. Pondération *f.*
lever ['li:və*] n. Techn., Autom. Levier *m.* ‖ Milit. Bascule *f.* (of a rifle). ‖ Techn. Raquette *f.* (of a watch). ‖ **Lever-handle,** n. Bec-de-cane. *m.* ‖ **Lever-scales,** n. Balance romaine *f.*
— v. tr. Déplacer à l'aide d'un levier. ‖ Fig. *To lever out,* déloger.
leverage ['levəridʒ] n. Action (or) puissance (*f.*) du levier ; *to bring leverage to bear on,* exercer des pesées sur (a door) ; chercher à prendre prise sur (s.o.).
leveret ['levərit] n. Zool. Levraut *m.*
leviable ['leviəbl] adj. Fin. Imposable (person) ; recouvrable, perceable (tax).
Leviathan [li'vaiəθən] n. Léviathan *m.*
levigate ['levigeit] v. tr. Med. Léviger.
levigation [ˌlevi'geiʃən] n. Med. Lévigation *f.*
levirate ['li:virit] n. Lévirat *m.*
levitate ['leviteit] v. intr. Se soulever par lévitation.
levitation ['levi'teiʃən] n. Lévitation *f.*
levite ['li:vait] n. Eccles. Lévite *m.*
levitical [li'vitikəl] adj. Lévitique.
Leviticus [-əs] n. Lévitique *m.*
levity ['leviti] n. Légèreté *f.* (lit. and fig.).
levulose ['levjulous] n. Chim. Lévulose *m.*
levy ['levi] n. Fin., Milit. Levée *f.*
— v. tr. Fin. Imposer (a fine) ; lever (taxes). ‖ Milit. Lever (troops). ‖ Fig. *To levy war on,* faire la guerre à.
lewd [lju:d] adj. Lascif, lubrique, impudique, vicieux. ‖ † Ignoble.
lewdly [-li] adv. Lascivement.
lewdness [-nis] n. Lascivité, lubricité *f.*
Lewis ['luis] n. Techn. Louve *f.* ‖ Milit. *Lewis gun,* fusil mitrailleur Lewis.
lexeme ['leksi:m] n. Gramm. Lexème *m.*
lexical ['leksikl] adj. Lexical.
lexicographer [ˌleksi'kɔgrəfə*] n. Lexicographe *s.*
lexicographical [ˌleksikə'græfikəl] adj. Lexicographique.
lexicography [ˌleksi'kɔgrəfi] n. Lexicographie *f.*
lexicological [ˌleksikə'lɔdʒikl] adj. Gramm. Lexicologique.
lexicologist [ˌleksi'kɔlədʒist] n. Lexicologue *m.*
lexicology [-'kɔlədʒi] n. Lexicologie *f.*
lexicon ['leksikən] n. Lexique *m.*
Leyden ['leidn] n. Geogr. Leyde *m.* ‖ Electr. *Leyden jar,* bouteille de Leyde.
liability [ˌlaiə'biliti] n. Jur. Responsabilité *f.* ‖ Fin. Pl. Passif *m.* ; engagements *m. pl.* ; dettes *f. pl.* ‖ Fig. Disposition, inclination *f.* (*to,* à).
liable ['laiəbl] adj. Jur. Responsable (*for,* de) ;

passible (*to*, de). ‖ Fig. Prédisposé, disposé, sujet (*to*, à). ‖ U. S. *We are liable to be in Chicago next week*, il se peut que nous soyons à Chicago la semaine prochaine.
liaise [li'eiz] v. intr. Milit. Faire la liaison.
liaison [li:'eizɔ:ŋ] n. Gramm., Culin., Milit., Fig. Liaison *f*. ‖ **Liaison-officer**, n. Milit. Officier (*m*.) de liaison. ‖ **Liaison-pilot**, n. Aviat. Pilote (*m*.) de liaison.
liana [li'ɑ:nə] n. Bot. Liane *f*.
liar ['laiə*] n. Menteur *s*.
lias ['laiəs] n. Geol. Lias *m*. (stratum); liais *m* (stone).
libation [lai'beiʃən] n. Libation *f*.
libel ['laibəl] n. Libelle, pamphlet *m*. ‖ Jur. Ecrit diffamatoire *m*. ‖ Jur., Naut., Eccles. Acte introductif (*m*.) d'instance. ‖ Fig. Action calomnieuse (or) peu flatteuse *f*. (*on*, *against*, contre).
— v. tr. (1). Jur., Fig. Diffamer. ‖ Jur., Naut., Eccles. Intenter une action contre.
libeller ['laibḷə*] n. Diffamateur *m*.; diffamatrice *f*.
libellist [-ist] n. Libelliste *s*.
libellous [-əs] adj. Diffamatoire, calomnieux.
liberal ['libərəl] adj. Libéral, large, généreux (person); large, généreux (reward). ‖ Libéral (arts, education, profession). ‖ Large, sans étroitesse (interpretation). ‖ Jur. Libéral (in politics).
— n. Jur. Libéral *m*.
liberalism [-izṃ] n. Libéralisme *m*.
liberality [ˌlibə'ræliti] n. Libéralité *f*. (generosity). ‖ Largeur (*f*.) d'esprit (broad-mindedness).
liberalization [ˌlibərəlai'zeiʃən] n. Fig. Elargissement *m*. (of views).
liberalize ['libərəlaiz] v. tr. Elargir (ideas); rendre libéral (people).
liberally [-i] adv. Libéralement.
liberate ['libəreit] v. tr. Milit., Jur., Chim. Libérer. ‖ Fin. Mobiliser.
liberation [ˌlibə'reiʃən] n. Milit., Jur. Libération *f*. ‖ Chim. Dégagement *m*. (of gas). ‖ Fin. Mobilisation *f*. (of capital).
liberator ['libəreitə*] n. Milit., Fig. Libérateur *m*.; libératrice *f*.
Liberia [lai'biəriə] n. Geogr. Libéria *m*.
libertarian [ˌlibə'tɛəriən] adj., n. Libertaire *s*.
liberticide [li'bɛ:tisaid] adj., n. Liberticide *m*.
libertinage ['libətinidʒ], **libertinism** [-izṃ] n. Libertinage *m*. ‖ † Libre pensée *f*.
libertine ['libətain] adj. Libertin. ‖ † De libre penseur.
— n. Libertin *s*. (See debauchee). ‖ † Libre penseur *m*.
liberty ['libəti] n. Liberté *f*. (*of*, de); *at liberty*, libre, en liberté; *at liberty to*, libre de. ‖ Libre disposition *f*. (*of*, de). ‖ Jur. Pl. Privilèges *m. pl.*; franchises *f. pl*. ‖ Naut. Permission *f*. (to a sailor); *liberty boat*, vedette de permissionnaires; U. S. *liberty ship*, cargo. ‖ Philos. Liberté *f*. (See freedom.) ‖ Pl. Libertés, privautés, familiarités *f. pl*. ‖ Fin. U. S. *Liberty bond*, bon de l'emprunt de la première guerre mondiale. ‖ Loc. *Liberty cap*, bonnet phrygien; *Liberty Hall*, la maison du bon Dieu, l'abbaye de Thélème.
libidinal [li'bidinəl] adj. Psych. Libidinal.
libidinous [li'bidinəs] adj. Libidineux.
libido [li'bi:dou] (pl. **libidos** [-z]) n. Psych. Libido *f*.
libra ['laibrə] (pl. **librae** [-i:]) n. † Livre *f*. ‖ Astron. Balance *f*.
librarian [lai'brɛəriən] n. Bibliothécaire *m*.
librarianship [-ʃip] n. Poste *m*. (or) science (*f*.) de bibliothécaire.
library ['laibrəri] n. Bibliothèque *f*.; *mobile library*, bibliothèque circulante; *newspaper library*, hémérothèque.
librate [lai'breit] v. intr. Osciller.

libratory ['laibrətori] adj. Oscillatoire.
libration [lai'breiʃən] n. Oscillation *f*. ‖ Astron. Libration *f*.
librettist [li'bretist] n. Theatr. Librettiste *s*.
libretto [li'bretou] (pl. **libretti** [-i]) n. Theatr. Livret *m*.
Libya ['libiə] n. Geogr. Libye *f*.
lice [lais]. See louse.
licence, U. S. **license** ['laisəns] n. Jur. Autorisation *f*.; permis *m*.; *dog licence*, taxe sur les chiens; *marriage licence*, dispense de bans. ‖ Comm. Licence *f*. (of import); *licence duty*, patente. ‖ Autom. *Driving licence*, permis de conduire; U. S. *license plate*, plaque d'immatriculation. ‖ Gramm., Fig. Licence *f*.
license v. tr. Autoriser (*to*, à); permettre (*to*, de). ‖ Jur. Autoriser la parution de (a book); donner un permis à (s.o.). ‖ Comm. Patenter (s.o.).
licensed [-t] adj. Jur., Comm. Patenté. ‖ Fin. Inscrit (broker). ‖ Aviat. Breveté. ‖ Fig. Privilégié.
licensee [ˌlaisən'si:] n. Jur. Titulaire (*s*.) d'un permis. ‖ Comm. Patenté *m*.
licenser ['laisənsə*] n. Fonctionnaire (*m*.) chargé de délivrer les permis. ‖ Jur. Concédant *m*. ‖ Theatr. Censeur *m*.
licentiate [lai'senʃiit] n. Licencié *s*.
licentious [lai'senʃəs] adj. Licencieux.
licentiously [-li] adv. Licencieusement.
licentiousness [-nis] n. Dévergondage *m*.
lichen ['laikən] n. Bot., Med. Lichen *m*.
licit ['lisit] adj. Licite.
licitly [-li] adv. Licitement.
lick [lik] v. tr. Lécher (s.o., sth., the walls); *to lick one's chops*, se lécher (or) pourlécher les babines. ‖ Fam. Lécher; *to lick the dust*, mordre la poussière; *to lick into shape*, dégrossir; *to lick s.o.'s boots*, lécher les bottes de qqn. ‖ Fam. Battre, enfoncer (to overcome); tanner les côtes à (to thrash). ‖ U. S. Fam. Venir à bout de (a problem).
— v. intr. *To lick up*, lécher.
— n. Coup (*m*.) de langue. ‖ Fam. *A lick and a promise*, un bout de toilette. ‖ Fam. Brin *m*.; U. S. *he won't do a lick of work*, il ne fait pas une once de travail. ‖ Fam. Coup *m*. (blow). ‖ Pop. Course *f*.; *at full lick*, à plein gaz.
lickerish [-əriʃ] adj. Friand, difficile (finicky). ‖ Avide (greedy). ‖ Débauché (lecherous).
lickety-split ['likəti,split] adv. Fam. Ventre à terre, à fond de train.
licking ['likiŋ] n. Lèchement *m*. ‖ Fam. Tripotée, raclée *f*. (See drubbing.)
lickspittle ['likspitḷ] n. Fam. Chien couchant *m*.; lèche-cul *m*. (pop.)
licorice ['likəris] n. See liquorice.
lictor ['liktə*] n. Licteur *m*.
lid [lid] n. Couvercle *m*. (for a box, pot). ‖ Med. Paupière *f*. ‖ Bot. Opercule *m*. ‖ Fam. Galurin *m*. (hat). ‖ Fam. *To put the lid on*, mettre le comble à; U. S. Serrer la vis à.
lido ['li:dou] (pl. **lidos** [-z]) n. Piscine découverte *f*. (swimming-pool); plage aménagée *f*. (beach).
lie [lai] n. Mensonge *m*.; *to tell lies*, mentir. ‖ Démenti *m*.; *experience gives him the lie*, l'expérience lui donne le démenti. ‖ **Lie-detector**, n. Détecteur de mensonges *m*.
— v. intr. (2). Mentir.
lie v. intr. (97). Etre couché (*on*, sur) [person]; *to lie asleep*, être endormi. ‖ Coucher (*with*, avec) [person]. ‖ Gésir, reposer (the dead); *here lies*, ci-gît; *to lie dead*, être étendu mort. ‖ Etre posé (or) étendu (things); *to lie on the table*, être déposé sur la table. ‖ S'étendre (coast, space); se trouver, être placé (or) situé (*to*, à) [land]; passer (road); *to lie across*, *along*, traverser, longer. ‖ Etre, se trouver; *to lie hidden*, être caché. ‖ Rester, demeurer, se trouver; *to lie helpless*, demeurer sans secours; *to lie still*, rester tranquille. ‖ Rester,

demeurer, séjourner (*in*, dans). ‖ MED. Etre alité. ‖ MILIT. Camper (troops). ‖ NAUT. Etre à l'ancre. ‖ SPORTS. Rester tapi (game). ‖ FIN Etre déposé (*at*, à) [money]. ‖ JUR. Se soutenir (action). ‖ FIG. Résider (*in*, dans) [choice, interest, remedy]. ‖ FIG. Appartenir, incomber (*with*, à); *as far as it lies with me*, autant que cela dépendra de moi (or) sera en mon pouvoir. ‖ **To lie about**, traîner. ‖ **To lie by**, rester à l'écart (person); demeurer en réserve (thing). ‖ **To lie down**, se coucher (*on*, sur); FAM. *To take it lying down*, encaisser sans piper mot. ‖ **To lie in**, MED. Etre en couches; FAM. Faire la grasse matinée. ‖ **To lie off**, NAUT. Rester au large; TECHN. Débrayer. ‖ **To lie over**, être ajourné; *it can lie over*, il n'y a pas péril en la demeure. ‖ **To lie to**, NAUT. Etre à la cape. ‖ **To lie up**, se retirer (person); MED. Etre alité; NAUT. Désarmer.
— n. Antre, repaire *m.* (of an animal). ‖ Configuration *f.* (of the land). ‖ NAUT. Gisement *m.* ‖ SPORTS. Position *f.* (of a ball). ‖ FAM. *To study the lie of the land*, repérer le terrain. ‖ **Lie-abed**, n. FAM. Flemmard, pantouflard *m.* ‖ **Lie-in**, n. FAM. Grasse matinée *f.; I shall treat myself to a lie-in tomorrow morning*, je vais me payer le luxe de dormir demain matin. ‖ **Lie-up**, n. Période d'inactivité; relâche *f.* (fam.).

Liechtenstein ['liktən,stain] n. GEOGR. Liechtenstein *m.*

lied [li:d] (pl. **lieder** [-ə*]) n. MUS. Lied *m.*

lief [li:f] adv. *I had as lief*, j'aimerais autant.

liege [li:dʒ] adj. † Suzerain (lord); lige (subject).
— n. † Suzerain (lord); vassal (subject).

lien ['li:ən] n. JUR. Droit (*m.*) de rétention; créance privilégiée *f.; vendor's lien*, privilège du vendeur.

lieu [lju:] n. Lieu *m.; in lieu of*, au lieu de, en remplacement (or) en guise de.

lieutenancy [lef'tenənsi], U. S. [lju'tenənsi]) n. † Lieutenance *f.* ‖ MILIT. Grade de lieutenant *m.*

lieutenant ([lef'tenənt], U.S. [lu:'tenənt]) n. MILIT., FIG. Lieutenant *m.* ‖ NAUT. Lieutenant de vaisseau *m.* ‖ **Lieutenant-colonel**, n. MILIT. Lieutenant-colonel (*m.*) commandant un bataillon. ‖ **Lieutenant-commander**, n. NAUT. Capitaine (*m.*) de corvette. ‖ **Lieutenant-general**, n. MILIT. Général (*m.*) de division. ‖ **Lieutenant-governor**, n. U. S. Vice-gouverneur *m.* ‖ **Lieutenant-junior-grade**, n. U. S. NAUT. Lieutenant en second *m.*

life [laif] (pl. **lives** [laivz]) n. Vie *f.* (quality, state); *to bring back to life*, ramener à la vie, ranimer; *to come to life*, reprendre conscience, revenir à la vie (or) à soi; *to take one's own life*, attenter à ses jours, se suicider. ‖ Vie *f.* (period); *to have a short life*, avoir la vie courte. ‖ Vie *f.* (activities); *military life*, la vie militaire. ‖ Vie *f.* (manner of living); *to lead a wild life*, mener une vie de débauche. ‖ Vie *f.* (reality); *to have seen life*, connaître la vie; *true to life*, conforme à la réalité vivante. ‖ Vie humaine *f.* (being); *a heavy toll of lives*, de grosses pertes, beaucoup de victimes. ‖ Vie, biographie *f.* (biography). ‖ ECCLES. *Eternal life*, vie éternelle. ‖ ARTS. *From life*, d'après nature; *still life*, nature morte. ‖ FIN. *Life annuity*, rente viagère; *life estate*, bien en viager; *life interest*, usufruit. ‖ ELECTR. Durée *f.* (of a bulb). ‖ FIG. Vie, âme *f.* (of the party). ‖ FAM. *For the life of me*, dussé-je y perdre la vie; *how's life?*, que devenez-vous? ‖ **Life-belt**, n. NAUT. Ceinture (*f.*) de sauvetage. ‖ **Life-blood**, n. FIG. Essence, partie vitale *f.* ‖ **Life-boat**, n. NAUT. Canot de sauvetage *m.* ‖ **Life-buoy**, n. NAUT. Bouée (*f.*) de sauvetage. ‖ **Life-cycle**, n. MED. Cycle (*m.*) de vie. ‖ **Life-giving**, adj. Vivifiant. ‖ **Life-guard**, n. Garde du corps *m.*; U. S. Maître nageur, sauveteur *m.* ‖ **Life-jacket**, n. NAUT., AVIAT. Gilet de sauvetage *m.* ‖ **Life-line**, n. NAUT. Ligne (*f.*) de sauvetage; U. S.

Voie (*f.*) d'approvisionnement. ‖ **Life-net**, n. Filet de sauvetage *m.* ‖ **Life-saver**, n. Sauveteur *m.;* CULIN. U. S. Bonbon acidulé *m.* ‖ **Life-saving**, n. Sauvetage *m.* ‖ **Life-size**, adj. ARTS. Grandeur nature. ‖ **Life-style**, n. Mode (or) style (*m.*) de vie. ‖ **Life-table**, n. Table de mortalité *f.*

lifeless [-lis] adj. Sans vie; terne.

lifelessly [-lisli] adv. Sans vie.

lifelessness [-lisnis] n. Manque (*m.*) de vie.

lifelike [-laik] adj. Vivant (picture); ressemblant, parlant, vivant (portrait).

lifelong [-lɔŋ] adj. De toujours, de toute la vie.

lifer [-ə*] n. FAM. Condamné (*s.*) à perpétuité (prisoner); condamnation à vie (or) à perpétuité *f.* (sentence).

lifetime [-taim] n. Vie, durée de la vie *f.; vivant m.*
— adj. A vie.

lift [lift] v. tr. Lever (one's arm, eyes); soulever (a weight). ‖ Elever, dresser (a spire). ‖ AGRIC. Arracher (potatoes); dépiquer (seedlings). ‖ MILIT. Allonger (the fire). ‖ MED. Remonter, rajeunir (s.o.'s face). ‖ SPORTS. Ramasser (the ball); remporter (the prize). ‖ U. S. JUR. Purger (a mortgage). ‖ FIG. Elever (heart, mind). ‖ FAM. Démarquer (a passage); piquer, rafler, faucher (s.o.'s purse); *to lift a story*, plagier. ‖ **To lift down**, descendre (*from*, de) [s.o., sth.]. ‖ **To lift off**, enlever. ‖ **To lift up**, lever (one's hands); relever (one's head); élever (one's voice).
— v. intr. Se lever, se soulever. ‖ Se gondoler, se boursoufler (floor). ‖ Se lever (fog); se dissiper (gloom); apparaître (land). ‖ AVIAT. Décoller. ‖ NAUT. S'élever à la lame.
— n. Haussement *m.* (of an arm); levée *f.* (of a weight). ‖ Elévation *f.* (in the ground); soulèvement *m.* (of waves). ‖ Port *m.* (of head). ‖ Ascenseur *m.* (for people); monte-charge *m.* (for things). ‖ TECHN. Hauteur de chute *f.* (of a canal-lock); hauteur (*f.*) de levage (of a crane); course *f.* (of a valve). ‖ NAUT. Balancine *f.* ‖ AVIAT. Force ascensionnelle *f.* (of a balloon); poussée *f.* (of a plane). ‖ CH. DE F. Rame *f.* ‖ AUTOM. *To give s.o. a lift*, conduire qqn d'un coup de voiture, faire profiter qqn de sa voiture. ‖ **Lift-attendant** (or) **-boy**, n. Liftier *m.*

lifter [-ə*] n. Souleveur *m.* ‖ U. S. FAM. Chapardeur *m.*

lifting [-iŋ] n. Soulèvement *m.* (of a weight). ‖ MILIT. Allongement *m.* (of fire). ‖ AVIAT. Sustentation *f.; lifting capacity*, portance. ‖ AGRIC. Arrachage *m.;* extraction en motte *f.* ‖ FAM. Démarquage, plagiat *m.* ‖ FAM. Chapardage *m.*

liftman ['liftmən] (pl. **liftmen**) n. Liftier, garçon d'ascenseur *m.*

ligament ['ligəmənt] n. MED. Ligament *m.*

ligamentous [,ligə'mentəs] adj. MED. Ligamenteux.

ligate [lai'geit] v. tr. MED. Ligaturer.

ligation [-ʃən] n. MED. Ligature *f.* (action).

ligature ['ligətʃuə*] n. Lien *m.* (tie). ‖ MED., GRAMM. Ligature *f.* ‖ MUS. Liaison *f.* (line, notes).
— v. tr. Lier. ‖ MED. Ligaturer.

light [lait] adj. Léger (burden); plat (purse); léger, fin (rain); léger (wind). ‖ MILIT. Léger (infantry, tank). ‖ CH. DE F. Haut le pied (engine); léger (rail); à voie droite (railway). ‖ ARCHIT., ARTS. Léger (drawing, tracery). ‖ MED. Léger (meal, sleep). ‖ CULIN. Léger (cake, wine). ‖ FIN. Au-dessous du poids (coin); léger (tax). ‖ MUS. Léger (music); *light opera*, opérette. ‖ GRAMM. Non (or) sous-accentué (syllable). ‖ FIG. Léger, frivole (conduct, woman); léger (error, punishment, sound); léger, agile (foot); délicat (hand, touch); léger, insouciant (heart, spirits); léger, amusant, distrayant (reading); léger, libre (talk); facile, peu fatigant (work); *to be light on one's feet*, avoir la démarche légère, être leste; *to make light of*, faire peu de

cas de, traiter de broutille (or) de bagatelle. ‖ FAM. *Light in the head,* au cerveau creux. ‖ **Light-armed,** adj. MILIT. Portant des armes légères. ‖ **Light-fingered,** adj. Aux doigts agiles (or) longs (fam.) ; *light-fingered people,* les pickpockets. ‖ **Light-handed,** adj. A la main légère ; peu chargé. ‖ **Light-handedness,** n. Délicatesse (or) légèreté (*f.*) du toucher. ‖ **Light-headed,** adj. MED. Délirant ; FIG. Etourdi (scatter-brained) ; divagant (wandering). ‖ **Light-hearted,** adj. Au cœur léger, insouciant. ‖ **Light-heeled,** adj. Leste, au pied léger. ‖ **Light-horseman,** n. MILIT. Soldat (*m.*) de la cavalerie légère. ‖ **Light-minded,** adj. Léger, frivole, volage. ‖ **Light-o'-love,** n. Femme légère *f.* ‖ **Light-weight,** n. SPORTS. Poids léger *m.* ; U. S. FAM. Personne (*f.*) de peu de poids ; petite bière *f.* — adv. Légèrement. ‖ CH. DE F. A vide (truck) ; *to run light,* aller haut le pied (engine). ‖ FIG. Sans peine.
— v. tr. Descendre. (See ALIGHT.) ‖ **To light into,** U. S. FAM. Tomber sur (s.o.) ; attaquer (one's work). ‖ **To light out,** U. S. FAM. Décamper.

light n. Lumière *f.* (*of,* de) ; *point of light,* point lumineux. ‖ Jour *m.* (daylight) ; *it is light,* il fait jour. ‖ Jour, éclairage *m. ; against the light,* à contre-jour ; *to give a bad light,* éclairer mal. ‖ Lumière *f.* (of an artificial source) ; lampe, lanterne, bougie *f. ; to bring in a light,* apporter de la lumière ; *to show s.o. a light,* éclairer qqn. ‖ Flamme *f.* ; *a light for a cigarette,* du feu pour allumer une cigarette. ‖ Feu *m. ; Bengal light,* feux de Bengale. ‖ ARCHIT. Jour *m.* ; fenêtre *f.* (window) ; vitre *f.* (windowpane) ; *pavement light,* dalle de verre. ‖ ARTS. Jour, éclairage *m. ; light and shade,* ombres et lumières, clair-obscur. ‖ MUS. *Lights and shades,* nuances. ‖ AUTOM., NAUT. Feu *m.* ‖ MILIT. *Lights out,* extinction des feux. ‖ ELECTR. Lumière, électricité *f.* ‖ PHYS. *Light wave,* onde lumineuse. ‖ COMM. *Advertising lights,* enseignes lumineuses. ‖ FIG. Lumière *f.* ; jour, éclairage *m.* (aspect) ; *in an unfavourable light,* sous un jour défavorable. ‖ FIG. Eclaircissement, jour *m.* (enlightenment) ; lumière, élucidation *f.* (illumination) ; connaissances, lumières *f. pl.* (knowledge) ; *a shining light,* une des lumières du temps ; *to shed light on,* éclairer, mettre en lumière. ‖ FAM. *To see the red light,* flairer le danger ; *to stand in one's own light,* rester dans son coin (or) dans l'ombre. ‖ **Light-buoy,** n. NAUT. Photophore *m.* ‖ **Light-shell,** n. MILIT. Obus éclairant *m.* ‖ **Light-year,** n. PHYS. Année de lumière *f.*
— adj. Eclairé, clair. ‖ Pâle, clair (colour).
— v. tr. (98). Allumer (a candle, fire). ‖ Eclairer (a room, street, s.o.) ; éclairer le chemin de (a plane, s.o.) ; *to light the way for,* éclairer (s.o.). ‖ FIG. Eclairer, illuminer (s.o.'s eyes, face). ‖ **To light up,** allumer.
— v. intr. Allumer, donner de la lumière. ‖ Prendre, s'allumer (match, fire). ‖ S'éclairer, s'illuminer (eyes, face). ‖ **To light up,** s'allumer ; FIG. S'éclairer.

lighted [-id] adj. Allumé (cigarette). ‖ Eclairé (street).

lighten [-ŋ] v. tr. Alléger (lit. and fig.).
— v. intr. S'alléger (lit. and fig.)

lighten [-ŋ] v. tr. Eclairer (a room). ‖ Eclaircir (a colour). ‖ FIG. Eclairer (s.o.'s face).
— v. intr. S'éclairer, s'éclaircir (sky). ‖ FIG. S'éclairer, s'illuminer (eyes).
— v. impers. Faire des éclairs.

lighter [-ə*] n. Allumeur *m.* (person). ‖ Allumoir *m.* (thing). ‖ Briquet *m. ; cigar-lighter,* allume-cigare.

lighter ['laitə*] n. NAUT. Chaland *m. ;* gabare *f.*
— v. tr. NAUT. Transporter par chaland, bateler

lighterage [-ridӡ] n. NAUT. Transport par chaland, gabarage, acconage *m.*

lighthouse ['laithaus] n. NAUT. Phare *m.* ‖ **Lighthouse-lamp,** n. Fanal *m.*

lighting [-iŋ] n. Allumage *m.* (of a lamp). ‖ Eclairage *m.* (of streets). ‖ ELECTR. *Lighting engineer,* éclairagiste. ‖ THEATR. *Lighting effects,* jeux de lumière. ‖ ARTS. Eclairage, jour *m.* (of a picture).

lightly [-li] adv. Légèrement. ‖ Joyeusement, d'un cœur léger (merrily). ‖ A la légère, avec légèreté (carelessly). ‖ De gaieté de cœur, capricieusement (wantonly).

lightness [-nis] n. Légèreté *f.* (lit. and fig.).

lightning [-niŋ] n. Eclair *m. ;* foudre *f.* ‖ **Lightning-arrester,** n. Parafoudre *m.* ‖ **Lightning-bug,** n. ZOOL. U. S. Luciole *f.* (See FIREFLY.) ‖ **Lightning-conductor** (or) **-rod,** n. Paratonnerre *m.*
— adj. Eclair (speed, raid, visit) ; surprise (strike) ; *lightning chess,* blitz.

lights [laits] n. CULIN. Mou *m.* (of veal).

lightship ['laitʃip] n. NAUT. Bâtiment-balise, bateau-feu (or) -phare *m.*

lightsome [-səm] adj. Lumineux.

lightsome [-səm] adj. Agile, leste, léger (nimble). ‖ Gracieux, pimpant (lively). ‖ Gai, enjoué (cheerful).

lightwood [-wud] n. Bois résineux (or) sec et inflammable *m.*

ligneous ['liɡniəs] adj. Ligneux.

lignification [ˌliɡnifiˈkeiʃən] n. Lignification *f.*

lignify ['liɡnifai] v. tr. (2). Lignifier.
— v. intr. Se lignifier.

lignite ['liɡnait] n. Lignite *m.*

lignum vitae ['liɡnəmˈvaiti:] n. BOT. U. S. Gaïac *m.*

Ligures [liˈɡjuəri:z] n. pl. GEOGR. Ligures *m. pl.*

likable ['laikəbl] adj. Sympathique (person) ; attirant, plaisant (thing).

like [laik] v. tr. Aimer, avoir de la sympathie pour, être attiré par (s.o.). ‖ Aimer, avoir du goût pour (sth.). ‖ Aimer, se satisfaire de, se plaire à, trouver du plaisir (or) de la satisfaction à ; *I should like a dozen pencils,* je voudrais une douzaine de crayons ; *I'd like a word with you,* j'aurais un mot à vous dire. † Plaire à.
— v. intr. Aimer, vouloir ; *as much as ever you like,* tant que vous voudrez ; *as you like,* comme vous voudrez, comme il vous plaira, à votre gré ; *do what you like with it,* faites-en ce qui vous conviendra.
— n. Goût *m.* ; préférence *f.* ‖ Inclinations *f. pl.*

like adj. Pareil, semblable, similaire, analogue, même, tel (similar). ‖ Equivalent, égal, semblable (equal). ‖ Disposé à ; *to feel like sleeping,* avoir envie de dormir. ‖ MATH., ELECTR. Semblable. ‖ **Like-minded,** adj. Du même avis.
— conj. FAM. Comme ; *do it like I tell you,* fais ça comme je t'ai dit. ‖ U. S., FAM. Comme si ; *he acted like he didn't know me,* il a fait semblant de ne pas me connaître.
— adv. Comme ; *a man like you,* un homme comme vous ; *to be nothing like so rich,* être loin d'être aussi riche ; *to work like mad,* travailler comme un possédé. ‖ FAM. Apparemment (likely) ; *that's something like,* voilà quelque chose de bien.
— prep. Comme ; *it looks like a fine day tomorrow,* demain paraît devoir être beau, il y a des chances pour qu'il fasse beau demain ; *something like twenty pounds,* quelque vingt livres ; *that's just like him,* ça lui ressemble bien, c'est bien de lui, le voilà bien ; *to be* (or) *look like,* ressembler à (s.o., sth.) ; *to sing like a bird,* chanter comme un oiseau.
— n. Semblable, pareil *s. ; and the like,* et le reste du même acabit ; *the like of him,* son pareil ; *to do the like,* en faire autant.

likelihood [-lihud] n. Vraisemblance, apparence *f. ; in all likelihood,* selon toute probabilité.

likely [-li] adj. Probable, vraisemblable, possible. ‖

Vraisemblable, digne de créance (credible). ‖ Susceptible, dans le cas (for, to, de) ; de nature (to, à) ; *she was not likely to succeed*, elle avait peu de chances de succès. ‖ Propre, approprié, convenable (for, à) [suitable]. ‖ Prometteur, doué, capable (promising).
— adv. *Very likely*, très probablement, vraisemblablement, à peu près certainement.

liken [-n] v. tr. Comparer (to, à) ; *to liken oneself to*, s'assimiler à.

likeness [-nis] n. Apparence *f.*; *in the likeness of a swan*, sous la forme (or) l'aspect d'un cygne. ‖ Ressemblance *f.* (to, avec) ; *to catch a likeness*, attraper la ressemblance. ‖ Portrait *m.*

likewise [-waiz] adv. De la même manière, de même, pareillement. ‖ Aussi, en outre, de plus (moreover).

liking ['laikiŋ] n. Goût, penchant *m.*; prédilection *f.* (for, pour) [sth.]. ‖ Goût, attrait, penchant *m.*; sympathie, amitié, affection, inclination *f.* (for, pour) [sth.]. ‖ Goût, gré *m.* (taste).

lilac ['lailək] n. Bot. Lilas *m.*
— adj. Lilas (colour).

lilaceous [,lili'eiʃəs] adj. Bot. Liliacé.

Lilliputian [,lili'pju:ʃiən] adj., n. Lilliputien *s.*

lilt [lilt] n. Chant rythmé *m.* (song). ‖ Cadence *f.* (rhythm).
— v. tr., intr. Chanter en rythmant.

lily ['lili] n. Bot. Lis *m.*; *lily of the valley*, muguet. ‖ Blas. Fleur (*f.*) de lis. ‖ U. S. Fam. Gogo *m.* ‖ **Lily-iron**, n. Sports. Harpon à dard mobile *m.* ‖ **Lily-livered**, adj. Fam. Froussard ; trouillard ; qui a les foies (pop.).
— adj. Blanc comme un lis, lilial.

limb [lim] n. Math., Astron. Limbe *m.*

limb n. Med. Membre *m.* ‖ Bot. Branche *f.*; rameau *m.* ‖ Geogr. Contrefort *m.* (of mountains). ‖ Gramm. Membre *m.* (of a sentence). ‖ Eccles. Bras *m.* (of a cross). ‖ Fam. Polisson *m.* (child); *limb of the law*, flic. ‖ Fam. *Out on a limb*, sur la corde raide.
— v. tr. Med. Démembrer, mutiler (body). ‖ Bot. Ébrancher (tree).

limbed [-d] adj. Membré.

limber ['limbə*] n. Milit. Avant-train *m.* (of a gun carriage).
— v. tr. Milit. Accrocher à l'avant-train.

limber adj. Leste, agile, preste, souple (person); souple, flexible (thing).
— v. tr. Assouplir ; *to limber up*, faire des exercices d'assouplissement.

limbo ['limbou] n. Eccles. Limbes *m. pl.* ‖ Fam. Oubli *m.* (oblivion) ; oubliette *f.* (prison).

lime [laim] n. Bot. Limon *m.*; lime, limette *f.*

lime n. Bot. Tilleul *m.* (linden). ‖ **Lime-tree**, n. Bot. Tilleul *m.*

lime n. Glu *f.* (birdlime). ‖ Chim. Chaux *f.* ‖ **Lime-burner**, n. Chaufournier *m.* ‖ **Lime-kiln**, n. Four (*m.*) à chaux. ‖ **Lime-twig**, n. Gluau *m.* ‖ **Lime-wash**, n. Lait (*m.*) de chaux ; badigeon *m.*
— v. tr. Prendre à la glu (birds) ; engluer (twigs). ‖ Agric. Chauler.

limelight ['laimlait] n. Lumière oxhydrique *f.* ‖ Theatr. Rampe *f.* ‖ Fig. *In the limelight*, en vedette, très en vue, au premier plan.

limen ['laimən] n. Philos. Seuil *m.*

limerick ['limərik] n. Poème humoristique et parfois scabreux en cinq vers *m.*

limestone ['laimstoun] n. Calcaire *m.*; castine *f.*

limit ['limit] n. Limite, borne *f.* (see BOUND) [lit. and fig.]. ‖ Fam. *He's the limit*, il est unique ; *that's the limit*, c'est le bouquet.
— v. tr. Limiter.

limitary [-əri] adj. Limité (limited). ‖ Servant de limite, limitatif (restrictive). ‖ Limitrophe, situé à la limite (border-line).

limitation [,limi'teiʃən] n. Limitation *f.* ‖ Restriction *f.* ‖ Jur. Prescription *f.*; *time limitation*, péremption.

limitative ['limitətiv], **limiting** [-iŋ] adj. Limitatif ; *limiting angle*, angle limite.

limited [-id] adj. Limité. ‖ Restreint, limité (edition). ‖ Fin. Anonyme, à responsabilité limitée (company) ; *limited partnership*, société en commandite. ‖ Ch. de F. Rapide ; U. S. de luxe (train).

limitless [-lis] adj. Illimité, sans limite.

limitrophe ['limitrouf] adj. Limitrophe (to, de).

limn [lim] v. tr. † Enluminer.

limner ['limnə*] n. Arts. Enlumineur *m.*

limnology [lim'nɔlədʒi] n. Limnologie *f.*

limousine ['limuzi:n] n. Autom. Limousine *f.*

limp [limp] v. intr. Boitiller, clocher, claudiquer ; *to limp along*, s'en aller en clopinant.
— n. Med. Boiterie, claudication *f.*

limp adj. Mou, flasque. ‖ Techn. Souple (binding). ‖ Fam. Mou, abattu ; *as limp as a rag*, comme une chiffe.

limpet ['limpit] n. Zool. Lepas *m.*; patelle *f.* ‖ Fam. Crampon *m.*

limpid ['limpid] adj. Limpide.

limpidity [lim'piditi] n. Limpidité *f.*

limpidly ['limpidli] adv. Limpidement.

limply ['limpli] adv. Mollement.

limpness [-nis] n. Mollesse *f.*

limy ['laimi] adj. Gluant, englué (sticky). ‖ Chim. Calcaire.

linage ['lainidʒ] n. Nombre (*m.*) de lignes (number) ; paiement (*m.*) à la ligne (payment).

linchpin ['linʃpin] n. Techn. Esse, cheville (*f.*) d'essieu.

linctus ['liŋktəs] n. Med. Sirop (*m.*) contre la toux, antitussique *m.*

lindane ['lindein] n. Chim., Agric. Lindane *m.* (pesticide).

linden ['lindən] n. Bot. Tilleul *m.* (See LIME.)

line [lain] n. Ligne *f*, trait *m.* (by a pencil, pen) ; ligne *f.* (in writing) ; *drop me a line*, envoyez-moi un mot. ‖ Vers *m.* (verse). ‖ Ligne *f.*; contour *m.* (outline). ‖ Ligne, rangée *f.* (row) ; *in a line*, à la file ; *in line*, en rang ; U. S. *to stand in line*, faire la queue ; *to toe the line*, se mettre en ligne. ‖ Ligne *f.*; alignement *m.*; *to fall into line*, s'aligner. ‖ Ligne, limite, délimitation *f.*; *to draw the line*, faire la démarcation, mettre une limite. ‖ Ligne, série, suite, liste *f.* (series). ‖ Ligne, coupe *f.*; mouvement *m.* (of a dress). ‖ Ligne *f.* (at the phone). ‖ Archit. Cordeau *m.*; *building line*, alignement (of the street). ‖ Techn. Tuyauterie *f.* (pipe). ‖ Electr. Ligne, canalisation *f.* ‖ Phys. Raie *f.* (of the spectrum). ‖ Math. Ligne *f.* ‖ Ch. de F. Ligne, voie *f.* ‖ Autom. *Line of route*, itinéraire. ‖ Aviat. Ligne *f.* ‖ Naut. Cordage *m.*; amarre *f.* (cord) ; ligne *f.*; *ship of the line*, vaisseau de ligne ; *shipping line*, compagnie de navigation. ‖ Milit. Ligne *f.*; *front line*, première ligne. ‖ Geogr. Ligne *f.*; équateur *m.*; *State line*, ligne frontière d'un État. ‖ Arts. Cimaise *f.* (cyma) ; ligne *f.* (in a picture). ‖ Theatr. Pl. Rôle, texte *m.* ‖ Jur. Ligne, lignée *f.* (lineage). ‖ Comm. Article *m.* ‖ Sports. Ligne *f.* (in fishing). ‖ Med. Trait *m.* (feature) ; ride *f.*; pli *m.* (on the forehead) ; ligne *f.* (of the hand). ‖ U. S. Queue, file d'attente *f.* ‖ Fig. Ligne *f.* (of conduct); *broad lines*, grandes lignes. ‖ Fig. Directive *f.*; *to work on the lines of*, travailler sous la conduite de. ‖ Fig. Harmonie *f.*; *to bring into line*, remettre d'aplomb (or) d'accord. ‖ Fig. Partie, spécialité, branche *f.*; rayon *m.*; *that's right in my line*, c'est tout à fait dans mes cordes ; *what's your line?*, que faites-vous ? ‖ Fig. Pl. Destin *m.*; situation, condition *f.*; *hard lines*, déveine, malchance. ‖ Fam. *All along the line*, sur toute la ligne, d'un bout à l'autre ; *to give s.o. line enough*, lâcher la bride à qqn ; *to hold the line*, tenir le coup ; *to toe the line*, rentrer dans l'obéissance

(or) le rang. ‖ Fam. Baratin *m.; to shoot a line,* galéger. ‖ **Line-drawing,** n. Arts. Dessin au trait *m.* ‖ **Line-engraving,** n. Arts. Taille-douce *f.* ‖ **Line-fishing,** n. Sports. Pêche à la ligne *f.* ‖ **Line-shooter,** n. Fam. Esbrouffeur, galégeur *m.* ‖ **Line-shooting,** n. U. S. Galéjade, tartarinade *f.* ‖ **Line-spacer,** n. Interligneur *m.* ‖ **Line-up,** n. U. S. Sports. Personnel *m.;* composition *f.* (of a team).
— v. tr. Rayer, régler, tracer des lignes (or) des traits sur. ‖ S'aligner le long de, longer en faisant la haie. ‖ Med. Sillonner, rider (face). ‖ **To line up,** Milit. Aligner.
— v. intr. **To line up,** s'aligner; U. S. faire la queue.
line v. tr. Doubler (a coat); fourrer (*with,* de) [a glove]. ‖ Tapisser, garni (*with,* de) [a trunk]. ‖ Milit. Chemiser (a gun). ‖ Arch. Revêtir (a wall). ‖ Techn. Tuber (a well). ‖ Naut. Renforcer (a sail). ‖ Fam. *To line one's pocket,* faire sa pelote, se garnir les poches; *to line one's stomach,* se caler les côtes, se remplir le jabot.
line v. tr. Zool. Couvrir (a bitch).
lineage ['linidʒ] n. Lignage *m.; lignée *f.
lineal ['liniəl] adj. En ligne directe.
lineament ['liniəmənt] n. Trait *m.*
linear ['liniə*] adj. Linéaire.
lineation [ˌlini'eiʃən] n. Lignes *f. pl.; tracé *m.
lineman ['lainmən] (pl. **linemen**) n. Electr. Poseur (*m.*) de lignes. ‖ Ch. de F. Garde-ligne *m.*
linen ['linin] n. Linge *m.; bed linen,* literie. ‖ Toile *f.* (cloth). ‖ **Linen-basket,** n. Panier à linge *m.* ‖ **Linen-closet,** n. U. S. Armoire (*f.*) à linge. ‖ **Linen-draper,** n. Comm. Marchand (*m.*) de nouveautés; calicot *m.* (fam.). ‖ **Linen-drapery,** n. Comm. Nouveautés *f. pl.;* blanc *m.* (drapery); lingerie *f.* (underwear). ‖ **Linen-room,** n. Lingerie *f.* ‖ **Linen-show,** n. Comm. Exposition (*f.*) de blanc. ‖ **Linen-warehouse,** n. Comm. Magasin de blanc *m.*
— adj. De lin (thread); *linen cloth,* toile de fil.
linenette [linə'net] n. Comm. Toile coton, lustrine *f.*
liner ['lainə*] n. Naut. Paquebot, navire (*m.*) de ligne. ‖ Aviat. Avion de transport *m.*
liner n. Doubleur *s.* (of coats). ‖ Techn. Manchon (or) revêtement intérieur *m.* ‖ Milit. Chemise *f.*
linesman ['lainzmən] (pl. **linesmen**) n. Electr. Poseur (*m.*) de lignes. ‖ Milit. Soldat (*m.*) de la ligne; lignard *m.* (fam.). ‖ Sports. Arbitre (*m.*) de ligne (or) de touche.
ling [liŋ] n. Zool. Lingue *f.* ‖ Culin. Merluche *f.,* merlu *m.*
ling n. Bot. Bruyère, callune *f.*
linger ['liŋgə*] v. intr. S'attarder, traîner (to delay); lambiner, flâner (to loiter). ‖ Persister (doubt, hope, use). ‖ **To linger on,** traîner. ‖ **To linger over,** s'attarder sur, prolonger.
lingerer [-rə*] n. Retardataire *s.* ‖ Lambin, traînard *s.*
lingerie ['lɛ̃:nʒəri:] n. Comm. Lingerie *f.* (women's).
lingering ['liŋgəriŋ] adj. Long, soutenu, prolongé (look). ‖ Med. Chronique (disease); lent (death). ‖ Fig. Persistant (hope).
lingo ['liŋgou] n. Gramm. Jargon *m.* ‖ Fam. Baragouin *m.*
lingua franca ['liŋgwə'fræŋka] n. † Lingua franca *f.,* sabir *m.* (spoken in the Levant). ‖ Gramm. Langue commune (ou) véhiculaire (ou) de relation *f.* (providing mutual understanding).
lingual ['liŋgwəl] adj. Med., Gramm. Lingual.
— n. Gramm. Linguale *f.*
linguist [-gwist] n. Linguiste *s.*
linguistic [liŋ'gwistik] adj. Linguistique.
linguistically [-əli] adv. Linguistiquement.
linguistics [-s] n. sg. Linguistique *f.*
liniment ['linimənt] n. Med. Liniment, baume *m.*
lining ['lainiŋ] n. Réglage, lignage *m.*
lining n. Doublure *f.* (of a coat); coiffe *f.* (of a hat).

Techn. Doublage, coffrage, revêtement intérieur *m.;* fourrure *f.* ‖ Fam. *A good lining for the stomach,* un bon calage de côtes.
link [liŋk] n. Anneau, chaînon, maillon *m.* (of a chain). ‖ Maille *f.* (of knitting work). ‖ Pl. Boutons (*m. pl.*) de manchette; jumelles *f. pl.* (cuff-links). ‖ Techn. Coulisse; tige (*f.*) d'assemblage. ‖ Autom. Bielle (*f.*) d'accouplement. ‖ Fig. Lien *m.;* liaison *f.; weak link,* point faible.
— v. tr. Lier, joindre, relier, réunir (*to, with,* à); *to link arms,* se donner le bras. ‖ Fig. Unir, relier, rattacher.
— v. intr. **To link in** (or) **up,** se lier, s'unir, se joindre (*with,* à). ‖ **To link on,** se lier, se joindre, s'attacher (*to,* à).
linkage [-idʒ] n. Chaînons *m. pl.* ‖ Autom. Timonerie *f.* ‖ Fig. Liaison *f.*
linking [-iŋ] n. Union, liaison *f.* ‖ Jur. *Linking arrangements,* apparentements (in politics).
links [-s] n. pl. Sports. Terrain de golf *m.* ‖ Geogr. Etendue sablonneuse *f.*
linnet ['linit] n. Zool. Linotte *f.*
lino ['lainou], **linoleum** [li'nouliəm] n. Lino, linoléum *m.*
linocut ['lainou,kʌt] n. Arts. Linogravure *f.*
Linotype ['lainotaip] n. Techn. Linotype *f.*
linotyper ['lainotaipə*] n. Techn. Linotypiste *s.*
linseed ['linsi:d] n. Bot., Med. Graine (*f.*) de lin; *linseed cake,* tourteau; *linseed meal, oil,* farine, huile de lin.
linsey-woolsey ['linzi'wulzi] n. Tiretaine *f.*
lint [lint] n. Med. Charpie *f.*
lintel ['lintl] n. Arch. Linteau *m.*
liny ['laini] adj. Strié, rayé (surface). ‖ Med. Ridé (face). ‖ Arts. Linéaire.
lion ['laiən] n. Zool., Astron., Blas. Lion *m.* ‖ Fig. Lion, vedette *f.* ‖ **Lion-hearted,** adj. Au cœur de lion.
lioness [-is] n. Zool. Lionne *f.*
lionet [-it] n. Zool. Lionceau *m.*
lionize [-aiz] v. tr. Traiter en vedette, mettre en vue (or) au premier plan.
lip [lip] n. Med. Lèvre *f.* (of mouth, wound). ‖ Zool. Babine *f.* ‖ Culin. Bec *m.* (of a saucepan); bord *m.* (of a vessel). ‖ Fam. Impertinence, insolence *f.* ‖ Loc. *To keep a stiff upper lip,* relever la tête, tenir le coup; *to lick one's lips,* se lécher les babines; *to open one's lips,* desserrer les dents, ouvrir la bouche; *to screw up one's lips,* pincer les lèvres. ‖ **Lip-language** (or) **-reading,** n. Lecture (*f.*) sur les lèvres. ‖ **Lip-read,** v. tr. Lire sur les lèvres. ‖ **Lip-service,** n. Eccles. Dévotion (*f.*) des lèvres; Fig. *To pay lip-service to the cause of peace,* servir en paroles la cause de la paix. ‖ **Lip-speaking,** n. Med. Phonomimie *f.*
— v. tr. (1). Effleurer des lèvres, tremper les lèvres dans (a cup). ‖ Baigner (the coast). ‖ Mus. Emboucher (a trumpet). ‖ Fig. Laisser tomber du bout des lèvres (a word).
lipid(e) ['laipid] n. Med. Lipide *m.*
lipped [-t] adj. Aux lèvres (person). ‖ A bec (pitcher).
lipsalve [-sɑ:v] n. Med. Pommade (*f.*) rosat. ‖ Fig. Pommade *f.*
lipstick [-stik] n. Rouge (*m.*) à lèvres, bâton de rouge *m.*
liquate [li'kweit] v. tr. Techn. Liquater.
liquefaction [ˌlikwi'fækʃən] n. Liquéfaction *f.*
liquefiable [ˌlikwi'faiəbl] adj. Liquéfiable.
liquefy ['likwifai] v. (2). Liquéfier.
— v. intr. Se liquéfier.
liquescent [li'kwesnt] adj. Liquescent.
liqueur [li'kjuə*] n. Liqueur *f.; liqueur wine,* vin de liqueur.
liquid ['likwid] adj. Phys. Liquide (air, state). ‖ Mus. Clair (sound). ‖ Fin. Disponible (assets);

liquide (debt). ‖ GRAMM. Liquide (consonant). ‖ FIG. Limpide (appearance); flottant (conviction).
— n. Liquide *m*. ‖ GRAMM. Liquide *f*.
liquidate [-eit] v. tr., intr. Liquider. ‖ FIN. Fixer, déterminer.
liquidation [ˌlikwi'deiʃən] n. Liquidation *f*.
liquidator ['likwideitə*] n. FIN. Liquidateur *m*.
liquidity [li'kwiditi] n. Liquidité *f*. ‖ FIG. Limpidité *f*.
liquidness ['likwidnis] n. PHYS., FIN. Liquidité *f*.
liquor ['likə*] n. Alcool, spiritueux *m.; liquor question*, la question de l'alcool; *liquor trade*, le commerce des boissons. ‖ CHIM. *Gas liquor*, eau ammoniacale. ‖ MED. Solution *f*. ‖ FAM. *In liquor*, dans les vignes du Seigneur.
— v. tr. MED. Traiter par une solution. ‖ *To liquor up*, FAM. U. S. Payer un coup à boire à.
— v. intr. *To liquor up*, FAM. U. S. Chopiner.
liquorice ['likəris] n. BOT., MED. Réglisse *f*.
liquorish ['likəriʃ] adj. FAM. Porté sur la bouteille.
lira ['liərə] (pl. **lire** [-i]) n. FIN. Lire *f*.
lisp [lisp] v. intr. Zézayer, bléser, zozoter. ‖ FAM. Gazouiller (child).
— v. tr. Dire en zézayant.
— n. Zézayement, blèsement *m.; to have a lisp*, zézayer. ‖ FIG. Murmure *m*. (of leaves, stream).
lisping [-iŋ] adj. Blèse. ‖ FIG. Gazouillant, murmurant.
lissom(e) ['lisəm] adj. Souple, flexible. (See LIMBER.) ‖ Agile, leste (nimble).
list [list]. See LISTEN.
list v. tr. † Vouloir, aimer (to choose).
— v. impers. Plaire (*to*, à).
list n. NAUT. Bande *f*. ‖ ARCHIT. Inclinaison *f*.
— v. intr. NAUT. Donner de la bande. ‖ ARCHIT. Pencher.
list n. Lisière *f*. (of cloth); bourrelet *m*. (of door). ‖ Liste *f*. (of names, numbers, words). ‖ Index, catalogue, tableau *m*. ‖ JUR. Rôle *m.; black list*, liste noire. ‖ FIN. *Assessment list*, rôle des impôts; *official list*, cote officielle. ‖ COMM. Bordereau *m.; list price*, prix courant. ‖ MILIT., NAUT. Annuaire *m.; on the active list*, en activité. ‖ CULIN. *Wine list*, carte des vins.
— v. tr. Mettre une lisière à (a cloth); mettre des bourrelets à (a door). ‖ Porter sur une liste (or) un tableau (names); cataloguer, énumérer (things).
— v. intr. † MILIT. Enrôler.
listel ['listl̩] n. ARCHIT. Listel *m*.
listen ['lisn̩] v. intr. Ecouter; *to cry to all who will listen*, crier à qui veut l'entendre. ‖ *To listen for*, chercher à entendre, essayer d'entendre. ‖ *To listen to*, écouter; *to listen in to*, écouter, suivre (a radio programme, a telephone conversation).
listener ['lisnə*] n. Auditeur *m.;* auditrice *f.; to be a good listener*, avoir l'art d'écouter. ‖ Ecouteur *s*. (pej.).
listening [-iŋ] n. Ecoute *f*. ‖ **Listening-post**, n. MILIT. Poste (*m*.) d'écoute.
listless ['listlis] adj. Apathique. ‖ Indifférent (*of*, à).
listlessness [-nis] n. Apathie, inertie, indifférence *f*.
lists [lists] n. pl. †. Lice *f.;* champ clos *m*.
lit [lit]. See LIGHT. ‖ **Lit-up**, adj. Eclairé, illuminé; U. S. POP. Allumé, éméché, paf, parti, gai.
litany ['litəni] n. ECCLES. Litanie *f*.
liter ['li:tə*] n. U. S. See LITRE.
literacy ['litərəsi] n. Fait (*m*.) de savoir lire et écrire.
literal [-əl] adj. Littéral (sense, translation). ‖ De lettre; *literal error*, faute d'impression. ‖ FIG. Terre à terre, prosaïque (mind); sans fard, cru (truth). ‖ **Literal-minded**, adj. Sans imagination, prosaïque.
— n. Coquille *f*. (misprint).
literalism [-əlizm̩] n. Littéralisme *m*.

literalist [-əlist] n. Personne (*f*.) qui prend tout à la lettre.
literality [ˌlitə'ræliti] n. Littéralité *f*.
literalize ['litərəlaiz] v. tr. Prendre à la lettre (to interpret). ‖ Traduire littéralement (to translate).
literally [-əli] adv. Littéralement, à la lettre. ‖ FAM. Littéralement, vraiment.
literary [-əri] adj. Littéraire (agent, property, style, word, work); de lettres (man).
literate [-it] adj. Sachant lire et écrire. ‖ † Lettré (erudite).
— n. ECCLES. Prêtre (*m*.) non diplômé de l'université.
literati [ˌlitə'rɑːti:] n. pl. Lettrés, gens (*m. pl.*) qui ont des lettres.
literature ['litərətʃə*] n. Littérature *f.;* œuvres littéraires *f. pl.* (writings). ‖ Carrière (*f*.) des lettres (profession). ‖ COMM. Documentation publicitaire; littérature *f*. (fam.).
litharge ['liθɑːdʒ] n. CHIM. Litharge *f*.
lithe [laið], **lithesome** [-səm] adj. Souple, flexible.
litheness [-nis] n. Souplesse *f*.
lithic ['liθik] adj. Lithique (industries). ‖ CHIM. Du lithium. ‖ MED. Lithiasique.
lithium ['liθiəm] n. CHIM. Lithium *m*.
lithochromy [ˌliθə'kroumi] n. Lithochromie *f*.
lithograph ['liθəgrɑːf] n. Lithographie *f*.
— v. tr. Lithographier.
lithographer [li'θɔgrəfə*] n. Lithographe *m*.
lithographic [ˌliθə'græfik] adj. Lithographique.
lithography [li'θɔgrəfi] n. Lithographie *f*.
lithopone ['liθəpoun] n. Lithopone *m*.
lithoprint [-print] v. tr. Lithographier.
— n. Livre lithographié *m*.
Lithuania [ˌliθju'einiə] n. GEOGR. Lituanie *f*.
Lithuanian [-ən] adj., n. GEOGR. Lituanien *s*.
litigant ['litigənt] adj. JUR. Litigant, plaidant.
— n. JUR. Plaideur *s*.
litigate [-eit] v. intr. JUR. Plaider.
— v. tr. Contester.
litigation [ˌliti'geiʃən] n. JUR. Litige *m*.
litigious [li'tidʒəs] adj. JUR. Procédurier (person); litigieux (point).
litigiously [-li] adv. D'une manière litigieuse. ‖ Par esprit procédurier (or) de chicane.
litigiousness [-nis] n. Esprit (*m*.) procédurier.
litmus ['litməs] n. CHIM. Tournesol *m*. ‖ **Litmus-paper**, n. Papier de tournesol *m*.
litotes ['laitoti:z] n. GRAMM. Litote *f*.
litre ['li:tə*] n. Litre *m*.
litter ['litə*] n. Litière *f*. (vehicle). ‖ MED. Civière *f*. (stretcher). ‖ ZOOL. Portée *f*. ‖ AGRIC. Litière *f*. ‖ FAM. Progéniture (*f*.) (children); ordures *f. pl.* (garbage); désordre, fouillis *m*. (jumble); production *f*. (literary works). ‖ **Litter-basket**, n. Corbeille (*f*.) à papier. ‖ **Litter-bin**, n. Boîte (*f*.) à ordures, poubelle *f*. ‖ **Litter-lout**, U. S. **litter-bug**, n. Personne (*f*.) qui jette des papiers sales, des détritus dans les lieux publics.
— v. tr. ZOOL. Mettre bas. ‖ AGRIC. Faire la litière de. ‖ FAM. Jeter le désordre dans (a room); encombrer, traîner sur (a table).
— v. intr. ZOOL. Mettre bas.
little ['litl̩] adj. Petit (child); *little ones*, les petits, les enfants. ‖ Petit (in amount, degree, size). [See SMALL.] ‖ Petit, bref, court (in distance, duration). ‖ Petit, faible (in force, importance). ‖ Peu de (in number); *a little money*, un peu d'argent; *little if any*, peu ou prou de; *little or no*, peu ou point de. ‖ ECCLES. Petit (hours, office). ‖ ASTRON. Petit (Bear). ‖ FIG. Petit, étroit, mesquin (mind).
— adv. Peu (not much). ‖ Guère, fort peu (not at all). ‖ *Little by little*, peu à peu, petit à petit; *a little*, un peu; *not a little*, beaucoup (amount); très (degree).
— n. Peu *m.; a little of*, un peu de; *the little he knows*, le peu qu'il sait. ‖ Peu de chose; *I had*

little to do with it, je n'y suis pas pour grand-chose ; *to make* (or) *think little of*, faire peu de cas de. ‖ Courte durée *f.; after, for a little*, après, pendant un petit moment ; *wait a little*, attendez quelques instants.

littleness [-nis] n. Petitesse. ‖ Fig. Mesquinerie, étroitesse, petitesse *f.*

littoral ['litərəl] n. Littoral *m.*
— adj. Du littoral. (See COASTAL.)

liturgical [li'tə:dʒikəl] adj. Eccles. Liturgique.

liturgics [-dʒiks] n. sg. Eccles. Liturgie *f.* (science).

liturgist [-dʒist] n. Eccles. Liturgiste *m.*

liturgy ['litədʒi] n. Eccles. Liturgie *f.* (ritual).

livable ['livəbl] adj. Logeable, habitable (house). ‖ Fig. Supportable (life, person) ; *livable with*, vivable (fam.) [person].

live [liv] v. Vivre (to be alive) ; vivre, durer (to remain alive) ; *the times we live in*, les temps qui courent. ‖ Vivre, mener une vie ; *to live well*, bien vivre ; *to live and let live*, ne pas s'occuper du voisin, se montrer tolérant. ‖ S'entretenir, subsister ; vivre (*by*, de [one's work] ; *on*, sur [one's capital] ; *on*, de [vegetables]) ; *to live on twenty pounds a month*, vivre avec vingt livres par mois. ‖ Habiter, loger, demeurer (*in*, dans) [see DWELL] ; habiter, cohabiter (*with*, avec) ; *to live together*, cohabiter, vivre en commun. ‖ Fig. Vivre, durer, persister (memory). ‖ **To live in**, coucher chez ses patrons, être à demeure. ‖ **To live on**, continuer à vivre ; Fig. Persister, vivre. ‖ **To live out**, ne pas être logé, coucher chez soi. ‖ **To live through**, vivre (difficult times) ; survivre à (a war). ‖ **To live up to**, vivre selon (one's ideals) ; remplir (one's promise).
— v. tr. Vivre, passer (one's life). ‖ Vivre (one's faith, a double life, a part) ; *to live a lie*, vivre dans le mensonge. ‖ **To live down**, faire oublier avec le temps (a lapse) ; surmonter à la longue (a sorrow).

live [laiv] adj. Vivant, en vie (alive). ‖ Ardent (coal) ; allumé (match) ; enflammé (spark). ‖ Vif, vivifiant (air) ; vif, brillant (colour). ‖ Techn. Tournant (axle) ; roulant (load) ; vif (steam) ; *live weight*, charge utile. ‖ Milit. Naturel (abatis) ; chargé (cartridge) ; non éclaté (shell). ‖ Electr. Electrisé, en charge, sous tension (conductor, wire). ‖ Radio. En direct (broadcast). ‖ Fig. D'actualité (question). ‖ Fam. *A live wire*, un type dynamique. ‖ **Livestock**, n. Agric. Bétail *m.* ; Jur. Cheptel *m.*

liveable ['livəbl] adj. See LIVABLE.

lived [-d] adj. A la vie ; *short-lived*, de vie courte, éphémère.

livelihood [-lihud] n. Vie, subsistance *f.* ; moyens (*m. pl.*) d'existence ; gagne-pain *m.*

liveliness [-linis] n. Vivacité, vie *f.* ; entrain *m.*

livelong ['livlɔŋ] adj. Tout le long de ; *the livelong day*, toute la sainte journée.

lively ['laivli] adj. Vivant (lifelike). ‖ Plein de vie, vigoureux (vigorous). ‖ Vivant, animé, plein d'entrain (animated). ‖ Joyeux, gai, enjoué (cheerful). ‖ Dégourdi, vif, pétillant (wide-awake). ‖ Vif, intense (vivid). ‖ Vif, vivifiant (brisk). ‖ Chim. Actif. ‖ Naut. Vif (boat). ‖ Sports. Elastique (ball) ; prompt à rebondir (ground). ‖ Fam. *To have a lively time*, en voir de vertes et de pas mûres.

liven [-ṇ] v. tr. Animer.
— v. intr. S'animer.

liver ['livə*] n. Vivant *m.* ; *plain liver*, homme rangé (or) de vie frugale. ‖ Viveur *m.* ; *fast, loose liver*, noceur, libertin.

liver n. Med. Foie *m.* ; *liver complaint*, maladie de foie. ‖ Culin. Foie *m.* ‖ Pop. *Liver wing*, aile droite (arm). ‖ **Liver-coloured**, adj. Brun-rouge (colour) ; Med. Jaune, olivâtre (complexion). ‖ **Liver-paste**, n. Culin. Mousse (*f.*) de foie gras. ‖ **Liver-pâté**, n. Culin. Pâté de foie *m.*

liverish [-riʃ] adj. Med. Hépatique.

livery ['livəri] n. † Ration *f.* (allowance). ‖ † Pension *f.* (for horses). ‖ Livrée *f.* (of a servant) ;

liveried, en livrée. ‖ Jur. Emancipation *f.* ; *livery of seisin*, saisine. ‖ **Livery-company**, n. † Corporation *f.* ‖ **Livery-stable**, n. Ecurie (*f.*) de louage.

livid ['livid] adj. Livide (*with*, de).

lividity [li'viditi], **lividness** ['lividnis] n. Lividité *f.*

living ['liviŋ] n. Vie, existence *f.* (state). ‖ Vie, subsistance *f.* ; moyens (*m. pl.*) d'existence (livelihood) ; *to make a living*, gagner sa vie (or) sa croûte (fam.). ‖ Culin. Nourriture *f.* ; *good living*, bonne chère. ‖ Eccles. Bénéfice *m.* ‖ Loc. *The living*, les vivants.
— adj. Vivant, en vie, vif (man) ; *living soul*, âme qui vive. ‖ D'être vivant ; *within living memory*, de mémoire d'homme. ‖ Vivant (image, language, picture). ‖ Vif (force, stream, water). ‖ Actif (institution). ‖ De vie (conditions). ‖ Suffisant pour vivre ; *living wage*, minimum vital, salaire de base. ‖ Ressemblant à la vie ; *living death*, mort vivante, vie pire que la mort. ‖ **Living-room**, n. Salle (*f.*) de séjour, living-room *m.* ‖ **Living-space**, n. Espace vital *m.*

Livy ['livi] n. Tite-Live.

lixiviate [lik'sivieit] v. tr. Techn. Lixivier.

lizard ['lizəd] n. Zool. Lézard *m.*

llama ['lɑ:mə] n. Zool. Lama *m.*

lo [lou] interj. † Las !, voici que.

loach [loutʃ] n. Zool. Loche *f.*

load [loud] n. Fardeau, faix *m.* ; charge *f.* (burden). ‖ Poids *m.* (weight). ‖ Charge *f.* ; chargement *m.* (of an animal, a vehicle). ‖ Naut. Cargaison *f.* ‖ Milit. Charge *f.* (of a gun). ‖ Techn. Puissance *f.* ; rendement *m.* (of an engine). ‖ Electr. Charge *f.* ‖ Fig. Poids *m.* (of cares) ; charge *f.* (of work). ; *to take a load off s.o.'s shoulders*, ôter un poids à qqn. ‖ Fam. Pl. Tas *m. pl.*, flopée *f.* (*of*, de). ‖ **Load-displacement**, n. Naut. Déplacement (*m.*) en charge. ‖ **Load-line**, n. Naut. Ligne de flottaison en charge *f.* ‖ **Load-shedding**, n. Electr. Délestage *m.*
— v. tr. Charger (an animal, a passenger, a person, a vehicle) ; *to load oneself with*, se charger de. ‖ Piper (the dice) ; plomber (a stick) ; alcooliser (the wine). ‖ Charger (a camera, a firearm). ‖ Fin. Majorer (a premium). ‖ Fig. Combler, couvrir, accabler (*with*, de). ‖ Fam. *To have a load on*, tenir une cuite.
— v. intr. Charger. ‖ Se charger (camera, gun).

loaded [-id] adj. Chargé (animal, gun, person, vehicle). ‖ Pipé (dice) ; plombé (stick). ‖ Med. Chargé (urine). ‖ Fin. Majoré (premium). ‖ U. S. Pop. Plein, saoul (drunk).

loader [-ə*] n. Chargeur *m.*

loading [-iŋ] n. Chargement *m.* ‖ Fin. Surprime *f.*

loadstar ['loudstɑ:*] n. Astron. Etoile polaire *f.*

loadstone [-stoun] n. Magnétite, pierre (*f.*) d'aimant.

loaf [louf] (pl. **loaves** [louvz]) n. Pain long *m.* ; miche *f.* ; *French loaf*, flûte. ‖ Pain de sucre *m.* (sugar-loaf).

loaf v. intr. Flânocher, traîner, baguenauder ; *to loaf about*, battre le pavé ; traîner ses guêtres.
— v. tr. *To loaf away the time*, passer son temps à traînailler.
— n. Flânerie *f.* ; baguenaudage *m.*

loafer [-ə*] n. Fainéant, clampin, baguenaudier, traînard *m.* (idler). ‖ Rôdeur, voyou *m.* (rascal). ‖ U. S. Mocassins *m. pl.* ; chaussures (*f. pl.*) de marche.

loam [loum] n. Agric. Terreau *m.* ‖ Geol., Techn. Glaise, argile, potée *f.* ‖ Archit. Torchis *m.*
— v. tr. Archit. Torcher.

loamy [-i] adj. Agric. Gras. ‖ Geol. Argileux.

loan [loun] n. Prêt *m.* ; *loan on trust*, prêt d'honneur ; on *loan*, à titre de prêt. ‖ Fin. Emprunt *m.* ‖ **Loan-bank**, n. Crédit municipal *m.* ‖ **Loan-collection**, n. Exposition (*f.*) d'objets prêtés. ‖ **Loan-**

office, n. FIN. Bureau de prêt (or) d'emprunt *m.* ‖ **Loan-society**, n. FIN. Société (*f.*) de crédit. ‖ **Loan-word**, n. GRAMM. Mot d'emprunt *m.* — v. tr. U. S. Prêter.

loath [louθ] adj. Répugnant, peu enclin (*to,* à); *nothing loath,* bien volontiers.

loathe [louð] v. tr. Avoir de l'aversion (or) de la répulsion (or) du dégoût pour; détester.

loathing [-iŋ] n. Répugnance, répulsion *f.*

loathsome [-səm] adj. Répugnant, repoussant, dégoûtant.

loathsomeness [-səmnis] n. Caractère répugnant *m.*

loaves [louvz]. See LOAF.

lob [lɔb] v. intr. (1). Se traîner, avancer d'un pas lourd. — v. tr. SPORTS. Lober (in tennis). — n. SPORTS. Lob *m.* (in tennis).

lobate ['loubeit] adj. BOT. Lobé.

lobby ['lɔbi] n. Couloir, corridor, vestibule *m.* ‖ JUR. Couloir *m.;* Salle (*f.*) des pas perdus (in Parliament). ‖ Lobby *m.,* groupe (*m.*) de pression. — v. tr. Faire pression sur (a person); faire passer (a bill). — v. intr. Faire pression.

lobbyist [-ist] n. Membre (*m.*) d'un lobby (or) d'un groupe de pression.

lobe [loub] n. MED. Lobe *m.*

lobectomy [lou'bektəmi] n. MED. Lobectomie *f.*

lobotomy [lou'bɔtəmi] n. MED. Lobotomie *f.*

lobster ['lɔbstə*] n. ZOOL., CULIN. Homard *m.; spiny lobster,* langouste.

lobular ['lɔbjulə*] adj. Lobulaire.

lobule [-ju:l] n. Lobule *m.*

local ['loukəl] adj. Local (colour, interest, time); restreint (outlook). ‖ De l'endroit; en ville (on a letter); *local quarrels,* querelles de clocher; *local road,* route vicinale. ‖ COMM. Fixe (agent); sur place (bill, purchases). ‖ MED. Local (anaesthetic); localisé (pain); topique, externe (remedy). ‖ CH. DE F. D'intérêt local (train). ‖ GRAMM. De lieu (adverb). — n. Informations régionales *f. pl.* (news); journal local *m.* (newspaper); timbre local *m.* (stamp). ‖ Personne (*f.*) du pays, indigène *m.* (person). ‖ Examen régional *m.* ‖ CH. DE F. Train d'intérêt local; tortillard (fam.) m. ‖ SPORTS. Equipe locale *f.* ‖ COMM. Agent local *m.* ‖ POP. Bistro du coin *m.* (pub). — [lou'kɑ:l] n. Localité *f.*

locale [lou'kɑ:l] n. Milieu *m.;* lieux *m. pl.*

localism ['loukəlizm] n. Coutume locale *f.* ‖ Régionalisme *m.;* esprit de clocher. ‖ GRAMM. Provincialisme *m.*

locality [lo'kæliti] n. Lieu (*m.*) où l'on se trouve; *I know his present locality,* je connais sa résidence actuelle. ‖ Localisation *f.* (geographical position); *sense of locality,* sens de l'orientation. ‖ Région *f.; in this locality,* dans ces parages. ‖ FAM. Localité *f.;* patelin *m.*

localization [,loukəlai'zeiʃən] n Localisation *f.*

localize ['loukəlaiz] v. tr. Localiser.

locally [-i] adv. Localement; sur les lieux.

locate [lo'keit] v. tr. Localiser, repérer. ‖ Etablir, situer, assigner. ‖ U. S. Situer, déterminer l'emplacement de; *to be located somewhere,* être domicilié quelque part. — v. intr. U. S. FAM. S'établir (*in,* à).

location [lou'keiʃən] n. Localisation *f.* ‖ Situation *f.;* emplacement *m.* (local position). ‖ Réserve, concession *f.* ‖ CINEM. Extérieurs *m. pl.*

locative ['lɔkətiv] adj., n. GRAMM. Locatif *m.*

loc. cit. Written abbr. for *loco citato,* ouvrage cité, loc. cit.

loch [lɔk] n. GEOGR. Loch *m.*

lock n. Mèche, bouche *f.* (curl); pl. Chevelure *f.* (hair). ‖ Flocon *m.* (of wool).

lock n. Serrure *f.; under lock and key,* sous clef. ‖

TECHN., CH. DE F. Verrou *m.* ‖ TECHN. Sac à air *m.,* poche (*f.*) d'air (air-lock). ‖ MILIT. Platine *f.* (of gun). ‖ AUTOM. Angle de braquage. ‖ SPORTS. Clef *f.* (in wrestling). ‖ NAUT. Ecluse *f.; to go through a lock,* sasser. ‖ FIG. Impasse *f.* ‖ **Lock-bolt,** n. Pêne *m.* ‖ **Lock-chamber,** n. NAUT. Chambre d'écluse *f.* ‖ **Lock-keeper,** n. NAUT. Eclusier *m.* ‖ **Lock-nut,** n. TECHN. Contre-écrou *m.* ‖ **Lock-out,** n. Lock-out *m.* ‖ **Lock-stitch,** n. Point (*m.*) de piqûre; point noué *m.* ‖ **Lock-up,** n. Fermeture *f.;* FIN. Immobilisation; FAM. Bloc, violon *m.* (prison). — v. tr. Fermer à clef (a door); enfermer (s.o., sth.). ‖ Etreindre; *to lock one's arms around s.o.'s neck,* nouer ses bras autour du cou de qqn. ‖ TECHN. Bloquer, caler. ‖ CH. DE F. Verrouiller. ‖ NAUT. Ecluser. ‖ MED. *Locked tooth,* dent barrée. ‖ FIG. Enfermer, enclore. ‖ **To lock away,** mettre sous clef, serrer. ‖ **To lock in,** enfermer à clef. ‖ **To lock out,** fermer dehors; COMM. Lock-outer. ‖ **To lock up,** fermer (a house); enfermer à clef; boucler (fam.) [s.o.]; FIN. Immobiliser, bloquer (capital); boucler (a stock). — v. intr. Fermer à clef (door). ‖ TECHN. Se bloquer (wheel); *to lock into,* s'engrener (or) s'enclaver dans.

lockage [-idʒ] n. NAUT. Eclusage *m.* ‖ JUR. Droits (*m. pl.*) d'éclusage.

locker [-ə*] n. Armoire (or) case (*f.*) fermant à clef. ‖ NAUT. Caisson *m.;* soute *f.* ‖ **Locker-room,** n. Vestiaire (*m.*) à cases individuelles.

locket [-it] n. Médaillon *m.*

lockjaw [-dʒɔ:] n. MED. Trisme *m.*

locking [-iŋ] n. Fermeture à clef *m.* ‖ TECHN. Bloquage, verrouillage *m.* ‖ NAUT. Eclusage *m.*

locksman [-smən] n. NAUT. Eclusier *m.*

locksmith [-smiθ] n. Serrurier *m.*

loco ['loukou] adj. U. S. POP. Cinglé, fêlé, toqué. (See BATTY.)

locomotion [,loukə'mouʃən] n. Locomotion *f.*

locomotive [,loukə'moutiv] adj. Locomotif (machine). ‖ Locomoteur *m.;* locomotrice *f.* (faculty). ‖ FAM. Voyageur, itinérant (person). — n. CH. DE F. Locomotive *f.*

locomotor [-ə *] adj., n. TECHN., MED. Locomoteur *m.;* locomotrice *f.*

locum (tenens) ['loukəm'(ti:nənz)] n. Remplaçant, suppléant, intérimaire *m.*

locus ['loukəs] (pl. **loci** ['lousai]) n. MATH. Lieu géométrique. ‖ ARCHIT. Situation, assise *f.* ‖ JUR. Scène *f.* (of a crime).

locust ['loukəst] n. ZOOL. Sauterelle *f.;* criquet *m.* ‖ BOT. Caroube *f.* ‖ **Locust-tree,** n. BOT. Caroubier; robinier *m.*

locution [lo'kju:ʃən] n. Locution *f.* ‖ Expression *f.* (way of speaking).

locutory ['lɔkjutəri] n. Parloir *m.*

lode [loud] n. Filon *m.;* veine *f.* (in mining).

lodestar ['loudstɑ:*] n. ASTRON. Etoile polaire *f.* ‖ FIG. Pôle (*m.*) d'attraction; phare *m.*

lodestone ['loudstoun] n. Magnétite *f.*

lodge [lɔdʒ] n. Loge *f.* (of a caretaker). ‖ Maisonnette *f.; shooting lodge,* pavillon de chasse. ‖ Loge *f.* (of Freemasons); groupe *m.* (of a trade union). ‖ ZOOL. Gîte *m.* ‖ U. S. Hutte *f.* (of American Indian). — v. tr. Loger, héberger, abriter (s.o.); *to lodge oneself,* se loger. ‖ Abriter, renfermer, contenir. ‖ MILIT. Loger (an arrow, a bullet); enfoncer (*in,* dans) [a sword]. ‖ JUR. Produire (a proof); *to lodge an appeal,* interjeter appel; *to lodge a complaint,* porter plainte; *to lodge in a gaol,* incarcérer. ‖ FIN. Déposer, confier (*with,* à) [money]. ‖ AGRIC. Coucher, verser (crops). ‖ FIG. Loger, introduire (an idea). — v. intr. Loger, être logé. ‖ MILIT. Se loger (arrow, bullet). ‖ AGRIC. Verser, se coucher (crops).

LOCOMOTIVES — LOCOMOTIVES

1. CHARGEMENT MÉCANIQUE DU CHARBON
   MECHANICAL STOKING
2. FOYER
   FIRE-BOX
3. ÉCHAPPEMENT DOUBLE
   DOUBLE CHIMNEY
4. RÉSERVOIR D'EAU 34ᵐ3
   WATER TANK 34ᵐ3
5. RÉCHAUFFEUR D'EAU
   WATER HEATER
6. CHAUDIÈRE TUBULAIRE
   TUBULAR BOILER
7. DÔME DE VAPEUR
   (STEAM-) DOME
8. SURCHAUFFEUR
   SUPERHEATER

9. RÉGULATEUR
   REGULATOR;THROTTLE
10. CYLINDRE
    CYLINDER
11. SORTIE DE LA VAPEUR
    STEAM EXHAUST
12. ROUE MOTRICE
    DRIVING WHEEL
13. BIELLE MOTRICE
    PISTON-ROD
14. BIELLE D'ACCOUPLEMENT
    CONNECTING ROD
15. SOUPAPE DE SÛRETÉ
    SAFETY VALVE
16. ÉCRAN LÈVE-FUMÉE
    SMOKE-DEFLECTOR

1. BOGGIE PORTEUR
   CARRYING BOGIE
2. ESSIEU MOTEUR
   DRIVING AXLE
3. ENGRENAGE RÉDUCTEUR
   REDUCING GEAR
4. FIL DE CONTACT
   CONTACT WIRE
5. PANTOGRAPHE
   PANTOGRAPH
6. DISJONCTEUR
   CIRCUIT-BREAKER
7. CONTACTEUR
   CONTACTOR

8. RÉSISTANCE DE DÉMAR-
   RAGE
   STARTING RESISTANCES
9. COMBINATEUR
   COMBINER
10. INVERSEURS
    REVERSORS
11. MOTEURS
    ENGINES
12. VENTILATEURS
    VENTILATING-FANS
13. COMPRESSEUR
    COMPRESSOR
14. CIRCULATION D'HUILE
    LUBRIFICATION

---

lodg(e)ment [-mənt] n. MILIT. Logement *m.*; mainmise *f.* ‖ COMM. Dépôt obstruant *m.*
lodger [-ə*] n. Locataire *s.* (in a rented room); sous-locataire *s.* (in s.o. else's home).
lodging [-iŋ] n. (act, place). ‖ Pl. Garni, appartement meublé *m.* ‖ JUR. Déposition *f.* (of a complaint). ‖ FIN. Dépôt *m.* (of money). ‖ **Lodging-house,** n. Asile *m.* (for the destitute); hôtel meublé *m.* (for workmen).
loess ['louis] n. Lœss *m.*
loft [lɔft] n. Grenier *m.*; soupente *f.* ‖ ARCHIT., ECCLES. Tribune *f.* ‖ ZOOL. Colombier, pigeonnier *m.*; *loft of pigeons,* vol de pigeons. ‖ SPORTS. Coup (*m.*) en hauteur.
— v. tr. ZOOL. Garder au pigeonnier.
loftily [-ili] adv. En hauteur. ‖ FIG. Avec hauteur.
loftiness [-inis] n. Hauteur, élévation *f.* ‖ FIG. Élévation *f.* (of feelings); hauteur, arrogance *f.* (haughtiness).
lofty [-i] adj. Haut. ‖ FIG. Elevé (feeling, style); hautain, arrogant (person). [See HAUGHTY.]
log [lɔg] n. Grosse bûche, bille, grume *f.*; rondin, tronc d'arbre *m.* ‖ NAUT. Loch *m.* ‖ CULIN. Bûche *f.* ‖ FAM. *King Log,* le roi soliveau. ‖ **Log-book,** n. NAUT. Journal de bord *m.*; AVIAT. Livre de vol *m.*; TECHN. Registre de travail *m.*; RADIO. Carnet (*m.*) d'écoute. ‖ **Log-hut,** n. Hutte (*f.*) en rondins. ‖ **Log-line,** n. NAUT. Ligne (*f.*) de loch. ‖ **Log-way,** n. Chemin (*m.*) de rondins.
— v. tr. (1). Tronçonner, débiter (wood). ‖ Abattre et débiter les arbres de (a region). ‖ NAUT. Filer.
log [lɔg] n. MATH. Logarithme, log. *m.*
logan ['lougən] n. Rocher branlant *m.*
loganberry ['lougənbəri] n. BOT., AGRIC. Framboise (*f.*) de Logan.
logarithm ['lɔgəriθm] n. MATH. Logarithme *m.*
logarithmic [,lɔgə'riθmik] adj. MATH. Logarithmique; des logarithmes (scale).
logarithmically [-əli] adv. MATH. Par les logarithmes.
loge [louʒ] n. THEATR. Loge *f.*
logger ['lɔgə*] n. U. S. Bûcheron *m.*

loggerhead ['lɔgəhed] n. NAUT. Boulet à brai *m.* ‖ ZOOL. Tortue de mer *f.* ‖ FAM. Tête (*f.*) de bois; lourdaud *m.* ‖ FAM. Désaccord *m.*; *at loggerheads with,* en bisbille avec.
loggia ['lɔdʒjə] n. ARCHIT. Loggia *f.*
logic ['lɔdʒik] n. Logique *f.*
logical [-əl] adj. Logique.
logically [-əli] adv. Logiquement.
logician [lɔ'dʒiʃən] n. Logicien *s.*
logistics [lɔ'dʒistiks] n. pl. MILIT. Logistique *f.*
logo ['lougou] (pl. **logos** [-z]) n. Insigne, emblème *m.*; marque *f.* (used in advertisement).
logogram ['lɔgogræm] n. Sténogramme *m.*
logography [lo'gɔgræfi] n. Logographie *f.*
logogriph ['lɔgogrif] n. Logogriphe *m.*
logomachy [lo'gɔməki] n. Logomachie *f.*
logotype ['lɔgou,taip] n. Insigne, emblème *m.*; marque *f.* (See LOGO.) ‖ TECHN. Logotype *m.* (in printing).
logroll ['lɔgrol] v. intr. U. S. Rouler le bois à flotter. ‖ U. S. FAM. S'allier politiquement.
logwood ['lɔgwud] n. BOT. Bois (*m.*) de campêche.
logy ['lougi] adj. U. S. Abruti, amorphe; vaseux (fam.).
loin [lɔin] n. MED. Rein *m.*; lombe *f.* ‖ CULIN. Aloyau *m.* (of beef); échine *f.* (of pork); longe *f.* (of veal). ‖ **Loin-chop,** n. CULIN. Côte première *f.* ‖ **Loin-cloth,** n. Pagne *m.*
loiter ['lɔitə*] v. intr. Flâner, flânocher, muser, musarder (to dawdle). ‖ S'attarder, traîner (to linger). ‖ JUR. Rôder.
— v. tr. **To loiter away,** perdre en flânant (one's time).
loiterer [-rə*] n. Flâneur; musard *s.* ‖ Traînard *m.* ‖ JUR. Rôdeur *s.*
loitering [-riŋ] adj. Flâneur.
loiteringly [-riŋli] adv. En flânant.
loll [lɔl] v. tr. Reposer (*on,* sur) [one's head]. ‖ **To loll out,** laisser pendre.
— v. intr. Se laisser aller, s'affaler, se vautrer (*in,* dans). ‖ **To loll about,** flânocher, tirer sa flemme. ‖ **To loll out,** pendre (tongue).

lollipop ['lɔlipɔp] n. Sucette *f*.
lollop ['lɔləp] v. intr. FAM. Flânocher, traînailler. (See LOITER.)
lolly ['lɔli] n. FAM. Sucette *f*. (sweet); esquimau *m*. (ice). ‖ POP. Fric, pognon, pèze *m*.; oseille *f*.
Lombard ['lʌmbəd] n. GEOGR. Lombard *s*. ‖ FIN. *Lombard Street*, quartier de la finance.
— adj. GEOGR. Lombard.
Lombardic [lʌm'bɑ:dik] adj. GEOGR., ARTS. Lombard, de Lombardie.
London ['lʌndən] n. GEOGR. Londres *m*.
— adj. GEOGR. Londonien, de Londres. ‖ BOT. *London pride*, désespoir-du-peintre.
Londoner [-ə*] n. GEOGR. Londonien *s*.
Londonize [-aiz] v. tr. Donner le genre londonien à.
lone [loun] adj. Solitaire (person, thing); isolé, désert (place). ‖ Seule (woman). ‖ Isolé, délaissé (lonesome).
loneliness [-linis] n. Solitude *f*. ‖ Isolement, sentiment d'abandon *m*.
lonely [-li] adj. Seul, solitaire (person); isolé, solitaire, désolé (place). ‖ Isolé, délaissé.
loner ['lounə*] n. FAM. Solitaire *s*. (animal, person).
lonesome [-səm] adj. Solitaire (alone). ‖ Isolé, délaissé (lonely).
lonesomeness [-səmnis] n. Isolement *m*.
long [lɔŋ] adj. Long (in dimension, space, time); *a long time*, longtemps; *to grow longer*, s'allonger. ‖ D'une longueur donnée; *three miles long*, long de trois milles. ‖ Long, étendu, à longue portée (far-reaching). ‖ Long, qui tarde; *to be long in coming*, tarder (or) être long à venir. ‖ Grand, considérable; *long vacation*, grandes vacances. ‖ FIN. De longueur (measure). ‖ FIN. Gros (bill, figure); élevé (price). ‖ SPORTS. *At long bowls*, à longue distance; *long odds*, pari risqué. ‖ CINEM. *Long shot*, plan général, scène filmée à distance. ‖ GRAMM. Long (syllable, vowel). ‖ RADIO. Grand (wave). ‖ FAM. *A long face*, une figure d'une aune, la mine longue; *a long tongue*, la langue trop longue; *in the long run*, à la longue; *long home*, la dernière demeure; *to have a long head*, savoir flairer le vent, avoir l'œil; *to make a long nose*, faire un pied de nez. ‖ FAM. *Long drink*, alcool à l'eau; *long shot*, pari risqué. ‖ **Long-bill**, n. ZOOL. Bécassine *f*. ‖ **Long-boat**, n. NAUT. Chaloupe *f*. ‖ **Long-bow**, n. † Arc *m*.; FAM. *To draw the long-bow*, galéger, raconter des craques. ‖ **Long-cloth**, n. COMM. Percale *f*. ‖ **Long-clothes**, n. Maillot *m*. ‖ **Long-distance**, adj. A longue distance; SPORTS. De fond (runner); U. S. Interurbain (on the phone). ‖ **Long-eared**, adj. A longues oreilles. ‖ **Long-headed**, n. MED. Dolicocéphale; FAM. Au nez creux. ‖ **Long-lived**, adj. A longue vie; FAM. Persistant (error). ‖ **Long-necked**, adj. Au long cou. ‖ **Long-range**, adj. A grand rayon d'action. ‖ **Long-shaped**, adj. Allongé (face). ‖ **Long-sighted**, adj. MED. Presbyte; ‖ FAM. A vue longue, prévoyant. ‖ **Long-sightedness**, n. MED. Presbytie *f*.; FAM. Prévoyance *f*. ‖ **Long-straws**, n. Courte paille *f*. (game). ‖ **Long-term**, adj. FIN. A longue date (loan); JUR. A long terme (policy); FIG. A longue échéance. ‖ **Long-winded**, adj. FAM. Verbeux (person); salivard (fam.); interminable (story).
— adv. Longtemps; *as long as*, tant que, pourvu que; *before long*, avant longtemps; *for long*, pendant longtemps; *how long*, combien de temps, depuis combien; *long ago*, il y a longtemps; *long before*, longtemps avant. ‖ Pendant; tout le long de; *his whole life long*, sa vie durant. ‖ Longtemps. ‖ FAM. *So long*, à bientôt; *he is not long for this world*, il ne fera pas de vieux os. ‖ **Long-drawn-out**, adj. Prolongé, long (sigh); délayé (story). ‖ **Long-forgotten**, adj. Oublié depuis longtemps. ‖ **Long-playing record**, n. Disque microsillon *m*. ‖ **Long-spun**, adj. Délayé, interminable. ‖

Long-suffering, adj. Endurant, patient; longanime.
— n. GRAMM. Longue *f*. ‖ FAM. *The long and the short of the matter*, l'affaire de long en large.
— v. intr. Soupirer (*after*, après); brûler, rêver, avoir grande envie (*for, to*, de) [see YEARN]; *I long to*, il me tarde de.
longanimity [,lɔŋgə'nimiti] n. Longanimité *f*.
longer ['lɔŋgə*] adv. comp. Plus longtemps; *how much longer*, combien de temps; *no longer*, plus; *ten hours longer*, dix heures de plus.
— adj. comp. See LONG.
longeron ['lɔndʒərən] n. AVIAT. Longeron *m*.
longevity [lɔn'dʒeviti] n. Longévité *f*.
longhand ['lɔŋhænd] n. Ecriture ordinaire *f*.
longies ['lɔŋi:z] n. pl. U. S. Pantalon d'enfant *m*.
longing [-iŋ] adj. Impatient, ardent, avide.
— n. Désir ardent *m.*; envie passionnée; nostalgie *f.* (*for, after*, de). ‖ MED. Envie *f*.
longingly [-iŋli] adv. Impatiemment.
longish [-iʃ] adj. Plutôt long; longuet (fam.).
longitude ['lɔndʒitju:d] n. Longitude *f*.
longitudinal [,lɔndʒi'tju:dinəl] adj. Longitudinal.
longshanks ['lɔŋʃæŋks] n. ZOOL. Echasse *f*. ‖ FAM. Longues-jambes *f. pl.*
longshore ['lɔŋʃɔ:*] adj. NAUT. Côtier.
longshoreman [-mən] (pl. **longshoremen**) n. Docker *m*. (in a port). ‖ Pêcheur (*m*.) d'huîtres (or) de moules (fisherman).
longsome ['lɔŋsəm] n. Long, ennuyeux.
longueur [lɔ̃gœ:r] n. Longueur *f*., temps mort *m*. (tedious passage).
longways [-weiz], **longwise** [-waiz] adv. En long, dans la longueur.
loo [lu:] n. Mouche *f*. (card game). ‖ **Loo-table**, n. Guéridon *m*.
loo n. FAM. Petit coin (ou) endroit, pipi-room *m*.
looby ['lu:bi] n. Lourdaud *m*.
loofah ['lu:fə] n. Luffa *m*. (plant); éponge végétale *f*. (sponge).
look [luk] v. intr. Regarder (in general). ‖ Ouvrir des yeux ronds (to gaze). ‖ Prendre garde; *to look where one is going*, faire attention où l'on va. ‖ Etre exposé, donner, ouvrir, s'orienter (to be facing). ‖ S'attendre (*to*, à) [to expect]. ‖ U. S. Tendre, viser (*to*, à). ‖ FAM. *Look here!*, eh là!, voyez un peu! ‖ **To look about**, regarder autour; *to look about for*, chercher du regard. ‖ **To look after**, s'occuper de, veiller sur, être attentif à (s.o.); entretenir, s'occuper de (sth.). ‖ **To look at**, regarder, porter ses regards sur; FIG. Considérer, envisager; FAM. *Fair to look at*, de physique agréable. ‖ **To look away**, détourner les yeux, regarder ailleurs. ‖ **To look back**, regarder en arrière (*upon*, vers). ‖ **To look down**, regarder à terre (or) en baissant les yeux; COMM. Baisser (price); *to look down on*, regarder de haut (person); dominer (place); U. S. FAM. *To look down one's nose*, regarder d'un air dédaigneux. ‖ **To look for**, s'attendre à, prévoir, envisager (to anticipate); chercher, être en quête de (to search). ‖ **To look forward**, s'attendre (*to*, à); être impatient (*to*, de). ‖ **To look in**, entrer en passant (*at, on*, chez) [to call]; regarder la télévision (at T.V.). ‖ **To look into**, parcourir (a book); examiner, prendre connaissance de (a question). ‖ **To look on**, regarder faire, être spectateur (to be an observer); donner sur (to command a view). ‖ **To look out**, regarder à l'extérieur (person); donner (*on*, sur) [room]; FAM. Faire attention, prendre garde; *to look out for*, guetter (s.o.), s'attendre à (sth.). ‖ **To look round**, jeter un coup d'œil circulaire. ‖ **To look up**, regarder en haut (or) en l'air; FAM. Se remonter, reprendre. ‖ **To look upon**, regarder, envisager, considérer.
— v. tr. Regarder (s.o., sth.). ‖ Traduire par son regard; *to look one's despair*, faire passer son désespoir dans ses yeux. ‖ Paraître; *to look one's years*, paraître son âge. ‖ Sembler, paraître, avoir l'aspect

de; *it looks like rain*, on dirait qu'il va pleuvoir; *to look a rascal*, avoir l'air d'un coquin; *to look the part*, avoir le physique de l'emploi. ‖ † S'assurer (*that*, que). ‖ FAM. *Look sharp*, vite !, dépêchez-vous. ‖ **To look down**, mater du regard. ‖ **To look over**, parcourir du regard ; *to look s.o. all over*, regarder qqn sur toutes les coutures. ‖ **To look through**, examiner attentivement, éplucher (papers). ‖ **To look up**, consulter (a list); chercher (*in*, dans) [a word] ; FAM. *To look s.o. up*, passer voir qqn. — n. Regard *m.* (glance); *to have a look at*, jeter un coup d'œil à. ‖ Air, aspect *m.; allure f.* (appearance); *by the look of it*, d'après les apparences; *I don't like the look of things*, cela ne me dit rien qui vaille. ‖ Ligne *f.; new-look*, new look. ‖ Physique agréable *m.; to have looks and youth*, avoir la beauté et la jeunesse. ‖ **Look-in**, n. Visite éclair *f.;* SPORTS. Chance *f.* ‖ **Look-out**, n. Guet *m.;* surveillance *f.;* affût *m.* (*for*, de); NAUT. Vigie *f.* (man); poste de guetteur *m.* (post); MILIT. Guetteur *m.* (man); poste (*m.*) d'observation (post); FAM. Perspective *f.* ‖ **Look-over**, n. Regard de haut en bas *m.* ‖ **Look-see**, n. FAM. Coup d'œil *m.* (pour contrôle). ‖ **Look-up**, n. Courte visite *f.*

looker [-ə*] n. Spectateur, assistant *m.* ‖ FAM. Jolie femme, beauté *f.* ‖ **Looker-on** (pl. *lookers-on*), n. Spectateur *m.;* spectatrice *f.*

looking [-iŋ] adj. A l'air de. ‖ **Looking-back**, n. PHILOS. Rétrospection *f.* ‖ **Looking-down**, n. Regard méprisant *m.* ‖ **Looking-for**, n. Recherche (*f.*) de. ‖ **Looking-glass**, n. Miroir *m.;* glace *f.* ‖ **Looking-over**, n. Examen *m.;* étude *f.*

loom [lu:m] n. TECHN. Métier de tisserand *m.* ‖ NAUT. Bras *m.* (of oar).

loom n. Vague silhouette *f.* — v. intr. Se dessiner, se profiler, s'estomper (*in*, dans); *to loom up out of*, se dégager de. ‖ FIG. Se dessiner, apparaître.

loon [lu:n] n. ZOOL. Plongeon *m.*

loony ['lu:ni] adj. FAM. Toqué, dingo *s.* ‖ **Loony-bin**, n. FAM. Asile (*m.*) d'aliénés.

loop [lu:p] n. Boucle *f.* (of cord, river); spire *f.* (of spiral). ‖ Picot *m.* (stitch). ‖ Agrafe *f.* (staple). ‖ AVIAT. Boucle *f.* ‖ CH. DE F. Boucle (or) ligne (*f.*) d'évitement ; voie (*f.*) de raccordement. ‖ SPORTS. Croisé *m.* (in skating). ‖ PHYS., ELECTR. Ventre *m.* — v. tr. Boucler, faire une boucle à (cord). ‖ Enrouler (*around*, autour de). ‖ ELECTR. Fermer (a circuit). ‖ AVIAT. *To loop the loop*, faire un looping. ‖ **To loop back**, mettre dans une embrasse (a drapery). ‖ **To loop up**, remonter en agrafant. — v. intr. Boucler ; faire des boucles (or) des méandres.

looper [-ə*] n. ZOOL. Chenille arpenteuse *f.*

loophole [-ˌhoul] n. ARCHIT. Meurtrière *f.* ‖ FAM. Echappatoire ; porte ouverte *f.* (*for*, à). — v. tr. ARCHIT. Ouvrir des meurtrières dans (a wall).

loose [lu:s] adj. Détaché, libre. ‖ Lâché (animal); vague (coat); lâche (cord, knot, texture); dénoué, flottant (hair); détaché, volant (sheet); branlant (stone); *to come* (or) *get loose*, se détacher, se desservir, se défaire. ‖ TECHN. Desserré (nut); mobile (plant); mou (rope); fou (wheel); *to work loose*, prendre du jeu, se desserrer. ‖ CHIM. Libre. ‖ GEOL. Friable (soil). ‖ MED. Relâché (bowels); gras (cough); flasque, mou (skin); branlant (tooth). ‖ COMM. En vrac (goods). ‖ FIN. *Loose cash*, menue monnaie. ‖ MILIT. Dispersé (order). ‖ FIG. Vague, décousu (idea); relâché, lâche (style); libre, loin du texte, approximatif (translation). ‖ FIG. Dissolu (life); relâché (morals); grossier (talk); facile (woman); *to let loose*, donner libre cours à. ‖ FAM. *At a loose end*, sans occupation; *at loose ends*, en pagaille ; *of loose build*, dégingandé ; *to have a loose tongue*, ne pas savoir tenir sa langue, avoir la langue trop longue. ‖ **Loose-fitting**, adj. Non ajusté,

vague. ‖ **Loose-jointed**, adj. Dégingandé. ‖ **Loose-leaf**, adj. A feuille volante. ‖ **Loose-tongued**, adj. A la langue déliée (or) longue. — v. tr. Délivrer, délier, détacher. ‖ Dénouer (hair, knots). ‖ Lâcher ; *to loose one's hold*, lâcher prise. ‖ NAUT. Larguer. ‖ ECCLES. Délier, absoudre. ‖ FIG. Démuseler (passions) ; délier (s.o.'s tongue). — n. Libre cours *m.* (*to*, à). ‖ FAM. *On the loose*, en goguette.

loosely [-li] adv. Au large, sans serrer, lâchement. ‖ Vaguement, sans précision. ‖ Librement, licencieusement.

loosen [-ṇ] v. tr. Défaire, desserrer, relâcher. ‖ TECHN. Desserrer, donner du jeu à (a nut). ‖ AGRIC. Ameublir (the soil). ‖ MED. Dégager (a cough); libérer (the bowels). ‖ FIG. Relâcher (discipline) ; délier (s.o.'s tongue). — v. intr. Se défaire, se détacher, se relâcher. ‖ TECHN. Se desserrer, prendre du jeu. ‖ MED. Se dégager.

looseness [-nis] n. Etat vague, relâchement *m.* ‖ Ampleur *f.* (of a coat). ‖ TECHN. Desserrage, jeu *m.* ‖ MED. Relâchement *m.* (of bowels); flaccidité *f.* (of skin); état branlant *m.* (of tooth). ‖ GEOL. Friabilité *f.* (of soil). ‖ FIG. Vague, décousu *m.; * imprécision *f.* ‖ FIG. Relâchement, dérèglement *m.* (of morals).

loot [lu:t] n. MILIT. Butin *m.* ‖ U. S. POP. Fric *m.* — v. tr. Piller.

looter [-ə*] n. Pillard *m.*

lop [lɔp] v. intr. (1). Tomber mollement. ‖ Bondir (animal). ‖ **Lop-eared**, adj. Aux oreilles pendantes. ‖ **Lop-sidedly**, adv. De guingois. — v. tr. Laisser pendre.

lop v. tr. (1). Elaguer (a branch); ébrancher, émonder (a tree). ‖ FIG. *To lop off*, abattre, trancher (a head). — n. Elagage *m.*

lop v. intr. (1). NAUT. Clapoter. — n. NAUT. Clapotis *m.*

lope [loup] v. intr. Courir avec souplesse. — n. Pas souple *m.*, grande foulée *f.*

loquacious [lou'kweiʃəs] adj. Loquace, disert.

loquaciously [-li] adv. Avec loquacité.

loquaciousness [-nis], **loquacity** [lou'kwæsiti] n. Loquacité *f.*

lord [lɔ:d] n. Seigneur *m.* (of a feudal estate). ‖ Maître, chef *m.* (ruler). ‖ Roi *m.* (magnate). ‖ Lord *m.* (title). ‖ Pl. Chambre (*f.*) des lords (Parliament). ‖ ECCLES. Seigneur *m.; Lord's Prayer*, Notre Père, oraison dominicale *m.* — interj. FAM. Seigneur !, Grand Dieu !, Dieu du ciel ! — v. tr. Créer lord (s.o.). ‖ *To lord it over*, dominer; *he lords it over everybody*, tout plie devant lui.

lordliness [-linis] n. Hauteur, arrogance, morgue *f.* (pride). ‖ Magnificence *f.;* grand genre *m.*

lordling [-liŋ] n. Nobliau *m.*

lordly [-li] adj. Hautain, altier, arrogant (lofty). ‖ Majestueux, de grand seigneur (noble).

lordship [-ʃip] n. Seigneurie *f.* (dominion, estate, title). ‖ Autorité *f.* (over, sur).

lore [lɔ:*] n. † Science *f.* (knowledge); doctrine *f.* (teaching).

lorgnette [lɔ:'njet] n. Face-à-main *m.* ‖ FAM. Lorgnette *f.*

lorn [lɔ:n] adj. † Désolé, solitaire.

lorry ['lɔri] n. Camion *m.* (See TRUCK.)

losable ['lu:zəbḷ] adj. Perdable.

lose [lu:z] v. tr. (99). Perdre, égarer (sth.); U. S. *Lost and found*, bureau des objets trouvés. ‖ Perdre, ne plus posséder ; *to lose one's temper*, perdre patience. ‖ Perdre (by death); *to lose one's daughter*, perdre sa fille. ‖ Perdre, ne plus suivre ; *to lose the way*, se perdre, se dérouter ; *not to lose a word of*, ne pas perdre un mot de. ‖ Perdre, manquer, laisser fuir (an opportunity). ‖ Perdre, gaspiller (one's time). ‖ Faire perdre, coûter (sth.); *to lose s.o. his*

job, faire perdre son emploi à qqn. ‖ MED. Perdre (a limb); ne pas pouvoir sauver (a patient); *to lose one's voice*, avoir une extinction de voix. ‖ NAUT. *To be lost at sea*, périr (or) être perdu en mer. ‖ TECHN. Retarder de (ten minutes). ‖ CH. DE F. Manquer (the train). ‖ FIG. Perdre; *he has not lost by it*, il n'y a rien perdu; *to lose oneself*, se perdre, se plonger, s'absorber (*in*, dans).
— v. intr. Perdre; *to lose heavily*, prendre une culotte (fam.). ‖ MILIT., SPORTS. Perdre. ‖ TECHN. Retarder (watch). ‖ LOC. *To get lost*, se perdre, s'égarer; U. S. *to lose out to*, perdre au profit de.

loser [-ə*] n. Perdant *s*. ‖ SPORTS. *Bad, good loser*, mauvais, beau joueur. ‖ FIN. *To be a loser*, subir une perte.

losing [-iŋ] adj. A perte (bargain); perdu d'avance, désespéré (game); mauvais (proposition); perdant (team).

loss [lɔs] n. Perte *f*. (of s.o., sth.); *at a loss*, à perte. ‖ Déperdition *f*. (of heat); *loss in transit*, déchet de route. ‖ Dommage *m.;* *to meet with a loss*, subir un préjudice. ‖ MED. Perte *f*. (of blood, sight); extinction *f*. (of voice). ‖ FIG. Embarras *m.;* *at a loss*, désorienté; *at a loss for an answer*, bien embarrassé pour répondre; *to be a dead loss*, être la cinquième roue d'un carrosse.

lost [lɔst]. See LOSE.

lot [lɔt] n. Sort, tirage au sort *m.;* *to cast* (or) *draw lots*, tirer au sort; *to cast in one's lot with*, tenter la fortune avec. ‖ Sort, destin, lot *m*. (fate); *it's the common lot*, tout le monde y passe. ‖ Lot *m.;* parcelle *f*. (of ground); lotissement *m*. (in city); *a corner lot*, un emplacement de coin. ‖ COMM. Lot *m*. (of goods); *in one lot*, en bloc. ‖ JUR. † Ecot *m*. ‖ FAM. Flopée *f.;* *lots of friends*, des tas d'amis. ‖ FAM. Type *m.;* *bad lot*, mauvais sujet.
— v. tr. (1). Lotir.
— v. intr. U. S. Tirer au sort.

loth [louθ] adj. See LOATH.

lotion [louʃən] n. Lotion *f*.

lottery [lɔtəri] n. Loterie *f*. (lit. and fig.). ‖ FIN. *Lottery bond*, bon à lot.

lotto [lɔtou] n. Loto *m*.

lotus [lɔtəs] n. Lotus *m*. ‖ **Lotus-eater**, n. † Lotophage *m.;* FAM. Songe-creux *m*.

loud [laud] adj. Vif (applause); sonore (bell, laugh); grand (cry); fort (noise, sound); haut, fort (voice); *to be loud in one's admiration*, manifester chaleureusement (or) crier son admiration; *to be loud in one's complaints*, se répandre en lamentations bruyantes. ‖ Véhément (denial); criant (lie). ‖ Vulgaire (behaviour, person); criard (colour); voyant, toquard (fam.) [costume]. ‖ **Loud-mouthed**, adj. Au verbe haut; gueulard (pop.). ‖ **Loud-speaker**, n. Haut-parleur *m*.
— adv. Haut, fort, à haute voix.

loudly [-li] adv. Fort, haut; à haute voix. ‖ Bruyamment (noisily). ‖ Hautement, énergiquement. ‖ D'une manière tapageuse (conspicuously).

loudness [-nis] n. Force *f*. (of a noise). ‖ Caractère bruyant *m*. (of a claim). ‖ Clinquant *m.;* allure tapageuse *f*. (of dress).

lough [lɔk] n. GEOGR. Lac; bras (*m*.) de mer.

lounge [laundʒ] v. intr. Flâner, badauder, traîner. (See SAUNTER.) ‖ S'étaler, s'affaler, se vautrer, paresser (*in*, dans). [See LOLL.]
— v. tr. *To lounge away*, perdre en flânerie.
— n. Flânerie *f*. ‖ Sofa, canapé, divan *m*. (couch). ‖ Chaise longue *f*. (chair). ‖ Salle (*f*.) de repos; hall *m*. (in hotel); petit salon *m*. (in house). ‖ **Lounge-car**, n. U. S. Voiture-salon *m*. ‖ **Lounge-chair**, n. Chaise longue *f*. ‖ **Lounge-lizard**, n. FAM. Danseur mondain, gigolo *m*.

lounger [-ə*] n. Flâneur *s*.

lour [laue*]. See LOWER.

louse [laus] (pl. **lice** [lais]) n. ZOOL. Pou *m*. ‖ FAM. Salaud *m*.
— v. tr. U. S. POP. **To louse up**, bousiller, bâcler.

lousy [lauzi] adj. Pouilleux. ‖ FAM. Piètre, miteux, moche; *lousy trick*, tour de cochon.

lout [laut] v. intr. † S'incliner.

lout n. Lourdaud, balourd *m*. (See BOOR.)

loutish [-iʃ] adj. Lourdaud. (See BOORISH.)

loutishness [-iʃnis] n. Gaucherie, rusticité *f*.

louvre [lu:və*] n. ARCHIT. Lucarne *f.;* *adjustable louvres*, aérateur. ‖ ARCHIT. Abat-vent *m*. ‖ NAUT. Jalousie *f*. ‖ AUTOM., AVIAT. Auvent *m*. ‖ **Louvreboard**, n. ARCHIT. Abat-vent, abat-son *m*.

lovable [lʌvəbl] adj. Très aimable, fort sympathique.

lovage [lʌvidʒ] n. BOT. Livèche *f*.

love [lʌv] n. Amour *m.;* *in love with*, amoureux (or) épris de; *love at first sight*, coup de foudre; *to make love to*, faire la cour à (to court), faire l'amour avec (to have intercourse with); *to marry for love*, faire un mariage d'amour; *a love affair*, une liaison. ‖ Mon amour, mon trésor *m.;* chéri *s*. (term of address). ‖ Amour, cupidon, angelot *m*. (Cupid). ‖ Amoureux *s*. (See FLAME); *an old love of his*, une de ses anciennes. ‖ Affection *f*. (for, pour); *my love to all*, mes vives amitiés à tous; *no love lost between them*, pas d'excès de sympathie entre eux; *with much love*, avec mes affectueuses pensées. ‖ Attrait, plaisir *m.;* *a labour of love*, une œuvre chère; *to work for love*, travailler pour la gloire (or) pour le roi de Prusse. ‖ SPORTS. Zéro *m*. (at tennis). ‖ **Love-child**, n. Enfant de l'amour *m*. ‖ **Love-feast**, n. ECCLES. Agape *f*. ‖ **Love-knot**, n. Faveur *f*. ‖ **Love-lorn**, adj. Languissant d'amour; délaissé. ‖ **Love-making**, n. Cour *f*. (courtship); amour *m*. (sexual intercourse). ‖ **Love-match**, n. Mariage d'amour *m*. ‖ **Love-potion**, n. Philtre d'amour *m*. ‖ **Love seat**, n. U. S. Causeuse *f*. ‖ **Love-song**, n. MUS. Romance *f*.
— v. tr. Aimer (one's husband, wife, parents). ‖ Aimer, avoir de l'amitié pour (one's friends). ‖ Aimer, être attaché à (an animal). ‖ FAM. Aimer, adorer, être passionné de (good music); *I should love to go with you*, j'aimerais aller avec vous.

lovelace [lʌvleis] n. Séducteur *m*.

loveless [lʌvlis] adj. Sans amour.

loveliness [-linis] n. Beauté, grâce *f*.

lovelock [-lɔk] n. Accroche-cœur *m*.

lovely [-li] adj. Beau; gracieux, charmant, attirant (exquisite). ‖ Agréable, aimable (enjoyable).
— n. FAM. Belle, beauté *f.;* *my lovely*, ma belle, ma jolie.

lover [-ə*] n. Amoureux *s*. (sweetheart). ‖ Amant *m*. (paramour). ‖ Amateur *m*. (of, de).

lovesick [-sik] adj. Féru d'amour.

lovey [lʌvi] n. Mon chou, trésor *m*. ‖ **Lovey-dovey**, adj. FAM. Tendre, sentimental; mièvre.

loving [-iŋ] adj. Aimant, affectueux (person). ‖ Amical, d'amitié, d'amour (act). ‖ **Loving-kindness**, n. Dilection, bonté *f*.

lovingly [-iŋli] adv. Affectueusement, tendrement.

lovingness [-iŋnis] n. Affection, tendresse *f*.

low [lou] v. tr., intr. Beugler.
— n. Beuglement *m*.

low adj. Bas (in degree, height, intensity, sonority); *to burn low*, baisser (fire, lamp); *in a low voice*, à voix basse. ‖ Petit (in quantity, stature); *to run low*, baisser (provisions). ‖ Récent (in date). ‖ Bas, peu profond (shallow). ‖ Décolleté (dress, neckline). ‖ GEOGR. Bas (latitude); *Low Countries*, Pays-Bas. ‖ NAUT. Bas (tide, water). ‖ FIN. Bas (cost, price, value, wages). ‖ ECCLES. Bas (Church, mass); *Low Sunday*, Quasimodo. ‖ MUS. Grave (note, sound). ‖ ARTS. Bas (relief). ‖ THEATR. *Low comedy*, farce. ‖ MED. Bas (pressure); *low diet*, diète; *to be very low*, être bien bas (patient). ‖ MATH. *Lowest common multiple*, plus petit commun multiple. ‖ TECHN. Faible (speed). ‖ GRAMM. Bas (German, Latin). ‖ U. S. AUTOM. *Low gear*, première vitesse. ‖ FIG. Profond (bow). ‖ FIG. Inférieur, peu évolué

(animal, race) ; piètre, pauvre, défavorable (opinion) ; humble, bas, modeste (origin) ; *to lie low,* se tenir coi, faire le mort. ‖ Fig. Abattu, déprimé, mélancolique ; *in low spirits,* sans entrain, découragé. ‖ Fig. Vil, bas (debased) ; vulgaire, grossier, trivial (vulgar). ‖ Fam. A court (*on,* de) ; *in low water,* à fond de cale, à sec. ‖ **Low-brow,** adj. Fam. Sans prétentions intellectuelles ; n. Fam. Manuel *m.* ‖ **Low-browed,** adj. Med. Au front bas ; Archit. A entrée basse ; Geol. Surplombant (rock). ‖ **Low-cost,** adj. Fin. Bon marché. ‖ **Low-down,** adj. Bas, au ras du sol ; Fig. Bas, vil ; n. Fam. *To give the low-down on,* tuyauter sur. ‖ **Low-frequency,** adj. Electr. A basse fréquence. ‖ **Low-key,** adj. Cinem. Sombre (picture). ‖ **Low-lifer,** n. U. S. Pop. Mufle *m.* (boor) ; canaille *f.* (ruffian). ‖ **Low-minded,** adj. D'esprit vulgaire. ‖ **Low-necked,** adj. Décolleté (dress). ‖ **Low-pitched,** adj. Bas, grave (voice) ; Archit. A faible pente (roof) ; au plafond bas (room) ; Fig. Peu élevé (ideal). ‖ **Low-pressure,** adj. A basse pression. ‖ **Low-rate,** adj. A tarif réduit. ‖ **Low-spirited,** adj. Déprimé, découragé, abattu, sans entrain (or) vitalité ; en perte de vitesse (fam.). ‖ **Low-water,** adj. Naut. *Low-water mark,* étiage.
— adv. Bas ; *to hit low,* toucher bas. ‖ Bas, à voix basse (in a low voice). ‖ Récemment (recently). ‖ Mus. Bas ; *to set lower,* baisser. ‖ Fin. Bon marché, à bas prix. ‖ Med. *To feed low,* se nourrir légèrement, se mettre à la diète. ‖ Fig. Petitement, modérément ; *to play low,* jouer petit jeu. ‖ Fig. Bas ; *to fall as low as to,* tomber assez bas pour. ‖ **Low-born,** adj. De naissance (or) d'origine très modeste. ‖ **Low-bred,** adj. Mal élevé, de piètre éducation. ‖ **Low-grade,** adj. Médiocre, de qualité inférieure. ‖ **Low-lying,** adj. Bas, de faible élévation (land, cloud). ‖ **Low-swung,** adj. Autom. Surbaissé.
— n. Autom. Première *f.* (low gear). ‖ Fin. Plancher *m.;* prices have reached a new low, les prix se sont encore effondrés. ‖ Geogr. Basse pression *f.*

lower [-ə*] adj. comp. (See Low.) ‖ Bas, inférieur (classes) ; *lower school,* petit collège. ‖ Geogr. Bas (Alps, California). ‖ Naut. Inférieur (deck) ; bas (sail). ‖ Jur. *Lower House,* Chambre basse. ‖ Techn. *Lower case,* bas de casse. ‖ Med. Inférieur (jaw) ; d'en bas (tooth).
— adv. Plus bas ; *the lower paid,* les salariés les plus mal payés.
— v. tr. Abaisser (in general). ‖ Baisser (voice). ‖ Med., Fin. Diminuer. ‖ Naut. Mettre à la mer (a boat) ; amener (a sail). ‖ Fig. Abaisser, diminuer, avilir ; *lowered in social status,* déclassé.
— v. intr. Baisser, s'abaisser. ‖ Fin. Baisser. ‖ Med. Décliner, baisser.

lower ['lauə*] v. intr. Se renfrogner, prendre un air sombre, regarder de travers. (See scowl.) ‖ Menacer (clouds) ; s'assombrir, se couvrir (sky).
— n. Figure renfrognée *f.;* regard de travers *m.*

lowering ['louəriŋ] adj. Menaçant.
— n. Abaissement *m.* (in general). ‖ Fin. Rabais *m.* (of prices) ; diminution *f.* (in taxation) ; *lowering of tariff walls,* abaissement des barrières douanières. ‖ Naut. Mise à la mer *f.* (of a boat) ; calage *m.* (of a sail).

lowering [-riŋ] adj. En baisse, en diminution.
lowermost [-moust] adj. Le plus bas.
lowland ['loulənd] n. Plaine *f.* ‖ Geogr. Pl. Basse Ecosse *f.*
— adj. De la plaine. ‖ Geogr. De la Basse Ecosse.
lowlander [-ə*] n. Geogr. Habitant (*s.*) de la Basse Ecosse.
lowliness ['loulinis] n. Humilité *f.*
lowly [-li] adj. Humble.
—adv. Humblement.
lowness [-nis] n. Petite altitude *f.* (in height). ‖ Petitesse *f.* (in stature). ‖ Fig. Condition modeste *f.*

‖ Fig. Dépression *f.;* abattement, découragement *m.* ‖ Fig. Bassesse, grossièreté *f.*
lox [lɔks] n. U. S. Culin. Saumon fumé et salé *m.*
loxygen ['lɔksidʒən] n. Chim. Oxygène liquide *m.*
loyal ['lɔiəl] adj. Loyal. ‖ Fidèle (*to,* envers).
loyalism [-izm] n. Loyalisme *m.*
loyalist [-ist] n. Loyaliste *m.*
loyally [-i] adv. Loyalement.
loyalty [-ti] n. Fidélité *f.* (*to,* à) [a king]. ‖ Solidarité *f.* (*to,* envers, vis-à-vis de) [one's comrades].
lozenge ['lɔzindʒ] n. Math., Blas. Losange *m.* ‖ Med. Pastille, tablette *f.*
lozenged [-d] adj. Math. En losange. ‖ Blas. Losangé.
L.S.D. [.eles'di:] abbr. *lysergic acid diethylamide,* L.S.D.
Ltd. Written abbr. for *limited,* s. a. r. l.
lubber ['lʌbə*] n. Lourdaud ; bêta ; argousin *m.*
lubberliness [-linis] n. Gaucherie, lourdeur *f.*
lubberly [-li] adv. Gauche, lourd, pataud.
— adv. Gauchement, lourdement.
lubricant ['l(j)u:brikənt] n. Techn. Lubrifiant *m.*
lubricate [-keit] v. tr. Techn. Lubrifier. ‖ Pop. Lubricated, rétamé (drunk).
lubrication [,l(j)u:bri'keiʃən] n. Techn. Lubrification *f.;* graissage *m.*
lubricator ['l(ju):brikeitə*] n. Techn. Graisseur *m.*
lubricity [lju:'brisiti] n. Onctuosité *f.* (of a lubricant). ‖ Fig. Lubricité *f.* (lewdness) ; duplicité *f.* (perfidy).
lubritorium [,lju:bri'tɔ:riəm] n. U. S. Station-graissage *f.*
luce [l(j)u:s] n. Zool. Brochet *m.*
lucency ['lju:snsi] n. Luminosité *f.*
lucent [-nt] adj. Lumineux. ‖ Translucide.
lucern(e) [lu:'sə:n] n. Bot. Luzerne *f.*
lucid ['lju:sid] adj. Clair, lumineux, transparent. ‖ Zool. Luisant. ‖ Fig. Lucide (mind, thinker) ; clair (style, talk).
lucidity [lju:'siditi] n. Clarté, luminosité, transparence *f.* ‖ Fig. Lucidité *f.* (of mind) ; clarté *f.* (of style).
lucidly ['lju:sidli] adv. Lumineusement. ‖ Fig. Lucidement ; clairement.
Lucifer ['lu:sifə*] n. Eccles. Lucifer *m.* ‖ Astron. Vénus *f.* ‖ Fam. Allumette-tison *f.* (match).
luck [lʌk] n. Chance ; veine *f.* (chance) ; *beginner's luck,* la veine des ignorants, aux innocents les mains pleines ; *stroke of luck,* coup de chance, bénédiction. ‖ Destin *m.;* chance *f.; it'll be bad luck if,* ce serait bien le diable (or) la déveine si ; *to be down on one's luck,* être dans la débine ; *to be out of luck,* avoir la déveine (or) le guignon ; *to spin a hard-luck story,* débiter une histoire lamentable (beggar).
luckily [-ili] adv. Par chance, heureusement.
luckiness [-inis] n. Chance, bonne fortune *f.*
luckless [-lis] adj. Malencontreux, fatal (event) ; malchanceux ; guignard (fam.) [person].
lucky [-i] adj. Heureux, favorable, propice (event) ; fortuné, favorisé par la chance ; veinard, chançard, verni (fam.) [person] ; dû à la chance (result) ; qui porte bonheur (thing) ; *it was lucky for you you did it,* bien vous en a pris ; *lucky charm,* porte-bonheur ; *lucky dip,* sac à surprise.
lucrative ['lu:krətiv] adj. Lucratif.
lucre ['lu:kə*] n. Lucre *m.*
lucubrate ['lu:kjubreit] v. intr. Composer pendant la nuit ; pondre (fam.).
lucubration [,lu:kju'breiʃən] r. Travail *m.* (or) composition (*f.*) nocturne. ‖ Pl. Elucubration *f.*
ludicrous ['lu:dikrəs] adj. Ridicule, risible, grotesque (see comic).
ludicrously [-li] adv. Ridiculement.
ludicrousness [-nis] n. Ridicule, grotesque *m.*
ludo ['lu:dou] n. Petits chevaux *m. pl.* (game).

luff [lʌf] v. intr. NAUT. Loger.
— v. tr. NAUT. Masquer, cacher; *to luff the helm*, faire une auloffée.
— n. NAUT. Lof *m.;* ralingue *f.* (of sail); épaule *f.* (of ship).

luffa ['lʌfə] n. See LOOFAH.

lug [lʌg] n. NAUT. Voile (*f.*) à bourcet; taille-vent *m.* ǁ **Lug-sail,** n. Taille-vent *m.*

lug v. tr. (1). Traîner (to drag). ǁ FIG. Introduire, insérer, amener (*in,* dans).
— v. intr. Tirer (*at,* sur).
— n. Traction *f.* ǁ MED. Oreille *f.* (Scottish). ǁ TECHN. Tenon, arrêtoir, ergot *m.*

luge [lju:dʒ] n. SPORTS. Luge *f.*
— v. tr. SPORTS. Luger.

luggage ['lʌgidʒ] n. CH. DE F. Bagages *m. pl.; luggage in advance,* bagages non accompagnés. ǁ U. S. Articles (*m. pl.*) de voyage. ǁ **Luggage-carrier,** n. CH. DE F. Porte-bagages *m.* ǁ **Luggage-porter,** n. Bagagiste *m.;* CH. DE F. Facteur *m.* ǁ **Luggage-rail,** n. AUTOM. Galerie *f.* ǁ **Luggage-trolley,** n. CH. DE F. Diable *m.* ǁ **Luggage-van,** n. CH. DE F. Fourgon (*m.*) aux bagages.
— N. B. *Luggage* est invariable et n'a pas de pluriel.
— adj. U. S. Cuir (colour).

lugger ['lʌgə*] n. NAUT. Lougre *m.*

lugubrious [lu:'gju:briəs] adj. Lugubre.

lugubriously [-li] adv. Lugubrement.

lug(worm) ['lʌg(,wə:m)] n. ZOOL. Ver (*m.*) de sable (or) des pêcheurs, arénicole *f.*

Luke [lu:k] n. Luc *m.*

lukewarm ['lu:kwɔ:m] adj. Tiède (lit. and fig.).

lukewarmness [-nis] n. Tiédeur *f.* (lit. and fig.).

lull [lʌl] v. tr. Bercer; *to lull to sleep,* endormir en berçant. ǁ NAUT. Calmer (sea, wind). ǁ FIG. Endormir.
— v. intr. Se calmer. ǁ NAUT. Calmir.
— n. NAUT. Accalmie; bonace *f.* ǁ FIG. Accalmie *f.;* moment de calme *m.*

lullaby ['lʌləbai] n. MUS. Berceuse *f.*

lumbago [lʌm'beigou] n. MED. Lumbago *m.*

lumbar ['lʌmbə*] adj., n. MED. Lombaire *f.*

lumber n. Objets hétéroclites *m. pl.;* bric-à-brac *m.* ǁ U. S. Bois (*m.*) de charpente. (See TIMBER.) ǁ FIG. Fatras *m.* ǁ **Lumber-mill,** n. Scierie *f.* ǁ **Lumber-room,** n. Fourre-tout, débarras, dépotoir, capharnaüm *m.* ǁ **Lumber-yard,** n. U. S. Chantier (*m.*) de bois d'œuvre.
— v. tr. Entasser en vrac, empiler (articles); encombrer, bourrer (*with,* de) [a room].
— v. intr. Débiter (wood).

lumber v. intr. *To lumber along,* avancer d'un pas pesant.

lumberer [-rə*] n. Bûcheron *m.*

lumberer [-rə˄] n. Lourdaud *m.*

lumbering [-riŋ] adj. Encombrant.
— n. Encombrement *m.* ǁ Exploitation (*f.*) de bois d'œuvre.

lumbering [-riŋ] adj. Lourd.

lumberjack [-,dʒæk] n. U. S. Bûcheron *m.*

lumberman [-mən] (pl. **lumbermen**) n. Bûcheron *m.*

lumbrical ['lʌmbrikəl] adj., n. MED. Lombrical *m.*

luminary ['lu:minəri] n. ASTRON. Astre, luminaire *m.* ǁ FIG. Lumière *f.*

luminescent [,lu:mi'nesənt] adj. Luminescent.

luminiferous [,lu:mi'nifərəs] adj. Resplendissant, illuminant, irradiant la lumière.

luminosity [,lu:mi'nɔsiti] n. Luminosité *f.*

luminous ['lu:minəs] adj. Lumineux. (See BRIGHT.)

luminously [-li] adv. Lumineusement.

luminousness [-nis] n. Luminosité *f.* (lit. and fig.).

lumme ['lʌmi] interj. POP. Zut alors!, fichtre!

lummox ['lʌməks] n. U. S. FAM. Balourd, godiche, godichon, pataud *s.*

lump [lʌmp] n. Tas, bloc *m.* ǁ Boulet *m.* (of coal);

motte *f.* (of earth); masse *f.* (of lead); bloc *m.* (of stone); morceau *m.* (of sugar). ǁ MED. Bosse *f.* ǁ COMM. *In the lump,* en bloc. ǁ FIN. *Lump sum,* somme globale; prix à forfait. ǁ FIG. Bloc, ensemble *m.;* masse *f.* ǁ FAM. Dadais, lourdaud *m.; great lump,* grand flandrin; *a lump in one's throat,* la gorge nouée.
— v. tr. Englober. entasser, réunir (*under,* sous).
— v. intr. Faire des mottes (earth). ǁ **To lump along,** marcher d'un pas lourd.

lump n. ZOOL. Lompe *m.*

lump v. tr. FAM. Encaisser; *if you don't like it, you can lump it,* si ça ne vous plaît pas, c'est le même prix (or) mettez votre mouchoir dessus.

lumpenproletariat [,lʌmpən,prouli'teəriət] n. Lumpenproletariat, sous-prolétariat *m.*

lumper [-ə*] n. NAUT. Débardeur *m.* ǁ ARCHIT. Petit entrepreneur à forfait *m.*

lumpish [-iʃ] adj. Balourd; lourdaud, godiche (clumsy). ǁ Lourd d'esprit (dull-witted).

lumpishness [-iʃnis] n. Gaucherie *f.* ǁ Lourdeur (*f.*) d'esprit.

lumpy [-i] adj. Plein de mottes (earth). ǁ CULIN. Grumeleux (sauce). ǁ MED. Plein de bosses. ǁ NAUT. Clapoteux (sea).

lunacy ['lu:nəsi] n. MED. Aliénation mentale, folie *f.* (See INSANITY.) ǁ FIG. Folie *f.*

lunar ['lu:nə*] adj. ASTRON. Lunaire (distance, month, year); lunaire, en forme de croissant (shape). ǁ MED. Semi-lunaire (bone).
— n. ASTRON. Etude de la lune *f.*

lunarian [lu:'nɛəriən] n. Habitant (*s.*) de la lune. ǁ Astronome (*m.*) qui observe la lune.

lunate ['lu:nit] adj. BOT. Luné.

lunatic ['lu:nətik] adj. MED. De fou, d'aliéné. ǁ FAM. Extravagant.
— n. MED. Aliéné, fou *s.; lunatic asylum,* asile d'aliénés. ǁ FAM. *Lunatic fringe,* la bande des extrémistes.

lunation [lu:'neiʃən] n. ASTRON. Lunaison *f.*

lunch [lʌnʃ] n. Déjeuner *m.* (mid-day meal). ǁ U. S. Casse-croûte *m* (snack). ǁ **Lunch-counter,** n. U. S. Snack-bar *m.* ǁ **Lunch-room,** n. U. S. Petit restaurant *m.* ǁ **Lunch-stall,** n. Cantine d'école *f.*
— v. intr. Déjeuner, luncher. ǁ U. S. Casser la croûte.
— v. tr. Faire déjeuner; offrir à déjeuner à.

luncheon ['lʌnʃən] n. Déjeuner *m.* (See LUNCH.) ǁ CH. DE F. Service *m.* ǁ U. S. Casse-croûte *m.;* collation *f.* (snack). ǁ **Luncheon-basket,** n. Panier-repas *m.*

luncheonette [,lʌnʃən'et] n. U. S. Snack-bar *m.*

luncher ['lʌnʃə*] n. Déjeuneur *s.*

lune [lu:n] n. MATH. Lunule *f.*

lunette [lu:'net] n. ARCHIT., MILIT. Lunette *f.*

lung [lʌŋ] n. MED. Poumon *m.; iron lung,* poumon d'acier. ǁ FAM. *At the top of one's lungs,* à pleins poumons.

lunge [lʌndʒ] n. Longe *f.*
— v. tr. Faire manœuvrer à la longe.

lunge n. Mouvement brusque (*m.*) en avant. ǁ SPORTS. Coup droit *m.;* botte *f.* (in fencing).
— v. intr. S'élancer brusquement en avant. ǁ SPORTS. Se fendre; pousser une botte (*at,* à). ǁ FIG. *To lunge out at,* lancer une estocade à.

lunger ['lʌŋə*] n. U. S. FAM. Tubard *m.*

lungwort ['lʌŋwɔ:t] n. BOT. Pulmonaire *f.*

lunula ['lu:njulə] (pl. **lunulae** [-i:]) n. MED., MATH. Lunule *f.*

lupercalia [,lu:pə:'keiljə] n. pl. Lupercales *f. pl.*

lupin, lupine ['lu:pin] n. BOT. Lupin *m.*

lupus ['lu:pəs] n. MED. Lupus *m.*

lurch [lə:tʃ] n. AUTOM. Embardée *f.* ǁ NAUT. Coup de roulis *m.;* embardée *f.*
— v. intr. AUTOM. Faire une embardée. ǁ NAUT.

Embarder, rouler. ‖ Aviat. Embarder. ‖ Fam. Vaciller, tituber.

lurch n. Fam. Panne *f.; to be left in the lurch,* rester en carafe; *to leave in the lurch,* laisser en plan (or) le bec dans l'eau, planter là.

lurcher [-ə*] n. Chapardeur *s.* (thief). ‖ Zool. Chien de braconnier *m.* (crossbred dog).

lure [ljuə*] n. Sports. Leurre *m.* ‖ Fig. Leurre, appât, piège *m.* ‖ Fig. Attrait *m.; attirance f.*
— v. tr. Sports. Leurrer. ‖ Fig. Leurrer, prendre au piège. ‖ Fig. Attirer, séduire.

lurid ['ljuərid] adj. Blafard, livide, blême (pale). ‖ Rougeoyant, flamboyant, feu, rouge-cuivré (glowing). ‖ Fig. Sombre (look); saisissant (news); tragique, sensationnel, hautement coloré (tale).

lurk [lə:k] v. intr. Se cacher, se tapir, s'embusquer. ‖ Fig. Se dissimuler.

lurker [-ə*] n. Individu (*m.*) aux aguets; mouchard *m.* (fam.).

lurking [-iŋ] adj. Fig. Caché, secret, intime. ‖ Lurking-place, n. Cachette *f.;* Sports. Affût *m.*

luscious ['lʌʃəs] adj. Culin. Succulent, délicieux, hautement savoureux (in general); fondant (fruit). ‖ Fig. Evocateur, savoureux, voluptueux, alanguissant (lascivious); douceâtre, édulcoré (sweet).

lusciousness [-nis] n. Culin. Succulence *f.* ‖ Fig. Edulcoration *f.;* volupté *f.*

lush [lʌʃ] adj. Bot. Plein de sève. ‖ Fam. Luxuriant, fleuri.

lush n. U. S. Pop. Pochard *s.*

lushy [-i] adj. Pop. Plein, soûl.

lust [lʌst] n. Luxure *f.; désir lascif m.* ‖ Eccles. Concupiscence *f.* ‖ Fig. Appétit *m.; soif, convoitise f.*
— v. intr. *To lust after* (or) *for,* désirer; Fig. Convoiter; avoir soif de.

luster ['lʌstə*] n. U. S. See LUSTRE.

lustful [-ful] adj. Luxurieux, lascif, lubrique (person). ‖ Plein de convoitise, allumé (look).

lustfully [-fuli] adv. Luxurieusement, lascivement.

lustfulness [-fulnis] n. Désir libidineux *m.; lascivité f.*

lustily [-ili] adv. Vigoureusement.

lustiness [-inis] n. Vigueur *f.*

lustral ['lʌstrəl] adj. Lustral.

lustrate [lʌs'treit] v. tr. † Purifier.

lustration [-ʃən] n. Lustration *f.*

lustre ['lʌstə*] n. Lustre *m.* (five years).

lustre n. Eclat, brillant, chatoiement *m.* (brilliance). ‖ Luisance *f.; lustre m.* (gloss). ‖ Cati *m.* (on a cloth); lustrine *f.* (glossy cloth). ‖ Vernis, brillant, glacis, lustre *m.* (on pottery); *lustre ware,* poterie mordorée. ‖ Lustre *m.* (chandelier); pendeloque *f.* (on a chandelier). ‖ Fig. Lustre *m.*
— v. tr. Lustrer (cloth, pottery).

lustreless [-lis] adj. Terne, mat. ‖ Fig. Sans éclat, terne.

lustrine ['lʌstrin] n. Lustrine *f.*

lustrous ['lʌstrəs] adj. Lustré (cloth, pottery). ‖ Fig. Chatoyant. (See BRIGHT.)

lustrum ['lʌstrəm] n. Lustre *m.* (five years).

lusty ['lʌsti] adj. Vigoureux, fort, bien bâti; costaud (fam.).

lutanist ['lu:tənist] n. Mus. Luthiste *s.*

lute [lu:t] n. Mus. Luth *m.* ‖ Lute-maker, n. Mus. Luthier *m.* ‖ Lute-player, n. Mus. Joueur (*s.*) de luth. ‖ Lute-string, n. Mus. Corde (*f.*) de luth.

lute n. Techn. Lut *m.*
— v. tr. Techn. Luter.

lutein ['lju:tiin] n. Chim. Lutéine *f.*

luteous ['lju:tiəs] adj. Orangé.

lutestring ['lju:tstriŋ] n. Fam. Lustrine *f.*

lutetium [lu'ti:ʃiəm] n. Chim. Lutécium *m.*

Lutheran ['lu:θərən] adj., n. Luthérien *s.*

lutheranism [-izm̩] n. Luthéranisme *m.*

lux [lʌks] (pl. **luces** ['lju:si:z]) n. Phys. Lux *m.*

luxate [lʌk'seit] v. tr. Med. Luxer.

luxation [-ʃən] n. Med. Luxation *f.*

luxe [luks] n. Luxe *m.; de-luxe hotel,* hôtel de grand luxe.

Luxembourg ['lʌksəmbə:g] n. Geogr. Luxembourg *m.* (province).

Luxemburg n. Geogr. Grand-duché de Luxembourg *m.*

luxuriance [lʌg'zjuəriəns] n. Luxuriance *f.*

luxuriant [-ənt] adj. Luxuriant.

luxuriate [-eit] v. intr. Bot. Pousser avec exubérance (or) à profusion. ‖ Fig. Prendre du bon temps; se complaire (*in,* dans); jouir délicieusement (*in,* de).

luxurious [-əs] adj. Luxueux, somptueux (splendid). ‖ Voluptueux, sensuel.

luxury ['lʌkʃəri] n. Luxe *m.; luxury article, tax, trade,* article, taxe, commerce de luxe. ‖ Pl. Plaisir *m.; douceur, délice, jouissance f.* ‖ † Volupté *f.*

lycanthropy [lai'kænθrəpi] n. Med. Lycanthropie *f.*

lyceum [lai'si:əm] n. † Lycée *m.* (at Athens). ‖ Auditorium *m.; salle (f.)* de conférences (lecture hall).

lycopod ['laikəpɔd] n. Bot. Lycopode *m.*

lye [lai] n. Chim. Lessive *f.*

lying ['laiiŋ] n. Mensonge *m.*
— adj. Mensonger, menteur.

lying n. Position couchée *f.* ‖ Repos *m.* (rest). ‖ Lit *m.;* couche *f.* (bed). ‖ Med. Décubitus *m.* ‖ Lying-in, n. Med. Couches *f. pl.*
— adj. Couché, étendu (person). ‖ Situé (place).

lyingly ['laiiŋli] adv. Mensongèrement.

lyke [laik] n. Cadavre *m.* (See LICH.) ‖ Lyke-wake, n. Veillée funèbre *f.*

lymph [limf] n. Med. Lymphe *f.*

lymphangitis [,limfæn'dʒaitis] n. Med. Lymphangite *f.*

lymphatic [lim'fætik] adj. Med., Fig. Lymphatique.
— n. Med. Vaisseau lymphatique *m.*

lymphocyte ['limfəsait] n. Med. Lymphocyte *m.*

lymphoid ['limfɔid] adj. Med. Lymphoïde.

lyncean [lin'siən] adj. De lynx (eye); à l'œil de lynx (person).

lynch [linʃ] v. tr. Lyncher.
— n. *Lynch law,* loi de Lynch.

lynching [-iŋ] n. Lynchage *m.*

lynx [liŋks] n. Zool. Lynx, loup-cervier *m.* ‖ Lynx-eyed, adj. A l'œil de lynx.

Lyons ['laiənz] n. Geogr. Lyon *m.*

lyre ['laiə*] n. Mus. Lyre *f.* ‖ Lyre-bird, n. Zool. Oiseau-lyre, ménure *m.*

lyric ['lirik] adj. Lyrique (poetry, poets).
— n. Poème lyrique *m.; pl.* poésie lyrique *f.* ‖ Theatr. Pl. Couplets (*m. pl.*) de revue.

lyrical [-əl] adj. Lyrique (ballads). ‖ Fam. Lyrique, dithyrambique.

lyricism ['lirisizm̩] n. Lyrisme *m.*

lyricist [-sist] n. Poète lyrique *m.* ‖ Parolier *m.* (song-writer).

lyrist ['laiərist] n. Mus. Joueur (*m.*) de lyre.

lysergic [li'sə:dʒik] adj. *Lysergic acid,* acide lysergique; *lysergic acid diethylamide,* L. S. D.

lysine ['laisin] n. Chim. Lysine *f.*

lysol ['laisɔl] n. (trade mark). Lysol, désinfectant (*m.*) à base de crésol.

M

m [em] n. M., m *m*. ‖ Mille *m*. (Roman numeral).
ma [mɑ:] n. Fam. Maman *f*.
M.A. [,em'ei] abbr. *Master of Arts*, see MASTER.
ma'am [mɑ:m] n. Madame *f*.
mac [mæk] n. Fam. Imper *m*. (mackintosh).
macabre [mə'kɑ:br] adj. Macabre; *macabre humour*, humour noir. ‖ Surnaturel.
macaco [mə'keikou], **macaque** [mə'kɑ:k] n. Zool. Macaque *m*. (monkey).
macaco n. Zool. Maki *m*. (lemur).
macadam [mə'kædəm] n. Macadam *m*.
— adj. En macadam.
macadamize [-aiz] v. tr. Macadamiser.
macaroni [,mækə'rouni] n. Culin. Macaroni *m*. ‖ † Muscadin *m*.
macaronic [-'rɔnik] adj. Macaronique.
— n. pl. Poème macaronique *m*.
macaroon [-ru:n] n. Culin. Macaron *m*.
macassar [mə'kæsə*] adj. De macassar (oil).
macaw [mə'kɔ:] n. Zool. Ara *m*. (See PARROT.)
Maccabeus [,mækə'bi:əs] adj. † Macchabée.
mace [meis] n. Milit., Jur., Sports. Masse *f*. ‖ **Mace-bearer,** n. Jur. Massier *m*.
mace n. Bot., Culin. Macis *m*.
Macedonia [,məse'dounjə] n. Geogr. Macédoine *f*.
macerate ['mæsəreit] v. tr. Faire macérer.
— v. intr. Macérer.
maceration [,mæsə'reiʃən] n. Macération *f*.
Mach (number) [mæk (nʌmbə*)] n. Aviat. Nombre (m.) de Mach; *mach one, two, etc.*, mach 1, 2, etc.
machete [mə'tʃeti] n. Machette *f*.
Machiavelli [,mækiə'veli] n. Machiavel *m*. ‖ Fig. Etre machiavélique *m*.
machiavellian [-iən] adj. Machiavélique.
machiavellism [-izm] n. Machiavélisme *m*.
machicolated [mə'tʃikəleitid] adj. Archit. A mâchicoulis.
machicolation [-ʃən] n. Archit. Mâchicoulis *m*.
machinable [mə'ʃi:nəbl] adj. Techn. Usinable.
machinate ['mækineit] v. intr. Comploter.
machination [,mæki'neiʃən] n. Machination *f*.
machinator ['mækineitə*] n. Machinateur *m*.; machinatrice *f*.
machine [mə'ʃi:n] n. Techn., Phys. Machine *f*. ‖ Aviat. Appareil *m*. ‖ Autom. Machine *f*. (bicycle, car). ‖ U. S. Leviers (*m. pl.*) de commande; noyau directeur *m*. (of a political party). ‖ Fig. Machine *f*.; automate *m*. ‖ **Machine-finish,** v. tr. Techn. Usiner. ‖ **Machine-gun,** n. Milit. Mitrailleuse *f*.; v. tr. Milit. Mitrailler. ‖ **Machine-gunner,** n. Milit. Mitrailleur *m*. ‖ **Machine-gunning,** n. Milit. Mitraillage *m*. ‖ **Machine-made,** adj. Fait à la machine, mécanique. ‖ **Machine-readable,** adj. Inform. En langage machine. ‖ **Machine-shop,** n. Techn. Atelier d'usinage *m*. (or) de construction; machinerie *f*. ‖ **Machine-stitch,** v. tr. Piquer à la machine. ‖ **Machine-tool,** n. Techn. Machine-outil *m*.
— v. tr. Coudre à la machine. ‖ Techn. Faire mécaniquement; usiner.
machinery [mə'ʃi:nəri] n. Techn. Machinerie *f*.; machines *f*. pl. ‖ Fig. Rouages, organes *m*. pl.; mécanisme, outillage *m*. ‖ Fig. Intervention (*f*.) du merveilleux (in literature).
machinist [-ist] n. Techn. Machiniste *m*. (designer).

mécanicien *m*. (mechanic); **mécanicienne** *f*. (sewing-machine operator).
machismo [mæt'ʃizmou] n. Machisme *m*.
macho ['mætʃou] (pl. **machos** [-z]) n. Macho *m*.
mackerel ['mækrəl] adj. Pommelé (sky).
mackerel n. Zool. Maquereau *m*.
mackintosh ['mækintɔʃ] n. Imperméable, mackintosh *m*. (raincoat). ‖ Tissu imperméable *m*.; gabardine *f*. (cloth).
mac(k)le ['mækl] n. Maculature *f*., macle *f*.
— v. tr. Maculer.
macramé ['mækrə,mei] n. Macramé *m*.
macrobiotic [,mækroubai'ɔtik] adj. Macrobiotique.
macrocephalic [,mækrosə'fælik] adj. Med. Macrocéphale.
macrocosm ['mækrokɔzm] n. Macrocosme *m*.
macro-economics [,mækro,i:kə'nɔmiks] n. sg. Macro-économie *f*.
macromolecule [,mækro'mɔli,kju:l] n. Phys., Chim. Macromolécule *f*.
macron ['meikrɔn] n. Gramm. Macron *m*.
macrophotography [,mækrofə'tɔgrəfi] n. Macrophotographie *f*.
macrophysics [,mækro'fiziks] n. sg. Phys. Macrophysique *f*.
macroscopic [,mækro'skɔpik] adj. Macroscopique.
macula ['mækjulə] (pl. **maculae** [-i:]) n. Macule *f*.
maculation [,mækju'leiʃən] n. Maculature *f*. (spot); maculage *m*. (spotting).
maculate ['mækjuleit] v. tr. Maculer.
mad [mæd] adj. Fou *m*.; folle *f*.; insensé (action); fou (person). ‖ Fou, hors de soi; *mad with fear*, fou de peur. ‖ Fou, furieux, en fureur; *to drive s.o. mad*, faire damner qqn, exaspérer qqn. ‖ Fou, possédé, acharné; *to work like mad*, travailler avec acharnement. ‖ Tout fou, extravagant (in gaiety). ‖ Fou, entiché, toqué (*about*, de); *mad about drawing*, passionné de dessin. ‖ Med. Enragé (dog); dément, aliéné (person). ‖ Fam. *Mad as a hatter*, fou à lier. ‖ **Mad-house,** n. Med., Fam. Maison (*f*.) de fous.
Madagascar [,mædə'gæskə*] n. Geogr. Madagascar *f*.
madam ['mædəm] n. Madame, Mademoiselle *f*. ‖ Pop. Tenancière de maison close *f*.
madcap ['mædkæp] n. Ecervelé *s*.; tête folle *f*.
madden [-n] v. tr. Rendre fou, exaspérer.
— v. intr. S'exaspérer, devenir fou.
madder ['mædə*] n. Bot., Comm. Garance *f*.
madding [-iŋ] adj. Affolé, éperdu; bruyant.
made [meid] pret., p.p. See MAKE. ‖ Culin. Elaboré, varié (dish); compliqué (gravy). ‖ Med. Charpenté. ‖ Fig. Arrivé (man). ‖ **Made-up,** ad. Composé (page); inventé (story); maquillé (woman). ‖ **Made-to-order,** ad. Comm. Fait sur mesure (dress).
Madeira [mə'diərə] n. Geogr. Madère *f*. ‖ Culin. Madère *m*. (wine); *Madeira cake*, gâteau de Savoie.
madly ['mædli] adv. Follement. ‖ En fureur. ‖ Eperdument, à la folie.
madman [-mən] (pl. **madmen**) n. Fou, dément, aliéné *m*.
madness ['mædnis] n. Folie *f*. (folly). ‖ Fureur, exaspération *f*. (fury). ‖ Folie *f*.; emballement *m*. (excitement). ‖ Med. Folie, démence, aliénation *f*. (insanity); rage *f*. (rabies). ‖ Fam. *There is method in his madness*, il n'est pas si fou qu'il en a l'air.
Madonna [mə'dɔnə] n. Madone *f*.

madras [mə'drɑ:s] n. COMM. Madras *m.*
madrepore ['mædripɔ:*] n. Madrépore *m.*
madrigal ['mædrigəl] n. Madrigal *m.*
Madrilenian [,mædri'li:niən] adj., n. GEOGR. Madrilène *s.*
madwoman ['mæd,wumən] (pl. **madwomen**) n. Folle, démente, aliénée *f.*
Maecenas [mi:'si:nəs] n. Mécène *m.*
Maelstrom ['meilstrɔm] n. GEOGR. Malstrom *m.* ‖ FIG. Tourbillon *m.*
maenad ['mi:næd] n. Ménade *f.*
maestro ['maistrou] n. MUS. Maestro *m.*
Mae-West ['mei'west] n. AVIAT. POP. Gilet de sauvetage *m.*
maffick ['mæfik] v. intr. Manifester joyeusement.
mafia ['mæfiə] n. Mafia *f.*
mafioso [,mæfi'ousou] n. Mafioso *m.*
mag [mæg] n. FAM. Magazine *m.*, revue *f.* ; hebdomadaire, hebdo *m.* (weekly).
magazine [,mægə'zi:n] n. Magazine, périodique *m.* ; revue *f.* (publication). ‖ MILIT. Magasin, dépôt *m.* (storeroom) ; magasin *m.* (of guns).
magazinist [-ist] n. Collaborateur (*m.*) d'une revue.
Magdalen ['mægdəlin] n. Madeleine *f.* (name). ‖ FAM. Repentie *f.*
— ['mɔ:dlin] adj. De la Madeleine (College).
Magdalenian [mægdə'li:niən] adj. GEOL. Magdalénien.
magenta [mə'dʒentə] adj., n. Magenta, fuchsia *m.* (colour).
maggot ['mægɔt] n. ZOOL. Asticot *m.* ‖ FAM. Lubie, toquade *f.*
maggoty [-i] adj. Plein de vers. ‖ FAM. Lunatique, fantaisiste.
Magi ['meidʒai]. See MAGUS.
Magian [-dʒiən] adj. Des rois mages.
— n. Roi mage *m.* (magus). ‖ Magicien *m.* (wizard).
magic ['mædʒik] adj. Magique.
— n. Magie *f.*
magical [-kl] adj. Magique.
magically [-əli] adv. Magiquement.
magician [mə'dʒiʃən] n. Magicien *s.*
Maginot-line ['mædʒinou'lain] n. MILIT. Ligne (*f.*) Maginot. ‖ **Maginot-minded,** adj. FAM. Persuadé de l'inviolabilité de la ligne Maginot ; obsédé par une idée défensive.
magisterial [,mædgis'tiəriəl] adj. Magistral, de maître. ‖ Autoritaire, dominateur. (See MASTERFUL.) ‖ JUR. En qualité de magistrat.
magisterially [-i] adv. Magistralement ; en maître. ‖ JUR. En qualité de magistrat.
magistracy ['mædʒistrəsi] n. JUR. Magistrature *f.*
magistral [mə'dʒistrəl] adj. MED., MILIT., FIG. Magistral.
magistrate ['mædʒistreit] n. JUR. Magistrat ; juge (*m.*) de paix ; *examining magistrate,* juge d'instruction.
magma ['mægmə] (pl. **magmata** [-tə]) n. CHIM., GEOL. Magma *m.*
Magna Carta ['mægnə'kɑ:tə] n. Grande Charte *f.*
magnanimity [,mægnə'nimiti] n. Magnanimité *f.*
magnanimous [mæg'næniməs] adj. Magnanime.
magnanimously [-məsli] adv. Magnanimement.
magnate ['mægneit] n. Magnat *m.* ; *oil magnate,* roi du pétrole, pétrolier.
magnesia [mæg'ni:ʒiə] n. CHIM., MED. Magnésie *f.*
magnesium [-ziəm] n. CHIM. Magnésium *m.*
magnet ['mægnit] n. PHYS., FIG. Aimant *m.*
magnetic [mæg'netik] adj. Magnétique (fluid, look, person). ‖ PHYS. Magnétique (axis, circuit, field, meridian, pole, tape) ; aimanté (needle) ; *magnetic deviation,* déviation de la boussole.
— n. pl. PHYS. Magnétisme *m.* (science).
magnetically [mæg'netikəli] adv. Magnétiquement.
magnetism ['mægnitizm] n. Magnétisme *m.* (force, property).

magnetite [-ait] n. Magnétite *f.*
magnetize [-aiz] v. tr. PHYS. Aimanter. ‖ MED. Magnétiser. ‖ FIG. Attirer.
magneto [mæg'ni:tou] n. ELECTR. Magnéto *f.* ‖ **Magneto-electric,** adj. ELECTR. Magnéto-électrique. ‖ **Magneto-shield,** n. AUTOM. Couvercle (*m.*) de magnéto.
magnetron ['mægni,trɔn] n. ELECTR. Magnétron *m.*
magnific(al) [mæg'nifik(əl)] adj. Magnifique.
magnification [,mægnifi'keiʃən] n. Glorification *f.* (of s.o.) ; amplification *f.* (of sth.). ‖ PHYS. Grossissement *m.*
magnificence [mæg'nifisns] n. Magnificence *f.*
magnificent [-nt] adj. Magnifique, somptueux. (See GRAND.)
magnificently [-ntli] adv. Magnifiquement.
magnifico [mæg'nifikou] n. † Grand, magnifique *m.* (Venitian lord). ‖ FAM. Ponte *m.*
magnifier ['mægnifaiə*] n. PHYS. Loupe *f.* ‖ FIG. Exagérateur *m.* ; exagératrice *f.*
magnify [-fai] v. tr. (2). PHYS. Grossir (an image) ; amplifier (a sound). ‖ † Magnifier, exalter. ‖ FIG. Grossir, exagérer, amplifier.
magnifying [-faiiŋ] adj. PHYS. Grossissant ; *magnifying glass,* loupe, verre grossissant.
magniloquence [mæg'niləkwəns] n. Grandiloquence ; emphase *f.*
magniloquent [-kwənt] adj. Grandiloquent.
magnitude ['mægnitju:d] n. ASTRON. Magnitude *f.* ‖ FIG. Ampleur *f.* (of a problem).
magnolia [mæg'nouljə] n. BOT. Magnolia *m.*
magnum ['mægnəm] n. Magnum *m.* (bottle). ‖ **Magnum-bonum,** n. BOT. Prune-abricot *f.* (plum) ; saucisse *f.* (potato).
magpie ['mægpai] n. ZOOL. Pie *f.* ‖ MILIT. Coup (*m.*) sur l'avant-dernier cercle de la cible. ‖ FAM. Jacasse *f.* (chatterbox).
Magus ['meigəs] (pl. **Magi** ['meidʒai]) n. Mage *m.* ; *Simon Magus,* Simon le Magicien ; *the Magi,* les Rois mages.
maharaja(h) [,mɑ:hə'rɑ:dʒə] n. Maharadjah *m.*
maharanee [-ni:] n. Maharani *f.*
mahatma [mə'hɑ:tmə] n. Mahatma *m.*
mah-jong(g) [,mɑ:'dʒɔŋ] n. Mah-jong *m.*
mahlstick ['mɔ:lstik] n. ARTS. Appui-main *m.*
mahogany [mə'hɔgəni] n. BOT., COMM. Acajou *m.* (colour, tree, wood).
— adj. En acajou (table). ‖ Acajou (colour).
Mahometan [mə'hɔmitən] adj., n. Mahométan *s.*
Mahometanism [-izm] n. Mahométanisme *m.*
mahout [mə'haut] n. Cornac *m.*
maid [meid] n. Vierge, jeune fille *f.* (maiden) ; *old maid,* vieille fille. ‖ Domestique, bonne *f.* (servant). ‖ ECCLES. *The Maid,* la Pucelle. ‖ **Maid-of-all-work,** n. Bonne (*f.*) à tout faire.
maiden ['meidn] n. Vierge, jeune fille *f.* (maid). ‖ † Guillotine *f.*
— adj. Non mariée (unmarried) ; virginal (virgin). ‖ De jeune fille ; *maiden name,* nom de jeune fille. ‖ BOT. Vierge, non taillé (plant). ‖ SPORTS. Pour chevaux inédits (races) ; inédit, qui n'a gagné aucun prix (horse). ‖ JUR. Blanc, sans cause à juger (session). ‖ NAUT. Premier (voyage). ‖ FIG. Vierge, premier, de débutant ; *maiden speech,* premier discours ; discours inaugural.
maidenhair [-hɛə*] n. BOT. Capillaire *m.*
maidenhead [-hed] n. Virginité *f.* (quality). ‖ MED. Hymen *m.*
maidenhood [-hud] n. Célibat *m.* (state, time).
maidenly [-li] adj. Virginal, pudique, modeste.
— adv. Modestement, pudiquement.
maidservant ['meid,sə:vənt] n. Servante *f.*
maieutics [mæ'ju:tiks] n. pl. Maïeutique *f.*
mail [meil] n. Cotte (*f.*) de mailles.

— v. tr. Revêtir d'une cotte de mailles. ‖ Fig. *The mailed fist*, la trique, la manière forte.

mail n. Courrier *m.* (letters). ‖ Poste *f.* (conveyance); *air mail services*, messageries aériennes; *Royal Mail*, Service des Postes. ‖ Ch. de f. Train postal *m.*; U. S. *railway mail clerk*, convoyeur des postes. ‖ Naut. *Indian mail*, malle des Indes. ‖ **Mail-bag,** n. Sac postal *m.* ‖ **Mail-boat,** n. Naut. Bateau-poste *m.* ‖ **Mail-car,** n. Ch. de f. Wagon postal *m.*; Fam. Voiture d'enfant. ‖ **Mail carrier,** n. U. S. Facteur *m.* ‖ **Mail catcher,** n. U. S. Ch. de f. Transporteur (*m.*) de sacs postaux. ‖ **Mail-coach,** n. Malle-poste *f.* ‖ **Mail-order,** n. Comm. Commande par poste *f.*; *mail-order firm*, entreprise de vente par correspondance. ‖ **Mail-plane,** n. Aviat. Avion postal *m.* ‖ **Mail-train,** n. Ch. de f. Train postal *m.* ‖ **Mail-van,** n. Ch. de. f. Fourgon postal *m.*
— v. tr. Envoyer par la poste; poster. ‖ Comm. *Mailing list*, fichier d'adresses (for advertising purposes).

mailbox [-,bɔks] n. U. S. Boîte (*f.*) aux lettres.

mailman [-mən] (pl. **mailmen**) n. U. S. Facteur *m.*

maim [meim] v. tr. Estropier, mutiler. ‖ Fam. Mutiler (a text).

main [mein] adj. Puissant, total; *by main force*, de vive force. ‖ Techn. Principal; *main sewer*, égout collecteur. ‖ Agric. Principal (crop). ‖ Ch. de f. Grand (line). ‖ Naut. Principal (deck); majeur (mast). ‖ Aviat. Sustentateur (wing). ‖ Milit. *Main body*, gros (of the army). ‖ Comm. *Main office*, bureau central, siège social. ‖ Gramm. Principal (clause). ‖ Fig. Saillant (feature); dominant (idea); *the main thing*, l'essentiel. ‖ **Main-brace,** n. Naut. Grand bras *m.* (of yard); Fam. *To splice the main-brace*, servir une tournée de rhum supplémentaire. ‖ **Main-traveled,** adj. U.S. Passant, à grosse circulation (road). ‖ **Main-yard,** n. Naut. Grand-vergue *f.*
— n. Force *f.*; *with might and main*, à tour de bras, de toutes ses forces. ‖ Principal, essentiel *m.*; *in the main*, en général, en gros, dans l'ensemble. ‖ Techn. Conduite (or) canalisation principale *m.* (pipe); grand collecteur *m.* (sewer). ‖ Electr. Câble (*m.*) de distribution, secteur *m.* ‖ Radio. *Mains set*, secteur. ‖ Naut. Grand mât (mast); haute mer *f.* (ocean).

mainland [-lənd] n. Geogr. Continent *m.*

mainline [-lain] v. intr. Pop. Se shooter.

mainly [-li] adv. Principalement. (See especially.)

mainmast [-mɑ:st] n. Naut. Grand mât *m.*

mainsail [-seil, -sḷ] n. Naut. Grand-voile *f.*

mainsheet [-ʃi:t] n. Naut. Grand-écoute *f.*

mainspring [-spriŋ] n. Techn. Grand ressort *m.* ‖ Fig. Principe déterminant, mobile principal *m.*

mainstay [-stei] n. Naut. Etai de grand mât *m.* ‖ Fig. Assise principale *f.*; fondement, essentiel *m.*

mainstream [-stri:m] n. Courant dominant *m.*, tradition, habitude *f.*; *in the mainstream of*, dans le droit fil de.
— adj. Traditionnel, ordinaire, habituel.

maintain [men'tein] v. tr. Entretenir, faire vivre, assurer la subsistance de, subvenir aux besoins de (one's family). [See support.] ‖ Techn., Med. Entretenir. ‖ Jur. Soutenir (a cause); maintenir (order); défendre (one's rights). ‖ Milit. Entretenir (an army); soutenir (a siege). ‖ Fig. Garder, conserver (an advantage); entretenir (friendship); maintenir, soutenir (an opinion); soutenir (one's reputation); observer (silence); *to maintain one's ground*, maintenir ses positions, ne pas céder un pouce de terrain.

maintainable [-əbḷ] adj. Tenable (position); soutenable (opinion).

maintenance ['meintinəns] n. Entretien *m.*; *maintenance allowance, order*, pension, obligation alimentaire. ‖ Techn. Entretien *m.*; *maintenance man*, dépanneur. ‖ Jur. Maintien *m.* (of order); défense *f.*

(of one's rights). ‖ Loc. *In maintenance of*, à l'appui de.

maintop ['meintɔp] n. Naut. Grand-hune *f.*; *maintop gallant*, grand perroquet; *maintop mast*, grand mât de hune; *maintop sail*, grand hunier.

Maintz [maintz] n. Geogr. Mayence *f.*

maison(n)ette [,meizə'net] n. Maison individuelle *f.*; appartement en duplex *m.*

maize [meiz] n. Bot. Maïs *m.*
— adj. Jaune maïs.

majestic [mə'dʒestik] adj. Majestueux.

majestically [-əli] adv. Majestueusement.

majesty ['mædʒəsti] n. Majesté *f.*

majolica [mə'dʒɔlikə] n. Majolique *f.*

major ['meidʒə*] adj. Majeur, plus grand. ‖ Philos., Eccles., Jur., Mus. Majeur. ‖ Autom. De priorité (road). ‖ U.S. Principal (study).
— n. Jur. Majeur *s.* (person). ‖ Philos. Majeure *f.* ‖ Milit. Commandant; chef de bataillon (or) d'escadrons *m.* ‖ U. S. Matière principale *f.* (at school). ‖ **Major-general,** n. Milit. Général (*m.*) de division.
— v. intr. U. S. Se spécialiser (in, dans) [a study].

majordomo [,meidʒə'doumou] n. Majordome *m.*

majority [mə'dʒɔriti] n. Majorité, majeure partie *f.* ‖ Jur. Majorité *f.* (in age, politics). ‖ Milit. Grade de commandant *m.*

majuscule ['mædʒə,skju:l] adj. Capital; *majuscule script*, écriture capitale (in palaeography).
— n. Capitale *f.* (in palaeography).

make [meik] v. tr. (100).

---

1. Fabriquer. — 2. Arranger. — 3. Provoquer. — 4. Effectuer. — 5. Causer. — 6. Formuler. — 7. Constituer. — 8. Etablir. — 9. Devenir. — 10. Former. — 11. Créer. — 12. Rendre. — 13. Représenter. — 14. Tirer. — 15. Apprécier. — 16. Tenir. — 17. Gagner. — 18. Essayer. — 19. Faire suivi de l'infinitif. — 20. Obliger. — 21. Culin. — 22. Math. — 23. Electr. — 24. Ch. de f. — 25. Milit. — 26. Naut. — 27. Sports. — 28. Jur. — 29. Fin. — 30. Eccles. — 31. Fam. — 32. To make after. — 33. To make down. — 34. To make of. — 35. To make out. — 36. To make over. — 37. To make up.

---

1. Faire, fabriquer; *to make barrels*, faire des tonneaux; *to make a machine*, construire une machine. ‖ 2. Faire, arranger; *to make the beds*, faire les lits. ‖ 3. Faire, provoquer; *to make haste*, se hâter; *to make a noise*, faire du bruit; *to make use of*, se servir de. ‖ 4. Faire, effectuer, exécuter (an attempt); *to make the distance*, effectuer (or) couvrir la distance; *to make way*, faire du chemin. ‖ 5. Causer, provoquer, produire, susciter; *to make a change*, provoquer un changement. ‖ 6. Faire, formuler (an offer, a proposal, a speech); *to make a complaint*, porter plainte; *to make an excuse*, présenter une excuse. ‖ 7. Faire, constituer; *to make pleasant reading*, être agréable à lire. ‖ 8. Faire, établir, fixer; *to make a rule that*, établir en principe que. ‖ 9. Faire, devenir; *to make a good leader*, faire un bon conducteur d'hommes. ‖ 10. Faire, former; *to make a fool of oneself*, se conduire sottement, se tourner en ridicule; *to make game of*, se moquer de. ‖ 11. Faire, créer; *to make s.o. a knight*, faire qqn chevalier; *to make s.o. president*, porter qqn à la présidence, élire qqn président. ‖ 12. Rendre; *this portrait makes you an old man*, ce portrait vous vieillit; *to make oneself uneasy*, s'en faire, se tourmenter; *to make s.o. hungry*, donner faim à qqn. ‖ 13. Faire, représenter; *he is not so bad as you make him*, vous le faites plus mauvais qu'il n'est. ‖ 14. Tirer; *to make the best of*, tirer le meilleur parti de; *to make little, much of*, faire peu, beaucoup de cas de. ‖ 15. Apprécier,

évaluer ; *he made the distance about forty miles,* il estima la distance à quarante milles environ ; *what do you make the time?,* quelle heure croyez-vous qu'il est ? ‖ **16.** Tenir ; *to make good a promise,* tenir une promesse. ‖ **17.** Se faire, gagner ; *to make many friends,* se faire beaucoup d'amis. ‖ **18.** Essayer ; *he made to speak, but he couldn't utter a word,* il tenta de parler mais il ne put prononcer un mot. ‖ **19.** Faire (with an infinitive) ; *to make do,* s'arranger, se contenter (*with,* de) ; *to make s.o. repeat a word,* faire répéter un mot à qqn. ‖ **20.** Faire, obliger à ; forcer à ; *he soon made his influence felt,* il eut bientôt fait sentir son influence ; *he was made to appear before the judge,* on l'a fait comparaître devant le juge ; *to make oneself hated,* se faire haïr ; *to make serious people respect one,* se faire respecter des gens sérieux. ‖ **21.** CULIN. Faire (a meal, tea). ‖ **22.** MATH. *Two halves make an entirety,* deux moitiés font un entier. ‖ **23.** ELECTR. Fermer (a circuit) ; effectuer, mettre (a contact). ‖ **24.** CH. DE F., FAM. *To make the train,* avoir le train, arriver à temps pour prendre le train. ‖ **25.** MILIT. Faire (peace, war). ‖ **26.** NAUT. Faire, filer (knots) ; approcher de, accoster à (land) ; *to make bad weather,* rencontrer gros temps ; *to make port,* arriver à bon port ; *to make sail,* faire voile. ‖ **27.** SPORTS. Battre, faire (the cards) ; faire (a trick) ; ramasser avec (a trump) ; *to make the team,* se faire admettre dans l'équipe. ‖ **28.** JUR. Faire (one's will) ; *to make default,* faire défaut. ‖ **29.** FIN. Gagner (money) ; faire (a purchase) ; *to make a fortune,* faire fortune ; *to make good a loss to,* dédommager qqn d'une perte. ‖ **30.** ECCLES. Créer, faire (man, world). ‖ **31.** U. S. POP. *To make a girl,* finir par tomber une fille ; *to make s.o.,* faire la fortune de qqn ; *to make sth.,* piquer (or) faucher qqch. ‖ **32.** **To make after,** pourchasser, poursuivre. ‖ **33. To make down,** retailler en plus petit, diminuer (a dress). ‖ **34. To make of,** considérer, comprendre, envisager (s.o.'s actions). ‖ **35. To make out,** dresser, établir, faire (an account, a list) ; établir (a conclusion) ; remplir (a form) ; déchiffrer (handwriting) ; comprendre (a problem) ; distinguer, apercevoir (sth.) ; *I can't make it out,* je n'y comprends rien ; *to make out that,* prétendre que ; *to make s.o. out,* faire (or) présenter (or) dépeindre qqn (to represent) ; comprendre qqn (to understand). ‖ **36. To make over,** céder, transmettre, léguer (*to,* à) ; U. S. transformer (a dress). ‖ **37. To make up,** faire, confectionner (a dress) ; recharger, garnir (the fire) ; dresser (a list) ; regagner (lost ground) ; maquiller, farder (oneself, s.o.'s face) ; faire (a parcel) ; rassembler, réunir (people) ; former, constituer, composer (a whole) ; U. S. repasser, se représenter à (an examination) ; TECHN. Mettre en page (a book) ; MED. Préparer (a potion) ; FIN. Régler (an account) ; faire (a balance-sheet) ; combler (a difference) ; compléter (a sum) ; *to make it up to s.o. for sth.,* dédommager (or) indemniser qqn de qqch. ; *to make up the even money,* faire l'appoint ; FIG. Arranger (an argument, differences) ; inventer, forger (a story) ; *to make it up again,* se réconcilier ; *to make up one's mind to,* se résoudre à. — v. intr. Aller, s'avancer ; faire route (*for, towards,* vers) ; se rendre (*for,* à). ‖ Agir (*against,* contre ; *for,* pour) ; *to make for,* être propice à, favoriser. ‖ Rendre ; *to make fast,* fixer solidement ; *to make ready,* apprêter, préparer. ‖ Se faire, se montrer, devenir ; *to make free with,* prendre des libertés avec ; *to make merry,* s'amuser ; *to make sure of,* s'assurer de. ‖ Faire mine de ; *to make as if to,* faire semblant de. ‖ NAUT. Baisser (ebb) ; monter (flood). ‖ ELECTR. *To make and break,* s'allumer et s'éteindre. ‖ U. S. POP. *To make like,* imiter, faire comme. ‖ **To make away,** s'éloigner ; *to make away with,* soustraire (money) ; gaspiller (one's fortune) ;

supprimer (s.o.) ; détruire, faire disparaître (sth.) ; *to make away with oneself,* se suicider, se détruire (fam.). ‖ **To make off,** décamper, détaler, déguerpir, filer. ‖ **To make out,** U. S. FAM. Aller, prospérer ; subsister. ‖ **To make up,** se maquiller ; *to make up for,* réparer (a fault) ; compenser (a loss) ; rattraper (lost time) ; suppléer à (sth. wanting) ; *to make up to,* s'approcher de ; FIG. Faire des avances à. — n. Stature *f.* (of a person). ‖ Façon *f.* (of a dress) ; forme *f.* (of an object). ‖ TECHN., CULIN. Fabrication *f.* ‖ COMM. Marque *f.* ‖ ELECTR. Fermeture *f.* ‖ FAM. *To be on the make,* se pousser, essayer de faire ses affaires (businessman) ; U. S. Etre en quête de bonnes fortunes (man). ‖ **Make-and-break,** n. ELECTR. Conjoncteur-disjoncteur *m.* ; adj. ELECTR. Intermittent (current). ‖ **Make-believe,** n. Faux-semblant, trompe-l'œil *m.* ; chimères *f. pl.* ; adj. FAM. Prétendu, de chiqué ; v. tr. faire semblant. ‖ **Make-do,** adj. De fortune. ‖ **Make-peace,** n. Pacificateur, médiateur *m.* ‖ **Make-up,** n. Confection *f.* (of dress) ; maquillage *m.* (of s.o.) ; arrangement *m.* (of sth.) ; TECHN. Mise (*f.*) en pages (in printing) ; FAM. Invention *f.* ‖ **Make-weight,** n. Complément de poids *m.* ; FAM. Bouche-trou *m.*

maker [-ə*] n. Faiseur *s.* (in dress-making). ‖ TECHN. Fabricant *m.* (of hats) ; constructeur *m.* (of machines). ‖ ECCLES. Créateur *m.* ‖ **Maker-up,** n. Maquilleur *m.* ; TECHN. Metteur *m.* en pages (in printing) ; COMM. Emballeur *m.*

makeshift [-ʃift] n. Moyen (*m.*) de fortune. ‖ FIG. Pis-aller, expédient ; truc *m.* (fam.). — adj. De fortune (dinner) ; de circonstance (government).

making [-iŋ] n. Confection *f.* (of dress). ‖ TECHN. Fabrication *f.* (in general). ‖ Construction *f.* (of machines). ‖ CULIN. Confection, fabrication *f.* ‖ FIN. Pl. Petits profits *m. pl.* ‖ FIG. Composition *f.* (of a book) ; élément (*m.*) de réussite (of s.o.). ‖ FAM. *To have the makings of,* avoir l'étoffe de.

malachite ['mæləˌkait] n. Malachite *f.*

maladjusted [ˌmælə'dʒʌstid] adj. TECHN. Mal ajusté. ‖ FIG. Inadapté.

maladjustment [-mənt] n. TECHN. Mauvais ajustement *m.* ‖ FIG. Inadaptation *f.* ; dérèglement *m.*

maladminister [ˌmæləd'ministə*] v. tr. U. S. Mal administrer.

maladministration [mælədˌminis'treiʃən] n. Mauvaise administration *f.*

maladroit ['mælədrɔit] adj. Maladroit. (See AWKWARD.)

maladroitly [-li] adv. Maladroitement.

maladroitness [-nis] n. Maladresse *f.*

malady ['mælədi] n. MED. Maladie *f.* (See DISEASE.)

Malaga ['mæləgə] n. GEOGR., CULIN. Malaga *m.*

Malagasy [ˌmælə'gæsi] adj., n. GEOGR. Malgache *s.*

malaise [mæ'leiz] n. Malaise *m.*

malapropism ['mæləprɔpizm] n. Impropriété d'expression *f.*

malapropos [ˌmæləprə'pou] adv. Mal à propos. — adj. Inopportun, inapproprié. — r Acte (*m.*) effectué mal à propos ; impair *m.*

malaria [mə'lɛəriə] n. MED. Malaria *f.* ; paludisme *m.* ‖ Malaria-stricken, adj. MED. Impaludé.

malarial [-əl] adj. MED. Paludéen (fever) ; de la malaria (mosquito).

malassimilation [mæləˌsimi'leiʃən] n. MED. Mauvaise assimilation *f.*

Malawi [mə'lɑːwi] n. GEOGR. Malawi *m.*

Malay [mə'lei] adj., n. GEOGR. Malais *s.*

Malaya [-jə] n. GEOGR. Malaisie *f.*

Malaysia [mə'leiziə] n. GEOGR. Malaysia *f.*

malcontent ['mælkənˌtent] adj., n. Mécontent *s.*

Maldives ['mɔːldaivz] n. pl. GEOGR. Maldives *f. pl.*

male [meil] adj. BOT., ZOOL., TECHN. Mâle. ‖ MED., GRAMM. Masculin. ‖ Loc. *Male friend,* ami. — n. Mâle *m.*

malediction [ˌmæli'dikʃən] n. Malédiction *f.*

maledictory [-təri] adj. De malédiction.

malefaction [,mæli'fækʃən] n. Méfait *m.*

malefactor ['mælifæktə*] n. Malfaiteur *m.;* malfaitrice *f.*

malefic [mə'lefik] adj. Maléfique.

maleficence [-fisns] n. Malfaisance *f.*

maleficient [-fisnt] adj. Malfaisant (*to*, pour); nuisible (*to*, à). ‖ Criminel.

malevolence [mə'levələns] n. Malveillance *f.*

malevolent [-lənt] adj. Malveillant.

malevolently [-ləntli] adv. Avec malveillance.

malfeasance [məl'fi:zns] n. JUR. Acte illégal *m.;* agissements coupables *m. pl.*

malfeasant [-znt] adj. JUR. Coupable.

malformation [,mælfɔ:'meiʃən] n. MED. Malformation *f.*

malfunction [mæl'fʌŋkʃən] n. Dérèglement, dysfonctionnement *m.*
— v. intr. Se dérégler, être déréglé.

Mali ['mɑ:li] n. GEOGR. Mali *m.*

malice ['mælis] n. Malice, malveillance, méchanceté *f.* ‖ Rancune *f.* (*to, towards*, envers) [grudge]. ‖ JUR. Intention délicteuse *f.; with malice prepense,* avec préméditation.

malicious [-ʃəs] adj. Méchant, malveillant. ‖ Rancunier, vindicatif. ‖ JUR. Volontairement coupable (act); délictueux (intention); arbitraire (prosecution).

maliciously [-ʃəsli] adv. Méchamment, dans l'intention de nuire. ‖ Par rancune. ‖ JUR. Dans une intention criminelle.

malign [mə'lain] adj. Malveillant (person); nuisible, pernicieux (thing). ‖ MED., ASTRON. Malin. ‖ FIG. Malfaisant.
— v. tr. Calomnier, diffamer.

malignancy [mə'lignənsi] n. Malignité, méchanceté *f.* ‖ MED. Malignité *f.*

malignant [-nənt] adj. Malveillant, méchant (person); pernicieux (thing). ‖ MED. Malin.
— n. † Réprouvé *s.*

malignantly [-nəntli] adv. Malignement.

malignity [-niti] n. MED., FIG. Malignité *f.*

Malines [mə'li:nz] n. GEOGR. Malines *f.; Malines lace,* dentelle de Malines. ‖ U. S. Tulle *m.* (fabric).

malinger [mə'liŋgə*] v. intr. Tirer au flanc.

malingerer [-re*] n. MILIT., FAM. Tireur au flanc *m.* (See GOLDBRICKER.)

malingering [-riŋ] n. MILIT., FAM. Tirage au flanc, carottage *m.*

mall [mɔ:l] n. Mail *m.* (game, lane, walk).

mallard ['mæləd] n. ZOOL. Malard, canard sauvage *m.*

malleability [,mæliə'biliti] n. Malléabilité *f.*

malleable ['mæliəbl] adj. Malléable. (See PLIABLE.)

mallet [,mælit] n. TECHN., SPORTS. Maillet *m.*

malleus [-iəs] n. MED. Marteau *m.* (of the ear).

mallow ['mælou] n. BOT. Mauve *f.*

malmsey ['mɑ:msi] n. Malvoisie *f.* (wine).

malnutrition ['mælnju:'triʃən] n. MED. Malnutrition *f.*

malodorant [mæ'loudorənt], **malodorous** [-əs] adj. Malodorant. (See STINKING.)

malpractice [mæl'præktis] n. JUR. Incurie *f.* ‖ TECHN. Malfaçon *f.*

malt [mɔlt] n. Malt *m.* ‖ **Malt-extract,** n. Extrait de malt *m.* ‖ **Malt-house,** n. Malterie *f.* ‖ **Malt-kin,** n. Touraille *f.* ‖ **Malt-liquor,** n. Bière *f.* ‖ **Malt-loft,** n. Germoir *m.* ‖ **Malt-sugar,** n. Maltose *m.*
— v. tr. Malter.
— v. intr. Se malter.

Malta [-ə] n. GEOGR. Malte *f.* ‖ MED. *Malta fever,* fièvre de Malte.

malted [-id] adj. CULIN. *Malted milk,* farine lactée.

Maltese [mɔl'ti:z] adj. GEOGR. Maltais. ‖ BLAS. De Malte (cross). ‖ ZOOL. *Maltese dog,* maltais, bichon.
— n. GEOGR., ZOOL. Maltais *s.*

Malthusianism [mɑl'θju:ziənizm] n. Malthusianisme *m.*

malting ['mɔltiŋ] n. Maltage *m.* (act); malterie *f.* (house).

maltose ['mɔltous] n. CHIM. Maltose *m.*

maltreat [mæl'tri:t] v. tr. Maltraiter.

maltreatment [-mənt] n. Mauvais traitement *m.*

maltster ['mɔ:ltstə*] n. Malteur *m.*

malvaceous [mæl'veiʃəs] adj. BOT. Malvacé.

malversation [,mælvə'seiʃən] n. Malversation *f.*

mamelon ['mæmələn] n. Mamelon *m.* (billock).

mameluke ['mæməlu:k] n. Mameluk *m.*

mamilla [mæ'milə] n. MED. Mamelon, bout du sein *m.*

mamillary [-ləri] adj. Mamillaire.

mamma [mə'mɑ:] n. FAM. Maman *f.*

mammal ['mæməl] n. ZOOL. Mammifère *m.*

mammalian [-ən] adj., n. ZOOL. Mammifère *m.*

mammary ['mæməri] adj. MED. Mammaire.

mammiferous [mæ'mifərəs] adj. ZOOL. Mammifère.

Mammon ['mæmən] n. Mammon *m.* ‖ FIG. Veau d'or *m.*

mammonism [-izm] n. FIG. Idolâtrie (*f.*) de l'argent.

mammoth ['mæməθ] n. ZOOL. Mammouth *m.*
— adj. Enorme; *mammoth sale,* vente monstre; *mammoth tank,* char géant, mastodonte.

mammy ['mæmi] n. FAM. Maman *f.* ‖ U. S. Nourrice noire *f.*

mampus ['mæmpəs] n. Multitude *f.*

man [mæn] (pl. **men**) n. Homme, être humain, individu *m.; personne *f.* (human being); *any man,* quelqu'un, n'importe qui; *as one man,* à l'unanimité, comme un seul homme. ‖ Humanité *f.;* homme *m.* (human race). ‖ Homme *m.* (adult male); *an old man,* un vieillard; *between man and man,* d'homme à homme; *man and boy,* de l'enfance à la maturité. ‖ Homme *m.* (manly man); *a man of the world,* un homme d'expérience; *to make a man of,* faire un homme de. ‖ Domestique *m.* (manservant); ‖ MILIT., NAUT. Ordonnance *f.* (or) *m.* (orderly); homme *m.* (sailor, soldier); navire *m.* (ship). ‖ TECHN. Ouvrier *m.* ‖ COMM. Employé, garçon *m.* ‖ SPORTS. Pion *m.* (in draughts); pièce *f.* (in chess); équipier, joueur *m.* (player). ‖ JUR. Citoyen, habitant *m.* (of, de); *the man Jones,* le sieur (or) le nommé Jones; *man of straw,* homme de paille. ‖ FAM. *My good man,* mon brave; *my little man,* mon petit bonhomme. ‖ FAM. Homme *m.* (husband, lover); *to live as man and wife,* vivre maritalement. ‖ **Man-about-town,** n. Boulevardier. ‖ **Man-at-arms,** n. † Homme (*m.*) d'armes. ‖ **Man-child,** n. Enfant mâle *m.* ‖ **Man-eater,** n. Mangeur (*m.*) d'hommes (animal); anthropophage, cannibale *m.* (person). ‖ **Man-hater,** n. Misanthrope *m.* ‖ **Man-hour,** n. Heure de main-d'œuvre ouvrière *f.* ‖ **Man-hunt,** n. Chasse à l'homme. ‖ **Man-made,** adj. Artificiel (satellite). ‖ **Man-of-war,** n. NAUT. Navire (*m.*) de guerre. ‖ **Man-sized,** adj. U. S. FAM. Costaud, de taille.
— v. tr. (1). MILIT. Servir (a battery); garnir (a fort, trench); armer (a gun). ‖ NAUT. Equiper (a boat); amariner (a prize); armer (the pumps); *to man ship,* faire passer l'équipage à la bande. ‖ **To man up,** pourvoir de main-d'œuvre (an industry).
— interj. U. S. POP. Tiens!, fichtre !

Man [mæn] n. GEOGR. *Isle of Man,* île (*f.*) de Man.

manacle ['mænəkl] n. JUR. Menotte *f.*
— v. tr. JUR. Passer les menottes à. ‖ FIG. Entraver.

manage ['mænidʒ] v. tr. Diriger, administrer, gérer (a company). ‖ Mener, conduire (business); *to manage one's own affairs,* conduire sa barque, faire son compte. ‖ Maîtriser, dompter (an animal); gouverner, tenir, mater (s.o.). ‖ Venir à bout de, mener à bien (a piece of work); *he managed it very cleverly,* il a très bien arrangé (or) goupillé ça (fam.). ‖ TECHN. Manier, manœuvrer (a tool). ‖ FIG. Ménager, manier habilement (s.o.).

— v. intr. S'y prendre, se tirer d'affaire, s'en tirer, s'arranger, se débrouiller; *to manage to,* trouver moyen de, s'arranger pour, parvenir à.
manageability [,mænidʒə'biliti], **manageableness** ['mænidʒəbḷnis] n. Maniabilité *f.* ‖ Docilité, souplesse *f.*
manageable ['mænidʒəbḷ] adj. Maniable (tool). ‖ Faisable (undertaking). ‖ Docile, maniable (person).
management [-mənt] n. Direction, administration, exploitation, gérance *f.* (of a company, factory). ‖ Direction *f.* (persons); « *under new management* », « changement de propriétaire ». ‖ Maniement *m.* (of persons, tools). ‖ Manège *m.;* manigance *f.* (contrivance); débrouillardise *f.* (skill).
manager [-ə*] n. Directeur, administrateur, gérant *m.; sales manager,* directeur commercial; *general manager,* directeur général. ‖ Administrateur *m.* (man); ménagère *f.* (woman) [in household affairs]. ‖ AGRIC. Régisseur *m.* ‖ JUR. *Receiver and manager,* syndic de faillite. ‖ SPORTS, THEATR. Manager, imprésario *m.* ‖ FIG. Chef *m.; to be a bad manager of men,* ne pas savoir comment manier les hommes.
manageress [-əris] n. Directrice, gérante *f.*
managerial [,mænə'dʒiəriəl] adj. Directorial; *managerial staff,* cadres supérieurs.
managing ['mænidʒiŋ] adj. Directeur, gérant; *managing director,* administrateur gérant; directeur technique; U. S. *managing editor,* rédacteur en chef. ‖ JUR. *Managing clerk,* premier clerc, principal. ‖ FIG. Entendu, actif.
— n. See MANAGEMENT.
manatee [,mænə'ti:] n. ZOOL. Lamantin *m.*
Manchu [mæn'tʃu:] adj., n. GEOGR. Mandchou *s.*
Manchuria [-riə] n. GEOGR. Mandchourie *f.*
manciple ['mænsipḷ] n. Econome *m.*
mandamus [mæn'deiməs] n. JUR. Commandement *m.*
mandarin ['mændərin] n. Mandarin *m.*
mandarin n. Mandarine *f.* (colour, fruit, liquor).
mandatary ['mændətəri] n. JUR. Mandataire *s.*
mandate ['mændeit] n. JUR. Mandat *m.* ‖ ECCLES. Mandement *m.* ‖ † Commandement *m.*
— v. tr. JUR. Mettre sous le mandat (*to,* de).
mandated [-id] adj. JUR. Placé sous mandat.
mandatory [-əri] adj. JUR. Impératif, comminatoire; *mandatory writ,* mandement.
— n. JUR. Mandataire *s.*
mandible ['mændibḷ] n. ZOOL. Mandibule *f.*
mandola [mæn'doulə] n. MUS. Mandore *f.*
mandolin(e) ['mændolin] n. MUS. Mandoline *f.*
mandragora [,mændrə'gɔːrə], **mandrake** ['mændreik] n. BOT. Mandragore *f.*
mandrel ['mændrəl], **mandril** [-dril] n. TECHN. Mandrin *m.*
mandrill ['mændril] n. ZOOL. Mandrill *m.*
manducate ['mændjukeit] v. tr. MED. Mâcher.
manducation [,mændju'keiʃən] n. MED. Mastication *f.* ‖ ECCLES. Manducation *f.*
manducatory ['mændjukətəri] adj. MED. Masticatoire.
mane [mein] n. Crinière *f.*
manege [mæ'neːʒ] n SPORTS Manège *m.* (academy); haute école *f.* (art, exercices).
manes ['meini:z] n. pl. Mânes *m. pl.*
maneuver [mə'nuːvə*] n., v. See MANŒUVRE.
manful ['mænful] adj. Viril, résolu, hardi.
manfully [-i] adv. Résolument.
manfulness [-nis] n. Virilité, résolution *f.*
manganate ['mæŋgənet] n. CHIM. Manganate *m.*
manganese [,mæŋgə'niːz] n. CHIM. Manganèse *m.*
mange [meindʒ] n. MED. Gale *f.*
mangel-wurzel ['mæŋgḷ'wəːzḷ], **mangold-wurzel** ['mæŋgould-] n. BOT. Betterave fourragère *f.*
manger ['meindʒə*] n. Mangeoire *f.* ‖ ECCLES. Crèche *f.* ‖ FAM. *A dog in the manger,* le chien du jardinier.

mangle ['mæŋgḷ] v. tr. Mutiler, déchiqueter. ‖ FIG. Mutiler (a text); estropier (a word). ‖ FAM. Massacrer.
mangle n. Calandre *f.*
— v. tr. Calandrer.
mangler [-ə*] n. Calandreur *s.*
mango ['mæŋgou] n. BOT. Mangue *f.* (fruit); manguier *m.* (tree).
mangosteen ['mæŋgəstiːn] n. BOT. Mangouste *f.* (fruit); mangoustan *m.* (tree).
mangrove ['mæŋgrouv] n. BOT. Mangle *f.* (fruit); manglier, palétuvier *m.* (tree).
mangy ['meindʒi] adj. MED. Galeux. ‖ FAM. Miteux, moche.
manhandle ['mæn,hændḷ] v. tr. TECHN. Manutentionner. ‖ FAM. Malmener.
manhattan [mæn'hætṇ] n. Manhattan *m.* (cocktail).
manhole ['mæn,houl] n. Trou d'homme *m.* (in general); regard *m.* (in a sewer).
manhood ['mænhud] n. Humanité *f.* (mankind). ‖ Age viril *m.;* maturité *f.* (state). ‖ Virilité *f.* (manliness).
mania ['meiniə] n. MED. Folie furieuse, démence *f.* ‖ FIG. Manie *f.* (*for,* de).
maniac [-æk] adj. MED. Fou furieux ♂. ‖ FIG. Maniaque, enragé *s.* (*for,* de); mordu *s.* (fam.).
maniacal [mæ'naiəkəl] adj. MED. Fou, de fou.
manic ['mænik] adj. PSYCH. Maniaque. ‖ **Manic-depressive,** adj. PSYCH. Maniaco-dépressif.
manicure ['mænikjuə*] n. Manucure *m.* (care); manucure *s.* (person).
— v. tr. Manucurer, faire les mains à.
manifest ['mænifest] adj. Manifeste, évident.
— n. NAUT. Manifeste *m.*
— v. tr. Manifester; *to manifest itself,* se manifester. ‖ NAUT. Faire figurer sur le manifeste.
— v. intr. Manifester (in politics). ‖ Se manifester (ghost).
manifestant [mæni'festənt] n. U. S. Manifestant *s.*
manifestation [,mænifes'teiʃən] n. Manifestation *f.*
manifestly ['mænifestli] adv. Manifestement.
manifesto [,mæni'festou] n. Manifeste *m.*
manifold ['mænifould] adj. A polycopier (papier); *manifold writer,* polygraphe, appareil (*m.*) à polycopier. ‖ FIG. Multiple, nombreux (duties); sous de nombreux rapports (villain); varié, divers, à formes variées (wisdom).
— n. Polycopie *f.* (document). ‖ TECHN. Tubulure *f.* (pipe); *oil manifold,* collecteur d'huile. ‖ MATH. Multiplicité *f.* ‖ PHILOS. Diversité *f.*
— v. tr. Polycopier.
manifolder [-ə*] n. TECHN. Appareil (*m.*) à polycopier; autocopiste *m.;* Ronéo *f.*
manifolding [-iŋ] n. Polycopie *f.* (act).
manikin ['mænikin] n. Mannequin *m.* ‖ MED. Figure anatomique *f.* ‖ FAM. Petit homme, homuncule; nabot *m.* (fam.).
manil(l)a [mə'nilə] n. GEOGR. Manille *f.; Manilla cheroot,* manille *m.* (cigar); *Manilla hemp,* chanvre de Manille; *Manilla paper,* papier bulle; *Manilla rope,* manille *f.* ‖ U. S. *Manilla folder,* chemise (for documents).
manille [mæ'nil] n. Manille *f.* (game).
manioc ['mæniɔk] n. BOT. Manioc *m.*
maniple ['mænipḷ] n. † ECCLES. Manipule *m.*
manipulate [mə'nipjuleit] v. tr. Manipuler, manier, manœuvrer. ‖ FAM. Tripoter (accounts); emberlificoter, entortiller (s.o.).
manipulation [mə,nipju'leiʃən] n. Manipulation *f.* ‖ FIN. Agiotage *m.*
manipulator [mə'nipjuleitə*] n. Manipulateur *m.* ‖ FIN. Agioteur *m.*

manitou ['mænitu:] n. Manitou *m.*
mankind [mæn'kaind] n. Humanité *f.;* genre humain *m.* (human race). — ['mænkaind] n. Hommes *m. pl.;* sexe fort *m.* (male sex).
manlike ['mænlaik] adj. D'homme, digne d'un homme (manly). ‖ Pareil à un homme; *manlike ape,* anthropoïde. ‖ FAM. Hommasse, masculin (woman).
manliness [-linis] n. Virilité *f.;* qualités viriles *f. pl.*
manly [-li] adj. Mâle, viril. ‖ D'homme, masculin.
manna ['mænə] n. ECCLES., BOT. Manne *f.*
manned [mænd] p. p. See MAN. ‖ ASTRONAUT. Habité (spacecraft).
mannequin ['mænikin] n. COMM. Mannequin *m.* (model, woman).
manner ['mænə*] n. Manière, façon *f.* (way); *by all, no manner of means,* certainement, en aucune façon; *in a manner,* dans un certain sens; *in a manner of speaking,* pour ainsi dire, façon de parler. ‖ Sorte, espèce *f.;* genre *m.* (kind); *all manner of things,* toute sorte de choses. ‖ Manière, façon, habitude *f.* (habit); *to the manner born,* créé et mis au monde pour ça. ‖ Allure, attitude, tenue *f.;* maintien, comportement *m.* (behaviour); *to have a bad manner,* n'avoir aucune aisance. ‖ Pl. Manières *f. pl.;* usages *m. pl.;* savoir-vivre *m.* (polite ways); *lack of manners,* manque d'éducation; *where are your manners?,* en voilà des façons?, d'où sortez-vous? ‖ Pl. Mœurs *f. pl.; comedy of manners,* comédie de mœurs. ‖ ARTS, MUS. Manière *f.;* style *m.; after the manner of,* à la manière de. ‖ GRAMM. Manière *f.*
mannered ['mænəd] adj. Aux manières; *ill-mannered,* mal élevé, sans éducation. ‖ ARTS, FIG. Maniéré.
mannerism ['mænərizm] n. Maniérisme *m.* ‖ ARTS. Genre *m.*
mannerless ['mænəlis] adj. Fruste, sans éducation.
mannerliness [-linis] n. Savoir-vivre *m.;* courtoisie *f.*
mannerly [-li] adj. Courtois, bien élevé.
mannikin ['mænikin] n. See MANIKIN.
mannish ['mæniʃ] adj. D'homme. ‖ Hommasse, garçonnier, masculin (woman).
mannishness [-nis] n. Allure hommasse (or) masculine *f.*
manœuvrability [mə,nu:vrə'biliti] n. AVIAT. Maniabilité *f.*
manœuvre [mə'nu:və*] n. MILIT., NAUT. Manœuvre *f.* ‖ FIG. Manœuvre, menée, manigance *f.; unsavoury manœuvres,* vilains procédés; *vote-catching manœuvre,* manœuvre électorale. — v. intr. MILIT., NAUT., FIG. Manœuvrer. — v. tr. MILIT., NAUT. Faire manœuvrer. ‖ FIG. Manœuvrer (s.o.); *to manœuvre s.o. into paying,* amener qqn habilement à payer.
manometer [mæ'nɔmitə*] n. TECHN. Manomètre *m.* ‖ MED., FAM. Sphygmomanomètre *m.*
manor ['mænə*] n. † Seigneurie *f.* ‖ **Manor-house,** n. ARCHIT. Manoir *m.*
manorial [mə'nɔ:riəl] adj. Seigneurial.
manpower ['mæn,pauə*] n. TECHN. Main-d'œuvre *f.* ‖ MILIT. Effectif, potentiel humain *m.*
manqué ['mɔŋkei] adj. Manqué (actor, writer, hero).
manrope ['mæn,roup] n. Garde-corps *m.*
mansard ['mænsɑ:d] n. ARCHIT. Comble brisé *m.* ‖ **Mansard-roofed,** adj. ARCHIT. Mansardé.
manse [mæns] n. Presbytère écossais *m.*
manservant ['mæn,sə:vənt] n. Domestique, valet *m.*
mansion ['mænʃən] n. Château, manoir *m.* (in the country); hôtel particulier *m.* (in town); *Mansion House,* résidence officielle du lord-maire de

Londres. ‖ Pl. Maison (*f.*) de rapport. ‖ ASTROL. Maison *f.*
manslaughter ['mæn,slɔ:tə*] n. JUR. Homicide involontaire *m.*
manslayer [-sleiə*] n. JUR. Meurtrier *s.*
mantel ['mæntl] n. Manteau (or) dessus (*m.*) de cheminée. ‖ **Mantel-board** (or) **-shelf,** n. Dessus (or) tablette de cheminée. ‖ **Mantel-tree,** n. Linteau (*m.*) de cheminée.
mantelet ['mæntlit] n. Mantelet *m.* (mantlet). ‖ MILIT. Pare-balles *m.*
mantelpiece ['mæntl̩pi:s] n. Manteau (*m.*) de cheminée; dessus *m.* (or) tablette (*f.*) de cheminée.
mantilla [mæn'tilə] n. Mantille *f.*
mantis ['mæntis] n. ZOOL. Mante *f.; praying mantis,* mante religieuse. ‖ **Mantis-crab** (or) **-shrimp,** n. ZOOL. Squille *f.*
mantle ['mæntl] n. Mante, cape *f.* ‖ TECHN. Manchon, manteau *m.;* chemise *f.* ‖ ARCHIT. Parement *m.* ‖ FIG. Manteau *m.* — v. tr. Envelopper d'une mante (or) cape. ‖ FIG. Couvrir, revêtir; voiler. — v. intr. Mousser, écumer (liquid). ‖ MED. Monter, affluer (blood); rougir (face).
mantlet [-lit] n. Mantelet *m.*
mantua ['mæntjuə] n. † Robe vague *f.*
Mantua n. GEOGR. Mantoue *f.*
manual ['mænjuəl] adj. Manuel (alphabet, gift, work); à bras (haulage). ‖ MILIT. *Manual exercise,* maniement des armes. ‖ JUR. *Under my sign manual,* signé de ma main. — n. Manuel *m.* (book). ‖ MUS. Clavier (*m.*) d'orgue.
manually [-i] adv. Manuellement, à la main.
manufactory [,mænju'fæktəri] n. TECHN. Manufacture, usine *f.*
manufacture [-ʃə*] n. TECHN. Fabrication *f.* (act); produit manufacturé *m.* (product). ‖ TECHN., FIG. Industrie *f.* (branch, production). — v. tr. TECHN. Fabriquer, manufacturer. ‖ FIG. Fabriquer en série (art, literature); fabriquer, monter (story).
manufacturer [-tʃərə*] n. TECHN. Fabricant, industriel *m.* ‖ FIG. Fabricant, fabricateur *m.*
manufacturing [-tʃəriŋ] adj. TECHN. Industriel. — n. TECHN. Fabrication *f.*
manumission [,mænju'miʃən] n. † Affranchissement *m.*
manumit [,mænju'mit] v. tr. (1). Affranchir.
manure [mə'njuə*] n. AGRIC. Fumier, engrais *m.; liquid manure,* purin; *manure heap,* fumier. — v. tr. AGRIC. Fumer, mettre de l'engrais dans.
manuscript ['mænjuskript] adj., n. Manuscrit *m.*
Manx [mæŋks] adj. GEOGR. De l'île de Man. ‖ ZOOL. Sans queue (cat). — n. Manx, mannois *m.* (language).
Manxman [-mən] (pl. **Manxmen**) n. GEOGR. Mannois *s.*
many ['meni] adj. Beaucoup de, bien des, un grand nombre de; de nombreux, maint, plusieurs (see MUCH); *as many opportunities as,* autant d'occasions que; *ever so many times,* je ne sais combien de fois; *how many books,* combien de livres; *many compliments,* beaucoup de compliments; *not so many trumps as,* pas autant d'atouts que; *of many kinds,* de toutes sortes; *so many apples that,* tant de pommes que; *too many flowers,* trop de fleurs. ‖ Nombreux; *not very many,* en petit nombre; *they were so many,* ils étaient si nombreux; *you are none too many to,* vous n'êtes pas trop nombreux pour. ‖ **Many a,** maint; *for many a week,* depuis des semaines; *many a time,* bien des (or) maintes fois. ‖ **Many-coloured,** adj. Multicolore. ‖ **Many-flowered,** adj. BOT. Multiflore. ‖ **Many-sided,** adj. MATH. Polygonal; FIG. Complexe (question); divers (talent). ‖ **Many-sidedness,** n. FIG.

Complexité *f.* (of a question); diversité *f.* (of a talent).
— N.B. Le comparatif de *many* est *more*, le superlatif *most*.
— pron. indef. Beaucoup, un grand (or) bon nombre (*of*, de).
— n. Foule, multitude *f.*; peuple *m.*; *the will of the many*, la volonté de la masse. ‖ Quantité *f.*; *a good many*, beaucoup de.

map [mæp] n. GEOGR. Carte *f.*; *map of the world*, mappemonde. ‖ FAM. *Off the map*, à l'autre bout du monde (place); n'ayant plus d'intérêt (question); *to put on the map*, faire connaître, mettre en vedette. ‖ U. S. FAM. Balle, bille, bobine, fiole *f.* (mug). ‖ **Map-maker**, n. GEOGR. Cartographe *s.* ‖ **Map-making**, n. GEOGR. Cartographie *f.* ‖ **Map-measurer**, n. Curvimètre *m.*
— v. tr. (1). GEOGR. Faire la carte de. ‖ FIG. To **map out**, organiser, monter, arranger.

maple ['meipl] n. BOT. Erable *m.*
— adj. D'érable (syrup, sugar).

maquette [mæ'ket] n. ARTS. Maquette *f.* (in sculpture).

maquis ['mæki] n. MILIT. Maquis *m.*; *member of the maquis*, maquisard; *to take to the maquis*, prendre le maquis. ‖ Maquisard *m.* (person).

mar [mɑ:*] v. tr. (1). Ruiner, gâcher (sth.). ‖ Défigurer, démolir (s.o.).

marabou ['mærəbu:] n. ZOOL., COMM. Marabout *m.*

marabout ['mærəbu:t] n. Marabout *m.*

maraschino [,mærəs'ki:nou] n. Marasquin *m.*; *maraschino cherries*, cerises au marasquin.

marasmus [mə'ræzməs] n. MED. Marasme *m.*

Marathon ['mærəθɔn] n. GEOGR., SPORTS. Marathon *m.*

maraud [mə'rɔ:d] v. intr. Marauder.
— v. tr. Piller. (See PLUNDER.)

marauder [-ə*] n. Maraudeur, malandrin *m.*

maravedi [,mærə'veidi] n. FIN. Maravedis *m.*

marble ['mɑ:bl] n. Marbre *m.* (statue, stone); *imitation marble*, similimarbre. ‖ Bille *f.* (ball); *to play at marbles*, jouer aux billes.
— adj. Du marbre; *marble cutter*, marbrier; *marble industry*, industrie marbrière. ‖ De marbre, en marbre (pavement, slab); *marble quarry*, marbrière. ‖ Marmoréen (whiteness).
— v. tr. Marbrer. ‖ CULIN. Persiller (meat).

marbleize [-bə,laiz] v. tr. U. S. Marbrer.

marbling [-bliŋ] n. Marbrure *f.*

marbly [-bli] adj. Marbré.

marc ['mɑ:k] n. Marc *m.* (brandy, grapes). ‖ AGRIC. Tourteau *m.*

marcasite ['mɑ:kə,sait] n. Marcassite *f.*

March [mɑ:tʃ] n. FAM. Mars *m.*

march n. GEOGR. Marche, frontière *f.*
— v. intr. *To march upon*, être limitrophe de (or) à la limite de, border.

march n. MILIT. Marche *f.*; *day's march*, étape; *march past*, défilé. ‖ MILIT. Pas *m.*; *double march*, pas gymnastique. ‖ MUS. Marche *f.* ‖ FIG. Marche, avance *f.*; cheminement, progrès *m.* ‖ FAM. *To steal a march on*, prendre de l'avance sur.
— v. intr. MILIT. Faire une marche; *to march past*, défiler. ‖ FIG. Avancer, marcher. ‖ FAM. *To march away* (or) *off*, *in*, *out*, partir, entrer, sortir.
— v. tr. MILIT. Faire marcher.

marching [-iŋ] n. MILIT. *Marching orders*, feuille de route.

marchioness ['mɑ:ʃənis] n. Marquise *f.*

marchpane ['mɑ:tʃpein] n. CULIN. Massepain *m.*

marconigram [mɑ:'kounigræm] n. Radiogramme, câble *m.*

mare [mɛə*] n. ZOOL. Jument *f.* ‖ *Mare's nest*, n. FAM. Redécouverte de l'Amérique *f.* ‖ *Mare's tail*, n. BOT. Prèle *f.*; NAUT. Cirrus *m.*

Margaret ['mɑ:gərit] n. Marguerite *f.*

margarine [,mɑ:dʒə'ri:n, mɑ:gə'ri:n] n. CULIN. Margarine *f.*

margay ['mɑ:gei] n. ZOOL. Chat-tigre *m.*

marge [mɑ:dʒ] n. FAM. Margarine *f.*

margin ['mɑ:dʒin] n. Bord *m.* (of a river, well); bord, lisière *f.* (of a wood). ‖ Marge *f.* (on a page); *bottom, head margin*, marge inférieure, supérieure; *in the margin*, en marge. ‖ Marge *f.*; écart *m.* (of prices, quantity, time); *to allow a margin for*, laisser une marge pour. ‖ FIN. Couverture, provision *f.* ‖ FIG. Limite *f.* ‖ **Margin-release**, n. TECHN. Déclenchemarge *m.*
— v. tr. Faire une marge à (a book). ‖ FIN. Déposer des provisions pour.

marginal [-inl] adj. Marginal (note). ‖ TECHN. *Marginal stop*, curseur de marge. ‖ AGRIC. Peu fertile (land). ‖ PHYS. Périphérique (rays). ‖ FIG. *Marginal case*, cas limite.

marginalia [,mɑ:dʒi'neiliə] n. Pl. Notes marginales *f. pl.*

marginate ['mɑ:dʒineit] adj. Marginé.

margrave ['mɑ:greiv] n. Margrave *m.*

marguerite [,mɑ:gə'ri:t] n. BOT. Marguerite *f.* (daisy); anthémis *f.* (Paris daisy).

Maria [mə'raiə] n. Marie *f.* ‖ FAM. *Black Maria*, panier à salade.

Marian ['mɛəriən] adj. De Marie.

marigold ['mærigould] n. BOT. Souci *m.*

marijuana [,mæriju'ɑ:nə], **marihuana** [,mæri'hwɑ:nə] n. Marijuana, marihuana *f.*

marina [mə'ri:nə] n. NAUT. Port (*m.*) de plaisance, marina *f.*

marinade [,mæri'neid] n. CULIN. Marinade *f.*
— v. tr. CULIN. Faire mariner.

marinate ['mærineit] v. tr. CULIN. Faire mariner.

marine [mə'ri:n] adj. NAUT. Marin (animal, barometer, engine); naval (forces); de marine (infantry); maritime (insurance).
— n. NAUT. *Mercantile* (or) *merchant marine*, marine marchande. ‖ ARTS. Marine *f.* ‖ MILIT. Marine *m.* ‖ FAM. *Tell that to the marines*, à d'autres!

mariner ['mærinə*] n. NAUT. Marin *m.*; *master mariner*, capitaine (of merchant ship).

marionette [,mæriə'net] n. Marionnette *f.* (puppet).

marital ['mæritl] adj. Conjugal, matrimonial (of marriage); *marital status*, situation de famille. ‖ Marital (of a husband).

maritime ['mæri,taim] adj. Maritime (plant, culture, province, climate); naval (power); de la mer (perils). ‖ JUR. Maritime (law).

marjoram ['mɑ:dʒərəm] n. BOT. Marjolaine *f.*

mark [mɑ:k] n. Mark *m.* (coin, weight).

mark n. Marque, trace *f.*; *to leave a mark on*, laisser une trace sur. ‖ Marque *f.*; repère, point de repère *m.* (guide mark). ‖ Note *f.* (rating); *good marks*, bons points, bonnes notes. ‖ Signe *m.*; *exclamation mark*, point d'exclamation; *punctuation marks*, signes de ponctuation; *question mark*, point d'interrogation. ‖ JUR. Croix, signature (*f.*) d'illettré; *to make one's mark*, faire une croix. ‖ JUR. Empreinte *f.* (finger-mark). ‖ FIN. Cote *f.* ‖ COMM. Marque *f.* (label). ‖ NAUT. Voyant *m.* (on buoy). ‖ SPORTS. Marque *f.* (at football); épigastre *m.* (in boxing); ligne (*f.*) de départ (in racing); put *m.*, cible *f.* (target); *to get off the mark*, démarrer. ‖ MED. Marque, tache *f.*; *up to the mark*, d'aplomb, en forme. ‖ FIG. Marque, preuve *f.*; signe, témoignage *m.* (indication). ‖ FIG. Marque, empreinte *f.* (on, sur) [influence]. ‖ FIG. But *m.* (aim); *beside the mark*, à côté de la question; *to hit the mark*, mettre dans le mille; *wide of the mark*, loin du but, loin de compte. ‖ FIG. Niveau *m.* (standard); *up to the mark*, à la hauteur. ‖ FIG. Marque, valeur, importance *f.* (eminence); *of mark*, marquant, de

marque; *to make one's mark,* faire sa place au soleil, se faire un nom, marquer. ‖ FAM. *Easy mark,* gogo, poire (see GULL); *save the mark,* excusez du peu; sauf votre respect.
— v. tr. Marquer, chiffrer (linen); marquer (notepaper, a passage). ‖ Coter, noter (an exercise). ‖ COMM. Etiqueter (goods); marquer (prices). ‖ FIN. Coter. ‖ SPORTS. Marquer (score). ‖ MILIT. *To mark time,* marquer le pas. ‖ MED. Marquer (skin). ‖ FIG. Marquer, désigner (*for,* pour) [to designate]; marquer, caractériser (to distinguish); marquer; dénoter, indiquer (to show). ‖ FIG. Observer (s.o.); remarquer, noter, faire attention à (sth.); *mark my words,* notez bien ce que je dis. ‖ FAM. *Mark you,* remarquez bien, mais par exemple, en revanche; *to mark time,* piétiner sur place. ‖ **To mark down,** FIN. Baisser (a price); SPORTS. Rembûcher (a stag). ‖ **To mark off,** mesurer (a distance); jalonner (a road); distinguer (*from,* de) [s.o., sth.]. ‖ **To mark out,** tracer (boundaries); borner (field); désigner (*for,* pour) [s.o., sth.]; distinguer (*from,* de) [s.o., sth.]. ‖ **To mark up,** FIN. Augmenter, surcharger (prices).

marked [-t] adj. Marqué, biseauté (card). ‖ FIG. Marqué, prononcé, accusé (change, tendency); marqué (man).

markedly [-idli] adv. D'une manière marquante.

marker [-ə*] n. Marqueur *s.* (person); marquoir *m.* (tool). ‖ SPORTS. Carnet-bloc *m.* (book); marqueur *s.* (person). ‖ **Marker-bomb,** n. AVIAT. Marqueur *m.*

market ['mɑ:kit] n. Marché *m.* (place); *market square,* carreau des halles, place du marché. ‖ Marché, débouché *m.* (demand); *ready market,* débit facile; *to have a good market for,* avoir une grosse demande sur. ‖ Marché *m.* (sale); *black, semi-black* (or) U. S. *grey market,* marché noir, gris; *to be in the market for,* être acheteur de; *to be on the market,* être en vente; *to put on the market,* mettre dans le commerce. ‖ Marché *m.* (mart, region); *the American market,* le marché américain. ‖ FIN. Marché *m.*; cours *m.* pl.; bourse *f.*; *at market price,* au cours, au prix courant; *market value,* valeur marchande; *outside market,* coulisse; U. S. *to play the stock market,* jouer à la bourse. ‖ FIG. Trafic, marché *m.*; *to make a market of,* trafiquer de. ‖ **Market-day,** n. Jour de marché *m.* ‖ **Market-garden,** n. AGRIC. Jardin maraîcher *m.* ‖ **Market-gardener,** n. AGRIC. Maraîcher *s.* ‖ **Market-gardening,** n. AGRIC. Culture maraîchère *f.* ‖ **Markethouse,** n. Halle *f.* ‖ **Market-maker,** n. FIN. Contrepartiste *m.* ‖ **Market-place,** n. Place (*f.*) du marché. ‖ **Market research,** n. COMM. Etudes (*f.* pl.) de marché. ‖ **Market-town,** n. Bourg *m.* ‖ **Market-woman,** n. Marchande (*f.*) des halles.
— v. intr. Faire son marché.
— v. tr. Vendre, mettre sur le marché.

marketable [-əbl] adj. Vendable, de bonne vente.

marketeer [,mɑ:ki'ti:ə*] n. *Black marketeer,* trafiquant du marché noir.

marketing ['mɑ:kitiŋ] n. Marketing *m.* (commercial technique); commercialisation, mise en vente *f.* (selling).

marking ['mɑ:kiŋ] n. Marquage *m.* ‖ Notes *f.* pl. (at school). ‖ FIN. Cotation *f.* ‖ Pl. Marques *f.* pl. ‖ **Marking-clerk,** n. FIN. Coteur *m.* ‖ **Marking-gauge,** n. Trusquin *m.* ‖ **Marking-ink,** n. Encre (*f.*) à marquer. ‖ **Marking-off,** n. Séparation *f.* ‖ **Marking-out,** n. Bornage *m.* (of a field); tracé *m.* (of a road); FIG. Détermination, délimitation *f.* ‖ **Marking-tool,** n. TECHN. Rouanne *f.*

marksman [-smən] (pl. **marksmen**) n. MILIT., SPORTS. Tireur (*m.*) d'élite. ‖ JUR. Illettré *m.*

marksmanship [-smənʃip] n. MILIT., SPORTS. Habileté (*f.*) au tir.

marl [mɑːl] n. AGRIC. Marne *f.* ‖ **Marl-pit,** n. Marnière *f.*
— v. tr. AGRIC. Marner.

marl v. tr. NAUT. Merliner.

marlin ['mɑ:lin] n. U. S., ZOOL. Marlin *m.*

marline [-in] n. NAUT. Merlin, lusin *m.*

marlin(e)spike [-inspaik] n. NAUT. Epissoir *m.*

marmalade ['mɑ:məleid] n. CULIN. Confiture (*f.*) d'oranges.

marmoreal [,mɑ:mɔ:'riəl] adj. Marmoréen.

marmoset ['mɑ:məzet] n. ZOOL. Ouistiti *m.*

marmot ['mɑ:mɔt] n. ZOOL. Marmotte *f.*

maroon [mə'ru:n] adj. Marron-roux.
— n. Marron *m.* (firework). ‖ Marron-roux *m.* (colour).

maroon n. Nègre marron *s.* (slave). ‖ NAUT. Personne abandonnée sur une île déserte *f.*
— v. tr. NAUT. Abandonner sur une île déserte.
— v. intr. Flâner, flânocher. (See LOITER.)

marque [mɑ:k] n. † NAUT. Marque *f.*

marquee [mɑ:'ki] n. Tente-marquise *f.*

Marquesas [mɑ:'keizəz] n. GEOGR. Marquises *f.* pl. (islands).

marquetry ['mɑ:kitri] n. Marqueterie *f.*

marquess, marquis ['mɑ:kwis] n. Marquis *m.*

marquisate [-it] n. Marquisat *m.*

marquise [mɑ'ki:z] n. Marquise *f.* (person, ring).

marriage ['mæridʒ] n. Mariage *m.; marriage articles,* contrat de mariage; *marriage bonds,* liens conjugaux; *marriage bureau,* agence matrimoniale; *marriage guidance,* assistance de conseillers conjugaux. ‖ ECCLES. *Marriage ceremony,* bénédiction nuptiale. ‖ Mariage *m.* (at cards). ‖ FIG. Mariage *m.; alliance,* symbiose *f.*

marriageable [-əbl] adj. Mariable, nubile, en âge de se marier.

married ['mærid] adj. Conjugal (life); marié (person).

marrow ['mærou] n. MED. *Spinal marrow,* moelle épinière. ‖ CULIN. Moelle *f.* ‖ BOT. *Vegetable marrow,* courge, courgette. ‖ FIG. Moelle, essence, quintessence *f.* (pith); vitalité, vigueur *f.* (vitality).

marrowbone [-boun] n. Os (*m.*) à moelle.

marrowfat [-fæt] adj. Cassé (pea).

marrowless [-lis] adj. Sans moelle (bone). ‖ FIG. Mou, flasque, sans ressort.

marrowy [-i] adj. Plein de moelle (bone). ‖ FIG. Substantiel.

marry ['mæri] v. tr. (2). Marier (*to,* à); *to get married,* se marier. ‖ Epouser, se marier avec. ‖ FAM. *To marry money,* épouser le sac.
— v. intr. Se marier; *to marry beneath one,* se mésallier; *to marry a second time,* se remarier.

Mars [mɑ:z] n. Mars *m.* (god, planet).

Marseilles [mɑ:'seilz] n. GEOGR. Marseille *f.* ‖ COMM. Piqué *m.* (fabric).

marsh [mɑ:ʃ] n. Marais, marécage; palus *m.* (†). ‖ **Marsh-fever,** n. MED. Fièvre paludéenne *f.; paludisme m.* ‖ **Marsh-gas,** n. Gaz (*m.*) des marais; CHIM. Méthane *m.* ‖ **Marsh-hen,** n. ZOOL. Sarcelle, poule d'eau *f.* ‖ **Marsh-mallow,** n. BOT. Guimauve *f.;* CULIN. Bonbon (*m.*) à la guimauve, pâte de guimauve *f.*

marshal ['mɑ:ʃəl] n. † MILIT. Maréchal *m.* ‖ JUR. Maître (*m.*) des cérémonies; *judge's marshal,* secrétaire d'un juge itinérant. ‖ U. S. Shérif *m.*
— v. intr. (1). Se ranger, se placer.
— v. tr. (1). Placer, disposer (a company). ‖ Introduire (*into,* dans) [s.o.]. ‖ MILIT. Ranger, mettre en rang. ‖ BLAS. Disposer.

marshalling [-iŋ] n. Ordonnancement *m.* ‖ CH. DE F. Triage *m.; marshalling yard,* gare de triage.

marshalship [-ʃip] n. MILIT. Maréchalat *m.*

marshy ['mɑ:ʃi] adj. Marécageux.

marsupial [mɑ:'sju:piəl] adj., n. ZOOL. Marsupial *m.*

mart [mɑ:t] n. COMM. Marché *m.* (centre); salle de vente *f.* (room).

marten ['mɑ:tin] n. ZOOL. Martre *f.*

martensite ['mɑ:tin,zait] n. TECHN. Martensite f.
martial ['mɑ:ʃəl] adj. Martial (appearance, law, person, spirit); *to declare martial law,* proclamer l'état de siège. ‖ ASTRON. De Mars, martien.
martially [-i] adv. Martialement.
Martian ['mɑ:ʃiən] n. ASTRON. Martien s.
martin ['mɑ:tin] n. ZOOL. Martinet m. (See MARTLET.)
martinet [,mɑ:ti'net] n. Chef très autoritaire m.; adjudant, gendarme, pète-sec m. (fam.).
martingale ['mɑ:tingeil] n. NAUT., SPORTS. Martingale f.
martini [mɑ:'ti:ni] n. Martini-gin m. (cocktail). ‖ Martini m. (vermouth) [nom déposé].
martlet ['mɑ:tlit] n. ZOOL. Martinet m. ‖ BLAS. Merlette f.
martyr ['mɑ:tə*] n. ECCLES., FIG. Martyr s.
— v. tr. ECCLES., FIG. Martyriser.
martyrdom [-dəm] n. ECCLES., FIG. Martyre m.
martyrize [-raiz] v. tr. ECCLES., FIG. Martyriser.
martyrology ['mɑ:tə,rɔlədʒi] n. ECCLES. Martyrologe m.
marvel ['mɑ:vəl] n. Merveille f.; *to work marvels,* faire merveille. ‖ Objet d'étonnement m.; *it's a marvel to me that,* cela m'étonne fort que.
— v. intr. (1). S'émerveiller (*at,* de) [to be full of wonder]. ‖ S'étonner (*at,* de) [to be astonished]. ‖ Se demander (*how,* comment; *why,* pourquoi) [to wonder].
marvellous [-əs] adj. Merveilleux, miraculeux. ‖ Etonnant, surprenant, extraordinaire.
marvellously [-əsli] adv. Merveilleusement. ‖ Etonnamment.
Marxist ['mɑ:ksist] adj., n. Marxiste s.
Mary ['mɛəri] n. Marie f.
marzipan ['mɑ:zi'pæn] n. CULIN. Massepain m. (See MARCHPANE.)
mascara [mæs'kɑ:rə] n. Mascara m.
mascle ['mæ:skl̩] n. † BLAS. Macle f.
mascot ['mɑskət] n. Mascotte f.
masculine ['mæskjulin] adj. Mâle (descent); masculin, hommasse (woman). ‖ GRAMM. Masculin (gender, noun, rhyme); *to be masculine,* être du masculin. ‖ FIG. Mâle, viril.
— n. GRAMM. Masculin m.
masculinity [,mæskju'liniti] n. Masculinité f.
maser ['meizə*] n. PHYS. Maser m.
mash [mæʃ] n. Fardeau m. (in brewing). ‖ AGRIC. Mash m.; pâtée f. ‖ CULIN. Purée f. ‖ FIG. Bouillie f. ‖ **Mash-tub** (or) **-tun,** n. Brassin m.; cuve-matière f.
— v. tr. Brasser (in brewing). ‖ CULIN. Ecraser; *mashed potatoes,* purée de pommes de terre. ‖ FIG. Mettre en bouillie (or) compote.
mash n. FAM. Béguin m. (person).
— v. tr. Faire le béguin de; *to be mashed on,* avoir le béguin pour, être entiché de.
masher [-ə*] n. FAM. Tombeur m.
masher n. Broyeur m. (tool).
mashie ['mæʃi] n. SPORTS. Mashie m.
mask [mɑ:sk] n. Masque m. (covering, disguise, figure, person); *death mask,* masque mortuaire. ‖ SPORTS. Face f. (of fox). ‖ ARCHIT. Mascaron m. ‖ TECHN. Cache m. (in photography). ‖ FIG. Masque m.
— v. tr. Masquer; *to mask one's face,* se masquer. ‖ MILIT., MED. Masquer. ‖ TECHN. Poser un cache à. ‖ FIG. Masquer, dissimuler, déguiser.
masker [-ə*] n. Masque m. (person).
masochism ['mæzəkizm] n. Masochisme m.
masochist [-kist] n. Masochiste s.
mason ['meisn̩] n. ARCHIT. Maçon m. ‖ JUR. Franc-maçon s.
— v. tr. ARCHIT. Maçonner.
masonic [mə'sɔnik] adj. JUR. Maçonnique.
masonry ['meisnri] n. ARCHIT. Maçonnerie f. (art, wall). ‖ JUR. Franc-maçonnerie f.

masque [mɑ:sk] n. THEATR. Masque m.
masquerade [,mɑ:skə'reid] n. Mascarade f. (act, troop); bal masqué m. (ball); déguisement, masque (costume). ‖ FIG. Mascarade f.; faux-semblant m.
— v. intr. Se masquer; se déguiser (*as,* en). ‖ FIG. Prendre un masque; se faire passer (*as,* pour).
masquerader [-ə*] n. Masque; carnaval m. (fam.) [person]. ‖ FIG. Fourbe, hypocrite s.
mass [mɑ:s] n. ECCLES. Messe f.; *high mass,* grand-messe; *low mass,* messe basse; *to attend, to say mass,* assister à, dire la messe.
mass [mæs] n. Masse, foule f. (of persons); pl. les masses populaires; *in the mass,* en bloc; *mass meeting,* meeting monstre. ‖ Masse f.; amas, tas m. (of things). ‖ PHYS. Masse f. ‖ TECHN. *Mass production,* production en série. ‖ MILIT. *Mass attack,* attaque massive; *mass formation,* formation en masse. ‖ JUR. Majorité f. (of the people). ‖ FAM. Collection f.; composé, assemblage m.; *he was a mass of bruises,* il n'était qu'un bleu. ‖ **Mass media,** n. pl. Mass media, médias m. pl. ‖ **Mass-observation,** n. Etudes et enquêtes sociales f. pl. ‖ **Mass-observer,** n. Spécialiste (s.) d'enquêtes sociales. ‖ **Mass-produce,** v. tr. Produire massivement, en série.
— v. tr. Masser.
— v. intr. Se masser.
massacre ['mæsəkə*] n. Massacre m.
— v. tr. Massacrer.
massage ['mæsɑ:ʒ] n. Massage m.
— v. tr. Masser.
masseur [mæ'sə*] n. Masseur m.
masseuse [mæ'sə:z] n. Masseuse f.
massicot ['mæsikɔt] n. CHIM. Massicot m.
massif ['mæsi:f] n. GEOL., GEOGR. Massif m.
massing ['mæsiŋ] n. Agglomération f.; attroupement m. (of persons); amoncellement, entassement m. (of things). ‖ MILIT. Concentration f.; rassemblement m. (of troops).
massive ['mæsiv] adj. Massif. ‖ GEOL. Aggloméré.
massively [-li] adv. Massivement.
massiveness [-nis] n. Massiveté f.
massy ['mæsi] adj. Massif.
mast [mɑ:st] n. NAUT. Mât m.; pl. mâts m. pl.; *mâture f.; *to sail before the mast,* être simple matelot. ‖ RADIO. Pylône m. ‖ **Mast-head,** n. NAUT. Tête (f.) de mât; *at the mast-head,* en vigie; v. tr. NAUT. Envoyer à la tête du mât. ‖ **Mast-hole,** n. NAUT. Etambrai m. ‖ **Mast-rope,** n. NAUT. Guinderesse f.
— v. tr. NAUT. Mâter (a ship); hisser (a yard).
mast n. Faines f. pl.; glands m. pl.; glandée f.
mastectomy [mæ'stektəmi] n. MED. Mammectomie, mastectomie f.
master ['mɑ:stə*] n. Maître m. (of animals, household, institution, slaves); maître, employeur m. (of servants); patron m. (of workmen). ‖ Principal, directeur m. (headmaster); maître, professeur m. (schoolteacher); *Master of Arts,* maître ès arts; diplômé d'études supérieures (in English modern universities); licencié ès lettres (in the case of Oxford and Cambridge, in American universities). ‖ Maître m. (expert); *past master in,* passé maître en. ‖ Monsieur m. (title for a boy, an employer); SPORTS. *Fencing master,* maître d'armes. ‖ NAUT. Maître à bord, patron, capitaine m. ‖ ARCHIT. *Master builder,* entrepreneur; *master mason,* maître maçon m. ‖ ARTS. Maître m. (person). ‖ JUR. Conseiller maître m.; *master of ceremonies,* maître de cérémonies; *Master of the Rolls,* conservateur des archives judiciaires. ‖ FIG. Maître m.; *to be master of oneself,* être maître (or) avoir la maîtrise de soi; *to be one's own master,* être son propre maître, ne dépendre que de soi-même, avoir son indépendance.
‖ **Master-at-arms,** n. NAUT. Capitaine (m.) d'armes. ‖ **Master-key,** n. Passe-partout m. ‖ **Master-mind,** n. Esprit supérieur m.; v. tr. U. S. FAM. Concevoir, diriger. ‖ **Master-sergeant,** n. U. S. MILIT.

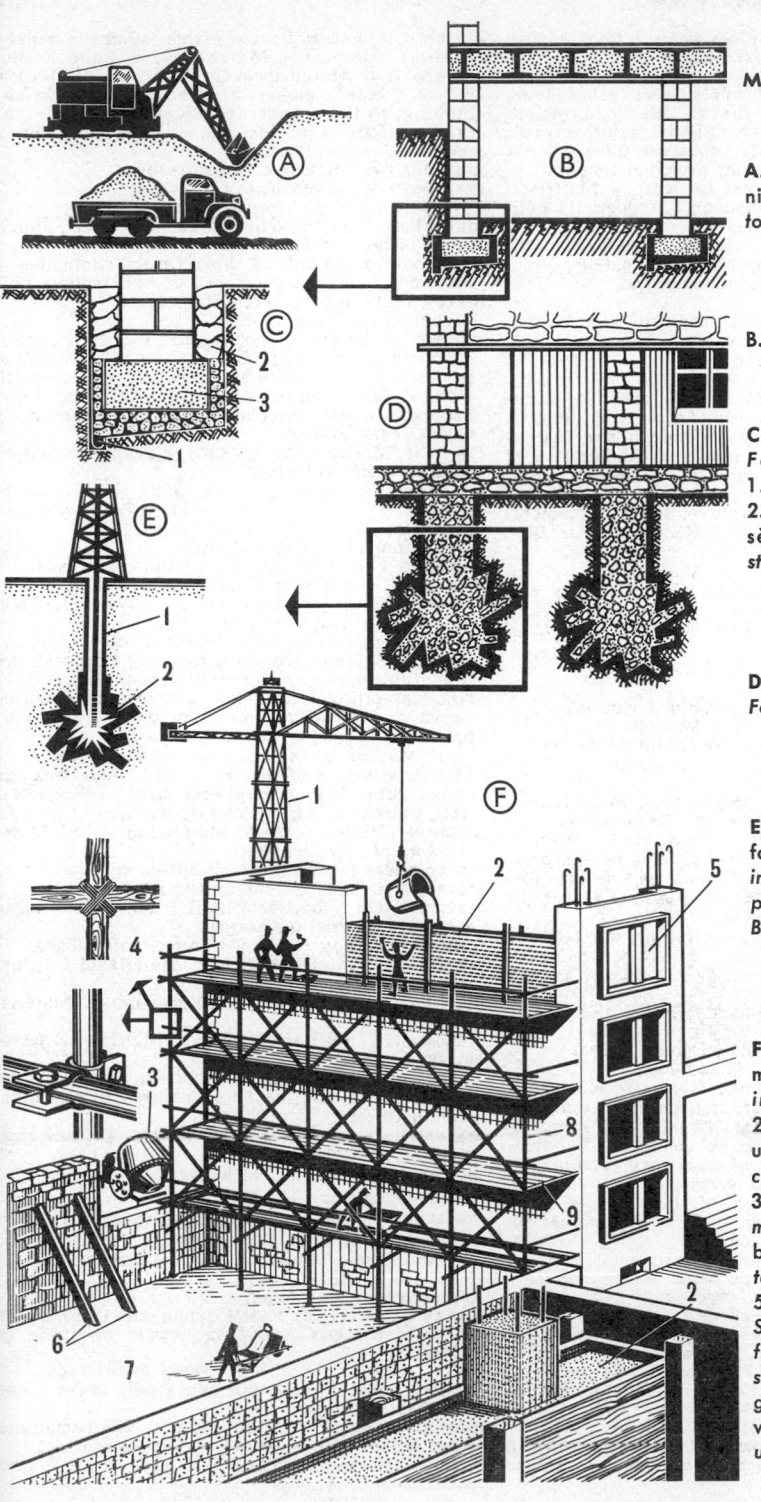

MASONRY
MAÇONNERIE

A. Fouille à la pelle mécanique. *Mechanical excavator (or power shovel) at work.*

B. Fondations. *Foundations.*

C. Fondations (détail). *Foundations (detail) :* 1. Drainage. *Drainage;* 2. Remplissage en pierre sèche. *Filling with dry stone;* 3. Assise en béton. *Concrete base.*

D. Fondations sur pieux. *Foundations supported on piles.*

E. Exécution d'un pieu de fondation profonde. *Driving of a deep-foundation pile :* 1. Trou de forage. *Boring hole;* 2. Assise en béton. *Concrete base.*

F. Édification d'un immeuble. *Erection ot a building :* 1. Grue. *Crane;* 2. Coulage du béton dans un coffrage. *Pouring of concrete into a frame;* 3. Bétonnière. *Concrete mixer;* 4. Détails d'assemblage d'échafaudage. *Details of scaffolding joint;* 5. Réserve pour fenêtre. *Space for window, window frame;* 6. Étançon. *Prop, stanchion;* 7. Fouille. *Digging, excavation;* 8. Baliveau. *Scaffolding pole, upright;* 9. Plat-bord. *Scaffold-board, platform.*

Sergent-chef *m.* ‖ **Master-singer**, n. † Mus. Maître chanteur *m.* ‖ **Master-stroke**, n. Fig. Coup de maître *m.*
— adj. Techn. Principal (joint); mère (gauge, lode, tap); maître (wheel). ‖ Electr. Maître, principal (switch). ‖ Theatr., Radio. Original (print, record). ‖ Fig. De maître (hand); directeur (idea, plan); magistral (mind); dominant, principal (passion).
— v. tr. Diriger, gouverner (to rule). ‖ Maîtriser, dominer, subjuguer (to subdue). ‖ Acquérir la maîtrise de (to become an expert in).
masterdom [-dəm] n. Empire *m.; autorité f.*
masterful [-ful] adj. Impérieux, dominateur.
masterly [-li] adj. De maître, magistral.
— adv. Magistralement.
mastermind [-,maind] n. U. S. Esprit supérieur *m.*
— v. tr. U. S. Etre la cheville ouvrière de; concevoir et diriger (operations).
masterpiece [-pi:s] n. Chef-d'œuvre *m.*
mastership [-ʃip] n. Maîtrise *f.* (ability); autorité *f.* (dominion). ‖ Fig. Maîtrise *f.* (of a subject).
mastery [-ri] n. Empire *m.;* domination *f.* (ascendancy). ‖ Supériorité *f.;* dessus *m.* (upper hand); *to gain the mastery over,* l'emporter sur. ‖ Maîtrise *f.* (act, skill).
mastic ['mæstik] n. Mastic *m.* (colour, cement, resin). ‖ Bot. Lentisque *m.* ‖ **Mastic-tree**, n. Bot. Lentisque *m.*
masticate ['mæstikeit] v. tr. Mastiquer.
mastication [,mæsti'keiʃən] n. Mastication *f.*
masticator ['mæstikeitə*] n. Masticateur *m.* (animal, machine, organ). ‖ Fam. Pl. Mandibules *f. pl.* (jaws).
masticatory [-əri] adj. Masticateur.
— n. Med. Masticatoire *m.*
mastiff ['mæstif] n. Zool. Mâtin, dogue *m.*
mastitis [mæs'taitis] n. Med. Mammite *f.*
mastodon ['mæstədɔn] n. Zool. Mastodonte *m.*
mastoid ['mæstɔid] adj. Med. Mastoïde.
— n. Fam. Mastoïdite *f.*
mastoiditis [,mæstɔi'daitis] n. Med. Mastoïdite *f.*
masturbate ['mæstəbeit] v. intr. Se masturber.
masturbation [,mæstə'beiʃən] n. Masturbation *f.*
mat [mæt] n. Natte (of straw); tapis *m.* (carpet); paillasson *m.* (door-mat); dessous (*m.*) de plat (or) d'assiette (table-mat); *electrically heated mat,* tapis chauffant. ‖ Naut. Paillet *m.*
— v. tr. (1). Couvrir de nattes (or) de tapis. ‖ Emmêler (hair).
— v. intr. S'emmêler.
mat(t) adj. Mat.
— n. Matité *f.* ‖ Surface mate *f.* ‖ Filet d'or mat *m* (border). ‖ Techn. Matrice *f.* (in printing).
— v. tr. (1). Matir (metal). ‖ Dépolir (glass).
matador ['mætədɔ:*] n. Matador *m.*
match [mætʃ] n. Egal, pair *m.; to be more than a match for s.o.,* dépasser qqn de cent coudrées; mettre qqn dans sa poche; *to meet one's match,* trouver son pareil (or) avec qui compter. ‖ Pendant, assortiment *m.; her hat and shoes are a good match,* son chapeau et ses chaussures sont bien assortis (or) vont bien ensemble. ‖ Mariage *m.; to make a match of it,* se marier. ‖ Parti *m.* (mate); *an excellent match,* un excellent parti. ‖ Sports. Match *m.* ‖ **Match-maker**, n. Marieur *s.* ‖ **Match-making**, n. Manie (*f.*) de faire des mariages. ‖ **Match-mark**, n. Point de repère *m.*
— v. tr. Egaler, être l'égal de (to be equal to). ‖ Correspondre à; *his looks match his character,* il a bien l'air de ce qu'il est. ‖ Rivaliser avec; *I can't match your story,* je n'en connais pas de meilleure que la vôtre! ‖ Assortir (a cloth); harmoniser (colours); apparier (gloves). ‖ Marier (*with,* à); *well matched,* bien assortis, formant un beau couple.
— v. intr. Aller (*with,* avec); être assorti (*with,* à). ‖ S'harmoniser, se marier (*with,* avec) [colours]; s'apparier (gloves).

match n. Allumette *f.; wax match,* allumette-bougie. ‖ Milit. Mèche *f.* ‖ **Match-box**, n. Boîte à allumettes *f.* ‖ **Match-lock**, n. Milit. Fusil (*m.*) à mèche. ‖ **Match-maker**, n. Allumettier *s.* ‖ **Match-making**, n. Fabrication des allumettes *f.* ‖ **Match-stick**, n. Fam. Allumette, baguette (*f.*) de tambour; mollet de coq *m.* (leg).
matcher [-ə*] n. Comm. Assortisseur *s.*
matchet [-it] n. Machette *f.*
matching [-iŋ] n. Assortiment *m.*
matchless [-lis] n. Sans pareil, inégalable, inimitable, incomparable.
matchwood [-wud] n. Bois (*m.*) d'allumettes. ‖ Echardes *f. pl.;* éclats (*m. pl.*) de bois (splinters).
mate [meit] n. Mat *m.* (checkmate).
— v. tr. Faire échec et mat.
mate n. Camarade *s.;* compagnon *m.;* compagne *f.* ‖ Copain *m.;* copine *f.* (fam.) [chum]. ‖ Conjoint *s.* (spouse). ‖ Zool. Mâle *m.;* femelle *f.* (of animals). ‖ Naut. Officier en second *m.* (of a merchant ship); *boatswain's mate,* second maître de manœuvre. ‖ Culin., Med. Aide *m.*
— v. tr. Marier (*with,* à) [s.o.]. ‖ Zool. Accoupler, apparier (*with,* à) [a bird].
— v. intr. Se marier, s'unir (*with,* à). ‖ Frayer (*with,* avec); tenir compagnie (*with,* à). ‖ Zool. S'accoupler (*with,* à).
maté ['mæte] n. Maté *m.* (tea).
mateless ['meitlis] adj. Sans compagnon, seul.
matelote [mæt'lɔt] n. Culin. Matelote *f.*
mater ['meitə*] n. Med. Mère *f.; pia mater,* pie-mère. ‖ Fam. *The mater,* ma mère.
material [mə'tiəriəl] adj. Matériel (object, possessions). ‖ Physique (comfort, force). ‖ Corporel, des sens (pleasures); matériel (interest, success). ‖ Notable, profond (change); considérable, énorme (service); *material to,* important pour. ‖ Jur. Pertinent (evidence); en rapport (*to,* avec).
— n. Matière *f.; raw material,* matière première. ‖ Matériau *m.; building materials,* matériaux de construction. ‖ Pl. Fournitures *f. pl.; office materials,* fournitures (or) articles de bureau. ‖ Etoffe *f.;* tissu *m.* (fabric). ‖ Milit. Matériel *m.* ‖ Fig. Matériaux *m. pl.* (*for,* de, pour).
materialism [-izm] n. Matérialisme *m.*
materialist [-ist] n. Matérialiste *s.*
materialistic [mə,tiəriə'listik] adj. Matérialiste (person); matériel (pleasures).
materialistically [-əli] adv. Avec matérialisme.
materiality [mə,tiəri'æliti] n. Matérialité *f.* ‖ Jur. Importance *f.*
materialization [,mətiəriəlai'zeiʃən] n. Matérialisation *f.*
materialize [mə'tiəriəlaiz] v. tr. Matérialiser (ectoplasm, an idea)
— v. intr. Se matérialiser (ectoplasm, idea); prendre forme (or) corps (idea); se réaliser (possibility); aboutir (project).
materially [-li] adv. Matériellement. ‖ Considérablement, sensiblement.
materiel [mə,tiəri'el] n. Milit. Matériel *m.*
maternal [mə'tə:nl] adj. Maternel.
maternally [-nəli] adv. Maternellement.
maternity [-niti] n. Maternité *f.*
— adj. Comm. Pour futures mamans (dress). ‖ Med. De grossesse (belt); d'accouchement (centre); *maternity hospital,* maternité.
matey ['meiti] adj. Fam. Copain, pote (*with,* avec).
— n. Mon vieux, vieux, mon pote *m.* (term of address).
math [mæθ] n. U. S. Fam. Math, maths *f. pl.*
mathematical [,mæθi'mætikəl] adj. Math., Philos. Mathématique.
mathematically [-i] adv. Math. Mathématiquement. ‖ Fam. Par a plus b; rigoureusement.
mathematician [,mæθəmə'tiʃən] n. Math. Mathématicien *s.*

MATHEMATICS AND PHYSICS (Symbols)
Symboles utilisés en mathématiques et en physique

a multiplié par b	$a.b$	a times b
a facteur de b	$a.b$	— — —
a sur b	$a/b\,;\ \dfrac{a}{b}$	a over b; a by b
a plus (moins) b	$a \overset{+}{-} b$	a plus (minus) b
a plus b sur c	$\dfrac{a+b}{c}$	a plus b by c
f de x (fonction)	$f(x)$	function x
A prime	A'	A prime
A seconde	A''	A double prime
a au carré	a^2	a squared
a puissance n	a^n	a to the nth power
racine carrée de a	$\sqrt{a}$	square root of a
racine cubique de a	$\sqrt[3]{a}$ •	cubic root of a
a égale b	$a = b$	a equals b
a plus grand que b	$a > b$	a greater than b
a plus petit que b	$a < b$	a less than b
a différent de b	$a \neq b$	a not equal to b
a identique à b	$a \equiv b$	a identically equal to b
a inférieur ou égal à b	$a \leqslant b$	a equal to or less than b
AB parallèle à CD	$AB /\!/ CD$	AB parallel to CD
élément de pile		cell
batterie à B. T. (basse tension)		L. T. battery (low-tension battery); U. S. A battery
condensateur		condenser
terre		earth; U. S. ground
antenne		aerial; U. S. antenna
interrupteur		switch
ampèremètre		ammeter
voltmètre		voltmeter
résistance fixe		fixed resistance
— ajustable		adjustable resistance
bobine de self		self-inductance
— à curseur		variable inductance
transformateur		transformer
génératrice de courant continu		D. C. generator
— — — alternatif		A. C. generator

mathematics [ˌmæθə'mætiks] n. sg. MATH. Mathématique f., mathématiques f. pl.

maths [mæθs] n. sg. FAM. Math, maths f. pl.

matinee ['mætinei] n. THEATR. Matinée f.; matinee idol, idole du public.

matins ['mætinz] n. pl. ECCLES. Matines f. pl.

mating ['meitiŋ] n. Union f. (of persons). ‖ ZOOL. Accouplement m.

matrass ['mætrəs] n. CHIM. Matras m.

matriarch ['meitri,ɑːk] n. Femme détenant l'autorité f. ‖ FIG. Maîtresse femme, matrone f.

matriarchal ['meitri'ɑːkəl] adj. Matriarcal.

matriarchy ['meitriɑːki] n. Matriarcat m.

matricide [-said] n. Matricide m. (act, person).

matriculate [mə'trikjuleit] v. tr. Immatriculer. — v. intr. S'immatriculer. ‖ Passer l'examen d'entrée.

matriculation [mə,trikju'leiʃən] n. Immatriculation f. (inscription); examen (m.) d'entrée (exam).

matrilineal [ˌmætri'liniəl] adj. Matrilinéaire; par les femmes.

matrilocal ['mætri,loukḷ] adj. Matrilocal.

matrimonial [ˌmætri'mounjəl] adj. Matrimonial. ‖ JUR. En matière de mariage.

matrimonially [-i] adv. Conjugalement.

matrimony ['mætriməni] n. Mariage m.; vie conjugale f. ‖ Mariage m. (card game).

matrix ['meitriks] (pl. **matrices** [-siz]) n. MED., GEOL., TECHN. Matrice f.

matron ['meitrən] n. † Matrone f. ‖ Mère de famille f.; matron of honour, dame d'honneur d'une mariée. ‖ Dame âgée f. (old lady). ‖ Intendante, économe f. (in an institution). ‖ MED. Surveillante f. (in a hospital).

matronage [-idʒ] n. † Etat (m.) de matrone; ensemble (m.) des matrones. ‖ Rôle (m.) d'une intendante (or) surveillante.

matronal [-ḷ] adj. † De matrone. ‖ Domestique, familial (duty).

matronly [-li] adj. † De matrone. ‖ Mûr, âgé; to look matronly, faire dame patronnesse.

matronship [-ʃip] n. Intendance f. (in an institution). ‖ MED. Poste (m.) de surveillante.

matter ['mætə*] n. Matière, substance f.; colouring matter, substance colorante. ‖ Objets, documents m. pl.; postal matter, lettres et colis postaux. ‖ PHYS. Matière f. ‖ MED. Pus m. ‖ TECHN. Copie f. (copy); plomb m. (type). ‖ FIG. Fond m. ‖

Fig. Objet, sujet *m.* (*for*, de); matière *f.* (*for*, à); *a laughing matter*, matière à rire; *reading matter*, choses à lire. ‖ Fig. Importance *f.; it makes no matter*, ça n'a pas d'importance; *no matter how, when*, n'importe quand, comment; *no matter how fast*, si vite que; *what matter*, qu'importe. ‖ Fig. Affaire, question *f.;* fait *m.; an easy matter*, chose facile; *matter of course*, question évidente, chose qui va de soi; *matter of fact*, question de fait; *as a matter of fact*, à vrai dire, de fait, effectivement; *as matters stand*, vu l'état actuel des choses; *for that matter*, à cet égard, quant à cela; à vrai dire; *in all matters of*, en tout ce qui concerne (or) touche; *in the matter of*, en matière de; *in this matter*, sur ce point, à ce sujet; *matter of habit, taste, time*, affaire (or) question d'habitude, de goût, de temps; *matter of history*, fait historique; *quite another matter*, une tout autre question. ‖ Fig. Difficulté *f.; there's sth. the matter*, il y a qqch. qui cloche; *there's sth. the matter with you*, vous avez qqch.; *what's the matter?*, qu'y a-t-il?; *what's the matter with you?*, qu'avez-vous?; qu'est-ce qui vous prend? ‖ **Matter-of-course**, adj. Naturel, qui va de soi, normal. ‖ **Matter-of-fact**, adj. Prosaïque, réaliste, positif, terre à terre. ‖ **Matter-of-factness**, n. Prosaïsme, réalisme, positivisme *m.*
— v. intr. Importer; *it doesn't matter*, ça n'a pas d'importance, ça ne fait rien, c'est un détail; *what does it matter to him?*, quelle importance cela a-t-il pour lui?; qu'est-ce que ça lui fait? (fam.). ‖ Med. Suppurer.

matterful [-ful] adj. Substantiel, dense, riche, plein (book).

Matterhorn ['mætəhɔːn] n. Geogr. Mont Cervin.

matting ['mætiŋ] n. Tressage *m.* (of straw). ‖ Nattes *f. pl.;* paillassons *m. pl.* ‖ Enchevêtrement *m.* (tangle).

matting n. Matage *m.* (of metal). ‖ Dépolissage *m.* (of glass).

mattins ['mætinz] n. pl. Eccles. Matines *f. pl.*

mattock ['mætək] n. Pioche-hache *f.*

mattress ['mætris] n. Matelas *m.; interior-sprung* (or) U. S. *inner-spring mattress*, matelas à ressort; *wool mattress*, matelas de laine. ‖ Sommier *m.; wire mattress*, sommier métallique.

maturate ['mætjuəreit] v. tr. Med. Faire mûrir.

maturation [,mætjuˈreiʃən] n. Agric., Med. Maturation *f.* ‖ Fig. Développement *m.*

maturative [məˈtjuərətiv] adj. Qui aide à la maturation.

mature [məˈtjuə*] adj. Fin. Echu. ‖ Fig. Mûr.
— v. tr. Agric., Fig., Med. Faire mûrir, mûrir.
— v. intr. Fin. Echoir. ‖ Fig. Mûrir.

maturely [-li] adv. Mûrement.

maturity [-riti] n. Agric., Fig. Maturité *f.* ‖ Fin. Echéance *f.*

matutinal [,mætjuˈtainl] adj. Matutinal, du matin.

maud [mɔːd] n. Plaid *m.* (or) couverture (*f.*) à rayures grises.

maudlin ['mɔːdlin] adj. Larmoyant, pleurard; gnangnan (fam.).

maul [mɔːl] n. Techn. Mail *m.; mailloche f.*
— v. tr. Malmener (s.o.). ‖ U. S. Fendre au mail (stumps). ‖ Fam. *To maul about*, peloter (a woman).

maulstick ['mɔːlstik] n. Arts. Appui-main *m.*

maunder ['mɔːndə*] v. intr. Divaguer (to drivel); errer, flâner (to wander).

Maundy ['mɔːndi] s. Eccles. Lavement (*m.*) des pieds; *Maundy Thursday*, Jeudi saint.

Mauritania [,mɔriˈteiniə] n. Geogr. Mauritanie *f.*

Mauritius [mɔˈriʃəs] n. Geogr. Ile Maurice *f.*

mauser ['mauzə*] n. Milit. Mauser *m.*

mausoleum [,mɔːsəˈliəm] n. Mausolée *m.*

mauvais quart d'heure [mouvɛkardœːr] n. Mauvais quart d'heure *m.*

mauve [mouv] adj., n. Mauve *m.* (colour).

maverick ['mævərik] n. U.S. Animal errant *m.* ‖ U. S. Fam. Indépendant, réfractaire (political dissenter).

mavis ['meivis] n. Zool. Grive *f.*

maw [mɔː] n. Zool. Jabot *m.* (of birds); caillette *f.* (of cows); poche (*f.*) d'air (of fish). ‖ Fam. Jabot *m.* (stomach).

mawkish ['mɔːkiʃ] adj. Fade (insipid); nauséeux, écœurant (nauseating). ‖ Fig. Sottement sentimental; bébête, gnangnan, à l'eau de rose (fam.).

mawkishly [-li] adv. Insipidement.

mawkishness [-nis] n. Fadeur; insipidité *f.* ‖ Fig. Sentimentalité à l'eau de rose; fadasserie *f.* (fam.).

mawworm ['mɔːwəːm] n. Med. Oxyure *m.* ‖ Fig. Tartufe *m.*

maxi ['mæksi] n. Jupe (*f.*) [or] manteau (*m.*) maxi.

maxilla [mækˈsilə] n. (pl. **maxillae** [-iː]) n. Med. Maxillaire supérieur *m.*

maxillary [-əri] adj. Med. Maxillaire.

maxim ['mæksim] n. Maxime *f.* (See SAYING.)

maxim n. Milit. Mitrailleuse (*f.*) Maxim.

maximal [-əl] adj. Maximum, maximal.

maximize [-aiz] v. tr. Porter au maximum.

maximum [-əm] (pl. **maxima** [-ə]) adj., n. Maximum *m.*

may [mei] n. Mai *m.; May Day*, premier mai, fête du travail; *May Queen*, reine de mai. ‖ Bot. Aubépine *f.* (flower). ‖ Pl. Epreuves (*f. pl.*) de mai (at Cambridge). ‖ **May-beetle** (or) **-bug**, n. Zool. Hanneton *m.* ‖ **May-fly**, n. Zool. Ephémère *m.*
— v. intr. Cueillir de l'aubépine. ‖ Fêter le premier mai.

may [mei] aux. defect. Pouvoir (probability); *it may be*, cela se peut, ce n'est pas impossible; *he may not come*, peut-être ne viendra-t-il pas, il se peut qu'il ne vienne pas. ‖ Pouvoir (possibility); *whatever you may say*, quoi que vous puissiez dire; *he may have made a mistake*, il a pu se tromper; *however hard he might try to conceive it*, quelque effort qu'il fît pour le concevoir. ‖ Pouvoir (permission); *I may not tell you*, je ne puis vous le dire (je n'y suis pas autorisé); *if I may*, si vous le permettez; *if I may say so*, si j'ose m'exprimer ainsi. ‖ Pouvoir bien; *I may as well do it*, je ferais aussi bien de le faire; *you might shut the door*, vous pourriez fermer la porte; *you may as well come*, vous feriez aussi bien de venir; *who may it be?*, qui ce peut-il bien être? ‖ Pouvoir (wish); *may he be happy!*, puisse-t-il être heureux! ‖ Pouvoir, avoir beau; *try as you may, you will not succeed*, vous avez beau essayer, vous ne réussirez pas. ‖ (Subjunctive); *be that as it may*, quoi qu'il en soit; *whoever you may be*, qui que vous soyez; *so that you may defend your interests*, afin que vous défendiez vos intérêts.

maybe [-biː] adv. Peut-être.

mayday [-dei] n. Naut., Aviat. Signal (*m.*) de détresse; S. O. S. *m.*

Mayfair ['meifə*] n. Mayfair; le faubourg Saint-Germain.

mayhem ['meihem] n. Jur. † Mutilation volontaire *f.* ‖ Pagaille *f.:* chahut, chaos, chambardement *m.*

mayonnaise [meiəˈneiz] n. Culin. Mayonnaise *f.*

mayor [mɛə*] n. Maire *m.*

mayoralty [-rəlti] n. Mandat de maire *m.* (office and term).

mayoress [-ris] n. Mairesse *f.*

maypole ['meipoul] n. Mai *m.* (pole). ‖ Fam. Echalas, escogriffe *m.;* asperge, perche *f.* (tall person).

mazard ['mæzəd] n. Bot. Guigne *f.* (cherry).

mazarine [,mæzəˈriːn] adj., n. Bleu foncé *m.*

maze [meiz] n. Labyrinthe, dédale *m.* ‖ Enchevêtrement *m.* ‖ Fig. Imbroglio *m.; in a maze*, désorienté.
— v. tr. Fig. Embarrasser, désorienter, égarer.

mazurka [məˈzəːkə] n. Mus. Mazurka *f.*

mazy ['meizi] adj. Sinueux, en dédale. ‖ Fig. Perplexe, désorienté (persons) ; embrouillé, enchevêtré, compliqué (things).

me [mi:] pron. pers. Moi, me ; *he gave it to me*, il me le donna ; *he came to me*, il vint à moi. ‖ Fam. *Ah me!*, pauvre de moi !

mead [mi:d] n. Hydromel *m*.

mead [mi:d], **meadow** ['medou] n. Prairie *f.* ; pré *m*. ‖ **Meadow-sweet**, n. Bot. Reine (*f.*) des prés.

meadowy [-i] adj. De prairie. ‖ Herbeux (grassy).

meagre ['mi:gə*] n. Zool. Bar *m*.

meagre adj. Maigre (lit. and fig.).

meagrely [-li] adv. Maigrement.

meagreness [-nis] n. Maigreur *f*. ‖ Fig. Pauvreté, médiocrité, rareté *f*.

meal [mi:l] n. Repas *m*. ‖ Agric. Traite *f*. ‖ **Meal ticket**, n. U. S. Ticket-repas *m*. ‖ **Meal-time**, n. Heure (*f.*) du repas.
— v. intr. Prendre son repas, manger (*with*, avec).

meal n. Farine *f*. ‖ **Meal-worm**, n. Ver (*m.*) de farine.

mealie ['mi:li] n. Agric. Maïs, épi de maïs *m*. (in South Africa).

mealiness [-inis] n. Caractère farineux *m*. ‖ Fig. Papelardise, cautèle *f*.

mealy [-li] adj. Farineux (potato). ‖ Med. Blême (complexion). ‖ **Mealy-mouthed**, adj. Fam. Benoît, patelin, papelard, cauteleux, doucereux, mielleux.

mean [mi:n] n. Milieu, moyen terme *m.* ; *golden mean*, le juste milieu. ‖ Math. Moyenne *f*. ‖ Pl. Moyen *m.* ; moyens *m. pl.* ; *a means to*, un moyen de ; *by all manner of means*, par tous les moyens ; *by all means*, mais certainement, faites donc, je vous en prie (when answering) ; *by any means*, par n'importe quel moyen ; *by means of*, au moyen de ; *by no means*, en aucune manière ; pas le moins du monde ; *he is by no means a scholar*, il n'est rien moins qu'un érudit. ‖ Fin. Moyens *m. pl.* ; ressources *f. pl.* ; *a man of means*, une personne fortunée, un homme riche ; *private means*, ressources personnelles.
— N. B. Au sens de « moyen », *means* se construit comme un sing. ; au sens de « ressources », il prend le verbe au pluriel.
— adj. Moyen (quality, quantity). ‖ Math. Moyen.

mean adj. Médiocre, piètre, pauvre (inferior) ; *the meanest slave*, le dernier esclave. ‖ Minable, misérable, humble. ‖ Mesquin, plat ; *it's mean of him*, c'est bien petit de sa part. ‖ Méprisable, bas, vil ; *mean character*, caractère vil ; *mean trick*, sale coup. ‖ Pingre ; rat (fam.) [stingy]. ‖ U. S. Désagréable ; *mean job*, fichu travail ; *mean weather*, sale temps ; *to feel mean*, se sentir mal en train.

mean v. tr. (101). Avoir l'intention, se proposer, être dans la disposition (*to*, de) [to intend] ; *what do you mean to do?*, que comptez-vous faire ? ‖ Avoir des intentions ; *he means no harm*, il n'a pas de mauvaises intentions ; *he means well by you*, il vous veut du bien. ‖ Vouloir, avoir la volonté de ; *he never meant it*, il ne l'a pas voulu (or) fait exprès ; *without meaning it*, sans le vouloir. ‖ Vouloir ; exiger ; *I mean you to speak*, j'entends que vous parliez. ‖ Destiner (*for*, à) ; *meant for a storeroom*, destiné à servir de réserve ; *that remark was meant for you*, c'est à vous que s'adressait cette remarque ; c'était une pierre dans votre jardin (fam.). ‖ Faire allusion à, désigner ; *do you mean him?*, est-ce à lui que vous faites allusion (or) de lui que vous parlez ? ‖ Vouloir dire, penser ; *what do you mean by it?*, qu'entendez-vous par là ? ; *you don't really mean it*, vous ne le pensez pas au fond. ‖ Vouloir dire, signifier ; *the French word « oui » means « yes »*, le mot français « oui » veut dire « yes », le sens du français « oui » est « yes ». ‖ Signifier, impliquer ; *it doesn't mean much*, ça ne signifie pas grand-chose ; *I can't tell*

you what it has meant to me, je ne saurais vous dire ce que cela a représenté pour moi ; *money doesn't mean happiness*, l'argent ne fait pas le bonheur ; *what does it mean?*, qu'est-ce à dire ? ‖ U. S. Fam. *To mean business*, avoir des intentions sérieuses, ne pas plaisanter.

meander [mi'ændə*] n. Méandre *m*. (of a stream). ‖ Arts. Frettes *f. pl.* ‖ Fig. Pl. Méandres *m. pl.*
— v. intr. Serpenter (stream). ‖ Errer, vagabonder (person).

meandrous [-drəs] adj. Sinueux.

meanie ['mi:ni] n. Fam. Radin *s.*, grippe-sou *m*. (miser) ; méchant *s.*, teigne *f*. (nasty person).

meaning ['mi:niŋ] adj. Intentionné ; disposé. ‖ Significatif, expressif.
— n. Intention *f*. (thought). ‖ Sens *m.* ; signification *f*. (sense).

meaningful [-ful] adj. Plein de sens, significatif.

meaningfully [-fuli], **meaningly** [-li] adv. Significativement.

meaningless [-lis] adj. Dépourvu de sens, sans signification.

meanly ['mi:nli] adv. Médiocrement, pauvrement, petitement, misérablement, piètrement. ‖ Bassement, vilement. ‖ Chichement, avec ladrerie.

meanness [-nis] n. Médiocrité, pauvreté, petitesse *f*. ‖ Bassesse, vilenie *f*. ‖ Ladrerie, mesquinerie *f*. (stinginess).

meant [ment] pret., p.p. See MEAN.

meantime ['mi:n'taim], **meanwhile** [-'wail] n. Intervalle *m*.
— adv. Dans l'intervalle (or) l'entre-temps, pendant ce temps, en attendant, d'ici là, sur ces entrefaites.

measles ['mi:zlz] n. sg. Med. Rougeole *f.* ; *German measles*, rubéole. ‖ Ladrerie *f*. (in pigs).

measly [-li] adj. Med. Rougeoleux, atteint de rougeole. ‖ Ladre (pig). ‖ Fam. De rien du tout, misérable, piètre, insignifiant.

measurability [,meʒərə'biliti] n. Mensurabilité *f*.

measurable ['meʒərəbl] adj. Mesurable, mensurable. ‖ Chim. Dosable.

measurably [-bli] adv. Sensiblement, notablement, appréciablement.

measure ['meʒə*] n. Mesures *f. pl.* (in dressmaking) ; *made to measure*, fait sur mesure. ‖ Math. Mesure *f.* ; *liquid, long, square measure*, mesure de capacité, de longueur, de surface. ‖ Math. Diviseur *m*. ‖ Chim., Mus. Mesure *f*. ‖ Jur. Mesure (or) voie légale *f*. ‖ Techn. Justification *f*. (in printing). ‖ Naut. Cubage *m*. ‖ Geol. Pl. Gisement, étage *m*. ‖ Fig. Mesure, limite *f.* ; *beyond measure*, démesurément ; *in a measure*, dans une certaine mesure ; *in a large measure*, en grande partie ; *in due measure*, avec mesure ; *in some measure*, jusqu'à un certain point. ‖ Fig. Mesure, modération *f.* ; *sense of measure*, pondération *f*. ‖ Fig. Mesure, valeur *f.* ; *to give one's measure*, faire ses preuves ; *to take the measure of s.o.*, jauger qqn. ‖ Fig. Mesure, disposition *f.* ; *to take drastic measures*, prendre des mesures rigoureuses, employer les grands moyens.
— v. tr. Mesurer (distance, length, time) ; métrer (wall) ; cuber (wood). ‖ Prendre les mesures de (s.o.) [in dressmaking] ; *to be measured for*, faire prendre ses mesures pour. ‖ *To measure swords*, se battre en duel, se mesurer avec qqn. ‖ Fig. Mesurer (one's strength, words) ; toiser (s.o.) ; mesurer, régler (one's spending). ‖ Fam. *To measure one's length*, s'étaler de tout son long. ‖ **To measure off**, mesurer (fabric). ‖ **To measure out**, mesurer (corn) ; distribuer (parts) ; verser (tea). ‖ **To measure up**, mesurer (wood) ; *to measure up to*, être au niveau de (or) à la hauteur de (a task) ; être l'égal de (s.o.).

measured ['meʒəd] adj. Mesuré (space, time) ; *with measured steps*, à pas comptés. ‖ Cadencé, rythmé, scandé (tread). ‖ Mesuré, modéré, pondéré (language). ‖ GRAMM. Mesuré (verse).

measureless [-lis] adj. Illimité, incommensurable. ‖ Démesuré, sans mesure.

measurement [-mənt] n. Mesurage *m.* ‖ TECHN. Arpentage *m.* (of ground). ‖ NAUT. Cubage *m.* ‖ COMM. Encombrement *m.* (of goods). ‖ Pl. Mesures, mensurations *f. pl.* (of s.o.).

measuring [-riŋ] n. Mesurage *m.; métrage m.* (of a fabric). ‖ TECHN. Arpentage *m.* ‖ CHIM. Dosage *m.* ‖ NAUT. Jaugeage *m.* ‖ **Measuring-chain,** n. Chaîne (*f.*) d'arpenteur. ‖ **Measuring-glass,** n. Verre gradué *m.* ‖ **Measuring-rod,** n. Mètre rigide *m.; réglette-jauge f.* ‖ **Measuring-tape,** n. Mètre ruban *m.* ‖ **Measuring-tube,** n. Tube pour dosage *m.* ‖ **Measuring-worm,** n. ZOOL. Chenille arpenteuse *f.*

meat [mi:t] n. † Nourriture *f.; manger m.* (food); repas *m.* (meal). ‖ CULIN. Viande *f.* ‖ FIG. Substance *f.* (of a story). ‖ FIG. *Meat and drink,* ce qui fait vivre. ‖ FAM. *That's not my meat,* ce n'est pas mes oignons. ‖ **Meat-safe,** n. Garde-manger *m.*

meatless [-lis] adj. Sans viande. ‖ ECCLES. Maigre (day, meal).

meatus [mi'eitəs] n. MED. Méat *m.*

meaty ['mi:ti] adj. De viande. ‖ Plein de viande. ‖ Charnu (fleshy). ‖ FIG. Plein de substance, nourri de faits, bein rempli. (See PITHY.)

Mecca ['mekə] n. GEOGR. La Mecque *f.* ‖ FIG. Terre d'élection *f.*

mechanic [mi'kænik] n. TECHN., AVIAT. Ouvrier mécanicien *m.* ‖ † Artisan *m.*

mechanical [-əl] adj. TECHN. Mécanique (art, power); mécanicien (civilisation, engineer). ‖ ARTS. Géométrique (drawing). ‖ FIG. Machinal, mécanique, automatique (actions).

mechanically [-əli] adv. TECHN. Mécaniquement. ‖ FIG. Machinalement, en automate.

mechanics [-s] n. sg. TECHN. Mécanique *f.* ‖ FIG. Mécanisme *m.*

mechanism ['mekənizm] n. TECHN., FIG. Mécanisme *m.* ‖ MUS. Technique *f.* ‖ PHILOS. Machinisme *m.* ‖ FIG. Système *m.* (defence mechanism).

mechanist [-nist] n. TECHN. Mécanicien monteur *m.* ‖ PHILOS. Machiniste *m.*

mechanization [,mekənai'zeiʃən] n. Mécanisation *f.*

mechanize ['mekənaiz] v. tr. Mécaniser. ‖ AGRIC. *Mechanized farming,* motoculture. ‖ MILIT. *Mechanized army,* armée motorisée.

mechanotherapy [,mekəno'θerəpi] n. MED. Mécanothérapie *f.*

Mechlin ['meklin] n. GEOGR. Malines *f.* ‖ COMM. Dentelle (*f.*) de Malines.

medal ['medl] n. Médaille *f.* ‖ FAM. *A putty medal,* une médaille en chocolat.

medalled [-d] adj. Médaillé.

medallic [mi'dælik] adj. De (or) en médaille.

medallion [-jən] n. Médaillon *m.*

medallist ['medlist] n. Médailliste *m.* (engraver); médaillé *m.* (recipient).

meddle ['medl] v. intr. S'ingérer (in, dans); se mêler, s'occuper (with, de) [to interfere]. ‖ Toucher, tripoter (with, à) [to temper].

meddler [-ə*] n. Intrigant, officieux, touche-à-tout *m.*

meddlesome [-səm], **meddling** ['medliŋ] adj. Intrigant, importun, curieux, indiscret; fouinard, qui met son nez partout (fam.).

meddling n. Immixtion, ingérance *f.* (in, with, dans).

media ['mi:diə] n. pl. Média, mass media *m. pl.* ‖ See MEDIUM.

medi(a)eval [,medi'i:vəl] adj. Médiéval, du Moyen Age. ‖ Moyenâgeux (suggestive of the Middle Ages).

medi(a)evalist [-ist] n. Médiéviste *s.*

medial ['mi:diəl] adj. Médial, médian (in the middle). ‖ Moyen (average).

median [-ən] adj. Médian. ‖ MATH. *Median line,* médiane. — n. MED. Veine médiane *f.*

mediant [-ənt] n. MUS. Médiante *f.*

mediastinum [,mi:diəs'tainəm] n. MED. Médiastin *m.*

mediate ['mi:diit] adj. Médiat. — [-eit] v. intr. S'entremettre, servir d'intermédiaire (person); servir de lien (things). ‖ Intervenir (*between,* entre). — v. tr. Obtenir par médiation (a result). ‖ Servir d'intermédiaire pour communiquer (an information, object).

mediation [,mi:di'eiʃən] n. Médiation *f.*

mediative ['mi:diətiv], **mediatory** [-əri] adj. Médiateur *m.; médiatrice f.*

mediator [-ə*] n. Médiateur *m.*

mediatrix [-rix] n. Médiatrice *f.*

medic ['medik] See MEDICO.

medicable ['medikəbl] adj. MED. Curable.

medical [-əl] adj. MED. Médical (attendance, profession); de médecine (book, school); sanitaire (store); en médecine (student); *medical department,* service de santé; *medical man,* membre du corps médical; *medical certificate,* certificat médical (clean bill of health), attestation de maladie (excusing absence from work). ‖ MILIT. *Medical officer,* médecin militaire, major, officier de santé; *medical unit,* formation sanitaire; U. S. *medical examiner,* médecin légiste. ‖ JUR. *Medical jurisprudence,* médecine légale. — n. FAM. Visite médicale *f.* (examination). ‖ FAM. Etudiant (*s.*) en médecine (student).

medically [-əli] adv. Médicalement.

medicament [me'dikəmənt] n. MED. Médicament *m.*

Medicare ['medi,keə*] n. U. S. Medicare *m.,* système (*m.*) d'assurance-maladie en faveur notamment des personnes âgées.

medicaster ['medi:kəstə*] n. Médicastre *m.*

medicate [-eit] v. tr. MED. Médicamenter (s.o.); rendre médicamenteux (sth.).

medicated [-eited] adj. Hydrophile (cotton); hygiénique (soap); médicinal (water); médicamenteux (wine).

medication [,medi'keiʃən] n. Médication *f.*

medicinal [me'disinl] adj. MED. Médicinal; médicamenteux.

medicinally [-li] adv. MED. Médicinalement; comme médicament.

medicine ['medsin] n. MED. Médecine *f.* (art, science); médicament, remède *m.* (drug); *patent medicines,* spécialités pharmaceutiques. ‖ Rite (or) objet magique *m.* (among savages). ‖ FAM. Purgatif *m.; purge f.* ‖ FAM. *To take one's medicine,* avaler la pilule. ‖ **Medicine-chest,** n. Pharmacie portative *f.* ‖ **Medicine-man,** n. Sorcier *m.* — v. tr. MED. Médicamenter, traiter.

medico ['medikou] n. FAM. Toubib *m.* (doctor); carabin *m.* (student). ‖ **Medico-legal,** adj. JUR. Médico-légal.

medieval [,medi'i:vəl]. See MEDIAEVAL.

mediocre ['mi:dioukə*] adj. Médiocre (quality).

mediocrity [,mi:di'ɔkriti] n. Médiocrité *f.* (quality). ‖ Médiocre *m.; médiocrité f.* (person).

meditate ['mediteit] v. intr. Méditer (on, sur). [See PONDER.] — v. tr. Envisager, projeter. ‖ Méditer, comploter.

meditation [,medi'teiʃən] n. Méditation *f.*

meditative ['meditətiv] adj. Méditatif.

meditatively [-li] adv. D'un air méditatif.

meditator ['mediteitə*] n. Penseur, songeur *s.*

Mediterranean [,meditə'reinijən] adj. GEOGR. Méditerranéen (climate); intérieur, Méditerranée (sea); entouré de terres (waters). — n. GEOGR. Méditerranéen *s.* (person); Méditerranée *f.* (sea).

MEDICINE (Vocabulary) — MÉDECINE (Vocabulaire)

sain (= solide)	sound	urticaire	nettle-rash, urticaria
sain (= plein de santé)	healthy	migraine	sick-headache, migraine
sain (= bon pour la santé)	wholesome	névralgie	neuralgia
malade	ill, sick	évanouissement	faint, fainting fit
maladif	sickly	s'évanouir	to faint
chétif, souffreteux	delicate	vertige	dizziness, giddiness, vertigo
indisposé	unwell	épuisement	exhaustion
souffrant	ailing	défaillance	breakdown
douloureux	painful	tomber sans connaissance	to fall senseless
enflammé	inflamed	perdre connaissance	to lose consciousness
endolori	aching	des sels	smelling salts
gravement malade	seriously ill	cicatrice	scar
douleur physique	pain, suffering	blessure, plaie	wound
indisposition	ailment	saigner	to bleed
rhume [de cerveau]	cold [in the head]	contusion	bruise
rhume [de poitrine]	cold [on the chest]	foulure	sprain, twist
toux	cough, coughing	bosse	bump [par un coup]
refroidissement	chill		hump [d'un bossu]
quinte de toux	fit of coughing	enflure	swelling
coqueluche	whooping-cough	ampoule	blister
grippe	influenza, « flu »	clou, furoncle	boil
bronchite	bronchitis	bouton	pimple
fièvre intermittente	ague	se faire vacciner	to be vaccinated
contagieux	infectious, contagious	vaccin	vaccine
s'aliter	to take to one's bed	vacciner	to vaccinate; to inoculate
éternuer	to sneeze	soulager	to relieve
tuberculose	tuberculosis, consumption	rechute	relapse
rhume des foins	hay fever	régime	diet
scarlatine	scarlet fever	diète	low (or) starvation diet
rougeole	measles	écharpe	arm-sling
diabète	diabetes	panser	to dress [une blessure]
goutte	gout		to tend [quelqu'un]
torticolis	stiff neck, torticollis	pansement	dressing, bandage
angine	angina, quinsy	guérison [d'une maladie]	recovery [from an illness]
oreillons	mumps	guérison [d'une plaie]	healing [of a wound]
variole	smallpox	indemne, sain et sauf	unharmed, unscathed, scatheless
indigestion	indigestion		
jaunisse	jaundice	entrer en convalescence	to convalesce
mal à la gorge	sore throat	se porter comme un charme	to be in the best of health

medium ['mi:diəm] n. Milieu *m.* (mean). ‖ Milieu *m.*; atmosphère, ambiance *f.* (environment). ‖ Intermédiaire, instrument, moyen *m.* (means); *advertising medium*, organe de publicité. ‖ Entremise *f.* (of s.o.); *by the medium of*, par le canal de. ‖ Médium *m.* (in spiritualism). ‖ PHYS. Véhicule *m.* ‖ ARTS. Moyen (*m.*) d'expression. ‖ CHIM. Agent *m.* ‖ MED. Véhicule *m.*; *culture medium*, bouillon de culture. ‖ FIN. *Medium of exchange*, agent monétaire.

— N. B. Deux pluriels : *media* et *mediums*.

— adj. Moyen (height). ‖ SPORTS. *Medium distance*, demi-fond. ‖ RADIO. Moyen (wave). ‖ **Medium-sized**, adj. De taille moyenne.

mediumistic [,mi:diəm'istik] adj. Médiumnique.

medlar ['medlə*] n. BOT. Nèfle *f.* (fruit); néflier *m.* (tree).

medley ['medli] n. Mélange, méli-mélo, pêle-mêle *m.*; mixture *f.* ‖ Mélange hétéroclite *m.* ‖ MUS. Pot-pourri *m.*

— adj. Mêlé, mélangé; hétéroclite.

— v. tr. Mélanger, mêler.

medulla [me'dʌlə] n. MED., BOT. Moelle *f.*

medullary [-ləri] adj. MED., BOT. Médullaire.

medusa [mi'dju:zə] n. †, ZOOL. Méduse *f.*

meed [mi:d] n. Récompense *f.* ‖ Tribut *m.* (of praise).

meek [mi:k] adj. Doux, résigné, patient. ‖ ECCLES. Doux, débonnaire.

meekly [-li] adv. Avec une humble douceur.

meekness [-nis] n. Douceur, mansuétude *f.* ‖ Résignation, patience *f.*

meerschaum ['miəʃəm] n. Ecume de mer *f.* (substance); pipe en écume de mer *f.* (pipe).

meet [mi:t] adj. † Séant, convenable.

meet v. tr. (102). Rencontrer (s.o.) [to come upon]. ‖ Aller au-devant de (s.o.); *to send s.o. to meet s.o.*, envoyer qqn à la rencontre de qqn. ‖ Croiser (s.o.) [to come across]. ‖ Faire la connaissance de (s.o.) [to become acquainted with]. ‖ S'entretenir avec (s.o.). ‖ Rencontrer, se mesurer avec (s.o.) [to fight with]. ‖ Frapper (the ear); *to meet s.o.'s eye*, rencontrer le regard de qqn. ‖ COMM. Faire honneur à (a bill). ‖ GEOGR. Se jeter dans (a river). ‖ AUTOM. Attraper, avoir (the bus). ‖ FIG. Rencontrer (a disaster); recevoir (one's reward); *to meet one's death*, trouver la mort. ‖ FIG. Affronter (a danger); faire face à (a difficulty, expenses); réfuter (an objection); *to meet a rebuke with a laugh*, accueillir une rebuffade en riant; *to meet trouble half-way*, aller chercher les ennuis. ‖ FIG. Satisfaire (demands, desires); satisfaire à, répondre à (requirements, wants); *to meet the case*, convenir, faire l'affaire.

— v. intr. Se rencontrer (to come together). ‖ Faire connaissance (to become acquainted). ‖ Se réunir, se toucher, se rejoindre (to be united). ‖ Se rencontrer, s'affronter (to conflict). ‖ FAM. *To make ends meet*, joindre les deux bouts, boucler son budget. ‖ **To meet up with**, U. S. Rencontrer. ‖ **To meet with**, subir, être victime de (an accident); trouver (a violent death); rencontrer (difficulties, obstacles, sth.); essuyer (a loss, a refusal); recevoir (a welcome).

— n. SPORTS. Rendez-vous (*m.*) de chasse.

meeting [-iŋ] n. Rencontre *f.* (coming together). ‖ Duel *m.*; rencontre *f.* ‖ Assemblée, réunion *f.* ‖ Meeting *m.* (of people). ‖ Séance *f.*; *open meeting*, séance publique; *to open the meeting*, ouvrir la séance. ‖ ECCLES. Assemblée (*f.*) des quakers; office religieux *m.* ‖ SPORTS. Courses *f. pl.* (race-meeting). ‖ **Meeting-house**, n. ECCLES. Temple (*m.*) des quakers. ‖ **Meeting-place**, n. Lieu (*m.*) de réunion.

meetness [-nis] n. A-propos *m.*

megalith ['megaliθ] n. Mégalithe *m.*

megalomania [,megələ'meinjə] n. MED. Mégalomanie *f.*

megalomaniac [-ək] n. MED. Mégalomane *s.*

megalosaurus ['megəlo'sɔ:rəs] n. ZOOL. Mégalosaure *m.*

megaphone ['megəfoun] n. Porte-voix *m.* ‖ SPORTS. Mégaphone *m.; megaphone steward,* annonceur, speaker.
— v. tr. U. S. Amplifier.

megaton [-tɔn] n. Mégatonne *f.*

megrim ['mi:grim] n. MED. Migraine *f.* ‖ Vertigo *m.* (in horses). ‖ FIG. Lubie *f.* (whim). ‖ Pl. Humeur noire *f.;* cafard *m.* (melancholy).

meiosis [mai'ousis] (pl. **meioses** [-si:z]) n. MED. Méiose *f.*

meiotic [mai'ɔtik] adj. MED. Méiotique.

melancholia [,melən'kouljə] n. MED. Hypocondrie *f.*

melancholic [,melən'kɔlik] adj. MED. Hypocondriaque. ‖ FIG. Mélancolique.

melancholically [-əli] adv. Mélancoliquement.

melancholy ['melənkɔli] n. Mélancolie *f.*
— adj. Mélancolique (person); attristant, triste (thing).

mélange [melɑ̃:ʒ] n. Mélange, amalgame *m.* (medley).

melanin ['melənin] n. MED. Mélanine *f.*

Melba toast ['melbə'toust] n. U. S. Biscotte *f.*

meld [meld] v. tr. U. S. Annoncer (a combination of cards).

mêlée, U. S. melee ['melei] n. Mêlée *f.*, corps à corps *m.* (brawl); escarmouche, échauffourée *f.* (skirmish); empoignade *f.* (argument); amas, monceau *m.* (muddle).

meliorable ['mi:liərəbḷ] adj. Améliorable.

meliorate [-reit] v. tr. Améliorer.
— v. intr. S'améliorer.

melioration [mi:liə'rei ʃən] n. Amélioration *f.*

meliorism ['mi:liərizm] n. PHILOS. Méliorisme *m.*

melissa [me'lisə] n. BOT. Citronnelle *f.* ‖ MED. *Melissa cordial* (or) *water,* eau de mélisse.

mellifluence [me'lifluəns] n. Onction, papelardise *f.*

mellifluous [-əs] adj. Mielleux, onctueux, douceureux.

mellow ['melou] adj. AGRIC. Meuble (soil). ‖ BOT. Fendant (fruit). [See RIPE.] ‖ CULIN. Moelleux (wine). ‖ FIG. Fondu (colour); mûri, mûr (person); moelleux (voice); *to grow mellow,* se mûrir. ‖ FAM. Pompette, gris (tipsy).
— v. tr. AGRIC. Ameublir. ‖ BOT. Mûrir (fruit). ‖ CULIN. Rendre moelleux, velouter (wine). ‖ FIG. Fondre (colours); mûrir (voice); adoucir (voice). ‖ FAM. Griser.
— v. intr. AGRIC. S'ameublir. ‖ BOT. Mûrir. ‖ CULIN. Se velouter. ‖ FIG. Se fondre, se patiner (colours); mûrir (person); prendre du moelleux (voice).

mellowness [-nis] n. AGRIC. Richesse *f.* ‖ BOT. Fondant *m.* (of fruit). ‖ CULIN. Moelleux *m.* (of wine). ‖ FIG. Fondu *m.* (of colours); maturité *f.* (of s.o.); moelleux *m.* (of a voice).

melodeon [mi'loudjən] n. MUS. Orgue expressif *m.* (organ); accordéon *m.*

melodic [mi'lɔdik] adj. MUS. Mélodique.

melodious [mi'loudjəs] adj. MUS. Mélodieux.

melodiously [-li] adv. Mélodieusement.

melodiousness [-nis] n. Musicalité *f.;* caractère mélodieux *m.* ‖ Mélodie, harmonie *f.*

melodist ['melədist] n. MUS. Mélodiste *s.*

melodize [-daiz] v. intr. MUS. Composer (or) chanter des mélodies.
— v. tr. MUS. Mettre en musique. ‖ Rendre mélodieux.

melodrama ['melodrɑ:mə] n. THEATR., FIG. Mélodrame *m.*

melodramatic [,melodrə'mætik] adj. Mélodramatique.

melodramatize [melə'dræmətaiz] v. tr. Mélodramatiser.

melody ['melədi] n. MUS. Mélodie *f.*

melomania [melo'meiniə] n. Mélomanie *f.*

melomaniac [-niæk] n. Mélomane *s.*

melon ['melon] n. BOT. Melon *m.; musk melon,* cantaloup. ‖ U. S. FAM. Part (*f.*) du gâteau (profits).

melt [melt] v. intr. Fondre (butter, metal, pear). ‖ Fondre, se dissoudre (solid). ‖ Se fondre, s'estomper (*into,* dans) (colours). ‖ FIG. Fléchir (decision); s'adoucir (feelings); s'attendrir (person); *to melt with pity,* se fondre de compassion. ‖ FAM. Fondre, se volatiliser (*into,* dans). ‖ **To melt away,** se dissiper (crowd); fondre (money, snow).
— v. tr. Faire fondre (butter); fondre (metals). ‖ FIG. Toucher, attendrir, émouvoir (s.o.). ‖ **To melt down,** envoyer à la fonte (scrap-iron).
— n. Fonte *f.*

melted [-id] adj. Fondu (butter, metal).

melting [-iŋ] adj. Fondant (butter, metal, snow); de fusion (point). ‖ Fondant, mûr (fruit). ‖ Torride, de plomb (sun). ‖ FIG. Attendri, apitoyé (voice); attendrissant (words). ‖ **Melting-pot,** n. Creuset *m.;* FAM. *To put back into the melting-pot,* mettre à la refonte.
— n. Fusion, fonte *f.* (of metals); fonte *f.* (of snow). ‖ FIG. Attendrissement *m.*

meltingly [-iŋli] adv. FIG. De façon attendrissante.

member ['membə*] n. MED., JUR., MATH., GRAMM., FIG. Membre *m.; ordinary member of the public,* simple particulier.

membership [-ʃip] n. Sociétariat *m.;* qualité (*f.*) de membre. ‖ COMM. Société *f.*

membrane ['membrein] n. Membrane *f.*

membraneous [mem'breinjəs], **membranous** ['membrənəs] adj. Membraneux.

memento [me'mentou] n. ECCLES. Mémento *m.* ‖ FIG. Souvenir *m.* (reminder).

memo ['memou] (pl. **memos** [-z]) n. FAM. Pensebête *m.* (for oneself). ‖ Note *f.;* papier, rapport *m.* (to someone else).

memoir ['memwɑ:*] n. Mémoire *m.;* étude, dissertation *f.* (essay). ‖ Notice biographique *f.* (in a newspaper). ‖ Pl. Mémoires *m. pl.* (autobiography); actes *m. pl.* (records of a learned society).

memorable ['memərəbḷ] adj. Mémorable.

memorably [-bli] adv. Mémorablement.

memorandum [,memə'rændəm] n. Mémorandum, mémoire *m.* ‖ JUR. Acte constitutif *m.* (of association). ‖ COMM. Bordeɪeau *m.* ‖ FAM. Note *f.*
— N. B. Deux pluriels : *memoranda, memorandums.*

memorial [mi'mɔ:riəl] adj. Mémoratif (faculty); commémoratif (festival, monument).
— n. Monument commémoratif *m.* ‖ JUR. Mémorial *m.* (diplomatic paper); requête officielle *f.* (petition); *memorial of a deed,* extrait pour enregistrement. ‖ U. S. *Memorial Day,* fête nationale du souvenir des morts de la guerre (May 30th).

memorialist [-ist] n. Mémorialiste *m.*

memorialize [-aiz] v. tr. Commémorer (s.o., sth.). ‖ Adresser une requête officielle à (to petition).

memorize ['meməraiz] v. tr. Consigner pour mémoire (a fact); conserver au souvenir (s.o.). ‖ Apprendre par cœur (to learn by heart).

memory ['meməri] n. Mémoire *f.* (faculty); *never within the memory of living man,* jamais de mémoire d'homme. ‖ Souvenir *m.* (recollection); *in memory of,* en mémoire de; *to bring away a pleasant memory of,* emporter une douce image de (or) un agréable souvenir de. ‖ Mémoire *f.* (remembrance); *of illustrious memory,* d'illustre (or) de glorieuse mémoire : *to keep the memory of s.o. alive,* entretenir la mémoire de qqn. ‖ INFORM. Mémoire *f.* (store).

men [men]. See MAN.

menace ['menəs] *n.* Menace *f.* (See THREAT.). ‖ FAM. Danger public *m.* (nuisance).
— *v. tr.* Menacer (*with*, de).
menacing [-iŋ] *adj.* Menaçant.
menacingly [-iŋli] *adv.* D'un air menaçant.
ménage [mei'nɑ:ʒ] *n.* Ménage *m.* (household). ‖ *Ménage à trois,* ménage à trois.
menagerie [me'nædʒəri] *n.* Ménagerie *f.*
mend [mend] *v. tr.* Raccommoder (clothes); repriser (socks). ‖ Réparer (roads, tools). ‖ Arranger (the fire). ‖ Hâter ; *to mend one's pace,* presser le pas. ‖ FIG. Réparer (a harm); *least said soonest mended,* moins on en dit mieux ça vaut. ‖ FIG. Améliorer (matters); *to mend one's ways,* changer de conduite, s'amender.
— *v. intr.* MED. S'améliorer (condition, situation); se corriger (fault); s'amender (person).
— *n.* Raccommodage *m.* (in material); reprise *f.* (in stockings). ‖ Réparation *f.* (of roads, tools). ‖ MED., FIG. Amélioration *f.; on the mend,* en voie d'amélioration.
mendable [-əbl] *adj.* Raccommodable (material); réparable (roads, tools). ‖ FIG. Améliorable (condition); amendable, corrigible (fault, person).
mendacious [men'deiʃəs] *adj.* Mensonger.
mendaciously [-li] *adv.* Mensongèrement.
mendacity [men'dæsiti] *n.* Propension (*f.*) au mensonge. ‖ Mensonge *m.* (lie).
mendelevium [‚mendi'li:viəm] *n.* CHIM. Mendélévium *m.*
mendicancy ['mendikənsi], **mendicity** [men'disiti] *n.* Mendicité *f.*
mendicant [-ənt] *adj., n.* Mendiant *m.*
menfolk ['men‚fouk] *n. pl.* Hommes *m. pl.* ; types *m. pl.* (fam.).
menhir ['menhiə*] *n.* Menhir *m.*
menial ['mi:niəl] *adj.* Servile, de domestique.
— *n.* Valet *m.* ‖ Laquais, larbin *m.* (pej.).
meningeal [me'nindʒiəl] *adj.* MED. Méningé.
meninges [-dʒi:z] *n. pl.* MED. Méninges *f. pl.*
meningitis [‚menin'dʒaitis] *n.* MED. Méningite *f.*
meniscus [me'niskəs] *n.* Ménisque *m.*
menopause ['menopɔ:z] *n.* MED. Ménopause *f.*
menorah [mi'nɔ:rə] *n.* ECCLES. Menorah *f.,* chandelier (*m.*) à sept branches.
menorrhagia [‚menə'reidʒiə] *n.* MED. Ménorragie *f.*
menorrhœa [-'riə] *n.* MED. Ménorrhée *f.*
menses ['mensi:z] *n. pl.* MED. Menstrues, règles, époques *f. pl.*
menstrual ['menstruəl] *adj.* MED. Menstruel. ‖ ASTRON. Mensuel.
menstruate [-eit] *v. intr.* MED. Avoir ses règles.
menstruation [‚menstru'eiʃən] *n.* MED. Menstruation *f.*
menstruum ['menstruəm] *n.* CHIM. Dissolvant *m.*
mensurability [‚menʃurə'biliti] *n.* Mensurabilité *f.*
mensurable ['mensurəbl] *adj.* Mensurable ; mesurable. ‖ MUS. Rythmé.
mensuration [‚mensjuə'reiʃən] *n.* Mesurage *m.* (act). ‖ MATH., MED. Mensuration *f.*
menswear ['menz‚weə*] *n.* COMM. Vêtements pour hommes *m. pl.* ; habillement masculin *m.*
mental ['mentl] *adj.* MED. Mental (age, deficiency); psychiatrique (hospital); des maladies mentales (specialist). ‖ MATH. *Mental arithmetic,* calcul mental. ‖ FIG. Intellectuel (culture); mental (reservation); *mental sphere,* domaine de l'esprit. ‖ FAM. Toqué (crazy).
mentality [men'tæliti] *n.* Mentalité *f.*
mentally ['mentəli] *adv.* Mentalement.
menthol ['menθɔl] *n.* Menthol *m.*
mentholated [-eitid] *adj.* Mentholé.
mention ['menʃən] *n.* Mention *f.*
— *v. tr.* Mentionner, citer ; faire mention de, parler de ; *not worth mentioning,* sans importance, qui

ne vaut pas la peine d'être signalé ; *not to mention,* sans parler de, sans compter. ‖ JUR. *To mention s.o. in one's will,* coucher qqn sur son testament. ‖ MILIT. *To mention in dispatches,* citer à l'ordre du jour. ‖ FAM. *Don't mention it,* je vous en prie, ce n'est rien, il n'y a pas de quoi ; de rien (pop.).
mentor ['mentə*] *n.* Mentor *m.*
menu ['menju] *n.* Menu *m.,* carte *f.* (See BILL OF FARE.)
meow [mi'au] *n., v. intr.* See MIAOW.
Mephistophelean L‚mefistofi'liən] *adj.* Méphistophélique.
mephitic [me'fitik] *adj.* Méphitique.
mercantile ['mə:kəntail] *adj.* COMM. Commercial (affaires); de commerce (establishment); commerçant (nation); mercantile (operations, system); négociable (paper); *mercantile agent,* commissionnaire en marchandises. ‖ JUR. Commercial (law). ‖ NAUT. Marchand (navy). ‖ FAM. Mercantile (pej.).
mercantilism [-izm] *n.* COMM. Système mercantile *m.* ‖ Mercantilisme *m.* (pej.).
mercenary ['mə:sinəri] *adj., n.* MILIT., FIG. Mercenaire *m.*
mercer ['mə:sə*] *n.* COMM. Marchand (*m.*) de tissus précieux et soieries.
mercerize [-raiz] *v. tr.* Merceriser.
mercerized [-raizd] *adj.* Mercerisé.
mercery [-ri] *n.* COMM. Soieries *f. pl.* (goods); commerce (*m.*) des soieries (trade).
merchandise ['mə:tʃəndaiz] *n.* Marchandise *f.* (See GOODS.) ‖ Pl. Présentoir *m.*
— *v. intr.* U. S. Commercer.
merchant ['mə:tʃənt] *n.* COMM. Négociant *m.*
— *adj.* JUR. *Law merchant,* droit commercial. ‖ NAUT. Marchand (marine, ship). ‖ FIN. *Merchant bank,* banque d'affaires.
merchantable [-əbl] *adj.* Négociable, vendable. (See MARKETABLE.)
merchantman [-mən] (pl. **merchantmen**) *n.* NAUT. Navire marchand *m.*
merciful ['mə:siful] *adj.* Miséricordieux (*to,* pour) [clement]. ‖ Pitoyable, compatissant (sympathetic).
mercifully [-i] *adv.* Miséricordieusement. ‖ Avec compassion.
mercifulness [-nis] *n.* Miséricorde *f.* ‖ Pitié, compassion *f.*
merciless ['mə:silis] *adj.* Impitoyable.
mercilessly [-li] *adv.* Impitoyablement.
mercilessness [-nis] *n.* Nature impitoyable *f.*
mercurial [mə:'kjuəriəl] *adj.* Eloquent ; habile, rusé ; commerçant, fripon (having qualities attributed to the god Mercury). ‖ Vif, éveillé, prompt ; changeant, versatile, inconstant (having qualities suggestive of mercury). ‖ CHIM. Mercuriel. ‖ ASTRON. De Mercure.
— *n.* MED. Préparation mercurielle *f.*
mercurialism [-izm] *n.* MED. Hydrargyrisme *m.*
mercuriality [mə:‚kjuəri'æliti] *n.* Habileté *f.;* esprit commerçant *m.* ‖ Vivacité ; versatilité *f.* (See MERCURIAL.)
Mercurochrome [mə:'kjuro‚kroum] *n.* U. S. CHIM., MED. Mercurochrome *m.*
mercury ['mə:kjuri] *n.* CHIM., ASTRON. Mercure *m.* ‖ Mercure *m.* (god).
mercy ['mə:si] *n.* Miséricorde, grâce, clémence *f.; to beg for mercy,* demander grâce. ‖ Merci *f.; at s.o.'s mercy,* à la merci de qqn. ‖ Pitié, compassion *f.; for mercy's sake,* par pitié ; *to have mercy on,* avoir pitié de ; *without mercy,* sans pitié ; *works of mercy,* œuvres charitables. ‖ Bienfait *m.;* chance *f.; it's a mercy that,* il est heureux que, c'est une chance que. ‖ MED. *Mercy killing,* euthanasie.
mere ['miə*] *n.* Lac *m.* (lake); marais *m.* (marsh); étang *m.* (pond).
mere *adj.* Pur, unique, seul ; *a mere glance,* un simple coup d'œil, rien qu'un coup d'œil.

merely [-li] adv. Purement et simplement; *she merely smiled*, elle se contenta de sourire.
meretricious [ˌmeri'triʃəs] adj. De courtisane. ‖ FIG. De mauvais aloi (interest); en clinquant (ornaments); boursouflé, tapageur (style).
meretrix ['meritriks] n. † Courtisane *f.*
merganser [məˈgænsə*] n. ZOOL. Harle *m.*
merge [mə:dʒ] v. tr. Fondre (*in*, dans); amalgamer (*in*, avec). ‖ Incorporer (*in*, dans).
— v. intr. Se fondre (*in*, dans); s'amalgamer (*in*, avec). ‖ S'incorporer (*in*, à); se confondre (*in*, avec).
mergence [-əns] n. Fusionnement *m.*
merger [-ə*] n. JUR., FIN. Fusion, unification *f.*
meridian [məˈridiən] n. GEOGR. Méridien *m.* ‖ ASTRON. Point culminant *m.* ‖ FIG. Zénith, apogée *m.*
— adj. ASTRON. De midi, méridien. ‖ FIG. De l'apogée.
meridional [-l] adj. ASTRON. D'un méridien. ‖ GEOGR. Méridional.
— n. GEOGR. Méridional *s.*
meringue [məˈræŋ] n. CULIN. Meringue *f.*
merino [məˈri:nou] n. ZOOL., COMM. Mérinos *m.*
merit ['merit] n. Mérite *m.* ‖ Pl. Valeur réelle *f.*; fond *m.* ‖ JUR. Pl. Bien-fondé *m.*
— v. tr. Mériter. (See DESERVE.)
meritocracy [ˌmeriˈtɔkrəsi] n. Méritocratie *f.*
meritorious [ˌmeriˈtɔ:riəs] adj. Méritoire (deed); méritant (person).
meritoriously [-li] adv. De façon méritoire.
merlin ['mə:lin] n. ZOOL. Emerillon *m.*
mermaid ['mə:meid] n. Sirène *f.*
merman [-mən] n. Triton *m.*
Merovingian [ˌmerəˈvindʒiən] adj., n. Mérovingien *s.*
merrily ['merili] adv. Gaiement, joyeusement.
merriment [-mənt] n. Gaieté, réjouissance *f.* ‖ Hilarité *f.* ‖ Pl. Divertissements *m. pl.*
merriness [-nis] n. Gaieté *f.*
merry ['meri] adj. Gai, joyeux (see GLAD); *to make merry*, s'amuser, se réjouir. ‖ † Plaisant, aimable. ‖ FAM. Gai, gris (tipsy). ‖ **Merry-andrew**, n. Paillasse, pitre *m.* ‖ **Merry-go-round**, n. Chevaux (*m. pl.*) de bois. ‖ **Merry-maker**, n. Membre (*m.*) d'une joyeuse compagnie; festoyeur *m.* ‖ **Merry-making**, n. Réjouissance *f.*; partie (*f.*) de plaisir.
merry n. BOT. Merise *f.*
merrythought [-θɔ:t] n. ZOOL. Lunette *f.*
mescal [mes'kal] n. BOT. Mezcal, mescal, peyotl *m.*
mescaline ['meskəli:n] n. CHIM. Mescaline *f.*
meseems [mi'si:mz] v. impers. † Il me semble.
mesentery ['mesəntəri] n. MED. Mésentère *m.*
mesh [meʃ] n. Maille *f.* (of net). ‖ Pl. Filet *m.* (net). ‖ TECHN. Engrenage *m.*; *in mesh*, en prise. ‖ CH. DE F. Pl. Réseau *m.* ‖ FIG. Engrenage *m.* (of circumstances); réseau *m.* (of intrigues). ‖ FIG. Pl. Rets, filets *m. pl.* (snares).
— v. tr. Prendre au filet. ‖ TECHN. Engrener. ‖ FIG. Prendre dans ses rets.
— v. intr. TECHN. S'engrener (*with*, avec).
mesial ['mi:ziəl] adj. MED. Médian.
mesmerism ['mezmərizm] n. Mesmérisme *m.*
mesmerist [-ist] n. Mesmérien *s.*
mesne [mi:n] adj. † *Mesne lord*, vavasseur. ‖ JUR. Intermédiaire *m.*
mesogaster [ˌmesoˈgæstə*] n. MED. Mésogastre *m.*
meson [mes'ɔn] n. PHYS. Méson *m.*
Mesopotamia [ˌmesəpəˈteimjə] n. GEOGR. Mésopotamie *f.*
Mesopotamian [-ən] adj., n. GEOGR. Mésopotamien *s.*
mess [mes] n. † Portion *f.*; brouet *m.*; *mess of pottage*, plat de lentilles. ‖ Pâtée *f.* (for dogs). ‖ MILIT. Mess *m.* (for officers); popote *f.*, ordinaire *m.* (for other ranks). ‖ NAUT. Table *f.* (for officers); plat *m.* (for ratings). ‖ FAM. Gâchis *m.*; *to*

make a mess of it, gâcher tout. ‖ FAM. Méli-mélo, fouillis *m.* (jumble); *to clear up the mess*, débrouiller l'écheveau. ‖ FAM. Pétrin *m.* (muddle); *to get out of a mess*, se dépatouiller. ‖ POP. U. S. Crétin *m.* ‖ **Mess-tin**, n. MILIT. Gamelle, cantine *f.*
— v. tr. FAM. Gâcher, bousiller. ‖ MILIT. Approvisionner.
— v. intr. MILIT. Manger au mess. ‖ NAUT. Faire table; *to mess together*, faire popote ensemble. ‖ **To mess about**, FAM. Tripoter. ‖ **To mess around**, U. S. POP. Lambiner.
message ['mesidʒ] n. Message *m.* (communication); *code, telephone message*, message chiffré, téléphoné. ‖ Commission *f.* (errand); *to run messages*, faire les courses. ‖ Message *m.* (of a philosopher, poet, politician); prédiction *f.* (of a prophet).
— v. tr. Envoyer par messager. ‖ Transmettre par signaux, signaler.
messenger ['mesindʒə*] n. Messager *m.* ‖ Courrier, commissionnaire *m.*; *office messenger*, coursier. ‖ NAUT. Tournevire *m.*
Messiah [mi'saiə] n. ECCLES. Messie *m.*
Messianic [ˌmesiˈænik] adj. ECCLES. Messianique.
messieurs ['mesəz] n. pl. COMM. Messieurs *m. pl.*
messmate ['mesmeit] n. MILIT. Camarade de mess *m.* ‖ NAUT. Camarade de plat *m.*
messy ['mesi] adj. Sale, souillé (dirty); salissant (soiling). ‖ Désordonné (disordered).
mestizo [mes'ti:zou] n. Métis *s.*
met [met] adj. FAM. Météorologique, météo; *the met office weather report*, le bulletin météo.
— n. FAM. *The Met*, l'office de météorologie britannique.
met adj. FAM. Métropolitain.
— n. U. S. FAM. *The Met*, le Met, l'Opéra de New York.
met [met] pret., p. p. See MEET.
metabolic [ˌmetəˈbɔlik] adj. MED. Métabolique.
metabolism [meˈtæbɔlizm] n. MED. Métabolisme *m.*
metacarpal [ˌmetəˈkɑ:pəl] adj. MED. Métacarpien.
metacarpus [-pəs] n. MED. Métacarpe *m.*
metage ['mi:tidʒ] n. Mesurage *m.*
metal ['metl] n. Métal *m.* ‖ TECHN. Empierrement *m.* (of a road); plomb *m.* (in printing); verre (*m.*) en fusion (for making glassware). ‖ CH. DE F. Ballast *m.*; pl. rails *m. pl.* ‖ † FIG. Etoffe *f.* (See METTLE.) ‖ **Metal-like**, adj. Métalliforme. ‖ **Metal-work**, n. TECHN. Serrurerie (*f.*) d'art; pl. Usine métallurgique. ‖ **Metal-worker**, n. TECHN. Serrurier d'art; métallurgiste *m.*
— adj. En (or) de métal, métallique.
— v. tr. (1). Empierrer (a road).
metalanguage ['metəˌlæŋgwidʒ] n. PHILOS., GRAMM. Métalangage *m.*, métalangue *f.* ‖ INFORM. Métalangage *m.*
metallic [mi'tælik] adj. Métallique.
metalling ['metliŋ] n. TECHN. Empierrement *m.*
metallize ['metəlaiz] v. tr. Métalliser (a surface). ‖ Vulcaniser (rubber).
metallography [ˌmetəˈlɔgrəfi] n. Métallographie *f.*
metalloid ['metəlɔid] adj., n. Métalloïde *m.*
metallurgic(al) [ˌmetəˈlə:dʒik(əl)] adj. Métallurgique.
metallurgist [meˈtælədʒist] n. Métallurgiste *m.*
metallurgy [-dʒi] n. Métallurgie *f.*
metamorphic [ˌmetəˈmɔ:fik] adj. De la métamorphose. ‖ GEOL. Métamorphique.
metamorphism [ˌmetəˈmɔ:fizm] n. Métamorphisme *m.*
metamorphose [-fouz] v. tr. Métamorphoser.
— v. intr. Se métamorphoser (*into, to*, en).
metamorphosis [-fəsis] n. Métamorphose *f.*

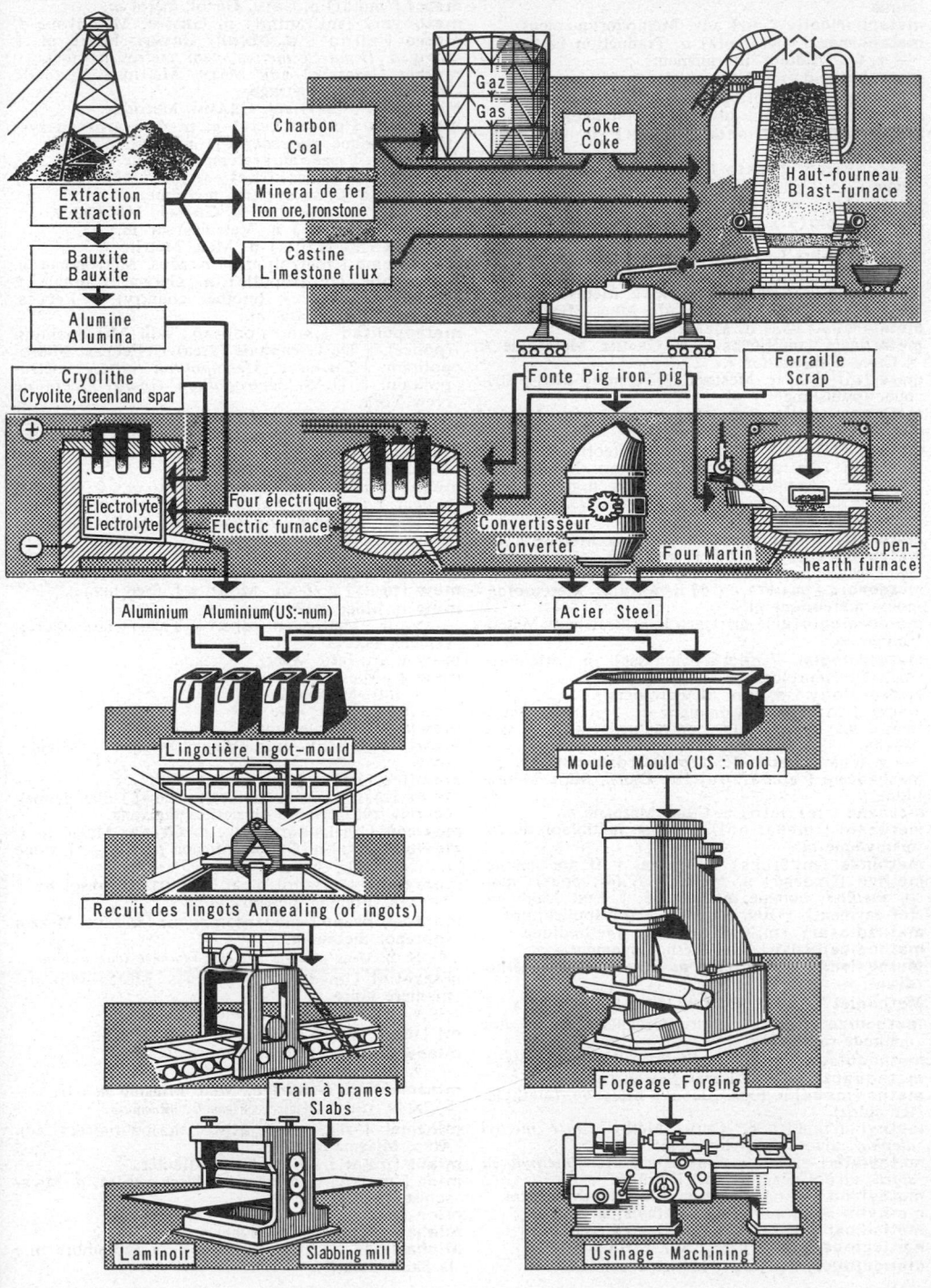

Gaz / Gas

Coke / Coke

Charbon / Coal

Minerai de fer / Iron ore, Ironstone

Castine / Limestone flux

Haut-fourneau / Blast-furnace

Extraction / Extraction

Bauxite / Bauxite

Alumine / Alumina

Cryolithe / Cryolite, Greenland spar

Fonte Pig iron, pig

Ferraille / Scrap

Electrolyte / Electrolyte

Four électrique / Electric furnace

Convertisseur / Converter

Four Martin

Open-hearth furnace

Aluminium Aluminium(US:-num)

Acier Steel

Lingotière Ingot-mould

Moule Mould (US : mold)

Recuit des lingots Annealing (of ingots)

Train à brames Slabs

Forgeage Forging

Laminoir

Slabbing mill

Usinage Machining

metaphor ['metəfə*] n. Métaphore f.; to mix metaphors, faire des métaphores incohérentes.
metaphoric(al) [,metə'fɔrik(əl)] adj. Métaphorique.
metaphorically [-əli] adv. Métaphoriquement.
metaphrase ['metəfreiz] n. Traduction littérale f.
— v. tr. Traduire littéralement.
metaphrastic [metə'fræstik] adj. Littéral.
metaphysical [,metə'fizikəl] adj. Métaphysique.
metaphysically [-i] adv. Métaphysiquement.
metaphysician [,metəfi'ziʃən] n. Métaphysicien s.
metaphysics [,metə'fiziks] n. sg. Métaphysique f.
metaplasm ['metəplæzm̩] n. MED. Métaplasme m.
metapsychic(al) [,metə'saikik(əl)] adj. Métapsychique.
metapsychics [-iks] n. sg. Métapsychique f.
metargon [me'tɑ:gən] n. CHIM. Métargon m.
metastasis [me'tæstəsis] n. MED. Métastase f.
metatarsal [,metə'tɑ:səl] adj. MED. Métatarsien.
metatarsus [-səs] n. MED. Métatarse m.
metathesis [me'tæθəsis] n. GRAMM. Métathèse f. || CHIM. Substitution f.
mete [mi:t] v. tr. Mesurer. || To mete out, distribuer (punishments).
metempsychosis [,metempsi'kousis] n. Métempsycose f.
meteor ['mi:tjə*] n. ASTRON. Météore m.
meteoric [,mi:ti'ɔrik] adj. ASTRON. Météorique. || U. S. Atmosphérique (phenomenon). || FIG. Comme un météore; meteoric promotion, avancement fulgurant.
meteorite ['mi:tjɔrait] n. ASTRON. Météorite m.
meteorograph ['mi:tiərə,grɑ:f] n. TECHN. Météorographe m.
meteoroid ['mi:tiə,rɔid] n. ASTRON. Météoroïde, corps météorique m.
meteorologic(al) [,mi:tjərə'lɔdʒik(əl)] adj. Météorologique.
meteorologist [,mi:tjə'rɔlədʒist] n. Météorologue; météorologiste; météo m. (fam.).
meteorology [-dʒi] n. Météorologie f.
meter [mi:tə*] n. Compteur m. || AUTOM. Parcmètre m.; meter maid, contractuelle. || U. S. See METRE.
— v. tr. Mesurer le débit (or) la consommation de.
methadone ['meθə,doun] n. CHIM., MED. Méthadone f.
methane ['mi:θein] n. CHIM. Méthane m.
methanol ['meθə, nɔl] n. CHIM. Méthanol, alcool méthylique m.
methinks [mi'θiŋks] v. impers. † Il me semble.
method ['meθəd] n. Méthode f. (of, pour); man of method, homme méthodique. || FIN. Mode m. (of payment). || JUR. Modalité f. (of application).
methodic(al) [mi'θɔdikəl] adj. Méthodique.
methodically [-li] adv. Méthodiquement.
Methodism ['meθədizm̩] n. ECCLES., FIG. Méthodisme m.
Methodist [-ist] n. ECCLES., FIG. Méthodiste s.
methodize [-daiz] v. tr. Organiser selon une méthode rigoureuse.
methodology [,meθə'dɔlədʒi] n. Méthodologie f.
methought [mi'θɔ:t] pret. See METHINKS.
meths [meθs] n. FAM. Alcool à brûler m. (methylated spirit).
methyl ['meθil] n. CHIM. Méthyle m.; methyl alcohol, alcool méthylique, méthanol.
methylate [-eit] v. tr. CHIM. Dénaturer; methylated spirit, alcool dénaturé (or) à brûler.
methylene [-li:n] n. CHIM., MED. Méthylène m.
methylic [-ik] adj. CHIM. Méthylique.
meticulosity [,metikju'lɔsiti] n. Méticulosité f.
meticulous [mi'tikjuləs] adj. Méticuleux.
meticulously [-li] adv. Méticuleusement.

métier ['metiei] n. Métier m., profession f. (trade); spécialité f., point fort m. (forte).
metis ['meitis] n. Métis s.
metol ['metɔl] n. CHIM. Génol, métol m.
metonymy [mi'tɔnimi] n. GRAMM. Métonymie f.
metre ['mi:tə*] n. MATH., GRAMM. Mètre m. || SPORTS. Hundred metres, cent mètres (sprint).
metric ['metrik] adj. MATH. Métrique (system); metric volume, métrage.
metric(al) [-(ə)l] adj. GRAMM. Métrique.
metricate ['metri,keit] v. tr. Convertir au système métrique, procéder à la métrisation de.
— v. intr. Passer au système métrique.
metrication [,metri'keiʃən] n. Métrisation f., conversion (f.) au système métrique.
metrics ['metriks] n. sg. GRAMM. Métrique f.
metrist ['metrist] n. Versificateur m.
metritis [me'traitis] n. MED. Métrite f.
metronome ['metrənoum] n. MUS. Métronome m.
metropolis [mi'trɔpəlis] n. GEOGR. Capitale f. (city); métropole f. (mother country). || ECCLES. Siège métropolitain m.
metropolitan [,metrə'pɔlitən] adj. Métropolitain (police). || De la capitale (area). || ECCLES. Métropolitain. || CH. DE F. Metropolitan railway, métropolitain. || U. S. Metropolitan Opera, Opéra de New York.
— n. GEOGR. Habitant (s.) de la capitale (or) de la métropole. || ECCLES. Métropolitain m. (in the Roman Catholic Church); métropolite m. (in the Orthodox Eastern Church).
mettle ['metl̩] n. Tempérament m. || Fougue, ardeur f.; to put s.o. on his mettle, piquer qqn au jeu. || Etoffe f.; to show one's mettle, faire ses preuves.
mettlesome [-səm] adj. Ardent, plein de fougue, vif (spirited).
mew [mju:] n. ZOOL. Mouette f. (See GULL.)
mew n. Mue, volière f.
— v. tr. Mettre en cage. || FAM. Claquemurer, boucler (s.o.).
mew v. tr., intr. Muer.
mew n. Miaulement m.
— v. intr. Miauler.
mewing [-iŋ] n. Mue f.
mewing n. Miaulement m.
mewl [mju:l] v. intr. Vagir (infant). || Miauler (cat).
mewling [iŋ] n. Vagissement m.
mews [mju:z] n. invar. Petite rue (f.) d'anciennes écuries transformées en petites maisons.
Mexican ['meksikən] adj., n. GEOGR. Mexicain s.
Mexico [-kou] n. GEOGR. Mexico f. (city); Mexique m. (country).
mezzanine ['mezəni:n] n. ARCHIT. Entresol m. || THEATR. Premier dessous m.
mezzo-soprano ['medzoso'prɑ:no] n. MUS. Mezzo-soprano, mezzo m.
— N. B. Deux pluriels : mezzo-sopranos (ou) soprani.
mezzotint ['medʒotint] n. ARTS. Mezzo-tinto m.; manière noire f.
— v. tr. ARTS. Graver en mezzo-tinto.
mi [mi:] n. MUS. Mi m.
miaow [mi'au] n. Miaou m.
— v. intr. Miauler.
miasma [mai'æzmə] n. MED. Miasme m.
— N. B. Deux pluriels : miasmas, miasmata.
miasmal [-əl], **miasmatic** [,maiəz'mætik] adj. MED. Miasmatique.
miaul [mi'ɔ:l] v. intr. FAM. Miauler.
mica ['maikə] n. Mica m. || Mica-schist, n. Mica-schiste m.
mice [mais]. See MOUSE.
Michael ['maikl] n. Michel m.
Michaelmas ['miklməs] n. Le 29 septembre m.; la Saint-Michel f.

mick [mik] n. FAM. Irlandais m. ‖ FAM. Catho s.

mickey [miki] n. FAM. Fiole f.; to take the mickey out of, faire marcher. ‖ U. S. POP. Mickey Finn, boisson droguée.

mickle ['mikl] adj. † Beaucoup de. (See MUCH.)

microampere [,maikro'æmpɛə*] n. ELECTR. Microampère m.

micro-analysis [,maikroə'nælizis] n. CHIM. Micro-analyse f.

microbe ['maikroub] n. MED. Microbe m.

microbial [mai'kroubiəl] adj. MED. Microbien.

microbicide [-said] n. MED. Microbicide m.

microbiology [,maikrobi'ɔlədʒi] n. MED. Microbiologie f.

microcephalic [,maikrose'fælik] adj., n. MED. Microcéphale m.

microchip ['maikro,tʃip] n. ELECTR. Microcircuit m.; pastille, tranche, puce f. (fam.).

microcircuit ['maikro,sə:kit] n. ELECTR. Microcircuit m.

microclimate ['maikro,klaimit] n. GEOGR. Microclimat m.

microcopy ['maikrou,kopi] n. Microreproduction f.

microcosm ['maikrokɔzm] n. Microcosme m.

microdot ['maikro,dɔt] n. Micropoint m.

microelectronics [,maikroilek'trɔniks] n. sg. ELECTR. Micro-électronique f.

microfiche ['maikro,fi:ʃ] n. Microfiche f.

microfilm [,maikro'film] n. Microfilm m.
— v. tr. Microfilmer.

micrograph ['maikro,græf] n. TECHN. Micrographie, image micrographique f.

micrography [-'græfi] n. Micrographie f.

microgroove ['gru:v] n. MUS. Microsillon m.

microhm ['maikroum] n. ELECTR. Microhm m.

micrometer [mai'krɔmitə*] n. TECHN. Micromètre, palmer m.; micrometer balance, microbalance.

micromillimeter [,maikro'milimi:tə*] n. Micromillimètre m.

micron ['maikrɔn] n. PHYS. Micron m.

micro-organism [,maikro'ɔ:gənizm] n. ZOOL., BOT. Micro-organisme m.

microphone ['maikrofoun] n. Microphone m.

microphonic [maikro'fɔnik], microphonous [-əs] adj. Microphone.

microphotograph [,maikro'foutəgrɑ:f] n. Microphotographie f.

microprint ['maikro,print] n. Micro-imprimé m.

microscope ['maikrəskoup] n. PHYS. Microscope m.

microscopic [,maikrəs'kɔpik] adj. Microscopique.

microscopical [-əl] adj. PHYS. De (or) au microscope.

microscopy [mai'krɔskəpi] n. Microscopie f.

microsecond ['maikro,sekənd] n. Microseconde f.

microtome ['maikro,toum] n. TECHN. Microtome m.

microwave ['maikro,weiv] n. PHYS. Onde ultra-courte f.

micturate ['miktjureit] v. intr. MED. Uriner.

micturition [,miktjuə'riʃən] n. MED. Miction f.

mid [mid] adj. A demi, à moitié, mi-; in mid air, entre ciel et terre. ‖ Mid-course, n. Milieu (m.) de carrière; mi-course f. ‖ Mid-iron, n. SPORTS. Fer moyen m. ‖ Mid-Lent, n. ECCLES. Mi-Carême f.
— prep. Au milieu de. (See AMID.)

midbrain [-brein] n. MED. Cerveau moyen m.

midday [-dei] n. Midi m. (See NOON.)
— adj. De midi.

midden [-midn] n. AGRIC. Fumier m. (See DUNG-HILL.) ‖ Débris archéologiques m. pl.

middle ['midl] n. Milieu m.; in the very middle of, au beau milieu de la. ‖ Mi-corps m.; round the middle, autour de la taille. ‖ FAM. In the middle of, au beau milieu de; in the middle of one's work, en plein travail.

— adj. Du milieu (table). ‖ Médial, intermédiaire (position). ‖ Moyen (Ages, height, latitude, size); middle course, parti moyen. ‖ GEOGR. Moyen (East); du milieu (Empire). ‖ ARCHIT. Mitoyen (wall). ‖ SPORTS. Moyen (weight). ‖ MED. Middle finger, médius. ‖ GRAMM. Moyen (voice); Middle English, moyen anglais; Middle Latin, latin médiéval. ‖ Middle-aged, adj. D'âge mûr, entre deux âges. ‖ Middle-class, n. Classe moyenne, bourgeoisic f.; adj. bourgeois. ‖ Middle-of-the-road, adj. U. S. FAM. Modéré (policy). ‖ Middle-sized, adj. De taille moyenne.
— v. tr. TECHN. Centrer. ‖ NAUT. Plier en deux.

middleman [-mən] (pl. middlemen) n. COMM. Intermédiaire s. ‖ FAM. Entremetteur m.

middling ['midliŋ] adj. Assez bien, passable; couci-couça (fam.). ‖ COMM. Moyen, ordinaire.
— adv. Assez bien, pas mal, passablement.

middlings [-z] n. pl. AGRIC. Recoupe f. ‖ TECHN. Mixtes m. pl. ‖ COMM. Marchandises (f. pl.) de qualité moyenne.

middy ['midi] n. FAM., NAUT. Aspirant m. ‖ COMM. Blouse-chemise f.

midge [midʒ] n. ZOOL. Moucheron m.

midget [-it] n. Nain s. (See DWARF.)
— adj. Miniature, mini. ‖ NAUT. Midget submarine, sous-marin de poche.

midi ['midi] n. Jupe (f.) [or] manteau (m.) midi (or) au genou.

Midland ['midlənd] adj. De l'intérieur du pays. ‖ GEOGR. Des Midlands.
— n. Centre du pays m. ‖ GEOGR. Pl. Midlands m. pl.

midmost [-moust] adv. Au plein milieu.
— n. Point central m.

midnight [-nait] n. Minuit m. ‖ FAM. To burn the midnight oil, travailler tard la nuit.

midriff [-rif] n. MED. Diaphragme m. ‖ COMM. Bare midriff ensemble, maillot deux-pièces. ‖ FAM. Creux de l'estomac m.

midship [-ʃip] n. NAUT. Milieu d'un navire m.

midshipman [-ʃipmən] (pl. midshipmen) n. NAUT. Aspirant, midship m.

midst [midst] n. Milieu m.; in our midst, au milieu de nous.
— prep. Parmi.

midsummer ['mid,sʌmə*] n. Solstice d'été m.; Midsummer Day, la Saint-Jean. ‖ Plein été, milieu de l'été m.; A Midsummer Night's Dream, « Le songe d'une nuit d'été ».

midway ['midwei] n. Mi-chemin m.
— adj., adv. A mi-chemin.

midwife ['midwaif] (pl. midwives [-waivz]) n. MED. Sage-femme f.

midwifery ['midwifri] n. MED. Obstétrique f.

midwinter ['mid'wintə*] n. Solstice d'hiver m. ‖ Plein hiver, cœur de l'hiver m.

mien [mi:n] n. Mine f.; air m.

miff [mif] n. FAM. Prise (f.) de bec, chamaillerie f. (tiff). ‖ Bouderie f.; to be in a miff, faire la tête (or) le nez.
— v. tr. FAM. Tracasser, mettre en rogne.

might [mait] n. Puissance, force f. (See STRENGTH.)

might. See MAY. ‖ Might-have-been, n. Ce qui aurait pu arriver (event); raté m. (person).

mightily [-ili] adv. Puissamment, avec force. ‖ FAM. Enormément, formidablement, supérieurement, fameusement.

mightiness [-inis] n. Puissance f.

mighty [-i] adj. Puissant, fort. ‖ FAM. Formidable, fameux.
— adv. FAM. Formidablement, bigrement; to be mighty sorry, regretter infiniment.

mignonette [,minjə'net] n. BOT. Réséda m.

migraine ['mi:grein] n. MED. Migraine f.

migrant ['maigrənt] n. Emigrant s. (person). ‖ ZOOL. Migrateur m.
— adj. See MIGRATORY.

migrate [mai'greit] v. intr. Emigrer.
migration [-ʃən] n. Emigration *f.* ‖ Zool. Migration *f.*
migrator [-tə*] n. Migrateur *m.*
migratory ['maigrətəri] adj. Emigrant (person); nomade (people). ‖ Zool. Migrateur *m.;* migratrice *f.*
Mikado [mi'kɑ:dou] n. Mikado *m.*
mike [maik] n. Fam. Microphone *m.*
mil [mil] n. Millième de pouce (unit of measure).
milady [mi'leidi] n. Milady *f.*
Milanese [,miln'ni:z] adj., n. Geogr. Milanais *s.*
milch [miltʃ] adj. Zool. Laitière (cow). ‖ Fig. *Milch* cow, vache à lait.
mild [maild] adj. Doux (beer, cheese, tobacco). ‖ Techn. Doux (steel). ‖ Geogr. Doux (weather); *mild climate,* climat doux, ciel clément. ‖ Med. Bénin *m.;* bénigne *f.* (disease); doux (medicine). ‖ Fig. Doux (look, person); léger (punishment); peu strict (rule). ‖ Fig. Modéré (exercise); d'estime (success).
milden [-n] v. tr. Adoucir.
— v. intr. S'adoucir.
mildew ['mildju:] n. Moisissure, piqûre *f.* (on leather, paper). ‖ Agric. Rouille, nielle *f.* (on plants); mildiou *m.* (on vine).
— v. tr. Piquer (leather, paper). ‖ Agric. Nieller (plants); frapper de mildiou (vine).
mildewy [-i] adj. Piqué (leather, paper). ‖ Agric. Niellé (plant); mildiousé (vine).
— v. intr. Se piquer (plants); Agric. Se nieller (plants); être mildiousé (vine).
mildly ['maildli] adv. Doucement, avec douceur. ‖ Faiblement, modérément. ‖ Med. Bénignement.
mildness [-nis] n. Douceur *f.* (of tobacco). ‖ Geogr. Douceur *f.* (of climate); clémence *f.* (of weather). ‖ Med. Bénignité *f.* (of a disease); douceur *f.* (of a medicine). ‖ Fig. Douceur *f.* (of nature, s.o.); légèreté *f.* (of a punishment).
mile [mail] n. Mille *m.* (measure).
mileage [-idʒ] n. Parcours (*m.*) en milles. ‖ Autom. Kilométrage *m.*
milestone ['mail,stoun] n. Borne milliaire (or) kilométrique *f.* ‖ Fig. Jalon, événement en jalon *m.* (in s.o.'s life).
milfoil ['milfɔil] n. Bot. Millefeuille *m.*
miliary ['miljəri] adj. Med. Miliaire.
milieu [mi:lʃø] n. Milieu social *m.*
militant ['militənt] adj. Combatif. ‖ Activiste. ‖ Eccles. Militant.
— n. Militant *s.*
militarily ['militərili] adv. Milit. Militairement.
militarism [-rizm] n. Militarisme *m.*
militarist [-rist] n. Militariste *m.*
militarize [-raiz] v. tr. Milit. Militariser.
military [-ri] adj. Milit. Militaire (attaché, police, service); *military man,* militaire. ‖ Jur. *Military law,* code de justice militaire.
— n. Armée *f.;* troupes *f. pl.* (collectively).
militate ['militeit] v. intr. † Combattre. ‖ Militer (*against,* contre); *in favour of,* en faveur de.
militia [mi'liʃə] n. † Milice *f.* ‖ Milit. Garde nationale *f.* ‖ U. S. Milit. Corps (*m.*) de réserve.
militiaman [-mən] (pl. **militiamen**) n. † Milicien *m.* ‖ Milit. Garde national *m.* ‖ U. S. Réserviste *m.*
milk [milk] n. Lait *m.* (of cow); *milk powder,* lait en poudre; *milk sugar,* lactose. ‖ Bot. *Coconut milk,* lait de coco. ‖ Med. Lacté (diet); de lait (fever, tooth). ‖ Fig. *Milk of human kindness,* la pleine générosité du cœur. ‖ Loc. *To cry over spilt milk,* gémir sur l'irréparable, pleurer sur le pot cassé. ‖ **Milk-and-water,** adj. Fam. Fade, délavé, insipide. ‖ **Milk-can,** n. Berthe *f.* (dairyman's); Culin. Boîte (*f.*) à lait. ‖ **Milk-float,** n. Camionnette (*f.*) de livraison du lait. ‖ **Milk-pan,** n. Jatte (*f.*) à lait. ‖ **Milk-toast,** n. Culin. Pain perdu *m.;* U. S.

Fam. Poule mouillée *f.;* emplâtre, empoté *m.* ‖ **Milk-white,** adj. D'une blancheur laiteuse.
— v. tr. Traire. ‖ Extraire (juice). ‖ Fig. Soutirer (ideas, money); *to milk s.o. for information,* soutirer des renseignements à qqn.
milker [-ə*] n. Trayeur *s.* ‖ Zool. Vache laitière *f.*
milkiness [-inis] n. Blancheur laiteuse *f.* (colour). ‖ Aspect laiteux *m.;* lactescence *f.* (appearance).
milking-machine [-iŋ mə'ʃi:n] n. Techn. Machine (*f.*) à traire, trayeuse *f.*
milkmaid [-meid] n. Agric. Trayeuse *f.* ‖ Comm. Laitière, crémière *f.*
milkman [-mən] (pl. **milkmen**) n. Comm. Laitier, crémier *m.*
milksop [-sɔp] n. Fam. Poule mouillée *f.;* mollasson; emplâtre, empoté *m.*
milkweed [-wi:d] n. Bot. Laiteron *m.*
milky [-i] adj. Laiteux. ‖ Astron. *Milky Way,* Voie lactée.
mill [mil] n. Moulin *m.* (for grinding coffee, grain, pepper). ‖ Manufacture, fabrique *f.* (factory); *textile mill,* manufacture de textile. ‖ Techn. Fraise *f.* (cutter); laminoir *m.* (rolling-mill). ‖ Culin. Moulin, moulinet *m.* (for vegetables). ‖ Fam. *To go through the mill,* passer par de sales moments, en voir de dures, en baver. ‖ **Mill-cake,** n. Agric. Tourteau *m.* ‖ **Mill-course** (or) **-race,** n. Bief *m.* ‖ **Mill-hand,** n. Ouvrier *m.* ‖ **Mill-hopper,** n. Trémie *f.* ‖ **Mill-owner,** n. Usinier *m.* ‖ **Mill-pond,** n. Retenue *f.;* réservoir *m.* ‖ **Mill-wheel,** n. Roue (*f.*) du moulin.
— v. tr. Moudre (coffee, grain, pepper). ‖ Culin. Battre (cream); broyer (vegetables). ‖ Techn. Fouler (cloth); fraiser (gears); bocarder (ore).
— v. intr. Tournoyer. ‖ Pop. Tabasser, bourrer.
millboard ['milbɔ:d] n. Carton-pâte *m.*
millenary ['milinəri] adj., n. Millénaire *m.*
millenium [mi'leniəm] n. Eccles. Millénium *m.* ‖ Fig. Age d'or *m.*
millepede ['milipi:d] n. Zool. Mille-pattes *m.*
miller ['milə*] n. Meunier *m.; miller's wife,* meunière. ‖ Minotier *m.* (of power-driven mill). Techn. Fraiseuse *f.* (machine); fraiseur *m.* (person). ‖ Zool. Hanneton *m.;* U. S. papillon (*m.*) de nuit.
millesimal [mi'lesiməl] adj., n. Millième *m.*
millet ['milit] n. Bot. Millet, mil *m.; black millet,* sorgho.
milliampere [mili'æmpɛə*] n. Electr. Milliampère *m.*
milliard ['miljəd] n. Milliard *m.*
millibar ['milibɑ:*] n. Millibar *m.*
milligram(me) [-græm] n. Milligramme *m.*
millilitre [-li:tə*] n. Millilitre *m.*
millimetre [-mi:tə*] n. Millimètre *m.*
milliner ['milinə*] n. Comm. Modiste *f.*
millinery [-nəri] n. Comm. Articles (*m. pl.*) de modes.
milling ['miliŋ] n. Mouture *f.* (act); minoterie *f.* (trade). ‖ Techn. Foulage *m.* (of cloth); fraisage *m.* (of gears); bocardage *m.* (of ore). ‖ **Milling-machine,** n. Techn. Fraiseuse *f.*
million ['miljən] n. Million *m.* ‖ Fam. *The million,* tout le populo; U. S. *to feel like a million,* être en pleine forme (or) gonflé à bloc.
— adj. Million; *forty million Frenchmen,* quarante millions de Français.
millionaire [,miljə'nɛə*] n. Millionnaire *s.*
millionth ['miljənθ] adj., n. Millionième *m.*
millstone ['mil,stoun] n. Meule *f.* (of mill). ‖ Archit. Meulière *f.* ‖ Fig. *A millstone round one's neck,* un boulet à traîner.
millwright ['milrait] n. Constructeur (*m.*) de moulins.
milometer [mai'lɔmitə*] n. Autom. Compteur (*m.*) de miles.
milord [mi'lɔ:d] n. Milord *m.*
milt [milt] n. Laitance *f.* (of fish); rate *f.* (of mammals).

milter [-ə*] n. Zool. Poisson laité *m.*
Miltonian [mil'tounjən], **Miltonic** [mil'tɔnik] adj. Miltonien.
mime [maim] n. Mime *m.*
— v. intr., tr. Mimer.
mimeograph ['mimiogrɑːf] n. Autocopiste *m.*
mimetic [mi'metik] adj. Zool. Mimétique. ‖ Fig. Imitatif.
mimic ['mimik] adj. Imitateur. ‖ Factice, simulé (mock).
— n. Mime *m.* ‖ Imitateur *m.; imitatrice f.*
— v. tr. (1). Imiter, copier; singer (fam.).
mimicry [-ri] n. Mimique *f.* (art). ‖ Imitation *f.* ‖ Zool., Bot. Mimétisme *m.*
mimosa [mi'mouzə] n. Bot. Mimosa *m.*
mina ['mainə] n. Zool. Mainate *m.*
minacious [mi'neiʃəs] adj. Menaçant.
minaret ['minəret] n. Minaret *m.*
minatory [-təri] adj. Comminatoire; menaçant.
mince [mins] n. Culin. Hachis, haché, *m.* ‖ **Mince-pie**, n. Culin. Tourte (*f.*) aux fruits en dés.
— v. tr. Culin. Hacher. ‖ Fig. Edulcorer; *not to mince matters,* appeler les choses par leur nom, ne pas mâcher ses mots, ne pas y aller par quatre chemins.
— v. intr. Minauder, faire des manières.
mincemeat [-miːt] n. Culin. Mélange (*m.*) de fruits aromatisés coupé en dés. ‖ † Culin. Hachis de viande *m.* (mince). ‖ Fam. *To make mincemeat of,* mettre en marmelade (or) en compote.
mincing [-iŋ] adj. Minaudier, grimacier.
— n. Grimaces, minauderies *f. pl.*
mind [maind] n. Esprit *m.; to enter s.o.'s mind,* venir à l'esprit de qqn. ‖ Esprit *m.;* intelligence *f.* ‖ Esprit *m.;* raison *f.; in one's right mind,* dans son bon sens; *sound in mind,* sain d'esprit. ‖ Idée, pensée *f.; it takes my mind off my work,* cela me change les idées. ‖ Opinion *f.;* avis *m.; to be of one mind,* être du même avis; *to speak one's mind,* dire ce qu'on pense. ‖ Décision, résolution *f.; to be of two minds,* être irrésolu; *to change one's mind,* changer d'avis (or) de dessein; *to make up one's mind,* se décider, se résoudre (*to,* à); *to know one's mind,* savoir ce qu'on veut. ‖ Envie, intention *f.; I have half a mind, a good mind to,* j'ai envie, bonne envie de; *nothing is farther from my mind,* rien n'est plus éloigné de mes intentions. ‖ Idée *f.;* goût *m.; to be to s.o.'s mind,* être au goût (or) au gré de qqn. ‖ Attention *f.; to keep one's mind on,* porter toute son attention sur; *to take one's mind off,* détourner son esprit de. ‖ Souvenir *m.;* mémoire *f.; that puts me in mind of sth.,* ça me dit (or) rappelle qqch.; *to bear in mind,* se rappeler; *to call to mind,* rappeler, remémorer; *to see in one's mind's eye,* évoquer, imaginer, avoir en tête. ‖ Philos. Esprit *m.;* âme *f.* ‖ **Mind-picture**, n. Représentation mentale *f.* ‖ **Mind-reading**, n. Lecture de pensée *f.*
— v. tr. Prêter attention à; *never mind her,* ne faites pas attention à elle. ‖ Faire attention à; *mind your language!,* surveillez (or) mesurez vos paroles!; *mind what you are about!,* attention à ce que vous faites! ‖ Penser à; *mind you phone him,* n'oubliez pas de lui téléphoner. ‖ Prendre garde; *mind yourself,* prenez garde à vous, méfiez-vous; *mind your backs!,* dégagez! ‖ Ecouter, obéir à; *if you had minded me,* si vous m'aviez écouté. ‖ Se soucier de, s'inquiéter de; *don't mind what people say,* moquez-vous du qu'en-dira-t-on; *never mind the consequences,* ne vous préoccupez pas des conséquences. ‖ Veiller sur; *to mind the baby,* surveiller le bébé; *to mind the shop,* garder la boutique. ‖ Se plaindre de, trouver à redire à; *do you mind my shutting the door?,* ça ne vous fait rien que je ferme la porte?; *I don't mind the cold,* je ne crains pas le froid. ‖ S'occuper de; *mind your own business,* mêlez-vous de vos affaires.

— v. intr. Ne pas oublier de; *he'll come, mind,* il viendra, songez-y. ‖ Remarquer; *and very difficult, mind you,* et très difficile, je vous assure (or) vous savez. ‖ Se soucier, s'inquiéter; *never mind,* ça ne fait rien, ne vous faites pas de souci, peu importe. ‖ Trouver à redire à; *if you don't mind,* si ça vous est égal, si vous n'y voyez pas d'inconvénient, si cela ne vous ennuie pas.
minded [-id] adj. Disposé (*to,* à); *if you are so minded,* si cela vous chante, si le cœur vous en dit. ‖ D'esprit; *commercially minded,* d'esprit commerçant.
mindful [-ful] adj. Attentif (*to,* à); soucieux (*of,* de); *to be mindful of others,* penser aux autres. ‖ Qui a le souvenir (*of,* de); *to be mindful of an event,* se rappeler un événement. ‖ Conscient (*of,* de); *to be mindful of the danger,* avoir conscience du danger.
mindless [-lis] adj. Inintelligent, sans esprit (senseless). ‖ Insouciant (*of,* de) [careless]; inattentif (*of,* à) [heedless]; oublieux (*of,* de) [forgetful].
mine [main] pron. poss. Le mien, la mienne; à moi; les miens, les miennes.
— adj. poss. † Mon, ma, mes.

A. Puits d'extraction. *Hoisting-shaft;* B. Puits d'aérage. *Ventilation shaft;* C. Station de chargement. *Loading-station;* D. Front de taille. *Working-face;* E. Convoyeur. *Conveyor, conveyer;* F. Ecluses d'aérage. *Air-vents;* H. Faille. *Fault;* I. Remblayage. *Packing;* K. Bure à matériel. *Blind shaft;* L. Bure hélicoïdale. *Twist-pit,* (U. S.) *spiral shaft;* M. Chevalement. *Pit-head gear,* (U. S.) *gallows, head frame;* N. Lavoir. *Buddle;* O. Cokerie. *Coking plant;* P. Bassin de décantation. *Decanting bed;* Q. Usine de récupération des sous-produits. *By-product recovery plant;* R. Ventilation. *Ventilation.*

mine n. Techn., Milit., Naut., Fig. Mine *f.* ‖ **Mine-clearer**, n. Milit. Démineur *m.* ‖ **Mine-detector**, n. Milit., Naut. Détecteur (*m.*) de mines. ‖ **Mine-field**, n. Région minière *f.;* Naut., Milit. Champ (*m.*) de mines. ‖ **Mine-layer**, Naut., Milit. Mouilleur (or) poseur (*m.*) de mines. ‖ **Mine-**

shaft, n. Puits (*m.*) de mine. ‖ **Mine-sweeper,** n. NAUT. Dragueur (*m.*) de mines. ‖ **Mine-worker,** n. Mineur, ouvrier (*m.*) de la mine.
— v. tr. Creuser (the earth); exploiter (minerals). ‖ Extraire (coal). ‖ MILIT., NAUT. Miner. ‖ FIG. Miner, saper.
— v. intr. Faire des sondages (*for,* pour trouver).
miner [-ə*] n. TECHN., MILIT. Mineur *m.*
mineral ['minərəl] adj., n. Minéral *m.*
mineralization [,minərəlai'zeiʃən] n. Minéralisation *f.*
mineralize ['minərəlaiz] v. tr. Minéraliser.
mineralogical [,minərə'lɔdʒikal] adj. Minéralogique.
mineralogist [,minə'rɔlədʒist] n. Minéralogiste *m.*
mineralogy [,minə'rælədʒi] n. Minéralogie *f.*
Minerva [mi'nə:və] n. Minerve *f.*
minestrone [,mini'strouni] n. CULIN. Minestrone *m.*
minever ['minivə*] n. ZOOL., COMM. Petit-gris *m.*
mingle ['miŋgl] v. tr. Mélanger, mêler.
— v. intr. Se mélanger, se mêler.
mingy ['mindʒi] adj. FAM. Radin, rapiat, mesquin (mean); minuscule (small).
mini ['mini] n. FAM. Minijupe *f.* (miniskirt).
miniature ['minjətʃə*] n. ARTS. Miniature *f.*
— adj. ARTS. De miniature; *miniature painter,* miniaturiste. ‖ TECHN. De petit format; très réduit; *miniature model,* maquette. ‖ FAM. En miniature (or) réduction; petit format.
miniaturist [-rist] n. ARTS. Miniaturiste *s.*
miniaturize [-raiz] v. tr. TECHN. Miniaturiser.
minibus ['mini,bʌs] n. Minibus, minicar *m.*
minicab [-,kæb] n. Voiture individuelle (*f.*) utilisée comme taxi.
minicar [-,kɑ:*] n. AUTOM. Petite voiture *f.*
minigroove ['minigru:v] n. MUS. Microsillon *m.*
minim ['minim] n. Jambage *m.* (in writing). ‖ Goutte *f.* (drop). ‖ MUS. Blanche *f.* ‖ ECCLES. Minime *m.*
minimal [-əl] adj. Minimum, minimal.
minimize [-aiz] v. tr. Réduire au minimum. ‖ FIG. Minimiser, sous-estimer.
minimum ['miniməm] (pl. **minima** [-ə]) n. Minimum *m.*
— adj. Minimal, minimum (fam.); *minimum wage,* salaire minimum.
mining ['mainiŋ] n. Mine *f.;* travail (*m.*) des mines.
minion ['minjən] n. † Mignon *s.* ‖ JUR. Séide *m.* (of the government). ‖ FIG. Favori *s.* ‖ FAM. *Minion of the law,* flic.
miniskirt ['mini,skə:t] n. Minijupe *f.*
minister ['ministə*] n. JUR. Ministre *m.* ‖ ECCLES. Pasteur, ministre *m.*
— v. intr. Subvenir aux besoins (*to,* de). ‖ Rendre service, aider (*to,* à). ‖ ECCLES. *To minister to,* desservir (a parish).
— v. tr. † Procurer.
ministerial [,minis'tiəriəl] adj. JUR. Ministériel (bench); exécutif (function); gouvernemental (team). ‖ ECCLES. De ministre, sacerdotal (duties). ‖ FIG. Servant d'agent; *to be ministerial to,* servir d'agent.
ministerialist [-ist] n. Ministériel *m.*
ministrant ['ministrənt] adj., n. ECCLES. Officiant *m.* ‖ FIG. Dispensateur *m.*
ministration [minis'treiʃən] n. ECCLES. Ministère *m.* ‖ MED. Administration *f.* ‖ FIG. Service *m.*
ministry ['ministri] n. JUR., FIG. Ministère *m.*
minium ['miniəm] n. CHIM. Minium *m.*
miniver ['minivə*] n. ZOOL., COMM. Petit-gris *m.*
mink [miŋk] n. ZOOL., COMM. Vison *m.*
minnow ['minou] n. ZOOL. Vairon *m.*
minor ['mainə*] adj. Cadet (brother, pupil). ‖ GEOGR., MUS., PHILOS., ECCLES. Mineur. ‖ FIG. De peu d'importance; petit, menu (expenses, repairs); secondaire (importance); subalterne, inférieur (part); mineur (poet).

— n. MUS. Mineur *m.* ‖ PHILOS. Mineure *f.* ‖ ECCLES. Frère mineur *m.* ‖ JUR. Mineur *s.* ‖ U. S. Matière secondaire *f.* (at school).
Minorca [mi'nɔ:kə] n. GEOGR. Minorque *f.*
minority [mai'nɔriti], [mi'nɔriti] n. Minorité *f.*
minotaur ['minətɔ:*] n. Minotaure *m.*
minster ['minstə*] n. ARCHIT. Cathédrale; abbatiale *f.*
minstrel ['minstrəl] n. Ménestrel *m.* ‖ U. S. MUS. Interprète (*m.*) de chants nègres; *minstrel show,* concert de chants nègres. (See MINSTRELSY.)
minstrelsy [-si] n. Art (or) groupe (*m.*) [or] chants (*m. pl.*) des ménestrels.
mint [mint] n. BOT., CULIN. Menthe *f.* ‖ **Mint-julep,** n. U. S. Whisky glacé (*m.*) à la menthe. ‖ **Mint-sauce,** n. CULIN. Sauce à la menthe *f.*
mint n. ARCHIT. Hôtel (*m.*) de la Monnaie. ‖ FAM. Mine *f.* (of documents); *a mint of money,* des sommes folles.
— v. tr. Frapper (see COIN); *to mint money,* battre monnaie. ‖ Monnayer (gold). ‖ FAM. Forger, créer (a word).
mintage [-idʒ] n. Monnayage *m.* (act); monnaies *f. pl.* (coins). ‖ FIG. Création *f.* (of a word).
minuet [,minju'et] n. MUS. Menuet *m.*
minus ['mainəs] prep. MATH. Moins. ‖ FIG. Sans.
— adj. En moins. ‖ MATH. Négatif (quantity); moins (sign). ‖ FAM. *A minus quantity,* quantité négligeable.
— n. MATH. Moins *m.* (sign); quantité négative *f.* ‖ FIG. Inconvénient, élément négatif *m.* (disadvantage).
minuscule [mi'nʌskju:l] adj., n. Minuscule *f.*
minute [mai'nju:t] adj. Menu, minime, infime (detail). ‖ Minutieux, très précis et détaillé (account).
minute ['minit] n. Minute *f.* (of a degree, of an hour). ‖ Minute *f.;* double, brouillon *m.* (duplicate). ‖ Pl. Compte rendu, procès-verbal *m.* (of a meeting). ‖ FAM. Minute *f.;* instant, moment *m.* ‖ **Minute-book,** n. JUR. Minutier; registre (*m.*) des procès-verbaux. ‖ **Minute-gun,** n. MILIT. Canon (*m.*) tirant toutes les minutes. ‖ **Minute-hand,** n. Aiguille (*f.*) des minutes.
— v. tr. Chronométrer, minuter. ‖ JUR. Faire une minute de, dresser le procès-verbal de; minuter. ‖ *To minute down,* prendre note (or) acte de.
minutely [-li] adj. De chaque minute.
— adv. A chaque minute.
minutely [mai'nju:tli] adv. Minutieusement.
minuteman [-mən] (pl. **minutemen**) n. U. S. Membre (*m.*) de la garde nationale (at the time of the Revolution). ‖ U. S. FIG. Franc-tireur *m.*
minuteness [-nis] n. Exiguïté *f.* (smallness). ‖ Minutie, parfaite exactitude *f.*
minutiae [mai'nju:ʃii:] s. pl. Infimes détails *m. pl.*
minx [miŋks] n. Espiègle, coquine *f.;* *sly minx,* fine mouche. ‖ Péronnelle, chipie *f.* (pej.).
Miocene ['maiosi:n] adj., n. GEOL. Miocène *m.*
miracle ['mirəkl] n. ECCLES., THEATR. Miracle *m.* ‖ FIG. Miracle, prodige *m.;* merveille *f.;* *miracle man,* homme miracle.
miraculous [mi'rækjuləs] adj. ECCLES. Miraculeux. ‖ FIG. Miraculeux, merveilleux, prodigieux.
miraculously [-li] adv. ECCLES., FIG. Miraculeusement; *miraculously healed,* miraculé.
mirage [mi'rɑ:ʒ] n. Mirage *m.*
mire ['maiə*] n. Bourbier *m.;* fondrière *f.* (bog). ‖ Fange, boue, bourbe *f.* (mud).
— v. tr. Embourber (to bog); souiller, crotter, tacher de boue (to soil).
mirror ['mirə*] n. Miroir *m.;* glace *f.* ‖ **Mirror image,** n. Image (*f.*) spéculaire (or) en miroir; FIG. Réplique *f.,* pendant exact *m.*
— v. tr. Refléter; *to be mirrored in,* se mirer dans.
mirth [mə:θ] n. Joie, gaieté *f.*
mirthful [-ful] adj. Gai, joyeux, rieur. (See MERRY.)

mirthfully ˈ[-fuli] adv. Gaiement.
mirthless [-lis] adj. Sans gaieté, morne.
miry [ˈmaiəri] adj. Bourbeux, boueux, fangeux (muddy). ‖ FIG. Bas, infect, souillé.
mis- [mis] pref. Mal. ‖ **Mis-shapen**, adj. Déformé (hat); difforme (limb, person). ‖ **Mis-spell**, v. tr. (148). Mal orthographier. ‖ **Mis-spelling**, n. Faute d'orthographe f. ‖ **Mis-spend**, v. tr. (149). Dépenser mal à propos (money); perdre (one's time). ‖ **Mis-state**, v. tr. Exposer d'une manière inexacte; dénaturer. ‖ **Mis-statement**, n. Rapport inexact m.; erreur (f.) de fait.
misadventure [ˌmisədˈventʃə*] n. Mésaventure f. ‖ JUR. Accident m.
misadvise [-ˈvai:z] v. tr. Mal conseiller.
misalliance [ˌmisəˈlaiəns] n. Mésalliance f.
misanthrope [ˈmisənθroup], **misanthropist** [miˈsænθrəpist] n. Misanthrope m.
misanthropic [ˌmisənˈθrɔpik] adj. Misanthropique.
misanthropy [miˈsænθrəpi] n. Misanthropie f.
misapplication [ˈmisˌæpliˈkeiʃən] n. Mauvaise application f.; emploi erroné m.
misapply [ˈmisəˌplai] v. tr. (2). Mal appliquer.
misapprehend [ˈmisˌəpriˈhend] v. tr. Mal comprendre (or) interpréter.
misapprehension [ˈmisˌəpriˈhenʃən] n. Mauvaise interprétation; fausse idée f.
misappropriate [ˈmisəˈprouprieit] v. tr. Détourner, distraire.
misappropriation [ˈmisəˌproupriˈeiʃən] n. Détournement, abus (m.) de confiance.
misbecome [ˌmisbiˈkʌm] v. tr. Convenir mal à.
misbecoming [-iŋ] adj. Peu convenable (to, à); malséant (to, pour).
misbegotten [ˈmisbiˈgɔtṇ] adj. JUR. Illégitime (child). ‖ BOT. Rabougri (plant).
misbehave [-ˈheiv] v. intr. Se conduire mal.
misbehavio(u)r [-ˈheivjə*] n. Mauvaise conduite, inconduite f.
misbelief [-ˌliːf] n. ECCLES. Fausse croyance, opinion erronée f.
misbeliever [-ˌliːvə*] n. Mécréant m.
miscalculate [misˈkælkjuleit] v. tr. Mal calculer.
miscalculation [ˈmisˌkælkjuˈleiʃən] n. MATH. Erreur (f.) de calcul. ‖ FIG. Faux calcul, mécompte m.
miscall [misˈkɔːl] v. tr. Appeler à tort (or) en se trompant. ‖ FAM. Injurier.
miscarriage [misˈkæridʒ] n. Perte f. (of a letter). ‖ JUR. *Miscarriage of justice*, erreur judiciaire; déni de justice. ‖ MED. Fausse couche f. ‖ FIG. Avortement, échec m. (of, de).
miscarry [-ˈkæri] v. tr. (2). S'égarer, se perdre (letter). ‖ MED. Faire une fausse couche. ‖ FIG. Avorter, échouer.
miscast [-ˈkɑːst] adj. THEATR. Désigné pour un rôle qui ne lui convient pas (actor); mal distribué (play).
miscegenation [ˌmisidʒiˈneiʃən] n. Fusion (f.) des races humaines, métissage m.
miscellanea [ˌmisəˈleinjə] n. pl. Mélanges m. pl.
miscellaneous [-əs] adj. Varié, divers (news). ‖ Diversement inspiré, produisant en des genres divers, éclectique (writer).
miscellany [ˈmisələni] n. Mélange m.
mischance [misˈtʃɑːns] n. Malchance, mésaventure f.; malheur m.
mischief [ˈmisˌtʃif] n. Tort, mal m. (harm); *to do s.o. a mischief*, causer du tort à qqn. ‖ Ennui m. (cause of annoyance); *the mischief of it is that*, le malheur c'est que. ‖ Méchanceté, mauvaise intention f.; *to be up to some mischief*, méditer quelque sale tour; *to get into mischief*, faire des bêtises (child). ‖ Zizanie, brouille f.; *to make mischief*, semer la discorde. ‖ FAM. Coquin, fripon s. (little rogue). ‖ **Mischief-maker**, n. Semeur (m.) de ziza-

nie; trouble-ménage; brandon (m.) de discorde. ‖ **Mischief-making**, adj. Malfaisant; n. Mauvais procédés (m. pl.) pour semer la discorde.
mischievous [ˈmisˌtʃivəs] adj. Malfaisant (person); nuisible (thing). ‖ Espiègle, malicieux (child); insupportable (pej.).
mischievously [-li] adv. Méchamment; nuisiblement. ‖ Malicieusement.
mischievousness [-nis] n. Méchanceté, malice f. (of s.o.); nature nuisible f. (of sth.). ‖ Espièglerie f.
miscibility [ˌmisiˈbiliti] n. Miscibilité f.
miscible [ˈmisibl] adj. Miscible (with, avec).
miscolo(u)r [msˈkʌlə*] v. tr. Présenter sous de fausses couleurs.
misconceive [miskənˈsiːv] v. intr. Avoir une conception fausse (of, de).
— v. tr. Mal comprendre.
misconception [ˈmisˌkənˈsepʃən] n. Conception erronée f. ‖ Malentendu m.
misconduct [misˈkɔndəkt] n. COMM. Mauvaise gestion f. ‖ JUR. Adultère m. ‖ FIG. Mauvaise conduite f.
— [ˌmiskənˈdʌkt] v. tr. COMM. Mal administrer. ‖ FIG. Mal conduire; *to misconduct oneself*, se conduire mal.
misconstruction [ˌmiskənsˈtrukʃən] n. Fausse interprétation f.
misconstrue [ˌmiskənˈstruː] v. tr. Mal interpréter. (See MISINTERPRET.)
miscopy [misˈkɔpi] v. tr. (2). Mal recopier, commettre une erreur en recopiant.
miscount [misˈkaunt] n. Erreur (f.) de calcul.
— v. tr., intr. Mal compter.
miscreant [ˈmiskriənt] n. † Mécréant s. ‖ FIG. Vaurien m.
miscreated [misˈkrieitid] adj. Difforme; *miscreated creature*, avorton.
misdate [-ˈdeit] v. tr. Mal dater.
misdeal [-ˈdiːl] v. tr. (45). Faire maldonne.
— n. Maldonne f.
misdeed [-ˈdiːd] n. Méfait m. ‖ JUR. Délit m.
misdemean [ˌmisdiˈmiːn] v. intr. Se conduire mal.
misdemeanant [-ənt] n. JUR. Délinquant s.
misdemeano(u)r [-ə*] n. Méfait m. ‖ JUR. Délit correctionnel m.
misdirect [misdaiˈrekt] v. tr. Mal diriger (a blow, one's studies); renseigner mal (s.o.). ‖ Mal adresser (a letter).
misdirection [-ʃən] n. Mauvais renseignement m. ‖ Erreur d'adresse f.
misdoing [ˈmisˈduːiŋ] n. Méfait m.
misdoubt [misˈdaut] v. tr. Se douter de, soupçonner.
mise [miːz] n. JUR. Accord m.
mise en scène [mizɑ̃sɛn] n. THEATR. Mise en scène f. (staging); décor, cadre m. (stage setting). ‖ FIG. Décor, cadre m. (surroundings of an event).
miser [ˈmaizə*] n. Avare s.
miserable [ˈmizərəbl] adj. Misérable, malheureux (person). ‖ Déplorable, pénible (event). ‖ Piteux, misérable, lamentable (dress, speech). ‖ Misérable, mesquin (salary).
misère [miˈzeə*] n. Misère f. (at cards).
miserere [ˌmizəˈriəri] n. MUS., ECCLES. Miserere m. ‖ Miséricorde f. (seat).
misericord [miˈzerikɔːd] n. Miséricorde f. (dagger, seat).
miserliness [ˈmaizəlinis] n. Avarice f.
miserly [-li] adj. Avare.
misery [ˈmizəri] n. Souffrance, violente douleur f. (pain). ‖ Misère f. (poverty). ‖ Détresse f. (distress).
misestimate [misˈestimeit] v. tr. Estimer mal.
misfeasance [-ˈfiːzəns] n. JUR. Abus (m.) de pouvoir.
misfire [-ˈfaiə*] n. AUTOM., MILIT. Raté m.
— v. intr. AUTOM. Avoir des ratés. ‖ MILIT. Faire long feu. ‖ FAM. Tomber à plat; cafouiller; foirer.

misfit ['misfit] n. Comm. Laissé-pour-compte *m.* ‖ Fam. Inadapté *s.*

misfortune [mis'fɔ:tʃn] n. Infortune *f.*; malheur *m.*

misgive [mis'giv] v. tr. (71). Provoquer l'appréhension chez, donner le pressentiment à.

misgiving [-iŋ] n. Inquiétude, appréhension *f.*; pressentiment *m.* (*about,* au sujet de).
— adj. Plein d'appréhension.

misgotten ['mis'gɔtn] adj. Mal acquis.

misgovern ['mis'gʌvən] v. tr. Mal gouverner.

misgovernment [-mənt] n. Mauvais gouvernement *m.* (of a country). ‖ Mauvaise administration *f.* (of business).

misguide ['mis'gaid] v. tr. Conseiller (or) diriger (or) orienter mal.

misguided [-id] adj. Malencontreux (attempt, conduct); dévoyé, fourvoyé (person).

mishandle [mis'hændl] v. tr. Malmener.

mishap [-'hæp] n. Désagrément, contretemps, ennui *m.*

mishear [-'hiə*] v. tr. (77). Entendre mal.

mishit ['mis,hit] n. Sports. Coup manqué *m.*
— [,mis'hit] v. tr. (81). Sports. Manquer son coup.

mishmash ['miʃ,mæʃ] n. Salmigondis *m.,* salade *f.* (hotchpotch).

misinform ['misin'fɔ:m] v. tr. Mal renseigner.

misinformation ['mis,infə'meiʃən] n. Faux renseignement *m.*

misinterpret ['misin'tə:prit] v. tr. Mal interpréter.

misinterpretation ['misin,tə:pri'teiʃən] n. Erreur d'interprétation *f.*

misjudge [mis'dʒʌdʒ] v. tr. Mal juger, se tromper sur.
— v. intr. Se tromper, juger mal.

misjudgment [-mənt] n. Jugement erroné *m.*

mislay [mis'lei] v. tr. (89). Egarer. ‖ Jur. Adirer.

mislead [-'lid] v. tr. (90). Abuser, tromper (to deceive). ‖ Fourvoyer, diriger mal (to misguide). ‖ Dévoyer, corrompre (to corrupt).

mismanage [mis,mænidʒ] v. tr. Mal gérer (or) administrer.

mismanagement [-mənt] n. Mauvaise administration *f.*

misname ['mis'neim] v. tr. Donner un nom inexact à.

misnomer [-noumə*] n. Jur. Erreur (*f.*) de nom. ‖ Gramm. Emploi d'un mot dans un sens erroné *m.*

misogamy [mi'sɔgəmi] n. Misogamie *f.*

misogynist [-dʒinist] n. Misogyne *m.*

misogyny [-dʒini] n. Misogynie *f.*

misplace ['mis'pleis] v. tr. Mal placer, déplacer, égarer (an object). ‖ Fig. Placer mal (one's affection); faire hors de propos (an observation).

misplaced [-t] adj. Mal placé, égaré (object). ‖ Fig. Mal compris (charity); déplacé (word).

misprint [mis'print] n. Faute d'impression; coquille *f.* (fam.).
— v. tr. Imprimer avec une coquille.

misprision [-'priʒən] n. Jur. Négligence coupable *f.*

mispronounce ['misprə'nauns] v. tr. Mal prononcer, écorcher (a word).

mispronunciation ['misprə,nʌnsi'eiʃən] n. Mauvaise prononciation *f.*

misquotation ['miskwou'teiʃən] n. Fausse citation *f.*

misquote [mis'kwout] v. tr. Citer inexactement.

misread ['mis'ri:d] v. tr. (108). Mal lire.

misreckoning [mis'rekəniŋ] n. Erreur (*f.*) de compte. ‖ Fig. Défaut (*m.*) de perspicacité.

misreport [,misri'pɔ:t] n. Compte rendu inexact (or) erroné *m.* (unintentional); compte rendu mensonger *m.* (deliberate).
— v. tr. Rapporter de façon inexacte.

misrepresent ['mis,repri'zent] v. tr. Mal représenter; dénaturer.

misrepresentation ['mis,reprizən'teiʃən] n. Présentation fausse, dénaturation *f.*

misrule [mis'ru:l] n. Mauvaise administration *f.*
— v. tr. Mal administrer.

miss [mis] v. tr. Manquer; louper, rater (fam.) [one's aim, blow]; *to miss the mark* (or) *point,* passer (or) toucher à côté. ‖ Manquer, rater (fam.) [a train, s.o.]. ‖ Manquer, sécher (fam.) [a lecture]. ‖ Manquer, laisser passer, ne pas saisir (an opportunity). ‖ Ne pas saisir (or) comprendre (a joke); manquer, ne pas trouver (s.o.'s house). ‖ Eprouver le manque de, regretter; *do you miss it?,* cela vous prive-t-il?; *I miss you,* vous me manquez (or) faites défaut; je m'ennuie de vous (fam.). ‖ *To miss out,* U. S. Fam. Rater; laisser passer (an opportunity).
— n. Echec *m.*; *we scored several near misses,* plusieurs de nos coups ont manqué de fort peu.

miss n. Mademoiselle *f.* (title). ‖ Comm. Fillette *f.*; *misses' size,* taille jeunes filles. ‖ Fam. Demoiselle, donzelle *f.*

missal ['misəl] n. Eccles. Missel *m.*

missile ['misail] n. Projectile *m.* ‖ Milit. Missile *m.* (self-propelling); *guided missile,* engin télécommandé.

missing ['misiŋ] adj. Manquant, égaré (thing). ‖ Milit. *Reported missing,* porté manquant (or) disparu. ‖ Aviat. Qui n'est pas rentré (plane). ‖ Fig. *Missing link,* chaînon manquant.
— n. Milit. *The missing,* les disparus.

mission ['miʃən] n. Eccles., Milit., Jur., Fig. Mission *f.*
— adj. Eccles. Des missions; *mission priest,* missionnaire; *mission priesthood,* sacerdoce missionnaire.

missionary ['miʃənəri] n., adj. Eccles. Missionnaire *m., adj.*

missioner [-ə] n. Missionnaire paroissial *m.*

missis, missus ['misiz] n. Pop. Patronne *f.* (used by servants). ‖ Pop. Bourgeoise *f.* (used by the husband).

Mississippi [misi'sipi] n. Geogr. Mississippi *m.*

missive ['misiv] adj., n. Missive *f.* (See letter.)

missy ['misi] n. U. S. Fam. Petite demoiselle *f.*

mist [mist] n. Brume *f.*; *Scotch mist,* bruine, crachin. ‖ Buée *f.*; brouillard *m.* (before the eyes). ‖ Fig. Pl. Brumes *f. pl.* (of past); *the mists of time,* la nuit des temps.
— v. intr. Se couvrir de brume (landscape). ‖ Se couvrir de buée (mirror). ‖ Se voiler (eyes).
— v. tr. Embrumer (a landscape); embuer (a mirror). ‖ Voiler, embuer (eyes).

mistakable [mis'teikəbl] adj. Sujet à erreur.

mistake [mis'teik] n. Erreur *f.* (fault); *to make the mistake of,* commettre l'erreur de, avoir le tort de. ‖ Erreur, méprise *f.* (misunderstanding); *to make a mistake,* se tromper. ‖ Gramm. Faute *f.*
— v. tr. (103). Mal comprendre (or) interpréter (words). ‖ Se méprendre (or) se tromper sur (s.o.); se tromper à propos de (sth.); *to mistake s.o. for,* prendre qqn pour, confondre qqn avec.
— v. intr. Se tromper, se méprendre.

mistaken [-ən] adj. Mal compris (or) interprété (words). ‖ Erroné, faux (idea); dans l'erreur (person); *to be mistaken about* (or) *as to,* se tromper sur. ‖ Jur. *Mistaken identity,* erreur sur la personne.

mister ['mistə*] n. Monsieur *m.* (titre précédant un nom propre et toujours abrégé en Mr.). ‖ Fam. M'sieu *m.*; *hey, mister!,* dites-donc, vous là-bas!
— v. tr. Donner du monsieur à (s.o.).

mistful ['mistful] adj. Embrumé, brumeux.

mistify [-ifai] v. tr. (2). Comm. Pulvériser en nuage, vaporiser.

mistily [-ili] adv. Dans un brouillard.

mistime ['mis'taim] v. tr. Faire à contretemps (sth.). ‖ Mal calculer, mal calculer le moment de.

mistiness ['mistinis] n. Brume *f.*; état brumeux *m.* ‖ Fig. Flou *m.*; grisaille *f.*

mistletoe ['misltou] n. Bot. Gui *m*.
mistook [mi'stuk] pret. See MISTAKE.
mistral [mis'trɑ:l] n. Mistral *m*. (wind).
mistranslate ['mis,trɑ:nsleit] v. tr. Mal traduire.
mistranslation ['mistrɑ:ns'leiʃən] n. Traduction erronée *f*.
mistreat [mis'tri:t] v. tr. U. S. Maltraiter.
mistreatment [-mənt] n. U.S. Mauvais traitement *m*.
mistress ['mistris] n. Maîtresse *f*. (housewife, paramour, teacher). ‖ † Madame *f*. (title).
mistrial [mis'traiəl] n. Jur. Procès (*m*.) entaché de nullité.
mistrust [mis'trʌst] n. Méfiance, défiance *f*. (in, of, de).
— v. tr. Se méfier (or) défier de.
mistrustful [-ful] adj. Méfiant (of, envers).
mistrustfully [-fuli] adv. Avec méfiance.
misty ['misti] adj. Brumeux, embrumé. ‖ Fig. Flou, vague.
misunderstand ['mis,ʌndə'stænd] v. tr. (183). Mal interpréter (or) comprendre. ‖ Se méprendre sur.
misunderstanding [-iŋ] n. Méprise *f.;* malentendu *m*. (mistake). ‖ Mésintelligence *f.;* désaccord *m*. (dissension).
misunderstood ['mis,ʌndə'stud] adj. Mal compris (or) interprété (word). ‖ Incompris (person).
misusage [mis'ju:zidʒ] n. Jur. Mauvais traitements *m. pl*.
misuse ['mis'ju:z] v. tr. Faire mauvais usage de, mésuser de. ‖ Maltraiter (to maltreat).
— ['mis'ju:s] n. Mauvais usage (or) emploi *m*. ‖ Jur. Abus *m*. (of authority). ‖ Gramm. Emploi abusif *m*. (of words).
misuser [-ə*] n. Jur. Abus *m*. (of benefit, liberty, privilege).
mite [mait] n. Obole *f*. (contribution). ‖ Eccles. Denier *m*. ‖ Zool. Mite *f*. ‖ Fam. Brin *m.;* miette *f*. (bit); gosse, mioche *m*. (child).
miter ['maitə*] n. U. S. See MITRE.
mitigate ['mitigeit] v. tr. Alléger (burden). ‖ Tempérer (climate); adoucir (cold). ‖ Atténuer (a fault); alléger, atténuer (pain, sorrow); mitiger, adoucir (a penalty); calmer, apaiser (wrath).
mitigation [,miti'geiʃən] n. Allègement *m*. (of a burden). ‖ Atténuation *f*. (of a fault); allègement *m*. (of a pain); mitigation *f*. (of a penalty); apaisement *m*. (of wrath).
mitigatory ['mitigeitəri] adj. Atténuant.
mitochondrion [,maitou'kɔndriən] (pl. **mitochondria** [-driə]) n. Med. Mitochondrie *f*.
mitosis [mai'tousis] (pl. **mitoses** [-si:z]) n. Med. Mitose *f*.
mitral ['maitrəl] adj. Med. Mitral.
mitre ['maitə*] n. Mitre *f*. (of chimney). ‖ Eccles. Mitre *f*. (of bishop). ‖ Archit. Onglet *m*. ‖ **Mitre-joint**, n. Assemblage à onglet *m*.
— v. tr. Eccles. Mitrer. ‖ Archit. Tailler (or) assembler à onglet.
mitt [mit] n. Sports, Fam. Gant *m*. ‖ Pop. Patte, pince *f*. (hand); to hand s.o. the frozen mitt, tourner le dos à qqn, battre froid à qqn.
mitten ['mitn] n. Mitaine *f*. ‖ U. S. Moufle *f*.
mittimus ['mitiməs] n. Jur. Mandat de dépôt *m*.
mity ['maiti] adj. Mité.
mix [miks] v. tr. Mélanger, mêler (with, à, avec). ‖ Culin. Malaxer (a cake); faire (a cocktail, mayonnaise); battre, retourner (a salad). ‖ Fig. Combiner (play and work). ‖ **To mix up**, bien mélanger; Fig. Embrouiller; to mix up in (or) with, impliquer dans, mêler à (to involve).
— v. intr. Se mélanger, se mêler. ‖ Se joindre, s'unir, se mêler (with, à).
— n. Fam. Mélange *m*. (of things, of people). ‖ Culin. Cake-mix, préparation (*f*.) pour gâteaux. ‖ Cinem. Mixage *m*. ‖ **Mix-up**, n. Quiproquo, malentendu *m*. (misunderstanding); pagaille *f*. (disorder); Fam. Bagarre *f*. (fight).

mixed [-t] adj. Mélangé, mêlé. ‖ Mixte (feeling, marriage, school). ‖ Culin. Panaché (ice, salad); assorti (sweets). ‖ Math. Fractionnaire (number). ‖ Fig. Perplexe, perdu (person); mêlé, composite (society).
mixer [-ə*] n. Techn. Malaxeur, mélangeur *m*. ‖ Culin. Mixeur. ‖ Cinem. Opérateur du son *m*. ‖ Fam. To be a bad mixer, n'être pas sociable; to be a good mixer, avoir du liant (or) de l'entregent.
mixing [-iŋ] n. Mélange *m*. ‖ Techn., Culin. Malaxage *m*. ‖ Cinem. Mixage *m*. ‖ Med. Mixtion *f*. ‖ Fig. Brassage, mélange *m*.
mixture ['mikstʃə*] n. Mélange, amalgame *m*. ‖ Med. Mixture *f*. ‖ Comm. Tissu chiné *m*. (cloth).
miz(z)en ['mizn] n. Naut. Artimon *m*. ‖ **Mizzenmast**, n. Naut. Mât d'artimon *m*.
mizzle ['mizḷ] n. Bruine *f*.
— v. intr. Bruiner. (See DRIZZLE.)
mizzle v. intr. Pop. Détaler.
mnemonic [ni:'mɔnik] adj. Mnémonique.
mnemonics [-iks] n. sg. Mnémonique, mnémotechnique *f*.
mnemotechnic [,ni:mo'teknik] adj. Mnémotechnique.
mo [mou] n. Fam. Moment, instant *m.;* wait a mo, attends un instant; half a mo, deux secondes.
M.O. [em'ou] abbr. Medical Officer, médecin militaire (or) des armées, officier de santé.
moan [moun] n. Plainte *f*. (complaint). ‖ Gémissement *m*. (sound).
— v. intr. Se plaindre, se lamenter. ‖ Gémir.
— v. tr. Pleurer (a dead person); déplorer, gémir sur (one's fate). ‖ Dire en gémissant.
moaning [-iŋ] adj. Gémissant.
— n. Gémissement *m*.
moat [mout] n. Fossé *m.;* douve *f*.
— v. tr. Entourer d'une douve.
mob [mɔb] n. Foule *f*. (crowd); cohue *f*. (unruly crowd). ‖ Populo *m.;* populace *f*. (masses). ‖ Canaille, racaille, pègre *f*. (rabble). ‖ **Mob-cap**, n. Charlotte *f*.
— v. tr. (1). Molester, malmener (to attack). ‖ Assiéger, entourer (to crowd around).
— v. intr. S'attrouper.
mobile ['moubail] adj. Mobile. ‖ Fig. Changeant (character); mobile (features).
— n. Arts. Mobile *m*.
mobility [mo'biliti] n. Mobilité *f*.
mobilization [,moubilai'zeiʃən] n. Milit., Fin. Mobilisation *f*.
mobilize ['moubilaiz] v. tr., intr. Milit., Fig., Fin. Mobiliser.
mobster ['mɔbstə*] n. Pop. Gangster *m*.
moccasin ['mɔkəsin] n. Mocassin *m*.
mocha ['moukə] n. Culin. Moka *m*. (coffee); mocha cake, moka.
— adj. Culin. Au café.
mock [mɔk] adj. Faux, factice, simulé, contrefait (see SHAM); mock modesty, fausse modestie. ‖ Comm. D'imitation, simili. ‖ Milit. Mock fight, combat simulé. ‖ **Mock-heroic**, adj. Héroï-comique, burlesque. ‖ **Mock-turtle soup**, n. Culin. Potage (*m*.) à la tortue.
— n. † Moquerie *f*. ‖ Objet (*m*.) de dérision (laughing-stock). ‖ Simulacre *m*. ‖ **Mock-up**, n. Maquette, réplique *f.;* Milit. Trompe-l'œil, truquage *m*.
— v. tr. Moquer, ridiculiser, tourner en dérision (to ridicule). ‖ Contrefaire, imiter, singer (to mimic). ‖ Défier, narguer (to defy). ‖ Tromper, leurrer (to deceive).
mockery ['mɔkəri] n. Moquerie, raillerie *f*. ‖ Objet (*m*.) de risée (laughing-stock). ‖ Simulacre, semblant *m*. (imitation). ‖ Parodie, comédie *f*. (travesty).
mocking [-iŋ] adj. Zool. Moqueur (bird).
— n. Moquerie *f*.

mockingly [-iŋli] adv. En se moquant.

mod [mɔd] abbr. *modern*, moderne ; *« mod cons »*, confort moderne, tout confort (in newspaper advertisement).

Mod n. Mod *m.*, jeune (*s.*) se signalant par le soin avec lequel il s'habille.

modal ['moudļ] adj. Philos., Jur., Gramm. Modal.

modality [mo'dæliti] n. Modalité *f.*

mode [moud] n. Mode, genre *m. ;* façon, manière *f.* (method). ‖ Mode *f.* (fashion). ‖ Mus., Philos., Gramm. Mode *m.* ‖ Culin. U. S. *A la mode*, à la mode (beef) ; couvert de crème glacée (pie).

model ['mɔdļ] n. Modèle *m. ; model maker*, modéliste. ‖ Maquette *f.* (of a monument, statue) ; *working model*, modèle réduit en état de fonctionner. ‖ Mannequin (person) ; patron (pattern) [in dress-making]. ‖ Naut. Gabarit *m.* ‖ Arts. Modèle *m.* Med. *Anatomical model*, écorché. ‖ Fig. Modèle *m.* (see example) ; *to take s.o. as one's model*, prendre modèle sur qqn.
— adj. Modèle (child, dwelling). ‖ En miniature, réduit (aircraft).
— v. tr. (1). Modeler (*after, on, upon*, sur). ‖ Prendre modèle (or) exemple (*on*, sur).
— v. intr. Présenter les modèles, faire le mannequin. ‖ Arts. Poser.

modeller [-ə*] n. Modeleur *s.*

modelling [-iŋ] n. Modelage *m.* ‖ Création (*f.*) de modèles.

Modena [mo'di:nə] n. Geogr. Modène *f.*

moderate ['mɔdərit] adj. Moyen (capacity, size). ‖ Modeste (drinker) ; frugal (meal). ‖ Fin., Comm. Modéré, modique (price). ‖ Fig. Modéré (advice, desire, opinion, person) ; mesuré (language) ; médiocre (work).
— n. Modéré *m.*
— [-eit] v. tr. Modérer, tempérer.
— v. intr. Se modérer.

moderately [-itli] adv. Modérément.

moderateness [-itnis] n. Comm. Modicité *f.* (of price). ‖ Fig. Modération *f.* (in opinions) ; médiocrité *f.* (in work).

moderation [,mɔdə'reiʃən] n. Frugalité *f.* (in eating). ‖ Fig. Modération, mesure, retenue *f. ;* in *moderation*, avec mesure. ‖ Pl. Premier examen du B. A. à Oxford.

moderator ['mɔdəreitə*] n. Président du jury d'examen *m.* (at the university). ‖ Eccles., Techn. Modérateur *m.*

modern ['mɔdən] adj. Moderne (art, Greek, history, person, thing) ; *modern languages*, les langues vivantes.
— n. Moderne *s.*

modernism [-izm] n. Modernisme *m.* (taste). ‖ Nouveauté *f.* (invention, usage). ‖ Eccles. Modernisme *m.* ‖ Gramm. Néologisme *m.* (idiom).

modernist [-ist] n. Eccles. Moderniste *m.*

modernistic [mɔdə'nistik] adj. Arts, Philos. Moderniste.

modernity [mɔ'də:niti] n. Modernité *f.*

modernization [,mɔdənai'zeiʃən] n. Modernisation *f.*

modernize ['mɔdənaiz] v. tr. Moderniser.
— v. intr. Se moderniser.

modest ['mɔdist] adj. Modeste, simple (unassuming). ‖ Modeste, réservé (shy). ‖ Modeste, chaste, pudique (pure) ; *a modest woman*, une femme honnête. ‖ Modeste, modéré (not excessive). ‖ Modeste, sans prétention (humble, quiet).

modestly [-li] adv. Modestement. ‖ Modérément.

modesty [-i] n. Modestie, simplicité *f.* (in appearance, behaviour, style). ‖ Modestie, réserve, pudeur *f.* (sense of decency). ‖ Modicité *f.* (moderation).

modicum ['mɔdikəm] n. Faible quantité *f. ;* peu *m.*

modifiable ['mɔdi,faiəbļ] adj. Modifiable. ‖ Atténuable.

modification [,mɔdifi'keiʃən] n. Modification *f.* ‖ Atténuation *f.*

modificative ['mɔdifikeitiv] adj., n. Gramm. Modificatif *m.*

modificatory [-təri] adj. Modificateur.

modifier ['mɔdifaiə*] n. Modificateur *m. ;* modificatrice *f.*

modify [-fai] v. tr. (2). Gramm., Fig. Modifier. ‖ Jur. Atténuer.

modish ['moudiʃ] adj. A la mode.

modiste [mo'di:st] n. Couturière *f.* (dressmaker) ; modiste *f.* (milliner).

Mods [mɔdz] n. pl. Fam. Premier examen (*m.*) du B. A. à Oxford (abbr. for *Moderations*).

modular ['mɔdjulə*] adj. Modulaire.

modulate ['mɔdjuleit] v. tr. Ajuster, adapter, approprier (*to*, à). ‖ Theatr., Radio, Mus. Moduler.
— v. intr. Radio, Mus. Moduler.

modulation [,mɔdju'leiʃən] n. Modulation *f.*

modulator ['mɔdjuleitə*] n. Radio, Mus. Modulateur *m.*

module ['mɔdju:l] n. Module *m.*

modulus ['mɔdjuləs] n. Math. Module *m.* ‖ Techn. Coefficient *m.*

modus ['moudəs] n. *Modus operandi*, manière de faire, technique, procédure. ‖ *Modus vivendi*, modus vivendi, compromis.

mog [mɔg], moggie ['mɔgi] n. Fam. Minet, matou *m.* (cat).

Mogul [mou'gʌl] adj. Mongol.
— n. Mongol *m.* ‖ Fam. *The Great Mogul*, le Grand Moghol. ‖ Fam. U. S. Huile *f. ;* gros bonnet *m.*

mohair ['mouhɛə*] n. Mohair *m.*

Mohammedan [mo'hæmidən] adj., n. Mahométan, musulman *s.*

Mohammedanism [-izm] n. Mahométisme *m.*

Mohican ['mouikən] n. Mohican *m.*

moiety ['mɔiəti] n. † Moitié *f.* ‖ Part, portion, fraction *f.* (share).

moire [mwɑ:*] n. Moire *f.*
— v. tr. Moirer.

moiré [-rei] adj., n. Moiré *m.*

moist [mɔist] adj. Humide, mouillé (eyes) ; moite (hand, skin). ‖ Humide (climate, heat). [See wet.] ‖ Med. Purulent (eczema).

moisten ['mɔisņ] v. tr. Humidifier. ‖ Mouiller, humecter, imbiber (*with*, de). ‖ Moitir (the skin).
— v. intr. S'humidifier ; s'humecter.

moistness ['mɔistnis] n. Moiteur *f.* (of skin). ‖ Humidité *f.* (of climate).

moisture [-ʃə*] n. Buée *f.* (on mirror). ‖ Humidité *f.* (See dampness.)

moisturize ['mɔistʃə,raiz] v. tr. Humecter, humidifier, hydrater ; *moisturizing cream*, crème hydratante.

moisturizer [-ə*] n. Crème hydratante *f.*

moke [mouk] n. Pop. Bourrin *m.* (donkey). ‖ Pop. Cornichon *m.* (silly ass).

molar ['moulə*] adj., n. Med. Molaire *f.*

molar adj. Phys. De la masse, molaire.

molasses [mə'læsiz] n. sg. Mélasse *f.* (See treacle.)

mold [mould]. See mould.

mole [moul] n. Med. Grain (*m.*) de beauté (on the face) ; nævus *m.* (on the skin).

mole n. Med. Môle *f.* (in uterus).

mole n. Phys., Chim. Mole *f.* (gram-molecule).

mole n. Zool. Taupe *f.* ‖ Mole-catcher, n. Taupier *m.* ‖ Mole-hill, n. Taupinière *f.* ‖ Mole-trap, n. Taupière *f.*

mole n. Môle *m.* (jetty).

molecular [mo'lekjulə*] adj. Phys. Moléculaire.

molecule ['mɔlikju:l] n. Phys. Molécule *f.*

moleskin ['moulskin] n. Velours de coton *m.* (cloth) ; taupe *f.* (fur). ‖ Pl. Pantalon de velours *m.*

molest [mə'lest] v. tr. Molester, malmener, rudoyer (to bully). ‖ Tourmenter, importuner (to annoy).

MONEY (Vocabulary) — L'ARGENT (Vocabulaire)

I. According to the social function.

bénéfice (ecclésiastique)	living
cachet (d'artistes sous contrat)	fee
droits (écrivains, auteurs)	royalties
gages (domestiques)	wages
honoraires (médecins)	fee
honoraires (avocats)	fee, retainer
indemnités (parlementaires)	emoluments
prêt, solde (militaires)	pay
provision (avoués)	retaining fee
salaire, paye (ouvriers, employés)	wages, pay
traitement (fonctionnaires)	salary
vacations (juges)	dues

II. General terms.

appointements, émoluments	perquisite, fee
rémunération, rétribution	payment
suppléments divers, allocations	grants, allowances
— allocations de chômage	unemployment benefit
— indemnités	compensation
— prime	bounty (mil.) ; bonus
— gratification	gratuity
— guelte	bonus, percentage
— commission	commission
— pourboire	tip

III. Different forms.

argent (liquide)	(ready) money
espèces	cash, hard cash
numéraire	specie
fonds	funds, cash
être en fonds	to be in funds (or) in cash
monnaie (petite)	change, small change
Monnaie (la)	the Mint
gain	gain, profit
bénéfice (net, brut)	(net, gross profit)
profits et pertes	profit and loss
revenu	income
capital immobilisé	fixed assets, capital
capital disponible	liquid assets
ressources	support, means, stand-by
avoir, avoirs	estate, property
bien, biens	estate
biens meubles	personal estate
biens immobiliers	real estate
valeurs	securities, stocks
valeur nominale	face value
devises	currency
encaisse	cash in hand, cash balance

IV. National money (ancient and recent).

obole	obol, obolus
sesterce	sesterce
denier	denarius, denier
liard	farthing
écu	crown
guinée (1813)	guinea
franc français (F)	French franc (Fr. Fr.)
livre sterling	pound sterling
billet de dix dollars	ten-dollar bill
livre (familier)	quid
shilling (familier)	bob
mark	mark
lire	lira
drachme	drachma
rouble	rouble
couronne (Scandin.)	crown
roupie (Inde)	rupee

V. Purchase and sale.

achat et vente	purchase and sale, dealing
acheteur et vendeur	buyer and seller
troc	barter
liquidation	clearance
concurrence	competition
concurrents	competitors
producteur	producer
consommateur	consumer
intermédiaire	middleman
denrée, marchandise	commodity
l'offre et la demande	supply and demand
chiffre d'affaires	turnover
prix de revient	cost price
prix de vente	selling price
mise de fonds	outlay
grossiste	wholesaler
détaillant	retail dealer, retailer
prix courant	price-list
monopole	monopoly
devis	estimate (pour le prix) specification (pour les matériaux)
échantillon	sample, pattern
expédition	forwarding
expéditeur	consigner ; shipper
destinataire	consignee ; adressee (lettre)
réceptionnement	acceptance
réceptionner	to take over
livraison	delivery
lettre de voiture	way-bill
cahier des charges	specification sheets
commerce intérieur	home trade
commerce extérieur	foreign trade
rentabilité	payability
mouvement d'affaires	activity; boom
baisse	slump
crise	depression, recession

VI. Book-keeping.

comptabilité en partie simple	single-entry book-keeping
comptabilité en partie double	double-entry book-keeping
doit, débit	debit, the debtor side
avoir, crédit	credit, the creditor side
comptable	book-keeper, accountant
expert comptable	chartered accountant, U. S. certified public accountant
inventaire	stock-taking
bilan	balance-sheet
grand livre	ledger
actif	assets
passif	liabilities
recettes	receipts
dépenses	outlays, expenditure
entretien	maintenance
frais d'entretien	maintenance expenses
frais d'exploitation	running expenses
frais généraux	overhead expenses
patente	licence
paiement comptant	cash payment
vente à tempérament	hire purchase
échéance	date of maturity
échoir; échu	to be due; due
faillite	failure, bankruptcy
solvabilité	solvency
facture pro forma	invoice
facture de paiement	bill

VII. Bank and Exchange.

billet de banque	(bank)note; U. S. bill
dépôt et retrait	deposit and withdrawal
lettre de change	bill of exchange
traite	draft, I. O. U.
billet à ordre	promissory note
chèque barré	crossed cheque
virement	transfer
talon	counterfoil ; stub (fam.)
coffre-fort	safe
reçu, quittance	receipt
action, actionnaire	share, share-holder
obligation, obligataire	bond, bond-holder
courtier	broker
agent de change	stock-broker
placer, placement	to invest, investment
intérêts simples, composés	simple, compound interest
coupon	warrant-coupon
cote, cours	quotation
baisse	fall, drop, decline
hausse	advance, rise
vente à terme	sale for the account
krach	crash, smash, collapse

molestation [,mɔles'teiʃən] n. Molestation *f.*
moll [mɔl] n. FAM. Môme, poule *f.* (woman). ‖ POP. Tapineuse *f.* (prostitute).
mollification [,mɔlifi'keiʃən] n. Adoucissement *m.*
mollify ['mɔlifai] v. tr. (2). Adoucir, apaiser, pacifier.
mollusc ['mɔləsk] n. ZOOL. Mollusque *m.*
mollycoddle ['mɔlikɔdl] n. FAM. Poule mouillée *f.;* mollasson *m.* (See MILKSOP.)
— v. tr. Dorloter, mignoter. (See CODDLE.)
Molotov ['mɔlə,tɔf] n. *Molotov cocktail,* cocktail Molotov.
molt [moult] n., v. U. S. See MOULT.
molten ['moultn] adj. En fusion. ‖ Fondu et coulé.
molybdenum [mɔlib'di:nəm] n. CHIM. Molybdène *m.*
mom [mɔm] n. U. S., FAM. Maman *f.*
moment ['moumənt] n. Moment, instant *m.* (period). ‖ Importance *f.; of great moment,* de haute importance. ‖ PHYS., MATH. Moment *m.* (of a force).
momentaneity [,mouməntə'ni:iti], momentariness ['mouməntərinis] n. Momentanéité *f.*
momentarily ['mouməntərili] adv. Momentanément.
momentary [-əri] adj. Momentané, passager. (See TRANSIENT.)
momentous [mo'mentəs] adj. Important, d'importance.
momentum [-əm] (pl. momenta [-ə]) n. TECHN., PHYS. Force d'impulsion *f.* ‖ FAM. Vitesse acquise *f.;* élan *m.*
momma ['mɔmə], mommy ['mɔmi] n. U. S., FAM. Maman *f.*
monac(h)al ['mɔnəkəl] adj. Monacal.
monachism [-kizm] n. Monachisme *m.*
Monaco ['mɔnə,kou] n. GEOGR. Monaco *f.*
monad ['mɔnæd] n. PHILOS., CHIM., ZOOL. Monade *f.*
monadic [mɔ'nædik] adj. PHILOS. Monadiste. ‖ CHIM. Univalent.
monarch ['mɔnək] n. Monarque *m.* (See KING.) ‖ ZOOL. Danaïde *f.*
monarchic(al) [mɔ'nɑ:kik(ə)l] adj. Monarchique.
monarchism ['mɔnəkizm] n. Monarchisme *m.*
monarchist [-ist] n. Monarchiste *s.*
monarchy [-i] n. Monarchie *f.*
monastery ['mɔnəstri] n. ECCLES. Monastère *m.*
monastic [mɔ'næstik] adj. ECCLES. Monastique, monacal.
monastically [-tikəli] adv. ECCLES. Monastiquement.
monasticism [-tisizm] n. Monachisme *m.* (system). ‖ Vie monastique *f.* (life).
monatomic [,mɔnə'tɔmik] adj. PHYS., CHIM. Monoatomique.
monaural [mɔ'nɔ:rəl] adj. TECHN. Monaural, monophonique. ‖ MED. Monaural.
Monday [mʌndi] n. Lundi *m.*
monetary ['mʌnitəri] adj. FIN. Monétaire.
monetization [,mʌniti'zeiʃən] n. FIN. Monétisation *f.*
monetize ['mʌnitaiz] v. tr. FIN. Monétiser.
money ['mʌni] n. FIN. Espèces *f. pl;* numéraire *m.* (coins, notes); *money payment,* paiement en espèces. ‖ FIN. Monnaie *f.; counterfeit money,* fausse monnaie. ‖ FIN. Argent *m.; money's worth,* valeur (or) contrepartie en argent ; *to make money,* gagner de l'argent, s'enrichir ; *to put money into,* placer de l'argent dans. ‖ FIN. Pl. Fonds, deniers *m. pl.; public moneys,* deniers publics; *with my own money,* de mes propres deniers. ‖ FAM. *Money for jam,* argent vite gagné ; *not everyone's money,* pas à la portée de toutes les bourses ; *there's money in it,* ça peut rapporter. ‖ **Money-bag,** n. Sacoche *f.;* FAM. Pl. Richard *m.* (person); sac *m.* (wealth). ‖ **Money-bill,** n. FIN. Loi (*f.*) de finances. ‖ **Money-box,** n. Tronc *m.* (for contributions); tirelire *f.* (for

savings). ‖ **Money-changer,** n. FIN. Changeur, cambiste *m.* ‖ **Money-grubber,** n. FAM. Grippe-sou *m.* ‖ **Money-lender,** n. Prêteur *m.;* COMM. Bailleur (*m.*) de fonds. ‖ **Money-maker,** n. Amasseur d'argent *m.* ‖ **Money-making,** adj. Lucratif, profitable (business); habile à gagner de l'argent (person); n. Gain *m.* (act). ‖ **Money-market,** n. FIN. Marché financier *m.;* bourse *f.* ‖ **Money-minded,** adj. Intéressé ; *to be money-minded,* être près de ses intérêts, penser argent. ‖ **Money-order,** n. FIN. Mandat *m.* ‖ **Money-spinner,** n. Mine (*f.*) d'or (fig.).
moneyed [-d] adj. Possédant (class) ; fortuné (person); pécuniaire (resources); *moneyed interest,* les capitalistes, les puissances d'argent.
moneyless [-lis] adj. Démuni d'argent.
monger ['mʌŋgə*] n. COMM., FAM. Marchand *s.*
Mongol ['mɔŋgɔl], Mongolian [mɔŋ'goulian] adj. Mongol, mongolien, mongolique.
— n. GEOGR., MED. Mongol *s.*
Mongolia [mɔŋ'goulia] n. GEOGR. Mongolie *f.*
mongolism ['mɔŋgə,lizm] n. MED. Mongolisme *m.*
mongoose ['mɔŋgu:s] n. ZOOL. Mangouste *f.*
mongrel ['mʌŋgrəl] n. MED., BOT. Métis *m.* ‖ ZOOL. Chien bâtard *m.*
— adj. BOT. Métis. ‖ ZOOL., FAM. Bâtard.
monies ['mʌniz] n. pl. FIN. Sommes *f. pl.; monies received,* recettes effectives.
monism ['mɔnizm] n. PHILOS. Monisme *m.*
monition [mo'niʃən] n. ECCLES. Monition *f.* ‖ JUR. Citation *f.* ‖ FIG. Avertissement *m.*
monitor ['mɔnitə*] n. Moniteur *m.* (at school). ‖ NAUT., TECHN. Monitor *m.* ‖ RADIO. Contrôleur d'enregistrement *m.* ‖ **Monitor-room,** n. RADIO. Cabine (*f.*) d'enregistrement (or) d'écoute.
— v. tr. Servir de moniteur à. ‖ RADIO. Contrôler.
monitorial [,mɔnit'ɔ:riəl] adj. De moniteur.
monitoring ['mɔnitəriŋ] n. RADIO. Service (*m.*) d'écoute.
monitory [-ri] adj. ECCLES. Monitoire. ‖ FIG. D'avertissement.
— n. ECCLES. Monitoire *m.*
monitress ['mɔnitris] n. Monitrice *f.* (at school).
monk [mʌŋk] n. ECCLES. Moine, religieux *m.*
monkery [-əri] n. FAM. Moinerie *f.*
monkey ['mʌŋki] n. ZOOL. Singe *m.* (ape); guenon *f.* (female ape). ‖ TECHN. Mouton *m.* ‖ TECHN. U. S. *Monkey wrench,* clé anglaise. ‖ FAM. Petit singe, gamin *m.* (kid). ‖ FAM. U. S. *Monkey business,* affaire louche, sale tour ; *monkey suit,* uniforme. ‖ **Monkey-jacket,** n. Veston court *m.* ‖ **Monkey-like,** adj. Simiesque. ‖ **Monkey-nut,** n. Cacahouète *f.* ‖ **Monkey-puzzle,** n. BOT. Araucaria *m.* ‖ **Monkey-tricks** (or) U. S. **shines,** n. pl. Singeries *f. pl.*
— v. tr. Singer.
— v. intr. Faire des singeries. ‖ **To monkey about,** baguenauder, flânocher. ‖ **To monkey with,** FAM. Tripoter.
monkeyish ['mʌŋkiiʃ] adj. De singe.
monkish ['mʌŋkiʃ] adj. De moine (pej.).
mono ['mɔnou] adj., n. TECHN., FAM. Mono adj., *f.*
monochord ['mɔnokɔ:d] n. MUS. Monocorde *m.*
monochromatic [,mɔnokrou'mætik] adj. PHYS. Monochromatique (light, radiation).
monochrome [-kroum] adj., n. ARTS. Monochrome *m.*
monocle ['mɔnəkl] n. Monocle *m.*
monocoque ['mɔnokɔk] n. AVIAT. Monocoque *m.*
monocotyledon ['mɔno,kɔti'li:dən] n. BOT. Monocotylédone *f.*
monoculture [-,kʌltʃə*] n. AGRIC. Monoculture *f.*
monocyte ['mɔnosait] n. MED. Monocyte *m.*
monodactylous [mɔno'dæktiləs] adj. ZOOL. Monodactyle.
monogamist [mə'nɔgəmist] n. Monogame *s.*
monogamy [-mi] n. Monogamie *f.*

monogram ['mɔnogræm] n. Monogramme m.
monograph [-grɑ:f] n. Monographie f.
monographer [-grɑ:fə*] n. Monographe m.
monolingual [,mɔno'liŋgwḷ] adj. Monolingue.
monolith ['mɔnoliθ] n. Monolithe m.
monologist [mə'nɔlədʒist] n. Monologueur s.
monologize [-dʒaiz] v. intr. Monologuer.
monologue ['mɔnəlɔg] n. Monologue m.
monomania [,mɔnə'meiniə] n. Monomanie f.
monomaniac [-ək] n. Monomane s.
monomer ['mɔnəmə*] n. Chim. Monomèrc m.
monomeric [,mɔnə'merik] adj. Chim. Monomère.
monometallism [mɔno'metəlizm̥] n. Fin. Monométallisme m.
monomial [mɔ'noumiəl] adj., n. Math. Monôme m.
monopetalous [,mɔno'petələs] adj. Bot. Mono-
pétale.
monophonic [-'fɔnik] adj. Techn. Monophonique,
monaural.
monoplane ['mɔnoplein] n. Aviat. Monoplan m.
monopolist [mə'nɔpəlist] n. Monopolisateur m.
monopolistic [mə,nɔpə'listik] adj. Monopolistique.
monopolization [mə,nɔpəlai'zeiʃən] n. Monopolisation f.
monopolize [mə'nɔpəlaiz] v. tr. Monopoliser.
monopoly [-li] n. Monopole m. (of, U. S. on, de).
monorail ['mɔnoreil] n. Ch. de F. Monorail m.
monoscope [-skoup] n. Radio. Monoscope m.
monosyllabic [,mɔnəsi'læbik] adj. Gramm. Monosyllabique.
monosyllable ['mɔno,silæbḷ] n. Gramm. Monosyllabe m.
monotheism ['mɔnoθi:izm̥] n. Monothéisme m.
monotheist [-θi:ist] n. Monothéiste s.
monotheistic [,mɔnoθi:'istik] adj. Monothéiste.
monotone ['mɔnotoun] adj. Monotone.
— n. Monotonie f. (in style); uniformité f.; ton
monotone m. (in voice).
monotonous [mə'nɔtənəs] adj. Monotone.
monotonously [-li] adv. Monotonement.
monotony [mə'nɔtəni] n. Monotonie f.
monotype ['mɔnotaip] n. Techn. Monotype f.
monovalence [,mɔno'veiləns] n. Chim. Monovalence f.
monovalent [-lənt] adj. Chim. Monovalent.
monoxide [mɔ'nɔksaid] n. Chim. Protoxyde m.
Monseigneur [mɔ̃seɲœ:r] n. Monseigneur m.
Monsignor [mɔn'si:njə*] n. Eccles. Monseigneur,
Monsignore m.
monsoon [mɔn'su:n] n. Mousson f.
monster ['mɔnstə*] adj., n. Monstre m.
monstrance ['mɔnstrəns] n. Eccles. Ostensoir m.
monstrosity [mɔns'trɔsiti], monstruousness
['mɔnstrəsnis] n. Monstruosité f.
monstrous ['mɔnstrəs] adj. Monstrueux (abnormal,
horrible, huge).
montage ['mɔntɑ:ʒ] n. Theatr., Radio. Montage m.
month [mʌnθ] n. Mois m. || Fin. Month's pay,
mois, salaire mensuel. || Fam. A month of Sundays,
une éternité, un temps fou.
monthly [-li] adj. Mensuel. || Fin. Monthly pay-
ment, mensualité.
— adv. Mensuellement, tous les mois.
— n. Revue mensuelle f. || Pl. Fam. Règles f. pl.
monticule ['mɔntikjul] n. Monticule m.
monument ['mɔnjumənt] n. Monument m. (building, memorial, work).
monumental [,mɔnju'mentḷ] adj. Monumental;
monumental mason, marbrier. || Fig. Monumental
(ignorance, literary work).
monumentalize [-əlaiz] v. tr. Commémorer par un
monument.
moo [mu:] v. intr. Meugler. (See Low.)
— n. Meuglement m. || Moo-cow, n. Fam. Vache f.
(child's word).

mooch [mu:tʃ] v. intr. Fam. Flânocher (to loiter);
rôdailler, rôder (to skulk).
— v. tr. Fam. Chaparder, piquer (to pilfer). || U. S.
Pop. Taper de (to cadge).
moocher [-ə*] n. U. S. Pop. Tapeur, parasite, pique-
assiette m.
mood [mu:d] n. Mus., Gramm. Mode m.
mood n. Disposition, humeur f.; état (m.) d'âme;
to be in a bad mood, être de mauvais poil (fam.);
to fall in with the mood of, se mettre au diapason
de. || Pl. Lubies f. pl.
moodily [-ili] adv. Avec maussaderie (or) humeur.
moodiness [-inis]. n. Maussaderie f. || Humeur chan-
geante, versatilité f.
moody [-i] adj. Maussade, morose. || D'humeur
changeante, versatile, lunatique.
moon [mu:n] n. Lune f.; moon rocket, fusée lunaire.
|| Astron. Lunaison f. || Fam. Once in a blue moon,
tous les trente-six du mois, quand les poules auront
des dents; à la saint-glinglin.
— v. intr. To moon about, muser, musarder.
— v. tr. To moon away, passer à rêver (or) à
muser.
moonbeam [-bi:m] n. Rayon (m.) de lune.
mooncalf [-kɑ:f] n. Idiot m.
moonish [-iʃ] adj. U. S. Fig. Lunatique, versatile.
moonless [-lis] adj. Sans lune.
moonlight [-lait] n. Clair (m.) de lune.
— adj. Au clair de lune (dancing); moonlight flit,
déménagement à la cloche de bois.
— v. intr. Fam. Travailler au noir.
moonlighter [-ə*] n. Fam. Travailleur (s.) au noir.
moonlit [-lit] adj. Eclairé par la lune.
moonrise [-raiz] n. Lever (m.) de la lune.
moonscape [-skeip] n. Paysage lunaire m.
moonshine [-ʃain] n. Clair (m.) de lune. || Fam.
Baliverne f. (nonsense). || U. S. Pop. Alcool (m.) de
contrebande.
moonshiner [-ʃainə*] n. U. S. Pop. Contrebandier
d'alcool m.
moonshiny [-ʃaini] adj. Eclairé par la lune. (See
Moonlit.) || Fam. Lunaire, chimérique, irréel.
moonstone [-stoun] n. Pierre de lune f.
moonstruck [-strʌk] adj. Fam. Lunatique (capricious); toqué (crazed); sidéré (flabbergasted).
moony [-i] adj. De la lune. || Semblable à la lune
(moon-like). || En croissant (crescent-shaped). ||
Fam. Dans la lune, rêveur.
moor [muə*] n. † Marécage m. (marsh). || Lande,
bruyère f. (heath). || Moor-cock, n. Zool. Lagopède,
coq (m.) de bruyère. || Moor-hen, n. Zool. Poule
d'eau, sarcelle f.
Moor n. Geogr. Maure m.; Mauresque f.
moor v. tr. Amarrer (a boat); mouiller (a mine).
— v. intr. Naut. S'amarrer.
moorage [-ridʒ] n. Naut. Amarrage; mouillage m.
(act, place); droits (m. pl.) d'ancrage (charge).
mooring [-riŋ] n. pl. Naut. Amarres f. pl. (cables);
amarrage m. (moorage).
— adj. Naut. D'amarrage.
Moorish ['muəriʃ] adj. Geogr. Mauresque.
moose [mu:z] n. Zool. U. S. Elan, orignal m.
moot [mu:t] n. † Assemblée f. || Jur. Débat m. (in
a law-school).
— adj. Discutable, qui se discute, à débattre (point).
— v. tr. Débattre, discuter (a point).
mop [mɔp] n. Balai (m.) à franges. || Ecouvillon m.
(baker's). || Naut. Faubert m. || Fam. Tignasse f.
(hair); Mrs. Mop, Mᵐᵉ Plumeau, femme de ménage.
— v. tr. (1). Balayer. || Ecouvillonner (the oven).
|| Naut. Fauberter. || Fam. To mop one's brow,
s'essuyer (or) s'éponger le front. || To mop up,
Milit. Nettoyer; Fam. Rafler, cueillir, ramasser
(profits); nettoyer, liquider (s.o.).
mope [moup] v. intr. Fam. Avoir le cafard, broyer du
noir, voir tout en noir.
— n. Fam. Cafardeux s. || Pl. Cafard noir m.

moped ['mouped] n. Cyclomoteur, vélomoteur *m.*; Mobylette *f.* (nom déposé).

mopish [-iʃ] adj. FAM. Cafardeux.

mopishly [-iʃli] adv. En broyant du noir, la mine longue.

mopishness [-iʃnis] n. Découragement *m.*; humeur sombre *f.*

mopping-up ['moupiŋ,ʌp] n. Epongeage *m.* ‖ MILIT., FAM. Nettoyage *m.*

moquette [mɔ'ket] n. Moquette *f.* (carpet).

moraine [mo'rein] n. GEOL. Moraine *f.*

moral ['mɔrəl] adj. Moral (certainty, courage, faculty, law, sense). ‖ Moral, qui a le sens moral, droit (man); honnête (woman). ‖ De morale (book). — n. Morale, moralité *f.* (lesson). ‖ Pl. Moralité *f.*; principes *m. pl.*; mœurs *f. pl.* (habits).

morale [mɔ'rɑ:l] n. Moral *m.*; état d'esprit *m.* (spirit); force d'âme *f.*; *to undermine the morale of,* démoraliser.

moralist ['mɔrəlist] n. Moraliste *m.*

moralistic [,mɔrə'listik] adj. Moraliste.

morality [mɔ'ræliti] n. Moralité *f.* (quality); caractère (or) sens moral *m.* ‖ Moralité *f.*; bonnes mœurs *f. pl.* (conduct). ‖ Instruction morale *f.*; pl. sermon *m.* (fam.). ‖ † PHILOS. Morale *f.*; pl. principes moraux *m. pl.* ‖ THEATR. Moralité *f.*

moralization [,mɔrəlai'zeiʃən] n. Moralisation *f.*

moralize ['mɔrəlaiz] v. tr. Chercher la morale de (a fable). ‖ Interpréter selon la morale (an event). ‖ Moraliser, donner le sens moral à (s.o.). — v. intr. Moraliser.

moralizer [-ə*] n. Moraliseur *s.*

morally ['mɔrəli] adv. Moralement (practically). ‖ Selon la morale, de façon morale (virtuously). ‖ Du point de vue moral (from a moral point of view).

morass [mo'ræs] n. Fondrière *f.*; marais *m.* (See BOG.) ‖ FAM. Marasme *m.*

moratorium [,mɔrə'tɔ:riəm] n. JUR. Moratorium, moratoire *m.*

— N. B. Deux pluriels : *moratoriums, moratoria.*

moratory ['mɔrətəri] adj. Moratoire.

morbid ['mɔ:bid] adj. MED. Pathologique (anatomy). ‖ FIG. Malsain (curiosity); morbide (desire, idea). ‖ FAM. Horrifiant, atroce (detail).

morbidezza [,mɔ:bi'detsa] n. ARTS. Morbidesse *f.*

morbidity [mo:'biditi], **morbidness** ['mɔ:bidnis] n. Morbidité *f.*

mordacious [mɔ:'deiʃəs] adj. Mordant, caustique.

mordacity [mɔ:'dæsiti], **mordancy** ['mɔ:dənsi] n. Causticité *f.* ‖ CHIM. Mordacité *f.*

mordant ['mɔ:dənt] adj. Mordant. ‖ MED. Aigu. — n. TECHN., CHIM. Mordant *m.*

more [mɔ:*] adj. Plus de, davantage de; *more flowers,* une plus grande quantité de fleurs, davantage de fleurs; *more mischief than ill-will,* plus d'espièglerie que de méchanceté; *no more nonsense!* assez de bêtises. ‖ En plus, de plus; *one week more,* une semaine de plus; *would you like some more?,* en voulez-vous encore? ‖ Plus que; *four is more than two,* quatre est plus grand que deux; *we are more than you,* nous sommes plus nombreux que vous.
— pron. Plus, davantage; *no more,* pas plus, pas davantage, rien de plus; *something more,* qqch. de plus; *the more he got, the more he asked,* plus il obtenait, plus il demandait; *you made yourself more of a hindrance than a help,* vous avez été plus gênant qu'utile.
— adv. Plus, davantage; plutôt; *more cunning than intelligent,* plus rusé qu'intelligent; *more than a hundred,* plus de cent; *more or less,* plus ou moins; *more... than, plus... que*; *neither more nor less,* ni plus ni moins; *no more... than,* pas plus... que; *once more,* une fois de plus; *the more powerful as,* d'autant plus puissant que; *to blush more and more,* rougir de plus belle; *to grow more and more wicked,* devenir de plus en plus méchant.

moreish ['mɔ:riʃ] adj. FAM. Bon, qui a un goût de revenez-y; *that's moreish,* c'est pas dégueulasse (pop.).

morel [mɔ'rel] n. BOT. Morille *f.* (mushroom); morelle *f.* (nightshade).

morello [mo'relou] n. BOT. Griotte *f.* (cherry).

moreover [mɔ:'rouvə*] adv. En outre, de plus, au reste, qui plus est.

mores ['mɔ:reiz] n. pl. Mœurs *f. pl.,* pratique sociale *f.* (of a community).

Moresque [mɔ'resk] adj. GEOGR. Mauresque.

morganatic [,mɔ:gə'nætik] adj. JUR. Morganatique.

morgue [mɔ:g] n. U. S. Morgue *f.* (mortuary). ‖ U. S. Archives (*f. pl.*) d'un journal.

moribund ['mɔribʌnd] adj. Moribond.

Mormon [mɔ:mən] n. Mormon *m.*

morn [mɔ:n] n. Matin *m.*

morning [-iŋ] n. Matin *m.*; *good morning,* bonjour; *in the morning,* le matin. ‖ Matinée *f.*; *all the morning,* toute la matinée. ‖ FIG. Aube, aurore *f.* ‖ FAM. Morning after, lendemain de bombe. — adj. Du matin (breeze, star). ‖ D'après-midi; *morning coat,* jaquette.

Moroccan [mə'rɔkən] adj., n. GEOGR. Marocain *s.*

Morocco [-kou] n. GEOGR. Maroc *m.* ‖ COMM. Maroquin *m.*; *Morocco dressing, goods,* maroquinerie.

moron ['mɔ:ərən] n. MED. Arriéré *s.* ‖ FAM. Crétin, idiot *m.*

morose [mə'rous] adj. Morose, maussade.

morosely [-li] adv. Maussadement.

moroseness [-nis] n. Morosité *f.*

morpheme ['mɔ:fi:m] n. GRAMM. Morphème *m.*

Morpheus ['mɔ:fjus] n. Morphée *m.*

morphia ['mɔ:fjə], **morphine** ['mɔ:fi:n] n. MED. Morphine *f.*

morphinomaniac ['mɔ:fino'meiniæk] n. MED. Morphinomane *s.*

morphologic(al) [,mɔ:fə'lɔdʒik(əl)] adj. GRAMM., MED. Morphologique.

morphology [mɔ:'fɔlədʒi] n. GRAMM., MED. Morphologie *f.*

Morris ['mɔris] adj., n. MUS. Champêtre (dance).

morrow ['mɔrou] n. Lendemain *m.*

morse [mɔ:s] n. ZOOL. Morse *m.*

Morse adj. RADIO. Morse *m.* — v. intr. Employer le morse.

morsel ['mɔ:səl] n. Morceau *m.* — v. tr. (1). Morceler.

mort [mɔ:t] n. SPORTS. Hallali *m.*

mortal ['mɔ:tl] adj. Mortel (enemy, hatred, man, remains). ‖ Mortel (disease, fight); *mortal to,* fatal à, mortel pour. ‖ ECCLES. Mortel (sin). ‖ FAM. Possible et imaginable, au monde; *it's no mortal good to anyone,* ce n'est strictement bon à personne. — n. Mortel *s.*

mortality [mɔ:'tæliti] n. Mortalité *s.* (nature, proportion); *mortality tables,* statistique de mortalité. ‖ Mortels *m. pl.* (mankind).

mortally ['mɔ:təli] adv. Mortellement.

mortar ['mɔ:tə*] n. MED., ARCHIT. Mortier *m.* ‖ Mortar-board, n. Bonnet carré, mortier *m.* (cap); ARCHIT. Planche (*f.*) à mortier. — v. tr. ARCHIT. Lier au mortier. ‖ MILIT. Pilonner.

mortgage ['mɔ:gidʒ] n. JUR., FIN. Hypothèque *f.*; *to raise a mortgage,* prendre une hypothèque. — v. tr. JUR. Hypothéquer.

mortgageable [-əbl] adj. JUR. Hypothécable.

mortgagee [,mɔ:gə'dʒi:] n. JUR. Créancier hypothécaire *m.*

mortgager ['mɔ:gədʒə*] n. JUR. Débiteur hypothécaire *m.*

mortice ['mɔːtis] n., v. intr. See MORTISE.
mortician [mɔːˈtiʃən] n. U. S. Entrepreneur de pompes funèbres. (See UNDERTAKER.)
mortification [ˌmɔːtifiˈkeiʃən] n. MED. Gangrène f. ‖ FIG. Mortification f. (humiliation, self-denial).
mortify ['mɔːtifai] v. tr. (2). MED. Gangrener. ‖ FIG. Mortifier.
— v. intr. MED. Se gangrener.
mortifying [-iŋ] adj. Mortifiant.
mortise ['mɔːtis] n. ARCHIT. Mortaise f. ‖ Mortise-gauge, n. TECHN. Trusquin m. ‖ Mortise-lock, n. TECHN. Serrure à encastrer (or) à mortaiser f.
— v. intr. ARCHIT. Mortaiser.
mortmain ['mɔːtmein] n. JUR. Mainmorte f.
mortuary ['mɔːtjuəri] adj. Mortuaire.
— n. Morgue f.
Mosaic [moˈzeiik] adj. Mosaïque, de Moïse.
mosaic adj. En (or) de mosaïque.
— n. Mosaïque f. ‖ AVIAT. Relevé photographique m.
— v. tr. Mosaïquer.
mosaicist [-isist] n. Mosaïste m.
Moscow ['mɔskou] n. GEOGR. Moscou m.
Moses ['mouziz] n. Moïse m.
mosey ['mouzi] v. intr. FAM. To mosey along, aller son petit bonhomme de chemin ; to mosey around, déambuler, flâner ; to mosey off, filer, se tirer.
Moslem ['mɔzləm] adj., n. Musulman s.
mosque [mɔsk] n. Mosquée f.
mosquito [mɔsˈkiːtou] n. ZOOL. Moustique m. ‖ Mosquito-bite, n. Piqûre (f.) de moustique. ‖ Mosquito-curtain (or) -net, n. Moustiquaire f.
moss [mɔs] n. BOT. Mousse f. ‖ † Marécage m. (bog). ‖ Moss-grown, adj. Moussu, couvert de mousse ; FAM. Vétuste ; vieux jeu. ‖ Moss-rose, n. BOT. Rose moussue f. ‖ Moss-trooper, n. Maraudeur m.
— v. tr. Couvrir de mousse.
mossback [-bæk] n. U. S. POP. Vieille baderne f.; rétrograde m.
mossiness [-inis] n. Aspect moussu m.
mossy [-i] adj. Moussu.
most [moust] adj. Le plus de ; he who made the most noise, celui qui a fait le plus de bruit. ‖ La plupart de ; for the most part, pour la plupart, en majeure partie ; in most cases, dans la majorité des cas.
— pron. La plupart ; most of my books, la plupart de mes livres. ‖ Le plus, le maximum m.; at the most, tout au plus ; to make the most of it, en tirer le meilleur parti possible. ‖ La plus grande partie ; most of the city, la plus grande partie de la ville.
— adv. Le plus ; most horrible, le plus horrible ; what I hope most, ce que j'espère le plus. ‖ Très, bien ; most likely, fort probablement ; a most beautiful evening, un très beau soir. ‖ U. S. FAM. Presque (almost).
mostly [-li] adv. Surtout, principalement (chiefly). ‖ Le plus souvent, la plupart du temps, généralement parlant, presque toujours (in the main). ‖ En majeure partie (for the most part).
mot [mou] n. Bon mot, mot d'esprit m. (witticism).
mote [mout] n. Grain (m.) de poussière. ‖ FAM. To see a mote in another's eye, voir la paille dans l'œil d'autrui.
motel ['moutel] n. Motel m.
motet [mouˈtet] n. MUS. Motet m.
moth [mɔθ] n. ZOOL. Phalène f. (or) m. (butterfly) ; mite f. (clothes moth). ‖ Moth-ball, n. Naphtaline, boule antimite f. ‖ Moth-eaten, adj. Mité ; to become moth-eaten, se miter. ‖ Moth-killer, n. Antimite m.
mother ['mʌðə*] n. Mère f. (parent) ; Mother's Day, fête des mères. ‖ ECCLES. Supérieure, mère f. ‖ CULIN. Mère f. (of vinegar). ‖ FIG. Mère f. ‖

FAM. Every mother's son of us, tous tant que nous sommes ; Mother Goose, ma Mère l'Oie. ‖ Mother-in-law, n. Belle-mère f. ‖ Mother-of-pearl, adj. En (or) de nacre ; n. invar. Nacre f.
— N. B. Noter le pluriel : mothers-in-law.
— adj. Maternel (love). ‖ Mère ; mother country, mère patrie ; mother tongue, langue maternelle (native) ; langue mère (original).
— v. tr. Servir de mère à. ‖ Attribuer la maternité de (upon, à) [a child]. ‖ Chérir, dorloter (to coddle). ‖ FIG. Donner naissance à. ‖ FAM. Se reconnaître l'auteur de.
motherhood ['hud] n. Maternité f.
motherland [-'lænd] n. Mère patrie, patrie f.
motherless [-lis] adj. Orphelin de mère.
motherliness [-linis] n. Attitude maternelle f.
motherly [-li] adj. Maternel.
mothy ['mɔθi] adj. Plein de mites, mité.
motif [mouˈtif] n. ARTS, MUS. Motif m.
motile ['moutail] adj. ZOOL. Doué de mouvement, mobile.
motility [mouˈtiliti] n. Motilité f.
motion ['mouʃən] n. Mouvement m. (act) ; to set in motion, mettre en mouvement (or) en marche. ‖ Mouvement, geste m. (gesture) ; to make motions to, faire des signes à. ‖ Marche f.; smooth motion, allure régulière. ‖ TECHN. Mouvement m. (of a clock) ; mécanisme m. (of a machine). ‖ MED. Selle f. ‖ JUR. Motion, proposition f.; to carry a motion, adopter une motion. ‖ AVIAT. Lost motion, perte de vitesse. ‖ THEATR., FAM. Motion picture, film ; pl. cinéma. ‖ FIG. Mouvement m.; impulsion f. ‖ Motion-camera, n. Ciné-caméra f.
— v. tr. Faire signe à (to, de).
— v. intr. Faire signe (to, à).
motional [-l] adj. De mouvement.
motionless [-lis] adj. Sans mouvement, immobile.
motivate ['moutiveit] v. tr. Motiver.
motive ['moutiv] adj. Moteur m.; motrice f. ‖ PHYS. Cinétique (energy).
— n. Motif m. (for acting) ; hidden motives, raisons cachées. ‖ Mobile m. (of an action) ; powerful motive, mobile puissant.
— v. tr. Motiver (an action).
motivity [mouˈtiviti] n. Motilité f. ‖ TECHN. Energie cinétique f. ‖ MED. Motricité f.
motley ['mɔtli] adj. Bigarré, bariolé (many-coloured). ‖ Mélangé, mêlé, panaché (heterogeneous).
— n. † Habit d'arlequin m. ‖ Livrée (f.) de bouffon (jester's coat). ‖ Bigarrure f. ‖ FAM. Salmigondis m.
motor ['moutə*] n. TECHN., ELECTR. Moteur m. (engine) ; motor-pump, motopompe. ‖ AUTOM. Auto f. (car). ‖ FIN. Pl. Actions (f. pl.) des constructions d'automobiles. ‖ MED. Nerf moteur m. ‖ Motor-bike, n. FAM. Moto f. ‖ Motor-boat, n. NAUT. Canot automobile. ‖ Motor-coach, n. Autocar m. ‖ Motor-driven, adj. Motorisé, à traction automobile. ‖ Motor-fuel, n. Carburant m. ‖ Motor-road, n. Autostrade f. ‖ Motor-school, n. Auto-école f. ‖ Motor-scooter, n. Scooter m. ‖ Motor-yacht, n. NAUT. Autoyacht m.
— adj. Moteur m.; motrice f.
— v. intr. Aller en auto (to, à). ‖ Faire de l'auto.
motorable [-rəbl] adj. Carrossable (road).
motorcade [-keid] n. U. S. Défilé (m.) de voitures.
motorcycle [-saikl] n. Motocyclette f.
motorcyclist [-saiklist] n. Motocycliste s.
motordrome [-droum] n. Autodrome m.
motoring [-riŋ] n. Automobilisme m.; school of motoring, auto-école.
motorist [-rist] n. Automobiliste s.
motorization [ˌmoutəraiˈzeiʃən] n. Motorisation f.
motorize ['moutəraiz] v. tr. Motoriser.

motorized [-d] adj. Motorisé. ‖ AGRIC. *Motorized farming,* motoculture.

motorless [-lis] adj. AVIAT. Sans moteur.

motorman [-mən] (pl. **motormen**) n. Wattman *m.*

motorway [-ˌwei] n. AUTOM. Autoroute *f.*

mottle [ˈmɔtl̩] n. Moucheture *f.* ‖ MED. Marbrure *f.* ‖ COMM. Laine chinée *f.*

mottled [-d] adj. Tacheté, moucheté, bigarré, pommelé. ‖ COMM. Chiné (cloth, wool) ; madré (soap). ‖ MED. Brouillé (complexion).

motto [ˈmɔtou] n. Devise *f.* (on a coat of arms, in life). ‖ Epigraphe *f.* (in a literary work). ‖ MUS. Motif *m.*

moufflon [ˈmuːflɔn] n. ZOOL. Mouflon *m.*

moujik [ˈmuːʒik] n. Moujik *m.*

mould [mould] n. AGRIC. Humus, terreau *m. ;* terre meuble *f.* ‖ **Mould-board,** n. AGRIC. Versoir *m.*
— v. tr. AGRIC. Butter.

mould n. ARTS. Moule *m.* ‖ ARCHIT. Moulures *f. pl.* (group) ; calibre, profil *m.* (pattern). ‖ CULIN. Moule *m.* ‖ TECHN. Matrice *f.* (in printing). ‖ NAUT. Gabarit *m.* ‖ FIG. Forme *(f.)* d'esprit ; *cast in a heroic mould,* de la trempe des héros.
— v. tr. ARTS., CULIN. Mouler. ‖ NAUT. Gabarier. ‖ FIG. Pétrir, façonner.

mould n. Moisissure *f. ;* moisi *m.*
— v. intr. Se moisir.

moulder [-ə*] v. intr. Tomber en poussière. ‖ FIG. S'effondrer. (See DECAY.)

moulder [-ə*] n. Mouleur *m.*

moulding [-iŋ] n. ARTS., CULIN. Moulage *m.* ‖ NAUT. Gabariage *m.* ‖ ARCHIT. *Plain moulding,* listeau. ‖ ELECTR. Baguette *f.*

mouldy [-i] adj. Moisi. ‖ CULIN. Persillé (cheese). ‖ FAM. Assommant (evening) ; mal en train, patraque (person).

moult [moult] v. intr. Muer.
— v. tr. Changer de (feathers, skin).
— n. Mue *f.*

mound [maund] n. BLAS. Globe *m.*

mound n. Monticule *m.* (hill). ‖ Tumulus *m.* (over a grave). ‖ Remblai *m.*
— v. tr. Remblayer. ‖ Mettre en tas.

mount [maunt] n. Mont *m. ;* montagne *f.* (mountain). ‖ Monture *f.* (horse, support). ‖ SPORTS. Monte *f.*
— v. intr. Monter (*on,* sur) ; *to mount up to,* s'élever jusqu'à. ‖ Augmenter, croître (to increase). ‖ SPORTS. Monter.
— v. tr. Monter (a hill, the stairs). ‖ Monter sur (a table, the throne). ‖ TECHN. Monter (an engine, a jewel, a pulley). ‖ MILIT. Monter (guard) ; armer (a gun). ‖ NAUT. Porter (guns). ‖ THEATR. Monter (a play). ‖ SPORTS. Monter (a horse).

mountain [ˈmauntin] n. Montagne *f.* ‖ MED. *Mountain cure,* cure d'altitude ; *mountain sickness,* mal des montagnes. ‖ MILIT. *Mountain artillery,* artillerie de montagne. ‖ FIG. Montagne *f. ;* monceau *m.* (heap).

mountaineer [ˌmauntiˈniə*] n. Montagnard *s.* ‖ SPORTS. Alpiniste *s.*

mountaineering [-riŋ] n. SPORTS. Alpinisme *m.*

mountainous [ˈmauntinəs] adj. Montagneux. ‖ FAM. Monumental.

mountebank [ˈmauntibæŋk] n. Saltimbanque. ‖ FIG. Charlatan *m.*

mountebankery [-əri] n. Charlatanisme *m.*

mounted [ˈmauntid] adj. Monté, à cheval (police, infantry).

mourn [mɔːn] v. intr. Porter le deuil ; *to mourn for,* déplorer (a loss) ; pleurer (s.o.).
— v. tr. Pleurer (s.o.) ; déplorer (sth.).

mourner [-ə*] n. Affligé *s.* ‖ Membre d'un cortège funèbre *m. ;* chief *mourner,* personne qui conduit le deuil. ‖ † Pleureur *s.*

mournful [-ful] adj. Affligé, désolé (person) ; lugubre, funèbre (thing).

mournfully [-fuli] adv. Lugubrement, très tristement.

mournfulness [-fulnis] n. Tristesse *f. ;* air funèbre *m.*

mourning [-iŋ] n. Affliction, désolation *f.* ‖ Deuil *m. ; deep, half mourning,* grand, demi-deuil ; *mourning for,* en deuil de. ‖ **Mourning-band,** n. Crêpe *m.*

mousaka [muˈsɑːkə] n. CULIN. Moussaka *f.*

mouse [maus] (pl. **mice** [mais]) n. ZOOL. Souris *f. ; field mouse,* mulot. ‖ NAUT. Guirlande *f.* (of a rope). ‖ FAM. Rat *m.* (person). ‖ U. S. POP. Œil au beurre noir *m.*
— v. intr. Faire la chasse aux souris (cat).
— v. tr. Chasser, tâcher d'attraper. ‖ NAUT. Aiguilleter.

mouser [-ə*] n. Chasseur (*m.*) de souris, bon ratier *m.*

mousetrap [-træp] n. Souricière *f.*

mousse [muːs] n. CULIN. Mousse *f.* ‖ COMM. Crêpe, Nylon *m.*

moustache [musˈtɑːʃ] n. Moustache *f.*

mousy [ˈmausi] adj. De souris. ‖ Plein de souris. ‖ FAM. Terne (hair) ; effacé (person).

mouth [mauθ] n. Bouche *f.* (of ass, horse, man) ; gueule *f.* (of dog, lion). ‖ Grimace *f.* ‖ Entrée *f.* (of a bag, hole, port) ; goulot *m.* (of a bottle) ; embouchure *f.* (of a channel, river) ; gueule *f.* (of a firearm, an oven) ; gueulard *m.* (of a blast furnace) ; dégorgement *m.* (of a sewer) ; trou *m.* (of a well). ‖ FAM. Bec *m. ; not to open one's mouth,* ne pas desserrer les dents ; *to give mouth to,* exprimer ; *to have a big mouth,* avoir une grande gueule ; *to be down in the mouth,* avoir l'air défrisé. ‖ **Mouth-filling,** adj. Ronflant ; dont on a plein la bouche. ‖ **Mouth-organ,** n. MUS. Harmonica *m.* ‖ **Mouth-wash,** n. Dentifrice *m.*
— [mauð] v. tr. Déclamer (to declaim) ; dégoiser (fam.). ‖ Happer ; prendre dans la bouche (to take). ‖ SPORTS. Assurer la bouche de (a horse).
— v. intr. Déclamer. ‖ Grimacer.

mouthful [ˈmauθful] n. Bouchée *f.*

mouthing [ˈmauðiŋ] n. Déclamation, harangue *f. ;* verbiage ; dégoisage *m.* (fam.).

mouthpiece [ˈmauθpiːs] n. Tuyau *m.* (of pipe). ‖ Cornet *m.* (of microphone, telephone) ; embout *m.* (of speaking-tube). ‖ MUS. Embouchure *f.* ‖ FIG. Porte-parole *m.* (See SPOKESMAN.)

mouthy [ˈmauði] adj. Déclamatoire (bombastic). ‖ FAM. Vantard, hâbleur (boasting) ; braillard, fort en gueule (noisy).

movability [ˌmuːvəˈbiliti], **movableness** [ˈmuːvəblnis] n. Mobilité *f.*

movable [ˈmuːvəbl̩] adj. Mobile. ‖ JUR. Mobilier (effects) ; meuble (property).
— n. pl. Mobilier *m. ;* effets personnels *m. pl.* ‖ JUR. Biens meubles *m. pl.*

move [muːv] v. tr. Remuer, bouger, déplacer (to change the position of). ‖ Mouvoir, remuer, mettre en mouvement (or) en marche (to set in motion). ‖ Provoquer, soulever, exciter (to stir up), ‖ Inciter, pousser, porter, (*to,* à) [to incite]. ‖ Émouvoir, toucher, affecter, remuer (to touch). ‖ JUR. Déposer, soumettre, mettre aux voix (a resolution) ; *to move that,* proposer que. ‖ MED. Relâcher (the bowels). ‖ **To move about,** déplacer, changer de place. ‖ **To move away,** écarter, ôter, éloigner. ‖ **To move back,** faire reculer ; pousser en arrière. ‖ **To move forward,** avancer ; faire avancer. ‖ **To move in,** emménager (furniture) ; faire entrer (s.o.). ‖ **To move on,** faire circuler (a crowd). ‖ **To move out,** déménager (furniture) ; déloger, faire sortir (s.o.) ; sortir (sth.). ‖ **To move round,** tourner. ‖ **To move up,** monter, faire monter.
— v. intr. Remuer, bouger, se mouvoir (to change place). ‖ Se déplacer, se mettre en mouvement, aller

(to be in motion). ‖ Marcher, avancer (to walk). ‖ Déménager, changer d'appartement (to move out). ‖ Agir ; se remuer, se démener (fam.) [to be active]. ‖ Evoluer (*in*, *on*, dans) [to spend one's time]. ‖ Jur. Déposer une motion (or) résolution, faire une proposition. ‖ Sports. Jouer (at chess). ‖ Fig. Avancer, progresser (to advance). ‖ **To move about**, aller et venir. ‖ **To move away**, s'éloigner, s'en aller, se retirer. ‖ **To move back**, reculer. ‖ **To move forward**, avancer, s'avancer. ‖ **To move in**, emménager. ‖ **To move off**, s'éloigner, s'en aller (person) ; s'ébranler (procession) ; Autom. Démarrer ; Ch. de f. S'ébranler. ‖ **To move on**, se remettre en marche (carriage) ; avancer, circuler (person). ‖ **To move out**, déménager. ‖ **To move up**, avancer, monter.
— n. Mouvement *m*.; *to make a move*, se lever, s'en aller. ‖ Déménagement *m*. (change of residence). ‖ Sports. Coup *m*. (act) ; tour *m*. (turn) [at chess, draughts]. ‖ Jur. Mesure, action *f*. ‖ Fig. Mouvement, pas *m*.; *to make the first move*, prendre les devants, faire les premiers pas. ‖ Fam. *To be always on the move*, être toujours par monts et par vaux ; *to be up to every move*, la connaître dans les coins.

movement [-mənt] n. Mouvement *m*. (act) ; mouvement, geste *m*. (gesture). ‖ Mouvement, déplacement *m*.; *night movement*, déplacement de nuit. ‖ Allées et venues *f*. *pl*.; agissements, faits et gestes *m*. *pl*. (activities). ‖ Sports, Milit., Techn., Mus., Arts, Jur. Mouvement *m*. ‖ Gramm. Mouvement *m*.; cadence *f*. ‖ Fin. Activité *f*. (Exchange) ; mouvement *m*. (in price). ‖ Radio. Défilement *m*. (in T. V.). ‖ Med. Selle *f*. (faeces). ‖ Comm. Transport *m*. (of goods). ‖ Fig. Mouvement *m*. (of anger).

mover [-ə*] n. Philos. Moteur, mobile *m*. ‖ Jur. Motionnaire, auteur (*m*.) d'une motion. ‖ U. S. Déménageur *m*. ‖ Fig. Inspirateur, animateur *m*.

movie [-i] n. U. S. Film *m*.; pl. cinéma *m*.

moving [-iŋ] adj. Mouvant ; mobile. ‖ Roulant (staircase). ‖ Moteur *m*.; motrice *f*. (force). ‖ Theatr. *Moving picture*, projection (or) vue (or) image cinématographique. ‖ Fig. Animateur ; *moving spirit*, âme, cheville ouvrière. ‖ Fig. Emouvant, touchant (affecting).
— n. Mouvement *m*. ‖ Déplacement *m*. ‖ Déménagement *m*. ‖ Naut. Déballage *m*. ‖ **Moving away**, n. Eloignement *m*. ‖ **Moving back**, n. Recul, retour en arrière *m*. ‖ **Moving forward**, n. Avancée *f*.; marche (*f*.) en avant. ‖ **Moving in**, n. Emménagement *m*. (into a house) ; Milit. Pénétration *f*. ‖ **Moving off**, n. Départ *m*. ‖ **Moving out**, n. Déménagement *m*. (from a house) ; Milit. Sortie *f*.

movingly [-iŋli] adv. De façon émouvante.

mow [mou] v. tr. (104). Agric., Fig. Faucher.

mower [-ə*] n. Tondeuse *f*. (lawn-mower) ; faucheuse *f*. (reaper) ; faucheur *s*. (person).

mowing [-iŋ] n. Agric. Fauchage *m*. (of hay) ; tonte *f*. (of lawn). ‖ **Mowing-machine**, n. Agric. Faucheuse *f*. ‖ **Mowing-time**, n. Fauchaison *f*.

Mozambique [,mouzəm'bi:k] n. Geogr. Mozambique *m*.

M.P. [em'pi:] abbr. *Member of Parliament*, membre du Parlement, parlementaire, député. ‖ Milit. Abbr. *Military police*, police militaire.

m.p.g. Written abbr. for *miles per gallon*, indication de la consommation d'essence en « miles par gallon ».

m.p.h. Written abbr. for *miles per hour*, indication de la vitesse en « miles par heure ».

Mr. ['mistə*] (pl. **Messrs** ['mesəz]) n. Equivalent de M., Monsieur ; *Mr. Jones*, M. Jones ; *Mr. Secretary*, M. le Secrétaire.

Mrs. ['misiz] (pl. **Mrs.** or **Mesdames** ['mei,dæm]) n. Equivalent de Mme, Madame.

Ms. [miz] n. Forme ambiguë entre « Miss » et « Mrs. ».

M. Sc. [emes'si:] abbr. *Master of Science*, maîtrise en sciences (diploma), titulaire d'une maîtrise en sciences (graduate).

much [mʌtʃ] adj. Beaucoup de, une grande quantité de ; *much attention*, beaucoup d'attention ; *as much courage as*, autant de courage que ; *how much bread*, combien de pain ; *not so much courage as*, pas autant de courage que ; *too much money*, trop d'argent.
— pron., n. Beaucoup ; *it doesn't matter much*, ça n'a pas grande importance ; *there is not much in it*, il n'y a pas grand-chose là-dedans ; *that was too much for him*, c'était trop pour lui ; *they were too much for him*, il n'était pas de taille à leur résister ; *they do not see much of one another*, ils ne se voient pas souvent ; *through much of the night*, pendant une bonne partie de la nuit ; *to make much of*, faire grand cas de, attacher beaucoup d'importance à ; *you have much to be thankful for*, vous avez tout lieu d'être reconnaissant ; *you are not much of a scholar*, vous n'êtes rien moins que calé, vous n'êtes pas un fameux savant. ‖ Fam. *It's a bit much*, c'est un peu trop fort ; *it isn't up to much*, c'est très quelconque ; *much he knows about it !*, surtout qu'il en sait bien qqch. !
— adv. Beaucoup ; *as much*, autant ; *as much again*, encore autant ; *as* (or) *so much as*, autant que ; *by that much*, de tout cela ; *how much*, combien ; *it is as much as saying that*, autant dire que ; *much as*, pour autant que ; *much the same*, environ (or) à peu près le même ; *much more*, beaucoup plus ; *much to my regret*, à mon vif regret ; *not so much as*, pas autant (or) tant que ; *quite as much as*, tout autant que ; *so much*, tant, tellement, si ; *so much that*, tant que ; *so much the better*, tant mieux ; *so much the less, the more, as*, d'autant moins, plus, que ; *so much so that*, à tel point que ; *too much*, trop ; *this, that much*, autant que, ceci, cela ; *very much*, beaucoup, grandement ; *without so much as*, sans même. ‖ Beaucoup, vivement (with a verb) ; *much to do*, beaucoup à faire. ‖ Très, fort (with a past part.) ; *much concerned*, très inquiet. ‖ Beaucoup (with a comp. or superl.) ; *much better*, beaucoup mieux ; *much the best*, de beaucoup le meilleur. ‖ Fam. *I expected as much*, je m'y attendais bien ; *he would not so much as open his mouth*, il n'a pas seulement daigné ouvrir la bouche ; *not much !*, plus souvent !, mon œil ! ; *so much for him !*, et voilà pour lui ! ; *so much for that !*, et d'une.

muchness [-nis] n. Quantité *f*. ‖ Fam. *Much of a muchness*, kif kif, bonnet blanc et blanc bonnet.

mucilage ['mju:silidʒ] n. Mucilage *m*. ‖ U. S. Colle *f*. (gum).

mucilaginous [,mju:si'lædʒinəs] adj. Mucilagineux.

muck [mʌk] n. Fumier *m*. (manure). ‖ Boue, gadoue *f*. (mud). ‖ Fam. Saleté, cochonnerie *f*. ‖ **Muckheap** (or) **-hill**, n. Tas de fumier *m*.
— v. tr. Salir, souiller. ‖ Fam. *To muck up*, cochonner, saloper.
— v. intr. **To muck about**, Fam. Traînailler.

mucker [-ə*] n. Fam. Billet de parterre *m*.; bûche *f*. (See cropper.)

muckrake [-reik] v. intr. Dévoiler des scandales.

muckraker [-reikə*] n. Déterreur (*m*.) de scandales.

muckworm [-wə:m] n. Zool. Ver de fumier *m*.

mucky [-i] adj. Sale, crotté.

mucosity [mju:'kɔsiti] n. Med. Mucosité *f*.

mucous ['mju:kəs] adj. Med. Muqueux ; *mucous membrane*, muqueuse.

mucus n. Med. Mucus *m*.; mucosité *f*.

mud [mʌd] n. Boue, fange ; gadoue *f*. (on a road) ; *stuck in the mud*, embourbé. ‖ Vase *f*.; limon *m*. (in a river). ‖ Archit. Torchis *m*.; *mud wall*, mur en torchis. ‖ Fig. Boue *f*. ‖ **Mud-bath**, n. Med. Bain (*m.*) de boue. ‖ **Mud-flap,** n. Garde-boue (*m.*) en caoutchouc. ‖ **Mud-flat,** n. Slikke, vasière littorale *f.* ‖ **Mud-pack,** n. Masque (*m.*) de beauté. ‖ **Mud-shovel,** n. Bogue *f.* ‖ **Mud-slinger,** n. Calomniateur *m.*; calomniatrice *f.* ‖ **Mud-slinging,** n. Attaques calomnieuses *f. pl.*

muddiness [-inis] n. Saleté *f.*; état boueux *m.* ‖ Aspect trouble *m.* (of a liquid). ‖ FIG. Confusion *f.*

muddle ['mʌdḷ] n. Désordre, fouillis, embrouilla-mini *m.* (jumble). ‖ FIG. Désarroi *m.* ‖ FAM. Pagaille *f.*; *a dreadful muddle,* la bouteille à l'encre. ‖ **Muddle-headed,** adj. Brouillon, confus, fumeux. ‖ **Muddle-headedness,** n. Confusion *f.*

— v. tr. Embrouiller, emmêler; mettre la pagaille dans; emberlificoter (fam.); *muddled at the start,* mal parti. ‖ FIG. Obscurcir (the brain); embrouiller (the ideas).

— v. intr. FAM. Tripatouiller, tripoter. ‖ **To muddle through,** se débrouiller tant bien que mal; se dépa-touiller (fam.); se démerder (obscene).

muddler [-ə*] n. Brouillon *m.* ‖ U. S. Marteau-mixer *m.* (swizzle-stick).

muddy [-i] adj. Boueux, fangeux (road); bourbeux, vaseux (river). ‖ Crotté, plein de boue (clothes). ‖ Terne, gris (light); trouble (liquid). ‖ MED. Ter-reux, brouillé (complexion). ‖ TECHN. Nuageux (diamond). ‖ FAM. Vague (thinking).

— v. tr. (2). Salir, crotter. ‖ Troubler (a liquid). ‖ MED. Brouiller (the complexion). ‖ FAM. Brouiller, obscurcir (the mind).

mudguard [-gɑ:d] n. AUTOM. Garde-boue *m.*

mudlark [-lɑ:k] n. FAM. Loupiot, poulbot *m.*

muesli ['mju:zli] n. CULIN. Muesli *m.*

muezzin [mu:'ezin] n. Muezzin *m.*

muff [mʌf] n. Manchon *m.*

muff n. SPORTS. Loupage, coup raté *m.* ‖ FAM. Cornichon, daim *m.*; andouille, noix *f.*

— v. intr. FAM. U. S. Foirer.

— v. tr. FAM. Louper, rater.

muffin ['mʌfin] n. CULIN. Petit gâteau mollet beurré et grillé *m.*; U. S. Pain moufflet *m.*

muffle ['mʌfl] n. Mufle *m.* (of cow).

muffle n. Moufle *f.* (glove). ‖ TECHN., CHIM. Moufle *m.*

— v. tr. Emmitoufler (to wrap); *to muffle oneself up,* s'emmitoufler. ‖ Assourdir, étouffer (to deaden).

muffler [-ə*] n. Cache-nez *m.* (scarf). ‖ AUTOM. Pot d'échappement *m.* ‖ MUS. Etouffoir *m.*

mufti ['mʌfti] n. Muphti *m.* ‖ MILIT., NAUT. Cos-tume civil *m.*; *in mufti,* en civil, en pékin.

mug [mʌg] n. Timbale *f.* ‖ MILIT. Tin mug, quart. ‖ FAM. Daim, cornichon *m.*; cruche *f.*; *what do you take me for, a mug?,* tu ne m'as pas regardé, non?; tu me prends pour une andouille? ‖ FAM. Bille, bobine, binette, bouille, trompette, fiole *f.* (phiz); *ugly mug,* gueule d'empeigne.

— v. tr. POP. U. S. Photographier.

— v. intr. THEATR. U. S. Exagérer les jeux de phy-sionomie.

mug v. tr. FAM. Bûcher, potasser, piocher.

mug v. tr. Agresser (or) attaquer dans la rue, voler.

mugger [-ə*] n. Auteur (*m.*) d'une agression.

mugginess ['mʌginis] n. Lourdeur, chaleur pesante *f.* (of weather).

mugging [-iŋ] n. Agression, attaque *f.* (robbery).

muggins ['mʌginz] (pl. **mugginses** or **muggins**) n. FAM. Imbécile, abruti, crétin, nigaud s.; *muggins will get landed with it again,* c'est encore ma pomme (or) mézigue qui va écoper.

muggy [-i] adj. Mou, chaud et humide (weather).

mugwort ['mʌgwɔ:t] n. BOT. Armoise *f.*

mugwump [-wʌmp] n. U. S. Indépendant *m.* (in politics). ‖ FAM. Grand manitou *m.*

mulatto [mju'lætou] adj., n. Mulâtre *m.*

mulattress [-tris] n. Mulâtresse *f.*

mulberry ['mʌlberi] n. BOT. Mûrier *m.* (bush); mûre *f.* (fruit).

mulch [mʌltʃ] n. AGRIC. Paillis *m.*

— v. tr. AGRIC. Pailler.

mulct [mʌlkt] n. JUR. Amende *f.*

— v. tr. JUR. Frapper d'une amende. ‖ FIG. Priver, dépouiller (of, de).

mule [mju:l] n. ZOOL. Mulet *m.* (he); mule *f.* (she). ‖ TECHN. Renvideur *m.* ‖ COMM. Mule *f.* (slipper). ‖ U. S. NAUT. Tracteur *m.* ‖ FAM. Mule *f.* ‖ **Mule-driver,** n. Muletier *m.* ‖ **Mule-jenny,** n. TECHN. Renvideur *m.*

muleteer [,mju:li'tiə*] n. Muletier *m.*

mulish ['mju:liʃ] adj. ZOOL. De mulet. ‖ FAM. Têtu comme une mule, entêté. (See STUBBORN.)

mulishly [-li] adv. Opiniâtrement.

mulishness [-nis] n. Obstination, opiniâtreté *f.*; entêtement *m.*

mull [mʌl] v. intr. U. S. FAM. *To mull over,* rumi-ner, ressasser.

— v. tr. CULIN. Chauffer et épicer.

mullah ['mʌlə] n. Mollah, mulla *m.*

mulled [mʌld] adj. CULIN. Chaud et épicé (wine).

mullein ['mʌlin] n. BOT. Molène *f.*

muller ['mʌlə*] n. TECHN., MED. Molette *f.*

mullet ['mʌlit] n. ZOOL. Mulet *m.* (fish); red *mullet,* rouget.

mulligan ['mʌligən] n. U. S. POP. Ragoût *m.*

mullion ['mʌliən] n. ARCHIT. Meneau *m.*

mullioned [-d] adj. ARCHIT. A meneaux.

multicoloured [,mʌlti'kʌləd] adj. Multicolore.

multicylinder [-'silində*] adj. Polycylindrique.

multifarious [-'fɛəriəs] adj. Extrêmement varié. ‖ Multiple. (See MANIFOLD.)

multifariousness [-'fɛəriəsnis] n. Extrême diver-sité, multiplicité *f.*

multiform ['mʌltifɔ:m] adj. Multiforme.

multilateral [,mʌlti'lætərəl] adj. Multilatéral.

multilingual [,mʌlti'liŋgwəl] adj. Multilingue, plurilingue.

multimillionaire [,mʌltimiljə'nɛə*] adj., n. Multimillionnaire, milliardaire s.

multimotored [,mʌlti'moutəd] adj. Multi-moteur.

multinational [-'næʃənḷ] adj. Multinational.

— n. FIN., COMM. Multinationale *f.*

multinomial [-'noumiəl] adj., n. MATH. Poly-nôme *m.*

multiparous [mʌl'tipərəs] adj. MED., ZOOL. Mul-tipare.

multipartite [mʌlti'pɑ:tait] adj. A divisions mul-tiples. ‖ JUR. Multipartite.

multiphase [-'feiz] adj. ELECTR. Multiphasé.

multiplane [-'plein] n. AVIAT. Multiplan *m.*

multiple ['mʌltipl] adj. Multiple. ‖ ELECTR. En parallèle, en batterie (connection). ‖ COMM. A suc-cursales multiples (store). ‖ AGRIC. Polysoc (plough). ‖ MED. En plaques (sclerosis).

— n. MATH. Multiple *m.*

multiplex [-pleks] adj. Multiple (manifold). ‖ ELECTR. Multiplex.

— v. tr. ELECTR. Envoyer par multiplex.

multipliable [-'plaiəbḷ], **multiplicable** [-plikəbḷ] adj. Multipliable.

multiplicand [,mʌltipli'kænd] n. MATH. Multipli-cande *m.*

multiplication ['mʌltipli'keiʃən] n. MATH. Multi-plication *f.*; *multiplication table,* table de multipli-cation. ‖ TECHN. Amplification *f.*

multiplicative [,mʌltipli'keitiv] adj. MATH. Multi-plicatif.

multiplicity ['mʌlti'plisiti] n. Multiplicité *f.*

multiplier ['mʌltiplaiə*] n. MATH., ELECTR. Mul-tiplicateur *m.*

multiply [-plai] v. tr. (2). MATH., TECHN., MED., ECCLES. Multiplier.

— v. intr. Se multiplier.

multiplying [-plaiiŋ] adj. Multipliant; multiplicatif. ‖ **Multiplying-gear,** n. TECHN. Multiplication *f.*
— n. Multiplication *f.*

multi-purpose [ˌmʌlti'pə:pəs] adj. A tous usages, polyvalent.

multiracial [-'reiʃəl] adj. Multiracial.

multi-storey [-'stɔ:ri] adj. A plusieurs étages, en hauteur (building); *multi-storey block,* tour.

multitude ['mʌltitju:d] n. Multitude *f.*

multitudinous [ˌmʌlti'tju:dinəs] adj. Très nombreux (numerous). ‖ Multiple, divers (manifold). ‖ En foule, à flots (crowded).

multivalence [-'veiləns] n. CHIM. Polyvalence *f.*

multivalent [-'veilənt] adj. CHIM. Polyvalent.

mum [mʌm] interj. Motus; *mum's the word!,* pas un mot!
— adj. Silencieux, coi; *to keep mum,* ne pas piper, la boucler (fam.).
— v. intr. (1). Parler par signes, mimer.

mum n. POP. Maman *f.* ‖ POP. Madame *f.* ‖ U.S. FAM. Chrysanthème *m.*

mumble ['mʌmbl] v. tr., intr. Marmonner, marmotter. ‖ † Mâchonner (to chew).
— n. Marmottement *m.*

mumbler [-ə*] n. Marmotteur *s.*

mumbling [-iŋ] adj. Marmottant.
— n. Marmottage *m.*

mumbo-jumbo ['mʌmbou'dʒʌmbou] n. Simagrées *f. pl.,* momerie *f.* (meaningless ritual). ‖ Charabia, galimatias *m.* (gibberish). ‖ Fétiche *m.* (idol).

mummer ['mʌmə*] n. THEATR. Mime *m.* ‖ FAM. Cabotin *m.*

mummery [-ri] n. THEATR. Pantomime *f.* ‖ FAM. Mômerie *f.*

mummification [ˌmʌmifi'keiʃən] n. Momification *f.*

mummify ['mʌmifai] v. tr. (2). Momifier.
— v. intr. Se momifier.

mummy ['mʌmi] n. FAM. Maman *f.*

mummy n. Momie *f.; mummy cloth,* bandelette.

mump [mʌmp] v. intr. Bouder.

mumpish ['mʌmpiʃ] adj. Boudeur, renfrogné.

mumps [mʌmps] n. pl. MED. Oreillons *m. pl.* ‖ † Bouderie *f.*

munch [mʌnʃ] v. tr. Mâcher. (See CHEW.)

mundane ['mʌndein] adj. Mondain, du monde, du siècle. (See WORLDLY.) ‖ De la terre, terrestre (earthly).

mundaneness [-nis] n. Mondanité *f.*

municipal [mju'nisipəl] adj. Municipal; *municipal corporation,* municipalité.

municipality [mjuːnisi'pæliti] n. Municipalité *f.*

municipalize [mjuː'nisipəlaiz] v. tr. Municipaliser.

munificence [mju'nifisns] n. Munificence *f.*

munificent [-ŋt] adj. Munificent.

munificently [-ŋtli] adv. Avec munificence.

muniment ['mjuːnimənt] n. JUR. Archives *f. pl.*

munition [mjuːˈniʃən] n. MILIT. Munition *f.* ‖ **Munition-factory,** n. Fabrique (*f.*) de munitions.
— v. tr. MILIT. Amunitionner.

mural ['mjuərəl] adj. Mural.
— n. ARTS. U.S. Peinture murale *f.*

muralist [-ist] n. ARTS. Fresquiste *s.*

murder ['mə:də*] n. Assassinat *m.* ‖ LOC. *Murder will out,* tôt ou tard la vérité se fait jour.
— v. tr. Assassiner. ‖ FAM. Massacrer.

murderer [-rə*] n. Meurtrier; assassin *m.*

murderess [-ris] n. Meurtrière *f.*

murderous [-rəs] adj. Homicide (act, intent); meurtrier (war, weapon).

mure [mjuə*] v. tr. *To mure up,* murer (a window). ‖ FAM. Claquemurer (s.o.).

murex ['mjuəreks] n. ZOOL. Murex *m.*

muriatic [ˌmjuəri'ætik] adj. CHIM. Muriatique.

murk [mə:k] adj. Obscur. (See DARK.)
— n. Ténèbres *f. pl.*

murkiness [-inis] n. Obscurité *f.*

murky [-i] adj. Obscur, ténébreux. (See GLOOMY.)

murmur ['mʌ:mə*] n. Murmure *m.*
— v. intr., tr. Murmurer.

murmuring [-iŋ] adj. Murmurant.
— n. Murmures *m. pl.*

murphy ['mə:fi] n. CULIN., POP. Patate *f.* (potato).

murrain ['mʌrin] n. MED. Epizootie *f.* ‖ † Peste *f.*

muscadine ['mʌskədin], **muscat** ['mʌskət], **muscatel** [ˌmʌskə'tel] n. Muscat *m.* (grape, wine).

muscidae ['mʌsidiː] n. pl. ZOOL. Muscidés *m. pl.*

muscle ['mʌsl] n. MED. Muscle *m.* (See BRAWN.) ‖ FAM. *Not to move a muscle,* ne pas ciller. ‖ **Muscle-man,** n. FAM. Athlète; costaud; type à biceps *m.* (pop.).
— v. intr. **To muscle in on,** U.S. FAM. S'immiscer dans; pénétrer à la force du poignet dans.

muscled [-d] adj. Musclé.

muscovado [ˌmʌskə'vɑ:dou] n. Cassonade *f.*

Muscovite ['mʌskəvait] adj., n. GEOGR. Moscovite *s.*
— n. COMM. Mica *m.*

Muscovy ['mʌskəvi] n. Moscovie *f.*

muscular ['mʌskjulə*] adj. MED. Musculaire (action, tissue); musclé (body).

muscularity [ˌmʌskju'læriti] n. MED. Musculosité *f.* (of a limb); muscularité *f.* (of tissue).

musculature ['mʌskjulətʃə*] n. MED. Musculature *f.*

muse [mju:z] n. Muse *f.*

muse v. intr. Méditer, réfléchir. (See PONDER.) ‖ Rêver, songer (on, à). ‖ Se laisser aller à rêver (on, sur, devant).
— n. † Rêverie *f.*

musette [mju:'zet] n. MUS. Musette *f.* ‖ **Musette bag,** n. MILIT. U.S. Musette *f.* (haversack).

museum [mju'ziəm] n. Musée *m.* (of art, antiquities); muséum *m.* (of natural history).

mush [mʌʃ] n. U.S. CULIN. Gaude *f.* ‖ RADIO. Brouillage *m.* ‖ FAM., CULIN. Bouillie *f.* ‖ POP. Niaiserie *f.; U.S. Mush talk,* fadaises.
— v. intr. U.S. POP. Se dire des niaiseries; se peloter. ‖ U.S. Voyager à pied dans la neige près d'un traîneau.

mushroom ['mʌʃrum] n. BOT. Champignon *m.*
— adj. De champignons (bed); aux champignons (hunt). ‖ ELECTR. A cloche (insulator). ‖ FAM. Champignon (town).
— v. intr. Chercher les champignons. ‖ S'aplatir comme un champignon (to flatten). ‖ U.S. Pousser comme un champignon; se propager, s'étendre.

mushrooming [-iŋ] n. Cueillette (*f.*) des champignons; *to go mushrooming,* aller à la chasse aux champignons.

mushy ['mʌʃi] adj. Mou, en bouillie (food); détrempé (ground). ‖ RADIO. Brouillé. ‖ FAM. Fade, niais, à l'eau de rose, à la guimauve.

music ['mju:zik] n. Musique *f.; cheap music,* musiquette; *to set to music,* mettre en musique (a poem). ‖ **Music-book,** n. Cahier (*m.*) à musique. ‖ **Music-folio,** n. Carton (*m.*) à musique. ‖ **Music-hall,** n. Music-hall *m.; U.S.* Auditorium *m.* ‖ **Music-lover,** n. Musicomane *s.* ‖ **Music-master,** n. Professeur (*m.*) de musique. ‖ **Music-paper,** n. Papier (*m.*) à musique. ‖ **Music-stand,** n. Pupitre *m.* ‖ **Music-stool,** n. Tabouret de piano *m.*

musical [-əl] adj. MUS. A musique (box); musical (ear, evening); de musique (instrument); musicien (person); mélodieux (verse). ‖ THEATR. *Musical comedy,* opérette.
— n. THEATR. Opérette *f.*

musicality [ˌmju:zi'kæliti] n. MUS. Musicalité *f.*

musically ['mju:zikəli] adv. MUS. Musicalement.

musicalness [-nis] s. Harmonie, mélodie *f*.
musician [mju:'ziʃən] n. Mus. Musicien *s*.
musicographer [,mju:zi'kɔgrəfə*] n. Mus. Musicographe *s*.
musicologist [-lɔdʒist] n. Mus. Musicologue *s*.
musicology [-lədʒi] n. Mus. Musicologie *f*.
musing ['mju:ziŋ] adj. Rêveur, songeur.
— n. Rêverie, songerie *f*.
musk [mʌsk] n. Musc *m*. ‖ **Musk-deer**, n. Zool. Musc *m*. ‖ **Musk-melon**, n. Bot. Cantaloup *m*. ‖ **Musk-rat**, n. Zool. Rat musqué, ondatra *m.;* Comm. Castor du Canada *m*. ‖ **Musk-rose**, n. Bot. Rose musquée *f*.
musket ['mʌskit] n. Milit. † Mousquet *m*.
musketeer [,mʌski'tiə*] n. Milit. † Mousquetaire *m*.
musketry ['mʌskitri] n. Milit. † Mousqueterie *f*.
musky ['mʌski] adj. Musqué.
Muslim ['mʌzlim] adj., n. Musulman *adj., s*. (See Moslem.)
muslin ['mʌzlin] n. Mousseline *f.; cambric muslin*, percale. ‖ U. S. Indienne *f*. (calico).
muslinet [,mʌzli'net] n. Mousseline (*f.*) de coton.
musquash ['mʌskwɔʃ]. See Musk-rat.
muss [mʌs] n. U. S. Désordre, fouillis *m*.
— v. tr. U. S. Chiffonner, froisser (a dress); ébouriffer (hair).
mussel ['mʌsl̩] n. Zool. Moule *f*.
Mussulman ['mʌslmən] adj., n. Musulman *s*.
mussy ['mʌsi] adj. U. S. En désordre (disorderly); sale (dirty); froissé (rumpled).
must [mʌst] v. defect. Falloir, être nécessaire de (necessity); *I must see him*, il faut que je le voie. ‖ Falloir, devoir (obligation); *if you wish to find him at home, you must arrive before five*, si vous voulez le trouver chez lui, il faudra arriver avant cinq heures; *what must we do?*, que faire? ‖ Devoir, falloir, être obligatoire de (compulsion); *I must pay her*, il faut que je la paie; je dois absolument la payer. ‖ Devoir (probability); *he must be a foreigner*, il doit être étranger; *you must know him*, vous le connaissez sans doute. ‖ Devoir (certainty, deduction); *it must be*, c'est plus que probable; *it must have rained while we were in*, il a dû pleuvoir pendant que nous étions à l'intérieur. ‖ Falloir, ne pas manquer de (fatality); *just as I was sleeping, he must turn on the radio*, juste comme je dormais, le voilà qui (or) il a fallu qu'il ouvre la radio!; *why must he be always talking?*, pourquoi faut-il qu'il parle sans cesse? ‖ Pouvoir, avoir le droit de (in negative sentences); *you mustn't touch the cake*, il ne faut pas toucher au gâteau.
— n. U. S. Impératif *m.; a helmet is an absolute must in the tropics*, le port d'un casque colonial est une nécessité absolue aux tropiques; *this book is a must*, c'est un livre qu'il faut lire.
— adj. U. S. Nécessaire, essentiel.
must n. Moût *m*. (before fermentation); vin doux *m*. (new wine).
must n. Moisi *m*.; moisissure *f*.
mustache [mə'stɑ:ʃ] n. U. S. See Moustache.
mustang ['mʌstæŋ] n. Zool. Mustang *m*.
mustard ['mʌstəd] n. Bot., Culin. Moutarde *f*. ‖ **Mustard-gas**, n. Milit. Ypérite *f*. ‖ **Mustard-maker**, n. Moutardier *m*. ‖ **Mustard-plaster** (or) **-poultice**, n. Med. Sinapisme, cataplasme sinapisé, autoplasme *m*. ‖ **Mustard-pot**, n. Culin. Pot (*m*.) à moutarde.
muster ['mʌstə*] n. Rassemblement *m*. (act); assemblée *f*. (meeting). ‖ Milit. Revue *f*. ‖ Naut. Appel *m*. ‖ Fam. Bande, troupe *f*. ‖ **Muster-roll**, n. Milit. Feuille (*f.*) d'appel, contrôles *m*. pl.; Naut. Rôle *m*.
— v. tr. Assembler, rassembler, réunir, grouper. ‖ Assembler (the crew); faire l'appel de (ratings). ‖ **To muster in**, U. S. Milit. Enrôler. ‖ **To**

muster out, U. S. Milit. Démobiliser. ‖ **To muster up**, Fig. Rassembler (strength).
— v. intr. S'assembler, se réunir.
mustering-in [-riŋ'in] n. U. S. Milit. Enrôlement *m*.
mustering-out [-riŋ'aout] n. U. S. Milit. Démobilisation *f*.
mustiness ['mʌstinis] n. Moisi, goût de moisi *m*.
musty ['mʌsti] adj. Moisi (bread); *to grow musty*, moisir. ‖ Renfermé, confiné (see Stuffy); *musty smell*, remugle. ‖ Fam. Vieux jeu.
mutability [,mju:tə'biliti] n. Mutabilité *f*. ‖ Inconstance *f*. (fickleness).
mutable ['mju:təbl] adj. Muable, variable, changeable. ‖ Changeant, inconstant (fickel). ‖ Gramm. Métaphonisable (vowel).
mutant ['mju:tnt] adj., n. Mutant *adj., m*.
mutate [mju:'teit] v. tr. Zool., Bot: Faire muter.
— v. intr. Zool., Bot. Muter.
mutation [mju:'teiʃən] n. Altération *f.;* changement *m*. ‖ Med. Mutation *f*. ‖ Gramm. Métaphonie *f*. (of a vowel).
mutatis mutandis [mu:'tɑ:tis mu:'tændis] adv. Mutatis mutandis.
mutative [-tiv] adj. Gramm. Métaphonique.
mute [mju:t] adj. Muet, silencieux (silent). ‖ Muet, incapable de parler. (See Voiceless.) ‖ Gramm. Sourd (consonant); muet (h, vowel).
— n. Med. Muet *m*. ‖ Mus. Sourdine *f*. ‖ Theatr. Personnage muet *m*. ‖ Gramm. Consonne sourde *f.;* voyelle muette *f*. ‖ Jur. Accusé (*m*.) qui refuse de se défendre.
— v. tr. Mus. Mettre la sourdine à.
mutely [-li] adv. En silence.
muteness [-nis] n. Med. Mutisme *m*. ‖ Fig. Mutisme, silence *f*.
mutilate ['mju:tileit] v. tr. Mutiler, estropier. (See Maim.) ‖ Fig. Mutiler, tronquer. (See Mangle.)
mutilation [,mju:ti'leiʃən] n. Mutilation *f*.
mutilator ['mju:tileitə*] n. Mutilateur *m.;* mutilatrice *f*.
mutineer [,mju:ti'niə*] n. Naut., Milit. Mutin *m*. ‖ Fig. Révolté *s*.
mutinous ['mju:tinəs] adj. Naut. Mutiné. ‖ Fig. En révolte, révolté, rebellé.
mutinously [-nəsli] adv. Séditieusement; avec révolte (or) rébellion.
mutiny [-ni] n. Naut., Milit. Mutinerie *f*. ‖ Fig. Révolte *f.;* soulèvement *m*.
— v. intr. (2). Naut., Milit. Se mutiner. ‖ Fig. Se révolter.
mutism ['mju:tizm̩] n. Mutisme *m*.
mutt [mʌt] n. Pop. Andouille *f.;* crétin *m*. (blockhead). ‖ U. S. Pop. Cabot *m*. (dog).
mutter ['mʌtə*] v. intr. Marmonner. (See Mumble.) ‖ Marmonner, grommeler, ronchonner, bougonner (to grumble). ‖ Gronder (thunder).
— v. tr. Marmotter, marmonner.
— n. Marmottement *m*. (mumbling). ‖ Grommellement *m*. (grumbling).
mutton ['mʌtn̩] n. Culin. Mouton *m.; leg of mutton*, gigot; *mutton fat*, graisse de mouton, suif. ‖ **Mutton-chop**, n. Culin. Côtelette (*f.*) de mouton; Pl. Fam. Côtelettes *f*. pl. (side-whiskers).
muttonhead [-'hed] n. Fam. Cornichon *m*.
mutual ['mju:tjuəl] adj. Mutuel (consent, effort, service). ‖ Réciproque (aid, conquest, hatred). ‖ Commun (consent, friend). ‖ Jur. Mutuel (insurance); *mutual benefit society*, société de secours mutuels, mutuelle; *mutual testament*, donation au dernier vivant; *on mutual terms*, à des conditions de réciprocité. ‖ Fin. *Mutual savings bank*, banque d'épargne mutuelle.
mutualism [-izm̩] n. Mutualisme *m*.
mutuality [,mjutju'æliti] n. Mutualité *f*.
muzzle ['mʌzl] n. Museau *m*. (nose). ‖ Muselière *f*. (strap). ‖ Milit. Gueule, bouche *f*. (of a gun).

‖ **Muzzle-loader,** n. MILIT. Arme (*f.*) qu'on charge par le canon. ‖ **Muzzle-velocity,** n. MILIT. Vitesse initiale *f.*
— v. tr. Museler (lit. and fig.).
muzzy ['mʌzi] adj. FAM. Flou (ideas); abruti, hébété (person).
my [mai] adj. poss. Mon *m.*; ma *f.*; mes *pl.*; *I broke my leg,* je me suis cassé une jambe.
— interj. *Oh! my!,* fichtre!, par exemple!
mycology [mai'kɔlədʒi] n. BOT. Mycologie *f.*
myelitis [,maiə'laitis] n. MED. Myélite *f.*
myeloma [,maiə'loumə] n. MED. Myélome *m.*
myna(h) ['mainə] n. ZOOL. Mainate *m.*
myocarditis [,maiokɑ:'daitis] n. MED. Myocardite *f.*
myocardium [maio'kɑ:diəm] n. MED. Myocarde *m.*
myope ['maioup] n. MED. Myope *s.*
myopia [mai'oupiə], **myopy** ['maioupi] n. MED. Myopie *f.*
myopic [mai'ɔpik] adj. MED. De myope, myope.
myositis [,maio'soutis] n. BOT. Myosotis *m.*
myriad ['miriəd] n. Myriade *f.*
— adj. Innombrable.
myriapod ['miriəpɔd] n. ZOOL. Myriapode *m.*
myrmidon ['mə:midən] n. Myrmidon *m.* ‖ FAM. Spadassin *m.* (ruffian); *myrmidons of the law,* sbires.
myrobalan [mai'rɔbələn] n. BOT. Myrobalan *m.*
myrrh [mə:*] n. Myrrhe *f.*
myrtle ['mə:tl̩] n. BOT. Myrte *m.* ‖ U. S. Pervenche *f.*
myself [mai'self] pron. Moi-même, en personne (emphatic); *I went myself,* j'y suis allé moi-même. ‖ Me (reflexive); *I hurt myself,* je me suis fait mal. ‖ Moi-même (my true self); *I am not myself,* je sors de mes gonds, je suis hors de moi, je ne me connais plus. ‖ FAM. *I am not feeling quite myself,* je ne me sens pas tout à fait d'aplomb.
mysterious [mis'tiəriəs] adj. Mystérieux.
mysteriously [-li] adv. Mystérieusement.
mysteriousness [-nis] n. Mystère *m.*; nature mystérieuse *f.*

mystery ['mistəri] n. ECCLES., THEATR., FIG. Mystère *m.* ‖ **Mystery-man,** n. Homme mystérieux *m.* ‖ **Mystery-play,** n. THEATR. Mystère *m.* ‖ **Mystery story,** n. U. S. Roman (*m.*) à sensation.
mystic ['mistik] adj. Magique (formula); occulte (power); ésotérique (rite); surnaturel (truth). ‖ Mystérieux, énigmatique. ‖ ECCLES. Mystique.
— n. Initié *s.* ‖ ECCLES. Mystique *m.*
mystical [-əl] adj. ECCLES. Mystique; *mystical theology,* mystique.
mystically [-əli] adv. ECCLES. Mystiquement.
mysticalness [-əlnis] n. ECCLES., PHILOS. Mysticité *f.*
mysticism ['mistisizm̩] n. ECCLES., PHILOS. Mysticisme *m.*
mystification [,mistifi'keiʃən] n. Mystification *f.*; tour *m.* (See HOAX.) ‖ Mystère *m.*; obscurité, complexité *f.* (of a question); perplexité *f.* (of a person).
mystify ['mistifai] v. tr. (2). Mystifier. (See HOAX.) ‖ Embrouiller, obscurcir, entourer de mystère (or) de complications (a question). ‖ Embrouiller, désorienter, intriguer (s.o.).
mystique [mi:s'tik] n. Mystique *f.*
myth [miθ] n. Mythe *m.*
mythic(al) [miθik(əl)] adj. Mythique.
mythicize ['miθisaiz] v. tr. Donner un sens mythique à.
mythographer [mi'θɔgrəfə*] n. Mythographe *s.*
mythologer [-lədʒə*], **mythologist** [-lədʒist] n. Mythologue *s.*
mythologic(al) [,miθə'lɔdʒik(əl)] adj. Mythologique.
mythologize [mi'θɔlədʒaiz] v. tr. Faire un mythe de. (See MYTHICIZE.)
— v. intr. Etudier la mythologie.
mythology [-dʒi] n. Mythologie *f.*
mythomania [,miθə'meiniə] n. MED. Mythomanie *f.*
mythomaniac [-ək] n. MED. Mythomane *s.*
myxomatosis [,miksəmə'tousis] n. MED. Myxomatose *f.*

N

n [en] n. N, n *m.* (letter). ‖ MATH. n (indefinite number); *to the nth power,* à la n-ième puissance, à la puissance n. ‖ PHYS. N, newton *m.* ‖ CHIM. N, azote *m.* ‖ GEOGR. N., nord *m.* (north); du nord (or) septentrional (northern).
nab [næb] v. tr. (1). FAM. Pincer, cueillir, coincer (s.o.); pincer, choper, chauffer (sth.); *to get nabbed,* se faire pincer.
nabob ['neibɔb] n. Nabab *m.*
nacelle [næ'sel] n. AVIAT. Nacelle *f.*
nacre ['neikə*] n. Nacre *f.* ‖ ZOOL. Pinne marine *f.*
nacr(e)ous [-kriəs] adj. Nacré. (See PEARLY.)
nadir ['neidiə*] n. ASTRON. Nadir *m.* ‖ FIG. Stade le plus bas *m.*
naevus ['ni:vəs] (pl. **naevi** [-vai]) n. MED. Nævus *m.*

nag [næg] n. FAM. Bidet, canasson *m.* (hack). ‖ U. S. FAM. Vieux tacot *m.* (jalopy).
nag n. Querelle, chamaillerie *f.*
— v. tr. Quereller, harceler, bousculer.
— v. intr. Criailler, vociférer (*at,* contre).
nagger [-ə*] n. Criarde, harpie *f.*
nagging [-iŋ] adj. Grognon, chamailleur, criard (person). ‖ MED. Harcelant (pain).
naiad ['naiæd] n. Naïade *f.*
nail [neil] n. MED. Ongle *m.* (of animal, bird, person). ‖ TECHN. Clou *m.*; *frost nail,* crampon à glace. ‖ FAM. *For want of a nail the shoe was lost,* pour un point Martin perdit son âne; *to hit the nail on the head,* enfoncer le clou, frapper juste; *to pay on the nail,* payer recta (or) rubis sur l'ongle. ‖ **Nail-brush,** n. Brosse (*f.*) à ongles. ‖ **Nail-claw**

(or) **-wrench,** n. Arrache-clou *m.* ‖ **Nail-clippers,** n. Coupe-ongles *m.* ‖ **Nail-maker** (or) **-smith,** n. Cloutier *m.* ‖ **Nail-making,** n. Clouterie *f.* ‖ **Nail-scissors,** n. pl. Ciseaux à ongles *m. pl.* ‖ **Nail-varnish** (or U. S.) **-enamel, -polish** n. Vernis (*m.*) à ongles.
— v. tr. Clouer (*on, to,* sur, à). ‖ Clouter (boots). ‖ Fig. *To nail a lie on the counter,* démasquer un mensonge. ‖ **To nail down,** clouer ; Fam. Coincer (s.o.). ‖ **To nail up,** clouer ; Agric. Palisser.
nailed [-d] adj. Cloué (case) ; clouté (shoe). ‖ Med. Onglé.
nailer [-ə*] n. Cloutier *m.* (nail-maker). ‖ Fam. Crack, as *m.* (person) ; truc formidable (thing).
nailery [-əri] n. Clouterie *f.*
nailing [-iŋ] n. Clouage *m.* (of case). ‖ Cloutage *m.* (of boots). ‖ Clous *m. pl.* (collectively).
naïve [nai'i:v] adj. Naïf.
naïvely [-li] adv. Naïvement ; avec ingénuité.
naïvety [nai'i:vtei] n. Naïveté *f.*
naja ['neidʒə] n. Zool. Naja *m.*
naked ['neikid] adj. Nu, dénudé (member, person) ; *stark naked,* nu comme un ver. ‖ Dénudé (landscape, tree) ; nu (wall). ‖ Nu (bulb, globe, sword). ‖ Jur. *Naked bond,* contrat sans garantie. ‖ Fig. Nu (truth) ; *to be visible to the naked eye,* se voir à l'œil nu.
nakedly [-li] adv. A nu. ‖ Fig. Sans fard, crûment.
nakedness [-nis] n. Nudité *f.* (lit. and fig.).
namby-pamby ['næmbi'pæmbi] adj. Fam. Sentimental, gnangnan, à l'eau de rose (novel) ; minaudier, maniéré, grimacier (person).
name [neim] n. Nom *m. ; Christian name* (or) U. S. *first name,* prénom ; *full name,* nom et prénoms ; *a good name,* un beau nom ; *his name is John,* il s'appelle Jean ; *Smith by name,* du nom de (or) dénommé Smith ; *to know only by name,* ne connaître que de nom ; *to speak in the name of,* parler au nom de. ‖ Appellation, dénomination *f. ; endearing names,* noms d'amitié. ‖ Comm. *Name of a firm,* raison sociale ; *registered name,* nom déposé. ‖ Fig. Célébrité, renommée *f. ; to make a name for oneself,* se faire un nom, atteindre à la notoriété. ‖ **Name-band,** n. U. S. Fam. Orchestre célèbre *m.* ‖ **Name-child,** n. Enfant (*m.*) qui porte le nom d'une personne qu'on a voulu honorer. ‖ **Name-day,** n. Fête *f.* (of s.o.). ‖ **Name-part,** n. Theatr., Cinem. Personnage (*m.*) qui donne son nom à la pièce (or) au film. ‖ **Name-plate,** n. Plaque d'entrée *f.*
— v. tr. Nommer, appeler. ‖ Appointer. ‖ Mentionner.
nameless [-lis] adj. Sans nom, inconnu (person). ‖ Anonyme (author, visitor). ‖ Fig. Sans nom, innommable (crime) ; sans nom, indicible (grief).
namely [-li] adv. A savoir, c'est-à-dire (to wit).
namesake [-seik] n. Homonyme *m.* (of s.o.).
naming [-iŋ] n. Dénomination *f.* ; choix d'un nom *m.*
Nancy ['nænsi] n. Annette, Nancy *f.* ‖ **Nancy-boy,** n. Fam. Tapette, tante *f.*
nankeen [næŋ'ki:n] n. Nankin *m.* (cloth). ‖ Comm. Porcelaine de Chine *f.*
— adj. Chamois, nankin (colour).
Nanking [næŋ'kiŋ] n. Geogr. Nankin *m.*
nanny ['næni] n. Nounou *f.*
nanny(-goat) [(-gout)] n. Chèvre, bique, biquette *f.*
nanosecond ['nænou,sekənd] n. Nanoseconde *f.*
nap [næp] n. Demi-sommeil, assoupissement *m.* (sleep). ‖ Somme *m.* (doze).
— v. intr. Somnoler, faire un somme. ‖ Fam. *To catch s.o. napping,* prendre la pie au nid.
nap n. Duvet *m.* ; peluche *f.* (of cloth) ; poil *m.* (of felt, velvet). ‖ Pl. Comm. Drap bourru *m.*
— v. tr. Lainer, molletonner.
nap n. Fam. Nap *m.* (at cards) ; tuyau increvable *m.* (at racing).
— v. tr. Sports. Donner gagnant (a horse).
napalm ['neipɑ:m] n. Napalm *m.*

nape [neip] n. Med. Nuque *f.*
naphtha ['næfθə] n. Naphte *m.* ‖ U. S. Pétrole *m.*
naphthalene [-li:n] n. Chim. Naphtaline *f.*
naphthol ['næfθɔl] n. Chim. Naphtol *m.*
napkin ['næpkin] n. Serviette *f.* ‖ Couche *f.* (for infant). ‖ **Napkin-ring,** n. Rond (*m.*) de serviette.
Napoleon [nə'pouliən] n. Napoléon *m.* ‖ U. S. Culin. Mille-feuilles *m.*
Napoleonic [nə,pouli'ɔnik] adj. Napoléonien.
nappy ['næpi] adj. Pelucheux (cloth). ‖ Mousseux (ale).
— n. Fam. Couche *f.* (for infant).
narcissism ['nɑ:sisizm] n. Narcissisme *m.*
narcissus [nɑ:'sisəs] n. Bot. Narcisse *m.*
narcosis [nɑ:'kousis] n. Med. Narcose *f.*
narcotic [nɑ:'kɔtik] adj., n. Med. Narcotique *m.*
narcotize [-taiz] v. tr. Narcotiser, administrer un narcotique à.
nard [nɑ:d] n. Bot., Med. Nard *m.*
narghile ['nɑ:gili] n. Narguilé *m.* (See hookah.)
nark [nɑ:k] n. Fam. Mouchard *m.*
— v. tr. Fam. Mettre en rogne.
narrate [næ'reit] v. tr. Raconter, narrer.
narration [nə'reiʃən] n. Relation *f.* (of event). ‖ Fin. Libellé *m.* (in book-keeping).
narrative ['nærətiv] n. Récit, conte *m. ;* histoire *f.* (story). ‖ Narration *f.* (account).
— adj. Narratif.
narrator [nə'reitə*] n. Narrateur *m.* ‖ Mus. Récitant *s.*
narratress [-tris] n. Narratrice *f.*
narrow ['nærou] adj. Etroit (in general) ; *to grow narrow,* se rétrécir. ‖ Gramm. Tendu (vowel). ‖ Fig. Minutieux, méticuleux (inspection) ; petit, faible (majority) ; étroit, borné (mind) ; étroit, strict (sense) ; *in narrow circumstances,* dans des conditions financières limitées, dans la gêne. ‖ Fam. *To have a narrow escape,* y échapper de justesse. ‖ **Narrow-minded,** adj. A l'esprit étroit. ‖ **Narrow-mindedness,** n. Etroitesse (*f.*) d'esprit.
— n. Naut. Etranglement, goulet *m.*
— v. tr. Rétrécir, resserrer. ‖ Restreindre, diminuer.
— v. intr. Se rétrécir, se resserrer.
narrowing [-iŋ] n. Rétrécissement *m.* ‖ Etranglement *m.* (of a road). ‖ Diminution *f.* (in knitting). ‖ Fig. Limitation *f.*
narrowish [-iʃ] adj. Assez étroit.
narrowly [-li] adv. Etroitement. ‖ Minutieusement, méticuleusement. ‖ Tout juste, de justesse.
narrowness [-nis] n. Etroitesse *f.* ‖ Minutie *f.* (of an inspection). ‖ Fig. Petitesse, étroitesse, limitation *f.*
narthex ['nɑ:θeks] n. Archit. Narthex *m.*
narwhal ['nɑ:wəl] n. Zool. Narval *m.,* licorne de mer *f.*
nasal ['neizl] adj. Med. Nasal. ‖ Gramm. Nasal ; *to lose its nasal sound,* se dénasaliser.
— n. † Nasal *m.* ‖ Gramm. Nasale *f.*
nasality [nei'zæliti] n. Nasalité *f.* (quality) ; nasillement *m.* (twang).
nasalization [,neizəlai'zeiʃən] n. Gramm. Nasalisation *f.*
nasalize ['neizəlaiz] v. tr. Gramm. Nasaliser.
— v. intr. Nasiller.
nascent ['næsnt] adj. Bot., Chim., Fig. Naissant. ‖ Med. Débutant.
nastily ['nɑ:stili] adv. Désagréablement. ‖ De façon dégoûtante.
nastiness [-nis] n. Goût désagréable *m.* (taste). ‖ Puanteur *f.* (odour). ‖ Obscénité *f.* ‖ Méchanceté *f.* (of a person). ‖ U. S. Saleté *f.*
nasturtium [nəs'tə:ʃəm] n. Bot. Capucine *f.* (flower) ; cresson (*m.*) de fontaine (watercress).
nasty ['nɑ:sti] adj. Nauséabond (odour) ; répugnant, infect (taste). ‖ Mauvais, sale (business, trick, weather) ; *a nasty job,* un fichu boulot (fam.). ‖ Méchant, mauvais, désobligeant (person). ‖ Indé-

cent, ordurier (language); impur (mind). ‖ MED. Sérieux, vilain.

natal ['neitl] adj. Natal; de naissance.

natality [nə'tæliti] n. Natalité *f.*

natation [nə'teiʃən] n. SPORTS. Natation *f.*

natatorial [neitə'tɔ:riəl], **natatory** ['neitətəri] adj. Natatoire.

natatorium [,neitə'tɔ:riəm] n. U. S. Piscine couverte *f.*

nation ['neiʃən] n. Nation *f.*

national ['næʃənl] adj. National. ‖ NAUT. De nation (flag). ‖ MILIT. *National service*, service national. ‖ MED. *National Health Service*, en Grande-Bretagne, service national de la santé, équivalent du système de Sécurité sociale.
— n. Pl. Nationaux, ressortissants *m. pl.* ‖ SPORTS. Steeple national *m.* ‖ **National-socialism,** n. National-socialisme *m.* ‖ **National-socialist,** n. National-socialiste *s.*

nationalism ['næʃənəlizm] n. Nationalisme *m.* ‖ Etatisme *m.* (in politics).

nationalist [-ist] n. Nationaliste *s.* ‖ Etatiste *s.* (in politics).

nationalistic [,næʃənə'listik] adj. Nationaliste.

nationality [,næʃə'næliti] n. Nationalité *f.* (nation, origin). ‖ Esprit (or) caractère national *m.* (character).

nationalization [,næʃənəlai'zeiʃən] n. Nationalisation *f.* (of an industry); naturalisation *f.* (of a person).

nationalize ['næʃənəlaiz] v. tr. Nationaliser (an industry). ‖ Naturaliser (s.o.).
— v. intr. Etre naturalisé.

nationally [-li] adv. Nationalement; sous l'angle national.

native ['neitiv] n. Natif, naturel *s.* (*of*, de). ‖ Indigène, autochtone *s.* ‖ ZOOL., BOT. Indigène *m.*
— adj. Natif, inné, naturel (qualities). ‖ Natal (country, land); maternel (language); de naissance (place). ‖ Du pays (customs). ‖ Indigène (inhabitant, State); originaire (*to*, de); *native labour*, main-d'œuvre indigène. ‖ CHIM. Naturel (albumin); natif (silver). ‖ **Native-born,** adj. Indigène.

nativity [nə'tiviti] n. ECCLES. Nativité *f.* ‖ ASTRON. Horoscope *m.*

N. A. T. O., Nato ['neitou] abbr. *North Atlantic Treaty Organization,* O. T. A. N., Organisation du traité de l'Atlantique Nord.

natron ['neitrən] n. Natron *m.*

natter ['nætə*] v. intr. FAM. Bavarder, jacasser.
— n. FAM. Bavardage *m.;* to have a natter, tailler une bavette.

natterjack ['nætə,dʒæk] n. ZOOL. Crapaud (*m.*) des roseaux (or) des joncs.

nattiness ['nætinis] n. Elégance *f.* (smartness). ‖ Dextérité *f.* (skill).

natty ['næti] adj. Coquet, élégant (smart). ‖ Habile, adroit (skilful). ‖ Habilement fait, commode (handy).

natural ['nætʃərəl] adj. Naturel (tone, size, state). ‖ De la nature (law); de ce monde (life). ‖ Naturel, inné, natif, foncier (quality); *natural to,* propre à. ‖ Naturel, normal (*that,* que). ‖ COMM. Grège, beige (wool). ‖ MUS. Naturel (note). ‖ PHYS. Propre (frequency); *natural philosophy,* physique. ‖ BOT., ZOOL. Naturel (history); *natural historian,* naturaliste. ‖ JUR. Naturel (child); *death from natural causes,* mort naturelle. ‖ **Natural-born,** adj. De naissance.
— n. † Innocent, demeuré *s.* ‖ MUS. Note naturelle *f.* (note); bécarre *m.* (sign). ‖ U. S. Personne douée *f.* (person); POP. solution parfaite *f.* (thing).

naturalism [-izm] n. Naturalisme *m.*

naturalist [-ist] n. PHILOS., ARTS. Naturaliste.

naturalistic [,nætʃərə'listik] adj. Naturaliste. ‖ ARTS. Naturiste.

naturalization [,nætʃərəlai'zeiʃən] n. Naturalisation *f.* ‖ BOT., ZOOL. Acclimatation *f.*

naturalize ['nætʃərəlaiz] v. tr. Naturaliser (*to,* en, dans). ‖ BOT., ZOOL. Acclimater. ‖ ARTS. Rendre naturel. ‖ PHILOS. Rationaliser.
— v. intr. BOT., ZOOL. S'acclimater. ‖ BOT. Herboriser (person).

naturalizing [-iŋ] n. BOT., ZOOL. Acclimatation *f.* ‖ BOT. Herborisation *f.*

naturally ['nætʃərəli] adv. Naturellement, par nature (or) tempérament. ‖ Naturellement, simplement. ‖ Naturellement, bien entendu (of course).

naturalness [-nis] n. Naturel *m.* ‖ Normal *m.;* norme *f.*

nature ['neitʃə*] n. Nature *f.* (of man, soil); nature, essence *f.;* ordre *m.* (of things); *to depend on the nature of,* tenir à la nature de. ‖ Naturel, tempérament, caractère *m.* (of persons); *by nature,* par (or) de nature, naturellement. ‖ Nature, sorte, espèce *f.;* *of such nature as to,* de nature à; *words in the nature of a threat,* des paroles à allure menaçante. ‖ Nature *f.; against nature,* contre nature; *in a state of nature,* à l'état naturel. ‖ MED. Fonctions naturelles *f. pl.* ‖ ARTS. *To draw from nature,* dessiner d'après nature.

naturism [-rizm] n. ARTS, PHILOS. Naturisme *m.*

naturist [-rist] n. ARTS, PHILOS. Naturiste *s.*

naught [nɔ:t] n. Néant *m.; all for naught,* en pure perte; *to come to naught,* échouer; aboutir à zéro; *to set at naught,* tenir pour rien. ‖ MATH. Zéro *m.*

naughtily [-ili] adv. Mal.

naughtiness [-inis] n. Méchanceté, mauvaise tenue *f.* (of a child). ‖ FAM. Crudité *f.* (of a story).

naughty [-i] adj. Méchant, vilain, polisson, pas sage (child). ‖ FAM. Leste, cru, salé (story).

nausea ['nɔ:siə] n. Nausée *f.* (lit. and fig.).

nauseate [-eit] v. tr. Prendre en dégoût (food). ‖ Ecœurer, donner la nausée à (s.o.).
— v. intr. Avoir des nausées, avoir envie de vomir. ‖ Etre écœuré (*at,* par).

nauseating [-eitiŋ], **nauseous** [-əs] adj. Dégoûtant, écœurant. ‖ MED. Nauséeux.

nauseousness [-əsnis] n. Nature écœurante *f.*

nautical ['nɔ:tikəl] adj. Marin (chart, mile); nautique (instrument); naval (matter); de marine (term).

nautically [-i] adv. Nautiquement.

nautilus ['nɔ:tiləs] (pl. **nautilusses** [-ləsis] or **nautili** [-,lai]) n. ZOOL. Nautile *m.* (pearly nautilus); *paper nautilus,* argonaute.

naval ['neivəl] adj. Naval (architecture, college, engagement); de marine (officer); maritime (power); *naval base,* base navale, port de guerre.

navally [-i] adv. Au point de vue naval.

nave [neiv] n. TECHN. Moyeu *m.*

nave n. ECCLES. Nef *f.;* vaisseau *m.*

navel ['neivəl] n. MED. Nombril, ombilic *m.; navel string,* cordon ombilical. ‖ FIG. Centre *m.* ‖ **Navel-orange,** n. AGRIC. Navel *f.*

navicert ['neivisə:t] n. Navicert *m.*

navicular [nə'vikjulə*] adj. MED. Naviculaire.

navigability [,nævigə'biliti], **navigableness** ['nævigəblnis] n. NAUT. Navigabilité *f.* ‖ AVIAT. Manœuvrabilité *f.*

navigable ['nævigəbl] adj. NAUT. De navigabilité (condition); navigable (river). ‖ AVIAT. Dirigeable, manœuvrable.

navigate [-geit] v. intr. NAUT. Naviguer.
— v. tr. NAUT. Naviguer sur, parcourir (seas); gouverner (a ship). ‖ AVIAT. Voyager dans (air); piloter (plane).

navigating [-geitiŋ] adj. NAUT., AVIAT. De navigation.
— n. Navigation *f.*

navigation [ˌnævi'geiʃən] n. NAUT., AVIAT. Navigation f.; *navigation laws*, code maritime.

navigational [-l̩] adj. De navigation.

navigator ['nævigeitə*] n. NAUT. Navigateur; officier (m.) des montres. ‖ AVIAT. Observateur (m.) de navigation; navigateur aérien m.

navvy ['nævi] n̂. Terrassier m.; *steam-navvy*, piocheuse.

— v. tr. (2). Faire des travaux de terrassement.

navy ['neivi] n. NAUT. Marine de guerre, flotte f.; forces navales f. pl.; *merchant navy*, marine marchande.

— adj. De la Marine (Department). ‖ Marine (blue).

nay [nei] adv. Non. ‖ Que non !, que dis-je !, voire !, et même.

— n. Non m.; *to say s.o. nay*, opposer un refus à qqn.

Nazarene [ˌnæzə'ri:n] n. Nazaréen s.

naze [ne:iz] n. GEOGR. Nez, cap m.

Nazi ['nɑ:tsi] adj., n. Nazi s.

Nazify [-fai] v. tr. (2). Nazifier.

Nazism ['nɑ:tsizm̩] n. Nazisme m.

N.B. [en'bi:] abbr. *nota bene*, N. B.

N.C.O. [ensi:'ou] abbr. *non-commissioned officer*, sous-officier.

neap [ni:p] adj. De morte-eau (tide).

— n. pl. Mortes-eaux f. pl.

— v. intr. Décroître; être aux mortes-eaux.

— v. tr. NAUT. *To get neaped*, amortir.

Neapolitan [niə'pɔlitən] adj., n. GEOGR. Napolitain s. ‖ CULIN. *Neapolitan ice-cream*, tranche napolitaine.

near ['niə*] adv. Près, à proximité (in space); *near at hand*, à portée de la main; *near by*, non loin, dans le voisinage; *to draw near to*, s'approcher de; *to live near to*, habiter près de. ‖ Près (in time); *near to Easter*, à l'approche de Pâques. ‖ Proche (in intimacy); *those near and dear to me*, mes proches. ‖ Près (event); *to be as near as could be to doing*, être à un cheveu de faire. ‖ Presque (nearly); *I am nothing near so rich*, je suis loin d'être aussi riche; *to be very near tipsy*, être presque gris. ‖ FAM. Avec économie. ‖ **Near-sighted**, adj. MED. Myope. ‖ **Near-sightedness**, n. MED. Myopie, vue basse f.

— prep. Près de, auprès de, dans le voisinage de (s.o., sth.); *come near me*, approchez-vous de moi. ‖ Près de, sur le point de; *near the end*, près de finir; *to come near being*, être sur le point (or) à deux doigts d'être. ‖ Près de; au niveau de; *the same or near it*, la même chose ou à peu près. ‖ D'imitation; *near antique*, imitation d'ancien; *near beer*, bière ersatz; *near silk*, soie artificielle. ‖ GEOGR. *Bihorel near Rouen*, Bihorel-lès-Rouen.

— adj. Intime (friend); proche (relative). ‖ Gauche (horse, side). ‖ Proche, prochain (event, time); proche (place); court, direct (road). ‖ Près de la vérité (guess); près de la réalité, frappant (resemblance); approchant (offer); près du texte (translation); *it was a near thing*, ç'a été juste, il s'en est fallu de peu; *near miss*, coup manqué de peu (or) collision évitée de justesse; *near silk*, simili soie. ‖ FIN. Délicat, minutieux (work). ‖ SPORTS. Disputé (race). ‖ GEOGR. *Near East*, Proche-Orient.

— v. tr. S'approcher de, approcher (s.o.) ‖ Approcher de (a place). ‖ FIG. Etre sur le point de; *to be nearing one's end*, être près de sa fin.

nearby [-'bai] adj. U. S. Proche.

— adv. U. S. Tout près.

nearly [-li] adv. Près, de près; *to be nearly acquainted with*, être en relations intimes avec; *to concern s.o. very nearly*, toucher qqn de très près. ‖ A peu près, presque; *nearly ten*, près de dix; *to be nearly home*, être presque arrivé chez soi; *very nearly*, peu s'en faut, tout près; *you nearly died*, vous avez failli mourir, il s'en est fallu de peu que vous ne mouriez.

nearness [-nis] n. Proximité f., voisinage m. (of place); proximité f. (of time). ‖ Intimité f. (of friends); étroitesse f. (of relationship). ‖ Fidélité f. (of translation). ‖ FAM. Ladrerie f.

neat [ni:t] n. ZOOL. Bœuf, bovin m.; bêtes à cornes f. pl.; bétail, cheptel m. ‖ CULIN. *Neat's tongue*, langue de bœuf.

neat adj. Pur, sec, sans eau, nature (drink). ‖ Simple, net, soigné; coquet, pimpant (clothes). [See SMART.] ‖ Net, propre, bien tenu (exercise-book); net (handwriting). ‖ Fin (ankle); bien fait, joli (leg). ‖ Propre, ordonné, adroit, habile, précis (person). ‖ Bien tourné (speech); élégant (style); bien fait, réussi (work). ‖ U. S. FAM. *That's neat*, chic alors.

neatherd [-hə:d] n. Vacher, bouvier m.

neatly [-li] adv. Avec netteté (or) soin. ‖ Avec goût. ‖ Adroitement, habilement.

neatness [-nis] n. Netteté f.; ordre, soin m. (in work). ‖ Goût m.; simple élégance f. (of dress). ‖ Finesse f. (of ankles); beauté f. (of legs). ‖ Ordre m.; habileté f. (of s.o.). ‖ Elégance (of style).

Nebuchadnezzar [ˌnebjukəd'nezə*] n. Nabuchodonosor m.

nebula ['nebjulə] (pl. **nebulae** [-li:]) n. ASTRON. Nébuleuse f. ‖ MED. Taie f. (on eye).

nebular [-ə*] adj. ASTRON. Nébulaire.

nebulosity [ˌnebju'lɔsiti] n. ASTRON. Nébulosité f.

nebulous ['nebjuləs] adj. ASTRON. Nébuleux. ‖ FAM. Flou, nébuleux, vague.

nebulously [-li] adv. Nébuleusement.

necessarily ['nesəsərili] adv. Obligatoirement, inévitablement, forcément, nécessairement.

necessary ['nesəsəri] adj. Inévitable, indispensable, nécessaire (for, to, à); *if it is necessary*, en cas de nécessité, s'il y a lieu; *it is necessary for you to do it*, il vous faut le faire, il faut que vous le fassiez; *to make it necessary for s.o. to*, rendre obligatoire pour qqn de.

— n. Pl. Nécessaire m. (see ESSENTIAL); *the bare necessaries*, le strict nécessaire; *the necessaries of life*, l'indispensable; *travel necessaries*, nécessaire de voyage. ‖ FAM. Frais inévitables m. pl.

necessitarian [ˌnəsesi'tɛəriən] adj., n. Déterministe s.

necessitarianism [-izm̩] n. Déterminisme m.

necessitate [nə'sesiteit] v. tr. Imposer, rendre obligatoire, nécessiter. (See ENTAIL.)

necessitous [-təs] adj. Nécessiteux. (See NEEDY.)

necessitousness [-təsnis] n. Gêne, indigence f.

necessity [nə'sesiti] n. Obligation, nécessité f.; *case of absolute necessity*, cas de force majeure; *of necessity*, obligatoirement, de toute nécessité; *out of necessity*, par la force des choses, par nécessité; *under the necessity of*, dans l'obligation de. ‖ Besoin m. (for, de); *there is no necessity for him to*, il n'a pas besoin de; U. S. *necessities of life*, nécessités de la vie. ‖ Dénuement m.; indigence f.; *to be in necessity*, être dans le besoin. ‖ PHILOS. *Doctrine of necessity*, déterminisme.

neck [nek] n. Cou m. (of animal, person). ‖ Encolure f. (of a dress); *low neck*, décolleté; *V-neck*, décolleté en pointe. ‖ Goulot m. (of a bottle). ‖ MED. Collet m. (of tooth); col m. (of womb); *stiff neck*, torticolis. ‖ CULIN. Collet m. (of mutton). ‖ GEOL. Langue f. (of land). ‖ TECHN. Gorge f. (of axle); étranglement m. (of pipe). ‖ CHIM. Col m. (of retort). ‖ SPORTS. Encolure f. (in horse-racing). ‖ FAM. *Neck and crop*, à corps perdu; *to give s.o. a pain in the neck*, enquiquiner qqn; *to get it in the neck*, écoper, trinquer; *to have a neck*, avoir du culot; *to fall on s.o.'s neck*, sauter au cou de qqn. ‖ U. S. POP. *Shot in the neck*, éméché, paf, parti. ‖ **Neck-band**, n. Col m.; encolure f. (of shirt). ‖ **Neck-deep**, adj. Jusqu'au cou. ‖ **Neck-flap**, n. Couvre-nuque m. ‖ **Neck-line** (or) **-opening**, n. Encolure f.; décolleté m. ‖ **Neck-slip**, n. Collier m.

(bottle). ‖ **Neck-tie**, n. Cravate *f.*; Fam. *Neck-tie party*, pendaison.
— v. tr. Fam. Siffler (to drink). ‖ U. S. Fam. Bécoter, peloter (to cuddle).
— v. intr. U. S. Fam. Se bécoter.
neckcloth [-klɔθ] n. Cache-col, tour de cou *m.*
neckerchief [-ətˌʃif] n. Foulard, tour de cou *m.*
necking [-iŋ] n. Archit. Gorge *f.* ‖ U. S. Fam. Câlineries *f. pl.*; bécotage *m.*
necklace [-lis] n. Collier *m.*
necklet [-lit] n. Collier *m.* (jewel). ‖ Collet *m.* (fur).
necrological [ˌnekrəˈlɔdʒikəl] adj. Nécrologique.
necrology [neˈkrɔlədʒi] n. Nécrologe *m.* (death-roll); nécrologie *f.* (obituary notice).
necromancer [ˈnekrɔmænsə*] n. Nécromancien *s.*
necromancy [-si] n. Nécromancie *f.*
necrophilia [ˌnekroˈfiliə] n. Nécrophilie *f.*
necropolis [neˈkrɔpəlis] n. Nécropole *f.*

— N. B. Deux pluriels : *necropolises, necropoles.*

necrosis [neˈkrousis] n. Med., Bot. Nécrose *f.*
necrotize [ˈnekrətaiz] v. intr. Se nécroser.
nectar [ˈnektə*] n. Nectar *m.*
nectarine [-rin] n. Agric. Brugnon *m.*
née, U. S. nee [nei] adj. Née, de son nom de jeune fille.
need [niːd] n. Besoin *m.* (necessity); *in case of need, if need be,* en cas de besoin, si besoin est, au besoin; *those most in need of,* ceux qui ont le plus besoin de; *to be in urgent need of,* avoir grand besoin de ; *to have need to do,* avoir besoin de (or) être obligé de faire. ‖ Difficulté *f.*; embarras *m.* (trouble); *in times of need,* aux heures difficiles, dans l'adversité. ‖ Besoin, dénuement *m.*; gêne, indigence *f.* (poverty); *to be in great need,* être dans la misère. ‖ Pl. Besoins *m. pl.* (wants); *to supply the needs of,* subvenir aux besoins de. ‖ Fam. Pl. Petits besoins *m. pl.*
— v. tr. Avoir besoin de (s.o., sth.). ‖ Réclamer, demander, exiger, vouloir, avoir besoin de, être obligé de ; *I need to do,* je suis obligé de faire, je dois faire, il faut que je fasse, j'ai besoin de faire ; *to need no saying,* aller sans dire.
— v. aux. Avoir besoin de, être obligé de ; *he need not do it,* il n'a pas besoin de le faire, il n'est pas tenu (or) obligé de le faire, il n'est pas indispensable (or) il est inutile qu'il le fasse ; *why need there be ?,* qu'est-il besoin de ?
— v. intr. Etre dans le besoin.
— v. impers. Falloir.
needed [-id] adj. Nécessaire.
needful [-ful] adj. Nécessaire *(for, to,* à).
— n. Nécessaire *m.*; *to supply the needful,* fournir le nécessaire ; foncer, casquer (fam.).
needfulness [-fulnis] n. Besoin *m.*
neediness [-inis] n. Gêne, indigence *f.*; besoin *m.*
needle [ˈniːdl̩] n. Aiguille *f.* ‖ Med. Aiguille *f.* ‖ Mus. Aiguille *f.* (of gramophone). ‖ Arts. *Engraving needle,* pointe sèche. ‖ Naut. Aiguille *f.* (of compass). ‖ Archit. Obélisque *f.* ‖ Geol. Aiguille *f.* ‖ Techn. *Touch needle,* toucheau *m.* ‖ Autom. Pointeau *m.* ‖ Fam. *To have the needle,* être de mauvais poil. ‖ **Needle-case,** porte-aiguilles *m.* ‖ **Needle-furze,** n. Bot. Genêt épineux *m.* ‖ **Needle-making,** n. Aiguillerie *f.* ‖ **Needle-point,** n. Pointe d'aiguille *f.*; Math. Pointe sèche *f.* ‖ **Needle-shaped,** adj. En aiguille. ‖ **Needle-threader,** n. Enfile-aiguilles *m.*
— v. tr. Coudre. ‖ Fam. Taquiner, asticoter, harceler. ‖ Fam. U. S. Corser (a drink).
— v. intr. Coudre.
needleful [-ful] n. Aiguillée *f.*
needless [ˈniːdlis] adj. Peu nécessaire, inutile, sans besoin, qui ne sert à rien.
needlessly [-li] adv. Sans besoin, inutilement.
needlessness [-nis] n. Inutilité *f.* (of sth.). ‖ Inopportunité *f.* (of a remark).
needlewoman [ˈniːdl̩ˌwumən] n. Femme (*f.*) habile aux travaux d'aiguille. ‖ Couturière à la journée ; lingère *f.*
needlework [-wəːk] n. Travaux (*m. pl.*) à l'aiguille ; ouvrages (*m. pl.*) de dame. ‖ Ouvrage *m.*; *needlework case,* trousse à ouvrage. ‖ Couture *f.* (at school).
needs [niːdz] adv. Nécessairement, de toute nécessité.
needy [-i] adj. Nécessiteux, besogneux.
— n. *The needy,* les nécessiteux.
neem [niːm] n. Bot. Margousier *m.*
ne'er [neə*] adv. Ne... jamais ; jamais. (See never.) ‖ **Ne'er-do-well, ne'er-do-weel,** n. Bon à rien *m.*
nefarious [niˈfɛəriəs] adj. Infâme.
nefariousness [-nis] n. Infamie *f.*
negate [niˈgeit] v. tr. Nier.
negation [niˈgeiʃən] n. Négation *f.* (See denial.)
negative [ˈnegətiv] adj. Négatif. ‖ Math. *Negative sign,* moins.
— n. Négative *f.*; *to answer in the negative,* répondre par la négative. ‖ Négatif *m.* (in photography). ‖ Gramm. Négation *f.*
— v. tr. Neutraliser (an effect) ; repousser, rejeter (a plan). ‖ Réfuter (an assumption) ; s'inscrire en faux contre (a statement). ‖ Naut. Annuler (a signal).
negatively [-li] adv. Négativement.
neglect [niˈglekt] n. Manque de soin *m.*; *out of neglect,* faute de précautions. ‖ Négligence *f.*; défaut (*m.*) d'attention. ‖ Manque (*m.*) de soins (or) d'égards (*of,* pour, envers, à l'égard de); *in total neglect,* dans un abandon total.
— v. tr. Manquer de soin, laisser aller ; *to neglect one's person,* se négliger. ‖ Négliger (one's duties, interests) ; *to neglect to come,* omettre de venir. ‖ Manquer de soins (or) d'égards pour, négliger, laisser à l'abandon.
neglected [-id] adj. Négligé, mal tenu (appearance). ‖ Abandonné, délaissé (person).
neglectful [-ful] adj. Négligent (careless). ‖ Oublieux (*of,* de) [remiss].
neglectfully [-fuli] adv. Négligemment.
négligé, negligee [ˈnegliˌʒei] n. Négligé *m.* (night-dress).
negligence [ˈneglidʒəns] n. Manque de soin *m.*; négligence *f.* (remissness) ; *a piece of negligence,* une négligence. ‖ Négligence, insouciance *f.* (carelessness).
negligent [-dʒənt] adj. Négligent, oublieux. (See neglectful.) ‖ Négligé, mal tenu, sans soin (slovenly). ‖ Négligent, insouciant (careless).
negligently [-dʒəntli] adv. Négligemment, avec négligence (or) insouciance.
negligible [-dʒəbl̩] adj. Négligeable.
negotiability [niˌgouʃiəˈbiliti] n. Négociabilité *f.*
negotiable [niˈgouʃiəbl̩] adj. Fin. Négociable ; *negotiable paper,* effet. ‖ Fam. Franchissable (obstacle) ; praticable (road).
negotiant [-ənt] n. Négociateur *m.*; négociatrice *f.*
negotiate [-eit] v. tr. Fin., Fig. Négocier. ‖ Autom. Prendre (a corner) ; monter (a hill). ‖ Fam. Venir à bout de.
— v. intr. *To negotiate for,* négocier, entreprendre des pourparlers pour.
negotiation [niˌgouʃiˈeiʃən] n. Négociation *f.* (*of,* de) ; *under negotiation,* en voie de négociations. ‖ Pourparlers *m. pl.* (with, avec) ; *to enter into negotiations with,* entrer en pourparlers avec, entamer des négociations avec. ‖ Autom. Prise *f.* (of a corner) ; montée *f.* (of a hill).
negotiator [niˈgouʃieitə*] n. Négociateur *m.*
negotiatress [-trəs], **negotiatrix** [-triks] n. Négociatrice *f.*
negress [ˈniːgris] n. Négresse *f.*
negrillo [niˈgrilə] n. Négrillon *s.*
Negro [ˈniːgrou] adj., n. Nègre *m.* ‖ Mus. *Negro spiritual,* negro spiritual.

negroid [-grɔid] adj. Négroïde.

negus ['ni:gəs] n. CULIN. Vin chaud et épicé *m.*

neigh [nei] n. Hennissement *m.*
— v. intr. Hennir.

neighbour ['neibə*] n. Voisin *s.* ‖ ECCLES. Prochain *m.*
— v. tr. Etre voisin de, avoisiner.
— v. intr. Voisiner (*with,* avec); être voisin (*with,* de).

neighbourhood [-hud] n. Voisinage *m.;* proximité *f.* (nearness); *in the neighbourhood of,* au voisinage de, près de. ‖ Voisinage *m.;* parages *m. pl.* (district). ‖ Environs, alentours *m. pl.* (vicinity). ‖ FAM. *In the neighbourhood of five,* aux alentours de cinq, cinq environ.

neighbouring [-iŋ] adj. Avoisinant, voisin.

neighbourliness [-linis] n. Rapports (*m. pl.*) de bon voisinage.

neighbourly [-li] adj. De bon voisinage (action, relations); bon voisin, serviable (person).

neighing ['neiiŋ] adj. Hennissant.
— n. Hennissement *m.*

neither ['naiθə*] adv., conj. Ni; *neither... nor,* ni... ni; *neither one nor the other,* ni l'un ni l'autre. ‖ Non plus, pas davantage; *I can't walk, neither can I run,* je ne peux pas marcher, et pas mieux courir.
— adj., pron. Ni l'un ni l'autre, aucun (*of,* de).

nelly ['neli] n. ZOOL. Pétrel géant *m.*

nelson ['nelsən] n. SPORTS. Prise Nelson, double prise de tête *f.*

nemesis ['nemisis] n. Nemesis *f.* (goddess). ‖ Justice distributive *f.; divine nemesis,* justice divine.

nenuphar ['nenjufɑ:*] n. BOT. Nénuphar *m.*

neo [ni:ou] pref. Néo. ‖ **Neo-classicism,** n. Néoclassicisme *m.* ‖ **Neo-colonialism,** n. Néocolonialisme *m.*

neodymium [.ni:ou'dimiəm] n. CHIM. Néodyme *m.*

neolithic [.ni:ou'liθik] adj. Néolithique.

neologism [ni'ɔlədʒizm̩] n. GRAMM. Néologisme *m.*

neologist [-dʒist] n. Néologiste *m.*

neon ['ni:ɔn] n. CHIM., ELECTR. Néon *m.; neon lamp, tube,* lampe, tube au néon; *neon-tube lighting,* éclairage au néon.

neonatal [.ni:ou'neitl̩] adj. MED. Néonatal.

neophyte ['ni:oufait] n. ECCLES., FIG. Néophyte *s.*

neoplasm ['ni:oplæzm] n. MED. Néoplasme *m.*

neoprene ['ni:o,pri:n] n. Néoprène *m.* (rubber).

Nepal [ni'pɔ:l] n. GEOGR. Népal *m.*

nephew ['nevju] n. Neveu *m.*

nephrite ['nefrait] n. Néphrite *f.* (jade).

nephritic [ne'fritik] adj. MED. Néphrétique.

nephritis [ne'fraitis] n. MED. Néphrite *f.; sufferer from nephritis,* néphrétique.

nepotism ['nepotizm] n. Népotisme *m.*

Neptune ['neptju:n] n. Neptune *m.*

Neptunian [nep'tju:niən] adj. Neptunien.

neptunium ['neptju:niəm] n. Neptunium *m.*

Nereid ['ni:əriid] n. Néréide *f.*

neroli ['ni:əroli] n. Néroli *m.*

nerval ['nə:vəl] adj. MED. Neural.

nervate [-vit] adj. BOT. Nervé.

nervation [nə:'veiʃən] n. BOT. Nervation *f.*

nerve [nə:v] n. MED. Nerf *m.; in a state of nerves,* fort énervé; *nerve specialist,* neurologue. ‖ BOT., ARCHIT. Nervure *f.* ‖ FAM. Nerf *m.; to get on s.o.'s nerves,* taper sur les nerfs (or) sur le système à qqn. ‖ FAM. Toupet, aplomb *m.; he has got a nerve,* en voilà un qui ne manque pas de culot (or) qui n'a pas froid aux yeux. ‖ **Nerve-cell,** n. MED. Cellule nerveuse *f.;* neurone *m.* ‖ **Nerve-centre,** n. MED. Centre nerveux *m.;* FIG. Point névralgique *m.* ‖ **Nerve-gas,** n. MILIT. Gaz neurotoxique *m.* ‖ **Nerve-impulse,** n. MED. Influx nerveux *m.* ‖ **Nerve-knot,** n. MED. Ganglion nerveux *m.* ‖ **Nerve-patient,** n.

MED. Névropathe *s.* ‖ **Nerve-racking,** adj. Exaspérant, horripilant, agaçant au plus haut point.
— v. tr. Donner du nerf (or) de la force à, fortifier. ‖ Encourager; *to nerve oneself to,* prendre son courage à deux mains pour.

nerveless [-lis] adj. Sans nerfs (or) force, inerte, mou. ‖ BOT. Sans nervures. ‖ MED. Sans nerfs.

nervelessness [-lisnis] n. Manque (*m.*) d'énergie, inertie *f.;* abattement *m.*

nerviness [-inis], **nervosity** [nə:'vɔsiti] n. Nervosité *f.* ‖ U. S. Toupet *m.* (nerve).

nervose ['nə:vous] adj. MED. Neural. ‖ BOT. Nervé.

nervous ['nə:vəs] adj. MED. Nerveux (disease, system); *central nervous system,* système nerveux central; *autonomic nervous system,* système neurovégétatif; *nervous breakdown,* dépression nerveuse. ‖ ARTS. Vigoureux, énergique. ‖ FIG. Emu, troublé, intimidé; traqueux (fam.); *to feel nervous,* se sentir mal à l'aise; avoir le trac (fam.). ‖ FIG. Excitable, irritable; inquiet, craintif (nervy).

nervously [-li] adv. Avec trouble (or) émotion, timidement.

nervousness [-nis] n. MED. Nervosité *f.;* état nerveux *m.* ‖ FIG. Emotion *f.;* trac *m.*

nervure ['nə:vjuə*] n. BOT. Nervure *f.*

nervy ['nə:vi] adj. Enervé, agacé, irrité (on edge). ‖ Nerveux, saccadé (jerky). ‖ FAM. Culotté, plein de toupet.

nescience ['neʃiəns] n. Ignorance *f.* ‖ PHILOS. Nescience *f.*

nescient [-ənt] adj. Ignorant (*of,* de). ‖ PHILOS. Nescient.
— adj., n. ECCLES. Agnostique *s.*

ness [nes] n. Promontoire, cap *m.*

nest [nest] n. Nid *m.* (of ants, birds, mice, wasps). ‖ Nichée *f.* (of birds); nestful. ‖ Série *f.; nest of drawers,* classeur (for office); chiffonnier (for room); *nest of shelves,* casier; *nest of tables,* table gigogne. ‖ CH. DE F. Epi *m.* ‖ TECHN. Faisceau *m.* ‖ **Nest-box,** n. Pondoir *m.* ‖ **Nest-egg,** n. Nichet *m.;* FAM. Boursicot, bas de laine *m.* (savings).
— v. intr. Se nicher, nicher, faire son nid (birds). ‖ TECHN. S'emboîter.
— v. tr. TECHN. Emboîter.

nestful [-ful] n. Nichée *f.*

nesting [-iŋ] adj. Nicheur (bird); des nids (time).
— n. TECHN. Emboîtage; emboîtement *m.*

nestle ['nesl] v. tr. Blottir, nicher.
— v. intr. Se blottir, se nicher, se pelotonner.

nestling ['nestliŋ] n. ZOOL. Oisillon *m.*

net [net] n. Filet *m.; butterfly net,* filet à papillons; *crayfish net,* balance à écrevisses; *game nets,* rets. ‖ Filet *m.; hair net,* filet, résille; *shopping net,* filet à provisions. ‖ Tulle *m.; spotted net,* tulle point d'esprit. ‖ SPORTS. Filet *m.* (at tennis). ‖ FIG. Piège *m.; to fall into the net,* tomber dans le panneau. ‖ **Net-fishing,** n. Pêche (*f.*) au filet.
— v. tr. Prendre au filet. ‖ Faire au filet (work). ‖ SPORTS. Envoyer au filet (the ball).
— v. intr. Faire du filet.

net adj. Net (price, weight, yield).
— v. tr. FIN. Rapporter (or) toucher net.

netful [-ful] n. Filet, plein filet *m.* (*of,* de).

nether ['neðə*] adj. Inférieur; *the nether world,* les régions infernales.

Netherlander [-ləndə*] n. GEOGR. Néerlandais, Hollandais *s.*

Netherlandish [-ləndiʃ] adj., n. Néerlandais, hollandais *m.*

Netherlands [-ləndz] n. pl. GEOGR. Pays-Bas *m. pl.;* Hollande *f.*

nethermost [-moust] adj. Le plus profond.

netlike ['netlaik] adj. Rétiforme.

nett [net] adj. Net (price, weight, yield). [See NET.]

netter [-ə*] n. Filetier *m.*

netting [-iŋ] n. Pose (*f.*) des filets. ‖ Fabrication (*f.*)

du filet. ‖ Tulle *f.* (cloth). ‖ Naut. Pl. Bastingages *m. pl.* ‖ **Netting-needle,** n. Navette *f.*

nettle ['netl] n. Bot. Ortie *f.* ‖ **Nettle-rash,** n. Med. Urticaire *f.* ‖ **Nettle-sting,** n. Piqûre d'ortie *f.*
— v. tr. Ortier ; *to nettle oneself,* se piquer avec des orties. ‖ Fam. Piquer au vif, agacer, égratigner, vexer (s.o.).

network ['netwə:k] n. Travail au filet *m.* ‖ Filet, ouvrage en filet *m.* ‖ Réseau *m.* (of railways, rivers, roads, telephones) ; *rail network,* réseau ferré. ‖ Radio. Chaîne *f.* ‖ Fam. Tissu *m.* (of lies).
— v. tr. Radio. Transmettre en chaîne.

neume [nju:m] n. Mus. Neume *m.*

neural ['njuərəl] adj. Med. Neural ; nerval.

neuralgia [njuə'ræld3ə] n. Med. Névralgie *f.*

neuralgic [njuə'ræld3ik] adj. Med. Névralgique.

neurasthenia [,njuərəs'θi:niə] n. Med. Neurasthénie, psychasthénie *f.*

neurasthenic [-ik] adj. Med. Neurasthénique, psychasthénique.

neurine ['njuərain] n. Med. Tissu nerveux *m.* ‖ Chim. Neurine, névrine *f.*

neuritis [njuə'raitis] n. Med. Névrite *f.*

neurologist [njuə'rɔləd3ist] n. Med. Neurologue *s.*

neurology [-d3i] n. Med. Neurologie *f.*

neuron ['njuərɔn] n. Med. Neurone *m.* (cell) ; système cérébro-spinal *m.* (system).

neuropath ['njuərɔpæθ] n. Med. Névropathe *s.*

neuropathology [,njuərɔpæ'θɔləd3i] n. Med. Neuropathologie *f.*

neuropathy [njuə'rɔpəθi] n. Med. Névropathie *f.*

neuroptera [njuə'rɔptərə] n. pl. Zool. Névroptères *m. pl.*

neurosis [njuə'rousis] (pl. **neuroses** [-si:z]) n. Med. Névrose *f.*

neuro-surgery [,njuərou'sə:d3əri] n. Med. Neurochirurgie *f.*

neurotic [njuə'rɔtik] adj., n. Med. Névrosé *s.*

neuroticism [-tisizm] n. Névrosisme *m.*

neuter ['nju:tə*] adj. Gramm., Zool. Neutre.
— n. Gramm. Neutre *m. ; in the neuter,* au neutre. ‖ Zool. Abeille stérile *f.* (bee) ; animal châtré *m.* (in general).
— v. tr. Châtrer.

neutral [-trəl] adj. Chim., Electr., Milit., Jur. Neutre. ‖ Fig. Neutre, indéterminé.
— n. Jur. Neutre *m.* (in politics). ‖ Autom. Point mort *m.* (of gear-shift).

neutralist [-ist] n. Neutraliste *m.*

neutrality [nju'træliti] n. Jur., Chim. Neutralité *f.*

neutralization [,nju:trəlai'zeiʃən] n. Neutralisation *f.*

neutralize ['nju:trəlaiz] v. tr. Chim., Electr., Jur., Fig. Neutraliser ; *to neutralize one another,* se neutraliser.

neutrino [nju:'tri:nou] (pl. **neutrinos** [-z]) n. Phys. Neutrino *m.*

neutron ['nju:trɔn] n. Phys. Neutron *m.* ‖ Milit. *Neutron bomb,* bombe à neutrons.

névé ['nevei] n. Geol. Névé *m.*

never ['nevə*] adv. Ne... jamais ; *he never came,* il n'est jamais venu. ‖ Jamais ; *never more,* jamais plus, plus jamais ; *never yet,* jamais encore. ‖ Pas du tout (emphatically) ; *she said never a word about it,* elle n'a pas dit un seul mot à ce sujet. ‖ Fam. Certainement pas. ‖ **Never-ceasing,** adj. Incessant. ‖ **Ne'er-do-well,** n. Fam. Propre à rien *m.* ‖ **Never-dying,** adj. Impérissable. ‖ **Never-ending,** adj. Sans fin, perpétuel, interminable. ‖ **Never-fading,** adj. Grand teint (cloth) ; Fig. Impérissable. ‖ **Never-failing,** adj. Intarissable (well) ; Med. Infaillible (remedy). ‖ **Never-never,** n. Achat à tempérament *m.* ‖ **Never-never land,** n. Fam. Pays imaginaire ; pays (*m.*) de légende. ‖ **Never-sweat,** n. Fam. Flemmard, cossard *s.*

— interj. Fam. Jamais de la vie !, pas possible !, que me dites-vous là !

nevermore [-'mɔ:*] adv. Plus jamais, jamais plus.

nevertheless [,nevəðə'les] adv. Néanmoins, toutefois, pourtant, malgré tout.

new [nju:] adj. Nouveau *m. ;* nouvelle *f.* (fashion, invention, play, suit, topic, year) ; *there is nothing new,* il n'y a rien de nouveau ; *to become a new man,* devenir un autre homme. ‖ Nouveau (at school) ; frais émoulu (*from,* de) ; *the new boys,* les nouveaux. ‖ Nouveau, novice (to business) ; *new to one's trade,* neuf dans le métier. ‖ Neuf (garment) ; *in new clothes,* habillé de neuf, en costume neuf. ‖ Neuf (country, district, idea). ‖ Culin. Frais (bread) ; pas fait (cheese) ; nouveau (potatoes, wine). ‖ Geogr. *New Caledonia, England, Guinea, Orleans, Zealand,* la Nouvelle-Calédonie, -Angleterre, -Guinée, -Orléans, -Zélande ; *New Hebrides,* les Nouvelles-Hébrides ; *New Yorker,* New-Yorkais ; *New Zealander,* Néo-Zélandais.
— adv. Nouvellement. ‖ **New-blown,** adj. Bot. Frais éclos. ‖ **New-born,** adj. Nouveau-né. ‖ **New-coined,** adj. Fin. Nouvellement frappé ; Fam. Nouveau, nouvellement forgé (word). ‖ **New-come,** adj. Nouvellement arrivé. ‖ **New-comer,** n. Nouveau venu, nouvel arrivant *s.* ‖ **New-fangled,** adj. Nouveau genre. ‖ **New-laid,** adj. Frais pondu, du jour (egg).

newel ['njuəl] n. Archit. Noyau *m.* (of stairs) ; pilastre *m.* (at bottom of handrail).

Newfoundland [,nju:fənd'lænd], [nju:'faundlənd] n. Geogr. Terre-Neuve *f.*
— [nju:'faundlənd] n. Zool. Terre-neuve *m.*

Newfoundlander [nju'faundlændə*] n. Geogr., Naut. Terre-neuvien *m.*

Newgate ['nju:git] n. Newgate (prison). ‖ Fam. *Newgate bird,* pilier de prison, gibier de potence.

newish [-iʃ] adj. Plutôt (or) assez nouveau.

newly [-li] adv. Nouvellement, récemment, dernièrement, fraîchement. ‖ **Newly-born,** adj. Nouvellement né, naissant ; *newly-born child,* nouveau-né. ‖ **Newly-weds,** n. pl. Nouveaux mariés *m. pl.*

newness [-nis] n. Nouveauté *f.* (See NOVELTY.) ‖ Etat de neuf *m.* (of garment). ‖ Inexpérience *f.* (of s.o.). ‖ Culin. Fraîcheur *f.* (of bread) ; défaut (*m.*) de maturité (of cheese) ; jeunesse *f.* (of wine).

news [nju:z] n. sg. Nouvelle *f. ;* nouvelles *f. pl. ; what's the news?,* quoi de neuf ? ; *sad piece of news,* triste nouvelle ; *to send news of oneself,* donner de ses nouvelles. ‖ Nouvelles, informations *f. pl. ;* communiqué *m. ; financial news,* chronique financière ; *news items,* échos, faits divers ; *news pictures,* reportage photographique. ‖ Actualité *f. ; to be in the news,* défrayer la chronique. ‖ Sujet (*m.*) de chronique (for news-writer). ‖ Radio. Journal parlé *m. ;* informations *f. pl.* ‖ Ciném. *News cinema,* ciné-actualités, cinéac ; *news film,* actualités. ‖ **News-agency,** n. Agence (*f.*) d'informations. ‖ **News-agent,** n. Agent (*m.*) d'information (in a news-agency) ; marchand (or) dépositaire (*s.*) de journaux (dealer). ‖ **News-board,** n. Voyant, panneau, tableau *m.* ‖ **News-boy,** n. Vendeur (*m.*) de journaux. ‖ **News-conference,** n. Conférence de presse *f.* ‖ **News-letter,** n. Bulletin (*m.*) d'information. ‖ **News-print,** n. Papier journal *m.* ‖ **News-reader,** n. Radio. Speaker (*m.*) des informations. ‖ **News-room,** n. Salle (*f.*) des journaux (in a library) ; salle de rédaction *f.* (in a newspaper office, a radio or television station). ‖ **News-sheet,** n. Feuille *f.* ‖ **News-stall** (or) U. S. **-stand,** n. Etalage (*m.*) de marchands de journaux ; kiosque (*m.*) à journaux. ‖ **News-vendor,** n. Marchand (*m.*) de journaux. ‖ **News-writer,** n. Journaliste *s.*

newscast [-kæst] n. Radio. U. S. Informations *f. pl.*

newscaster [-kæstə*] n. Radio. Speaker-rédacteur (*m.*) des informations.

newsdealer [-di:lə*] n. U. S. Marchand (òr) dépositaire (s.) de journaux.

newsman [-mən] (pl. **newsmen**) n. Vendeur (s.) de journaux. ‖ U. S. Journaliste m.

newsmonger [-,mʌŋgə*] n. Colporteur (s.) de nouvelles, potinier s.

newspaper [-peipə*] n. Journal m.; daily, weekly newspaper, quotidien, hebdomadaire.

newsprint [-print] n. Papier de journal m.

newsreel [-ri:l] n. U. S. Bande (f.) d'actualités.

newsroom [-rum] n. U. S. Service (m.) des informations (newspaper office).

newsy ['nju:zi] n. U. S. FAM. Vendeur (m.) de journaux.

newt [nju:t] n. ZOOL. Triton m.

newton ['nju:tn] n. PHYS. Newton m. (unit).

next [nekst] adj. Prochain, voisin, le plus proche (place); next to, contigu à, attenant à; à côté de. ‖ Prochain, suivant (time); the next day, le lendemain; the next day but one, le surlendemain; the next morning, le lendemain matin; next year, l'année prochaine; the next year, l'année suivante. ‖ Suivant, prochain (in order); next number, prochain numéro; who comes next?, à qui le tour?, qui vient ensuite?; to come next to s.o., venir immédiatement après qqn. ‖ Premier, plus proche; the next time I sing, la prochaine fois que je chanterai; the next thing is to, la première chose à faire c'est de; the next best thing would be to, à défaut, le mieux serait de. ‖ COMM. The next larger size, la taille (or) pointure au-dessus; what next, please?, et avec cela? ‖ FAM. For next to nothing, pour trois fois rien; next to nobody, presque personne. ‖ LOC. Next door, la maison d'à côté; next door but one, deux maisons à côté de chez moi; next neighbours, voisins de porte; to live next door to, habiter à côté de chez (or) porte à porte avec; the people next door, les gens d'à côté; the next of kin, les proches parents, la famille.
— adv. Après, ensuite (in place, order); la prochaine fois (in time).
— prep. Près de, à côté de (s.o., sth.). ‖ FAM. The thing next my heart, la chose qui me tient le plus à cœur.

nexus ['neksəs] n. Connexion f.

N.H.S. [eneitʃ'es] abbr. National Health Service, en Grande-Bretagne, service national de la santé, équivalent du système de Sécurité sociale.

N.I. [en'ai] abbr. National Insurance, système britannique d'assurances sociales.

Niagara [nai'ægərə] n. GEOGR. Niagara m.; Niagara Falls, Chutes du Niagara.

nib [nib] n. Bec f. (of pen). ‖ TECHN. Pointe f. (of tool).
— v. tr. (1). Munir d'une plume. ‖ Tailler en bec.

nibbed [-d] adj. A bec. ‖ TECHN. A pointe.

nibble ['nibl] n. Grignotage, grignotement m. ‖ Tout petit morceau m. (bit). ‖ SPORTS. Touche f. (in fishing).
— v. tr. Grignoter. ‖ TECHN. Grignoter, gruger.
— v. intr. Grignoter; to nibble at one's food, chipoter, manger du bout des dents. ‖ SPORTS. Mordre (at the bait).

nibs [nibz] n. FAM. His nibs, Sa Majesté, Sa Seigneurie.

Nicaragua [,nikə'rægjuə] n. GEOGR. Nicaragua m.

nice [nais] adj. Difficile, délicat (finicky); difficile, exigeant, scrupuleux, méticuleux (punctilious) [person]. ‖ Subtil (distinction); minutieux, méticuleux (enquiry); délicat (experiment, point). ‖ Juste (ear); aiguisé, vif (eye); fin (taste). ‖ Aimable, gentil (to, avec, envers) [character, person]; it is nice of him to, c'est gentil de sa part de; nice people, des gens bien (or) comme il faut. ‖ Agréable, délicieux (evening); to be nice and warm, être agréablement au chaud (person); faire une chaleur agréable (weather). ‖ Joli, charmant; to say nice things, dire de jolies choses. ‖ CULIN. Bon, réussi (dinner). ‖ FAM. Nice mess, beau pétrin. ‖ Nice-looking, adj. Beau, plaisant.

nicely [-li] adv. Soigneusement, minutieusement, avec soin (carefully). ‖ Justement, exactement (exactly). ‖ Gentiment, aimablement (kindly). ‖ Agréablement, délicieusement (pleasantly). ‖ Joliment (prettily).

niceness [-nis] n. Exigence, méticulosité f. (punctiliousness). ‖ Difficulté, délicatesse f. (difficulty). ‖ Subtilité, finesse f. (fineness). ‖ Subtilité, acuité f. (quickness). ‖ Gentillesse, amabilité f. (kindness); agrément m. (pleasantness).

nicety [-iti] n. Précision, exactitude f. (exactness). To a nicety, à la perfection; au poil (fam.). ‖ Subtilité f. (fineness). ‖ Pl. Niceties, détails insignifiants, finesses, minuties.

niche [nitʃ] n. ARCHIT., FIG. Niche f.
— v. tr. Mettre dans une niche (in wall).
— v. intr. Se nicher.

Nichrome ['nai,kroum] n. TECHN. Alliage (m.) nickel-chrome, Nichrome m. (nom déposé).

Nick [nik] n. FAM. Nicolas m. ‖ FAM. Old Nick, le diable.

nick n. Entaille, encoche, coche f. (in plank). ‖ Onglet m. (for opening penknife); fente f. (in screwhead). ‖ Brèche f. (in edge of blade). ‖ In the nick of time, à point nommé, au bon moment; fort à propos; à pic (fam.).
— v. tr. Entailler, encocher, cocher (a plank). ‖ Fendre (a screw-head). ‖ Anglaiser (a horse's tail). ‖ Ebrécher (a blade). ‖ Biseauter (cards); gagner (in game). ‖ FAM. Deviner; to nick it, piger. ‖ POP. Pincer (s.o.); chauffer, faucher, carotter (sth.).
— v. intr. ZOOL. Se croiser (with, avec). ‖ SPORTS. To nick in, couper.

nickel ['nikl] n. Nickel m. ‖ U. S. FAM. Pièce (f.) de cinq cents. ‖ Nickel-in-the-slot machine, .n. U. S. Appareil à sous m. ‖ Nickel-plate, v. tr. Nickeler. ‖ Nickel-plater, n. Nickeleur m. ‖ Nickel-plating, n. Nickelage m.
— v. tr. Nickeler.

nickelling [-iŋ] n. Nickelage m. (act); nickelure f. (result).

nicker ['nikə*] n. invar. POP. Livre f. (pound).

nickname ['nikneim] n. Surnom, sobriquet m. ‖ Diminutif m. (shortened name).
— v. tr. Surnommer. ‖ Appeler par son diminutif.

nicotian [ni'kouʃən] adj. Nicotique.

nicotine ['nikəti:n] n. CHIM. Nicotine f.

nicotinism [-izm] n. MED. Tabagisme m.

nict(it)ate ['nikt(it)eit] v. intr. Ciller.

nict(it)ation [,rikt(it)'teiʃən] n. Cillement m.

nidify ['nidifai] v. intr. (2). Faire son nid, nidifier.

nidus ['naidəs] (pl. **niduses** [-iz], **nidi** ['naidai]) n. ZOOL. Nid m. (of insects). ‖ MED., FIG. Foyer m.

niece [ni:s] n. Nièce f.

niellist [ni'elist] n. Nielleur s.

niello [ni'elou] n. Nielle m. (enamel); niellure f. (work); to inlay with niello, nieller. ‖ Niello-work, n. Niellure f.

nielloed [-d] adj. Niellé.

niff [nif] n. FAM. Puanteur f.
— v. intr. FAM. Puer, empester.

niffy [-i] adj. Puant.

nifty ['nifti] adj. FAM. Pimpant.

Niger ['naidʒə*] n. GEOGR. Niger m. (state, river).

Nigeria [nai'dʒiəriə] n. GEOGR. Nigeria m.

niggard ['nigəd] adj., n. Avare s. (See MISER.)

niggardliness [-linis] n. Avarice, pingrerie f.

niggardly [-li] adj. Pingre; rapiat, rat (fam.) [person]. ‖ Mesquin, piètre (portion).
— adv. Avec mesquinerie, chichement, parcimonieusement.

nigger ['nigə*] n. Nègre m.; négresse f.; noir s. ‖

FAM. *Nigger in the wood-pile,* anguille sous roche. ‖ **Nigger-brown,** adj. Tête-de-nègre.
— v. tr. Noircir.

niggle [nigl] v. intr. Tatillonner, couper les cheveux en quatre. ‖ ARTS. Pignocher.

niggler [-ə*] n. Tatillon, vétilleur *s.* ‖ ARTS. Pignocheur *s.*

niggling [-iŋ] adj. Insignifiant (detail); tatillon (person). ‖ ARTS. Fignolé, pignoché.

nigh [nai] adv., prep. Près. (See NEAR.)

night [nait] n. Nuit *f.; by night,* nuitamment, de nuit; *last night,* cette nuit, la nuit dernière; *in the night,* pendant la nuit; *night and day,* nuit et jour; *to have a good night,* passer une bonne nuit. ‖ Soir *m.; last night,* hier soir; *the night before,* la veille au soir. ‖ Nuit, obscurité *f.; at night,* à la nuit; *night is falling,* la nuit tombe. ‖ COMM. *Night's lodging,* nuit, logement pour la nuit (at an inn). ‖ THEATR. Représentation *f.; first night,* première. ‖ MUS. Soirée musicale *f.* ‖ FIG. Nuit *f.;* ténèbres *f. pl.* ‖ LOC. *The Arabian Nights,* « Les Mille et Une Nuits ». ‖ FAM. *To make a night of it,* passer la nuit en bombe. ‖ **Night-bell,** n. Sonnette de nuit *f.* ‖ **Night-bird,** n. ZOOL. Nocturne, oiseau (*m.*) de nuit; FAM. Noctambule *m.* ‖ **Night-blind,** adj. Nyctalope. ‖ **Night-cap,** n. Bonnet (*m.*) de nuit; FAM. Posset *m.* ‖ **Night-club,** n. Boîte de nuit *f.* ‖ **Night-dress,** n. Chemise de nuit, robe à dormir *f.* ‖ **Night-driver,** n. AUTOM. Routier (*m.*) conduisant de nuit. ‖ **Night-fighter,** adj. AVIAT. De nuit (pilot). ‖ **Night-gown,** n. Chemise de nuit *f.* ‖ **Night-haunt,** n. Boîte de nuit *f.* ‖ **Night-lamp,** n. Veilleuse *f.* ‖ **Night-piece,** n. ARTS. Effet (*m.*) de nuit. ‖ **Night-prowler,** n. Noctambule (person); rôdeur *m.* (ruffian). ‖ **Night-shelter,** n. Asile (*m.*) de nuit. ‖ **Night-shift,** n. TECHN. Equipe de nuit *f.* ‖ **Night-shirt,** n. Chemise de nuit *f.* (for men). ‖ **Night-time,** n. Nuit *f.; at night-time,* la nuit. ‖ **Night-watch,** n. Garde de nuit *f.* (act, person); veille de nuit *f.;* NAUT. Quart (*m.*) de nuit. ‖ **Night-watchman,** n. Veilleur (*m.*) de nuit. ‖ **Night-work,** n. Travail (*m.*) de nuit.

nightery [-ri] n. POP. U. S. Boîte de nuit *f.*

nightfall [-fɔ:l] n. Tombée (*f.*) du jour; crépuscule *m.;* nuit tombante *f.; at nightfall,* à la brune.

nightie [-i] n. FAM. Chemise de nuit *f.*

nightingale [-iŋgeil] n. ZOOL., FIG. Rossignol *m.*

nightjar [-dʒɑ:*] n. ZOOL. Engoulevent *m.*

nightly [-li] adj. De nuit (happening at night). ‖ De tous les soirs, de toutes les nuits.
— adv. Chaque soir; toutes les nuits.

nightman [-mən] (pl. **nightmen**) n. Vidangeur *m.*

nightmare [-mɛə*] n. Càuchemar *m.* (lit. and fig.).

nightmarish [-mɛəriʃ] adj. Cauchemardesque.

nightshade [-,ʃeid] n. BOT. Morelle *f.; deadly nightshade,* belladone.

nigrescence [nai'gresəns] n. Noirceur *f.*

nigrescent [-ənt] adj. Nigrescent.

nigrite ['naigrait] n. ELECTR. Nigrite *f.*

nigritude ['nigritju:d] n. Noirceur *f.*

nihilism [,nai(h)ilizm] n. Nihilisme *m.*

nihilist [-ist] n. Nihiliste *s.*

nihilistic [-istik] adj. Nihiliste.

nihility [-iti] n. Néant *m.* ‖ FAM. Rien *m.;* broutille, vétille, misère *f.*

nil [nil] n. Rien *m.* ‖ Néant *m.* (on an official form). ‖ SPORTS. Zéro *m.*

Nile [nail] n. GEOGR. Nil *m.*

nimble ['nimbl] adj. Agile, leste, preste (person); ingambe (old person). ‖ Prompt (*at, in,* à). ‖ FIG. Délié, prompt (mind). ‖ **Nimble-footed,** adj. Aux pieds agiles. ‖ **Nimble-minded,** adj. A l'esprit prompt.

nimbleness [-nis] n. Agilité *f.* ‖ FIG. Promptitude, vivacité *f.*

nimbus ['nimbəs] n. Nimbe *m.* (halo). ‖ Nimbus *m.* (rain, cloud). ‖ ARTS. Auréole *f.*
— N. B. Deux pluriels : *nimbuses, nimbi.*

Nimrod ['nimrɔd] n. Nemrod *m.*

nincompoop ['ninkəmpu:p] n. FAM. Crétin, serin, cornichon *m.*

nine [nain] adj., n. Neuf *m.* ‖ † *The Nine,* les neuf sœurs. ‖ MATH. *To cast out the nines,* faire la preuve par neuf. ‖ FAM. *Dressed up to the nines,* en tralala. ‖ **Nine-hole-course,** n. SPORTS. Neuf trous *m.*

ninefold [-fould] adj., adv. Multiplié par neuf.

ninepin [-pin] n. Quille *f.* (See SKITTLE.) ‖ Pl. Jeu (*m.*) de quilles (set).

nineteen [-'ti:n] adj., n. Dix-neuf *m.*

nineteenth [-'ti:nθ] adj., n. Dix-neuvième *m.*

ninetieth [-tiiθ] adj., n. Quatre-vingt-dixième *m.*

ninety [-ti] adj., n. Quatre-vingt-dix *m.* ‖ Pl. FAM. *The nineties,* entre quatre-vingt-dix et cent ans (age); les années 90 (years). ‖ **Ninety-one,** adj. Quatre-vingt-onze. ‖ **Ninety-nine,** adj. Quatre-vingt-dix-neuf; MED. *To say ninety-nine,* dire trente-trois.

ninny ['nini] n. FAM. Nigaud *s.* (person).

ninth [nainθ] adj., n. Neuvième *m.*

ninthly [-li] adv. Neuvièmement.

niobium [nai'oubiəm] n. CHIM. Niobium *m.*

nip [nip] n. FAM. Goutte, rincette *f.;* pousse-café *m.* (See DRAM, TOT.)
— v. intr. (1). FAM. Siroter.

Nip. n. FAM. U. S. Japonais *m.*

nip n. Pincement, pinçon *m.* (pinch). ‖ Etranglement *m.* (narrowing). ‖ NAUT. Portage *m.;* étrive *f.* ‖ AGRIC. Morsure (*f.*) du froid; piquant, vif *m.* (in the air). ‖ GEOGR. Dentelure, déchiqueture *f.* (of coast-line).
— v. tr. (1). Pincer. (See PINCH.) ‖ NAUT. Etuver. ‖ AGRIC. Brûler, brouir (a plant); *nipped by the frost,* gelé, éborgné. ‖ Mordre, piquer (fingers, cold). ‖ FIG. *To nip in the bud,* tuer dans l'œuf. ‖ FAM. Chiper, chauffer, faucher.
— v. intr. **To nip around,** être étrivé (rope). ‖ **To nip in,** FAM. Entrer vivement. ‖ **To nip off,** s'esquiver, sortir vite.

nipped-in [-tin] adj. Ceintré (waist).

nipper [-ə*] n. Pince, pincette, tenaille *f.* (tool). ‖ ZOOL. Pince *f.* ‖ FAM. Mioche, gosse *m.*

nippiness [-inis] n. Agilité, prestesse *f.* ‖ Fraîcheur *f.* (of cold).

nipping [-iŋ] adj. Pinçant (cold, tool); mordant (remark, wind).

nipple ['nipl] n. MED. Mamelon, bout du sein *m.* ‖ Tétine *f.* (of feeding-bottle). ‖ GEOGR. Mamelon *m.* ‖ TECHN. AUTOM. Raccord *m.* ‖ **Nipple-cactus,** n. BOT. Mamillaire *f.*

Nipponese ['nipəni:z] adj., n. GEOGR. Nippon.

nippy ['nipi] adj. FAM. Preste, rapide; *to be nippy about it,* se grouiller (or) dérouiller. ‖ FAM. Vif, mordant (cold).

nirvana [niə'vɑ:nə] n. Nirvâna *m.*

nisei ['nisei] n. U. S. Citoyen américain (*s.*) né de parents japonais.

nisi ['naisai] conj. JUR. Sous condition (decision); provisoire (decree).

nit [nit] n. ZOOL. Lente *f.* ‖ FAM. U. S. Propre à rien *m.*

niter ['naitə*] n. U. S. See NITRE.

nitrate ['naitreit] n. CHIM. Nitrate *m.*
— v. tr. CHIM. Nitrater.

nitrated [-id] adj. CHIM. Nitré, nitraté.

nitration [nai'treiʃən] n. CHIM. Nitration *f.*

nitre ['naitə*] n. CHIM. Nitre *m.* (See SALTPETRE.) ‖ **Nitre-bed,** n. Nitrière *f.*

nitric [-trik] adj. CHIM. Nitrique; *nitric oxide,* bioxyde d'azote.

nitride [-tráid] n. CHIM. Nitrure m.
— v. tr. Nitrurer.
nitrification [,naitrifi'keiʃən] n. Nitrification f.
nitrify ['naitrifai] v. tr. (2). Nitrifier.
— v. intr. Se nitrifier.
nitrile [-trail] n. CHIM. Nitrile m.
nitrite [-trait] n. CHIM. Nitrite m.
nitrobenzene [,naitro'benzi:n] n. CHIM. Nitrobenzène m.
nitrocellulose [-'seljulous] n. Nitrocellulose f.
— adj. Cellulosique.
nitrogelatine [-'dʒeləti:n] n. Gélatine-dynamite f.
nitrogen ['naitrodʒən] n. CHIM. Azote, nitrogène m.
— adj. CHIM. Nitrogène.
nitrogenous [nai'trodʒinəs] adj. CHIM. Azoté.
nitro-glycerine ['naitro,glisə'ri:n] n. CHIM.
Nitroglycérine f.
nitrous ['naitrəs] adj. CHIM. Nitreux, azoteux,
d'azote.
nitty ['niti] adj. Couvert de lentes.
nitty-gritty ['niti'griti] n. FAM. Fond (or) cœur
du problème m., réalité concrète f., détails pratiques
m. pl. ; to get down to the nitty-gritty, en venir aux
choses sérieuses.
— adj. Concret, pratique (situation, details).
nitwit ['nitwit] n. FAM. Âne, nigaud, crétin s.
nival ['naivəl] adj. BOT. Nivéal. ‖ Nival.
niveous ['ni:viəs] adj. Neigeux, nivéen.
nix [niks] n. FAM. Nib de nib m. ; peau de balle f.
no [nou] adj. Aucun, nul, pas de ; no man, aucun
homme, personne ; no admittance, entrée interdite ;
no smoking, défense de fumer. ‖ Peu, pas, nullement ; it's no small matter, ce n'est pas rien. ‖
SPORTS. No ball, balle nulle. ‖ FAM. No go!, pas
mèche!, je ne marche pas! ‖ No-account, adj. U.S.
FAM. Négligeable, sans importance. ‖ No-load, adj.
TECHN. A vide. ‖ No-man's land, n. Zone neutre f.
— adv. Non ; to say no, dire non. ‖ Ne... pas ; to
be no wiser than, ne pas être plus sage que.
— n. Non m. ‖ Vote négatif (or) défavorable m.
(in voting).
No. Written abbr. for number, Nº (or) nº, numéro.
Noachian [nou'eikiən] adj. De Noé.
Noah ['nouə] n. Noé m.
nob [nɔb] n. FAM. Citrouille, fiole f. (head).
nob n. FAM. Richard, aristo m. ; the nobs, la haute.
nobble ['nɔbl̩] v. tr. Acheter, corrompre (s.o.);
capter (votes). ‖ FAM. Faucher, rafler (money) ; pincer (s.o.). ‖ FAM., SPORTS. Droguer (to drug) ; écloper (to lame) [a horse].
nobby ['nɔbi] adj. FAM. Chic, rupin.
nobelium [nou'bi:liəm] n. CHIM. Nobélium m.
nobiliary [nou'biljəri] adj. Nobiliaire.
nobility [-iti] n. Noblesse f.
noble ['noubl̩] adj. Noble (birth, person, soul). ‖
Superbe, magnifique, imposant (building, mountain).
‖ Noble-minded, adj. Magnanime, généreux.
— n. Aristocrate, noble m.
nobleman [-mən] (pl. noblemen) n. Gentilhomme ;
noble m.
noblemindedness [noubl̩'maindidnis] n. Grandeur (or) noblesse d'âme f.
nobleness ['noubl̩nis] n. Noblesse f. (of birth). ‖
Majesté f. (of a building). ‖ FIG. Grandeur, noblesse
f. (of mind).
noblewoman [-wumən] (pl. noblewomen [-wi-
mən]) n. Aristocrate f.
nobly ['noubli] adv. Noblement. ‖ Superbement.
nobody ['noubədi] pron. Personne, nul ; nobody
knows it, nul (or) personne ne le sait.
— n. FAM. Nullité f. ; zéro, rien du tout m. ‖ FAM.
Inconnu s.
nook [nɔk] n. Encoche, coche f.
— v. tr. Encocher.
nock n. NAUT. Empointure f.

noctambulism [nɔk'tæmbjulizm] n. Noctambulisme m. ‖ MED. Somnambulisme m.
noctambulist [-ist] n. Noctambule s. ‖ MED. Somnambule s.
nocturn ['nɔktə:n] n. ECCLES. Nocturne m.
nocturnal [nɔk'tə:nəl] adj. Nocturne. (See NIGHTLY.)
— n. pl. ZOOL. Nocturnes m. pl.
nocturne ['nɔktə:n] n. MUS. Nocturne m. ‖ ARTS.
Effet (m.) de nuit.
nocuous ['nɔkjuəs] adj. Nocif.
nod [nɔd] n. Signe (m.) de tête (assent) ; to answer
with a nod, opiner. ‖ Signe (m.) de tête (bow) ; to
give a nod, saluer en inclinant la tête. ‖ Dodelinement (m.) de la tête (from sleepiness) ; the land of
Nod, le pays des Songes.
— v. tr. (1). Incliner (one's head) ; to nod assent,
faire signe que oui.
— v. tr. (1). Faire un signe de tête (to, à) ; all
heads nodded in approval, tous opinèrent. ‖ Dodeliner de la tête (to wag one's head). ‖ Sommeiller,
somnoler (to doze). ‖ S'incliner, pencher (to bend).
‖ Ballotter (to toss). ‖ Chanceler (to totter).
nodal ['noudl̩] adj. PHYS. Nodal.
nodding ['nɔdiŋ] adj. Dodelinant (head). ‖ Ballot-
tant, dansant (plume). ‖ Chancelant (building).
— n. Signe (m.) de tête. ‖ Dodelinement m. ‖ Balancement m.
noddle ['nɔdl̩] n. FAM. Ciboulot, citron m. (See
NUT, PATE.)
— v. tr. FAM. Branler (one's head).
node [noud] n. ASTRON., MATH., PHYS., ELECTR.,
BOT. Nœud m. ‖ MED. Nodosité f.
nodose [no'dous] adj. Noueux.
nodosity [no'dɔsiti] n. Nodosité f. (See KNOTTINESS.)
nodular ['nɔdjulə*] adj. MED., GEOL. Nodulaire.
nodule ['nɔdju:l] n. MED., BOT., GEOL. Nodule m.
nodulose [,nɔdju'lous] adj. BOT., GEOL. Noduleux.
nodus ['noudəs] (pl. nodi [-ai]) n. FIG. Nœud m.
Noel [nou'el] n. † Noël m.
noetic [no'etik] adj., n. Intellectuel s.
— n. pl. Science de l'intelligence f.
nog [nɔg] n. Cheville f. (peg). ‖ BOT. Chicot m. (on
tree). ‖ ARCHIT. Soliveau m.
— v. tr. (1). Cheviller. ‖ ARCHIT. Hourder.
nog n. Bière forte f.
noggin ['nɔgin] n. Pot, quart m.
nohow ['nouhau] adv. FAM. Aucunement, en
aucune façon. ‖ POP. Mal fichu.
noise [nɔiz] n. Bruit m. ; to make a noise, faire
du bruit. ‖ Tintamarre, boucan m. (din). ‖ Son,
bruit m. ; clanging noise, bruit métallique. ‖ Friture f. (on the telephone). ‖ RADIO. Bruit de fond
m. ‖ MED. Pl. Bourdonnements m. pl. (in the ears).
— v. tr. Ebruiter, faire du bruit autour de ; noised
abroad, publié à grand bruit.
noiseless [-lis] adj. Sans bruit, silencieux. ‖ TECHN.
Insonorisé.
noiselessly [-lisli] adv. Silencieusement, sans bruit.
noiselessness [-lisnis] n. Silence m. ‖ TECHN. Fonctionnement silencieux m.
noisily [-ili] adv. Bruyamment.
noisiness [-inis] n. Tintamarre, vacarme m. (din).
‖ Nature bruyante, turbulence f. (boisterousness).
noisome [-nɔisəm] adj. Puant, fétide. (See STINK-
ING.) ‖ BOT. Nuisible.
noisomeness [-nis] n. Puanteur, fétidité f. ‖ BOT.
Nocivité f.
noisy ['nɔizi] adj. Bruyant (child, crowd, street). ‖
Criard, voyant (colour). ‖ FIG. Enflé, pompeux,
tapageur (style).
nomad ['noumæd] adj., n. Nomade s.
nomadic [no'mædik] adj. Nomade.
nomadism ['nɔmədizm] n. Nomadisme m.
nomadize [-aiz] v. intr. Vivre en nomade.
nom de plume [nɔmdə'plu:m] n. Nom (m.) de
guerre ; pseudonyme m. (See PEN-NAME.)

nomenclature [nou'menklətʃə*] n. Nomenclature *f*.

nominal ['nɔminļ] adj. Nominal, de nom. ‖ FIN. Fictif (prices, value). ‖ TECHN. Nominal (horsepower). ‖ MILIT. Nominatif (roll).

nominalism [-əlizm̩] n. PHILOS. Nominalisme *m*.

nominalist [-əlist] n. PHILOS. Nominaliste *s*.

nominally [-əli] adv. Nominalement.

nominate [-eit] v. tr. Nommer, appeler (to name, to mention). ‖ Nommer, désigner (to appoint). ‖ Fixer, déterminer (to fix). ‖ Proposer (to put up).

nomination [,nɔmi'neiʃən] n. Nomination, présentation (for an appointment).

nominative ['nɔminətiv] adj. Désigné (member). ‖ GRAMM. Nominatif.
— n. GRAMM. Nominatif *m*.

nominator ['nɔmineitə*] n. Présentateur *m*.

nominee [nɔmi'ni:] n. Personne dénommée *f*. (for an annuity); candidat agréé *s*. (for a post).

nomogram ['nɔməgræm] n. MATH. Abaque *m*.

non [nɔn] pref. Non *m*. ‖ **Non-absorbent**, adj. Non perméable. ‖ **Non-acceptance**, n. FIN. Non-acceptation *f*. ‖ **Non-accomplishment**, n. Inaccomplissement *m*. ‖ **Non-activity**, n. Non-activité *f*. ‖ **Non-adjustable**, adj. Non réglable. ‖ **Non-aggression**, n. Non-agression *f*. ‖ **Non-alcoholic**, adj. Non alcoolisé. ‖ **Non-alignement**, n. Non-alignement *m*. ‖ **Non-appearance**, n. JUR. Non-comparution *f*. ‖ **Non-attendance**, n. Non-assistance, absence *f*. ‖ **Non-belligerence**, n. Non-belligérance *f*. ‖ **Non-beneficed**, adj. ECCLES. Habitué (priest). ‖ **Non-com**, n. MILIT., FAM. Sous-off *m*. ‖ **Non-combatant**, adj., n. MILIT. Non combattant *adj.*, non-combattant *m*. ‖ **Non-commissioned**, adj. MILIT. Non breveté; *non-commissioned officer*, sous-officier. ‖ **Non-committal**, adj. Qui n'engage à rien; qui ne se compromet pas, réservé; normand (fam.). ‖ **Non-completion**, n. Non-achèvement *m*. ‖ **Non-compliance**, n. Refus (*m*.) d'obéissance. ‖ **Non-compressible**, adj. Incompressible. ‖ **Non-concur**, v. tr. JUR. U. S. Rejeter. ‖ **Non-concurrence**, n. JUR. Non-concurrence *f.*; *non-concurrence of sentences*, cumul de peines. ‖ **Non-conducting**, adj. PHYS. Non conducteur; ELECTR. Isolant. ‖ **Non-conductor**, n. PHYS. Non-conducteur *m.*; ELECTR. Isolant *m*. ‖ **Non-consent**, n. Défaut de consentement *m*. ‖ **Non-contributory**, adj. FIN. Sans cotisation versée par le bénéficiaire (pension scheme). ‖ **Non-corrodible**, adj. Inoxydable. ‖ **Non-dazzle**, adj. AUTOM. Code, non-aveuglant (headlight). ‖ **Non-delivery**, n. Non-livraison; non-réception *f*. ‖ **Non-detachable**, adj. Indémontable. ‖ **Non-directional**, adj. PSYCH. Non-directif. ‖ **Non-effective**, adj. Ineffectif; MILIT. En non-activité. ‖ **Non-ego**, n. PHILOS. Non-moi *m*. ‖ **Non-event**, n. Evénement insignifiant *m.*, petite péripétie *f*. ‖ **Non-existence**, n. PHILOS. Non-être *m*. ‖ **Non-existent**, adj. Non existant. ‖ **Non-explosive**, adj. Inexplosif. ‖ **Non-fading**, adj. COMM. Bon teint (colour). ‖ **Non-feasance**, n. JUR. Délit (*m*.) par abstention. ‖ **Non-ferrous**, adj. Non ferreux. ‖ **Non-fiction**, n. Littérature non romanesque *f.*; adj. Non romanesque. ‖ **Non-flying**, adj. AVIAT. Non volant. ‖ **Non-fouling**, adj. TECHN. Inencrassable. ‖ **Non-freezing**, adj. Incongelable. ‖ **Non-fulfilment**, n. Non-exécution *f*. ‖ **Non-greasy**, adj. Qui ne graisse pas. ‖ **Non-halation**, adj. Antihalo. ‖ **Non-inflammable**, adj. Ininflammable. ‖ **Non-interference**, n. Non-intervention *f*. ‖ **Non-iron**, adj. Qui ne se repasse pas (fabric, garment). ‖ **Non-juring**, adj. Inassermenté (priest). ‖ **Non-ladder**, adj. Indémaillable (stocking). ‖ **Non-metal**, n. CHIM. Non-métal, métalloïde *m*. ‖ **Non-metallic**, adj. CHIM. Non métallique. ‖ **Non-mobile**, adj. MILIT. Sédentaire. ‖ **Non-moral**, adj. Amoral. ‖ **Non-negotiable**, adj. FIN. Non négociable. ‖ **Non-observance**, n. Inobservance *f*. ‖ **Non-official**, adj. Officieux. ‖ **Non-oxidizing**, adj. Inoxydable. ‖ **Non-payment**, n. Non-paiement *m*. ‖ **Non-perfor-**

mance, n. Non-exécution *f*. ‖ **Non-profit-making**, U. S. **non-profit**, adj. A but non lucratif (organization). ‖ **Non-proliferation**, n. Non-prolifération *f*. ‖ **Non-provided**, adj. Libre (school). ‖ **Non-recurring**, adj. FIN. Extraordinaire (expenditure). ‖ **Non-removable**, adj. Inamovible. ‖ **Non-residence**, n. Non-résidence *f*. (in general); externat *m*. (at school). ‖ **Non-resident**, adj. Non résident; n. Non-résident *m*. (in general); externe *m*. (at school); voyageur de passage *m*. (in a hotel). ‖ **Non-returnable**, adj. COMM. Perdu (packing). ‖ **Non-reversible**, adj. Irréversible. ‖ **Non-sectarian**, adj. Impartial. ‖ **Non-sinkable**, adj. NAUT. Insubmersible. ‖ **Non-skid**, adj. AUTOM. Antidérapant. ‖ **Non-smoker**, n. Non-fumeur *m*. ‖ **Non-starter**, n. FIG., FAM. Entreprise (*f.*) vouée à l'échec; raté, tocard *s*. (person); SPORTS. Non-partant m. ‖ **Non-stick**, adj. Qui n'attache pas (pan). ‖ **Non-stop**, adj. CH. DE F. Direct; AVIAT. Sans escale; THEATR. Permanent. ‖ **Non-stretching**, adj. Inextensible. ‖ **Non-success**, n. Insuccès *m.*; non-réussite *f*. ‖ **Non-transferable**, adj. Personnel (ticket). ‖ **Non-U**, adj. FAM. Pas distingué, qui manque de classe. ‖ **Non-unionist**, n. Non-syndiqué *s*. ‖ **Non-viable**, adj. MED. Non viable. ‖ **Non-violence**, n. Non-violence *f*. ‖ **Non-violent**, adj. Non-violent.

nonage ['nounidʒ] n. Minorité *f*.

nonagenarian [,nounədʒi'nɛəriən] n. Nonagénaire *s*.

nonagon ['nɔnə,gɔn] n. MATH. Nonagone, ennéagone *m*.

nonce [nɔns] n. Occasion *f.; for the nonce,* pour la circonstance. ‖ **Nonce-word**, n. GRAMM. Création verbale occasionnelle *f*.

nonchalance ['nɔnʃələns] n. Indifférence nonchalante *f.*; nonchaloir *m*.

nonchalant [-ənt] adj. Indifférent, nonchalant, négligent.

nonconformist [,nɔnkən'fɔ:mist] adj., n. ECCLES. Non-conformiste *s*.

nonconformity [-miti] n. ECCLES. Non-conformisme *m*.

nondescript ['nɔndiskript] adj. Indéfinissable, quelconque (person); indescriptible (thing).

none [nʌn] pron. Aucun; *none at all*, pas un seul; *none of that*, pas de ça; *none of them*, aucun d'eux (or) d'entre eux; nul (or) personne parmi eux. ‖ Personne, nul; *none but you saw him*, nul autre que vous ne l'a vu, vous seul l'avez vu. ‖ Pas, point, aucun (emphatically).
— adv. Pas; *to be none the wiser for it*, n'être pas plus sage pour autant; *they are none too generous*, ils ne sont pas excessivement généreux. ‖ **None the less**, adv. Néanmoins, toutefois, pourtant, ne... pas moins.

nonentity [nɔ'nentiti] n. Néant *m*. ‖ FAM. Nullité *f*. (person); *only a few nonentities*, quatre pelés et un tondu.

nonesuch ['nʌn,sʌtʃ] n. See NONSUCH.

nonet [nɔ'net] n. MUS. Nonetto *m*.

nonetheless [,nʌnðə'les] adv. See NONE.

nonpareil ['nɔnpərəl] adj. Sans pareil, qui n'a pas son pareil, inégalé.
— n. Modèle *m.*, parangon (†) *m*.

nonplus ['nɔn'plʌs] n. Perplexité *f*.
— v. tr. (1). Déconcerter, dérouter; désemparer.

nonsense ['nɔnsəns] n. Absurdité, sottise, bêtise, imbécillité, ineptie, ânerie *f.; he will stand no nonsense*, il ne plaisante pas sur ce chapitre; *no nonsense!*, pas de bêtises!; *with no nonsense*, en tout bien tout honneur.

nonsensical [-ikəl] adj. Absurde, inepte, bête, sot.

nonsensically [-ikəli] adv. Absurdement, stupidement.

non sequitur ['nɔn 'sekwitə*] n. Illogisme *m.*, manque (*m*.) de suite (in reasoning).

nonsuch ['nʌn,sʌtʃ] n. Personne (or) chose

exceptionnelle (or) sans pareille *f.* ‖ Bot. Minette, lupuline *f.*

noodle ['nu:dl] n. Fam. Nouille *f.* (person).

noodles [-z] n. pl. Culin. Nouilles *f. pl.*

nook [nuk] n. Coin *m. ; breakfast nook,* coin-repas.

noon [nu:n] n. Midi *m.*

noonday [-dei] n. Midi *m.* ‖ Fig. Faîte *m.*
— adj. De midi (sun).

noose [nu:s] n. Nœud coulant *m.* (running knot). ‖ Collet *m.* (snare). ‖ Lasso *m.* ‖ Corde *f.* (hangman's halter) ; *to put one's head in a noose* (fam.), se jeter dans la gueule du loup.
— v. tr. Prendre au lasso (or) au collet (entrap). ‖ Faire un nœud coulant à.

nopal ['noupəl] n. Bot. Nopal *m.*

nope [noup] adv. Fam. Non.

nor [nɔ:*] conj. Ni ; *neither... nor,* ni... ni ; *neither John nor Peter,* ni Jean ni Pierre ; *she neither eats nor drinks,* elle ne mange ni ne boit. ‖ Ni... non plus ; *nor I,* ni moi non plus. ‖ Et... pas davantage ; *nor had he promised to come,* et il n'avait pas davantage promis de venir.

Nordic ['nɔ:dik] adj. Nordique.

noria ['nɔ:riə] n. Noria *f.*

norm [nɔ:m] n. Norme *f.*

normal [-əl] adj. Normal, ordinaire, commun (person, thing) ; normal (school). ‖ Math. Perpendiculaire (to, à). ‖ Electr., Techn. De régime. ‖ Chim. Neutre (salt) ; titré (solution).
— n. Normale *f. ;* état normal *m.* ‖ Math. Perpendiculaire *f.*

normalcy [-əlsi] n. U. S. Normalité *f. ;* état normal *m.*

normality [nɔ:'mæliti] n. Normalité *f.*

normalization [,nɔ:məlai'zei ʃən] n. Normalisation *f.*

normalize ['nɔ:məlaiz] v. tr. Normaliser.

normally [-əli] adv. Normalement.

Norman ['nɔ:mən] adj., n. Geogr. Normand *s.* ‖ Archit. Roman *m.*

Normandy [-di] n. Geogr. Normandie *f.*

Normanesque [,nɔ:mə'nesk] adj. Archit. Roman.

normative ['nɔ:mətiv] adj. Normatif.

Norse [nɔ:s] adj., n. Norrois, nordique *m.* ‖ Norvégien *m.*

Norseland ['nɔ:slənd] n. Geogr. Norvège *f.*

Norseman ['nɔ:smən] (pl. **Norsemen**) n. Norvégien *m.* ‖ Scandinave *m.*

north [nɔ:θ] n. Nord *m.*
— adv. Au nord (of, de). ‖ Du nord, vers le nord (with movement).
— adj. Au nord (aspect). ‖ Du nord, septentrional. ‖ Geogr. Du nord (America) ; Nord (cape). ‖ **North-east,** adj., adv., n. Nord-est *m.* ‖ **North-eastern,** adj. Du nord-est. ‖ **North-west,** adj., adv., n. Nord-ouest *m.* ‖ **North-western,** adj. Du nord-ouest.

northbound ['nɔ:θ,baund] adj. En direction du nord.

northeaster [,nɔ:θ'i:stə*] n. Vent du nord-est *m. ;* nordé (or) nordet *m.* (naut.).

norther ['nɔ:ðə*] n. U. S. Vent du nord *m.*

northerly [-əli] adj. Au nord (aspect) ; vers le nord (direction) ; nord (latitude) ; du nord (wind).
— n. Vent du nord.
— adv. Vers le nord.

northern ['nɔ:ðən] adj. Du nord, septentrional ; *northern lights,* aurore boréale.

northerner [-ə*] n. Septentrional *m. ;* personne (*f.*) du nord. ‖ U. S. Nordiste *m.*

northernmost [-moust] adj. Le plus au nord.

northing ['nɔ:ðiŋ] n. Naut. Chemin nord *m.*

northland ['nɔ:θlənd] n. Nord du pays *m.* ‖ Pl. Pays (*m. pl.*) du nord.

Northman [-mən] (pl. **Northmen**) n. Scandinave *m.*

Northumbrian [nɔ:'θʌmbriən] adj., n. Geogr. Northumbrien.

northward ['nɔ:θwəd] adj. Au nord, du nord.
— n. Nord *m. ;* direction (*f.*) nord.

northwards [-z] adv. Vers le nord.

Norway ['nɔ:wei] n. Norvège *f.*

Norwegian [nɔ:'wi:dʒən] adj., n. Norvégien *s.*

nor'-wester [,nɔ:'westə*] n. Vent du nord-ouest, norois *m.*

nose [nouz] n. Nez *m. ; to blow one's nose,* se moucher. ‖ Museau *m.* (of animal) ; nez *m.* (of dog). ‖ Odorat, nez *m. ; to have a good nose,* avoir le nez fin. ‖ Arôme, bouquet *m.* (odour). ‖ Culin. *Parson's* (or) U. S. *pope's nose,* croupion, sot-l'y-laisse. ‖ Techn. Bec *m.* ‖ Naut., Aviat. Nez *m.* ‖ Ch. de f. Pointe *f.* ‖ Fig. Flair *m.* (*for,* pour). ‖ Fam. *To lead by the nose,* mener par le bout du nez ; *to look down one's nose,* faire un nez ; *to make a long nose at,* faire un pied de nez à ; *to poke one's nose into,* fourrer son nez dans ; *to turn up one's nose at,* faire la nique à. ‖ **Nose-bag,** n. Musette *f.* (for horse) ; Med. *Nose-bag mask,* masque médical. ‖ **Nose-band,** n. Muserolle *f.* ‖ **Nose-bleeding** (or) U. S. **-bleed,** n. Med. Saignement de nez *m.* ‖ **Nose-cap,** n. Milit. Coiffe *m.* ‖ **Nose-cone,** n. Nez *m.* (of plane) ; ogive *f.* (of missile). ‖ **Nose-dive,** n. Aviat. Piqué *m. ;* v. intr. Aviat. Descendre en piqué. ‖ **Nose-key,** n. Techn. Contre-clavette *f.* ‖ **Nose-lift,** n. Aviat. Cabrage *m.* ‖ **Nose-piece,** n. † Nasal *m.* (of armour) ; Techn. Bec *m. ;* Phys. Porte-objectifs *m.* ‖ **Nose-pipe,** n. Techn. Ajutage *m.* ‖ **Nose-sprayer,** n. Med. Insufflateur *m.* ‖ **Nose-wheel,** n. Aviat. Roue (*f.*) avant, train (*m.*) avant. ‖ **Nose-wiper,** n. Fam. Tire-jus *m.*
— v. tr. Flairer, sentir. ‖ **To nose out,** flairer, dépister, découvrir par son flair.
— v. intr. **To nose about,** fureter, fouiner. ‖ **To nose after,** chercher en fouinant. ‖ **To nose at,** flairer. ‖ **To nose down,** Aviat. Piquer du nez. ‖ **To nose in,** Fam. S'immiscer. ‖ **To nose out,** Geol. Affleurer. ‖ **To nose up,** Aviat. Monter en piqué.

nosegay [-gei] n. Bouquet parfumé *m.*

nosey ['nouzi] adj. See Nosy.

nosh [nɔʃ] v. tr. Pop. Grignoter, casser une petite croûte (to eat between meals, nibble). ‖ Bouffer, becqueter, boulotter (to eat).
— n. Pop. En-cas, casse-croûte *m.* (snack) ; bouffe *f.* (food, meal). ‖ **Nosh-up,** n. Gueuleton *m.,* bouffe *f.*

nostalgia [nɔs'tældʒiə] n. Nostalgie *f.* (See Homesickness.)

nostalgic [-dʒik] adj. Nostalgique.

nostril ['nɔstril] n. Med. Narine *f.* ‖ Zool. Naseau *m.*

nostrum ['nɔstrəm] n. Orviétan *m. ;* panacée *f.*

nosy ['nouzi] adj. au gros nez. ‖ Malodorant (smelly). ‖ Culin. Parfumé (tea). ‖ Fam. Fureteur ; *Nosy Parker,* U. S. *nosy Ned,* furet, fouinard.

not [nɔt] adv. Pas ; *not a word,* pas un mot. ‖ Ne... pas (or) point ; *not at all,* pas du tout ; *not to come,* ne pas venir ; *she will not come,* elle ne viendra pas. ‖ Non ; *not guilty,* non coupable ; *not you !,* pas vous !, vous non (or) certainement pas ! ; *I hope not,* j'espère que non.

notability [,noutə'biliti] n. Notabilité *f.* (notableness, person).

notable ['noutəb] adj. Notable, important, appréciable, considérable (worthy of note). ‖ Notable, éminent, distingué (eminent).
— n. Notable *m.* (person).

notableness [-nis] n. Notabilité *f.*

notably [-i] adv. Notablement.

notarial [no'tɛəriəl] adj. Jur. Notarial (charge) ; notarié (deed).

notarize ['noutə,raiz] v. tr. U. S., Jur. Authentifier ; *notarized,* notarié.

notary ['noutəri] n. Jur., Eccles. Notaire *m.*

notation [nou'tei ʃən] n. Notation *f.* ‖ Math. Numération *f.*

notch [nɔtʃ] n. Encoche, coche, entaille ƒ. (in general). ‖ Ébréchure ƒ. (in a blade). ‖ TECHN. Dent ƒ. (in a wheel). ‖ MILIT. Cran m. ‖ GEOGR. Col m. — v. tr. Encocher, cocher, entailler. ‖ Ebrécher (a blade). ‖ TECHN. Denter (a wheel). ‖ ARCHIT. Assembler à entailles. ‖ **To notch up,** cocher.

note [nout] n. Note, marque ƒ.; signe m.; note of infamy, marque d'infamie. ‖ Note ƒ.; to make a note of it, en prendre note; to take due note of, prendre bonne note de. ‖ Note, annotation ƒ.; commentaire m. (on, sur) [a book]. ‖ Note ƒ. (minute); diplomatic note, mémorandum, note diplomatique. ‖ Billet, petit mot m. (short letter). ‖ Remarque ƒ.; nothing of note, rien de notable (or) à signaler; worthy of note, digne d'attention. ‖ GRAMM. Point m. (of exclamation, interrogation). ‖ FIN. Billet m., coupure ƒ. (bank-note). ‖ FIN. Billet, bon m.; advice note, lettre d'avis; discount note, bordereau d'escompte; note of hand, reconnaissance de dette. ‖ MUS. Note ƒ.; U. S. whole note, half note, quarter note, eighth note, sixteenth note, ronde, blanche, noire, croche, double croche. ‖ FIG. Renom m.; man of note, notabilité, personnage de marque. ‖ **Note-book,** n. Carnet, calepin, agenda m. (pocket-book); cahier m. (for schoolboy); bloc-notes m. (for short-hand-writer). ‖ **Note-case,** n. Portefeuille, porte-billets m. ‖ **Note-pad,** n. Bloc-notes, bloc-correspondance m. ‖ **Note-paper,** n. Papier (m.) à lettres. — v. tr. Noter, relever, constater; prendre acte (or) note de. ‖ **To note down,** noter, inscrire.

noted [-id] adj. Eminent, distingué (person); remarquable (thing). ‖ Notable, remarquable (for, par).

noter [-ə*] n. Noteur, enregistreur s.

noteworthiness [-,wə:ðinis] n. Importance ƒ.

noteworthy [-wə:ði] adj. Remarquable, notable, important, digne d'attention.

nothing ['nʌθiŋ] pron. Rien; nothing but, rien que; to see nothing, ne rien voir. ‖ Rien de; nothing else matters, rien d'autre n'importe, tout le reste n'est rien; nothing much, pas grand-chose; nothing more, rien de plus; nothing new, rien de nouveau; there is nothing for it but to, il n'y a rien d'autre à faire qu'à. ‖ Loc. Nothing doing, rien à faire; to be nothing if not intelligent, être intelligent avant tout; to do nothing of the sort, n'en faire rien. — n. Rien m.; as if nothing had happened, comme si de rien n'était; for nothing, gratuitement (free of charge); pour rien (in vain); sans raison (groundlessly); for next to nothing, pour trois fois rien. ‖ Rien, objet (m.) d'indifférence; to be nothing to, n'être rien pour, être indifférent à; to make nothing of, ne pas se soucier de (not to care about); ne rien comprendre à (not to understand); ne pas faire cas de (not to value). ‖ Rien, néant m.; to come to nothing, aboutir à zéro, faire fiasco, venir à rien. ‖ Rien m., vétille ƒ.; a mere nothing, un zéro (person); une bagatelle, une broutille (thing). — adv. Pas du tout, aucunement, en rien; nothing less than, rien moins que.

nothingness [-nis] n. Néant m. ‖ FAM. Insignifiance ƒ.

notice ['noutis] n. Avis m.; notification ƒ.; advance notice, préavis; to give notice of, avertir de. ‖ Instructions ƒ. pl.; notice to pay, avertissement; to serve a notice on, signifier un arrêt à; until further notice, jusqu'à nouvel ordre. ‖ Délai m.; at a moment's notice, à l'instant, sur-le-champ, d'un moment à l'autre; at short notice, à bref délai. ‖ Congé m.; to give notice to, donner son congé à (an employee); donner sa démission (an employer); donner ses huit jours à (one's master); to give notice upon, donner congé à (a tenant). ‖ Avis, placard m.; affiche ƒ. (on a wall). ‖ Notice, note; petite annonce ƒ.; entrefilet m. (in a newspaper); notice of a book, compte rendu d'un livre. ‖ Attention, note ƒ.; to attract notice, se faire remarquer; to bring to notice,

faire remarquer; to take notice of, prendre note (or) connaissance de, faire (or) prêter attention à, prendre garde à. ‖ **Notice-board,** n. Tableau d'affichage m. (in schools); écriteau m. (on a wall); AUTOM. Panneau (m.) de signalisation. — v. tr. Observer, remarquer, constater, s'apercevoir de (to remark); he noticed her hesitate (or) hesitating, il remarqua qu'elle hésitait. ‖ Faire attention à, prendre garde à (to take care to). ‖ Donner congé à (a tenant). ‖ Faire le compte rendu de (a book); donner la revue de (a play).

noticeable [-əbl] adj. Notable, digne de remarque (noteworthy). ‖ Appréciable, perceptible, sensible, palpable, notable (tangible).

notifiable ['noutifaiəbl] adj. MED. A déclarer obligatoirement (disease).

notification [,noutifi'keiʃən] n. Notification ƒ.; avis m. (see INFORMATION); will friends please accept this as the only notification, le présent avis tiendra lieu de faire-part.

notify ['noutifai] v. tr. (2). Annoncer, notifier, faire connaître (a fact); aviser, avertir (s.o.). ‖ Convoquer (a candidate); to be notified, recevoir sa collante (candidate); to be notified of, recevoir notification de. ‖ JUR. Déclarer (a birth); to notify s.o. of a decision, signifier un arrêt à.

notion ['nouʃən] n. Notion, idée ƒ.; to have no notion of, ne pas avoir la moindre idée de. ‖ Opinion, idée ƒ.; to have a notion that, avoir le sentiment que. ‖ Caprice m.; lubie, fantaisie ƒ.; as the notion takes her, selon que ça la prend. ‖ U. S. COMM. Pl. Mercerie ƒ. (haberdashery); inventions pratiques ƒ. pl. (gadgets).

notional [-l] adj. Imaginaire. ‖ PHILOS. Spéculatif. ‖ U. S. Capricieux. ‖ GRAMM. A sens plein (verb).

notoriety [,noutə'raiəti] adj. Notoriété ƒ. (repute); notabilité ƒ. (person).

notorious [no'tɔːriəs] adj. Notoire, insigne, de notoriété publique, reconnu.

notoriously [-li] adv. Notoirement.

notoriousness [-nis] n. Notoriété ƒ.

notwithstanding. [,nɔtwiθ'stændiŋ] prep. Cependant, malgré, nonobstant, en dépit de. — adv. Néanmoins, pourtant, toutefois, quand même, malgré tout. — conj. Quoique, bien que.

nougat ['nuːgɑ:] n. Nougat m.

nought [nɔːt]. See NAUGHT.

noumenon ['naumənən] (pl. **noumena** [-ə]) n. PHILOS. Noumène m.

noun [naun] n. GRAMM. Nom, substantif m. — adj. GRAMM. Substantival.

nourish ['nʌriʃ] v. tr. Nourrir; alimenter (on, with, de). ‖ FIG. Nourrir, bercer.

nourishing [-iŋ] adj. Nourrissant, nutritif.

nourishment [-mənt] n. Alimentation ƒ. (of, de) [act]; nourriture ƒ. (food). ‖ FIG. Pâture ƒ. (of the mind).

nous [naus] n. PHILOS. Intellect, esprit m. ‖ FAM. Jugeote ƒ.

nouveau riche [nuvo 'riːʃ] n. Nouveau riche m.

nova ['nouvə] n. ASTRON. Nova ƒ.

novation [no'veiʃən] n. JUR. Novation ƒ.

novel ['nɔvəl] n. Roman m.; saga novel, roman-fleuve.

novel adj. Nouveau et original.

novelette [,nɔvə'let] n. Nouvelle, bluette ƒ.; roman (m.) à treize sous, roman rose m.

novelist ['nɔvəlist] n. Romancier s.

novelistic [nɔvə'listik] adj. Du roman.

novelize ['nɔvəlaiz] v. tr. Romancer.

novella [nou'velə] n. Nouvelle ƒ. récit m. (short novel).

novelty ['nɔvəlti] adj. Innovation ƒ. (change); nouveauté ƒ. (newness). ‖ COMM. Nouveauté, fantaisie ƒ.

November [no'vembə*] n. Novembre m.

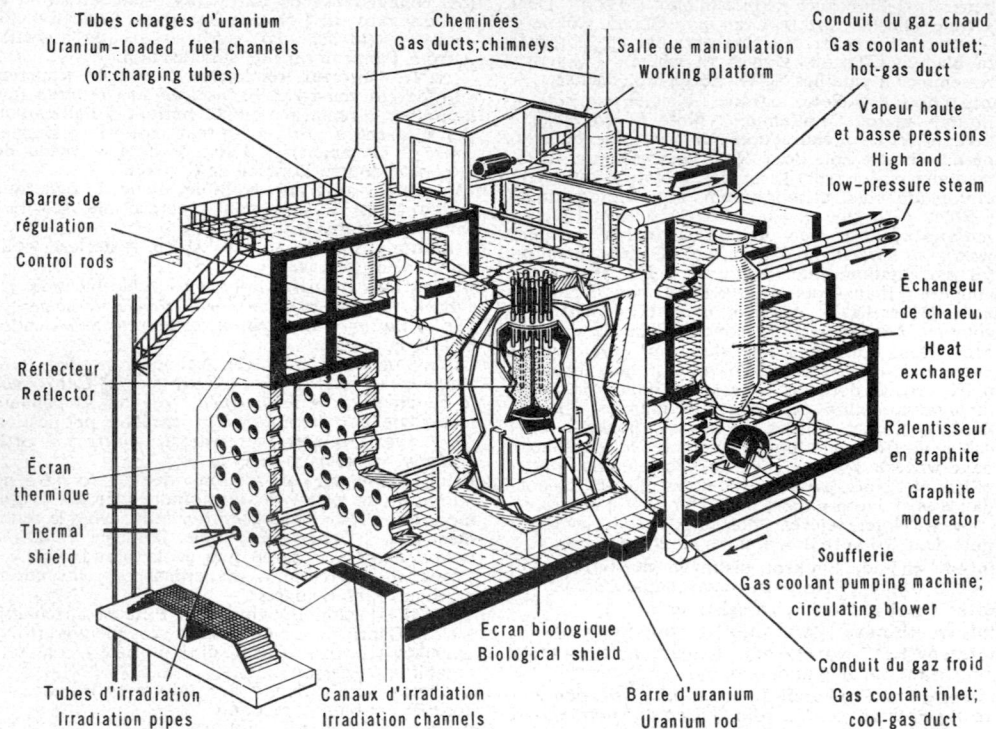

Tubes chargés d'uranium
Uranium-loaded fuel channels
(or: charging tubes)

Cheminées
Gas ducts; chimneys

Salle de manipulation
Working platform

Conduit du gaz chaud
Gas coolant outlet;
hot-gas duct

Vapeur haute
et basse pressions
High and
low-pressure steam

Barres de
régulation
Control rods

Échangeur
de chaleur
Heat
exchanger

Réflecteur
Reflector

Ralentisseur
en graphite

Graphite
moderator

Écran
thermique
Thermal
shield

Soufflerie
Gas coolant pumping machine;
circulating blower

Ecran biologique
Biological shield

Conduit du gaz froid
Gas coolant inlet;
cool-gas duct

Tubes d'irradiation
Irradiation pipes

Canaux d'irradiation
Irradiation channels

Barre d'uranium
Uranium rod

---

novena [no'vinə] n. ECCLES. Neuvaine *f.*
novercal [no'və:kəl] adj. De belle-mère.
novice ['nɔvis] n. ECCLES., FAM. Novice *m.*
noviciate [no'viʃieit] n. ECCLES. Noviciat *m.* ‖ FAM. Apprentissage *m.*
novocaine ['nouvokein] n. MED. Novocaïne *f.*
now [nau] adv. Maintenant, à présent, en ce moment, actuellement (presently) ; *as for now,* quant à présent ; *until now,* jusqu'à présent ; *up to now,* jusqu'ici. ‖ Maintenant, immédiatement, tout de suite, dans un moment, sur-le-champ (at once). ‖ Alors, à ce moment-là (then) ; *by now,* à l'heure actuelle ; *even now,* déjà, même maintenant ; *just now,* tout à l'heure ; *now and then,* de temps en temps, par moments ; *now... now,* tantôt... tantôt. ‖ Or (explanatory).
— interj. Donc, eh bien, et alors ; *now ! now !,* voyons ! voyons ! ; *now then !,* allons !, attention ! ; *well now !,* eh bien !
— conj. Maintenant que.
— n. Moment présent *m. ; from now on,* dès à présent, à partir de maintenant ; *in a week from now,* d'aujourd'hui en huit, d'ici une semaine.
nowadays [-ədeiz] adv. Aujourd'hui, à l'heure qu'il est (or) actuelle, de nos jours.
nowed [noud] adj. BLAS. Noué.
Nowel [nou'el] n. † Noël *m.*
nowhere ['nou(h)wɛə*] adv. Nulle part, en aucun endroit. ‖ SPORTS. Distancé, battu. ‖ LOC. *She is nowhere near as pretty as you,* il s'en faut de beaucoup qu'elle soit aussi jolie que vous.
— n. Néant, lieu indéfinissable *m.*
nowise ['nouwaiz] adv. Aucunement, en aucune manière.
nowt [naut] n. POP. Rien. (See NOTHING.)
noxious ['nɔkʃəs] adj. Nuisible, nocif (in general).

‖ BOT., CHIM. Délétère. ‖ MED. Contagieux, malsain. ‖ FIG. Pernicieux, malfaisant.
noxiously [-li] adv. De façon nuisible ; pernicieusement.
noxiousness [-nis] n. Nocivité *f.*
nozzle ['nɔzl] n. Lance *f.* (for watering). ‖ Bec *m.* (of bellows) ; suceur *m.* (of vacuum-cleaner). ‖ MED. Canule *f.* ‖ AUTOM. *Spray nozzle,* gicleur. ‖ MILIT. Lance *f.* (of flame-thrower). ‖ **Nozzle-man,** n. MILIT. Porte-lance *m.*
nr. Written abbr. for *near,* près de.
nth [enθ] adj. *n*ième (degree).
nuance [nju:'ãs] n. Nuance *f.*
nub [nʌb] n. Petit morceau *m.* ‖ U. S. Noyau, cœur *m.* (of the matter). ‖ † Bosse *f.*
— adj. Concassé (sugar).
nubbly [-li] adj. En petits morceaux. ‖ Bossué.
nubile ['nju:bil] adj. Nubile. (See MARRIAGEABLE.)
nubility [nju'biliti] n. Nubilité *f.*
nucha ['nju:kə] n. MED. Nuque *f.*
nuclear ['nju:kliə*] adj. PHYS. Nucléaire, atomique (energy, physics, bomb, warfare, ship) ; nucléaire, de l'atome (fission, fusion) ; *nuclear reactor,* réacteur nucléaire, pile atomique ; *nuclear power,* puissance nucléaire (energy, country). ‖ **Nuclear-powered,** adj. Nucléaire, atomique (ship).
nuclease [-eis] n. CHIM. Nucléase *f.*
nucleate [-eit] v. tr. Grouper en noyau.
— v. intr. Former un noyau.
— adj. Nucléé.
nucleic [-ik] adj. MED. *Nucleic acid,* acide nucléique *m.*
nucleolar [-ələ*] adj. Nucléolaire.
nucleolus [nju'kliələs] (pl. **nucleoli** [-əlai]) n. MED. Nucléole *m.*
nucleon [-ən] n. PHYS. Nucléon *m.*

nucleonics [nju:kli'ɔniks] n. sg. Atomistique *f.*
nucleus [nju:kliəs] (pl. **nuclei** [-ai]) n. PHYS., MED., ASTRON., NAUT., FIG. Noyau *m.*
nude [nju:d] adj. Nu (member). ‖ ARTS. *Nude figure,* nu. ‖ COMM. Teinte chair (stockings). ‖ JUR. Unilatéral.
— n. Nudité *f.* (figure). ‖ ARTS. Nu *m.; studies from the nude,* nus.
nudge ['nʌdʒ] n. Coup de coude *m.*
— v. tr. Pousser du coude.
nudism ['nju:dizm] n. Nudisme *m.*
nudist [-ist] n. Nudiste *s.*
nudity [-iti] n. Nudité *f.* ‖ ARTS. Nu *m*
nugatory ['nju:gətəri] adj. Futile (trifling). ‖ Sans effet, vain, inefficace (ineffective).
nugget ['nʌgit] n. Pépite *f.* (of gold).
nuisance ['nju:səns] n. Ennui, désagrément *m.;* contrariété *f.;* empoisonnement, embêtement *m.* (fam.); *it is a nuisance for him to,* cela l'ennuie bien de; *what a nuisance!,* que c'est contrariant!, comme c'est ennuyeux!; quelle scie! (fam.). ‖ JUR. Acte dommageable *m.;* nuisance *f.* ‖ FAM. Poison, fléau *m.* (person); *what a public nuisance he is!,* quelle calamité publique que cet homme!, quel embêteur il fait!
nuke [nju:k] n. U. S. POP. Bombe (or) arme nucléaire *f.*
— v. tr. U. S. POP. Lâcher la bombe sur.
null [nʌl] adj. JUR. Nul (act); caduc (legacy); *null and void,* nul et non avenu. ‖ FIG. Nul (person); sans effet, inutile (thing).
nullification [,nʌlifi'keiʃən] n. Annulation *f.*
nullifidian [,nʌli'fidiən] n. Athée *s.*
nullify ['nʌlifai] v. tr. (2). Annuler, infirmer.
nulliparous [nʌ'lipərəs] adj. MED. Nullipare.
nullity ['nʌliti] n. JUR. Nullité *f.* (of an act, a marriage); caducité *f.* (of a legacy). ‖ FIG. Nullité *f.* (character, person).
N.U.M. [enju:'em] abbr. *National Union of Mineworkers,* en Grande-Bretagne, syndicat national des mineurs.
numb [nʌm] adj. Engourdi, gourd. ‖ **Numb-fish,** n. ZOOL. Torpille *f.*
— v. tr. Engourdir.
numbed [-d] adj. Engourdi (with, par) [cold]; glacé (with, par) [fear].
number ['nʌmbə*] n. Nombre *m.; a large number of,* nombre de, de nombreux, un grand nombre de; *ten in number,* au nombre de dix; *to swell the number,* grossir le nombre. ‖ Groupe *m.; of our number,* des nôtres, de notre groupe. ‖ Pl. Nombre *m.* (numerousness); *numbers being equal,* à nombre égal. ‖ Numéro *m.* (of a house, ticket); *at number ten,* au numéro dix. ‖ Numéro *m.;* livraison *f.* (of a periodical). ‖ Numéro *m.; telephone number,* numéro de téléphone (or) d'appel. ‖ Pl. Nombres, vers *m. pl.;* poésie *f.* ‖ AUTOM. Numéro *m.* (of a car). ‖ MATH. Nombre, chiffre *m.* ‖ COMM. Numéro *m.* ‖ GRAMM. Nombre *m.* ‖ THEATR. Numéro *m.* (item). ‖ MILIT. Matricule *m.* (of man, rating). ‖ CHIM. Indice *m.* (in analysis). ‖ MUS. Pl. Mesures *f. pl.; vocal number,* tour de chant. ‖ ECCLES. Pl. Nombres *m. pl.* (book). ‖ FAM. *His number is up,* son compte est bon; *number one,* bibi (myself); *to take care of number one,* prendre soin de sa petite personne. ‖ **Number-board,** n. SPORTS. Tableau *m.* ‖ **Number-card,** n. SPORTS. Dossard *m.* ‖ **Number-plate,** n. AUTOM. Plaque d'immatriculation *f.*
— v. tr. Compter, dénombrer (to reckon up). ‖ Compter, comprendre, compter au nombre de (to include). ‖ Compter, se monter à; s'élever à, se chiffrer à (to amount to). ‖ Numéroter (car, street).
— v. intr. MILIT. Se numéroter.
numberer [-rə*] n. Compteur *s.* ‖ Numéroteur *s.*
numbering [-riŋ] n. Dénombrement, compte *m.* (of

persons, things). ‖ Numérotage *m.* (of cars, houses, streets). ·‖ **Numbering-machine** (or) **-stamp,** n. Numéroteur *m.* (in general); folioteuse *f.* (for ledgers); composteur *m.* (dater).
numberless [-lis] adj. Innombrable, sans nombre. (See COUNTLESS.)
numbles ['nʌmblz] n. ZOOL. Entrailles *f.*
numbness ['nʌmnis] n. Engourdissement *m.* (lit. and fig.).
numerable ['nju:mərəbl] adj. Dénombrable.
numeral [-əl] adj. Numéral.
— n. MATH. Numéral; chiffre, nombre *m.*
numerary [-əri] adj. Numéraire.
numerate [-it] adj. Qui a une formation mathématique.
numeration [,nju:mə'reiʃən] n. MATH. Numération *f.*
numerator ['nju:məreitə*] n. MATH. Numérateur *m.*
numerical [nju'merikəl] adj. Numérique.
numerically [-əli] adv. Numériquement.
numerous ['nju:mərəs] adj. Nombreux (many). ‖ Cadencé (in poetry).
numerously [-li] adv. En nombre. ‖ Harmonieusement.
numerousness [-nis] n. Nombre *m.* (numbers). ‖ Cadence *f.;* nombre *m.* (in poetry).
numismatic [,nju:miz'mætik] adj. Numismatique.
numismatics [-iks] n. sg. Numismatique *f.*
numismatist [nju:'mizmətist] n. Numismate *s.*
nummary ['nʌməri] adj. FIN. Monétaire, numéraire.
numskull ['nʌmskʌl] n. FAM. Benêt, bêta, idiot *m.*
nun [nʌn] n. ECCLES. Religieuse, nonne, sœur *f.* ‖ COMM. *Nun's thread,* coton à broder.
nunciature ['nʌnʃiətʃə*] n. ECCLES. Nonciature *f.*
nuncio ['nʌnʃiou] n. ECCLES. Nonce *m.*
nuncupative ['nʌnkjupeitiv] adj. JUR. Nuncupatif.
nunhood ['nʌnhud] n. ECCLES. Etat (*m.*) de religieuse.
nunnery [-əri] n. ECCLES. Couvent, monastère *m.;* nonnerie *f.* (fam.).
N.U.P.E. ['nju:pi] abbr. *National Union of Public Employees,* en Grande-Bretagne, syndicat national des employés du secteur public.
nuptial ['nʌpʃəl] adj. Nuptial.
— n. pl. Noces *f. pl.*
nurse [nə:s] n. Nourrice *f.; at nurse,* en nourrice; *to put out to nurse,* mettre en nourrice. ‖ Bonne (*f.*) d'enfants (nursemaid). ‖ MED. Infirmière; garde-malade *f.; male nurse,* infirmier. ‖ ZOOL. Ouvrière *f.* (ant, bee). ‖ **Nurse-child,** n. Nourrisson *s.*
— v. tr. Nourrir, allaiter (an infant). ‖ Câliner, cajoler (a child). ‖ MED. Soigner (a disease, s.o.). ‖ BOT. Soigner (plants). ‖ AGRIC. Prendre soin de, diriger, gérer (an estate). ‖ SPORTS. Grouper (the balls at billiards); serrer (a horse). ‖ FIG. Nourrir (a hope, project); soigner (one's public).
nurseling ['nə:sliŋ] n. See NURSLING.
nursemaid [-meid] n. Bonne (*f.*) d'enfant.
nursery [-əri] n. Nursery, chambre (*f.*) d'enfants. ‖ Garderie *f.; day nursery,* crèche; *public nursery,* pouponnière; *nursery school,* école maternelle; *nursery rhyme,* comptine; *nursery tale,* conte de nourrice. ‖ AGRIC. Pépinière *f.; nursery man,* pépiniériste. ‖ ZOOL. Alevinier, vivier *m.* ‖ SPORTS. *Nursery slopes,* pentes (*f. pl.*) pour les débutants (skiing). ‖ FIG. Pépinière *f.* (of scientists, of artists).
nurseryman [-ərimən] (pl. **nurserymen**) n. AGRIC. Pépiniériste *m.*
nursey [-i] n. FAM. Nounou *f.*
nursing [-iŋ] adj. Allaitant, qui nourrit (mother). ‖ Nourricier (father). ‖ MED. Infirmier, des infirmières; *nursing home,* maison de santé (mental hospital); clinique (surgical hospital); maison de repos (for rest-cure).
— n. Allaitement *m.* (of an infant); bercement *m.*

(of a child). ‖ MED. Soins *m. pl.; to do nursing,* être infirmière (or) garde-malade. ‖ AGRIC. Culture *f.;* entretien *m.* ‖ FIG. Entretien *m.*
nursling [-liŋ] n. Nourrisson *m.* ‖ FAM. Poulain *m.*
nurture ['nə:tʃə*] n. Nourriture *f.* (act, food).
— v. tr. Nourrir (lit. and fig.). ‖ Instruire, éduquer.
nurturer [-rə*] n. Nourricier *s.*
N.U.S. [enju:'es] abbr. of *National Union of Students,* en Grande-Bretagne, union nationale des étudiants.
nut [nʌt] n. Noix *f.* (in general); noisette *f.* (hazelnut). ‖ TECHN. Ecrou *m.* ‖ MUS. Talon *m.* (of bow); sillet *m.* (of violin). ‖ NAUT. Tenon *m.* ‖ COMM. Tête-de-moineau *f.* (coal). ‖ CULIN. Gâteau rond *m.* ‖ FAM. Caboche, ciboule *f.* (head). ‖ FAM. Pl. Toqué, maboul, sonné (person); *he is nuts,* il est cinglé; *to be dead nuts on,* être toqué de; *to go nuts,* perdre la boule. ‖ U. S. *Nuts!,* des nèfles!, des prunes!, des dattes! ‖ **Nut-brown,** adj. Noisette (colour); châtain (hair). ‖ **Nut-case,** n. POP. Dingue, cinglé, malade *s.;* zinzin *m.* ‖ **Nut-cracker,** n. Casse-noix, casse-noisettes *m.* ‖ **Nut-house,** n. POP. Asile *m.,* maison (*f.*) de fous. ‖ **Nut-oil,** n. CULIN. Huile de noix *f.* ‖ **Nut-tree,** n. BOT. Noisetier, coudrier *m.*
nutmeg [-meg] n. Noix de muscade *f.* ‖ **Nutmegtree,** n. BOT. Muscadier *m.*
nutria ['nju:triə] n. Ragondin, castor du Chili *m.*
nutrient ['nju:triənt] adj. Nutritif.
nutriment ['nju:trimənt] n. Eléments nutritifs, aliments *m. pl.*
nutrition [nju'triʃən] n. Nutrition *f.* ‖ Alimentation *f.*

nutritional [-əl] adj. Alimentaire.
nutritionist [-ist] n. Diététicien *s.*
nutritious [nju'triʃəs] adj. Nutritif.
nutritiousness [-nis] n. Nutritivité *f.*
nutritive ['nju:tritiv] adj. Nutritif, nourrissant.
— n. Aliment, élément nutritif *m.*
nutshell ['nʌt,ʃəl] n. Coquille de noix *f.* ‖ FAM. *In a nutshell,* en un mot.
nuttiness ['nʌtinis] n. Goût (*m.*) de noisette.
nutting [-iŋ] n. Cueillette (*f.*) des noisettes.
nutty [-i] adj. Plein de noix (or) de noisettes. ‖ A goût de noisette (taste). ‖ FIG. Savoureux. ‖ FAM. Entiché (*on, upon,* de). ‖ U. S. POP. Cinglé, dingo, sonné, fêlé, toqué.
nuzzle ['nʌzl̩] v. intr. Fouiller du groin, fouiner (pig). ‖ Renifler, flairer (dog). ‖ FAM. Se blottir, pelotonner (*against,* contre).
nyctalopia [niktə'loupiə] n. Nyctalopie *f.*
Nylon ['nailən] n. (trade mark). Nylon *m.; Nylon stockings,* bas en Nylon.
nymph [nimf] n. Nymphe *f.*
nymphae [-i:] n. pl. ZOOL. Nymphes *f. pl.*
nymphaea [nim'fi:ə] n. BOT. Nymphéa, nénuphar *m.* (See WATER-LILY.)
nymphean [-ən] adj. De nymphe.
nymphet ['nimfit] n. Nymphette *f.*
nympho ['nimfou] (pl. **nymphos** [-z]) n. POP. Nymphomane *f.*
nymphomania [,nimfə'meiniə] n. MED. Nymphomanie *f.*
nymphomaniac [nimfo'meiniæk] n. MED. Nymphomane *f.*

O

o [ou] n. O, o *m.* ‖ Rond *m.* (circle); zéro *m.* (nought). ‖ CHIM. Oxygène *m.*
— interj. O, oh!, ah!
o' [ə] prep. See OF.
oaf [ouf] n. FAM. Ballot, nigaud, bêta *m.*
oafish ['oufiʃ] adj. Stupide, rustre.
oafishness [-nis] n. Sottise *f.*
oak [ouk] n. BOT. Chêne *m.* ‖ **Oak-bark,** n. MED. Ecorce (*f.*) de chêne. ‖ **Oak-leaf,** n. Feuille (*f.*) de chêne. ‖ **Oak-mast,** n. Glandée *f.* ‖ **Oak-wood,** n. Chênaie *f.* (grove); chêne *m.* (wood).
— adj. De (or) en chêne (furniture). ‖ Chêne (colour).
oaken [-ən] adj. En chêne.
oakum [-əm] n. Etoupe, filasse *f.*
O.A.P. [ouei'pi:] abbr. *old age pension,* pension de retraite; *old age pensioner,* retraité.
oar ['ɔ:*] n. NAUT. Rame *f.;* aviron *m.; to ply the oars,* souquer; *to rest on one's oars,* lever les avirons. ‖ NAUT. Rameur *m.* (oarsman). ‖ FAM. *To lie* (or) *rest on one's oars,* se reposer sur ses lauriers.
— v. intr. NAUT. Ramer.
— v. tr. NAUT. Faire aller à la rame.
oarsman [-zmən] (pl. **oarsmen**) n. NAUT. Rameur *m.*
oarsmanship [-zmənʃip] n. NAUT. Science (*f.*) de l'aviron.

oarswoman [-zwumən] (pl. **oarswomen**) n. NAUT. Rameuse *f.*
oasal [o'eisəl] adj. Oasien.
oasis [o'eisis] (pl. **oases** [-i:z]) n. GEOGR., FIG. Oasis *f.*
oast [oust] n. AGRIC. Four (*m.*) à sécher le houblon. ‖ **Oast-house,** n. Séchoir à houblon *m.*
oat [out] n. BOT. Avoine *f.; wild oats,* folle avoine. ‖ CULIN. *Rolled oats,* flocons d'avoine. ‖ FAM. *To sow one's wild oats,* jeter sa gourme. ‖ **Oat-grass,** n. Folle avoine *f.*
oatcake [-,keik] n. CULIN. Galette d'avoine *f.*
oaten [-n] adj. D'avoine.
oath [ouθ] n. Serment *m.; to break one's oath,* se parjurer; *to swear an oath,* faire un serment; *to take an oath,* prêter serment; *to take one's Bible oath on it,* en jurer par la Bible. ‖ JUR. On oath, sous serment (declaration); assermenté (witness); *to administer the oath to,* faire prêter serment à. ‖ FAM. Juron *m.* ‖ **Oath-bound,** adj. Tenu par serment. ‖ **Oath-breaker,** n. Parjure *s.* (person). ‖ **Oath-breaking,** n. Parjure *m.* (act).
oatmeal [-mi:l] n. CULIN. Farine d'avoine *f.*
O.A.U. [ouei'ju:] abbr. *Organization of African Unity,* Organisation de l'unité africaine, O. U. A.
obbligato [,ɔbli'gɑ:tou] adj. MUS. Obligé, obbligato.
— n. MUS. Partie obligée *f.*

obduracy [ˈɔbdjurəsi] n. Entêtement *m.;* obstination *f.* (stubbornness). ‖ Endurcissement *m.;* inflexibilité *f.* (hardness). ‖ ECCLES. Impénitence *f.*
obdurate [-rit] adj. Obstiné, entêté (stubborn). ‖ Endurci (hardened). ‖ Invétéré, enraciné (confirmed). ‖ Inflexible. ‖ ECCLES. Impénitent.
obedience [oˈbiːdjəns] n. Obéissance *f.* (*to,* à); *to compel obedience from,* se faire obéir de. ‖ COMM. Conformité *f.; in obedience to your orders,* selon vos ordres. ‖ ECCLES. Obédience *f.*
obedient [-ənt] adj. Obéissant, soumis (*to,* à).
obediently [-əntli] adv. Avec obéissance. ‖ COMM. *Yours obediently,* toujours à vos ordres.
obeisance [oˈbeisəns] n. † Salut *m.* ‖ Hommage *m.*
obeliscal [ɔbiˈliskəl] adj. Obéliscal.
obelisk [ˈɔbilisk] n. ARCHIT. Obélisque *m.* ‖ TECHN. Obèle *f.*
obese [oˈbiːs] adj. Obèse.
obesity [-iti] n. Obésité *f.*
obey [oˈbei] v. tr. Obéir à (impulse, orders, s.o.). — v. intr. Obéir.
obeyer [-ə*] n. JUR. *Obeyer of the laws,* personne respectueuse de la loi.
obfuscate [ˈɔbfʌskeit] v. tr. † Assombrir. ‖ FIG. Obscurcir, brouiller, troubler.
obi [ˈoubi] n. Obi *m.*
obit [ˈoubit] n. ECCLES. Obit *m.; obit book,* obituaire. ‖ Notice nécrologique *f.*
obituarist [oˈbitjuərist] n. Nécrologue *m.*
obituary [-əri] n. Obituaire, nécrologe *m.* — adj. Nécrologique; *obituary column,* nécrologie.
object [ˈɔbdʒekt] n. Objet *m.;* chose *f.* (thing). ‖ GRAMM. Objet, régime, complément *m.* ‖ FIG. Objet, but *m.;* fin *f.* (end); *to accomplish one's object,* arriver à ses fins; *with this object,* dans cette intention, dans ce but. ‖ FIG. Objet, sujet *m.* (*for, of,* de). ‖ FAM. *There is no object in,* ça ne sert à rien de. ‖ **Object-glass,** n. PHYS. Objectif *m.* ‖ **Object-lesson,** n. Leçon (*f.*) de choses; FIG. Exemple, modèle *m.*
— [əbˈdʒekt] v. intr. Faire des objections (*to,* à); trouver à redire, s'élever (*to,* contre) [sth.]. ‖ Répugner, s'opposer (*to,* à); *do you object to his coming?,* voyez-vous un inconvénient à ce qu'il vienne? ‖ JUR. Récuser (a witness).
objectify [ɔbˈdʒektifai] v. tr. (2). PHILOS. Objectiver.
objection [-ʃən] n. Objection *f.* (*to,* a, contre); *to raise objections,* faire des objections, soulever des difficultés. ‖ Inconvénient *m.; if he has no objection,* s'il n'y voit pas d'inconvénient, si cela ne lui fait rien, s'il n'est pas d'avis contraire.
objectionable [-ʃənəbl̩] adj. Répréhensible, critiquable (criticizable). ‖ Choquant, désagréable (unpleasant).
objectionableness [-ʃənəbl̩nis] n. Nature choquante (or) critiquable *f.*
objectionably [-ʃənəbli] adv. De façon désagréable (or) critiquable.
objectional [-ʃənəl] adj. D'objection.
objective [-tiv] adj. PHILOS., MED. Objectif. ‖ GRAMM. Régime. ‖ FIG. Apparent (truth). — n. Objectif *m.* ‖ GRAMM. Régime *m.*
objectively [-tivli] adv. Objectivement.
objectiveness [-tivnis], **objectivity** [ˌɔbdʒekˈtiviti] n. Objectivité *f.*
objectivism [ɔbˈdʒekti,vizm] n. Objectivisme *m.*
objectless [ˈɔbdʒektlis] adj. Sans but (or) objet.
objector [əbˈdʒektə*] n. Contradicteur *m.; conscientious objector,* objecteur de conscience; protestataire.
objet d'art [ɔbˈʒɛˈdaːr] n. Objet d'art, bibelot *m.*
objurgate [ˈɔbdʒəːgeit] v. tr. Faire des objurgations à.
objurgation [ˌɔbdʒəːˈgeiʃən] n. Objurgation *f.*
objurgatory [ɔbˈdʒəːgətəri] adj. Objurgatoire.
oblate [ˈɔbleit] adj. MATH. Aplati.

oblate n. ECCLES. Oblat *s.*
oblation [ɔˈbleiʃən] n. ECCLES. Oblation *f.*
obligate [ˈɔbligeit] v. tr. Obliger, contraindre, soumettre à une obligation.
obligation [ɔbliˈgeiʃən] n. Obligation *f.; to be under an obligation to,* être tenu de; *to put s.o. under an obligation,* imposer une obligation à qqn. ‖ Dette de reconnaissance *f.;* obligations *f.* pl. (*to, envers*); *to remain under an obligation to,* rester l'obligé de. ‖ COMM. Engagement *m.; without obligation,* sans engagement.
obligatory [ˈɔbligətəri] adj. Obligatoire; *to make it obligatory upon s.o. to,* rendre obligatoire pour qqn de, imposer à qqn de.
oblige [oˈblaidʒ] v. tr. Obliger, astreindre, contraindre (*to,* à) [to compel]. ‖ Obliger, rendre service à (to assist); *to be obliged to s.o. for,* être redevable (or) reconnaissant à qqn de; *to oblige s.o. with money,* rendre service à qqn en lui donnant de l'argent; *please oblige me with a light,* voudriez-vous avoir l'obligeance de me donner du feu. — v. intr. Rendre service, êtꞔ obligeant.
obligee [ˌɔbliˈdʒiː] n. Obligé *s.* (person under obligation). ‖ JUR. Obligataire *s.*
obliger [oˈblaidʒə*] n. Personne (*f.*) à qui l'on a des obligations.
obliging [-iŋ] adj. Obligeant, complaisant.
obligingly [-iŋli] adv. Obligeamment, avec complaisance.
obligingness [-iŋnis] n. Obligeance *f.*
obligor [ˌɔbliˈgɔː*] n. JUR. Obligé *s.*
oblique [oˈbliːk] adj. Oblique (in general). ‖ FAM. Indirect, détourné (ways). — n. Barre oblique (or) de fraction *f.* ‖ MED. Oblique, muscle oblique *m.* — v. intr. MILIT. Obliquer (*to,* à).
obliquely [-li] adv. Obliquement.
obliquity [-witi] n. Obliquité *f.* ‖ FAM. Duplicité, tortuosité *f.*
obliterate [oˈblitəreit] v. tr. Effacer, gratter, enlever. ‖ Oblitérer (a stamp). ‖ MED. Oblitérer (a duct).
obliterating [-iŋ] adj. Oblitérateur *m.;* oblitératrice *f.*
obliteration [ˌɔblitəˈreiʃən] n. Grattage *m.* (act); rature *f.* (result). ‖ Oblitération *f.* (of a duct, a stamp).
obliterator [oˈblitəreitə*] n. Effaceur *s.*
oblivion [oˈbliviən] n. Oubli *m.* ‖ JUR. Amnistie *f.*
oblivious [-əs] adj. Oublieux (*of,* de). ‖ FAM. Ignorant; *to be totally oblivious of,* ignorer absolument.
obliviousness [-əsnis] n. Oubli *m.*
oblong [ˈɔblɔŋ] adj. Oblong. — n. Rectangle *m.*
obloquy [ˈɔbləkwi] n. Critique malveillante *f.; public obloquy,* vindicte publique. ‖ Déshonneur *m.* (shame).
obnoxious [ɔbˈnɔkʃəs] adj. Détestable, exécrable, odieux (odious). ‖ Déplaisant, désagréable (unpleasant). ‖ Antipathique (*to,* à); détesté (*to,* par).
obnoxiously [-li] adv. Désagréablement.
obnoxiousness [-nis] n. Nature odieuse *f.*
obnubilation [ˌɔbnjubiˈleiʃən] n. MED. Obnubilation *f.*
oboe [ˈoubou] n. MUS. Hautbois *m.; tenor oboe,* cor anglais. ‖ **Oboe-player,** n. MUS. Hautboïste *m.*
oboist [-ist] n. MUS. Hautboïste *s.*
obol [ˈɔbɔl] n. Obole *f.*
obscene [ɔbˈsiːn] adj. Osé, grossier, malsonnant, inconvenant. ‖ Obscène.
obscenely [-li] adv. De façon obscène (or) osée.
obscenity [-iti] n. Obscénité *f.* ‖ FAM. Parole (or) attitude osée *f.*
obscurantism [ˌɔbskjuəˈræntizm] n. Obscurantisme *m.*
obscurantist [-tist] adj., n. Obscurantiste *s.*

obscuration [,ɔbskjuə'reiʃən] n. Obscurcissement *m.* ‖ ASTRON. Occultation *f.*

obscure [ɔb'skjuə*] adj. Obscur, sombre; *to become obscure,* s'obscurcir. ‖ FIG. Obscur, retiré (hidden); obscur, inconnu (undistinguished). ‖ FIG. Obscur, peu clair (abstruse).
— v. tr. Obscurcir, assombrir, voiler. ‖ FIG. Obscurcir, voiler (to dim); éclipser (to overshadow).

obscurely [-ḷi] adv. Obscurément.

obscureness [-nis], **obscurity** [-riti] n. Obscurité *f.* (lit. and fig.).

obsequies ['ɔbsikwiz] n. pl. Funérailles, obsèques *f. pl.*

obsequious [əb'si:kwiəs] adj. Obséquieux.

obsequiously [-li] adv. Obséquieusement.

obsequiousness [-nis] n. Obséquiosité *f.*

observance [əb'zə:vəns] n. Observance, observation *f.; religious observances,* pratiques religieuses.

observant [-ənt] adj. Observateur *m.;* observatrice *f.;* d'observation (mind). ‖ Respectueux (*of,* de); attentif (*of,* à) [one's duty].

observantly [-əntli] adv. Avec attention.

observation [,ɔbzə:'veiʃən] n. Observation *f.; under observation,* en observation; sous surveillance. ‖ Observation, remarque *f.;* commentaire *m.* ‖ MED., MILIT. Observation *f.* ‖ NAUT. *To take an observation,* faire le point. ‖ ASTRON. Visée, observation *f.;* sondage *m.* ‖ U. S. CH. DE F. *Observation car,* voiture panoramique.

observatory [ob'zə:vətəri] n. ASTRON. Observatoire *m.*

observe [ob'zə:v] v. tr. Observer, se soumettre à (to obey). ‖ Observer, regarder, étudier (to look at). ‖ Observer, noter, remarquer (to notice); *I observe him stop* (or) *stopping,* j'ai remarqué qu'il s'arrêtait. ‖ Observer, surveiller (to watch). ‖ Dire (to say).
— v. intr. Observer. ‖ Faire une remarque (*on,* au sujet de, sur).

observer [-ə*] n. Observateur *m.;* observatrice *f.*

obsess [ob'ses] v. tr. Obséder (*with,* par); *to be obsessed by,* vivre dans la hantise (or) l'obsession de.

obsessing [-iŋ] adj. Obsédant.

obsession [əb'seʃən] n. Obsession, hantise, idée fixe *f.*

obsessional [-əl] adj. MED. D'obsession.

obsessionist [-ist] n. Obsédé *s.*

obsessive [ob'sesiv] adj. Obsessif.

obsidian [ob'sidiən] n. Obsidienne *f.*

obsidional [-əl] adj. Obsidional.

obsolescence [ɔbsə'lesəns] n. Vieillissement *m.* ‖ MED. Décrépitude *f.*

obsolescent [-ənt] adj. Vieillissant, qui devient désuet. ‖ Atrophié.

obsolete ['ɔbsəli:t] adj. Suranné, démodé (clothes); effacé (inscription); aboli (institution); périmé (ticket). ‖ AUTOM. Démodé. ‖ NAUT. Déclassé. ‖ GRAMM. Inusité, vieilli. ‖ MED. Obsolète. ‖ TECHN. Hors d'usage.

obsoleteness [-nis] n. Désuétude *f.*

obstacle ['ɔbstəkḷ] n. Obstacle *m.; to put obstacles in the way of,* susciter des obstacles à (s.o.); mettre obstacle à (sth.). ‖ SPORTS. Obstacle *m.* (in racing); chicane *f.* (in ski-ing).

obstetrical [ɔb'stetrikəl] adj. MED. Obstétrical.

obstetrics [-triks] n. sg. MED. Obstétrique *f.*

obstinacy ['ɔbstinəsi] n. Obstination, opiniâtreté *f.;* entêtement *m.* ‖ MED. Persistance *f.*

obstinate [-nit] adj. Obstiné (*in,* à). ‖ Opiniâtre, entêté, têtu (stubborn). ‖ MED. Persistant.

obstinately [-nitli] adj. Obstinément.

obstreperous [ob'strepərəs] adj. Bruyant, turbulent (boisterous). ‖ Rouspéteur (quarrelsome).

obstreperousness [-nis] n. Tapage, vacarme *m.* ‖ Turbulence; rouspétance *f.* (fam.).

obstruct [ob'strʌkt] v. tr. Obstruer, boucher, engorger (a pipe); encombrer (a street); entraver (movements); gêner (the traffic, the view); embâcler (water-way). [See BLOCK.]

obstruction [-ʃən] n. Engorgement *m.* (of a pipe); encombrement *m.* (of traffic); entrave *f.* (in movements). ‖ JUR. Obstruction *f.* (in politics); *to practise obstruction,* faire de l'obstruction. ‖ MED. Occlusion *f.* (of the bowels).

obstructionism [-ʃənizm] n. Obstructionnisme *m.*

obstructionist [-ʃənist] n. Obstructionniste *s.*

obstructive [-tiv] adj. Obstructif. ‖ JUR. Obstructionniste, d'obstruction. ‖ MED. Obstructif.

obstructiveness [-tivnis] n. Obstruction *f.;* obstructionnisme *m.*

obstructor [-ə*] n. Empêcheur *s.*

obstruent ['ɔbstruənt] adj. MED. Obstruant.

obtain [ob'tein] v. tr. Obtenir, se procurer (to get). ‖ FIN. Réaliser (rates).
— v. intr. Prévaloir, régner, être en vigueur.

obtainable [-əbḷ] adj. Procurable, qu'on peut obtenir.

obtainment [-mənt] n. Obtention *f.*

obtrude [ob'tru:d] v. tr. Mettre en avant; *to obtrude oneself on,* s'imposer à, se pousser auprès de.
— v. intr. *To obtrude on* (or) *upon,* importuner, agir en intrus (or) s'imposer auprès de.

obtrusion [ob'tru:ʒən] n. Intrusion, importunité *f.*

obtrusive [-siv] adj. Intrus, importun. ‖ Important, prétentieux, qui se met en avant. ‖ Pénétrant (odour).

obtrusively [-sivli] adv. Avec importunité, en intrus, indiscrètement.

obtrusiveness [-sivnis] n. Importunité *f.*

obturate ['ɔbtjureit] v. tr. Obturer.

obturating [-iŋ] adj. Obturateur *m.;* obturatrice *f.*

obturation [,ɔbtjuə'reiʃən] n. Obturation *f.*

obturator ['ɔbtjureitə*] adj., n. Obturateur *m.*

obtuse [ob'tju:s] adj. MATH., FIG. Obtus. ‖ **Obtuse-angled,** adj. MATH. obtusangle.

obtuseness [-nis] n. Fait (*m.*) d'être obtus. ‖ FIG. Manque (*m.*) de compréhension (or) d'intelligence.

obverse ['ɔbvə:s] adj. FIG. Obvers. ‖ BOT. Renversé.
— n. Avers *m.* (of a medal). ‖ FIG. Envers, opposé *m.*

obvert [ob'və:t] v. tr. PHILOS. Retourner.

obviate ['ɔbvieit] v. tr. Obvier à (a difficulty); prévenir, devancer (an objection).

obvious ['ɔbviəs] adj. Evident, clair, patent, manifeste, visible; *it was the obvious thing to do,* cela s'imposait; *to be glaringly obvious,* crever les yeux. ‖ Voyant; tape-à-l'œil (fam.) [showy].
— n. Evidence *f.; to deny the obvious,* nier l'évidence.

obviously [-li] adv. Manifestement, évidemment, visiblement, de façon patente.

obviousness [-nis] n. Evidence *f.*

ocarina [,ɔkə'ri:nə] n. MUS. Ocarina *m.*

occasion [o'keiʒən] n. Raison *f.;* sujet, motif *m.* (cause); *he has no occasion to be alarmed,* il n'a pas besoin (or) lieu de s'inquiéter; *to give occasion to,* donner lieu (or) occasion à. ‖ Occasion *f.;* cas *m.; should the occasion arise,* le cas échéant. ‖ Occasion, circonstance *f.* (juncture); *for the occasion,* pour la circonstance; *on occasion,* à l'occasion, de temps à autre; *on another occasion,* une autre fois. ‖ Occasion *f.* (*to,* de). [See OPPORTUNITY.] ‖ Cérémonie *f.*
— v. tr. Occasionner, provoquer, déterminer, causer, susciter (to cause). ‖ Pousser, déterminer (to induce).

occasional [-əl] adj. Occasionnel (cause). ‖ D'occasion, intermittent, occasionnel (visitor). ‖ De circonstance (poem, verse). ‖ Volant (chair; table).

occasionally [-əli] adv. Occasionnellement; de temps en temps.

occident ['ɔksidənt] n. Occident *m*.
occidental [ɔksi'dentəl] adj. Occidental. (See WESTERN.)
occipital [ɔk'sipitl̩] adj., n. MED. Occipital *m*.
occiput ['ɔksipʌt] n. MED. Occiput *m*.
occlude [o'klu:d] v. tr. Obstruer, fermer. ‖ CHIM., MED. Occlure.
— v. intr. MED. S'emboîter (teeth).
occlusion [-ʃən] n. Occlusion, fermeture *f*. ‖ CHIM., MED. Occlusion *f*. ‖ MED. Emboîtement *m*. (of teeth).
occult [o'kʌlt] adj. Occulte.
— v. tr. ASTRON. Occulter.
— v. intr. S'éclipser.
occultation [,ɔkəl'teiʃən] n. ASTRON. Occultation *f*.
occultism [ɔ'kʌltizm] n. Occultisme *m*.
occultist [-ist] n. Occultiste *s*.
occultness [-nis] n. Nature occulte *f*.
occupancy ['ɔkjupənsi] n. Possession, occupation *f*.
occupant [-ənt] n. Occupant *s*. (of a house). ‖ Possesseur, titulaire *m*. (of a job).
occupation [,ɔkju'peiʃən] n. Occupation *f*. (tenure); *fit for occupation*, habitable, occupable. ‖ Occupation *f*.; travail *m*. (employment); *to give occupation to*, donner de l'occupation à. ‖ Occupation, profession *f*.; métier *m*. (pursuit); *what's his occupation?*, qu'est-ce qu'il fait? ‖ MILIT. Occupation *f*. (by troops); *reserved occupation*, affectation spéciale.
occupational [-l̩] adj. De métier, professionnel. ‖ MED. Professionnel (disease); rééducatif (therapy).
occupier ['ɔkjupaiə*] n. Occupant, locataire *s*.
occupy [-pai] v. tr. (2). Occuper, habiter (a house). ‖ Occuper (a place, seat, space). ‖ Occuper, donner du travail (s.o.). ‖ Occuper (s.o.'s attention, time); occuper, tenir (a post, rank). ‖ MILIT. Occuper.
occur [o'kə:*] v. intr. (1). Arriver, avoir lieu, se produire, se présenter, survenir (to happen); *to occur again*, se reproduire, se représenter, s'offrir de nouveau. ‖ Se rencontrer, se présenter, se trouver (to be met with). ‖ Venir à l'esprit, se présenter; *it occurred to him that*, l'idée lui vint que.
occurrence [-rəns] n. Fait (*m*.) de se produire; *of frequent occurrence*, fréquent, qui arrive souvent. ‖ Fait, événement, incident *m*. (event). ‖ GEOL. Venue *f*. (of metal). ‖ ECCLES. Occurrence *f*.
occurrent [-rənt] adj. Occurrent, qui se produit.
ocean ['ouʃən] n. NAUT., GEOGR. Océan *m*. ‖ FIG. Mer *f*. ‖ FAM. Pl. Flopée *f*. ‖ U. S. Mer *f*.; *by the ocean*, au bord de la mer. ‖ **Ocean-going**, adj. NAUT. Long-courrier; *ocean-going submarine*, sous-marin croiseur.
— adj. Océanique, de l'océan (wave); *ocean sea*, mer océane. ‖ NAUT. Au long cours (voyage). ‖ U. S. Par mer (transportation).
Oceania [ouʃi'einjə] n. GEOGR. Océanie *f*.
Oceanian [-ən] adj., n. GEOGR. Océanien *s*.
oceanic [ouʃi'ænik] adj. Océanique.
oceanographer [,ouʃiən'ɔgrəfə*] n. Océanographe *m*.
oceanography [-fi] n. Océanographie *f*.
ocellate ['ɔselet] adj. ZOOL. Ocellé.
ocellus [ɔ'seləs] n. ZOOL. Ocelle *m*.
ocelot ['ousilɔt] n. ZOOL. Ocelot *m*.
ochre ['oukə*] n. Ocre *f*.
— v. tr. Ocrer.
o'clock [ə'klɔk] n. See CLOCK.
octad ['ɔktæd] n. Huitaine *f*. ‖ CHIM. Corps octovalent *m*.
octagon ['ɔktəgən] n. MATH. Octogone *m*.
octagonal [ɔk'tægənəl] adj. MATH. Octogonal.
octahedral [ɔktə'hi:drəl] adj. Octaédrique.
octahedron [-drən] n. MATH. Octaèdre *m*.
octane ['ɔktein] n. CHIM. Octane *m*.; *high-octane*

fuel, supercarburant; *octane number*, indice d'octane.
octavalent [,ɔktə'veilənt] adj. CHIM. Octavalent, de valence huit.
octave ['ɔkteiv] n. MUS., SPORTS, ECCLES. Octave *f*.
octavo [ɔk'teivou] adj., n. In-octavo *m*.
octennial [ɔk'tenjəl] adj. Durant huit ans; arrivant tous les huit ans.
octet [ɔk'tet] n. Huitain *m*. ‖ MUS. Octuor *m*.
October [ɔk'toubə*] n. Octobre *m*.
octogenarian [,ɔktodʒe'nɛəriən] adj., n. Octogénaire *s*.
octopod ['ɔktopɔd] n. ZOOL. Poulpe *m*.
— N. B. Deux pluriels : *octopods, octopoda*.
octopus [-pəs] n. ZOOL. Pieuvre *f*.
— N. B. Deux pluriels : *octopuses, octopodes*. On emploie aussi *octopi*, pluriel peu grammatical.
octoroon [,ɔktə'ru:n] n. Octavon *s*.
octosyllabic [,ɔktosi'læbik] adj. Octosyllabique, octosyllabe.
— n. Vers octosyllabe *m*.
octosyllable [,ɔkto'siləbl̩] n. Octosyllabe *m*. (verse, word).
octuple ['ɔktjupl̩] adj. Octuple.
— v. tr. Octupler.
ocular ['ɔkjulə*] adj., n., PHYS. Oculaire *m*.
oculist [-list] n. MED. Oculiste *s*.
odalisque ['oudəlisk] n. Odalisque *f*.
odd [ɔd] adj., Impair (number). ‖ Environ; *thirty thousand odd*, trente mille et quelques. ‖ Dépareillé (unmatched); déparié (unpaired). ‖ Quelconque; *at odd times*, de-ci de-là. ‖ A tout faire, de peine (man); *odd jobs*, bricolage, petits travaux. ‖ Bizarre, curieux, étrange (queer). ‖ ASTRON. *Odd day*, bissextil. ‖ FIN. *Odd money*, appoint. ‖ COMM. *Odd lot*, solde; *odd size*, taille (or) pointure non courante. ‖ **Odd-numbered**, adj. Impair.
oddity [-iti] n. Bizarrerie, étrangeté, singularité *f*. (quality). ‖ Curiosité *f*. (thing). ‖ Original *s*. (person).
oddments [-mənts] n. pl. COMM. Fins de séries, occasions *f*. *pl*.; articles soldés *m*. *pl*. (see REMNANTS); défets *m*. *pl*. (in book-trade).
oddness [-nis] n. Imparité *f*. ‖ FIG. Bizarrerie, étrangeté *f*.
odds [ɔdz] n. pl. Inégalité *f*.; *overwhelming odds*, supériorité écrasante. ‖ Chances *f*. *pl*.; *the odds are against me*, les chances sont contre moi. ‖ SPORTS. Cote *f*. (on a horse); *to give odds to*, donner de l'avance à, céder des points à (an opponent). ‖ Pari *m*.; *the odds are that*, on peut parier que. ‖ FAM. Différence *f*.; *what's the odds?*, quelle importance cela a-t-il?, qu'est-ce que ça fait? ‖ FAM. Bisbille *f*.; *to be at odds with*, être mal avec. ‖ LOC. *Odds and ends*, bribes, bouts, morceaux (bits); bibelots (curios); restes (food); *a few odds and sods*, quatre pelés et un tondu.
ode [oud] n. Ode *f*.
Odeum [ou'di:əm] n. Odéon *m*.
odious ['oudjəs] adj. Odieux, haïssable, exécrable, détestable.
odiously [-li] adv. Odieusement.
odium ['oudjəm] n. Odieux *m*. (odiousness). ‖ Réprobation *f*. (upon, sur).
odograph ['oudə,grɑ:f] n. Odographe *m*.
odometer [ɔ'dɔmitə*] n. TECHN. Odomètre *m*. ‖ U. S., AUTOM. Compteur kilométrique *m*.
odontologist [,ɔdɔn'tɔlədʒist] n. MED. Odontologiste *s*.
odontology [-dʒi] n. MED. Odontologie *f*.
odoriferous [,oudə'rifərəs] adj. Odoriférant.
odorous ['oudərəs] adj. Odorant (having a smell); parfumé (sweet-smelling).
odo(u)r ['oudə*] n. Odeur *m*. (See SMELL.) ‖ Parfum *m*. (fragrance). ‖ ECCLES. *In the odour of sanctity*, en odeur de sainteté. ‖ FAM. *To be in bad odour*, ne pas être en odeur de sainteté, être mal

vu ; *to be in good odour with,* être dans les bonnes grâces (or) les petits papiers de.
odourless [-lis] adj. Inodore.
Odyssey ['ɔdisi] n. Odyssée *f.* (lit. and fig.).
O. E. C. D. [oui:si:'di:] abbr. *Organization for Economic Co-operation and Development,* Organisation de coopération et de développement économique, O. C. D. E.
oecology [i:'kɔlədʒi] n. See ECOLOGY.
oecumenical [,i:kju'menikəl] adj. ECCLES. Œcuménique.
oedema [i:'di:mə] n. invar. MED. Œdème *m.*
oedematous [i:'demətəs] adj. MED. Œdémateux.
Oedipus ['i:dipəs] n. Œdipe *m.*
— adj. PHILOS. D'Œdipe (complex).
oenology [i:'nɔlədʒi] n. Œnologie *f.*
oesophagus [i:'sɔfəgəs] (pl. **oesophagi** [-gai]) n. MED. Œsophage *m.*
oestrogen ['i:strədʒən] n. MED. Œstrogène *m.*
oestrogenic [,i:strə'dʒenik] adj. MED. Œstrogène.
oestrus ['i:strəs] n. MED. Œstrus *m.*
œuvre [œ:vr] n. Œuvre *f.,* œuvres complètes *f.* pl. ; œuvre *m.*
of [ɔv, əv] prep. De (possession) ; *the light of the sun,* la lumière du soleil. ‖ De (cause, origin) ; *it's very kind of you,* c'est très aimable de votre part ; *of necessity,* nécessairement ; *of set purpose,* de propos délibéré ; *to die of thirst,* mourir de soif. ‖ De (quality) ; *poor of spirit,* pauvre d'esprit. ‖ De (quantity) ; *enough of delays,* assez de délais ; *it is not much of a fib,* ce n'est pas un gros mensonge. ‖ De, dès (time) ; *a visit of a fortnight,* un séjour de quinze jours ; *call on me of an evening,* venez un soir ; *of late,* récemment ; *of old,* d'autrefois. ‖ Pour (opinion) ; *to have doubts of s.o.,* avoir des doutes sur qqn. ‖ En (material, specialty) ; *a ring of gold,* un anneau en or ; *doctor of science,* docteur ès sciences. ‖ De (distance) ; *within a mile of the town,* à moins d'un mille de la ville. ‖ A, de (characteristic) ; *a fine figure of a man,* un beau type d'homme, un homme bien bâti ; *he of the green coat,* l'homme à l'habit vert ; *to be of pleasing appearance,* avoir un aspect agréable. ‖ De, au sujet de (about) ; *to hear of s.o.,* entendre parler de qqn. ‖ Entre, parmi (out of) ; *he of all men,* lui entre tous ; *this day of all days,* ce jour parmi tous les autres jours. ‖ De (intensive) ; *the memory of her,* son souvenir ; *the virtue of virtues,* la vertu par excellence. ‖ Par, de (agency) ; *beloved of all,* aimé de tous. ‖ De, à, envers (after adj., v.) ; *capable of,* capable de ; *careless of,* indifférent à ; *to buy of,* acheter à ; *to dream of,* rêver de ; *to know of,* avoir des informations sur ; *to smell of,* sentir. ‖ U. S. *A quarter of ten,* dix heures moins le quart.
off [ɔ:f] prep. De (removal) ; *get off the chair,* levez-vous de la chaise ; *it threw him off his balance,* cela lui fit perdre l'équilibre ; *not far off each other,* non loin l'un de l'autre ; *one year off,* à un an de là ; *to be off one's head,* avoir perdu l'esprit. ‖ De (origin) ; *to dine off potatoes,* dîner de pommes de terre ; *to be off eggs,* être dégoûté des œufs ; SPORTS. *Off side,* hors-jeu. ‖ NAUT. Au large de ; à la hauteur de. ‖ FAM. *Day off,* jour de congé ; *time off,* du temps libre, des loisirs ; *to have an afternoon off,* avoir campos l'après-midi. ‖ **Off-centre,** adj. Désaxé, décentré, décalé. ‖ **Off-chance,** n. U. S. Chance improbable *f.* ‖ **Off-hand,** adv. Immédiatement, sur-le-champ, impromptu (at once) ; sans façon, cavalièrement, avec désinvolture (cavalierly) ; adj. Immédiat, spontané, impromptu (extemporaneous) ; cavalier, sans façon, désinvolte, dégagé (with, vis-à-vis de) [casual]. ‖ **Off-handedness,** n. Désinvolture, attitude cavalière *f.* ; sans-gêne *m.* ‖ **Off-key,** adj., adv. Faux. ‖ **Off-licence,** n. Licence (*f.*) autorisant la vente de boissons alcoolisées à

emporter ; magasin (*m.*) de vins et spiritueux. ‖ **Off-limits,** n. U. S., MILIT. « Défense d'entrer ». ‖ **Off-line,** adj. INFORM. Non connecté, autonome. ‖ **Off-load,** v. tr. Déposer, débarquer. ‖ **Off-peak,** adj. CH. DE F., AUTOM., ELECTR. En dehors des heures de pointe, aux heures creuses. ‖ **Off-position,** n. ELECTR. Rupture (*f.*) de circuit. ‖ **Off-print,** n. Tiré à part *m.* ‖ **Off-putting,** adj. Repoussant, rebutant, rébarbatif (repellent) ; déconcertant (disconcerting). ‖ **Off-scourings,** n. pl. Rebut, déchet *m.* ‖ **Off-shore,** adv. NAUT. Au large ; adj. NAUT. Du côté de la terre ; TECHN. Off-shore. ‖ **Off-stage,** adj., adv. THEATR. Dans les coulisses ; CINEM. Off, hors champ. ‖ **Off-street,** adj. AUTOM. En dehors de la voie publique (parking). ‖ **Off-the-face,** adj. Relevé (hat). ‖ **Off-the-record,** adj. Non destiné à la publication, confidentiel.
— adv. Au loin (away) ; *farther off,* plus loin ; *two miles off,* à deux milles de là. ‖ Au loin (departure) ; *to be* (or) *go off,* s'en aller, partir ; filer (fam.). ‖ Enlevé, ôté (removal) ; *hats off !,* chapeaux bas ! découvrez-vous ! ; *with my coat off,* ayant posé la veste, en manches de chemise. ‖ ELECTR. Fermé, coupé. ‖ CULIN. Eventé (beer) ; avancé (meat). ‖ THEATR. A la cantonade. ‖ NAUT. Au large. ‖ FAM. *Badly off for,* à court de ; *well off,* argenté, à son aise. ‖ LOC. *Off and on,* de temps à autre, par intervalles (or) moments ; *right* (or) *straight off,* immédiatement, tout de suite ; illico (fam.).
— adj. Extérieur ; *off side,* verso. ‖ De congé, férié (day). ‖ Sans entrain ; *off season,* morte-saison. ‖ COMM. A domicile (consumption) ; à emporter (goods). ‖ TECHN. Hors champ. ‖ U. S. Toqué (fam.).
— v. intr. NAUT. Prendre le large.
offal ['ɔfəl] n. Déchets, détritus, débris *m.* pl. ‖ Ordures *f.* pl. (See REFUSE). ‖ CULIN. Abats *m.* pl.
offcut [-kʌt] n. Découpure *f.*
offence [o'fens] n. Froissement *m.* ; blessure *f.* ; *to cause offence to,* blesser, froisser ; *to take offence at,* se formaliser de, se scandaliser de ; *without offence to you,* soit dit sans vous offenser. ‖ ECCLES. Offense, faute *f.* ; péché *m.* ‖ JUR. Acte délictueux *m.* ; infraction *f.* ; *minor offence,* tort léger, contravention ; *second* (or) *old offence,* récidive. ‖ MILIT. Attaque *f.*
offenceless [-lis] adj. Sans péché, innocent. ‖ Inoffensif.
offend [o'fend] v. intr. JUR. *To offend against the law,* commettre un délit ; *to offend against a regulation,* enfreindre un règlement. ‖ ECCLES., FAM. Pécher (against, contre).
— v. tr. Blesser, froisser, désobliger, offenser (to vex). ‖ Choquer, scandaliser, offusquer (to shock)
offender [-ə*] n. Offenseur *m.* ‖ ECCLES. Pécheur *m.* ; pécheresse *f.* ‖ JUR. Délinquant, contrevenant *m.* ; *old offender,* récidiviste.
offending [-iŋ] adj. offensant.
offense [o'fens] n. U. S. See OFFENCE.
offensive [o'fensiv] adj. Blessant, désobligeant (vexing). ‖ Choquant, offusquant (shocking). ‖ Offensant, injurieux (insulting). ‖ Déplaisant, désagréable, répugnant (unpleasant). ‖ Grossier, malsonnant (obscene). ‖ Brusque, rogue (rude). ‖ MILIT. Offensif.
— n. MILIT. Offensive *f.* ; *to switch over to the offensive,* passer à l'offensive.
offensively [-li] adv. De façon blessante (or) choquante (or) injurieuse. ‖ Désagréablement. ‖ Grossièrement.
offensiveness [-nis] n. Caractère blessant (or) choquant (or) injurieux (or) déplaisant (or) grossier *m.*
offer ['ɔfə*] n. Offre *f.* (in general). ‖ Demande (*f.*) en mariage. ‖ COMM. Offre *f.* ; *is that your final offer ?,* est-ce votre dernier mot ? ‖ † Tentative *f.* (at, pour).
— v. tr. Offrir ; *to offer s.o. sth.,* offrir qqch. à qqn. ‖ Offrir, proposer ; *to offer to do,* offrir de

faire, s'offrir à faire. ‖ Formuler, exprimer ; *to offer a remark,* faire une remarque. ‖ Offrir, présenter ; *to offer possibilities,* offrir des possibilités. ‖ Tenter, faire mine de ; *to offer to strike,* esssayer de frapper. ‖ THEATR. *To offer to go,* faire mine de sortir, esquisser une sortie ; « *offers to go »,* fausse sortie. ‖ MILIT. Prêter (*to,* à) [one's flank]. ‖ COMM. Faire (conditions) ; offrir, mettre en vente (goods). ‖ FAM. Présenter (at an examination).
— v. intr. S'offrir, se présenter.

offerer [rə*] n. Offreur *s.* ‖ COMM. Offrant *m.*

offering [-riŋ] n. Offre *f.* (act, thing). ‖ ECCLES. Offrande *f.*

offertory ['ɔfətəri] n. ECCLES. Offrande *f.* (collection) ; offertoire *m.* (oblation).

office ['ɔfis] n. Office *m. ; through s.o.'s good offices,* grâce aux bons offices de qqn. ‖ Devoir *m. ; to perform the last offices to,* rendre les derniers devoirs à. ‖ Office *m. ;* fonction, charge *f. ; public office,* fonctions publiques ; *to hold, to take office,* rester en, entrer en fonctions. ‖ Fonction ministérielle *f. ; to be called to office,* recevoir un portefeuille. ‖ Administration *f. ; Government office,* ministère ; *Foreign, War Office,* ministère des Affaires étrangères, de la Guerre. ‖ Service, bureau *m. ; head office,* bureau central, siège social. ‖ Bureau, cabinet *m. ; manager's office,* bureau du directeur. ‖ ARCHIT. Pl. Communs *m. pl.* (of a house). ‖ ECCLES. Office *m. ; Holy Office,* Saint-Office. ‖ **Office-bearer,** U. S. **Office-holder,** n. Fonctionnaire *s.* ‖ **Office-boy,** n. Coursier ; sauteruisseau *m.* (fam.). ‖ **Office-building,** n. Immeuble (*m.*) de bureaux. ‖ **Office hours,** n. pl. Heures (*f. pl.*) de bureau. ‖ **Office-seeker,** n. FAM. Politicien (*m.*) qui convoite un portefeuille. ‖ **Office-work,** n. Travail de bureau *m.*

officer [-ə*] n. Fonctionnaire *s. ; police officer,* agent de police, sergent de ville, gardien de la paix. ‖ Membre *m.* (of a society). ‖ Officier *m.* (of an Order, in the Salvation Army). ‖ MILIT. Officier *m. ; field officer,* officier supérieur. ‖ NAUT. Officier *m. ; executive officer,* second. ‖ AVIAT. Officier *m.*
— v. tr. MILIT. Fournir des cadres à, encadrer. ‖ MILIT. Commander.

officering [-əriŋ] n. MILIT. Encadrement *m.* ‖ Commandement *m.*

official [o'fiʃəl] adj. Officiel, administratif. ‖ Officiel, authentique. ‖ Officiel, en titre. ‖ MED. Officinal. ‖ ECCLES. Official.
— n. Fonctionnaire, employé de l'Etat *m. ; higher, minor, senior officials,* haut, petit, moyen fonctionnaire. ‖ Pl. Cadres (*m. pl.*) d'une administration.

officialdom [-dəm] n. Bureaucratie *f. ;* fonctionnarisme *m.*

officialese [o,fiʃə'li:z] n. Jargon administratif *m.*

officially [o'fiʃəli] adv. Officiellement.

officialty [-ʃəlti] n. ECCLES. Officialité *f.*

officiant [-ʃənt] n. ECCLES. Officiant *m.* (at service) ; desservant *m.* (in parish).

officiate [-ʃieit] v. intr. ECCLES. Officier (at a service) ; *to officiate in a parish,* desservir une paroisse. ‖ FAM. Remplir les fonctions (as, de).

officinal [,ɔfi'sainl] adj. MED. Officinal.

officious [o'fiʃəs] adj. Officieux (unofficial). ‖ Officieux, trop empressé (over-zealous).

officiously [-li] adv. Officieusement.

officiousness [-nis] n. Officiosité *f.*

offing ['ɔfiŋ] n. NAUT. Large *m.* ‖ FIG. *In the offing,* en perspective.

offish ['ɔfiʃ] adj. Fier, distant.

offset ['ɔfset] n. BOT. Rejeton *m.* ‖ GEOL. Contrefort *m.* ‖ ARCHIT. Ressaut *m. ;* saillie *f.* ‖ TECHN. Décalage, décentrement *m. ;* courbure *f.* (of a pipe) ; Offset *m.* (in printing). ‖ MATH. Ordonnée *f.* ‖ FIN., FIG. Compensation *f.* (*to,* à). ‖ FAM. Repoussoir *m.* (to s.o.'s beauty).

— v. tr. (122). TECHN. Décaler, décentrer. ‖ FIN., FIG. Compenser.
— v. intr. BOT. Pousser des surgeons. ‖ TECHN. Maculer (in printing).
— adj. TECHN. Décalé, décentré, désaxé, déporté.

offshoot ['ɔf:ʃu:t] n. BOT. Rejeton *m.*

offside ['ɔf'said] adj., adv. SPORTS. Hors jeu.

offspring [-spriŋ] n. Progéniture, descendance *f.*

offtake [-teik] n. TECHN., COMM. Ecoulement *m.*

oft [ɔft] adv. † Souvent.

often ['ɔfən] adv. Souvent, maintes fois, fréquemment ; *as often as,* chaque fois que ; *how often,* combien de fois ; tous les combien. ‖ FAM. *Every so often,* de temps en temps, par moments.

oftentimes [-taimz] adv. † Souventefois.

ogee ['oudʒi:] n. ARCHIT. Cimaise, doucine *f.*

ogival [ou'dʒaivəl] adj. ARCHIT. Ogival, en ogive.

ogive ['oudʒai:v] n. ARCHIT. Ogive *f.*
— adj. ARCHIT. En ogive (pointed).

ogle ['ougl] n. Œillade *f.*
— v. tr. Lorgner, reluquer ; faire les yeux doux à, faire de l'œil à.
— v. intr. Jouer de la prunelle.

ogler [-ə*] n. Reluqueur *s.*

Ogpu ['ɔgpu:] n. Guépéou *f.*

ogre ['ougə*] n. Ogre *m.*

ogr(e)ish ['ougriʃ] adj. D'ogre.

ogress ['ougris] n. Ogresse *f.*

oh [ou] interj. Oh ; ô.

ohm [oum] n. PHYS., ELECTR. Ohm *m.*

O.H.M.S. [oueiʃem'es] abbr. *On Her (or) His Majesty's Service,* au service de Sa Majesté.

oidium [ou'idiəm] n. Oïdium *m.*

oil [ɔil] n. Huile *f.* (in general). ‖ Pétrole *m. ; fuel (or) crude oil, oil fuel,* mazout ; *paraffin oil,* pétrole lampant. ‖ MED. Huile, essence *f.* ‖ CULIN., ARTS, ECCLES. Huile *f.* ‖ FAM. *To pour oil on the flames,* jeter de l'huile sur le feu ; *to pour oil on the troubled waters,* calmer la tempête ; *to strike oil,* trouver le filon. ‖ U. S. FAM. Flatterie *f.* ‖ **Oil-bearing,** adj. BOT. Oléagineux ; GEOL. Pétrolifère. ‖ **Oil-bomb,** n. Bombe (*f.*) à mazout. ‖ **Oil-can,** n. Bidon (*m.*) à huile ; burette *f.* ‖ **Oil-colour,** n. Peinture à l'huile *f.* (product). ‖ **Oil-concession,** n. Concession pétrolière *f.* ‖ **Oil-cruet,** n. Huilier *m.* ‖ **Oil-cup,** n. Godet graisseur *m.* ‖ **Oil-duct,** n. Conduite d'huile *f.* ‖ **Oil-engine,** n. Moteur à pétrole *m.* ‖ **Oil-feeder,** n. Burette à huile *f.* ‖ **Oil-field,** n. Terrain (or) gisement pétrolifère *m.* ‖ **Oil-fired,** adj. Chauffé au mazout. ‖ **Oil-king,** n. FAM. Roi du pétrole *m.* ‖ **Oil-lamp,** n. Lampe (*f.*) à huile (or) à pétrole. ‖ **Oil-paint,** n. Peinture à l'huile *f.* (product). ‖ **Oil-painting,** n. ARTS. Peinture à l'huile *f.* (act, picture). ‖ **Oil-seed,** n. Graine (*f.*) de lin. ‖ **Oil-separator,** n. Déshuileur *m.* ‖ **Oil-shale,** n. Schiste bitumineux *m.* ‖ **Oil-sheet,** GEOL. Nappe (*f.*) de pétrole. ‖ **Oil-slick,** n. NAUT. Marée noire *f.* ‖ **Oil-stove,** n. Poêle à mazout *m.* ‖ **Oil-tank,** n. Bac à pétrole *m. ;* réservoir (*m.*) d'huile. ‖ **Oil-tanker,** n. NAUT. Pétrolier *m.* ‖ **Oil-tempering,** n. Huilage *m.* ‖ **Oil-tree,** n. BOT. Ricin *m.* ‖ **Oil-well,** n. Puits de pétrole *m.*
— v. tr. Huiler, graisser. ‖ CULIN. Huiler (a pan). ‖ FAM. *To oil one's tongue,* prendre un ton doucereux ; *to oil the wheels,* mettre du beurre dans les épinards. ‖ **To oil up,** encrasser d'huile.
— v. intr. CULIN. Fondre (butter). ‖ NAUT. Faire le plein de mazout.

oilcake [-keik] n. AGRIC. Tourteau *m.*

oilcloth [-klɔθ] n. Toile huilée *f.* (for raincoat). ‖ Toile cirée *f.* (for table). ‖ Linoléum *m.* (for floors).

oiled [-d] adj. Huilé, graissé (tool). ‖ Huilé (paper) ; en toile huilée (raincoat). ‖ FAM. Plein, rétamé.

oiler [-ə*] n. Graisseur *m.* (person). ‖ Godet graisseur *m.* (oil-cup) ; burette à huile *f.* (oil-feeder).

OIL

PÉTROLE (I)

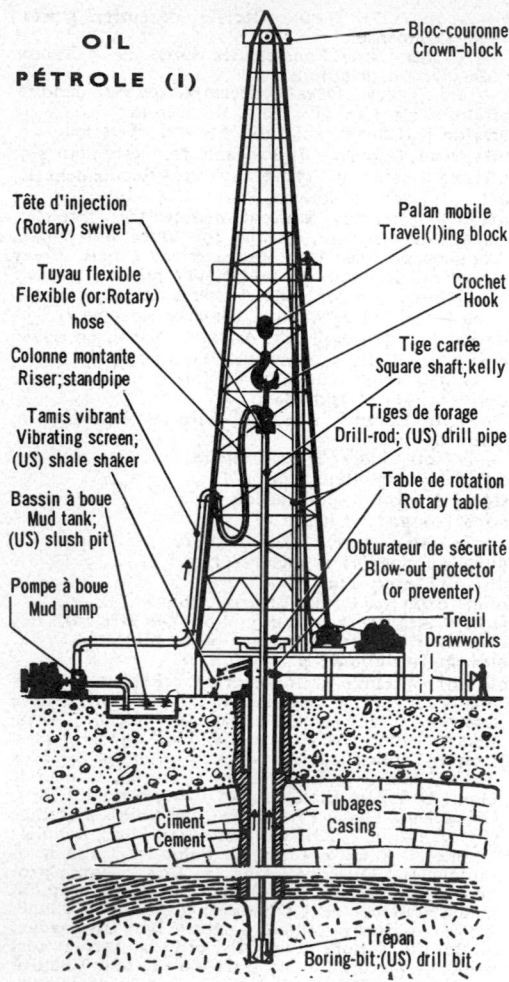

Tête d'injection (Rotary) swivel — Bloc-couronne Crown-block

Palan mobile Travel(l)ing block

Tuyau flexible Flexible (or:Rotary) hose

Crochet Hook

Tige carrée Square shaft;kelly

Colonne montante Riser;standpipe

Tiges de forage Drill-rod; (US) drill pipe

Tamis vibrant Vibrating screen; (US) shale shaker

Table de rotation Rotary table

Bassin à boue Mud tank; (US) slush pit

Obturateur de sécurité Blow-out protector (or preventer)

Pompe à boue Mud pump

Treuil Drawworks

Tubages Casing

Ciment Cement

Trépan Boring-bit;(US) drill bit

---

oiliness [-inis] n. Aspect huileux (or) graisseux m. ‖ Fig. Onctuosité, onction f.

oiling [-iŋ] n. Huilage, graissage m.

oilman [-mən] (pl. **oilmen**) n. Comm. Huilier, droguiste m. ‖ Techn. Graisseur m. ‖ U. S. Pétrolier m.

oilskin [-skin] n. Toile cirée (or) huilée f. ‖ Naut. Ciré m.

oilstone [-stouŋ] n. Affiloir m.
— v. tr. Affiler, affûter.

oily [-i] adj. Huileux, graisseux. ‖ Fam. Onctueux, doucereux, mielleux.

ointment ['ɔintmənt] n. Onguent m.; pommade f.

O. K., U. S. **okay** [ou'kei] interj. Fam. D'accord, très bien, parfait, correct; it's O. K., ça colle!
— n. Fam. Approbation f.; accord m.
— v. tr. U. S. Approuver.

okapi [ou'kɑ:pi] n. Zool. Okapi m.

okra ['oukrə] n. Bot., Agric. Okra, gombo m.

old [ould] adj. Vieux; old age, âge, vieillesse, vieux jours. ‖ Vieux, âgé (person); old man, vieillard, vieil homme; old maid, vieille fille; old woman, femme âgée, vieille; to grow old, vieillir, prendre de l'âge. ‖ Âgé; he is ten years old, il a dix ans; how old is he?, quel âge a-t-il?; to be old enough

---

to, avoir l'âge de, être assez grand pour. ‖ Vieux, ancien (long-established); old trick, tour classique. ‖ Vieux, habile, expérimenté (experienced); to be an old hand, connaître le métier, être un vieux de la vieille. ‖ Ancien (former); in the old days, autrefois; old boy, ancien élève; of old, de jadis, d'autrefois; depuis longtemps. ‖ Culin. Rassis (bread); vieux (wine). ‖ Eccles. Vieil (man); Ancien (Testament); old in sin, pécheur endurci. ‖ Geogr. Ancien (world). ‖ Fam. Any old thing, ce qui vous tombera sous la main; at any old time, n'importe quand; old chap (or) boy, mon vieux; the old man, le patron (boss), le paternel (father). ‖ Fam. Old salt, vieux loup de mer. ‖ **Old-age pensions,** n. Jur. Fonds (m.) vieillesse; retraite (f.) des vieux. ‖ **Old-clothes-man,** n. Fripier, marchand (m.) d'habits (or) aux puces. ‖ **Old-established,** adj. Ancien. ‖ **Old-fashioned,** adj. Vieux jeu, arriéré (ideas, person); démodé, suranné, vieillot, à l'ancienne mode (things). ‖ **Old-maidish,** adj. De vieille fille. ‖ **Old-style,** adj. Vieux style, à l'ancienne mode. ‖ **Old-time,** adj. D'autrefois, antique. ‖ **Old-timer,** n. Fam. Un vieux (m.) de la vieille. ‖ **Old-world,** adj. Des temps antiques, de l'Antiquité; Geogr. De l'Ancien Monde; Fam. Vieillot.

olden [-ən] adj. D'autrefois.
— v. tr., intr. Vieillir.

oldie [-i] n. Fam. Petit vieux m.; petite vieille f. (person). ‖ Vieux succès m.

oldish [-iʃ] adj. Vieillot; plutôt ancien.

oldster [-stə*] n. Fam. Vieux m.; vieille f.

oleaginous [,ouli'ædʒinəs] adj. Bot. Oléagineux. ‖ Fam. Onctueux, doucereux.

oleander [,ouli'ændə*] n. Bot. Laurier-rose m.

oleaster [-'æstə*] n. Bot. Olivier sauvage m.

olefin(e) ['ouli,fi:n] n. Chim. Oléfine f.

oleiferous [,ouli'ifərəs] adj. Bot. Oléifère f.

olein ['ouliin] n. Chim. Oléine f.

oleomargarine [,oulio'mɑ:dʒə'ri:n] n. U. S. Margarine f.

oleometer [ouli'ɔmitə*] n. Phys. Oléomètre m.

oleum ['ouliəm] n. Chim. Oléum m.

olfaction [ɔl'fækʃən] n. Med. Olfaction f.

olfactive [-tiv], **olfactory** [-təri] adj. Med. Olfactif.

oligarchy ['ɔligɑ:ki] n. Oligarchie f.

oliphant ['ɔlifənt] n. Mus. Olifant m.

olivaceous [,ɔli'veiʃəs] adj. Olivâtre.

olivary ['ɔlivəri] adj. Med. Olivaire.

olive ['ɔliv] n. Bot. Olive f. (fruit); olivier m. (tree). ‖ Culin. Olive f. (fruit); beef olive, paupiette. ‖ Comm. Olive f. (button). ‖ Eccles. Mount of Olives, mont des Oliviers. ‖ **Olive-branch,** n. Rameau d'olivier m. ‖ **Olive-coloured,** adj. Olivâtre. ‖ **Olive-drab,** adj. U. S. Gris-vert olive. ‖ **Olive-green,** adj. Vert olive. ‖ **Olive-grove,** n. Olivaie f. ‖ **Olive-grower,** n. Agric. Oléiculteur m. ‖ **Olive-harvest,** n. Agric. Olivaison f. ‖ **Olive-moulding,** n. Archit. Olive f. ‖ **Olive-oil,** n. Culin. Huile d'olive f. ‖ **Olive-shell,** n. Zool. Olive f. ‖ **Olive-wood,** n. Olivaie f. (grove); olivier m. (wood).
— adj. Olive (colour); olivâtre (complexion).

Oliver [-ə*] n. Olivier m.

olivet [-et] n. Comm. Olive; olivette f.

Olympiad [o'limpiæd] n. Olympiade f.

Olympian [-iən] adj., n. Olympien s.

Olympic [-ik] adj. Olympique.

Olympus [-əs] n. Olympe m.

Oman [ou'mɑ:n] n. Geogr. Oman m.

ombudsman ['ɔmbudzmən] (pl. **ombudsmen**) n. Jur. Ombudsman, médiateur m.

omega ['oumigə] n. Oméga m.

omelet(te) ['ɔmlit] n. Culin. Omelette f.

omen ['oumen] n. Augure, présage m.
— v. tr. Augurer, présager.

[Top diagram — English labels]

Gusher; (US) well head

Unrectified petrol; (US) natural gasoline

Liquefied petroleum gas

Pre-heater; stripping plant

Crude oil

Reforming

Chemical treatment

Straight-run oil (or gasoline)

Chemical treatment

Cracked gas

Cracking

Cracked oil

Fuel-oil

Light gas oil

Heavy gas oil

Lubricating oil-stock

Condenser

Fuels

Residual fuels, residues

Clay absorbers

Pipe-line

Fractionating column or tower

De-paraffining (or: dewaxing) treatment

Heater

Refinery storage

Storage tank

Filling station, pumping station

Asphalt plant

Rock-gas, natural gas

Liquefield petroleum gas

Aviation grade petrol

(US: gasoline) Petrol

Solvents

Paraffin (US: kerosene)

Gas oil

Distillate fuel oil

Cracked gas

Industrial fuel oil

Lubricating oils

Petroleum wax paraffin wax

Bitumen asphalt

Waxes, wax polishes boots polishes, insulators

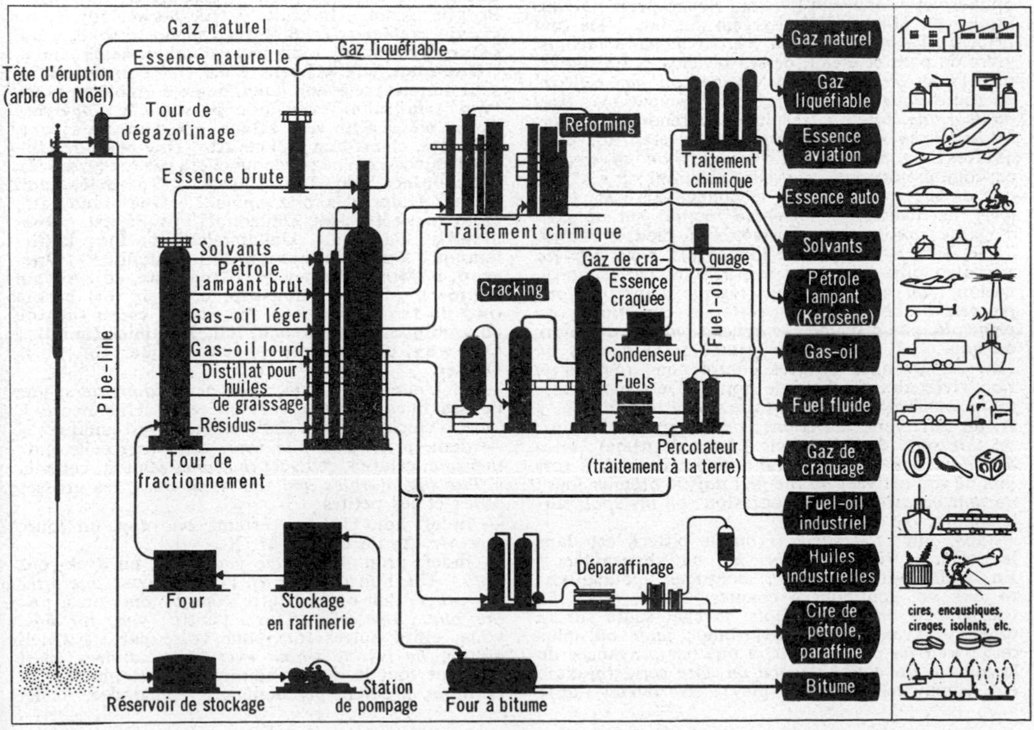

[Bottom diagram — French labels]

Tête d'éruption (arbre de Noël)

Gaz naturel

Essence naturelle

Gaz liquéfiable

Tour de dégazolinage

Essence brute

Reforming

Traitement chimique

Solvants

Traitement chimique

Pétrole lampant brut

Cracking

Gaz de cra-quage

Essence craquée

Fuel-oil

Gas-oil léger

Gas-oil lourd

Distillat pour huiles de graissage

Condenseur

Fuels

Résidus

Percolateur (traitement à la terre)

Pipe-line

Tour de fractionnement

Déparaffinage

Four

Stockage en raffinerie

Réservoir de stockage

Station de pompage

Four à bitume

Gaz naturel

Gaz liquéfiable

Essence aviation

Essence auto

Solvants

Pétrole lampant (Kerosène)

Gas-oil

Fuel fluide

Gaz de craquage

Fuel-oil industriel

Huiles industrielles

Cire de pétrole, paraffine

Bitume

cires, encaustiques, cirages, isolants, etc.

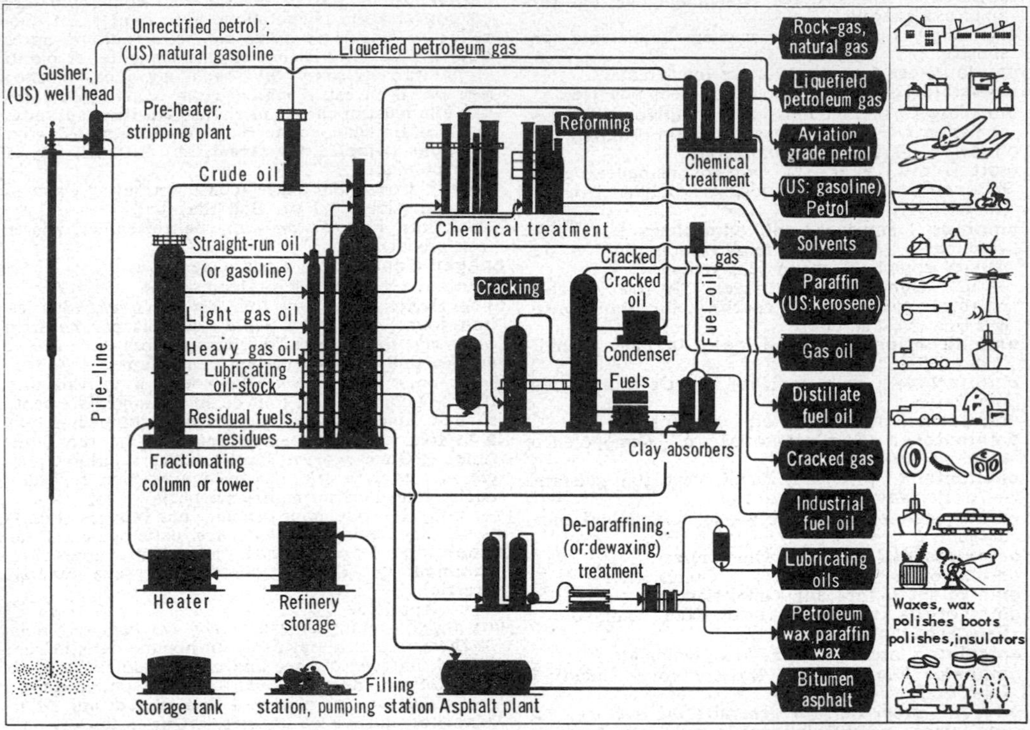

omentum [ou'mentəm] n. Med. Epiploon *m*.
ominous ['ɔminəs] adj. Inquiétant, de mauvais augure, menaçant.
ominously [-li] adv. De manière inquiétante (or) sinistre.
ominousness [-nis] n. Nature inquiétante *f*.
omissible [o'misibl] adj. Qu'on peut omettre.
omission [-ʃən] n. Omission *f*. ‖ Oubli *m*. ‖ Eccles. Omission *f*. ‖ Techn. Bourdon *m*. (in printing).
omissive [-siv] adj. D'omission.
omit [o'mit] v. tr. (1). Omettre, manquer de (to miss out). ‖ Omettre, négliger, oublier (*to*, de) [to fail].
omnibus ['ɔmnibəs] (pl. **omnibuses** [-iz]) adj. Omnibus. ‖ Loc. *Omnibus edition*, édition des œuvres complètes en un seul volume.
— n. † Omnibus *m*. (carriage). ‖ Autom. Autobus *m*. (bus); car *m*. (motor coach). ‖ **Omnibus-route**, n. Ligne (*f*.) d'autobus.
omnidirectional [,ɔmnidi'rekʃənl]] adj. Omnidirectionnel.
omnifarious [,ɔmni'fɛəriəs] adj. De tous genres, très variés.
omniform ['ɔmnifɔ:m] adj. Omniforme.
omnipotence [ɔm'nipətəns] n. Omnipotence, toute-puissance *f*.
omnipotent [-tənt] adj. Omnipotent, tout-puissant.
— n. Eccles. Tout-puissant *m*.
omnipresence ['ɔmni'prezəns] n. Omniprésence, ubiquité *f*.
omnipresent [-ənt] adj. Omniprésent.
omniscience [ɔm'nisjəns] n. Omniscience *f*.
omniscient [-ənt] adj. Omniscient.
omnivorous [ɔm'nivərəs] adj. Zool. Omnivore. ‖ Fam. Dévorant.
omoplate ['oumopleit] n. Med. Omoplate *f*.
omphalos ['ɔmfələs] n. Bosse *f*. (of a shield). ‖ Fam. Centre *m*.
on [ɔn] prep. Sur (in general); *on one leg*, sur une jambe; *on the wall*, sur le mur; *new book on Shakespeare*, nouveau livre sur Shakespeare; *he has money on him*, il a de l'argent sur lui. ‖ De (out of); *to live on bread and water, on one's income*, vivre de pain et d'eau, de ses revenus. ‖ En (movement); *on a journey*, en voyage; *on our way to*, en route pour. ‖ En, sur, pour (occupation); *bent on learning English*, résolu à apprendre l'anglais; *he had been there on business*, il y était allé pour affaires; *on holiday*, en vacances; *on an errand*, en commission. ‖ A, de, sur (position); *it's a new one on me*, celle-là je ne la connaissais pas; *on a level*, de niveau; *on an equal footing*, sur un pied d'égalité; *on foot, on horseback*, à pied, à cheval. ‖ De, sur, à propos de (influence); *have pity on me*, ayez pitié de moi. ‖ De, à, sous, par (subordination); *on approval*, sous réserve d'approbation; *on certain conditions*, à certaines conditions; *on principle*, par principe; *to depend on s.o.*, dépendre de qqn. ‖ A, sur, contre (attack); *the attacks on s.o.*, les critiques dirigées contre qqn; *to live on s.o.*, vivre aux crochets de qqn. ‖ De (belonging); *to be on the committee*, faire partie du comité. ‖ A, de, sur, vers (direction); *on the right*, à droite; *on this side*, de ce côté-ci. ‖ Le (time); *on a fine day*, par un beau jour; *on his arrival*, à (or) lors de son arrivée; *on the first day*, le premier jour; *on that occasion*, à cette occasion; *on the spot*, sur-le-champ.
— adv. Sur; *the steak is on*, le bifteck est dans la poêle. ‖ Vêtu; *with her hat on*, chapeautée. ‖ En continuant; *to go on*, continuer, poursuivre; *to sing on*, continuer à chanter. ‖ Sur, vers; *the cat jumped on to the table*, le chat sauta sur la table. ‖ Avant, plus tard (time); *later on*, plus tard; *well on in the night*, à une heure avancée de la nuit. ‖ En action; *to be on*, être serré (brake); être commencé, se jouer (play); être ouvert (tap);

to have sth. on, avoir qqch. à faire. ‖ En communication; *to be put on to s.o. on the phone*, être en conversation téléphonique avec qqn. ‖ En querelle; *to be always on to s.o.*, être toujours après qqn. ‖ Fam. *And so on*, et ainsi de suite, et patati et patata; *it's simply not on*, il n'y a pas mèche; *he's on*, il en est, il marche; *she is neither on nor off*, elle n'est ni chèvre ni chou. ‖ **On-line**, adj. adv. Inform. En ligne, connecté. ‖ **On-shore**, adj. Naut. Du large (wind). ‖ **On-street**, adj. Autom. Sur la voie publique.
— adj. Comm. Sur place (consumption). ‖ Sports. Gauche (side). ‖ Fam. Bon (days).
— v. intr. Fam. *To on with*, mettre, enfiler, passer (one's coat).
onager ['ɔnəgə*] n. Zool. Onagre *m*.
onanism ['ɔnənizm] n. Onanisme *m*.
once [wʌns] adv. Une fois; *once a week*, tous les huit jours; *once in a while*, une fois par hasard; *once and for all*, une fois pour toutes; *once more*, encore une fois; encore un coup (fam.). ‖ Autrefois; *once upon a time there was*, il y avait une fois. ‖ Loc. *At once*, tout de suite, immédiatement, sur-le-champ; aussitôt, à l'instant (immediately); à la fois, en même temps, ensemble (at the same time). ‖ **Once-over**, n. Fam. Examen rapide et précis *m*.; *to give sth. the once-over*, bien regarder qqch., jeter l'œil du maître sur qqch.
— conj. Dès que, pour peu que; une fois que (fam.).
— n. Une seule fois; *that once*, cette seule fois-là.
oncoming ['ɔn,kʌmiɳ] adj. Qui approche; imminent. ‖ Autom. Qui vient en sens inverse (traffic).
— n. Approche *f*.
one [wʌn] num. adj. Un; *there was only one man in the street*, il n'y avait qu'un homme dans la rue. ‖ Seul, unique; *his one and only*, sa dulcinée; *with one voice*, d'une seule voix; ‖ A l'unisson, en unité; *to become one*, se marier. ‖ **One-armed**, adj. Med. Manchot, qui n'a qu'un bras. ‖ **One-cylinder**, adj. Techn. Monocylindrique. ‖ **One-eyed**, adj. Med. Borgne; Zool. Uninoculé. ‖ **One-horse**, adj. A un cheval (vehicle); U. S. Fam. *One-horse town*, trou. ‖ **One-legged**, adj. Med. Qui n'a qu'une seule jambe. ‖ **One-man**, adj. Manœuvré par (or) constitué d'un seul homme; *one-man band*, homme orchestre; *one-man exhibition*, exposition personnelle; *one-man show*, pièce à un seul acteur, one-man-show; *one-man dog*, chien d'un seul maître. ‖ **One-off**, adj. Unique (object); qui ne se renouvellera pas (occurrence). ‖ **One-piece**, adj. D'une pièce. ‖ **One-price**, adj. Comm. Uniprix, à prix unique. ‖ **One-sided**, adj. D'un seul côté; Jur. Unilatéral; Fig. Partial. ‖ **One-sidedly**, adv. Jur. Unilatéralement; Fig. Partialement. ‖ **One-sidedness**, n. Fig. Partialité *f*. ‖ **One-step**, n. Mus. One-step *m*. ‖ **One-time**, adj. Ancien (former). ‖ **One-upmanship**, n. Désir (or) besoin (*m*.) de faire mieux que son voisin, esprit (*m*.) de compétition. ‖ **One-track**, adj. Routinier (mind). ‖ **One-way**, adj. Autom. A sens unique; Ch. de f. D'aller.
— n. Unité *f*. ‖ Un *m*.; *one of his daughters*, une de ses filles; *such a one*, un tel. ‖ Une heure *f*. (one o'clock). ‖ Pop. *He's a one*, il est unique!
— dem. pron. *The one who*, celui (or) celle qui; *this one*, celui-ci, celle-ci; *that one*, celui-là, celle-là. ‖ *The big marbles and the small ones*, les grosses billes et les petites.
— indef. adj. Un, un certain; *one day*, un jour; *one Mr. X*, un certain M. X.
— indef. pron. Un; *have you one?*, en avez-vous un? ‖ Un, l'un; *one of us*, l'un de nous; *one after the other*, l'un après l'autre; *one by one*, un à un; *the one... the other*, l'un... l'autre; *you, for one*, vous, entre autres (or) pour votre part. ‖ Quelqu'un; *he is one whom everybody admires*, c'est qqn que tout le monde admire; *he was not one to grumble*, il n'était pas homme à se plaindre. ‖ On;

one ought to be satisfied with one's lot, on doit se contenter de son sort. ‖ **One's,** son, sa, ses ; *when one has read a few pages, one's opinion is formed,* quand on a lu quelques pages, on a formé son opinion.

oneness [-nis] n. Unité *f.* ‖ Unicité *f.* ‖ FIG. Accord *m.*

onerous ['ɔnərəs] adj. FIN. Onéreux. ‖ FIG. Lourd.

onerously [-li] adv. A titre onéreux, onéreusement.

onerousness [-nis] n. Onérosité *f.*

oneself [wʌn'self] pron. Soi-même (emphatic) ; *to see sth. oneself,* voir qqch. soi-même (or) de ses propres yeux. ‖ Se (reflexive) ; *to enjoy oneself,* s'amuser. ‖ Soi ; *to speak of oneself,* parler de soi ; *to take sth. upon oneself,* prendre qqch. sur soi.

ongoing ['ɔn,gouiŋ] adj. En cours (in progress) ; continu (developing).

onion ['ʌnjən] n. BOT., CULIN. Oignon *m.* ; *Spring onion,* petit oignon ; *Welsh onion,* ciboule. ‖ FAM. *To know one's onions,* connaître son affaire. ‖ **Onion-skin,** n. BOT. Pelure (*f.*) d'oignon ; COMM. Papier pelure *m.*

oniony [-i] adj. Ayant goût (or) odeur d'oignon.

onlooker ['ɔn,lukə*] n. Spectateur *m.* ; spectatrice *f.* ; assistant *m.* ; badaud *m.* (pej.).

only ['ounli] adj. Seul, unique.
— adv. Seulement, simplement, rien que, ne... que ; *not only... but,* non seulement... mais encore ; *one child only,* rien qu'un enfant, un seul enfant ; *you have only to take it,* vous n'avez qu'à le prendre. ‖ FAM. Encore, seulement ; *only last week,* la semaine dernière encore, pas plus tard que la semaine dernière. ‖ **Only-begotten,** adj. ECCLES. Unique (Son).
— conj. Mais, seulement ; *only that,* si ce n'est que.

onomastic [ɔno'mæstik] adj. Onomastique.

onomatopoeia [,ɔnɔmæto'piːə] n. Onomatopée *f.*

onomatopoe(t)ic [-(t)ik] adj. Onomatopéique.

onrush ['ɔnrʌʃ] n. Ruée *f.*

onset [-set] n. MED. Attaque *f.* ‖ MILIT. Assaut *m.* ; attaque *f.* ‖ CHIM. Départ *m.* ‖ FIG. Abord *m.* ; *at the onset,* de prime abord ; *from the onset,* dès l'abord.

onside [,ɔn'said] adj., adv. SPORTS. Pas hors jeu.

onslaught [-slɔːt] n. MED., MILIT., FIG. Attaque *f.*

ontogenesis [,ɔnto'dʒenisis] n. MED. Ontogenèse *f.*

ontological [,ɔnto'lɔdʒikəl] adj. Ontologique.

ontology [-dʒi] n. PHILOS. Ontologie *f.*

onus ['ounəs] n. JUR., FIG. Charge *f.*

onward ['ɔnwəd] adj. En avant, progressif.

onwards [-z] adv. En avant ; *from today onwards,* à partir d'aujourd'hui, dorénavant.

onyx ['ɔniks] n. Onyx *m.*

oodles ['uːdlz] n. pl. FAM. Flopée *f.* (*of,* de).

oof [uːf] n. FAM. Galette, oseille *f.* ; pognon, grisbi, pèze *m.*

oogenesis [,ouə'dʒenisis] n. MED. Ovogenèse *f.*

oolite ['ouəlait] n. Oolithe *m.*

oomph [umf] n. U. S. POP. Montant, sex-appeal *m.*

oops [ups] interj. Hop-là!, et hop!

ooze [uːz] n. Vase, boue *f.* ; limon *m.* (mud). ‖ Suintement *m.* ; fuite *f.* (oozing). ‖ TECHN. Jusée *f.*
— v. intr. Suinter, sourdre (*from,* de). ‖ S'infiltrer, filtrer (*through,* dans). ‖ FAM. *To ooze with pride,* suer l'orgueil. ‖ *To ooze away,* fuir, diminuer. ‖ **To ooze out,** FIG. Transpirer, percer.

oozing [-iŋ] adj. Suintant ; dégoulinant (fam.).
— n. Suintement *m.*

oozy [-i] adj. Bourbeux, vaseux (muddy). ‖ Suintant.

opacity [o'pæsiti] n. Opacité *f.* ‖ FIG. Lourdeur, opacité *f.* (See OBTUSENESS.)

opal ['oupəl] n. Opale *f.*
— adj. Opale, opalin.

opalescence [oupə'lesns] n. Opalescence *f.*

opalescent [-nt] adj. Opalescent, opalisé.

opaline ['oupəlain] adj. Opalin.
— ['oupəliːn] n. Opaline *f.*

opaque [ou'peik] adj. Opaque ; *to become opaque,* s'opacifier. ‖ FIG. Lourd.

O. P. E. C. ['ou,pek] abbr. *Organization of Petroleum Exporting Countries,* Organisation des pays exportateurs de pétrole, O. P. E. P.

open ['oupən] adj. Ouvert ; *wide open,* grand ouvert. ‖ Ouvert ; *to be unable to keep one's eyes open,* dormir debout. ‖ Ouvert, accessible (*to,* à) [s.o., sth.] ; *to keep open house,* tenir table ouverte. ‖ Ouvert, libre ; *in the open,* à ciel ouvert ; en plein air ; en pleine campagne ; à la belle étoile ; au grand jour. ‖ MED. Libre (bowels) ; dilaté (pore) ; ouvert (wound) ; *to lay a wound open,* mettre une plaie à nu. ‖ ELECTR. Ouvert (circuit). ‖ FIN. Ouvert (account) ; non barré (cheque). ‖ JUR. Non conclu (contract) ; vacant (job) ; public (letter, trial) ; flottant (policy). ‖ COMM. A jour (embroidery). ‖ AGRIC. Meuble (soil) ; *on open ground,* en pleine terre. ‖ BOT. Ouvert (flower). ‖ SPORTS. Dégagé (play) ; ouvert (season) ; *open race,* omnium. ‖ AUTOM. Découvert (car, corner) ; libre, non encombré, ouvert (road). ‖ MILIT. Ouvert (city) ; dispersé (order) ; de mouvement (warfare). ‖ NAUT. Non ponté (boat) ; doux (weather) ; *on the open sea,* en haute mer, au grand large ; *open to the wind,* exposé au vent. ‖ GRAMM. Ouvert (vowel). ‖ FIG. Déclaré (enemy) ; ouvert, franc (person). ‖ FIG. Exposé (*to,* à) [calumny] ; ouvert, accessible (*to,* à) [pity]. ‖ FIG. Libre, dégagé, sans opinion préconçue (mind) ; en suspens, non réglé (question) ; *to keep a day open for,* réserver un jour pour ; *to leave the matter open,* réserver la question, laisser la question pendante. ‖ FIG. Loisible, permis ; *it is open to you to,* vous avez la faculté de (or) toute la liberté de. ‖ **Open-air,** adj. En (or) de plein air ; THEATR. De verdure (theatre) ; MED. *Open-air treatment,* cure d'air. ‖ **Open-armed,** adj. A bras ouverts. ‖ **Open-cast,** adj. TECHN. A ciel ouvert, à découvert. ‖ **Open-ended,** adj. Non limitatif, libre. ‖ **Open-eyed,** adj. Les yeux grands ouverts (or) écarquillés ; FIG. Très conscient, les yeux bien ouverts. ‖ **Open-faced,** adj. Au visage ouvert. ‖ **Open-handed,** adj. Généreux ; qui a toujours la main à la poche (fam.). ‖ **Open-handedly,** adv. Libéralement, à pleines mains. ‖ **Open-handedness,** n. Libéralité, générosité *f.* ‖ **Open-heart,** adj. MED. A cœur ouvert (surgery). ‖ **Open-hearted,** adj. Ouvert, franc, expansif, bon, cordial, généreux. ‖ **Open-heartedness,** n. Franchise ; cordialité *f.* ‖ **Open-jaw,** adj. En ciseaux. ‖ **Open-minded,** adj. A l'esprit ouvert, libéral, sans parti pris. ‖ **Open-mindedness,** n. Largeur (*f.*) d'esprit, libéralité *f.* ‖ **Open-mouthed,** adj. Bouche bée. ‖ **Open-necked,** adj. A col ouvert. ‖ **Open-plan,** adj. ARCHIT. Sans cloisons (space, architecture). ‖ **Open-work,** adj. Ajouré, à jour ; n. Jours *m. pl.* ; TECHN. Exploitation (*f.*) à ciel ouvert.
— v. tr. Ouvrir (in general). ‖ Ouvrir (eyes, hands, mouth) ; *to open one's legs,* écarter les jambes. ‖ Ouvrir, creuser, pratiquer (a hole) ; ouvrir, percer (a road). ‖ ELECTR. Ouvrir (a circuit). ‖ AGRIC. Défricher (ground). ‖ ARCHIT. Dégager (a vista). ‖ COMM. Ouvrir, monter (a shop). ‖ FIN. Ouvrir (an account). ‖ JUR. Exposer (a case) ; inaugurer (an institution) ; ouvrir, entamer (negociations) ; ouvrir (session). ‖ MILIT. Ouvrir (fire, front, ranks). ‖ FIG. Ouvrir, épancher (one's heart) ; dévoiler (one's intentions). ‖ **To open out,** ouvrir, élargir, agrandir (a hole) ; ouvrir, déployer (a sheet). ‖ **To open up,** ouvrir (a mine, a road, a shop).
— v. intr. S'ouvrir (door) [*into, on to,* sur]. ‖ COMM. S'ouvrir (shop). ‖ BOT. S'ouvrir, s'épanouir. ‖ FIG. S'ouvrir, commencer (*with,* par). ‖ **To open out,** s'étendre (prospects) ; FIG. *To open out to,* ouvrir son cœur à. ‖ **To open up,** COMM. Ouvrir une maison ; FIG. *To make s.o. open up,* délier la langue de qqn.

openable [-əbl̩] adj. Ouvrable. ‖ THEATR. Praticable.

opener [-ə*] n. Ouvreur s. ‖ COMM. Débouchoir, décapsulateur m. (for bottle).

opening [-iŋ] n. Ouverture f. ‖ ARTS. Vernissage m. ‖ THEATR. Opening night, première.
— adj. MED. Purgatif.

openly [-li] adv. Ouvertement, franchement.

openness [-is] n. Aspect découvert m. ‖ NAUT. Douceur m. (of weather). ‖ FIG. Franchise; libéralité; ouverture (f.) d'esprit.

opera ['ɔp(ə)rə] n. MUS., THEATR. Opéra m.; comic opera, opéra bouffe; grand opera, opéra; light opera, opérette. ‖ **Opera-cloak,** n. Manteau du soir m. ‖ **Opera-glasses,** n. Jumelles f. pl. ‖ **Opera-hat,** n. Gibus, claque, haut-de-forme m. ‖ **Opera-house,** n. Opéra m.

operable ['ɔpərəbl̩] adj. MED. Opérable.

operate [-reit] v. intr. MED. Opérer; to operate on s.o. for sth., opérer qqn de qqch. ‖ JUR. Agir, jouer, opérer. ‖ TECHN. Fonctionner. ‖ FIN. Jouer, spéculer (for, à).
— v. tr. MED. Opérer, accomplir (a cure). ‖ TECHN. Actionner, faire fonctionner. ‖ U. S. Diriger, exploiter, tenir.

operatic [,ɔpə'rætik] adj. THEATR. D'opéra.
— n. pl. FAM. Opéra (m.) d'amateurs.

operating ['ɔpəreitiŋ] adj. MED. Opérateur, qui opère. ‖ ECCLES. Opérant (grace). ‖ U. S. De marche (costs); exploitant, gérant (staff). ‖ **Operating-room,** n. MED. Salle d'opération f.; THEATR. Cabine de projection f. ‖ **Operating-table,** n. MED. Table d'opération f.
— n. MED. Action f. (of a remedy); fait (m.) d'opérer (by a surgeon). ‖ TECHN. Fonctionnement m.; manœuvre f. ‖ U. S. Exploitation f.

operation [,ɔpə'reiʃən] n. MED. Opération f.; illegal operation, manœuvre abortive; emergency operation, opération à chaud. ‖ JUR. Application, mise à l'exécution, action f. (of a law); to be in operation, être en vigueur. ‖ MATH., FIN., MILIT. Opération f. ‖ FIG. Opération, action f.

operational [-əl] adj. MILIT. Des opérations, d'opération. ‖ TECHN. En état de marche.

operative ['ɔpərətiv] adj. Opératif. ‖ MED. Opératoire. ‖ JUR. Opérant (decree); exécutoire (obligation); to become operative, entrer en vigueur. ‖ TECHN. Pratique, actif, ouvrier.
— n. TECHN. Ouvrier s.; skilled operatives, ouvriers spécialisés. ‖ U. S. Détective privé m.

operator [-eitə·] n. Opérateur m.; opératrice f. ‖ MED. Opérateur m. ‖ CINEM. Opérateur, projectionniste m. ‖ NAUT. Wireless operator, radio. ‖ TECHN. Ouvrier m. (workman); téléphoniste s.; télégraphiste s. ‖ U. S. AUTOM. Conducteur, chauffeur m. ‖ U. S. Propriétaire (or) exploitant (m.) de mines; usinier m.

operculum [-ləm] (pl. **opercula** [-lə]) n. Opercule m.

operetta [,ɔpə'retə] n. MUS., THEATR. Opérette f.

ophidian [o'fidiən] adj., n. ZOOL. Ophidien m.

ophthalmia [ɔf'ælmiə] n. MED. Ophtalmie f.

ophthalmic [-mik] adj. MED. Ophtalmologique (hospital); ophtalmique (remedy).

ophthalmologic(al) [,ɔfθælmə'lɔdʒik(əl)] adj. MED. Ophtalmologique.

ophthalmologist [,ɔfθæl'mɔlədʒist] n. MED. Ophtalmologiste s.

ophthalmology [-dʒi] n. MED. Ophtalmologie f.

ophthalmoscope [ɔf'θælmə,skoup] n. MED. Ophtalmoscope m.

opiate ['oupiit] adj. MED. Opiacé.
— n. MED. Opiat m. ‖ **Opiate-monger,** n. FAM. Bourreur de crâne m.
— v. tr. MED. Opiacer.

opine [o'pain] v. intr. Opiner; formuler l'avis, penser (that, que).

opinion [o'pinjən] n. Opinion f.; in my opinion, à mon avis; matter of opinion, question d'appréciation; to be of (the) opinion that, estimer que; I have my own opinion just the same, je n'en pense pas moins; public opinion, le qu'en-dira-t-on. ‖ Opinion, idée, estime f.; to have a high opinion of, avoir fort bonne opinion de, tenir en haute estime, faire grand cas de. ‖ JUR. Counsel's opinion, consultation d'avocat.

opinionated [-eitid] adj. Opiniâtre, entêté, obstiné, attaché à ses opinions.

opinionativeness [-eitivnis] n. Opiniâtreté f.; dogmatisme, entêtement (m.) dans ses opinions.

opiomaniac [,oupio'meiniək] n. MED. Opiomane s.

opium ['oupjəm] n. Opium m.; opium den, fumerie d'opium. ‖ **Opium-fiend,** n. FAM. Opiomane s. ‖ **Opium-poisoning,** n. MED. Thébaïsme m. ‖ **Opium-smoker,** n. Fumeur (s.) d'opium.

Oporto [o'pɔ:tou] n. GEOGR. Porto m.

opossum [ə'pɔsəm] n. ZOOL. Opossum m.; sarigue f.

opotherapy [ɔpo'θerəpi] n. MED. Opothérapie f.

opponens [ɔ'pounenz] adj., n. MED. Opposant m.

opponent [ə'pounənt] adj. Opposé. ‖ MED. Opposant.
— n. Opposant, adversaire, antagoniste s. (See ADVERSARY.) ‖ COMM. Concurrent s.

opportune ['ɔpətju:n] adj. Opportun, à propos.

opportunely [-li] adv. Opportunément, à propos, à point; à pic (fam.).

opportuneness [-nis] n. Opportunité f.; à-propos m.

opportunism [-izm̩] n. Opportunisme m.

opportunist [-ist] n. Opportuniste s. (See TIME-SERVER.)

opportunity [,ɔpə'tjuniti] n. Occasion f. (for, de); to make an opportunity of, se ménager une occasion de; to miss, to take an opportunity, laisser passer, saisir une occasion. ‖ A-propos m. (opportuneness).

opposable [ə'pouzəbl̩] adj. Opposable (to, à).

oppose [ə'pouz] v. tr. Opposer (to, à); élever (to, contre) [to set over]. ‖ Mettre en opposition, contraster (to contrast). ‖ S'opposer à, mettre opposition (or) obstacle à, contrecarrer (to set oneself against).

opposed [-d] adj. Opposé, antagoniste; hostile (to, à). ‖ Opposé, en contradiction (to, avec); contraire (to, à).

opposer [-ə*] n. Opposant s.

opposing [-iŋ] adj. Opposé, opposant, adverse, antagoniste.

opposite ['ɔpəzit] adj. En face; opposé, face (to, à); vis-à-vis (to, de) [facing]. ‖ Contraire, opposé (from, to, à); in the opposite direction, en sens inverse; to take the opposite view, prendre le contre-pied de. ‖ PHYS. Contraire (pole). ‖ FAM. Opposite number, homologue, complément, pendant.
— n. Opposé, contraire m. (contrary). ‖ Contre-pied m. (reverse). ‖ Opposite m.
— adv. En face.
— prep. En face de, vis-à-vis de; opposite each other, en face l'un de l'autre.

opposition [,ɔpo'ziʃən] n. Opposition f. (to, à) [antagonism]. ‖ Opposition, résistance f. (to, à). ‖ JUR. Opposition f. (in politics). ‖ COMM. Concurrence f. (to, avec).

oppositive [-tiv] adj. Contrastant.

oppress [o'pres] v. tr. Opprimer (to crush); oppresser (to weigh down). ‖ MED. Oppresser, étouffer.

oppressed [-d] adj. MED. Opprimé.
— n. pl. Opprimés m. pl.

oppression [ə'preʃən] n. Oppression f. (crushing). ‖ MED. Oppression f.; accablement m. ‖ MED. Oppression f.; étouffement m.

oppressive [-siv] adj. Opprimant, oppressif (oppressing). ‖ Lourd, accablant, étouffant.

oppressively [-sivli] adj. De manière opprimante (or) accablante.

oppressiveness [-sivnis] n. Tyrannie, disposition tyrannique *f.*; caractère oppressif *m.* ‖ Lourdeur *f.*; accablement, poids *m.* (of atmosphere).

oppressor [-sə*] n. Oppresseur, opprimant *s.*

opprobrious [ə'proubriəs] adj. Infamant.

opprobriousness [briəsnis] n. Nature injurieuse (or) infamante *f.*

opprobrium [-briəm] n. Opprobre *m.*

oppugn [o'pju:n] v. tr. Attaquer, s'en prendre à.

oppugner [-ə*] n. Assaillant, adversaire *s.*

opt [ɔpt] v. intr. Opter (*for*, pour).

optative ['ɔptətiv] adj., n. GRAMM. Optatif *m.*

optic ['ɔptik] adj. MED. Optique.

optical [-əl] adj. PHYS. Optique, d'optique.

optician [ɔp'tiʃən] n. Opticien *m.*

optics ['ɔptiks] n. sg. PHYS. Optique *f.*

optimal ['ɔptiməl] adj. Optimal, optimum.

optimism ['ɔptimizm] n. Optimisme *m.*

optimist [-ist] n. Optimiste *s.*

optimistic [ɔpti'mistik] adj. Optimiste.

optimistically [-əli] adv. Avec optimisme.

optimize [-maiz] v. tr. Optimiser.

optimum [-məm] adj., n. Optimum *m.*

option ['ɔpʃən] n. Option *f.* ‖ Latitude, faculté, liberté *f.*; *to have no option but to*, n'avoir pas d'autre alternative que de. ‖ FIN. Option *f.* (*on*, sur); *giver, taker of an option*, optionnaire, optant; *option deal*, opération à prime. ‖ JUR. Substitution *f.* (of fine); faculté *f.* (of purchase).

optional [-əl] adj. A option (course of study). ‖ Facultatif (in general).

opulence ['ɔpjuləns] n. Opulence *f.* (See WEALTH.)

opulent [-lənt] adj. Opulent (wealthy). ‖ Abondant, copieux (plentiful). ‖ Plantureux, opulent (buxom).

opulently [-ləntli] adv. Avec opulence.

opus ['oupəs] n. MUS. Opus *m.* ‖ FIG. *Opus magnum*, grand œuvre *m.*, œuvre principale *f.*

opuscule [ɔ'pʌskju:l] n. Opuscule *m.*

or [ɔ:*] conj. Ou; *a millionaire five or six times over*, cinq ou six fois millionnaire. ‖ Ni (with negation); *he cannot walk or run*, il ne peut marcher ni courir. ‖ Ou, ou bien, sinon (otherwise); *speak or else look out*, il faut parler ou gare!

oracle ['ɔrək||] n. Oracle *m.* ‖ FAM. *To be Sir Oracle*, se prendre pour un oracle.

oracular [ɔ'rækjulə*] adj. D'oracle. ‖ Dogmatique, sentencieux.

oral ['ɔ:rəl] adj. Oral. ‖ JUR. Testimonial (evidence). ‖ MED. Par voie buccale (or) orale (administration); oral (cavity).
— n. FAM. Oral *m.* (viva voce).

orange ['ɔrindʒ] n. BOT. Orange *f.* (fruit); agrume *m.* (collectively); oranger *m.* (tree). ‖ **Orange-blossom**, n. Fleur (*f.*) d'oranger. ‖ **Orange-girl**, n. Orangère *f.* ‖ **Orange-seller**, n. COMM. Oranger *m.*
— adj. Orange, orangé.

Orange adj., n. GEOGR. Orange *m.*

orangeade ['ɔrindʒ'eid] n. Orangeade *f.*

Orangeism ['ɔrindʒizm] n. Orangisme *m.*

Orangeman [-mən] n. Orangiste *m.*

orangery [-ri] n. Orangerie *f.*

orang-(o)utang [o'ræŋu'tæŋ] n. ZOOL. Orang-outan *m.*

orate [o'reit] v. intr. FAM. Laïusser, phraser.

oration [o'reiʃən] n. Allocution *f.*; laïus *m.* (fam.). ‖ ECCLES. *Funeral oration*, oraison funèbre. ‖ GRAMM. Discours *m.*

orator ['ɔrətə*] n. Orateur *m.*; *woman orator*, oratrice.

Oratorian [,ɔrə'tɔːriən] adj., n. ECCLES. Oratorien *s.*

oratoric(al) [-ik(əl)] adj. Oratoire (delivery, talent). ‖ FAM. Phraseur (person); verbeux (speech).

oratorio [,ɔrə'tɔːriou] n. MUS. Oratorio *m.*

oratory ['ɔrətəri] n. Art oratoire *m.*; *pulpit oratory*, éloquence de la chaire. ‖ ECCLES. Oratoire *m.*

oratress ['ɔrətris] n. Oratrice *f.*

orb [ɔ:b] n. Orbe, globe *m.* ‖ BLAS. Monde *m.*

orbed [-d] adj. Rond.

orbicular [ɔ:'bikjulə*] adj. Orbiculaire.

orbit ['ɔ:bit] n. ASTRON., MED., FIG. Orbite *f. to go* (or) *swing into orbit*, se placer sur son orbite.
— v. tr. Tourner autour de (the earth).

orbital [-əl] adj. ASTRON. Orbital. ‖ MED. Orbitaire. ‖ FAM. De ceinture (road).

orc [ɔ:k] n. ZOOL. Epaulard *m.*

orchard ['ɔ:tʃəd] n. AGRIC. Verger *m.*

orcharding [-iŋ] n. AGRIC. Fructiculture *f.*

orchardist [-ist] n. AGRIC. Fructiculteur, producteur (*m.*) de fruits.

orchestra ['ɔ:kəstrə] n. MUS., THEATR. Orchestre *m.*

orchestral [ɔ:'kestrəl] adj. MUS. Orchestral.

orchestrate ['ɔ:kəstreit] v. tr. MUS., FIG. Orchestrer.

orchestration [,ɔ:kes'treiʃən] n. MUS., FIG. Orchestration *f.* (See SCORING.)

orchid ['ɔ:kid] n. BOT. Orchidée *f.*

orchil ['ɔ:tʃil] n. BOT. Orseille *f.*

orchis ['ɔ:kis] n. BOT. Orchis *m.*

orchitis [ɔ:'kaitis] n. MED. Orchite *f.*

ordain [ɔ:'dein] v. tr. JUR. Ordonner, prescrire, décréter, décider. ‖ ECCLES. Ordonner. ‖ FIG. Fixer, déterminer (an event); destiner (s.o.).

ordainer [-ə*] n. Ordonnateur *m.*; ordonnatrice *f.* ‖ ECCLES. Ordinant *m.*

ordaining [-iŋ] n. ECCLES. Ordination *f.*

ordeal [ɔ:'diəl] n. † Ordalie *f.*; jugement de Dieu *m.* ‖ FIG. Dure épreuve *f.* ‖ **Ordeal-tree**, n. BOT. Tanghinia *m.*

order ['ɔ:də*] n. Ordre, arrangement *m.*; disposition *f.*; *out of order*, en désordre; *to set in order*, mettre en ordre. ‖ Ordre *m.*; règle *f.*; *in order*, en règle (passport); *to put one's affairs in order*, mettre ses affaires en ordre. ‖ Ordre, rang *m.*; *of the first order*, du premier ordre. ‖ Ordre *m.*; suite, succession *f.*; *chronological order*, ordre chronologique. ‖ Ordre *m.* (of knighthood); décoration *f.* (medal). ‖ Ordre, avis *m.*; *until further order*, jusqu'à nouvel ordre. ‖ Ordre, commandement *m.*; instruction, consigne *f.*; *to give orders to*, donner des ordres à. ‖ Ordre *m.*; discipline *f.*; *law and order*, ordre public. ‖ Ordre, régime *m.* (of events, things); classe *f.* (of society). ‖ ECCLES. Ordre *m.* (holy, monastic); *order of service*, office; *to take Holy Orders*, entrer dans les ordres. ‖ ARCHIT., BOT. Ordre *m.* ‖ COMM. Commande *f.*; *made to order*, fait sur commande; *to place an order with*, passer une commande à; *to put on order*, commander. ‖ FIN. Bonne forme *f.* (of account); ordonnancement *m.* (for payment); mandat *m.* (on a bank); *cheque to the order of*, chèque à l'ordre de. ‖ JUR. Arrêt *m.*; décision; injonction *f.* (of the court); ordonnance *f.* (of the judge); *departmental order*, arrêté ministériel; *Order in Council*, décret-loi. ‖ TECHN. Etat *m.*; *in working order*, en état de marche (or) de fonctionner; *out of order*, en mauvais état, en panne, détraqué, déréglé. ‖ MILIT. Ordre *m.* (of battle); consigne *f.* (instructions); *in gala order*, en grande tenue; *to come to the order*, reposer armes. ‖ FAM. *It's a large order*, ce n'est pas une petite affaire; *out of order*, détraqué, patraque, mal fichu (unfit). ‖ **Order-blank** (or) **-slip**, n. COMM. Bon (*m.*) de commande. ‖ **Order-book**, n. COMM. Carnet (or) livre (*m.*) de commande.
— v. tr. Mettre en ordre, ordonner, ranger (to arrange). ‖ Régler; *to order one's own life*, disposer de sa vie. ‖ Ordonner à, commander à (*to*, de) [s.o.]. ‖ Désigner (*to*, pour) [s.o.]. ‖ MED. Ordonner,

prescrire. ‖ Comm. Commander. ‖ To order about, faire aller et venir, faire virevolter (fam.). ‖ To order away, renvoyer, faire partir. ‖ To order back, rappeler, faire revenir. ‖ To order down, in, off, out, up, faire descendre, entrer, partir, sortir, monter.

orderer [-rə*] n. Ordonnateur *m.* ‖ Directeur *m.*

orderless [-lis] adj. Sans ordre, en désordre.

orderliness [-linis] n. Ordre, calme *m.;* tenue, discipline *f.* ‖ Ordre, goût de l'ordre *m.* ‖ Esprit (*m.*) de méthode.

orderly [-li] adj. Ordonné, en ordre, rangé (well-ordered). ‖ Méthodique, ordonné, soigneux (careful). ‖ Calme, discipliné, posé, pondéré (cool). ‖ Milit. De semaine (duty, officer); de rapport (room).
— n. Milit. Planton *m.* ‖ Med. *Hospital orderly,* ambulancier; U. S. infirmier. ‖ *Street orderly,* cantonnier urbain, balayeur de rues.

ordinal ['ɔ:dinəl] adj., n. Math., Eccles. Ordinal *m.*

ordinance ['ɔ:dinəns] n. Jur. Ordonnance *f.;* arrêté, décret ministériel *m.;* U. S. arrêté municipal *m.* ‖ Eccles. Rite *m.; Sacred Ordinance,* Eucharistie.

ordinand [-ænd] n. Eccles. Ordinand *m.*

ordinant [-ənt] n. Eccles. Ordinant *m.*

ordinariness ['ɔ:dinərinis] n. Caractère commun *m.;* banalité *f.*

ordinary [-əri] adj. Ordinaire, habituel, courant, coutumier (usual); *in the ordinary way,* d'habitude, en temps ordinaire; comme d'habitude. ‖ Ordinaire, quelconque, commun, banal (common). ‖ Moyen, commun, typique (average). ‖ Jur. Ordinaire (ambassador). ‖ Comm. Attitré (agent).
— n. Ordinaire *m.;* norme *f.; out of the ordinary,* peu commun, sortant de l'ordinaire. ‖ Culin. Table (*f.*) d'hôte (bill); ordinaire *m.* (meal). ‖ Eccles. Ordinaire *m.* (bishop, rite). ‖ Blas. Pièce honorable *f.* ‖ Comm. *Purveyor in ordinary to,* fournisseur attitré de.

ordinate [-it] n. Math. Ordonnée *f.*

ordination [,ɔ:di'neiʃən] n. Agencement, arrangement *m.* ‖ Eccles. Ordonnance *f.* (of God); ordination *f.* (of priests).

ordnance ['ɔ:dnəns] n. Milit. Artillerie *f.* (artillery); service du matériel *m.*
— adj. Milit. Topographique; *Ordnance Survey,* service cartographique; *ordnance survey map,* carte d'état-major.

ordure ['ɔ:djuə*] n. Ordure *f.* ‖ Fam. Grossièretés *f. pl.*

ore ['ɔ:*] n. Minerai *m.* ‖ Ore-bearing, adj. Métallifère.

oregano [.ɔri'gɑ:nou] n. Culin. Origan *m.*

organ ['ɔ:gən] n. Mus. Orgue *m.;* orgues *f. pl.; American, street, theatre organ,* orgue de salon, de Barbarie, de cinéma. ‖ Med., Jur. Organe *m.* ‖ Organ-builder, n. Mus. Facteur (*m.*) d'orgues. ‖ Organ-case (or) -chest, n. Mus. Buffet d'orgue *m.* ‖ Organ-grinder, n. Mus. Joueur (*s.*) d'orgue de Barbarie. ‖ Organ-loft, n. Archit. Tribune *f.* ‖ Organ-pipe n. Mus. Tuyau d'orgue *m.* ‖ Organ-screen, n. Archit. Jubé *m.* ‖ Organ-stop, n. Mus. Jeu d'orgue *m.*

organdie ['ɔ:gəndi] n. Organdi *m.*

organic [ɔ:'gænik] adj. Med. Organisé (being); organique (disease, life). ‖ Chim. Organique. ‖ Fig. Organique, systématique (whole).

organically [-əli] adv. Med. Organiquement. ‖ Fig. Foncièrement.

organism ['ɔ:gənizm] n. Med. Organisme *m.* ‖ Fig. Organisation *f.*

organist [-ist] n. Mus. Organiste *s.*

organization [,ɔ:gənai'zeiʃən] n. Organisation *f.;* agencement *m.* ‖ Organisme *m.; charity organization,* œuvre de charité; *youth organization,* organisme de jeunesse.

organize ['ɔ:gənaiz] v. tr. Organiser (entertainment, leisure, society).
— v. intr. S'organiser. ‖ Jur. *Right to organize,* droit d'association.

organizer [-ə*] n. Organisateur *m.;* organisatrice *f.*

organizing [-iŋ] n. Organisation *f.*

orgasm ['ɔ:gæzm] n. Med. Orgasme *m.* ‖ Fig. Point culminant, paroxysme *m.*

orgeat ['ɔ:ʒɑ:] n. Culin. Orgeat *m.*

orgiastic [,ɔ:dʒi'æstik] adj. Orgiaque.

orgy ['ɔ:dʒi] n. Orgie *f.* (profusion, revel).

oriel ['ɔ:riəl] adj. Archit. En saillie, en encorbellement (window).

orielled [-d] adj. Archit. A fenêtres en encorbellement.

orient ['ɔ:riənt] n. Orient *m.* (See East.) ‖ Orient *m.;* eau *f.* (of a pearl). ‖ Geogr. *The Orient,* l'Orient.
— adj. Oriental.
— v. tr. Orienter.

oriental [-əl] adj., n. Oriental *s.* (See Eastern.)

orientalism [-əlizm] n. Orientalisme *m.*

orientalist [-əlist] n. Orientaliste *s.*

orientalize [-əlaiz] v. tr. Orientaliser.
— v. intr. S'orientaliser.

orientate ['ɔ:rienteit] v. tr. Orienter (building); *to orientate oneself,* s'orienter.

orientation [,ɔ:rien'teiʃən] n. Orientation *f.*

orienteering [-'tiəriŋ] n. Sports. Course d'orientation *f.*

orifice ['ɔrifis] n. Orifice *m.*

oriflamme ['ɔriflæm] n. Oriflamme *f.*

origan ['ɔrigən], origanum [ɔ'rigənəm] n. Bot. Origan *m.*

origin ['ɔridʒin] n. Origine *f.* (beginning, birth, source). ‖ Comm. Origine, provenance *f.*

original [o'ridʒinəl] adj. Original, premier, primitif (first). ‖ Original, pittoresque, nouveau (new). ‖ Eccles. Originel (sin).
— n. Original *m.* (person, text).

originality [,ɔridʒi'næliti] n. Originalité *f.*

originally [o'ridʒinəli] adv. A l'origine, originairement (at the beginning); originellement (at the source). ‖ Originalement (in a novel manner).

originate [-eit] v. tr. Donner naissance à, promouvoir, créer, faire naître.
— v. intr. Provenir, dériver, être issu, tirer son origine (from, in, de). [See Derive.]

origination [,ɔridʒi'neiʃən] n. Création *f.* (act); naissance *f.* (result). ‖ Origine *f.* (source).

originative [o'ridʒineitiv] adj. Créateur *m.;* créatrice *f.;* inventif.

originator [-ə*] n. Créateur, promoteur *m.;* créatrice, promotrice *f.* (person). ‖ Point de départ, mobile originel *m.* (reason).

oriole ['ɔ:rioul] n. Zool. Loriot *m.*

orison ['ɔrizən] n. Eccles. Oraison *f.*

Orkneys ['ɔrkniz] n. pl. Geogr. Orcades *f. pl.*

Orlando [ɔ:'lændou] n. Roland *m.* (in history); Orlando *m.* (in Shakespeare).

orlop ['ɔ:lɔp] n. Naut. Faux pont *m.*

ormer ['ɔ:mə*] n. Zool. Ormeau *m.*

ormolu ['ɔ:molu:] n. Similor, or moulu *m.*

ornament ['ɔ:nəmənt] n. Ornement *m.;* garniture *f.* ‖ Autom. Enjoliveur *m.* ‖ Mus. Pl. Agréments *m. pl.*
— v. tr. Orner, ornementer (with, de).

ornamental [,ɔ:nə'mentəl] adj. Ornemental, décoratif, d'ornementation; *ornamental wall, water,* mur bahut, pièce d'eau.

ornamentalist [-ist] n. Archit., Arts. Ornemaniste *s.*

ornamentation [,ɔ:nəmen'teiʃən] n. Ornementation, décoration *f.;* embellissement *m.* (act, things).

ornamenter ['ɔ:nəmentə*] n. Décorateur *m.;* décoratrice *f.*

ornamentist [,ɔ:nə'mentist] n. ARCHIT., ARTS. Ornemaniste *m*.

ornate [ɔ:'neit] adj. Orné, ornementé, paré. ‖ FIG. Enjolivé, fleuri (style).

ornateness [-nis] n. Enjolivement *m*.

orneriness ['ɔ:nərinis] n. U. S. FAM. Méchante humeur *f*. (cantankerousness).

ornery ['ɔ:nəri] adj. U. S. FAM. Entêté, têtu (stubborn); hargneux, teigneux (cantankerous); vache, sale, de cochon (treacherous) ‖ Quelconque, ordinaire (common).

ornithological [,ɔ:niθə'lɔdʒikəl] adj. ZOOL. Ornithologique.

ornithologist [,ɔ:ni'θɔlədʒist] n. ZOOL. Ornithologue *s*.

ornithology [-dʒi] n. ZOOL. Ornithologie *f*.

ornithorhynchus [,ɔ:niθə'riŋkəs] n. ZOOL. Ornithorynque *m*.

orography [ɔ'rɔgrəfi] n. Orographie *f*.

orotund ['ɔrotʌnd] adj. Sonore; ronflant (fam.).

orphan ['ɔ:fən] n. Orphelin *s*. ‖ JUR. Enfant assisté *m*.
— adj. Orphelin.

orphanage [-idʒ] n. Orphelinage *m*. (orphanhood). ‖ Orphelinat *m*. (home).

orphaned [-d] adj. Orphelin.

orphanhood [-hud] n. Orphelinage *m*.

orphanize [-aiz] v. tr. Rendre orphelin.

orphic [-fik] adj. ARTS. Orphique. ‖ FIG. Enchanteur.

orphrey ['ɔ:frei] n. Orfroi *m*.

orpiment ['ɔ:pimənt] n. Orpiment *m*.

orris ['ɔris] n. Galon d'or *m*.

orris n. BOT. Iris *m*.

orthicon ['ɔ:θikən] n. RADIO. Orthicon *m*.

orthocentre [,ɔ:θo'sentə*] n. MATH. Orthocentre *m*.

orthochromatism [-'kroumætizṃ] n. Orthochromatisme *m*.

orthodontics [,ɔ:θo'dɔntiks] n. sg. MED. Orthodontie *f*.

orthodontist [-'dɔntist] n. MED. Orthodontiste *s*.

orthodox ['ɔ:θədɔks] adj. ECCLES., FIG. Orthodoxe.

orthodoxy [-i] n. ECCLES., FIG. Orthodoxie *f*.

orthoepic [,ɔ:θou'epik] adj. GRAMM. Orthoépique, d'une prononciation correcte.

orthoepy ['ɔ:θou,epi] n. GRAMM. Orthoépie, phonétique normative *f*.

orthogenesis [,ɔ:θo'dʒenəsis] n. MED. Orthogénèse *f*.

orthographical [,ɔ:θo'græfikəl] adj. GRAMM. Orthographique.

orthography [ɔ:'θɔgrəfi] n. GRAMM. Orthographe *f*. ‖ MATH. Projection orthogonale *f*.

orthopaedic [ɔ:θo'pi:dik] adj. MED. Orthopédique.

orthopaedics [-diks] n. sg. MED. Orthopédie *f*.

orthopaedist [-dist] n. MED. Orthopédiste *m*.

orthopter [ɔ:'θɔptə*] n. ZOOL. Orthoptère *m*.

orthopterous [-tərəs] adj. ZOOL. Orthoptère.

orthoptic [-tik] adj. MED. De vision normale.

ortolan ['ɔ:tələn] n. ZOOL. Ortolan *m*.

oryx ['ɔriks] n. ZOOL. Oryx *m*.

Oscar ['ɔskə*] n. Oscar *m*. (name, prize). ‖ U. S. POP. Feu *m*. (revolver).

oscillate ['ɔsileit] v. intr. Osciller.
— v. tr. Faire osciller.

oscillating [-iŋ] adj. TECHN. Oscillant (cylinder). ‖ ELECTR. Oscillateur (coil); oscillatoire (current).
— n. Oscillation *f*.

oscillation [,ɔsi'leiʃən] n. Oscillation *f*.

oscillator ['ɔsileitə*] n. Oscillateur *m*.

oscillatory [-əri] adj. ELECTR. Oscillatoire, oscillant.

oscillograph ['ɔsilogrɑ:f] n. ELECTR. Oscillographe *m*.

oscilloscope [ə'siloskoup] n. RADIO. Oscilloscope *m*.

osculant ['ɔskjulənt] adj. ZOOL. Voisin, apparenté.

oscular [-lə*] adj. MED. Osculaire. ‖ MATH. Osculateur. ‖ FAM. Bécoteur.

osculate [-leit] v. intr. ZOOL. S'apparenter (with, à); avoir des caractères communs (with, avec). ‖ MATH. To osculate with, baiser (a line). ‖ FAM. Se bécoter.
— v. tr. MATH. Baiser. ‖ FAM. Bécoter.

osculation [,ɔskju'leiʃən] n. MATH. Osculation *f*. ‖ FAM. Embrassades *f. pl.*; bécotages *m. pl.*

osculatory ['ɔskjulətəri] adj. MATH. Osculateur.

osier ['ouʒə*] n. Osier *m*. ‖ Osier-bed, n. Oseraie *f*.

osiery ['ouʒiəri] n. Oseraie *f*. (holt). ‖ Vannerie *f*. (basket-work).

osmium ['ɔzmiəm] n. CHIM. Osmium *m*.

osmose ['ɔzmous], **osmosis** [ɔz'mousis] n. PHYS. Osmose *f*.

osmotic [ɔz'mɔtik] adj. PHYS. Osmotique (pressure).

osprey ['ɔsprei] n. ZOOL. Orfraie *f*. ‖ COMM. Aigrette *f*.

ossature ['ɔsətʃə*] n. ARCHIT. Carcasse *f*. ‖ MED. Ossature *f*.

osseous ['ɔsiəs] adj. MED., ZOOL. Osseux.

Ossianic [ɔsi'ænik] adj. Ossianique.

ossicle ['ɔsikl] n. MED. Osselet *m*.

ossification [,ɔsifi'keiʃən] n. MED. Ossification *f*.

ossifrage ['ɔsifridʒ] n. ZOOL. Orfraie *f*.

ossify ['ɔsifai] v. tr. (2). Ossifier.
— v. intr. S'ossifier.

ossuary ['ɔsjuəri] n. Ossuaire *m*.

osteitis [ɔsti'aitis] n. MED. Ostéite *f*.

ostensible [ɔs'tensibl] adj. Soi-disant, prétendu.

ostensibly [-sibli] adv. En apparence, sous un prétexte, censément.

ostensive [-siv] adj. Ostensible, visible. (See CONSPICUOUS.) ‖ PHILOS. Evident (reason); spécieux (proof).

ostensory [-səri] n. ECCLES. Ostensoir *m*.

ostentation [,ɔsten'teiʃən] n. Ostentation *f*.; apparat, faste *m*.

ostentatious [-ʃəs] adj. Plein d'ostentation; paradant (fam.).

ostentatiously [-ʃəsli]] adv. Avec ostentation.

ostentatiousness [-ʃəsnis] n. Ostentation *f*.

osteo-arthritis [,ɔstioɑ:'θraitis] n. MED. Ostéoarthrite *f*.

osteologist [ɔsti'ɔlədʒist] n. MED. Ostéologue *f*.

osteology [-dʒi] n. MED. Ostéologie *f*.

osteomyelitis [,ɔstio,maiə'laitis] n. MED. Ostéomyélite *f*.

osteopath ['ɔstiopæθ] n. MED. Ostéopathe *m*.

osteopathy [,ɔsti'ɔpəθi] n. MED. Ostéopathie *f*.

ostler ['ɔslə*] n. Palefrenier, valet (*m*.) d'écurie.

ostracism ['ɔstrəsizṃ] n. Ostracisme *m*.

ostracize [-saiz] v. tr. Frapper d'ostracisme.

ostreiculture ['ɔstriikʌltjə*] n. Ostréiculture *f*.

ostrich ['ɔstritʃ] n. ZOOL. Autruche *f*. ‖ Ostrich-feather, n. Plume d'autruche *f*. ‖ Ostrich-like, adj. FAM. D'autruche (stomach).

Ostrogoth ['ɔstrogɔθ] adj., n. GEOGR. Ostrogoth.

otalgia [ɔ'tældʒiə] n. MED. Otalgie *f*.

otary ['outəri] n. ZOOL. Otarie *f*.

other ['ʌðə*] adj. Autre; *have you other resources?*, avez-vous d'autres ressources?; *other people*, d'autres, autrui. ‖ Autre (indefinite); *some author or other*, un auteur quelconque, quelque auteur; *some day or other*, un jour ou l'autre. ‖ Autre, différent; *quite other reasons*, des raisons tout autres.
— pron. Autre; *no other than*, nul autre que; *others*, d'autres, autrui; *some other*, quelqu'un d'autre; *the others*, les autres; *some... others*, les uns... les autres. ‖ Autre; *devoted to each other*, dévoués l'un à l'autre.

— adv. Autrement ; *he could not do other than,* il n'a pas pu faire autrement que.

otherwise [-waiz] adv. Autrement (*than,* que) ; différemment (differently) ; *except as otherwise provided,* sauf disposition contraire. ‖ Autrement, au cas contraire, sans quoi (or else). ‖ A d'autres égards, autrement, sous d'autres aspects, par ailleurs (in other respects).

otherworldliness [-'wə:ldlinis] n. Détachement du monde.

otherworldly [-'wə:ldli] adj. Détaché du siècle.

otic ['outik] adj. Med. *Otic bone,* osselet, rocher.

otiose ['ou ̗ious] adj. Oiseux. ‖ † Oisif.

otiosely [-li] adv. Oiseusement. ‖ † Oisivement.

otioseness [-nis] n. Inutilité *f.* ; caractère oiseux *m.*

otitis [ou'taitis] n. Med. Otite *f.*

otologist [ou'tɔlədʒist] n. Med. Otologiste *m.*

otology [-dʒi] n. Med. Otologie *f.*

otoscope ['outoskoup] n. Med. Otoscope *m.*

otter ['ɔtə*] n. Zool. Loutre *f.* ‖ Naut. Otter *m.* ‖ **Otter-skin,** n. Comm. Loutre *f.*

Ottoman ['ɔtəmən] n. Geogr. Ottoman *s.* ‖ Comm. Ottomane *f.* (divan).

oubliette [u:bli'et] n. Archit. Oubliettes *f. pl.*

ouch [autʃ] interj. Aïe.

ought [ɔ:t] v. aux. Devoir ; *you ought to help him,* vous devriez l'aider. ‖ Falloir ; *to sleep more than one ought,* dormir plus qu'il ne faut. ‖ Devoir, avoir des chances de ; *that ought to succeed,* ça devrait réussir. ‖ Devoir, avoir avantage à ; *you ought to have seen that,* vous auriez dû voir ça.

ought n. See AUGHT.

ouija-board ['wi:dʒə'bɔ:d] n. Ouija-ja *m.*

ounce [auns] n. Math. Once *f.* (measure, weight).

ounce n. Zool. Once *f.* ; lynx *m.*

our ['auə*] poss. adj. Notre ; *our enemies,* nos ennemis.

ours [̗auəz] poss. pron. Le nôtre *m.* ; la nôtre *f.* ; les nôtres *pl.* ; *a friend of ours,* un de nos amis. ‖ A nous ; *it is not ours to,* il ne nous appartient pas de, ce n'est pas à nous de.

ourself [̗auə'self] (pl. **ourselves** [-'selvz]) pers. pron. Nous-même.

oust [aust] v. tr. Jur. Evincer. ‖ Fam. Déloger, débusquer, faire déguerpir (or) déloger. (See EJECT.)

ouster [-ə*] n. Jur. Eviction *f.*

out [aut] adv. Dehors ; *out there,* là-bas ; *to go out,* sortir ; *to put s.o. out,* mettre qqn dehors ; *to be out,* être sorti ; *to dine out,* dîner en ville. ‖ De sortie ; *day out,* jour de sortie ; *truth will out,* la vérité se dégage toujours. ‖ En dehors ; *inside out,* à l'envers, sens dessus dessous. ‖ Au-dehors ; *to lean out,* se pencher au-dehors. ‖ Au-dehors, visible ; *the secret is out,* le secret est dévoilé ; *the sun is out,* le soleil est sorti. ‖ Dans l'erreur ; *to be out in one's accounts,* s'être trompé dans ses comptes ; *to be far* (or) *a long way out,* être loin du compte, se tromper de beaucoup. ‖ Eteint (fire, gas, light). ‖ Achevé ; *before the year is out,* avant la fin de l'année. ‖ Jusqu'au bout ; *to have one's cry out,* pleurer son content ; *to hear out,* entendre jusqu'au bout. ‖ Ch. de f. *Voyage out,* voyage aller. ‖ Autom. *All out,* à plein gaz, à toute vitesse. ‖ Comm. En tournée (traveller). ‖ Jur. Expiré (lease). ‖ Milit. Tiré (sword) ; sur pied (troops). ‖ Naut. Filé (rope) ; déployé (sail) ; bas (tide) ; *out at sea,* en mer. ‖ Zool. Eclos (bird). ‖ Bot. Epanoui (flower). ‖ Med. Luxé (joint). ‖ Sports. Hors jeu (ball) ; knock-out (boxer) ; éliminé (player) ; *all out,* à fond. ‖ Fam. *Out after* (or) *for,* en quête de ; *to put oneself out for,* se décarcasser pour. ‖ **Out-and-out,** adj. Convaincu, achevé, parfait ; *out-and-out fool,* triple sot ; adv. Absolument, complètement. ‖ **Out-and-outer,** n. Fam. Convaincu, outrancier *s.* (person) ; parfait mensonge (or) menteur *m.* (lie, lier). ‖ **Out-building,** n. Annexe, dépendance *f.* ‖

Out-devil, v. tr. Surpasser en diablerie. ‖ **Out-dweller,** n. Banlieusard *s.* ‖ **Out-Herod,** v. tr. *To out-Herod Herod,* être plus royaliste que le roi. ‖ **Out-of-date,** adj. Démodé ; périmé, dépassé. ‖ **Out-of-fashion,** adj. Démodé, passé de mode. ‖ **Out-of-school,** adj. Extra-scolaire (activity). ‖ **Out-of-the-way,** adj. Ecarté, détourné (place) ; Fin. Exorbitant (price) ; Fig. Peu commun. ‖ **Out-of-work,** n. Chômeur *s.* ‖ **Out-patient,** n. Med. Malade (*s.*) non hospitalisé ; *out-patient department,* service de consultation externe ; *out-patient psychiatric clinic,* clinique psychiatrique de jour. ‖ **Out-relief,** n. Jur. Secours (*m. pl.*) à domicile. ‖ **Out-size,** adj. De taille exceptionnelle ; *out-size shop,* magasin spécialisé dans les grandes tailles. ‖ **Out-talk,** v. tr. Etre plus bavard (or) convaincant que. ‖ **Out-vote,** v. tr. Jur. Battre, l'emporter sur. ‖ **Out-worker,** n. Ouvrier (*s.*) à domicile.

— interj. *Out with you !,* sortez ! ; *out with it !,* alors crache-le, accouche !

— adj. Extérieur (part) ; *out at elbows,* aux coudes troués, rapé, élimé. ‖ Comm. Hors série (size) ; *out-sizes,* grandes tailles ; *to be entirely out of,* être entièrement démuni de.

— n. Extérieur *m.* ; *ins and outs,* coins et recoins, aîtres, êtres (of a house). ‖ Techn. Bourdon *m.* (in printing).

— adv. pl. *Out and away,* de beaucoup, sans contredit, assurément.

— prep. phr. *Out of,* hors de, en dehors de (place) ; *to be out of place,* ne pas être à sa place. ‖ Hors de ; *out of breath,* essoufflé, hors d'haleine ; *out of the question,* hors de question. ‖ Sans ; *out of money, work,* sans argent, travail. ‖ Par ; *out of curiosity,* par curiosité. ‖ Outre ; *out of measure,* outre mesure. ‖ Loin de ; *out of sight, out of mind,* loin des yeux, loin du cœur. ‖ Dans ; *to take a cigarette out of s.o.'s case,* prendre une cigarette dans l'étui de qqn. ‖ Parmi ; *one criticism out of many,* une critique parmi beaucoup d'autres. ‖ Sur ; *in nine cases out of ten,* neuf fois sur dix. ‖ Du fond de ; *out of the corner of one's eye,* du coin de l'œil ; *out of the fog,* du fond du brouillard. ‖ A bout de ; *out of patience,* à bout de patience. ‖ Comm. *Out of print,* épuisé (book). ‖ Fam. *Out of one's senses,* détraqué, tapé.

— v. tr. Sports. Mettre out (ball) ; mettre knock-out (a boxer) ; mettre hors jeu (a player). ‖ Fam. Descendre (to kill) ; sortir (to oust).

outback [-bæk] adv. A l'intérieur du pays (in Australia).

— adj. De l'intérieur.

— n. Intérieur *m.*

outbalance [aut'bæləns] v. tr. Contrebalancer, l'emporter sur.

outbid [aut'bid] v. tr. (20). Surenchérir. ‖ Fig. Renchérir sur (*in,* en) [s.o.].

outbidder [-ə*] n. Surenchérisseur *s.*

outbidding [-iŋ] n. Surenchère *f.*

outblaze [aut'bleiz] v. tr. Eclipser.

outboard ['autbɔ:d] adj. Naut. Extérieur (cabin) ; hors-bord (motor). ‖ Techn. Extérieur.

— adv. Vers l'extérieur. ‖ Naut. Hors bord.

outbrave [aut'breiv] v. tr. Braver (danger) ; être plus brave que (s.o.).

outbreak ['autbreik] n. Geol. Eruption *f.* (of volcano) ; *outbreak of fire,* incendie, sinistre. ‖ Milit. Déchaînement *m.* (of war). ‖ Med. Manifestation *f.* (of epidemic). ‖ Fig. Explosion *f.* ; accès, débordement *m.* ; *new outbreak,* recrudescence.

outburst [-bə:st] n. Accès, déchaînement, débordement *m.* (of temper). ‖ Elan *m.* (of generosity) ; éclat *m.* (of laughter).

outcast [-kɑ:st] adj., n. Banni, proscrit, réprouvé *s.* ; paria *m.*

outclass [aut'klɑ:s] v. tr. Sports. Surclasser.

outcome ['autkʌm] n. Issue, fin *f.* ; aboutissement, résultat *m.*

outcrop [-krɔp] n. GEOL., PHILOS. Affleurement *m.*
— v. intr. GEOL. Affleurer.
outcry [-krai] n. Clameur *f.;* tollé *m.*
outdare [aut'dɛə*] v. tr. Braver (danger); dépasser en hardiesse (s.o.).
outdated [-'deitid] adj. Démodé.
outdistance [-'distəns] v. tr. SPORTS. Distancer.
outdo [aut'du:] v. tr. (47). Surpasser (*in*, en).
outdoer [-ə*] n. Renchérisseur *s.*
outdoor ['autdɔ:*] adj. Extérieur, au-dehors (life). ‖ De plein air (games). ‖ De ville (clothes). ‖ JUR. A domicile (relief). ‖ CINEM. *Outdoor scenes,* extérieurs.
outdoors [-dɔ:z] adv. Au-dehors; en plein air; dehors.
— n. Plein (or) grand air *m.;* grands espaces *m. pl.*
outer ['autə*] adj. Extérieur, externe (side). ‖ De dessus (clothes). ‖ MILIT. *Outer flank,* aile marchante. ‖ SPORTS, FAM. Knock-out.
— n. Cercle extérieur (*m.*) d'une cible. ‖ Coup (*m.*) dans le cercle extérieur d'une cible.
outermost [-moust] adv. Le plus en dehors, extérieur; le plus éloigné, extrême, maximum.
outface [aut'feis] v. tr. Toiser du regard.
outfall ['autfɔ:l] n. Déversoir *m.* (of a sewer). ‖ GEOGR. Embouchure *f.*
outfight [aut'fait] v. tr. (57). Surpasser dans la lutte.
outfit ['autfit] n. SPORTS. Attirail *m.* ‖ Trousseau *m.* (clothes). ‖ TECHN. Nécessaire *m.* ‖ MED. Trousse *f.* ‖ MILIT. Equipement *m.* ‖ MILIT., FAM. Unité *f.*
outfitter [-ə*] n. COMM. Costumier, marchand (*m.*) de confections.
outfitting [-iɳ] n. Equipement *m.* ‖ COMM. Confection *f.*
outflank [aut'flæɳk] v. tr. MILIT. Tourner (a town); déborder (troops). ‖ FAM. Entortiller.
outflow ['autflou] n. Coulée *f.* (of lava); décharge *f.* (of a sewer); écoulement *m.* (of water). ‖ FIG. Epanchement *m.*
outfly [aut'flai] v. tr. (61). Dépasser en vol.
outgeneral [-dʒenərəl] v. tr. MILIT. Dépasser en tactique (or) stratégie.
outgoer ['autgouə*] n. Sortant *s.*
outgoing [-iɳ] adj. Sortant. ‖ Démissionnaire (official). ‖ TECHN. De sortie (pipe). ‖ NAUT. Descendant (tide). ‖ CH. DE F. Partant (train). ‖ FIG. Ouvert, affable (person).
— n. Sortie *f.* ‖ Pl. Débours *m. pl.*
outgrow [aut'grou] v. tr. (74). Dépasser en hauteur, être plus grand que (s.o.). ‖ Devenir trop grand pour (one's clothes). ‖ Perdre en grandissant (a habit).
outgrowth ['autgrouθ] n. Excroissance *f.* ‖ FIG. Aboutissement, résultat *m.*
outguess [,aut'ges] v. tr. Anticiper les réactions de, percer (or) déjouer les intentions de.
outhaul ['authɔ:l] n. NAUT. Drisse *f.*
outhouse [-haus] n. Appentis *m. pl.* ‖ Pl. Dépendances *f. pl.;* communs *m. pl.* ‖ U. S. Cabinets; lieux (*m. pl.*) d'aisance.
outing [-iɳ] n. Sortie *f.; to go for an outing,* partir en promenade.
outjockey [aut'dʒɔki] v. tr. FAM. Rouler, avoir.
outlander ['aut,lændə*] n. Etranger *s.*
outlandish [aut'lændiʃ] adj. † Etranger. ‖ Ecarté (place). ‖ Bizarre, étrange (manner).
outlandishness [-nis] n. Etrangeté *f.*
outlast [aut'lɑ:st] v. tr. Durer plus longtemps que.
outlaw ['autlɔ:] n. Hors-la-loi *m.*
— v. tr. Mettre hors-la-loi.
outlawed [-d] adj. Proscrit, banni.
outlawry [-ri] n. Proscription *f.*
outlay ['autlei] n. FIN. Débours *m. pl.; capital outlay,* frais d'installation, mise de fonds initiale.
outlet [-lət] n. Sortie *f.* ‖ TECHN. Ecoulement, dégor-

geoir, déversoir *m.* ‖ COMM. Débouché *m.* ‖ AVIAT. *Jet outlet,* tuyère d'éjection. ‖ U. S. ELECTR. Prise (*f.*) de courant. ‖ FIG. Exutoire *m.* (*for,* à, pour).
outline [-lain] n. Contour, profil *m.* (of a thing). ‖ Silhouette, ligne *f.* (of s.o.). ‖ Canevas, schéma, plan, topo *m.;* ébauche *f.; main outlines,* grandes lignes. ‖ Sigle, sténogramme *m.* (in shorthand writing). ‖ ARTS. Tracé, dessin au trait *m.*
— v. tr. Découper, détacher, profiler, silhouetter; *to be outlined against,* se profiler sur. ‖ Esquisser, ébaucher, tracer les grandes lignes de (a plot, scheme). ‖ ARTS. Délinéer, tracer.
outlining [-lainiɳ] n. Contour *m.;* délinéation *f.* ‖ Ebauchage *m.;* esquisse *f.*
outlive [aut'liv] v. tr. Survivre à.
outlook ['autluk] n. Guet *m.; on the outlook,* aux aguets. ‖ FIG. Perspective, vue *f.;* horizon *m.*
outlying [-laiiɳ] adj. Ecarté, détourné.
outmanœuvre [-'nu:və*] v. tr. Contre-manœuvrer; déjouer les menées de.
outmarch [aut'mɑ:tʃ] v. tr. Dépasser, devancer, marcher plus vite que.
outmatch [-'mætʃ] v. tr. SPORTS. Surpasser, l'emporter sur.
outmoded [-'moudid] adj. Démodé, passé de mode.
outmost ['autmoust] adj. Extrême; le plus éloigné.
outnumber [aut'nʌmbə*] v. tr. Surpasser en nombre.
outpace [-'peis] v. tr. Dépasser, distancer.
outplay [-'plei] v. tr. SPORTS. Surpasser, battre au jeu. ‖ FAM. Dominer.
outpoint [-'pɔint] v. tr. SPORTS. Battre aux points.
outpost ['autpoust] n. MILIT. Avant-poste *m.*
outpouring [-pɔ:riɳ] n. Epanchement *m.* (of heart). ‖ Débordement, flot *m.* (of abuses).
output [-put] n. TECHN. Rendement, débit *m.;* production *f.* ‖ FIN. Rendement *m.* ‖ ELECTR. Puissance fournie, puissance *f.* (power); borne de sortie *f.* (terminal). ‖ INFORM. Sortie *f.,* output *m.*
outrage ['autreidʒ] n. Outrage *m.; to commit an outrage against* (or) *on,* faire subir un outrage à. ‖ Atteinte *f.;* outrage *m.* (*against,* à) [common sense, good taste, religion]. ‖ JUR. Attentat *m.*
— v. tr. Faire outrage à (the law, nature). ‖ Outrager, violenter (a woman).
outrageous [aut'reidʒəs] adj. Outrageux, abusif. ‖ Outrageant (accusation); révoltant, scandaleux, abominable (behaviour); criant, flagrant, choquant (injustice). ‖ FIN. Exorbitant (price). ‖ FAM. Horrible, affreux.
outrageously [-li] adv. Outrageusement, abusivement (immoderately). ‖ Scandaleusement, abominablement (glaringly).
outrageousness [-nis] n. Nature outrageante *f.* (of an accusation). ‖ Abomination, vilenie *f.* (of behaviour). ‖ FIN. Exorbitance *f.*
outrange [aut'reindʒ] v. tr. MILIT. Porter plus loin que (gun). ‖ FIG. Surpasser (s.o.).
outrank [-'ræɳk] v. tr. Etre hiérarchiquement supérieur à. ‖ FIG. Dépasser, prévaloir sur.
outré [u:trei] adj. Outré.
outride [aut'raid] v. tr. (111). Dépasser à cheval, chevaucher plus vite que. ‖ NAUT. Etaler.
outrider ['aut,raidə] n. Membre (*m.*) d'une escorte; *a motorcycle outrider,* un motard de l'escorte.
outrig ['autrig] n. NAUT. Epatement *m.*
outrigger ['autrigə*] n. NAUT. Outrigger *m.* (boat); porte-en-dehors *m.* (bracket); arc-boutant *m.* (spar); balancier *m.* (of dug-out canoe). ‖ AVIAT. Longeron de support *m.*
outright [aut'rait] adv. Net, sur le coup (on the spot). ‖ Carrément, crûment, rondement, nettement, sans mâcher les mots (bluntly). ‖ FIN. A prix forfaitaire, en bloc.
— ['autrait] adj. Absolu, total (sheer). ‖ Carré,

net, rond (straightforward). || Fin. Forfaitaire (purchase); à forfait (sale).

outrightness [aut'raitnis] n. Franchise brutale, netteté *f.* ; franc-parler *m.*

outrival [aut'raivəl] v. tr. (1). L'emporter sur.

outrun [aut'rʌn] v. tr. (114). Gagner de vitesse. || Fig. Dépasser, outrepasser.

outrunner ['autrʌnə*] n. Avant-coureur *m.*

outrush ['autrʌʃ] n. Fuite *f.* (of gas); jaillissement *m.* (of water).

outsail [aut'seil] v. tr. Naut. Dépasser.

outsell [-'sel] v. tr. (120). Comm. Se vendre mieux que (commodity); vendre plus que (seller).

outset ['autset] n. Début, commencement, principe *m.* ; *at the outset,* au départ. || Naut. Courant en direction du large.

outshine [aut'ʃain] v. tr. (126). Eclipser.

outside [aut'said] n. Extérieur *m.* (of s.o., sth.); *on the outside,* au- (or) en dehors. || Maximum, bout *m.* ; *at the outside,* tout au plus. || Impériale *f.* (of bus, tram); plate-forme *f.* (of a Paris bus). || Sports. Ailier *m.*
— ['autsaid] adj. Extérieur, du dehors (in general). || De l'impériale (on bus). || A domicile (worker). || Fin. Maximum (price); coulissier (transaction); *outside broker,* coulissier. || Fig. Du dehors (opinion). || Fam. Ultime, suprême (chance).
— adv. A l'extérieur, dehors, au- (or) en dehors ; *from outside,* du dehors. || Sur l'impériale (on bus). || A la terrasse (at a café).
— prep. A l'extérieur de, hors de, en dehors de (a place, a question). || Pop. *To get outside (of) a meal,* venir à bout d'un repas.

outsider [-ə*] n. Fin. Coulissier *m.* || Sports. Outsider *m.* (horse); ailier *m.* (man). || Fam. Profane *s.* (in art, law, science); horsein *m.* ; *a rank outsider,* une espèce de voyou.

outsit [aut'sit] v. tr. (136). Prolonger sa visite plus longtemps que.

outskirts ['autskə:ts] n. pl. Abords *m. pl.* (of a town); lisière, orée *f.* (of a wood). || Périphérie *f.* (of a city).

outsmart [aut'smɑ:t] v. tr. Fam. Rouler, être plus malin que.

outspoken [aut'spoukən] adj. Carré, net.

outspokenly [-li] adv. Carrément, rondement.

outspokenness [-nis] n. Franchise brutale *f.*

outspread ['autspred] adj. Déployé.
— n. Déploiement *m.*

outstanding [aut'stændiŋ] adj. Saillant, dominant, marquant (feature, matter). || Eminent, hors ligne, de premier plan (person). || En suspens. || Fin. A recouvrer (debts); échu (interest); en retard (payment).

outstandingly [-li] adv. Eminemment.

outstare [aut'stɛə*] v. tr. Faire baisser les yeux à.

outstay [-stei] v. tr. Rester plus longtemps que (see OUTSIT); *to outstay one's welcome,* s'incruster (fam.).

outstretched ['autstretʃt] adj. Tendu (arm); ouvert (hand).

outstrip [aut'strip] v. tr. (1). Distancer, gagner de vitesse ; enfoncer (fam.). || Fig. Dépasser.

outvalue [aut'vælju:] v. tr. Avoir plus de valeur que, surpasser en valeur.

outvie [-'vai] v. tr. Dépasser ; *to outvie each other,* rivaliser.

outvote [-'vout] v. tr. Obtenir plus de voix que (or) la majorité contre.

outwalk [-'wɔ:k] v. tr. Dépasser à la marche, être meilleur marcheur que.

outward ['autwəd] adj. En dehors (direction). || Extérieur, du dehors. || Ch. de F., Naut. D'aller. || Med. Externe (application).
— adv. Vers l'extérieur, au dehors ; en dehors (see OUTWARDS). || **Outward-bound,** adj. Naut. En partance.
— n. Extérieur *m.*

outwardly [-li] adv. Extérieurement.

outwardness [-nis] n. Extériorité *f.*

outwards [-z] adv. Au-dehors ; en dehors.

outwear [aut'wɛə*] v. tr. (186). User entièrement (to wear out). || Se débarrasser de (to get rid of). || Durer plus longtemps que (to wear better).

outweigh [-'wei] v. tr. Peser plus que. || Fig. Avoir plus de poids que.

outwit [-'wit] v. tr. (1). Dépasser en finesse, mettre en défaut la sagacité de. || Dépister.

outwork ['autwə:k] n. Archit. Hors-d'œuvre *m.* || Milit. Ouvrage avancé *m.* || Techn. Travail à domicile *m.*
— v. tr. Dépasser en rendement.

ouzel ['u:zl] n. Zool. *Ring ouzel,* merle à plastron ; *water ouzel,* cingle plongeur.

ova ['ouvə] n. pl. See OVUM.

oval ['ouvəl] adj., n. Ovale *m.*

ovalization [,ouvəlai'zeiʃən] n. Ovalisation *f.*

ovalize ['ouvəlaiz] v. tr. Ovaliser.
— v. intr. S'ovaliser.

ovarian [o'vɛəriən] adj. Med., Bot. Ovarien.

ovariotomy [,ouvɛəri'ɔtəmi] n. Med. Ovariotomie *f.*

ovary ['ouvəri] n. Med., Bot. Ovaire *m.*

ovate ['ouvit] adj. Zool. Ové.

ovation [o'veiʃən] n. Ovation *f.*

oven ['ʌvn] n. Culin. Four *m.* ; *in a quick, slow oven,* à feu vif, doux. || Techn. Etuve *f.* || Fam. Etuve *f.*; étouffoir, four *m.* || **Oven-ready,** adj. Culin. Tout préparé, prêt à cuire.

ovenware ['ʌvn,wɛə*] n. Porcelaine (*f.*) à feu.

over ['ouvə*] prep. Sur, au-dessus de ; *over the piano,* sur le piano ; *to hang over s.o.'s head,* être suspendu sur la tête de ; *we flew over France,* nous avons survolé la France. || A travers ; *all over the world,* dans le monde entier. || Par-dessus ; *to throw over,* jeter par-dessus. || Sur, de ; *to gain the ascendancy over,* prendre l'ascendant sur ; *to triumph over all difficulties,* triompher de toutes les difficultés. || De l'autre côté de ; *the house over the street,* la maison de l'autre côté de la rue. || En, durant ; *over night,* en une nuit, pendant la nuit. || Au-delà de ; *from over the sea(s),* par-delà les mers. || Au-dessus de, plus de ; *to be over sixty,* avoir dépassé soixante ans ; *to sleep for over two hours,* dormir plus de deux heures. || Occupé à ; *over his newspaper,* en train de lire son journal ; *over her tea,* tout en prenant son thé.
— adv. Dessus, sur tout. || Partout, entièrement ; *aching all over,* tout courbatu. || Entièrement, complètement ; *to read over,* lire jusqu'au bout. || De suite, en répétant ; *over and over,* d'une façon répétée, à plusieurs reprises, maintes fois. || Par-dessus ; *to boil over,* tomber en bouillant ; *to lean over,* se pencher. || A la renverse ; *to fall over,* faire la culbute, tomber (person) ; se renverser (thing). || Dans l'autre sens ; *to turn over,* se retourner (in bed) ; tourner, voir au verso (a document). || De l'autre côté ; *over against,* en face de ; *over from,* venant de ; *to cross over,* traverser ; *over there,* là-bas. || Davantage ; *seven and over,* sept et plus. || De trop, en trop ; *to have sth. over,* avoir qqch. en trop ; *what is left over,* le reste, l'excédent, le restant, ce qui reste. || Passé, achevé ; *the worse was over,* le pire était passé ; *to get it over with,* pour en finir avec. || **Over-abundant,** adj. Surabondant. || **Over-active,** adj. Hyperactif, suractif ; Med. *Over-active thyroid,* hyperthyroïdie. || **Over-activity,** n. Hyperactivité, suractivité *f.* || **Over-all,** adj. Total, d'ensemble (length) ; Autom. *Over-all length,* encombrement. || **Over-anxious,** adj. Trop désireux (or) empressé (*to,* de) ; très angoissé, hyperangoissé. || **Over-cautious,** adj. Trop prudent, timoré. || **Over-compensation,** n. Psych. Surcompensation *f.* || **Over-confidence,** n. Outrecuidance *f.* (in oneself);

confiance exagérée *f.* (in s.o.). ‖ **Over-confident,** adj. Outrecuidant, présomptueux ; trop confiant (*in,* en) ; *to be over-confident,* ne douter de rien. ‖ **Over-cooked,** adj. CULIN. Trop cuit. ‖ **Over-curious,** adj. Trop curieux, indiscret, inquisiteur. ‖ **Over-daring,** n. Excès (*m.*) d'audace ; adj. Trop audacieux, témé-raire. ‖ **Over-develop,** v. tr. Développer excessi-vement. ‖ **Over-eager,** adj. Trop empressé (or) zélé ; trop impatient (or) désireux (*to,* de). ‖ **Over-elaborate;** adj. Trop compliqué ; trop fouillé ; tara-biscoté (fam.). ‖ **Over-emphasis,** n. Trop grande insistance *f.* ‖ **Over-emphasize,** v. tr. Trop insister sur, s'obnubiler sur ; exagérer l'importance de. ‖ **Over-estimate,** n. Surestimation *f.* ; v. tr. Surest-mer. ‖ **Over-expose,** v. tr. Surexposer. ‖ **Over-exposure,** n. Surexposition *f.* ‖ **Over-familiar,** adj. Trop familier. ‖ **Over-fatigue,** n. Excès (*m.*) de fatigue, v. tr. Surmener. ‖ **Over-indulge,** v. tr. Gâter, être trop indulgent pour (s.o.) ; donner libre cours à (a passion) ; v. intr. Faire des abus (*in,* de). ‖ **Over-indulgence,** n. Excès (*m.*) d'indulgence (*of,* envers) ; abus, excès m. (*in,* de). ‖ **Over-inflate,** v. tr. Gonfler excessivement. ‖ **Over-insure,** v. tr. Assurer au-delà de sa valeur. ‖ **Over-issue,** n. FIN. Surémission *f.* ‖ **Over-many,** adj. Trop de. ‖ **Over-nice,** adj. Trop difficile ; FIG. Trop subtil. ‖ **Over-nicety,** n. Subtilité, chinoiserie *f.* ‖ **Over-popu-lated,** adj. Surpeuplé. ‖ **Over-population,** n. Surpeuplement m. ‖ **Over-pressure,** n. TECHN. Surpression *f.* ; FIG. Surmenage m. ‖ **Over-react,** v. intr. Réagir trop vivement (or) avec excès. ‖ **Over-refine,** v. tr. Trop raffiner. ‖ **Over-refi-nement,** n. Excès de raffinement m. ; préciosité *f.* ‖ **Over-rider,** n. AUTOM. Banane *f.* ‖ **Over-ripe,** adj. Trop fait, avancé (cheese) ; trop mûr (fruit). ‖ **Over-scrupulous,** adj. Trop scrupuleux, pointilleux, tatil-lon. ‖ **Over-sexed,** adj. Qui a une forte libido ; *he is over-sexed,* c'est un obsédé sexuel. ‖ **Over-simplifi-cation,** n. Simplification abusive, schématisation *f.* ‖ **Over-simplify,** v. tr. Simplifier à l'extrême, sché-matiser. ‖ **Over-subscribed,** adj. FIN. Souscrit au-delà de l'offre de titres. ‖ **Over-train,** v. tr. SPORTS. Surentraîner ; claquer (fam.) ; v. intr. SPORTS. Se cla-quer à l'entraînement. ‖ **Over-training,** n. SPORTS. Surentraînement m. ‖ **Over-use,** n. Emploi excessif m. ; v. tr. Employer avec excès. ‖ **Over-value,** v. tr. Surestimer. ‖ **Over-zealous,** adj. Trop zélé.
— n. Jeté m. (in knitting). ‖ FIN. Excédent m. ; *cash overs,* excédents de caisse. ‖ TECHN. Pl. Passe *f.* ; exemplaires (*m. pl.*) de passe.

overact [ouvə'rækt] v. tr. THEATR. Charger.
overacting [-iŋ] n. THEATR. Charge *f.*
overage [ouvə'ridʒ] n. U. S. Surplus m.
overall ['ouvərɔ:l] n. Blouse *f.* (child's, woman's). ‖ Pl. Bleus m. pl. ; salopette, combinaison *f.* (worker's).
overarm ['ouvər,ɑ:m] adj. SPORTS. *Overarm stroke,* coupe indienne, overarm stroke (in swim-ming) ; *overarm serve,* service par en dessus (at tennis).
— adv. Par en dessus.
overawe [,ouvər'ɔ:] v. tr. Intimider, faire peur à.
overbalance [,ouvə'bæləns] v. tr. Peser davan-tage que. ‖ Surpasser.
— v. intr. Se renverser, perdre l'équilibre.
— n. Excédent m.
overbear [ouvə'bɛə*] v. tr. (9). Renverser (s.o.). ‖ FIG. Intimider (s.o.) ; passer outre à (s.o.'s wishes) ; l'emporter sur, surclasser (sth.).
overbearing [-riŋ] adj. Impérieux, tranchant, auto-ritaire.
overbid [,ouvə'bid] v. tr. (20). Enchérir sur.
overbidder [-ə*] n. Surenchérisseur s.
overblown [,ouvə'bloun] adj. Passé (storm). ‖ BOT. Trop ouvert (flower).
overboard ['ouvəbɔ:d] adv. NAUT. Par-dessus bord ; *man overboard!,* un homme à la mer ! ‖ FAM. Par-dessus bord, à l'abandon.

overbodied [,ouvə'bɔdid] adj. AUTOM. A carros-serie exagérée.
overbold [-'bould] adj. Trop confiant, arrogant (person) ; téméraire (person, action).
overbook [-'buk] v. tr. Vendre plus de places qu'il n'y en a de disponibles dans.
overbrim [ouvə'brim] v. tr., intr. (1). Déborder, dépasser le bord.
overbuild [-'bild] v. tr. (28). Trop construire dans.
overbuilt [-'bilt] adj. Trop construit, aux agglo-mérations trop denses.
overburden ['ouvə,bə:dən] n. Surcharge m.
— [,ouvə'bə:dən] v. tr. Surcharger (*with,* de). ‖ FIG. Accabler ; *not overburdened with scruples,* peu encombré de scrupules.
overbuy [ouvə'bai] v. tr. (31). FIN. Acheter incon-sidérément.
overcall [ouvə'kɔ:l] n. Annonce supérieure *f.* (at cards).
— v. tr. Monter sur l'annonce de.
overcast ['ouvəkɑ:st] n. Surjet m.
— [ouvə'kɑ:st] v. tr. Surjeter (a seam). ‖ Obscur-cir, couvrir (the sky). ‖ FIG. Assombrir (mind).
— adj. Obscurci, couvert (sky, weather). ‖ FIG. Assombri, voilé.
overcharge ['ouvətʃɑ:dʒ] n. Surcharge m. ‖ COMM. Prix surfait m. ; majoration excessive *f.*
— [,ouvə'tʃɑ:dʒ] v. tr. Surcharger (*with,* de). ‖ COMM. Faire payer trop cher à, voler (s.o.) ; faire payer (or) compter trop cher (sth.).
— v. intr. **To overcharge on,** majorer.
overclothe [-'klouð] v. tr. (38). Trop couvrir (*with,* de) ; *to overclothe oneself,* trop s'habiller, se couvrir trop.
overcloud [-'klaud] v. tr. Couvrir. ‖ FIG. Assom-brir. (See OVERCAST.)
— v. intr. Se couvrir. ‖ FIG. S'assombrir.
overcoat ['ouvəkout] n. Pardessus m. ‖ MILIT. Capote *f.*
overcolour [,ouvə'kʌlə*] v. tr. Enjoliver, exagérer.
overcome [,ouvə'kʌm] v. tr. (39). Vaincre, l'em-porter sur, venir à bout de, triompher de, maîtriser ; *to overcome one's grief,* surmonter son chagrin, prendre le dessus.
overcrossing ['ouvəkrɔsiŋ] n. CH. DE F. Passage supérieur m.
overcrowd [,ouvə'kraud] v. tr. Bonder ; remplir excessivement (*with,* dé). ‖ Surpeupler (a town).
overcrowding [-iŋ] n. Encombrement m. ; sur-charge *f.* ‖ Surpeuplement m.
overdecorate [ouvə'dekəreit] v. tr. Décorer (or) orner avec excès. ‖ FIG. Trop enjoliver.
overdo [ouvə'du:] v. tr. (47). Exagérer, outrer (to exaggerate). ‖ CULIN. Faire trop cuire.
overdone [-'dʌn] adj. Exagéré, outré, excessif. ‖ Surmené, épuisé ; claqué, éreinté, esquinté (fam.). ‖ CULIN. Trop cuit.
overdose ['ouvə'dous] n. MED. Dose excessive *f.*
overdraft [-drɑ:ft] n. FIN. Découvert m.
overdraw [ouvə'drɔ:] v. tr. (48). FIN. *To be over-drawn,* avoir du découvert ; *to overdraw one's account,* tirer à découvert. ‖ FIG. Trop enjoliver.
overdress [-'dres] v. tr. Habiller avec une élégance outrée.
— v. intr. S'habiller d'une manière voyante.
overdress ['ouvə,dres] n. Robe chasuble, cha-suble *f.*
overdrive ['ouvədraiv] n. AUTOM. Vitesse surmul-tipliée ; surmultiplication *f.*
— [ouvə'draiv] v. tr. (51). Surmener, trop fati-guer.
overdue [ouvə'dju:] adj. FIN. Echu, arriéré. ‖ CH. DE F., NAUT. En retard. ‖ FIG. Attendu depuis longtemps.
overeat [ouvər'i:t] v. tr., intr. Manger avec excès.
overeating [-'i:tiŋ] n. Excès (*m.*) de nourriture.
overexcite [,ouvərek'sait] v. tr. Surexciter.

overexcitement [-mənt] n. Surexcitation; effervescence f.

overexert [,ouvərig'zə:t] v. tr. Tendre excessivement; *to overexert oneself*, aller au-delà de (or) dépasser ses forces, se surmener.
— v. intr. Se surmener.

overexertion ['ouvərig'zə:/ən] n. Surmenage m.

overfall ['ouvəfɔ:l] n. Dégorgeoir m. ‖ NAUT. Raz de courant m.

overfeed [ouvə'fi:d] v. tr. (55). Suralimenter (on, de, par).
— v. intr. Se suralimenter; se nourrir avec excès.

overfeeding [-iŋ] n. Suralimentation f.

overflight ['ouvə,flait] n. AVIAT. Survol m.

overfloat [ouvə'flout] v. tr. Surnager.

overflow ['ouvəflou] n. Débordement m. (act); trop-plein m. (pipe); inondation f. (result). ‖ Rejet, enjambement m. (in prosody).
— v. tr. Déborder (container); inonder (river).
— v. intr. Déborder (with, de) [liquid]. ‖ Regorger (with, de) [people]. ‖ Dégorger (gutter). ‖ FIG. *To overflow with gratitude*, déborder de reconnaissance, se confondre en remerciements; *to overflow with riches*, regorger de richesses.

overflowing [-iŋ] adj. Débordant (lit. and fig.). ‖ Comble, bondé (room).

overfly [,ouvə'flai] v. tr. (61). AVIAT. Survoler (a place); franchir (a limit).

overfraught [-'frɔ:t] adj. Surchargé (with, de).

overfree [-'fri:] adj. Trop libre (with, avec).

overfulfil, U. S. **overfulfill** [-ful'fil] v. tr. (1). Remplir au-delà des prévisions (a plan).

overfull [-'ful] adj. Trop plein (of, with, de).

overgarment ['ouvəgɑ:mənt] n. Vêtement de dessus m.

overgeared [ouvə'gi:əd] adj. AUTOM. A vitesse surmultipliée.

overgild [-'gild] v. tr. (69). Surdorer.

overgrow [-'grou] v. tr. (74). Trop grandir pour (child); *to overgrow oneself*, grandir trop vite. ‖ BOT. Envahir, recouvrir.

overgrown [-'groun] adj. Qui a trop grandi, trop grand pour son âge (child). ‖ BOT. Envahi (with, par); recouvert (with, de).

overgrowth [-'grouθ] n. Croissance trop rapide f. ‖ BOT. Luxuriance f.

overhand ['ouvəhænd] adj. NAUT. Simple (knot). ‖ TECHN. Renversé (stope). ‖ SPORTS. Au-dessus de la tête.

overhang ['ouvəhæŋ] n. Saillie f.; surplomb m.
— [-'hæŋ] v. tr. (75). Surplomber, faire saillir au-dessus de. ‖ FIG. Planer sur, être suspendu sur.

overhanging ['ouvə'hæŋiŋ] adj. Surplombant.
— ['ouvəhæŋiŋ] n. Porte-à-faux m.

overhaul ['ouvəhɔ:l] n. Examen minutieux m. ‖ TECHN. Réfection f.; démontage m.
— [,ouvə'hɔ:l] v. tr. Examiner minutieusement. ‖ Réviser, démonter, vérifier. ‖ NAUT. Dépasser (a ship); affaler (tackle).

overhead [ouvə'hed] adv. Au-dessus de la tête, en haut, au-dessus.
— adj. Aérien (cable); suspendu (system); en dessus (valve). ‖ Vertical (lighting). ‖ FIN. Général (expenses); forfaitaire (price).
— n. FIN. Frais généraux m. pl.

overhear [-'hiə*] v. tr. (77). Surprendre (conversation).

overheat [-'hi:t] v. tr. Surchauffer. ‖ FIG. Echauffer.
— v. intr. TECHN. Chauffer.

overjoy [-'dʒɔi] v. tr. Remplir de joie.

overkill ['ouvə,kil] n. MILIT. Surcapacité (f.) de tuer; sursaturation (f.) d'armes.

overladen [,ouvə'leidn̩] adj. Surchargé (with, de).

overland [-'lænd] adv. Par terre.
— ['ouvəlænd] adj. Voyageant par terre. ‖ De terre (route).

overlap ['ouvəlæp] n. Chevauchement m. ‖ ARCHIT. Recouvrement m.; imbrication f.
— [ouvə'læp] v. intr., tr. (1). Chevaucher. (See OVERLIE.) ‖ Dépasser, déborder. ‖ Empiéter sur, déborder sur.

overlay ['ouvəlei] n. Couvre-lit m. (coverlet); matelas m. (mattress). ‖ TECHN. Housse f.
— [,ouvə'lei] v. tr. (89). Recouvrir (with, de). ‖ ARCHIT. Incruster (wall). ‖ TECHN. Acérer (steel).

overlaying [-'leiiŋ] n. Recouvrement m. ‖ ARCHIT. Incrustation f. ‖ TECHN. Acérage m.

overleaf [-'li:f] adv. Au verso.

overleap [-'li:p] v. tr. (92). Sauter, franchir; *to overleap oneself*, être emporté trop loin par son élan.

overlie [-'lai] v. tr. (97). Couvrir, empiéter sur, chevaucher. (See OVERLAP.) ‖ Etouffer (a baby).

overload ['ouvəloud] n. Surcharge f.
— [,ouvə'loud] v. tr. Surcharger.

overlook [ouvə'luk] v. tr. Donner sur, ouvrir sur, avoir vue sur (to command a view). ‖ Laisser échapper, perdre de vue (to neglect); passer sur, passer sous silence, fermer les yeux sur (to wink at). ‖ Surveiller (to look after). ‖ Jeter le mauvais œil à (to cast a spell on).

overlooker ['ouvəlukə*] n. Espion s. (spy); surveillant s. (supervisor).

overlord ['ovəlɔ:d] n. Suzerain m.

overlordship [ovə'lɔ:dʃip] n. Suzeraineté f.

overly ['ouvəli] adv. Trop, excessivement.

overlying [-'laiiŋ] n. Empiètement, chevauchement, recouvrement m. ‖ Etouffement m.

overman [-mən] (pl. **overmen**) n. TECHN. Contremaître m. (in general); porion m. (in a mine).

overmaster [ouvə'mɑ:stə*] v. tr. Maîtriser, dominer.

overmastering [-təriŋ] adj. Dominant; dominateur. ‖ Irrésistible.

overmatch [ouvə'mætʃ] v. tr. Surclasser, avoir l'avantage sur; être trop fort pour; *to be overmatched*, avoir trouvé son maître, avoir affaire à trop forte partie.

overmuch ['ouvə'mʌtʃ] adv. Trop, excessivement.
— adj. Excessif.

overnight [-'nait] adv. La veille. ‖ La nuit, du jour au lendemain; *to stay overnight with friends*, passer la nuit chez des amis.
— adj. De la veille. ‖ COMM. *Overnight charge*, hébergement d'une nuit; *overnight case*, petite valise pour court déplacement.

overpass [-'pɑ:s] v. tr. Traverser (a country). ‖ Dépasser, aller au-delà de (the limits). ‖ Surpasser, dépasser (s.o.). ‖ † Laisser passer. (See OVERLOOK.)
— n. Passage supérieur m., passerelle f. (bridge).

overpast [-'pɑ:st] adj. Passé depuis longtemps.

overpay [-'pei] v. tr. (105). Trop payer.

overpayment [-'peimənt] n. Paiement excessif m.; surpaye f.

overpeople [-'pi:pl̩] v. tr. Surpeupler.

overpitch ['pitʃ] v. tr. SPORTS. Lancer trop loin. ‖ FAM. Exagérer, porter à un ton trop élevé.

overplacement [-'pleismənt] n. Superposition f.

overplay [-'plei] v. tr. THEATR. Charger (to overact). ‖ FIG. Surestimer, exagérer l'importance de (to over-emphasize). ‖ LOC. *To overplay one's hand*, surestimer son jeu (at cards), trop présumer de ses forces (fig.).

overplus ['ouvəplʌs] n. Surplus m.

overpower [ouvə'pauə*] v. tr. Subjuguer, dominer, dompter; écraser (fam.).

overpowering [-riŋ] adj. Accablant; écrasant; dominant.

overpraise [ouvə'preiz] v. tr. Louer exagérément, faire un éloge excessif de, surfaire.

overprint [-'print] n. Surimpression f. ‖ Surcharge f.
— v. tr. Surimprimer. ‖ Surcharger (a stamp).

overproduce [,ouvəprə'djus] v. tr. Aboutir à une surproduction de, produire en excès.
overproduction [-'dʌkʃən] n. Surproduction *f.*
overrate [ouvə'reit] v. tr. Surestimer (to over-value). ‖ Fɪɴ. Surtaxer.
overreach [-'riːtʃ] v. tr. Dépasser, distancer ; *to overreach oneself,* surestimer ses forces.
override [-'raid] v. tr. (111). Parcourir à cheval (a place) ; piétiner sous les sabots (s.o.). ‖ Surmener, épuiser (a horse). ‖ Jᴜʀ. Outrepasser ; *to override one's commission,* commettre un abus de pouvoir. ‖ Fɪɢ. L'emporter sur, passer avant ; passer outre à.
overrule [-'ruːl] v. tr. Contresigner, superviser, diriger en chef. ‖ Jᴜʀ. Négliger, passer outre à (to disregard) ; annuler (to rescind). ‖ Fɪɢ. Avoir le dessus sur (or) raison de.
overrun ['ouvərʌn] n. Tᴇᴄʜɴ. Report *m.* ‖ Aᴜᴛᴏᴍ. Poussée *f.*
— [ouvə'rʌn] v. tr. (114). Faire des incursions dans, dévaster, parcourir (a country) ; *overrun with,* envahi par. ‖ Inonder (a field). ‖ Fatiguer excessivement ; *to overrun oneself,* se claquer à la course. ‖ Cʜ. ᴅᴇ ꜰ. Brûler (a signal). ‖ Eʟᴇᴄᴛʀ. Survolter. ‖ Tᴇᴄʜɴ. Remanier (a line).
— v. intr. Déborder, inonder (water). ‖ Aᴜᴛᴏᴍ. Marcher en roue libre. ‖ Tᴇᴄʜɴ. Chasser (printed line).
overrunner [ouvə'rʌnə*] n. Envahisseur *m.*
overrunning [-iŋ] n. Envahissement *m.* (by people). ‖ Inondation *f.* (by flood). ‖ Eʟᴇᴄᴛʀ. Survoltage *m.* ‖ Tᴇᴄʜɴ. Remaniement *m.*
oversea ['ouvəsi:] adj. D'outre-mer. ‖ Fɪɴ. Extérieur (debt).
— adv. Outre-mer.
overseas [-z] adv. Outre-mer.
oversee [ouvə'si:] v. tr. (117). Surveiller.
overseer ['ouvəsi:ə*] n. Surveillant *s.* (overlooker). ‖ Tᴇᴄʜɴ. Contremaître *m.* (foreman) ; prote *m.* (in printing).
oversell [ouvə'sel] v. tr. (120). Fɪɴ. Faire la survente de.
oversensitive [-'sensitiv] adj. Hypersensible.
oversew [ouvə'sou] v. tr. Surjeter ; *oversewn hem,* ourlet à jour.
— N. B. Prét. *oversewed ;* p. p. *oversewn.*
overshade [-'ʃeid] v. tr. Ombrager.
overshadow [-'ʃædou] v. tr. Ombrager, obscurcir. ‖ Fɪɢ. Eclipser. (See ᴏᴜᴛsʜɪɴᴇ.)
overshoes ['ouvəʃu:z] n. pl. Caoutchoucs *m.* pl. (rubbers).
overshoot [ouvə'ʃu:t] v. tr. (128). Outrepasser ; dépasser (the mark). ‖ Sᴘᴏʀᴛs. Dépeupler (a covert).
— m. Dépassement *m.*
oversight ['ouvəsait] n. Inadvertance, étourderie *f. ; through an oversight,* par mégarde. ‖ Surveillance *f.* (supervision).
oversize [-'saiz], **oversized** [-'saizd] adj. Au-dessus des dimensions normales, trop grand ; surchargé (class) ; trop nombreux (family).
oversleep [ouvə'sli:p] v. intr. (138). Dépasser l'heure du réveil, dormir au-delà de l'heure voulue.
oversleeve ['ouvəsli:v] n. Garde-manche *m.*
overspend [ouvə'spend] v. tr. (149). Dépasser, excéder (budget) ; épuiser (strength).
— v. intr. Trop dépenser.
overspill ['ouvə,spil] n. Trop-plein, excédent *m.* ‖ Gᴇᴏɢʀ. Excédent démographique (*m.*) des grandes agglomérations ; *overspill town,* ville-satellite.
overspread [ouvə'spred] v. tr. (155). Recouvrir (with, de). ‖ Couvrir, se répandre sur (sth.).
overstaff [-'stɑ:f] v. tr. Doter d'un personnel pléthorique ; *this office is overstaffed,* il y a trop d'employés dans ce bureau.
overstate [-'steit] v. tr. Outrer, exagérer.
overstatement [-'steitmənt] n. Exagération, outrance *f.* (act). ‖ Déclaration exagérée *f.*

overstay [-'stei] v. tr. (158). Rester au-delà de.
overstep [-'step] v. tr. (1). Dépasser, franchir.
overstimulation [,ouvəstimju'leiʃən] n. Mᴇᴅ. Surexcitation *f.*
overstitch ['ouvəstitʃ] n. Surjet *m.*
overstock ['ouvəstɔk] n. Cᴏᴍᴍ. Stock excessif *m. ;* surcharge *f.*
— [,ouvə'stɔk] v. tr. Cᴏᴍᴍ. Encombrer par un stock excessif (with, de) ; surapprovisionner. ‖ Aɢʀɪᴄ. Constituer un cheptel trop important pour (a farm) ; peupler à l'excès (a pond).
overstocking [-'stɔkiŋ] n. Cᴏᴍᴍ. Surstockage, encombrement *m.*
overstrain ['ouvəstrein] n. Surtension *f.* ‖ Fɪɢ. Surmenage *m.*
— [,ouvə'strein] v. tr. Surtendre. ‖ Fɪɢ. Tirer sur (an argument) ; épuiser (s.o.) ; *to overstrain oneself,* se surmener.
overstress ['ouvəstres] n. Tᴇᴄʜɴ. Surcharge *f.*
— [,ouvə'stres] v. tr. Tᴇᴄʜɴ. Surcharger. ‖ Fɪɢ. Mettre trop l'accent sur.
overstride [ouvə'straid] v. tr. (164). Faire des foulées plus longues que (s.o.) ; enjamber (sth.).
overstrung [-'strʌŋ] adj. Surexcité.
overswollen [-'swoulən] adj. Gonflé.
overt ['ouvət] adj. Non déguisé, évident, manifeste. ‖ Public.
overtake [ouvə'teik] v. tr. (174). Rattraper (s.o.). ‖ Sᴘᴏʀᴛs. Dépasser, distancer. ‖ Aᴜᴛᴏᴍ. Doubler. ‖ Fɪɢ. Frapper, atteindre, surprendre.
overtaking [-iŋ] n. Aᴜᴛᴏᴍ. Dépassement *m. ; no overtaking,* défense de doubler.
overtask [ouvə'tɑ:sk] v. tr. Accabler de besogne, surmener.
overtax [-'tæks] v. tr. Fɪɴ. Surtaxer, surimposer ; accabler d'impôts. ‖ Fɪɢ. Accabler, épuiser ; *to overtax one's strength,* abuser de ses forces.
overtaxation [,ouvətæk'seiʃən] n. Fɪɴ. Surimposition *f. ;* excès (*m.*) d'impôts.
overthrow ['ouvəθrou] n. Chute, ruine *f.*
— [ouvə'θrou] v. tr. (180). Renverser, verser. ‖ Fɪɢ. Jeter à bas, démolir.
overthrust ['ouvəθrʌst] n. Gᴇᴏʟ. Chevauchement *m.*
— [ouvə'θrʌst] v. intr. (181). Gᴇᴏʟ. Chevaucher.
overtime ['ouvətaim] ñ. Heures supplémentaires *f. pl. ;* surtemps *m.*
— adv. En heures supplémentaires.
overtire [ouvə'taiə*] v. tr. Fatiguer à l'excès.
overtly [-li] adv. Ouvertement, à visage découvert.
overtness ['ouvətnis] n. Franchise ; nature ouverte *f.*
overtone [-toun] n. Mᴜs. Harmonique *m.*
overtop [ouvə'tɔp] v. tr. (1). Dominer, dépasser en hauteur. ‖ Fɪɢ. Dépasser.
overtrump [-'trʌmp] v. tr. Surcouper.
overture ['ouvətjuə*] n. Jᴜʀ., Mᴜs. Ouverture *f.*
overturn [-tə:n] n. Gᴇᴏʟ. Renversement.
— [ouvə'tə:n] v. tr. Renverser, faire verser. ‖ Nᴀᴜᴛ. Faire chavirer. ‖ Aᴜᴛᴏᴍ. Faire capoter.
— v. intr. Verser (carriage). ‖ Nᴀᴜᴛ. Chavirer. ‖ Aᴜᴛᴏᴍ., Aᴠɪᴀᴛ. Capoter.
overturning [ouvə'tə:niŋ] n. Renversement *m.* ‖ Nᴀᴜᴛ. Chavirage *m.* ‖ Aᴜᴛᴏᴍ., Aᴠɪᴀᴛ. Capotage *m.*
overvaluation ['ouvə,vælju'eiʃən] n. Fɪɴ. Surévaluation *f.* ‖ Fɪɢ. Estime exagérée *f.*
overvalue ['ouvə'vælju:] n. Fɪɴ. Survaleur *f.*
— v. tr. Fɪɴ., Fɪɢ. Surestimer. (See ᴏᴠᴇʀʀᴀᴛᴇ.)
overvoltage [-'voultidʒ] n. Eʟᴇᴄᴛʀ. Surtension *f.*
overweening [-'wi:niŋ] adj. Suffisant, vaniteux, outrecuidant (person) ; insensé (orgueil).
overweight ['ouvəweit] n. Excédent *m.* (luggage, weight). [See ᴏᴠᴇʀʙᴀʟᴀɴᴄᴇ.]
— adj. Constituant un excédent.
— [ouvə'weit] v. tr. Surcharger.
overwhelm [ouvə'hwelm] v. tr. Ensevelir, envahir,

recouvrir (a place). ‖ Fig. Ecraser, accabler; *overwhelmed by s.o.'s kindness,* confondu de reconnaissance envers qqn; *overwhelmed with work,* débordé de travail.

overwhelming [-iŋ] adj. Ecrasant, accablant.
— n. Recouvrement *m.* ‖ Fig. Ecrasement, accablement *m.*

overwhelmingly [-iŋli] adv. De manière écrasante.

overwork ['ouvə'wə:k] n. Travail supplémentaire *m.* ‖ Travail excessif, surmenage *m.*
— [,ouvə'wə:k] v. tr. Surmener, accabler de travail. ‖ Fig. Abuser de.
— v. intr. Se surmener, travailler excessivement; se fatiguer les méninges (fam.).

overworking [ouvə'wə:kiŋ] n. Surmenage *m.*

overworld ['ouvəwə:ld] n. Monde supérieur *m.*

overwrought [ouvə'rɔ:t] adj. Trop travaillé. ‖ Surmené, nerveusement épuisé.

ovidae ['ouvidi:] n. pl. Zool. Ovidés *m. pl.*

oviduct ['ɔvi.dʌkt] n. Med. Oviducte *m.*

oviform ['ouvifɔ:m] adj. Ovoïde.

ovine ['ouvain] adj. Zool. Ovin.

oviparous [o'vipərəs] adj. Zool. Ovipare.

oviposit [ouvi'pɔzit] v. tr. Zool. Pondre.

oviposition [,ouvipo'ziʃən] n. Zool. Ponte *f.*

ovoid ['ouvɔid] adj. Ovoïde.
— n. pl. Comm. Boulets *m. pl.* (coal).

ovoidal ['ouvɔidəl] adj. Ovoïdal.

ovolo ['ouvəlo] (pl. **ovoli** [-li:]) n. Archit. Ove; boudin *m.*

ovulate ['ɔvju,leit] v. intr. Med. Ovuler.

ovulation [,ɔvju'leiʃən] n. Med. Ovulation *f.*

ovule ['ouvju:l] n. Med. Ovule *m.*

ovum ['ouvəm] (pl. **ova** [-ə]) n. Med. Ovule *m.* ‖ Archit. Ove *m.*

ow [au] interj. Aïe, ouïe, ouille.

owe [ou] v. tr. Devoir (*to,* à) [sth.] (lit. and fig.). ‖ Sports. Rendre.

owing [iŋ] adj. Dû (*to,* à); motivé (*to,* par).
— prep. phr. **Owing to,** à cause de, en raison de.

owl [aul] n. Zool. Hibou *m.; barn* (or) *screech owl,* effraie; *brown owl,* chat-huant; *horned owl,* duc. ‖ Fam. *Wise owl,* Sage.
— adj. U. S. Fam. *Owl bus,* dernier autobus; *owl train,* train de nuit.

owlery [-əri] n. Nid (*m.*) de hibou.

owlet [-it] n. Zool. Jeune hibou *m.*

owlish [-iʃ] adj. Zool. De hibou. ‖ Fam. Sage.

own [oun] v. tr. Posséder, être possesseur de (to possess). ‖ Avouer, convenir (to admit). ‖ Reconnaître (to acknowledge). ‖ Jur. Reconnaître (a child).
— v. intr. Convenir (*to,* de). ‖ Fam. *To own up,* avouer, se mettre à table.
— adj. Propre, à soi; *his own brother,* son propre frère; *to make one's own dresses,* faire ses robes soi-même.
— n. Propre avoir; mien, tien, sien *m.; an aroma of their own,* un parfum spécial (or) du cru (or) authentique (or) bien à eux; *for reasons of my own,* pour des raisons bien à moi; *to come into one's own,* rentrer en possession de son bien; *to make sth. one's own,* s'approprier qqch. ‖ Les miens, les tiens, les siens *m. pl.* (relatives). ‖ Propre compte *m.; on one's own,* de son propre chef.

owner [-ə*] n. Possesseur *m.; joint owner,* copos-

sesseur. ‖ Comm. Propriétaire *s.* ‖ Jur. *Rightful owner,* ayant droit.

ownerless [-lis] adj. Sans propriétaire. ‖ Perdu, sans maître (dog).

ownership [-ʃip] n. Possession *f.* ‖ Jur. Propriété *f.*

ox [ɔks] (pl. **oxen** [-ən]) n. Zool. Bœuf *m.; Indian ox,* zébu. ‖ **Ox-bird,** n. Zool. Bécasseau *m.* ‖ **Ox-cart,** n. Char (*m.*) à bœufs. ‖ **Ox-eye,** n. Œil-de-bœuf *m.;* Zool. Mésange charbonnière *f.;* Bot. Grande marguerite *f.* ‖ **Ox-pecker,** n. Pique-bœuf, aiguillon *m.* ‖ **Ox-tail,** n. Culin. Queue (*f.*) de bœuf. ‖ **Ox-tongue,** n. Langue (*f.*) de bœuf.

oxalate ['ɔksəlit] n. Chim. Oxalate *m.*

oxalic [ɔk'sælik] adj. Chim. Oxalique.

Oxford ['ɔksfəd] adj. Geogr. D'Oxford; *Oxford man,* Oxonien, actuel (or) ancien étudiant d'Oxford. ‖ Techn. A croisillons (frame). ‖ Eccles. D'Oxford (Movement). ‖ Comm. *Oxford shirting,* oxford.
— n. Geogr. Oxford *m.*

oxherd [-hə:d] n. Bouvier *s.*

oxhide [-haid] n. Cuir de bœuf *m.*

oxhorn [-hɔ:n] n. Corne (*f.*) de bœuf.

oxidant ['ɔksidənt] n. Chim. Oxydant *m.*

oxidation [,ɔksi'deiʃən] n. Chim. Oxydation *f.*

oxide ['ɔksaid] n. Chim. Oxyde *m.*

oxidizable [ɔksi'daizəbl] adj. Chim. Oxydable.

oxidize ['ɔksidaiz] v. tr. Chim. Oxyder.
— v. intr. Chim. S'oxyder.

Oxonian [ɔk'sounjən] adj. Oxonien, d'Oxford.
— n. Etudiant (*m.*) d'Oxford.

oxyacetylene ['ɔksiə'setili:n] adj. Oxyacétylénique; *oxyacetylene welding,* soudure autogène.

oxygen ['ɔksidʒən] n. Chim. Oxygène *m.* ‖ Med. *Oxygen cylinder* (or) U. S. *tank,* ballon d'oxygène; *oxygen tent,* tente à oxygène.

oxygenate [ɔk'sidʒəneit] v. tr. Chim. Oxygéner.

oxygenation [,ɔksidʒə'neiʃən] n. Chim. Oxygénation *f.*

oxygenizable [-'naizəbl̩] adj. Chim. Oxygénable.

oxygenize [ɔk'sidʒenaiz] v. tr. Chim. Oxygéner.

oxyhydrogen ['ɔksi'haidrədʒən] adj. Chim. Oxhydrique.

oxymoron [,ɔksi'mɔ:rɔn] n. Gramm. Oxymoron *m.*

oyer ['ɔiə*] n. Jur. Audition (*f.*) aux assises.

oyes, oyez [ou'jes] interj. Oyez!

oyster ['ɔistə*] n. Zool. Huître *f.* ‖ Fam. Tombeau *m.* (discreet person). ‖ Pop. Crachat *m.* ‖ **Oyster-bank,** n. U. S. Banc (*m.*) d'huîtres. ‖ **Oyster-bed,** n. Banc (*m.*) d'huîtres; huîtrière *f.* ‖ **Oyster-breeder,** n. Ostréiculteur *m.* ‖ **Oyster-breeding,** n. Ostréiculture *f.* ‖ **Oyster-dealer, oyster-man,** n. Comm. Ecailler *m.* ‖ **Oyster-farm,** n. Parc (*m.*) à huîtres. ‖ **Oyster-farming,** n. Industrie ostréicole *f.* ‖ **Oyster-knife,** n. Ouvre-huîtres *m.* ‖ **Oyster-opener,** n. Ouvre-huîtres *m.* (knife); écailler *s.* (person). ‖ **Oyster-plant,** n. Bot. Salsifis *m.* ‖ **Oyster-shell,** n. Coquille d'huître *f.* ‖ **Oyster-woman,** n. Comm. Ecaillère *f.*

oz(a)ena [o'zi:nə] n. Med. Ozène *m.*

ozone [o'zoun] n. Chim. Ozone *m.* ‖ U. S. Air pur, plein air *m.*

ozonize ['ouzonaiz] v. tr. Chim. Ozoniser.

ozonometer [ouzo'nɔmitə*] n. Ozonomètre *m.*

ozotype ['ouzotaip] n. Ozotype *m.*

P

p [pi:] n. P, p *m.; to mind one's P's and Q's,* tourner sept fois sa langue dans la bouche avant de parler.

p. Written abbr. for *page,* page, p. ‖ [pi:] abbr. *penny* (or) *pence,* penny, pence; *this newspaper costs 15 p.,* ce journal coûte 15 pence.

pa [pɑ:] n. FAM. Papa *m.*

P. A. [pi:'ei] abbr. *public address (system),* sonorisation, sono. ‖ Abbr. *per annum,* par an.

pabulum ['pæbjuləm] n. Aliment *m.; nourriture f.* ‖ FIG. *Mental pabulum,* nourriture de l'esprit.

pace [peis] n. Allure, démarche *f.;* pas *m.* (gait); *at a quick pace,* d'un pas rapide; *at a slow pace,* lentement, à pas lents; *at a walking pace,* au pas. ‖ Pas *m.* (measure); enjambée *f.;* pas *m.* (step). ‖ FIG. *To go the pace,* mener la vie à grandes guides; *to put s.o. through his paces,* voir ce dont qqn est capable; *he can't keep pace with things,* il est dépassé par les événements.
— v. intr. Aller un pas, marcher; *to pace up and down,* faire les cent pas. ‖ Aller à l'amble (horse).
— v. tr. Mesurer en pas (to measure). ‖ Arpenter (a room). ‖ SPORTS. Régler l'allure de.

pacemaker ['peis,meikə*] n. SPORTS. Entraîneur *m.* (in cycling); lièvre *m.* (in athletics). ‖ MED. Centre de l'automatisme cardiaque *m.* (area in heart); pacemaker, stimulateur cardiaque *m.* (electronic device). ‖ FIG. Chef (*m.*) de file (leader).

pachyderm ['pækidə:m] n. ZOOL. Pachyderme *m.*

pachydermatous [,pæki'də:mətəs] adj. ZOOL. Pachyderme. ‖ FIG. Coriace.

pacific [pə'sifik] adj. Paisible, pacifique.

Pacific n. GEOGR. Pacifique, océan Pacifique *m.*

pacification [,pæsifi'keiʃən] n. Pacification *f.*

pacifier [-faiə*] n. Pacificateur *m.;* pacificatrice *f.* ‖ U. S. Sucette *f.* (for babies).

pacifism ['pæsifizm̩] n. Pacifisme *m.*

pacifist [-fist] n. Pacifiste *s.*

pacify [-fai] v. tr. (2). Apaiser, calmer, pacifier.

pack [pæk] n. Ballot *m.* (pedlar's); paquet *m.* ‖ Meute *f.* (of hounds); bande *f.* (of wolves). ‖ MILIT. Sac *m.* ‖ MED. Enveloppement humide *m.* ‖ SPORTS. Jeu *m.* (of cards); mêlée *f.* (at rugby). ‖ FIG. Tas, tissu *m.* (of lies); ramassis *m.* (of thieves); foule *f.* (of troubles). ‖ **Pack-animal,** n. Bête de somme *f.* ‖ **Pack-horse,** n. Cheval (*m.*) de bât. ‖ **Pack-ice,** n. Glace de banquise *f.* ‖ **Pack-saddle,** n. Bât *m.*
— v. tr. Emballer, empaqueter. ‖ Mettre dans une valise (clothing); encaquer (herrings); mettre en boîte (meat); mettre en balles (wool); *to pack a trunk,* faire une malle. ‖ Bâter (a horse). ‖ Bourrer, remplir (*with,* de) [a space]; *closely packed,* tassé; *packed room,* salle comble. ‖ CH. DE F. Bourrer, tasser. ‖ TECHN. Garnir (a piston). ‖ U. S. Porter (a pistol). ‖ FIG. Composer, trier (a committee, a jury). ‖ MED. Faire un enveloppement humide à (a patient). ‖ FAM. *To pack s.o. off,* envoyer promener qqn. ‖ **To pack up,** emballer; FAM. *To pack up one's bits and pieces,* prendre ses cliques et ses claques.
— v. intr. Emballer; empaqueter. ‖ FAM. Expédier; *to send s.o. packing,* envoyer qqn à la balançoire. ‖ **To pack off,** plier bagage. ‖ **To pack up,** faire sa malle (or) sa valise. (fam.) ‖ **To pack together,** se serrer.

package ['pækidʒ] n. Emballage *m.* (packing); colis, paquet *m.* (parcel). ‖ U. S. Sachet *m.* (of needles); *package store,* magasin de spiritueux non consommables sur place. ‖ **Package deal,** n. COMM. Contrat global *m.;* FIG. Marché *m.* ‖ **Package tour,** n. Voyage organisé *m.*

packer [-ə*] n. Emballeur *m.; automatic packer,* emballeuse automatique.

packet [-it] n. Colis, paquet *m.* ‖ Sachet *m.* (of needles). ‖ **Packet-boat,** n. NAUT. Paquebot *m.*

packing [-iŋ] n. Emballage, empaquetage *m.* (of a parcel). ‖ Bourrage, remplissage *m.* (of a space). ‖ TECHN. Garniture *f.* (of a piston). ‖ **Packing-case,** n. Caisse (*f.*) d'emballage. ‖ **Packing-needle,** n. Carrelet d'emballeur *m.* ‖ **Packing-ring,** n. TECHN. Segment *m.* (of a piston).

packthread [-,θred] n. Ficelle *f.*

pact [pækt] n. Pacte, traité *m.*

pad [pæd] n. POP. Chemin *m.;* route *f.; on the pad,* sur le trimard.
— v. tr. POP. *To pad it, to pad the hoof,* prendre le train onze, aller à pattes.
— v. intr. Aller à pied, cheminer.

pad n. Bourrelet, coussin, tampon *m.* ‖ Mantelet *m.;* Sellette *f.* (of harness). ‖ Tampon encreur (for inking). ‖ Buvard *m.* (blotting-pad); bloc-correspondance *m.* (writing-pad). ‖ ZOOL. Coussin charnu *m.* (of a dog); patte *f.* (of a rabbit). ‖ SPORTS. Jambière *f.* (for cricket); plastron *m.* (for fencing). ‖ TECHN. Mandrin *m.* (of a brace). ‖ MED. *Electric pad,* thermoplasme, cataplasme électrique.
— v. tr. Capitonner (a chair); ouater (clothing); rembourrer (a cushion); matelasser, capitonner (a door); *padded cell,* cellule matelassée, cabanon. ‖ FIG. Bourrer, délayer (a speech). ‖ **To pad out,** FAM. Tirer à la ligne; *to pad out a book,* allonger la sauce, faire du remplissage.

padding [-iŋ] n. Ouate *f.;* rembourrage, remplissage *m.* ‖ FIG. Remplissage; bla-bla-bla *m.* (fam.).

paddle ['pædl] n. NAUT. Pagaie *f.* (of a canoe); promenade (*f.*) en périssoire (voyage). ‖ Aube, palette *f.* (of a water-wheel). ‖ **Paddle-boat,** n. Bateau (*m.*) à aubes. ‖ **Paddle-valve,** n. Vannelle *f.* ‖ **Paddle-wheel,** n. Roue (*f.*) à palettes.
— v. tr. NAUT. Pagayer. ‖ FIG. *To paddle one's own canoe,* se débrouiller tout seul. ‖ U. S. FAM. Fesser (a child).
— v. intr. Patauger, barboter. (See DABBLE.)

paddler ['pædlə*] n. Pagayeur *s.*

paddock ['pædək] n. Enclos *m.* ‖ SPORTS. Pesage *m.*

paddy ['pædi] n. Paddy, riz (*m.*) non décortiqué. ‖ **Paddy-field,** n. Rizière *f.*

paddy n. POP. Rogne *f.; in a paddy,* en colère. ‖ **Paddy-waggon,** n. U. S. POP. Voiture cellulaire *f.;* panier (*m.*) à salade (fam.).

padlock ['pædlɔk] n. Cadenas *m.*
— v. tr. Cadenasser, fermer au cadenas (a door).

padre ['pɑ:drei] n. MILIT., NAUT., FAM. Aumônier *m.*

paean ['pi:ən] n. Péan *m.*

paediatrician [,pi:diə'triʃən], **paediatrist** [-'ætrist] n. MED. Pédiatre *s.*

paediatrics [,pi:di'ætriks] n. sg. MED. Pédiatrie *f.*

pagan ['peigən] adj., n. Païen *s.* (See HEATHEN.)

paganism [-izm̩] n. Paganisme *m.*

paganize [-aiz] v. tr. Paganiser.

page [peidʒ] n. Page *m.* (at court). ‖ Groom, chasseur *m.* (in a hotel). ‖ **Page-boy,** n. Chasseur, groom *m.*
— v. tr. Envoyer chercher; demander par haut-parleur (in a hotel, an airport).

page n. Page *f.* (of a book).
— v. tr. Paginer (a book).
pageant ['pædʒənt] n. Cortège (or) spectacle historique *m.* ‖ Pompe *f.;* déploiement fastueux *m.* (exhibition). ‖ Aviat. *Air pageant,* fête de l'air.
pageantry [-ri] n. Apparat *m.;* pompe *f.* (display). ‖ Spectacle *m.* (spectacle).
paginate ['pædʒineit] v. tr. Paginer.
pagination [,pædʒi'neiʃən] n. Pagination *f.*
pagoda [pə'goudə] n. Archit. Pagode *f.*
pah! [pɑ:] interj. Pouah!
paid [peid] adj. A gages. (See pay.) ‖ **Paid-up,** adj. Jur., Fin. Libéré (policy).
pail [peil] n. Seau *m.* (See bucket.) ‖ Naut. Baille *f.*
pailful [-ful] n. Seau, plein seau *m.*
paillasse ['pæli,æs] n. Paillasse *f.*
pain [pein] n. Chagrin *m.;* douleur, peine, souffrance *f.* (mental); douleur *f.* (physical). ‖ Peine, punition *f.* (punishment); *under pain of,* sous peine de. ‖ Pl. Peine *f.; to take pains,* se donner du mal (or) de la peine. ‖ Fam. *To give s.o. a pain in the neck,* enquiquiner qqn. ‖ **Pain-killer,** n. Med. Anodin, calmant, antalgique *m.*
— v. tr. Affliger, faire de la peine à (s.o.) [mentally]; *it pains me to,* il m'en coûte de. ‖ Faire mal à (s.o.) [physically].
painful [-ful] adj. Difficile, laborieux, pénible (task). ‖ Douloureux (wound).
painfully [-fuli] adv. Douloureusement; péniblement.
painfulness [-fulnis] n. Douleur *f.*
painless [-lis] adj. Indolore; *painless childbirth,* accouchement sans douleur. ‖ Sans peine.
painstaking ['peinzteikiη] adj. Assidu, soigneux, appliqué (person); soigné (work).
— n. Soin *m.;* application *f.*
paint [peint] n. Peinture *f.; box of paints,* boîte de couleurs; *coat of paint,* couche de peinture; « *wet paint* », « prenez garde à la peinture ». ‖ Fard *m.* (make-up). ‖ **Paint-box,** n. Boîte (*f.*) de couleurs. ‖ **Paint-brush,** n. Pinceau *m.*
— v. tr. Couvrir de peinture, peindre; *to paint sth. red,* peindre qqch. en rouge. ‖ Dépeindre, décrire (to depict). ‖ Farder (the face). ‖ Arts. Peindre. ‖ Med. Badigeonner (the throat). ‖ Fam. *To paint the town red,* faire la nouba.
— v. intr. Mettre du rouge, se farder (to make up). ‖ Arts. Peindre, faire de la peinture.
painter [-ə*] n. Peintre *m.*
painter n. Naut. Amarre *f.*
painting [-iη] n. Arts. Peinture *f.; painting in oils,* peinture à l'huile. ‖ Arts. Tableau *m.* (picture). ‖ Med. Badigeonnage *m.* ‖ Fig. Description, peinture *f.*
paintwork ['peintwə:k] n. Peintures *f. pl.* (of a building).
pair [pɛə] n. Paire *f.* (of stockings); *pair of pants, of trousers,* caleçon, pantalon. ‖ Couple *m.;* paire *f.* (of animals); *carriage and pair,* voiture à deux chevaux. ‖ Couple *m.* (of people); *the happy pair,* l'heureux couple, les deux conjoints. ‖ Fam. *Another pair of shoes,* une autre paire de manches.
— v. tr. Accoupler, apparier, mettre par paires (gloves, shoes). ‖ **To pair off,** arranger deux par deux, assortir par deux.
— v. intr. S'accoupler, s'apparier. ‖ **To pair off,** s'arranger deux par deux; Jur. S'entendre avec un adversaire pour s'absenter en même temps (in Parliament).
pajamas [pə'dʒæməz] n. pl. U. S. Pyjama *m.*
Pakistan [,pɑ:ki'stɑ:n] n. Geogr. Pakistan *m.*
Pakistani [-'stɑ:ni] n., adj. Geogr. Pakistanais *adj., s.*
pal [pæl] n. Fam. Camarade *s.;* copain *m.;* copine *f.* (See buddy.)
— v. intr. **To pal up,** se lier (with, avec).

palace ['pæləs] n. Palais *m.*
paladin ['pælədin] n. Paladin *m.*
palaeographer [,pæli'ɔgrəfə*] n. Paléographe *m.*
palaeographic [,pælio'græfik] adj. Paléographique.
palaeography [,pæli'ɔgrəfi] n. Paléographie *f.*
palaeolithic [,pælio'liθik] adj. Paléolithique.
palaeontology [,pæliən'tɔlədʒi] n. Paléontologie *f.*
palaeozoic [,pælio'zouik] adj., n. Paléozoïque, primaire *adj., m.*
palais ['pælei] n. *Palais de danse,* dancing.
palankeen, palanquin ['pælən'ki:n] n. Palanquin *m.*
palatable ['pælətəbl̩] adj. Agréable au palais, savoureux. ‖ Fig. Agréable (*to,* à).
palatal ['pælətl̩] adj. Gramm. Palatal.
— n. Gramm. Palatale *f.*
palatalisation [,pælətəlai'zeiʃən] n. Gramm. Palatalisation *f.*
palate ['pælit] n. Med. Palais *m.; soft palate,* palais mou. ‖ Fig. Palais; goût *m.; pleasures of the palate,* plaisirs de la table.
palatial [pə'leiʃəl] adj. Magnifique, grandiose, splendide.
palatinate [pə'lætinit] n. Palatinat *m.*
palatine ['pælətain] adj. Palatin; *the Palatine Hill,* le mont Palatin.
palaver [pə'lɑ:və*] n. Palabre *f.*‖ Fam. Bavardage *m.* (gossip); embobelinage (soft soap).
— v. intr. Palabrer. ‖ Fam. Bavarder (to chatter).
— v. tr. Flagorner (to wheedle).
pale [peil] s. Pieu *m.* (of a fence). ‖ Blas. Pal *m.* ‖ Fig. Bornes, limites *f. pl.; withih the pale,* dans le giron (or) sein (*of,* de).
pale [peil] adj. Pâle, blême; *deadly pale,* pâle comme la mort; *pale blue,* bleu pâle. ‖ Culin. Blanc (ham). ‖ **Pale-face,** n. Blanc *m.;* blanche *f.* ‖ **Pale-faced,** adj. Au visage pâle.
— v. intr. Pâlir, devenir pâle.
paleness [-nis] n. Pâleur *f.*
paleo- [pælio-] pref. U. S. See palaeo-.
palette ['pælit] n. Arts. Palette *f.*
palfrey ['pɔ:lfri] n. Palefroi *m.*
palimpsest ['pælimpsest] n. Palimpseste *m.*
palindrome ['pælin,droum] adj., n. Palindrome *adj., m.*
paling ['peiliη] n. Palissade *f.*
palinode ['pælinoud] n. Palinodie *f.*
palisade [,pæli'seid] n. Palissade *f.*
— v. tr. Palissader, entourer d'une palissade.
palish ['peiliʃ] adj. Pâlot; un peu pâle.
pall [pɔ:l] n. Poêle *m.;* drap mortuaire *m.* ‖ Eccles. Pallium *m.* ‖ Fig. Voile *m.* (of smoke); manteau *m.* (of snow). ‖ **Pall-bearer,** n. Porteur (*s.*) d'un cordon du poêle.
pall v. intr. Devenir fade (or) insipide (*on,* pour); *it never palls on you,* on ne s'en dégoûte jamais.
— v. tr. Rassasier (appetite); blaser, émousser (senses).
palladium [pə'leidiəm] n. Chim. Palladium *m.*
pallet ['pælit] n. Palette *f.* (potter's). ‖ Arts. Palette *f.* (artist's). [See palette.] ‖ Techn. Cliquet *m.* (of rachet wheel); palette *f.* (of a clock, for stocking goods). ‖ Mus. Soupape *f.* (of organ).
palliasse ['pæli,æs] n. Paillasse *f.*
palliate ['pælieit] v. tr. Med. Pallier. ‖ Fig. Atténuer, pallier.
palliation [,pæli'eiʃən] n. Med. Palliation *f.* ‖ Fig. Atténuation *f.*
palliative ['pæliətiv] adj., n. Palliatif *m.*
pallid ['pælid] adj. Pâle, blême (face); blafard (light). [See pale.]
pallidness [-nis], **pallor** ['pælə*] n. Pâleur *f.*
pally ['pæli] adj. Fam. Copain (with, avec).
palm [pɑ:m] n. Bot. Palme *f.* (branch); palmier *m.* (tree). ‖ Eccles. *Palm Sunday,* dimanche des

Rameaux. ‖ Fig. *To bear the palm*, remporter la palme. ‖ **Palm-grove**, n. Bot. Palmeraie *f.* ‖ **Palm-oil**, n. Huile de palme *f.* ‖ **Palm-tree**, n. Bot. Palmier *m.*

palm n. Paume *f.* (of the hand). ‖ Zool. Empaumure *f.* (of a stag). ‖ Naut. Patte *f.* (of an anchor). ‖ Fam. *To grease s.o.'s palm*, graisser la patte à qqn. ; *to know like the palm of one's hand*, connaître comme sa poche. ‖ **Palm-greasing**, n. Fam. Graissage (*m.*) de patte.
— v. tr. Escamoter (a card). ‖ *To palm off*, faire passer (*on*, à) [a bad coin].

palmate ['pælmit] adj. Palmé.
palmer ['pɑ:mə*] n. Pèlerin *m.*
palmetto [pæl'metou] n. Bot. Palmier nain *m.*; palmette *f.*
palmiped ['pælmiped] adj., n. Palmipède *m.*
palmist ['pɑ:mist] n. Chiromancien *s.*
palmistry [-ri] n. Chiromancie *f.*
palmy ['pɑ:mi] adj. Fig. Heureux ; *in my palmy days*, dans mes beaux jours.
palp [pælp] n. Zool. Palpe *f.*
palpability [,pælpə'biliti], **palpableness** ['pælpəbḷnis] n. Palpabilité *f.* ‖ Fig. Evidence *f.*
palpable ['pælpəbḷ] adj. Palpable. ‖ Fig. Evident.
palpably [-i] adv. Fig. Evidemment.
palpate ['pælpeit] v. tr. Med. Palper.
palpitate ['pælpiteit] v. intr. Palpiter.
palpitation [,pælpi'teiʃən] n. Palpitation *f.*
palsy ['pɔ:lzi] n. Med. Paralysie *f.*
palter ['pɔ:ltə*] v. intr. Biaiser, tergiverser, ergoter (*with*, avec) [s.o.]. ‖ Marchander (*with*, sur) [sth.]. ‖ Badiner ; *to palter with a question*, traiter une question à la légère.
paltriness ['pɔ:ltrinis] n. Mesquinerie *f.*
paltry ['pɔ:ltri] adj. Mesquin, misérable, méchant.
paludal ['pæljudəl] adj. Paludéen.
palynology [,pæli'nɔlədʒi] n. Bot. Palynologie *f.*
pampas [pæmpəs] n. pl. Pampas *f. pl.*
pamper ['pæmpə*] v. tr. Choyer, mignoter, gâter.
pamphlet ['pæmflit] n. Brochure *f.* ; opuscule *m.* ; *scurrilous pamphlet*, pamphlet.
pamphleteer [,pæmfli'tiə*] n. Auteur (*m.*) de brochures. ‖ Pamphlétaire *m.* (scurrilous).
pan [pæn] n. Culin. Casserole *f.*, poêlon *m.* ; *pots and pans*, batterie de cuisine. ‖ Geol. Cuvette *f.* ‖ Milit. † Bassinet *m.* (of a musket). ‖ Techn. Bassin *m.* (of a balance). ‖ Cuvette *f.* (of W. C.). ‖ Fig. *Flash in the pan*, feu de paille. ‖ Fam. U. S. Binette, bille *f.* (face). ‖ **Pan-scrubber** (or) **scraper**, n. Eponge métallique *f.* ; tampon (*m.*) à vaisselle.
— v. tr. *To pan out*, laver à la batée (in mining).
— v. intr. *To pan out*, Fig. Réussir.
pan v. intr. Cinem. Faire un panoramique.
— n. Cinem. Panoramique *m.*
Pan n. Pan *m.* ‖ **Pan-pipe**, n. Flûte (*f.*) de Pan.
panacea [,pænə'siə] n. Panacée *f.* (See CURE-ALL.).
panache [pə'næʃ] n. Panache *m.*
Panama [,pænə'mɑ:] n. Geogr. Panama *m.* ; *Panama Canal*, canal du Panama ; *Panama hat*, panama, chapeau de Panama.
Pan-American [,pænə'merikən] adj. Panaméricain.
pancake ['pænkeik] n. Culin. Crêpe *f.* ‖ Aviat. Descente (*f.*) à plat. ‖ Techn. *Pancake coil*, galette. ‖ Fam. *As flat as a pancake*, plat comme une galette.
— v. intr. Aviat. Descendre à plat, plaquer.
panchromatic [,pænkrou'mætik] adj. Techn. Panchromatique.
pancreas ['pæŋkriəs] n. Med. Pancréas *m.*
pancreatic [,pæŋkri'ætik] adj. Med. Pancréatique.
panda ['pændə] n. Zool. Panda *m.* ‖ *Panda car*, voiture de police.

pandemic [pæn'demik] adj. Pandémique.
pandemonium [,pændi'mounjəm] n. Pandémonium *m.*
pander ['pændə*] n. Entremetteur, proxénète ; maquereau *m.* (pop.).
— v. intr. *To pander to*, se prêter à ; encourager (a vice).
— v. tr. Servir d'entremetteur à.
Pandora [pæn'dɔ:rə] n. Pandore *f.* ; *Pandora's box*, boîte de Pandore.
p. and p. [pi:ənd'pi:] abbr. *postage and packing*, emballage et port.
pane [pein] n. Carreau *m.*, vitre *f.*
panegyric [,pæni'dʒirik] n. Panégyrique *m.*
— adj. Elogieux.
panegyrical [-əl] adj. Elogieux.
panegyrist [-ist] n. Panégyriste *m.*
panegyrize ['pænədʒiraiz] v. tr. Faire le panégyrique de. (See EULOGIZE.)
panel ['pænl] n. Panneau *m.* (in a door, a dress). ‖ Med. Liste (*f.*) des médecins des assurances sociales. ‖ Jur. Tableau *m.* (or) liste (*f.*) du jury. ‖ Autom., Aviat. *Instrument panel*, planche de bord. ‖ Fam. Groupe *m.* ‖ **Panel-discussion**, n. Discussion (*f.*) par un groupe d'orateurs. ‖ **Panel-doctor**, n. Med. Médecin (*m.*) des assurances sociales. ‖ **Panel-heating**, n. Chauffage par rayonnement. ‖ **Panel-patient**, n. Med. Malade assuré social *s.*
— v. tr. (1). Archit. Garnir de boiseries (a room) ; lambrisser (a wall). ‖ Garnir de panneaux (a dress).
pang [pæŋ] n. Angoisse *f.* ; serrement (*m.*) de cœur ; *pangs of death*, affres de la mort.
panhandle ['pæn,hændḷ] n. U. S. Enclave territoriale *f.*, territoire (*m.*) qui fait saillie.
— v. tr. U. S. Fam. Mendier, mendigoter.
— v. intr. U. S. Fam. Faire la manche.
panhandler [-ə*] n. U. S. Fam. Mendigot *m.*
panic ['pænik] n. Bot. Millet *m.*
panic adj. Panique (terror).
— n. Affolement *m.* ; panique *f.* ; *to get into a panic*, prendre les choses au tragique, s'affoler. ‖ **Panic-monger**, n. Semeur (*s.*) de panique. ‖ **Panic-stricken**, adj. Affolé, pris de panique.
— v. tr. U. S. Semer la panique dans. ‖ Theatr. Secouer (the audience).
— v. intr. U. S. Etre pris de panique.
panicky [-i] adj. Alarmiste (report) ; qui s'affole facilement ; paniquard (fam.) [person].
panjandrum [pæn'dʒændrəm] n. Fam. Gros bonnet ; ponte *m.*
pannier ['pæniə*] n. Panier *m.* (basket). ‖ Panier *m.* (pack). ‖ *Pannier dress*, robe à paniers.
pannikin ['pænikin] n. Gobelet *m.* ; récipient (*m.*) en fer-blanc.
panoply ['pænəpli] n. Panoplie *f.*
panorama [,pænə'rɑ:mə] n. Panorama *m.*
panoramic [-ræmik] adj. Panoramique ; *panoramic view*, panorama.
pansy ['pænzi] m. Bot. Pensée *f.* ‖ Pop. Tapette, tante *f.*
pant ['pænt] v. intr. Battre du flanc, panteler (animal) ; palpiter (heart) ; haleter (person) ; *to pant for breath*, chercher à reprendre haleine. ‖ Fig. Aspirer (*for*, à) ; soupirer (*for*, après).
— v. tr. *To pant out*, dire d'une voix haletante.
— n. Halètement *m.* ; palpitation *f.*
pantaloon [,pæntə'lu:n] n. Theatr. Pantalon. ‖ Comm. pl. *Pair of pantaloons*, pantalon.
pantechnicon [pæn'teknikən] n. Voiture (*f.*) de déménagement.
pantheism ['pænθiizm] n. Panthéisme *m.*
pantheist [-ist] n. Panthéiste *s.*
pantheistic [,pænθi'istik] adj. Panthéiste.
Pantheon [pæn'θi:ən] n. Panthéon *m.*
panther ['pænθə*] n. Zool. Panthère *f.*
panties ['pæntiz] n. pl. Fam. Culotte, petite

culotte *f.* ; slip *m.* ‖ **Pantie-belt** (or U. S.) **-girdle**, n. Gaine-culotte *f.*
pantihose ['pænti,houz] n. Collant *m.*
pantile ['pæntail] n. Carreau hollandais *m.* ‖ ARCHIT. Tuile flamande *f.*
pantograph ['pæntə,grɑ:f] n. TECHN., CH. DE F. Pantographe *m.*
pantomime ['pæntəmaim] n. Mime *m.* ‖ THEATR. Pantomime, revue-féerie *f.*
— v. tr. Mimer.
— v. intr. S'exprimer en pantomime.
pantry ['pæntri] n. Office *f.* ‖ Dépense *f.*
pants [pænts] n. pl. Caleçon *m.* ‖ U. S., FAM. Pantalon *m.*
panty-waist ['pæntiweist] n. U. S. POP. Femmelette *f.*
panzer ['pænzə] adj. MILIT. Blindé.
panzers [-zəz] n. pl. MILIT. Blindés *m. pl.* ; arme blindée *f.* (troops).
pap [pæp] n. † Téton *m.* ‖ Mamelon *m.* (of a mountain).
pap n. Pulpe *f.* ‖ CULIN. Bouillie *f.*
papa [pə'pɑ:] n. Papa *m.*
papacy ['peipəsi] n. ECCLES. Papauté *f.*
papal ['peipəl] adj. Papal.
papaw ['pɔ:,pɔ:] n. BOT. Papaye *f.* (fruit) ; papayer *m.* (tree). ‖ U. S. BOT. Asimine *f.* (fruit) ; asiminier *m.* (tree).
paper ['peipə*] n. Papier *m.* ; *paper industry,* industrie du papier ; *old papers,* paperasses ; *to put down on paper,* coucher par écrit. ‖ Pl. Pièce *f.* ; document *m.* (document) ; *to send in one's papers,* donner sa démission. ‖ Journal *m.* (newspaper) ; *evening paper,* journal du soir ; *sports paper,* journal sportif ; *weekly paper,* hebdomadaire. ‖ Mémoire *m.* ; étude *f.* (study) ; *to read a paper,* faire une conférence (*on,* sur). ‖ MILIT. *Call-up papers,* ordre d'appel. ‖ NAUT. *Ship's papers,* papiers de bord. ‖ FIG. *On paper,* sur le papier, en théorie. ‖ **Paper-basket,** n. Corbeille (*f.*) à papier. ‖ **Paper-chase,** n. SPORTS. Rallye-paper *m.* ‖ **Paper-clip** (or) **-fastener,** n. Agrafe, pince *f.* ; trombone *m.* ‖ **Paper-hanger,** n. Tapissier *m.* ‖ **Paper-hanging,** n. Tapissage ; collage (*m.*) de papier peint. ‖ **Paper-knife,** n. Coupe-papier *m. invar.* ‖ **Paper-mill,** n. Papeterie, fabrique (*f.*) de papier. ‖ **Paper-weight,** n. Presse-papiers *m. invar.* ‖ **Paper-work,** n. Paperasserie *f.*
— adj. De papier, en papier. ‖ FIG. Sur le papier, en théorie.
— v. tr. Tapisser, couvrir de papier. ‖ FIG. *To paper over,* camoufler ; *to paper over the cracks,* colmater les brèches (fig.).
paperback [-,bæk] n. Livre broché, livre (*m.*) de poche.
— adj. Broché, au format de poche.
papier mâché [,pæpjei'mæʃei] n. Papier mâché *m.*
papilionaceae [pə,pilio'neisii:] n. pl. BOT. Papilionacées *f. pl.*
papilionaceous [-ʃəs] adj. BOT. Papilionacé.
papilla [pə'pilə] n. Papille *f.*
papillary [-əri] adj. Papillaire.
papism ['peipizm] n. ECCLES. Papisme *m.*
papist [-ist] n. ECCLES. Papiste *s.*
papistic(al) [pə'pistik(əl)] adj. ECCLES. Papiste.
papistry ['peipistri] n. ECCLES. Papisme *m.*
papoose [pə'pu:s] n. Enfant indien *m.*
paprika ['pæprikə] n. CULIN. Paprika *m.*
Papua ['pæpjuə] n. GEOGR. Papouasie *f.*
papula ['pæpjulə] (pl. **papulae**) n. MED., BOT. Papule *f.*
papyrus [pə'pairəs] n. Papyrus *m.*
— N. B. Deux pluriels : *papyruses, papyri.*
par [pɑ:*] n. Egalité *f.* ; *to be on a par with,* aller de pair avec, être à l'égal de. ‖ FIN. Pair *m.* ; *above, below par,* au-dessus, au-dessous du pair ; *at par,* au pair. ‖ U. S. SPORTS. Normale (*f.*) du parcours

(in golf). ‖ FAM. *To feel below par,* ne pas se sentir dans son assiette.
par n. FAM. Paragraphe, alinéa *m.*
para ['pærə] n. FAM. Para *m.* (parachutist). ‖ Abbr. *paragraph,* paragraphe, alinéa.
parable ['pærabl] n. Parabole *f.*
parabola [pə'ræbələ] n. MATH. Parabole *f.*
parabolic(al) [,pærə'bɔlik(əl)] adj. Parabolique.
paracetamol [,pærə'si:tə,mɔl] n. MED. Paracétamol *m.*
parachute [,pærə'ʃu:t] n. AVIAT. Parachute *m.* ; *parachute drop,* parachutage ; *parachute flare,* fusée-parachute.
— v. intr. AVIAT. Descendre en parachute.
parachuting [-iŋ] n. AVIAT. Parachutage *m.*
parachutist ['pærə,ʃu:tist], [,pærə'ʃu:tist] n. AVIAT. Parachutiste *s.*
paraclete ['pærəkli:t] n. ECCLES. Paraclet *m.*
parade [pə'reid] n. Parade *f.* ; étalage *m.* ; *to make a parade of,* faire parade (or) étalage (or) montre de. ‖ Esplanade, promenade publique *f.* ‖ Défilé *m.* ; *fashion parade,* présentation de collections. ‖ SPORTS. Parade *f.* ‖ MILIT. Défilé (of troops) ; parade, revue *f.*
— v. tr. Faire parade de ; afficher. ‖ MILIT. Assembler ; faire défiler.
— v. intr. Parader. ‖ MILIT. Défiler.
paradigm ['pærədaim] n. GRAMM. Paradigme *m.*
paradisaical [,pærədi'zaiəkəl], **paradisiac** [,pærə'disiæk] adj. Paradisiaque.
paradise ['pærədais] n. Paradis *m.* ; *earthly paradise,* paradis terrestre. ‖ ZOOL. *Bird of paradise,* oiseau de paradis. ‖ FIG. *To live in a fool's paradise,* se nourrir d'illusions.
paradox ['pærədɔks] n. Paradoxe *m.*
paradoxical [,pærə'dɔksikəl] adj. Paradoxal.
paradoxically [-əli] adv. Paradoxalement.
paraffin ['pærəfin] n. Pétrole *m.* ; *paraffin lamp,* lampe à pétrole ; *paraffin oil,* pétrole. ‖ MED. Paraffine *f.* ; *liquid paraffin,* huile de paraffine ; *paraffin wax,* paraffine solide.
— v. tr. Paraffiner.
paragon ['pærəgən] n. Parangon, modèle *m.*
paragraph ['pærəgrɑ:f] n. Paragraphe, alinéa *m.* ; *new paragraph,* à la ligne. ‖ Entrefilet, écho *m.* (in a newspaper).
— v. tr. Diviser en paragraphes (or) en alinéas.
paragraphist [-ist] n. Echotier *m.*
Paraguay ['pærə,gwai] n. GEOGR. Paraguay *m.*
parakeet ['pærəki:t] n. ZOOL. Perruche *f.*
parallactic [,pærə'læktik] adj. PHYS., ASTRON. Parallactique.
parallax ['pærə,læks] n. PHYS., ASTRON. Parallaxe *f.*
parallel ['pærəlel] adj. MATH. Parallèle (*with,* à). ‖ ELECTR. *In parallel,* en parallèle. ‖ FIG. Analogue (*to, with,* à).
— n. MATH. Parallèle *f.* ‖ GEOGR. Parallèle *m.* ‖ FIG. Parallèle *m.* (*between,* entre) ; *without parallel,* sans pareil.
— v. tr. Comparer, mettre en parallèle (two things). ‖ Egaler, être comparable à (sth.).
parallelepiped [,pærələ'lepiped] n. MATH. Parallélépipède *m.*
parallelism ['pærəlelizm] n. Parallélisme *m.*
parallelogram [,pærə'leləgræm] n. MATH. Parallélogramme *m.*
paralyse ['pærəlaiz] v. tr. Paralyser.
paralysis [pə'ræləsis] (pl. **paralyses** [-si:z]) n. MED. Paralysie *f.*
paralytic [,pærə'litik] adj., n. MED. Paralytique *s.*
paramagnetic [,pærəmæg'netik] adj. PHYS. Paramagnétique.
— n. PHYS. Substance paramagnétique *f.*
paramagnetism [-'mægni,tizm] n. PHYS. Paramagnétisme *m.*

paramedical [‚pærə'medikļ] adj. Paramédical.
parameter [pə'ræmitə*] n. Math., Fig. Paramètre m.
paramilitary [pærə'militri] adj. Paramilitaire.
paramount ['pærəmaunt] adj. Suprême (importance); souverain (lord).
paramour ['pærəmuə*] n. Amant m.; maîtresse f.
paranoia [‚pærə'nɔiə] n. Med. Paranoïa f.
paranormal [‚pærə'nɔ:məl] adj. Paranormal.
parapet ['pærəpit] n. Parapet, garde-fou m. ‖ Milit. Parapet m. ‖ Archit. Parapet walk, chemin de ronde.
paraph ['pærəf] n. Paraphe, parafe m.
paraphernalia [‚pærəfə'neiljə] n. pl. Attirail m.; affaires f. pl. ‖ Fam. Saint-frusquin, barda m.
paraphrase ['pærəfreiz] n. Paraphrase f.
— v. tr. Paraphraser.
paraplegia [‚pærə'pli:dʒiə] n. Med. Paraplégie f.
paraplegic [-dʒik] adj., n. Med. Paraplégique s. (See spastic.)
parapsychology [‚pærəsai'koulədʒi] n. Parapsychologie f.
parasite ['pærəsait] n. Zool., Bot., Fig. Parasite m.
parasitic [‚pærə'sitik] adj. Parasite.
parasitism ['pærəsaitizm] n. Parasitisme m.
parasol [‚pærə'sɔl] n. Ombrelle f.
parathyroid [‚pærə'θairɔid] n. Med. Parathyroïde f.
paratrooper ['pærətrupə*] n. Aviat. Parachutiste militaire m.
paratroops [-trups] n. Aviat. Parachutistes m. pl.; infanterie (f.) de l'air.
paratyphoid [‚pærə'taifɔid] adj. Med. Paratyphoïde (fever); paratyphique (bacillus, sufferer).
— n. Med. Paratyphoïde f.
paravane ['pærəvein] n. Naut. Paravane m.; paramines m. invar.
parboil ['pɑ:bɔil] v. tr. Culin. Faire bouillir (or) cuire à demi; étourdir (meat); blanchir (vegetables).
parcel ['pɑ:sļ] n. Paquet, colis m.; parcels office, bureau des messageries; parcel post, service des colis postaux. ‖ Fin. Paquet m. (of shares). ‖ Comm. Lot m. (of goods). ‖ Jur. Parcelle f. (of land). ‖ Fam. Tas m.; bande f. (of fools); tas m. (of lies). ‖ Parcel-delivery, n. Factage m.
— v. tr. Naut. Limander. ‖ To parcel out, morceler, diviser. ‖ To parcel up, emballer.
parch [pɑ:tʃ] v. tr. Rôtir, griller; parching wind, vent dévorant. ‖ Dessécher, altérer.
— v. intr. Se dessécher.
parchment [['pɑ:tʃmənt] n. Parchemin m.
pard [pɑ:d] n. † Léopard m.
pard [pɑ:d], pardner ['pɑ:dnə*] n. U. S. Pop. Pote m., copain s.
pardon ['pɑ:dņ] n. Pardon m.; to beg s.o.'s pardon, demander pardon à qqn. ‖ Eccles. Indulgence f.
— v. tr. Pardonner, excuser.
pardonable [-əbļ] adj. Pardonnable, excusable.
pardoner [-ə*] n. Eccles. Vendeur (m.) d'indulgences.
pare [pɛə*] v. tr. Peler, éplucher (an apple); ébarber (the edges of a book); couper, rogner (the nails). ‖ To pare down, rogner.
paregoric [‚pærə'gɔrik] adj., m. Med. Parégorique m.
parent ['pɛərənt] n. Père m. (or) mère f.; parent metal, métal de base; parent rock, roche mère; parent tree, souche. ‖ Fig. Cause, origine f. ‖ Parent-ship, n. Naut. Navire ravitailleur m.
parentage [-idʒ] n. Parenté, naissance f.
parental [pə'rentļ] adj. Paternel et maternel; des parents.
parentally [-əli] adv. En père, en mère.

parenthesis [pə'renθisis] (pl. parentheses [-i:z]) n. Parenthèse f.; in parenthesis, entre parenthèses.
parenthesize [-saiz] v. tr. Mettre entre parenthèses.
parenthetic(al) [pærən'θetik(əl)] adj. Entre parenthèses.
parenthetically [-əli] adv. Entre parenthèses.
par excellence [pɑ:r'eksələns] adv. Par excellence.
parget ['pɑ:dʒit] v. tr. Archit. Crépir, plâtrer.
— n. Archit. Crépi, revêtement (m.) de plâtre.
parhelion [pɑ:'hi:ljən] (pl. parhelia [-jə]) n. Astron. Parhélie m.
pariah ['pɛəriə] n. Paria m.
parietal [pə'raiitļ] adj. Med. Pariétal.
paring ['pɛəriŋ] n. Epluchure f.
pari passu [‚pæri 'pæsu:] adv. De pair, de concert.
parish ['pæriʃ] n. Eccles. Paroisse f.; Parish school, école paroissiale; parish hall, salle des œuvres; parish priest, curé; pasteur. ‖ Commune f. (civil); parish council, conseil municipal; to go on the parish, tomber à la charge de la commune; parish-pump politics, politique de clocher.
parishioner [pə'riʃənə*] n. Eccles. Paroissien s.
Parisian [pə'rizjən] adj., n. Parisien s.
parity ['pæriti] n. Egalité f. ‖ Fin. Parité f.
park [pɑ:k] n. Parc m. ‖ Autom. Car park, parc à voitures. ‖ Milit. Gun park, parc d'artillerie.
— v. tr. Autom. Garer, parquer. ‖ Agric. Parquer (sheep). ‖ Milit. Mettre dans un parc (artillery).
— v. intr. Autom. Stationner.
parka ['pɑ:kə] n. Parka m.
parkin [-in] n. Culin. Croquignole d'avoine f.
parking [-iŋ] n. Autom. Stationnement m.; no parking, stationnement interdit, défense de stationner. ‖ Parking-lot, n. U. S. Parking, parc de stationnement m. ‖ Parking-meter, n. Parcmètre m. ‖ Parking-ticket, n. Contravention (f.) pour stationnement interdit; contredanse f. (fam.).
parkway [-wei] n. U. S. Route de plaisance f.
parky ['pɑ:ki] adj. Fam. Frisquet; it's parky, this morning, ça pince, ce matin.
parlance ['pɑ:ləns] n. Langage, parler m.; in common parlance, en langage courant.
parley ['pɑ:li] n. Pourparlers m. pl.; conférence f.; to hold a parley with, parlementer avec.
— v. intr. Parlementer (with, avec).
parliament ['pɑ:ləmənt] n. Parlement m.; Houses of Parliament, les Chambres.
parliamentarian [‚pɑ:ləmən'tɛəriən], parliamentary [‚pɑ:lə'mentəri] adj. Parlementaire; parliamentary elections, élections législatives.
parlo(u)r ['pɑ:lə*] n. Petit salon m. (in a house); bar parlour, salon particulier (of an inn). ‖ Eccles. Parloir m. (of a convent). ‖ U. S. Salon m. (shop); beauty parlor, salon de beauté, boutique d'une esthéticienne. ‖ Parlor car, n. U. S. Ch. de f. Wagon-salon m. ‖ Parlour game, n. Jeu (m.) de société. ‖ Parlour maid, n. Femme de chambre f.
parlous ['pɑ:ləs] adj. Précaire, alarmant, périlleux.
Parmesan [‚pɑ:mi'zæn] adj., n. Culin. Parmesan m.
Parnassian [pɑ:'næsiən] adj. Parnassien.
Parnassus [-əs] n. Parnasse m.
parochial [pə'roukjəl] adj. Eccles. Paroissial. ‖ Jur. Communal. ‖ Fig. Local; de clocher (pej.).
parochialism [-izm] n. Esprit de clocher m.
parodist ['pærədist] n. Parodiste m.
parody [-i] n. Parodie f.; pastiche m.
— v. tr. Parodier.
parole [pə'roul] n. Parole (f.) d'honneur; on parole, sur parole.
— v. tr. Libérer sur parole (a prisoner). ‖ U. S. Libérer conditionnellement.
parolee [pærou'li:] n. U. S. Libéré (s.) sur parole.
parotid [pə'rɔtid] adj., n. Med. Parotide f.

paroxysm ['pærəksizm̩] n. MED. Paroxysme. ‖ FIG. Crise *f*.

parquet ['pɑːkei] n. Parquet *m*.; *parquet flooring*, parquetage.

parr [pɑː*] n. ZOOL. Saumoneau, parr *m*.

parricide ['pærisaid] n. Parricide *m*. (crime); parricide *s*. (person).

parrot ['pærət] n. ZOOL. Perroquet *m*. ‖ MED. *Parrot disease* (or) *fever*, psittacose. ‖ **Parrot-fashion**, adv. A la manière d'un perroquet. ‖ **Parrot-fish**, n. ZOOL. Perroquet (*m*.) de mer.

parry ['pæri] n. SPORTS. Parade *f*.
— v. tr. Parer, détourner (a blow). ‖ FIG. Tourner (a difficulty); éluder (a question).

parse [pɑːz] v. tr. GRAMM. Faire l'analyse grammaticale de.

parsec ['pɑːsek] n. ASTRON. Parsec *m*.

Parsee [pɑːˈsiː] adj., n. Parsi *s*.

parsimonious [ˌpɑːsiˈmounjəs] adj. Parcimonieux, lésineur; regardant (stingy).

parsimoniously [-li] adv. Parcimonieusement, avec parcimonie.

parsimony ['pɑːsiməni] n. Parcimonie *f*.

parsing ['pɑːziŋ] n. GRAMM. Analyse grammaticale *f*.

parsley ['pɑːsli] n. BOT. Persil *m*.

parsnip ['pɑːsnip] n. BOT. Panais *m*.

parson ['pɑːsn̩] n. ECCLES. Curé *m*. (priest); pasteur *m*. (protestant). ‖ FAM. *Parson's nose*, croupion; sot-l'y-laisse.

parsonage [-idʒ] n. ECCLES. Presbytère *m*.; cure *f*.

part [pɑːt] n. Partie, part *f*.; *for my part*, pour ma part, quant à moi; *for the most part*, pour la plupart, pour la plus grande partie, en général, le plus souvent; *in part*, partiellement; *in these parts, in this part of the world*, dans ces parages; *on his part*, de sa part; *to be part and parcel of*, faire partie intégrante de; *to have a part in*, y être pour qqch.; *to have no part in*, n'y être pour rien; *to take part*, prendre part (in, à); *to take sth. in good part*, prendre qqch. en bonne part. ‖ Fascicule, livraison *m*. (of a publication). ‖ Parti *m*. (side); *to take s.o.'s part*, prendre parti pour qqn. ‖ Raie *f*. (in the hair). ‖ Pl. Dons *m. pl.*; *a man of parts*, homme de talent. ‖ TECHN. Pièce *f*.; *spare parts*, pièces de rechange. ‖ GRAMM. Partie *f*.; *parts of speech*, parties du discours; *principal parts*, temps principaux (of a verb). ‖ MUS. Partie *f*.; *orchestral parts*, parties d'orchestre. ‖ GEOGR. Pl. Région *f*.; endroit, lieu *m*.; *in foreign parts*, à l'étranger. ‖ THEATR. Rôle *m*.; *to get right inside a part*, entrer dans la peau d'un personnage; *to take* (or) *play a part*, jouer un rôle. ‖ MED. Pl. Parties *f. pl.* ‖ **Part-exchange**, n. COMM. Reprise *f*.; *that garage wouldn't take my old car in part-exchange*, ce garage n'a pas accepté de reprendre ma vieille voiture. ‖ **Part-owner**, n. Copropriétaire *s*. ‖ **Part-song**, n. MUS. Chant (*m*.) à plusieurs voix. ‖ **Part-time**, adj., adv. A mi-temps; *part-time job*, emploi à mi-temps, mi-temps.
— adv. En partie, partiellement; à moitié.
— v. tr. Séparer, fendre, diviser en deux parties; *to part one's hair*, se faire une raie. ‖ NAUT. Rompre (a cable). ‖ † Partager.
— v. intr. Se séparer, se diviser en deux parties (crowd). ‖ Se quitter, se séparer (two people). ‖ S'éloigner, se séparer (*from*, de). ‖ Se dessaisir, se départir, se défaire (*with*, de); céder; abandonner (sth.). ‖ NAUT. Se rompre, céder (cable).

partake [pɑːˈteik] v. intr. (174). Prendre part, participer (*in*, or, à); *to partake of a meal*, prendre un repas (oneself); partager un repas (with others). ‖ Tenir, avoir qqch. (*of*, de) [to smack of]. ‖ ECCLES. *To partake of the Sacrament*, s'approcher des sacrements.

partaker [-ə*] n. Participant *m*. (*in*, à).

parterre [pɑːˈtɛə*] n. THEATR., AGRIC. Parterre *m*.

parthenogenesis ['pɑːθinoˈdʒenisis] n. Parthénogenèse *f*.

Parthian ['pɑːθiən] adj. GEOGR. De Parthe; *Parthian shot*, la flèche du Parthe.

partial ['pɑːʃəl] adj. Partial (*to, towards*, envers) [biased]; injuste (unjust). ‖ Partiel, en partie (in part). ‖ MATH. Partiel. ‖ FAM. *To be partial to*, avoir un faible pour.

partiality [ˌpɑːʃiˈæliti] n. Partialité *f*.; favoritisme *m*. (bias). ‖ Partialité, prédilection *f*.; penchant *m*. (*for*, pour) [liking].

partially ['pɑːʃeli] adv. Partialement, avec partialité (with bias). ‖ Partiellement, en partie (in part).

participant [pɑːˈtisipənt] n. Participant *s*.

participate [-peit] v. intr. Prendre part, participer (*in*, à). ‖ Avoir qqch., tenir (*of*, de).

participation [pɑːˌtisiˈpeiʃən] n. Participation *f*.

participator [pɑːˈtisipeitə*] n. Participant *s*.

participial [ˌpɑːtiˈsipiəl] adj. GRAMM. Participial.

participle ['pɑːtisip̩l] n. GRAMM. Participe *m*.

particle ['pɑːtik̩l] n. Paillette *f*. (of metal); parcelle *f*. (of sand). ‖ PHYS. Atome *m*.; molécule *f*. ‖ FIG. Brin, grain *m*. (of common sense). ‖ GRAMM. Particule *f*.

particoloured ['pɑːtiˌkʌləd] adj. Bigarré, panaché.

particular [pɑˈtikjulə*] adj. Personnel, individuel (personal); *particular friend*, ami intime; *particular interests*, intérêts particuliers. ‖ Méticuleux, minutieux, exigeant, difficile (fastidious); *particular about one's food*, difficile pour la nourriture. ‖ Particulier, spécial (special); *for a particular reason*, pour une raison précise; *to take particular care over it*, y mettre un soin particulier.
— n. Détail *m*.; particularité *f*.; *in every particular*, en tout point; *in particular*, en particulier. ‖ Pl. Détails *m. pl.*; *full particulars*, tous les détails (or) renseignements.

particularism [pɑˈtikjulərizm̩] n. Particularisme *m*.

particularist [-ist] n. Particulariste *m*.

particularity [pɑˌtikjuˈlæriti] n. Méticulosité, minutie *f*. (meticulousness); particularité *f*. (speciality).

particularization [pɑˌtikjuləraiˈzeiʃən] n. Particularisation *f*.

particularize [pɑˈtikjuləraiz] v. tr. Particulariser, spécifier, détailler.
— v. intr. Préciser, spécifier.

particularly [-ləli] adv. Particulièrement, spécialement, exceptionnellement (especially). ‖ Individuellement (individually). ‖ Particulièrement, en particulier (in particular).

parting ['pɑːtiŋ] n. Départ *m*. (departure); *parting gift*, cadeau d'adieu. ‖ Séparation *f*. (separation); *parting of the ways*, bifurcation des chemins. ‖ Rupture *f*. (of a cable). ‖ Raie *f*. (in the hair). ‖ FIG. *At the parting of the ways*, au carrefour, à la croisée des chemins.

partisan [ˌpɑːtiˈzæn], ['pɑːtizən] n. Partisan *m*. ‖ FIG. *Partisan spirit*, esprit de parti.

partisan n. MILIT. Pertuisane *f*.

partisanship [-ʃip] n. Esprit de parti *m*.

partition [pɑːˈtiʃən] n. Division *f*.; partage, démembrement *m*. (of a country); morcellement *m*. (of land). ‖ Cloison *f*. (wall).
— v. tr. Diviser; partager, démembrer (a country); morceler (land); cloisonner (a room).

partitive [pɑːˈtitiv] adj., n. GRAMM. Partitif *m*.

partly [pɑːtli] adv. Partiellement, en partie.

partner ['pɑːtnə*] n. Associé, partenaire *s*.; compagnon *m*.; compagne *f*. ‖ COMM. Associé *m*.; *sleeping partner*, bailleur de fonds, commanditaire. ‖ Cavalier, danseur *m*.; danseuse *f*. (dancing-partner). ‖ SPORTS. Partenaire *m*.
— v. tr. S'associer à, être associé à (s.o.).

partnership [-ʃip] n. Association *f*. ‖ COMM. *Part-*

nership firm, société en nom collectif ; *to go into partnership*, s'associer (*with*, avec).

partridge ['pɑːtridʒ] n. Zool. Perdrix *f.*; *rock partridge*, bartavelle ; *young partridge*, perdreau *m.* ‖ Culin. Perdreau *m.*

parturition [,pɑːtjuə'riʃən] n. Med. Parturition *f.*

party ['pɑːti] n. Groupe *m.*; troupe, bande, partie *f.* (group) ; *party line*, ligne de postes groupés. ‖ Parti *m.* (political party) ; *party line*, directives du parti ; *party politics*, politique de parti. ‖ Réunion, réception *f.*; *a tea, dinner party*, un thé, un dîner ; *evening party*, soirée ; *to give a party*, recevoir, donner une réception ; U. S. *party boy*, fêtard, coureur de parties joyeuses. ‖ Milit. Détachement *m.* (of troops). ‖ Jur. Partie *f.* (to a contract) ; *all parties concerned*, tous les intéressés ; *contracting parties*, parties contractantes ; *third party*, un tiers, une tierce personne ; *to become a party to*, signer (a contract). ‖ Pop. Individu *m.*; *old party*, vieux bonhomme, vieille dame. ‖ Loc. *To be (a) party to*, être complice de, y être pour qqch. ‖ **Party-wall**, n. Archit. Mur mitoyen *m.*
— adj. De parti (leader) ; partisan (quarrel). ‖ A postes groupés (line).

parvenu ['pɑːvənjuː] n. Parvenu *s.*

parvis ['pɑːvis] n. Parvis *m.*

Paschal ['pɑːskəl] adj. Pascal.

pasha ['pɑːʃə] n. Pacha *m.*

pasque-flower ['pɑːsk,flauə*] n. Bot. Anémone, passe-fleur *f.*

pasquinade [,pæskwi'neid] n. Pasquinade *f.*

pass [pɑːs] n. Geogr. Col, défilé *m.* ‖ Passe *f.* (of a conjuror). ‖ Laissez-passer *m.* (document). ‖ Situation *f.*; état *m.* (situation). ‖ Naut. Passe *f.* ‖ Sports. Passe *f.* (in fencing, football). ‖ Ch. de f. Titre (*m.*) de circulation. ‖ Theatr. Billet (*m.*) de faveur. ‖ Fig. *To sell the pass*, trahir, vendre la mèche. ‖ **Pass-book**, n. Fin. Carnet (*m.*) de banque ; échéancier *m.* ‖ **Pass-key**, n. Passepartout *m. invar.* ‖ **Pass-mark**, n. Moyenne *f.* (in examination).
— v. intr. Avoir cours, passer (coin). ‖ Passer, disparaître (disappear). ‖ Défiler ; se dérouler (procession). ‖ Avoir cours, être accepté (theory). ‖ Passer, s'écouler (time). ‖ Etre considéré (*for*, comme) ; être tenu (*for*, pour) ; passer (*for*, pour) [to be considered]. ‖ Arriver, se passer, avoir lieu (to happen). ‖ Etre reçu (in examination). ‖ Sports. Passer, renoncer (at cards). ‖ **To pass along**, circuler, passer son chemin. ‖ **To pass away**, disparaître (to disappear) ; trépasser, mourir (to die). ‖ **To pass by**, passer, passer à côté ; se dérouler. ‖ **To pass off**, se passer, se dérouler. ‖ **To pass on**, passer son chemin (to continue) ; mourir (to die). ‖ **To pass out**, Fam. s'évanouir ; tomber dans les pommes (fam.). ‖ **To pass over**, s'éloigner (storm).
— v. tr. Passer, franchir (to cross over). ‖ Passer, faire passer (false money). ‖ Dépasser (to overtake). ‖ Passer, passer devant, passer à côté de (to pass by). ‖ Passer, transmettre, faire passer (to transmit). ‖ Milit. *To pass in review*, passer en revue. ‖ Sports. Passer (a ball) ; dépasser (a runner). ‖ Culin. *To pass through a sieve*, passer. ‖ Jur. *To pass sentence*, prononcer le jugement. ‖ Autom. Doubler (a vehicle). ‖ Fig. Réussir à (an examination) ; prononcer (a judgement) ; émettre (an opinion) ; voter (a resolution) ; dépasser (to surpass) [s.o.] ; passer (the time). ‖ **To pass across**, traverser. ‖ **To pass along**, passer par. ‖ **To pass off**, faire passer. ‖ **To pass on**, faire circuler (news) ; *to pass a document on to*, faire passer un document à. ‖ **To pass over**, franchir, traverser. ‖ **To pass round**, faire circuler. ‖ **To pass through**, traverser ; Jur. Passer en douane.

passable ['pɑːsəbl̩] adj. Passable, assez bon (good enough). ‖ Traversable (river) ; praticable (road).

passably [-əbli] adv. Passablement.

passage ['pæsidʒ] n. Passage *m.*; action (*f.*) de passer (action). ‖ Couloir, corridor *m.* (in house). ‖ Passage *m.*; ruelle *f.* (alley). ‖ Passage *m.* (of a book) ; *selected passages*, morceaux choisis. ‖ Couloir, corridor *m.* ‖ Jur. Adoption *f.* (of a law, of a measure). ‖ Naut. Traversée *f.* ‖ Fig. Passage *m.*; transition *f.* ‖ Fig. *Passage of arms*, passe d'armes, échange d'arguments. ‖ **Passage-way**, n. Passage *m.*; ruelle *f.*

passenger [-indʒə*] n. Naut., Aviat. Voyageur ; passager *s.* ‖ Ch. de F. *Passenger train*, train de voyageurs ; *by passenger train*, en grande vitesse. ‖ Autom. Passager *s.*; *passenger seat*, siège des passagers. ‖ Fig. Non-valeur *f.*, poids mort *m.*

passer ['pɑːsə*], **passer-by** [-'bai] (pl. **passers-by**) n. Passant *s.*

passim ['pæsim] adv. Passim.

passing ['pɑːsiŋ] adj. Ephémère, passager (ephemeral) ; fait en passant, fortuit (fortuitous) ; *passing events*, actualités. ‖ **Passing-bell**, n. Glas *m.* ‖ **Passing-grade**, n. U. S. Moyenne *f.* (mark).
— n. Passage *m.* ‖ Autom. Doublement *m.* ‖ Fig. Mort *f.*; trépas *m.* (death) ; écoulement *m.*, fuite *f.* (of time).
— adj. Extrêmement ; *passing fair*, très beau, de toute beauté.

passion ['pæʃən] n. Colère, fureur *f.*; courroux, emportement *m.* (anger) ; *fit of passion*, accès de colère ; *to fly into a passion*, s'emporter. ‖ Passion *f.*; amour *m.* (love) ; *to conceive a passion for*, s'éprendre de. ‖ Passion *f.*; goût *m.* (taste) ; *ruling passion*, passion dominante ; *to have a passion for*, avoir la passion de. ‖ Eccles. Passion *f.*; *Passion week*, semaine sainte. ‖ **Passion-flower**, n. Bot. Passiflore *f.* ‖ **Passion-play**, n. Theatr. Mystère (*m.*) de la Passion.

passionate [-it] adj. Emporté, irascible (person, temper). ‖ Ardent, passionné, véhément (person, speech).

passionately [-itli] adv. Passionnément.

passive ['pæsiv] adj. Passif, soumis, inactif ; *passive resistance*, résistance passive. ‖ Gramm. Passif (voice).
— n. Gramm. Passif *m.*

passively [-li] adv. Passivement. ‖ Gramm. Au passif.

passiveness [-nis], **passivity** [pæ'siviti] n. Passivité, inertie *f.*

Passover ['pɑːs,ouvə*] n. Eccles. Pâque *f.* (Jewish).

passport ['pɑːspɔːt] n. Passeport *m.*

password [-wəːd] n. Mot (*m.*) de passe.

past [pɑːst] adj. Passé ; *for some time past*, depuis quelque temps ; *the past week*, la semaine dernière. ‖ Sortant, ancien (chairman). ‖ Gramm. Passé ; *in the past tense*, au passé ; *past participle*, *tense*, participe, temps passé.
— n. Passé *m.*; *as in the past*, comme par le passé ; *in the past*, autrefois, au temps passé ; *to relieve the past*, faire revivre le passé. ‖ **Past-master**, n. Maître passé *m.* (of a guild) ; ancien maître *m.* (of a freemasons' lodge). ‖ Fam. *To be a past-master*, être passé maître (*at*, *in*, en, dans).
— prep. Au-delà de, plus loin que (beyond) ; *just past that house*, un peu plus loin que cette maison. ‖ Plus de (more than) ; *she is past forty*, elle a plus de quarante ans (or) quarante ans passés ; *it is past ten*, il est plus de dix heures. ‖ Hors de (outside, unaffected by) ; *past endurance*, insupportable ; *you are past praying for*, les prières ne peuvent plus vous sauver.
— adv. Devant, auprès ; *to hasten past*, passer en hâte ; *two hours went past*, deux heures passèrent.

pasta ['pæstə] n. Culin. Pâtes *f. pl.*

paste [peist] n. Culin. Pâte *f.*; *anchovy paste*,

beurre d'anchois. ‖ COMM. Strass *m.* (jewellery). ‖ MED. *Tooth-paste,* pâte dentifrice.
— v. tr. Coller. ‖ **To past up,** afficher.
pasteboard [-bɔ:d] n. Carton *m.*
pastel ['pæstəl] n. ARTS. Pastel *m.* ‖ ÇOMM. *Pastel shades,* tons pastels.
pastel n. BOT. Pastel *m.*
pastellist [-ist] n. ARTS. Pastelliste *s.*
pastern ['pæstə:n] n. Paturon *m.*
pasteurize ['pæstəraiz] v. tr. Pasteuriser, stériliser.
pasticcio [pæs'titʃou], **pastiche** [-'ti:ʃ] n. ARTS, MUS. Pastiche *m.*
pastil ['pæstil], **pastille** [pæs'ti:l] n. Pastille *f.*
pastime ['pɑ:staim] n. Passe-temps *m. invar.;* divertissement *m.; distraction f.; jeu m.*
pastor ['pɑ:stə*] n. ECCLES. Pasteur *m.*
pastoral [-rəl] adj. Pastoral, champêtre (scenery). ‖ AGRIC. De pâture; *pastoral land,* pâturages. ‖ ECCLES. Pastoral (letter); de pasteur.
— n. ARTS. Bergerie. ‖ MUS. Pastourelle, pastorale *f.* ‖ ECCLES. Lettre pastorale *f.*
pastry ['peistri] n. CULIN. Pâte *f.* (dough); pâtisserie *f.* (cake). ‖ **Pastry-board,** n. CULIN. Planche à pâtisserie *f.* ‖ **Pastry-cook,** n. Pâtissier *m.* ‖ **Pastry-shop,** n. Pâtisserie *f.*
pasturage ['pɑ:stjuridʒ] n. AGRIC. Pâturage *m.* (feeding); pâture *f.* (field).
pasture [-tʃə*] n. AGRIC. Pâture *f.; pré, pâturage m.* ‖ **Pasture-land,** n. Pâturages *m. pl.*
— v. intr. Paître.
— v. tr. Paître, faire paître.
pasty ['pæsti] n. CULIN. Pâté *m.*
pasty adj. Pâteux. ‖ **Pasty-faced,** adj. Au teint de papier mâché.
pat [pæt] n. Petite tape *f.; caresse f.* ‖ Coquille *f.* (of butter).
— v. tr. Taper, tapoter, donner une tape à. ‖ Flatter, caresser (a dog). ‖ FIG. *To pat s.o. on the back,* passer la main dans le dos à qqn ; *to pat oneself on the back,* se féliciter, se congratuler.
— adj. Tout prêt, à propos ; *pat answer,* réponse bien tapée.
— adv. A propos, à point ; *to answer pat,* répondre à pic (or) du tac au tac. ‖ Fermement ; *to stand pat,* ne pas en démordre, y tenir mordicus.
patch [pætʃ] n. Morceau *m.;* pièce *f.* (mend). ‖ Tampon, couvre-œil *m.* (eye-patch). ‖ Tache *f.* (of colour); parcelle *f.* (of land); pan, carré *m.* (of sky); flaque *f.* (of snow, water); carré, plant *m.* (of vegetables). ‖ † Mouche *f.* (on the face). ‖ AUTOM. Rustine, pastille *f.* (on an inner-tube). ‖ FAM. *Not to be a patch on,* ne pas venir à la cheville de ; *to strike a bad patch,* avoir la déveine. ‖ **Patch-test,** n. MED. Test *(m.)* d'allergie.
— v. tr. Rapiécer, raccommoder (clothing). ‖ AUTOM. Réparer, poser une rustine à (an innertube). ‖ **To patch up,** rapetasser (clothing) ; rafistoler (a machine); FIG. Arranger (a quarrel).
patchouli [pæt'ʃu:li] n. Patchouli *m.*
patchwork [-wə:k] n. Patchwork *m.*
— adj. Bigarré (landscape); fait de pièces et de morceaux (quilt).
patchy [-i] adj. Fait de pièces et de morceaux. ‖ FIG. Inégal.
pate [peit] n. FAM. Ciboule, caboche *f.*
pâté ['pætei] n. CULIN. Pâté *m.; pâté de foie gras,* foie gras.
patella [pə'telə] n. MED. Rotule *f.* ‖ BOT. Patella *f.*
patellar [-ə*] adj. MED. Rotulien (reflex).
paten ['pætən] n. ECCLES. Patène *f.*
patent ['peitənt] adj. COMM. Breveté (invention); verni (leather). ‖ MED. *Patent medicine,* spécialité pharmaceutique. ‖ JUR. *Letters patent,* lettres patentes. ‖ FIG. Evident, clair, patent, manifeste.
— n. COMM. Patente *f.,* brevet *(m.)* d'invention ;

infringement of patent, contrefaçon ; *patent office,* bureau des brevets d'invention ; *to take out a patent,* prendre un brevet.
— v. tr. COMM. Faire breveter.
patentee [,peitən'ti:] n. COMM. Détenteur *(m.)* d'un brevet.
patently [-li] adv. Clairement, manifestement.
pater ['peitə*] n. FAM. Papa *m.; the pater,* mon pater (fam.) ; le paternel (pop.).
paterfamilias ['peitəfə'miliəs] n. Père *(m.)* de famille.
paternal [pə'tə:nl] adj. Paternel.
paternalism [-izm] n. Paternalisme *m.*
paternally [-əli] adv. Paternellement.
paternity [-iti] n. Paternité *f.* ‖ FIG. Origine, source, provenance *f.*
paternoster ['pætə'nɔstə*] n. ECCLES. Patenôtre *f.,* pater *m.*
path [pɑ:θ] n. Sentier, chemin *m.* ‖ Allée *f.* (in a garden). ‖ Course *f.* (of a river); *mountain path,* sentier de montagne. ‖ MILIT. Trajectoire *f.* (of bullet). ‖ FIG. Chemin, sentier *m.; voie f.* ‖ **Pathfinder,** n. Pionnier, éclaireur *m.*
pathetic [pə'θetik] adj. Touchant, pitoyable, attendrissant, triste. ‖ Pathétique. ‖ Désespéré (attempt).
pathetically [-əli] adv. Pathétiquement.
pathless ['pɑ:θlis] adj. Sans chemin frayé.
pathogen ['pæθə,dʒen] n. MED. Agent pathogène *m.*
pathogenic [,pæθə'dʒenik] adj. MED. Pathogène (producing disease); pathogénique (pertaining to pathogenesis).
pathologic(al) [,pæθə'lɔdʒik(əl)] adj. MED. Pathologique.
pathologist [pə'θɔlədʒist] n. MED. Pathologiste *m.*
pathology [-dʒi] n. MED. Pathologie *f.*
pathos ['peiθɔs] n. Pathétique *m.*
pathway ['pɑ:θwei] n. Sentier, chemin *m.* ‖ Trottoir *m.* (in street).
patience ['peiʃəns] n. Patience *f.; I have no patience with him,* il m'exaspère ; *out of patience,* à bout de patience ; *to have patience,* prendre patience ; *to possess one's soul in patience,* patienter. ‖ SPORTS. Réussite *f.* (at cards) ; *to play patience,* faire des réussites.
patient ['peiʃənt] adj. Patient, endurant.
— n. MED. Malade, patient *s.*
patiently [-li] adv. Patiemment, avec patience.
patina ['pætinə] n. Patine *f.*
patinated [-eitid] adj. Patiné.
patois ['pætwɑ:] n. GRAMM. Patois *m.*
patrial ['peitriəl] adj. JUR. D'ascendance britannique (et autorisé, de ce fait, à résider en GrandeBretagne).
— n. JUR. Personne *(f.)* d'ascendance britannique.
patriarch ['peitriɑ:k] n. Patriarche *m.*
patriarchal [,peitri'ɑ:kəl] adj. Patriarcal.
patriarchate ['peitriɑ:kit], **patriarchy** [-ki] n. Patriarcat *m.*
patrician [pə'triʃən] adj., n. Patricien *s.*
patricide ['pætrisaid] n. JUR. Patricide *m.* (act); patricide *s.* (person).
patrilineal [,pætri'liniəl] adj. Patrilinéaire.
patrilocal [-'loukl] adj. Patrilocal.
patrimonial [,pætri'mounjəl] adj. Patrimonial.
patrimony ['pætriməni] n. Patrimoine *m.* (See HERITAGE.) ‖ ECCLES. Revenu *(m.)* d'une église.
patriot ['peitriət] n. Patriote *s.*
patriotic [,pætri'ɔtik] adj. Patriotique.
patriotically [-əli] adv. Patriotiquement ; en patriote.
patriotism ['peitriətizm] n. Patriotisme *m.*
patrol [pə'troul] n. MILIT., NAUT. Patrouille *f.; to go on (a) patrol,* faire des patrouilles. ‖ U. S. Secteur *m.* (of a policeman). ‖ **Patrol-boat,** n. Patrouil-

leur *m.* ‖ **Patrol car,** n. U. S. Voiture de police *f.*
‖ **Patrol wagon,** n. U. S. Voiture cellulaire *f.*
— v. intr. Patrouiller.
— v. tr. Parcourir en patrouille.
patrolman [-mən] (pl. **patrolmen**) n. U. S. Agent-
patrouilleur *m.*
patron ['peitrən] n. Protecteur *m.* (of the arts);
patron *m.* (of a charity); habitué *s.* (of the cinema).
‖ COMM. Client *s.* (client). ‖ ECCLES. *Patron saint,*
saint patron.
patronage ['pætrənidʒ] n. Patronage, appui *m.;*
protection *f.; under patronage of,* sous les auspices
de. ‖ COMM. Clientèle *f.* ‖ ECCLES. Droit (*m.*) de
disposer d'un bénéfice.
patroness ['peitrənis] n. Patronne, protectrice *f.*
patronize ['pætrənɑiz] v. tr. Protéger, patronner
(an artist). ‖ Traiter avec condescendance (s.o.). ‖
COMM. Donner sa clientèle à, se fournir chez.
patronizing [-iŋ] adj. Protecteur.
patronizingly [-iŋli] adv. D'un air protecteur.
patronymic [ˌpætrə'nimik] adj. Patronymique.
— n. Patronyme *m.*
patten ['pætn] n. Patin, socque *m.*
patter ['pætə*] n. Bavardage; baratin, boniment
m. (chatter). ‖ THEATR. Parlé *m.*
— v. tr. Bredouiller, marmotter.
— v. intr. Caqueter, bavarder; baratiner (fam.).
patter ['pætə*] n. Petit bruit *m.* (of feet); crépitement *m.* (of hail); fouettement *m.* (of the rain);
grésillement *m.* (of snow).
— v. intr. Trottiner, marteler (footsteps); crépiter
(hail); fouetter (rain); grésiller (snow).
pattern ['pætən] n. Exemple, modèle *m.* (example).
‖ Patron *m.* (in dressmaking). ‖ ARTS. Dessin,
motif *m.* ‖ COMM. Echantillon *m.* ‖ TECHN. Gabarit
m. ‖ PHILOS. Pattern, schème *m.* ‖ U. S. Arrangement *m.;* disposition, tendance *f.* ‖ **Pattern-
book,** n. COMM. Livre d'échantillons *m.* ‖ **Pattern-
bombing,** n. AVIAT. Bombardement (*m.*) en masse.
‖ **Pattern-shop,** n. TECHN. Atelier (*m.*) de modèles.
— v. tr. *To pattern oneself on,* prendre pour
modèle, se modeler sur. ‖ ARTS. Orner de motifs.
patty ['pæti] n. CULIN. Petit pâté *m.*
paucity ['pɔːsiti] n. Rareté, pénurie *f.;* manque
m. (of money); disette *f.* (of news).
paunch ['pɔːnʃ] n. Panse, bedaine *f.;* bedon *m.*
— v. tr. Eventrer, étriper.
pauper ['pɔːpə*] n. Indigent *s.; pauper's grave,*
fosse commune.
pauperism [-rizm] n. Paupérisme *m.*
pauperize [-raiz] v. tr. Réduire à l'indigence.
pause [pɔːz] n. Pause *f.;* arrêt *m.;* hésitation *f.;*
to give pause to, faire hésiter. ‖ MUS. Point
d'orgue *m.*
— v. intr. Hésiter, faire une pause; s'arrêter (*on,*
upon, sur).
pave [peiv] v. tr. Paver. ‖ FIG. *To pave the way,*
préparer le chemin, frayer la voie (*for,* pour);
ouvrir la voie (*for,* à).
pavement [-mənt] n. Pavé, pavage, dallage *m.*
(material); trottoir *m.* (streetwalk). ‖ U. S. Chaussée
f. (roadway). ‖ **Pavement-artist,** n. Bohème (*m.*)
qui fait des tableaux sur le trottoir.
pavilion [pə'viljən] n. Pavillon *m.*
paving ['peiviŋ] n. Pavage, dallage *m.* ‖ **Paving-
stone,** n. Pavé *m.*
paviour [-jə*] n. Paveur *m.*
paw [pɔː] n. Patte *f.* ‖ FAM. *Keep your paws off!,*
bas les pattes!
— v. tr. Donner un coup de patte à; *to paw the
ground,* piaffer (horse). ‖ FAM. Tripoter, peloter.
— v. intr. Piaffer (horse).
pawkiness ['pɔːkinis] n. Ruse, finasserie *f.*
pawky [-i] adj. Rusé, finaud.
pawl [pɔːl] n. Cliquet, linguet *m.*
pawn [pɔːn] n. SPORTS, FIG. Pion *m.*
pawn n. Gage, nantissement *m.; in pawn,* en

gage; chez ma tante (fam.). ‖ **Pawn-ticket,** n.
Reconnaissance *f.*
— v. tr. Mettre en gage; déposer au mont-de-piété.
pawnbroker [-broukə*] n. Prêteur (*m.*) sur gages.
pawnshop [-ʃɔp] n. Officine (*f.*) de prêteur sur
gages. ‖ Mont-de-piété, crédit municipal *m.*
pawpaw ['pɔː,pɔː] n. See PAPAW.
pax [pæks] n. ECCLES. Paix *f.* (tablet); baiser (*m.*)
de paix (kiss).
— interj. FAM. Pouce!
pay [pei] n. Appointements *m. pl.* (of a civil-
servant); salaire *m.* (of an office-worker); paie,
paye *f.* (of a workman); *equal pay,* égalité des
salaires; *holidays with pay,* congés payés; *in the
pay of,* à la solde de. ‖ MILIT. Solde *f.* (officer's);
prêt *m.* (soldier's). ‖ **Pay-bed,** n. MED. Lit (*m.*)
d'hôpital dont le coût n'est pas pris en charge par
la Sécurité sociale. ‖ **Pay-claim,** n. Demande (*f.*)
d'augmentation de salaire, revendication salariale *f.*
‖ **Pay-day,** n. Jour (*m.*) de paie. ‖ **Pay-desk,** n.
Caisse *f.*, comptoir-caisse *m.;* guichet *m.* ‖ **Payload,** n. Charge payante *f.;* AVIAT. Poids utile *m.*
Pay off, n. U. S. FAM. Paie *f.* (act, time); bouquet
m. (climax). ‖ **Pay-packet** (or U. S.) -**envelope,** n.
Enveloppe, paie *f.* ‖ **Pay-phone** (or U. S.) -**station,**
n. Taxiphone *m.*, cabine publique *f.* ‖ **Pay-roll,** n.
Liste (*f.*) des salariés d'une entreprise; *to be on the
pay-roll,* faire partie du personnel. ‖ **Pay-slip,** n.
Feuille de paie *f.*
— v. tr. (105). Payer (s.o., a sum of money); *to pay
s.o. to do sth.,* payer qqn pour faire qqch.; *to
pay s.o. a sum,* payer une somme à qqn. ‖ Régler
(a bill); payer, solder (a debt); acquitter (duty). ‖
MILIT. Solder (troops). ‖ FIN. Donner (a dividend);
rapporter (an interest); *pay as you earn,* retenue
à la source. ‖ FIG. *To pay s.o. a compliment,* faire
un compliment à qqn; *to pay court to,* faire sa
cour à; *to pay homage to,* rendre hommage à; *to
pay s.o. one's respects,* présenter ses respects à qqn;
to pay a visit, faire une (or) rendre visite. ‖ FAM
To pay s.o. in his own coin, rendre à qqn la monnaie de sa pièce; *to pay a visit,* aller au petit coin;
to rob Peter to pay Paul, découvrir saint Paul pour
couvrir saint Pierre. ‖ **To pay away,** NAUT. Laisser
filer (a cable). ‖ **To pay back,** rendre (money);
rembourser (s.o.). ‖ **To pay for,** payer; *to pay
for sth. with one's life,* payer qqch. de sa vie. ‖
To pay in, verser (*to,* à); *to pay a sum into an
account,* verser une somme à un compte. ‖ **To pay
off,** rembourser (a creditor); régler, acquitter (a
debt); MILIT. Licencier (troops); NAUT. Débarquer (a crew); désarmer (a ship); FAM. *To pay
off old scores,* régler de vieux comptes. ‖ **To pay
out,** régler son compte à (s.o.); NAUT. Laisser filer
(a cable). ‖ **To pay up,** solder, régler, acquitter.
— v. intr. Payer, verser de l'argent. ‖ COMM. Rapporter, être avantageux; *it pays,* ça rapporte, ça
paie. ‖ **To pay off,** FAM. Avoir du succès; être
rentable.
payable ['peiəbl] adj. FAM. Payable (*to,* à).
P.A.Y.E. [piːeiwaiˈiː] abbr. *pay-as-you-earn,* prélèvement direct de l'impôt sur le salaire, retenue de
l'impôt à la source.
payee [peiˈiː] n. Bénéficiaire *s.*
payer ['peiə*] n. Payeur, payant *s.*
paying [-iŋ] n. Remboursement (of a creditor);
règlement *m.* (of a debt); paiement, versement *m.*
(of money).
— adj. Payant (person); *paying guest,* pensionnaire, invité payant. ‖ COMM. Rémunérateur (business).
paymaster ['pei,mɑːstə*] n. Payeur, caissier *m.* ‖
NAUT. Commissaire *m.* ‖ MILIT. Trésorier *m.*
payment [ˈpeimənt] n. Paiement, payement *m.;
cash payment,* paiement, payement comptant;
payment in full, liquidation. ‖ FIG. Récompense *f.;*
prix *m.*

payola [pei'oulǝ] n. Arrosage *m.* (bribery); pot-de-vin *m.*, enveloppe *f.* (bribe).
P.C. [pi:'si:] abbr. *police constable*, agent de police, policier.
p. c. Written abbr. for *per cent*, pour cent, p. 100. ‖ Written abbr. for *postcard*, carte postale.
pct. U. S. Written abbr. for *per cent*, pour cent, p. 100.
pea [pi:] n. BOT., CULIN. Pois *m.; green peas*, petits pois; *sweet pea*, pois de senteur. ‖ LOC. *Like two peas in a pod*, comme les deux doigts de la main; *to be as like as two peas*, se ressembler comme deux gouttes d'eau; *to jump about like a pea on a drum*, se démener comme un diable dans un bénitier. ‖ **Pea-jacket**, n. NAUT. Vareuse *f.* ‖ **Pea-pod**, n. Cosse *f.* ‖ **Pea-shooter**, n. Sarbacane *f.* ‖ **Pea-soup**, n. CULIN. Potage Saint-Germain. ‖ **Pea-souper**, n. FAM. Purée *(f.)* de pois (fog).
peace [pi:s] n. Paix *f.; peace with honour*, paix honorable; *to make peace*, faire la paix. ‖ Paix *f.*, ordre public *m.* (public order); *breach of the peace*, attentat à l'ordre public. ‖ Calme *m.*, tranquillité *f.* (tranquillity); *peace of mind*, tranquillité d'âme; *to give s.o. no peace*, ne laisser ni paix ni trêve à qqn; *to hold one's peace*, se taire; *to live in peace*, vivre en paix. ‖ **Peace-loving**, adj. Pacifique. ‖ **Peace-offering**, n. Offrande propitiatoire *f.* ‖ **Peace-pipe**, n. Calumet *(m.)* de paix. ‖ **Peace-treaty**, n. Traité *(m.)* de paix.
peaceable ['pi:sǝbl] adj. Pacifique.
peaceableness [-nis] n. Calme *m.*, tranquillité *f.*
peaceably [-i] adv. Pacifiquement; en paix.
peaceful ['pi:sful] adj. Paisible, tranquille, calme; pacifique.
peacefully [-i] adv. Paisiblement; pacifiquement.
peacefulness [-nis] n. Tranquillité *f.*, calme *m.*
peacemaker ['pi:s,meikǝ*] n. Pacificateur, médiateur, conciliateur *s.*
peach [pi:tʃ] n. BOT. Pêche *f.* (fruit); pêcher *m.* (tree). ‖ **Peach-blossom**, n. Fleur *(f.)* de pêcher.
peach v. intr. FAM. Moucharder; *to peach on*, donner (s.o.).
peacock ['pi:kɔk] n. ZOOL. Paon *m.*
peafowl ['pi:faul] n. ZOOL. Paon *m.; paonne f.*
peahen ['pi:hen] n. ZOOL. Paonne *f.*
peak [pi:k] n. Visière *f.* (of a cap). ‖ Pic *m.;* cime *f.* (of a mountain). ‖ NAUT. Bec *m.* (of an anchor); pic, coqueron *m.* (of a ship). ‖ CH. DE F. *Peak hours*, heures de pointe (or) d'affluence. ‖ ELECTR. Pointe *m.; peak-load*, maximum de charge. ‖ FIG. Comble, summum *m.*
— v. intr. Plafonner.
peaked [-t] adj. A pointe. ‖ A visière (cap). ‖ Tiré, fatigué (face).
peaky [-i] adj. FAM. Hâve; *to look a bit peaky*, avoir les traits tirés, être un peu pâlot.
peal [pi:l] n. Sonnerie *f.;* carillon *m.* (of bells); coup, grondement *m.* (of thunder). ‖ Éclat *m.* (of laughter).
— v. intr. Carillonner, retentir (bells); grondeɪ (thunder). ‖ Éclater (laughter).
— v. tr. Sonner, faire retentir.
peanut ['pi:nʌt] n. BOT. Arachide; cacahouète *f.* ‖ Peanut butter, n. Crème *f.* de cacahouète. ‖ Peanut gallery, n. U. S. THEATR. Poulailler *m.*
pear [pɛǝ*] n. Poire *f.; prickly pear*, figue de Barbarie. ‖ **Pear-shaped**, adj. Piriforme, en forme de poire. ‖ **Pear-tree**, n. BOT. Poirier *m.*
pearl [pǝ:l] n. Perle *f.* ‖ FIG. Perle *f.* (person). ‖ LOC. *To cast pearls before swine*, donner de la confiture aux chiens. ‖ **Pearl-barley**, n. Orge perlé *m.* ‖ **Pearl-diver** (or) **-fisher**, n. Pêcheur *(m.)* de perles. ‖ **Pearl-grey**, adj., n. invar. Gris perle. ‖ **Pearl-oyster**, n. Huître perlière *f.* ‖ **Pearl-shell**, n. Coquille nacrée *f.*
— v. intr. Perler, former des gouttelettes.
pearly [-i] adj. Perlé, nacré.

peasant ['pezǝnt] n. Paysan *m.;* paysanne *f.*
peasantry [-ri] n. Paysannat *m.;* paysannerie *f.*
pease [pi:z] n. Pois *m. pl.* ‖ **Pease-pudding**, CULIN. Purée *(f.)* de pois.
peat [pi:t] n. Tourbe *f.* ‖ **Peat-bog**, n. Tourbière *f.*
peaty ['pi:ti] adj. Tourbeux.
pebble [pebl] n. Caillou *m.* ‖ Galet *m.* (on beach). ‖ **Pebble-dash**, n. Crépi moucheté *m.* ‖ **Pebble-weave**, n. Granité *m.* (material).
pebbly ['pebli] adj. Caillouteux; *pebbly beach*, plage à galets.
pecan [pi'kæn] n. BOT. Caryocar, pekea *m.* (tree); noix pécan *f.* (nut).
peccadillo [,pekǝ'dilou] n. Peccadille, vétille *f.*
peccancy ['pekǝnsi] n. Vice *m.*
peccant [-ǝnt] adj. Coupable.
peccary [-ǝri] n. ZOOL. Pécari *m.*
peck [pek] n. Coup de bec *m.* ‖ FAM. Bécot (kiss). — v. tr. Picoter, becqueter; frapper avec le bec (bird). ‖ FAM. Baisoter, bécoter (kiss). ‖ **To peck at**, picoter; FAM. becqueter; *to have sth. to peck at*, avoir qqch. à se mettre sous la dent. ‖ **To peck out**, crever à coups de bec (the eyes).
peck n. Picotin *m.* (of oats). ‖ FIG. Tas *m.; a peck of troubles*, bien des malheurs.
pecker [-ǝ*] n. FAM. *To keep one's pecker up*, ne pas lâcher pied, tenir bon.
peckish [-iʃ] adj. FAM. Affamé; *to feel peckish*, avoir la dent, se sentir le ventre creux.
Pecksniff ['peksnif] n. Tartufe, cafard *m.*
pectin [pektin] n. CHIM. Pectine *f.*
pectoral ['pektǝrǝl] adj., n. MED. Pectoral *m.*
peculate ['pekjuleit] v. intr. Détourner des fonds.
peculation [,pekju'leiʃǝn] n. Péculat, détournement de fonds *m.*
peculator ['pekjuleitǝ*] n. Concussionnaire, dilapidateur *(m.)* des deniers publics.
peculiar [pi'kju:liǝ*] adj. Particulier, propre (to, à). ‖ Spécial, particulier (special). ‖ Bizarre, étrange, singulier (strange); *he's a bit peculiar*, c'est un excentrique, il a un grain.
peculiarity [pi,kju:li'æriti] n. Particularité, singularité *f.;* trait distinctif *m.; special peculiarities*, signes particuliers; *to have one's little peculiarities*, avoir ses petites manies.
peculiarly [pi'kju:ljǝli] adv. Particulièrement (particularly). ‖ Étrangement (strangely).
pecuniary [pi'kju:njǝri] adj. Pécuniaire; *pecuniary troubles*, ennuis d'argent.
pedagogic(al) [,pedǝ'gɔgik(ǝl)] adj. Pédagogique.
pedagogics [-iks] n. pl. Pédagogie *f.*
pedagogue ['pedǝgɔg] n. Pédagogue *m.*
pedagogy [-gɔdʒi] n. Pédagogie *f.*
pedal ['pedl] n. Pédale *f.* ‖ **Pedal-boat** (or) **-craft**, n. Pédalo *m.* ‖ **Pedal-car**, n. Vélocar *m.* ‖ **Pedal-pusher**, n. U. S. FAM. Corsaire *m.*
— v. intr. Pédaler (cyclist). ‖ MUS. Mettre la pédale.
pedant ['pedǝnt] n. Pédant *s.*
pedantic [pi'dæntik] adj. Pédantesque.
pedantically [-ǝli] adv. Pédantesquement; en pédant, avec pédantisme.
pedantry ['pedǝntri] n. Pédanterie *f.;* pédantisme *m.*
peddle ['pedl] v. intr. Faire le colportage.
— v. tr. Colporter (goods, gossip, ideas); se livrer au trafic de (drugs).
peddler ['pedlǝ*] n. Petit trafiquant *m.* (of drugs). ‖ U. S. See PEDLAR.
peddling ['pedliŋ] n. Colportage *m.*
pederast ['pedǝræst] n. Pédéraste *m.*
pederasty ['pedǝ,ræsti] n. Pédérastie *f.*
pedestal ['pedistl] n. Piédestal; socle *m.* (plinth). ‖ FIG. Piédestal *m.; to put s.o. on a pedestal*, mettre qqn sur un piédestal. ‖ **Pedestal-table**, n. Guéridon *m.*

pedestrian [pə'destriən] n. Piéton *m.* ‖ Pl. FAM. Piétaille *f.*
— adj. Pédestre; à pied. ‖ AUTOM. *Pedestrian crossing*, passage clouté; *pedestrian precinct*, zone piétonne (or) piétonnière. ‖ FIG. Prosaïque (style).
pediatrician [pi:diə'triʃən], **pediatrist** [-trist] n. MED. Pédiatre *m.*
pediatrics [pi:di'ætrics] n. sg. U. S. MED. Pédiatrie *f.*
pedicab ['pedikæb] n. U. S. Vélotaxi *m.*
pedicure ['pedi,kjuə*] n. Pédicurie *f.* (treatment). ‖ Pédicure *s.* (person).
pedigree ['pedigri:] n. Arbre généalogique *m.*; généalogie *f.* ‖ Pedigree *m.* (of a dog); *pedigree dog*, chien de race.
pediment ['pedimənt] n. ARCHIT. Fronton *m.*
pedlar ['pedlə*] n. Colporteur, porteballe *m.*
pedometer [pi'dɔmitə*] n. Podomètre *m.*
peduncle [pe'dʌŋkl] n. BOT. Pédoncule *m.*
pee [pi:] n. FAM. Pipi *m.*; *to go for (or) to have a pee*, aller faire pipi.
— v. intr. FAM. Faire pipi.
peek [pi:k] n. U. S. Coup d'œil *m.* (glimpse). ‖ U. S. *Peek-a-boo!*, coucou!; cache-cache.
— v. intr. Jeter un coup d'œil sur (to peep).
peel [pi:l] n. Pelure *f.* (of apple); zeste *m.* (of lemon); peau, écorce *f.* (of orange).
— v. tr. Peler (an apple); éplucher (a potato); écorcer (a stick). ‖ U. S. *To keep one's eyes peeled*, ouvrir l'œil. ‖ **To peel off**, enlever (the skin); FAM. Se dépouiller de (one's clothes).
— v. intr. Se peler (fruit); s'écailler (paint). ‖ **To peel off**, s'écailler (paint); AVIAT. Se détacher; FAM. Se déshabiller.
peeler ['pi:lə*] n. Eplucheur, couteau éplucheur *m.* (knife). ‖ TECHN. Eplucheuse *f.* (mechanical device).
peeler n. † FAM. Sergent (*m.*) de ville, argousin *m.*
peeling ['pi:liŋ] n. Epluchure *f.* ‖ Décorticage *m.* (of an almond). ‖ Desquamation *f.*; peeling *m.* (of the face).
peep [pi:p] n. Piaulement, pépiement *m.* (of a bird); petit cri aigu *m.* (of a mouse).
— v. intr. Piauler, pépier (bird); pousser de petits cris aigus (mouse).
peep n. Coup d'œil *m.*; regard furtif *m.*; *to have a peep at*, regarder à la dérobée. ‖ LOC. *At peep of day*, au point du jour. ‖ **Peep-hole**, n. Judas *m.*
— v. intr. **To peep at**, regarder à la dérobée.
peeper ['pi:pə*] n. Curieux, indiscret *s.*; voyeur *m.* (Peeping Tom). ‖ Pl. FAM. Mirettes *f. pl.*, quinquets *m. pl.* (eyes).
peer [piə*] n. Pair, égal *m.*; pareil *s.* (equal); *to be tried by one's peers*, être jugé par ses pairs. ‖ Pair *m.* (rank).
— v. intr. **To peer at**, scruter du regard; *to peer into s.o.'s face*, dévisager qqn avec insistance.
peerage [-ridʒ] n. Pairie *f.*
peeress [-ris] n. Pairesse *f.*
peerless ['piəlis] adj. Sans égal, sans pareil; incomparable.
peerlessly [-li] adv. Incomparablement.
peeve [pi:v] n. FAM. Tuile *f.*, barbe *f.*, embêtement *m.* (bother); grogne, rogne *f.* (bad humour).
peeved [-d] adj. Embêté; en rogne.
peevish ['pi:viʃ] adj. Revêche, irritable, hargneux, grincheux. ‖ Maussade.
peevishly [-li] adv. Avec maussaderie (or) humeur.
peevishness [-nis] n. Maussaderie, mauvaise humeur *f.*
peewit ['pi:wit] n. ZOOL. Vanneau *m.*
peg [peg] n. Pince (*f.*) à linge (clothes-peg); patère *f.* (hat-peg); piquet *m.* (tent-peg). ‖ Fausset *m.* (of cask). ‖ Fer *m.* (of a top). ‖ MUS. Cheville *f.* (of a violin). ‖ FAM. Doigt *m.* (of whisky); *to be a square peg in a round hole*, ne pas être taillé pour ça; *to come down a peg*, baisser d'un cran, mettre de l'eau dans son vin; *to take down a peg*, remettre à sa

place, rabattre le caquet à. ‖ **Peg-leg**, n. Jambe (*f.*) de bois. ‖ **Peg-top**, n. Toupie *f.*; *peg-top trousers*, fuseaux.
— v. tr. (1). Cheviller. ‖ FIN. Stabiliser (the exchange). ‖ SPORTS. Marquer (the score). ‖ **To peg down**, fixer avec des piquets. ‖ **To peg out**, piqueter, délimiter (a claim).
— v. intr. **To peg away**, persévérer, travailler ferme; *to peg away at*, piocher. ‖ **To peg out**, SPORTS. Terminer sa partie; FAM. Passer l'arme à gauche, lâcher la rampe, claquer.
Pegasus ['pegəsəs] n. Pégase *m.*
pejorative ['pi:dʒərətiv] adj., n. Péjoratif *m.*
peke [pi:k] n. FAM., ZOOL. Pékinois *m.*
Pekinese [,pi:ki'ni:z] n. ZOOL., GEOGR. Pékinois *m.*
pelage ['pelidʒ] n. Pelage *m.*
pelagic [pe'lædʒik] adj. En pleine (or) haute mer (fishing). ‖ BOT., ZOOL. Pélagique.
pelargonium [,pelə'gouniəm] n. BOT. Pélargonium *m.*
pelf [pelf] n. FAM. Fafiot, pèze *m.* (See OOF.)
pelican ['pelikən] n. ZOOL. Pélican *m.*
pelisse [pe'li:s] n. Pelisse *f.*
pellagra [pə'leigrə] n. MED. Pellagre *f.*
pellet ['pelit] n. Boulette *f.* (of bread, of paper). ‖ Petit plomb, grain de plomb *m.* (of a gun). ‖ MED. Pilule *f.*
pellicle ['pelikl] n. Pellicule *f.*
pellitory ['pelitəri] n. BOT. Pariétaire *f.*; *pellitory of Spain*, pyrèthre *m.*
pell-mell ['pel'mel] adv. Pêle-mêle.
— adj. Confus; en confusion, en désordre.
pellucid [pe'lju:sid] adj. Transparent. ‖ FIG. Clair, lucide (mind); limpide (style).
pellucidity [,pelju:'siditi] n. Transparence *f.* ‖ FIG. Clarté, lucidité *f.*
pelmet ['pelmit] n. Lambrequin *m.*
pelota [pe'loutə] n. SPORTS. Pelote basque *f.*
pelt [pelt] n. Grêle *f.* (of stones); *at full pelt*, à plein gaz, à toute vitesse.
— v. tr. Cribler de; *to pelt with stones*, lancer une grêle (or) une volée de pierres à.
— v. intr. Tomber à verse (rain); *pelting rain*, pluie battante. ‖ **To pelt down**, tomber à seaux.
pelt [pelt] n. Peau *f.* (of an animal).
peltry [-ri] n. Pelleterie *f.*
pelvic [pelvik] adj. MED. Pelvien.
pelvis [-is] n. MED. Bassin *m.*
pen [pen] m. AGRIC. Enclos, parc *m.*
— v. tr. (106). Parquer.
pen [pen] n. Plume *f.*; stylo *m.* (fountain-pen); *ball-point pen*, crayon à bille; *quill pen*, plume d'oie; *to push a pen*, gratter du papier; *to put pen to paper*, mettre la main à la plume. ‖ FIG. Plume *f.*; *to have a ready pen*, avoir la plume facile; *to live by one's pen*, vivre de sa plume. ‖ **Pen-and-ink**, adj. A la plume. ‖ **Pen-friend**, n. Correspondant *s.* ‖ **Pen-name**, n. Pseudonyme littéraire *m.* ‖ **Pen-nib**, n. Bec (*m.*) de plume. ‖ **Pen-pusher**, n. FAM. Scribouillard, gratte-papier, plumitif, écrivaillon *m.* ‖ **Pen-tray**, n. Plumier *m.*
— v. tr. (1). Ecrire, rédiger.
pen n. ZOOL. Cygne femelle *f.*
pen n. U. S. POP. Taule *f.* (penitentiary).
penal ['pi:nl] adj. JUR. Pénal (code); pénitentiaire (colony); punissable, sanctionnable (offence); *penal servitude for life*, travaux forcés à perpétuité.
penalize [-əlaiz] v. tr. JUR. Infliger une pénalité à. ‖ SPORTS. Pénaliser (a player).
penally [-əli] adv. Pénalement.
penalty ['penlti] n. JUR. Peine, pénalité *f.*; *under penalty of death*, sous peine de mort. ‖ SPORTS. Pénalité *f.* (in rugby); penalty *m.* (in football); *penalty area*, surface de réparation. ‖ FIG. Rançon *f.*; conséquences *f. pl.*; *penalty of fame*, rançon de la gloire; *to pay the penalty*, supporter les conséquences (*of*, de).

penance [-əns] n. Pénitence f. (for, de, pour).
penates [pe'neiti:z] n. pl. Pénates m. pl.
pence [pens] n. pl. See PENNY.
penchant ['pentʃənt] n. Penchant m. (for, pour).
pencil ['pensl̩] n. Crayon m.; in pencil, au crayon; indelible pencil, crayon à encre indélébile; pencil drawing, dessin au crayon; propelling pencil, porte-mine. ‖ Eyebrow pencil, crayon pour les sourcils. ‖ PHYS. Faisceau m. (of light-rays). ‖ **Pencil-box**, n. Plumier m. ‖ **Pencil-cap**, n. Protège-pointe m. ‖ **Pencil-case**, n. Porte-mine; porte-crayon m. invar. ‖ **Pencil-mark**, n. Trait au crayon m. ‖ **Pencil-sharpener**, n. Taille-crayon m. invar.
— v. tr. (1). Crayonner (a note); marquer au crayon (sth.). ‖ To pencil one's eyebrows, se faire les sourcils au crayon.
pendant ['pendənt] n. Pendeloque f. (of a chandelier); pendentif m. (of a necklace); anneau m. (of a watch). ‖ ARCHIT. Cul-de-lampe m. ‖ NAUT. Flamme f.; guidon m. ‖ ARTS. Pendant m. (of a picture).
pendent adj. Suspendu, pendant, surplombant, retombant. ‖ JUR. Pendant, en suspens, non jugé.
pendentive [pen'dentiv] n. ARCHIT. Pendentif m.
pending ['pendiŋ] adj. Pendant; still pending, encore en suspens.
— prep. En attendant; pendant, durant.
pendulous [-juləs] adj. Pendant (lip); suspendu (nest). ‖ Balançant, oscillant (movement).
pendulum [-juləm] n. Pendule, balancier m. ‖ FIG. Swing of the pendulum, mouvement de balancier.
penetrability [ˌpenitrə'biliti] f. Pénétrabilité f.
penetrable ['penitrəbl̩] adj. Pénétrable.
penetrate [-eit] v. tr. Pénétrer, traverser, passer à travers. ‖ FIG. Percer (the shadows); découvrir (a thought).
— v. intr. Pénétrer (into, dans; through, à travers).
penetrating [-eitiŋ] adj. Pénétrant.
penetration [ˌpeni'treiʃən] n. Pénétration f.
penetrative ['penitreitiv] adj. Pénétrant.
penguin ['peŋgwin] n. ZOOL. Manchot; pingouin m.
penholder ['penhouldə*] n. Porte-plume m. invar.
penicillin [ˌpeni'silin] n. MED. Pénicilline f.
peninsula [pi'ninsjulə] n. GEOGR. Péninsule, presqu'île f.
peninsular [-ə*] adj. GEOGR. Péninsulaire. ‖ MILIT. D'Espagne (war).
penis ['pi:nis] n. Pénis m.
penitence ['penitəns] n. Pénitence f.; repentir m.
penitent [-tənt] adj. Pénitent, repentant.
— n. Pénitent s.
penitential [ˌpeni'tenʃəl] adj. ECCLES. De pénitence (psalms).
— n. ECCLES. Pénitentiel m.
penitentiary [-ʃəri] n. Maison (f.) de correction. ‖ ECCLES. Pénitencerie; penitentiary priest, pénitencier. ‖ U. S. Pénitencier m.
— adj. ECCLES. Pénitentiaire. ‖ U. S. JUR. Entraînant la réclusion.
penitently ['penitəntli] adv. Avec repentir, d'un air contrit.
penknife ['pennaif] n. Canif m.
penmanship ['penmənʃip] n. Ecriture, calligraphie f.
pennant [-ənt], **pennon** [-ən] n. Pennon m.; banderole f. ‖ NAUT. Flamme f.
penniless [-ilis] adj. Dénué de ressources; sans le sou; misérable, indigent.
penn'orth [-əθ]. See PENNYWORTH.
penny [peni] (pl. **pence** [pens], **pennies** ['peniz]) n. Penny m.; pièce (f.) de deux sous. ‖ FAM. To spend a penny, se retirer un instant, aller au petit coin. ‖ LOC. A penny for your thoughts, à quoi pensez-vous?; in penny numbers, au numéro; par

pièces détachées; not to be a penny the wiser, n'en être pas plus avancé, n'en savoir pas plus long qu'avant; not to have a penny to bless oneself with, n'avoir pas un radis; penny dreadful, roman à treize sous; to cost a pretty penny, coûter un joli denier; to earn an honest penny, gagner honnêtement son argent; to look twice at every penny, prendre garde à un sou; to make a pretty penny out of it, en tirer un joli bénéfice; to turn up like a bad penny, vous revenir comme une pièce fausse. ‖ **Penny-a-liner**, n. Journaliste (m.) à deux sous la ligne; échotier m. ‖ **Penny-in-the-slot machine**, n. Distributeur automatique m. ‖ **Penny-piece**, n. Pièce (f.) de deux sous; not to have a penny-piece, n'avoir pas un rond. ‖ **Penny-whistle**, n. Flûtiau à bon marché m. ‖ **Penny-wise**, adj. Qui regarde à un sou; to be penny-wise and pound-foolish, économiser un franc et en jeter mille.
pennyweight [-'weit] n. 1,55 gramme (approx.).
pennyworth [-wə:θ] n. To buy a pennyworth of, acheter pour deux sous de.
penology [pi:'nɔlədʒi] n. JUR. Pénologie f.
pension ['penʃən] n. Pension, retraite f.; old age pension scheme, fonds vieillesse; retiring (or) retirement pension, pension de retraite; to apply to be retired on (a) pension, demander sa mise à la retraite. ‖ Pension f. (board and lodging).
— v. tr. Pensionner. ‖ **To pension off**, mettre à la retraite.
pensionable [-əbl̩] adj. Donnant droit à une retraite.
pensional [-əl] adj. De pension; pensional deductions, retenues pour la retraite.
pensionary [-əri] n. Pensionné s.
pensioner [-ə*] n. Retraité, pensionné s. ‖ Invalide m. (in institution).
pensive ['pensiv] adj. Pensif, songeur.
pensively [-li] adv. Pensivement; d'un air pensif.
pensiveness [-nis] n. Rêverie, songerie f.
pent [pent] adj. **Pent in, up**, enfermé; parqué. ‖ FIG. **Pent up**, refoulé (emotions).
pentacle [-əkl] n. Pentacle m.
pentagon [-əgən] n. MATH., U. S. ARCHIT. Pentagone m.
pentahedron [pentə'hi:drən] n. MATH. Pentaèdre m.
pentameter [pen'tæmitə*] n. Pentamètre m.
pentane [pentein] n. CHIM. Pentane m.
Pentateuch ['pentətju:k] n. ECCLES. Pentateuque m.
pentathlon [pen'tæθlən] n. SPORTS. Pentathlon m.
pentavalent [ˌpentə'veilənt] adj. CHIM. Pentavalent, quintivalent.
Pentecost ['pentikɔst] n. ECCLES. Pentecôte f.
penthouse ['penthaus] n. ARCHIT. Appentis, hangar m. (building). ‖ Auvent, abri extérieur m. (over a door). ‖ Appartement (m.) sur toit (on roof).
pentode ['pentoud] n. ELECTR., RADIO. Pent(h)ode f.
pentothal ['pentəθəl] n. MED. Pentothal m.
penult [pe'nʌlt], **penultimate** [-imit] adj. Pénultième, avant-dernier.
— n. Pénultième f.
penumbra [pe'nʌmbrə] n. Pénombre f.
penurious [pi'njuəriəs] adj. Parcimonieux, ladre (parcimonious). ‖ Pauvre (poor). ‖ Mesquin, sordide (shabby).
penuriously [-li] adv. Parcimonieusement. ‖ Pauvrement. ‖ Mesquinement, sordidement.
penury ['penjuəri] n. Manque m.; pénurie f. (of, de) [lack]. ‖ Misère, pauvreté, indigence f. (poverty).
peony ['piəni] n. BOT. Pivoine f.
people ['pi:pl̩] n. Gens m. pl.; on (in general); what will people say?, qu'en dira-t-on? ‖ Sujets m. pl. (of a king); ressortissants m. pl. (of a coun-

try). ‖ Gens *m. pl.; personnes f. pl.; monde m.* (persons); *honest people,* d'honnêtes gens; *how many people?,* combien de personnes?; *many people,* beaucoup, beaucoup de monde. ‖ Populace *f.; public,* peuple *m.* (populace); *man of the people,* homme du peuple; *the common people,* le peuple; le populo (pej.). ‖ Parents *m. pl.; famille f.* (relations); *to write to one's people,* écrire chez soi (or) aux siens. ‖ Peuple *m.; nation f.* (nation).
— N. B. *People* est invariable au sens collectif; il prend le pluriel *peoples* au sens de « nation ».
— v. tr. Peupler.

pep [pep] n. FAM. Allant *m.; vitalité f.*
— v. tr. *To pep up,* animer (a discussion); corser (a play); ragaillardir (s.o.).

pepper ['pepə*] n. Poivre *m.; Cayenne pepper,* poivre de Cayenne. ‖ FAM. Vinaigre *m.* (in skipping). ‖ **Pepper-and-salt,** adj. Marengo (cloth); poivre et sel (hair). ‖ **Pepper-mill,** n. Moulin à poivre *m.* ‖ **Pepper-pot,** U. S. **Pepper shaker,** n. Poivrière *f.*
— v. tr. Poivrer, saupoudrer. ‖ MILIT. Canarder. ‖ FIG. Cribler (*with,* de).

peppercorn ['pepəkɔ:n] n. Grain de poivre *m.* ‖ JUR. *Peppercorn rent,* loyer nominal.

peppermint [-mint] n. Menthe poivrée *f.* ‖ **Peppermint-drop,** n. Pastille de menthe *f.*

peppery [-ri] adj. Poivré. ‖ FIG. Emporté, irascible.

pepsin ['pepsin] n. CHIM., MED. Pepsine *f.*

peptic [-tik] adj. MED. Digestif.

peptide [-taid] n. CHIM. Peptide *m.*

peptone [-toun] n. CHIM., MED. Peptone *f.*

per [pə:*] prep. Par; *per hour,* à l'heure; de l'heure; *per annum,* par an; *per cent,* pour cent : *per pound,* la livre. ‖ COMM. *As per invoice,* suivant facture.

peradventure [,pərəd'ventʃə*] adv. † Par hasard; peut-être.
— n. *Beyond a peradventure,* sans aucun doute, à n'en pas douter.

perambulate [pə'ræmbjuleit] v. tr. Parcourir.

perambulation [pə,ræmbju'leiʃən] n. Parcours *m.*

perambulator [pə'ræmbjuleitə*] n. Voiture (*f.*) d'enfant.

perceivable [pə'si:vəbl] adj. Perceptible.

perceive [pə'si:v] v. tr. Percevoir (to hear, to see). ‖ S'apercevoir de, remarquer (*that,* que) [to notice]. ‖ Comprendre, percevoir, saisir (to understand).

percentage [pə'sentidʒ] n. Pourcentage *m.*

perceptibility [pə,septi'biliti] n. Perceptibilité *f.*

perceptible [pə'septibl] adj. Perceptible; sensible.

perceptibly [-tibli] adv. D'une manière perceptible, sensiblement.

perception [-ʃən] n. Perception; sensibilité *f.*

perceptive [-tiv] adj. Perceptif.

perceptivity [,pə:sep'tiviti] n. Faculté (*f.*) de percevoir.

perch [pə:tʃ] n. ZOOL. Perche *f.*

perch n. Perchoir *m.* (for bird). ‖ Perche *f.* (measure).
— v. intr. Percher, se percher, se poser, jucher (*on,* sur).

perchance [pə'tʃɑ:ns] adv. † Peut-être; par hasard, d'aventure.

percipient [pə:'ʃipiənt] adj. Percepteur *m.; perceptrice f.; conscient.*
— n. Sujet télépathique *m.*

percolate ['pə:kəleit] v. tr., intr. Passer, filtrer.

percolation [,pə:kə'leiʃən] n. Filtrage *m.*

percolator ['pə:kəleitə*] n. Filtre; percolateur *m.*

percuss [pə:'kʌs] v. tr. Percuter.

percussion [-'kʌʃən] n. Percussion *f.; choc m.; percussion cap,* capsule de fulminate. ‖ MED. Percussion *f.* ‖ MUS. Percussion; batterie *f.*

percussive [-'kʌsiv] adj. Percutant.

perdition [-'diʃən] n. Perdition, perte, ruine *f.* ‖ ECCLES. Perdition, damnation *f.*

peregrinate ['perigrineit] v. intr. Pérégriner.

peregrination [,perigri'neiʃən] n. Pérégrination *f.*

peregrine ['perigrin] n. ZOOL. Pèlerin *m.* (falcon).

peremptorily [pə'rəmptərili] adv. Péremptoirement, impérieusement; d'un ton décisif.

peremptoriness [-tərinis] n. Caractère décisif *m.*

peremptory [-təri] adj. Péremptoire, tranchant; décisif; absolu.

perennial [pə'renjəl] adj. Durable, perpétuel. ‖ BOT. Vivace (plant). ‖ FIG. Eternel.
— n. BOT. Plante vivace *f.*

perfect ['pə:fikt] adj. Complet, achevé, parfait, fini (complete). ‖ Parfait, sans défaut, impeccable (faultless). ‖ U. S. Absolu; *perfect loss,* perte sèche. ‖ GRAMM. Parfait; *perfect tense,* parfait, passé composé. ‖ FIG. Parfait, véritable; *to be a perfect stranger,* être absolument inconnu.
— n. GRAMM. Parfait *m.; in the perfect,* au parfait.
— [pə'fekt] v. tr. Parfaire, achever, compléter, finir, perfectionner, rendre parfait.

perfectibility [pə,fekti'biliti] n. Perfectibilité *f.*

perfectible [pə'fektibl] adj. Perfectible.

perfection [-ʃən] n. Achèvement, accomplissement *m.* (completion). ‖ Perfection *f.* (faultlessness); *to perfection,* à souhait; *to fall short of perfection,* ne pas réaliser la perfection.

perfectionism [-ʃə,nizm] n. Perfectionnisme *m.*

perfectionist [pə'fekʃənist] n. Perfectionniste *s.*

perfective [pə'fektiv] n., adj. GRAMM. Perfectif, accompli *m., adj.*

perfectly ['pə:fiktli] adv. Parfaitement.

perfectness [-nis] n. Perfection, excellence *f.*

perfervid [pə:'fə:vid] adj. Ardent, exalté.

perfervidly [-li] adv. Avec exaltation.

perfidious [pə:'fidiəs] adj. Perfide; traître *m.; traîtresse f.*

perfidiously [-li] adv. Perfidement, traîtreusement.

perfidiousness [-nis] n. Perfidie *f.*

perfidy ['pə:fidi] n. Perfidie *f.*

perforate ['pə:fɔreit] v. tr. Perforer. ‖ Percer (to pierce).
— v. intr. Pénétrer (*into,* dans).

perforated [-id] adj. Perforé.

perforation [,pə:fə'reiʃən] n. Perforation *f.*

perforator ['pə:fəreitə*] n. Perforateur *m.*

perforce [pə'fɔ:s] adv. Forcément.

perform [-'fɔ:m] v. tr. S'acquitter de, remplir (a duty, a function); tenir (a promise); célébrer (a rite); accomplir (a task). ‖ MED. Faire (an operation). ‖ THEATR. Remplir (a part); jouer, représenter (a play). ‖ MUS. Exécuter (music).
— v. intr. THEATR. Jouer; *performing dog,* chien savant.

performable [-əbl] adj. Faisable.

performance [-əns] n. Acte; exploit *m.* (deed). ‖ Célébration *f.* (of a rite); accomplissement *m.* (of a task). ‖ SPORTS. Performance *f.* ‖ TECHN. Marche *f.; fonctionnement m.* (of a machine). ‖ AVIAT. Rendement *m.* (of an aircraft). ‖ THEATR. Séance *f.* (at a cinema); représentation *f.* (of a play); *first performance,* première; *no performance to-night,* ce soir relâche.

performer [-ə*] n. THEATR. Artiste; acteur *m.; actrice f.* ‖ MUS. Exécutant *s.*

perfume ['pə:fju:m] n. Parfum *m.*
— [pə'fju:m] v. tr. Parfumer.

perfumer [pə'fju:mə*] n. Parfumeur *m.*

perfumery [-əri] n. Parfumerie *f.*

perfunctorily [pə'fʌŋktərili] adv. Négligemment, avec négligence; superficiellement; pour la forme; par manière d'acquit.

perfunctoriness [-inis] n. Négligence *f.*

perfunctory [-i] adj. Négligent; superficiel; fait pour la forme.

pergola ['pə:gələ] n. Tonnelle *f.*
perhaps [pə'hæps] adv. Peut-être; *perhaps not*, peut-être que non.
perianth ['periænθ] n. Bot. Périanthe *m.*
pericarditis [,perikɑ:'daitis] n. Med. Péricardite *f.*
pericardium [-'kɑ:diəm] n. Med. Péricarde *m.*
pericarp ['perikɑ:p] n. Bot. Péricarpe *m.*
perigee ['peridʒi:] n. Astron. Périgée *m.*
perihelion [,peri'hi:ljən] n. Astron. Périhélie *m.*
peril ['peril] n. Péril, danger *m.; at your peril*, à vos risques et périls; *in peril of*, en danger de.
perilous [-əs] adj. Périlleux. (See dangerous.)
perilously [-əsli] adv. Périlleusement, dangereusement.
perimeter [pə'rimitə*] n. Math., Milit. Périmètre *m.*
perineum [,peri'ni:əm] n. Med. Périnée *m.*
period ['piəriəd] n. Période, époque *f.;* espace de temps *m.;* durée *f.; bright period*, éclaircie. ‖ Epoque *f.; period furniture*, meubles de style (or) d'époque. ‖ Astron. Période *f.; cycle m.* ‖ Gramm. Phrase, période *f.* (phrase); *well-rounded period*, phrase bien tournée. ‖ Gramm. Pause *f.;* point *m.* (punctuation). ‖ Med. Phase *f.;* stade *m.* (of a disease). ‖ Med. Pl. Règles, époques *f. pl.* ‖ Math. Période *f.* ‖ U. S. Cours *m.* (at school).
periodic [,piəri'ɔdik] adj. Périodique (event). ‖ Ample, bien balancé (style). ‖ Chim. *Periodic table*, tableau périodique.
periodical [-əl] adj. Périodique.
— n. Périodique *m.;* publication périodique *f.*
periodically [-əli] adv. Périodiquement.
periodisation [,piəriədai'zeiʃən] n. Périodisation *f.*
periosteum [,peri'ɔstiəm] n. Med. Périoste *m.*
peripatetic [,peripə'tetik] adj. Philos. Péripatétique (doctrine); péripatéticien (school). ‖ Fig. Ambulant.
peripheral [pə'rifərəl] adj. Math. Périphérique, circonférentiel.
periphery [-əri] n. Math. Périphérie *f.*
periphrasis [pə'rifrəsis] (pl. **periphrases** [-i:z]) n. Gramm. Périphrase, circonlocution *f.*
periphrastic [,peri'fræstik] adj. Gramm. Périphrastique.
periscope ['periskoup] n. Objectif périscopique *m.* (photography). ‖ Naut. Périscope *m.*
perish ['periʃ] v. intr. Périr, mourir (person). ‖ Se détériorer (substance). ‖ Fam. *To perish with cold*, mourir de froid.
— v. tr. Détériorer, faire périr.
perishable [-əbl] adj. Périssable. ‖ Ephémère; de courte durée. ‖ Comm. *Perishable goods*, denrées périssables.
— n. pl. Comm. Denrées périssables *f. pl.*
peristaltic [,peri'stæltik] adj. Med. Péristaltique.
peristyle ['peristail] n. Archit. Péristyle *m.*
peritoneum [,peritə'ni:əm] n. Med. Péritoine *m.*
peritonitis [-'naitis] n. Med. Péritonite *f.*
periwig ['periwig] n. Perruque *f.*
periwinkle [-winkl] n. Bot. Pervenche *f.*
periwinkle n. Zool. Bigorneau *m.*
perjure ['pə:dʒə*] v. tr. *To perjure oneself*, se parjurer.
perjurer [-ʒərə*] n. Parjure *s.*
perjury [-ʒəri] n. Parjure *m.* ‖ Jur. Faux serment *m.; to commit perjury*, faire un faux serment.
perk [pə:k] v. intr. **To perk up**, se ranimer, redresser la tête, se requinquer (fam.).
— v. tr. **To perk up**, Fam. Requinquer.
perk n. Fam. See perquisite.
perkily [-ili] adv. D'un air éveillé (or) dégagé (or) effronté.
perky [-i] adj. Eveillé; dégagé; effronté (air).
perm [pə:m] n. Fam. Permanente, indéfrisable *f.*
— v. tr. Fam. Onduler; *to have one's hair permed*, se faire faire une permanente.

perm n. Fam. Permutation *f.*
permafrost ['pə:mə,frɔst] n. Geogr. Permafrost *m.*
permanence ['pə:mənəns] n. Permanence, stabilité; durée *f.*
permanency [-ənsi] n. Permanence, stabilité *f.* ‖ Poste fixe, emploi permanent *m.* (job, post).
permanent [-ənt] adj. Permanent; *permanent address*, résidence (or) adresse fixe; *permanent post*, poste fixe, emploi inamovible; *permanent wave*, permanente, indéfrisable. ‖ Ch. de f. *Permanent way*, voie ferrée.
— n. Fam. Permanente *f.*
permanently [-əntli] adv. De manière permanente.
permanganate [pə'mæŋgənit] n. Chim. Permanganate *m.*
permeability [,pə:miə'biliti] n. Perméabilité *f.*
permeable ['pə:miəbl] adj. Perméable.
permeate [-ieit] v. tr. Pénétrer, saturer, filtrer à travers.
— v. intr. Pénétrer, se répandre, s'infiltrer, s'insinuer (*through*, à travers).
permeation [,pə:mi'eiʃən] n. Pénétration *f.*
permissible [pə'misibl] adj. Permis, tolérable.
permission [-ʃən] n. Permission *f.*
permissive [-siv] adj. Permissif (tolerant). ‖ Facultatif (optional).
permissiveness [pə'misivnis] n. Permissivité *f.*
permit ['pə:mit] n. Permis *m.;* autorisation *f.; to take out a permit*, se faire délivrer un permis. ‖ Jur., Comm. Passe-avant, congé *m.; export* (or) *import permit*, permis de sortie (or) d'entrée.
— [pə'mit] v. tr. (1). Permettre (*to*, de); autoriser (*to*, à); *to permit s.o. to do sth.*, permettre à qqn de faire qqch.
— v. intr. Permettre, admettre.
permutable [pə'mju:təbl] adj. Permutable.
permutation [,pə:mju'teiʃən] n. Permutation *f.*
permute [pə'mju:t] v. tr. Math. Permuter.
pernicious [pə:'niʃəs] adj. Med., Fig. Pernicieux.
perniciously [-li] adv. Pernicieusement.
pernickety [pə'nikiti] adj. Méticuleux, pointilleux. ‖ Difficile, délicat. ‖ Délicat, minutieux (work).
perorate ['perəreit] v. intr. Pérorer.
peroration [,perə'reiʃən] n. Péroraison *f.*
peroxide [pə'rɔksaid] n. Chim. Peroxyde *m.; hydrogen peroxide*, eau oxygénée. ‖ Fam. *Peroxide blonde*, décolorée.
peroxided [-id] adj. Oxygéné (hair).
perpendicular [,pə:pen'dikjulə*] adj. Math., Archit. Perpendiculaire (*to*, à). ‖ Archit. Flamboyant (Gothic).
— n. Fil (*m.*) à plomb. ‖ Math. Perpendiculaire *f.; out of perpendicular*, hors d'aplomb; en porte à faux.
perpendicularly [-ləli] adv. Perpendiculairement.
perpetrate ['pə:pitreit] v. tr. Perpétrer, commettre.
perpetration [,pə:pi'treiʃən] n. Perpétration *f.*
perpetrator ['pə:pitreitə*] n. Auteur *m.*
perpetual [pə'petjuəl] adj. Perpétuel.
perpetually [-əli] adv. Perpétuellement; sans cesse.
perpetuate [-eit] v. tr. Perpétuer, éterniser.
perpetuation [pə,petju'eiʃən] n. Perpétuation *f.*
perpetuity [,pə:pi'tjuiti] n. Perpétuité *f.; in, in perpetuity*, à perpétuité. ‖ Fin. Rente perpétuelle *f.*
perplex [pə'pleks] v. tr. Rendre perplexe; plonger dans la perplexité.
perplexed [-st] adj. Perplexe, confus (look); perplexe, embarrassé (person).
perplexedly [-sidli] adv. Avec perplexité, confusément.
perplexity [-siti] n. Perplexité, confusion *f.;* embarras *m.*
perquisite ['pə:kwizit] n. Casuel; revenant-bon *m.* (additional fee). ‖ Pourboire *m.;* gratification *f.*

(tip). ‖ Pl. FAM. Petits profits *m. pl.;* gratte *f.* (pickings).

perron ['perən] n. ARCHIT. Perron *m.*

perry ['peri] n. Poiré *m.*

persecute ['pə:sikju:t] v. tr. Harceler, tourmenter, poursuivre. ‖ Persécuter (heretics, minorities).

persecution [,pə:si'kju:ʃən] n. Persécution *f.*

persecutor ['pə:sikju:tə*] n. Persécuteur *m.;* persécutrice *f.*

perseverance [,p:si'viərəns] n. Persévérance *f.; by sheer perseverance,* à la force du poignet, à force de persévérance.

persevere [-'viə*] v. intr. Persévérer, persister *(with,* dans); persister *(in,* à).

persevering [-riŋ] adj. Persévérant, assidu.

perseveringly [-riŋli] adv. Avec persévérance.

Persia ['pə:ʃə] n. GEOGR. Perse *f.* (See IRAN.)

Persian [-ʃən] adj. Perse (ancient); persan (modern). ‖ De Perse (carpet). ‖ ZOOL. Persan (cat). ‖ GEOGR. Persique (gulf).
— n. Perse *s.* (ancient); Persan *s.* (modern). ‖ GRAMM. Persan *m.*

persiflage ['pə:si,flɑ:ʒ] n. Persiflage *m.*

persimmon [pə:'simən] n. BOT. Plaqueminier, persimmon *m.* (tree); plaquemine *f.,* kaki *m.* (fruit).

persist [pə'sist] v. intr. Persister, s'obstiner *(in,* dans, à).

persistence [-əns], **persistency** [-ensi] n. Persistance, persévérance, obstination; permanence *f.*

persistent [-ənt] adj. Persistant.

persistently [-əntli] adv. Avec persistance:

person ['pə:sņ] n. Personne *f.;* individu *m.; in person,* en personne; *to be delivered to the addressee in person,* à remettre en mains propres. ‖ GRAMM. Personne *f.; in the first person,* à la première personne.

persona [pə:'sounə] (pl. **personae** [-ni:]) n. PSYCH. Persona *f.* ‖ *Persona grata, non grata,* persona grata, non grata.

personable [-əbļ] adj. Beau *m.;* belle *f.;* bien fait.

personage [-idʒ] n. Personnage *m.;* personne *f.* ‖ THEATR. Personnage *m.*

personal [-ļ] adj. Personnel; *personal column,* petite correspondance (in a newspaper); *personal liberty,* liberté individuelle; *to make personal remarks,* faire des personnalités. ‖ JUR. *Personal estate* (or) *property,* biens mobiliers. ‖ GRAMM. Personnel (pronoun).

personality [,pə:sə'næliti] n. Personnalité *f.;* caractère propre *m.* (character); *to lack personality,* manquer de personnalité. ‖ Personne *f.;* personnage *m.* (person). ‖ Pl. Personnalités *f. pl.* (personal remarks).

personalization [,pə:sənəlai'zeiʃən] n. Personnification *f.* (of inanimate objects). ‖ Personnalisation *f.* (of one's possessions).

personalize ['pə:sənə,laiz] v. tr. Personnifier (inanimate objects). ‖ Personnaliser (one's possessions).

personally ['pə:sņəli] adv. En personne; *to do sth. personally,* faire qqch. en personne. ‖ Personnellement; pour ma part; quant à moi; en ce qui me concerne (for my part).

personalty [-əlti] n. JUR. Biens mobiliers *m. pl.*

personate ['pə:səneit] v. tr. Se faire passer pour (s.o.). ‖ THEATR. Jouer; jouer le rôle de.

personation [,pə:sə'neiʃən] n. JUR. Usurpation *(f.)* d'identité.

personification [pə:,sɔnifi'keiʃən] n. Personnification *f.*

personify [pə:'sɔnifai] v. tr. (2). Personnifier.

personnel [pə:sə'nel] n. Personnel *m.; personnel department, manager,* service, chef du personnel. ‖ MILIT. *Personnel carrier,* véhicule de transport de troupes.

perspective [pə'spektiv] n. Perspective, vue *f.* ‖

FIG. Perspective *f.; in its true perspective,* sous son vrai jour,
— adj. Perspectif, en perspective.

Perspex ['pə:speks] n. Perspex *m.*

perspicacious [,pə:spi'keiʃəs] adj. Perspicace.

perspicaciously [-'keiʃəsli] adv. Avec perspicacité (or) pénétration.

perspicacity [-'kæsiti] n. Perspicacité, clairvoyance *f.*

perspicuity [-'kjuiti] n. Clarté, netteté *f.*

perspicuous [pə'spikjuəs] adj. Clair.

perspicuously [-li] adv. Clairement.

perspiration [,pə:spi'reiʃən] n. Transpiration, sueur *f.; dripping with perspiration,* en nage.

perspire [pəs'paiə*] v. intr. Transpirer; suer. (See SWEAT.)

persuade [pə'sweid] v. tr. Persuader, convaincre *(of,* de) [sth.].

persuasion [-ʒən] n. Persuasion *f.* ‖ Conviction, croyance *f.* (conviction). ‖ ECCLES. Croyance religieuse *f.* (belief); secte *f.* (denomination).

persuasive [-ziv] adj. Persuasif.

persuasively ['zivli] adv. D'une façon persuasive.

pert [pə:t] adj. Effronté, hardi, impertinent (bold); mutin (saucy).

pertain [pə:'tein] v. intr. Etre du ressort, être le propre *(to,* de) [to belong]. ‖ Avoir rapport, se rattacher *(to,* à) [to refer].

pertinacious [,pə:ti'neiʃəs] adj. Obstiné, entêté, opiniâtre.

pertinaciously [-li] adv. Obstinément, opiniâtrement; avec entêtement.

pertinaciousness [,pə:ti'neiʃəsnis], **pertinacity** [-'næsiti] n. Obstination *f.;* entêtement *m.;* opiniâtreté *f.*

pertinence ['pərtinəns], **pertinency** [-ənsi] n. Justesse *f.;* à propos *m.*

pertinent [-ənt] adj. Pertinent, juste, approprié; à-propos.

pertinently [-əntli] adv. Pertinemment; avec justesse; avec à-propos.

pertly ['pə:tli] adv. Avec effronterie (or) impertinence. ‖ D'un air mutin.

pertness [-nis] n. Effronterie, impertinence *f.*

perturb [pə'tə:b] v. tr. Agiter, troubler, inquiéter.

perturbation [,pə:tə'beiʃən] n. Perturbation, inquiétude *f.;* trouble *m.*

Peru [pə'ru:] n. GEOGR. Pérou *m.*

peruke [pə'ru:k] n. Perruque *f.*

perusal [pə'ru:zəl] n. Examen *m.* (examination). ‖ Lecture *f.* (reading).

peruse [-'ru:z] v. tr. Examiner (examine). ‖ Lire attentivement (read).

Peruvian [pə'ru:viən] adj., n. Péruvien.

pervade [pə'veid] v. tr. Pénétrer, imprégner. ‖ FIG. Animer; s'emparer de.

pervading [-iŋ] adj. Répandu, pénétrant.

pervasion [pə:'veiʒən] n. Pénétration *f.*

pervasive [-siv] adj. Pénétrant.

perverse [pə:'və:s] adj. Obstiné, entêté, revêche, contrariant (obstinate). ‖ Pervers, perverti, dépravé (perverted).

perversely [-'və:sli] adv. Avec perversité; de manière à contrarier.

perversion [-'və:ʃən] n. Perversion *f.* ‖ Dénaturation *f.* (of facts).

perversity [-'və:siti] n. Perversité *f.;* caractère contrariant *m.*

pervert [pə:'və:t] v. tr. Dépraver, pervertir (s.o.). ‖ Fausser (words). ‖ Dépraver, dénaturer (taste). ‖ ECCLES. Détourner de ses croyances (s.o.).
— ['pə:və:t] n. Perverti, dévoyé *s.* ‖ ECCLES. Apostat *m.* ‖ MED. *Sexual pervert,* inverti.

pervious ['pə:viəs] adj. Perméable.

peseta [pə'seitə] n. Peseta *f.*

pesky ['peski] adj. U. S. FAM. Fichu, sacré (confounded); enquiquinant, rasant, canulant, maudit (annoying).

pessary ['pesəri] n. MED. Pessaire *m.*

pessimism [pesimizm] n. Pessimisme *m.*

pessimist [-ist] n. Pessimiste *s.*

pessimistic [-istik] adj. Pessimiste.

pest [pest] n. Insecte nuisible *m.* ‖ FIG. Fléau *m.*

pester [-ə*] v. tr. Tourmenter, importuner. ‖ FAM. assommer; *he pesters the life out of me,* il me casse les pieds, il me bassine.

pesticide ['pesti‚said] n. CHIM., AGRIC. Pesticide *m.*

pestiferous [pes'tifərəs] adj. Nuisible. ‖ FIG. Pernicieux. ‖ FAM. Assommant.

pestilence ['pestiləns] n. Peste *f.*

pestilent ['pestilənt], **pestilential** [‚pesti'lenʃəl] adj. Pesteux, pestilent (of the plague). ‖ FIG. Catastrophique, calamiteux (destructive); pernicieux, pestilentiel (pernicious).

pestilently [-əntli] adv. D'une façon pernicieuse.

pestle ['pesl] n. Pilon *m.*
— v. tr. Pilonner.

pet [pet] n. Animal favori *m.; pet dog,* chien familier. ‖ Enfant gâté *s.; he's a real pet,* c'est un vrai chou; *my pet,* mon petit loup; *pet aversion,* bête noire; *pet subject,* dada, cheval de bataille; *to make a pet of,* choyer.
— v. tr. (1). Choyer, gâter, chouchouter. ‖ U. S. Caresser; peloter (fam.).

pet n. Accès (*m.*) de mauvaise humeur; *to be in a pet,* être de mauvaise humeur; bouder.

petal ['petl] n. BOT. Pétale *m.*

petard [pe'tɑ:d] n. Pétard *m.* ‖ FIG. *Hoist with one's own petard,* pris à son propre piège.

Peter ['pi:tə*] n. Pierre *m.* ‖ NAUT. *Blue Peter,* pavillon de partance. ‖ ECCLES. *Peter's pence,* denier de Saint-Pierre.

peter v. intr. *To peter out,* s'épuiser (mine); se tarir (stream); FAM. Partir en fumée.

petersham ['pi:təʃəm] n. Manteau (*m.*) de ratine (coat); ratine *f.* (material); gros grain *m.* (ribbon).

petiole ['petioul] n. BOT. Pétiole *m.*

petite [pə'ti:t] adj. De petite stature, menu (woman). ‖ *Petite bourgeoisie,* petite bourgeoisie.

petition [pi'tiʃən] n. Pétition, supplique *f.* ‖ JUR. Requête *f.; petition for divorce,* demande de divorce; *to file a petition,* déposer son bilan.
— v. tr. Adresser (or) présenter une pétition à.

petitioner [-ə*] n. Solliciteur *s.* ‖ JUR. Requérant *s.*

petrel ['petrəl] n. ZOOL. Pétrel *m.; stormy petrel,* oiseau des tempêtes.

petrifaction [‚petri'fækʃən] n. Pétrification *f.*

petrify ['petrifai] v. tr. (2). Pétrifier. ‖ FIG. Pétrifier (*with,* de).
— v. intr. Se pétrifier.

petrochemical [‚petrou'kemikl] adj. Pétrochimique.
— n. Produit pétrochimique *m.*

petrochemistry [-'kemistri] n. Pétrochimie *f.*

petrography [pe'trogrəfi] n. Pétrographie *f.*

petrol ['petrol] n. Essence *f.; high-grade petrol,* supercarburant. ‖ **Petrol-can,** n. Bidon *m.* ‖ **Petrol-lorry,** n. Camion-citerne *m.* ‖ **Petrol pump,** n. Pompe à essence *f.* ‖ **Petrol-voucher,** n. Chèque-essence *m.*

petroleum [pə'trouljəm] n. Pétrole *m.; petroleum jelly,* vaseline *f.*

petrology [pi'trolədʒi] n. Pétrologie *f.*

petrous ['petrəs] adj. Pierreux.

petticoat ['petikout] n. Jupon *m.; Petticoat government,* régime du cotillon. ‖ FAM. Femme *f.* ‖ **Petticoat-chaser,** n. U. S. FAM. Coureur (*m.*) de cotillons.

pettifog ['petifog] v. intr. (1). Avocasser.

pettifogger [-ə*] n. Avocassier *m.*

pettifogging [-iŋ] adj. Chicanier.

pettily ['petili] adv. Petitement.

pettiness [-nis] n. Petitesse, mesquinerie *f.*

petting ['petiŋ] n. FAM. U. S. Bécotage, batifolage; pelotage *m.*

pettish ['petiʃ] adj. Irritable; de mauvaise humeur, maussade, revêche.

pettishly [-li] adv. Avec dépit; avec humeur.

pettishness [-nis] n. Irritabilité *f.;* dépit *m.*

petty ['peti] adj. Petit, insignifiant, sans importance; *petty monarch,* roitelet. ‖ NAUT. *Petty officer,* contremaître, officier marinier. ‖ FIN., COMM. *Petty cash,* petite monnaie; *petty expenses,* menus frais. ‖ JUR. *Petty larceny,* larcin; *petty sessions,* session des juges de paix. ‖ **Petty-minded,** adj. Mesquin.

petulance ['petjuləns] n. Irritabilité *f.*

petulant [-ənt] adj. Irritable.

petunia [pi'tju:njə] n. BOT. Pétunia *m.*

pew [pju:] n. Banc (*m.*) d'église.

pewit ['pi:wit] n. ZOOL. Vanneau *m.*

pewter ['pju:tə*] n. Etain *m.*

pewterer [-ərə*] n. Potier d'étain *m.*

peyote [pei'outi] n. Peyotl *m.*

pH [pi:'eitʃ] n. CHIM. pH *m.*

phaeton ['feitn] n. Phaéton *m.*

phagocyte ['fægosait] n. MED. Phagocyte *m.*

phalanx ['fælæŋks] n. Phalange *f.*

phallic ['fælik] adj. Phallique.

phallus ['fæləs] n. Phallus *m.*
— N. B. Deux pluriels : *phalli, phalluses.*

phantasm ['fæntæzm] n. † Fantôme *m.* ‖ Chimère, illusion *f.* ‖ MED. Phantasme *m.*

phantasmagoria [‚fæntæsmə'gɔ:riə] n. Fantasmagorie *f.*

phantasmagoric [-rik] adj. Fantasmagorique.

phantasmal [fæn'tæzməl], **phantasmic** [-mik] adj. Fantomatique, fantômal.

phantasy ['fæntəsi] n. See FANTASY.

phantom ['fæntəm] n. Fantôme *m.*
— adj. Fantôme, imaginaire. ‖ MED. Fantôme (limb); nerveuse (pregnancy). ‖ ELECTR. Fantôme (circuit).

Pharaoh ['fæərou] n. Pharaon *m.*

Pharisaic [‚færi'seiik] adj. Pharisaïque.

Pharisee ['færisi:] n. Pharisien *m.*

pharmaceutical [‚fɑ:mə'sju:tikəl] adj. Pharmaceutique.

pharmaceutics [-'sju:tiks] n. sg. Pharmaceutique *f.* (pharmacy). ‖ Pl. Produits pharmaceutiques *m. pl.* (remedies).

pharmacist ['fɑ:məsist] n. Pharmacien *s.*

pharmacology [-'kɔlədʒi] n. Pharmacologie *f.*

pharmacopoeia [‚fɑ:məko'pi:ə] n. Pharmacopée *f.;* codex *m.*

pharmacy ['fɑ:məsi] n. Pharmacie *f.*

pharyngeal [fə'rindʒiəl] adj. MED. Pharyngien.

pharyngitis [‚færin'dʒaitis] n. MED. Pharyngite *f.*

pharyngoscope [fə'riŋgə‚skoup] n. MED. Pharyngoscope *m.*

pharynx ['færiŋks] n. MED. Pharynx *m.*

phase [feiz] n. Phase, période *f.* ‖ ELECTR. Phase *f.*
— v. tr. Programmer, réaliser progressivement. ‖ *To phase in, out,* introduire, supprimer progressivement (or) par étapes (or) par paliers.

Ph. D. [pi:eitʃ'di:] abbr. *Doctor of Philosophy,* doctorat (degree); docteur, titulaire d'un doctorat (person).

pheasant ['feznt] n. ZOOL. Faisan *m.; hen pheasant,* faisane; *young pheasant,* faisandeau.

phenobarbital [‚fi:nou'bɑ:bitl], **phenobarbitone** [-‚toun] n. MED. Phénobarbital *m.*

phenol ['fi:nɔl] n. CHIM. Phénol *m.*

phenomenal [fi'nɔminl] adj. Phénoménal. ‖ FIG. Prodigieux, extraordinaire.

phenomenology [fi‚nɔmə'nɔlədʒi] n. Phénoménologie *f.*

phenomenon [fi'nɔminən] n. Phénomène *m.*

phenotype ['fi:nou‚taip] n. Phénotype *m.*

phenyl ['fi:nail] n. CHIM. Phényle m.
pheromone ['ferə,moun] n. ZOOL. Phéromone f.
phew [fju:] interj. Pouah!
phial ['faiəl] n. Fiole f.
philander [fi'lændə*] v. intr. Flirter; faire la cour.
philanderer [-ərə*] n. Flirteur, coureur m.
philanthropic [,filən'θrɔpik] adj. Philanthropique.
philanthropist [fi'lænθrəpist] n. Philanthrope m.
philanthropy [-əpi] n. Philanthropie f.
philatelic [filə'telik] adj. Philatélique.
philatelist [fi'lætəlist] n. Philatéliste s.
philately [-əli] n. Philatélie f.
philharmonic [,filhɑː'mɔnik] adj. MUS. Philharmonique.
Philippines ['fili,pi:nz] n. pl. GEOGR. Philippines f. pl.
Philistine ['filistain] n. Philistin m. ‖ FAM. Béotien m.
philological [filə'lɔdʒikəl] adj. Philologique.
philologist [fi'lɔlədʒist] n. Philologue m.
philology [-dʒi] n. Philologie f.
philosopher [fi'lɔsəfə*] n. Philosophe m.; moral philosopher, moraliste; philosopher's stone, pierre philosophale.
philosophical [,filə'sɔfikəl] adj. Philosophique. ‖ FAM. Philosophe, résigné (resigned).
philosophically [-əli] adv. Philosophiquement.
philosophize [fi'lɔsəfaiz] v. intr. Philosopher.
philosophy [-fi] n. Philosophie f.; moral philosophy, morale.
philtre ['filtə*] n. Philtre m.
phiz [fiz] n. FAM. Binette, bouille, fiole f. (face).
phlebitis [fli'baitis] n. MED. Phlébite f.
phlebotomize [fli'bɔtəmaiz] v. intr. MED. Faire une saignée.
phlebotomy [-əmi] n. MED. Phlébotomie, saignée f.
phlegm [flem] n. MED., FIG. Flegme m.
phlegmatic [fleg'mætik] adj. Flegmatique.
phlegmatically [-əli] adv. Flegmatiquement.
phlox [flɔks] n. BOT. Phlox m.
phobia ['foubiə] n. Phobie f.
Phoebus ['fi:bəs] n. Phébus m.
Phoenicia [fi'niʃiə] n. GEOGR. Phénicie f.
Phoenician [-iən] adj., n. Phénicien s.
phoenix ['fi:niks] n. Phénix m.
phone [foun] n. FAM. Téléphone m.; phone box, cabine téléphonique. ‖ **Phone-in**, n. RADIO. Emission (f.) à laquelle les auditeurs (or) les téléspectateurs participent par des appels téléphoniques.
— v. tr., intr. FAM. Téléphoner.
phoneme ['founi:m] n. GRAMM. Phonème m.
phonemics [fə'ni:miks] n. sg. GRAMM. Phonologie f.
phonetic [fə'netik] adj. Phonétique.
phonetically [-əli] adv. Phonétiquement.
phonetician [foune'tiʃən] n. Phonéticien m.
phonetics [[fə'netiks] n. sg. GRAMM. Phonétique f.
phoney ['founi] adj. FAM. A la noix, à la gomme; phoney war, drôle de guerre; it's phoney, c'est de la blague.
— n. FAM. Charlatan m.
phonic ['founik, fɔnik] adj. Phonique.
phonograph ['founəgrɑːf] n. Phonographe m.
phonology [fə'nɔlədʒi] n. GRAMM. Phonologie f.
phony ['founi] adj., n. U. S. See PHONEY.
phosgene ['fɔsdʒi:n] n. CHIM. Phosgène m.
phosphate [-feit] n. CHIM. Phosphate m.
phosphatic [fɔs'fætik] adj. CHIM. Phosphatique.
phosphide [-faid] n. CHIM. Phosphure m.
phosphor ['fɔsfə*] n. Substance luminescente f.
phosphorescence [,fɔsfə'resn̩s] n. Phosphorescence f.
phosphorescent [-resn̩t] adj. Phosphorescent.
phosphoric ['fɔsfɔrik] adj. CHIM. Phosphorique.
phosphorous ['fɔsfərəs] adj. Phosphoreux.
phosphorus ['fɔsfərəs] n. CHIM. Phosphore m.
phosphuretted [fɔs'fjuretid] adj. Phosphoré.

photo ['foutou] (pl. **photos** [-ouz]) n. FAM. Photo f. ‖ **Photo-finish**, n. SPORTS. Course (f.) dans laquelle le classement est déterminé par la photo-finish; FIG. Compétition serrée f.
— v. tr. FAM. Photographier.
photocell [-sel] n. Cellule photo-électrique f.
photochemistry [,fouto'kemistri] n. Photochimie f.
photocomposition [-,kɔmpə'ziʃən] n. U. S. TECHN. Photocomposition f. (in printing).
photocopier ['fouto,kɔpiə*] n. Photocopieur m., photocopieuse f.
photocopy [-,kɔpi] n. Photocopie f.
— v. tr. (2). Photocopier.
photoelectric [,foutoi'lektrik] adj. Photoélectrique (cell).
photogenic [-'dʒenik] adj. Photogénique.
photograph ['foutəgrɑːf] n. Photographie f.; to take a photograph, faire une photographie.
— v. tr. Photographier; to be photographed, se faire photographier.
— v. intr. To photograph well, être photogénique.
photographer [fə'tɔgrəfə*] n. Photographe m.; street photographer, photo-stoppeur.
photographic [,fouto'græfik] adj. Photographique; photographic library, photothèque.
photography [fə'tɔgrəfi] n. Photographie f.
photogravure [,fouto'greivjuə*] n. Photogravure, héliogravure f.
photolithography [-li'θɔgrəfi] n. Photolitho f.
photomap ['foutomæp] n. Carte photographique aérienne f.
photometer [fə'tɔmitə*] n. Photomètre m.
photometry [-tri] n. Photométrie f.
photomontage [,foutomɔn'tɑːʒ] n. Photomontage m.
photon ['foutɔn] n. PHYS. Photon m.
photophobia [,fouto'foubiə] n. MED. Photophobie f.
photosensitive [-'sensitiv] adj. Photosensible.
photosetting ['fouto,setiŋ] n. TECHN. Photocomposition f. (in printing).
photosphere [-,sfiə*] n. ASTRON. Photosphère f.
photostat [-,stæt] n. Photostat m.; photocopie f.
— v. tr. Photocopier.
photosynthesis [,fouto'sinθisis] n. BOT. Photosynthèse f.
phototype ['fouto,taip] n. TECHN. Phototype m.
phrasal ['freizl̩] adj. GRAMM. Phrasal verb, verbe à postposition.
phrase [freiz] n. Locution, expression f. ‖ MUS. Phrase f. ‖ **Phrase-book**, n. Recueil (m.) d'expressions. ‖ **Phrase-monger**, n. FAM. Phraseur s.
— v. tr. Rédiger (a letter); exprimer (a thought).
phraseology [,freizi'ɔlədʒi] n. Phraséologie f.
phratry ['freitri] n. Phratrie f.
phrenological [,frenə'lɔdʒikəl] adj. Phrénologique.
phrenologist [fri'nɔlədʒist] n. Phrénologue m.
phrenology [-dʒi] n. Phrénologie f.
phthisic ['θaisik] adj. MED. Phtisique.
phthisis ['θaisis] n. MED. Phtisie f.
phut [fʌt] n. Son mat m.
— adv. FAM. To go phut, péter, claquer (machine); tomber à l'eau, aller à vau-l'eau (undertaking), faire fiasco (business).
phylactery [fi'læktəri] n. Phylactère m.
phyletic [fai'letik] adj. BOT., ZOOL. Phylétique.
phylloxera [,filok'siərə] n. Phylloxéra m.
phylum ['failəm] (pl. **phyla** [-lə]) n. BOT., ZOOL. Phylum m.
physic ['fizik] n. MED. Médicament, remède m.; drogue f. (fam.).
physical [-əl] adj. Physique (culture, force). ‖ Matériel (impossibility). ‖ PHYS. Physique (science).
physically [-əli] adv. Physiquement.
physician [fi'ziʃən] n. Médecin m. (See DOCTOR.)

physicist ['fizisist] n. Physicien s.
physics ['fiziks] n. pl. Physique ƒ.
physiognomist [‚fizi'ɔnəmist] n. Physionomiste m.
physiognomy [-'ɔnəmi] n. Physionomie ƒ.
physiological [‚fizio'lɔdʒikəl] adj. Physiologique.
physiologist [‚fizi'ɔlədʒist] n. Physiologiste s.
physiology [-dʒi] n. Physiologie ƒ.
physiotherapist [‚fizio'θerəpist] n. Physiothérapiste m.
physiotherapy [-i] n. Physiothérapie ƒ.
physique [fi'zi:k] n. Structure ƒ. (of a body). ‖ Physique m. (of a person).
phytozoon [‚faitə'zouən] (pl. **phytozoa** [-ə]) n. Zoophyte m.
pi [pai] n. Pi m.
piacular [pi'ækjulə*] adj. Expiatoire.
pia mater ['paiə'meitə] n. MED. Pie-mère m.
pianist ['piənist] n. MUS. Pianiste s.
piano ['pjænou], **pianoforte** [‚pjæno'fɔ:ti] n. MUS. Piano m.; grand, upright piano, piano à queue, droit ; to play (on) the piano, jouer du piano. ‖ **Piano-maker**, n. Facteur (m.) de pianos. ‖ **Piano-stool**, n. Tabouret de piano m. ‖ **Piano-tuner**, n. Accordeur de piano m. ‖ **Piano-wire**, n. Corde (ƒ.) de piano.
— ['pjɑ:nou] adv. MUS. Piano ; doucement.
pianola [piə'noulə] n. MUS. Piano mécanique m.; Pianola m. (nom déposé).
piastre [pi'æstə*] n. Piastre ƒ.
piazza [pi'ætsə] n. Place ƒ. ‖ U. S. Véranda ƒ.
pibroch ['pi:brɔk] n. MUS. Air (m.) de cornemuse.
pica ['paikə] n. Cicéro m. (in typography).
picador ['pikə'dɔ:*] n. Picador m.
picaresque [‚pikə'resk] adj. Picaresque.
picalilli ['pikəlili] n. CULIN. Sorte de macédoine en rémoulade ƒ.
piccaninny ['pikənini] n. Négrillon s. ‖ Gosse s. (kiddy).
piccolo ['pikəlou] n. MUS. Petite flûte ƒ.
pick [pik] n. Pioche ƒ.; pic m. ‖ **Pick-and-shovel**, adj. FAM. U. S. Qui met la main à la pâte, pratique (scientist) ; fatigant, pénible (work).
pick n. Choix m.; to have (or) take one's pick, faire son choix. ‖ Elite ƒ.; the pick of the bunch, le dessus du panier.
— v. tr. Choisir (to choose) ; to pick one's words, choisir ses mots ; to pick one's way, marcher avec précaution. ‖ Défaire, effilocher (rags) ; to pick oakum, faire de la filasse. ‖ Crocheter (a lock) ; to pick pockets, voler à la tire. ‖ Sonder, curer ; to pick one's teeth, se curer les dents. ‖ Ronger (a bone). ‖ Chercher (to seek) ; to pick acquaintance with, faire connaissance avec ; to pick a quarrel with, chercher querelle à. ‖ AGRIC. Cueillir (fruit) ; piocher (the ground). ‖ LOC. To have a bone to pick with, avoir maille à partir avec ; to pick s.o.'s brains, exploiter les connaissances de qqn ; to pick holes in, dénigrer ; to pick to pieces, déchirer à belles dents. ‖ **To pick off**, enlever, cueillir, arracher (fruit) ; MILIT. Abattre un à un. ‖ **To pick out**, trier, choisir, désigner ; dénicher, dégoter (fam.) ; ARTS. Echampir. ‖ **To pick over**, trier (rags). ‖ **To pick up**, ramasser (from the ground) ; dénicher (a curio) ; apprendre (to learn) ; recueillir (a shipwrecked sailor) ; prendre (a traveller) ; RADIO. Capter (a message). ‖ **Pick-a-back**, adv. Sur les épaules, sur le dos. ‖ **Pick-me-up**, n. Cordial, remontant ; ravigotant m. (fam.). ‖ **Pick-up**, n. MUS. Pick-up m.; AUTOM. Reprise ƒ.; FAM. Traînée ƒ.
— v. intr. Becqueter, béqueter, picoter (birds). ‖ Manger du bout des dents (person) ; to pick at one's food, faire le dégoûté ; to pick and choose, chipoter, pignocher. ‖ To pick up, reprendre des forces ; se retaper (fam.). ‖ **To pick up with**, faire la connaissance de.
pickaninny [‚pikə'nini] n. See PICCANINNY.

pickaxe [-æks] n. Pioche ƒ.
picker [-ə*] n. Cueilleur, récolteur s.
picket [-it] n. Pieu, piquet m. ‖ MILIT. Piquet, poste, détachement m.; fire picket, piquet d'incendie. ‖ FIG. Strike picket, piquet de grève.
— v. tr. Mettre au piquet (a horse). ‖ Entourer de piquets de grève (a factory).
picking [-iŋ] n. Cueillette ƒ.; cueillage m. (of fruit). ‖ Triage m. (selection). ‖ Crochetage m. (of a lock). ‖ Pl. Restes m. pl. (left over). ‖ Gratte ƒ. (perks).
pickle [pikl] n. CULIN. Saumure, marinade ƒ. ‖ Pl. Conserves (ƒ. pl.) au vinaigre. ‖ FAM. Gâchis m.; in a (sorry) pickle, dans de beaux draps.
— v. tr. Mariner (brine) ; conserver dans le vinaigre.
picklock ['piklɔk] n. Rossignol m. (of a burglar) ; crochet m. (of a locksmith). ‖ Crocheteur m. (person).
pickpocket [-‚pɔkit] n. Pickpocket ; voleur (m.) à la tire.
picnic [-nik] n. Pique-nique m.
— v. intr. Faire un pique-nique.
picric ['pikrik] adj. CHIM. Picrique.
Pict [pikt] n. Picte m.
pictogram ['piktə‚græm], **pictograph** [-‚græf] n. Pictogramme m.
pictographic [‚piktə'græfik] adj. Pictographique.
pictorial [pik'tɔ:riəl] adj. Pittoresque (description) ; illustré (periodical) ; en images (writing).
— n. Illustré, journal illustré m.
pictorially [-i] adv. Au moyen d'images.
picture ['piktʃə*] n. Gravure, image ƒ. (engraving) ; illustration ƒ. (in a magazine). ‖ Peinture ƒ.; tableau m. ‖ U. S. Photographie f. ‖ CINEM. Film m.; talking pictures, cinéma parlant. ‖ FIG. To be a picture of one's father, être tout le portrait de son père ; to be the picture of health, respirer la santé ; to conjure up a mental picture of sth., se représenter (or) visualiser qqch. ‖ **Picture-book**, n. Livre (m.) d'images. ‖ **Picture-gallery**, n. Musée (m.) de peinture, pinacothèque ƒ. ‖ **Picture-goer**, n. Habitué (s.) du cinéma. ‖ **Picture-place**, n. Cinéma m. ‖ **Picture postcard**, n. Carte postale illustrée ƒ. ‖ **Picture window**, n. Fenêtre panoramique ƒ.
— v. tr. Dépeindre, décrire, représenter ; to picture to oneself, s'imaginer, se représenter.
picturesque [‚piktʃə'resk] adj. Pittoresque.
picturesquely [-'reskli] adv. Pittoresquement.
picturesqueness [-'resknis] n. Pittoresque m.
piddle ['pidl] v. intr. FAM. Faire pipi.
pidgin ['pidʒin] n. Pidgin English, jargon, petit nègre m. ‖ FAM. That's not my pidgin, ce n'est pas mes oignons.
pie [pai] n. ZOOL. Pie ƒ.
pie n. CULIN. Pâté m.; shepherd's pie, hachis aux pommes de terre ; meat pie, pâté de viande. ‖ CULIN. U. S. Tarte ƒ. ‖ FAM. To eat humble pie, filer doux, aller à Canossa ; to have had a finger in the pie, y avoir trempé. ‖ **Pie-dish**, n. CULIN. Tourtière ƒ. (for tarts) ; terrine ƒ. (for meat).
pie n. Pâte ƒ.; pâté m. (typography).
piebald ['paibɔ:ld] adj. Pie (horse). ‖ FIG. Bigarré.
piece [pi:s] n. Pièce, partie ƒ. (part) ; fragment, morceau m. (bit) ; all in one piece, tout d'une pièce ; in pieces, en morceaux, en fragments ; piece of furniture, meuble ; piece of land, parcelle de terrain ; to take to pieces, défaire (a dress) ; démonter (a machine). ‖ MILIT. Pièce ƒ. (of artillery) ; fowling piece, canardière ƒ. ‖ FIN. Pièce, pièce de monnaie ƒ. (coin) ; a sixpenny piece, pièce de six pence. ‖ MUS. Pièce ƒ. (of music). ‖ COMM. By the piece, à la pièce, à la tâche. ‖ FIG. Piece of advice, folly, insolence, news, conseil, étour-

derie, insolence, nouvelle. ‖ Loc. *To be all of a piece*, être du même acabit ; *to fly into pieces*, voler en éclats ; *to give s.o. a piece of one's mind*, dire son fait à qqn. ‖ **Piece-work**, n. Comm. Travail (*m.*) à la pièce. ‖ **Piece-worker**, n. Comm. Ouvrier (*s.*) à la pièce (or) à la tâche.
— v. tr. Joindre, assembler. ‖ **To piece together**, unir, joindre.

piecemeal [-miːl] adv. Pièce à pièce, morceau par morceau, par morceaux.
— adj. Fragmentaire, parcellaire, décousu.

piecrust ['paikrʌst] n. Culin. Croûte (*f.*) de pâté. ‖ Fam. *Piecrust promise*, promesse à la noix.

pied [paid] adj. Bigarré, panaché, bariolé.

pied-à-terre [pjeta'tɛːr] n. Pied-à-terre *m. invar.*

Piedmont ['piːdmɔnt] n. Geogr. Piémont *m.*

Piedmontese [,piːdmɔn'tiːz] n. adj. Geogr. Piémontais *s.*

pieman ['paimən] n. Marchand (*m.*) de petits pâtés.

pier [piə*] n. Jetée *f.* ; jetée-promenade *f.* ‖ Archit. Pile *f.* (of bridge) ; pied-droit *m.* (of door). ‖ **Pier-glass**, n. Trumeau *m.*

pierce [piəs] v. tr. Percer, transpercer, pénétrer. ‖ **To pierce through**, transpercer.

piercing ['piəsiŋ] adj. Perçant. ‖ Aigu (sharp).

piercingly [-li] adv. D'une manière perçante.

pietism ['paiətizm] n. Eccles. Piétisme *m.*

pietistical [-tistikəl] adj. Confit en dévotion.

piety [-ti] n. Piété *f.*

piezo-electric [pai,iːzoi'lektrik] adj. Piézo-électrique.

piezo-electricity [-ilek'trisiti] n. Piézo-électricité *f.*

piezometer [,paii'zɔmitə*] n. Piézomètre *m.*

piffle ['pifl] n. Fam. Baliverne, foutaise *f.*
— v. intr. Fam. Dire des bêtises.

piffling [-liŋ] adj. Futile. ‖ Insignifiant (detail).

pig [pig] n. Cochon, porc, pourceau *m.* ; *pig breeding*, industrie porcine ; *suckling pig*, cochon de lait. ‖ Culin. *Roast pig*, cochon de lait rôti. ‖ Techn. Gueuse *f.* (of iron) ; saumon *m.* (of lead). ‖ Fig. *To buy a pig in a poke*, acheter chat en poche. ‖ Fam. Cochon *m.* ‖ **Pig-iron**, n. Saumon (*m.*) de fonte. ‖ **Pig-tail**, n. Natte *f.*) de Chinois.
— v. intr. (1). Fam. *To pig it*, vivre comme des cochons.

pigeon ['pidʒən] n. Pigeon *m.* ; pigeonne *f.* ; *homing pigeon*, pigeon voyageur ; *wild pigeon*, ramier. ‖ Sports. *Clay pigeon*, pigeon artificiel. ‖ Fam. Pigeon *m.* ; dupe *f.* (dupe). ‖ **Pigeon-chested**, adj. A la poitrine bombée. ‖ **Pigeon-fancier**, n. Sports. Colombophile *s.* ‖ **Pigeon-hole**, n. Case *f.* (for papers) ; casier, fichier *m.* (set) ; v. tr. caser ; classer (to file). ‖ **Pigeon-house** (or) **-loft**, n. Colombier *m.* ‖ **Pigeon-shooting**, n. Sports. Tir aux pigeons *m.* ‖ **Pigeon-toed**, adj. Aux pieds tournés en dedans.

pigeon n. See pidgin.

pigeonry [-ri] n. Pigeonnier *m.*

piggery ['pigəri] n. Fam. Porcherie *f.*

piggish [-iʃ] adj. Sale, malpropre (dirty). ‖ Glouton, goinfre (greedy).

piggishness [-iʃnis] n. Saleté, malpropreté *f.* (dirtiness). ‖ Gloutonnerie, goinfrerie *f.* (greediness).

piggy, piggie ['pigi] n. Petit cochon *m.* ; *piggy bank*, tirelire.

piggyback [-,bæk] adv. Sur les épaules, sur le dos. (See pick-a-back.)
— n. *To give s.o. a piggyback*, porter qqn sur son dos (or) sur les épaules.

pigheaded [pig'hedid] adj. Entêté, têtu, obstiné.

piglet ['piglit], **pigling** [-liŋ] n. Petit cochon, porcelet *m.*

pigman [-mən] (pl. pigmen) n. Agric. Porcher *m.*

pigment ['pigmənt] n. Pigment *m.*

pigmentation [,pigmən'teiʃən] n. Pigmentation *f.*

pigmy ['pigmi] n., adj. See pygmy.

pigskin ['pigskin] n. Peau (*f.*) de porc.

pigsticker [-stikə*] n. Egorgeur de porcs *m.* ‖ Coupe-choux *m. invar.* ‖ Sports. Chasseur de sangliers *m.*

pigsticking [-stikiŋ] n. Sports. Chasse (*f.*) au sanglier.

pigsty [-stai] n. Agric. Porcherie *f.* ‖ Fig. Bouge *f.*

pigswill [-swil] m. Pâtée (*f.*) pour les porcs ; branée *f.*

pigtail [-teil] n. Queue, natte *f.*

pigwash [-wɔʃ] n. Eaux grasses *f. pl.* ‖ Fam. Lavasse *f.*

pike [paik] n. Zool. Brochet *m.*

pike n. Pique *f.* ‖ Geogr. Pic *m.*

pike n. Barrière (*f.*) de péage. (See turnpike.)

pikestaff [-stɑːf] n. Hampe de pique *f.* ; *plain as a pikestaff*, clair comme le jour.

pilaff [pi'lɑːf] n. Culin. Pilaf *m.*

pilaster [pi'læstə*] n. Archit. Pilastre *m.*

pilau, pilaw [pi'lɔː] n. Culin. Pilaf *m.*

pilchard ['piltʃəd] n. Zool. Pilchard *m.*

pile [pail] n. Pieu *m.* (stake). ‖ Pilotis *m.* (under building) ; *row of piles*, pilotis. ‖ **Pile-driver**, n. Sonnette, batterie *f.*

pile n. Tas, monceau *m.*, pile *f.* ‖ Bûcher *m.* (funeral). ‖ Archit. Edifice, bâtiment *m.* ‖ Milit. Faisceau *m.* ‖ Electr., Phys. Pile *f.* ‖ Fam. *To make one's pile*, faire sa pelote. ‖ **Pile-up**, n. Amoncellement, entassement *m.* ; Autom. Carambolage *m.*
— v. tr. Empiler, amonceler, entasser. ‖ Milit. *To pile arms*, former les faisceaux. ‖ Fam. *To pile it on*, exagérer. ‖ **To pile up**, entasser, empiler, amonceler.
— v. intr. *To pile up*, s'amonceler, s'entasser.

pile n. Poil *m.* (of a carpet).

piles [pailz] n. pl. Med. Pl. Hémorroïdes *f. pl.*

pilewort ['pailwəːt] n. Bot. Ficaire *f.*

pilfer ['pilfə*] v. tr., intr. Chaparder.

pilferer [-ərə*] n. Chapardeur *s.*

pilfering [-əriŋ] n. Chapardage, barbotage *m.*

pilgrim ['pilgrim] n. Pèlerin *s.*

pilgrimage [-idʒ] n. Pèlerinage *m.*

piliferous [pai'lifərəs] adj. Bot. Pilifère.

pill [pil] n. Med. Pilule *f.* ‖ Fig. Pilule *f.* ; *bitter pill*, dragée amère. ‖ Fam. Raseur *m.* (bore). ‖ **Pill-box**, n. Med. Boîte à pilules *f.* ; Milit. Abri (*m.*) en béton. ‖ **Pill bug**, n. U. S. Zool. Cloporte *m.*

pillage ['pilidʒ] n. Pillage *m.*
— v. tr. Piller, saccager, mettre à sac.

pillager [-ə*] n. Pillard, saccageur *s.*

pillaging [-iŋ] adj. Pillard.

pillar ['pilə*] n. Pilier *m.* ; colonne *f.* ‖ Colonne *f.* (of smoke, of water). ‖ Fig. Pilier *m.* (of the Church) ; *driven from pillar to post*, renvoyé de Pierre à Paul. ‖ **Pillar-box**, n. Borne postale, boîte (*f.*) aux lettres ; *pillar-box red*, rouge drapeau.

pillion ['piljən] n. Coussinet *m.* (of a horse) ; siège arrière, tansad *m.* (of a motor-cycle) ; *to ride pillion*, monter en croupe. ‖ **Pillion-passenger** (or) **-rider**, n. Passager (*s.*) de derrière.

pillory ['piləri] n. Pilori *m.*
— v. tr. (2). Mettre au pilori. ‖ Fig. Exposer au ridicule.

pillow ['pilou] n. Oreiller *m.* ‖ Techn. Coussinet *m.* ‖ **Pillow-case** (or) **-slip**, n. Taie (*f.*) d'oreiller. ‖ **Pillow-fight**, n. Bataille (*f.*) d'oreillers. ‖ **Pillow-lace**, n. Dentelle (*f.*) au fuseau.
— v. tr. Servir d'oreiller à (sth.) ; *to pillow one's head in one's arms*, reposer la tête sur ses bras.

pillowy [-i] adj. Moelleux, doux.

pilose ['pailous], **pilous** [-ləs] adj. Pileux, poilu.

pilot ['pailət] n. Naut. Pilote *m.* ‖ Aviat. Pilote *m.* ; *second pilot*, co-pilote. ‖ Fig. Guide *m.* ‖ **Pilot-balloon**, n. Ballon pilote *m.* ‖ **Pilot-boat**, n. Naut. Bateau pilote *m.* ‖ **Pilot-coat** (or) **-jacket**, n.

NAUT. Vareuse *f.* ‖ **Pilot-engine,** n. CH. DE F. Locomotive pilote (or) estafette *f.* ‖ **Pilot-fish,** n. ZOOL. Pilote *m.* ‖ **Pilot-flag,** n. NAUT. Pavillon de pilote *m.* ‖ **Pilot-flame,** n. Veilleuse *f.* ‖ **Pilot-jet,** n. AUTOM. Gicleur de ralenti *m.* ‖ **Pilot-lamp,** n. Lampe témoin *f.* ‖ **Pilot-light,** n. Veilleuse *f.*; AVIAT. Feu pilote *m.* ‖ **Pilot-officer,** n. AVIAT. Sous-lieutenant aviateur *m.*
— v. tr. NAUT., AVIAT., FIG. Piloter.
pilotage [-id3] n. Pilotage *m.*; droits (*m. pl.*) de pilotage.
pilotless [-lis] adj. AVIAT. Sans pilote, robot (plane).
pilule ['pilju:l] n. Petite pilule *f.*
pimento [pi'mentou] n. BOT., CULIN. Piment *m.*
pimp [pimp] n. Entremetteur *s.*
— v. intr. Servir d'entremetteur (*for*, à).
pimpernel ['pimpənəl] n. BOT. Mouron *m.*
pimple ['pimpl] n. Bouton *m.*
pimply [-i] n. Boutonneux.
pin [pin] n. Epingle *f.*; *safety-pin*, épingle de sûreté (or) de nourrice. ‖ NAUT. *Belaying pin*, cabillot. ‖ TECHN. Cheville, goupille *f.*; clavette *f.*, goujon *m.* ‖ ELECTR. Fiche (*f.*) de prise de courant. ‖ CULIN. *Rolling-pin*, rouleau à pâtisserie. ‖ SPORTS. Drapeau de trou *m.* (at golf); quille *f.* (at ninepins). ‖ FIG. *For two pins*, pour un peu; *not to care a pin*, s'en moquer comme de l'an quarante; *pins and needles*, fourmillements; fourmis (in one's legs); *to be on pins and needles*, être sur des charbons ardents; *you could have heard a pin drop*, on aurait entendu voler une mouche. ‖ FAM. Pl. Guibolles, quilles, flûtes *f. pl.* ‖ **Pin-frog,** n. Pique-fleurs *m.* ‖ **Pin-head,** n. Tête d'épingle *f.*; U. S. POP. Crétin *m.* ‖ **Pin-hole,** n. Trou (*m.*) d'épingle; sténopé *m.* (in photography). ‖ **Pin-money,** n. Argent (*m.*) de poche. ‖ **Pin-prick,** n. Piqûre d'épingle *f.*; FIG. Coup (*m.*) d'épingle. ‖ **Pin-stripe,** n. Rayure (*f.*) fine (or) de tennis (in cloth). ‖ **Pin-up (girl),** n. Pin-up *f.* ‖ **Pin-wheel,** n. Roue des chevilles *f.* (of a clock); soleil *m.* (fireworks).
— v. tr. (1). Epingler, attacher avec une épingle. ‖ TECHN. Cheviller, goupiller. ‖ ARCHIT. Etayer (a wall). ‖ FIG. Clouer, coller; *to pin one's hopes on*, mettre toutes ses espérances dans; *to pin s.o.'s arms*, lier les bras à qqn. ‖ **To pin down,** lier. ‖ **To pin-point,** mettre le doigt sur, localiser. ‖ **To pin up,** épingler (the hair); attacher avec une punaise (on the wall).
pinafore ['pinəfɔ:*] n. Tablier (*m.*) d'enfant; sarrau *m.*
pinaster ['painæstə*] n. BOT. Pinastre, pin maritime *m.*
pinball ['pin,bɔ:l] n. Flipper *m.*
pince-nez ['pæns,nei] n. Pince-nez *m. invar.*
pincer ['pinsə] n. Pince *f.* (of a crab). ‖ Pl. Tenaille *f.*, tenailles *f. pl.* ‖ MILIT. *Pincer movement*, mouvement en tenailles.
pinch [pinʃ] n. Pinçon, pincement *m.*; *to give s.o. a pinch*, pincer qqn. ‖ Pincée *f.* (of salt); prise *f.* (of snuff). ‖ FIG. Morsure *f.* (of hunger); *at* (or) U. S. *in a pinch*, au besoin, en cas de besoin; *to feel the pinch*, tirer le diable par la queue; *when it comes to the pinch*, au moment critique.
— v. tr. Pincer. ‖ Blesser (feet). ‖ FAM. Pincer, chauffer (to catch). ‖ POP. Chiper, chaparder, chauffer, piquer (to steal). ‖ **To pinch off,** BOT. épincer (a bud).
— v. intr. Etre étroit (shoe). ‖ FIG. *Where the shoe pinches*, où le bât blesse. ‖ FAM. *To pinch and scrape*, liarder, pignoter.
pinchbeck ['pinʃbek] n. Similor, doublé *m.*; toc *m.* (fam.).
— adj. En doublé; en toc (fam.).
pinched ['pinʃt] adj. Tiré, hâve (features). ‖ FAM. *Pinched for money*, à court d'argent; *pinched with hunger*, tenaillé par la faim.

pincushion ['pin,kuʃən] n. Pelote à épingles *f.*
Pindaric [pin'dærik] adj. Pindarique.
pine [pain] n. Pin *m.* ‖ **Pine-cone,** n. Pomme (*f.*) de pin. ‖ **Pine-grove** (or) **-wood,** n. Pinède *f.* ‖ **Pine-kernel,** n. Pignon *m.*; pigne *f.*
pine v. intr. Languir, dépérir; *to pine for*, soupirer après (or) pour; *to pine for news*, se miner à attendre des nouvelles. ‖ **To pine away,** languir, dépérir; se consumer (*with*, de) [grief].
pineal ['piniəl] adj. MED. Pinéal.
pineapple ['pain,æpl] n. Ananas *m.*
pinetum ['paini:təm] n. Sapinière, pinède *f.*
pinfold ['pinfould] n. Fourrière *f.* ‖ Parc *m.*
— v. tr. Mettre en fourrière. ‖ Parquer.
ping [piŋ] n. Sifflement *m.* (of a bullet).
— v. intr. Siffler (bullet). ‖ AUTOM. U. S. Cogner, cliqueter.
Ping-Pong ['piŋpɔŋ] n. SPORTS. Ping-Pong *m.*
pinion ['pinjən] n. Aileron *m.*; aile, plume d'aile *f.*
— v. tr. Couper le bout de l'aile à (a bird). ‖ Lier (the arms); lier les bras à (s.o.).
pinion n. TECHN. Pignon; *pinion wheel*, roue à pignon.
pink [piŋk] v. tr. Toucher avec une épée. ‖ Denteler les bords de (a dress). ‖ **To pink out,** orner.
pink v. intr. AUTOM. Cliqueter (engine).
— n. AUTOM. Cliquetis *m.*
pink n. BOT. Œillet *m.* ‖ Rose *m.* (colour); *hunting pink*, rouge chasseur. ‖ POP. *To be in the pink,* se porter comme un charme.
— adj. Rose.
pinkie [-i] n. U. S. Auriculaire, petit doigt *m.*
pinkish [-iʃ] adj. Rosâtre, rosé.
pinko [-ou] (pl. **pinkos** [-ouz]) n. FAM. Gauchisant *s.*
pinnace ['pinəs] n. NAUT. Grand canot *m.*; pinasse *f.*
pinnacle ['pinəkl] n. ARCHIT. Pinacle, couronnement *m.* ‖ GEOGR. Cime *f.*; pic *m.* (of a mountain). ‖ FIG. Apogée, faîte, comble *m.*
pinnate ['pinət] adj. BOT. Pinné, penné.
pinnule ['pinjul] n. BOT. Foliole *f.* ‖ TECHN. Pinnule *f.*
pinny ['pini] n. FAM. Tablier *m.*
pint [paint] n. Pinte *f.* (measure). ‖ **Pint-sized,** adj. FAM. Riquiqui, minuscule.
pinta [-ə] n. FAM. Pinte (*f.*) [or] demi-litre (*m.*) de lait.
pintle ['pintl] n. NAUT. Aiguillot *m.* (of a rudder). ‖ TECHN. Cheville ouvrière *f.*
pioneer [,paiə'niə*] n. Pionnier *m.* ‖ **Pioneer-work,** n. Travail de pionnier; défrichage *m.*
— v. intr. Etre un pionnier (or) à l'avant-garde (*in*, dans, en matière de).
— v. tr. Ouvrir, défricher (road, way); être à l'avant-garde de, être l'instigateur de (programme, course of action).
pious ['paiəs] adj. Pieux.
piously [-li] adv. Pieusement.
pip [pip] n. ZOOL. Pépie *f.* (in fowls). ‖ FAM. Cafard *m.*
pip n. Point *m.* (on a playing-card). ‖ RADIO. Pl. Top *m.*
pip n. Pépin *m.* (of a fruit). ‖ **Pip-squeak,** n. U. S. POP. Nabot *m.*
pip v. tr. (1). SPORTS. Battre, vaincre (a competitor). ‖ FAM. Recaler (a candidate); rater (an exam).
pipe [paip] n. Pipe *f.* (for smoking); *pipe of peace*, calumet de paix. ‖ Filet (*m.*) de voix (sound). ‖ Conduite *f.*; tuyau, conduit *m.* (tube). ‖ Pipe *f.* (of wine). ‖ MED. Tube *f.* ‖ MUS. Chalumeau *m.* ‖ FIG., FAM. *Put that in your pipe and smoke it!*, mettez cela dans votre poche et votre mouchoir par-dessus! ‖ **Pipe-clay,** n. Terre de pipe *f.*; craie (*f.*) de tailleur; v. tr. Passer à la craie. ‖ **Pipe-cleaner,** n. Cure-pipe *m.* ‖ **Pipe-dream,** n. Rêve *m.*; utopie, chimère *f.* ‖ **Pipe-line,** n. Conduite *f.*; pipe-

line *m.* || **Pipe-organ,** n. Mus. Grandes orgues *f. pl.* || **Pipe-rack,** n. Râtelier (*m.*) à pipes. || **Pipe-wrench,** n. Pince (*f.*) à tube.
— v. tr. Naut. Siffler (an order); *to pipe all hands,* rassembler tout le monde. || Mus. Jouer sur un chalumeau (a tune). || Lisérer, garnir d'un passepoil (a dress). || Transporter par tuyau (a liquid).
— v. intr. Mus. Jouer du chalumeau (or) de la cornemuse. || **To pipe down,** Fam. Mettre la sourdine, baisser le diapason. || **To pipe up,** se faire entendre.
piper [-ə*] n. Mus. Cornemuseur *m.* || Fig. *To pay the piper,* payer les violons.
pipette [pi'pet] n. Pipette *f.*
piping ['paipiŋ] n. Mus. Son (*m.*) du chalumeau (or) de la cornemuse. || Passepoil *m.* (on a dress). || Tuyauterie; canalisation *f.* (of water).
— adj. *Piping hot,* tout chaud, bouillant.
pipit ['pipit] n. Zool. Pipi(t) *m.;* farlouse *f.*
pipkin ['pipkin] n. Poêlon *m.*
pippin ['pipin] n. Reinette *f.* (apple).
piquancy ['pi:kənsi] n. Goût piquant *m.* || Fig. Piquant *m.*
piquant ['pi:kənt] adj. Piquant. || Fig. Mordant.
piquantly [-li] adv. D'une manière piquante.
pique [pi:k] n. Pique, rancune *f.;* ressentiment *m.*
— v. tr. Piquer, exciter (s.o.'s curiosity). || Piquer, dépiter, irriter (s.o.).
piquet [pi'ket] n. Sports. Piquet *m.*
piracy ['pairəsi] n. Piraterie *f.* || Fig. Contrefaçon *f.;* plagiat *m.*
Piraeus [pai'ri:əs] n. Geogr. Le Pirée *m.*
piranha [pi'rɑ:njə] n. Zool. Piranha *m.*
pirate ['pairət] n. Pirate, corsaire, flibustier *m.* || Fig. Contrefacteur, plagiaire *m.*
— v. tr. Contrefaire. || Démarquer, plagier (a book).
piratical [pai'rætikəl] adj. De pirate. || Plagiaire.
piratically [-i] adv. En pirate.
pirogue [pi'roug] n. Pirogue *f.*
pirouette [,piru'et] n. Pirouette *f.*
— v. intr. Pirouetter.
piscatorial [piskə'tɔ:riəl], **piscatory** ['piskətəri] adj. De la pêche.
Pisces ['pisi:z] n. Astron. Poissons *m. pl.*
pisciculture ['pisikʌltʃə*] n. Pisciculture *f.*
piscina [pi'sainə, pi'si:nə] (pl. **piscinae**) n. Vivier *m.* || Eccles. Piscine sacrée *f.*
pish [piʃ] interj. Fi !, Bah !
— v. intr. Dire « fi ».
piss [pis] n. Pop. Pisse *f.;* *to have a piss,* aller pisser. || Fig. *To take the piss out of,* se foutre de.
— v. intr. Pop. Pisser. || **To piss about** (or) **around,** Fig. Déconner. || **To piss off,** Fig. Se tirer, se barrer, foutre le camp.
— v. tr. Pop. Pisser (blood); mouiller, pisser dans (trousers); *it is pissing down,* il pleut comme vache qui pisse. || **To piss off,** Fig. Emmerder ; *I am pissed off,* j'en ai marre, j'en ai ras le bol.
pissed [-t] adj. Pop. Bourré (drunk); *to get pissed,* se poivrer, se cuiter, prendre une biture. || Loc. *Pissed as a newt, pissed out of one's head,* soûl comme une barrique, rond comme une queue de pelle.
pistachio [pis'tɑ:ʃiou] n. Pistache *f.* (nut); pistachier *m.* (tree).
pistil ['pistil] n. Bot. Pistil *m.*
pistol ['pistl̩] n. Pistolet, colt *m.* || **Pistol-shot,** n. Coup de pistolet *m.*
piston ['pistən] n. Piston *m.* || **Piston-ring,** n. Segment de piston *m.* || **Piston-rod,** n. Tige (*f.*) de piston. || **Piston-stroke,** n. Coup de piston *m.*
pit [pit] n. Fosse *f.;* trou *m.* || Arène *f.* (cockpit). || Piège *m.;* trappe *f.* (trap). || Carrière *f.* (quarry). || puits *m.* (mine shaft). || Med. Creux *m.* (of the stomach); trou *m.;* marque *f.* (pockmark). || Autom. *Inspection pit,* fosse à réparations. || Theatr. Parterre *m.* || U. S. Bourse (*f.*) de commerce. || Fig. *To dig a pit for,* tendre un piège à. || **Pit-boy,** n.

Galibot *m.* || **Pit-head,** n. Carreau *m.* (of a mine). || **Pit-prop,** n. Etai (*m.*) de mine.
— v. tr. (1). Mettre en parc, faire battre (a cock). || Piquer, trouer (a metal). || Med. Grêler. || Fig. *To pit oneself against,* se mesurer contre.
pit n. U. S. Noyau *m.* (of fruit).
— v. tr. (1). U. S. Dénoyauter.
pit-a-pat ['pitəpæt] adv. *To go pit-a-pat,* trottiner (feet); palpiter, battre (heart); crépiter (rain).
pitch [pitʃ] n. Poix *f.* || Brai *m.* (coal-tar) || Fig. *Pitch black,* noir d'ébène ; *pitch dark,* noir comme dans un four. || **Pitch-pine,** n. Pitchpin *m.*
— v. tr. Brayer, enduire de poix.
pitch n. Jet, lancement *m.* (of a stone). || Place habituelle (of a hawker). || Naut. Tangage *m.* || Archit. Hauteur sous clef *f.* (of an arch); degré (*m.*) de pente (of a roof). || Mus. Ton, diapason *m.* || Sports. Terrain *m.* || Techn. Pas, écartement *m.* (of a thread). || Aviat. Pas *m.* (of a propellor). || Fig. Degré *m.;* *at its highest pitch,* à son comble ; *to such a pitch,* à tel point. || **Pitch-pipe,** n. Mus. Diapason (*m.*) de bouche. || **Pitch-and-toss,** n. Jeu (*m.*) de pile ou face.
— v. tr. Asseoir (a camp); dresser (a tent). || Lancer (to throw). || Milit. Ranger (a battle); *pitched battle,* bataille rangée. || Pop. Raconter (a story). || **To pitch into,** Fam. Rentrer dedans (to abuse, to beat). || **To pitch on** (or) **upon,** arrêter son choix sur (s.o., sth.).
— v. intr. Naut. Tanguer. || **To pitch in,** Fam. S'atteler au boulot, s'y coller.
pitchblende ['pitʃblend] n. Pechblende *f.*
pitcher ['pitʃə*] n. Cruche *f.;* broc *m.* || **Pitcher-plant,** n. Bot. Népenthès *m.*
pitcher n. Sports. Lanceur *m.* (at baseball).
pitchfork [-fɔ:k] n. Agric. Fourche *f.*
— v. tr. Lancer avec une fourche. || Fam. *To pitch-fork s.o. into a job,* bombarder qqn dans un poste.
pitching [-iŋ] n. Lancement *m.* || Naut. Tangage *m.*
pitchpin [-pin] n. Pitchpin *m.*
pitchy ['pitʃi] adj. Noir (or) collant comme de la poix.
piteous ['pitiəs] adj. Piteux, pitoyable.
piteously [-li] adv. Piteusement.
piteousness [-nis] n. Etat piteux *m.*
pitfall [pitfɔ:l] n. Piège *m.;* trappe *f.* || Fig. Piège *m.*
pith [piθ] n. Moelle *f.;* *pith helmet,* casque colonial *m.* || Ziste *m.* (of an orange). || Fig. Essence, moelle *f.* (essence); vigueur, énergie *f.* (vigour).
pithecanthrope [,piθi'kænθroup] n. Pithécanthrope *m.*
pithily ['piθili] adv. Avec vigueur. || Avec concision.
pithiness [-inis] n. Vigueur *f.* || Concision *f.*
pithy [-i] adj. Plein de moelle. || Fig. Vigoureux; substantiel, concis. || Fig. Savoureux; plein de suc (aphorism).
pitiable ['pitiəbl̩] adj. Pitoyable ; minable.
pitiably [-i] adv. Pitoyablement.
pitiful ['pitiful] adj. Compatissant, plein de pitié (compassionate); lamentable, pitoyable, piteux (lamentable).
pitifully [-i] adv. Avec compassion (compassionately); à faire pitié (lamentably).
pitiless ['pitilis] adj. Impitoyable ; sans pitié.
pitilessly [-li] adv. Sans pitié.
pitman ['pitmən] n. (pl. **pitmen**) n. Mineur, houilleur *m.* || (Pl. **pitmans**) U. S. Bielle *f.*
piton ['pitən] n. Sports. Piton *m.* || **Piton-hammer,** n. Marteau-piolet *m.*
pittance ['pitəns] n. Pitance *f.;* *mere pittance,* portion congrue.
pitter-patter ['pitə,pætə*] adv. See PIT-A-PAT.

pituitary [pi'tju:itəri] adj. MED. *Pituitary gland* (or) *body*, glande pituitaire, hypophyse.
— n. MED. Hypophyse *f.*

pity ['piti] n. Compassion, pitié *f.; for pity's sake*, par pitié ; de grâce ; *to feel pity for*, avoir pitié de ; *to take pity on*, prendre pitié de. ‖ Dommage *m.*; *it's a thousand pities*, c'est grand dommage ; *the more's the pity*, c'est d'autant plus malheureux, ce n'en est que plus fâcheux.
— v. tr. (2). Plaindre, avoir pitié de (s.o.).

pitying [-iŋ] adj. Compatissant.

pityingly [-iŋli] adv. Avec pitié, avec compassion.

pivot ['pivət] n. Pivot, axe *m.* ‖ **Pivot-bridge,** n. Pont tournant *m.*
— v. tr. Faire pivoter.
— v. intr. Pivoter.

pivotal [-l] adj. *Pivotal state*, État pivot ; *pivotal trades*, métiers essentiels.

pixie, pixy [piksi] n. Fée *f.; lutin m.*

pizza ['pi:tsə] n. CULIN. Pizza *f.*

pizzeria [,pi:tsə'ri:ə] n. Pizzeria *f.*

pizzle ['pizl] n. *Bull's pizzle*, nerf de bœuf.

placard ['plækɑ:d] n. Affiche *f.*
— v. tr. Afficher.

placate [plə'keit] v. tr. Apaiser, calmer.

place [pleis] n. Lieu, endroit *m.; localité f.* (place) ; place *f.* (town square) ; *from place to place*, de-ci de-là ; *in all places*, partout, en tous lieux ; *in another place*, ailleurs ; *market place*, place du marché ; *place of refuge*, lieu de refuge ; *watering place*, station balnéaire, ville d'eau. ‖ Côté, endroit *m.; all over the place*, de tous les côtés. ‖ Lieu, édifice *m.; maison f.* (building) ; *my place*, chez moi ; *place in the country*, maison de campagne ; *place of amusement*, lieu de divertissement ; *place of business*, maison de commerce ; *place of worship*, édifice religieux. ‖ Emploi, poste *m.; place f.* (employment) ; *to fill* (or) *take s.o.'s place*, remplacer qqn. ‖ Rang *m.; place f.* (rank) ; *high place*, rang élevé ; *to know one's place*, savoir se tenir à sa place ; *to put s.o. in his place*, remettre qqn à sa place. ‖ Place *f.; a place for everything and everything in its place*, une place pour chaque chose et chaque chose à sa place ; *to change places*, changer de places ; *to lay a place for*, mettre un couvert pour. ‖ MILIT. *Fortified place*, place forte. ‖ MATH. *Decimal place*, décimale. ‖ SPORTS. *To back a horse for a place*, jouer un cheval placé. ‖ FIG. *If I were in your place*, à votre place ; *this is no place for ladies*, ce n'est pas un endroit convenable pour des dames ; *to look out of place*, avoir l'air dépaysé ; *to take place*, avoir lieu, arriver, se passer ; *to take the place of everything*, tenir lieu de tout. ‖ **Place-kick,** n. SPORTS. Coup d'envoi *m.* ‖ **Place-mat,** n. Set (*m.*) de table. ‖ **Place-name,** n. Nom de lieu, toponyme *m.* ‖ **Place-setting,** n. Couvert *m.*
— v. tr. Placer, mettre. ‖ FIN. Placer (money). ‖ COMM. Passer (an order). ‖ FIG. Se rappeler, remettre (s.o.). ‖ FIG. Placer ; *to be awkwardly placed*, se trouver dans une situation difficile ; *to place a matter in s.o.'s hands*, remettre une affaire entre les mains de qqn.
— v. intr. SPORTS. Finir placé (in horse-racing).

placebo [plə'si:bou] (pl. **placebos** [-z]) n. MED. Placebo *m.*

placenta [plə'sentə] n. MED. Placenta *m.*

placer ['pleisə*] n. Placer, gisement aurifère *m.*

placid ['plæsid] adj. Placide, calme, paisible, tranquille, serein.

placidity [plə'siditi] n. Placidité *f.: calme m.*

placidly ['plæsidli] adv. Avec calme ; tranquillement ; avec placidité.

placket ['plækit] n. Fente, poche *f.*

plage [plɑ:ʒ] n. Plage mondaine *f.*

plagiarism ['pleidʒərizm̩] n. Plagiat ; démarquage *m.* (of a book).

plagiarist [-ist] n. Plagiaire *m.*

plagiarize [-aiz] v. tr. Plagier (an author) ; démarquer (a book).

plagiary [-i] n. Plagiat *m.*

plague [pleig] n. MED. Peste *f.* ‖ FIG. Fléau *m.; calamité, plaie f.* ‖ FAM. *A plague on him!* la peste soit de lui ! ‖ **Plague-spot,** n. Foyer (*m.*) d'infection. ‖ **Plague-stricken,** adj. Frappé de la peste (country) ; pestiféré (person).
— v. tr. FIG. Tourmenter ; embêter, raser, bassiner (fam.) ; *to plague the life out of*, casser les pieds à ; *to plague with questions*, assommer de questions.

plaice [pleis] n. ZOOL. Carrelet *m.*

plaid [plæd] n. Tissu écossais, plaid *m.*
— adj. En tissu écossais, écossais.

plain [plein] adj. Clair, évident (clear) ; *to make one's meaning plain*, bien se faire comprendre. ‖ Simple (simple) ; *in plain clothes*, en civil ; *plain and purl*, mailles à l'endroit et à l'envers ; *plain answer*, réponse carrée ; *plain dealing*, procédés honnêtes ; *plain speaker*, Saint Jean Bouche d'Or ; *plain speaking*, franchise ; *plain truth*, la vérité toute nue ; *under plain cover*, sous pli discret. ‖ Laid, sans attraits (unattractive). ‖ GRAMM. *Plain infinitive*, infinitif sans to. ‖ CULIN. Simple (food) ; au naturel (without seasoning) ; *plain cooking*, cuisine bourgeoise ; *plain chocolate*, chocolat à croquer. ‖ **Plain-clothes,** adj. En civil (policeman). ‖ **Plain-sailing,** n. NAUT. Navigation (*f.*) sans problème ; FIG. parcours (*m.*) sans embûches ; *it's all plain sailing from now on*, à partir de maintenant, tout va marcher comme sur des roulettes. ‖ **Plain-spoken,** adj. Franc, qui a son franc-parler.
— adv. Simplement, clairement, franchement ; distinctement.
— n. Plaine *f.*

plainly [-li] adv. Simplement, clairement, franchement ; distinctement ; *to put it plainly*, pour parler clair ; *to speak plainly*, parler sans détours.

plainness [-nis] n. Clarté *f.* (clearness) ; simplicité *f.* (simplicity) ; manque (*m.*) de beauté (unattractiveness).

plainsong [-sɔŋ] n. MUS. Plain-chant *m.*

plaint [pleint] n. Lamentation, plainte *f.; gémissement m.* ‖ JUR. Plainte *f.*

plaintiff [-if] n. JUR. Demandeur *m.; demanderesse f.; plaignant s.*

plaintive [-iv] adj. Plaintif.

plaintively [-ivli] adv. Plaintivement.

plait [plæt] n. Tresse, natte *f.* (hair). ‖ Pli *m.* (fold).
— v. tr. Tresser, natter. ‖ Plier.

plan [plæn] n. Plan, projet *m.; according to plan*, selon les prévisions ; *to draw up a plan*, dresser un plan ; *to upset s.o.'s plans*, déranger les combinaisons (or) les projets de qqn. ‖ MILIT. Plan *m.* (of campaign). ‖ MATH., ARCHIT. Plan *m.; projection f.*
— v. tr. (1). ARCHIT. Faire le plan de (a building). ‖ FIG. Projeter, combiner ; *to plan for the future*, préparer l'avenir.

planar ['pleinə*] adj. MATH. Plan. ‖ ÉLECTR. Planar ; *planar diode, process*, diode, méthode planar.

plane [plein] n. BOT. Platane *m.*

plane n. Rabot *m.* (tool). ‖ **Plane-iron,** n. Fer de rabot *m.*
— v. tr. Raboter.

plane n. MATH. Plan *m.* ‖ AVIAT. Avion *m.* (aeroplane) ; plan *m.; surface portante f.* (of an aeroplane). ‖ FIG. Plan, niveau *m.; on the same plane as*, au même niveau que.
— adj. Plan, plat. ‖ MATH. *Plane geometry*, géométrie plane. ‖ **Plane-table,** n. Planchette *f.*
— v. intr. **To plane down,** AVIAT. Descendre en vol plané.

planet ['plænit] n. ASTRON. Planète *f.*

planetarium [,plæni'tɛəriəm] n. Planétarium *m.*
— N. B. Deux pluriels : *planetariums, planetaria.*

planetary [-əri] adj. ASTRON. Planétaire.
plangent ['plændʒənt] adj. Retentissant.
planimeter [plæ'nimitə*] n. Planimètre *m.*
planimetry [-tri] n. Planimétrie *f.*
planish ['plæniʃ] v. tr. Planer, polir au marteau (metal). ‖ Satiner (a photograph).
planisher [-ə*] n. Planoir *m.*
planisphere ['plænisfiə*] n. Planisphère *m.*
plank [plæŋk] n. Planche *f.; madrier*, ais *m.* ‖ NAUT. Bordage *m.* ‖ FIG. Article, paragraphe *m.* (in a political programme).
— v. tr. Planchéier. ‖ **To plank down**, FAM. Allonger (money).
planking [-iŋ] n. Planchéiage *m.*
plankton [-tən] n. Plancton *m.*
planned [plænd] adj. Dirigé (economy).
planner ['plænə*] n. Planificateur *s.; town planner*, urbaniste; *programme planner*, programmateur.
planning [-iŋ] n. Planification *f.;* planisme, dirigisme *m.; family planning*, contrôle des naissances; *town planning*, urbanisme.
plant [plɑ:nt] n. BOT. Plante *f.* ‖ TECHN. Outillage, matériel *m.;* installation *f.* (in a factory). ‖ POP. Coup monté *m.* ‖ **Plant-louse**, n. ZOOL. Puceron *m.*
— v. tr. AGRIC. Planter. ‖ FIG. *To plant an idea in s.o.'s mind*, implanter une idée dans l'esprit de qqn. ‖ FAM. Coller, flanquer (a blow); planquer (stolen goods); *to plant oneself in front of*, se planter (or) se camper devant. ‖ **To plant out**, v. tr. Repiquer.
plantain ['plæntin] n. BOT. Plantain *m.*
plantain n. Banane (*f.*) des Antilles. ‖ Bananier *m.* (tree).
plantation [plɑ:n'teiʃən] n. Plantation *f.* ‖ Colonisation *f.* (act); colonie *f.* (colony).
planter ['plɑ:ntə*] n. Cultivateur *m.* ‖ Planteur, colon *m.* (in the colonies).
plantigrade ['plæntigreid] n. ZOOL. Plantigrade *m.*
plaque [plɑ:k] n. Plaque *f.*
plash [plæʃ] n. Flaque d'eau *f.*
plash n. Clapotement, flac *m.* (noise).
— v. intr. Clapoter.
plasm [plæzm] n. Protoplasme *m.; U. S.* plasma *m.*
plasma ['plæzmə] n. Plasma *m.*
plaster ['plɑ:stə*] n. Plâtre *m.* ‖ MED. Emplâtre *m.; court plaster*, taffetas d'Angleterre; *mustard plaster*, cataplasme sinapisé; *plaster of Paris*, gypse, plâtre à mouler; *sticking-plaster*, taffetas gommé. ‖ **Plaster-cast**, n. MED. Plâtre *m.*
— v. tr. ARCHIT. Plâtrer. ‖ MED. Plâtrer (a limb); mettre un emplâtre à (a wound). ‖ FAM. *Plastered*, plein, saoul, noir (drunk).
plasterboard ['plɑ:stə,bɔ:d] n. TECHN. Plasterboard, placoplâtre *m.*
plastered ['plɑ:stəd] adj. POP. Bourré, paf, rond.
plasterer ['plɑ:stərə*] n. Plâtrier *m.*
plastic ['plæstik] adj. COMM. Plastique; *plastic goods*, matières plastiques. ‖ ARTS. Plastique (arts); *plastic clay*, terre à modeler; ‖ MED. *Plastic surgery*, chirurgie plastique (or) esthétique. ‖ TECHN. *Plastic explosive*, plastic; *plastic bomb*, charge de plastic. ‖ FIG. Plastique, malléable, souple.
— n. Plastique *m.* ‖ Pl. Matière plastique; industrie plastique *f.*
plasticine ['plæsti,si:n] n. (trade mark). Plasticine, pâte (*f.*) à modeler.
plasticity [plæs'tisiti] n. Plasticité *f.*
plastron ['plæstrən] n. Plastron *m.*
plate [pleit] n. Assiette *f.; dinner, soup plate*, assiette plate, creuse. ‖ Planche, gravure, estampe *f.* (engraving). ‖ Plaque *f.* (photography). ‖ Argenterie *f.* (silver). ‖ AUTOM. *Number plate*, U. S. *license plate*, plaque matricule. ‖ ARCHIT. Sablière *f.* (of a roof). ‖ SPORTS. Coupe *f.;* prix *m.* (horseracing). ‖ CULIN. *Hot plate*, chauffe-plat. ‖ ECCLES. Plateau (*m.*) de quête. ‖ POP. pl. Ripatons

m. pl. (feet). ‖ **Plate-glass**, n. Glace (*f.*) sans tain (or) de vitrage. ‖ **Plate-layer**, n. CH. DE F. Ouvrier (*m.*) de la voie; poseur (*m.*) de voie. ‖ **Plate-lunch**, n. U. S. FAM. Déjeuner avec un plat garni *m.* ‖ **Plate-rack**, n. Egouttoir *m.;* égoutte- (or) porte-assiettes *m. invar.* ‖ **Plate-warmer**, n. Chauffe-assiettes *m. invar.*
— v. tr. Plaquer (*with*, de); *to plate with gold, nickel, silver*, dorer, nickeler, argenter.
plateau ['plætou] n. GEOGR. Plateau *m.*
— N. B. Deux pluriels : *plateaux, plateaus.*
plateful ['pleitful] n. Assiettée *f.*
platen ['plætn̩] n. Plateau *m.* (of a machine-tool); platine *f.* (of a printing-press); rouleau *m.* (of a typewriter).
plater ['pleitə*] n. Plaqueur *m.* ‖ SPORTS. Cheval de second ordre *m.*
platform ['plætfɔ:m] n. Estrade, plate-forme *f.* ‖ CH. DE F. Quai, trottoir *m.; arrival, departure platform*, quai d'arrivée, de départ. ‖ JUR. Programme électoral *m.* (of a political party).
plating ['pleitiŋ] n. Placage, plaqué *m.*
platinize ['plæti,naiz] v. tr. TECHN. Platiner.
platinum [-əm] n. Platine *m.* ‖ **Platinum-blonde**, n. Blonde platinée *f.* (person); blond-platine (shade).
platitude ['plætitju:d] n. Platitude, banalité *f.;* lieu commun *m.*
platitudinarian [-i'nɛəriən] n. Débiteur (*m.*) de lieux communs.
— adj. Banal, plat.
platitudinize [,plæti'tju:dinaiz] v. intr. Débiter des lieux communs, dire des banalités.
platitudinous [-əs] adj. Banal, plat.
Plato ['pleitou] n. Platon *m.*
platonic [plə'tɔnik] adj. Platonicien (doctrine). ‖ Platonique (love).
Platonist ['pleitənist] n. Platonicien *m.*
platoon [plə'tu:n] n. MILIT. Section *f.;* peloton *m.* (†).
platter ['plætə*] n. † Ecuelle *f.* ‖ MILIT. Gamelle *f.* ‖ U. S. Plat *m.; platée f.* ‖ U. S. FAM. Disque *m.* (record).
platypus ['plætipəs] n. Ornithorynque *m.*
plaudits ['plɔ:dits] n. pl. Applaudissements *m. pl.*
plausibility [,plɔ:zi'biliti] n. Plausibilité *f.*
plausible ['plɔ:zibl̩] adj. Vraisemblable, plausible (argument). ‖ Spécieux, jésuitique (specious). ‖ Enjôleur, beau parleur (person).
plausibly [-i] adv. Plausiblement; spécieusement.
play [plei] n. Action, activité *f.;* jeu *m.* (action); *in full play*, en pleine activité; *to bring, to come into play*, mettre, entrer en jeu. ‖ Amusement, divertissement, jeu *m.* (amusement); *child's play*, jeu d'enfant; *in play*, en plaisantant, pour rire; *play upon words*, jeu de mots. ‖ Jeu *m.* (gambling); *at play*, au jeu. ‖ Mouvement, jeu *m.* (movement); *play of light*, jeu de lumière. ‖ THEATR. Pièce *f.;* spectacle *m.* ‖ TECHN. Jeu *m.* (in a bearing). ‖ SPORTS. *In play, out of play*, en jeu, hors jeu. ‖ FIG. *Influences in play*, influences en jeu; *to give full play to*, donner libre cours à; U. S. *to make a play for*, mettre tout en œuvre pour obtenir, jouer le grand jeu pour obtenir (sth.). ‖ **Play-actor**, n. THEATR., FIG. Comédien *m.* ‖ **Play-actress**, n. THEATR., FIG. Comédienne *f.* ‖ **Play-back**, n. Retour (*m.*) en arrière, reproduction *f.* (of tape, of film); *play-back head*, tête de lecture. ‖ **Play-bill**, n. THEATR. Affiche *f.;* programme *m.* ‖ **Play-group**, n. Garderie *f.* (for young children). ‖ **Play-off**, n. SPORTS. Belle *f.;* match décisif *m.* ‖ **Play-room**, n. Nursery *f.* ‖ **Play-pen**, n. Parc (*m.*) pour enfants.
— v. intr. Jouer, folâtrer, prendre ses ébats, s'ébattre (animals, children). ‖ Jouer (fountain). ‖ SPORTS. *To play at cards, at football*, jouer aux cartes, au football; *to play for love, for money*, jouer pour l'honneur, pour de l'argent; *to be played*, se jouer (match). ‖ MUS. *To play (on) the piano*,

jouer du piano. ‖ FIG. *To play fair*, jouer franc jeu ; *to play for time*, gagner du temps ; *to play into s.o.'s hands*, faire le jeu de qqn ; *to play on words*, jouer sur les mots ; *to play truant* (or) U. S. *hookey*, faire l'école buissonnière ; *to play with fire, with s.o.'s affections*, jouer avec le feu, avec l'affection de qqn. ‖ **To play about**, faire des bêtises (with, avec). ‖ **To play off**, SPORTS. Rejouer un match ; jouer la belle. ‖ **To play on**, continuer de jouer. ‖ **To play up**, faire de son mieux ; U. S. *to play up to s.o.*, flatter qqn.

— v. tr. Faire, jouer ; *to play a trick, a joke on*, faire une farce (or) jouer un tour à. ‖ THEATR. Jouer (a part) ; *to play Hamlet*, jouer Hamlet, tenir le rôle de Hamlet. ‖ SPORTS. Jouer (a card) ; jouer à (football, tennis) ; disputer (a match) ; jouer contre (another team). ‖ MUS. Jouer de (an instrument) ; jouer (a piece). ‖ FIG. *To play the fool*, faire l'imbécile ; *to play the game*, jouer le jeu ; *to play s.o. false*, trahir qqn. ‖ **To play along**, embobiner, entortiller (to manipulate). ‖ **To play down**, minimiser. ‖ **To play off**, *to play s.o. off against s.o.*, opposer qqn à qqn. ‖ **To play up**, faire valoir, donner toute son importance à ; FAM. agacer, faire marcher (s.o.).

playboy [-bɔi] n. Playboy *m.*

player [-ə*] n. Joueur *s.* ‖ MUS. Exécutant *s.* ‖ THEATR. Acteur *m.* ; actrice *f.* ‖ SPORTS. Joueur, équipier *m.* ‖ **Player-piano**, n. MUS. Piano mécanique *m.*

playfellow [-felou] n. Camarade de jeu *m.*

playful [-ful] adj. Enjoué, folâtre, badin.

playfully [-fuli] adv. En jouant, en badinant (or) batifolant.

playfulness [-fulnis] n. Badinage, enjouement *m.*

playgoer [-gouə*] n. Amateur (*m.*) de théâtre ; habitué (*s.*) des spectacles.

playground [-graund] n. Cour de récréation *f.*

playhouse [-haus] n. Théâtre *m.* ‖ U. S. Maison de récréation *f.*

playing card [-iŋ kɑːd] n. Carte (*f.*) à jouer.

playing field [-iŋ fiːld] n. Terrain (*m.*) de sport.

playlet [-let] n. THEATR. Petite pièce, piécette *f.*

playmate [-meit] n. Camarade de jeu *m.*

plaything [-θiŋ] n. Jouet *m.*

playtime [-taim] n. Récréation *f.*

playwright [-rait] n. Auteur dramatique, dramaturge *m.*

plea [pliː] n. Excuse *f.* ; prétexte *m.* ; *on the plea of*, sous prétexte de. ‖ JUR. Défense *f.*

plead [pliːd] v. intr. Plaider, intercéder (*for*, pour ; *with*, auprès de). ‖ JUR. Plaider (guilty).

— v. tr. Invoquer, alléguer (an excuse). ‖ JUR. Plaider.

pleadable [-əbl] adj. Plaidable.

pleader [-ə*] n. Plaideur *m.*

pleading [-iŋ] n. Plaidoirie *f.*

— adj. Implorant.

pleadingly [-iŋli] adv. D'un ton suppliant.

pleasant ['pleznt] adj. Agréable, aimable ; *pleasant evening*, bonne soirée.

pleasantly [-li] adv. Agréablement.

pleasantness [-nis] n. Agrément, charme *m.*

pleasantry [-tri] n. Plaisanterie *f.*

please [pliːz] v. tr. Plaire à, faire plaisir à, contenter (s.o.) ; *hard to please*, difficile, exigeant ; *may it please your Majesty to*, que votre Majesté daigne ; *please God!*, Dieu le veuille !, plaise à Dieu ! *to be pleased to*, se plaire à, être heureux de ; *to please oneself*, faire à sa guise ; *to please the ear*, flatter l'oreille ; *please yourself*, faites comme bon vous semblera (or) comme vous l'entendrez.

— v. intr. Plaire, être agréable, faire plaisir ; *do as you please*, faites à votre guise (or) comme bon vous semble ; *if you please*, s'il vous plaît ; *please be seated*, veuillez vous asseoir ; asseyez-vous, je vous en prie ; *please don't do that*, de grâce, ne faites pas cela.

pleased [-d] adj. Content, satisfait (with, de).

pleasing [-iŋ] adj. Agréable.

pleasingly [-iŋli] adv. Agréablement.

pleasurable ['pleʒərəbl] adj. Agréable.

pleasurably [-i] adv. Agréablement.

pleasure ['pleʒə] n. Plaisir *m.* ; *at s.o.'s pleasure*, au gré de qqn ; *pleasure resort*, ville de plaisir ; *pleasure trip*, voyage d'agrément ; *to afford great pleasure to*, faire grand plaisir à ; *to take pleasure in*, éprouver du plaisir à ; *what is your pleasure?*, qu'y a-t-il pour votre service ? ; *with pleasure*, avec plaisir, volontiers. ‖ JUR. Bon plaisir (Queen's). ‖ **Pleasure-boat**, n. Bateau (*m.*) de plaisance. ‖ **Pleasure-ground**, n. Jardin d'agrément *m.* ‖ **Pleasure-loving**, adj. Qui aime le plaisir. ‖ **Pleasure-trip**, n. Voyage d'agrément *m.*

pleat [pliːt] n. Pli *m.* ; *box pleat*, pli creux.

— v. tr. Plisser, faire des plis à (a skirt).

plebeian [pli'biːən] adj., n. Plébéien, roturier *s.*

plebiscite ['plebisit] n. Plébiscite *m.*

plebs [plebs] n. Plèbe *f.* ‖ FAM. Populo *m.*

plectrum ['plektrəm] n. MUS. Plectre *m.*

pledge [pledʒ] n. Gage, nantissement *m.* ; *to put in pledge*, mettre en gage, engager ; *to take out of pledge*, dégager. ‖ Toast *m.* ; santé *f.* (toast). ‖ Vœu *m.* ; promesse *f.* (vow) ; *to sign the pledge*, faire vœu de tempérance.

— v. tr. Mettre en gage, engager. ‖ Boire à la santé de, porter un toast à (s.o.) [toast]. ‖ Engager, donner (one's word).

pledget [-it] n. MED. Plumasseau ; tampon (*m.*) de charpie.

Pleiad ['plaiəd] n. Pléiade *f.*

— N. B. Deux pluriels : *Pleiades, Pleiads*.

pleistocene ['plaistəsiːn] adj. Pléistocène.

plenary ['pliːnəri] adj. Entier, absolu. ‖ JUR. Plénier.

plenipotentiary [ˌplenipə'tenʃəri] n. Plénipotentiaire *m.*

plenitude ['plenitjuːd] n. Plénitude *f.*

plenteous ['plentjəs] adj. Abondant.

plenteously [-li] adv. Abondamment.

plenteousness [-nis] n. Abondance *f.*

plentiful ['plentiful] adj. Abondant, copieux.

plenty ['plenti] n. Abondance *f.* ; *horn of plenty*, corne d'abondance ; *in plenty*, à foison, en suffisance ; *land of plenty*, pays de cocagne ; *plenty of*, quantité de ; *to have plenty of time, to live on*, avoir largement le temps, de quoi vivre.

— adv. FAM. Grandement, largement.

plenum ['pliːnəm] n. PHYS. Plein *m.*

pleonasm ['pliːənæzm] n. Pléonasme *m.*

pleonastic [ˌpliːə'næstik] adj. Pléonastique.

plesiosaurus ['pliːsiə'sɔːrəs] n. Plésiosaure *m.*

plethora ['pleθərə] n. Pléthore *f.*

plethoric [ple'θɔrik] adj. Pléthorique.

pleura ['pluərə] n. MED. Plèvre *f.*

pleurisy ['pluərisi] n. MED. Pleurésie *f.*

pleuritic [pluə'ritik] adj. Pleurétique.

plexiglass ['pleksiˌglɑːs] n. (trade mark). TECHN. Plexiglas *m.*

plexus ['pleksəs] n. MED. Plexus *m.*

— N. B. Deux pluriels : *plexus, plexuses*.

pliability [ˌplaiə'biliti] n. Flexibilité *f.* ‖ FIG. Souplesse, docilité *f.*

pliable ['plaiəbl], **pliant** [-ənt] adj. Flexible. ‖ FIG. Souple, docile, malléable.

pliancy ['plaiənsi] n. Flexibilité *f.* ‖ FIG. Malléabilité *f.*

pliantly [-li] adv. Avec souplesse. ‖ FIG. Docilement.

pliers ['plaiəz] n. pl. Pinces *f.* pl.

plight [plait] v. tr. Engager ; *plighted lovers*, fiancés ; *plighted word*, parole engagée ; *to plight one's troth*, s'engager, engager sa foi.

plight n. État *m.* ; condition *f.* ; *in a sorry plight*, dans un triste état ; dans de beaux draps (fam.).

plimsoll ['plimsəl] n. Chaussure de gymnastique *f.*. tennis *m. invar.*

Plimsoll n. NAUT. *Plimsoll line* (or) *mark,* marque de franc-bord.

plinth [plinθ] n. ARCHIT. Plinthe *f.*; socle *m.*

pliocene ['plaiəsi:n] adj. Pliocène.

plod [plɔd] v. intr. (1). Marcher péniblement, cheminer lourdement. ‖ **To plod on,** persévérer.
— n. Marche pénible *f.*

plodder [-ə*] n. Travailleur *s.*; bûcheur, piocheur *s.* (fam.).

plodding [-iη] adj. Pesant, lourd (step). ‖ Persévérant (person).

plonk [plɔŋk] n., v. See PLUNK.

plonk n. FAM. Pinard *m.* (wine); picrate, gros rouge *m.* (cheap wine).

plop [plɔp] n. Plouf *m.*
— v. intr. Faire plouf, tomber en faisant plouf.
— adv. Avec un plouf, en faisant plouf.

plosive ['plousiv] n., adj. GRAMM. Occlusive *f.*, *adj. f.*

plot [plɔt] n. Parcelle *f.* (of land). ‖ Intrigue *f.* (of a novel). ‖ Complot *m.*, conspiration *f.* (conspiration); *the Gunpowder Plot,* la conspiration des Poudres; *to hatch a plot,* ourdir un complot. ‖ MATH. Tracé *m.* ‖ THEATR. *Lighting plot,* jeux de lumière durant une représentation.
— v. tr. (1). Relever; *plotting paper,* papier quadrillé; *to plot on the map,* pointer sur la carte. ‖ Comploter, conspirer. ‖ MATH. Tracer.
— v. intr. Conspirer, comploter.

plotter [-ə*] n. Conspirateur *m.*; conspiratrice *f.*

plough [plau] n. AGRIC. Charrue *f.* ‖ ASTRON. Chariot *m.* ‖ FIG. *To put one's hand to the plough,* se mettre à l'ouvrage. ‖ **Plough-land,** AGRIC. Terre (*f.*) de labour. ‖ **Plough-stock** (or) **-tail,** n. AGRIC. Mancheron (*m.*) de charrue.
— v. tr. AGRIC. Labourer (a field); creuser (a furrow). ‖ FIG. Fendre, sillonner. ‖ **To plough in,** AGRIC. Enterrer en labourant (a crop). ‖ **To plough up,** AGRIC. Passer la charrue dans (a field).
— v. intr. AGRIC. Labourer.

ploughman [-mən] (pl. **ploughmen** [-men]) n. AGRIC. Laboureur *m.*

ploughshare [-ʃεə*] n. AGRIC. Soc (*m.*) de charrue.

plover ['plʌvə*] n. ZOOL. Pluvier *m.*

plow [plau]. U. S. See PLOUGH.

ploy [plɔi] n. FAM. Coup, truc, stratagème *m.*; feinte *f.* (manœuvre). ‖ FAM. Affaire *f.* (occupation).

pluck [plʌk] n. Action (*f.*) d'arracher d'un coup sec. ‖ CULIN. Fressure *f.* ‖ FAM. Cran, cœur, courage *m.*
— v. tr. Plumer (a bird); épiler (the eyebrows); arracher (feathers); cueillir (a flower); *to pluck s.o. by the sleeve,* tirer qqn par la manche. ‖ FAM. *To be plucked,* être recalé (at exam.). ‖ **To pluck out,** arracher. ‖ **To pluck up,** arracher; FIG. ressaisir; *to pluck up courage,* reprendre courage; prendre son courage à deux mains (fam.).

pluckily [-ili] adv. Avec courage.

plucky [-i] adj. Courageux; crâne (fam.); *to be plucky,* avoir du cran, n'avoir pas froid aux yeux.

plug [plʌg] n. Tampon, bouchon *m.*; bonde *f.* ‖ Chique *f.* (of tobacco). ‖ Chasse d'eau (of a W. C.); *to pull the plug,* tirer la chasse. ‖ ELECTR. Fiche, prise *f.* ‖ AUTOM. Bougie *f.* ‖ FAM. Réclame *f.* ‖ **Plug-hole,** n. Trou d'écoulement *m.*
— v. tr. (1). Boucher, tamponner. ‖ FAM. Faire l'article pour; enfoncer dans la tête du public. ‖ POP. Tirer une balle dans la peau de (s.o.) [to shoot]. ‖ **To plug in,** ELECTR. Brancher. ‖ **To plug up,** boucher.
— v. intr. **To plug away,** FAM. Turbiner, bûcher, piocher, buriner.

plum [plʌm] n. Prune *f.*; *plum tree,* prunier. ‖ FIG. Morceau de choix *m.*, aubaine *f.* ‖ FAM. *The plums,* les meilleurs filons (jobs). ‖ **Plum-cake,**

n. CULIN. Cake *m.* ‖ **Plum-duff,** n. CULIN. Pudding (*m.*) aux raisins. ‖ **Plum-pudding,** n. CULIN. Plum-pudding *m.*

plumage ['plu:midӡ] n. Plumage *m.*

plumb [plʌm] n. Plomb *m.* (of a plumb-line). ‖ Aplomb *m.*; *out of plumb,* hors d'aplomb. ‖ NAUT. Sonde *f.* ‖ **Plumb-bob,** n. Plomb *m.* (of a plumb-line). ‖ **Plumb-line,** n. Fil à plomb *m.* ‖ **Plumb-rule,** n. Niveau à plomb *m.*
— adj. Vertical, droit, d'aplomb, à plomb.
— adv. FAM. En plein, exactement, juste; *to fall plumb on one's head,* tomber en plein sur la tête. ‖ U. S. FAM. Complètement; *plumb crazy,* totalement fou, fou à lier.
— v. tr. Sonder (the depths). ‖ Vérifier l'aplomb de, remettre d'aplomb (sth.).

plumbago [-'beigou] n. Plombagine *f.*

plumber ['plʌmə*] n. Plombier *m.*

plumbic ['plʌmbik] adj. CHIM. Plombique.

plumbiferous [plʌm'bifərəs] adj. Plombifère.

plumbing [-iη] n. Plomberie *f.* ‖ Tuyauterie *f.*; *modern plumbing,* tout-à-l'égout.

plume [plu:m] n. Panache, plumet *m.*, aigrette *f.*
— v. tr. Orner de plumes. ‖ FIG. *To plume oneself,* se piquer, se targuer (on, de).

plummer-block ['plʌmə,blɔk] n. TECHN. Palier *m.*

plummet ['plʌmit] n. Plomb *m.* ‖ NAUT. Sonde *f.*
— v. intr. Tomber en chute libre, s'effondrer; dégringoler (fam.).

plummy ['plʌmi] adj. Abondant en prunes. ‖ FAM. De choix, de première bourre (work); traînant, caverneux (voice).

plump [plʌmp] adj. Grassouillet, potelé, rebondi, dodu; rondouillard (fam.).
— v. intr. Tomber lourdement. ‖ **To plump for,** FAM. Choisir, donner sa voix à (a candidate).
— v. tr. Jeter brusquement; flanquer (fam.); *to plump oneself down,* se laisser tomber, s'affaler. ‖ **To plump up,** secouer (a pillow).
— n. Chute lourde *f.*; *to fall with a plump,* tomber comme une masse.
— adv. Pesamment, lourdement.

plumpness [-nis] n. Embonpoint *m.*

plunder ['plʌndə*] n. Butin *m.* (booty). ‖ Pillage *m.* (of a town).
— v. tr. Piller, saccager, mettre à sac.

plunderer [-ərə*] n. Pillard *m.*

plunge [plʌndӡ] n. Plongeon *m.* ‖ FIG. *To take the plunge,* faire le plongeon.
— v. tr. Plonger, enfoncer, immerger (into, dans). ‖ COMM. *Plunging neckline,* décolleté plongeant. ‖ FIG. Plonger, jeter (into, dans).
— v. intr. Plonger, se jeter. ‖ NAUT. Tanguer (ship).

plunger [-ə*] n. Plongeur *m.* ‖ U. S. Spéculateur *m.*

plunk [plʌŋk] v. intr. Tomber avec un bruit sourd, chuter; *to plunk down in,* se laisser choir (or) s'affaler dans. ‖ Sonner, tinter, résonner (guitar, rain).
— v. tr. Poser bruyamment (an object); allonger (money). ‖ Faire sonner (or) tinter (or) résonner (a guitar).
— n. Bruit sourd *m.* (of drops of water); son, tintement *m.* (of guitar).

pluperfect ['plu:'pə:fikt] n., adj. GRAMM. Plus-que-parfait *m.*

plural ['pluərəl] n., adj. GRAMM. Pluriel *m.*; *in the plural,* au pluriel.

pluralism [-izm̩] n. Cumul *m.*

pluralist [-ist] n. Cumulard *m.* (fam.).

plurality [pluə'ræliti] n. Cumul *m.* (of offices). ‖ Majorité *f.* (majority).

plus [plʌs] prep. Plus.
— adj. En plus, de plus. ‖ **Plus-fours,** n. Culotte (*f.*) de golf.
— n. MATH. Plus *m.* (sign).

plush [plʌʃ] n. Peluche *f.*
— adj. See PLUSHY.

plushy [-i] adj. Pelucheux. ‖ FAM. Rupin.

Pluto ['plu:tou] n. Pluton m.

plutocracy ['plu:'tɔkrəsi] n. Ploutocratie f.

plutocrat ['plu:təkræt] n. Ploutocrate m.

plutocratic [plu:to'krætik] adj. Ploutocratique.

plutonium [plu:'touniəm] n. CHIM. Plutonium m.

pluvial ['plu:viəl] adj. Pluvieux.

pluviometer [,plu:vi'ɔmitə*] n. Pluviomètre m.

ply [plai] n. Pli m. (of material); toron, brin m. (of rope).

— v. tr. (2). Manier, se servir de : to ply the needle, manier (or) faire courir l'aiguille; to ply the oars, faire force de rames; to ply s.o. with drink, verser à boire sans arrêt à qqn; to ply s.o. with questions, presser qqn de questions; to ply a trade, exercer un métier.

— v. intr. Faire le trajet (or) le service (or) la navette (between, entre).

plywood [-wu:d] n. Contre-plaqué m.

P.M. [pi:'em] abbr. Prime Minister, Premier ministre.

p.m. abbr. post meridiem, de l'après-midi (or) du soir; at 7 p.m., à 7 h du soir, à 19 h.

pneumatic [nju:'mætik] adj. Pneumatique; pneumatic drill, foreuse à air comprimé.

pneumonia [nju'mounjə] n. MED. Pneumonie f.

po [pou] (pl. **pos** [-z]) n. FAM. Pot m. (chamber pot). || **Po-faced,** adj. FAM. A l'air pincé, avec une figure d'enterrement.

P.O. [pi:'ou] abbr. Post office, poste; P.O. box, boîte postale.

poach [poutʃ] v. tr. CULIN. Pocher (eggs).

poach v. tr. Braconner (game). || SPORTS. Chiper (at tennis). || FIG. To poach on s.o.'s preserves, picorer dans l'assiette de qqn, marcher sur les platebandes de qqn.

— v. intr. Braconner.

poacher [-ə*] n. Braconnier m. || SPORTS. Chipeur.

poaching [-iŋ] n. Braconnage m.

pochette [pɔ'ʃet] n. Pochette f.

pock [pɔk] n. MED. Pustule de petite vérole f. || **Pock-mark,** MED. Marque de petite vérole. || **Pock-marked,** MED. Grêlé (face).

pocket ['pɔkit] n. Poche f.; breast pocket, poche intérieure; pocket edition, édition de poche. || Sac m. (of hops). || Poche f., sac m. (of ore). || SPORTS. Blouse f. (of a billiard-table). || AVIAT. Air pocket, trou d'air m. || MILIT. Poche f. (of troops). || MED. Poche f. (under the eyes). || FAM. To be in pocket, être en veine; to be out of pocket, y être de sa poche; en être pour son argent; to have s.o. in one's pocket, avoir qqn dans sa manche. || **Pocket-battleship,** n. NAUT. Cuirassé (m.) de poche. || **Pocket-book,** n. Calepin; portefeuille m. (note-book); U. S. sac (m.) à main (hand-bag). || **Pocket calculator,** n. Calculatrice de poche f. || **Pocket-comb,** n. Peigne (m.) de poche. || **Pocket-handkerchief,** n. Mouchoir (m.) de poche. || **Pocket-knife,** n. Canif m. || **Pocket-lamp,** n. Lampe de poche f. || **Pocket-money,** n. Argent (m.) de poche. || **Pocket veto,** n. U. S. Veto présidentiel de fait m.

— v. tr. Empocher, mettre dans sa poche; to pocket money, empocher, palper (fam.). || SPORTS. Blouser (at billiards). || FIG. To pocket one's pride, mettre son orgueil dans sa poche. || FAM. Chiper (to steal).

pocketful [-ful] n. Pochée, pleine poche f.

pod [pɔd] n. Gousse, cosse f.; senna pods, follicules de séné.

— v. intr. (1). Former des cosses.

— v. tr. Ecosser.

podge [pɔdʒ] n. FAM. Rondouillard s.; magot m.

podginess [-inis] n. FAM. Embonpoint m.

podgy [-i] adj. FAM. Potelé, rondelet.

podiatrist [pɔ'di:ətrist] n. U. S. Pédicure s.

podiatry [pɔ'di:ətri] n. U. S. Pédicurie f.

podium ['poudiəm] n. Podium m.

poem ['pouim] n. Poème m.

poet ['pouit] n. Poète m.

poetaster [,pouitæstə*] n. Poétaillon, rimailleur m.

poetess ['pouitis] n. Poétesse, femme poète f.

poetic [po'etik], **poetical** [-əl] adj. Poétique.

poetically [-əli] adv. Poétiquement.

poeticize [po'etisaiz] v. tr., intr. Poétiser.

poetics [po'etiks] n. sg. Poétique f.

poetize ['pouitaiz] v. intr. Faire des vers.

poetry ['pouitri] n. Poésie f.; piece of poetry, poésie; to write poetry, faire des vers.

pogrom ['pɔgrəm] n. Pogrom(e) m.

poignancy ['pɔinənsi] n. Mordant m.; acuité f. || FIG. Piquant m.

poignant [-t] adj. Mordant, aigu, poignant. || CULIN. Piquant, relevé (sauce). || U. S. Emouvant (moving).

poignantly [-li] adv. D'une façon poignante (or) U. S. émouvante.

poinsettia [pɔin'setiə] n. BOT. Poinsettia m.

point [pɔint] n. Point m.; cardinal points, les points cardinaux; points of the compass, rose des vents, aire de vent. || Point m. (of departure, of view). Particularité, caractéristique f. (of an animal). || Point, détail m. (of an argument, of a story); I see no point in, j'estime inutile de; in point of fact, en fait, à vrai dire; in point of numbers, sous le rapport du nombre; beside the point, à côté de la question; on that, this point, à cet égard; off the point, hors de propos, étranger à la question; to carry one's point, avoir gain de cause; to come to the point, venir au fait; to make a point, faire ressortir un argument; to the point, à propos. || Trait m. (of character); that's not my strong point, ce n'est pas mon fort; to have one's good points, avoir ses bons côtés. || Cas m. (of conscience); question f. (of fact); point m. (of honour); to make a point of, se faire un cas de conscience (or) un devoir de; to make it a point of pride not to complain, se faire un point d'orgueil de ne pas se plaindre. || Pointe f. (of a needle); bec m. (of a pen); rayon m. (of a star). || Point, instant m. (of time); on the point of death, à l'article de la mort; to be on the point of doing sth., être sur le point de faire qqch. || PHYS. Degré, point m.; boiling point, point d'ébullition. || MATH. Point m. (of intersection); decimal point, virgule; six point five, six virgule cinq. || MILIT. Pointe f. (of an advance-guard). || SPORTS. To score points, marquer des points; to win on points, gagner aux points. || COMM., FIN. Point m. || ELECTR. Prise (f.) de courant. || CH. DE F. Pl. Aiguilles f. pl. || GEOGR. Promontoire m. || BLASON. Point m. || GRAMM. Point m. (of punctuation). || **Point-blank,** adj. Direct, sans correction (fire); de but en blanc, à brûle-pourpoint (question); net, catégorique (refusal); adv. Catégoriquement (bluntly); à brûle-pourpoint; à bout portant (straight). || **Point-duty,** n. On point-duty, de service; à station fixe; policeman on point-duty, agent-vigie. || **Point-to-point,** n. SPORTS. Steeple-chase m.

— v. tr. Tailler en pointe, munir d'une pointe (a stick); aiguiser (a tool). || Tendre (a finger); braquer, pointer (a weapon). || Indiquer, montrer (the way). || TECHN. Jointoyer (brickwork). || FIG. Donner du piquant à (a remark). || **To point out,** montrer (or) indiquer du doigt; FIG. Signaler, faire remarquer. || **To point up,** U. S. Accentuer, souligner, faire ressortir.

— v. intr. To point at, montrer du doigt. || **To point to,** être dirigé vers; désigner (a direction); indiquer (the hour).

pointed ['pɔintid] adj. Pointu, effilé; à pointe. || ARCHIT. Pointed arch, ogive. || FIG. Mordant, sarcastique (remark).

pointedly [-li] adv. FIG. D'un ton mordant.

pointedness [-nis] n. FIG. Mordant m.

pointer ['pɔintə*] n. Baguette f. (stick). || Aiguille f. (of a dial). || ZOOL. Chien d'arrêt m. || FAM. Tuyau m. (tip).

pointing [-iŋ] n. ARCHIT. Jointoiement *m*.
pointless [-lis] adj. Emoussé, épointé ; sans pointe.
‖ FIG. Inutile (action) ; sans sel (joke) ; ridicule (remark).
pointsman [-smən] (pl. **pointsmen**) n. CH. DE F. Aiguilleur *m*.
poise [pɔiz] n. Equilibre *m*. ‖ Port *m*. (of the head). ‖ FIG. Poids, équilibre *m*. ; pondération *f*.
— v. tr. Tenir en équilibre.
— v. intr. Etre en équilibre.
poison ['pɔizn] n. Poison *m*. ; *to take poison*, s'empoisonner. ‖ **Poison-gas**, n. Gaz asphyxiant *m*. ‖ **Poison-pen**, n. FAM. Corbeau ; auteur (*m*.) de lettres anonymes.
— v. tr. Empoisonner. ‖ FIG. Corrompre, contaminer, pervertir.
poisoner [-ə*] n. Empoisonneur *m*.
poisoning [-iŋ] n. Empoisonnement *m*.
poisonous [-əs] adj. Venimeux (animal) ; asphyxiant (gas) ; vénéneux (plant). ‖ FIG. Empoisonné.
poke [pouk] n. Sac *m*. ; poche *f*.
poke n. Poussée *f*. ; coup *m*. (with the finger). ‖ **Poke-bonnet**, n. Cabriolet *m*.
— v. tr. Pousser, piquer, enfoncer ; *to poke s.o. in the ribs*, donner à qqn une bourrade (or) un coup de coude dans les côtes. ‖ Attiser, tisonner (the fire). ‖ FIG. *To poke fun at*, se moquer de ; se payer la tête de, se ficher de (s.o.) [fam.] ; *to poke one's nose into*, fourrer son nez dans.
poker [-ə*] n. Tisonnier *m*. ‖ FAM. *As stiff as a poker*, raide comme un piquet. ‖ **Poker-work**, n. Pyrogravure *f*.
poker n. SPORTS. Poker *m*. ‖ **Poker-face**, n. Visage impassible *m*.
poky [-i] adj. Misérable (lodgings).
Poland ['poulənd] n. GEOGR. Pologne *f*.
polar ['poulə*] adj. Polaire (circle) ; *polar bear*, ours blanc ; *polar lights*, aurore boréale.
— s. MATH. Polaire *f*.
polarimeter [ˌpoulə'rimitə*] n. PHYS. Polarimètre *m*.
polariscope [po'læriskoup] n. PHYS. Polariscope m.
polarity [po'læriti] n. Polarité *f*.
polarization [ˌpoulərai'zeiʃən] n. Polarisation *f*.
polarize ['poulərɑiz] v. tr. Polariser.
— v. intr. Se polariser.
pole [poul] n. Poteau *m*. ; *greasy pole*, mât de cocagne ; *telegraph pole*, poteau télégraphique. ‖ Timon *m*. (carriage). ‖ Montant *m*. (of a tent). ‖ Perche *f*. ‖ FAM. *Up the pole*, timbré, toqué, cinglé. ‖ **Pole-vaulting**, n. SPORTS. Saut (*m*.) à la perche.
— v. tr. Pousser à la perche ; *to pole one's way*, faire avancer le bateau à la perche.
pole n. Pôle *m*. ‖ GEOGR. *North, South Pole*, pôle nord, pôle sud. ‖ ASTRON. *Pole star*, étoile polaire. ‖ ELECTR. Pôle *m*.
Pole n. GEOGR. Polonais *s*.
pole-axe [-æks] n. Merlin *m*.
— v. tr. Assommer.
polecat [-kæt] n. ZOOL. Putois *m*. ‖ U. S. Mouffette *f*.
polemic [pə'lemik] adj. Polémique *f*.
polemics [-iks] n. sg. Polémique *f*.
police [pə'li:s] n. Police *f*. ; *police officer*, agent de police ; *police station*, poste de police, commissariat ; gendarmerie (rural) ; *river police*, police fluviale ; *police dog*, chien policier ; *police state*, Etat policier. ‖ **Police-court**, n. Tribunal (*m*.) de simple police.
— v. tr. Policer. ‖ Contrôler ; superviser.
policeman [-mən] (pl. **policemen**) n. Agent (*m*.) de police ; sergent (*m*.) de ville. ‖ Gendarme *m*. (only rural).
policewoman [-wumən] (pl. **policewomen** [-wimən]) n. Femme-agent *f*.
policy ['pɔlisi] n. Politique *f*. ; *foreign policy*, poli-

tique étrangère. ‖ Conduite *f*. ; *honesty is the best policy*, l'honnêteté est la meilleure politique ; *our policy is to*, nous avons pour principe de.
policy n. Police *f*. (insurance policy) ; *to take out a policy*, prendre une police. ‖ **Policy-holder**, n. Assuré *s*.
polio ['pouliou] n. FAM., MED. Polio *f*.
poliomyelitis ['poulioumaiə'laitis] n. MED. Poliomyélite *f*.
polish ['pɔliʃ] n. Poli, brillant, lustre *m*. (of a surface) ; *high polish*, poli brillant ; *to take the polish off*, ternir. ‖ *Boot* (or) U. S. *shoe polish*, cirage, crème à chaussures ; *floor polish*, cire à parquet ; *furniture polish*, encaustique à meubles ; *liquid metal polish*, produit d'entretien pour les cuivres ; *nail polish*, vernis pour ongles ; *stove polish*, pâte pour fourneaux. ‖ FIG. Politesse *f*. ; belles manières *f*. *pl*. ; vernis *m*.
— v. tr. Cirer (the floor, shoes) ; astiquer (leather) ; lisser (stone) ; polir (wood). ‖ FIG. Raffiner, polir (s.o.). ‖ **To polish off**, expédier, terminer rapidement (work) ; FAM. *To polish s.o. off*, en finir avec qqn ; régler le compte de qqn. ‖ **To polish up**, faire reluire ; astiquer ; FIG. Dégourdir (a boor) ; dérouiller (a language) ; châtier ; fignoler (fam.) [one's style].
Polish ['pouliʃ] adj. GEOGR. Polonais.
polisher ['pouliʃə*] n. Polisseur *s*. (person). ‖ Polissoir *m*. (machine).
politburo ['pɔlit,bjuərou] n. Politburo, bureau politique *m*.
polite [pə'lait] adj. Poli, courtois ; *polite society*, le beau monde.
politely [-li] adv. Poliment ; avec politesse.
politeness [-nis] n. Politesse *f*.
politic ['pɔlitik] adj. Politique, avisé, judicieux, prudent. ‖ *The body politic*, le corps politique.
political [pə'litikəl] adj. Politique (economy, geography, party) ; *political jobbery*, politicaillerie.
politically [-i] adv. Politiquement.
politician [ˌpɔli'tiʃən] n. Homme politique *m*. ‖ Politicien *m*. (pej.).
politico [pə'liti,kou] (pl. **politicos** [-z]) n. FAM. Politicien *s*., homme politique *m*.
politics ['pɔlitiks] n. sg. Politique *f*.
polity ['pɔliti] n. Constitution politique *f*. ‖ Etat *m*.
polka ['pɔlkə] n. Polka *f*. ‖ **Polka-dotted**, adj. COMM. A pois (material).
poll [poul] n. Tête *f*. (head). ‖ Vote, scrutin *m*. ; *to go to the poll* (or) U. S. *polls*, aller aux urnes. ‖ Sondage *m*. (Gallup). ‖ **Poll-tax**, n. Capitation *f*.
— v. tr. Ecorner (cattle) ; étêter (a tree). ‖ Obtenir (a vote).
— v. intr. Voter (in an election).
Poll [pɔl] n. (*Pretty*) *Poll*, Jacquot (parrot).
pollard [-əd] n. Animal (*m*.) sans cornes. ‖ Têtard *m*. (tree).
— v. tr. Etêter (a tree).
pollen ['pɔlən] n. Pollen *m*.
pollinate [-ineit] v. tr. Couvrir de pollen.
polling ['pouliŋ] n. Action (*f*.) de voter ; élections *f*. *pl*. ‖ **Polling-booth**, n. Isoloir *m*. ; bureau de scrutin *m*. ‖ **Polling-station**, n. Centre de vote *m*.
pollinization [pɔlinai'zeiʃən] n. BOT. Pollinisation *f*.
polliwog ['pɔliwɔg] n. U. S. ZOOL. Têtard *m*.
pollster [-stə*] n. U. S. Enquêteur public *m*.
pollutant [pə'lu:tnt] adj., n. Polluant adj., *m*.
pollute [po'lju:t] v. tr. Polluer, souiller, rendre impur. ‖ FIG. Corrompre, profaner.
pollution [-ʃən] n. Pollution, contamination *f*.
polo ['poulou] n. SPORTS. Polo *m*. ; *polo shirt*, polo.
polonaise [ˌpɔlə'neiz] n. Polonaise *f*. (dress, dance).
polonium [pə'louniəm] n. CHIM. Polonium *m*.
polony [pə'louni] n. CULIN. Saucisson *m*.

poltergeist ['pɔltə,gaist] n. Esprit frappeur (or) follet, lutin m.
poltroon [pɔl'tru:n] n. Poltron m.
polyandrous [pɔli'ændrəs] adj. Polyandre.
polyandry ['pɔliændri] n. Polyandrie f.
polyanthus [,pɔli'ænθəs] n. BOT. Primevère f.
polyatomic [,pɔliə'tɔmik] adj. CHIM. Polyatomique.
polybasic [,pɔli'beisik] adj. CHIM. Polybasique.
polychromatic [,pɔlikro'mætik] adj. Polychrome.
polychrome ['pɔlikroum] adj. Polychrome.
— n. Polychromie f.
polyclinic [,pɔli'klinik] n. MED. Polyclinique f.
polyester ['pɔli,estə*] n. CHIM. Polyester m.
polyethylene [,pɔli'eθi,li:n] n. CHIM. Polyéthylène m.
polygamist [po'ligəmist] n. Polygame m.
polygamous [-əs] adj. Polygame.
polygamy [-i] n. Polygamie f.
polyglot ['pɔliglɔt] adj., n. Polyglotte s.
polygon ['pɔligən] n. MATH. Polygone m.
polygonal [po'ligɔnəl] adj. MATH. Polygonal.
polygonum [-gənəm] n. BOT. Renouée f.
polyhedral ['pɔli'hi:drəl], polyhedric [-'hedrik] adj. Polyèdre, polyédrique.
polyhedron ['hi:drən] n. MATH. Polyèdre m.
polymath ['pɔli,mæθ] n. Savant m., personne (f.) au savoir encyclopédique.
polymer ['pɔlimə*] n. CHIM. Polymère m.
polymeric [,pɔli'merik] adj. CHIM. Polymère.
polymerization [pə,limərai'zei∫ən] n. CHIM. Polymérisation f.
polymerize ['pɔlimə,raiz] v. tr. CHIM. Polymériser.
polymorphic [,pɔli'mɔ:fik], polymorphous [-'mɔ:fəs] adj. Polymorphe.
polymorphism [-'mɔ:fizm̩] n. Polymorphisme m.
polymorphonuclear [-,mɔ:fou'nju:kliə*] adj. MED. Polynucléaire.
Polynesia [,pɔli'ni:ʒə] n. GEOGR. Polynésie f.
Polynesian [-'ni:ʒən] adj., n. GEOGR. Polynésien adj., s.
polynomial [-'noumiəl] adj., n. MATH. Polynôme m.
polyp(e) ['pɔlip] n. Polype m.
polyphase ['pɔlifeiz] adj. ELECTR. Polyphasé.
polyphonic [,pɔli'fɔnik], polyphonous [pɔ'lifənəs] adj. MUS. Polyphonique. ‖ GRAMM. Polyphone (letter).
polyphony [pə'lifəni] n. MUS., GRAMM. Polyphonie f.
polypod ['pɔli,pɔd] n., adj. ZOOL. Polypode m.
polypropylene [,pɔli'proupi,li:n] n. CHIM. Polypropylène m.
polypus ['pɔlipəs] (pl. polipi [-pai]) n. MED. Polype m.
polysemic [,pɔli'si:mik], polysemous [-'si:məs] adj. GRAMM. Polysémique.
polysemy [,pɔli'si:mi] n. GRAMM. Polysémie f.
polystyrene [-'stairi:n] n. CHIM. Polystyrène m.
polysyllabic [,pɔlisi'læbik] adj. Polysyllabique.
polysyllable ['pɔlisiləbl̩] n. Polysyllabe m.
polytechnic [-'teknik] adj. Polytechnique.
polytheism ['pɔliθi:izm̩] n. Polythéisme m.
polytheist [-θi:ist] n. Polythéiste m.
polythene ['pɔli,θi:n] n. CHIM. Polyéthylène m. ‖ COMM. Polythene bag, sac en plastique.
polyurethane [,pɔli'juərə,θein] n. CHIM. Polyuréthane m.
polyvalence [,pɔli'veiləns], polyvalency [-ənsi] n. CHIM. Polyvalence f.
polyvalent [-ənt] adj. CHIM. Polyvalent.
polyvinyl [,pɔli'vainil] adj. CHIM. Polyvinylique; de polyvinyle.
pom [pɔm] n. See POMMY.
pomade [pə'mɑ:d] n. Pommade f.
— v. tr. Pommader.

pomander [po'mændə*] n. Sachet parfumé m.
pomegranate ['pɔmigrænət] n. BOT. Grenade f. (fruit); grenadier m. (tree).
pommel ['pʌml] n. Pommeau m.
— v. tr. Rosser, bourrer de coups.
pommy, pommie ['pɔmi] n. POP. Anglais, British s. (in Australian slang).
pomp [pɔmp] n. Pompe f.; faste, apparat m.; pomp and circumstance, grand apparat.
pom-pom ['pɔmpɔm] n. MILIT. Canon-mitrailleuse m.
pompon ['pɔmpɔn] n. Pompon m.
pomposity [pɔm'pɔsiti] n. Suffisance, emphase f.
pompous ['pɔmpəs] adj. Fastueux. ‖ Prétentieux, suffisant (person); ampoulé, emphatique; pompier (fam.) [style].
pompously [-li] adv. Pompeusement.
ponce [pɔns] n. POP. Souteneur, maquereau m.; proxénète s. (pimp). ‖ POP. Tapette f. (pansy).
— v. intr. POP. Faire le maquereau, vivre de proxénétisme (to pimp). ‖ POP. To ponce around (or) about, se donner des airs de tapette.
poncho ['pɔnt∫ou] (pl. ponchos [-z]) n. Poncho m.; pèlerine (or) cape (f.) de cycliste.
pond [pɔnd] n. Bassin m.; pièce d'eau f. ‖ Mare f.; étang m. (in a meadow); abreuvoir m. (on a farm). ‖ Vivier m. (fish-pond).
ponder ['pɔndə*] v. tr. Considérer, peser; réfléchir à (or) sur (sth.).
— v. intr. Méditer, réfléchir.
ponderable [-ərəbl̩] adj. Pondérable.
ponderous [-ərəs] adj. Massif, pesant, lourd (object). ‖ FIG. Ennuyeux, laborieux (task).
ponderously [-ərəsli] adv. Pesamment.
pone [poun] n. U. S. Pain de maïs m.
pong [pɔŋ] n. FAM. Infection, puanteur f.
— v. intr. FAM. Empester; puer, chlinguer (pop.).
pongee [pɔn'dʒi:] n. Pongé m.
poniard ['pɔnjəd] n. † Poignard m.
— v. tr. Poignarder.
pontiff ['pɔntif] n. Pontife m. ‖ ECCLES. Prélat, évêque m.
pontifical [pɔn'tifikəl] adj. ECCLES. Pontifical.
— n. pl. ECCLES. Ornements pontificaux m. pl.
pontificate [-'tifikit] n. ECCLES. Pontificat m.
— [-'tifikeit] v. intr. FAM. Pontifier.
pontify ['pɔntifai] v. intr. (2). FAM. Pontifier; faire l'important.
pontoneer [,pɔntə'niə*] n. MILIT. Pontonnier m.
pontoon [pɔn'tu:n] n. Ponton m. ‖ Pontoon-bridge, n. Pont (m.) de bateaux.
pontoon n. Vingt-et-un (at cards).
pony ['pouni] n. Poney m. ‖ POP. Vingt-cinq livres sterling. ‖ U. S. Corrigé m. (at school). [See CRIB.] ‖ Pony-carriage, n. Panier m. ‖ Pony-tail hair-do, n. Queue (f.) de cheval.
pooch [pu:t∫] n. U. S. FAM. Cabot, clebs m.
poodle ['pu:dl̩] n. ZOOL. Caniche m.
poof [puf] n. POP. Pédé m.; tapette, tante f.
pooh [pu:] inter. Bah! Peup! ‖ Pooh-pooh, v. tr. Faire fi de, se moquer de; dédaigner, dénigrer.
pool [pu:l] n. Mare f. (pond); piscine f. (swimming-pool). ‖ Mare f. (of blood); flaque f. (of water).
pool n. SPORTS. Cagnotte f. (at cards); poule f. (billiards); football pool, concours de pronostics de football. ‖ COMM. Pool; syndicat industriel (or) commerçant; typists' pool, équipe de dactylos.
— v. tr. Mettre en commun. ‖ COMM. Mettre en syndicat; former un pool de.
poop [pu:p] n. NAUT. Poupe f. (stern); dunette f. (poop-deck). ‖ Poop-deck, n. NAUT. Dunette f. ‖ Poop-rail, n. NAUT. Rambarde f.
— v. tr. Embarquer par l'arrière (a wave). ‖ Balayer la dunette de (a ship).
poop n. U. S. FAM. Tuyau m. (tip).
pooped [pu:pt] adj. FAM. Vanné, crevé, raplapla.
poor [puə*] adj. Pauvre, indigent (indigent); a poor

man, *woman*, un pauvre, une pauvresse. ‖ Médiocre, peu brillant, piètre, de mauvaise qualité (mediocre) ; *poor excuse*, *opinion*, piètre excuse, opinion ; *poor health*, petite santé ; *poor soil*, sol maigre (or) peu fertile ; *to be poor at sth.*, être faible en qqch. ‖ Malheureux, pauvre, à plaindre (unfortunate) ; *poor fellow*, pauvre diable ; *poor me!*, pauvre de moi ! ‖ **Poor-box**, n. Tronc (*m.*) pour les pauvres. ‖ **Poor-house**, n. Asile (*m.*) des indigents. ‖ **Poor-law**, n. Loi sur l'assistance publique *f.* ‖ **Poor-relief**, n. Assistance publique *f.* ‖ **Poor-spirited**, adj. Pusillanime, timoré.

poorly ['puəli] adv. Pauvrement ; médiocrement.
— adj. Souffrant, indisposé ; en mauvaise santé ; patraque (fam.).

poorness ['puənis] n. Pauvreté *f.* ; insuffisance *f.*

pop [pɔp] n. Crac ; bruit sec ; bruit (*m.*) de bouchon qui saute. ‖ FAM. Boisson pétillante (or) gazeuse *f.* ‖ POP. *In pop*, au clou, chez ma tante. ‖ **Pop-corn**, n. Maïs éclaté *m.* ‖ **Pop-eyed**, adj. FAM. Aux yeux saillants (or) en boules de loto. ‖ **Pop-gun**, n. Pistolet d'enfant *m.* ‖ **Pop-shop**, n. POP. Mont-de-piété *m.* ; clou *m.*
— v. tr. Crever (a balloon) ; faire sauter (a cork). ‖ U. S. Faire éclater (corn). ‖ FAM. Mettre brusquement ; *to pop one's head in the door*, passer tout à coup la tête à la porte ; *to pop the question*, faire sa demande en mariage, se déclarer. ‖ POP. Mettre au clou (to pawn). ‖ **To pop off**, FAM. *To pop off a pistol*, lâcher un coup de pistolet.
— v. intr. Eclater, péter ; crever (balloon) ; sauter (cork). ‖ **To pop back**, AUTOM. Pétarader. ‖ **To pop in**, entrer en passant. ‖ **To pop off**, FAM. Déguerpir (to depart) ; clamser (to die). ‖ **To pop out**, sortir brusquement ; *his eyes were popping out of his head*, les yeux lui sortaient de la tête. ‖ **To pop up**, FAM. Apparaître, surgir ; émerger brusquement.
— adv., int. Paf!, pan!, crac! ; *to go pop*, sauter.

pop n. FAM. Papa *m.* (father).

pop n. FAM. Pop *m.* (pop music).
— adj. Pop ; *pop art*, pop art ; *pop music*, pop music (or) pop.

pope [poup] n. ECCLES. Pope *m.* (Greek Orthodox Church) ; papè *m.* (Roman Catholic Church). ‖ CULIN. *Pope's eye*, noix ; U. S. *Pope's nose*, croupion. ‖ SPORTS. *Pope Joan*, nain jaune (at cards).

popedom [-dəm] n. Papauté *f.*

popery [-əri] n. Papisme *m.*

popinjay ['pɔpindʒei] n. † Perroquet *m.* ‖ Fat, freluquet *m.* (person).

popish ['poupiʃ] adj. Papiste.

poplar ['pɔplə*] n. BOT. Peuplier *m.*

poplin ['pɔplin] n. Popeline *f.*

popliteal [pɔp'litiəl] adj. MED. Poplité.

popper ['pɔpə*] n. FAM. Bouton-pression *m.*, pression *f.* (press-stud).

poppet ['pɔpit] n. NAUT. Colombier *m.* ‖ TECHN. Poupée *f.* ‖ FAM. Chéri *s.* ‖ **Poppet-valve**, n. TECHN. Clapet *m.*

popple ['pɔpl] v. intr. Clapoter, s'agiter, onduler.
— n. Clapotement *m.* ; ondulation *f.*

poppy ['pɔpi] n. BOT. Pavot *m.* ; *corn poppy*, coquelicot.

poppycock ['pɔpi,kɔk] n. FAM. Sottise, bêtise, ânerie *f.*

popsy, **popsie** ['pɔpsi] n. FAM. Poule, poulette *f.* (girl).

populace ['pɔpjuləs] n. Populace *f.*

popular [-ə*] adj. Populaire ; du peuple ; *popular fallacy*, erreur courante ; *popular phrase*, expression populaire (or) vulgaire. ‖ MUS. De charme (singer) ; en vogue, à succès (song). ‖ COMM. *At popular prices*, à la portée de toutes les bourses.

popularity [,pɔpju'læriti] n. Popularité *f.*

popularize ['pɔpjuləraiz] v. tr. Populariser, vulgariser.

popularly [-li] adv. Populairement.

populate [,pɔpjuleit] v. tr. Peupler.

population [,pɔpju'leiʃən] n. Population *f.* ; *increase in population*, accroissement démographique.

populism ['pɔpjulizm] n. Populisme *m.*

populist [-ist] adj., n. Populiste *adj.*, *s.*

populous ['pɔpjuləs] adj. Populeux ; très peuplé.

porcelain ['pɔ:slin] n. Porcelaine *f.*

porch [pɔ:tʃ] n. Porche, portique *m.* ‖ Marquise *f.* (portico). ‖ U. S. POP. Véranda *f.* ‖ **Porch-climber**, n. U. S. POP. Rat d'hôtel *m.*

porcine ['pɔ:sain] adj. Porcine.

porcupine ['pɔ:kjupain] n. ZOOL. Porc-épic *m.* ; *porcupine-fish*, hérisson de mer.

pore [pɔ:*] n. Pore *m.*

pore v. intr. S'absorber, être plongé (*over*, dans).

pork [pɔ:k] n. CULIN. Porc *m.* ; viande (*f.*) de porc ; *fresh*, *salt pork*, porc frais, salé ; *pork chop*, côtelette de porc. ‖ **Pork-barrel**, n. U. S. FAM. Assiette au beurre *f.* ‖ **Pork-butcher**, n. Charcutier *s.* ; *pork-butcher shop*, charcuterie. ‖ **Pork-pie**, n. CULIN. Pâté de porc *m.* ‖ **Pork-rind**, n. Couenne *f.* ‖ **Pork-sausage**, n. CULIN. Saucisse *f.*

porker ['pɔ:kə*] n. Porc à l'engrais ; goret *m.*

porkling [-kliŋ] n. Porcelet ; goret *m.*

porky [-ki] adj. FAM. Gras à lard ; obèse.

porn [pɔ:n] n. FAM. Porno *m.* (pronography).

porno ['pɔ:nou] adj., n. FAM. Porno *adj.*, *m.*

pornographer [pɔ:n'ɔgrəfə*] n. Pornographe.

pornographic [,pɔ:no'græfik] adj. Pornographique.

pornography [pɔ:'nɔgrəfi] n. Pornographie *f.*

porosity [pɔ:'rɔsiti] n. Porosité *f.*

porous ['pɔ:rəs] adj. Poreux.

porphyry ['pɔ:firi] n. Porphyre *m.*

porpoise ['pɔ:pəs] n. ZOOL. Marsouin *m.*

porridge ['pɔridʒ] n. CULIN. Bouillie d'avoine *f.*

porringer ['pɔrindʒə*] n. Ecuelle *f.* ; bol *m.*

port [pɔ:t] n. Port *m.* ; *free port*, port franc ; *home port*, port d'attache ; *port installations*, installations portuaires ; *to reach port*, arriver à bon port.

port n. NAUT. Sabord *m.* ‖ TECHN. Orifice *m.* ; lumière *f.* ‖ **Port-hole**, n. NAUT. Hublot *m.*

port n. NAUT. Bâbord *m.* ; *on the port side*, *to port*, à bâbord.
— v. tr. NAUT. Mettre à bâbord (the helm).
— v. intr. NAUT. Venir sur bâbord.

port v. tr. MILIT. *Port arms!* portez armes !

port n. Porto *m.* (wine).

portable ['pɔ:təbl] adj. Portatif.
— n. Appareil portatif *m.*

portage ['pɔ:tidʒ] n. COMM. Port, transport *m.* ; frais (*m. pl.*) de port.

portal ['pɔ:təl] n. Portail *m.*

portal adj. MED. Porte (vein).

portcullis [pɔ:t'kʌlis] n. Herse *f.*

Porte [pɔ:t] n. *The Sublime Porte*. la Sublime Porte.

portend [pɔ:'tend] v. tr. Présager, prédire, augurer.

portent ['pɔ:tent] n. Présage *m.* ‖ Prodige *m.*

portentous [pɔ:'tentəs] adj. De mauvais augure ; sinistre. ‖ Monstrueux, prodigieux.

portentously [-li] adv. Sinistrement. ‖ Prodigieusement, extraordinairement.

porter ['pɔ:tə*] n. Portier, concierge *m.* (of a building).

porter n. Portefaix, porteur *m.* ; *railway porter*, porteur, facteur. ‖ Conducteur *m.* (in a sleeper). ‖ Porter *m.* ; bière brune *f.* (beer).

porterage ['pɔ:təridʒ] n. COMM. Factage *m.* ; prix de transport *m.*

portfolio [pɔ:t'fouljou] n. Serviette *f.* (brief case). ‖ JUR. *Minister without portfolio*, ministre sans portefeuille.

portico ['pɔ:tikou] n. Portique *m.*

portion ['pɔ:ʃən] n. Portion, ration *f.* (of food) ; portion *f.* (of a whole). ‖ Dot *f.* (dowry). ‖ Destinée *f.* ; sort, lot, destin *m.* (lot). ‖ JUR. Quote-part ; part *f.* (of an inheritance).
— v. tr. **To portion out**, partager, distribuer, répartir. ‖ Doter.

portionless [-lis] adj. Sans dot.

portliness ['pɔ:tlinis] n. Embonpoint *m.* ; corpulence *f.*

portly [-li] adj. Gros, corpulent.

portmanteau [pɔ:t'mæntou] n. Valise *f.* ‖ GRAMM. *Portmanteau word*, mot gigogne, mot-valise, amalgame.

portrait ['pɔ:trət] n. ARTS. Portrait *m.* ; *half-length, full-length portrait*, portrait en buste, en pied ; *to sit for one's portrait*, faire faire son portrait.

portraitist [-ist] n. ARTS. Portraitiste *s.*

portraiture [-ʃə*] n. ARTS. Portrait *m.* ‖ FIG. Description *f.*

portray [pɔ:'trei] v. tr. Dépeindre, décrire.

portrayal [-əl] n. Description, représentation *f.*

portress ['pɔ:tris] n. Portière *f.*

Portugal ['pɔ:tjugl] n. GEOGR. Portugal *m.*

Portuguese [,pɔ:tju'gi:z] adj., n. GEOGR. Portugais *adj., s.* ‖ **Portuguese man-of-war**, n. ZOOL. Physalie, galère *f.*

pose [pouz] n. Pose, attitude *f.* ‖ FIG. Pose, affectation *f.*
— v. tr. Poser (a question). ‖ ARTS. Faire prendre la pose à (a model).
— v. intr. ARTS. Prendre une pose (model). ‖ FAM. Poser ; *to pose as*, se faire passer pour.

poser [-ə*] n. Question embarrassante. ‖ FAM. Colle *f.* (puzzler).

poseur [pou'zə:*] n. Poseur *m.*
— N. B. Le féminin, en anglais comme en français, est *poseuse.*

posh [pɔʃ] adj. POP. Chic, chouette, bath.

posit ['pɔzit] v. tr. Enoncer, poser en principe.

position [pə'ziʃən] n. Position *f.* ; *cramped position*, fausse position. ‖ Position *f.* ; emplacement *m.* ; *in position*, en position, à sa place ; *out of position*, déplacé. ‖ Place *f.* (in class). ‖ Guichet *m.* (at the post-office). ‖ Emploi *m.* ; place, poste *f.* (post) ; *position of trust*, poste de confiance ; *to occupy a position*, remplir une fonction. ‖ Rang social *m.* (rank) ; *in a high position*, haut placé ; *to fill one's position*, tenir son rang ; *to know one's position*, savoir garder les distances. ‖ MILIT. Position *f.* ‖ NAUT. Lieu *m.* (of a ship). ‖ AVIAT. *Pilot's, navigator's position*, poste de pilotage, du navigateur. ‖ PHILOS. Point (*m.*) de vue. ‖ FIG. Etat *m.*, situation *f.* ; *false position*, position fausse ; *in my position*, à ma place ; *to be in a position to*, être à même de ; *to take up a position*, prendre position (in an argument). ‖ **Position-light**, n. NAUT. Feu (*m.*) de position.
— v. tr. Situer, mettre en position.

positive ['pɔzitiv] adj. Convaincu, certain, assuré (*of*, de) [convinced]. ‖ Positif, authentique (fact) ; vrai (miracle) ; formel (order) ; manifeste (proof). ‖ PHILOS. Positif ; *positive turn of mind*, esprit positif. ‖ MATH., ELECTR., GRAMM. Positif.
— n. Positif *m.*

positively [-li] adv. Positivement, formellement. ‖ Assurément, sûrement, certainement.

positiveness [-nis] n. Certitude, assurance *f.*

positivism [-izm] n. PHILOS. Positivisme *m.*

positivist [-ist] n. PHILOS. Positiviste *s.*

positron ['pɔzi,trɔn] n. PHYS. Positron *m.*

positronium [,pɔzi'trouniəm] n. PHYS. Positronium *m.*

posse ['pɔsi] n. Foule *f.* (crowd). ‖ Troupe *f.*, détachement *m.* (police).

possess [pə'zes] v. tr. Posséder ; être possesseur (or) en possession de (sth.) ; *possessed by*, sous le coup de (fear) ; *possessed of*, doué de (a quality) ;

possessed with, obsédé (or) possédé par (an idea) ; *to possess oneself*, se contenir ; *to possess oneself of sth.*, s'emparer de qqch. ; *what possessed you to do that?*, qu'est-ce qui vous a pris d'agir ainsi?, quelle idée avez-vous eue?, je vous demande un peu ! ‖ ECCLES. *Possessed by a devil*, possédé du démon.

possession [-'zeʃən] n. Possession, jouissance *f.* ; *immediate possession*, jouissance immédiate (of a house) ; *possession is nine points of the law*, possession vaut titre. ‖ Objet possédé *m.* ; possession *f.* (object). ‖ Pl. Possessions, colonies *f. pl.* (colonies). ‖ ECCLES. Possession *f.*

possessive [-'zesiv] adj. Possessif. ‖ FAM. Abusif (mother).
— n. GRAMM. Possessif *m.*

possessor [-'zesə*] n. Possesseur *m.* ‖ JUR. *Owner possessor*, détenteur de biens propres.

possibility [,pɔsi'biliti] n. Possibilité *f.* ; *within the bounds of possibility*, dans l'ordre des choses possibles. ‖ Eventualité *f.* (event) ; *to foresee all the possibilities*, envisager toutes les éventualités.

possible ['pɔsibl] adj. Possible ; *as far as possible*, dans la mesure du possible ; *as much as possible*, autant que possible ; *if possible*, si possible, si faire se peut. ‖ COMM. *Possible losses*, pertes éventuelles.
— n. Possible *m.* ‖ SPORTS. *To score a possible*, faire le maximum (at shooting).

possibly [-i] adv. Selon ce qui est possible ; peut-être bien ; *I cannot possibly come*, il m'est impossible de venir.

possum ['pɔsəm] n. ZOOL. Opossum *m.* ‖ FAM. *To play possum*, se tenir coi, faire le mort.

post [poust] n. Poteau, montant *m.* ‖ SPORTS. Poteau (*m.*) d'arrivée (winning-post) ; *to be left at the post*, manquer le départ. ‖ LOC. *As deaf as a post*, sourd comme un pot.
— v. tr. Afficher, placarder (a notice).

post n. Poste *f.* ; courrier *m.* ; *by post*, par la poste ; *by return of post*, par retour du courrier ; *to miss the post*, manquer la levée ; *to take a letter to the post* (or) *post-office*, porter une lettre à la poste. ‖ **Post-bag**, n. Sac postal *m.* ‖ **Post-box**, n. Boîte (*f.*) à (or) aux lettres. ‖ **Post-boy**, n. † Postillon *m.* ‖ **Post-chaise**, n. † Chaise de poste *f.* ‖ **Post-code**, n. Code postal *m.* ‖ **Post-free**, adj. Franco ; en franchise. ‖ **Post-haste**, adv. A toute allure, en toute hâte ; dare-dare (fam.) ; *to travel post-haste*, courir la poste. ‖ **Post-horn**, n. Trompe *f.* ‖ **Post-horse**, n. Cheval (*m.*) de poste. ‖ **Post-office**, n. Bureau (*m.*) de poste ; *post-office clerk*, postier ; *post-office savings bank*, caisse d'épargne postale. ‖ **Post-paid**, adj. Affranchi (letter) ; port payé (parcel). ‖ **Post-time**, n. Heure (*f.*) du courrier.
— v. tr. Poster, mettre à la poste, jeter à la boîte aux lettres (a letter). ‖ FIN. *To post to the profit and loss account*, passer à profits et pertes. ‖ FIG. *To keep s.o. posted*, tenir qqn au courant. ‖ U. S. FAM. Mettre au courant.

post n. Situation *f.* ; poste, emploi *m.* (job). ‖ MILIT. Poste *m.* ; *listening post*, poste d'écoute ; *last post*, sonnerie de la retraite (or) aux morts.
— v. tr. MILIT. Poster, placer (a sentry).

post pref. Post-. ‖ **Post-date**, n. Postdate *f.* ; v. tr. Postdater. ‖ **Post-graduate**, adj. Postérieur à la licence, du troisième cycle ; n. Etudiant (*s.*) du troisième cycle. ‖ **Post-meridiem**, adv. De l'après-midi, du soir ; *at three p.m.*, à 3 heures de l'après-midi ; *at ten p.m.*, à 10 heures du soir. ‖ **Post-mortem**, adj., adv. Après décès ; n. MED. Autopsie *f.* ; U. S. FAM. Discussion (*f.*) après le fait. ‖ **Post-war**, adj. D'après guerre.

postage [-idʒ] n. Affranchissement *m.* ; *postage-due stamp*, timbre-taxe ; *postage paid*, port payé. ‖ **Postage-stamp**, n. Timbre-poste *m.*

postal [-əl] Postal (union) ; *postal order*, U. S.

postal money order, mandat-poste; *postal reply coupon,* coupon-réponse.
postcard [-kɑ:d] n. Carte postale *f.*
poster [-ə*] n. Affiche *f.* (notice); afficheur, colleur (*m.*) d'affiches (person). ‖ **Poster-designer,** n. Affichiste *s.*
poste restante ['poust ri'stænt] n. Poste restante *f.*
posterior [pɔs'tiəriə*] adj. Postérieur (*to,* à). — n. FAM. Postérieur, derrière *m.*
posteriorly [-li] adv. Postérieurement.
posterity [pɔs'teriti] n. Postérité *f.*
postern ['poustə:n] n. Poterne; porte (*f.*) de derrière; porte dérobée *f.*
postface ['poustfəs] n. Postface *f.*
posthumous ['pɔstjuməs] adj. Posthume.
posthumously [-li] adv. Posthumement.
postilion [pɔs'tiljən] m. Postillon *m.*
postman ['poustmən] (pl. **postmen**) n. Facteur *m.; railway postman,* convoyeur des postes.
postmark [-mɑ:k] n. Timbre (*m.*) d'oblitération; *letter with a London postmark,* lettre portant le timbre de Londres (or) timbrée de Londres.
postmaster [-,mɑ:stə*] n. Receveur (*m.*) des postes; *Postmaster General,* ministre des Postes et Télécommunications.
postmistress [-,mistris] n. Receveuse des postes *f.*
postpone [poust'poun] v. tr. Remettre, ajourner, différer; renvoyer à plus tard (see DELAY).
postponement [-mənt] n. Remise (*f.*) à plus tard; renvoi, ajournement *m.*
postposition [,poustpə'ziʃən] n. GRAMM. Postposition *f.*
postpositive [-'pɔzitiv] adj. GRAMM. Postpositif.
postprandial ['poust'prændiəl] adj. Après le repas, postprandial.
postscript [-skript] n. Post-scriptum *m.* ‖ Postface *f.* (of a book). ‖ RADIO. Commentaire (*m.*) après les informations.
postulant ['pɔstjulənt] n. Postulant *s.*
postulate [-julit] n. Postulat *m.* — [-juleit] v. tr. Poser en postulat; considérer comme admis. — v. intr. **To postulate for,** réclamer, postuler, stipuler.
posture [-ʃə*] n. Posture, pose, attitude *f.;* maintien *m.* — v. tr. Mettre dans une posture; poser (a model). — v. intr. Prendre une posture.
posy ['pouzi] n. Bouquet (*m.*) de fleurs.
pot [pɔt] n. Pot *m.;* marmite *f.; pots and pans,* batterie de cuisine. ‖ Pot (*m.*) de chambre (chamberpot). ‖ SPORTS, FAM. Coupe *f.* ‖ FIG. *To keep the pot boiling,* faire bouillir la marmite. ‖ FAM. *Big pot,* huile, grosse légume, gros bonnet; *pots of money,* des flopées d'argent, un argent fou; *to go to pot,* aller à la dérive. ‖ **Pot-bellied,** adj. Ventru, pansu. ‖ **Pot-belly,** n. Panse, bedaine *f.* ‖ **Pot-boiler,** n. Littérature alimentaire *f.* ‖ **Pot-boy,** n. Garçon de cabaret *m.* ‖ **Pot-herb,** n. Herbe potagère *f.* ‖ **Pot holder,** n. U. S. Manique *f.* ‖ **Pot-hole,** n. Marmite *f.* (cavern); cassis *m.* (in a road). ‖ **Pot-holer,** n. FAM. Spéléologue *m.* ‖ **Pot-holing,** n. FAM. Spéléologie *f.* ‖ **Pot-hook,** n. CULIN. Crémaillère *f.* ‖ **Pot-hunter,** n. SPORTS, FAM. Chasseur (*m.*) qui tire tous les gibiers; concurrent (*s.*) qui vise à gagner un prix. ‖ **Pot-luck,** n. *To take pot-luck,* manger à la fortune du pot. ‖ **Pot-plant,** n. Plante (*f.*) en pot. ‖ **Pot-shot,** n. *To take a pot-shot,* tirer au jugé, au pifomètre (pop.). — v. tr. CULIN. Conserver; mettre en terrine (foodstuffs); *potted meat,* viande en terrine. ‖ BOT. Empoter, mettre en pot (plants). ‖ SPORTS. Blouser (at billiards). ‖ FAM. Tuer, abattre (game). — v. intr. Tirer (*at,* sur); lâcher un coup de feu (*at,* à).
pot n. POP. Hasch *m.,* herbe *f.*

potable ['poutəbl] adj. Potable.
potash ['pɔtæʃ] n. CHIM. Potasse *f.*
potassium [pə'tæsjəm] n. CHIM. Potassium *m.*
potation [pou'teiʃən] n. Boisson *f.* (drink, drinking); breuvage *m.* (drink). ‖ Pl. Libations *f. pl.*
potato [pə'teitou] n. Pomme de terre *f.; baked, boiled, mashed potatoes,* pommes de terre au four, à l'anglaise, en purée; *sweet potato,* patate. ‖ **Potato-blight,** n. Maladie (*f.*) des pommes de terre. ‖ **Potato-beetle** (or) **-bug,** n. Doryphore *m.* ‖ **Potato-chipper,** n. CULIN. Friteuse *f.* ‖ **Potato-chips,** n. pl. CULIN. Frites *f. pl.;* U. S. Chips *n. pl.*
poteen [pɔ'ti:n] n. Alcool (*m.*) distillé en fraude en Irlande; gnôle *f.*
potency ['poutənsi] n. Force, puissance *f.*
potent [-ənt] adj. Convaincant (argument); fort (drink); puissant (person); violent (poison); efficace (remedy).
potentate [-enteit] n. Potentat *m.*
potential [pə'tenʃəl] adj. Potentiel, possible, en puissance. ‖ MILIT. *Potential strength,* effectif mobilisable. — n. Possibilité *f.* ‖ ELECTR., GRAMM., MILIT. Potentiel *m.*
potentially [-i] adv. Potentiellement; en puissance.
potentiometer [pə,tenʃi'ɔmitə*] n. ELECTR. Potentiomètre *m.*
potently ['poutəntli] adv. Puissamment.
pother ['pɔðə*] n. Confusion *f.,* vacarme, tumulte *m.; to make a pother about sth.,* faire des histoires.
potion ['pouʃən] n. MED. Dose *f.* ‖ † Potion *f.; love potion,* philtre d'amour.
pot-pourri [,pou'puəri] n. Fleurs (*f. pl.*) aromatiques dans un pot-pourri. ‖ Pot-pourri *m.* (medley).
potsherd ['pɔtʃə:d] n. † Tesson *m.*
pottage ['pɔtidʒ] n. † Potage, brouet *m.* ‖ FIG. *To sell one's birthright for a mess of pottage,* vendre son droit d'aînesse pour un plat de lentilles.
potter ['pɔtə*] n. Potier *m.*
potter v. intr. S'amuser à des riens; travailler sans suite. ‖ Lambiner, traînasser. ‖ **To potter about,** bricoler.
pottery [-ri] n. Poterie *f.; art du potier m.* (art). ‖ Vaisselle de terre *f.* (vessel).
potting-shed ['pɔtiŋ,ʃed] n. AGRIC. Serre, resserre *f.*
potty ['pɔti] adj. Petit, insignifiant (small); toqué, timbré (stupid).
potty n. FAM. Pot *m.* (chamber-pot); *potty trained,* qui va au pot, propre (child).
pouch [pautʃ] n. Petit sac *m.;* poche *f.* ‖ Blague *f.* (for tobacco). ‖ Poche *f.* (under the eyes). ‖ ZOOL. Poche ventrale *f.* (of a marsupial). ‖ U. S. JUR. *Diplomatic pouch,* valise diplomatique. ‖ MILIT. Giberne *f.* — v. tr. Empocher. ‖ Faire bouffer (a dress). — v. intr. Bouffer (dress).
pouf(fe) [pu:f] n. Pouf *m.* (seat).
poulp [pu:lp] n. Poulpe *m.; pieuvre f.*
poult [poult] n. Poulet *m.* (chicken); dindonneau *m.* (turkey).
poulterer [-ərə*] n. Marchand (*m.*) de volaille.
poultice ['poultis] n. MED. Cataplasme *m.; mustard poultice,* sinapisme. — v. tr. MED. Mettre un cataplasme à.
poultry ['poultri] n. Volaille *f.* ‖ **Poultry-farm,** n. AGRIC. Élevage (*m.*) de volaille. ‖ **Poultry-yard,** AGRIC. n. Basse-cour *f.*
pounce [pauns] n. Action (*f.*) de s'abattre sur; *to make a pounce,* s'élancer, se jeter, s'abattre (*on, upon, at,* sur). — v. intr. Fondre, se jeter, s'abattre (*on,* sur).
pounce n. Sandaraque *f.* ‖ ARTS. Ponce *f.* — v. tr. ARTS. Poncer.
pound [paund] n. Fourrière *f.* — v. tr. Mettre en fourrière (animals).
pound n. Livre *f.* (money); *pound sterling,* livre sterling. ‖ Livre *f.* (weight); *to sell by the pound,*

vendre à la livre. ‖ Loc. *A question of pounds, shillings and pence,* une question de gros sous.
pound v. tr. Piler, broyer, pilonner (sugar). ‖ Bourrer de coups ; tabasser (fam.) [s.o.].
— v. intr. **To pound along** (or) **on,** avancer d'un pas lourd. ‖ **To pound away,** frapper dur (*at,* sur).
poundage [-idჳ] n. Commission *f.*
pounder [-ə*] n. Pilon *m.*
pour [pɔ:*] v. tr. Verser (liquid) ; couler (metal). ‖ Fig. Epancher, déverser. ‖ **To pour off,** décanter. ‖ **To pour out,** verser ; Fig. *To pour out one's troubles,* épancher ses chagrins.
— v. intr. Tomber à torrents (rain). ‖ **To pour down,** tomber à verse (rain). ‖ **To pour in, out,** entrer, sortir à flots.
pourer ['pɔ:rə*] n. Couleur *m.*
pouring [-iŋ] adj. Torrentiel (rain).
pout [paut] n. Moue *f.*
— v. intr. Bouder, faire la moue (or) la lippe.
pouter [-ə*] n. Boudeur *s.* ‖ Zool. Pigeon boulant *m.*
poverty ['pɔvəti] n. Pauvreté, indigence *f. ; extreme poverty,* misère ; *to cry poverty,* pleurer misère. ‖ Fig. Manque *m.,* pénurie, disette *f.* ‖ **Poverty-stricken,** adj. Indigent, dans la misère.
P.O.W. [,pi:ou'dʌblju:] abbr. *prisoner of war,* prisonnier de guerre.
powder ['paudə*] n. Poudre *f.* ‖ U. S. Fam. *To take a powder,* prendre la poudre d'escampette. ‖ **Powder-box,** n. Boîte à poudre *f.* ‖ **Powder-keg,** n. Milit., Fig. Poudrière *f.* ‖ **Powder-magazine,** Milit. Poudrière *f.* ‖ **Powder-puff,** n. Houppe, houpette *f.* ‖ **Powder room,** n. U. S. Toilettes (*f. pl.*) pour dames.
— v. tr. Réduire en poudre ; pulvériser. ‖ Saupoudrer (*with,* de) ; *to powder one's face,* se poudrer.
powdery [-əri] adj. Poudreux. ‖ Friable.
power ['pauə*] n. Autorité *f. ;* pouvoir *m.* (authority) ; *in power,* au pouvoir ; *power of life and death,* droit de vie et de mort ; *the powers that be,* les autorités ; *to do all in one's power,* faire tout ce qui est en son pouvoir ; *to fall into s.o.'s power,* tomber au pouvoir de qqn ; *to have power over,* avoir autorité sur ; *to have s.o. in one's power,* avoir qqn sous sa coupe ; *with full powers,* de pleine autorité. ‖ Faculté, capacité *f. ;* talent *m.; mental powers,* facultés intellectuelles ; *power of speech,* talent oratoire. ‖ Puissance, force *f.* (strength). ‖ Possibilité *f. ; with power to,* avec faculté de. ‖ Puissance *f.* (nation) ; *the Great Powers,* les grandes puissances. ‖ Jur. *Power of attorney,* procuration *f.;* Math. Puissance *f. ; to the third power,* à la troisième puissance. ‖ Techn. Puissance, force, énergie *f. ; motive power,* force motrice ; *water power,* énergie hydraulique. ‖ Electr. *Electric power,* énergie électrique. ‖ Loc. *To do a power of good,* faire un bien énorme. ‖ **Power-axle,** n. Techn. Essieu moteur *m.* ‖ **Power-brakes,** n. pl. Servo-freins *m. pl.* ‖ **Power-consumption,** n. Energie consommée *f.* ‖ **Power-dive,** v. intr. Aviat. Piquer à plein gaz. ‖ **Power-hammer,** n. Marteau-pilon *m.* ‖ **Power-house,** n. U. S. Centrale électrique *f. ;* U. S. Pop. Foyer (*m.*) d'énergie. ‖ **Power-plant,** n. Groupe (or) installation électrogène. ‖ **Power-politics,** n. Politique de la force armée *f.* ‖ **Power-rail,** Ch. de f. Rail conducteur *m.* ‖ **Power-station,** n. Electr. Centrale électrique *f.* ‖ **Power-stroke,** n. Techn. Détente *f.* (of motor).
powerful [-ful] adj. Puissant ; efficace.
powerfully [-fuli] adv. Puissamment.
powerless [-lis] adj. Impuissant. ‖ Inefficace.
powerlessness [-lisnis] n. Impuissance *f.* ‖ Inefficacité *f.*
pow-wow ['pauwau] n. Palabre *f.*
— v. intr. Discuter, palabrer.
pox [pɔks] n. Med. Variole *f.* ‖ Pop. Vérole *f.*

practicability [,præktikə'biliti] n. Praticabilité *f.*
practicable ['præktikəbl] adj. Praticable, carrossable. (See PASSABLE.) ‖ Praticable, exécutable, réalisable, possible, faisable. ‖ Theatr. Praticable.
practical [-əl] adj. Pratique (in general). ‖ Chim., Techn. Appliqué. ‖ Fig. Entendu (experienced) ; pratique, positif (matter-of-fact). ‖ Fam. *Practical joke,* mauvaise plaisanterie, brimade, mauvais tour ; *with practical unanimity,* avec la quasi-unanimité.
— n. Séance (or) épreuve (*f.*) de travaux pratiques (at school, university).
practically [-əli] adv. Pratiquement. ‖ Fam. Virtuellement, pour ainsi dire, en fait.
practicalness [-əlnis] n. Caractère (or) sens pratique *m.*
practice ['præktis] n. Pratique *f.* (in general) ; *in practice,* pratiquement ; *to put into practice,* mettre en pratique. ‖ Habitude *f. ; in accordance with the usual practice,* selon les usages. ‖ Entraînement *m.;* pratique, expérience *f.; in practice,* bien entraîné ; *out of practice,* rouillé, qui n'a plus la main. ‖ Techn. Technique *f.* ‖ Sports, Aviat. Entraînement *m.* ‖ Med. Clientèle *f.* (of a doctor) ; exercice *m.* (of medecine). ‖ Jur. Procédure *f.* (of the courts) ; étude *f.* (of a lawyer). ‖ Mus. Etude *f.* ‖ **Practice-firing,** n. Milit. Exercice de tir *m.*
— v. U. S. See PRACTISE.
practician [præk'ti/n] n. Praticien *s.*
practise ['præktis] v. tr. Pratiquer, mettre en pratique. ‖ Exercer (a profession). ‖ Mus. Etudier ; *to practise the scales,* faire des gammes. ‖ Sports. Entraîner.
— v. intr. Med. Exercer. ‖ Mus. Faire des exercices, travailler.
practised [-t] adj. Expérimenté (*in,* dans) ; habile, exercé (*in,* à).
practising [-iŋ] adj. Med. Traitant. ‖ Jur. En exercice. ‖ Eccles. Pratiquant.
— n. Exercice *m.* (of a profession). ‖ Mus. Exercices *m. pl.* ‖ Sports. Entraînement *m.* ‖ Fig. Pratique *f.* (of virtue).
practitioner ['prækti/nə*] n. Med. Praticien *m.; general practitioner,* omnipraticien, médecin de médecine générale ; *local practitioner,* médecin de quartier.
praesidium [pri'sidiəm] n. Praesidium, présidium *m.*
praetor ['pri:tə*] n. Préteur *m.*
praetorian [pri:'tɔ:riən] adj., n. Prétorien *m.*
praetorium [pri:'tɔ:riəm] n. Prétoire *m.*
pragmatic [præg'mætik] adj. Pragmatique.
pragmatical [-əl] adj. Vaniteux, outrecuidant, suffisant. ‖ Dogmatique. ‖ Philos. Pragmatique.
pragmatically [-əli] adv. Avec suffisance (or) dogmatisme. ‖ Philos. Pragmatiquement.
pragmatism ['prægmətizm] n. Pédanterie *f. ;* dogmatisme *m.* ‖ Réalisme *m.* ‖ Philos. Pragmatisme *m.*
pragmatist [-tist] n. Philos. Pragmatiste *m.*
pragmatize [-taiz] v. tr. Rationaliser.
prairie ['prɛəri] n. U. S. Prairie, savane *f.* (grassland). ‖ **Prairie-dog,** n. Zool. Cynomys *m.*
praise [preiz] n. Eloge *m. ;* louange *f.*
— v. tr. Louer, faire l'éloge de. (See COMMEND, LAUD.) ‖ Eccles. Louer, glorifier. ‖ Fam. *To praise to the skies,* porter aux nues (or) au pinacle ; *to praise up,* vanter, louanger.
praiser [-ə*] n. Louangeur *s.* (adulator) ; laudateur, prôneur *m.* (lauder).
praiseworthy [-,wə:ði] adj. Louable, digne d'éloges. (See COMMENDABLE.)
pram [præm] n. Naut. Prame *f.* ‖ Fam. Voiture (*f.*) d'enfant (perambulator).
prance [prɑ:ns] v. intr. Zool. Piaffer, caracoler (horse). ‖ Fam. Se pavaner, se rengorger (person) ; piaffer (with impatience).
prandial ['prændiəl] adj. Med. Prandial.

prang [præ*ɳ*] v. tr. Autom., Aviat. Accrocher, bousiller (in an accident). ‖ Fam., Milit. Bombarder, arroser.
— n. Autom., Aviat. Accrochage *m.* (accident). ‖ Fam., Milit. Raid *m.*
prank [præɳk] n. Frasque, équipée *f.* (escapade). ‖ Farce, niche, gaminerie *f.* (joke).
prank v. tr. Orner, parsemer (*with*, de).
prankish [-i*ʃ*] adj., Techn., Fam. Capricieux.
praseodymium [ˌpreiziou'dimiəm] n. Chim. Praséodyme *m.*
prate [preit] v. intr. Jacasser, bavarder. ‖ Dire des niaiseries.
prater [-ə*] n. Bavard *s.*
prattle ['prætl] n. Babil *m.* (of children); bavardage, papotage *m.* (of women).
— v. intr. Babiller, gazouiller (children); papoter, jaser, jacasser (women).
prattler [-ə*] n. Babillard; bavard *s.*
prattling [-i*ɳ*] adj. Babillard (bird, child); jaseur (brook); bavard (person).
— n. Babillage; bavardage *m.*
prawn [prɔ:n] n. Zool. Bouquet *m.;* crevette *f.*
— v. intr. Pêcher la crevette.
praxis ['præksis] n. Gramm. Exemple *m.* ‖ Fig. Coutume *f.*
pray [prei] v. tr. Prier (*for*, pour); *to pray s.o. to do*, prier qqn de faire.
— v. intr. Prier; *to pray to s.o.*, prier qqn.
prayer [-ə*] n. Eccles. Orant *s.* ‖ Fig. Suppliant *s.*
prayer [prɛə*] n. Prière, demande *f.* ‖ Eccles. Prière, oraison *f.; at one's prayers*, en prière; *to say one's prayers*, faire sa prière. ‖ **Prayer-book**, n. Eccles. Livre (*m.*) de prières; eucologe *m.* (in general); rituel anglican *m.* (Book of Common Prayer). ‖ **Prayer-mill** (or) **-wheel**, n. Moulin (*m.*) à prières. ‖ **Prayer-stool**, n. Prie-Dieu *m.*
prayerful [-əful] adj. Pieux.
pre [pri:] pref. Pré-, d'avance, à l'avance, antérieurement, au préalable. ‖ **Pre-acquaint**, v. tr. Informer à l'avance (*with*, de); familiariser (*with*, avec). ‖ **Pre-acquaintance**, n. Information préalable *f.* ‖ **Pre-cited**, adj. Précité. ‖ **Pre-combustion**, n. Précombustion *f.* ‖ **Pre-condemn**, v. tr. Condamner d'avance. ‖ **Pre-contract**, n. Contrat préalable *m.;* v. tr. Précontracter. ‖ **Pre-election**, adj. Préélectoral. ‖ **Pre-eminence**, n. Prééminence *f.* ‖ **Pre-eminent**, adj. Prééminent; exceptionnel (*in*, par). ‖ **Pre-eminently**, adv. De façon prééminente. ‖ **Pre-empt**, v. tr. Préempter, acquérir d'avance. ‖ **Pre-emption**, n. Préemption *f.* ‖ **Pre-emptive**, adj. Préemptif. ‖ **Pre-emptor**, n. Acquéreur (*m.*) par préemption. ‖ **Pre-engage**, v. tr. Engager (or) retenir d'avance; n. Pré-engagement, engagement préalable (or) antérieur *m.* ‖ **Pre-establish**, v. tr. Préétablir. ‖ **Pre-examination**, n. Examen préalable *m.* ‖ **Pre-exist**, v. tr. Préexister. ‖ **Pre-existence**, n. Préexistence *f.* ‖ **Pre-existent**, adj. Préexistant. ‖ **Pre-ignition**, n. Autom. Préallumage *m.* ‖ **Pre-judicial**, adj. Préjudiciel. ‖ **Pre-ordain**, v. tr. Préordonner. ‖ **Pre-pack**, v. tr. Préemballer. ‖ **Pre-package**, n. Préemballage *m.* ‖ **Pre-raphaelite**, adj., n. Arts. Préraphaélite *adj., s.* ‖ **Pre-record**, v. tr. Préenregistrer; *pre-recorded tape*, bande préenregistrée; *prerecorded programme*, émission en différé. ‖ **Pre-release**, adj. Theatr. D'avant-première, de première vision. ‖ **Pre-school**, adj. Préscolaire. ‖ **Pre-shrunk**, adj. Irrétrécissable. ‖ **Pre-war**, adj. D'avant guerre; *pre-war period*, avant-guerre.
preach [pri:t*ʃ*] v. tr. Eccles. Prêcher. ‖ Fam. *To preach down, up*, dénigrer, prôner.
— v. intr. Eccles. Prêcher, faire un sermon. ‖ Fam. *To preach to deaf ears*, prêcher dans le désert.
preacher [-ə*] n. Eccles. Prédicateur *m.* (priest); *the Preacher*, l'Ecclésiaste. ‖ Fam. Prêcheur *s.*
preachify [-ifai] v. intr. (2). Fam. Prêcher. (See SERMONIZE.)

preaching [-i*ɳ*] adj. Eccles., Fam. Prêcheur.
— n. Eccles. Prédication *f.;* sermon, prêche *m.* ‖ Fam. Prêcherie *f.*
preachy [-i] adj. Fam. Prêcheur, sermonneur.
preadmonish [pri:æd'məni*ʃ*] v. tr. Avertir à l'avance.
preamble [pri:'æmbl] n. Préambule, préliminaire *m.* ‖ Préface *f.* (of a book). ‖ Jur. Attendus *m. pl.*
— v. tr. Faire le préambule de.
— v. intr. Faire un préambule.
preannounce [pri:ə'nauns] v. tr. Annoncer à l'avance.
prearrange [pri:ə'reindʒ] v. tr. Arranger d'avance.
prebend ['prebənd] n. Eccles. Prébende *f.*
prebendary [-əri] n. Eccles. Prébendier *m.*
precarious [pri'kɛəriəs] adj. Précaire, incertain, douteux. ‖ Jur. Précaire.
precariously [-li] adv. Précairement.
precariousness [-nis] n. Précarité *f.;* état précaire *m.*
precarium [pri'kɛəriəm] n. Jur. Précaire *m.*
precast [pri:kɑ':st] adj. Coulé à l'avance (concrete); préfabriqué (house).
precatory ['prekətəri] adj. Gramm., Jur. Précatif.
precaution [pri'kɔ:*ʃ*ən] n. Précaution *f.; by way of precaution*, par mesure de précaution. ‖ Milit. *Air-raid precautions*, défense passive (or) contre avions (civil defence).
precautionary [-əri] adj. De précaution. ‖ Préventif (alert).
precede [pri'si:d] v. tr. Précéder (to go before). ‖ Faire précéder (*with*, de). ‖ Avoir la préséance sur (to have precedence of).
precedence ['presidəns] n. Préséance *f.* (*of*, sur); *to yield precedence to*, s'effacer devant, céder le pas à. ‖ Jur. Priorité *f.*
precedent [-dənt] n. Précédent *m.; to become a precedent*, constituer un précédent. ‖ Tradition, coutume *f.* ‖ Jur. Jurisprudence *f.*
— adj. Précédent, antérieur.
precedented ['presiˌdentid] adj. Qui a un précédent; *not precedented*, sans précédent.
precedential [presi'den*ʃ*əl] adj. Constituant un précédent. ‖ Préliminaire. (See PRECURSIVE.)
precent [pri'sent] v. intr. Eccles. Mus. Tenir le rôle de premier chantre.
— v. tr. Eccles. Mus. Chanter, entonner.
precentor [-ə*] n. Eccles. Mus. Premier chantre *m.* (cantor); maître (*m.*) de chapelle (choir-master).
precentorship [-ə*ʃ*ip] n. Eccles. Mus. Maîtrise *f.*
precept ['pri:sept] n. Précepte *m.* ‖ Jur. Mandat *m.* ‖ Fin. Feuille de contributions *f.*
preceptor [-ə*] n. † Précepteur *m.* (See TUTOR.) ‖ U. S. Répétiteur *m.*
preceptorial [ˌpri:sep'tɔ:riəl] adj. Préceptoral.
preceptorship [pri'septə*ʃ*ip] n. Préceptorat *m.* (See TUTORSHIP.)
precession [pri'se*ʃ*ən] n. Astron. Précession *f.*
precinct [pri'siɳkt] n. Enceinte *f.* (enclosure). ‖ Pl. Alentours, environs *m. pl.* ‖ U. S. Circonscription électorale *f.*
preciosity [ˌpre*ʃ*i'ositi] n. Préciosité *f.*
precious ['pre*ʃ*əs] adj. Précieux, de valeur. ‖ Précieux, affecté (mannered). ‖ Précieux, utile (*to*, à) [valuable]. ‖ Précieux, cher (*to*, à) [dear]. ‖ Fam. *A precious fool*, un fameux imbécile; *precious little hope*, petit (or) maigre espoir.
— n. Fam. *My precious*, mon trésor.
— adv. Fam. Fameusement.
preciously [-li] adv. Précieusement. ‖ Avec préciosité. ‖ Fam. Fameusement.
preciousness [-nis] n. Grande valeur *f.;* caractère précieux *m.* ‖ Préciosité, affectation *f.*
precipice ['presipis] n. Précipice *m.*
precipitable [pri'sipitəbl] adj. Chim. Précipitable.

precipitancy [-tənsi] n. Précipitation *f.* (haste); empressement *m.* (zeal).
precipitant [-tənt] n. CHIM. Précipitant *m.*
precipitate [-tit] n. CHIM. Précipité *m.*
— adj. Précipité, hâtif. ‖ Précipité, irréfléchi.
— [-teit] v. tr. Précipiter (*into*, dans) [s.o., sth.]. ‖ Condenser (dew, rain). ‖ CHIM. Précipiter. ‖ FIG. Précipiter, hâter.
— v. intr. CHIM. Se précipiter.
precipitately [-titli] adv. Précipitamment.
precipitation [pri,sipi'teiʃən] n. CHIM., PHYS., FIG. Précipitation *f.*
precipitous [pri'sipitəs] adj. Escarpé, à pic.
precipitously [-li] adv. A pic, abruptement.
precipitousness [-nis] n. Escarpement, à pic *m.*
précis ['preisi:] n. invar. Abrégé, résumé *m.* (of a document, letter, report). ‖ **Précis-writing**, n. Rédaction (*f.*) de résumé; compte rendu (*m.*) de lecture.
precise [pri'sais] adj. Précis, exact.
precisely [-li] adv. Avec précision; de façon précise. ‖ Exactement, ponctuellement. ‖ Précisément, justement.
preciseness [-nis] n. Précision *f.* (accuracy). ‖ Méticulosité *f.*
precision [pri'siʒən] n. Précision *f.*
— adj. De précision (instruments, tools).
preclude [pri'klu:d] v. tr. Empêcher, mettre dans l'impossibilité, priver (*from*, de). ‖ Ecarter, prévenir, exclure. (See AVERT.)
preclusive [pri'klu:siv] adj. Excluant; *preclusive of a misunderstanding*, qui prévient un malentendu.
precocious [pri'kouʃəs] adj. Précoce. (See FORWARD.)
precociously [-li] adv. Précocement.
precociousness [-nis], **precocity** [pri'kɔsiti] n. Précocité *f.*
precognition ['pri:kɔg'niʃən] n. JUR. Instruction *f.* ‖ PHILOS. Préconnaissance *f.* (See FOREKNOWLEDGE.)
precognosce [,pri:kɔg'nɔs] v. tr. JUR. Instruire.
preconceive ['pri:kən'si:v] v. tr. Préconcevoir.
preconceived [-d] adj. Préconçu (idea).
preconception ['prikən'sepʃən] n. Idée préconçue *f.* (prejudice); préconception *f.* (prenotion).
preconcerted [-'sə:tid] adj. Préconcerté, arrêté antérieurement.
preconization [,pri:,konai'zeiʃən] n. ECCLES. Préconisation *f.*
preconize ['pri:kənaiz] v. tr. ECCLES., FIG. Préconiser.
preconizer [-ə*] n. Préconisateur *m.;* préconisatrice *f.*
preconstruction [pri:kən'strʌkʃən] n. Préconstruction *f.* (See PREFABRICATION.)
precordial [pri:'kɔ:diəl] adj. MED. Précordial.
precursive [pri'kə:siv], **precursory** [-əri] adj. Préliminaire (precedential); précurseur, avant-coureur (premonitory).
precursor [-ə*] n. Précurseur *m.*
precursory [-əri] adj. See PRECURSIVE.
predacious, U. S. predaceous [pri'deiʃəs] adj. ZOOL. Prédateur; de proie, rapace.
predacity [pre:dæsiti] n. Rapacité *f.*
predate ['pri:'deit] v. tr. Précéder, avoir lieu avant. ‖ Antidater. (See FOREDATE.)
predator ['predətə*] n. ZOOL. Prédateur *m.*
predatory [-əri] adj. ZOOL. Prédateur; de proie, rapace. ‖ FIG. Prédateur; pillard.
predecease [,pri:di'si:s] v. tr. JUR. Prédécéder.
— n. JUR. Prédécès *m.*
predecessor ['pri:disesə*] n. Prédécesseur *m.* ‖ Aïeul *s.* (forefather).
predestinate [pri'destinit] adj., n. Prédestiné *s.*
— [-eit] v. tr. Prédestiner (*to*, à). [See FOREDOOM.]
predestination [pri,desti'neiʃən] n. Prédestination *f.*

predestine [pri'destin] v. tr. Destiner d'avance (*to*, à). ‖ ECCLES. Prédestiner.
predeterminate ['pri:di'tə:minit] adj. ECCLES. Prédéterminé.
predetermination ['pri:di,tə:mi'neiʃən] n. Détermination antérieure *f.* ‖ ECCLES. Prédétermination *f.*
predetermine ['pri:di'tə:min] v. tr. Déterminer au préalable. ‖ ECCLES. Prédéterminer.
predial ['pri:diəl] adj. JUR. Foncier (property); prédial (servitude).
predicable ['predikəbl] adj. PHILOS. Prédicable.
— n. PHILOS. Catégorème *m.* ‖ Pl. Universaux *m. pl.*
predicament [pri'dikəmənt] n. PHILOS. Prédicament *m.* ‖ FIG. Mauvaise posture *f.; the human predicament*, la condition humaine.
predicant ['predikənt] adj. ECCLES. Prêcheur.
predicate [-it] n. GRAMM. Attribut *m.* ‖ PHILOS. Prédicat *m.*
— [-eit] v. tr. Affirmer.
predication [,predi'keiʃən] n. † Prédication *f.* ‖ GRAMM. Attribution *f.* ‖ PHILOS. Affirmation *f.*
predicative [pre'dikətiv] adj. Affirmatif. ‖ GRAMM. Attributif. ‖ PHILOS. Prédicatif.
predicatory ['predikətəri] adj. ECCLES. Prêcheur.
predict [pri'dikt] v. tr. Prédire. (See FORETELL.)
prediction [pri'dikʃən] n. Prédiction *f.*
predictive [-tiv] adj. Prophétique.
predictor [-tə*] n. Prédiseur *s.* ‖ Prophète *m.* (of, de). ‖ TECHN. Viseur automatique *m.*
predikant ['predikənt] n. ECCLES. Prédicant *m.*
predilection [,pri:di'lekʃən] n. Prédilection *f.* (*for*, pour).
predispose ['pri:dis'pouz] v. tr. Prédisposer (*to*, à).
predisposition ['pri:,dispə'ziʃən] n. Prédisposition *f.* (*to*, à). [See LIABILITY.]
predominance [pri'dɔminəns] n. Prédominance *f.*
predominant [-ənt] adj. Prédominant.
predominantly [-əntli] adv. De manière prédominante.
predominate [-eit] v. intr. Prédominer; prévaloir. (See PREVAIL.)
predominating [-eitiŋ] adj. Prédominant.
preen [pri:n] v. tr. ZOOL. *To preen its feathers*, se lisser les plumes. ‖ FAM. *To preen oneself*, faire des mines (girl); faire la roue (man).
prefab [pri:'fæb] adj. FAM. Préfabriqué.
prefabricate [pri:'fæbrikeit] v. tr. Préfabriquer.
prefabrication ['pri:,fæbri'keiʃən] n. Préfabrication *f.*
preface ['prefəs] n. Préface *f.* (of a book). [See FOREWORD.] ‖ Exorde *m.* (of a speech). ‖ ECCLES. Préface *f.*
— v. tr. Préfacer (a book). ‖ Servir de prélude à (an event). ‖ Citer en introduction (sth.), faire précéder (*with*, de) [words].
prefatory ['prefətəri] adj. Liminaire (page); préliminaire (remarks).
prefect ['pri:fekt] n. Préfet *m.*
prefectorial [,pri:fek'tɔ:riəl] adj. Préfectoral.
prefecture ['pri:fektjuə*] n. Préfecture *f.*
prefer [pri'fə*] v. tr. (1). Préférer (*to*, à); aimer mieux (*to*, que). ‖ JUR. Intenter (an action); adresser (a petition); formuler (a request); *to prefer a charge*, porter une accusation (*against*, contre).
preferable ['prefərəbl] adj. Préférable (*to*, à).
preferably [-əbli] adv. Préférablement.
preference [-əns] n. Préférence *f.* (*for*, pour; *over*, sur); *in preference to*, préférablement à, de préférence à. ‖ Préférence, chose préférée *f.* ‖ Droit (*m.*) de priorité.
— adj. FIN. Privilégié (stock); préférentiel (tariff).
preferential [,prefə'renʃəl] adj. Privilégié (creditor, debt); préférentiel (tariff); *preferential treatment*, tour de faveur.
preferment [pri'fə:mənt] n. Avancement *m.;* promotion *f.* (*to*, à).

prefiguration [pri:‚figju'reiʃən] n. Préfiguration ƒ.
prefigure [pri:'figə*] v. tr. Préfigurer. ‖ Se figurer d'avance.
prefix ['pri:fiks] n. GRAMM. Préfixe m. ‖ JUR. Titre m.
— [pri:'fiks] v. tr. GRAMM. Préfixer. ‖ FIG. Faire précéder (to, de). [See PREFACE.]
preformation [pri:fɔ:'meiʃən] n. Préformation ƒ.
pregnable ['pregnəbl] adj. MILIT. Prenable. ‖ FIG. Controversable.
pregnancy ['pregnənsi] n. MED. Gestation, grossesse ƒ. ‖ AGRIC. Fertilité ƒ. ‖ FIG. Portée ƒ. (of an event); fécondité ƒ. (of mind).
pregnant [-ənt] adj. MED. Enceinte. ‖ ZOOL. Pleine. ‖ FIG. Gros, plein (with, de).
preheater [pri:'hi:tə*] n. TECHN. Réchauffeur.
prehensile [pri'hensàil], **prehensive** [-siv] adj. ZOOL. Préhensile.
prehension [-ʃən] n. Préhension ƒ. (See GRIPPING.) ‖ FIG. Fait (m.) de saisir.
prehistoric ['pri:‚his'tɔrik] adj. Préhistorique.
prehistory ['pri:'histəri] n. Préhistoire ƒ.
prejudge ['pri:'dʒʌdʒ] v. tr. Préjuger (a question). ‖ Juger d'avance (s.o.).
prejudgment [-mənt] n. Jugement prématuré m. ‖ Opinion préconçue ƒ. (prejudice).
prejudice ['predʒudis] n. JUR. Préjudice m. (see DETRIMENT); to the prejudice of, au préjudice de; without prejudice to, sans préjudice de. ‖ FIG. Préjugé m., prévention ƒ.
— v. tr. JUR. Porter préjudice à. ‖ FIG. Prévenir (against, contre).
prejudiced [-t] adj. Plein de préjugés. ‖ Prévenu (against, contre; in favour of, en faveur de).
prejudicial [‚predʒu'diʃəl] adj. Préjudiciable, nuisible, dommageable (to, à).
prelacy ['preləsi] n. ECCLES. Prélature ƒ.; épiscopat m.
prelate ['prelit] n. ECCLES. Prélat m.
prelatic(al) [pre'lætik(əl)] adj. ECCLES. Episcopal; hiérarchisé (Church).
prelect [pri'lekt] v. intr. Faire une conférence (on, sur; to, à).
prelection [-'lekʃən] n. Conférence ƒ.
prelector [-'lektə*] n. Conférencier m.
prelibation ['pri:lai'beiʃən] n. Avant-goût m.
prelim [pri:'lim] n. FAM. Premier examen (m.) dans certaines universités britanniques. ‖ Pl. Pages (ƒ. pl.) de titre (of book).
preliminarily [-li] adv. Préliminairement, au préalable; en guise de préliminaire.
preliminary [pri'liminəri] adj. Préliminaire, préalable; préparatoire, introductoire.
— n. Préliminaire m. (of, to, de).
prelude ['prelju:d] n. Prélude m. (to, à).
— [pri'lju:d] v. intr. Précéder, préluder à. ‖ Laisser prévoir.
— v. intr. Préluder.
prelusive [pri'lju:siv] adj. Préliminaire.
premature [‚premə'tjuə*] adj. Prématuré. (See UNTIMELY.)
prematurely [-li] adv. Prématurément.
premeditate [pri'mediteit] v. tr. Préméditer.
premeditation [pri‚medi'teiʃən] n. Préméditation ƒ.
premier ['premjə*] adj. FAM. Premier.
— n. Premier ministre m. (in England, in France); président du Conseil m. (in France).
première [prə'mjɛə*] n. THEATR. Vedette ƒ. (actress); première ƒ. (play); première danseuse (or) dancer, danseuse étoile.
premise ['premis] n. PHILOS. Prémisse ƒ. ‖ JUR. Pl. Intitulé m. ‖ ARCHIT. Pl. Locaux, immeubles m. pl.; on the premises, sur les lieux, sur place.
— [pri'maiz] v. tr. PHILOS. Poser en prémisse (or)

en principe. ‖ MED. Débuter par. ‖ FIG. Faire précéder (with, de). [See PREFACE.]
premium ['pri:mjəm] n. FIN. Prime ƒ.; Exchange premium, agio. ‖ FIG. Prime ƒ. (on, à).
premolar [pri:'moulə*] adj. MED. Prémolaire.
premonish [pri'mɔniʃ] v. tr. Avertir à l'avance.
premonition [‚pri:mə'niʃən] n. Prémonition ƒ. ‖ MED. Signe avant-coureur m.
premonitory [pri'mɔnitəri] adj. Prémonitoire.
premonstrant [pri'mɔnstrənt] adj., n. ECCLES. Prémontré m.
prenatal [pri:'neitəl] adj. Prénatal. (See ANTE-NATAL.)
prenotion [pri:'nouʃən] n. Prénotion ƒ. (See PRE-CONCEPTION.)
prenuptial [pri:'nʌpʃl] adj. Prénuptial.
preoccupant [pri'ɔkjupənt] n. Occupant antérieur s.
preoccupation [pri‚ɔkju'peiʃən] n. Préoccupation ƒ.; souci m. (care). ‖ Préoccupation, absorption ƒ. (abstractedness). ‖ Préoccupation, occupation antérieure ƒ. (preoccupancy).
preoccupy [pri'ɔkjupai] v. tr. (2). Préoccuper (mind, s.o.). ‖ Occuper antérieurement (a house).
prep [prep] n. FAM. Etude ƒ.; prep room, salle d'étude. ‖ FAM. Ecole préparatoire ƒ.
prepaid [pri:'peid] adj. Payé d'avance. ‖ Affranchi (letter); carriage prepaid, franco de port.
preparation [‚prepə'reiʃən] n. CULIN., MED., FIG. Préparation ƒ. ‖ Pl. Préparatifs, apprêts m. pl. ‖ FAM. Etude ƒ. (at school).
preparative [pri'pærətiv] adj. Préparatoire.
— adv. En vue (to, de).
— n. Acte préparatoire m. ‖ Pl. Préparatifs m. pl.
preparatively [-tivli] adv. En préparation, en vue (to, de).
preparatory [-təri] adj. Préparatoire.
— adv. Préalablement (to, à); en vue (to, de).
prepare [pri'pɛə*] v. tr. Préparer, arranger, organiser (to make ready). ‖ Elaborer, rédiger (to write). ‖ Préparer (for, à) [to train]. ‖ CULIN. Préparer. ‖ TECHN. Apprêter.
— v. intr. Se préparer, s'apprêter, se disposer (for, to, à); se mettre en devoir (to, de).
preparedness [-ridnis] n. Fait (or) état (m.) d'être prêt. ‖ MILIT. State of preparedness, état d'alerte préventive.
preparer [-ə*] n. Préparateur m.; préparatrice ƒ. (See MAKER.) ‖ TECHN. Apprêteur m.
prepay ['pri:'pei] v. tr. (105). Payer d'avance. ‖ Affranchir (letter).
prepayable [-əbl] adj. Payable d'avance. ‖ Affranchissable (letter).
prepayment [-mənt] n. Paiement (m.) d'avance. ‖ Affranchissement m. (of a letter).
prepense [pri'pens] adj. JUR. Prémédité; with malice prepense, avec préméditation.
preponderance [pri'pɔndərəns] n. Prépondérance ƒ. (on, over, sur).
preponderant [-ənt] adj. Prépondérant.
preponderantly [-əntli] adv. De façon prépondérante; preponderantly socialist, à prépondérance socialiste.
preponderate [-eit] v. intr. L'emporter (over, sur). ‖ Etre prépondérant.
preposition [‚prepo'ziʃən] n. GRAMM. Préposition ƒ.
prepositional [-əl] adj. GRAMM. Prépositif (phrase); prépositionnel (use).
prepositionally [-əli] adv. GRAMM. Comme préposition.
prepositive [pri'pɔzitiv] adj. GRAMM. Prépositif.
prepossess [‚pri:po'zes] v. tr. Pénétrer, imprégner (with, de) [to imbue]. ‖ Obséder, posséder, hanter (to dominate). ‖ Prévenir (against, contre; in favour of, en faveur de) [to predispose].

prepossessed [-t] adj. Pénétré, imbu (*with*, de). ‖ Prévenu (*against*, contre).

prepossessing [-iŋ] adj. Aimable, avenant, attirant, engageant (appearance, face); *he has a prepossessing manner*, son abord prévient en sa faveur.

prepossessingness [-iŋnis] n. Nature attirante *f.*

prepossession [ˌpriːpoˈzeʃən] n. Préjugé *m.*; prévention *f.* (See PREJUDICE.)

preposterous [priˈpostərəs] adj. Absurde, saugrenu, déraisonnable, extravagant.

preposterously [-li] adv. Absurdement.

preposterousness [-nis] n. Absurdité *f.*

prepotency [priˈpoutənsi] n. Prédominance *f.* ‖ MED. Prépotence *f.*

prepotent [-ənt] adj. Prédominant. ‖ MED. Dominant.

preprint [ˈpriːprint] n. Texte imprimé *m.* (of a speech); tiré à part *m.* (of a book).

prepuce [ˈpriːpjuːs] n. MED. Prépuce *m.*

prerequisite [priːˈrekwizit] n. Condition préalable *f.* (See PRECONDITION.) ‖ U. S. Cours préparatoire au cours supérieur *m.*
— adj. Préalablement nécessaire.

prerogative [priˈrogətiv] n. Prérogative *f.* (See PRIVILEGE.)

presage [ˈpresidʒ] n. Présage *m.* (portent). ‖ Pressentiment *m.* (forewarning).
— [priˈseidʒ] v. tr. Présager, laisser présager, faire prévoir (to portend). ‖ Augurer, prédire (to predict). ‖ Pressentir, avoir le pressentiment de (to foresee)
— v. intr. Constituer un présage.

presageful [ˈpresidʒful] adj. Présageant; *presageful of good*, de bon augure.

presanctified [priːˈsæŋktifaid] adj., n. pl. ECCLES. Présanctifié *m.*

presbyopia [ˌprezbiˈoupiə] n. MED. Presbytie *f.*

presbyopic [-ik] adj. MED. Presbyte (person); presbytique (sight).

presbyter [ˈprezbitə*] n. ECCLES. Prêtre *m.* (in Episcopal Church); Ancien *m.* (in Presbyterian Church).

Presbyterian [ˌprezbiˈtiəriən] adj., n. ECCLES. Presbytérien *s.*

presbyterianism [-izm̩] n. ECCLES. Presbytérianisme *m.*

presbytery [ˈprezbitəri] n. ARCHIT. Chœur *m.* ‖ ECCLES. Presbytère *m.* (residence); consistoire *m.* (Church Court).

prescience [ˈpreʃiəns] n. Prescience *f.*

prescient [-ənt] adj. Prescient.

prescientific [ˈpriːˌsaiənˈtifik] adj. Antérieur aux découvertes de la science moderne.

prescind [priˈsind] v. tr. Retrancher (*from*, de).
— v. intr. Faire abstraction (*from*, de).

prescribe [priˈskraib] v. tr. Prescrire, imposer (conduct, time). ‖ JUR. Prescrire, stipuler. ‖ MED. Prescrire.
— v. intr. **To prescribe for**, MED. Faire une ordonnance pour; JUR. Prescrire.

prescript [ˈpriːskript] n. Prescription *f.*

prescriptible [priˈskriptibl̩] adj. Prescriptible.

prescription [-ʃən] n. JUR., FIG. Prescription *f.*; usage *m.* ‖ MED. Ordonnance *f.*

prescriptive [-tiv] adj. De prescription. ‖ JUR. Consacré par l'usage.

presence [ˈprezn̩s] n. Présence *f.*; *in presence of*, en présence de, par-devant; *to be admitted to the Presence*, être reçu en audience par le roi. ‖ Allure, prestance *f.*; aspect, extérieur *m.* (bearing); *of good presence*, qui représente bien. ‖ FIG. *Presence of mind*, présence d'esprit. ‖ **Presence-chamber**, n. Salle d'audience *f.*

present [-n̩t] adj. Présent (*at*, à); *all present*, toutes les personnes présentes; *the present letter*, la présente (fam.). ‖ Actuel; *at the present time*, à présent; *the present year*, cette année, l'année en cours.
‖ Présent, en question; *in the present case*, dans le cas que nous intéresse. ‖ GRAMM. Présent. ‖ FIN. Appelé (capital). ‖ FIG. *Present to the mind*, présent à l'esprit. ‖ **Present-day**, adj. D'aujourd'hui, contemporain, d'actualité.
— n. Présent, temps présent *m.*; époque actuelle *f.*; *for the present*, pour le moment. ‖ JUR. Pl. Présente *f.*

present [ˈprezn̩t] n. Cadeau, présent, don *m.* (see GIFT); *give him sth. useful as a present*, faites-lui cadeau de qqch. d'utile; *to make s.o. a present of sth.*, offrir qqch. à qqn. ‖ COMM. *For a present*, pour offrir.

present [priˈzent] v. tr. Présenter (*to*, à) [to introduce]; *to present oneself at an examination*, se présenter à un examen. ‖ Présenter, offrir (to show); *to present difficulties*, présenter des difficultés. ‖ Présenter, soumettre (to submit). ‖ Présenter, étaler, déployer (to state). ‖ Donner, offrir (*to*, à) [to offer]; *to present s.o. with sth.*, faire cadeau de qqch. à qqn. ‖ FIN. Présenter (an invoice). ‖ JUR. Déposer (a bill, a complaint). ‖ MILIT. *Present arms!*, présentez armes! ‖ THEATR. Donner (a play).

presentable [priˈzentəbl̩] adj. Présentable (person); sortable, montrable, acceptable (fam.). ‖ Portable, présentable, mettable (clothing).

presentation [ˌprezənˈteiʃən] n. Présentation *f.* (of, de; to, à) [in general]. ‖ Remise *f.* (of a gift); souvenir *m.* (gift). ‖ FIN., MED., ECCLES. Présentation *f.* ‖ **Presentation-copy**, n. Spécimen; exemplaire (*m.*) du service de presse.

presentative [priˈzentətiv] adj. ECCLES. Collatif. ‖ FIG. Suggestif, évocateur, représentatif.

presentee [ˌprezənˈtiː] n. Personne présentée *f.* (to, à). ‖ Personne (*f.*) à laquelle on remet un souvenir. ‖ Débutante *f.* (at Court). ‖ ECCLES. Collataire *m.*

presenter [priˈzentə*] n. Présentateur *m.*; présentatrice *f.* ‖ Personne (*f.*) qui remet un souvenir. ‖ ECCLES. Présentateur *m.*

presentient [priˈsenʃiənt] adj. Saisi du pressentiment (of, de).

presentiment [priˈzentimənt] n. Pressentiment *m.*

presentive [-tiv] adj. Evocateur *m.*; évocatrice *f.*

presently [ˈprezn̩tli] adv. Tout à l'heure; dans un instant; bientôt.

presentment [priˈzentmənt] n. Présentation *f.* (in general). ‖ ECCLES., THEATR. Représentation *f.* ‖ JUR. Déclaration (*f.*) du jury. ‖ FIG. Description *f.*

preservability [ˌprizəːvəˈbiliti] n. Possibilités (*f. pl.*) de conservation.

preservable [priˈzəːvəbl̩] adj. Conservable.

preservation [ˌprezəːˈveiʃən] n. Conservation *f.* ‖ FIG. Préservation *f.* (protection); maintien *m.* (upholding).

preservative [priˈzəːvətiv] adj. Préservatif; préservateur *m.*; préservatrice *f.* (See PROTECTIVE.)
— n. Préservatif *m.* ‖ MED., COMM. Antiputride *m.*

preservatize [-taiz] v. tr. Conserver par antiputride.

preserve [priˈzəːv] n. CULIN. Confiture *f.* ‖ SPORTS. *Game preserve*, chasse gardée. ‖ FIG. *To encroach* (or) *trespass on s.o.'s preserves*, marcher sur les brisées (or) plates-bandes de qqn.
— v. tr. Préserver (*from*, de); protéger (*from*, contre). ‖ CULIN. Conserver, mettre en conserve. ‖ SPORTS. Garder; conserver (game). ‖ FIG. Conserver, garder (memory, traditions); maintenir (peace); observer (silence).

preserved [-d] adj. CULIN. Conservé, en conserve (meat); confit (fruit); *preserved food*, conserves. ‖ ARCHIT. En état de conservation. ‖ FAM. *Well preserved*, bien conservé (person).

preserver [-ə*] n. Préservateur *m.*; préservatrice *f.* (from, de). ‖ COMM. Préservatif *m.*; *dress-preservers*, dessous-de-bras.

preserving [-iŋ] n. Préservation *f.* (act). ‖ CULIN. Conservation *f.* (of fruit, meat); confection (*f.*) des

confitures. ‖ **Preserving-fruit,** n. CULIN. Fruit (*m.*) pour confitures (or) conserves. ‖ **Preserving-pan,** n. CULIN. Bassine (*f.*) à confitures.
preside [pri'zaid] v. intr. Présider. ‖ **To preside at,** présider, présider à ; MUS. Tenir (the organ).
presidency ['prezidənsi] n. Présidence *f.* ‖ Directorat *m.* (of a college). ‖ U. S. Rectorat *m.* (of a university).
president [-dənt] n. Président *m.* (in general). ‖ Secrétaire général *m.* (of a trade union). ‖ Directeur *m.* (of a college). ‖ U. S. Recteur *m.* (of a university).
presidential [prezi'denʃəl] adj. Présidentiel.
presidentship ['prezidəntʃip] n. Présidence *f.* ‖ Directorat *m.* ‖ U. S. Rectorat *m.*
presidium [pri'sidiəm] n. Présidium, praesidium *m.*
press [pres] n. Pression *f.; serrement m. (squeez*ing). ‖ Foule, mêlée, presse *f.* (crowd). ‖ Presse, urgence *f.* (urgency). ‖ Presse, hâte *f.* (haste). ‖ Armoire *f.* (clothes-press). ‖ Presse *f.* (pressing-machine ; printing-press) ; *rotary press,* rotative. ‖ Impression *f.* (printing) ; *in the press,* sous presse ; *to pass for press,* donner le bon à tirer. ‖ Presse *f.* (newspapers) ; *press-campaign,* campagne de presse ; *to write for the press,* faire du journalisme. ‖ Presse *f.; to have a bad press,* avoir mauvaise presse. ‖ Imprimerie *f.* (printing-office). ‖ **Press-agency,** n. Agence de presse *f.* ‖ **Press agent,** n. Agent (*m.*) de publicité, chargé (*s.*) de relations publiques. ‖ **Press attaché,** n. Attaché (*s.*) de presse. ‖ **Press-box,** n. Tribune de la presse *f.* ‖ **Press-button,** n. Bouton-pression *m.* ‖ **Press-clipping,** n. U. S. Coupure de presse *f.* ‖ **Press-copy,** n. Exemplaire du service (*m.*) de presse (book) ; COMM. Copie *f.* ‖ **Press-cutting,** n. Coupure de presse *f.; press-cutting agency,* Argus de la presse. ‖ **Press-gallery,** n. Tribune de la presse *f.* ‖ **Press-house,** n. Pressoir *m.* ‖ **Press-mark,** n. Cote *f.* ‖ **Press-proof,** n. Dernière épreuve, tierce, bonne feuille *f.* ‖ **Press release,** n. Bulletin (or) communiqué (*m.*) de presse. ‖ **Press-stone,** n. TECHN. Marbre *m.* ‖ **Press-stud,** n. Bouton-pression *m.* ‖ **Press-up,** n. SPORTS. Traction *f.; to do press-ups,* faire des pompes (fam.).
— v. tr. Presser, appuyer sur. ‖ Presser, serrer, étreindre (to clasp). ‖ Presser, serrer, exprimer (to squeeze). ‖ Repasser, donner un coup de fer à (to iron). ‖ Presser, harceler, talonner (to beset) ; *to press s.o. for,* insister auprès de qqn pour avoir. ‖ Insister sur, appuyer sur (to dwell on) ; *to press one's advantage,* pousser son avantage. ‖ Imposer (*on, upon,* à) [to thrust on]. ‖ TECHN. Calandrer (fabric) ; pressurer (grapes) ; emboutir, estamper (metal) ; satiner (paper) ; fouler (hides). ‖ **To press back,** refouler. ‖ **To press down,** AUTOM. Appuyer sur, enfoncer. ‖ **To press in,** enfoncer. ‖ **To press on,** faire tenir en appuyant ; FIG. Activer. ‖ **To press out,** repasser (a crease) ; exprimer (juice).
— v. intr. Presser (to be urgent). ‖ Se presser, se serrer, s'entasser (to crowd). ‖ Appuyer (*on,* sur). ‖ FIG. Peser (*on,* sur). ‖ **To press on,** presser le pas, se dépêcher ; *to press on with,* activer.
press v. tr. NAUT. Enrôler de force. ‖ MILIT. Réquisitionner.
— n. NAUT. Enrôlement forcé *m.* ‖ **Press-gang,** n. Presse *f.*
pressed [-t] adj. Appuyé, serré (*against,* contre). ‖ Pressé, serré, comprimé. ‖ TECHN. Embouti, estampé. ‖ FIG. *Pressed for,* à court de ; *pressed for time,* très pressé.
presser [-ə*] n. Pressoir *m.* (for grapes) ; presseur *s.* (person). ‖ CULIN. Presse *f.* (for meat). ‖ **Presser-bar,** n. Pied-de-biche *m.*
pressful [-ful] n. Pressée *f.*
pressing [-iŋ] adj. Pressant, urgent (need, danger, business), pressant, empressé, instant (invitation).

— n. TECHN. Pièce emboutie *f.,* embouti *m.* (part of vehicle) ; gravure *f.* (gramaphone record).
pressingness [-iŋnis] n. Urgence *f.*
pressman [-mən] n. Journaliste *m.* ‖ TECHN. Presseur, pressureur *m.*
pressure ['preʃə*] n. PHYS., TECHN. Pression *f.* ‖ AUTOM. *Tyre pressure,* gonflage. ‖ ELECTR. Tension *f.* ‖ MED. *Blood pressure,* tension artérielle ; *high, low blood pressure,* hypertension, hypotension. ‖ COMM. Presse *f.* (of business) ; *at full pressure,* à plein rendement. ‖ FIG. Pression, poussée, influence *f.; under pressure,* sous la contrainte ; *under the pressure of,* sous le coup de. ‖ **Pressure-cooker,** n. CULIN. Autocuiseur, autoclave *m.; co*cotte Minute (trade mark) *f.* ‖ **Pressure-gauge,** n. TECHN. Manomètre *m.* ‖ **Pressure group,** n. FIG. Groupe (*m.*) de pression. ‖ **Pressure-oiler,** n. AUTOM. Servo-graisseur *m.* ‖ **Pressure-reducer,** n. TECHN. Détendeur *m.* ‖ **Pressure-suit,** n. ASTRONAUT. Combinaison pressurisée *f.*
pressurize [-raiz] v. tr. Pressuriser.
prestidigitation [,prestididʒi'teiʃən] n. Prestidigitation *f.*
prestidigitator [presti'didʒiteitə*] n. Prestidigitateur *m.*
prestige [pres'ti:ʒ] n. Prestige *m.* (glamour, reputation).
— adj. De prestige, prestigieux.
prestigious [-'tidʒəs] adj. Prestigieux.
presto ['prestou] adv. MUS. Presto.
— interj. *Hey presto,* et hop!, et le tour est joué !
prestress ['pri:'stres] n. ARCHIT. Précontrainte *f.*
— [pri':stres] v. tr. Précontraindre.
presumable [pri'zju:məbl] adj. Présumable (*of,* de la part de).
presumably [-əbli] adv. Probablement, vraisemblablement.
presume [pri'zju:m] v. tr. Présumer, supposer (to assume) ; *to presume s.o. guilty,* présumer de la culpabilité de qqn. ‖ Prendre la liberté, se permettre (*to,* de).
— v. intr. Etre présomptueux ; *to presume too much,* trop présumer de soi ; *to presume too much on,* trop présumer de, surestimer. ‖ Se targuer (*on,* de) [to avail oneself of]. ‖ Abuser (*on,* de) [to impose upon].
presumer [-ə*] n. Présomptueux *s.*
presuming [-iŋ] adj. Présomptueux.
presumption [pri'zʌmpʃən] n. Présomption *f.* (evidence, presumptuousness).
presumptive [-tiv] adj. Présomptif (heir) ; *presumptive evidence,* preuve par présomption.
presumptuous [-tjuəs] adj. Présomptueux. (See PRESUMING.)
presumptuously [-tjuəsli] adv. Présomptueusement.
presuppose [pri:sə'pouz] v. tr. Présupposer. (See IMPLY.)
presupposition [,pri:sʌpə'ziʃən] n. Présupposition *f.*
pretence, U. S. **pretense** [pri'tens] n. Affectation, simulation *f.; semblant m.; to make a pretence of,* faire semblant de. ‖ Prétexte *m.; under the pretence of,* sous couleur de. ‖ JUR. Procédé frauduleux *m.* ‖ FIG. Prétention *f.; to make pretence to,* avoir des prétentions à. ‖ FIG. Prétention, vanité *f.*
pretend [pri'tend] n. FAM. Simulacre *m.*
— v. tr. Simuler, feindre (sth.). ‖ Faire semblant (or) mine, feindre, jouer la comédie (*to,* de) ; *to pretend to be,* se donner pour, se prétendre. ‖ Prétendre (to set up) ; *to pretend to be,* avoir la prétention d'être ; se piquer d'être.
— v. intr. Avoir des prétentions (*to,* à). ‖ Prétendre (*to,* à).
pretender [-ə*] n. Simulateur *m.; simulatrice f.* ‖ Prétendant *s.* (*to,* à).
pretense [pri'tens] n. U. S. See PRETENCE.

pretension [pri'ten͡ʃən] n. Prétention *f.* (*to*, à) [claim]. ‖ Titre *m.;* prétention légitime *f.* ‖ Prétention, vanité *f.* (pretentiousness).
pretentious [-ʃəs] adj. Prétentieux (conceited, showy). ‖ Snob.
pretentiously [-ʃəsli] adv. Prétentieusement.
pretentiousness [-ʃəsnis] n. Prétention, vanité *f.*
preterhuman ['pri:tə'hju:mən] adj. Surhumain.
preterite ['pretərit] adj., n. GRAMM. Prétérit *m.*
— adj. D'autrefois, de jadis.
preterition [pri:tə'riʃən] n. GRAMM., JUR. Prétérition *f.*
pretermission [-'miʃən] n. GRAMM., JUR. Prétérition *f.* ‖ FIG. Interruption *f.; without pretermission*, sans solution de continuité.
pretermit [-'mit] v. tr. (1). Omettre, négliger. ‖ Interrompre, suspendre. ‖ FAM. Cesser.
preternatural [-'nætjurəl] adj. Surnaturel.
preternaturalism [-'nætjurəlizm̩] n. ECCLES. Surnaturalisme *m.*
pretext ['pri:tekst] n. Prétexte *m.* (*for*, pour); *to make a pretext of sth. in order to*, prendre prétexte de qqch. pour; *under the pretext of*, sous prétexte de.
— [pri:'tekst] v. tr Prétexter. (See PLEAD.)
prettification [pritifi'keiʃən], **prettifying** ['pritifaiiŋ] n. Enjolivement *m.*
prettify ['priti,fai] v. tr. (2). Enjoliver.
prettily ['pritili] adv. Joliment (finely); gentiment (nicely); délicatement (tactfully).
prettiness [-nis] n. Joliesse *f.* (beauty). ‖ Gentillesse *f.* (sweetness of manner). ‖ Préciosité, mignardise *f.* (in style).
pretty ['priti] adj. Joli, beau (good-looking); gentil, gracieux (nice); adroit, habile (skilful). ‖ FAM. Joli, beau, fameux.
— adv. Assez, passablement, à peu près. ‖ FAM. *To be sitting pretty*, être bien placé, avoir le filon.
— n. Colifichet *m.* (trinket). ‖ COMM. Pl. Lingerie (*f.*) de luxe.
pretzel ['pretsəl] n. CULIN. Bretzel *m.*
prevail [pri'veil] v. intr. Prévaloir (*against*, contre; *over*, sur); l'emporter (*over*, sur). ‖ Prédominer, dominer, régner (*in*, dans). ‖ **To prevail upon**, déterminer, décider, amener (*to*, à) [s.o.]. ‖ MED. Sévir, courir (epidemic).
prevailing [-iŋ] adj. Prédominant, dominant.
prevalence ['prevələns] n. Prédominance *f.*
prevalent [-lənt] adj. Prédominant. ‖ MED. Qui court, répandu.
prevaricate [pri'værikeit] v. intr. Biaiser (to equivocate). ‖ Mentir (to lie).
prevaricating [-iŋ] adj. Menteur.
prevarication [,priværi'keiʃən] n. Equivoques *f. pl.;* faux-fuyants *m. pl.* (quibbling). ‖ Mensonge *m.* (lie).
prevaricator [pri'værikeitə*] n. Barguigneur, biaiseur *s.* (equivocator); menteur *s.* (liar).
prevenient [pri'vi:njənt] adj. Antérieur, préalable (*to*, à). ‖ MED. Préventif (*of*, de). ‖ ECCLES. Prévenant.
prevent [pri'vent] v. tr. Empêcher (*from*, de) [to hinder]; *I was prevented*, j'ai eu un empêchement. ‖ Prévenir, détourner (to avert). ‖ Prévenir, parer à, obvier à (to ward off). ‖ † ECCLES. Prévenir (to anticipate).
preventable [-əbl̩] adj. Evitable.
preventative [-ətiv] n., adj. See PREVENTIVE.
preventer [-ə*] n. Empêcheur *s.* (person); empêchement *m.* (thing). ‖ NAUT. *Preventer brace*, faux étai; *preventer tack*, fausse amure.
prevention [pri'venʃən] n. Empêchement *m.* (obstacle). ‖ Prévention *f.;* mesures (*f. pl.*) de prévention; *accident prevention campaign*, campagne préventive contre les accidents; *prevention of*

unemployment, mesures de précaution contre le chômage.
preventive [pri'ventiv] adj. MED. Préventif. ‖ JUR. Douanier (officer).
— n. MED., COMM. Préventif *m.*
preventively [-li] adv. Préventivement.
preventorium [priven'tɔ:riəm] n. MED. Préventorium *m.*
preview [pri:'vju:] n. Exhibition préalable *f.* ‖ CINEM. Première vision, avant-première *f.*
— v. tr. CINEM. Visionner (a film).
previous ['pri:vjəs] adj. Antérieur, préalable (*to*, à). ‖ Précédent, d'avant. ‖ FAM. Pressé.
— adv. COMM. Au préalable; antérieurement, préalablement (*to*, à).
previously [-li] adv. Préalablement, antérieurement (*to*, à). ‖ Précédemment, auparavant.
previousness [-nis] n. Antériorité *f.* ‖ U. S. FAM. Hâte *f.*
previse [pri'vaiz] v. tr. Prévoir. ‖ Prévenir.
prevision [pri:'viʒən] n. Prévision *f.*
prey [prei] n. Proie *f.; a prey to*, en proie à.
— v. intr. **To prey upon**, faire sa proie de, s'acharner sur, ravager. ‖ FIG. **To prey on**, miner, ronger, obséder.
preyer [-ə*] n. Ravageur *m.* (*upon*, de).
preying [-iŋ] adj. Dévastateur. ‖ ZOOL. Féroce (animal); de proie (bird).
price [prais] n. COMM. Prix *m.; cost, fair trade, full price*, prix coûtant, imposé, fort. ‖ FIN. Cours *m.; price of money*, taux de l'escompte. ‖ SPORTS. Cote *f.* ‖ FIG. Prix *m.; valeur f.; beyond price*, inestimable, sans prix. ‖ FAM. *What price?*, eh bien?, qu'en dites-vous de? ‖ **Price-cutting**, n. Rabais *m.;* réduction *f.* ‖ **Price-fixing**, n. Entente (*f.*) sur les prix (between manufacturers); FIN. Contrôle (*m.*) [or] réglementation (*f.*) des prix (by government). ‖ **Price-list**, n. Tarif *m.*
— v. tr. COMM. Etablir un prix pour (goods); demander le prix de. ‖ FIG. Evaluer, estimer, apprécier.
priced [-t] adj. COMM. A prix marqué.
priceless [-lis] adj. Sans prix, inestimable (see INVALUABLE). ‖ FAM. Impayable; *he's priceless*, il est unique.
pricelessness [-lisnis] adj. Valeur inappréciable *f.*
pricey ['praisi] adj. FAM. Chérot *adj. m.;* cher, coûteux.
prick [prik] n. Piqûre *f.* (of a needle). ‖ † FIG. Aiguillon *m.* ‖ ARG. Bite *f.* (penis); con *s.*, couillon *m.* (bastard). ‖ **Prick-eared**, adj. ZOOL. Aux oreilles droites (dog); FIG. A l'oreille tendue (person).
— v. tr. Piquer (pins, sth.). ‖ Faire (a hole) [*in*, dans]. ‖ Crever (a balloon). ‖ Enclouer (a horse). ‖ SPORTS. Eperonner. ‖ MED. Percer, ponctionner, crever (an abscess). ‖ NAUT. *To prick the chart*, faire le point. ‖ FAM. *To prick the bubble of*, dégonfler. ‖ **To prick out**, AGRIC. Repiquer; ARTS. Reproduire en piquant (a design). ‖ **To prick up**, dresser; *to prick up its ears*, dresser les oreilles (dog); *to prick up one's ears*, dresser l'oreille (person).
— v. intr. SPORTS. Piquer des deux (on horseback). ‖ MED. Fourmiller (limbs). ‖ CULIN. Se piquer (wine). ‖ **To prick out**, pointer (stars).
pricker [-ə*] n. Poinçon *m.* ‖ Roulette (*f.*) à piquer (wheel). ‖ ARTS. Piquoir *m.* ‖ SPORTS. Piqueur *m.* ‖ FIG. Aiguillon *m.*
pricket [-it] n. ZOOL. Daguet *m.* ‖ ECCLES. Broche *f.* (of chandelier).
pricking [-iŋ] adj. Piquant.
— n. Piquage *m.* ‖ MED. Ponction *f.* (of an abscess); fourmillement *m.* (of a limb). ‖ FIG. Pl. Remords *m. pl.* ‖ **Pricking-wheel**, n. Roulette (*f.*) à piquer.
prickle [prikl̩] n. BOT. Epine *f.* (See THORN.) ‖ ZOOL. Piquant *m.*
— v. tr. Piquer, picoter.
— v. intr. MED. Fourmiller.

prickling [-iŋ] n. Fourmillement, picotement *m*.
prickly [-i] adj. Bot. Epineux; *prickly pear*, figuier (or) figue de Barbarie. ‖ Zool. Armé de piquants. ‖ Med. Fourmillant, picotant. ‖ Fig. Epineux, délicat. ‖ Fam. *To be prickly*, gratter (beard).
prickwood ['prikwud] n. Bot. Fusain *m*.
pride [praid] n. Orgueil *m*. (defect); *to take pride in*, tirer vanité de. ‖ Fierté *f*. (quality); *to take a pride in*, être fier de. ‖ Sports. Fougue *f*. (of a horse); troupe *f*. (of lions). ‖ Bot. *London pride*, désespoir du peintre. ‖ Fig. Apogée *f*.; sommet *m*. (See Acme.)
— v. tr. *To pride oneself*, s'enorgueillir, se glorifier, se vanter (*on, upon*, de); être fier (*on, upon*, de).
prier ['praiə*] n. Fam. Fouineur *s*.
priest [priːst] n. Eccles. Prêtre *m*. ‖ **Priest-ridden**, adj. Bigot, cagot; dominé par le clergé.
priestcraft [-krɑːft] n. Cléricalisme *m*.
priestess [-is] n. Prêtresse *f*.
priesthood [-hud] n. Eccles. Clergé *m*. (clergy); prêtrise *f*. (orders); *to enter the priesthood*, prendre la soutane, se faire prêtre.
priestly [-li] adj. Sacerdotal; de prêtre.
prig [prig] n. Poseur, faiseur *m*.) de chichis (attitudinizer). ‖ Petit saint *m*. (hypocrite). ‖ Fam. Chapardeur *s*.
— v. tr. (1). Chaparder, chauffer, piquer.
priggish [-iʃ] adj. Poseur, pédant; plein de soupe (fam.) [pedantic]. ‖ Collet monté (prudish).
priggishness [-iʃnis] n. Pose, pédanterie *f*. ‖ Pruderie, bégueulerie *f*. (prudishness).
prim [prim] adj. Compassé, guindé (manner, person); forcé, pincé (smile). ‖ Coquet, bien entretenu (or) dessiné (garden).
— v. tr. (1). *To prim oneself up*, se pomponner; *to prim up one's mouth*, faire la bouche en cœur.
prima ballerina ['priːmə ‚bælə'riːnə] n. Danseuse étoile *f*.
primacy ['praiməsi] n. Primauté *f*.; primat *m*. ‖ Eccles. Primatie *f*.
prima donna ['priːmə 'dɔnə] n. Mus. Prima donna, cantatrice *f*. ‖ Fig. Monstre sacré *m*., diva *f*. (temperamental person).
— N. B. Deux pluriels : *prima donnas, prime donne*.
prima facie ['praimə 'feiʃi] adv. A première vue, de prime abord.
— adj. Apparemment valable (or) légitime (reason, solution). ‖ Jur. *Prima facie evidence*, élément ayant force probante.
primal ['praiməl] adj. Primitif. ‖ Fig. Fondamental, primordial.
primally [-əli] adv. Primitivement. ‖ Essentiellement, principalement.
primarily [-ərili] adv. Primitivement, originairement. ‖ Principalement.
primary [-əri] adj. Primitif, originel. ‖ Primaire (colour, school). ‖ Electr., Astron., Med., Geol. Primaire. ‖ Gramm. Primitif. ‖ Philos. Premier (cause, importance). ‖ U. S. Jur. Primaire (election). ‖ Fig. Principal, essentiel.
— n. Electr., Geol. Primaire *m*. ‖ Astron. Planète *f*. ‖ U. S. Jur. Primaire *f*. (election). ‖ Zool. Rémige primaire *f*.
primate [-it] n. Eccles. Primat *m*.
primate n. Zool. Primate *m*.
prime [praim] adj. Premier, primordial, principal. ‖ Premier, primitif, originel. ‖ Math., Astron. Premier. ‖ Techn. *Prime mover*, motrice. ‖ Comm. De première qualité, de premier choix. ‖ Jur. Premier (Minister). ‖ Philos. Premier (cause); *prime mover*, primum mobile *m*. âme, animateur.
— n. Commencement *m*. (of the world). ‖ Printemps (*m*.) de la vie; *in one's prime*, dans la fleur de l'âge. ‖ Meilleur, nec plus ultra *m*.; fine fleur *f*.; dessus du panier *m*. ‖ Eccles. Prime *f*. ‖ Math. Nombre premier *m*. (number); prime *f*. (sign). ‖ Mus. Son fondamental *m*. ‖ Phys. Atome simple *m*.

— v. tr. Techn. Amorcer (pump). ‖ Arts. Imprimer (canvas). ‖ Milit. Amorcer (fuse). ‖ Fig. Mettre au courant (*with*, par). ‖ Fam. *To prime up*, abreuver, saouler (*with*, de).
— v. intr. Techn., Astron. Primer.
primeness [-nis] n. Comm. Qualité supérieure *f*.
primer [-ə*] n. Amorce *f*. (fuse); amorceur *m*. (person). ‖ Arts. Apprêteur *m*.; *primer coat*, couche d'impression.
primer [-ə*, 'primə*] n. Premier livre, livre élémentaire *m*.; premiers éléments *m*. pl.
primeval [prai'miːvəl] adj. Primitif. ‖ Bot. Vierge (forest).
priming ['praimiŋ] n. Amorçage *m*. (of a pump). ‖ Amorce *f*. (for firearms). ‖ Apprêt *m*., impression *f*. (for canvas, for wall); enduit *m*. (for wood).
primipara [prai'mipərə] (pl. **primiparae** [-riː]) n. Med. Primipare *f*.
primiparous [prai'mipərəs] adj. Med. Primipare.
primitive ['primitiv] adj. Arts, Gramm., Geol., Techn., Eccles., Fig. Primitif.
— n. Arts. Primitif *m*.
primitiveness [-nis] n. Nature primitive *f*.
primness ['primnis] n. Allure compassée (or) confite *f*. ‖ Ordre méticuleux *m*.
primogenitor [praimo'dʒenitə*] n. Premier ancêtre *m*. ‖ Fam. Aïeul *s*.
primogeniture [-tʃə*] n. Primogéniture *f*. ‖ Jur. Succession par primogéniture *f*.; droit (*m*.) d'aînesse.
primordial [prai'mɔːdiəl] adj. Primitif, originel (primeval). ‖ Essentiel (prime).
primordially [-i] adv. Primitivement. ‖ Primordialement. ‖ Fondamentalement.
primp [primp] adj. U. S. Fam. Chic.
— v. intr. S'attifer; *to primp up*, se pomponner. (See Prink.)
primrose ['primrouz], **primula** ['primjulə] n. Bot. Primevère *f*.
primus ['praiməs] n. (trade mark). Réchaud de camping *m*.
prince [prins] n. Prince *m*. ‖ Fam. Pl. Grands *m*. pl. (of this world).
princedom [-dəm] n. Principauté *f*.
princely [-li] adj. Princier.
princess [-is] n. Princesse *f*. ‖ Comm. *Princess dress*, robe princesse.
principal ['prinsipəl] adj. Principal (in general). ‖ Gramm., Math., Theatr. Principal. ‖ Culin. De résistance (dish). ‖ Jur. Principal, premier (clerk).
— n. Comm., Techn. Directeur, patron *m*. (manager). ‖ Comm. Commettant *m*. (in transaction). ‖ Fin. Principal *m*. (of a debt). ‖ Jur. Auteur *m*. (of a crime). ‖ Milit. Adversaire *m*. (in a duel). ‖ Mus. Soliste *s*. ‖ Theatr. Premier rôle *m*. ‖ Directeur *m*. (of a school).
principality [prinsi'pæliti] n. Principauté *f*.
principally ['prinsipəli] adv. Principalement.
principalship [-əlʃip] n. Directorat *m*.
principate ['prinsipit] n. Principat *m*.
principle ['prinsipl] n. Principe *m*. (beginning, element, rule, truth); *to lay it down as a principle that*, poser en principe que. ‖ Jur. Loi *f*. (of population).
principled [-d] adj. A principes (person). ‖ Arts. Appuyé sur des principes.
prink [priŋk] v. tr. Parer, pomponner (s.o.). ‖ Zool. Lisser (feathers).
— v. intr. Fam. Faire du genre. ‖ Fam. *To prink up*, se pomponner. (See Primp.)
print [print] n. Empreinte, marque, trace *f*.; *finger print*, empreinte digitale. ‖ Texte imprimé *m*.; *in print*, imprimé, paru; *out of print*, épuisé; *to find oneself in print*, se voir imprimer (writer). ‖ Impression *f*.; caractères *m*. pl.; *small print*, petits caractères. ‖ Imprimé *m*. (printed matter). ‖ Tirage

m. ; blue print, photocopie bleue, photocalque. ‖ Epreuve photographique *f. ; to take a print from,* tirer une épreuve de. ‖ Imprimé *m.* (cotton); indienne *f.* (fabric). ‖ Moule *m. ; butter print,* moule à beurre. ‖ Arts. Estampe *f.* ‖ **Print-out,** n. Inform. Sortie sur imprimante *f. ;* listing, listage *m.* ‖ **Print-room,** n. Arts. Cabinet (*m.*) d'estampes. ‖ **Print-works,** n. Imprimerie (*f.*) pour étoffes.
— v. tr. Imprimer (*on, upon,* sur); empreindre, marquer. ‖ Imprimer, tirer (a book); *to have a book printed,* se faire imprimer, donner un livre à l'impression (writer). ‖ Ecrire en caractères d'imprimerie (a letter). ‖ Imprimer (cloth). ‖ Tirer (a negative). ‖ **To print out,** Inform. Sortir sur imprimante, lister.
— v. intr. Etre à l'impression (book). ‖ *To print well,* donner une bonne épreuve (negative).
printable [-əbl̩] adj. Imprimable.
printed [-id] adj. Imprimé (cloth, seal, text); *printed matter,* imprimés. ‖ Electr. *Printed circuit,* circuit imprimé.
printer [-ə*] n. Imprimeur *m.* (of books, cloth). ‖ Typographe *m. ; printer's error,* faute d'impression, coquille ; *printer's reader,* correcteur. ‖ Inform. Imprimante *f.*
printery [-əri] n. U. S. Imprimerie *f.*
printing [-iŋ] n. Impression *f.* (act); typographe (art). ‖ Ecriture (*f.*) en caractères d'imprimerie. ‖ Tirage *m.* (in photography). ‖ **Printing-frame,** n. Techn. Châssis *m.* ‖ **Printing-ink,** n. Encre d'imprimerie *f.* ‖ **Printing-machine** (or) **-press,** n. Techn. Presse *f.* ‖ **Printing-office,** n. Imprimerie *f.*
printless [-lis] adj. Sans empreinte.
prior ['praiə*] adj. Précédent. ‖ Antérieur (*to,* à).
— adv. *Prior to,* avant, antérieurement à, préalablement à.
— n. Eccles. Prieur *m.*
prioress [-ris] n. Eccles. Prieure *f.*
priority [prai'ɔriti] n. Antériorité *f.* ‖ Priorité *f.* (*over,* sur).
— adj. Prioritaire. ‖ Fin. *Priority share,* action privilégiée.
priorship ['praiəʃip] n. Eccles. Priorat *m.*
priory [-ri] n. Eccles. Prieuré *m.*
prise [praiz] v. tr. Ouvrir au levier, forcer. (See PRIZE.) ‖ Fig. Arracher ; *to prise a piece of news out of s.o.,* arracher une information à qqn.
prism ['prizm] n. Phys., Math. Prisme *m.* ‖ Pl. Couleurs (*f. pl.*) du prisme. ‖ Fam. *Prunes and prisms,* prononciation affectée.
prismatic [priz'mætik] adj. Prismatique (colour); prismé (cristal) ; à prisme (sight).
prismy ['prizmi] adj. Irisé.
prison ['prizn̩] n. Prison *f.* (place); *sent to prison,* conduit au dépôt, écroué, détenu, incarcéré, emprisonné. ‖ Prison, détention *f.* (punishment); *prison register,* registre d'écrou. ‖ Milit. *Prison camp,* camp de prisonniers. ‖ **Prison-breaker,** n. Evadé (*s.*) de prison. ‖ **Prison-breaking,** n. Evasion *f.* ‖ **Prison-house,** n. Maison (*f.*) d'arrêt. ‖ **Prison-van,** n. Voiture cellulaire *f. ;* panier (*m.*) à salade (fam.). ‖ **Prison-yard,** n. Cour de prison *f.*
— v. tr. Emprisonner.
prisoner [-ə*] n. Jur. Détenu, prisonnier *s. ; prisoner at the bar,* accusé, prévenu. ‖ Milit. Prisonnier *m. ; to take prisoner,* faire prisonnier. ‖ Sports. *Prisoner's base,* barres, jeux de barres. ‖ Fig. Prisonnier *s.*
prissy ['prisi] adj. Bégueule, collet monté, chichiteux. (See PRIGGISH.)
pristine ['pristi:n] adj. Primitif, de jadis.
prithee ['priði] interj. † Je t'en prie.
privacy ['praivəsi] n. Retraite *f. ;* isolement *m. ; to live in privacy,* vivre à l'écart. ‖ Intimité *f. ; married in strict privacy,* marié dans la plus stricte intimité. ‖ Secret *m.* (in affairs).
private ['praivit] adj. Particulier (car, entrance, house, lesson); particulier, réservé (office, room);

private pupil, élève en leçons particulières, tapir. ‖ Privé (life, property); *private fishing,* pêche réservée. ‖ Isolé, retiré (place). ‖ Secret (matter); réservé (person). ‖ Dans l'intimité (marriage) ; intime, privé (party). ‖ Intime, personnel (opinion, use). ‖ Confidentiel (interview, letter). ‖ Milit. Simple (soldier). ‖ Jur. *Private agreement* (or) *contract,* acte sous seing privé ; *private citizen,* simple particulier. ‖ Med. Intime (hygiene); sexuel (parts). ‖ Theatr. A bureaux fermés (performance).
— n. Intimité, vie privée *f.* ‖ Jur. Séance privée *f. ; in private,* à huis clos. ‖ Milit. Simple soldat *m.* ‖ Med. Pl. Parties *f. pl.*
privateer [praivə'ti:ə*] n. Naut. Corsaire *m.* (person, ship).
— v. intr. Naut. Faire la course.
privateering [-riŋ] n. Naut. Course, expédition *f.*
privately ['praivitli] adv. En privé (or) particulier, confidentiellement. ‖ En personne, personnellement. ‖ Privément, en tant que particulier.
privation [prai'veiʃən] n. Privation *f.* ‖ Philos. Manque *m.*
privative ['praivətiv] adj. Gramm. Privatif. ‖ Fig. Négatif.
privet ['privit] n. Bot. Troène *m.*
privilege ['privilidʒ] n. Privilège, avantage *m. ;* prérogative *f. ; privilege of age,* bénéfice de l'âge. ‖ Jur. *Parliamentary privilege,* immunité parlementaire.
privileged [-d] adj. Privilégié (favoured). ‖ Dispensé par privilège (*from,* de); possédant le privilège (*to,* de).
privity ['priviti] n. Connaissance *f.* (*to,* de). ‖ Jur. Lien de droit *m.*
privy ['privi] adj. Instruit, mis au courant, averti (*to,* de). ‖ Privé, secret. ‖ Jur. Privé ; *Lord Privy Seal,* lord du Sceau privé, garde du petit Sceau.
— n. Complice *s.* (abettor). ‖ Jur. Ayant droit *m.* ‖ Fam. Cabinets *m. pl.*
prize [praiz] n. Prix *m.* (reward); *to award a prize to,* primer. ‖ Lot *m.* (in a lottery); *first prize,* gros lot. ‖ **Prize day,** n. U. S. Jour (*m.*) des prix. ‖ **Prize-giving,** n. Distribution (*f.*) des prix. ‖ **Prize-list,** n. Palmarès *m.* ‖ **Prize-ox,** n. Bœuf primé *m.* ‖ **Prize-winner,** n. Gagnant, lauréat *s.* ‖ **Prize-winning,** adj. Primé, couronné (novel).
— v. tr. Priser, estimer, apprécier.
— adj. U. S. Primé, couronné (prize-winning).
prize n. Naut. Prise *f. ;* butin *m.* ‖ Fam. Aubaine *f.*
— v. tr. Naut. Capturer (a ship).
prize n. Techn. Point d'appui *m.* (fulcrum); pesée *f.* (leverage).
— v. tr. *To prize open,* ouvrir au levier.
— v. intr. Exercer une pesée (*against,* sur).
pro [prou] prep., n. Pour *m. ; pros and cons,* les pour et les contre.
pro adj., n. Sports. Fam. Professionnel *s.*
pro- pref. Pro- ; vice-. ‖ **Pro-British,** adj. Anglophile, pro-anglais. ‖ **Pro-German,** adj. Germanophile, pro-allemand. ‖ **Pro-rector,** n. Pro-recteur *m.*
P.R.O. [pi:ɑ:'rou] abbr. *public relations officer,* responsable des relations publiques.
probabilism ['prɔbəbilizm] n. Philos. Probabilisme *m.*
probability [,prɔbə'biliti] n. Probabilité *f.* (likelihood); vraisemblance *f.* (verisimilitude). ‖ Math. Probabilité *f.*
probable ['prɔbəbl̩] adj. Probable (likely). ‖ Vraisemblable (credible).
— n. Candidat probable *s.*
probably [-əbli] adv. Probablement ; vraisemblablement ; en toute probabilité.
probate ['proubit] n. Jur. Homologation *f.* (of a will); testament authentique *m.* (will).
— v. tr. Jur. U. S. Homologuer.
probation [pro'beiʃən] n. Stage *m. ; on probation,*

stagiaire. ‖ Jur. *On probation,* en liberté surveillée. ‖ Eccles. Probation *f.*
probationary [-əri] adj. De stage. ‖ Eccles. De probation.
probationer [-ə*] n. Stagiaire *s.* ‖ Jur. Délinquant *(s.)* en liberté surveillée. ‖ Eccles. Novice *s.*
probative ['proubətiv] adj. Probant. (See conclusive.)
probe [proub] n. Med. Sondage *m.* (act); sonde *f.* (Instrument). ‖ Techn. Nettoie-bec *m.* ‖ Fam. Enquête *f.*
— v. tr. Med. Sonder. ‖ Fam. Sonder (s.o.); scruter (sth.).
— v. intr. Fig. Pénétrer, fouiller *(into,* dans).
prober [-ə*] n. Med. Sondeur *s.* ‖ Fam. Fouilleur, inquisiteur *m.;* fouinard *m.* (fam.).
probing [-iŋ] adj. Serré; inquisiteur; pénétrant.
probity ['prɔbiti] n. Probité *f.*
problem ['prɔbləm] n. Math. Problème *m.* ‖ Theatr. Thèse *f.* ‖ Milit. Thème *m.* ‖ Med. *Problem child,* enfant difficile. ‖ Fig. Problème *m.;* question *f.*
problematic(al) [‚prɔble'mætik(əl)] adj. Problématique. (See questionable.)
proboscis [pro'bɔsis] n. Zool. Trompe *f.* ‖ Fam. Pif *m.* (nose).
procedural [pro'si:dʒərəl] adj. De procédure (matters).
procedure [-dʒə*] n. Procédé *m.;* façon *(f.)* d'agir (dealing). ‖ Jur. Procédure *f.* (regulations).
proceed [pro'si:d] v. intr. Poursuivre son chemin, continuer à marcher, avancer. ‖ Se rendre, aller *(to,* à); marcher, se diriger *(to,* vers). ‖ Agir, procéder (to go on); *how do you proceed?,* comment vous y prenez-vous? ‖ Se mettre, procéder *(to,* à). ‖ Se poursuivre, continuer, avancer; *to be proceeding,* être en cours. ‖ Provenir, venir, sortir *(from,* de) [a place]. ‖ Découler, dériver *(from,* de) [to originate]. ‖ Jur. *To proceed against,* plaider contre, poursuivre; *to proceed to,* en venir à, se livrer à, recourir à (violence); *to proceed with,* retenir (a charge). ‖ Philos. Procéder *(by,* par). ‖ Eccles. Procéder *(from,* de). ‖ **To proceed with,** continuer, poursuivre.
proceeding [-iŋ] n. Procédé *m.;* manière *(f.)* d'agir (dealing). ‖ Procédé, acte *m.; suspicious proceedings,* démarches louches. ‖ Pl. Débats; travaux *m. pl.* (of a society); réunion *f.* (meeting); actes *m. pl.;* compte rendu *m.* (publication). ‖ Jur. Poursuites *f. pl.;* procès *m.; to take proceedings against,* entamer des poursuites contre, intenter un procès à.
proceeds ['prousi:dz] n. pl. Comm. Produit, montant *m.* (of a sale); bénéfices *m. pl.*
process [prə'ses] v. intr. Fam. Défiler, avancer en cortège.
process l'prouses] n. Processus *m.* (course, method, progress). ‖ Déroulement, développement *m.; in process of,* en cours (or) en train de (or) voie de. ‖ Procédé *m.;* méthode *f.* ‖ Jur. Action en justice *f.;* procès *m.* ‖ Med. Processus, procès *m.* ‖ Bot. Proéminence *f.* ‖ Geol. Eminence *f.* ‖ Techn. Similigravure *f.* ‖ Chim. Réaction *f.* ‖ Fig. Processus *m.;* marche *f.* (of thought). ‖ **Process-engraver,** n. Photograveur, similigraveur *m.* ‖ **Process-server,** n. Jur. Huissier *m.* ‖ **Process-work,** n. Phototypie; similigravure *f.*
— v. tr. Techn. Traiter, transformer, apprêter. ‖ Jur. Poursuivre. ‖ Arts. Prendre en phototypie.
processing [-iŋ] n. Traitement *m.;* transformation *f.; food-processing industry,* industrie alimentaire. ‖ **Processing tax,** n. U. S. Impôt *(m.)* sur l'industrialisation des denrées.
procession [pro'seʃən] n. Cortège *m.* ‖ Eccles. Procession *f.* ‖ Fam. Procession *f.;* défilé *m.* (string).
— v. intr. Défiler. ‖ Eccles. Processionner, faire la procession.
— v. tr. Passer en procession dans.
processional [-əl] adj. Processionnel.

processionally [-əli] adv. Processionnellement, en procession.
processionary [-əri] adj. Zool. Processionnaire (caterpillar).
processionist [-ist] n. Membre du cortège *m.*
processionize [-aiz] v. intr. Processionner.
proclaim [pro'kleim] v. tr. Proclamer, élire (to elect). ‖ Proclamer, déclarer, publier (to publish). ‖ Jur. Publier (the banns); promulguer (an edict); interdire (a meeting).
proclaimer [-ə*] n. Proclamateur *m.;* proclamatrice *f.*
proclamation [‚prɔklə'meiʃən] n. Proclamation *f.* ‖ Jur. Publication *f.* (of banns); interdiction *f.* (of a meeting).
proclitic [pro'klitik] adj., n. Gramm. Proclitique *m.*
proclivity [pro'kliviti] n. Propension, tendance, inclination *f.;* penchant *m. (to,* à).
proconsul [pro'kɔnsəl] n. Proconsul *m.*
proconsulate [-it] n. Proconsulat *m.*
procrastinate [pro'kræstineit] v. intr. Remettre au lendemain, atermoyer, temporiser, lanterner (fam.).
procrastination [‚prɔkræsti'neiʃən] n. Remise *(f.)* au lendemain; temporisation *f.*
procrastinative [pro'kræstinətiv] adj. Dilatoire (act); temporisateur (person).
procrastinator [-neitə*] n. Temporisateur *s.;* lanterne *f.* (fam.).
procreate ['proukrieit] v. tr. Procréer.
procreation [proukri'eiʃən] n. Procréation *f.*
procreative ['proukrieitiv] adj. Procréateur *m.;* procréatrice *f.*
proctor ['prɔktə*] n. Censeur *m.* ‖ Jur. Avoué *m.; Queen's proctor,* procureur de la reine. ‖ U. S. Surveillant *m.* (of an examination).
procumbent [pro'kʌmbənt] adj. A plat ventre. (See prone.) ‖ Bot. Procombant.
procurable [prə'kjuərəbl] adj. Procurable.
procuration [‚prɔkju'reiʃən] n. Jur., Eccles. Procuration *f.* ‖ Jur. Proxénétisme *m.* ‖ Fin. Acquisition *f.*
procurator ['prɔkjureitə*] n. Jur. Procureur, fondé *(m.)* de pouvoirs (proxy). ‖ † Procurateur *m.*
procuratory [-rətəri] adj. Jur. De procuration, pour pouvoir.
procure [pro'kjuə*] v. tr. Procurer *(for,* à). ‖ Jur. Entraîner à la prostitution (a woman).
— v. intr. Se procurer, obtenir (to get). ‖ Jur. Faire du proxénétisme.
procurement [-mənt] n. Acquisition *f. (of,* de). ‖ Jur. Proxénétisme *m.* ‖ U. S. Approvisionnement *m.*
procurer [-rə*] n. Personne *(f.)* qui procure. ‖ Jur. Proxénète, entremetteur *m.* (See pander.)
procuress ['prɔkjuris] n. Jur. Entremetteuse, procureuse *f.* (bawd).
prod [prɔd] n. Coup *(m.)* donné du bout des doigts. ‖ Coup *(m.)* de pointe. ‖ Aiguillon, objet pointu *m.*
— v. tr., intr. Pousser, presser. ‖ Fig. Aiguillonner, activer *(into,* à).
prodigal ['prɔdigəl] adj., n. Prodigue *s. (of,* de).
prodigality [‚prɔdi'gæliti] n. Prodigalité *f.*
prodigalize ['prɔdigəlaiz] v. tr. Prodiguer.
prodigally [-əli] adv. Prodigalement.
prodigious [pro'didʒəs] adj. Prodigieux. ‖ Fam. Fabuleux, stupéfiant.
prodigiously [-li] adv. Prodigieusement. ‖ Fam. Formidablement.
prodigiousness [-nis] n. Prodigiosité *f.*
prodigy ['prɔdidʒi] n. Prodige *m.* (See marvel.)
prodrome ['prɔdrom] n. Prodrome *m. (to,* de).
produce ['prɔdju:s] n. Agric. Produit *m.* ‖ Comm. Denrées *f. pl.;* produits *m. pl.;* U. S. *produce merchant,* fruitier, marchand des quatre-saisons. ‖ Milit., Naut. Matériel réformé *m.*
— [pro'dju:s] v. tr. Présenter, montrer, produire (to bring forward). ‖ Fournir, donner (to give). ‖ Tirer, faire sortir *(from,* de). ‖ Produire, causer,

provoquer, créer, engendrer (to bring about). ‖ AGRIC. Produire. ‖ FIN. Rapporter. ‖ MATH. Prolonger (a line). ‖ TECHN. Produire, fabriquer. ‖ THEATR. Mettre en scène (a play). ‖ CINEM. Faire sortir, produire (a film). ‖ JUR. Produire (a witness).

producer [pro'dju:sə*] n. Producteur *m.* ‖ TECHN. Gazogène *m.* ‖ THEATR. Metteur (*m.*) en scène. ‖ CINEM. Cinéaste *m.*

producible [-ibl̥] adj. Productible. ‖ MATH. Prolongeable.

producive [-iv] adj. Productif.

product ['prɔdʌkt] n. COMM., MATH. Produit *m.* ‖ FIG. Production *f.* (of literature, nature).

production [pro'dʌkʃən] n. Production, présentation *f.* ‖ Production, génération *f.* ‖ Production *f.;* rendement *m.* (output). ‖ Production, denrée *f.;* produit *m.* (product). ‖ Production, œuvre *f.* (work). ‖ TECHN. Fabrication *f.; joint production committee,* comité d'entreprise. ‖ CINEM., THEATR. Production *f.* (of a film); mise en scène *f.* (of a play).

productive [-tiv] adj. Productif. ‖ AGRIC. Fertile (*of,* en). ‖ FIG. Fécond.

productively [-tivli] adv. Avec profit.

productiveness [-tivnis], **productivity** [,prodək'tiviti] n. Productivité *f.;* rapport *m.*

proem ['prouəm] n. Proème *m.*

prof [prɔf] n. FAM. Prof (*s.*), professeur *m.* (at a university).

profanation [,prɔfə'neiʃən] n. Profanation *f.* (See DESECRATION.)

profane [pro'fein] adj. Profane (act, art, person). ‖ Impie, sacrilège; *profane word,* juron. ‖ Grossier, qui jure (or) sacre (person).
— v. tr. Profaner (a church); blasphémer (the name of God).

profanely [-li] adv. De façon profane. ‖ Avec impiété. ‖ Grossièrement.

profaner [-ə*] n. Profanateur *m.;* profanatrice *f.*

profanity [pro'fæniti] n. Caractère profane *m.* ‖ Impiété *f.* ‖ Juron, blasphème *m.* (oath).

profess [pro'fes] v. tr. Professer (doctrine, esteem, opinion, religion). ‖ Déclarer, affirmer (*that,* que); *to profess to be,* se dire, se prétendre, se faire passer pour. ‖ Professer (history, medicine); exercer (a trade). ‖ ECCLES. Faire profession de.

professed [-t] adj. Avéré, déclaré, manifeste (avowed). ‖ Prétendu, soi-disant (alleged). ‖ Professionnel (by profession). ‖ ECCLES. Profès.

professedly [-idli] adv. Ouvertement, manifestement (openly). ‖ Soi-disant, prétendument (supposedly).

profession [prə'feʃən] n. Profession, déclaration *f.* (*of,* de). ‖ Profession, profession libérale *f.; métier m.* (trade); *by profession,* de profession. ‖ Profession *f.;* membres (*m. pl.*) de la profession; *medical profession,* corps médical. ‖ THEATR. Théâtre *m.*

professional [-əl] adj. Professionnel, du métier. ‖ De métier, de carrière. ‖ Par profession, professionnel (by profession). ‖ Expert, spécialiste diplômé. ‖ Appartenant à une profession libérale; *the professional classes,* les membres des professions libérales. ‖ SPORTS. Professionnel.
— n. Personne (*f.*) du métier, spécialiste; professionnel *s.* ‖ SPORTS. Professionnel *s.*

professionalism [-ə,lizm̥] n. Professionnalisme *m.*

professionality [,profeʃə'næliti] n. Caractère professionnel *m.*

professionalize [pro'feʃənəlaiz] v. tr. Faire un métier de. ‖ SPORTS. Professionnaliser.

professionally [-əli] adv. En professionnel. ‖ Par profession. ‖ En tant que spécialiste; dans l'exercice de sa profession.

professor [pro'fesə*] n. Adepte *s.* (of a doctrine). ‖ Professeur *m.* (at a university). ‖ MED. Professeur; chef (*m.*) de clinique.

professorate [pro'fesərit], **professoriate** [,pro-

fe'sɔ:riit] n. Professorat *m.* ‖ Corps professoral *m.* (body).

professorial [,profe'sɔ:riəl] adj. Professoral.

professorially [-əli] adv. Professoralement.

professorship [pro'fesəʃip] n. Professorat *m.* ‖ Chaire *f.* (*of,* de); *appointed to a professorship of history,* nommé à une chaire d'histoire.

proffer ['prɔfə*] n. Offre *f.*
— v. tr. Offrir (*to,* à).

profferer [-rə*] n. Offrant *s.*

proficiency [pro'fiʃənsi] n. Capacité, compétence *f.*

proficient [-ʃənt] adj. Compétent, expert (*in,* en); versé (*in,* dans).

profile ['proufail] n. Silhouette *f.* (of the body); profil *m.* (of the face); *in profile,* de profil. ‖ Courte biographie, physionomie littéraire *f.;* portrait *m.* ‖ ARCHIT., AVIAT. Profil *m.* ‖ TECHN. Calibre, chantournement *m.*
— v. tr. Profiler; *to be profiled,* se profiler. ‖ TECHN. Profiler, chantourner.

profiling [-iŋ] n. Profilage *m.*

profilist [-ist] n. Silhouetteur *m.*

profit ['prɔfit] n. Profit, avantage *m.; with profit,* avec fruit. ‖ COMM., FIN. Profit, bénéfice *m.; to make a profit on,* faire du bénéfice sur. ‖ **Profit-balance,** n. FIN. Solde bénéficiaire *m.* ‖ **Profit-earning,** adj., FIN., COMM. Rentable. ‖ **Profit-seeking,** adj. Intéressé (person); à but lucratif (society); n. Profit-sharing, adj. Intéressé aux bénéfices; n. Coparticipation (*f.*) aux bénéfices. ‖ **Profit-taker,** n. FIN. Profiteur *m.* ‖ **Profit-taking,** n. Prise (*f.*) de bénéfices. ‖ **Profit-tax,** n. FIN. Impôt (*m.*) sur les bénéfices.
— v. tr. Profiter à, être avantageux pour.
— v. intr. Profiter, bénéficier (*by,* de).

profitable [-əbl] adj. Profitable (*to,* à).

profitableness [-əblnis] n. Caractère avantageux, profit *m.* (*of,* de).

profitably [-əbli] adv. Profitablement; avantageusement; à profit.

profiteer [,prɔfi'ti:ə*] n. Profiteur *s.* (pej.).
— v. intr. Agir en profiteur (or) mercanti.

profiteering [-riŋ] n. Mercantilisme *m.*

profitless ['prɔfitlis] adj. Sans profit.

profligacy ['prɔfligəsi] n. Débauche *f.;* dévergondage *m.;* paillardise *f.* (fam.) [debauchery]; prodigalité, dissipation *f.* (lavishness). ‖ FAM. Profusion *f.*

profligate [-git] adj., n. Débauché, libertin *s.* (dissolute); prodigue *s.* (prodigal).

profligately [-gitli] adv. D'une manière dissolue.

pro forma ['prou 'fɔ:mə] adj., adv. Pour la forme.
— adj. COMM. *Pro forma invoice,* facture pro forma.

profound [pro'faund] adj. Profond (difference, interest, obscurity, scholarship, wisdom); approfondi (study). [See DEEP.]
— n. Profondeurs *f. pl.*

profoundly [-li] adv. Profondément.

profoundness [-nis], **profundity** [pro'fʌnditi] n. Profondeur *f.*

profuse [pro'fju:s] adj. Prodigue (*in, of,* de) [person]; abondant, multiple (thing). ‖ MED. Profus (perspiration).

profusely [-li] adv. A profusion, abondamment.

profuseness [-nis] n. Profusion *f.*

profusion [prə'fju:ʒən] n. Profusion, foison, abondance *f.* (abundance). ‖ Profusion, libéralité *f.* (lavishness).

progenitor [pro'dʒenitə*] n. Ancêtre, aïeul *m.* (See PRIMOGENITOR.) ‖ Original, archétype *m.* (of a manuscript).

progenitress [-tris] n. Aïeule *f.*

progeniture [-tʃə*] n. Engendrement *m.* (act); progéniture *f.* (offspring).

progeny ['prɔdʒəni] n. Progéniture *f.* (offspring).

‖ Descendants *m. pl.;* lignée *f.* (issue). ‖ Fam. Suite *f.;* résultat *m.*
progesterone [prou'dʒestə,roun] n. Med. Progestérone *f.*
prognathic [prɔg'næθik], **prognathous** [-neiθəs] adj. Med. Prognathe.
prognose [prɔg'nouz] v. tr. Med. Pronostiquer.
prognosis [prɔgnousis] (pl. **prognoses** [-i:z]) n. Med. Prognose *f.;* pronostic *m.*
prognostic [prɔg'nɔstik] adj. Med. Pronostique. — n. Med. Symptôme *m.* ‖ Fig. Pronostic *m.*
prognosticate [-eit] v. tr. Pronostiquer.
prognostication [,prɔgnɔsti'keiʃən] n. Pronostication *f.* (act); pronostic *m.* (result). ‖ Pressentiment *m.* (foreboding).
prognosticative [prɔg'nɔstikətiv] adj. *Prognosticative of,* augurant, présageant, faisant pronostiquer.
prognosticator [-eitə*] n. Pronostiqueur *s.*
prognosticatory [-ətəri] adj. Med., Fig. Symptomatique (*of,* de).
program ['prougræm] n. Inform. Programme *m.* ‖ U. S. See programme. — v. tr. (1). Inform. Programmer. ‖ U. S. See programme.
program(me) ['prougram] n. Theatr., Jur., Fig. Programme *m.* (of concert, party). ‖ Radio. Emissions *f. pl.;* rubrique *f.;* programme *m.* ‖ **Programme-music,** n. Mus. Musique descriptive *f.* ‖ **Programme-seller,** n. Theatr. Vendeur (*s.*) de programmes. — v. tr. (1). Theatr., Radio., Fig. Programmer.
programmer [-ə*] n. Inform. Programmeur *s.* (person). ‖ Techn. Programmateur *m.* (device).
programming [-iŋ] n. Programmation *f.* — adj. Inform. De programmation (language).
progress ['prougres] n. Marche (*f.*) en avant; avancement *m.* (forward movement). ‖ Cheminement, cours *m.* (development); *progress of events,* cours des événements; *in progress,* en cours. ‖ Progrès, avancement *m.* (improvement); *to make great progress,* faire de grands progrès. ‖ Etape *f.* (of a career, life). ‖ † Voyage *m.* ‖ **Progress report,** n. Bulletin (*m.*) sur l'état des travaux; Med. Bulletin (*m.*) de santé. — [pro'gres] v. intr. S'avancer, progresser (*towards,* vers) [to advance]. ‖ Progresser, faire des progrès (*with,* dans) [to improve]. ‖ Faire une tournée (official).
progression [pro'greʃən] n. Progression, marche (*f.*) en avant (moving forward). ‖ Math., Mus. Progression *f.*
progressionism [-izm̩] n. Progressisme *m.*
progressionist [-ist], **progressist** [pro'gresist] adj., n. Progressiste *s.*
progressive [pro'gresiv] adj. Du progrès (age); progressif (movement); progressiste (party). — n. Progressiste *s.*
progressively [-li] adv. Progressivement.
progressiveness [-nis] n. Progressivité *f.*
prohibit [pro'hibit] v. tr. Prohiber, défendre, interdire. ‖ Empêcher (*from,* de).
prohibition [prouhi'biʃən] n. Prohibition, interdiction *f.* (*from,* de). ‖ U. S. Prohibition *f.; prohibition party,* parti prohibitionniste.
prohibitionism [-izm̩] n. Prohibitionnisme *m.*
prohibitionist [-ist] adj., n. Prohibitionniste *s.;* sec *m.* (fam.).
prohibitive [pro'hibitiv] adj. Fin. Prohibitif.
prohibitory [-əri] adj. Jur. Prohibitif.
project ['prɔdʒekt] n. Projet *m.* ‖ U. S. Programme *m.* — [pro'dʒekt] v. tr. Projeter (to plan). ‖ Projeter, lancer (to throw). ‖ Cinem. Projeter (a picture). ‖ Math. Tracer la projection de (a figure). ‖ Fig. Extérioriser. ‖ Fam. Transplanter, transporter. — v. intr. Se projeter (to stand out). ‖ Déborder, saillir, sortir, dépasser (*from,* de); s'avancer (*into,* dans).

projectile [pro'dʒektail], ['prɔdʒiktail] adj., n. Projectile *m.* (See missile.)
projecting [-iŋ] adj. En saillie, saillant, dépassant.
projection [pro'dʒekʃən] n. Projection *f.;* lancement, jet *m.* (throwing forward). ‖ Projection *f.* (of beam). ‖ Cinem. *Projection apparatus,* projecteur; *projection room,* cabine de projection. ‖ Math., Naut. Projection *f.* ‖ Archit. Saillie *f.;* ressaut; porte-à-faux *m.* ‖ Geogr. Planisphère *m.* ‖ Fig. Image *f.* (of life); conception *f.* (of a plan).
projectionist [-ist] n. Cinem. Projectionniste *m.*
projective [pro'dʒektiv] adj. Math. Descriptif (geometry); de projection (plane); projectif (property). ‖ Fig. Extériorisant.
projector [-ə*] n. Projecteur *s.* (planner). ‖ Techn. Projecteur, appareil (*m.*) de projection.
projecture [pro'dʒektʃə*] n. Archit. Projecture *f.*
prolapse ['proulæps] n. Med. Prolapsus *m.;* descente, ptôse *f.* — v. intr. Med. Descendre, se ptôser.
prole [proul] n. Fam. Prolo *m.* — adj. Fam. Prolétaire, de prolo.
prolegomena [,proule'gɔminə] n. pl. Prolégomènes *m. pl.*
proletarian [,proule'tɛəriən] adj. Prolétarien; prolétaire; de prolétaire. — n. Prolétaire *s.*
proletarianism [-izm̩] n. Prolétariat *m.* (condition, opinions).
proletarianize [-aiz] v. tr. Prolétariser.
proletariat [,proule'tɛəriət] n. Prolétariat *m.* (class).
proliferate [pro'lifəreit] v. intr., tr. Proliférer.
proliferation [,prolifə'reiʃən] n. Prolifération *f.*
prolific [pro'lifik] adj. Prolifique.
prolification [,prolifi'keiʃən] n. Prolifération *f.* ‖ Fécondité *f.* ‖ Procréation *f.*
prolificness [pro'lifiknis] n. Fécondité *f.*
prolix ['prouliks] adj. Prolixe. (See diffuse, verbose.)
prolixity [pro'liksiti] n. Prolixité *f.*
prolixly [-li] adv. Prolixement, avec prolixité.
prolocutor [pro'lɔkjutə*] n. Eccles. Président *m.* ‖ † Porte-parole *m.*
prologue ['proulɔg] n. Prologue *m.* (*to,* de). — v. tr. Faire un prologue à.
prolong [pro'lɔŋ] v. tr. Prolonger (in space, time).
prolongation [,proulɔŋ'geiʃən] n. Prolongement *m.* (in space); prolongation *f.* (in time).
prom [prɔm] n. U. S. Fam. Bal *m.*
promenade [,prɔmə'nɑ:d] n. Promenade *f.* (place, walk). ‖ Theatr. Promenoir *m.* ‖ Mus. *Promenade concert,* concert-promenade. ‖ Naut. *Promenade deck,* U. S. Pont-promenade. — v. intr. Parader, déambuler. (See ambulate.) — v. tr. Promener (s.o.). ‖ Se promener dans (or) sur. ‖ Exhiber, faire étalage de (to show).
promenader [-ə*] n. Promeneur *s.*
Prometheus [pro'mi:θjus] n. Prométhée *m.*
promethium [-θiəm] n. Chim. Prométhéum *m.*
prominence ['prɔminəns] n. Proéminence *f.* (projection, protuberance). ‖ Importance *f.; to bring into prominence,* faire ressortir; *to come into prominence,* prendre de l'importance.
prominent [-nənt] adj. Proéminent, saillant (projecting). ‖ Fig. Eminent, marquant, important (outstanding); en relief, en vue, saillant (striking).
promiscuity [,promis'kju:iti] n. Promiscuité *f.*
promiscuous [pro'miskjuəs] adj. Mêlé (mass). ‖ Fam. Au hasard, fait au petit bonheur. ‖ Fam. Très libre, peu farouche (person).
promiscuously [-li] adv. En promiscuité. ‖ Pêlemêle. ‖ Au petit bonheur, au hasard.
promise ['prɔmis] n. Promesse *f.* (assurance). ‖ Promesse, espérance *f.; of great promise,* qui pro-

met beaucoup (person); qui se révèle très prometteur (thing).
— v. tr. Promettre; *to promise s.o. sth.* (or) *sth.
to s.o.*, promettre qqch. à qqn; *to promise oneself
sth.*, se promettre qqch. ‖ Promettre (*to*, de); faire
augurer (or) prévoir. ‖ Loc. *To promise the moon*,
promettre monts et merveilles.
promised [-t] adj. Promis.
promisee [,prɔmi'si:] n. Jur. Détenteur (*m.*) d'une
promesse.
promising ['prɔmisiŋ] adj. Prometteur.
promissory ['prɔmisəri] adj. Promissoire. ‖ Comm.
Promissory note, billet à ordre.
promontoried ['prɔməntərid] adj. Geogr. A promontoire.
promontory [-ri] n. Geogr. Promontoire *m.* (See
HEADLAND.) ‖ Med. Promontoire *m.*; protubérance *f.*
promote [prɔ'mout] v. tr. Promouvoir, nommer
(*to*, à). ‖ Jur. Promouvoir (a bill). ‖ Fin. Fonder
(a company). ‖ Chim. Provoquer (a reaction). ‖
U. S. Faire du battage pour. ‖ Fig. Fomenter,
susciter, provoquer (disorder, hatred); encourager
(projects, progress); contribuer à (a result).
promoted [-id] adj. Promu, nommé (*to*, à).
promoter [-ə*] n. Promoteur, instigateur *m.*; instigatrice *f.* (see ORIGINATOR). ‖ Fin. Fondateur *m.* ‖
Sports. Organisateur *m.*
promoting [-iŋ] n. Promotion *f.* ‖ Fin. Fondation *f.*
‖ Chim. Amorçage *m.* ‖ Fig. Provocation *f.* (of
disorder); encouragement *m.* (of progress).
promotion [prɔ'mouʃən] n. Promotion *f.*; avancement *m.* (see PREFERMENT); *promotion list*, tableau
d'avancement. ‖ Fin. Fondation *f.* ‖ U.S. Réclame *f.*
promotive [-tiv] adj. Favorable (*of*, à); *promotive
of*, suscitant, encourageant, favorisant (sth.).
prompt ['prɔm(p)t] adj. Prompt, hâtif (hasty);
prompt, immédiat (ready). ‖ Fin. Comptant. ‖ Comm.
Livrable sans délai et comptant.
— n. Fin. Délai-limite *m.*
— adv. Fam. Pile, ric-rac; *at six o'clock prompt*, à
six heures pile.
prompt n. Suggestion *f.* ‖ Theatr. Réplique souf-
flée *f.* ‖ *Prompt-box*, n. Theatr. Trou du souffleur
m. ‖ *Prompt-side*, n. Theatr. Côté jardin *m.*
— v. tr. Suggérer (*to* à) [to suggest]. ‖ Pousser,
inciter, porter (*to*, à) [to instigate]. ‖ Theatr. Souffler, souffler son rôle à. ‖ Fam. *To prompt s.o. with
sth.*, souffler qqch. à qqn.
prompter [-ə*] n. Instigateur *m.*; instigatrice *f.*
(*to*, de). ‖ Theatr., Fam. Souffleur *s.*
prompting [-iŋ] n. Suggestion, instigation *f.* (*to*, à).
‖ Theatr., Fam. Fait (*m.*) de souffler.
promptitude [-itju:d], **promptness** [-nis] n.
Promptitude, diligence *f.* (*to*, *in*, à).
promptuary [-juəri] n. Manuel *m.*
promulgate ['prɔməlgeit] v. tr. Promulguer. (See
ENACT.) ‖ Répandre (news).
promulgation [,prɔməl'geiʃən] n. Promulgation *f.*
promulgator ['prɔməlgeitə*] n. Promulgateur *m.*;
promulgatrice *f.*
prone [proun] adj. Prostré, couché sur le ventre,
étendu face contre terre. ‖ Geogr. En pente, abrupt,
en descente. ‖ Fig. Porté, prédisposé, enclin (*to*, à).
proneness [-nis] n. Inclination, prédisposition *f.*
(*to*, à). [See PROPENSITY.]
prong [prɔŋ] n. Dent *f.* (of a fork). ‖ Techn.
Griffe *f.*
— v. tr. Enfourcher, enfoncer la fourche dans.
pronged [-d] adj. A fourchons.
pronominal [pro'nɔminəl] adj. Gramm. Pronominal.
pronominally [-əli] adv. Gramm. Pronominalement.
pronoun ['prounaun] n. Gramm. Pronom *m.*
pronounce [prɔ'nauns] v. tr. Déclarer, décréter. ‖
Prononcer, articuler (a word). ‖ Jur. Prononcer
(sentence).
— v. intr. Prononcer (to articulate). ‖ Se déclarer,

se prononcer (*for*, pour). ‖ Jur. Prononcer, statuer
(*on*, sur).
pronounceable [-əbl] adj. Prononçable.
pronounced [-t] adj. Prononcé, marqué. (See
DECIDED, MARKED.)
pronouncedly [-idli]' adv. De façon prononcée,
d'une manière accusée.
pronouncement [-mənt] n. Déclaration *f.*
pronto ['prɔntou] adv. U. S. Fam. Illico.
pronunciamento [pro,nʌnsiæ'mentou] n. Manifeste *m.*
pronunciation [prə,nʌnsi'eiʃən] n. Prononciation *f.*
proof [pru:f] n. Preuve *f.* (*of*, de); *by way of proof*,
comme preuve, en guise de preuve. ‖ Jur. Preuve *f.*;
proof of death, constatation de décès; *proof of
identify*, papiers, pièces d'identité. ‖ Techn. Epreuve
f.; essai *m.* (test); épreuve *f.* (in printing). ‖ **Proof-
correction**, n. Correction (*f.*) sur épreuves. ‖ **Proof-
reader**, n. Lecteur-correcteur *s.* ‖ **Proof-reading**,
n. Correction (*f.*) d'épreuves. ‖ **Proof-sheet**, n.
Epreuve *f.*
— adj. A l'épreuve (*against*, de); résistant (*against*,
à). ‖ Fig. A l'abri (*against*, de); insensible (*against*,
à); cuirassé (*against*, contre).
— v. tr. Rendre résistant (or) inattaquable (in general). ‖ Imperméabiliser (to waterproof). ‖ Techn.
Tirer une épreuve de.
proofless [-lis] adj. Dénué de preuves.
prop [prɔp] n. Appui, support *m.* ‖ Archit. Etançon, étai, étrésillon *m.* ‖ Agric. Rame *f.* (for peas);
tuteur *m.* (for plants). ‖ Fam. Pilier, soutien *m.* ‖
Prop-word, n. Mot d'appui *m.*
— v. tr. (1). Soutenir; appuyer (*against*, contre);
to prop oneself against, se caler contre. ‖ Agric.
Ramer (peas); tuteurer (plants); échalasser (vine).
‖ Techn. Boiser (a mine). ‖ Archit., Fig. Etayer.
prop n. Theatr., Fam. Accessoire *m.*
prop n. Aviat., Fam. Hélice *f.* (propeller). ‖ **Prop-
jet**, n. Turbopropulseur *m.*
propaedeutic(s) [,proupi:'dju:tik(s)] n. sg. (or)
pl. Propédeutique *f.*
propaedeutic(al) [-(əl)] adj. Propédeutique.
propaganda [,propə'gændə] n. Propagande *f.* ‖
Eccles. Propagation de la foi *f.*
propagandism [-izm] n. Propagandisme *m.*
propagandist [-ist] n. Propagandiste *s.* ‖ Eccles.
Missionnaire *m.*
propagandize [-aiz] v. intr. Faire de la propagande.
propagate ['prɔpəgeit] v. tr. Propager, transmettre,
répandre. (See SPREAD.)
— v. intr. Se propager.
propagation [,prɔpə'geiʃən] n. Propagation *f.*
propagative ['prɔpəgeitiv] adj. Propagateur *m.*;
propagatrice *f.*
propagator [-ə*] n. Propagateur *m.*; propagatrice *f.*
‖ Agric. Germoir *m.*
propane ['proupein] n. Chim. Propane *m.*
propel [pro'pel] v. tr. (1). Propulser, faire avancer.
‖ Fam. Pousser.
propellant [-ənt] n. Propulseur *m.* ‖ Propergol *m.*
propellent [-ənt] adj. Propulseur.
propeller [-ə*] n. Propulseur *m.* ‖ Naut., Aviat.
Hélice *f.*; *feathered propeller*, hélice en drapeau. ‖
Propeller-shaft, n. Naut. Arbre porte-hélice *m.*;
Aviat. Arbre à cardan *m.*; Autom. Arbre (*m.*) de
transmission.
propelling [-iŋ] adj. *Propelling pencil*, porte-mine
à mine rétractable.
propense [pro'pens] adj. Porté (*to*, à).
propensity [-iti] n. Propension, tendance *f.*; penchant *m.* (*for*, *to*, à); *propensity for lying*, disposition au mensonge.
proper ['prɔpə*] adj. Propre, particulier, spécial
(*to*, à) [peculiar]. ‖ Propre, juste, authentique
(appropriate). ‖ Opportun, convenable, indiqué,

utile; *at the proper time*, en temps voulu, au bon moment. ‖ Bon; *in proper condition*, en bon état; *to deem proper to*, juger bon (or) à propos de. ‖ Convenable, comme il faut, bienséant (decent); *to do the proper thing by*, agir comme il convient envers. ‖ GRAMM. Propre (noun, sense, word); correct (use). BLAS. Au naturel (lion). ‖ ECCLES. Du jour (psalms). ‖ FAM. Vrai, réel, parfait; *proper idiot*, parfait crétin.
— n. ECCLES. Propre *m.*

properly [-li] adv. Bien, comme il faut, convenablement, correctement. ‖ JUR. De bon droit. ‖ GRAMM. Proprement, au sens propre; *properly so called*, proprement dit. ‖ FAM. Proprement, absolument.

properness [-nis] n. Convenance *f.*

propertied ['prɔpətid] adj. Possédant.

property [-ti] n. Propriété *f.* (right, ownership). ‖ Propriété *f.*; biens *m. pl.*; *damage to property*, dégâts matériels; *personal property*, biens personnels; *public property*, propriété publique. ‖ Propriété *f.*; domaine *m.* (estate). ‖ Propriété *f.*; immeuble *m.* (house). ‖ Propriété, caractéristique *f.* (peculiar quality). ‖ CHIM., MED., BOT. Propriété *f.* ‖ THEATR. Accessoire *m.*; pl. Réserve (*f.*) d'accessoires et décors. ‖ **Property-horse**, n. THEATR. Cheval-jupon *m.* ‖ **Property-man**, n. THEATR. Accessoiriste *m.* ‖ **Property-room**, n. THEATR. Magasin (*m.*) des accessoires. ‖ **Property-tax**, n. FIN. Impôt foncier *m.*

prophecy ['prɔfisi] n. Prophétie *f.* (act, utterance).

prophesier [-saiə*] n. Prophète *m.*; prophétesse *f.*

prophesy [-sai] v. intr. Prophétiser, faire des prophéties.
— v. tr. Prédire, prophétiser.

prophet ['prɔfit] n. Prophète *m.*

prophetess [-is] n. Prophétesse *f.*

prophetic(al) [prɔ'fetik(əl)] adj. Prophétique.

prophetically [-əli] adv. Prophétiquement.

prophylactic [‚prɔfi'læktik] adj., n. MED. Prophylactique *m.* ‖ U. S. Contraceptif; préservatif *m.*

prophylaxis [-sis] n. MED. Prophylaxie *f.*

propinquity [prɔ'piŋkwiti] n. Proximité *f.* (in space). [See VICINITY.] ‖ Proximité, prochaineté *f.* (in time). ‖ JUR. Parenté proche *f.* (relationship). ‖ FIG. Ressemblance, affinité *f.* (of ideas).

propionic [‚proupi'ɔnik] adj. CHIM. *Propionic acid*, acide propionique.

propitiable [prɔ'piʃiəbl] adj. Qui peut devenir propice. ‖ Qu'on peut se faire pardonner.

propitiate [-eit] v. tr. Rendre propice. ‖ Calmer, apaiser.

propitiation [‚propiʃi'eiʃən] n. Propitiation *f.*

propitiative [prɔ'piʃieitiv] adj. Expiatoire.

propitiatory [-ətəri] adj., n. Propitiatoire *m.*

propitious [prɔ'piʃəs] adj. Propice (to, à).

propitiously [-li] adv. Favorablement.

propitiousness [-nis] n. Caractère propice *m.*

proponent [prɔ'pounənt] n. U. S. Auteur, proposeur *m.*

proportion [prɔ'pɔːʃən] n. Proportion *f.*; rapport *m.*; *in proportion to*, au prorata de, par rapport à. ‖ Proportion, mesure *f.*; *in proportion as*, à mesure que; *in proportion to*, en raison de. ‖ Proportion, harmonie *f.*; *in due proportion*, bien proportionné; *out of proportion*, disproportionné, hors de proportion (with, avec). ‖ Pl. Proportions, dimensions *f. pl.* (size). ‖ FIN. Part *f.* (of expenses, profits); *in equal proportions*, à parts égales. ‖ CHIM. MED. FIG. ‖ MATH., MUS., ARCHIT. Proportion *f.*
— v. tr. Proportionner (to, à). ‖ CHIM., MED. Doser. ‖ TECHN. Chercher les dimensions de.

proportionable [-əbl] adj. Proportionné, en proportion.

proportionably [-əbli] adv. Proportionnellement.

proportional [-əl] adj. Proportionnel, proportionné (to, à); en proportion, en raison (to, de).

proportionalism [-əlizm] n. Représentation proportionnelle *f.*

proportionalist [-əlist] n. Proportionnaliste *s.*

proportionality [‚propɔː*ʃə'næliti] n. Proportionnalité *f.*

proportionally [pro'pɔːsənəli] adv. Proportionnellement (to, à); en proportion (to, de).

proportionate [-it] adj. Proportionné (to, à).

proportionately [-itli] adv. Proportionnellement; *proportionately speaking*, toutes proportions gardées.

proportioning [-iŋ] n. CHIM., MED. Dosage *m.* ‖ TECHN. Recherche (*f.*) des dimensions.

proportionment [-mənt] n. Fait (*m.*) de proportionner; distribution proportionnelle *f.*

proposable [prə'pouzəbl] adj. Proposable.

proposal [-əl] n. Proposition *f.* ‖ Demande (*f.*) en mariage. ‖ ECCLES. Promesse (*f.*) de mariage. ‖ U. S. TECHN. Soumission *f.* ‖ FIG. Projet *m.*

propose [pro'pouz] v. tr. Proposer (an object); poser (a problem). ‖ Proposer (a candidate, motion); *to propose the health of*, boire à la santé de, porter un toast à. ‖ Se proposer, avoir l'intention (to, de) [to intend].
— v. intr. Se proposer, avoir un dessein. ‖ Faire une demande en mariage; *to propose to*, faire sa demande à.

proposer [-ə*] n. Proposeur *s.*

proposition [‚propə'ziʃən] n. Proposition *f.* ‖ GRAMM., PHILOS., MATH., MUS. Proposition *f.* ‖ FAM. Affaire *f.*; *a different proposition*, une autre question.
— v. tr. U. S. POP. Faire une proposition douteuse à.

propositional [-əl] adj. PHILOS. De la proposition; par syllogisme.

propound [pro'paund] v. tr. Proposer, émettre (an idea, a theory); poser (a problem, question). ‖ JUR. Faire homologuer (a will).

propounder [-ə*] n. Auteur, proposeur *m.*

proprietary [prə'praiətəri] adj. De propriétaire (care); possédant (classes); de propriété (rights). ‖ ECCLES. Privé (chapel). ‖ MED. *Proprietary medicines*, spécialités pharmaceutiques.
— n. Propriété *f.*; droit (*m.*) de propriété. ‖ Propriétaires *m. pl.* (collectively).

proprietor [-tə*] n. Propriétaire *s.*

proprietorship [-təʃip] n. Propriété *f.* (See OWNERSHIP.)

proprietress [-tris] n. Propriétaire *f.*

propriety [-ti] n. Convenance, correction *f.* (of manners); *breach of propriety*, incorrection, manque de savoir-vivre; *an instinct for propriety*, le sens des convenances. ‖ Opportunité *f.* (of an action). ‖ GRAMM. Propriété *f.* (of a word).

propulsion [pro'pʌlʃən] n. Propulsion *f.*

propulsive [-siv] adj. Propulsif; propulseur.

propyl ['proupil] n. CHIM. Propyle *m.*

pro rata ['prou 'rɑːtə] adj., adv. Au prorata.

prorogation [‚prourə'geiʃən] n. JUR. Prorogation *f.* (of Parliament).

prorogue [pro'roug] v. tr. JUR. Proroger.
— v. intr. JUR. Se proroger.

prosaic [pro'zeiik] adj. FIG. Prosaïque.

prosaically [-əli] adv. Prosaïquement.

prosaicness [-nis], **prosaism** ['prouzeiizm] n. Prosaïsme *m.* (See PROSINESS.)

prosaist ['prouzeiist] n. Prosateur *m.* (prose-writer). ‖ FIG. Esprit prosaïque *m.*

proscenium [pro'siːniəm] n. † Proscenium *m.* ‖ THEATR. Avant-scène *f.*

proscribe [pros'kraib] v. tr. Proscrire.

proscriber [-ə*] n. Proscripteur *m.*

proscript ['prouskript] n. Proscrit *s.*

proscription [pros'kripʃən] n. Proscription *f.*

proscriptive [-tiv] adj. De proscription.
prose [prouz] n. Prose *f*. ‖ Tirade *f*.; long discours *m*. (speech). ‖ Thème *m*. (at school). ‖ Eccles. Prose *f*. ‖ Fig. Prosaïsme *m*. ‖ **Prose-writer,** n. Prosateur *m*.
— v. tr. Mettre en prose.
— v. intr. Fam. Débiter du bla-bla-bla, phraser.
prosector [pro'sektə*] n. Prosecteur *m*.
prosecutable ['prɔsikju:təbḷ] adj. Jur. Qui peut être intenté (action); poursuivable (person).
prosecute ['prɔsikju:t] v. tr. Intenter (an action); poursuivre (a claim); mener (an inquiry); poursuivre en justice (s.o.). ‖ Fig. Exercer (a profession); poursuivre (studies); effectuer (a voyage).
prosecution [,prɔsi'kju:ʃən] n. Jur. Accusation *f*.; ministère public *m*. (public prosecutor); poursuites *f. pl.* (proceedings). ‖ Fig. Exercice *m*. (of a profession); poursuite *f*. (of studies).
prosecutor ['prɔsikjutə*] n. Jur. Ministère public, procureur *m*. (attorney); plaignant *s*. (plaintiff).
prosecutrix [,prɔsi'kju:triks] n. Jur. Plaignante *f*.
proselyte ['prɔsilait] n. Prosélyte *s*.
— v. intr. U. S. Faire du prosélytisme.
proselytism [-itizm̩] n. Prosélytisme *m*.
proselytize [-itaiz] v. tr. Faire un prosélyte de.
— v. intr. Faire du prosélytisme.
proser ['prouzə*] n. Fam. Raseur, phraseur *m*.
prosify ['prouzifai] v. tr. (2). Prosaïser.
— v. intr. Faire de la prose assommante; phraser.
prosiness [-nis] n. Prosaïsme *m*.
prosodic [pro'sɔdik] adj. Prosodique.
prosodist ['prɔsədist] n. Prosodiste *m*.
prosody [-di] n. Prosodie *f*.
prosopopoeia [,prɔsoupə'pi:jə] n. Gramm. Prosopopée *f*.
prospect ['prɔspekt] n. Vue, perspective *f*.; paysage *m*. (vista). ‖ Vue; perspective *f*. (outlook). ‖ Pl. Perspectives, espérances *f. pl.*; avenir *m*. (future, promise). ‖ Techn. Prélèvement *m*. (of ore). ‖ U. S. Comm. Client éventuel *s*. ‖ U. S. Fam. Parti *m*. (for possible marriage). ‖ **Prospect-glass,** n. Jumelle, longue-vue *f*.
— [prɔs'pekt] v. intr. Prospecter; *to prospect for*, chercher. ‖ Promettre.
— v. tr. Prospecter.
prospecting ['prɔspektiŋ] n. Prospection *f*. (act).
prospective [pro'spektiv] adj. Prospectif. ‖ Jur. A effet futur, d'avenir. ‖ Comm. Eventuel, possible. ‖ Fig. Futur, en perspective, d'approche.
prospectively [-ivli] adv. Dans l'avenir, plus tard. ‖ Fig. En perspective.
prospector [-ə*] n. Prospecteur *s*.; *oil, gold prospector*, chercheur de pétrole, d'or.
prospectus [-əs] (pl. **prospectuses** [-əsiz]) n. Prospectus *m*. ‖ Fin. Appel pour emprunt *m*.
prosper ['prɔspə*] v. intr. Prospérer (business); réussir (person). [See thrive.]
— v. tr. Faire prospérer.
prosperity [prɔs'periti] n. Prospérité *f*.
prosperous ['prɔspərəs] adj. Prospère (business); prospère, de prospérité (look); favorable (wind).
prosperousness [-nis] n. Prospérité *f*. (of, de).
prostate ['prɔsteit] n. Med. Prostate *f*.
prostatic [prɔs'tætik] adj. Med. Prostatique.
prostatitis [,prɔstə'taitis] n. Med. Prostatite *f*.
prosthesis ['prɔsθisis] n. Med. Prothèse *f*. ‖ Gramm. Prosthèse *f*.
prostitute ['prɔstitju:t] n. Prostituée *f*.
— v. tr. Prostituer; *to prostitute oneself*, se prostituer.
prostitution [,prɔsti'tju:ʃən] n. Prostitution *f*.
prostitutor ['prɔstitjutə^] n. Prostituteur *m*.
prostrate ['prɔstrit] adj. Prosterné (before, to, devant) [bowing]. ‖ Couché, gisant (prone). ‖ Med. Prostré. ‖ Bot. Procombant. ‖ Fig. Effondré, anéanti.

— [prɔs'treit] v. tr. Etendre; *to prostrate oneself*, se prosterner. ‖ Med., Fig. Abattre, accabler.
prostration [prɔs'treiʃən] n. Prosternation *f*.; prosternement *m*. ‖ Med. Prostration *f*. ‖ Fig. Accablement, effondrement *m*.
prostyle ['proustail] n. Archit. Prostyle *m*.
prosy ['prouzi] adj. Monotone (life); ennuyeux; raseur (fam.) [person]; prosaïque (style).
protactinium [,proutæk'tiniəm] n. Chim. Protactinium *m*.
protagonism [pro'tægənizm̩] n. Protagonisme *m*.
protagonist [-nist] n. Protagoniste *s*.
protean [prou'ti:ən] adj. Protéiforme, changeant.
protect [pro'tekt] v. tr. Protéger (against, from, contre). ‖ Comm. Faire provision pour (a bill of exchange). ‖ Jur. Protéger. ‖ Naut. Cuirasser (a cruiser). ‖ Fig. Sauvegarder (interests); patronner (s.o.).
protecting [-iŋ] adj. De protection; protecteur *m*.; protectrice *f*.
protection [pro'tekʃən] n. Protection *f*. (against, contre). ‖ Abri *m*. (place). ‖ Jur. Protection *f*. ‖ Naut. Blindage *m*. ‖ **Protection-deck,** n. Naut. Pont blindé *m*. ‖ **Protection-racket,** n. Chantage (*m*.) à la protection contre les gangs.
protectionism [-izm̩] n. Jur. Protectionnisme *m*.
protectionist [-ist] n. Jur. Protectionniste *m*.
protective [pro'tektiv] adj. Protecteur, préservateur *m*.; protectrice, préservatrice *f*. ‖ Jur. Protecteur (duty); *protective custody*, détention préventive. ‖ Milit. De couverture (troops). ‖ Fin. Chargé des intérêts de.
protectively [-li] adv. De façon protectrice. ‖ Jur. Au moyen de la protection.
protectiveness [-nis] n. Caractère protecteur *m*.
protector [pro'tektə] n. Protecteur *m*. (device, person). [See patron.]
protectorate [-ərit] n. Protectorat *m*.
protectress [-ris] n. Protectrice *f*.
protégé ['prouteʒei] n. Protégé *s*.
protein ['proutiin] n. Chim., Med. Protéine *f*.
pro tempore [prou 'tempəri] adj. Provisoire, intérimaire.
— adv. Provisoirement, par intérim.
protest ['proutest] n. Protestation *f*. (action, declaration). ‖ Jur. *Under protest*, sous réserve. ‖ Comm. Protêt *m*. ‖ Naut. *Ship's protest*, rapport de mer. ‖ Fam. *Under protest*, à son corps défendant.
— [pro'test] v. tr. Protester de (one's innocence); protester (that, que). ‖ Comm. Protester (a bill). ‖ U. S. Protester contre (a decision).
— v. intr. Protester (against, contre).
Protestant ['prɔtestənt] adj., n. Eccles. Protestant *s*.
Protestantism [-izm̩] n. Eccles. Protestantisme *m*.
protestation [,prɔtes'téiʃən] n. Protestation *f*.
protester [prə'testə*] n. Protestataire *s*. (See objector.)
prothesis ['prɔθisis] n. Eccles. Prothèse *f*.
protocole ['proutokɔl] n. Jur. Protocole *m*. (State etiquette).
protohistory [,prouto'histəri] n. Protohistorique *f*.
proto-Indo-European ['prouto'indou,juərə'pi:ən] n. Gramm. Proto-indo-européen *m*.
protomartyr [-'mɑ:tə*] n. Eccles. Protomartyr *m*.
proton ['prouton] n. Phys. Proton *m*.
protonotary [,prouto'noutəri] n. Eccles. Protonotaire *m*.
protoplasm ['proutoplæzm̩] n. Med. Protoplasme *m*.
protoplast ['proutoplɑ:st] n. Med. Protoplaste *m*. ‖ Fig. Prototype *m*.
prototype ['proutətaip] n. Prototype *m*.
protoxide [pro'tɔksaid] n. Chim. Protoxyde *m*.
protozoa [,proutə'zouə], **protozoans** [-əns] n. pl. Med. Protozoaires *m. pl.*

protract [proˈtrækt] v. tr. JUR. Prolonger, faire durer. ‖ TECHN. Relever.

protractile [-ail] adj. ZOOL. Extensile.

protraction [proˈtrækʃən] n. JUR. Prolongation *f.;* longueurs *f. pl.* ‖ TECHN. Relevé *m.* ‖ MED. Protraction *f.*

protractor [-tə*] n. MED. Protracteur *m.* ‖ MATH. Rapporteur *m.* ‖ FAM. Lanterneur *m.*

protrude [prəˈtruːd] v. tr. Sortir, faire sortir, amener en avant.
— v. intr. Avancer, dépasser, déborder, faire saillie. (See PROJECT.)

protruding [-iɳ] adj. Saillant (eyes); bombé (forehead); proéminent (jaw). ‖ MED. Hernié (bowel).

protrusion [proˈtruːʒən] n. Saillie *f.* ‖ MED. Protrusion *f.*

protuberance [proˈtjuːbərəns] n. Protubérance *f.*

protuberant [-ənt] adj. Protubérant.

proud [praud] adj. Orgueilleux, altier; *to be proud of,* s'enorgueillir de, tirer vanité de. ‖ Fier (legitimately); *to be proud to,* être fier (or) heureux de, trouver sa fierté à. ‖ Imposant, superbe, majestueux (stately). ‖ MED. Fongueux (flesh). ‖ TECHN. Saillant (rivet). ‖ **Proud-hearted,** adj. Au cœur fier.

proudly [-li] adv. Orgueilleusement. ‖ Fièrement.

provable [ˈpruːvəb̬l] adj. Prouvable.

provableness [-əb̬lnis] n. Démontrabilité *f.*

provably [-əbli] adv. De façon prouvable.

prove [pruːv] v. tr. † TECHN. Éprouver. ‖ TECHN. Tirer une épreuve de. ‖ MATH. Faire la preuve de (a sum). ‖ JUR. Justifier (damages); prouver (sth.); homologuer (a will). ‖ FIG. Prouver, établir, démontrer; *to prove oneself,* faire ses preuves.
— v. intr. Se montrer, s'affirmer, s'avérer, se révéler, paraître. ‖ U. S. *Proving ground,* terrain d'essai. ‖ **To prove up,** U. S. Réunir les documents (*on,* pour obtenir).

provenance [ˈprɔvinəns] n. Provenance *f.* (place of origin).

provender [ˈprɔvəndə*] n. AGRIC. Fourrage *m.* ‖ FAM. Provende *f.*
— v. tr. AGRIC. Affourrager (cattle); donner de l'avoine à (horses).

prover [ˈpruːvə*] n. TECHN. Compte-fils *m.* (device); tireur (*m.*) d'épreuves (person).

proverb [ˈprɔvə:b] n. Proverbe *m.*

proverbial [proˈvə:biəl] adj. Proverbial; *to become proverbial,* passer en proverbe.

proverbially [-əli] adv. Proverbialement.

provide [proˈvaid] v. intr. Se prémunir, se pourvoir, prendre des précautions (*against,* contre); parer, obvier (*against,* à); *to provide for,* prévoir (an eventuality). ‖ Pourvoir, subvenir (*for,* aux besoins de) [s.o.]; *to provide for oneself,* se suffire.
— v. tr. Pourvoir, nantir, munir (*with,* de) [s.o.]. ‖ Fournir, ménager (sth.); *not to provide a decent living,* ne pas nourrir son homme; *to provide a topic of conversation,* défrayer la conversation.

provided [-id] adj. Pourvu, nanti, muni (*with,* de); *well provided for,* bien renté, les poches bien garnies. ‖ Préparé, prêt (*for,* à) [an eventuality]. ‖ Décidé, conclu; *unless otherwise provided,* sauf conventions contraires.
— conj. Pourvu, à condition (*that,* que).

providence [ˈprɔvidəns] n. Prévoyance *f.* ‖ ECCLES. Providence; protection providentielle *f.*

provident [-ənt] adj. Prévoyant (person); de prévoyance (society); *provident fund,* caisse de prévoyance. ‖ Économe, prévoyant. (See SPARING.)

providential [ˌprɔviˈdenʃəl] adj. Providentiel.

providentially [-əli] adv. Providentiellement.

provider [proˈvaidə*] n. Pourvoyeur, fournisseur *s.*

province [ˈprɔvins] n. Province *f.* ‖ JUR. Juridiction *f.* ‖ FIG. Département, rayon, domaine *m.*

provincial [proˈvinʃəl] adj. Provincial, de province.
— n. ECCLES. Provincial *m.*

provincialism [-izm̩] n. GRAMM. Provincialisme *m.* ‖ FIG. Esprit de clocher *m.*

provinciality [ˌprɔvinʃiˈæliti] n. Provincialité *f.*

provision [proˈviʒən] n. Mesures prises *f. pl.* (*against,* contre; *for,* pour); *to make provision for,* pourvoir à, prendre des dispositions (or) des précautions pour. ‖ CULIN. Pl. Provisions *f. pl.;* vivres *m. pl.* ‖ FIN. Prestation *f.* (of capital); réserve *f.* (*for,* pour). ‖ JUR. Clause *f.* (of an act); *to fall within the provisions of the law,* tomber sous le coup de la loi.
— v. tr. Approvisionner, ravitailler.

provisional [-əl] adj. Provisoire, temporaire. ‖ JUR. Provisionnel.

provisionally [-əli] adv. Provisoirement, temporairement, à titre provisoire. ‖ JUR. Provisionnellement.

provisionment [-mənt] n. Approvisionnement *m.*

proviso [proˈvaizou] n. JUR. Clause restrictive, condition formelle *f.*

provisory [proˈvaizəri] adj. JUR. Conditionnel (clause); provisoire (government).

Provo [ˈprouvou] (pl. **Provos** [-z]) n. Membre (*m.*) de l'I. R. A. provisoire.

provocation [ˌprɔvəˈkeiʃən] n. Provocation *f.* ‖ Stimulant *m.* (*to,* à). ‖ Irritation *f.;* accès (*m.*) de colère (fit of anger). ‖ FAM. Provocation, aguicherie, agacerie *f.*

provocative [proˈvɔkətiv] adj. Provocateur *m.;* provocatrice *f.;* provocatif. ‖ FAM. Provocant, aguichant (alluring).
— n. Aphrodisiaque *m.* ‖ MED. Stimulant *m.*

provoke [proˈvouk] v. tr. Pousser, inciter (*to,* à) [to induce]. ‖ Provoquer, exciter, faire naître (to cause). ‖ Fâcher, agacer, contrarier, ennuyer (to annoy).

provoker [-ə*] n. Provocateur *m.;* provocatrice *f.*

provoking [-iɳ] adj. Contrariant, énervant, agaçant; fâcheux, désolant.

provost [ˈprɔvəst] n. Principal *m.* (at a university). ‖ † Prévôt *m.* ‖ JUR. Maire *m.* (in Scotland).
— [proˈvou] n. MILIT. Prévôt *m.*

provostal [proˈvɔstəl] adj. Prévôtal.

provostry [ˈprɔvəstri] n. Prévôté *f.*

provostship [-ʃip] n. Principalat *m.* ‖ † Prévôté *f.* ‖ JUR. Fonction (*f.*) de maire.

prow [prau] n. NAUT. Proue *f.*

prowess [ˈprauɛs] n. Prouesse *f.* (deed, valour).

prowl [praul] v. intr., tr. Rôder.
— n. Chasse *f.* (for animals). ‖ Fait (*m.*) de rôder. ‖ **Prowl car,** n. U. S. Voiture de patrouille *f.*

prowler [-ə*] n. Rôdeur *s.*

proximate [ˈprɔksimit] adj. Proche. ‖ Approximatif. ‖ PHILOS. Prochain (cause). ‖ CHIM. Immédiat (analysis).

proximately [-li] adv. Promptement. ‖ Approximativement. ‖ Immédiatement.

proximity [prɔkˈsimiti] n. Proximité *f.* (*of, to,* de).

proximo [ˈprɔksimou] adv. Prochain, du mois prochain.

proxy [ˈprɔksi] n. JUR. Procuration *f.;* pouvoir *m.* (act); mandataire; fondé (*s.*) de pouvoir (person); vote émis par mandataire *m.* (vote).

prude [pruːd] n. Prude, mijaurée *f.*

prudence [ˈpruːdəns] n. Prudence, circonspection. (See CAUTION.)

prudent [-ənt] adj. Prudent, circonspect, avisé.

prudential [pruˈdenʃəl] adj. De prudence. ‖ FIN. Industriel (insurance). ‖ U. S. De gestion (committee).
— n. pl. Attitude prudente *f.;* mesures (*f. pl.*) de prudence.

prudentialism [-izm̩] n. Excès (*m.*) de prudence; attitude timorée *f.*

prudently [ˈpruːdəntli] adv. Prudemment.

prudery [ˈpruːdəri], **prudishness** [-iʃnis] n. Pruderie; pudibonderie *f.*

prudish [-iʃ] adj. Prude. (See PRIGGISH.)
prudishly [-iʃli] adv. Avec pruderie.
pruinose ['pruinous] adj. BOT. Pruineux.
prune [pru:n] n. BOT., CULIN. Pruneau m. ‖ U. S. FAM. Repoussoir m. (ugly); bêta m. (silly).
— adj. Prune (colour).
prune v. tr. AGRIC. Tailler, émonder, élaguer. (See TRIM.) ‖ FAM. Couper dans, faire des coupures dans (a text).
prunella [pru'nelə] n. BOT. Prunelle f.
prunella n. MED. Muguet m.
pruner ['pru:nə*] n. Emondeur, élagueur m.
pruning [-iŋ] n. AGRIC. Taille f.; élagage, émondage m. ‖ Pl. Emondes f. pl. ‖ Pruning-bill, n. Serpette f. ‖ Pruning-hook, n. Emondoir m.
prurience ['pruəriəns] n. Luxure f. ‖ † FAM. Démangeaison f.
prurient [-ənt] adj. Lascif.
prurigo [pru'raigou] n. MED. Prurigo m.
pruritus [pru'raitəs] n. MED. Prurit m.
Prussia ['prʌʃə] n. GEOGR. Prusse f.
Prussian [-ən] adj., n. GEOGR. Prussien s. ‖ COMM. Prussian blue, bleu de Prusse.
prussiate ['prʌʃiit] n. CHIM. Prussiate. (See CYANIDE.)
prussic ['prʌsik] adj. CHIM. Prussique.
pry [prai] n. TECHN. Levier-barre m.
— v. tr. (2). Soulever au levier.
Pry n. Paul Pry, curieux, fureteur s.
pry v. intr. (2). Fureter; chercher à pénétrer; mettre son nez (fam.) [into, dans].
prying [-iŋ] adj. Fureteur, inquisiteur. ‖ Curieux, indiscret.
pryingly [-iŋli] adv. Curieusement, avec indiscrétion; en furetant.
P.S. [pi:'es] abbr. postscript, post-scriptum, P.-S.
psalm [sɑ:m] n. ECCLES. Psaume m. ‖ Psalm-book, n. Psautier m.
psalmist [-ist] n. ECCLES. Psalmiste m.
psalmodic [sæl'mɔdik] adj. Psalmodique.
psalmodize ['sɑ:modaiz] v. tr., intr. Psalmodier.
psalmody [-di] n. Psalmodie f.
psalter ['sɑ:ltə*] n. ECCLES. Psautier m.
psaltery [-əri] n. MUS. Psaltérion m.
psephology [se'fɔlədʒi] n. Sociologie électorale f.
pseud [sju:d] adj., n. FAM. Prétentieux, poseur adj., s.
pseudo ['sju:dou] préf. Pseudo-.
— adj. Insincère, inauthentique.
pseudonym ['sju:dɔnim] n. Pseudonyme m.
pseudonymous [sju'dɔniməs] adj. Pseudonyme.
pshaw [ʃɔ:] interj. Peuh!, pouh!
— v. tr. Dédaigner.
— v. intr. Manifester son dédain.
psht [pʃ:t] interj. Chut!
psittacism ['sitəsizm] n. Psittacisme m.
psittacosis [,sitə'kousis] n. MED. Psittacose f.
psora ['sɔ:rə] n. MED. Gale f.
psoriasis [sɔ'raiəsis] n. MED. Psoriasis m.
psst [pst] interj. Psitt!
psych [saik] v. tr. U. S. FAM. Analyser (to psychoanalyse). ‖ Intimider (to frighten). ‖ To psych out, percer, analyser les mobiles de (a person); décortiquer (a problem). ‖ To psych up, se préparer psychologiquement (for, à).
psyche ['saiki:] n. Psyché f.
psychedelic [,saiki'delik] adj., n. Psychédélique adj., m.
psychiatric [saiki'ætrik] adj. MED. Psychiatrique.
psychiatrist [sai'kaiətrist] n. MED. Psychiatre m.
psychiatry [-tri] n. MED. Psychiatrie f.
psychic ['saikik] adj. Psychique; métapsychique.
— n. Médium m.
psychics [-s] n. pl. Métapsychique f.
psychism ['saikizm] n. Psychisme m.
psychist [-ist] n. Psychiste; métapsychiste s.

psychoanalyse [saikou'ænəlaiz] v. tr. MED. Psychanalyser.
psychoanalysis [,saikouə'næləsis] n. MED. Psychanalyse f.
psychoanalyst [,saikou'ænəlist] n. MED. Psychanalyste s.
psychoanalytic (al) [,saikouənæ'litik(əl)] adj. MED. Psychanalytique.
psycholinguistics [,saikouliŋ'gwistiks] n. sg. Psycholinguistique f.
psychological [,saiko'lɔdʒikəl] adj. Psychologique. ‖ FAM. Psychologique, critique, décisif.
psychologically [-dʒikəli] adv. Psychologiquement.
psychologist [sai'kɔlədʒist] n. Psychologue s.
psychology [-dʒi] n. Psychologie f.
psychometry [sai'kɔmitri] n. Psychométrie f.
psychomotor [,saiko'moutə*] adj. Psychomoteur.
psychoneurosis [,saikonju'rousis] n. MED. Psychonévrose f.
psychopathology [,saikopə'θɔlədʒi] n. MED. Psychopathologie f.
psychopath ['saiko'pæθ] n. MED. Psychopathe s.
psychopathic [,saiko'pæθik] adj. Psychopathique (illness); psychopathe (person).
psychopathy [sai'kɔpəθi] n. Psychopathie f.
psychophysiology [,saikou,fizi'ɔlədʒi] n. Psychophysiologie f.
psychosis [sai'kousis] (pl. psychoses [-i:z]) n. MED. Psychose f.
psychosomatic [-,sou'mætik] adj. Psychosomatique.
psychosurgery [,saiko'sə:dʒəri] n. Psychochirurgie f.
psychotherapeutics [saikou,θerə'pju:tiks] n. sg. MED. Psychothérapeutique f.
psychotherapist [,saiko'θerəpist] n. MED. Psychothérapeute s.
psychotherapy [-pi] n. MED. Psychothérapie f.
psychotic [sai'kɔtik] adj., n. MED. Psychotique adj., s.
psychotropic [,saiko'trɔpik] adj. MED. Psychotrope; a psychotropic drug, un psychotrope.
ptarmigan ['tɑ:migən] n. ZOOL. Lagopède m.
pterodactyl [,pterə'dæktil] n. ZOOL. Ptérodactyle m.
P.T.O. [pi:ti:'ou] abbr. please turn over, tournez, s'il vous plaît, T. S. V. P.
ptosis ['tousis] n. MED. Ptôse f.
pub [pʌb] n. FAM. Bistrot m. ‖ Pub-crawl, n. FAM. Vadrouille, godaille, tournée (f.) des bistrots. ‖ Pub-crawler, n. FAM. Vadrouilleur, godailleur, coureur (m.) de bistrots.
puberty ['pju:bəti] n. MED. Puberté f.
pubes [pju:bi:z] n. MED. Pubis m.
pubescence [pju'besn̩s] n. BOT. Pubescence f. ‖ MED. Puberté f.
pubescent [-nt] adj. BOT. Pubescent. ‖ MED. Pubère.
pubic ['pju:bik] adj. MED. Pubien.
pubis ['pju:bis] (pl. pubes [-i:z]) n. MED. Pubis m. (bone).
public ['pʌblik] adj. Public (lecture, life, man, works); public dinner, banquet; public school, école secondaire (or) privée; U. S. école primaire communale; public transport, transports en commun; public servant, fonctionnaire; public utility, service public; public spirit, esprit social, civisme; to make public, rendre public, publier. ‖ Municipal (library); public holiday, fête légale. ‖ Public-address system, n. Sonorisation, sono f. ‖ Public-house, n. Bar, débit (m.) de boissons. (See PUB.) ‖ Public Record Office, n. Archives nationales britanniques f. pl. ‖ Public relations, n. Relations (f. pl.) avec le public (gen.); relations publiques, public-relations f. pl. (of a company); public relations officer, chargé de relations publiques. ‖ Public-spirited, adj. D'esprit social, dévoué au bien public.
— n. Public m.; in public, en public, publiquement.

publican [-ən] n. Cabaretier, débitant (*m.*) de boissons. ‖ ECCLES. Publicain *m.*

publication [ˌpʌbli'keiʃən] n. Publication, parution *f.* (of a book); publication *f.* (work). ‖ JUR. Publication *f.* (of banns); promulgation *f.* (of a law).

publicist ['pʌblisist] n. Publiciste, journaliste *m.* ‖ Spécialiste de droit international *m.* ‖ Publicitaire, agent (*m.*) de publicité (publicity agent).

publicity [pʌb'lisiti] n. Publicité *f.* (see ADVERTISING); *publicity bureau*, agence de publicité; *publicity agent*, publicitaire.

publicize [ˌpʌbli'saiz] v. tr. Faire connaître au public, divulguer.

publish ['pʌbliʃ] v. tr. Publier, faire paraître, sortir (a book); *just published*, vient de paraître; *now publishing*, en cours de publication, sous presse; *published*, paru en librairie. ‖ JUR. Publier (the banns). ‖ FIG. Publier, divulguer (news).

publisher [-ə*] n. Editeur *m.* ‖ U. S. *Newspaper publisher*, propriétaire de journal.

publishing [-iŋ] n. Publication *f.*
— adj. D'édition.

puce [pju:s] adj. Puce (colour).

puck [pʌk] n. Lutin, puck *m.*

puck n. ZOOL. Engoulevent *m.*

puck n. SPORTS. Galine *f.*

pucker ['pʌkə*] n. Fronce, grigne *f.* (crease). ‖ Ride *f.* (wrinkle).
— v. tr. Froncer, faire goder. (See COCKLE.) ‖ Rider (face); *to pucker one's brows*, froncer le sourcil.
— v. intr. Froncer, goder, grigner. ‖ Se rider; se contracter.

puckish [-iʃ] adj. De lutin.

pud [pud] n. FAM., CULIN. Pudding *m.*; dessert *m.*

pudding ['pudiŋ] n. CULIN. Pudding *m.* (cake); *black pudding*, boudin. ‖ NAUT. Emboudinure *f.*; boudin *m.* ‖ **Pudding-face**, n. FAM. Face de lune *f.* ‖ **Pudding-head**, n. FAM. Crétin *m.* ‖ **Pudding-stone**, n. TECHN., GEOL. Poudingue *m.*
— v. tr. NAUT. Emboudiner.

puddle ['pʌdl̩] n. Petite mare; flaque *f.* ‖ TECHN. Corroi *m.*
— v. intr. Barboter, patauger. ‖ FAM. Faire un beau gâchis.
— v. tr. Troubler (water). ‖ TECHN. Corroyer (clay); puddler (iron).

puddling [-iŋ] n. TECHN. Puddlage *m.*

puddly [-i] adj. Bourbeux.

pudency ['pju:dənsi], **pudicity** [pju'disiti] n. Pudicité *f.*

pudenda [pju'dendə] n. pl. MED. Parties *f. pl.*

pudge [pʌdʒ] n. FAM. Personne boulotte *f.*

pudgy [-i] adj. Rondouillard.

puerile ['pjuərail] adj. Puéril. (See CHILDISH.)

puerility [pjuə'riliti] n. Puérilité *f.*

puerperal [pju'ə:pərəl] adj. MED. Puerpéral.

puff [pʌf] n. Bouffée *f.* (of air, smoke); jet *m.* (of steam). ‖ Chou *m.* (of ribbon); bouillon *m.* (on a skirt); bouffant *m.* (of a sleeve). ‖ Houpette, houppe *f.* (for powder). ‖ CULIN. Feuilleté *m.* (cake). ‖ U. S. Edredon *m.* ‖ FAM. Battage, tam-tam, boniment *m.* (blurb); souffle *m.* (breath). ‖ **Puff-ball**, n. BOT. Vesse-de-loup *f.* ‖ **Puff-box**, n. Boîte à poudre *f.* ‖ **Puff-paste**, n. CULIN. Feuilletage *m.*; pâte feuilletée *f.* ‖ **Puff-puff**, n. FAM. Teuf-teuf *m.*
— v. intr. Souffler. ‖ Jeter des bouffées (of smoke, steam); *to puff at one's pipe*, tirer sur sa pipe.
— v. tr. Lancer (or) jeter des bouffées de (smoke, steam). ‖ Tirer sur (a pipe). ‖ **To puff out**, faire bouffer (a skirt); émettre (smoke). ‖ **To puff up**, gonfler (lit. and fig.).

puffed [-t] adj. Bouffant (sleeve). ‖ CULIN. Gonflé (rice). ‖ FAM. Essoufflé, haletant. ‖ **Puffed up**, adj. Bouffi (face); FIG. Gonflé (*with*, de) [person]; boursouflé (style).

puffin [pʌfin] n. ZOOL. Macareux.

puffiness ['pʌfinis] n. MED. Bouffissure *f.* ‖ FIG. Boursouflure *f.*

puffy [-i] adj. Bouffi (eye, face, person). ‖ Bouffant (skirt, sleeve). ‖ Essoufflé, poussif (person).

pug [pʌg] n. ZOOL. Carlin *m.* (dog). ‖ **Pug-nose**, n. Nez camus *m.* ‖ **Pug-nosed**, adj. Camus, camard.

pug n. Glaise *f.*
— v. tr. Pétrir, malaxer (clay). ‖ ARCHIT. Hourder.

pugilism ['pju:dʒilizm] n. SPORTS. Pugilat *m.* (See BOXING.)

pugilist [-ist] n. SPORTS. Pugiliste *m.* (See BOXER.)

pugnacious [pʌg'neiʃəs] adj. Batailleur, pugnace.

pugnaciousness [-nis], **pugnacity** [pʌg'næsiti] n. Nature querelleuse, pugnacité *f.*

puisne ['pju:ni] adj. Postérieur (*to*, à). ‖ JUR. Conseiller (judge).

puke [pju:k] n. POP. Dégobillage *m.*
— v. intr. POP. Dégobiller, dégueuler.

puking [-iŋ] n. POP. Dégobillage *m.*

pukka ['pʌkə] adj. FAM. *A pukka sahib*, un vrai monsieur.

pulchritude ['pʌlkritju:d] n. Beauté *f.*

pule [pju:l] v. intr. ZOOL. Pépier (bird); piailler (chicken). ‖ FAM. Vagir (baby); piauler (child).

puling [-iŋ] n. Pépiement *m.* (of bird); piaillement *m.* (of chicken). ‖ FAM. Piaulement *m.* (of child); vagissement *m.* (of infant).
— adj. FAM. Vagissant (baby); piauleur (child).

pull [pull] n. Traction *f.*; tirage *m.* (act); *to give a pull*, exercer une traction, tirer. ‖ Effort (*m.*) de traction; tirage *m.*; tirée *f.* (fam.). ‖ Poignée *f.* (of drawer). ‖ PHYS. Force d'attraction *f.* (of a magnet). ‖ SPORTS. Coup tiré *m.* (golf); coup d'aviron *m.* (rowing). ‖ U. S. Rendement *m.* ‖ FAM. Soutien, appui, piston *m.*; *to have the pull of* (or) *over*, avoir barre sur; *to have pull*, avoir du piston. ‖ FAM. Bouffée *f.* (of smoke); lampée *f.* (of wine). ‖ **Pull-back**, adj. TECHN. De rappel (spring); n. Entrave *f.* ‖ **Pull-off**, n. Détente *f.* ‖ **Pull-out**, adj. A coulisse (slide); n. AVIAT. Ressource *f.* ‖ **Pull-over**, n. Pull-over, pull *m.* ‖ **Pull-up**, n. Arrêt *m.* (act); auberge (*f.*) de routiers (inn); SPORTS. Rétablissement *m.*
— v. tr. Tirer (in general). ‖ Tirer, traîner (to drag). ‖ SPORTS. Renvoyer (the ball); faire marcher (a boat); manier (oar); retenir (race-horse). ‖ U. S. COMM. Attirer (custom). ‖ TECHN. Tirer (a proof). ‖ FAM. *To pull the strings*, être par-derrière, tirer les ficelles; *to pull a face*, faire une grimace; *to pull s.o.'s leg*, monter un bateau à qqn. ‖ **To pull about**, traîner, tirailler; FAM. Malmener. ‖ **To pull away**, entraîner, tirer (s.o.); tirer, arracher (sth.). ‖ **To pull back**, tirer en arrière, repousser; FAM. Retarder. ‖ **To pull down**, baisser, rabattre (a hat); abattre, raser, démolir (a house); FIG. Abattre, décourager (s.o.); FAM. Dénicher (a job); renverser (government). ‖ **To pull in**, rentrer (in general); SPORTS. Retenir (a horse). ‖ **To pull off**, retirer, enlever, ôter (in general); SPORTS. Remporter (a prize); FAM. Enlever, emporter, décrocher. ‖ **To pull on**, mettre, enfiler. ‖ **To pull out**, sortir, tirer; MED. Arracher, extraire (teeth). ‖ **To pull over**, enfoncer, tirer sur; renverser. ‖ **To pull round**, MED. Remettre en forme; ranimer. ‖ **To pull through**, tirer d'affaire (s.o.); mener à terme (sth.). ‖ **To pull together**, remettre d'aplomb. ‖ **To pull up**, tirer; hisser; faire monter (in general); lever, relever, retrousser; AGRIC. Arracher; SPORTS. Arrêter net (horse); FAM. Rabrouer (s.o.).
— v. intr. Tirer (*at*, sur). Tirer, tomber mal (dress). ‖ SPORTS. Souquer, nager (boat); se braquer (horse). ‖ AUTOM. Tirer. ‖ FAM. *To pull different ways*, tirer à hue et à dia; *to pull with*, influencer. ‖ **To pull ahead**, SPORTS. Se détacher. ‖ **To pull in**, CH. DE F. Entrer en gare. ‖ **To pull out**, CH. DE F. Quitter la gare; AUTOM. Sortir, se dégager; NAUT. Ramer au large; U. S. FAM. Se défiler. ‖ **To pull over**,

Autom. Se ranger, se replier. ‖ **To pull through,** en réchapper, s'en tirer, se remettre. ‖ **To pull together,** s'entendre. ‖ **To pull up,** s'arrêter ; Sports. Faire des tractions ; Fig. Stopper, mettre un frein, se réduire.

puller [-ə*] n. Tireur s. ‖ Sports. Rameur s. ‖ Techn. Démonteur ; extracteur m.

pullet ['pulit] n. Zool. Poulette f. ‖ Culin. Poulet m. ; poularde f.

pulley ['puli] n. Poulie f. ‖ **Pulley-block,** n. Moufle f.

pulling ['pulin] n. Tirage m. ; traction f. ‖ Techn. Tirage m. (in printing). ‖ Sports. Maniement m. (of oar). ‖ **Pulling back,** n. Tirage (m.) en arrière. ‖ **Pulling down,** n. Démolition f. (of a house) ; Fig. Renversement m. ‖ **Pulling in,** n. Ch. de F. Arrivée en gare f. ‖ **Pulling off,** n. Enlèvement m. ‖ **Pulling out,** n. Méd. Arrachage m. ; Ch. de F. Démarrage m. ‖ **Pulling through,** n. Fam. Dépatouillage m.

Pullman ['pulmən] n. Ch. de F. Voiture-salon m. (parlour-car) ; Voiture-lit m. (sleeper).

pullulate ['pʌljuleit] v. intr. Pulluler. (See swarm.) ‖ Bot. Pousser, germer. ‖ Fig. Se répandre.

pullulation [,pʌlju'leiʃən] n. Pullulation f. ; pullulement m. ‖ Bot. Pousse, germination f. ‖ Fig. Expansion f.

pulmometer [pʌl'mɔmetə*] n. Méd. Spiromètre m.

pulmonaria [,pʌlmo'nɛəriə] n. Bot. Pulmonaire f.

pulmonary ['pʌlmənəri] adj. Méd. Pulmonaire (artery, disease) ; poitrinaire, tuberculeux (person). ‖ Zool. Poumoné.

Pulmotor ['pʌlmoutə*] n. U. S. Méd. Appareil (m.) pour respiration artificielle.

pulp [pʌlp] n. Bot., Méd. Pulpe f. ‖ Techn. Pâte f. (for paper). ‖ Fam. *Crushed to a pulp,* en capilotade, en compote. ‖ U. S. Pl. Revue (f.) [or] roman (m.) populaire. ‖ **Pulp-fiction,** n. U. S. Fam. Roman populaire m. ‖ **Pulp-magazine,** n. U. S. Revue (f.) à bon marché.
— v. tr. Réduire en pâte. ‖ Décortiquer (to husk). ‖ Mettre au pilon (books). ‖ Méd. Pulper.

pulpit ['pulpit] n. Eccles. Chaire f. ‖ Naut. Balcon m.
— adj. Eccles. De la chaire (oratory).

pulpitarian [,pulpi'tɛəriən] n. Fam. Prêcheur m.

pulpiteer [,pulpi'tiːə*] n. Fam. Prêcheur m.
— v. intr. Prêcher sans cesse.

pulpiteering [-rin] n. Fam. Prêcherie f.

pulsar ['pʌl,sɑ:*] n. Astron. Pulsar m.

pulsate [pʌl'seit] v. intr. Méd., Fig. Battre, palpiter.

pulsatile [-ətail] adj. Méd. Pulsatile ; de percussion.

pulsation [pʌl'seiʃən] n. Méd. Pulsation f. ‖ Electr. Battement m.

pulsatory ['pʌlsətəri] adj. Pulsatoire.

pulse [pʌls] n. Méd., Fig. Pouls m. ; *to feel s.o.'s pulse,* tâter le pouls à qqn. ‖ Méd. Pulsation f. (of heart). ‖ Phys. Pouls m. (of radar) ; vibration f. (of waves).
— v. intr. Méd., Fig. Battre, palpiter.

pulse n. Bot. Légumineuses f. pl.

pultaceous [pʌl'teiʃəs] adj. Pultacé.

pulverizable ['pʌlvəraizəbl] adj. Pulvérisable.

pulverization [,pʌlvərai'zeiʃən] n. Pulvérisation f.

pulverize ['pʌlvəraiz] v. tr. Vaporiser (a liquid) ; pulvériser (a solid). ‖ Fig. Pulvériser.
— v. intr. Se vaporiser (liquid) ; se pulvériser (solid).

pulverizer [-ə*] n. Pulvérisateur m. (for liquid) ; broyeur m. (for solids).

pulverulence [pʌl'verjuləns] n. Pulvérulence f.

pulverulent [-ənt] adj. Pulvérulent. (See powdery.)

puma ['pjuːmə] n. Zool. Puma m. (See cougar.)

pumice ['pʌmis] n. Pierre ponce f.
— v. tr. Poncer.

pumiceous [pju'miʃəs] adj. Ponceux.

pummel ['pʌməl] v. tr. (1). Rosser, bourrer de coups, piler.

pummelling [-in] n. Raclée f.

pump [pʌmp] n. Techn., Autom., Naut. Pompe f. ; *to give a pump,* donner un coup de pompe. ‖ **Pump-barrel,** n. Barillet m. ‖ **Pump-priming,** n. Amorçage m. ‖ **Pump-room,** n. Buvette f. (at spa).
— v. tr. Pomper ; *to pump dry,* assécher. ‖ Fam. Cuisiner (a prisoner) ; tirer les vers du nez à (s.o.). ‖ **To pump out,** assécher. ‖ **To pump up,** pomper ; Autom. Gonfler (tyre).
— v. intr. Pomper. ‖ Fam. Battre.

pump n. Escarpin, soulier vernis m.

pumped [-t] adj. Sports. Essouflé. ‖ **Pumped out,** Fam. Pompé.

pumping [-in] adj. D'extraction, d'épuisement (engine, shaft, station).
— n. Pompage m. ‖ Fam. Questionnaire astucieux ; art (m.) de tirer les vers du nez.

pumpkin ['pʌmpkin] n. Bot. Citrouille f. ; potiron m.

pun [pʌn] n. Calembour, jeu (m.) de mots.
— v. intr. (1). Faire des jeux de mots.

pun v. tr. (1). Techn. Piler, pilonner.

punch [pʌnʃ] n. Techn. Poinçon m. (hand punch) ; chasse-clous m. (nail punch) ; découpoir à l'emporte-pièce m. (hollow punch) ; poinçonneuse f. (machine) ; pointeau m. ‖ Inform. *Punch(ed) card, tape,* carte, bande perforée. ‖ **Punch-mark,** n. Repère m.
— v. tr. Poinçonner ; perforer ; découper à l'emporte-pièce ; *punched cards,* cartes perforées. ‖ **To punch out,** chasser ; découper à l'emporte-pièce.

punch n. Coup de poing m. ‖ Sports. Punch m. ‖ Fam. Nerf, allant, punch m. ; *punch line,* chute (of a joke). ‖ **Punch-drunk,** adj. Fam. Abruti de coups.
— v. tr. Donner des coups de poing à, cogner sur.

punch n. Culin. Punch m.

Punch n. Polichinelle m. ‖ Theatr. *Punch and Judy show,* guignol.

puncheon ['pʌntʃən] n. Baril m. (cask). ‖ U. S. Archit. Lame (f.) de parquet ; tronçon fendu m.

puncher ['pʌntʃə*] n. Poinçonneur m. (person) ; poinçonneuse f. ; emporte-pièce m. (tool).

Punchinello [,pʌntʃi'nelou] n. Theatr. Polichinelle m.

punching ['pʌntʃin] n. Poinçonnage, découpage (act) m. ‖ Découpure f. (result). ‖ **Punching-machine,** n. Poinçonneuse ; découpeuse f.

punching n. Coups (m.) de poing. ‖ **Punching-ball,** n. Sports. Punching-ball m.

punctilio [pʌŋk'tiliou] n. Formalisme m. ‖ Vétille f.

punctilious [-əs] adj. Pointilleux, vétilleux (particular). ‖ Formaliste, cérémonieux, attaché aux usages. ‖ Chatouilleux, pointilleux (on, sur).

punctiliousness [-əsnis] n. Méticulosité f. ‖ Formalisme, attachement au protocole m.

punctual ['pʌŋktjuəl] adj. Ponctuel, exact (in, à, en, dans).

punctuality [,pʌŋktju'æliti] n. Ponctualité, exactitude f.

punctually ['pʌŋktjuəli] adv. Ponctuellement.

punctuate [-eit] v. tr. Gramm., Fig. Ponctuer.

punctuation [,pʌŋktju'eiʃən] n. Gramm. Ponctuation f.

punctum ['pʌŋktəm] (pl. **puncta** [-ə]) n. Méd., Zool. Point m.

puncture ['pʌŋktʃə*] n. Perforation f. ‖ Méd. Ponction f. ‖ Autom. Crevaison f. ‖ **Puncture-patch,** n. Autom. Rustine f. ‖ **Puncture-proof,** adj. Autom. Increvable.
— v. tr. Perforer. ‖ Méd. Ponctionner. ‖ Autom. Crever.
— v. intr. Autom. Crever.

pundit ['pʌndit] n. Pandit m. ‖ Fam. Ponte m.

pungency ['pʌndʒənsi] n. Saveur (or) odeur

piquante *f.* ‖ MED. Acuité, vivacité *f.* ‖ FIG. Acuité *f.* (of sorrow); mordant *m.; *causticité *f.* (of words).

pungent [-ənt] adj. BOT. Piquant. ‖ CULIN. Piquant, relevé. ‖ MED. Aigu, vif. ‖ FIG. Déchirant, poignant (sorrow); mordant, caustique (words).

pungently [-əntli] adv. De façon mordante.

Punic ['pju:nik] adj. Punique.

puniness ['pju:ninis] n. Débilité, chétivité *f.*

punish ['pʌniʃ] v. tr. Punir (for, de). [See DISCIPLINE.] ‖ SPORTS. Bourrer de coups, malmener (a boxer). ‖ AUTOM. Fatiguer (the engine).

punishable [-əbl] adj. Punissable. ‖ JUR. Délictueux; *punishable by,* passible de.

punisher [-ə*] n. Punisseur *s.* ‖ SPORTS. Cogneur *m.*

punishing [-iŋ] n. Punition *f.*
— adj. FAM. Dur, épuisant.

punishment [-mənt] n. Punition *f.* (See CHASTISEMENT.) ‖ JUR. Peine *f.* ‖ SPORTS. Correction *f.; he can stand* (or) *take punishment,* il sait encaisser.

punitive ['pju:nitiv] adj. Punitif.

Punjab [pʌn'dʒɑ:b] n. GEOGR. Pendjab *m.*

Punjabi [-i] adj. GEOGR. Du Pendjab.
— n. GEOGR. Habitant (s.) du Pendjab. ‖ GRAMM. Pendjabi *m.*

punk [pʌŋk] n. Amadou *m.* (tinder). ‖ FAM. Insanité, ineptie *f.* (nonsense). ‖ FAM. Voyou *m.* (young ruffian); punk *s.* (punk rock fan).
— adj. FAM. Punk (rock, fashion). ‖ U. S. Pourri (wood). ‖ U. S. POP. Mal fichu (person); moche (thing).

punner ['pʌnə*] n. TECHN. Hie *f.* (See BEETLE.)

punnet ['pʌnit] n. COMM. Petit panier *m.,* barquette *f.* (for soft fruit).

punster ['pʌnstə*] n. Faiseur (s.) de calembour.

punt [pʌnt] n. NAUT. Bachot *m.* (boat); coup (*m.*) de perche (or) de gaffe (pole-stroke). ‖ **Punt-gun,** n. Canardière *f.* ‖ **Punt-pole,** n. NAUT. Perche *f.*
— v. tr. NAUT. Conduire à la perche; yoler (boat); transporter en bachot (person).

punt n. SPORTS. Coup (*m.*) de volée.
— v. tr. SPORTS. Envoyer d'un coup de volée.
— v. intr. SPORTS. Donner un coup de volée.

punt v. intr. Ponter (at cards). ‖ SPORTS. Parier. ‖ FIN. Boursicoter.

punter [-ə*] n. Parieur *s.,* ponte *m.* (at cards); parieur *s.* (at races). ‖ POP. Micheton *m.* (of a prostitute).

puny ['pju:ni] adj. Menu, chétif, malingre.

pup [pʌp] n. ZOOL. Chiot, petit chien *m.* ‖ FAM., COMM. Rossignol *m.*
— v. tr., intr. ZOOL. Mettre bas.

pupa ['pju:pə] (pl. **pupae** [-i:]) n. ZOOL. Chrysalide *f.*

pupate [pju:'peit] v. intr. ZOOL. Se muer en chrysalide, nymphoser.

pupil ['pju:pil] n. MED. Pupille *f.* (of the eye).

pupil n. Ecolier, élève *s.* ‖ JUR. Pupille *s.*

pupillage [-idʒ] n. Fait (*m.*) d'être élève; scolarité *f.* ‖ JUR. Minorité *f.* (nonage); tutelle, pupillarité *f.* (wardship).

pupillarity [,pjupi'læriti] n. JUR. Pupillarité *f.*

pupillary ['pjupiləri] adj. D'écolier, d'élève. ‖ JUR. Pupillaire.

pupillary adj. MED. Pupillaire.

puppet ['pʌpit] n. THEATR. Marionnette *f.* ‖ FAM. Pantin *m.* ‖ **Puppet-government,** n. FAM. Gouvernement fantoche *m.* ‖ **Puppet-player,** n. THEATR. Marionnettiste *m.* ‖ **Puppet-show,** n. THEATR. Spectacle (or) théâtre (*m.*) de marionnettes.

puppeteer [,pʌpi'ti:ə*] n. THEATR. Marionnettiste *m.*

puppetry ['pʌpitri] n. FAM. Bande (*f.*) de pantins.

puppy ['pʌpi] n. ZOOL. Chiot, jeune chien *m.* (See PUP.) ‖ FAM. Jeune gandin *m.* ‖ **Puppy-cake** (or) U. S. **biscuit,** n. Gâteau de chien *m.* ‖ **Puppy love,** n. U. S. FAM. Premier amour *m.*

puppyhood [-hud] n. ZOOL. Jeunesse (*f.*) du chien. ‖ FAM. Vertes années *f. pl.*

puppyish [-iʃ] adj. FAM. Naïf et prétentieux.

puppyism [-izm] n. FAM. Naïveté prétentieuse *f.*

purblind ['pə:blaind] n. MED. Myope, qui voit très mal. ‖ FAM. Aveugle, borné, étroit.

purblindness [-nis] n. MED. Myopie, vue très basse *f.* ‖ FAM. Etroitesse (*f.*) de vue.

purchasable ['pə:tʃesəbl] adj. Achetable.

purchase ['pə:tʃəs] n. COMM. Achat *m.; *acquisition *f.* ‖ Prise *f.; *point d'appui *m.* ‖ TECHN. Palan *m.* ‖ NAUT. Cartahu *m.; *apparaux *m. pl.* ‖ **Purchase-price,** n. COMM. Prix d'achat *m.*
— v. tr. COMM. Acheter, acquérir, faire l'acquisition de.
— v. intr. COMM. Faire des achats (or) des emplettes.

purchaser [-ə*] n. COMM. Acheteur, acquéreur *s.* ‖ FIN. Adjudicataire *m.* (at auction); preneur *m.* (of a bill of exchange).

purchasing [-iŋ] adj. COMM. Acquéreur (party); d'achat (power). ‖ FIN. Adjudicataire.
— n. COMM. Achat *m.*

pure ['pjuə*] adj. Pur. ‖ **Pure-blood, pure-bred,** adj., n. Pur-sang *m.; *de race pure *f.* ‖ **Pure-minded,** adj. A l'esprit pur, chaste.

purgation [pə:'geiʃən] n. MED., ECCLES. Purgation *f.*

purgative ['pə:gətiv] adj. MED. Purgatif.

purgatorial [,pə:gə'tɔ:riəl] adj. ECCLES. Du purgatoire, purificateur.

purgatory ['pə:gətəri] n. ECCLES. Purgatoire *m.*
— adj. ECCLES. Purificateur.

purge [pə:dʒ] n. MED. Purgation *f.* (act); purge *f.; *purgatif *m.* (remedy). ‖ TECHN. Purge, vidange *f.* ‖ JUR. Epuration *f.* (in politics). ‖ **Purge-cork,** n. TECHN. Purgeur *m.* ‖ **Purge-organizer,** n. JUR. Epurateur *m.*
— v. tr. MED. Purifier (blood); purger (s.o.). ‖ TECHN. Purger, nettoyer. ‖ CULIN. Faire dégorger (fish). ‖ JUR. Epurer (in politics); *to purge an offence,* purger sa peine; *to purge oneself of,* se laver, de, se disculper de. ‖ FIN. Assainir (finances). ‖ ECCLES. *To purge away,* expier.

purger [-ə*] n. Purificateur *s.* (device, person).

purging [-iŋ] adj. MED. Purgatif. ‖ TECHN. Purgeur.
— n. MED. Purification; purge *f.* ‖ TECHN. Nettoyage *m.* ‖ JUR. Epuration *f.* ‖ FIN. Assainissement *m.* ‖ ECCLES. Expiation *f.*

purification [,pjuərifi'keiʃən] n. ECCLES., FIG. Purification *f.* ‖ FIN. Assainissement *m.*

purificatory ['pjuərifikeitəri] adj. Purificatoire.

purifier ['pjuərifaiə*] n. Purificateur *m.; *purificatrice *f.* ‖ TECHN. Epurateur *m.*

purify [-fai] v. tr. (2). Purifier (from, of, de). ‖ MED. Purifier, dépurer. ‖ TECHN. Epurer.
— v. intr. Se purifier. ‖ MED. Se dépurer. ‖ TECHN. S'épurer.

purifying [-faiiŋ] adj. Purifiant.

purism ['pjuərizm] n. Purisme *m.*

purist [-ist] n. Puriste *s.*

puristical [pjuə'ristikəl] adj. Puriste.

Puritan ['pjuəritən] adj., n. Puritain *s.*

puritanical [pjuəri'tænikəl] adj. Puritain; de puritain.

puritanism ['pjuəritənizm] n. Puritanisme *m.*

purity ['pjuəriti] n. Pureté *f.*

purl [pə:l] Picot *m.* ‖ **Purl-stitch,** n. Maille (*f.*). à l'envers.
— v. tr. Faire des picots à. ‖ Faire une maille à l'envers.

purl n. Gazouillement *m.* (of a stream).
— v. intr. Murmurer, gazouiller.

purler [-ə*] n. FAM. Bûche *f.* (See CROPPER.)

purlieu ['pə:lju:] n. Limites, bornes *f. pl.* (bounds). ‖ Pl. Alentours, environs, abords *m. pl.* ‖ JUR. Confins *m. pl.*

purlin ['pə:lin] n. ARCHIT. Panne *f.*
purling [-iŋ] adj. Murmurant, gazouillant.
purloin [pə:'lɔin] v. tr. Subtiliser, soustraire.
purloiner [-ə*] n. Détourneur *s.*
purloining [-iŋ] n. Détournement *m.*
purple [pə:pl̩] adj. † Pourpre. ‖ Violet, violacé, cramoisi. ‖ FIG. *Purple passage*, morceau de bravoure. ‖ **Purple-wood**, n. Palissandre *m.*
— n. Pourpre *f.* ‖ Violet *m.* ‖ MED. Pl. Purpura *m.* ‖ AGRIC. Pl. Nielle *f.*
— v. tr. Empourprer.
— v. intr. S'empourprer.
purplish [-iʃ] adj. Violacé, purpurin, cramoisi.
purport ['pə:pə:t] n. Teneur *f.;* sens *m.* (of a document); portée *f.* (of a word). ‖ COMM. Objet *m.* (of a letter).
— [pə:'pɔ:t] v. tr. Etre censé; viser à; *to purport to be*, se présenter comme, avoir la prétention d'être. ‖ Impliquer, laisser entendre (or) supposer.
purportedly [pə:'pɔ:tidli] adv. Visant à.
purportless ['pə:pə:tlis] adj. Sans portée.
purpose ['pə:pəs] n. Dessein *m.;* intention *f.; for the purpose of*, dans le dessein de, afin de; *on purpose*, exprès, délibérément. ‖ Résolution, volonté, énergie *f.; infirm of purpose*, irrésolu, indécis, sans volonté. ‖ But *m.;* fin *f.; for all purposes*, à tous usages; *for my purpose*, pour ce que je veux en faire; *for that purpose*, dans ce but; *for the above purposes*, aux effets ci-dessus; *to serve s.o.'s purpose*, faire l'affaire de qqn, répondre aux désirs de qqn. ‖ Propos, fait *m.; to speak to the purpose*, parler à propos. ‖ Utilité *f.; for all pratical purposes*, pratiquement; *to good purpose*, avec fruit; *to no purpose*, vainement; *to some purpose*, utilement. ‖ JUR. *For the purpose of*, au sens de (an article). ‖ **Purpose-built**, adj. ARCHIT. Construit en vue d'une utilisation précise. ‖ **Purpose-made**, adj. Fabriqué exprès.
— v. tr. Se proposer de, avoir l'intention de, compter.
purposeful [-ful] adj. Réfléchi (act); avisé, réfléchi, pondéré (person). ‖ Entêté, tenace (stubborn).
purposefully [-fuli] adv. Avec une intention arrêtée, intentionnellement.
purposefulness [-fulnis] n. Réflexion *f.;* discernement *m.* ‖ Ténacité *f.*
purposeless [-lis] adj. Inutile, vain, sans objet (or) but.
purposely [-li] adv. De propos délibéré, à dessein, exprès, volontairement.
purposive [-iv] adj. Voulu, délibéré, fait exprès, intentionnel (act); résolu, décidé (person). ‖ MED. Remplissant une fonction.
purpura ['pə:pjurə] n. MED. Purpura *m.* ‖ ZOOL. Pourpier *m.*
purpure ['pə:puə*] n. BLAS. Pourpre *m.*
purr [pə:*] n. ZOOL. Ronron *m.* (of a cat). ‖ TECHN. Ronflement *m.* ‖ AVIAT. Vrombissement *m.*
— v. intr. ZOOL. Ronronner, faire ronron. ‖ TECHN. Ronfler. ‖ AVIAT. Vrombir.
purse [pe:s] n. Bourse *f.; well-lined purse*, gousset bien garni. ‖ COMM. Porte-monnaie *m.* ‖ ZOOL., BOT., MED. Bourse *f.* ‖ FIN. *Public purse*, trésor. ‖ U. S. Sac (*m.*) à main. ‖ FAM. *Beyond s.o.'s purse*, trop cher pour qqn. ‖ **Purse-strings**, n. Cordons (*m. pl.*) de la bourse.
— v. tr. Plisser (one's brow); froncer (one's eyebrows); pincer (one's lips).
purser [-ə*] n. NAUT. Commissaire *m.*
pursership [-ə/ip] n. NAUT. Commissariat *m.*
purslane ['pə:slen] n. BOT. Pourpier *m.*
pursuable [pə:'sjuəbl] adj. Poursuivable.
pursuance [-əns] n. Exécution, poursuite *f.* (of a plan); *in pursuance of*, conformément à; par suite de; en application de.
pursuant [-ənt] adv. Conformément (*to*, à), suivant.

pursue [pə:'sju] v. tr. Poursuivre (an animal, enemy). ‖ FIG. Rechercher, tendre vers (happiness); suivre (a line of conduct); exercer (a profession); continuer, poursuivre (one's studies, way).
pursuer |-ə*| n. Poursuivant *s.* ‖ JUR. Plaignant *s.*
pursuit [pə:'sju:t] n. Poursuite *f.; in pursuit of*, à la poursuite de. ‖ Profession, carrière *f.;* métier *m.* ‖ Occupation *f.;* travail *m.* ‖ AVIAT. Chasse, poursuite. ‖ FIG. Poursuite, recherche *f.* (of happiness). ‖ **Pursuit-plane**, n. AVIAT. Chasseur, avion (*m.*) de chasse.
pursy ['pə:si] adj. Poussif, essoufflé (short-winded). ‖ Ventru, bedonnant (portly).
pursy n. Bridé (eye); pincé (lips). ‖ FAM. Au gousset garni, à la bourse pleine.
purulence ['pjuəruləns] n. MED. Purulence *f.* (act); pus *m.* (result).
purulent [-ənt] adj. MED. Purulent.
purvey [pə'vei] v. tr. Fournir.
— v. intr. Etre le fournisseur (*for*, de).
purveyance [-əns] n. Approvisionnement *m.* (act). ‖ JUR. Pourvoirie *f.*
purveyor [-ə*] n. Fournisseur, approvisionneur *s.* ‖ † Officier (*m.*) de bouche.
purview ['pə:vju:] n. Portée (*f.*) du regard (of s.o.). ‖ JUR. Articles *m. pl.* ‖ FIG. Portée *f.* (of a book); limites *f. pl.* (of an enquiry); domaine *m.* (of s.o.)
pus [pʌs] n. MED. Pus *m.*
push [puʃ] n. Poussée *f.; with one push*, d'un seul coup. ‖ ARCHIT. Poussée *f.* (of a vault). ‖ MILIT. Poussée en masse *f.* ‖ FIG. Moment critique (or) décisif *m.* (emergency); *when it comes to the push*, à l'instant crucial. ‖ FAM. Initiative *f.;* dynamisme, entregent *m.* (drive). ‖ FAM. Coup de collier *m.* (effort); *to make a push to*, en mettre un coup pour. ‖ U. S. FAM. Clique *f.* ‖ **Push-and-pull**, adj. à tirette; CH. DE F. En navette. ‖ **Push-button**, n. ELECTR., TECHN. Poussoir *m.;* adj. U. S. Déclenché automatiquement; presse-bouton (warfare). ‖ **Push-cart**, n. Poussette; U. S. Voiture (*f.*) des quatre-saisons. ‖ **Push-chair**, n. Poussette *f.* (for baby). ‖ **Push-off**, n. FAM. Impulsion *f.* ‖ **Push-over**, n. U. S. Adversaire aisément convaincu *s.* (person); jeu d'enfant *m.* (thing). ‖ **Push-pin**, n. Punaise *f.* (nail). ‖ **Push-push**, n. Pousse-pousse *m.* ‖ **Push-stroke**, n. SPORTS. Queutage *m.* ‖ **Push-up**, n. U. S., SPORTS. Traction *f.* (See PRESS-UP.)
— v. tr. Pousser (s.o., sth.). ‖ Presser sur, appuyer sur (the button). ‖ COMM. Pousser la vente de (goods); pousser (the sale); activer (trade); *to push one's wares*, vanter sa marchandise, faire l'article. ‖ FIG. Pousser, étendre (to extend); pousser, pistonner (to recommend); pousser, presser, harceler (to urge on); *to push oneself*, se pousser. ‖ **To push away, back**, repousser. ‖ **To push forward**, pousser en avant, faire avancer. ‖ **To push in**, enfoncer. ‖ **To push on**, pousser, activer, exciter (*to*, à). ‖ **To push out**, pousser dehors, faire sortir; BOT. Pousser; NAUT. Mettre à l'eau. ‖ **To push over**, faire tomber. ‖ **To push through**, faire traverser; JUR. Faire passer (a bill); FIG. Amener à bonne fin. ‖ **To push to**, pousser (the door). ‖ **To push up**, repousser, relever; FIG. Pistonner, pousser.
— v. intr. Pousser (*against*, sur). ‖ Avancer, pousser; *to push one's way into*, se pousser dans. ‖ **To push forward**, avancer. ‖ **To push in**, s'introduire de force. ‖ **To push off**, NAUT. Pousser au large. ‖ **To push on**, avancer; pousser (*to*, jusqu'à); FAM. Donner un coup de pouce (*with*, à). ‖ **To push through**, s'ouvrir un chemin.
pusher [-ə*] n. Personne (*f.*) qui pousse. ‖ TECHN. Pousseuse *f.* ‖ AVIAT. Avion (*m.*) à hélice propulsive. ‖ FAM. Arriviste *s.*
pushful [-ful] adj. Arriviste.
pushfulness [-fulnis] n. Arrivisme *m.*
pushing [-iŋ] adj. Arriviste.
pushy [-i] adj. U. S. FAM. Arriviste; arrogant.

pusillanimity [,pju:silə'nimiti] n. Pusillanimité *f*.
pusillanimous [,pju:si'læniməs] adj. Pusillanime.
puss [pus] n. ZOOL. Minet *s*. ‖ FAM. Coquine *f*. ‖ U. S. FAM. Frimousse *f*.; *nasty puss*, gueule d'empeigne, sale gueule. ‖ **Puss-in-the-corner**, n. SPORTS. Quatre coins *m. pl.*
pussy [-i] n. ZOOL. Minet *s*. ‖ BOT. Chaton *m*.
pussyfoot [-fut] n. FAM. Patte pelue *f*. ‖ Prohibition *f*.; prohibitionniste *m*.
— v. intr. Faire patte de velours. ‖ U. S. Ne pas se compromettre, répondre en Normand.
pustulate ['pʌstjuleit] v. intr. MED. Bourgeonner, être plein de pustules.
— v. tr. MED. Couvrir de pustules.
pustule [-tju:l] n. MED. Pustule *f*.
pustulous ['pʌstjuləs] adj. MED. Pustuleux.
put [put] n. SPORTS. Lancement *m*. ‖ FIN. Prime (*f*.) à livrer, option de vente *f*. ‖ **Put-up**, adj. Truqué; *put-up job*, coup monté.
— v. tr. (107). Mettre, placer, poser (*in, into, dans; on*, sur) [in general]. ‖ Mettre, employer (*to*, à) [a use]. ‖ Mettre; *to put a stop to*, faire cesser, mettre un terme à. ‖ Mettre, placer, désigner; *to put s.o. to a trade*, faire apprendre un métier à qqn. ‖ Mettre, pousser; *to put s.o. out of patience*, pousser qqn à bout. ‖ Mettre, décider; *let's put it that you were not there*, mettons que vous n'y étiez pas. ‖ Remettre; *to put the matter right*, remettre les choses d'aplomb; *to put s.o. in his place, on the right road*, remettre qqn à sa place, dans le droit chemin. ‖ Soumettre; *to put s.o. through an examination, to a test*, faire subir à qqn un examen, un test. ‖ Exposer (a case); présenter, soumettre (a proposal, resolution); poser (a question); *not to know how to put it*, ne pas savoir comment s'exprimer. ‖ Traduire, rendre, mettre (*into*, en) [a text]. ‖ Estimer, évaluer; *I put it at seven pounds*, je l'estime à sept livres. ‖ MILIT. *To put to flight*, mettre en fuite. ‖ SPORTS. Lancer (the weight). ‖ THEATR. *To put on the stage*, monter, mettre en scène. ‖ FIN. Mettre, placer (*into*, dans; *on*, sur) [money]; employer (*in*, à, en) [a sum]. ‖ **To put about**, faire courir, mettre en circulation (to circulate); inquiéter, tourmenter (to worry); NAUT. Faire virer de bord. ‖ **To put across**, faire passer de l'autre côté; U. S. FAM. Faire avaler. ‖ **To put aside**, mettre de côté; FIG. Renoncer à. ‖ **To put away**, serrer, ranger, rentrer, placer (to place); FIN. Mettre de côté; FIG. Eloigner, chasser; FAM. Coffrer (to jail); mettre au clou (to pawn); engloutir (to wolf). ‖ **To put back**, replacer, remettre en place, reposer (to replace); retarder (to set back); rejeter en arrière (to throw back). ‖ **To put by**, FIN. Economiser, mettre de côté; FIG. Eluder. ‖ **To put down**, déposer, poser; MATH. Poser (a number); AUTOM. Déposer (a passenger); NAUT. Mouiller (a buoy); FIG. Attribuer, imputer (to ascribe); interdire, suffoquer, intimider (to disconcert); estimer, évaluer (to estimate); humilier, rabaisser (to humble); supprimer, faire cesser (to put an end to); réprimer (to repress); rabrouer (to snub); noter, inscrire (to write down); *to put s.o. down as fifty*, donner cinquante ans à qqn. ‖ **To put forth**, BOT. Pousser, mettre; FIG. Publier (to bring about); émettre, proposer (to express); déployer (to show). ‖ **To put forward**, avancer; FIG. Mettre en avant, pousser, pistonner (to back); émettre, avancer, exprimer (to express); FAM. *To put one's best foot forward*, partir du pied droit. ‖ **To put from**, rejeter, écarter. ‖ **To put in**, AGRIC. Semer, planter; JUR. Présenter (a claim); FAM. Dire, placer (a word). ‖ **To put off**, enlever, retirer, ôter (to doff); FIG. Dérouter, démonter (to disconcert); dégoûter, écœurer (to disgust); décourager, rebuter (to dispirit); détourner, éloigner (to divert); éloigner, indisposer, repousser (to estrange); endormir, ballotter, user de faux-fuyants avec (to hum-

bug); se débarrasser de (to get rid of); ajourner, différer, remettre (to postpone). ‖ **To put on**, mettre, enfiler, prendre (to don); *to put s.o. on the telephone*, donner la communication à qqn; ELECTR. Allumer (the light); AUTOM. Serrer, mettre (brakes); augmenter (speed); SPORTS. Mettre, miser (on a horse); FIN. Augmenter (price); THEATR. Monter (a play); MUS. Mettre, faire marcher (the gramophone); CULIN. Servir (a dish); faire chauffer (a pan); FIG. Mettre, placer, désigner (to appoint); faire jouer, simuler (to feign); prendre, affecter (to pretend); FAM. *To put it on*, le faire à la pose. ‖ **To put out**, expulser, mettre dehors (to eject); éteindre (to extinguish); publier, sortir (to issue); sortir, montrer, faire voir (to show); avancer, étendre, tendre (to stretch out); MILIT. Arborer (flags); NAUT. Mettre à l'eau (a boat); FIN. Placer (money); MED. Crever (an eye); décrocher (s.o.'s jaw); démettre, luxer (s.o.'s shoulder); FAM. Fâcher, ennuyer, contrarier (to annoy); gêner, déranger (to bother); dérouter, démonter, interloquer (to disconcert). ‖ **To put through**, TECHN. Mettre en communication (*to*, avec); FIG. Mener à bonne fin. ‖ **To put to**, atteler; FAM. *To be hard put to it*, avoir du tintouin. ‖ **To put together**, assembler, unir, rassembler; TECHN. Assembler, monter; MATH. Additionner; FIG. Comparer (facts); rassembler (thoughts). ‖ **To put up**, lever, relever (to draw up); accrocher, poser, mettre (to hang up); loger, coucher, héberger (to lodge); emballer, faire un paquet de (to pack); afficher, coller (to post up); MILIT. Opposer (resistance); rengainer (sword); AUTOM. Garer (car); TECHN. Raccrocher (the receiver); SPORTS. Faire lever (a partridge); ARCHIT. Bâtir, construire (house); FIN. Avancer, fournir (money); augmenter, majorer (prices); *to put up for auction*, mettre à prix; JUR. Présenter (a candidate); faire (a petition); THEATR. Représenter (a play); ECCLES. Faire (a prayer); FIG. Pousser, inciter (to incite); mettre au courant (*to*, de); tuyauter (*to*, sur) [to inform]; FAM. Monter (a dirty trick); bâtir (a yarn); *to put one's feet up*, pantoufler. ‖ **To put upon**, FAM. Entortiller, manœuvrer (s.o.).
— v. intr. NAUT. *To put into port*, faire relâche; *to put to sea*, appareiller. ‖ **To put back**, NAUT. Rentrer au port. ‖ **To put by**, économiser. ‖ **To put forth**, BOT. Pousser. ‖ **To put in**, NAUT. Faire escale (or) relâche; JUR. Poser sa candidature (*for*, à). ‖ **To put off**, remettre, atermoyer; NAUT. Pousser au large. ‖ **To put up**, s'accommoder, s'arranger (*with*, de); se résigner (*with*, à); *hard to put up with*, dur à avaler (or) encaisser (fam.).
putative ['pju:tətiv] adj. JUR. Putatif. (See SUPPOSED.)
putatively [-li] adv. JUR. Putativement.
putlog ['pʌtlɔg] n. ARCHIT. Boulin *m*.
putrefaction [,pju:tri'fækʃən] n. Putréfaction *f*.
putrefiable ['pju:trifaiəbl] adj. Putréfiable.
putrefy [-fai] v. tr. (2). Putréfier, pourrir.
— v. intr. Se putréfier, pourrir. ‖ MED. Suppurer, se gangrener. ‖ FIG. Se corrompre.
putrefying [-faiiŋ] adj. En putréfaction.
putrescence [pju'tresns] n. Putrescence *f*.
putrescent [-nt] adj. Putrescent.
putrescible [pju'tresibl] adj. Putrescible.
putrid ['pju:trid] adj. En putréfaction, en pourriture. ‖ MED. Putride.
putridity [pju:'triditi], **putridness** ['pju:tridnis] n. Pourriture, putridité *f*.
putsch [putʃ] n. Putsch *m*.
putt [pʌt] n. SPORTS. Coup roulé *m*.
— v. tr. SPORTS. Poter.
puttee [pʌ'ti:] n. MILIT. Bande molletière *f*.
putter ['putə*] n. Metteur, poseur *m*. ‖ TECHN. Moulineur *m*. ‖ SPORTS. Lanceur *m*.
putter ['pʌtə*] n. SPORTS. Poteur *m*. (club); joueur (*s*.) qui réussit bien les coups roulés (golfer).

putter v. intr. U. S. See POTTER. Bricoler (to potter).

putting [ˈputiŋ] n. Mise, pose *f*. ‖ FIN. Délivrement *m*.; délivrance *f*. ‖ NAUT. *Putting to sea*, appareillage. ‖ SPORTS. *Putting the shot* (or) *weight*, lancement du poids. ‖ FIG. Présentation *f*. ‖ **Putting away**, n. Rangement *m*.; FIN. Economie *f*.; FIG. Eloignement, rejet *m*. ‖ **Putting back**, n. Remise en place *f*.; MILIT. Ajournement *m*.; NAUT. Retour au port *m*.; FIG. Retardement *m*. ‖ **Putting by**, n. FIN. Economie, mise (*f*.) de côté; FIG. Eloignement, détournement *m*. ‖ **Putting down**, n. Dépôt *m*.; inscription *f*.; NAUT. Mouillage *m*.; FIG. Abaissement *m*. (of pride); apaisement *m*. (of rebellion). ‖ **Putting forth**, n. Publication *f*.; BOT. Poussée *f*.; FIG. Déploiement *m*. ‖ **Putting forward**, n. Avancement *m*. (of a clock); FIG. Exposition, mise (*f*.) en avant. ‖ **Putting in**, n. Introduction *f*.; JUR. Production *f*. (of a document); NAUT. Escale *f*. ‖ **Putting off**, n. Renvoi *m*.; remise *f*.; FIN. Désintéressement *m*. ‖ **Putting on**, n. Mise *f*.; revêtement *m*. (of clothes); AUTOM. Serrement *m*.; FIN. Augmentation *f*.; TECHN. Avancement *m*. (of clock); ELECTR. Allumage *m*.; RADIO. Mise en marche *f*.; FIG. Affectation *f*. ‖ **Putting out**, n. Avancement *m*. (of arm); extinction *f*. (of fire); expulsion *f*. (of s.o.); FIN. Placement *m*.; MED. Luxation *f*. ‖ **Putting through**, n. TECHN. Mise en communication *f*.; FIG. Réussite *f*. ‖ **Putting to**, n. Attellement *m*. ‖ **Putting together**, n. Assemblage *m*. (of pieces); empaquetage, emballage *m*.; FIG. Rapprochement *m*.; collation *f*. (of facts). ‖ **Putting up**, n. Pose, mise *f*.; accrochage *m*. (hanging up); hébergement, logement *m*. (lodging); emballage *m*. (packing); FIN. Hausse, augmentation *f*.; JUR. Publication *f*. (of banns); affichage *m*. (of bills); présentation *f*. (of a candidate); AUTOM. Garage *m*.; ARCHIT. Construction, érection *f*.; SPORTS. Levée (of game).

putty [ˈpʌti] n. Mastic *m*. (glazier's); potée *f*. (jeweller's). ‖ **Putty-coloured**, adj. Mastic. ‖ **Putty-knife**, n. TECHN. Couteau (*m*.) à mastiquer. — v. tr. Mastiquer.

puttying [-iŋ] n. Masticage *m*.

puzzle [ˈpʌzļ] n. Embarras *m*.; incertitude *f*. ‖ Enigme *f*.; problème *m*.; *Chinese puzzle*, casse-tête chinois; *cross-word puzzle*, mots croisés; *jig-saw puzzle*, puzzle, jeu de patience; *to be a puzzle to*, dérouter (s.o.). — v. tr. **To puzzle out**, déchiffrer (a letter); FIG. Eclaircir (a mystery); résoudre (a problem). — v. intr. Se creuser les méninges (*about, over*, au sujet de).

puzzler [-ə*] n. FAM. Colle *f*.

puzzling [-iŋ] adj. Embarrassant, intrigant.

PVC [piːviːˈsiː] abbr. *polyvinyl chloride*, chlorure de vinyle. ‖ COMM. *PVC mack*, ciré.

Pygmean [pigˈmiːən] adj. Pygméen.

Pygmy [ˈpigmi] n. Pygmée *m*. — adj. Pygméen.

pyjamas [ˈpidʒɑːməz] n. pl. Pyjama *m*. ‖ **Pyjama-clad**, adj. En pyjama. ‖ **Pyjama-coat**, n. Veste (*f*.) de pyjama.

pylon [ˈpailən] n. TECHN., ELECTR., ARCHIT. Pylône *m*.

pylorus [paiˈlɔːrəs] n. MED. Pylore *m*.

pyorrhea [paiəˈriːə] n. MED. Pyorrhée *f*.

pyosis [ˈpaiousis] n. MED. Suppuration *f*.

pyramid [ˈpirəmid] n. ARCHIT., MATH. Pyramide *f*.

pyramidal [piˈræmidəl] adj. Pyramidal.

pyre [ˈpaiə*] n. Bûcher funéraire *f*.

Pyrenean [ˌpirəˈniːən] adj. GEOGR. Pyrénéen.

Pyrenees [-ˈniːz] n. pl. GEOGR. Pyrénées *f*. pl.

pyrethrum [paiˈriːθrəm] n. BOT., MED. Pyrèthre *m*.

pyretic [paiˈretik] adj. Pyrétique.

Pyrex [ˈpaireks] n. CULIN. Pyrex *m*.

pyridine [ˈpairidain] n. MED., CHIM. Pyridine *f*.

pyrites [paiˈraitiːz] n. pl. Pyrite *f*.

pyrography [paiˈrɔgrəfi], **pyrogravure** [ˌpairoˈgrævjuə*] n. ARTS. Pyrogravure *f*.

pyrolysis [paiˈrɔlisis] (pl. **pyrolyses** [-iːz]) n. Pyrolyse *f*.

pyromania [ˌpairoˈmeiniə] n. MED. Pyromanie *f*.

pyromaniac [-iək] n. MED. Incendiaire *s*.

pyrometer [paiˈrɔmitə*] n. PHYS. Pyromètre *m*.

pyrotechnic [ˌpairoˈteknik] adj. Pyrotechnique; *pyrotechnic display*, feu d'artifice.

pyrotechnics [-niks] n. sg. Pyrotechnique *f*. ‖ Feu d'artifice *m*. (firework display). — N. B. Au sens de « feu d'artifice », *pyrotechnics* peut être singulier ou pluriel.

pyrotechnist [-nist] n. Artificier *m*.

pyrotechny [-ni] n. Pyrotechnie *f*.

pyroxylin(e) [paiˈrɔksilin] n. CHIM. Pyroxyle, fulmicoton *m*.

pyrrhic [ˈpirik] adj. Pyrrhique. ‖ FAM. A la Pyrrhus (victory).

Pythagoras [paiˈθægərəs] n. Pythagore *m*.

Pythagorean [paiˌθægəˈriːən] adj. Pythagoricien.

Pythia [ˈpiθiə] n. Pythie *f*.

Pythian [-ən] adj. Pythien.

python [ˈpaiθən] n. ZOOL. Python *m*.

python n. Lutin, lare *m*.

pythoness [-is] n. Pythonisse *f*.

pyx [piks] n. ECCLES. Ciboire *m*. ‖ FIN. Contrôle *m*. ‖ **Pyx-cloth**, n. ECCLES. Custode *f*.

pyxidium [pikˈsidiəm] (pl. **pyxidia** [-ə]) n. BOT. Pyxide *f*.

pyxis [ˈpiksis] (pl. **pixides** [-idiːz]) n. ECCLES., BOT. Pyxide *f*. ‖ MED. Cavité cotyloïde *f*.

q [kjuː] n. Q, q *m*.
Qatar [kæˈtɑː*] n. GEOGR. Qatar *m*.
Q.E.D. [kjuːiːˈdiː] abbr. *quod erat demonstrandum*, ce qu'il fallait démontrer, C.Q.F.D.

qua [kwei] adv. En qualité de, en tant que.
quack [kwæk] n. Coin-coin *m*. — v. intr. Crier comme un canard, faire coin-coin. ‖ FAM. Jacasser.

quack n. Charlatan *m.; quack doctor,* charlatan; *quack remedy,* remède de charlatan.
— v. intr. Faire le charlatan, plastronner.
— v. tr. Faire de la réclame (or) du battage pour; faire mousser (fam.).

quackery ['kwækəri] n. Charlatanisme *m.*

quackish [-iʃ] adj. De charlatan.

quad [kwɔd] n. See QUADRANGLE, QUADRAT. ‖ Pl. FAM. Quadruplés (born at a birth).

quadragenarian [ˌkwɔdrədʒiˈnɛəriən] adj., n. Quadragénaire *s.*

Quadragesima [ˌkwɔdrəˈdʒesimə] n. ECCLES. Quadragésime *f.; Quadragesima Sunday,* dimanche de la Quadragésime.

quadrangle ['kwɔdræŋgl] n. MATH. Quadrilatère, tétragone *m.* ‖ ARCHIT. Cour *f.* (of a college).

quadrangular [-gjulə*] adj. MATH. Quadrangulaire.

quadrant [kwɔdrənt] n. Quadrant, quart de cercle *m.* ‖ TECHN. Secteur *m.*

quadrat [-rit] n. TECHN. Cadrat *m.*

quadrate ['kwɔdrit] adj. MED. Carré, rectangulaire.
— [kwɔ'dreit] v. tr. Rendre carré. ‖ Faire cadrer *(to, with,* avec). ‖ MATH. Réduire au carré équivalent; *to quadrate the circle,* faire la quadrature du cercle.
— v. intr. Cadrer *(with,* avec).

quadratic [kwɔ'drætik] adj. MATH. Quadratique; *quadratic equation,* équation quadratique (or) du second degré.
— n. MATH. Equation *(f.)* du second degré.

quadrature ['kwɔdritʃə*] n. MATH., ASTRON. Quadrature *f.*

quadrennial [kwɔ'drenjəl] adj. Quadriennal.

quadri ['kwɔdri] pref. Quadri. ‖ **Quadrilateral,** adj. MATH. Quadrilatéral; MATH. Quadrilatère *m.* ‖ **Quadripartite,** adj. Quadriparti, quadripartite. ‖ **Quadrisyllabic,** adj. GRAMM. Quadrisyllabique. ‖ **Quadrisyllable,** n. GRAMM. Quadrisyllabe *m.* ‖ **Quadrivalence,** n. Quadrivalence *f.* ‖ **Quadrivalent,** adj. Quadrivalent, tétravalent.

quadrille [kwɔ'dril] n. MUS. Quadrille *m.*

quadrillion [kwɔ'driljən] n. Quadrillion *m.*

quadroon [kwə'dru:n] n. Quarteron *s.*

quadrumanous [kwə'dru:mənəs] adj., n. ZOOL. Quadrumane *m.*

quadruped ['kwɔdruped] adj., n. ZOOL. Quadrupède *m.*

quadruple ['kwɔdrupl̩] adj., n. Quadruple *m.*
— v. tr. Quadrupler.
— v. intr. Se quadrupler.

quadruplet [-plit] n. Quadruplé *s.*

quadruplicate [kwɔ'dru:plikit] adj. Quadruplé.
— n. Quatre exemplaires *m.*
— [-keit] v. tr. Quadrupler. ‖ Tirer quatre exemplaires de.

quadrupole ['kwɔdrupoul] n. ELECTR. Quadripôle *m.*

quaestor ['kwi:stə*] n. Questeur *m.*

quaff [kwɔf] v. tr., intr. FAM. Déglutir, siffler, lamper.

quag [kwæg], **quaggery** [-əri]. See QUAGMIRE.

quaggy [-i] adj. Marécageux.

quagmire [-maiə*] n. Fondrière *f.; marécage; terrain marécageux *m.* (bog). ‖ FIG. Mauvaise passe *f.; pétrin *m.* (fam.).

quail [kweil] n. ZOOL. Caille *f.* ‖ **Quail-call** (or) **-pipe,** n. SPORTS. Courcaillet *m.*

quail v. intr. Trembler, reculer, faiblir.
— v. tr. Faire trembler, intimider.

quaint [kweint] adj. † Attrayant, piquant, gracieux. ‖ D'une originalité plaisante, original, pittoresque. ‖ Singulier, bizarre. (See QUEER.) ‖ D'un archaïsme piquant, qui a un caractère vieillot.

quaintly [-li] adv. † Avec élégance, artistiquement. ‖ D'une manière originale (or) pittoresque. ‖ Singulièrement, bizarrement.

quaintness [-nis] n. † Elégance *f.* ‖ Originalité *f.* ‖ Singularité, bizarrerie *f.* ‖ Cachet *(m.)* d'antiquité.

quake [kweik] v. intr. Trembler *(for, with,* de).
— n. FAM. Tremblement *(m.)* de terre.

Quaker [-ə*] n. ECCLES. Quaker *m.* ‖ FAM. *Quaker-meeting,* réunion morne, colloque de muets.

Quakeress [-ərəs] n. Quakeresse *f.*

Quakerism [-ərizm̩] n. Quakérisme *m.*

qualification [ˌkwɔlifiˈkeiʃən] n. Modification, réserve, restriction *f.; statement with qualifications,* déclaration contenant des restrictions. ‖ Aptitude, compétence, capacité *f.* ‖ Conditions requises *f. pl.; titres justificatifs (or) nécessaires *m. pl.;* diplôme *m.; to appoint according to qualifications,* recruter sur titres. ‖ Qualification *f.* (description). ‖ JUR. Habileté *f.*

qualify ['kwɔlifai] v. tr. (2). Qualifier *(as,* de) [to describe]. ‖ Qualifier *(for,* pour) [to entitle]; rendre apte *(for,* à); *to be qualified to,* être qualifié (or) compétent pour, avoir qualité pour, être apte à. ‖ Modifier, atténuer (to mitigate); *in a qualified sense,* dans un sens restreint; *to qualify one's acceptance,* accepter sous réserve. ‖ JUR. Habiliter. ‖ COMM. *Qualified acceptance,* acceptation sous condition.
— v. intr. Se rendre apte *(for,* à); se qualifier, obtenir les titres *(for,* pour); *to qualify as a doctor,* être reçu médecin.

qualifying [-iŋ] adj. Qualificatif; *qualifying examination,* examen d'entrée, certificat d'aptitude. ‖ FIN. Statutaires (shares). ‖ SPORTS. *Qualifying round,* série éliminatoire.

qualitative ['kwɔlitətiv] adj. Qualitatif.

quality [-ti] n. Qualité *f.* (degree of excellence); *of good, poor quality,* de bonne, de mauvaise qualité; *of the best quality,* de premier choix. ‖ Qualité (status); *a lady of quality,* une dame de qualité. ‖ Qualité *f.;* don *m.* (mental or moral attribute). ‖ MUS. Qualité. ‖ FAM. *The quality,* la fine fleur, le gratin.
— adj. De qualité, de qualité supérieure; *quality papers,* la presse sérieuse.

qualm [kwɔ:m] n. MED. Nausée *f.* ‖ FIG. Appréhension *f.* ‖ FIG. Scrupule *m.* (of conscience).

qualmish [-iʃ] adj. MED. Nauséeux. ‖ FIG. Inquiet, mal à l'aise, plein d'appréhension. ‖ FIG. Scrupuleux; à la conscience inquiète.

quandary ['kwɔndəri] n. Grand embarras *m.; impasse *f.; in a quandary,* pris dans un dilemme.

quantify [kwɔntifai] v. tr. (2). MATH. Déterminer la quantité de. ‖ PHILOS., PHYS. Quantifier.

quantitative [-tətiv] adj. MATH., GRAMM. Quantitatif.

quantity [-ti] n. Quantité, somme *f.;* volume, nombre *m.; to buy in large quantities,* acheter en grande quantité. ‖ Quantité, abondance *f.* ‖ GRAMM. Quantité (of vowel sounds). ‖ MATH. Quantité; *unknown quantity,* inconnue. ‖ TECHN. Série *f.; quantity production,* fabrication en série. ‖ ARCHIT. *Quantity surveyor,* métreur m. ‖ FAM. Tas *m.* (heap).

quantize ['kwɔntaiz] v. tr. PHYS. Quantifier.

quantum ['kwɔntəm] (pl. **quanta** [-tə]) n. Quantum *m.* (share). ‖ PHYS. Quantum *m.; quantum mechanics,* mécanique quantique; *quantum theory,* théorie des quanta.

quarantine ['kwɔrənti:n] n. NAUT., FIG. Quarantaine *f.; quarantine service,* service de santé.
— v. tr. Mettre en quarantaine.
— v. intr. Se mettre en quarantaine.

quark [kwɑ:k] n. PHYS. Quark *m.*

quarrel ['kwɔrəl] n. † MILIT. Carreau *(m.)* d'arbalète.

quarrel n. Motif *(m.)* de plainte (*against, with,* con re); *I have no quarrel with him,* je n'ai rien à lui reprocher. ‖ Querelle, altercation, dispute, brouille *f.; to pick a quarrel with s.o.,* chercher querelle à qqn. ‖ Différend *m.; to espouse s.o.'s

quarrel, épouser la querelle de qqn, embrasser la cause de qqn, prendre le parti de qqn.
— v. intr. Se plaindre (*for*, de) [sth.]; *to quarrel with*, faire des reproches à (s.o.); trouver à redire à (sth.). ‖ Se quereller, se disputer, se brouiller, se fâcher (*with*, avec).

quarrelling [-iŋ] n. Querelle, dispute *f.*
— adj. Querelleur.

quarrelsome [-səm] adj. Querelleur, batailleur, belliqueux. ‖ Irascible.

quarrelsomeness [-səmnis] n. Caractère batailleur *m.;* humeur belliqueuse *f.*

quarry ['kwɔri] n. † Curée *f.* ‖ SPORTS. Proie *f.;* gibier poursuivi *m.* ‖ FAM. Individu traqué *m.*

quarry n. TECHN. Carrière *f.* ‖ FIG. Mine *f.* ‖ Quarry-stone, n. Moellon *m.*
— v. intr. TECHN. Exploiter une carrière. ‖ FIG. Faire des recherches.
— v. tr. TECHN. Extraire. ‖ FIG. Extraire, puiser.

quarryman [-mən] (pl. **quarrymen**) n. TECHN. Carrier *m.*

quart [kwɔːt] n. Quart de gallon, litre *m.* (approx.).

quart n. SPORTS. Quatrième *f.* (in card games); quarte *f.* (in fencing).

quartan ['kwɔːtn] adj. MED. Quarte.
— n. MED. Fièvre quarte *f.*

quarter ['kwɔːtə*] n. Quart *m.* (of an hour); *a quarter to six*, six heures moins le quart ; *a quarter to*, moins le quart ; *a quarter past seven*, sept heures et quart. ‖ Quart *m.* (of a pound); *a pound and a quarter*, une livre et quart. ‖ Quatre cents mètres *m. pl.* (fourth of a mile). ‖ Trimestre *m.* (of a year). ‖ Quartier *m.* (of a town); *slum quarter*, zone. ‖ Endroit, côté *m.; from all quarters*, de toutes parts. ‖ Pl. Résidence *f.; to shift one's quarters*, changer de domicile. ‖ Milieu *m.; in high quarters*, en haut lieu ; *responsible quarters*, milieux autorisés. ‖ ZOOL. Pl. Arrière-train *m.* (of an animal). ‖ CULIN. Quartier *m.* (of beef). ‖ BLAS. Quartier *m.* ‖ ASTRON. Quartier *m.* (of moon). ‖ JUR. Terme *m.* (of rent). ‖ NAUT. Hanche *f.* (of ship); direction *f.* (of the wind); pl. branle-bas *m.* ‖ MILIT. Quartier, cantonnement *m.; at close quarters*, corps à corps; *winter quarters*, quartiers d'hiver. ‖ U. S. Vingt-cinq cents *m. pl.* ‖ FIG. Quartier *m.; to give quarter*, faire quartier. ‖ **Quarter-binding,** n. Demi-reliure *f.* ‖ **Quarter-cask,** n. Quartaut *m.* ‖ **Quarter-day,** n. JUR. Terme, jour du terme *m.* ‖ **Quarter-deck,** n. NAUT. Gaillard d'arrière *m.* ‖ **Quarter-final,** n. SPORTS. Quart (*m.*) de finale. ‖ **Quarter-light,** n. AUTOM. Déflecteur *m.* ‖ **Quarter-note,** n. MUS. Noire *f.* ‖ **Quarter-sessions,** n. pl. JUR. Assises trimestrielles *f. pl.* ‖ **Quarter-wind,** n. NAUT. Vent grand largue *m.*
— v. tr. Diviser (or) partager en quatre. ‖ BLAS., † JUR. Ecarteler. ‖ MILIT. Cantonner. ‖ NAUT. Assigner un poste à. ‖ FAM. Installer.
— v. intr. Loger, s'installer (*at, with*, chez). ‖ SPORTS. Quêter (hounds). ‖ NAUT. Souffler grand largue. ‖ ASTRON. Changer de quartier (moon).

quarterage [-ridʒ] n. FIN., JUR. Paiement trimestriel, terme *m.*

quartering [-riŋ] n. Division (*f.*) en quatre. ‖ SPORTS. Quête *f.* ‖ NAUT. Désignation (*f.*) des postes de combat. ‖ MILIT. Cantonnement *m.* ‖ TECHN. Equarrissage *m.* (of a log). ‖ BLAS. Ecartelure *f.* ‖ ARCHIT. Chevron *m.*
— adj. NAUT. Grand largue (wind).

quarterly [-li] adj. Trimestriel.
— n. Publication trimestrielle *f.*
— adv. Trimestriellement, tous les trois mois.

quartermaster [-.mɑːstə*] n. NAUT. Second maître timonier *m.* ‖ MILIT. Intendant militaire *m.* ‖ † MILIT. Quartier-maître *m.* ‖ **Quatermaster-Corps,** n. U. S. MILIT. Service (*m.*) de l'Intendance. ‖ **Quatermaster-general,** n. MILIT. Intendant géné-

ral *m.* ‖ **Quartermaster-sergeant,** n. MILIT. Maréchal des logis-chef (in artillery); sergent-chef (in infantry).

quartern [-n] n. Quinze centilitres *m. pl.* (fourth of a pint); trois livres et demie *f. pl.* (fourth of a stone). ‖ Pain (*m.*) de quatre livres (loaf).

quarterstaff [-stɑːf] (pl. **quarterstaves** [-steivz]) n. SPORTS. Bâton (*m.*) d'escrime.

quartet [kwɔː'tet] n. MUS. Quatuor *m.*

quarto ['kwɔːtou] n. In-quarto *m.*

quartz [kwɔːtz] n. Quartz *m.*

quartzite [-ait] n. Quartzite *m.*

quasar ['kweizɑː*] n. ASTRON. Quasar *m.*

quash [kwɔʃ] v. tr. JUR. Annuler (an indictment).

quash v. tr. Etouffer (a feeling, an uprising).

quasi ['kweisai] adv. Quasi, presque. ‖ **Quasistellar object,** n. ASTRON. Objet (*m.*) quasi-stellaire.

quatercentenary [,kwætəsen'tiːnəri] adj. Du quatrième centenaire.
— n. Quatrième centenaire *m.*

quaternary [kwə'təːnəri] adj. Quaternaire.
— n. Ensemble (*m.*) de quatre (set). ‖ GEOL. Quaternaire *m.*

quaternion [-njən] n. MATH. Quaternion *m.*

quatrain ['kwɔtrən] n. Quatrain *m.*

quatrefoil ['kætrəfɔil] n. ARCHIT., BLAS. Quatrefeuilles *m.*

quattrocentist [,kwætro'tʃentist] n. ARTS. Artiste (or) écrivain italien (*m.*) du XVe siècle.
— adj. ARTS. Du XVe siècle italien.

quattrocento [-tou] n. ARTS. XVe siècle italien *m.*

quaver ['kweivə*] v. intr. Trembloter, chevroter (voice). ‖ MUS. Faire un trémolo.
— v. tr. Dire en chevrotant. ‖ MUS. Triller.
— n. Chevrotement, trémolo *m.* ‖ MUS. Croche *f.* (note); trille *m.* (trill).

quaveringly [-riŋli] adv. En chevrotant.

quay [kiː] n. NAUT. Quai *m.* (See WHARF.)

quayage [-idʒ] n. Droits (*m.*) de quai (wharfage).

quean [kwiːn] n. † Traînée, gueuse *f.*

queasiness ['kwiːzinis] n. Nausées *f. pl.* ‖ FIG. Scrupules *m. pl.*

queasy [-zi] adj. Nauséeux, répugnant (food); dégoûté (person); *to feel queasy*, avoir envie de rendre. ‖ FIG. Scrupuleux.

Quebec [kwi'bek] n. GEOGR. Québec *m.*

Quebecker [-ə*], **Québécois** [kebe'kwa] adj., n. GEOGR. Québécois *adj.*, *s.*

queen [kwiːn] n. Reine *f.; Queen Elizabeth*, la reine Elisabeth. ‖ SPORTS. Reine *f.* (in cards, chess). ‖ BOT. *Queen of the meadows*, reine-des-prés. ‖ ZOOL. Reine *f.* (of bees). ‖ FIG. Reine *f.* (flower, place, woman). ‖ FAM. *Queen Anne is dead*, passez au déluge! ‖ **Queen-bee,** n. ZOOL. Reine (*f.*) des abeilles; U. S. FAM. Présidente active *f.* ‖ **Queen-mother,** n. Reine mère *f.*
— v. tr. Faire reine (a woman). ‖ SPORTS. Damer. ‖ FAM. *To queen it*, pontifier, jouer à la reine.
— v. intr. SPORTS. Aller à dame.

queenhood [-hud] n. Royauté d'une femme ; dignité de reine *f.*

queenliness [-linis] n. Majesté *f.*

queenly [-li], **queenlike** [-laik] adj. Majestueux, royal, de reine.

queer [kwiə*] adj. Drôle, étrange, bizarre (odd). ‖ Douteux, suspect, louche (suspicious). ‖ MED. Mal à l'aise, souffrant, indisposé (out of sorts). ‖ FAM. Excentrique, bizarre. ‖ FAM. Inverti.
— v. tr. Gâcher, démolir (to spoil). ‖ Déranger; *to queer s.o.'s pitch*, mettre les bâtons dans les roues à qqn. ‖ Rendre malade. ‖ U. S. *To queer oneself*, se mettre dans le pétrin.
— n. U. S. POP. Fausse monnaie *f.* ‖ FAM. Tapette *f.* (homosexual).

queerish [-riʃ] adj. Plutôt bizarre, singulier. ‖ FAM. Patraque, mal fichu.

queerly [-li] adv. Etrangement.

queerness [-nis] n. Bizarrerie *f.* ‖ Malaise *f.*

quell [kwel] v. tr. Etouffer, réprimer. (See QUASH.)

quench [kwenʃ] v. tr. Eteindre (fire, light); étancher (thirst). ‖ TECHN. Tremper (hot steel). ‖ ELECTR. Etouffer (spark). ‖ FIG. Etouffer (desire); refroidir (enthusiasm); réprimer (emotion); contenir (speed). ‖ FAM. Clouer le bec à (s.o.).

quenchable [-əbl̩] adj. Extinguible.

quencher [-ə*] n. FAM. Rafraîchissement; verre *m.*

quenchless [-lis] adj. Inextinguible.

quenelle [kə'nel] n. CULIN. Quenelle *f.*

querist ['kwiərist] n. Questionneur *s.*

quern [kwəːn] n. Moulin à bras *m.* (hand-mill). ‖ CULIN. Moulin *m.* (for pepper, spices). ‖ **Quern-stone**, n. Meule (*f.*) de moulin.

querulous ['kwerуləs] adj. Grognon, ronchon; rouspéteur (fam.).

querulously [-li] adv. En récriminant (or) ronchonnant.

querulousness [-nis] n. Maussaderie, mauvaise humeur, tendance (*f.*) à récriminer.

query ['kwiəri] n. Question *f.*; point (*m.*) à élucider.
— v. intr. Poser des questions; *to query if,* chercher à savoir si.
— v. tr. Questionner (s.o.); douter de, mettre en question (sth.).

quest [kwest] n. † Enquête *f.* ‖ SPORTS. Quête *f.* (of hounds). ‖ FIG. Quête, poursuite *f.*
— v. intr. SPORTS. Quêter.
— v. tr. Se mettre en quête de.

question ['kwestʃən] n. Question *f.* (asking); *to ask* (or) *put a question,* poser une question. ‖ Question *f.*; point *m.* (subject); *begging the question,* pétition de principe; *it is not out of the question that,* il n'est pas exclu que; *out of the question,* hors de question; *that's not the question,* ce n'est pas la question; *to ventilate a question,* retourner une question dans tous les sens. ‖ Doute *m.; beyond question,* hors de doute; *there is no question of his veracity,* sa sincérité ne fait pas de doute. ‖ Affaire, question *f.* (matter); *a question of money,* une question d'argent. ‖ JUR. Question *f.* (before an assembly); *to put the ques:'on,* mettre la question aux voix. ‖ † Question *f.* (torture). ‖ FAM. *Question!,* c'est à voir, cela reste à savoir. ‖ **Question-mark,** n. Point (*m.*) d'interrogation. ‖ **Question-master,** n. RADIO. Questionneur, meneur de jeu *m.*
— v. tr. Questionner, poser des questions à, interroger (interrogate). ‖ Mettre en question (or) en doute, contester, douter de (to doubt); *it is not to be questioned that,* il n'y a aucun doute que. ‖ Se demander (whether, si); *I question whether he will come,* je ne sais trop s'il viendra.

questionable [-əbl̩] adj. Discutable, contestable, incertain (doubtful). ‖ Douteux, trouble, suspect, pas net (shady).

questionably [-əbli] adv. D'une manière contestable (or) suspecte.

questionless [-lis] adj. Indiscutable, incontestable, indubitable. (See UNQUESTIONABLE.)

questionnaire [kwestio'nɛə*] n. Questionnaire *m.*

queue [kjuː] n. Queue *f.* (of hair, wig). ‖ Queue, file *f.* (line); *to fall in at the end of the queue,* se mettre à (or) prendre la queue.
— v. intr. *To queue up,* faire la queue.

quibble ['kwibl̩] n. † Calembour *m.* ‖ Argutie *f.* (cavilling); faux-fuyant *m.* (evasion).
— v. intr. User de faux-fuyants, se défiler (to equivocate). ‖ Chicaner, ergoter (to split hairs).

quibbler [-ə*] n. † Faiseur (*m.*) de calembours. ‖ Sophiste, casuiste *m.* (equivocater). ‖ Ergoteur, coupeur (*m.*) de cheveux en quatre (caviller).

quibbling [-iŋ] n. Casuistique *f.*; arguties *f. pl.* (cavilling); dérobades *f. pl.* (evasion).
— adj. Evasif (argument); ergoteur (person).

quiche [kiːʃ] n. CULIN. Quiche *f.*

quick [kwik] adj. † Vif, vivant (living). ‖ Vif, prompt (look, reply). ‖ Rapide; *it is quicker to go through the garden,* c'est plus court de passer par le jardin. ‖ AGRIC. Vif (hedge). ‖ MED. Rapide (pulse). ‖ MILIT. Accéléré (step). ‖ FIG. Vif, prompt (mind); fin (sense); vif, impatient, emporté (temper). ‖ U. S. FAM. *Quick on the draw,* impulsif, prompt à la détente. ‖ **Quick-change,** adj. THEATR. A transformations rapides; AUTOM. A changement rapide. ‖ **Quick-eared,** adj. A l'oreille fine. ‖ **Quick-eyed,** adj. A l'œil perçant. ‖ **Quick-freeze,** v. tr. Surgeler; n. Surgélation *f.* ‖ **Quick-handed,** adj. A la main leste. ‖ **Quick-sighted,** adj. A la vue perçante; FIG. Perspicace. ‖ **Quick-tempered,** adj. Vif, emporté, coléreux. ‖ **Quick-witted,** adj. D'esprit prompt, spirituel.
— adv. Vite, rapidement (quickly). ‖ **Quick-firing,** adj. MILIT. A tir rapide.
— n. Vif *m.; to cut to the quick,* blesser au vif.

quicken [-ən] v. tr. † Ranimer, raviver. ‖ Accélérer, hâter (one's pace). ‖ MED. Accélérer (the pulse). ‖ MUS. Presser (the tempo). ‖ FIG. Stimuler, exciter (appetite, desire, person).
— v. intr. S'accélérer (pace). ‖ MED. Bouger (foetus); sentir remuer l'enfant (pregnant woman). ‖ FIG. Se ranimer (hope).

quickie [-i] n. CINEM. FAM. Court métrage (*m.*) de qualité inférieure. ‖ U. S. FAM. Chose vite faite *f.*

quicklime [-laim] n. Chaux vive *f.*

quickly [-li] adv. Rapidement, promptement, vite. ‖ Sans délai, tout de suite. ‖ Prestement, vivement.

quickness [-nis] n. Vitesse, rapidité *f.* ‖ MED. Finesse *f.* (of ear); fréquence *f.* (of pulse); acuité *f.* (of sight). ‖ FIG. Promptitude, vivacité *f.* (of mind); vivacité *f.;* emportement *m.* (of temper).

quicksand [-sænd] n. Sable mouvant *m.*

quickset [-set] n. BOT. Aubépine *f.* (hawthorn); haie vive *f.* (hedge).
— adj. Vive (hedge).

quicksilver [-,silvə*] n. CHIM. Vif-argent, mercure *m.* ‖ FAM. Vif-argent *m.*
— v. tr. Etamer (a mirror).

quicksilvering [-,silvəriŋ] n. Etamage *m.* (act); tain *m.* (result).

quid [kwid] n. invar. POP. Livre sterling *f.*

quid n. Chique *f.* (of tobacco).

quiddity [-iti] n. † Qualité essentielle *f.* ‖ FIG. Nuance subtile, argutie *f.*

quidnunc ['kwidnʌŋk] n. Curieux (*s.*) à l'affût de nouvelles.

quid pro quo ['kwidprou'kwou] n. Equivalent *m.; to return a quid pro quo,* rendre la monnaie de la pièce. ‖ † Quiproquo *m.*

quiescence [kwai'esn̩s] n. Tranquillité *f.*

quiescent [-n̩t] adj. Inactif, en repos (motionless). ‖ GRAMM. Quiescent.

quiet ['kwaiət] n. Calme *m.;* tranquillité, paix, quiétude *f.* (peace). ‖ Tranquillité *f.;* silence *m.* ‖ Repos *m.* (rest). ‖ FAM. *All quiet on the Western Front,* à l'ouest rien de nouveau; *on the quiet,* en douce; sans raffut.
— adj. Tranquille, immobile (still). ‖ Silencieux, paisible, tranquille (silent). ‖ Calme, tranquille, doux (gentle). ‖ Paisible, pacifique, en paix, en repos (peaceful). ‖ Reposant, délassant, apaisant (soothing). ‖ Tranquille, sans souci (or) inquiétude (carefree). ‖ Caché, dissimulé (secret). ‖ Modeste, réservé (unobtrusive). ‖ Sobre, discret (not pretentious). ‖ COMM. Calme.
— v. tr. Calmer, apaiser.

quieten [-ən] v. tr., intr. See QUIET.

quietism [-izm̩] n. Quiétisme *m.*

quietist [-ist] n. Quiétiste *m.*

quietly [-ly] adv. Tranquillement, paisiblement.

quietness [-nis] n. Tranquillité *f.*

quietude [-ju:d] n. Quiétude *f.*

quietus [kwai'i:təs] n. FIN. Quitus *m.* ‖ FIG. Coup (*m.*) de grâce.

quiff [kwif] n. Banane *f.* (in man's hairstyle); accroche-cœur *m.* (kiss-curl).

quill [kwil] n. Plume d'oie *f.* (pen); cure-dent *m.* (tooth-pick). ‖ ZOOL. Tuyau *m.* (of a feather); piquant *m.* (of a hedgehog). ‖ SPORTS. Flotteur *m.* (in fishing). ‖ TECHN. Bobine *f.;* fourreau *m.* ‖ MED. Tuyau *m.* (of cinchona). ‖ MUS. Pipeau, chalumeau *m.* ‖ **Quill-driver,** n. FAM. Gratte-papier, plumitif *m.* ‖ **Quill-feather,** n. Penne *f.*
— v. tr Tuyauter, rucher.
— v. intr. † Bobiner.

quillet [-it] n. † Argutie *f.*

quilling [-iŋ] n. Tuyautage, ruché *m.* (act); ruche *f.* (result).

quilt [kwilt] n. Couverture piquée *f.* (coverlet); couvre-pied, édredon américain *m.* (eiderdown).
— v. tr. Piquer (to sew up); ouater, capitonner, rembourrer (to pad).

quilting [-iŋ] n. Ouatage, rembourrage, capitonnage *m.* (act); piqué *m.* (material).

quin [kwin] n. FAM. Quintuplé *s.*

quinary ['kwainəri] adj. MATH. Quinaire.

quince [kwins] n. BOT. Coing *m.* (fruit); cognassier *m.* (tree).

quincentenary [ˌkwinsen'ti:nəri] adj. Du cinquième centenaire.
— n. Cinquième centenaire *m.*

quincuncial [kwin'kʌnʃəl] adj. En quinconce.

quincunx ['kwinkʌŋks] n. Quinconce *f.*

quinine [kwi'ni:n] n. MED. Quinine *f.*

quinquagenarian [ˌkwiŋkwədʒi'nɛəriən] adj., n. Quinquagénaire *s.*

quinquagesima [-'dʒesimə] n. ECCLES. Quinquagésime *f.*

quinquennial [kwiŋ'kwenjəl] adj. Quinquennal.

quinquennium [-iəm] n. Quinquennat *m.*

quinquina [kwiŋ'ki:nə] n. MED., BOT. Quinquina *m.*

quinsy [kwinzi] n. MED. Esquinancie, angine *f.*

quint [kwint] n. SPORTS, MUS. Quinte *f.*

quintal [-]] n. Quintal *m.*

quintan [-ən] adj., n. MED. Quinte *f.*

quinte [kɛ:t] n. SPORTS. Quinte *f.*

quintessence [kwin'tesns] n. Quintessence *f.*

quintessential [ˌkwinti'senʃəl] adj. Quintessentiel.

quintet(te) [kwin'tet] n. MUS. Quintette *m.*

quintillion [kwin'tiljən] n. MATH. Quintillion *m.*

quintuple ['kwintjupl] adj., n. MATH. Quintuple *m.*
— v. tr., intr. Quintupler.

quintuplet [ˌkwintjuplit] n. Quintuplé *s.*

quip [kwip] n. Raillerie *f.;* quolibet *m.*
— v. tr., intr. Railler.

quire [kwaiə*] n. Main *f.* (of paper); in quires, en feuilles, non broché.

quire n. † Chœur *m.* (See CHOIR.)

quirk [kwə:k] n. Raillerie *f.;* sarcasme *m.* (quip). ‖ Faux-fuyant *m.;* échappatoire *f.* (equivocation). ‖ Mot d'esprit *m.* (sally). ‖ Paraphe *m.* (following signature); fioriture *f.* (to handwriting). ‖ ARCHIT. Gorge *f.*

quirk n. AVIAT. FAM. Novice *m.*

quisling ['kwizliŋ] n. Collaborateur, traître *m.*

quit [kwit] adj. Quitte (*for,* pour); *quit of,* débarrassé de.
— v. tr. (1). † S'acquitter (*of,* de). ‖ Lâcher, quitter, abandonner (to give up); lâcher (to let go). ‖ Quitter, s'en aller de (to depart from); quitter, laisser (to leave). ‖ U. S. Cesser, arrêter de (to stop).
— v. intr. U. S. S'en aller, partir (to go away). ‖ U. S. Lâcher la partie (to give up).

quitch [kwitʃ] n. BOT. Chiendent *m.*

quitclaim ['kwitkleim] n. JUR. Renonciation (*f.*) à ses droits.
— v. tr. JUR. Renoncer à un droit sur.

quite [kwait] adv. Tout à fait, complètement, entièrement (entirely). ‖ Absolument, parfaitement (positively). ‖ Vraiment, réellement (truly). ‖ FAM. Extrêmement, très (very). ‖ FAM. *Not quite,* plutôt douteux, pas très convenable. ‖ FAM. Assez, passablement; *quite a few,* un bon nombre; *quite a while,* un bon moment.

quits [kwits] adj. Quitte (*with,* avec).

quittance ['kwitəns] n. FIN., COMM. Quittance *f.* ‖ † Remise *f.* ‖ FIG. Rétribution *f.* (repayment); représailles *f. pl.* (reprisal).

quitter ['kwitə*] n. U. S. Lâcheur *s.*

quiver ['kwivə*] n. Carquois *m.*

quiver v. intr. Battre (eyelids); trembler, frémir (leaves, lips); trembler, frémir, frissonner (person); trembloter, trembler, vibrer (voice); palpiter (wings).
— v. tr. *To quiver its wings,* battre des ailes.
— n. Battement *m.* (of eyelids, wings); frémissement *m.* (of leaves); frisson, frémissement, tremblement *m.* (of person); tremblotement, chevrotement *m.* (of voice).

quivering [-riŋ] adj. Battant (eyelids); frémissant (leaves); frémissant, frissonnant, tremblant (person); tremblotant (voice).
— n. See QUIVER.

qui vive [ˌki: 'vi:v] n. *On the qui vive,* sur le qui-vive.

Quixote ['kwiksot] n. Don Quichotte *m.*

Quixotic [kwik'sotik] adj. De Don Quichotte.

quixotism ['kwiksotizm] n. Donquichottisme *m.*

quiz [kwiz] n. † Original *s.* (eccentric). ‖ Plaisanterie *f.* (joke); mystification *f.* (hoax). ‖ Railleur, gouailleur *m.* (joker). ‖ U. S. Colle *f.;* examen *m.* (questioning).
— v. tr. Se moquer de, railler (to gibe at). ‖ U. S. Poser des colles à.

quizzical ['kwizikəl] adj. Railleur, moqueur, persifleur (bantering). ‖ Cocasse, drôle. (See COMIC.) ‖ U. S. FAM. Plein d'esprit critique; embarrassé (perplexed).

quizzing [-iŋ] adj. Railleur. ‖ **Quizzing-glass,** n. Lorgnon *m.*
— n. Persiflage *m.* ‖ U. S. Examen *m.*

quod [kwod] n. FAM. Bloc *m.;* taule *f.;* *to put in quod,* fourrer dedans.
— v. tr. FAM. Fourrer au bloc.

quoin [koin] n. ARCHIT. Voussoir *m.* (of an arch); angle, coin *m.* (of a wall). ‖ TECHN. Cale *f.* ‖ MILIT. Coussin *m.* ‖ **Quoin-stone,** n. ARCHIT. Pierre (*f.*) d'angle.
— v. tr. Caler, coincer.

quoining [-iŋ] n. Calage *m.*

quoit [koit] n. Palet *m.*
— v. tr. Lancer.

quondam ['kwondəm] adj. D'autrefois, ancien.

quorum ['kwo:rəm] n. Quorum *m.; we had a quorum,* le quorum fut atteint.

quota ['kwoutə] n. FIN. Quote-part *f.; taxable quota,* quotité imposable.

quotable ['kwoutəbl] adj. Citable. ‖ FIN. Cotable.

quotation [kwo'teiʃən] n. Citation *f.* ‖ FIN. Cours *m.;* cote *f.* ‖ TECHN. Cadrat *m.* ‖ GRAMM. *Quotation marks,* guillemets.

quote [kwout] v. tr. Citer (an example, a text); rappeler (a number). ‖ FIN. Coter. ‖ COMM. Etablir (a price); indiquer un prix (or) un tarif à (s.o.). ‖ GRAMM. Mettre entre guillemets.
— v. intr. Citer; faire des citations (*from,* de, d'après). ‖ COMM. Indiquer un prix; donner le tarif.
— n. FAM. Citation *f.* ‖ FAM., COMM. Estimation (*f.*) de coût, devis *m.* ‖ FAM. GRAMM. Guillemet *m.; in quotes,* entre guillemets.

quoth [kwouθ] v. def. † *Quoth he,* dit-il.

quotidian [kwo'tidiən] adj. Quotidien, journalier

(daily). ‖ Banal, monotone, de tous les jours (every-day).
— n. MED. Fièvre quotidienne *f.*

quotient ['kwouʃənt] n. MATH. Quotient *m.*
q. v. [kju:'vi:] abbr. *quod vide*, voir ce mot (in cross references).

R

r [ɑ:*] n. R, r *m.* ‖ LOC. *The three Rs,* la lec-ture, l'écriture et l'arithmétique (reading, writing, (a)rithmetic).
rabbet ['ræbit] n. TECHN. Feuillure, rainure *f.* ‖ NAUT. Râblure *f.* ‖ **Rabbet-plane,** n. TECHN. Guil-laume *m.*
— v. tr. TECHN. Feuiller (a plank); assembler à guillaume (two planks).
rabbi ['ræbai], **rabbin** ['ræbin] n. ECCLES. Rab-bin *m.; Chief Rabbi,* Grand rabbin.
rabbinic(al) [ræ'binik(əl)] adj. ECCLES. Rabbi-nique.
rabbit ['ræbit] n. ZOOL. Lapin *m.; doe rabbit,* lapine; *wild rabbit,* lapin de garenne. ‖ CULIN. *Buck rabbit,* rôtie au fromage surmontée d'un œuf; *stewed rabbit,* lapin en gibelotte; *Welsh rabbit,* toast au fromage. ‖ SPORTS. Mazette *f.* (at tennis). ‖ **Rabbit-breeding,** n. AGRIC. Cuniculi-culture *f.* ‖ **Rabbit-farm,** n. AGRIC. Elevage (*m.*) de lapins. ‖ **Rabbit-hutch,** n. Cabane (*f.*) à lapins, clapier *m.* ‖ **Rabbit-punch,** n. SPORTS. Coup (*m.*) sur la nuque. ‖ **Rabbit-warren,** n. Garenne *f.*
— v. intr. Chasser le lapin.
rabbity [-i] adj. De lapin (taste). ‖ FAM. Chétif, malingre (personne).
rabble ['ræbl] n. Cohue, foule *f.* (crowd); populo *m.* (fam.). ‖ Canaille, racaille, populace, tourbe, lie populaire *f.* (riff-raff). ‖ **Rabble-rouser,** n. Agita-teur; fomentateur (*m.*) de révolte.
rabble n. TECHN. Râble, ringard *m.*
— v. tr. TECHN. Brasser (molten metal).
rabblement [-mənt] n. Tumulte *m.* ‖ Cohue *f.*
Rabelaisian [,ræbə'leiziən] adj., n. Rabelaisien *s.*
Rabelaisianism [-izm̩] n. Gauloiserie *f.*
rabid ['ræbid] adj. ZOOL. Enragé (dog). ‖ MED. Rabique (virus). ‖ FIG. Féroce, farouche (hate); dévorant (hunger, thirst); enragé, forcené (oppo-nent); fanatique (supporter).
rabidity [rə'biditi], **rabidness** ['ræbidnis] n. ZOOL. Rage *f.* ‖ FIG. Fureur, violence *f.*
rabies ['reibii:z] n. MED. Rage, hydrophobie *f.*
rac(c)oon [rə'ku:n] n. ZOOL. Raton laveur *m.*
race [reis] n. GEOGR. Raz *m.* (in sea); courant fort *m.* (in stream). ‖ ASTRON. Cours *m.* (of a star, of time). ‖ TECHN. Bief *m.* (mill-race). ‖ TECHN. Voie (*f.*) de roulement. ‖ SPORTS. Course *f.; to run a race,* disputer une course; *to run a race with,* lutter de vitesse avec. ‖ FIG. Carrière *f.* (span of life); *his race is run,* il est arrivé au terme de sa vie. ‖ **Race-card,** n. Programme (*m.*) des courses. ‖ **Race-goer,** n. Turfiste *m.* ‖ **Race-meeting,** n. Réu-nion (*f.*) de courses. ‖ **Race-track,** n. Piste *f.;* U. S. champ (*m.*) de course.
— v. intr. Aller (or) courir à toute allure (or) vitesse; galoper; *to race along,* aller grand train. ‖ SPORTS. Lutter de vitesse (*against, with,* avec);

to race against time, courir contre la montre. ‖ TECHN. S'emballer (engine); s'affoler (propeller). ‖ **To race about,** faire tout au grand galop.
— v. tr. Faire marcher à toute allure; conduire (or) entraîner à toute vitesse; *to race s.o. off one's feet,* faire trotter qqn au point qu'il ne tienne plus sur ses jambes. ‖ Faire lutter de vitesse avec; faire courir (*against,* contre). ‖ Lutter de vitesse avec (action); arriver le premier (result). ‖ SPORTS. Faire courir (a horse). ‖ TECHN. Emballer (an engine). ‖ FAM. *To race away a fortune,* manger une fortune aux courses.
race n. Race *f.; the human race,* la race humaine. ‖ Lignée *f.; true to race,* extrêmement racé. ‖ **Race-hatred,** n. Haine raciale *f.* ‖ **Race relations,** n. pl. Rapports (*m. pl.*) entre les races (or) les groupes ethniques; *race relations board,* commission contre la discrimination raciale. ‖ **Race-riot,** n. Emeute raciale *f.*
racecourse [-kɔ:s] n. SPORTS. Champ (*m.*) de courses.
racehorse [-hɔ:s] n. Cheval (*m.*) de course; *to keep racehorses,* faire courir.
raceme [rə'si:m] n. BOT. Grappe *f.* (flower cluster).
racer [-ə*] n. SPORTS. Avion (or) bateau (or) che-val *m.* (or) bicyclette (or) motocyclette (or) voiture (*f.*) de course; coureur *m.* (person).
rachidian [rə'kidiən] adj. BOT. Rachidien.
rachis ['reikis] (pl. **rachides** ['rækidi:z]) n. BOT., MED. Rachis *m.*
rachitic [rə'kitik] adj. MED. Rachitique.
rachitis [rə'kaitis] n. MED. Rachitisme *m.*
racial ['reiʃəl] adj. De race, racial.
racialism [-izm̩] n. Racisme *m.*
racialist [-ist] n. Raciste *s.*
raciness ['reisinis] n. Goût de terroir *m.;* bou-quet *m.* (of wine). ‖ Verve *f.;* piquant *m.* (of lan-guage).
racing [-iŋ] adj. Qui court à toute vitesse. ‖ SPORTS. De course (bicycle, car); *racing people,* turfistes. ‖ SPORTS. Qui fait courir (person). ‖ TECHN. Emballé (engine); affolé (propeller).
— n. SPORTS. Courses *f. pl.* ‖ TECHN. Emballement *m.* (of an engine); affolement *m.* (of a propeller). ‖ **Racing-track,** n. Piste *f.*
racism ['reisizm̩] n. U. S. Racisme *m.*
racist [-ist] n. U. S. Raciste *s.*
rack [ræk] n. Moutons *m. pl.* (clouds).
— v. intr. Se disperser, fuir devant le vent (clouds).
rack n. Destruction *f.; to go to rack and ruin,* s'en aller à la dérive (business, person); tomber en ruine (house).
rack n. SPORTS. Traquenard *m.* (horse's gait).
— v. intr. SPORTS. Traquenarder.
rack v. tr. Soutirer (wine).

rack n. Etagère *f.;* garage, soutien-vélos *m.* (bicycle-rack); classeur *m.* (filing-system); claie *f.* (for fruit); portemanteau *m.* (hat-rack); filet *m.* (luggage-rack); casier *m.* (pigeon-hole); égouttoir *m.* (plate-rack). ‖ Autom. *Roof rack,* galerie *f.* ‖ Aviat. *Bomb rack,* lance-bombes. ‖ Agric. Ridelle *f.* (of cart); râtelier *m.* (for fodder). ‖ † Chevalet (*m.*) de torture. ‖ Techn. *Rack and pinion,* crémaillère *f.* ‖ Fig. Supplice *m.;* torture *f.; on the rack,* à la torture; sur le gril (fam.); *to put on the rack,* mettre au supplice. ‖ **Rack-railway,** n. Ch. de F. Chemin (*m.*) de fer à crémaillère. ‖ **Rack-rent,** n. Loyer (*m.*) exorbitant; v. tr. Imposer un loyer exorbitant à (a tenant). ‖ **Rack-renter,** n. propriétaire abusif *m.;* locataire pressuré *m.* ‖ **Rack-wheel,** n. Techn. Roue dentée *f.*
— v. intr. Agric. Garnir les râteliers.
— v. tr. † Infliger le supplice du chevalet à. ‖ Agric. Placer dans un râtelier (fodder); placer sur une claie (fruit). ‖ Techn. Déplacer au moyen de la crémaillère. ‖ Comm. Imposer un loyer exorbitant à (a lessee); fixer à un taux exorbitant (a rent). ‖ Fig. Mettre au supplice (or) à la torture; *to rack one's brains,* se creuser la cervelle, se torturer les méninges; *racked by hunger, remorse,* tenaillé par la faim, le remords. ‖ **To rack back,** U. S. Fam. Enguirlander.

racket ['rækit] n. Sports. Raquette *f.* (bat). ‖ Comm. Raquette *f.* (snow-shoe). ‖ Pl. Sports. Rackets *m.* (game). ‖ U. S. Palette *f.;* battoir *m.* (in table-tennis). ‖ **Racket-press,** Sports. Presse-raquette *m.*

racket n. Tumulte, tapage, vacarme *m.;* boucan, chahut, chambard, foin *m.* (fam.). ‖ Epreuve *f.* (ordeal). ‖ Dissipation *f.; to go on the racket,* faire la bombe (or) la noce. ‖ Fam. Affaire *f.* (or) métier louche *m.;* combine *f.;* truc *m.* (dodge); escroquerie *f.;* chantage, racket *m.* (fraud); *drug racket,* trafic des stupéfiants; *to be in on the racket,* être dans le coup. ‖ Loc. *To stand the racket,* payer la note (to bear the expense); payer les pots cassés (to pay the piper); prendre le risque (to run the risk); tenir le coup (to stick it out).
— v. intr. **To racket about,** Fam. Faire du boucan (to make a row); mener joyeuse vie, faire la noce (to have a gay time).

racketeer [,ræki'ti:ə*] n. Racketter, escroc, gangster *m.;* combinard *m.*

racketer ['ræki t*] n. Fam. Tapageur (roisterer); noceur *s.* (fast liver).

racking ['rækiŋ] adj. Med. Exténuant (cough); fou (headache); atroce (pain). ‖ Comm. Exorbitant (rent).

racking n. Agric. Soutirage *m.* (of wine).

racoon [rə'ku:n] n. See RACCOON.

racquet ['rækit] n. See RACKET.

racy ['reisi] adj. Parfumé, qui sent le terroir (wine). ‖ Zool. De race (animal). ‖ Fig. Vif, plein de verve (person); vigoureux, piquant (style). ‖ Fam. Salé (story).

radar ['reidɑ :*] n. Radio. Radar, radiodétecteur *m.; radar operator,* radariste; *radar scanner,* balai; *radar screen,* écran de radar.

radial ['reidiəl] adj. Med., Math., Techn. Radial. ‖ **Radial(-ply),** adj. Autom. Radial (tyre).
— n. Med. Radiale *f.* (artery); radial *m.* (muscle, nerve). ‖ Techn. Moteur (*m.*) en étoile.

radial adj. Med. Du radium.

radian ['reidiən] n. Math. Radian, radiant *m.*

radiance [-əns] n. Rayonnement, éclat *m.* ‖ Phys. Radiation *f.;* rayonnement *m.*

radiant [-ənt] adj. Rayonnant, resplendissant. (See EFFULGENT.) ‖ Radieux (beauty, face); brillant (eyes); *to be radiant with joy,* rayonner de joie. ‖ Bot. Rayonnant. ‖ Phys. Rayonnant, radiant (heat). ‖ Astron. Radiant.
— n. Phys. Point radiant; foyer rayonnant *m.* ‖ Astron. Radiant *m.*

radiantly [-əntli] adv. Avec éclat *m.* ‖ Fig. D'un air radieux.

radiate [-it] adj. Zool. Radié.
— [-eit] v. intr. Rayonner (*from,* de) [lines, roads]. ‖ Phys. Rayonner; irradier; radier.
— v. tr. Phys. Dégager, répandre. ‖ Radio. Transmettre, diffuser, émettre. ‖ Fig. Irradier, répandre.

radiation [reidi'ei ʃən] n. Irradiation *f.* (of heat); rayonnement *m.* (light). ‖ Phys. Radiation *f.* (of radium). ‖ Med. *Radiation sickness,* mal des rayons.

radiator ['reidieitə*] n. Techn. Radiateur *m.* ‖ **Radiator-cap,** n. Autom. Bouchon de radiateur *m.* ‖ **Radiator-muff,** n. Autom. Couvre-radiateur *m.*

radical ['rædikəl] n. Math., Jur., Gramm. Radical *m.*
— adj. Math., Jur., Gramm. Radical. ‖ Fig. Radical, fondamental, essentiel (change, error, principle), avancé (ideas); radical (measure); foncier, absolu (thorough).

radicalism [-izm] n. Radicalisme *m.*

radically [-i] adv. Radicalement.

radices ['reidi,si:z] n. pl. See RADIX.

radicle ['rædik l] n. Bot. Radicule; radicelle *f.* ‖ Chim. Radical *m.*

radii ['reidi,ai] n. pl. See RADIUS.

radio [reidio] n. Radio. Poste de radio *m.;* radio, T. S. F. *f.* (radio set); radio, T. S. F. *f.* (wireless). ‖ Radio. Radio *m.* ‖ Med. Radiographie, radio *f.* ‖ **Radio-active,** adj. Phys. Radio-actif. ‖ **Radio-activity,** n. Phys. Radio-activité *f.* ‖ **Radioastronomy,** n. Astron. Radioastronomie *f.* ‖ **Radiobeacon,** n. Radiobalise *f.;* radiophare *m.* ‖ **Radio cab,** n. Radio-taxi *m.* ‖ **Radio-carbon,** n. Radiocarbone *m.; radio-carbon dating,* datation au radiocarbone. ‖ **Radio-chemistry,** n. Radiochimie *f.* ‖ **Radio-compass,** n. Radiocompas *m.* ‖ **Radio-control,** n. Radioguidage, téléguidage *m.;* v. tr. Radioguider, téléguider. ‖ **Radio-element,** n. Phys. Radioélément *m.* ‖ **Radio-engineer,** n. Ingénieur (*m.*) radio. ‖ **Radio ham,** n. Radioamateur *m.* ‖ **Radio-operator,** n. Radiotélégraphiste (or) -téléphoniste *m.* ‖ **Radio-sonde,** n. Techn. Radiosonde *f.* ‖ **Radio source,** n. Astron. Radiosource *f.* ‖ **Radio telescope,** n. Astron. Radiotélescope *m.* ‖ **Radio wave,** n. Radio. Onde radio (or) radioélectrique *f.*

radiogram [-græm] n. Radio. Combiné radiophono *m.* (radio set); radiogramme *m.* (wireless telegram).

radiograph ['reidiogrɑ:f] n. Med. Radiographie *f.;* radio *f.* (fam.).
— v. tr. Med. Radiographier.

radiographic ['reidio'græfik] adj. Radiographique.

radiography [reidi'ogrəfi] n. Med. Radiographie *f.* ‖ Techn. Radiotélégraphie *f.*

radioisotope [,reidio'aisətoup] n. Radio-isotope *m.*

radiolocate [,reidiolou'keit] v. tr. Repérer par radar.

radiolocation [,reidiolou'kei ʃən] n. Radar *m.;* radiorepérage *m.;* radiodétection *f.*

radiological [,reidio'lɔdʒikəl] adj. Med. Radiologique.

radiologist [,reidi'ɔlədʒist] s. Med. Radiologue *s.*

radiology [-dʒi] n. Med. Radiologie *f.*

radiometer [,reidi'ɔmitə*] n. Phys. Radiomètre *m.*

radiometry [-tri] n. Phys. Radiométrie *f.*

radiophone ['reidiofoun] n. Techn. Radiophone; photophone *m.*

radiophonic [,reidiə'fɔnik] adj. Mus. Electro-acoustique.

radiophony [,reidi'ɔfəni] n. Radiophonie *f.*

radioscopic [,reidio'skɔpik] adj. Med. Radioscopique.

radioscopy [,reidi'ɔskəpi] n. Med. Radioscopie *f.*

radiotelegram [,reidio'teligræm] n. RADIO. Radiotélégramme, radio *m.*
radiotelegraph [-grɑ:f] n. RADIO. Appareil (*m.*)
de radiotélégraphie.
radiotelegraphic [,reidioteli'græfik] adj. Radio-
télégraphique.
radiotelegraphy [,reidiotə'legrəfi] n. Radiotélégraphie *f.*
radiotelephone [,reidio'telifoun] n. Radiotélé-
phone *m.*
— v. tr. Radiotéléphoner.
radiotelephony [,reidiotə'lefəni] n. Radiotéléphonie, T. S. F. *f.*
radiotherapy [,reidio'θerəpi] n. MED. Radiothérapie *f.*
radiothermy ['reidio,θə:mi] n. MED. Radio-
thermie *f.*
radish ['rædiʃ] n. BOT. Radis *m.; bunch of
radishes*, botte (*f.*) de radis. || **Radish-bed**, n.
AGRIC. Ravière *f.* || **Radish-dish**, n. Ravier *m.*
radium ['reidiəm] n. Radium *m.; radium emanation*, émanation de radium, radon.
radiumtherapy ['reidiəm'θerəpi] n. MED. Radiumthérapie *f.*
radius ['reidiəs] (pl. **radii** [-ai]) n. MATH. Rayon
m.; radius vector, rayon vecteur. || AUTOM. *Steering
radius*, rayon de braquage. || AVIAT. *Cruising radius*,
autonomie. || MED. Radius *m.* || FIG. Rayon *m.;
within a radius of*, dans un rayon de.
radix ['reidiks] (pl. **radices** [-si:z]) n. MATH.
Base *f.*
radon ['reidɔn] n. PHYS. Radon.
raffia ['ræfiə] n. Raphia *m.; made of raffia*, en
raphia.
raffish ['ræfiʃ] adj. FAM. Bravache (flashy); débauché (rakish); canaille (roguish).
raffle ['ræfl] n. Loterie, tombola *f.*
— v. intr. Prendre un billet de tombola (*for*, pour).
— v. tr. Mettre en tombola.
raft [rɑ:ft] n. Amas flottant *m.* || NAUT. Radeau
m. || AGRIC. Train de bois *m.* || ARCHIT. Châssis
(*m.*) de fondation.
— v. tr. Transporter sur un radeau (to carry by
raft); traverser sur un radeau (to cross on a raft);
faire un radeau de (to build a raft of).
— v. intr. Conduire un radeau (or) un train de
bois.
raft [ræft] n. U. S. FAM. Tas *m.; tapée, tripotée,
flopée *f.*
rafter [-ə*] n. ARCHIT. Chevron *m.* || Pl. Chevron-
nage *m.* (system).
— v. tr. ARCHIT. Chevronner. || AGRIC. Labourer
en billons.
raftsman [-smən] (pl. **raftsmen**) n. Flotteur *m.*
(on a timber-raft).
rag [ræg] n. Chiffon, lambeau *m.; loque *f.; to tear
to rags*, mettre en lambeaux. || Pl. COMM. Chiffons
*m. pl.; drilles *f. pl.* (for papermaking). || Pl. Vête-
ments *m. pl.; in one's glad rags*, sur son trente et
un; *not to have a rag to put on one's back*, ne
rien avoir à se mettre sur le dos. || Pl. Haillons
*m. pl.; guenilles *f. pl.; in rags*, déguenillé, dépe-
naillé; *in rags and tatters*, tout en loques. || FIG.
Lambeau, petit morceau *m.* (scrap, shred); brin *m.;
parcelle *f.* (de vérité). || FAM. Drapeau (flag); canard
*m.; feuille (*f.*) de chou (newspaper); *to feel like
a wet rag*, se sentir mou comme une chiffe; *it's
like a red rag to him*, il voit rouge quand on lui
parle de ça. || U. S. FAM. *To chew the rag*, tailler
une bavette. || **Rag-and-bone-man**, n. Chiffonnier
m. || **Rag-bag**, n. Sac (*m.*) aux chiffons; FAM.
Souillon *f.* (slattern). || **Rag-book**, n. Livre (*m.*)
d'images sur toile. || **Rag-doll**, n. Poupée (*f.*) en
chiffons. || **Rag-fair**, n. Marché (*m.*) aux puces. ||
Rag-merchant, n. Chiffonnier (*m.*) en gros. || **Rag-
paper**, n. Papier (*m.*) de chiffons. || **Rag-picker**,
n. Chiffonnier *s.; biffin *m.* (fam.). || **Rag-sorter**,
n. TECHN. Trieur (*s.*) de chiffons.
rag n. GEOL. Calcaire oolithique *m.* || ARCHIT.
Grande ardoise *f.*
rag n. Farce *f.* (joke); chahut *m.* (noise); brimade
f. (on a student); *students' rag*, canular; monôme.
— v. intr. (1). Chahuter, faire du tapage.
— v. tr. Brimer (a fellow-student); chahuter (a
master). || Laver la tête à (to scold); taquiner, faire
enrager (to tease).
ragamuffin ['rægəmʌfin] n. Galopin, polisson,
garnement *m.* (ruffian); va-nu-pieds *m.; gamin des
rues *m.* (urchin).
rage [reidʒ] n. Rage, fureur *f.; to fly into a rage*,
entrer en fureur, sortir de ses gonds. || Ardeur *f.*
(of battle); fureur, violence *f.; déchaînement *m.* (of
the weather). || Passion, manie *f.* (passion); vogue
f.; to be all the rage, faire fureur; *he is all the rage*,
on se l'arrache.
— v. intr. Etre en fureur, tempêter (*against*, contre).
|| Divaguer, dérailler (to be mad). || FIG. Sévir
(epidemic, war); être démonté (sea); faire rage,
être déchaîné (wind).
ragged ['rægid] adj. Déchiqueté (cloud, rock);
raboteux, rocailleux (ground). || En lambeaux, en
loques (clothes); en guenilles, en haillons, dégue-
nillé, dépenaillé (person). || FIG. Qui manque d'en-
semble (chorus, team); inégal, imparfait (performance, work); haché, raboteux (style); rauque,
discordant (voice). || U. S. *On the ragged edge of*,
à l'extrême limite de, tout au bord de.
raggedly [-li] adv. En haillons, en loques (in rags).
|| FIG. Inégalement; *to sing raggedly*, manquer
d'ensemble vocal.
raggedness [-nis] n. Délabrement *m.* (of clothing);
aspect déguenillé *m.; guenilles *f. pl.* (of s.o.). ||
Inégalités, rugosités, anfractuosités *f. pl.* (of ground).
|| FIG. Manque (*m.*) d'ensemble (of a chorus, team);
inégalité *f.* (of style).
ragger ['rægə*] n. FAM. Chahuteur *m.*
raggle-taggle ['rægl-'tægl] n. Canaille, racaille,
populace *f.*
raging ['reidʒiŋ] n. Fureur *f.*
— adj. Furieux, en fureur, acharné (person); *in a
raging temper*, dans une colère bleue. || Furieux,
démonté (sea); déchaîné (wind). || Féroce (appe-
tite); brûlant (fever); fou (headache); dévorant
(hunger); ardent (thirst).
raglan ['ræglən] n., adj. Raglan *m.*
ragout [ræ'gu] s. CULIN. Ragoût *m.*
ragtag [-tæg] n. *The ragtag and bobtail*, quatre
pelés et un tondu.
ragtime ['rægtaim] n. U. S. MUS. Air syncopé *m.*
— adj. U. S. FAM. Syncopé, fougueux.
raid [reid] n. MILIT. Raid, coup (*m.*) de main. ||
AVIAT. Raid *m.* || JUR. Incursion, razzia *f.* (by ban-
dits); *police raid*, rafle (on a district); descente de
police (on a gambling-den).
— v. intr. MILIT., AVIAT. Faire un raid. || JUR.
Faire une razzia (or) une incursion (bandits);
faire une rafle (or) une descente (police).
— v. tr. MILIT. Faire une incursion dans (a coun-
try); razzier (a tribe); piller (a village). || AVIAT.
Bombarder. || JUR. Faire une descente (or) une
rafle dans.
raider [-ə*] n. Maraudeur, pillard *m.* || NAUT. Croi-
seur (*m.*) de course (cruiser); corsaire *m.* (priva-
teer); *surface raider*, corsaire de surface. || MILIT.
Commando *m.* || AVIAT. Avion ennemi *m.; « Raiders
Past » signal*, signal de fin d'alerte.
rail [reil] n. Balustrade *f.* (of a balcony); étrésillon
m. (brace, strut); parapet *m.* (of a bridge); ridelle
f. (of a cart); barreau *m.* (of a chair, fence, window); barre *f.* (hand-rail); garde-fou *m.* (on a high
building); rampe *f.* (stair-rail); accoudoir, appui

m. (of a window). ‖ Naut. Lisse *f.* (bulwark-rail); rambarde *f.; bastingages m. pl.* (hand-rail); *guard rail,* filière. ‖ Ch. de F. Chemin de fer *m.; voie ferrée f.* (method of transport); rail *m.* (track); *to run off the rails,* dérailler; *to send by rail,* envoyer par chemin de fer. ‖ Pl. Techn. Traverse, banc de traverse *f.* (of a door). ‖ Pl. Fin. Chemins (*m. pl.*) de fer (shares). ‖ U. S. Fam. *To sit on the rail,* se réserver. ‖ Fam. *To be off the rails,* être détraqué; *to run off the rails,* dérailler. ‖ **Rail-car,** n. Ch. de F. Autorail *m.; automotrice,* micheline *f.* ‖ **Rail-chair,** n. Techn. Coussinet de rail *m.* ‖ **Rail-gauge,** n. Techn. Gabarit d'écartement *m.* ‖ **Rail-head,** n. Ch. de F. Tête de ligne; Milit. Gare (*f.*) de ravitaillement; Techn. Champignon de rail *m.*
— v. tr. Ch. de F. Envoyer par chemin de fer (a parcel); poser des rails sur (a track). ‖ Archit. Munir d'une barre d'appui (or) d'un garde-fou. ‖ **To rail in,** enclore d'une barrière (or) d'une grille. ‖ **To rail off,** séparer par une barrière (or) une grille. ‖ **To rail round,** entourer d'une barrière (ou) d'une grille.

rail n. Zool. Râle *m.* (bird).

rail v. intr. *To rail at* (or) *against,* déblatérer contre, invectiver contre, s'en prendre à.

railer [-ə*] n. Dénigreur *s.* (detractor); déblatéreur *s.* (grouser).

railing ['reiliŋ] n. Clôture *f.; iron railing,* grille. ‖ Garde-fou *m.;* balustrade *f.* (of a balcony); parapet *m.* (of bridge); rampe *f.* (of staircase).

railing n. Injures, insultes, invectives *f. pl.*

railingly [-li] adv. En termes injurieux (insultingly); d'une façon railleuse (mockingly).

raillerie ['reiləri] n. Raillerie *f.*

railroad ['reilroud] n. U. S. Chemin de fer *m.* (see RAILWAY); *railroad pass,* carte de circulation.
— v. tr. U. S. Transporter par chemin de fer. ‖ Fam. Faire voter rapidement (a motion); persuader de force (s.o.) [*into,* de].

railroader [-ə*] n. U. S. Cheminot *m.*

railway ['reilwei] n. Ch. de F. Chemin de fer *m.; voie ferrée f.;* ligne (*f.*) de chemin de fer. ‖ U. S. Ligne *f.* (for light vehicles).
— adj. De chemin de fer (guide); ferroviaire (lines); par chemin de fer (transport); *railway carriage,* wagon *m.; railway crossing,* croisement de voies; passage à niveau (level-crossing); *railway engine,* locomotive; *railway porter,* facteur; *railway station,* gare; *railway system,* réseau de chemin de fer. ‖ **Railway-car,** n. U. S. Wagon *m.* ‖ **Railway-cutting,** n. Déblai *m.* ‖ **Railway-embankment,** n. Remblai.

railwayman [-mən] (pl. **railwaymen**) n. Employé des chemins de fer, cheminot *m.*

raiment ['reimənt] n. † Arroi *m.;* vêtements *m. pl.*

rain [rein] n. Pluie *f.; drizzling rain,* bruine; *in the rain,* à (or) sous la pluie; *it looks like rain,* on dirait qu'il va pleuvoir. ‖ Bot. *Golden rain,* cytise. ‖ Fig. Pluie *f.* (of bullets, of congratulations, of questions); flot *m.* (of tears). ‖ **Rain-chart,** n. Carte pluviométrique *f.* ‖ **Rain-cloud,** n. Nimbus *m.* ‖ **Rain-gauge,** n. Techn. Pluviomètre *m.* ‖ **Rain-shower,** n. Averse *f.* ‖ **Rain-water,** n. Eau de pluie *f.* ‖ **Rain-worm,** n. Zool. Ver (*m.*) de terre.
— v. impers. Pleuvoir; *it is raining,* il pleut; *to rain buckets, torrents,* pleuvoir à seaux, à torrents, tomber des cordes. ‖ Fig. Pleuvoir (bullets, presents). ‖ Loc. *It never rains but it pours,* un malheur n'arrive jamais seul.
— v. intr. Pleuvoir (blows); couler (tears).
— v. tr. *To rain blows on,* faire pleuvoir une grêle de coups sur.

rainbow [-bou] n. Arc-en-ciel *m.* ‖ **Rainbow-coloured,** adj. Irisé.

raincoat [-kout] n. Imperméable, manteau (*m.*) de pluie. (See WATERPROOF.)

raindrop [-drɔp] n. Goutte de pluie *f.*

rainfall [-fɔ:l] n. Chute de pluie; précipitation; averse *f.* (shower). ‖ Cote de pluviosité *f.; annual rainfall,* quantité de pluie annuelle.

raininess [-inis] n. Pluviosité *f.;* temps pluvieux *m.*

rainless [-lis] adj. Sec, sans pluie.

rainproof [-pru:f] adj., n. Imperméable *m.*
— v. tr. Imperméabiliser.

raintight [-tait] adj. See RAINPROOF.

rainwear [-wɛə*] n. Vêtements (*m. pl.*) de pluie.

rainy [-i] adj. Pluvieux (climate, weather); des pluies (season); *it is rainy,* le temps est à la pluie. ‖ Fig. *Rainy day,* période difficile; *to be provided for against a rainy day,* avoir gardé une poire pour la soif.

raise [rei:z] n. Relance *f.* (at cards). ‖ U. S. Fam. Augmentation *f.* (in wages).
— v. tr. Relever (shop-blind, window-blind); *to raise the window,* relever le châssis (in a house) [or] la glace (in a train). ‖ Lever, soulever (an object, a weight); *to raise one's glass to one's lips,* porter son verre à la bouche; *to raise one's hat to s.o.,* saluer qqn. ‖ Lever, relever (one's arm, eyes, head). ‖ Relever, remettre debout (to make stand up). ‖ Lever, élever, mettre debout, dresser (to erect). ‖ Elever, porter (to a dignity). ‖ Bâtir, construire, édifier (a building); élever (a monument); ériger (a statue). ‖ Remonter (to heighten); surélever (a building); rehausser (a piece of ground). ‖ Extraire (coal); remonter à la surface (sunken ship). ‖ Créer, occasionner (to cause); provoquer (a disturbance); soulever (a question); faire naître (a suspicion). ‖ Soulever, exciter (a crowd); élever, formuler (an objection, a protest); hausser (one's tone); élever (one's voice). ‖ Ranimer (s.o.'s hopes); *to raise s.o.'s spirits,* remonter le moral à qqn. ‖ Augmenter (to increase); rehausser, ajouter à (a reputation); élever (the temperature). ‖ Evoquer, faire apparaître (a ghost). ‖ Soulever, faire voler (a cloud of dust). ‖ Naut. Lever (the anchor); guinder (a mast); renflouer (a ship). ‖ Milit. Lever (an army, a blockade, a siege); promouvoir (an officer). ‖ Eccles. Ressusciter (*from,* d'entre). ‖ Jur. Lever (taxes). ‖ Med. Donner (blisters). ‖ Culin. Faire lever (bread). ‖ Agric. Elever, faire l'élevage de (livestock); produire, faire pousser, cultiver (vegetables). ‖ Mus. *To raise the pitch of,* monter. ‖ Arts. Relever (a colour). ‖ Fin. Elever, relever (charges, fees, prices); rassembler, réunir (funds); émettre, contracter (a loan); se procurer (money); *to raise money on,* emprunter sur. ‖ Techn. Garnir (cloth). ‖ Fam. *Fit to raise the dead,* capable de réveiller un mort; *to raise Cain* (or) *merry hell* (or) *a stink,* causer du grabuge (to cause ructions); faire un boucan de tous les diables (to make a din); *to raise the wind,* trouver l'argent. ‖ **To raise up,** Med. Lever, soulever (a patient); Eccles. Susciter (a prophet).

raisin ['reizṇ] n. Culin. Raisin sec *m.*

raising ['reiziŋ] n. Relèvement *m.* (in general). ‖ Elévation *f.* (of one's voice). ‖ Evocation *f.* (of ghosts). ‖ Milit., Jur. Levée *f.* ‖ Naut. Guindage *m.* ‖ Eccles. Résurrection *f.* ‖ Archit. Erection *f.* (action); surélévation *f.* (of a building); relèvement *m.* (of a wall). ‖ Agric. Elevage *m.* (of cattle); culture *f.* (of plants). ‖ Fin. Relèvement *m.;* augmentation *f.* ‖ Techn. Extraction *f.* (of coal). ‖ Fig. Rehaussement *m.*

raison d'être [rɛzɔ̃ 'dɛtr] n. Raison (*f.*) d'être.

raj [rɑ:dʒ] n. Gouvernement *m.; the British raj in India,* le gouvernement britannique en Inde.

rajah ['rɑ:dʒə] n. Rajah *m.*

rake [reik] n. Fourgon, crochet à feu *m.* ‖ Agric. Râteau *m.;* ratissoire *f.* ‖ Fam. Démêloir *m.* (comb). ‖ **Rake-off,** n. U. S. Fam. Ristourne *f.; to get a rake-off,* faire de la gratte.
— v. tr. Attiser (a fire). ‖ Gratter, racler (to score).

‖ Milit. Balayer (ground); prendre d'enfilade (troops). ‖ Agric. Ratisser (crops, leaves); râteler (hay). ‖ Fig. Fouiller, chercher dans (to search); embrasser du regard (visually); dominer (window). ‖ **To rake away,** enlever au râteau. ‖ **To rake in,** Fam. Ratisser; emmagasiner (money). ‖ **To rake out,** gratter, décendrer (a stove). ‖ **To rake over,** égratigner (a flower-bed); repasser (a path); U. S. Fam. *To rake over the coals,* enguirlander. ‖ **To rake up,** attiser, réveiller (an old quarrel); revenir sur (the past).
— v. intr. Agric. Ratisser. ‖ Fig. Fouiller, fureter (*in,* dans).

rake n. Naut. Inclinaison *f.* (of funnels); élancement *m.* (of the stem); quête *f.* (of the stern-post). ‖ Archit. Pente *f.* (of floor).
— v. tr. Naut. Incliner vers l'arrière.
— v. intr. Archit. Etre en pente. ‖ Naut. Etre incliné.

rake n. Débauché, viveur, coureur *m.* ‖ Fam. Dépenaillé *m.*

raking [-iŋ] n. Agric. Ratissage *m.* ‖ Fig. Fouille *f.* ‖ Pop. *A raking over the coals,* une bonne engueulade.
— adj. Milit. D'enfilade (fire).

rakish [-iʃ] adj. Naut. Elancé (bow); aux formes élancées (ship).

rakish adj. Cavalier, cascadeur, désinvolte, effronté (air); débauché, dissolu (person).

rakishness [-iʃnis] n. Débauche *f.*; libertinage *m.* ‖ Effronterie *f.* (jauntiness).

râle [rɑːl] n. Med. Râle *m.*

rally ['ræli] n. Réunion *f.*; rally *m.* (mass-meeting); ralliement *m.* (reassembly); *youth rally,* réunion de la jeunesse. ‖ Med., Sports. Reprise *f.*; passe (*f.*) de jeu (in tennis). ‖ Comm. Reprise *f.* (of prices). ‖ Autom. Rallye *m.*
— v. tr. (2). Rassembler, réunir (supporters). ‖ Ranimer, rappeler (to revive); *to rally one's spirits,* reprendre courage.
— v. intr. Se rassembler, se réunir (supporters). ‖ Se grouper (round, autour de). ‖ Se ranimer, se réveiller. (courage).

rally v. tr. Railler; se moquer·(*on,* de).

rallying [-iŋ] n. Ralliement *m.*

rallying adj. Railleur (bantering).

rallyingly [-iŋli] adv. En raillant, d'un ton railleur.

ram [ræm] n. Zool., Astron., Milit. Bélier *m.* ‖ Naut. Eperon *m.* (of a ship); navire à éperon *m.* (ship). ‖ Techn. Bélier *m.* (hydraulic); pilon, mouton *m.* (of a steam-hammer); piston *m.* (of a pump); bourre d'argile *f.* (tamping); chariot (*m.*) porte-outils (for tools). ‖ Pop. Coureur, tombeur *m.* (Don Juan). ‖ **Ram-jet,** n. Aviat. Statoréacteur *m.* ‖ **Ram-pump,** n. Techn. Pompe foulante *f.*
— v. tr. (1). Cogner, heurter violemment; *to ram one's head against a wall,* se cogner la tête contre un mur. ‖ Aviat., Naut. Eperonner. ‖ Milit. Tasser (a cartridge); refouler (a shell). ‖ Autom. Tamponner. Techn. Bourrer (to block up); battre, damer, tasser, pilonner (to force down); enfoncer (with a pile-driver). ‖ Fig. Faire entrer de force (*in, into,* dans); *to ram home,* pousser à fond (an argument). ‖ Fam. Fourrer (*into,* dans) [clothes]. ‖ **To ram down,** tasser (earth); enfoncer (to drive in, to push on). ‖ **To ram in,** enfoncer. ‖ **To ram up,** boucher (a hole).

ramadan [ræmə'dæn] n. Eccles. Ramadan *m.*

ramble ['ræmbl̩] n. Flânerie, promenade *f.*; *to go for a ramble,* faire une balade (fam.). ‖ Propos incohérents *m. pl.*
— v. intr. Errer de-ci de-là, vagabonder, se promener. ‖ Fig. Divaguer; radoter (old man); *to ramble off into digressions,* se lancer dans des digressions.

rambler [-ə*] n. Promeneur *s.* (walker). ‖ Divaga-

teur *m.*; divagatrice *f.* ‖ Radoteur *s.* (old person). ‖ Agric. Rosier grimpant, rambler *m.*

rambling [-iŋ] adj. A bâtons rompus (conversation); errant (existence); décousu, incohérent (speech); vagabond (thoughts); *rambling talk,* divagations. ‖ Agric. Grimpant, rampant (plant). ‖ Archit. Bâti sans plan.
— n. Vagabondages *m. pl.* ‖ Fig. Divagations *f. pl.*; radotages *m. pl.*

rambunctious [ræm'bʌŋkʃəs] adj. U. S. Turbulent, exubérant, fougueux.

ramekin, ramequin ['ræməkin] n. Culin. Ramequin *m.*

ramification [,ræmifi'keiʃən] n. Ramification *f.*

ramify ['ræmifai] v. intr. (2). Se ramifier.
— v. tr. Ramifier.

rammer ['ræmə*] n. Techn. Pilon, mouton *m.* (for piles); demoiselle, hie *f.* (paviour's). ‖ Milit. Refouloir *m.*

rammish ['ræmiʃ] adj. Puant; à odeur de bouc.

ramose [ræ'mous] adj. Bot. Rameux.

ramp [ræmp] n. Plan incliné, talus *m.*; pente, rampe *f.* ‖ Autom. Pont élévateur *m.* ‖ Ch. de f., Archit. Rampe *f.* ‖ Fam. Majoration (*f.*) injustifiée des prix (price-increase); coup monté *m.* (stunt); escroquerie *f.* (swindle).
— v. intr. Se dresser menaçant sur ses pattes de derrière (lion). ‖ Archit. Ramper. ‖ Fig. Enrager, tempêter; fulminer, râler (fam.).
— v. tr. Archit. Construire en rampe (or) pente.

rampage [ræm'peidʒ] v. intr. Se démener comme un fou (to rush about); tempêter (to storm).
— n. Fam. Exaspération, rage *f.*; *on the rampage,* déchaîné, dans une colère bleue.

rampageous [-əs] adj. Violent, furieux, déchaîné. ‖ Fig. Criard, voyant (colour).

rampancy ['ræmpənsi] n. Violence *f.* ‖ Exubérance *f.*; déchaînement *m.*

rampant [-ənt] adj. Agressif (fierce); violent, déchaîné, effréné (unrestrained); *to be rampant,* sévir (plague); s'étaler (vice). ‖ Vigoureux, exubérant, luxuriant (flourishing); vigoureux, fougueux (high-spirited). ‖ Archit., Blas. Rampant.

rampart ['ræmpɑːt] n. Archit. Rempart *m.*

ramrod ['ræmrɔd] n. Milit. Ecouvillon *m.* (of a gun); baguette *f.* (of a rifle). ‖ Loc. *Straight as a ramrod,* droit comme un i.

ramshackle ['ræmʃækl̩] adj. Croulant, ruineux, délabré; *ramshackle old car,* vieille guimbarde, vieux clou, casserole (fam.).

ran [ræn] pret. See Run.)

ranch [rɑːnʃ, U. S. ræntʃ] n. U. S. Ranch *m.*
— v. intr. U. S. Diriger (or) exploiter un ranch.

rancher [-ə*] n. U. S. Propriétaire de ranch *m.* (owner); cowboy *m.* (employee).

rancid ['rænsid] adj. Rance; *to go rancid,* rancir.

rancidity [ræn'siditi], **rancidness** ['rænsidnis] n. Rancissure *f.*; rance *m.*

rancorous ['ræŋkərəs] adj. Rancunier, rancuneux, plein de rancœur (or) d'aigreur.

rancour [-ə*] n. Rancune, rancœur *f.*; ressentiment *m.*

rand [rænd] n. Techn. Trépointe (*f.*) du talon. ‖ Geogr. Rand *m.*

random ['rændəm] adj. Fait au hasard, fortuit (choice); *random shot,* balle perdue.
— n. *At random,* à l'aveuglette (blindly); au hasard, sans but précis (haphazardly); *to talk at random,* parler à tort et à travers.

randy ['rændi] adj. Remuant (boisterous); grossier (coarse). ‖ Allumé (eye); lascif, luxurieux (person); émoustillé, porté sur la bagatelle (fam.).

ranee ['rɑːniː] n. Maharani *f.*

rang ['ræŋ] pret. See Ring.

range [reindʒ] n. Milit., Naut. Portée *f.* (of a fire-arm); champ de tir *m.* (for rifles); polygone *m.* (for artillery); *to correct the range,* rectifier le tir; *high.*

low range, grande, petite hausse ; *at long range*, à longue portée. ‖ NAUT. Bitture (of cable). ‖ ARCHIT. Rangée *f.* (of houses). ‖ GEOGR. Région, zone, superficie *f.* (area of land) ; chaîne *f.* (of mountains). ‖ MATH. Direction *f.* ; alignement *m.* ‖ MUS. Etendue *f.* ; diapason *m.* ‖ CULIN. Fourneau à gaz *m.* (gas-range) ; fourneau (*m.*) de cuisine (kitchenrange). ‖ U. S. AGRIC. Grand pâturage *m.* ‖ FIG. Portée *f.* (scope) ; *within the range of*, à la portée de. ‖ FIG. Gamme *f.* (of colours) ; série *f.* (of patterns) ; écart *m.* (of speeds) ; choix *m.* (of subjects). ‖ FIG. Champ (*m.*) d'activité ; rayon (*m.*) d'action ; sphère *f.* (of activity) ; cercle *m.* (of ideas) ; étendue *f.* (of knowledge) ; champ *m.* (of studies) ; *range of vision*, champ visuel. ‖ FIG. Champ libre *m.* ; *to give free range to*, donner libre essor à (one's imagination) ; *the whole range*, toute la lyre (or) gamme. ‖ **Range-finder**, n. MILIT. Télémètre *m.* ‖ **Range-pole**, n. ARCHIT. Jalon *m.* ‖ **Range-table**, n. MILIT. Table (*f.*) de tir.

— v. intr. Disposer en ligne, ranger, aligner (to set in a row). ‖ Ranger ; *to range oneself on the side of*, se ranger du côté de. ‖ Ranger, mettre en ordre (or) place (to arrange) ; ranger, classer (to classify). ‖ Parcourir (to rove over). ‖ NAUT. Elonger (the cable) ; longer (the coast).

— v. intr. Se ranger, se placer ; être classé (to be classed) ; s'aligner (to be in a line) ; *to range along*, longer. ‖ S'étendre ; *to range from 26 to 32*, aller (or) varier de 26 à 32. ‖ Errer, vagabonder (to rove) ; circuler librement ; *to range over*, parcourir (country). ‖ MILIT. *To range over*, porter à, avoir une portée de.

ranger [-ə*] n. † Rôdeur, vagabond *m.* ‖ JUR. Garde forestier ; conservateur (*m.*) des forêts. ‖ ZOOL. Limier *m.* (dog). ‖ Pl. U. S. Gendarmerie montée *f.*

rank [ræŋk] n. Rang *m.* ; classe, condition *f.* (social rank) ; *person of rank*, personne de haut rang ; *people of all ranks*, gens de toutes conditions. ‖ Rang *m.* ; place *f.* ; *of the very first rank*, de tout premier plan. ‖ MILIT. Rang ; grade *m.* ; *rank and file*, hommes de troupe ; *to rise from the ranks*, sortir du rang. ‖ AUTOM. Stationnement *m.* (for taxis) ; station *f.* (of taxis) ; *at the head of the rank*, en tête de file. ‖ MUS. Rang *m.* (of organpipes). ‖ FIG. *The rank and file*, la masse, le peuple, le tout venant.

— v. tr. Ranger, placer, classer ; *to rank among the great*, compter parmi les grands. ‖ MILIT. Ranger (soldiers). ‖ U. S. Avoir le pas sur (to outrank).
— v. intr. Se ranger, prendre rang, se classer ; *to rank above, below*, être supérieur, inférieur à ; *to rank with*, aller de pair avec. ‖ **To rank off**, MILIT. Partir en marche.

rank adj. Absolu, complet (deceit) ; pur (disgrace) ; flagrant, criant (injustice) ; grossier (lie) ; fieffé (pedant) ; vrai (poison). ‖ Grossier, répugnant, immonde, ignoble (foul). ‖ Fétide (fetid) ; rance (rancid) ; fort (strong) ; *to smell rank*, sentir fort, ‖ AGRIC. Dru, touffu, vigoureux (grass) ; plantureux, trop fort (or) riche (land) ; luxuriant, exubérant (vegetation).

ranker [-ə*] n. MILIT. Officier sorti du rang *m.* (officer) ; simple soldat *m.* (soldier).

rankle ['ræŋkl] v. intr. † MED. S'enflammer. ‖ FIG. S'envenimer ; rester sur le cœur ; laisser une rancœur ; *it rankled with him*, il en était ulcéré.

rankly ['ræŋkli] adv. Vigoureusement, surabondamment (prolifically). ‖ Avec une odeur fétide (smelly). ‖ Grossièrement (grossly).

rankness [-nis] n. Vigueur, exubérance, luxuriance *f.* (of vegetation). ‖ Odeur fétide *f.* (smell) ; rancidité *f.* (taste). ‖ Grossièreté *f.* (grossness).

ransack ['rænsæk] v. tr. Fouiller (to search thoroughly). ‖ Piller, saccager, mettre à sac (to pillage).

ransom ['rænsəm] n. Rançon *f.* ; *to hold to ransom*, rançonner.
— v. tr. Rançonner (to demand ransom for) ; racheter, payer rançon pour (to pay ransom for).

ransoming [-iŋ] n. Rançonnement *m.* (demanding). ‖ Rachat *m.* (paying).

rant [rænt] n. Rodomontade *f.* (bombast). ‖ Divagation *f.* (declamation).
— v. intr. Emboucher la trompette (to declaim) ; extravaguer, divaguer (to rave) ; tempêter, tonitruer (to storm).
— v. tr. Déclamer avec extravagance.

rantam ['ræntæm] n. FAM. *To go on the rantam*, faire la noce.

ranter ['ræntə*] n. Déclamateur forcené, énergumène *m.*

ranunculus [rə'nʌŋkjuləs] n. BOT. Renoncule *f.*

rap [ræp] n. Tape *f.* ; petit coup sec *m.* ; *there was a rap at the door*, on frappa à la porte. ‖ FIG. *To give s.o. a rap on the knuckles*, donner sur les doigts à qqn, remettre qqn à sa place. ‖ FAM. *To take the rap*, ramasser la tape.
— v. intr. Frapper, cogner, donner un coup sec.
— v. tr. Frapper, donner un coup sec à ; *to rap the door, the table*, frapper à la porte, sur la table. ‖ **To rap out**, débiter vite ; lâcher (an oath) ; lancer (a retort).

rap n. † Pièce fausse *f.* ‖ LOC. *Not to be worth a rap*, ne pas valoir tripette ; *not to care a rap*, s'en ficher éperdument, s'en balancer.

rapacious [rə'peiʃəs] adj. Rapace.

rapaciously [-li] adv. Avec rapacité.

rapaciousness [-nis], **rapacity** [rə'pæsiti] n. Rapacité *f.*

rape [reip] n. † Rapt ; enlèvement *m.* ‖ JUR. Viol *m.*
— v. tr. † Enlever. ‖ JUR. Violer.

rape n. AGRIC. Colza *m.* (for oil) ; navette *f.* (for sheep). ‖ **Rape-oil**, n. Huile (*f.*) de colza (or) de navette. ‖ **Rape-seed**, n. Graine (*f.*) de colza.

rape n. Marc de raisin *m.* (grape pulp). ‖ Râpé *m.* (wine).

rapid ['ræpid] n. GEOGR. Rapide *m.*
— adj. Rapid ; prompt. ‖ Raide, rapide (slope). ‖ MILIT. Accéléré (fire). ‖ **Rapid-fire**, adj. MILIT. À tir rapide.

rapidity [rə'piditi] n. Rapidité *f.*

rapier ['reipiə*] n. Rapière *f.*

rapine ['ræpain] n. Rapine *f.*

rapist ['reipist] n. JUR. Violeur *s.*, auteur d'un viol *m.*

rappee [ræ'pi:] n. Tabac râpé *m.*

rapport [ræ'pɔ:*] n. Rapport ; *in rapport with*, en rapport avec (relation) ; en harmonie avec (sympathy).

rapporteur [ræpɔ:'tə:*] n. Rapporteur.

rapprochement [raprɔʃ'mɑ̃] n. Rapprochement *m.* (between states).

rapscallion [ræp'skæljən] n. Vaurien *s.*

rapt [ræpt] adj. Profond (attention) ; ravi, enchanté, transporté, extasié (look, person) ; absorbé (in meditation, study, thought).

raptorial [ræp'tɔ:riəl] adj. ZOOL. De proie.

rapture [-ʃə*] n. Ravissement, transport, enchantement *m.* ; extase, griserie *f.* (see ECSTASY) ; *to go into raptures over*, s'extasier sur.

raptured [-ʃəd] adj. Ravi, transporté.

rapturous [-ʃərəs] adj. Frénétique, enthousiaste (applause) ; d'extase, de ravissement (cries) ; ravi, transporté, extasié (people).

rare [rɛə*] adj. Rare (atmosphere). ‖ Exceptionnel (extraordinary) ; rare, précieux (precious) ; peu commun (seldom found) ; *to grow rare*, se raréfier. ‖ CHIM. Rare (earths). ‖ FAM. Impayable (amusing) ; fameux (excellent) ; pas banal (unusual).

rare adj. U. S. CULIN. Saignant.

rarebit ['rɛəbit] n. CULIN. *Welsh rarebit*, toast au fromage.

rarefaction [,rɛəri'fæk,ʃən] n. Raréfaction *f.*

rarefiable ['rɛərifaiəbl̩] adj. Raréfiable

rarefy [-fai] v. tr. (2). Raréfier. ‖ FIG. Affiner. — v. intr. Se raréfier.

rarely ['rɛəli] adv. Rarement. ‖ FAM. Fameusement, formidablement.

rareness [-nis] n. Rareté *f.*

raring ['rɛəriŋ] adj. FAM. Piaffant d'impatience; *raring to go*, brûlant d'envie de partir.

rarity ['rɛəriti] n. Rareté *f.* ‖ Objet rare *m.* (object).

rascal ['rɑ:skəl] n. Coquin, fripon, polisson *s.*; garnement *m.*

rascaldom [-dəm] n. Coquinerie *f.* (trick). ‖ Pègre *f.*; milieu *m.* (rabble).

rascally [-i] adj. Fripon (person); vilain, de coquin (trick); *my rascally son*, mon coquin de fils.

rash [ræʃ] n. MED. Eruption *f.*; taches rouges *f.* pl. (in measles); boutons *m.* pl. (spots).

rash adj. Inconsidéré, irréfléchi (action); impétueux, téméraire (person); imprudent (promise, words).

rasher [-ə*] n. CULIN. Tranche (*f.*) de lard.

rashly [-li] adv. Imprudemment, inconsidérément, sans réflexion (to act); à la légère (to speak).

rashness [-nis] n. Imprudence, témérité, impétuosité; précipitation imprudente *f.*

rasp [rɑ:sp] n. Grincement *m.* (noise). ‖ TECHN. Râpe *f.*
— v. tr. TECHN. Râper (wood). ‖ CULIN. Chapeler (bread). ‖ FIG. Irriter; racler, écorcher (s.o.'s ears). ‖ **To rasp away**, enlever à la râpe; CULIN. Chapeler. ‖ **To rasp out**, lâcher d'une voix rauque (an oath, order).
— v. intr. Crisser, grincer (sound). ‖ Parler d'une voix âpre.

raspberry ['rɑ:zbəri] n. BOT. Framboise *f.*; *raspberry bush* (or) *cane*, framboisier. ‖ FAM. Rebuffade *f.*; *to get a raspberry from*, se faire rabrouer par.

rasping ['rɑ:spiŋ] n. Râpage *m.* (act). ‖ Crissement, grincement *m.* (sound). ‖ Pl. Râpure *f.* (gratings). ‖ Pl. CULIN. Chapelure *f.*
— adj. Qui râpe (tool). ‖ Grinçant (sound); âpre, rauque (voice).

raster ['ræstə*] n. TECHN. Trame *f.* (on T. V. screen).

rat [raet] n. ZOOL. Rat *s.*; *extermination of rats*, dératisation. ‖ Jaune *m.* (worker). ‖ Renégat *s.* (renegade). ‖ U. S. POP. Faux frère *m.* (betrayer); crépon *m.* (hair pad). ‖ FAM. Lâcheur *s.* (quitter). ‖ LOC. *Like a drowned rat*, trempé comme une soupe; *to smell a rat*, soupçonner quelque anguille sous roche, subodorer quelque sale histoire. ‖ **Rat-catcher**, n. Chasseur (*m.*) de rats. ‖ **Rat-catching**, n. Chasse (*f.*) aux rats. ‖ **Rat-poison**, n. Mort-aux-rats *f.* ‖ **Rat race**, n. FIG. Ronde infernale *f.* (of life); foire d'empoigne *f.* (of business). ‖ **Rat's-tail**, n. TECHN. Queue-de-rat *f.* (file). ‖ **Rat-trap**, n. Ratière *f.*; U. S. FIG. Souricière *f.*
— interj. Pl. Zut!; sans blague! (surprised disbelief).
— v. intr. Attraper des rats, dératiser. ‖ Faire le jaune (workman). ‖ FAM. Quitter le navire (to let one's side down); tourner casaque (to turn coat); *to rat on a pal*, donner un copain.

ratable ['reitəbl̩] adj. See RATEABLE.

ratafia [rætə'fiə] n. Ratafia *m.*

ratatouille [rætə'twi:] n. CULIN. Ratatouille *f.*

ratch [rætʃ] n. Roue (*f.*) à cliquet.
— v. tr. TECHN. Encliqueter. ‖ Denter.

ratchet [-it] n. TECHN. Encliquetage *m.* (act); cliquet *m.* (catch). ‖ **Ratchet-wheel**, n. TECHN. Roue (*f.*) à cliquet.

rate [reit] n. Régime, taux *m.* (of consumption); *at the rate of 500 litres per day*, à raison de 500 litres par jour; *rate of flow*, débit moyen (of electricity,

water). ‖ Catégorie, classe *f.*; ordre *m.*; *first rate*, de premier ordre. ‖ Allure, vitesse, cadence *f.*; train *m.* (speed); *at a terrific rate*, à une allure vertigineuse, d'un train d'enfer. ‖ MED. Fréquence *f.* (of the pulse). ‖ FIN. Proportion *f.*; pourcentage *m.* (ratio); prix *m.* (cost); taux *m.* (of discount, interest); cours *m.* (of exchange); prime *f.* (of insurance); taux, tarif *m.* (of salaries); *basic salary rate*, salaire de base; *rate of living*, train de vie. ‖ Pl. FIN. Taxes municipales, contributions *f.* pl.; impôts, *m.* pl. ‖ LOC. *At any rate*, en tout cas, de toute façon; *at that rate*, à ce compte-là, dans ce cas. ‖ **Rate-aided**, adj. Subventionné par la commune. ‖ **Rate-collector**, n. Receveur municipal *m.* ‖ **Rate-office**, n. Recette municipale *f.*
— v. intr. Etre classé (*as*, comme).
— v. tr. Estimer, apprécier, évaluer (to estimate). ‖ Considérer (or) regarder comme; *to rate among one's friends*, compter au nombre de ses amis. ‖ AUTOM., NAUT. Classer. ‖ FIN. Taxer; *what is the house rated at?*, quel est le loyer imposable de la maison? ‖ U. S. Mériter (to deserve).

rate v. tr. Tancer (*for doing*, pour avoir fait); passer un savon à, engueulander (fam.).

rateable [-əbl̩] adj. Evaluable. ‖ FIN. Imposable.

ratepayer [-peiə*] n. Contribuable *s.* (See TAXPAYER.)

rather ['rɑ:ðə*] adv. Plutôt, plus exactement; *or rather*, ou plutôt, ou pour mieux dire. ‖ Plutôt, de préférence; *I'd much rather, I would rather stay*, je préférerais de beaucoup, j'aimerais mieux rester; *I would rather not*, je n'y tiens pas. ‖ Plutôt, passablement; assez (fairly); légèrement (slightly); quelque peu (somewhat); *rather better*, un peu mieux; *to look rather silly*, avoir l'air plutôt bête. ‖ FAM. *Do you know him? Rather!*, le connaissez-vous? Plutôt! (or) je vous crois!
— interj. FAM. En effet!, un peu!, bien sûr!

ratification [rætifi'keiʃən] n. Ratification *f.*

ratify ['rætifai] v. tr. (2). Ratifier.

rating ['reitiŋ] n. Estimation, évaluation *f.* ‖ U. S. Classement *m.* (of a pupil). ‖ AUTOM. Classement *m.* (of a boat); spécialité, classe *f.* (of a man); matelot *m.* (sailor). ‖ SPORTS. Classe, catégorie *f.* ‖ JUR. Cote, répartition *f.* ‖ ELECTR. Conditions normales de fonctionnement.

rating n. FAM. Engueulade *f.*

ratio ['reiʃiou] n. Proportion, raison *f.*; rapport *m.*; *in direct, indirect ratio to*, en raison directe, inverse de.

ratiocinate [,ræti'ɔsineit] v. intr. Raisonner.

ratiocination [,rætiɔsi'neiʃən] n. Raisonnement *m.*

ration ['ræʃən] n. Ration *f.*; *iron rations*, réserve de vivres; *off the ration*, en vente libre; *on the ration*, rationné. ‖ **Ration-book**, n. Carte (*f.*) d'alimentation (or) de ravitaillement; *clothing ration-book*, carte d'habillement (or) de textile; *ration-book holder*, rationnaire.
— v. tr. Rationner (food); distribuer des rations à (people).

rational [-l] adj. Rationnel, fondé sur (or) conforme à la raison. ‖ Raisonnable, sensé (argument, person); raisonné (explanation); logique (solution); rationaliste (tendencies). ‖ MATH. Rationnel. ‖ FAM. Pratique.

rationale [ræʃio'nɑ:li] n. Exposé raisonné *m.* (account); raison d'être, raison fondamentale *f.* (principle).

rationalism ['ræʃnəlizm] n. Rationalisme *m.*

rationalist [-ist] adj., n. Rationaliste *s.*

rationalistic [,ræʃnə'listik] adj. Rationaliste.

rationality [,ræʃə'næliti] n. Rationalité *f.*

rationalization [,ræʃnəlai'zeiʃən] n. Rationalisation *f.*

rationalize ['ræʃnəlaiz] v. tr. Rationaliser. ‖ MATH. Rendre rationnelle.

rationally [-əli] adv. Rationnellement; raisonnablement; logiquement.

rationing [-iŋ] n. Rationnement m.; *rationing by the purse*, rationnement par hausse de prix.

rattan [ræ'tæn] n. Rotin m.

rat-tat ['ræt'tæt] n. Toc-toc m. (on the door); ran-tan-plan m. (on the drum).

ratten ['rætn] v. tr. Saboter le matériel de.

ratter ['rætə*] n. ZOOL. Ratier m. (dog). ‖ FAM. Lâcheur m.

rattle ['rætl̩] n. Hochet m. (child's); crécelle f. (football fan's). ‖ Bruit (m.) de ferraille (of a bicycle); bruit m. (of a car); cliquetis (of chains); claquement m. (of a door); grésillement m. (of hail); crachotis m. (of a loud-speaker); crépitement m. (of rifle-fire); tapotis m. (of a typewriter). ‖ MED. Râle m. ‖ ZOOL. Sonnette f. (of a rattle-snake). ‖ FAM. Caquetage m. (chatter); tapette f.; moulin (m.) à paroles (chatterbox); vacarme, potin, boucan m. (shindy). ‖ **Rattle-brained** (or **-pated**, adj. FAM. Etourdi, écervelé.
— v. intr. Ferrailler (bicycle); cliqueter (machinery); crépiter (rifle-fire); trembler (windows); *to rattle at the door*, cogner à (or) secouer la porte. ‖ MED. Râler. ‖ **To rattle along**, rouler avec fracas. ‖ **To rattle away**, partir avec fracas (coach); FAM. Dégoiser (to talk). ‖ **To rattle down**, dégringoler avec fracas. ‖ **To rattle off**, partir avec fracas. ‖ **To rattle on**, continuer à rouler avec fracas (train); FAM. Dégoiser (to talk).
— v. tr. Faire résonner (or) s'entrechoquer; faire claquer (castanets); agiter (dice); faire cliqueter (keys); FAM. Ebranler, affoler (s.o.). ‖ **To rattle off**, jouer au grand galop (a piece of music); expédier, torcher (a piece of work); débiter comme un moulin (a speech). ‖ **To rattle up**, NAUT. Lever vivement (the anchor).

rattler [-ə*] n. FAM. Type formidable m. (person); chose épatante f. (thing). ‖ U. S. ZOOL. Serpent (m.) à sonnettes. ‖ U. S. FAM. Tacot m. (car).

rattlesnake [-sneik] n. ZOOL. Serpent (m.) à sonnettes; crotale m.

rattletrap [-træp] n. AUTOM. Tacot, tapecul m.; vieille bagnole (or) guimbarde f. (See CROCK.) ‖ Pl. FAM. Vieilleries f. pl. ‖ POP. Gueuloir m.; gueule f.

rattling [-iŋ] adj. Résonnant, crépitant. ‖ Rapide, vif (speed). ‖ FAM. Epatant, au poil, du tonnerre.

ratty ['ræti] adj. Infesté de rats (place); de rat (smell). ‖ FAM. Grincheux, en rogne (angry). ‖ U. S. POP. Délabré, moche (dilapidated).

raucous ['rɔːkəs] adj. Rauque.

raucousness [-nis] n. Raucité f.

ravage ['rævidʒ] n. Ravage m.; dévastation f.; *ravages of time*, outrage des ans, injure du temps.
— v. intr., tr. Ravager.

ravaging [-iŋ] adj. Ravageur.

rave [reːiv] v. intr. Etre en délire, délirer, divaguer, déraisonner (person); être déchaîné (wind). ‖ S'emporter, tempêter, fulminer, pester (at, contre). ‖ Etre fou, raffoler (about, de); s'extasier (about, sur); s'enthousiasmer (about, de, pour).
— n. FAM. U. S. Eloge enthousiaste m.; *rave review*, compte rendu dithyrambique.

ravel ['rævl̩] v. intr. S'embrouiller, s'enchevêtrer. ‖ **To ravel out**, s'effilocher.
— v. tr. Emmêler, embrouiller, enchevêtrer. ‖ **To ravel out**, effilocher (material); démêler (threads); FIG. Débrouiller (a difficulty).
— n. Emmêlement m. ‖ Effilochure f.

ravelin ['rævlin] n. MILIT. Demi-lune f.

ravelling ['rævliŋ] n. Effilochage m. (action); effilochure f. (product).

raven ['reivn̩] n. ZOOL. Corbeau m.
— adj. Noir comme un corbeau.

raven ['rævn̩] v. tr. Manger voracement, dévorer.
— v. intr. Rôder en quête d'une proie (animal);

to raven for, être affamé de (to be hungry for); chercher avec voracité (to hunt for). ‖ Vivre de rapine (person).

ravenous [-əs] adj. Vorace, féroce (appetite); dévorant (hunger); affamé (person); *to be ravenous*, avoir l'estomac dans les talons. ‖ † Rapace.

ravenously [-əsli] adv. Voracement; *to be ravenously hungry*, avoir une faim de loup.

ravenousness [-əsnis] n. Voracité f. ‖ Appétit dévorant m.

ravine [rə'viːn] n. GEOL. Ravine f.

ravined [-d] adj. GEOL. Raviné.

raving ['reiviŋ] n. Délire m.; divagation f.
— adj. Délirant; *raving mad*, fou furieux.

ravioli [rævi'ouli] n. pl. CULIN. Ravioli m. pl.

ravish ['ræviʃ] v. tr. Enlever (s.o.); ravir, emporter (s.o., sth.); violer (a woman). ‖ Ravir, enchanter, transporter. (See ENRAPTURE.)

ravisher [-ə*] n. Ravisseur s.

ravishing [-iŋ] adj. Ravissant.

ravishingly [-iŋli] adv. A ravir, de façon ravissante.

ravishment [-mənt] n. Enlèvement, rapt m. (carrying away); viol m. (rape). ‖ FIG. Ravissement m.

raw [rɔː] adj. Pur (alcohol); cru (hide); brut (metal); grège (silk); *raw materials*, matières premières. ‖ CULIN. Cru (food). ‖ MILIT. Non aguerri (troops). ‖ MED. Sensible, à fleur de peau (nerves); à vif (wound). ‖ ARTS. Cru (colours). ‖ FIG. Vif (air); froid et humide (weather). ‖ FIG. Novice, inexpérimenté (inexperienced); mal dégrossi, inculte (uncouth). ‖ FAM. Cru (story); *it's a raw deal*, il y a de l'abus, c'est dur à avaler; *to give s.o. a raw deal*, en faire voir de dures à qqn; *raw spirits*, tord-boyaux.
— n. Point sensible m. ‖ FIG. *To touch on the raw*, piquer au vif. ‖ U. S. LOC. *In the raw*, brut, fruste; nu.

rawboned [-bound] adj. Décharné (man); efflanqué (horse).

rawhide [-haid] adj. De cuir vert (whip).

rawness [-nis] n. Crudité f. (of fruit). ‖ Froid humide m. (weather). ‖ FIG. Inexpérience f.

ray [rei] n. PHYS. Radiation f.; rayon m. ‖ MATH., BOT., ZOOL. Rayon m. ‖ FIG. Rayon m.; lueur f. (of hope).

ray n. ZOOL. Raie f.; *electric ray*, torpille f.

rayon ['reiən] n. COMM. Rayonne, soie artificielle f.

raze [reiz] v. tr. Raser, démolir (to demolish); rayer, effacer (to erase); érafler (to graze).

razor [-ə*] n. Rasoir m. ‖ **Razor-backed**, adj. En dos d'âne (hill). ‖ **Razor-bill**, n. ZOOL. Manchot m. ‖ **Razor-blade**, n. Lame (f.) de rasoir. ‖ **Razor-edge**, adj. En lame de couteau; n. Fil de rasoir m.; FIG. *On the razor-edge*, sur la corde raide. ‖ **Razor-fish** (or) **-shell**, n. ZOOL. Couteau m. ‖ **Razor-strop**, n. Cuir à rasoir m.

razz [ræz] v. tr. U. S. FAM. Mettre en boîte.

razzia ['ræziə] n. Razzia f.

razzle ['ræzl̩] n. FAM. Bombe, bombance, noce f. (See SPREE.); *on the razzle*, en goguette. ‖ **Razzle-dazzle**, n. FAM. Bombe f.; U. S. FAM. Clinquant m.

Rd. Written abbr. for *road*, route, rue.

re [riː] prep. COMM. Concernant, touchant, au sujet de, à propos de.

re pref. Re-, ré-, r-. ‖ **Re-act**, v. tr. THEATR. Rejouer (a play). ‖ **Re-dress**, v. tr. Rhabiller (s.o.); THEATR. Changer les costumes de (a play); TECHN. Réapprêter (skins); ravaler (a wall). ‖ **Re-echo**, v. intr. Résonner, retentir; v. tr. Répéter, renvoyer en écho. ‖ **Re-edify**, v. tr. Réédifier. ‖ **Re-edit**, v. tr. Rééditer. ‖ **Re-edition**, n. Réédition f. ‖ **Re-educate**, v. tr. MED. Rééduquer; mal dégrossi, inculte. ‖ **Re-education**, n. Rééducation f. ‖ **Re-elect**, v. tr. Réélire. ‖ **Re-election**, n. Réélection f. ‖ **Re-eligible**, adj. Rééligible. ‖

reasoning [-iŋ] adj. Doué de raison.
— n. Raisonnement *m.;* dialectique *f.* ‖ Discussion *f.*
reasonless [-lis] adj. Dénué de raison.
reassemble ['riə'sembḷ] v. tr. Rassembler. ‖ TECHN. Remonter.
— v. intr. Se rassembler.
reassert ['ri:ə'sə:t] v. tr. Réaffirmer.
reassume ['ri:ə'sju:m] v. tr. Reprendre ; réassumer (responsibility).
reassure [,riə'ʃuə*] v. tr. Rassurer, tranquilliser. ‖ FIN. Réassurer.
reave [ri:v] v. intr. Commettre des ravages.
— v. tr. Ravager (to plunder). ‖ Arracher (to tear away).
— N. B. Noter le pret. et le p.p. poétiques *reft.*
rebate ['ri:beit] n. COMM. Rabais, escompte *m.;* réduction *f.*
rebate v. tr. Diminuer, rabattre. ‖ Emousser.
rebec(k) ['ri:bek] n. MUS. Rebec *m.*
rebel ['rebḷ] adj. Insurgé.
— n. Insurgé, rebelle *s.;* mutin *s.* (mutiner).
— [ri'bel] v. intr. (1). Se rebeller, se révolter, se soulever.
rebellion [ri'beljən] n. Rébellion *f.*
rebellious [-əs] adj. MILIT. Insubordonné. ‖ MED., FIG. Rebelle.
rebelliously [-əsli] adv. Avec révolte.
rebirth [ri:'bə:θ] n. Renaissance *f.;* renouveau *m.*
rebore ['ri:,bɔ:*] v. tr. TECHN. Réaléser (bore of cylinder).
reborn ['ri:'bɔ:n] adj. Réincarné ; né de nouveau.
rebound [ri:'baund] n. Rebondissement *m.* ‖ MILIT. Ricochet *m.* (of a bullet).
— [ri'baund] v. intr. Rebondir. ‖ FIG. Rebondir ; retomber (*upon*, sur).
rebroadcast ['ri:brɔ:dkæ:st] n. RADIO. Retransmission *f.*
— v. tr. RADIO. Retransmettre.
rebuff [ri'bʌf] n. Rebuffade *f.* ‖ Echec, déboire *m.*
— v. tr. Rebuter, repousser ; rembarrer (fam.).
rebuild ['ri:'bild] v. tr. Rebâtir, reconstruire.
rebuilder [-ə*] n. Reconstructeur *m.*
rebuilding [-iŋ] n. Reconstruction *f.*
rebuke [ri'bju:k] n. Reproche, blâme *m.*
— v. tr. Réprimander, blâmer ; *to rebuke s.o. for sth.,* reprocher qqch. à qqn.
rebukingly [-iŋli] adv. Avec reproche, sévèrement.
rebus ['ri:bəs] n. Rébus *m.*
rebut [ri'bʌt] v. tr. (1). Rejeter (a claim) ; repousser, rebuter (s.o.).
recalcitrant [ri'kælsitrənt] adj. Récalcitrant.
recalcitrate [-treit] v. intr. Regimber.
recall [ri'kɔ:l] n. Révocation, annulation *f.; past recall,* irrévocable. ‖ MILIT. Rappel *m.* (of reservists). ‖ U. S. Invalidation (*f.*) d'un député.
— v. tr. Rappeler, évoquer, faire revivre (see RECOLLECT). ‖ Se rappeler, se souvenir de (s.o.). ‖ Ranimer ; *to recall to life,* rappeler à la vie. ‖ JUR. Rappeler (an ambassador) ; révoquer (a decision, a judgment) ; revenir sur (a promise) ; rétracter (one's words). ‖ MILIT. Rappeler (a reservist).
recant [ri'kænt] v. intr. Se rétracter.
— v. tr. Rétracter ; *to recant one's opinion,* se déjuger, reviser son opinion.
recantation [,ri:kæn'teiʃən] n. Rétractation *f.*
recap ['ri:'kæp] v. intr. FAM. Récapituler ; *to recap,* en résumé, pour nous résumer.
recap v. tr. Rechaper.
recapitulate [,ri:kə'pitjuleit] v. tr. Récapituler ; reprendre (the facts).
recapitulation ['ri:kə,pitju'leiʃən] n. Récapitulation *f.*
recapitulatory ['ri:kə'pitjulətəri] adj. Récapitulatif.
recapture ['ri:'kæptʃə*] n. Reprise *f.*
— v. tr. Reprendre.

recast ['ri:'kɑ:st] n. TECHN. Refonte *f.* (of metal). ‖ MATH. Nouveau calcul *m.* ‖ THEATR. Nouvelle distribution *f.*
— v. tr. (32). TECHN. Refondre. ‖ MATH. Recalculer. ‖ THEATR. Redistribuer. ‖ FIG. Refondre, remanier.
recce ['reki] n. MILIT., FAM. Reconnaissance *f.*
— v. tr. MILIT., FAM. Reconnaître.
recede [ri'si:d] v. intr. Reculer, s'éloigner (person, thing). ‖ NAUT. Descendre (tide). ‖ MILIT. Se retirer. ‖ MED. Fuir, être fuyant (forehead) ; *his hair is receding,* il a le front dégarni. ‖ FIN. Baisser, décliner. ‖ *To recede from,* revenir sur.
receipt [ri'si:t] v. tr. COMM. Acquitter.
— n. Réception *f.* (of a letter) ; *to acknowledge receipt of,* accuser réception de ; *to pay on receipt,* payer à la réception. ‖ COMM. Recette *f.* (amount) ; pl. recettes, entrées *f. pl.;* encaissements *m. pl.* ‖ COMM. Reçu, récépissé *m.;* quittance *f.* ‖ CULIN. Recette *f.* (See RECIPE.) ‖ **Receipt-book,** n. Livre (*m.*) de quittances ; CULIN. Livre (*m.*) de recettes. ‖ **Receipt-form,** n. Quittance *f.* ‖ **Receipt-stamp,** n. Timbre-quittance *m.*
receivability [,risi:və'biliti] n. Recevabilité *f.*
receivable [-əbḷ] adj. Recevable.
receive [ri'si:v] v. tr. Recevoir. ‖ Recevoir, accueillir (to welcome). ‖ Encaisser (a punch) ; essuyer (a refusal). ‖ FIN. Toucher (money, a salary). ‖ JUR. Receler (stolen goods) ; *to receive fifteen days,* écoper de quinze jours de prison. ‖ RADIO. Capter (a transmission). ‖ SPORTS., COMM. Réceptionner.
— v. intr. Recevoir. ‖ ECCLES. Communier. ‖ JUR. Faire du recel. ‖ RADIO. Prendre une émission.
receiver [-ə*] n. Destinataire *s.* (of a letter). ‖ JUR. Liquidateur, séquestre *m.* (liquidator) ; receveur *m.* (tax-collector) ; receleur *s.* (of stolen goods) ; *receiver's office,* recette *f.; official receiver,* syndic de faillite. ‖ COMM. Consignataire *s.* (consignee) ; réceptionnaire *s.* (receiving-clerk). ‖ ELECTR. Récepteur *m.* (of telephone) ; *to lift the receiver,* décrocher. ‖ RADIO. Poste récepteur *m.* ‖ TECHN. Réservoir *m.* ‖ CHIM., PHYS. Ballon, récipient *m.*
receiving [-iŋ] adj. De réception. ‖ RADIO. Récepteur *m.,* réceptrice *f.*
— n. Réception *f.* ‖ JUR. *Receiving of stolen goods,* recel.
recency ['ri:snsi] n. Caractère récent *m.;* date récente *f.*
recension [ri:'senʃən] n. Révision *f.;* texte révisé *m.* ‖ Recension *f.;* compte rendu *m.* (review).
recent ['ri:snt] adj. Récent ; nouveau (development).
recently [-li] adv. Récemment ; tout dernièrement ; *as recently as,* pas plus tard que ; *until quite recently,* jusqu'à ces derniers temps.
receptacle [ri'septəkḷ] n. Réceptacle *m.* ‖ TECHN. Récipient *m.*
reception [ri'sepʃən] n. Réception *f.* (act, party) ; accueil *m.* (welcome) ; *to have a favourable reception,* être bien accueilli (book). ‖ RADIO. Réception *f.* ‖ **Reception-area,** n. Aire de réception *f.* ‖ **Reception-clerk,** n. Employé (*s.*) à la réception. ‖ **Reception-desk,** n. Réception *f.* (in a hotel). ‖ **Reception-order,** n. MED. Permis d'internement *m.* (commitment). ‖ **Reception-room,** n. Pièce (*f.*) de réception.
receptionist [-ist] n. Réceptionniste *s.*
receptive [ri'septiv] adj. Réceptif.
receptivity [,risep'tiviti] n. Réceptivité *f.*
recess [ri'ses] n. Récréation *f.* (at school). ‖ JUR. Vacances *f. pl.;* ajournement *m.* ‖ MED. Fosse, dépression *f.* ‖ ARCHIT. Renfoncement *m.* (in general) ; alcôve *f.* (for a bed) ; embrasure *f.* (of a door) ; niche *f.* (for a statue). ‖ GEOGR. Recul *m.* (of water). ‖ FIG. Recoin, repli *m.*
— v. intr. U. S. JUR. Suspendre les séances, s'ajourner.
— v. tr. ARCHIT. Pratiquer un renfoncement dans

(to make a recess); mettre en retrait (to put into a recess).

recession [ri'seʃən] n. Recul, éloignement *m.* ‖ MED., GEOL. Régression *f.* ‖ U. S. FIN. Mouvement (*m.*) de baisse; récession *f.*

recessive [ri'sesiv] adj. Rétrograde. ‖ GRAMM. Remontant. ‖ BOT. Récessif.

recharge [,ri:'tʃɑːdʒ] v. tr. Recharger; *to recharge one's batteries*, recharger ses batteries (lit., fig.).

rechauffe [rei'ʃoufei] n. CULIN., FAM. Réchauffé *m.*

recherché [rə'ʃɛəʃei] adj. FIG. Recherché.

recidivism [ri'sidivizm] n. Récidive *f.*

recidivist [-ist] n. Récidiviste *s.*

recipe ['resipi] n. CULIN. Recette *f.* ‖ MED. Ordonnance *f.* ‖ FIG. Recette *f.;* moyen, expédient *m.*

recipient [ri'sipiənt] adj. Qui reçoit. ‖ Réceptif (receptive).
— n. Donataire *s.* ‖ Bénéficiaire *s.* (of a cheque). ‖ Titulaire *s.* (of a prize). ‖ Destinataire *s.* (of a letter). ‖ JUR. Ayant droit *m.*

reciprocal [ri'siprəkəl] n. MATH. Réciproque *f.;* inverse *m.*
— adj. Réciproque. (See MUTUAL.) ‖ GRAMM. Réciproque. ‖ MATH. Réciproque; inverse (ratio).

reciprocally [-kəli] adv. Réciproquement.

reciprocate [-keit] v. tr. Echanger, donner en retour (aid); retourner, répondre à (good wishes). ‖ TECHN. Donner un mouvement alternatif à.
— v. intr. Retourner le compliment; rendre la pareille. ‖ TECHN. Avoir un mouvement alternatif (or) de va-et-vient.

reciprocation [ri,siprə'keiʃən] n. Réciprocité *f.;* retour *m.* (of a compliment). ‖ TECHN. Alternance *f.;* va-et-vient *m.*

reciprocity [,resi'prɔsiti] n. Réciprocité *f.*

recital [ri'saitl] n. Récit *m.;* narration *f.;* énumération *f.* (of details); récitation *f.* (of poetry). ‖ MUS. Récital *m.;* audition *f.* ‖ JUR. Exposé *m.*

recitation [resi'teiʃən] n. Récitation *f.* ‖ U. S. Classe *f.* (period); *recitation room,* salle de classe.

recitative [,resitə'tiːv] n. MUS. Récitatif *m.*

recite [ri'sait] v. intr. Réciter, déclamer; dire un monologue.
— v. tr. Enumérer (details); exposer, relater (facts); réciter, déclamer (poetry). ‖ U. S. Répondre.

reciter [-ə*] n. Récitateur *m.;* récitatrice *f.;* déclamateur *m.;* déclamatrice *f.;* diseur *s.* ‖ Livre (*m.*) de récitations (book).

reck [rek] v. intr., tr. † Se soucier de; *he recks but little of it,* peu lui importe, il n'en a cure.

reckless [-lis] adj. Inconsidéré (headlong); insouciant (heedless). ‖ Téméraire, imprudent (rash); *reckless driver,* chauffard.

recklessly [-lisli] adv. Inconsidérément. ‖ Imprudemment.

recklessness [-lisnis] n. Insouciance *f.* (heedlessness); témérité, imprudence *f.* (rashness).

reckon ['rekən] v. tr. Compter, calculer, supputer (to calculate); compter (to count); *reckoning everything,* tout compris, tout compte fait. ‖ Regarder (or) considérer comme (to consider as). ‖ Compter (among, au nombre de, au rang de, dans, parmi). ‖ **To reckon up,** additionner, calculer, faire le compte (or) le décompte de.
— v. intr. Compter, calculer. ‖ Régler un compte, compter (with, avec); *you'll have to reckon with,* vous aurez affaire à. ‖ Compter (from, de, à partir de); *reckoning from yesterday,* à compter d'hier. ‖ Estimer, juger (to estimate); supposer, imaginer (to suppose); croire, penser (to think). ‖ Compter (on, upon, sur).

reckoner [-ə*] n. Calculateur *m.;* calculatrice *f.* ‖ Barème *m.*

reckoning [-iŋ] n. Calcul, compte *m.* (calculations); *to be out in one's reckoning,* s'être trompé dans ses

calculs. ‖ Estimation *f.* (judgment); *to the best of my reckoning,* autant que j'en puis juger. ‖ Règlement (*m.*) de comptes. ‖ COMM. Note *f.* (at an hotel); addition *f.* (at a restaurant). ‖ NAUT. Estime *f.*

reclaim [ri'kleim] n. † Past (or) *beyond reclaim,* perdu à tout jamais (person, thing).
— v. intr. Réclamer (against, contre).
— v. tr. Réformer, amender, convertir, régénérer; tirer (from, de); *reclaimed woman,* repentie. ‖ AGRIC. Amender. ‖ TECHN. Récupérer.

reclaimable [-əbl] adj. AGRIC., FIG. Amendable. ‖ TECHN. Récupérable.

reclamation [,reklə'meiʃən] n. Réclamation *f.* (claiming-back). ‖ AGRIC., FIG. Amendement *m.* ‖ TECHN. Récupération *f.*

recline [ri'klain] v. tr. Appuyer, reposer (one's head).
— v. intr. Etre couché (or) étendu, se reposer. ‖ Reposer (head).

reclothe ['ri:'klo:uð] v. tr. Rhabiller.

recluse [ri'klu:s] adj., n. Reclus *s.*

reclusion [ri'klu:ʒən] n. Réclusion *f.*

recognition [,rekəg'niʃən] n. Reconnaissance *f.* (acknowledgment); *in recognition of,* en reconnaissance de. ‖ Reconnaissance *f.* (identification); *beyond recognition,* méconnaissable. ‖ Attention; considération *f.* ‖ AVIAT. Identification *f.*

recognizable [,rekəg'naizəbl] adj. Reconnaissable.

recognizance [ri'kɔgnizəns] n. JUR. Engagement *m.* (promise); caution *f.* (sum).

recognize ['rekəgnaiz] v. tr. Reconnaître (by, à); identifier (by, par). ‖ Saluer, faire un signe de reconnaissance à (to show signs of knowing). ‖ Reconnaître, accepter, admettre (as, pour). ‖ Reconnaître, avouer, concéder (to admit); reconnaître, apprécier (to appreciate); se rendre compte de (to realize). ‖ JUR. Reconnaître (a child, government). ‖ COMM. Accréditer (an agent). ‖ U. S. Donner la parole à (a speaker).

recoil [ri'kɔil] n. Recul *m.;* reculade *f.* (retreat). ‖ Rebondissement *m.* (rebound); détente *f.* (of a spring). ‖ MILIT. Recul *m.* ‖ FIG. Dégoût *m.,* horreur *f.* (from, de); répugnance *f.* (from, pour).
— v. intr. Reculer. ‖ Se détendre (spring). ‖ MILIT. Reculer (gun, soldiers). ‖ FIG. Reculer (from, devant); avoir horreur (from, de); se révolter (from, contre); se refuser (from, à); retomber (on, sur).

recollect ['rikə'lekt] v. tr. Assembler de nouveau.

recollect [,rekə'lekt] v. tr. Se rappeler, se souvenir de. ‖ Rassembler (one's courage); *to recollect oneself,* se recueillir.

recollection [,rekə'lekʃən] n. Souvenir *m.* (thing remembered). ‖ Mémoire *f.; to the best of my recollection,* autant que je m'en souvienne; *within my recollection,* aussi loin que remontent mes souvenirs. ‖ Recueillement *m.* (mystical contemplation).

recomfort [ri'kʌmfət] v. tr. Réconforter.

recommence [,rekə'mens] v. intr. Recommencer.

recommend [rekə'mend] v. tr. Recommander, conseiller (to, à) [sth.]. ‖ Recommander à, conseiller à (to, de) [s.o.]; *not to be recommended,* à déconseiller. ‖ Recommander, confier (to, à) [to commit]. ‖ Recommander, parler en faveur de, appuyer (a candidate); *he has little to recommend him,* il n'a pas grand-chose pour lui.

recommendable [-əbl] adj. Recommandable.

recommendation [,rekəmen'deiʃən] n. Recommandation *f.*

recommendatory [rekə'mendətəri] adj. De recommandation *f.*

recompense ['rekəmpens] n. Châtiment *m.* (punishment); récompense *f.* (for, de) [reward]; rétribution *f.* (retribution). ‖ Compensation *f.;* dédommagement *m.* (for damage).
— v. tr. Châtier (to punish); récompenser (for, de)

[to reward]. ‖ Compenser, réparer (damage) ; dédommager (s.o.).

recompose ['ri:kəm'pouz] v. tr. Calmer de nouveau (s.o.) ; rarranger (sth.). ‖ Chim. Recomposer.

reconcilable ['rekənsailəbl̩] adj. Réconciliable (person). ‖ Conciliable (with, avec).

reconcile [-sail] v. tr. Arranger (a dispute) ; réconcilier, raccommoder (person) ; to become reconciled, se réconcilier. ‖ Concilier, accorder, rendre compatible (with, avec) [things]. ‖ Eccles. Réconcilier. ‖ Fig. To become reconciled to, se faire à (to get used to) ; être réconcilié avec, se résigner à (to resign oneself to).

reconcilement [-sailmənt], **reconciliation** ['rekənsili'eiʃən] n. Arrangement m. (of a dispute) ; conciliation f. (of opinions) ; réconciliation f. (of two persons).

recondite ['rekəndait] adj. Abstrus, abscons (obscure) ; profond (profound).

reconditely [-li] adv. D'une manière abstruse.

reconditeness [-nis] n. Obscurité ; abstraction f. ‖ Profondeur f.

recondition ['ri:kən'diʃən] v. tr. Techn. Remettre à neuf, reconditionner.

reconduct ['ri:kən'dʌkt] v. tr. Reconduire.

reconnaissance [ri'kɔnisəns] n. Milit. Reconnaissance f.

— adj. Milit., Aviat. De reconnaissance.

reconnoitre [,rekə'nɔitə*] n. Milit. Reconnaissance f.

— v. tr. Reconnaître.

— v. intr. Faire une reconnaissance. ‖ Fig. Explorer, reconnaître le terrain.

reconnoitrer [-tərə*] n. Eclaireur m.

reconquer ['ri:'kɔŋkə*] v. tr. Reconquérir (from, sur).

reconsider ['ri:kən'sidə*] v. tr. Envisager (or) examiner de nouveau, reconsidérer. ‖ Revenir sur (a decision) ; reviser (a judgment).

reconsideration ['ri:kən,sidə'reiʃən] n. Remise (f.) en question ; nouvel examen m. ‖ Révision f.

reconsolidate ['ri:kən'sɔlideit] v. tr. Reconsolider.

reconstituent [-'stitjuənt], **reconstructive** [-strʌktiv] adj., n. Reconstituant m.

reconstitute ['ri:kɔnstitju:t] v. tr. Reconstituer. ‖ Culin. Réhydrater.

reconstitution ['ri:kɔnsti'tju:ʃən] n. Reconstitution f.

reconstruct ['ri:kn'strʌkt] v. tr. Archit. Reconstruire, rebâtir. ‖ Jur. Reconstituer (a crime). ‖ Fig. Rebâtir, refondre.

reconstruction [-ʃən] n. Archit. Reconstruction, réfection, restauration f. ‖ Jur. Reconstitution f. ‖ U. S. Réorganisation f. ‖ Fig. Refonte f.

reconversion ['ri:kən'və:ʃən] n. Techn. Reconversion f.

reconvert ['ri:kən'və:t] v. tr. Reconvertir.

reconvey ['ri:kən'vei] v. tr. Transporter de nouveau. ‖ Jur. Rétrocéder.

reconveyance ['ri:kɔn'veiəns] n. Jur. Rétrocession f.

recopy ['ri:'kɔpi] v. tr. (2). Recopier.

record ['rekɔ:d] adj. Jamais atteint ; record attendance figure, affluence, chiffre record ; at record speed, à une vitesse record.

— n. Document, souvenir, monument m. (historical). ‖ Mention f. ; rapport, récit m. ; to be on record, être authentique (fact) ; there is no record of it in history, l'histoire n'en fait pas mention ; to go on record, se déclarer publiquement. ‖ Dossier m. (file) ; fiche f. (record card) ; registre m. (register) ; record of attendance, registre de présence ; to have a good record, être bien noté (at the office) ; avoir de bonnes notes (at school). ‖ Etat de service, certificat m. (testimonial). ‖ Minute f. (of an act) ; procès-verbal m. (of evidence) ; rapport officiel m. (official report). ‖ Pl. Annales, archives f. pl. ; Public Record Office, Archives. ‖ Jur. Enregistrement m. (of a fact) ; casier judiciaire m. (police record). ‖ Sports. Record m. ; to break the record, battre le record ; world distance record, record du monde de distance. ‖ Radio. Disque m. (gramophone record) ; enregistrement m. (recording) ; record library, discothèque. ‖ Techn. Courbe enregistrée f. ‖ Fam. Off the record, en secret, à titre confidentiel ; off-the-record statement, déclaration officieuse. ‖ **Record-dealer**, n. Disquaire m. ‖ **Record-holder**, n. Sports. Recordman m. (pl. recordmen) ; recordwoman f. (pl. recordwomen) ‖ **Record-player**, n. Radio. Tourne-disque, pick-up, électrophone m.

record [ri'kɔ:d] v. intr. Radio. Enregistrer.

— v. tr. Enregistrer, prendre acte (to register) ; relater, rapporter (to relate). ‖ Jur. Recenser (population) ; to record one's vote, voter. ‖ Radio. Enregistrer.

recordable [-əbl̩] adj. Digne de mention. ‖ Radio. Enregistrable.

recorder [-ə*] n. Jur. Juge « recorder » m. (judge) ; archiviste s. ; greffier m. (registrar). ‖ Theatr. Sound recorder, appareil d'enregistrement du son. ‖ Radio. Artiste (s.) qui enregistre (artist) ; enregistreur, appareil enregistreur m. (machine) ; tape recorder, magnétophone. ‖ Mus. Flûte (f.) à bec.

recording [-iŋ] n. Narration f. (narration) ; enregistrement m. (noting down). ‖ Radio. Enregistrement m.

— adj. Jur. Chargé du recensement (official). ‖ Eccles. The Recording Angel, l'ange qui tient le grand livre. ‖ Radio. Qui enregistre (artist) ; enregistreur (instrument) ; d'enregistrement (session, studio, van) ; de magnétophone (tape).

recount [ri'kaunt] v. tr. Raconter.

recount [ri:'kaunt] v. tr. Recompter.

recoup [ri'ku:p] v. intr. Récupérer ses pertes.

— v. tr. Dédommager, indemniser (for, de). ‖ Jur. Défalquer, déduire.

recoupment [-mənt] n. Dédommagement m. ‖ Récupération f. (of losses). ‖ Jur. Défalcation f.

recourse [ri'kɔ:s] n. Recours m. (to, à).

recover ['ri:kʌvə*] v. tr. Recouvrir.

recover [ri'kʌvə*] v. intr. Se redresser, se ressaisir. ‖ Jur. Avoir gain de cause. ‖ Med. Se remettre, se rétablir (from an illness) ; revenir à soi, reprendre connaissance (to regain consciousness). ‖ Jur. Right to recover, droit de reprise.

— v. tr. Retrouver (sth. lost) ; repêcher (sth. floating) ; rattraper (lost time). ‖ Reprendre (to reclaim) ; reconquérir (to reconquer) ; rentrer en possession de (to regain possession of) ; regagner (to win back) ; to recover oneself, se ressaisir, se reprendre (to full oneself together) ; retrouver son équilibre (to regain one's balance) ; se redresser, se relever (to regain one's position). ‖ Se remettre de, se relever de (to get over) ; réparer (losses). ‖ Med. Faire revenir (a fainting person) ; retrouver (one's appetite) ; recouvrer (one's reason) ; to recover one's breath, reprendre haleine ; to recover consciousness, revenir à soi, reprendre ses esprits. ‖ Jur. Recouvrer ; récupérer, faire rentrer (a debt) ; to recover damages, obtenir des dommages-intérêts.

recoverable [-rəbl̩] adj. Récupérable. ‖ Med. Guérissable, curable.

recovery [-ri] n. Redressement m. (of one's position) ; récupération f. (of sth. lost). ‖ Jur. Obtention f. (of damages). ‖ Med. Guérison f. ; rétablissement m. ; past recovery, dans un état désespéré (patient). ‖ Fin. Reprise f. (of business) ; recouvrement m. (of a debt) ; redressement m. (of prices). ‖ Sports. Remise en garde f. (in fencing) ; to make a brilliant recovery, se ressaisir brillamment (at golf, at tennis). ‖ Fig. Rétablissement m. ; past recovery, sans remède, irrémédiable (situation).

recreant ['rekriənt] adj., n. Lâche *m*. (cowardly) ; traître *m*. (false).

recreate ['ri:kri'eit] v. tr. Recréer.

recreate ['rekrieit] v. intr. Se distraire, se divertir. — v. tr. Récréer, amuser, distraire, divertir.

recreation ['rekri'eiʃən] n. Récréation, distraction, détente *f*. ; divertissement, amusement *m*.

recreation ['ri:,kri'eiʃən] n. Nouvelle création *f*.

recreative ['rekrieitiv] adj. Récréatif.

recriminate [ri'krimineit] v. intr. Récriminer.

recrimination [ri,krimi'neiʃən] n. Récrimination ; rouspétance *f*. (fam.).

recriminative [ri'kriminətiv], **recriminatory** [-təri] adj. Récriminatoire ; récriminateur *m*. ; récriminatrice *f*.

recrudesce [,ri:kru:'des] v. intr. Reprendre de plus belle ; subir une recrudescence.

recrudescence [-ns] n. Recrudescence *f*.

recrudescent [-nt] adj. Recrudescent.

recruit [ri'kru:t] n. Recrue *f*. ‖ MILIT. Recrue *f*. ; conscrit *m*. ; bleu *m*. (fam.). — v. intr. Se réapprovisionner. ‖ MED. Reprendre des forces ; se remettre. — v. tr. Recruter ; fournir des recrues à (to enlist). ‖ Renforcer (to reinforce) ; to recruit supplies, se réapprovisionner. ‖ MILIT. Recruter. ‖ MED. Restaurer, rétablir (s.o.'s health) ; remonter (s.o.).

recruiter [-ə*] n. Recruteur *m*.

recruiting [-iŋ], **recruitment** [-mənt] n. MILIT. Recrutement *m*. ‖ MED. Rétablissement *m*. (of s.o.) ; réparation *f*. (of s.o.'s strength). ‖ **Recruiting-sergeant**, n MILIT. Sergent recruteur *m*. — adj. MILIT. Recruiting board, conseil de révision ; recruiting office (or) station, bureau de recrutement.

rectal ['rektəl] adj. MED. Rectal.

rectangle ['rektæŋgl] n. MATH. Rectangle *m*.

rectangular [rek'tæŋgjulə*] adj. MATH. Rectangle, rectangulaire.

rectifiable ['rektifaiəbl] adj. Rectifiable. ‖ Réparable (mistake).

rectification [,rektifi'keiʃən] n. Rectification *f*.

rectifier ['rektifaiə*] n. Rectificateur *m*. ; rectificatrice *f*. ‖ ELECTR. Redresseur *m*.

rectify [-fai] v. tr. (2). Rectifier, corriger. ‖ Modifier (to alter). ‖ MATH., CHIM. Rectifier. ‖ ELECTR. Redresser.

rectilineal [,rekti'linjəl], **rectilinear** [-ə*] adj. Rectiligne.

rectitude ['rektitju:d] n. Rectitude *f*.

recto ['rektou] n. Recto *m*. (of a page).

rector ['rektə*] n. Directeur *m*., principal *m*. (of a school) ; recteur *m*. (of a university). ‖ ECCLES. Curé *m*. (in the Anglican church) ; supérieur *m*. (of a religious order).

rectorate ['rektərət] n. Rectorat *m*.

rectorial [rek'tɔ:riəl] adj. Rectoral.

rectory ['rektəri] n. ECCLES. Presbytère *m*.

rectum ['rektəm] n. MED. Rectum.

recumbency [ri'kʌmbənsi] n. Position couchée *f*. (or) de repos.

recumbent [-ənt] adj. Couché. (See PRONE.) ‖ ARTS. Recumbent figure, gisant.

recuperate [ri'kju:pəreit] v. intr. MED. Se rétablir, se remettre ; récupérer (fam.). — v. tr. MED. Recouvrer (one's health) ; rétablir, guérir (s.o.). ‖ TECHN. Récupérer (waste products).

recuperation [ri,kju:pə'reiʃən] n. MED. Rétablissement *m*. ‖ TECHN. Récupération *f*.

recuperative [ri'ku:pərətiv] adj. MED. Régénérateur *m*. ; régénératrice *f*.

recuperator [-reitə*] n. TECHN. Récupérateur *m*. -

recur [ri'kə:*] v. intr. (1). Revenir, reparaître. ‖ Se reproduire, se répéter (event) ; se représenter (occasion) ; se renouveler (question). ‖ Revenir (to, à) [the memory] ; revenir, se reporter (to, à) [a subject]. ‖ MATH. Se reproduire (figures).

recurrence [-rəns] n. Retour *m*. ; réapparition *f*. ‖ Récurrence *f*.

recurrent [-rənt] adj. Qui revient, périodique. ‖ MED., BOT. Récurrent. — n. MED. Artère récurrente *f*. ; nerf récurrent *m*.

recusant [ri'kju:zənt] adj., n. Réfractaire *s*. (against, à). ‖ † ECCLES. Récusant *s*.

recut ['ri:'kʌt] v. tr. Retailler, recouper. ‖ Aviver (a blade).

recycle [,ri:'saikl] v. tr. TECHN. Recycler, récupérer.

red [red] n. Rouge *m*. ; couleur (ou) teinte rouge *f*. ‖ SPORTS. Bille rouge *f*. (in billiards). ‖ FIN. Déficit *m*. ‖ FAM. Rouge *s*. (in politics). ‖ LOC. To see red, voir rouge ; U. S. To be in the red, être en déficit. — adj. Rouge (colour). ‖ Roux *m*., rousse *f*. (beard, hair) ; rouge, injecté (eyes) ; vermeil (lips, mouth) ; red with anger, rouge de colère ; to turn red, rougir. ‖ Rouge (flag) ; de l'extrême gauche (politician). ‖ CHIM. Red lead, minium. ‖ AUTOM. To run past (or) U. S. to go through a red light, brûler un feu rouge. ‖ CULIN. Saur (herring) ; rouge ; saignant (meat). ‖ GEOGR. Rouge (Sea). ‖ GEOL. Rose (marble). ‖ ZOOL. Red Admiral, vulcain. ‖ FIG. Sanglant (threats) ; red light, signe de danger ; to see the red light, se rendre compte du danger. ‖ LOC. It's like a red rag to a bull, ça lui fait l'effet du rouge au taureau ; to paint the town red, faire la tournée des grands-ducs. ‖ **Red-bearded**, adj. A la barbe rousse. ‖ **Red-blooded**, adj. Vigoureux. ‖ **Red-breasted**, adj. ZOOL. A gorge rouge (bird). ‖ **Red-cap**, n. MILIT., FAM. Soldat (*m*.) de la police militaire ; U. S. CH. DE F. Porteur *m*. ‖ **Red-faced**, adj. Rubicond, rougeaud, au visage enluminé. ‖ **Red-gum**, n. BOT. Red-gum tree, eucalyptus résineux. ‖ **Red-handed**, adj. En flagrant délit, sur le fait ; la main dans le sac (fam.). ‖ **Red-hat**, n. MILIT.. FAM. Officier d'état-major. ‖ **Red-head**, n. Roux *m*., rousse *f*. ; rouquin *s*. (fam.). ‖ **Red-headed**, adj. Roux, rouquin. ‖ **Red-heat**, n. Rouge *m*. ‖ **Red-hot**, adj. Chauffé au rouge ; FIG. Chauffé à blanc ; radical (politician) ; red-hot blonde, blonde incendiaire. ‖ **Red-legged**, adj. ZOOL. Aux pattes rouges (bird). ‖ **Red-letter**, adj. A marquer d'une pierre blanche ; red-letter day, jour de fête ; jour mémorable. ‖ **Red-light**, adj. Malfamé ; réservé (quarter). ‖ **Red-nosed**, adj. Au nez rouge. ‖ **Red-rimmed**, adj. Eraillé, cerné de rouge (eyes). ‖ **Red-roofed**, adj. Au toit rouge. ‖ **Red-tape**, n. FIG. Formalités (or) chinoiseries administratives *f*. *pl*. ; paperasserie, bureaucratie tatillonne *f*. ‖ **Red-tapedom** (or) **-tapism**, n. Paperasserie *f*. ; rond-de-cuirisme *m*. ‖ **Red-tape-minded**, adj. Enroutiné, encroûté. ‖ **Red-tapist**, n. Bureaucrate tatillon, rond-de-cuir *m*.

redact [ri'daekt] v. tr. Rédiger ; préparer pour la publication.

redaction [-ʃən] n. Rédaction ; révision *f*.

redactor [-tə*] n. Rédacteur *m*.

redan [ri'daen] n. MILIT. Redan *m*.

redbreast ['redbrest] n. ZOOL. Rouge-gorge *m*.

redbrick ['red,brik] n. En Grande-Bretagne, université (*f*.) de fondation récente.

redden ['redn] v. tr. Rougir. — v. intr. Roussir (foliage) ; rougir (person) ; rougeoyer (sky).

reddish [-iʃ] adj. Rougeâtre.

redecorate [,ri:'dekəreit] v. tr. Repeindre, retapisser, refaire (a room, a house). — v. intr. Refaire les peintures, poser de nouveaux papiers.

redecoration [,ri:dekə'reiʃən] n. Réfection (*f*.) des peintures, pose (*f*.) de nouveaux papiers.

redeem [ri'di:m] v. tr. Racheter (to buy back). ‖ JUR. Purger (a mortgage) ; regagner (one's rights). ‖ ECCLES. Racheter, sauver (mankind). ‖ FIN. Dégager, retirer (from pawn) ; honorer (a bill) ; amortir

551 REDEEMABLE — REEK

(a debt). ‖ U. S. Fin. Convertir en espèces (a bank-note). ‖ Fig. Racheter, compenser (a failing); rattraper (lost time); tenir (a promise).
redeemable [-əbḷ] adj. Rachetable. ‖ Fin. Amortissable (debt); récupérable (from pawn).
redeemer [-ə*] n. Racheteur s. ‖ Eccles. Rédempteur m. ‖ Fam. Sauveur m.
redemption [ri'dempʃən] n. Rachat m. ‖ Jur. Purge f. (of a mortgage); sale with power of redemption, vente à réméré. ‖ Eccles. Rédemption f. ‖ Fin. Dégagement m. (from pawn); amortissement m. (of a debt); rachat, remboursement m. (of a loan); redemption fund, caisse d'amortissement. ‖ Fig. Past redemption, irréparable, irrémédiable.
redemptive [-tiv] adj. Rédempteur m.; rédemptrice f.
redemptorist [-tərist] n. Eccles. Rédemptoriste m.
redeploy [ˌri:di'plɔi] v. tr. Redéployer (troops, workers); restructurer (labour).
redeployment [-'plɔimənt] n. Redéploiement m.; redeployment of labour, restructuration de l'emploi.
redevelop [ˌri:di'veləp] v. tr. Remodeler (an area). ‖ Redévelopper.
redhibitory [red'hibitəri] adj. Jur. Rédhibitoire.
rediffusion [ˌri:di'fju:ʒən] n. Techn. Retransmission (f.) par câble, télédistribution f.
redintegrate [re'dintigreit] v. tr. Renouveler (to renew). ‖ Réintégrer (s.o.); rétablir dans son intégrité (sth.).
redintegration [reˌdinti'greiʃən] n. Renouvellement m. ‖ Rétablissement m.; réintégration f.
redirect ['ri:dai'rekt] v. tr. Faire suivre (a letter) [see Forward].
redirection [-'rekʃən] n. Réexpédition f.
rediscover ['ri:dis'kʌvə*] v. tr. Redécouvrir.
rediscovery [-əri] n. Redécouverte f.
redistribute ['ri:dis'tribjut] v. tr. Redistribuer. ‖ Répartir de nouveau.
redistribution ['ri:distri'bjuʃən] n. Redistribution f. ‖ Nouvelle répartition f.
redness ['rednis] n. Rougeur f. ‖ Rousseur f. (of hair).
redo [ri:'du:] v. tr. (47). Refaire (a piece of work); refaire, repeindre, retapisser (a room); recoiffer, repeigner (one's hair).
redolence ['redələns] n. Senteur f. (See scent.)
redolent [-ənt] adj. Odorant, parfumé. ‖ Exhalant des effluves (of, de); to be redolent of spring, embaumer le printemps. ‖ Fig. Evocateur (of, de).
redouble ['ri'dʌbḷ] n. Surcontre m. (at bridge).
— v. tr. Replier; plier en quatre (cloth). ‖ Surcontrer.
redouble [ri'dʌbḷ] v. intr. Redoubler.
— v. tr. Redoubler de.
redoubling [-iŋ] n. Redoublement m.
redoubt [ri'daut] n. Milit. Redoute f.
redoubtable [-əbḷ] adj. Redoutable.
redound [ri'daund] v. intr. Contribuer (to, à). ‖ Rejaillir (upon, sur).
redox ['ri:dɔks] n. Chim. Oxydoréduction f.
— adj. Chim. D'oxydoréduction, redox.
redress [ri'dres] n. Réparation f.; redressement m.; beyond redress, irréparable; to seek redress at s.o.'s hands, demander justice à qqn.
— v. tr. Rétablir (balance). ‖ Corriger, remédier à (an abuse); réparer (a wrong). ‖ Secourir (to aid); soulager (to relieve).
redresser [-ə*] m. Redresseur s. (of wrongs).
redshank ['red.ʃæŋk] n. Zool. Chevalier m.
redskin ['redskin] n. Peau-Rouge m.
redstart [-stɑ:t] n. Zool. Rouge-queue m. (bird).
reduce [ri'dju:s] v. intr. Med. Maigrir.
— v. tr. Réduire (to, à, en) [ashes, dust]. ‖ Réduire, ramener (to, à) [obedience]. ‖ Réduire, contraindre

(to, à) [begging, despair]. ‖ Rédiger, consigner par écrit (to put into writing). ‖ Appauvrir (to impoverish); réduire, diminuer (to lessen); affaiblir (to weaken); in reduced circumstances, dans la gêne. ‖ Abaisser, ravaler (to lower). ‖ Raccourcir (in length); amincir (in width). ‖ Autom. Ralentir (speed). ‖ Milit. Réduire (a fort, a region); to reduce to the ranks, casser. ‖ Med. Faire maigrir (a fat person); réduire (a fracture); résoudre (a swelling). ‖ Culin. Faire réduire (a sauce). ‖ Math., Chim. Réduire. ‖ Fin. Réduire (prices); at reduced prices, au rabais. ‖ Techn. Ralentir (output).
reducer [-ə*] n. Réducteur m.
reducible [-ibḷ] adj. Réductible.
reduction [ri'dʌkʃən] n. Réduction f. (to another state). ‖ Raccourcissement m. (in length); diminution f. (in width). ‖ Autom. Ralentissement m. (of speed). ‖ Milit. Reduction to the ranks, cassation. ‖ Jur. Relaxation f. (of a sentence); reduction of taxes, dégrèvement. ‖ Med. Réduction f. (of a fracture); amaigrissement m. (of a person); résolution f. (of a swelling). ‖ Math. Réduction f. ‖ Fin. Réduction, baisse, diminution f. (of prices, of wages). ‖ Comm. Remise (on, sur) [an article]. ‖ Electr. Diminution f. (of voltage). ‖ Phys. Baisse f. (in temperature). ‖ Techn. Démultiplication f. (in mechanics); atténuation f. (in photography).
redundancy [ri'dʌndənsi], **redundance** [-əns] n. Surabondance f., excès m. ‖ Redondance f. (of word, of information); verbosité, prolixité f. (of style). ‖ Pl. Redondances, répétitions, redites f. pl. ‖ Suppression (f.) d'emplois, licenciement m. (sacking); chômage m. (unemployment); redundancy payment, indemnité de licenciement. ‖ Techn. Système (m.) de rechange (or) de relais.
redundant [-ənt] adj. Superflu, de trop, faisant double emploi. ‖ Redondant (word, information), pléonastique (expression), plein de redondances (or) de redites (style). ‖ En surnombre (staff no longer needed), frappé de licenciement (staff laid-off); made redundant, licencié (or) au chômage pour raison économique. ‖ Techn. De rechange, de relais (mechanical or electronical component).
reduplicate [ri'dju:plikit] adj. Redoublé. ‖ Bot. Rédupliqué.
— [-keit] v. tr. Redoubler.
reduplication [riˌdju:pli'keiʃən] n. Redoublement m.; répétition f. ‖ Gramm. Redoublement m.
reduplicative [ri'dju:plikətiv] adj. Gramm. Réduplicatif.
redwing ['redwiŋ] n. Zool. Mauvis m.
redwood [-wud] n. Bot. Séquoia m.
redye ['ri:'dai] v. tr. Reteindre, faire reteindre.
reed [ri:d] n. Bot. Roseau m. ‖ Mus. Pipeau, chalumeau m. (pipe); anche f. (of a wind-instrument); pl. instruments à anche. ‖ Techn. Peigne f. (of a loom). ‖ Archit. Pl. Chaume f. ‖ Fig. Broken reed, planche pourrie. ‖ **Reed-organ**, n. Mus. Harmonium m. ‖ **Reed-pipe**, n. Mus. Tuyau (m.) d'anches. ‖ **Reed-stop**, n. Mus. Jeux (m.) d'anches.
— v. tr. Mus. Munir d'une anche. ‖ Archit. Couvrir de chaume.
reedy [-i] adj. † De roseaux (bed). ‖ Plein de roseaux (ground). ‖ Mince (person). ‖ Nasillard (instrument, voice).
reef [ri:f] n. Naut. Récif, banc m. ‖ Techn. Reef m. ‖ Fig. Ecueil m.
reef v. tr. Naut. Rentrer (a mast); prendre un ris dans (a sail).
— n. Naut. Ris m. ‖ Fam. To let out a reef, desserrer sa ceinture. ‖ **Reef-knot**, n. Naut. Nœud plat m.
reefer [-ə*] n. Naut. Caban m. (jacket); aspirant m. (midshipman); matelot (m.) qui prend les ris (sailor). ‖ U. S. Pop. Cigarette (f.) à marijuana.
reek [ri:k] n. Fumée f. (smoke); vapeur f. (vapour). ‖ Odeur f. (smell); relent m. (of tobacco).
— v. intr. Fumer (sth. burning). ‖ Ruisseler (with,

de) [blood]. ‖ Sentir mauvais, empester (to smell); *to reek of,* puer, empester, empoisonner. ‖ FIG. Exhaler ; *to reek with crime,* suer le crime.

reeking [-iŋ] adj. Fumant. ‖ Puant.

reeky [-i] adj. Enfumé ; fumeux.

reel [ri:l] n. Bobine *f.* (of cotton, of thread). ‖ Chancellement *m.;* titubation *f.* (staggering). ‖ CINEM. Bande *f.*, rouleau *m.* ‖ MUS. Reel, branle écossais *m.* ‖ SPORTS. Moulinet *m.* (of fishing-rod). ‖ TECHN. Touret *m.* (drum); dévidoir *m.; bobine f.* (spool). ‖ LOC. *Off the reel,* tout d'un trait, sans s'arrêter. ‖ **Reel-holder,** n. TECHN. Porte-bobines *m.*
— v. intr. Tournoyer (to whirl). ‖ MUS. Danser le reel. ‖ MED. Avoir le vertige (to feel giddy); chanceler, tituber (to stagger); *to reel down the street,* descendre la rue en titubant. ‖ FIG. Etre ébranlé; *his mind reeled at the thought,* cette pensée lui donna le vertige.
— v. tr. Bobiner. ‖ **To reel in,** ramener. ‖ **To reel off,** dévider; FIG. Dévider; dégoiser (fam.). ‖ **To reel up,** ramener.

reeling [-iŋ] n. Bobinage *m.; dévidage m.* ‖ Chancellement *m.; titubation f.*
— adj. Qui tourne (head). ‖ Chancelant, titubant (gait, person). ‖ Qui fait chanceler (blow).

reeve [ri:v] n. Bailli *m.*

reeve v. tr. NAUT. Capeler (a rope); passer à travers (a shoal).
— N. B. Ce verbe peut faire *rove* au pret. et au p.p.

ref [ref] n. FAM. SPORTS. Arbitre *m.*

reface [,ri:'feis] v. tr. Refaire la façade de, rhabiller (a building).

refashion ['ri:'fæʃən] v. tr. Refaçonner.

refection [ri'fekʃən] n. CULIN. Collation *f.* ‖ MED. Réfection *f.* ‖ FIG. Rafraîchissement *m.*

refectory [ri'fektəri] n. Réfectoire *m.*

refer [ri'fə:*] v. intr. (1). Se rapporter, avoir rapport (or) trait (*to*, à) [to have relation]. ‖ S'en rapporter, se reporter, s'adresser (*to*, à); *to refer to,* consulter (an authority). ‖ Faire allusion (*to*, à); faire mention (*to*, de); *he never refers to it,* il n'y fait jamais allusion, il n'en parle jamais. ‖ COMM. *Referring to your letter,* comme suite à votre lettre.
— v. tr. Soumettre (*to*, à) [a question]; *to refer a question to s.o.'s judgment,* se référer à l'avis de qqn; *to refer oneself to,* s'en rapporter à, s'en référer à, s'en remettre à. ‖ Renvoyer (*to*, à) [s.o.]; *I have been referred to you,* on m'a dit de m'adresser à vous. ‖ Référer ; attribuer (*to*, à) [to attribute]; rapporter, rattacher (*to*, à) [to connect]. ‖ Ajourner (a candidate). ‖ JUR. Renvoyer (*to*, devant) [a matter]. ‖ FIN. *To refer a cheque to drawer,* refuser d'honorer un chèque.

referable [-əbl] adj. Attribuable; rattachable (*to*, à).

referee [,refə'ri:] v. intr., tr. Arbitrer.
— n. Répondant *m.* ‖ SPORTS, JUR. Arbitre *m.* ‖ FIN. Avaliste *m.*

reference ['refrəns] n. Référence, recommandation *f.* (certificate); référence *f.* (person); *to take up s.o.'s references,* prendre des renseignements sur qqn. ‖ Rapport *m.;* relation *f.* (*to*, avec) [connection]. ‖ Allusion *f.* (*to*, à); mention *f.* (*to*, de). ‖ Référence *f.;* renvoi *m.* (*to*, à); *reference book,* ouvrage à consulter ; *reference mark,* renvoi *m.* (in a book); repère (on a map). ‖ JUR. Renvoi *m.* (of an affair); compétence *f.* (of a court); répondant *m.* (person). ‖ ECCLES. *Reference Bible,* concordance biblique. ‖ LOC. *In* (or) *with reference to,* comme suite à (a letter); quant à, à propos de, en ce qui concerne, relativement à (a subject); *without reference to,* sans tenir compte de, sans égard pour.

referendum [refə'rendəm] n. Référendum *m.*

referential [-ʃəl] adj. De référence.

refill ['ri:'fil] v. tr. Remplir de nouveau.
— v. intr. Se remplir à nouveau. ‖ AUTOM. Faire le plein ; *refilling station,* poste d'essence.

— ['ri:fil] n. Objet (*m.*) de rechange (in general); cartouche *f.* (for a ball-point pen); pellicule (*f.*) de rechange (for a camera); pile (*f.*) de rechange (for an electric torch); feuilles (*f. pl.*) de rechange (for a note-book); mine (*f.*) de rechange (for a propelling pencil).

refine [ri'fain] v. tr. TECHN. Affiner (metals); épurer (oil); raffiner (sugar). ‖ FIG. Raffiner, épurer.
— v. intr. TECHN. S'affiner (metals); s'épurer (oil); se raffiner (sugar). ‖ FIG. Renchérir (*on, upon,* sur); se raffiner (manners); s'épurer (morals).

refinement [-mənt] n. TECHN. Affinage *m.* (of metals); épuration *f.* (of oil); raffinage *m.* (of sugar); perfectionnement *m.* (improvement). ‖ FIG. Raffinement *m.,* délicatesse *f.* (of character, feeling); raffinement *m.,* subtilité *f.* (subtlety).

refiner [-ə*] n. TECHN., FIG. Raffineur *m.*

refinery [-əri] n. TECHN. Affinerie *f.* (for metals); raffinerie *f.* (for sugar).

refit ['ri:'fit] v. intr. (1). NAUT. Se radouber.
— v. tr. Réparer, remettre en état. ‖ NAUT. Radouber. ‖ TECHN. Remonter (a factory); rajuster (a machine).
— ['ri:fit] n. NAUT. Radoub *m.* ‖ TECHN. Remontage *m.;* rajustement *m.*

reflate [,ri:'fleit] v. tr. FIN. Relancer (the economy).

reflation [,ri:'fleiʃən] n. FIN. Relance *f.*

reflect [ri'flekt] v. tr. PHYS. Renvoyer (heat, sound); réfléchir, refléter (an image, light). ‖ FIG. Refléter (personality); faire retomber (or) rejaillir (*on,* sur) [blame, discredit]; *reflected glory,* gloire qui rejaillit sur autrui.
— v. intr. PHYS. Réfléchir. ‖ FIG. Se dire, penser, se faire la réflexion (*that,* que); *to reflect on* (or) *upon,* faire tort à, nuire à la réputation de ; porter atteinte à (to harm); penser à, méditer sur, réfléchir à (to ponder); *to reflect upon,* blâmer, critiquer faire des réflexions désobligeantes sur (to criticize); adresser des reproches à (to reproach).

reflectingly [-iŋli], **reflectively** [-ivli] adv. Avec réflexion, d'un air réfléchi.

reflection [ri'flekʃən] n. Reflet *m.;* image *f.* ‖ Réflexion *f.* (meditation); *on reflection,* toute réflexion faite. ‖ Réflexion désobligeante; critique *f.* (censure); reproche *m.* (reproach); atteinte *f.* (on s.o.'s honour); *to cast reflections on,* blâmer. ‖ PHYS. Réflexion ; réverbération *f.* ‖ Pl. Réflexions, remarques, considérations *f. pl.;* commentaires *m. pl.* (*on, upon,* sur).

reflective [-tiv] adj. Réfléchi (person). ‖ PHYS. Réflecteur, réfléchissant (surface). ‖ GRAMM. Réfléchi (verb).

reflectiveness [-tivnis] n. Caractère réfléchi *m.*

reflector [-tə*] n. Réflecteur *m.* ‖ AUTOM. Rétroviseur *m.* (driving-mirror); catadioptre *m.* (of a bicycle).

reflex ['ri:fleks] n. Reflet *m.* ‖ MED. Réflexe *m.* ‖ FIG. Reflet *m.*
— adj. BOT. Réfléchi. ‖ MED. Réflexe. ‖ PHYS. Réfléchi, réflexe; *reflex camera,* appareil reflex. ‖ RADIO. Monté en reflex. ‖ MATH. Plein (angle).

reflexed [-t] adj. BOT., PHYS. Réfléchi.

reflexibility [ri,fleksi'biliti] n. Réflexibilité *f.*

reflexible [ri'fleksib] adj. Réflexible.

reflexion [-ʃən] n. See REFLECTION.

reflexive [-siv] adj. GRAMM. Réfléchi.
— n. GRAMM. Verbe (or) pronom réfléchi *m.*

reflexively [-sivli] adv. GRAMM. Au sens réfléchi ; à la forme réfléchie.

refloat ['ri:'flout] v. tr. NAUT. Renflouer. ‖ FIN. Emettre de nouveau (a loan). ‖ FIG. Remettre à flot.

refluence ['refluəns] n. Reflux *m.*

refluent [-ənt] adj. Qui reflue.

reflux ['ri:flʌks] n. Reflux *m.* ‖ Jusant *m.* (of the tide).

reforest [,ri:'fɔrest] v. tr., intr. Reboiser. (See REAFFOREST.)

reforge ['ri:'fɔ:dʒ] v. tr. Reforger.

reform ['ri:'fɔ:m] v. intr. Se reformer.
— v. tr. Reformer ; rallier.

reform [ri'fɔ:m] n. Réforme *f.* ‖ U. S. *Reform school,* maison de redressement.
— v. intr. Se réformer.
— v. tr. Réformer (abuses, s.o.) ; *to reform oneself,* se réformer, s'amender, se corriger. ‖ Réformer, apporter des réformes à (social services).

reformable [-əbl̩] adj. Réformable, corrigible.

reformation [,refə'meiʃən] n. Réforme *f.* ‖ ECCLES. Réforme *f.* ‖ FIG. Amendement, changement (m.) de conduite, conversion *f.*

reformative [ri'fɔ:mətiv] adj. De réforme.

reformatory [-ətəri] adj. Réformateur *m.;* réformatrice *f.;* de réforme. ‖ JUR. *Reformatory school,* maison de correction.
— s. JUR. Maison (f.) de correction (or) de redressement ; établissement (m.) d'éducation surveillée.

reformer [-ə*] n. Réformateur *m.;* réformatrice *f.* ‖ Réformiste *s.* (in politics). ‖ ECCLES. Partisan (m.) de la Réforme.

refract [ri'frækt] v. tr. PHYS. Réfracter ; *refracting telescope,* lunette d'approche.

refraction [ri'frækʃən] n. PHYS. Réfraction *f.*

refractive [-tiv] adj. PHYS. Réfractif, réfringent ; de réfraction (index).

refractivity [,rifræk'tiviti] n. Réfringence *f.*

refractor [ri'fræktə*] n. PHYS. Milieu réfringent *m.;* dispositif (m.) de réfraction.

refractoriness [-tərinis] n. Récalcitrance *f.;* caractère rebelle m.

refractory [-təri] adj. Réfractaire, rebelle, récalcitrant, insoumis. ‖ CHIM. Réfractaire. ‖ MED. Opiniâtre.

refrain [ri'frein] n. MUS. Refrain m.

refrain v. tr. † Refréner, retenir.
— v. intr. Se retenir, s'abstenir, s'empêcher, se garder (from, de).

refrangible [ri'frændʒibl̩] adj. PHYS. Réfrangible.

refresh [ri'freʃ] v. intr. Se rafraîchir (to drink) ; se restaurer (to eat) ; se reposer, se délasser (to rest).
— v. tr. Rafraîchir (to cool). ‖ Rafraîchir, restaurer (by drinking and eating) ; délasser, reposer (s.o.) ; retaper (fam.). ‖ FIG. Rafraîchir (the memory).

refresher [-ə*] n. JUR. Honoraires (m. pl.) d'encouragement. ‖ FIG. Rafraîchissement m. (of the memory) ; *refresher course,* cours de perfectionnement. ‖ FAM. Rafraîchissement m. (drink, food) ; *to have a refresher,* boire un pot.

refreshing [-iŋ] adj. Rafraîchissant. ‖ Réconfortant (sight) ; délassant, reposant (sleep).

refreshment [-mənt] n. Rafraîchissement, repos, délassement m. (rest). ‖ CULIN. Rafraîchissement, en-cas m. ; *to have some refreshment,* prendre qqch. ‖ **Refreshment-bar,** n. Buvette *f.* ‖ **Refreshment-room,** n. CH. DE F. Buffet m.

refrigerant [ri'fridʒərənt] adj., n. Réfrigérant m.

refrigerate [-reit] v. intr. Etre réfrigéré.
— v. tr. Réfrigérer, refroidir. ‖ Frigorifier (meat).

refrigeration [ri,fridʒə'reiʃən] n. Réfrigération, frigorification *f.*

refrigerator [ri'fridʒəreitə*] n. Réfrigérateur m. (of freezing-apparatus). ‖ Glacière *f.* (apparatus) ; chambre frigorifique *f.* (room). ‖ NAUT. Frigorifiques m. pl.
— adj. *Refrigerator van* (or) *car,* wagon frigorifique.

refrigeratory [-təri] adj., n. CHIM. Réfrigérant m.

refringent [ri'frindʒənt] adj. PHYS. Réfringent.

reft [reft] pret., p. p. See REAVE.

refuel ['ri:'fjuəl] v. intr. NAUT. Se ravitailler en combustible. ‖ AVIAT. Faire le plein d'essence.

refuge ['refju:dʒ] v. intr. S'abriter, se réfugier.
— v. tr. Abriter, donner asile à.

— n. Refuge, asile, abri m. ; *to take refuge,* se réfugier (in, dans).

refugee [,refju:'dʒi:] n. Réfugié s.

refulgence [ri'fʌldʒəns] n. Eclat m. ; splendeur *f.*

refulgent [-dʒənt] adj. Eclatant, resplendissant.

refund ['ri:'fʌnd] n. Remboursement m. ‖ FIN. Ristourne *f.*
— [ri'fʌnd] v. intr. Rembourser.
— v. tr. Rembourser, rendre (money) ; *to refund postage,* couvrir les frais d'envoi. ‖ FIN. Ristourner.

refundable [-əbl̩] adj. Remboursable.

refundment [-mənt] n. Remboursement m. ‖ FIN. Ristourne *f.*

refurbish [,ri:'fə:biʃ] v. tr. Remettre à neuf ; retaper (fam.).

refurnish ['ri:'fə:niʃ] v. tr. Remeubler (to furnish again) ; refournir (to redeliver).

refusable [ri'fju:zəbl̩] adj. Refusable.

refusal [-əl] n. Refus m. (to, de) ; *he will take no refusal,* il n'admet pas de refus ; les refus ne le rebutent pas. ‖ JUR. Droit (m.) de préemption (option) ; déni m. (of justice). ‖ COMM. Non-acceptation *f.* (of goods).

refuse [ri'fju:z] v. intr. Refuser, opposer un refus. ‖ SPORTS. Ne pas fournir la couleur (at cards) ; refuser de sauter (horse).
— v. tr. Refuser (a candidate, an offer). ‖ Rejeter, repousser (a request) ; opposer un refus à (s.o.) ; *to be refused sth.,* essuyer un refus, se voir refuser qqch. ; *to refuse s.o. sth.,* refuser qqch. à qqn ; *to refuse to do,* refuser de faire (or) se refuser à faire (sth.). ‖ MILIT. Refuser. ‖ SPORTS. Refuser de sauter (horse).

refuse ['refjus] adj. De rebut, de déchet.
— n. Ordures *f. pl.;* détritus m. pl. ; *household refuse,* ordures ménagères ; *refuse bin,* poubelle, boîte à ordures ; *refuse dump,* terrain de décharge. ‖ Déchets m. pl. (of food).

refutable ['refjutəbl̩] adj. Réfutable.

refutal [-l̩], **refutation** [,refju'teiʃən] n. Réfutation *f.* (See DISPROOF.)

refute [ri'fju:t] v. tr. Réfuter (an accusation) ; confondre (an accuser).

refuter [-ə*] n. Réfutateur *m.;* réfutatrice *f.*

regain ['ri:'gein] v. tr. Recouvrer, récupérer (see RECOVER) ; *to regain one's good name,* rétablir sa réputation. ‖ Regagner (a place) ; rejoindre (s.o.). ‖ MED. Recouvrer (one's strength) ; reprendre (consciousness).

regainable [-əbl̩] adj. Recouvrable, récupérable, regagnable.

regal ['ri:gəl] adj. Royal, de roi ; digne d'un roi. (See KINGLY.)

regale [ri'geil] v. intr. Se régaler (with, on, de).
— v. tr. Régaler (with, de). ‖ FIG. Réjouir.

regalia [ri'geiliə] n. pl. Insignes m. pl. ‖ Insignes royaux m. pl. (royal insignia) ; bijoux (m. pl.) de la couronne (Crown Jewels).

regality [ri'gæliti] n. Royauté, souveraineté *f.* ‖ Pl. Droits régaliens m. pl.

regard [ri'gɑ:d] n. † Regard m. (look). ‖ Attention, considération *f.* (to, pour) ; égard, souci m. ; *having regard to,* eu égard à, en raison de ; *to pay regard to,* avoir égard à, faire attention à. ‖ Rapport, sujet m. ; *in this regard,* à ce sujet ; *in* (or) *with regard to,* quant à, en ce qui concerne, vis-à-vis de. ‖ Respect m. ; considération, déférence *f.* ; *out of regard for,* par égard pour ; *to have great regard for,* avoir beaucoup d'estime pour. ‖ Pl. Amitiés *f. pl.;* compliments, respects m. pl.; souvenir m.
— v. tr. Regarder, considérer, observer (to look at). ‖ Avoir de la considération pour, estimer, respecter (to have respect for). ‖ Craindre (to fear). ‖ Faire attention à, tenir compte de (to take into account). ‖ Regarder, concerner (to concern) ; *as regards,* quant à ; *that does not regard me,* cela ne me concerne pas. ‖ Regarder, considérer, envisager (as,

comme); tenir (*as*, pour); *to regard as finished*, tenir pour fait; *to regard in the light of a disaster*, considérer comme un désastre.

regardant [-ənt] adj. BLAS. Regardant.

regardful [-ful] adj. Attentif (*of*, à); soigneux (*of*, de) [careful]. ‖ Plein d'égards (*of*, pour) [respectful].

regardfully [-fuli] adj. Avec soin. ‖ Avec beaucoup d'égards.

regarding [-iŋ] prep. Quant à, concernant, touchant, au sujet de, relativement à.

regardless [-lis] adj. Inattentif, indifférent (*of*, à); insouciant (*of*, de). [See IRRESPONSIVE.]
— adv. Sans se soucier, sans se préoccuper (*of*, de); *regardless of expense*, sans regarder à la dépense. ‖ FAM. Sans se laisser arrêter; *to press on regardless*, y aller tête baissée.

regardlessness [-lisnis] n. Indifférence, insouciance *f*.

regarnish ['ri:'gɑ:niʃ] v. tr. Regarnir.

regatta [ri'gætə] n. SPORTS. Régate(s) *f*. (*pl*.)

regency ['ri:dʒənsi] n. Régence *f*.

regenerate [ri'dʒenereit] v. tr. Régénérer.
— v. intr. Se régénérer. ‖ Se reproduire (to grow again).

regeneration [ri,dʒenə'reiʃən] n. Régénération *f*.

regenerative [ri'dʒenərətiv] adj. Régénérateur *m*.; régénératrice *f*.

regenerator [ri'dʒenəreitə*] n. Régénérateur *m*.; régénératrice *f*. ‖ TECHN. Régénérateur *m*.

regent ['ri:dʒənt] adj., n. Régent *s*.; *prince regent*, prince régent.

regicidal [,redʒi'saidl̥] adj. Régicide.

regicide ['redʒisaid] n. Régicide *s*.

regild ['ri:'gild] v. tr. (69). Redorer.

régime, regime [re'ʒi:m] n. JUR. Régime *m*.

regimen ['redʒimen] n. GRAMM., MED. Régime *m*.

regiment ['redʒimənt] v. tr. Enrégimenter.
— n. † Régime *m*. (government). ‖ MILIT. Régiment *m*.

regimental [redʒi'mentl̥] n. MILIT. Uniforme *m*.; *in full regimentals*, en grande tenue.
— adj. MILIT. Du régiment, régimentaire.

region ['ri:dʒən] n. Région *f*. ‖ FAM. *To cost something in the region of £200*, coûter dans les 200 livres. ‖ LOC. *The lower regions*, les Enfers.

regional [-l̥] adj. Régional.

regionalism [-lizm̥] n. Régionalisme *m*.

register ['redʒistə*] n. Registre *m*. (list). ‖ NAUT. Registre (*m*.) de visite, certificat (*m*.) de nationalité, lettres de mer *f*.; *Lloyd's register*, le Véritas; U. S. *Navy Register*, liste navale. ‖ JUR. Registre *m*.; liste *f*. (electoral); liste de contrôle *f*. (police); *land register*, matrice cadastrale; *public registers*, actes publics; *Register office*, bureau de l'état civil. ‖ MUS. Registre *m*.; étendue *f*. ‖ TECHN. Compteur, enregistreur *m*. (apparatus); registre *m*. (in printing). ‖ U. S. Bouche de chaleur (or) de ventilation *f*.
— v. intr. JUR. Se faire inscrire, s'inscrire (as an alien, on an electoral list, at a hotel, a university). ‖ COMM. S'inscrire (*with*, chez). ‖ TECHN. Coïncider exactement (parts); être en registre (in printing). ‖ U. S. MED. *Registered nurse*, infirmière diplômée d'Etat. ‖ FAM. Etre enregistré; *what he was told hasn't registered*, il n'a pas pigé.
— v. tr. Enregistrer, inscrire; prendre note de; *to register oneself*, se faire inscrire. ‖ Recommander (a letter). ‖ CH. DE F. Enregistrer (luggage). ‖ AUTOM. Immatriculer (a car). ‖ JUR. Déclarer (a birth); déposer (a trade-mark). ‖ TECHN. Faire coïncider (parts); enregistrer (rainfall); marquer (temperature); mettre en registre (in printing). ‖ FAM. Exprimer, refléter, traduire (happiness, surprise).

registrable ['redʒistrəbl̥] adj. Enregistrable.

registrar [,redʒis'trɑ:*] n. Archiviste *s*. (of a university). ‖ JUR. Officier (*m*.) de l'état civil; greffier *m*. (at court); *Registrar's office*, bureau de l'état

civil; *to get married before the Registrar*, se marier civilement. ‖ U. S. *Registrar's office*, secrétariat (of a university).

registration [,redʒis'treiʃən] n. Enregistrement *m*.; inscription *f*. ‖ Recommandation *f*. (of a letter). ‖ CH. DE F. Enregistrement *m*. (of luggage). ‖ MILIT. Recensement *m*. ‖ AUTOM. *Registration number*, numéro minéralogique; *registration plate*, plaque de police. ‖ MUS. Registration *f*. ‖ JUR. Dépôt *m*. (of a trade-mark).

registry ['redʒistri] n. Enregistrement *m*.; inscription *f*. ‖ NAUT. Certificat (*m*.) d'immatriculation; *port of registry*, port d'attache. ‖ JUR. Bureau de l'état civil (or) de l'enregistrement *m*.; *receiver of registry fees*, receveur de l'enregistrement.

regive ['ri:'giv] v. tr. Redonner.

reglet ['reglət] n. Réglette *f*. ‖ ARCHIT. Réglet *m*.

regnal ['regnəl] adj. Du règne (year).

regnant ['regnənt] adj. Régnant (sovereign, queen). ‖ FIG. Régnant, dominant (idea, opinion).

regorge ['ri:'gɔ:dʒ] v. intr. Refluer.
— v. tr. Dégorger, vomir (to vomit up). ‖ Ravaler (to swallow again).

regrate ['ri:'greit] v. tr. COMM. Regratter.

regress [ri'gres] v. intr. Retourner en arrière. ‖ ASTRON., FIG. Rétrograder.
— ['ri:'gres] n. Retour (*m*.) en arrière; régression, rétrogression *f*.

regression [ri'greʃən] n. Régression *f*.

regressive [-siv] adj. Régressif.

regressively [-sivli] adv. Régressivement.

regret [ri'gret] n. Regret *m*.; *much to my regret*, à mon grand regret; *with regret*, à regret (against one's wishes); avec regret (with sorrow).
— v. tr. (1). Regretter (sth. lost). ‖ Regretter, avoir le regret de (to long for). ‖ Regretter, être désolé (or) ennuyé (or) fâché de, avoir le regret de (see DEPLORE); *it is to be regretted that*, il est regrettable que.

regretful [-ful] adj. De regret (attitude); plein de regrets (person).

regretfully [-fuli] adv. Avec (or) à regret.

regrettable [-əbl̥] adj. Regrettable.

regrettably [-əbli] adv. Regrettablement.

regroup ['ri:'gru:p] v. tr. Regrouper. ‖ Remembrer (lands).

regulable ['regjuləbl̥] adj. Réglable.

regular ['regjulə*] n. MILIT. Soldat régulier *m*. (or) de carrière. ‖ ECCLES. Régulier, religieux *m*. ‖ FAM. Habitué *s*.
— adj. Régulier (features, footsteps); uniforme (surface). ‖ Fidèle (reader); habituel (hour); permanent (staff). ‖ Réglé, exact, ponctuel (person); *as regular as clockwork*, réglé comme du papier à musique. ‖ Régulier, en règle, dans les formes (according to rule); réglé, régulier (life); *to make regular*, régulariser. ‖ MILIT. Régulier (army, soldier); de carrière (officer). ‖ ECCLES., MED., GRAMM. Régulier. ‖ COMM. Normal, ordinaire (price); *regular customer*, habitué, bon client. ‖ FAM. Vrai, véritable; *he's a regular ass, a regular bore*, c'est un âne bâté, une vraie scie. ‖ U. S. FAM. Régulier; *regular guy*, chic type.
— adv. POP. See REGULARLY.

regularity [,regju'læriti] n. Régularité *f*. ‖ MED. Régularité intestinale *f*.

regularization [,regjulərai'zeiʃən] n. Régularisation *f*.

regularize ['regjuləraiz] v. tr. Régulariser.

regularly [-li] adv. Régulièrement. ‖ Vraiment, véritablement.

regulate ['regjuleit] v. tr. Régler; *to be regulated by*, se régler sur. ‖ Réglementer (people).

regulation [,regju'leiʃən] n. JUR. Règlement, arrêté *m*.; ordonnance *f*. ‖ NAUT. Régulation *f*. ‖

TECHN. Réglage *m.* ‖ AUTOM. *Regulation lamp,* lampe code.
— adj. Réglementaire. ‖ MILIT. D'ordonnance (boots) ; réglementaire (uniform).
regulative ['regjuleitiv] adj. Régulateur *m. ;* régulatrice *f.*
regulator [-tə*] n. Régulateur *m.,* régulatrice *f.* (person). ‖ TECHN. Régulateur *m.*
regulus ['regjuləs] n. ZOOL. Roitelet huppé *m.* ‖ ASTRON. Régulus *m.* ‖ TECHN. Culot *m.*
regurgitate [ri'gə:dʒiteit] v. intr. Regorger.
— v. tr. Régurgiter.
regurgitation [ri,gə:dʒi'teiʃən] n. Régurgitation *f.* ‖ MED. *Mitral regurgitation,* insuffisance mitrale.
rehabilitate ['ri:ə'biliteit] v. tr. Réhabiliter.
rehabilitation ['ri:ə,bili'teiʃən] n. Réhabilitation *f.* ‖ Reconstruction, réorganisation *f.* (of a country). ‖ MED. Rééducation *f.* ‖ JUR. Reclassement *m.* ‖ FIN. Assainissement *m.* (of the market).
rehandle ['ri:'hændḷ] v. tr. Traiter à nouveau (a question).
rehandle [ri:'hændḷ] v. tr. TECHN. Remettre un manche à.
rehash ['ri:'haeʃ] n. Réchauffé *m.* ‖ U. S. Rabâchage *m. ;* rengaine *f.*
— v. tr. Réchauffer. ‖ U. S. Rabâcher, ressasser, seriner.
rehearsal [ri'hə:səl] n. Enumération, relation *f. ;* récit détaillé *m.* ‖ THEATR. Répétition *f. ; dress rehearsal,* répétition générale (or) en costume.
rehearse [ri'hə:s] v. intr. THEATR. Répéter.
— v. tr. Enumérer, raconter en détail. ‖ THEATR. Répéter. ‖ JUR. Reconstituer (a crime).
reheat ['ri:hi:t] v. tr. Réchauffer.
reheater ['ri:'hi:tə*] n. TECHN. Réchauffeur *m.*
rehouse ['ri:'ha:uz] v. tr. Reloger ; recaser (fam.).
reify ['ri:ə,fai] v. tr. (2). U. S. Concrétiser (an abstraction).
reign [rein] v. intr. Régner (*over,* sur).
— n. Règne *m. ; in the reign of,* sous le règne de ; *the reign of despotism,* le régime du bon plaisir.
reigning [-iŋ] adj. Régnant (sovereign). ‖ SPORTS. *Reigning champion,* tenant du titre.
reimbursable [,ri:im'bə:səbḷ] adj. Remboursable.
reimburse [,ri:'im'bə:s] v. tr. Rembourser.
reimbursement [-mənt] n. Remboursement *m.*
reimport ['ri:im'po:t] v. tr. Réimporter.
reimport ['ri:'impo:t], **reimportation** [,ri:impo:'teiʃən] n. Réimportation *f.*
reimpose [,ri:im'pouz] v. tr. Imposer de nouveau (a duty, an obligation).
reimpression [,ri:im'preʃən] n. Réimpression *f.*
rein [rein] n. Rêne, bride *f. ; to hold the reins,* tenir les rênes (or) la bride. ‖ Brassière *f.* (for leading a child). ‖ FIG. *To give rein to,* lâcher la bride à (one's anger) ; donner libre cours (or) carrière à, se laisser entraîner par (one's imagination) ; *to keep a tight rein on,* tenir la bride serrée à (s.o.).
— v. intr. Ralentir (to slow up) ; s'arrêter (to stop).
— v. tr. **To rein back,** reculer. ‖ **To rein in,** retenir, contenir. ‖ **To rein up,** arrêter.
reincarnate ['ri:in'kɑ:neit] v. tr. Réincarner.
reincarnation ['ri:,inkɑ:'neiʃən] n. Réincarnation *f.*
reindeer ['reindi:ə*] n. invar. ZOOL. Renne *m.*
reinforce [,ri:in'fo:s] n. Renfort *m.*
— v. tr. TECHN., FIG. Renforcer. ‖ ARCHIT. Armer (concrete).
reinforcement [-mənt] n. Renforcement *m.* (action) ; renfort *m.* (material). ‖ Pl. MILIT. Renfort *m.* ‖ FIG. Renfort *m.*
reingratiate [,ri:in'greiʃieit] v. tr. Faire rentrer en grâce ; *to reingratiate oneself with,* rentrer en grâce auprès de.

reinless ['reinlis] adj. Sans rênes, débridé (horse). ‖ FIG. Sans frein, effréné.
reinsert [,ri:in'sə:t] v. tr. Réinsérer, réintroduire, replacer (*in, into,* dans).
reinstall [,ri:in'sto:l] v. tr. Réinstaller.
reinstate [,ri:in'steit] v. tr. Rétablir (*in,* dans).
reinstatement [-mənt] n. Rétablissement *m.* ‖ Réintégration *f.* (*in,* dans).
reinsure ['ri:in'ʃuə*] v. tr. JUR. Réassurer.
reinter ['ri:in'tə:*] v. tr. (1). Renterrer.
reinterrogate ['ri:in'terougeit] v. tr. Réinterroger.
reintroduce ['ri:'intrə'dju:s] v. tr. Présenter de nouveau (s.o.) ; réintroduire (sth.).
reinvest ['ri:in'vest] v. tr. Revêtir à nouveau (*with,* de). ‖ MILIT., FIN. Réinvestir.
reinvestment [-mənt] n. Réinvestiture *f.* ‖ MILIT., FIN. Nouvel investissement *m.*
reinvigorate ['ri:in'vigəreit] v. tr. Revigorer ; ravigoter (fam.).
reissue ['ri:'iʃju] n. Réédition *f.* ‖ FIN. Nouvelle émission *f.*
— v. tr. Rééditer (book). ‖ FIN. Emettre de nouveau.
reiterate [ri':itəreit] v. tr. Réitérer.
reiteration [ri:,itə'reiʃən] n. Réitération *f.*
reiterative [ri:'itərətiv] adj. Réitératif.
reject ['ri:dʒekt] n. Rebut *m.* (See REFUSE.) ‖ MILIT. Conscrit ajourné *m.* ‖ COMM. Article de rebut *m. ; export reject,* article impropre à l'exportation.
— [ri'dʒekt] v. tr. Rejeter, repousser (a possibility). ‖ Econduire (a suitor). ‖ Refuser (a candidate), repousser (a plea). ‖ MED. Rejeter, évacuer. ‖ MILIT. Ajourner.
rejectable [ri'dʒektəbḷ] adj. A rejeter ; rejetable.
rejection [ri'dʒekʃən] n. Rejet *m.* (of a bill) ; refus *m.* (of an offer). ‖ Pl. MED. Déjections *f. pl.* ‖ Pl. TECHN. Rebuts *m. pl.*
rejoice [ri'dʒɔis] v. tr. Réjouir, ravir, enchanter ; *to be rejoiced to,* se réjouir de.
— v. intr. Se réjouir, être ravi (*at, over,* de). ‖ **To rejoice in,** FAM. Jouir de, posséder (sth.) ; *he rejoiced in the name of Brown,* il s'honorait du nom de Brown.
rejoicing [-iŋ] n. Réjouissance, allégresse, liesse, jubilation *f.* ‖ Pl. Fête *f. ;* réjouissances *f. pl.*
— adj. Réjouissant (news) ; plein d'allégresse (or) de joie, en liesse (person).
rejoicingly [-iŋli] adv. Avec joie.
rejoin [ri'dʒɔin] v. intr. Répliquer (to reply).
— v. tr. Rejoindre (to meet). ‖ MILIT. Rejoindre, rallier.
rejoin ['ri:'dʒɔin] v. tr. Rejoindre, réunir.
— v. intr. Se rejoindre.
rejoinder [-də*] n. JUR. Réplique, riposte *f.* ‖ FAM. Repartie *f. ; neat rejoinder,* réponse heureuse.
rejuvenate [ri'dʒu:vineit] v. tr., intr. Rajeunir.
rejuvenesce [ri,dʒu:və'nes] v. intr. Rajeunir.
rejuvenescence [-ṇs] n. Rajeunissement *m.*
rejuvenescent [-ṇt] adj. Rajeunissant.
rekindle [ri'kindḷ] v. tr. Rallumer.
— v. intr. Se rallumer, se ranimer.
relapse Lri'læps] n. Rechute *f.* (*into,* dans). ‖ MED. Rechute *f. ; to have a relapse,* faire une rechute, rechuter. ‖ ECCLES. Relaps *s.*
— v. intr. Retomber (*into,* dans). ‖ MED. Rechuter. ‖ ECCLES. Etre relaps.
relate [ri'leit] v. intr. Se rapporter, avoir rapport, être relatif (*to,* à).
— v. tr. Relater (details) ; conter, raconter (a story) ; *strange to relate!,* chose curieuse!, étrange à dire ! ‖ Apparenter (two breeds) ; établir un rapport entre (two facts) ; rattacher (*to,* à) [a category].
related [-id] adj. Apparenté, allié (*to,* à) ; rattaché (*to,* à) ‖ PHILOS. Connexe. ‖ MUS. Relatif. ‖ CHIM. Apparenté.
relater [-ə*] n. Conteur *s. ;* narrateur *m.,* narratrice *f.*
relation [ri'leiʃən] n. Relation *f. ;* rapport, récit *m.*

(description). ‖ Parent s. (person); parenté f. (relationship). ‖ Relation f.; rapport m. (business, social); accointance f. (pejorative); friendly relations, relations d'amitié. ‖ Rapport m.; it bears no relation to the facts, cela n'a aucun rapport avec les faits. ‖ MED. Pl. Rapports sexuels m. pl. ‖ COMM. Public relations, contact (or) rapports avec le public.

relationship [-ʃip] n. Parenté f. (of families). ‖ Rapport m. (with, avec) [s.o., sth.].

relative ['relətiv] n. Parent s. ‖ GRAMM. Relatif m. — adj. Relatif (to, à); par rapport (to, à) [compared with]; dépendant (to, de) [depending on]. — adv. POP. Relativement (to, à).

relatively [-li] adv. Relativement.

relativism [-izm̩] n. PHILOS. Relativisme m.

relativist [-ist] n. Relativiste s.

relativity [,relə'tiviti] n. PHILOS., PHYS., FIG. Relativité f.

relax [ri'læks] v. intr. Se détendre, se délasser, se relaxer (person). ‖ Se détendre (to become less tense); se relâcher (to become less severe). ‖ Se relâcher (in, dans) [one's efforts]. — v. tr. Détendre, relâcher, desserrer (one's grip). ‖ JUR. Mitiger (a sentence). ‖ MED. Relâcher (the bowels); relaxer (one's limbs); enflammer (the throat). ‖ FIG. Détendre, délasser, distraire (the mind); se relâcher dans (one's efforts); relâcher (one's discipline).

relaxation [,rilæk'seiʃən] n. Récréation f., délassement m. (recreation); repos m. (rest). ‖ Détente f. (of the mind); relaxation f. (of the muscles); Relâchement m. (of discipline). ‖ JUR. Mitigation f. (of a sentence).

relay ['ri:'lei] v. tr. (89). Poser de nouveau, reposer.

relay [ri'lei] v. intr. Etre relayé, se relayer. — v. tr. RADIO. Relayer. ‖ TECHN. Munir de relais. — n. Relais m. (of horses, of men); relève f. (of workmen). ‖ ELECTR., SPORTS. Relais m. ‖ RADIO. Emission relayée f. ‖ Relay-race, n. SPORTS. Course (f.) à relais. ‖ Relay-station, n. RADIO. Relais m.

relearn ['ri:'lə:n] v. tr. Rapprendre.

releasable [ri'li:səbl] adj. AVIAT. Largable. ‖ CINEM. Projetable. ‖ TECHN. Qui peut se déclencher.

release [ri'li:s] n. Délivrance, libération f.; élargissement m. (setting free). ‖ Dispense, exemption, libération f. (from a commitment). ‖ Soulagement m. (from pain). ‖ Autorisation (f.) de publier (news); press release, communiqué de presse. ‖ AVIAT. Lâchage m. (of a bomb). ‖ MILIT. Démobilisation; mise en disponibilité f. (from the Forces). ‖ JUR. Cession f., transfert m. (of land); relaxation f. (of a prisoner). ‖ CINEM. Mise en circulation, location f. (of a film). ‖ COMM. Mise en vente f. ‖ COMM. Acquit, reçu m.; quittance f. ‖ TECHN. Déclenchement, débrayage, déclic m. (action, device); émission f.; échappement m. (of steam). ‖ Release-valve, n. TECHN. Soupape de sûreté. — v. tr. Délivrer, libérer, mettre en liberté, élargir (to set free). ‖ Dégager (one's foot, hand). ‖ Dispenser, libérer (from a commitment). ‖ Décharger (from a burden); soulager (from pain, sorrow). ‖ Faire sortir (a book); autoriser la publication de (news). ‖ AVIAT. Lâcher (a bomb); larguer (a fuel tank). ‖ MILIT. Démobiliser; mettre en disponibilité. ‖ JUR. Remettre (a debt); transférer (land); relâcher (a prisoner). ‖ CINEM. Mettre en circulation (or) en location. ‖ COMM. Mettre en vente. ‖ TECHN. Déclencher, débrayer.

releasee [rili:'si:] n. JUR. Cessionnaire s.

releaser [ri:'li:sə*] n. CINEM. Distributeur m. ‖ TECHN. Déclencheur m.

releasor n. JUR. Cédant s.

relegable ['relegəbl] adj. Relégable (to, à).

relegate [-geit] v. tr. Bannir (s.o.); reléguer (sth.). ‖ Renvoyer (to an expert). ‖ SPORTS. Reléguer, déclasser (a team).

relegation [,reli'geiʃən] n. Bannissement m. (of s.o.); relégation f. (of s.o., sth.). ‖ Renvoi m. (to an expert). ‖ SPORTS. Renvoi (m.) à la division inférieure.

relent [ri'lent] v. intr. S'adoucir, se laisser attendrir.

relentingly [-iŋli] adv. Avec moins de rigueur.

relentless [-lis] adj. Inflexible, implacable.

relentlessly [-li] adv. Inflexiblement.

relentlessness [-nis] n. Inflexibilité f.

relevance ['relivəns], relevancy [-ənsi] n. A-propos m.; pertinence f. ‖ Rapport m. (to, avec).

relevant [-ənt] adj. A propos, pertinent. ‖ Ayant rapport, applicable (to, à); to be relevant, entrer en ligne de compte. ‖ Significatif (facts); utile (information). ‖ JUR. Relevant documents, pièces justificatives.

relevantly [-əntli] adv. Pertinemment.

reliability [ri,laiə'biliti] n. Sécurité f. (of a machine); sûreté f. (of memory, of a person); honnêteté f. (honesty). ‖ ELECTR. Fiabilité f.

reliable [ri'laiəbl] adj. TECHN. Bon, de tout repos. ‖ FIG. Sûr; solide; sur qui on peut compter, digne de confiance (person); efficient, sérieux (secretary); bon, digne de foi (source).

reliance [ri'laiəns] n. Confiance f. (on, en).

reliant [-ənt] adj. Confiant (on, en). ‖ Dépendant (on, de).

relic ['relik] n. Relique f., reste m. (from the past). ‖ ECCLES. Relique f. ‖ Pl. Restes m. pl., dépouille f. (corpse). ‖ FAM. Ancêtre, croulant s.; vieux schnock m.

relict [-t] n. † Veuve f. ‖ GEOL., ZOOL., BOT. Relique f.

relief [ri'li:f] n. Aide, assistance f.; secours m. (aid); relief fund, caisse de secours. ‖ Soulagement m. (moral, physical); dérivatif m. (from, à) [one's sorrow]. ‖ Relief m.; valeur f.; to bring out in relief, mettre en relief; to stand out in relief against, se détacher sur. ‖ MILIT. Délivrance f. (of a town); relève f. (of a guard). ‖ AUTOM., CH. DE F. Relief coach, train, car, train supplémentaire; relief road, dérivation, route de délestage. ‖ JUR. Réparation f., redressement m. (of a wrong); basic relief, dégrèvement de base; relief from taxation, dégrèvement. ‖ ARTS. High, low relief, haut-, bas-relief. ‖ GEOGR. Relief m.; relief map, carte en relief. ‖ Relief-cock, n. TECHN. Décompresseur m.

relievable [ri'li:vəbl] adj. MED. Remédiable (illness); qu'on peut soulager (pain). ‖ MILIT. Secourable (position).

relieve [ri'li:v] v. tr. Soulager; dissiper (anxiety); to feel relieved, se sentir soulagé; to relieve s.o.'s mind, tranquilliser qqn; to relieve one's feelings, s'épancher. ‖ Soulager, secourir (to help). ‖ Remédier à (a situation). ‖ Dissiper (boredom); égayer (colours, life). ‖ MED. To relieve oneself, se soulager. ‖ MILIT. Relever (a sentry); délivrer (a town). ‖ TECHN. Réduire (the pressure). ‖ FAM. Soulager, délester (of, de) [s.o.].

relievo [ri'li:vou] n. ARTS. Relief m.

religion [ri'lidʒən] n. Religion f. ‖ Secte religieuse f. ‖ FAM. To take to religion, donner dans la dévotion.

religionism [-izm̩] n. Bigoterie f.

religionist [-ist] n. Bigot s.

religiosity [ri,lidʒi'ositi] n. Religiosité f.

religious [ri'lidʒəs] n. invar. ECCLES. Religieux s. — adj. ECCLES. De piété (book); religieux, pieux (person); de religion (wars). ‖ FAM. Religieux, scrupuleux (care).

religiously [-li] adv. ECCLES., FAM. Religieusement.

religiousness [-nis] n. Piété, dévotion f. ‖ Caractère religieux m. ‖ FAM. Religiosité f.

reline [,ri:'lain] v. tr. Refaire la doublure de, redoubler.

relinquish [ri'liŋkwiʃ] v. tr. Abandonner (hope); renoncer à (one's rights). ‖ Lâcher (to release).

relinquishment [-mənt] n. Abandon m. (of, de); renonciation f. (of, à).
reliquary ['relikwəri] n. Eccles. Reliquaire m.
relish ['reliʃ] n. Culin. Goût m.; saveur f. (of a dish); soupçon m. (of garlic); hors-d'œuvre, amuse-gueule m. (hors-d'œuvre); condiment, assaisonnement m. (seasoning); to eat with relish, se régaler. ‖ Fig. Piquant, ragoût, attrait m. (enjoyable quality). ‖ Fig. Penchant m. (for, pour); to do sth. with relish, se délecter à faire qqch.; to have a relish for, raffoler de.
— v. intr. Avoir un léger goût (of, de).
— v. tr. Goûter, apprécier (to enjoy). ‖ Culin. Assaisonner, relever. ‖ Fig. Se délecter à.
relive ['riː'liv] v. tr. Revivre.
reload ['riː'loud] v. tr. Recharger.
reloading [-iŋ] n. Rechargement m.
relocate [ˌriː'loukeit] v. tr. Situer à nouveau. ‖ Déplacer, transférer (a population, a factory); to relocate outside a city, décentraliser.
relocation [ˌriːlou'keiʃən] n. Transfert m.; décentralisation f. (outside a city).
reluct [ri'lʌkt] v. intr. Montrer de la répugnance (at, against, pour).
reluctance [-əns] n. Répugnance f.; to make a show of reluctance, se faire prier; with reluctance, à contrecœur. ‖ Electr. Reluctance f.
reluctant [-ənt] adj. Faire à regret (or) à contrecœur (action); répugnant, peu disposé (to, à) [person].
reluctantly [-əntli] adj. A son corps défendant.
rely [ri'lai] v. intr. (2). Compter, faire fond (on, upon, sur); s'en rapporter, se fier (on, upon, à); avoir confiance (on, upon, en).
remain [ri'mein] n. Reste m. ‖ Pl. Restes; débris; vestiges m. pl.; ruines f. pl. ‖ Pl. Restes m. pl.; mortal remains, dépouille mortelle.
— v. tr. Rester (in general); the fact remains that, il n'en reste pas moins vrai que; that remains to be seen, c'est ce que nous verrons. ‖ Rester, demeurer (to stay).
remainder [-ə*] v. tr. Comm. Solder.
— n. Reste m. (part); autres m. pl. (people). ‖ Jur. Réversion f. ‖ Pl. Comm. Invendus soldés m. pl. (books); fin de série f. (clothes).
remake ['riː'meik] v. tr. Refaire.
— n. Cinem. Remake m.
remaking ['riː'meikiŋ] n. Réfection f.
remand [ri'mɑː:nd] n. Jur. Renvoi (m.) à une autre audience; remand home, prison préventive.
— v. tr. Jur. Renvoyer; he was remanded for a week, son cas a été remis à huitaine. ‖ Jur. Person remanded in custody, préventionnaire; remanded in custody, en prison préventive.
remanence ['remənəns] n. Electr. Rémanence f.
remanent [-ənt] adj. Electr. Rémanent.
remark [ri'mɑː:k] n. Remarque, attention f. (notice). ‖ Remarque, observation f., commentaire m. (comment); réflexion f., propos m. (pej.).
— v. intr. Faire des remarques (or) observations (on, sur).
— v. tr. Remarquer, observer (to notice). ‖ Remarquer, faire remarquer (or) observer (to say).
remarkable [-əbl] adj. Remarquable.
remarkably [-əbli] adv. Remarquablement.
remarriage ['riː'mæridʒ] n. Remariage m.
remarry ['riː'mæri] v. intr. (2). Se remarier.
— v. tr. Se remarier avec. ‖ Remarier (registrar).
remediable [ri'miːdiəbl] adj. Remédiable.
remedial [-əl] adj. Réparateur m.; réparatrice f. ‖ Med. Curatif.
remediless ['remidilis] adj. Irrémédiable. ‖ Med. Sans remède.
remedy ['remidi] n. Med., Fig. Remède m. (for, à). ‖ Jur. Recours m. ‖ Fin. Tolérance f. (of the Mint).
— v. tr. (2). Med., Fig. Remédier à.
remelt ['riː'melt] v. tr. Refondre.

remember [ri'membə*] v. tr. Se rappeler, se souvenir de (see Recollect); se rappeler (that, que); easily remembered, facile à retenir; I remember seeing it, je me rappelle l'avoir vu; something to remember s.o. by, un souvenir de qqn. ‖ Retrouver; to remember oneself, se reprendre. ‖ Rappeler; remember me to your parents, rappelez-moi au bon souvenir de vos parents. ‖ Eccles. Commémorer (the dead). ‖ Fam. Remember the guide, n'oubliez pas le guide.
remembrance [-brəns] n. Souvenir m.; mémoire f. (memory, thing remembered). ‖ Mémoire f. (period of time); within the remembrance of man, de mémoire d'homme. ‖ Eccles. Remembrance Day, le jour de l'Armistice de 1918. ‖ Pl. Amitiés f. pl.; meilleur souvenir m.; compliments m. pl. (to, à).
remind [ri'maind] v. tr. Faire penser (of, à) [s.o.]; to remind s.o. of sth., rappeler qqch. à qqn. ‖ Rappeler, évoquer; he reminds me of his father, il me rappelle son père; that reminds me!, à propos!
reminder [-ə*] n. Mémento, mémorandum m. ‖ Comm. Rappel m.
reminisce [ˌremi'nis] v. intr. Raconter ses souvenirs. (See Recollect.)
reminiscence [-ns] n. Réminiscence f.
reminiscent [-nt] adj. Qui se souvient vaguement (of, de). ‖ Fam. Reminiscent of, qui fait penser à, évocateur de.
remiss [ri'mis] adj. Négligent, insouciant.
remissible [ri'misibl] adj. Rémissible.
remission [ri'miʃən] n. Diminution, atténuation f. ‖ Jur. Remise f. ‖ Eccles., Med. Rémission f.
remissness [ri'misnis] n. Négligence, insouciance f.
remit [ri'mit] v. intr. (1). Se relâcher, se calmer.
— v. tr. Remettre (to, à) [a question]. ‖ Relâcher (to relax). ‖ Eccles. Remettre, pardonner (sins). ‖ Jur. Différer; renvoyer. ‖ Comm. Remettre, faire parvenir (to, à).
remittal [-l] n. Remise f. (of a debt). ‖ Eccles. Rémission f. (for, de). ‖ Jur. Renvoi m. (of case); remise f. (of a sentence).
remittance [-əns] n. Comm. Versement m.; remise f.
remittee [rimi'tiː] n. Comm. Destinataire s.
remittent [ri'mitnt] adj. Med. Rémittent (disease, fever). ‖ Fig. Irrégulier, intermittent.
— n. Med. Maladie (or) fièvre rémittente f.
remitter [-ə*] n. Jur. Renvoi m. ‖ Comm. Remetteur m.
remnant ['remnənt] n. Reste, restant m. (see Remain). ‖ Débris, bout m.; bribe f. (of food). ‖ Vestige m. (of a custom). ‖ Comm. Coupon m. (of material); pl. soldes m. pl.; remnant sale, coupons en solde, solde de coupons.
remodel ['riː'mɔdl] v. tr. Réorganiser. ‖ Techn., Arts. Remodeler. ‖ Fig. Remanier, refondre.
remould [ˌriː'mould] v. tr. U. S. See Remould.
remonstrance [ri'mɔnstrəns] n. Remontrance f. ‖ Protestation f.
remonstrant [-ənt] adj. Qui proteste (person); de remontrance (or) protestation (tone).
— n. Protestataire m. ‖ Sermonneur s. ‖ Eccles. Remontrant m.
remonstrate [-eit] v. tr. Faire observer (or) remarquer.
— v. intr. Protester (against, contre). ‖ Faire des remontrances (upon, au sujet de; with, à).
remonstrative [ri'mɔnstrətiv] adj. De remontrance; de protestation.
remorse [ri'mɔː:s] n. Remords m. (at, de; for, pour); a feeling of remorse, un remords. ‖ Pitié f.
remorseful [-ful] adj. Plein de remords.
remorsefully [-fuli] adj. Avec remords.
remorseless [-lis] adj. Sans remords. ‖ Impitoyable (pitiless).
remorselessly [-lisli] adv. Sans remords. ‖ Sans pitié, impitoyablement.

remote [ri'mout] adj. Eloigné (*from*, de). ‖ Reculé (antiquity, period); lointain (country); retiré, écarté (spot). ‖ Faible, léger, lointain, vague (slight); *I haven't the remotest idea*, je n'ai pas la moindre idée. ‖ Distant, d'un abord difficile (stand-offish). ‖ TECHN. *Remote control*, commande à distance.

remotely [-li] adv. Loin, au loin, dans le lointain. ‖ De loin (related). ‖ Vaguement, faiblement.

remoteness [-nis] n. Eloignement *m.* ‖ Degré éloigné *m.* (of relationship). ‖ Attitude distante, réserve *f.* (aloofness).

remould [,ri:'mould] v. tr. Remodeler, refaçonner. ‖ AUTOM. Rechaper (to retread).
— ['ri:,mould] n. AUTOM. Pneu rechapé *m.*

remount [ri'mount] n. Cheval (*m.*) de rechange. ‖ MILIT. Remonte *f.*
— v. intr. Remonter à cheval. ‖ FIG. Remonter (*to*, à).
— v. tr. Remonter (a hill). ‖ Enfourcher de nouveau (a bicycle); remonter sur (a horse). ‖ MILIT. Rémonter.

removability [ri,mou:və'biliti] n. Amovibilité *f.*

removable [ri'mou:vəbl̩] adj. Amovible (official). ‖ Transportable (machine); mobile (object); détachable (piece).

removal [-əl] n. Enlèvement *m.* (taking away). ‖ Déménagement *m.* (of furniture); changement (*m.*) de domicile (change of address); *removal to a house*, emménagement. ‖ Déplacement *m.* (of an official). ‖ MED. Ablation *f.* ‖ FIG. Suppression *f.* (of an evil); soulagement *m.* (of suffering). ‖ FAM. Liquidation *f.* (murder).

remove [ri'mou:v] n. Distance *f.* ‖ Degré (*m.*) de parenté (relationship). ‖ Accès (*m.*) à la classe supérieure (in a school); *not to get one's remove*, redoubler une classe. ‖ † Déménagement *m.* ‖ CULIN. Service *m.*
— v. intr. Déménager.
— v. tr. Enlever, effacer, faire partir (a stain). ‖ Déménager (one's furniture). ‖ Retirer (one's hat); éloigner (sth. in the way). ‖ Transporter (to carry); retirer (to lead away). ‖ Déplacer (an official). ‖ MED. Lever (a bandage); opérer l'ablation de (a tumour); *removing cream*, crème à démaquiller; *to remove to hospital* (or) U. S. *to the hospital*, transporter à l'hôpital, hospitaliser. ‖ FIG. Supprimer (a difficulty); chasser (a doubt); écarter (an obstacle).

remover [-ə*] n. Déménageur *m.* (person); dissolvant *m.* (thing).

remunerate [ri'mju:nəreit] v. tr. Rémunérer.

remuneration [ri,mju:nə'rei∫ən] n. Rémunération *f.* (*for*, de).

remunerative [ri'mju:nərətiv] adj. Rémunérateur *m.*, rémunératrice *f.*

renaissance [ri'neisəns] n. ARTS. Renaissance *f.*

renal ['ri:nəl] adj. MED. Rénal.

rename [,ri:'neim] v. tr. Donner un nouveau nom à, rebaptiser.

renascence [ri'næsn̩s] n. Renaissance *f.*; renouveau *m.*

renascent [-n̩t] adj. Renaissant.

rend [rend] v. intr. (109). Se déchirer, se fendre.
— v. tr. Fendre (the air); déchirer (s.o.'s heart); *to rend one's hair*, s'arracher les cheveux.

render ['rendə*] v. tr. Rendre, donner en retour; *to render thanks to*, rendre grâces à. ‖ Rendre (homage, a service). ‖ Donner, fournir (to give); *to render an account of*, rendre compte de. ‖ Rendre (to make); *to render s.o. happy*, rendre qqn heureux. ‖ Rendre, traduire (into another language). ‖ † Rendre, restituer (*into*, à) ‖ MILIT. Rendre (a fortress); livrer (a prisoner); *to render oneself to*, se rendre à. ‖ JUR. Rendre (a judgment). ‖ ARTS, MUS. Rendre, interpréter. ‖ CULIN. Faire fondre. ‖ ARCHIT. Plâtrer; crépir.

rendering [-riŋ] n. Interprétation *f.* (interpreta-tion); traduction, version *f.* (translation). ‖ MILIT. Reddition *f.* ‖ ARCHIT. Crépi *m.*

rendezvous ['rᾶ:deivu:] n. Rendez-vous *m.*

rendition [ren'di∫ən] n. MILIT. Reddition *f.* ‖ U. S. Interprétation *f.*; traduction *f.* (translation); rendement *m.* (yield).

renegade ['renigeid] n. Renégat *s.*
— v. intr. ECCLES. Apostasier. ‖ FAM. Tourner casaque; *to renegade from*, renier.

reneg(u)e [ri'ni:g] v. intr. Renoncer (in cards). ‖ U. S. FAM. Renoncer, faire machine en arrière.

renew [ri'nju:] v. tr. Renouveler; *renewed outbreaks of unrest*, recrudescence de troubles; *to renew acquaintance with*, renouer connaissance avec; *to renew one's subscription*, se réabonner. ‖ JUR. Reconduire.

renewable [-əbl̩] adj. Renouvelable.

renewal [-əl] n. Renouvellement, remplacement *m.*; *renewal of subscription*, réabonnement. ‖ Reprise *f.* (of a activity).

rennet ['renit] n. Présure *f.*

rennet n. BOT. Reinette *f.* (apple).

renounce [ri'nauns] n. Renonce *f.*
— v. intr. Renoncer (in cards).
— v. tr. Renoncer à, abandonner (a right). ‖ Renier, désavouer (a friend, one's party); répudier (one's principles); dénoncer (a treaty).

renouncement [-mənt] n. Renoncement *m.* (*of*, à). ‖ Désaveu *m.* (of one's party).

renovate ['renoveit] v. tr. Renouveler, rénover; rajeunir; restaurer.

renovation [,renou'vei∫ən] n. Rénovation *f.*

renovator ['renouveitə*] n. Rénovateur *m.*; rénovatrice *f.*

renown [ri'naun] n. Renom *m.*; renommée *f.*

renowned [-d] adj. Renommé, réputé (*for*, pour); célèbre (*for*, par). [See FAMOUS.]

rent [rent] n. Déchirure *f.*; accroc *m.* (tear). ‖ Fissure *f.* ‖ FIG. Rupture *f.*; schisme *m.*
— pret., p. p. See REND.

rent v. intr. Se louer, être loué.
— v. tr. Louer; prendre en location (a house); fixer un loyer à (s.o.).
— s. Loyer *m.*; *quarter's rent*, terme. ‖ Prix (*m.*) de location (of a piano). ‖ AGRIC. Affermage *m.* ‖ **Rent-day**, n. Jour du terme *m.* ‖ **Rent-free**, adj. Exempt de loyer; adv. Sans payer de loyer.

rentability [,rentə'biliti] n. Rentabilité *f.*

rentable ['rentəbl̩] adj. Qu'on peut louer.

rental [-l] n. Montant du loyer, loyer *m.* ‖ U. S. *Rental library*, livres en location. ‖ Etat (*m.*) des loyers, revenu (*m.*) en loyers (ou) fermages.

renter [-ə*] n. Locataire *s.* (of a flat); fermier *m.* (of land). ‖ Loueur *s.* (lessor).

renunciation [ri,nʌnsi'ei∫ən] n. Reniement, désaveu *f.* (*of*, de). ‖ Renonciation *f.*; renoncement *m.* (*of*, à) [self-denial].

reoccupation ['ri:ɔkju'pei∫ən] n. Réoccupation *f.*

reoccupy ['ri:ɔkjupai] v. tr. (2). Réoccuper.

reopen ['ri:oupn̩] v. tr., v. intr. Rouvrir.

reorder [,ri:'ɔ:də*] v. tr. COMM. Passer une nouvelle commande de, commander à nouveau. ‖ Réorganiser.

reorganization [ri,ɔ:gənai'zei∫ən] n. Réorganisation *f.*

reorganize [ri'ɔ:gənaiz] v. tr. Réorganiser.
— v. intr. Se réorganiser.

reorient ['ri:'ɔ:rient] v. tr. Réorienter.

rep [rep] n. COMM. Reps *m.*

rep n. FAM. COMM. Représentant, V. R. P. *m.*

rep n. FAM. THEATR. Répertoire *m.*; *he acts in rep*, il fait partie d'une compagnie à répertoire.

repaint ['ri:'peint] v. tr. Repeindre.

repair [ri'pɛə*] n. † Fréquentation *f.* (*to*, de). ‖ Endroit fréquenté *m.* (place).
— v. intr. † Se rendre (*to*, à).

repair v. tr. Réparer; raccommoder. ‖ NAUT. Radouber. ‖ FIG. Réparer.
— n. Réparation *f.;* raccommodage *m.* (of clothes); *beyond repair,* irréparablement abîmé. ‖ Etat *m.; in bad repair,* en mauvais état; *to keep in repair,* entretenir. ‖ Pl. NAUT. Radoub *m.* ‖ TECHN. Réparation *f.; repair outfit,* nécessaire à outils; *repair shop,* atelier de réparations; *under repair,* en réparation.
repaper [,ri:'peipə *] v. tr. Refaire les papiers peints de, retapisser.
reparable ['repərəbl] adj. Réparable.
reparation [,repə'reiʃən] n. Réparation *f.*
reparative ['repərətiv] adj. Réparateur *m.;* réparatrice *f.*
repartee [,repɑː'tiː] n. Repartie, réplique *f.*
repartition [,riːpɑː'tiʃən] n. Répartition *f.*
repass ['riː'pɑːs] v. intr. Repasser (to pass again).
— v. tr. Repasser devant (a house); repasser, retraverser (a river). ‖ Repasser (to hand back). ‖ JUR. Voter de nouveau (a law).
repast [ri'pɑːst] n. Repas *m.*
repatriate [riː'pætrieit] v. tr.·Rapatrier.
repatriation [riː'pætri'eiʃən] n. Rapatriement *m.*
repay [ri'pei] v. intr. (105). Faire un remboursement *m.*
— v. tr. Rendre, rembourser (a sum of money); rembourser *(for,* de) [s.o.]. ‖ Récompenser (an effort). ‖ Rendre (a blow).
repayable [-əbl] adj. Remboursable.
repayment [-mənt] n. Remboursement *m.* ‖ FIG Récompense *f.*
repeal [ri'piːl] n. JUR. Révocation *f.* (of a decree); abrogation *f.* (of a law); annulation *f.* (of a sentence).
— v. tr. JUR. Révoquer (a decree); abroger (a law); annuler (a sentence).
repealable [-əbl] adj. Révocable; abrogeable.
repeat [ri'piːt] n. Répétition *f.* ‖ MUS. Reprise *f.* ‖ THEATR. Bis *m.* ‖ COMM. Commande identique *f.*
— v. intr. Se répéter. ‖ MED. Remonter, causer des renvois (food). ‖ TECHN. Etre à répétition.
— v. tr. Répéter; renouveler (to do again). ‖ Redire, répéter (to say again); *to repeat oneself,* se répéter. ‖ Réciter (by heart). ‖ ARTS. Reproduire. ‖ THEATR. Répéter. ‖ U. S. Redoubler (a class).
repeatedly [-idli] adv. A plusieurs reprises.
repeater [-ə*] n. Montre à répétition *f.* ‖ NAUT. Répétiteur *m.* ‖ MATH. Fraction périodique *f.* ‖ MILIT. Fusil *(m.)* à répétition. ‖ RADIO. Répétiteur, relais amplificateur, traducteur *m.* ‖ U. S. JUR. Récidiviste *m.* ‖ U. S. Redoublant *s.* (at school).
repeating [-iŋ] adj. A répétition (rifle, watch). ‖ NAUT. Répétiteur. ‖ MATH. *Repeating decimal,* fraction périodique.
repel [ri'pel] v. tr. (1). Repousser.
repellent [-lənt] adj. Répulsif. ‖ FIG. Repoussant, répugnant.
— n. Produit insecticide *m.* (insect-repellent). ‖ U. S. Tissu imperméable *m.* (waterproof fabric).
repent [ri'pent] v. intr. Se repentir *(of,* de).
— v. tr. Se repentir de; regretter. ‖ † *To repent oneself of,* se repentir de.
repentance [-əns] n. Repentir *m.; stool of repentance,* sellette.
repentant [-ənt] adj. Repentant.
repeople ['riː'piːpl] v. tr. Repeupler.·
repeopling [-iŋ] n. Repeuplement *m.*
repercussion ['riːpə:'kʌʃən] n. Répercussion *f.*
repercussive [-siv] adj. Répercutant.
repertoire ['repətwɑː*] n. THEATR., MUS. Répertoire *m.*
repertory [-təri] n. Répertoire *m.*
repetend [,repi'tend] n. Refrain *m.* ‖ MATH. Période *f.*

répétiteur [repeti'tœ:r] n. MUS. Maître de chant *m.* (of an opera singer).
repetition [,repi'tiʃən] n. Répétition; redite *f.* ‖ Réitération *f.* (of an action); renouvellement *m.* (of an effort). ‖ Récitation *f.* ‖ Collationnement *m.* (of a telegram). ‖ ARTS. Reproduction *f.* ‖ MUS. Reprise *f.* ‖ **Repetition-compound**, n. GRAMM. Composé *(m.)* par réduplication. ‖ **Repetition-paid**, adj. Collationné (telegram).
repetitive [ri'petitiv] adj. Plein de répétitions (book); rabâcheur (person).
repine [ri'pain] v. intr. Etre mécontent, se plaindre *(at, against,* de); murmurer *(at, against,* contre).
repining [-iŋ] adj. Mécontent (person); dolent (tone).
— n. Plaintes, murmures *f. pl.*
replace [ri'pleis] v. tr. Replacer, remettre en place (to put back in place). ‖ Remplacer *(by,* par); substituer *(by,* à) [to substitute].
replaceable [-əbl] adj. Remplaçable.
replacement [-mənt] n. Remise en place *f.;* remplacement *m.* (action); remplaçant *m.* (person). ‖ TECHN. Pièce *(f.)* de rechange. ‖ AUTOM. *Replacement engine,* moteur reconditionné.
replant ['riː'plɑːnt] v. tr. Replanter.
replate ['riː'pleit] v. tr. TECHN. Replaquer; redorer (with gold); réargenter (with silver).
replay ['riː'plei] v. tr. Rejouer.
— n. SPORTS. Match rejoué *m.*
replenish [ri'pleniʃ] v. tr. Remplir, faire le plein *(with,* de); *to replenish one's stock with,* se réapprovisionner en.
replenishment [-mənt] n. Remplissage *m.* ‖ Réapprovisionnement *m.*
replete [ri'pliːt] adj. Rempli, plein, gorgé *(with,* de).
repletion [ri'pliːʃən] n. Réplétion, satiété *f.*
replevin [ri'plevin] n. JUR. Mainlevée *f.*
replevy [-i] v. tr. (2). JUR. Obtenir la mainlevée de.
replica ['replikə] n. Fac-similé, double *m.,* reproduction, copie *f.* (of a document); réplique *f.* (of a painting).
replicate [-keit] adj. BOT. Replié.
— v. tr. Faire une copie de. ‖ Replier.
replication [,repli'keiʃən] n. Réplique *f.*
replunge ['riː'plʌndʒ] v. tr. Replonger.
— v. intr. Replonger. ‖ FIG. Se replonger.
reply [ri'plai] v. intr., tr. (2). Répondre; répliquer (quickly).
— n. Réponse *f.;* réplique *f.; reply paid,* réponse payée. ‖ COMM. *In reply to,* en réponse à (a letter). ‖ **Reply-coupon**, n. Coupon-réponse *m.*
repolish ['riː'pɔliʃ] v. tr. Repolir.
report [ri'pɔːt] n. Nouvelle *f.* (news); rumeur *f.,* bruit *m.* (rumour); *as report has it,* selon les bruits qui courent. ‖ Rapport *m. (on,* sur); procès-verbal *m.* (of a debate); compte rendu *m.* (of a speech); exposé *m.* (on a subject). ‖ Bulletin *m.* (made regularly); *to make a progress report,* faire un état périodique (or) un rapport sur l'état de la question; *stock-market report,* bulletin des cours de la Bourse; *terminal, weather report,* bulletin trimestriel, météorologique; U. S. *report card,* bulletin scolaire. ‖ Renom *m.;* réputation *f.; of good report,* de bonne réputation. ‖ MILIT. Détonation *f.* ‖ MED. *Sick report,* rôle des malades. ‖ JUR. Procès-verbal *m.; to draw up a report against,* dresser procès-verbal à.
— v. intr. Faire un reportage (for a broadcast, a newspaper). ‖ Donner son opinion (or) impression *(on,* sur). ‖ Rapporter, faire un rapport *(on,* sur); donner un compte rendu *(on,* de). ‖ Se présenter *(to,* à) [s.o.]. ‖ MED. *To report sick,* se faire porter malade. ‖ MILIT. *To report to one's unit,* rallier son unité.
— v. tr. Rapporter (s.o.'s words). ‖ Dire, déclarer (to declare); signaler, annoncer (to pass on the information); raconter, relater (to relate). ‖ Rap-

porter, répandre le bruit que ; *he is reported to have escaped yesterday*, on dit qu'il s'est échappé hier ; il se serait échappé hier. ‖ Faire un reportage sur (for a newspaper) ; faire un rapport sur (a project) ; faire un compte rendu de (a speech) ; *to report progress*, faire un rapport sur l'état de la question. ‖ *To report oneself*, se présenter (to a superior). ‖ Dénoncer (to denounce).

reportage [ripɔ:'tɑ:ʒ] n. Reportage *m.*

reported [ri'pɔ:tid] adj. GRAMM. *Reported speech*, style indirect. ‖ MILIT. *Reported missing*, porté manquant.

reporter [-ə] n. Reporter *m.; journaliste m.; our reporter in London*, notre correspondant (or) envoyé spécial à Londres ; *reporters' gallery*, tribune de la presse. ‖ Rapporteur, auteur d'un rapport *m.* ‖ JUR. Sténographe *m.* (for official records).

reposal [ri'pouzəl] n Action (*f.*) de placer.

repose [ri'pouz] v. intr. Reposer (to lie) ; se reposer (to take rest). ‖ FIG. Reposer, être fondé (*on*, sur). — v. tr. Reposer. ‖ FIG. Placer (one's confidence). — n. Repos *m.* (rest) ; sommeil *m.* (sleep). ‖ ECCLES. *Repose of the Virgin*, dormition de la Sainte Vierge. ‖ FIG. Repos, calme *m.; * sérénité *f.*

reposeful [-ful] adj. Reposant, calme.

repository [ri'pɔzitəri] n. COMM. Dépôt, magasin *m.; furniture repository*, garde-meuble. ‖ ELECTR. Caveau *m.* ‖ FIG. Dépositaire *s.* (of secrets).

repossess ['ri:pə'zes] v. tr. Rentrer en possession de (sth.) ; *to repossess oneself of*, reprendre possession de.

repoussé [rə'pu:se] adj., n. TECHN. Repoussé *m.*

repp [rep] n. COMM. Reps *m.*

reprehend [,repri'hend] v. tr. Réprimander, blâmer. (See REBUKE.)

reprehensible [-sibḷ] adj. Répréhensible.

reprehensibleness [-sibḷnis] n. Caractère répréhensible *m.*

reprehensibly [-sibli] adv. De façon répréhensible.

reprehension [,repri'henʃən] n. Réprimande *f.*

represent [,repri'zent] v. tr. Représenter (to be a representative of). ‖ Représenter, dépeindre (to depict) ; décrire (to describe) ; signaler (to point out) ; représenter (to portray), symboliser, figurer (to symbolize). ‖ THEATR. Jouer (a character) ; représenter (a play).

representable [-əbḷ] adj. Représentable.

representation [,reprizen'teiʃən] n. Représentation *f.* (act, image). ‖ Représentation *f.* (by ambassadors) ; *joint representation*, démarche collective (*to*, auprès de). ‖ Représentation, reproduction *f.* (presentation). ‖ Pl. Représentations *f. pl.; * remontrance courtoise *f.* (*to*, à). ‖ JUR. *Proportional representation*, représentation proportionnelle. ‖ THEATR. Représentation *f.* ‖ COMM. Représentants *m. pl.; * représentation *f.*

representational [,reprizen'teiʃənḷ] adj. Représentatif. ‖ ARTS. Figuratif, de la représentation du réel.

representative [,repri'zentətiv] n. Représentant *m.* (commercial, political). ‖ U. S. Député, représentant *m.* — adj. Représentatif (*of*, de).

representatively [-li] adv. Par représentation.

repress ['ri:'pres] v. tr. Presser de nouveau.

repress [ri'pres] v. tr. Réprimer, retenir. ‖ MED., FIG. Refouler.

repression [ri'preʃən] n. Répression *f.* ‖ MED., FIG. Refoulement *m.* (unconscious).

repressive [-siv] adj. Répressif ; de répression (measures).

reprieve [ri'pri:v] v. tr. JUR. Surseoir à l'exécution de. ‖ FIG. Accorder un délai à. — n. JUR. Sursis *m.; * commutation de la peine capitale *f.; right of reprieve*, droit de grâce. ‖ FIG. Délai, répit *m.*

reprimand ['reprimɑ:nd] n. Réprimande *f.* (See REBUKE.) — v. tr. Réprimander. ‖ JUR. Blâmer publiquement.

reprint [ri:'print] v. tr. Réimprimer ; *book that is reprinting*, livre en réimpression. — ['ri:print] n. Réimpression *f.; cheap reprint*, édition populaire ; *separate reprint*, tiré à part.

reprisals [ri'praizəls] n. pl. Représailles *f. pl.; as reprisals for*, en représailles de ; *to make reprisals*, user de représailles.

reprise [ri'praiz] n. JUR. Reprise *f.*

reproach [ri'proutʃ] v. tr. Adresser (or) faire des reproches à (*about, concerning*, au sujet de) [s.o.] ; blâmer (s.o., sth.) ; *to reproach s.o. for doing sth.*, reprocher à qqn d'avoir fait qqch. ; *to reproach s.o. with sth.*, reprocher qqch. à qqn ; faire grief à qqn de qqch. — n. Cause (*f.*) de déshonneur ; *to be a reproach to*, être la honte de. ‖ Honte *f.; * opprobre *m.* (disgrace). ‖ Reproche, blâme *m.* (See REBUKE.) ‖ ECCLES. Pl. Impropères *m. pl.*

reproachable [-əbḷ] adj. Reprochable.

reproachful [-ful] adj. Réprobateur *m.; * réprobatrice *f.*

reproachfully [-fuli] adv. Avec reproche.

reprobate ['reprobeit] v. tr. ECCLES., FIG. Réprouver. — [-bit] adj. ECCLES., FIG. Réprouvé. ‖ FAM. Dépravé. — n. ECCLES., FIG. Réprouvé *s.* ‖ FAM. Vaurien *m.; old reprobate*, vieux marcheur.

reprobation [,repro'beiʃən] n. Réprobation *f.*

reproduce [,ri:prə'dju:s] v. tr. Reproduire. — v. intr. Se reproduire.

reproducer [-ə*] n. Reproducteur *m.; * reproductrice *f.*

reproducible [-ibḷ] adj. Reproductible.

reproduction [,ri:prə'dʌkʃən] n. Reproduction *f.; reproduction rate*, taux de survie. ‖ Reproduction, copie *f.*

reproductive [-tiv] adj. Reproductif ; reproducteur *m.; * reproductrice *f.*

reproof ['ri:'pru:f] v. tr. Réimperméabiliser (a coat).

reproof [ri'pru:f] n. Reproche *m.* (See REBUKE.)

reproval [ri'pru:vəl] n. Reproche, blâme *m.*

reprove [ri'pru:v] v. tr. Réprimander, blâmer. ‖ † Réprouver.

reprovingly [-iŋli] adv. D'un air (or) ton réprobateur.

reprovision ['ri:prə'viʒən] v. tr. Réapprovisionner. — v. intr. Se réapprovisionner.

reptant ['reptənt] adj. ZOOL. Rampant.

reptile ['reptail] n. ZOOL. Reptile *m.* ‖ FAM. Chien couchant *m.* — adj. Rampant ; *the reptile press*, la presse vendue.

reptilian [rep'tiliən] n. ZOOL. Reptile *m.* — adj. ZOOL. Reptilien.

republic [ri'pʌblik] n. République *f.*

republican [-ən] adj., n. Républicain *s.*

republicanism [-nizm] n. Républicanisme *m.*

republicanize [-naiz] v. tr. Républicaniser.

republish ['ri:'pʌbliʃ] v. tr. Republier, rééditer.

repudiate [ri'pju:dieit] v. tr. JUR. Refuser d'honorer (a contract) ; répudier (a wife). ‖ FIG. Désavouer, renier, repousser. — v. intr. JUR. Renier une dette publique.

repudiation [ri,pju:di'eiʃən] n. JUR. Répudiation *f.* (divorce) ; refus (*m.*) de reconnaître une dette publique (by a government). ‖ FIG. Répudiation *f.; * désaveu, reniement *m.*

repugnance [ri'pʌgnəns] n. Incompatibilité (*between*, avec). ‖ Répugnance, antipathie, aversion *f.* (*against, to*, pour).

repugnant [-ənt] adj. Incompatible, inconciliable (*with*, avec). ‖ Répugnant (*to*, à) ; *to be repugnant*

to, répugner à. ‖ Répugnant (person); écœurant (fam.); dégueulasse (pop.).

repulse [ri'pʌls] v. tr. Repousser, rejeter (to reject). ‖ Repousser, rebuter (to rebuff). ‖ Milit. Repousser. — n. Milit. Echec *m.* ‖ Fig. Rebuffade *f.* (rebuff); refus *m.* (refusal).

repulsion [-ʃən] n. Répulsion, répugnance, aversion *f.* ‖ Phys. Répulsion *f.*

repulsive [-siv] adj. Froid, distant (stand-offish). ‖ Repoussant, répugnant, dégoûtant, écœurant, révoltant (disgusting). ‖ Phys. Répulsif. ‖ **Repulsive-looking,** adj. D'un aspect repoussant; *a repulsive-looking creature,* un affreux.

repulsiveness [-sivnis] n. Caractère repoussant *m.* ‖ Phys. Force répulsive *f.*

repurchase ['ri:'pə:tʃəs] n. Rachat *m.* — v. tr. Racheter.

reputability [ˌrepjutə'biliti] n. Honorabilité *f.*

reputable ['repjutəbl] adj. Honorable, estimable, estimé.

reputation [ˌrepju:'teiʃən] n. Réputation *f.*

repute [ri'pju:t] n. Réputation, renommée *f.;* renom *m.* (see Fame); *in repute,* réputé; *of ill repute,* mal famé (place). — v. tr. Etre réputé; *to be reputed to be stingy,* passer pour avare.

reputed [-id] adj. Supposé, prétendu.

request [ri'kwest] v. tr. Demander (qqch.); demander à, prier *(to,* de) [qqn]; inviter *(to,* à) [qqn]. — n. Demande, prière, requête *f.; by popular request,* à la demande générale; *on request,* sur demande. ‖ Faveur, vogue *f.; to be in request,* être très recherché; *he is much in request,* on se l'arrache. ‖ Autom. *Request stop,* arrêt facultatif, « faire signe au machiniste ». ‖ Radio. *Request programme,* émission composée de disques demandés par les auditeurs.

requiem ['rekwi.em] n. Mus. Requiem *m.*

require [ri'kwaiə*] v. tr. Exiger, réclamer, requérir (to demand); *to require s.o. to do sth.,* exiger de qqn qu'il fasse qqch., sommer qqn de faire qqch.; *to require sth. of s.o.,* exiger qqch. de qqn; *within the required time,* dans les délais prescrits. ‖ Exiger, demander, vouloir, nécessiter; avoir besoin de (to have need of); *he has all he requires,* il a tout ce dont il a besoin; *if required,* s'il le faut; *when required,* au besoin; *to require great care,* demander beaucoup de soin.

requirement [-mənt] n. Réclamation *f.* (demand); exigence, nécessité *f.;* besoin *m.* (need); *to meet s.o.'s requirements,* répondre aux désirs (or) satisfaire aux exigences de qqn. ‖ Condition requise *f.* (condition). ‖ U. S. Pl. Cours obligatoires *m. pl.*

requisite ['rekwizit] adj. Requis, indispensable. — n. Condition requise *f.* (condition). ‖ Chose nécessaire (or) indispensable *f.* ‖ Comm. Pl. Accessoires *m. pl.; toilet requisites,* objets de toilette.

requisition [ˌrekwi'ziʃən] v. tr. Réquisitionner. — n. Demande *f.* (request). ‖ Milit. Réquisition *f.; to call into requisition,* réquisitionner.

requital [ri'kwaitl] n. Récompense *f. (for,* de). ‖ Vengeance *f.;* représailles *f. pl.* (retaliation).

requite [ri'kwait] v. tr. Récompenser, payer de retour (an action); récompenser *(for,* de) [s.o.]; *requited love,* amour partagé. ‖ Venger (an insult).

reredos ['riədɔs] n. Eccles. Retable *m.*

rerun [ˌri:'rʌn] v. tr. (114). Repasser, ressortir (in a cinema); rediffuser (on T. V.). — ['ri:.rʌn] n. Reprise *f.* (in a cinema); rediffusion *f.* (on T. V.).

resale ['ri:'seil] n. Revente *f.*

rescind [ri'sind] v. tr. Jur. Révoquer (an act); annuler (a decision); casser (a judgment); abroger (a law).

rescission [ri'siʒən] n. Jur. Rescision *f.* (of an act); annulation *f.* (of a decision); abrogation *f.* (of a law).

rescript ['ri:skript] n. Nouvelle transcription *f.* ‖ Jur. Rescrit *m.*

rescue ['reskju:] n. Secours, sauvetage *m.;* délivrance *f.; to the rescue!,* au secours!; *rescue party, work,* équipe, travaux de sauvetage; *rescue squad,* équipe de secours. ‖ Jur. Délivrance par la force *f.* — v. tr. Secourir, porter secours à. ‖ Sauver, délivrer, tirer *(from,* de). ‖ Jur. Délivrer de force.

rescued [-d] adj. Sauvé, délivré. — n. Rescapés *s. pl.*

rescuer [-ə *] n. Sauveteur *m.;* libérateur *m.;* libératrice *f.* ‖ Med. Secouriste *s.*

research [ri'sə:tʃ] v. intr. Faire des recherches. — s. Recherche *f.* (on, sur); *research worker,* chercheur.

researcher [-ə*] n. Chercheur *s.*

reseat [ˌri:'si:t] v. tr. Recapitonner, rempailler, refaire le fond de (a chair); refaire les sièges de (a theatre, a church). ‖ Changer de place, rasseoir (a person); *to reseat oneself,* se rasseoir. ‖ Techn. Refaire le siège de (a valve).

resect [ri'sekt] v. tr. Med. Réséquer.

resection [ri'sekʃən] n. Med. Résection *f.*

reseda [ri'si:də] adj., n. Bot. Réséda *m.*

resell ['ri:'sel] v. tr. (120). Revendre.

resemblance [ri'zembləns] n. Ressemblance *f.* (to, avec). [See Likeness.]

resemble [ri'zembl] v. tr. Ressembler à; *to resemble one another,* se ressembler.

resembling [-iŋ] adj. Ressemblant.

resent [ri'zent] v. tr. Etre froissé (or) blessé de (to feel displeasure); être indigné de, s'offenser de (to feel indignation).

resentful [-ful] adj. Rancunier, plein de ressentiment. ‖ Irrité, outré *(of,* de).

resentment [-mənt] n. Ressentiment *m.*

reservation [ˌrezə'veiʃən] n. Réserve *f.; mental reservation,* restriction mentale; *with reservation,* sous bénéfice d'inventaire. ‖ Location, réservation *f.* (booking); cabine (or) chambre (or) place retenue *f.* (cabin, room, seat). ‖ Jur. Réservation *f.* ‖ U. S. Terrain réservé *m.;* réserves *f. pl.* (park).

reserve [ri'zə:v] v. tr. Réserver *(for,* pour); (to reserve oneself for, se réserver pour. ‖ Mettre en réserve (to keep for a purpose); mettre de côté (to set aside). ‖ Réserver, retenir (to book). — n. Réserve, restriction *f.; with all reserve,* sous toutes réserves. ‖ Milit., Agric., Fin. Réserve *f.* ‖ Comm. *Reserve price,* prix minimum. ‖ Fig. Réserve *f.* (attitude).

reserved [-d] adj. Réservé; loué (seat). ‖ Naut. *Reserved list,* cadre de réserve. ‖ Comm. *All rights reserved,* tous droits de reproduction réservés. ‖ Fig. Réservé (person).

reservedly [-idli] adv. Avec réserve.

reservist [-ist] n. Milit. Réserviste *m.*

reservoir ['rezəvwɑ:*] n. Réservoir *m.*

reset ['ri:'set] v. tr. (122). Remettre en place, replacer. ‖ Remettre à l'heure (one's watch). ‖ Med. Remettre (a limb). ‖ Techn. Remonter (a precious stone). ‖ Agric. Replanter.

resettle ['ri:'setl] v. tr. Remettre. ‖ Réinstaller; recaser (fam.).

reshape [ˌri:'ʃeip] v. tr. Remodeler, restructurer.

reship ['ri:'ʃip] v. tr., intr. Naut. Rembarquer.

reshuffle ['ri:'ʃʌfl] v. tr. Rebattre (cards). ‖ Fig. Remanier (the Cabinet). — n. Nouveau battement *m.* ‖ Fig. *Cabinet reshuffle,* remaniement ministériel.

reside [ri'zaid] v. intr. Résider (in, dans) [person]. ‖ Résider (in, dans); appartenir (in, à) [quality]. ‖ Etre acquis (or) dévolu (in, à) [rights].

residence ['rezidəns] n. Résidence, demeure, habitation *f.; gentleman's residence,* maison de maître. ‖ Résidence *f.;* séjour *m.* (stay). ‖ Jur. Domicile *m.; residence permit,* permis de séjour.

residency [-ənsi] n. Résidence *f.*

resident [-ənt] n. Habitant; pensionnaire s. ‖ Résident m. (official).
— adj. Résidant. ‖ A demeure (official); fixe (population). ‖ Appartenant (in, à). ‖ MED. Resident physician, interne; médecin à demeure.
residential [,rezi'denʃəl] adj. Résidentiel.
residual [ri'zidjuəl] n. MATH. Reste m. ‖ CHIM. Résidu m.
— adj. Restant. ‖ CHIM. Résiduel, résiduaire.
residuary [-əri] adj. JUR. Residuary legatee, légataire universel. ‖ CHIM. Résiduel, résiduaire.
residue ['rezidju:] n. Reste m. ‖ JUR. Reliquat m. (of an inheritance). ‖ MATH., CHIM. Résidu m.
residuum [ri'zidjuəm] (pl. **residua** [-juə]) n. Reste m. ‖ CHIM. Résidu m. (See RESIDUE.)
resign [ri'zain] v. intr. Donner sa démission, démissionner (from, de).
— v. tr. Résigner (one's office); se démettre de, donner sa démission de (one's post). ‖ Abandonner (to, à) [sth.]. ‖ ECCLES. Remettre (to, à) [one's soul]. ‖ FIG. Soumettre; to resign oneself to, se résigner à.
resignation [,rezig'neiʃən] n. Démission f.; to hand in one's resignation, donner sa démission. ‖ JUR. Abandon m. (of a right). ‖ FIG. Résignation, acceptation f.
resignedly [ri'zainidli] adv. Avec résignation.
resile [ri'zail] v. intr. PHYS. Rebondir.
resilience [ri'ziliəns], **resiliency** [-i] n. Rebondissement m. (act); élasticité f. (quality). ‖ FIG. Ressort moral m.
resilient [-ənt] adj. Rebondissant, élastique. ‖ FIG. Energique, vif.
resin ['rezin] v. tr. Résiner.
— n. Résine f. ‖ **Resin-tapper**, n. Résinier m. ‖ **Resin-tapping**, n. Résinage m.
resinous ['rezinəs] adj. Résineux.
resipiscence [,resi'pisəns] n. Résipiscence f.
resist [ri'zist] v. tr. Résister à; no woman could resist him, il ne trouvait pas de cruelles. ‖ Résister à la tentation de.
— v. intr. Résister, offrir de la résistance, faire opposition.
resistance [-əns] n. Résistance f.; to offer no resistance, se laisser faire. ‖ MILIT. Resistance fighter, movement, résistant, résistance. ‖ TECHN., ELECTR. Résistance f. ‖ FAM. To take the line of least resistance, aller au plus facile, suivre la loi du moindre effort. ‖ **Resistance-box**, n. ELECTR. Rhéostat m.; boîte de résistance f.
resistant [-ənt] adj. Résistant.
resistivity [,rizis'tiviti] n. ELECTR. Résistivité f.
resistless [ri'zistlis] adj. Irrésistible. ‖ Sans résistance, incapable de résister (unresisting).
resistlessly [-li] adv. Irrésistiblement.
resistor [-ə*] n. ELECTR. Résistance f.
resit [ri:'sit] v. tr. (136). Repasser, se représenter à (an examination).
resole ['ri:'soul] v. tr. TECHN. Ressemeler.
resoling [-iŋ] n. TECHN. Ressemelage m.
resoluble ['rezəljubļ] adj. Résoluble (problem). ‖ CHIM. Décomposable (into, en).
resolute ['rezəlju:t] adj. Résolu, déterminé.
resolutely [-li] adv. Résolument.
resoluteness [-nis] n. Résolution, fermeté f.
resolution [,rezə'lju:ʃən] n. Résolution, détermination, décision f. (act, quality); lack of resolution, manque de fermeté (or) caractère; to make a resolution, prendre une résolution. ‖ MED., MATH., CHIM., JUR. Résolution f. ‖ RADIO. Picture resolution, définition d'une image télévisée.
resolutive ['rezəljutiv] n. Résolutif m.
— adj. JUR. Résolutoire. ‖ MED. Résolutif.
resolvability [,rizɔlvə'biliti] n. Résolubilité f.
resolvable [ri'zɔlvəbļ] adj. Résoluble.
resolve [ri'zɔlv] n. Résolution, détermination f.
— v. intr. Se résoudre, se dissoudre (into, en). ‖

MED. Se résoudre; se résorber. ‖ FIG. Se résoudre, se décider, se déterminer (to, upon, à).
— v. tr. † Décider (s.o.). ‖ Résoudre, transformer (into, en). ‖ Résoudre, décider (to, de); this being resolved upon, cela une fois résolu (or) décidé. ‖ Dissiper (a doubt); résoudre (a problem). ‖ MUS., MED., PHYS. Résoudre.
resolvedly [-idli] adv. Résolument.
resolvent [ri'zɔlvənt] adj., n. Résolvant m.
resonance ['rezənəns] n. Résonance f.
resonant [-ənt] adj. Résonnant.
resonator [-eitə*] n. Résonateur m.
resorb [ri'zɔ:b] v. tr. Résorber.
resorcin [ri'zɔ:sin] n. CHIM. Résorcine f.
resorption [ri'sɔ:pʃən] n. Résorption f.
resort [ri'zɔ:t] v. intr. To resort to, fréquenter (to frequent); se rendre à, aller à (to go). ‖ FIG. Recourir, avoir recours (to, à).
— n. Concours m.; affluence f. (thronging). ‖ Lieu de séjour m. (place); bathing, seaside resort, station balnéaire, plage; health, winter resort, station climatique, hivernale. ‖ FIG. Recours m. (to, à); in the last resort, en dernier ressort.
resound [ri'zaund] v. tr. Faire résonner. ‖ † Chanter (praises).
— v. intr. Résonner; retentir (with, de). ‖ FIG. Avoir du retentissement.
resounding [-iŋ] adj. Retentissant.
resource [ri'sɔ:s] n. Ressource f. (resourcefulness). ‖ Ressource f. (see EXPEDIENT); as a last resource, en dernier ressort. ‖ Récréation, distraction f. (amusement). ‖ Pl. FIN. Ressources f. pl.
resourceful [-ful] adj. Plein de ressources; débrouillard (fam.).
resourceless [-lis] adj. Sans ressources (without money). ‖ Peu débrouillard, empoté.
respect [ris'pekt] v. tr. Respecter, estimer, éprouver du respect pour (to feel esteem for). ‖ Concerner, avoir rapport (or) trait à (to relate to); as respects, quant à, concernant. ‖ Respecter (the law).
— n. Respect m.; out of respect for, par respect (or) égard pour. ‖ Considération, déférence f. (esteem). ‖ Point de vue m.; in one respect, sous un certain rapport; in other respects, à d'autres égards; in some respects, en quelque sorte. ‖ Rapport m.; to have respect to, concerner, se rapporter à; with respect to, en ce qui concerne, quant à. ‖ Considération f.; égard m.; attention f. (of, to pour); to have respect to, avoir égard à, se soucier de, tenir compte de; without respect of persons, sans acception de personnes. ‖ Pl. Respects, hommages, devoirs m. pl.
respectability [ris,pektə'biliti] n. Respectabilité f., honorabilité f. ‖ Convenance, décence f.; bienséances f. pl. (decency). ‖ Pl. FAM. Gens honorables m. pl.
respectable [ris'pektəbļ] adj. Respectable, honorable, estimable (worthy of respect). ‖ Respectable, considérable (considerable). ‖ Passable, assez bon (not to be disdained). ‖ Honnête, digne, comme il faut (decent); convenable (presentable).
respectably [-bli] adv. Respectablement, honorablement. ‖ Convenablement, comme il faut. ‖ Passablement, pas mal (fairly well).
respecter [-ə*] n. To be no respecter of, ne pas respecter (laws); ne pas faire acception de (persons).
respectful [-ful] adj. Respectueux (towards, envers, à l'égard de, pour).
respectfully [-fuli] adv. Respectueusement.
respecting [-iŋ] prep. Relativement à, à propos de, quant à, touchant, concernant, en ce qui concerne. (See CONCERNING.)
respective [-iv] adj. Respectif.
respectively [-ivli] adv. Respectivement.
respirable ['respirəb] adj. Respirable.
respiration [,respi'reiʃən] n. MED. Respiration f.

respirator ['respireitə*] n. MED. Respirateur *m*. ‖ MILIT. Masque à gaz *m*.

respiratory [-əri] adj. MED. Respiratoire.

respire [ris'paiə*] v. intr., tr. MED. Respirer.

respite ['respit] n. Répit *m*.; *no respite*, pas de cesse. ‖ JUR. Sursis, délai *m*. (*for*, de, pour).
— v. tr. Accorder un répit à. ‖ MED. Soulager momentanément. ‖ JUR. Accorder un sursis à (the accused); surseoir à l'éxécution de (a condemned prisoner); différer (a judgment).

resplendence [ris'plendəns], **resplendency** [-ənsi] n. Resplendissement *m*.

resplendent [-ənt] adj. Resplendissant.

respond [ris'pɔnd] n. ECCLES. Répons *m*.
— v. intr. Répondre (*to*, à). ‖ Obéir; réagir [*to*, à]. ‖ U. S. JUR. Etre responsable.

respondent [-ənt] n. Répondant *s*. ‖ JUR. Défendeur *m*.; défenderesse *f*.
— adj. Répondant; réagissant (*to*, à).

response [ris'pɔns] n. Réponse *f*.; *to meet with a warm response*, recevoir un accueil chaleureux. ‖ Réaction *f*.

responsibility [ris,pɔnsi'bility] n. Responsabilité *f*.; *on one's responsibility*, sous sa propre responsabilité.

responsible [ris'pɔnsibl] adj. Digne de confiance, sur qui on peut compter (person); autorisé (quarters). ‖ Comportant des responsabilités (post). ‖ Chargé (*for*, de); responsable (*for*, de; *to*, envers); *to be directly responsible to*, relever directement de. ‖ Responsable (*for*, de) [one's actions]. ‖ FIN. Solvable. ‖ FAM. Auteur (*for*, de).

responsions [-ʃənz] n. pl. Premier (*m*.) des trois examens d'admissibilité au B. A. (à l'université d'Oxford).

responsive [-siv] adj. Sensible. ‖ Vibrant (audience) [*to*, à]. ‖ TECHN. Nerveux (motor).

responsively [sivli] adv. En réponse. ‖ Avec sympathie (or) réciprocité de sentiments.

responsiveness [-sivnis] n. Sensibilité, sympathie *f*. ‖ TECHN. Nervosité *f*.

responsory [-səri] n. ECCLES. Répons *m*.

respray [,ri:'sprei] v. tr. TECHN. Repeindre au pistolet, refaire la laque de (a car).

rest [rest] v. intr. Se reposer; *not to rest till*, n'avoir de cesse que; *to rest easy*, dormir sur ses deux oreilles. ‖ Reposer, demeurer (to remain). ‖ Etre fondé (*on*, sur) [to be founded on]; reposer, s'appuyer (*on*, sur) [to lean on]. ‖ FIG. Tomber, se poser, s'arrêter (*on*, sur) [to come to rest on]; se fier (*on*, à); s'appuyer, se reposer (*on*, sur) [to rely on]. ‖ FAM. *To rest upon one's oars*, s'endormir (fam.).
— v. tr. Faire (or) laisser reposer; *to rest oneself*, se reposer; *God rest his soul!*, Dieu lui donne le repos! ‖ Poser, appuyer (to lean). ‖ FIG. Fonder.
— n. Repos *m*.; *at rest*, au repos. ‖ Repos, sommeil *m*. (sleep). ‖ Repos, calme *m*.; *to set one's heart at rest*, se tranquilliser. ‖ Arrêt *m*.; pause *f*.; *to come to rest*, s'immobiliser. ‖ Asile, foyer *m*. (rest-home). ‖ ECCLES. Repos *m*. (death); *to lay s.o. to rest*, enterrer qqn. ‖ MUS. Silence *m*.; *crotchet* (or) U. S. *quarter rest*, soupir; *quaver rest*, demi-soupir; *semibreve* (or) U. S. *eighth* (or) U. S. *whole rest*, pause. ‖ TECHN. Appui, support *m*. ‖ **Rest-camp**, n. MILIT. Cantonnement de repos. ‖ **Rest-cure**, n. MED. Cure de repos. ‖ **Rest-house**, n. Auberge, hôtellerie *f*. (inn); maison (*f*.) de repos (for workers). ‖ **Rest-room**, n. U. S. Toilette *f*.

rest v. intr. Rester, demeurer; *and there the matter rests*, les choses en sont là. ‖ Appartenir, tenir, incomber (*with*, à).
— n. Reste, restant *m*. (remainder); *the rest*, les autres (people). ‖ FIN. Réserve *f*. ‖ COMM. Arrêté *m*. ‖ FAM. *And all the rest of it*, et tout le tremblement; et patati et patata.

restart ['ri:'stɑ:t] v. intr., Recommencer, reprendre; remettre ça (fam.). ‖ TECHN. Repartir.
— v. tr. Recommencer, reprendre. ‖ TECHN. Remettre en marche.

restate ['ri:'steit] v. tr. Répéter.

restaurant ['restərənt] n. Restaurant *m*. ‖ **Restaurant-car**, n. CH. DE F. Wagon-restaurant *m*.

restaurateur [,restərə'tə:*] n. Restaurateur *s*. (restaurant-keeper).

restful ['restful] adj. Reposant (giving rest); paisible, tranquille (quiet).

restfully [-i] adv. Paisiblement, tranquillement.

restfulness [-nis] n. Tranquillité *f*.

restitute ['restitju:t] v. tr. Restituer.

restitution [,resti'tju:ʃən] n. Restitution *f*.; *to make restitution of*, restituer. ‖ Réparation, compensation *f*. ‖ PHYS. Retour (*m*.) d'une forme primitive.

restive ['restiv] adj. Rétif. ‖ Nerveux (uneasy).

restively [-li] adv. Avec nervosité.

restiveness [-nis] n. Humeur rétive *f*. ‖ Nervosité *f*. (uneasiness).

restless [restlis] adj. Agité (sea). ‖ Remuant, turbulent (child). ‖ MED. Blanc, d'insomnie (night); agité (patient). ‖ FIG. Agité, inquiet (mind); *to get restless*, s'impatienter, ne pas tenir en place.

restlessly [-li] adv. Sans repos. ‖ Avec turbulence. ‖ Avec inquiétude. ‖ Nerveusement, fébrilement, fiévreusement.

restlessness [-nis] n. Turbulence, agitation *f*. ‖ MED. Insomnie *f*. ‖ FIG. Agitation, fièvre, fébrilité, nervosité *f*.

restock ['ri:'stɔk] v. tr. AGRIC. Repeupler (*with*, de) [forest]; reboiser (land). ‖ COMM. Remonter, réapprovisionner (*with*, en).

restorable [ris'tɔ:rəbl] adj. Rétablissable. ‖ ARTS, TECHN. Restaurable.

restoration [,restɔ'reiʃən] n. Remise en place *f*. (putting back); restitution *f*. (returning). ‖ Réintégration *f*. (*to*, dans); *restoration to favour*, rentrée en grâce. ‖ Rétablissement *m*. (of a text). ‖ MED., JUR. Rétablissement *m*. ‖ ARTS, ARCHIT., TECHN. Restauration *f*.

restorative [ris'tɔ:rətiv] adj. n. MED. Fortifiant, reconstituant *m*.

restore [ris'tɔ:*] v. tr. Rendre, restituer (to give back). ‖ Remettre (*to*, à); *to restore to its former condition*, remettre en état. ‖ Réintégrer (*to*, dans) [a post]. ‖ Rétablir (*to*, dans) [order; a text; s.o.]. ‖ MED. Rétablir (s.o.'s health); *restored to health*, guéri. ‖ ARTS, ARCHIT., TECHN. Restaurer.

restorer [-rə*] n. Personne (*f*.) qui restitue (returner). ‖ ARTS, TECHN. Restaurateur *m*.; restauratrice *f*. ‖ MED. Fortifiant *m*.

restrain [ris'trein] v. tr. Entraver (s.o.'s activities); retenir, empêcher (*from*, de). ‖ JUR. Détenir (in custody). ‖ FIG. Réprimer, contenir (one's anger); maîtriser (one's emotions); retenir (one's tears); *to restrain oneself*, se contraindre, se contenir.

restrainable [-əbl] adj. Qui peut être contenu.

restraint [ris'treint] n. Restriction, contrainte, entrave *f*.; frein *m*. ‖ JUR. Contrainte (*f*.) par corps; emprisonnement *m*. ‖ MED. Internement *m*. (of a lunatic); *to put under restraint*, interner. ‖ COMM. *Restraint of trade*, atteinte (or) restriction à la liberté du commerce. ‖ FIG. Contrainte, réserve, retenue *f*.; *to throw off all restraint*, s'émanciper.

restrict [ris'trikt] v. tr. Restreindre, limiter. ‖ AUTOM. *Restricted area*, zone de vitesse limitée.

restriction [ris'trikʃən] n. COMM., PHILOS., FIG. Restriction *f*.

restrictive [-tiv] adj. Restrictif. ‖ GRAMM. Limitatif (clause).

restrictively [-tivli] adv. Avec restriction.

restructure [,ri:'strʌktʃə*] v. tr. Restructurer.

result [ri'zʌlt] n. Résultat *m.;* conséquence *f.; as a result of,* par suite de. ‖ MATH. Résultat *m.*
— v. intr. Résulter, provenir, s'ensuivre *(from,* de). ‖ To result **in,** aboutir à, avoir pour résultat de.
resultant [-ənt] adj. Résultant.
— n. MATH. Résultante *f.*
resultful [-ful] adj. Fructueux.
resultless [-lis] adj. Sans résultat.
resume [ri'zju:m] v. intr. Reprendre.
— v. tr. Reprendre, se remettre à (sth. interrupted). ‖ Reprendre possession de; *to resume one's seat,* se rasseoir. ‖ Récapituler.
résumé ['reizju:mei] n. Résumé *m.*
resumption [ri'zʌmpʃən] n. Reprise *f.*
resurface ['ri:'sə:fis] v. tr. TECHN. Remettre en état (a road).
— v. intr. NAUT. Remonter à la surface, faire surface (submarine).
resurgence [ri'sə:dʒəns] n. Résurrection *f.*
resurgent [-ənt] adj. Renaissant.
resurrect [,rezə'rekt] v. intr., tr. Ressusciter.
resurrection [,rezə'rekʃən] n. ECCLES., FIG. Résurrection *f.*
resuscitate [ri'sʌsiteit] v. intr., tr. Ressusciter.
resuscitation [ri,sʌsi'teiʃən] n. Résurrection *f.*
ret [ret] v. intr., tr. Rouir (flax).
retable [ri'teibl] n. ECCLES. Retable *m.*
retail ['ri:teil] n. COMM. Détail *m.;* vente *(f.)* au détail; *retail dealer,* marchand au détail; *retail price,* prix de détail; *to sell retail,* vendre au détail.
— [ri'teil] v. tr. COMM. Détailler, vendre au détail. ‖ FAM. Colporter (scandal).
— v. intr. Se détailler, se vendre au détail.
retailer [-ə*] n. COMM. Détaillant *s.* ‖ FAM. Colporteur *s.*
retain [ri'tein] v. tr. Contenir (to hold back); retenir, maintenir (to maintain). ‖ Conserver, garder (to keep). ‖ Engager (to hire). ‖ Garder le souvenir de, garder en mémoire (to remember). ‖ JUR. Retenir (a lawyer).
retainer [-ə*] n. Chose *(f.)* [or] personne *(f.)* qui conserve. ‖ † Suivant *m.* (of a noble); pl. suite *f.* ‖ JUR. Provisions *f. pl.*
retake [,ri:'teik] v. tr. (174). Reprendre. ‖ CINEM. Tourner de nouveau, refaire (a shot, a scene).
— ['ri:,teik] n. Nouvelle prise *(f.)* de vue(s).
retaliate [ri'tælieit] v. intr. Rendre la pareille (on, à); user de représailles (on, envers).
— v. tr. Rendre, payer de retour. ‖ JUR. Retourner (upon, contre) [an accusation].
retaliation [ri,tæli'eiʃən] n. Revanche *f.;* représailles *f. pl.;* esprit *(m.)* de revanche; *law of retaliation,* loi du talion.
retaliatory [ri'tæliətəri] adj. De représailles.
retard [ri'tɑ:d] v. intr. Retarder. ‖ Tarder (person).
— v. tr. Retarder.
— n. NAUT., AUTOM. Retard *m.*
retardation [,ri:tɑ:'deiʃən] n. Retard, retardement *m.* ‖ Ralentissement *m.* (slowing). ‖ NAUT. Retard *m.* ‖ PHYS. Retardation *f.*
retardative [ri'tɑ:dətiv], **retardatory** [-ətəri] adj. Retardateur.
retarded [-id] adj. Retardé. ‖ MED. *Mentally retarded,* arriéré; demeuré (fam.).
retardment [-mənt] n. Retardement, retard *m.*
retch [ri:tʃ] n. MED. Haut-le-cœur *m.*
— v. intr. MED. Avoir des haut-le-cœur.
retell ['ri:tel] v. tr. (177). Redire; raconter de nouveau.
retention [ri'tenʃən] n. Conservation *f.;* maintien *m.* ‖ PHILOS., MED. Rétention *f.*
retentive [-tiv] adj. Qui retient; *to be retentive of,* conserver, retenir. ‖ FIG. Fidèle (memory).
retentiveness [-tivnis] n. Faculté *(f.)* de retenir. ‖ FIG. Fidélité *f.* (of the memory).

rethink [,ri:'θiŋk] v. tr. (178). Repenser, reconsidérer.
— ['ri:,θiŋk] n. Réexamen *m.*
reticence ['retisəns] n. Réticence *f.*
reticent [-ənt] adj. Réticent.
reticently [-əntli] adv. Avec réticence.
reticle ['retikl] n. PHYS. Réticule *m.*
reticular [re'tikjulə*] adj. Réticulaire.
reticulate [re'tikjuleit] v. tr. Diviser en réseau.
— [-it] adj. Réticulé.
reticule ['retikju:l] n. Réticule *m.*
reticulum [-ləm] n. Réticulum *m.*
retighten ['ri:'taitn] v. tr. Resserrer.
retina ['retinə] n. MED. Rétine *f.*
retinal [-əl] adj. MED. Rétinien.
retinitis [,reti'naitis] n. MED. Rétinite *f.*
retinue ['retinju:] n. Suite *f.*
retire [ri'taiə*] n. MILIT., MUS. Retraite *f.*
— v. tr. JUR. Mettre à la retraite. ‖ MILIT. Faire replier (troops). ‖ FIN. Retirer (from circulation).
— v. intr. Se retirer (to withdraw); aller se coucher (to retire to bed); *to retire into oneself,* se replier sur soi-même. ‖ JUR. Prendre sa retraite; *to apply to be retired on a pension,* demander sa mise à la retraite. ‖ COMM. Se retirer (from business). ‖ MILIT. Se replier.
retired [ri'taiəd] adj. Retiré (life). ‖ Retiré, écarté, peu fréquenté (spot). ‖ JUR. A la retraite, retraité (civil servant, officer); de retraite (pay). ‖ COMM. Retiré des affaires.
retiredness [-ədnis] n. Vie retirée *f.* ‖ Amour *(m.)* de la solitude; réserve *f.;* effacement *m.*
retirement [-əmənt] n. Recul *m.;* retraite *f.* ‖ JUR. Retraite *f.* ‖ MILIT. Repliement *m.* ‖ SPORTS. Abandon *m.* (from a match). ‖ FIN. Retrait *m.* ‖ FIG. Effacement *m.;* retraite *f.*
retiring [-əriŋ] adj. Où l'on se retire; *retiring room,* cabinet particulier. ‖ Qui se retire; sortant (president). ‖ De retraite (pension). ‖ FIG. Effacé (modest); farouche (shy).
retold ['ri:'tould] pret., p. p. See RETELL.
retort [ri'tɔ:t] v. intr. Répliquer, riposter.
— v. tr. Répliquer, riposter, rétorquer, retourner. ‖ Payer de retour, rendre.
— n. Réplique, riposte *(to,* à).
retort v. tr. CHIM. Distiller en vase clos.
— n. CHIM. Cornue *f.*
retorted [-id] adj. Recourbé.
retortion [ri'tɔ:ʃən] n. Renversement *m.* ‖ JUR. Rétorsion *f.;* représailles *f. pl.*
retouch ['ri:'tʌtʃ] n. Retouche *f.*
— v. tr. Retoucher.
retrace [ri'treis] v. tr. Retracer; reconstituer (the past); remonter à l'origine de (sth.). ‖ LOC. *To retrace one's steps,* revenir sur ses pas, rebrousser chemin.
retract [ri'trækt] v. intr. Se rétracter. ‖ AVIAT. S'escamoter, rentrer.
— v. tr. Rentrer (claws). ‖ AVIAT. Escamoter (the under-carriage). ‖ FIG. Retirer, rétracter, revenir sur (a promise, statement).
retractable [-əbl] adj. AVIAT. Escamotable.
retractation [,ri:træk'teiʃən] n. Rétractation *f.* ‖ MED. Recul *m.* (of the tongue).
retractile [ri'træktail] adj. Rétractile.
retraction [-ʃən] n. Rétraction *f.* ‖ FIG. Rétractation *f.*
retranslate ['ri:trɑ:ns'leit] v. tr. Retraduire.
retransmission [-'miʃən] n. RADIO. Retransmission *f.* (of a broadcast); réexpédition *f.* (of a telegram).
retransmit [-'mit] v. tr. RADIO. Retransmettre (a broadcast); réexpédier (a telegram).
retread ['ri:tred] v. tr. (182). Fouler de nouveau. ‖ Suivre de nouveau (a path); retourner à (a place).

retread ['ri:'tred] v. tr. AUTOM. Rechaper (a tyre).
— ['ri:,tred] n. AUTOM. Pneu rechapé *m.*
— N. B. Au sens de « rechaper », le verbe *retread* est régulier.

retreat [ri'tri:t] v. tr. SPORTS. Ramener (in chess).
— v. intr. Se retirer; s'éloigner; reculer. ‖ MILIT. Reculer, battre en retraite. (See RETIRE.) ‖ MED. *Retreating chin,* menton fuyant.
— n. Recul *m.;* retraite *f.* (in general); régression *f.* (of the sea). ‖ Retraite *f.;* abri, asile *m.; retreat house,* maison de retraite. ‖ MILIT., ECCLES. Retraite *f.*

retrench [ri'trenʃ] v. intr. Faire des économies.
— v. tr. Réduire, diminuer (to reduce); restreindre (to restrict). ‖ Faire des coupures dans (a book); supprimer (a passage). ‖ MILIT. Retrancher.

retrenchment [-mənt] n. Retranchement *m.;* suppression *f.* ‖ MILIT. Retranchement *m.* ‖ FIN. Réduction (*f.*) de dépenses.

retrial [,ri:'traiəl] n. JUR. Nouveau procès *m.*

retribution [,retri'bju:ʃən] n. Récompense *f.* (reward). ‖ Châtiment *m.; the Day of Retribution,* le jour du châtiment.

retributive [ri'tribjutiv], **retributory** [-təri] adj. De récompense. ‖ De châtiment.

retrievable [ri'tri:vəbl] adj. Récupérable (object); recouvrable (property). ‖ FIG. Réparable (error).

retrieval [-əl] n. Récupération *f.* (of an object); recouvrement *m.* (of property). ‖ FIG. Réparation *f.* (of an error); rétablissement *m.* (of one's position); *beyond retrieval,* irréparable.

retrieve [ri'tri:v] n. Rétablissement *m.*
— v. intr. SPORTS. Rapporter (game-dog).
— v. tr. Retrouver, récupérer (an object); recouvrer (property). ‖ Tirer, sauver *(from,* de) [danger]. ‖ SPORTS. Rapporter (dead game). ‖ FIG. Réparer (an error); rétablir (one's reputation).

retriever [-ə*] n. ZOOL. Retriever *m.*

retroact [,ri:tro'ækt] v. intr. Réagir. ‖ JUR. Avoir un effet rétroactif.

retroaction [-ʃən] n. Réaction *f.* ‖ JUR. Rétroaction *f.*

retroactive [-tiv] adj. Rétroactif.

retroactively [-tivli] adv. Rétroactivement.

retrocede [,ri:tro'si:d] v. tr. Rétrocéder.
— v. intr. Rétrograder. ‖ MED. Remonter.

retrocession [-'seʃən] n. Rétrogradation *f.* ‖ JUR., MED. Rétrocession *f.*

retrocessive [-'sesiv] adj. Rétrocessif.

retroflex ['retrofleks] adj. GRAMM. Rétroflexe.

retroflexion [,ri:tro'flekʃən] n. MED. Rétroflexion *f.*

retrogradation [,retrogrə'deiʃən] n. Dégénérescence *f.* ‖ ASTRON. Rétrogradation *f.*

retrograde ['retrogreid] adj. Rétrograde.
— v. intr. Rétrograder.

retrogress [,ri:tro'gres] v. intr. Rétrograder. ‖ Dégénérer.

retrogression [-ʃən] n. Mouvement rétrograde *m.* ‖ FIG. Dégénérescence *f.*

retrogressive [-siv] adj. Rétrogressif, rétrograde. ‖ Dégénérescent.

retro-rocket ['retrou,rɔkit] n. ASTRONAUT. Rétrofusée *f.*

retrospect ['retrospekt] n. Examen rétrospectif *m.;* vue rétrospective *f.; in retrospect,* en rétrospective.

retrospection [,retro'spekʃən] n. Rétrospection *f.;* examen rétrospectif *m.*

retrospective [-tiv] adj. Rétrospectif. ‖ JUR. A effet rétroactif.
— n. U. S. Rétrospective, exposition rétrospective *f.*

retrospectively [-tivli] adv. Rétrospectivement. ‖ JUR. Rétroactivement.

retroversion [,retro've:ʃən] n. MED. Rétroversion *f.*

retry [,ri:'trai] v. tr. (2). JUR. Juger de nouveau;

the case was retried, l'affaire est repassée en jugement.

return [ri'tə:n] v. intr. Revenir (to come back); retourner (to go back); rentrer (to return home). ‖ Retourner, revenir *(to,* à) [a former owner (or) state].
— v. tr. Rapporter (to bring back); rendre (to give back); remettre (to put back); restituer (to restore); renvoyer, retourner (to send back). ‖ Déclarer (to declare); répondre, répliquer (to reply). ‖ Répondre à; rendre (a compliment, visit); opposer (a denial); s'acquitter de (obligations); *to return good for evil,* rendre le bien pour le mal; *to return s.o.'s love,* répondre à l'affection de qqn. ‖ JUR. Elire (an M. P.); déclarer (guilty); rendre, prononcer (a verdict). ‖ FIN. Estimer, évaluer (a sum of money); *to return one's income to the tax authorities,* faire sa déclaration au fisc. ‖ PHYS. Renvoyer (sound).
— n. Retour *m.* (coming back); *many happy returns of the day,* mes meilleurs vœux pour votre anniversaire; *on his return,* dès son retour; *return to school,* rentrée des classes. ‖ Retour, renvoi *m.* (sending back). ‖ Restitution *f.* (of sth. lost). ‖ Remise en place *f.* (putting back). ‖ Echange *m.* (exchange); récompense *f.* (for, de) [recompense]. ‖ Pl. Tabac blond *m.* (tobacco). ‖ CH. DE F. Aller et retour *m.* (ticket); *return journey,* voyage de retour. ‖ JUR. Proclamation (*f.*) des résultats (of an election); élection *f.* (of an M. P.); recensement *m.* (of the population); exposé, relevé *m.* (report); statistique *f.* (statistics); *Board of Trade returns,* statistique commerciale; *nil return,* état néant. ‖ FIN. Déclaration *f.* (of income); remboursement *m.* (of a sum); *to send in one's return of income,* envoyer sa déclaration d'impôts. ‖ COMM. Rendu *m.* (object); reprise (*f.*) des invendus, vente (*f.*) avec facilité de retour (selling); pl. bouillon *m.* (unsold newspapers). ‖ COMM. Ristourne *f.* (of a sum overpaid); bénéfice, profit *m.* (profit); pl. rentrées, recettes *f. pl.* (receipts). ‖ SPORTS. Riposte *f.; return match,* revanche. ‖ TECHN. Rapport, rendement *m.* (productivity); course (*f.*) de retour (of a piston).

returnable [-əbl] adj. Qu'on peut rendre, restituable. ‖ JUR. Eligible (candidate). ‖ COMM. *Non returnable,* perdu (packing).

returned [-d] adj. De retour (person). ‖ Renvoyé à l'expéditeur (letter, packet). ‖ JUR. Libéré (convict). ‖ COMM. *Returned article,* rendu.

returning [-iŋ] adj. *Returning officer,* président du bureau de vote.

reunion ['ri:'ju:njən] n. Réunion *f.*

reunite ['ri:ju:'nait] v. intr. Se réunir de nouveau.
— v. tr. Réunir, rassembler. ‖ FIG. Réunir.

reusable [,ri:'ju:zəbl] adj. Réutilisable.

reuse [,ri:'ju:z] v. tr. Réutiliser; remployer (or) réemployer.
— ['ri:,ju:s] n. Réutilisation *f.;* remploi (or) réemploi *m.*

rev [rev] n. AUTOM. FAM. Tour *m.*
— v. intr. AUTOM. FAM. *To rev up,* s'emballer.
— v. tr. AUTOM. FAM. *To rev up,* faire s'emballer.

revalorization ['ri:,vælərai'zeiʃən] n. FIN. Revalorisation *f.*

revalorize ['ri:'væləraiz] v. tr. FIN. Revaloriser.

revaluation ['ri:,vælju:'eiʃən] v. tr. FIN. Réévaluation *f.*

revalue ['ri:'vælju:] v. tr. Réévaluer.

revamp ['ri:'væmp] v. tr. Remettre une empeigne à (a shoe). ‖ U. S. FAM. Renflouer.

revanchism [ri'væntʃizm] n. Revanchisme *m.*

revanchist [-ist] n. Revanchard *s.*

revarnish ['ri:'vɑ:niʃ] v. tr. TECHN. Revernir.

reveal [ri:'vi:l] n. ARCHIT. Jouée *f.;* listel *m.*

reveal v. tr. Révéler, laisser voir, découvrir (to show). ‖ FIG. Révéler, divulguer, mettre à jour.

revealer [-ə*] n. Révélateur m.; révélatrice f.
revealment [-mənt] n. Révélation f. (See DISCLOSURE.)
reveille [ri'væli], U. S. ['revəli] n. MILIT. Diane f.
revel ['revl] n. Divertissement m.; fête f. ‖ Ebats m. pl. ‖ Bacchanale; partie fine f. (orgy). ‖ Pl. Menus plaisirs m. pl.
— v. tr. (1). To revel away, gaspiller en plaisirs.
— v. intr. Se divertir, se réjouir, s'ébattre. ‖ FIG. Se délecter (in, à); faire ses délices, se griser (in, de). ‖ FAM. Faire bombance (or) ripaille.
revelation [,revi'leiʃən] n. Révélation f. ‖ ECCLES. Apocalypse f.
reveller 'revələ*] n. Viveur, noceur s.
revendication [ri,vendi'keiʃən] n. Revendication f.
revenge ri'vendʒ] v. tr. Venger (s.o., sth.); to revenge oneself, to be revenged, se venger (on, sur); tirer vengeance (on, de).
— n. Vengeance f.; in revenge, pour se venger; to take revenge on s.o. for sth., se venger de qqch. sur qqn. ‖ Revanche f. (chance to retaliate).
revengeful [-ful] adj. Vindicatif (vindictive). ‖ Vengeur m.; vengeresse f. (avenging).
revengefully [-fuli] adv. Par vengeance.
revengefulness [-fulnis] n. Esprit vindicatif m.
revenger [-ə*] n. Vengeur m.; vengeresse f.
revenue ['revinju:] n. FIN. Revenu m. ‖ JUR. Fisc m. (administration); revenue office, bureau de perception; revenue officer, agent des douanes; revenue stamp, timbre fiscal; Public Revenue, Trésor public.
reverberant [ri'və:bərənt], **reverberative** [-rətiv] adj. Réverbérant.
reverberate [-reit] v. tr. PHYS. Réfléchir (heat, light); renvoyer (sound).
— v. intr. PHYS. Réverbérer (heat, light); résonner (sound).
reverberation [ri,və:bə'reiʃən] n. PHYS. Réverbération f. (of heat, of light); répercussion f. (of sound).
reverberator [ri'və:bəreitə*] n. Réflecteur m.
reverberatory [-təri] adj. TECHN. A réverbère.
— n. TECHN. Four à réverbère m.
revere [ri'viə*] v. tr. Révérer, vénérer.
reverence ['revərəns] n. Respect m.; vénération f.; to bow in reverence, révérer, vénérer; saving your reverence, révérence parler. ‖ ECCLES. Your Reverence, monsieur l'abbé.
reverend [-ənd] n. ECCLES. Ecclésiastique m.
— adj. Vénérable. ‖ ECCLES. Révérend; the Rev. John Smith, le Révérend John Smith (Anglican Church); M. l'abbé Smith (Roman Catholic Church); Most Reverend, Révérendissime; the Right Rev. Bishop of, Son Excellence Monseigneur l'évêque de.
reverent [-ənt] adj. Respectueux.
reverential [revə'renʃəl] adj. Révérenciel.
reverently [-əntli] adv. Respectueusement.
reverie ['revəri] n. Rêverie f.
revers [ri'viə*] n. Revers m. (of coat).
—N. B. Ce mot est invariable dans l'orthographe; au pl., dans la prononciation, on entend le son final [-z].
reversal [ri'və:səl] n. Renversement m.; inversion f. ‖ JUR. Annulation f. (of a judgment). ‖ TECHN. Reversal finder, viseur redresseur. ‖ FIG. Revirement m. (of opinion).
reverse [ri'və:s] adj. Contraire, opposé, inverse (to, à); reverse side, revers. ‖ MILIT. De revers (fire). ‖ GEOGR. Reverse slope, contre-pente. ‖ TECHN. Reverse motion, marche arrière.
— n. Contraire, opposé, inverse m.; he is the reverse of polite, il n'est rien moins que poli. ‖ Revers m. (of a coin, medal); verso m. (of printed form). ‖ Défaite f. (defeat); revers m. (of fortune). ‖ AUTOM., FIG. To go into reverse, faire marche arrière.
— v. intr. AUTOM. Faire marche arrière. ‖ MUS.

Renverser (in dancing). ‖ TECHN. Renverser la marche (of a machine).
— v. tr. Renverser, retourner. ‖ Transposer. ‖ MILIT., NAUT. Renverser. ‖ AUTOM. To reverse one's car, faire marche arrière. ‖ JUR. Annuler, casser (a decision). ‖ TECHN. To reverse the engine, faire machine en arrière. ‖ FIG. Bouleverser (a situation).
reversely [-li] adj. Inversement.
reverser [-ə*] n. ELECTR. Inverseur m.
reversibility [ri,və:si'biliti] n. Réversibilité f.
reversible [ri'və:sibl] adj. Réversible. ‖ JUR. Révocable (decision). ‖ COMM. A double face, sans envers (material).
reversing [-siŋ] adj. AUTOM. Reversing light, feu de marche arrière.
reversion [-ʃən] n. JUR. Réversion f.; retour m. (of property); held in reversion, grevé d'un droit de retour. ‖ MED. Retour m.; reversion to type, réversion. ‖ TECHN. Inversion f. (in photography).
reversionary [-ʃənəri] adj. JUR., FIN. Réversible. ‖ MED. Atavique.
revert [ri'və:t] v. intr. Revenir (to, à).
— v. tr. Porter en arrière.
revertibility [ri,və:ti'biliti] n. JUR. Réversibilité f.
revertible [ri'və:tibl] adj. JUR. Réversible.
revet [ri'vet] v. tr. (1). ARCHIT. Revêtir.
revetment [-mənt] n. ARCHIT. Revêtement m.
revictual ['ri':vitl] v. intr. Se ravitailler.
— v. tr. Ravitailler.
review [ri'vju:] v. intr. Faire de la critique littéraire.
— v. tr. Revoir, examiner; passer en revue (past events). ‖ Faire la critique (or) le compte rendu de, rendre compte de (a book). ‖ MILIT., NAUT. Passer en revue. ‖ JUR. Réviser (a trial).
— n. Examen m.; revue f.; recensement m. (of past events). ‖ Revue f. (publication). ‖ Revue, critique, recension f.; compte rendu m. (of a book); review copy, exemplaire de service de presse. ‖ JUR. Révision, revision f. (of a trial).
reviewal [-əl] n. Critique f.; compte rendu m. (of a book).
reviewer [-ə*] n. Critique m.
revile [ri'vail] v. tr. Injurier, insulter. (See ABUSE.)
— v. intr. Etre injurieux; invectiver (against, contre).
reviler [-ə*] n. Insulteur m.
reviling [-iŋ] adj. Injurieux.
revisable [ri'vaizəbl] adj. Révisable.
revisal [-əl] n. Révision f.
revise [ri'vaiz] n. TECHN. Epreuve en page f.; second revise, troisième épreuve.
— v. tr. Revoir, réviser, corriger (to correct); reviser (to modify). ‖ Repasser, reviser, revoir (school-work).
reviser [-ə*] n. Réviseur m.; correcteur m.; correctrice f.
revision [ri'viʒən] n. Révision f.
revisionism [ri'viʒə,nizm] n. Révisionnisme m.
revisionist [-ist] n. Révisionniste s.
revisit ['ri':vizit] v. tr. Revisiter, retourner voir.
revisory [ri'vaizəri] adj. De révision.
revitalize ['ri':vaitəlaiz] v. tr. Revivifier.
revivable [ri'vaivəbl] adj. Que l'on peut ranimer.
revival [-əl] n. MED. Retour (m.) à la vie; retour (m.) des forces. ‖ JUR. Remise en vigueur f. (of a law). ‖ ARTS. Renaissance f. ‖ THEATR., COMM. Reprise f. ‖ ECCLES., FIG. Réveil, renouveau m.; U.S. revival meeting, réunion pieuse en vue du réveil de la foi.
revive [ri'vaiv] v. intr. MED. Reprendre vie. ‖ ARTS. Renaître. ‖ COMM. Reprendre (trade). ‖ FIG. Se réveiller; se ranimer (feelings); renaître (hopes).
— v. tr. Rétablir, rénover (a custom); remettre en vogue (a fashion). ‖ Ranimer (the conversation); ranimer, faire revivre (feelings, memories); réveil-

ler (a wish). ‖ Remonter (to cheer up). ‖ MED. Rappeler à la vie; ranimer. ‖ JUR. Remettre en vigueur. ‖ THEATR. Reprendre (a play).
reviver [-ə*] n. Chose (f.) [or] personne (f.) qui ranime; ravigoteur m. (fam.). ‖ COMM. Encaustique f. ‖ FAM. Petit verre; requinquant m. (fam.); *to have an early morning reviver*, tuer le ver.
revivification [ri,vivifi'kei ʃən] n. Revivification f.
revivify [ri'vivifai] v. tr. (2). Revivifier.
reviviscence [,revi'visn̩s] n. Reviviscence f.
revocable ['revəkəbl̩] adj. Révocable.
revocation [,revə'kei ʃən] n. JUR. Révocation f. (of a decree); retrait m. (of a licence).
revocatory ['revəkətəri] adj. Révocatoire.
revoke [ri'vouk] n. Renonce f. (at cards).
— v. intr. Renoncer (at cards).
— v. tr. JUR. Révoquer, abroger (a decree); contremander, annuler (an order); retirer (a licence).
revolt [ri'voult] n. Révolte f. (see REBELLION); *to rise in revolt*, se soulever (*against*, contre); *to stir up to revolt*, soulever.
— v. intr. Se révolter (*against*, contre; *at*, à); se révolter, s'insurger, se soulever, se rebeller (*against*, contre).
revolting [-iŋ] adj. Révolté, insurgé (rebellious). ‖ FIG. Révoltant (repulsive).
revoltingly [-iŋli] adv. De façon révoltante.
revolute [,revə'lju:t] adj. BOT. Révoluté.
revolution [,revə'lju:ʃən] n. Révolution f. (political, social). ‖ ASTRON. Révolution f. ‖ TECHN. Rotation f. (round an axis); tour m. (of a wheel); *revolution counter*, compte-tours.
revolutionary [-ri] n. Révolutionnaire s.
— adj. Révolutionnaire. ‖ TECHN. Giratoire.
revolutionize [-aiz] v. tr. Révolutionner.
revolve [ri'vɔlv] v. tr. Faire tourner. ‖ FIG. Tourner et retourner dans son esprit (problem); ruminer, ressasser (thought).
— v. intr. Tourner (wheel). ‖ Revenir (seasons).
revolver [-ə*] n. Revolver m.
revolving [-iŋ] adj. Qui revient, de retour (year). ‖ ASTRON. Qui tourne (planet). ‖ TECHN. Rotatif, pivotant, à rotation; tournant (bookcase, door, light); à pivot (crane).
revue [ri'vju:] n. Revue f.
revuist [-ist] n. THEATR. Revuiste s.
revulsion [ri'vʌl ʃən] n. MED. Révulsion f. ‖ FIG. Brusque revirement m.
revulsive [-siv] adj. MED. Révulsif.
reward [ri'wɔ:d] v. tr. Récompenser. ‖ Rémunérer.
— n. Récompense f.; *as a reward for*, en récompense de. ‖ Rémunération f.; *ten pounds reward*, dix livres de récompense.
rewardable [-əbl̩] adj. Digne de récompense.
rewarding [-iŋ] adj. Rémunérateur m.; rémunératrice f. ‖ Qui en vaut la peine, gratifiant (experience); qui vaut le déplacement (film).
rewind [,ri:'waind] v. tr. (190). Remonter (a watch); TECHN. rembobiner (film); rebobiner (wire).
rewire [,ri:'waiə*] v. tr. ELECTR. Refaire l'installation électrique.
rewrite ['ri:'rait] v. tr. (195). Récrire, remanier. ‖ FAM. U. S. *Rewrite man*, remanieur.
Rexine ['reksi:n] n. COMM. Similicuir f.
rhabdomancy ['ræbdə'mænsi] n. Rabdomancie f.
Rhaetic ['ri:tik] adj., n. GEOL. Rhétien m.
Rhaeto-romanic ['ri:touro'mænik] adj. Rhéto-roman.
rhapsodic(al) [ræp'sɔdik(əl)] adj. Rhapsodique.
rhapsodist ['ræpsədist] n. Rhapsodiste m.
rhapsodize [-daiz] v. intr. S'extasier (*over*, sur).
rhapsody [-di] n. Rhapsodie f. ‖ FAM. Dithyrambe m.
rhea ['riə] n. ZOOL. Nandou m.
Rheims [ri:ms] n. GEOGR. Reims.
Rhemish ['ri:mi ʃ] adj. GEOGR. Rémois, de Reims.

Rhenish ['reni ʃ] n. Vin (m.) du Rhin.
— adj. GEOGR. Rhénan; du Rhin (wine).
rheostat ['riəstæt] n. ELECTR. Rhéostat m.
rhesus ['ri:səs] adj. MED. *Rhesus factor*, facteur rhésus.
rhetor ['ri:tə:*] n. Rhéteur m.
rhetoric ['retərik] n. Rhétorique; éloquence f. (eloquence). ‖ Déclamation, emphase (pej.).
rhetorical [ri'tɔrikəl] adj. De rhétorique. ‖ De pure forme (question); emphatique (style).
rhetorician [,retə'ri ʃən] n. PHILOS. Rhétoricien m. ‖ Rhéteur m. (pej.).
rheum [ru:m] n. MED. Chassie f. (in the eyes); mucosités f. pl. (in the nose).
rheumatic [ru:'mætik] n. MED. Rhumatisant s. ‖ Pl. FAM. Rhumatismes m. pl.
— adj. MED. Rhumatismal (disease); rhumatisant (person); *rheumatic fever*, rhumatisme articulaire aigu.
rheumatism ['ru:mətizm̩] n. MED. Rhumatisme m.
rheumatoid [-tɔid] adj. MED. Rhumatoïde; *rheumatoid arthritis*, rhumatisme articulaire.
rheumatologist [,ru:mə'tɔlədʒist] n. MED. Rhumatologue s.
rheumatology [-'tɔlədʒi] n. MED. Rhumatologie f.
rheumy ['ru:mi] adj. MED. Chassieux (eyes).
rhinal ['rainəl] adj. MED. Nasal.
Rhine ['rain] n. GEOGR. Rhin m.
Rhineland [-lənd] n. GEOGR. Rhénanie f.
Rhinelander [-ləndə*] n. GEOGR. Rhénan s.
Rhinestone [-stoun] n. Caillou du Rhin, faux diamant m.
rhinitis [ri'naitis] n. MED. Rhinite f.
rhino ['rainou] n. POP. Pèze, galette f.
rhino n. ZOOL., FAM. Rhinocéros m.
rhinoceros [rai'nɔsərəs] n. ZOOL. Rhinocéros m.
rhinoplasty ['reinoplæsti] n. MED. Rhinoplastie f.
rhizome ['raizoum] n. BOT. Rhizome m.
Rhodesia [ro'di:ziə] n. GEOGR. Rhodésie f.
Rhodesian [-ən] adj., n. GEOGR. Rhodésien s.
Rhodian ['roudiən] adj., n. GEOGR. Rhodien s.
rhodium ['roudiəm] n. CHIM. Rhodium m.
rhododendron [,roudə'dendrən] n. BOT. Rhododendron m.
rhomb [rɔm] n. See RHOMBUS.
rhombic ['rɔmbik] adj. MATH. Rhombique.
rhombohedral [,rɔmbo'hi:drəl] adj. MATH. Rhomboédrique.
rhombohedron [-drən] MATH. Rhomboèdre m.
rhomboid ['rɔmbɔid] adj., n. MATH., MED. Rhomboïde m.
rhombus ['rɔmbəs] (pl. **rhombuses** [-əsiz], **rhombi** [-ai]) n. MATH. Rhombe, losange m. ‖ Rhomboèdre m.
Rhone [roun] n. GEOGR. Rhône m.
rhubarb ['ru:bɑ:b] n. BOT., MED. Rhubarbe f.
rhumb [rʌm] n. NAUT. Rumb, rhumb m. ‖ **Rhumb-line**, n. NAUT. Loxodromie f.
rhyme [raim] s. Rime f.; *rhyme scheme*, agencement des rimes, versification. ‖ Pl. Vers m. pl.; poésie f.; *to put into rhyme*, mettre en vers. ‖ LOC. *Without rhyme or reason*, sans rime ni raison.
— v. intr. Faire des vers; rimailler (pej.). ‖ Rimer (*with*, avec).
— v. tr. Mettre en vers. ‖ Faire rimer (two words).
rhymed [-d] adj. Rimé; *rhymed couplets*, rimes plates.
rhymer [-ə*] n. Rimeur m.
rhymester [-stə*] n. Rimailleur m.
rhyming [-iŋ] adj. Rimé (words).
— n. Versification f.; *rhyming dictionary*, dictionnaire de rimes.
rhythm [riðm] n. Rythme m.
rhythmic(al) ['riθmik(əl)] adj. Rythmique, cadencé.
rhythmically [-i] adv. Avec rythme.

rib [rib] v. tr. NAUT. Garnir de membrures. ‖ TECHN. Garnir de nervures (a book). ‖ U. S. Taquiner.
— n. MED. Côte ƒ. ‖ AVIAT. Travée ƒ. ‖ NAUT. Membre *m.;* membrure ƒ. ‖ MUS. Eclisse ƒ. ‖ ARCHIT. Nervure, ƒ. (of fan-vaulting); ogive ƒ. (arch). ‖ CULIN. Côte ƒ. (of beef). ‖ TECHN. Côte ƒ. (in knitting); nervure ƒ. (of a book); baleine ƒ. (of umbrella). ‖ BOT. Nervure ƒ. (of leaf). ‖ FAM. Moitié ƒ. (wife).

ribald ['ribəld] n. † Ribaud *m.* ‖ Grossier personnage *m.*
— adj. Grivois, ordurier.

ribaldry [-ri] n. Grivoiserie ƒ.; paillardise ƒ.

ribband ['ribənd] n. NAUT. Lisse ƒ. ‖ See RIBBON.

ribbon ['ribən] n. Ruban *m.* ‖ Pl. Lambeaux *m. pl.* (tatters). ‖ FIG. Ruban *m.* (of road). ‖ FAM. Pl. Guides ƒ. *pl.* (driving reins). ‖ **Ribbon-brake,** n. TECHN. Frein à ruban *m.* ‖ **Ribbon-development,** n. ARCHIT. Extension urbaine en bordure de route ƒ. ‖ **Ribbon-reverse,** n. Renversement du ruban *m.* (in typewriting). ‖ **Ribbon-saw,** n. TECHN. Scie (ƒ.) à ruban. ‖ **Ribbon-trade,** n. COMM. Rubanerie ƒ.

ribboned [-d] adj. Enrubanné.

riboflavine [,raibo'fleivin] n. MED. Riboflavine ƒ.

ribonucleic [,raibounju:'kli:ik] adj. MED. *Ribonucleic acid,* acide ribonucléique.

rice [rais] n. BOT. Riz *m.* ‖ CULIN. Riz *m.; ground rice,* farine de riz. ‖ **Rice-field,** n. Rizière ƒ. ‖ **Rice-growing,** n. AGRIC. Riziculture ƒ.; adj. rizier. ‖ **Rice-paper,** n. Papier de riz *m.* ‖ **Rice-pudding,** n. CULIN. Riz au lait *m.* ‖ **Rice-water,** m. Eau (ƒ.) de riz. ‖ **Rice-wine,** n. Saké *m.*
— v. tr. U. S. CULIN. Réduire en une purée riziforme (cooked potatoes).

ricer [-ə*] n. U. S. CULIN. Presse-purée *m.*

rich [ritʃ] n. Riches; richards (fam.) *m. pl.*
— adj. Riche (person); *to grow rich,* s'enrichir; *to make s.o. rich,* enrichir qqn. ‖ Riche (in, en) [abundant]. ‖ Luxueux (luxurious); superbe, splendide, magnifique (magnificent); somptueux (sumptuous). ‖ AGRIC. Gras (pastures); riche, fertile (soil). ‖ CULIN. Riche, nutritif (food); crémeux, gras (pastries); généreux (wine). ‖ TECHN. Riche (mixture). ‖ FIG. Lourd, chargé (aroma); chaud, riche, vif (colour); chaud (perfume); ample, chaud, étoffé (voix). ‖ FAM. Fameux, impayable, crevant, marrant (amusing).

riches [-iz] n. pl. Richesses ƒ. *pl.* (See WEALTH.)

richly [-li] adv. Richement, somptueusement, magnifiquement. ‖ Abondamment, amplement, grandement, largement. ‖ FAM. Joliment.

richness [-nis] n. Richesse ƒ. (of a person). ‖ Abondance ƒ. (abundance); luxe *m.* (luxury); magnificence, somptuosité ƒ. (magnificence). ‖ AGRIC. Richesse, fertilité ƒ. ‖ CULIN. Richesse ƒ. (of food); générosité ƒ. (of wine). ‖ FIG. Chaleur ƒ. (of a colour, perfume, voice).

rick [rik] v. tr. AGRIC. Mettre en meules.
— n. AGRIC. Meule ƒ.

rick n. MED. Effort *m.; rick in the neck,* torticolis.
— v. tr. MED. *To rick one's back,* se donner un tour de reins.

rickets ['rikits] n. invar. MED. Rachitisme *m.*
— N. B. *Rickets* se construit avec un verbe au *sing.* ou au *plur.*

rickety [-iti] adj. MED. Rachitique. ‖ FIG. Branlant, boiteux, bancal (shaky). ‖ FAM. Faible, débile, chancelant (weak).

rickshaw ['rikʃɔ:] n. Pousse-pousse *m.* ‖ AUTOM. *Bicycle rickshaw,* vélo-pousse. ‖ **Rickshaw boy** (or) **man,** n. Pousse-pousse *m.*

ricochet ['rikɔʃei] n. Ricochet *m.*
— v. intr. Ricocher.
— v. tr. MILIT. Exécuter un tir à ricochet sur.

rictus ['riktəs] n. MED. Rictus *m.*

rid [rid] v. tr. (110). Débarrasser, défaire (of, de)

[s.o.]; *to get rid of,* renvoyer (to dismiss); se débarrasser de (to free oneself from); supprimer (to kill); éconduire (to show out) [s.o.]; se débarrasser de (sth.).

riddance ['ridəns] n. Débarras *m.*

ridden ['ridn]. See RIDE.

riddle ['ridl] n. TECHN. Crible *m.*
— v. tr. TECHN. Cribler, passer au crible. ‖ FIG. Cribler (with, de).

riddle n. Enigme, devinette ƒ.; *to ask s.o. a riddle,* poser une énigme à qqn; *to speak in riddles,* parler par énigmes.
— v. intr. Parler par énigmes.
— v. tr. Deviner, trouver la clef de, résoudre l'énigme de.

riddler [-ə*] n. TECHN. Cribleur s.

ride [raid] n. Tour *m.;* promenade ƒ.; *to go for a ride,* aller se promener à bicyclette (or) à cheval (or) en voiture. ‖ Trajet, voyage *m.* (journey); *it's only a short ride by bus,* il n'y en a pas pour longtemps par l'autobus. ‖ Allée cavalière ƒ. (in a wood). ‖ U. S. POP. *To take s.o. for a ride,* faire marcher qqn (to dupe); embarquer qqn pour sa dernière promenade, emmener qqn faire un tour (to kidnap and murder).
— v. tr. (111). Monter (a horse); *to ride a bicycle, donkey,* monter à bicyclette, à dos d'âne; *to ride to death,* crever (a horse). ‖ Traverser à cheval (a country, a town). ‖ SPORTS. Courir (a race). ‖ NAUT. Voguer sur (the waves). ‖ ZOOL. Monter. ‖ FIG. Opprimer, dominer (to oppress); *ridden by fear,* hanté par la peur; *to ride to death,* ressasser (an idea, a theory); *to ride rough-shod over all opposition,* piétiner toute opposition. ‖ **To ride across,** v. tr. Traverser (à bicyclette, à cheval, en voiture). ‖ **To ride down,** v. tr. Piétiner, passer sur le corps à.
— v. intr. Monter, monter du cheval; *to ride astride,* monter à califourchon. ‖ Chevaucher, faire un trajet à cheval, se promener à cheval; *they rode all the way,* ils firent tout le trajet à cheval. ‖ Aller (on a camel, à dos de chameau; *on a bicycle,* à bicyclette). ‖ Se laisser monter (horse); *to ride well,* être une bonne monture. ‖ Etre à cheval (on a broomstick, on s.o.'s back); être à califourchon (on s.o.'s knee). ‖ Voyager, faire un trajet (in a vehicle). ‖ Voguer (clouds). ‖ NAUT. Flotter, voguer; *to ride at anchor,* être mouillé (or) à l'ancre. ‖ SPORTS. Peser en selle. ‖ TECHN. Chevaucher (to overlap); travailler (to work out of position). ‖ U. S. FAM. *To let things ride a few more weeks,* laisser courir les choses quelques semaines de plus. ‖ **To ride along,** passer. ‖ **To ride away,** partir. ‖ **To ride back,** retourner. ‖ **To ride by,** passer. ‖ **To ride in,** entrer. ‖ **To ride off,** partir. ‖ **To ride on,** continuer sa route. ‖ **To ride out,** sortir; NAUT. *To ride out the storm,* étaler la tempête; FIG. Surmonter la crise. ‖ **To ride up,** arriver; remonter.

rideable [-əbl] adj. Que l'on peut monter (horse). ‖ Praticable (path).

rider [-ə*] n. Cavalier s. (of a horse). ‖ Cycliste s. (on a bicycle); motocycliste s. (on a motorcycle); voyageur s. (in a vehicle). ‖ Ecuyer *m.* (in a circus). ‖ Note annexe ƒ.; papillon *m.* ‖ JUR. Avenant *m.;* clause additionnelle ƒ. (of a bill); codicille *m.* (of a will). ‖ SPORTS. Jockey *m.* ‖ MATH. Problème (*m.*) d'application.

ridge [ridʒ] v. tr. Sillonner, canneler. ‖ AGRIC. Labourer en sillons (ground); butter (plants). ‖ ARCHIT. Enfaîter (a roof).
— v. intr. Se rider; se couvrir de crêtes (or) de stries.
— n. Arête, strie ƒ. (on a rock); ride ƒ. (on sand). ‖ NAUT. Ecueil, banc *m.* ‖ GEOGR. Chaîne ƒ. (of hills); crête, arête ƒ. (of mountains). ‖ MED. Arête ƒ. (of the nose). ‖ AGRIC. Billon *m.* ‖ ARCHIT. Crête

f.; faîtage *m.* (of a roof). ‖ **Ridge-piece** (or) **pole,** n. ARCHIT. Faîtage *m.* ‖ **Ridge-plough,** n. AGRIC. Buttoir *m.* ‖ **Ridge-tile,** n. ARCHIT. Tuile faîtière *f.*

ridgy [-i] adj. Sillonné de stries, ridé. ‖ Côtelé, en arêtes, dentelé.

ridicule ['ridikju:l] v. tr. Ridiculiser, tourner en ridicule. (See DERIDE, MOCK.)
— n. Dérision, raillerie, moquerie *f.; to invite ridicule,* prêter à rire.

ridiculous [ri'dikjuləs] n. Ridicule *m.*
— adj. Risible, plaisant; *to make ridiculous,* ridiculiser; *to make oneself ridiculous,* se rendre quelque peu ridicule; *the ridiculous side of,* le côté risible de.

ridiculously [-li] adv. Ridiculement.

ridiculousness [-nis] n. Ridicule *m.*

riding adj. Monté (on horseback). ‖ NAUT. Mouillé (anchored). ‖ TECHN. Qui travaille (cable).
— n. Allée cavalière *f.* (riding path). ‖ AUTOM. Suspension *f.* ‖ NAUT. Mouillage *m.* ‖ SPORTS. Equitation *f.* ‖ TECHN. Chevauchement *m.* ‖ **Riding-boots,** n. pl. Bottes (*f. pl.*) de cheval. ‖ **Riding-breeches,** n. pl. Culotte (*f.*) de cheval. ‖ **Riding-habit,** n. SPORTS. Costume de cheval *m.;* amazone *f.* ‖ **Riding-light,** n. NAUT. Feu (*m.*) de position. ‖ **Riding-master,** n. Maître (*m.*) d'équitation. ‖ **Riding-school,** n. Manège *m.;* école d'équitation *f.* ‖ **Riding-whip,** n. Cravache *f.*

rife [raif] adj. Abondant (with, en). ‖ Répandu; *to be rife,* se répandre, sévir.

riffle ['rifl] n. Riffle *m.*

riff-raff ['rifraef] n. Canaille, racaille, pègre *f.*

rifle ['raifl] v. tr. Vider (a drawer); piller (a place); dévaliser (s.o.).

rifle v. tr. MILIT. Tirer sur; fusiller. ‖ TECHN. Rayer (a gun-barrel).
— n. MILIT. Fusil *m.* ‖ SPORTS. Carabine de chasse *f.* ‖ Pl. MILIT. Fusiliers *m. pl.* ‖ **Rifle-range,** n. MILIT. Portée (*f.*) de fusil (distance); champ (or) stand de tir *m.* ‖ **Rifle-shot,** n. MILIT. Portée (*f.*) de fusil (distance); tireur *m.* (marksman); coup de fusil *m.* (shot).

rifleman [-mən] (pl. **riflemen**) n. MILIT. Fusilier, carabinier m.

rift [rift] n. Fente, fissure, crevasse *f.; rift in the clouds,* éclaircie.

rig [rig] n. NAUT. Gréement *m.* ‖ TECHN. Equipement *m.;* installation *f.; oil rig,* derrick *m.,* plateforme (*f.*) de forage. ‖ U.S. Attelage *m.* ‖ FAM. Accoutrement *m.* ‖ **Rig-out,** n. FAM. Toilette *f.;* accoutrement *m.*
— v. tr. NAUT. Gréer; monter. ‖ **To rig out,** FAM. Attifer, nipper, fringuer, frusquer, accoutrer. ‖ **To rig-up,** monter, installer.

rig n. Tour *m.;* farce *f.* (joke); coup monté *m.* (piece of trickery). ‖ FIN. Coup (*m.*) de bourse.
— v. tr. Truquer. ‖ FIN. *To rig the market,* provoquer une hausse (or) baisse artificielle.

rigadoon [,rigə'du:n] n. MUS. Rigaudon *m.*

rigger ['rigə*] n. NAUT. Gréeur *m.* ‖ TECHN. Monteur-régleur *m.* ‖ TECHN. Poulie de commande *f.;* tambour *m.* ‖ U. S. FAM. Palissade (*f.*) de chantier de construction.

rigger n. Tripoteur *m.*

rigging [-iŋ] n. NAUT. Gréage *m.* (action); gréement *m.* (system); capelage *m.* (of a mast). ‖ AVIAT. Gréement *m.* ‖ TECHN. Montage *m.*

rigging [-iŋ] n. Tripotage *m.*

right [rait] adj. Droit; *on the right-hand side,* à droite; *to be someone's right hand,* être le bras droit de qqn. ‖ Bon (morally good). ‖ Juste, exact, correct; *the right time,* l'heure exacte; *that's right,* c'est juste; *you are right,* vous avez raison. ‖ Préférable, meilleur (best); voulu (desired); juste, bon, équitable (fair, just); approprié, convenable (most appropriate); *have I done the right thing?,* ai-je fait ce qu'il fallait?; *I thought it right to tell you,*

j'ai cru bon de vous le dire; *it is only right for him to know that,* il n'est que juste qu'il le sache; *on the right road,* dans le bon chemin; *to come at the right moment,* tomber bien; *to put right,* mettre sur la bonne voie (s.o.); rectifier (sth.). ‖ En bon état, en ordre (in good order). ‖ MED. En bonne santé; *to be in one's right mind,* avoir toute sa raison; *to be on the right side of forty,* ne pas avoir encore quarante ans; *to feel right again,* se sentir de nouveau sur pied (fam.). ‖ COMM. *Right side down, up,* à l'envers, à l'endroit. ‖ MATH. Droit (angle, line). ‖ U. S. *Is that right?,* vraiment?, est-ce possible? ‖ POP. *A bit of all right,* une fille épatante (girl); un truc épatant (sth.). ‖ LOC. *All right! right-o!,* d'accord!, bon!, entendu!, convenu!, ça y est!; *are you all right?,* ça va?; *he's all right,* c'est un type bien; *right enough!,* effectivement!, bien sûr!, je veux bien!, c'est vrai. ‖ **Right-about,** n. Demi-tour (*m.*) à droite; adv. *To turn right-about,* faire demi-tour; adj. *Right-about turn,* demi-tour à droite. ‖ **Right-angled,** adj. MATH. Rectangle, rectangulaire; à angle droit. ‖ **Right-hand,** de droite, à droite; TECHN. A droite (screw); FIG. *His right-hand man,* son bras droit. ‖ **Right-handed,** adj. Droitier (person); SPORTS. Du droit (punch). ‖ **Right-hander,** n. Droitier *s.;* SPORTS. Coup du droit *m.* ‖ **Right-minded,** adj. A l'esprit droit; sain d'esprit. ‖ **Right-winger,** n. SPORTS. Ailier droit *m.*
— v. intr. NAUT. Se redresser, se relever.
— v. tr. AUTOM., NAUT. Redresser. ‖ JUR. Réparer (an injustice); faire justice à (s.o.); redresser (a wrong). ‖ FIG. Corriger, rectifier (an error).
— adv. Droit, directement (straight). ‖ A droite; *right and left,* à droite et à gauche, de droite et de gauche; de tous les côtés. ‖ Tout à fait (exactly); *right against the wall,* tout contre le mur; *right away,* sur-le-champ, tout de suite; de ce pas (at once); du premier coup (at the first try); *right here,* ici même; *right in the middle,* au beau (or) en plein milieu; *right now,* tout de suite. ‖ Tout à fait, complètement (quite); *right at the back of the class,* tout au fond de la classe. ‖ Bien, équitablement, avec justice (justly); *it serves him right,* c'est bien fait pour lui. ‖ Bien, juste, exactement, correctement (accurately); très, fort (very); bien, comme il faut (well). ‖ MILIT. *Eyes right!,* tête droite! ‖ NAUT. *Right ahead,* droit debout (or) devant. ‖ ECCLES. Très (Reverend).
— n. Bien, bon *m.; right and wrong,* le bien et le mal. ‖ Droite *f.; côté droit m.; on my right,* à ma droite. ‖ JUR. Droite *f.* (in politics). ‖ MILIT. *By the right!,* guide à droite! ‖ JUR. Droit *m.;* justice *f.; loss of civil rights,* dégradation nationale (or) civique; *in one's own right,* de son propre chef; *right of pardon,* droit de grâce; *to have a right to,* avoir droit à (sth.); avoir le droit de (do sth.); *to know the rights of a case,* connaître les tenants et les aboutissants d'une affaire; *what right have you to enter?,* de quel droit entrez-vous?; *within one's right,* dans son droit. ‖ SPORTS. Coup (*m.*) du droit (in boxing). ‖ LOC. *To put to rights,* arranger, remettre en ordre; redresser (a wrong).

righteous [-ʃəs] adj. Vertueux, juste, droit. ‖ Juste, justifié (act, anger).

righteously [-ʃəsli] adv. Vertueusement.

righteousness [-ʃəsnis] n. Vertu, rectitude, droiture, honnêteté *f.*

rightful [-ful] adj. Equitable (conduct). ‖ JUR. Légitime.

rightfully [-fuli] adv. Equitablement. ‖ JUR. Légitimement, à juste titre, à bon droit.

rightly [-li] adv. Comme il faut (correctly); exactement (exactly); justement, avec justice, à juste titre, à bon droit (justly); avec sagesse, sagement, vertueusement (wisely); *rightly or wrongly,* à tort ou à raison.

rightness [-nis] n. Justesse, exactitude f. (of an answer). ‖ Justesse, rectitude f. ‖ JUR. Bien-fondé m. (of a claim).

righto ['rait'ou] interj. FAM. D'accord!, dac!

rigid ['ridʒid] adj. Rigide, raide. ‖ FIG. Rigide, intransigeant.

rigidity [ri'dʒiditi] n. Rigidité, raideur f. ‖ FIG. Rigidité, intransigeance f.

rigidly ['ridʒidli] adv. Rigidement. ‖ FIG. Strictement, rigoureusement.

rigmarole ['rigməroul] n. Galimatias m.; propos incohérents m. pl.; chapelet (m.) de sottises; litanie, tartine f. (fam.).

rigor ['rigə:*] n. MED. Frissons m. pl. (trembling); rigor mortis, rigidité cadavérique. ‖ U. S. See RIGOUR.

rigorism ['rigərizm] n. Rigorisme m.

rigorist [-ist] n. Rigoriste s.

rigorous [-əs] adj. Rigoureux.

rigorously [-əsli] adv. Rigoureusement.

rigour ['rigə*] n. Rigueur, sévérité, dureté f. (harshness). ‖ Rigueur, austérité f. (austerity). ‖ Rigueur f. (of weather). ‖ MATH. Rigueur, exactitude, précision f.

rile [rail] v. tr. FAM. Exaspérer, agacer.

rill [ril] n. Ruisseau, ruisselet m.
— v. intr. Ruisseler.

rim [rim] v. tr. Border. ‖ TECHN. Janter (a wheel).
— n. Bord, rebord m. ‖ Monture f. (of spectacles); jante f. (of a wheel).

rime [raim] n. Rime f. (See RHYME.)

rime [raim] n. Givre, frimas m.; gelée blanche f.
— v. tr. Givrer, couvrir de givre (or) frimas.

rimy [-i] adj. Givré.

rind [raind] v. tr. BOT. Ecorcer.
— n. BOT. Ecorce f. ‖ CULIN. Couenne f. (of bacon); croûte f. (of cheese); pelure f. (of fruit).

rinderpest ['rindəpest] n. MED. Peste bovine f.

ring [riŋ] n. Son m. (sound); sonnerie f. (of bells); tintement m. (of metal). ‖ Coup (m.) de sonnette (or) de timbre; to hear a ring at the door, entendre sonner à la porte. ‖ Appel téléphonique, coup de téléphone (or) de fil m. (telephone-ring). ‖ Intonation f.; timbre m. (of the voice). ‖ ECCLES. Jeu (m.) de cloches.
— v. tr. (112). Sonner, faire sonner (bells). ‖ Faire sonner (or) tinter (coins). ‖ FIG. Chanter (s.o.'s praises). ‖ To ring back, rappeler (at the telephone). ‖ To ring down, v. tr. THEATR. Sonner pour la chute de (the curtain). ‖ To ring in, v. tr. Carillonner l'arrivée de; to ring out the Old Year, réveillonner le 31 décembre. ‖ To ring up, v. tr. Donner un coup de téléphone à; THEATR. To ring up the curtain, frapper les trois coups.
— v. intr. Sonner, tinter (bells, coins); vibrer (voice). ‖ Sonner (person); to ring for the lift (or) U. S. elevator, appeler l'ascenseur; to ring for s.o., sonner qqn. ‖ Résonner, retentir (to re-echo). ‖ MED. Tinter, bourdonner (ears). ‖ FIG. To ring false, true, sonner faux, juste. ‖ To ring off, v. intr. Raccrocher, couper (at the telephone).

ring v. tr. Entourer, encercler, cerner. ‖ CULIN. Couper en rondelles. ‖ AGRIC. Baguer (a bird, a tree); mettre un anneau au nez de (a bull).
— v. intr. Décrire des cercles.
— n. Anneau m. (in general); anneau m.; bague f. (for a finger); rond m. (serviette-ring); wedding ring, alliance. ‖ Cercle m. (of people); sitting in a ring, assis en rond. ‖ U. S. POP. Gang m. ‖ MED. Cerne m.; to have rings round the eyes, avoir les yeux battus (or) cernés. ‖ SPORTS. Ring m. (boxing-ring); piste f. (circus-ring); the ring, les bookmakers; les boxeurs (boxers); la boxe (boxing). ‖ COMM. Groupe, cartel m. ‖ BOT. Cerne, cercle m. ‖ TECHN. Segment m. ‖ FAM. To make rings around s.o., enfoncer qqn dans les grandes largeurs. ‖ Ring-

bolt, n. TECHN. Piton m. ‖ **Ring-craft,** n. SPORTS. Technique de la boxe f. ‖ **Ring-dove,** n. ZOOL. Ramier m. ‖ **Ring-finger,** n. MED. Annulaire m. ‖ **Ring-road,** n. Route de ceinture f.

ringer [-ə*] n. Sonneur, carillonneur m. ‖ U. S. SPORTS. Cheval (m.) substitué à un autre (in a race). ‖ FAM. Double, sosie m.

ringing [-iŋ] adj. Sonnant, tintant (bell); sonore, retentissant (cry, voice).
— n. Son m.; sonnerie f. (of bells). ‖ MED. Bourdonnement, tintement m. (in the ears).

ringleader [-,li:də*] n. Meneur m.

ringlet [-lit] n. Petit anneau m. ‖ Bouclette, frisette f. (of hair).

ringworm [-wə:m] n. MED. Teigne f.

rink [riŋk] n. SPORTS. Patinoire f. (ice-rink); skating m. (roller-skating-rink).

rinse [rins] n. Rinçage m.
— v. tr. Rincer; to rinse one's hands, se passer les mains à l'eau.

rinsing [-iŋ] n. Rinçage m. ‖ Pl. Rinçures f. pl.

riot ['raiət] v. intr. S'ameuter. ‖ Faire du tapage (or) vacarme (to make a row). ‖ Raffoler (in, de); s'adonner complètement (in, à).
— n. JUR. Emeute f.; pl. troubles f. pl.; Riot Act, loi contre les attroupements; to read the Riot Act, faire les trois sommations légales. ‖ THEATR. To be a riot, faire fureur (play). ‖ FIG. Orgie; débauche f. (of colours). ‖ FAM. To read the Riot Act to, passer un savon à (s.o.); to run riot, être déchaîné (person); pousser follement (vegetation). ‖ **Riot call,** n. U. S. FAM. Appel (m.) à Police Secours. ‖ **Riot squad,** n. U. S. FAM. Equipe (f.) de Police Secours.

rioter [-ə*] n. Emeutier m. ‖ Noceur m.

riotous [-əs] adj. Séditieux. ‖ Turbulent, tumultueux (boisterous); dissolu, débauché (profligate); tapageur (rowdy).

rip [rip] n. Rosse f. (horse); vaurien m. (person).

rip n. Déchirure f. (See TEAR.) ‖ **Rip-cord,** n. AVIAT. Cordelette (f.) de déclenchement, tirette f. (of a parachute); corde de déchirure f. (of a balloon). ‖ **Rip-off,** n. POP. Vol m. (lit., fig.); it's a rip-off, c'est du vol!, quelle arnaque! ‖ **Rip-saw,** n. TECHN. Scie (f.) à refendre.
— v. intr. Se déchirer; se fendre. ‖ FAM. To let rip, exploser (person); to rip along, marcher à plein gaz; let her rip! fonce!, appuie sur le champignon! (car). ‖ To rip away, v. intr. Se déchirer.
— v. tr. (1). Déchirer (to tear); éventrer (to tear open). ‖ Refendre (wood). ‖ ARCHIT. Enlever les tuiles de (a roof). ‖ To rip away, arracher, déchirer. ‖ To rip off, arracher, déchirer; POP. Dévaliser, détrousser (to rob), escroquer, arnaquer (to swindle), faucher, piquer (to steal). ‖ To rip out, arracher; FAM. Lâcher (an oath). ‖ To rip up, défaire (a seam); fendre (wood); éventrer (s.o.); FIG. Raviver.

rip n. NAUT. Clapotis m.

riparian [rai'pɛəriən] adj., n. Riverain s.

ripe [raip] adj. CULIN. Mûr (apple); fait (cheese). ‖ MED. Mûr (abscess). ‖ FIG. Rouge, vermeil (lips). ‖ FIG. Mûr (for, pour); prêt (for, à); a ripe old age, un bel âge.

ripely [-li] adv. Mûrement.

ripen [-ən] v. tr. Mûrir, faire mûrir.
— v. intr. Mûrir (lit. and fig.).

ripeness [-nis] n. Maturité f.

riposte [ri'post] n. Riposte f.
— v. intr. Riposter.

ripper [ripə*] n. Eventreur m. ‖ TECHN. Scie (f.) à refendre. ‖ FAM. Type sensationnel m. (person); truc formidable m. (thing).

ripping [-iŋ] adj. FAM. Epatant, sensationnel.

rippingly [-li] adv. FAM. Epatamment.

ripple ['ripl] v. intr. Se rider (water). ‖ Murmurer,

gazouiller (stream); clapoter (tide). ‖ Onduler (hair). ‖ Perler, s'égrener (laughter).
— v. tr. Rider, faire rider.
— n. Ride *f.* (on the water). ‖ Gazouillement; clapotis *m.* ‖ Ondulation *f.* (of hair). ‖ Murmure *m.* (of conversation); *ripple of laughter*, rire perlé qui s'égrène, cascade de rires. ‖ **Ripple-mark**, n. Ride *f.* (on sand).

rippled [-d] adj. Ridé, ondulé; *rippled silk fabric*, cloqué de soie.

ripply [-i] adj. Couvert de rides.

rise ⌊raiz⌋ n. Ascension *f.* (act); éminence, hauteur, élévation *f.* (hill); côte *f.* (slope). ‖ Jur. Avancement *m.;* promotion, élévation *f.* ‖ Theatr. Lever *m.* (of the curtain). ‖ Mus. Hausse *f.* ‖ Geogr. Crue *f.* (of a river); flux *m.* (of the tide). ‖ Phys. Augmentation *f.* (of pressure); hausse *f.* (of temperature). ‖ Fin. Relèvement *m.* (of the Bank Rate); hausse *f.* (of prices); augmentation *f.* (in prices, salary). ‖ Fig. Source, origine *f.; to give rise to*, produire, engendrer, susciter, provoquer, donner lieu à. ‖ Fam. *To take* (or) *to get a rise out of*, se payer la tête de, faire marcher (s.o.).
— v. tr. (113). Sports. Faire lever (bird); faire mordre (fish).
— v. intr. Se relever (to pick oneself up); se lever (to get out of bed, to stand up). ‖ Monter (to slope up). ‖ S'élever, se dresser (to be erect). ‖ Monter, s'élever; *to rise above a given temperature*, dépasser une température donnée. ‖ Se lever (wind); *the squall rose into a tempest*, le grain devint tempête. ‖ S'élever (in rank); *to rise from nothing*, partir de rien. ‖ Se soulever, se révolter (to revolt). ‖ Avoir sa source (*from*, dans) [to originate]. ‖ Jur. Lever la séance (meeting). ‖ Eccles. *To rise from the dead*, ressusciter des morts. ‖ Mus. Monter. ‖ Geogr. Se relever (ground); être en crue (river); monter (tide); prendre sa source (*in*, dans); ‖ Astron. Se lever (star). ‖ Sports. Mordre (fish); se lever (game-birds). ‖ Culin. Lever (dough). ‖ Fin. Monter (prices). ‖ Fig. Croître, grandir (anger, hopes); *to rise to the occasion*, se montrer à la hauteur de la situation.

risen [rizn] p. p. See rise.

riser ⌊-ə*⌋ n. Personne (*f.*) qui se lève (early, late); *to be an early riser*, être matinal; *to be a late riser*, aimer faire la grasse matinée. ‖ Techn. Colonne montante *f.* (of gas, water); contre-marche *f.* (of a stair-case).

risibility [ˌrizi'biliti] n. Risibilité *f.*

risible ⌊'rizibl⌋ adj. † Rieur. ‖ Risible (laughable); du rire (of laughter).

rising ⌊'raiziŋ⌋ n. Elévation *f.* (of ground). ‖ Révolte *f.;* soulèvement *m.* ‖ Jur. Clôture *f.* ‖ Eccles. Résurrection *f.* ‖ Theatr., Astron. Lever *m.* ‖ Fin. Augmentation, hausse *f.*
— adj. Qui monte. ‖ Qui se lève (wind). ‖ Astron. Levant. ‖ Fig. Croissant (anger); nouveau, montant (generation). ‖ Loc. *He is rising ten*, il va sur ses dix ans.

risk [risk] v. tr. Risquer, hasarder (one's money). ‖ Risquer, courir le risque de; se risquer à faire (sth.); *to risk it*, tenter le coup.
— n. Risque, péril, aléa *m.; at your own risk*, à vos risques et périls. ‖ Risques *m. pl.* (in insurance).

riskiness ⌊-inis⌋ n. Aléas; risques et périls *m. pl.*

risky [-i] adj. Risqué, aléatoire, hasardeux. ‖ Risqué, dangereux.

risotto [ri'zɔtou] n. Culin. Risotto *m.*

risqué [-ei] adj. Osé, risqué, scabreux.

rissole ⌊'risoul⌋ n. Culin. Rissole, croquette *f.*

rite [rait] n. Rite *m.;* cérémonie *f.*

ritual ⌊'ritjuəl⌋ adj., n. Rituel *m.*

ritualism [-izm] n. Ritualisme *m.*

ritualist [-ist] n. Ritualiste *s.*

ritualistic [ˌritjuə'listik] adj. Ritualiste.

ritually ⌊'ritjuəli⌋ adj. Rituellement.

ritzy ⌊'ritsi⌋ adj. Fam. Chic, super-chic, sélect.

rival ⌊'raivəl⌋ adj., n. Rival *s.* (See competitor.)
— v. tr. (1). Rivaliser avec.
— v. intr. Rivaliser, être en rivalité (*with*, avec).

rivalize [-laiz] v. intr. Rivaliser (*with*, avec).

rivalry [-ri] n. Rivalité *f.* ‖ Emulation *f.*

rive [raiv] v. intr. Eclater, se fendre.
— v. tr. Fendre. ‖ **To rive away** (or) **off**, arracher.
— N. B. Le p. p. est *rived* ou *riven*.

river ⌊'rivə*⌋ n. Geogr. Fleuve *m.;* rivière *f.* ‖ Fig. Fleuve *m.* ‖ U. S. Pop. *To sell down the river*, emmener en bateau. ‖ **River-bank**, n. Bord (*m.*) du fleuve (or) de la rivière. ‖ **River-basin**, n. Bassin fluvial *m.* ‖ **River-bed**, n. Lit (*m.*) de rivière. ‖ **River-borne**, adj. Transporté par voie d'eau. ‖ **River-fish**, n. Poisson (*m.*) d'eau douce. ‖ **River-head**, n. Source *f.* ‖ **River-horse**, n. Zool. Hippopotame *m.* ‖ **River-keeper**, n. Sports. Garde-pêche *m.* ‖ **River-port**, n. Port fluvial *m.* ‖ **River-side**, n. Bord (*m.*) du fleuve (or) de la rivière; adj. Au bord de l'eau.

river ⌊'raivə*⌋ n. Techn. Fendeur *s.* (person).

riverain ⌊'rivərein⌋ adj., n. Riverain *s.* (riparian).

riverine [-ain] adj. Riverain. ‖ Fluvial.

riverman ⌊'rivəmən⌋ n. Naut. Batelier *m.*

riverside [ˌrivə'said] n. Rive *f.;* bord de l'eau *m.*
— ⌊'rivəsaid⌋ adj. Situé au bord d'une rivière.

riverway ⌊'rivəwei⌋ n. Voie fluviale *f.*

rivet ⌊'rivit⌋ n. Techn. Rivet *m.* ‖ **Rivet-joint**, n. Techn. Assemblage (*m.*) par rivets.
— v. tr. Techn. River, riveter. ‖ Fig. Retenir (the attention); cimenter (a friendship); river, fixer (one's eyes).

riveter [-ə*] n. Techn. Riveteuse *f.* (machine); riveur *m.* (person).

rivet(t)ing [-iŋ] n. Techn. Rivetage *m.* ‖ **Riveting-hammer**, n. Techn. Rivoir *m.* ‖ **Riveting-machine**, n. Techn. Riveteuse *f.*

Riviera [ˌrivi'eərə] n. Geogr. Côte d'Azur *f.* (in France); Riviera italienne *f.* (in Italy).

rivulet ⌊'rivjulit⌋ n. Ruisselet, filet (*m.*) d'eau.

rix-dollar [ˌriks'dɔlə*] n. Rixdale *f.*

R. N. A. [ɑːen'ei] abbr. *Ribonucleic acid*, acide ribonucléique, A. R. N.

roach [routʃ] n. Zool. Gardon *m.*

roach n. U. S. Zool. Blatte *f.*, cafard *m.* (cockroach). ‖ U. S. Pop. Mégot de joint *m.*

road [roud] n. Route *f.; road transport*, transports routiers. ‖ Rue *f.* (in a town). ‖ Autom. *It's your road*, vous avez la priorité. ‖ Naut. Rade *f.* ‖ U. S. Chemin de fer *m.; on the road*, en voyage. ‖ Fig. Voie *f.; on the road to success*, sur le chemin du succès. ‖ U. S. Fam. *To hit the road*, déguerpir. ‖ **Road-block**, n. Barrage (*m.*) sur route. ‖ **Road-hog**, n. Fam. Chauffard *m.* ‖ **Road-holding**, n. Tenue de route *f.* ‖ **Road-house**, n. Guinguette *f.;* relais *m.* ‖ **Road-labourer**, n. Cantonnier *m.* ‖ **Road-map**, n. Carte routière *f.* ‖ **Road-metal**, n. Matériaux (*m. pl.*) d'empierrement. ‖ **Road-roller**, n. Rouleau compresseur *m.* ‖ **Road sign**, n. Panneau (*m.*) de signalisation. ‖ **Road-surveyor**, n. Agent voyer *m.* ‖ **Road test**, n. Essai (*m.*) sur route. ‖ **Road-trials**, n. Compétitions routières *f. pl.* ‖ **Road-works**, n. pl. Travaux (*m. pl.*) de voirie; « attention travaux » (warning sign).

roadman [-mən] n. Cantonnier *m.*

roadside [-said] adj. Situé au bord de la route (hotel). ‖ Autom. De fortune (repairs).

roadside [ˌroud'said] n. Accotement, bord (*m.*) de la route; *roadside inn*, guinguette.

roadstead ⌊'roudsted⌋ n. Naut. Rade *f.*

roadster [-stə*] n. Cheval (*m.*) de fatigue (horse). ‖ Bicyclette routière *f.* (bicycle). ‖ Autom. Roadster *m.* ‖ Naut. Navire (*m.*) en rade.

roadway [-wei] n. Chaussée *f.*

roadworthy [-wə:ði] adj. En état de rouler, en bon état (car).

roam [roum] v. tr. Parcourir, errer dans (or) par ; *to roam the streets*, polissonner dans les rues (child). — v. intr. Errer, rôder ; *to roam about*, errer de-ci de-là, vagabonder ; traîner (fam.). — n. Promenade *f.*

roan [roun] n. Basane *f.* (for bookbinding).

roan adj., n. Rouan *m.*

roar [rɔ:*] n. Hurlement *m. ;* clameurs *f. pl.* ‖ Gros éclat *m.* (of laughter) ; *to set in a roar*, désopiler. ‖ ZOOL. Mugissement *m.* (of a bull) ; rugissement *m.* (of a lion). ‖ FIG. Ronflement *m.* (of a fire) ; grondement *m.* (of gunfire, of thunder) ; mugissement *m.* (of the wind). — v. tr. Hurler (an order) ; brailler, beugler (a song). — v. intr. Rugir, vociférer, hurler. ‖ *To roar with laughter*, rire à gorge déployée, se tordre. ‖ ZOOL. Mugir (bull) ; rugir (lion). ‖ FIG. Gronder (gunfire, thunder) ; mugir, hurler (wind).

roarer [-ə*] n. Cheval cornard *m.* (horse). ‖ U. S. TECHN., FAM. Puits jaillissant *m.*

roaring [-iŋ] n. See ROAR. — adj. Hurlant, beuglant. ‖ ZOOL. Mugissant (bull) ; rugissant (lion). ‖ FAM. Epatant ; *a roaring trade*, des affaires du tonnerre.

roast [roust] adj. CULIN. Rôti (meat) ; tranche *f.* (of meat) ; *roast beef*, rosbif. ‖ FIG. Rôti, grillé. — n. CULIN. Rôti *m.* — v. intr. CULIN. Rôtir. ‖ FIG. Griller. — v. tr. CULIN. Faire cuire sur le plat (egg) ; rôtir, faire rôtir (meat) ; torréfier (coffee). ‖ TECHN. Griller, calciner (minerals). ‖ FIG. *To roast oneself*, se rôtir, se griller. ‖ FAM. Railler, blaguer, chiner (to banter). ‖ U. S. FAM. Ereinter (to criticize).

roaster [-ə*] n. Rôtisseur *m.* (person). ‖ CULIN. Rôtissoire *f.* (apparatus) ; brûloir *m.* (for coffee) ; volaille (*f.*) à rôtir (fowl).

roasting [-iŋ] adj. Brûlant. — n. CULIN. Rôtissage *m.* (of meat) ; torréfaction *f.* (of coffee). ‖ TECHN. Grillage *m.* ‖ FAM. Raillerie *f.* ‖ FAM. U. S. Savon *m.* ‖ **Roasting-jack**, n. CULIN. Tournebroche *m.*

rob [rɔb] v. intr. (1). Voler. — v. tr. Voler, détrousser (s.o.) ; piller (to pillage) ; *to rob s.o. of sth.*, voler (or) dérober qqch. à qqn.

robber [-ə*] n. Voleur *s.*

robbery [-əri] n. Vol *m.*

robe [roub] v. intr. Revêtir sa robe. — v. tr. Revêtir d'une robe ; parer. — n. Vêtement *m.* (in general) ; robe *f.* (of a baby) ; U. S. *night robe*, chemise de nuit. ‖ Robe *f.* (of office) ; *Master of the Robes*, Intendant (*m.*) de la garde-robe. ‖ U. S. Couverture *f.*, plaid *m.* (rug).

robin [ˈrɔbin] n. *Robin Hood*, Robin des Bois. ‖ ZOOL. Rouge-gorge *f.* ‖ U. S. Grive migratrice *f.* ‖ **Robin-redbreast**, n. ZOOL. Rouge-gorge *m.*

robot [ˈroubɔt] n. Robot *m.* — adj. Automatique. ‖ **Robot-pilot**, n. AVIAT. Pilote automatique *m.*

roburite [ˈroubərait] n. CHIM. Roburite *f.*

robust [roˈbʌst] adj. Robuste, vigoureux.

robustious [-ʃəs] adj. Violent ; bruyant. (See BOISTEROUS.)

robustly [-li] adj. Vigoureusement, avec robustesse.

robustness [-nis] n. Robustesse, vigueur *f.*

rocambole [ˈrɔkəmboul] n. BOT. Rocambole *f.*

rock [rɔk] adj. Rupestre (drawings). — n. Roc *m.* ‖ U. S. Pierre *f.* (stone). ‖ GEOL. Roche *f.* ; rocher *m.* ‖ NAUT. Ecueil *m.* ‖ GEOGR. Rocher *m.* (of Gibraltar). ‖ CULIN. Bâtons (*m. pl.*) de sucrerie. ‖ FAM. *To be on the rocks*, être à la côte (or) décavé (or) à fond de cale. ‖ U. S. POP. *To have rocks in one's head*, être cinglé. ‖ Pl. U. S. POP. Fric *m.* (oof). ‖ **Rock-basin**, n. GEOL. Bassin

géologique *m.* ‖ **Rock-bed**, n. GEOL. Lit (or) fond (*m.*) de roche. ‖ **Rock-bottom**, n. GEOL. Fond rocheux *m. ;* FAM. Fin fond *m. ;* adj. Le plus bas, défiant toute concurrence (price). ‖ **Rock-bound**, adj. Hérissé de rochers (coast). ‖ **Rock-cake**, n. CULIN. Rocher *m.* ‖ **Rock-climber**, n. SPORTS. Varappeur *s.* ‖ **Rock-climbing**, n. SPORTS. Montée en varappe *f.* ‖ **Rock-crystal**, n. Cristal (*m.*) de roche. ‖ **Rock-drill**, n. TECHN. Foreuse, perforatrice *f.* ‖ **Rock-English**, n. Patois (*m.*) de Gibraltar. ‖ **Rock-face**, n. Varappe *f.* ‖ **Rock-fish**, n. ZOOL. Rascasse *f.* ‖ **Rock-lobster**, n. ZOOL. Langoustine. ‖ **Rock-melon**, n. AGRIC. Cantaloup *m.* ‖ **Rock-oil**, n. TECHN. Naphte minéral *m.* ‖ **Rock-ribbed**, adj. NAUT. Rocheux, hérissé de rochers (coast) ; U. S. Intransigeant (policy). ‖ **Rock-salt**, n. Sel gemme *m.* ‖ **Rock-water**, n. Eau de roche *f.*

rock n. Balancement *m.* ‖ MUS. *Rock and roll*, rock and roll ; rock'n'roll (fam.). — v. tr. Balancer ; faire osciller. ‖ Ebranler (to shake). ‖ Bercer (a child) ; *to rock to sleep*, endormir en berçant. ‖ NAUT. Ballotter (a ship). ‖ TECHN. Basculer (a lever) ; travailler au berceau (ore). ‖ FIG. Bercer. — v. intr. Se bercer, se balancer. ‖ Vaciller, osciller. ‖ Trembler, vibrer. ‖ MUS. *To rock and roll*, danser le rock'n'roll. ‖ FAM. *To rock with laughter*, se tordre, se gondoler, se bidonner.

rocker [-ə*] n. Berceur *s.* ‖ Bascule *f.* ‖ Rocking-chair *m.* ‖ TECHN. Berceau *m.* ‖ FAM. *To go off one's rocker*, se détraquer. ‖ **Rocker-arm**, n. TECHN. Basculeur *m.*

rocker n. POP. Rocker, blouson noir *m.*

rockery [-əri] n. Jardin (*m.*) de rocaille.

rocket [ˈrɔkit] n. Fusée *f.* ‖ MILIT. Roquette *f.* ‖ FAM. Savon *m. ; to send s.o. a rocket*, envoyer une lettre d'engueulade à qqn. ‖ **Rocket-apparatus**, n. Fusée porte-amarre *f.* ‖ **Rocket-fighter, -plane**, n. AVIAT. Chasseur-, avion-fusée *m.* ‖ **Rocket-gun**, n. MILIT. Lance-amarre, lance-fusée *m.* — v. intr. Se lancer comme un éclair ; *to rocket past*, passer comme une flèche. ‖ Monter en flèche.

Rockies [ˈrɔkiz] n. pl. GEOGR. Montagnes Rocheuses *f. pl.*

rocking [ˈrɔkiŋ] n. Balancement *m.* ‖ Tremblement *m.* ‖ TECHN. Basculage *m.* — adj. A bascule (horse). ‖ **Rocking-arm**, n. TECHN. Basculeur *m.* ‖ **Rocking-chair**, n. Rocking-chair *m.*

rocky [-i] adj. Rocheux (mountains) ; rocailleux (road). ‖ FIG. Rocailleux, raboteux.

rococo [rəˈkoukou] adj., n. Rococo *m.*

rod [rɔd] n. Baguette *f.* ‖ Verge *f.* (of office, for punishment). ‖ Perche *f.* (measure). ‖ Tringle *f.* (of curtains, stairs). ‖ SPORTS. Canne à pêche *f.* ‖ FAM. *To have a rod in pickle for*, garder un chien de sa chienne pour ; *to rule s.o. with a rod of iron*, mener qqn à la trique (or) à la baguette. ‖ **Rod-bacterium**, n. MED. Bâtonnet *m.*

rode [roud] pret. See RIDE.

rodent [ˈroudənt] adj., n. ZOOL. Rongeur *m.*

rodeo [rouˈdeiou] n. Rodéo *m.*

rodomontade [ˈrɔdəmənˈteid] n. Rodomontade *f.* (See BRAGGING.)

roe [rou], **roebuck** [-bʌk] n. ZOOL. Chevreuil *m.*

roe n. ZOOL. Œufs *m. pl.* (hard) ; *soft roe*, laite, laitance.

roentgen [ˈrɔntgən] n. PHYS. Röntgen *m.* (unit).

roentgenography [ˌrɔntgəˈnɔgrəfi] n. Radiographie *f.*

roentgenology [-ˈnɔlədʒi] n. Radiologie *f.*

rogations [roˈgeiʃəns] n. pl. ECCLES. Rogations *f. pl.*

Roger [ˈrɔdʒə*] n. Roger. ‖ NAUT. *The Jolly Roger*, le pavillon noir.

roger v. tr. ARG. Baiser, sauter. — interj. FAM. Entendu, compris, d'accord.

rogue [roug] n. Coquin, fripon s.; chenapan m. (rascal). ‖ Coquin, fripon, malin, espiègle, polisson s. (mischievous). ‖ SPORTS. Cheval qui refuse m. ‖ ZOOL. Solitaire m.

roguery [-əri] n. Gredinerie, malhonnêteté f. (of a person). ‖ Espièglerie f. (of a child).

roguish [-iʃ] adj. De coquin, de gredin, malhonnête. ‖ Coquin, fripon, malin, espiègle, polisson (mischievous).

roguishly [-iʃli] adj. Comme un gredin. ‖ Malicieusement; avec espièglerie.

roister ['rɔistə*] v. intr. FAM. Faire du chahut.

roisterer [-rə*] n. FAM. Tapageur s.

roistering [-riŋ] n. FAM. Tapage, chahut m.
— adj. Tapageur, chahuteur, bruyant.

role, rôle [roul] n. Rôle m. (actor's part, social function).

roll n. Rouleau m. (of paper); bâton m. (stick); carotte f. (of tobacco). ‖ Roulement m. (of thunder). ‖ Balancement m. (gait). ‖ Déroulement m. (of a phrase). ‖ MILIT. Appel m.; to call the roll, faire l'appel. ‖ NAUT. Houle f. (of the sea); roulis m. (of a ship). ‖ AVIAT. Vol en tonneau m. ‖ MED. Bourrelet m. (of fat). ‖ JUR. Etat, rôle m.; liste f.; to strike off the rolls, rayer du tableau. ‖ MUS. Roulement m. (of a drum). ‖ ARCHIT. Volute f. ‖ CULIN. Petit pain m. (loaf); coquille f. (of butter). ‖ CINEM. Bobine f. (of camera-film); galette f. (of cinema-film). ‖ TECHN. Rouleau, cylindre m. ‖ **Roll-back,** n. U. S. FAM. Baisse f. (of prices). ‖ **Roll-bar,** n. AUTOM. Arceau (m.) de sécurité (on sportscar). ‖ **Roll-call,** n. Appel m. ‖ **Roll-on,** n. Gaine f.; corset m. ‖ **Roll-top desk,** n. Bureau à cylindre m.
— v. intr. Rouler (in general). ‖ Rouler sa bosse (to travel). ‖ Gronder (thunder). ‖ Se balancer, se dandiner; se déhancher (in walking). ‖ Se rouler, se retourner, se vautrer (in, dans; on, sur). ‖ AVIAT., NAUT., MUS. Rouler. ‖ TECHN. Se laminer (metals). ‖ FAM. To be rolling in money, rouler sur l'or. ‖ **To roll about,** v. intr. Rouler çà et là. ‖ **To roll along,** rouler; FAM. S'amener (to arrive). ‖ **To roll away,** s'éloigner. ‖ **To roll by,** passer. ‖ **To roll down,** rouler de haut en bas (object); couler (tears). ‖ **To roll in,** entrer lourdement (person); déferler (waves); FAM. S'entasser (money). ‖ **To roll off,** dégringoler. ‖ **To roll on,** continuer de rouler; s'écouler (time). ‖ **To roll out,** sortir en titubant. ‖ **To roll over,** se retourner. ‖ **To roll round,** tourner (earth). ‖ **To roll up,** monter en spirale (smoke); se rouler (into a ball); FAM. S'amener, rappliquer.
— v. tr. Rouler (a ball, cigarette); enrouler (to roll up); to roll one's eyes, rouler les yeux; to roll one's r's, rouler les r, grasseyer. ‖ CULIN. Etendre au rouleau (dough); rouler (roast). ‖ ZOOL. To roll itself into a ball, se rouler en boule. ‖ TECHN. Rouler (the grass); laminer (metals); cylindrer (a road). ‖ **To roll about,** rouler çà et là. ‖ **To roll along,** rouler le long de. ‖ **To roll away,** éloigner. ‖ **To roll back,** rouler en arrière. ‖ **To roll down,** descendre. ‖ **To roll in,** faire entrer. ‖ **To roll on,** passer, enfiler (one's pullover). ‖ **To roll out,** rouler dehors; FIG. Faire ronfler (verse). ‖ **To roll over,** retourner. ‖ **To roll up,** rouler, enrouler; retrousser (one's sleeves).

roller [-ə*] n. Rouleau m. ‖ NAUT. Lame de houle f. ‖ MED. Bande roulée f. ‖ TECHN. Laminoir m. (for metals); rouleau, cylindre m.; road roller, rouleau compresseur. ‖ **Roller-blind,** n. Store m. ‖ **Roller coaster,** n. U. S. Scenic railway m.; montagnes russes f. pl. ‖ **Roller-skate,** v. intr. SPORTS. Patiner sur roulettes. ‖ **Roller-skates,** n. pl. SPORTS. Patins (m. pl.) à roulettes. ‖ **Roller-skating,** n. SPORTS. Patinage (m.) à roulettes, skating m. ‖ **Roller-towel,** n. Essuie-mains (m.) à rouleau.

rollick ['rɔlik] n. Gaieté exubérante f. ‖ Ebats m. pl.
— v. intr. Faire la fête. ‖ Folâtrer.

rolling ['rouliŋ] adj. Roulant, qui roule (stone). ‖ Ondulé (ground). ‖ NAUT. Houleux (sea); qui roule (ship). ‖ CH. DE F. Rolling stock, matériel roulant. ‖ FIG. To be a rolling stone, rouler sa bosse un peu partout.
— n. Roulement m. ‖ NAUT. Roulis m. ‖ TECHN. Laminage, cylindrage m. ‖ **Rolling-mill,** n. TECHN. Laminerie f. (building); laminoir m. (machine). ‖ **Rolling-pin,** n. CULIN. Rouleau (m.) à pâtisserie.

roly-poly ['rouli'pouli] adj. FAM. Dodu, rondelet, potelé. (See PLUMP.)
— n. CULIN. Bûche à la confiture f. ‖ FAM. Poupard m.

Romaic [ro'meiik] adj., n. Romaïque m.

romaine [rou'mein] n. AGRIC. Romaine f. (cos lettuce).

Roman ['roumən] n. GEOGR. Romain s.
— adj. GEOGR. Romain. ‖ MED. Aquilin (nose).

romance [ro'mæns] n. † Roman (m.) d'aventures (or) de chevalerie. ‖ Conte bleu m.; aventure merveilleuse, histoire romanesque f. (story). ‖ Evénement romanesque m. (event); idylle f. (love); to say good-bye to romance, renoncer à l'amour; dételer (fam.). ‖ Charme m. (charm); romance of the sea, poésie de la mer. ‖ MUS. Romance f.
— adj. GRAMM. Roman (language).
— v. intr. Exagérer, broder.

romancer [-ə*] n. † Conteur s. ‖ FAM. Enjoliveur, brodeur m.

Romanesque [,roumə'nesk] adj., n. ARTS. Roman m.

Romania [ro'meinjə] n. GEOGR. Roumanie f.

Romanist ['roumənist] adj., n. Romaniste s.

Romanize ['roumənaiz] v. tr. Romaniser. ‖ GRAMM. Transcrire en caractères romains.
— v. intr. ECCLES. Romaniser, tendre au catholicisme.

Romanizer [-ə*] n. Romanisant s.

Romansch [ro'mænʃ] adj., n. Romanche m.

romantic [ro'mæntik] n. Romantique s.
— adj. Romanesque. ‖ ARTS. Romantique. ‖ U. S. Romantic lead, jeune premier.

romantically [-əli] adv. De façon romanesque. ‖ En romantique.

romanticism [ro'mæntisizm] n. Romantisme m.

romanticist [-ist] n. Romantique s.

romanticize [-aiz] v. tr. Romancer.
— v. intr. Donner dans le romanesque.

Romany ['rɔməni] n. Romanichel m.
— adj. De romanichel.

Rome [roum] n. GEOGR. Rome f.

Romish [-iʃ] adj. ECCLES. Papiste.

romp [rɔmp] n. Jeu bruyant m.; gambades, diableries f. pl. (playing). ‖ Enfant turbulent s. (child); garçon manqué m. (girl).
— v. intr. S'ébattre; se dépenser; faire le diable à quatre. ‖ FAM. To romp home (or) in, gagner dans un fauteuil.

romper [-ə*] n. Batifoleur s. ‖ Pl. Barboteuse f. (clothing).

rompish [-iʃ], **rompy** [-i] adj. Turbulent, bruyant (boy); garçonnier (girl).

rondeau ['rɔndou] n. Rondeau m.

rondo ['rɔndou] n. MUS. Rondo m.

roneo ['rouniou] n. TECHN. Ronéo f.
— v. tr. TECHN. Ronéotyper.

röntgen ['rɔntgən] n. See ROENTGEN.

rood [ru:d] n. Quart d'arpent m. ‖ ECCLES. Croix f. ‖ **Rood-screen,** n. ECCLES. Jubé m.

roof [ru:f] v. tr. ARCHIT. Couvrir. ‖ FIG. Abriter, loger (s.o.).
— n. ARCHIT. Toit, comble m.; toiture f. ‖ AUTOM. Toit m. (of a car); impériale f. (of an omnibus). ‖ AVIAT. Plafond m. ‖ ECCLES. Ciel m. (of an altar). ‖ MED. Palais m. (of the mouth). ‖ FIG. Voûte f. ‖ FAM. To raise the roof, faire un boucan de tous les diables. ‖ **Roof-garden,** n. ARCHIT. Jardin (m.) sur

un toit en terrasse. ‖ **Roof-light,** n. AUTOM. Plafonnier *m.* ‖ **Roof-rack,** n. AUTOM. Galerie *f.*

roofer [-ə*] n. ARCHIT. Couvreur *m.*

roofless [-lis] n. *The roofless,* les sans-abri.
— adj. Sans toit. ‖ FIG. Sans abri.

rook [ruk] n. Tours *f.* (in chess).
— v. intr. Roquer (in chess).

rook n. ZOOL. Freux *m.;* corneille *f.*
— v. tr. FAM. Escroquer, empiler.

rookery [-əri] n. ZOOL. Colonie (*f.*) de freux (birds); colonie *f.* (of penguins, seals). ‖ FAM. Repaire *m.*

rookie ['ruki] n. MILIT., FAM. Bleu *m.*

room [rum] n. Place *f.; espace m.* (space); *to make room for,* faire place à ; *to take up too much room,* prendre trop de place. ‖ Pièce, salle, chambre *f.;* bureau *m.; pl.* logement, appartement *m.; room and board,* le gîte et le couvert; *bachelor's rooms,* garçonnière. ‖ NAUT. Soute *f.;* cambuse *f.* ‖ FIG. Sujet; lieu *m.;* occasion; raison *f.; there is room for improvement,* on peut faire mieux encore. ‖ **Room clerk,** n. U. S. Employé (*s.*) à la réception (in a hotel). ‖ **Room-mate,** n. Compagnon (*s.*) de chambre; co-thurne *m.* (fam.). ‖ **Room-service,** n. Service (*m.*) dans les chambres; garçon d'étage *m.* ‖ **Room temperature,** n. Température ambiante *f.; wine at room temperature,* vin chambré.
— v. intr. U. S. Vivre en garni. ‖ Partager une chambre (*with,* avec).

roomer ['ru:mə*] n. U. S. Locataire (*s.*) d'une chambre; sous-locataire *s.*

roomette [ru:m'eit] n. U. S. CH. DE F. Chambrette (*f.*) de sleeping.

roomful ['rumful] n. Chambrée, pleine salle *f.*

roomily ['ru:mili] adv. Spacieusement.

roominess [-inis] n. Dimensions spacieuses *f. pl.*

rooming [-iŋ] adj. U. S. A appartements meublés.

roomy [-i] adj. Spacieux (See COMMODIOUS.)

roost [ru:st] n. AGRIC. Juchoir, perchoir *m.; to go to roost,* se jucher. ‖ FAM. *To come home to roost,* faire choc en retour; *to go to roost,* aller faire dodo ; *to rule the roost,* faire la loi.
— v. intr. AGRIC. Se jucher, se percher. ‖ FAM. Loger, percher.

rooster [-ə*] n. ZOOL. Coq *m.*

root [ru:t] v. tr. ZOOL. Fouiller (pig). ‖ FIG. *To root out* (or) *up,* dénicher, déterrer.
— v. intr. ZOOL. Fouger (boar); fouiller avec le groin (pig). ‖ FIG. Fouiller, fouiner dans.

root v. tr. AGRIC. Enraciner. ‖ FAM. *To root s.o. to the spot,* clouer qqn sur place. ‖ *To root for,* U. S. SPORTS, FAM. Applaudir, encourager. ‖ *To root out* (or) *up,* déraciner, arracher ; FIG. Extirper.
— v. intr. AGRIC. S'enraciner, prendre racine.
— n. BOT. Racine *f.; to pull up by the roots,* déraciner. ‖ MUS. Note fondamentale *f.* ‖ GRAMM., MATH., MED. Racine *f.* ‖ FIG. Origine, cause, source, base *f.; to go to the root of,* aller au fond de ; *to pull up by the roots,* extirper ; *to take root,* prendre racine ; *root and branch,* entièrement, de fond en comble. ‖ **Root-bound,** adj. Profondément enraciné. ‖ **Root-cutter,** n. AGRIC. Coupe-racines *m.* ‖ **Root-sign,** n. MATH. Radical *m.* ‖ **Root-word,** n. GRAMM. Mot racine (or) souche *m.*

rootedly [-idli] adv. Profondément.

rooter [-ə*] n. U. S. FAM. Partisan, fanatique *m.*

rootlet [-lit] n. BOT. Radicelle *f.*

rooty [-i] adj. Plein de racines.

rope [roup] n. Corde *f.* ‖ Cordon *m.* (of a bell). ‖ Collier *m.* (of pearls). ‖ NAUT. Cordage, filin *m.* ‖ CULIN. Graisse, viscosité *f.* (in beer, in wine); chapelet *m.* (of onions). ‖ SPORTS. Cordée *f.* (of mountaineers); *pl.* cordes *f. pl.* (in boxing); *first on the rope,* premier de cordée ; *on a doubled rope,* en rappel ; *to put on the rope,* s'encorder. ‖ FAM. *To give s.o. plenty of rope,* lâcher la bride à qqn ; *to know the ropes,* connaître les ficelles, être à la coule ; *to learn the ropes,* se dégourdir. ‖ Rope-

dancer (or) **-walker,** n. Equilibriste, funambule, danseur (*s.*) de corde. ‖ **Rope-house,** n. Corderie *f.* ‖ **Rope-ladder,** n. Echelle de corde *f.* ‖ **Ropemaker,** n. Cordier *m.* ‖ **Rope-railway,** n. Funiculaire *m.* ‖ **Rode-soled,** adj. A semelles de corde.
— v. tr. Corder, encorder, attacher avec une corde. ‖ NAUT. Ralinguer. ‖ SPORTS. Tirer, retenir (a horse); encorder (mountaineers); *to rope down,* faire une descente en rappel ; U. S. Prendre au lasso. ‖ **To rope in,** entourer de cordes ; FAM. Prendre dans une rafle (to capture); enrôler (to get s.o.'s support); embobeliner (to bamboozle).
— v. intr. CULIN. Se corder, durcir.

ropeway [-wei] n. TECHN. Téléphérique *m.*

ropiness ['roupinis] n. Viscosité *f.* (of beer).

ropy [-i] adj. Visqueux.

roquet ['rouke] n. SPORTS. Touche *f.*
— v. tr., intr. SPORTS. Roquer (in croquet).

rosaceous [rou'zeiʃəs] adj. BOT. Rosacé.

rosarium [rou'zɛəriəm] s. AGRIC. Roseraie *f.*

rosary ['rouzəri] n. AGRIC. Roseraie *f.* ‖ ECCLES. Rosaire *m.* (fifteen sets); chapelet *m.* (five sets).

rose [rouz] pret. See RISE.

rose n. Rose *m.* (colour). ‖ BOT. Rose *f.* ‖ MED. Erysipèle *m.* ‖ ARCHIT., ELECTR. Rosace *f.* ‖ AGRIC. Pomme *f.* (of watering-can). ‖ FIG. *Bed of roses,* lit de roses ; *under the rose,* sous le manteau. ‖ LOC. *The Wars of the Roses,* la guerre des Deux-Roses. ‖ **Rose-bay,** n. BOT. Rhododendron ; laurier-rose *m.* ‖ **Rose-bed,** n. AGRIC. Massif (*m.*) de rosiers. ‖ **Rose-bowl,** n. Coupe (*f.*) à fleurs. ‖ **Rose-bush,** n. BOT. Rosier *m.* ‖ **Rose-colour,** n. Rose *m.* ‖ **Rosecoloured,** adj. Couleur de rose *f.; to see everything through rose-coloured spectacles,* voir tout en rose. ‖ **Rose-diamond,** n. Rose *f.* ‖ **Rose-garden,** n. AGRIC. Roseraie *f.* ‖ **Rose-leaf,** n. Feuille *f.* (or) pétale (*m.*) de rose. ‖ **Rose-like,** adj. Rosacé, rosé. ‖ **Rose-pink,** adj., n. Rose, rosé *m.* ‖ **Rose-red,** n. Vermillon *m.;* adj. Vermeil. ‖ **Rose-tree,** n. BOT. Rosier *m.* ‖ **Rose-water,** n. Eau de rose *f.* ‖ **Rose-window,** n. ARCHIT. Rosace *f.*

rosé ['rouzei] n. Rosé *m.* (wine).

roseate [-iit] adj. Rosé.

rosebud [-bʌd] n. BOT., FIG. Bouton (*m.*) de rose.

rosemary ['rouzməri] n. BOT. Romarin *m.*

roseola [,rouzi'oulə] n. MED. Roséole *f.*

rosette [ro'zet] n. I. Rosette *f.* ‖ ARCHIT., ELECTR. Rosace *f.*

rosewood ['rouzwud] n. Palissandre *m.*
— adj. De (or) en palissandre.

Rosicrucian [,rouzi'kru:ʃən] n. Rose-croix *m.*
— adj. Rosicrucien.

rosin ['rozin] n. Colophane *f.* (See COLOPHONY.)
— v. tr. Colophaner.

roster [rostə*] n. MILIT. Tableau de service *m.; promotion roster,* tableau d'avancement.

rostral ['rostrəl] adj. Rostral.

rostrate [-eit], **rostrated** [-eitid] adj. Rostré.

rostrum [-əm] n. Tribune *f.* ‖ † Rostre *m.*

rosy ['rouzi] adj. De rose, couleur de rose. ‖ Vermeil (cheek). ‖ FIG. Riant (colours, future).

rot [rot] v. tr. (1). Pourrir, décomposer, putréfier. ‖ MED. Carier (a tooth). ‖ POP. Blaguer (to chaff).
— v. intr. Pourrir, se décomposer, se putréfier (see DECAY); *to rot away, off,* tomber en pourriture. ‖ MED. Se carier. ‖ FIG. Pourrir, croupir. ‖ FAM. Blaguer.
— interj. POP. Foutaises ! ; c'est de la blague !
— n. Pourriture, décomposition, putréfaction *f.* ‖ MED. Carie *f.; liver rot,* douve du foie. ‖ FIG. Démoralisation *f.* ‖ POP. Foutaises *f. pl.;* couillonnades *f. pl.* (pop.). ‖ **Rot-gut,** n. POP. Tord-boyaux *m.* (spirits). ‖ **Rot-proof,** adj. Imputrescible.

rota ['routə] n. Liste *f.;* tableau *m.* ‖ ECCLES. Rote *f.*

rotary [routəri] adj. Rotatif, rotatoire. ‖ U. S. Rond-point *m.* (circus); *Rotary Club,* Rotary Club.

‖ **Rotary-press**, n. TECHN. Rotative *f*. ‖ **Rotary-printer**, n. TECHN. Rotativiste *m*.
rotate [ro'teit] v. intr. Tourner ; pivoter.
— v. tr. Tourner, faire tourner. ‖ Faire à tour de rôle (work). ‖ AGRIC. Alterner (crops).
rotation [ro'teiʃən] n. Rotation *f*. (turning) ; tour *m*. (turn). ‖ Retour (*m*.) périodique ; *by* (or) *in rotation*, à tour de rôle. ‖ AGRIC. *Rotation of crops*, assolement.
rotative ['routətiv] adj. Rotatif, rotatoire. ‖ AGRIC. En assolement.
rotator [ro'teitə*] n. MED. Rotateur *m*.
rote [rout] n. Routine *f*. ; *by rote*, par cœur (by heart) ; machinalement, comme un moulin (fam.) [by repetition].
rotogravure [ˌroutougrə'vjuə*] n. TECHN. Rotogravure *f*. (in printing).
rotor ['routə*] n. Rotor *m*. ‖ AUTOM. Balai rotatif *m*. ‖ NAUT. *Rotor ship*, navire à rotors.
rotten ['rɔtn] adj. Pourri, putréfié. ‖ Gâté (fruit). ‖ MED. Carié, gâté (tooth). ‖ FIG. Corrompu, pourri, véreux. ‖ FAM. Lamentable, pitoyable (feeble) ; crasseux (dirty) ; *to feel rotten*, se sentir fichu ; *what rotten luck!*, quelle guigne! ; manque de pot ! (pop.).
rottenness [-nis] n. Pourriture *f*. ‖ FAM. Caractère lamentable *m*.
rotter [-ə*] n. FAM. Sale type, salaud *m*.
rotund [ro'tʌnd] adj. Rond, arrondi (figure) ; rondelet (person). ‖ FIG. Ronflant (style). [See BOMBASTIC.]
rotunda [-ə] n. ARCHIT. Rotonde *f*.
rotundity [-iti] n. Rotondité, rondeur *f* . ; embonpoint *m*. ‖ FIG. Redondance *f*.
rouble ['ru:bḷ] n. Rouble *m*.
roué ['ru:ei] n. FAM. Débauché *m*. ; *old roué*, vieux marcheur.
rouge ['ru:ʒ] n. Rouge *m*.
— v. tr. Farder, mettre du rouge à.
— v. intr. Se mettre du rouge.
rough [rʌf] n. Terrain accidenté *m*. ‖ TECHN. *In the rough*, à l'état brut. ‖ FIG. Mauvais côté (*m*.) des choses ; *to take the rough with the smooth*, prendre la vie comme elle vient. ‖ FAM. Voyou, apache *m*.
— adv. Rudement, brutalement.
— v. tr. Ebouriffer (feathers, hair). ‖ Ferrer à glace (a horse). ‖ TECHN. Dépolir (glass). ‖ FAM. Malmener ; *to rough it*, manger de la vache enragée ; U. S. coucher sur la dure. ‖ **To rough down**, dégrossir. ‖ **To rough-dry**, faire sécher sans repassage (laundry). ‖ **To rough-handle**, FAM. Malmener, écharper. ‖ **To rough in** (or) **out**, ébaucher. ‖ **To rough out**, dégrossir. ‖ **To rough up**, U. S. Malmener.
— adj. Inégal (in general). ‖ Accidenté (ground) ; rocailleux (path) ; raboteux (road). ‖ Rugueux (paper, skin, tongue). ‖ Sommaire, approximatif ; *rough draft*, brouillon ; *at a rough estimate*, à vue d'œil ; approximativement ; *rough guess*, approximation ; *rough sketch*, ébauche, esquisse, croquis. ‖ Dur, rude (work) ; *rough work*, le plus gros, le gros ouvrage. ‖ Sommaire (justice) ; rude, fruste, grossier, mal dégrossi (manners) ; dur, brusque (voice). ‖ Violent, brutal (treatment) ; *to give s.o. a rough handling*, tabasser qqn. ‖ NAUT. Mauvais, mouvementé (crossing) ; gros, houleux (sea) ; gros, mauvais (weather) ; violent (wind). ‖ SPORTS. Brutal (play). ‖ CULIN. Apre (wine). ‖ TECHN. Brut (diamond, state) ; non rogné (edges of a book) ; gros (linen) ; en grume (timber). ‖ GRAMM. *Rough breathing*, esprit rude. ‖ Loc. *It's rough on him*, il n'a vraiment pas de chance, tout lui tombe dessus. ‖ **Rough-and-ready**, adj. Sans façon, nature (person) ; fruste (method) ; fait à la hâte (work). ‖ **Rough-and-tumble**, n. Mêlée *f*. ; adj. Désordonné (fight) ; mouvementé (life). ‖ **Rough-cast**, v. tr. ARCHIT. Crépir ; adj., n. Crépi *m*. ‖ **Rough-coated**, adj. ZOOL. A poil dur (dog) ; à long poil (horse). ‖ **Rough-grained**, adj.

A gros grain. ‖ **Rough-hewn**, adj. Taillé à coups de serpe ; FIG. Ebauché. ‖ **Rough-house**, n. FAM. Chahut (row) *m*. ; U. S. POP. Voyouterie *f*. (hooliganism). ‖ **Rough-rider**, n. Dresseur (*m*.) de chevaux. ‖ **Rough-riding**, n. SPORTS. Moto-cross *m*. ‖ **Rough-spoken**, adj. Bourru.
roughage [-idʒ] n. MED. Ballast *m*., aliment (*m*.) favorisant le transit intestinal.
roughen [-n] v. tr. Rendre rude (or) rugueux.
— v. intr. Devenir rude (or) rugueux. ‖ Grossir (sea).
roughish [-iʃ] adj. Assez rude. ‖ NAUT. Plutôt houleux (sea).
roughly [-li] adv. Rudement, brutalement, brusquement (harshly). ‖ Grossièrement (made). ‖ Approximativement, à peu près (more or less) ; sommairement (summarily) ; en gros, grosso modo (on the whole).
roughneck [-nek] n. U. S. FAM. Mal dégrossi *s*. ‖ U. S. POP. Dur *m*.
roughness [-nis] n. Rudesse, rugosité *f*. ‖ Inégalité *f*. (of the ground) ; mauvais état *m*. (of a road). ‖ NAUT. Agitation *f*. (of the sea). ‖ CULIN. Apreté *f*. (of a wine). ‖ FIG. Brusquerie, rudesse *f*. (of manners, of the voice) ; brutalité *f*. (of treatment).
roughshod [-ʃɔd] adj. Ferré à glace (horse). ‖ FIG. *To ride roughshod over s.o.*, piétiner qqn.
roulade [ru'lɑ:d] n. MUS. Roulade *f*. ‖ U. S. CULIN. Paupiette *f*.
roulette [ru'let] n. Roulette *f*.
Roumania [ru'meinjə] n. GEOGR. Roumanie *f*.
Roumanian [-jən] adj., n. GEOGR. Roumain *s*.
round [raund] n. Rond, cercle *m*. (in general). ‖ Ronde, révolution *f*. ; série, succession *f*. ‖ Cycle *m*. ; *caught in the daily round of work*, pris dans l'engrenage des travaux journaliers ; *daily round*, train-train quotidien. ‖ Tour *m*. ; tournée *f*. (circuit) ; *to be on one's rounds*, être en tournée ; *to go the rounds*, faire le tour de la ville (rumour). ‖ Salve *f*. (of applause) ; tournée *f*. (of drinks). ‖ MILIT. Cartouche *f*. (cartridge) ; décharge, salve *f*. (salvo) ; coup *m*. (shot). ‖ MILIT. Tournée d'inspection *f*. (of an officer) ; ronde *f*. (of soldiers). ‖ MUS. Canon perpétuel *m*. ‖ ARTS. Bosse *f*. ‖ SPORTS. Round *m*. (in boxing) ; tournée *f*. (of golf). ‖ CULIN. *Round of beef*, gîte à la noix ; *round of toast*, rôtie ; *round of veal*, rouelle de veau.
— adj. Rond, circulaire. ‖ Rond, cylindrique ; sphérique. ‖ Rond, arrondi (rounded) ; voûté (shoulders). ‖ Bon, fort (big) ; gros (oath) ; vif (pace) ; rondelet (sum) ; sonore (voice). ‖ **Round-eyed**, adj. Aux yeux ronds ; *to gaze round-eyed at*, regarder en écarquillant les yeux. ‖ **Round-hand**, adj., n. Ronde *f*. (writing). ‖ **Round-house**, n. † Corps (*m*.) de garde ; NAUT. Poulaine *f*. ; U. S. CH. DE F. Rotonde *f*. ‖ **Round-shouldered**, adj. MED. Voûté ; au dos rond. ‖ **Round-table**, adj. Autour du tapis vert (conference). ‖ **Round-top**, n. NAUT. Hune *f*. ‖ **Round-trip**, n. U. S. CH. DE F. Voyage aller et retour *m*. ; adj. Circulaire (ticket).
— adv. Autour, tout autour (see AROUND) ; *round about*, aux alentours ; *the only hotel for miles round*, le seul hôtel à plusieurs milles à la ronde ; *orchard with a wall all round*, verger clos de murs. ‖ De tour, de circonférence ; *to be four feet round*, avoir quatre pieds de tour. ‖ En tournant ; *to pass sth. round*, faire circuler (or) passer qqch ; *there is just enough to go round*, il y en a juste assez pour faire le tour ; *he offered drinks all round*, il paya une tournée générale ; *it's a long way round*, cela fait un grand détour ; *go round by the other way*, faites le tour par l'autre chemin ; *to invite s.o. round*, inviter qqn à venir chez soi. ‖ Loc. *Taken all round*, dans l'ensemble.
— prep. Autour de (movement, position) ; *sitting round the table*, assis autour de la table. ‖ De l'autre côté de (beyond, past) ; *to go round*, tourner (a

corner); contourner (an obstacle); *just round the corner*, juste après le coin de la rue. ‖ Naut. *To sail round*, doubler (a cape). ‖ Fam. *To talk round a subject*, tourner autour du pot.
— v. intr. S'arrondir. ‖ **To round on**, s'en prendre à, tomber sur (to attack); vendre, donner (to denounce).
— v. tr. Arrondir. ‖ Couper (a dog's ears). ‖ Autom. Prendre (a turning). ‖ Naut. Doubler (a cape); contourner (an obstacle). ‖ **To round off**, arrondir; achever. ‖ **To round up**, rassembler (cattle); Fam. Faire une rafle de, cueillir (suspects).
roundabout [-əbaut] adj. Indirect, détourné (lit. and fig.); *roundabout means*, détours, biais; *roundabout phrase*, circonlocution.
— n. Détour *m.* ‖ Manège *m.* (at a fair). ‖ Autom. Sens giratoire *m.*; rond-point *m.* (circus). ‖ Fig. Circonlocution *f.*
roundel [-l] n. Rondeau *m.* ‖ Mus. Ronde *f.*
roundelay [-əlei] n. Mus. Rondeau *m.*
rounder [-ə*] n. Techn. Outil à arrondir *m.* ‖ Pl. Sports. Balle (*f.*) au camp. ‖ U. S. Fam. Fêtard *m.*
Roundhead [-hed] n. Tête ronde *f.*
roundish [-iʃ] adj. Assez rond; rondelet.
roundly [-li] adv. En forme de rond. ‖ Fig. Rondement; carrément.
roundness [-nis] n. Rondeur, rotondité *f.* ‖ Fig. Rondeur; ampleur *f.*
roundup [-ʌp] n. U. S. Rassemblement *m.* (of cattle). ‖ Fam. Rafle *f.* (of suspects).
rouse [rauz] n. Milit. Réveil *m.*
— v. intr. Se réveiller. ‖ Sortir de sa torpeur.
— v. tr. Activer (the fire). ‖ Activer; secouer (from indifference); réveiller, éveiller (from sleep); *to rouse to action*, inciter à agir. ‖ Irriter, provoquer, exciter (to make angry). ‖ Susciter (admiration); exciter, stimuler (a feeling); soulever (indignation). ‖ Naut. Haler. ‖ Sports. Faire lever (birds).
rouser [-ə*] n. Personne (or) chose (*f.*) qui réveille. ‖ Techn. Agitateur *m.*
rousing [-iŋ] adj. Qui éveille (or) excite. ‖ Emouvant (appeal); chaleureux (applause); frénétique (cheers); vibrant (speech). ‖ Fam. Gros (lie).
roustabout ['raustə,baut] n. Manœuvre (*m.*) dans l'exploitation d'un gisement pétrolier. ‖ U.S. Homme de pont *m.* (deckhand); débardeur *m.* (longshoreman); manœuvre *m.* (labourer).
rout [raut] v. tr. Milit. Mettre en déroute.
— n. Bande *f.* (of revellers). ‖ Milit. Déroute, débandade *f.* ‖ Jur. Attroupement *m.* ‖ † Raout *m.*
rout v. intr. Fouiller la terre, fouir. (See ROOT.) ‖ Fouiner, fourrager, farfouiller (to rummage).
— v. tr. **To rout out**, extirper, extraire.
route [ruːt] n. Route *f.*; itinéraire *m.* ‖ Ligne *f.*; parcours *m.* (bus-route). ‖ **Route-map**, n. Autom. Carte routière *f.*
— v. tr. Expédier, faire passer (*via, through*, via, par).
— [raut] n. Milit. Route *f.* ‖ **Route-march**, n. Milit. Marche (*f.*) d'entraînement.
routine [ruː'tiːn] n. Routine *f.*; *the daily routine*, le train-train quotidien; *routine enquiries*, constatations d'usage; *routine duties* (or) *work* (or) *service*, affaires courantes, travail courant. ‖ Milit. Emploi (*m.*) du temps; *routine patrol*, ronde. ‖ Inform. Programme *m.* ‖ Theatr. Numéro *m.*
routinish [-iʃ] adj. Routinier.
routinism [-izm̩] n. Routine *f.*; encroûtement *m.* (fam.).
routinist [-ist] n. Routinier *s.*
rove [rouv] n. Fam. *To be on the rove*, vagabonder.
— v. tr. Parcourir (a country); errer dans (street). ‖ Naut. Ecumer (the seas).
— v. intr. Errer, rôder, vagabonder. ‖ Errer (eyes).

rover [-ə*] n. Vagabond, rôdeur *s.* ‖ Eclaireur; routier *m.* ‖ Naut. Pirate, écumeur (*m.*) de mer.
row [rou] n. Rangée *f.*; rang *m.*; *in a row*, en rang; *in rows*, par rangs. ‖ Autom. File *f.* (of cars). ‖ Agric. Ligne *f.* (of vegetables).
row n. Naut. Promenade (*f.*) en barque; partie (*f.*) de canotage; *to go for a row*, faire une promenade en canot. ‖ **Row-boat**, n. Naut. Bateau (*m.*) à rames.
— v. tr. Naut. Faire aller à la rame (or) à l'aviron (a boat); transporter en canot (s.o.); *to row s.o. across* (or) *over the river*, faire passer la rivière à qqn en canot. ‖ Sports. *To row a race*, faire une course d'aviron; *to row stroke*, être chef de nage.
— v. intr. Ramer. ‖ Naut. Nager.
row v. intr. Fam. Se disputer (*with*, avec).
— v. tr. Fam. Sonner les cloches à.
— n. Fam. Altercation, querelle *f.* ‖ Fam. Savon *m.*; *to get into a row*, se faire secouer. ‖ Fam. Boucan, barouf, ramdam *m.*; *to kick up a row*, faire du barnum (or) du raffut.
rowan ['rauən] n. Bot. Sorbe *f.* (berry); sorbier *m.* (tree).
rowdiness ['raudinis] n. Tapage *m.*; turbulence *f.*
rowdy [-i] n. Chahuteur, tapageur *m.* (See RUMBUSTIOUS.) ‖ Voyou *m.*
— adj. Tapageur; *to be rowdy*, chahuter.
rowdyism [-iizm̩] n. Tapage, chahut *m.*
rowel ['rauəl] n. Molette *f.* (of spur). ‖ Med. Rouelle *f.*
— v. tr. Med. Eperonner. ‖ Med. Appliquer une rouelle à (a horse).
rower ['rouə*] n. Rameur *s.* ‖ Naut. Nageur *m.*
rowing [-iŋ] n. Canotage *m.* ‖ Naut. Nage *f.* ‖ **Rowing-boat**, n. Bateau (*m.*) à rames. ‖ **Rowing-club**, n. Sports. Cercle d'aviron *m.*
rowlock [-lɔk] n. Naut. Tolet *m.*; dame *f.*
royal ['rɔiəl] adj. Royal; du roi (of the king); de de la reine (of the queen); U. S. *royal blue*, bleu de roi. ‖ Naut. De cacatois (mast). ‖ Bot. Royal (fern). ‖ Techn. *Royal octavo*, in-8° raisin. ‖ Fig. Royal, princier.
— n. Naut. Cacatois *m.* ‖ Sports. Cerf (*m.*) à douze andouillers. ‖ Pl. Milit. Régiment du Roi *m.*
royalism [-izm̩] n. Royalisme *m.*
royalist [-ist] n. Royaliste *s.*
royally [-i] adv. Royalement.
royalty [-ti] n. Royauté *f.* ‖ Membre (*m.*) de la famille royale; personnages royaux *m. pl.* (collectively). ‖ Fin. Droits (*m. pl.*) d'auteur (paid to an author); redevance *f.* (to an inventor).
rozzer ['rɔzə*] n. Pop. Flic, poulet *m.*
r.p.m. [ɑː'piː'em] abbr. *revolutions per minute*, tours par minute, tr/min.
rub [rʌb] n. Frottement *m.*; friction *f.*; *to give sth. a rub up*, donner un coup de torchon à, épousseter, astiquer. ‖ Fam. *There's the rub*, voilà le hic.
— v. intr. Se frotter, se frictionner (person); frotter (thing). ‖ S'user (clothes). ‖ **To rub along**, vivoter; se tirer d'affaire; *to rub along together*, bien s'accorder. ‖ **To rub up**, se frotter (*against*, à, contre).
— v. tr. (1). Frotter (*against, on*, contre sur). ‖ Astiquer (to polish). ‖ Med. Frictionner. ‖ Archit. Poncer (a drawing); prendre un frottis de (an inscription). ‖ Fam. *To rub up the wrong way*, prendre à rebrousse-poil. ‖ **To rub down**, bouchonner (a horse); frictionner (s.o.); frotter (sth). Techn. Frotter, adoucir. ‖ **To rub in**, faire pénétrer en frottant; Fam. *Don't rub it in!*, n'insistez pas; *to rub it in*, appuyer sur la chanterelle. ‖ **To rub off**, faire disparaître. ‖ **To rub out**, effacer; U. S. Pop. Liquider, expédier, descendre, ôter le goût du pain à (s.o.). ‖ **To rub up**, frotter, astiquer, fourbir (to polish); Fig. Rafraîchir (a memory); *to rub up one's French*, dérouiller son français.
rub-a-dub-dub [rʌbə,dʌbdʌb] n. Rataplan *m.*

rubber ['rʌbə*] v. tr. Techn. Caoutchouter. — adj. En caoutchouc (ball); *rubber band*, élastique. ‖ Comm. *Rubber goods*, articles d'hygiène en caoutchouc. ‖ Fin. Sans provision (check). — n. Frotteur *s.* (person); frottoir *m.* (thing). ‖ Gomme *f.* (eraser). ‖ Caoutchouc *m.* ‖ U. S. Pl. Caoutchoucs *m. pl.* (overshoes). ‖ U. S. Pop. Préservatif *m.* ‖ **Rubber-covered,** adj. Sous caoutchouc. ‖ **Rubber-neck,** n. U. S. Badaud *m.; v.* intr. U. S. Badauder; *rubber-neck tourist*, touriste voyageant en autocar. ‖ **Rubber-stamp,** n. Tampon *m.;* adj. U. S. Fam. Béni-oui-oui; *rubber-stamp Parliament*, Parlement ratificateur. ‖ **Rubber-tree,** n. Bot. Arbre (*m.*) à gomme. ‖ **Rubber-tyred,** adj. Caoutchouté.

rubber n. Rob, robre *m.* (in cards).
rubberize [-raiz] v. tr. Techn. Caoutchouter.
rubbery [-ri] adj. Techn. Caoutchouteux.
rubbing [rʌbiŋ] n. Frottement *m.; friction f.;* frottage *m.* ‖ Med. Frictions *f. pl.* ‖ Techn. Frottis *m.* ‖ **Rubbing-away,** n. Usure *f.* ‖ **Rubbing-down,** n. Usure *f.* (wear); bouchonnage *m.* (of a horse). ‖ **Rubbing-up,** n. Astiquage *m.*
rubbish ['rʌbiʃ] n. Détritus, débris, rebuts, déchets *m. pl.* (see refuse); ordures, immondices *f. pl.* ‖ Décombres *m. pl.* (from building). ‖ Camelote *f.* (trash); *good riddance of bad rubbish!*, bon débarras! ‖ Fam. Bêtises, sottises, balivernes *f. pl.; to talk rubbish*, dire des imbécillités. ‖ **Rubbish-bin,** n. Boîte (*f.*) aux ordures, poubelle *f.* ‖ **Rubbish-cart,** n. Tombereau *m.* ‖ **Rubbish-dump,** n. Dépotoir *m.* ‖ **Rubbish-heap,** n. Monceau (*m.*) de détritus. ‖ **Rubbish-shoot,** n. Dépotoir *m.* (dump); vide-ordures *m.* (in building).
rubbishy [-i] adj. Sans valeur, de camelote.
rubble ['rʌbl̩] n. Archit. Blocaille *f.;* moellons *m. pl.* (masonry); brocaille *f.* (for roads).
rube [ru:b] n. U. S. Fam. Péquenot, cul-terreux *m.*
rubefacient [,ru:bi'feiʃənt] adj., n. Med. Rubéfiant *m.*
rubefaction [-'fækʃən] n. Med. Rubéfaction *f.*
rubefy ['ru:bifai] v. tr. Med. Rubéfier.
rubella [ru'belə] n. Med. Rubéole *f.*
rubicund ['ru:bikənd] adj. Rubicond.
rubidium [ru:'bidiəm] n. Chim. Rubidium *m.*
rubied ['ru:bid] adj. Couleur de rubis.
rubiginous [ru:'bidʒinəs] adj. Rubigineux.
ruble ['ru:bl̩] n. Rouble *m.*
rubric ['ru:brik] n. Rubrique *f.*
rubrical [-əl] adj. De rubrique.
rubricate [-eit] v. tr. Rubriquer.
ruby ['ru:bi] n. Rubis *m.* ‖ Couleur (*f.*) de rubis. ‖ Techn. Corps 5 1/2 *m.* (type). ‖ Fig. Sang *m.* (blood); vin rouge *m.* (wine). — adj. Couleur de rubis; vermeil (lips); vineux, rubicond (nose).
ruche [ru:ʃ] n. Ruche *f.* (in dressmaking).
ruching [-iŋ] n. U. S. Ruché *m.* (frilling).
ruck [rʌk] n. Sports. Peloton *m.* ‖ Fig. *The common ruck*, le vulgum pecus.
ruck n. Pli, froncis *m.* (in dress-making). — v. intr. Se froisser, se chiffonner. — v. tr. Plisser; froisser, chiffonner.
ruckle ['rʌk̩l] n. Med. Râle *m.* — v. intr. Med. Râler.
rucksack ['rʌksæk] n. Sac de camping (or) à dos *m.*
ruckus ['rʌkəs] n. U. S. Fam. Echauffourée *f.*
ruction ['rʌkʃən] n. Fam. Grabuge *m.*
rudder ['rʌdə*] n. Gouvernail *m.* ‖ **Rudder-bar,** n. Naut. Barre (*f.*) du gouvernail; Aviat. Palonnier, gouvernail (*m.*) de direction. ‖ **Rudder-post,** n. Naut. Etambot *m.*
ruddiness ['rʌdinis] n. Rougeur *f.;* teint enluminé *m.*
ruddy ['rʌdi] adj. Coloré, haut en couleur (complexion). ‖ Rougeâtre; rouge (glow). ‖ Fam. Satané, sacré. — v. intr. (2). Rougeoyer.

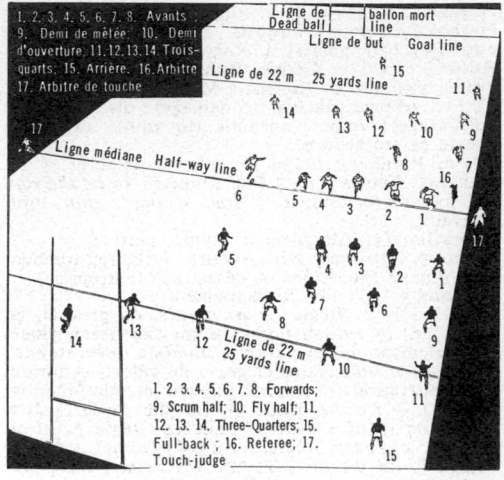

1. 2. 3. 4. 5. 6. 7. 8. Forwards; 9. Scrum half; 10. Fly half; 11. 12. 13. 14. Three-Quarters; 15. Full-back; 16. Referee; 17. Touch-judge

rude [ru:d] adj. Grossier, rudimentaire, primitif (primitive). ‖ Robuste (robust). ‖ Brusque (sudden); rude, violent (violent). ‖ Mal élevé, fruste (badly brought-up); grossier (coarse); impoli (impolite); *to make rude remarks*, dire des grossièretés.
rudely [-li] adv. Grossièrement, rudimentairement (primitively). ‖ Brusquement (suddenly); violemment (violently). ‖ Grossièrement (coarsely); impoliment (impolitely).
rudeness [-nis] n. Caractère primitif *m.* (primitiveness). ‖ Rudesse *f.* (lack of refinement). ‖ Grossièreté, impolitesse *f.* (impoliteness).
rudiment ['ru:dimənt] n. Med. Rudiment *m.* ‖ Pl. Rudiments, éléments *m. pl.;* notions élémentaires *f. pl.*
rudimentary [,ru:di'mentəri] adj. Rudimentaire.
rue [ru:] n. Bot. Rue *f.*
rue v. tr. Regretter amèrement, se repentir de.
rueful [-ful] adj. Triste, lugubre; *the Knight of the Rueful Countenance*, le Chevalier de la Triste Figure.
ruefully [-fuli] adv. Tristement, lugubrement.
ruefulness [-fulnis] n. Tristesse *f.;* air triste *m.*
ruff [rʌf] n. Coupe *f.* (at cards). — v. intr., tr. Couper (at cards).
ruff n. † Fraise *f.* (collar). ‖ Zool. Collier *m.* (of a bird); pigeon capucin *m.* (bird).
ruffian ['rʌfjən] n. Apache, bandit *m.*
ruffianism [-izm] n. Actes (*m. pl.*) de brigandage; voyouterie *f.*
ruffianly [-li] adj. D'apache (appearance); brutal, à tête d'apache (person).
ruffle ['rʌfl̩] n. Rides *f. pl.* (ripple). ‖ Ruche *f.;* jabot plissé (in dress-making). ‖ Zool. Collier *m.* — v. intr. Se hérisser (feathers); s'ébouriffer (hair). ‖ Se rider (water). — v. tr. Ebouriffer (feathers, hair). ‖ Agiter, rider, troubler (water). ‖ Froisser, chiffonner (to crease). ‖ Fig. Contrarier, froisser (s.o.).
rug [rʌg] n. Tapis *m.;* U. S. *Oriental rug*, tapis d'Orient. ‖ Descente (*f.*) de lit (bedside rug); couverture (*f.*) de voyage (travelling-rug).
rugby ['rʌgbi] n. Sports. Rugby *m.; rugby player*, rugbyman; *Rugby League*, rugby à treize.
rugged ['rʌgid] adj. Rugueux (bark); accidenté (ground); raboteux (road); anfractueux, déchiqueté (rock). ‖ Rude, bourru (character); rude (features); fruste, grossier (style). ‖ U. S. Robuste.
ruggedly [-li] adv. Rudement.

ruggedness [-nis] n. Aspérité, rugosité *f.* ‖ Anfractuosité *f.* (of rocks). ‖ Fig. Rudesse *f.*

rugger ['rʌgə*] n. Fam. Rugby *m.*

rugose [,ru'gous], **rugous** ['ru:gəs] adj. Rugueux.

rugosity [ru:'gɔsiti] n. Rugosité *f.*

Ruhr ['ruə*] n. Geogr. Ruhr *f.*

ruin ['ruin] v. tr. Ruiner. ‖ Med. Détruire (health). ‖ Fig. Abîmer, gâcher (to damage); discréditer (to disparage); ruiner, anéantir (to ruin); causer la perte de (to seduce). — n. Ruine *f.; to go to ruin*, se délabrer. ‖ Pl. Archit. Ruines *f. pl.* ‖ Fig. Ruine *f.; to be the ruin of*, perdre (or) ruiner. ‖ Pop. *Mother's ruin*, tord-boyaux.

ruination [rui'neiʃən] n. Ruine, perte *f.*

ruinous ['ruinəs] adj. Archit. Délabré, tombant en ruine. ‖ Fig. Ruineux, désastreux (entreprise).

ruinously [-li] adv. Ruineusement.

rule [ru:l] n. Règle *f.; as a rule*, en général, en principe; *by rule of thumb*, d'une façon empirique. ‖ Règlement *m.* (regulation); *standing rules*, statuts; *to work to rule*, faire la grève du zèle. ‖ Autorité, administration *f.;* empire, pouvoir *m.* (domination, power). ‖ Autom. Code *m.* (of the road). ‖ Jur. Décision *f.* (of a court). ‖ Eccles. Règle *f.* (of an order). ‖ Sports. Règle, loi *f.* (of a game). ‖ Math. Règle *f.* (of three). ‖ Techn. Mètre *m.;* règle graduée *f.* (for measuring); filet *m.* (in typography). — v. intr. Fin. Se pratiquer; *to rule high*, se maintenir (prices). ‖ **To rule over**, régner sur. — v. tr. Gouverner (a country, a people); régner sur (a nation). ‖ Conseiller, guider (to advise); diriger, mener (to lead); Tracer à la règle (a line); régler (paper). ‖ Jur. Décider, déclarer. ‖ Fig. Contenir, maîtriser (one's passions). ‖ **To rule off**, tirer une ligne au-dessous de; Comm. Clore, arrêter. ‖ **To rule out**, écarter, exclure.

ruler [-ə*] n. Souverain *s.;* maître *m.* ‖ Techn. Règle *f.* (instrument); régleur *m.* (person).

rulership [-əʃip] n. Empire, pouvoir *m.;* autorité, domination *f.*

ruling [-iŋ] adj. Souverain; dirigeant (classes); dominant (passion). ‖ Fin. Pratiqué, actuel (price). — n. Gouvernement *m.* (action). ‖ Jur. Décision *f.*

rum [rʌm] n. Rhum *m.* ‖ Alcool, spiritueux *m.*

rum adj. Fam. Rigolo, bizarre; *rum customer*, drôle de numéro.

Rumania [ru'meinjə] n. Geogr. Roumanie *f.*

Rumanian [-ən] adj., n. Geogr. Roumain *s.*

rumba ['rʌmbə] n. Mus. Rumba *f.*

rumble ['rʌmbl] n. Roulement *m.* (of a cart); grondement *m.* (of thunder). ‖ Med. Borborygme *m.* ‖ **Rumble-seat**, n. Autom. Spider *m.* — v. tr. *To rumble out*, grommeler (a remark). — v. intr. Rouler bruyamment (cart); gronder (thunder). ‖ Med. Faire des borborygmes.

rumble v. tr. Pop. Voir venir (s.o.); subodorer (sth.).

rumbustious [rʌm'bʌstʃəs] adj. Fam. Turbulent, bruyant, chahuteur.

rumen ['ru:men] n. Zool. Panse *f.*

ruminant ['ru:minənt] adj., n. Zool. Ruminant *m.*

ruminate [-eit] v. intr., v. tr. Zool., Fig. Ruminer.

rumination [,ru:mi'neiʃən] n. Rumination *f.*

ruminative ['ru:mineitiv] adj. Méditatif; absorbé.

rummage ['rʌmidʒ] v. tr. Fouiller. — v. intr. Fouiller (*among, in*, dans; *for*, pour trouver). — n. Fouille *f.* (search). ‖ Objets divers *m. pl.; rummage sale*, déballage.

rummy ['rʌmi] adj. Fam. Rigolo, bizarre. (See RUM.)

rummy n. Rami *m.* (card-game).

rumour ['rumə*] n. Rumeur *f.;* bruit *m.; rumour has it that, there are rumours that*, on dit que, le bruit court que. ‖ **Rumor-mongering**, n. U. S. Colportage (*m.*) de fausses nouvelles. — v. tr. Répandre le bruit de; *it is rumoured that*, le bruit court que.

rump [rʌmp] n. Zool. Croupion *m.* (of a bird); croupe *f.* (of a quadruped). ‖ Culin. Culotte *f.* (of beef). ‖ Fam. Postérieur *m.* ‖ Loc. *The Rump Parliament*, le Parlement Croupion.

rumpish [-iʃ] adj. Fam. Bruyant.

rumple ['rʌmpl] v. tr. Ebouriffer (s.o.'s hair). ‖ Froisser, chiffonner (material). ‖ Fam. Contrarier (to annoy).

rumpsteak ['rʌmp'steik] n. Culin. Romsteck *m.*

rumpus ['rʌmpəs] n. Fam. Chahut, potin, boucan, barouf *m.* (shindy). ‖ Fam. Prise (*f.*) de bec; *to have a rumpus with*, s'engueuler avec. ‖ **Rumpus room**, n. U. S. Salle (*f.*) de jeux (or) de récréation.

run [rʌn] n.

---

1. Action de courir. — 2. Course. — 3. Elan. — 4. Ruée. — 5. Série. — 6. Cadence. — 7. Vogue. — 8. Direction. — 9. Démaillage. — 10. Disposition. — 11. Généralité. — 12. Promenade. — 13. Autom., Ch. de f. — 14. Naut., Aviat. — 15. Milit. — 16. Theatr. — 17. Sports. — 18. Geol. — 19. Techn. — 20. Fin. — 21. Comm. — 22. Fam. — 23. Run-around. — 24. Run-down. — 25. Run-proof. — 26. Run-up.

---

1. Action (*f.*) de courir; *at a run*, au pas de course; *to be always on the run*, être tout le temps à courir; *to break into a run*, prendre le pas de course. ‖ 2. Course *f.; to have a long run*, courir longtemps. ‖ 3. Elan *m.; to take a short run*, prendre un faible élan. ‖ 4. Ruée *f.* (rush). ‖ 5. Durée *f.;* succession, suite, série, marche *f.* (of events); *in the long run*, à la longue; *ordinary run of things*, train-train habituel. ‖ 6. Cadence *f.;* rythme *m.* (of a phrase). ‖ 7. Vogue *f.* (popularity). ‖ 8. Direction *f.;* tendance *f.* (tendency). ‖ 9. Echelle, maille filée *f.;* démaillage *m.* (in a stocking). ‖ 10. Libre accès *m.* (*of*, à); entière disposition (*of*, de) [unrestricted use]. ‖ 11. Généralité *f.; common run of mankind*, commun des mortels; *run of the mill*, tout venant. ‖ 12. Course, excursion, promenade *f.;* tour *m.; to go for a run in the car*, faire un petit tour en voiture; *trial run*, course d'essai. ‖ 13. Autom., Ch. de f. Trajet, parcours *m.; it's only half an hour's run*, il n'y a qu'une demi-heure de chemin de fer (or) voiture pour y aller. ‖ 14. Naut., Aviat. Parcours *m.; landing run*, parcours à l'atterrissage. ‖ 15. Milit. *To be on the run*, s'enfuir; *to keep the enemy on the run*, harceler l'ennemi. ‖ 16. Theatr. Carrière *f.; to have a long run*, tenir longtemps l'affiche. ‖ 17. Sports. Point *m.* (in cricket); descente, piste *f.* (for winter sports). ‖ 18. Geol. Coulée *f.;* éboulement *m.* (of ground). ‖ 19. Techn. Veine *f.* (of gold); marche *f.* (of a machine). ‖ 20. Fin. Tendance *f.* (of the market). ‖ 21. Comm. Catégorie *f.* (of goods). ‖ 22. Fam. *To be on the run*, être recherché par la police; *to give s.o. a run for his money*, en donner à qqn pour son argent; *to keep on the run*, mener tambour battant, ne pas laisser refroidir. ‖ 23. **Run-around**, n. U. S. Fam. *To give the run-around*, esquiver, éviter. ‖ 24. **Rundown**, n. Diminution, réduction *f.* (reduction); examen, passage (*m.*) en revue (analysis); adj. Fatigué, épuisé (person); délabré (thing). ‖ 25. **Run-proof**, adj. U. S. Indémaillable (stocking). ‖ 26. **Run-up**, n. Sports. Elan *m.;* Fig. Préparatif *m.*, préliminaires *m. pl.*

— v. tr. (114).

---

1. Couvrir. — 2. Courir. — 3. Promener. — 4. Tracer. — 5. Enfoncer. — 6. Autom. — 7. Naut., Ch. de f. — 8. Milit. — 9. Jur. — 10. Med. — 11. Sports. — 12. Comm. — 13. Techn. — 14. Fig. — 15. To run down. — 16. To run in. — 17. To run off. — 18. To run on. — 19. To run out. — 20. To run over. — 21. To run through. — 22. To run up.

1. Couvrir (a distance). ‖ **2.** Courir (the streets). ‖ **3.** Promener (*over,* sur) [one's fingers, hand]. ‖ **4.** Tracer (a line); *to run one's pencil through a word,* biffer (or) rayer un mot. ‖ **5.** Enfoncer (to drive in); pousser (to push); *to run s.o. close,* serrer qqn de près. ‖ **6.** AUTOM. Entretenir; posséder (fam.) [a car]; *cheap to run,* économique. ‖ **7.** NAUT., CH. DE F. Mettre en service, assurer le service de (a ship, train); *to run a ship aground,* mettre un navire à la côte. ‖ **8.** MILIT. Forcer (a blockade); *to run a sword through,* transpercer d'un coup d'épée, passer une épée à travers le corps de. ‖ **9.** JUR. Faire la contrebande de, passer en contrebande. ‖ **10.** MED. *To run a temperature,* faire de la température, avoir de la fièvre. ‖ **11.** SPORTS. Chasser (a fox); faire courir (a horse); courir (a race). ‖ **12.** COMM. Vendre (goods); diriger, administrer (an enterprise); exploiter (a factory); tenir (a hotel); éditer, gérer (a publication). ‖ **13.** TECHN. Faire aller (or) marcher (or) fonctionner (a machine); couler (molten metal). ‖ **14.** FIG. Courir, s'exposer à (a risk). ‖ **15.** To run down, renverser (to knock over); écraser (to run over); NAUT. Couler (a ship); SPORTS. Mettre aux abois (a stag); JUR. Découvrir la retraite de (a suspect); FAM. Décrier, dénigrer, déblatérer contre (s.o.); éreinter, démolir (sth.). ‖ **16.** To run in, introduire (a liquid); TECHN. Roder (a motor); FAM. Fourrer au bloc (a suspect). ‖ **17.** To run off, rédiger en vitesse (an article); réciter d'un trait (a poem); SPORTS. Faire courir (a race); PHYS. Faire écouler (a liquid); TECHN. Couler (metal). ‖ **18.** To run on, THEATR. Amener (a decor); TECHN. Faire suivre (in printing). ‖ **19.** To run out, laisser filer (a line); SPORTS. Mettre hors jeu (in cricket); *to run oneself out,* être à bout de souffle. ‖ **20.** To run over, parcourir des yeux (a text); AUTOM. Ecraser, passer sur le corps à. ‖ **21.** To run through, faire répéter (to rehearse); MILIT. Transpercer. ‖ **22.** To run up, hisser (a flag); FIN. Laisser accumuler (a debt); laisser monter (prices); ARCHIT. Construire (a house).
— v. intr. (114).

---

1. Courir. — 2. Passer. — 3. Fuir. — 4. Dégoutter. — 5. Se répandre. — 6. S'étendre. — 7. Se transmettre. — 8. Trotter. — 9. Etre conçu. — 10. AUTOM. — 11. NAUT. — 12. JUR. — 13. MED. — 14. SPORTS. — 15. THEATR. — 16. AGRIC. — 17. FIN. — 18. COMM. — 19. TECHN. — 20. FAM. — 21. LOC. — 22. To run about. — 23. To run across. — 24. To run after. — 25. To run against. — 26. To run along. — 27. To run at. — 28. To run away. — 29. To run back. — 30. To run by. — 31. To run down. — 32. To run for. — 33. To run in. — 34. To run into. — 35. To run off. — 36. To run on. — 37. To run out. — 38. To run over. — 39. To run round. — 40. To run through. — 41. To run up. — 42. To run upon.

---

1. Courir; *to run to help s.o.,* voler au secours de qqn; *to run to meet s.o.,* courir au-devant de qqn. ‖ **2.** Aller, passer (to pass); glisser (to slide). ‖ **3.** Fuir; *to run for it,* se sauver. ‖ **4.** Dégoutter (to drip); couler (to flow); ruisseler (to stream); s'étaler, déteindre (colour); couler (cheese, liquids); baver (pen); se démailler (stockings). ‖ **5.** Courir, se répandre (news). ‖ **6.** S'étendre, courir (round a room) [picture-rail]. ‖ **7.** Se transmettre; *it runs in the family,* cela tient de famille. ‖ **8.** Trotter; *that time keeps running through my head,* cet air me trotte dans la tête. ‖ **9.** Etre conçu; *the message ran thus,* le message était rédigé en ces termes; *so the story runs,* selon l'histoire. ‖ **10.** AUTOM. Rouler (car); circuler, faire le service (public vehicle); *to run into a tree,* rentrer dans un arbre. ‖ **11.** NAUT. Filer (so many knots); *a heavy sea was running,* la mer était grosse; *to run into port,* entrer au port;

se réfugier dans le port. ‖ **12.** JUR. Etre valide (or) en vigueur (decree); *the two sentences to run concurrently,* avec confusion des deux peines. ‖ **13.** MED. Suppurer (abscess); pleurer (eyes); couler (nose); *to run with sweat,* ruisseler de sueur. ‖ **14.** SPORTS. Courir. ‖ **15.** THEATR. Se jouer, tenir l'affiche (play). ‖ **16.** AGRIC. Ramper, grimper (plant); *to run to seed,* monter en graine. ‖ **17.** FIN. Se monter, s'élever (*to,* à) [amount]. ‖ **18.** COMM. Courir (to be valid). ‖ **19.** TECHN. Marcher, fonctionner (machine); tourner (wheel). ‖ **20.** FAM. *I can't run to a new suit,* je ne peux pas me payer un complet nouveau. ‖ **21.** LOC. *To run high,* être déchaîné (passions); être échauffé (tempers); *to run short,* s'épuiser (rations); *to run short of money,* être à court d'argent. ‖ **22.** To run about, courir çà et là. ‖ **23.** To run across, traverser en courant; rencontrer par hasard (to meet). ‖ **24.** To run after, courir après. ‖ **25.** To run against, se heurter contre (to bump); rencontrer par hasard (to meet). ‖ **26.** To run along, longer, border; FAM. *Run along!,* filez! ‖ **27.** To run at, se jeter sur, attaquer. ‖ **28.** To run away, s'emballer (horse); se sauver, s'enfuir (person); *to run away with,* enlever (s.o., sth.); FAM. *Don't run away with the idea that,* n'allez pas vous mettre en tête que. ‖ **29.** To run back, retourner en courant. ‖ **30.** To run by, passer devant en courant. ‖ **31.** To run down, descendre en courant (person, thing); couler (water); s'arrêter faute d'être remonté (watch). ‖ **32.** To run for, U. S. Se présenter à, poser sa candidature pour. ‖ **33.** To run in, entrer en courant. ‖ **34.** To run into, s'exposer au (danger); se jeter dans (river); AUTOM. Entrer en collision avec, tamponner (car). FIN. S'élever à (a sum); *to run into debt,* s'endetter. ‖ **35.** To run off, s'écouler (liquid); se sauver, s'enfuir (person); *to run off the rails,* dérailler; *to run off the subject,* faire une digression. ‖ **36.** To run on, continuer (lecture); continuer sa course (person); passer, s'écouler (time); TECHN. Suivre sans alinéa (paragraph); enjamber (verse); être lié (words). ‖ **37.** To run out, couler (liquid); s'écouler, tirer à sa fin (period); sortir en courant (person); se dérouler (rope); s'épuiser (stocks); *to run out of,* manquer de, être à bout de (sth.). ‖ **38.** To run over, déborder (liquid); parcourir, jeter un coup d'œil sur (a text); AUTOM. Ecraser, passer sur (s.o.); FAM. *To run over to,* faire un saut jusque chez (the baker's). ‖ **39.** To run round, courir autour de; *to run round to,* faire un saut jusque chez. ‖ **40.** To run through, traverser en courant (person); traverser, passer à travers (thing); parcourir, jeter un coup d'œil sur (a text); FIN. Gaspiller, manger (a fortune); ‖ **41.** To run up, arriver en courant; monter en courant (the stairs); FIN. Monter (prices); *to run up against,* rencontrer à l'improviste. ‖ **42.** To run upon, rencontrer à l'improviste.

runabout ['rʌnə,baut] n. AUTOM. Voiturette *f.* ‖ U. S. Vagabond *m.*

runaway ['rʌnəwei] n. Fugitif. ‖ MILIT. Fuyard, déserteur (soldier). ‖ FAM. *To catch a runaway in his hide-out,* trouver la pie au nid.
— adj. Fugitif (person). ‖ Emballé (horse). ‖ Parti à la dérive (car). ‖ Facile (victory). ‖ Clandestin (marriage).

rune [ru:n] n. Rune *f.*

rung [rʌn] p. p. See RING.

rung n. Bâton, barreau *m.* (of a chair); échelon *m.* (of a ladder).

runic ['ru:nik] adj. Runique.

runnel ['rʌnl] n. Rigole *f.*

runner ['rʌnə*] n. Coureur *s.* ‖ Messager, courrier *m.* ‖ Racoleur *m.* (of a hotel). ‖ Coulisseau *m.* (of a drawer). ‖ Chemin *m.* de table (table-runner). ‖ U. S. CH. DE F. Mécanicien *m.* ‖ SPORTS. Lame *f.* (of a skate); patin *m.* (of a sledge). ‖ ZOOL. Râle (*m.*) d'eau. ‖ BOT. Coulant, stolon *m.*; *runner bean,* haricot à rames. ‖ FIN. Contrepartiste; démarcheur *m. ;* U. S. encaisseur *m.* ‖ Techn. Chariot, trolley *m. ;* curseur *m.* (cursor) ; poulie *f.* (pulley) ; couronne mobile (of a turbine) ; roue (wheel). ‖ Milit. Agent (*m.*) de transmission. ‖ **Runner-up,** premier (*m.*) des ajournés ; Sports. Second *m.*

running [-iŋ] n. Course *f. ; to be in the running,* avoir des chances d'arriver ; *to be out of the running,* ne plus compter. ‖ Ecoulement *m.* (of a liquid) ; ruissellement *m.* (of water). ‖ Circulation *f.* (of buses, trains). ‖ Jur. Contrebande *f.* ‖ Med. Suppuration *f.* ‖ Comm. Direction *f.* (of a firm). ‖ Techn. Marche *f. ;* fonctionnement *m.* (of a machine). ‖ **Running-board,** n. Autom. Marchepied *m.* ‖ **Running-down,** n. Fam. Dénigrement, éreintage *m.* ‖ **Running-track,** n. Sports. Piste *f.*
— adj. Courant (person, title). ‖ Vif, coulant (stream). ‖ Coulant (style) ; *running hand,* cursive. ‖ De suite ; *twice running,* deux fois de suite, à deux reprises. ‖ Milit. En retraite (fight) ; roulant (fire). ‖ Naut. Coulant (knot). ‖ Med. Suppurant (sore) ; *running cold,* rhume de cerveau carabiné. ‖ Fin. Courant (account, expenses). ‖ Techn. *Running block,* poulie mobile. ‖ Radio. *Running commentary,* reportage en direct.

runny [-i] adj. Qui coule (nose) ; qui pleure (eye) ; qui fond (butter) ; trop liquide (sauce) ; baveux (omelette).

runt [rʌnt] n. Zool. Bovin (*m.*) de petite race (cattle) ; rosse *f.* (horse). ‖ Fam. Nabot, avorton *m.* (person) ; *little runt,* riquiqui.

runty [-i] adj. U. S. Rabougri.

runway ['rʌnwei] n. Techn. Piste, rampe *f. ; overhead runway,* transporteur aérien. ‖ Aviat. Piste (*f.*) d'envol.

rupee [ru:'pi:] n. Roupie *f.*

rupture ['rʌptʃə*] n. Rupture *f.* ‖ Med. Hernie *f.*
— v. intr. Se rompre.
— v. tr. Rompre. ‖ Med. *To rupture oneself,* se donner une hernie.

rural ['ruərəl] adj. Rural, rustique, champêtre ; *rural dwellers,* les ruraux. ‖ Jur. Rural (postman) ; *rural policeman,* garde champêtre.

ruralism [-izm] n. Rusticité *f.* ‖ U. S. Gramm. Régionalisme *m.*

ruralize [-aiz] v. intr. Vivre à la campagne.
— v. tr. Rendre rural.

ruse [ru:z] n. Ruse *f.*

rush [rʌʃ] n. Paille *f.* (for chair-seats). ‖ Bot. Jonc *m.* ‖ **Rush-bed,** n. Bot. Jonchaie *f.* ‖ **Rush-bottomed,** adj. A fond de paille (chair). ‖ **Rush-mat,** n. Natte (*f.*) de jonc.
— v. tr. Agric. Joncher. ‖ Techn. Joncer (chairs).

rush n. Course précipitée, ruée *f. ; rush hours,* heures d'affluence ; *to make a rush at,* se jeter sur. ‖ Rush, moment (*m.*) de presse (haste) ; *rush order,* commande urgente. ‖ Bouffée *f.* (of air). ‖ Milit. Bond, assaut *m.* ‖ Med. Afflux *m.* (of blood) [*to,* à]. ‖ Electr. Accélération *f.* (of current). ‖ U. S. Cinem. Projection (*f.*) d'essai, rushes *m. pl.*
— v. tr. Entraîner (or) pousser vivement ; *to rush s.o. to hospital,* transporter qqn d'urgence à l'hôpital ; *don't let me rush you,* prenez votre temps. ‖ Dépêchez (to hurry) ; exécuter d'urgence (an order) ; *rushed off one's feet,* débordé. ‖ Milit. Prendre d'assaut (a position). ‖ Jur. Faire passer à la hâte (a bill). ‖ Fam. Estamper ; *he rushed me £ 5 for it,* il m'a extorqué cinq livres pour ça. ‖ **To rush up,** faire venir d'urgence ; Archit. Bâtir à la hâte.
— v. intr. Se précipiter, se ruer, se jeter, s'élancer. ‖ Med. *The blood rushed to his face,* le sang lui monta au visage. ‖ **To rush about,** courir çà et là. ‖ **To rush at,** se jeter sur. ‖ **To rush back,** retourner brusquement. ‖ **To rush down,** descendre précipitamment (person) ; dévaler (stream). ‖ **To rush**

into, se jeter dans (an affair) ; surgir à (one's memory) ; faire irruption dans (a room). ‖ **To rush out,** sortir précipitamment. ‖ **To rush through,** lire à la hâte (a book) ; visiter au pas de course (a museum) ; traverser à toute vitesse (a town) ; expédier (one's work). ‖ **To rush up,** accourir (to arrive) ; monter à toute vitesse (the stairs).

rushed [-d] adj. Débordé (person) ; fait à la va-vite, expédié (work).

rushing [-iŋ] n. Précipitation *f.*
— adj. Impétueux (torrent).

rushy [-i] adj. De jonc. ‖ Couvert de joncs.

rusk [rʌsk] n. Culin. Biscotte *f.*

russet ['rʌsit] adj. Roux, roussâtre (colour).
— n. Roux *m.* (colour). ‖ Agric. Reinette grise *f.* (apple) ; rousselet *m.* (pear).

russety [-i] adj. Roussâtre.

Russia ['rʌʃə] n. Geogr. Russie *f.* ‖ Comm. Cuir (*m.*) de Russie.

Russian [-ən] n. Geogr., Gramm. Russe *s.*

Russianize [-aiz] v. tr. Russifier.

Russophile ['rʌsofil] adj., n. Russophile *s.*

Russophobe [-foub] adj., n. Russophobe *s.*

rust [rʌst] v. intr. Se rouiller. ‖ S'encroûter.
— v. tr. Rouiller.
— n. Rouille *f. ; to rub the rust off,* se dérouiller (person) ; dérouiller (thing). ‖ **Rust-coloured,** adj. Roux. ‖ **Rust-preventer,** n. Antirouille *m.* ‖ **Rust-proof,** adj. Inoxydable.

rustic ['rʌstik] n. Paysan, campagnard *s.* (countryman) ; rustre *m.* (pej.).
— adj. Rustique, champêtre.

rustically [-əli] adv. Rustiquement.

rusticate [-eit] v. intr. Se retirer à la campagne.
— v. tr. Renvoyer temporairement (a student). ‖ Archit. Rustiquer.

rustication [,rʌsti'keiʃən] n. Vie à la campagne *f.* ‖ Renvoi temporaire *m.* (of a student).

rusticity [,rʌs'tisiti] n. Rusticité *f.*

rustiness ['rʌstinis] n. Rouille, rouillure *f.* ‖ Fig. Rouille *f.*

rustle ['rʌsl] n. Frou-frou *m.* (of a dress) ; bruissement *m.* (of leaves) ; froissement *m.* (of paper).
— v. intr. Bruire, froufrouter ; faire un bruit de papier froissé.
— v. tr. Faire bruire ; froufrouter ; froisser. ‖ U. S. Se démener, se remuer.

rustler [-ə*] n. U. S. Voleur (*m.*) de bétail. ‖ U. S. Débrouillard ; type expéditif *m.*

rustless ['rʌstlis] adj. Sans rouille. ‖ Inoxydable.

rusty [-i] adj. Rouillé ; *to get rusty,* se rouiller. ‖ Couleur de rouille. ‖ Med. Rauque, éraillé (voice). ‖ Fig. Rouillé.

rut [rʌt] n. Ornière *f.* ‖ Fig. Ornière *f. ; in a rut,* enrouliné ; *to get, to put into a rut,* s'encroûter, encroûter.
— v. tr. (1). Sillonner d'ornières.

rut n. Zool. Rut *m.*
— v. intr. Zool. Etre en rut.

rutabaga [,ru:tə'bɑ:gə] n. Bot. Rutabaga *m.* (See swede.)

ruthenium [ru:'θi:niəm] n. Chim. Ruthénium *m.*

ruthless ['ru:θlis] adj. Impitoyable, cruel.

ruthlessly [-li] adv. Impitoyablement.

ruthlessness [-nis] n. Caractère impitoyable *m.*

rutilant ['ru:tilənt] adj. Rutilant.

rutted ['rʌtid], **rutty** [-i] adj. Défoncé, plein d'ornières (road).

Rwanda [ru'ændə] n. Geogr. Rwanda, Ruanda *m.*

rye [rai] n. Agric. Seigle *m.* ‖ U. S. Whisky *m.* ‖ **Rye-grass,** n. Agric. Ray-grass *m.* (See darnel.)

ryepeck ['raipek] n. Naut. Perche (*f.*) d'amarrage.

ryot ['raiət] n. Paysan indien *s.*

S

s [es] n. S, s. (letter). ‖ Geogr. Abbr. *South*, sud ;
abbr. *Southern*, du sud, méridional. ‖ Fin. † Abbr.
shilling, shilling.

's [s,z] = *is*. (See BE.)

's [s] gen. poss. *The boy's books*, les livres du garçon ; *the boys' books*, les livres des garçons.

Saar [sɑ:*] n. Geogr. Sarre *f.* ; *Saar region*, région
sarroise.

sabbath ['sæbəθ] n. Sabbat *m.* (witches'). ‖ Eccles.
Dimanche *m.* (Sunday) ; sabbat *m.* (of the Jewish
week).

sabbatical [sə'bætikəl] adj. Eccles. Sabbatique. ‖
Loc. *Sabbatical year*, année de congé sabbatique
(granted to university teachers).

saber ['seibə*] n. U. S. See SABRE.

sable ['seibl] n. Zool., Comm. Zibeline *f.*

sable n. Blas. Sable *m.* ‖ Couleur noire *f.* ‖ Pl.
Vêtements (*m. pl.*) de deuil.
— adj. Noir. ‖ Blas. De sable.

sabot ['sæbou] n. Sabot *m.*

sabotage ['sæbotɑ:ʒ] n. Sabotage *m.*
— v. tr. Saboter.

saboteur [sæbo'tœ*] n. Saboteur *m.*

sabre ['seibə*] n. Sabre *m.* ‖ **Sabre-rattling,** n.
Menace d'intervention militaire *f.*
— v. tr. Sabrer.

saburral [sæ'bʌrəl] adj. Med. Saburral (tongue).

sac [sæk] n. Robe sac *f.* (dress). ‖ Med., Zool.,
Bot. Sac *m.*

saccharin ['sækərin] n. Chim., Culin. Saccharine *f.*

saccharine [-,rain] adj. Saccharin. ‖ Fig. Mielleux.

sacerdotal [sæsə'doutl] adj. Sacerdotal.

sachem ['sætʃəm] n. U. S. Sachem *m.* ‖ U. S. Fam.
Gros bonnet *m.*

sachet ['sæʃei] n. Sachet de parfum, sultan *m.*

sack [sæk] n. Sac *m.* (bag, content). ‖ Fam. Sac,
paquet *m.* ; *to get the sack*, recevoir son paquet, se
faire balancer ; *to give the sack to*, débarquer,
balancer. ‖ U. S. Fam. Pieu *m.* (bed). ‖ **Sack-hoist,**
n. Monte-sacs *m.* ‖ **Sack-race,** n. Course (*f.*) en sac.
— v. tr. Ensacher, mettre en sac. ‖ Fam. Balancer,
saquer, dégommer ; *to be sacked*, recevoir son
paquet.

sack n. Milit. Sac, pillage *m.*
— v. tr. Milit. Saccager, mettre à sac.

sackbut ['sæk,bʌt] n. Mus. Saquebute, saque-
boute *f.*

sackcloth [-klɔθ] n. Toile (*f.*) à sacs (or) d'emballage ; serpillière, grosse toile *f.* ‖ Fig. Bure *f.*

sackful [-ful] n. Sachée *f.* ; plein sac *m.*

sacral ['seikrəl] adj. Med. Du sacrum, sacré.

sacrament ['sækrəmənt] n. Eccles. Sacrement *m.* ;
Holy Sacrament, saint sacrement. ‖ † Serment *m.*

sacramental [,sækrə'mentl] adj. Sacramental.
— n. pl. Eccles. Sacramentaux *m. pl.*

sacred ['seikrid] adj. Sacré. ‖ Consacré (*to*, à). ‖
Eccles. Saint (history) ; majeur (order) ; sacré
(vessel) ; *Sacred Heart*, Sacré-Cœur. ‖ Mus. Religieux (music) ; spirituel (concert). ‖ Fig. Sacré,
inviolable (oath).

sacredness [-nis] n. Caractère sacré *m.* ‖ Inviolabilité *f.*

sacrifice ['sækrifais] n. Sacrifice *m.* ; immolation *f.*
(of a victim). ‖ Victime, offrande *f.* ‖ Sacrifice,
renoncement *m.* ; abnégation *f.* ; *at the sacrifice of*,
aux dépens de. ‖ Comm. *At a sacrifice*, à perte.
— v. tr. Sacrifier, immoler, offrir en sacrifice (a

victim). ‖ Renoncer à ; sacrifier (one's interests). ‖
Comm. Sacrifier, vendre à perte.
— v. intr. Sacrifier, faire des offrandes *f.* ‖ Faire
des sacrifices (to economize).

sacrificial [sækri'fiʃəl] adj. Eccles. Sacrificatoire.
‖ Comm. Au-dessous du prix coûtant ; à perte (sale).

sacrilege ['sækrilidʒ] n. Sacrilège *m.*

sacrilegious [sækri'li:dʒəs] adj. Sacrilège.

sacrilegist [-dʒist] n. Sacrilège *s.*

sacristan ['sækristən] n. Eccles. Sacristain *m.*

sacristy [-ti] n. Eccles. Sacristie *f.*

sacro-lumbar [,sækro'lʌmbə*] adj. Med. Sacro-
lombaire.

sacrosanct ['sækrosæŋkt] adj. Sacro-saint.

sacrum ['seikrəm] n. Med. Sacrum *m.*

sad [sæd] adj. Triste, malheureux ; déprimé, mélancolique (person) ; lugubre, morne (place) ; *sadder
but wiser*, désenchanté. ‖ Cruel (loss) ; déplorable
(mistake) ; fâcheux, navrant, affligeant, désolant
(news).

sadden ['sædn] v. tr. Attrister, rendre triste,
déprimer.
— v. intr. S'attrister, devenir mélancolique.

saddle ['sædl] n. Selle *f.* (of a bicycle, a horse) ;
sellette *f.* (of a harness) ; *in the saddle*, en selle ;
to be thrown from the saddle, vider les étriers. ‖
Culin. Selle *f.* (of mutton). ‖ Naut. Collier *m.* (of
a boom). ‖ Geogr. Col *m.* ‖ **Saddle-bag,** n. Sacoche
de selle *f.* ‖ **Saddle-blanket** (or) **-cloth,** n. Couverture *f.* (or) tapis (*m.*) de selle. ‖ **Saddle-bow,** n.
Fourche (*f.*) d'arçon ; pommeau *m.* ‖ **Saddle-horse,**
n. Cheval (*m.*) de selle.
— v. tr. Seller (a horse). ‖ Fig. Charger (*with*, de) ;
to saddle s.o. with one's own misdeeds, mettre ses
propres méfaits sur le dos de qqn.

saddleback [-bæk] n. Dos d'âne *m.* ; toit *m.* (or)
montagne (*f.*) en dos d'âne ; ensellement *m.* ‖
Cheval ensellé *m.*
— adj. En dos d'âne. ‖ Ensellé.

saddler [-ə*] n. Sellier *m.*

saddlery [-əri] n. Sellerie *f.*

sadism ['seidizm] n. Sadisme *m.*

sadist [-ist] n. Sadique *s.*

sadistic [sei'distik] adj. Sadique.

sadly ['sædli] adv. Tristement, avec tristesse (melancholically). ‖ Douloureusement, cruellement (grievously). ‖ Pitoyablement, misérablement. ‖ Fam.
Sérieusement, bigrement.

sadness [-nis] n. Tristesse, mélancolie *f.*

sado-masochism [,seido'mæsə,kizm] n. Sado-
masochisme *m.*

sado-masochist [-,kist] n. Sadomasochiste *s.*

sado-masochistic [,seidou,mæsə'kistik] n.
Sadomasochiste *adj.*

safari [sə'fɑ:ri] n. Safari *m.* ; *to go on safari*, faire
un safari. ‖ Comm. *Safari jacket*, saharienne.

safe [seif] n. (pl. **safes**) n. Coffre-fort *m.* ; caisse *f.*
(strong-box). ‖ Garde-manger *m.* (food-store).
— adj. Sain et sauf (person) ; intact, en bon état
(thing). ‖ En lieu sûr ; en sécurité, en sûreté, à l'abri
(secure). ‖ Prudent, modéré, raisonnable (cautious) ;
sûr, certain (trustworthy). ‖ Fin. Sûr, sans risque ;
de tout repos (investment) ; *safe custody*, dépôt en
garde (for securities). ‖ Jur. *Safe in jail*, hors d'état
de nuire. ‖ Fam. *To be on the safe side*, se tenir à
carreau. ‖ **Safe-breaker,** n. Perceur (*m.*) de coffres-
forts. ‖ **Safe-conduct,** n. Sauf-conduit *m.* ‖ **Safe-
deposit vault,** n. Cave *f.* (or) service (*m.*) des
coffres. ‖ **Safe-keeping,** n. Garde, bonne garde *f.*

safeguard [-gɑ:d] n. Sauvegarde *f*.
— v. tr. Sauvegarder.
safely [-li] adv. En sûreté, sans danger. ‖ Sain et sauf, à bon port, sans mal, sans accident. ‖ Sans crainte (or) hésitation.
safeness [-nis] n. Sûreté, sécurité *f*. (of a place, a transaction). ‖ TECHN. Solidité *f*. (of a mechanism).
safety [-ti] n. Sûreté, sécurité *f*.; absence (*f*.) de danger (or) de risques. ‖ **Safety-belt**, n. Ceinture de sécurité *f*. ‖ **Safety-catch**, n. Cran (*m*.) de sûreté. ‖ **Safety curtain**, n. THEATR. Rideau de fer *m*. ‖ **Safety-device**, n. Dispositif (*m*.) de sûreté, organe (*m*.) de sûreté. ‖ **Safety-fuse**, n. Mèche de sûreté *f*.; cordon Bickford *m*.; ELECTR. Fusible, plomb *m*. ‖ **Safety-glass**, n. AUTOM. Glace Sécurit *f*. ‖ **Safety-match**, n. Allumette suédoise *f*. ‖ **Safety-measure**, n. Mesure de précaution *f*. ‖ **Safety net**, n. Filet, filet d'acrobate *m*. ‖ **Safety-pin**, n. Epingle de nourrice (or) de sûreté *f*. ‖ **Safety-razor**, n. Rasoir (*m*.) de sûreté. ‖ **Safety-valve**, n. Soupape de sûreté *f*.
saffron ['sæfrən] n., adj. CULIN. Safran *m*.
sag [sæg] v. intr. Pencher (to bend); s'affaisser, fléchir (to sink). ‖ FIN. Fléchir (market); baisser (prices). ‖ NAUT. Etre dépalé.
— v. tr. Courber, affaisser, faire fléchir.
— n. Courbure *f*.; affaissement *m*. ‖ Flèche *f*. (of a telegraph wire). ‖ NAUT. Dérive *f*. ‖ FIG. Fléchissement *m*.; baisse *f*.
saga ['sɑ:gə] n. Saga *f*. ‖ **Saga-novel**, n. Roman-fleuve *m*.
sagacious [sə'geiʃəs] adj. Intelligent, sagace, avisé.
sagacity [sə'gæsiti] n. Sagacité *f*.
sage [seidʒ] n. BOT., CULIN. Sauge *f*.
sage adj. Sage, prudent (conduct, person). ‖ Solennel, grave.
— n. Sage *m*.
sagely [-li] adv. Avec sagesse (or) prudence.
sageness [-nis] n. Sagesse *f*. (See WISDOM.)
sagging ['sægiŋ] adj. Fléchissant. ‖ FIN. Creux (market); en baisse (prices).
Sagittarius [sædʒi'tɛəriəs] n. ASTRON. Sagittaire *m*.
sago ['seigou] (pl. **sagos** [-ɔ:z]) n. BOT., CULIN. Sagou *m*.
said [sed]. See SAY. ‖ JUR. Dit, susdit (act, document, person).
sail [seil] n. NAUT. Voile *f*. ‖ Voilure *f*., voiles *f*. pl. (collectively); *full sail*, toutes voiles dehors; *to get under* (or) *to set sail*, mettre à la voile. ‖ Voile *f*., vaisseau *m*. (boat). ‖ Promenade (or) croisière à voile *f*.; *to go for a sail*, faire une promenade en bateau à voile. ‖ Voyage (or) trajet (*m*.) en mer. ‖ TECHN. Aile *f*. (of a windmill). ‖ FAM. *To take the wind out of s.o.'s sails*, obliger qqn à en rabattre, dégonfler qqn; *to shorten* (or) *to take in sail*, baisser pavillon. ‖ **Sail-cloth**, n. Toile à voile *f*. ‖ **Sail-maker**, n. Voilier *m*. ‖ **Sail-plane**, n. AVIAT. Planeur *m*.
— v. intr. NAUT. Naviguer, faire voile, voguer; *to sail close to the wind*, serrer le vent. ‖ NAUT. Mettre à la voile (sailing-ship); partir (steamship). ‖ AVIAT., ZOOL. Planer, voguer, glisser (balloon, bird). ‖ FAM. Avancer toutes voiles dehors (person); *to sail in*, débarquer, arriver, entrer.
— v. tr. NAUT. Manœuvrer, commander (a boat); naviguer sur, parcourir en bateau (the seas).
sailer [-ə*] n. NAUT. Voilier *m*. (ship); *good sailer*, bon marcheur.
sailing [-iŋ] n. NAUT. Manœuvre *f*. (of a boat); navigation *f*. (science, skill). ‖ NAUT. Départ *m*. ‖ FAM. *To be all plain sailing*, ne pas faire un pli.
sailor [-ə*] n. NAUT. Matelot, marin *m*.; *sailor's home*, abri du marin; *sailor's knot*, régate (of a necktie); *sailor hat*, jean-bart (child's), canotier *m*. (lady's).
sainfoin ['sænfɔin] n. BOT. Sainfoin *m*.

saint [seint, sint, snt] adj. ECCLES., FIG. Saint.
— [seint] n. ECCLES., FIG. Saint *s*.; *All Saints' Day*, la Toussaint. ‖ FAM. *She's no saint*, ce n'est pas un prix de vertu.
— v. tr. Canoniser.
sainted ['seintid] adj. Pieux, sanctifié (person); sacré, consacré, sanctifié (place). ‖ FAM. *My sainted aunt!*, Dieu du ciel!
sake [seik] n. *For the sake of, for ...'s sake*, pour, par égard pour, pour l'amour de, à cause de; *for God's sake*, pour l'amour de Dieu; *for mercy's* (or) *pity's sake*, par pitié; *for my sake*, pour moi; *for both our sakes*, pour nous deux. ‖ Dans le but de, en vue de, pour; *art for art's sake*, l'art pour l'art.
sake ['sake] n. Saké *m*. (rice wine).
sal [sæl] n. BOT. Sal *m*.
sal n. MED. Sel *m*.; *sal ammoniac, volatile*, sel ammoniac, volatil.
salaam [sə'lɑ:m] interj. Salam (Muslim salutation).
salable ['seiləbl] adj. COMM. Vendable, de vente possible.
salacious [sə'leiʃəs] adj. Salace (person); salé (story).
salad ['sæləd] n. BOT., CULIN. Salade *f*.; *fruit salad*, salade de fruits; *lettuce salad*, laitue; *salad oil*, huile de table. ‖ FIG. *Salad days*, vertes années. ‖ **Salad-bowl**, n. Saladier *m*. ‖ **Salad-dressing**, n. CULIN. Assaisonnement (*m*.) pour la salade, vinaigrette *f*.
salamander ['sæləmændə*] n. ZOOL. Salamandre *f*. ‖ CULIN. Four (*m*.) de campagne. ‖ TECHN. Loup *m*.
salami [sə'lɑ:mi] n. CULIN. Salami *m*.
salary ['sæləri] n. Traitement *m*.; appointements *m*. pl.; rémunération *f*.; *to draw a fixed salary*, toucher un traitement fixe.
— v. tr. Payer des appointements à; *high salaried*, bien rétribué (job).
sale [seil] n. COMM. Vente *f*.; débit *m*.; mise en vente *f*.; *for sale*, à vendre. ‖ Vente (*f*.) aux enchères (auction). ‖ Occasions *f*. pl. (bargain sale). ‖ *Sales check*, facture; *sale contract*, contrat de vente; *sale goods*, soldes; *white sale*, exposition de blanc. ‖ FIN. *Cash, credit sale*, vente au comptant, à crédit; *sale for the account*, vente à terme. ‖ JUR. *Compulsory sale*, adjudication forcée. ‖ **Sale-price**, n. Prix (*m*.) de vente. ‖ **Sales talk**, n. U. S. Boniment *m*. ‖ **Sale-value**, n. Valeur marchande *f*.
salesclerk [-klə:k] n. U. S. Vendeur *m*.
salesgirl [-gə:rl] n. U. S. Vendeuse *f*.
salesman [-mən] (pl. **salesmen**) n. Vendeur, commis *m*. (in a shop). ‖ Courtier, représentant, placier *m*. (agent); marchand *m*. (dealer); *travelling salesman*, voyageur de commerce, commis voyageur.
salesmanship [-mənʃip] n. COMM. Art (*m*.) de vendre.
salesroom [-rum] n. COMM. Salle (*f*.) de vente.
saleswoman [-wumən] (pl. **saleswomen** [-wimin]) n. Vendeuse *f*.
salic ['sælik] adj. Salique (law).
salicylate [sə'lisilet] n. CHIM. Salicylate *m*.
salicylic [,sæli'silik] adj. CHIM. Salicylique.
salience ['seiljəns] n. Projection, saillie *f*. (of a configuration). ‖ Saillant *m*., saillie *f*. (part).
salient [-ənt] adj. † Bondissant; jaillissant. ‖ Saillant, en saillie (angle). ‖ FIG. Frappant (argument); saillant (feature).
— n. Saillant *m*.
saliferous [sə'lifərəs] adj. GEOL. Salifère *f*.
salina [sə'lainə] n. Salin *m*.
saline ['seilain] adj. Salin, salé (lake, spring); salant (marsh). ‖ CHIM. Salin.
— [sə'lain] n. Saline *f*.; marais salant *m*. ‖ CHIM., MED. Sel purgatif *m*.
saliva [sə'laivə] n. MED. Salive *f*.
salivary ['sælivəri] adj. MED. Salivaire.
salivate [-veit] v. tr. MED. Faire saliver.
— v. intr. MED. Saliver.

sallow ['sælou] n. Bot. Saule m.
sallow adj. Blême, blafard, jaune.
— n. Teint blafard (or) jaune m.
— v. intr., tr. Jaunir, pâlir.
sallowish [-ish] adj. Jaunâtre, au teint brouillé.
sallowness [-nis] n. Teint jaunâtre m.; pâleur maladive f.
sally [sæli] n. Sortie, courte excursion f. ‖ Milit. Sortie f. ‖ Fig. Sursaut, élan m. (of activity, emotion); saillie f. (of wit); boutade, pointe (f.) d'esprit (witty remark).
— v. intr. (2). To sally forth, sortir, partir en promenade, se mettre en route. ‖ Milit. To sally out, faire une sortie. ‖ Sally-port, n. Milit. Poterne (f.) de sortie.
salmagundi [sælmə'gʌndi] n. Culin., Fig. Salmigondis m.
salmi ['sælmi] n. Culin. Salmis m.
salmon ['sæmən] n. Zool., Culin. Saumon m.; young salmon, saumoneau. ‖ Salmon-colour, n. Couleur (f.) saumon. ‖ Salmon-trout, n. Zool. Truite saumonée f.
— adj. Saumon.
salmonella [,sælmə'nelə] n. Med. Salmonelle f.
salon ['sælɔ̃:] n. Salon m. (reception-room, social gathering). ‖ Arts. Salon m. (exhibition). ‖ U. S. Beauty salon, institut de beauté.
saloon [sə'lu:n] n. Salon m. (of a hotel); billiard saloon, salle de billard; hairdressing saloon, salon de coiffure. ‖ U. S. Débit (m.) de boisson, cabaret m. (pub). ‖ Naut. Salon m.; saloon deck, pont de première classe. ‖ Autom. Conduite intérieure f.; seven-seater saloon, familiale. ‖ Milit. Saloon rifle, carabine de salon. ‖ Saloon-bar, n. Bar m. ‖ Saloon-car, n. Ch. de F. Wagon-salon m. ‖ Saloon keeper, n. U. S. Cabaretier m. (See Publican.)
salpingitis [sælpin'dʒaitis] n. Med. Salpingite f.
salsify ['sælsifi] n. Bot., Culin. Salsifis m.
salt [sɔlt] n. Sel m.; kitchen salt, gros sel; rock, sea salt, sel gemme, marin; table salt, sel fin (or) de table; in salt, salé, conservé dans le sel. ‖ Saline f.; marais salant, pré salé m. (marsh). ‖ Salière f. (container); to eat s.o.'s salt, manger à la table de qqn. ‖ Chim. Sel m.; chlorure de sodium m.; Glauber's salt, sel de Glauber, sulfate de soude. ‖ Med. Smelling salts, sels. ‖ Naut. Old salt, vieux loup de mer. ‖ Eccles. Salt of the earth, sel de la terre. ‖ Fig. Sel, piquant m. (spiciness). ‖ Fam. Salt of the earth, l'élite, la crème, le « nec plus ultra »; not to be worth one's salt, ne pas valoir son sel; with a grain of salt, avec circonspection. ‖ Salt-box, n. Boîte (f.) à sel. ‖ Salt-cellar, n. Salière f. ‖ Salt-lake, n. Lac salé; chott m. (in North Africa). ‖ Salt-lick, n. Pain salé m.; saunière f.; U. S. Terrain salifère m. ‖ Salt-marsh, n. Marais salant m.; saline f. ‖ Salt-mill, n. Egrugeoir m. ‖ Salt-mine, n. Mine (f.) de sel. ‖ Salt shaker, n. U.S. Salière f. ‖ Salt-sprinkler, n. Salière f. ‖ Salt-tax, n. † Gabelle f. ‖ Salt-water, n. Eau salée f.; salt-water fish, poisson (m.) de mer. ‖ Salt-works, n. Salines f. pl.; raffinerie (f.) de sel.
— adj. Salé; salt marsh, marais salant; salt meadow, pré salé. ‖ Culin. Salé (butter). ‖ Fig. Amer, douloureux (tears).
— v. tr. Culin. Saler. ‖ Chim. Traiter par des sels. Comm. Forcer (an account). ‖ Fam. To salt away, faire des conserves de, mettre à gauche (money).
S.A.L.T. [sɔlt] abbr. Strategic Arms Limitation Talks, pourparlers sur la limitation des armes stratégiques, S. A. L. T.
saltation [sæl'teiʃən] n. Bonds, sauts m. pl.; gambade f. ‖ Fig. Brusque changement m. (or) saute d'idée f.
salter ['sɔltə*] n. Saunier m. ‖ Saleur m. ‖ Comm. Marchand (m.) de salaisons.
saltern [-ən] n. Saline f.

salting [-iŋ] n. Salage m., salaison f. ‖ Salting-tub, n. Saloir m.
saltire ['sɔ:ltaiə*] n. Blas. Sautoir m.
saltish [-iʃ] adj. Plutôt salé.
saltless [-lis] adj. Fade, qui manque de sel.
saltness [-nis] n. Salure f. ‖ Salinité f. (of sea-water).
saltpetre [-,pi:tə*] n. Chim. Salpêtre m.; saltpetre works, salpêtrière.
saltwort [-wə:t] n. Bot. Soude f.
salty [-i] adj. Salé, saumâtre. ‖ Fig. Salé (bill); salé, corsé (joke).
salubrious [sə'lu:briəs] adj. Salubre.
salubrity [-ti] n. Salubrité f.
salutary ['sæljutəri] adj. Salutaire.
salutation [sælju'teiʃən] n. Salutation f. ‖ Eccles. Angelic Salutation, salutation angélique, Ave Maria.
salutatory [-təri] adj. De salutation.
— n. U.S. Discours d'adieu m.
salute [sə'lu:t] n. Salut m.; salutation f. ‖ Milit., Naut. Salve f. (of guns); salut m. (of the hand). ‖ Sports. Salut m. (in fencing). ‖ † Accolade f.
— v. tr. Saluer, adresser un salut à. ‖ Milit., Naut. Saluer. ‖ Fig. Accueillir, saluer (an arrival); frapper (the attention). ‖ † Accoler.
salvable ['sælvəbl] adj. Susceptible d'être sauvé. ‖ Eccles. En état de grâce.
salvage ['sælvidʒ] n. Sauvetage m. (act); objets (or) biens sauvés m. pl. (objects); salvage plant, appareils de renflouage. ‖ Techn. Récupération f. (of materials). ‖ Salvage-vessel, n. Naut. Bateau sauveteur m.; dock de sauvetage m. (for submarines).
— v. tr. Sauver, procéder au sauvetage de. ‖ Autom. Récupérer (a car).
salvation [sæl'veiʃən] n. Préservation f.; salut m. ‖ Comm. Relèvement m. (economic). ‖ Eccles. Salut m.; Salvation Army, Armée du Salut.
salvationist [-ist] n. Salutiste s.
salve [sɑ:v] n. Med. † Onguent, baume m.; pommade f. ‖ Fig. Baume, apaisement m.
— v. tr. Med. Appliquer un onguent (or) une pommade sur; dissimuler (a defect). ‖ Naut. Sauver (objects, ship). ‖ Fig. Résoudre (a difficulty); dissiper (a misunderstanding); endormir (remorse); sauver (a reputation); panser (wounded pride).
salver ['sælvə*] n. Plateau m.
salvo ['sælvo] n. Restriction, réserve f. ‖ Restriction mentale, excuse f.; échappatoire f.; faux-fuyant m.
salvo n. Milit., Fig. Salve f.
salvor ['sælvə*] n. Naut. Sauveteur m.
Sam [sæm] n. Samuel m.; Uncle Sam, l'Oncle Sam.
Samaritan [sə'mæritən] adj., n. Eccles. Samaritain s.
samarium [sə'meəriəm] n. Chim. Samarium m.
samba ['sæmbə] n. Samba f.
sambo ['sæmbou] n. Fam. Moricaud m.
same [seim] adj. Même; the very same thing, une seule et même chose; to be one and the same person, n'être qu'une seule et même personne. ‖ Jur. That (or) this same, ce même, le susdit, ledit. ‖ Loc. At the same time, en même temps, au même moment (time), à la fois (simultaneously); at the same time that, au moment même où; in the same way, de même; to amount to (or) to be one and the same thing, revenir au même.
— Syn. : IDENTICAL, SIMILAR, VERY.
— pron. The same, le même, la même, les mêmes; the same to you, à vous de même, pareillement; all (or) just the same, tout de même, quand même, malgré tout, néanmoins; it's all (or) just the same, c'est tout un, c'est tout comme; it's all the same to me, cela m'est indifférent, ça m'est égal; if it's all the same to you, si cela ne vous fait rien; to think the same of, penser la même chose de; I would have done the same, j'aurais fait de même; to still look

the same, n'avoir pas changé. ‖ JUR. Le susdit, la susdite, les susdits, les susdites. ‖ FAM. *Same here,* et moi de même, pour moi aussi.

sameness [-nis] n. Ressemblance, identité *f.* (similarity). ‖ Uniformité, monotonie *f.* (lack of variety).

samite ['sæmait] n. Samit, brocart, lamé d'or *m.*

samizdat [səmiz'dat] n. Samizdat *m.*

samlet ['sæmlit] n. ZOOL. Saumoneau *m.*

Samoa [sə'mouə] n. GEOGR. Samoa *m.*

samovar ['sæmə,vɑ:ʳ] n. Samovar *m.*

Samoyed ['sæmojed] n. GEOGR., ZOOL. Samoyède *m.*

samp [sæmp] n. U. S. BOT. Gruau de maïs *m.*

sampan ['sæmpæn] n. NAUT. Sampan *m.*

samphire ['sæmfaiəʳ] n. BOT. Salicorne *m.*

sample ['sɑ:mpl] n. Echantillon *m.* (of fabric); prise *f.;* prélèvement *m.* (of ore); essai *m.* (of wine). ‖ Exemple, spécimen *m.;* catégorie *f.* (cross-section). ‖ MED. Prise *f.;* prélèvement *m.* ‖ BOT. *Sample area,* parcelle d'essai; *sample tree,* arbre type. ‖ **Sample-card,** n. COMM. Carte (*f.*) d'échantillons. ‖ **Sample-post,** n. Echantillon (*m.*) sans valeur (postal indication).
— v. tr. COMM. Echantillonner; prendre (or) donner un échantillon de (a fabric); lotir (ore). ‖ FIG. S'assurer de la valeur de. ‖ FAM. Goûter, déguster (drink, food).

sampler [-əʳ] n. Modèle (*m.*) de broderie. ‖ COMM. Courtier, échantillonneur *m.* ‖ BOT. Baliveau *m.*

sampling [-iŋ] n. Echantillonnage *m.* (of fabric); lotissage (of ore). ‖ FAM. Dégustation *f.* (of food).

Samson ['sæmsən] n. Samson *m.* ‖ FAM. Hercule *m.*

samurai ['sæmuːrai] n. invar. Samouraï *m.*

sanative ['sænətiv], **sanatory** ['sænətəri] adj. Sanitaire, sain, salutaire (clean, hygienic); curatif, guérisseur (health-restoring).

sanatorium [,sænə'tɔːriəm] (pl. **sanatoria** [-ə]) n. MED. Sanatorium *m.*

sanctification [,sæŋktifi'keiʃən] n. ECCLES. Sanctification *f.*

sanctify ['sæŋktifai] v. tr. (2). ECCLES. Consacrer (a day); sanctifier (a person).

sanctimonious [,sæŋkti'mounjəs] adj. Cagot, bigot, cafard, papelard; confit en dévotion; *sanctimonious knave,* bon apôtre.

sanctimoniousness [-nis], **sanctimony** ['sæŋktimoni] n. Papelardise, bigoterie, cagoterie *f.*

sanction ['sæŋkʃən] n. Sanction, approbation *f.,* consentement *m.* (assent); autorisation *f.* (of an author); consécration *f.* (by usage). ‖ JUR. Ordonnance *f.,* décret *m.* (edict); sanction *f.* (punishment).
— v. tr. Approuver, autoriser, encourager (an action); sanctionner, ratifier (a law); accompagner de sanctions (an order).

sanctity [-titi] n. ECCLES. Sainteté *f.* ‖ FIG. Caractère sacré *m.* (of an oath, a promise).

sanctuary [-tjueri] n. ECCLES. Sanctuaire, temple *m.,* église *f.* (church); sanctuaire *m.* (sacrarium). ‖ JUR. Asile, refuge *m.; right of sanctuary,* immunité, droit d'asile. ‖ ZOOL. Refuge *m.* (for wild-life). ‖ SPORTS. Période d'interdiction *f.* (out of the hunting season). ‖ MILIT. Refuge-abri *m.*

sanctum [-təm] n. ECCLES. Sanctuaire, saint (*m.*) des saints. ‖ FAM. Sanctuaire, antre *m.,* turne *f.* (private den).

sand [sænd] n. Sable *m.;* sables *m. pl.;* banc de sable *m.* (on ocean floor); *fine* (or) *scouring sand,* sablon. ‖ Pl. Sables *m. pl.;* grains (*m. pl.*) de sable; grève, plage *f.* (beach, seashore). ‖ MED. *Urinary sand,* sable, gravier. ‖ FIG. Temps *m.;* instants *m. pl.;* vie *f.* ‖ FIG. Sable *m.; to build on sand,* bâtir sur le sable. ‖ U. S. FAM. Cran *m.,* étoffe *f.* (grit). ‖ **Sand-bar,** n. Banc de sable *m.; ensablement *m.* (at a river's mouth). ‖ **Sand-bath,** n. TECHN. Bain de sable *m.* ‖ **Sand-blast,** n. TECHN. Sableuse *f.;* jet de sable *m.* ‖ **Sand-box,** n. Seau à pâté de sable *m.* (for children); sablier *m.* (for ink-drying). ‖ CH. DE F. Sablière *f.;* SPORTS. Caisse (*f.*) à sable (on

golf-links). ‖ **Sand-dune** (or) **hill,** n. Dune *f.* ‖ **Sand-glass,** n. Sablier *m.* ‖ **Sand-man,** n. COMM. Sablonnier *m.;* FAM. Marchand de sable *m.* ‖ **Sand-pit,** n. Sablière *f.* ‖ **Sand-pump,** n. Désensableur *m.* ‖ **Sand-soap,** n. Savon minéral *m.* ‖ **Sand-storm,** n. Simoun *m.;* tempête (*f.*) de sable.
— v. tr. Sabler, ensabler. ‖ Frotter avec du sable. ‖ Mêler de sable (flour, sugar). ‖ Passer au papier de verre (to sandpaper).

sandal ['sændl] n. Sandale *f.* (shoe); barrette *f.* (strap).
— v. tr. Chausser de sandales.

sandal n. BOT. Santal *m.* ‖ **Sandal-wood,** n. BOT. Bois de santal *m.*

sandarac ['sændəræk] n. CHIM. Réalgar *m.*

sandbag ['sændbæg] n. Sac de sable *m.* (for ballast). ‖ Matraque *f.,* assommoir *m.* (cosh). ‖ MILIT. Sac (*m.*) à terre.
— v. tr. Garnir (or) étayer de sacs de terre. ‖ FAM. Assommer.

sanders ['sɑːndəs] n. BOT. Santal *m.*

sandpaper ['sændpeipəʳ] n. Papier-émeri, papier de verre *m.*
— v. tr. Passer au papier de verre.

sandpiper [-paipəʳ] n. ZOOL. Bécasseau *m.*

sandstone [-stoun] n. Grès *m.*

sandwich ['sæn(d)witʃ] (pl. **sandwiches** [-iz]) n. CULIN. Sandwich *m.; ham sandwich,* sandwich au jambon. ‖ **Sandwich-board,** n. COMM. Panneau d'homme-sandwich *m.* ‖ **Sandwich counter,** n. U. S. Buffet *m.* ‖ **Sandwich course,** n. Enseignement (*m.*) théorique coupé de stages dans une entreprise. ‖ **Sandwich-loaf,** n. CULIN. Pain (*m.*) de mie. ‖ **Sandwich-man,** n. COMM. Homme-sandwich *m.*
— v. tr. CULIN. Faire un sandwich avec. ‖ FIG. Intercaler, introduire (*between,* entre; *in,* dans).

sandy ['sændi] adj. Sablonneux, de sable; *sandy bottom,* fond de sable. ‖ Blond roux (colour).

sane [sein] adj. MED. Sain d'esprit; bien équilibré (mind); *to be sane,* avoir toute sa raison. ‖ FIG. Sensé, raisonnable (idea).

Sanforized ['sænfəraizd] adj. U. S. Rendu irrétrécissable (fabric).

sang [sæŋ] pret. See SING.

sang-froid [sɑ̃ frwa] n. Sang-froid, flegme *m.*

Sangrail ['sæŋgreil], **Sangreal** [sæn'griəl] n. Saint Graal *m.*

sanguinarily ['sæŋgwinərili] adv. Sanguinairement.

sanguinary [-əri] adj. Sanglant (accident, battle). ‖ Altéré de sang (bloodthirsty). ‖ Sanguinaire, barbare (law).

sanguine ['sæŋgwin] adj. De sang (rain). ‖ MED. Rouge, rubicond, congestionné (complexion); sanguin (temperament). ‖ FIG. Confiant; optimiste; *to feel sanguine about,* envisager avec optimisme.
— v. tr. Ensanglanter, teinter de sang.

sanguineness [-nis] n. Optimisme *m.;* confiance *f.*

sanguineous [sæŋ'gwiniəs] adj. MED. Sanguin. ‖ FIG. Rouge sang.

sanguinolent [-nɔlənt] adj. Sanguinolent.

Sanhedrim ['sænidrim] n. ECCLES. Sanhédrin *m.*

sanify ['sænifai] v. tr. (2). Assainir, améliorer les conditions sanitaires de.

sanitarian [sæni'tɛəriən] n. Hygiéniste *m.*
— adj. Sanitaire, hygiénique, d'hygiène.

sanitarium [-əm] n. U. S. MED. Sanatorium *m.;* centre (*m.*) de postcure.

sanitary ['sænitəri] adj. Sanitaire, d'hygiène (in general); hygiénique, périodique (towel, U. S. napkin); *sanitary engineering,* technique (or) matériel sanitaire. ‖ MILIT. Sanitaire (cordon).

sanitate [-teit] v. tr. Assainir. See SANIFY.

sanitation [sæni'teiʃən] n. Amélioration de l'hygiène *f.;* assainissement *m.* (of a town). ‖ Aménagements sanitaires *m. pl.; modern sanitation,* tout-à-l'égout. ‖ U. S. Science de l'hygiène *f.*

sanity ['sæniti] n. MED. Santé mentale. ‖ FIG. Modération, raison *f.; rectitude f.* (of judgment); bon sens, jugement sain *m.*

sank [sæŋk] pret. See SINK.

San Marino [sæn mə'ri:nou] n. GEOGR. Saint-Marin *m.*

Sanskrit ['sænskrit] n. Sanskrit *m.*

Santa Claus ['sæntə'klɔ:z] n. Père Noël, saint Nicolas *m.*

santon ['sæntən] n. Santon *m.*

santonica [sæn'tɔnikə] n. BOT. Santonine *f.*

santonin ['sæntonin] n. MED., CHIM. Santonine *f.*

São Tomé [sæn tu'me] n. GEOGR. São Tomé *m.*

sap [sæp] n. BOT. Sève *f.* ‖ **Sap-wood,** n. BOT. Aubier *m.*
— v. tr. BOT. Tirer la sève de. ‖ FIG. Affaiblir, épuiser, dévitaliser.

sap n. MILIT., FIG. Sape *f.*
— v. intr. (1). MILIT., FIG. Saper.
— v. tr. MILIT. Saper, miner. ‖ MED. Affaiblir, miner (the health). ‖ FIG. Saper, ébranler peu à peu (a belief).

sap v. intr. (1). Potasser, bûcher.
— n. FAM. Gourde *f.; ballot m.*

sapajou ['sæpədʒu:] n. ZOOL. Sapajou *m.*

sapid ['sæpid] adj. Sapide. ‖ FIG. Savoureux, piquant, intéressant.

sapience ['seipiəns] n. † Sapience *f.* ‖ Sagesse *f.* ‖ Pédantisme *m.; pédanterie f.*

sapient [-ənt] adj. Sage, sagace, savant. ‖ Pédant.

sapiential [seipi'enʃəl] adj. ECCLES. De la sagesse ; *sapiential books,* livres sapientiaux.

sapiently ['seipiəntli] adv. Sagement.

sapless ['sæplis] adj. BOT. Desséché, sans sève (plant); stérile (soil). ‖ FIG. Sans vigueur (character); fade, banal, insipide (idea).

sapling ['sæpliŋ] n. BOT. Jeune arbre ; baliveau *m.* ‖ Pl. Boisage *m.* (in a forest). ‖ ZOOL. Levron *m.* ‖ FIG. Adolescent *m.*

saponaceous [,sæpə'neiʃəs] adj. Savonneux, saponacé. ‖ FIG. Onctueux, mielleux.

saponification [,sæpənifi'keiʃən] n. Saponification *f.*

saponify [sæ'pɔnifai] v. tr. (2). Saponifier.
— v. intr. Se saponifier.

saponin ['sæpənin] n. CHIM. Saponine *f.*

sapper ['sæpə*] n. MILIT. Sapeur *m.; taupin m.* (fam.); pl. génie *m.*

Sapphic ['sæfik] adj. Saphique (stanza, verse). ‖ MED. Lesbien.
— n. pl. Vers saphiques *m. pl.*

sapphire ['sæfaiə] n. Saphir *m.* ‖ ZOOL. Colibri *m.*
— adj. Saphir, bleu saphir adj. invar.

sapphirine [-irin] adj. Saphirin, de saphir.

sappiness ['sæpinis] n. BOT. Richesse en sève *f.* ‖ FAM. Nigauderie; inexpérience *f.*

sappy [-i] adj. BOT. Plein de sève. ‖ FAM. Nigaud, naïf ; inexpérimenté, jeune.

saraband ['særəbænd] n. MUS. Sarabande *f.*

Saracen ['særəsn] n. GEOGR. Sarrasin *s.*
— adj. Sarrasin. ‖ BOT. *Saracen corn,* sarrasin, blé noir.

sarcasm ['sɑ:kæzm̩] n. Sarcasme *m.; raillerie f.* (remark); esprit sarcastique *m.* (spirit).

sarcastic [sɑ:'kæstik] adj. Sarcastique, ironique, mordant ; *sarcastic remark,* sarcasme.

sarcastically [-əli] adv. Sarcastiquement.

sarcelle [sɑ:'sel] n. ZOOL. Sarcelle *f.*

sarcocele ['sɑ:kəsel] n. MED. Sarcocèle *s.*

sarcoma [sɑ:'koumə] n. MED. Sarcome *m.*
— N. B. Deux pluriels : *sarcomas, sarcomata.*

sarcophagus [sɑ:'kɔfəgəs] n. Sarcophage *m.*
— N. B. Deux pluriels : *sarcophaguses, sarcophagi.*

sard ⌊sɑ:d⌋ n. Sardoine *f.; sarde m.*

sardine [sɑ:'di:n] n. ZOOL., CULIN. Sardine *f.* ‖ FAM. *Packed like sardines,* serrés comme des harengs.

sardine ['sɑ:dain] n. Sardoine *f.* (stone).

Sardinia [sɑ:'dinjə] n. GEOGR. Sardaigne *f.*

Sardinian [-ən] adj., n. GEOGR. Sarde *s.*

sardonic [sɑ:'dɔnik] adj. MED. Sardonien. ‖ FIG. Sardonique (laugh).

sardonyx ['sɑ:dəniks] n. Sardoine *f.*

sargasso [sɑ:'gæsou] n. BOT. Sargasse *f.* ‖ GEOGR. *Sargasso Sea,* mer des Sargasses.

sarge [sæ:dʒ] n. FAM., MILIT. Sergent *m.*

sari, saree ['sɑ:ri] n. Sari *m.*

sarmentose ['sɑ:mentous], **sarmentous** [sɑ:'mentəs] adj. BOT. Sarmenteux.

sarong [sɑ:'rɔŋ] n. Sarong, pagne *m.*

sarsaparilla [sɑ:səpə'rilə] n. BOT., CHIM. Salsepareille *f.*

sarsenet ['sɑ:snit] n. Taffetas (*m.*) pour doublure.

sartorial [sɑ:'tɔ:riəl] adj. De tailleur ; *sartorial artist,* artiste tailleur. ‖ Vestimentaire (elegance).

sash [sæʃ] n. Large ceinture nouée *f.* ‖ MILIT. Ceinture ; écharpe *f.*

sash n. Châssis *m.* (of a window); fenêtre *f.* (window). ‖ **Sash-cord,** n. Cordon de châssis *m.* ‖ **Sash-window,** n. Fenêtre à guillotine *f.*

sass [sæs] n. U. S. FAM. Culot, toupet *m.; insolence f.* (See SAUCE.)

Sassenach ['sæsə,næk] n. Anglais *s.* (derogatory Scottish term).

sassy ['sæsi] adj. U. S. FAM. Culotté, gonflé, effronté. (See SAUCY.)

sat [sæt] pret., p. p. See SIT.

Satan ['seitən] n. Satan *m.*

Satanic [sə'tænik] adj. Satanique.

Satanism ['seitənizm] n. Satanisme *m.*

satchel ['sætʃəl] n. Carton, cartable *m.* (for books); sacoche *f.* (for clothes). ‖ SPORTS. Gibecière *f.* (for game); sacoche *f.* (saddle-bag).

sate [seit] v. tr. Assouvir (an appetite, a passion); rassasier (s.o.). ‖ FIG. Blaser, dégoûter.

sate [seit] † pret. See SIT.

sateen [sæ'ti:n] n. Satinette *f.*

satellite ['sætəlait] n. ASTRON., FIG. Satellite *m.*
— adj. Satellite; *satellite state,* pays satellite, satellite; *satellite town,* cité satellite.

satiate ['seiʃieit] v. tr. Rassasier, assouvir ; gorger. ‖ FIG. Blaser (with, de).
— [-it] adj. Rassasié.

satiation [,seiʃi'eiʃən], **satiety** [sə'taiəti] n. Satiété *f.; to the point of satiety,* jusqu'à satiété.

satin ['sætin] n. Satin *m.; satin finish,* apprêt satiné (of paper). ‖ **Satin-paper,** n. Papier satiné *m.* ‖ **Satin-stitch,** n. Plumetis *m.* ‖ **Satin-wood,** n. BOT. Bois de citronnier *m.*
— adj. En satin ; *satin slippers,* souliers de satin.
— v. tr. Satiner.

satinette [sæti'net] n. Satinette *f.* (cotton); satinade *f.* (silk).

satiny [-i] adj. Satiné.

satire ['sætaiə*] n. Satire *f.* (literary). ‖ Ironie, raillerie *f.; sarcasme m.*

satiric(al) [sə'tirik(əl)] adj. Satirique (literature); sarcastique, railleur, moqueur (person).

satirist ['sætərist] n. Satirique *m.* ‖ Esprit mordant *m.; railleur m.* (person).

satirize [-raiz] v. tr. Satiriser, faire la satire de.

satisfaction [sætis'fækʃən] n. Satisfaction *f.; contentement, plaisir m. (at, with,* de); *to give satisfaction to,* contenter, satisfaire ; *to express satisfaction at* (or) *over,* se féliciter de ; *to note with satisfaction,* être heureux de noter. ‖ Réparation *f.* (of an insult); dédommagement *m.* (of a wrong); *to give s.o. satisfaction,* rendre raison à qqn. ‖ Information, édification *f.* (through persuasion); *proved to his satisfaction,* prouvé de manière à le convaincre. ‖ Assouvissement *m.* (of the appetite); apaisement *m.* (of curiosity, desire). ‖ COMM. Désintéressement (of a creditor); règlement, paiement, acquittement *m.; liquidation f.* (of a debt). ‖ Exécution *f.* (of a promise); accomplissement *m.* (of a requirement); *to enter satisfaction,* enregistrer l'acquittement d'une obligation. ‖ ECCLES. Satisfaction *f.*

satisfactorily [sætis'fæktərili] adv. De manière satisfaisante.

satisfactoriness [-inis] n. Caractère satisfaisant *m.*

satisfactory [-i] adj. Qui donne satisfaction (pupil); satisfaisant (reason, result); *to bring to a satisfactory conclusion,* mener à bien; *to give a satisfactory account of,* justifier de; *not to be satisfactory,* laisser à désirer. ‖ ECCLES. Satisfactoire, expiatoire.

satisfy ['sætisfai] v. tr. (2). Satisfaire, contenter, donner des sujets de satisfaction à (s.o.). ‖ Satisfaire (an ambition); répondre à (expectations, a need); assouvir (one's hatred); remplir (a requirement); *to satisfy the examiners,* être reçu (in an examination). ‖ Satisfaire (an appetite); assouvir (one's curiosity); *to be satisfied to,* trouver suffisant de, se contenter de. ‖ Convaincre, assurer (to persuade); dissiper, éclaircir, lever (a doubt); *to satisfy oneself that,* s'assurer que, être édifié sur le point de. ‖ Faire réparation à, satisfaire (one's honour). ‖ COMM. Satisfaire, désintéresser (a creditor); régler, payer, liquider (a debt); s'acquitter de (an obligation).
— v. intr. Satisfaire, donner satisfaction, être satisfaisant.

satisfying [-iŋ] adj. Satisfaisant; convaincant (argument). ‖ CULIN. Nourrissant.

satisfyingly [-iŋli] adv. De façon satisfaisante.

satrap ['sætræp] n. Satrape *m.*

saturable ['sætjurəbl] adj. Saturable.

saturate [-reit] v. tr. Saturer, imprégner, imbiber, tremper (*with*, de).
— [-rit] adj. Saturé.

saturation [sætju'reiʃən] n. CHIM. Saturation *f.; saturation point,* point de saturation. ‖ Imprégnation *f.;* trempage *m.* ‖ ELECTR. *Saturation voltage,* tension de saturation. ‖ COMM. *To reach saturation point,* être saturé (market). ‖ GEOL. *Zone of saturation,* nappe bathydrique.

Saturday ['sætədei] n. Samedi *m.*

Saturn ['sætə:n] n. ASTRON. Saturne *m.*

Saturnalia [sætə:'neiljə] n. Saturnales *f. pl.*

Saturnalian [-jən] adj. Des Saturnales. ‖ FIG. Orgiaque.

Saturnian [sæ'tə:niən] adj. ASTRON. De Saturne. ‖ Saturnien (age, verse).
— n. Vers saturnien *m.* ‖ Saturnien *m.*

saturnic [-nik] adj. MED. Saturnin.

saturnine [-nain] nadj. MED. *Saturnine poisoning,* saturnisme. ‖ CHIM. Saturnin; de plomb. ‖ FIG. Taciturne, sombre (temperament).

saturnism [-nizm] n. MED. Saturnisme *m.*

satyr ['sætə*] n. Satyre *m.*

satyric [sə'tirik] adj. Satyrique.

sauce [sɔ:s] n. CULIN. Sauce *f.; apple sauce,* compote de pommes; *chocolate sauce,* crème au chocolat; *shrimp sauce,* beurre de crevettes; *tomato sauce,* sauce tomate, coulis de tomate; *vinegar sauce,* vinaigrette, sauce piquante. ‖ FIG. Condiment, assaisonnement *m.; sel m.* (of danger). ‖ FIG. Insolence, impertinence, effronterie *f.* ‖ U. S. FAM. *Apple sauce,* flagornerie, pommade *f.;* allons donc!, je n'en crois rien! (interj.). ‖ **Sauce-boat,** n. Saucière *f.* ‖ **Sauce-cook,** n. Saucier *m.*
— v. tr. CULIN. Accompagner d'une sauce; assaisonner (*with*, de). ‖ FIG. Etre insolent avec.

saucebox [-bɔks] n. FAM. Effronté *s.*

saucepan [-pən] n. CULIN. Casserole *f.;* poêlon *m.; double saucepan,* bain-marie.

saucer ['sɔ:sə*] n. Soucoupe *f.* ‖ NAUT. Saucier *m.,* écuelle *f.* (of a capstan). ‖ ARTS. Godet *m.* ‖ AVIAT. *Flying saucer,* soucoupe volante. ‖ LOC. *Eyes as*

big as saucers, des yeux en boules de loto. ‖ **Saucer-eyed,** adj. Aux yeux en boule de loto.

saucily ['sɔ:sili] adv. Insolemment. ‖ FAM. Avec chic, coquettement.

sauciness [-nis] n. Impertinence, insolence, effronterie *f.;* toupet *m.* ‖ NAUT. Coquetterie *f.* ‖ FAM. Chic *m.* (of a hat).

saucy ['sɔ:si] adj. Effronté, impertinent, insolent. ‖ Gamin, mutin (gesture); mutin, affriolant (smile). ‖ Coquet, chic (hat). ‖ NAUT. Pimpant (ship).

Saudi ['sɔ:di] adj., n. GEOGR. Saoudien *adj., s.* ‖ **Saudi Arabia,** n. GEOGR. Arabie Saoudite *f.*

sauerkraut ['sauə*kraut] n. CULIN. Choucroute *f.*

sauna ['sɔ:nə] n. Sauna *m.*

saunter ['sɔ:ntə*] v. intr. Flâner, flânocher (to loiter); se balader; déambuler (to stroll).
— n. Flânerie *f.* (act); pas (*m.*) de promenade (gait).

saunterer [-rə*] n. Flâneur, museur *s.*

saurian ['sɔ:riən] adj., n. ZOOL. Saurien *m.*

sausage ['sɔsidʒ] n. CULIN. Saucisson *m.* (dry, preserved); saucisse *f.* (for cooking). ‖ MILIT. *Sausage balloon,* ballon d'observation, saucisse. ‖ **Sausage-meat,** n. CULIN. Chair à saucisse *f.* ‖ **Sausage-roll,** n. CULIN. Friand *m.*

sauté ['soutei] adj., n. CULIN. Sauté *adj., m.*
— v. tr. CULIN. Sauter, faire sauter.

savable ['seivəbl] adj. Récupérable.

savage ['sævidʒ] adj. Sauvage, de sauvage (customs, race). ‖ Féroce (animal); sauvage, cruel, brutal (blow); en rage, furieux (person).
— n. Sauvage, barbare *s.* (native); brute *f,* sauvage *m.* (person).
— v. tr. Attaquer sauvagement (of a dog), piétiner (of a horse). ‖ FIG. Ereinter, démolir (to criticize).

savagely [-li] adv. En sauvage. ‖ Furieusement; sauvagement, brutalement (brutally).

savageness [-nis], **savagery** [-ri] n. Etat sauvage *m.;* sauvagerie *f.* ‖ Fureur *f.* (anger); cruauté, sauvagerie *f.* (cruelty).

savanna(h) [sə'vænə] n. AGRIC. Savane *f.* ‖ U. S. Savannah *f.*

savant ['sævənt] n. Erudit, savant *m.*
— N. B. Le féminin, en anglais comme en français, est *savante.*

savate [sæ'væt] n. SPORTS. Savate *f.;* chausson *m.*

save [seiv] v. tr. Sauver (*from,* de) [a life, a person]; *to save from death,* arracher à la mort; *to save s.o. from falling,* empêcher qqn de tomber. ‖ Préserver, délivrer (*from,* de); garantir (*from,* contre). ‖ Sauver, sauvegarder (appearances); sauver, protéger (one's honour); *to save the situation,* se montrer à la hauteur des circonstances. ‖ Ménager (one's clothing); économiser, épargner, mettre de côté (one's money); gagner (time); éviter, épargner (trouble); garder (stamps). ‖ MED. Ménager (one's health). ‖ COMM. Economiser (labour); recueillir, capter (waste products). ‖ SPORTS. *To save the goal,* arrêter le ballon (in football). ‖ ECCLES. Sauver (the soul); *to be saved,* faire son salut. ‖ NAUT. Ne pas manquer (the tide). ‖ LOC. *God save the mark!,* Dieu me pardonne!; *God save the Queen!,* vive la reine! ‖ **Save-all,** n. Brûle-tout *m.*
— v. intr. Economiser, épargner, faire des économies, mettre de l'argent de côté. ‖ SPORTS. Arrêter le ballon (in football).
— n. SPORTS. Arrêt du ballon *m.* (in football).
— prep. Sauf, excepté, à l'exception de, hormis, sans compter, en dehors de; *save on that point,* à cela près.
— conj. *Save that,* sauf que, sinon que, à moins que.

saver [-ə*] n. Sauveur, libérateur *m.;* libératrice *f.* ‖ Personne (*f.*) qui économise. ‖ TECHN. Economiseur *m.* (device).

savin ['sævin] n. BOT. Sabine *f.*

saving ['seiviŋ] n. Sauvetage *m.;* action (*f.*) de sauver. ‖ COMM. Economie *f.* (of labour, time).

MED. Fait (m.) de ménager (one's health). ‖ FIN. Pl. Economies f. pl.; épargne f.; pécule m. ‖ ECCLES. Salut m. (of souls). ‖ **Savings-bank,** n. FIN. Caisse d'épargne f.
— adj. Econome, ménager (person); économique, qui économise (thing); *labour-saving device,* économiseur de main-d'œuvre. ‖ NAUT. *Life-saving,* de sauvetage (apparatus). ‖ ECCLES. Justifiant (grace). ‖ JUR. Restrictif (clause).
— prep. Sauf; excepté, hormis; si ce n'est.

savio(u)r [ˈseivjə*] n. Sauveur m. ‖ ECCLES. *Our Saviour,* Notre Sauveur.

savoir-faire [ˈsævwɑ:* ˈfeə*] n. Savoir-faire, doigté m.; diplomatie f.

savor [ˈseivə*] n. U. S. See SAVOUR.

savory [ˈseivəri] n. BOT., CULIN. Sariette f.

savour [ˈseivə*] n. Saveur f.; goût, arôme, parfum m. ‖ FIG. Arrière-goût, soupçon m.; pointe, trace f.
— v. tr. Savourer, goûter.
— v. intr. **To savour of,** sentir, avoir un goût de; FAM. Donner l'idée de, sentir.

savouriness [-rinis] n. Saveur, succulence, sapidité f.; bon goût m.

savourless [-lis] adj. Insipide, fade, sans saveur.

savoury [-ri] adj. Savoureux, succulent, appétissant. ‖ CULIN. Salé, piquant (unsweetened); *savoury herbs,* plantes aromatiques.
— n. CULIN. Plat épicé m.; mets relevés m. pl.; poisson fumé (or) salé m.

Savoy [səˈvɔi] n. GEOGR. Savoie f. ‖ CULIN. Chou frisé m.

savvy [ˈsævi] v. intr., tr. POP. Piger.
— n. POP. Jugeote f.; savoir m.
— adj. U. S. POP. Malin, roublard.

saw [sɔ:]. See SEE.

saw n. Dicton m. (See SAYING.)

saw Scie f.; *power saw,* scie mécanique. ‖ **Saw-file,** n. TECHN. Tiers-point m. ‖ **Saw-horse,** n. Chevalet m. ‖ **Saw-mill,** n. Scierie f. ‖ **Saw-pit,** n. Fosse (f.) de scieur de long. ‖ **Saw-toothed,** adj. Serrate, en dents de scie.
— v. tr. (115). Scier; *to saw through,* tronçonner (a log); scier, débiter en sciant (a board, a plank); sciotter (marble, stone). ‖ **Sawn-off** (or) U. S. **sawed-off shotgun,** n. Fusil à canon tronçonné.

sawbones [-bounz] n. FAM. Carabin m. (physician); charcutier m. (surgeon).

sawdust [-dʌst] n. Sciure f.

sawfish [-fiʃ] n. ZOOL. Poisson-scie m.

sawyer [-jə*] n. Scieur de long m. ‖ U. S. Arbre (m.) immergé gênant la navigation.

sax [sæks] n. Hache (f.) d'ouvrage. ‖ MUS., FAM. Saxe m.

saxhorn [ˈsækshɔ:n] n. MUS. Saxhorn m.

saxifrage [ˈsæksifridʒ] n. BOT. Saxifrage f.

Saxon [ˈsæksn] adj. Saxon. ‖ ARCHIT. Teutonique roman.
— n. Saxon s.

Saxony [-əni] n. GEOGR. Saxe f. ‖ Laine fine f.

saxophone [ˈsæksəfoun] n. MUS. Saxophone m.

say [sei] v. tr. (116). Dire (a sentence, a word); *to say again,* répéter, redire; *to say nothing,* se taire, ne rien dire; *to say the least,* le moins qu'on puisse dire; *much may be said on,* il y a beaucoup à dire sur. ‖ Réciter (a lesson). ‖ Dire, affirmer (an opinion); *you don't say!,* pas possible! ‖ Dire, penser (to like, to thing); *what do you say to it?,* qu'en dites-vous?, qu'en pensez-vous? ‖ Mettre (to estimate); *let's say about fifty yards,* mettons cinquante mètres environ. ‖ JUR. Alléguer. ‖ ECCLES. Dire (a prayer). ‖ LOC. *I say!,* dites donc! (to draw attention); fichtre! (in admiration, astonishment); *as they say,* comme dit l'autre, comme on dit; *say no more,* pas un mot de plus, n'en dites pas davantage; *to say the word,* donner l'ordre (to command); dire oui (to a marriage proposal); *that is to say,* c'est-à-dire; *that goes without saying,* cela va sans

dire (or) de soi; *you said it,* vous l'avez dit; *so to say,* pour ainsi dire.
— n. Dire, mot m.; parole f.; *to have one's say,* dire son mot (or) ce qu'on a à dire. ‖ Droit (m.) de donner son opinion; *to have a say in the matter,* avoir voix au chapitre, avoir son mot à dire.

saying [-in] n. Proverbe, adage m.; maxime f. ‖ Action (or) possibilité (f.) de dire; *saying and doing,* faire et dire; *there's no saying where we'll find it,* impossible de dire où nous le trouverons.

sbirro [ˈzbirou] (pl. **sbirri** [-i]) n. Sbire m.

sc. Written abbr. for *scilicet,* c'est-à-dire, c.-à-d.

scab [skæb] n. MED. Croûte, escarre f. ‖ ZOOL., MED., BOT. Gale f. ‖ TECHN. Dartre f. ‖ FAM. Canaille, racaille f.; salaud m. ‖ FAM. Jaune m. (blackleg).
— v. intr. MED. Former une croûte, se cicatriser. ‖ TECHN. Dartrer. ‖ FAM. Trahir ses camarades; remplacer un gréviste.

scabbard [ˈskæbəd] n. Gaine f. (of a dagger); fourreau m. (of a sword).

scabbiness [ˈskæbinis] n. MED. Etat galeux m. (of animals); état croûteux (of a wound). ‖ TECHN. Etat dartreux m. ‖ FAM. Ladrerie f.

scabby [ˈskæbi] adj. MED. Galeux (animal); croûteux, scabieux (wound). ‖ TECHN. Dartreux. ‖ FAM. Ladre, pingre, mesquin (person); sordide, méprisable (thing).

scabies [ˈskeibii:z] n. MED. Gale f.

scabious [-əs] adj. MED. Galeux.
— n. BOT. Scabieuse f.

scabrous [ˈskeibrəs] adj. Raboteux, rugueux. ‖ FIG. Scabreux, risqué.

scads [skædz] n. U. S. POP. Des tas m. pl.; des quantités industrielles f. pl. (lot); pèze m. (money).

scaffold [ˈskæfəld] n. ARCHIT. Echafaudage m. ‖ JUR. Echafaud m. ‖ THEATR. † Estrade f. (platform); tribunes f. pl. (seats). ‖ TECHN. Engorgement m.
— v. tr. ARCHIT. Dresser un échafaudage contre (or) autour de.
— v. intr. TECHN. S'engorger.

scaffolder [-ə*] n. ARCHIT. Echafaudeur m.

scaffolding [-iŋ] n. ARCHIT. Echafaudage m.; *fixed scaffolding,* sapine. ‖ **Scaffolding-pole,** n. Ecoperche, étamperche f.

scalable [ˈskeiləbl] adj. Qu'on peut escalader.

scalable adj. TECHN. Détartrable.

scalar [ˈskeilə*] adj. MATH. Scalaire.
— n. MATH. Grandeur scalaire f., scalaire m.

scald [skɔ:ld] v. tr. MED. Ebouillanter, échauder; *to be scalded to death,* mourir de ses brûlures. ‖ CULIN. Echauder (meat, milk); blanchir (vegetables); ébouillanter (a vessel).
— n. MED. Echaudure f. ‖ CULIN. Echaudage m. ‖ **Scald-head,** n. MED. Teigne f.

scalding [-iŋ] n. MED. Echaudage, ébouillantage m. ‖ CULIN. Cuisson (f.) jusqu'au point d'ébullition (of milk); blanchiment m. (of vegetables). ‖ **Scalding (-hot),** adj. Brûlant. ‖ **Scalding-room** (or) **-tube,** n. Echaudoir m.

scale [skeil] n. ZOOL. Ecaille f. (of fish). ‖ BOT. Teigne f. (of trees). ‖ MED. Squame f. (on skin); tartre m. (of teeth). ‖ CHIM. Oxyde m. (of copper, iron). ‖ TECHN. Tartre, entartrage, dépôt calcaire m. (on a boiler); pl. battitures f. pl. (on cast metal).
— v. tr. BOT. Exfolier. ‖ MED. Exfolier (bone); desquamer (skin); détartrer (teeth). ‖ CULIN. Ecailler (fish). ‖ TECHN. Entartrer (to cover with scales); détartrer, décaper (to scrape scales from).
— v. intr. S'écailler; s'effeuiller (colour); se déplâtrer (plaster). ‖ MED. S'exfolier (bone); se desquamer (skin). ‖ BOT. S'exfolier. ‖ TECHN. S'entartrer.

scale n. Plateau m. (for weighing); *to turn the scale,* faire pencher la balance. ‖ Pl. Balance f.; trébuchet m. (for gold); *kitchen* (or) *shop scales,*

balance à plateaux; *platform scales*, bascule. ‖ SPORTS. Pesage *m.* ‖ ASTRON. Balance *f.*
— v. tr. Peser.
— v. intr. Peser, avoir un poids de. ‖ **To scale in**, SPORTS. Passer au pesage (race-horse).

scale n. Echelle *f.* (of degrees); série, suite *f.* (of numbers); graduation *f.* (of a thermometer). ‖ Etendue *f.* (of a calamity); envergure *f.* (of an enterprise). ‖ COMM., FIN. Tarif *m.; gamme f.* (of prices); échelle *f.;* barème *m.* (of salaries); *tax on a descending scale*, impôt régressif. ‖ JUR. *Costs on the higher scale*, le maximum des frais. ‖ TECHN. *Standard scale*, échelle des calibres. ‖ RADIO. *Wavelength scale*, cadran des longueurs d'onde. ‖ GEOGR. Echelle *f.* (of a map); *on a large, small scale*, en grand, en petit; *large-scale map*, carte à grande échelle. ‖ TECHN. Cadran gradué, *m.; règle divisée f.* (of measurements); *diagonal scale*, échelle de proportion. ‖ MUS. Gamme *f.* ‖ ARTS. Echelle *f.* (of colours); gamme *f.* (of nuances); *scale drawing*, dessin à l'échelle. ‖ FIG. *Social scale*, échelle sociale. **Scale-paper**, n. Papier quadrillé *m.*
— v. tr. Faire l'ascension de (a mountain); escalader (a wall). ‖ ARTS. Tracer à l'échelle (a map). ‖ **To scale down**, réduire l'échelle de.

scaled [-d] adj. ZOOL. Ecaillé. ‖ MED. Squameux (skin). ‖ MATH. Ecaillé (triangle).

scalene ['skeili:n] adj. MATH., MED. Scalène.
— n. MATH. Triangle scalène *m.* ‖ MED. Scalène *m.*

scaler ['skeilə*] n. Ecailleur *m.* (of fish). ‖ TECHN. Nettoyeur *m.* (employee); piqueur, batteur *m.* (implement). ‖ MED. Rugine *f.*

scaliness [-inis] n. MED. Squamosité *f.*

scaling [-iŋ] n. CULIN. Ecaillage *m.* ‖ MED. Détartrage *m.* ‖ TECHN. Désincrustation *f.* (of a boiler); entartrage *m.* (on a boiler).

scaling n. SPORTS. Escalade *f.* ‖ FIN. Graduation *f.* ‖ ARTS. Dessin (or) tracé (*m.*) à l'échelle.

scallawag ['skæləwæg] n. See SCALLYWAG.

scallion ['skæljən] n. BOT. Ciboule, échalote *f.*

scallop ['skɔləp] n. ZOOL. Peigne *m.;* coquille Saint-Jacques *f.* ‖ CULIN. Coquille (*f.*) au gratin. ‖ ARTS. Découpure, dentelure *f.;* découpe *f.*, feston *m.* ‖ BLAS. Coquille *f.*
— v. tr. CULIN. Faire gratiner en coquilles. ‖ ARTS. Denteler, découper.

scalloped [-d] adj. CULIN. Gratiné, au gratin. ‖ ARTS. Dentelé (design); découpé (embroidery). ‖ ARCHIT. En écailles (moulding).

scallywag ['skæliwæg] n. FAM. Vaurien, garnement, chenapan *m.*

scalp [skælp] n. MED. Epicrâne, cuir chevelu *m.* ‖ GEOGR. Sommet pelé *m.* (of a mountain). ‖ U. S. Scalpe *m.* (in Indian warfare); ‖ **Scalp-hunter**, n. Chasseur (*m.*) de têtes; FAM. Ereinteur *m.* (critic).
— v. tr. MED. Ruginer. ‖ COMM. Mévendre. ‖ FIN. Boursicoter. ‖ FAM. Ereinter.

scalpel [-əl] n. MED. Scalpel *m.*

scalper [-ə*] n. U. S. Chasseur (*m.*) de têtes. ‖ U. S. COMM., FIN. Trafiqueur; boursicoteur *m.*

scaly ['skeili] adj. ZOOL. Ecailleux. ‖ MED. Squameux. ‖ TECHN. Tartreux (boiler); lamellé, lamelleux, paillé (metal). ‖ POP. Mesquin, chiche (action); minable, piètre (appearance).

scamp [skæmp] n. Garnement, chenapan *m.; little scamp*, petit polisson.
— v. tr. Bâcler, bousiller, torchonner. (See BOTCH.)

scamper [-ə*]n. Bâcleur, bousilleur *m.*

scamper n. Course allègre (or) rapide *f.*
— v. intr. FAM. Courir allègrement; *to scamper away*, détaler; *to scamper through*, traverser (or) parcourir au galop.

scampi [-pi] n. ZOOL. Langoustine *f.*

scan [skæn] n. Regard scrutateur *m.*
— v. tr. Examiner, scruter (a face); promener un regard sur (a group); sonder (the horizon); toiser

(s.o.) [from head to foot]. ‖ Feuilleter, parcourir rapidement, jeter un coup d'œil sur (a book). ‖ Scander, mesurer (verse). ‖ RADIO. Balayer.
— v. intr. Se scander (poetry).

scandal ['skændl] n. Scandale, opprobre *m.;* honte, affaire scabreuse *f.; to create a scandal*, faire un esclandre. ‖ Médisance *f.; cancans m. pl.* (gossip); *to talk scandal*, cancaner; *to talk scandal about*, médire de, cancaner sur; casser du sucre sur le dos de (fam.). ‖ JUR. Diffamation *f.;* atteinte (*f.*) à la dignité du tribunal. ‖ **Scandal-monger**, n. Cancanier *m.;* mauvaise langue *f.;* colporteur (*m.*) d'histoires scandaleuses.

scandalize [-aiz] v. tr. Scandaliser (see SHOCK); *to be scandalized*, se scandaliser.

scandalous [-əs] adj. Scandaleux, honteux, odieux (conduct, happening); mauvais (tongue); *it's scandalous*, c'est une honte; *scandalous gossip*, chronique scandaleuse; *scandalous thing*, indignité. ‖ JUR. Calomnieux, diffamatoire (accusation, statement).

scandalously [-li] adv. Scandaleusement.

scandalousness [-nis] n. Indignité, infamie *f.* (of an action, of conduct); caractère scandaleux *m.* (of a spectacle).

Scandinavia [,skændi'neivjə] n. GEOGR. Scandinavie *f.*

Scandinavian [-ən] adj., n. GEOGR. Scandinave *s.*

scanner ['skænə*] n. Scrutateur *m.*, scrutatrice *f.* ‖ Sondeur *s.* (of a thought). ‖ Prosodiste *s.* ‖ RADIO. Scanner *m.*

scanning [-iŋ] adj. Scrutateur *m.;* scrutatrice *f.*
— n. Scansion *f.* (of verse). ‖ Examen minutieux *m.* ‖ RADIO. Balayage *m.*, exploration *f.*

scansion ['skænʃən] n. Scansion *f.*

scansorial [skæn'sɔ:riəl] adj., n. ZOOL. Grimpeur *s.*

scant [skænt] adj. Sommaire (attire); faible, bien juste (measure, weight); maigre (success); pauvre (vegetation); *to be scant of*, avoir peu de; *scant of speech*, peu communicatif, avare de paroles. ‖ MED. *Scant of breath*, hors d'haleine, essoufflé, poussif. ‖ NAUT. Pointu (wind).
— v. intr. NAUT. Refuser (wind).
— v. tr. *To scant s.o. of sth.*, mesurer qqch. à qqn avec parcimonie.

scanties [-iz] n. U. S. Slip (*m.*) de dame.

scantily [-ili] adv. Maigrement, chichement, de façon insuffisante. ‖ Etroitement. ‖ Sommairement, à la légère (dressed).

scantiness [-inis] n. Etroitesse *f.* (of a garment); insuffisance *f.* (of measure, quantity, weight); exiguïté *f.* (of resources); pauvreté *f.* (of vegetation).

scantling [-liŋ] n. Petite quantité *f.* ‖ Volige *f.;* madrier *m.; building scantling*, échantillon de construction. ‖ TECHN. Chantier *m.* (for barrel-manufacturing). ‖ NAUT. Pl. Echantillons *m. pl.*

scantly [-li] adv. Insuffisamment; chichement, mesquinement.

scanty [-i] adj. Restreint, tout juste suffisant, peu abondant. ‖ Maigre (meal); rare (vegetation).

scape [skeip] n. BOT. Hampe *f.* ‖ ZOOL. Scape *m.* (of an antenna); tuyau *m.* (of a feather). ‖ ARCHIT. Fût *m.* (of a column).

scapegoat ['skeipgout] n. ECCLES. Bouc émissaire *m.* ‖ FAM. Bouc émissaire, lampiste *m.*

scapegrace [-greis] n. Garnement, mauvais sujet *m.* ‖ Enfant incorrigible *m.;* désespoir (*m.*) de la famille (fam.).

scapula ['skæpjulə] (pl. **scapulae** [-i:]) n. MED. Omoplate *f.*

scapular [-ə*] adj. ZOOL. Scapulaire. ‖ MED. De l'omoplate; scapulaire; thoracique.
— n. ECCLES. Scapulaire *m.* ‖ ZOOL. Rémige scapulaire *f.*

scapulary [-əri] adi. ECCLES. Scapulaire.

scar [skɑ:*] n. MED. Cicatrice *f.* (in general); balafre *f.* (on the face). ‖ BOT. Hile *m.* ‖ **Scar-face,** n. MED. Balafré *m.* ‖ **Scar-tissue,** n. MED. Tissu cicatriciel *m.*
— v. tr. MED. Balafrer (the face); laisser une cicatrice sur (the skin).
— v. intr. To scar **over,** se cicatriser.
scar [skɑ:*] n. Rocher escarpé *m.*
scarab ['skærəb], **scarabaeus** [skærə'biəs] n. ZOOL. Scarabée *m.*
scarce [skɛəs] adj. Rare, peu abondant (see RARE); *to become* (or) *grow scarce,* se faire rare; *to be scarce of,* être à court de. ‖ FAM. *To make oneself scarce,* s'esquiver, s'éclipser, se défiler.
scarcely [-li] adv. Presque pas, à peine, ne... guère (see HARDLY); *scarcely ever,* presque jamais; *to have scarcely any time,* n'avoir guère de temps; *to be scarcely able to walk,* pouvoir à peine marcher; *to be scarcely able to believe,* avoir du mal (or) de la peine à croire; *I scarcely know,* je ne sais pas trop. ‖ Certainement pas, probablement pas (expressing incredulity); *you can scarcely have finished,* vous n'avez sûrement pas fini.
scarceness [-nis], **scarcity** [-iti] n. Manque *m.;* rareté, disette, pénurie *f.* ‖ Raréfaction *f.* (of labour); *scarcity of money,* crise financière.
scare [skɛə*] n. Panique *f.; to create a scare,* semer la panique; *to give s.o. a scare,* faire une peur terrible à qqn; *scare headline,* manchette sensationnelle. ‖ **Scare-monger,** n. Alarmiste, paniquard *m.,* semeur (*s.*) de panique.
— v. tr. Effarer, effrayer, épouvanter (s.o.) [see FRIGHTEN]; *to scare away,* effaroucher, faire fuir en effrayant (a wild animal).
— v. intr. U. S. Prendre peur, s'effaroucher.
scarecrow [-krou] n. Epouvantail *m.* ‖ FAM. Epouvantail *m.* (fright); *dressed like a scarecrow,* dépenaillé.
scared [-d] adj. Terrifié, épouvanté; *scared out of one's wits,* fou d'épouvante; *to be scared to death,* mourir de peur.
scarf [skɑ:f] n. Echarpe *f.;* cravate *f.* (cravat); fichu, cache-col, cache-nez *m.* (muffler); foulard *m.* (silk); carré *m.* (square). ‖ U. S. Chemin (*m.*) de table (runner). ‖ ECCLES. Etole *f.* ‖ MILIT. Echarpe *f.* ‖ **Scarf-skin,** n. MED. Epiderme *m.;* cuticule *f.*
— N. B. Deux pluriels : *scarfs, scarves.*
scarf n. ARCHIT. Assemblage (*m.*) à mi-bois; enture *f.* ‖ TECHN. Chanfrein (*m.*) de soudure.
— v. tr. NAUT. Enter. ‖ TECHN. Amorcer.
scarification [skɛərifi'keiʃən] n. MED. Scarification *f.* ‖ AGRIC. Extirpation *f.*
scarificator ['skɛərifikeitə*] n. MED. Scarificateur *m.*
scarifier [-faiə*] n. MED. Scarificateur *m.* ‖ AGRIC. Extirpateur *m.* ‖ TECHN. *Road scarifier,* piocheuse scarificatrice.
scarify [fai] v. tr. (2). MED. Scarifier. ‖ AGRIC. Ecroûter, ameublir. ‖ FAM. Ereinter (by criticism).
scarifying [-faiiŋ] adj. FIG. Cinglant (reproach).
— n. MED. Scarifiage *m.* ‖ AGRIC. Ecroûtage *m.* ‖ FIG. Ereintement *m.*
scarlatina [skɑ:lə'ti:nə] n. MED. Scarlatine *f.*
scarlet ['skɑ:lit] adj. Ecarlate (colour); coquelicot (dress); *to blush scarlet,* s'empourprer (cheeks); devenir cramoisi (person). ‖ MED. *Scarlet fever* (or) *rash,* scarlatine. ‖ ECCLES. *Scarlet hat,* chapeau de cardinal. ‖ BOT. *Scarlet pimpernel,* mouron rouge. ‖ FAM. *Scarlet woman,* prostituée.
— n. Ecarlate *f.* ‖ ECCLES. Pourpre *f.*
scarp [skɑ:p] n. GEOGR. Escarpement *m.* (of a hill). ‖ MILIT. Escarpe *f.*
— v. tr. Rendre escarpé (or) abrupt.
scarp n. BLAS. Echarpe *f.*
scarped [-d] adj. Abrupt, à pic. ‖ MILIT. Escarpé.

scarper ['skɑ:pə*] v. intr. POP. Se débiner, se tailler, se barrer, se calter.
scarred [skɑ:d] adj. MED. Balafré (face); plein de cicatrices, couturé (skin); grêlé (by smallpox); *scarred over,* cicatrisé.
scarus ['skɛərəs] n. ZOOL. Scare; perroquet (*m.*) de mer.
scary ['skɛəri] adj. U. S. Peureux, timide (frightened); épouvantable, effroyable (frightening).
scat [skæt] interj. FAM. Filez!, ouste!
scathe [skeiδ] v. tr. Nuire à. ‖ Foudroyer (by lightning). ‖ FIG. Cingler, blesser (by criticism).
— n. Dommage *m.* ‖ FIG. Blessure *f.*
scatheless [-lis]. † adj. Indemne.
scathing [-iŋ] adj. FIG. Acerbe, cinglant, caustique, mordant (comment); sanglant, virulent (criticism); âpre (irony).
scatological [skætə'lɔdʒikəl] adj. Scatologique.
scatology [skə'tɔlədʒi] n. Scatologie *f.* ‖ MED. Coprologie *f.*
scatophage ['skætəfeidʒ] n. ZOOL. Scatophage *m.*
scatter ['skætə*] n. Eparpillement *m.,* dispersion *f.*
— v. tr. Faire envoler (birds); dissiper (clouds); disperser (a crowd); éparpiller (leaves); disséminer (news); *to scatter papers on the floor,* joncher le plancher de papiers; *city scattered with parks,* ville parsemée de parcs. ‖ AGRIC. Epandre (fertilizer); semer (seeds). ‖ MILIT. Disperser (the enemy); écarter, éparpiller (shot). ‖ **Scatter-brain,** n. FAM. Etourdi, évaporé, écervelé *s.;* tête de linotte *f.* ‖ **Scatter-brained,** adj. FAM. Etourdi, écervelé; *to be scatter-brained,* n'avoir pas de plomb dans la cervelle, avoir une tête de linotte.
— v. intr. S'éparpiller, se disperser, se débander.
scatty ['skæti] adj. FAM. Qui n'a rien dans le citron, écervelé.
scavenge ['skævindʒ] v. tr. Vider (dust-bins, garbage-cans); ramasser (rubbish); balayer (the streets). ‖ TECHN. Balayer, refouler. ‖ MILIT. Ecouvillonner.
— v. intr. Fouiller dans les poubelles. ‖ ZOOL. Se nourrir d'ordures (beetle).
scavenger [-ə*] n. Eboueur, boueux, balayeur (*m.*) des rues. ‖ Egoutier *m.* (sewer-worker). ‖ ZOOL. Coprophage *m.* ‖ **Scavenger-beetle,** n. ZOOL. Nécrophore *m.;* fouille-merde *m.* (pop.).
scavenging [-iŋ], **scavengery** [-əri] n. Enlèvement (*m.*) des ordures (refuse disposal); balayage *m.* (street-cleaning). ‖ TECHN. Balayage *m.* ‖ MILIT. Ecouvillonnage *m.*
scenario [si'nɛə:rio] n. CINEM. Scénario *m.* ‖ THEATR. Canevas *m.* (of a play). ‖ **Scenario-writer,** n. Scénariste *m.*
scene [si:n] n. Scène *f.;* spectacle *m.* (sight); décor, cadre, paysage *m.;* vue, perspective *f.* (surroundings, view); *change of scene,* changement d'air. ‖ THEATR. Scène *f.* (locale, subdivision); décor (scenery); *the scene is laid in Paris,* l'action se situe (or) se passe à Paris; *the scene changes,* l'action change de théâtre. ‖ JUR. Lieux *m. pl.* (of a crime); théâtre, lieu *m.* (of events). ‖ MILIT. Théâtre *m.* (of operations). ‖ FIG. *Behind the scenes,* en sous-main, dans les coulisses; *the political scene,* la scène politique; *what goes on behind the scenes,* le dessous des cartes. ‖ FIG. Incident, drame *m.;* scène, histoire, querelle *f.; to make a scene,* faire une scène (or) un esclandre. ‖ **Scene-dock,** n. THEATR. Remise (*f.*) à décors. ‖ **Scene-painter,** n. THEATR. Brosseur (*m.*) de décors. ‖ **Scene-shifter,** n. THEATR. Machiniste *m.*
scenery [-əri] n. Vue *f.;* paysage *m.* ‖ THEATR. Scène *f.; décors m. pl.*
scenic [-ik] adj. THEATR. Scénique, théâtral. ‖ ARTS. Scénique. ‖ FIG. Théâtral, spectaculaire.
scenography [si:'nɔgrəfi] n. Scénographie *f.* ‖ ARTS. Dessin (*m.*) en perspective.
scent [sent] n. Parfum *m.;* senteur *f.* (fragrance);

odeur *f.* (smell). ‖ Parfum *m.* (liquid) ; *to use scent,* se parfumer. ‖ Odorat, flair *m.* (sense of smell) ; *to have no scent,* n'avoir pas de nez (animal). ‖ Sports. Fumet, vent *m.* (smell) ; piste, voie, trace *f.* (track) ; *on the right scent,* sur la piste ; *to lose* (or) *be thrown off the scent,* perdre le pied ; *to throw off the scent,* dépister. ‖ Fig. *To get scent of,* avoir vent de ; *to put on a false scent,* aiguiller sur une fausse piste ; *to throw off the scent,* dérouter (the police). ‖ **Scent-bag,** n. Sachet à parfums *m.*; Zool. Poche à sécrétion odoriférante *f.* ‖ **Scent-bottle,** n. Flacon (*m.*) de parfum. ‖ **Scent-spray,** n. Vaporisateur *m.*
— v. tr. Parfumer, embaumer (the air) ; imprégner (*with,* de) [a garment]. ‖ Sports. Flairer, sentir (a quarry). ‖ Fam. Flairer, subodorer (trouble).
— v. intr. Sentir, flairer. ‖ Avoir de l'odorat (or) du nez.
scented [-id] adj. Parfumé, embaumé, imprégné (*with,* de). ‖ Bot. Odoriférant (garden) ; odorant (herb). ‖ Zool. *Keen-scented,* au nez fin (hound).
scentless [-lis] adj. Inodore, sans parfum (flower). ‖ Sports. Sans fumet.
scepsis ['skepsis] n. Philos. Scepticisme *m.*
sceptic ['skeptik] n. Sceptique *s.*
sceptical [-əl] adj. Sceptique.
sceptically [-əli] adv. En sceptique, avec scepticisme, sceptiquement.
scepticism ['skeptisizm] n. Scepticisme *m.*
sceptre ['septə*] n. Sceptre *m.*
schedule ['ʃedju:l] (U. S. ['skedju:l]) n. Comm. Nomenclature *f.* (of accounts) ; liste officielle *f.* (of charges) ; inventaire *m.* (of machines) ; barème *m.* (of prices) ; cédule *f.* (of taxes). ‖ Jur. Bilan *m.* (of bankruptcy) ; bordereau *m.* (memorandum) ; annexe *f.* (of a statute). ‖ U. S. Ch. de f. Horaire, indicateur *m.*; *on schedule,* selon l'horaire. ‖ U. S. Calendrier *m.* (of events) ; plan *m.* (of a work project) ; *according to schedule,* selon les prévisions.
— v. tr. Classer (*as,* comme). ‖ Jur. Ajouter comme annexe, inscrire (an item). ‖ U. S. Inscrire au programme (an event) ; dresser le plan de (a job) ; *scheduled to speak,* prévu comme orateur. ‖ Ch. de f. Inscrire à l'horaire (a train).
scheduled [-d] adj. Fin. Selon le tarif (prices) ; cédulaire (taxes). ‖ Ch. de f. Indiqué (hour, train). ‖ U. S. *To be scheduled,* figurer au programme (event).
schema ['ski:mə] (pl. **schemata** [-tə]) n. Schéma *m.* ‖ Gramm. Figure (*f.*) de mots. ‖ Philos. Schème *m.*
schematic [ski:'mætik] adj. Schématique.
schematize ['ski:mətaiz] v. tr. Schématiser.
scheme [ski:m] n. Combinaison *f.*; arrangement *m.*; *scheme of things,* ordre de la nature. ‖ Plan, projet *m.*; étude *f.* ‖ Système, barème *m.* (of test grades). ‖ Exposé *m.* (outline) ; plan, topo *m.* (schema). ‖ Arts. *Colour scheme,* combinaison (*f.*) de couleurs. ‖ Milit. Plan *m.* (of demobilization) ; thème *m.* (of exercise). ‖ Jur. *Scheme of composition,* concordat préventif à la faillite. ‖ Fig. Machination, intrigue, cabale *f.*; complot *m.*; *shady scheme,* combine.
— v. intr. Comploter, intriguer, ruser ; *to scheme for,* briguer (a job) ; *to scheme to do sth.,* combiner de faire qqch.
— v. tr. Combiner, machiner (a plot). ‖ **Scheme-arch,** n. Archit. Arc surbaissé.
schemer [-ə*] n. Intrigant, comploteur *m.*; machinateur, *m.*; machinatrice *f.*; *to be a clever schemer,* savoir nager (fam.). ‖ Faiseur (*m.*) de plans, bâtisseur (*m.*) de projets.
scherzo ['skeətsou] (pl. **scherzos** [-ɔ:z]) n. Mus. Scherzo *m.*
schism ['sizm] n. Eccles. Schisme *m.*
schismatic [siz'mætik] adj., n. Eccles. Schismatique *s.*

schist [ʃist] n. Schiste *m.*
schistose ['ʃistous], **schistous** [-əs] adj. Schisteux.
schizo ['skitsou] (pl. **schizos** [-ɔ:z]) adj., n. Fam. Schizo, schizophrène *adj., s.*
schizogenesis [,skaidzo'ʒenəsis] n. Fissiparité *f.*
schizoid ['skitsɔid] adj., n. Med. Schizoïde *adj., s.*
schizophrenia [,skitzo'fri:niə] n. Med. Schizophrénie *f.*
schizophrenic [-'fri:nik] adj. Med. Schizophrène.
schmaltz [ʃmælts] n. U. S. Mus. Fam. Musique sentimentale *f.*
schnapps [ʃnæps] n. Culin. Schnaps *m.*
schnorkel ['ʃnɔ:kl] n. Naut. Schnorchel *m.* ‖ Sports. Tuba *m.*
scholar ['skɔlə*] n. Elève, écolier *s.* (school-boy or -girl) ; élève, disciple *m.* (follower) ; *apt scholar,* persone qui apprend facilement. ‖ Erudit, savant, intellectuel, homme (*m.*) d'étude ; *fine scholar,* fin lettré ; *Greek, Latin scholar,* helléniste, latiniste. ‖ Boursier *s.* (scholarship holder).
scholarly [-li] adj. Savant (literature) ; érudit (person) ; d'érudition (work).
scholarship [-ʃip] n. Savoir *m.*; érudition, science *f.* ‖ Humanisme *m.* (in the humanities) ; connaissance *f.* (in languages). ‖ Bourse (*f.*) d'études (award) ; *to win a scholarship,* obtenir une bourse.
scholastic [sko'læstik] adj. Dans l'enseignement (post) ; de l'enseignement (profession) ; scolaire (year). ‖ Pédant (manner, speech). ‖ Philos. Scolastique.
— n. Philos. Scolastique *m.*
scholasticism [-tisizm] n. Philos. Scolastique *f.*
scholium ['skouliəm] n. Scolie *f.*
— N. B. Deux pluriels : *scholiums, scholia.*
school [sku:l] n. Ecole *f.*; *high school,* école secondaire, collège, U. S. établissement d'enseignement secondaire correspondant au second cycle des lycées ; *non-provided* (or) U. S. *private school,* école libre ; *public school,* grande école d'enseignement secondaire, U. S. école communale ; *secondary school,* école secondaire. ‖ Ecole *f.*; classes *f. pl. lower, middle, upper school,* petites, moyennes, hautes (or) grandes classes. ‖ Classe, école *f.* (school ing) ; *to be in* (or) *at school,* être en classe ; *to go to school,* aller en classe (or) à l'école ; *school fees,* frais scolaires. ‖ Ecole, académie *f.*; cours, institut *m.* (for specialized or technical training) ; faculté, section *f.* (of a college, university) ; *evening* (or) *night school,* école (or) classe (or) cours du soir ; *summer school,* cours de vacances (or) d'été. ‖ Eccles. *Denominational* (or) U. S. *parochial school,* école confessionnelle ; *Sunday school,* catéchisme. ‖ Milit. Ecole *f.* ‖ Techn. *Technical* (or) *trade school,* école des arts et métiers (or) professionnelle (or) industrielle ; *school of mines,* école des mines. ‖ Arts. *Art school,* académie d'art ; *the French school,* l'école française (manner, theory). ‖ Mus. *Dancing school,* académie (or) cours de danse ; *music school,* conservatoire de musique (institution) ; méthode de musique (manual). ‖ Autom. *Driving school,* auto-école. ‖ Sports. *Fencing school,* salle d'escrime. ‖ Philos. Ecole *f.*; disciples *m. pl.* (of a great master) ; école *f.* (of thought). ‖ Fig. Ecole *f.* (of adversity) ; *gentleman of the old school,* homme de la vieille école. ‖ **School-book,** n. Livre scolaire (or) de classe. ‖ **School-day,** n. Jour (*m.*) de classe ; pl. Vie scolaire *f.*; années (*f. pl.*) d'école. ‖ **School-house,** n. Ecole, maison d'école *f.*; pensionnat *m.* (boarding-school). ‖ **School-ma'am,** n. Fam. Maîtresse d'école, institutrice *f.* ‖ **School-mate,** n. Condisciple, camarade (*s.*) de classe (or) d'école. ‖ **School-teacher,** n. Maître *m.* (or) maîtresse (*f.*) d'école ; instituteur *m.*; institutrice *f.*
— v. tr. Envoyer à l'école, instruire ; former (an

animal, a child). ‖ Discipliner (a gesture, one's voice); *to school s.o. to do sth.*, entraîner qqn à faire qqch.; *to school oneself to routine*, s'astreindre à la routine. ‖ THEATR., FIG. *To school s.o. in a part*, apprendre son rôle à qqn.

school [sku:l] n. ZOOL. Banc *m.* (of fish); bande *f.* (of porpoises).
— v. intr. ZOOL. Aller par bancs (fish); se réunir en bande (porpoises).

schoolboy [-bɔi] n. Ecolier, élève *m.*

schooled [-d] adj. Dressé (animal); formé, entraîné, rompu (child); acquis, discipliné (patience).

schoolfellow [-felou] n. Camarade (*s.*) d'école; condisciple *s.*; compagne *f.*

schoolgirl [-gə:l] n. Ecolière, élève *f.*; *schoolgirl complexion*, teint frais de petite pensionnaire.

schooling [-iŋ] n. Instruction, éducation *f.*; enseignement *m.*; études *f. pl.*

schoolman [-mən] (pl. **schoolmen**) n. PHILOS. Scolastique *m.*; *the Schoolmen*, l'Ecole. ‖ U. S. Professeur *m.*

schoolmaster [-mɑ:stə*] n. Instituteur, maître (*m.*) d'école (primary); professeur *m.* (secondary). ‖ Directeur *m.* (headmaster).

schoolmistress [-mistris] n. Institutrice, maîtresse d'école *f.* (primary); professeur *m.* (secondary). ‖ Directrice *f.* (headmistress).

schoolroom [-rum] n. Salle de classe, classe *f.*

schooner ['sku:nə*] n. NAUT. Goélette *f.*; schooner *m.* ‖ **Schooner-rigged**, adj. NAUT. Gréé en goélette.

schooner n. U. S. Chope *f.* (of beer).

schottische [ʃɔ'ti:ʃ] n. MUS. Scottish *f.*

sciagram ['saiəgræm] n. ARTS. Sciographie *f.* (process); silhouette *f.* (result). ‖ MED. Skiagramme *m.*

sciagraph [-grɑ:f] n. MED. Skiagramme *m.* ‖ ARCHIT. Sciographie *f.*; coupe verticale *f.*

sciagraphy [sai'ægrəfi] n. MED. Skiagraphie *f.* ‖ ARTS., ASTRON. Sciographie *f.*

sciatic [sai'ætik] adj. MED. Sciatique.

sciatica [-tikə] n. MED. Sciatique *f.*

science ['saiəns] n. Science *f.*; savoir *m.*; connaissances *f. pl.*; *physical sciences*, sciences physiques; *social science*, sciences sociales (or) humaines. ‖ **Science fiction**, n. Science-fiction *f.*

scienter [sai'entə*] adv. JUR. A bon escient.
— n. *To prove a scienter*, prouver qu'un acte a été commis à bon escient.

scientific [saiən'tifik] adj. Scientifique. ‖ Etudié, recherché (cruelty); de précision (instruments); de science (person). ‖ SPORTS. Qui boxe scientifiquement (boxer).

scientist ['saiəntist] n. Homme de science, savant *m.*; *Christian Scientist*, scientiste chrétien.

scientology [,saiən'tɔlədʒi] n. ECCLES. Scientologie *f.*

sci-fi ['sai'fai] n. Science-fiction, S.-F. *f.*

scilicet ['sili,set] adv. C'est-à-dire.

scimitar ['simitə*] n. Cimeterre *m.*

scintilla [sin'tilə] n. Soupçon, fragment, impondérable *m.*; parcelle *f.*; miette *f.* (fam.). ‖ Indice infime *m.* (of evidence); étincelle *f.* (of genius).

scintillant ['sintilənt], **scintillating** [-leitiŋ] adj. Scintillant, étincelant.

scintillate [-leit] v. intr. Scintiller, étinceler.

scintillation [,sinti'leiʃən] n. ASTRON. Scintillation *f.* ‖ FIG. Pétillement *m.* (of wit).

sciolism ['saiolizm] n. Demi-savoir *m.*; demi-science *f.*

sciolist [-list] n. Demi-savant, faux savant *m.*

scion ['saiən] n. BOT. † Surgeon *m.* ‖ BOT. Scion, greffon *m.* ‖ FIG. Héritier, rejeton *m.*

scirrhosity [si'rɔsiti] n. MED. Squirrosité *f.*

scirrhous ['sirəs] adj. MED. Squirrheux.

scirrhus n. MED. Squirre *m.*

scissile ['sisil] adj. Scissile, fissile.

scission ['siʃən] n. Coupage *m.* (with a cutting-

edge); cisaillement *m.* (with scissors). ‖ FIG. Scission, division *f.*

scissor [sizə*] n. Pl. Ciseaux *m. pl.*; *three pairs of scissors*, trois ciseaux; *to work with scissors and paste*, travailler à coups de ciseaux. ‖ CH. DE F. *Scissors crossing*, traversée bretelle. ‖ TECHN. *Hoisting scissors*, louve à pinces. ‖ SPORTS. Coup (*m.*) de ciseaux (in swimming); *scissors jump*, saut en coup de ciseaux; *scissors stop*, arrêt en ciseaux (in skiing). ‖ **Scissor-bill**, n. ZOOL. Bec-en-ciseaux *m.*
— v. tr. Cisailler.

scissoring [-riŋ] n. Cisaillement *m.*

sclaff [sklæf] n. SPORTS. Coup éraflant *m.* (in golf).
— v. tr. SPORTS. Erafler.

sclera ['skliərə] n. MED. Sclérotique *f.*

scleroderma [,skliəro'də:mə] n. MED. Sclérodermie *f.*

sclerometer [skliə'rɔmitə*] n. PHYS. Scléromètre *m.*

sclerosed ['skliərouzd] adj. MED. Sclérosé.

sclerosis [skliə'rousis] n. MED. Sclérose *f.*; *disseminated* (or) *insular sclerosis*, sclérose en plaques.

sclerotic [-'rɔtik] adj. MED. Sclérotique.

sclerotitis [,skliərou'taitis] n. MED. Sclérotite *f.*

sclerous ['skliərəs] adj. MED. Scléreux.

scoobs [skɔbz] n. pl. Limaille *f.* (of metal); sciure *f.* (sawdust); copeaux *m. pl.* (wood chips). ‖ Scorie *f.* (dross).

scoff [skɔf] n. Sarcasme *m.*; raillerie *f.* (act); objet (*m.*) de risée (laughing-stock).
— v. intr. Se moquer. ‖ **To scoff at**, mépriser (a danger); faire les gorges chaudes de, railler (s.o.); *to be scoffed at*, recueillir des railleries, être un objet de risée.

scoff n. POP. Bouffe, tortore *f.*
— v. tr. POP. Bâfrer, bouffer.

scoffer [-ə*] n. Railleur *s.*

scoffing [-iŋ] adj. Railleur, moqueur.
— n. Raillerie, moquerie *f.*

scold [skould] n. Grondeuse *f.*; femme criarde (or) querelleuse *f.*; ronchonneuse, bougone *f.* (fam.).
— v. intr. Grogner, gronder, criailler, ronchonner.
— v. tr. Gronder, morigéner, tancer.

scolding [-iŋ] adj. Grondeur, bougon, criard, ronchonneur.
— n. Criaillerie *f.* ‖ Gronderie, réprimande, semonce *f.* (reproaches).

scolia ['skouliə] n. ZOOL. Scolie *f.*

scolion ['skouliən] n. MUS. Scolie *m.*

scoliosis [skouli'ousis] n. MED. Scoliose *f.*

scollop ['skɔləp] n. See SCALLOP.

scolopendra [,skɔlo'pendrə] n. ZOOL. Scolopendre *f.*

scomber ['skɔmbə*] n. ZOOL. Maquereau *m.*

sconce [skɔns] n. Bougeoir *m.* ‖ Flambeau *m.* (on a piano); applique *f.* (on a wall). ‖ Bobèche *f.* (of a candle-holder); coin du feu *m.* (of a fireplace).

sconce n. MILIT. Fort détaché, fortin *m.* ‖ **Sconce-piece**, n. Iceberg (*m.*) à ras d'eau.

scone [skɔn] n. CULIN. Galette (*f.*) au lait.

scoop [sku:p] n. Pelle à main *f.*; couteau *m.* (for cheese); main *f.* (in a grocery shop); louche *f.* (for ice-cream); nacelle *f.* (for weighing); *coal scoop*, seau à charbon. ‖ Coup (*m.*) de pelle; action *f.* (or) geste (*m.*) d'enlever à la pelle (or) à la louche. ‖ NAUT. Ecope *f.* ‖ MED. Curette, gouge *f.*; *aural scoop*, cure-oreille. ‖ CH. DE F. Cuiller *f.* (of a locomotive); ‖ TECHN. Godet *m.* (of a dredger); cuiller (*f.*) de graissage (of an engine). ‖ FAM. Reportage exclusif *m.*; primeur d'une nouvelle sensationnelle *f.* (in journalism). ‖ POP. Rafle *f.*; coup de filet; gros bénéfice *m.*; *to make a scoop*, réussir un coup. ‖ **Scoop-net**, n. Epuisette, drague *f.*
— v. tr. **To scoop out**, excaver (earth); évider (vegetables); écoper (water); gouger (wood). ‖ **To scoop up**, ramasser à la pelle (sand); écoper

(water). ‖ Fam. *To scoop the other papers*, publier une nouvelle à sensation avant les autres journaux. ‖ Pop. Rafler (a profit).
scooped [-d] adj. **Scooped-out**, creux, évidé, en cuillère. (See SCOOP.)
scooper [-ə*] n. Personne (*f.*) qui puise (or) creuse. ‖ Techn. Outil (*m.*) à évider ; échoppe *f.* ‖ Med. Curette *f.* ‖ Zool. Avocette *f.*
scoot [sku:t] v. intr. Pop. Détaler. (See SCAMPER.)
scooter ['sku:tə*] n. Trottinette, patinette *f.* (for children). ‖ Autom. Scooter *m.* ‖ U. S. Naut. Bateau (*m.*) à voiles et à patins.
scope [skoup] n. Etendue, portée *f.* ; rayon *m.* (of an action) ; domaine propre *m.* (of a branch of knowledge) ; capacité *f.* (of intellect) ; envergure *f.* (of an undertaking) ; plan *m.* (of work) ; *beyond s.o.'s scope*, hors de la compétence (or) du rayon de qqn. ‖ Espace, champ *m.* (of activity) ; *to give free scope to*, donner carrière à ; *to have full scope*, avoir ses coudées franches. ‖ Naut. *Riding scope*, touée.
scorbutic [skɔ:'bju:tik] adj., n. Med. Scorbutique *s.*
scorbutus [-təs] n. Med. Scorbut *m.* (See SCURVY.)
scorch [skɔ:tʃ] n. Med. Brûlure superficielle *f.* ‖ Roussissement *m.* ‖ Autom. Course (*f.*) à plein gaz.
— v. tr. Med. Brûler légèrement. ‖ Culin. Roussir. ‖ Agric. Griller (buds) ; rôtir, dessécher (grass). ‖ Fig. Blesser, égratigner (by sarcasm).
— v. intr. Roussir, se brûler, se griller. ‖ Autom. Faire de l'excès de vitesse, brûler la route.
scorched [-t] adj. Culin. Roussi, légèrement brûlé. ‖ Med. Adusté (face). ‖ Bot. Desséché (grass) ; grillé (plant). ‖ Milit. *Schorched earth policy*, tactique (or) politique de la terre brûlée.
scorcher [-ə*] n. Fam. Journée torride *f.* ‖ U. S. Autom. Pédalard *m.* (cyclist) ; chauffard *m.* (motorist). ‖ Pop. Remarque (*f.*) caustique (or) à l'emporte-pièce. ‖ Pop. Chose (or) personne épatante *f.*
scorching [-iŋ] adj. Torride (heat) ; brûlant (wind). ‖ Fig. Caustique, cinglant, mordant (criticism) ; brûlant (glance).
— n. Culin. Roussissement *m.* ‖ Agric. Dessèchement *m.* ‖ Autom. Vitesse excessive *f.*
score [skɔ:*] n. Coche, entaille, marque *f.* ; trait *m.* ‖ Incision *f.* (on leather) ; strie *f.* (on rock) ; encoche *f.* (on a tally) ; trait (*m.*) de repère (on a tree). ‖ Pl. Grand nombre *m.* ; grandes quantités *f. pl.* ; masse *f.* (of people) ; tas *m. pl.* (of times). ‖ Comm. Compte *m.* ; ardoise *f.* (fam.). ‖ Med. Eraflure, entaille *f.* (on the skin). ‖ Math. Vingt, vingtaine. ‖ Sports. Marque *f.* ; compte (or) total (*m.*) des points ; *to keep the score*, compter (or) marquer les points ; *what's the score?*, quelle est la marque?, où en est le jeu ? ‖ Mus. Partition *f.* ; *full, vocal score*, partition d'orchestre, de chant ; *piano score*, réduction pour piano. ‖ Techn. Grippure *f.* (on a bearing) ; rayure *f.* (on a cylinder) ; gorge *f.* (of a pulley). ‖ Fig. Point, sujet, compte *m.* ; question *f.* ; *on that score*, à cet égard. ‖ U. S. Pop. *To know the score*, en connaître un bout, être dégourdi. ‖ **Score-board**, n. Ardoise *f.* (in a pub) ; Sports. Tableau *m.* ‖ **Score-card**, n. Sports. Carton *m.* ; carte (*f.*) du parcours (in golf). ‖ **Score-game**, n. Sports. Concours (or) match (*m.*) par coups (in golf). ‖ **Score-sheet**, n. Carnet *m.* (or) feuille (*f.*) de marque.
— N. B. *Score*, précédé d'un numéral, reste invariable.
— v. tr. Entailler, encocher. ‖ Rayer (the ground) ; inciser (leather) ; strier (a rock) ; souligner (a sentence) ; faire des coches à (a tally) ; *to score out*, rayer, barrer, biffer, supprimer. ‖ Med. Couturer. ‖ Comm. Porter en compte, enregistrer (a debt) ; inscrire sur l'ardoise (in a pub). ‖ Techn. Buriner (an engraving plate) ; gratteler (a metal plate). ‖ Sports. Marquer (a goal) ; compter, gagner (points) ; *no score*, aucun but enregistré ; *to score no tricks*,

être capot (at bridge). ‖ Mus. Noter (an air) ; orchestrer (a piece).
— v. intr. Sports. Marquer les points (scorekeeper) ; marquer des points (player, team) ; gagner (winner). ‖ Fig. Avoir l'avantage ; se tailler un succès.
scored [-d] adj. Rayé (cylinder) ; affouillé (gun barrel) ; sillonné (mountain side) ; strié (rock) ; barré, biffé (word). ‖ Med. Couturé (skin) [with scars] ; creusé, labouré (with wrinkles).
scorer [-:rə*] n. Marqueur *s.*
scoria ['skɔ:riə] (pl. **scoriae** [-i:]) n. Scorie *f.* ; mâchefer *m.*
scorify [-fai] v. tr. (2). Scorifier.
scoring ['skɔ:riŋ] n. Encochage *m.* ; incision *f.* (on leather) ; striage *m.* (of rock). ‖ Med. Eraflement *m.* ‖ Comm. Inscription *f.* ; enregistrement *m.* (of a debt). ‖ Mus. Notation *f.* (of an air) ; orchestration *f.* (of a composition) ; arrangement *m.* (for different instruments). ‖ Cinem. Sonorisation *f.* ‖ Sports. Marque *f.* (of points) ; *scoring board*, tableau ; boulier (for billiards). ‖ U. S. Fam. Savon *m.* (scolding). ‖ **Scoring-book**, n. Milit. Carnet de tir *m.*
scorn [skɔ:n] n. Dédain, mépris *m.*
— v. tr. Dédaigner, mépriser ; faire fi de (advice) ; rejeter (a suggestion) ; *to scorn to do sth.*, trouver indigne de soi de faire qqch.
scorner [-ə*] n. Railleur *s.*
scornful [-ful] adj. Méprisant ; dédaigneux (see DISDAINFUL) ; *to be scornful of*, dédaigner, mépriser.
scornfully [-fuli] adv. Dédaigneusement, avec mépris, d'un air méprisant.
scornfulness [-fulnis] n. Dédain, mépris *m.* ; caractère dédaigneux *m.* (of a reply).
scorning [-iŋ] n. Dédain *m.* (of, pour) ; mépris *m.* (of, de, pour).
Scorpio ['skɔ:piou] n. Astron. Scorpion *m.*
scorpion [-ən] n. Zool., Astron. Scorpion *m.*
Scot [skɔt] n. Geogr. Ecossais *s.*
scot n. Ecot *m.* ; *to pay one's scot*, payer son écot. ‖ **Scot-free**, adj. Sans frais (free from payment) ; sain et sauf, indemne (unharmed) ; *to get sth. scot-free*, recevoir (or) procurer qqch. gratis.
Scotch [skɔtʃ] adj. Geogr. Ecossais ; d'Ecosse. ‖ Zool. *Scotch terrier*, Scotch-terrier ; **Scotch tape**, n. U. S. Ruban adhésif, « Scotch » *m.*
— n. Geogr. Ecossais *m. pl.* ‖ Gramm. Ecossais *m.* (language). ‖ Fam. Whisky écossais, scotch *m.*
scotch n. Cale *f.* ; sabot d'arrêt *m.*
— v. tr. Caler.
scotch n. Entaille *f.* (incision) ; trait *m.* (mark). ‖ Sports. Ligne de limite *f.* (in hopscotch).
— v. tr. Mettre hors de combat (or) hors d'état de nuire. ‖ Fig. Barrer, biffer ; annuler (an event).
Scotchman [-mən] (pl. **Scotchmen**) n. Geogr. † Ecossais *m.* ‖ Naut. Défense (*f.*) de gréement.
Scotchwoman [-wumən] (pl. **Scotchwomen**) n. Geogr. Ecossaise *f.*
scoter ['skotə*] n. Zool. Macreuse *f.*
Scotland ['skɔtlənd] n. Geogr. Ecosse *f.* ‖ Jur. *Scotland Yard*, la Sûreté.
Scots [skɔts] adj. Geogr. Ecossais ; *Scots Guards*, Garde écossaise.
— n. pl. Ecossais *m. pl.*
Scotsman [-mən] (pl. **Scotsmen**) n. Geogr. Ecossais *m.*
Scotswoman [-wumən] (pl. **Scotswomen**) n. Geogr. Ecossaise *f.*
Scott [skɔt] interj. *Great Scott!*, Grand Dieu !
Scot(t)icism [-isizm] n. Idiotisme écossais *m.*
Scottie [-i] n. Zool., Fam. Scotch-terrier *m.* ‖ Fam. Ecossais *m.*
Scottish [-iʃ] adj. Geogr. Ecossais.
scoundrel ['skaundrəl] n. Scélérat, vaurien, gredin *m.* ; misérable *s.* ; canaille, fripouille *f.* (fam.).

scoundrelism [-izm̩] n. Scélératesse, canaillerie *f*.
scoundrelly [-i] adj. Scélérat, canaille.
scour ['skauə*] n. Nettoyage, récurage *m*. ‖ Dégraissant *m*. (for wool). ‖ Tᴇᴄʜɴ. Chasse *f*. (of a flushing cistern); force érosive *f*. (of a stream). ‖ Mᴇᴅ. Diarrhée *f*.
— v. tr. Lessiver (clothing); nettoyer, astiquer (a floor); dessuinter (hides); décaper, fourbir (metal); récurer (a pan); dégraisser, dessuinter (wool). ‖ Nettoyer à grande eau (a ditch); affouiller, dégrader (a river bank); donner une chasse d'eau à (a sewer). ‖ Aɢʀɪᴄ. Nettoyer (corn). ‖ Nᴀᴜᴛ. Curer (a port). ‖ Mᴇᴅ. Purger.
scour v. tr. Ecumer, sillonner (a territory, a town); éplucher, passer au crible (a document).
— v. intr. Courir (or) parcourir dans tous les sens (*for*, *after*, à la recherche de).
scourer [-rə*] n. Nettoyeur, récureur *s*.; cureur *s*. (of a ditch); balayeur *s*. (of leather); décapeur *s*. (of metal); dégraisseur *s*. (of wool); pot-scourer, cure-casseroles.
scourge [skə:dʒ] n. Fouet *m*.; *Russian scourge*, knout. ‖ Discipline *f*. (for self-flagellation). ‖ Fɪɢ. Fléau *m*.
— v. tr. Fouetter, flageller; *to scourge oneself*, se donner la discipline. ‖ Aɢʀɪᴄ. Epuiser (the soil). ‖ Fɪɢ. Opprimer, être un fléau pour.
scourger [-ə*] n. Fouetteur *s*. ‖ Fɪɢ. Oppresseur *s*.; fléau *m*.
scouring ['skauriŋ] n. Lessivage *m*. (of clothing); nettoyage *m*. (of a floor); balayage *m*. (of leather); décapage *m*. (of metal); récurage *m*. (of a pot). ‖ Nettoyage (*m*.) à grande eau (of a ditch); affouillement *m*. (of a river-bank). ‖ Aɢʀɪᴄ. Nettoiement *m*. (of corn). ‖ Nᴀᴜᴛ. Curage *m*. (of a port). ‖ Mᴇᴅ. Purgation *f*. ‖ **Scouring-brick** (or) **-stone**, n. Brique anglaise *f*. ‖ **Scouring-machine**, n. Machine (*f*.) à nettoyer (or) à décaper.
scouse [skaus] n. Fᴀᴍ. Habitant (*s*.) de Liverpool. ‖ Gʀᴀᴍᴍ. Dialecte (*m*.) de Liverpool.
— adj. Fᴀᴍ. De Liverpool.
scout [skaut] n. Mɪʟɪᴛ. Eclaireur *m*.; *scout car*, automobile de reconnaissance. ‖ Nᴀᴜᴛ. *Scout ship*, vedette, croiseur, éclaireur; *submarine scout*, patrouilleur contre sous-marins. ‖ Aᴠɪᴀᴛ. Avion (or) dirigeable (*m*.) de reconnaissance. ‖ Zᴏᴏʟ. Pingouin commun *m*. ‖ Domestique *m*. (at Oxford). ‖ Sᴘᴏʀᴛs. See ғɪᴇʟᴅᴇʀ. ‖ *Boy Scout*, boy-scout. ‖ **Scout-master**, n. Chef-scout, scoutmestre *m*. ‖ **Scout-mistress**, n. Cheftaine *f*.
— v. intr. Mɪʟɪᴛ. Aller en reconnaissance; éclairer le terrain (or) la marche; *to scout around for*, chercher.
— v. tr. Repousser avec mépris (or) avec dédain (a suggestion).
scouting [-iŋ] n. Mɪʟɪᴛ. Reconnaissance *f*.; éclairage *m*. ‖ Nᴀᴜᴛ. *Scouting vessel*, éclaireur. ‖ Aᴠɪᴀᴛ. Reconnaissance aérienne *f*.; *photo-reconnaissance f*.; *scouting plane*, appareil de reconnaissance. ‖ Scoutisme *m*. (for Boy Scouts).
scow [skau] n. Nᴀᴜᴛ., Fᴀᴍ. Chaland *m*.; *ferry scow*, toue.
scowl [skaul] n. Air maussade *m*.; mine renfrognée *f*. ‖ Froncement (*m*.) de sourcils (frown).
— v. intr. Se renfrogner, prendre un air maussade, faire grise mine; froncer les sourcils (to frown); *to scowl at*, regarder de travers. ‖ Fɪɢ. Menacer (height); s'assombrir, s'obscurcir (sky).
scowling [-iŋ] adj. Menaçant, maussade, renfrogné (look, person); torve (eyes).
scrabble ['skræbl̩] v. intr. **To scrabble about**, gratter çà et là, jouer des pieds et des mains. ‖ **To scrabble for**, chercher à quatre pattes.
— v. tr. See sᴄʀɪʙʙʟᴇ.
scrag [skræg] n. Personne maigre *f*.; bête efflanquée *f*. ‖ Cou décharné *m*. (of an animal); nuque *f*. (of a person). ‖ Bᴏᴛ. Excroissance *f*. (of a branch);

souche *f*. (of a tree trunk). ‖ Gᴇᴏʟ. Terrain rocailleux *m*.; éperon *m*. (of a rock formation). ‖ Cᴜʟɪɴ. Collet *m*. (of mutton).
— v. tr. Pendre, garrotter; tordre le cou à. ‖ Sᴘᴏʀᴛs, Fᴀᴍ. Cravater.
scragginess [-inis] n. Maigreur *f*. (of a body). ‖ Rugosité, anfractuosité *f*. (of a rock mass). ‖ Bᴏᴛ. Nodosité *f*. (of a branch); rabougrissement *m*. (of a tree trunk).
scraggy ['skrægi] adj. Décharné, émacié (person); long et maigre (neck). ‖ Bᴏᴛ. Noueux (branch); rabougri (tree). ‖ Gᴇᴏʟ. Anfractueux (rock).
scram [skræm] v. intr. U. S. Pᴏᴘ. Décamper, se barrer, se tailler, se débiner.
scramble ['skræmbl̩] n. Ascension (or) escalade (*f*.) à quatre pattes. ‖ Bousculade, mêlée *f*.; curée *f*. (for jobs); lutte *f*. (for a living); *to fling oneself into the scramble*, se ruer à la curée; *to throw pennies for a scramble*, jeter des sous à la volée. ‖ Sᴘᴏʀᴛs. Moto-cross *m*.
— v. intr. Aller à quatre pattes; *to scramble up a hill*, escalader une colline en rampant. ‖ Jouer des pieds et des mains; *to scramble for sth.*, se battre pour avoir qqch.; *to scramble into one's clothes*, enfiler ses habits à la six-quatre-deux.
— v. tr. Rᴀᴅɪᴏ. Brouiller. ‖ Cᴜʟɪɴ. *Scrambled eggs*, œufs brouillés.
scrambling [-iŋ] n. Mêlée, lutte *f*.
— adj. Sans méthode, en désordre; à la va-comme-je-te-pousse (fam.).
scran [skræn] n. Fᴀᴍ. Restes, bouts *m*. *pl*.
scrap [skræp] n. Petit morceau, fragment *m*. ‖ Bribe *f*. (of conversation); parcelle *f*. (of ground); bout, brin, chiffon *m*. (of paper). ‖ Découpure *f*. (for an album); coupure *f*. (of a newspaper article). ‖ Cᴜʟɪɴ. Fritons *m*. *pl*. (of fat); rogatons *m*. *pl*. (of food); restes, reliefs *m*. *pl*. (of a meal); débris *m*. *pl*. (of poultry). ‖ Pl. Bouts *m*. *pl*.; bribes *f*. *pl*. (of cloth); démolitions *f*. *pl*. (of buildings); riblons *m*. *pl*.; ferraille *f*. (from a foundry); déchets, débris *m*. *pl*. (of metal). ‖ Fɪɢ. Fiche *f*. (of comfort). ‖ **Scrap-book**, n. Album (*m*.) de découpures. ‖ **Scrap-dealer** (or) **-merchant**, n. Ferrailleur *m*.; Aᴜᴛᴏᴍ. Casseur *m*. ‖ **Scrap-heap**, n. Tas (*m*.) de ferraille; Fɪɢ. Rancart *m*., poubelle *f*. ‖ **Scrap-iron** (or) **-metal**, n. Ferraille *f*. ‖ **Scrap-yard**, n. Chantier (*m*.) de ferrailleur; Aᴜᴛᴏᴍ. Cimetière (*m*.) de voitures.
— v. tr. Mettre au rebut; envoyer à la ferraille. ‖ Mɪʟɪᴛ. Réformer (equipment). ‖ Fɪɢ. Mettre au rancart (a project).
scrap n. Pᴏᴘ. Querelle, dispute *f*.; bagarre *f*. (brawl). ‖ Mɪʟɪᴛ. Echauffourée *f*.; engagement *m*. ‖ Sᴘᴏʀᴛs, Fᴀᴍ. Match *m*. (in boxing).
— v. intr. Se colleter, se prendre aux cheveux, se flanquer une peignée.
scrape [skreip] n. Coup de racloir (or) de grattoir *m*.; grattage *m*.; trait *m*. (of a pen). ‖ Grincement *m*. (noise). ‖ Mᴜs. Coup d'archet *m*. ‖ Cᴜʟɪɴ. Mince couche *f*. (of butter on bread). ‖ Fᴀᴍ. Difficulté, mauvaise affaire *f*.; mauvais pas *m*.; *to get into a scrape*, s'attirer des ennuis, se mettre dans de beaux draps; *to get out of a scrape*, se tirer d'affaire, sortir d'embarras.
— v. tr. Erafler, écorcher. ‖ Gratter, racler; décaper (an embankment); dépiler, écharner (leather); décrasser (metal); raturer (parchment); regratter (a wall); *to scrape away* (or) *off* (or) *out*, enlever en grattant (or) en raclant; *to scrape down*, diminuer en grattant; gratter (or) racler du haut en bas. ‖ Aʀᴛs. Boësser (an engraving plate); riper (a sculpture). ‖ Mᴇᴅ. Ruginer (a bone); *to scrape one's finger*, s'érafler le doigt; *to scrape out*, prélever (a vesicle). ‖ Cᴜʟɪɴ. Gratter (a vegetable). ‖ Nᴀᴜᴛ. Nettoyer (a hull); *to scrape the bottom*, talonner. ‖ Sᴘᴏʀᴛs. Racler (a golf ball). ‖ Fᴀᴍ. *To scrape one's plate*, faire plat net; *to scrape together*,

amasser sou à sou (a sum of money); *to scrape up an acquaintance with*, réussir à lier connaissance avec; *to scrape the fiddle*, racler du violon. — v. intr. Frôler; frotter (*against*, contre); *to scrape through*, arriver tout juste à passer par. ‖ Grincer, racler (noisily). ‖ Faire une révérence; *to bow and scrape*, faire des courbettes. ‖ Mus. *To scrape on a violin*, racler du violon, jouailler. ‖ Fig. *To scrape along*, s'en tirer péniblement, vivoter; *to scrape clear of*, friser, se tirer de justesse de (a danger); *to scrape through*, réussir de justesse (in an examination).

scraper [-ə*] n. Gratteur, racleur s. (person). ‖ Racloir, grattoir *m.*, raclette *f.* (implement); gratte *f.* (for paint). ‖ Techn. Paroir *m.* (for book-binding); alumelle *f.* (in carpentry); raclette *f.* (for chimney-sweeping); curette *f.* (in mines); écorcheuse *f.* (for road surfacing); ébarboir *m.* (for zinc-working). ‖ Agric. Ratissoire *f.* ‖ **Scraper-mat**, n. Décrottoir *m.*

scraping [-iŋ] adj. Qui gratte, qui racle. ‖ Grinçant (noise); *scraping sound*, grincement. ‖ Obséquieux (bow, salute); avare, ladre (person). — n. Grattage, raclage *m.;* dépilage *m.* (of leather); décapage *m.* (of metal); décrottage *m.* (of shoes); regrattement *m.* (of a wall). ‖ Techn. Décapage *m.* (of an embankment); raturage *m.* (of parchment). ‖ Arts. Ripage *m.* ‖ Pl. Echarnures *f. pl.* (of leather); grattures *f. pl.* (of metal); raclures *f. pl.* (of wood). ‖ Mus. Grincement *m.* (of a violin). ‖ Med. Eraflement *m.* ‖ Culin. Grattage *m.* (action); pl. raclures *f. pl.* (peelings); restes *m. pl.*, bribes *f. pl.* (remains); *pan scrapings*, raclons. ‖ Fam. *Bowing and scraping*, multiples courbettes. ‖ Fam. Economies (*f. pl.*) de bout de chandelle.

scrapper ['skræpə*] n. Sports. Pugiliste *m.* ‖ Fam. Bagarreur s.

scrappiness [-inis] n. Caractère batailleur *m.* (of a person); caractère décousu *m.* (of a style).

scrappy [-i] adj. Morcelé, fragmenté. ‖ Culin. Composé de restes (meal). ‖ U. S. Plein de cran. ‖ Fig. Hétéroclite (collection); plein de lacunes (education); décousu (speech, style).

scratch [skrætʃ] n. Raie, éraflure *f.* (on film); striation *f.* (on rock); rayure *f.* (on a table). ‖ Grattement *m.* (action). ‖ Bruit grinçant *m.;* frottement *m.* (of a match); grincement *m.* (of a pen). ‖ Griffonnage, gribouillage *m.* (handwriting). ‖ Med. Egratignure, éraflure *f.;* coup (*m.*) de griffe (by an animal); coup (*m.*) d'ongle (by a person). ‖ Sports. Scratch *m.* (in a race). ‖ U. S. Cinem. Titre provisoire *m.* (of a film). ‖ Fam. *To come up to scratch*, s'exécuter; se montrer à la hauteur; *to start from scratch*, partir de rien. ‖ **Scratch-awl**, Traçoir *m.* ‖ **Scratch man**, n. Sports. Scratch *m.* ‖ **Scratch pad**, n. U. S. Bloc-notes *m.* ‖ **Scratch-player**, n. Joueur classé à zéro *m.* (in tennis). ‖ **Scratch-race**, n. Sports. Course scratch *f.* ‖ **Scratch-test**, n. Med. Test (*m.*) d'allergie. ‖ **Scratch-weed**, n. Bot. Grateron *m.* ‖ **Scratch-work**, n. Arts. Graffiti *m. pl.* — v. tr. Rayer (glass); creuser (a hole); strier (rock); gratter (the soil). ‖ Frotter (a match). ‖ Griffonner, gribouiller (to scrawl); *to scratch off* (or) *out*, rayer, effacer, biffer; *to scratch out s.o.'s eyes*, arracher les yeux à qqn; *to scratch together*, ramasser sou à sou (a sum of money); arriver tout juste à réunir (a team). ‖ Med. Se gratter (a part of the body); égratigner, érafler, griffer, écorcher (the skin). ‖ Arts. Dessiner à traits superficiels; graver (ivory). ‖ Sports. Déclarer forfait pour (a horse); décommander (a race). ‖ Fam. Contremander (an engagement); *to scratch s.o.'s back*, gratter qqn où ça le démange, chatouiller l'épiderme à qqn. — v. intr. Griffer, égratigner. ‖ Se gratter. ‖ Gratter, grincer (pen); accrocher (surface). ‖ Sports.

Renoncer à concourir. ‖ Fam. *To scratch along*, vivoter. — adj. Disparate; hétéroclite (collection); improvisé, sommaire (meal). ‖ Sports. De fortune, sans homogénéité (team).

scratcher [-ə*] n. Gratteur s. (person); grattoir *m.* (tool).

scratching [-iŋ] n. Coup (*m.*) de griffe (or) d'ongle. ‖ Rayage *m.;* striation *f.* (of a surface). ‖ Rayage *m.;* radiation *f.* (striking out). ‖ Frottement *m.* (of a match). ‖ Grincement *m.* (of a pen). ‖ Med. Grattement *m.* (of a part of the body); écorchement, éraflement *m.* (of the skin). ‖ Mus. Bruit (*m.*) de surface (on a record).

scratchy [-i] adj. Grinçant (noise); rugueux (surface). ‖ Arts. Hésitant, lâché (sketch). ‖ Mus. Inégal, manquant d'ensemble (performance). ‖ Sports. Disparate, non homogène (team). ‖ Fam. Chatouilleux, irritable, de mauvaise humeur (person).

scrawl [skrɔ:l] n. Griffonnage, gribouillage *m.;* pattes (*f. pl.*) de mouche. — v. tr. et intr. Griffonner, gribouiller.

scrawler [-ə*] n. Griffonneur, gribouilleur s.; barbouilleur (*m.*) de papier.

scrawny ['skrɔ:ni] adj. U. S. See scraggy.

scray [skrei] n. Zool. Sterne *f.*

scream [skri:m] n. Cri perçant *m.* (of fright); hurlement *m.* (of pain); *to give a scream*, pousser un cri perçant. ‖ Grand éclat *m.* (of laugther). ‖ Pop. Type désopilant *m.* (person); truc tordant *m.* (thing); *it's a scream*, c'est marrant; *he's a scream*, il est roulant. — v. intr. Crier, pousser des cris perçants; hurler (with pain); *to scream with laughter*, rire aux larmes; *to scream with terror*, pousser des cris de terreur. ‖ Zool. Trompeter (eagle); brailler (peacock). ‖ Ch. de f. Siffler (locomotive). — v. tr. Crier à tue-tête (an order); brailler (a song).

screamer [-ə*] n. Crieur, braillard s. ‖ Zool. Oiseau au cri perçant *m.* ‖ U. S. Pop. Histoire (or) pièce désopilante; manchette sensationnelle *f.*

screaming [-iŋ] adj. Ch. de f. Sifflant (locomotive). ‖ Fam. Tordant, marrant, bidonnant, désopilant (anecdote); voyant (colours); criard, braillard (person); perçant (sound).

screamline [-lain] v. tr. U. S. Fam. Titrer en gros caractères.

scree [skri:] n. Geol. Eboulis *m.*

screech [skri:tʃ] n. Cri aigu (or) perçant *m.* — v. intr. Pousser des cris aigus. ‖ Mus. Chanter d'une voix vrillante. — v. tr. Crier d'une voix aigre (or) perçante. ‖ **Screech-owl**, n. Zool. Chat-huant *m.*

screechy [-i] adj. Criard.

screed [skri:d] n. Harangue, tirade *f.* ‖ Techn. Cueillie *f.* ‖ Fam. Tartine *f.* (letter); kyrielle *f.* (of claims).

screen [skri:n] n. Ecran *m.*; *draught* (or) *folding screen*, paravent; *fire screen*, garde-feu, pare-étincelles. ‖ Med. Garde-vue *m.* ‖ Archit. Clôture *f.;* jubé *m.* (of a chancel). ‖ Milit., Naut. Rideau *m.* ‖ Electr. Ecran *m.; aerial screen*, antenne de compensation. ‖ Techn. Tamis, crible *m.* (for gravel); claie *f.* (for sand). ‖ Autom., Aviat. Pare-brise *m.* ‖ Agric. Brise-vent *m.* ‖ Cinem. Ecran *m.; to show on the screen*, projeter; *screen rights*, droits d'adaptation cinématographique; *screen test*, bout d'essai. ‖ Fig. Masque *m.* (of gaiety); voiles *m. pl.* (of night). ‖ **Screen-play**, n. Cinem. Scénario *m.* ‖ **Screen-printing**, n. Techn. Sérigraphie *f.* ‖ **Screen-writer**, n. Cinem. Scénariste s. — v. tr. Munir d'un écran; *to screen off*, cacher (or) abriter derrière un paravent. ‖ Mettre à couvert; abriter, protéger (from danger); garantir (from the wind); *to screen from blame*, soustraire à la censure. ‖ Electr. Blinder (a lamp). ‖ Milit.

Dérober (a battery). ‖ TECHN. Egaliser (coal); tamiser, cribler (gravel, sand). ‖ AGRIC. Cribler (grain). ‖ CINEM. Porter à l'écran (a novel). ‖ FIG. Couvrir (s.o.); trier (candidates); cacher, masquer, dissimuler (a defect).

screener [-ə*] n. Tamiseur s.

screening [-iŋ] n. Protection f. (from, contre). ‖ TECHN. Criblage m. (of coal); tamisage m. (of sand). ‖ AGRIC. Criblage m. ‖ RADIO., ELECTR. Compensation f. (of an aerial); blindage m. (of a lamp). ‖ Pl. Poussier m.; criblure f. ‖ FIG. Triage m.

screw [skru:] n. Vis f.; endless (or) perpetual (or) worm screw, vis sans fin. ‖ Tour (m.) de vis; to give another screw, donner un autre tour de vis. ‖ Cornet m.; papillote f. (of candy). ‖ NAUT. Hélice f.; rigging screw, ridoir. ‖ AVIAT. Air, helicopter screw, hélice propulsive, sustentatrice. ‖ SPORTS. Effet m. (in billiards). ‖ FAM. Appointements m. pl. ‖ POP. Pingre, grigou m. (miser); pressureur m. (oppressor). ‖ POP. Carcan m.; rosse, carne f. (old nag); garde-chiourme m. (warder). ‖ LOC., FAM. To have a screw loose, être timbré, avoir un grain; there's a screw loose somewhere, il y a qqch. qui cloche quelque part. ‖ Pl. FAM. Poucettes f. pl.; to put the screw on s.o., serrer la vis à qqn. ‖ **Screw-bolt,** n. Boulon fileté m. ‖ **Screw-coupling,** n. Manchon (m.) à vis (or) à union. ‖ **Screw-cutting,** n. Taraudage m. ‖ **Screw-driven,** adj. A hélice. ‖ **Screw-driver,** n. Tournevis m. ‖ **Screw-eye,** n. Piton m. ‖ **Screw-hook,** n. Crochet (m.) à vis. ‖ **Screw-lamp-holder,** n. ELECTR. Douille à vis f. ‖ **Screw-jack,** n. Cric m. ‖ **Screw-propeller,** n. NAUT., AVIAT. Hélice f. ‖ **Screw-steamer,** n. NAUT. Navire (m.) à hélice. ‖ **Screw-tap,** n. Taraud m. ‖ **Screw-wrench,** n. Clef anglaise f.
— v. tr. Visser; fixer au moyen de vis; to screw off, dévisser; to screw tight, visser à bloc; to screw up, resserrer. ‖ Contracter (one's features); tourner (one's neck); to screw one's face into a smile, grimacer un sourire. ‖ TECHN. Fileter (a pipe); tarauder (a pipe). ‖ SPORTS. Donner de l'effet à (a billiard ball); couper (a tennis ball). ‖ FIG. Pressurer, exploiter (s.o.); extorquer, arracher (from, out of, à) [sth.]; to screw up one's courage, rassembler son courage. ‖ POP. Entuber (to cheat); cambrioler (to burgle). ‖ ARG. Baiser, tringler; get screwed, screw you!, va te faire foutre! ‖ **To screw up,** U. S. FAM. Bousiller.
— v. intr. Se visser (knob, nut); tourner (tap). ‖ Se tortiller (person). ‖ Dévier (projectile).

screwball [-bɔ:l] adj., n. U. S. Détraqué.

screwed [-d] adj. Fileté, à vis (bolt); taraudé (handle). ‖ FAM. Eméché, pompette, paf. ‖ U. S. FAM. Fichu.

screwing [-iŋ] n. Vissage m.; serrage m. (of a bolt). ‖ U. S. FAM. To take a screwing, être coulé (or) vissé. ‖ **Screwing off** (or) **out,** n. Dévissage. ‖ **Screwing up,** n. Vissage (of a lid); crispation f. (of the features).

screwy ['skru:i] adj. Fourbu (horse). ‖ POP. Cinglé, dingue, givré (crazy); givré, poivré (drunk).

scribble ['skribl] v. tr. Carder.

scribble n. Griffonnage, gribouillage m.; pattes (f. pl.) de mouche (fam.). ‖ Billet (m.) écrit à la hâte.
— v. tr. Griffonner, gribouiller. (See SCRAWL.)
— v. intr. Griffonner, gribouiller; noircir du papier. ‖ Ecrivailler (columnist).

scribbler [-ə*] n. Griffonneur, gribouilleur s. ‖ Gratte-papier; écrivaillon m.

scribbling [-iŋ] n. Griffonnage, gribouillage m.; scribbling block (or) pad, bloc-notes.

scribe [skraib] n. Scribe m. ‖ TECHN. Tracelet m. (tool).
— v. tr. Tracer. ‖ Pointer, repérer (a centre). ‖ Trusquiner (a line).

scriber [-ə*] n. Pointe (f.) à tracer, trusquin m.

scrimmage ['skrimidʒ] n. Mêlée, bousculade, bagarre f. ‖ SPORTS. Mêlée f. (in rugby).
— v. intr. Se quereller, se bousculer. ‖ S'empresser, s'activer.
— v. tr. SPORTS. Mettre en mêlée.

scrimp [skrimp] v. intr. Lésiner.
— v. tr. Lésiner sur. ‖ Saboter, bâcler (a piece of work).

scrimpy [-i] adj. Etriqué (garment); parcimonieux, chiche (person).

scrimshank ['skrim,ʃæŋk] v. intr. MILIT., FAM. Tirer au flanc, tirer au cul.

scrimshanker [-ə*] n. MILIT., FAM. Tire-au-flanc, tire-au-cul m. invar.

scrip [skrip] n. FIN. Certificat provisoire (m.) d'actions. ‖ U. S. MILIT. Coupures f. pl. (of dollar currency in occupied countries).

script [skript] n. Manuscrit m.; copie f. (of an examination). ‖ Ecriture f.; print script, script writing, écriture en caractères d'imprimerie. ‖ JUR. Original m. (of a document). ‖ CINEM. Scénario m. ‖ **Script-writer,** n. CINEM. Scénariste s.
— v. tr. Ecrire le scénario de.

scriptural ['skriptʃərəl] adj. ECCLES. Scripturaire.

scripture [-tʃə*] n. ECCLES. Ecritures f. pl.; Holy Scripture, Ecriture Sainte. ‖ Citation biblique f. (text).

scrivener ['skrivnə*] n. † Ecrivain public. ‖ JUR. Notaire m. ‖ FIN. Changeur m. ‖ FAM. Plumitif m.

scrofula ['skrɔfjulə] n. MED. Scrofule f.

scrofulous [-ləs] adj. MED. Scrofuleux.

scroll [skroul] n. Rouleau m. (of paper). ‖ ARTS. Arabesque f.; cartouche m. (for engraving); banderole f. (for an inscription). ‖ ARCHIT. Volute f. ‖ BLAS. Listel m. ‖ MUS. Crosse f. (of a violin). ‖ FAM. Fioriture f.; parafe m. (following a signature). ‖ **Scroll-work,** n. ARTS. Arabesques f. pl.
— v. tr. Mettre en rouleau (paper). ‖ ARTS. Enjoliver, ornementer.

scrotum ['skroutəm] (pl. **scrota** [-ə]) n. MED. Scrotum m.

scrounge [skraundʒ] v. tr. POP. Barboter; rabioter (to pilfer); écornifler (to sponge).
— v. intr. FAM. To scrounge from (or) U. S. on, vivre aux crochets de.

scrounger [-ə*] n. POP. Chapardeur; écornifleur s.

scrounging [-iŋ] n. POP. Barbotage, écorniflage m.

scrub [skrʌb] n. BOT. Arbuste rabougri m.; brousse f.; broussailles f. pl. ‖ Vieille brosse usée f. ‖ Barbe courte f.; petite moustache drue f. ‖ Nettoyage (m.) à la brosse; récurage m. ‖ U. S. SPORTS. Joueur novice (or) n'appartenant pas à l'équipe régulière. ‖ ZOOL. Petite race bovine f. ‖ FAM. Personne malingre f.; avorton m. ‖ **Scrub-broom,** n. NAUT. Goret m. ‖ **Scrub-team,** n. U. S. SPORTS. Equipe (f.) de joueurs de deuxième ordre.
— adj. U. S. Rabougri, malingre, chétif.
— v. tr. (1). Frotter, nettoyer à la brosse; récurer (a pan). ‖ NAUT. Goreter; briquer (a deck). ‖ CHIM. Laver (a gas).
— v. intr. Faire un nettoyage à la brosse. ‖ Faire de gros travaux.

scrubber [-ə*] n. Brosse f.; éponge métallique f., récureur m. (implement); laveur s. (person). ‖ CHIM. Epurateur, scrubber m.

scrubbing [-iŋ] n. Nettoyage (m.) à la brosse; récurage m. (of utensils). ‖ NAUT. Goretage m.; briquetage m. (of a deck). ‖ CHIM. Lavage m. (of a gas). ‖ **Scrubbing-board,** n. Planche à laver f. ‖ **Scrubbing-brush,** n. Brosse (f.) en chiendent.

scrubby [-i] adj. BOT., ZOOL. Rabougri, chétif (animal, plant); court et dru (beard); insignifiant, chétif, malingre (person); broussailleux (terrain).

scrubwoman [-wumən] (pl. **scrubwomen** [-wimin]) n. U. S. Femme (f.) de ménage pour gros travaux.

scruff [skrʌf] n. MED. Nuque *f.*; *to take by the scruff of the neck*, saisir par la peau du cou (an animal); prendre au collet (a person).

scruffy ['skrʌfi] adj. Débraillé, négligé (person); crasseux, mal tenu (place). ‖ MED. Pelliculeux (scalp); dartreux, squameux (skin).

scrum [skrʌm] n. Mêlée, bousculade *f.* ‖ SPORTS. Mêlée *f.*; *set, loose scrum*, mêlée fermée, ouverte. ‖ **Scrum-half**, n. SPORTS. Demi (*m.*) de mêlée.

scrummage [-idʒ] n. See SCRUM.

— v. intr. Se bousculer. ‖ SPORTS. Faire une mêlée.

scrump [skrʌmp] v. intr. FAM. Chaparder des pommes (from an orchard).

scrumptious ['skrʌmpʃəs] adj. POP. Epatant; délicieux (food).

scrumpy ['skrʌmpi] n. Cidre *m.* (from South-West England).

scrunch [skrʌntʃ]. See CRUNCH.

scruple ['skru:pl] n. Scrupule *m.* (measure). ‖ FIG. Scrupule *m.* (of conscience). ‖ FAM. Grain, soupçon *m.*

— v. intr. Avoir (or) se faire des scrupules; *to scruple to*, se faire scrupule de, hésiter à.

scrupulous [-əs] adj. Scrupuleux, consciencieux. ‖ Exact, méticuleux, minutieux (performance).

scrupulously [-əsli] adv. Scrupuleusement, consciencieusement; méticuleusement.

scrupulousness [-əsnis] n. Scrupulosité, minutie *f.* ‖ Esprit scrupuleux *m.*; scrupules *m. pl.*

scrutator [skru:'teitə*] n. Scrutateur *m.*; scrutatrice *f.*

scrutineer [ˌskru:ti'niə*], **scrutinizer** ['skru:tinaizə*] n. Scrutateur *m.*; scrutatrice *f.*

scrutinize ['skru:tinaiz] v. tr. Scruter; dévisager avec insistance (a person); sonder, examiner à fond (a proposal). ‖ Vérifier, pointer (election results).

scrutinizing [-iŋ] adj. Scrutateur *m.*; scrutatrice *f.*; inquisiteur *m.*; inquisitrice *f.*

— n. Examen minutieux *m.* ‖ Pointage *m.* (of election results).

scrutiny ['skru:tini] n. Regard attentif; examen rigoureux *m.*; recherche minutieuse *f.* ‖ Pointage *m.* (of the vote).

scuba ['skju:bə] n. Scaphandre autonome *m.* ‖ **Scuba-diving**, n. SPORTS. Plongée (*f.*) en scaphandre autonome.

scud [skʌd] n. NAUT. Diablotins *m. pl.* (clouds); rafale *f.* (squall). ‖ FAM. Course rapide; fuite *f.*

— v. intr. (1). NAUT. Galoper (clouds); filer (ship). ‖ FAM. Détaler.

scuff [skʌf] v. intr. Traîner les pieds. ‖ S'érafler (leather).

— v. tr. Frotter, racler (by dragging the feet); érafler (shoes). ‖ AUTOM. User (a tyre tread).

— n. FAM. Babouche *f.*

scuffle ['skʌfl] n. Mêlée, échauffourée, bagarre *f.*; colletage *m.*

— v. intr. Traîner les pieds. ‖ Se bousculer; se colleter, se bagarrer (*with*, avec).

scull [skʌl] n. NAUT. Aviron de couple *m.*; godille *f.*

— v. intr. NAUT. Ramer en couple; godiller.

— v. tr. NAUT. Faire avancer à la godille.

sculler [-ə*] n. NAUT. Canot (*m.*) à godille (boat); godilleur *s.* (person).

scullery ['skʌləri] n. Arrière-cuisine, laverie *f.* ‖ **Scullery-maid**, n. Plongeuse *f.*

scullion ['skʌljən] n. Marmiton, plongeur *m.*

sculp(t) [skʌlp(t)] v. tr., intr. ARTS. Sculpter.

sculptor [-tə*] n. ARTS. Sculpteur *m.*

sculptress [-tris] n. ARTS. Femme sculpteur *f.*

sculptural [-ʃərəl] adj. ARTS. Sculptural. ‖ Plastique (beauty).

sculpture [-ʃə*] n. ARTS. Sculpture *f.*; statuaire *f.* (in marble); ciselure *f.* (on metal).

— v. intr. ARTS. Sculpter, faire de la sculpture.

— v. tr. ARTS. Sculpter (a figure, a surface); ciseler (metal) [*in, out of*, dans].

sculpturesque [ˌskʌlptʃə'resk] adj. ARTS. Sculptural (in general); plastique (beauty).

sculpturing ['skʌlptʃəriŋ] n. ARTS. Sculptage *m.*

scum [skʌm] n. CULIN. Ecume, mousse *f.* (on milk); chapeau *m.* (on wine). ‖ TECHN. Scories, crasses *f. pl.* ‖ FAM. Canaille, racaille *f.*; lie *f.*; rebut *m.* (of society).

— v. intr. (1). Ecumer, se couvrir d'écume.

scumble ['skʌmbl] n. ARTS. Glacis, frottis *m.*

— v. tr. ARTS. Glacer; frotter (a colour); estomper (an outline).

scummy ['skʌmi] adj. Ecumeux, couvert d'écume. ‖ TECHN. Recouvert de scories (metal). ‖ FAM. Bas, méprisable (act, person).

scunner ['skʌnə*] n. Aversion, répulsion *f.*; *to take a scunner at, against*, avoir de l'aversion pour, prendre en grippe.

scupper ['skʌpə*] n. NAUT. Dalot *m.*

— v. tr. NAUT. Saborder (a boat); surprendre et massacrer (a crew). ‖ FIG. Saboter (a plan).

scurf [skə:f] n. MED. Farines *f. pl.* (of an eruption); pellicules *f. pl.* (on the scalp). ‖ BOT. Teigne *f.* ‖ TECHN. Tartre *m.*

scurfy [-i] adj. MED. Pelliculeux (scalp); dartreux, squameux (skin).

scurrility [skʌ'riliti] n. Bassesse, goujaterie *f.* (of an act, a person); vulgarité, grossièreté *f.* (of a statement).

scurrilous ['skʌriləs] adj. Outrageant (accusation); vil, indigne, ignoble, méprisable (act, person); grossier, vulgaire, ordurier (language). ‖ FAM. Rosse; *scurrilous story*, rosserie, vacherie.

scurry ['skʌri] n. Galopade, débandade *f.*; sauve-qui-peut *m.* (of a crowd). ‖ Tourbillon *m.* (of dust, snow).

— v. intr. (2). Prendre ses jambes à son cou; *to scurry away* (or) *off*, déguerpir, décamper, détaler (fam.); se cavaler (pop.).

scurvily ['skə:vili] adv. Indignement, bassement.

scurvy ['skə:vi] n. MED. Scorbut *m.* ‖ **Scurvy-grass**, n. BOT. Cochléaria *m.*

— adj. FAM. Bas, vil, indigne, ignoble, méprisable; *scurvy action*, turpitude *f.*; *scurvy fellow*, goujat; *scurvy trick*, goujaterie. ‖ FAM. Rosse. (See SCURRILOUS.)

scut [skʌt] n. ZOOL. Couette *f.* (of a rabbit). ‖ POP. Mufle *m.*

scutcheon ['skʌtʃən] n. See ESCUTCHEON.

scutcher ['skʌtʃə*] n. TECHN. Ecang *m.* (implement); écangueur *s.* (person).

scute [skju:t] n. ZOOL. Ecaille *f.* (of a reptile).

scuttle ['skʌtl] n. Seau à charbon *m.* ‖ AGRIC. Corbeille *f.*

scuttle n. NAUT. Ecoutillon *m.* (ladder); hublot *m.* (port-hole). ‖ AUTOM. Bouclier avant *m.* ‖ U. S. Trappe *f.* (in a roof). ‖ **Scuttle-butt**, n. NAUT. Charnier *m.*; U. S. On-dit, bavardage *m.*

— v. tr. NAUT. Saborder; envoyer par le fond; *to scuttle one's ship*, se saborder.

scuttle n. Galopade, débandade *f.* ‖ LOC. *Policy of scuttle*, politique d'abandon.

— v. intr. Courir précipitamment; *to scuttle away* (or) *off*, détaler, décamper, déguerpir (person); débouler (rabbit).

scuttling [-iŋ] n. NAUT. Sabordement *m.*

scutum ['skju:təm] n. (pl. *scuta* [-ə]) n. † MILIT. Scutum *m.* ‖ ZOOL. Ecusson *m.* (of an insect); écaille *f.* (of a tortoise). ‖ MED. Rotule *f.*

scythe [saið] n. AGRIC. Faux *f.*

— v. tr. AGRIC. Faucher.

'sdeath [zdeθ] interj. Morbleu!

sea [si:] n. Mer *f.*; *at sea*, en mer; *by sea*, par mer; *by the sea*, au bord de la mer; *sea air*, air marin. ‖ Vague, lame *f.*; *to ship a sea*, embarquer un paquet de mer. ‖ Houle *f.*; gros temps *m.*; *heavy, rough sea*, mer grosse, agitée. ‖ NAUT. *Sea battle*, bataille navale; *to go to sea*, se faire marin (person); prendre le large (ship). ‖ COMM. *Sea* *transport,* messageries maritimes. ‖ Fɪɢ. Mer *f.* (of clouds); multitude *f.* (of difficulties). ‖ Fᴀᴍ. *To be all at sea,* avoir perdu le nord, être désorienté (or) désaxé (or) déboussolé, ne plus s'y reconnaître; *to be half seas over,* avoir du vent dans les voiles. ‖ **Sea-air,** adj. D'air marin *m.;* Mᴇᴅ. *Sea-air cure,* thalassothérapie. ‖ **Sea-anchor,** n. Nᴀᴜᴛ. Ancre flottante *f.* ‖ **Sea-anemone,** n. Bᴏᴛ. Actinie *f.* ‖ **Sea-arm,** n. Bras (*m.*) de mer. ‖ **Sea-baths,** n. pl. Bains (*m. pl.*) de mer. ‖ **Sea-biscuit,** n. Cᴜʟɪɴ. Biscuit (*m.*) de mer; cassant *m.* (fam.). ‖ **Sea-born,** adj. Né de la mer. ‖ **Sea-borne,** adj. Cᴏᴍᴍ. Transporté par mer (goods); maritime (trade). ‖ **Sea-calf,** n. Zᴏᴏʟ. Veau marin, phoque *m.* ‖ **Sea-captain,** n. Nᴀᴜᴛ. Capitaine (*m.*) de vaisseau. ‖ **Sea-coast,** n. Côte *f.;* rivage marin, littoral *m.* ‖ **Sea-cow,** n. Zᴏᴏʟ. Lamantin, morse *m.* ‖ **Sea-dog,** n. Zᴏᴏʟ. Chien (*m.*) de mer (fish); phoque *m.* (seal); Nᴀᴜᴛ. Loup (*m.*) de mer (sailor). ‖ **Sea-eel,** n. Zᴏᴏʟ. Congre *m.;* anguille de mer *f.* ‖ **Sea-elephant,** n. Eléphant (*m.*) de mer. ‖ **Sea-fight,** n. Combat naval *m.* ‖ **Sea-fish,** n. Zᴏᴏʟ. Poisson (*m.*) [or] poissons (*m. pl.*) de mer. ‖ **Sea-floor,** n. Fond sous-marin *m.* ‖ **Sea-foam,** n. Ecume de la mer *f.* ‖ **Sea-food,** n. Cᴜʟɪɴ. Fruits (*m. pl.*) de mer (shell-fish). ‖ **Sea-fowl,** n. Zᴏᴏʟ. Oiseau (*m.*) [or] oiseaux (*m. pl.*) de mer. ‖ **Sea-front,** n. Front (*m.*) de mer. ‖ **Sea-god,** n. Dieu marin, triton *m.* ‖ **Sea-goddess,** n. Néréide *f.* ‖ **Sea-green,** adj. Vert de mer; glauque. ‖ **Sea-hog,** n. Zᴏᴏʟ. Marsouin *m.* ‖ **Sea-horse,** Cheval marin *m.;* Zᴏᴏʟ. Hippocampe *m.* (hippocampus); morse *m.* (walrus). ‖ **Sea-king,** n. Roi (*m.*) de la mer. ‖ **Sea-legs,** n. Fᴀᴍ. Pied marin *m.;* *to get one's sea-legs,* prendre le pied marin, s'amariner. ‖ **Sea-level,** n. Niveau (*m.*) de la mer. ‖ **Sea-line,** n. Horizon *m.;* ligne (*f.*) d'horizon. ‖ **Sea-lion,** n. Zᴏᴏʟ. Otarie *f.* ‖ **Sea-lord,** n. Lord (*m.*) de l'Amirauté. ‖ **Sea-mark,** n. Nᴀᴜᴛ. Amer *m.;* balise *f.* ‖ **Sea-mew,** n. Zᴏᴏʟ. Mouette *f.* ‖ **Sea-mile,** n. Nᴀᴜᴛ. Mille marin *m.* ‖ **Sea-needle,** n. Zᴏᴏʟ. Orphie, aiguille de mer *f.* ‖ **Sea-nettle,** n. Bᴏᴛ. Méduse *f.* ‖ **Sea-pass,** n. Nᴀᴜᴛ. Certificat (*m.*) de neutralité. ‖ **Sea-pay,** n. Fɪɴ. Solde à la mer *f.* ‖ **Sea-pie,** n. Zᴏᴏʟ. Pie de mer *f.;* Cᴜʟɪɴ. Pâté (*m.*) de viande salée et de légumes. ‖ **Sea-plant,** n. Bᴏᴛ. Plante marine *f.* ‖ **Sea-risk,** n. Fortune (*f.*) de mer. ‖ **Sea road,** n. U. S. Nᴀᴜᴛ. Route de navigation *f.* ‖ **Sea-room,** n. Evitage *m.* ‖ **Sea-rover,** n. Pirate, flibustier, forban *m.* ‖ **Sea-salt,** n. Sel marin *m.* ‖ **Sea-scout,** n. Boy-scout marin *m.* ‖ **Sea-shell,** n. Coquille de mer *f.;* coquillage *m.* ‖ **Sea-shore,** n. Rivage, littoral, bord (*m.*) de la mer, côte, plage *f.* ‖ **Sea-sick,** adj. Mᴇᴅ. *To be sea-sick,* avoir le mal de mer. ‖ **Sea-sickness,** n. Mᴇᴅ. Mal (*m.*) de mer. ‖ **Sea-trip,** n. Excursion (or) promenade en mer, croisière (*f.*) d'agrément. ‖ **Sea-urchin,** n. Zᴏᴏʟ. Oursin *m.* ‖ **Sea-view,** n. Vue sur la mer *f.* ‖ **Sea-voyage,** n. Traversée *f.;* voyage (or) trajet (*m.*) par (or) en mer. ‖ **Sea-wall,** n. Digue *f.,* endiguement *m.* ‖ **Sea-water,** n. Eau de mer *f.* ‖ **Sea-way,** n. Nᴀᴜᴛ. Sillage *m.* (of a boat); levée *f.* (of the sea); U. S. Route de navigation *f.* ‖ **Sea-wind,** n. Brise (*f.*) de mer. ‖ **Sea-wolf,** n. Zᴏᴏʟ. Bar *m.* (fish); Fᴀᴍ. Ecumeur (*m.*) de mer (pirate). ‖ **Sea-wrack,** n. Bᴏᴛ. Varech, fucus *m.*

seaboard [-bɔːd] n. Littoral, rivage, bord (*m.*) de la mer, côte *f.*

seafarer [-fɛərə*] n. Nᴀᴜᴛ. Marin *m.*

seafaring [-fɛəriŋ] adj. Nᴀᴜᴛ. Navigant, de mer (ship); *sea-faring man,* marin.

seagoing [-gouiŋ] adj. Nᴀᴜᴛ. Marin, navigant, qui va en mer (person); de haute mer, de long cours (ship). ‖ Cᴏᴍᴍ. Maritime (trade).

seagull [-gʌl] n. Zᴏᴏʟ. Mouette *f.;* goéland *m.*

seal [siːl] n. Zᴏᴏʟ. Phoque, veau marin *m.*
— v. intr. Sᴘᴏʀᴛs. Pêcher (or) chasser le phoque.

seal n. Sceau *m.* (on documents); cachet *m.* (on envelopes); *Great Seal,* grand sceau, sceau de l'Etat; *Privy Seal,* petit sceau. ‖ Plomb *m.* (of customs inspector). ‖ Jᴜʀ. Scellé *m.* ‖ Cᴏᴍᴍ. Cachet *m.;* capsule *f.* (on a bottle); plomb *m.* (on a container). ‖ Tᴇᴄʜɴ. Joint *m.* (or) rondelle (*f.*) étanche; liquide obturateur *m.* (in a siphon). ‖ Fɪɢ. Autorisation *f.; to set one's seal to,* donner son approbation à. ‖ Fɪɢ. Empreinte *f.* (of death); cachet *m.* (of distinction); sceau *m.* (of genius); gage *m.;* preuve *f.* (of love). ‖ **Seal-ring,** n. Chevalière *f.*
— v. tr. Sceller, apposer un sceau sur (a document); cacheter (an envelope); *sealed letter,* pli clos; *sealed orders,* Plomber (after customs inspection). ‖ Jᴜʀ. Apposer les scellés sur. ‖ Cᴏᴍᴍ. Confirmer (a bargain); cacheter (a bottle); souder (a tin). ‖ Cᴜʟɪɴ. Saisir (a steak). ‖ Aʀᴄʜɪᴛ. Sceller (a beam); fixer (a clamp); colmater (a crevice). ‖ Mɪʟɪᴛ., Nᴀᴜᴛ. Adopter officiellement (a design). ‖ Tᴇᴄʜɴ. Assurer l'étanchéité de (a joint); obturer (a shaft, a window); sceller (a tube). ‖ Aᴜᴛᴏᴍ. Boucher (a puncture). ‖ Fɪɢ. Confirmer (a decision); régler (a destiny); sceller (s.o.'s lips).

sealer [-ə*] n. Sᴘᴏʀᴛs. Chasseur (or) pêcheur (*m.*) de phoques (person); navire (*m.*) équipé pour la pêche aux phoques (ship).

sealer n. Scelleur *s.* ‖ Tᴇᴄʜɴ. Pince (*f.*) à sceller. ‖ U. S. Vérificateur (*m.*) des poids et mesures.

sealing [-iŋ] n. Scellage *m.* (of a document); cachetage *m.* (of an envelope). ‖ Plombage *m.* (of luggage). ‖ Tᴇᴄʜɴ. Fermeture hermétique, obturation *f.* ‖ Aʀᴄʜɪᴛ. Scellement, fixage *m.* (of a beam); colmatage *m.* (of a crevice). ‖ **Sealing-wax,** n. Cire à cacheter *f.*

sealskin [-skin] n. Zᴏᴏʟ. Peau (*f.*) de phoque. ‖ Cᴏᴍᴍ. Peau (*f.*) de phoque.

seam [siːm] n. Couture *f.; French seam,* couture double. ‖ Fissure *f.* (in rock). ‖ Tᴇᴄʜɴ. Joint *m.* (in metal); agrafe *f.;* agrafage *m.* (welding). ‖ Gᴇᴏʟ. Couche *f.* (of coal); veine *f.,* gisement, filon *m.* (of ore). ‖ Nᴀᴜᴛ. Couture *f.,* (of a deck). ‖ Mᴇᴅ. Couture, balafre *f.* (on the face); ride profonde *f.* (wrinkle). ‖ **Seam-stitch,** n. Maille (*f.*) à l'envers.
— v. tr. Faire une couture à, piquer une couture dans; *to seam up,* assembler, réunir par une couture (parts of a garment). ‖ Couturer, fissurer (a rock). ‖ Tᴇᴄʜɴ. Agrafer (metal). ‖ Mᴇᴅ. Couturer, marquer de cicatrices; balafrer (face).

seaman ['siːmən] (pl. **seamen**) n. Nᴀᴜᴛ. Marin, matelot *m.* (ordinary); navigateur *m.* (skilled).

seamanlike [-laik] adj. Nᴀᴜᴛ. De marin; d'un bon marin, manœuvrier.

seamanship [-ʃip] n. Nᴀᴜᴛ. Manœuvre *f.;* matelotage *m.*

seamless ['siːmlis] adj. Sans soudure (metal); sans couture (stocking).

seamstress [-stris] n. Couturière *f.*

seamy [-i] adj. Plein de coutures; *seamy side,* envers. ‖ *Seamy side of life,* vilain côté de la vie, revers de la médaille.

seance ['seans] n. Séance, session *f.* (of a society). ‖ Séance (*f.*) de spiritisme.

seaplane ['siːplein] n. Aᴠɪᴀᴛ. Hydravion *m.; seaplane base,* hydroaéroport.

seaport [-pɔːt] n. Nᴀᴜᴛ. Port (*m.*) de mer.

sear [siə*] adj. Desséché, flétri; sec (leaf). ‖ Fɪɢ. Desséché (conscience, heart).
— v. tr. Marquer au fer rouge (an animal). ‖ Aɢʀɪᴄ. Dessécher, flétrir (grain, plants); faner (leaves). ‖ Mᴇᴅ. Cautériser (a wound). ‖ Fɪɢ. Endurcir (the conscience); dessécher (the heart). ‖ **Searing-iron,** n. Cautère *m.*
— v. tr. Se faner, se dessécher, se flétrir.

search [səːtʃ] n. Recherche, quête *f.* (in general); fouille *f.* (of a drawer); *in search of,* à la recherche de, en quête de; *to make a search,* faire des recher-

ches. ‖ Visite *f.* (by a customs officer). ‖ JUR. Perquisition *f.* (of a house); fouille *f.* (of a prisoner); *house search,* visite domiciliaire; *search warrant,* mandat de perquisition. ‖ **Search-party,** n. Expédition (*f.*) de secours.
— v. tr. Chercher (or) fouiller dans (a drawer); scruter, sonder (a face). ‖ JUR. Visiter (luggage); faire une perquisition dans (a house); fouiller (a prisoner). ‖ MED. Sonder (a wound). ‖ FIG. Sonder (one's heart); scruter (one's memory).
— v. intr. Faire des recherches (or) des fouilles, fouiller. ‖ U. S. Perquisitionner. ‖ **To search after** (or) **for,** chercher, aller à la recherche de. ‖ **To search into,** rechercher, approfondir. ‖ **To search over,** parcourir.
searcher [-ə*] n. Chercheur *s.*; investigateur *m.*; investigatrice *f.* ‖ Visiteur *m.* (customs officer). ‖ JUR. Perquisitionneur *m.* ‖ MED. Sonde *f.*
searching [-iŋ] adj. Approfondi (inquiry); attentif, minutieux, rigoureux (inspection); scrutateur, perçant (look); pénétrant (study, wind). ‖ MED. Efficace (remedy).
— n. Recherche, enquête *f.*; examen *m.*; fouilles *f. pl.* ‖ Visite *f.* (of luggage). ‖ JUR. Perquisition *f.* (of premises); fouille *f.* (of a prisoner).
searchingly [-iŋli] adv. Minutieusement.
searchlight [-lait] n. ELECTR. Lumière (*f.*) d'un projecteur (beam); projecteur *m.* (projector).
seascape ['si:skeip] n. Panorama marin *m.* ‖ ARTS. Marine *f.*
seaside [-said] n. NAUT. Bord (*m.*) de la mer; *seaside resort,* station balnéaire.
season ['si:zn] n. Saison, époque *f.*; *late season,* arrière-saison. ‖ Epoque, période *f.,* temps *m.*; *holiday season,* période des vacances; *in due season,* en temps voulu. ‖ THEATR. Saison théâtrale *f.* ‖ COMM. *Between season,* demi-saison; *busy season,* fort de la saison; *dead* (or) *dull* (or) *off-season,* morte-saison. ‖ AGRIC. *In season,* de saison. ‖ ZOOL. *In season,* en chaleur. ‖ SPORTS. *Open season,* saison de la chasse (or) de la pêche. ‖ FIG. *In season and out of season,* à tout propos et hors de propos; *in season,* opportun; *out of season,* déplacé, hors de saison (remark). ‖ **Season-ticket,** n. Carte (*f.*) d'abonnement.
— v. tr. Acclimater, endurcir, mûrir (a person); préparer, traiter, abreuver (a wine vat); mûrir, laisser se faire (wine); conditionner, dessécher (wood). ‖ CULIN. Assaisonner (with garlic, vinegar); épicer, relever (with spices). ‖ MILIT. Aguerrir (troops). ‖ NAUT. Amariner (sailors). ‖ FIG. Saler (an anecdote); atténuer, tempérer (a judgment); assaisonner (a speech).
— v. intr. S'acclimater, s'aguerrir (person). ‖ Se sécher (timber); se faire (wine). ‖ MILIT. S'aguerrir (troops). ‖ NAUT. S'amariner (sailors).
seasonable [-əbl] adj. De saison, qui convient à la saison. ‖ FIG. A propos, opportun.
seasonableness [-əblnis] n. Opportunité *f.*; à-propos *m.*
seasonably [-əbli] adv. Opportunément, à propos; en temps utile.
seasonal [-əl] adj. Des saisons. ‖ COMM., MED. Saisonnier. ‖ TECHN. Embauché pour les travaux de saison (worker).
seasoner [-ə*] n. Personne (*f.*) qui assaisonne. ‖ CULIN. Condiment *m.*; épice *f.* ‖ NAUT. Marin saisonnier *m.*
seasoning [-iŋ] n. Acclimatement *m.* (of a person). ‖ Maturation *f.* (of a wine); avinage *m.* (of a winecask); séchage *m.* (of wood). ‖ CULIN. Assaisonnement, condiment *m.* ‖ MILIT. Aguerrissement *m.* ‖ NAUT. Amarinage *m.* ‖ FIG. Modération *f.* (of judgment); assaisonnement *m.* (of a story).
seat [si:t] n. Siège *m.*; fauteuil *m.* (armchair); banc *m.* (bench); chaise *f.* (chair); *to take a seat,* s'asseoir, prendre un siège; *to keep one's seat,* rester

assis. ‖ Selle *f.* (on a bicycle). ‖ Siège, fond *m.* (of a chair); fond *m.* (of trousers). ‖ *Country seat,* maison de campagne. ‖ JUR. Centre *m.* (of a government); chef-lieu *m.* (of justice); siège *m.* (in Parliament); mandat *m.* (Parliamentary term). ‖ TECHN. Chaise *f.* (of a bearing); assiette, selle *f.* (of a cylinder); alvéole *m.* (of a diamond); assiette *f.* (of a machine). ‖ AUTOM. Banquette *f.* (of a bus); assise *f.* (of a car); siège *m.* (for the driver); *emergency* (or) U. S. *jump seat,* strapontin. ‖ CH. DE F. Place assise *f.*; banquette *f.*; *take your seats!,* en voiture! ‖ AVIAT. Baquet *m.* (for pilot). ‖ NAUT. Banc *m.* (of a rower). ‖ MILIT. Théâtre *m.* (of operations). ‖ THEATR. Place assise *f.*; gradin *m.* (in an amphitheatre); fauteuil *m.* (in stalls, in a box); *folding seat,* strapontin. ‖ MED. Siège *m.* (of an illness). ‖ SPORTS. Assiette *f.* (in equitation); *to have a good seat,* bien se tenir en selle. ‖ FIG. Centre *m.* (of learning); foyer *m.* (of science). ‖ U.S. FAM. *To be in the driver's seat,* mener le jeu. ‖ FAM. Séant, postérieur *m.* ‖ **Seat-belt,** n. Ceinture de sécurité, ceinture *f.*
— v. tr. Asseoir, faire asseoir (s.o.); *to seat oneself,* s'asseoir. ‖ Fournir de chaises (an auditorium). ‖ ARCHIT. Etablir, asseoir (a foundation). ‖ THEATR. Placer (audience). ‖ AUTOM. Contenir (a number of persons). ‖ TECHN. Ajuster.
— v. intr. *To be seated,* s'asseoir (action); être assis (state); *please be seated,* veuillez vous asseoir, asseyez-vous je vous prie. ‖ MED. *To be seated in,* avoir son siège dans. ‖ TECHN. *To seat on,* porter sur, reposer sur.
seating [-iŋ] n. Attribution (*f.*) des places assises; disposition *f.* (of guests); *seating accommodation* (or) *capacity,* nombre de places assises. ‖ Matériaux (*m. pl.*) pour sièges. ‖ TECHN. Portage *m.*; ber *m.* (of a boiler); embase *f.* (of a machine); assiette *f.* (of a part); siège *m.* (of a valve).
seaward ['si:wəd] adj. NAUT. Du large (breeze); qui porte au large (tide).
— n. Côté (*m.*) du large.
— adv. Vers le large.
seaweed [-wi:d] n. BOT. Algue, herbe marine *f.*
seaworthiness ['si:wə:ðinis] n. NAUT. Navigabilité *f.* (of a ship).
seaworthy [-i] adj. NAUT. En état de naviguer, capable de tenir la mer.
sebaceous [si'beiʃəs] adj. MED. Sébacé (gland).
seborrh(o)ea [səbɔ:'ri:ə] n. MED. Séborrhée *f.*
sebum ['si:bəm] n. MED. Sébum *m.*
sec [sek] n. FAM. Seconde *f.*; *I won't be a sec,* j'en ai pour deux secondes.
secant ['si:kənt] adj. MATH. Sécant.
— n. MATH. Sécante *f.*
secateurs ['sekətəz] n. pl. Sécateur *m.*
secede [si'si:d] v. intr. Se séparer, faire sécession. ‖ ECCLES. Faire scission.
seceder [-ə*] n. Scissionnaire, séparatiste *s.* ‖ ECCLES. Dissident *s.*
secession [si'seʃən] n. Sécession, scission *f.* ‖ ECCLES. Dissidence *f.* ‖ U. S. *War of Secession,* Guerre de Sécession.
secessionist [-ist] n. U. S. Sécessionniste *s.*
seclude [si'klu:d] v. tr. Eloigner du monde, tenir éloigné (or) écarté; *to seclude oneself,* vivre à l'écart (or) dans l'isolement, se confiner. ‖ ZOOL. Interner (carrier pigeons).
secluded [-id] adj. Retiré, effacé, cloîtré (existence); écarté, retiré (retreat).
seclusion [si'klu:ʒən] n. Retraite, solitude *f.,* isolement *m.*; *in seclusion,* retiré, solitaire. ‖ Lieu retiré *m.*, retraite *f.* ‖ ZOOL. Internement *m.* (of pigeons).
second ['sekənd] adj. Deuxième; second; *in the second place,* en second lieu, secondo, deuxièmement; *twenty-second,* vingt-deuxième; *on the second floor,* au deuxième étage, au second; U. S. au pre-

mier étage ; *second marriage*, secondes noces. ‖
Deux (chapters, dates, monarchs) ; *every second
day*, tous les deux jours. ‖ Nouveau ; *on second
thoughts*, à la réflexion, réflexion faite. ‖ Autre,
second ; *second self*, seconde nature, autre soi-
même. ‖ Inférieur, secondaire (quality) ; *to be
second to no one*, n'être inférieur à personne ; *to
be second to s.o.*, venir après qqn (in priority). ‖
CH. DE F. *Second class*, deuxième classe, seconde.
‖ AUTOM. Deuxième (gear). ‖ MILIT. *Second lieutenant*, sous-lieutenant. ‖ NAUT. En second (lieutenant). ‖ MUS. Deuxième (violin). ‖ SPORTS.
Second team, équipe seconde. ‖ MED. *Second sight*,
seconde vue ; *to be in one's second childhood*, être
retombé en enfance. ‖ JUR. Issu de germain (cousin). ‖ FAM. *Second fiddle*, sous-fifre. ‖ **Second-
best**, adj. Numéro deux ; de tous les jours (garment) ; n. pis-aller *m. ; to come off second best*,
se faire battre. ‖ **Second-class**, adj. De deuxième
qualité, de second ordre, seconde classe (goods,
hotel). ‖ **Second-generation**, adj. De la seconde
génération. ‖ **Second-hand**, adj. D'occasion (book,
car) ; usagé (clothing) ; de revente (market) ; *second-
hand book-seller*, bouquiniste ; *second-hand dealer*,
revendeur, brocanteur ; *to have one's information at
second-hand*, tenir ses renseignements de seconde
main (or) d'un tiers. ‖ **Second-rate**, adj. De second
ordre, de qualité inférieure (or) moyenne.
— v. tr. Seconder, soutenir. ‖ Appuyer (a proposition) ; appuyer la motion de (a speaker). ‖ MILIT.
[se'kɔnd]. Mettre en disponibilité (a soldier) ;
seconded personnel, personnel détaché.
— n. Second, deuxième *s.* (in rank, in a series). ‖
Seconde *f.* (60th of a minute) ; *in a split second*,
en un tiers de seconde, en un rien de temps ; *just a
second*, attendez un instant. ‖ Témoin, second *m.*
(in a duel). ‖ MILIT. *Second in command*, commandant en second. ‖ NAUT. *Second in command*, officier en second. ‖ COMM. Marchandise de deuxième
qualité *f.* ‖ ASTRON., MATH. Seconde *f.* ‖ MUS.
Deuxième partie *f.* (of a composition) ; seconde *f.*
(interval). ‖ SPORTS. Second, soigneur *m.* (in boxing). ‖ **Second-hand**, n. Aiguille *(f.)* des secondes,
trotteuse *f.*
secondarily ['sekəndərili] adv. Secondairement,
en second.
secondary ['sekəndəri] adj. Secondaire ; peu
important (question). ‖ Supérieur (education,
school). ‖ ELECTR. D'accumulateurs (battery) ;
induit (current). ‖ PHYS. Secondaire (optical image).
‖ ASTRON. *Secondary planet*, satellite. ‖ JUR. Indirect (evidence). ‖ GRAMM. Dérivé (meaning) ; secondaire (stress). ‖ ECCLES. Second (cause).
— n. Subalterne, subordonné *m.* ‖ ELECTR., GEOL.
Secondaire *m.* ‖ ASTRON. Satellite *m.* ‖ ECCLES.
Membre secondaire du chapitre *m.*
seconder [-ə*] n. Deuxième parrain *m.* (of a candidate). ‖ Supporter *m.* (of a motion).
secondly [-li] adv. Deuxièmement ; secundo (fam.).
secrecy ['si:krəsi] n. Secret *m. ; in secrecy*, en
secret ; *under pledge of secrecy*, sous le sceau du
secret ; *there is no secrecy about it*, on n'en fait
pas mystère. ‖ Discrétion *f.*
secret ['si:krit] n. Secret *m. ;* confidence *f.* (of
lovers) ; *as a secret*, en confidence ; *open secret*,
secret de Polichinelle. ‖ Pl. Mystères *m. pl.* (of
nature). ‖ Pl. MED. Parties *f. pl.* ‖ ECCLES. Secrète
f. ‖ † Chemise de maille *f.*
— adj. Secret, caché ; retiré (place) ; dérobé (stairway). ‖ MILIT. Secret (agent, service). ‖ COMM.
Secret partner, commanditaire, bailleur de fonds.
‖ MED. *Secret parts*, parties. ‖ FIG. Peu communicatif, secret, renfermé (person) ; secret (society).
secretarial [,sekrə'tɛəriəl] adj. De secrétaire ; de
secrétariat.
secretariat [-riit] n. Secrétariat *m.*
secretary ['sekrətri] n. Secrétaire *s. ; honorary*,

private secretary, secrétaire honoraire, particulier.
‖ Chancelier *m.* (of a consulate) ; secrétaire *s.* (of
an embassy) ; ministre *m.* (in the government) ;
Secretary of State, ministre à portefeuille ; U. S.
ministre des Affaires étrangères. ‖ Secrétaire *m.*
(desk). ‖ ZOOL. Secrétaire, serpentaire *m.*
secretaryship [-ʃip] n. Secrétariat *m.*
secrete [si'kri:t] v. tr. Soustraire à la vue ; *to
secrete oneself*, s'enfermer. ‖ MED. Sécréter. ‖ JUR.
Receler.
secretion [si'kri:ʃən] n. Action de cacher *f.* ‖
MED. Sécrétion *f.* ‖ JUR. Recel *m.*
secretive [-tiv] adj. MED. Sécréteur *m. ;* sécrétrice
f. ‖ FIG. Renfermé, secret, cachottier.
secretiveness [-tivnis] n. Caractère cachottier *m. ;*
nature secrète *f.*
secretory [-təri] adj. MED. Sécrétoire ; sécréteur
m., sécrétrice *f.*
— n. MED. Organe sécréteur *m.*
sect [sekt] n. Secte *f.*
sectarian [sek'tɛəriən] adj., n. Sectaire *s.*
sectarianism [-izm̦] n. Sectarisme *m.*
sectary ['sektəri] n. ECCLES. Schismatique *s.*
sectile ['sektail] adj. Sectile, sécable.
section ['sekʃən] n. Sectionnement, coupage *m. ;*
section, division, coupe *f.* (action). ‖ Portion, section, partie, division *f.* (part) ; compartiment *m.*
(of a drawer) ; tranche *f.* (slice) ; tronçon *m.* (of a
tube). ‖ Classe *f.* (of population). ‖ Rubrique *f.* (of
a newspaper) ; paragraphe, alinéa *m. ;* partie *f.* (of a
text) ; *comic section*, page humoristique. ‖ JUR.
Article *m.* (of a law). ‖ ARTS, AUTOM., ARCHIT.
Profil *m. ;* coupe *f.* (of metal). ‖ TECHN. Profilé *m.* (of metal) ;
élément *m.* (of a sectional boiler). ‖ CH. DE F. Secteur, tronçon *m.* (of track) ; compartiment *m.* (of a
sleeper). ‖ MATH. Section *f.* ‖ AVIAT. Patrouille *f.*
‖ MILIT. Section *f.* (of artillery) ; escouade *f.* (of
infantry). ‖ CULIN. Portion *f.* (of cheese) ; part *f.*
(of cake) ; tranche *f.* (of orange). ‖ COMM. Rayon
m. (of a department store). ‖ U. S. Quartier *m.*
(of town).
— v. tr. Sectionner.
sectional [-ḷ] adj. D'une catégorie, d'une classe,
d'un parti, d'une région (interests). ‖ Quadrillé
(paper). ‖ ARTS. De section (area, surface) ; en
coupe, en profil (design). ‖ TECHN. En sections ;
sectionnel (boiler) ; démontable (bookcase) ; profilé
(metal).
sectionalism [-ḷizm̦] n. U. S. Régionalisme *m.*
sector ['sektə*] n. TECHN., ASTRON., MILIT., COMM.
Secteur *m.* ‖ MATH. Compas (*m.*) de proportion.
secular [ˈsekjulə*] adj. Séculaire, de longue date
(ancient, historical) ; Temporel, du monde, du
siècle (temporal) ; laïque (education) ; séculier, civil
(history) ; mondain (life). ‖ ECCLES. Séculier (priest).
‖ ASTRON. Séculaire (variation). ‖ MUS. Profane ;
séculaire (hymn). ‖ JUR. Temporel (justice). ‖ FIG.
Durable (renown).
— n. ECCLES. Séculier, prêtre séculier *m.*
secularism [-rizm̦] n. Sécularisme *m. ;* mondanité
f. ‖ Politique de la laïcité *f.* (in education). ‖ PHI-
LOS. Matérialisme *m.*
secularist [-rist] n. Partisan (*m.*) de la laïcité. ‖
PHILOS. Matérialiste, libre penseur *m.*
secularization [,sekjuləri'zeiʃən] n. Laïcisation
f. (of a school). ‖ ECCLES. Désaffectation *f.* (of a
church) ; sécularisation *f.* (of a domain).
secularize ['sekjuləraiz] v. tr. Laïciser (a school).
‖ ECCLES. Désaffecter (a church) ; séculariser (a
domain).
secund ['si:kənd] adj. BOT., ZOOL. Unilatéral.
securable [si'kjuərəbl] adj. Procurable, trouvable.
secure [si'kjuə*] adj. Tranquille, en paix, sans
inquiétude (mentally) ; sauf, en sûreté, à l'abri
(physically). ‖ Ferme, solide, qui offre toute sécurité ; *to make secure*, fermer (or) fixer solidement.
‖ MILIT. En lieu sûr (prisoner) ; *secure from attack*,

à l'abri des attaques. ‖ Fin. Sûr, de tout repos (investment). ‖ Archit. Fixé (beam); assujetti (door); solide (foundation). ‖ Naut. Bien amarré (boat). ‖ Fig. Assuré, certain (future); ferme (hope). — v. tr. Mettre en sûreté (or) à l'abri; préserver *(from,* de); *to secure oneself against,* se garantir contre. ‖ Mettre en lieu sûr (or) sous clef. ‖ Se saisir de, s'emparer de, s'assurer de, mettre la main sur. ‖ Avoir, obtenir, acquérir, se procurer (to get); réserver (a seat); s'assurer (a service); assurer, procurer *(for,* à). ‖ Comm. Nantir (a creditor); garantir (a loan). ‖ Techn. Immobiliser, fixer (or) attacher solidement; accorer (a barrel); bien fermer (a door); arrimer (a load); bloquer (a screw); verrouiller (a shutter). ‖ Milit. Fortifier (a garrison); garder (a pass); mettre en lieu sûr (a prisoner); mettre à l'abri (troops); *to secure arms,* mettre l'arme sous le bras gauche. ‖ Jur. Ecrouer, mettre sous les verrous (a prisoner). ‖ Naut. Saisir (an anchor); amarrer (a boat). ‖ Agric. Rentrer (a crop).

securely [-li] adv. Sûrement, sans danger, en sécurité. ‖ Techn. Fermement, solidement. ‖ Fig. Avec confiance, sans crainte.

security [-riti] n. Sécurité, sûreté f. ‖ Protection, garantie f. *(against,* contre). ‖ Techn. Stabilité f.; solidité f. (of an installation); *security device,* dispositif de sûreté. ‖ Fin. Valeur f., titre m.; (pl.) fonds m. pl.; portefeuille m. (bond, share, stock); garantie, action m., cautionnement, nantissement m. (for a debt, a loan); *government securities,* fonds d'Etat; *on security,* sur gage. ‖ Jur. Garantie f. (act); garant, répondant m. (person); *Security Council,* Conseil de sécurité; *social security scheme,* Sécurité sociale, assurances sociales; *to lodge security,* déposer un cautionnement; *to be security for,* se porter garant (or) caution (or) fort pour, répondre de. ‖ Fig. Certitude f. (of judgment).

sedan [si'd ə n] n. U.S. Autom. Conduite intérieure, limousine f. ‖ **Sedan-chair,** n. Chaise (f.) à porteurs. ‖ **Sedan-cloth,** n. Sedan m.

sedate [si'deit] adj. Sobre, discret (furnishings). ‖ Fig. Calme (conduct); posé (person); rassis (temperament).

sedate v. tr. Med. Administrer un sédatif à, placer sous calmant.

sedately [-li] adv. Posément, calmement.

sedateness [-nis] n. Allure posée f.; équilibre, calme m.

sedation [si'dei ʃ ə n] n. Med. Sédation f.

sedative ['sedətiv] adj., n. Med. Sédatif m.

sedentarily ['sedntərili] adv. Sédentairement.

sedentariness [-inis] n. Vie sédentaire f., sédentarisme m.

sedentary [-i] adj. Sédentaire. ‖ Arts. Assis. ‖ Zool. Sédentaire. — n. Sédentaire s.

sedge [sedʒ] n. Laîche f. ‖ **Sedge-warbler,** n. Zool. Fauvette (f.) des marais.

sedgy [-i] adj. Bot. Couvert de joncs.

sediment ['sedimənt] n. Sédiment, dépôt m. ‖ Boue f. (of ink); lie f. (of wine). ‖ Chim. Résidu m. ‖ Geol. Alluvionnement m. ‖ Med. Sédiment m.

sedimentary [sedi'mentəri] adj. Geol. Sédimentaire.

sedimentation [,sedimen'tei ʃ ə n] n. Sédimentation f.

sedition [sə'di ʃ ə n] n. Sédition f.

seditious [- ʃ əs] adj. Séditieux.

seduce [si'dju:s] v. tr. Corrompre, dépraver (to corrupt). ‖ Séduire (a woman). ‖ Séduire, attirer (to attract).

seducer [-ə*] n. Séducteur m.; séductrice f. ‖ Corrupteur m.; corruptrice f.

seduction [si'dʌk ʃ ə n] n. Corruption f., entraînement au mal m. ‖ Séduction f. (of women). ‖ Charme, attrait m., séduction f. (attractiveness).

seductive [-tiv] adj. Séduisant, attrayant. ‖ Alléchant (offer); aguichant (smile).

seductiveness [-tivnis] n. Séduction f. (of a glance, a woman); caractère alléchant m. (of an offer).

seductress [-tris] n. Séductrice, ensorceleuse f.

sedulity [si'dju:liti], **sedulousness** ['sedju:ləs-nis] n. Assiduité, application f.; empressement m.

sedulous ['sedjuləs] adj. Assidu, appliqué, diligent, empressé.

sedulously [-li] adv. Assidûment, diligemment.

see [si:] n. Eccles. Archevêché m. (of an archbishop); siège épiscopal, évêché m. (of a bishop); *Holy* (or) *Papal See,* Saint-Siège, siège apostolique.

see v. tr. (117). Voir; apercevoir (to perceive); regarder (to watch); *to see again,* revoir; *to see s.o. working,* voir travailler qqn; *to see sth. done,* voir faire qqch.; *to see the sights,* visiter les monuments. ‖ S'apercevoir de, observer, remarquer (in general); reconnaître (an error); comprendre (a joke); saisir (a nuance); apprécier (a thought); voir, se rendre compte de (a truth). ‖ Envisager, juger, considérer; *as far as I can see,* autant que je puis en juger; *as I see it,* à ce qu'il me paraît; *do as you see fit,* faites comme bon vous semble. ‖ Avoir une entrevue avec; accorder un entretien à; fréquenter, avoir des relations avec (friends); recevoir (visitors); *to go and see s.o.,* aller (or) passer voir qqn.; *to see no one,* ne recevoir personne, n'être visible pour personne. ‖ Accompagner, reconduire; *to see s.o. to the door* (or) *out, home,* accompagner qqn jusqu'à la porte, jusque chez lui; *to see s.o. off,* voir partir qqn, venir dire au revoir à qqn; *to see s.o. through,* aider (or) assister (or) soutenir qqn, prêter son appui à qqn; *to see sth. through,* mener qqch. jusqu'au bout. ‖ Milit. To see service, servir, faire campagne. ‖ Med. Consulter (the doctor); *to see the light,* naître, voir le jour. ‖ Fig. Assister à, passer par, éprouver, subir; connaître (changes); faire l'expérience de (life); *to have seen better days,* avoir connu des jours meilleurs; *to have seen the world,* avoir beaucoup vécu; *to see the light,* comprendre, se rendre compte; se convertir. ‖ Fig. Voir, savoir; *to see one's way clear to do sth.,* savoir comment s'y prendre pour faire qqch.; voir le moyen de faire qqch.; *that remains to be seen,* qui vivra verra, cela reste à voir. ‖ Fam. To see stars, voir trente-six chandelles.

— v. intr. Voir. ‖ Comprendre, se rendre compte; *as far as I can see,* autant que je puis en juger. ‖ Réfléchir; *I'll see about it,* j'y songerai; *let me see,* voyons un peu. ‖ Med. To see poorly, avoir une vue défectueuse. ‖ Fam. *See here!,* dites donc!, voyons! ‖ **To see after** (or) to, s'occuper de, être attentif à; *to see to it that all is ready,* veiller à ce que (or) s'assurer que tout soit prêt. ‖ **To see through,** voir clair dans, deviner les dessous de (a gesture); pénétrer, percer (a mystery); pénétrer les intentions de, voir clair dans le jeu de (s.o.).

seed [si:d] n. Agric., Bot. Graine f. (in general); pépin m. (of a fruit); semence f., semences f. pl. (for sowing); *to go to seed,* s'affricher (field), monter en graine (plant). ‖ Zool. Frai m. (of an oyster). ‖ Med. Sperme m.; semence f. ‖ Fig. Progéniture f. ‖ Fig. Cause f., principe m., germes m. pl. (of discord). ‖ Fam. *To go to seed,* monter en graine (person). ‖ Culin. Gâteau à l'anis (or) au carvi m. ‖ **Seed-cake,** n. Culin. Gâteau à l'anis (or) au carvi m. ‖ **Seed-corn,** n. Bot. Blé (m.) de semence. ‖ **Seed-drill,** n. Agric. Semoir m. ‖ **Seed-lobe,** n. Bot. Cotylédon m. ‖ **Seed-pearl,** n. Petite perle f. ‖ **Seed-plot,** n. Agric. Semis m.; Fig. Foyer m. (of revolt). ‖ **Seed-time,** n. Semaison f., temps (m.) des semailles. ‖ **Seed-trade,** n. Comm. Graineterie f. ‖ **Seed-vessel,** n. Bot. Péricarpe m.

— v. intr. Agric. Monter en graine; grener (cereals). ‖ S'égrener.

— v. tr. Agric. Semer, ensemencer. ‖ Epépiner, égruger (a fruit). ‖ Sports. Trier (players).

seeder [-ə*] n. AGRIC. Semoir m. ‖ TECHN. Epépineuse f. ‖ ZOOL. Poisson qui fraye m.

seediness [-inis] n. Usure f., état râpé m. (of a garment); aspect m. (or) tenue (f.) minable (of s.o.).

seedless [-lis] adj. BOT. Asperme; sans pépins (fruit).

seedling [-liŋ] n. BOT. Jeune plant m.; élève f. ‖ AGRIC. Semis m.

seedsman [-zmən] (pl. **seedsmen**) n. COMM. Grainetier m. ‖ AGRIC. Grainier m.

seedy [-i] adj. AGRIC., BOT. Plein de graines, grenu; monté en graine. ‖ FIG. Râpé, usé (garment); minable, miteux (person). ‖ FAM. Vaseux, patraque; to look seedy, avoir une mine de papier mâché.

seeing [-iŋ] conj. Etant donné que, vu que, considérant.
— n. Vue, vision f. ‖ LOC. Seeing is believing, voir c'est croire.
— adj. Voyant. ‖ ZOOL. Seeing-eye dog, chien d'aveugle.

seek [si:k] v. tr. (118). Chercher, aller à la recherche de, essayer (or) s'efforcer de trouver ; to seek death, se faire tuer. ‖ Chercher à atteindre, poursuivre (an aim); demander (counsel, satisfaction); rechercher (a criminal); briguer (a favour); être en quête de (work). ‖ Aller (or) se rendre (or) se retirer à (a retreat); aller trouver (s.o.); to seek shelter, se réfugier sous un abri. ‖ NAUT. S'efforcer d'atteindre (land). ‖ SPORTS. Quêter (game).
— v. intr. Chercher, se livrer à des recherches. ‖ To seek after (or) for, chercher, rechercher, poursuivre. ‖ To seek out, tâcher de découvrir, faire choix de. ‖ To seek through, fouiller, explorer. ‖ To seek to, essayer (or) tenter de, chercher (or) s'efforcer à.

seeker [-ə*] n. Chercheur s.

seem [si:m] v. intr. Sembler, paraître; it seems to me that, il me semble que, à mon avis, selon moi; so it seems, à ce qu'il paraît, paraît-il; it seems not, il paraît que non; to seem interesting, sembler intéressant; to seem honest, paraître honnête; to seem to be working, avoir l'air de travailler. ‖ Avoir l'impression que (to feel as if); I seemed to be sinking, j'avais l'impression de sombrer.

seeming [-iŋ] adj. Apparent, de façade, soi-disant.
— n. Apparence f., aspect, semblant m.

seemingly [-iŋli] adv. En apparence, apparemment, autant qu'il paraisse.

seemliness [-linis] n. Grâce, beauté f. (attractiveness); convenance, bienséance f. (correctness).

seemly [-li] adj. Joli, gracieux (attractive); approprié, bienséant, convenable (correct).

seep [si:p] v. intr. Suinter, filtrer, s'infiltrer.

seer [si:ə*] n. Voyant, prophète s. ‖ MED. Voyant m.

seersucker ['si:ə‚sʌkə] n. Seersucker m.

seesaw ['si:'sɔ:] n. Bascule f.
— v. intr. Jouer à la bascule. ‖ TECHN. Osciller. ‖ FIG. Hésiter, balancer.
— adj. De bascule, de va-et-vient (motion).

seethe [si:ð] v. intr. (119). CULIN. Bouillonner. ‖ FIG. S'agiter, bouillonner; foisonner, grouiller.

seething [-iŋ] adj. Bouillonnant; tourmenté (waters). ‖ FIG. En effervescence (or) fermentation (country); grouillant, foisonnant (crowd, mass); seething with excitement, en ébullition.

segment ['segmənt] n. MATH., ARCHIT. Segment m. ELECTR. Segment m., lame f. (of a commutator). ‖ CULIN. Tranche f. (of an orange). ‖ **Segment-gear** (or) **-wheel**, n. TECHN. Secteur denté m.
— v. tr. Segmenter.
— v. intr. ZOOL. Se segmenter.

segmental [seg'mentl] adj. Segmentaire. ‖ ARCHIT. Surbaissé (arch).

segmentation [‚segmən'teiʃən] n. Segmentation f.

segmented ['segmentid] adj. Segmenté. ‖ TECHN. A facettes (mirror). ‖ CULIN. A tranches (orange).

segregate ['segrəgeit] v. tr. Séparer, isoler, mettre à part.
— v. intr. Se diviser, se dissocier. ‖ Se cristalliser.
— [-git] adj. Isolé. ‖ ZOOL. Simple, séparé.

segregation [‚segrə'geiʃən] n. Ségrégation f.

segregationist [-ist] n. Ségrégationniste s.

segregative ['segrəgeitiv] adj. Ségrégatif.

seigneur [sein'jə*], **seignor** [sei'njɔr] n. Seigneur m.

seigniory [-ri] n. Seigneurie f.

seine [sein] n. SPORTS. Seine, senne f.
— v. tr., intr. SPORTS. Pêcher à la seine.

seism ['saizm] n. Séisme m.

seismic [-ik] adj. Sismique, séismique.

seismograph [-əgrɑ:f] n. Sismographe m.

seismology [saiz'mɔlədʒi] n. Sismologie f.

seizable ['si:zəbl̩] adj. Saisissable.

seize [si:z] v. tr. Saisir; s'emparer de, mettre la main sur; se saisir de (to take hold of). ‖ JUR. Arrêter, appréhender (a person); saisir (property). ‖ MILIT. Enlever (a fortress). ‖ NAUT. Amarrer. ‖ MED. Prendre, saisir. ‖ FIG. Comprendre, saisir (a meaning); sauter sur (an opportunity).
— v. intr. Se saisir, s'emparer (upon, de). ‖ MED. To be seized by, être pris de (an attack). ‖ TECHN. Gripper, coincer; to seize up, se caler.

seizin [-in] n. JUR. Saisine f.

seizure ['si:ʒə*] n. MILIT., NAUT. Prise, capture f. (of a fortress, a ship); mainmise f. (of, sur) [a territory]. ‖ JUR. Arrestation f. (of a person); saisie f. (of property). ‖ MED. Attaque f. ‖ TECHN. Grippure f.; calage m.

sejant ['si:dʒənt] adj. BLAS. Séant.

seldom ['seldəm] adv. Rarement, peu souvent; to be seldom seen, se faire rare.

select [si'lekt] v. tr. Choisir, faire choix de (from, parmi). ‖ COMM. Trier. ‖ SPORTS. Sélectionner.
— adj. Choisi, de choix. ‖ D'élite, très fermé, très chic (club). ‖ AGRIC. De premier choix (produce).

selection [si'lekʃən] n. Choix m. (act). ‖ Collection f.; recueil (m.) de morceaux choisis (literary). ‖ ZOOL. Sélection f.

selective [-tiv] adj. Sélectif. ‖ ELECTR. Sélecteur.

selectivity [-tiviti] n. Qualité sélective f. ‖ RADIO. Sélectivité f.

selectman [-tmən] (pl. **selectmen**) n. U.S. Conseiller municipal m.

selector [si'lektə*] n. Sélectionneur s. ‖ RADIO., TECHN. Sélecteur m.

selenate ['seli‚neit] n. CHIM. Séléniàte m.

selenic [si'lenik] adj. CHIM. Sélénique.

selenium [si'li:niəm] n. CHIM. Sélénium m.

self [self] (pl. **selves** [selvz]) n. Personnalité, individualité f.; a shadow of his former self, l'ombre de ce qu'il était autrefois; one's better self, notre meilleur côté; my second self, un autre moi-même, mon alter ego; to be one's old self, être rétabli (or) retapé; avoir repris du poil de la bête (fam.). ‖ Egoïsme, intérêt personnel m. (self-centredness). ‖ PHILOS. Moi, ego m. ‖ COMM. A moi-même (on cheques). ‖ BOT. Fleur de couleur uniforme f.
— adj. De même (fabric, trimming). ‖ **Self-abasement**, n. Dégradation f.; avilissement m. ‖ **Self-absorbed**, adj. Egocentrique. ‖ **Self-abuse**, n. Onanisme m. ‖ **Self-accusation**, n. Autocritique, auto-accusation f. ‖ **Self-acting**, adj. TECHN. Automatique. ‖ **Self-addressed**, adj. Self-addressed envelope, enveloppe à son nom et à son adresse. ‖ **Self-adjusting**, adj. TECHN. A réglage automatique. ‖ **Self-advertisement**, n. Cabotinage, battage m. ‖ **Self-analysis**, n. Introspection, auto-analyse f. ‖ **Self-apparent**, adj. Evident. ‖ **Self-approving**, adj. Content de soi; suffisant (smile). ‖ **Self-asserting** (or) **-assertive**, adj. Autoritaire, arrogant, impérieux. ‖ **Self-assurance**, n. Assurance, f.; aplomb m. ‖ **Self-assured**, adj. Sûr de soi. ‖ **Self-binder**,

n. AGRIC. Moissonneuse-lieuse *f.* ‖ **Self-centred,** adj. Egocentrique. ‖ **Self-closing,** adj. A fermeture automatique. ‖ **Self-cocking,** adj. A armement automatique (gun). ‖ **Self-colour,** n. Couleur naturelle *f.* ; BOT. Couleur uniforme *f.* ; adj. Armuré (design) ; uni, ton sur ton (fabric). ‖ **Self-command,** n. Maîtrise (*f.*) de soi, empire sur soi-même, sang-froid *m.* ‖ **Self-communion,** n. Recueillement *m.* ‖ **Self-conceit,** n. Suffisance, vanité *f.* ‖ **Self-confessed,** adj. *She is a self-confessed alcoholic,* de son propre aveu, elle est alcoolique. ‖ **Self-confidence,** n. Confiance (*f.*) en soi. ‖ **Self-confident,** adj. Sûr de soi, plein d'assurance ; qui ne doute de rien (presumptuous). ‖ **Self-conscious,** adj. Contraint, emprunté (manner) ; gêné, embarrassé, qui se sent observé (person) ; *to make s. o. self-conscious,* intimider qqn. ‖ **Self-consciousness,** n. Contrainte, gêne *f.* ; embarras ; respect humain *m.* ; PHILOS. Conscience *f.* ‖ **Self-contained,** adj. Indépendant (accommodation) ; réservé, renfermé, peu communicatif (person) ; TECHN. Indépendant, autonome. ‖ **Self-contempt,** n. Mépris pour soi-même *m.* ‖ **Self-contradictory,** adj. En contradiction avec soi-même. ‖ **Self-control,** n. Sang-froid, empire sur soi-même *m.* ; maîtrise (*f.*) de soi. ‖ **Self-cooker,** n. CULIN. Autocuiseur *m.* ‖ **Self-created,** adj. Qui s'est créé (or) que l'on a créé soi-même. ‖ **Self-critical,** adj. Qui se critique ; *be a little more self-critical,* fais un peu plus ton autocritique. ‖ **Self-criticism,** n. Autocritique *f.* ‖ **Self-deception** (or) **-deceit,** n. Illusion *f.* ‖ **Self-defeating,** adj. Inopérant, qui a l'effet inverse. ‖ **Self-defence,** n. JUR. Instinct (*m.*) de conservation ; corps défendant *m.* ; légitime défense *f.* ; SPORTS. Autodéfense *f.* ; *noble art of self-defence,* noble art. ‖ **Self-delusion,** n. Illusion *f.* ‖ **Self-denial,** n. Abnégation *f.*, renoncement, oubli de soi *m.* ‖ **Self-dependent,** adj. Confiant en soi, indépendant. ‖ **Self-depreciation,** n. Modestie exagérée *f.* ‖ **Self-destruction,** n. Suicide *m.* ‖ **Self-determination,** n. Autodétermination *f.* ‖ **Self-discipline,** n. Autodiscipline *f.* ‖ **Self-distrust,** n. Défiance (*f.*) de soi. ‖ **Self-educated,** adj. Autodidacte. ‖ **Self-effacing,** adj. Discret, qui aime à s'effacer. ‖ **Self-employed,** adj. Indépendant (worker). ‖ **Self-esteem,** n. Amour-propre *m.* ; estime (*f.*) de soi. ‖ **Self-evident,** adj. Evident, qui va de soi, qui saute aux yeux ; de La Palisse (truth) [fam.]. ‖ **Self-examination,** n. Examen (*m.*) de conscience. ‖ **Self-excitation,** n. ELECTR. Auto-excitation *f.* ‖ **Self-explanatory,** adj. Qui s'explique de soi-même. ‖ **Self-expression,** n. Expression de sa propre personnalité *f.* ‖ **Self-fecundation** (or) **-fertilization,** n. Autofécondation *f.* ‖ **Self-feeding,** adj. TECHN. A alimentation (or) remplissage automatique. ‖ **Self-fertilizing,** adj. BOT. A pollinisation directe. ‖ **Self-flattery,** n. Complaisance (*f.*) envers soi-même. ‖ **Self-forgetful,** adj. Oublieux de soi ; altruiste. ‖ **Self-forgetfulness,** n. Oubli de soi, *m.* ; abnégation *f.* ‖ **Self-governing,** adj. Autonome. ‖ **Self-government,** n. Gouvernement personnel *m.* ; indépendance, autonomie *f.* ‖ **Self-help,** n. Effort (or) secours personnel *m.* ; *self-help restaurant,* restaurant libre service. ‖ **Self-humiliation,** n. Abaissement volontaire *m.* ; ECCLES. Anéantissement *m.* ‖ **Self-importance,** n. Infatuation, suffisance *f.* ‖ **Self-important,** adj. Important, vaniteux, présomptueux, suffisant. ‖ **Self-induction,** n. ELECTR. Self-induction, inductance, self *f.* ‖ **Self-indulgence,** n. Complaisance (or) faiblesse (*f.*) envers soi-même ; satisfaction égoïste (*f.*) de ses désirs, sybaritisme *m.* ‖ **Self-indulgent,** adj. Qui s'écoute, qui ne se refuse rien, sybarite. ‖ **Self-inflicted,** adj. Que l'on s'inflige à soi-même ; MED. Volontaire (injury). ‖ **Self-interest,** n. Intérêt personnel *m.* ‖ **Self-justification,** n. Justification de sa propre conduite *f.* ‖ **Self-knowledge,** n. Connaissance (*f.*) de soi-même. ‖ **Self-loading,** adj. A chargement automatique (firearm). ‖ **Self-locking,** adj. A fermeture automatique. ‖ **Self-love,** n. Egoïsme, amour de soi, amour-

propre *m.* ‖ **Self-lubricating,** adj. TECHN. Autolubrifiant. ‖ **Self-made,** adj. *Self-made man,* fils de ses œuvres, self-made man. ‖ **Self-portrait,** n. ARTS. Autoportrait *m.* ‖ **Self-possessed,** adj. Maître de soi, flegmatique, plein de sang-froid. ‖ **Self-possession,** n. Calme, sang-froid *m.* (See COMPOSURE.) ‖ **Self-preservation,** n. ZOOL. Conservation *f.* ; JUR. Légitime défense *f.* ; instinct (*m.*) de conservation. ‖ **Self-propelled,** adj. TECHN. Autopropulsé. ‖ **Self-propelling,** adj. TECHN. Autopropulseur, automoteur *m.* ; automotrice *f.* ‖ **Self-raising,** adj. Avec poudre levante incorporée (flour). ‖ **Self-recording** (or) **-registering,** adj. Enregistreur. ‖ **Self-regard,** see SELF-RESPECT. ‖ **Self-regulating,** adj. TECHN. A autoréglage ; autorégulateur *m.* ; autorégulatrice *f.* ‖ **Self-reliance,** n. Assurance, confiance (*f.*) en soi. ‖ **Self-renunciation,** n. Renoncement *m.* ; abnégation *f.* ‖ **Self-reproach,** n. Repentir, remords, reproche intérieur *m.* ‖ **Self-respect,** n. Respect de soi *m.* ; dignité personnelle *f.* ‖ **Self-respecting,** adj. Qui a le respect de soi. ‖ **Self-restraint,** n. Retenue *f.* ; empire sur soi *m.* ‖ **Self-righteous,** adj. Pharisaïque. ‖ **Self-righteousness,** n. Pharisaïsme *m.* ‖ **Self-righting,** adj. NAUT. A redressement automatique, inchavirable. ‖ **Self-sacrifice,** n. Sacrifice de soi *m.* ; immolation personnelle *f.* ‖ **Self-same,** adj. Identique, exactement le même. ‖ **Self-satisfaction,** n. Contentement de soi *m.* ; suffisance, fatuité *f.* ‖ **Self-satisfied,** adj. Content de soi, suffisant. ‖ **Self-sealing,** adj. TECHN. Auto-obturateur (tank). ‖ **Self-seeking,** adj. Egoïste ; n. Egoïsme *m.* ; recherche (*f.*) de soi. ‖ **Self-service,** n. Self-service *m.* ; *self-service restaurant,* restaurant libre service, self-service, self. ‖ **Self-starter,** n. AUTOM. Démarreur automatique *m.* ‖ **Self-styled,** adj. Soi-disant, prétendu. ‖ **Self-sufficiency,** n. Indépendance *f.* ; vanité, présomption, suffisance *f.* (pejorative). ‖ **Self-sufficient** (or) **-sufficing,** adj. Indépendant ; suffisant, présomptueux. ‖ **Self-suggestion,** n. Autosuggestion *f.* ‖ **Self-supporting,** adj. Qui subvient à ses besoins, qui vit de son travail ; COMM. Qui couvre ses frais. ‖ **Self-surrender,** n. Abdication de sa volonté *f.* ‖ **Self-taught,** adj. Autodidacte. ‖ **Self-willed,** adj. Entêté, obstiné, opiniâtre. ‖ **Self-winding,** adj. TECHN. A remontage automatique.

selfish [-iʃ] adj. Egoïste, intéressé ; personnel (motive). ‖ Avare (stingy).

selfishness [-iʃnis] n. Egoïsme *m.* ‖ Avarice *f.* (stinginess).

selfless [-lis] adj. Désintéresé, sans egoïsme, altruiste.

selflessness [-lisnis] n. Désintéressement, altruisme, oubli de soi *m.*

sell [sel] v. tr. (120). COMM. Vendre ; placer (goods) ; *to sell cheap, retail,* vendre à bon marché, au détail ; *to sell off,* liquider, écouler, solder ; *to sell out,* épuiser, réaliser (a stock). ‖ FIN. *To sell for delivery, short,* vendre à couvert, à découvert (shares). ‖ JUR. *To sell up,* faire saisir (property). ‖ FIG. Trahir (one's country). ‖ POP. Amener à la balançoire, monter le coup à (s.o.). — v. intr. Se vendre ; trouver acquéreur ; *to sell out,* vendre son fonds, tout liquider ; *sold out,* épuisé (edition). ‖ POP. *To be sold on,* être toqué de. — n. POP. Blague, fumisterie *f.*

seller [-ə*] n. COMM. Vendeur, marchand, débitant *s.* ; *best-seller,* super-succès de librairie ; *quick seller,* article d'écoulement facile. ‖ FIN. Réalisateur *m.* ; réalisatrice *f.* (of bonds).

sellotape ['selə,teip] n. (trademark) Scotch *m.* (nom dép.), ruban adhésif transparent *m.* — v. tr. Coller avec du Scotch, scotcher.

seltzer-water ['seltsə*;'wɔːtə*] n. Eau (*f.*) de Seltz.

selvage, selvedge ['selvidʒ] n. Lisière *f.* (of a fabric) ; gâche *f.* (of a lock).

selves [selvz] n. pl. See SELF.

semantic [si'mæntik] adj. GRAMM. Sémantique.
semantically [-tikəli] adv. GRAMM. Sémantiquement.
semanticist [-tisist] n. Sémanticien s.
semantics [-tiks] n. sg. GRAMM. Sémantique f.
semaphore ['seməfɔ:*] n. Sémaphore m.
semasiology [,seməsi'ɔlədʒi] n. GRAMM. Sémasiologie f.
semblance ['sembləns] n. Apparence f.; air, aspect, semblant m.; in semblance, en apparence.
semen ['si:mən] n. MED. Sperme m.
semester [sə'mestə*] n. U. S. Semestre m. (school half-year).
semi ['semi] pref. Semi, demi. ‖ **Semi-annual**, adj. Semestriel. ‖ **Semi-barbarian**, adj. A demi barbare. ‖ **Semi-circular**, adj. Demi-circulaire. ‖ **Semi-conscious**, adj. A demi conscient. ‖ **Semi-darkness**, n. Demi-jour m. ‖ **Semi-detached**, adj. ARCHIT. Jumeau, accolé (houses). ‖ **Semi-diameter**, n. MATH. Demi-diamètre m. ‖ **Semi-final**, n. SPORTS. Demi-finale f. ‖ **Semi-finalist**, n. SPORTS. Joueur (s.) en demi-finale. ‖ **Semi-literate**, adj. A demi illettré. ‖ **Semi-obscurity**, n. Demi-obscurité f. ‖ **Semi-official**, adj. Semi-officiel, officieux. ‖ **Semi-opaque**, adj. Semi-opaque. ‖ **Semi-precious**, adj. Fin (stone). ‖ **Semi-skilled**, adj. Semi-skilled worker, ouvrier spécialisé, O. S. ‖ **Semi-transparent**, adj. Semi- (or) demi-transparent. ‖ **Semi-tropical**, adj. Subtropical.
semi n. FAM. Pavillon jumelé m.
semibreve [-'bri:v] n. MUS. Ronde f.
semicolon [-'koulən] n. GRAMM. Point-virgule m.
semiconductor [,semikən'dʌktə*] adj., n. ELECTR. Semi-conducteur adj., m.
semilunar [-'lu:nə*] adj. Semi-lunaire.
seminal ['seminəl] adj. Séminal.
seminar ['seminə*] n. Séminaire m. (of students).
seminarist [-rist] n. ECCLES. Séminariste m.
seminary [-ri] n. Institution f. ‖ Collège m. ‖ ECCLES. Séminaire m.
semination [,semi'neiʃən] n. BOT. Sémination f.
semiology [,si:mi'ɔlədʒi], **semiotics** [si:mi'ɔtiks] n. MED., GRAMM. Sémiologie, sémiotique f.
semiquaver ['semikweivə*] n. MUS. Double croche f.
Semite ['semait] adj., n. Sémite s.
Semitic [sə'mitik] adj. Sémitique.
semitone ['semitoun] n. MUS. Demi-ton m.
semivowel ['semi'vouəl] n. GRAMM. Semi-voyelle f.
semolina [semə'li:nə] n. CULIN. Semoule f.
sempiternal [sempi'tə:nl] adj. Sempiternel.
senate ['senit] n. Sénat m.
senator [-ə*] n. Sénateur m.
senatorial [,senə'tɔ:riəl] adj. Sénatorial.
senatorship ['senətəʃip] n. Sénatoriat m.
send [send] v. tr. (121). Envoyer (a letter); joindre (an enclosure); expédier (a package). ‖ Faire devenir (to make); to send s.o. mad, rendre qqn fou. ‖ Envoyer avec violence, lancer, repousser; to send s. o. packing, envoyer bouler qqn. ‖ TECHN. Lancer, projeter (a rocket). ‖ COMM. To send in, rendre (an accounting); to send up, faire hausser (prices). ‖ BOT. To send forth, pousser, produire (buds, leaves). ‖ FAM. To send s.o. packing (or) about his business, envoyer promener qqn. ‖ **To send away**, renvoyer, chasser, congédier, remercier (an employee); expédier, faire partir (a package). ‖ **To send down**, faire descendre; exclure (a student); NAUT. Dégréer (a yard-arm). ‖ **To send forth**, émettre, exhaler, répandre (an exhaust, an odour). ‖ **To send in**, faire passer (a calling-card); envoyer, remettre (a resignation); faire entrer (s.o.). ‖ **To send off**, renvoyer, chasser; expédier (a letter); assister au départ de (a departing friend). ‖ **To send out**, mettre à la porte (s.o.); exhaler, répandre (an odour). ‖ **To send up**, mettre en ascension, enlever (a balloon); faire monter (s.o., sth.).

— v. intr. † Envoyer un message (or) un messager (to, à). ‖ Accorder, envoyer (fate, God). ‖ **To send after**, envoyer à la recherche (or) à la poursuite de, faire suivre. ‖ **To send for**, envoyer chercher, faire venir, faire appeler (a person); faire prendre (sth.). ‖ NAUT. Tanguer fortement, acculer, lever le nez. ‖ **Send-off**, n. Manifestation (or) fête (f.) d'adieu.
sender [-ə*] n. Expéditeur m.; expéditrice f.; return to sender, retour à l'expéditeur. ‖ Signaleur s. (of a signal). ‖ COMM. Expéditionnaire s.; remettant m. (of a money-order). ‖ TECHN. Manipulateur, transmetteur m. ‖ RADIO. Morse sender, clef Morse.
Senegal [seni'gɔ:l] n. GEOGR. Sénégal m.
Senegalese [,senigə'li:z] adj., n. GEOGR. Sénégalais s.
senescence [si'nesns] n. Sénescence f.
senescent [-nt] adj. Sénescent.
seneschal ['seniʃəl] n. Sénéchal m.
senile ['si:nail] adj. Sénile.
senility [se'niliti] n. Sénilité.
senior ['si:njə*] adj. Aîné, plus âgé; Smith senior, Smith père (or) l'aîné. ‖ Plus ancien, supérieur, premier, principal (in grade, rank); senior clerk, premier commis, commis principal; premier clerc (in law office); senior partner, associé principal; senior citizen, personne du troisième âge. ‖ MILIT. Supérieur (officer). ‖ U. S. Senior year, dernière année d'études.
— n. Aîné s.; doyen s. (in age). ‖ Ancien s. (at school). ‖ U. S. Etudiant de dernière année.
seniority [,si:ni'ɔriti] n. Priorité (or) supériorité (f.) par l'âge; doyenneté f. ‖ Ancienneté f.; droit (m.) d'ancienneté (in rank).
senna ['senə] n. BOT. Séné m.
sennit ['senit] n. NAUT. Tresse f.
sensation [,sensei'ʃən] n. Sensation, impression f.; sentiment m. (physical feeling). ‖ Effet sensationnel m.; to create a sensation, faire sensation, soulever l'émoi; faire du bruit.
sensational [sen'seiʃənl] adj. Sensationnel, à sensation, à effet (event, novel); à gros effets (writer). ‖ MED. Des sensations. ‖ PHILOS. Sensualiste.
sensationalism [-izm] n. Recherche (f.) du sensationnel; goût (m.) de l'épate (fam.). ‖ PHILOS. Sensualisme m.
sense [sens] n. Sens m.; the five senses, les cinq sens. ‖ Sens m.; sensualité f.; pleasures of the senses, plaisirs des sens. ‖ Sentiment m.; conscience f. (discernment); sens m. (of honour, humour); moral sense, sens moral. ‖ Bon sens, jugement sain m.; common sense, sens commun; person of sense, personne sensée; to talk sense, parler raisonnablement (or) selon le bon sens. ‖ Sens m.; signification f.; in a sense, dans un certain sens (or) une certaine mesure; to make no sense, n'avoir pas de sens, ne rien signifier, ne rimer à rien; in every sense of the word, dans toute la force (or) l'acception du terme. ‖ Opinion f.; vues f. pl. (of an assembly). ‖ MED. Equilibre mental m.; to be out of one's senses, avoir perdu le sens (or) la raison (or) la tête. ‖ MED. Connaissance f.; to lose, to regain one's senses, perdre, reprendre connaissance; sense of hearing, of smell, of sight, odorat; sense organs, organes des sens; sense of pain, sensation de douleur. ‖ FIG. Sixth sense, sixième sens, instinct, intuition.
— v. tr. Sentir intuitivement, pressentir, avoir le sens de. ‖ PHILOS. Percevoir par les sens.
senseless [-lis] adj. Insensé, déraisonnable, dénué de sens (act, behaviour); qui n'a pas le sens commun (person). ‖ MED. Insensible (insensitive); inanimé, sans connaissance (unconscious).
senselessness [-lisnis] n. Manque de bon sens m.; bêtise f. ‖ MED. Insensibilité f.
sensibility [,sensi'biliti] n. Emotivité f. ‖ Sensibilité f. (emotional, physical).
sensible ['sensibl] adj. Sensible, perceptible, apparent, visible. ‖ Assez considérable, appréciable, sen-

sible (difference, quality). ‖ Conscient (aware); *to be sensible of,* se rendre compte de. ‖ Judicieux (choice); commode, pratique, rationnel (clothing); sensé, raisonnable. sage (decision. person).

sensibleness [-nis] n. Raison *f.;* bon sens, jugement *m.*

sensibly [-i] adv. Raisonnablement, avec bon sens. ‖ Sensiblement, d'une manière appréciable.

sensitive [ˈsensitiv] adj. Sensible, impressionnable, sensitif (person); ombrageux (public opinion). ‖ MED. Sensible, sensitif. ‖ COMM. Instable (market). ‖ TECHN. Sensibilisé (paper); impressionnable (photographic plate); sensible (scales). ‖ BOT. *Sensitive plant,* sensitive.
— n. MED. Sujet sensible *m.* (to hypnosis).

sensitiveness [-nis] n. Sensibilité *f.* ‖ Sensitivité, délicatesse *f.* (of feelings). ‖ TECHN. Impressionnabilité *f.*

sensitize [ˈsensitaiz] v. tr. Sensibiliser, rendre sensible.

sensor [ˈsensə*] n. TECHN. Senseur, capteur *m.*

sensorial [senˈsɔːriəl] adj. MED. Sensoriel.

sensory [ˈsensəri] adj. Sensitif, des sens. ‖ MED. Sensoriel.

sensual [ˈsensjuəl] adj. Sensuel, des sens (enjoyment, pleasures); sensuel (person).

sensualism [-izm̩] n. Sensualité *f.* ‖ PHILOS. Sensualisme *m.*

sensualist [-ist] n. Personne sensuelle *f.;* voluptueux *s.* ‖ PHILOS. Sensualiste *m.*

sensuality [ˌsensjuˈæliti] n. Sensualité *f.*

sensuous [ˈsensjuəs] adj. Capiteux (charm). ‖ Des sens, voluptueux (enjoyment). ‖ Sensuel (poetry, style). ‖ PHILOS. Provenant des sens, matérialiste.

sensuousness [-nis] n. Volupté *f.* ‖ Sensualité *f.* (in poetry).

sentence [ˈsentens] n. † Sentence, maxime *f.;* avis *m.* ‖ GRAMM. Phrase *f.;* proposition *f.* (subordinate). ‖ JUR. Jugement, arrêt *m.;* sentence *f.; commutation of sentence,* commutation de peine.
— v. tr. JUR. Condamner.

sentential [senˈtenʃəl] adj. GRAMM. De (or) d'une phrase.

sententious [-ʃəs] adj. Sentencieux, dogmatique.

sententiousness [-ʃəsnis] n. Dogmatisme; ton sentencieux *m.*

sentient [ˈsenʃənt] adj. Sensible.

sentiment [ˈsentimənt] n. Sentiment *m.* ‖ Avis, sentiment *m.* (opinion). ‖ Souhait, vœu *m.* (wish). ‖ Sentimentalité, sensibilité *f.* ‖ Sensiblerie *f.* (mawkishness).

sentimental [ˌsentiˈmentl̩] adj. Sentimental. ‖ THEATR. Sentimental, larmoyant (comedy).

sentimentalism [-əlizm] n. Sentimentalisme *m.*

sentimentalist [-əlist] n. Sentimentaliste *s.* ‖ Personne sentimentale *f.*

sentimentality [ˌsentimenˈtæliti] n. Sentimentalité *f.* ‖ Sensiblerie *f.* (mawkish).

sentimentalize [ˌsentiˈmentəlaiz] v. intr. Faire du sentiment.
— v. tr. Rendre sentimental (or) larmoyant.

sentinel [ˈsentinl̩] n. MILIT. Sentinelle *f.;* factionnaire *m.; to stand sentinel,* monter la garde.

sentry [ˈsentri] n. MILIT., NAUT. Sentinelle *f.;* factionnaire *m.; to go on sentry,* prendre la garde. ‖ **Sentry-box,** n. Guérite *f.* ‖ **Sentry-go,** n. Faction *f.*

sepal [ˈsiːpəl] n. BOT. Sépale *m.*

separability [ˌsepərəˈbiliti] n. Séparabilité *f.*

separable [ˈsepərəbl̩] adj. Séparable.

separate [ˈsepərit] adj. Séparé, détaché, à part (column); particulier (entrance, room); isolé, à l'écart (existence); indépendant (interests). ‖ TECHN. Détaché (machine part).
— [-reit] v. tr. Séparer, diviser. ‖ Détacher, décoller *(from,* de). ‖ Trier (to sort out). ‖ Mettre à l'écart, isoler. ‖ CULIN. Ecrémer (milk). ‖ TECHN. Départir (metals); dédoubler (wire).
— v. intr. Se séparer, se détacher, s'éloigner *(from,* de); rompre *(from,* avec). ‖ Se quitter (to take leave); se disperser (to scatter). ‖ JUR. Se séparer (man and wife).
— [ˈsepritз] n. pl. Coordonnés *m. pl.* (clothes).

separately [ˈsepəritli] adv. Séparément, à part. ‖ Un à un, un à la fois.

separation [ˌsepəˈreiʃən] n. Séparation *f.;* rupture *f.* (political). ‖ Triage *m.* (of ore). ‖ CULIN. Ecrémage *m.* (of milk). ‖ AUTOM. Décollage, décollement *m.* (of tyre-tread). ‖ MILIT. *Separation allowance,* allocation militaire. ‖ JUR. *Separation from bed and board,* séparation de corps et de biens. ‖ ECCLES. Scission *f.* ‖ PHYS. Ecart *m.* (of lenses).

separatism [ˈsepərətizm] n. Séparatisme *m.*

separatist [-tist] n. Séparatiste *s.*

separative [-tiv] adj. Séparatif.

separator [ˈsepəreitə*] n. TECHN. Séparateur *m.*

sepia [ˈsiːpjə] n. ARTS. Sépia *f.* ‖ ZOOL. Seiche *f.*

sepoy [ˈsiːpɔi] n. Cipaye *m.*

sepsis [ˈsepsis] n. MED. Septicémie *f.*

septangular [sepˈtæŋgjulə*] adj. MATH. Heptagonal.

September [sepˈtembə*] n. Septembre *m.*

septennate [sepˈtenit] n. Septennat *m.*

septet(te) [sepˈtet] n. MUS. Septuor *m.*

septic [ˈseptik] adj. MED. Septique (tank); infecté (wound).

septicaemia [septiˈsiːmiə] n. MED. Septicémie *f.*

septicity [sepˈtisiti] n. MED. Septicité *f.*

septime [ˈseptiːm] n. SPORTS. Septime *f.* (in fencing).

septivalent [ˌseptiˈveilənt] adj. CHIM. Heptavalent.

septuagenarian [ˌseptjuədʒiˈnɛəriən] adj., n. Septuagénaire *s.*

Septuagesima [ˌseptjuəˈdʒesimə] n. ECCLES. Septuagésime *f.*

Septuagint [ˈseptjuədʒint] n. ECCLES. Version (*f.*) des Septante.

septum [ˈseptəm] (pl. **septa** [-tə]) n. MED. Septum *m.*

septuor [ˈseptjuə*] n. MUS. Septuor *m.*

septuple [ˈseptjupl̩] adj., n. Septuple *m.*

septuplet [sepˈtjuːplit] n. Septuplé *s.* ‖ MUS. Septolet *m.*

sepulchral [siˈpʌlkrəl] adj. Sépulcral; tumulaire (stone); *sepulchral vault,* caveau. ‖ FIG. Caverneux, sépulcral (voice).

sepulchre [ˈsepəlkə*] n. Sépulcre *m.*
— v. tr. Ensevelir, mettre au tombeau.

sepulture [-tʃə*] n. Sépulture *f.*

sequacious [siˈkweiʃəs] adj. Cohérent (argument); suivi (speech). ‖ Servile (imitator).

sequel [ˈsiːkwəl] n. Continuation, suite *f.* ‖ Conséquence *f.;* résultat *m.*

sequence [-kwəns] n. Suite, série, succession *f.* (of events). ‖ Ordre *m.* (historical); enchaînement *m.* (logical). ‖ Séquence *f.* (at cards). ‖ MUS., CINEM., ECCLES. Séquence *f.* ‖ GRAMM. Concordance *f.* (of tenses).

sequent [-kwənt] adj. Conséquent, résultant (effect); successif, consécutif (event, thought).

sequential [siˈkwenʃəl] adj. Séquentiel. ‖ INFORM. *Sequential access,* accès séquentiel.

sequester [siˈkwestə*] v. tr. Isoler, écarter; *to sequester oneself,* se retirer, se confiner. ‖ Confisquer, s'approprier (possessions). ‖ JUR. Séquestrer (a person); mettre sous séquestre (property).

sequestrate [-treit] v. tr. JUR. Mettre sous séquestre.

sequestration [ˌsiːkwesˈtreiʃən] n. Retraite *f.;* éloignement du monde *m.* (of a person). ‖ Confiscation, appropriation *f.* (of property). ‖ JUR. Séquestration *f.* (of a person); mise (*f.*) sous séquestre (of property).

sequestrator ['si:kwestreitə*] n. JUR. Séquestre *m.*

sequestrum [si:'kwestrəm] (pl. **sequestra** [-trə]) n. MED. Séquestre *m.*

sequin ['si:kwin] n. Sequin *m.*

sequoia [si'kwɔiə] n. BOT. Séquoia *m.*

seraglio [se'rɑ:liou] n. Sérail, harem *m.*

seraph ['seræf] (pl. **seraphim** [-fim]) n. ECCLES. Séraphin *m.*

seraphic [sə'ræfik] adj. ECCLES. Séraphique.

Serb [sə:b], **Serbian** [-jən] adj., n. GEOGR. Serbe *s.* ‖ Serbe *m.* (language).

Serbia [-jə] n. GEOGR. Serbie *f.*

serenade [,seri'neid] n. MUS. Sérénade *f.*
— v. tr. Donner une sérénade à.

serenader [,seri'neidə*] n. MUS. Donneur (*m.*) de sérénade.

serendipity [,serən'dipiti] n. Génie (*m.*) de faire des trouvailles heureuses.

serene [sə'ri:n] adj. Tranquille, paisible, serein (person, regard); calme, serein (sea); serein, clair (sky). ‖ *His Serene Highness*, Son Altesse Sérénissime.
— n. Etendue de mer calme *f.;* espace de ciel serein *m.*

serenely [-li] adv. Avec sérénité, tranquillement.

serenity [si'reniti] n. Sérénité, tranquillité *f.;* calme *m.* ‖ Sérénité *f.* (royal title).

serf [sə:f] n. Serf *m.;* serve *f.*

serfage [-idʒ], **serfdom** [-dəm] n. Servage *m.*

serge [sə:dʒ] n. Serge *f.; cotton serge*, sergé.

sergeant ['sɑ:dʒənt] n. Sergent, exempt *m.* ‖ Brigadier *m.* (of police). ‖ MILIT. Maréchal des logis *m.* (cavalry); sergent *m.* (infantry); *quartermaster sergeant*, sergent-fourrier. ‖ **Sergeant-at-arms**, n. MILIT. Sergent (*m.*) d'armes. ‖ **Sergeant-at-law**, n. JUR. Avocat *m.* ‖ **Sergeant-major**, n. MILIT. Sergent major, maréchal des logis chef *m.*

serial ['siəriəl] adj. D'une série, en série. ‖ D'ordre, matricule (number). ‖ Périodique; *serial novel*, roman-feuilleton; *serial rights*, droits de reproduction en feuilleton; *serial writer*, feuilletoniste.
— n. Publication périodique *f.;* roman-feuilleton *m.* ‖ Feuilleton télévisé, sérial *m.* (on T. V.).

serialize [-aiz] v. tr. Arranger en série. ‖ Publier en feuilleton (a novel). ‖ COMM., TECHN. Fabriquer en série.

serially [-i] adv. En (or) par série. ‖ En feuilleton (novel).

seriate ['siərieit] v. tr. Sérier.
— [-it] adj. Sérié, en série.

seriatim [,siəri'eitim] adv. Successivement, point par point.

sericate ['serikeit], **sericeous** [se'riʃəs] adj. BOT., ZOOL. Soyeux.

sericulture [,seri'kʌltʃə*] n. Sériciculture *f.*

series ['siəri:z] n. Série *f.* (of articles); suite *f.* (of errors, monarchs); *in series*, en série, de suite. ‖ ARTS. Gamme, échelle *f.* (of colours). ‖ CHIM. *Series of reactions*, réactions caténaires. ‖ ELECTR. *Series connection*, montage en série. ‖ **Series-winding**, n. Enroulement (*m.*) en série.

serin ['serin] n. ZOOL. Serin *m.*

seringa [sə'riŋgə] n. BOT. Seringa *m.*

serio-comic ['siəriou'kɔmik] adj. Héroï-comique.

serious ['siəriəs] adj. Sérieux, grave, réfléchi. ‖ Sensible (damage); gros (error); lourd (loss); grave (mistake). ‖ Sérieux, sincère (earnest); *to be serious*, ne pas plaisanter. ‖ MED. Grave, sérieux (illness). ‖ **Serious-minded**, adj. Réfléchi, sérieux.

seriously [-li] adv. Sérieusement, avec sérieux; *to take seriously*, prendre au sérieux. ‖ Sincèrement, plaisanterie à part; sans blague (fam.). ‖ MED. Gravement, dangereusement, grièvement.

seriousness [-nis] n. Sérieux *m.;* gravité *f.*

sermon ['sə:mən] n. ECCLES. Sermon *m.;* prône *m.* (Catholic); prêche *m.* (Protestant). ‖ FAM. Sermon *m.*

sermonize [-aiz] v. tr. FAM. Sermonner.
— v. intr. FAM. Prêcher.

sermonizer [-aizə*] n. Sermonneur *s.*

serological [,sirɔ'lɔdʒikəl] adj. MED. Sérologique.

serologist [si'rɔlədʒist] n. MED. Sérologiste *s.*

serology [si'rɔlədʒi] n. MED. Sérologie *f.*

serosity [siə'rɔsiti] n. MED. Sérosité *f.*

serotherapy [,siəro'θerəpi] n. MED. Sérothérapie *f.*

serotinous [si'rɔtinəs] adj. BOT. Tardif.

serous ['siərəs] adj. MED. Séreux.

serpent ['sə:pənt] n. ZOOL. Serpent *m.; young serpent*, serpenteau. ‖ MUS., ASTRON. Serpent *m.* ‖ **Serpent-charmer**, n. Charmeur (*s.*) de serpents. ‖ **Serpent-eater**, n. ZOOL. Serpentaire *m.* ‖ **Serpent-like**, adj. Sinueux, serpentin.

serpentine [-ain] adj. ZOOL. De serpent. ‖ FIG. Serpentin (dance); sinueux, tortueux (road). ‖ FIG. Perfide; vipérin.
— n. Serpentine *f.*
— v. intr. Serpenter.

serrate ['sereit] adj. Serratiforme, en dents de scie; dentelé.
— [sə'reit] v. tr. Découper en dents de scie; denteler; *serrated edge*, denture.

serration [ser'eiʃən] n. BOT. Dentelure *f.*

serried ['serid] adj. Serré, pressé.

serrulate ['serjuleit] adj. BOT. Serrulé, denticulé.

serum ['siərəm] n. MED. Sérum *m.; protective serum*, immunisant.

serval ['sə:vəl] n. ZOOL. Serval *m.*

servant ['sə:vənt] n. Domestique *s.;* serviteur *m.;* servante *f.* (see DOMESTIC); *general servant*, bonne à tout faire. ‖ Pl. Domesticité *f.;* gens (*m. pl.*) de maison (in private service); personnel *m.* (in a hotel). ‖ Employé *s.* (in industry, government); *civil servant*, fonctionnaire; *public servant*, agent d'un service public; *servants and agents*, préposés. ‖ Serviteur *m.* (epistolary form). ‖ TECHN. *Servant apparatus*, appareil commandé. ‖ MILIT. Ordonnance *f.* (of an officer). ‖ **Servant-girl**, n. Domestique, servante, bonne *f.;* U. S. serveuse *f.*

serve [sə:v] v. tr. Servir, être au service de; rendre service à, être utile à (to be of service). ‖ Répondre à (a need); servir (a purpose); *to serve the purpose*, faire l'affaire; *to serve the purpose of*, remplacer, tenir lieu de, jouer le rôle de. ‖ Suffire à, satisfaire, contenter (a number of people). ‖ Traiter; *to serve s. o. badly*, mal agir envers qqn. ‖ Remplir, exercer, s'acquitter de (an assignment, a function). ‖ Faire (an apprenticeship); accomplir (a probationary period); purger, subir (a term of punishment). ‖ Fournir, alimenter (with, en); pourvoir (with, de). ‖ CULIN. Dresser, accommoder (with, de) [a dish]; *to serve up*, servir (a meal); *dinner is served*, Madame est servie. ‖ TECHN. Servir (a machine). ‖ MILIT. Faire (one's time); servir (a gun). ‖ NAUT. Fourrer (gear). ‖ ZOOL. Servir, saillir, couvrir, monter (a mare). ‖ CH. DE F. Faire le service de, desservir (a locality). ‖ ECCLES. Servir. ‖ JUR. Subir (a sentence); signifier, notifier (a subpoena). ‖ SPORTS. Servir. ‖ FAM. *Serves you right!*, c'est bien fait pour vous!, c'est pain bénit!, ça vous fera les pieds! ‖ *To serve out*, se venger de, rendre la pareille à (an enemy); distribuer (rations).
— v. intr. Servir, rendre service, être utile. ‖ Etre esclave (in bondage); être domestique (in private service). ‖ Faire l'affaire, suffire; *to serve as*, servir de, tenir lieu de; *to serve to*, servir à. ‖ MILIT., NAUT. Servir, faire son service. ‖ SPORTS. Servir. ‖ JUR. *To serve on the jury*, être du jury.
— n. SPORTS. Service *m.*

server [-ə*] n. Personne qui sert *f.;* serveur *s.* (person); plateau *m.* (utensil). ‖ ECCLES. Servant *m.* ‖ SPORTS. Serveur, servant *s.*

service ['sə:vis] n. Service *m.; civil* (or) *public service*, administration ; *secret service*, service secret. ‖ Fonction *f.*; service *m.* (action). ‖ Service *m.* (domestic, feudal) ; *to go into* (or) *take service*, entrer en service ; *to take into one's service*, prendre à son service. ‖ Disposition *f.; at your service*, à votre service. ‖ Assistance *f.*; bon office *m.; to do* (or) *render a service*, rendre un service. ‖ Utilité, aide *f.; to be of service*, rendre service, être utile, servir à qqch. ‖ Service *m.* (crockery) ; *coffee service*, service à café. ‖ MILIT., NAUT. Pl. Armée, aviation et marine *f.; branch of the service*, arme ; *compulsory service*, service obligatoire ; *service families*, familles de militaires ; *service stripe*, chevron, brisque. ‖ NAUT. Fourrure *f.* (of gear). ‖ COMM. *At your service*, dévoué à vos ordres ; *service charge*, service ; *service not included*, service (or) pourboire non compris. ‖ ECCLES. Office *m.; burial service*, service funèbre. ‖ JUR. Signification *f.* ‖ CH. DE F., SPORTS. Service *m.* ‖ FAM. *To have seen service*, avoir fait de l'usage, en avoir vu de dures. ‖ **Service area,** n. AUTOM. Aire (*f.*) de service. ‖ **Service-book,** n. ECCLES. Paroissien *m.* ‖ **Service industry,** n. Ensemble (*m.*) des services, secteur tertiaire *m.* ‖ **Service-lead,** n. ELECTR. Branchement d'abonné *m.* ‖ **Service module,** n. ASTRONAUT. Module de service *m.* ‖ **Service-rifle,** n. MILIT. Fusil (*m.*) d'ordonnance. ‖ **Service road,** n. AUTOM. Route (*f.*) d'accès. ‖ **Service-station,** n. AUTOM. Station-service *f.* ‖ **Service-tank,** n. AUTOM. Nourrice *f.* ‖ **Service-uniform,** n. MILIT. Uniforme réglementaire *m.*
— v. tr. TECHN., AUTOM. Entretenir, réparer.
serviceable [-əbl̩] adj. Serviable (person) ; commode, pratique, utile (thing). ‖ Durable, de bon usage, solide (clothing).
serviceableness [-əblnis] n. Serviabilité *f.; empressement m.* (of a person) ; utilité, commodité *f.* (of an implement). ‖ Solidité, utilité *f.* (of clothing).
serviceman [-mən] (pl. **servicemen**) n. MILIT. Militaire *m.*
servicewoman [-wumən] (pl. **servicewomen** [-wimin]) n. MILIT. Femme-soldat *f.*
serviette [sə:vi'et] n. Serviette de table *f.*
servile ['sə:vail] adj. Servile, de domestique (condition). ‖ Asservissant (yoke) ; asservi (race). ‖ Rampant, vil, abject (flattery) ; servile (imitation). ‖ ECCLES., GRAMM. Servile.
servilely [-li] adv. Avec servilité.
servility [sə:'viliti] n. Servilité *f.; abjection, bassesse f.*
serving ['sə:viŋ] n. Service *m.* (of a master). ‖ CULIN. Portion *f.* (of a dish) ; service *m.* (of a meal). ‖ ZOOL. Saillie *f.* ‖ SPORTS. Service *m.* ‖ JUR. Signification *f.* ‖ NAUT. Fourrage *m.* ‖ **Serving-man,** n. Serviteur, domestique *m.*
servitor ['sə:vitə*] n. Serviteur *m.* ‖ † Boursier *m.* (at Oxford).
servitude [-tju:d] n. Servitude *f.; esclavage, asservissement m.* ‖ JUR. Servitude *f.; penal servitude,* travaux forcés.
servo- [sə:vo] pref. Servo-. ‖ **Servo-assisted,** adj. Servoassisté, servocommandé. ‖ **Servo-brake,** n. AUTOM. Servofrein *m.* ‖ **Servo-control,** n. TECHN. Servocommande *f.* ‖ **Servo-mechanism,** n. TECHN. Servomécanisme *m.* ‖ **Servo-motor,** n. TECHN. Servomoteur *m.*
sesame ['sesəmi] n. BOT. Sésame *m.* ‖ LOC. *Open sesame !,* Sésame ouvre-toi !
session ['sefən] n. Séance *f.*; session *f.* (of Parliament) ; *to be in session,* siéger. ‖ Année universitaire *f.*; U. S. semestre (or) trimestre universitaire *m.* ‖ JUR. Session *f.*; assises *f. pl.*
sesterce ['sestə:s] n. Sesterce *m.*
set [set] v. tr. (122). Poser, placer, mettre (to put) ; disposer, placer (chairs) ; poster (a guard) ; proposer, exposer (a problem). ‖ Mettre en plis, faire une

mise en plis à (hair). ‖ Régler (a clock) ; mettre (the table) ; dresser (a trap). ‖ Serrer (one's teeth) ; *to set s.o.'s teeth on edge,* agacer les dents à qqn. ‖ Attribuer, attacher (importance, value) ; *to set a price on s.o.'s head,* mettre à prix la tête de qqn. ‖ Proposer, imposer ; donner (an example) ; régler (a pace). ‖ Mettre ; *to set eyes on,* voir, apercevoir ; *to set fire to,* mettre le feu à, incendier ; *to set foot on,* mettre le pied sur ; *to set oneself against,* s'opposer résolument à, se mettre en travers de ; *to set oneself to,* se mettre à, entreprendre de ; *to set one's hand to,* apposer sa signature à (a document) ; mettre la main à (a task) ; *to set one's heart* (or) *one's mind on,* mettre tout son effort à ; *to set one's wits to,* s'appliquer à trouver une solution à (a problem). ‖ Diriger, lancer, lâcher (on, sur) [a dog, the police] ; lancer (the fashion). ‖ Fixer, immobiliser, faire prendre (or) durcir (cement) ; nouer (a fruit) ; cailler (milk). ‖ Mettre (followed by an attributive or an adverbial expression) ; *to set free,* libérer ; *to set going,* mettre en marche (or) en train (or) en mouvement (or) en route ; *to set laughing,* faire rire ; *to set right,* détromper, éclairer, désabuser (a person) ; redresser, mettre de l'ordre dans, ranger (things) ; *to set thinking,* faire réfléchir, donner à réfléchir à ; *to set at variance* (or) *by the ears,* brouiller, désunir, mettre aux prises ; *to set in order,* ranger, mettre en ordre (or) de l'ordre dans ; *to set s.o. on his feet,* remettre qqn sur pieds (or) d'aplomb ; *to set on fire,* incendier, allumer, mettre le feu à ; *to set to rights,* remettre en place (or) en ordre. ‖ JUR. *To set aside,* annuler (a decree) ; casser (a judgment) ; rejeter (a request) ; mettre de côté. ‖ **To set back,** empêcher, gêner ; retarder (a clock). ‖ **To set by,** économiser, note de, inscrire ; déposer (passengers) ; recueillir (s.o.'s words). ‖ **To set down,** noter, prendre, laisser de côté (a scruple) ; *to set sth. down to,* attribuer qqch. à. ‖ **To set forth,** montrer, déployer, produire ; déclarer, faire savoir (an announcement) ; exposer, énoncer (an opinion). ‖ **To set off,** rehausser, faire valoir, mettre en valeur (an effect) ; faire exploser (fireworks) ; mettre en train (s.o.). ‖ **To set on,** pousser, exciter (to, à) [s.o.] ; *to be set on,* aspirer à, avoir à cœur de, avoir jeté son dévolu sur. ‖ **To set out,** proclamer, publier (an announcement). ‖ COMM. Montrer, étaler, exhiber (goods) ; TECHN. Espacer, écarter (print) ; AGRIC. Tracer (a garden plot) ; semer (seeds), planter (trees). ‖ **To set up,** développer (the body) ; FIG. Faire entendre (a claim, a protest) ; pousser (a cry) ; fonder (an institution) ; établir, procurer une situation à (a person) ; causer, provoquer (a quarrel) ; placer bien en vue, mettre en évidence (a sign) ; élever, ériger, dresser (a statue) ; avancer, lancer, proposer (a theory) ; *to set oneself up again,* se remplumer (fam.) ; *to set up shop,* s'établir (shopkeeper) ; *to set s.o. up with,* fournir (or) approvisionner qqn de (or) en.
— v. intr. Se figer, prendre ; faire prise (cement). ‖ Devenir fixe (eyes) ; se durcir (facial expression). ‖ Tomber (drapery, garment) ; ‖ ZOOL. Tomber en arrêt, arrêter (gun-dog). ‖ ASTRON. Se coucher (sun). ‖ COMM. *To set up,* s'établir (in a business). ‖ MED. Devenir rigide (corpse) ; se serrer (jaw, teeth). ‖ BOT., AGRIC. Se nouer (fruit). ‖ NAUT. Porter, se diriger (current) ; *to set in, out,* monter, descendre (tide) ; *to set in,* se lever (wind). ‖ CULIN. Prendre (jelly). ‖ FIG. S'affermir, se former (character) ; décliner, pâlir (fame). ‖ **To set about,** se mettre en devoir de, se mettre à, entreprendre. ‖ **To set forth** (or) **off,** partir, se mettre en route. ‖ **To set in,** commencer (rain) ; se lever, s'établir (wind). ‖ **To set on,** commencer, s'y mettre ; attaquer, monter à l'attaque. ‖ **To set to,** s'y mettre, y aller de tout son cœur. ‖ **To set up for,** se poser en, s'ériger en, se donner pour ; faire profession de, se targuer de.

— adj. Fixé (date, time); établi, prescrit (form, manner); fixe (weather). ‖ Préparé, apprêté; *all set,* fin prêt. ‖ Immobile; figé (smile); rigide, serré (teeth). ‖ MILIT. Rangé (battle). ‖ FIG. Immuable, bien arrêté (opinion); délibéré (purpose); étudié (speech). ‖ **Set-in,** adj. Rapporté (sleeve).
— n. Assortiment *m.*; série, collection *f.* ‖ Service *m.* (of dishes); garniture *f.* (of a dressing table); attelage *m.* (of horses); parure *f.* (of jewelry); trousse *f.* (of tools); collection *f.* (of volumes); série *f.* (of weights); *set of furniture,* ameublement, mobilier. ‖ Groupe *m.* (of people); clique, bande *f.* (pejorative); classe *f.*; clan, cercle *m.* (social stratum); catégorie *f.* (of thinkers, writers); *fast set,* monde où l'on s'amuse; *smart set,* gratin (fam.). ‖ Tournure *f.* (of mind); direction, tendance *f.* (of opinion). ‖ Configuration *f.*; disposition *f.* (of drapery); chute *f.* (of a garment). ‖ Figure *f.* (in a quadrille). ‖ Attitude *f.*; maintien, port *m.* (of the head). ‖ Epaisseur *f.* (of a printing character). ‖ AGRIC. Plant *m.*; jeune fruit *m.* ‖ GEOL. Configuration *f.* (of a mountain range). ‖ MED. *Set of features,* physionomie; *set of teeth,* denture, dentition; *set of false teeth,* dentier; râtelier (fam.). ‖ NAUT. Direction *f.* (of the current); jeu *m.* (of oars). ‖ ARCHIT. Assiette *f.* (of a beam); gauchissement, affaissement *m.* (under pressure). ‖ TECHN. Jeu *m.* (of machine parts); châssis *m.* (of a mine); chasse *f.* (of a saw); cadre *m.* (of timber). ‖ RADIO. Poste, appareil (*m.*) de T.S.F.; radio *f.* ‖ ZOOL. Couvée *f.* (of eggs); arrêt *m.* (of a gun-dog). ‖ SPORTS. Set *m.* (in tennis). ‖ **Set-back,** n. Déception, déconvenue *f.*; revers (*m.*) de fortune; MED. Rechute *f.*; COMM. Recul *m.*; FIN. Tassement *m.* (of stocks). ‖ **Set-nut,** n. TECHN. Contre-écrou *m.* ‖ **Set-off,** n. COMM. Compensation *f.*; JUR. Demande reconventionnelle *f.*; ARCHIT. Saillie *f.* ‖ **Set-out,** n. Début *m.*; mise (*f.*) en train (or) en route; équipement *m.*; préparatifs *m. pl.*; étalage, déploiement *m.* (display). ‖ **Set-piece,** n. CULIN. Pièce montée *f.*; TECHN. Pièce (*f.*) d'artifice. ‖ **Set-pin,** n. TECHN. Goupille (*f.*) de calage. ‖ **Set-screw,** n. TECHN. Vis de pression *f.* ‖ **Set-square,** n. ARTS. Equerre *f.* ‖ **Set-to,** n. Pugilat *m.*; bagarre *f.*; SPORTS. Assaut *m.* (in fencing); FAM. Prise (*f.*) de bec; *to have a set-to,* s'empoigner. ‖ **Set-up,** n. Port, maintien *m.* (of the body); TECHN. Mise en position *f.* (of a surveying instrument); FIG. Organisation *f.*; situation, structure *f.*; fonctionnement; U. S. FAM., SPORTS. Match (*m.*) de boxe simulé.

setaceous [siːˈteiʃəs] adj. ZOOL. Sétacé.
setiferous [siːˈtifərəs] adj. ZOOL. Sétifère.
setness [ˈsetnis] n. Compassement *m.* (of conduct, behaviour); fermeté *f.* (of an intention); détermination *f.* (of a purpose); opiniâtreté *f.* (of views). ‖ Rigidité *f.* (of features); fixité *f.* (of a stare).
seton [ˈsiːtṇ] n. MED. Séton *m.*
settee [seˈtiː] n. Causeuse *f.*; *back-to-back settee,* boudeuse.
setter [ˈsetə*] n. TECHN. Poseur *m.* (of bricks); monteur, sertisseur *m.* (of gems). ‖ ZOOL. Setter *m.*
setting [-iŋ] n. Pose *f.*; montage *m.*; incrustation, insertion *f.* ‖ Composition *f.* (in typesetting). ‖ TECHN. Durcissement *m.*; solidification *f.*; prise *f.* (of cement); affilage *m.* (of a tool). ‖ TECHN. Monture *f.* (for a gem); montage, sertissage *m.* (act). ‖ MED. Réduction *f.* (of a fracture); remboîtement *m.* (of a limb). ‖ MUS. Mise en musique *f.* (of words). ‖ THEATR. Mise en scène *f.* ‖ ASTRON. Coucher *m.* (of the sun). ‖ FIG. Cadre, milieu, entourage *m.* (of an existence, a person); déclin *m.* (of fame). ‖ **Setting-rule,** n. Filet à composer *m.* ‖ **Setting-stick,** n. Composteur *m.* ‖ **Setting-up,** n. Instauration *f.* (of an organization).
settle [ˈsetḷ] n. Banc à haut dossier *m.*
settle v. tr. Etablir, installer (s.o.). ‖ Décider, déterminer, convaincre. ‖ Ramener le calme dans (or)

chez; calmer (agitation); apaiser, dissiper (doubts). ‖ Stabiliser, rendre immuable; fixer, arrêter (a date); trancher, résoudre (a difficulty); régler (a dispute); décider (an issue); conclure (a question). ‖ Régler, mettre ordre à (one's affairs). ‖ Coloniser, s'établir dans (a territory). ‖ COMM. Payer, régler (an account, a debt). ‖ JUR. Constituer, assigner (an annuity, an inheritance). ‖ CHIM., CULIN. Laisser reposer, faire déposer (dregs, sediment); clarifier (a liquid). ‖ FIG. Arrêter, fixer (an opinion); stabiliser (the weather). ‖ FAM. Régler son compte à, faire son affaire à (s.o.).
— v. intr. S'installer, se fixer, s'établir, élire domicile (*in, a, dans*). ‖ Se stabiliser, s'immobiliser, s'arrêter. ‖ Se calmer, s'apaiser (excitement, wind); se mettre au beau (weather). ‖ S'appliquer; *to settle to a task,* se mettre à une tâche. ‖ S'arranger, rentrer dans l'ordre (business matters); *to get settled,* s'organiser (in a new house). ‖ ARCHIT. Se tasser (foundation). ‖ COMM. Régler, payer une note. ‖ CHIM., CULIN. Déposer, se précipiter (dregs, sediment); reposer, se clarifier (liquid). ‖ ZOOL. Se poser, se percher (bird). ‖ FAM. *It's all settled,* c'est du tout cuit. ‖ **To settle down,** s'assagir, se ranger; s'établir, se marier; *to settle down in Paris,* se fixer (or) s'établir à Paris. ‖ **To settle on, upon,** se décider pour, opter pour, fixer son choix sur.
settlement [-mənt] n. Etablissement *m.*; installation, fixation *f.* ‖ Colonie *f.*; colonisation *f.* ‖ Œuvre sociale *f.* (community centre). ‖ Arrangement, accommodement *m.* (of an argument); règlement *m.* (of a dispute). ‖ COMM. Règlement *m.* (of an account, a debt); établissement *m.* (of a business). ‖ FIN. Liquidation *f.*; *full settlement,* solde de tout compte. ‖ ARCHIT. Tassement *m.* (of foundations). ‖ JUR. Pension, rente *f.* (pension); dot *f.*; douaire *m.* (dower); constitution *f.* (of an annuity, an endowment); contrat *m.* (of marriage); *Act of Settlement,* loi de succession au trône (in England); *judicial settlement,* procédure judiciaire; *marriage settlement,* contrat de mariage; *to make a settlement,* constituer une dot. ‖ U. S. Localité *f.*
settler [-ə*] n. Colon *m.* ‖ Décideur *s.* (of an argument). ‖ FAM. Coup (or) argument décisif *m.*
seven [ˈsevṇ] adj., n. Sept *m.*
sevenfold [-fould] adj. Septuple.
seventeen [-ˈtiːn] adj., n. Dix-sept *m.*
seventeenth [ˈtiːnθ] adj. Dix-septième. ‖ Dix-sept (in dates, titles).
— n. Dix-septième *m.*
seventh [-θ] adj. Septième. ‖ Sept (in dates, titles).
— n. Septième *m.* ‖ MUS. Septième *f.*
seventhly [-θli] adv. Septièmement.
seventieth [-tiiθ] adj., n. Soixante-dixième *m.*
seventy [-ti] adj., n. Soixante-dix *m.*
sever [ˈsevə*] v. tr. Séparer, diviser, couper, retrancher; détacher (*from,* de). ‖ Couper, sectionner. ‖ JUR. Disjoindre. ‖ FIG. Cesser (connections); rompre (friendship).
— v. intr. Se séparer (persons); rompre, se casser en deux (thing).
several [ˈsevrəl] adj. Plusieurs; *several times,* plusieurs fois. ‖ Séparé, différent, divers, distinct, respectif. ‖ JUR. Divis (property); individuel (responsibility). ‖ COMM. *Joint and several bond,* obligation solidaire.
— pron. Plusieurs; *several of them,* plusieurs d'entre eux.
severally [-i] adv. Séparément, individuellement, respectivement. ‖ JUR. *Jointly and severally,* conjointement et solidairement.
severalty [-ti] n. JUR. Possession individuelle *f.*; *in severalty,* en propre.
severance [ˈsevrəns] n. Séparation, désunion, disjonction *f.* ‖ Interruption *f.* (of communications); rupture *f.* (of relations).
severe [siˈviə*] adj. Sévère, dur (attitude); rigou-

reux (sentence). ‖ Violent, pénible, douloureux (blow); rude, rigoureux (climate); intense (heat) ‖ Sévère, rigoureux (examination); dur (expérience); grave (failure); minutieux (inquiry). ‖ Ironique, sarcastique, mordant (remark). ‖ Arts, Archit. Austère, sévère, sobre. ‖ Med. Grave, sérieux (illness); aigu, vif (pain).

severely [-li] adv. Sévèrement, avec sévérité. ‖ Rudement, durement, violemment. ‖ Ironiquement. ‖ Arts. Sobrement. ‖ Med. Gravement (ill); grièvement (wounded).

severity [si'veriti] n. Sévérité, dureté f. (of character); rigueur f. (of a punishment); to use severity, sévir. ‖ Rigueur f. (of a climate); rudesse f. (of treatment). ‖ Caractère minutieux (or) rigoureux m. (of an examination); difficulté f. (of an ordeal). ‖ Med. Gravité f. (of an illness); violence, acuité f. (of a pain). ‖ Arts. Sobriété f.

sew [sou] v. tr. Coudre; to sew on, coudre (a button); to sew up, coudre, faire un point à (a tear). ‖ Brocher (a book). ‖ Med. Coudre, suturer (a wound).
— v. intr. Coudre, faire de la couture.
— N. B. Le p.p. est sewn en Grande-Bretagne. Aux Etats-Unis on emploie sewed.

sewage ['sju:idʒ] n. Eaux (f. pl.) d'égouts. ‖ **Sewage-farm** (or) **-fields**, n. Champs (m. pl.) d'épandage. ‖ **Sewage-works**, n. Station (f.) d'épuration des eaux usées.
— v. intr. Agric. Engraisser, fumer.

sewer ['souə*] n. Couseur s. ‖ Brocheur s. (of books).

sewer ['sjuə*] n. Egout m.; main sewer, égout collecteur. ‖ Fig. Cloaque m. (of vice). ‖ **Sewer-gas**, n. Gaz méphitique m. ‖ **Sewer-man**, n. Egoutier m. ‖ **Sewer-rat**, n. Zool. Rat d'égout m.

sewerage [-ridʒ] n. Eaux (f. pl.) d'égouts. ‖ Système (m.) d'égouts.

sewing ['souiŋ] n. Couture f. ‖ Brochage m. (of books). ‖ Med. Suture f. ‖ **Sewing-machine**, n. Machine à coudre f.

sewn [soun] p. p. See sew.

sex [seks] n. Sexe m. ‖ Sexualité f. ‖ Fam. Rapport m.; to have sex with, coucher avec. ‖ **Sex-appeal**, n. Sex-appeal m. ‖ **Sex-kitten**, n. Allumeuse f. ‖ **Sex-life**, n. Vie amoureuse f. ‖ **Sex-maniac**, n. Obsédé sexuel s. ‖ **Sex-starved**, adj. Fam. Frustré sur le plan sexuel, refoulé.
— adj. Sexuel (education, instinct, chromosome).
— v. tr. Déterminer le sexe de.

sexagenarian ['seksədʒi'nɛəriən] adj. n. Sexagénaire s.

sexagenary [,seksə'dʒi:nəri] adj. De soixante, qui va par soixante, sexagésimal.

Sexagesima [-'dʒesima] n. Eccles. Sexagésime f.

sexagesimal [-'dʒesiməl] adj. Sexagésimal.

sexed [sekst] adj. Bot., Zool. Sexué. ‖ Fam. To be highly sexed, avoir du tempérament.

sexivalent [,seksi'veilənt] adj. Chim. Hexavalent.

sexless ['sekslis] adj. Zool., Bot. Asexué.

sexology [sek'sɔlədʒi] n. Sexologie f.

sextain ['sekstən] n. Sixtain m.

sextant ['sekstənt] n. Naut. Sextant m.

sextette [seks'tet] n. Mus. Sextuor m.

sextodecimo ['sekstou'desimou] n. In-16, inseize m. (book, size).

sexton ['sekstən] n. Eccles. Sacristain m. ‖ Fam. Fossoyeur m.

sextuple [seks'tju:pl] adj., n. Sextuple m.

sextuplet [-plit] n. Sextuplé s. ‖ Mus. Sextolet m.

sexual ['seksjuəl] adj. Sexuel.

sexuality [,seksju'æliti] n. Sexualité f.

sexually ['seksjuəli] adv. Sexuellement.

sexy ['seksi] adj. Fam. Capiteuse, excitante, affriolante, croustillante, troublante (woman); to be sexy, avoir du chien (or) du sex-appeal.

Seychelles [sei'ʃel] n. pl. Geogr. Seychelles f. pl.

sez [sez] v. intr. Representation of says; sez he, qu'i' m' dit; sez you!, que tu dis!

S.F. [es'ef] abbr. science fiction, science-fiction, S.-F.

shabbily ['ʃæbili] adv. Mesquinement, vilainement, petitement (manner of behaving). ‖ Pauvrement, misérablement (manner of dressing).

shabbiness [-nis] n. Mesquinerie, petitesse f. (of behaviour). ‖ Parcimonie, avarice f. (stinginess). ‖ Apparence miteuse f.; état râpé (or) élimé m. (of clothing); piètre état m. (of furniture).

shabby ['ʃæbi] adj. Mesquin, méprisable, vil (behaviour, character). ‖ Parcimonieux, avare, chiche, pingre (person). ‖ Pauvre, minable, (furniture); râpé, usé, élimé (clothing); minable, pauvrement vêtu (person).

shabrack ['ʃæbræk] n. Chabraque f.

shack [ʃæk] n. Cabane, hutte f.
— v. intr. U. S. Pop. To shack up with, se coller avec.

shackle ['ʃækl] n. Boucle f.; maillon (m.) d'assemblage (of a cable, chain); anse, branche f. (of a padlock). ‖ Pl. Fers m. pl. (of a prisoner). ‖ Autom. Jumelle f. ‖ Ch. de f. Manille f. ‖ Naut. Cigale f. (of an anchor). ‖ Fig. Pl. Entraves f. pl. (of convention).
— v. tr. Mettre les fers à, entraver (a prisoner). ‖ Maniller, mailler (a chain). ‖ Naut. Etalinguer. ‖ Ch. de f. Accoupler. ‖ Fig. Entraver.

shaddock ['ʃædək] n. Bot. Pamplemousse m.

shade [ʃeid] n. Ombre f.; in the shade, à l'ombre. ‖ Pl. Ombrage, lieu ombragé m. (place); ombres f. pl.; obscurité f.; voiles m. pl.; ténèbres f. pl. (of night). ‖ Ombre f.; fantôme m. (ghost). ‖ Nuance f. (of a meaning, an opinion). ‖ Ombre. trace f.; soupçon, brin m.; tantinet m. (fam.) [touch]. ‖ Ecran m. (screen); globe de verre m. (for clocks); abat-jour m. (for lamps). ‖ U. S. Store m. (window-blind). ‖ Arts. Nuance f.; ton m. (hue); ombre f. (in painting). ‖ Naut. Tente f. ‖ Fig. Ombre, obscurité f.; put in (or) into the shade by; éclipsé par. ‖ Fam. Of every shade and hue, de tout poil.
— v. tr. Ombrager, donner de l'ombre à. ‖ Voiler, cacher, masquer, estomper, atténuer (a light). ‖ Arts. Estomper (an outline); nuancer, ombrer (a painting); to shade off, dégrader. ‖ Comm. Réduire légèrement (prices). ‖ Fig. Voiler, assombrir (features); nuancer (a meaning).
— v. intr. Arts. Se dégrader; se fondre (off, into, en).

shaded [-id] adj. Ombragé, à l'ombre. ‖ Arts. Ombré (dessin); hachuré (map).

shadeless [-lis] adj. Sans ombre.

shadily [-ili] adv. Avec de l'ombre. ‖ Fam. D'une manière louche (or) équivoque.

shadiness [-inis] n. Ombre, f.; ombrage m. ‖ Fam. Aspect louche, caractère véreux m. (of a business); réputation suspecte f.; manque (m.) d'honnêteté (of a person).

shading [-iŋ] n. Action (f.) d'ombrer. ‖ Arts. Nuancement m.; ombres f. pl. (of a drawing).

shadow ['ʃædou] n. Ombre, obscurité f. (darkness). ‖ Ombre f. (silhouette); to cast a shadow, projeter une ombre. ‖ Fantôme, spectre m.; ombre f. (ghost). ‖ Soupçon m.; ombre f. (touch). ‖ Protection, ombre f.; abri m. (shelter). ‖ Reflet m.; ombre, illusion f.; to pursue a shadow, courir après une ombre. ‖ Med. Cerne m.; to have shadows under the eyes, avoir les yeux cernés. ‖ Fig. Voile m. (of sadness); ombre, obscurité f. (of solitude). ‖ Fam. Filateur m. (detective); ombre f. (inseparable companion).
— v. tr. Couvrir d'ombre, obscurcir. ‖ Fam. Filer, suivre comme une ombre. ‖ **Shadow-box**, v. intr. Sports. S'entraîner contre un adversaire imagi-

naire. ‖ **Shadow-show,** n. THEATR. Ombres chinoises *f. pl.*

shadower [-ə*] n. Filateur *m.*

shadowing [-iŋ] n. FAM. Filature; *f.;* pistage *m.*

shadowless [-lis] adj. Sans ombre.

shadowy [-i] adj. Peu éclairé, sombre, ténébreux (dark); ombragé, ombreux (shaded). ‖ FIG. Chimérique (dream); vague, indistinct (outline, smile); indécis (plan).

shady ['ʃeidi] adj. Ombragé, ombreux; couvert (path). ‖ FAM. Louche, équivoque, trouble, véreux, interlope (dealings); *shady character,* individu suspect. ‖ FAM. *On the shady side of fifty,* sur le mauvais versant de la cinquantaine.

shaft [ʃɑ:ft] n. Flèche *f.;* dard, trait *m.* (arrow); hampe *f.* (of a lance); *Cupid's shafts,* traits de l'Amour. ‖ Rayon, trait *m.* (of light); sillon *m.* (of lightning); éclair *m.* (of thunder). ‖ Tige *f.* (of a chandelier). ‖ ARCHIT. Flèche *f.* (of a bell-tower); tige *f.;* fût *m.* (of a column); souche *f.* (of a chimney). ‖ ZOOL. Tuyau *m.* (of a feather). ‖ TECHN. Brancard *m.* (of a carriage, a wagon); cheminée *f.* (of a blast furnace); puits *m.* (of a mine). ‖ U. S. Cage *f.* (of an elevator). ‖ MED. Corps *m.* (of the tibia). ‖ AUTOM., NAUT. Arbre *m.;* axe *m.* ‖ FIG. Flèche *f.;* trait *m.* ‖ **Shaft-horse,** n. ZOOL. Limonier *m.*

shafting [-iŋ] n. TECHN. Arbres (*m. pl.*) de transmission.

shag [ʃæg] v. tr. POP. Vider, pomper (to exhaust).

shag [ʃæg] n. Tignasse *f.* (hair). ‖ Peluche, panne *f.* (textiles); tabac bleu *m.* (tobacco). ‖ BOT. Broussaille *f.* ‖ ZOOL. Cormoran huppé *m.*

shagginess [-inis] n. Aspect ébouriffé *m.* (of hair); longueur (or) rudesse (*f.*) de poil (of an animal's coat).

shaggy [-i] adj. Poilu; hirsute (beard); en broussailles (eyebrows); pelucheux (fabric); ébouriffé (hair). ‖ A longs poils rudes (animal's coat). ‖ BOT. Broussailleux (field); touffu (hedge); velu (leaf). ‖ FAM. *Shaggy dog story,* histoire loufoque, loufoquerie.

shagreen [ʃə'gri:n] n. Chagrin *m.;* peau (*f.*) de chagrin.

shah [ʃɑ:] n. Shah *m.*

shake [ʃeik] v. tr. (123). Secouer (a carpet); faire trembler (or) osciller, ébranler (a table); agiter violemment, brandir (a stick); *to shake hands with,* serrer la main à, donner une poignée de main à; *to shake one's head,* hocher (or) secouer la tête; faire un signe de tête négatif. ‖ FIG. Emouvoir, bouleverser, troubler; ébranler (s.o.'s confidence); diminuer la valeur de (s.o.'s reputation); *that shook him,* ça l'a fait tiquer. ‖ **To shake down,** faire tomber en secouant; tasser en secouant; étendre (blanket, straw). ‖ **To shake out,** faire sortir en secouant, secouer (a bag, garment); dérouler (a flag). ‖ **To shake up,** mêler en agitant; secouer, tapoter (a pillow).

— v. intr. Trembler violemment, être secoué (or) ébranlé. ‖ Chanceler (building); branler (door); trembloter, chevroter (voice). ‖ MUS. Faire des trilles. ‖ NAUT. Fouetter (mast); ralinguer (sail).

— n. Secousse *f.;* ébranlement, tremblement *m.* ‖ Poignée *f.;* serrement *m.* (of the hand); hochement, signe négatif *m.* (of the head). ‖ MED. Pl. Fièvre *f.* ‖ MUS. Trille *m.* ‖ FAM. Instant *m.;* seconde *f.; in two shakes,* en deux temps trois mouvements. ‖ POP. *It's no great shakes,* ça ne casse rien. ‖ **Shake-down,** n. FAM. Plumard (*m.*) de fortune (bed); U. S. Rançon *f.* (by a racketeer); v. tr. U. S. FAM. Rançonner; ‖ **Shake-up,** n. FAM. Grand remaniement *m.* (of personnel).

shaker [-ə*] n. Secoueur *s.* (person). ‖ Mixeur *m.; cocktail-shaker,* shaker. ‖ ECCLES. Trembleur, shaker *m.*

Shakespearian [ʃeiks'piəriən] adj. Shakespearien.

shakily ['ʃeikili] adv. D'une voix chevrotante (speaking); à pas chancelants (walking); d'une main tremblante (writing). ‖ En tremblant (or) branlant.

shakiness [-nis] n. Manque (*m.*) de stabilité (or) de solidité (of a building); tremblement *m.* (of the hand); faiblesse *f.* (of health); instabilité *f.* (of a situation).

shako ['ʃeikou] n. MILIT. Shako *m.*

shaky ['ʃeiki] adj. Tremblant, branlant, peu solide (building); tremblé (handwriting); mal affermi (situation); mal assuré, tremblotant (voice). ‖ MED. Tremblant (hand); chancelant; détraqué, patraque (fam.) [health].

shale [ʃeil] n. Schiste argileux *m.* ‖ **Shale-oil,** n. Huile (*f.*) de schiste.

shall [ʃæl] v. aux. defect. (Future); *I shall go,* j'irai. ‖ (Command); *you shall do it,* vous le ferez; *he shall not leave,* je défends qu'il parte. ‖ (Necessity, obligation); *shall I stay?,* voulez-vous que je reste? ‖ (Question); *shall we sing?,* si nous chantions?

shallop ['ʃæləp] n. NAUT. Chaloupe, péniche *f.*

shallot [ʃə'lɔt] n. BOT. Echalote *f.*

shallow ['ʃælou] adj. Plat (recipient); peu profond (water). ‖ AGRIC. Superficiel (soil). ‖ NAUT. *Shallow draught,* faible tirant; *shallow water,* hautsfonds. ‖ FIG. Superficiel, sans profondeur (knowledge); frivole, qui manque de fond (person); futile, creux (talk). ‖ **Shallow-minded,** adj. A l'esprit superficiel; *to be shallow-minded,* manquer de profondeur d'esprit.

— n. pl. NAUT. Haut-fond *m.*

— v. tr. Rendre moins profond.

— v. intr. Devenir moins profond.

shallowness [-nis] n. Manque (or) défaut (*m.*) de profondeur. ‖ FIG. Futilité *f.* (of conversation); caractère superficiel *m.* (of knowledge).

shalt [ʃælt] v. aux. † Second person singular of *shall.*

shaly ['ʃeili] adj. Schisteux.

sham [ʃæm] v. tr. Feindre, simuler; *to sham sleep,* faire semblant de dormir.

— v. intr. Simuler, feindre, faire semblant, jouer la comédie.

— n. Feinte, simulation *f.;* frime *f.;* trompe-l'œil, chiqué *m.* (fam.). ‖ Supercherie, imposture, comédie *f.* (action); imposteur, farceur *s.* (person). ‖ COMM. Imitation, camelote *f.;* faux, toc *m.* (article).

— adj. Feint, simulé (illness); d'emprunt (learning); faux, vain (title). ‖ COMM. Factice, truqué, postiche, de camelote, en toc (jewelry). ‖ MILIT. *Sham battle,* combat simulé, petite guerre. ‖ FIN. Fictif (dividend).

shaman ['ʃæmən] n. Chaman *m.*

shamanism ['ʃæmə,nizm] n. Chamanisme *m.*

shamateur ['ʃæmətə:*] n. SPORTS. Amateur marron *m.*

shamble ['ʃæmbl] v. intr. Marcher en traînant les pieds, aller à pas traînants (or) incertains.

shambles ['ʃæmblz] n. sg. (or) pl. Abattoir *m.* ‖ FIG. Scène (*f.*) de carnage. ‖ FAM. *A shambles,* une belle pagaille.

shame [ʃeim] n. Honte *f.; to bring shame upon,* faire honte à; *to cry shame,* crier au scandale; *for shame!,* quelle honte!, quelle horreur!; *it's a shame,* c'est dommage, c'est une honte; *to put to shame,* faire honte à; *to have lost all sense of shame,* avoir toute honte bue, être sans vergogne. ‖ Déshonneur *m.;* infamie, ignominie *f.* (scandal).

— v. tr. Faire honte à, mortifier, humilier.

shamefaced [-'feist] adj. Confus, timide; honteux (manner). ‖ Pudique, modeste.

shamefacedly [-feisidli] adv. Timidement, d'une manière gênée.

shamefacedness [-'feisidnis] n. Confusion, timidité excessive *f.*

shameful [-ful] adj. Honteux, scandaleux, infâme, indigne, déshonorant. (See DISGRACEFUL.)

shamefully [-fuli] adv. Honteusement, scandaleusement, d'une manière indigne.

shamefulness [-fulnis] n. Honte, infamie, indignité f.

shameless [-lis] adj. Honteux, scandaleux, indigne (action); éhonté, effronté (behaviour, person); dévergondé, sans vergogne (person).

shamelessly [-lisli] adv. Effrontément, d'une manière éhontée.

shamelessness [-lisnis] n. Impudeur, effronterie, impudence f.

shammer ['ʃæmə*] n. Imposteur s., simulateur m.; simulatrice f.

shampoo [ʃæm'pu:] n. Shampooing m.; dry shampoo, shampooing sec.
— v. tr. Shampooiner; faire un shampooing à.

shamrock ['ʃæmrɔk] n. BOT. Trèfle d'Irlande f.

shandy ['ʃændi] adj., n. CULIN. Panaché m. ‖ Bière panachée f.

shandygaff [-gæf] n. Bière panachée f.

shanghai ['ʃæŋhai] v. tr. NAUT., FAM. Enrôler de force. ‖ FAM. Obliger, contraindre (into, à).

shank [ʃæŋk] n. MED. Jambe f.; tibia m. ‖ ZOOL. Canon m. (of a horse). ‖ CULIN. Jarret m. (of beef); manche m. (of mutton). ‖ BOT. Queue f. (of a flower); tige f. (of a plant). ‖ TECHN. Tige f. (of a rivet); branche f. (of scissors); manche m. (of a tool). ‖ ARCHIT. Fût m. (of a column). ‖ NAUT. Verge f. (of an anchor). ‖ FAM. To go on Shanks' mare (or) pony, prendre le train onze.
— v. intr. To shank off, BOT. Tomber (fruit); se flétrir par la tige (plant).

shan't [ʃɑ:nt] v. aux. Contraction of shall not.

shantung [ʃæn'tʌŋ] n. Chantoung, shantung m.

shanty ['ʃænti] n. Baraque, bicoque, cabane f. ‖ Shanty-town, n. FAM. Bidonville m.

shanty n. NAUT. Chant (m.) de marins.

shape [ʃeip] n. Forme, configuration f.; in the shape of, sous la (or) en forme de; out of shape, déformé. ‖ Forme f. (for hat-making); façon, coupe f. (of a garment). ‖ Silhouette, ombre, forme indistincte f. (apparition). ‖ Condition normale, forme f., bon ordre (or) état m.; to take shape, prendre tournure (or) forme; prendre corps (conviction); se dessiner (plan). ‖ CULIN. Moule m.; chocolate shape, crème au chocolat. ‖ FIG. Forme, manière, sorte f.; in no shape or form, sous aucune forme, d'aucune façon. ‖ FAM. In good shape, en bonne forme; in poor shape, mal en point.
— v. tr. Former, façonner, créer. ‖ Modeler, donner une forme à (clay); profiler (a mould); tailler (stone); toupiller (wood); shaped like, en forme de. ‖ ARTS. Contourner (ceramics); tournasser (on a lathe). ‖ FIG. Pétrir (s.o.'s character); former, esquisser (a plan); to shape one's course, diriger ses pas, se diriger (towards, vers).
— v. intr. Se développer, se former, prendre forme; to shape well, prendre bonne tournure (business); s'annoncer favorablement (harvest).

shapeless [-lis] adj. Informe, sans forme; difforme.

shapelessness [-lisnis] n. Manque (m.) de forme; difformité f.

shapeliness [-linis] n. Beauté de forme f., belles proportions f. pl., galbe m.

shapely [-li] adj. Beau, bien proportionné, bien fait de sa personne; bien tourné (or) balancé (fam.).

shaper [-ə*] n. Façonneur s. ‖ TECHN. Emboutissoir m. (machine); emboutisseur s. (person). ‖ ARTS. Calibreur s. (of ceramics). ‖ FIG. Auteur, organisateur m. (of a plan).

shaping [-iŋ] n. Façonnement, façonnage, ajustage m. (of a garment). ‖ FIG. Formation f. (of character); conception, mise (f.) au point (of a plan).

shard [ʃɑ:d], **sherd** [ʃə:d] n. Tesson m. ‖ ZOOL. Elytre m.

share [ʃɛə*] n. AGRIC. Soc m. (of a plough).

share n. Part, portion f.; lion's share, part du lion; share and share alike, à parts égales; to come in for a share of, avoir sa part de; to fall to s.o.'s share, échoir en partage à qqn; to go shares with, partager avec; to have a share in, contribuer à, prendre part à l'accomplissement de. ‖ Ecot m. (assessment, contribution). ‖ FIN. Apport m. (of capital); participation, quote-part f.; part f. (of a founder); action f.; titre m. (of stock). ‖ Share-certificate, n. FIN. Titre m. ‖ Share-cropper, n. U. S. AGRIC. Métayer m. ‖ Share-warrant, n. FIN. Titre au porteur m.
— v. tr. Partager, diviser en parts, répartir (sth.); avoir sa part (in, of, de).
— v. intr. Partager, faire un partage; to share and share alike, avoir parts égales; to share in, avoir sa part de, prendre part à, participer à.

shareholder [-.houldə*] n. FIN. Actionnaire, détenteur (m.) de titres; sociétaire s.

sharer [-ə*] n. Partageant s. ‖ Participant s.

shark [ʃɑ:k] n. ZOOL. Requin m.; basking shark, pèlerin m. ‖ FIG. Grec m. (at cards); requin m. (in finances); escroc m. (swindler). ‖ U. S. FAM. As m.

sharking [-iŋ] n. FAM. Escroquerie f.

sharp [ʃɑ:p] adj. Tranchant, bien affilé (knife); aigu, acéré, pointu (needle); sharp edge, tranchant. ‖ Pointu, effilé (roof). ‖ Pénétrant, vif, piquant, glacé (cold, wind). ‖ Âcre, piquant (odour, taste). ‖ Brusque (change, transition); violent, marqué (contrast, opposition); raide (incline, slope). ‖ Perçant, aigu (cry); sec (noise); aigre (voice). ‖ Acerbe, violent (argument); amer, mordant, aigre, cinglant (criticism); cuisant (defeat); sévère (reproof); acéré, bien affilé (tongue). ‖ Aiguisé, vorace, grand (appetite); violent (feeling); vif, amer (regret); cuisant (remorse). ‖ Prompt, vif, alerte, rapide (pace, trot). ‖ En éveil, vigilant, attentif (awareness); fin, subtil, pénétrant (mind). ‖ MILIT. Rude, vif, violent (combat, struggle). ‖ MED. Perçant (eyesight); angulaire (features); fin (hearing); violent, aigu, cuisant (pain). ‖ ARTS. Vif, net (silhouette). ‖ MUS. Dièse. ‖ AUTOM. Brusque (curve). ‖ FAM. Rusé, astucieux (person); peu scrupuleux, malhonnête (practice, procedure). ‖ POP. Dégourdi, malin; as sharp as a needle (or) U. S. tack, fin comme l'ambre. ‖ U. S. FAM. Coquet (dress).
— adv. Exactement, précis, tapant (hour, time). ‖ Net (stopping); brusquement (turning). ‖ Vivement; look sharp! vite! ‖ MUS. En diésant, trop haut. ‖ Sharp-cut, adj. Net, nettement découpé. ‖ Sharp-edged, adj. A arête vive. ‖ Sharp-looking, adj. Eveillé, à l'air intelligent (person); chic, bien coupé (garment). ‖ Sharp-sighted, adj. Pénétrant, sagace, qui voit clair. ‖ Sharp-witted, adj. A l'esprit vif; perspicace.
— n. Aiguille fine f. ‖ MUS. Dièse m. ‖ U. S. FAM. Connaisseur m.
— v. tr. MUS. Diéser. ‖ FAM. Duper (s.o.); filouter (sth.) [from, à].
— v. intr. Tricher au jeu.

sharpen [-n] v. tr. Affiler, aiguiser, affûter (a blade). ‖ Appointer, tailler (a pencil). ‖ Rendre acerbe (a voice). ‖ MUS. Diéser. ‖ CULIN. Relever (a sauce). ‖ FIG. Aiguiser (the appetite); exciter (a desire); aviver, aggraver (an enmity); affiner (the intelligence). ‖ FAM. Dégourdir (s.o.).
— v. intr. Devenir plus aigu (noise); devenir plus âpre, vif (faculties). ‖ FIG. S'aiguiser (faculties).

sharper [-ə*] n. Escroc, aigrefin, chevalier d'industrie, aventurier m. ‖ Tricheur, entôleur m. (at cards).

sharply [-li] adv. Nettement, d'une façon tranchée (defined, divided). ‖ En pointe, avec une arête vive; sharply pointed, à pointe acérée (or) fine. ‖ A pic, en pente raide, raidement (sloping); brusquement, court (turning). ‖ Avec brusquerie, d'un ton acerbe, d'une voix cassante (answering); vivement, violemment, rudement, sévèrement, vertement (criticizing). ‖ Fort (freezing); raide (hitting); attentivement (listening); avec un bruit sec (sounding); à vive allure, allégrement (walking). ‖ MED. Vivement, avec une douleur vive (suffering).

sharpness [-nis] n. Aiguïté *f.* (of an angle); acuité *f.* (of an edge, a noise, a voice). ‖ Brusquerie *f.* (of a gesture); rapidité, vivacité *f.* (of a pace). ‖ Netteté *f.* (of a contrast, an outline). ‖ Raideur *f.* (of a slope); brusque virage (or) crochet *m.* (of a turning). ‖ Apreté, rigueur *f.* (of the cold); âcreté *f.* (of an odour). ‖ Violence *f.* (of an argument); acerbité, aigreur *f.* (of temper); sévérité, âpreté *f.* (of tone). ‖ Subtilité, vivacité, pénétration *f.* (of mind). ‖ Vivacité *f.* (of feeling); acuité *f.* (of remorse). ‖ MED. Acuité *f.* (of eyesight, pain); finesse *f.* (of hearing). ‖ CULIN. Acidité *f.* (of a fruit); piquant *m.* (of a sauce).

sharpshooter [-ʃuːtə*] n. MILIT. Tireur (*m.*) d'élite.

shatter ['ʃætə*] v. tr. Fracasser, mettre en morceaux, briser en éclats. ‖ MED. Détraquer, délabrer (health); ébranler (nerves). ‖ FIG. Briser, ruiner, anéantir (hopes).
— v. intr. Se fracasser, se mettre en morceaux.

shave [ʃeiv] v. tr. Raser; faire la barbe à (s.o.). ‖ Se raser, se faire la barbe. ‖ TECHN. Planer, doler. ‖ FIG. Raser, friser, effleurer.
— v. intr. Se raser, se faire la barbe.
— n. Acte (*m.*) de raser; barbe *f.*; *to get a shave,* se faire raser; *to give s.o. a shave,* raser qqn; *to have a shave,* se raser, se faire raser. ‖ Effleurement *m.* (action); coup effleurant *m.*; *to have a close shave,* échapper à un cheveu près. ‖ TECHN. Plane *f.* (of wood).

shaveling [-liŋ] n. † Tonsuré, prestolet *m.* ‖ U. S. Jouvenceau *m.*

shaven [-n] adj. Rasé; *clean-shaven,* rasé de près.

shaver [-ə*] n. Barbier *m.* ‖ FAM. *Little* (or) *young shaver,* gosse, gamin, moutard.

shaving [-iŋ] n. Barbe, action (*f.*) de raser (or) de se raser. ‖ TECHN. Planage *m.* (action). ‖ TECHN. Ebarbure *f.* (of metal); copeau *m.* (of wood). ‖ **Shaving-bowl,** n. Plat (*m.*) à barbe. ‖ **Shaving-brush,** n. Blaireau *m.* ‖ **Shaving-cream,** n. Crème (*f.*) à raser. ‖ **Shaving-soap** (or) **-stick,** n. Savon (*m.*) à barbe.

shawl [ʃɔːl] n. Châle *m.*

shawm [ʃɔːm] n. MUS. Chalumeau, pipeau *m.*

she [ʃiː] pron. Elle; *it is she,* c'est elle; *she is his aunt,* c'est sa tante; *she who works,* celle qui travaille. ‖ NAUT. Il (boat). ‖ **She-bear,** n. Ourse *f.* ‖ **She-cat,** n. Chatte *f.* ‖ **She-devil,** n. Démon (*m.*) femelle. ‖ **She-monkey,** n. Guenon *f.*
— n. ZOOL. Femelle *f.*; *it's a she,* c'est une femelle.

sheaf [ʃiːf] (pl. **sheaves** [ʃiːvz]) n. Botte *f.* ‖ Liasse *f.* (of papers). ‖ MILIT. Faisceau *m.* (of arrows). ‖ AGRIC. Gerbe *f.* (of flowers).
— v. tr. Mettre en bottes (or) en gerbes (or) en faisceaux (or) en liasses. ‖ AGRIC. Engerber, enjaveler (grain); mettre en bottes.

shear [ʃiə*] v. tr. (124). Tondre (animals, cloth); couper (a branch); ciseler (velvet). ‖ TECHN. Cisailler (metal). ‖ FIG. Priver, dépouiller. ‖ FAM. Tondre, plumer, écorcher (to fleece).
— v. intr. Tondre. ‖ Se cisailler (beam).
— N. B. En américain, le p.p. *sheared* s'emploie au sens propre. *shorn* au sens figuré.
— n. Pl. Cisailles *f. pl.* (scissors). ‖ TECHN. Cisaillement *m.* ‖ **Shear-legs,** n. TECHN. Bigue *f.*

shearer [-rə*] n. Tondeur *m.*

shearing [-riŋ] n. Tonte *f.*

shearling [-liŋ] n. ZOOL. Mouton d'un an *m.*

shearwater [-,wɔːtə*] n. ZOOL. Puffin *m.*

sheath [ʃiːθ] n. Gaine *f.* (for a knife); étui *m.* (for scissors); fourreau *m.* (for a sword, an umbrella). ‖ TECHN. Manchon protecteur *m.* ‖ ZOOL. Etui *m.* ‖ BOT. Gaine *f.* ‖ MED. Gaine *f.* (of an artery);

enveloppe *f.* (of an organ); condom *m.* (male preservative). ‖ ELECTR. Ecran *m.* ‖ **Sheath-dress,** n. Fourreau *m.* ‖ **Sheath-knife,** n. Couteau (*m.*) à gaine.

sheathe [ʃiːð] v. tr. Engainer (a knife); rengainer (a sword). ‖ Envelopper, revêtir d'une enveloppe. ‖ ARCHIT. Recouvrir (a roof). ‖ NAUT. Doubler, souffler (a ship's bottom). ‖ TECHN. Armer (a cable).

sheave [ʃiːv] n. TECHN. Cache-entrée *m.* (of a keyhole); réa *m.* (of a pulley).

sheaves [ʃiːvz]. See SHEAF.

Sheba ['ʃiːbə] n. *The Queen of Sheba,* la reine de Saba.

shebang [ʃi'bæŋ] n. U. S. POP. Fourbi *m.*

shebeen [ʃə'biːn] n. Débit (*m.*) de boissons qui vend de l'alcool sans licence (in Ireland).

shed [ʃed] n. Hangar *m.*; appentis *m.* (lean-to); auvent *m.* (open); remise *f.*, dépôt *m.* (for tools). ‖ Baraque, hutte, cabane *f.* ‖ AGRIC. Etable *f.* ‖ CH. DE F. Hangar (*m.*) à locomotives; dépôt de matériel roulant *m.*
— v. tr. (125). Répandre, verser. ‖ Se défaire de, abandonner, se dépouiller de (clothing, possessions). ‖ Diffuser, répandre (light); déverser (water). ‖ BOT. Perdre (leaves). ‖ ZOOL. Jeter, laisser tomber (horns); dépouiller (shell); changer de (skin). ‖ FIG. Répandre (happiness, tears); *to shed light on,* éclairer (a question). ‖ FAM. Semer (s.o.).
— v. intr. ZOOL. Muer; perdre son poil.

shedder [-ə*] n. Verseur *s.* (person). ‖ ZOOL. Animal (*m.*) qui mue.

sheen [ʃiːn] n. Luminosité *f.*; éclat, brillant, chatoiement *m.* (of a jewel); lustre, luisant, reflet *m.* (of silk); miroitement *m.* (of water).

sheep [ʃiːp] (pl. **sheep**) n. invar. ZOOL. Mouton *m.*; *lost sheep,* brebis perdue. ‖ FAM. Bêta, nigaud *m.* ‖ ECCLES. Ouailles *f. pl.* ‖ FIG. *Black sheep,* brebis galeuse. ‖ FAM. *To make sheep's eyes at,* faire les yeux doux à. ‖ **Sheep-dip,** n. Bain parasiticide *m.* ‖ **Sheep-dog,** n. ZOOL. Chien de berger *m.* ‖ **Sheep-farmer,** n. AGRIC. Eleveur (*m.*) de moutons. ‖ **Sheep-fold,** n. Bercail *m.*, bergerie *f.* ‖ **Sheep-pox,** n. MED. Clavelée *f.* ‖ **Sheep-run,** n. Pâturage *m.* ‖ **Sheep-shearing,** n. AGRIC. Tonte (*f.*) des moutons, tonte.

sheepish [-iʃ] adj. Penaud, décontenancé; niais.

sheepishly [-iʃli] adv. D'un air niais (or) penaud.

sheepishness [-iʃnis] n. Air penaud *m.*; timidité niaise *f.*

sheepman [-mən] (pl. **sheepmen**) n. U. S. Eleveur (*m.*) de moutons.

sheepskin [-skin] n. Peau (*f.*) de mouton (hide); basane *f.* (leather). ‖ FAM. Peau (*f.*) d'âne (diploma).

sheer [ʃiə*] adj. Perpendiculaire; à pic (cliff); accore (coast). ‖ Transparent, fin, diaphane (fabric). ‖ FIG. Vrai, véritable, simple, complet; absolu (impossibility); seul (necessity); pur (nonsense); *by sheer force,* de vive force; *in sheer desperation,* en désespoir de cause; *sheer madness,* folie pure (or) douce.
— adv. Complètement, tout à fait; droit (forward). ‖ Perpendiculairement, à pic, à plomb.
— v. intr. Se dresser (or) descendre à pic.

sheer n. NAUT. Embardée *f.* ‖ NAUT. Tonture *f.* ‖ **Sheer-rail,** n. Liston *m.* ‖ **Sheer-strake,** n. Vibord *m.*
— v. intr. NAUT. Faire une embardée; embarder; *to sheer off,* passer à bonne distance (*from,* de). ‖ FAM. S'écarter, prendre le large.

sheet [ʃiːt] n. Drap *m.* (bed linen); *winding sheet,* linceul; *as white as a sheet,* pâle comme un linge. ‖ Feuille *f.* (of glass, lead, paper, rubber); nappe, lame *f.* (of fire, metal, water); couche *f.* (of ice, snow); tôle *f.* (of metal); *proof sheet,* épreuve. ‖ COMM. Etat *m.*; bulletin *m.* (for orders); bordereau *m.* (for sales); *balance sheet,* bilan, inventaire. ‖ NAUT. Ecoute *f.*; *fore-sheet,* gaillard; *main sheet.*

écoute de grand-voile ; *stern-sheet*, chambre. ‖ Fam. U. S. Feuille *f. ;* canard *m.* (newspaper). ‖ Fam. *To be three sheets in the wind*, avoir du vent dans les voiles, tenir une cuite. ‖ **Sheet-anchor, n.** Naut. Ancre (*m.*) de veille ; Fig. Ancre (*m.*) de salut. ‖ **Sheet-copper, n.** Feuille (*f.*) de cuivre. ‖ **Sheet-glass, n.** Verre (*m.*) à vitres. ‖ **Sheet-iron, n.** Tôle *f.* ‖ **Sheet-lightning, n.** Eclair (*m.*) de chaleur. ‖ **Sheet-steel, n.** Tôle (*f.*) d'acier.
— v. tr. Couvrir (or) envelopper d'un drap (or) d'une bâche. ‖ Recouvrir comme d'une nappe. ‖ Ensevelir (in a winding-sheet).

sheeting [-iŋ] n. Toile (*f.*) pour draps.

sheik [ʃeik] n. Cheik *m.* ‖ Pop. Bourreau (*m.*) des cœurs ; tombeur *m.*

shekel [ˈʃekl] n. Sicle *m.* ‖ Pl. Fam. Galette *f.*

shelf [ʃelf] (pl. **shelves** [ʃelvz]) n. Tablette *f. ;* planche *f.* (closet) ; rayon *m.* (cupboard, library) ; plateau *m.* (oven) ; pl. étagère *f.* (set of shelves). ‖ Geol. Rebord *m.*, saillie, corniche *f.* (of a cliff) ; récif *m.* (underwater) ; *continental shelf*, plateau (or) banc continental. ‖ Naut. Bauquière *f.* ‖ Fam. *To be on the shelf*, avoir coiffé sainte Catherine, monter en graine. ‖ **Shelf-life, n.** Durée (*f.*) limite de stockage. ‖ **Shelf-mark, n.** Cote *f.* (on library book).

shell [ʃel] n. Coquille *f.* (of an egg). ‖ Zool. Carapace *f.* (of a lobster) ; coquille *f.* (of a mollusc) ; écaille *f.* (of a tortoise) ; *sea shell*, coquillage. ‖ Bot. Coque, coquille *f.* (of a nut) ; gousse, cosse *f.* (of peas). ‖ Archit. Carcasse *f.* (of a building). ‖ Naut. Yole *f.*, canot (*m.*) de course (boat) ; coque *f.* (of a ship). ‖ Milit. Obus *m.* (shrapnel) ; coquille *f.* (of a sword). ‖ Techn. Corps cylindrique *m. ;* enveloppe *f.* (of a boiler) ; caisse *f.* (of a drum) ; chape *f.* (of a pulley). ‖ Fig. Extérieur *m. ;* apparence, forme vide *f.* ‖ Fig. Grandes lignes *f. pl. ;* ébauche *f.* (of a plan). ‖ Fam. Coquille *f. ; to come out of, to withdraw into one's shell*, sortir de, rentrer dans sa coquille. ‖ **Shell-egg, n.** Comm. Œuf frais *m.* ‖ **Shell-fire, n.** Milit. Bombardement (or) tir (*m.*) par obus. ‖ **Shell-fish, n.** Zool. Crustacé ; coquillage *m. ;* Culin. Coquillages, fruits (*m. pl.*) de mer. ‖ **Shell-proof, adj.** Milit. Blindé. ‖ **Shell-shock, n.** Med. Psychose traumatique *f. ;* commotion *f.* (or) ébranlement nerveux (*m.*) par éclatement d'obus. ‖ **Shell-work, n.** Arts. Décoration (*f.*) en coquillages.
— v. tr. Couvrir d'une carapace. ‖ Culin. Retirer de sa coquille (or) de sa carapace (fish) ; écaler, décortiquer (nuts) ; écosser, égrener (peas). ‖ Milit. Bombarder, canonner.
— v. intr. **To shell off**, s'écailler. ‖ **To shell out**, Pop. abouler, casquer.

shellac [ʃeˈlæk] n. Gomme laque *f. ;* laque (*f.*) en feuilles.
— v. tr. Laquer. ‖ U. S. Pop. Tabasser.

shellacking [-iŋ] n. U. S. Pop. Rossée, raclée *f.*

shelling [ˈʃeliŋ] n. Décorticage *m.* (of nuts) ; écaillage *m.* (of oysters) ; égrenage *m.* (of peas) ; épluchage *m.* (of shrimps). ‖ Milit. Bombardement *m.*

shelter [ˈʃeltə*] n. Abri, lieu de refuge *m. ;* asile *m.* (for the homeless) ; abrivent *m.* (for a sentry) ; *night shelter*, asile de nuit ; *playground shelter*, préau *m. ; under shelter*, à l'abri, à couvert ; *to find* (or) *to take shelter*, s'abriter, trouver asile.
— v. tr. Abriter (or) protéger (*from*, contre, de). ‖ Mettre à l'abri à couvert. ‖ Donner asile à, recueillir.
— v. intr. S'abriter, se mettre à couvert.

shelterless [-lis] adj. Sans abri (or) refuge.

shelve [ʃelv] v. tr. Garnir de rayonnages (a wall). ‖ Mettre sur un rayon (books). ‖ Fam. Classer, enterrer, mettre en sommeil, laisser dormir (a question) ; remiser, mettre au rancart (s.o., sth.).
— v. intr. Aller en pente douce.

shelves [-z] n. pl. See SHELF.

shelving [-iŋ] n. Aménagement (*m.*) des rayons. ‖ Arrangement *m.* (of books). ‖ Rayonnages *m. pl.* tablettes *f. pl.* ‖ Fam. Classement ; enterrement *m.* (fam.) [of a question] ; mise (*f.*) au rancart (of s.o.).

shemozzle [ʃiˈmɔzl] n. Pop. Boucan, ramdam *m.* (row) ; bagarre *f.* (brawl) ; pagaille, pagaïe *f.* (muddle).

shenanigan [ʃiˈnænigən] n. U. S. Fam. Cirque, tohu-bohu *m.* (rumpus). ‖ U. S. Fam. Roublardise *f.*

shepherd [ˈʃepəd] n. Berger, pâtre *m. ; shepherd boy, girl*, petit pâtre, jeune bergère. ‖ Comm. *Shepherd's check*, pied-de-poule (textile). ‖ Eccles. Pasteur *m.* ‖ Culin. *Shepherd's pie*, hachis de viande enrobé de pommes de terre.
— v. tr. Garder, surveiller (animals). ‖ Fig. Guider, veiller sur (children).

shepherdess [-is] n. Bergère *f.*

sherbet [ˈʃə:bət] n. Sorbet *m.*

shereef, sherif [ʃeˈrif] n. Chérif *m.*

sheriff [ˈʃerif] n. Jur. Shérif *m. ; sheriff's officer*, huissier. ‖ U. S. Chef (*m.*) de la police (of a county).

sherry [ˈʃeri] n. Xérès *m.*

Shetland [ˈʃetlʌnd] n. Geogr. Archipel (*m.*) des Shetland. ‖ Comm. Shetland *m.*

shibboleth [ˈʃiboleθ] n. Schibboleth *m.* ‖ Fam. Mot d'ordre *m. ;* doctrine *f.* (of a party).

shield [ʃi:ld] n. Milit. Bouclier, écu *m.* (of a knight) ; pare-balles, pare-éclats, masque *m.* (against shrapnel). ‖ Ecusson *m.* (of a pocket-knife). ‖ Techn. Tôle protectrice *f.*, volet (or) écran protecteur *m. ;* contre-porte *f.* (of a furnace) ; cuirasse *f.* (of miner's lamp). ‖ Blas. Ecu *m.* ‖ Autom. *Sun-shield*, pare-soleil. ‖ **Shield-budding, n.** Agric. Ecussonnage *m.*
— v. tr. Protéger, défendre (*from*, de, contre) ; mettre à l'abri (*from*, de). [See PROTECT.] ‖ Techn. Masquer. ‖ Electr. Blinder. ‖ Fig. Couvrir (s.o.).

shieldless [-lis] adj. Sans bouclier. ‖ Fig. Sans défense.

shift [ʃift] n. Changement *m. ;* modification *f.* ‖ Renverse *f.* (of current) ; saute *f.* (of wind). ‖ Journée (*f.*) de travail ; période (*f.*) de relève (for workers). ‖ Equipe *f.* (of employees) ; *to work in shifts*, se relayer. ‖ Moyen, expédient *m. ;* ressource *f. ; to make shift to* (or) *with*, trouver moyen de, s'arranger (or) s'accommoder de, se tirer d'affaire avec ; *at one's last shift*, à bout de ressources. ‖ Subterfuge, détour, faux-fuyant, artifice *m. ;* ruse, échappatoire *f.* ‖ Fin. Déplacement *m.* (of prices). ‖ Archit. Décalage *m.* ‖ Geol. Faille *f.* ‖ Mus. Changement (*m.*) de position (in violin playing). ‖ † Linge (or) vêtement (*m.*) de rechange ; chemise de femme *f.*
— v. tr. Déplacer, changer de place, remuer, bouger. ‖ Changer de, remplacer par un autre, substituer un autre à. ‖ Theatr. Changer (the scenery). ‖ Naut. Changer (the helm). ‖ Milit. Déplacer (fire). ‖ Ch. de f. Décaler (a train schedule). ‖ U. S. Autom. *To shift gears*, changer de vitesse. ‖ Fig. Rejeter (blame, responsibility) ; *to shift one's ground*, changer ses batteries.
— v. intr. Changer de place (or) de direction ; remuer, bouger, se déplacer. ‖ Tourner, sauter (wind). ‖ Theatr. Changer (scene). ‖ Naut. Se désarrimer (cargo). ‖ Fam. Equivoquer, biaiser, finasser (to dodge) ; *to shift for oneself*, se débrouiller (or) se dépatouiller tout seul.

shiftiness [-inis] n. Fausseté *f.*

shiftless [-lis] adj. Paresseux, peu débrouillard, sans initiative ; mou *m.*, molle *f.*

shifty [-i] adj. Faux, sournois, fuyant (glance) ; rusé, retors, roublard (person).

shill [ʃil] n. U. S. Pop. Entraîneur, compère *m.* (of a gambler).

shillelagh [ʃəˈleilə] n. Gourdin *m.* (in Ireland).

shilling [ˈʃiliŋ] n. Fin. Shilling *m.*

shilly-shallier ['ʃili,ʃæliə*] n. FAM. Tergiversateur *m.*, tergiversatrice *f.*
shilly-shally ['ʃili,ʃæli] n. FAM. See SHILLY-SHALLYING.
— adj. FAM. Indécis, hésitant.
— v. intr. FAM. Hésiter, tergiverser, tourner autour du pot.
shilly-shallying [-iŋ] n. FAM. Indécision, irrésolution, tergiversation *f.*; atermoiements *m. pl.*
shim [ʃim] n. TECHN. Cale, pièce d'épaisseur *f.*
— v. tr. TECHN. Caler.
shimmer ['ʃimə*] n. Lueur *f.*; chatoiement, miroitement, reflet tremblant *m.*
— v. intr. Luire, chatoyer, miroiter.
shimmy ['ʃimi] n. MUS. Shimmy *m.* (dance). ‖ AUTOM. U. S. Shimmy *m.* (wobble). ‖ FAM. Liquette *f.*
— v. intr. (2). Danser le shimmy. ‖ FAM. Tanguer (car); se déhancher (person).
shin [ʃin] n. MED. Devant (*m.*) du tibia. ‖ ZOOL. Canon *m.* (of a horse). ‖ CULIN. Jarret *m.* (of veal). ‖ CH. DE F. Eclisse *f.* ‖ **Shin-bone**, n. Tibia *m.* ‖ **Shin-guard** (or) **-pad**, n. SPORTS. Protège-tibia *m.*, jambière *f.*
— v. intr. *To shin down*, dégringoler ; *to shin up*, grimper à, se hisser sur.
— v. tr. Donner des coups de pied dans les jambes de (s.o.).
shindig ['ʃindig] n. U. S. POP. Sauterie, « party » *f.*
shindy ['ʃindi] n. Tapage, chahut, boucan *m.* (noise); bagarre *f.* (row). ‖ U. S. POP. Sauterie *f.*
shine [ʃain] n. Eclat, brillant *m.* ‖ Luisant *m.* (on worn fabric). ‖ Beau temps *m.*; *in rain or shine*, par tous les temps. ‖ Brillant *m.* (on shoes); U. S. *my shoes need a shine*, mes chaussures ont besoin d'un coup de cirage. ‖ FAM. *To take the shine out of*, faire la pige à. ‖ U. S. FAM. *To take a shine to*, se toquer de, s'enticher de (s.o.).
— v. intr. (126). Luire, reluire (surface). ‖ ASTRON. Briller (sun); *the moon is shining*, il fait clair de lune ; *the sun is shining*, il fait du soleil ; *to shine on*, éclairer, illuminer. ‖ FIG. Rayonner, resplendir (face); briller, être brillant (in society). ‖ U. S. FAM. *To shine up to*, passer la main dans le dos à.
— v. tr. Faire reluire (or) briller (by polishing). ‖ U. S. (p.p., pret. **shined**). Polir (leather); cirer (shoes).
shiner [-ə*] n. Cireur, décrotteur *m.* (of shoes). ‖ POP. Jaunet *m.*; pl. pognon, fric *m.* ‖ U. S. POP. Œil poché (or) au beurre noir *m.*
shingle ['ʃingl] n. Bardeau *m.* ‖ Coupe à la garçonne *f.* ‖ U. S. COMM. FAM. Enseigne *f.*; *to hang out one's shingle*, s'établir (in business).
— v. tr. Essenter (a roof). ‖ Couper les cheveux à la garçonne à (s.o.).
shingle n. Galets *m. pl.* (on the beach).
shingle v. tr. TECHN. Cingler, tringler (iron).
shingles ['ʃinglz] n. pl. MED. Zona *m.*
shingly ['ʃingli] adj. Couvert de galets, caillouteux.
shininess ['ʃaininis] n. Luisance *f.* ‖ Lustrage *m.*
shinny ['ʃini] v. intr. U. S. FAM. *To shinny up*, grimper à.
Shintoism ['ʃintouizm] n. Shintoïsme *m.*
shinty ['ʃinti] n. SPORTS. Jeu (*m.*) proche du hockey sur gazon.
shiny ['ʃaini] adj. Brillant, luisant. ‖ Lustré (from wear).
ship [ʃip] n. NAUT. Navire *m.* (merchant); bâtiment, vaisseau *m.* (war); bateau *m.* (fam.); *to take ship*, s'embarquer; *on board ship*, à bord. ‖ MED. *Hospital ship*, navire hôpital. ‖ CULIN. *Ship's biscuit*, biscuit de mer. ‖ FAM. *Ship of the desert*, chameau; *ship of State*, char de l'Etat. ‖ **Ship-broker**, n. NAUT. Courtier maritime *m.* ‖ **Ship-canal**, n. Canal maritime *m.* ‖ **Ship-chandler**, n. Entrepreneur (*m.*) de marine; fournisseur (*m.*) de la Marine.
— v. tr. NAUT. Embarquer (a cargo, passengers,

water); enrôler (a crew); monter (a mast); armer, border (the oars). ‖ COMM. Envoyer, expédier (goods by rail or by sea).
— v. intr. S'embarquer, embarquer (passenger). ‖ NAUT. Armer sur un vaisseau.
shipboard [-bɔ:d] n. NAUT. Bord *m.*; *on shipboard*, à bord.
shipbuilder [-bildə*] n. Constructeur (*m.*) de navires.
shipbuilding [-bildiŋ] n. NAUT. Construction navale *f.*
shipload [-loud] n. NAUT. Cargaison *f.*, chargement *m.*; *by the shipload*, par bateaux entiers.
shipmaster [-mɑ:stə*] n. NAUT. Capitaine marchand *m.* ‖ Patron de navire *m.* (owner).
shipmate [-meit] n. Camarade (or) compagnon de bord *m.*
shipment [-mənt] n. Embarquement *m.*; expédition *f.* (by rail or sea). ‖ Chargement *m.* (goods shipped); livraison *f.* (goods delivered).
shipowner [-ounə*] n. Armateur *m.*
shipper [-ə*] n. COMM. Affréteur, expéditeur *m.*; expéditrice *f.*
shipping [-iŋ] m. Embarquement *m.*; mise (*f.*) à bord (of a cargo); enrôlement *m.* (of a crew). ‖ Navires marchands; bâtiments *m. pl.* (of a country, in a port). ‖ Navigation *f.*; *shipping routes*, routes de navigation. ‖ Marine marchande *f.*; *shipping trade*, affaires maritimes. ‖ TECHN. Montage *m.* ‖ **Shipping-agency**, n. Agence maritime *f.* ‖ **Shipping-agent**, n. Agent maritime *m.* ‖ **Shipping-articles**, n. pl. Conditions (*f. pl.*) d'embarquement. ‖ **Shipping-bill**, n. Connaissement *m.* ‖ **Shipping-charges**, n. pl. Frais (*m. pl.*) de mise à bord. ‖ **Shipping-clerk**, n. COMM. Expéditionnaire *m.* ‖ **Shipping-company**, n. Compagnie (*f.*) de navigation. ‖ **Shipping-intelligence** (or) **-news**, n. Nouvelles maritimes *f. pl.*; renseignements (*m. pl.*) sur les mouvements maritimes. ‖ **Shipping-master**, n. Agent maritime, enrôleur *m.* ‖ **Shipping-measurements**, n. pl. NAUT. Cubage *m.* ‖ **Shipping-office**, n. Agence maritime *f.*; inscription maritime *f.* (for sailors). ‖ **Shipping-room**, n. U. S. COMM. Salle d'expédition *f.*
shipshape [-ʃeip] adj. NAUT. Bien étarqué. ‖ FAM. Bien tenu (or) arrangé, en bon ordre.
— adv. En marin; comme il faut.
shipway [-wei] n. NAUT. Cale (*f.*) de lancement.
shipwreck [-rek] n. NAUT. Naufrage *m.*; *to have a shipwreck*, faire naufrage. ‖ FIG. Ruine *f.*; naufrage *m.*
— v. tr. Faire naufrager; *to be shipwrecked*, faire naufrage.
— v. intr. Faire naufrage, naufrager.
shipwright [-rait] n. NAUT. Constructeur (*m.*) de navires.
shipyard [-jɑ:d] n. NAUT. Chantier (*m.*) de constructions navales.
shire [ʃaiə*] n. Comté *m.* (in England). ‖ **Shire-town**, n. Chef-lieu de comté *m.*
shirk [ʃə:k] v. tr. Manquer à, se dérober à, se soustraire à (an assignment); esquiver, éluder (a duty, a question). ‖ FAM. Sécher (school); renâcler devant (a task).
— v. intr. Se dérober. ‖ MILIT. Tirer au flanc. ‖ FAM. Se défiler.
shirker [-ə*] n. Renâcleur, flanchard *s.* ‖ MILIT. Tireur au flanc *m.*
shirr [ʃə:*] v. tr. Bouillonner (a skirt). ‖ U. S. CULIN. Cuire au four (eggs).
shirred [-d] adj. Caoutchouté (ribbon); à fronces (skirt). ‖ U. S. CULIN. Cuit au four (egg).
shirt [ʃə:t] n. Chemise *f.* (man's); blouse *f.*; chemisier *m.* (woman's). ‖ FAM. *To lose one's shirt*, perdre jusqu'à son dernier sou. ‖ **Shirt-blouse**, n. Chemisier *m.* (woman's). ‖ **Shirt-front**, n. Plastron

(*m.*) de chemise. ‖ **Shirt-maker,** n. Chemisier *m.*
‖ **Shirt-sleeve,** n. Manche *f.*; adj. U. S. FAM. A la
bonne franquette. ‖ **Shirt-tails,** n. pl. Pans (*m. pl.*)
de chemise.

shirting ['ʃəːtiŋ] n. Shirting *m.*

shirtless [-lis] adj. Sans chemise.

shirtwaist [-weist] n. U. S. Chemisier *m.*

shirty [-i] adj. POP. En rogne, de mauvais poil.

shish kebab ['ʃiːʃ kəˈbæb] n. CULIN. Chiche-
kebab *m.*, brochette *f.*

shit [ʃit] n. ARG. Merde *f.* (excrement); *to have a
shit,* aller chier. ‖ ARG. Merdeux, salaud *m.*; salope *f.* (bastard). ‖
ARG. Hasch *m.* (hashish). ‖ Pl. ARG. Chiasse *f.*
(diarrhoea). ‖ LOC. *Not to give a shit,* s'en foutre
complètement.
— interj. Merde!
— adj. Merdique; *a shit job,* un boulot à la con.
— v. intr. (1). ARG. Chier.

shitty ['ʃiti] adj. ARG. Merdique, dégueulasse.

shiver ['ʃivə*] n. Eclat, fragment, morceau *m.* ‖
Pierre schisteuse *f.*
— v. tr. Briser en éclats, fracasser.
— v. intr. Se briser. voler en éclats.

shiver n. Frisson, tremblement *m.*
— v. intr. Frissonner, grelotter, trembler (*with,*
de). [See SHAKE.] ‖ NAUT. Ralinguer (sail). ‖ LOC.
Shiver my timbers!, Mille tonnerres!
— v. tr. NAUT. Faire faséyer (a sail).

shivery [-ri] adj. Frissonnant, fiévreux.

shoal [ʃoul] n. GEOL. Haut-fond, banc de sable *m.*
(See BAR.) ‖ FIG. Traquenard, danger caché *m.*
— adj. Peu profond (water).
— v. intr. Diminuer de profondeur (or) de fond.

shoal n. ZOOL. Banc voyageur *m.* (of fish); bande *f.*
(of porpoises). ‖ FAM. Tas *m.*; bande *f.* (of persons).
— v. intr. ZOOL. Aller par bancs (fish).

shoat [ʃout] n. U. S. ZOOL. Porcelet *m.*

shock [ʃɔk] n. Choc, heurt, coup *m.*; secousse *f.*
‖ Impact *m.* (of a collision). ‖ GEOL. Séisme *m.*;
secousse *f.* (of an earthquake). ‖ MILIT. Rencontre
f.; choc, assaut *m.* ‖ ELECTR. Choc *m.*; secousse
f. ‖ MED. Traumatisme *m.*; commotion *f.*; *surgical
shock,* choc opératoire. ‖ FIG. Coup, choc *m.* ‖
Shock-absorber, n. AUTOM. Amortisseur *m.*;
AVIAT. Sandow *m.* ‖ **Shock-proof,** adj. Résistant
aux chocs, anti-choc. ‖ **Shock-tactics,** n. MILIT.
Tactique (*f.*) de choc. ‖ **Shock-therapy,** n. PSYCH.
Thérapeutique (*f.*) de choc (by means of drugs);
traitement (*m.*) par électrochoc (by means of an
electric shock). ‖ **Shock-troops,** n. MILIT. Troupes
(*f. pl.*) de choc. ‖ **Shock wave,** n. PHYS., AVIAT.
Onde (*f.*) de choc.
— v. tr. Choquer, scandaliser, effaroucher; *to be
shocked,* se scandaliser, se choquer. ‖ Bouleverser;
révolter, frapper d'indignation; remplir d'horreur.
‖ Blesser (the ear). ‖ MED. Choquer, commotionner.

shock n. Tignasse, toison *f.* (head of hair). ‖ **Shock-
headed,** adj. Ebouriffé.

shock n. AGRIC. Meulon *m.* (of wheat).
— v. tr. Moyetter (wheat).

shocker [-ə*] n. FAM. Horreur *f.* (person, thing).
‖ Surprise pénible *f.*; coup rude *m.* (blow). ‖ FAM.
Roman sensationnel, livre à scandale *m.*; pièce
grand-guignolesque *f.*

shocking [-iŋ] adj. Choquant, scandaleux, horrifiant (behaviour); atterrant (news); affreux,
épouvantable (spectacle); abominable, exécrable
(weather).
— adv. FAM. See SHOCKINGLY.

shockingly [-iŋli] adv. Affreusement, horriblement,
épouvantablement, d'une manière odieuse (behaving); excessivement, extrêmement (expensive).

shod [ʃɔd] p. p. See SHOE.

shoddy ['ʃɔdi] n. Drap (*m.*) de laine d'effilochage.
‖ COMM. Camelote, pacotille *f.*

— adj. D'effilochage. ‖ COMM. De camelote, de
pacotille.

shoe [ʃuː] n. Soulier *m.*; chaussure *f.*; *court, house,
wooden shoes,* escarpins, chaussons; sabots; *to put
on, to take off one's shoes,* se chausser, se déchausser. ‖ Fer *m.* (horseshoe); *to cast a shoe,* perdre un
fer, se déferrer. ‖ AUTOM. Sabot *m.* (of a brake).
‖ TECHN. Patin *m.* ‖ NAUT. Savate, semelle *f.* (of an
anchor); sole *f.* (of a rudder). ‖ NAUT. Semelle *f.*
(of a gun-carriage). ‖ LOC. *To put the shoe on the
right foot,* s'en prendre à celui qui le mérite; *that's
where the shoe pinches,* c'est là que le bât le
blesse; *in your shoes,* à votre place. ‖ **Shoe-buckle,**
n. Boucle (*f.*) de soulier. ‖ **Shoe-cream,** n. Crème-
cirage *m.* ‖ **Shoe-horn,** n. Chausse-pied *m.*; corne
f. ‖ **Shoe-lace,** n. Lacet de soulier *m.* ‖ **Shoe-
leather,** n. Cuir (*m.*) pour souliers. ‖ **Shoe-polish,**
n. Cirage *m.* ‖ **Shoe-repairman,** n. Cordonnier *m.*
‖ **Shoe-repair shop,** n. Cordonnerie *f.* ‖ **Shoe-
shine,** n. U. S. Cirage *m.*; *shoe-shine boy,* décrotteur. ‖ **Shoe-shop,** U. S. **Shoe-store,** n. Magasin
(*m.*) de chaussures. ‖ **Shoe-string,** n. Lacet *m.*;
U. S. CULIN. *Shoe-string potatoes,* pommes paille,
croustilles; FAM. *To start on a shoe-string,* monter
une affaire avec quelques fafiots. ‖ **Shoe-tree,** n.
Embauchoir *m.*; forme *f.*
— v. tr. (127). Chausser. ‖ ZOOL. Ferrer (horses).
‖ TECHN. Garnir d'une ferrure (or) d'une semelle
(or) d'un patin; bander, embattre (a wheel). ‖ NAUT.
Brider (an anchor).

shoeblack [-blæk] n. Cireur, décrotteur *m.*

shoeblacking [-blækiŋ] n. U. S. Cirage noir (*m.*)
pour chaussures.

shoeing [-iŋ] n. Ferrage *m.*; ferrure *f.* (of a horse).
‖ TECHN. Pose (*f.*) d'un patin (or) d'un sabot.

shoemaker [-meikə*] n. Cordonnier *m.* (cobbler).
‖ Bottier *m.* (bootmaker).

shone [ʃɔn] p. p. See SHINE.

shoo [ʃuː] interj. Ch! (to chickens); allez!, filez!
(to children).
— v. tr. Faire ch! à; *to shoo away,* chasser, faire
enfuir.

shook [ʃuk] pret. See SHAKE.

shoot [ʃuːt] n. Course rapide *f.* (of a propelled
object); élan, bond (*m.*) en avant (of a ball). ‖
Dépôt *m.* (dumping ground). ‖ MILIT., NAUT. Tir,
exercice de tir *m.* ‖ SPORTS. Partie de chasse *f.*
‖ BOT. Rejeton; scion *m.*; pousse *f.* ‖ GEOL. Coulée
(*f.*) de minerai. ‖ TECHN. Déversoir, plan incliné
m.; manche *f.* (for coal); coulisseau *m.* (for parcels); coulisse *f.* (for rubbish). ‖ MED. Elancement
m. (of pain).
— v. intr. (128). S'élancer, se lancer, se précipiter,
aller comme un trait, être projeté comme une
flèche; *to shoot ahead* (or) *forward,* s'élancer en
avant; *to shoot ahead of,* devancer; *to shoot down,
up,* descendre, monter à toute vitesse; *to shoot out,*
jaillir (flame); *to shoot past,* passer comme un
éclair; *to shoot through,* traverser comme une
flèche. ‖ MILIT. Tirer (with a bow, a gun); lancer
un projectile. ‖ SPORTS. Chasser; *to be out shooting,*
être parti à la chasse. ‖ SPORTS. Raser le sol
(cricket ball); shooter (in football). ‖ ASTRON. Filer
(star). ‖ MED. Lanciner, élancer (pain). ‖ BOT. Pousser, bourgeonner (bud, tree); germer (plant). ‖
CINEM. Tourner. ‖ **To shoot away,** tirer sans
désemparer.
— v. tr. (128). Lancer, envoyer, décocher (a projectile); projeter, jeter brusquement (by violent
motion). ‖ Atteindre, toucher, blesser (to hit);
tuer (to kill). ‖ Passer rapidement sous (a bridge);
franchir, descendre (rapids). ‖ Déverser (coal). ‖
ELECTR. Darder (a beam, a ray). ‖ TECHN. Pousser
à fond (a lock). ‖ BOT. Pousser (branches). ‖ MILIT.
Tirer, faire partir (an arrow, bullet, missile); tirer
un coup de (a gun); fusiller, passer par les armes
(a prisoner). ‖ MED. *Shot through the arm,* le bras

traversé d'une balle. ‖ Med., Fam. Faire une piqûre à. ‖ Sports. Chasser, tirer (game) ; jeter, tendre (a fishing-net) ; chasser dans (a wood) ; marquer (a goal) ; caler (a marble). ‖ Cinem. Tourner (a film). ‖ Naut. To shoot the sun, prendre la hauteur du soleil. ‖ Fam. To shoot a line, galéjer ; to shoot the moon, déménager à la cloche de bois ; I'll be shot if, je veux bien être pendu si, le diable m'emporte si. ‖ U. S. Fam. To shoot the breeze, tailler une bavette, faire un brin de causette ; U. S. To shoot the works, tenter le coup. ‖ Loc. To shoot away, emporter par une balle (or) un obus ; épuiser (munitions). ‖ To shoot down, Aviat., Sports. Abattre, descendre (enemy, game). ‖ To shoot forth, Bot. Pousser (buds). ‖ To shoot off, emporter par une balle (or) par un obus. ‖ To shoot out, sortir (one's horns) ; tirer, darder (one's tongue) ; Bot. Pousser (buds). ‖ To shoot up, cribler de projectiles, faire pleuvoir une grêle de balles sur.

shooter [-ə*] n. Chasseur, tireur s. ‖ Techn. Instrument de lancement m. ; arme (f.) de tir ; U. S. arme (f.) à feu ; six-shooter, revolver à six coups. ‖ Sports. Marqueur de but m. (in basket-ball) ; balle rasante f. (in cricket).

shooting [-iŋ] n. Décochement m. (of an arrow) ; action (f.) de tirer (a gun) ; action (f.) de fusiller. ‖ Blessure (or) mort (f.) par un coup de fusil ; Franchissement m. (of rapids). ‖ Sports. Chasse (f.) au fusil ; shooting season, saison de la chasse. ‖ Milit. Tir m. ; fusillade f. ‖ Bot. Pousse f. (of branches) ; bourgeonnement m. (of buds). ‖ Med. Elancement m. (of a pain). ‖ Cinem. Prise (f.) de vues, tournage m. (of a film) ; indoor, outdoor shooting, intérieurs, extérieurs. ‖ Astron. Shooting star, étoile filante. ‖ **Shooting-box,** n. Pavillon (or) rendez-vous (m.) de chasse. ‖ **Shooting-brake** (or) **-break,** n. Autom. Break m. ‖ **Shooting-gallery,** n. Stand de tir m. ‖ **Shooting-licence,** n. Permis (m.) de chasse. ‖ **Shooting-party,** n. Sports. Partie de chasse f. ‖ **Shooting-range,** n. Champ de tir m. ; Milit. Polygone (m.) d'artillerie ; Cinem. Distance (f.) de prise de vues. ‖ **Shooting-script,** n. Cinem. Découpage m. ‖ **Shooting-stick,** n. Canne-siège f.

shop [ʃɔp] n. Comm. Magasin m. ; boutique f. (in general) ; rayon m. (in a department store) ; débit m. (for tobacco, wine) ; to keep, to shut up shop, tenir, fermer boutique. ‖ U. S. Techn. Atelier m. (workshop). ‖ Fin. Introducteurs m. pl. ‖ Fam. Maison ; boîte f. ‖ Fam. Affaires f. pl. ; to talk shop, parler affaires (or) métier (or) boutique. ‖ **Shop-assistant,** n. Employé, vendeur, commis s. ‖ **Shop-boy,** n. Garçon (m.) de courses, petit commis m. ‖ **Shop-floor,** n. Atelier (m.) de fabrication (place) ; ouvriers s. pl. (workers). ‖ **Shop-girl,** n. Vendeuse, commise, demoiselle (f.) de magasin. ‖ **Shop-lifter,** n. Voleur (s.) à l'étalage. ‖ **Shop-soiled,** adj. Comm. Défraîchi. ‖ **Shop-steward,** n. Délégué d'atelier, représentant syndical m. ‖ **Shop-talk,** n. Jargon de métier m. ‖ **Shop-walker,** n. Inspecteur (m.) de magasin ; chef de rayon m. ‖ **Shop-window,** n. Vitrine, devanture f. ; étalage m. ‖ **Shop-worn,** adj. Défraîchi.
— v. intr. Faire des achats (or) des emplettes (or) des courses.
— v. tr. Pop. Coffrer, faire coffrer (s.o.).

shopkeeper [-ki:pə*] n. Comm. Commerçant, marchand m. ; boutiquier m. (pej.) ; détaillant, débitant m. (retailer).

shopman [-mən] (pl. **shopmen**) n. Comm. Vendeur m. (employee) ; petit commerçant, boutiquier m. (proprietor).

shopper [-ə*] n. Client, acheteur s.

shopping [-iŋ] n. Achats m. pl. ; emplettes f. pl. ; shopping bag, filet (or) sac à provisions ; shopping cart, chariot, caddie ; shopping centre, quartier commerçant ; to go shopping, courir les magasins, faire ses courses.

shore [ʃɔ:*] n. Geol. Rivage, littoral m. ; côte f. ; bord m. (of the sea) ; bord m. ; rive f. (of a river) ; plage f. (sandy beach). ‖ Naut. Terre f. ; in, off, on shore, près de la côte, au large, à terre. ‖ **Shore patrol,** n. U. S. Milit. Patrouille (f.) de garde-côte.
— v. tr. Débarquer (a cargo) ; échouer (a ship).

shore n. Techn. Etai, étançon m. ‖ Naut., Archit. Epontille f. ; accore m.
— v. tr. Techn. To shore up, étayer, étançonner. ‖ Naut. Accorer, épontiller.

shoreless [-lis] adj. Fig. Sans bords, sans bornes.

shorn [ʃɔ:n]. See shear.

short [ʃɔ:t] adj. Court (in general). ‖ Court, petit (distance) ; in a short time, bientôt, après un court laps de temps, dans peu de temps ; short waist, taille haute (of a dress) ; to grow short, se raccourcir (days). ‖ Court, direct ; short cut, raccourci, chemin de traverse ; to take a short cut, prendre au plus court. ‖ Court, bref (discourse) ; short story, nouvelle, conte. ‖ Petit, trapu (person) ; of short stature, de petite taille. ‖ Incomplet, insuffisant ; to be short of, manquer de, être à court de ; to give short weight, ne pas donner le poids. ‖ Brusque, vif, peu endurant (nature, temper) ; sec, raide, peu poli (person) ; to be short with, parler sèchement à, être cassant avec. ‖ Comm. A courte échéance (bill, payment) ; à court terme (loan) ; short bill, effet. ‖ Fin. A découvert (sale) ; short account, découvert, position à la baisse. ‖ Med. Short sight, wind, myopie, essoufflement ; short of breath, poussif. ‖ U. S. Cinem. Short subject, court métrage. ‖ Culin. Croustillant (bread) ; sablé (crust) ; brisé (pastry). ‖ U. S. Techn. Aigre, cassant (clay, iron). ‖ Naut. Court (waves). ‖ Gramm. Bref (sound) ; inaccentué (syllable). ‖ Agric. Déficitaire (crop). ‖ Fig. To take short views, avoir des vues courtes. ‖ Fam. Dick is short for Richard, Dick est le diminutif de Richard. ‖ Loc. To make short work of, expédier, se débarrasser rapidement de ; to make a long story short, pour abréger. ‖ **Short change,** n. Monnaie inexacte f. ; v. tr. Ne pas rendre assez de monnaie à ; truander, empiler (fam.). ‖ **Short-circuit,** n. Electr. Court-circuit m. ; v. tr. Court-circuiter. ‖ **Short-handed,** adj. A court de personnel (or) de main-d'œuvre. ‖ **Short list,** n. Liste (f.) de candidats retenus après présélection ; v. tr. Retenir la candidature de, présélectionner. ‖ **Short-lived,** adj. Bref, éphémère, de courte durée (emotion) ; qui meurt prématurément, qui vit peu de temps (person). ‖ **Short-range,** adj. A court terme (forecast) ; à courte portée (gun). ‖ **Short-sighted,** adj. Med. Myope, à la vue courte (or) basse ; Fig. A courte vue. ‖ **Short-sightedness,** n. Med. Myopie f. ; Fig. Imprévoyance f. ; manque (m.) de perspicacité. ‖ **Short-spoken,** adj. A la parole brève (or) tranchante. ‖ **Short-staffed,** adj. A court de personnel ; to be short-staffed, manquer de personnel. ‖ **Short-story writer,** n. Nouvelliste s. ‖ **Short-tempered,** adj. Vif, coléreux, emporté. ‖ **Short-wave,** adj. Radio. A ondes courtes. ‖ **Short-winded,** adj. Med. Poussif, facilement essoufflé, à l'haleine courte.
— adv. Court, de court, net, brusquement ; to cut s.o. short, couper la parole à qqn ; to stop short, s'arrêter net, demeurer court. ‖ En deçà ; to come (or) to fall short of, être (or) rester au-dessous de, n'être pas à la hauteur de, manquer à (one's duty), ne pas atteindre (one's mark), être loin de valoir (a model) ; to fall short, rester en deçà, être insuffisant ; to run short, être insuffisant, s'épuiser ; to be nothing short of robbery, être un vol ni plus ni moins, être bel et bien un vol. ‖ Short of, à l'exception de, à part, en laissant de côté ; short of stealing, he would do anything, il est capable de tout, sauf de voler. ‖ Fin. A courte échéance (borrowing) ; à découvert (selling).
— n. Abréviation f. ; diminutif m. (of a name) ; surnom m. (nickname) ; for short, par abréviation. ‖ Résumé, abrégé m. ; in short, bref, en un mot,

en deux mots. ‖ Pl. Short *m.* (outer garment); slip *m.* (underwear). ‖ GRAMM. Brève *f.* ‖ COMM. Déficit *m.* ‖ FIN. Vente (*f.*) à découvert; baissier *m.* (person). ‖ U. S. CINEM. Court métrage *m.* ‖ FAM. ELECTR. Court-jus *m.*

shortage [-idʒ] n. Manque *m.; insuffisance f.;* quantité manquante *f.* ‖ Pénurie (*f.*) de personnel; rareté de la main-d'œuvre *f.* (labour shortage). ‖ Crise *f.* (of paper); disette *f.* (of provisions); *housing shortage,* crise du logement. ‖ COMM. Tare *f.* (of cash). ‖ FIN. *To make up the shortage,* combler le déficit.

shortbread [-bred], **shortcake** [-keik] n. CULIN. Sablé, gâteau sec *m.;* croquignole *f.*

shortcoming ['ʃɔ:t'kʌmiŋ] n. Manque, déficit *m.;* insuffisance *f.* ‖ Pl. FIG. Défauts, points faibles *m. pl.;* imperfections, faiblesses *f. pl.* (of a person).

shorten ['ʃɔ:tn̩] v. tr. Raccourcir, diminuer, rapetisser (a garment); abréger (a task, a text). ‖ Réduire (rations). ‖ NAUT. *To shorten sail,* diminuer de voile (or) de toile.
— v. intr. Se raccourcir, se rapetisser, diminuer.

shortening [-iŋ] n. Raccourcissement, rapetissement *m.* ‖ FIN. Amoindrissement *m.* (of credit). ‖ CULIN. Matière grasse *f.* (for pastry).

shortfall ['ʃɔ:t,fɔ:l] n. Déficit, manque *m.*

shorthand ['ʃɔ:thænd] n. Sténographie *f.; to write shorthand,* sténographier. ‖ **Shorthand-typist,** n. Sténo-dactylographe *s.* ‖ **Shorthand-writer,** n. Sténographe *s.*

shortie [-i] adj. See SHORTY.

shortish [-iʃ] adj. Assez (or) plutôt court. ‖ Trapu, courtaud (person).

shortly [-li] adv. Brièvement (briefly); sèchement (irritably); bientôt, prochainement, sous peu (soon).

shortness [-nis] n. Brièveté, courte durée *f.* (duration); manque (*m.*) de longueur, petitesse *f.* (length, size). ‖ Manque *m.* (of money); insuffisance *f.* (of provisions). ‖ Brusquerie, sécheresse *f.* (of manner). ‖ MED. *Shortness of breath,* manque de souffle (*m.*); *shortness of sight,* myopie.

shorty, shortie ['ʃɔ:ti] n. FAM. Demi-portion *f.,* avorton *m.* (person).
— adj. *Shorty nightdress,* chemise de nuit ultra-courte.

shot [ʃɔt]. See SHOOT.

shot n. Projectile *m.;* plomb *m.;* plombs *m. pl.;* boulet *m.* (of a cannon); balle *f.* (of a gun); *small shot,* petit plomb. ‖ Action (*f.*) de tirer (at a target); *at a shot,* d'un seul coup, du premier coup; *to have a flying shot at,* tirer au vol sur. ‖ Coup, coup de feu *m.;* décharge *f.* (detonation); *pistol shot,* coup de pistolet; *without firing a shot,* sans coup tirer. ‖ Tireur *s.* (person); *good shot,* bon fusil. ‖ CINEM. prise de vues *f.;* plan *m.; close, distance, long shot,* premier plan, lointain, plan général; *exterior shots,* extérieurs. ‖ SPORTS. Shoot *m.* (in basketball); *your shot,* à vous de jouer. ‖ MED. Piqûre *f.* ‖ Tentative *f.;* essai *m.; to have a shot at,* essayer. ‖ LOC. *To be off like a shot,* partir comme une flèche, filer comme un dard; *to do sth. like a shot,* faire qqch. sans une seconde d'hésitation. ‖ FAM. *Big shot,* huile, gros bonnet; *a long shot,* une chance sur mille. ‖ FAM. Goutte *f.* (of whisky). ‖ **Shot-gun,** n. Fusil (*m.*) de chasse; FAM. *shot-gun wedding,* mariage forcé. ‖ **Shot-proof,** adj. A l'épreuve des projectiles.
— N. B. Au sens de « munition », *shot* est invariable; dans les autres sens, il prend le pluriel.
— v. tr. (1). MILIT. Charger à plomb (a gun). ‖ TECHN. Grenailler (metal). ‖ SPORTS. Plomber (a fishing line).
— adj. COMM. Changeant (silk). ‖ FAM. Paf, parti, éméché. ‖ U. S. FAM. Réduit à zéro (chances).

should [ʃud]. See SHALL.

shoulder ['ʃouldə*] n. Epaule *f.; breadth of shoulders,* carrure; *round shoulders,* dos rond; *to sling sth. over one's shoulder,* porter qqch. en bandoulière; *to stand head and shoulders above s.o.,* dépasser qqn de la tête. ‖ Ressaut *m.* (of ground); épaulement *m.* (of a hill); contrefort *m.* (of a mountain). ‖ CULIN. Epaule *f.* ‖ ARCHIT. Epaulement *m.* ‖ TECHN. Embase *f.* (of a bolt); arrêtoir *m.* (of a tenon). ‖ NAUT. Epaulette *f.* ‖ CH. DE F. Contrefort *m.* ‖ AUTOM. Accotement *m.; hard shoulder,* accotement stabilisé, bande de dégagement d'urgence; *soft shoulder,* accotement non stabilisé. ‖ LOC. *Shoulder to shoulder,* coude à coude, côte à côte; *to put one's shoulder to the wheel,* pousser à la roue, en mettre un coup; *to give s.o. the cold shoulder,* battre froid à qqn; *to rub shoulders with,* fréquenter, côtoyer, frayer avec; *to tell s.o. sth. straight from the shoulder,* ne pas s'embarrasser pour dire ce qu'on pense à qqn. ‖ **Shoulder-bag,** n. Sac (*m.*) à bandoulière. ‖ **Shoulder-belt,** n. Baudrier *m.;* bandoulière *f.* ‖ **Shoulder-blade,** n. MED. Omoplate *f.* (of a person); ZOOL. Paleron *m.* (of an animal). ‖ **Shoulder-braid,** n. Fourragère *f.* ‖ **Shoulder-joint,** n. MED. Articulation de l'épaule *f.* ‖ **Shoulder-knot,** n. Aiguillette *f.* ‖ **Shoulder-pad,** n. Epaulette *f.* (inside garment). ‖ **Shoulder-piece,** n. MILIT. Crosse *f.* (of a light gun). ‖ **Shoulder-sash,** n. Bandoulière *f.* ‖ **Shoulder-strap,** n. Bandoulière *f.* (of a bag); brassière *f.* (of a knapsack); épaulette, bretelle, patte d'épaule *f.* (on underwear).
— v. tr. Pousser de l'épaule; *to shoulder one's way through a crowd,* se frayer un passage dans la foule à coups d'épaules. ‖ Prendre sur l'épaule, charger sur le dos (a burden). ‖ MILIT. *To shoulder arms,* se mettre au port d'armes. ‖ ARCHIT. Epauler (a beam). ‖ FIG. Endosser (a responsibility); charger de, assumer la charge de (a task).

shout [ʃaut] v. intr. Crier, pousser des cris; *to shout at s.o.,* s'adresser à qqn en criant; *to shout for joy,* crier de joie; *to shout for s.o.,* appeler qqn de toutes ses forces; *to shout like mad,* s'égosiller.
— v. tr. Crier (a name); vociférer, déblatérer (an insult); exprimer par des cris (or) par des clameurs (an opinion); *to shout down,* huer; *to shout oneself hoarse,* s'enrouer à force de crier.
— n. Cri *m.;* clameur *f.; shouts of applause,* acclamations. ‖ Eclat *m.* (of laughter).

shove [ʃʌv] v. tr. Pousser; bousculer (by pushing). ‖ FAM. Fourrer (sth. into a drawer); *to shove the responsibility on to,* coller la responsabilité à.
— v. intr. *To shove through,* se frayer un chemin à travers (a crowd); *to shove by* (or) *past s.o.,* passer près de qqn en le bousculant. ‖ NAUT. *To shove off,* pousser au large. ‖ FAM. *To shove along* (or) *off,* filer, se trotter, se sauver.
— n. FAM. Poussée *f.;* ramponneau *m.*

shovel ['ʃʌvl̩] n. Pelle *f.; coal, steam shovel,* pelle à charbon, à vapeur. ‖ **Shovel-hat,** n. ECCLES. Chapeau (*m.*) à larges bords.
— v. tr. Pelleter. ‖ FAM. Bâfrer (one's food).

shovelful [-ful] n. Pelletée *f.*

shoveller [-ə*] n. Pelleteur *s.* ‖ ZOOL. Souchet *m.*

show [ʃou] v. tr. (129). Montrer, faire voir, offrir à la vue, exposer, exhiber; *to show one's face,* se montrer; montrer son nez (fam.). ‖ Marquer (one's age, the hour, time); indiquer (a place, the way); tracer (a road). ‖ Révéler, laisser voir; accuser (an improvement). ‖ Témoigner de (appreciation, gratitude); montrer (capacities); faire preuve de (courage, intelligence); déployer (daring); manifester, marquer, révéler (emotion); *to show fight,* faire mine de résister; *to show reason,* exposer ses raisons; *to show oneself in one's true colours,* se montrer sous son vrai jour. ‖ Expliquer, enseigner; montrer à (s.o.); *to show s.o. how to read,* apprendre à lire à qqn. ‖ Exposer (an animal). ‖ COMM. Présenter (a brand of goods); étaler, mettre

en vitrine (in a display window); *what can I show you, ladies?*, que désirent ces dames? ‖ FIN. Se solder par (a loss); faire ressortir (profit). ‖ CINEM. Projeter (on the screen); présenter (to the public). ‖ SPORTS. *To show one's hand*, montrer son jeu, étaler ses cartes. ‖ NAUT. *To show a light*, porter un feu. ‖ ARTS. Représenter, figurer (an object). ‖ MATH. Démontrer. ‖ JUR. Faire apparoir (one's right). ‖ **To show down,** reconduire en bas. ‖ **To show in,** faire entrer (a visitor). ‖ **To show off,** faire montre (or) parade de, étaler. ‖ **To show out,** reconduire (a visitor). ‖ **To show up,** faire monter (a guest); mettre en vue (a thing); démasquer, dénoncer, dévoiler (treachery).
— v. intr. Se montrer, se voir, être visible, paraître, se laisser voir (to be visible). ‖ Passer, dépasser (petticoat, slip). ‖ Faire voir, révéler, prouver (to prove). ‖ CINEM. Passer (film). ‖ **To show off,** aimer à paraître, parader, se pavaner; faire du fla-fla (or) de l'épate (fam.). ‖ **To show through,** transparaître. ‖ **To show up,** se dessiner, ressortir (against a background); se silhouetter (on the horizon); faire son apparition, se présenter, faire acte de présence, s'amener (fam.) [to be present].
— n. Apparence *f.;* semblant, simulacre *m.; to make a show of,* faire semblant (or) mine de; *to put up a show of resistance,* manifester quelques velléités de résistance. ‖ Exposition *f.;* étalage *m.;* concours *m.; agricultural show,* comice agricole; *dog, flower show,* exposition canine, d'horticulture; *horse show,* concours hippique; *motor show,* salon de l'auto. ‖ Parade, ostentation *f.;* étalage, apparat *m.* (display); *to be fond of show,* aimer la parade; *to make a show of,* faire parade de, afficher (knowledge, wealth). ‖ Levée *f.* (of hands); *by show of hands,* à main levée (vote). ‖ THEATR. Spectacle *m.;* film *m.* (cinema); pièce *f.* (play); attractions *f. pl.* (variety, vaudeville); *dumb show,* pantomime. ‖ COMM. *On show,* exposé. ‖ FAM. Affaire *f.; to boss* (or) *to run the show,* faire marcher (or) être à la tête de l'affaire. ‖ FAM. Rendement *m.; bad show,* mauvais travail; *good show!,* bravo!, parfait! ‖ **Show-bill,** n. THEATR. Affiche *f.* ‖ **Show-boat,** n. U. S. THEATR. Bateau-théâtre *m.* ‖ **Show-business,** n. Art (*m.*) de montrer des spectacles. ‖ **Show-card,** n. COMM. Pancarte *f.;* affiche, étiquette *f.* (in a shop-window); carte (*f.*) d'échantillons (sample). ‖ **Show-case,** n. Etalage *m.* (in a museum); vitrine *f.* (in a shop). ‖ **Show-down,** n. Cartes (*f. pl.*) sur table (at cards); FAM. Déballage *m.* (of intentions); moment critique, tournant décisif *m.* ‖ **Show-flat,** n. Appartement modèle *m.* ‖ **Show-girl,** n. THEATR. Figurante, girl *f.* ‖ **Show-off,** n. FAM. M'as-tu-vu, poseur *s.* ‖ **Show-piece,** n. Clou, joyau *m.* (of a collection); modèle, modèle du genre *m.* (of its kind). ‖ **Show-place,** n. Lieu (*m.*) d'intérêt touristique. ‖ **Show-room,** n. COMM. Salon (*m.*) de démonstration (or) d'exposition. ‖ **Show-window,** n. U. S. COMM. Etalage *m.,* vitrine *f.*

shower [´ʃauə*] n. Averse *f.* (rain); chute *f.* (of hail); *April shower,* giboulée de mars; *heavy shower,* ondée. ‖ Douche *f.; hot and cold shower,* douche écossaise. ‖ Gerbe *f.* (of sparks). ‖ FIG. Volée, grêle *f.* (of blows); avalanche *f.* (of insults); averse, pluie *f.* (of letters); volée *f.* (of stones). ‖ U.S. Réception (*f.*) où chacun apporte un cadeau. ‖ FAM., MILIT. Bande (*f.*) de crétins. ‖ **Shower-bath,** n. Bain-douche *m.,* douche *f.* ‖ **Shower-proof,** adj. Imperméable.
— v. intr. Pleuvoir; tomber à verse (or) par ondées (or) comme la grêle.
— v. tr. Verser, déverser; faire tomber par ondées. ‖ FIG. Combler (*with,* de) [attention]; *to shower with blows,* faire pleuvoir une grêle de coups sur.

shower [´ʃouə*] n. Exposeur *s.* ‖ COMM. Exposant *s.* (exhibitor); démonstrateur *m.;* démonstratrice *f.* (seller).

showery [´ʃauəri] adj. Pluvieux.

showily [´ʃouili] adv. Avec ostentation (displayed); d'une manière voyante (dressed); avec un luxe criard (furnished).

showiness [-inis] n. Prétention, ostentation *f.;* clinquant *m.:* caractère voyant *m.* (of colours); luxe criard *m.* (of furnishings).

showing [-iŋ] n. Présentation *f.* (display). ‖ Prestation, performance *f.* (performance). ‖ Déclaration *f.,* témoignage *m.; on your own showing,* d'après vos dires. ‖ CINEM. Projection, présentation *f.*

showman [-mən] (pl. **showmen**) n. THEATR. Organisateur (*m.*) de spectacles; directeur (*m.*) de cirque: montreur (*m.*) de curiosités.

shown [-n] p. p. See SHOW.

showy [-i] adj. Prétentieux, voyant, criard, tapageur; tape-à-l'œil (fam.). ‖ Fastueux, plein d'ostentation (ceremony).

shrank [ʃræŋk] pret. See SHRINK.

shrapnel [´ʃræpnl] n. MILIT. Shrapnel *m.* ‖ FAM. Eclat d'obus *m.*

shred [ʃred] n. Petit morceau, lambeau, fragment *m.;* torn to shreds, en lambeaux, déchiqueté. ‖ FIG. Parcelle, ombre *f.;* grain, brin *m.; to tear to shreds,* démolir entièrement, ne rien laisser subsister de (an argument).
— v. tr. (130). Déchiqueter, mettre en lambeaux. ‖ Tailler (cloth). ‖ CULIN. Déchiqueter (meat); couper finement en long (vegetables). ‖ TECHN. Délisser, effilocher (paper, rags).

shrew [ʃruː] n. Mégère, harpie *f.* ‖ **Shrew-mouse,** n. ZOOL. Musaraigne *f.*

shrewd [ʃruːd] adj. † Dur, douloureux (blow); sévère, âpre (cold). ‖ Sagace, perspicace, malin, pénétrant (person); judicieux (reasoning); fin, subtil (wit) [see ACUTE, CUTE]; *to make a shrewd guess,* avoir de fortes raisons pour deviner.

shrewdly [-li] adv. Finement, avec perspicacité.

shrewdness [-nis] n. Sagacité, perspicacité, pénétration, finesse *f.*

shrewish [-iʃ] adj. Acariâtre, querelleur.

shrewishly [-iʃli] adv. D'une manière acariâtre.

shrewishness [-iʃnis] n. Humeur acariâtre *f.*

shriek [ʃriːk] v. intr. Crier, pousser un cri perçant (or) déchirant; *to shriek with laughter,* rire haut.
— v. tr. Crier; *to shriek out a cry for help,* appeler au secours à tue-tête.
— n. Cri perçant (or) déchirant *m.*

shrift [ʃrift] n. † Confession et absolution *f.* ‖ LOC. *Short shrift,* jugement (or) châtiment expéditif.

shrike [ʃraik] n. ZOOL. Pie-grièche *f.*

shrill [ʃril] adj. Aigu (cry); aigre, criard, strident (sound); perçant, pointu (voice).
— v. intr. Rendre (or) avoir un son aigu.
— v. tr. **To shrill forth,** donner cours en cris aigus à (one's grief). ‖ **To shrill out,** lancer d'une voix criarde (insults); chanter d'une voix perçante (or) aiguë (a song).

shrillness [-nis] n. Acuité, stridence *f.*

shrilly [-li] adv. Sur un ton aigu; avec un son strident.

shrimp [ʃrimp] n. ZOOL. Crevette grise *f.;* salicoque *f.* ‖ FAM. Gringalet, aztèque, avorton, riquiqui, moucheron *m.*
— v. intr. Pêcher la crevette.

shrimper [-ə*] n. Pêcheur (*m.*) de crevettes.

shrine [ʃrain] n. ECCLES. Châsse *f.* (casket); chapelle *f.* (chapel); lieu saint (place); tombeau, mausolée *m.* (tomb). ‖ U. S. Sanctuaire, basilique *f.* (of the Immaculate Conception). ‖ FIG. Sanctuaire *m.* (of art); haut lieu *m.*

shrink [ʃriŋk] v. intr. (131). Rétrécir, se rétrécir, rapetisser, resserrer. ‖ Rentrer (cloth). ‖ TECHN. Se contracter (metal); travailler (wood). ‖ MED. Rapetisser, se tasser (person). ‖ FIN. Amoindrir, diminuer (income). ‖ FIG. **To shrink away** (or) **back,** reculer, se dérober; *to shrink from doing,*

répugner à faire. ‖ FIG. *To shrink into oneself,* rentrer dans sa coquille, se replier sur soi-même. — v. tr. Rétrécir, faire rétrécir (cloth) ; contracter (metal).
— n. Rétrécissement *m.* (of material). ‖ U. S. FAM. Psy, psychanalyste *s.* ‖ **Shrink-proof** (or) **-resistant,** adj. Irrétrécissable.

shrinkable [-əbl] adj. Rétrécissable.

shrinkage [-idʒ] n. Rétrécissement, raccourcissement *m.* ‖ Rentrée *f.* (of cloth) ; contraction *f.* (of metal, wood) ; retrait *m.* (of metal).

shrinking [-iŋ] adj. Qui diminue (or) se rétrécit. ‖ FIG. Timide, craintif ; *shrinking violet,* grand timide.

shrinkingly [-iŋli] adv. Timidement, craintivement ; avec répugnance.

shrive [ʃraiv] v. tr. (132). ECCLES. † Confesser, absoudre ; *to shrive oneself,* se confesser.

shrivel ['ʃrivl] v. intr. Se ratatiner, se rider, se plisser, se dessécher ; se parcheminer, se racornir, se recroqueviller. (See WIZEN.)
— v. tr. Rider, ratatiner, dessécher, recroqueviller (an apple, the skin) ; racornir (leather) ; brûler (a plant).

shroud [ʃraud] n. Linceul, suaire *m.* ‖ TECHN. Bouclier *m.* ‖ NAUT. Haubans *m. pl.* ‖ FIG. Voiles *m. pl.* (of the night).
— v. tr. Ensevelir, envelopper d'un linceul. ‖ FIG. Cacher, voiler, abriter.

Shrove [ʃrouv] adj. *Shrove Tuesday,* Mardi gras.

shrovetide [-taid] n. Jours gras *m. pl.*

shrub [ʃrʌb] n. BOT. Arbrisseau, arbuste *m.*

shrub n. CULIN. Grog (*m.*) aux fruits.

shrubbery [-əri] n. BOT. Bosquet *m.*

shrubby [-i] adj. BOT. Couvert d'arbustes. ‖ Ressemblant à un arbuste ; *shrubby tree,* arbrisseau.

shrug [ʃrʌg] v. tr. Hausser (one's shoulders).
— n. Haussement (*m.*) d'épaules.

shrunk [ʃrʌŋk] p. p. See SHRINK.

shrunken ['ʃrʌŋkn̩] adj. Rétréci, raccourci. ‖ Rentré (cloth) ; réduit (head) ; contracté (metal) ; ratatiné, racorni (skin).

shuck [ʃʌk] n. U. S. BOT. Bogue *f.* (of a chestnut) ; spathe *f.* (of corn) ; cosse, gousse *f.* (of peas) ; brou *m.;* écale *f.* (of walnuts). ‖ Pl. U. S. FAM. *Not worth shucks,* qui ne vaut pas un radis.
— v. tr. U. S. Eplucher (corn) ; écosser (peas) ; décortiquer (nuts) ; écailler (oysters). ‖ U. S. FAM. *To shuck off,* mettre au rancart.
— interj. Pl. U. S. Des prunes !, zut !

shudder ['ʃʌdə*] v. intr. Frissonner (with cold) ; frémir, trembler (with horror) [with, de]. (See SHAKE.)
— n. Frisson, frémissement *m.*

shuddering [-riŋ] adj. Frissonnant, frémissant.
— n. Frisson, frémissement *m.*

shuffle ['ʃʌfl] v. tr. Faire glisser (or) passer (from one position to another). ‖ Mêler, brouiller, jeter pêle-mêle (or) en désordre (files, papers). ‖ Traîner (the feet). ‖ Battre (a pack of cards). ‖ **To shuffle off,** se dérober à (one's responsibilities) ; *to shuffle off this mortal coil,* dépouiller cette enveloppe mortelle, quitter cette triste vie.
— v. intr. Changer de place (or) de position. ‖ Traîner les pieds (or) les jambes, marcher d'un pas traînant. ‖ Battre les cartes. ‖ FIG. Changer d'attitude, équivoquer, tergiverser.
— n. Déplacement, changement (*m.*) de place. ‖ Mouvement (or) pas traînant *m.;* démarche traînante *f.* ‖ Désordre *m.;* confusion *f.* ‖ Battement, mélange *m.* (of playing cards). ‖ Frottement (*m.*) des pieds (in dancing). ‖ FIG. Tergiversation *f.;* faux-fuyant *m.*

shuffling [-iŋ] adj. Traînant (gait) ; qui traîne les pieds (person). ‖ FIG. Evasif, équivoque (statement).
— n. Marche traînante *f.* ‖ Entremêlement, embrouillement *m.,* confusion *f.*

shufflingly [-iŋli] adv. En traînant les pieds, d'un pas traînant. ‖ FIG. D'une manière équivoque, en biaisant ; de façon évasive.

shun [ʃʌn] v. tr. (1). Eviter, fuir, esquiver. ‖ S'éloigner de, éviter (society).

shunt [ʃʌnt] v. tr. CH. DE F. Garer, manœuvrer, aiguiller (a train). ‖ ELECTR. Dériver, shunter (a circuit) ; bifurquer (a current). ‖ FIG. Détourner (a discussion) ; différer, ajourner, remettre (a plan).
— v. intr. CH. DE F. Se garer (train).
— n. CH. DE F. Manœuvre *f.* ‖ ELECTR. Dérivation *f.;* shunt *m.; shunt circuit,* circuit dérivé.

shunter [-ə*] n. CH. DE F. Gareur (*m.*) de trains. ‖ ELECTR. Dérivateur *m.*

shush [ʃuʃ] v. tr. Faire taire (s.o.).
— interj. Chut !

shut [ʃʌt] v. tr. (133). Fermer ; clore (see CLOSE) ; *to shut the door in s.o.'s face,* fermer la porte au nez de qqn ; *to shut s.o.'s mouth,* clore le bec à qqn. ‖ FIG. *To shut one's ears to the truth,* refuser d'entendre la vérité. ‖ **To shut down,** rabattre (a cover) ; fermer (a factory, a window). ‖ **To shut in,** enfermer ; entourer, encercler (a place) ; *to shut oneself in,* s'enfermer ; *to shut one's finger in the door,* se pincer (or) se prendre le doigt dans la porte. ‖ **To shut off,** couper (the engine) ; isoler (s.o.) ; couper, fermer (water) ; *to shut oneself off,* se séparer, s'isoler. ‖ **To shut out,** exclure (the air, s.o.) ; empêcher de voir (the light, a view) ; empêcher, mettre obstacle à, rendre impossible (a plan) ; mettre dehors (or) à la porte (s.o.). ‖ **To shut to,** bien fermer, pousser à fond (a door, a lock). ‖ **To shut up,** enfermer (s.o., sth.) ; *to shut oneself up,* s'enfermer, se confiner, se calfeutrer, se claquemurer ; *to shut up shop,* fermer boutique (fam.) ; FAM. *To shut s.o. up,* faire taire qqn ; couper le sifflet à qqn (fam.).
— v. intr. Se fermer, fermer. ‖ **To shut down,** se fermer, s'arrêter (factory). ‖ **To shut to,** fermer (or) se fermer bien. ‖ **To shut up,** FAM. la boucler, fermer son bec ; *shut up !,* la ferme ! ‖ **Shut-in,** n. U. S. Reclus *s.; the shut-ins,* les confinés.

shutter [-ə*] n. Volet *m.;* contrevent *m.* (outside) ; persienne *f.* (slatted, Venetian). ‖ Obturateur *m.* (of a camera). ‖ AUTOM. Volet *m.* ‖ TECHN. Vanne *f.*

shuttle ['ʃʌtl] n. Navette *f.* ‖ **Shuttle-service,** n. AUTOM., CH. DE F. Navette *f.* ‖ **Shuttle-winder,** n. TECHN. Dévidoir (*m.*) de machine à coudre.
— v. intr. Faire la navette.
— v. tr. Transporter en navette (passengers). ‖ FIG. Expédier, envoyer ; *shuttled from one office to another,* expédié d'un bureau à un autre.

shuttlecock [-kɔk] n. SPORTS. Volant *m.* (See BATTLEDORE.)

shy [ʃai] adj. Timide, réservé. (See BASHFUL.) ‖ *To be shy of,* se défier (or) méfier de ; ne tenir guère à ; *to fight shy of,* éviter. ‖ Craintif, farouche, peureux (animal) ; ombrageux (horse). ‖ NAUT. Pointu (wind). ‖ FIG. Fugitif, difficile à saisir. ‖ U. S. FAM. *To be shy of money,* être à court d'argent.
— v. intr. ZOOL. Faire un écart (horse). ‖ FAM. *To shy at,* avoir peur de, s'effaroucher de.
— n. Ecart *m.* (of a horse).

shy [ʃai] v. tr. (2). Lancer, jeter (a stone).
— v. intr. Lancer une pierre (at, à, sur).
— n. Jet, lancement *m.* (of a stone). ‖ FIG. Essai, tentative *f.*

Shylock ['ʃailɔk] n. Shylock *m.* ‖ FIG. Vautour *m.*

shyly ['ʃaili] adv. Timidement, craintivement, modestement.

shyness [-nis] n. Timidité, modestie, réserve *f.* ‖ ZOOL. Caractère ombrageux *m.* (of a horse).

shyster ['ʃaistə*] n. Canaille *f.;* homme (*m.*) d'affaires véreux ; *shyster lawyer,* avocat de bas étage.

si [siː] n. MUS. Si *m.*

Siam ['sai'æm] n. GEOGR. Siam m. (See THAILAND.)
Siamese ['saiə'mi:z] adj., n. GEOGR. Siamois s. ‖ MED. *Siamese twins*, frères siamois, sœurs siamoises.
Siberia [sai'biəriə] n. GEOGR. Sibérie f.
Siberian [-ən] adj., n. GEOGR. Sibérien s.
sibilant ['sibilənt] adj. GRAMM. Sifflant.
— n. GRAMM. Sifflante f.
sibilate [-eit] v. intr., tr. Prononcer en sifflant.
sibilation [sibi'leiʃən] n. Sibilation f.
siblings ['sibliŋs] n. pl. Enfants (m. pl.) de mêmes parents.
sibyl ['sibl] n. Sibylle f.
sibylline ['sibilain] adj. Sibyllin.
sic [sik] adv. Sic.
siccative ['sikətiv] n. adj. Siccatif m.
sice [sais] n. Six m. (in dice).
Sicilian [si'siljən] adj., n. GEOGR. Sicilien s.
Sicily ['sisili] n. GEOGR. Sicile f.
sick [sik] v. tr. FAM. Lancer (*on*, après) [a dog].
sick adj. MED. Malade (see ILL); *sick person*, malade; *sick with the flu*, malade (or) atteint de la grippe; *to fall sick*, tomber malade. ‖ MED. Nauséeux; *sick headache*, migraine; *to be sick*, vomir, rendre; *to feel sick*, avoir mal au cœur (or) des nausées, U. S. être malade. ‖ FIG. Nostalgique; *to be sick for*, languir de, soupirer après, avoir la nostalgie de. ‖ FAM. Ecœuré, dégoûté; *to be sick of*, en avoir assez de, être saturé de; en avoir plein le dos de (fam.). ‖ **Sick-bay**, n. NAUT. Hôpital de bord m.; infirmerie f. ‖ **Sick-bed**, n. Lit (m.) de douleur. ‖ **Sick-benefit**, n. Indemnité journalière f. ‖ **Sick-berth**, n. NAUT. Poste (m.) des blessés (or) des malades. ‖ **Sick-leave**, n. Congé (m.) de maladie. ‖ **Sick-list**, n. Liste (f.) des malades; *on the sick-list*, porté malade. ‖ **Sick-pay**, n. Indemnité patronale f. ‖ **Sick-room**, n. Chambre (f.) de malade. ‖ **Sick-ward**, n. Salle (f.) des malades.
— n. pl. *The sick*, les malades s. pl.
— v. tr. FAM. *To sick up*, vomir, rendre.
sicken [-ən] v. intr. MED. Tomber malade; dépérir, s'affaiblir; languir (*with*, de); avoir le cœur soulevé, être écœuré (*at*, par); se lasser, se dégoûter (*of*, de). ‖ AGRIC. S'étioler, dépérir (plant). ‖ FIG. Etre dégoûté (*at*, de).
— v. tr. Rendre malade, donner mal au cœur à. ‖ FIG. Ecœurer, dégoûter.
sickening [-əniŋ] adj. MED. Ecœurant. ‖ FIG. Ecœurant, dégoûtant.
sickish [-iʃ] adj. MED. Indisposé; nauséeux. ‖ FIG. Légèrement écœurant (scent, taste).
sickle ['sikl] n. AGRIC. Faucille f. ‖ ASTRON. Lion m.
sickliness ['siklinis] n. MED. Etat maladif m.; mauvaise santé, santé fragile f.; pâleur f. (of a complexion); langueur f. (of a gaze). ‖ AGRIC. Etiolement m. (of a plant). ‖ FIG. Sentimentalité outrée f. (of literature); caractère écœurant m. (of a scent); fadeur f. (of sentiments).
sickly [-li] adj. MED. Pâle, terreux (complexion); languissant (gaze); maladif, souffreteux (person). ‖ MED. Malsain, insalubre (climate). ‖ AGRIC. Etiolé, débile (plant). ‖ FIG. Pâle, faible (colour, light, smile); écœurant (scent); blafard (sunshine); fade (taste). ‖ FIG. Maladif, morbide (sensitivity); exagéré (sentimentality). ‖ **Sickly-sweet**, adj. Douceâtre.
sickness [-nis] n. MED. Maladie f. (in general); mal m. (air, sea). ‖ MED. Nausées f. pl.; mal au cœur m. ‖ **Sickness benefit**, n. Indemnité journalière f.
side [said] n. Côté m.; *left, right side*, côté gauche, droit; *right, wrong side*, endroit, envers (of cloth); *to hold (or) split one's sides with laughter*, se tenir les côtes de rire. ‖ Pente f., versant, penchant m. (of a hill); bord m. (of a road). ‖ Parti, côté, bord m. (in an argument); *to take sides*, se ranger d'un côté, sortir de la neutralité. ‖ Ligne (f.) de descendance généalogique, côté m. (of a family); *on the distaff side*, du côté maternel. ‖ ZOOL. Flanc m. (of an animal). ‖ CULIN. Flèche f. (of bacon). ‖ COMM. *Credit, debit side*, côté avoir, doit. ‖ JUR. *The other side*, la partie adverse. ‖ SPORTS. Effet m. (in billiards); équipe f. (team). ‖ FIG. Morgue, hauteur, suffisance f.; *to put on side*, poser, faire des manières. ‖ LOC. *From all sides*, de tous les côtés, de toutes parts; *from side to side*, d'un côté à l'autre, de-ci de-là; *on all sides*, de tous côtés, de côté et d'autre; partout; *on both sides*, des deux côtés; *side by side*, côte à côte; *the other side of the picture*, l'envers de la médaille. ‖ FAM. *To be on the wrong side of sixty*, avoir doublé le cap de la soixantaine. ‖ FAM. *On the side*, par-dessus le marché; *profits on the side*, gratte. ‖ **Side-altar**, n. ECCLES. Autel latéral m. ‖ **Side-arm**, n. MILIT. Baïonnette, épée f. ‖ **Side-burns**, n. pl. U. S. Favoris m. pl.; côtelettes f. pl. ‖ **Side-car**, n. AUTOM. Side-car m. ‖ **Side-conflict**, n. Conflit secondaire m. ‖ **Side-dish**, n. CULIN. Plat d'accompagnement m. ‖ **Side-door**, n. Porte (f.) latérale (or) de service, petite porte. ‖ **Side-drum**, n. MUS. Tambour m. ‖ **Side-entrance** (or) **-entry**, n. Entrée latérale f. ‖ **Side-face**, n. Profil m.; adj., adv. De profil. ‖ **Side-glance**, n. Coup d'œil oblique, regard de côté m. ‖ **Side-issue**, n. Question (f.) d'intérêt secondaire. ‖ **Side-kick**, n. U. S. POP. Copain m. ‖ **Side-light**, n. ELECTR. Eclairage de côté m.; NAUT. Feux (m. pl.) de côté; FIG. Aperçu indirect, éclaircissement m. ‖ **Side-line**, n. CH. DE F. Voie secondaire f.; FIG. Occupation (f.) [or] talent (m.) secondaire; seconde spécialité f.; violon d'Ingres m. (See HOBBY.) ‖ **Side-note**, n. Note marginale f. ‖ **Side-pocket**, n. Poche (f.) de côté. ‖ **Side-rail**, n. Garde-fou m.; CH. DE F. Contre-rail m.; main courante f. (on a locomotive); NAUT. Rambarde f. ‖ **Side-road**, n. Chemin (m.) de traverse. ‖ **Side-saddle**, n. Selle (f.) de femme; *to ride side-saddle*, monter en amazone. ‖ **Side-seat**, n. Siège (m.) de côté. ‖ **Side-show**, n. THEATR. Attraction secondaire f.; spectacle forain m. (at a circus); FAM. Evénement secondaire m. ‖ **Side-slip**, n. AUTOM. Dérapage m.; AVIAT. Glissade (f.) sur l'aile; BOT. Pousse (f.) d'arbre; v. intr. AUTOM. Déraper; AVIAT. Glisser sur l'aile; FIG. Donner un coup de barre. ‖ **Side-splitting**, adj. FAM. Convulsif, homérique (laugh); crevant, marrant, désopilant (spectacle). ‖ **Side-step**, n. Ecart m.; AUTOM. Marchepied m.; MILIT., SPORTS. Pas de côté m.; v. intr. Faire un pas de côté; SPORTS. Esquiver; v. tr. FIG. Eviter (an issue, a problem). ‖ **Side-stroke**, n. Coup de côté m.; SPORTS. Nage (f.) sur le côté. ‖ **Side-track**, n. CH. DE F. Voie (f.) de garage; FIG. Question (f.) d'intérêt secondaire; *to get on a side-track*, s'écarter du sujet; v. tr. CH. DE F. Aiguiller sur une voie de garage; FIG. Ecarter, remettre à plus tard (an issue); FAM. Donner le change à; semer (s.o.). ‖ **Side-view**, n. Vue (f.) de profil (or) de côté. ‖ **Side-walk**, n. Contre-allée f.; U. S. Trottoir m. (pavement). ‖ **Side-wall**, n. Paroi latérale f. (of a shaft); AUTOM. Flanc m. (of a tyre). ‖ **Side-wheeler**, n. NAUT. Bateau (m.) à aubes (paddle-boat). ‖ **Side-whiskers**, n. pl. Favoris m. pl. ‖ **Side-wind**, n. Vent de côté m.; FIG. Source (or) influence indirecte f.
— v. intr. *To side with*, se ranger du côté de, prendre parti pour, faire cause commune avec.
sideboard [-bɔ:d] n. Buffet m.; desserte, crédence f. ‖ FAM. Pl. Favoris m. pl.
sidelong [-lɔŋ] adj. De côté, oblique; du coin de l'œil (glance).
— adv. Obliquement, de côté.
sidereal [sai'diəriəl] adj. ASTRON. Sidéral.
siderurgy [sidə'rə:dʒi] n. Sidérurgie f.
sidesman ['saidzmən] (pl. **sidesmen**) n. ECCLES. Marguillier adjoint, quêteur m.
sideward [-wəd] adj. De côté, latéral.
sidewards [-wədz] adv. De côté, latéralement.

sideways [-weiz], **sidewise** [-waiz] adv. De côté, latéralement. ‖ En crabe (walking).
— adj. Latéral, de côté.

siding [-iŋ] n. CH. DE F. Voie (f.) de garage; embranchement m.

sidle ['saidl] v. intr. Avancer de biais, marcher de côté.

siege [si:dʒ] n. MILIT., FIG. Siège m.; to lay siege to, assiéger, mettre le siège devant; to raise the siege, lever le siège. ‖ **Siege-gun**, n. MILIT. Pièce (f.) de siège. ‖ **Siege-works**, n. pl. Travaux (m. pl.) de siège.

Sienna [si'enə] n. GEOGR. Sienne f. ‖ ARTS. Terre de Sienne f.

sierra [si'erə] n. Sierra f.

Sierra Leone [si'eərə li'ouni] n. GEOGR. Sierra Leone f.

siesta [si'estə] n. Sieste f.

sieve [siv] n. Crible m. (coarse); tamis m. (fine); sas m. (industrial); to pass through a sieve, tamiser. ‖ AGRIC. Van m. ‖ FAM. Bavard s.; écumoire f.
— v. tr. Passer au crible (or) au tamis, tamiser.

sift [sift] v. tr. Passer au crible (or) au tamis, tamiser; cribler (gravel, sand). ‖ AGRIC. Vanner (grain). ‖ CULIN. Sasser, passer (flour). ‖ FIG. Passer au crible (evidence); approfondir (an issue); to sift out, dégager (the truth).
— v. intr. Filtrer (dust); se tamiser (light).

sifter [-ə*] n. Tamiseur, cribleur s. (person). ‖ Cribleuse f. (machine); tamis, crible m. (sieve).

sigh [sai] n. Soupir m.; to breathe a sigh, laisser échapper un soupir.
— v. intr. Soupirer; pousser un soupir.
— v. tr. To sigh forth (or) out, exprimer en soupirant, exhaler dans un soupir.

sighingly [-iŋli] adv. En soupirant.

sight [sait] n. Vue f.; aperçu m., vision f. (perception); to catch (or) get sight of, apercevoir, découvrir, entrevoir; to come into, to go out of, sight, apparaître, disparaître; to know by sight, connaître de vue; to lose sight of, perdre de vue; out of sight, caché aux regards; at first sight, on sight, à première vue, au premier coup d'œil; to translate at sight, traduire à livre ouvert; love at first sight, coup de foudre; to be in sight of, pouvoir apercevoir; to be unable to bear the sight of s.o., ne pas pouvoir voir qqn en peinture (or) sentir qqn (fam.). ‖ Vue f., spectacle m.; the sights, les curiosités, les monuments publics; to make a sight of oneself, se rendre ridicule, se fagoter. ‖ Action (f.) de viser; to take sight, viser. ‖ MED. Vue f.; long, short sight, presbytie, myopie; to lose one's sight, perdre la vue, devenir aveugle; second sight, seconde vue. ‖ COMM. Vue f.; payable at sight, payable à vue; sight bill, effet à vue. ‖ MUS. To read at sight, déchiffrer, jouer à vue. ‖ NAUT. Pinnule f. (of an alidade); to heave into sight, paraître (ship); to be in sight of shore, pouvoir discerner la terre. ‖ PHYS. Lumière f. (of a sextant); mire f. (of an observatory); viseur m. (of a telescope). ‖ JUR. In the sight of the law, aux yeux de la loi. ‖ MILIT. Mire f. (of a gun); back, front sight, hausse, guidon; to take sight, viser. ‖ FIG. Jugement m.; vue f. (way of looking at); to find favour in s.o.'s sight, trouver grâce aux yeux de qqn. ‖ FAM. A sight better, beaucoup mieux; a sight for sore eyes, un spectacle délicieux. ‖ LOC. Out of sight, out of mind, loin des yeux, loin du cœur. ‖ **Sight-bar** (or) **-rule**, n. Alidade, aiguille (f.) de mire. ‖ **Sight-hole**, n. Regard m. (peep-hole); lumière f. (of a sextant). ‖ **Sight-line**, n. Ligne (f.) de mire. ‖ **Sight-reading**, n. Lecture à vue f.; MUS. Déchiffrement m.
— v. tr. Apercevoir, aviser. ‖ NAUT. To sight land, venir en vue de la terre. ‖ TECHN. Munir d'une mire (or) d'un viseur. ‖ COMM. Voir (a bill). ‖ ASTRON.

Viser, observer (a star). ‖ MILIT. Pointer (a rifle); mirer (a target).
— v. intr. Viser; sighting shot, coup de réglage.

sighted [-id] adj. Qui voit; the sighted, les voyants.

sightless [-lis] adj. MED. Aveugle. ‖ FIG. Invisible (poetically).

sightlessness [-lisnis] n. MED. Cécité f.

sightliness [-linis] n. Charme m.; beauté, grâce f.

sightly [-li] adj. Agréable à regarder, charmant, gracieux.

sightseeing [-si:iŋ] n. Visite (f.) des curiosités; tourisme urbain m.

sightseer [-si:ə*] n. Excursionniste, touriste, curieux s.

sigillate ['sidʒileit] adj. BOT. Sigillé.

sigma ['sigmə] n. Sigma m.

sigmoid ['sigmɔid] adj. MED. Sigmoïde.

sign [sain] n. Signe m.; symbole, indice m., marque f. ‖ Indication, preuve f.; signe m. (of anger, of rain); trace f. (record); to show signs of, révéler des traces de (past); manifester des signes de (future). ‖ Présage m.; signe m. (in heaven). ‖ Geste, signe m. (signal); to give (or) make a sign to s.o. to begin, faire signe à qqn de commencer; to talk by signs, parler par signes. ‖ COMM. Enseigne f.; neon sign, enseigne au néon. ‖ AUTOM. Road, traffic sign, poteau indicateur, de signalisation. ‖ MATH. Signe m. ‖ ECCLES. Signe m. (of the cross); to make the sign of the cross, se signer. ‖ ASTRON. Signe m. (of the zodiac). ‖ MUS. Symbole m. ‖ **Sign-language**, n. Langage (m.) par signes. **Sign-manual**, n. Signature f., seing m.
— v. tr. Signer (one's name, a statement); apposer sa signature à (a treaty); to sign oneself, signer. ‖ Faire signe; indiquer par signes; faire mine (by a play of the features). ‖ ECCLES. To sign oneself, se signer. ‖ COMM. Viser (an account); souscrire (a letter of credit). ‖ To sign away, JUR. Céder, signer l'abandon de (property). ‖ To sign on, embaucher (an employee).
— v. intr. Signer, donner sa signature. ‖ Faire signe de (by gestures). ‖ To sign off, RADIO. Terminer une émission. ‖ To sign on, s'embaucher. ‖ To sign up for, s'inscrire à (a class).

signal ['signl] n. Signal m.; to give, to make a signal, donner, faire un signal. ‖ Avertisseur m. (alarm). ‖ RADIO. Indicatif m. ‖ NAUT., MILIT. pl. Transmissions f.; Signal Corps, service des transmissions. ‖ CH. DE F. Block signal, disque de fermeture. ‖ **Signal-book**, n. Code (m.) de signaux. ‖ **Signal-box**, n. Poste (m.) à signaux. ‖ **Signal-lamp** (or) **-light**, n. Lampe (f.) de signal; NAUT. Fanal m.; TECHN. Lampe (f.) témoin. ‖ **Signal-man**, n. CH. DE F. Aiguilleur m.; NAUT. Signaleur m. ‖ **Signal-mast** (or) **-post**, n. Mât (or) poteau (m.) de signaux. ‖ **Signal-station**, n. Sémaphore m.; NAUT. Poste (m.) de timonerie.
— v. intr. Donner un signal, faire des signaux, signaler. ‖ Faire signe (to, à) [s.o.]. ‖ AUTOM. Mettre le bras (before stopping).
— v. tr. Signaler (a ship, train, turn). ‖ Faire signe à (s.o.)
— adj. Remarquable, insigne (achievement); éclatant (success).

signalize [-əlaiz] v. tr. Signaler, distinguer, marquer.

signaller [-ələ*] n. Signaleur s.

signalling [-əliŋ] n. Avertissement m., signalisation f.; transmission (f.) de signaux. ‖ AUTOM. Signalling device, signalisateur.

signally [-əli] adv. D'une façon insigne, remarquablement.

signatory [-ətəri] adj. et n. Signataire s.

signature ['signətˌrə*] n. Signature f.; visa m. (on administrative documents); stamped signature, griffe; to put one's signature on, apposer sa signature à. ‖ COMM. Marque f. ‖ JUR. Joint signature,

signature collective. ‖ Mus. *Key signature*, armature, armure. ‖ Radio. *Signature tune*, indicatif musical.

signboard ['sainbɔ:d] n. Tableau, panneau *m.* ‖ Comm. Enseigne *f.*

signer ['sainə*] n. Signataire *s.*

signet ['signət] n. Sceau, cachet *m.* ‖ **Signet-ring**, n. Chevalière *f.*

significance [sig'nifikəns] n. Signification *f.* (of a gesture); importance, portée, conséquence *f.* (of an incident). [See MEANING.]

significant [-ənt] adj. Significatif (glance); important, d'importance, de grande portée (incident).

significantly [-əntli] adv. D'une manière significative; d'un air entendu (smiling).

signification [signifi'kei∫ən] n. Signification *f.*; sens *m.*

significative [sig'nifikətiv] adj. Significatif (of, de).

signify ['signifai] v. tr. (2). Signifier, être le signe de, indiquer (to indicate). ‖ Vouloir dire, signifier, avoir le sens de. (See MEAN.) ‖ Signifier (one's consent); faire connaître (an opinion).
— v. intr. Importer; *it doesn't signify*, cela n'a aucune importance.

signpost ['sainpoust] n. Poteau indicateur; signal routier *m.*

silage ['sailidʒ] n. Agric. Ensilage, ensilotage *m.*
— v. tr. Ensiler, ensiloter.

silence ['sailəns] n. Silence *m.*; *to call for, to keep silence*, réclamer, garder le silence. ‖ Calme, silence *m.* (of the night). ‖ Loc. *Silence means assent*, qui ne dit mot consent.
— v. tr. Faire taire (dogs); imposer silence à, réduire au silence (persons); amortir, étouffer (a sound).

silencer [-ənsə*] n. Techn. Amortisseur *m.* ‖ Autom. Silencieux; pot d'échappement *m.*

silent [-ənt] adj. Silencieux, muet; *to become silent*, se taire; *to keep silent*, garder le silence. ‖ Taciturne, silencieux, peu communicatif; tranquille. ‖ Insonore, silencieux. ‖ U. S. Comm. *Silent partner*, commanditaire. ‖ Cinem., Gramm. Muet.

silently [-əntli] adv. Silencieusement, en silence, sans bruit.

Silenus ['sai'li:nəs] n. Silène *m.*

Silesia [sai'li:siə] n. Geogr. Silésie *f.* ‖ Comm. Silésienne *f.* (cloth).

silhouette [,silu:'et] n. Silhouette *f.* ‖ **Silhouette-target**, n. Cible-silhouette *f.*
— v. tr. Silhouette.
— v. intr. *To be silhouetted*, se silhouetter, se profiler, se dessiner.

silica ['silikə] n. Silice *f.*

silicate [-keit] n. Chim. Silicate *m.*

siliceous [si'li∫əs] adj. Chim. Siliceux.

silicic [-sik] adj. Chim. Silicique.

silicify [-sifai] v. tr. (2). Silicifier, pétrifier. ‖ Techn. Silicatiser.
— v. intr. Se silicifier, se pétrifier.

silicon ['silikən] n. Chim. Silicium *m.*

silicone [-koun] n. Chim. Silicone *m.*

silicosis [sili'kousis] n. Med. Chalicose, cailloute *f.*

siliquose ['silikwous], **siliquous** [-kwəs] adj. Bot. Siliqueux.

silk [silk] n. Soie *f.*; *silk culture*, sériciculture. ‖ ‖ **Silk-finish**, n. Similisage *m.* ‖ **Silk-hat**, n. Haut-de-forme *m.* ‖ **Silk-mill**, n. Filature (*f.*) de soie. ‖ **Silk-paper**, n. Papier (*m.*) de soie. ‖ **Silk-reel**, n. Dévidoir (*m.*) de cocons. ‖ **Silk-screen**, n. Arts. Sérigraphie *f.*; *silk-screen print*, sérigraphe. ‖ **Silk-worm**, n. Zool. Ver (*m.*) à soie.
— adj. De soie (cloth, garment); *silk fabrics*, soieries.

silken [-ən], **silky** [-i] adj. Soyeux. ‖ Fig. Doucereux, mielleux, onctueux.

silkiness [-inis] n. Nature soyeuse *f.*; ‖ Fig. Moelleux *m.*; onction *f.*

sill [sil] n. Seuil *m.* (of a door); rebord, appui *m.* (of a window). ‖ Archit. Sablière basse *f.* ‖ Techn. Seuil, heurtoir *m.* (of a hydraulic lock); sole *f.* (of a mining gallery). ‖ Geol. Filon-couche *m.*

sillabub ['siləbʌb] n. Culin. Sorte (*f.*) de sabayon.

silliness ['silinis] n. Sottise, bêtise, niaiserie *f.*

silly [-i] adj. Sot, niais, bête (act, person); stupide, saugrenu (remark); *silly girl* (or) *woman*, petite oie, bécasse, sotte; *silly thing*, bêtise, sottise, balourdise. ‖ Fam. *Silly ass!*, imbécile!; *to be knocked silly*, voir trente-six chandelles.
— n. Sot, niais, nigaud *m.*; bêta, serin *m.* (fam.).

silo ['sailou] n. Agric. Silo *m.*
— v. tr. Agric. Ensiler, ensiloter.

silt [silt] n. Vase *f.*; limon *m.*; boues *f. pl.*; *deposition of silt*, envasement.
— v. tr. *To silt up*, envaser, ensabler.
— v. intr. *To silt up*, s'envaser, s'ensabler.

silver ['silvə*] n. Argent *m.* (metal); *German* (or) *nickel silver*, maillechort. ‖ Argent *m.*; monnaie (*f.*) d'argent (coins). ‖ Argenterie *f.* (silver-ware).
— adj. En argent (coin); d'argent (paper). ‖ Argenté (hair); *silver gilt*, vermeil. ‖ Chim. *Silver solution*, solution argentique. ‖ Bot. Argenté (fir). ‖ Fig. Argentin (sound). ‖ Loc. *Born with a silver spoon in one's mouth*, né coiffé. ‖ **Silver-fish**, n. Zool. Argentine *f.* (fish); lépisme, poisson d'argent *m.* (insect). ‖ **Silver-foil**, n. Feuille (*f.*) d'argent. ‖ **Silver-fox**, n. Zool. Renard argenté *m.* ‖ **Silver-grey**, n. Gris argenté *m.* ‖ **Silver-lining**, n. Fig. Rayon d'espoir *m.* ‖ **Silver-plate**, n. Argenterie *f.* (in general); vaisselle (*f.*) d'argent (hollow-ware). ‖ **Silver-plated**, adj. Argenté, plaqué d'argent. ‖ **Silver-tongued**, adj. Eloquent, à la langue dorée. ‖ **Silver-ware**, n. Argenterie *f.*
— v. tr. Argenter; étamer (a mirror).
— v. intr. S'argenter, blanchir (hair).

silversmith [-smiθ] n. Orfèvre *m.*; argentier (†) *m.*

silverweed [-wi:d] n. Bot. Argentine *f.*

silvery [-ri] adj. Argenté. ‖ Fig. Argentin (laugh).

silviculture ['silvi,kʌltʃə*] n. Sylviculture *f.*

simian ['simiən] adj. Zool. Simiesque, simien.
— n. Simien, singe *m.*

similar ['similə*] adj. Ressemblant. ‖ Approchant. ‖ Analogue (instance); semblable (tastes). ‖ Math. Similaire (product); semblable (triangle).
— n. Semblable; pareil *m.*

similarity [simi'læriti] n. Ressemblance, similarité *f.* (See LIKENESS.)

similarly [-li] adv. Semblablement, pareillement; de même.

simile ['simili] n. Gramm. Comparaison *f.*

similitude [si'militju:d] n. Similitude, ressemblance *f.*

simmer ['simə*] v. intr. Culin. Mijoter, bouillotter, frémir (liquid); mitonner (soup). ‖ Fig. Frémir, bouillir (with, de) [person]; fermenter (revolt).
— v. tr. Culin. Faire mijoter (stew); amener à ébullition (water).
— n. Culin. Faible ébullition *f.*; frémissement *m.* ‖ Fig. Ebullition, colère contenue *f.*

simmering [-riŋ] n. Culin. Cuisson (*f.*) à petits bouillons, bouillottement *m.* ‖ Fig. Bouillonnement *m.* (of anger); ferment *m.* (of revolt).

simoniac [sai'mouniæk] n. Eccles. Simoniaque *m.*

simon-pure ['saimən-'pjuə*] adj. U. S. Authentique.

simony ['saiməni] n. Eccles. Simonie *f.*

simoon [si'mu:n], U. S. **simoom** n. Simoun *m.*

simper ['simpə*] n. Sourire affecté *m.*
— v. intr. Minauder.
— v. tr. Prononcer en minaudant.

simpering [-riŋ] n. Minauderie *f.*
— adj. Minaudier.

simperingly [-riŋli] adv. En minaudant.

simple ['simpl] adj. Simple; naturel, sans affectation (person); *simple folk*, les humbles, les petites

gens; *simple soul*, bonne âme. ‖ Facile, simple (problem). [See EASY.] ‖ Crédule, naïf, niais, simple (simple-minded). ‖ Pur, pur et simple, simple (mere); *to be a simple workman*, n'être qu'un ouvrier. ‖ GRAMM. Indépendant (sentence); simple, non composé (tense). ‖ MATH. *Simple addition*, addition de nombres d'un seul chiffre; *simple equation*, équation du premier degré. ‖ BOT., COMM., CHIM., TECHN., MED. Simple. ‖ ZOOL. *Simple eye*, ocelle. ‖ **Simple-hearted**, adj. Simple, franc, ingénu. ‖ **Simple-minded**, adj. Naïf, candide; simple d'esprit. ‖ **Simple-mindedness**, n. Naïveté *f.*; simplicité (*f.*) d'esprit.
— n. Semple *m.* (of a loom). ‖ BOT., MED. Simple *m.*; herbe médicinale *f.*

simpleness [-nis] n. Simplicité *f.* ‖ FIG. Candeur, naïveté *f.*; simplicité (*f.*) d'esprit.

simpleton [-tən] n. Nigaud, niais, bêta *m.*; nouille, gourde *f.* (fam.).

simplicity [sim'plisiti] n. Facilité, simplicité *f.* (easiness); simplicité *f.*; naturel *m.* (naturalness). ‖ Candeur, franchise *f.* ‖ Naïveté *f.*

simplify ['simplifai] v. tr. (2). Simplifier.

simply [-i] adv. Simplement; absolument (purely). ‖ Sans affectation (or) recherche (naturally). ‖ Tout simplement, purement et simplement (merely); *it is simply pouring*, il pleut à verse.

simulacrum [simju'leikrəm] n. Simulacre, semblant *m.*

simulate ['simjuleit] v. tr. Simuler, feindre (an illness); affecter (indifference); prendre l'aspect de (s.o., sth.).

simulation [simju'leiʃən] n. Simulation, feinte *f.*

simultaneity [ˌsiməltə'neiiti], **simultaneousness** [ˌsiməl'teinjəsnis] n. Simultanéité *f.*

simultaneous [siməl'teinjəs] adj. Simultané; concomitant (with, avec); qui a lieu en même temps (with, que).

simultaneously [-li] adv. Simultanément. ‖ En même temps (with, que).

sin [sin] n. ECCLES. Péché *m.* ‖ FIG. Infraction *f.*; manquement *m.* (against, à).
— v. intr. Pécher. ‖ FIG. *To sin against*, enfreindre, commettre une infraction à; manquer à.

sinapism ['sinəpizm] n. MED. Sinapisme *m.*

since [sins] adv. Depuis (time); *long since*, depuis longtemps, il y a longtemps; *ever since*, depuis lors.
— prep. Depuis; *to have been up since dawn*, être levé dès l'aube; *I have been working since yesterday*, je travaille depuis hier; *since seeing them*, depuis que je les ai vus.
— conj. Depuis que; que; *since I have been working*, depuis que je travaille. ‖ Puisque, vu que, étant donné que (because); *since it is late*, puisqu'il est tard.

sincere [sin'siə*] adj. Sincère, franc (person); vrai, réel (sentiment).

sincerely [-li] adv. Sincèrement; *yours sincerely*, cordialement à vous.

sincerity [sin'seriti] n. Sincérité *f.* ‖ Franchise, bonne foi *f.*

sine [sain] n. MATH. Sinus *m.*

sinecure ['sainəkjuə*] n. Sinécure *f.*

sine die ['saini 'daii] adv. Sine die.

sine qua non ['saini kwei 'nɔn] n. Condition (*f.*) sine qua non.

sinew ['sinju:] n. MED. Tendon *m.*; muscle *m.* ‖ Pl. Muscles *m. pl.*; nerf *m.*; force, vigueur *f.* ‖ CULIN. Croquant, tirant *m.* (in meat). ‖ FIG. Nerf *m.* (of war).

sinewless [-lis] adj. MED. Sans tendons. ‖ FIG. Mou.

sinewy [-i] adj. MED. Musclé, nerveux, vigoureux. ‖ CULIN. Tendineux.

sinful ['sinful] adj. ECCLES. Coupable; *sinful person*, pécheur, pécheresse. ‖ FIG. Scandaleux (loss, waste).

sinfulness [-nis] n. Péché *m.* (act); culpabilité *f.* (guilt); caractère coupable *m.* (of an act).

sing [siŋ] v. tr. (134). MUS. Chanter. ‖ NAUT. *To sing out*, crier (a command). ‖ FIG. *To sing the praises of*, chanter les louanges de.
— v. intr. Chanter; siffler (wind). ‖ ZOOL. Bourdonner (insect). ‖ MED. Bourdonner (ears). ‖ NAUT. *To sing out*, crier un commandement. ‖ U. S. POP. Se mettre à table, manger le morceau. (See SQUEAL.) ‖ FAM. *To sing another tune*, déchanter, changer de gamme; *to sing small*, se dégonfler, filer doux, rabattre son caquet.

Singapore [ˌsiŋə'pɔ:*] n. GEOGR. Singapour *m.*

singe [sindʒ] v. tr. Roussir. ‖ CULIN. Flamber (poultry). ‖ FIG. *To singe one's wings*, se brûler les ailes.
— v. intr. Se roussir.
— N. B. Noter l'orthographe du p. prés. *singeing*.
— n. Marque de brûlure, roussissure *f.*

singeing [-iŋ] n. Brûlage léger *m.* ‖ CULIN. Flambage *m.*

singer ['siŋgə*] n. MUS. Chanteur *s.*; cantatrice *f.* ‖ ZOOL. Chanteur *m.*

singing [-iŋ] n. MUS. Chant *m.* ‖ MED. Bourdonnement *m.* (in the ears). ‖ FIG. Sifflement *m.* (of an arrow, the wind).

single ['siŋgl] adj. Seul, unique (one only). ‖ Simple (opposite of double); *in single rank*, sur un rang. ‖ Séparé, particulier, individuel; *single bed*, lit d'une personne; *single room*, chambre particulière. ‖ Sans aide, seul; *single combat*, combat singulier. ‖ Non marié; *single person*, célibataire. ‖ Sincère, honnête; *single heart*, cœur droit. ‖ JUR. Uninominal (ballot). ‖ BOT. Simple (flower). ‖ CH. DE F. Simple (ticket); *single line*, voie unique. ‖ COMM. *Single entry book-keeping*, comptabilité en partie simple. ‖ FIN. Seul et même (loan); unique (premium). ‖ SPORTS. *Single court*, court de simple. ‖ TECHN. *Single parts*, pièces détachées. ‖ **Single-acting**, adj. TECHN. A simple effet. ‖ **Single-barrelled**, adj. A un coup (gun). ‖ **Single-blessedness**, n. FAM. Célibat *m.* ‖ **Single-breasted**, adj. Droit, à un seul rang de boutons (coat). ‖ **Single-cylinder**, adj. Monocylindrique. ‖ **Single-handed**, adj. Maniable d'une seule main (instrument); sans aide, tout seul (person). ‖ **Single-hearted**, adj. Sincère, honnête, franc, loyal. ‖ **Single-minded**, adj. Qui n'a qu'un but. ‖ **Single-mindedness**, n. Unité d'intention *f.* ‖ **Single-phase**, adj. ELECTR. Monophasé. ‖ **Single-seater**, n. AVIAT. Monoplace *m.* ‖ **Single-track**, adj. CH. DE F. A voie unique; FIG. Qui ne peut suivre qu'une seule idée (mind).
— n. SPORTS. Coup *m.* (baseball); simple *m.* (tennis); *women's singles*, simple dames.
— v. tr. *To single out*, choisir, remarquer, distinguer (as, comme; for, pour). ‖ AGRIC. Séparer (plants).

singleness [-nis] n. Probité, honnêteté, droiture *f.* ‖ Sincérité *f.* (of heart); *singleness of mind*, suite dans les idées; *with singleness of purpose*, en vue d'un seul but. ‖ Unicité *f.* ‖ Célibat *m.*

singlestick [-stik] n. SPORTS. Canne *f.*; bâton *m.*

singlet ['siŋglit] n. Gilet (*m.*) de corps (or) de flanelle. ‖ SPORTS. Maillot *m.*

singleton ['siŋgltən] n. Elément isolé *m.*; singleton *m.* (in cards). ‖ MATH. Singleton *m.*

singly [-li] adv. Séparément, un à un, individuellement; *working singly*, opérant isolément. ‖ Seul, sans aide. ‖ † Seulement, uniquement.

singsong ['siŋsɔŋ] n. Ton monotone *m.* ‖ MUS. Chant monotone *m.*
— adj. Traînant, monotone.

singular ['siŋgjulə*] adj. Insigne (outstanding); singulier, surprenant (surprising); rare, extraordinaire (unusual). ‖ Singulier, bizarre, étrange (peculiar). ‖ Individuel, pris isolément (individual). ‖ GRAMM., MATH. Singulier.

— n. GRAMM. Singulier *m.; in the singular,* au singulier.

singularity [siŋgju'læriti] n. Singularité *f.* ‖ Particularité *f.* ‖ Bizarrerie, étrangeté *f.* ‖ Caractère unique *m.*

singularize ['siŋgjulɘraiz] v. tr. Singulariser.

singularly [-li] adv. Singulièrement. ‖ Remarquablement. ‖ Etrangement.

sinister ['sinistɘ*] adj. Sinistre. ‖ Mauvais, menaçant, sinistre (air, countenance). ‖ BLAS. Sénestre.

sink [siŋk] v. intr. (135). S'enfoncer, descendre au-dessous d'un niveau ; *to sink out of sight,* disparaître. ‖ Sombrer, couler (under water) ; *to sink like a stone,* couler à pic. ‖ S'abaisser, baisser, pencher (head, shoulders). ‖ Baisser (level) ; descendre, s'abaisser (slope). ‖ S'affaisser, se tasser (earth, foundations). ‖ Diminuer, décroître (daylight) ; se faire plus bas (noise). ‖ Tomber, se laisser tomber, s'abattre, s'écrouler (animal, person) ; *to sink to one's knees,* tomber à genoux. ‖ Pénétrer (*into,* dans) ; tomber (*into,* dans) ; *to sink into a deep sleep,* plonger dans un profond sommeil ; *to sink into an armchair,* s'effondrer dans un fauteuil. ‖ NAUT. Sombrer, couler au fond (ship). ‖ ASTRON. Baisser, disparaître sous l'horizon (moon, sun). ‖ MED. S'affaiblir, décliner, baisser (strength) ; se creuser (cheeks) ; devenir cave (eyes) ; se serrer, défaillir (heart). ‖ FIN. Baisser, être en baisse (prices). ‖ FIG. Tomber (*into,* dans) [oblivion] ; *to sink in,* faire impression (meaning). ‖ FIG. Faiblir (courage) ; sombrer, s'écrouler (hope) ; s'abattre (spirits) ; *to sink under a burden,* succomber sous un fardeau. ‖ LOC. *Sink or swim,* advienne que pourra !, vogue la galère !

— v. tr. Enfoncer, faire descendre lentement ; plonger (under the surface, into the water). ‖ Abaisser, laisser tomber, faire pencher ; *to sink one's voice,* baisser la voix. ‖ Affaisser (floor, foundation, ground) ; faire baisser, abaisser le niveau de (a lake). ‖ Enfoncer, faire pénétrer (a stake). ‖ Foncer (a mine-shaft) ; creuser (a well). ‖ Graver en creux (a medal). ‖ NAUT. Mouiller (a mine) ; couler (a ship). ‖ FIN. Amortir, éteindre (a debt) ; placer à fonds perdus, immobiliser (money). ‖ FIN. Faire baisser, réduire (prices). ‖ FIG. Supprimer (a disagreement) ; dissimuler, tenir secret (a fact) ; négliger (interests).

sink n. Evier, bac d'évier *m.* (in a kitchen). ‖ TECHN. Cône d'avancement *m.* (in a mine). ‖ FIG. Cloaque, bourbier *m.; sink of iniquity,* cloaque de tous les vices. ‖ **Sink-hole,** n. Puisard *m.*

sinker [-ɘ*] n. Plomb *m.* (for immersing). ‖ NAUT. Crapaud d'amarrage *m.* ‖ TECHN. Ouvrier fonceur *m.* (shaft-sinker) ; puisatier *m.* (well-digger). ‖ SPORTS. Plomb *m.* (for fishing). ‖ U. S. FAM., CULIN. Pet-de-nonne *m.* (doughnut).

sinking [-iŋ] n. Descente *f.; enfoncement m.* ‖ Enlisement *m.* (in the mire). ‖ Tassement, affaissement *m.* (of the ground). ‖ Abaissement *m.* (of a level). ‖ TECHN. Creusage, forage *m.* (of a mineshaft, a well) ; enfoncement *m.* (of a stake). ‖ NAUT. Envoi par le fond *m.* (act) ; engloutissement *m.* (result). ‖ FIN. Amortissement *m.* (of a debt) ; placement (*m.*) à fonds perdus (of a sum of money). ‖ MED. Défaillance *f.* (fainting) ; abaissement *m.* (of the voice). ‖ **Sinking-fund,** n. FIN. Caisse (*f.*) d'amortissement.

sinless ['sinlis] adj. Sans péché, pur, innocent.

sinlessness [-nis] n. Innocence, pureté *f.*

sinner ['sinɘ*] n. Pécheur *m.; pécheresse f.*

Sinologist [si'nɔlɘdʒist] n. Sinologue *s.*

Sinology [si'nɔlɘdʒi] n. Sinologie *f.*

sinter ['sintɘ*] n. GEOL. Travertin *m.*

— v. tr., intr. Agglomérer. ‖ Fritter.

sinuate ['sinjuit] adj. Sinué.

sinuosity [ˌsinju'ɔsiti] n. Sinuosité *f.*

sinuous ['sinjuɘs] adj. Sinueux.

sinus ['sainɘs] (pl. **sinuses** [-iz]) n. MED. Sinus *m.*

sinusitis [ˌsainɘ'saitis] n. MED. Sinusite *f.*

sip [sip] v. tr. (1). Siroter, boire à petits coups, savourer, déguster.

— n. Petit coup *m.; goutte f.*

siphon ['saifɘn] n. Siphon *m.* ‖ Siphon (*m.*) à eau de Seltz (bottle).

— v. tr. Siphonner.

— v. intr. Se transvaser, s'écouler au moyen d'un siphon.

siphonage [-idʒ] n. Siphonnement, siphonage *m.*

sippet ['sipit] n. CULIN. Pain trempé *m.; mouillette f.* (for eggs) ; croûton *m.* (as a garnish).

sir [sɘ:*] n. Monsieur *m.* ‖ MILIT. *Yes, sir,* oui, capitaine ; oui, monsieur (to an equal or to an inferior) ; oui, mon capitaine ; oui, mon colonel (to a superior officer). ‖ Monsieur *m.* (in a letter). ‖ Sir *m.* (English title). ‖ Sire *m.* (to a king) ; Monseigneur *m.* (to a prince).

— N. B. Au pluriel, on emploie *Sirs* ou *Gentlemen. Sir* (titre anglais) doit toujours être suivi du prénom.

sire ['saiɘ*] n. † Père, aïeul *m.* ‖ Sire *m.* (to a king). ‖ ZOOL. Père *m.* (of a horse).

— v. tr. ZOOL. Etre le père de, engendrer.

siren ['saiɘrɘn] n. ZOOL., TECHN., NAUT. Sirène *f.* ‖ FIG. Sirène, femme fatale *f.*

siriasis [si'raiɘsis] n. MED. Insolation *f.*

Sirius ['siriɘs] n. ASTRON. Sirius *m.*

sirloin ['sɘ:lɔin] n. CULIN. Aloyau *m.*

sirocco [si'rɔkou] n. Sirocco *m.*

sirup ['sirɘp] n. U. S. See SYRUP.

sis [sis] n. FAM. Frangine *f.*

sisal ['sisɘl] n. BOT. Sisal *m.*

siskin ['siskin] n. ZOOL. Tarin *m.*

sissy ['sisi] n. FAM. Poule mouillée, lopette *f.* (milksop) ; homme efféminé *m.*, tapette *f.* (pansy).

— adj. FAM. Trouillard (cowardly) ; qui fait fille, efféminé (effeminate).

sister ['sistɘ*] n. Sœur *f.* ‖ *The Three Sisters,* les Parques. ‖ ECCLES. Religieuse, sœur *f.* ‖ MED. Infirmière en chef, surveillante *f.* (in a hospital). ‖ NAUT. *Sister ships,* navires jumeaux. ‖ FIG. *Sister members,* consœurs, collègues ; *sister nations,* nations sœurs. ‖ **Sister-in-law,** n. Belle-sœur *f.*

sisterhood [-hud] n. Fraternité *f.* ‖ ECCLES. Communauté (*f.*) de femmes.

sisterly [-li] adv., adj. De sœur.

Sistine ['sistain] adj. ARCHIT. Sixtine (chapel).

sistrum ['sistrɘm] (pl. **sistra** [-ɘ]) n. MUS. Sistre *m.*

Sisyphus ['sisifɘs] n. Sisyphe *m.*

sit [sit] n. Ajustement *m.* (of a garment).

— v. intr. (136). S'asseoir (to sit down) ; être (or) rester assis (to be sitting) ; *please sit down,* veuillez vous asseoir ; *to sit quietly* (or) *still,* rester tranquille. ‖ Aller, tomber (garment). ‖ Se tenir habituellement (in a place). ‖ Etre situé (or) placé, se trouver (wind). ‖ JUR. Siéger, être en jugement (court) ; être en séance (Parliament) ; *to sit on the jury,* faire partie du jury. ‖ ZOOL. Se poser, se percher, être perché (birds) ; couver (on eggs). ‖ SPORTS. Se tenir en selle (horseman). ‖ ARTS. Poser (for a portrait). ‖ MILIT. Mettre le siège (*before,* devant). ‖ FIG. *To sit at home,* être inactif, ne pas bouger ; *to sit heavy on s.o.'s conscience* (or) *stomach,* peser sur la conscience (or) sur l'estomac de qqn ; *to sit in judgment,* se donner des airs de juge ; *to sit in state,* trôner. ‖ FAM. *To be sitting pretty,* être comme un coq en pâte. ‖ **To sit down,** s'asseoir, prendre un siège ; *to sit down to a meal,* se mettre à table ; FIG. *To sit down under an insult,* encaisser une insulte sans piper. ‖ **To sit for,** représenter (an electoral district) ; se présenter à (an examination). ‖ **To sit on** (or) **upon,** siéger pour juger (a case) ; étouffer (an idea) ; faire partie de (a committee) ; se réunir pour régler (a question) ;

faire taire (s.o.). ‖ **To sit tight,** ne pas céder, ne pas se laisser ébranler. ‖ **To sit up,** se dresser sur son séant ; se tenir droit (while seated) ; ne pas se coucher, veiller tard ; POP. *To make s.o. sit up,* secouer (or) faire buriner qqn. ‖ **Sit-down strike,** n. Grève (*f.*) sur le tas. ‖ **Sit-in,** n. Sit-in *m.*

— v. tr. † S'asseoir ; *to sit oneself down,* s'asseoir. ‖ Asseoir (a child). ‖ SPORTS. Monter, être à cheval sur, se tenir en selle sur (a horse). ‖ **To sit out,** ne pas prendre part à (a dance) ; rester jusqu'à la fin de (a meeting).

sitar [si'tɑ:] n. MUS. Sitar *m.*

sitcom ['sit,kɔm] n. FAM. Comédie de situation *f.*

site [sait] n. Site *m.* ‖ Emplacement *m.* (of a building) ; *building site,* terrain à bâtir. ‖ *Launching site,* aire de lancement.

— v. tr. Situer (to locate) ; placer, fixer l'emplacement de (to provide with a site).

sitter [ˈsitə*] n. Personne assise *f.* ‖ ARTS. Modèle *s.* ‖ CH. DE F. Voyageur assis *m.* ‖ ZOOL. Poule couveuse *f.* ‖ SPORTS. Gibier posé *m.* ‖ FAM. Jeu d'enfant *m.* (child's play) ; gardien (*s.*) d'enfant.

sitting [-iŋ] n. Posture assise *f.* ‖ Séance, réunion *f.* (of an assembly) ; session *f.* (of Parliament). ‖ ARTS. Pose *f.* ; *at one sitting,* en une seule séance. ‖ JUR. Audience *f.* (of a court). ‖ ZOOL. Couvée *f.* (of eggs) ; couvaison *f.* (by the hen). ‖ ECCLES. Siège réservé *m.* ‖ FAM. *At a sitting,* d'un trait.

— adj. Assis ; *in a sitting posture,* sur son séant, assis. ‖ ZOOL. Couveuse (hen). ‖ SPORTS. Posé (game). ‖ JUR. En séance (court) ; siégeant (judge) ; occupant (tenant). ‖ **Sitting-room,** n. Salle (*f.*) de séjour, petit salon *m.* (in a house) [see PARLOUR] ; place (*f.*) pour s'asseoir, places assises *f. pl.* (space). ‖ **Sitting war,** n. U. S. Drôle de guerre *f.*

situate ['sitjueit] v. tr. Situer.

— adj. Situé. ‖ JUR. Sis.

situation [,sitju'eiʃən] n. Situation *f.* ; emplacement, site *m.* ‖ COMM. Place, position *f.* ; poste, emploi *m.* (job) ; *situations wanted, vacant,* demandes, offres d'emplois. ‖ THEATR. Situation *f.*

sitz-bath [ˈsitsbɑ:θ] n. Bain de siège *m.*

six [siks] adj., n. MATH. Six *m.* ; *six o'clock,* six heures ; *he is six,* il a six ans. ‖ FIN. *Three and six,* trois shillings et six pence. ‖ LOC. *Six of one and half-a-dozen of the other,* bonnet blanc et blanc bonnet, kif-kif ; *at sixes and sevens,* en pagaille. ‖ **Six-shooter,** n. Arme (*f.*) à six coups. ‖ **Six-sided,** adj. Hexagone.

sixfold [-fould] adj. Sextuple.

— adv. Au sextuple.

sixpence [-pəns] n. Six pence *m. pl.* ; pièce (*f.*) de six pence.

sixpenny [-pəni] adj. A (or) de six pence.

sixte [sikst] n. SPORTS. Sixte *f.* (in fencing).

sixteen [,siks'ti:n] adj., n. Seize *m.*

sixteenth [-θ] adj., n. Seizième *m.* ‖ Seize *m.* (dates, titles). ‖ U. S. MUS. *Sixteenth note,* double croche.

sixth [siksθ] adj. Sixième.

— n. Sixième *m.* ‖ MUS. Sixte *f.*

sixthly [-li] adv. Sixièmement.

sixtieth ['sikstiəθ] adj., n. Soixantième *m.*

sixty [-ti] adj., n. Soixante *m.*

sizable ['saizəbl] adj. D'une bonne grosseur ; de la grosseur voulue. ‖ FIG. D'une certaine importance.

sizar ['saizə*] n. Boursier *m.* (at certain colleges).

size [saiz] n. Grandeur, grosseur, dimension *f.* ; taille *f.* (of an animal, a person) ; format *m.* (of a book). ‖ COMM. Numéro *m.* (of an article) ; taille *f.* (of a garment) ; pointure *f.* (of gloves, shoes) ; encolure *f.* (of shirt-collars) ; *to take the size of,* mesurer. ‖ TECHN. Format *m.* (of books, paper) ; calibre *m.* (of a cartridge) ; size *f.* (for weighing pearls). ‖ ARTS. *Life size,* grandeur naturelle. ‖ FAM. *That's about the size of it,* c'est à peu près ça.

— v. tr. Classer (or) arranger par ordre de dimen-

sions. ‖ Mettre à la dimension voulue. ‖ TECHN. Ajuster, calibrer (machine parts) ; égaliser (shot). ‖ **To size up,** prendre les dimensions de, estimer la taille de ; FAM. Juger, apprécier (s.o.).

size n. TECHN. Colle *f.* ; apprêt, encollage *m.*

— v. tr. Apprêter, coller, encoller.

sizeable [-əbl] adj. See SIZABLE.

sized [-d] adj. D'une certaine taille.

sizzle ['sizl] v. intr. Grésiller.

— n. Grésillement *m.*

skald [skɔ:ld] n. Scalde *m.*

skate [skeit] n. ZOOL. Raie *f.* (fish).

skate n. U. S. POP. Sale coco *m.* (person). ‖ ZOOL. Rosse *f.* (nag).

skate n. Patin *m.*

— v. intr. Patiner. ‖ FIG. *To skate on thin ice,* avancer sur un terrain dangereux.

skateboard [-,bɔ:d] n. Skateboard *m.*, planche (*f.*) à roulettes.

skater [-ə*] n. SPORTS. Patineur *s.*

skating [-iŋ] n. SPORTS. Patinage *m.* ‖ **Skating-rink,** n. Patinoire *f.* ; skating *m.*

skedaddle [ski'dædl] v. intr. Décamper, déguerpir.

— n. Débandade *f.*

skein [skein] n. Echeveau *m.* ‖ ZOOL. Vol *m.* (of wild geese). ‖ FAM. *Tangled skein,* embrouillamini.

skeletal ['skelətl] adj. Squelettique.

skeleton [-n] n. MED. Squelette *m.* ; ossature *f.* ‖ ARCHIT. Charpente, carcasse *f.* ‖ FIG. Plan, cadre, canevas *m.* (of a book). ‖ FAM. *A living skeleton,* un vrai squelette ; *a skeleton in the cupboard* (or) U. S. *in the closet,* un secret de famille, une tare secrète ; *skeleton at the feast,* rabat-joie.

— adj. *Skeleton key,* crochet ; rossignol (fam.) [burglar's] ; *skeleton staff,* personnel réduit. ‖ MILIT. *Skeleton army,* armée-cadre ; *skeleton map,* carte muette.

skeletonize [-naiz] v. tr. Squelettiser. ‖ FIG. Réduire au strict minimum.

skene [ski:n] n. Couteau-poignard *m.*

skep [skep] n. Panier d'osier *m.* ; harasse *f.* ‖ ZOOL. Ruche en paille *f.*

skepsis ['skepsis] n. U. S. See SCEPSIS.

sketch [sketʃ] n. ARTS. Croquis, dessin *m.* ; esquisse. ébauche *f.* ‖ THEATR. Sketch *m.* ; saynète *f.* ‖ FIG. Etude *f.* ; aperçu, résumé *m.* ; *character sketch,* portrait littéraire. ‖ **Sketch-book,** n. ARTS. Carnet (or) album (*m.*) de croquis. ‖ **Sketch-map,** n. Carte-croquis *f.*

— v. tr. ARTS. Esquisser, croquer, ébaucher.

— v. intr. Faire des croquis (or) esquisses.

sketcher [-ə*] n. ARTS. Dessinateur *m.* ; dessinatrice *f.*

sketchiness [-inis] n. Ebauchage, manque (*m.*) de détails.

sketchy [-i] adj. Sommaire ; ébauché, non fini. ‖ Imprécis (features) ; vague (idea) ; rudimentaire (knowledge).

skew [skju:] adj. Biais (arch, bridge) ; oblique (section) ; *skew chisel,* biseau. ‖ **Skew-eyed,** adj. MED. Louche, qui louche. ‖ **Skew-wheel,** n. TECHN. Roue hyperboloïde *f.*

— n. Biais *m.* ; obliquité *f.*

— v. intr. Biaiser, obliquer.

skewbald [-bɔ:ld] adj. ZOOL. Pie (horse).

skewer ['skjuə*] n. CULIN. Brochette *f.* ‖ FAM. Broche *f.* (sword).

— v. tr. CULIN., FAM. Embrocher.

ski [ski:] n. SPORTS. Ski *m.* ‖ **Ski-jump,** n. Saut (*m.*) à skis. ‖ **Ski-lift,** n. Remonte-pente *m. invar.* ‖ **Ski-run,** n. SPORTS. Piste (*f.*) de ski, piste. ‖ **Ski-tip,** n. Spatule *f.*

— N. B. Le pluriel est *ski* ou *skis.*

— v. intr. Faire du ski ; *to ski across,* passer en ski.

skid [skid] n. Cale *f.* ; chantier *m.* (for barrels). ‖ TECHN. Chaîne (*f.*) à enrayer ; sabot (*m.*) de roue. ‖ NAUT. Défense (*f.*) en bois. ‖ AUTOM. Dérapage

m.; embardée *f.* ‖ AVIAT. Patin *m.*; *tail skid*, béquille arrière. ‖ U. S. FAM. *On the skids*, en perte de vitesse.
— v. tr. Caler (a barrel); enrayer, bloquer (a wheel). ‖ NAUT. Protéger au moyen de défenses en bois.
— v. intr. AUTOM. Déraper; faire une embardée.
skiddoo [ski'du:] interj. U. S. FAM. Décampez!, vingt-deux!
skier ['skiə*] n. SPORTS. Skieur *s.*
skiff [skif] n. NAUT. Esquif *m.*; yole *f.*; skiff *m.*
skilful ['skilful] adj. Adroit, habile, ingénieux.
skilfully [-i] adv. Adroitement, habilement.
skilfulness [-nis] n. Habileté, adresse *f.*
skill [skil] n. Habileté, adresse, dextérité, ingéniosité *f.*; *technical skill*, compétence. ‖ U. S. Métier (or) art pratique *m.*
skilled [skild] adj. Habile. ‖ Spécialisé, expérimenté (labour); qualifié (worker).
skillet ['skilit] n. CULIN. Poêlon (*m.*) à trois pieds; U.S. poêle *f.*
skillfull ['skilful] adj. U.S. See SKILFUL.
skilly ['skili] n. CULIN. Soupe claire *f.*
skim [skim] v. tr. CULIN. Ecrémer (milk); écumer, dégraisser (soup). ‖ FIG. Effleurer (a subject), raser (surface).
— v. intr. **To skim along**, glisser, passer légèrement. ‖ AVIAT. *To skim along the ground, the water*, faire du rase-mottes, hydroplaner. ‖ FIG. Parcourir, lire en diagonale; *to skim over* (or) *through*, feuilleter. ‖ **Skim-milk**, n. CULIN. Lait écrémé *m.*
skimmer [-ə*] n. CULIN. Ecrémeur *s.* (person); écrémoir *m.* (for milk); écumoire *f.* (for soup). ‖ ZOOL. Bec-en-ciseaux *m.*
skimp [skimp] v. tr. Lésiner sur, être chiche de; *to skimp s.o. in sth.*, fournir qqn chichement de qqch.; donner qqch. au compte-gouttes à qqn (fam.). ‖ Bâcler, saboter (work).
— v. intr. Lésiner (*on*, sur). ‖ Bâcler son travail. (See BOTCH.)
skimpiness [-inis] n. Insuffisance *f.* (of a portion). ‖ Aspect étriqué *m.* (of a garment).
skimpy [-i] adj. Lésineur, chiche (person). ‖ Etriqué (garment); insuffisant, maigre (portion); bâclé (work).
skin [skin] n. MED. Peau *f.*; *outer, true skin*, épiderme, derme. ‖ ZOOL. Peau, dépouille *f.* ‖ COMM. Peau *f.*; pl. peausserie *f.* ‖ BOT. Peau *f.*; pelure *f.* (on a fruit, an onion). ‖ CULIN. Peau *f.* (on milk); robe *f.* (of a sausage); outre *f.* (gourd). ‖ NAUT. Carène, coque *f.* (of a ship). ‖ TECHN. Croûte *f.* (on an ingot). ‖ AVIAT. Revêtement *m.* (of a fuselage). ‖ FIG. *To have a thick skin*, avoir la peau dure; *to have a thin skin*, réagir en écorché vif, être susceptible. ‖ LOC. *He's got her under his skin*, il l'a dans la peau; *to be only skin and bones*, n'avoir que la peau et les os; *to save one's skin*, sauver sa peau; *wet to the skin*, trempé jusqu'aux os; *to escape by the skin of one's teeth*, y échapper de justesse; *to strip to the skin*, se mettre à poil. ‖ **Skin-deep**, adj. Superficiel; à fleur de peau (beauty). ‖ **Skin-disease**, n. MED. Dermatose *f.* ‖ **Skin-diver**, n. SPORTS. Plongeur *s.*, amateur (*m.*) de plongée sous-marine. ‖ **Skin-diving**, n. SPORTS. Plongée sous-marine *f.* ‖ **Skin-flick**, n. POP., CINEM. Film porno *m.*, porno *m.* ‖ **Skin-game**, n. FAM. Escroquerie *f.* ‖ **Skin-grafting**, n. MED. Greffe épidermique *f.* ‖ **Skin-test**, n. MED. Cuti-réaction *f.* ‖ **Skin-tight**, adj. Collant.
— v. tr. MED. Ecorcher, dépouiller, enlever la peau de; *to skin one's elbow*, s'écorcher le coude. ‖ CULIN. Dépouiller, dépiauter, écorcher (an animal); peler, éplucher (vegetables). ‖ NAUT. Revêtir (a ship). ‖ TECHN. Décroûter (a casting). ‖ FAM. Ecorcher (s.o.); *to skin a flint*, tondre un œuf.
— v. intr. MED. *To skin over*, se cicatriser (wound). ‖ U. S. FAM. *To skin through*, se faufiler par (an opening); passer tout juste (an exam).

skinflint [-flint] n. FAM. Grippe-sou, grigou *m.*
skinful [-ful] n. FAM. *To have a skinful*, tenir une bonne cuite.
skinless [-lis] adj. Sans peau.
skinner [-ə*] n. Ecorcheur *s.* ‖ Peaussier, pelletier *m.* (skin-dresser). ‖ COMM. Marchand (*m.*) de fourrures.
skinniness [-inis] n. Maigreur, émaciation *f.*
skinny [-i] adj. Efflanqué, étique (horse); maigrichon, décharné (person).
skint [skint] adj. POP. Fauché, dans la dèche.
skip [skip] n. Petit saut *m.*; gambade *f.* ‖ MUS. Saut *m.*
— v. intr. Sauter, sautiller; bondir, gambader. ‖ Sauter à la corde. ‖ FIG. Faire des omissions; sauter des passages (in a text); *to skip around*, papillonner (from one subject to another); *I'm skipping over several items*, j'en passe. ‖ POP. Décamper, décaniller.
— v. tr. FIG. Passer, sauter, omettre.
skip n. TECHN. Cage *f.*, skip *m.* (in a mine). ‖ Benne *f.*, skip *m.* (for builders' refuse).
skipjack ['skipdʒæk] n. Grenouille sauteuse *f.* (toy). ‖ ZOOL. Tape-marteau *m.* (beetle).
skipper ['skipə*] n. Sauteur *s.* ‖ ZOOL. Brochet saurien *m.*
skipper n. NAUT. Patron, capitaine *m.* (of small craft). ‖ SPORTS. Capitaine *m.* (of a team).
— v. tr. NAUT. Commander. ‖ SPORTS. Etre le capitaine de.
skipping [-iŋ] n. Saut (*m.*) à la corde. ‖ Sautage *m.* (in printing). ‖ **Skipping-rope**, n. Corde (*f.*) à sauter.
skirl [skə:l] n. MUS. Son aigu (*m.*) de la cornemuse.
— v. intr. MUS. Jouer (bagpipe).
skirmish ['skə:miʃ] n. MILIT. Escarmouche, échauffourée *f.*
— v. intr. MILIT. Escarmoucher.
skirmisher [-ə*] n. MILIT. Escarmoucheur, tirailleur *m.*
skirret ['skirit] n. BOT. Chervis *m.*
skirt [skə:t] n. Jupe *f.*; *divided skirt*, jupe-culotte. ‖ Pans *m. pl.*, basque *f.* (of a coat); jupe *f.* (of a frock-coat). ‖ Pl. Bord *m.*, extrémité *f.* (of a city); lisière, orée *f.* (of the forest). ‖ POP. Typesse, gonzesse *f.* (woman).
— v. tr. Border, suivre le bord de, contourner (a hill); longer, serrer (a wall). ‖ NAUT. Côtoyer.
— v. intr. *To skirt along*, suivre le bord de.
skirting [-iŋ] n. Tissu (*m.*) pour jupes. ‖ TECHN. Plinthe *f.*
skit [skit] n. THEATR. Courte pièce satirique, pasquinade *f.*
skitter ['skitə*] v. intr. Trottiner; *to skitter off*, détaler, déguerpir; *to skitter across the water*, effleurer l'eau en éclaboussant. ‖ SPORTS. Pêcher à la dandinette.
skittish [-iʃ] adj. ZOOL. Ombrageux, peureux (horse). ‖ FIG. Capricieux, fantasque; volage (person); évaporé (woman).
skittishness [-iʃnis] n. Instabilité *f.*; pétulance; légèreté *f.*
skittle ['skitl] n. SPORTS. Quille *f.*; jeu (*m.*) de quilles. ‖ FIG. *Not all beer and skittles*, pas tout rose.
skive [skaiv] v. tr. Tailler en feuilles minces (leather); décharner (a pelt). ‖ Polir (a diamond).
skiver [-ə*] n. Doleur, drayeur *m.* (person); doloir *m.* (tool). ‖ Feuille mince (*f.*) de cuir.
skivvy ['skivi] n. FAM. Bonniche *f.* ‖ Pl. U. S. Sous-vêtements *m. pl.* (for men).
skua ['skju:ə] n. ZOOL. Skua *m.*
skulduggery [skʌl'dʌgəri] n. U. S. FAM. Roublardise *f.*; montage de coup *m.*
skulk [skʌlk] v. intr. Se cacher, se dissimuler. ‖ Rôder en se dissimulant (to prowl). ‖ Fainéanter (to idle). ‖ MILIT., FAM. Tirer au flanc.

— n. Fainéant, feignant *m.* ‖ Rôdeur sournois *s.* ‖ MILIT. Embusqué *m.* ‖ ZOOL. Bande, troupe *f.* (of foxes).

skull [skʌl] n. MED. Crâne *m.* ‖ LOC. *Skull and cross-bones*, tête de mort. ‖ **Skull-cap**, n. Calotte *f.*

skunk [skʌŋk] n. ZOOL. Mouffette *f.*; putois (*m.*) d'Amérique. ‖ COMM. Skunks, sconse *m.* ‖ FAM. Salaud, chameau *m.*

sky [skai] n. ASTRON. Ciel *m.* (pl. cieux). ‖ ARTS. Ciel *m.* (pl. ciels); plafond *m.*, corniche *f.* (in a gallery). ‖ FIG. Contrée *f.*, climat, ciel *m.* (clime). ‖ FIG. Pl. Cieux *m. pl.*; *to praise to the skies*, tresser des guirlandes à, porter aux nues. ‖ **Sky-blue**, adj., n. Bleu ciel *m.* ‖ **Sky-diving**, n. SPORTS. Parachutisme sportif *m.* ‖ **Sky-high**, adv. Très haut; *to blow sky-high*, complètement anéantir; adj. Vertigineux, exorbitant. ‖ **Sky-line**, n. Ligne (*f.*) d'horizon, horizon *m.*; profil *m.* (of a city). ‖ **Sky-rocket**, n. Fusée volante *f.*; v. intr. FIN. Monter en flèche (prices). ‖ **Sky-sail**, n. NAUT. Contre-cacatois *m.* ‖ **Sky-way**, n. AVIAT. Route aérienne *f.* ‖ **Sky-writing**, n. Ecriture (*f.*) dans le ciel.

— v. tr. ARTS. Accrocher au plafond (an exhibition). ‖ SPORTS. Lancer en chandelle (a ball).

Skye n. GEOGR. Ile (*f.*) de Skye. ‖ **Skye-terrier**, n. ZOOL. Skye-terrier *m.*

skyjack ['skai,dʒæk] v. tr. FAM. Détourner (a plane).

skyjacker [-ə*] n. FAM. Pirate de l'air *m.*

skylark ['skailɑ:k] n. ZOOL. Alouette (*f.*) des champs.

— v. intr. FAM. Faire le fou, batifoler, chahuter. (See FROLIC.)

skylight [-lait] n. Lucarne, fenêtre à tabatière *f.* ‖ NAUT. Claire-voie *f.*

skyscape [-skeip] n. ARTS. Etude (*f.*) de ciel.

skyscraper [-skreipə*] n. Gratte-ciel *m. invar.*

skyward [-wəd] adj., adv. Vers le ciel.

slab [slæb] n. Plaque, tranche *f.* (of marble); table *f.* (of slate); dalle *f.* (of stone); dosse *f.* (of wood). ‖ TECHN. Brame *f.* (of metal). ‖ CULIN. Grosse tranche *f.* (of cake); tablette *f.* (of chocolate); pavé *m.* (of gingerbread).

— v. tr. Trancher (marble, stone); enlever les dosses de (a tree-trunk). ‖ Daller (a terrace).

slack [slæk] adj. Mou, lâche, mal tendu (rope). ‖ Nonchalant, mou; flemmard (fam.) [person]; mou (weather). ‖ NAUT. Lent (ship); *slack water*, étale. ‖ TECHN. Desserré (screw). ‖ COMM. *Slack season*, morte-saison. ‖ CH. DE F. *Slack hours*, heures creuses. ‖ TECHN. *To be slack*, avoir du jeu.

— adv. Mollement; doucement, lentement; incomplètement, imparfaitement.

— n. Mou, battant *m.* (of a rope). ‖ Pl. Pantalon *m.* ‖ TECHN. Jeu *m.* (of a screw). ‖ COMM. Ralentissement *m.*; morte-saison *f.*

— v. tr. Relâcher, détendre. ‖ Ralentir (an activity, a pace). ‖ TECHN. Eteindre, amortir (lime); desserrer (a screw). ‖ NAUT. *To slack off*, larguer, filer (a cable); mollir (a rope).

— v. intr. Prendre du lâche (or) du mou (rope). ‖ TECHN. Prendre du jeu (screw). ‖ FAM. Se reposer, se détendre; flemmarder (fam.); *to slack off*, s'endormir, se relâcher. ‖ **Slack-rope**, n. Corde lâche *f.*; voltige *f.*; *slack-rope performer*, voltigeur.

slack n. TECHN. Fines *f. pl.* (coal dust).

slacken [-ŋ] v. tr. Détendre, relâcher, mollir, donner du mou à (a rope). ‖ Ralentir (an activity); *to slacken speed*, diminuer de vitesse. ‖ TECHN. Desserrer (a screw). ‖ LOC. Lâcher (the reins).

— v. intr. Se détendre, se relâcher; prendre du mou (rope). ‖ TECHN. Se desserrer (screw). ‖ NAUT. Mollir (wind). ‖ COMM. Diminuer, fléchir (business). ‖ FIN. S'engourdir (market). ‖ FIG. Se ralentir, diminuer (activities).

slacker [-ə*] n. MILIT. Tireur au flanc *m.* ‖ FAM. Flemmard *m.*

slackly [-li] adv. Mollement. ‖ FIG. Négligemment.

slackness [-nis] n. Mou *m.* (of a rope). ‖ TECHN. Jeu *m.* (of a screw). ‖ FIN. Engourdissement *m.* (of the market). ‖ COMM. Stagnation *f.*; fléchissement *m.* (of business). ‖ MED. Détente *f.* (of muscles). ‖ FIG. Relâchement *m.* (of discipline); désœuvrement *m.*; mollesse *f.* (of s.o.).

slag [slæg] n. Scories *f. pl.*; crasses *f. pl.*; mâchefer *m.* (from a blast furnace). ‖ Lave *f.* (volcanic). ‖ **Slag-heap**, n. Terril, crassier *m.*

— v. intr. (1). Se scorifier.

slaggy ['slægi] adj. Scoriacé.

slain [slein]. See SLAY.

slake [sleik] v. tr. Apaiser, étancher (a thirst). [See QUENCH.] ‖ TECHN. Eteindre (lime). ‖ FIG. Assouvir (a desire for revenge).

slakeless ['sleiklis] adj. Inextinguible (thirst). ‖ FIG. Insatiable (desire for revenge).

slalom ['slɑ:lɔm] n. SPORTS. Slalom *m.*

slam [slæm] v. tr. Claquer, faire claquer (a door); *to slam down*, jeter avec violence, flanquer par terre (an object).

— v. intr. Claquer (door). ‖ Faire chelem (or) la vole (at cards).

— n. Claquement *m.* (of a door). ‖ Chelem *m.* (at cards). ‖ U. S. FAM. Succès *m.*

slander ['slɑ:ndə*] n. Calomnie *f.* ‖ JUR. Diffamation *f.*; *slander action*, procès en diffamation.

— v. tr. Calomnier, diffamer.

slanderer [-rə*] n. Calomniateur *m.*; calomniatrice *f.* ‖ JUR. Diffamateur *m.*; diffamatrice *f.*

slanderous [-rəs] adj. Calomnieux, diffamatoire.

slanderously [-rəsli] adv. Calomnieusement.

slang [slæŋ] n. Argot *m.*; langue verte *f.*

— v. tr. FAM. Engueuler; *to slang one another*, s'enguirlander.

slangy [-i] adj. D'argot, argotique (language); argotier, parlant argot (person).

slant [slɑ:nt] n. Pente, inclinaison *f.* ‖ Biais, biseau *m.* ‖ NAUT. *Slant of wind*, petite brise favorable. ‖ U. S. FIG. Point (*m.*) de vue, manière (*f.*) de voir.

— v. intr. Etre en pente, incliner, s'incliner; être oblique (or) de biais.

— v. tr. Incliner, mettre en pente; faire aller obliquement. ‖ U. S. FIG. Donner un biais spécial à (a question).

— adj. Penché, incliné, oblique. ‖ **Slant-eyed**, adj. Aux yeux bridés.

slanting [-iŋ] adj. En pente, incliné; oblique (direction); qui tombe en oblique (rain). ‖ Couché, incliné (handwriting).

slantingly [-iŋli], **slantwise** [-waiz] adv. Obliquement, de biais.

slap [slæp] n. Claque, tape *f.* (on the back). ‖ Gifle, claque, calotte *f.* (in the face).

— v. tr. Donner une claque (or) une tape à; *to slap in the face*, gifler, souffleter, calotter; *to slap on the back*, allonger une tape sur le dos à.

— adv. Tout à coup, tout droit, en plein; *to run slap into*, se heurter en plein contre. ‖ **Slap-bang**, adv. Brusquement, violemment; à corps perdu. ‖ **Slap-dash**, adj. Impétueux, irréfléchi (act, person); bâclé, sans soin (work); adv. d'un seul coup, à la volée. ‖ **Slap-happy**, adj. FAM. Cinglé, toqué. ‖ **Slap-stick**, n. THEATR. Batte (*f.*) d'Arlequin; arlequinades *f. pl.* ‖ **Slap-up**, adj. FAM. Chic, dernier cri (hat); de premier ordre (meal).

slash [slæʃ] n. Entaille, estafilade *f.* ‖ Balafre *f.* (on the face). ‖ Crevé *m.* (in dressmaking).

— v. tr. Frapper à grands coups (with a cane, sword); taillader (to gash). ‖ Balafrer (the face). ‖ Faire des crevés dans (a dress). ‖ Faire claquer (a whip). ‖ Cingler (a horse). ‖ Abattre (trees). ‖ FIN. Réduire (wages). ‖ FIG. Rogner dans, amputer,

taillader (a text); éreinter, esquinter (by criticism);
slashing critic, éreinteur.
— v. intr. Frapper d'estoc et de taille; sabrer, ferrailler. ‖ Frapper à tort et à travers.
slat [slæt] n. Lame, latte, lamelle *f.* ‖ Traverse *f.* (of a bedstead).
slate [sleit] n. Ardoise *f.* ‖ Fig. *Clean slate*, table rase; *policy of the clean slate*, politique du coup d'éponge. ‖ **Slate-blue**, adj., n. Bleu ardoise *m.* ‖ **Slate-clay**, n. Schiste argileux *m.* ‖ **Slate-coloured**, adj. Ardoisé. ‖ **Slate-quarry**, n. Ardoisière *f.*
— adj. Gris ardoise (colour). ‖ Couvert en ardoise (roof).
— v. tr. Couvrir d'ardoises (or) en ardoise. ‖ U. S. Fig. Inscrire sur la liste (a candidate); inscrire au programme (an event).
slate v. tr. Fam. Critiquer, éreinter.
slater [-ə*] n. Couvreur *m.* ‖ Zool. Cloporte *m.*
slattern ['slætə:n] n. Souillon *f.*
slatterliness [-linis] n. Désordre *m.;* malpropreté, saleté *f.*
slatternly [-li] adj. Malpropre, négligé.
slaty ['sleiti] adj. Ardoisier, schisteux (soil). ‖ Ardoisé (slate-coloured).
slaughter ['slɔ:tə*] n. Abattage *m.* (of animals). ‖ Boucherie *f.;* massacre, carnage *m.* (of people). ‖ **Slaughter-house**, n. Abattoir *m.*
— v. tr. Abattre (animals). ‖ Tuer, massacrer, abattre (people).
slaughterer [-rə*] n. Abatteur, assommeur *m.* (of animals). ‖ Tueur, massacreur *m.* (of people).
Slav [slɑ:v] adj., n. Geogr. Slave *s.*
slave [sleiv] n. Esclave *s.; to make a slave of,* réduire en esclavage; *white-slave trade,* traite des blanches. ‖ Fig. *To be a slave to duty,* ne connaître que son devoir. ‖ **Slave-ship**, n. Naut. Négrier *m.* ‖ **Slave-state**, n. Etat esclavagiste *m.* ‖ **Slave-trade**, n. Traite (*f.*) des Noirs. ‖ **Slave-trader**, n. Négrier, marchand (*m.*) d'esclaves.
— v. intr. Fam. Trimer, trimarder, bûcher, buriner.
slaver [-ə*] n. Négrier *m.* ‖ *White-slaver*, proxénète. ‖ Naut. Négrier *m.* (ship).
slaver ['slævə*] v. intr. Med. Baver.
— n. Med. Bave, salive *f.* ‖ Fig. Léchage (*m.*) de bottes.
slavery ['sleivəri] n. Esclavage *m.* ‖ *White slavery*, traite des blanches, proxénétisme. ‖ Fig. Asservissement *m.* (to a habit). ‖ Fam. Travail tuant *m.*
slavery ['slævəri] adj. Med. Baveux. ‖ Fam. De basse flatterie.
slavey ['sleivi] n. Fam. Petite bonne à tout faire, cendrillon *f.*
Slavic ['slɑ:vik] adj. Slave.
— n. Slave *m.* (language).
slavish ['sleiviʃ] adj. D'esclave. ‖ Fig. Vil, bas, abject; servile (imitation).
slavishly [-li] adv. En esclave, servilement.
slavishness [-nis] n. Servilité *f.* ‖ Fig. Bassesse *f.*
Slavonian [slə'vouniǝn] adj., n. Geogr. Slave *s.*
Slavonic [slə'vɔnik] adj. Slave.
— n. Langue slave *f.;* slave, slavon *m.*
slaw [slɔ:] n. U. S. Culin. Salade (*f.*) de choux.
slay [slei] v. tr. (137). Tuer, massacrer, abattre.
slayer [-ə*] n. Tueur, meurtrier *m.*
sleazy ['sli:zi] adj. Mince, léger, de camelote.
sled [sled] n. Traîneau *m.*
— v. intr. Aller en traîneau.
sledge [sledʒ] n. Traîneau *m.* ‖ † Claie *f.* (for executions).
— v. intr. Aller en traîneau.
sledge-hammer [-hæmə*] n. Techn. Marteau de forgeron *m.;* masse *f.*
sleek [sli:k] adj. Lisse, luisant, poli (hair). ‖ Fig. Mielleux, onctueux, doucereux (manner, person).
— v. tr. Lisser, polir.
sleekness [-nis] n. Luisant, poli *m.* ‖ Fig. Onctuosité, onction *f.*

sleep [sli:p] n. Sommeil *m.; to go to sleep,* s'endormir; *to put to sleep,* endormir; *my hand has gone to sleep,* j'ai la main engourdie (or) des fourmis dans la main. ‖ Somme *m.* (nap). ‖ Fig. *Last sleep,* dernier sommeil, éternel repos. ‖ **Sleepwalker**, n. Med. Somnambule *s.* ‖ **Sleep-walking**, n. Med. Somnambulisme *m.*
— v. intr. (138). Dormir, être endormi; *to sleep light,* avoir le sommeil léger. ‖ Coucher; passer la nuit; *to sleep with,* coucher avec. ‖ Dormir de son dernier sommeil (after death). ‖ Fig. *He can't sleep for worrying over it,* il n'en dort plus; *to sleep on a question,* consulter son oreiller; *sleep on it!,* la nuit porte conseil!
— v. tr. Faire coucher; coucher (s.o.). ‖ *To sleep oneself sober,* se dessoûler en dormant, cuver son vin. ‖ Loc. *To sleep the hours away,* passer son temps à dormir; *to sleep the sleep of the just,* dormir du sommeil du juste.
sleeper [-ə*] n. Dormeur *s.; to be a heavy, light sleeper,* avoir le sommeil profond, léger. ‖ Zool. Animal hibernant *m.* ‖ Archit. Gîte *m.* (of a floor); patin *m.* (of a staircase). ‖ Ch. de f. Couchette *f.* (berth); wagon-lit, sleeping *m.* (coach); traverse *f.* (rail). ‖ U. S. Fam. Triomphateur imprévu *m.*
sleepily [-ili] adv. D'un air endormi.
sleepiness [-inis] n. Envie (*f.*) de dormir; somnolence *f.* ‖ Assoupissement *m.*
sleeping [-iŋ] adj. Dormant, endormi. ‖ Comm. *Sleeping partner,* commanditaire, bailleur de fonds.
— n. Sommeil *m.* ‖ **Sleeping-bag**, n. Sac de couchage *m.* ‖ **Sleeping-car**, n. Ch. de f. Wagon-lit, sleeping *m.* ‖ **Sleeping-draught** (or) -**pill**, n. Med. Somnifère *m.* ‖ **Sleeping-sickness**, n. Med. Encéphalite, maladie (*f.*) du sommeil.
sleepless [-lis] adj. Sans sommeil, d'insomnie; *sleepless night,* nuit blanche. ‖ Med. Insomniaque (person). ‖ Fig. Toujours en éveil, inlassable (energy, mind).
sleeplessness [-lisnis] n. Med. Insomnie *f.*
sleepy [-i] adj. Somnolent; *to be sleepy,* avoir sommeil. ‖ Bot. Blet (fruit). ‖ Fig. Inactif, endormi, engourdi. ‖ **Sleepy-head**, n. Endormi; fainéant *m.*
sleet [sli:t] n. Neige fondue *f.;* grésil *m.*
— v. intr. Grésiller, tomber de la neige fondue.
sleety [-i] adj. De grésil.
sleeve [sli:v] n. Manche *f.; short sleeve,* mancheron; *to roll* (or) *turn up one's sleeves,* retrousser ses manches. ‖ Techn. Manchon *m.;* fourreau *m.* (of a cylinder). ‖ Autom. Boîte *f.* (of an axle). ‖ Fig. *To have sth. up one's sleeve,* avoir un atout en réserve; *to laugh up one's sleeve,* rire sous cape. ‖ **Sleeve-board**, n. Jeannette *f.* (ironing); passe-carreau *m.* (tailoring).
sleeveless [-lis] adj. Sans manches.
sleigh [slei] n. Traîneau *m.* ‖ **Sleigh-bell**, n. Grelot *m.;* clochette *f.* ‖ **Sleigh-ride**, n. Promenade (*f.*) en traîneau.
— v. intr. Aller en traîneau.
— v. tr. Transporter en traîneau.
sleight [slait] n. Habileté, adresse, dextérité *f.* ‖ **Sleight-of-hand**, n. Prestidigitation *f.;* tours (*m. pl.*) de passe-passe; escamotage *m.*
slender ['slendə*] adj. Svelte, élancé (figure); délié (hand); menu (person); fin, mince, fluet (waist); *to become slender,* s'amincir. ‖ Fig. Faible (hope); médiocre (intelligence); modique, exigu, modeste (resources).
slenderize [-raiz] v. tr. U. S. Amincir.
slenderness [-nis] n. Minceur, ténuité, sveltesse. ‖ Fig. Faiblesse *f.* (of hope); modicité *f.* (of resources).
sleuth [slu:θ], **sleuth-hound** [-haund] n. Zool. Limier *m.* ‖ U. S. Fam. Détective, limier *m.;* pl. Sûreté *f.* (police).
— v. intr. U. S. Fam. Jouer au détective; filer qqn.

slew [slu:]. See SLAY.
slew v. tr. Faire pivoter. ‖ NAUT. Dériver.
— v. intr. Pivoter, virer.
— n. Mouvement (m.) de rotation sur soi-même.
slew n. U. S. FAM. Tas m.; floppée f.
slice [slais] n. CULIN. Tranche f. (of bread, cake);
aiguillette f. (of chicken); darne f. (of fish); côte,
tranche f. (of melon); round slice, rondelle; slice of
bread and butter, tartine beurrée. ‖ CULIN. Ecu-
moire f. (implement); truelle f. (fish slicer). ‖ TECHN.
Coup en biseau m. ‖ SPORTS. Coup (m.) déviant à
droite (in golf). ‖ FIG. Part f. (of luck).
— v. tr. Découper en tranches. ‖ FIG. Fendre (air,
water).
— v. intr. SPORTS. Faire dévier la balle à droite (in
golf). ‖ **Slice-bar,** n. TECHN. Lance (f.) à feu (for
heating).
slick [slik] adj. Glissant (slippery). ‖ Lisse, luisant
(sleek). ‖ Simple, absolu. ‖ FAM. Habile, adroit;
slick customer, fin matois, fine mouche. ‖ FAM. Chic,
tiré à quatre épingles.
— n. Flaque (f.) de mazout (on the road); nappe
(f.) de mazout (on the sea).
— adv. Vite, vivement, prestement. ‖ Complètement, exactement; to cut slick through, couper net.
— v. tr. TECHN. Lisser.
— v. intr. U. S. FAM. To slick up, se pomponner,
se faire beau.
slicker [-ə*] n. U. S. Imperméable m. ‖ U. S. FAM.
Roublard m.
slide [slaid] v. intr. (139). Glisser (over, sur). ‖ Se
glisser (into or out of a place). ‖ TECHN. Coulisser
(mechanism). ‖ MUS. Passer (melody, voice). ‖ FIG.
Passer insensiblement, glisser, se laisser aller; to
slide over a subject, glisser sur un sujet; to let slide,
laisser aller à la dérive. ‖ FIG. To slide away (or)
by, s'écouler; passer.
— v. tr. Glisser, faire glisser. ‖ TECHN. Lancer
(timber). ‖ FIG. Couler (a glance).
— n. Glissade f.; glissement m. ‖ Eboulement m.
(landslide). ‖ SPORTS. Glissoire f. (for children);
piste inclinée f.; plan de glissement m. (ski-jump).
‖ TECHN. Timber slide, glissoir. ‖ TECHN. Glissement
m. (act); coulant m.; glissière, coulisse (device);
course f. (of a piston). ‖ TECHN. Couvercle (m.) à
coulisse, tiroir m. ‖ PHYS. Plaque f. (of a camera,
microscope); châssis (m.) pour plaques (for viewing); colour, lantern slide, vue en couleurs, de projection. ‖ MATH. Réglette f. (of a slide-rule). ‖ MUS.
Coulé m.; glissade f. (on the violin). ‖ **Slide-box,**
n. TECHN. Boîte (f.) à tiroir. ‖ **Slide-bridge,** n.
Pont roulant m. ‖ **Slide-fastener,** n. Fermeture
(f.) à crémaillère. ‖ **Slide-projector,** n. Projecteur
cinématographique m. ‖ **Slide-rule,** n. MATH. Règle
à calcul. ‖ **Slide-trombone,** n. MUS. Trombone (m.)
à coulisse.
slider [-ə*] n. Glisseur s. (person). ‖ ELECTR. Curseur m. ‖ TECHN. Coulant; coulisseau m.; coulisse f.
sliding [-iŋ] n. Glissement m. ‖ TECHN. Coulisse-
ment m.
— adj. Glissant, à coulisse. ‖ **Sliding-door,** n.
Porte à coulisse f. ‖ **Sliding-panel,** n. Panneau
mobile m. ‖ **Sliding-scale,** n. Echelle mobile f. ‖
Sliding-seat, n. AUTOM. Siège amovible m.; SPORTS.
Banc à glissière (in racing-skiff).
slight [slait] adj. Mince, frêle, menu; élancé, svelte
(figure). ‖ F I G. Insignifiant, peu considérable
(damage); piètre, faible (intelligence); léger (mistake); petit (pause); not the slightest idea, pas la
moindre idée.
— n. Mésestime f.; manque (m.) d'égard; affront m.
— v. tr. Méconnaître (a duty); faire peu de cas de,
manquer d'égards envers (s.o.).
slighting [-iŋ] adj. Méprisant, dédaigneux.
slightly ['slaitli] adv. Légèrement, faiblement, un
peu; slightly built, élancé; frêle.

slightness [-nis] n. Minceur, ténuité f. ‖ Sveltesse
f. (of build). ‖ FIG. Insignifiance f. (of damage);
légèreté f. (of an error); faiblesse f. (of a difference).
slim [slim] adj. Mince, svelte, élancé (figure); to
grow, to make slimmer, s'amincir, amincir. ‖ U. S.
FIG. Léger, mince (chance, hope).
— v. tr. Faire maigrir.
— v. intr. Se faire maigrir; maigrir.
slime [slaim] n. Vase f.; limon m. ‖ Pl. Boues
f. pl.; schlamms m. pl. (in mining). ‖ Bitume liquide
m. ‖ ZOOL. Humeur visqueuse f. (of fish); bave f.
(of snails).
— v. tr. Couvrir de vase.
— v. intr. To slime out of (or) through sth., s'en
tirer par des moyens ignobles (or) en pataugeant
dans la boue.
sliminess [-inis] n. Nature vaseuse (or) visqueuse
f. ‖ FAM. Servilité, obséquiosité f.
slimness ['slimnis] n. Minceur, sveltesse f. ‖ FIG.
Faiblesse f. (of chances).
slimy ['slaimi] adj. Vaseux, limoneux. ‖ Gras
(mud); gluant, visqueux (paste). ‖ FIG. Obséquieux,
mielleux.
sling [sliŋ] n. Fronde f. ‖ Bandoulière, courroie f.
(for carrying); bretelle f. (for a gun). ‖ MED.
Echarpe f. ‖ NAUT. Saisine f.; yard sling, suspente.
‖ TECHN. Elingue, cravate f. (for hoisting). ‖ **Sling-
back,** n. Chaussure à bride, sandale f. ‖ **Sling-shot,**
n. U. S. Lance-pierres m. invar.; fronde f. (toy).
— v. tr. (140). Lancer, jeter. (See TOSS.) ‖ Suspendre au moyen d'une courroie (or) d'une chaîne;
to carry slung over one's shoulder, porter en bandoulière. ‖ TECHN. Elinguer (a cask); brayer, brider
(a stone). ‖ NAUT. Accrocher (a hammock). ‖ U. S.
FAM. To sling it, en débiter (or) raconter.
sling n. Grog au gin (or) au rhum m.
slinger [-ə*] n. Frondeur s. ‖ Lanceur, jeteur s.
(thrower).
slink [sliŋk] v. intr. (141). To slink away (or) off,
s'en aller furtivement.
— v. tr. ZOOL. Avorter.
— n. ZOOL. Avorton m.
slinky [-i] adj Collant (garment).
slip [slip] v. intr. Glisser (by accident); to slip from
s.o.'s grasp, échapper des mains (or) glisser entre
les doigts de qqn. ‖ Entrer furtivement, se glisser,
se couler (into a room); se faufiler (through a
crowd); to slip into a dress, passer (or) enfiler une
robe. ‖ Glisser (or slide along). ‖ TECHN. To slip
home, se fermer à fond (bolt). ‖ FIG. Faire une
erreur (or) un faux pas; faillir; to slip from the
path of virtue, s'écarter du droit chemin; to slip
into bad habits, tomber dans de mauvaises habitudes. ‖ FIG. To slip by, s'échapper (opportunity);
s'écouler (time). ‖ FIG. To slip away (or)
off, s'éclipser, s'esquiver; to let slip, laisser échapper (an opportunity, a remark, secret). ‖ FAM. To
slip along, filer; to slip along to the station, faire
un saut jusqu'à la gare.
— v. tr. Se débarrasser de, se dégager de (a chain);
to slip off, ôter, enlever, retirer; to slip on, mettre,
enfiler, passer (a dress). ‖ Passer (around, autour
de) [one's arm]. ‖ Glisser furtivement, placer
secrètement (into, dans) [sth.]. ‖ ZOOL. Lâcher (a
hound); mettre bas prématurément (its young); to
slip the hounds, laisser courre. ‖ BOT. Couper pour
faire des boutures (a branch). ‖ NAUT. Filer (an
anchor, a cable). ‖ TECHN. Pousser (a bolt). ‖ FIG.
It slipped my memory, j'ai oublié. ‖ FAM. To slip
one over on, jouer une farce à (s.o.).
— n. Glissade f. (slide, sliding). ‖ Combinaison f.;
dessous (m.) de robe (underwear); pillow-slip, taie
d'oreiller. ‖ Bande f.; bout m. (of paper). ‖ Coulant
m. (of a purse). ‖ Placard m. (proof-slip). ‖ BOT.
Bouture f. ‖ NAUT. Cale f.; on the slips, sur cale.
‖ THEATR. Pl. Coulisses f. pl. ‖ ARTS. Barbotine f.
(in ceramics). ‖ SPORTS. Laisse f. (for hounds). ‖

FIG. Erreur, faute *f.*; faux pas *m.*; *slip of the tongue*, lapsus. ‖ FAM. *A mere slip of a girl*, une gamine. ‖ LOC. *To give s.o. the slip*, fausser compagnie à (or) dérouter qqn; *there's many a slip 'twixt the cup and the lip*, il y a loin de la coupe aux lèvres. ‖ **Slip-carriage**, n. CH. DE F. Wagon détaché *m.* ‖ **Slip-cover**, n. Housse *f.* ‖ **Slip-knot**, n. Nœud coulant *m.* ‖ **Slip-over**, adj. A enfiler (dress); n. Pull-over *m.* (jersey, sweater). ‖ **Slip-road**, n. AUTOM. Bretelle *f.* ‖ **Slip-rope**, n. NAUT. Amarre (*f.*) en double. ‖ **Slip-up**, n. Echec, contretemps *m.*; FAM. Gaffe, bévue *f.*

slipper [-ə*] n. Pantoufle *f.*; *Turkish slipper*, babouche. ‖ Chausson *m.* (for babies). ‖ TECHN. Patin *m.* (of a brake). ‖ **Slipper-bath**, n. Baignoire-sabot *f.*

slippered [-əd] adj. En pantoufles.

slipperiness [-ərinis] n. Nature glissante *f.* ‖ FIG. Finasserie, ruse *f.*

slippery [-əri] adj. Glissant (surface). ‖ COMM. Incertain, instable (business). ‖ FIG. Rusé, matois (person); délicat, scabreux (subject).

slippy [-i] adj. POP. Glissant; *to be* (or) *look slippy*, se grouiller.

slipshod [-ʃɔd] adj. En savates. ‖ FIG. Négligé (manner, work).

slipslop [-slɔp] n. Lavasse *f.* ‖ FIG. Fadasserie, mièvrerie *f.* (emotions); littérature sentimentale *f.*; roman rose *m.* (novel).

slipway [-wei] n. NAUT. Cale *f.*

slit [slit] n. Fente, fissure, rainure *f.* ‖ Déchirure *f.* (tear). ‖ Ajour *m.* (in needlework). ‖ MED. Incision *f.*; *to have slits of eyes*, U. S. *to have eyes like slits*, avoir les yeux bridés.
— v. tr. (142). Déchirer (a cloth); éventrer (a sack); *to slit s.o.'s throat*, égorger qqn. ‖ Fendre (a skirt). ‖ TECHN. Refendre (leather); découper en lanières (metal). ‖ MED. Faire une incision dans.
— v. intr. Se fendre, se déchirer; craquer (to split).
— adj. Fendu (skirt). ‖ Déchiré (torn). ‖ **Slit-eyed**, adj. Aux yeux bridés.

slither ['sliðə*] v. intr. Glisser en perdant l'équilibre. ‖ Traîner les pieds. ‖ ZOOL. Onduler (snake).

sliver ['slivə*] n. Petit morceau *m.* (bit); tranche mince *f.* (slice). ‖ Eclat *m.* (splinter). ‖ SPORTS. Amorce *f.* (for bait).
— v. tr. Fendre. ‖ Couper en tranches. ‖ Arracher (*from*, de) [a small piece].
— v. intr. Se fendre; se morceler. ‖ S'arracher; se détacher (*from*, de).

slob [slɔb] n. Vase *f.*; limon *m.* ‖ U. S. FAM. Rustaud (boor); cochon *m.* (dirty pig).

slobber ['slɔbə*] n. MED. Bave, salive *f.* ‖ FIG. Sentimentalisme fade *m.*
— v. tr. MED. Baver sur. ‖ FAM. Bâcler (a job).
— v. intr. MED. Baver. ‖ FIG. Larmoyer, faire preuve de sentimentalisme.

slobbery [-ri] adj. MED. Baveux, mouillé. ‖ FIG. Larmoyant (sentimentality); bâclé (work).

sloe [slou] n. BOT. Prunelle *f.* ‖ **Sloe-gin**, n. Liqueur de prunelle, Prunellia *f.* ‖ **Sloe-tree**, n. BOT. Prunellier *m.*

slog [slɔg] n. Coup violent *m.* ‖ FAM. Corvée *f.*; boulot, turbin *m.*
— v. tr. Frapper dur, taper ferme. ‖ SPORTS. Cogner sur (a boxer).
— v. intr. Frapper à tort et à travers; *to slog along*, marcher d'un pas lourd; *to slog away at*, bûcher.

slogan ['slougən] n. † Cri (*m.*) de guerre. ‖ COMM. Slogan *m.* ‖ FIG. Mot d'ordre *m.*

slogger ['slɔgə*] n. SPORTS. Cogneur. ‖ FAM. Bûcheur, turbineur *m.*

sloop [slu:p] n. NAUT. Petite corvette *f.* (aviso); sloop *m.* (sailing-vessel).

slop [slɔp] n. † Mare (*f.*) de liquide renversé. ‖ Fange, boue *f.* ‖ Pl. Eau sale; lavasse *f.*; rinçures, eaux (*f. pl.*) de vaisselle (or) de toilette. ‖ CULIN.

Pl. Aliments liquides *m. pl.*; lavasse *f.* (drink); bouillon *m.* (soup). ‖ FIG. Sensiblerie *f.*; sentimentalisme *m.* ‖ **Slop-basin**, n. Vide-tasses *m.* ‖ **Slop-pail**, n. Seau (*m.*) de toilette.
— v. intr. (1). Renverser un liquide, faire des saletés en renversant un liquide; *to slop over*, déborder, se renverser (liquide). ‖ FIG. *To slop over*, se répandre en effusions.
— v. tr. Renverser, répandre, faire déborder (a liquid); inonder, salir (a surface).
— n. pl. † Hauts-de-chausses bouffants *m. pl.* ‖ Pl. Vêtements (*m. pl.*) de confection. ‖ NAUT. Effets (*m. pl.*) d'habillement. ‖ **Slop-room**, n. NAUT. Magasin d'habillement *m.* ‖ **Slop-shop**, n. Magasin (*m.*) de confections; friperie *f.* ‖ **Slop-work**, n. Confection *f.*; FAM. Travail bousillé, bousillage *m.*

slop n. POP. Flic, poulet *m.*

slope [sloup] n. Pente, inclinaison, déclivité *f.* ‖ Talus *m.* (continental); versant *m.* (of a hill). ‖ Dénivellation, différence (*f.*) de niveau (of the ground). ‖ Direction oblique *f.*; biais *m.* ‖ CH. DE F. Rampe *f.* ‖ MATH. Pente, inclinaison *f.* (of a curve). ‖ MILIT. *At* (or) *to the slope*, sur l'épaule (rifle).
— v. intr. Etre en pente; pencher, être incliné; *to slope down, up*, descendre, monter. ‖ Etre en biais. ‖ POP. *To slope around, off*, flânocher, décamper.
— v. tr. Pencher, incliner. ‖ Taluter (a ditch); biseauter (a plank); déverser (a wall). ‖ MILIT. *To slope arms*, mettre l'arme sur l'épaule.

sloping [-iŋ] adj. En pente, incliné. ‖ En talus (ground); en déclive (surface). ‖ Oblique, de biais. ‖ Couché (handwriting).

slopingly [-iŋli] adv. En pente, de biais, obliquement.

sloppiness ['slɔpinis] n. Fait (*m.*) d'être inondé de flaques. ‖ Saleté, malpropreté *f.* (of a place, a person); manque d'ordre *m.* (of a person). ‖ FIG. Mollesse *f.* (of character); négligence *f.* (of a style). ‖ FIG. Sentimentalité larmoyante *f.*

sloppy [-i] adj. Boueux, bourbeux, plein de flaques (road); mouillé, inondé (with liquid) [table]. ‖ Trop ample, mal ajusté (garment). ‖ Mou, flasque (person); avachi (waistline). ‖ FAM. Fadasse, larmoyant (literature); négligé, débraillé (method); bâclé (work); *sloppy sentimentality*, sensiblerie.

slosh [slɔʃ]. See SLUSH.

slot [slɔt] n. Cannelure *f.*; fente *f.* (in a money-box). ‖ THEATR. Trappillon *m.* ‖ TECHN. Entaille, encoche, rainure, mortaise *f.*; lumière *f.* (in a piston-wall). ‖ **Slot-machine**, n. Appareil (*m.*) à sous (or) à jetons (for games of chance); distributeur automatique *m.* (for chocolates, cigarettes).
— v. tr. Entailler, encocher, mortaiser. ‖ Tailler une fente dans.

sloth [slouθ] n. Paresse, fainéantise, indolence *f.* ‖ ZOOL. Paresseux *m.*

slothful [-ful] adj. Paresseux, indolent. (See LAZY.)

slothfully [-fuli] adv. Paresseusement, avec indolence.

slouch [slautʃ] v. intr. S'avachir, se négliger, avoir une allure lourde, marcher d'un pas traînant. ‖ Pencher négligemment (head); s'affaisser (épaules).
— v. tr. Rabattre le bord de (a hat).
— n. Démarche lourde, allure mollasse *f.*; *to walk with a slouch*, traîner le pas. ‖ Position rabattue *f.* (of a hat). ‖ POP. Maladroit *m.* ‖ **Slouch-hat**, n. Chapeau mou (or) rabattu *m.*

sloucher [-ə*] n. Lourdaud, fainéant; avachi *m.*

slough [slau] n. Bourbier *m.*; fondrière *f.* ‖ FIG. *Slough of despond*, abîme du désespoir.

slough [slʌf] n. ZOOL. Dépouille *f.* (of a reptile). ‖ MED. Escarre *f.*
— v. intr. ZOOL. Muer (reptile). ‖ MED. S'escarrifier.
— v. tr. ZOOL. Se dépouiller de (the skin). ‖ FIG. *To slough off*, se débarrasser de (a habit).

sloughy ['slaui] adj. Boueux, marécageux.
sloughy ['slʌfi] adj. ZooL. Pareil à une dépouille de serpent. ‖ MED. Couvert d'une escarre.
Slovak ['slouvæk] adj., n. GEOGR. Slovaque s.
sloven ['slʌvn̩] n. Souillon f. ‖ FAM. Bousilleur m.
Slovene ['slouvi:n], **Slovenian** [slo'vi:njən] adj., n. GEOGR. Slovène s.
slovenliness ['slʌvənlinis] n. Saleté, malpropreté f.; laisser-aller, manque (m.) de tenue. ‖ Négligence f.; manque de soin m. (in work).
slovenly [-li] adj. Sale, malpropre, mal tenu. ‖ Négligent, sans soin. ‖ FIG. Débraillé (style); bousillé (work).
slow [slou] adj. Lent; paresseux (current); ralenti (pace); *slow speed*, petite vitesse. ‖ Qui met du temps à, long à (person); *to be slow in doing*, tarder à faire. ‖ Lent à comprendre, d'esprit lourd; arriéré (backward). ‖ En retard (clock); *to be five minutes slow*, retarder de cinq minutes. ‖ MED. Lent, paresseux (digestion); rare (pulse). ‖ CH. DE F. Omnibus (train). ‖ FIG. Ennuyeux, qui manque d'entrain. ‖ FAM. Rasant (conversation); endormi (village). ‖ Slow-coach, U. S. Slow-poke, n. Lambin m.; chenille, tortue f. (fam.). ‖ Slow-down, adj. Perlé (strike). ‖ Slow-match, n. TECHN. Mèche à combustion f. ‖ Slow-motion, n. CINEM. Ralenti m. (film). ‖ Slow-witted, adj. A l'esprit lourd, de compréhension lente. ‖ Slow-worm, adj. ZooL. Orvet m.
— adv. Lentement, doucement; *to go slow*, faire la grève perlée.
— v. intr. **To slow down** (or) **up**, ralentir, diminuer de vitesse; FIG. mollir (person).
— v. tr. **To slow down** (or) **up**, ralentir, ralentir la marche de; **slowing down**, décélération.
slowly [-li] adv. Lentement, avec lenteur. ‖ AUTOM. *Drive slowly*, au pas!, ralentir!
slowness [-nis] n. Lenteur f. ‖ Retard m. (of a clock). ‖ Stagnation f. (of a compass). ‖ FIG. Intelligence lente; lenteur (f.) d'esprit. ‖ FAM. Manque d'entrain m. (of a conversation, a town).
slub [slʌb] v. tr. Boudiner (wool).
— n. Laine boudinée f.
sludge [slʌdʒ] n. Vase, fange f. ‖ TECHN. Boue f.
sludgy [-i] adj. Vaseux, bourbeux, fangeux. ‖ TECHN. Boueux.
slue [slu:]. [See SLEW.
slug [slʌg] n. MILIT., TECHN. Lingot m. ‖ Ligne-block f. (in linotype). ‖ U. S. Jeton m. (for telephones, slot-machines). ‖ U. S. FAM. Bon coup m. (hard blow); goutte f. (of whisky).
slug v. tr. U. S. FAM. Tabasser.
slug n. ZooL. Limace f. ‖ Slug-a-bed, n. FAM. Cossard, flemmard m.
sluggard [-ə:d] n. Paresseux, fainéant m.
sluggish [-iʃ] adj. Paresseux, fainéant, mou (person); paresseux (river). [See INDOLENT.] ‖ MED. Engorgé, paresseux (liver); lent (pulse).
sluggishly [-iʃli] adv. Paresseusement.
sluggishness [-iʃnis] n. Paresse, fainéantise, mollesse f. (of s.o.); lenteur f. (of a stream). ‖ MED. Engorgement m.; paresse f. (of the liver); lenteur f. (of the pulse).
sluice [slu:s] n. Ecluse f.; bonde f. (of a pond); pale f. (of a reservoir). ‖ Canal (m.) de décharge (for overflow); bief m. (of a water-mill). ‖ Masse d'eau (f.) contenue par une vanne. ‖ Sluice m. (in gold-mining). ‖ Rinçage (m.) à grande eau. ‖ Sluice-gate (or) -valve, n. Vanne f.
— v. tr. Vanner; lâcher les vannes de (a reservoir). ‖ Rincer, laver à grande eau. ‖ Débourber (a sewer). ‖ Munir d'une vanne.
— v. intr. **To sluice out**, couler (or) se répandre à flots.
slum [slʌm] n. Taudis m. ‖ Pl. Bas quartiers m. pl.; zone f. ‖ Slum-clearance, n. Abolissement (m.) des taudis.
— v. intr. Visiter les taudis.

slumber ['slʌmbə*] n. Sommeil, assoupissement; somme m.; *to fall into a slumber*, s'endormir, s'assoupir. (See SLEEP.)
— v. intr. Dormir; sommeiller, être assoupi.
slumberous [-rəs] adj. Somnolent, assoupi (sleepy). ‖ Qui invite au sommeil, endormant (soporific). ‖ FIG. Endormi (town).
slummer ['slʌmə*] n. Visiteur (s.) des taudis.
slummy [-i] adj. De taudis (area); sordide (street).
slump [slʌmp] n. FIN. Effondrement m. (in prices); dégringolade f. (of exchange rates). ‖ COMM. Dépression f.; *slump in business*, crise des affaires.
— v. intr. Tomber lourdement; *to slump down on a sofa*, s'écrouler sur un divan. ‖ FIN. S'effondrer, dégringoler (fam.) [prices].
slur [slə:*] v. tr. (1). Mal articuler (or) prononcer. ‖ Maculer (type). ‖ MUS. Lier (notes); couler (a passage). ‖ FIG. Dire du mal de, déconsidérer, déprécier. ‖ **To slur over**, passer sous silence, glisser sur (a detail).
— v. intr. Bredouiller. ‖ S'estomper, se brouiller (outline, silhouette). ‖ MUS. Lier.
— n. Bredouillement m.; mauvaise articulation f. ‖ Macule f. (in typesetting). ‖ MUS. Liaison f.; coulé m. ‖ FIG. Insinuation malveillante; insulte f., affront (insult); tache f. (on a reputation); *to cast a slur on*, porter atteinte à la réputation de.
slurp [slə:p] v. tr. FAM. Manger (or) boire bruyamment.
— n. FAM. Borborygme m.
slurry ['slʌri] n. Boue f.; coulis m. (of cement); schlamm m. (of coal dust).
slush [slʌʃ] n. Boue liquide f.; neige à demi fondue f.; gadoue f. ‖ FIG. Sentimentalité larmoyante f. ‖ Slush fund, n. U. S. Fonds secrets (m. pl.) destinés à verser des pots-de-vin, caisse noire f.
— v. intr. **To slush around**, patauger, barboter (in mud).
slushy [-i] adj. Boueux, bourbeux; couvert de neige fondante. ‖ FAM. D'une sentimentalité fadasse.
slut [slʌt] n. Souillon, salope f. (slattern). ‖ Coureuse, catin f. (trollop).
sluttish [-iʃ] adj. Sale, malpropre. ‖ De salope.
sly [slai] adj. Rusé, adroit, fin. ‖ Malin, espiègle. ‖ Sournois, en dessous; en cachette, en secret (act); *on the sly*, sans rien dire à personne, en tapinois. ‖ FAM. Sly dog, fin matois, rusé compère; *sly minx*, fine mouche (or) lame. ‖ Sly-boots, n. FAM. Petit coquin, espiègle; finaud s.
slyly [-li] adv. Adroitement, avec finesse (or) ruse. ‖ Sournoisement, en cachette. ‖ Malicieusement, ironiquement.
slyness [-nis] n. Finesse, ruse f. ‖ Sournoiserie f. ‖ Malice, espièglerie f.
smack [smæk] n. NAUT. Bateau (m.) de pêche.
smack n. Léger goût, arrière-goût. ‖ Bouquet m. (of a liqueur). ‖ FIG. Soupçon, grain m.; trace f.
— v. intr. **To smack of**, avoir un léger goût (or) arrière-goût de, sentir. ‖ FIG. *To smack of,* donner une impression de, sentir.
smack n. Claquement m. (of lips, a whip). ‖ Tape f. (with the hand); gifle f.; soufflet m. (slap). ‖ FAM. Gros baiser, bécot m. (kiss).
— v. tr. Faire claquer (one's lips, a whip). ‖ Taper, claquer (with the hand); gifler, donner une claque à (to slap).
— v. intr. Claquer, retentir (kiss).
— adv. En plein, vlan!, paf!
smacker [-ə*] n. FAM. Claque (or) gifle retentissante f. ‖ FAM. Gros baiser, bécot m., bise f. ‖ POP. Livre f.; dollar m.
smacking [-iŋ] adj. Qui claque. ‖ Vigoureux, énergique. ‖ Bon, frais (breeze).
small [smɔ:l] adj. Petit; exigu (area); modique (income); fluet (voice); menu (waist); *small letters*, minuscules. ‖ Petit, peu nombreux; restreint (com-

mittee) ; *in small numbers,* en petit nombre. ‖ De courte durée ; *a small time,* peu de temps. ‖ COMM. *Small change,* petite monnaie ; *small shopkeeper,* petit commerçant. ‖ NAUT. *Small craft,* canots, barques. ‖ CULIN. Léger. ‖ MILIT. Menu (shot). ‖ FIG. Peu important, insignifiant, léger, faible ; *small matter,* question insignifiante, bagatelle ; *small wonder,* guère (or) pas étonnant. ‖ FIG. Petit, mesquin, peu généreux ; *it is small of her,* c'est mesquin de sa part. ‖ FIG. Humble, obscur ; *small people,* petites gens ; *to live in a small way,* avoir un train de maison réduit, vivre modestement. ‖ FAM. Penaud ; *to feel small,* n'être pas fier, être dans ses petits souliers ; *to look small,* avoir l'air penaud ; *to make s.o. feel small,* rabattre le caquet à qqn ; *to make oneself small,* rentrer la tête dans les épaules. ‖ LOC. *Small fry,* menu fretin ; *small hours,* petit matin ; *small talk,* papotage, menus propos. ‖ **Small-arms,** n. pl. MILIT. Armes portatives *f. pl.* ‖ **Small-clothes,** n. pl. † Culotte collante *f.* ‖ **Small-minded,** adj. A l'esprit mesquin. ‖ **Small-scale,** adj. Réduit (model). ‖ **Small-sword,** n. SPORTS. Epée d'escrime, rapière *f.* ‖ **Small-time,** adj. U. S. FAM. De troisième ordre. ‖ **Small-town-ish,** adj. Provincial. ‖ **Small-wares,** n. pl. Mercerie *f.*
— n. MED. *Small of the back,* chute des reins, bas du dos. ‖ Pl. Menu *m.* (coal). ‖ Pl. Examen préliminaire *(m.)* d'admissibilité à Oxford.
— adv. Menu, en petits caractères (writing). ‖ LOC. *To sing small,* déchanter, baisser le ton.

smallish [-iʃ] adj. Plutôt petit ; petiot (person).
smallness [-nis] n. Petitesse *f.* (of dimensions). ‖ Exiguïté *f.* (of an area) ; modicité *f.* (of an amount). ‖ FIG. *Smallness of mind,* mesquinerie, petitesse d'esprit. ‖ FIG. Petitesse, insignifiance *f. ;* peu *(m.)* d'importance.
smallpox [-pɔks] n. MED. Petite vérole, variole *f.*
smalt [smɔlt] n. Smalt *m.*
smaltine ['smɔltain] n. Smaltine *f.*
smarm [smɑ:m] v. tr. FAM. Faire de la lèche à. ‖ **To smarm down,** aplatir (one's hair).
smarmy ['smɑ:mi] adj. FAM. Flagorneur, lèche-bottes (person) ; obséquieux, suave (manners).
smart [smɑ:t] n. Cinglure *f.* (of a lash). ‖ MED. Douleur cuisante *f.* ‖ FIG. Cinglure (*f.*) (of an insult).
— adj. Vif, cinglant, cuisant (blow, lash) ; sec (blow, stroke). ‖ Vif, vigoureux, énergique ; *smart box on the ear,* bonne gifle ; *to go at a smart pace,* aller bon pas ; *smart reprimand,* verte semonce. ‖ Alerte, éveillé ; habile, adroit, débrouillard, dégourdi (fam.) ; rusé, madré (pejorative) ; *to act smart,* faire le malin ; *smart answer,* réponse spirituelle (or) bien envoyée ; *smart practice,* conduite peu scrupuleuse, escroquerie ; *smart trick,* bon tour ; truc ingénieux. ‖ MED. Cuisant (pain). ‖ U. S. FAM. Formidable. ‖ FAM. Elégant, chic, coquet, pimpant (dress) ; dernier cri, à la mode (fad) ; stylé (servant) ; *smart set* (or) *society,* beau monde, monde chic ; haute gomme *f.,* gratin *m.* (fam.) ; *Parisian smart set,* le Tout-Paris. ‖ **Smart-Alec,** n. FAM. Poseur, m'as-tu-vu, gommeux *m.*
— v. intr. MED. Picoter (eyes) ; éprouver une douleur cuisante (person) ; cuire, brûler (wound). ‖ FIG. *To smart under,* souffrir de (an injustice) ; ressentir vivement (an insult) ; *you'll smart for this,* il vous en cuira.
smarten [-n] v. tr. Embellir, donner du chic à (a dress) ; *to smarten oneself up,* se faire beau, se pomponner, se bichonner. ‖ FAM. Dégourdir, dégrossir, déluter (s.o.).
— v. intr. **To smarten up,** s'embellir, prendre du chic. ‖ FAM. Se dégourdir, se dégrossir, se déniaiser, se déluter.
smarting [-iŋ] n. Sensation de brûlure, douleur cuisante *f. ;* picotement *m.* (of the eyes).
smartly [-li] adv. Promptement, vivement ; preste-

ment (at a fast pace). ‖ Vigoureusement, énergiquement ; violemment. ‖ Adroitement, habilement ; finement, spirituellement (wittily). ‖ Elégamment, coquettement, avec chic.
smartness [-nis] n. Violence *f.* (of a blow, lashing). ‖ Vivacité, prestesse *f.* (of a gesture). ‖ Intelligence, habileté *f.* (cleverness). ‖ Finesse *f.* (of mind) ; à-propos, esprit *m.* (of a reply). ‖ Elégance, coquetterie *f. ;* chic *m.* (style).
smash [smæʃ] n. Fracassement *m. ; to fall with a smash,* tomber avec un fracas terrible. ‖ AUTOM., CH. DE F. Collision *f. ;* tamponnement *m.* ‖ FIN. Faillite ; débâcle ; déconfiture *f. ;* krach *m.* ‖ U. S. *Brandy smash,* cognac glacé à la menthe. ‖ SPORTS. Smash *m.* (tennis). ‖ **Smash-and-grab,** adj. FAM. *Smash-and-grab robbery,* vol avec bris de vitrine. ‖ **Smash-up,** n. AUTOM., CH. DE F. Collision *f.*
— v. tr. Briser, fracasser, réduire en miettes. ‖ MILIT. Détruire, démolir, anéantir (the enemy). ‖ SPORTS. Smasher (a tennis ball). ‖ FIG. Ecraser, ruiner ; pulvériser (a record).
— v. intr. Eclater (or) s'écraser en morceaux, se briser ; se fracasser. ‖ AUTOM. *To smash into,* emboutir. ‖ FIN. Faire faillite, s'effondrer.
— adv. FIN. *To go smash,* faire faillite. ‖ AUTOM. *To run smash into,* s'emboutir contre.
— adj. THEATR. *To be a smash hit,* avoir un succès fou.
smasher [-ə*] n. Briseur, écraseur *m.* ‖ Coup *(m.)* de massue (blow) ; chute (or) collision fracassante *f.* (smash). ‖ FIG. Argument-massue *m.*
smashing [-iŋ] adj. FAM. Terrible, formidable, super, extra.
smattering ['smætəriŋ] n. Connaissance superficielle *f. ;* notions *f. pl.*
smear [smiə*] n. Tache, souillure *f. ;* barbouillage *m.* ‖ FIG. Atteinte (*f.*) à la réputation ; *smear campaign,* campagne de calomnies.
— v. tr. Tacher, salir, souiller. ‖ Etaler (an ink stain). ‖ Enduire, barbouiller (with, de) [to coat]. ‖ FIG. Salir (s.o.)
— v. intr. S'estomper (outline) ; s'étaler (stain). (See SMUDGE.)
smeary [-ri] adj. Taché, barbouillé. ‖ Graisseux, gras.
smectite ['smektait] n. Smectite *f.*
smell [smel] n. Odeur ; senteur *f. ;* parfum *m.* (aroma) ; mauvaise odeur *f.* (stench). ‖ MED. Odorat *m.* (sense) ; *keen sense of smell,* odorat fin. ‖ ZOOL. Flair, nez *m.* (of a hound). ‖ CULIN. Fumet *m.* (of wine).
— v. tr. (143). Sentir, humer, flairer, respirer le parfum de. ‖ MED. Avoir l'odorat fin. ‖ FAM. *To smell a rat,* se douter de qqch., flairer quelque anguille sous roche ; *to smell trouble,* avoir le nez creux. ‖ FAM. **To smell out,** découvrir en flairant ; détecter, dépister.
— v. intr. Sentir, avoir un parfum ; sentir mauvais ; *to smell of,* sentir ; *to smell sweet,* sentir bon. ‖ MED. Avoir bon odorat. ‖ FIG. *To smell of,* sentir, fleurer, avoir les apparences de, suggérer la pensée de.
smeller [-ə*] n. Flaireur *s.* ‖ Chose (or) personne (*f.*) qui sent mauvais. ‖ POP. Pif, blair *m.* (nose).
smelliness [-inis] n. Mauvaise odeur, puanteur *f.*
smelling-salts [-iŋsɔlts] n. Sels volatils *m. pl.*
smelly [-i] adj. Malodorant, puant.
smelt [smelt] v. tr. TECHN. Extraire par fusion (metal) ; fondre (ore).
smelt n. ZOOL. Eperlan *m.*
smelt pret., p. p. See SMELL.
smidgen, smidgin ['smidʒən] n. U. S. FAM. Chouia *m.,* larme *f.* (drink) ; miette *f.* (food).
smile [smail] v. intr. Sourire (at, on, à). ‖ **To smile at,** FIG. Sourire de, montrer du mépris pour. ‖ **To smile on** (or) **upon,** FIG. Sourire à, être favorable à.
— v. tr. Exprimer par un sourire ; *to smile one's*

encouragement, encourager par un sourire. ‖ Sourire de (in a certain manner) ; *to smile a sad smile,* sourire tristement, avoir un sourire triste. ‖ **To smile away,** dissiper en souriant, écarter d'un sourire.
— n. Sourire *m. ; with a smile,* avec un sourire, en souriant.

smilingly [-iŋli] adv. En souriant.

smirch [smə:tʃ] v. tr. Tacher, salir, souiller. ‖ Noircir (to blacken).
— n. Tache, salissure, souillure *f.* ‖ Noircissure *f.*

smirk [smə:k] n. Sourire affecté (or) niais *m. ;* minauderie *f.*
— v. intr. Sourire d'un air affecté ; minauder.

smite [smait] v. tr. (144). Férir. ‖ Frapper. ‖ Venir à (the mind). ‖ Eccles. Battre, vaincre. ‖ Fig. *To be smitten with,* être pris de (ambition, desire) ; être affligé de (remorse) ; être épris de, se coiffer de (s.o.) ; être frappé de (terror). ‖ **To smite down,** abattre.
— v. intr. *To smite together,* s'entrechoquer. ‖ **To smite on** (or) **upon,** frapper (or) tomber (or) venir battre sur.
— n. Coup *m.* ‖ Fam. Essai *m. ;* tentative *f.*

smiter [-ə*] n. Frappeur *s.*

smith [smiθ] n. Forgeron *m. ; shoeing smith,* maréchal-ferrant ; *smith's shop,* forge, maréchalerie.

smithereens [smiðəˈri:ns] n. pl. Morceaux *m. pl.,* miettes *f. pl. ; to smash to smithereens,* briser en mille morceaux ; mettre en capilotade (fam.).

smithy ['smiði] n. Forge *f. ; shoeing smithy,* maréchalerie.

smitten ['smitn]. See SMITE.

smock [smɔk] n. † Chemise *f.* (woman's). ‖ Tablier *m.* (child's) ; blouse *f.* (peasant's) ; blouse-tablier *f.,* sarrau *m.* (woman's).

smocking ['smɔkiŋ] n. Fronces *f. pl. ;* smocks *m. pl. ;* nids (*m. pl.*) d'abeilles.

smog [smɔg] n. Brouillard fumeux *m.*

smoke [smouk] n. Fumée *f.* ‖ Fam. Cigarette *f.,* cigare *m.* ‖ Fig. *To go up in smoke,* piquer une colère bleue ; *to end in smoke,* n'aboutir à rien. ‖ **Smoke-bell** (or) **-consumer,** n. Fumivore *m.* ‖ **Smoke-black,** n. Noir (*m.*) de fumée. ‖ **Smoke-bomb,** n. Bombe fumigène *f.* ‖ **Smoke-dried,** adj. Fumé. ‖ **Smoke-free,** adj. Désenfumé. ‖ **Smoke-grey,** adj., n. Gris fumé *m.* ‖ **Smoke-helmet,** n. Casque (*m.*) pare-fumée. ‖ **Smoke-sail,** n. Naut. Masque (*m.*) à fumée. ‖ **Smoke-screen,** n. Rideau (*m.*) de fumée. ‖ **Smoke-stack,** n. Naut., Ch. de F. Cheminée *f.*
— v. intr. Fumer. ‖ Se fumer (cigar, cigarette). ‖ Fam. Fumer (with anger).
— v. tr. Fumer. ‖ Enfumer, noircir de fumée (to blacken or fill with smoke) ; *smoked glasses,* verres fumés. ‖ Culin. Fumer (fish, ham) ; boucaner (meat). ‖ Fam. Griller (a cigarette) ; avoir des soupçons sur (s.o.) ; détecter, flairer, soupçonner (sth.). ‖ **To smoke out,** enfumer (insects).

smokeless [-lis] adj. Sans fumée.

smoker [-ə*] n. Fumeur *s.* ‖ Ch. de F. Compartiment (*m.*) de fumeurs.

smokiness [-inis] n. Etat (or) aspect fumeux *m. ;* atmosphère fumeuse *f.* ‖ Culin. Goût (*m.*) de fumée.

smoking [-iŋ] adj. Fumant.
— n. Emission de fumée *f.* ‖ Action (*f.*) de fumer ; *no smoking,* défense de fumer. ‖ Fumigation, action (*f.*) d'enfumer (insects). ‖ Culin. Fumage *m.* ‖ **Smoking-carriage,** (or) U. S. **-car,** n. Ch. de F. Voiture (*m.*) de fumeurs. ‖ **Smoking-compartment,** n. Ch. de F. Compartiment (*m.*) pour fumeurs. ‖ **Smoking-jacket,** n. Veston d'intérieur *m.* ‖ **Smoking-mixture,** n. Mélange *m.* de tabacs. ‖ **Smoking-room,** n. Fumoir *m.*

smoky [-i] adj. Fumeux (atmosphere) ; brumeux

(horizon). ‖ Qui fume (chimney). ‖ Rempli de fumée, enfumé (city). ‖ Noirci par la fumée, enfumé (surface).

smolder ['smouldə*] v. intr., n. U. S. See SMOULDER.

smolt [smoult] n. Zool. Jeune saumon *m.*

smooch [smu:tʃ] v. intr. Fam. Se bécoter, se faire des mamours.

smooching [-iŋ] n. Fam. Bécotage *m. ;* fricassée (*f.*) de museaux.

smooth ꞁsmu:ðꞁ adj. Sans aspérités (or) rugosités ; lisse (bark, hair) ; sans rides (brow) ; poli (glass). ‖ Soyeux, moelleux (pelt) ; doux (skin). ‖ Imberbe (hair-free). ‖ Techn. Doux, régulier (mechanism). ‖ Naut. Calme, uni, plat (sea) ; par mer calme (voyage). ‖ Culin. Moelleux (taste, wine). ‖ Fig. Coulant, facile (style). ‖ Fig. Flatteur, caressant, doucereux (language) ; doux, onctueux, mielleux (voice). ‖ Fig. Sans heurts, paisible (life) ; poli, aimable (manner) ; facile, égal (temper). ‖ **Smooth-bore,** n. Milit. Fusil (*m.*) à canon lisse ; canon (*m.*) à âme lisse. ‖ **Smooth-chinned,** adj. Imberbe ; rasé de près. ‖ **Smooth-cut,** n. Taille douce *f.* (of a file). ‖ **Smooth-faced,** adj. Imberbe ; Fig. A l'air patelin (or) mielleux. ‖ **Smooth-running,** adj. A marche douce (or) régulière. ‖ **Smooth-shaven,** adj. Rasé de près. ‖ **Smooth-spoken** (or) **-tongued,** adj. Aux paroles doucereuses ; patelin ; enjôleur. ‖ **Smooth-tempered,** adj. Au caractère égal.
— n. Partie lisse *f.* ‖ Action (*f.*) de lisser. ‖ Naut. Accalmie, embellie *f.*
— v. tr. (also **smoothe**). Lisser (feathers, hair) ; égaliser (a surface) ; planer, aplanir (wood). ‖ Adoucir (an angle) ; Dérider (one's brow) ; effacer (wrinkles). ‖ Fig. Adoucir, rendre moins pénible (an existence) ; aplanir, niveler, enlever les obstacles de (a way) ; *to smooth away* (or) *over,* aplanir (difficulties). ‖ **To smooth down,** Fig. apaiser, calmer. ‖ **To smooth over,** Fig. pallier, atténuer, voiler.
— v. intr. **To smooth down,** se calmer, s'apaiser.

smoothie [-i] n. U. S. Fam. Chattemite *f. ;* flagorneur *m.*

smoothing [-iŋ] n. Lissage *m.* (of feathers) ; égalisation *f.* (of a surface) ; aplanissage *m.* (of wood). ‖ **Smoothing-iron,** n. Fer à repasser *m.* ‖ **Smoothing-plane,** n. Rabot *m.*

smoothly [-li] adv. Doucement, sans secousses (gently). ‖ Uniment, sans inégalités (evenly).

smoothness [-nis] n. Douceur *f. ;* satiné *m.* (of skin) ; égalité *f.* (of a surface). ‖ Techn. Bon fonctionnement *m.* (of an engine) ; douceur *f.* (of a mechanical function). ‖ Naut. Calme *m.* (of the sea). ‖ Fig. Air doucereux *m.* (of s.o.) ; coulant *m.* (of a style).

smote [smout] pret. See SMITE.

smother ['smʌðə*] n. Brouillard épais *m. ;* nuage (*m.*) de fumée (or) de poussière. ‖ Cendres fumantes *f. pl.*
— v. tr. Etouffer, suffoquer. ‖ Couvrir (a fire). ‖ Eteindre, étouffer (a noise) ; retenir (a scream) ; étouffer (a yawn). [See STIFLE.] ‖ Fig. Etouffer (a scandal) ; accabler (with, de) [s.o.] ; *to smother with attention,* accabler de prévenances.
— v. intr. Etre étouffé, suffoquer.

smothering [-riŋ] n. Etouffement *m. ;* suffocation *f.* ‖ Fig. Suppression *f.* (of liberty).
— adj. Suffocant, écrasant. [See STIFLING.]

smoulder ['smouldə*] v. intr. Couver (lit. and fig.).
— n. Feu (*m.*) qui couve ; combustion lente *f.*

smudge [smʌdʒ] v. tr. Salir, tacher, souiller, barbouiller. ‖ Brouiller (an outline). ‖ Agric. Protéger par un feu fumigène (an orchard). ‖ Fig. Ternir, salir (a reputation).
— v. intr. Baver (ink) ; se brouiller (outline) ; s'écraser (pencil mark). [See SMEAR.]
— n. Petite tache, saleté *f. ;* barbouillage *m.* ‖ Agric. Feu fumigène *m.*

smug [smʌg] adj. Suffisant, béat (expression) ; content (or) satisfait de soi (person).

smuggle ['smʌgl̩] v. tr. Faire passer en contrebande (or) en fraude. ‖ **To smuggle away** (or) **out**, escamoter, faire disparaître.
— v. intr. Faire la contrebande ; frauder.

smuggler [-ə*] n. Contrebandier, fraudeur m.

smuggling [-iŋ] n. Contrebande, fraude f.

smugness [-nis] n. Suffisance f. ; contentement de soi ; air avantageux m.

smut [smʌt] n. Flocon (m.) [or] tache (f.) de suie. ‖ AGRIC. Charbon m. ; suie, nielle f. (on wheat). ‖ FIG. Grivoiseries f. pl.
— v. tr. Tacher de suie ; noircir.
— v. intr. AGRIC. Se nieller (wheat).

smuttiness [-inis] n. Saleté, noirceur f. ‖ AGRIC. Niellure f. ‖ FIG. Grossièreté, grivoiserie f.

smutty [-i] adj. Taché de suie ; sale, noirci. ‖ AGRIC. Niellé (wheat). ‖ FIG. Grossier, obscène, grivois.

snack [snæk] n. Part, portion f. ‖ CULIN. Repas léger, goûter ; casse-croûte m. ; dînette f. ‖ **Snack-bar,** m. Snack-bar m.
— v. intr. Casser la croûte, manger sur le pouce.

snaffle ['snæfl̩] n. SPORTS. Filet m.
— v. tr. POP. Chiper, chaparder. ‖ POP. Pincer, arrêter (a thief).

snafu ['snæfu] n. U. S. FAM. Micmac, gâchis m. ; salade f.

snag [snæg] n. AGRIC. Moignon m. (of a branch) ; chicot m. (stump). ‖ MED. Chicot m. (of a tooth). ‖ NAUT. Chicot m. (tree). ‖ Fil tiré m. (in a stocking). ‖ FIG. Ecueil, obstacle, hic m. ; pierre (f.) d'achoppement.
— v. tr. (1). Accrocher (a stocking). ‖ NAUT. Heurter, toucher (a submerged obstacle) ; mettre en état de navigation (a waterway). ‖ AGRIC. Essoucher (a field).

snaggy [-i] adj. NAUT. Semé d'obstacles immergés. ‖ AGRIC. Hérissé de souches.

snail ['sneil] n. ZOOL. Escargot, colimaçon m. ‖ LOC. At a snail's pace, à pas de tortue.

snake [sneik] n. ZOOL. Serpent m. ; common (or) grass snake, couleuvre. ‖ LOC. Snake in the grass, serpent caché sous les fleurs ; to cherish a snake in one's bosom, réchauffer un serpent dans son sein. ‖ **Snake-charmer,** n. Charmeur (s.) de serpents. ‖ **Snake fence,** n. U. S. Clôture (f.) en lattes croisées. ‖ **Snake-like,** adj. Anguiforme, ophidien. ‖ **Snake-root,** n. BOT. Serpentaire f. ‖ **Snake-stone,** n. Ammonite f. ‖ **Snake-weed,** n. BOT. Bistorte f.
— v. intr., v. tr. Serpenter.

snaky [-i] adj. Infesté de serpents. ‖ ZOOL. De serpent, couleuvrin. ‖ FIG. Serpentant, sinueux.

snap [snæp] v. tr. Casser net, briser (or) rompre avec un bruit sec. ‖ Fermer avec un bruit sec ; to snap shut, fermer brusquement. ‖ Happer (or) saisir (or) enlever d'un coup de dents. ‖ Prendre un instantané de (in photography). ‖ To snap one's fingers, faire claquer les doigts ; to snap one's fingers at, narguer, faire la nique à (s.o.) ; se moquer de (a danger, threat). ‖ **To snap off,** enlever (by biting) ; briser (by grasping) ; FAM. To snap s.o.'s nose off, manger le nez à qqn. ‖ **To snap out,** exprimer avec aigreur ; donner d'un ton sec (an order) ; to snap out of it, se remettre d'aplomb. ‖ **To snap up,** happer, ramasser vivement ; FIG. Enlever (a bargain) ; interrompre brusquement, reprendre sèchement (s.o.).
— v. intr. Casser net, se briser, rompre. ‖ Se fermer avec un bruit sec (clasp). ‖ Partir (pistol) ; claquer (whip). ‖ Faire mine de mordre. ‖ **To snap at,** chercher à mordre, donner un coup de dents à ; FIG. Se jeter sur, sauter sur (an opportunity) ; parler sur un ton hargneux à, reprendre avec aigreur (s.o.). ‖ **To snap off,** se briser, se détacher subitement.

— n. Cassure, rupture soudaine f. ‖ Bruit sec m. ; claquement m. (of the fingers, a whip). ‖ Coup (m.) de dents ; mouvement brusque (m.) pour mordre ; to make a snap at, tenter de mordre. ‖ Bouchée f. ; morceau m. (bite). ‖ Chiquenaude f. (of the fingers). ‖ Agrafe f. (of a bracelet) ; bouton-pression, pression f. (on a dress) ; fermoir m. (on a purse). ‖ Cold snap, froid brusque, courte période de froid. ‖ Jeu (m.) de cartes enfantin. ‖ Instantané m. (photograph). ‖ CULIN. Petit gâteau sec, biscuit croquant m. ‖ THEATR. Engagement (m.) de courte durée. ‖ FIG. Vivacité, prestesse f. (of gait) ; brio m. (of style). ‖ U. S. FAM. Jeu d'enfant, coup facile m.
— adj. Inopiné, imprévu, à l'improviste, au pied levé. ‖ Pris sans réflexion (decision). ‖ U. S. FAM. Facile ; snap course, cours tout mâché. ‖ **Snap-bolt,** n. Verrou (m.) automatique (or) à ressort. ‖ **Snap-link,** n. Fermoir (m.) de chaîne. ‖ **Snap-lock,** n. Serrure (f.) à ressort.
— adv. Avec un claquement (or) bruit sec.

snapdragon [-drægən] n. BOT. Gueule-de-loup f.

snapper [-ə*] n. Teigne, personne hargneuse f. ‖ ZOOL. Perche rouge f.

snappish [-iʃ] adj. Hargneux, irritable, acariâtre.

snappishly [-iʃli] adv. D'un ton hargneux, d'une humeur bourrue.

snappishness [-iʃnis] n. Humeur hargneuse f. ; caractère acariâtre m.

snappy [-i] adj. Energique, plein d'allant (or) de sève. ‖ Plein de sel, spirituel (phrase) ; vif (style). ‖ Froid et sec (weather). ‖ Acariâtre, hargneux, bourru (temper). ‖ FAM. Make it snappy !, grouillez-vous ! ‖ POP. Elegant, chic (clothes).

snapshot [-ʃɔt] n. Instantané m. (photograph).

snare ['snɛə*] n. Piège, lacet, filet, collet m. ‖ FIG. Piège m.
— v. tr. Prendre au piège ; attraper (s.o.).

snarl [snɑːl] v. intr. S'embrouiller, s'emmêler.
— v. tr. Embrouiller, emmêler, enchevêtrer. ‖ TECHN. Repousser.
— n. Enchevêtrement m. ‖ FIG. Confusion f. ; brouillamini m. ‖ U. S. FAM. Traffic snarl, embouteillage.

snarl v. intr. Montrer les dents ; grogner (animal). ‖ Grogner, parler d'un ton hargneux (person).
— v. tr. Dire en grognant (or) d'un ton hargneux.
— n. Grognement m. (of an animal). ‖ Ton (or) propos hargneux m.

snarler [-ə*] n. Grognon m.

snarling [-iŋ] n. Grognement, grondement m.
— adj. Grognant, hargneux.

snatch [snætʃ] v. tr. Saisir brusquement, s'emparer vivement de, agripper. ‖ JUR. Voler. ‖ U. S. FAM. Enlever, kidnapper. ‖ To snatch (a kiss) ; to snatch forty winks, piquer un roupillon. ‖ **To snatch away** (or) **off,** arracher, emporter vivement. ‖ **To snatch from,** arracher à, ravir à. ‖ **To snatch up,** ramasser vivement.
— v. intr. **To snatch at,** faire un mouvement pour saisir, tâcher de saisir ; FIG. Saisir au vol (an opportunity). ‖ Snatch-and-grab, n. Vol (m.) à l'esbroufe.
— n. Geste vif (m.) pour saisir ; action (f.) de saisir. ‖ U. S. FAM. Rapt d'enfant, kidnapping m. ‖ FIG. Courte période f. ; petit intervalle m. ; to work by snatches, travailler d'une façon décousue. ‖ FIG. Bribe f. ; fragment m. (of a conversation). ‖ **Snatch-block,** n. NAUT. Galoche f.

snazzy ['snæzi] adj. POP. Bath, chouette, qui en jette drôlement.

sneak [sniːk] v. intr. Se glisser furtivement (or) honteusement. ‖ FAM. Moucharder, rapporter, cafarder. ‖ **To sneak away** (or) **off,** partir furtivement, s'esquiver, s'éclipser. ‖ **To sneak in,** entrer à la dérobée, se faufiler dans. ‖ **To sneak out,** se glisser furtivement hors de, sortir en sournois.
— v. tr. Chiper, barboter, chaparder.

— n. Pleutre, pied-plat m. ‖ Fam. Mouchard, rapporteur m. ‖ Sneak-thief, n. Chapardeur s.

sneakers [-əz] n. pl. U. S. Chaussures (f. pl.) de tennis (or) de gymnastique.

sneaking [-iŋ] adj. Furtif, sournois, en dessous. ‖ Secret (admiration) ; caché, inavoué (desire). ‖ Servile. rampant.

sneakingly [-iŋli] adv. Furtivement, en cachette, à la dérobée. ‖ Sournoisement, en dessous. ‖ Servilement, avec bassesse.

sneer ['sniə*] n. Ricanement, sourire moqueur (or) méprisant m. ‖ Sarcasme, persiflage m.
— v. intr. Ricaner, sourire d'un air moqueur (or) méprisant. ‖ To sneer at, se moquer de, se gausser de, railler.
— v. tr. To sneer down, faire taire à force de railleries.

sneerer [-rə*] n. Ricaneur, moqueur, persifleur, railleur s.

sneeringly [-iŋli] adv. En ricanant, d'un air méprisant, de façon sarcastique.

sneeze [sni:z] v. intr. Eternuer. ‖ Fam. It's not to be sneezed at, il ne faut pas cracher dessus.
— n. Eternuement m.

snick [snik] v. tr. Entailler, encocher ; faire une entaille dans. ‖ Sports. Faire dévier légèrement (a cricket ball).
— n. Petite entaille (or) encoche f. ‖ Sports. Coup léger (m.) qui fait dévier la balle (at cricket).

snicker [-ə*] U. S. See snigger.

snide [snaid] adj. Fam. Vachard (remark). ‖ Fam. Faux, factice, en toc (jewel).

sniff [snif] v. tr. Renifler ; flairer, sentir ; humer (snuff). ‖ Med. To sniff up, aspirer.
— v. intr. Renifler ; flairer. ‖ To sniff at, sentir, flairer ; Fam. Faire la grimace devant, cracher sur.
— n. Reniflement m. ; to take a sniff of, sentir un peu. ‖ Bouffée f. (of air).

sniffle [-l] v. intr. Etre enchifrené ; renifler.
— n. Enchifrènement m. ; to have the sniffles, avoir un début de rhume, être enchifrené.

sniffy [-i] adj. Fam. Dédaigneux, méprisant, arrogant. ‖ Malodorant.

snifter ['sniftə*] n. Fam. Verre (m.) à dégustation (glass) ; goutte f. ; petit verre m. (nip).

snigger ['snigə*] n. Ricanement, petit rire sournois (or) narquois m. ‖ Rire grivois m.
— v. intr. Rire d'un rire contenu (or) narquois, ricaner.

snip [snip] v. tr. Couper ; to snip off, détacher d'un coup de ciseaux.
— n. Coup (m.) de ciseaux. ‖ Petite entaille (or) encoche f. (notch). ‖ Petit bout m. (of cloth, paper). ‖ Fam. Tailleur m. ‖ Pop. Affaire avantageuse, occasion f. ‖ U. S. Fam. Gamin m. ; personne insignifiante f.

snipe [snaip] n. Zool. Bécassine f.
— v. intr. Chasser la bécassine. ‖ Milit. To snipe at, canarder.
— v. tr. Milit. Tuer ; descendre (fam.) [from ambush].

sniper ['snaipə*] n. Milit. Tireur embusqué ; canardeur m. (fam.).

snippet ['snipit] n. Petit morceau, bout m. ; coupe f. ‖ Fig. Bribe f. ‖ U. S. Fam. Gamin m. (kid).

snippety [-i], snippy ['snipi] adj. Morcelé, fragmentaire ; insignifiant. ‖ Fig. Dédaigneux, méprisant (person, remark).

snitch [snitʃ] v. tr. Pop. Chaparder.
— v. intr. Pop. Vendre la mèche ; moucharder ; to snitch on s.o., donner qqn.
— n. Pop. Pif m. (nose).

snivel ['snivəl] n. Morve ; goutte (f.) au nez. ‖ Fig. Pleurnicherie f.
— v. intr. Avoir la goutte au nez ; être morveux. ‖ Fig. Pleurnicher.

sniveller [-ə*] n. Pleurnicheur m. ; chialeur, reniflard m. (fam.).

snob [snɔb] n. Poseur, fat, snob m. ‖ Milit. Cordonnier m.

snobbery [-əri], snobbishness [-iʃnis] n. Morgue, pose, affectation f.

snobbish [-iʃ] adj. Poseur, prétentieux, fiérot.

snog [snɔg] v. intr. Pop. Se peloter.

snood [snu:d] n. Résille f. (for the hair).

snook [snu:k] n. Zool. Brochet (m.) de mer.

snook n. Fam. To cock a snook, faire un pied de nez.

snooker ['snu:kə*] n. Sorte (f.) de billard.
— v. tr. Coincer, bloquer. ‖ Fig. Mettre dans une mauvaise posture.

snoop [snu:p] v. intr. U. S. Fam. Fouiner, fureter.

snooty ['snu:ti] adj. Fam. Bêcheur, prétentieux (person) ; snob (place).

snooze [snu:z] n. Petit somme m.
— v. intr. Sommeiller ; pioncer (fam.).

snore [snɔ:*] n. Ronflement m.
— v. intr. Ronfler.

snorer [-rə*] n. Ronfleur s.

snorkel ['snɔ:kl] n. See schnorkel.

snort [snɔ:t] v. intr. S'ébrouer, renâcler (horse) ; renifler bruyamment, ronfler, pousser un ronflement (person). ‖ Ronfler, tousser (engine).
— v. tr. Dire en reniflant de colère (or) en renâclant ; grogner (an answer).
— n. Ebrouement m. (of a horse). ‖ Grognement, reniflement m. (of a person). ‖ U. S. Pop. Petit verre m. ; goutte, larme f. (of liquor).

snorter [-ə*] n. Cheval (m.) qui s'ébroue. ‖ Renâcleur, grogneur s. ‖ Pop., Naut. Bourrasque carabinée f. ‖ Pop. Truc terrible m. ; a snorter of a shot, un tir génial ; this job's a real snorter, c'est une vraie vacherie, ce boulot.

snot [snɔt] n. Med. Morve f. ‖ Fam. Morveux s. (person). ‖ Snot-rag, n. Pop. Tire-jus m. (handkerchief).

snotty [-i] adj. Morveux.
— n. Naut. Morveux m. (midshipman).

snout [snaut] n. Zool. Museau m. ; boutoir m. (of a boar) ; mufle m. (of a bull) ; groin m. (of a pig). ‖ Techn. Bec, ajutage m. ; tuyère f.

snow [snou] n. Neige f. ; driven snow, neige vierge ; snow region, région névéenne. ‖ Chim. Carbonic acid (or) U. S. dioxide snow, neige carbonique. ‖ Pop. Neige, coco, schnouff f. ; U. S. drogue f. ‖ Fig. Snows of yesteryear, neiges d'antan. ‖ Snow-bird, n. Zool. Pinson (m.) des neiges. ‖ Snow-blindness, n. Med. Cécité (f.) des neiges. ‖ Snow-boot, n. Snow-boot m. ‖ Snow-bound, adj. Bloqué par la neige. ‖ Snow-capped (or) -covered, adj. Couronné de neige, enneigé. ‖ Snow-drift, n. Amas (m.) de neige, congère f. ‖ Snow-fall, n. Chute de neige f. ‖ Snow-field, n. Champ (m.) de neige. ‖ Snow-flake, n. Flocon (m.) de neige. ‖ Snow-goggles, n. pl. Lunettes (f. pl.) d'alpiniste. ‖ Snow-line, n. Limite (f.) des neiges perpétuelles. ‖ Snow-man, n. Bonhomme (m.) de neige. ‖ Snow-plough, n. Chasse-neige m. ‖ Snow-shoe n. Raquette f. ‖ Snow-storm, n. Tempête de neige f., blizzard m. ‖ Snow-white, adj. Blanc comme la neige ; n. Blanche-Neige f. (in fairy-tale).
— v. intr. Neiger, tomber de la neige.
— v. tr. Faire pleuvoir en neige. ‖ Fig. Snowed under by (or) with, écrasé de (debts), accablé de, débordé de (work).

snowball [-bɔ:l] n. Boule de neige f. ‖ Culin., Bot. Boule-de-neige f. ‖ Snowball-tree, n. Bot. Boule-de-neige f.
— v. intr. Fig. Faire boule de neige (debts, problems).
— v. tr. Lancer des boules de neige à, bombarder de boules de neige.

snowdrop [-drɔp] n. Bot. Perce-neige f.

snowy [-i] adj. Neigeux (climate) ; de neige (season) ; couvert de neige (surface). ‖ FIG. De neige, blanc comme la neige (colour).

snub [snʌb] n. Rebuffade, mortification, avanie ƒ. ; affront, camouflet m. ‖ NAUT. Arrêt soudain m. (of a rope).
— v. tr. (1). Rabrouer, rembarrer, remettre à sa place, rabattre le caquet à. ‖ Traiter avec froideur ; feindre de ne pas voir. ‖ NAUT. Casser l'erre de (a ship).

snub adj. Camard, camus, retroussé (nose). ‖ **Snub-nosed**, adj. Au nez camard, camard.

snubber [-ə*] n. U. S. Amortisseur de choc m.

snuff [snʌf] v. tr. Eteindre, moucher (a candle) ; to snuff out, éteindre avec les doigts. ‖ FIG. Détruire, éteindre (ambition, hope).
— n. Mouchure ƒ., champignon m. (of a candle).

snuff n. Tabac à priser m. ; pinch of snuff, prise ; to take snuff, priser. ‖ LOC. To be up to snuff, être dégourdi (or) dessalé.
— v. tr., intr. Priser. ‖ **Snuff-box**, n. Tabatière ƒ. ‖ **Snuff-coloured**, adj. De couleur tabac, cachou. ‖ **Snuff-taker**, n. Priseur s.

snuffer [-ə*] n. Priseur s. (person). ‖ Pl. Mouchette ƒ. (implement).

snuffle [-ḷ] v. intr. MED. Renifler. ‖ MED. Etre enchifrené, avoir le nez bouché. ‖ Nasiller (in speaking).
— v. tr. Nasiller.
— n. MED. Reniflement m. ; enchifrènement m. ‖ Ton nasillard m. ‖ FIG. Langage hypocrite m.

snuffy ['snʌfi] adj. Sali par le tabac (clothing) ; peu soigné (person).

snug [snʌg] adj. Douillet (bed) ; très ajusté (garment) ; confortable (house) ; bien au chaud (person) ; bien abrité (site). ‖ NAUT. Abrité (harbour) ; paré à tout événement (ship). ‖ FIG. Gentil, coquet (income, sum) ; gentil (job).
— v. tr. (1). To snug oneself, se calfeutrer, s'acagnarder douillettement, se câliner. ‖ NAUT. To snug down, parer (a ship).

snuggery [-əri] n. Pièce confortable ƒ. ; endroit douillet m.

snuggle ['snʌgḷ] v. intr. Se pelotonner, se serrer (against, up to, contre, tout près de).
— v. tr. Serrer dans ses bras ; dorloter (a child).

snugly ['snʌgli] adv. Confortablement, douillettement, commodément, à l'aise ; chaudement.

snugness ['snʌgnis] n. Confort, bien-être m. ; ambiance chaude et douillette ƒ. ‖ Fait (m.) d'être très ajusté (garment).

so [sou] adv. Ainsi, de cette manière, comme ceci (or) cela ; so it seems, il paraît que c'est ainsi ; is that so?, vraiment ?, pas possible ! ; so be it ainsi soit-il. ‖ De même, de la même manière, ainsi ; so help me God, ainsi Dieu me soit en aide. ‖ Tellement, si ; so happy, si heureux ; so busy, tellement occupé ; so much, so many, tant de, tellement de ; be so kind as to, ayez la bonté de. ‖ Aussi, si (in a negative comparison) ; not so kind as his wife, pas si bon que sa femme ; they did not stay so long, ils ne sont pas restés si longtemps. ‖ Aussi, et ... aussi ; he wrote, and so did she, il a écrit et elle aussi ; you are tired and so am I, vous êtes fatigué et moi aussi. ‖ Le, ce (pronoun) ; I hope so, je l'espère bien, j'espère que oui ; I think so, je crois que oui, je le crois ; I told you so, je vous l'ai bien dit. ‖ **So far**, jusqu'ici, jusqu'à présent, jusque-là (until now) ; so far as, autant que, dans la mesure où ; so far as I care, pour ce qui me concerne ; so far as I know, autant que je sache. ‖ **So many**, tant de, tellement de ; so many men, so many points of view, autant de personnes, autant de points de vue différents ; in so many words, textuellement, en propres termes ; they are just so many thieves, ce ne sont ni plus ni moins que des voleurs. ‖ **So much**, tant, une quantité donnée ; tant de, tellement de ; they get so much per day, on leur donne (or) les paie tant par jour ; what he said was so much nonsense, ce qu'il a dit n'était rien d'autre que des bêtises ; she did not so much as answer, elle n'a même pas répondu ; so much for that, et voilà pour cela, et d'une ! (fam.). ‖ **So that**, afin que ; de sorte que, si bien que ; I came early, so that you could go, je suis venu de bonne heure, de sorte que (or) pour que vous puissiez partir ; he stays home so as to rest, il reste chez lui afin de se reposer. ‖ LOC. Ever so, infiniment (grateful) ; if so, s'il en est ainsi ; just so, quite so, parfaitement, nous sommes d'accord ; or so, environ, approximativement (measure, weight) ; and so forth, et ainsi de suite, et cætera. ‖ So long, au revoir, à bientôt, à un de ces jours.
— conj. Aussi, donc, par conséquent ; he told me everything, so don't worry, il m'a tout dit, donc ne vous inquiétez pas ; I overslept, so nothing is ready, je me suis réveillé trop tard, par conséquent rien n'est prêt. ‖ **So-called**, adj. Ainsi nommé ; soidisant ; prétendu ; the so-called temperate zone, la zone dite tempérée ; to be properly so-called, être ainsi appelé à juste titre ; so-called experts, soidisant (or) prétendus experts. ‖ **So-and-so**, n. FAM. Machin m. ; individu, type m. (pejorative) ; Mr. So-and-so, M. Un tel, M. Chose. ‖ **So-so**, adj., adv. Ni bien ni mal, comme ci comme ça ; couci-couça (fam.).

so n. See SOH.

soak [souk] v. tr. Tremper, faire baigner (in a liquid). ‖ Imbiber, saturer, tremper (to drench) ; soaked through, trempé jusqu'aux os ; to soak in, imprégner de, baigner de. ‖ FIG. To soak in (or) up, absorber, s'imbiber de (knowledge, sunlight). ‖ U. S. FAM. Rosser. ‖ U. S. POP. Faire casquer, estamper (to charge excessively) ; saouler (to intoxicate).
— v. intr. Baigner, tremper (in a liquid). ‖ S'infiltrer, pénétrer, imprégner (liquid). ‖ S'imbiber, se détremper (bread). ‖ FAM. Biberonner, pomper dur (to drink).
— n. Trempe, action (ƒ.) de tremper. ‖ Imbibition ƒ. ‖ CHIM. Bain m. ‖ FAM. Beuverie ƒ. (drinking bout) ; entonnoir, poivrot m. (drunkard).

soakage [-idʒ] n. Eau d'infiltration ƒ. ‖ Imbibition, infiltration ƒ.

soaker [-ə*] n. Pluie battante ƒ. ‖ FAM. Poivrot m.

soaking [-iŋ] n. Trempe ƒ. ; trempage, baignage, m. ‖ FAM. To get a soaking in the rain, être trempé, se faire tremper.
— adj. Détrempé (garments) ; trempé (person).

soap [soup] n. Savon m. ; cake of soap, savon, pain de savon, savonnette ; soft soap, savon noir. ‖ FAM. Soft soap, pommade, lèche ; U. S. no soap, rien à faire. ‖ **Soap-boiler**, n. Savonnier m. (person) ; chaudière (ƒ.) à savon (utensil). ‖ **Soap-box**, n. Caisse (ƒ.) à savon ; soap-box orator, harangueur, laïusseur, orateur de carrefour. ‖ **Soap-bubble**, n. Bulle (ƒ.) de savon. ‖ **Soap-dish**, n. Porte-savon m. ‖ **Soap-flakes**, n. pl. Savon (m.) en paillettes. ‖ **Soap-opera**, n. RADIO. Mélo m. ‖ **Soap-stone**, n. Stéatite ƒ. ‖ **Soap-suds**, n. pl. Eau (ƒ.) de savon. ‖ **Soap-works**, n. Savonnerie ƒ.
— v. tr. Savonner.

soapiness [-inis] n. Nature savonneuse ƒ. ‖ FIG. Onction ƒ.

soapy [-i] adj. Savonneux, plein de savon. ‖ FIG. Doucereux, onctueux, mielleux.

soar [sɔ:*] v. intr. Monter (or) s'élever dans les cieux, prendre son essor. ‖ Planer dans les airs.

soaring [-iŋ] n. Essor m. ‖ AVIAT., ZOOL. Planement m. (of an aeroplane, a bird). ‖ AVIAT. Vol (m.) plané (or) à voiles (of a glider). ‖ COMM. Hausse, élévation ƒ. (of costs).

sob [sɔb] v. intr. (1). Sangloter.
— v. tr. **To sob out**, sangloter, dire en sanglotant ; to sob oneself to sleep, s'endormir en sanglotant.

— n. Sanglot *m*. ‖ **Sob-stuff,** n. FAM. Littérature (or) pièce larmoyante *f*.

sobbingly [-iŋli] adv. En sanglotant.

sober [-ə*] adj. Discret (attire) ; peu voyant, sobre (colour). ‖ A jeun, sobre (temperate) ; qui n'est pas sous l'influence de l'alcool (or) pas ivre (not drunk) ; dessoûlé, dégrisé (sobered up). ‖ FIG. Sobre, modéré, tempéré ; grave (expression) ; réel (fact) ; sensé (judgment) ; rassis (mind) ; réfléchi (opinion) ; simple (truth).

— v. tr. Dégriser ; dessoûler (fam.). ‖ Calmer, rendre raisonnable, modérer.

— v. intr. **To sober down** (or) **up,** se dégriser ; se dessoûler (fam.) [intoxicated person] ; s'assagir, se calmer, devenir raisonnable (reckless person).

soberly ['sɔbə:li] adv. Sobrement, modérément. ‖ Sérieusement, raisonnablement. ‖ Calmement, tranquillement, posément. ‖ Discrètement, de couleurs sobres.

soberness [-nis], **sobriety** [sə'braiəti] n. Modération, tempérance *f*. ‖ État (*m*.) de sobriété. ‖ FIG. Sobriété *f*. (of attire, colours, speech) ; calme, sérieux *m. ;* **gravité** *f*. (of mind).

sobriquet ['soubri.kei] n. Sobriquet *m*.

soccer ['sɔkə*] n. SPORTS. Football (*m*.) association.

sociability [,souʃə'biliti] n. Sociabilité *f*.

sociable ['souʃəbl] adj. Sociable ; amical, intime (gathering) ; de compagnie agréable (people). ‖ ZOOL. Sociétaire (animal).

— n. Confident *m*. (chair).

sociableness [-nis] n. Sociabilité *f*.

sociably [-i] adv. Amicalement, en bonne entente.

social ['souʃəl] adj. Vivant en société. ‖ Social (contract, insurance, problem) ; *social system*, société. ‖ Mondain, social ; *social events*, mondanités ; *social rank*, rang dans la société. ‖ U. S. *Social butterfly*, mondaine très répandue ; *social climber*, parvenu. ‖ ZOOL. Social (animal). ‖ **Social Democracy,** n. Social-démocratie *f*. ‖ **Social Democrat,** n. Social-démocrate *s*. ‖ **Social science,** n. Sciences humaines (or) sociales *f. pl*. ‖ **Social scientist,** n. Spécialiste (*s*.) des sciences humaines. ‖ **Social security,** n. Aide sociale *f*. ‖ **Social services,** n. Services sociaux *m. pl*. ‖ **Social worker,** n. Assistante sociale *f. ;* social workers, travailleurs sociaux.

— n. FAM. Réunion sans cérémonie *f*.

socialism [-izm] n. Socialisme *m*.

socialist [-ist] n. Socialiste *s*.

socialistic [,souʃə'listik] adj. Socialiste.

socialite ['souʃəlait] n. FAM. Mondain *s*.

sociality [souʃi'æliti] n. Socialité *f*. ‖ Sociabilité *f*. (sociableness).

socialize ['souʃəlaiz] v. tr. Socialiser.

— v. intr. U. S. FAM. *To socialize with*, frayer avec, fréquenter.

society [sə'saiəti] n. Société *f*. ‖ Compagnie *f*. (of s.o.). ‖ Monde *m. ; fashionable society*, beau monde ; gratin (fam.) ; *society gossip*, mondanités. ‖ COMM. Société, association ; œuvre *f*. (charitable).

socio- [,sousio] pref. Socio-. ‖ **Socio-cultural,** adj. Socioculturel. ‖ **Socio-economic,** adj. Socio-économique. ‖ **Socio-linguistic,** adj. Sociolinguistique. ‖ **Socio-linguistics,** n. sg. Sociolinguistique *f*.

sociological [,sousio'lɔdʒikəl] adj. Sociologique.

sociologist [,sousi'ɔlədʒist] n. Sociologue *s*.

sociology [-dʒi] n. Sociologie *f*.

sociometric [,sousiə'metrik] adj. Sociométrique.

sociometry [,sousi'ɔmitri] n. Sociométrie *f*.

sock [sɔk] n. Chaussette *f*. ‖ Semelle intérieure *f*. (of a shoe). ‖ † THEATR. Brodequin, socque *m*.

sock n. POP. Coup, gnon *m*.

— v. tr. POP. Flanquer un pain à (s.o.). ‖ Lancer (a brick, stone) [at s.o.].

socket ['sɔkit] n. Cavité *f*. ‖ ELECTR. Douille *f*. ‖ TECHN. Baril *m*. (of a brace) ; bobèche *f*. (of a candlestick) ; sabot *m*. (of a caster). ‖ MED. Cavité articulaire, glène *f*. (of a bone) ; orbite *f*. (of the eye) ; alvéole *m*. (of a tooth). ‖ **Socket-joint,** n. Joint (*m*.) à rotule.

socle ['sɔkl̩] n. ARCHIT. Socle *m*.

Socrates ['sɔkrati:z] n. Socrate *m*.

Socratic [sɔ'krætik] adj. Socratique.

sod [sɔd] n. BOT. Gazon *m. ;* motte (*f*.) de gazon. ‖ FAM. Terre *f. ; under the sod*, enterré.

— v. tr. *To sod over*, gazonner, couvrir de mottes de gazon.

sod n. POP. Salaud, connard *m*. (bastard). ‖ POP. Type, bougre *m*. (chap).

— v. tr. POP. *Sod you*, je t'emmerde ; *sod it !*, merde alors !

— v. intr. POP. **To sod off,** aller se faire foutre.

soda ['soudə] n. CHIM. Soude *f*. ‖ COMM. *Washing soda*, carbonate de soude. ‖ CULIN. *Baking soda*, bicarbonate de soude. ‖ U. S. CULIN. *Ice-cream soda*, mélange de glaces et d'eau de Seltz. ‖ **Soda-fountain,** n. Bar *m. ;* buvette *f. ;* débit (*m*.) de boissons non alcoolisées. ‖ **Soda jerk(er),** n. U. S. FAM. Serveur (*m*.) de boissons non alcoolisées. ‖ **Soda-water,** n. Eau (*f*.) de Seltz, soda *m*.

sodality [so'dæliti] n. ECCLES. Sodalité, confrérie, congrégation *f*.

sodden ['sɔdn̩] adj. Saturé, détrempé. ‖ CULIN. Mou, mal cuit, pâteux (bread). ‖ FIG. Abruti (with liquor).

— v. tr. Tremper, détremper, saturer, imbiber.

— v. intr. Etre détrempé, s'imprégner d'humidité.

sodic ['soudik] adj. CHIM. Sodique.

sodium [-djəm] n. CHIM. Sodium *m*.

sodomite ['sɔdəmait] n. Sodomite *s*.

sodomy [-i] n. Sodomie *f*.

soever [so'eva*] adv. Que ce soit.

sofa ['soufə] n. Sofa, canapé, divan *m*. ‖ **Sofa-bed,** n. Canapé-lit *m*.

soft [sɔft] adj. Mou, moelleux (bed) ; gras (coal) ; doux (iron) ; tendre (rock) ; inconsistant, liquide (mud). ‖ Doux, lisse (to the touch) ; mou (collar, hat) ; fin, flou (hair) ; souple (leather) ; doux (silk). ‖ Tiède, doux, mou (air, weather) ; *soft rain*, pluie douce. ‖ Doux (to the ear) ; ouaté, feutré (footstep). ‖ Doux, calme, paisible, tranquille (sleep). ‖ CULIN. Non alcoolisé, sucré (drink) ; doux (water) ; moelleux (wine). ‖ ARTS. Doux, délicat, atténué (colour, light) ; mou, flou, peu accentué (outline). ‖ MUS. Doux (note, voice) ; sourd (pedal). ‖ MED. Flasque, mou (muscle) ; *soft palate*, voile du palais ; *to go soft*, ramollir (muscle). ‖ ZOOL. *Soft roe*, laitance. ‖ COMM. *Soft goods*, textiles, tissus. ‖ U. S. FIN. *Soft currency*, billets de banque, traites. ‖ GRAMM. Doux, voisé (consonant) ; *soft breathing*, esprit doux (in Greek). ‖ SPORTS. Mou (wicket). ‖ FIG. Aimable (answer) ; compatissant (heart) ; affable, conciliant (person). ‖ FIG. Faible, sans énergie (character, person). ‖ FIG. Sot, niais, simple ; *to go soft*, perdre la boule. ‖ FAM. *Soft job*, bon fromage, filon ; *to be soft on*, avoir un faible (or) le béguin pour ; *to have a soft life* (or) *time*, se la couler douce ; *to say soft nothings*, dire des douceurs. ‖ **Soft-boiled,** adj. CULIN. Mollet (egg). ‖ **Soft-focus,** adj. Flou (photography). ‖ **Soft-headed** (or) **-witted,** adj. FAM. Faible d'esprit ; niais, nigaud. ‖ **Soft-hearted,** adj. Au cœur tendre. ‖ **Soft-pedal,** v. intr. U. S. FAM. Atténuer ; gazer (fam.) ; v. tr. Atténuer, parler doucement de ; gazer sur (fam.). ‖ **Soft-sawder,** n. U. S. FAM. Pommade, lèche *f*. ‖ **Soft-soap,** n. Savon noir *m. ;* FAM. Pommade, lèche *f. ;* v. tr. FAM. Passer de la pommade à. ‖ **Soft-solder,** v. tr. TECHN. Souder à l'étain ; n. Soudure tendre *f*. ‖ **Soft-spoken,** adj. Doucereux, mielleux. ‖ **Soft-tack,** n. NAUT. Pain *m*.

— adv. Doucement, sans bruit.

— interj. Chut ! doucement !

soften ['sɔfn̩] v. tr. Amollir, ramollir; assouplir (leather); détremper, adoucir (steel). ‖ Assouplir (hair); adoucir (skin). ‖ Adoucir (the temperature, a voice, water). ‖ ARTS. Estomper, adoucir (a contour, design); atténuer (a colour). ‖ MILIT. Affaiblir, énerver, user la résistance de (troops). ‖ MED. Ramollir (muscles); atténuer (pain). ‖ FIG. Adoucir, rendre calme et paisible (existence, manners); attendrir, émouvoir (s.o.).
— v. intr. S'amollir, se ramollir. ‖ S'assouplir, devenir soyeux (hair); s'adoucir (skin). ‖ MILIT. S'affaiblir, s'efféminer (troops). ‖ ARTS. S'atténuer, se fondre, s'adoucir (colour). ‖ FIG. S'atténuer, se calmer (emotions); s'adoucir, s'attendrir (person).

softener [-ə*] n. Appareil pour amollir m. (device); ramollissant m. (substance).

softening [-iŋ] n. Amollissement m. ‖ Assouplissement m. (of leather); détrempe f. (of steel). ‖ MED. Ramollissement m. (of the brain). ‖ FIG. Attendrissement m.

softie ['sɔfti] n. See SOFTY.

softish ['sɔftiʃ] adj. Un peu mou (or) tendre, mollet. ‖ Assez doux (or) compatissant. ‖ Un peu niais (or) nigaud. ‖ FAM. Pépère, de tout repos (job).

softness [-nis] n. Douceur f. (of fabric, skin); moelleux m. (of wool). ‖ Tiédeur, douceur f. (of climate). ‖ FIG. Mollesse f. (of character); douceur, affabilité f. (of manner, speech). ‖ FAM. Sottise, niaiserie f.

softy [-i] n. FAM. Niais, nigaud m. ‖ FAM. Mollasson m.; lavette, mauviette, poule mouillée f.

soggy l'sɔgi] adj. Saturé, détrempé. ‖ Lourd (atmosphere). ‖ CULIN. Pâteux (bread).

soh [sou] n. MUS. Sol m. invar.

soil [sɔil] v. tr. Salir, souiller, tacher, maculer.
— v. intr. Se salir, se tacher.
— n. Souillure, saleté f. (See SPOT, STAIN.)

soil n. Sol, terrain, terroir m.; terre f. ‖ Glèbe f. (feudal). ‖ FIG. Contrée f.; pays m.; native soil, pays natal. ‖ **Soil science,** n. Pédologie f.

soil v. tr. Mettre au vert.

soil v. intr. ZOOL. Prendre souille (boar); battre l'eau (deer).

soirée ['swɑːrei] n. Soirée f. (social gathering).

sojourn ['sɔdʒən] n. Séjour m.
— v. intr. Séjourner, faire un séjour.

sojourner [-ə*] n. Personne (f.) de passage, touriste s.

sol [sɔl] n. MUS. Sol m.

solace ['sɔləs] v. tr. Consoler (s.o.); soulager, adoucir (s.o.'s grief).
— n. Consolation f.; soulagement m.

solanum [sou'leinəm] n. BOT. Solanée f.

solar ['soulə*] adj. ASTRON., MED. Solaire. ‖ PHYS. Solar battery, cell, pile solaire, photopile.

solarium [sou'lɛəriəm] n. Solarium m.

solarize ['souləraiz] v. tr. Griller, solariser (a photographic plate).

sold [sould]. See SELL.

solder ['sɔdə*] n. Soudure f.; hard solder, brasure; soft solder, claire soudure.
— v. intr., v. tr. Souder, ressouder.

soldering [-riŋ] n. Soudure f.; soudage; brasage tendre m. ‖ **Soldering-iron,** n. Fer (m.) à souder.

soldier ['souldʒə*] n. MILIT. Soldat, militaire m.; common (or) private soldier, simple soldat, homme de troupe; old soldier, vieux routier, vétéran; to become a soldier, se faire soldat, entrer dans l'armée, endosser l'uniforme; toy soldier, soldat de plomb. ‖ NAUT., FAM. Marin (m.) d'eau douce. ‖ POP. Hareng saur, gendarme m.
— v. intr. Etre soldat (or) militaire. ‖ NAUT. Tirer au flanc.

soldierly [-li] adj. MILIT. De soldat, martial. ‖ Soldatesque.

soldiery [-ri] n. MILIT. Soldats, militaires m. pl.; troupe, garnison f. ‖ Soldatesque f. (pejorative).

sole [soul] n. Semelle f. (of a shoe); inner sole, première. ‖ MED. Plante (f.) du pied. ‖ TECHN. Sole f. (of a mine); semelle f. (of a plane). ‖ AGRIC. Fond, plancher m. (of a plough). ‖ ARCHIT. Plate-forme f. (of a building).
— v. tr. Mettre une semelle à; ressemeler (shoes).

sole n. ZOOL. Sole f.; lemon-sole, limande.

sole adj. Seul, unique. ‖ JUR. Universel (legatee); exclusif (right). ‖ COMM. Exclusif (agent).

solecism ['sɔlisizm] n. GRAMM. Solécisme m.; faute de grammaire f. ‖ FIG. Manque (m.) de savoir-vivre; faute (f.) de goût; impair m.

solely [-li] adv. Uniquement, seulement.

solemn ['sɔləm] adj. Solennel; grave (expression, matter); sérieux (fact). ‖ JUR. Solemn agreement, contrat solennel.

solemnity [sɔ'lemniti], **solemnness** ['sɔlemnis] n. Solennité, gravité f. (of an event); gravité f.; sérieux m. (of an expression); solennité f. (of a speech). ‖ Fête (or) cérémonie solennelle f.

solemnization [,sɔləmnai'zeiʃən] n. Solennisation, célébration f.

solemnize ['sɔləmnaiz] v. tr. Solenniser (an event); célébrer (a marriage). ‖ Rendre solennel (an occasion); donner de la solennité à (a place).

solemnly [-li] adv. Solennellement, avec solennité; gravement.

solen ['soulən] n. ZOOL. Couteau m. (fam.).

solenoid ['sɔliːnɔid] n. ELECTR. Solénoïde m.

sol-fa ['sɔl'fɑː] v. tr. Solfier.
— n. Solfège m.

solfeggio [sɔl'fedʒiou] n. MUS. Solfège m.

solicit [sə'lisit] v. tr. Solliciter, faire appel à (s.o.); demander avec insistance, solliciter, quémander (sth.). ‖ Postuler (employment); briguer (votes). ‖ Racoler, raccrocher (as a prostitute does).
— v. intr. Racoler (prostitute).

solicitation [sə,lisi'teiʃən], **soliciting** [sə'lisitiŋ] n. Sollicitation f. ‖ Racolage, raccrochage m. (by a prostitute).

solicitor [sə'lisitə*] n. JUR. Solicitor, homme (m.) d'affaires dont les fonctions s'apparentent à celles de l'avocat et du notaire. ‖ U. S. JUR. Conseiller (m.) juridique d'une municipalité. ‖ U. S. COMM. Placier, démarcheur, représentant m. ‖ **Solicitor-general,** n. Avocat général, procureur général m.

solicitous [-əs] adj. Soucieux, désireux (of, de). ‖ Préoccupé, inquiet (about, de).

solicitously [-əsli] adv. Avec sollicitude. ‖ Avec trouble, anxieusement.

solicitude [-juːd] n. Sollicitude f.; souci m. (anxiety); empressement m. (eagerness).

solid ['sɔlid] adj. Solide, substantiel (food); résistant (rock); to become solid, se solidifier. ‖ Solide, durable, bien construit, fort (building, structure); of solid build, bien charpenté (or) découplé (person). ‖ Massif (gold, silver). ‖ Plein, sans interligne (typography). ‖ AUTOM. Plein (tyre). ‖ MATH. Cube, polyédrique, solide (angle); dans l'espace (geometry); de volume (measure). ‖ ARTS. Uni, uniforme (colour). ‖ FIG. Solide, effectif (argument); sérieux, posé (person); soutenu (work); solid sense, solide bon sens. ‖ FIG. Plein; four solid days, quatre bonnes journées, quatre journées d'affilée. ‖ FIG. Unanime (opinion, vote); to be (or) to go solid for, être unanimement en faveur de.
— n. Solide m. ‖ MATH. Corps solide m. ‖ **Solid-forged,** adj. TECHN. Monobloc. ‖ **Solid-hoofed,** adj. ZOOL. Solipède. ‖ **Solid-state** adj. PHYS. De l'état solide; ELECTR. A semi-conducteurs.

solidarity [,sɔli'dæriti] n. Solidarité f.

solidifiable [sə,lidi'faiəbl̩] adj. Qui peut se solidifier. ‖ Congelable.

solidification [sə,lidifi'keiʃən] n. Solidification f.

solidify [sə'lidifai] v. tr. (2). Solidifier.
— v. intr. Se solidifier.
solidity [-iti] n. Solidité, consistance *f*. ‖ JUR. Solidarité *f*. ‖ FIG. Fermeté, force *f*. (of an argument).
solidly ['sɔlidli] adv. Solidement. ‖ Fermement. ‖ A l'unanimité.
solidness [-nis] n. Solidité *f*. ‖ FIG. Unanimité *f*. (of a vote).
solidungular [,sɔli'dʌŋgjulə*], **solidungulate** [-julit] adj. ZOOL. Solipède.
solidus ['sɔlidəs] n. † Solidus *m*. (Roman coin). ‖ FIN. Shilling *m*.
soliloquize [sə'lilɔkwaiz] v. intr. Soliloquer, parler tout seul.
soliloquy [-kwi] n. Soliloque *m*.
soliped ['sɔliped] adj., n. ZOOL. Solipède *m*.
solipsism ['sɔlip,sizm] n. PHILOS. Solipsisme *m*.
solitaire [,sɔli'tɛə*] n. Solitaire *m*. (diamond, game). ‖ U. S. Patience *f*. (card game).
solitarily ['sɔlitərili] adv. Solitairement.
solitariness [-inis] n. Solitude *f*.; isolement *m*.
solitary [-i] adj. Solitaire, qui se sent seul (person); retiré, isolé (place). ‖ Seul, unique; *not a solitary one*, pas un seul. ‖ JUR. *Solitary confinement*, prison cellulaire, réclusion.
— n. ECCLES. Solitaire, anachorète *m*.
solitude ['sɔlitjuːd] n. Solitude *f*.; isolement *m*. ‖ Solitude *f*.; désert *m*. (place).
solmizate ['sɔlmizeit] v. intr., tr. MUS. Solfier.
solo ['soulou] n. MUS. Solo *m*. ‖ AVIAT. Vol (*m*.) en solo.
— N. B. Deux pluriels : *solos, soli*.
— adj. Solo (performance). ‖ MUS. Solo. ‖ AVIAT. En solo. ‖ SPORTS. En solitaire.
— adv. En solo; en solitaire.
soloist [-ist] n. MUS. Soliste *s*.
Solomon ['sɔləmən] n. ECCLES. Salomon *m*.
Solomon Islands ['sɔləmən 'ailendz] n. pl. GEOGR. Iles Salomon *f*. pl.
Solon ['soulon] n. Solon *m*. ‖ FAM. Législateur *m*.
solstice ['sɔlstis] n. ASTRON. Solstice *m*.
solstitial [sɔl'stiʃəl] adj. ASTRON. Solsticial.
solubility [,sɔlju'biliti] n. CHIM. Solubilité *f*. ‖ MATH., FIG. Résolubilité *f*.
soluble ['sɔljubl] adj. CHIM. Soluble; dissoluble. ‖ MATH., FIG. Résoluble.
solution [sə'luːʃən] n. CHIM. Solution *f*.; dissolution *f*.; *developing, fixing solution*, révélateur, fixateur; *standard solution*, liqueur titrée. ‖ PHILOS. Solution *f*. (of continuity). ‖ MATH. Résolution, solution *f*. ‖ FIG. Solution *f*.; dénouement *m*.
solvability [,sɔlvə'biliti] n. CHIM. Solubilité *f*. ‖ MATH., FIG. Résolubilité *f*.
solvable ['sɔlvəbl] adj. CHIM. Soluble. ‖ MATH., FIG. Résoluble.
solve [sɔlv] v. tr. † Dénouer, démêler. ‖ MATH. Résoudre. ‖ FIG. Résoudre, solutionner (a difficulty); résoudre, trouver le mot de (a puzzle).
solvency ['sɔlvənsi] n. Solvabilité *f*.
solvent [-ənt] adj. CHIM. Dissolvant. ‖ COMM., JUR. Solvable.
— n. CHIM. Dissolvant *m*.
Somalia [sou'mɑliə] n. GEOGR. Somalie *f*.
somatic [sou'mætik] adj. Somatique.
somatology [,soumə'tɔlədʒi] n. Somatologie *f*.
sombre ['sɔmbə*] adj. Sombre (lit. and fig.).
sombrely [-li] adv. Sombrement.
some [sʌm] adj. Quelque, quelconque; certain; *some other*, quelque autre; *some day*, un jour ou l'autre, un de ces jours; *some way or other*, d'une manière quelconque. ‖ Du, de la, des, quelques; *some tea and hot water*, du thé et de l'eau chaude; *some old papers*, de vieux papiers; *some students were waiting for me*, quelques étudiants m'attendaient. ‖ Quelque, pas mal de (a considerable amount); *some distance off*, à quelque distance; *that will take some time*, cela prendra pas mal de

temps; *give some thought to it*, apportez-y un peu de réflexion. ‖ POP. Un fameux, un pas ordinaire; *some luck!*, tu parles d'une veine!; *some meal!*, un repas formidable!; *some wind!*, quel vent!
— adv. Quelque, environ; *some few*, un petit nombre de; *some 5,000 people*, quelque cinq mille personnes. ‖ U. S. FAM. Plutôt, pas mal (somewhat).
— pron. indéf. Une certaine quantité (or) partie, un peu; *some of that paper*, une certaine quantité de ce papier; *some of the time*, une partie du temps; *would you like some wine?*, un peu de vin? ‖ En; *do you want some?*, en voulez-vous? ‖ Pl. Quelques-uns, quelques-unes, les uns, les unes, certains; d'aucuns (†); *some of my friends*, quelques-uns de mes amis; *some stayed, some left*, les uns sont restés, d'autres sont partis; *some of them*, certains d'entre eux. ‖ U. S. *And then some!*, et comment!
somebody [-bɔdi] pron. indéf. Quelqu'un; on; *somebody else*, quelqu'un d'autre; *somebody is calling you*, on vous appelle. ‖ FAM. Personnage *m*.; *to believe oneself to be somebody*, se croire quelqu'un.
somehow [-hau] adv. Tant bien que mal; dans un sens (in a way); *somehow or other*, d'une manière ou d'une autre, je ne sais comment (or) pourquoi.
someone [-wʌn]. See SOMEBODY.
someplace [-pleis] U. S. See SOMEWHERE.
somersault ['sɔməsɔlt] n. Culbute *f*. ‖ SPORTS. Saut périlleux *m*. ‖ AUTOM. Capotage, panache *m*.
— v. intr. SPORTS. Faire la culbute (or) le saut périlleux. ‖ AUTOM. Capoter.
something ['sʌmθiŋ] pron. indéf. Quelque chose; *something else*, quelque chose d'autre; *he said something or other*, il a dit je ne sais plus quoi. ‖ *Something of*, quelque chose comme, un semblant (or) un peu de; *to be something of a coward*, être quelque peu poltron; *to see something of someone*, voir qqn de temps en temps.
— adv. Un peu, quelque peu; tant soit peu, légèrement, dans une certaine mesure; *to be something under fifty*, avoir un peu moins de 50 ans. ‖ FAM. *That is something like!*, parfait!, à la bonne heure!
sometime [-taim] adv. Autrefois, jadis (formerly); *sometime next week*, dans le courant de la semaine prochaine.
— adj. Ci-devant, d'autrefois; ex- (former).
sometimes [-taimz] adv. Quelquefois, parfois; *sometimes... sometimes*, tantôt... tantôt.
somewhat [-(h)wɔt] adv. Quelque peu, un peu, tant soit peu, légèrement; *somewhat cold*, assez froid.
— pron. Un peu, quelque chose; *to be somewhat of a bore*, être quelque peu casse-pieds; *somewhat of a crisis*, en quelque sorte une crise.
somewhere [-wɛə*] adv. Quelque part; *somewhere else*, ailleurs, autre part; *somewhere about* (or) *around here*, quelque part par ici, dans les environs; *somewhere in the world*, de par le monde; *somewhere or other*, je ne sais où.
somnambulate [sɔm'næmbjuleit] v. intr. MED. Faire du somnambulisme.
somnambulism [-lizm] n. MED. Somnambulisme *m*.
somnambulist [-list] n. MED. Somnambule *s*.
somnambulistic [sɔm,næmbju'listik] adj. MED. Somnambulique.
somniferous [sɔm'nifərəs] adj. MED. Somnifère *f*.
somniloquist [sɔm'nilɔkwist] n. MED. Somniloque *s*.
somnolence ['sɔmnələns] n. Somnolence *f*.
somnolent [-lənt] adj. Somnolent.
son [sʌn] n. Fils *m*.; garçon *m*. (fam.). ‖ ECCLES. *Son of God, of man*, Fils de Dieu, de l'homme. ‖ FAM. *Every mother's son of them*, tous tant qu'ils sont. ‖ **Son-in-law**, n. Gendre *m*. ‖ **Son of a bitch**, n. ARG. Salaud, salopard, fumier, fils (*m*.) de pute.
sonant ['sounənt] adj. GRAMM. Sonore.
— n. GRAMM. Consonne sonore *f*.
sonar ['sounɑ:*] n. NAUT. Sonar *m*.

sonata [sə'nɑːtə] n. Mus. Sonate *f.*
sonatina [ˌsɔnə'tiːnə] n. Mus. Sonatine *f.*
sonde [sɔnd] n. Phys. Sonde *f.*
sone [soun] n. Phys. Sone *m.*
song [sɔŋ] n. Mus. Chant *m.* (act); chanson *f.* (piece of music); *song without words,* romance sans paroles. ‖ Zool. Ramage, chant *m.* (of birds). ‖ Eccles. Cantique *m.; Song of Songs,* Cantique des Cantiques. ‖ Fig. Poésie *f.;* vers *m. pl.;* poème *m.* ‖ Loc. *To buy sth. for a song,* acheter qqch. pour une bouchée de pain; *to make a song about it,* en faire tout un plat. ‖ **Song-bird,** n. Zool. Oiseau chanteur *m.* ‖ **Song-book,** n. Recueil (*m.*) de chansons. ‖ **Song-writer,** n. Chansonnier *s.*
songless [-lis] adj. Qui ne chante pas, sans voix. ‖ Muet (forest).
songster [-stə*] n. Mus. Chanteur *m.* ‖ Zool. Oiseau chanteur *m.* ‖ Fig. Poète *m.*
songstress [-stris] n. Mus. Chanteuse, cantatrice *f.* ‖ Poétesse *f.*
sonic ['sɔnik] adj. Phys. Sonique (speed). ‖ Aviat. *Sonic bang* (or) *boom,* bang supersonique ; *sonic barrier,* mur du son. ‖ Naut. Acoustique (depth-finder). ‖ Techn. Acoustique (mine).
soniferous [sou'nifərəs] adj. Sonore, résonnant. ‖ Qui propage le son.
sonnet ['sɔnit] n. Sonnet *m.*
sonneteer [ˌsɔni'tiə*] n. Sonnettiste *s.*
sonny ['sʌni] n. Fam. Fiston *m.*
sonofabitch [ˌsʌnəvə'bitʃ] n. See son of a bitch.
sonometer [sə'nɔmitə*] n. Phys. Sonomètre *m.*
sonority [sə'nɔriti] n. Phys. Sonorité *f.*
sonorous ['sɔnərəs] adj. Sonore.
soon [suːn] adv. Bientôt, tôt ; *soon after,* peu après ; *it will begin soon,* cela commencera sous peu ; *so soon,* si tôt. ‖ *As soon as, so soon as,* aussitôt que, dès que ; *I will come as soon as I can,* je viendrai aussitôt (or) dès que je pourrai. ‖ Volontiers (expressing preference) ; *I would just as soon leave,* j'aimerais autant (or) mieux partir.
sooner [-ə*] adv. Plus tôt ; *the sooner the better,* le plus tôt sera le mieux ; *no sooner said than done,* sitôt dit sitôt fait. ‖ Plutôt (rather) [*than,* que] ; *I would sooner leave,* j'aimerais autant (or) mieux partir.
soot [sut] n. Suie *f.*
— v. tr. **To soot up,** encrasser de suie.
— v. intr. S'encrasser par la suie.
sooth [suːθ] n. † Vérité *f.*
soothe [suːð] v. tr. Med. Calmer (nerves, pain). ‖ Fig. Apaiser, calmer (s.o.'s anger) ; flatter (s.o.'s vanity).
soothing [-iŋ] adj. Med., Fig. Calmant.
soothsayer ['suːθˌseiə*] n. Devin *m.;* devineresse *f.*
sooty ['suti] adj. Fuligineux. ‖ Noir (or) couvert de suie ; charbonneux.
sop [sɔp] n. Culin. Pain trempé *m.;* pl. soupe (*f.*) au lait. ‖ Fig. Appât *m.; to give a sop to Cerberus,* faire un don propitiatoire ; *to throw a sop to,* donner un os à ronger à.
— v. tr. Tremper, faire tremper. ‖ *To sop up,* éponger.
sophism ['sɔfizm] n. Sophisme *m.*
sophist [-ist] n. Sophiste *m.*
sophistic [sə'fistik] adj. Sophistique.
sophistically [-əli] adv. Sophistiquement.
sophisticate [-eit] v. tr. Tromper par des sophismes. ‖ Comm. Frelater (wine). ‖ Fig. Falsifier (a document) ; sophistiquer (a subject) ; altérer (a text). ‖ Fig. Sophistiquer, rendre artificiel.
sophisticated [-eitid] adj. Raffiné, recherché (refined) ; sophistiqué (unduly refined) ; subtil (subtle). ‖ Techn. Perfectionné, sophistiqué.
sophistication [ˌsəfisti'keiʃən] n. Sophistication, tromperie (*f.*) par des sophismes. ‖ Comm.

Falsification *f.;* frelatage *m.* ‖ Fig., Techn. Sophistication *f.*
sophistry ['sɔfistri] n. Sophisme *m.* (arguments) ; sophistique *f.* (art).
sophomore ['sɔfəmɔː*] n. U. S. Etudiant (*s.*) de deuxième année.
soporiferous [ˌsəpə'rifərəs] adj. Soporifère, soporatif.
soporific [-fik] adj., n. Soporifique *m.*
soporous ['sɔpərəs] adj. Med. Soporeux.
sopping ['sɔpiŋ] adj. Fam. Trempé (garment) ; mouillé jusqu'aux os (person).
— adv. Fam. *Sopping wet,* complètement trempé.
soppy ['sɔpi] adj. Fam. Trempé, détrempé (ground) ; larmoyant, à l'eau de rose (story) ; sentimental, fleur bleue (person) ; *to be soppy on,* avoir le béguin pour.
sopranist [sə'prɑːnist], **soprano** [-no] n. Mus. Soprano *m.*
— N. B. *Soprano* a deux pluriels : *sopranos, soprani.*
sorb [sɔːb] n. Bot. Sorbier *m.* ‖ **Sorb-apple,** n. Bot. Sorbe *f.*
sorbet ['sɔːbit] n. Culin. Sorbet *m.*
sorcerer ['sɔːsərə*] n. Sorcier *m.*
sorceress [-is] n. Sorcière *f.*
sorcery [-i] n. Sorcellerie *f.*
sordid ['sɔːdid] adj. Sale, dégoûtant, crasseux. ‖ Bas, vil, sordide ; *sordid lodging,* taudis. ‖ Zool. Sale (colouring).
sordidly [-li] adv. Sordidement ; bassement.
sordidness [-nis] n. Saleté *f.* ‖ Bassesse, sordidité *f.* (of character). ‖ Avarice, ladrerie *f.*
sordino [sɔː'diːnou] n. Mus. Sourdine *f.*
sore [sɔː*] adj. Med. Douloureux, endolori, sensible, enflammé, irrité ; *to have a sore finger,* avoir un bobo au doigt. ‖ Fig. Grand, cruel (distress) ; urgent (need) ; chagriné (person) ; pénible, douloureux (subject) ; *sore at heart,* désolé. ‖ Fam. Fâché, en colère ; *to get sore,* se fâcher. ‖ **Sore-head,** n. Fam. Rouspéteur, grincheux *s.*
— Med. Plaie *f.;* écorchure *f.;* bobo *m.* (fam.). ‖ Fig. Chagrin, souvenir douloureux *m.; to reopen an old sore,* raviver d'anciennes blessures.
— adv. † Péniblement, douloureusement, cruellement.
sorely [-li] adv. Med. Grièvement, gravement. ‖ Fig. Fort, cruellement, durement ; *sorely pressed,* aux abois.
soreness [-nis] n. Med. Endolorissement *m.;* sensibilité *f.* ‖ Fig. Chagrin *m.;* peine *f.* ‖ Fig. Irritabilité *f.;* amertume *f.* ‖ U. S. Fam. Colère *f.*
sorghum ['sɔːgəm] n. Bot. Sorgho *m.*
sorority [sə'rɔriti] n. U. S. Club très fermé (*m.*) d'étudiantes.
sorrel ['sɔrəl] n. Bot., Culin. Oseille *f.*
sorrel adj., n. Zool. Alezan *m.* (horse).
sorrily ['sɔrili] adv. Tristement. ‖ Pauvrement, mal, misérablement (pitifully).
sorriness [-nis] n. Pauvreté *f.;* état pitoyable *m.*
sorrow ['sɔrou] n. Chagrin *m.;* peine, douleur, affliction, tristesse *f.; to my sorrow,* à mon regret. ‖ **Sorrow-stricken,** adj. Accablé de chagrin.
— v. intr. S'affliger, s'attrister, avoir du chagrin (or) de la peine ; *to sorrow after* (or) *for,* s'affliger de, déplorer.
sorrowful [-ful] adj. Attristé, mélancolique, désolé (air) ; triste, chagrin (person). ‖ Attristant, affligeant, pénible (news).
sorrowfully [-fuli] adv. Tristement, avec chagrin.
sorry ['sɔri] adj. Chagrin, navré, désolé, peiné ; *to be sorry about* (or) *for,* regretter ; *to feel sorry for,* plaindre ; *I'm sorry,* pardon (excusing oneself) ; je suis désolé (expressing grief). ‖ Pauvre, piteux, triste, minable, misérable (appearance) ; *in a sorry plight,* dans une triste situation.
sort [sɔːt] n. Genre *m.;* sorte, espèce, catégorie *f.; of all sorts,* de toutes sortes. ‖ Manière, façon *f.;*

in a sort, en quelque sorte, dans une certaine mesure. ‖ Classe, condition *f.;* état *m.* (of mankind). ‖ Cru *m.* (of wine). ‖ Sorte *f.* (in typesetting). ‖ Autom. Marque *f.* ‖ Loc. *A sort of artist, an artist of sorts,* une espèce d'artiste; *a good sort,* un brave type; *nothing of the sort,* il n'en est rien; *sth. of the sort,* qqch. d'approchant; *in some sort,* jusqu'à un certain point; *to be out of sorts,* n'être pas dans son assiette, être mal en train (or) de mauvaise humeur. ‖ Fam. *To sort of remember sth.,* avoir comme un vague souvenir de qqch.
— v. tr. Assortir; classer par catégories (or) par espèces. ‖ Trier, faire le tri de. ‖ Comm. Lotir.

sorter [-ə*] n. Trieur *s.* (person). ‖ Trieuse *f.* (machine).

sortie ['sɔːti] n. Milit. Sortie *f.* ‖ Aviat. Vol, départ *(m.)* d'avions.

sortilege ['sɔːtilidʒ] n. Tirage au sort *m.* ‖ Sortilège, maléfice *m.*

SOS [,esou'es] n. S.O.S. *m.*

sot [sɔt] n. Alcoolique *s.*

sottish [-iʃ] adj. Abruti par l'alcool.

sottishness [-iʃnis] n. Abrutissement *(m.)* par l'alcoolisme.

sotto voce ['sɔtou 'voutʃi] adv. A voix basse.

souffle ['suːfl] n. Med. Souffle *m.*

soufflé ['suːflei] adj., n. Culin. Soufflé adj., *m.*

sough [sau] n. Murmure, soupir *m.*
— v. intr. Soupirer, murmurer, susurrer.

sought [sɔːt] pret., p. p. See Seek. ‖ Sought-after, adj. Très recherché (or) couru (or) en vogue.

soul [soul] n. Ame *f.; with all one's soul,* de toute son âme; *unable to call one's soul one's own,* entièrement dominé, dans un état d'esclavage absolu. ‖ Ame *f.* (part); animateur *m.;* animatrice *f.* (person); *the life and soul of,* le boute-en-train de (a party). ‖ Ame, sensibilité, chaleur, énergie *f.;* sentiment *m.* (in literature). ‖ Personnification *f.; to be the soul of discretion,* être la discrétion même. ‖ Etre vivant *m.;* personne, âme *f.; I don't see a soul,* je ne vois pas âme qui vive (or) pas un chat (fam.). ‖ Eccles. *All Souls' Day,* jour des Morts. ‖ Fam. Type *m.; good soul,* bonne âme (or) pâte; *poor soul,* pauvre créature. ‖ Soul-destroying, adj. Abrutissant, mortel pour l'âme. ‖ Soul-stirring, adj. Emouvant.

soulful [-ful] adj. Plein d'âme; expressif (eyes). ‖ Sentimental.

soulfully [-fuli] adv. Avec âme; avec expression (or) sentiment.

soulless [-lis] adj. Sans âme, terre à terre. ‖ Bas, vil. ‖ Abrutissant.

sound [saund] adj. Med. Sain, bien portant (body, mind); robuste (constitution); profond (slumber); *sound in mind,* sain d'esprit; *to be sound in wind and limb,* avoir bon pied bon œil, se porter comme un charme. ‖ Naut. Solide, en bon état (ship). ‖ Comm. Non endommagé, en bon état; sain (perishables); sans tare (timber). ‖ Fin. Solide (business, situation); solide, solvable (firm, house). ‖ Jur. Valable (title). ‖ Fig. Sain, valable, solide (argument); orthodoxe (doctrine); juste (objection). ‖ Fam. Magistral, vigoureux, en règle (whipping).
— adv. Profondément (asleep); *to sleep sound,* dormir à poings fermés.

sound n. Son, bruit *m.* ‖ Phys. *Science of sound,* acoustique. ‖ Fig. Impression produite *(f.)* par une déclaration; *not to like the sound of,* avoir une mauvaise impression de. ‖ Sound-barrier, n. Aviat. Mur du son *m.* ‖ Sound-board, n. Mus. Sommier *m.* (of an organ); table d'harmonie *f.* (of a piano). ‖ Soundbox, n. Caisse de résonance *f.;* Cinem. Cabine (*f.*) de son. ‖ Sound-damping, n. Insonorisation *f.* ‖ Sound-detector, n. Géophone, détecteur acoustique *m.* ‖ Sound-effects, n. pl. Cinem., Theatr. Bruitage *m.,* effets sonores *m. pl.* ‖ Sound-engi-

neer, n. Ingénieur du son *m.* ‖ Sound-hole, n. Mus. Ouïe *f.* (of a violin). ‖ Sound-post, n. Mus. Ame *f.* (of a violin). ‖ Sound-proof, v. tr. Insonoriser; adj. Insonorisé; isolant. ‖ Sound-track, n. Cinem. Bande sonore *f.* ‖ Sound-wave, n. Onde sonore *f.*
— v. intr. Sonner, résonner; retentir. ‖ Tinter, sonner (bell). ‖ Autom. Retentir (horn). ‖ Gramm. Se prononcer (letter). ‖ Fig. Sonner; paraître, sembler, donner l'impression de; *to sound strange,* sembler bizarre. ‖ To sound off, parler haut; parler net.
— v. tr. Faire sonner (or) résonner (or) tinter. ‖ Sonner (an alarm, a bell, trumpet). ‖ Milit. Sonner (a retreat). ‖ Autom. *To sound the horn,* klaxonner, corner. ‖ Gramm. Prononcer (a letter). ‖ Med. Ausculter (lungs). ‖ Ch. de f. Vérifier l'état de (a wheel). ‖ Fig. Proclamer, faire retentir; chanter (s.o.'s praises); *to sound a warning,* donner l'alarme.

sound v. tr. Naut., Med. Sonder. ‖ Fig. *To sound out,* sonder, pressentir, tâter le pouls à (s.o.); interroger (one's conscience).
— v. intr. Naut. Sonder, jeter la sonde. ‖ Zool. Plonger au fond.
— n. Med. Sonde *f.*

sound n. Geogr. Détroit, goulet; bras *(m.)* de mer; *the Sound,* le Sund. ‖ Zool. Vessie natatoire *f.*

sounder [-ə*] n. Electr. Parleur, sonneur *m.;* récepteur au son *m.* (in telegraphy).

sounder n. Naut. Sondeur *m.*

sounding [-iŋ] adj. Sonore, sonnant. ‖ Fig. Pompeux, creux (phrases); imposant, ronflant (title).
— n. Son, bruit *m.;* retentissement *m.* ‖ Med. Auscultation *f.* ‖ Techn. Percussion *f.* ‖ Autom. *Sounding of the horn,* klaxonnement, usage de l'avertisseur. ‖ Sounding-board, n. Abat-voix *m.*

sounding [-iŋ] n. Naut. Sondage *m.* (of depths). ‖ Naut. Pl. Sondes *f. pl.;* fonds *m. pl.* ‖ Med., Fig. Sondage *m.* ‖ Sounding-lead, n. Plomb *(m.)* de sonde. ‖ Sounding-line, n. Ligne de sonde *f.* ‖ Sounding-machine, n. Sondeur *m.*

soundless [-lis] adj. Silencieux, muet, sans bruit (noiseless).

soundless [-lis] adj. Insondable, sans fond (bottomless).

soundly [-li] adv. Sainement, bien, profondément (to sleep). ‖ Sainement, judicieusement, logiquement (to argue). ‖ Fam. Bien, de la bonne manière (to thrash).

soundness [-nis] n. Med. Bonne santé *f.;* bon état *m.* (of body, mind); profondeur *f.* (of sleep). ‖ Comm. Bon état *m.;* bonne condition *f.* (of goods). ‖ Fin. Solvabilité, solidité *f.* (of a business). ‖ Fig. Solidité *f.* (of an argument); orthodoxie *f.* (of a doctrine); justesse, sûreté *f.* (of judgment).

soup [suːp] n. Culin. Soupe *f.;* potage *m.; clear, thick, vegetable soup,* consommé, crème, potage aux légumes; *drink your soup,* mangez votre soupe. ‖ Fam. *In the soup,* dans la panade. ‖ Fam., Aviat. Brouillard *m.* ‖ Soup-kitchen, n. Soupe populaire *f.* ‖ Soup-ladle, n. Louche *f.* ‖ Soup-plate, n. Assiette creuse (or) à soupe *f.* ‖ Soup-ticket, n. Bon *(m.)* de soupe. ‖ Soup-tureen, n. Soupière *f.*
— v. tr. U. S. Autom. Fam. *To soup up,* pousser (a motor).

soupçon [sup'sɔ̃] n. Soupçon *m.,* pointe *f.*

sour [saua*] adj. Sur, aigre, acide; vert (grapes); suri, tourne (milk); *to turn sour,* tourner (milk). ‖ Med. *Sour stomach,* acidité stomacale, aigreurs d'estomac. ‖ Fig. Revêche (air); aigri, grincheux, acariâtre (person); acerbe, amer (remark). ‖ Sourpuss, n. U. S. Fam. Grincheux *s.*
— n. Techn. Eau acidulée *f.* ‖ *Whisky sour,* cocktail à base de whisky et de jus de citron.
— v. intr. Surir, s'aigrir. ‖ Tourner (milk). ‖ Fig. S'aigrir, devenir revêche (disposition, person).
— v. tr. Surir, aigrir, rendre acide. ‖ Faire tourner (milk). ‖ Med. Rendre acide. ‖ Fig. Rendre amer, aigrir (s.o.).

source [sɔːs] n. Source *f*. (of a river). ‖ MED. Foyer *m*. (of infection). ‖ Origine, source *f*. ‖ **Source-book**, n. Recueil (*m*.) de textes originaux. ‖ **Source material**, n. U. S. Sources originales *f. pl*.
sourish [ˈsauəriʃ] adj. Aigrelet. suret.
sourly [-li] adv. Aigrement, d'un air revêche.
sourness [-nis] n. Aigreur, acidité *f*. ‖ FIG. Amertume, humeur acariâtre *f*.
souse [saus] n. CULIN. Marinade *f*. ‖ FAM. Douche, saucée *f*. (in the rain). ‖ U. S. FAM. Soiffard *m*. (See SOAK.)
— v. tr. CULIN. Faire mariner. ‖ FAM. Plonger, tremper (in a liquid solution); arroser (s.o., sth.).
— v. intr. CULIN. Mariner.
soutane [suːˈtæn] n. Soutane *f*. (of Roman Catholic priest).
south [sauθ] n. Sud *m*.; *to the south of*, au sud de. ‖ Midi *m*. (of France).
— adj. Sud, du sud; *South America*, Amérique du Sud; *South American*, sud-américain; *South Africa*, Afrique du Sud; *South African*, sud-africain; *South Pole*, pôle Sud. ‖ Exposé au sud (room). ‖ Méridional (country).
— adv. Au sud, vers le sud; *due south*, droit vers le sud. ‖ **South-bound**, adj. En direction du sud. ‖ **South-east**, n. Sud-est *m*. ‖ **South-easter**, n. Vent du sud-est *m*. ‖ **South-west**, **sou'west**, n. Sud-ouest *m*. ‖ **South-wester**, **sou'wester**, n. Vent du sud-ouest *m*.; suroît *m*.
— v. intr. ASTRON. Passer le méridien. ‖ NAUT. Faire route vers le sud.
southerly [ˈsʌðəli] adj. Du sud; au midi (exposure); austral (latitude).
— adv. Vers le sud; du sud (wind).
— n. Vent du sud *m*.
southern [ˈsʌðən] adj. Du sud, au sud. ‖ Au midi, méridional (exposure). ‖ Du midi, méridional (France). ‖ ASTRON. *Southern Cross*, Croix du Sud. ‖ U. S. Sudiste (army, States).
— N. B. Le comp. est *more southern;* le superl. *southmost* ou *southernmost*.
southerner [-ə*] n. Habitant (*s*.) du sud. ‖ Méridional *s*. (in France). ‖ U. S. Sudiste *s*.
southernmost [-moust] adj. Le plus au sud.
southernwood [-wud] n. BOT. Citronnelle *f*.
southward [ˈsauθwəd] adj. Tourné vers le sud, du côté du sud.
— n. Sud *m*.
southwards [-z] adv. Vers le sud.
souvenir [ˈsuːvəˈniːə*] n. Souvenir *m*. (See KEEPSAKE.)
sovereign [ˈsɔvrin] adj. Souverain, suprême; de souveraineté (rights). ‖ MED. Infaillible, souverain (remedy). ‖ FIG. Souverain, absolu (contempt).
— n. Souverain, monarque *m*. ‖ FIN. Souverain *m*.
sovereignly [-li] adv. Souverainement.
sovereignty [-ti] n. Souveraineté *f*.
Soviet [ˈsouviet] n. Soviet *m*.
— adj. Soviétique; *the Soviet Union*, l'Union soviétique.
sovietologist [souviəˈtɔlədʒist] n. Soviétologue *s*.
sow [sou] v. tr. (145). AGRIC. Semer, ensemencer (*with*, en) [a field]; semer (seed). ‖ FIG. Semer, répandre (revolt, terror); parsemer, semer (*with*, de).
— v. intr. Semer, faire des semailles. ‖ Se préparer (revolt).
sow [sau] n. ZOOL. Truie *f*. ‖ TECHN. Gueuse *f*. ‖ **Sow-thistle**, n. BOT. Laiteron *m*.
sower [ˈsouə*] n. AGRIC., FIG. Semeur *s*.
sowing [-iŋ] n. Semailles *f. pl*.; ensemencement *m*. ‖ **Sowing-machine**, n. Semoir *m*. ‖ **Sowing-time**, n. Semaison *f*.; temps (*m*.) des semailles.
sown [soun] p. p. See sow.
soy [ˈsɔiə] n. CULIN. *Soy sauce*, sauce soja.

soya bean [ˈsɔiə ˈbiːn], U. S. **soybean** [ˈsɔi,biːn] n. AGRIC. Soja, soya *m*.
sozzled [ˈsɔzəld] adj. POP. Rond, beurré, paf.
spa [spɑː] n. Source minérale *f*. ‖ Ville d'eau, station thermale *f*.
space [speis] n. Espace *m*.; étendue, surface *f*. (area); place *f*.; espace *m*. (cubic); *to occupy* (or) *take up space*, prendre de la place. ‖ Intervalle, écartement *m*. (between two objects). ‖ Intervalle, espace de temps *m*.; *for a space*, pendant quelque temps; *short space*, court intervalle. ‖ TECHN. Espace *m*. (between letters); intervalle *m*. (between lines); *double space*, interligne double. ‖ ASTRONAUT. Espace *m*.; *space flight, travel*, vol, voyage spatial; *space probe, shuttle*, sonde, navette spatiale; *space medecine*, médecine aérospatiale; *space station*, station orbitale; *space walk*, sortie dans l'espace. ‖ **Space age**, n. Ere spatiale *f*.; adj. FIG. Ultra-moderne, futuriste. ‖ **Space-bar**, n. Barre (*f*.) d'espacement (on a typewriter). ‖ **Space opera**, n. U. S. Film (*m*.) d'aventures interplanétaires. ‖ **Space-saving**, adj. Qui fait gagner de la place, gain de place. ‖ **Space-time continuum**, n. PHYS. Continuum espace-temps *m*.
— v. tr. Espacer; disposer à des intervalles réguliers. ‖ COMM., MILIT. Echelonner.
— v. intr. Espacer (typewriter).
spacecraft [-,krɑːft] n. ASTRONAUT. Engin spatial *m*.
spaceman [-,mæn] n. ASTRONAUT. Astronaute *m*.
spaceship [-,ʃip] n. ASTRONAUT. Vaisseau spatial *m*.
spacesuit [-,suːt] n. ASTRONAUT. Scaphandre spatial *m*.
spacious [ˈspeiʃəs] adj. Spacieux, vaste, grand (abode); ample (garment). [See COMMODIOUS.]
spaciously [-li] adv. Spacieusement.
spaciousness [-nis] n. Etendue *f*.; vastes dimensions *f. pl*. ‖ Logeabilité *f*. (of an apartment, a vehicle).
spade [speid] n. Pelle *f*. (child's). ‖ AGRIC. Bêche *f*. ‖ LOC. *To call a spade a spade*, appeler un chat un chat. ‖ **Spade-work**, n. Gros travail *m*. ‖ FIG. Défrichage, débroussaillement *m*.
— v. tr. Bêcher.
spade n. Pique *m*. (in card games); *the six of spades*, le six de pique. ‖ U. S. FAM. *In spades*, franchement, carrément. ‖ POP. Nègre *m*., négresse *f*.; négro *m*. (péj.).
spadeful [-ful] n. Pleine bêche, pelletée *f*.
spaghetti [spəˈgeti] n. CULIN. Spaghetti *m. pl*.
— N. B. *Spaghetti* est sing. en anglais.
Spain [spein] n. GEOGR. Espagne *f*.
spalt [spɔlt] n. Spalt *m*.
spam [spæm] n. (trade mark). CULIN. Porc (*m*.) en boîte.
span [spæn] v. tr. (1). Franchir, traverser, enjamber (a river). ‖ Mesurer à l'empan. ‖ NAUT. Brider. ‖ FIG. Couvrir, embrasser (a period of time).
— n. Ouverture *f*. (of an arch); volant *m*. (of a beam); travée, portée *f*. (of a bridge, roof). Empan *m*. ‖ Hangar couvert (*m*.) à double pente. ‖ AVIAT. Envergure *f*. (of a plane). ‖ NAUT. Brague *f*. ‖ AGRIC. Paire *f*. (or) couple *m*. (of harnessed oxen). ‖ FIG. Court espace de temps *m*.; *mortal span*, séjour terrestre. ‖ **Span-roof**, n. Toit (*m*.) à double pente. ‖ **Span-worm**, n. ZOOL. Chenille arpenteuse (or) géomètre *f*.
span adj. See SPICK.
span pret. See SPIN.
spandrel [ˈspændrəl] n. ARCHIT. Tympan *m*.
spangle [ˈspæŋgl] n. Paillette *f*. ‖ BOT. *Oak spangle*, galle.
— v. tr. Pailleter.
spangly [-i] adj. Pailleté, étincelant.
Spaniard [ˈspænjəd] n. GEOGR. Espagnol *s*.

spaniel ['spænjəl] n. Zool. Epagneul *m.* ‖ Fam. Chien couchant *m.*

Spanish ['spæniʃ] adj. Geogr. Espagnol ; *Spanish Main*, Terre-Ferme *f.; *mer des Caraïbes. ‖ Comm. De Cordoue (leather). ‖ Med. *Spanish fly*, cantharide.
— n. Espagnol *m.* (language).

spank [spæŋk] v. tr. Fesser, donner une fessée à.
— v. intr. Aller au grand trot.
— n. Fessée *f.*

spanker [-ə*] n. Fouetteur *s.* ‖ Zool. Cheval rapide *m.*

spanker n. Naut. Brigantine *f.* ‖ **Spanker-boom,** n. Bôme *f.*

spanking [-iŋ] n. Fessée *f.*
— adj. Naut. *Spanking breeze*, bonne brise. ‖ Fam. Fameux, épatant.

spanless ['spænlis] adj. Sans bornes, incommensurable.

spanner ['spænə*] n. Personne (*f.*) qui mesure. ‖ Techn. Clef (*f.*) à écrous ; *adjustable spanner*, clef anglaise (or) à molette.

spar [spɑ:*] n. Naut. Espar *m.* ‖ Aviat. Longeron *m.; wing spar*, poutrelle. ‖ **Spar-deck,** n. Spardeck *m.*
— v. tr. Naut. Garnir d'espars. ‖ Aviat. Munir de longerons.

spar v. intr. (1). Sports. Se battre (cocks) ; s'entraîner à la boxe (persons). ‖ Fig. Se disputer, se chamailler.
— n. Sports. Combat de coqs ; combat d'entraînement d'un boxeur ; assaut (*m.*) de boxe amicale.

spar n. Spath *m.*

sparable ['spærəbl̩] n. Clou carré (*m.*) sans tête.

spare ['spɛə*] adj. Frugal, maigre (diet). ‖ Maigre, fluet, mince, sec (person). ‖ Disponible, de trop, inutilisé ; *spare time*, temps disponible, moments perdus, loisirs. ‖ De réserve, de rechange, en surnombre (extra) ; *spare room*, chambre d'ami. ‖ Fin. *Spare capital*, fonds disponibles. ‖ Autom. De secours (tyre). ‖ Techn. De rechange (parts). ‖ **Spare-ribs,** n. pl. Culin. Côtes découvertes *f. pl.* (of pork).
— n. Autom., Techn. Pièce (*f.*) détachée (or) de rechange.
— v. tr. Epargner, ménager (see economize) ; *to spare no expense*, ne pas regarder à la dépense ; *to spare no trouble*, ne pas marchander sa peine ; *not to spare oneself*, payer de sa personne ; *to spare oneself*, se ménager. ‖ Eviter ; *to spare oneself difficulty*, s'épargner des difficultés. ‖ Se priver de, se passer de ; *to have nothing to spare*, n'avoir que le strict nécessaire ; *to have room and to spare*, avoir de la place à revendre ; *to have time to spare*, avoir du temps devant soi. ‖ Epargner (s.o.'s life) ; *to spare s.o. one's complaints*, faire grâce à qqn de ses plaintes.
— v. intr. Economiser, épargner.

sparely [-li] adv. Frugalement, maigrement ; *sparely built*, sec comme un coup de trique.

sparing [-riŋ] adj. Frugal, ménager, économe, parcimonieux. (See thrifty.) ‖ Fig. Avare (of praise) ; sobre (of words).

sparingly [-riŋli] adv. Frugalement, maigrement. ‖ Sobrement, modérément.

sparingness [-riŋnis] n. Epargne, frugalité, parcimonie *f.*

spark [spɑ:k] n. Etincelle *f.* ‖ Flammèche *f.* (of burning wood). ‖ Naut., Fam. Pl. Radiotélégraphiste *m.* ‖ Autom. Etincelle (*f.*) d'allumage. ‖ Fig. Lueur, parcelle *f.* (of intelligence) ; souffle *m.* (of life) ; *spark of wit*, trait d'esprit, saillie. ‖ **Spark-arrester,** n. Ch. de f. Pare-étincelles *m.* ‖ **Spark-gap,** n. Radio. Eclateur, déflagrateur *m.; Electr. Pont d'allumage *m.* ‖ **Spark plug,** n. U. S. Autom. Bougie *f.*
— v. intr. Jeter (or) produire des étincelles.
— v. tr. Techn. Allumer (a motor).

spark n. Fam. Beau cavalier, élégant *m.; gay spark*, joyeux luron.

sparking–plug [-iŋplʌg] n. Autom. Bougie *f.*

sparkle ['spɑ:kl̩] v. intr. Etinceler, briller, scintiller (*with*, de) ; pétiller (fire) ; chatoyer (jewel) ; miroiter (lights). ‖ Mousser (wine). ‖ Fig. Etinceler (*with*, de) [anger, wit].
— n. Etincelle, lueur *f.; étincellement *m.* ‖ Feux *m. pl.* (of a diamond) ; pétillement *m.* (of eyes). ‖ Fig. Vivacité (*f.*) d'esprit.

sparkler ['spɑ:klə*] n. Chose qui étincelle *f.* ‖ Fam. Diamant, brillant *m.* ‖ U. S. Allumette japonaise *f.*

sparkless ['spɑ:klis] adj. Sans étincelle.

sparklet [-lit] n. Petite étincelle *f.*

sparkling [-liŋ] adj. Etincelant, brillant. ‖ Mousseux (wine).

sparklingly [-liŋli] adv. Avec éclat, d'une manière étincelante.

sparrer ['spɑ:rə*] n. Sports. Boxeur *m.*

sparring [-riŋ] n. Sports. Boxe amicale *f.* ‖ **Sparring-match,** n. Sports. Assaut (*m.*) de boxe amical. ‖ **Sparring-partner,** n. Sports. Partenaire d'entraînement *m.*

sparrow ['spærou] n. Zool. Moineau, passereau *m.* ‖ **Sparrow-hawk,** n. Zool. Epervier *m.*

sparry ['spɑ:ri] adj. Spathique.

sparse [spɑ:s] adj. Clairsemé, rare (hair) ; épars, éparpillé (houses) ; peu dense (population).

sparsely [-li] adv. Peu abondamment ; sans densité.

spasm ['spæzm] n. Med. Convulsion *f.* (clonic) ; spasme *m.* (functional) ; accès *m.* (of coughing) ; angine *f.* (of the chest). ‖ Fig. Accès *m.* (of anger, fright) ; affre *f.* (of grief) ; *to work in spasms*, travailler par à-coups.

spasmodic [spæz'mɔdik] adj. Med. Spasmodique (in general) ; convulsif, involontaire (movement). ‖ Fig. Fait par à-coups (work).

spasmodically [-əli] adv. Med. Convulsivement, d'une façon spasmodique. ‖ Fig. Par à-coups, irrégulièrement.

spastic ['spæstik] adj. Med. Spasmodique (paralysis).
— n. Med. Paraplégique *s.*

spat [spæt] See spit.

spat n. Demi-guêtre *f.*

spat n. Zool. Frai *m.* (of oysters).
— v. intr. Frayer (oyster).

spat n. U. S. Fam. Prise (*f.*) de bec.

spate [speit]. Crue *f.* (of a river). ‖ Fam. Flot *m.; marée, avalanche *f.; a spate of*, un tas de.

spathe [speið] n. Bot. Spathe *f.*

spatial ['speiʃəl] adj. De l'espace. ‖ Spatial (coordinates).

spatio-temporal [,speiʃiou'tempərəl] adj. Spatio-temporel.

spatter ['spætə*] v. tr. Eclabousser (*with*, de). ‖ Asperger (liquid).
— v. intr. Tomber en éclaboussant, gicler.
— n. Eclaboussement *m.; éclaboussure, aspersion *f.*

spatterdash [-dæʃ] n. Guêtre *f.*

spatula ['spætjulə] n. Culin., Med. Spatule *f.*

spatular [-ə*], **spatulate** [-it] adj. Spatulé.

spavin ['spævin] n. Zool. Eparvin *m.*

spawn [spɔ:n] n. Zool. Frai *m.; œufs *m. pl.* (of fish). ‖ Bot. Blanc *m.* (of mushrooms). ‖ Fam. Progéniture *f.; rejeton *m.*
— v. tr. Zool. Déposer (eggs). ‖ Fam. Avoir, engendrer, produire, donner naissance à.
— v. intr. Zool. Eclore (eggs) ; frayer (fish). ‖ Fam. Se multiplier, se reproduire.

spawning [-iŋ] n. Zool. Frai *m.* (act). ‖ **Spawning-place,** n. Frayère *f.* ‖ **Spawning-season,** n. Fraie *f.; époque (*f.*) du frai.

spay [spei] v. tr. Zool. Châtrer (a female).

speak [spi:k] v. intr. (146). Parler ; *to speak to*, parler à, adresser la parole à, s'adresser à, s'entre-

tenir avec (*about*, *of*, de). ‖ S'exprimer ; *to speak out*, parler net (to express oneself) ; parler fort (to speak loudly). ‖ Mus. Chanter (violin). ‖ Arts. Parler, être ressemblant (portrait). ‖ Zool. Donner de la voix (dog). ‖ Fig. *To speak well for*, être une preuve de, plaider en faveur de. ‖ Loc. *To speak back to*, répondre à, riposter à (in anger) ; *to speak badly, well of*, dire du mal, du bien de ; *so to speak*, pour ainsi dire ; *to be nothing to speak of*, ne pas valoir la peine d'en parler.
— v. tr. Parler, employer (a language) ; *to speak French*, parler français. ‖ Prononcer, dire (a word) ; *to speak comfort to*, adresser des paroles de consolation à ; *to speak sense*, dire des choses sensées ; *to speak the truth*, dire la vérité ; *her eyes spoke volumes*, ses yeux en disaient long, son regard était éloquent. ‖ Naut. Héler, arraisonner (a ship). ‖ Fig. Indiquer, montrer : proclamer ; *his deeds speak his courage*, ses actes révèlent son courage.
‖ **Speak-easy**, n. U. S. Fam. Débit clandestin *m*.
speaker [-ə*] n. Parleur, orateur *s*. personne (*f*.) qui parle. ‖ Président *m*. (of a meeting, in Parliament). ‖ Gramm. Locuteur *m*. ; locutrice *f*. ‖ Techn., Fam. Haut-parleur *m*., baffle *f*.
speakership [-ʃip] n. Présidence *f*. (in Parliament).
speaking [-iŋ] adj. Parlant, qui parle ; *speaking acquaintance*, simple connaissance ; *not on speaking terms*, brouillé, en froid. ‖ Arts. Vivant, parlant (likeness, portrait).
— n. Action (*f*.) de parler. ‖ Déclamation *f*. ; *public speaking*, art oratoire. ‖ Loc. *Generally speaking*, généralement parlant ; *strictly speaking*, à proprement parler, en serrant les choses de près. ‖ **Speaking-trumpet**, n. Porte-voix *m*. ‖ **Speaking-tube**, n. Tuyau acoustique *m*.
spear ['spiə*] n. Lance *f.* ; javelot *m.* ; javeline *f*. (weapon). ‖ Sports. Harpon *m*. (for fishing) ; épieu *m*. (for hunting). ‖ Bot. Brin *m*. (of grass) ; tige *f*. (of willow). ‖ Fig. *Spear side*, branche mâle (of a family). ‖ **Spear-grass**, n. Bot. Chiendent *m.* ; U. S. Pâturin *m*. ‖ **Spear-head**, n. Fer (*m*.) de lance ; Milit. U. S. Pointe *f*.
— v. intr. Bot. *To spear up*, monter.
spearman [-mən] (pl. **spearmen**) n. Lancier *m.* ; porteur de javelot *m*.
spearmint [-mint] n. Bot., Culin. Menthe verte *f*.
spec [spek] n. Fam. Hypothèse *f* ; *on spec*, à tout hasard.
special ['speʃəl] adj. Particulier, spécial ; *special correspondent*, envoyé spécial (of a newspaper) ; *special feature*, particularité (of s.o.) ; article spécial *m*. (in a newspaper) ; *special delivery letter*, lettre expresse. ‖ Tout particulier, exceptionnel (especial) ; *special care*, soin particulier. ‖ Comm. De faveur (price). ‖ Med. Topographique (anatomy). ‖ Ch. de f. Spécial (train). ‖ Jur. Bénévole (constable) ; *special licence*, dispense, autorisation spéciale.
— n. Edition spéciale *f*. (of a newspaper). ‖ Ch. de f. Train spécial *m*.
specialism [-izm] n. Spécialisation *f*.
specialist [-ist] n. Spécialiste *s*.
speciality [,speʃi'æliti] n. Particularité *f*. ‖ Spécialité *f*. (field of study) ; fort *m*. (fam.). ‖ Comm. Spécialité *f*.
specialization [,speʃəlai'zeiʃən] n. Spécialisation *f*. ‖ Zool., Med. Différenciation *f*.
specialize ['speʃəlaiz] v. tr. Particulariser, spécialiser ; désigner (or) adapter à un but spécial. ‖ Zool. Adapter (an organ) ; différencier (organisms).
— v. intr. Se spécialiser (*in*, dans) [a field of research]. ‖ Zool. Se différencier (species).
specially [-i] adv. Particulièrement, spécialement ; surtout. ‖ Dans un but particulier.
specialty [-ti] n. Jur. Contrat (*m*.) sous seing privé. ‖ Comm., Fig. Spécialité *f*.
specie ['spi:ʃi:] n. invar. Numéraire *m*., espèces *f. pl*. ‖ Comm. *To pay in specie*, payer en espèces.
— N. B. *Specie* est un collectif qui ne prend aucun article.

species [-z] n. invar. Zool. Espèce *f*. ‖ Fig. Sorte, espèce, catégorie *f.* ; genre *m*.
specific [spə'sifik] adj. Spécifique. ‖ Phys. *Specific gravity*, poids spécifique. ‖ Zool., Med. Spécifique. ‖ Fig. Déterminé (aim) ; explicite (order) ; précis (statement). ‖ Fig. Distinct, particulier, personnel, propre.
— n. Med. Spécifique *m*. (*for*, contre).
specifically [-əli] adv. Spécifiquement. ‖ Précisément, de façon précise.
specification [,spesifi'keiʃən] n. Spécification *f*. ‖ Comm. Mémoire descriptif *m*. (for a patent) ; prescriptions, stipulations *f. pl*. (for work to be done). ‖ Pl. Comm. Cahier (*m*.) des charges (of a bidder) ; stipulations *f. pl*. (of a contract). ‖ Jur. *Specification of charge*, chef d'accusation.
specificity [,spesi'fisiti] n. Med. Spécificité *f*.
specify ['spesifai] v. tr. (2). Spécifier, désigner. ‖ Préciser (conditions) ; *unless otherwise specified*, sauf indication contraire.
specimen ['spesimən] n. Spécimen *m.* ; échantillon, exemple *m*. (sample). ‖ Exemplaire *m*. (copy). ‖ Med. *To take a blood specimen*, faire une prise de sang. ‖ Fam. *Queer specimen*, drôle de particulier.
specious ['spi:ʃəs] adj. Spécieux, trompeur (appearance) ; captieux (argument).
speck [spek] n. Petite tache *f.* ; point *m*. (of colour) ; grain, brin, atome *m*. (of dust) ; mouche *f*. (of mud) ; grumeau *m*. (of salt). ‖ Tavelure, tache *f*. (on fruit). ‖ Fig. **Brin** *m*. (of consolation).
— v. tr. Tacheter, moucheter.
speckle ['spekl] n. Moucheture, tache *f*. (small spot) ; tache (*f*.) de rousseur (freckle).
speckled ['spekəld] adj. Moucheté, tacheté.
specs [speks] n. pl. Fam. Lunettes *f. pl*. ‖ † Besicles *f. pl*.
spectacle ['spektəkl] n. Spectacle *m.* ; *to make a spectacle of oneself*, se donner en spectacle. ‖ Pl. Lunettes *f. pl.* ; *three pairs of spectacles*, trois paires de lunettes. ‖ † Besicles *f. pl*. ‖ **Spectacle-case**, n. Etui (*m*.) à lunettes. ‖ **Spectacle-maker**, n. Lunetier *m*.
spectacled [-d] adj. Portant des lunettes. ‖ Zool. A lunettes (snake).
spectacular [spek'tækjulə*] adj. Spectaculaire ; impressionnant. ‖ Theatr. A grand spectacle (play, show). ‖ Fam. Théâtral.
spectator ['spek'teitə*] n. Spectateur *m.* ; spectatrice *f.* ; pl. assistance *f*. ‖ Témoin *m*. (of an accident).
spectatress [-tris] n. Spectatrice *f*.
specter ['spektə*] n. U. S. See SPECTRE.
spectral ['spektrəl] adj. Spectral, fantomal, fantomatique. ‖ Phys. Spectral (analysis) ; du spectre (colours).
spectre ['spektə*] n. Spectre, fantôme, revenant *m*. (See GHOST.)
spectrogram ['spektro,græm] n. Phys. Spectrogramme *m*.
spectrograph [-,græf] n. Phys. Spectrographe *m*.
spectrographic [,spektro'græfik] adj. Phys. Spectrographique.
spectrography [spek'trogræfi] n. Phys. Spectrographie *f*.
spectrology [spek'trolədʒi] n. Spectrologie *f*.
spectrometer [-mitə*] n. Phys. Spectromètre *m*.
spectroscope ['spektrəskoup] n. Spectroscope *m*.
spectroscopic [,spektro'skopik] adj. Spectroscopique.
spectroscopy [spek'troskəpi] n. Spectroscopie *f*.
spectrum ['spektrəm] (pl. **spectra** [-ə]) n. Astron., Phys. Spectre *m*. ‖ **Spectrum-analysis**, n. Analyse spectrale *f*.
specular ['spekjulə*] adj. Spéculaire (ore). ‖ Miroitant, réfléchissant (surface).

SPECTACLE

theatre, stage	théâtre, scène	property man	accessoiriste
pit; U. S. orchestra	parterre	prompt side (P. S.)	côté jardin
orchestra stall; U. S. seat	fauteuil d'orchestre	opposite prompt side (O. P.)	côté cour
dressing-room [d'artiste]	loge	scene-shifter	machiniste
box [de spectateur]		flies	cintres
dress circle; balcony	balcon; 2e balcon	dance, ballet	danse, ballet
the « gods »	le poulailler	ballet-dancer	danseur, danseuse
first night, première	première	prima ballerina	première danseuse
dress rehearsal	répétition générale	dancing star	danseuse étoile
understudy	doublure	film	film
encore	bis	pictures, U. S. movies	cinéma
interval; entr'acte	entracte	to double, to dub	doubler
play-bill	affiche	caption	sous-titre
applause	applaudissements	dubbing	doublage
hissing	sifflets	leading lady	jeune première
queue, U. S. line	queue, file	leading man	jeune premier
to queue, U. S. line up	faire la queue	screen	écran
house full!; U. S. sold out!	complet!	script	scénario
prompter ['s box]	souffleur (trou du)	(animated) cartoon	dessin animé
footlights	feux de rampe	documentary (film)	documentaire
wings	coulisses	slow motion	ralenti
behind the scenes	derrière les coulisses	to film	tourner un film
scenery, sets	décors	to adapt a novel	adapter un roman
stage manager	régisseur	(stage) director	réalisateur
properties; props	accessoires	close-up	gros plan

speculate [-leit] v. intr. Spéculer, faire de la théorie pure ‖ Méditer. ‖ Se livrer à des conjectures (*about*, *on*, sur). ‖ FIN. Jouer; spéculer (*in*, sur) [stocks].
speculation [spekju'leiʃən] n. Spéculation, méditation *f.* (*on*, sur); contemplation *f.* (*on*, de); conjecture, théorie, hypothèse *f.* ‖ FIN. Spéculation *f.*
speculative ['spekjulətiv] adj. Spéculatif. ‖ Méditatif, contemplatif (glance). ‖ Conjectural, théorique (assumption). ‖ FIN. Spéculatif.
speculator ['spekjuleitə*] n. Spéculatif, penseur *s.* ‖ FIN. Spéculateur *m.*; spéculatrice *f.*
speculum ['spekjuləm] n. MED. Spéculum *m.* ‖ PHYS. Miroir *m.* (of a telescope); ZOOL. Ocelle *f.*
sped [sped]. See SPEED.
speech [spiːtʃ] n. Conférence *f.* (lecture); discours *m.*; allocution, harangue *f.* (talk); speech, laïus *m.* (fam.); *to deliver* (or) *make a speech*, faire (or) prononcer un discours. ‖ Paroles *f. pl.*; propos *m. pl.* (remarks). ‖ Langue *f.*; langage, parler *m.* (of a people, a region). ‖ Parole *f.* (faculty); *to lose the power of speech*, perdre la parole. ‖ Parole, élocution, manière (*f.*) de parler; *to be slow of speech*, s'exprimer lentement; *to have a speech impediment*, avoir un défaut de prononciation. ‖ GRAMM. Discours *m.*; *figure of speech*, figure de rhétorique (or) de style; *parts of speech*, parties du discours. ‖ JUR. *Barrister's speech*, plaidoirie. ‖ MUS. Sonorité *f.*; qualité (*f.*) du son (of an organ). ‖ **Speech-defect**, n. MED. Difficulté d'élocution *f.* ‖ **Speech-disorder**, n. MED. Maladie (*f.*) [or] trouble (*m.*) de la parole. ‖ **Speech-making,** n. Discours *m. pl.*; allocutions *f. pl.* ‖ **Speech therapy**, n. MED. Orthophonie *f.*
speechifier [-ifaiə*] n. FAM. Discoureur, péroreur *s.*
speechify [-ifai] v. intr. (2). Discourir, pérorer, palabrer, épiloguer.
speechless [-lis] adj. Incapable de parler, sans voix, interloqué. (See MUTE). ‖ Muet (*with*, de) [emotion].
speechlessly [-lisli] adv. Sans voix, sans pouvoir parler.
speechlessness [-lisnis] n. Mutisme *m.* ‖ MED. Aphonie *f.*
speed [spiːd] n. Vitesse, rapidité, célérité, vélocité *f.*; *to make speed*, se presser, se dépêcher, faire diligence. ‖ AVIAT. *Air speed*, vitesse aérodynamique. ‖ LOC. *At top speed*, à toute vitesse, à

toute allure, à pleins gaz, à fond de train (car); à bride abattue, au grand galop, ventre à terre (horse); à toutes rames (rowing-boat); à toutes jambes (runner); à toute vapeur (train).
— v. tr. (147). † Expédier, dépêcher. ‖ Lancer (an arrow); souhaiter bon voyage (or) bon retour à (s.o.). ‖ † Faire réussir, favoriser; *God speed you*, que Dieu vous aide. ‖ **To speed up**, accélérer, améliorer; TECHN. Régler la vitesse de.
— v. intr. Aller vite, se hâter, se presser; *to speed off*, partir à toute vitesse. ‖ AUTOM. Faire de la vitesse. ‖ † Prospérer, réussir. ‖ **Speed-boat**, n. NAUT. Bateau glisseur, motoglisseur, hydroglisseur *m.* ‖ **Speed-demon**, n. AUTOM. Chauffard *m.* ‖ **Speed-indicator**, n. TECHN. Indicateur (*m.*) de vitesse; compte-tours *m.*; régleur (*m.*) de vitesse (on a gramophone). ‖ **Speed-limit**, n. Vitesse maximum *f.* ‖ **Speed-merchant**, n. AUTOM. Chauffard *m.* ‖ **Speed-way**, n. Piste *f.* (for racing); U. S. Autoroute *f.* (highway).
speeder [-ə*] n. TECHN. Contrôleur (*m.*) de vitesse.
speedily [-ili] adv. Rapidement, vite; en toute hâte. ‖ Promptement.
speediness [-inis] n. Vitesse, rapidité, célérité *f.* ‖ Promptitude *f.*
speedometer [spiː'dɔmitə*], **speedo** ['spiːdou] n. AUTOM. Indicateur (*m.*) de vitesse, compteur *m.*
speedster ['spiːdstə*] n. AUTOM., FAM. Conducteur (*s.*) qui a toujours le pied au plancher, fou (*s.*) du volant (driver); bolide *m.* (car).
speedwell ['spiːd,wel] n. BOT. Véronique *f.*
speedy ['spiːdi] adj. Rapide, vite. ‖ Prompt.
speiss [spais] n. TECHN. Speiss *m.*
spelaean [spiː'liːən] adj. Des cavernes.
spel(a)eologist [,spiːli'ɔlədʒist] n. Spéléologue *m.*
spel(a)eology [-dʒi] n. Spéléologie *f.*
spell [spel] n. Charme, sortilège *m.* (enchantment); incantation *f.*; sort, maléfice *m.* (evil spell); *to break the spell*, rompre le charme; *to cast a spell over*, jeter un sort sur, ensorceler; *under a spell*, envoûté. ‖ Attrait, charme *m.*, attirance *f.* (attraction). ‖ **Spell-binder**, n. FAM. Fascinateur, orateur fascinant *m.* ‖ **Spell-bound**, adj. Enchanté, ensorcelé; FIG. Fasciné.
spell v. tr. (148). Epeler. ‖ Orthographier (in writing). ‖ Former, écrire (a word) [by letters]. ‖ FIG. Signifier, équivaloir à (doom).
— v. intr. Epeler. ‖ Mettre l'orthographe, orthographier; *to learn how to spell*, apprendre l'ortho-

graphe. ‖ S'écrire (word) ; *how is it spelt?* (or) U. S. *spelled?*, comment cela s'écrit-il ?

spell n. Période courte *f.* ; intervalle, petit moment, temps *m.* ; *cold spell*, passe de froid. ‖ Comm. Relais *m.* ; relève *f.* ; *spell of duty*, tour de service ; *to take spells*, se relayer ; *at a spell*, tout d'un trait. — v. tr. U. S. Relever, relayer, remplacer (s.o. on duty).

speller [-ə*] n. Abécédaire, syllabaire *m.* (book). ‖ *To be a bad, good speller*, ne pas savoir, savoir l'orthographe.

spelling [-iŋ] n. Epellation *f.* ‖ Orthographe *f.* ; *literal spelling*, orthographe d'usage. ‖ **Spelling-bee**, n. Concours (*m.*) d'orthographe. ‖ **Spelling-book**, n. Abécédaire, livre (*m.*) de lecture.

spelt [spelt] n. Bot. Epeautre *m.*

spelt pret., p. p. See SPELL.

spelter [ˈspeltə*] n. Comm. Zinc *m.*

spencer [ˈspensə*] n. Naut. Voile goélette *f.*

spencer n. Spencer *m.* (garment).

spend [spend] v. intr. (149). Dépenser, faire des dépenses. ‖ Fig. S'user, se consumer, se gaspiller. — v. tr. Dépenser (effort, money) ; *to spend one's breath*, dépenser sa salive ; *without spending a penny*, sans bourse délier. ‖ Consommer, épuiser (ammunition, provisions) ; *to spend itself*, s'épuiser (anger, storm) ; *spent bullet*, balle morte ; *spent with fatigue*, épuisé de fatigue. ‖ Employer (care) ; passer (time) ; *to be far spent*, être écoulé (day). ‖ Dissiper (a fortune) ; gaspiller (money, time) ; *to spend money like water*, faire valser les écus, jeter son argent par les fenêtres.

spender [-ə*] n. Dépensier ; gaspilleur *s.* (waster).

spending [-iŋ] n. Dépense *f.* ; *spending power*, pouvoir d'achat.

spendthrift [-θrift] n. Dépensier, prodigue *s.* ; panier percé *m.* (fam.). — adj. Dépensier ; dilapidateur *m.* ; dilapidatrice *f.*

spent [spent] See SPEND.

sperm [spə:m] n. Med. Sperme *m.* ; semence *f.* ‖ Zool. *Sperm whale*, cachalot.

spermaceti [ˌspə:məˈseti] n. Zool. Spermaceti, blanc (*m.*) de baleine.

spermary [ˈspə:məri] n. Glande séminale *f.*

spermatic [spə:ˈmætik] adj. Spermatique.

spermatozoon [ˌspə:mətəˈzouən] (pl. **spermatozoa** [-ə]) n. Spermatozoïde *m.*

spermicidal [ˌspə:miˈsaidəl] adj. Spermicide.

spermicide [ˈspə:miˌsaid] n. Spermicide *m.*

spew [spju:] v. tr., intr. Vomir ; dégobiller (fam.). ‖ Cracher.

sphagnum [ˈsfægnəm] (pl. **sphagna** [-æ]) n. Bot. Sphaigne *f.*

sphenoid [ˈsfi:nɔid] adj. Med. Sphénoïde. — n. Med. Os sphénoïde *m.*

sphere [sfiə*] n. Sphère *f.* ; globe *m.* ‖ Math. Sphère *f.* ‖ Astron. Sphère *f.* ; ciel *m.* ‖ Naut. Voyant *m.* (of a lightship). ‖ Fig. Sphère *f.* ; cadre, milieu *m.* ; champ *m.* (of activity) ; domaine *m.* (of authority) ; zone *f.* (of influence) ; *sphere of authority*, compétence.

spheric [ˈsferik] adj. Math. Sphérique. ‖ Fig. Des sphères, du firmament (poetic). — n. pl. Math. Trigonométrie sphérique *f.*

spherical [-əl] adj. Sphérique. ‖ Math. Sphérique, de la sphère. ‖ Techn. A rotule (joint).

sphericity [sfeˈrisiti] n. Sphéricité *f.*

spheroid [ˈsfiərɔid] n. Sphéroïde *m.*

spherometer [sfiərˈɔmitə*] n. Sphéromètre *m.*

sphincter [ˈsfiŋktə*] n. Med. Sphincter *m.*

sphinx [sfiŋks] n. Sphinx *m.* — N. B. Deux pluriels : *sphinxes, sphinges.*

sphygmograph [ˈsfigməgrɑ:f] n. Med. Sphygmographe *m.*

sphygmus [ˈsfigməs] n. Med. Pouls *m.* ; pulsation *f.*

spica [ˈspaikə] n. Bot. Epi *m.* ‖ Med. Spica *m.*

spicate [-it] adj. Bot. En forme d'épi, à épi. ‖ Zool. A ergot, spiciforme.

spice [spais] n. Culin. Epice *f.* ; aromate, condiment *m.* ‖ Fig. Piment *m.* (of adventure) ; pointe *f.* (of irony) ; grain *m.* (of malice) ; *to give spice to*, pimenter (an anecdote). — v. tr. Culin. Epicer, aromatiser. ‖ Fig. Pimenter, relever (a story).

spicebush [-buʃ] n. Bot. Benjoin *m.*

spicery [-əri] n. Culin. Epices *f.* pl. ‖ † Epicerie *f.* (cupboard).

spicily [-ili] adv. Fig. D'une manière piquante (or) crue ; lestement.

spiciness [-nis] n. Culin. Goût épicé *m.* ‖ Fig. Piquant, sel *m.*

spick [spik] adj. *Spick and span*, net comme un sou neuf, bien astiqué (clean) ; tiré à quatre épingles (neat).

spicy [ˈspaisi] adj. Culin. Epicé (in general) ; aromatique, parfumé, relevé (seasoned). ‖ Fig. Piquant, croustillant, salé ; pimenté (expression) ; corsé, croustillant, cru, leste, grivois (story). ‖ Fam. Pimpant, chic.

spider [ˈspaidə*] n. Zool. Araignée *f.* ‖ Techn. Armature *f.* (of a mould) ; croisillon *m.* (of a wheel) ; crochet *m.* (of a well). ‖ U. S. Culin. Trépied *m.* ; sauteuse (*f.*) sur trépied (pan). ‖ **Spider-crab**, n. Zool. Araignée de mer *f.* ‖ **Spider('s)-web**, n. Toile d'araignée *f.*

spidery [-dəri] adj. Qui ressemble à une araignée ; *spidery handwriting*, pattes de mouche. ‖ Infesté d'araignées (place).

spiel [spi:l] n. U. S. Fam. Baratin, bourrage de crâne *m.* — v. intr. U. S. Fam. Baratiner. — v. tr. U. S. Fam. Dégoiser.

spifflicate [ˈspiflikeit] v. tr. Pop. Ecraser, anéantir ; écrabouiller (fam.).

spiffy [ˈspifi], **spiffing** [ˈspifiŋ] adj. Fam. Au poil, du tonnerre (excellent) ; chic (stylish).

spigot [ˈspigət] n. Cannelle *f.* ; fausset *m.* (of a barrel).

spik [spik] n. U. S. Pop. Latino-Américain, métèque *s.* (péj.).

spike [spaik] n. Pointe *f.* ; piquant *m.* (on barbed wire) ; lance *f.* (on a railing). ‖ Clou (*m.*) à large tête (nail). ‖ Ch. de f. Crampon *m.* ‖ Bot. Epi *m.* (ear) ; lavande *f.* (lavender). ‖ **Spike-drawer**, n. Techn. Pied-de-biche *m.* ‖ **Spike-heel**, n. Talon aiguille *m.* — v. tr. Clouer. ‖ Armer (or) hérisser de pointes (a gate). ‖ Milit. Enclouer (a cannon). ‖ U. S. Fam. Corser à l'alcool (a drink). — v. intr. Bot. Former des épis.

spikenard [-nɑ:d] n. Bot. Nard indien, spicanard *m.* ‖ Med. Nard *m.*

spiky [-i] adj. Armé (or) hérissé de pointes (or) de piquants. ‖ Aigu, pointu.

spile [spail] n. Fausset *m.* (of a cask). ‖ Archit. Pilotis *m.* ‖ Naut. Epite, cheville *f.* — v. tr. Percer pour ajuster un fausset. ‖ Archit. Piloter.

spill [spil] v. tr. (150). Répandre, renverser (a liquid). ‖ Désarçonner (a horseman) ; verser (passengers). ‖ Naut. Etouffer (a sail). ‖ Pop. Divulguer ; cracher (fam.) [a secret] ; *to spill the beans*, vendre la mèche, se mettre à table. — v. intr. Se répandre, se renverser, s'écouler, se déverser ; *to spill over*, déborder. — N. B. L'anglais préfère *spilt* aux pret. et p.p., l'américain *spilled*. — n. Chute, culbute *f.* ; *to take a spill*, ramasser une pelle (or) une bûche (fam.). ‖ **Spill-way**, n. Passe-déversoir *m.*

spill n. Brindille, longue allumette *f.*, tortillon de papier *m.* (for lighting a fire).

spillikin [ˈspilikin] n. Jonchet *m.*

spilt [spilt]. See SPILL.

spin [spin] v. tr. (151). Filer (thread, wool). ‖ Faire tourner (a dancing partner, top); faire tournoyer (or) pivoter (an object); *to spin a coin,* jouer à pile ou face. ‖ ZOOL. Filer, tisser (a spider's-web). ‖ SPORTS. Pêcher à la cuiller. ‖ FIG. *To spin out,* faire traîner en longueur, prolonger (a discussion); délayer, allonger (a story); passer, faire passer (time); *to spin a yarn,* raconter une longue histoire. — v. intr. Filer. ‖ Tourner (coin, top); tournoyer (suspended object); *to send s.o. spinning against the wall,* envoyer rouler (or) dinguer (fam.) qqn contre le mur. ‖ S'affoler (compass). ‖ AVIAT. Descendre en vrille. ‖ SPORTS. Pêcher à la cuiller. ‖ AUTOM. Patiner (tyres); *to spin along,* filer à toute vitesse; *to spin round,* faire un tête-à-queue. ‖ FIG. *My head is spinning,* la tête me tourne. — n. Tournoiement *m.;* rotation *f.* ‖ SPORTS. *To put spin on a ball,* donner de l'effet à une balle. ‖ AUTOM. *To go for a spin,* se balader en voiture.

spina bifida ['spainə 'bifidə] n. MED. Spina-bifida *m.*

spinach ['spinidʒ] n. CULIN. Epinards *m. pl.* ‖ BOT. Epinard *m.*

spinal ['spainl] adj. MED. Spinal, vertébral; *spinal column,* colonne vertébrale; *spinal cord,* cordon médullaire, moelle épinière; *spinal curvature,* déviation de la colonne vertébrale, scoliose.

spindle ['spindl̩] n. Fuseau *m.* ‖ Broche *f.* (of a spinning-machine) ‖ TECHN. Aiguille *f.* (of an injector); arbre *m.* (of a lathe); axe *m.* (of a pump); tige *f.* (of a valve). ‖ NAUT. Mèche *f.* (of the capstan); pivot *m.* (of the compass). ‖ **Spindle-shanked,** adj. FAM. Aux mollets de coq. ‖ **Spindle-shaped,** adj. Fuselé. ‖ **Spindle-tree,** n. BOT. Fusain *m.* — v. intr. S'élever en fuseau. ‖ BOT. Monter. — v. tr. Rouler en fuseau. ‖ TECHN. Façonner à la toupilleuse.

spindrift ['spindrift] n. Embrun *m.;* embruns *m. pl.;* poussière d'eau *f.*

spine [spain] n. BOT. Epine *f.* ‖ MED. Epine dorsale, colonne vertébrale *f.* ‖ ZOOL. Piquant *m.* ‖ TECHN. Dos *m.* (of a book). ‖ GEOGR. Arête *f.* (between slopes). ‖ **Spine-chilling,** adj. Terrifiant, qui vous glace jusqu'à la moelle.

spined [-d] adj. Epineux, à piquants. ‖ ZOOL. Vertébré.

spineless [-lis] adj. Sans épines (or) piquants. ‖ ZOOL. Invertébré. ‖ FIG. Mou, flasque; invertébré (fam.).

spinet ['spinit] n. MUS. Epinette *f.*

spinnaker ['spinəkə*] n. NAUT. Spinnaker *m.*

spinner ['spinə*] n. Fileur *s.* ‖ Métier (*m.*) à filer. ‖ ZOOL. Araignée fileuse *f.* ‖ TECHN. Repousseur au tour *m.* ‖ SPORTS. Cuiller *f.* (for fishing). ‖ FIG. Débiteur, conteur *s.* (of yarns).

spinneret [-rit] n. ZOOL., TECHN. Filière *f.*

spinney ['spini] n. BOT. Boqueteau *m.*

spinning ['spiniŋ] n. Filature *f.* (by machine); filage *m.* (by spinning-wheel). ‖ Tournoiement *m.;* rotation *f.* ‖ Affolement *m.* (of a compass needle). ‖ AVIAT. Vrille *f.* ‖ AUTOM. Patinage *m.* (of tyres). ‖ TECHN. Repoussage au tour *m.* ‖ SPORTS. Pêche (*f.*) à la cuiller. ‖ **Spinning-factory** (or) -**mill**, n. Filature *f.* ‖ **Spinning-frame** (or) -**machine**, n. Métier (*m.*) à filer. ‖ **Spinning-jenny**, n. Jenny *m.* ‖ **Spinning-song**, n. MUS. Chanson de toile *f.* ‖ **Spinning-top**, n. Toupie hollandaise *f.;* sabot *m.* ‖ **Spinning-wheel**, n. Rouet *m.*

spinose ['spainous], **spinous** [-əs] adj. Epineux, piquant.

spinster ['spinstə*] n. † Fileuse, filandière *f.* ‖ Célibataire *f.* (civil status); vieille fille *f.* (fam.).

spinsterhood [-hud] n. Célibat, état civil (*m.*) de femme célibataire.

spinule ['spainjuːl] n. BOT., ZOL. Spinule *f.*

spiny ['spaini] adj. Epineux, armé de piquants (or) d'épines. ‖ ZOOL. *Spiny lobster,* langouste. ‖ FIG. Epineux (problem).

spiracle ['spairəkl] n. BOT. Stomate *m.* ‖ ZOOL. Stigmate *m.* (of insects); évent *m.* (of whales).

spiraea [spai'riːə] n. BOT. Spirée *f.*

spiral ['spaiərəl] adj. En spirale; tournant, en colimaçon (stairway). ‖ TECHN. A ressort, à hélice (balance); à spirale (clutch); hélicoïdal (gear, wheel); à boudin, spiral (spring). ‖ AVIAT. En spirale (dive). ‖ MED. Rampant (bandage). — n. Spirale; hélice *f.;* hélicoïde *m.* ‖ Spire *f.* ‖ AVIAT. Montée (or) descente en spirale *f.* ‖ FIN. Montée en flèche (of prices). — v. intr. Tourner en spirale; vriller; tirebouchonner (fam.). ‖ AVIAT. *To spiral up, down,* monter, descendre en spirale.

spirant ['spaiərənt] n. Spirante *f.* — adj. GRAMM. Spirant (consonant).

spire ['spaiə*] n. ARCHIT. Flèche *f.* (of a church). ‖ BOT. Brin *m.* (of grass); cime *f.* (of a tree). — v. intr. S'élever en flèche; pousser en hauteur.

spire n. Spirale *f.* ‖ TECHN. Spire *f.;* tour *m.* (of a helix).

spirit ['spirit] n. Esprit *m.;* âme, essence *f.; present in spirit,* présent en esprit. ‖ Esprit *m.* (incorporeal being); spectre, revenant, fantôme *m.* (ghost); fée, elfe *f.;* lutin *m.* (sprite); *evil spirit,* esprit malin, mauvais esprit; *spirit of Liberty,* génie de la Liberté; *familiar spirit,* esprit familier. ‖ Esprit *m.;* animateur *m.;* animatrice *f.;* âme *f.* (person); *kindred spirit,* âme sœur; *leading spirit,* âme, chef; *meneur m.* (of a revolt); cheville ouvrière (of an undertaking). ‖ Esprit *m.;* disposition *f.; to enter into the spirit of,* s'adapter à, se mettre en harmonie avec (work); *in a spirit of mischief,* par espièglerie; *public spirit,* civisme. ‖ Caractère, cœur, courage; cran *m.* (fam.); *man of spirit,* homme de caractère; *to lack spirit,* manquer de cran. ‖ Pl. Ardeur, fougue, énergie *f.;* feu, entrain *m.; good, high spirits,* gaieté, entrain; *full of animal spirits,* plein de vie (or) d'entrain; *low* (or) *poor spirits,* abattement, découragement; *to keep up one's spirits,* ne pas se laisser abattre. ‖ ECCLES. Esprit, pur esprit *m.; Holy Spirit,* Esprit Saint, Saint-Esprit. ‖ CHIM. Alcool *m.;* esprit *m.* (of salts, wine); essence *f.* (of turpentine); *methylated spirits,* alcool à brûler. ‖ CULIN. Pl. Alcool (*m.*) de bouche, spiritueux *m. pl.; raw spirits,* alcool pur. ‖ JUR. *Spirit of the law,* esprit de la loi. ‖ **Spirit-lamp,** n. Lampe (*f.*) à alcool. ‖ **Spirit-level,** n. Niveau (*m.*) à bulle d'air. ‖ **Spirit-room,** n. NAUT. Cale (*f.*) à vin. — v. tr. Animer, encourager, exciter (to incite). ‖ *To spirit away* (or) *off,* faire disparaître comme par enchantement (s.o.); escamoter, subtiliser (sth.).

spirited [-id] adj. Animé, vivant, plein d'entrain (person). ‖ Animé (conversation); fougueux (horse); allant (music); intrépide (person); plein de verve (style); courageux (undertaking).

spiritedly [-idli] adv. Avec animation.

spiritedness [-idnis] n. Ardeur, verve, vigueur, fougue *f.;* entrain, feu, courage *m.*

spiritless [-lis] adj. Sans énergie (or) courage (or) caractère (lacking energy). ‖ Sans force (or) vigueur; mou (flabby). ‖ Sans entrain; terne (not lively). ‖ Triste, déprimé, abattu (depressed).

spiritlessly [-lisli] adv. Sans énergie (or) caractère. ‖ Faiblement, mollement. ‖ Sans entrain.

spiritlessness [-lisnis] n. Manque (*m.*) de caractère (or) de courage (or) d'entrain (or) de vigueur. ‖ Mollesse, léthargie *f.*

spiritual ['spiritjuəl] adj. Spirituel, immatériel, incorporel. ‖ ECCLES. Spirituel, de l'esprit. ‖ JUR.

Ecclésiastique (court); spirituel (lord). ‖ Mus. Sacré, spirituel. ‖ Fig. Mental, intellectuel.
— n. U. S. Mus. *Negro spirituals*, chants religieux des Noirs.

spiritualism [-izm̩] n. Spiritisme *m.* ‖ Philos. Spiritualisme *m.*

spiritualist [-ist] n. Spirite *s.* ‖ Philos. Spiritualiste *s.*

spirituality [ˌspiritjuˈæliti] n. Eccles. Spiritualité *f.* ‖ Jur., Eccles. Pl. Biens et revenus ecclésiastiques *m. pl.*

spiritualization [ˌspiritjuəlaiˈzeiʃən] n. Spiritualisation *f.*

spiritualize [ˈspiritjuəlaiz] v. tr. Spiritualiser. ‖ Donner un sens spirituel à.

spiritually [-i] adv. Spirituellement. ‖ En esprit.

spiritualness [-nis] n. Spiritualité *f.*

spirituous [ˈspiritjuəs] adj. Spiritueux, alcoolique; *spirituous liquors*, spiritueux.

spirometer [ˌspaiəˈrɔmitə*] n. Spiromètre *m.*

spirt, spurt [spəːt] v. intr. Saillir, jaillir, gicler; *to spirt up*, jaillir, gicler. (See squirt.)
— v. tr. Faire jaillir (or) gicler.
— n. Jaillissement, jet *m.;* giclée *f.*

spiry [ˈspaiəri] adj. Elancé, en flèche.

spit [spit] n. Culin. Broche *f.* ‖ Geol. Pointe (*f.*) de sable (or) de terre.
— v. tr. (1). Culin. Embrocher. mettre à la broche.

spit n. Med. Crachat *m.;* salive *f.* ‖ Zool. Crachement *m.* (of a cat). ‖ Fam. Crachin *m.* (drizzle). ‖ Loc. *He is the spit and image of his father*, c'est son père tout craché (or) décalqué.
— v. intr. (152). Cracher, expectorer. ‖ Zool. Cracher, félir (cat). ‖ Techn. Avoir des retours de flamme (motor). ‖ Fam. Crachoter (pen); crachiner (rain). ‖ Fig. *To spit upon*, cracher sur, faire fi de.
— v. tr. Med. Cracher; *to spit out*, cracher, recracher. ‖ Fam. Cracher. sortir (words); *spit it out!*, siffle-le!

spit n. Profondeur (*f.*) d'une bêche.

spitball [-bɔl] n. Fam. U. S. Boulette (*f.*) de papier mâché.

spite [spait] n. Rancune, malveillance *f.; from* (or) *out of spite*, par méchanceté; *to have a spite against*, garder rancune à, en vouloir à; garder une dent à (fam.). ‖ Dépit *m.; in spite of*, malgré, en dépit de; *in spite of the fact that*, quoique, bien que; *in spite of everyone*, envers et contre tous.
— v. tr. Contrarier, ennuyer, vexer.

spiteful [-ful] adj. Rancunier, malveillant, vindicatif (person); venimeux (tongue); *spiteful remark*, rosserie.

spitefully [-fuli] adv. Par dépit, par rancune.

spitefulness [-fulnis] n. Rancune, rancœur, malveillance, méchanceté *f.;* caractère rancunier *m.*

spitfire [ˈspitfaiə*] n. Aviat. Spitfire *m.* ‖ Fam. Rageur *m.*

spitter [-ə*] n. Cracheur *s.*

spitting [-iŋ] n. Med. Expectoration *f.;* crachement *m.*

spittle [ˈspitl] n. Med. Crachat *m.;* salive *f.*

spittoon [spiˈtuːn] n. Crachoir *m.*

spiv [spiv] n. Fam. B.O.F., trafiquant du marché noir; chevalier (*m.*) d'industrie.

splash [splæʃ] n. Eclaboussement *m.* (act); éclaboussure *f.* (stain). ‖ Clapotement, clapotage, clapotis *m.* (of waves). ‖ Plouf, flac *m.* (noise). ‖ Zool. Tache *f.;* bariolage *m.* (on plumage). ‖ Arts. Eclaboussure *f.* (of colour). ‖ Techn. Projection d'huile *f.; splash lubrication*, graissage par barbotage. ‖ Fam. Poudre (*f.*) de riz. ‖ Loc. *To make a splash*, faire du bruit, faire sensation. ‖ **Splash-board**, n. Autom. Garde-boue *m.* ‖ **Splash-down**, n. Astronaut. Amerrissage *m.* (of spacecraft).
— v. tr. Eclabousser (*with*, de); *to splash about*,

faire jaillir (or) gicler. ‖ Fig. Prodiguer (money); mettre en manchette (news).
— v. intr. Jaillir en éclaboussures, éclabousser; *to splash into the water*, tomber dans l'eau en faisant flac; *to splash up*, gicler. ‖ Clapoter (waves). ‖ Barboter, patauger; patouiller (fam.) [in mud, water]. ‖ **To splash about**, barboter (in a pool).

splasher [-ə*] n. Eclabousseur *m.* (person). ‖ Ch. de f. Garde-boue *m.* ‖ Techn. Plongeur *m.* (lubricating); tablier *m.* (shield).

splashy [-i] adj. Boueux, bourbeux. ‖ Arts. Barbouillé (sketch). ‖ Fam. Eclatant, voyant, tapageur (colour, dress); d'un luxe criard (jewelry); ostentatoire (person). [See flashy.]

splatter [ˈsplætə*] v. tr. Eclabousser (*with*, de) [s.o., sth.]; faire une aspersion de (a liquid).
— v. intr. Eclabousser. ‖ Clapoter (waves).

splay [splei] v. tr. Epauler (a horse). ‖ Archit. Ebraser, évaser (a window frame); délarder (an opening).
— v. intr. Archit. *To splay out*, s'évaser.
— n. Archit. Ebrasure *f.;* ébrasement *m.*
— adj. Plat et large. ‖ Med. Plat et tourné en dehors (foot).

spleen [spliːn] n. Med. Rate *f.* ‖ Fig. Mélancolie, humeur noire *f.;* spleen *m.; fit of spleen*, accès de tristesse, moment de cafard; ‖ Fig. Mauvaise humeur *f.;* dépit, fiel *m.; to vent one's spleen*, décharger sa bile (*on*, contre, sur).

spleenful [-ful], **spleeny** [-i] adj. Fig. Atrabilaire, hypocondriaque; morose (moody); rancunier, hargneux (spiteful).

splendent [ˈsplendənt] adj. Luisant, brillant.

splendid [ˈsplendid] adj. Splendide, magnifique, superbe, merveilleux. ‖ Fam. Epatant.

splendidly [-li] adv. Splendidement, magnifiquement; *to get along splendidly with*, s'accorder le mieux du monde avec.

splendiferous [splenˈdifərəs] adj. Fam. Epatant, mirobolant.

splendour [ˈsplendə*] n. Splendeur, magnificence *f.;* éclat *m.*

splenetic [spliˈnetik] adj. Med. Splénique. ‖ Fig. Atrabilaire, hypocondriaque; morose.
— n. Med. Remède (*m.*) contre la splénite (remedy); malade (*s.*) de la rate (patient). ‖ Fig. Hypocondriaque *s.*

splenic [ˈsplenik] adj. Med. Splénique.

splice [splais] v. tr. Techn. Episser (a cable); enter (wood). ‖ Cinem. Réparer (two lengths of film). ‖ Fam. *To get spliced*, se mettre la corde au cou (to marry).
— n. Techn. Epissure *f.* (in cable); enture *f.* (in wood).

spline [splain] n. Techn. Languette, clavette *f.* (between wheel and axle-shaft); cannelure, rainure, nervure *f.* (slot).
— v. tr. Techn. Claveter; canneler.

splint [splint] n. Med. Eclisse, attelle *f.;* gouttière *f.* (cradleshaped). ‖ Techn. Brin d'osier *m.* (for basket-weaving).
— v. tr. Med. Eclisser, mettre une attelle à. ‖ **Splint-bone**, n. Med. Péroné *m.;* Zool. Canon *m.*

splinter [ˈsplintə*] v. tr. Fendre, briser (in slivers). ‖ Faire voler en éclats.
— v. intr. Se fendre, éclater. ‖ Voler en éclats.
— n. Eclat *m.* (sliver). ‖ Eclat *m.* (of a bomb); écharde *f.* (of wood). ‖ Med. Esquille *f.* (of a bone). ‖ **Splinter-bone**, n. Med. Péroné *m.* ‖ **Splinter group**, n. Faction *f.*, groupe scissionniste *m.* ‖ **Splinter-proof**, adj. A l'épreuve des éclats (bombproof); se brisant sans éclats (glass).

splintery [-əri] adj. Eclatable. ‖ Med., Geol. Esquilleux.

splinting [-iŋ] n. Med. Eclissage *m.*

split [split] v. tr. (153). Fendre. ‖ Dédoubler (a hide); cliver (rock); déchirer (a skirt); écuisser

(a tree); faire éclater (wood). ‖ Diviser; couper en deux (an apple); partager (money, work). ‖ Désunir, diviser, créer une scission dans (a party). ‖ Fin. Partager, fractionner (shares). ‖ Loc. *To split the difference,* couper la poire en deux; *to split hairs,* couper les cheveux en quatre, discuter sur des pointes d'aiguille; *to split one's sides with laughter,* se tenir les côtes de rire. ‖ Loc. U. S. *To split one's ticket,* partager son vote entre divers candidats. ‖ ‖ **To split up,** disperser (a meeting); partager (money, work); Chim. Dédoubler (a compound); Math. Décomposer (a fraction); Phys. Désintégrer (the atom).
— v. intr. Se fendre; se cliver (rock); se déchirer (skirt); se déliter (stone); éclater (wood). ‖ Se diviser, se désunir (group, party). ‖ Naut. Se briser (ship). ‖ Med. *My head is splitting,* ma tête éclate, j'ai un mal de tête atroce. ‖ Fam. Cafarder; *to split on s.o.,* donner qqn. ‖ **To split up,** se fractionner; Phys. Se dédoubler (ion); Fam. Rompre, divorcer (couple).
— n. Fente *f.* ‖ Fissure, cassure, crevasse *f.* (in rock); déchirure *f.* (in a skirt); éclat *m.* (in wood). ‖ Division, rupture, scission *f.* (in a group). ‖ Pl. Grand écart *m.* (acrobatic); *to do the splits,* faire le grand écart. ‖ Culin. *Banana split,* banane à la crème. ‖ Comm. Quart (*m.*) de bouteille; demi *m.* (of beer); demi-bouteille *f.* (of wine). ‖ Med. Gerçure *f.* (of the skin).
— adj. Fendu (rock); déchiré (skirt). ‖ Med. *Split cloth,* bandage à plusieurs chefs; *split personality,* dédoublement de la personnalité. ‖ Culin. Cassé (peas). ‖ Techn. Fendu (pin); brisé (ring). ‖ Sports. *Split shot,* coup roqué (in croquet). ‖ Gramm. *Split infinitive,* disjonction de « to » à l'infinitif anglais. ‖ **Split-level,** adj. A deux niveaux (house, room). ‖ **Split-second,** adj. Fam. Ultra-rapide (intervention); *split-second hand,* aiguille des secondes.

splitter [-ə*] n. Fendeur *s.*

splitting [-iŋ] n. Fendage, éclatement *m.* ‖ Phys. Désintégration *f.* (of the atom).
— adj. Med. Atroce (headache).

splotch [splɔtʃ] n. Tache *f.* (of colour); souillure *f.;* barbouillage *m.* (of dirt).

splotchy [-i] adj. Taché, sali, barbouillé. ‖ Med. Marbré, brouillé (complexion).

splurge [splə:dʒ] v. intr. Battre l'eau. (See SPLASH.) ‖ U. S. Fam. Dépenser l'argent à la pelle; épater le bourgeois.
— n. Eclaboussement *m.;* déluge *m.* ‖ Fam. Epate, esbroufe *f.*

splutter ['splʌtə*] v. intr. Bredouiller, bafouiller, cafouiller (fam.) [stutter]. ‖ Crachoter (pen); postillonner (person). ‖ Techn. Cracher (collector); cafouiller (motor).
— v. tr. Eclabousser, répandre. ‖ *To splutter out,* bredouiller.
— n. Bredouillement *m.* ‖ Techn. Crachement *m.* (of a collector, pen); bafouillage *m.* (of a motor).

splutterer [-rə*] n. Bredouilleur *s.* ‖ Fam. Postillonneur *s.*

spluttering [-riŋ] n. Bredouillement, bafouillage *m.* ‖ Techn. Cafouillage *m.* ‖ Fam. Postillons *m. pl.*

spoil [spɔil] n. pl. Butin *m.;* dépouilles *f. pl.* (booty). ‖ Profit *m.;* avantages *m. pl.;* share of the spoils, part du gâteau. ‖ U. S. Assiette (*f.*) au beurre; *spoils system,* système des postes aux petits copains. ‖ Techn. Terril *m.*
— v. tr. (154). † Spolier, dépouiller (the enemy); saccager (a town). ‖ Abîmer; gâter, altérer (food, wine); avarier, détériorer, endommager (goods); gâcher (a piece of work). ‖ Couper (the appetite); déparer (the beauty of sth.). ‖ Med. Nuire à; *to spoil one's eyes,* s'abîmer les yeux. ‖ Fig. Gâter (a child); *to spoil the fun for,* gâcher la joie de. ‖ Fam. Faire son affaire à (to kill). ‖ **Spoil-sport,**

n. Empêcheur de danser en rond, rabat-joie *m.* (wet blanket).
— v. intr. Se gâter, se perdre, s'abîmer, s'avarier, se détériorer. ‖ Fam. *To be spoiling for a fight,* brûler de se battre.

spoilage [-idʒ] n. Pourriture *f.* (of food). ‖ Techn. Gâche *f.,* déchets (*m. pl.*) de tirage.

spoiler [-ə*] n. Pillard *s.;* spoliateur *m.;* spoliatrice *f.* ‖ Gâcheur *s.* ‖ Aviat. Spoiler *m.* ‖ Autom. Spoiler, becquet *m.*

spoiling [-iŋ] n. Pillage *m.;* spoliation *f.* (plundering). ‖ Détérioration, avarie *f.* (of food).

spoilsman [-zmən] (pl. **spoilsmen**) n. U. S. Chacal, profiteur, rat dans son fromage *m.*

spoke [spouk] n. Echelon *m.* (of a ladder); rai, rayon *m.* (of a wheel). ‖ Naut. Poignée *f.* (of rudder gear). ‖ Fig. Bâton *m.; to put a spoke in s.o.'s wheel,* mettre des bâtons dans les roues à qqn. ‖ **Spoke-bone,** n. Med. Radius *m.*
— v. tr. Mettre des rayons à. ‖ Mettre un bâton dans (a wheel).

spoke, spoken [-ŋ]. See SPEAK.

spokesman ['spouksmən] (pl. **spokesmen**) n. Porte-parole, interprète, représentant *m.*

spoliate ['spoulieit] v. tr. Spolier, dépouiller. ‖ Piller (to plunder).

spoliation [,spouli'eiʃən] n. Pillage *m.* ‖ Spoliation *f.;* dépouillement *m.* ‖ Jur. Destruction *f.* (of documents).

spoliator ['spoulieitə*] n. Pilleur *s.* ‖ Spoliateur *m.;* spoliatrice *f.* ‖ Destructeur *m.;* destructrice *f.*

spondee ['spɔndi:] n. Spondée *m.*

sponge [spʌndʒ] n. Eponge *f.* ‖ Coup (*m.*) d'éponge (act). ‖ Zool., Bot. Eponge *f.* ‖ Milit. Ecouvillon *m.* ‖ Culin. Pâte molle *f.; chocolate sponge,* mousse au chocolat. ‖ Techn. Eponge métallique *f.* ‖ Fam. Pique-assiette, écornifleur *m.* ‖ Loc. *To pass the sponge over,* passer l'éponge sur; *to throw up the sponge,* jeter l'éponge, abandonner la partie. ‖ **Sponge-bag,** n. Trousse de toilette *f.* ‖ **Sponge-bath,** n. Tub *m.* ‖ **Sponge-cake,** n. Culin. Biscuit (*m.*) de Savoie. ‖ **Sponge-cloth,** n. Tissuéponge *m.* ‖ **Sponge-finger,** n. Culin. Biscuit (*m.*) à la cuiller. ‖ **Sponge rubber,** n. Caoutchoucmousse *m.,* mousse *f.*
— v. tr. Eponger. ‖ Med. Lotionner (a wound). ‖ Milit. Ecouvillonner. ‖ Fam. Ecornifler, soutirer (a dinner). ‖ Fig. *To sponge out,* effacer le souvenir (or) la trace de, passer l'éponge sur.
— v. intr. Pêcher les éponges. ‖ Fig. Ecornifler, faire le pique-assiette; *to sponge on s.o.,* vivre aux crochets de qqn.

sponger [-ə*] n. Pêcheur (*s.*) d'éponges. ‖ Fig. Ecornifleur, parasite, pique-assiette *m.*

sponginess [-inis] n. Spongiosité, porosité *f.*

sponging [-iŋ] n. Nettoyage (*m.*) à l'éponge. ‖ Pêche (*f.*) des éponges. ‖ Med. Lotionnement *m.* ‖ Milit. Ecouvillonnage *m.* ‖ Fig. Ecorniflerie *f.;* parasitisme *m.*

spongy [-i] adj. Spongieux. ‖ Poreux. ‖ Med. Caverneux (tissue).

sponson ['spɔnsṇ] n. Naut. Encorbellement *m.;* jardin *m.* (of a paddle-box). ‖ Aviat. Nageoire *f.*

sponsor ['spɔnsə*] n. Répondant, garant *m.;* caution *f.* (*for,* de). ‖ Parrain *m.;* marraine *f.* (of a child, a club member). ‖ Theatr., Radio. Commanditaire *m.* ‖ U. S. *Thesis sponsor,* directeur de thèse.
— v. tr. Etre le garant de, répondre pour. ‖ Radio. Subventionner par des fonds privés (programmes).

spontaneity [spɔntə'ni:iti] n. Spontanéité *f.*

spontaneous [spɔn'teinjəs] adj. Spontané (combustion, generation); automatique (motion). ‖ Fig. Naturel, spontané.

spontaneously [-li] adv. Spontanément.

spontaneousness [-nis] n. Spontanéité *f.*

spontoon [spɔn'tu:n] n. Esponton *m.*

spoof [spu:f] v. tr. FAM. Filouter, attraper. ‖ Faire marcher, mettre en boîte (see FOOL); *you were spoofed*, on vous a eu.
— n. FAM. Fumisterie, attrape *f.; canard m.*

spoofer [-ə*] n. FAM. Blagueur *s.;* pince-sans-rire *m.*

spook [spu:k] n. FAM. Spectre, revenant, fantôme *m.;* apparition *f.* (See GHOST.)

spooky [-i] adj. De fantôme, de spectre, de revenant. ((See GHOSTLY.) ‖ Hanté (house).

spool [spu:l] n. Bobine *f.* (of a camera); tambour *m.* (of a fishing-reel); canette *f.* (of a sewing-machine). ‖ U. S. Peloton *m.* (of thread).
— v. tr. Bobiner; *to spool off, on,* débobiner, bobiner.

spoon [spu:n] n. Cuiller, cuillère *f.; basting spoon,* louche. ‖ SPORTS. Spoon *m.* (golf-club). ‖ NAUT. Rame (*f.*) à pale incurvée. ‖ **Spoon-bait,** n. SPORTS. Cuiller *f.* ‖ **Spoon-bill,** n. ZOOL. Spatule *f.* " **Spoon-fed,** adj. Nourri à la cuiller; FAM. Subventionné (enterprise).
— v. tr. *To spoon out* (or) *up,* prendre avec une cuiller, ramasser à la cuiller. ‖ SPORTS. Pêcher à la cuiller. ‖ SPORTS. Pousser (a croquet ball); prendre en cuiller (a golf ball). ‖ **To spoon-feed,** v. tr. Nourrir à la cuiller; FIG. Subventionner; FAM. Mâcher la besogne à.
— v. intr. FAM. Se faire des mamours.

spoondrift [-drift] n. Embrun *m.;* embruns *m. pl.*

spoonerism ['spu:nərizm] n. Contrepèterie *f.*

spoonful ['spu:nful] n. Cuillerée *f.*

spoony [-i] adj. FAM. Niais, bête. ‖ FAM. Amoureux; *to be spoony on,* avoir le béguin pour.
— n. FAM. Nigaud, niais *m.*

spoor [spuə*] n. Trace, piste *f.;* foulées *f. pl.*
— v. intr., tr. Suivre à la trace.

sporadic [spɔ'rædik] adj. MED. Sporadique. ‖ FIG. Isolé, rare.

sporadically [-əli] adv. Sporadiquement.

sporadicalness [-əlnis] n. Sporadicité *f.*

spore [spɔ:*] n. BOT., ZOOL. Spore *f.*

sporran ['spɔrən] n. Bourse *f.*, petit sac (*m.*) de peau (worn with Scottish national costume).

sport [spɔ:t] n. SPORTS. Jeu de plein air *m.; athletic sports,* athlétisme; *field sports,* chasse, pêche, courses de chevaux; *to go in for sport,* s'adonner aux sports. ‖ ZOOL., BOT. Monstre *m.* ‖ FIG. Plaisanterie, moquerie *f.; in sport,* pour rire, par plaisanterie; *to make sport of,* se moquer de, tourner en ridicule. ‖ FAM. Chic type *m.* ‖ **Sports-jacket,** n. Veste (*f.*) de sport.
— v. intr. Jouer, se divertir, s'amuser. ‖ ZOOL., BOT. Produire une variété anormale.
— v. tr. FAM. Arborer, exhiber, étaler.

sporting [-iŋ] adj. De sport; de chasse (gun). ‖ Sportif (magazine, person); *sporting man,* amateur de courses, fervent de sport. ‖ COMM. U. S. *Sporting goods,* articles de sport. ‖ FIG. Sportif, franc jeu (attitude); aléatoire, minime (chance); large, libéral (offer).
— n. ZOOL., BOT. Production (*f.*) de variétés anormales.

sportive [-iv] adj. Gai, folâtre, badin.

sportively [-ivli] adv. Gaiement.

sportiveness [-ivnis] n. Enjouement *m.*

sportscar [-skɑ:*] n. AUTOM. Voiture (*f.*) de sport.

sportsman [-smən] (pl. **sportsmen**) n. Sportif, sportsman *m.;* amateur (*m.*) de sports. ‖ FIG. Beau joueur *m.*

sportsmanlike [-smənlaik] adj. Digne d'un sportsman.

sportsmanship [-smənʃip] n. Pratique (*f.*) des sports; qualités sportives *f. pl.* ‖ FIG. Conduite sportive *f.*

sportswoman [-swumən] (pl. **sportswomen** [-wimin]) n. Sportive *f.*

sporty [-i] adj. FAM. Chic (decent); voyant (gaudy).

spot [spɔt] n. Tache, souillure, macule *f.* (grime). ‖ Endroit, lieu, point *m.* (site); *in spots,* par endroits; *to arrive on the spot,* arriver sur les lieux. ‖ Tache, moucheture *f.* (of colour); pois *m.* (polka-dot). ‖ Tavelure *f.* (on fruit). ‖ COMM. Pl. Marchandises (*f. pl.*) sur place; marchandises (*f. pl.*) payables (or) livrables dès la vente; *spot cash,* argent comptant; *spot cotton,* coton payé comptant; *spot prices,* prix sur place. ‖ MED. Bouton, grain *m.* (on the skin); *beauty spot,* grain de beauté; *spots before the eyes,* mouches devant les yeux. ‖ SPORTS. Mouche *f.* (in billiards). ‖ ZOOL. Pl. Moucheture *f.* (of a leopard). ‖ FAM. Spot *m,* ‖ U. S. POP. Situation *f.* ‖ FAM. Goutté *f.* (of whisky); brin *m.* (of work); *spot of trouble,* petit ennui. ‖ FIG. Tache *f.* (on a reputation); *weak spot,* point sensible, faible. ‖ LOC. *On the spot,* sur-le-champ, sans désemparer (immediately); sur les lieux, à l'endroit même (there). ‖ POP. *To put s.o. on the spot,* flanquer qqn dans le bain (to accuse); laisser qqn sur le carreau (or) terrain (to murder).
— v. tr. Tacher, souiller; salir (with dirt). ‖ Tacheter, moucheter (with colour). ‖ FAM. Repérer, dégotter, détecter (sth.); piger (the winner).
— v. intr. Se tacher, être salissant. ‖ **Spot-check,** n. Contrôle-surprise *m.;* v. tr. Vérifier à intervalles irréguliers. ‖ **Spot-news,** n. Dernière heure *f.* ‖ **Spot-remover,** n. Détachant *m.*

spotless [-lis] adj. Sans tache, immaculé (lit. and fig.).

spotlessness [-lisnis] n. Propreté, netteté *f.* ‖ FIG. Pureté *f.*

spotlight [-lait] n. ELECTR. Feu de projecteur *m.* ‖ THEATR. Projecteur, spot *m.;* rampe *f.* ‖ FIG. Publicité *f.*
— v. tr. THEATR. Diriger les projecteurs sur. ‖ FIG. Monter en épingle.

spotted [-id] adj. Taché, sali (with dirt). ‖ Tacheté, moucheté (with colour); à pois (dotted). ‖ ZOOL. Madré (leopard); tacheté, tavelé (panther). ‖ MED. *Spotted fever,* méningite cérébro-spinale.

spotter [-ə*] n. Personne (*f.*) qui repère. ‖ AVIAT. Avion (*m.*) de réglage de tir.

spotty [-i] adj. Taché, couvert de taches. ‖ Moucheté, tacheté (marked).

spouse [spauz] n. Epoux *m.;* épouse *f.* ‖ JUR. Conjoint *s.*

spout [spaut] v. intr. Jaillir; gicler. ‖ ZOOL. Souffler, lancer un jet d'eau (whale). ‖ FAM. Pérorer, laïusser.
— v. tr. Faire jaillir, lancer en un jet. ‖ FAM. Déclamer, dégoiser (insults). ‖ POP. U. S. Mettre au clou (to spawn).
— n. Gouttière; gargouille *f.;* tuyau (*m.*) de descente (for rain-water). ‖ Goulot *m.* (of a nozzle); dégorgeoir *m.* (of a pump); bec *m.* (of a teapot). ‖ Jet *m.;* colonne *f.* (of liquid). ‖ TECHN. Trémie *f.* ‖ POP. U. S. *Up the spout,* chez ma tante. ‖ **Spout-hole,** n. Lumière *f.* (of a pump); ZOOL. Event *m.* (of a whale).

spouter [-ə*] n. FAM. Péroreur, laïusseur *m.*

spouting [-iŋ] n. Jaillissement *m.* ‖ FAM. Déclamation, harangue *f.*

sprain [sprein] n. MED. Entorse, foulure *f.*
— v. tr. Fouler, donner une entorse à; *to sprain one's ankle,* se fouler la cheville.

sprang [spræŋ]. See SPRING.

sprat [spræt] n. ZOOL., CULIN. Sprat *m.* ‖ FAM. Gringalet *m.*

sprawl [sprɔ:l] v. intr. S'étendre, s'étaler, se vautrer. ‖ Etre étalé de tout son long; *to go sprawling,* se flanquer par terre, tomber les quatre fers en l'air. ‖ Se traîner, ramper à plat ventre (to crawl). ‖ S'en aller dans tous les sens (handwriting); couvrir la

page (news article). ‖ Bot. Ramper, se ramifier (plant).
— v. tr. Etendre (or) écarter d'une manière disgracieuse (one's legs). ‖ Espacer sans ordre (persons, things).
— n. Attitude affalée *f.*
sprawling [-iŋ] adj. Vautré (person). ‖ Informe et zigzaguant (handwriting).
spray [sprei] n. Bot. Branche *f.* ; rameau *m.* (flowering) ; brin *m.* (of mimosa). ‖ Barrette *f.* (of diamonds).
spray [sprei] n. Embrun *m.* ; écume, poussière d'eau *f.* ‖ Techn. Gicleur, atomiseur ; vaporisateur *m.* (for perfume).
— v. tr. Pulvériser, vaporiser (a liquid). ‖ Asperger, arroser. ‖ Agric. Bassiner, vaporiser. ‖ Techn. *To spray paint on,* peindre au pistolet. ‖ **Spray-gun,** n. Techn. Pistolet, pulvérisateur *m.* (for painting).
— v. intr. Se vaporiser. ‖ **To spray out,** gicler, se répandre en brouillard.
sprayer [-ə*] n. Vaporisateur, pulvérisateur *m.* (atomizer). ‖ Brûleur *m.* (for fuel oil) ; pistolet pneumatique *m.* (for paint). ‖ Arroseuse *f.* (sprinkler).
spraying [-iŋ] n. Pulvérisation, vaporisation *f.* ‖ Arrosage *m.*
spread [spred] v. tr. (155). Etaler, étendre (cloth) ; déployer (a flag) ; tendre (a net). ‖ Etaler, étendre, répandre (to extend) ; éparpiller (to scatter). ‖ Parsemer (an area) ; couvrir, recouvrir (a table) [with, de]. ‖ Naut. Déployer (sails) ; filer (oil on water). ‖ Culin. Tartiner (butter on bread). ‖ Comm. *To spread out,* étaler (goods). ‖ Zool. Déployer (wings). ‖ Mus. Arpéger (a chord). ‖ Med. Propager (an infection). ‖ Fig. Colporter, faire circuler (news) ; répandre, propager (a rumour) ; semer (panic, terror). ‖ Fam. *To spread oneself,* se surpasser (in performing a task) ; plastronner, se pavaner (to give oneself airs).
— v. intr. Se déployer, s'étendre, s'étaler. ‖ S'étendre (desert, stain) ; s'élargir (river). ‖ Se répandre, s'éparpiller, se disséminer, se disperser. ‖ Gagner, se communiquer (to, à) [fire]. ‖ Comm. *To spread out,* se développer ; établir des succursales (business). ‖ Med. Se propager (epidemic). ‖ Milit. S'écarter (shot). ‖ Fig. Se généraliser (ideas) ; se propager, se répandre (news, rumour).
— n. Etendue *f.* (of an area). ‖ Comm. Expansion *f.* ; développement *m.* (of an enterprise). ‖ Med. Propagation *f.* (of a disease). ‖ Bot. Développement du branchage *m.* (of a tree). ‖ Zool. Envergure *f.* (of wings). ‖ Archit. Largeur, ouverture *f.* (of a vault). ‖ Naut. *Spread of sail,* envergure, épatement. ‖ Fin. U. S. Différence *f.* (between prices). ‖ Fig. Diffusion *f.* (of education) ; développement *m.* ; expansion *f.* (of ideas). ‖ Fam. Festin *m.* ; gueuleton *m.* (pop). ‖ Fam. *Middle-aged spread,* rotondité de la cinquantaine.
— adj. Ecarté (fingers) ; ouvert (fan). ‖ Bot. Epanoui, ouvert (flower). ‖ Zool. Etendu (wing). ‖ Culin. Servi, mis (table). ‖ Mus. Arpégé (chord). ‖ **Spread-eagle,** n. Naut. Homme assujetti (*m.*) jambes et bras écartés (for punishment) ; Blas. Aigle éployée *f.* ; Sports. Grand aigle (in skating) ; Fin. U. S. Opération (*f.*) à cheval ; Culin. Volaille ouverte en deux et grillée *f.* ; adj. U. S. Chauvin ; vantard, grandiloquent.
spreader [-ə*] n. Techn. Etendeur, étaleur *m.* ; épandeuse *f.* ‖ Fig. Colporteur *s.* (of news).
spree [spri:] n. Bamboche, bombe *f.* ; *to be on the spree,* faire la noce ; tirer une bordée.
sprig [sprig] n. Brin *m.* ; petite branche, brindille, broutille *f.* ‖ Ramage *m.* (in embroidery). ‖ Barrette, aigrette *f.* (of diamonds). ‖ Techn. Petit clou sans tête. ‖ Fam. Jeune homme *m.* ; rejeton *m.* (pejorative).
— v. tr. (1). Orner de ramages (muslin).

sprightliness ['spraitlinis] n. Vivacité, animation *f.* ; enjouement *m.*
sprightly [-li] adj. Vif, éveillé, animé, enjoué. ‖ Pétillant, sémillant (wit).
spring [spriŋ] v. intr. (156). Bondir, sauter, s'élancer ; *to spring at,* se jeter sur ; *to spring forward,* se précipiter (or) s'élancer en avant ; *to spring out of,* sauter de ; *to spring to s.o.'s aid,* se précipiter au secours de qqn ; *to spring over,* sauter ; *tears sprang to his eyes,* les larmes lui vinrent aux yeux ; *to spring to one's feet,* se lever d'un bond. ‖ Faire ressort ; *to spring back,* revenir en arrière en se détendant (branch) ; *to spring open,* s'ouvrir subitement. ‖ Sourdre, jaillir (oil, water) ; *to spring into existence,* naître, apparaître soudainement. ‖ Tirer son origine, naître, provenir (from, de) ; avoir sa source (from, dans) ; *to spring from an ancient lineage,* descendre d'une vieille famille. ‖ Naut. Se fendre, craquer (mast). ‖ Archit. Naître (vault). ‖ Bot. Pousser, commencer à pousser (leaves) ; *to spring up,* poindre (plant). ‖ Techn. Jouer, gauchir (beam). ‖ Sports. *To spring into the saddle,* sauter en selle. ‖ Milit. *To spring to arms,* voler aux armes ; *to spring to the attack,* bondir à l'assaut. ‖ Loc. *Hope springs eternal in the human breast,* l'espoir au cœur humain reste toujours vivace. ‖ **To spring up,** se dresser (or) se lever vivement (person) ; prendre naissance (rumour) ; s'élever (storm).
— v. tr. Sauter, franchir (a ditch, hedge). ‖ Faire sauter (a mine). ‖ Techn. Faire jouer (a lock, spring, trap) ; fendre (a raquette) ; faire déjeter (timber). ‖ Sports. Lever (a covey). ‖ Naut. Contracter (a leak) ; faire craquer (a mast). ‖ Fam. Proposer (or) présenter à l'improviste, sortir (an idea, plan) ; faire (on, à) [a surprise] ; *to spring a question,* poser une question inattendue. ‖ Pop. U. S. Faire sortir de prison (legally or illegally).
— n. Bond, saut, élan *m.* ; *to take a spring,* prendre son élan. ‖ Détente *f.* (springing back). ‖ Source *f.* (of water). ‖ Printemps *m.* (springtime) ; *in the spring,* au printemps. ‖ Med. Elasticité *f.* (of muscles). ‖ Techn. Gauchissement *m.* (of a beam) ; ressort *m.* (of a bed, car, watch) ; *to act as a spring,* faire ressort. ‖ Archit. Naissance, retombée *f.* (of a vault) ; escape *f.* (of a column). ‖ Naut. Embossure ; cassure *f.* (of a mast). ‖ Autom. Pl. Suspension *f.* ; *spring clip,* bride. ‖ Fig. Source, origine, cause *f.* ; motif, principe *m.* (of a belief) ; mobile *m.*, source d'action *f.* (motivation). ‖ **Spring-balance,** balance *f.* (or) peson (*m.*) à ressort. ‖ **Spring-bed,** n. Lit à sommier élastique *m.* ‖ **Spring-board,** n. Tremplin *m.* ‖ **Spring-cleaning,** n. Grand nettoyage de printemps *m.* ‖ **Spring-fever,** n. Med. Malaise (*m.*) des premières chaleurs. ‖ **Spring-gun,** n. Piège à fusil *m.* ‖ **Spring-head,** n. Source *f.* ‖ **Spring-lock,** n. Serrure (*f.*) à ressort. ‖ **Spring-mattress,** n. Sommier élastique *m.* ‖ **Spring-tide,** n. Naut. Marée (*f.*) de vives eaux (or) de syzygie. ‖ **Spring-valve,** n. Techn. Soupape (*f.*) à ressort. ‖ **Spring-water,** n. Eau de source *f.* ‖ **Spring-wheat,** n. Bot. Blé de mars *m.*
springbok ['spriŋ͵bʌk] n. Zool. Springbok *m.*
springe [sprindʒ] n. Lacet, lacs *m.* (for birds) ; collet *m.* (for rabbits).
springer ['spriŋə*] n. Sauteur *s.* ‖ Zool. Springbok *m.* (antelope) ; springer *m.* (dog) ; épaulard *m.* (grampus). ‖ Archit. Sommier *m.* (of an arcade) ; naissance *f.* (of a vault).
springiness [-inis] n. Elasticité *f.*
springing [-iŋ] adj. Elastique, dansant (gait).
— n. Bonds, sauts *m. pl.* ‖ Jaillissement *m.* (of water). ‖ Techn. Gauchissement *m.* ‖ Archit. Naissance *f.* (of a vault). ‖ Bot. Germination *f.* (of a plant).
springless [-lis] adj. Sans ressort. ‖ Sans printemps (climate). ‖ Sans sources (desert). ‖ Fig. Lourd (gait) ; sans énergie (or) ressort (person).

springlet [-lit] n. Petite source *f.*
springlike [-laik] adj. Printanier.
springtime [-taim] n. Printemps ; renouveau *m.*
springy [-i] adj. Elastique ; moelleux (carpet) ; alerte (gait) ; à ressort (mattress).
sprinkle ['spriŋkl] v. tr. Répandre en gouttelettes (or) en poussière. ‖ Répandre, jeter (sand). ‖ Asperger, arroser, bassiner (with water). ‖ CULIN. Saupoudrer (with sugar). ‖ TECHN. Jasper (the edge of a book). ‖ FIG. Semer, parsemer (to strew).
— v. intr. Tomber en gouttes (or) en pluie fine (or) en poussière.
— n. Petite pluie fine *f.* ‖ Petite quantité (*f.*) répandue çà et là. ‖ CULIN. Pincée *f.* (of salt).
sprinkler [-ə*] n. AGRIC. Appareil d'arrosage *m.* ‖ ECCLES. Goupillon *m.*
sprinkling [-iŋ] n. Aspersion *f. ;* arrosage *m.* ‖ Légère couche *f.* (of sand). ‖ CULIN. Saupoudrage *m.* ‖ ECCLES. Aspersion *f.* ‖ FIG. Bribes, *f. pl.* (of knowledge) ; petit nombre *m.* (of people) ; notions *f. pl.* (of a subject). ‖ **Sprinkling-can,** n. U. S. Arrosoir *m.* ‖ **Sprinkling-cart,** n. U. S. Arroseuse *f.*
sprint [sprint] n. Course de vitesse *f.* ‖ SPORTS. Sprint *m.*
— v. intr. Faire une course de vitesse. ‖ SPORTS. Sprinter.
— v. tr. Courir à toute vitesse (a distance).
sprinter [-ə*] n. SPORTS. Sprinter. *m.*
sprit [sprit] n. NAUT. Livarde *f.*
sprite [sprait] n. Esprit, lutin, elfe *m.*
sprocket ['sprɔkit] n. TECHN. Dent *f.* (of a chain, pinion). ‖ **Sprocket-wheel,** n. TECHN. Pignon (*m.*) de chaîne.
sprout [spraut] v. intr. BOT. Bourgeonner (branch) ; pousser, pointer (plant) ; germer (seed).
— v. tr. BOT. Pousser. ‖ FAM. Laisser pousser (a moustache).
— n. BOT. Pousse *f. ;* bourgeon, germe *m.* ‖ CULIN. Pl. *Brussels sprouts,* choux de Bruxelles.
spruce [spru:s] adj. Pimpant, soigné ; tiré à quatre épingles (fam.).
— v. intr. *To spruce up,* se parer ; se pomponner ; s'attifer, s'astiquer (fam.).
— v. tr. *To spruce up,* pomponner ; *all spruced up,* pimpant ; sur son trente et un (fam.).
spruce n. BOT. Epicéa, spruce *m. ; white spruce,* sapinette *f.*
spruceness [-nis] n. Mise pimpante, élégance coquette *f.*
sprue n. MED. Psilosis *m.*
sprung [sprʌŋ]. See SPRING.
spry [sprai] adj. Alerte, actif, vif, plein d'entrain (nimble). ‖ FAM. Soigné, pimpant (spruce).
spud [spʌd] n. AGRIC. Sarcloir *m.* ‖ FAM. Trapu *m.* ‖ FAM. CULIN. Patate *f.*
— v. tr. AGRIC. Sarcler.
spuddy [-i] adj. FAM. Rondouillard, potelé.
spume [spju:m] n. NAUT. Ecume *f.* ‖ MED. Spume *f.*
— v. intr. NAUT. Ecumer.
spumous [-əs], **spumy** [-i] adj. Ecumeux.
spun [spʌn] pret., p. p. See SPIN.
— adj. Filé (glass) ; *spun gold,* fil d'or ; *spun yarn,* bitord.
spunk [spʌŋk] n. † Amadou *m.* ‖ FAM. Cran *m.* (See PLUCK.) ‖ POP. Sperme *m.*
spunky [-i] adj. FAM. Entreprenant ; plein de cran.
spur [spə*] n. ZOOL., AGRIC., GEOL., MILIT., SPORTS. Eperon *m.* ‖ CH. DE F. Embranchement *m.* ‖ ARCHIT. Entretoise *f.* ‖ FIG. Eperon, aiguillon, stimulant *m.* (of necessity) ; *on the spur of the moment,* sous l'inspiration du moment ; *to need the spur,* être apathique (or) indolent. ‖ LOC. *To put* (or) *set spurs to,* donner de l'éperon à, piquer des deux. ‖ **Spur-chuck,** n. TECHN. Mandrin (*m.*) à trois pointes ; griffe *f.* ‖ **Spur-gear,** n. Engrenage droit *m.* ‖ **Spur-wheel,** n. Roue droite *f.*
— v. tr. (1). Eperonner (a horse). ‖ Chausser d'épe-

rons (a horseman). ‖ FIG. *To spur on,* pousser, inciter, aiguillonner, talonner.
— v. intr. *To spur forward* (or) *on,* jouer des éperons, piquer des deux.
spurge [spə:dʒ] n. BOT. Euphorbe *f. ; spurge laurel,* daphné lauréole.
spurious [spjuəriəs] adj. Faux *m.* (money) ; simulé, feint (sentiments). ‖ Apocryphe (document) ; controuvé (text). ‖ † Illégitime, bâtard (child).
spuriously [-li] adv. Faussement ; par contrefaçon.
spuriousness [-nis] n. Fausseté *f. ;* caractère falsifié *m.* (of a text). ‖ † Illégitimité *f.* (of a child).
spurn [spə:n] v. tr. Repousser du pied. ‖ FIG. Dédaigner, mépriser.
— n. FIG. Mépris, refus méprisant, dédain *m.*
spurt [spə:t] n. Effort soudain, sursaut (*m.*) d'énergie ; coup de collier *m.* (fam.). ‖ SPORTS. Emballage, démarrage *m. ; final spurt,* pointe finale.
— v. intr. Faire un effort supplémentaire. ‖ SPORTS. S'emballer, démarrer.
spurt n., v. See SPIRT.
sputnik ['sputnik] n. Spoutnik *m.*
sputter ['spʌtə*] v. intr. Postillonner, crachoter. (See SPLUTTER.) ‖ Bredouiller, bafouiller. ‖ Grésiller (candle) ; pétiller, grésiller (wood) ; *to sputter out,* s'éteindre en grésillant.
— v. tr. Dire en postillonnant (or) en bredouillant.
— n. Grésillement *m.* (noise) ; bredouillement, bredouillage *m.* (incoherent speech).
sputum ['spju:təm] (pl. **sputa** [-ə]) n. MED. Crachat *m. ;* expectorations *f. pl.*
spy [spai] n. Espion *s.* ‖ FAM. *Police spy,* mouchard.
— v. tr. (2). Apercevoir, découvrir, remarquer. ‖ *To spy out,* découvrir par ruse (a secret) ; explorer en secret (a terrain).
— v. intr. Epier, espionner. ‖ *To spy into,* examiner de près, scruter ; chercher à pénétrer (a secret). ‖ *To spy upon,* épier, espionner, guetter. ‖ **Spyglass,** n. PHYS. Longue-vue, lunette (*f.*) d'approche. ‖ **Spy-hole,** n. Judas *m.* (in a door) ; regard *m.* (in machinery).
spying [-iŋ] n. Espionnage *m.*
squab [skwɔb] n. ZOOL. Pigeonneau. ‖ AUTOM. Coussin *m.* ‖ FAM. Poussah *m.*
— adj. ZOOL. Sans plumes. ‖ FAM. Courtaud, boulot, trapu (person). ‖ **Squab-chicken,** n. ZOOL. Poussin (*m.*) sans plumes.
— adv. Comme une masse, en faisant pouf.
squabble ['skwɔbl] v. intr. Se chamailler, se chicaner.
— v. tr. Faire chevaucher (printing characters).
— n. Chamaillerie, prise (*f.*) de bec.
squabbler [-ə*] n. Querelleur *s.*
squabbling [-iŋ] n. Chamaillerie *f.*
squabby [-i] adj. FAM. Courtaud, trapu, boulot.
squad [skwɔd] n. MILIT. Peloton *m. ;* escouade *f. ; firing squad,* peloton d'exécution. ‖ U. S. SPORTS. Equipe *f.* ‖ U. S. *Squad car,* voiture de police.
squadron ['skwɔdrən] n. MILIT. Escadron *m.* ‖ AVIAT. Groupe *m. ;* escadrille *f.* ‖ NAUT. Escadre *f.*
squali ['skweilai] n. ZOOL. Squales *m.*
squalid ['skwɔlid] adj. Sale, malpropre, crasseux (clothing) ; sordide, misérable (lodging).
squalidity [skwɔ'liditi], **squalidness** ['skwɔlidnis] n. Malpropreté, saleté ; misère *f.*
squalidly ['skwɔlidli] adv. Sordidement, misérablement.
squall [skɔ:l] v. intr., tr. Crier, brailler, piailler.
— n. Bourrasque, rafale *f.* ‖ NAUT. Grain *m. ; light squall,* risée. ‖ FAM. Grabuge, coup de chien *m.*
squaller [-ə*] n. Criard, braillard *s.*
squalling [-iŋ] n. Criaillerie *f.*
squally [-i] adj. NAUT. A grains, à rafales.
squalor ['skwɔlə*] n. Saleté, crasse *f. ;* sordidité *f.*
squama ['skweimə] (pl. **squamae** [-i:]) n. ZOOL. Squame *f.* ‖ BOT. Ecaille *f.*

squamous [-əs] adj. Squameux.
squander ['skwɔndə*] v. tr. Dilapider (a fortune); gaspiller (money, time).
squanderer [-rə*] n. Dissipateur, gaspilleur s.
squandering [-riŋ] n. Gaspillage m.
square [skwɛə*] n. Carré m.; case f. (of a chess-board); carreau m. (of a window). ‖ MATH. Carré m. ‖ TECHN. Equerre f. (for surveying). ‖ MILIT. Carré m. (in battle); terrain (m.) de manœuvre (parade ground). ‖ ARCHIT. Surface (f.) de cent pieds carrés (flooring); place f. (in a city); square m. (with garden). ‖ U. S. Bloc (or) pâté (m.) de maisons. ‖ CULIN. Carré m. (of cake). ‖ COMM. Silk square, carré de soie, foulard. ‖ FAM. Bourgeois (m.) formaliste (or) arriéré; raseur m. ‖ U. S. POP. Repas substantiel m. ‖ LOC. To be on the square, être loyal, jouer franc jeu; être franc-maçon (fam.).
— adj. Carré (house, table); de forme rectangulaire (outline); d'équerre, à angles droits (sides of a box). ‖ NAUT. Plat (knot); carré (sail). ‖ MATH. Carré (foot, number, root); de surface, de superficie (measure). ‖ SPORTS. A quatre; square dance, danse à quatre couples. ‖ TECHN. Plat; square joint, assemblage à plat. ‖ MED. Anguleux (build); carré (chin, shoulders); of square frame, trapu. ‖ CULIN. Solide, substantiel (meal). ‖ FIG. Net, catégorique (refusal). ‖ FIG. Honnête, franc, loyal; square dealing, procédés honnêtes, franc jeu. ‖ FIG. En bon ordre, en règle, rangé (orderly); to get things square, mettre ses affaires en ordre; to get square with, régler ses comptes avec. ‖ FAM. He's a square peg in a round hole, c'est un inadapté; il n'est pas taillé pour ce qu'il fait. ‖ Square-built, adj. Bâti en carré (building); trapu (person). ‖ Square-necked, adj. Décolleté en carré (dress). ‖ Square-rigged, adj. NAUT. Gréé en carré. ‖ Square-shouldered, adj. Aux épaules carrées. ‖ Square-toed, adj. A bout carré (shoe); FAM. formaliste et arriéré (person).
— v. tr. Carrer, rendre carré. ‖ Ecarter (elbows); élargir, carrer (shoulders). ‖ TECHN. Equarrir, dresser (stone); équerrer (timber). ‖ MATH. Faire la quadrature de (the circle); porter au carré, former le carré de (a number). ‖ NAUT. To square the yards, brasser carré. ‖ FIN. Régler, balancer (an account). ‖ JUR. Acheter, suborner (a witness). ‖ FIG. Ajuster, adapter, accommoder; faire cadrer (a theory); to square accounts, régler ses comptes (with, avec); to square matters, arranger les choses, mettre tout le monde d'accord.
— v. intr. To square together (or) with each other, se raccorder (edges). ‖ FIG. Cadrer, s'accorder (with, avec); correspondre (with, à). ‖ To square up, SPORTS. Prendre l'attitude d'un boxeur, se mettre en posture de combat; FIG. Régler ses comptes (with, avec).
— adv. Carrément, en carré, à angles droits (to, with, avec); d'équerre (to, with, avec); square in the stomach, en plein dans le ventre. ‖ FIG. Honnêtement, correctement.
squared [-d] adj. Quadrillé, à carreaux (paper); équarri (stone, wood). ‖ MATH. Elevé au carré.
squarely [-li] adv. A angles droits, en carré. ‖ FIG. Honnêtement, loyalement.
squareness [-nis] n. Forme carrée f. ‖ FIG. Loyauté, franchise f.
squaring [-iŋ] n. Equarrissage m. ‖ Quadrillage m. ‖ MATH. Quadrature f.
squarish [-iʃ] adj. A peu près carré.
squash [skwɔʃ] v. tr. Ecraser, aplatir. (See SQUELCH.) ‖ FAM. Couper le sifflet à, clore le bec à.
— v. intr. To squash into, entrer en s'écrasant dans, s'empiler dans.
— n. Ecrasement, aplatissement m. ‖ Cohue, presse f. (crowd). ‖ Floc, bruit mou m. (noise). ‖ CULIN. Lemon squash, citron pressé. ‖ BOT. Courge f.
squashy [-i] adj. Mou, qui s'écrase facilement;

boueux, bourbeux (earth). ‖ CULIN. A pulpe molle (fruit).
squat [skwɔt] v. intr. (1). S'accroupir (action); être accroupi (or) assis sur ses talons (position). ‖ ZOOL. Se tapir, se ramasser sur soi-même (animal). ‖ JUR. Occuper une propriété sans titre légal.
— adj. Accroupi, assis sur les talons. ‖ FAM. Trapu, courtaud.
— n. Accroupissement m. ‖ FAM. Courtaud s.
squatter [-ə*] n. Personne accroupie f. ‖ JUR. Squatter s.
squaw [skwɔ:] n. Femme peau-rouge, squaw f.
squawk [skwɔ:k] n. Cri rauque m. ‖ FIG. Coup (m.) de gueule, gueulante f.
— v. intr. Pousser un cri rauque. ‖ FIG. Râler, grogner, pousser une gueulante.
squeak [skwi:k] n. Petit cri aigu m. ‖ Couic m. (of a mouse); vagissement m. (of a rabbit). ‖ Grincement, crissement m. (of a hinge); craquement m. (of shoes). ‖ FAM. To have a narrow squeak, s'en tirer à moins une.
— v. intr. Pousser un cri aigu, couiner. ‖ Glapir. ‖ Grincer, crisser (hinge); craquer (shoes). ‖ U. S. POP. Cracher le morceau, se mettre à table (to squeal).
— v. tr. Glapir.
squeaker [-ə*] n. Glapisseur s. ‖ Chose (f.) qui grince. ‖ ZOOL. Pigeonneau m.; jeune oiseau m. ‖ POP. Cafard m. (informer).
squeal [skwi:l] v. intr. Piailler, glapir (small animal); crier (pig). ‖ FAM. Glapir, protester, crier (to protest). ‖ POP. Chanter, se mettre à table (to inform); to squeal on, donner (one's accomplices).
— v. tr. Glapir.
— n. Cri aigu (or) perçant m. ‖ FAM. Protestation, réclamation f.
squealer [-ə*]. See SQUEAKER.
squeamish ['skwi:miʃ] adj. MED. Sujet aux nausées (person); délicat (stomach); to feel squeamish, avoir mal au cœur, se sentir barbouillé (or) nauséeux. ‖ FIG. Délicat, difficile, dégoûté (over-fastidious); trop scrupuleux (over-scrupulous); pudibond (prudish).
squeamishness [-nis] n. MED. Disposition (f.) aux nausées. ‖ FIG. Goût difficile m.; délicatesse f. (of conscience).
squeegee ['skwi:'dʒi:] n. Raclette (f.) [or] racloir (m.) en caoutchouc. ‖ NAUT. Râteau de pont m.
squeezable ['skwi:zəbl] adj. Compressible, comprimable. ‖ FIG. Pressurable.
squeeze [skwi:z] v. tr. Serrer, presser, comprimer; to squeeze s.o.'s hand, serrer la main à qqn; to squeeze one's finger, se pincer le doigt; to squeeze in one's waist, se serrer la taille. ‖ ARTS., TECHN. Prendre l'empreinte de. ‖ CULIN. Presser (une orange). ‖ FAM. Embrasser, étreindre, serrer sur son cœur. ‖ FAM. Exercer une pression sur, serrer la vis à; faire marcher; to squeeze money from, pressurer, extorquer de l'argent à. ‖ To squeeze into, faire entrer (by force); to squeeze oneself into, entrer de force dans. ‖ To squeeze out, exprimer, faire sortir, produire (with an effort); obtenir (a confession); soutirer, extorquer (money); verser (a tear); exprimer (water). ‖ To squeeze through, faire passer à travers par la force; to squeeze oneself through, se frayer un passage à travers.
— v. intr. To squeeze into, s'introduire de force dans. ‖ To squeeze out, sortir de force (or) en se serrant. ‖ To squeeze through, se frayer un passage avec difficulté à travers, passer en se faufilant à travers; FAM. Passer tout juste (an examination). ‖ To squeeze together (or) up, se serrer, se presser, s'entasser.
— n. Compression f. ‖ Etreinte, embrassade f. ‖ Pression f. (of the hand). ‖ Presse, cohue f. (in a crowd); it's a tight squeeze, ça tient tout juste. ‖ SPORTS. Squeeze play, squeeze (in baseball). ‖

TECHN. Serrage *m.* ‖ ARTS. Empreinte *f.* ‖ CULIN. Pressée *f.; quelques gouttes *f. pl.* (of a lemon). ‖ FAM. Soutirage, pressurage *m.* (exaction).

squeezer [-ə*] n. TECHN. Compresseur *m.* ‖ CULIN. Presse *f.* ‖ FAM. Extorqueur *m.* (of money); oppresseur *m.* (of the public).

squelch [skweltʃ] v. tr. Ecraser. ‖ FIG. Réprimer, étouffer (a revolt). ‖ FAM. Clore le bec à, couper le sifflet à; aplatir (s.o.).
— v. intr. Gicler, faire flic flac (wet shoes); *to squelch through the mud*, marcher en faisant gicler la boue, patouiller dans la boue.
— n. Giclement *m.* (of mud); flic-flac *m.* (of wet shoes). ‖ Lourde chute (*f.*) sur qqch. de mou. ‖ FAM. Réplique désarçonnante *f.*

squib [skwib] n. Pétard *m.* ‖ TECHN. Canette *f.* (of a detonator). ‖ FAM. Petite annonce, courte légende *f.* (caption); brocard *m.* (lampoon).
— v. tr. FAM. Brocarder.

squid [skwid] n. ZOOL. Calmar, encornet *m.*

squiffy ['skwifi] adj. FAM. Eméché, pompette, parti, paf, brindezingue.

squiggle ['skwigl] n. Arabesque, fioriture *f.* (curlicue); gribouillage, gribouillis *m.* (scrawl).

squill [skwil] n. BOT. Scille *f.* ‖ ZOOL. Squille *f.*

squint [skwint] v. intr. Regarder en fronçant le sourcil. ‖ MED. Loucher. ‖ **To squint at**, regarder de côté, loucher sur.
— v. tr. MED. Fermer à moitié (eyes).
— n. MED. Strabisme *m.;* loucherie *f.* ‖ FAM. Regard oblique, coup d'œil *m.; to take a squint at*, jeter un coup d'œil sur.
— adj. MED. Louche, qui louche. ‖ **Squint-eyed**, adj. MED. Strabique; FIG. Au regard malveillant.

squire [skwaiə*] n. Ecuyer *m.* ‖ Grand propriétaire terrien *m.;* châtelain, seigneur du village *m.* ‖ FAM. Cavalier servant *m.* (lady's escort).
— v. tr. Accompagner, escorter, servir de cavalier à (a lady).

squirearchy [-rɑ:ki] n. Ensemble (or) gouvernement (*m.*) des grands propriétaires terriens.

squireship [-ʃip] n. Condition (*f.*) [or] rang (*m.*) de squire.

squirm [skwə:m] v. intr. Se tordre, se tortiller. ‖ FIG. Etre gêné (or) intimidé; se crisper (under a rebuke).
— n. Tortillement *m.* (act, motion).

squirrel ['skwirəl] n. ZOOL. Ecureuil *m.*
— v. tr. *To squirrel away*, amasser, entasser.

squirt [skwə:t] v. intr. Jaillir, gicler. (See SPOUT, SPIRT.)
— v. tr. Projeter, faire gicler. ‖ Seringuer, injecter.
— n. Seringue *f.* (implement). ‖ Jet *m.;* giclée *f.* (of liquid). ‖ FAM. Freluquet; petit merdeux *m.* (pop.). ‖ **Squirt-gun**, n. Pistolet à eau.

squirting [-iŋ] n. Seringage *m.* ‖ Jaillissement, giclement *m.*

squish [skwiʃ] v. intr. Gicler.
— n. Giclement *m.*

squishy [-i] adj. Mou et giclant, détrempé, bourbeux. (See SQUASHY.)

Sri Lanka ['sri 'læŋkə] n. GEOGR. Sri Lanka *m.*

St. Written abbr. for *Saint*, saint, Sᵗ. ‖ Abbr. *street*, rue.

stab [stæb] v. tr. (1). Poignarder (s.o.); percer (s.o.'s heart). ‖ FIG. Blesser à mort.
— v. intr. Donner un coup de poignard (*at*, à). ‖ FIG. Porter un coup mortel (*at*, à).
— n. Coup de poignard (or) de couteau *m.* ‖ FIG. Coup mortel *m.* ‖ FAM. Coup d'essai *m.; to have a stab at*, s'essayer à.

stabber [-ə*] n. Poignardeur, assassin *m.* ‖ TECHN. Tire-point *m.*

stabbing [-iŋ] adj. Perçant. ‖ MED. Lancinant, en coup de couteau.

stability [stə'biliti] n. Fermeté, solidité, consistance *f.* (personal); stabilité *f.* (of things).

stabilization [ˌsteibiliˈzeiʃən] n. Stabilisation *f.*

stabilize ['steibilaiz] v. tr. Stabiliser.

stabilizer [-ə*] n. AVIAT. Stabilisateur; ballonnet d'hydravion *m.* ‖ CHIM. Stabilisant *m.*

stable ['steibl] adj. Stable (chair, equilibrium); stable, fixe (job); *to become stable*, se stabiliser. ‖ Ferme (conviction); stable (government); constant, équilibré, solide (person). ‖ CHIM. Stable.

stable n. AGRIC., SPORTS. Ecurie *f.* ‖ **Stable-boy**, n. AGRIC. Palefrenier *m.;* SPORTS. Lad *m.* ‖ **Stable-call**, n. MILIT. MUS. Pansage *m.*
— v. tr. Mettre à l'écurie.
— v. intr. Etre à l'écurie. ‖ FAM. Percher, nicher.

stabling [-iŋ] n. Logement (*m.*) à l'écurie. ‖ Ecuries *f. pl.* (collectively).

stably ['steibli] adv. Stablement.

staccato [stəˈkɑ:tou] n. MUS. Staccato *m.*
— adj. MUS. En staccato. ‖ FIG. Saccadé.
— adv. MUS. Staccato. ‖ FIG. D'une manière saccadée.

stack [stæk] n. AGRIC. Meule *f.* ‖ MILIT. Faisceau *m.* ‖ ARCHIT. Corps *m.* (of chimney). ‖ CH. DE F., NAUT. Cheminée *f.* ‖ MATH. Corde *f.* (measure). ‖ U. S. Etagère, bibliothèque *f.* (bookshelves). ‖ FAM. Tas *m.;* pile *f.*
— v. tr. AGRIC. Mettre en meule. ‖ MILIT. Mettre en faisceaux. ‖ FAM. Empiler, entasser; *to be stacked with*, regorger de. ‖ U. S. FAM. *To stack the cards*, donner le coup de pouce en dessous pour orienter le jeu.

stactometer [stækˈtɔmitə*] n. PHYS. Stalagmomètre *m.*

staddle ['stædl] n. Baliveau *m.*
— v. tr. Baliver.

stadium ['steidiəm] (pl. **stadia** [-iə]; U. S. **stadiums**) n. MED., SPORTS. Stade *m.*

staff [stɑ:f] n. Bâton *m.; pilgrim's staff*, bourdon. ‖ EECLES. Crosse *f.* (of a bishop). ‖ NAUT. Mât *m.* (of flag); bois *m.* (of spear). ‖ MILIT., NAUT. Etat-major *m.; Staff College*, Ecole supérieure de guerre. ‖ Personnel *m.; teaching staff*, personnel enseignant. ‖ FIG. Soutien *m.; the staff of life*, le pain vital. ‖ **Staff-officer**, n. MILIT. Officier (*m.*) d'état-major.
— (pl. **staves** [stei:vz]; U. S. **staffs**) n. MUS. Portée *f.*
— v. tr. Pourvoir de personnel.

staff n. ARCHIT. Staff *m.*

stag [stæg] n. ZOOL. Cerf *m.* (hart); mâle *m.* (of the caribou). ‖ FAM. Homme (*m.*) qui fait cavalier seul. ‖ **Stag-beetle**, n. ZOOL. Cerf-volant *m.* ‖ **Stag-hunting**, n. SPORTS. Chasse (*f.*) à courre. ‖ **Stag party**, n. U. S. FAM. Réunion (*f.*) d'hommes.

stage [steidʒ] n. ARCHIT. Echafaudage *m.* ‖ NAUT. Plate *f.* (floating stage); débarcadère *m.* (landing stage). ‖ PHYS. Platine *f.* (of a microscope); étage *m.* (of a rocket). ‖ THEATR. Théâtre *m.* (art, profession); scène *f.* (platform); *to go on the stage*, monter sur les planches. ‖ Etape *f.* (distance); relais *m.* (place) [on a journey]; *by easy stages*, à petites étapes. ‖ AUTOM. Fare range, section (in a bus). ‖ FIG. Phase, période *f.;* degré *m.* (oi development, evolution); *by stages*, par paliers (or) échelons (or) degrés. ‖ FIG. Scène *f.;* champ *m.* (of activities). ‖ **Stage-coach**, n. Diligence *f.* ‖ **Stage-coachman**, n. Postillon *m.* ‖ **Stage-craft**, n. THEATR. Habileté scénique *f.* ‖ **Stage-direction**, n. THEATR. Indication scénique *f.* ‖ **Stage-door**, n. THEATR. Entrée (*f.*) des artistes. ‖ **Stage-effect**, n. THEATR. Effet théâtral *m.* ‖ **Stage-fright**, n. Trac *m.* ‖ **Stage-hand**, n. THEATR. Machiniste *m.* ‖ **Stage-manager**, n. THEATR. Régisseur *m.* ‖ **Stage-play**, n. THEATR. Pièce (*f.*) de théâtre. ‖ **Stage-player**, n. THEATR. Acteur *m.* ‖ **Stage-properties**, n. pl. THEATR. Accessoires *m. pl.* ‖ **Stage-struck**, adj. Passionné de théâtre. ‖ **Stage-whisper**, n. THEATR. Aparté *m.;* FIG. Chuchotement (*m.*) manquant de discrétion.
— v. tr. THEATR. Monter, mettre en scène.
— v. intr. THEATR. Se prêter à la mise en scène.

staged [-d] adj. Archit. A gradins, en étages.

stager [-ə*] n. Fam. *Old stager*, vieux routier.

stagey [-i] adj. See STAGY.

staggard ['stægəd] n. Cerf (*m.*) de quatre ans.

stagger ['stægə*] v. intr. Chanceler, tituber. || Fig. Fléchir, vaciller.
— v. tr. Faire chanceler. || Techn. Disposer en quinconces. || U. S. Echelonner; *staggered holidays*, congés échelonnés. || Aviat. Décaler (wings). || Fig. Désarçonner;· renverser (fam.) [s.o.].
— n. Allure chancelante *f.*

staggerer [-rə*] n. Fam. Coup d'assommoir, argument décisif *m.*; nouvelle renversante *f.*

staggering [-riŋ] adj. Chancelant, titubant. || Fam. Renversant, époustouflant.

staggers ['stægəz] n. sg. Zool. Vertigo *m.* || Fam. Vertige *m.*

staging ['steidʒiŋ] n. Etape *f.* || Theatr. Mise en scène *f.* || Archit. Echafaudage *m.*

stagnancy ['stægnənsi] n. Stagnation *f.* || Fig. Marasme *m.*

stagnant [-ənt] adj. Stagnant.

stagnate [-eit] v. intr. Se figer (blood); stagner, croupir (water). || Fig. Stagner, être immobilisé.

stagnation [stæg'neiʃən] n. Stagnation *f.*

stagy ['steidʒi] adj. Théâtral.

staid [steid] adj. Sérieux, posé, rassis.

staidness [-nis] n. Gravité *f.*; sérieux *m.*

stain [stein] v. tr. Tacher. || Colorer; *stained glass*, vitre de couleur; *stained glass window*, vitrail. || Teindre, teinter (to dye). || Fig. Souiller, ternir.
— v. intr. Se tacher.
— n. Tache *f.* (lit. and fig.).

stainable [-əbl] adj. Tachant.

stainer [-ə*] n. Teinturier *m.* (person); colorant *m.* (substance).

stainless [-lis] adj. Sans tache (lit. and fig.). || Inoxydable (steel).

stair [stɛə*] n. Marche *f.* (step). || Pl. Escalier *m.*; *below stairs*, en bas; chez les domestiques, à l'office (fam.). || Fam. *To climb the golden stairs*, monter au ciel. || **Stair-carpet**, n. Tapis d'escalier *m.* || **Stair-rod**, n. Tringle (*f.*) de tapis d'escalier.

staircase [-keis] n. Escalier *m.*

stake [steik] n. Pieu, poteau *m.* (post); jalon *m.* (rod). || Bûcher *m.*; *condemned to the stake*, condamné au bûcher. || Enjeu *m.* (gaming); *put down your stakes*, faites vos jeux. || Sports. Prix *m.* |; Agric. Echalas *m.* || Techn. Tasseau *m.* || U. S. Fin. Fonds réservés *m.* pl. || Fig. Enjeu *m.*; *his life is at stake*, sa vie est en jeu, il y va de sa vie. || U. S. Fam. *To pull up stakes*, déplacer ses pénates, déménager. || **Stake-money**, n. Mise *f.*; enjeu *m.*
— v. tr. Garnir (or) étayer de pieux (or) piquets. || Attacher à un piquet. || Agric. Ramer. || Fig. Jouer, hasarder, mettre en jeu. || **To stake off** (or) **out**, jalonner.

stakeholder [-houldə*] n. Dépositaire (*m.*) d'enjeux.

stalactite ['stæləktait] n. Stalactite *f.*

stalagmite ['stæləgmait] n. Stalagmite *f.*

stale [steil] adj. Vicié, confiné (air); de renfermé (smell). || Culin. Eventé (beer, wine); rassis (bread); pas frais (egg). || Comm. Défraîchi (goods). || Fin. Prescrit (cheque); plat (market). || Jur. Périmé. || Sports. Surentraîné. || Fig. Rebattu (joke); défraîchi (news); vieux, vieilli, rebattu (subject); usé (talent); *that's stale news*, c'est déjà vieux.
— v. tr. Culin. Eventer. || Fig. Déflorer, enlever tout son sel à.

stale n. Zool. Urine *f.*
— v. intr. Zool. Uriner.

stalemate [-meit] n. Sports. Pat *m.* (in chess). || Fig. Impasse *f.*
— v. tr. Faire pat. || Fig. Conduire à une impasse.

staleness [-nis] n. Odeur (*f.*) de renfermé. || Culin. Event *m.*; état rassis *m.* || Sports. Surentraînement *m.* || Fig. Banalité *f.*

stalinism ['stɑ:li,nizm] n. Stalinisme *m.*

stalinist [-,nist] n. Stalinien *s.*

stalk [stɔ:k] v. tr. Sports. Traquer. || Fam. Filer (s.o.).
— v. intr. Marcher dignement (or) à pas comptés.
— n. Démarche digne *f.* || Sports. Chasse (*f.*) à l'affût.

stalk n. Pied *m.* (of a glass); tuyau *m.* (of pipe). || Bot. Trognon *m.* (of a cabbage); tige, queue *f.* (of flower).

stalker [-ə*] n. Sports. Chasseur (*m.*) à l'affût.

stalking-horse [-iŋ'hɔ:s] n. Cheval d'abri *m.* || Fig. Paravent *m.*

stalky [-i] adj. Bot. A longue tige.

stall [stɔ:l] n. Stalle *f.* (in a stable); étable *f.* (stable). || Autom. Box *m.* (in a garage). || Comm. Etal, éventaire *m.* (at a market); stand *m.* (at an exhibition); *newspaper stall*, kiosque à journaux. || Eccles. Stalle *f.* || Theatr. Fauteuil d'orchestre *m.* || **Stall-feed**, v. tr. Agric. Engraisser à l'étable.
— v. tr. Mettre à l'étable (cattle). || Garnir de stalles (a stable). || Autom. Caler. || Aviat. Mettre en perte de vitesse.
— v. intr. S'embourber (cart). || Autom. Caler (engine). || Aviat. Se mettre en perte de vitesse. || Fig. *To stall for time*, gagner du temps. || **To stall off**, différer.

stallage [-idʒ] n. Droit (*m.*) de place (at a market).

stallion ['stæljən] n. Zool. Etalon *m.*

stalwart ['stɔ:lwət] adj. Robuste, vigoureux; costaud (fam.). || Fig. Ferme, résolu, déterminé.
— n. Costaud *m.*

stalwartness [-nis] n. Robustesse *f.* || Fig. Résolution *f.*

stamen ['steimen] n. Bot. Etamine *f.*
— N. B. Deux pluriels : *stamens, stamina.*

stamina ['stæminə] n. Résistance, endurance *f.*

staminal [-əl] adj. Bot. Staminal. || Med. Energétique.

staminate ['stæmineit] adj. Bot. Staminé.

stammer ['stæmə*] v. intr., tr. Med. Bégayer. || Fam. Balbutier, bafouiller.
— n. Med. Bégaiement *m.* || Fam. Bafouillage *m.*

stammerer [-rə*] n. Med. Bègue *s.*

stammering [-riŋ] adj. Med. Bégayant (articulation); bègue (person).

stammeringly [-riŋli] adv. En bégayant.

stamp [stæmp] v. tr. Poinçonner (gold); frapper, estamper (metal, paper). || Estampiller, viser (a document); timbrer (a letter). || Techn. Estamper, emboutir (metal); broyer, concasser, bocarder (ore). || Fig. Marquer, signaler, classer (as, comme) [s.o.]; imprimer, graver (on, sur) [sth.]. || **To stamp out**, Techn. Découper à l'emporte-pièce; Fig. Ecraser.
— v. intr. Trépigner, taper du pied.
— n. Empreinte *f.* (mark). || Timbre, timbre-poste *m.* (postage). || Jur. Estampille *f.*; visa *m.* (on a document). || Comm. Estampille *f.* || Techn. Estampe *f.*; coin; poinçon; pilon *m.*; broyeuse *f.* (tool). || Fig. Coin *m.* (of genius). || Fam. Catégorie, nature *f.*; *of the same stamp*, de la même trempe; du même acabit (pej.). || **Stamp-collector**, n. Collectionneur (*m.*) de timbres. || **Stamp-duty**, n. Droit de timbre *m.* || **Stamp-machine**, n. Distributeur automatique (*m.*) de timbres-poste; Techn. Estampeuse *f.* || **Stamp-mill**, n. Techn. Bocard *m.*

stampede [stæm'pi:d] n. Débandade *f.*; sauve-qui-peut *m.* (flight). || Ruée *f.* (rush).
— v. intr. Etre saisi de panique; fuir à la débandade. || Se ruer.
— v. tr. Provoquer la panique (or) la ruée de.

stamper ['stæmpə*] n. Techn. Estampeuse; poinçonneuse *f.* (machine) ; timbreur ; frappeur ; estampeur *m.* (person).

stamping [-in] n. Piétinement ; trépignement *m.* ‖ Estampillage *m.* (of metal). ‖ Timbrage *m.* ‖ Bocardage *m.* (of ore). ‖ **Stamping-ground,** n. FAM. Terrain favori, lieu (*m.*) d'élection. ‖ **Stamping-mill,** n. TECHN. Bocard *m.*

stance [stæns] n. SPORTS. Position, posture *f.*

stanch [stɑːntʃ] adj., v. tr. See STAUNCH.

stanchion ['stɑːnʃən] n. Etai, étançon *m.* ‖ Montant *m.* ‖ NAUT. Epontille *f.*
— v. tr. Etayer. ‖ Attacher à un montant. ‖ NAUT. Epontiller.

stand [stænd] v. intr. (157). Se tenir debout (on one's feet). ‖ Rester immobile, s'arrêter (stationary). ‖ Se lever (to an upright position). ‖ Se mettre, se placer, se tenir ; *to stand in the doorway,* se tenir à la porte ; *to stand in the rain,* rester sous la pluie. ‖ Rester, demeurer ; *to stand still,* rester tranquille. ‖ Durer, demeurer ; *to stand fast,* tenir bon. ‖ Rester valable, tenir (offer). ‖ Dépendre ; *it stands to reason that,* il va sans dire que. ‖ Maintenir ; ne pas démordre de ; *to stand to it that,* soutenir que. ‖ Se trouver, être ; *how do they stand in the matter of clothes ?,* où en sont-ils au point de vue vestimentaire ? ; *that's how it stands,* c'est comme ça ; *to stand first,* être au premier rang ; *to stand in awe of,* avoir peur de ; *to stand for nothing,* n'être compté pour rien ; *to stand ready to,* être prêt à. ‖ CHIM. Déposer. ‖ CULIN. Infuser (tea). ‖ NAUT. Faire route (ship). ‖ MILIT. *To stand sentry,* monter la garde. ‖ FIN. *To stand to lose,* s'attendre à perdre. ‖ SPORTS. Tomber en arrêt (hound). ‖ FAM. *Stand and deliver,* la bourse ou la vie ; *to stand on one's own feet,* voler de ses propres ailes ; U. S. *to stand pat,* refuser de bouger. ‖ **To stand about,** flâner, traîner. ‖ **To stand against,** résister à. ‖ **To stand at,** s'arrêter à, reculer (or) hésiter devant. ‖ **To stand away,** s'éloigner, s'écarter (*from,* de). ‖ **To stand back,** se tenir en retrait ; se reculer. ‖ **To stand by,** se tenir prêt, être présent sans intervenir (absolutely) ; se tenir près de (s.o.) ; NAUT. Se tenir paré ; FIG. Accepter (a decision) ; rester fidèle à (a promise) ; faire cause commune avec, prendre le parti de (s.o.). ‖ **To stand down,** se retirer. ‖ **To stand for,** signifier, vouloir dire (sth.) ; défendre, soutenir (a cause) ; remplacer (s.o., sth.) ; COMM., JUR. Représenter ; NAUT. Faire route vers ; U. S. FAM. Supporter, tolérer. ‖ **To stand in,** s'associer, se joindre (*with,* à) ; CINEM., FAM. Figurer (*for,* pour) ; FIN. Coûter ; NAUT. Mettre le cap (*for,* sur) ; courir (*to,* à). ‖ **To stand off,** se tenir à l'écart ; s'éloigner ; chômer (employee) ; NAUT. Courir au large ; FAM. Tergiverser. ‖ **To stand on,** NAUT. Continuer sa route ; FIG. Attacher de l'importance à, insister sur ; *to stand on one's dignity,* se retrancher dans sa dignité. ‖ **To stand out,** avancer, faire saillie (house) ; se détacher, se profiler (mountain) ; NAUT. Prendre le large ; FIG. S'opposer, résister (*against,* à) ; entrer en lutte (*with,* avec) ; FAM. *To stand out a mile,* crever les yeux. ‖ **To stand up,** se lever, se mettre debout ; FIG. Résister, tenir tête, faire face (*against,* à) ; tenir pied, résister (*to,* à) ; ne pas se laisser rebuter (*to,* par).
— v. tr. Mettre, placer, poser ; *to stand on end,* mettre debout. ‖ Endurer, supporter, résister à ; supporter (the cold) ; soutenir (a shock). ‖ Tenir ; *to stand one's ground,* ne pas lâcher pied, ne pas reculer. ‖ Courir (one's chance). ‖ MILIT. Soutenir (fire, a siege). ‖ JUR. *To stand one's trial,* subir son jugement, être jugé. ‖ FAM. Payer (a round of drinks) ; souffrir, encaisser, voir (s.o.) ; *he can't stand it any longer,* il en a plein le dos. ‖ **To stand up,** U. S. FAM. Poser un lapin à (s.o.).
— n. Aplomb *m.* ; *to take a firm stand,* se camper sur ses jambes. ‖ Position (*f.*) debout, station *f.* ;

to take one's stand behind a tree, se poster derrière un arbre. ‖ Support, pied, socle *m.* (of lamp). ‖ Guéridon *m.* ‖ Portemanteau *m.* (for coats and hats). ‖ CULIN. Dessous-de-plat *m. ; cruet, liqueur stand,* huilier, cabaret. ‖ COMM. Etal, stand *m.* ‖ SPORTS., MUS. Estrade, tribune *f. ;* stand *m.* ‖ MUS. Kiosque (*m.*) à musique (band-stand). ‖ COMM. Station *f. ;* stationnement *m.* ‖ AGRIC. Récolte (*f.*) sur pied. ‖ TECHN. Banc *m.* ‖ U. S. JUR. *To take the stand,* venir à la barre. ‖ U. S. *Highway stand,* guinguette. ‖ FIG. Position *f. ; to maintain one's stand,* s'en tenir à sa position initiale ; *to take one's stand on,* se fonder sur (a principle). ‖ FIG. Résistance, opposition *f. ; to make a stand against,* s'élever contre (an abuse) ; résister à (s.o.). ‖ **Stand-by** n. Ressource *f.* (money) ; soutien, partisan, défenseur *m.* (person) ; *on stand-by,* en réserve, prêt à intervenir ; AVIAT. Liste d'attente *f. ; to be on stand-by,* attendre une place libre à l'aéroport. ‖ **Stand-camera,** n. Appareil photographique à pied *m.* ‖ **Stand-in,** n. CINEM. Doublure *f.* ‖ **Stand-off-half,** n. SPORTS. Demi (*m.*) d'ouverture. ‖ **Stand-offish,** adj. Distant, froid, réservé. ‖ **Stand rest,** n. U. S. FAM. Appui *m.* ‖ **Stand-out,** n. U. S. Original *m.* ‖ **Stand-to,** n. MILIT. Alerte *f.* ‖ **Stand-up,** adj. Droit (collar) ; debout (lunch) ; rangé (fight).

standard ['stændəd] n. MILIT., BOT., FIG. Etendard *m.* ‖ FIN. Etalon *m.* (money) ; titre *m.* (of a silver coin) ; taux *m.* (of wages) ; *standard of living,* niveau (or) standard de vie. ‖ TECHN. Conduite *f.* (of gas) ; support, pied *m.* (of a lathe). ‖ AGRIC. Arbre de plein-vent *m.* ‖ CHIM. Titre *m.* (of a solution). ‖ COMM. *Up to standard,* conforme à l'échantillon, répondant à toutes les exigences. ‖ FIG. Degré *m.* (of knowledge) ; niveau *m.* (of an examination, intelligence, morality) ; modèle, type *m.* (of taste). ‖ **Standard-bearer,** n. MILIT. Porte-étendard *m.* ‖ **Standard-lamp,** n. Lampadaire *m.*
— adj. Etalon (measure). ‖ Sur pied (or) socle (lamp). ‖ FIN. Au titre (gold). ‖ COMM. Standard, normal, moyen, courant (in general). ‖ AGRIC. De plein-vent (tree). ‖ AUTOM. De série (car.). ‖ CHIM. Réactif (paper). ‖ FIG. Classique (author, book) ; définitif (edition) ; standard (model) ; *standard French,* le français courant.

standardization [ˌstændədaiˈzeiʃən] n. Etalonnement *m.* ‖ CHIM. Titrage *m.* ‖ COMM. Standardisation, uniformisation, production en série *f.* ‖ FIN. Péréquation *f.* ‖ TECHN. Normalisation *f.*

standardize ['stændədaiz] v. tr. Prendre pour étalon (or) type. ‖ CHIM. Titrer. ‖ COMM. Standardiser, faire en série.

standee [stænˈdiː] n. U. S. THEATR., FAM. Spectateur debout *m.*

stander ['stændə*] n. Voyageur debout *s.*

standing [-iŋ] n. Station (*f.*) debout. ‖ Durée *f. ; friend of long standing,* ami de longue date. ‖ Position *f. ; a man of some standing,* un homme considéré. ‖ COMM. Standing *m. ;* importance, surface *f.* (of a firm).
— adj. Debout (person) ; en pied (statue) ; stagnant (water). ‖ AGRIC. Sur pied (crop). ‖ MILIT. Permanent (army, camp). ‖ NAUT. Fixe (rope). ‖ FIN. Fixe (price) ; *standing expenses,* frais généraux. ‖ JUR. Permanent (committee). ‖ TECHN. Inactif (engine). ‖ AUTOM. En stationnement. ‖ SPORTS. A pieds joints (jump). ‖ FIG. Etabli, courant (custom) ; classique (joke) ; fixe, immuable (rule). ‖ **Standing-order,** n. Commande permanente *f.* (regular order) ; FIN. Virement automatique *m. ; to place a standing order,* faire une demande de prélèvement automatique ; Pl. Règlements (*m. pl.*) en vigueur. ‖ **Standing-room,** n. CH. DE F., THEATR. Places (*f. pl.*) debout.

standpat ['stændpæt] adj. U. S. FAM. Immobiliste.

standpatter [-ə*] n. U. S. FAM. Immobiliste *m.*

standpipe [-paip] n. TECHN. Colonne montante *f*.
standpoint ['-point] n. Point (*m*.) de vue.
standstill [-stil] n. MILIT. Stabilisation, accalmie *f*. ‖ COMM. Calme plat ; marasme *m. ;* stagnation *f*. ‖ FIG. Immobilisation *f. ;* arrêt complet, point mort *m. ;* panne *f*. (fam.).
stank [stæŋk]. See STINK.
stannary ['stænəri] n. Mine (*f*.) d'étain.
stannic [-ik] adj. CHIM. Stannique.
stanniferous [stæ'nifərəs] adj. Stannifère.
stanza ['stænzə] n. Stance, strophe *f*. ‖ ARCHIT. Loge *f*.
staphylococcus [,stæfilə'koukəs] n. MED. Staphylocoque *m*.
staple ['steipl] n. Cavalier *m*. (nail) ; crampon *m*. ‖ Broche, agrafe *f*. (for bookbinding). ‖ Gâche *f*. (bolt-staple).
— v. tr. Maintenir avec un cavalier (or) un crampon. ‖ Fixer avec une agrafe. ‖ Brocher au fil métallique.
staple n. TECHN. Fibre *f*. (of cotton, flax, wool) ; qualité *f*. (fineness). ‖ COMM. Denrée (or) production principale *f*. (product) ; denrée de base *f*. (item of trade) ; matière première *f*. (raw material) ; *staple commodity*, objet (or) denrée de première nécessité ; *staple industry*, industrie principale ; *staple trade*, commerce régulier. ‖ FIG. Fond, sujet principal *m*. ‖ **Staple-fibre**, n. Fibranne *f*.
stapler [-ə*] n. Agrafeuse *f*.
star [stɑ:*] n. ASTRON. Etoile *f. ;* astre *m*. ‖ Etoile *f*. (emblem, ornament). ‖ Astérisque *m*. ‖ CINEM. Star, étoile, vedette *f*. ‖ THEATR. Etoile f. ; *dancing star*, danseuse étoile. ‖ FIG. Etoile, destinée *f*. ‖ **Star-chamber**, n. † Chambre étoilée *f*. ‖ **Star-dust**, n. Poussière (*f*.) d'étoiles ; FAM. Illusion *f*. ‖ **Star-fish**, n. ZOOL. Etoile de mer *f*. ‖ **Star-gaze**, v. intr. FAM. Bayer aux corneilles, être dans la lune. ‖ **Star-gazer**, n. Astronome *m. ;* FAM. Rêvasseur *m*. ‖ **Star-lighting**, n. Diminution (*f*.) de l'éclairage urbain. ‖ **Star-shell**, n. MILIT. Fusée éclairante *f*. ‖ **Star-spangled**, adj. MILIT. Etoilé (banner). ‖ **Star-stone**, n. Astérie *f*. (sapphire). ‖ **Star-turn**, n. THEATR. Clou *m*.
— v. tr. (1). Etoiler, consteller. ‖ Marquer d'un astérisque. ‖ CINEM., FIG. Mettre en vedette.
— v. intr. CINEM. Ftre en vedette.
starboard ['stɑ:bəd] n. NAUT. Tribord *m*.
— v. tr. NAUT. Mettre à tribord (the helm).
— v. intr. NAUT. Venir sur tribord.
starch [stɑ:tʃ] n. Amidon *m*. ‖ Empois *m*. (paste). ‖ CULIN. Fécule *f*. (potato starch). ‖ FIG. Raideur, allure compassée *f*.
— adj. FIG. Raide, compassé.
— v. tr. Amidonner, empeser.
starchiness [-inis] n. Allure compassée *f*.
starchy [-i] adj. Amidonné, empesé. ‖ CULIN. Féculent, contenant de l'amidon ; *starchy food*, féculents. ‖ FIG. Guindé, compassé, raide.
stardom ['stɑ:dəm] n. FAM. Vedettariat *m*.
stare [stɛə*] v. intr. Regarder fixement. ‖ Ecarquiller les yeux, ouvrir de grands yeux. ‖ Sauter aux yeux. ‖ **To stare at**, regarder fixement, fixer son regard sur ; regarder en ouvrant de grands yeux ; *to stare at each other*, se dévisager.
— v. tr. Regarder fixement, fixer ; *to stare s.o. up and down*, toiser qqn. ‖ FAM. *It's staring you in the face*, ça vous saute aux yeux.
— n. Regard fixe (or) ahuri (or) hagard *m. ;* yeux écarquillés *m. pl.*
staring [-riŋ] adj. Ecarquillé, grand ouvert ; fixe (eye). ‖ Voyant, criard (colour).
staringly [-riŋli] adv. Fixement ; d'un œil ahuri (or) hagard. ‖ De façon voyante.
stark [stɑ:k] adj. Raide, rigide *f*. ‖ Résolu, décidé. ‖ FAM. Pur, absolu, total.
— adv. Tout à fait, entièrement, complètement ; *stark naked*, tout nu.

starkers [-əz] adj. POP. A poil (naked).
starlet [-lit] n. CINEM. Starlette *f*.
starlight [-lait] n. Lumière (*f*.) des étoiles.
— adj. Etoilé (night).
starling ['stɑ:liŋ] n. ZOOL. Sansonnet, étourneau *m*.
starling n. TECHN. Pilotis *m. pl*.
starry ['stɑ: i] adj. Etoilé. ‖ Etincelant. ‖ **Starry-eyed**, adj. Idéologue, peu pratique.
start [stɑ:t] v. intr. Sursauter, tressaillir, tressauter. ‖ Sauter ; *to start back*, faire un bond en arrière ; *to start aside*, faire un écart, se jeter de côté. ‖ S'ouvrir, se découdre (seam). ‖ Partir (*for*, pour) ; *to start on a journey*, partir en voyage. ‖ Commencer, débuter ; *to start with melon*, commencer par un melon ; *to start by doing*, commencer par faire ; *to start in life*, débuter dans la vie. ‖ TECHN. Démarrer (machine) ; sauter (rivet). ‖ NAUT. Entamer (a water-cask). ‖ **To start again**, recommencer ; FAM. Repartir du pied droit. ‖ **To start in**, FAM. Débuter. ‖ **To start off**, commencer ; partir ; AUTOM. Démarrer ; CH. DE F. S'ébranler. ‖ **To start out**, partir, se mettre en route ; *his eyes were starting out of his head*, les yeux lui sortaient de la tête. ‖ **To start up**, se lever brusquement (person) ; TECHN. Démarrer (engine) ; FIG. Surgir, se présenter (difficulty, idea).
— v. tr. Commencer, se mettre à ; *to start singing*, se mettre à chanter ; *to start everybody laughing*, provoquer le rire général, faire rire tout le monde. ‖ Ouvrir, découdre, faire craquer (a seam). ‖ SPORTS. Lever (a hare) ; lancer (a stag) ; donner le signal du départ à (a race). ‖ TECHN. Mettre en marche, lancer (a clock, an engine, a machine) ; faire sauter (a screw). ‖ ELECTR. Amorcer (a dynamo). ‖ CH. DE F. Faire partir (a train). ‖ COMM. Lancer, fonder (a business house). ‖ FIG. Lancer (*in, on*, dans) [s.o.]. ‖ FIG. Entamer (a conversation) ; émettre (a doubt) ; faire naître (a quarrel, rumour) ; soulever (a question) ; amorcer (a subject).
— N. B. Se construit avec l'infinitif ou la forme en *-ing*.
— n. Tressaillement, sursaut, tressaut, brusque mouvement *m. ; by fits and starts*, par à-coups. ‖ Départ, début, commencement *m. ; to get a good start in life*, prendre un bon démarrage dans la vie. ‖ SPORTS. Avance *f*. (advantage) ; point de départ *m*. (place) [in a race] ; *to give s.o. a ten yard start* donner à qqn dix yards d'avance. ‖ FAM. Rum (or) *odd start*, drôle d'aventure, événement bizarre.
starter [-ə*] n. Débutant *s. ;* personne (*f*.) qui part ; *to be a slow starter*, être lent à démarrer (or) se mettre en route. ‖ SPORTS. Partant *m*. (competitor) ; starter *m*. (signal-giver). ‖ AUTOM., AVIAT. Démarreur *m*. ‖ FIG. Promoteur *m*. (of a discussion) ; auteur *m*. (of an objection). ‖ FAM. Amorce *f. ;* moyen de lancement *m*.
starting [-iŋ] n. Sursaut, tressaut *m*. ‖ Commencement, départ *m*. ‖ TECHN. Mise en marche *f*. ‖ **Starting-block**, n. SPORTS. Starting-block *m*. ‖ **Starting-line**, n. SPORTS. Ligne (*f*.) de départ. ‖ **Starting-pistol**, n. SPORTS. Pistolet, pistolet de starter *m*. ‖ **Starting-point**, n. Point de départ *m*. ‖ **Starting-post**, n. Poteau de départ *m*. ‖ **Starting-price**, n. SPORTS. Cote (*f*.) de départ ; FIN. Prix initial *m*.
startle [stɑ:tl] v. tr. Faire sursauter, surprendre.
startler [-ə*] n. FAM. Nouvelle sensationnelle *f*.
startling [-iŋ] adj. Sensationnel, saisissant ; suffocant (fam.).
starvation [stɑ:'veiʃən] n. Famine ; privation (*f*.) de nourriture. ‖ MED. Inanition *f*.
— adj. de famine (wages).
starve ['stɑ:v] v. intr. Etre affamé ; mourir de faim. ‖ FIG. Etre privé (or) sevré, manquer (for, de). ‖ FAM. Mourir de faim ; la crever (pop.).
— v. tr. Affamer, faire mourir de faim. priver de

nourriture. (See FAMISH.) ‖ MILIT. Réduire par la famine (a town). ‖ FIG. Priver (*of*, de).

starveling [-liŋ] adj. Affamé, famélique (animal, person). ‖ FAM. De famine (wages).
— n. Affamé, meurt-de-faim *m.* (person). ‖ Animal famélique *m.*

stash [stæʃ] v. tr. U. S. FAM. *To stash away*, planquer, mettre à gauche (money).
— n. U. S. FAM. Planque *f.* (hiding-place); stock *m.*, réserve *f.* (hidden thing); magot *m.* (hidden money).

state [steit] n. Etat *m.* (in general); *to be in a bad state*, être en mauvais état. ‖ Rang *m.;* qualité, condition *f.* (social status). ‖ Apparat *m.;* pompe *f.* (display); *to lie in state*, être exposé solennellement (body). ‖ Etat *m.* (government, nation); *Church and State*, l'Eglise et l'Etat; *States General*, Etats généraux; *the United States*, les Etats-Unis. ‖ FAM. *To get into a state*, se frapper, se mettre dans tous ses états.
— adj. D'apparat, de parade; *State apartments*, grandes pièces de réception; *State carriage*, voiture officielle de cérémonie. ‖ D'Etat (documents); *to establish State control over*, étatiser. ‖ U. S. *State Department*, ministère des Affaires étrangères. ‖ **State-room**, n. Pièce (*f.*) d'apparat; NAUT. Cabine (*f.*) de luxe; U. S. CH. DE F. Voiture-couchette spéciale *f.*
— v. tr. Fixer, déterminer, spécifier (a condition, date, time). ‖ Exposer, formuler (*on*, sur) [one's opinion]; *to state one's name and status*, décliner ses noms et ses qualités. ‖ Affirmer, assurer, déclarer (*that*, que). ‖ FIN. Spécifier (an account). ‖ MATH. Poser (a problem).

statecraft [-krɑ:ft] n. Habileté politique; diplomatie, politique *f.*

stateliness [-linis] n. Majesté, dignité imposante *f.*

stately [-li] adj. Majestueux, imposant. ‖ FAM. *Stately home*, château.

statement [-mənt] n. Déclaration, affirmation, assertion *f.* ‖ Exposé, rapport, compte rendu *m.; official statement to the press*, communiqué à la presse. ‖ Récit *m.;* relation *f.* (of an event). ‖ COMM. Relevé *m.* (of account); *monthly statement*, fin de mois, bilan mensuel.

statesman ['steitsmən] (pl. **statesmen**) n. Homme d'Etat.

statesmanlike [-laik] adj. D'homme d'Etat.

statesmanship [-ʃip] n. Habileté politique *f.*

static ['stætik] adj. PHYS. Statique.
— n. pl. PHYS. Statique *f.* ‖ U. S. RADIO. Parasites *m. pl.*

station ['steiʃən] n. Poste *m.;* place *f.* (location); *to take up one's station*, se placer, prendre son poste. ‖ Poste *m.; first-aid station*, poste sanitaire d'urgence; *postal station*, centre postal; *police station*, poste de police. ‖ Station *f.; weather station*, station météorologique. ‖ ECCLES. *Stations of the Cross*, stations du chemin de croix. ‖ NAUT. *Naval station*, station navale, port militaire. ‖ MILIT. Poste *m.; military station*, garnison. ‖ CH. DE F. Gare *f.; goods* (or) U. S. *freight station*, gare de marchandises. ‖ AUTOM. *Bus station*, terminus d'autobus; *petrol* (or) U. S. *service station*, poste d'essence. ‖ RADIO. Poste *m.* ‖ FIG. Position *f.;* rang *m.; station in life*, condition sociale. ‖ **Station-house**, n. Poste (*m.*) de police. ‖ **Station-master**, n. CH. DE F. Chef (*m.*) de gare. ‖ **Station-rod**, n. TECHN. Tige *f.* ‖ **Station-signal**, n. RADIO. Indicatif du poste *m.* ‖ **Station-wagon**, n. U. S. AUTOM. Station-wagon *m.;* canadienne *f.*
— v. tr. Poster, placer.
— v. intr. MILIT. Tenir garnison (*at*, à). ‖ NAUT. Etre en station (*at*, à).

stationary [-əri] adj. Stationnaire. ‖ TECHN. Fixe. ‖ AUTOM. En stationnement.

stationer [-ə*] n. Papetier *m.; stationer's shop*, papeterie.

stationery [-ri] n. Papeterie *f.;* fournitures (*f. pl.*) de bureau.

statism ['steitizm] n. Etatisme *m.*

statistic [stə'tistik] adj. Statistique.
— n. Statistique *f.* (numerical fact).

statistical [-əl] adj. Statistique.

statistician [,stætis'tiʃən] n. Statisticien *s.*

statistics [stə'tistiks] n. sg. Statistique *f.* (science).

stator ['steitə*] n. ELECTR. Stator *m.*

statoscope ['stætə,skoup] n. TECHN., AVIAT. Statoscope *m.*

statuary ['stætjuəri] adj. Statuaire, de statue.
— n. ARTS. Statuaire *f.* (art, statues); statuaire *m.* (artist).

statue ['stætju:] n. Statue *f.*

statued [-d] adj. Statufié (person); orné de statues (place).

statuesque [,stætju'esk] adj. Sculptural.

statuette [-'et] n. Statuette *f.*

stature ['stætʃə*] n. Stature *f.*

status ['steitəs] n. Statut *m.*, position sociale *f.* (of individual in society); place *f.*, rang, standing *m.* (superior position); *status symbol*, symbole d'appartenance sociale, marque de standing. ‖ Situation *f.*, état *m.* (state of affairs). ‖ JUR. Statut *m.* ‖ **Status quo**, n. Statu quo *m.*

statute ['stætju:t] n. JUR. Ordonnance *f.;* décret *m.* (by a legislative body). ‖ Pl. Statuts, règlements *m. pl.* ‖ **Statute-book**, n. JUR. Code *m.* ‖ **Statute-law**, n. JUR. Droit écrit *m.*

statutory [-ri] adj. Réglementaire; fixé par la loi. ‖ Statutaire.

staunch [stɔ:nʃ] adj. Ferme, solide (courage); sûr, dévoué (friend). ‖ NAUT. Etanche.
— v. tr. MED. Etancher (blood); étancher le sang de (a wound).

staunchness [-nis] n. Fermeté *f.* ‖ Dévouement *m.;* loyauté *f.* ‖ NAUT. Etanchéité *f.*

stave [steiv] n. Bâton *m.* (stick). ‖ Douve *f.* (of a cask); bâton *m.* (of a chair); échelon *m.* (of a ladder). ‖ Stance, strophe *f.* (of a poem). ‖ MUS. Portée, mesure *f.*
— v. tr. Garnir de douves (a cask). ‖ **To stave in**, défoncer (a cask). ‖ **To stave off**, détourner, conjurer.
— v. intr. Se défoncer.

staves [steivz] n. pl. MUS. See ʃTAFF.

stay [stei] v. tr. (158). Arrêter, retarder (progress); *to stay one's hand*, se retenir. ‖ JUR. Différer, surseoir à (a judgment).
— v. intr. Rester, demeurer, séjourner (in a place); *to stay at a hotel*, descendre à l'hôtel. ‖ Arrêter (to halt); attendre (to wait); *stay a little*, attendez un peu. ‖ SPORTS. Tenir le coup, tenir (to continue). ‖ **To stay away**, s'absenter, être absent. ‖ **To stay down**, redoubler (at school). ‖ **To stay in**, rester chez soi, ne pas sortir (person); être en retenue (at school). ‖ **To stay on**, rester encore. ‖ **To stay out**, rester dehors, ne pas rentrer. ‖ **To stay up**, veiller, ne pas se coucher.
— n. Séjour *m.* (in a town); visite *f.* (with friends). ‖ JUR. Sursis *m.; an appeal is not a stay*, l'appel n'est pas suspensif. ‖ † Entrave *f.* ‖ **Stay-at-home**, adj., n. Casanier *s.*

stay n. Support, soutien *m.* ‖ ARCHIT. Etai *m.* ‖ Pl. Corset *m.* ‖ FIG. Soutien, appui *m.* ‖ **Stay-lace**, n. Lacet de corset *m.* ‖ **Stay-maker**, corsetier *s.*

stay n. NAUT. Hauban *m.* (guy); étai *m.* (of mast). ‖ **Stay-rope**, n. Câble de haubanage *m.*
— v. tr. NAUT. Haubaner, étayer (a mast); faire virer (a ship).

stayer [-ə*] n. Personne (*f.*) qui arrête. ‖ SPORTS. Coureur de fond, stayer *m.*

staysail [-sl] n. NAUT. Voile (*f.*) d'étai.

stead [sted] n. † Place *f.;* in s.o.'s stead, au lieu (or) à la place de qqn; *to stand s.o. in good stead*, être très utile à qqn.

steadfast ['stedfɑ:st] adj. Ferme, inébranlable, constant ; stable, solide.
steadfastly [-fɑ:stli] adv. Fermement.
steadfastness [-fɑ:stnis] n. Fermeté, ténacité, constance ; stabilité *f.*
steadily [-ili] adv. Fermement, solidement ; constamment. ‖ Régulièrement ; de façon soutenue (or) unie. ‖ Avec sagesse.
steadiness [-inis] n. Fermeté, sûreté *f.* (of hand, mind). ‖ Régularité *f.* (in action). ‖ Persévérance *f.* ‖ FIN. Tenue, stabilité *f.* (of prices).
steady [-i] adj. Ferme, sûr (hand, mind). ‖ Régulier, soutenu (action, progress) ; persévérant, régulier (worker). ‖ Sérieux, posé (person). ‖ MILIT. Nourri (fire). ‖ SPORTS. Régulier (play). ‖ FIN. *Steady tone,* tendance soutenue.
— n. TECHN. Support *m.* (for a tool).
— v. tr. (2). Affermir, assurer (hand) ; calmer, assagir (s.o.). NAUT. Appuyer (a ship).
— v. intr. S'affermir. ‖ S'assagir.
steak [steik] n. CULIN. Tranche *f.* (of fish or meat) ; bîfteck *m.* (beef).
steal [sti:l] v. tr. (159). Voler, dérober (sth.). ‖ Jeter (*at, sur*) [a glance]. ‖ FAM. *To steal a march on,* gagner de vitesse.
— v. intr. Voler. ‖ FIG. *To steal about* (or) *around,* se glisser, agir à la dérobée ; *to steal in, out,* entrer, sortir furtivement.
— n. U. S. FAM. Occasion (*f.*) bon marché.
stealer [-ə*] n. Voleur *s.*
stealth [stelθ] n. *By stealth,* à la dérobée, en cachette, en tapinois, furtivement.
stealthily [-ili] adv. A la dérobée.
stealthiness [-inis] n. Nature furtive *f.*
stealthy [-i] adj. Furtif (glance) ; *with stealthy treaa,* à pas de loup.
steam [sti:m] n. Buée, vapeur *f.* (from boiling water). ‖ Vapeur, pression *f.* (lit. and fig.); *to let off steam,* ouvrir les soupapes. ‖ FAM. *Under my own steam,* par mes propres moyens. ‖ **Steam-boiler,** n. Chaudière à vapeur *f.* ‖ **Steam-engine,** n. Machine à vapeur *f.* ‖ **Steam-gauge,** n. TECHN. Indicateur (*m.*) de pression. ‖ **Steam-hammer,** n. TECHN. Marteau-pilon (*m.*) à vapeur. ‖ **Steam-heating,** n. Chauffage (*m.*) à la vapeur. ‖ **Steam-roller,** n. Rouleau compresseur *m.* (lit., fig.) ; v. intr. Balayer (the opposition), imposer (a bill). ‖ **Steam table,** n. U. S. CULIN. Table (*f.*) à compartiments chauffés à la vapeur. ‖ **Steam turbine,** n. TECHN. Turbine (*f.*) à vapeur.
— v. tr. Passer à la vapeur, étuver. ‖ CULIN. Cuire à l'étuvée.
— v. intr. Dégager de la vapeur, fumer. ‖ Monter en vapeur. ‖ TECHN. Marcher à la vapeur. ‖ **To steam ahead,** FAM. Faire des progrès rapides, marcher à toute vapeur.
steamboat [-bout] n. NAUT. Bateau (*m.*) à vapeur.
steamer [-ə*] n. NAUT. Steamer ; paquebot *m.* ‖ CULIN. Marmite à étuvée *f.*
steamship [-ʃip] n. NAUT. Vapeur *m.*
steamy [-i] adj. Plein de buée. ‖ Vaporeux.
stearate ['sti:əreit] n. CHIM. Stéarate *m.*
stearic [sti'ærik] adj. CHIM. Stéarique.
stearin(e) ['stiərin] n. Stéarine *f.*
steatite ['stiətait] n. Stéatite *f.*
steed [sti:d] n. ZOOL. Coursier *m.*
steel [sti:l] n. Acier *m.* (metal). ‖ Busc *m.* (in a corset). ‖ MILIT. Fer *m.* (sword) ; *with cold steel,* à l'arme blanche. ‖ **Steel-clad,** adj. Bardé de fer. ‖ **Steel-grey,** adj. Gris acier. ‖ **Steel-hearted,** adj. FIG. Au cœur de fer. ‖ **Steel-wool,** n. Laine (*f.*) d'acier. ‖ **Steel-works,** n. Aciérie *f.*
— v. tr. Aciérer. ‖ FIG. Cuirasser, endurcir ; *to steel one's heart* (or) *oneself against,* se cuirasser contre.
steeliness [-inis] n. Inflexibilité *f.*
steely [-i] adj. D'acier. ‖ FIG. Dur, d'acier.
steelyard [-jɑ:d] n. Romaine *f.* (balance).

steep [sti:p] v. tr. Tremper, faire infuser. ‖ Rouir (hemp). ‖ Mouiller (linen). ‖ FIG. Plonger, baigner (*in,* dans).
— v. intr. Tremper, infuser. ‖ Rouir.
— n. Macération, trempe *f.* (action) ; bain *m.* (result). ‖ Rouissage *m.* (of hemp). ‖ Mouillage *m.* (of linen).
steep adj. Escarpé, raide, à pic, abrupt (slope). ‖ FAM. Exorbitant (price) ; invraisemblable (story).
— n. Escarpement, à-pic *m.*
steepen [-ən] v. tr. Raidir. ‖ FIN. Augmenter, durcir (prices).
— v. intr. S'escarper, devenir plus raide (slope). ‖ FIN. Augmenter.
steeper [-ə*] n. Trempoire *f.*
steeple ['sti:pl] n. ARCHIT. Clocher *m.* (church tower) ; flèche *f.* (spire). ‖ **Steeple-crowned,** adj. En pain de sucre (hat).
steeplechase [-tʃeis] n. SPORTS. Steeple, steeplechase *m.*
steeply [-li] adv. En pente raide, à pic.
steepness [-nis] n. Raideur *f.* (of slope).
steer [stiə*] n. ZOOL. Bouvillon *m.*
steer v. tr. Diriger (*to,* vers) [one's steps]. ‖ NAUT. Gouverner. ‖ AUTOM. Conduire. ‖ FIG. *To steer the ship of State,* tenir le gouvernail de l'Etat.
— v. intr. NAUT. Etre à la barre (sailor) ; gouverner (ship). ‖ **To steer for,** faire route sur, cingler vers.
— n. U. S. FAM. Tuyau *m.* (advice).
steerage [-idʒ] n. NAUT. Entrepont ; avant-carré *m.* ‖ **Steerage-passenger,** n. NAUT. Passager (*m.*) de troisième classe. ‖ **Steerage-way,** n. NAUT. Erre (*f.*) pour gouverner.
steerer [-ə*], **steersman** [-zmən] n. NAUT. Timonier, homme (*m.*) de barre. ‖ U. S. FAM. *Steerer,* tuyauteur.
steering [-iŋ] n. NAUT. Manœuvre de la barre *f.* ‖ AUTOM. Conduite *f.* ‖ **Steering committee,** n. Comité directeur *m.* ‖ **Steering-indicator,** n. Axomètre *m.* ‖ **Steering-wheel,** n. NAUT. Roue (*f.*) du gouvernail ; AUTOM. Volant *m.*
steeve [sti:v] n. NAUT. Inclinaison *f.* (of bowsprit).
— v. tr. NAUT. Incliner.
stein [stain] n. U. S. Chope *f.*
stele ['sti:li] (pl. **stelae** [-i:]) n. Stèle *f.*
stellar ['stelə*] adj. Stellaire.
stellate [-eit] adj. BOT. Etoilé, radié.
stem [stem] v. tr. (1). Arrêter, contenir, endiguer, refouler (lit. and fig.).
stem n. BOT. Tige *m.* (of flower) ; queue *f.* (of fruit) ; pétiole *f.* (of leaf) ; tronc *m.* (of tree). ‖ Pied *m.* (of glass) ; tuyau *m.* (of pipe) ; remontoir *m.* (of watch). ‖ BLAS. Branche, souche *f.* ‖ GRAMM. Radical, thème *m.* ‖ NAUT. Etrave *f.* ‖ SPORTS. Chasse-neige *m.* (in skiing). ‖ FIG. *From stem to stern,* de bout en bout, de fond en comble. ‖ **Stem-turn,** n. SPORTS. Virage (*m.*) en chasse-neige.
— v. tr. Egrapper ; écôter.
— v. intr. U. S. Dériver, naître (*from,* de).
stembogen ['stem'bougən] n. Stembogen *m.*
stemless [-lis] adj. Sans tiges.
stemlet [-lit] n. Petite tige *f.*
stemma ['stemə] (pl. **stemmata** [ste'mɑ:tə]) n. BLAS. Arbre généalogique *m.* ‖ ZOOL. Ocelle *m.*
stench [stenʃ] n. Puanteur *f.* ‖ **Stench-trap,** n. Siphon *m.*
stencil ['stensl] n. Pochoir *m.* (sheet) ; travail au pochoir *m.* (work). ‖ Stencil *m.* (in typewriting).
— v. tr. (1). Faire au pochoir. ‖ Tirer au stencil.
Sten-gun ['sten'gʌn] n. MILIT. Fusil automatique *m.*
stenograph ['stenəgrɑ:f] n. Sténographie *f.* (symbol, text). ‖ Sténotype *f.* (machine).
stenographer [ste'nəgrəfə*], **stenographist** [-ist] n. Sténographe ; sténo (fam.) *s.*
stenographic [steno'græfik] adj. Sténographique.

stenographically [-əli] adv. Sténographiquement.
stenography [ste'nɔgrəfi] n. Sténographie *f.*
stenotype ['stenotaip] n. Sténotype *f.*
stenotypist [,steno'taipist] n. Sténotypiste *s.*
stenotypy ['stenotaipi] n. Sténotypie *f.*
Stentor ['stentə*] n. Stentor *m.*
stentorian [sten'tɔ:riən] adj. De stentor.
step [step] n. Pas *m.* (in walking); *step by step*, pas à pas; *with measured steps*, à pas comptés. ‖ Pas *m.* (stride); *to make a long step towards*, faire un grand pas vers. ‖ Pas *m.; empreinte (f.)* de pas (footprint); *to follow in s.o.'s steps*, marcher sur les pas de qqn; *to retrace one's steps*, revenir sur ses pas. ‖ Pas *m.; démarche f.* (fait). ‖ Pas *m.; allure, cadence f.; to be, to keep in step*, être, marcher au pas. ‖ Marche *f.* (of stairs). ‖ Seuil *m.* (of doorway). ‖ Echelon *m.* (of ladder); marche-pied *m.* (of a vehicle). ‖ Pl. Escalier *m.; flight of steps*, perron, escalier; *pair of steps*, escabeau. ‖ MILIT. *Quick step*, pas accéléré. ‖ NAUT. Emplanture *f.* ‖ TECHN. Gradin *m.* ‖ MUS. Pas *m.* ‖ FIG. Démarche *f.; false step*, pas de clerc. ‖ FIG. Mesure *f.; to take steps*, prendre des dispositions, aviser. ‖ FIG. Etape *f.; the first step in one's career*, les débuts dans sa carrière. ‖ **Step-cone**, n. TECHN. Cône-poulie *m.* ‖ **Step-dance**, n. Danse *(f.)* de caractère. ‖ **Step-joint**, n. ARCHIT. Joint à recouvrement *m.* ‖ **Step-ladder**, n. Escabeau *m.* ‖ **Step-like**, adj. En gradins.
— v. intr. (1). Faire des pas; *to step short*, faire des petits pas. ‖ Faire un pas; *to step forward*, faire un pas en avant; *to step into*, monter dans. ‖ Marcher; *to step on s.o.'s toes*, marcher sur les pieds de qqn. ‖ **To step aside**, s'écarter, se ranger; FIG. Faire une digression. ‖ **To step back**, reculer. ‖ **To step down**, descendre. ‖ **To step in**, entrer; FIG. S'interposer. ‖ **To step on it**, U. S. FAM. Se grouiller, mettre les gaz. ‖ **To step out**, sortir; FAM. Allonger le pas; *to step out of line*, s'écarter de la ligne d'action. ‖ **To step up**, monter; s'approcher *(to*, de).
— v. tr. MUS. Danser. ‖ NAUT. Arborer (a mast). ‖ **To step off**, mesurer. ‖ **To step up**, FAM. Augmenter, intensifier.
stepbrother [-,brʌðə*] n. Demi-frère *m.*
stepchild [-,tʃaild] n. Beau-fils *m.; belle-fille f.;* enfant *(m.)* d'un premier lit.
stepdaughter [-,dɔ:tə*] n. Belle-fille *f.*
stepfather [-,fɑ:ðə*] n. Beau-père; parâtre *m.* †.
stepmother ['step,mʌðə*] n. Belle-mère; marâtre *f.*
stepmotherly [-li] adj. De marâtre.
steppe [step] n. Steppe *f.*
stepped [stept] adj. A marches. ‖ A gradins (or) étages; en échelons.
stepper [-ə*] n. Steppeur *m.* (horse).
stepping [-iŋ] n. Marche *f.; pas m.* ‖ **Stepping-stone**, n. FIG. Marchepied, tremplin *m.*
stepsister ['step,sistə*] n. Demi-sœur *f.*
stepson [-,sʌn] n. Beau-fils *m.*
stereo ['steriou] adj. FAM., MUS. Stéréo *adj. invar.*
— n. FAM., MUS. Stéréo *f.* (stereophony); chaîne stéréo *f.* (stereo set).
stereochemistry [stiəriə'kemistri] n. Stéréochimie *f.*
stereogram ['steriə,græm] n. RADIO. Compact *(m.)* stéréo. ‖ TECHN. Stéréogramme *m.*
stereograph [-,grɑ:f] n. TECHN. Stéréographe *m.*
stereometer [-'mitə*] n. Stéréomètre *m.*
stereophonic [,steriə'fɔnik] adj. RADIO. Stéréophonique.
stereophony [,steri'ɔfəni] n. RADIO. Stéréophonie *f.*
stereoscope ['stiəriəskoup] n. Stéréoscope *m.*
stereoscopic [,stiəriə'skɔpik] adj. Stéréoscopique.

stereotype ['stiəriətaip] n. Clichage *m.* (act); cliché *m.* (result).
— v. tr. Clicher, stéréotyper. ‖ FIG. Stéréotyper.
stereotypy [-i] n. Stéréotypie *f.*
sterile ['sterail] adj. AGRIC., ZOOL., MED., FIG. Stérile.
sterility [ste'riliti] n. Stérilité *f.*
sterilization [,sterilai'zeiʃən] n. Stérilisation *f.*
sterilize ['sterilaiz] v. tr. AGRIC., ZOOL. Stériliser.
sterilizer [-ə*] n. Stérilisateur *m.*
sterling ['stə:liŋ] n. FIN. Sterling *m. invar.; pound sterling*, livre sterling; *sterling area, balance*, zone, balance sterling.
— adj. FIN., massif (silver). ‖ FIG. De bon aloi, solide.
stern [stə:n] n. NAUT. Arrière *m.* ‖ ZOOL. Arrière-train (of an animal). ‖ FAM. Derrière *m.* ‖ **Stern-post**, n. NAUT. Etambot *m.* ‖ **Stern-way**, n. NAUT. Culée *f.*
stern adj. Sombre (air); sévère, austère (character, person); sévère, rigoureux (punishment); triste (reality).
sternly [-li] adv. Avec austérité; sévèrement; rigoureusement.
sternmost [-moust] adj. NAUT. Le plus en arrière.
sternness [-nis] n. Austérité; sévérité, rigueur *f.*
sternum ['stə:nəm] (pl. **sterna** [-ə]) n. MED. Sternum *m.*
sternutation [,stə:nju'teiʃən] n. Eternuement *m.*
sternutatory [stə:'nju:tətəri] adj. n. Sternutatoire *m.*
steroid ['steroid] n. MED. Stéroïde *m.*
steroidal [ste'rɔidəl] adj. MED. Stéroïde.
sterol ['sterɔl] n. MED. Stérol *m.*
stertorous ['stə:tərəs] adj. MED. Stertoreux, ronflant.
stet [stet] v. intr. Rétablir (on proof or manuscript).
stethoscope ['steθəskoup] n. MED. Stéthoscope *m.*
stetson ['stetsn] n. Stetson, chapeau texan *m.*
stevedore ['sti:vdɔ*] n. Débardeur, arrimeur *m.* (labourer); entrepreneur de chargement et déchargement *m.*
— v. tr. NAUT. Arrimer (the cargo); arrimer la cargaison de (a ship).
stew [stju:] v. tr. CULIN. Faire une compote de (fruit); faire un ragoût de (meat); *stewed fruit*, fruits cuits, compote de fruits.
— v. intr. CULIN. Mijoter. ‖ FAM. Cuire, étouffer; *to stew in one's own juice*, mariner dans son jus.
— n. CULIN. Compote *f.* (of fruit); civet *m.* (of hare); ragoût *m.* (of mutton). ‖ FAM. Bouleversement *m.; to be in a stew*, être dans tous ses états. ‖ FAM. Etuve *f.* ‖ **Stew-pan** (or) **pot**, n. CULIN. Cocotte *f.*
stew n. Vivier *m.* (for fish); parc *m.* (for oysters).
steward [stju:əd] n. Régisseur, intendant *m.* ‖ Délégué *m.; shop-steward*, représentant syndical. ‖ SPORTS. Commissaire *m.* ‖ NAUT., AVIAT. Steward *m.*
stewardess [-is] NAUT. Stewardesse *f.* ‖ AVIAT. Hôtesse *(f.)* de l'air.
stewardship [-ʃip] n. Intendance, régie *f.* ‖ Gestion *f.*
sthenic ['sθenik] adj. MED. Sthénique.
stibium ['stibiəm] n. Antimoine *m.*
stick [stik] v. tr. (160). Enfoncer (a knife); piquer (a pin); *to stick a flower in one's hair*, piquer une fleur dans ses cheveux. ‖ Saigner, égorger (a pig); poignarder (s.o.). ‖ Planter, ficher (on a spike). ‖ Piquer, garnir, hérisser *(with*, de). ‖ Coller (a stamp); *to stick a postage stamp on a letter*, timbrer une lettre. ‖ Mettre; fourrer (fam.); *stick it in the corner*, mettez ça dans le coin. ‖ FAM. Souffrir, sentir (s.o.); supporter (sth.); *to stick it*, tenir le coup; *to stick it on*, exagérer, saler la note: *to*

stick it out, tenir jusqu'au bout. || **To stick down,** inscrire, mettre (*on,* sur); FAM. Fourrer, flanquer. || **To stick out,** bomber (one's chest); passer (one's head); tirer (one's tongue). || **To stick up,** afficher (a bill); dresser (one's ears); POP. Attaquer à main armée; *stick' em up!,* haut les mains!
— v. intr. Se ficher, s'enfoncer (knife); s'enfoncer (pin). || Se coller, coller (stamp). || S'embourber (in the mud). || Rester, se fixer (in a place). || Rester, subsister (*in,* dans). || TECHN. Se coincer, se bloquer, se caler. || CULIN. Attacher (*to,* à). || FAM. S'accrocher; *he sticks like a leech,* il se cramponne; il ne décolle pas; *he sticks there for hours,* il ne démarre pas; *stick to it!,* ne lâchez pas!; *to stick to one's guns,* ne pas en démordre. || **To stick at,** reculer devant, achopper contre (a difficulty); s'acharner sur (a task); *to stick at nothing,* être capable de tout. || **To stick by** (or) **to,** s'attacher à, rester fidèle à (a friend). || **To stick on,** adhérer (stamp); FAM. Se cramponner (person); *to stick on a horse,* tenir à cheval. || **To stick out,** dépasser, sortir, faire saillie; FAM. S'obstiner, s'entêter (*for,* à). || **To stick up,** se dresser; FAM. *To stick up for,* prendre fait et cause pour; *to stick up to,* tenir tête à.
— n. Petit rameau *m.;* branchette *f.* (twig). || Brindille *f.;* bois sec *m.* (for fuel). || Bâton *m.;* baguette *f.* || Verge *f.* (rod); *to get the stick,* recevoir le fouet. || Canne *f.* (walking stick). || Bâton *m.* (of chewing gum); barre *f.* (of chocolate). || MUS., MILIT. Baguette *f.* || AVIAT. Manche à balai *m.* || NAUT. Vergue *f.* || SPORTS. Crosse *f.* (in hockey). || TECHN. Composteur *m.* || AGRIC. Rame *f.* || CULIN. Branche *f.* (of celery); tige *f.* (of rhubarb). || FAM. *Rum* (or) *odd stick,* drôle de particulier. || **Stick-in-the-mud,** adj. FAM. Empoté, mal dégourdi; vieux jeu; n. FAM. Empoté; vieux numéro *m.* || **Stick-up,** adj. Droit (collar); n. FAM. Hold-up *m.*
sticker [-ə*] n. Colleur *m.* (of bills). || Couteau; surin *m.* (pop.) [knife]. || U. S. Etiquette *f.* (label). || FAM. Crampon, pot de colle (person); colle *f.* (question).
stickiness [-inis] n. Adhésivité, viscosité *f.*
sticking [-iɲ] adj. Collant. || **Sticking-plaster,** n. Taffetas gommé, sparadrap *m.*
— n. Adhérence *f.;* collage *m.* (*to,* à). || TECHN. Coincement, grippage *m.*
stickleback ['stiklbæk] n. ZOOL. Epinoche *f.*
stickler ['stiklə*] n. FAM. Adhérent (or) partisan farouche *s.; to be a stickler for,* être à cheval sur (etiquette).
stickpin [-pin] n. U. S. Epingle de cravate *f.* (See BREAST-PIN.)
sticky [stiki] adj. Collant, gluant. || Adhésif, adhérent. || MILIT. Adhérent (bomb). || FAM. Pointilleux, tatillon.
stiff [stif] adj. Dur (brush); raide, rigide (cardboard); empesé (shirt-front). || CULIN. Dur, ferme (paste). || Raide (slope, stairs). || AGRIC. Glaiseux (soil). || TECHN. Grippé. || MED. Ankylosé (joint); raide (limb, walk); courbatu (person). || FIG. Dur (examination); raide, gourmé, compassé (manner, person); opiniâtre (resistance); raide (style). || FAM. Raide (drink), salé (price); *a stiff yarn,* une raide. || **Stiff-fronted,** adj. Empesé (shirt). || **Stiff-necked,** adj. Intraitable, irréductible; opiniâtre; U. S. FAM. Collet monté.
— n. MED., FAM. Macchabée *m.* || FIN., FAM. Billet *m.* || FAM. *Big stiff,* gros bêta.
stiffen [-ɲ] v. tr. Raidir. || Baleiner (a bodice); empeser (a shirt-front). || MILIT. Renforcer. || CULIN. Corser (a drink); durcir, raffermir (a paste); lier (a sauce). || FIG. Raidir, durcir (s.o.); rendre plus dur (sth.).
— v. intr. Se raidir. || Durcir.
stiffener [-nə*] n. Contrefort *m.* (of boots). || Renfort *m.* || FAM. Gnole *f.*

stiffening [-niɲ] n. Empois *m.* || Renfort *m.* || Raidissement *m.*
stiffly [-li] adv. Avec raideur.
stiffness [-nis] n. Raideur *f.* (lit. and fig.). || Dureté, fermeté *f.*
stifle ['staifl] v. tr., intr. Etouffer (lit. and fig.); *to stifle one's grief,* faire taire sa douleur.
stifling [-iɲ] adj. Etouffant, caniculaire (heat).
stigma ['stigmə] n. † Marque (*f.*) au fer rouge. || BOT., MED. Stigmate *m.* || MED. Stigmate *m.;* nævus *m.* || FIG. Stigmate *m.;* flétrissure *f.*
stigmata [stig'mɑ:tə] n. pl. ECCLES. Stigmates *m. pl.*
stigmatic [stig'mætik] adj. Stigmatique.
— n. ECCLES. Stigmatisé *s.*
stigmatist ['stigmətist] n. ECCLES. Stigmatisé *s.*
stigmatization [,stigmətai'zeiʃən] n. Stigmatisation *f.*
stigmatize ['stigmətaiz] v. tr. Stigmatiser.
stile [stail] n. Montant *m.* (of a door).
stile n. Echalier *m.* (steps). || Tourniquet *m.* (turnstile).
stiletto [sti'letou] n. Stylet *m.* (dagger). || Poinçon *m.* (instrument); *stiletto heel,* talon aiguille.
still [stil] adj. Calme, immobile, tranquille (quiet). || Silencieux, sans bruit (silent). || Dormant, stagnant (water). || Naturel, non champagnisé (wine). || ARTS. *Still life,* nature morte. || **Still-born,** adj. MED., FIG. Mort-né.
— n. Calme, silence *m.* || CINEM. Photographie *f.*
— v. tr. Calmer, apaiser, tranquilliser. || Faire taire.
— v. intr. Se calmer, s'apaiser. || Se taire.
— adv. Encore, toujours (continually). || Pourtant, cependant, toutefois, néanmoins (nevertheless). || Encore (with a comparative); *still more,* encore plus; *still colder,* encore plus froid.
still n. CHIM. Alambic *m.* || **Still-room,** n. CHIM. Salle (*f.*) des alambics; ARCHIT. Office *m.*
— v. tr. CHIM., FIG. Distiller.
stillage [-idʒ] n. CHIM. Châssis *m.*
stilling [-iɲ] n. Chantier *m.* (for cask).
stilling n. CHIM. Distillation *f.*
stillness [-nis] n. Calme, silence, repos *m.;* paix, tranquillité *f.*
stilly [-i] adj. Calme, silencieux.
— adv. Paisiblement, avec calme.
stilt [stilt] n. Echasse *f.* || **Stilt-walker,** n. ZOOL. Echassier *m.*
stilted [-id] adj. ARCHIT. Surhaussé. || FIG. Guindé, compassé, gourmé.
stiltedness [-idnis] n. Raideur *f.* (of s.o.); emphase *f.* (of style).
stimulant ['stimjulənt] adj., n. MED. Stimulant *m.* || FAM. Alcool *m.*
stimulate [-eit] v. tr. Stimuler (lit. and fig.).
stimulation [,stimju'leiʃən] n. Stimulation *f.*
stimulative ['stimjulətiv] adj. Stimulateur.
stimulus ['stimjuləs] (pl. **stimuli** [-ai]) n. Stimulant *m.* || BOT. Stimule *m.* || MED. Stimulus *m.* || FIG. Coup de fouet *m.*
stimy ['staimi] n., v. tr. (2). See STYMIE.
sting [stiɲ] v. tr. (161). Piquer. || FIG. Blesser, piquer au vif. || POP. Arnaquer, entuber.
— v. intr. Piquer. || MED. Cuire, picoter.
— n. ZOOL. Aiguillon, dard *m.* (of a bee); crochet *m.* (of a snake); Poil urticant *m.* || MED. Cuisson, douleur cuisante *f.* || FIG. Mordant *m.* (of an attack, a remark); aiguillon *m.* (of conscience); morsure *f.* (of hunger); âpre blessure *f.* (of an insult); *to give a sting to,* acérer. || **Sting-fish,** n. ZOOL. Vive *f.* || **Sting(ing)-nettle,** n. BOT. Ortie dioïque, grande ortie *f.*
stinger [-ə*] n. FAM. Coup cinglant *m.*
stingily [,stindʒili] adv. Chichement.
stinginess [-nis] n. Avarice, pingrerie, ladrerie *f.*
stingless ['stiɲlis] adj. Sans aiguillon.
stingo ['stiɲgou] n. Bière forte *f.* || FAM. Brio *m.*

stingy ['stindʒi] adj. Avare, ladre, pingre, chiche.
stink [stiŋk] v. intr. (162). Puer, empester, sentir mauvais ; *to stink of,* puer, empester.
— v. tr. **To stink out,** chasser par la puanteur.
‖ U. S. **To stink up,** faire sentir mauvais.
— n. Puanteur, odeur infecte *f.* ‖ Pl. FAM. Chimie *f.* ‖ FAM. *To raise a stink,* faire du chambard (or) une histoire. ‖ **Stink-bomb,** n. MILIT. Bombe puante *f.* ‖ **Stink-pot,** n. Pot à feu *m. ;* POP. Type puant *m.* ‖ **Stink-trap,** n. Siphon *m.*
stinker [-ə*] n. Type puant ; chameau *m. ;* peste *f.* (person) ; chose puante, infection *f.* (thing). ‖ Pot à feu *m.* ‖ FAM. Sale type *m.* (person) ; sale corvée *f.* (work).
stinking [-iŋ] adj. Puant, empesté. ‖ FIG. Puant.
— adv. FAM. *Stinking rich,* vachement riche, plein aux as.
stint [stint] v. tr. Mesurer, lésiner sur (sth.). ‖ Rationner, restreindre (s.o.) ; *to stint s.o. of sth.,* mesurer (or) refuser qqch. à qqn ; *to stint oneself,* se mettre à la portion congrue.
— n. Restriction *f.* ‖ Besogne assignée, tâche journalière (or) convenue *f.* (work).
stintless [-lis] adj. Prodigué, donné sans restriction (or) largement.
stipe [staip] n. BOT. Stipe *m.*
stipend ['staipend] n. ECCLES., JUR. Traitement *m.*
stipendiary [stai'pendjəri] adj. Rémunéré, appointé.
— n. Salarié *s.* ‖ JUR. Magistrat appointé *m.*
stipple ['stipl] v. tr. Pointiller.
— n. Pointillé *m.*
stipulate ['stipuleit] adj. BOT. Stipulé.
stipulate v. tr. Stipuler.
— v. intr. Convenir expressément (*for,* de) ; stipuler (*that,* que).
stipulated [-id] adj. Stipulé. ‖ Conventionnel (place) ; prescrit (time).
stipulation [,stipju'leiʃən] n. Stipulation *f.*
stipule ['stipju:l] n. BOT. Stipule *f.*
stir [stə*] v. tr. (1). Remuer, mouvoir (a limb) ; *not to stir a finger,* ne pas remuer un pouce. ‖ Attiser (the fire). ‖ FIG. Exciter, soulever (s.o.'s anger) ; émouvoir, troubler, remuer (s.o.). ‖ **To stir up,** remuer, agiter ; FIG. Exciter (courage, curiosity) ; fomenter (discord, revolution) ; attiser (hatred) ; aiguillonner, exciter, secouer (s.o.).
— v. intr. Remuer, bouger.
— n. Mouvement *m.* ‖ Action (*f.*) de remuer. ‖ Agitation *f. ;* remue-ménage *m.* ‖ FIG. Emoi *m. ;* sensation *f.*
stir n. POP. Cabane, taule (or) tôle *f.*
stirabout [-ə,baut] n. CULIN. Bouillie *f.* (of oatmeal). ‖ FAM. Remue-ménage, *m.*
stirless [-lis] adj. Immobile.
stirps [stə:ps] (pl. **stirpes** [-i:z]) n. JUR. Souche *f.* ‖ ZOOL. Famille *f.*
stirrer ['stə:rə*] n. Personne remuante *f.* ‖ CHIM. Agitateur *m.* ‖ CULIN. Batteur, mixer *m. ;* mouvette *f.* ‖ FIG. Fomentateur, fauteur *m.*
stirring [-iŋ] adj. Actif, remuant, turbulent (child). ‖ FIG. Sensationnel (event) ; actif, agité, mouvementé (life) ; émouvant, remuant (speech).
stirrup ['stirəp] n. SPORTS, TECHN. Etrier *m.* ‖ **Stirrup-bone,** n. MED. Etrier *m.* ‖ **Stirrup-cup,** n. FAM. Coup de l'étrier *m.* ‖ **Stirrup-leather,** n. Etrivière *f.* ‖ **Stirrup-pump,** n. Pompe à main portative *f.*
stitch [stitʃ] n. Point *m.* (in needlework, tapestry) ; maille *f.* (in knitting). ‖ MED. Point de suture ; *stitch in the side,* point de côté. ‖ FAM. *To be in stitches,* se tenir les côtes (to laugh). ‖ **Stitch-wheel,** n. Roulette *f.*
— v. tr. Coudre, piquer. ‖ Brocher (a book). ‖ MED. Suturer. ‖ **To stitch up,** recoudre.
— v. intr. Coudre.

stitchwort [-wə:t] n. BOT. Stellaire *f.*
stiver ['staivə*] n. FAM. Sou *m.*
stoat [stout] n. ZOOL. Hermine *f.*
stochastic [stɔ'kæstik] adj. Stochastique.
stock [stɔk] n. † BOT. Souche *f. ;* tronc *m.* ‖ TECHN. Base *f.* (of an anvil) ; bois *m.* (of a plane) ; manche *m.* (of a tool, whip). AGRIC. Mancheron *m.* (of plough) ; ente *f.* (in grafting) ; *live-stock,* cheptel. ‖ BOT. Giroflée *f.* ‖ CULIN. Consommé, concentré pour bouillon. ‖ THEATR. *Stock of plays,* répertoire. ‖ CH. DE F. Matériel *m.* ‖ MILIT. Fût *m.* (of rifle). ‖ NAUT. Pl. Chantier *m. ;* cale (*f.*) de construction. ‖ FIN. Réserve *f.* (of money) ; valeurs, actions *f. pl. ;* titres, fonds *m.* pl. (bonds) ; *to take in stocks,* prendre des titres en report. ‖ COMM. Col dur, col-cravate *m.* (collar) ; matière première *f.* (raw material) ; stock, fonds, approvisionnement *m.* réserve *f.* (supply) ; *to have in stock,* avoir en magasin (or) à la réserve ; *to take stock,* faire l'inventaire. ‖ ECCLES. Plastron noir *m.* (of clergyman). ‖ Pl. † Pilori *m. ;* ceps *m. pl.* (punishment). ‖ FIG. Souche *f.* (of a family) ; fonds *m.* (of knowledge). ‖ FAM. *Your stock is going up,* vos actions montent. ‖ **Stock-book,** n. FIN. Magasinier *m.* ‖ **Stock-breeding,** n. AGRIC. Elevage *m.* ‖ **Stock-broker,** n. FIN. Agent de change *m.* ‖ **Stock-car,** n. AUTOM., SPORTS. Stock-car *m. ;* U. S. CH. DE F. Wagon (*m.*) à bestiaux. ‖ **Stock-Exchange,** n. FIN. Bourse (*f.*) des valeurs. ‖ **Stock-farm,** n. AGRIC. Ferme (*f.*) d'élevage. ‖ **Stock-fish,** n. Stockfisch *m.* ‖ **Stock-holder,** n. FIN. Actionnaire *m.* ‖ **Stock-in-trade,** n. COMM. Stock en magasin *m. ;* TECHN. Outillage *m. ;* FAM. Bagage, répertoire *m.* ‖ **Stock-jobber,** n. FIN. Courtier (*m.*) en valeurs. ‖ **Stock-list,** n. FIN. Cours (*m. pl.*) de la Bourse, cote *f.* ‖ **Stock-market,** n. FIN. Marché *m.* ‖ **Stock-pile,** n. Stock *m.,* réserve *f. ;* v. tr. stocker. ‖ **Stock-piling,** n. Stockage *m.* ‖ **Stock-pot,** n. CULIN. Faitout, pot-au-feu *m.* ‖ **Stock-room,** n. Réserve, arrière-boutique *f.* ‖ **Stock-still,** adj. Immobile comme une borne. ‖ **Stock-taking,** n. COMM. Inventaire *m.* ‖ **Stock-yard,** n. AGRIC. Parc (*m.*) à bestiaux.
— adj. COMM. Courant, de série. ‖ THEATR. Du répertoire. ‖ FAM. Courant, consacré, classique, habituel.
— v. tr. COMM. Emmagasiner, recevoir en stock, stocker (goods) ; approvisionner, monter, fournir (*with,* de) [shop]. ‖ AGRIC. Engranger (a crop). ‖ NAUT. Enjaler (an anchor). ‖ FIG. Meubler (one's memory).
— v. intr. AGRIC. Bourgeonner.
stockade [stɔ'keid] n. Palissade, palanque *f.*
stockholder ['stɔkhouldə*] n. FIN. Actionnaire *s.*
stockinet(te) [stɔki'net] n. Sorte (*f.*) de jersey.
stocking ['stɔkiŋ] n. Bas *m.* ‖ ZOOL. Balzane *f.* ‖ **Stocking-foot,** n. Pied de bas *m. ; in stocking-feet,* marchant sur ses bas, sans souliers, déchaussé. ‖ **Stocking-stitch,** n. Point de jersey *m.* ‖ **Stocking-trade,** n. COMM. Bonneterie *f.*
stockist [-ist] n. COMM. Stockiste *m.*
stocky [-i] adj. FAM. Costaud, trapu.
stodge ['stɔdʒ] v. tr. FAM. *To stodge oneself,* s'empiffrer ; se bourrer (*with,* de).
— n. FAM. Etouffe-chrétien *m.* (food). ‖ FAM. Barbe *f.* (dull matter) ; raseur *s.* (dull person).
stodgy [-i] n. CULIN. Pâteux (bread) ; bourratif, lourd (food). ‖ FIG. Indigeste (book).
stoic [stouik] adj., n. PHILOS. Stoïcien *adj., s.* ‖ FIG. Stoïque *adj., s.*
stoical [-əl] adj. FIG. Stoïque.
stoically [-əli] adv. Stoïquement.
stoichiometry, stoicheiometry [,stɔiki'ɔmi-tri] n. CHIM. Stœchiométrie *f.*
stoicism ['stouisizm] n. Stoïcisme *m.*
stoke [stouk] v. tr. Chauffer (a boiler) ; garnir (fire).
— v. intr. **To stoke up,** chauffer ; FAM. S'empiffrer, bouffer.

stokehold [-hould] n. NAUT. Chaufferie *f.*
stoker [-ə*] n. NAUT., CH. DE F. Chauffeur *m.*
‖ TECHN. Chargeur automatique *m.*
stole [stoul] n. † Stole *f.* ‖ ECCLES. Etole *f.* ‖
COMM. Echarpe, étole *f.*
stole n. † Chaise percée *f.*
stole pret. See STEAL.
stolid ['stɔlid] adj. Flegmatique, impassible. ‖
Lourd, passif.
stolidly [-li] adv. Flegmatiquement.
stolidness [-nis] n. Flegme *m.*
stomach ['stɔmək] n. MED., ZOOL. Estomac *m.;*
on an empty stomach, à jeun, l'estomac vide; le
ventre creux (fam.); *to turn the stomach*, soulever
le cœur. ‖ FAM. Ventre *m.* (belly). ‖ FAM. Envie *f.;*
goût *m.* (*for*, de); cran, estomac *m.* (*for*, pour);
to put some stomach into, donner du cœur au
ventre à. ‖ **Stomach-ache**, n. MED. Mal d'estomac
(or) de ventre *m.* ‖ **Stomach-pump**, n. MED. Pompe
stomacale *f.* ‖ **Stomach-tube**, n. MED. Sonde stomacale *f.*
— v. tr. FAM. Digérer (sth.).
stomachal [-l] adj. MED. Stomacal.
stomachful [-ful] n. FAM. Ventrée *f.*
stomachic [sto'mækik] adj., n. MED. Stomachique *m.*
stomatitis [ˌstoumə'taitis] n. MED. Stomatite *f.*
stomatology [-'tɔlədʒi] n. MED. Stomatologie *f.*
stomp [stɔmp] v. intr. Marcher bruyamment (or)
en tapant les pieds.
stone [stoun] n. Pierre *f.; stone wall*, mur de
pierre. ‖ Pierre précieuse, pierrerie, gemme *f.;*
semi-precious stone, pierre fine. ‖ Grêlon *m.* (hail-
stone). ‖ MATH. Stone *m.* ‖ BOT. Noyau *m.* (of
peach). ‖ MED. Pierre *f.* (calculus, disease). ‖ FAM.
To cast a stone at, jeter la pierre à; *to have a
heart of stone*, avoir une pierre à la place du cœur;
to leave no stone unturned, ne rien négliger pour
aboutir; remuer ciel et terre. ‖ **Stone-blind**, adj.
Complètement aveugle. ‖ **Stone-break**, n. BOT.
Saxifrage *m.* ‖ **Stone-breaker**, n. TECHN. Concasseur *m.* (machine); casseur (*m.*) de pierres (person).
‖ **Stone-broke**, adj. U. S. FAM. Fauché, sans un,
dans la dèche. ‖ **Stone-coal**, n. Anthracite *m.* ‖
Stone-cold, adj. Complètement froid; *stone-cold
sober*, pas du tout bourré. ‖ **Stone-coloured**, adj.
Gris pierre. ‖ **Stone-cutter**, n. Tailleur (*m.*) de
pierre. ‖ **Stone-dead**, adj. Raide mort. ‖ **Stone-deaf**,
adj. Sourd comme un pot. ‖ **Stone-fruit**, n. BOT.
Drupe *f.; fruit* (*m.*) à noyau. ‖ **Stone-mason**, n.
Tailleur (*m.*) de pierre. ‖ **Stone-pit**, n. Carrière de
pierre *f.* ‖ **Stone-work**, n. ARCHIT. Maçonnerie *f.*
— N. B. *Stone* (poids) est invariable.
— adj. En pierre.
— v. tr. Lapider (s.o.). ‖ Enoyauter (fruit). ‖ TECHN.
Empierrer, paver.
stoned [-d] adj. POP. Bourré, rond (on alcohol);
défoncé (on drugs).
stonewall [-wɔ:l] v. intr. SPORTS. Jouer serré. ‖
FAM. Faire de l'obstruction.
— adj. Impassible.
stoneware [-wɛə*] n. Grès *m.;* poterie (*f.*) de
grès.
stoniness [-inis] n. Nature pierreuse *f.* ‖ FIG.
Dureté *f.*
stony [-i] adj. Pierreux (road). ‖ FIG. Dur, de
pierre (heart); glacial (look, politeness). ‖ **Stony-
broke**, adj. FAM. Dans la dèche, décavé.
stood [stud] pret., p.p. See STAND.
stooge [stu:dʒ] n. FAM., THEATR. Comparse *m.* ‖
U. S. FAM. Nègre, prête-nom *m.*
— v. intr. FAM. Faire le nègre.
stook [stuk] n. AGRIC. Moyette *f.*
— v. tr. AGRIC. Mettre en moyettes.
stool [stu:l] n. Tabouret *m.* (seat). ‖ † Garde-robe
f. (water-closet). ‖ MED. Pl. Selles *f. pl.* (fæces);

to go to stool, aller à la selle. ‖ BOT. Plante mère
f. ‖ SPORTS. Appeau *m.* ‖ ARCHIT. Rebord *m.* (of
a window). ‖ **Stool-ball**, n. SPORTS. Balle (*f.*) au
camp. ‖ **Stool-pigeon**, n. SPORTS. Appeau *m.;*
U. S. FAM. Mouchard, indicateur (informer).
— v. intr. AGRIC. Rejetonner; tabler. ‖ MED. Aller
à la selle.
stoop [stu:p] n. U. S. Perron *m.* ‖ Véranda *f.*
stoop v. intr. Se courber, se baisser. ‖ Etre voûté,
avoir le dos rond. ‖ FIG. Faire des bassesses;
s'abaisser, se ravaler, descendre (*to*, à).
— v. tr. Courber (one's back); baisser, pencher,
courber (one's head).
— n. Dos rond *m.;* attitude voûtée *f.* ‖ **Stoop-
shouldered**, adj. Voûté.
stop [stɔp] v. tr. (1). Boucher (a hole); aveugler
(a leak); obstruer, obturer (a pipe); combler (a
gap); barrer (the way). ‖ Arrêter, stopper (a movement, s.o., watch). ‖ Cesser (visits, work); *stop it!,*
assez!, finissez!, cela suffit!; *without stopping*, sans
dételer. ‖ Couper (electricity, gas, water). ‖ Supprimer (s.o.'s holidays); *to stop s.o.'s allowance*,
couper les vivres à qqn. ‖ Empêcher (*from*, de)
[s.o.]; *to stop sth. being done*, empêcher que qqch.
se fasse. ‖ FIN. Suspendre (payment); opérer une
retenue sur (wages). ‖ MED. Plomber (a tooth);
étancher (a wound). ‖ GRAMM. Ponctuer. ‖ **To stop
down**, diaphragmer (a lens). ‖ **To stop up**, boucher.
— v. intr. Arrêter, s'arrêter, stopper (car, person,
train). ‖ Cesser (noise, rain, work). [See CEASE.]
‖ S'arrêter (watch). ‖ FAM. Rester. ‖ **To stop away**,
ne pas venir. ‖ **To stop behind**, rester en arrière. ‖
To stop off, U. S. S'arrêter, descendre (*at*, à).
‖ **To stop up**, U. S. Passer; *to stop up to see*,
rendre visite à.
— n. Arrêt *m.* (act, halt); *request stop*, arrêt facultatif; *to make a stop*, s'arrêter; faire une pause.
‖ TECHN. Arrêtoir, butoir *m.; marginal stop*, curseur de marge, margeur. ‖ PHYS. Diaphragme *m.*
‖ NAUT. Genope *f.* ‖ MUS. Clé *f.* (of clarinet);
trou *m.* (of flute); touche *f.* (of guitar); jeu *m.* (of
organ). ‖ GRAMM. Point *m.* ‖ FAM. Terme *m.; to
come to a dead stop*, arriver au point mort, s'arrêter complètement. ‖ **Stop-bolt**, n. Arrêtoir *m.* ‖
Stop-gap, n. FAM. Bouche-trou *m.* ‖ **Stop-go**, adj.
FIN. *Stop-go policy*, politique de coups de frein et
d'accélérateur alternés, politique de stop-(and-)go. ‖
Stop-lamp, n. AUTOM. Stop *m.* (on vehicle). ‖ **Stop-
press news**, n. FAM. Dernière heure *f.* (in a
newspaper). ‖ **Stop-signal**, n. CH. DE F. Signal
d'arrêt *m.* ‖ **Stop-valve**, n. Soupape (*f.*) d'arrêt *m.*
‖ **Stop-watch**, n. Compte-secondes, chronomètre à
déclic, compteur de temps *m.*
stopcock [-kɔk] n. Robinet d'arrêt *m.*
stopoff [-ˌɔf] **stopover** [-ˌouvə*] n. Halte, étape
f. ‖ AVIAT. Escale *f.*
stoppage [-idʒ] n. Arrêt *m.* (of traffic, work). ‖
Obstruction *f.*, engorgement *m.* (of a pipe). ‖ FIN.
Suspension *f.* (of payment); retenue *f.* (on wages).
‖ MED. Occlusion *f.*
stopper [-ə*] n. Bouchon (*m.*) en verre. ‖ TECHN.
Taquet, arrêtoir *m.* ‖ NAUT. Bosse *f.* ‖ FAM. Terme
m.; to put a stopper on, mettre fin à.
— v. tr. Boucher. ‖ NAUT. Bosser.
stopping [-iŋ] n. Arrêt *m.* ‖ Suppression, suspension *f.* ‖ Obturation *f.;* bouchage *m.* ‖ Barrage *m.*
(of a road). ‖ MED. Plombage *m.* (of a tooth). ‖
FIN. Opposition *f.* (*of*, sur) [a cheque].
storage ['stɔ:ridʒ] n. COMM. Emmagasinage *m.*
(act); magasinage *m.* (charges); *storage capacity*,
capacité d'entreposage; entrepôts, magasins *m. pl.*
(space). ‖ ELECTR. Emmagasinage *m.* ‖ INFORM.
Mise en mémoire, mémorisation *f.; storage device*,
mémoire. ‖ **Storage-battery**, n. ELECTR. Accumulateur. ‖ **Storage-cell**, n. ELECTR. Elément d'accu *m.*
store [stɔ:*] n. Provision, réserve *f.* (*for*, pour).

‖ COMM. Boutique *f. ;* Pl. Grand magasin *m. ; village store,* épicerie de village. ‖ MILIT. Pl. Matériel ; approvisionnement *m. ;* munitions *f. pl.* ‖ FIG. Réserve *f. ; in store,* en réserve. ‖ FAM. *To set great, little store by,* faire grand cas, peu de cas de. ‖ **Store cake,** n. U. S. Gâteau de pâtissier *m.* ‖ **Store-cattle,** n. AGRIC. Bétail à l'engrais, *m.* ‖ **Store food,** n. U. S. Plats cuisinés *m. pl.* ‖ **Store-keeper,** n. Magasinier *m. ;* U. S. Commerçant, boutiquier *m.* ‖ **Store-room,** n. Resserre *f. ;* NAUT. Cambuse *f. ;* magasin, coqueron *m. ;* AVIAT. Soute *f.* ‖ **Store-ship,** n. NAUT. Ravitailleur *m.* — v. tr. Mettre en réserve. ‖ COMM. Emmagasiner, entreposer (goods) ; mettre au garde-meuble (furniture). ‖ AGRIC. Engranger, rentrer (crop). ‖ MILIT. Approvisionner (*with,* de). ‖ INFORM. Mettre en mémoire, mémoriser. ‖ FIG. Enrichir, meubler (*with,* de) [one's mind]. ‖ **To store up,** mettre en réserve (or) de côté (lit. and fig.).

storehouse [-haus] n. Magasin, entrepôt, dépôt *m.* ‖ FIG. Mine *f.* (of information).

stor(e)y ['stɔːri] n. Etage *m.* ‖ FAM. *To be weak in the upper storey,* déménager, avoir un grain.
— N. B. L'américain préfère l'orthographe *story.*

storiated ['stɔːrieitid] adj. ARCHIT., ARTS. Historié.

storied ['stɔːrid] adj. ARTS. Historié. ‖ FAM. Narré, relaté dans l'histoire.

stork [stɔːk] n. ZOOL. Cigogne *f.*

storm [stɔːm] n. Orage *m. ;* tempête *f.* ‖ MILIT. Assaut *m.* ‖ FIG. Torrent *m.* (of abuse) ; grêle, pluie, averse *f.* (of arrows). ‖ FIG. Tempête *f. ;* troubles *m. pl.* ‖ **Storm-beaten,** adj. Battu par la tempête. ‖ **Storm-belt** (or) **-zone,** n. Zone orageuse *f.* ‖ **Storm-centre** n. Centre du cyclone *m. ;* FIG. Foyer (*m.*) de troubles. ‖ **Storm-cloud,** n. Nuage orageux *m. ;* FIG. Nuage (*m.*) annonciateur de la tempête. ‖ **Storm-jib,** n. NAUT. Tourmentin *m.* ‖ **Storm-lantern,** n. Lanterne-tempête *f.* ‖ **Storm-sail,** n. NAUT. Voile de cape *f.* ‖ **Storm-signal,** n. Signal (*m.*) de tempête. ‖ **Storm-tossed,** adj. Ballotté par la tempête. ‖ **Storm-trooper,** n. MILIT. Membre (*m.*) d'une colonne d'assaut. ‖ **Storm-window,** n. Contre-fenêtre *f.*
— v. intr. Tomber à verse (rain) ; souffler en tempête (wind). ‖ FAM. Tempêter (*at,* contre).
— v. tr. MILIT. Monter à l'assaut de ; prendre d'assaut.

stormily [-ili] adv. Orageusement.

storminess [-inis] n. Caractère orageux *m.*

storming [-iŋ] n. MILIT. Assaut *m.* ‖ FAM. Fureur *f.* ‖ **Storming-party,** n. MILIT. Troupe (*f.*) d'assaut.

stormless [-lis] adj. Sans orages.

stormproof [-pruːf] adj. A l'épreuve de la tempête ; anticyclone.

stormy [-i] adj. Orageux (cloud) ; battu par la tempête (coast) ; orageux, tempétueux (rain, wind) ; orageux, démonté, en furie (sea). ‖ FIG. Orageux (discussion, life.)

story ['stɔːri] n. Histoire *f. ;* récit, conte *m.* (narration) ; *short story,* nouvelle, conte. ‖ Intrigue *f.* (plot). ‖ Version, relation *f.* (account). ‖ Rumeur *f. ; so the story goes,* d'après les on-dit. ‖ Papier, article *m.* (in a newspaper). ‖ FAM. Histoire *f. ;* conte *m.* (fib). ‖ **Story-book,** n. Livre (*m.*) de contes. ‖ **Story-teller,** n. Conteur *s. ;* FAM. Menteur, monteur (*s.*) de bateaux. (See FIBBER.) ‖ **Story-telling,** n. Art (*m.*) de conter ; FAM. Histoires *f. pl.*

story. See STOREY.

stoup [stuːp] n. ECCLES. Bénitier *m.* ‖ † Cruche *f.*

stout [staut] n. Stout *m.*

stout adj. Solide, résistant (firm). ‖ Solide, fort ; costaud (fam.) [sturdy] ; *stout of build,* solidement charpenté. ‖ Gros, corpulent, puissant (fat). ‖

Vaillant, ferme, résolu (undaunted). ‖ **Stout-hearted,** adj. Intrépide. ‖ **Stout-heartedness,** n. Intrépidité, vaillance *f.*

stoutish [-iʃ] adj. Replet.

stoutly [-li] adv. Solidement. ‖ Fermement, énergiquement. ‖ Vaillamment, résolument.

stoutness [-nis] n. Vigueur, force *f.* ‖ Corpulence *f. ;* embonpoint *m.*

stove [stouv] n. Poêle *m.* (for heating). ‖ Calorifère *m.* ‖ CULIN. Fourneau *m.* ‖ AGRIC. Serre chaude *f.* ‖ TECHN. Etuve *f.* ‖ **Stove-pipe,** n. Tuyau de poêle *m.* (pipe) ; FAM. Huit-reflets *m.* (hat).
— v. tr. AGRIC. Forcer, pousser. ‖ TECHN. Etuver.

stow [stou] v. tr. Ranger. ‖ NAUT. Saisir (the anchor) ; arrimer (a cargo). ‖ FAM. Fourrer ; *stow it !,* la ferme ! ; *to stow sth. full of,* bourrer qqch. de ; *to stow it away,* croûter, briffer.

stowage [-idʒ] n. Rangement *m.* ‖ NAUT. Arrimage *m.* (act) ; frais (*m. pl.*) d'arrimage (charge) ; espace utile *m.* (place).

stowaway [-əwei] n. Passager clandestin *s.*

strabismus [strə'bizməs] n. MED. Strabisme *m.*

straddle ['strædl] v. intr. Ecarquiller les jambes, se tenir les jambes écartées. ‖ FAM. Ménager la chèvre et le chou, répondre en normand.
— v. tr. Enfourcher (a horse). ‖ Chevaucher, être à califourchon sur (a chair). ‖ Enjamber, être à cheval sur (a river). ‖ MILIT. Encadrer.
— n. Ecartement (*m.*) des jambes. ‖ Chevauchement *m.* ‖ FIN. Opération (*f.*) à cheval. ‖ FAM. Politique (*f.*) de la chèvre et du chou.

straddler [-ə*] n. U. S. FAM. Normand *m.*

strafe [strɑːf] n. MILIT., FAM. Marmitage *m.*
— v. tr. MILIT., FAM. Marmiter.

strafing [-iŋ] n. MILIT. Marmitage *m.*

straggle ['strægl] v. intr. S'écarter, traîner, rester en arrière. ‖ Se disperser, s'éparpiller (persons). ‖ Etre disséminé (or) épars (or) détaché (houses) ; *to straggle along the street,* s'égrener le long de la rue. ‖ **To straggle off,** se détacher (or) se disperser par petits groupes.

straggler [-ə*] n. Traînard *s.* ‖ † Rôdeur *m.* ‖ AGRIC. Gourmand *m.* (branch).

straggling [-iŋ] adj. Disséminé, épars, détaché.

straight [streit] adj. Droit, rectiligne ; *in a straight line,* en droite ligne. ‖ Droit (back) ; raide (hair) ; *straight eye,* coup d'œil juste. ‖ D'aplomb (picture) ; *to set one's tie straight,* rectifier sa cravate. ‖ En ordre (room) ; *to put things straight,* arranger (or) rectifier les choses. ‖ SPORTS. Classique (dive). ‖ *straight thrust,* coup droit (in fencing). ‖ CULIN. Sec (whisky). ‖ FIG. Franc (answer) ; honnête (dealings) ; clair et précis, simple (definition) ; droit, honnête, franc, carré (person). ‖ **Straight-faced,** adj. Imperturbable, impassible. ‖ **Straight-haired,** adj. Aux cheveux raides. ‖ **Straight-lined,** adj. Rectiligne. ‖ **Straight-out,** adj. Droit, direct.
— adv. Droit, directement ; *to keep straight on,* continuer tout droit. ‖ Juste ; *to shoot straight,* tirer juste. ‖ FIG. Directement, carrément ; *to speak straight out,* parler sans détours. ‖ POP. Vrai !, sans blague ! ‖ LOC. *Straight away,* sur-le-champ ; *straight off,* immédiatement, au pied levé ; au débarqué, au débotté ; tout de go ; *straight out,* carrément, sans détours.
— n. Ligne droite *f. ; to cut on the straight,* couper droit fil. ‖ Aplomb *m. ; out of the straight,* de travers. ‖ Séquence *f.* (at poker). ‖ SPORTS. Ligne droite *f.*

straighten [-n] v. tr. Redresser (sth.). ‖ Ranger, mettre en ordre (a room). ‖ Rectifier (one's tie). ‖ FIG. Arranger (one's affairs).
— v. intr. Se redresser. ‖ FIG. S'arranger.

straightforward [streit'fɔːwəd] adj. Droit, franc (conduct) ; carré, direct, sans détours, franc (language, person).

straightforwardly [-li] adv. Sans détours.
straightforwardness [-nis] n. Loyauté, droiture ; rondeur *f*.
straightness ['streitnis] n. Rectitude *f*.
straightway [-wei] adv. Aussitôt, sur-le-champ.
strain [strein] v. tr. Tendre (a rope). ‖ Serrer (s.o.) ; *to strain s.o. to one's bosom*, serrer qqn sur son cœur. ‖ Tendre (one's ears) ; fatiguer, forcer (one's voice) ; *to strain one's eyes*, s'abîmer les yeux ; *to strain oneself*, se surmener. ‖ MED. Fouler (a limb) ; *to strain one's ankle*, se fouler la cheville ; *to strain oneself*, faire un faux mouvement. ‖ ARCHIT. Forcer (a beam). ‖ CULIN. Couler, passer, filtrer (a liquid). ‖ JUR. Violer (the law). ‖ FIG. Forcer (the meaning) ; abuser de, outrepasser (one's powers) ; tendre (relations) ; *to strain every nerve to*, tendre tous ses efforts pour.
— v. intr. Peiner, faire effort (*after*, pour atteindre). ‖ Filtrer (liquid). ‖ Tirer (*at*, sur). ‖ ARCHIT. Fatiguer (beam). ‖ TECHN. Gauchir. ‖ NAUT. Fatiguer.
— n. Tension *f*. (on a rope). ‖ ARCHIT. Gauchissement *m*.; déformation *f*. ‖ MED. Foulure *f*.; effort *m*. (sprain) ; *mental strain*, surmenage ; *to show signs of strain*, donner des signes de fléchissement. ‖ Pl. Accents *m*. pl. (in poetry). ‖ GRAMM. Ton, style *m*. (in a speech). ‖ MUS. Pl. Accords *m*. pl. ‖ FIG. Effort *m*.; tension *f*.
strained [-d] adj. Trop tendu (rope). ‖ Filtré (liquid). ‖ MED. Foulé (ankle) ; forcé (heart) ; tendu (nerves). ‖ FIG. Forcé, contraint.
strainer [-ə*] n. Filtre *m*. ‖ CULIN. Passoire *f*. ‖ TECHN. Epurateur *m*.
strait [streit] adj. † Etroit. ‖ Strait-jacket, n. Camisole de force. ‖ Strait-laced, adj. Prude ; collet-monté.
— n. pl. GEOGR. Détroit *m*. ‖ FAM. Indigence, gêne *f*.
straiten [-n] v. tr. Resserrer. ‖ FAM. Mettre dans la gêne ; *in straitened circumstances*, dans le besoin.
strand [strænd] n. Toron *m*. (of rope). ‖ Brin *m*. (of thread). ‖ BOT., ZOOL. Fibre *f*.
— v. tr. Toronner. ‖ Décorder.
strand n. Plage, grève *f*. (shore). ‖ Strand *m*. (in London). ‖ NAUT. Estran *m*.
— v. tr. NAUT. Echouer.
— v. intr. NAUT. S'échouer.
stranded [-id] adj. NAUT. Echoué. ‖ FAM. Le bec dans l'eau, en plan ; décavé.
strange [streindʒ] adj. † Etranger (foreign). ‖ Etranger, inconnu (*to*, à) [unknown]. ‖ Etranger, nouveau (to the work). ‖ Etrange, bizarre, singulier (queer) ; *to feel strange*, se sentir dépaysé. ‖ Etrange, surprenant, étonnant (astonishing).
strangely [-li] adv. Etrangement, bizarrement. ‖ Etonnamment.
strangeness [-nis] n. Etrangeté, bizarrerie, singularité *f*. ‖ Nouveauté *f*.
stranger [strein3ə*] n. Etranger *s*. (foreigner, newcomer, unknown person). ‖ Etranger *s*. (*to*, à) ; novice *s*. (*to*, dans). ‖ FAM. *You are quite a stranger!*, en voilà un revenant !, on ne vous voit plus !
strangle ['stræŋgl] v. tr. Etrangler. ‖ FIG. Etouffer.
— n. pl. MED. Gourme *f*. (of animals).
stranglehold [-hould] n. Prise (*f*.) à la gorge ; *to have a stranglehold on*, tenir à la gorge. ‖ FIG Etau *m*.
strangler [stræŋglə*] n. Etrangleur *s*. ‖ AUTOM. Etrangleur *m*.
strangulate ['stræŋgjuleit] v. tr. MED. Etrangler.
strangulation [,stræŋgju'leiʃən] n. Strangulation *f*. ‖ MED. Etranglement *m*.
strap [stræp] n. Courroie, lanière (of leather) *f*. ‖ Bande, patte *f*. (of material). ‖ Bracelet en cuir *m*. (watch-strap). ‖ Tirant *m*. (on boots) ; barrette *f*. (on shoes) ; sous-pied *m*. (of trousers). ‖ TECHN.

Collier *m*.; bride, bande *f*. ‖ Strap-hang, v. intr. FAM. Voyager debout en se tenant à la courroie. ‖ Strap-hanger, n. Voyageur debout *m*.
— v. tr. (1). Sangler, lier avec une courroie. ‖ MED. Bander. ‖ FAM. Fouetter à la courroie.
strappado [strə'peidou] n. † Estrapade *f*.
— v. tr. † Estrapader.
strapper ['stræpə*] n. FAM. Gaillard *s*.
strapping [-iŋ] n. FAM. Bien découplé.
— n. Action (*f*.) de sangler. ‖ Courroies *f*. pl. ‖ MED. Sparadrap *m*. ‖ FAM. Fouettée *f*.
strass [stræs] n. Strass *m*.
strata ['strɑ:tə] n. pl. See STRATUM.
stratagem ['strætədʒəm] n. Stratagème *m*.
strategic [strə'ti:dʒik] adj. MILIT. Stratégique.
strategically [-əli] adv. Stratégiquement.
strategics [-s] n. pl. Stratégie *f*.
strategist ['strætidʒist] n. Stratège *m*.
strategy [-dʒi] n. Stratégie *f*.; *grand strategy*, haute stratégie.
strath [stræθ] n. Vallée *f*.
stratification [,strætifi'keiʃən] n. Stratification *f*.
stratiform ['strætifɔ:m] adj. Stratiforme.
stratify [-fai] v. tr. (2). Stratifier.
stratocracy [strə'tɔkrəsi] n. Stratocratie *f*.
stratocruiser ['strɑ:tou'kru:zə*] n. AVIAT. Avion (*m*.) de ligne stratosphérique.
stratosphere ['strɑ:təsfi:ə*] n. Stratosphère *f*. ‖ Stratosphere-balloon, n. Ballon stratosphérique *m*.
stratum ['strɑ:təm] (pl. strata [-ə]) n. GEOL. Strate *f*. ‖ FIG. Couche *f*.
stratus ['strɑ:təs] n. Stratus *m*. (cloud).
straw [strɔ:] n. Paille *f*.; *straw hat*, chapeau de paille. ‖ Fétu, brin (*m*.) de paille (stalk). ‖ Chalumeau *m*., paille *f*. (drinking). ‖ FIG. *Man of straw*, homme de paille, prête-nom. ‖ FAM. Fétu *m*. (trifle) ; *not to be worth a straw*, ne pas valoir une guigne ; *to cling to a straw*, se raccrocher à une paille. ‖ LOC. *To draw straws*, tirer à la courte paille ; *the last straw*, le couronnement, le bouquet, la goutte d'eau qui fait déborder le vase. ‖ Straw-coloured, adj. Paille, jaune paille. ‖ Straw-mat, n. Paillasson *m*. ‖ Straw-mattress, n. Paillasse *f*. ‖ Straw-vote, n. U. S. Vote d'essai *m*.
— v. tr. Pailler.
strawberry ['strɔ:bəri] n. BOT. Fraise *f*. (fruit) ; fraisier *m*. (plant). ‖ Strawberry-blonde, n. U. S. Rousse *f*. ‖ Strawberry-mark, n. MED. Fraise *f*.; nævus *m*. ‖ Strawberry-tree, n. BOT. Arbousier *m*.
strawy ['strɔ:i] adj. De paille ; pailleux. ‖ Jaune paille.
stray [strei] v. intr. S'égarer, s'éloigner ; *to stray from the right road*, s'écarter de la bonne route. ‖ Errer, vagabonder.
— n. Animal errant *m*. ‖ Enfant abandonné *m*. ‖ ELECTR. Dispersion *f*. ‖ JUR. Biens (*m*. pl.) en déshérence. ‖ U.'S. RADIO. Pl. Friture *f*.
— adj. Errant, perdu (animal). ‖ Isolé, épars (houses). ‖ MILIT. Egaré, perdu (bullet). ‖ FIG. Fortuit.
streak [stri:k] n. Raie, rayure, bande *f*. ‖ Trait *m*.; coulée *f*. (of light) ; traînée, bande *f*. (of smoke) ; *streak of lightning*, éclair. ‖ Filon *m*. (of ore).
— v. tr. Rayer, strier, zébrer, sillonner (*with*, de).
streaky [-i] adj. Rayé, strié, zébré, sillonné. ‖ CULIN. Entrelardé (bacon). ‖ MED. Vergeté (complexion).
stream [stri:m] n. Ruisseau, cours (*m*.) d'eau (brook) ; fleuve *m*.; rivière *f*. (river). ‖ Courant *m*.; *against the stream*, contre le courant ; *down-, up-stream*, en aval, amont. ‖ Torrent *m*. (of lava) ; flot *m*. (of light) ; jet *m*. (of liquid). ‖ FIG. Torrent *m*. (of blood, tears). ‖ FAM. *To go with the stream*, suivre le mouvement, marcher avec le courant.
— v. intr. Couler. ‖ Flotter (hair, flag). ‖ Ruisseler

(*with*, de). ‖ **To stream in**, **out**, entrer, sortir à flots.
— v. tr. Verser à flots, laisser couler. ‖ NAUT. Mouiller.

streamer [-ə*] n. Banderole *f.* (ribbon). ‖ Serpentin *m.* (paper). ‖ NAUT. Flamme *f.* ‖ ASTRON. Pl Lumière polaire *f.* ‖ U. S. Titre en bandeau *m.* (newspaper headline).

streaming [-iŋ] adj. Ruisselant (*with*, de). ‖ Flottant (hair, flag).

streamlet [-lit] n. Ru, petit cours d'eau *m.*

streamline [-lain] v. tr. AUTOM., AVIAT. Profiler, caréner. ‖ FIG. Rationaliser, simplifier, moderniser (a measure, a system).

streamlined [-laind] adj. AUTOM. Aérodynamique. ‖ AVIAT. Fuselé, profilé, caréné.

street [stri:t] n. Rue *f.* ‖ FAM. *On the street*, sur le pavé ; *that's right up my street*, c'est tout à fait dans mes cordes ; *to walk the streets*, battre le pavé (person) ; faire le trottoir (prostitute). ‖ **Street-Arab**, (or) **-urchin**, n. FAM. Titi, poulbot, gamin (*m.*) des rues. ‖ **Street-floor**, n. U. S. Rez-de-chaussée *m.* ‖ **Street-guide**, n. Plan (*m.*) des rues. ‖ **Street-lamp**, n. Réverbère *m.* ‖ **Street-sweeper**, n. Balayeuse *f.* (machine) ; balayeur (*m.*) des rues (person). ‖ **Street-walker**, n. FAM. Péripatéticienne *f.*

streetcar [ˌ-kɑ:*] n. U. S. Tramway *m.*

strength [streŋθ] n. MED. Force *f.* ‖ MILIT. Effectifs *m. pl.; on the strength*, sur les contrôles. ‖ TECHN. Solidité, résistance *f.* ‖ CHIM. Teneur *f.; alcoholic strength*, degré d'alcool, teneur en alcool. ‖ FIG. Nombre *m.; in full strength*, au grand complet. ‖ FIG. Force, vigueur, solidité *f.; on the strength of*, sur la foi de, en s'autorisant de.

strengthen [-n] v. tr. MED. Fortifier. ‖ MILIT. Renforcer. ‖ TECHN. Consolider, renforcer. ‖ FIG. Renforcer, raffermir.
— v. intr. MED. Se fortifier. ‖ FIG. Se raffermir, se corser.

strengthless [-lis] adj. Dénué de forces, faible, débilité.

strenuous ['strenjuəs] adj. Acharné (conflict, effort) ; intense, actif (life) ; actif, énergique, infatigable (person) ; fatigant (profession) ; ardu (work).

strenuously [-li] adv. Energiquement.

strenuousness [-nis] n. Energie, activité *f.; zèle *m.*

streptococcal [-əl] adj. MED. Par le streptocoque (infection).

streptococcus ['strepto'kɔkəs] n. MED. Streptocoque *m.*

streptomycin [-'maisin] n. MED. Streptomycine *f.*

stress [stres] n. Tension *f.; effort *m.* ‖ Poussée, pression, contrainte *f.* ‖ Insistance *f.; to lay stress on*, insister sur, mettre l'accent sur. ‖ TECHN. Effort, travail *m.;* force, charge *f.* ‖ MED. Stress, choc, état (*m.*) d'alarme ; agression, commotion, perturbation *f.; mal-être *m.; under the stress of violent emotion*, en proie à une violente émotion. ‖ GRAMM. Accent tonique *f.* ‖ **Stress-disease**, MED. Surtension *f.;* état de choc *m.* ‖ **Stress-limit**, n. TECHN. Limite (*f.*) de travail (or) de charge. ‖ **Stress-unit**, n. TECHN. Unité de charge *f.*
— v. tr. Insister sur. (See EMPHASIZE.) ‖ TECHN. Fatiguer. ‖ GRAMM. Accentuer.

stressless [-lis] adj. GRAMM. Inaccentué.

stressor [-ə*] n. MED. Agresseur ; excitant ; stimulus ; agent stressant *m.*

stretch [stretʃ] v. tr. Tendre (a rope, spring). ‖ Etendre (one's arm) ; *to stretch one's legs*, allonger (or) se dégourdir (or) se dérouiller les jambes ; *to stretch oneself*, s'étirer. ‖ Déployer (one's wings). ‖ Etirer (elastic, gloves) ; élargir (shoes). ‖ FIG. Forcer (the law, meaning, truth) ; faire violence à (one's principles). ‖ **To stretch out**, allonger ; *to stretch out one's hand*, tendre la main ; *to stretch s.o. out*, étendre qqn (fam.).

— v. intr. S'étendre (country, road). ‖ S'allonger, s'étirer (elastic) ; se détendre (rope) ; s'élargir (shoes). ‖ S'étirer (person). ‖ FAM. Tirer sur la ficelle, exagérer. ‖ **To stretch out**, s'étendre (country) ; tendre la main (person) [*to*, pour] ; s'allonger (procession) ; NAUT. Souquer aux avirons ; FAM. Allonger le compas.

— n. Allongement, étirage *m.* (of rope). ‖ Déploiement *m.;* envergure *f.* (of wings). ‖ Extension *f.* (of arms). ‖ Etendue *f.* (of country) ; ruban *m.* (of road). ‖ GRAMM. Extension *f.* (of meaning). ‖ FIG. Effort *m.* (of imagination). ‖ FAM. *At a stretch*, tout d'une traite, à la file, sans débrider. ‖ POP. *To do a stretch*, faire de la taule, tirer son temps.

— adj. Extensible, élastique.

stretcher [-ə*] n. Baguette *f.* (for gloves) ; forme *f.* (for shoes) ; tendeur *m.* (for trousers). ‖ Traverse *f.* (for awning) ; bâton *m.* (of chair). ‖ MED. Brancard *m.;* civière *f.* ‖ ARTS. Châssis, cadre *m.* ‖ NAUT. Marchepied *m.* ‖ ARCHIT. Tirant, entrait *m.* ‖ FAM. Blague, craque, galéjade *f.* ‖ **Stretcher-bearer**, n. MED. Brancardier *m.*

stretchy [-i] adj. Elastique, qui prête.

strew [stru:] v. tr. (163). Semer, éparpiller, répandre (*over*, sur). ‖ Joncher, parsemer, couvrir (*with*, de).

— N. B. On trouve également le p.p. *strewn.*

stria ['straiə] (pl. **striae** ['straii]) n. Strie *f.*

striate [-it] adj. Strié.
— v. tr. Strier.

stricken ['strikən] adj. Frappé, touché. ‖ Blessé, navré, affligé. ‖ MED. Atteint (*with*, de). ‖ U. S. Rayé, annulé (deleted).

strickle ['strikl] n. AGRIC. Pierre (*f.*) à aiguiser. ‖ TECHN. Trousse *f.*
— v. tr. TECHN. Trousser.

strict [strikt] adj. Strict, précis, exact. ‖ Strict, sévère. ‖ Strict, rigoureux, absolu.

strictly [-li] adv. Exactement, précisément, étroitement. ‖ Strictement, sévèrement. ‖ Rigoureusement, strictement.

strictness [-nis] n. Précision, rigueur, exactitude *f.* ‖ Sévérité *f.*

stricture [-ʃə*] n. MED. Rétrécissement *m.* ‖ Pl. Critiques *f. pl.*

stride [straid] v. intr. (164). Marcher à grands pas (or) à grandes enjambées. ‖ **To stride along**, avancer à grands pas. ‖ **To stride over**, enjamber.
— v. tr. Arpenter (the street). ‖ Enjamber (an obstacle). ‖ Chevaucher, enfourcher (a horse). ‖ Se tenir à califourchon sur, chevaucher (a chair).
— n. Enjambée, foulée *f.; grand pas *m.* (step). ‖ Allure, vitesse *f.* (speed) ; *to hit one's stride*, prendre la cadence ; *to take sth. in one's stride*, faire qqch. sans le moindre effort (or) sur l'élan. ‖ FIG. Essor, progrès *m.*

strident ['straidnt] adj. Strident.

stridulant ['stridjulənt] adj. ZOOL. Stridulant.

stridulate [-leit] v. tr. ZOOL. Striduler.

stridulation [ˌstridju'leiʃən] n. ZOOL. Stridulation *f.*

strife [straif] n. Lutte *f.; conflit, différend *m.; domestic strife*, querelles de ménage.

strike [straik] n. Coup *m.* (blow). ‖ Grève *f.; to go on strike*, se mettre en grève, débrayer. ‖ Direction *f.* (of ore). ‖ TECHN. Frappe ; matrice *f.* (in coins). ‖ TECHN. Rencontre *f.* (oil-field). ‖ SPORTS. Touche *f.* (in fishing). ‖ FAM. Coup (*m.*) de veine. ‖ **Strike-breaker**, n. Jaune, briseur (*m.*) de grève. ‖ **Strike-pay**, n. Allocation (*f.*) aux grévistes.
— v. tr. (165). Porter (a blow) [*to*, à] ; *without striking a blow*, sans coup férir. ‖ Frapper, porter la main sur (s.o.) ; frapper (sth.) ; *to strike aside*, écarter d'un coup ; *to strike s.o. dead*, foudroyer qqn. ‖ Heurter, cogner, buter (one's elbow) [*against*, contre]. ‖ Enfoncer (a knife, nail) [*into*, dans]. ‖

Percer (the fog) ; *the cold struck him to the bone,* le froid le pénétra jusqu'à la moelle. ‖ Allumer, craquer, gratter, frotter (a match). ‖ Faire jaillir (light) ; tirer, faire naître (or) jaillir (sparks) [*from, out of,* de]. ‖ Sonner (the hour). ‖ Tomber sur, arriver à (the main road) ; tomber sur, découvrir (a track). ‖ Naut. Heurter (the rocks) ; amener (a sail) ; *to strike the bottom,* talonner. ‖ Milit. Lever (camp) ; plier (tents) ; conclure (a truce). ‖ Math. Etablir (an average) ; tracer (a circle) ; tirer (a line). ‖ Fin. Arrêter (an account) ; établir (a balance). ‖ Comm. Conclure (a bargain). ‖ Jur. Conclure (an agreement) ; constituer (a committee, a jury). ‖ Techn. Frapper (a coin) ; battre (the iron) ; *to strike work,* se mettre en grève (workers). ‖ Autom. Tamponner (s.o.). ‖ Mus. Plaquer (a chord) ; toucher de (the harp). ‖ Sports. Ferrer (fish) ; harponner (whale). ‖ Bot. Faire prendre (cuttings) ; *to strike roots,* prendre racine. ‖ Fig. Frapper (ear, fancy) ; attirer (eyes) ; frapper, impressionner (s.o.) ; *the thought struck me that,* l'idée me vint que, il me vint à l'idée que. ‖ Fig. Frapper (s.o.) [*with,* de] ; imprimer (terror) [*into,* dans, chez] ; *struck dumb,* frappé de mutisme. ‖ Fam. *That strikes me as rather silly,* cela me semble assez sot ; *to be struck all of a heap,* tomber des nues ; *to be struck on,* en pincer pour ; *to strike oil,* trouver le filon. ‖ To strike down, abattre, terrasser. ‖ To strike off, rayer (a name) [*from,* de] ; trancher (s.o.'s head) ; improviser (a speech) ; Techn. Tirer (copies) ; Fin. Déduire (a sum). ‖ To strike out, rayer, barrer, biffer (a name, word) ; ouvrir (a road) ; faire jaillir (sparks) ; Fig. Inventer, monter (a plan). ‖ To strike through, rayer, biffer (a word). ‖ To strike up, Sports. Relever d'un coup sec (sword) ; Mus. Attaquer (a piece) ; entonner (a song) ; Jur. Conclure (an agreement) ; Fig. Nouer, entamer (a conversation) ; contracter (a friendship) ; *to strike up an acquaintance with,* faire (or) lier connaissance avec.
— v. intr. Frapper ; *to strike back,* rendre les coups ; *to strike hard,* frapper un grand coup. ‖ Tenter de porter un coup (*at,* à). ‖ Frapper, tomber (light) [*on, upon,* sur]. ‖ Sonner (clock). ‖ Prendre, se diriger (*across,* à travers) ; s'enfoncer (*into,* dans). ‖ Pénétrer (cold) ; percer (sun). ‖ Prendre (match). ‖ Bot. S'enfoncer (roots) [*into,* dans]. ‖ Zool. Foncer, mordre (snake). ‖ Naut. Talonner (to strike bottom). ‖ Techn. Se mettre en grève (worker). ‖ Fig. Mettre le doigt, tomber (*on, upon,* sur) [a difficulty]. ‖ To strike out, frapper ; porter un coup (*at,* à) ; s'élancer ; se mettre en route ; Fam. *To strike out for oneself,* voler de ses propres ailes. ‖ To strike up, Mus. Préluder, commencer à jouer.

strikebound [-,baund] adj. Paralysé par la grève.

striker [-ə*] n. Gréviste *m.* ‖ Techn. Frappeur *m.* (device, person). ‖ Milit. Percuteur *m.*

striking [-iŋ] adj. Frappant, saisissant, impressionnant. ‖ Remarquable, notable.
— n. Frappement, fait (*m.*) de frapper ; coups *m. pl.* ‖ Frappe *f.* (of coins). ‖ Sonnerie *f.* (of clock). ‖ Grèves *f. pl.* ‖ Striking-distance, n. Portée *f.*

strikingly [-iŋli] adv. De façon frappante.

strikingness [-nis] n. Caractère frappant *m.*

string ⌊striŋ⌋ n. Ficelle *f.* (twine). ‖ Cordon, lacet *m.* (lace). ‖ Collier *m.* (of pearls). ‖ Mus. Corde *f.* (of instrument) ; pl. cordes *f. pl.* (instruments). ‖ Bot. Fil *m.* (in beans). ‖ Sports. Marque *f.* (in billiards). ‖ Geol. Veinule *f.* ‖ Eccles. *String of beads,* chapelet. ‖ Autom. File *f.* (of cars). ‖ Naut. Train *m.* (of barges). ‖ Ch. de f. Rame *f.* (of carriages). ‖ Culin. Chapelet *m.* (of onions). ‖ Fig. Chapelet *m.* (of abuse, pearls) ; kyrielle *f.* (of children) ; file *f.* (of people). ‖ Fam. On a string, le bec dans l'eau ; *a second string,* une seconde corde à

son arc ; *to get s.o. to pull the strings,* se faire pistonner ; *to pull the strings,* tirer les ficelles ; *to touch a string,* toucher la corde sensible. ‖ String-band, n. Mus. Orchestre (*m.*) à cordes. ‖ String-bean, Bot., Culin. Haricot *m.* ; U. S. Fam. Asperge *f.* (person). ‖ String-piece, n. Archit. Poutrelle *f.*
— v. tr. (166). Ficeler (a parcel). ‖ Enfiler (pearls). ‖ Bander (a bow). ‖ Culin. Enlever les fils de (beans). ‖ Mus. Mettre des cordes à (a violin). ‖ Fig. Tendre (the nerves). ‖ To string along, U. S. Fam. Faire marcher ; *to string along with,* suivre, adhérer à. ‖ To string up, Fam. Pendre haut et court.
— v. intr. Filer (glue). ‖ To string along with, U. S. Fam. Collaborer avec, suivre.

stringency ['strinʒənsi] n. Rigueur *f.* ‖ Fin. *Financial stringency,* resserrement monétaire.

stringent ⌊-ənt⌋ adj. Fin. Tendu (market). ‖ Fig. Rigoureux (rules).

stringer ['striŋə*] n. Archit. Longeron *m.* ‖ Geol. Veinule *f.* (of ore).

stringiness [-inis] n. Viscosité *f.* (of a liquid) ; nature filandreuse *f.* (of meat).

stringy [-i] adj. Visqueux (liquid) ; filandreux (meat).

strip [strip] v. tr. (1). Déshabiller, dévêtir (s.o.) ; dénuder, mettre à nu (sth.) ; *to strip the bed,* défaire le lit. ‖ Dépouiller, démunir (of, de). ‖ Ebrancher, effeuiller (a tree) ; écorcer (a trunk). ‖ Naut. Dépeler (a mast) ; dégréer (a ship). ‖ Electr. Dénuder (wire). ‖ Techn. Dégarnir. ‖ Fig. Déposséder. ‖ To strip off, enlever, arracher, ôter.
— v. intr. Se déshabiller, se dévêtir ; *to strip naked* (or) *to the skin,* se dénuder. ‖ Bot. S'effeuiller (tree) ; s'écorcer (trunk). ‖ Techn. Foirer (screw).

strip n. Bande *f.* (of material, paper) ; ruban *m.* (of metal). ‖ Langue, bande *f.* ; bout *m.* (of land). ‖ Bande dessinée *f.* (in newspaper). ‖ Agric. Planche *f.* ‖ Cinem. Bande *f.* ‖ Aviat. *Landing strip,* piste d'atterrissage. ‖ Strip-lighting, n. Lampe à incandescence *f.* ‖ Strip mining, n. U. S. Exploitation minière (*f.*) à ciel ouvert. ‖ Strip-tease, n. Theatr. Déshabillage, strip-tease *m.* ‖ Strip-teaser, n. Theatr. Effeuilleuse *f.*

stripe [straip] n. Rayure, raie, zébrure *f.* ‖ Bande *f.* (on trousers). ‖ Milit. Galon *m.* ‖ Arts. Filet *m.* ‖ U. S. Fam. Acabit, type *m.* (kind).

striped [-t] adj. Rayé, zébré. ‖ Med. Strié.

stripling ['stripliŋ] n. Adolescent *m.* ‖ Fam. Gringalet *m.*

stripper ['stripə*] n. Techn. Décapant *m.* (for paint, varnish). ‖ Fam. Effeuilleuse, strip-teaseuse *f.*

strive [straiv] v. intr. (167). S'efforcer, tenter (to, de). [See TRY.] ‖ Lutter, se débattre (against, contre) [to struggle]. ‖ Rivaliser (with, avec) [to compete].

stroboscope ['stroubə,skoup], **strobe** [stroub] n. Stroboscope *m.*

strode [stroud]. See STRIDE.

stroke [strouk] n. Coup *m.* (blow). ‖ Trait *m.* (of the pen) ; *up-stroke,* délié. ‖ Coup *m.* (of the hour). ‖ Arts. Coup *m.* (of pencil) ; touche *f.* (in painting). ‖ Med. Attaque *f.* ‖ Sports. Coup *m.* ; nage *f.* (in rowing) ; chef (*m.*) de nage (oarsman) ; brasse *f.* (in swimming) ; coup *m.* (at tennis). ‖ Techn. Course *f.* (of the piston). ‖ Fig. Coup, trait *m.* (of genius) ; *witty stroke,* trait d'esprit. ‖ Fam. *Not to do a stroke of work,* ne pas faire une once de travail, ne pas en ficher une ramée. ‖ Stroke-oar, n. Naut. Aviron d'arrière *m.*
— v. tr. Sports. Etre chef de nage de.

stroke v. tr. Caresser (a cat). ‖ Fam. *To stroke s.o. down,* amadouer qqn ; *to stroke s.o. the wrong way,* prendre qqn à rebrousse-poil.
— n. Caresse *f.*

strokingly [-iŋli] adv. De façon caressante.

stroll [stroul] v. intr. Flâner, flânocher. ‖ Déam-

buler, se balader (fam.). ‖ THEATR. *Strolling players,* acteurs ambulants.
— v. tr. Parcourir, déambuler dans (the streets).
— n. Tour *m.;* petite promenade *f.*
stroller [-ə*] n. Flâneur *s.* ‖ Promeneur *s.* ‖ THEATR. Acteur ambulant *m.* ‖ U. S. Voiture (*f.*) d'enfant, poussette *f.*
strong [strɔŋ] adj. Fort, solide (durable). ‖ Fort, vigoureux, robuste, solide (robust). ‖ Fort, nombreux; *forty strong,* au nombre de quarante. ‖ Fort, puissant (powerful); fort, violent, impétueux (violent). ‖ Fort, énergique, décidé (decided); fort, sévère, énergique (drastic). ‖ Fort, frappant, convaincant (persuasive); zélé, convaincu, actif (zealous). ‖ Fort; calé (fam.) [competent]. ‖ GRAMM. Fort (verb). ‖ CULIN. Rance (butter); fort (cheese, drink). ‖ FIN. Ferme (market). ‖ ELECTR. Intense (current). ‖ MUS. Fort (beat). ‖ MILIT. Bien défendu, fort. ‖ FAM. Fort; *that's too strong !,* c'est trop fort !; *to use the strong arm,* employer la force armée. ‖ **Strong-box,** n. Coffre-fort *m.* ‖ **Strong-minded,** adj. Résolu, décidé. ‖ **Strong-room,** n. FIN. Chambre (*f.*) des coffres.
— adv. Fort; *still going strong,* toujours solide; *to go strong,* marcher bon train.
stronghold [-hould] n. MILIT. Forteresse *f.* ‖ FIG. Forteresse, citadelle *f.;* bastion *m.*
strongish [-iʃ] adj. Assez fort.
strongly [-li] adv. Fortement.
strontia(n) ['strɔnʃiə(n)] n. CHIM. Strontiane *f.*
strontium [-əm] n. CHIM. Strontium *m.*
strop [strɔp] n. Cuir-affiloir *m.*
— v. tr. (1). Affiler sur le cuir (a razor). ‖ NAUT. Estroper (a block).
strophanthin [stro'fænθin] n. MED. Strophantine *f.*
strophe ['stroufi] n. † Strophe *f.*
stroppy ['strɔpi] adj. FAM. De mauvais poil, mal luné, à cran.
strove [strouv] pret. See STRIVE.
struck [strʌk] pret., p.p. See STRIKE.
structural ['strʌktʃərəl] adj. Structurel. ‖ GEOL., GRAMM., PSYCH. Structural. ‖ CHIM. De constitution (formula). ‖ TECHN. De construction (steel); *structural engineering,* ponts et chaussées.
structuralism ['strʌktʃərə,lizm] n. Structuralisme *m.*
structuralist [-list] adj., n. Structuraliste *adj., s.*
structurally [-li] adv. Structurellement.
structure [-tʃə*] n. Structure *f.* (of a country). ‖ ARCHIT. Edifice, bâtiment; ouvrage d'art *m.* ‖ BOT., MED. Structure *f.* ‖ PHYS. Composition *f.* (of the atom). ‖ FIG. Echafaudage *m.* (of arguments); structure *f.* (of a play); *social structure,* édifice social, structure sociale.
structureless [-tʃəlis] adj. GEOL. Amorphe. ‖ FIG. Sans structure.
strudel ['strudəl] n. CULIN. Chausson (*m.*) aux fruits.
struggle ['strʌgl] v. intr. Lutter, combattre, se battre (*against, with,* contre); être aux prises (*with,* avec); *to struggle against circumstances,* nager contre le courant. ‖ Se débattre, se démener, s'agiter. ‖ **To struggle along,** avancer péniblement. **To struggle for,** se disputer, lutter pour acquérir. ‖ **To struggle in** (or) **out** (or) **through,** se frayer péniblement un passage pour entrer (ou) sortir (ou) traverser. ‖ **To struggle up,** grimper péniblement; se lever avec difficulté.
— n. Lutte *f.;* combat *m.;* mêlée *f.* ‖ FIG. Lutte *f.;* effort *m.*
struggler [-ə*] n. Lutteur *s.*
struggling [-iŋ] adj. Qui se débat; qui cherche à percer.
— n. Lutte *f.*
strum [strʌm] v. intr. MUS. Jouailler.
— v. tr. MUS. Jouailler de.

struma ['struːmə] (pl. **strumae** [-iː]) n. MED. Ecrouelles, scrofules *f. pl.*
strumous [-əs] adj. MED. Scrofuleux.
strumpet ['strʌmpit] n. FAM. Catin *f.*
strung [strʌŋ] adj. FIG. *Highly strung,* les nerfs tendus, nerveux. (See STRING.)
strut [strʌt] v. intr. (1). Se pavaner, se rengorger.
— n. Démarche orgueilleuse *f.*
strut n. ARCHIT. Entretoise *f.;* étrésillon, montant *m.*
— v. tr. ARCHIT. Entretoiser.
struthious ['struːθjəs] adj. ZOOL. D'autruche.
strutter ['strʌtə*] n. FAM. Gonflé, crâneur *s.*
strychnia ['striknjə], **strychnine** [-niːn] n. CHIM. Strychnine *f.*
stub [stʌb] n. Bout, mégot *m.* (of cigar). ‖ Bout *m.* (of pencil). ‖ BOT. Souche *f.* ‖ TECHN. Mentonnet *m.* ‖ MED. Chicot *m.* (of tooth). ‖ FIN. Talon *m.* (of cheque).
— v. tr. (1). AGRIC. Essoucher (a field); arracher (roots). ‖ FAM. *To stub one's foot against,* buter contre; *to stub out one's cigarette,* écraser le bout de sa cigarette pour l'éteindre.
stubble ['stʌbl] n. AGRIC. Chaume *m.;* éteule *f.* ‖ FAM. Barbe (*f.*) de plusieurs jours (beard); cheveux (*m. pl.*) en brosse (hair).
stubbly [-i] adj. AGRIC. Couvert de chaume. ‖ FAM. De plusieurs jours (beard); en brosse (hair).
stubborn ['stʌbən] adj. Entêté, têtu, obstiné (person). ‖ Acharné, tenace, opiniâtre (effort). ‖ Rebelle, intraitable, à quoi l'on se heurte en vain (thing). ‖ ZOOL. Rétif (horse). ‖ AGRIC. Ingrat (soil). ‖ MED. Rebelle (fever).
stubbornly [-li] adv. Obstinément.
stubbornness [-nis] n. Obstination, opiniâtreté *f.;* entêtement *m.*
stubby ['stʌbi] adj. AGRIC. Couvert de chicots. ‖ BOT. Tronqué. ‖ FIG. Trapu (person).
stucco ['stʌkou] n. Stuc *m.*
— v. tr. Stuquer.
stuck [stʌk] adj. See STICK. ‖ **Stuck-up,** adj. Gourmé, affecté; *stuck-up woman,* mijaurée, poseuse.
stud [stʌd] n. Clou (*m.*) à grosse tête (or) doré. ‖ Clou *m.* (on pedestrian crossing). ‖ Crampon *m.* (on football boots). ‖ Bouton *m.* (on a shirt). ‖ TECHN. Goujon, tourillon *m.* ‖ ELECTR. Plot *m.* ‖ NAUT. Etai *m.* ‖ ARCHIT. Montant *m.* ‖ **Stud-hole,** n. Boutonnière *f.* ‖ **Stud-work,** n. ARCHIT. Colombage *m.*
— v. tr. (1). Clouter (a piece of furniture). ‖ Ferrer (boots). ‖ Parsemer, joncher (*with,* de).
stud n. SPORTS. Ecurie *f.* ‖ **Stud-book,** n. Stud-book *m.* ‖ **Stud-farm,** n. Haras *m.* ‖ **Stud-horse,** n. Etalon *m.*
studding ['stʌdiŋ] n. ARCHIT. Lattis *m.* ‖ **Studding-sail,** n. NAUT. Bonnette *f.*
student ['stjuːdənt] n. Etudiant *s.* (at a school). ‖ Savant, lettré, homme (*m:*) d'étude (scholar). ‖ Amateur (*m.*) d'études. ‖ **Student lamp,** n. U. S. Lampe ajustable *f.*
— adj. Estudiantin.
studentship [-ʃip] n. Temps (*m.*) d'études. ‖ Bourse (*f.*) d'études.
studied ['stʌdid] adj. Etudié, voulu.
studio ['stuːdiou] n. Atelier *m.* ‖ U. S. Salon *m.; music studio,* salon de musique. ‖ RADIO. Studio *m.* ‖ **Studio couch,** n. U. S. Canapé-lit *m.*
studious ['stjuːdiəs] adj. Studieux. ‖ Attentif, appliqué, empressé (*to,* à); désireux (*to,* de).
studiously [-li] adv. Studieusement. ‖ Attentivement. ‖ Volontairement.
studiousness [-nis] n. Amour (*m.*) de l'étude. ‖ Empressement, zèle *m.*
study ['stʌdi] n. Etude *f.* (act, process, product). ‖ Rêverie *f.; brown study,* méditation, songerie. ‖ Bureau, cabinet, studio *m.* (room); salle d'étude

f. (at school); U. S. *study hall*, salle d'études. ‖ Mus., Arts. Etude *f.* ‖ Theatr. *Good study*, acteur qui apprend vite ses rôles. ‖ Loc. *His face was a study*, il fallait voir sa tête.
— v..tr. (2). Etudier (a science). ‖ Etudier, observer (s.o.). ‖ Rechercher, viser (*to do*, à faire). ‖ **To study out**, approfondir, méditer sur (a question); résoudre (a problem).
— v. intr. Faire des études. ‖ S'étudier, s'appliquer (*to*, à). ‖ **To study for**, préparer (an examination). ‖ **To study under**, être l'élève de (s.o.).

stuff [stʌf] n. Etoffe *f.;* tissu *m.* ‖ Matériaux *m. pl.;* matières *f. pl.* ‖ Naut. Galipot *m.; small stuff*, lusin. ‖ Culin. *Green stuff*, légumes. ‖ Fig. Etoffe, essence *f.; full of good stuff*, étoffé (book); *to do one's stuff*, se montrer à la hauteur. ‖ Fam. Fatras *m.; nasty stuff*, saletés; *nice bit of stuff*, jolie fille; *silly stuff*, balivernes, sottises; *that's the stuff!* ça c'est tapé! ‖ Pop. Grisbi, pèze, pognon *m.* (money).
— v. tr. (1). Bourrer, remplir. ‖ Gaver (a goose). ‖ Empailler (a dead animal). ‖ Entasser, empiler, fourrer (*into*, dans) [sth.]. ‖ Culin. Farcir. ‖ **To stuff up**, boucher; Fam. Faire marcher (s.o.).
— v. intr. Se gaver, s'empiffrer. ‖ Fam. Monter un bateau. ‖ U. S. Fam. *Stuffed shirt*, poseur.

stuffer [-ə*] n. Empailleur *m.*

stuffiness [-inis] n. Manque d'air *m.* ‖ Fam. Esprit étroit *m.*

stuffing [-iŋ] n. Rembourrage, bourrage *m.* (action); bourre *f.;* rembourrage *m.* (material). ‖ Empaillage *m.* ‖ Culin. Farce *f.*

stuffy [-i] adj. Confiné, lourd (air); mal aéré, sentant le renfermé (room). [See FUGGY.] ‖ U. S. Fam. En rogne. ‖ Fam. A l'esprit étroit; collet monté.

Stuka ['stu:kə] n. Aviat. Stuka *m.*

stultify ['stʌltifai] v. tr. (2). Rendre ridicule, ridiculiser (to make ridiculous). ‖ Démentir, contredire, réduire à néant (to make worthless).

stum [stʌm] n. Moût *m.*
— v. tr. (1). Muter, soufrer.

stumble ['stʌmbl] v. intr. Broncher (horse). ‖ Trébucher, faire un faux pas (person). ‖ Se heurter, buter (*against*, contre) [an obstacle]. ‖ Tomber (*across, upon*, sur) [s.o.]. ‖ Achopper (*over*, sur) [a difficulty]. ‖ Bafouiller; *to stumble through one's recitation*, ânonner sa récitation.
— n. Faux pas *m.* ‖ Bronchement *m.*

stumbling [-iŋ] adj. Qui bronche (horse). ‖ Trébuchant (person). ‖ Hésitant (speech). ‖ **Stumbling-block**, n. Pierre (*f.*) d'achoppement.
— n. Bronchement *m.* ‖ Faux pas *m.* ‖ Hésitation *f.;* ânonnement *m.*

stumblingly [-iŋli] adv. En trébuchant.

stump [stʌmp] n. Bout *m.* (of cigar, pencil). ‖ Bot. Souche *f.* (of tree). ‖ Med. Moignon *m.* (of arm); chicot *m.* (of tooth). ‖ Arts. Estompe *f.* ‖ Fam. Tournée électorale *f.* ‖ Fam. Pl. Guiboles *f. pl.* (legs); *stir your stumps*, dérouille-toi, grouille-toi. ‖ **Stump-orator** (or) **-speaker**, n. Orateur de carrefour *m.*
— v. intr. Clopiner; *to stump in, out*, entrer, sortir en clopinant. ‖ Faire une tournée électorale. ‖ **To stump up**, Fam. Casquer.
— v. tr. Sports. Mettre hors jeu. ‖ Arts. Estomper. ‖ Fam. Coller (a candidate); *to be stumped on*, sécher sur (a question). ‖ Fam. **To stump up**, abouler, cracher (a sum).

stumper [-ə*] n. Fam. Colle *f.;* rébus *m.*

stumpiness [-inis] n. Allure trapue *f.*

stumpy [-i] adj. Trapu (person); court (thing). ‖ Agric. Plein de souches.

stun [stʌn] v. tr. (1). Etourdir, assommer. ‖ Fam. Abrutir, abasourdir; *stunned with surprise*, assis, suffoqué.

stung [stʌŋ]. See STING.

stunk [stʌŋk]. See STINK.

stunner ['stʌnə*] n. Fam. Type épatant *m.* (person); chose formidable *f.* (thing). ‖ U. S. Fam. Fille (*f.*) du tonnerre.

stunning [-iŋ] adj. Fam. Epatant, formid., du tonnerre.

stunt [stʌnt] n. Tour (*m.*) de force. ‖ Nouvelle sensationnelle *f.* (in newspaper). ‖ Aviat. Acrobatie *f.* ‖ Fam. Montage publicitaire *m.* ‖ **Stunt man**, n. Cinem. Acrobate-doublure, casse-cou, cascadeur *m.*

stunt v. tr. Arrêter (s.o.'s growth).

stunted [-id] adj. Rabougri; *to become stunted*, se rabougrir.

stupe [stju:p] n. Med. Compresse *f.*
— v. tr. Med. Mettre une compresse sur.

stupefaction [,stju:pi'fækʃən] n. Stupéfaction *f.*

stupefactive [-'fæktiv] adj. Med. Stupéfiant.

stupefier ['stju:pifaiə*] n. Med. Stupéfiant *m.*

stupefy [-fai] v. tr. (2). Abrutir, hébéter. ‖ Fig. Stupéfier, abasourdir; méduser (fam.).

stupendous [stju'pendəs] adj. Prodigieux. ‖ Fam. Formidable.

stupendously [-li] adv. Prodigieusement.

stupid ['stjupid] adj. Abruti, hébété (stupefied). ‖ Stupide, bête, idiot (foolish). ‖ Ennuyeux, triste, morne (dull).

stupidity [-iti] n. Abrutissement *m.* ‖ Stupidité, bêtise *f.*

stupidly [-li] adv. Stupidement.

stupor ['stju:pə*] n. Stupeur *f.*

sturdily ['stə:dili] adv. Avec robustesse. ‖ Hardiment, résolument.

sturdiness [-inis] n. Robustesse *f.* ‖ Hardiesse, résolution *f.*

sturdy [-i] adj. Robuste, vigoureux. ‖ Fig. Hardi, résolu, ferme.

sturdy [-i] n. Tournis *m.* (in sheep).

sturgeon ['stə:dʒən] n. Zool. Esturgeon *m.*

stutter ['stʌtə*] v. tr., intr. Bégayer.
— n. Bégaiement.

stutterer [-rə*] n. Bègue *s.*

sty [stai] n. Porcherie *f.* ‖ Fam. Taudis *m.*
— v. tr. (2). Mettre à la porcherie.

sty(e) n. Med. Orgelet *m.*

Stygian ['stidʒiən] adj. Du Styx (shore). ‖ Ténébreux (night).

style [stail] n. Style *m.* (instrument). ‖ Style *m.* (of an author, period). ‖ Genre *m.;* manière, façon *f.; in good style*, de bon ton, avec goût; *style of living*, train de maison, manière de vivre; *to do things in style*, bien faire les choses. ‖ Genre *m.;* manière, école *f.* ‖ Distinction *f.;* chic *m.; she has style*, elle a beaucoup de cachet. ‖ Titre *m.; to assume the style of*, s'intituler. ‖ Comm. Mode *f.* (fashion); raison sociale *f.* (name of a firm); modèle, type *m.* (pattern). ‖ Mus. Aiguille *f.* (of gramophone). ‖ Bot. Style *m.* ‖ Fam. *In fine style!*, de la belle façon; *that's the style!*, bravo, c'est tout à fait ça!
— v. tr. Qualifier, appeler; *to style oneself*, s'intituler.

stylet [-it] n. Stylet *m.*

styliform [-ifɔ:m] adj. Bot. Styliforme.

stylish [-iʃ] adj. Chic, élégant. (See FASHIONABLE.)

stylishly [-iʃli] adv. A la mode; avec chic.

stylist [-ist] n. Styliste *m.*

stylistic [stai'listik] adj. De style.
— n. pl. Stylistique *f.*

stylite ['stailait] n. Stylite *m.*

stylization [staili'zeiʃən] n. Stylisation *f.*

stylize ['stailaiz] v. tr. Styliser.

stylograph [-grɑ:f] n. Stylographe *m.*

stylographic [,stailə'græfik] adj. Stylographique.

styloid ['stailɔid] adj. Med. Styloïde; *styloid process*, apophyse styloïde.

stylus ['stailəs] n. Style *m.* (writing device).

stymie ['staimi] v. tr. FAM. Contrecarrer, gêner (a plan); coincer (a person).
styptic ['stiptik] adj., n. MED. Styptique *m.*
styrene ['stairi:n] n. CHIM. Styrène, styrolène *m.*
suable ['sjuəbl] adj. JUR. Poursuivable en justice.
suasion ['swei3ən] n. Persuasion *f.*
suave [swɑ:v] adj. Suave (fragrance). ‖ Affable, très aimable. ‖ Doucereux (pej.).
suavely [-li] adv. Suavement. ‖ Avec une extrême amabilité.
suavity [-itı] n. Suavité *f.* ‖ Extrême amabilité *f.* ‖ Politesse doucereuse *f.*
sub [sʌb] pref. Sous. ‖ **Sub-agent,** n. Sous-agent *m.* ‖ **Sub-basement,** n. Deuxième sous-sol *m.* ‖ **Sub-branch,** n. BOT., ZOOL. Sous-embranchement *m.;* COMM., FIN. Sous-succursale *f.* ‖ **Sub-director,** n. Sous-directeur *m.* ‖ **Sub-edit,** v. tr. Corriger (an article). ‖ **Sub-editor,** n. Secrétaire (*m.*) de rédaction. ‖ **Sub-machine-gun,** n. MILIT. Mitraillette *f.* ‖ **Sub-station,** n. RADIO. Poste de réseau clandestin *m.;* U. S. Bureau de quartier *m.* (branch section).
subacid [sʌb'æsid] adj. Aigrelet.
subagency [sʌb'eid3ənsi] n. Sous-agence *f.*
subalpine [-'ælpain] adj. GEOGR. Subalpin.
subaltern ['sʌbltən] adj. Subalterne. ‖ PHILOS. Subalterne.
— n. Subalterne, subordonné *s.* ‖ MILIT. Sous-lieutenant, lieutenant *m.*
subaqua [,sʌb'ækwə] adj. SPORTS. Sous-marin.
subaquatic [,sʌbə'kwætik] adj. Subaquatique.
subarctic [sʌb'ɑ:ktik] adj. GEOGR. Presque arctique.
subastral [-'æstrəl] adj. Sublunaire.
subatomic [,sʌbə'tɔmik] adj. PHYS. Subatomique.
subaudition [sʌb,ɔ:'diʃən] n. Sous-entente *f.*
subaxillary [,sʌbək'siləri] adj. Sous-axillaire.
subclass ['sʌbklɑ:s] n. Sous-classe *f.*
subcommission ['sʌbkə,miʃən] n. Sous-commission *f.*
subcommittee [-,miti] n. Sous-comité *m.*
subconscious ['sʌb'kɔnʃəs] adj. Subconscient.
— n. PHILOS. Subconscient *m.*
subconsciously [-li] adv. Inconsciemment, de façon subconsciente.
subconsciousness [-nis] n. Subconscience *f.*
subcontinent [sʌb'kɔntinənt] n. GEOGR. Sous-continent *m.*
subcontract [sʌb'kɔntrækt] n. Sous-traité *m.*
— ['sʌbkən,trækt] v. intr. Sous-traiter.
subcontractor [-ə*] n. Sous-entrepreneur, sous-traitant *m.*
subcontrary [sʌb'kɔntrəri] adj. MATH., PHILOS. Sub-contraire.
subculture ['sʌb,kʌltʃə*] n. Subculture *f.*
subcutaneous [sʌb,kju'teinjəs] adj. MED. Sous-cutané.
subdeacon [sʌb'di:kən] n. ECCLES. Sous-diacre *m.*
subdeaconry [-ri] n. ECCLES. Sous-diaconat *m.*
subdean ['sʌb'di:n] n. Sous-doyen *m.*
subdelegate [sʌb'deligit] n. Subdélégué *s.*
— [-geit] v. tr. Subdéléguer.
subdivide ['sʌbdi'vaid] v. tr. Subdiviser.
— v. intr. Se subdiviser.
subdivision [-,viʒən] n. Subdivision *f.*
subdominant ['sʌb'dɔminənt] n. MUS. Sous-dominante *f.*
subdue [səb'dju:] v. tr. Subjuguer, soumettre (a country). ‖ Adoucir, atténuer (a colour, light); baisser (voice). ‖ Amortir (pain). ‖ Dompter, maîtriser, réprimer (one's passion).
suberous [-əs] adj. BOT. Subéreux.
subfamily ['sʌb,fæmili] n. BOT., ZOOL. Sous-famille *f.*
subgenus ['sʌb'd3i:nəs] n. BOT. Sous-genre *m.*
subheading [-'hediꞧ] n. Sous-titre *m.*
subhuman [-'hju:mən] adj. Inférieur (animal). ‖

FIG. Sous-humain (condition); indigne d'un homme, bestial (behaviour).
subinspector ['sʌbin'spektə*] n. Sous-inspecteur *m.*
subinspectress [-tris] n. Sous-inspectrice *f.*
subjacent [sʌb'd3eisənt] adj. Sous-jacent.
subject ['sʌbd3ikt] adj. Assujetti, soumis (*to,* à) [submitted]. ‖ Sujet, porté, enclin (*to,* à) [liable]. ‖ LOC. *Subject to,* sous réserve de, sauf.
— n. Sujet *m.;* sujette *f.* (of a king). ‖ Sujet, thème *m.;* matière *f.* (subject); *enough on that subject,* assez sur ce chapitre. ‖ Sujet, motif *m.;* raison, cause *f.* (*for,* de) [reason]. ‖ MED., PHILOS., GRAMM. Sujet *m.* ‖ MUS. Motif *m.* ‖ **Subject-matter,** n. Sujet, thème *m.*
— [sʌb'd3ekt] v. tr. Subjuguer, asservir, soumettre, assujettir (*to,* à) [a country, s.o.]; *to subject oneself to,* se plier à (a rule). ‖ Soumettre, livrer (*to,* à) [an examination]. ‖ Exposer, livrer (*to,* à) [criticism].
subjection [sʌb'd3ekʃən] n. Subjugation *f.* ‖ Assujettissement *m.;* sujétion *f.* ‖ Fait (*m.*) de soumettre à.
subjective [-tiv] adj. PHILOS., ARTS. Subjectif. ‖ GRAMM. Sujet (case); subjectif (genitive).
subjectively [-tivli] adv. Subjectivement.
subjectivism [-tivizm] n. PHILOS. Subjectivisme *m.*
subjectivity [,sʌbʒek'tiviti] n. Subjectivité *f.*
subjoin [sʌb'd3ɔin] v. tr. Adjoindre.
sub judice [-'d3u:disi] adj. JUR. En instance.
subjugate ['sʌbd3ugeit] v. tr. Subjuguer.
subjugation [,sʌb3u'geiʃən] n. Subjugation *f.* (act); asservissement *m.* (result).
subjugator ['sʌb3ugeitə*] n. Asservisseur *m.*
subjunctive [səb'd3ʌꞧktiv] adj., n. GRAMM. Subjonctif *m.*
subkingdom [sʌb'kiꞧdəm] n. ZOOL., BOT. Sous-règne, clade *m.*
sublease ['sʌb'li:s] n. Sous-location *f.*
— v. tr. Sous-louer (by lessee or lessor).
sublessee ['sʌb,le'si:] n. Sous-locataire *s.*
sublessor [-'sə:*] n. Sous-bailleur *s.*
sublet [sʌb'let] v. tr. (96). Sous-louer.
sublieutenant ['sʌb,lef'tenənt] n. MILIT. Sous-lieutenant *m.* ‖ NAUT. Enseigne de vaisseau *m.*
sublimate ['sʌblimit] adj. CHIM. Sublimé. ‖ FIG. Raffiné, sublimisé.
— n. CHIM. Sublimé *m.*
— [-meit] v. tr. CHIM., PHILOS. Sublimer. ‖ FIG. Raffiner, sublimiser, idéaliser.
sublimation [,sʌbli'meiʃən] n. CHIM., PHILOS. Sublimation *f.*
sublime [sə'blaim] adj. Sublime (act, beauty, work); majestueux, imposant (scenery). ‖ Suprême, supérieur, sans pareil, inégalé (imprudence). ‖ MED. Epidermique.
— n. Sublime *m.*
— v. tr. CHIM. Sublimer. ‖ FIG. Sublimer, idéaliser.
— v. intr. CHIM., FIG. Se sublimer.
sublimely [-li] adv. Sublimement. ‖ Suprêmement.
subliminal [sʌb'liminl] adj. PSYCH. Subliminal (perception, advertising).
sublimity [sə'blimiti] n. Sublimité *f.*
sublingual [sʌb'liꞧgwəl] adj. Sublingual.
sublunar ['sʌb'lu:nə*] adj. Sublunaire.
submarine ['sʌbməri:n] adj., n. NAUT. Sous-marin *m.* ‖ **Submarine-pen,** n. NAUT. Abri sous-marin *m.*
submaxillary [sʌb,mæk'siləri] adj. MED. Sous-maxillaire.
submediant [sʌb'mi:diənt] n. MUS. Sus-dominante *f.*
submerge [sʌb'mə:d3] v. tr. Plonger (*into,* dans). ‖ Inonder, noyer, submerger (land). ‖ NAUT. Submerger (a ship). ‖ FIG. Noyer, submerger.
— v. intr. NAUT. Plonger. ‖ FAM. *The submerged tenth,* les économiquement faibles.
submergence [-əns] n. Submersion *f.*

submersible [sʌb'mə:sibl] adj., n. NAUT. Submersible *m*.
submersion [-ʃən] n. Submersion *f*.
submission [sʌb'miʃən] n. Soumission *f*. (*to*, à) [an authority, s.o.]. ‖ Docilité, soumission *f*. (quality). ‖ Soumission *f*. (*to*, à) [an examination]; présentation *f*. (of documents). ‖ JUR. Thèse *f*.
submissive [-siv] adj. Soumis. ‖ Docile.
submissively [-sivli] adv. Avec soumission.
submissiveness [-sivnis] n. Soumission, docilité *f*.
submit [səb'mit] v. intr. (1). Se soumettre, se résigner (*to*, à).
— v. tr. Soumettre (*to*, à) [s.o.'s judgment]. ‖ Faire observer (or) remarquer, alléguer, représenter, soutenir (*that*, que).
subnormal ['sʌb'nɔ:məl] adj. Au-dessous de la normale; *mentally subnormal*, déficient mental.
— n. MATH. Sous-normale *f*.
subnuclear [sʌb'nju:kliə*] adj. PHYS. Subnucléaire.
suborbital [-'ɔ:bitl] adj. MED. Sous-orbitaire. ‖ ASTRONAUT. Sous-orbital, suborbital.
suborder ['sʌb,ɔ:də*] n. ZOOL., BOT. Sous-ordre *m*.
subordinate [sə'bɔ:dnit] adj. Subordonné, subalterne, inférieur. ‖ GRAMM. Subordonné.
— n. Subordonné *s*.
— [-neit] v. tr. Subordonner (*to*, à).
subordination [sə,bɔ:di'neiʃən] n. Subordination *f*.
suborn [sʌ'bɔ:n] v. tr. Suborner.
subornation [,sʌbə:'neiʃən] n. Subornation *f*.
suborner [sʌ'bɔ:nə*] n. Suborneur *m*.
subplot ['sʌb,plɔt] n. THEATR. Intrigue secondaire, intrigue dans l'intrigue *f*.
subpoena [sʌb'pi:nə] n. JUR. Citation *f*.
— v. tr. JUR. Citer, assigner.
— N. B. Pret. et p.p. : *subpoenaed*.
subprefect [sʌb'pri:fekt] n. Sous-préfet *m*.
subprefecture [-fekt ʃə*] n. Sous-préfecture *f*.
subrent ['sʌb'rent] v. tr. Sous-louer.
subreption [sʌb'repʃən] n. Subreption *f*.
subrogate ['sʌbrɔgeit] v. tr. JUR. Subroger.
subrogation [,sʌbrə'geiʃən] n. JUR. Subrogation *f*.
subroutine ['sʌbru:,ti:n] n. INFORM. Sous-programme *m*.
subscribe [sʌb'skraib] v. tr. Apposer (*to*, au bas de) [one's name]. ‖ Signer (a document). ‖ Souscrire, verser en souscription (a sum).
— v. intr. Souscrire, consentir, donner son assentiment (*to*, à). [See AGREE.] ‖ Souscrire, verser une cotisation (*to*, à) [a club]; s'inscrire (*for*, pour) [a sum]. ‖ Souscrire (*to*, à) [a book]; s'abonner (*to*, à) [a periodical].
subscriber [-ə*] n. Soussigné *s*. ‖ Souscripteur, cotisant *m*. (to a book); abonné *s*. (to a magazine).
subscript ['sʌbskript] adj. GRAMM. Souscrit.
subscription [sʌb'skripʃən] n. Signature *f*. ‖ Souscription *f*. (to a book); abonnement *m*. (to a magazine). ‖ Assentiment *m*.; adhésion *f*. (to an opinion).
subsellium [sʌb'seljəm] (pl. **subsellia** [-jə]) n. ARCHIT., ECCLES. Miséricorde *f*.
subsequence ['sʌbsikwəns] n. Postérité *f*. (condition). ‖ Conséquence *f*. (happening).
subsequent [-ənt] adj. Subséquent, postérieur (*to*, à). ‖ Consécutif.
subsequently [-əntli] adv. Par la suite; subséquemment; postérieurement.
subserve [səb'sə:v] v. tr. Favoriser.
subservience [-iəns] n. Utilité *f*. (*to*, à). ‖ Asservissement *m*. (*to*, à). ‖ Obséquiosité, servilité *f*.
subservient [-iənt] adj. Utile (*to*, à). ‖ Soumis, asservi (*to*, à). ‖ Obséquieux, plat.
subset ['sʌb,set] n. MATH. Sous-ensemble *m*.
subside [səb'said] v. intr. Baisser, diminuer

(flood); déposer (liquid); tomber au fond, se déposer (sediment). ‖ Céder, se calmer (storm); tomber (wind); s'affaisser (building, ground). ‖ S'écrouler, se tasser, s'effondrer, s'affaler (person). ‖ FIG. S'apaiser, tomber (anger, excitement). ‖ FAM. Baisser pavillon. ‖ To subside into, revenir à; devenir, se changer en.
subsidence ['sʌbsidəns] n. Baisse *f*. (of flood); dépôt *m*.. précipitation *f*. (of sediment). ‖ Apaisement *m*. (of storm). ‖ Affaissement, tassement *m*. (of building, ground). ‖ Effondrement *m*. (of s.o.). ‖ FIG. Apaisement *m*. (of anger); déguisement *m*. (of passions).
subsidiarily [səb'sidjərili] adv. Subsidiairement.
subsidiary [-i] adj. Subsidiaire. ‖ MILIT. Mercenaire.
— n. Auxiliaire *s*.
subsidize ['sʌbsidaiz] v. tr. Subventionner; *to be subsidized from* (or) *out of*, émarger à. ‖ Fournir des subsides à.
subsidy [-i] n. Subside *m*. (to a government, a king); subvention *f*. (to a private enterprise).
subsist [səb'sist] v. intr. Subsister, persister (to continue). ‖ Subsister, vivre (*on*, de) [to live].
— v. tr. Faire vivre, entretenir, assurer la subsistance de.
subsistence [-ens] n. Persistance, subsistance *f*. ‖ Subsistance *f*.; moyens (*m. pl.*) d'existence; entretien *m*.
subsistent [-ənt] adj. Subsistant.
subsoil ['sʌbsɔil] n. GEOL. Sous-sol *m*.
— v. tr. AGRIC. Sous-soler.
subsoiler [-ə*] n. AGRIC. Fouilleuse *f*.
subsonic [sʌb'sɔnik] adj. AVIAT. Subsonique.
subspecies ['sʌb'spi:ʃi:z] n. ZOOL., BOT. Sous-espèce *f*.
substance ['sʌbstəns] n. Substance, matière *f*. (matter). ‖ Consistance, densité, corps *m*. (consistency). ‖ Solidité, réalité *f*. (true meaning). ‖ Substance, essence *f*.; fond *m*. (content). ‖ Avoir *m*.; fortune *f*. (wealth); *a man of substance*, un homme riche; qqn. qui a de quoi (fam.). ‖ PHILOS. Substance *f*.
substandard [sʌb'stændəd] adj. Inférieur au niveau moyen.
substantial [sʌb'stænʃəl] adj. Substantiel, réel, vrai (true). ‖ Substantiel, solide, sérieux (firm). ‖ Substantiel, considérable, consistant, important (ample). ‖ Valable, solide (noteworthy). ‖ Riche, cossu (wealthy).
substantialism [-izm̩] n. Substantialisme *m*.
substantiality [səb,stænʃi'æliti] n. Substantialité, réalité *f*.
substantially [səb'stænʃəli] adv. Substantiellement. ‖ Sensiblement.
substantiate [-ʃieit] v. tr. Etablir (a charge); justifier (a claim); *non-substantiated*, non appuyé de preuves.
substantiation [səb,stænʃi'eiʃən] n. Justification *f*.; fait (*m*.) d'appuyer de preuves.
substantival [,sʌbstən'taivəl] adj. GRAMM. Substantival.
substantive ['sʌbstəntiv] adj. GRAMM. Substantif. ‖ JUR. Positif. ‖ FIG. Autonome, indépendant.
— n. GRAMM. Substantif, nom *m*.
substantively [-li] adv. Substantivement.
substitute ['sʌbstitju:t] n. Suppléant, remplaçant *s*. (person). ‖ COMM. Succédané, ersatz *m*. (goods); contrefaçon *f*. (imitation). ‖ MILIT. Remplaçant *m*. ‖ ECCLES. Substitut *m*.
— adj. De remplacement (product); remplaçant (person).
— v. tr. Substituer (*for*, à) [sth.].
— v. intr. To substitute for, remplacer, suppléer (s.o.).
substitution [,sʌbsti'tju:ʃən] n. CHIM., JUR., FIG. Substitution *f*.

substratum ['sʌb'strɑ:təm] (pl. **substrata** [-ə])
n. AGRIC. Sous-sol *m*. ‖ PHILOS. Substratum *m*. ‖
FIG. Fonds *m*.
substructure ['sʌb'strʌktʃə*] n. ARCHIT. Infrastructure *f*. ‖ FIG. Soubassement *m*.; base *f*.
subsume [səb'sju:m] v. tr. Subsumer.
subtenancy ['sʌb'tenənsi] n. Sous-location *f*.
subtenant [-ənt] n. Sous-locataire *s*.
subtend [sʌb'tend] v. tr. MATH. Sous-tendre.
subterfuge ['sʌbtəfju:dʒ] n. Subterfuge *m*. ‖ †
Echappatoire *f*.
subterranean [,sʌbtə'reinjən] adj. Souterrain.
subtilization [,sʌbtili'zeiʃən] n. CHIM. Sublimation *f*. ‖ FIG. Raffinement *m*. ‖ FAM. Ergotage,
alambiquage *m*.
subtilize ['sʌbtilaiz] v. tr. CHIM. Sublimer, subtiliser. ‖ FIG. Raffiner. ‖ FAM. Subtiliser à l'excès ;
alambiquer.
— v. intr. FAM. Couper les cheveux en quatre,
ergoter.
subtitle ['sʌb'taitl] n. Sous-titre *m*.
— v. tr. Sous-titrer.
subtitling [-iŋ] n. Sous-titrage *m*.
subtle ['sʌtl] adj. CHIM., MED. Subtil (air, poison).
‖ FIG. Mystérieux (charm, wink) ; ingénieux
(device) ; subtil (distinction, mind, problem) ; fin,
habile, rusé (person) ; raffiné (policy).
subtlety [-ti] n. Subtilité, finesse *f*.
subtly [-i] adv. Subtilement.
subtonic ['sʌb'tɔnik] n. MUS. Sous-tonique *f*.
subtotal [sʌb'toutl] n. Total partiel *m*.
subtract [səb'trækt] v. tr. MATH., FIG. Soustraire
(*from*, de, à). [See DEDUCT.]
subtraction [-ʃən] n. MATH., FIG. Soustraction *f*.
subtractive [-tiv] adj. MATH. Soustractif.
subtrahend ['sʌbtrəhend] n. MATH. Nombre (*m*.)
à soustraire.
subtropical ['sʌb'trɔpikəl] adj. GEOGR. Presque
tropical, subtropical.
suburb ['sʌbə:b] n. Faubourg *m*. ‖ Pl. Banlieue *f*.
suburban [sə'bə:bən] adj. De faubourg ; de banlieue. ‖ De bourgeois ; *to become suburban*, s'embourgeoiser.
suburbanite [-ait] n. FAM. Banlieusard *s*.
suburbia [sə'bə:biə] n. FAM. Banlieue *f*. ; univers (*m*.) des petits-bourgeois de banlieue.
subvention [səb'venʃən] n. Subvention *f*.
subversion [səb'və:ʃən] n. Subversion *f*. ; renversement *m*.
subversive [-siv] adj. Subversif.
— n. Agent subversif, agitateur *s*.
subvert [səb'və:t] v. tr. Renverser.
subway ['sʌbwei] n. Passage souterrain *m*. ‖ U.S.
Métro *m*. ‖ **Subway rider**, n. U.S. Usager du
métro *m*.
subzero [sʌb'ziərou] adj. Au-dessous de zéro
(temperature).
succedaneous [,sʌksi'deinjəs] adj. Succédané.
succedaneum [-əm] (pl. **succedanea** [-ə]) n. Succédané *m*.
succeed [sək'si:d] v. tr. Succéder à.
— v. intr. Succéder (*to*, à). ‖ Avoir du succès, réussir (*in*, à).
success [sək'ses] n. † Issue *f*. ; résultat *m*. (end). ‖
Succès *m*. ; réussite *f*. ; *to be a success*, avoir du
succès ; *to make sth. a success*, faire réussir qqch.
successful [-ful] adj. Couronné de succès
(attempt) ; reçu, élu (candidate) ; favorisé par le
succès, qui réussit, heureux (person) ; *successful
union*, mariage réussi.
successfully [-fuli] adv. Avec succès.
succession [sək'seʃən] n. Succession, série, suite
f. (sequence) ; *in succession*, à la file, consécutivement, de suite. ‖ Succession *f*. (act, right) [*to*, à] ;
in succession to, en remplacement de. ‖ Descen-

dance, postérité *f*. ; descendants *m*. pl. (heirs). ‖
JUR. Succession *f*. ; héritage *m*. ; *succession duties*,
droit de succession.
successional [-l] adj. Successif. ‖ JUR. Successoral.
successive [sək'sesiv] adj. Successif, consécutif.
successively [-li] adv. Successivement.
successor [sək'sesə*] n. Successeur *s*. (*to*, *of*, de).
succinct [sək'siŋkt] adj. Succinct. (See CONCISE.)
succinctly [-li] adv. Succinctement.
succinctness [-nis] n. Concision *f*.
succory ['sʌkəri] n. BOT. Chicorée *f*.
succo(u)r ['sʌkə*] v. tr. Secourir, aider. (See
HELP.)
— n. Secours *m*. ; aide *f*. ‖ MILIT. † Renforts *m*. pl.
succubus ['sʌkjubəs] (pl. **succubi** [-ai]) n. Succube *m*.
succulence ['sʌkjuləns] n. Succulence *f*.
succulent [-ənt] adj. CULIN., FIG. Succulent. ‖
BOT. Gras (plant).
— n. BOT. Plante grasse *f*.
succumb [sə'kʌm] v. intr. Succomber (*to*, à) ;
mourir (*to*, de) [to die]. ‖ Succomber (*to*, à) ; être
écrasé (*to*, par) [to be overcome]. ‖ Succomber,
céder (*to*, à) [to yield].
succursal [sʌ'kə:səl] adj. ECCLES. De secours
(chapel) ; annexe (church).
— n. COMM. Succursale *f*.
such [sʌtʃ] adj., pron. Tel ; *his friends thought
him such*, ses amis le considéraient comme tel ;
until such moment as, jusqu'au moment où ; *such kindness*, une telle bonté ; *such a man*, un tel homme. ‖
Semblable, pareil ; *just such eyes*, les mêmes yeux.
‖ De ce genre, tel ; *any such reason*, toute raison de
cet ordre. ‖ Si ; *such a beautiful child*, un si bel
enfant ; *such foolish people*, des gens si sots. ‖ Tel,
si grand ; *he is such a liar*, il est tellement menteur.
‖ Tel (indefinite) ; *the way to such and such a place*,
le chemin pour aller à tel ou tel endroit. ‖ *Such as*,
tel que, comme ; *books such as these*, des livres
comme ceux-ci ; *such a friend as John*, un ami tel
que Jean ; *such as you see me*, tel que vous me
voyez. ‖ **Such as**, ceux qui, tels qui, les... qui (relative) ; *such as laugh today may weep tomorrow*,
ceux qui rient aujourd'hui pourraient bien pleurer
demain ; *such criticism as I heard concerning this
book is exaggerated*, les critiques que j'ai entendu
formuler sur ce livre sont outrées. ‖ **Such as to**,
suffisant pour. ‖ **Such that**, tel (or) si que ; *the
noise is such that I am deafened by it*, le bruit
est tel que j'en suis étourdi ; *they are such mean
people that everybody despises them*, ce sont des
gens si avares que tout le monde les méprise. ‖
All such, tous ceux-là. ‖ **As such**, comme tel. ‖
Not such... as, pas aussi... que ; *he is not such
a happy man as I*, il n'est pas aussi heureux que
moi, il ne connaît pas le même bonheur que moi.
suchlike [-laik] adj. De ce genre.
— pron. FAM. Autres choses du même genre.
suck [sʌk] v. tr. Sucer (bone, liquid, orange) ; *to
suck one's fingers*, se sucer les doigts. ‖ Gober (an
egg). ‖ Prendre (the breast). ‖ Boire (dew). ‖ ZOOL.
Butiner (flowers). ‖ FAM. Sucer, vider (s.o.) ; *like a
sucked orange*, comme un citron pressé. ‖ **To suck
down**, aspirer, engloutir (a swimmer). ‖ **To suck
in**, aspirer (air) ; absorber (knowledge) ; engloutir
(a swimmer) ; boire (words). ‖ **To suck up**, absorber, pomper, boire, s'imbiber up.
— v. intr. Sucer. ‖ Téter (baby). ‖ TECHN. Aspirer
(pump). ‖ **To suck up**, FAM. Lécher les bottes
(*to*, de).
— n. Succion *f*. (act) ; sucée *f*. (result). ‖ Tétée *f*.
(for babies). ‖ FAM. *Sucks !*, bien pris !, coincé !
sucker [-ə*] n. Suceur *s*. ‖ ZOOL. Rémora *m*. (fish) ;
cochon de lait *m*. (pig). ‖ ZOOL. Suçoir *m*. (of
insect) ; ventouse *f*. (of leech). ‖ BOT. Surgeon,
rejeton *m*. ‖ TECHN. Piston *m*. ; tuyau (*m*.) d'aspi-

ration (pipe). ‖ Fam. Blanc-bec *m.* ‖ U. S. Fam. Gobeur, gogo, ballot *m.; poire f.* (dupe).
— v. tr. Bot. Ebouturer.
— v. intr. Bot. Drageonner ; rejetonner.
sucking [-iŋ] adj. De lait (calf). ‖ Au sein (child).
suckle ['sʌkḷ] v. tr. Allaiter, nourrir (a baby).
suckling [-iŋ] n. Allaitement *m.* (act); nourrisson *m.* (baby).
sucrose ['sju:krous] n. Chim. Saccharose *m.*
suction ['sʌkʃən] n. Aspiration *f.* (of air, liquid); succion *f.* (of liquid). ‖ **Suction-gas**, n. Chim. Gaz pauvre *m.* ‖ **Suction-plant**, n. Techn. Gazogène *m.* ‖ **Suction-pump**, n. Pompe aspirante *f.* ‖ **Suction-valve**, n. Clapet (*m.*) d'aspiration.
suctorial [sʌk'tɔ:riəl] adj. Zool. Suceur.
Sudan [su:'dæn] n. Geogr. Soudan *m.*
Sudanese [ˌsu:də'ni:z] adj., n. Geogr. Soudanais *s.*
sudarium [sju:'dɛəriəm] n. Eccles. Sainte Face, véronique *f.*
sudation [sju:'deiʃən] n. Sudation *f.*
sudatorium [ˌsju:də'tɔ:riəm] (pl. **sudatoria** [-ə]) n. Bain (*m.*) de vapeur (or) turc.
sudatory ['sju:dətəri] adj., n. Med. Sudorifique *m.* ‖ Bain turc *m.*
sudden ['sʌdn̩] adj. Soudain, subit, brusque. ‖ Loc. *All of a sudden*, subitement, tout à coup, brusquement ; subito (fam.).
suddenly [-li] adv. Soudain, tout à coup.
suddenness [-nis] n. Soudaineté *f.*
sudoriferous [ˌsju:də'rifərəs] adj. Med. Sudoripare.
sudorific [-fik] adj., n. Med. Sudorifique *m.*
suds [sʌdz] n. pl. Eau (or) mousse (*f.*) de savon.
sue [sju:] v. tr. † Supplier, prier. ‖ Demander la main de (a young lady). ‖ Jur. Poursuivre en justice.
— v. intr. Faire sa cour (to woo). ‖ Jur. Intenter un procès (or) une action. ‖ **To sue for**, implorer, solliciter, demander ; *to sue to s.o. for sth.*, solliciter qqch. de qqn.
suede [sweid] n. Comm. Suède *m.* (for gloves, jackets) ; daim *m.* (for shoes).
suet [sju:it] n. Culin. Graisse fine (*f.*) de rognon.
suety [-i] adj. Graisseux.
suffer ['sʌfə*] v. tr. Souffrir, supporter, endurer, ressentir (pain). ‖ Essuyer (an affront); subir (a defeat). ‖ Supporter, souffrir, tolérer (s.o., sth.).
— v. intr. Souffrir (patient, victim). ‖ Fig. Pâtir, souffrir *(from, de).* ‖ Fig. Subir sa peine ; mourir (to die).
sufferable [-əbḷ] adj. Supportable.
sufferance [-rəns] n. Tolérance *f.*
sufferer [-rə*] n. Victime *f. (from, de).* ‖ Med. Patient, malade *s.*
suffering [-riŋ] adj. Souffrant.
— n. Souffrance *f.*
suffice [sə'fais] v. intr. Etre suffisant, suffire.
— v. tr. Satisfaire, suffire à.
sufficiency [sə'fiʃənsi] n. Suffisance, quantité suffisante *f.* ‖ Aisance *f.* (wealth).
sufficient [-ənt] adj. Suffisant *(for,* pour); *he has sufficient*, il en a assez, cela lui suffit.
sufficiently [-li] adv. Suffisamment.
suffix ['sʌfiks] n. Gramm. Suffixe *m.*
— v. tr. Gramm. Suffixer.
suffocate ['sʌfəkeit] v. tr., intr. Suffoquer, étouffer (lit. and fig.).
suffocating [-iŋ] adj. Suffocant, étouffant.
suffocation [ˌsʌfə'keiʃən] n. Suffocation *f.*
suffragan ['sʌfrəgən] adj., n. Eccles. Suffragant *m.* (to, de).
suffrage ['sʌfridʒ] n. Jur., Eccles., Fig. Suffrage *m.*
suffragette [ˌsʌfrə'dʒet] n. Suffragette *f.*

suffragist ['sʌfrədʒist] n. Partisan (*m.*) du vote des femmes.
suffuse [sə'fju:z] v. tr. Se répandre sur (colour, light); *suffused with tears*, baigné de larmes.
suffusion [-ʒən] n. Coloration *f.* (blush). ‖ Fait (*m.*) de baigner. ‖ Med. Suffusion *f.*
Sufism ['su:fizm̩] n. Soufisme *m.*
sugar ['ʃugə*] n. Culin. Sucre *m.; burnt sugar*, caramel. ‖ Fam. Douceurs *f. pl.;* miel *m.; to be all sugar*, être tout sucre et miel. ‖ **Sugar-almond**, n. Dragée *f.* ‖ **Sugar-basin** (or) U. S. **bowl**, n. Sucrier *m.* ‖ **Sugar-beet**, n. Bot. Betterave sucrière. ‖ **Sugar-boiler** (or) **maker**, n. Sucrier *m.* (person). ‖ **Sugar-candy**, n. Sucre candi *m.* ‖ **Sugar-cane**, n. Bot. Canne (*f.*) à sucre. ‖ **Sugar-coat**, v. tr. Dorer (the pill). ‖ **Sugar daddy**, n. U. S. Fam. Vieux protecteur ; papa gâteau *m.* ‖ **Sugar-dredger**, n. Fam. Saupoudroir *m.* ‖ **Sugar-industry**, n. Industrie sucrière *f.* ‖ **Sugar-loaf**, n. Pain de sucre *m.;* adj. Fam. En pain de sucre. ‖ **Sugar maple**, n. U. S. Bot. Erable (*m.*) à sucre. ‖ **Sugar orchard**, n. U. S. Bosquet (*m.*) [or] plantation (*f.*) d'érables à sucre. ‖ **Sugar-refinery**, n. Raffinerie *f.* ‖ **Sugar-refining**, n. Raffinage du sucre *m.* ‖ **Sugar-tongs**, n. Pince (*f.*) à sucre.
— v. tr. Sucrer. ‖ Fig. Dorer (the pill); sucrer, adoucir (one's words).
sugariness [-rinis] n. Saveur sucrée *f.* ‖ Fig. Douceur mielleuse *f.*
sugary [-ri] adj. Sucré. ‖ Fig. Sucré, doucereux, mielleux (person); sentimental, à l'eau de rose (story).
suggest [sə'dʒest] v. tr. Suggérer, inspirer (a desire, an idea); suggérer, insinuer, laisser supposer (to intimate). ‖ Evoquer, donner l'idée de, faire penser à (to prompt). ‖ Impliquer, supposer (to imply).
suggestibility [sə,dʒesti'biliti] n. Suggestibilité *f.*
suggestible [sə'dʒestibḷ] adj. Suggestible (person); proposable (thing).
suggestion [-ʃən] n. Suggestion *f.* (act, thought). ‖ Suggestion, proposition *f.* (proposal). ‖ Idée, pensée *f.* (idea). ‖ Pointe, nuance *f.* (hint).
suggestive [-tiv] adj. Suggestif ; *suggestive of*, évocateur de, faisant penser à.
suggestively [-tivli] adv. De façon suggestive.
suicidal [sjui'saidḷ] adj. Du suicide (mania); au suicide (tendency). ‖ Fam. *It is suicidal to*, c'est un vrai suicide de.
suicide ['sjuisaid] n. Suicide *m.* (act); *to attempt suicide*, attenter à ses jours. ‖ Suicidé *s.* (person).
suint [swint] n. Culin. Suint *m.*
suit [sju:t] n. Cour *f.* (wooing); demande (*f.*) en mariage. ‖ Requête *f.* (to, à, auprès de). ‖ Couleur *f.* (at cards); *to follow suit*, jouer la couleur. ‖ Ensemble, assortiment, jeu *m.* (set, series). ‖ Comm. Costume, complet *m.* (man's); tailleur *m.* (woman's). ‖ Jur. Action, poursuite *f.;* procès *m.; at the suit of*, à la diligence de. ‖ **Suit-case**, n. Mallette, valise *f.*
— v. tr. Adapter, approprier, accommoder (to, à); *to suit the word to the action*, accorder la parole à l'action. ‖ Convenir à ; arranger (s.o.); *that suits me best*, c'est ce qui me convient le mieux (or) qui fait le mieux mon affaire; *suit yourself*, faites à votre idée. ‖ Aller à, seoir à; *this hat doesn't suit you*, ce chapeau ne vous va pas. ‖ Pourvoir; *to be suited with*, avoir trouvé (a servant, situation).
— v. intr. Convenir, aller, faire l'affaire. ‖ Aller (with, avec); convenir (with, à).
suitability [ˌsju:tə'biliti], **suitableness** ['sju:t-əblnis] n. Convenance, appropriation *f.*
suitable ['sju:təbḷ] adv. Convenable, approprié, idoine. ‖ Approprié, adapté (to, à); en accord, en rapport (to, avec).
suitably [-i] adv. Convenablement. ‖ Conformément (to, à); en conformité (to, avec).

suite [swi:t] n. Suite *f.* (of a king). ‖ Série *f.; suite of furniture*, ameublement, mobilier ; *suite of rooms*, appartement. ‖ Mus. Suite *f.*

suiting ['sju:tiŋ] n. Tissu (*m.*) pour hommes.

suitor [-ə*] n. Prétendant, soupirant, amoureux *m.* (lover). ‖ Jur. Plaideur *s.*

sulfa drug ['sʌlfə'drʌg], **sulfonamide** [sʌl'fɔnəmaid] n. U. S. Med. Sulfamide *m.*

sulfur ['sʌlfɔ*] n. U. S. See SULPHUR.

sulk [sʌlk] n. Bouderie, maussaderie *f.; to be in the sulks*, bouder, faire la tête.
— v. intr. Bouder.

sulkiness [-inis] n. Bouderie *f.;* caractère boudeur (or) maussade *m.*

sulky [-i] adj. Boudeur ; *to be sulky with*, faire la tête à (s.o.).

sullen ['sʌlən] adj. Maussade, morose, sombre (person) ; triste, lugubre, sombre (thing). ‖ Rétif (horse) ; obstiné (silence). ‖ Menaçant (cloud).

sullenly [-li] adv. Maussadement, d'un air renfrogné. ‖ Silencieusement.

sullenness [-nis] n. Maussaderie, humeur sombre *f.* ‖ Taciturnité *f.*

sully ['sʌli] v. tr. (2). Souiller, salir (lit. and fig.).

sulpha-series ['sʌlfə'siəri:z] n. Med. Série (*f.*) de sulfamides.

sulphate ['sʌlfit] n. Chim. Sulfate *m.*

sulphide [-faid] n. Chim. Sulfure *m.*

sulphite [-fait] n. Chim. Sulfite *m.*

sulphonamide [sʌl'fɔnəmaid] n. Med. Sulfamide *m.*

sulphur ['sʌlfə*] n. Chim. Soufre *m.; sulphur mine*, soufrière ; *sulphur water*, eau sulfureuse.
— v. tr. Soufrer.

sulphurate [-reit] v. tr. Sulfurer, soufrer.

sulphuration [,sʌlfju'reiʃən] n. Agric. Sulfurage *m.* ‖ Techn. Soufrage *m.*

sulphurator [-tə*] n. Agric. Soufreuse *f.* ‖ Techn. Soufroir *m.*

sulphureous [sʌl'fjuəriəs] adj. Sulfureux.

sulphuretted [sʌl'fjuretid] adj. Chim. Sulfuré.

sulphuric [sʌl'fjuərik] adj. Chim. Sulfurique.

sulphurize ['sʌlfjuraiz] v. tr. Sulfurer ; soufrer.

sulphurous [-əs] adj. Chim. Sulfureux.

sulphury [-i] adj. Soufre, jaune soufre.

sultan ['sʌltən] n. Sultan *m.*

sultana [sʌl'tɑ:nə] n. Sultane *f.* ‖ Culin. Raisin (*m.*) de Smyrne.

sultanate ['sʌltənit] n. Sultanat *m.*

sultaness [-is] n. Sultane *f.*

sultriness ['sʌltrinis] n. Chaleur lourde et étouffante, lourdeur *f.*

sultry ['sʌltri] adj. Lourd, étouffant, caniculaire.

sum [sʌm] n. Arith. Calcul, problème (*m.*) d'arithmétique. ‖ Math. Somme *f.;* total, montant *m.* ‖ Fin. Somme *f.* (of money) ; *a nice* (or) U. S. *tidy little sum*, un joli denier. ‖ Fig. Fond *m.; in sum*, en somme, somme toute. ‖ **Sum-total**, n. Math. Somme totale *f.;* montant global *m.;* Fig. Substance intime *f.*
— v. tr. (1). Math. Additionner, faire le total de, totaliser. ‖ **To sum up**, Math. Additionner ; Jur. Résumer ; Fig. Faire la somme de ; Fam. Juger, jauger (s.o.).

sumac(h) ['su:mæk] n. Bot. Sumac *m.*

summarily ['sʌmərili] adv. Sommairement.

summarize [-raiz] v. tr. Résumer.

summary [-ri] adj., n. Sommaire *m.*

summation [sə'meiʃən] n. Math. Addition *f.*

summer ['sʌmə*] n. Eté *m.; summer time*, heure d'été. ‖ Fig. Printemps *m.* ‖ **Summer-house**, n. Cabinet (*m.*) de verdure ; pavillon *m.* ‖ **Summer-time**, n. Eté *m.* (season).
— adj. D'été (clothing) ; estival (resort) ; *summer holidays*, grandes vacances.
— v. intr. Passer l'été. ‖ Agric. Estiver.
— v. tr. Agric. Estiver (cattle).

summersault ['sʌməsɔ:lt]. See SOMERSAULT.

summit ['sʌmit] n. Geogr., Fig. Sommet, faîte *m.*

summon ['sʌmən] v. tr. Appeler (a servant). ‖ Jur. Convoquer (Parliament) ; citer (a witness). ‖ Milit. Sommer (a town to surrender). ‖ **To summon up**, rassembler (one's courage).

summons ['sʌmənz] (pl. **summonses** [-iz]) n. Convocation *f.* ‖ Jur. Citation ; assignation *f.*
— v. tr. Jur. Citer.

sump [sʌmp] n. Fosse d'aisance *f.* ‖ Techn. Puisard *m.* ‖ Autom. Carter *m.* ‖ Fam. Dépotoir *m.*

sumpter ['sʌmptə*] n. † Bête (*f.*) de somme.

sumption ['sʌmʃən] n. Philos. Majeure *f.*

sumptuary ['sʌmptjuəri] adj. Jur. Somptuaire.

sumptuous [-əs] adj. Somptueux, fastueux, splendide, magnifique.

sumptuously [-əsli] adv. Somptueusement.

sumptuousness [-əsnis] n. Somptuosité *f.*

sun [sʌn] n. Soleil *m.* (heavenly body, light) ; *in the sun*, au soleil. ‖ Astre *m.* (star). ‖ Jour *m.* (day) ; année *f.* (year) [in poetry]. ‖ Naut. *With the sun*, dans le sens des aiguilles d'une montre. ‖ Med. *Touch of the sun*, coup de soleil. ‖ Fig. Etoile *f.* ‖ **Sun-bath**, n. Bain de soleil *m.* ‖ **Sun-blind**, n. Store *m.* ‖ **Sun-blinkers**, n. pl. Lunettes (*f. pl.*) de soleil. ‖ **Sun-dial**, n. Cadran solaire *m.* ‖ **Sun-dress**, n. Robe de plage *f.;* bain de soleil *m.* ‖ **Sun-glasses**, n. pl. Verres fumés *m. pl.;* lunettes (*f. pl.*) de soleil. ‖ **Sun-hat**, n. Chapeau de soleil *m.* ‖ **Sun-helmet**, n. Casque colonial *m.* ‖ **Sun-lamp**, n. Cinem. Sunlight *m.;* U. S. Med. Lampe (*f.*) à rayons ultraviolets ; ‖ **Sun-myth**, n. Mythe solaire *m.* ‖ **Sun-parlor**, n. U. S. Solarium *m.* ‖ **Sun-ray**, adj. Med. Héliothérapique ; *sun-ray treatment*, héliothérapie. ‖ **Sun-roof**, n. Autom. Toit ouvrant *m.* ‖ **Sun-spot**, n. Tache solaire *f.* ‖ **Sun-tan**, n. Bronzage, hâle *m.* ‖ **Sun-tanned**, adj. Bronzé, hâlé. ‖ **Sun-up**, n. Lever du soleil *m.* ‖ **Sun-worship**, n. Culte (*m.*) du soleil. ‖ **Sun-worshipper**, n. Adorateur (*s.*) du soleil.
— v. tr. (1). Exposer au soleil, insoler ; *to sun oneself*, se chauffer au soleil, prendre un bain de soleil.

sunbathe [-,beiδ] v. intr. Prendre un bain de soleil, se faire bronzer.

sunbeam [-bi:m] n. Rayon de soleil *m.*

sunburn [-bə:n] n. Hâle *m.*

sunburnt [-bə:nt] adj. Hâlé, bronzé.

sunda [-sʌndə] n. Geogr. Sonde *f.*

sundae ['sʌndei] n. U. S. Culin. Glace (*f.*) au sirop (or) aux fruits.

Sunday ['sʌndi] n. Dimanche *m.; as long as a month of Sundays*, long comme un jour sans pain.
— adj. Du dimanche (clothes, school) ; dominical (calm, rest). ‖ **Sunday-go-to-meeting**, adj. U. S. Fam. Du dimanche (clothes).

sunder ['sʌndə*] v. tr. Séparer, couper en deux.

sundew ['sʌndju:] n. Bot. Drosera *m.*

sundown ['sʌndaun] n. Coucher du soleil *m.*

sundowner [-ə*] n. Chemineau *m.* (tramp). ‖ Fam. Apéritif *m.* (drink).

sundry ['sʌndri] adj. Divers, différent ; *all and sundry*, tous sans exception.
— n. pl. Comm. Articles divers *m. pl.* ‖ Fin. Frais divers *m. pl.*

sundryman [-mən] n. Comm. Marchand (*m.*) de fournitures diverses.

sunfish ['sʌnfiʃ] n. Zool. Poisson-lune *m.*

sunflower [-flauə*] n. Bot. Soleil, tournesol *m.*

sung [sʌŋ] p. p. See SING.

sunk [sʌŋk] pret., p. p. See SINK.

sunken ['sʌŋkən] adj. Creux, encaissé (road). ‖ Creux, cave (eyes). ‖ Naut. Immergé, submergé.

sunless ['sʌnlis] adj. Sans soleil.

sunlight [-lait] n. Lumière (*f.*) du soleil. ‖ **Sun-light-lamp**, n. Cinem. Sunlight *m.*

sunlit [-lit] adj. Ensoleillé.

sunnily [-ili] adv. Avec enjouement.
sunniness [-inis] n. Ensoleillement *m.* ‖ Fig. Enjouement *m.; nature gaie f.*
sunny [-i] adj. Ensoleillé (day, house, place); *it is sunny,* il fait du soleil. ‖ Exposé au soleil (side). ‖ Fig. Radieux, rayonnant, enjoué (person); *on the sunny side of forty,* du bon côté de la quarantaine; *to see the sunny side of everything,* voir tout en rose, voir le bon côté des choses.
sunproof [pru:f] adj. Inaltérable au soleil.
sunrise [-raiz] n. Lever du soleil *m.*
sunset [-set] n. Coucher du soleil *m.* ‖ Fig. Déclin *m.* (of life).
sunshade ['-ʃeid] n. Ombrelle *f.* (carried); parasol *m.* (for tables). ‖ Autom. Pare-soleil *m.*
sunshine [-ʃain] n. Soleil *m.; clarté (f.)* du soleil; *in the bright sunshine,* en plein soleil. ‖ Temps ensoleillé *m.* ‖ Autom. *Sunshine roof,* toit ouvrant. ‖ Fig. Rayonnement *m.,* gaieté rayonnante *f.*
sunshiny [-ʃaini] adj. Ensoleillé.
sunstroke [-strouk] n. Med. Insolation *f.*
sunstruck [-strʌk] adj. Med. Frappé d'insolation.
sup [sʌp] v. intr. (1). Souper (*with,* avec).
— v. tr. Prendre (broth). ‖ Donner à souper à, faire souper (s.o.).
— n. Gorgée *f.*
super ['sju:pə*] n. Theatr., Fam. Figurant *s.*
super adv. Au-dessus; de dessus; plus.
— adj. Fam. Excellent, formidable. ‖ **Super-duper,** adj. Fam. Mirobolant.
superable ['sju:pərəbl̩] adj. Surmontable.
superabound [ˌsju:pərə'baund] v. intr. Surabonder, foisonner (*in, with,* de).
superabundance [-əns] n. Surabondance *f.*
superabundant [-ənt] adj. Surabondant.
superabundantly [-əntli] adv. Surabondamment.
superadd ['sju:pə'æd] v. tr. Surajouter.
superannuate [sju:pə'rænjueit] v. tr. Retraiter, mettre à la retraite (s.o.). ‖ Fam. Mettre au rancart, remiser (sth.).
superannuated [-id] adj. Retraité (person). ‖ Démodé, suranné (thing).
superannuation ['sju:pəˌrænju'eiʃən] n. Mise à la retraite *f.* ‖ Caractère démodé *m.* ‖ Jur. *Superannuation fund,* caisse des retraites.
superb [sju'pə:b] adj. Superbe.
superbly [-li] adv. Superbement.
supercargo ['sju:pə'kɑ:gou] n. Naut. Subrécargue *m.*
supercharger [-'tʃɑ:dʒə*] n. Techn. Surcompresseur *m.*
superciliary [ˌsju:pə:'siliəri] adj. Med. Sourcilier.
supercilious [-iəs] adj. Sourcilleux, dédaigneux, hautain.
superciliously [-iəsli] adv. Avec hauteur, dédaigneusement.
superciliousness [-iəsnis] n. Hauteur *f.;* dédain *m.;* mine dédaigneuse *f.*
superconductivity [ˌsju:pəˌkɔndʌk'tiviti] n. Phys. Supraconduction, supraconductibilité, supraconductivité *f.*
superconductor [ˌsju:pəkən'dʌktə*] n. Phys. Supraconducteur *m.*
super-ego [ˌsju:pə'i:gou] n. Psych. Surmoi *m.*
supereminence [-'reminəns] n. Prééminence *f.*
supereminent[ˌsju:pə'reminənt]adj. Prééminent.
supererogation [ˈsju:pəˌrero'geiʃən] n. Surérogation *f.*
supererogatory ['sju:pərə'rɔgətəri] adj. Surérogatoire.
superexcellent [ˌsju:pə'reksələnt] adj. Excellentissime.
superfetation ['sju:pəfi'teiʃən] n. Med., Fig. Superfétation *f.*
superficial [ˌsju:pə'fiʃəl] adj. Superficiel. ‖ Fig. Superficiel, tout en surface; *to be superficial,* manquer de profondeur.

superficially [-i] adv. Superficiellement.
superficies [ˌsju:pə'fiʃˌi:z] n. Superficie *f.*
superfine ['sju:pə'fain] adj. Comm. Surfin. ‖ Fig. Trop subtil, très raffiné.
superfluity [-'fluiti] n. Superfluité *f.* (excess, state); superflu *m.* (quantity).
superfluous [sju:'pə:fluəs] adj. Superflu.
superfluously [-li] adv. De façon superflue.
superfortress ['sju:pə'fɔ:tris] n. Aviat. Superforteresse *f.*
superheat [ˌsju:pə'hi:t] v. tr. Surchauffer.
superheater [-ə*] n. Techn. Surchauffeur *m.*
superheterodyne [ˌsju:pə'hetərəˌdain], **superhet** ['sju:pəˌhet] n., adj. Radio. Superhétérodyne *m., adj.*
superhighway [-'haiwei] n. U. S. Autoroute *f.*
superhuman [-'hju:mən] adj. Surhumain.
superhumanly [-'hju:mənli] adv. Surhumainement, de façon surhumaine.
superimpose ['sju:pərim'pouz] v. tr. Superposer. ‖ Cinem. Surimprimer.
superincumbent ['sju:pərin'kʌmbənt] adj. Superposé. ‖ Surplombant.
superintend [ˌsju:pərin'tend] v. tr. Surveiller, diriger. ‖ Présider à.
superintendence [-əns] n. Surveillance, direction *f.*
superintendent [-ənt] n. Surveillant, directeur *m.* ‖ Officier de paix, inspecteur *m.* ‖ † Surintendant *m.* ‖ U. S. Concierge, gardien *m.*
superior [sju'piəriə*] adj. Supérieur (*to,* à) [s.o.]; au-dessus (*to,* de) [sth.]; *to be superior to flattery,* rester insensible à la flatterie. ‖ Comm., Techn., Milit. Supérieur. ‖ Fam. Supérieur, condescendant.
— n. Supérieur *s.*
superiority [sju,piəri'ɔriti] n. Supériorité *f.*
superiorly [sju'piəriərli] adv. De manière supérieure. ‖ Avec un air supérieur. ‖ Bot. Au-dessus.
superlative [sju'pə:lətiv] adj. Suprême (quality). ‖ Gramm. Superlatif.
— n. Gramm. Superlatif *m.*
superman ['sju:pəmæn] (pl. **supermen**) n. Surhomme *m.*
supermarket [-'mɑ:kit] n. Supermarché *m.*
supernaculum[sju:pə'nækjuləm]adv. Rubis sur l'ongle.
— n. Vin de choix *m.*
supernal [sju:'pə:nl̩] adj. Céleste.
supernatant [ˌsju:pə'neitənt] adj. Surnageant.
supernatural [ˌsju:pə'nætʃrəl] adj. Surnaturel.
supernaturally [-i] adv. Surnaturellement.
supernaturalness [-nis] n. Surnaturel *m.*
supernormal [ˌsju:pə'nɔ:məl] adj. Supranormal.
supernova [-'nouvə] n. Astron. Supernova *f.*
supernumerary [-'nju:mərəri] adj. Supplémentaire.
— n. Surnuméraire *s.* ‖ Theatr. Figurant *s.*
supernutrition [ˌsju:pənju'triʃən] n. Suralimentation *f.*
superphosphate [ˌsju:pə'fɔsfeit] n. Superphosphate *m.*
superposable [ˌsju:pə'pouzəbl̩] adj. Superposable.
superpose [-'pouz] v. tr. Superposer.
superposition [ˌsju:pəpə'ziʃən] n. Superposition *f.* (on, sur).
superpower ['sju:pəˌpauə*] n. Superpuissance *f.*
supersaturate [ˌsju:pə'sætjureit] v. tr. Sursaturer.
supersaturation ['sju:pəˌsætju'reiʃən] n. Sursaturation *f.*
superscribe [-'skraib] v. tr. Apposer une suscription (or) une indication sur (a parcel). ‖ Mettre l'adresse sur (a letter).
superscription [-'skripʃən] n. Inscription *f.* ‖ En-tête *m.* (on document); suscription *f.* (on letter).
supersede [-'si:d] v. tr. Remplacer (*by,* par). ‖ Supplanter, évincer, détrôner, prendre la place de (s.o.).

supersedeas [-'si:diəs] n. JUR. Suspension *f*.
supersensible [-'sensibl̩] adj. Suprasensible.
supersensitive [-'sensitiv] adj. Hypersensible.
supersonic [-'sounik] adj. Supersonique.
supersports [-'spɔːts] adj. AUTOM. Grand sport (car).
superstition [-'stiʃən] n. Superstition *f*.
superstitious [-stiʃəs] adj. Superstitieux.
superstitiously [-stiʃəsli] adv. Superstitieusement.
superstratum [-'strɑːtəm] (pl. **superstrata** [strɑːtə]) n. GEOL. Couche supérieure *f*.
superstructure ['sju:pə,strʌktʃə*] n. ARCHIT., NAUT. Superstructure *f*. ‖ FIG. Edifice *m*.
supersubtle [-'sʌtl̩] adj. Trop subtil.
supertanker ['sju:pə,tæŋkɔ*] n. NAUT. Supertanker *m*.
supertax ['sju:pətæks] n. U. S. FIN. Surtaxe *f*.
superterrestrial ['sju:pətə'restriəl] adj. Supraterrestre.
supertonic ['sju:pə'tɔnik] adj. MUS. Sus-tonique *f*.
supervene [,sju:pə'vi:n] v. intr. Survenir.
supervise ['sju:pəvaiz] v. tr. Contrôler, superviser ; surveiller. ‖ Diriger.
supervision [,sju:pə'viʒən] n. Contrôle *m. ;* surveillance *f*. ‖ Direction *f*.
supervisor ['sju:pə,vaizɔ*] n. Surveillant *s*. ‖ Directeur (or) patron (*s.*) de thèse (at university).
supinate ['sju:pineit] v. tr. Montrer la paume de (one's hand).
supinator ['sju:pineitə*] n. MED. Supinateur *m*.
supine ['sju:pain] n. GRAMM. Supin *m*.
supine [sju:'pain] adj. Couché sur le dos. ‖ FIG. Indolent, mou.
supinely [-li] adv. Sur le dos. ‖ FIG. Avec indolence, nonchalamment.
supineness [-nis] n. MED. Supination *f*. ‖ FIG. Indolence, mollesse *f*.
supper ['sʌpə*] n. Souper *m*. ‖ ECCLES. Last Supper, Cène ; *the Lord's Supper*, la communion.
supplant [sə'plɑ:nt] v. tr. Supplanter.
supplanter [-ə*] n. Supplanteur *m*.
supple ['sʌpl̩] adj. Souple, flexible ; *to become supple*, s'assouplir. ‖ FIG. Souple, conciliant. ‖ FIG. Servile, obséquieux (pej.).
— v. tr. Assouplir.
— v. intr. S'assouplir.
supplement ['sʌplimənt] n. Supplément.
— [sʌpli'ment] v. tr. Compléter, augmenter.
supplemental [,sʌpli'mentl̩] adj. MATH. Supplémentaire (angle). ‖ MED. Résiduel (air).
supplementary [-təri] adj. Supplémentaire.
suppleness ['sʌplnis] n. Souplesse *f*. (lit. and fig.). ‖ FIG. Servilité, obséquiosité *f*.
suppletory ['sʌplitəri] adj. GRAMM. Supplétif. ‖ JUR. Supplétoire.
suppliant ['sʌpliənt] adj., n. Suppliant *s*.
suppliantly [-li] adv. Avec supplication.
supplicate ['sʌplikeit] v. tr. Supplier (*to*, de) [s.o.]. ‖ Implorer (sth.).
— v. intr. *To supplicate for*, implorer pour obtenir (sth.).
supplicating [-iŋ] adj. Suppliant.
supplicatingly [-iŋli] adv. En suppliant.
supplication ['sʌpli'keiʃən] n. Supplication *f*. (act, prayer). ‖ Supplique *f*. (petition).
supplicatory ['sʌplikətəri] adj. Suppliant, de supplication.
supplier [sə'plaiə*] n. Fournisseur, pourvoyeur *s*.
supply [sə'plai] v. tr. (2). Fournir (goods). ‖ Approvisionner (*with*, en) [s.o.]. ‖ TECHN. Alimenter (a machine). ‖ MILIT. Ravitailler, amunitionner. ‖ FIG. Suppléer à (a deficiency) ; réparer, compenser (a loss) ; répondre à, subvenir à (a need) ; fournir (proofs) ; occuper par intérim (s.o.'s place).
— v. intr. *To supply for*, remplacer, suppléer, assurer l'intérim de (s.o.).

— n. Approvisionnement *m*. (act) ; *to bring supplies to*, ravitailler en vivres. ‖ Provision *f*. (reserve). ‖ Suppléance *f*. (post). ‖ MILIT. Fournitures *f. pl*. ‖ COMM. *Supply and demand*, l'offre et la demande ; *supply department*, intendance. ‖ FIN. Pl. Crédits budgétaires *m. pl*. ‖ FAM. Pl. Vivres *m. pl*. ; pension *f*. (of a young man).
— adj. D'alimentation (pipe, channel) ; remplaçant, suppléant (teacher). ‖ MILIT. D'approvisionnement, de ravitaillement.
support [sə'pɔ:t] v. tr. Supporter, soutenir, maintenir (sth., a weight). ‖ Soutenir, entretenir, faire vivre, subvenir aux besoins de (one's family) ; *to support oneself*, gagner sa vie, se suffire. ‖ FIG. Soutenir, étayer (a charge, theory) ; soutenir, appuyer (a candidate, motion, statement) ; supporter, endurer (fatigue, ordeal) ; soutenir (reputation) ; soutenir, défendre (s.o.) ; soutenir, remonter (s.o.'s courage) ; corroborer (suspicions).
— n. Support, appui *m*. (act, thing) ; *to give support to*, soutenir, appuyer. ‖ FIG. Soutien *m*. (of one's family) ; appui *m*. (of s.o.) ; *collection in support of*, quête en faveur de.
supportable [-əbl̩] adj. Soutenable (theory) ; supportable (trial).
supportably [-əbli] adv. Tolérablement.
supporter [-ə*] n. Support, appui *m*. (thing). ‖ Partisan, défenseur *m*. (person). ‖ SPORTS. Supporter *m*. ‖ BLAS. Tenant *m*.
supportless [-lis] adj. Sans soutien.
supposable [sə'pouzəbl̩] adj. Supposable.
suppose [sə'pouz] v. tr. Supposer (in general). ‖ Supposer, imaginer, présumer (to think). ‖ Présupposer, laisser supposer, faire croire à (to presuppose). ‖ Présumer ; *he is not supposed to know it*, il est censé l'ignorer ; *to be supposed to be haunted*, passer pour hanté ; U. S. *I am supposed to have a new car*, je dois avoir une nouvelle voiture.
— adv. Si, en supposant que, supposez que ; *suppose he writes to me first*, s'il m'écrit le premier.
supposed [-d] adj. Présumé, censé, supposé. ‖ Prétendu, soi-disant.
supposedly [-idli] adv. Probablement ; soi-disant.
supposition [,sʌpə'ziʃən] n. Supposition *f. ; on the supposition that*, à supposer que, dans l'hypothèse où.
suppositional [-l̩] adj. Hypothétique.
supposititious [sə,pozi'tiʃəs] adj. Hypothétique. ‖ JUR. Supposé.
suppository [sə'pozitəri] n. MED. Suppositoire *m*.
suppress [sə'pres] v. tr. Supprimer (in general). ‖ Etouffer (cough, sob) ; réprimer (laugh). ‖ Dissimuler (a fact) ; taire, ne pas révéler (a name). ‖ Interdire (a publication). ‖ Caviarder (to bluepencil). ‖ Dominer (one's feelings, passions) ; étouffer (news, scandal) ; réprimer (revolt).
suppressible [-ibl̩] adj. Supprimable. ‖ Maîtrisable ; dissimulable.
suppression [sə'preʃən] n. Suppression *f*. ‖ Répression *f*. (of anger, revolt) ; refoulement *m.,* domination *f*. (of emotions) ‖ Dissimulation *f*. (of facts, truth).
suppressive [sə'presiv] adj. Répressif.
suppressor [-ə*] n. Personne (*f.*) qui supprime (or) réprime. ‖ Dissimulateur *m*. ‖ TECHN. *Noise suppressor*, silencieux. ‖ RADIO. Antiparasite *m*.
suppurate ['sʌpjuəreit] v. intr. MED. Suppurer.
suppuration [,sʌpjuə'reiʃən] n. MED. Suppuration *f*.
suppurative ['sʌpjuərətiv] adj. MED. Suppuratif.
supracostal ['sju:prə'kɔstəl] adj. MED. Surcostal.
suprahepatic [,sju:prəhe'pætik] adj. MED. Sushépatique.
supramundane [,sju:prə'mʌndein] adj. Supramondain.
supranational [-'næʃnəl] adj. Supranational.
suprarenal [-'ri:nəl] adj. MED. Surrénal.

suprasensible [-'sensibl] adj. Suprasensible.
supremacy [sju'preməsi] n. Suprématie *f.*
supreme [sju'pri:m] adj. Suprême, souverain (dominant). ‖ Suprême, ultime (final).
supremely [-li] adv. Suprêmement.
supremo [sju'pri:mou] n. FAM. Grand chef (or) manitou *m.*
sura ['suərə] n. Surate *f.*
surah ['sjuərə] n. Surah *m.* (material).
surbase [sə:'beis] v. tr. ARCHIT. Surbaisser.
surcharge ['sə:tʃɑ:dʒ] n. Surcharge *f.* (load), ‖ Surtaxe *f.* (on a letter); surcharge *f.* (on a postage-stamp). ‖ FIN. Majoration *f.*
— [sə:'tʃɑ:dʒ] v. tr. Surcharger. ‖ Taxer (a letter); surcharger (a stamp). ‖ FIN. Surimposer.
surcingle [sə:'siŋgl] n. Sous-ventrière *f.* (harness). ‖ ECCLES. Ceinture *f.* (of a cassock).
surcoat ['sə:kout] n. † Surcot *m.*
surd [sə:d] adj. MATH. Irrationnel. ‖ GRAMM. Sourd. (See VOICELESS.)
— n. MATH. Quantité irrationnelle *f.* ‖ GRAMM. Consonne sourde *f.*
sure [ʃuə*] adj. Sûr, certain, assuré, convaincu (person); *to make sure of*, s'assurer de. ‖ Sûr, certain, infaillible (action); sûr, certain, indubitable (fact); *it is by no means sure that*, il n'est pas dit que. ‖ Sûr, de confiance (friend); sûr, sans danger (road). ‖ FAM. *Be sure to come*, venez sans faute; *don't be too sure*, il ne faut jurer de rien.
— adv. Sûrement, bien sûr, assurément; *as sure as*, aussi vrai que; *sure enough*, bien sûr, pour sûr, effectivement.
surely [-li] adv. Sûrement, à coup sûr. ‖ Sûrement, certainement. ‖ FAM. Sans doute, je suppose; *surely you don't believe that*, vous ne croyez pas cela, je pense.
sureness [-nis] n. Sûreté *f.* (of hand). ‖ Certitude *f.*
surety [-ti] n. Certitude *f.* ‖ JUR. Caution *f.*; garant *s.*; *to stand surety for*, se porter caution pour (or) garant de. ‖ **Surety-bond**, n. Cautionnement *m.*
suretyship [-tiʃip] n. Cautionnement *m.*
surf [sə:f] n. Ressac *m.*, brisants *m. pl.* (waves); écume *f.* (foam). ‖ **Surf-board**, n. SPORTS. Planche (*f.*) à surf. ‖ **Surf-riding**, n. SPORTS. Surf *m.*
— v. intr. Faire du (or) pratiquer le surf.
surface ['sə:fəs] n. Surface *f.* ‖ FIG. Extérieur *m.*; apparence, surface *f.*; *on the surface*, en surface, superficiellement.
— adj. De surface (water). ‖ NAUT. *Surface raider*, corsaire de surface. ‖ PHYS. Superficiel (tension). ‖ TECHN. A ciel ouvert (work). ‖ U. S. Par terre, par eau (mail).
— v. tr. TECHN. Polir la surface de; dégauchir (wood); revêtir (*with*, de) [a road].
— v. intr. NAUT. Faire surface.
surfeit ['sə:fit] n. Satiété, indigestion *f.*; *to have a surfeit of*, être rassasié de. ‖ FIG. Dégoût *m.*
— v. tr. Gorger, rassasier, repaître (*with*, de). ‖ FIG. Dégoûter, écœurer (*with*, de).
— v. intr. Se gorger, s'empiffrer. ‖ FIG. Etre dégoûté (or) écœuré (*with*, de).
surfy ['sə:fi] adj. Ecumant; battu de brisants.
surge [sə:dʒ] v. intr. Etre houleux (sea); bondir, s'enfler (waves). ‖ NAUT. Choquer (cable); monter sur les vagues (ship). ‖ TECHN. Galoper (engine). FIG. Monter, bouillonner (anger); se répandre, déborder (crowd).
— v. tr. Filer (a cable).
— n. Houle *f.* ‖ FIG. Houle, vague *f.*; bouillonnement *m.*
surgeon ['sə:dʒən] n. MED. Chirurgien *m.* ‖ MILIT. Médecin-major *m.*
surgery [-ri] n. MED. Chirurgie *f.* ‖ Cabinet *m.* (consulting-room). ‖ Dispensaire *m.*; clinique *f.* (dispensary). ‖ **Surgery-hours**, n. pl. Heures (*f. pl.*) de consultation.

surgical [-ikəl] adj. MED. Chirurgical, de chirurgie (instruments). ‖ Orthopédique (appliances, boots).
surgically [-ikəli] adv. MED. Chirurgicalement.
Surinam [,suəri'næm] n. GEOGR. Surinam *m.*
surliness ['sə:linis] n. Maussaderie *f.*; caractère revêche *m.*
surly ['sə:li] adj. Revêche, hargneux. ‖ Bourru, maussade.
surmise [sə:'maiz] n. Conjecture, supposition *f.*
— v. tr., intr. Conjecturer (*from*, de); supposer.
surmount [sə:'maunt] v. tr. Surmonter. ‖ FIG. Vaincre, surmonter.
surmountable [-əbl] adj. Surmontable.
surmullet [sə:'mʌlit] n. ZOOL. Rouget *m.*
surname ['sə:neim] n. Nom (*m.*) de famille. ‖ † Surnom *m.* (nickname).
— v. tr. Nommer, dénommer. ‖ Surnommer.
surpass [sə:'pɑ:s] v. tr. Surpasser (*in*, en); l'emporter sur (s.o.); *to surpass oneself*, se surpasser. ‖ Dépasser (s.o.'s hopes).
surpassing [-iŋ] adj. Eminent, nonpareil, incomparable, sans égal.
surpassingly [-iŋli] adv. Extrêmement, extraordinairement.
surplice ['sə:plis] n. ECCLES. Surplis *m.*
surpliced [-t] adj. ECCLES. En surplis.
surplus ['sə:pləs] n. Surplus, excédent, surnombre *m.* ‖ U. S. Boni *m.*
— adj. En surplus; *surplus copies*, exemplaires de passe. ‖ COMM. *Surplus stock*, stock soldé. ‖ FIN. *Surplus dividend*, superdividende; *surplus value*, valeur excédentaire.
surplusage [-idʒ] n. Surplus *m.*; surabondance *f* ‖ JUR. Redondance *f.*
surprise [sə'praiz] n. Surprise *f.*; *taken by surprise*, pris au dépourvu (or) à l'improviste. ‖ Surprise *f.*; étonnement *m.*; *much to my surprise*, à mon grand étonnement. ‖ Surprise *f.* (event); *to give s.o. a surprise*, faire une surprise à.
— adj. Inattendu, fait à l'improviste (visit). ‖ MILIT. Brusqué (attack). ‖ **Surprise-party**, n. Surprise-partie *f.*
— v. tr. Surprendre, prendre par surprise; *to surprise in the act*, prendre sur le fait; *to surprise s.o. into doing*, obliger qqn par surprise à faire. ‖ Surprendre, étonner; *to be surprised at*, être surpris de, s'étonner de. ‖ FIG. Surprendre (a secret).
surprisedly [-idli] adv. Avec surprise.
surprising [-iŋ] adj. Surprenant, étonnant.
surprisingly [-iŋli] adv. Etonnamment.
surrealism [sə:'ri:əlizm] n. ARTS. Surréalisme *m.*
surrealist [-ist] n. ARTS. Surréaliste *s.*
surrealistic [sə,ri:əl'istik] adj. ARTS. Surréaliste.
surrender [sə'rendə*] v. tr. MILIT. Livrer, rendre; *to surrender oneself*, se rendre. ‖ JUR. Abandonner, céder, renoncer à, se désister de (*to*, en faveur de) [property, rights]. ‖ COMM. Livrer au prix officiel. ‖ FIG. Abandonner (*to*, à).
— v. intr. MILIT. Se rendre. ‖ JUR. Se constituer prisonnier.
— n. MILIT. Remise *f.* (of prisoners); reddition *f.* (of soldiers, town). ‖ JUR. Abandon *m.*; renonciation, cession *f.* (of, de).
surreptitious [,sʌ.əp'tiʃəs] adj. Subreptice.
surreptitiously [-li] adv. Subrepticement.
surrogate ['sʌrəgit] n. Succédané *m.* (thing); remplaçant *s.* (person). ‖ PSYCH. Substitut *m.*
surround [sə'raund] v. tr. Entourer. ‖ MILIT. Cerner.
surroundings [-iŋs] n. pl. Entourage, milieu, cadre *m.* (of a person). ‖ Environs, alentours *m. pl.* (of a place).
surtax ['sə:tæks] n. FIN. Surtaxe *f.*
— v. tr. FIN. Surtaxer.

surveillance [sə:'veiljəns] n. JUR., MED. Surveillance *f*.

survey [sə:'vei] v. tr. Arpenter (a field); cadastrer (a parish); faire le relevé de, lever le plan de (a town). ‖ Inspecter, surveiller (public works). ‖ Contempler, embrasser du regard (the landscape). ‖ FIG. Examiner, étudier (a question).
— ['sə:vei] n. Arpentage; relevé, levé de plan *m*. ‖ Inspection, surveillance *f*. ‖ AVIAT. *Aerial survey*, levé aérophotogrammétrique. ‖ MILIT. *Survey company*, section topographique. ‖ FIG. Aperçu *m*. (of a subject); tour d'horizon *m*. ‖ FIG. Examen *m*.; étude, enquête *f*.

surveying [sə:'veiŋ] n. Arpentage *m*.; topographie *f*. ‖ Inspection, surveillance *f*. ‖ NAUT. *Naval surveying*, hydrographie.
— adj. Topographique (instruments); hydrographique (ship); *surveying wheel*, compte-pas.

surveyor [-ə*] n. Arpenteur; ingénieur topographe *m*.; *highway* (or) *road surveyor*, ingénieur du service vicinal, agent voyer. ‖ Inspecteur *m*.; *surveyor of taxes*, contrôleur des contributions directes.

survival [sə'vaivəl] n. Survivance *f*. (act, thing); *survival of the fittest*, sélection naturelle.

survive [sə'vaiv] v. tr. Survivre à (person); résister à (thing).
— v. intr. Survivre (person). ‖ Subsister (thing); *only three houses survive*, il ne reste que trois maisons.

survivor [-ə*] n. Survivant *s*.

sus [sʌs] n. POP. Suspect *s*.; soupçon *m*.
— v. tr. POP. **To sus out,** jauger (a person); se faire une idée de (a situation); *to sus it*, renifler (or) flairer qqch. de louche.

Susan ['su:zn] n. Suzanne *f*.

susceptibility [sə,septi'biliti] n. Susceptibilité *f*. ‖ Sensibilité *f*. (*to*, à). ‖ MED. Prédisposition *f*. (*to*, à).

susceptible [sə'septibl] adj. Susceptible, facilement froissé. ‖ Susceptible (*of*, de). ‖ Sensible (*to*, à). ‖ MED. Prédisposé (*to*, à).

suspect [sə*'pekt] v. tr. Soupçonner, se douter de; flairer (fam.) [to surmise]. ‖ Soupçonner, suspecter (*of*, de) [s.o.]. ‖ Soupçonner, se méfier de, douter de (to distrust).
— v. intr. Soupçonner; *I suspected as much*, je m'en doutais.
— ['sʌspekt] adj., n. Suspect *s*.

suspend [sə*'pend] v. tr. Suspendre (sth.). ‖ Suspendre, interrompre (an activity, payment, traffic). ‖ Suspendre, surseoir à (judgment, proceedings, sentence); suspendre (an official). ‖ Loc. *In a state of suspended animation*, en syncope (lit.); en veilleuse (fig.).

suspender [-ə*] n. Suspensoir *m*. ‖ Pl. Fixe-chaussettes *m*. (for men); jarretelles *f*. *pl*. (for women). ‖ Pl. U. S. Bretelles *f*. *pl*. ‖ **Suspender-belt,** n. Porte-jarretière *m*.

suspense [sə*'pens] n. Incertitude *f*.; *to keep in suspense*, tenir en haleine. ‖ JUR. Surséance *f*. ‖ CINEM. Suspense *m*.

suspension [-ʃən] n. Suspension *f*. (action, state). ‖ FIN., COMM., MILIT., CHIM., JUR. Suspension *f*. ‖ ECCLES. Suspense *f*. ‖ GRAMM. *Points of suspension*, U. S. *suspension points*, points de suspension. ‖ **Suspension-bridge,** n. Pont suspendu *m*. ‖ **Suspension-scales,** n. Romaine *f*.

suspensive [-siv] adj. JUR. Suspensif.

suspensory [-səri] adj. MED. Suspenseur. ‖ JUR. Suspensif.
— n. Suspensoir *m*.

suspicion [sə*'piʃən] n. Soupçon *m*.; suspicion *f*. ‖ FAM. Soupçon *m*.; ombre, trace *f*.
— v. tr. U. S. FAM. Soupçonner.

suspicious [-ʃəs] adj. Soupçonneux, défiant (suspecting). ‖ Suspect, louche (suspect).

suspiciously [-əsli] adv. Soupçonneusement. ‖ De façon suspecte.

suspiciousness [-əsnis] n. Méfiance, suspicion *f*.; caractère soupçonneux *m*. ‖ Caractère suspect *m*.

suss [sʌs] n., v. tr. See SUS.

sustain [sə*'tain] v. tr. Soutenir, supporter (a load). ‖ Soutenir (the body); entretenir (life); faire vivre, sustenter (s.o.). ‖ Soutenir, appuyer, étayer (a theory). ‖ Soutenir (a comparison, an effort, a reputation, s.o.'s courage). ‖ Subir, éprouver, essuyer (losses). ‖ MILIT. Soutenir (an attack, a siege). ‖ THEATR. Tenir (a part). ‖ MUS. Soutenir (a note). ‖ JUR. Recevoir, admettre (an objection); faire droit à (s.o.).

sustainable [-əbl] adj. Soutenable.

sustaining [-iŋ] adj. MED. Fortifiant. ‖ ARCHIT. De soutènement. ‖ TECHN. Portant (force).
— n. ARCHIT. Soutènement *m*.

sustenance ['sʌstinəns] n. Subsistance *f*.; *means of sustenance*, moyens de subsistance, possibilités de vie. ‖ Aliments *m*. *pl*.; nourriture *f*. (food). ‖ Valeur nutritive *f*. (in food); *there is more sustenance in meat*, la viande est plus nourrissante.

susurrate [sju*'sʌreit] v. intr. Susurrer.

sutler ['sʌtlə*] n. MILIT. Cantinier *s*.; vivandière *f*.

suttee [sʌ'ti:] n. Sâti *m*. (practice); sâti *f*. (widow).

sutural ['sju:tʃərəl] adj. MED. Sutural, de suture.

suture [-tʃə*] n. MED. Suture *f*.
— v. tr. MED. Suturer.

suzerain ['su:zərein] n. Suzerain *m*.

suzerainty [-ti] n. Suzeraineté *f*.

s. v. Written abbr. for *sub verbo*, à l'entrée (or) au mot; *see s. v. «dog»*, voir au mot «chien».

svelte [svelt] adj. Svelte, élancé.

swab [swɔb] v. tr. (1). NAUT. Fauberter. ‖ MED., MILIT. Ecouvillonner.
— n. NAUT. Faubert *m*. ‖ MILIT., MED. Ecouvillon *m*.

Swabian ['sweibiən] adj., n. GEOGR. Souabe *s*.

swaddle ['swɔdl] v. tr. Emmailloter.

swaddling [-iŋ] n. Emmaillotement *m*. ‖ **Swaddling-clothes,** n. Maillot *m*.; langes *f*. *pl*.; FAM. Enfance *f*.

swag [swæg] n. Balancement *m*. ‖ POP. Rafle *f*.; butin *m*. (plunder). ‖ U. S. Ballot *m*. (bundle).
— v. tr. (1). Balancer.

swage [sweidʒ] n. TECHN. Emboutissoir *m*.
— v. tr. Emboutir.

swagger ['swægə*] v. intr. Se carrer, se pavaner, faire l'avantageux; plastronner, crâner (fam.). ‖ Fanfaronner; se vanter (*about*, de).
— v. tr. Intimider par des rodomontades.
— n. Air avantageux (or) conquérant *m*. ‖ Allure cavalière (or) dégagée *f*. ‖ Fanfaronnade, rodomontade *f*. (See BOAST.)
— adj. Chic. ‖ **Swagger-cane** (or) **-stick,** n. MILIT. Jonc, stick *m*. ‖ **Swagger-coat,** n. COMM. Manteau trois quarts *m*.

swaggerer [-rə*] n. Crâneur, flambard *m*. ‖ Matamore, fanfaron *m*.

swain [swein] n. † Berger *m*. ‖ FAM. Soupirant *m*.

swallow ['swɔlou] v. tr. Avaler (drink, food). ‖ FIG. Rétracter (words). ‖ FAM. Avaler, encaisser (an insult); avaler, gober (a story); *to swallow it*, monter à l'échelle.
— v. intr. MED. Avaler, déglutir.
— n. Déglutition *f*. (act); gosier *m*. (throat). ‖ Gorgée *f*. (of drink); bouchée *f*. (of food). ‖ TECHN. Gorge de poulie *f*.

swallow n. ZOOL. Hirondelle *f*. ‖ **Swallow-dive,** n. SPORTS. Saut de l'ange *m*. ‖ **Swallow-tail,** n. TECHN. Queue-d'aronde *f*.; FAM. Queue-de-pie *f*. (coat).

swam [swæm] pret. See SWIM.

swami ['swɑ:mi] n. Swami *s*. (Hindu teacher).

swamp [swɔmp] n. Marécage m.
— v. tr. Embourber (in marsh, mud). ‖ Inonder, submerger (by water). ‖ Fig. Submerger, noyer, engloutir, couler (to ruin). ‖ Fam. Submerger, déborder (with work).
swampy [-i] adj. Marécageux.
swan [swɔn] n. Zool., Fig. Cygne m. ‖ Fam. Black swan, oiseau rare. ‖ **Swan-dive**, n. U. S. Sports. Saut de l'ange m. ‖ **Swan-neck**, n. Col de cygne m. ‖ **Swan's-down**, n. Comm. Cygne m. (for powder puff); molleton m. (fabric). ‖ **Swan-skin**, n. U. S. Flanelle de laine f. ‖ **Swan-song**, n. Chant du cygne m. (lit. and fig.).
swank [swæŋk] n. Pose, épate f.; bluff m. ‖ Poseur m. (person).
— v. intr. Crâner, poser, faire de l'esbroufe (or) le fier. (See SWAGGER.)
swanker [-ə*] n. Flambard, crâneur, poseur, bluffeur s.
swanky [-i] adj. Snob, poseur.
swannery ['swɔnəri] n. Elevage (m.) de cygnes (place).
swap [swɔp] v. tr., intr. Fam. Troquer.
sward [swɔ:d] n. Gazon m.
— v. tr. Gazonner.
swarf [swɑ:f] n. Limaille f.
swarm [swɔ:m] n. Zool. Essaim m. ‖ Fig. .Nuée, foule f.; essaim, vol, pullulement m.
— v. intr. Zool. Essaimer. ‖ Fig. S'attrouper, accourir en foule. ‖ Fig. Pulluler, fourmiller, grouiller (with, de).
— v. tr. Fig. Envahir, inonder.
swarm v. tr. Escalader, grimper à.
swarthiness ['swɔ:ðinis] n. Teint basané m.
swarthy [-i] adj. Basané, bistré, bronzé.
swash [swɔʃ] n. Clapoter, clapotement m.
— v. intr. Clapoter (water).
— v. tr. Clapoter contre (the rocks). ‖ Faire gicler (or) jaillir (water).
swashbuckler ['swɔʃ,bʌklə*] n. Matamore, bretteur, ferrailleur m.
swashbuckling [-iŋ] n. Rodomontade f. ‖ Panache (m.) des bretteurs.
swastika ['swɔstikə] n. Svastika m.; croix gammée f.
swat [swɔt] v. tr. (1). Ecraser (an insect). ‖ Fam. Cogner, taper sur (a person).
swath [swɔ:θ] n. Agric. Andain m. ‖ Fam. U. S. To cut a swath, faire de l'épate.
swathe [sweið] v. tr. Emmailloter.
— n. Bandelette f.; bandage m.
swatter ['swɔtə*] n. Tapette (f.) pour tuer les insectes.
sway [swei] v. intr. Incliner, pencher; s'incliner, se pencher (to lean). ‖ Osciller, se balancer, se dodeliner (to swing). ‖ Fig. Hésiter, balancer, osciller, vaciller.
— v. tr. Faire pencher, incliner (to cause to lean). ‖ Faire osciller, balancer (to cause to swing). ‖ Brandir (a cudgel, a sword); tenir (a sceptre). ‖ Fig. Gouverner, diriger (to dominate). ‖ Influencer (s.o.); influer sur (sth.); to sway s.o. from, détourner qqn de. ‖ To sway up, Naut. Hisser.
— n. Balancement m.; oscillation f. ‖ Fig. Domination f.; empire m. (over, sur).
swaying [-iŋ] adj. Oscillant; swaying gait, dandinement.
Swaziland ['swɑ:zi,lænd] n. Geogr. Swaziland m.
swear [swɛə*] v. tr. (168). Jurer (sth.); to swear an oath, faire un serment. ‖ Jurer, faire serment, promettre (to, de). ‖ Déclarer sous la foi du serment (sth.). ‖ To swear away, faire perdre par faux témoignage; to swear away s.o.'s life, faire condamner qqn à mort sur faux serment. ‖ To swear in, assermenter; faire prêter serment à (s.o., a witness); to be sworn in, prêter serment; to swear s.o. to

secrecy, faire jurer le secret à qqn. ‖ To swear off, jurer de s'abstenir de.
— v. intr. Jurer, prêter serment (on, sur). ‖ Jurer, sacrer, dire des jurons (to curse). ‖ Fam. Jurer, affirmer. ‖ To swear at, injurier. ‖ To swear by, jurer par; Fam. Vanter, jurer par, monter en épingle. ‖ To swear off, jurer de renoncer à. ‖ To swear to, Jur. Déclarer sous serment (sth.).
— n. Jurons m. pl. ‖ **Swear-word**, n. Fam. Juron, gros mot m.
swearer [-rə*] n. Personne (f.) qui prête serment. ‖ Jureur m.
sweat [swet] n. Sueur, transpiration f. (liquid); sudation, suée f. (state); to be in a sweat, être en eau (or) en nage. ‖ Transpiration f.; suintement m. (on a wall). ‖ Fig. Sueur f. ‖ Fam. Suée, corvée f. (hard work). ‖ **Sweat-cloth**, n. Tapis (m.) de selle. ‖ **Sweat-duct**, n. Med. Canal sudorifère m. ‖ **Sweat-gland**, n. Med. Glande sudoripare f. ‖ **Sweat-shirt**, n. Chemisier-tricot m. ‖ **Sweat-shop**, n. Fam. Atelier de pressurage (m.) où les ouvriers sont exploités.
— v. intr. (169). Suer, transpirer (animal, person). ‖ Suer, suinter, exsuder (wall). ‖ Fam. Avoir des sueurs froides (person); trimer, turbiner, suer sang et eau (worker).
— v. tr Suer (blood); faire suer (s.o.). ‖ Suer, laisser suinter (water). ‖ Bouchonner (a horse by rubbing). ‖ Techn. Faire ressuer. ‖ Med. Faire transpirer. ‖ Fam. Exploiter, pressurer (workers). ‖ To sweat in (or) on, Techn. Souder. ‖ To sweat out, Med. Guérir par sudation; Fam. To sweat it out, en baver, traverser une sale période.
sweater [-ə*] n. Comm. Sweater, pull-over m. ‖ Med. Sudorifique m. ‖ Fam. Exploiteur m.
sweatiness [-inis] n. Moiteur f.
sweating [-iŋ] n. Sudation, suée f. (of a person). ‖ Suintement m. (of a wall). ‖ Fam. Exploitation f. ‖ **Sweating-bath**, n. Bain (m.) de vapeur. ‖ **Sweating-room**, n. Etuve f. ‖ **Sweating-system**, n. Exploitation (f.) des ouvriers.
sweaty [-i] adj. En sueur (body); moite (hand). ‖ Plein de sueur (clothes); de sueur (odour). ‖ Fig. Epuisant (work).
Swede [swi:d] n. Geogr. Suédois s. ‖ Bot. Rutabaga m.
Sweden [-n] n. Geogr. Suède f.
Swedish [-iʃ] adj., n. Suédois m.
sweep [swi:p] v. intr. (170). Balayer (broom). ‖ S'étendre, s'étaler (plain). ‖ Se mouvoir rapidement (or) majestueusement (person). ‖ Naut. To sweep for mines, draguer des mines. ‖ To sweep across, traverser, balayer. ‖ To sweep along, avancer vivement; suivre rapidement (the road). ‖ To sweep around, décrire une courbe autour; Naut. Virer. ‖ To sweep by, passer vite (or) noblement. ‖ To sweep down, s'abattre, fondre (on, sur); descendre, dévaler (to, vers). ‖ To sweep in, entrer vivement (or) majestueusement. ‖ To sweep up, arriver (or) monter vivement (or) majestueusement.
— v. tr. Balayer (the dust, ground, room). ‖ Ramoner (the chimney). ‖ Promener (one's eyes); passer (over, sur) (one's hand). ‖ Balayer, parcourir (the horizon). ‖ Balayer, ravager (a country). ‖ Balayer, emporter, entraîner, enlever (out of, hors de) [s.o., sth.]. ‖ Balayer, écarter (from, de). ‖ To sweep along, entraîner, emporter; Fig. Entraîner, transporter, enthousiasmer; emballer (fam.). ‖ To sweep away, balayer; Fig. Balayer; liquider (fam.). ‖ To sweep down, entraîner, emporter. ‖ To sweep off, emporter, faire disparaître; rafler (fam.). ‖ To sweep out, donner un coup de balai à. ‖ To sweep up, entasser en balayant (the dust).
— n. Courbe, boucle f. (of a river, road). ‖ Geste circulaire m. (of the arm). ‖ Etendue f. (of plain). ‖ Balayage; coup de balai m. (sweeping). ‖ Ramo-

neur *m.* (chimney-sweep). ‖ ARCHIT. Courbure *f.* ‖ NAUT. Drague *f.* (for mines); aviron (*m.*) de galère (or) de queue (oar). ‖ MILIT. Portée *f.* (of a gun); *offensive sweep*, randonnée, offensive. ‖ FIG. Portée *f.* (of an argument). ‖ FIG. Coup de balai *m.; to make a clean sweep of*, se débarrasser de, faire table rase de. ‖ FAM. Coup de filet *m.; to make a clean sweep of*, rafler; *within the sweep of the net*, dans le cercle du filet. ‖ **Sweep-back**, n. AVIAT. Flèche (*f.*) à l'arrière. ‖ **Sweep-net**, n. Epervier *m.;* seine *f.*

sweeper [-ə*] n. Balayeur *m.* (person). ‖ Ramoneur *m.* (chimney-sweep). ‖ Balai mécanique *m.* (machine).

sweeping [-iŋ] adj. Qui balaie, balayant (movement). ‖ Vigoureux (blow); circulaire (glance); large (gesture). ‖ ARTS. Elancé (line). ‖ COMM. Imbattable, incroyable (reduction). ‖ FIG. Catégorique, absolu, radical. ‖ **Sweeping-machine**, n. Balayeuse *f.*
— n. Balayage *m.* (act). ‖ Pl. Balayures *f. pl.* (result). ‖ Ramonage *m.* ‖ FIG. Pl. Rebut *m.;* lie *f.* (of society).

sweepingly [-iŋli] adv. Catégoriquement.

sweepstake [-steik] n. SPORTS. Sweepstake *m.*

sweet [swi:t] adj. Doux, harmonieux, mélodieux, suave (to the ear); agréable, délicieux, reposant (to the sight); embaumé, doucement parfumé, pur (to the smell); doux, sucré (to the taste); *to smell sweet*, sentir bon. ‖ TECHN. Doux, uni, sans à-coup. ‖ CULIN. Frais (fish); doux, potable (water); doux, sucré (wine); U. S. *sweet corn*, maïs doux; *sweet course*, plats sucrés; *to have a sweet tooth*, aimer les douceurs (or) sucreries (or) friandises. ‖ FIG. Doux, aimable, gracieux, charmant, gentil; *to say sweet nothings to*, dire des douceurs (or) fadaises à. ‖ **Sweet-briar**, n. BOT. Eglantier *m.* ‖ **Sweet pea**, n. BOT. Pois (*m.*) de senteur. ‖ **Sweet-potato**, n. BOT. Patate douce *f.* ‖ **Sweet-shop**, n. COMM. Confiserie *f.* ‖ **Sweet-smelling**, adj. Parfumé. ‖ **Sweet-talker**, n. Endormeur, beau parleur *m.*
— n. Sucreries *f. pl.;* sucreries *f. pl.;* plats sucrés *m. pl.* ‖ Pl. Doux parfum *m.* ‖ Pl. Charmes *m. pl.;* délices *f. pl.* ‖ FIG. Pl. Plaisirs, agréments *m. pl.;* douceur *f.* (of life). ‖ FAM. Chéri *s.*

sweetbread [-b. ed] n. CULIN. Ris (*m.*) de veau.

sweeten [-n] v. tr. Sucrer (a liquid). ‖ Purifier (air, water). ‖ FIG. Adoucir.
— v. intr. S'adoucir.

sweetener [-nə*] n. Edulcorant *m.* ‖ FIG. Adoucissement *m.*

sweetening [-niŋ] n. Sucrage *m.;* édulcoration *f.* ‖ FIG. Adoucissement *m.*

sweetheart [-hɑ:t] n. Amoureux *s.*

sweetie [-i] n. FAM. Bonbon *m.* ‖ FAM. Amoureux *s.* ‖ **Sweetie-pie**, n. FAM. Chou, chéri *m.*

sweeting [-iŋ] n. BOT. Pomme douce *f.* ‖ † Chérie *f.*

sweetish [-iʃ] adj. Douceâtre, plutôt sucré.

sweetly [-li] adv. Doucement. ‖ Harmonieusement. ‖ Gentiment, agréablement.

sweetmeat [-mi:t] n. Bonbon *m.* ‖ Pl. Sucreries, friandises, douceurs *f. pl.*

sweetness [-nis] n. Douceur *f.*

swell [swell] v. intr. (171). Enfler, gonfler; s'enfler, se gonfler (*with*, de). ‖ Se renfler, onduler (ground). ‖ MED. Enfler, se tuméfier. ‖ NAUT. Se soulever (sea). ‖ CULIN. Lever (dough). ‖ FIG. S'enfler (murmur); augmenter; grossir (number). ‖ FIN. Grossir. ‖ FAM. Se gonfler, bouffir (person) [with pride]. ‖ **To swell out**, bomber.
— v. tr. Enfler, gonfler.
— n. Gonflement *m.* ‖ Ondulation *f.* (of ground). ‖ MED. Enflure *f.* ‖ NAUT. Houle *f.* ‖ MUS. Crescendo; son amplifié *m.* (sound); soufflet *m.* (of organ). ‖ FAM. Rupin *m.; the swells*, les gens huppés, le gratin.

— adj. FAM. Chic, épatant, huppé. ‖ **Swell-head**, n. U. S. Enflé *m.*

swelling [-iŋ] n. Gonflement *m.* ‖ Crue *f.* (of a river). ‖ MED. Enflure *f.* ‖ NAUT. Soulèvement *m.* (of waves). ‖ AUTOM. Hernie *f.* (on tyre).

swelter ['sweltə*] v. intr. Etre étouffant (air). ‖ Etouffer; être en nage (person).
— n. Chaleur étouffante *f.* ‖ Suée *f.* (sweat).

swept [swept] pret., p. p. See SWEEP. ‖ **Sweptback**, adj. AVIAT. En flèche, fuyant (wing).

swerve [swə:v] v. intr. Faire un écart (horse). ‖ Dévier (*from*, de) [person]. ‖ AUTOM. Faire une embardée. ‖ SPORTS. Crocheter (footballer).
— v. tr. Faire dévier. ‖ AUTOM. Faire faire une embardée à.
— n. Ecart *m.* ‖ Déviation *f.*

swift [swift] adj. Rapide (fast). ‖ Rapide, prompt (undelayed). ‖ Prompt, vif (quick). ‖ **Swift-footed**, adj. Au pied léger. ‖ **Swift-handed**, adj. Habile, aux mains déliées. ‖ **Swift-winged**, adj. Au vol rapide.
— adv. Vite, promptement, rapidement.
— n. ZOOL. Martinet *m.* ‖ TECHN. Dévidoir *m.*

swifter [-ə*] n. NAUT. Ceinture *f.* (of boat); raban *m.* (of capstan bar).

swiftly [-li] adv. Rapidement, vite.

swiftness [-nis] n. Rapidité, promptitude *f.*

swig [swig] v. tr., intr. (1). FAM. Lamper.
— n. FAM. Lampée *f.*

swill [swil] v. tr. Laver à grande eau. ‖ FAM. Lamper, siffler, descendre, entonner.
— v. intr. FAM. Entonner, lamper.
— n. Lavage (*m.*) à grande eau. ‖ Eaux grasses *f. pl.* (kitchen waste). ‖ FAM. Lampée *f.* (draught); ordure *f.* (literature).

swim [swim] v. intr. (172). Flotter, surnager (*on*, sur). ‖ SPORTS, NAUT. Nager; *to swim for it*, se sauver à la nage. ‖ MED., FAM. Tourner (head); se brouiller (vision). ‖ FIG. Nager (*in*, dans); ruisseler, être inondé (*with*, de).
— v. tr. Faire nager (a dog). ‖ SPORTS. Nager, parcourir à la nage (a distance); traverser à la nage (a river); lutter de vitesse à la nage avec (s.o.).
— n. SPORTS. Nage *f.* (action); eaux poissonneuses *f. pl.* (water). ‖ MED., FAM. Etourdissement *m.* ‖ FAM. *To be in the swim*, être dans le train. ‖ **Swimsuit**, n. Costume de bain *m.*

swimmer [-ə*] n. SPORTS. Nageur *s.* ‖ ZOOL. Vessie natatoire *f.*

swimmeret [-ərit] n. ZOOL. Patte natatoire *f.*

swimming [-iŋ] n. SPORTS. Natation, nage *f.* ‖ MED., FAM. Etourdissement *m.* ‖ **Swimming-bath** (or) **-pool**, n. Piscine *f.* ‖ **Swimming-belt**, n. Ceinture de natation *f.* ‖ **Swimming-bladder**, n. ZOOL. Vessie natatoire *f.*
— adj. Ruisselant, noyé de larmes (eyes). ‖ SPORTS. Nageant. ‖ FAM. Qui tourne (head).

swimmingly [-iŋli] adv. FAM. Comme sur des roulettes, à souhait.

swindle ['swindl] v. tr. Escroquer. ‖ FAM. Filouter, empiler.
— n. Escroquerie *f.* ‖ FAM. Filouterie *f.*

swindler [-ə*] n. Escroc, aigrefin *m.* ‖ FAM. Empileur *m.*

swine [swain] n. invar. ZOOL. Porc, cochon, pourceau *m.* ‖ POP. Cochon, salaud *m.* ‖ **Swine-herd**, n. Porcher *m.*

swinery [-əri] n. Porcherie *f.*

swing [swiŋ] v. intr. (173). Se balancer (to sway); *to swing to and fro*, se balancer. ‖ Osciller, ballotter (to oscillate). ‖ Pivoter, tourner (to pivot). ‖ Marcher d'un pas rythmé (to walk); *to swing down the street*, descendre la rue en scandant le pas. ‖ Jouer à la balançoire, se balancer. ‖ NAUT. Eviter (ship). ‖ **To swing for**, FAM. Etre pendu pour. ‖ **To swing on**, pivoter sur, tourner sur. ‖ **To swing round**, faire volte-face (person). AUTOM. Virer; MILIT.

Pivoter. ‖ **To swing to**, se refermer (door) ; Naut. *To swing to the anchor*, rappeler sur son ancre. — v. tr. Balancer (s.o., sth.) ; *to swing one's hips*, se dandiner. ‖ Mettre en branle (the bells) ; faire osciller (a pendulum) ; faire tournoyer, brandir (one's sword). ‖ Suspendre (a hammock, lamp). ‖ Mener à bien (the election). ‖ Milit. Faire pivoter (the troops) ; *to swing the lead*, tirer au flanc, se faire porter pâle. ‖ Naut. Faire éviter. ‖ Aviat. Lancer (the screw). ‖ Autom. Braquer (the wheels) ; *to swing a car right round*, faire faire un tête-à-queue à une voiture. — n. Balancement *m.* (act) ; balançoire *f.* (device). ‖ Oscillation *f.* (of a pendulum). ‖ Pas rythmé *m.* (walk). ‖ Mus. Swing *m.* (jazz) ; rythme *m.* (rhythm). ‖ Sports. Swing *m.* ‖ Fig. Carrière *f. ; in full swing*, en plein épanouissement (or) rendement, battant son plein. ‖ Fam. *To get the swing of*, attraper le coup de main pour. ‖ U. S. Fam. *Swing round the circle*, tournée électorale. ‖ **Swing-back**, n. Fig. Revirement *m.* ‖ **Swing-bridge**, n. Balançoire-bateau *f.* ‖ **Swing-bridge**, n. Pont tournant *m.* ‖ **Swing-cot**, n. Bercelonnette *f.* ‖ **Swing-door**, n. Porte (*f.*) va-et-vient. ‖ **Swing-gate**, n. Tourniquet *m. ;* barrière pivotante *f.* ‖ **Swing-round**, n. Autom. Tête-à-queue *m.* ‖ **Swing shift**, n. U. S. Techn. Equipe (*f.*) de relève mi-jour, mi-nuit. ‖ **Swing-wing**, adj. Aviat. A flèche variable ; n. aile (*f.*) [or] avion (*m.*) à flèche variable.

swingeing ['swindʒiŋ] adj. Violent, à assommer un bœuf (blow). ‖ Fig. Ecrasant (majority, taxation), énorme (damage, lie) ; *swingeing cuts*, coupes sombres.

swinging ['swiŋiŋ] n. Balancement *m.* ‖ Naut. Evitage *m.* — adj. Balançant, oscillant. ‖ Rythmé ; balancé ; au rythme large (verse).

swingingly [-li] adv. Rythmiquement, de façon entraînante.

swingle ['swiŋgl] n. Ecang *m.* — v. tr. Ecanguer.

swingletree [-tri:] n. Palonnier *m.*

swinish ['swainiʃ] adj. De pourceau ; de goinfre. ‖ Sale, immonde.

swinishness [-nis] n. Goinfrerie *f.* ‖ Saleté, grossièreté *f.*

swipe [swaip] v. tr., intr. Sports. Frapper à toute volée. ‖ Fam. Claquer. ‖ Fam. Chiper, barboter. — n. Sports. Coup (*m.*) à toute volée. ‖ Fam. Claque *f.*

swipes [swaips] n. pl. Fam. Bibine *f.* (drink).

swirl [swə:l] v. intr. Tourbillonner, tournoyer. — v. tr. Faire tourbillonner (or) tournoyer. — n. Tourbillon *m.* (of dust) ; remous *m.* (of water).

swish [swiʃ] v. tr. Cingler, fouetter (*with*, avec) [the air, s.o.]. ‖ Faire siffler (a stick, whip). ‖ Zool. *To swish its tail*, battre de la queue. ‖ **To swish off**, couper d'un coup de badine. — v. intr. Froufrouter (silk) ; *to swish in*, entrer dans un froufrou soyeux. ‖ Bruire (water). ‖ Siffler (whip). ‖ Provoquer des giclements ; *to swish through the mud*, passer en faisant gicler la boue. — n. Froufrou *m.* (of silk) ; bruissement *m.* (of water) ; sifflement *m.* (of whip). ‖ Giclement *m.* (of mud). ‖ Coup de fouet *m.* (stroke).

swish adj. Fam. Super-chic.

Swiss [swis] adj. Geogr. Suisse. — n. invar. Geogr. Suisse *m. ;* Suissesse *f.*

switch [switʃ] n. Badine, baguette *f. ; riding switch*, stick, houssine. ‖ Coup (*m.*) de badine (stroke). ‖ Ch. de f. Aiguille *f.* ‖ Electr. Commutateur, interrupteur *m.* ‖ U. S. Changement (*m.*) de position (or) de direction. ‖ **Switch-plate**, n. Ch. de f. Plaque de manœuvre *f.* ‖ **Switch tower**, n. Ch. de f. U. S. Cabine (*f.*) à signaux. — v. tr. Cingler, fouetter (the air, s.o., sth.). ‖ Arracher (*out of*, de). ‖ Ch. de f., Fig. Aiguiller (*on to*,

sur). ‖ Fam. Echanger (places). ‖ **To switch off**, Electr. Couper (the current) ; Ch. de f. Aiguiller (a train). ‖ **To switch on**, Electr. Mettre en circuit ; allumer (the light) ; Radio. Ouvrir (the radio). — v. intr. **To switch around**, U. S. Changer de position (or) de direction. ‖ **To switch off**, Electr. Couper le courant, éteindre ; Radio. Tourner le bouton (wireless) ; couper la communication (phone). ‖ **To switch on**, Electr. Donner le courant, allumer ; Autom. Mettre le contact.

switchback [-bæk] n. Sports, Fam. Montagnes russes *f. pl.*

switchboard [-bɔ:d] n. Electr. Tableau de distribution ; standard téléphonique *m.* ‖ **Switchboard-operator**, n. Standardiste *s.*

switchman [-mən] n. Ch. de f. U. S. Aiguilleur *m.*

Switzerland ['switsələnd] n. Geogr. Suisse *f.*

swivel ['swivl] n. Pivot *m.* ‖ Naut. Emerillon *m.* ‖ **Swivel-block**, n. Poulie (*f.*) à émerillon. ‖ **Swivel-bridge**, n. Pont tournant *m.* ‖ **Swivel-eyed**, adj. Med. Strabique, bigle. ‖ **Swivel-point**, n. Techn. Joint (*m.*) à rotule. ‖ **Swivel-seat**, n. Fauteuil tournant *m.* — v. intr. (1). Pivoter. — v. tr. Faire pivoter.

swiz(z) [swiz] n. Fam. Arnaque, entourloupe *f.* (swindle) ; déception *f.* (disappointment).

swizzle ['swizl] n. U. S. Cocktail *m.* ‖ **Swizzle-stick**, n. Marteau à champagne, moser *m.*

swollen ['swoulən] p. p. See swell. ‖ **Swollen-headed**, adj. Fam. Enflé, puant.

swoon [swu:n] v. intr. Med. S'évanouir, se trouver mal, perdre connaissance, tomber en syncope. (See faint.) ‖ Mus., Fig. S'éteindre, mourir. — n. Med. Evanouissement *m. ;* syncope *f.*

swoop [swu:p] v. intr. Zool. S'abattre, fondre (*on*, sur). — n. Zool. Attaque, descente *f.* ‖ Aviat. Abattée *f.* ‖ Fig. Attaque *f.*

swoosh [swuʃ] n. Bruissement, frou-frou *m.* (of silk) ; vrombissement *m.* (of wings, of car) ; sifflement, crissement *m.* (of skis). — v. intr. Froufrouter, bruisser ; vrombir ; siffler, crisser.

swop [swɔp] v. tr., intr. (1). Fam. Troquer. — n. Fam. Troc *m.*

sword [sɔ:d] n. Epée *f. ;* sabre *m.* ‖ Jur., †, Milit. Glaive *m.* ‖ Fig. Armes *f. pl. ; by fire and sword*, par le fer et le feu. ‖ **Sword-belt**, n. Ceinturon *m.* ‖ **Sword-cut**, n. Coup de sabre *m.* ‖ **Sword-dance**, n. Danse (*f.*) du sabre. ‖ **Sword-fish**, n. Zool. Espadon *m.* ‖ **Sword-knot**, n. Dragonne *f.* ‖ **Sword-play**, n. Sports. Escrime *f. ;* Fig. Joute oratoire *f.* ‖ **Sword-stick**, n. Canne à épée *f.*

swordsman [-zmən] (pl. **swordsmen**) n. Epéiste, tireur *m. ;* lame *f.*

swordsmanship [-zmənʃip] n. Sports. Habileté à l'escrime *f.*

swore [swɔ:*] pret., **sworn** [swɔ:n] p. p. See swear.

swot [swɔt] v. intr. (1). Fam. Bûcher, potasser. — n. Fam. Bûcheur, fort en thème *m.* (person) ; turbin, boulot *m.* (study).

swum [swʌm] p. p. See swim.

swung [swʌŋ] pret., p. p. See swing.

sybarite ['sibərait] adj., n. Sybarite *m.*

sybaritism ['sibəritizm] n. Sybaritisme *m.*

sycamore [sikəmɔ:*] n. Bot. Sycomore *m.*

syconium [sai'kouniəm] n. Bot. Sycone *m.*

sycophancy ['sikəfənsi] n. Flagornerie *f.*

sycophant [-ənt] n. † Sycophante *m.* ‖ Fam. Flagorneur *m.*

syllabary ['siləbəri] n. Syllabaire *m.*

syllabic [si'læbik] adj. Gramm. Syllabique.

syllabify [-bifai] v. tr. (2). Syllabiser.

syllabism [-izm] n. Gramm. Syllabisme *m.*

syllable ['siləbl] n. Gramm. Syllabe *f.* — v. tr. Prononcer en détachant les syllabes.

syllabub ['silə,bʌb] n. CULIN. See SILLABUB.
syllabus[-əs]n. Programme m. ‖ECCLES. Syllabus m.
syllepsis [si'lepsis] n. GRAMM. Syllepse f.
syllogism ['silədʒizm̩] n. PHILOS. Syllogisme m.
syllogize [-dʒaiz] v. intr. Faire des syllogismes.
sylph [silf] n. † Sylphe m. ‖ FAM. Sylphide f. ‖ Sylph-like, adj. FAM. Gracile, de sylphide.
sylvan ['silvən] adj. Sylvestre.
sylviculture ['silvi,kʌltʃə*] n. Sylviculture f.
symbiosis [,simbi'ousis] n. Symbiose f.
symbol ['simbəl] n. MATH., CHIM., FIG. Symbole m.
symbolic(al) [sim'bɔlik(əl)] adj. Symbolique.
symbolically [-i] adv. Symboliquement.
symbolism ['simbəlizm̩] n. Symbolisme m.
symbolist [-ist] n. Symboliste s.
symbolization [,simbəlai'zeiʃən] n. Symbolisation f.
symbolize ['simbəlaiz] v. tr. Symboliser, représenter. ‖ Traiter symboliquement.
symcentre ['simsentə*] n. Centre (m.) de symétrie.
symmetric(al) [si'metrik(əl)] adj. Symétrique.
symmetrically [-i] adv. Symétriquement.
symmetrize ['simitraiz] v. intr. Rendre symétrique.
symmetry [-tri] n. Symétrie f.
sympathetic [,simpə'θetik] adj. Sensible, altruiste, non égoïste. ‖ Compatissant (person). ‖ Exprimant la sympathie ; de sympathie (glance, smile, words). ‖ Marquant de la sympathie, bien disposé (audience, person); *to be sympathetic to a plan*, se montrer en faveur d'un plan. ‖ Sympathique (ink). ‖ MED. Sympathique ; *sympathetic nerve*, grand sympathique. ‖ PHYS. Vibrant par résonance.
— n. MED. Grand sympathique m.
sympathetically [-li] adv. Avec compassion (or) sympathie. ‖ PHYS. Par résonance.
sympathize ['simpəθaiz] v. intr. Compatir, exprimer sa sympathie. ‖ Partager la douleur (*with*, de) [s.o.]; s'associer (*with*, à) [s.o.'s joy]. ‖ Comprendre; *to sympathize with s.o. in his attitude*, comprendre le point de vue de qqn.
sympathizer [-ə*] n. Partisan m. (*with*, de) [a cause]. ‖ Personne (f.) qui compatit (*with*, avec) [s.o.].
sympathy ['simpəθi] n. Compassion, pitié f. (*for*, pour). ‖ Sympathie, compréhension f. (*between*, entre). ‖ Sympathie f.; accord de pensée; *in sympathy with*, en sympathie avec, du côté de. ‖ MED. Sympathie f. ‖ PHYS. Résonance f.
symphonic [sim'fɔnik] adj. MUS. Symphonique.
symphony ['simfəni] n. MUS. Symphonie f.; *symphony concert, orchestra*, concert, orchestre symphonique.
symphysis ['simfisis] n. ZOOL., MED. Symphyse f.
symposium [sim'pouziəm] (pl. **symposia** [-iə]) n. Festin, banquet m. ‖ Conférence f.; recueil (m.) d'articles. ‖ Colloque m.
symptom ['simptəm] n. MED. Symptôme m. ‖ FIG. Signe, indice m.
symptomatic [,simptə'mætik] adj. MED., FIG. Symptomatique.
synagogue ['sinəgɔg] n. Synagogue f.
synchroflash ['siŋkrouflæʃ] adj., n. Synchroflash m.
synchromesh ['siŋkrou,meʃ] n. AUTOM. Synchronisation f.
— adj. AUTOM. Synchronisé.
synchronic [siŋ'krɔnik] adj. Synchronique.
synchronism ['siŋkrənizm̩] n. Synchronisme m. ‖ RADIO. *Irregular synchronism*, drapeau.
synchronization [,siŋkrənai'zeiʃən] n. Synchronisation f.
synchronize ['siŋkrənaiz] v. tr. Synchroniser.
synchronizer [-aizə*] n. Synchroniseur m.
synchronous [-əs] adj. Synchrone.
synchrotron ['siŋkrə,trɔn] n. PHYS. Synchrotron m.
synclinal [siŋ'klainəl] adj. GEOL. Synclinal.

syncline ['siŋklain] n. GEOL. Synclinal m.
syncopate ['siŋkəpeit] v. tr. MUS., GRAMM. Syncoper.
syncopation [,siŋkə'peiʃən] n. GRAMM., MUS. Syncope f.
syncope ['siŋkəpi] n. GRAMM., MUS., MED. Syncope f.
syncretism ['siŋkretizm̩] n. PHILOS. Syncrétisme m.
syncretist [-ist] n. PHILOS. Syncrétiste s.
syndic ['sindik] n. Syndic m., administrateur s. (government official). ‖ Membre (m.) d'un comité administratif (in university).
syndicalism [-əlizm̩] n. Syndicalisme m.
syndicalist [-əlist] n. Syndicaliste s.
syndicalistic [,sindik]'istik] adj. Syndicaliste.
syndicate ['sindikit] n. Syndicat, consortium m. (of commercial firms); syndicat m. (of individuals). ‖ Agence (f.) vendant des articles, des photos, des bandes dessinées pour une publication simultanée dans plusieurs journaux.
— ['sindi,keit] v. tr. Créer un syndicat (or) un consortium de. ‖ Publier simultanément dans plusieurs journaux.
syndrome ['sindrəmi] n. MED. Syndrome m.
synecdoche [sin'ekdəki] n. Synecdoque f.
synergy ['sinə:dʒi] n. MED. Synergie f.
synod ['sinəd] n. ECCLES. Synode m.
synodical [si'nɔdikəl] adj. ECCLES., ASTRON. Synodique.
synonym ['sinənim] n. GRAMM. Synonyme m.
synonymic [,sinə'nimik] adj. Synonymique.
synonymous [si'nɔniməs] adj. Synonyme (*with*, de).
synonymy [-i] n. Synonymie f.
synopsis [si'nɔpsis] (pl. **synopses** [-i:z]) n. Tableau synoptique m. ‖ Précis, aide-mémoire m. ‖ ECCLES. Synopse f. ‖ CINEM. Synopsis m.
synoptic [-tik] adj. Synoptique.
synovia [si'nouviə] n. MED. Synovie f.
synovial [-l] adj. MED. Synovial.
syntactic [sin'tæktik] adj. GRAMM. Syntaxique.
syntax ['sintæks] n. Syntaxe f.
synthesis [sin'θisis] (pl. **syntheses** [-i:z]) n. CHIM., FIG. Synthèse f.
synthetic [sin'θetik] adj. Synthétique.
— n. Ersatz m. ‖ Pl. Plastiques m. pl.
synthetically [-əli] adv. Synthétiquement.
synthetize ['sinθetaiz] v. tr. Synthétiser.
syntonic [sin'tɔnik] adj. RADIO. Syntonique.
syntonism ['sintənizm̩] n. RADIO. Syntonie f.; accord m.
syntonization [,sintənai'zeiʃən] n. RADIO. Syntonisation f.
syntonize ['sintənaiz] v. tr. RADIO. Syntoniser.
syphilis ['sifilis] n. MED. Syphilis f.
syphilitic [,sifi'litik] adj. MED. Syphilitique.
syphon ['saifn̩] n. See SIPHON.
Syria ['siriə] n. GEOGR. Syrie f.
Syriac [-iæk] adj., n. GRAMM. Syriaque adj., m.
Syrian [-iən] adj., n. GEOGR. Syrien s.
syringa [si'riŋgə] n. BOT. Seringa m.
syringe ['sirindʒ] n. MED. Seringue f.
— v. tr. MED. Seringuer (the ears); injecter (a liquid).
syrinx ['siriŋks] n. † Syringe f. ‖ MUS. Syrinx f., flûte (f.) de Pan. ‖ MED. Trompe (f.) d'Eustache.
— N. B. Deux pluriels : *syrinxes, syringes.*
syrup ['sirəp] n. Sirop m.
syrupy [-i] adj. Sirupeux.
system ['sistim] n. ASTRON., PHILOS., MED. Système m. ‖ TECHN. Réseau m. ‖ MUS. Groupe m. ‖ FIG. Méthode f.
systematic [,sistə'mætik] adj. Systématique. (See ORDERLY.)
systematically [-əli] adv. Systématiquement.
systematization [,sistəmatai'zeiʃən] n. Systématisation f.

systematize ['sistimətaiz] v. tr. Systématiser.
systemic [sis'temik] adj. MED. De l'organisme, organique.

systole ['sistəli] n. MED. Systole *f*.
systyle ['sistail] adj. ARCHIT. Systyle.
syzygy ['sizidʒi] n. ASTRON. Syzygie *f*.

T

t [ti:] n. T, t *m*. ‖ FAM. *To a T*, à la perfection. ‖ **T-bone, T-bone steak,** n. CULIN. Steak (*m*.) T-bone. ‖ **T-iron,** n. TECHN. Fer (*m*.) en té. ‖ **T-junction,** n. AUTOM. Jonction (or) intersection (*f*.) en T. ‖ **T-shirt,** n. Tee- (or) T-shirt *m*.

ta [tɑ:] interj. FAM. Merci, m'ci.

tab [tæb] n. Ferret *m*. (of shoe-lace); oreillette *f*. (of cap); attache, patte *f*. (of coat). ‖ Etiquette *f*. (label). ‖ MILIT. Ecusson *m*. ‖ AVIAT. Déflecteur *m*.; *trimming tab,* fletner, compensateur. ‖ U. S. FAM. Note, facture *f*. (bill); *to keep tab(s) on,* ne pas perdre de vue.

tabard ['tæbəd] n. † Tabard *m*.

tabby ['tæbi] n. COMM. Moire *f*. ‖ ZOOL. Phalène *f*. (butterfly); chat (*m*.) de gouttière (cat).
— v. tr. Moirer.

tabernacle ['tæbənækl] n. ECCLES., NAUT. Tabernacle *m*. ‖ ARCHIT. Stalle (*f*.) à dais.
— v. tr. FIG. Abriter.

tabes ['teibi:z] n. MED. Tabès *m*.; *tabes dorsalis,* ataxie locomotrice.

tabescence [tə'besn̥s] n. MED. Tabescence *f*.

tabetic [tə'betik] adj., n. MED. Tabétique *s*.

tablature ['tæblətʃə*] n. MUS. Tablature *f*.

table ['teibl] n. Table *f*. (piece of furniture); *to be at table,* être à table; *to lay the table,* mettre le couvert. ‖ Table *f*. (food); *table wine,* vin de table; *to keep a good table,* avoir une bonne table. ‖ Tablée *f*. (people); *to set all the table laughing,* faire rire toute la table. ‖ Table *f*.; tableau *m*. ‖ TECHN., AVIAT., MATH., ECCLES. Table *f*. ‖ GEOGR. Plateau *m*. ‖ MED. Paume *f*. (of the hand). ‖ CH. DE F. Indicateur *m*. (time-table). ‖ FIG. *To turn the tables,* renverser (or) retourner la situation. ‖ **Table-altar,** n. ECCLES. Autel improvisé *m*. ‖ **Table-centre,** n. Centre (*m*.) de table. ‖ **Table-cloth,** n. Nappe *f*. (for meals); tapis (*m*.) de table. ‖ **Table-companion,** n. Convive, commensal *m*. ‖ **Table-cover,** n. Tapis (*m*.) de table. ‖ **Table-d'hôte meal,** n. Repas à prix fixe *m*. ‖ **Table-land,** n. GEOGR. Plateau *m*. ‖ **Table-leaf,** n. Rallonge *f*. ‖ **Table-linen,** n. Linge (*m*.) de table. ‖ **Table-spoon,** n. Cuillère à bouche *f*. ‖ **Table-spoonful,** n. Cuillerée à bouche *f*. ‖ **Table-talk,** n. Propos (*m*. *pl*.) de table. ‖ **Table-tennis,** n. SPORTS. Ping-pong *m*. ‖ **Table-turning,** n. Fait (*m*.) de faire tourner les tables. ‖ **Table-water,** n. Eau de table *f*.
— v. tr. Déposer (a bill); *to table a motion of confidence,* poser la question de confiance. ‖ U. S. Ajourner, classer. ‖ TECHN. Emboîter. ‖ NAUT. Renforcer (a sail).

tableau ['tæblou] (pl. **tableaux** [-lou]) n. Tableau *m*., représentation pittoresque *f*.; *what a tableau!,* vous voyez le tableau!; *tableau vivant,* tableau vivant. ‖ THEATR. Tableau *m*.; *tableau curtains,* rideaux à l'italienne.

tableful [-ful] n. Tablée *f*.

tablet [-it] n. † Tablette *f*. ‖ Plaque commémorative *f*. ‖ COMM. Tablette *f*. (of chocolate); pain *m*. (of soap). ‖ MED. Comprimé *m*. ‖ U. S. Bloc-correspondance *m*.

tabloid ['tæblɔid] n. † MED. Comprimé *m*. ‖ Tabloïd *m*. (newspaper).

taboo [tə'bu] adj., n. Tabou *m*.
— v. tr. Déclarer tabou; proscrire; *tabooed,* interdit, à l'index.

tabor ['teibə*] n. MUS. Tambourin *m*.

tabouret ['tæbərit] n. † Tabouret *m*. (stool). ‖ Tambour *m*. (for embroidery).

tabular ['tæbjulə*] adj. Tabulaire. ‖ En tableaux.

tabulate [-eit] v. tr. Disposer en tableaux; classer, cataloguer.

tabulator [-eitə*] n. Tabulateur *m*.

tachograph ['tækə,grɑːf] n. TECHN. Tachygraphe *m*.

tachometer [tə'kɔmitə*] n. TECHN. Tachymètre, compte-tours *m*.

tachycardia [,tæki'kɑːdjə] n. MED. Tachycardie *f*.

tachymeter [tə'kimetə*] n. Tachéomètre *m*.

tacit ['tæsit] adj. † Taciturne, muet. ‖ Tacite.

tacitly [-li] adv. Tacitement.

taciturn ['tæsitə:n] adj. Taciturne.

taciturnity [,tæsi'tə:niti] n. Taciturnité *f*.

tack [tæk] n. Semence *f*. (nail). ‖ Point de bâti *m*.; faufilure *f*. (stitch). ‖ NAUT. Amure *f*. (clew-line); bordée *f*. ‖ JUR. Clause additionnelle *f*. ‖ FAM. Voie, tactique *f*.; *to be on the wrong tack,* faire fausse route; *to get down to brass tacks,* en venir au fait, discuter le fond de l'affaire.
— v. tr. Clouer. ‖ Bâtir, faufiler. ‖ JUR. Annexer (*to,* à).
— v. intr. NAUT. Virer de bord; louvoyer. ‖ FAM. Changer ses batteries.

tack n. SPORTS. Sellerie *f*. (harnesses, saddles). ‖ **Tack-room,** n. Sellerie *f*.

tack n. FAM. Graille, bouffe *f*. ‖ NAUT., FAM. *Hard tack,* biscuit de marin; *soft tack,* pain.

tackle ['tækl] n. Attirail, fourniment *m*.; engins *m*. *pl*. (implements). ‖ Treuil, appareil de levage *m*. ‖ NAUT. Palan *m*. ‖ SPORTS. Placage; accrochage *m*.
— v. tr. NAUT. Amarrer. ‖ SPORTS. Tenter de plaquer. ‖ FIG. Etre aux prises avec (a difficulty); se lancer dans (a subject). ‖ FAM. Empoigner (s.o.). ‖ U. S. FAM. Taper (*for,* de) [s.o.].
— v. intr. FAM. S'atteler (*to,* à).

tacky ['tæki] adj. Prêt à coller; gluant (sticky). ‖ U. S. FAM. Râpé, minable (shabby).

tact [tækt] n. Tact, doigté *m*. ‖ MUS. Battement *m*.

tactful [-ful] adj. Délicat (hint); plein de tact, qui a du doigté (or) de la délicatesse (person).

tactic ['tæktik] n. Tactique *f*. (piece of tactics).

tactical ['tæktikəl] adj. MILIT. Tactique; *tactical bombardment,* bombardement systématique; *tactical importance,* valeur stratégique. ‖ FIG. Adroit.

tactician [tæk'tiʃən] n. MILIT. Tacticien *m.*
tactics ['tæktiks] n. sg. MILIT., FIG. Tactique *f.*
tactile ['tæktail] adj. MED. Tactile. ‖ FIG. Tangible.
tactless [-lis] adj. Sans tact.
tactlessness [-lisnis] n. Manque de tact *m.*
tactual ['tæktjuəl] adj. Tactile (test).
tactually [-əli] adv. Par le toucher.
tadpole ['tædpoul] n. ZOOL. Têtard *m.*
tael [teil] n. Tael *m.*
taenia ['ti:niə] (pl. **taeniae** [-ii:]) n. MED. Ténia *m.* (tapeworm); bandage *m.* (dressing).
taffeta ['tæfitə] n. Taffetas *m.*
taffrail ['tæf,reil] n. NAUT. Lisse (*f.*) de couronnement, rambarde (*f.*) arrière.
taffy ['tæfi] n. U. S. Caramel *m.* (toffee). ‖ U. S. Flagornerie *f.* (flattery).
Taffy n. FAM. Gallois *m.*
tafia ['tæfiə] n. Tafia *m.*
tag [tæg] n. Ferret *m.* (of shoelace); *to lose its tag,* se déferrer. ‖ Tirant *m.* (of boot). ‖ Etiquette *f.* (label). ‖ Bout *m.* (end). ‖ SPORTS. Chat perché *m.* (game). ‖ MUS. Refrain *m.;* rengaine *f.* ‖ THEATR. Allocution (*f.*) au baisser de rideau. ‖ FIG. Aphorisme, cliché *m.; old tag,* dicton. ‖ **Tag-day,** n. U. S. Jour (*m.*) de collecte publique. ‖ **Tag-line,** n. U. S. Amusante moralité *f.* ‖ **Tag question,** n. GRAMM. Reprise interrogative *f.*
— v. tr. (1). Ferrer (a lace). ‖ Rimer, aligner. ‖ Accrocher, attacher (*on, to,* à); *to tag together,* coudre, lier. ‖ SPORTS. Attraper. ‖ FIG. *To tag along with,* suivre.
tail [teil] n. ZOOL., AVIAT., ASTRON. Queue *f.* ‖ Queue, natte *f.* (hair). ‖ Basque, queue *f.* (of a coat); pan *m.* (of a shirt); pl. jaquette *f.;* habit, frac *m.* ‖ Pile *f.* (of a coin); *heads or tails,* pile ou face. ‖ Fin *f.;* bout *m.* (end). ‖ Suite, escorte *f.* (retinue). ‖ File, queue *f.* (of people waiting). ‖ Queue *f.* (at school). ‖ ARCHIT. Bas *m.* ‖ FAM. *To turn tail,* tourner les talons, prendre la poudre d'escampette. ‖ **Tail-board,** n. AUTOM. Hayon *m.* ‖ **Tail-braid,** n. Ganse *f.* ‖ **Tail-coat,** n. Habit *m.* ‖ **Tail-dive,** n. AVIAT. Glissade sur la queue *f.* ‖ **Tail-end,** n. Queue *f.;* bout *m.;* SPORTS. *At the tail-end,* en queue. ‖ **Tail-fin,** n. ZOOL. Nageoire caudale *f.;* AVIAT. Plan (*m.*) de dérive. ‖ **Tail-gate,** n. Porte aval *f.* (of a lock); AUTOM. Hayon *m.;* v. tr. U. S. AUTOM. Coller au pare-chocs de, suivre de trop près. ‖ **Tail-light,** n. AUTOM. Feu arrière *m.* ‖ **Tail-piece,** n. ARTS. Cul-de-lampe *m.;* MUS. Cordier *m.* (of violin); FAM. Dernier paragraphe *m.* (in a gossip column). ‖ **Tail-plane,** n. AVIAT. Plan fixe *m.* ‖ **Tail-spin,** n. AVIAT. Vrille *f.; tail-spin fall,* chute en vrille. ‖ **Tail-unit,** n. AVIAT. Empennage *m.*
— v. tr. Mettre une queue à. ‖ Encastrer (*in,* dans). ‖ Attacher (*on, to,* à). ‖ FAM. Enlever la queue de (a fruit). ‖ U. S. FAM. Suivre (s.o.).
— v. intr. Marcher sur les talons (*after,* de). ‖ *To tail away,* s'espacer, s'égrener; finir en queue de poisson.
tail n. JUR. Clause de substitution *f.*
— adj. JUR. *Estate tail,* bien substitué.
tailless [-lis] adj. Sans queue.
tailor ['teilə*] n. Tailleur *m.* ‖ **Tailor-made,** adj. Tailleur (suit).
— v. intr. Etre tailleur.
— v. tr. Faire (a costume); habiller (s.o.).
tailoring [-riŋ] n. Métier (or) ouvrage (*m.*) de tailleur.
tain [tein] n. Tain *m.*
taint [teint] n. Corruption *f.* ‖ Tache, souillure *f.* (of sin); stigmate *m.* (of vice). ‖ Trace *f.* (of infection). ‖ MED. Tare *f.*
— v. tr. Corrompre, infecter, souiller, vicier; *his vulgarity has tainted her,* sa vulgarité a déteint sur elle. ‖ CULIN. Gâter (food).
— v. intr. Se corrompre, se vicier; ‖ CULIN. Se gâter (food).

taintless [-lis] adj. Sans tache.
take [teik] v. tr. (174).

---

1. Prendre, saisir. — 2. Prendre, capturer. — 3. Prendre, enlever. — 4. Prendre, emporter. — 5. Porter, apporter. — 6. Contenir, renfermer. — 7. Porter, supporter. — 8. Se procurer, obtenir. — 9. Faire, accomplir. — 10. Prendre, acheter. — 11. Prendre, emprunter. — 12. Prélever, ôter. — 13. Prendre, extraire. — 14. Prendre, relever. — 15. Emmener, conduire. — 16. Comprendre. — 17. Prendre, considérer. — 18. Surprendre, prendre. — 19. Prendre, demander. — 20. Prendre, se donner. — 21. Prendre, exiger. — 22. Prendre, rechercher. — 23. Gagner, obtenir. — 24. Profiter de. — 25. Prendre, accepter. — 26. Recevoir. — 27. Eprouver, ressentir. — 28. Prendre, formuler. — 29. Prendre, assumer. — 30. Faire, assurer. — 31. Admettre, apprécier. — 32. Prendre, se permettre. — 33. Prendre, charmer. — 34. GRAMM. — 35. CULIN. — 36. MILIT. — 37. MED. — 38. SPORTS. — 39. AUTOM. — 40. TECHN. — 41. ARTS. — 42. FIN. — 43. To take about. — 44. To take along. — 45. To take away. — 46. To take back. — 47. To take down. — 48. To take in. — 49. To take into. — 50. To take off. — 51. To take on. — 52. To take out. — 53. To take over. — 54. To take up.

---

1. Prendre, saisir, tenir; *to take by the throat,* saisir à la gorge; *to take in one's hand,* prendre à la main. ‖ 2. Prendre, s'emparer de, capturer; *to take s.o. prisoner,* faire qqn prisonnier. ‖ 3. Prendre, enlever; *the thief took my watch,* le voleur m'a pris ma montre; *to take sth. from the drawer,* retirer qqch. du tiroir, prendre qqch. dans le tiroir. ‖ 4. Prendre, emporter; *take your gloves with you,* prenez vos gants. ‖ 5. Porter, apporter; *to take a parcel to the post office,* apporter un paquet à la poste. ‖ 6. Contenir, renfermer; *to take ten passengers,* contenir dix voyageurs. ‖ 7. Porter, supporter; *to take a heavy load,* supporter de lourdes charges. ‖ 8. Se procurer, obtenir, prendre; *to take a chair,* prendre une chaise; *to take cover,* se mettre à l'abri. ‖ 9. Faire, accomplir, exécuter; *to take a walk,* faire une promenade. ‖ 10. Prendre, acheter, louer; *to take a cottage for the summer,* louer une villa pour l'été; *to take three daily newspapers,* prendre trois quotidiens. ‖ 11. Prendre, emprunter; *to take a train,* prendre un train; *to take the wrong road,* se tromper de chemin. ‖ 12. Prélever, soustraire, retrancher, ôter; *to take a shilling off the price,* diminuer le prix d'un shilling. ‖ 13. Prendre, extraire; *the cover illustration is taken from,* l'illustration de la couverture est empruntée à; *to take a line from a poem,* extraire (or) sortir un vers d'un poème. ‖ 14. Prendre, relever; *to take notes,* prendre des notes; *to take s.o.'s photograph,* faire la photographie de qqn. ‖ 15. Emmener, conduire; *this road will take you to the town,* cette route vous mènera à la ville; *to take s.o. to dinner,* emmener dîner qqn. ‖ 16. Comprendre, interpréter; *to take a joke in earnest,* prendre une plaisanterie au sérieux; *to take s.o. (up) the wrong way,* mal comprendre qqn. ‖ 17. Prendre, considérer; *I am not the girl you take me for,* je ne suis pas celle que vous croyez; *to take the matter seriously,* prendre la chose avec gravité; *to take s.o. to be an intelligent person,* prendre qqn pour intelligent. ‖ 18. Prendre, surprendre; *to take s.o. unawares,* prendre qqn au dépourvu. ‖ 19. Prendre, exiger, demander; *it takes money to make money,* il faut avoir de l'argent pour en gagner. ‖ 20. Prendre, s'imposer, se donner; *to take action,* intervenir; *to take a vow,* faire un vœu; *to take a wife,* prendre femme. ‖

21. Prendre, exiger ; *to take a long time,* prendre beaucoup de temps ; *to take a lot of sugar,* consommer (or) demander beaucoup de sucre. ‖ **22.** Prendre, demander, rechercher ; *to take advice,* prendre conseil. ‖ **23.** Gagner, obtenir ; *to take first prize,* remporter le premier prix. ‖ **24.** Profiter de, saisir ; *to take an opportunity,* saisir (or) sauter sur une occasion. ‖ **25.** Prendre, accepter ; *to take it easy,* se la couler douce (fam.) ; *to take a job,* accepter un emploi ; *to take no denial,* ne pas tolérer de refus. ‖ **26.** Recevoir, subir, supporter ; *to take a beating,* recevoir une raclée. ‖ **27.** Eprouver, ressentir, *to take a dislike to,* prendre en grippe (s.o.) ; *to take pity on,* prendre pitié de. ‖ **28.** Prendre, former ; *to take a resolution,* prendre une détermination. ‖ **29.** Prendre, assumer ; *to take all the responsibility,* se charger de toute la responsabilité, tout prendre sur soi. ‖ **30.** Faire, assurer ; *to take the French class,* faire la classe de français. ‖ **31.** Mettre, admettre, apprécier ; *you may take it from me,* vous pouvez m'en croire. ‖ **32.** Prendre, se permettre ; *to take liberties with,* prendre des libertés avec. ‖ **33.** Prendre, captiver, charmer, séduire ; *to be taken with,* être pris (or) séduit par. ‖ **34.** GRAMM. Vouloir, demander (a mood). ‖ **35.** CULIN. Prendre, absorber (food) ; *do you take coffee ?,* prenez-vous du café ? ; *to take a meal,* faire un repas. ‖ **36.** MILIT. Prendre (a fortress). ‖ **37.** MED. Prendre, contracter ; attraper (fam.) [a disease] ; prendre (medicine) ; *to take s.o. to the hospital,* transporter qqn à l'hôpital. ‖ **38.** SPORTS. Tenir (a bet) ; prendre (an animal, a bird, fish, an opponent's piece) ; franchir (an obstacle) ; *to take punishment,* encaisser. ‖ **39.** AUTOM. Prendre (a corner). ‖ **40.** TECHN. Prendre (dye, polish). ‖ **41.** ARTS. Prendre, faire, représenter. ‖ **42.** FIN. Gagner. ‖ **43. To take about,** promener, sortir, accompagner dans une sortie (s.o.). ‖ **44. To take along,** emporter. ‖ **45. To take away,** emmener, retirer *(from,* de) [s.o.] ; enlever, emporter (s.o. by death) ; enlever, ôter *(from,* de) [sth.]. ‖ **46. To take back,** revenir sur, reprendre (one's word) ; reconduire, remmener (s.o.) ; reporter *(to,* à) [sth.] ‖ **47. To take down,** prendre (notes) ; noter, inscrire, mettre par écrit (a name) ; descendre, décrocher (a picture) ; démolir (a wall) ; TECHN. Démonter (a machine) ; FAM. Avaler (food) ; remettre à sa place (s.o.). ‖ **48. To take in,** rétrécir, diminuer, rentrer (a dress, seam) ; faire rentrer, s'approvisionner en (goods) ; diminuer (knitting) ; embrasser du regard (a landscape) ; prendre (lodgers) ; recueillir (orphans) ; faire entrer, introduire (s.o.) ; prendre (water) ; comprendre, englober, inclure (to include) ; AGRIC. Rentrer (the harvest) ; NAUT. Prendre (a reef) ; carguer (sail) ; FIN. Reporter (stock) ; FIG. Comprendre, saisir, apprécier, se rendre compte de (a situation) ; FAM. Avaler, gober (a story) ; rouler, empaumer, avoir, mettre dedans (s.o.). ‖ **49. To take into,** mettre dans ; *to take s.o. into one's confidence,* mettre qqn dans le secret ; *to take it into one's head to,* se mettre dans la tête de. ‖ **50. To take off,** faire disparaître, supprimer (an after-effect) ; recevoir (a message) ; décrocher (the receiver) ; quitter, ôter, enlever, retirer (one's clothes, sth.) ; détourner, lever *(from,* de) [one's eyes] ; MED. Amputer (a leg) ; NAUT. Débarquer (passengers) ; FIN. Rabattre *(from,* sur) [a sum] ; FIG. Distraire, détourner *(from,* de) [one's attention] ; *to take s.o.'s mind off his grief,* distraire qqn de sa douleur ; FAM. Singer, imiter, contrefaire (s.o.) ; *to take oneself off,* se sauver ; se débiner ; *to take s.o. off s.o.'s hands,* débarrasser (or) défaire qqn de qqn. ‖ **51. To take on,** prendre, revêtir (a form, quality) ; assumer (a responsibility) ; se charger de, entreprendre (a task) ; embaucher, engager (a workman) ; accompagner (or) mener plus loin (s.o.) ; SPORTS. Relever, tenir (a bet) ; se mesurer

avec, jouer contre (s.o.) ; CH. DE F. Prendre (passengers). ‖ **52. To take out,** retirer (one's luggage) ; enlever (a stain) ; faire sortir, sortir (s.o.) ; sortir (sth.) ; FIN. Enlever, ôter (a sum) ; JUR. Prendre (a patent) ; contracter (an insurance policy) ; COMM. *To take it out in,* se payer en ; MED. Arracher (a tooth) ; FAM. Ereinter, mettre à plat (s.o.) ; *I'll take it out of him,* il me la paiera. ‖ **53. To take over,** faire une reprise de (furniture) ; faire traverser (s.o.) ; COMM. Reprendre (a business) ; prendre livraison de (a car) ; JUR. Exproprier (a building) ; AUTOM. Transporter (goods) ; passer (s.o.) ; prendre (the watch) ; MILIT. Relever (a trench). ‖ **54. To take up,** ramasser, prendre (a book) ; enlever (a carpet) ; établir (one's residence) ; occuper, tenir (space) ; raccourcir, remonter (a sleeve) ; relever (a stitch) ; prendre, absorber (water) ; TECHN. Dépaver (a street) ; compenser (wear) ; AUTOM. Amortir (bumps) ; AUTOM., CH. DE F. Prendre (passengers) ; FIN. Honorer (a bill) ; lever (an option) ; souscrire à (shares) ; JUR. Arrêter (a thief) ; CINEM. Enrouler (the film) ; SPORTS. Tenir (a bet) ; relever (a challenge) ; FIG. Embrasser (a career) ; reprendre (a conversation) ; adopter, retenir (an idea) ; aborder (a matter, question) ; adopter (a method) ; comprendre (s.o.'s idea. s.o.) ; prendre, occuper (s.o.) ; absorber (s.o.'s attention) ; occuper, absorber, remplir (time) ; relever (a statement) ; se mettre à (study) ; FAM. Reprendre, relever, rabrouer (s.o.).
— v. intr. Prendre (fire). ‖ *To take well,* être photogénique (person). ‖ Prendre, avoir du succès, réussir (novel, play, theory). ‖ AGRIC., MED. Prendre. ‖ **To take after,** ressembler à, tenir de. ‖ **To take from,** diminuer, déprécier, nuire à. ‖ **To take off,** prendre son élan ; partir *(from,* de) ; AVIAT. Décoller. ‖ **To take to,** prendre goût à (a game) ; prendre, se livrer à (a habit) ; mordre à (a science) ; se prendre de sympathie pour, sympathiser avec (s.o.) ; prendre, avoir recours à (sth.) ; *to take to flight,* prendre la fuite ; *to take to writing,* se mettre à écrire, se faire écrivain. ‖ **To take up,** s'améliorer (weather) ; *to take up with,* se lier avec (friends) ; se mettre en ménage (or) se coller avec (fam.) [a lover].
— n. SPORTS. Prise *f.* ‖ FIN. Recette *f.* ‖ **Take-down,** adj. TECHN. Démontable ; n. FAM. Affront *m.* ‖ **Take-home,** adj. U. S. Net (pay). ‖ **Take-in,** n. FAM. Attrape-nigaud *m. ;* carotte *f.* ‖ **Take-off,** n. Départ m. (of a rocket) ; SPORTS. Elan *m.* (jump) ; AVIAT. Décollage *m. ;* FAM. Caricature, charge *f.* ‖ **Take-over,** n. FIN. Reprise, prise *(f.)* de contrôle, absorption *f. ; take-over bid,* offre publique d'achat, O. P. A. ‖ **Take-up,** n. TECHN. Tendeur *m. ;* CINEM. Enroulement *m.* (act) ; enrouleuse *f.* (machine).

taker [-ə*] n. Preneur *s.* ‖ FIN. Vendeur *m.* ‖ SPORTS. Tenant *m.* (of a bet). ‖ **Taker-in,** n. FAM. Carotteur, monteur de coup *s.* ‖ **Taker-off,** n. FAM. Singe, imitateur *m.*

taking [-iŋ] n. Prise *f.* (action). ‖ FIN. Pl. Recette *f.* ‖ MED. Prélèvement *m.,* prise *f.* (of blood). ‖ **Taking-in,** n. Diminution *f.* (in knitting). ‖ **Taking-off,** n. Elan *m. ;* AVIAT. Décollage *m.* ‖ **Taking-out,** n. TECHN., MED. Extraction *f.*
— adj. Attrayant, prenant, séduisant. ‖ FAM. Contagieux ; *that's taking,* ça s'attrape.

talc [tælk] n. CHIM. Talc *m.* ‖ MED. *Talcum powder,* talc.
— v. tr. MED. Talquer.

talcose [-ous] adj. Talqueux.

tale [teil] n. Conte, récit *m.* (story). ‖ Histoire *f. ;* rapport mensonger, ragot *m.* (gossip) ; *to tell tales,* rapporter ; cafarder (fam.). ‖ † Compte ; total *m.*

talebearer [-,bɛərə*] n. Rapporteur *s. ;* cafard *m.* (fam.). ‖ Cancanier *s.*

talebearing [-,bɛəriŋ] n. Rapportage ; cafardage *m.* (fam.). ‖ Cancans *m. pl.*

talent ['tælənt] n. Talent *m*. (faculty). ‖ Don *m*. (aptitude). ‖ † FIN. Talent *m*. ‖ **Talent-scout,** n. CINEM. Dénicheur (*m*.) de vedettes.

talented |-id] adj. De talent ; talentueux, doué.

tales ['teili:z] n. JUR. Jurés suppléants *m. pl.*

talesman [-mən] n. JUR. Juré suppléant *m*.

taleteller ['teil,telə*] n. Conteur *s*. ‖ FAM. Rapporteur *s.; *cafard *m*. (fam.).

talion ['tæliən] n. Talion *m*.

taliped ['tæliped] adj., n. MED. Pied-bot *m*. (person).

talipes [-i:z] n. MED. Pied bot *m*. (foot).

talisman ['tælizmən] n. Talisman *m*.

talismanic [,tælis'mænik] adj. Magique.

talk |tɔ:k] v. intr. Parler, dire (to express oneself) ; *to talk by signs,* parler par signes. ‖ Parler (*to*, à) ; causer, s'entretenir (avec) [to converse]. ‖ Bavarder, causer (to chatter) ; *to talk for the sake of talking,* parler pour ne rien dire. ‖ Jaser, parler (to gossip). ‖ FAM. *I'll talk to him,* je vais lui passer un savon ; *to talk through one's hat,* dire des bêtises. ‖ **To talk about,** parler de, discuter de ; *to know what one is talking about,* savoir ce qu'on a dit. ‖ **To talk at,** faire allusion à, parler pour (s.o.). ‖ **To talk back,** FAM. Répliquer, répondre. ‖ **To talk down to,** se mettre à la portée de (one's audience) [pej.]. ‖ **To talk on,** continuer à parler, poursuivre.

— v. tr. Dire, raconter ; *to talk nonsense,* dire des sottises. ‖ Parler (slang, Spanish). ‖ Parler de, discuter de, s'entretenir de (a subject). ‖ Agir par la parole sur (s.o.) ; *to talk oneself hoarse,* s'enrouer à force de parler ; *to talk s.o. into agreement,* amener qqn à (or) persuader qqn de conclure un accord ; *to talk s.o. out of doing sth.,* décourager (or) dissuader qqn de faire qqch. ‖ **To talk away,** faire passer en parlant (fear, time). ‖ **To talk down,** faire taire (s.o.) ; AVIAT. Donner les instructions d'atterrissage à. ‖ **To talk out,** discuter à fond (sth.). ‖ **To talk over,** gagner, persuader (s.o.) ; débattre, discuter (sth.). ‖ **To talk round,** tourner autour de (a question) ; persuader, gagner à son avis, convaincre (s.o.). ‖ **To talk up,** FAM. Vanter ; faire mousser (s.o., sth.).

— n. Mots *m. pl.; action and talk,* les actes et les paroles ; *to end in talk,* finir en queue de poisson. ‖ Bruit ; racontar, potin *m.; there is some talk of,* on dit que, il est question de. ‖ Sujet de commérage *m.; to be the talk of the town,* défrayer la chronique. ‖ Conversation *f.;* entretien *m.; to engage s.o. in talk,* lier conversation avec qqn. ‖ Causerie *f.; to give a talk on the radio,* parler à la radio.

talkative [-ətiv] adj. Bavard.

talkativeness [-ətivnis] n. Loquacité *f*.

talkee-talkee ['tɔ:ki'tɔ:ki] n. † Petit nègre *m*. ‖ FAM. Papotage *m*. (gossip).

talker ['tɔ:kə*] n. Causeur *s.; brilliant talker* beau parleur. ‖ Bavard *s*. ‖ FAM. Hâbleur *m*.

talkie [-i] n. FAM. Cinéma parlant *m*.

talking [-iŋ] adj. Qui parle (bird). ‖ CINEM. Parlant. ‖ FIG. Expressif, parlant (look) ; *talking point,* sujet d'entretien.

— n. Paroles *f. pl.;* propos *m. pl.* ‖ Bavardage *m*. ‖ **Talking-to,** n. FAM. Aubade *f.;* savon *m*.

tall [tɔ:l] adj. Grand (person) ; haut, grand, élevé (thing) ; *how tall is he?,* quelle est sa taille ?. combien mesure-t-il ? ‖ FAM. Outré, exagéré ; *tall story,* histoire marseillaise ; *tall talk,* hâblerie.

— adv. *To talk tall,* se vanter.

tallage ['tælidʒ] n. † FIN. Taille *f*.

tallboy ['tɔ:lbɔi] n. Commode *f.;* chiffonnier *m*. (furniture).

tallness [-nis] n. Taille élevée *f*. (of s.o.) ; hauteur *f*. (of sth.).

tallow ['tælou] n. Suif *m*. ‖ **Tallow-chandler,** n. Fabricant (or) marchand (*m*.) de chandelles. ‖

Tallow-faced, adj. Blême, blafard. ‖ **Tallow-tree,** n. BOT. Arbre à suif *m*.

— v. tr. Suiffer.

tallowy [-i] adj. Suiffeux. ‖ FAM. Blafard, terreux.

tally ['tæli] n. Taille *f*. (stick). ‖ Encoche, coche *f*. (notch). ‖ Pointage *m*. (of goods, names). ‖ Etiquette *f*. (tag). ‖ JUR. Contrepartie *f*. (of a document). ‖ COMM. Nombre-mesure *f*. (score). ‖ **Tally-clerk,** n. Pointeur *s*. ‖ **Tally-sheet,** n. Bordereau *m*.

— v. tr. Pointer (goods, names).

— v. intr. Contrôler. ‖ Concorder (accounts). ‖ Correspondre (*with*, à) ; concorder, cadrer, s'accorder (*with*, avec).

tally-ho [-'hou] interj., n. Taïaut *m*.

— v. intr. Crier taïaut.

tallyman [-mən] (pl. **tallymen**) n. Pointeur *m*. ‖ COMM. Marchand à tempérament *m*.

Talmud ['tælmʌd] n. Talmud *m*.

Talmudic [tæl'mʌdik] adj. Talmudique.

talon ['tælən] n. ZOOL. Serre *f*. (of bird of prey) ; griffe *f*. (of tiger). ‖ TECHN. Ergot *m*. (in a lock). ‖ SPORTS, FIN., ARCHIT. Talon *m*. (at cards, of cheque-book, moulding).

talus ['teiləs] (pl. **tali** [-ai]) n. MED. Astragale *m*.

tamable ['teiməbl] adj. See TAMEABLE.

tamandua [,tæmən'duə] n. ZOOL. Tamandua *m*.

tamanoir ['tæmənwɑ:*] n. ZOOL. Tamanoir *m*.

tamarack ['tæməræk] n. BOT. Mélèze (*m*.) d'Amérique.

tamarin ['tæmərin] n. ZOOL. Tamarin *m*.

tamarind ['tæmərind] n. BOT. Fruit du tamarinier *m*. (fruit) ; tamarinier *m*. (tree).

tamarisk ['tæmərisk] n. BOT. Tamaris *m*.

tambour ['tæmbuə*] n. ARCHIT., MILIT., MUS. Tambour *m*. ‖ TECHN. Métier, tambour *m*. (frame).

— v. tr., intr. Broder au tambour.

tambourine [,tæmbə'ri:n] n. MUS. Tambour (*m*.) de basque ; tambourin *m*. ‖ ZOOL. Tambour *m*.

tame [teim] v. tr. Apprivoiser, domestiquer (an animal) ; dompter (a wild horse). ‖ FIG. Dompter, mater, brider.

— adj. ZOOL. Apprivoisé, domestique. ‖ BOT., AGRIC. Cultivé. ‖ FIG. Dompté (person) ; plat, fade, terne (style).

tameable [-əbl] adj. Domptable.

tameless [-lis] adj. Indomptable.

tamely [-li] adv. Servilement, avec soumission. ‖ Platement, de façon terne.

tameness [-nis] n. Docilité, soumission *f*. ‖ FIG. Pusillanimité *f*. (of s.o.) ; platitude, banalité *f*. (of style).

tamer [-ə*] n. Dompteur *m*.

Tamil ['tæmil] adj., n. GRAMM. Tamil, tamoul *m*.

tammy ['tæmi] n. Etamine *f*. (fabric).

tammy n. CULIN. Tamis *m.; *passoire *m*.

tam-o'-shanter [,tæmə'ʃæntə*] n. Béret écossais *m*.

tamp [tæmp] v. tr. TECHN. Bourrer (a drill hole) ; damer (the ground).

tamper ['tæmpə*] v. intr. **To tamper with,** sudoyer, suborner, tenter de corrompre (s.o.) ; toucher à, tripoter (sth.) ; altérer, falsifier (a text) ; trifouiller, tripatouiller (fam.).

tamperer [-rə*] n. Suborneur *m*. (with, de) [persons] ; falsificateur *m*. (with, de) [texts].

tampion ['tæmpiən] n. MILIT. Tampon *m*. (of gun).

tampon ['tæmpən] n. Crépon *m*. (hair). ‖ MED., ARTS. Tampon *m*.

— v. tr. MED. Tamponner.

tamtam ['tæmtæm] n. Tam-tam *m*.

tan [tæn] adj. Feu (animal) ; gold (shoes) ; jaune, havane (thing).

— n. Tan *m*. ‖ Hâle *m*. (on the skin). ‖ Couleur (*f*.) feu (or) havane ; gold *m*. (colour). ‖ **Tan-house,**

n. Magasin (*m.*) d'écorces. ‖ **Tan-yard**, n. Tannerie *f.*
— v. tr. Tanner (hide). ‖ Bronzer, hâler, basaner (skin). ‖ FAM. Etriller, flanquer une tannée à (s.o.).
— v. intr. Se tanner (hide). ‖ Se bronzer, se hâler, se basaner (skin).

tanager ['tænədʒə*] n. ZOOL. Tangara *m.*

tandem ['tændəm] adj., adv. En tandem.
— n. Tandem *m.* (bicycle, team).

tang [tæŋ] n. Queue *f.* (of a file); soie *f.* (of a knife). ‖ FIG. Saveur *f.*

tang n. Tintement, tintamarre; bruit vibrant *m.*
— v. tr. Faire tinter (or) retentir. ‖ LOC. *To tang bees*, faire poser un essaim en faisant du tintamarre.

tangency ['tændʒənsi] n. Tangence *f.*

tangent [-ənt] adj. MATH. Tangent. ‖ TECHN. Tangentiel.
— n. MATH., FIG. Tangente *f.* ‖ FAM. *To go off at a tangent*, filer par la tangente.

tangential [tæn'dʒenʃəl] adj. Tangentiel.

Tangerine ['tændʒə'ri:n] adj. De Tanger.

tangerine n. COMM. Mandarine *f.*

tangibility [,tændʒi'biliti] n. Tangibilité *f.*

tangible ['tændʒibl] adj. Tangible, palpable. ‖ JUR. Matériel. ‖ FIG. Tangible.

tangibly [-i] adv. De façon tangible.

Tangier(s) [tæn'dʒiə(z)] n. GEOGR. Tanger *m.*

tangle [tæŋgl] v. tr. Enchevêtrer, entortiller, embrouiller (lit. and fig.).
— v. intr. S'enchevêtrer, s'entortiller, s'embrouiller.
— n. Enchevêtrement, fouillis *m.* ‖ AUTOM. Embouteillage *m.* ‖ FAM. Embrouillamini *m.*

tangle n. BOT. Algue *f.* ‖ NAUT. Drague *f.*

tangly [-i] adj. Embrouillé, enchevêtré. ‖ BOT. Plein d'algues.

tango ['tæŋgou] n. MUS. Tango *m.*

tangy ['tæŋi] adj. CULIN. Epicé, relevé. ‖ FIG. Savoureux, piquant.

tank [tæŋk] n. Réservoir *m.*; citerne *f.* ‖ AUTOM. Réservoir *m.* ‖ MILIT. Tank, char *m.* ‖ **Tank-buster**, n. MILIT. Canon antichar *m.* ‖ **Tank-car**, n. Wagon-citerne *m.* ‖ **Tank-engine** (or) locomotive, n. CH. DE F. Locomotive-tender *f.* ‖ **Tank-ship** (or) vessel, n. NAUT. Bateau-citerne *m.* ‖ **Tank-transporter**, n. MILIT. Porte-chars *m.* ‖ **Tank-truck**, n. U. S. Camion-citerne *m.*
— v. intr. **To tank up**, MILIT. Faire le plein; POP. Picoler; *to be tanked up*, être bourré.

tankage [-idʒ] n. Frais (*m. pl.*) d'emmagasinage *m.* (charge); capacité *f.* (capacity). ‖ AGRIC. Engrais *m.*

tankard [-əd] n. Chope *f.*

tanker [-ə*] n. NAUT. Pétrolier, bateau-citerne *m.*

tanner ['tænə*] n. Tanneur *m.*

tannery ['tænəri] n. Tannerie *f.*

tannic ['tænik] adj. CHIM. Tannique.

tannin ['tænin] n. Tanin, tannin *m.*

tanning ['tæniŋ] n. Tannage *m.* ‖ FAM. Raclée, dégelée *f.*

tansy ['tænzi] n. BOT. Tanacetum *m.*, tanaisie *f.*

tantalize ['tæntəlaiz] v. tr. Tenter, infliger le supplice de Tantale à.

tantalizing [-iŋ] adj. Tentant, torturant, provocant.

tantalum [-əm] n. CHIM., ELECTR. Tantale *m.*

Tantalus [-əs] n. Tantale *m.* ‖ COMM. Coffret (*m.*) à liqueurs. ‖ ZOOL. Tantale *m.*

tantamount ['tæntəmaunt] adj. Equivalent (*to*, à).

tantara [tæn'tɑ:rə] n. MUS. Taratata *m.*

tantrum ['tæntrəm] n. Accès (*m.*) de colère.

Tanzania [,tænzə'niə] n. GEOGR. Tanzanie *f.*

Taoism ['tɑ:ouizm] n. Taoïsme *m.*

Taoist [-ist] n. Taoïste *s.*

tap [tæp] n. Robinet *m.*; *cold-water tap*, robinet d'eau froide. ‖ Cannelle *f.* (of cask); *on tap*, en perce. ‖ ELECTR. Branchement *m.* ‖ TECHN. Taraud *m.* ‖ FAM. Boisson *f.* (drink); bar *m.*; buvette *f.*

(place); *to be on tap*, être toujours disponible (or) prêt (or) disposé. ‖ **Tap-room**, n. Buvette *f.*
— v. tr. (1). Mettre en perce (a cask); tirer (wine). ‖ Faire une prise à (a river). ‖ AGRIC. Entailler (a tree). ‖ TECHN. Couler (metal); tarauder (nut). ‖ ELECTR. Brancher sur; placer des écoutes sur (a telephone); écouter, surveiller (a conversation). ‖ MED. Percer (an abscess); ponctionner (a cavity). ‖ FAM. Taper (s.o.) [*for*, de]. ‖ FIG. Drainer (capital, talent), exploiter (resources).

tap n. Tape *f.* (blow). ‖ Petit coup *m.* (sound). ‖ MILIT. U. S. Pl. Extinction (*f.*) des feux. ‖ TECHN. Rondelle (*f.*) de cuir pour talon de chaussure.
— v. tr. (1). Taper, tapoter; donner un petit coup à. ‖ TECHN. Relever (a shoe-heel). ‖ **Tap-dance**, n. Danse (*f.*) à claquettes.
— v. intr. Taper, frapper un petit coup.

tape [teip] n. Ganse *f.* (for garments). ‖ Bolduc *m.* (for parcels). ‖ Ruban *m.* (of paper, steel). ‖ SPORTS. Bande d'arrivée *f.* ‖ FAM. Arrivée *f.* ‖ **Tape-machine**, n. Printing; récepteur morse, téléimprimeur *m.* ‖ **Tape-line, tape-measure**, n. Mètre-ruban, centimètre *m.* ‖ **Tape-recorder**, n. Magnétophone *m.* ‖ **Tape-recording**, n. Enregistrement sur magnétophone *m.*
— v. tr. Mettre une ganse à, border (a dress). ‖ Ficeler (a parcel). ‖ Mesurer au cordeau (land). ‖ ELECTR. Guiper. ‖ MILIT. Repérer. ‖ FAM. Jauger (s.o.); *I've got the situation taped*, j'ai la situation bien en main.

taper [-ə*] n. Longue chandelle *f.* ‖ Fuseau *m.* (form). ‖ ECCLES. Cierge *m.*
— adj. Mince, effilé, fuselé.
— v. intr. S'effiler; finir en pointe.
— v. tr. Effiler, fuseler, terminer en pointe.

tapering [-iŋ] adj. Effilé, fuselé; *tapering trousers*, fuseaux.

tapestried ['tæpistrid] adj. Tapissé.

tapestry [-tri] n. Tapisserie *f.* ‖ Cretonne (*f.*) d'ameublement. ‖ **Tapestry-carpet**, n. Tapis bouclé *m.* ‖ **Tapestry-weaver**, n. Tapissier *m.*

tapeworm ['teipwə:m] n. MED. Ténia, ver solitaire *m.*

tapioca [,tæpi'oukə] n. CULIN. Tapioca *m.*

tapir ['teipə*] n. ZOOL. Tapir *m.*

tapper ['tæpə*] n. Manipulateur *m.* ‖ Taraudeuse *f.*

tappet ['tæpit] n. TECHN. Taquet *m.* ‖ AUTOM. Culbuteur *m.*

tapster ['tæpstə*] n. Garçon de bar; cabaretier *m.*

tar [tɑ:*] n. Goudron *m.* ‖ NAUT., FAM. Loup (*m.*) de mer. ‖ **Tar-spraying**, n. Goudronnage *m.*
— v. tr. (1). Goudronner. ‖ FIG. Flétrir.

taradiddle ['tærədidl] n. FAM. Sornette, blague *f.*

tarantella [,tærən'telə] n. MUS. Tarentelle *f.*

tarantula [tə'ræntjulə] n. ZOOL. Tarentule *f.*

taraxacum [tə'ræksəkəm] n. BOT. Pissenlit *m.* ‖ MED. Taraxacum *m.*

tarboosh [tɑ:'bu:ʃ] n. Tarbouch(e) *m.*

tardigrade ['tɑ:digreid] adj., n. ZOOL. Tardigrade *m.*

tardily ['tɑ:dili] adv. Avec nonchalance. ‖ Sans empressement. ‖ Tardivement. ‖ U. S. En retard.

tardiness [-nis] n. Lenteur, nonchalance *f.* ‖ Manque d'empressement *m.* ‖ Retard *m.*

tardy ['tɑ:di] adj. Lent, nonchalant. ‖ Peu empressé. ‖ Tardif (belated). ‖ U. S. En retard.

tare [tɛə*] n. BOT. Ivraie *f.*

tare n. COMM. Tare *f.*
— v. tr. Tarer.

targe [tɑ:dʒ] n. † Targe *f.*

target ['tɑ:git] n. MILIT. Cible *f.* ‖ TECHN. Voyant *m.* ‖ U. S. CH. DE F. Disque *m.* ‖ FIG. Cible *f.*; but, objectif *m.*

tariff ['tærif] n. Tarif, barème *m.*
— v. tr. Tarifer.

tarlatan ['tɑ:lətən] n. Tarlatane *f.*

tarmac ['tɑ:mæk] n. (trade mark). TECHN. Tarmacadam *m.* (material). ‖ AUTOM. Chaussée *f.* (road surface). ‖ AVIAT. Piste (*f.*) en dur.
— v. tr. Tarmacadamiser.
— N.B. Remarquer l'orthographe du prét. et du p. p. *tarmacked.*
tarn [tɑ:n] n. Petit lac (*m.*) de montagne.
tarnish ['tɑ:niʃ] v. tr. Ternir (lit. and fig.).
— v. intr. Se ternir.
— n. Ternissure *f.*
tarnishable [-əbl] adj. Ternissable.
tarot ['tærou] adj., n. Tarot *m.; tarot cards,* tarot.
tarpaulin [tæ:'pɔ:lin] n. Bâche goudronnée *f.* ‖ NAUT. Prélart *m.* ‖ FAM. NAUT. Mathurin *m.*
— adj. En toile goudronnée; *tarpaulin bridge,* passerelle de bâches.
tarpon ['tɑ:pən] n. ZOOL. Tarpon *m.*
tarragon ['tærəgən] n. BOT. Estragon *m.*
tarred ['tɑ:d] adj. Goudronné, bitumé. ‖ FAM. *All tarred with the same brush,* tous du même tonneau.
tarrock ['tærək] n. ZOOL. Mouette *f.*
tarry ['tɑ:ri] adj. Goudronneux. ‖ Couvert de goudron, suintant.
tarry ['tæri] v. intr. (2). Demeurer, rester. (See STAY.) ‖ Tarder, s'attarder (to be late). ‖ **To tarry for,** attendre.
tarsal ['tɑ:sl̩] adj. MED. Tarsien.
tarsus [-əs] (pl. **tarsi** [-ai]) n. MED., ZOOL. Tarse *m.*
tart [tɑ:t] n. CULIN. Tourte *f.* (with crust); tarte *f.* (without crust). ‖ FAM. Poule *f.* ‖ **Tart-dish,** n. CULIN. Tourtière *f.*
— v. tr. **To tart up,** FAM. Attifer (person); retaper (a house, an object); *to tart oneself up,* s'attifer, s'habiller de façon tape-à-l'œil, se maquiller outrageusement.
tart adj. Acide, aigre, aigrelet. (See SOUR.) ‖ Vert (wine). ‖ FAM. Mordant (answer); aigre, acariâtre (disposition).
tartan ['tɑ:tən] n. Tartan *m.* (coat); écossais *m.* (fabric).
— adj. Ecossais.
tartan n. NAUT. Tartane *f.*
Tartar ['tɑ:tə*] n. GEOGR. Tartare (or) Tatar *m.* ‖ FAM. Dur de dur *m.* (man); virago *f.* (woman); *to catch a Tartar,* tomber sur un bec.
tartar n. Tartre *m.* (on bottle, teeth).
tartaric [tɑ:'tærik] adj. CHIM. Tartrique.
Tartarus [tɑ:tərəs] n. Tartare *m.* (abyss).
tartlet ['tɑ:tlit] n. CULIN. Tartelette *f.*
tartly ['tɑ:tli] adv. Avec aigreur.
tartness [-nis] n. Aigreur *f.* (lit. and fig.).
tartrate ['tɑ:treit] n. CHIM. Tartrate *m.*
Tarzan ['tɑ:zən] n. Tarzan *m.* ‖ U. S. FAM. Costaud *m.*
task [tɑ:sk] n. Travail *m.; * tâche, besogne *f.* ‖ Devoir *m.* (of a pupil). ‖ LOC. *To take s.o. to task for sth.,* réprimander qqn pour qqch., reprocher qqch. à qqn. ‖ **Task-force,** n. MILIT. Détachement spécial (*m.*) des forces de terre, de l'air et de mer. ‖ **Task-work,** n. Travail (*m.*) à la tâche.
— v. tr. Imposer une tâche à. ‖ Mettre à l'épreuve.
taskmaster [-ˌmɑ:stə*] n. Surveillant *m.* ‖ FIG. Tyran *m.*
tassel ['tæsəl] n. Gland *m.* (on curtain); pompon *m.* (on tam-o'-shanter). ‖ Signet *m.* (in a book). ‖ BOT. Aigrette *f.* (of maize).
— v. tr. (1). Garnir de glands. ‖ AGRIC. Ecimer (maize).
tastable ['teistəbl̩] adj. Qu'on peut goûter. ‖ Savoureux.
taste [teist] v. tr. Goûter, déguster. ‖ Goûter de, goûter à (to take a little of). ‖ † Goûter, apprécier (to enjoy). ‖ FIG. Goûter de.
— V. intr. Goûter, déguster (person). ‖ Avoir un goût (thing). ‖ **To taste of,** avoir un goût de, sentir; FIG. Goûter de.

— n. Goût *m.* (sense). ‖ Dégustation *f.* (act). ‖ Goût *m.; * saveur *f.* (flavour). ‖ Bouchée, gorgée *f.* (quantity). ‖ FIG. Goût *m.* (faculty, judgment); goût, penchant *m.; * inclination *f.* (*for,* pour) [preference]; *in good taste,* de bon goût. ‖ FAM. Aperçu, échantillon *m.*
tasteful [-ful] adj. De goût (person); de bon goût, savoureux (thing).
tastefully [-fuli] adv. Avec goût.
tastefulness [-fulnis] n. Bon goût *m.*
tasteless [-lis] adj. Sans saveur, fade. ‖ Sans goût.
taster [-ə*] n. Dégustateur *m.; * dégustatrice *f.* ‖ Tâte-vin *m.* (cup). ‖ Sonde *f.* (for cheese). ‖ FAM. Lecteur *m.* (publisher's reader).
tasty [-i] adj. CULIN. FAM. Savoureux, succulent. ‖ FAM. De bon goût.
tat [tæt] v. intr. (1). Faire de la frivolité.
— v. tr. Exécuter en frivolité (lacework).
tat n. FAM. Camelote, cochonnerie *f.* (shoddy goods).
tat, See TIT.
tata [tæ'tɑ:] interj. FAM. Salut!, Ciao!
tater ['teitə*] n. POP. Patate *f.* (potato).
tatter ['tætə*] n. Lambeau *m.* ‖ Pl. Loques *f. pl.; * haillons *m. pl.*
tatterdemalion [ˌtætədi'meiljən] n. Loqueteux *m.*
tattered ['tætəd] adj. Loqueteux, déguenillé, dépenaillé, en haillons (person); en lambeaux, en loques, tout déchiré (thing).
tatting ['tætiŋ] n. Frivolité *f.* (lace).
tattle ['tætl̩] n. Bavardage *m.* (chatter). ‖ Commérage *m.; * cancans *m. pl.* (gossip).
— v. intr. Bavarder. ‖ Cancaner, jaser.
tattler [-ə*] n. Bavard, cancanier *s.* ‖ ZOOL. Chevalier *m.*
tattoo [tə'tu:] n. MILIT. Retraite *f.*
— v. intr. Tambouriner.
tattoo v. tr. Tatouer.
— n. Tatouage *m.*
tatty ['tæti] adj. FAM. Minable, miteux.
tau [tɔ:] n. Tau *m.* ‖ **Tau-cross,** n. Croix (*f.*) de Saint-Antoine.
taught [tɔ:t] pret., p. p. See TEACH.
taunt [tɔ:nt] adj. NAUT. Elancé (mast).
taunt n. Sarcasme, brocard *m.; * raillerie, insulte *f.* ‖ Objet de sarcasme *m.*
— v. tr. Railler, bafouer, critiquer de façon insultante, couvrir de sarcasmes.
taunting [-iŋ] adj. Méprisant; injurieux, insultant; sarcastique.
taurine ['tɔ:rain] adj. ZOOL. De taureau, tauresque.
Taurus [-əs] n. ASTRON. Taureau *m.*
taut [tɔ:t] adj. NAUT. Etarqué (rope); paré (ship). ‖ FAM. Tendu (nerves); crispé (smile).
tauten [-n̩] v. tr. NAUT. Raidir.
tautologic(al) [ˌtɔ:tə'lɔdʒik(əl)] adj. Tautologique.
tautology [tɔ:'tɔlədʒi] n. Tautologie *f.*
tavern ['tævən] n. † Taverne *f.* ‖ Cabaret *m.* ‖ **Tavern-keeper,** n. Cabaretier *m.; * † tavernier *m.*
taw [tɔ:] v. tr. Mégir (hides).
taw n. Grosse bille (*f.*) de verre.
tawdrily ['tɔ:drili] adv. D'un luxe voyant.
tawdriness [-nis] n. Clinquant *m.* (of jewelry). ‖ Luxe tapageur *m.*
tawdry ['tɔ:dri] adj. Clinquant, voyant, criard.
— n. Clinquant *m.*
tawer ['tɔ:ə*] n. Mégissier *m.*
tawery [-ri] n. Mégisserie *f.*
tawny ['tɔ:ni] adj. Fauve, feu (colour); hâlé, basané, bronzé (skin).
taws(e) [tɔ:z] n. Martinet, fouet *m.*
tax [tæks] n. FIN. Impôt *m.; * taxe, contribution *f.; * amusement tax, impôt sur les spectacles; *purchase tax,* taxe de luxe. ‖ FIG. Charge, épreuve *f.* (*on,* pour). ‖ **Tax-collector,** n. FIN. Percepteur *m.* ‖

Tax-deductible, adj. Déductible des impôts. ‖ **Tax-evasion,** U. S. **tax-dodging,** n. FIN. Fraude fiscale *f.* ‖ **Tax-free,** adj. Net (or) exempt d'impôts. ‖ **Tax haven,** n. Paradis fiscal *m.* ‖ **Tax-office,** n. Perception *f.* ‖ **Tax-ridden,** adj. Ecrasé d'impôts.
— v. tr. FIN. Taxer, imposer. ‖ FIG. Mettre à l'épreuve (or) à contribution. ‖ FIG. Taxer, accuser (*with,* de). ‖ U. S. Compter, prendre (to charge).
taxable [-əbḷ] adj. FIN. Imposable.
taxation [tæk'seiʃən] n. FIN. Taxation *f.;* prélèvement *m.* (act); impôts *m. pl.* (taxes).
taxi ['tæksi] n. AUTOM. Taxi *m.* ‖ **Taxi-driver,** n. AUTOM. Chauffeur de taxi *m.* ‖ **Taxi-girl,** n. FAM. Entraîneuse *f.* ‖ **Taxi-rank** (or) U. S. **stand,** n. AUTOM. Station (*f.*) de taxis.
— v. intr. AVIAT. Rouler au sol. ‖ AUTOM. Aller en taxi.
taxidermist ['tæksidə:mist] n. Naturaliste *m.*
taxidermy [-i] n. Taxidermie *f.*
taximeter [tæk'simitə*] n. Taximètre *m.*
taxiplane ['tæksiplein] n. AVIAT. Avion-taxi *m.*
taxonomic(al) [,tæksə'nɔmik(əl)] adj. Taxinomique.
taxonomist [tæk'sɔnəmist] n. Taxinomiste *s.*
taxonomy [tæk'sɔnəmi] n. Taxinomie *f.*
taxpayer ['tækspeiə*] n. FIN. Contribuable *m.*
T. B. [,ti:'bi:] abbr. *tuberculosis,* tuberculose.
te [ti:] n. See TI.
tea [ti:] n. BOT., CULIN. Thé *m.; Indian tea,* thé de Ceylan. ‖ MED. Infusion, tisane *f. : camomile tea,* camomille. ‖ FIG. Thé, goûter *m.* (meal, reception). ‖ FAM. *That's not my cup of tea,* ce n'est pas mes oignons (or) mon rayon. ‖ **Tea-ball** (or) **infuser,** n. Boule (*f.*) à thé. ‖ **Tea-caddy,** n. Boîte (*f.*) à thé. ‖ **Tea-cloth,** n. Nappe (*f.*) à thé. ‖ **Tea-cosy,** n. Couvre-théière *m.* ‖ **Tea-cup,** n. Tasse (*f.*) à thé. ‖ **Tea-dance,** n. Thé dansant *m.* ‖ **Tea-leaf,** n. Feuille (*f.*) de thé; *tea-leaves,* thé, feuilles de thé. ‖ **Tea-party,** n. Thé *m.* ‖ **Tea-poisoning,** n. MED. Théisme *m.* ‖ **Tea-pot,** n. Théière *f.* ‖ **Tea-room** (or) **-shop,** n. Salon de thé *m.* ‖ **Tea-rose,** n. Bot. Rose thé *f.* ‖ **Tea-service** (or) **-set,** n. Service à thé *m.* ‖ **Tea-spoon,** n. Cuiller (*f.*) à café. ‖ **Tea-strainer,** n. Passe-thé *m.* ‖ **Tea-trolley,** U. S. **tea wagon,** n. Table roulante *f.* ‖ **Tea-urn,** n. Samovar *m.*
— v. intr. Prendre le thé.
— N. B. Noter les pret. et p. p. *tea'd.*
teach [ti:tʃ] v. tr. (175). Instruire (s.o.); enseigner (sth.); *to teach s.o. sth.,* enseigner (or) apprendre qqch. à qqn. ‖ **Teach-in,** n. Colloque, séminaire *m.*
— v. intr. Enseigner, être professeur.
teachable [-əbḷ] adj. Ouvert, apte à apprendre, docile (person); enseignable (thing).
teachableness [-əbḷnis] n. Aptitude (*f.*) à apprendre (of s.o.); caractère enseignable *m.* (of sth.).
teacher [-ə*] n. Maître, instituteur *m.;* maîtresse, institutrice *f.;* professeur, enseignant *s.; to spend five years as a teacher,* faire cinq ans de professorat.
teachership [-ʃip] n. Professorat *m.*
teaching [iŋ] n. Enseignement *m.* (art, doctrine, instruction, profession). ‖ **Teaching hospital,** n. Centre hospitalo-universitaire, C. H. U. *m.* ‖ **Teaching-machine,** n. Machine (*f.*) à enseigner.
teak [ti:k] n. BOT. Teck, tek *m.*
teal [ti:l] n. ZOOL. Sarcelle *f.*
team [ti:m] n. Attelage *m.* ‖ SPORTS. Equipe *f.;* team *m.* ‖ TECHN. Equipe *f.* ‖ **Team-spirit,** n. Esprit (*m.*) d'équipe. ‖ **Team-work,** n. Travail (*m.*) en équipe.
— v. tr. Atteler ensemble (horses). ‖ SPORTS. Faire jouer (*with,* avec), associer (*with,* à). ‖ FIG. Associer (*with,* à), faire travailler en collaboration (*with,* avec).
— v. intr. **To team up,** s'associer, se joindre (*with,* à).
teamster [-stə*] n. Charretier *m.* ‖ U. S. Camionneur *m.*

teapoy ['ti:pɔi] n. Petite table (*f.*) à thé.
tear ['tɛə*] v. tr. (176). Déchirer, lacérer; *to tear a hole in,* faire un trou à. ‖ Arracher (*from,* à, de; *out of,* de). ‖ Séparer (*from,* de). ‖ **To tear away,** arracher; *to tear s.o. away from,* décoller qqn de (fam.). ‖ **To tear down,** arracher (a poster). ‖ **To tear off,** arracher (a label); faire sauter (a wrapper). ‖ **To tear out,** arracher, déchirer (a page); *to tear s.o.'s eyes out,* arracher les yeux à qqn. ‖ **To tear up,** déchirer (a letter); AGRIC. Labourer (the ground); arracher (a tree).
— v. intr. Se déchirer. ‖ Tirer (*at,* sur). ‖ **To tear along,** filer précipitamment. ‖ **To tear around,** se précipiter.
— n. Déchirure *f.;* trou, accroc *m.* ‖ FAM. Rage *f.* (anger); allure, vitesse *f.* (speed). ‖ **Tear-off,** adj. Perforé (leaf); *tear-off calendar,* éphéméride. ‖ **Tear-proof,** adj. Indéchirable.
tear [tiə*] n. Larme *f.;* pleur *m.* ‖ FAM. Larme *f.* (drop). ‖ **Tear-duct,** n. MED. Conduit (or) canal lacrymal *m.* ‖ **Tear-gas,** n. MILIT. Gaz lacrymogène *m.* ‖ **Tear-jerker,** n. Mélo *m.* ‖ **Tear-stained,** adj. Marqué de larmes (face).
tearaway ['tɛərə,wei] n. Voyou *m.*
— adj. Fougueux, impétueux.
tearful ['tiəful] adj. Affligeant (event); en larmes (person). ‖ Larmoyant (pej.).
tearfully [-fuli] adv. En pleurant.
tearing ['tɛəriŋ] adj. Déchirant. ‖ FAM. Ravageur, furieux; *tearing rage,* colère bleue.
— n. Déchirement *m.* ‖ MED. Déchirure *f.* (of a muscle).
tearless ['tiəlis] adj. Sans larmes; aux yeux secs.
tease [ti:z] v. tr. TECHN. Effilocher (a fabric); peigner, carder (wool). ‖ FIG. Taquiner, tracasser, harceler; asticoter (fam.).
— n. Taquinerie *f.* (act); taquin *s.* (person). ‖ FAM. Allumeuse *f.* (woman).
teasel [-ḷ] n. BOT. Cardère *f.* ‖ TECHN. Carde *f.*
teaser [-ə*] n. Taquin *s.* ‖ FAM. Casse-tête *m.* ‖ U. S. FAM. Amorce *f.*
teasing [-iŋ] adj. Taquin (person); persifleur (tone).
teat [ti:t] n. MED. Mamelon, bout de sein *m.* ‖ ZOOL. Tétine *f.;* trayon *m.* ‖ TECHN. Téton *m.*
tec [tek] n. FAM. Détective *m.*
tech [tek] n. FAM. Ecole technique *f.*
technetium [tek'ni:ʃiəm] n. CHIM. Technétium *m.*
technic ['teknik] adj., n. Technique *f.*
technical [-əl] adj. Technique; *technical school,* école professionnelle.
technicality [,tekni'kæliti] n. Technicité *f.* ‖ Mot (or) aspect technique *m.* (technical difficulty). ‖ Point de détail *m.* (in rules). ‖ JUR. Vice (*m.*) de forme.
technically [-əli] adv. Techniquement; en termes techniques.
technician [tek'niʃən], **technicist** ['teknisist] n. Technicien *s.*
technicolor ['teknikʌlə*] adj., n. CINEM. Technicolor *m.*
technics ['tekniks] n. sg. Technologie *f.*
technique [tek'ni:k] n. Technique *f.*
technocracy [tek'nɔkrəsi] n. Technocratie *f.*
technocrat ['teknə,kræt] n. Technocrate *s.*
technocratic [,teknə'krætik] adj. Technocratique.
technological [,teknə'lɔdʒikəl] adj. Technologique.
technology [-dʒi] n. Technologie *f.*
techy ['tetʃi] adj. See TETCHY.
tectonic [-nik] adj. Architectonique. ‖ GEOL. Tectonique.
tectonics [-niks] n. sg. Architectonique *f.* ‖ GEOL. Tectonique *f.; plate tectonics,* tectonique des plaques.
tectrices [tek'traisi:z] n. pl. ZOOL. Tectrices *f. pl.*
ted [ted] v. tr. (1). AGRIC. Faner.

tedder [-ə*] n. AGRIC. Faneuse *f.* (machine); faneur *s.* (person).

Teddy ['tedi] n. Edouard *m.* (name). ‖ **Teddy-bear**, n. FAM. Nounours *m.; teddy-bear cloth*, peluche. ‖ **Teddy-boy**, n. FAM. Zazou *m.*

tedious ['ti:diəs] adj. Ennuyeux, fastidieux, lassant, assommant.

tediously [-li] adv. Fastidieusement, de façon assommante.

tediousness [-nis], **tedium** ['ti:diəm] n. Ennui *m.*

tee n. SPORTS. Tertre de départ, dé, tee *m.* (in golf).
— v. tr. SPORTS. Surélever (the ball).
— v. intr. To tee off (or) up, SPORTS. Commencer à jouer ; U. S. FAM. Se mettre en branle.

teehee. See TEHEE.

teem [ti:m] v. intr. † Enfanter ‖ Abonder (*with*, en); fourmiller, pulluler, grouiller, regorger (*with*, de).

teeming [-iŋ] adj. Grouillant (crowd); torrentiel (rain); bondé (street).

teen-age ['ti:n'eidʒ] adj. COMM. Pour adolescents.

teen-ager [-ə*] n. FAM. Adolescent *s.*

teens ['ti:nz] n. pl. Années (*f. pl.*) de l'adolescence *f.* (de 13 à 19 ans).

teeny-bopper ['ti:ni,bɔpə*] n. FAM. Minette *f.*

teeny(-weeny) ['ti:ni('wi:ni)], **teensy (weensy)** ['ti:nsi('wi:nsi)] adj. FAM. Tout petit, minuscule.

teepee ['ti:pi:] n. Tipi *m.*

teeter ['ti:tə*] v. intr. U. S. Basculer; chanceler.

teeter-totter [-'tɔtə*] n. U. S. Balançoire *f.*

teeth [ti:θ]. See TOOTH.

teethe [ti:ð] v. intr. MED. Percer (or) faire ses dents.

teething [-iŋ] n. MED. Dentition *f.*

teetotal [ti:'toutl] adj. Abstinent (person); anti-alcoolique (society). ‖ FAM. Absolu, entier.

teetotalism [-izm] n. Abstention (*f.*) de boissons alcooliques ; antialcoolisme *m.*

teetotaller [-ə*] n. Abstinent *s.*

teetotum [ti:'toutəm] n. Toton *m.*

tegular ['tegjulə*] adj. Tégulaire.

tegument ['tegjumənt] n. Tégument *m.*

tegumental [,tegju'mentəl], **tegumentary** [-əri] adj. Tégumentaire.

tehee [ti:'hi:] n. Rire étouffé *m.*
— v. intr. Pouffer.

telamon ['teləmən] n. ARCHIT. Atlante, télamon *m.*

telautograph [te'lɔ:təgrɑ:f] n. Télautographe *m.*

telecamera [teli'kæmərə] n. Appareil (*m.*) de téléphotographie.

telecast ['telikɑ:st] v. tr., intr. (32). Téléviser.
— n. RADIO. Emission de télévision *f.*

telecinema [,teli'sinimə] n. Télécinéma *m.*

telecommunication [,telikəmju:ni'keiʃən] n. Télécommunications *f. pl.*

telecontrol [,telikən'troul] n. Commande à distance *f.*

telefilm ['teli,film] n. Téléfilm *m.*

telegenic [,teli'dʒenik] adj. Télégénique.

telegram ['teligræm] n. Télégramme *m.; dépêche f.*

telegraph [-grɑ:f] n. Télégraphe *m.; telegraph boy* (or) *messenger*, télégraphiste (facteur); *telegraph operator*, télégraphiste (receveur). ‖ † Sémaphore *m.* ‖ SPORTS. Tableau d'affichage *m.*
— adj. Télégraphique (line, pole, wire).
— v. intr., tr. Télégraphier. ‖ FAM. Appeler par signes.

telegrapher [ti'legrəfə*] n. U. S. Télégraphiste *m.*

telegraphese [,teligrə'fi:z] n. Style télégraphique *m.*

telegraphic [,teli'græfik] adj. Télégraphique (address, message order, style).

telegraphically [-li] adv. Télégraphiquement.

telegraphist [ti'legrəfist] n. Télégraphiste *m.*

telegraphy [ti'legrəfi] n. Télégraphie *f.; wireless telegraphy*, télégraphie sans fil.

telekinesis [,telikai'ni:sis] n. PSYCH. Télékinésie *f.*

telemeter [ti'lemitə*] n. Télémètre *m.*

teleologic(al) [,teliə'lɔdʒik(!)] adj. PHILOS. Téléologique, finaliste.

teleology [,teli'ɔledʒi] n. PHILOS. Téléologie *f.*

telepathic [,teli'pæθik] adj. Télépathique.

telepathically [-əli] adv. Par télépathie.

telepathy [ti'lepəθi] n. Télépathie *f.*

telephone ['telifoun] n. Téléphone *m.* ‖ **Telephone-bell**, n. Sonnerie (*f.*) du téléphone. ‖ **Telephone book (or) directory**, n. Annuaire du téléphone, annuaire, Bottin *m.* ‖ **Telephone-booth**, n. Cabine téléphonique *f.* ‖ **Telephone-call**, n. Appel *m.* (or) communication (*f.*) téléphonique. ‖ **Telephone-exchange**, n. Central téléphonique *m.* ‖ **Telephone-girl**, **telephone-operator**, n. Téléphoniste, standardiste *f.* ‖ **Telephone-number**, n. Numéro de téléphone *m.* ‖ **Telephone-receiver**, n. Récepteur *m.* ‖ **Telephone-wire**, n. Fil téléphonique *m.*
— v. tr., intr. Téléphoner.

telephonic [,teli'fɔnik] adj. Téléphonique.

telephonically [-əli] adv. Par téléphone, téléphoniquement.

telephonist [ti'lefənist] n. Téléphoniste *s.*

telephony [-i] n. Téléphonie *f.*

telephotographic [,teli,foutə'græfik] adj. Téléphotographique.

telephotography [,telifə'tɔgrəfi] n. Téléphotographie *f.*

telephoto-lens [-lenz] n. Téléobjectif *m.*

teleprinter ['teliprintə*] n. Téléimprimeur, télétype *m.*

teleprompter ['teli,prɔmptə*] n. Téléprompteur *m.*

telescope ['teliskoup] n. Télescope *m.; longue-vue f.*
— v. tr. Télescoper, emboîter. ‖ FAM. Résumer.
— v. intr. Se télescoper.

telescopic [,telis'kɔpik] adj. Télescopique. ‖ FAM. Condensé.

telescopy [ti'leskəpi] n. Télescopie *f.*

teletype ['teli,taip], U. S. **teletypewriter** [,teli'taip,raitə*] n. Télétype, téléimprimeur, téléscripteur *m.*

teleview ['telivju:] v. tr. RADIO. Voir à la télévision.

televiewer [-ə*] n. Téléspectateur *m.; téléspectatrice f.*

televise ['telivaiz] v. tr. Téléviser.

television ['teliviʒən] n. Télévision *f.; television set*, appareil de télévision *m.*

telex ['teleks] n. Télex *m.*
— v. tr. Télexer, transmettre par télex (message); contacter par télex (person).

tell [tel] v. tr. (177). Dire, raconter (a story). ‖ Dire, faire connaître, énoncer; *I can't tell you how*, je ne saurais vous dire comment; *to tell the facts*, exposer les faits; *to tell the truth*, dire la vérité; à vrai dire. ‖ Indiquer, montrer (the way). ‖ Révéler, dénoter, dire; *her face told her joy*, la joie se peignait sur son visage. ‖ Discerner, déterminer, distinguer; *he can't tell the difference*, il ne peut pas voir la différence; *to tell s.o. by*, reconnaître qqn à; *to tell right from wrong*, démêler le bien du mal. ‖ Dire, assurer, affirmer (*that*, que). ‖ † Compter; *to tell one's beads*, dire son chapelet. FAM. *You're telling me!*, à qui le dites-vous! ‖ To tell off, MILIT. Affecter, désigner; FAM. Rembarrer, rabrouer. ‖ **Tell-tale**, adj. Révélateur; n. Dénonciateur, rapporteur *m.;* bavard *s.;* TECHN. Indicateur, contrôleur *m.;* NAUT. Axiomètre *m.*
— v. intr. Parler (*of*, de). ‖ FIG. Porter, influer (*on*, sur). ‖ To tell against, desservir, témoigner contre. ‖ To tell on, FAM. Dénoncer; rapporter contre (fam.). ‖ To tell over, dénombrer.

teller [-ə*] n. Conteur *s.;* narrateur *m.;* narratrice *f.* ‖ Scrutateur *m.* (of votes). ‖ FIN. Caissier *m.*

telling [-iŋ] adj. Fort, efficace, qui porte (argument); bien assené (blow).

tellurian [te'ljuəriən] adj. Tellurien.
telluric [te'ljuərik] adj. Chim., Med. Tellurique.
tellurium [te'ljuəriəm] n. Chim. Tellure *m.*
telly ['teli] n. Fam. Télé *f.* (television).
telpher ['telfə*] adj., n. Téléphérique; transporteur monorail *m.*
telpherage [-ridʒ] n. Téléphérage *m.*
temerity [ti'meriti] n. Témérité *f.*
temp ['temp] n. Fam. Intérimaire *s.*
temper ['tempə*] v. tr. Techn. Tremper (steel). ‖ Archit. Gâcher (mortar). ‖ Mus. Accorder. ‖ Fig. Tempérer, adoucir (an action); maîtriser, contenir (passions).
— v. intr. Techn. Se tremper.
— n. Techn. Trempe *f.* ‖ Fig. Tempérament, caractère *m.; to have a good temper,* avoir bon caractère. ‖ Fig. Calme, sang-froid *m.; out of temper,* en colère; *to lose one's temper,* se mettre en colère. ‖ Fig. Humeur *f.; in a bad temper,* de mauvaise humeur.
tempera ['tempərə] n. Arts. Tempera *f.*
temperament ['tempərəmənt] n. Med., Mus. Tempérament *m.*
temperamental [ˌtempərə'mentl̩] adj. Med. Constitutionnel (disease); cyclothymique (person). ‖ Fam. Instable.
temperance ['tempərəns] n. Tempérance *f.* (in drinking). ‖ Retenue, modération *f.* (in speech).
temperate [-it] adj. Tempéré (climate); tempérant, sobre (person). ‖ Fig. Modéré.
temperately [-itli] adv. Modérément.
temperateness [-itnis] n. Douce température *f.* (climate). ‖ Tempérance *f.* ‖ Fig. Modération *f.*
temperature ['temprətʃə*] n. Phys., Med. Température *f.* ‖ **Temperature-chart,** n. Med. Feuille de température *f.*
tempest ['tempist] n. Tempête, tourmente *f.;* ouragan *m.* ‖ Fig. Tempête *f.* (of applause).
tempestuous [tem'pestjuəs] adj. Tempêtueux, orageux.
Templar ['templə*] n. Templier *m.* ‖ Membre (*m.*) d'une société de tempérance.
template. See Templet.
temple ['templ̩] n. Temple *m.*
temple n. Med. Tempe *f.* ‖ **Temple-bone,** n. Med. Os temporal *m.*
templet ['templit] n. Gabarit, calibre *m.* ‖ Patron *m.* (pattern).
tempo ['tempou] n. Mus. Tempo *m.* ‖ Fig. Rythme *m.*
temporal ['tempərəl] adj. Med. Temporal. ‖ Gramm., Fig. Temporel.
— n. Med. Temporal *m.*
temporality [ˌtempə'ræliti] n. Eccles. Temporel *m.* ‖ Jur. Caractère provisoire *m.*
temporarily ['tempərərili] adv. Temporairement.
temporariness [-rinis] n. Jur. Caractère provisoire *m.*
temporary [-ri] adj. De passage (guest); temporaire, provisoire, transitoire (measure); intérimaire, à titre temporaire (post).
temporization [ˌtempərai'zeiʃən] n. Temporisation *f.* ‖ Compromis *m.* ‖ Adaptation (*f.*) aux circonstances.
temporize ['tempəraiz] v. intr. Temporiser, gagner du temps (to procrastinate). ‖ Accepter un compromis (*with,* avec). ‖ S'adapter aux circonstances.
temporizer [-ə*] n. Temporisateur *m.* ‖ Opportuniste *s.*
tempt [tempt] v. tr. Tenter, pousser, inciter (*to,* à). ‖ Tenter, séduire (to attract). ‖ Eccles. Tenter.
temptation [temp'teiʃən] n. Tentation *f.*
tempter ['temptə*] n. Tentateur *m.*
tempting [-iŋ] adj. Tentant, alléchant, séduisant. ‖ Culin. Appétissant. ‖ Eccles. Tentateur (devil).
temptress [-ris] n. Tentatrice *f.*
ten [ten] adj., n. Dix *m.*

tenable ['tenəbl̩] adj. Occupable (post); soutenable (theory). ‖ Milit. Tenable.
tenace ['teneis] n. Impasse, tenace *f.* (at cards).
tenacious [ti'neiʃəs] adj. Tenace. ‖ Attaché (*of,* à); opiniâtre (*of,* dans).
tenaciously [-li] adv. Avec ténacité.
tenacity [ti'næsiti] n. Ténacité *f.* ‖ Attachement *m.* (*of,* à). ‖ Techn. Cohésion *f.* (of a metal).
tenancy ['tenənsi] n. Location *f.* (act); durée de location *f.* (time).
tenant ['tenənt] n. Locataire *s.* (in a house). ‖ **Tenant-farmer,** n. Fermier à bail, tenancier *m.*
— v. tr. Louer.
tenantable [-əbl̩] adj. Habitable (house); locatif (repair).
tenantless [-lis] adj. Sans locataire, non loué.
tench [tenʃ] n. Zool. Tanche *f.*
tend [tend] v. intr. Aller, se diriger (*towards,* vers) [road]. ‖ Fig. Tendre, incliner (*to,* à); être susceptible (*to,* de); tendre, se diriger (*to,* vers).
tend v. tr. Garder (cattle). ‖ Med. Soigner, veiller sur (a patient). ‖ Techn. Surveiller (a machine). ‖ Naut. Faire éviter (a ship).
— v. intr. **To tend on,** † Servir.
tendency ['tendənsi] n. Tendance *f.*
tendential [-ʃəl] adj. A tendance, tendancieux.
tendentious [ten'denʃəs] adj. Tendancieux, partisan, partial.
tendentiously [-li] adv. Tendancieusement, partialement.
tendentiousness [-nis] n. Caractère tendancieux *m.,* partialité *f.*
tender ['tendə*] n. Garde *m.* ‖ Naut., Ch. de f. Tender *m.; seaplane tender,* ravitailleur d'hydravions. ‖ U. S. Fam. Barman *m.*
tender adj. Tendre (age, caress, grass, meat); sensible (feet, point). ‖ Emu (condolences, regrets); affectueux (congratulations, sympathy); tendre, affectueux (person). ‖ Délicat (conscience, subject). ‖ Soucieux, soigneux, jaloux (*of,* de). ‖ **Tender-hearted,** adj. Compatissant, au cœur tendre.
tender v. tr. Offrir (one's congratulations, resignation). ‖ Fin. *To tender money,* faire une offre réelle. ‖ Jur. Déférer (an oath); présenter (a plea).
— v. intr. Comm. Soumissionner (*for,* pour; *to,* auprès de).
— n. Offre *m.* ‖ Fin. Offre réelle *f.; legal tender,* cours légal; *to be legal tender,* avoir cours. ‖ Comm. Soumission *f.*
tenderer [-rə*] n. Comm. Soumissionnaire *m.*
tenderfoot [-fut] n. Nouveau venu *s.* ‖ U. S. Louveteau *m.* (boy scout). ‖ Fam. Novice, néophyte *m.*
tenderloin [-lɔin] n. Culin. Filet *m.*
tenderly [-li] adv. Tendrement.
tenderness [-nis] n. Tendreté, sensibilité *f.* ‖ Tendresse, affection *f.* ‖ Délicatesse *f.* (of conscience, of a subject). ‖ Soin *m.* (*of,* de).
tendinous ['tendinəs] adj. Tendineux.
tendon ['tendən] n. Med. Tendon *m.*
tendril ['tendril] n. Bot. Vrille *f.;* crampon *m.*
tenebrous ['tenibrəs] adj. † Ténébreux.
tenement ['tenəmənt] n. Logement *m.* ‖ Jur. Tenure *f.;* fonds *m.* ‖ **Tenement-house,** n. Maison ouvrière, maison (*f.*) de rapport.
tenesmus [ti'nezməs] n. Med. Ténesme *m.*
tenet ['ti:nət] n. Doctrine *f.;* principe *m.*
tenfold ['tenfould] adj. Décuple.
— adv. Dix fois plus.
tenner ['tenə*] n. Fam. Billet (*m.*) de 10 livres (or) de 10 dollars.
tennis ['tenis] n. Sports. Tennis *m.* (lawn-tennis); jeu (*m.*) de paume (real tennis). ‖ **Tennis-court,** n. Sports. Court *m.* ‖ **Tennis-shoe,** n. Chaussure (*f.*) de tennis.
tenon ['tenən] n. Techn. Tenon *m.* ‖ **Tenon-joint,** n. Assemblage (*m.*) à tenon et mortaise.
— v. tr. Techn. Assembler à tenon.

tenor ['tenə*] n. FIN. Echéance f. ‖ MUS. Ténor m. ‖ JUR. Teneur f. (of a document). ‖ FIG. Cours m. (of events).
tenorino [,tenə'ri:nou] n. MUS. Ténorino m.
tenpins ['tenpinz] n. U. S. Jeu (m.) de quilles.
tense [tens] n. GRAMM. Temps m.
tense adj. Tendu (lit. and fig.).
— v. tr. Tendre (muscles). ‖ **To tense up**, tendre; FIG. Rendre nerveux, contracter.
— v. intr. **To tense up**, se contracter; FIG. Se contracter, se crisper.
tensely [-li] adv. Avec tension.
tenseness [-nis] n. Tension f.
tensibility [,tensi'biliti] n. Extensibilité f.
tensile ['tensail] adj. Extensible. ‖ TECHN. De traction; *tensile strength*, résistance à la tension.
tension ['tenʃən] n. Tension f. ‖ TECHN. Traction f. ‖ ELECTR., FIG. Tension f. ‖ **Tension-bar**, n. AUTOM. Tendeur m.
tensional [-əl] adj. De tension.
tensor [-ə*] n. MED. Tenseur m.
tent [tent] n. Tente f. **Tent-cloth**, n. Toile de tente. ‖ **Tent-peg**, n. Piquet (m.) de tente. ‖ **Tent-stitch**, n. Petit point m.
— v. tr. Tenter.
— v. intr. Vivre sous la tente, camper.
tent n. MED. Mèche f.
— v. tr. MED. Mettre une mèche dans.
tentacle ['tentəkl] n. ZOOL. Tentacule m. ‖ BOT. Filament m.
tentacular [ten'tækjulə*] adj. Tentaculaire.
tentative ['tentətiv] adj. Expérimental, fourni à titre d'essai (or) de suggestion. ‖ Provisoire, suggéré (conclusion); *tentative offer*, ouverture. ‖ Timide, hésitant, indécis.
— n. Tentative f.
tentatively [-li] adv. A titre d'essai; avec une certaine hésitation.
tenter ['tentə*] n. TECHN. Elargisseuse f. (machine); surveillant m. (person). ‖ **Tenter-hook**, n. Clou à crochet m.; FAM. *To be on tenter-hooks*, être sur le gril (or) sur des charbons ardents.
tenth [tenθ] adj. Dixième (part, time). ‖ Dix (chapter, date, king).
— n. MATH. Dixième m. ‖ MUS. Dixième f. ‖ ECCLES. Dîme f. ‖ FIN. Décime m.
tenthly [-li] adv. Dixièmement.
tenuity [te'njuiti] n. Ténuité, minceur, finesse f. (of a thread). ‖ CHIM. Raréfaction f. (of air, gas). ‖ FIG. Faiblesse f. (of style).
tenuous ['tenjuəs] adj. Ténu, mince, fin. ‖ CHIM. Raréfié. ‖ FIG. Ténu, subtil (distinction); faible, pauvre (style).
tenure ['tenjuə*] n. † Tenure f. ‖ JUR. Possession f.; *fixity of tenure*, stabilité d'emploi.
tepee ['ti:pi:] n. See TEEPEE.
tepefy ['tepifai] v. tr. (2). Faire tiédir.
— v. intr. Tiédir.
tepid ['tepid] adj. Tiède (lit. and fig.).
tepidity [te'piditi] n. Tiédeur f. (lit. and fig.).
tepidly ['tepidli] adv. Tièdement.
teratology [,terə'tɔlədʒi] n. Tératologie f.
terbium ['tə:biəm] n. CHIM. Terbium m.
tercel(et) ['tə:sl(et)] n. ZOOL. Tiercelet m.
tercentenary [,tə:sen'ti:nəri] n. Tricentenaire m.
tercet ['tə:sit] n. Tercet m. ‖ MUS. Triolet m.
terebinth ['terebinθ] n. BOT. Térébinthe m.
terebra ['terebrə] (pl. **terebrae** [-i]) n. ZOOL. Tarière f.
terebrant [-ənt] adj. ZOOL. Térébrant m.
teredo [te'ri:dou] n. ZOOL. Taret m.
tergal ['tə:gəl] adj. Tergal (See DORSAL.)
tergiversate ['tə:dʒivə:seit] v. intr. Tergiverser.
tergiversation [,tə:dʒivə:'seiʃən] n. Tergiversation f.; recherche (f.) des faux-fuyants.
tergiversator ['tə:dʒivə:seitə*] n. Tergiversateur m.; tergiversatrice f.

term [tə:m] n. Terme m.; fin f. (end); *to set a term to*, mettre un terme à. ‖ Terme m.; durée f.; *short-term transaction*, opération à court terme; *term of copyright*, durée du copyright; *term of notice*, délai de préavis pour congé. ‖ Trimestre m. (at school); *beginning of the term*, rentrée scolaire, reprise des cours; *Easter term*, second trimestre. ‖ Pl. Conditions f. pl.; arrangement m.; *to come to terms*, venir à composition; *to make terms*, conclure un arrangement, s'arranger, s'entendre. ‖ Pl. Termes, rapports m. pl.; relations f. pl.; *not to be on the best of terms*, être en froid; *on good terms with*, en bons termes avec; *to be on speaking terms with*, être en relations avec, voir, parler à (s.o.). ‖ FIN. Terme m.; échéance f. (of a bill); *term of payment*, délai de paiement. ‖ FIN. Pl. Conditions f. pl.; prix m.; *on easy terms*, avec facilités de paiement; *terms of payment*, conditions de paiement. ‖ JUR. Session f. ‖ MATH., PHILOS. Terme m. ‖ GRAMM. Terme, mot m.; expression f.; *in no uncertain terms*, carrément, nettement, sans fard. ‖ **Term paper**, n. U. S. Dissertation f. ‖ **Term-time**, n. Période scolaire f.
— v. tr. Appeler, qualifier.
termagant ['tə:məgənt] n. Tervagant m. (deity). ‖ FAM. Virago, harpie f.
— adj. Revêche, acariâtre (shrewish). ‖ Querelleur (quarrelsome).
terminable ['tə:minəbl] adj. Terminable. ‖ JUR. Résiliable.
terminal [-l] adj. De démarcation (line); délimitant (mark). ‖ Trimestriel. ‖ BOT. Terminal. ‖ CH. DE F. De tête de ligne; *terminal point*, terminus. ‖ CINEM. Final. ‖ MILIT. *Terminal leave*, congé libératoire.
— n. ELECTR. Borne f. ‖ GRAMM. Terminaison f. ‖ CH. DE F. Terminus m. ‖ AVIAT., NAUT. Terminal m.; *air terminal*, aérogare. ‖ INFORM., TECHN. Terminal m.
terminate ['tə:mineit] adj. Final. ‖ MATH. Exact.
— v. tr. Borner, délimiter (to bound). ‖ Achever, terminer (to end).
— v. intr. Se terminer (in, par).
termination [,tə:mi'neiʃən] n. Fin f. (end). ‖ GRAMM. Terminaison f. (See ENDING.) ‖ MED. Interruption f. (of pregnancy).
terminism ['tə:minizm] n. ECCLES. Terminisme m. ‖ PHILOS. Nominalisme m.
terminological [tə:mi:nə'lɔdʒikəl] adj. Terminologique.
terminology [,tə:mi'nɔlədʒi] n. Terminologie f.
terminus ['tə:minəs] n. ARTS. Dieu Terme m. ‖ CH. DE F. Terminus m.
— N. B. Deux pluriels : *terminuses, termini*.
termitary ['tə:mitəri] n. ZOOL. Termitière f.
termite ['tə:mait] n. ZOOL. Termite m.
termless [-'tə:mlis] adj. Illimité, sans fin.
termly [-li] adv. Par terme (or) trimestre.
tern [tə:n] n. ZOOL. Sterne f.
ternary ['tə:nəri] adj. Ternaire.
terneplate [-pleit] n. Tôle plombée f.
terra ['terə] n. Terre f. ‖ **Terra-cotta**, n. ARTS. Terre cuite f. ‖ **Terra-firma**, n. Terre ferme f.; plancher (m.) des vaches (fam.). ‖ **Terra-incognita**, n. Terre inconnue f., territoire vierge m. (land); FIG. Terrain inconnu m.
terrace ['teris] n. GEOL. Terrasse f.; terre-plein m. ‖ ARCHIT. Terrasse f. (flat roof); rangée (f.) de maisons semblables f. (row).
— v. tr. Disposer en terrasse (a garden). ‖ Terrasser (a hillside).
terraced [-t] adj. Suspendu (garden). ‖ GEOL. En terrasse.
terrain [tə'rein] n. MILIT. Terrain m.
Terramycin [-maisin] n. (trade mark). MED. Terramycine f.
terrane [tə'rein] n. GEOL. Terrain m.

terraneous [tə'reiniəs] adj. Bot. Terrestre.
terrapin ['terəpin] n. Zool. Tortue aquatique *f*.
terrazzo [te'rætsou] n. Granito *m*.
terrene [te'ri:n] adj. Terrestre.
terrestrial [tə'restriəl] adj. Terrestre.
terrible ['teribl] adj. Terrible.
terribly [-i] adv. Terriblement.
terrier ['teriə*] n. Zool., Jur. Terrier *m*. ‖ Milit., Fam. Territorial *m*.
terrific [tə'rifik] adj. Terrifiant, terrible. ‖ Fam. Epoustouflant, mirobolant.
terrify ['terifai] v. tr. (2). Terrifier. (See FRIGHTEN.)
terrine [te'ri:n] n. Culin. Terrine *f*.
territorial [,teri'tɔ:riəl] adj. Régional (industry); territorial (waters). ‖ Agric. Terrien. ‖ Milit. Territorial.
— n. Agric. Propriétaire terrien *m*. ‖ Milit. Territorial *m*.
territoriality [,teritɔ:ri'æliti] n. Territorialité *f*.
territory ['teritəri] n. Territoire *m*.
terror ['terə*] n. Terreur *f*. (see FEAR); *deadly terror*, épouvante. ‖ Terreur *f*.; objet (*m*.) de terreur (person, thing). ‖ Fam. Diable, enfant terrible *m*. ‖ **Terror-stricken**, adj. Terrifié, saisi de terreur.
terrorism [-rizm] n. Terrorisme *m*.
terrorist [-rist] n. Terroriste *s*.
terrorize [-raiz] v. tr. Terroriser.
terry ['teri] n. Tissu bouclé *m*. ‖ **Terry-cloth**, n. U. S. Tissu-éponge *m*.
terse [tə:s] adj. Concis, succinct. (See CONCISE.)
tersely [-li] adv. Avec concision.
terseness [-nis] n. Concision *f*.
tertian ['tə:ʃən] adj. Tierce.
— n. Med. Fièvre tierce *f*.
tertiary ['tə:ʃəri] adj., n. Geol., Eccles. Tertiaire *m*.
tervalent [tə:'veilənt] adj. Trivalent.
terylene ['terə,li:n] n. (trade mark) Chim. Térylène *m*.
tessellated ['tesileitid] adj. Arts. Mosaïqué. ‖ Bot. Tessellé.
tessellation [,tesi'leiʃən] n. Formation en mosaïque *f*. (art); mosaïque *f*. (work).
test [test] n. Zool. Test *m*.
test n. Epreuve *f*. (see TRIAL); *to stand the test*, soutenir l'épreuve. ‖ Essai *m*.; *control test*, contre-essai. ‖ Test *m*.; *intelligence test*, test. ‖ Examen *m*.; *terminal test*, composition trimestrielle. ‖ Essai *m*.; épreuve *f*.; réactif (*for*, *of*, de). ‖ Med. *Blood test*, examen du sang. ‖ Autom. *Driving test*, examen du permis de conduire. ‖ Aviat. *Flight test*, vol d'essai; *test pilot*, pilote d'essai. ‖ Jur. *Test case*, précédent, cas (*m*.) faisant jurisprudence. ‖ Fig. Critérium, critère *m*.; pierre de touche *f*. ‖ **Test-bench**, n. Banc d'essai *m*. ‖ **Test drive**, n. Autom. Essai *m*., essai de route. ‖ **Test-glass** (or) **-tube**, n. Chim. Eprouvette *f*. ‖ **Test-match**, n. Sports. Match international, test-match *m*. (in cricket or rugby). ‖ **Test-paper**, n. Examen blanc *m*.; composition *f*.; Chim. Papier réactif *m*.
— v. tr. Eprouver, expérimenter. ‖ Chim. Traiter au réactif. ‖ Techn. Essayer, coupeller (gold); analyser (water). ‖ Fig. Eprouver, mettre à l'épreuve.
— v. intr. **To test for**, Chim. Faire la réaction de. ‖ **To test with**, Chim. Faire la réaction à.
testament ['testəmənt] n. Jur., Eccles. Testament *m*.
testamentary [,testə'mentəri] adj. Jur. Testamentaire.
testate ['testeit] adj. Jur. Ayant testé.
testator [tes'teitə*] n. Jur. Testateur *m*.
testatrix [-riks] n. Jur. Testatrice *f*.
tester ['testə*] n. Essayeur *m*.
tester n. Ciel de lit *m*. ‖ **Tester-bed**, n. Lit à baldaquin *m*.
testicle ['testikl] n. Med. Testicule *m*.
testifier ['testifaiə*] n. Témoin *m*.

testify [-fai] v. tr. (2). Jur. Déclarer, attester, affirmer. ‖ Fig. Faire preuve de, témoigner de.
— v. intr. Jur. Déposer. ‖ **To testify to**, attester, affirmer ; témoigner de.
testimonial [,testi'mounjəl] n. Attestation *f*.; certificat *m*. (text). ‖ Cadeau (*m*.) en témoignage d'estime (gift).
testimony ['testiməni] n. Jur. Témoignage *m*.; déposition *f*. ‖ Eccles. *Tables of the testimony*, Tables de la Loi. ‖ Fig. Témoignage *m*.
testiness ['testinis] n. Susceptibilité *f*. ‖ Irritabilité *f*.
testis ['testis] (pl. **testes** [-ti:z]) n. Med. Testicule *m*.
testudo [tes'tju:dou] n. Zool., † Milit. Tortue *f*.
testy ['testi] adj. Susceptible, chatouilleux. ‖ Irritable.
tetanic [ti'tænik] adj. Med. Tétanique.
tetanize ['tetənaiz] v. tr. Med. Tétaniser.
tetanus ['tetənəs] n. Med. Tétanos *m*.
tetany [-ni] n. Med. Tétanie *f*.
tetchy ['tetʃi] adj. Fam. Irritable, comme un crin, d'humeur noire.
tête-à-tête [,teitə'teit] n. Tête-à-tête *m*. invar. (conversation). ‖ Tête-à-tête, confident *m*. (sofa).
— adj. En tête-à-tête (dinner, talk).
— adv. Tête-à-tête, seul à seul.
tether ['teðə*] n. Longe *f*. ‖ Fam. *At the end of one's tether*, au bout de son rouleau.
— v. tr. Attacher à la longe.
tetrachloride [,tetrə'klɔ:raid] n. Chim. Tétrachlorure *m*.
tetrachord ['tetrəkɔ:d] n. Mus. Tétracorde *m*.
tetrad ['tetrəd] n. Quatre *m*. (number, series). ‖ Chim. Tétrade *f*.
tetraethyl [,tetrə'eθil] adj. Chim. Tétraéthyle (lead).
tetragon ['tetrəgən] n. Math. Quadrilatère *m*. ‖ Astron. Tétragone *m*.
tetrahedral [-'hi:drəl] adj. Math. Tétraédrique.
tetrahedron [-'hi:drən] n. Math. Tétraèdre *m*.
tetrarch ['tetrɑ:k] n. Tétrarque *m*.
tetravalent [tetrə'veilənt] adj. Chim. Quadrivalent.
tetter ['tetə*] n. Med. Affection cutanée *f*.; dartres *f*. pl.; *crusty tetter*, impétigo ; *scaly tetter*, psoriasis.
Teucrian ['tju:kriən] adj., n. Geogr. Troyen *s*.
Teuton ['tju:tən] n. Geogr. Teuton *s*.
Teutonic [tju:'tɔnik] adj. Gramm. Teutonique, germanique.
text [tekst] n. Texte *m*. ‖ **Text-book**, n Manuel classique *m*. ‖ **Text-hand**, n. Grosse *f*. (hand-writing).
textile ['tekstail] adj. Textile. ‖ Tissé (woven).
— n. Textile *m*.
textual ['tekstjuəl] adj. De texte (error); littéral (note); textuel (quotation).
textually [-i] adv. Concernant le texte. ‖ Textuellement.
texture ['tekstʃə*] n. Tissu *m*.; texture *f*. (of a fabric); grain *m*. (of wood). ‖ Med. Contexture *f*. (of body); grain *m*. (of the skin). ‖ Fig. Contexture, structure *f*.
Thailand ['tailənd] n. Thaïlande *f*., Siam *m*.
thalamus ['θæləməs] n. Thalamus *m*.
thaler ['tɑ:lə*] n. invar. Thaler *m*.
thalidomide [θə'lidə,maid] n. Thalidomide *f*.; *thalidomide child*, enfant victime de la thalidomide.
thallium ['θæljəm] n. Chim. Thallium *m*.
Thames [temz] n. Geogr. Tamise *f*.
than [ðæn] conj. Que; *other*, *rather than*, autre, plutôt que. ‖ Que; *taller than John*, plus grand que Jean; *to arrive earlier than*, arriver plus tôt que. ‖ De; *more than a pound*, plus d'une livre.
— prep. Comparé auquel; *a writer than whom there is none finer*, un écrivain auprès duquel il n'y a pas meilleur.
thane [θein] n. † Thane *m*.

thank [θæŋk] v. tr. Remercier (*for*, de) ; *thank you*, merci. ‖ Etre obligé ; *I will thank you to*, je vous serais reconnaissant de. ‖ **Thank-you**, n. Merci, remerciement *m*.
— n. pl. See THANKS.

thankful [-ful] adj. Reconnaissant (*to*, à).

thankfully [-fuli] adv. Avec reconnaissance.

thankfulness [-fulnis] n. Reconnaissance, gratitude *f*.

thankless [-lis] adj. Ingrat (person, task).

thanklessly [-lisli] adv. Avec ingratitude.

thanklessness [-lisnis] n. Ingratitude *f*. (of a person) ; nature ingrate *f*. (of a task).

thanks [θæŋks] n. pl. Remerciements *m. pl.* ; *thanks!*, merci ; *to give thanks to*, remercier. ‖ Grâces *f. pl.* ; *thanks to*, grâce à ; *to return thanks*, rendre grâces. ‖ **Thanks-offering**, n. Sacrifice (*m.*) d'action de grâces.

thanksgiving [ˈθæŋks,giviŋ] n. Action (*f.*) de grâces. ‖ U. S. Fête (*f.*) d'action de grâces (fourth Thursday of November).

that [ˈðæt] (pl. **those** [ðouz]) demons. adj. Ce, cet, cette ; ce...-là ; *that man is the thief*, cet homme est le voleur ; *those pens are bad*, ces plumes-là sont mauvaises. ‖ FAM. *That certain smile*, un certain sourire ; *that boy!*, oh! ce garçon !
— demons. pron. Ce, cela, ça (person, thing) ; *for all that*, malgré tout ; *that's that*, et voilà ; *that won't do here*, pas de ça ici ! ; *what do you say of that?*, qu'en dites-vous, que dites-vous de cela ? ‖ Celui-là, celle-là (pl. ceux-là, celles-là) ; *don't take these gloves, take those*, ne prenez pas ces gants-ci, prenez ceux-là ! *that is what you asked for*, voilà ce que vous avez demandé ; *what book do you want? That one*, quel livre voulez-vous ? Celui-là. ‖ Celui, celle (pl. ceux, celles) ; *that of my friend*, celui de mon ami. ‖ FAM. *At that*, là, sur ce point ; tout bien considéré ; soit dit en passant.
— adv. Aussi, si ; *I can't see that far ahead*, je ne peux pas voir si loin. ‖ FAM. Tellement, si ; *I was that tired I couldn't speak*, j'étais si fourbu que je ne pouvais parler.
— relat. pron. invar. Qui, que, lequel, laquelle, lesquels, lesquelles ; *the fact that you are referring to*, le fait auquel vous vous référez ; *the book that you know*, le livre que vous connaissez. ‖ Où, que ; *the time that I saw him*, la fois où je l'ai vu.
— conj. Que ; *I think that you are right*, je crois que vous avez raison ; *it is not that I love you less*, ce n'est pas que je vous aime moins ; *light the lamp that I may read my letter*, allumez la lampe, que je puisse lire ma lettre. ‖ Afin que, pour que, parce que, puisque ; *I'm sorry that I cannot help you*, je suis désolé de ne pouvoir vous aider ; *in that she was my friend*, parce qu'elle était mon amie ; *they died that we might live*, ils sont morts pour que nous puissions vivre ; *they ran so fast that I couldn't catch them*, ils couraient si vite que je n'ai pu les rattraper. ‖ Si ; *oh, that this day were over!*, oh, si ce jour était passé !

thatch [θætʃ] n. Chaume *m*. (for roof). ‖ FAM. Cheveux *m. pl.* ; *he has lost his thatch*, il est entièrement déplumé.
— v. tr. Couvrir de chaume.

thaumaturge [ˈθɔːmətəːdʒ] n. Thaumaturge *m*.

thaw [θɔː] v. intr. Fondre, dégeler (ice, snow). ‖ FAM. Se dégeler (person).
— v. tr. Faire dégeler.
— n. Dégel *m*. ‖ Fonte *f*. (of snow).

the [ðə] before a consonant, [ði] before a vowel, [ðiː] emphatically) def. art. Le, la, les ; *at the, to the*, au, à l', à la, aux ; *from the, of the*, du, de l', de la, des ; *the story ended*, l'histoire s'acheva ; *the President of the French Republic*, le président de la République française. ‖ Ce, cette, ces ; *he was absent at the time*, il était absent à cette époque. ‖ Le (stressed) ; *it is « the » restaurant in town*, c'est

« le » restaurant de la ville. ‖ (Not translated) ; *Charles the First*, Charles Iᵉʳ.
— adv. Plus, d'autant, ne ...que ; *the more he gets, the more he wants*, plus il obtient, plus il demande ; *they were all the more anxious because*, ils étaient d'autant plus inquiets que.

theatre [ˈθiətə*] n. THEATR. Théâtre *m*. (art, playhouse, technique). ‖ ARCHIT., MED. Amphithéâtre *m*. ‖ MILIT. Théâtre *m*. (of war). ‖ **Theatre-goer**, n. Habitué (*s.*) du théâtre.

theatrical [θiːætrikəl] adj. THEATR., FIG. Théâtral.
— n. pl. Spectacle *m. ; amateur theatricals*, théâtre d'amateurs.

theatrically [-i] adv. De manière théâtrale.

thee [ðiː] pers. pr. Te, toi. (See THOU.)

theft [θeft] n. Vol *m*.

theic [ˈθiːik] n. MED. Intoxiqué (*s.*) du thé.

theine [-iːn] n. CHIM. Théine *f*.

their [ðɛə*] poss. adj. Leur, leurs.

theirs [-z] poss. pr. Le leur, la leur, les leurs ; à eux, à elles ; *that book is theirs*, ce livre est à eux ; *theirs are better*, les leurs sont meilleurs.

theism [ˈθiːizm] n. Théisme *m*. (See DEISM.)

theist [-ist] n. Théiste *s*.

them [ðem] pers. pr. Les, eux, elles ; *to them*, leur, à eux, à elles ; *one of them*, l'un d'entre eux. ‖ POP. *That's them*, c'est eux.

thematic [θiˈmætik] adj. MUS., GRAMM. Thématique.

theme [θiːm] n. Thème, sujet *m. ; to be the theme of conversation*, défrayer la conversation. ‖ Dissertation, rédaction *f*. (essay). ‖ GRAMM., MUS. Thème *m*. ‖ **Theme-song**, n. MUS. Leitmotiv *m. ;* RADIO. U. S. Indicatif *m*.

themselves [ðemˈselvz] pers. pr. Eux-mêmes, elles-mêmes (intensive) ; *they went themselves*, ils y sont allés eux-mêmes. ‖ Se (reflexive) ; *to wash oneself*, se laver.

then [ðen] adv. Alors, à cette époque (at that time). ‖ Donc, dans ce cas, par conséquent (in that case). ‖ Ensuite, puis (next in time). ‖ Puis, et puis, et aussi (moreover). ‖ LOC. *But then*, en ce cas, mais alors ; *now... then*, tantôt... tantôt ; *now and then*, de temps en temps ; *there and then*, séance tenante ; *what then?*, et après ?
— adj. De cette époque ; *the then director*, le directeur d'alors.
— n. Ce temps-là *m. ; before then*, avant ce moment-là ; *between now and then*, d'ici là ; *from then on*, depuis lors ; *till then*, jusqu'alors, jusque-là.

thenar [ˈθiːnə*] n. MED. Plante *f*. (of the foot) ; paume *f*. (of the hand).
— adj. MED. Thénar (eminence).

thence [ðens] adv. † De là. ‖ Pour cette raison, par conséquent, donc.

thenceforth [-ˈfɔːθ], **thenceforward** [-ˈfɔːwəd] adv. Dès lors, désormais.

theocracy [θiˈɔkrəsi] n. Théocratie *f*.

theodicy [θiˈɔdisi] n. Théodicée *f*.

theodolite [θiˈɔdəlait] n. TECHN. Théodolite *m*.

theogony [-ˈɔgəni] n. Théogonie *f*.

theologian [θiɔˈloudʒiən] n. Théologien *s*.

theological [-ˈlɔdʒikəl] adj. Théologique.

theologize [θiˈɔlədʒaiz] v. intr. Faire de la théologie.

theology [-dʒi] n. Théologie *f*.

theophany [θiˈɔfəni] n. Théophanie *f*.

theorbo [θiˈɔːbou] n. MUS. T(h)éorbe *m*.

theorem [ˈθiərem] n. MATH. Théorème *m*.

theoretical [θiəˈretikəl] adj. Théorique.

theoretically [-i] adv. Théoriquement.

theoretician [ˌθiəreˈtiʃən] n. Théoricien *s*.

theoretics [ˌθiəˈretiks] n. sg. Théorie *f*., conceptions théoriques *f. pl.*

theorist [ˈθiərist] n. Théoricien *s*.

theorize [-raiz] v. intr. Théoriser, bâtir des théories.

theory [-ri] n. Théorie *f*.
theosophic(al) [θiə'sɔfik(əl)] adj. Théosophique.
theosophist [θi'ɔsəfist] n. Théosophe *s*.
theosophy [-fi] n. Théosophie *f*.
therapeutic [θerə'pju:tik] adj. MED. Thérapeutique.
therapeutics [-tiks] n. sg. MED. Thérapeutique *f*.
therapeutist [-tist] n. MED. Thérapeute *s*.
therapist ['θerəpist] n. Praticien *m.*, thérapeute *s.; occupational therapist*, ergothérapeute ; *speech therapist*, orthophoniste.
therapy ['θerəpi] n. MED. Thérapie *f*.
theratron ['θerətrən] n. Bombe (*f.*) au cobalt, thératron *m*.
there [δɛə*] adv. Là, y, en ce lieu, à cet endroit ; *will you go there?*, voulez-vous y aller ? ‖ Là, sur ce point, à ce sujet ; *there you are wrong*, à cet égard, vous vous trompez. ‖ Que voilà ; *that girl there*, cette jeune fille-là. ‖ Là-bas ; *hurry up there*, dépêchez-vous là-bas. ‖ *There is*, il y a, il est (unstressed) ; *there is very little time*, il y a fort peu de temps ; *there are two girls here*, il y a deux filles ici. ‖ *There is*, voilà (stressed) ; *there he comes*, le voilà qui vient ; *there's a good chap!*, en voilà un chic type!, tu seras bien chic! ‖ FAM. *I have been there*, j'y ai passé ; *he's not all there*, il est un peu dérangé.
— interj. Là, voilà! ; *there, that's done!*, là, c'est fait. ‖ Allons ; *there, there, don't worry*, allons, ne vous tracassez pas.
thereabout(s) [-əbaut(s)] adv. Dans ces parages, aux environs, près de.là (place). ‖ A peu près, environ (amount, degree, weight).
thereafter [δɛər'ɑ:ftə*] adv. † Par la suite ; après cela ; par la suite.
thereat [-'æt] adv. † Là-dessus, sur ce point.
thereby [-'bai] adv. De ce fait ; par là ; de cette manière ; par ce moyen.
therefore [-'fɔ:*] adv. Donc, par conséquent, c'est pourquoi. (See CONSEQUENTLY.)
therefrom [-'frɔm] adv. † De là.
therein [-'in] adv. Dedans, là-dedans. ‖ † A ce sujet ; à cet égard.
thereof [-'ɔv] adv. De cela, en.
thereon [-'ɔn] adv. † Dessus, là-dessus.
thereto [-'tu:] adv. † Y, à cela. ‖ En outre (besides).
thereupon [-'əpɔn] adv. Sur ce, là-dessus, sur quoi. ‖ Sur ce sujet, là-dessus, à cet égard. ‖ † Dessus.
therewith [-'wiδ], **therewithal** [wi'δɔ:l] adv. † Avec cela, en outre ; par-dessus le marché (fam.).
therm [θə:m] n. PHYS. Thermie *f*. (unit).
thermal [-əl] adj. Thermique (capacity, unit) ; thermal (spring).
thermality [-iti] n. Thermalité *f*.
thermic [ik] adj. Thermique.
— n. GEOGR., AVIAT. Ascendance thermique *f.*, thermique *m*.
thermion [-iən] n. PHYS. Thermion *m*.
thermionic [θə:mi'ɔnik] adj. PHYS. Thermoïonique, thermoélectronique (current, tube, valve).
thermocouple ['θə:mou,kʌpl] n. Thermocouple, couple thermoélectrique *m*.
thermodynamic [,θə:moudai'næmik] adj. Thermodynamique.
thermodynamics [-s] n. sg. Thermodynamique *f*.
thermoelectric(al) [,θə:moui'lektrik(!)] adj. Thermoélectrique.
thermoelectricity [,θə:mouilek'trisiti] n. Thermoélectricité *f*.
thermogenesis [,θə:mou'dʒenisis] n. MED. Thermogenèse *f*.
thermolysis [θə:'mɔlisis] n. PHYS. Thermolyse *f*.
thermometer [θə:'mɔmitə*] n. Thermomètre *m*.
thermometrical [,θə:mə'metrikəl] adj. Thermométrique.
thermometry [θə:'mɔmitri] n. Thermométrie *f*.

thermonuclear [,θə:mə'nju:kliə*] adj. PHYS. Thermonucléaire.
thermoplastic [-'plæstik] adj. Thermoplastique.
thermoregulator [,θə:mə'regjuleitə*] n. Thermostat, thermorégulateur *m*.
thermos ['θə:məs] adj. *Thermos bottle* (or) *flask*, bouteille Thermos (or) isolante.
thermoscope [-skoup] n. Thermoscope *m*.
thermoscopic [,θə:mə'skɔpik] adj. Thermoscopique.
thermosetting [-'setiŋ] adj. Thermodurcissable.
thermostat ['θə:məstæt] n. Thermostat *m*.
thermostatic [,θə:mə'stætik] adj. Thermostatique.
thermostatics [-s] n. sg. Thermostatique *f*.
thermotherapy [-'θeˈəpi] n. Thermothérapie *f*.
theroid ['θi:ərɔid] adj. Bestial.
thesaurus [θi'sɔ:rəs] (pl. **thesauri** [-ai]) n. Trésor, gros recueil *m*.
these [δi:z]. See THIS.
thesis ['θi:sis] (pl. **theses** [-si:z]) n. Thèse *f*. (doctoral treatise). ‖ Thèse, proposition *f*.
theurgy [θi'ə:dʒi] n. Théurgie *f*.
thews [θju:z] n. pl. Nerfs, muscles *m. pl.* ‖ FIG. Force, énergie *f*.
thewy ['θjui] adj. Musclé, fort.
they [δei] pers. pr. Ils, elles, eux ; *it is they*, ce sont eux ; *they are generous*, ils sont généreux ; *they are English*, ce sont des Anglais. ‖ Ceux, celles ; *they who believe*, ceux qui croient. ‖ On, *they say it's true*, on dit que c'est vrai.
thiamine ['θaiə,mi:n] n. MED. Thiamine *f*.
thick [θik] adj. Epais (board, wall) ; *to be three inches thick*, avoir trois pouces d'épaisseur, être épais de trois pouces. ‖ Gros (pipe, rod). ‖ Epais, boueux (ink, writing) ; épais (liquid, soup) ; gras (type). ‖ Epais, dense (darkness, fog) ; couvert, chargé (weather). ‖ Epais, tassé (corn) ; épais, dense, touffu (forest). ‖ Touffu (eyebrow) ; épais (hair). ‖ Lourd (head) ; pâteux (voice). ‖ Plein, rempli, garni (*with*, de). ‖ FAM. Intime, très lié (*with*, avec). ‖ FAM. Fort ; *it's a bit thick!*, c'est un peu raide. ‖ **Thick-head**, n. Crétin *m*. ‖ **Thick-headed**, adj. A la tête dure. ‖ **Thick-lipped**, adj. Lippu. ‖ **Thick-set**, adj. Trapu (person) ; épais (thing). ‖ **Thick-skinned**, adj. A la peau dure ; FIG. Qui n'a pas l'épiderme sensible.
— adv. Dru, épais ; en couche épaisse. ‖ FAM. *To lay it on thick*, ne pas y aller avec le dos de la cuiller, en donner bon poids.
— n. Gras *m*. (of the thumb). ‖ Cœur, milieu *m*. (of the forest). ‖ Vif *m*. (of a discussion) ; fort *m*. (of the fight). ‖ FAM. *Through thick and thin*, contre vent et marées, malgré tous les obstacles.
thicken [-ən] v. tr. Epaissir.
— v. intr. S'épaissir. ‖ FAM. *The plot thickens*, ça se corse.
thicket ['θikit] n. Fourré, hallier ; bosquet *m*.
thickish ['θikiʃ] adj. Assez épais (or) dense. ‖ Plutôt couvert (weather).
thickly [-li] adv. En couche épaisse ; dru. ‖ D'une voix empâtée.
thickness [-nis] n. Epaisseur *f*. (of board, forest, hair) ; densité *f*. (of fog) ; consistance *f*. (of a liquid); empâtement *m*. (of the voice) ; état nuageux, aspect chargé *m*. (of weather).
thief [θi:f] (pl. **thieves** [θi:vz]) n. Voleur *m*. ‖ FAM. *As thick as thieves*, amis comme cochons (or) comme larrons en foire.
thieve [θi:v] v. tr., intr. Voler. (See STEAL.)
thievish [-iʃ] adj. Voleur, de voleur.
thievishness [-iʃnis] n. Friponnerie *f.*; goût du vol *m*.
thigh [θai] n. MED. Cuisse *f*. ‖ **Thigh-bone**, n. MED. Fémur *m*.
thill [θil] n. Brancard *m*. ‖ **Thill-horse**, n. Limonier *m*.

thimble ['θimbḷ] n. Dé (*m.*) à coudre. ‖ TECHN. Bague, virole *f.*

thimbleful [-ful] n. Dé, plein dé *m.*

thimblerig [-rig] n. Tour (*m.*) des gobelets.
— v. tr. Escamoter. ‖ FAM. Monter (business); escroquer (s.o.).

thimblerigger [-rigə*] n. Escamoteur *m.* ‖ FAM. Escroc *m.*

thin [θin] adj. Mince (in general). ‖ Mince, léger (cloth); mince, ténu (thread); *thin stroke*, délié. ‖ Rare, clairsemé (beard); grêle (voice). ‖ Raréfié (air); clairsemé (population). ‖ Mince, maigre (face, person); *thin as a wafer*, plat comme une galette; *to grow thinner*, amincir, maigrir. ‖ CULIN. Clair (liquid, soup); long (sauce); faible (wine). ‖ FIG. Faible, maigre (argument, excuse). ‖ FAM. *To have a thin time*, en voir de grises. ‖ **Thin-skinned**, adj. A la peau mince; FAM. Susceptible, à l'épiderme sensible.
— adv. En couche mince (spread); en tranches minces (cut).
— v. intr. S'éclaircir (cheveux). ‖ **To thin (out)**, s'éclaircir, se disperser (crowd); s'éclaircir (mist); diminuer d'intensité (traffic).
— v. tr. Eclaircir (hair, vegetation). ‖ **To thin (down)**, éclaircir, allonger (paint, sauce). ‖ **To thin out**, réduire, faire baisser (population).

thing [θiŋ] n. Chose *f.*; objet *m.; the big things in the room*, les gros objets de la pièce. ‖ Pl. Vêtements, habits *m. pl.*; affaires *f. pl.* (clothes). ‖ Pl. Outils, ustensiles *m. pl.* (implements); *tea things*, service à thé. ‖ JUR. Pl. Biens *m. pl.; things personal*, biens mobiliers. ‖ COMM. *It's not the thing*, ça ne se fait pas, c'est passé de mode; *the latest thing in hats*, chapeau dernier cri. ‖ FIG. Chose *f.; as things are*, dans l'état actuel des choses; *for one thing*, tout d'abord, et d'une; *for another thing*, d'autre part, et de deux; *it's just one of those things*, ce sont des choses qui arrivent; *it would be a good thing to*, il serait bon de; *not a thing has been overlooked*, pas un détail n'a été négligé; *the thing is to succeed*, la grande affaire (or) le tout c'est de réussir; *that's the very thing*, c'est juste ce qu'il faut; *to expect great things of*, attendre monts et merveilles de; *to make a good thing out of*, tirer profit de. ‖ FAM. Etre *m.* (person); *poor little thing*, pauvre petite créature. ‖ FAM. Truc, machin *m.* (thingumabob). ‖ FAM. *How are things?*, alors comment ça va?; *not to feel quite the thing*, se sentir patraque; *to know a thing or two*, connaître le bout de gras, être à la coule.

thingum(a)bob ['θiŋəmibɔb], **thingumajig** [-midʒig], **thingummy** [-əmi] n. FAM. Truc, bidule, machin *m.*

think [θiŋk] v. intr. (178). Penser, réfléchir; *to think aloud*, penser tout haut. ‖ Penser, croire, estimer; *I think so*, je le crois, c'est mon avis. ‖ Penser, trouver; *I can't think why*, je me demande pourquoi. ‖ **To think about**, songer à; *to give s.o. sth. else to think about*, donner des distractions à qqn. ‖ **To think of**, penser à, envisager; *to think of everything*, songer à tout, tout prévoir; *when I come to think of it*, à la reflexion. ‖ *To think of*, penser à, se souvenir de; *I never thought of telling you*, je n'ai pas pensé à vous le dire. ‖ *To think of*, songer à, compter, se proposer de, projeter; *he thought of going for a ride*, il pensait aller faire un tour à cheval; *I couldn't think of it*, ce n'est pas à envisager, il ne saurait en être question. ‖ *To think of*, considérer, songer à; *to think of one's neighbour*, penser à son prochain. ‖ *To think of*, penser à, trouver; *to think of the right word*, trouver le mot juste. ‖ *To think of*, penser de, considérer, estimer, juger; *to think better of it*, se raviser; *to think badly, well of*, avoir mauvaise, bonne opinion de; *what do you think of him?*, que dites-vous (or) pensez-vous de lui?
— v. tr. Penser, croire, supposer; *one would have*

thought that, c'était à croire que; *who would have thought it?*, qui l'eût dit? ‖ Penser, concevoir, imaginer; *and to think he has gone away!*, dire qu'il est parti!; *you can't think what I mean*, vous ne pouvez comprendre (or) imaginer ce que je veux dire. ‖ Penser à, songer à; *did you think to bring your book*, avez-vous pensé à apporter votre livre? ‖ Penser, trouver, juger, considérer; *I think he is honest*, je le crois honnête; *to think it funny*, trouver drôle; *to think nothing of*, ne pas attacher d'importance à. ‖ S'attendre à; *I little thought to see you again*, je ne pensais plus vous revoir. ‖ Résoudre par la pensée; *to think one's way out of a dilemma*, sortir d'un dilemme à force d'y réfléchir. ‖ Se mettre par la pensée; *to think oneself into a state of exhaustion*, s'épuiser en réflexions. ‖ Entretenir; *to think sombre thoughts*, nourrir des idées noires. ‖ **To think away**, faire passer par la réflexion; *to think one's time away*, passer son temps à réfléchir. ‖ **To think out**, élaborer, édifier, combiner (a plan); considérer (a question); *well thought out*, bien combiné (plan). ‖ **To think over**, réfléchir à; *to think sth. over*, délibérer au sujet de qqch., peser qqch.; *on thinking it over*, à y bien regarder. ‖ **To think up**, inventer.
— n. FAM. *To have a think about it*, y réfléchir; *give it a good think*, penses-y sérieusement; *you've got another think coming*, compte là-dessus et bois de l'eau, tu peux toujours courir.

thinkable [-əbḷ] adj. Imaginable, concevable.

thinker [-ə*] n. Penseur *s.*

thinking [-iŋ] n. Fait (*m.*) de penser (act). ‖ Opinion *f.*; avis *m.*
— adj. Pensant, qui pense.

thinly ['θiŋli] adv. Maigrement, de façon mince. ‖ Peu, maigrement.

thinner [-ə*] n. TECHN. Diluant *m.*

thinness [-nis] n. Minceur *f.* (of paper, thread, wall). ‖ Légèreté *f.* (of material, wine). ‖ Fluidité *f.* (of liquid, soup). ‖ Rareté *f.* (of hair). ‖ Minceur, maigreur *f.* (of s.o.). ‖ FIG. Faiblesse, pauvreté *f.* (of an argument).

thinnish [-iʃ] adj. Plutôt mince (or) fin (or) clair (or) léger. ‖ Maigrichon. ‖ FIG. Assez faible.

third [θəːd] adj. Troisième (in general). ‖ Tiers (estate); tierce (person). ‖ Trois (chapter, date, kings). ‖ **Third-rate**, adj. De troisième ordre.
— n. Tiers *m.* ‖ MATH., ASTRON., MUS. Tierce *f.*

thirdly [-li] adv. Troisièmement.

thirst [θəːst] n. Soif *f.* (lit. and fig.).
— v. intr. Avoir soif. ‖ FIG. Etre altéré, avoir soif (*after, for*, de).

thirstily ['-ili] adv. Avidement.

thirstiness [-inis] n. Soif habituelle *f.*

thirsty [-i] adj. Altéré; assoiffé; *to be thirsty*, avoir soif; *to make thirsty*, altérer. ‖ Desséché, sec (earth). ‖ FIG. Altéré, avide (*for*, de). [See CRAVING.] ‖ FAM. Qui donne soif (work).

thirteen [θəːtiːn] adj., n. Treize *m.*

thirteenth [-θ] adj. Treizième. ‖ Treize (chapter, date, king).
— n. Treizième *m.*

thirty ['θəːti] adj., n. Trente *m.; in one's thirties*, dans les trente ans.

this [ðis] (pl. **these** [ðiːz]) demons. adj. Ce, cette, ces...-ci; *these cakes taste good*, ces gâteaux ont bon goût; *this table*, cette table-ci. ‖ Voici, il y a; *he has been in London these three years*, voici trois ans qu'il est à Londres, il est à Londres depuis trois ans.
— demonstr. pron. Celui-ci, celle-ci (pl. ceux-ci, celles-ci); *this is John*, celui-ci c'est Jean. ‖ Ceci; *I can see this more clearly than that*, je peux voir ceci plus clairement que cela.
— adv. Comme ceci; *this far*, jusqu'ici, jusqu'à présent. ‖ FAM. *It was this big*, c'était grand comme ça!

thisness [-nis] n. PHILOS. Eccéité *f*.
thistle ['θisl] adj. BOT. Chardon *m*.
thistly [-i] adj. Couvert de chardons. ‖ Piquant, hérissé.
thither ['ðiðə*] adv. † Là.
thitherward [-wəd] adv. † De ce côté-là.
thole [θoul] v. tr. † Endurer. ‖ Permettre.
thole [θoul], **thole-pin** [-,pin] n. NAUT. Tolet *m*.
thomism ['toumizm̩] n. PHILOS. Thomisme *m*.
thomist [-ist] n. PHILOS. Thomiste *s*.
thong [θɔŋ] n. Courroie, sangle, lanière *f*.
— v. tr. Sangler.
thoracic [θə'ræsik] adj. MED. Thoracique.
thorax ['θɔ:ræks] n. MED. Thorax *m*. ‖ † Cuirasse *f*.
thorite ['θɔ:rait] n. Thorite *f*.
thorium [-riəm] n. CHIM. Thorium *m*.
thorn [θɔ:n] n. † Thorn *m*. (letter). ‖ BOT. Epine *f*. ‖ FAM. *Don't keep me on thorns,* ne me faites pas languir. ‖ **Thorn-bush,** n. BOT. Buisson (*m*.) d'épines.
thornback [-bæk] n. ZOOL. Raie bouclée *f*.
thorny [-i] adj. Epineux.
thoron ['θourɔn] n. CHIM. Thoron *m*.
thorough ['θʌrə] adj. Complet, total, absolu (complete) ; minutieux (inspection) ; approfondi (knowledge) ; *to be thorough in one's work,* travailler consciencieusement. ‖ U. S. *Thorough brace,* soupente (of a carriage). ‖ **Thorough-bass,** n. MUS. Basse chiffrée, harmonie *f*.
— prep † A travers.
— adj. † Par le travers, de part en part.
thoroughbred [-bred] adj. De race pure (dog) ; pur sang (horse) ; racé (person).
— n. Animal (*m*.) de race ; pur-sang *m*. (horse) ; personne racée *f*.
thoroughfare [-fɛə*] n. Voie de communication, grande rue, artère *f*. ; *no thoroughfare,* rue barrée ; entrée interdite.
thoroughgoing [-gouiŋ] adj. Parfait.
thoroughly [-li] adv. Entièrement, totalement, complètement.
thoroughness [-nis] n. Perfection *f*. ; caractère achevé ; fignolage *m*. (of a work).
thorp [θɔ:p] n. Hameau *m*.
those [ðouz] pl. See THAT.
thou [ðau] pers. pr. Tu, toi.
— v. tr., intr. Tutoyer.
thou [θau] n. FAM. Mille *m*. (thousand) ; millième *m*. (thousandth). ‖ TECHN. Millième (*m*.) de pouce (measure).
— N. B. Deux pluriels : *thous, thou.*
though [ðou] conj. Même si, quand même (even if) ; bien que, quoique (although). ‖ **As though,** comme si. ‖ **What though,** qu'importe que, alors même que, même si.
— adv. Pourtant, tout de même (however). ‖ Vraiment, en vérité (indeed).
thought [θɔ:t] pret., p. p. See THINK.
thought n. Pensée *f*. (faculty). ‖ Pensée, réflexion, méditation *f*. (act). ‖ Pensée, réflexion, idée *f*. (idea). ‖ Pensée, idée *f*. ; dessein, projet *m*. (intention). ‖ Pensée, préoccupation *f*. ; souci *m*. (care). ‖ Pensée, opinion *f*. ; avis *m*. (opinion). ‖ Opinion, conception *f*. ; principe *m*. (principle). ‖ FAM. Brin, tantinet, tout petit peu *m*. ‖ **Thought-reading,** n. Lecture de pensée *f*. ‖ **Thought-transference,** n. Télépathie *f*. ‖ **Thought-wave,** n. Onde télépathique *f*.
thoughtful [-ful] adj. Pensif, rêveur, méditatif (thinking). ‖ Réfléchi, attentif (heedful). ‖ Prévenant, attentif, plein d'attentions (considerate). ‖ Soucieux, méditatif (anxious). ‖ Profond, grave (serious) [book, essay].
thoughtfully [-fuli] adv. Pensivement. ‖ Avec réflexion. ‖ Avec prévenance. ‖ Soucieusement.

thoughtfulness [-fulnis] n. Méditation, songerie, rêverie *f*. ‖ Réflexion, gravité *f*. ; air pensif *m*. ‖ Prévenance *f*. ; attentions *f*. *pl*.
thoughtless [-lis] adj. Etourdi, irréfléchi, inconsidéré. ‖ Sans prévenance (or) attentions, insouciant (*of,* de) ; manquant d'égards (*of,* pour).
thoughtlessly [-lisli] adv. Etourdiment, insouciamment ; à la légère.
thoughtlessness [-lisnis] n. Irréflexion, étourderie *f*. ‖ Manque (*m*.) de prévenance, insouciance *f*.
thousand ['θauzənd] adj. Mille (number) ; mil (in dates). ‖ FAM. Mille, millier *m*.
— n. Mille *m*. *invar.*
thousandth [-θ] adj., n. Millième *m*.
thraldom ['θrɔ:ldəm] n. Esclavage *m*.
thrall [θrɔ:l] n. Esclavage *m*. (bondage) ; esclave *s*. (slave).
— v. tr. Asservir.
thrash [θræʃ] v. tr. Rosser, rouer de coups ; flanquer une dégelée à (fam.) [s.o.]. ‖ AGRIC. Battre. ‖ **To thrash out,** discuter à fond (a matter) ; retourner (a question) ; démêler (truth).
thrashing [-iŋ] n. Dégelée, raclée, volée, frottée, tournée, pile *f*. (See DRUBBING). ‖ AGRIC. Battage *m*.
thrasonical [θrə'sɔnikəl] adj. Fanfaron.
thread [θred] n. Fil *m*. (of cotton, metal, silk). ‖ TECHN. Filet, pas *m*. (of screw). ‖ GEOL. Veine *f*. ‖ FIG. Fil *m*. (of life, a story). ‖ **Thread-counter,** n. Compte-fils *m*. ‖ **Thread-cutter,** n. Taraudeuse *f*. ‖ **Thread-like,** adj. Filiforme. ‖ **Thread-mark,** n. Filigrane *m*. (on banknotes).
— v. tr. Enfiler (a needle, pearls). ‖ Parsemer (*with,* de). ‖ TECHN. Fileter. ‖ FIG. *To thread one's way through,* se faufiler à travers.
threadbare [-bɛə*] adj. Elimé, usé jusqu'à la corde (cloth). ‖ Elimé, râpé, miteux (person). ‖ FIG. Usé, rebattu, rabaché.
threadbareness [-bɛənis] n. Usure *f*. ‖ FIG. Banalité *f*. ; caractère banal *m*.
threader [-ə*] n. TECHN. Taraudeuse *f*.
thready [-i] adj. Fibreux, filamenteux. ‖ Ténu (voice). ‖ MED. Filiforme.
threat [θret] n. Menace *f*. (*to,* pour).
threaten [-n̩] v. tr. Menacer (*with,* de) [s.o.] ; menacer de (punishment). ‖ Présager, faire craindre (sth. dangerous). ‖ FIG. Menacer ; *threatened with extinction,* en passe de disparaître (race).
— v. intr. Menacer (person) ; menacer, être menaçant (storm).
threatening [-niŋ] adj. Menaçant.
— n. Menaces *f*. *pl*.
three [θri:] adj., n. Trois *m*. ; *the Big Three,* les Trois Grands. ‖ **Three-cornered,** adj. Tricorne (hat) ; triangulaire (table). ‖ **Three-decker,** n. NAUT. Navire (*m*.) à trois ponts ; U. S. A trois couches (sandwich). ‖ **Three-dimensional,** adj. Tridimensionnel, à trois dimensions. ‖ **Three-engined,** adj. Trimoteur. ‖ **Three-legged,** adj. A trois pieds. ‖ **Three-master,** n. NAUT. Trois-mâts *m*. ‖ **Three-phase,** adj. ELECTR. Triphasé. ‖ **Three-ply,** adj. Contre-plaqué (wood) ; à trois brins (wool). ‖ **Three-point landing,** n. AVIAT. Atterrissage parfait *m*. ; FAM. Brillante conclusion *f*. ‖ **Three-pole,** ELECTR. Tripolaire. ‖ **Three-power,** adj. A trois, tripartite. ‖ **Three-quarter,** adj. De trois quarts (portrait) ; *three-quarter length coat,* manteau trois quarts ; n. SPORTS. Trois-quarts *m*. ‖ **Three-storied,** adj. A trois étages.
threefold [-fould] adj. Triple.
— adv. Triplement.
threepence [-pəns] n. FIN. Trois pence *m*. *pl*. (sum). ; adj. De trois pence.
threescore [-skɔ:*] adj. Soixante.
threesome [-səm] n. Trio, groupe (*m*.) de trois. ‖ SPORTS. Partie (*f*.) à trois.
— adj. A trois.
threnody ['θri:nədi] n. Thrène *m*.

thresh [θreʃ] v. tr. AGRIC. Battre.
thresher [-ə*] n. AGRIC. Batteuse f.
threshing [-iŋ] n. AGRIC. Battage m. ‖ **Threshing-floor**, n. AGRIC. Aire f. ‖ **Threshing-machine**, n. AGRIC. Batteuse f.
threshold ['θreʃould] n. Seuil m.
threw [θru] pret. See THROW.
thrice [θrais] adv. Trois fois.
thrift [θrift] n. Economie, épargne f. ‖ BOT. Statice m.
thriftily [-ili] adv. Avec économie, frugalement.
thriftiness [-inis] n. Economie, épargne f. ‖ BOT. Vigueur f.
thriftless [-lis] adj. Dépensier.
thriftlessness [-lisnis] n. Prodigalité f.
thrifty [-i] adj. Econome, ménager. ‖ U. S. Prospère ; avantageux.
thrill [θril] v. tr. Faire frémir (or) frissonner (with, de) ; émouvoir, bouleverser, empoigner, électriser. — v. intr. Frémir, frissonner, palpiter (with, de). ‖ **To thrill through**, pénétrer. — n. Frisson, frémissement m. ‖ MED. Frémissement m. ‖ FAM. Récit sensationnel m.
thriller [-ə*] n. Roman (or) spectacle (m.) à sensation, thriller m.
thrilling [-iŋ] adj. Saisissant, empoignant, bouleversant, palpitant.
thrillingly [-iŋli] adv. De façon émouvante.
thrive [θraiv] v. intr. (179). MED., BOT. Se développer, grandir. ‖ FIG. Prospérer, réussir.
thriven ['θrivn̩] p. p. See THRIVE.
thriving [-iŋ] adj. Vigoureux. ‖ FIG. Prospère, florissant.
throat [θrout] n. MED. Gorge f.; sore throat, mal de gorge. ‖ NAUT. Collet m. (of anchor). ‖ TECHN. Gueulard m. ‖ GEOGR. Gorge f. ‖ FAM. To jump down s.o.'s throat, sauter à la gorge de qqn, tomber sur le dos de qqn (to attack) ; to ram sth. down s.o.'s throat, imposer qqch. à qqn. ‖ **Throat-wash**, n. MED. Gargarisme m.
throaty [-i] adj. Guttural.
throb [θrɔb] v. intr. (1). MED. Battre, palpiter (heart) ; élancer (finger). ‖ TECHN. Vrombir (engine). — n. MED. Battement m.; palpitation f. ‖ TECHN. Vrombissement m. ‖
throbbing [-iŋ] adj. MED. Palpitant. ‖ TECHN. Vrombissant. ‖ FIG. Vibrant, frémissant.
throe [θrou] n. MED. Douleurs f. pl. (of childbirth) ; affres f. pl. (of death). ‖ FIG. Tourments m. pl.; affres f. pl.
thrombosis [θrɔm'bousis] n. MED. Thrombose f.
throne [θroun] n. Trône m. ‖ ECCLES. Pl. Trônes m. pl. (angels). — v. tr. Mettre sur le trône. ‖ FAM. To throne it, trôner.
throng [θrɔŋ] n. Foule, cohue, presse f. (crowd). — v. intr. Accourir en foule ; affluer. ‖ Se bousculer, se presser (round, autour de). — v. tr. Encombrer, remplir, envahir.
throstle ['θrɔsl̩] n. ZOOL. Grive f.
throttle ['θrɔtl̩] n. Gosier m. ‖ TECHN. Régulateur ; obturateur m.; soupape (f.) de réglage. ‖ AUTOM. At full throttle, à pleins gaz. ‖ **Throttle-control**, n. TECHN. Commande (f.) des gaz. — v. tr. Etrangler. ‖ FIG. Juguler.
through [θru:] prep. Au travers de, à travers, par ; to pass through, traverser, passer par. ‖ D'un bout à l'autre, à travers, pendant toute la durée de ; all through his life, sa vie durant. ‖ Par l'intermédiaire (or) l'entremise de ; to send through the post, envoyer par la poste. ‖ Grâce à, à cause de, par ; it's all through me that, c'est à cause de moi que. — adv. A travers, par ; to let sth. through, laisser passer qqch.; are you through?, êtes-vous reçu ? (at an examen) ; U. S. avez-vous fini ? ‖ D'un bout à l'autre, jusqu'au bout ; through and through, d'un bout à

l'autre, de bout en bout ; to know s.o. through and through, connaître qqn à fond ; to hear a concert through, entendre un concert jusqu'au bout. ‖ De part en part ; soaked through, mouillé jusqu'aux os. ‖ Directement ; to run straight through to London, aller directement à Londres (train). ‖ En communication téléphonique ; to get through to, mettre en communication avec ; to put through to, passer à (s.o.). — adj. TECHN. Passant (tenon). ‖ CH. DE F. Pourvu d'un billet direct (passenger) ; direct (ticket, train) ; through traffic, transit. ‖ FAM. To be through with, en avoir fini avec. ‖ **Through-communication**, n. CH. DE F. Intercommunication.
throughout [θru:'aut] adv. D'un bout à l'autre, de bout en bout, entièrement. — prep. D'un bout à l'autre de.
throve [θrouv] pret. See THRIVE.
throw [θrou] v. tr. (180). Jeter, lancer (a ball, missile). ‖ Jeter, projeter, pousser ; to throw oneself into, se jeter dans. ‖ Jeter, projeter, répandre ; to throw one's shadow on to, projeter son ombre sur. ‖ Jeter, lancer, plonger, mettre ; to throw difficulties in the way of, semer des difficultés sur le chemin de, mettre en difficultés. ‖ Jeter, rejeter ; to throw the blame on, rejeter le blâme sur. ‖ Jeter (dice) ; to throw open the door, ouvrir la porte toute grande. ‖ SPORTS. Renverser, terrasser (an opponent) ; désarçonner (a rider). ‖ ZOOL. Mettre bas (rabbits) ; to throw its feathers (or) its skin, muer. ‖ TECHN. Tourner, façonner au tour. ‖ FAM. To be thrown upon, tomber à la charge de. ‖ **To throw about**, gaspiller (one's money) ; jeter de-ci de-là (things) ; to throw oneself about, se démener. ‖ **To throw away**, jeter (a cigarette) ; exposer (one's life) ; perdre (one's time). ‖ **To throw back**, rejeter, renvoyer (a ball) ; réfléchir, mirer (an image) ; to be thrown back upon, être obligé de se rabattre sur. ‖ **To throw down**, abattre (one's cards, trees) ; jeter de haut en bas (stones) ; démolir (a wall) ; to throw oneself down, se jeter à terre ; CHIM. Déposer (sediment) ; LOC. To throw down one's tools, se mettre en grève, débrayer. ‖ **To throw in**, jeter dans (or) dedans (s.o., sth.) ; placer, introduire (a word) ; COMM. Ajouter par-dessus le marché. ‖ **To throw off**, se débarrasser de (a bore) ; rompre avec (a friend) ; quitter (one's clothes) ; jeter (the mask) ; se départir de (one's reserve) ; écrire vite (a story). ‖ **To throw on**, enfiler, mettre vite (one's clothes) ; jeter sur soi (a coat). ‖ **To throw out**, se défausser de (a card) ; bomber (one's chest) ; répandre (heat, light, smell) ; jeter dehors, expulser, chasser (s.o.) ; faire ressortir, mettre en relief (sth.) : ARCHIT. Construire en saillie ; MILIT. Envoyer en avant ; AGRIC. pousser, jeter (roots) ; JUR. rejeter (a bill) ; AUTOM. To throw out the clutch, débrayer. ‖ To throw over, abandonner, repousser, se débarrasser de (s.o.). ‖ **To throw up**, faire ressortir (colour) ; lever (hands) ; jeter en l'air (sth.) ; ouvrir (a sash-window) ; ARCHIT. Construire à la hâte ; MED., FIG. Vomir ; FIG. Abandonner, renoncer à (one's claims) ; se démettre de, démissionner de (one's post) ; to feel like throwing everything up, avoir envie de tout plaquer. — v. intr. Jeter, lancer. ‖ Jeter les dés. ‖ **To throw back**, retourner au type primitif. ‖ **To throw off**, SPORTS. Laisser courre ; FIG. Commencer. ‖ **To throw up**, vomir. — n. Jet, lancement, lancer m.; action (f.) de lancer ; throw of the dice, coup de dés. ‖ SPORTS. Jet m. (of the javelin) ; lancer m. (in fishing) ; mise à terre f. (in wrestling). ‖ GEOL. Rejet m. ‖ TECHN. Excentricité, déviation f.; bras m. (of crankshaft). ‖ U. S. Jeté de lit m. ‖ **Throw-away sheet**, n. Prospectus m. ‖ **Throw-back**, n. Mouvement en arrière, recul m.; MED. Retour atavique m.; régression f. ‖ **Throw-off**, n. SPORTS. Laisser-courre m. ‖ **Throw-out**, n. COMM. Rebut m.; ELECT. Interrup-

teur automatique *m.;* TECHN. Débrayage automatique *m.* ‖ **Throw-over gear,** n. AUTOM. Train baladeur *m.*

thrower [-ə*] n. Joueur *s.* (of dice). ‖ ARTS. Tourneur *m.* ‖ SPORTS. Lanceur *m.*

thru [θru:] U. S. See THROUGH.

thrum [θrʌm] n. Penne *f.* (of a loom). ‖ NAUT. Pl. Lardage *m.*
— v. tr. (1). Franger. ‖ NAUT. Larder.

thrum v. intr. (1). Tambouriner, tapoter (*on,* sur). ‖ MUS. Pincer de (a guitar).
— n. Tapotement *m.*

thrush [θrʌʃ] n. ZOOL. Grive *f.*

thrush n. MED. Muguet *m.*

thrust [θrʌst] v. tr. (180). Pousser violemment (or) fortement (s.o., sth.); *to thrust sth. under s.o.'s nose,* fourrer qqch. sous le nez de qqn. ‖ Enfoncer, plonger (*into,* dans) [one's hands, a knife]. ‖ Imposer (*upon,* à) [one's opinion]; *to thrust sth. upon s.o.,* obliger qqn à accepter qqch.; *to thrust oneself upon,* imposer sa présence à, se jeter à la tête de. ‖ **To thrust in,** introduire, enfoncer (sth.); placer (a word); fourrer (fam.). ‖ **To thrust out,** allonger, étendre (one's legs); chasser, expulser (s.o.). ‖ **To thrust through,** transpercer, percer; *to thrust one's way through the crowd,* se frayer un chemin en fendant la foule.
— v. intr. Pousser vivement. ‖ SPORTS. Tirer, porter une botte à (in fencing). ‖ FIG. *To thrust and parry,* faire assaut d'esprit, engager une joute avec qqn. ‖ **To thrust at,** frapper de la pointe (or) d'estoc, allonger un coup à. ‖ **To thrust past,** repousser pour passer.
— n. Forte poussée *f.* ‖ Coup (*m.*) de pointe. ‖ TECHN., ARCHIT., MILIT. Poussée *f.* ‖ SPORTS. Botte; estocade *f.* ‖ GÉOL. Chevauchement *m.*

thruster [-ə*] n. TECHN. Servomoteur *m.* ‖ FAM. Arriviste *s.*

thud [θʌd] v. intr. Tomber avec un bruit sourd.
— n. Bruit sourd, floc *m.*

thug [θʌg] n. Bandit, étrangleur *m.* ‖ Séide, sicaire *m.*

thulium [ˈθjuːliəm] n. CHIM. Thulium *m.*

thumb [θʌm] n. MED. Pouce *m.* ‖ FAM. *By rule of thumb,* par routine; *I know it by the pricking of my thumb,* mon petit doigt me l'a dit; *her fingers are all thumbs,* elle ne sait pas se servir de ses mains; *thumbs down!,* rien ne va plus; *thumbs up!,* chouette alors!, d'accord!; *under s.o.'s thumb,* sous la coupe de qqn. ‖ **Thumb-index,** n. Touche, encoche *f.;* onglet *m.* (of book). ‖ **Thumb-print,** n. Empreinte (*f.*) de pouce. ‖ **Thumb-stall,** n. Poucier *m.*
— v. tr. Feuilleter (a book). ‖ FAM. Faire de l'autostop auprès de (a motorist). ‖ FAM. *To thumb one's nose at,* faire un pied de nez à.

thumbnail [-neil] adj. En raccourci, minuscule; concis; *thumbnail sketch,* croquis minuscule; description en raccourci.
— n. Ongle du pouce *m.*

thumbtack [-tæk] n. U. S. Punaise *f.* (drawing pin).

thump [θʌmp] v. tr. Cogner, marteler. ‖ Frapper.
— v. intr. Cogner (*at, on,* sur).
— n. Coup violent *m.*

thumper [-ə*] n. Cogneur *m.* ‖ FAM. *That's a thumper!,* celle-là est raide!, en voilà une forte!

thumping [-iŋ] adj. FAM. Énorme (lie).

thunder [θʌndə*] n. Tonnerre *m.* (noise). ‖ FIG. Tonnerre *m.* (of applause); foudre *f.* (of the Church). ‖ FAM. *To steal s.o.'s thunder,* couper ses effets à qqn. ‖ **Thunder-clap,** n. Coup de tonnerre *m.;* FIG. Coup (*m.*) de massue; effet foudroyant *m.* ‖ **Thunder-cloud,** n. Nuage orageux *m.* ‖ **Thunder-shower,** n. Pluie (*f.*) d'orage.
— v. intr. Tonner (lit. and fig.). ‖ **To thunder forth,** pleuvoir, crépiter (applause). ‖ **To thunder**

out, fulminer, tempêter, tonner (*against,* contre). ‖ **To thunder past,** passer avec un bruit de tonnerre.
— v. tr. ECCLES. Fulminer. ‖ FAM. Tonner.

thunderbolt [-boult] n. Coup (*m.*) de foudre (lit. and fig.).

thundering [-riŋ] adj. Tonnant (voice).
— adv. FAM. Formidablement, bigrement; *a thundering good meal,* un festin du tonnerre.

thunderous [-rəs] adj. Orageux (weather). ‖ Crépitant (applause); tonnant (voice).

thunderpeal [-piːl] n. U. S. Coup de tonnerre *m.*

thunderstruck [-strʌk] adj. Foudroyé. ‖ FIG. Terrassé, interdit, pétrifié.

thundery [-ri] adj. Orageux.

thurible [ˈθjuəribl] n. Encensoir *m.*

thurifer [-fə*] n. Thuriféraire *m.*

Thursday [ˈθəːzdi] n. Jeudi *m.*

thus [ðʌs] adv. Ainsi, de cette façon, comme ceci (in this manner). ‖ Ainsi, à ce point, si (to this degree). ‖ Donc, ainsi, par conséquent (therefore).

thuya [ˈθjuːə] n. BOT. Thuya *m.*

thwack [θwæk] v. tr. FAM. Frapper sèchement, donner un grand coup à.
— n. FAM. Coup sec *m.*
— interj. Vlan!

thwart [θwɔːt] adj. † Transversal.
— v. tr. FIG. Contrecarrer, contrarier.
— n. NAUT. Banc *m.* (in a boat).

thy [ðai] poss. adj. Ton, ta, tes. (See THOU.)

thyme [taim] n. BOT. Thym *m.;* *wild thyme,* serpolet.

thymol [ˈθaiməl] n. CHIM. Thymol *m.*

thymus [θaiməs] n. MED. Thymus *m.*

thyroid [ˈθairɔid] adj., n. MED. Thyroïde *f.*

thyrsus [ˈθəːsəs] (pl. **thyrsi** [-sai]) n. Thyrse *m.*

thyself [ðaiˈself] pr. † Toi-même, te.

ti [tiː] n. MUS. Si *m. invar.*

tiara [tiˈɑːrə] n. Tiare *f.*

Tiber [ˈtaibə*] n. GEOGR. Tibre *m.*

Tibet [tiˈbet] n. GEOGR. Tibet *m.*

Tibetan [-ən] n. GEOGR. Tibétain *s.*

tibia [ˈtibiə] n. MED. Tibia *m.*
— N. B. Deux pluriels : *tibias, tibiae.*

tic [tik] n. MED. Tic *m.*

titch [titʃ] n. FAM. See TITCH.

tick n. FAM. Crédit *m.; on tick,* à crédit.
— v. tr. FAM. Faire crédit.

tick n. ZOOL. Tique *f.*

tick n. COMM. Toile (*f.*) à matelas.

tick v. intr. Faire tic tac, battre (clock). ‖ **To tick over,** AVIAT. Tourner au ralenti; FAM. Marcher au ralenti (business).
— v. tr. Cocher (on a list). ‖ **To tick off,** cocher, pointer; FAM. rembarrer, rabrouer (s.o.).
— n. Tic-tac *m.* ‖ Coche *f.;* pointage *m.* (on a list). ‖ FAM. Instant *m.; in a tick,* dans une seconde.

ticker [-ə*] n. RADIO. Ticker *m.* ‖ FAM. Cœur *m.* (heart); toquante *f.* (watch).

ticket [ˈtikit] n. CH. DE F., AUTOM. Ticket *m.* (in bus'tube). ‖ CH. DE F. Billet *m.* (in train). ‖ THEATR. Billet *m.; cloak-room ticket,* numéro de vestiaire. ‖ COMM. Étiquette *f.* ‖ Fiche; carte (*f.*) de lecteur; *pawn ticket,* reconnaissance du mont-de-piété; MILIT. *To get one's ticket,* être libéré. ‖ JUR. *Ticket of leave,* bulletin de libération conditionnelle. ‖ NAUT., AVIAT. Brevet *m.* ‖ U. S. Liste (*f.*) des candidats aux élections; *to vote a straight ticket,* voter pour la liste entière. ‖ U. S. Papillon de procès-verbal *m.; to give a ticket,* verbaliser. ‖ FAM. *That's the ticket,* c'est ça tout juste, ça colle parfaitement. ‖ **Ticket-agency,** n. Agence de location théâtrale *f.* ‖ **Ticket-clerk,** n. Distributeur (*m.*) de billets. ‖ **Ticket-collector,** n. CH. DE F. Contrôleur *m.* ‖ **Ticket-office,** n. CH. DE F. Guichet (*m.*) de distribution des billets. ‖ **Ticket-punch,** n. CH. DE F.

Poinçonneuse *f.* ‖ **Ticket-punching,** n. Poinçonnage *m.* ‖ **Ticket window,** n. U. S. Guichet *m.*
— v. tr. Comm. Etiqueter.
ticketing [-iŋ] n. Comm. Etiquetage *m.*
ticking ['tikiŋ] n. Comm. Toile (*f.*) à matelas.
tickle ['tikl] v. tr. Chatouiller (s.o.). ‖ Sports. Pêcher à la main (the trout). ‖ Fig. Chatouiller, exciter (curiosity); flatter (the palate). ‖ U. S. Fam. Enthousiasmer, exciter (to excite); donner envie de rire à (to excite amusement in).
— v. intr. Chatouiller; *my hand tickles,* la main me démange.
— n. Chatouillement *m.;* chatouille *f.* (fam.).
tickler [-ə*] n. Techn. Titillateur *m.* ‖ Fig. Sujet épineux *m.;* question embarrassante *f.* ‖ U. S. *Memory tickler,* pense-bête.
tickling [-iŋ] adj. Chatouillant. ‖ Med. D'irritation (cough).
— n. Chatouillement *m.*
ticklish [-iʃ] adj. Chatouilleux; *to be ticklish,* craindre la chatouille. ‖ Fig. Epineux, délicat, scabreux (question); susceptible, chatouilleux (person).
tidal ['taidl] adj. Naut. De marée (basin); d'échouage (harbour); *tidal wave,* mascaret (in estuary); barre de flot (on river); raz de marée, vague de fond (on sea). ‖ Med. De respiration (air). ‖ Fig. *Tidal wave,* vague, marée.
tidbit ['tid,bit] n. U. S. See TITBIT.
tiddler ['tidlə*] n. Fam. Petit poisson *m.* (small fish); épinoche *f.* (stickleback). ‖ Fam. Moutard *m.,* mioche *s.*
tiddl(e)y ['tidli] adj. Fam. Pompette, éméché (slightly drunk).
tiddly adj. Fam. Minuscule (very small). ‖ **Tiddly-winks,** n. sg. Jeu (*m.*) de puce.
tide [taid] n. † Saison, époque *f.* ‖ Période, journée *f.* (of work). ‖ Naut. Marée *f.; at high, low tide,* à marée haute, basse. ‖ Fig. Issue *f.* (of battle); vague *f.* (of discontent); courant *m.* (of public opinion); cours *m.* (of time). ‖ Fam. *To take the tide at the flood,* profiter de l'occasion. ‖ **Tide-gate,** n. Naut. Ecluse *f.* ‖ **Tide-mark,** n. Naut. Ligne (*f.*) des hautes eaux; laisse de haute mer *f.* ‖ **Tide-power,** n. Energie (or) force de la marée *f.; tide-power plant,* usine marémotrice. ‖ **Tide-table,** n. Table (*f.*) des marées.
— v. intr. Naut. Faire marée. ‖ **To tide in,** Naut. Entrer avec le flot. ‖ **To tide out,** Naut. Sortir avec le jusant.
— v. tr. **To tide over,** venir à bout de (a difficulty); *this sum will tide me over,* cette somme va me remettre à flot (or) me dépanner.
tideless [-lis] adj. Sans marée.
tidily ['taidili] adv. Soigneusement, proprement.
tidiness [-nis] n. Ordre *m.;* netteté, propreté *f.* ‖ Tenue nette *f.* (of dress).
tidings ['taidiŋz] n. pl. Nouvelles *f. pl.*
tidy ['taidi] adj. Net, soigné, propre, bien tenu (dress). ‖ Ordonné, bien tenu (room); ordonné, soigneux (person). ‖ Fam. Fameux (price, shot); *pretty tidy,* pas mal, passablement.
— n. Voile de fauteuil *m.* ‖ Vide-poche *m.*
— v. tr. (2). Mettre en ordre, ranger (a room). ‖ Nettoyer (to clean).
— v. intr. **To tidy up,** tout remettre en place; faire un brin de toilette.
tie [tai] v. tr. (2). Attacher, lier. ‖ Attacher (one's apron, shoes); faire (a knot); nouer, faire un nœud à (a ribbon). ‖ Archit. Relier. ‖ Mus. Lier. ‖ Fig. Enchaîner, river, attacher, lier, suspendre (*to,* à). ‖ **To tie down,** attacher, lier (*to,* à). ‖ **To tie up,** attacher (a dog); emballer, empaqueter, envelopper (goods); attacher, ficeler (a parcel); attacher, trousser (one's skirt); ligoter (s.o.); Med. Bander, panser (a wound); Fin. Bloquer, immobiliser (a sum); Jur. Rendre inaliénable (a succession); Fig. Rete-

nir, entraver; Fam. *Tied up,* empêché, retenu (person).
— v. intr. Sports. Etre à égalité (*with,* avec).
— n. Lien *m.;* attache *f.* (in general); cordon, lacet *m.* (of shoes). ‖ Cravate *f.* (neck-tie). ‖ Archit. Entretoise *f.* ‖ Mus. Liaison *f.* ‖ Naut. Itague *f.* ‖ Sports. Match (*m.*) à égalité; match de championnat *m.* ‖ U. S. Ch. de f. Traverse *f.* ‖ Fig. Lien *m.* (of blood, marriage); attache *f.* (of family). ‖ **Tie-bar,** n. Archit. Tirant *m.;* Ch. de f. Entretoise *f.* ‖ **Tie-clip,** n. Fixe-cravate *m.* ‖ **Tie-in,** adj. U. S. Conditionnel (sale). ‖ **Tie-pin,** n. Epingle de cravate *f.* ‖ **Tie-up,** n. Comm. Entente, union *f.;* U. S. blocage (*m.*) de la circulation (traffic); arrêt de travail *m.* (work); Fig. Impasse *f.*
tier ['tiə*] n. Etage *m.;* rangée superposée *f.* ‖ Gradin *m.* (of an amphitheatre). ‖ Terrasse *f.* (on a plateau).
— v. tr. Etager.
tierce [tiəs] n. Mus., Sports, Eccles. Tierce *f.* ‖ Comm. † Tierçon *m.*
tiff [tif] n. Fam. Chamaillerie, pique, brouillerie *f.*
— v. intr. Fam. Prendre la mouche, être à cran, se monter, prendre mal les choses.
tiffany ['tifəni] n. Gaze *f.*
tiffin ['tifin] n. Déjeuner léger *m.,* collation *f.*
tig [tig] n. *Long tig,* chat perché (game).
tige [ti:ʒ] n. Archit. Fût *m.* ‖ Bot. Tige *f.*
tiger ['taigə*] n. Zool., Fig. Tigre *m.* ‖ **Tiger-cat,** n. Zool. Chat-tigre *m.*
tigerish [-riʃ] adj. De tigre.
tight [tait] adj. Etanche (container); hermétique (joint); imperméable (partition). ‖ Raide, tendu (cord); solide, serré (knot); bloqué, serré à bloc (nut). ‖ Collant, ajusté (clothes); bien monté (furniture); trop petit (or) étroit (shoes). ‖ Sports. Serré (match). ‖ Fin. Trop juste (market); rare (money). ‖ Fam. Rond, plein (tipsy). ‖ Fam. *In a tight corner,* dans une mauvaise passe; *to keep a tight hand on,* tenir serré, brider. ‖ **Tight-drawn,** adj. Pincé (lips). ‖ **Tight-fisted,** adj. Fam. Serré, rapiat, près de ses sous. ‖ **Tight-fitting,** adj. Collant (clothes); fermant hermétiquement (door). ‖ **Tight-laced,** adj. Serré dans son corset; Fam. Collet monté. ‖ **Tight-lipped,** adj. Fam. Cadenassé.
— adv. Bien, fort, serré. ‖ U. S. Fam. *To sit tight,* tenir bon, se cramponner à ses positions.
— n. pl. Maillot, collant *m.*
tighten [-n] v. tr. Serrer (one's belt); rectifier (one's tie). ‖ Resserrer, serrer (a screw); tendre (a spring).
— v. intr. Se serrer, se resserrer.
tightly [-li] adv. Serré fortement, étroitement.
tightness [-nis] n. Etanchéité; herméticité; imperméabilité *f.* ‖ Tension, raideur *f.;* serrage *m.* (of a cord). ‖ Etroitesse *f.* (of clothes, grasp, knot). ‖ Fin. Rareté *f.* (of money). ‖ Med. Oppression *f.* (of the chest).
tightwad [-wæd] n. U. S. Fam. Grigou, grippe-sou, pignouf *m.*
tigress [taigris] n. Zool., Fig. Tigresse *f.*
Tigris n. Geogr. Tigre *m.*
tike [taik]. See TYKE.
tilbury ['tilbəri] n. Tilbury *m.*
tilde ['tilde] n. Gramm. Tilde *m.*
tile [tail] n. Archit. Tuile *f.* (for roof); carreau *m.* (paving). ‖ Fam. Galurin *m.* (hat); haut-de-forme *m.* (top hat). ‖ Zool. *Tile-cat,* n. Zool. Chat (*m.*) de gouttière.
— v. tr. Archit. Couvrir de tuiles (house); carreler (floor). ‖ Fig. Tuiler (in freemasonry); exiger le secret de (s.o.).
tiler [-ə] n. Archit. Couvreur; carreleur *m.* ‖ Fig. Tuilier *m.* (freemason).
tilery [-əri] n. Tuilerie *f.*
tiling [-iŋ] n. Toiture (*f.*) en tuiles; carrelage *m.*
till [til] n. Tiroir-caisse *m.*

till n. GEOL. Moraine f.

till prep. Jusqu'à, à; *good-bye till tomorrow*, à demain; *till next year*, jusqu'à l'année prochaine. || **Not till**, pas avant.

— conj. Jusqu'à ce que; *wait till the rain stops*, attendez qu'il ne pleuve plus. || **Not till**, pas avant que; *it was not long till he realized*, il ne mit pas longtemps à comprendre.

till [til] v. tr. AGRIC. Cultiver, labourer.

tillable [-əbl] adj. AGRIC. Arable, labourable.

tillage [-idʒ] n. AGRIC. Labourage, *m.*, culture *f.*

tiller [-ə*] n. AGRIC. Cultivateur *m.*

tiller n. BOT. Rejeton, baliveau *m.*

tiller n. NAUT. Barre *f.*

tilt [tilt] n. Bâche *f.* || NAUT. Tendelet *m.*

— v. tr. Bâcher. NAUT. Couvrir d'un tendelet.

tilt v. intr. S'incliner, pencher. || NAUT. Donner de la bande. || **To tilt at**, jouter contre; FIG. Rompre une lance avec; allonger un coup de patte à (fam.). || **To tilt over**, se renverser, verser. || **To tilt up**, se redresser, se relever, basculer en se redressant.

— v. tr. Pencher, incliner. || Culbuter, renverser (a car). || TECHN. Marteler. || **To tilt back**, rejeter en arrière (one's hat); rabattre (a seat). || **To tilt over**, renverser, faire basculer. || **To tilt up**, redresser.

— n. Pente, inclinaison *f.* || † Joute *f.* || NAUT. Bande *f.*, gîte *f.* || GEOL. Relèvement *m.* || FAM. *At full tilt*, à fond de train; *to run full tilt into*, se jeter tête baissée contre.

tilth [tilθ] n. AGRIC. Culture *f.*; couche arable *f.*

timbal ['timbəl] n. MUS. Timbale *f.*

timber ['timbə*] n. Bois (*m.*) de construction (building timber). || Poutre *f.*; madrier *m.*; arbres (*m. pl.*) de haute futaie (standing timber). || NAUT. Couple *m.* || U. S. FAM. Trempe *f.* || **Timber-merchant**, n. Marchand de bois *m.* || **Timber-raft**, n. Train de bois *m.* || **Timber-work**, n. Construction (*f.*) en bois; charpente *f.*

— v. tr. Boiser.

— v. intr. Faire du bois.

timbre n. MUS. Timbre *m.*

timbrel ['timbrəl] n. MUS. Tambourin *m.*

time [taim] n. Temps *m.*; *Father Time*, le Temps; *a long time ago*, il y a longtemps; *it's a long time since*, il y a belle lurette que. || Temps *m.*, période, époque *f.*; *a man of the times*, un homme de son siècle; *in Caesar's time*, au temps de César; *mediaeval times*, la période médiévale; *times are hard*, les temps sont durs. || Temps *m.*; période, durée *f.*; *a time of sorrow*, une triste période, une période de chagrin. || Temps, moment *m.*; *a good time was had by all*, tous ont pris du bon temps (or) s'en sont payé. || Temps, terme *m.*; *my time is close at hand*, mon heure approche; *my time is almost over*, mon temps est presque achevé, j'ai fait mon temps. || Temps *m.* (of apprenticeship, of imprisonment); *she is near her time*, elle est près d'accoucher. || Temps, loisir *m.*; *to have no time for reading*, n'avoir pas le temps de lire; *to have time on one's hands*, avoir du temps de reste. || Temps, rythme *m.*; *to mark time*, marquer le temps (or) le pas. || Temps, délai *m.*; *to leave s.o. little time*, prendre qqn de court; *within the required time*, dans les délais prescrits. || Temps *m.*, heure *f.*; *at the time they arrived*, à l'heure où ils arrivèrent; *on time*, à l'heure, à temps; *what time is it?*, quelle heure est-il? || Temps, moment convenable *m.*; *it is time to get up*, il est temps de se lever; *now is the time to act*, l'heure est venue d'agir. || Fois *f.*; *the first time in history*, pour la première fois dans les annales. || ASTRON. Temps *m.*; *solar time*, temps solaire. || TECHN. *Idle time*, temps improductif. || MUS. Mesure *f.*; *in strict time*, en mesure. || MUS. Tempo *m.* || SPORTS. Temps *m.* (winner's); *in quick time*, au pas accéléré; *to keep the time*, chronométrer; *to race against time*, courir contre la montre. || CULIN. *Cooking time*, temps de cuisson. || THEATR. Temps *m.* || FAM. *To have a high old time*, faire la bringue; *to have a rough time*, en voir de dures. || LOC. *After a long, short time*, longtemps, peu après; *another time*, une autre fois; *at all times*, en tout temps, à tout moment; *at no time*, jamais; *at the present time*, à l'heure qu'il est; *at this time of day*, à l'heure actuelle (or) qu'il est; *at times*, parfois, de temps à autre; *between times*, entre-temps; *every time that*, chaque fois que; *four times running*, quatre fois de suite; *from that time*, depuis lors; *from time to time*, de temps en temps; *from some time past*, depuis quelque temps; *if at any time*, si à l'occasion; *in due time and place*, en temps et lieu; *in his own good time*, à son heure; *in no time*, en moins de rien; *this time last year*, il y a un an à pareille époque. || **Time-bargain**, n. FIN. Marché à terme *m.* || **Time-bill**, n. COMM. Effet à court terme *m.* || **Time-bomb**, n. MILIT. Bombe (*f.*) à retardement. || **Time-book**, U. S. **time-card**, n. Registre (*m.*) de présence. || **Time-clock**, n. Horloge enregistreuse *f.* || **Time-consuming**, adj. Qui prend (or) fait perdre du temps. || **Time-exposure**, n. Pose *f.* (in photogr.). || **Time-honoured**, adj. Séculaire, consacré par l'usage. || **Time-lag**, n. Délai, décalage *m.*; MED. Latence *f.*, temps (*m.*) de réaction. || **Time-limit**, n. Délai *m.*, limite (*f.*) de temps. || **Time-saving**, adj. Economiseur de temps, qui fait gagner du temps. || **Time-server**, n. Opportuniste *s.* || **Time-sharing**, n. INFORM. Temps partagé, partage de temps, time-sharing *m.* || **Time-sheet**, n. Feuille de présence *f.* || **Time-switch**, n. ELECTR. Minuterie *f.* || **Time-table**, n. Emploi du temps; horaire *m.*; CH. DE F. Indicateur *m.* || **Time-tested**, adj. Eprouvé par le temps. || **Time-work**, n. Travail (*m.*) à l'heure.

— v. tr. Mesurer, calculer, régler; fixer l'heure de. || SPORTS. Chronométrer.

— v. intr. S'accorder (with, avec).

timekeeper [-,ki:pə*] n. Pointeur *s.* (person); chronomètre (*m.*) de précision (watch).

timekeeping [-,ki:piŋ] n. Pointage; chronométrage *m.*

timeless [-lis] adj. Sans fin; éternel.

timeliness [-linis] n. Opportunité *f.*

timely [-li] adj. Opportun, à propos, de saison.

timepiece [-pi:s] n. Pendule *f.* (clock); montre *f.*, chronomètre *m.* (watch).

timer [-ə*] n. Chronométreur *m.* || TECHN. Synchronisateur *m.*

timid ['timid] adj. Timide (shy); craintif, appréhensif (timorous).

timidity [ti'miditi], timidness ['timidnis] n. Timidité, nature craintive *f.*

timidly ['timidli] adv. Timidement.

timing ['taimiŋ] n. Moment, horaire *m.* (of an event); synchronisation *f.* (of two events), minutage *m.* (of an operation); sens du rythme, tempo *m.* (of an actor, a musician); coordination *f.* (of a boxer, a tennis player). || Chronométrage *m.* (with a stopwatch). || TECHN., AUTOM. Réglage *m.*; *timing gear*, engrenage de distribution.

timorous ['timərəs] adj. Timoré, craintif, peureux.

timorousness [-nis] n. Nature craintive (or) timorée, timidité peureuse *f.*

timpani ['timpənai] n. pl. MUS. Timbales *f.* pl.

tin [tin] n. Etain *m.* (métal). || Fer-blanc *m.*; *drinking tin*, timbale. || Boîte (*f.*) en fer-blanc (or) de conserve (see CAN); *sardine tin*, boîte à sardines. || Bidon *m.*; *petrol tin*, bidon à essence. || CULIN. Tourtière *f.* (for tarts); *cake tin*, moule à gâteaux. || POP. Fric *m.* (money). || **Tin-bearing**, adj. Stannifère. || **Tin-fish**, n. NAUT., FAM. Sous-marin *m.* || **Tin-foil**, n. Feuille (*f.*) d'étain. || **Tin-hat**, n. MILIT. FAM. Casque *m.* || **Tin-kettle**, n. Bouilloire (*f.*) en étain; FAM. Casserole *f.* (piano). || **Tin-opener**, n. Ouvre-boîte *m.* || **Tin-pan**, n. CULIN.

Tourtière *f.*; moule (*m.*) à pâtisserie; FAM. *Tin-Pan Alley*, rue des marchands de musique populaire. ‖ **Tin-plate**, n. Fer-blanc *m.*; v. tr. Etamer. ‖ **Tin-shop**, n. Ferblanterie *f.* ‖ **Tin-tack**, n. Semence (*f.*) de tapissier.
— adj. En étain. ‖ De fer-blanc. ‖ De plomb (soldier).
— v. tr. (1). Etamer. ‖ Mettre en boîtes, conserver.
tinctorial [tiŋk'tɔːriəl] adj. Tinctorial.
tincture ['tiŋktʃə*] n. Couleur, teinte *f.* (hue). ‖ MED. Teinture *f.* ‖ FIG. Teinture *f.* (of a science).
— v. tr. Teinter. ‖ FIG. Donner une teinture (or) nuance à.
tinder ['tində*] n. Amadou *m.*
tindery [-ri] adj. Inflammable.
tine [tain] n. AGRIC. Pointe, dent *f.* (of a fork). ‖ ZOOL. Andouiller, cor *m.*
ting [tiŋ] n. Tintement *m.* ‖ **Ting-a-ling**, n. Drelin-drelin *m.*
— v. intr. Tinter.
tinge [tindʒ] v. tr. Teinter, colorer, nuancer (*with*, de) [lit. and fig.].
— n. Teinte, nuance *f.*
tingle ['tiŋgl] v. intr. Fourmiller, picoter, cuire (skin). ‖ Tinter, bourdonner (ears). ‖ FAM. Démanger; gratter (fam.).
— n. Fourmillement, picotement *m.* ‖ Tintement, bourdonnement *m.*
tinker ['tiŋkə*] n. Rétameur *m.* (person). ‖ FAM. Bousilleur *s.* (botcher); bricoleur *s.* (jack-of-all-trades). ‖ FAM. *Not worth a tinker's damn,* qui ne vaut pas un radis.
— v. tr. Etamer, rétamer. ‖ FAM. Rafistoler.
— v. intr. **To tinker at**, bricoler à; retaper tant bien que mal.
tinkle ['tiŋkl] v. intr. Tinter.
— v. tr. Faire tinter.
— n. Tintement *m.* (of a bell). ‖ Chanson *f.* (of a spring). ‖ FAM. Bruit (*m.*) de casserole, timbre fêlé (of a piano); coup de fil *m.* (on the phone).
tinman ['tinmən], **tinner** [-ə*]. See TINSMITH.
tinned [-d] adj. Etamé. ‖ En (or) de conserve.
tinnitus [ti'naitəs] n. MED. Tintement (*m.*) d'oreilles.
tinny ['tini] adj. Grêle (sound); d'étain (taste).
tinsel ['tinsəl] n. Lamé, clinquant *m.*; paillettes *f. pl.* ‖ FIG. Clinquant *m.*
— adj. Clinquant, voyant, faux.
— v. tr. (1). Orner de paillettes (or) de clinquant. ‖ FIG. Donner un faux éclat à.
tinsmith ['tinsmiθ] n. Ferblantier, étameur *m.*
tinstone [-stoun] n. Cassitérite *f.*
tint [tint] n. Teinte, nuance *f.* ‖ ARTS. Hachures *f. pl.*; grisé *m.*
— v. tr. Teinter. ‖ ARTS. Ombrer, hachurer.
tintinnabulate [,tinti'næbjuleit] v. intr. Tintinnabuler, tinter.
tintinnabulation [,tinti,næbju'leiʃən] n. Tintinnabulement *m.*
tinty ['tinti] adj. Criard, de teintes éclatantes.
tinware ['tinwɛə*] n. Ferblanterie *f.*
tiny ['taini] adj. Menu, minuscule, tout petit; *tiny tot*, bambin.
tip [tip] n. Bout *m.*; pointe *f.* (of branch, nose, toes). ‖ TECHN. Bout, embout *m.* (cap). ‖ CULIN. Pointe *f.* (of asparagus).
— v. tr. (1). Mettre un bout à.
tip v. tr. (1). Effleurer, toucher à peine (to tap). ‖ Donner un pourboire à (a porter, waiter). ‖ Incliner, baisser (one's hat); faire pencher (the scales). ‖ Faire basculer, renverser, verser (*into*, dans). ‖ SPORTS. Tuyauter. ‖ **To tip off**, vider (a glass); faire tomber (s.o., sth.). ‖ FAM. Tuyauter (s.o.). ‖ **To tip out**, verser, déverser. ‖ **To tip over**, renverser. ‖ **To tip up**, culbuter, faire basculer; NAUT. Incliner.
— v. intr. Donner un pourboire (or) de l'argent.

‖ Basculer, culbuter, se renverser. ‖ NAUT. Chavirer. ‖ **To tip over**, se renverser, se retourner. ‖ To tip up, basculer.
— n. Pourboire *m.*; gratification; pièce *f.* (fam.). ‖ Petit coup *m.*; poussée légère *f.* (tap). ‖ Décharge *f.*; *rubbish tip*, dépotoir, fosse à ordures. ‖ Tas, monceau *m.* (of rubbish). ‖ SPORTS. Tuyau *m.* ‖ FAM. Truc *m.* ‖ **Tip-car**, n. Wagonnet (*m.*) à bascule. ‖ **Tip-cart**, n. Tombereau *m.* ‖ **Tip-iron**, n. U. S. Démonte-pneu *m.* ‖ **Tip-lorry**, n. Camion (*m.*) à benne basculante. ‖ **Tip-up**, adj. Basculant.
tippet ['tipit] n. † Pèlerine *f.* ‖ Palatine *f.*, collet *m.* (fur).
tipple ['tipl] v. intr. FAM. Sucer, picoler.
— v. tr. Siroter, buvoter.
— n. Boisson alcoolique *f.*
tippler [-ə*] n. FAM. Soiffard *s.*
tipsiness ['tipsinis] n. Ivresse *f.*
tipster ['tipstə*] n. SPORTS. Tuyauteur *m.*
tipsy ['tipsi] adj. FAM. Eméché, parti (person); d'ivrogne (smile). ‖ **Tipsy-cake**, U. S. **tipsy pudding**, n. CULIN. Baba (*m.*) au madère et à la crème.
tiptoe ['tip'tou] n. Pointe (*f.*) du pied; *on tiptoe*, sur la pointe des pieds.
— v. intr. Marcher sur la pointe des pieds.
tiptop [-'tɔp] n. Sommet *m.* ‖ FIG. Perfection *f.*
— adj. Parfait; chic, bath (fam.).
tirade [ti'reid] n. Tirade *f.*
tire ['taiə*]. See TYRE.
tire v. tr. Fatiguer (to exhaust). ‖ Ennuyer, lasser (to bore).
— v. intr. Se fatiguer, se lasser (*of*, de).
tired [-d] adj. Fatigué, las (weary). ‖ Assommé, ennuyé (bored).
tiredness [-dnis] n. Fatigue *f.*
tireless [-lis] adj. Infatigable, inlassable.
tirelessly [-lisli] adv. Infatigablement.
tiresome [-səm] adj. Fatigant, épuisant (exhausting). ‖ Lassant, fastidieux, agaçant (boring); ennuyeux, assommant (tedious).
tirewoman [-,wumən] (pl. **tirewomen** [-wimin]) n. Soubrette *f.*
tiro ['tairou] n. Apprenti, commerçant, débutant, novice *m.* (*in*, à).
tisane [ti'zæn] n. Tisane *f.*
tissue ['tisju:] n. Tissu léger *m.* (gauze); papier (*m.*) de soie (paper); *facial tissue*, papier-linge. ‖ MED., FIG. Tissu *m.*
tit [tit] n. Mamelle *f.* ‖ POP. Nichon, téton *m.*
tit n. ZOOL. Mésange *f.*
tit n. *Tit for tat*, un rendu pour un prêté; à bon chat bon rat; *to give s.o. tit for tat*, procéder avec qqn du tac au tac.
Titan ['taitən] n. Titan *m.*
titanesque ['taitə'nesk] adj. Titanesque.
titanic [tai'tænik] adj. De titan, gigantesque, colossal.
titanic adj. CHIM. Titanique.
titanium [tai'teiniəm] n. CHIM. Titane *m.*
titbit ['titbit] n. Bon morceau *m.*; friandise *f.*; *dainty titbit*, morceau de roi.
titch [titʃ] n. FAM. Demi-portion *f.*, moustique *m.*
titchy [-i] adj. FAM. Minuscule, microscopique.
titer ['taitə*] n. U.S. See TITRE.
titfer [-fə*] n. FAM. Galurin, bibi *m.*
tithe [taið] n. JUR. Dîme *f.* ‖ FAM. Dixième, quart, brin *m.*
— v. tr. Soumettre à la dîme (s.o.). ‖ Payer la dîme sur (a field).
tithing [-iŋ] n. Paiement (or) prélèvement (*m.*) de la dîme.
titillate ['titileit] v. tr. Chatouiller, titiller. ‖ Emoustiller.
titillation [,titi'leiʃən] n. Titillation *f.*; chatouillement *m.* ‖ Emoustillement *m.*
titivate ['titiveit] v. tr. FAM. Attifer, pomponner, bichonner.
— v. intr. Se pomponner, se faire beau.

titlark ['titlɑ:k] n. Zool. Pipit *m*.
title ['taitl̩] n. Titre *m*. (distinction, division, heading, page). ‖ Jur. Titre, droit *m*. (*to*, à). ‖ Fin. Titre *m*. (of gold). ‖ Eccles., Sports. Titre *m*. ‖ Cinem. *Credit titles*, générique. ‖ **Title-deed,** n. Jur. Titre (*m*.) de propriété. ‖ **Title-page,** n. Page (*f*.) de titre. ‖ **Title-role,** n. Theatr., Cinem. Rôle-titre *m*.
— v. tr. Titrer.
titled [-d] adj. Titré.
titleless [-lis] adj. Sans titre.
titmouse ['titmaus] (pl. **titmice** [-mais]) n. Zool. Mésange *f*.
titrate ['titreit] v. tr. Chim. Titrer.
titre ['taitə*] n. Chim. Titre *m*. (of a solution).
titter [titə*] n. Rire étouffé *m*.
— v. intr. Rire en catimini.
tittle ['titl̩] n. Iota *m*.
tittle-tattle ['titl̩tætl̩] n. Potins, cancans, commérages, bavardages *m. pl*.
— v. intr. Cancaner, bavarder.
tittup ['titəp] v. intr. Fringuer (horse).
titubation [,titju'beiʃən] n. Med. Titubation *f*.
titular ['titjulə*] adj., n. Titulaire *s*.
tizzy ['tizi] n. Fam. Panique *f*., affolement *m.; to be in, all of a tizzy*, être sens dessus dessous, être dans tous ses états.
tmesis ['tmi:sis] n. Gramm. Tmèse *f*.
T. N. T. [,ti:en'ti:] abbr. *trinitrotoluene*, trinitrotoluène, T. N. T.
to [tu] prep. A; *akin to*, apparenté à; *he came to where I was sitting*, il vint où j'étais assis; *he has talked to me*, il m'a parlé; *a man to know*, un homme à connaître; *what do you say to it?*, qu'avez-vous à répondre à cela? ‖ De; *glad to see you*, heureux de vous voir; *in proportion to*, en proportion de; *to take a fancy to*, s'engouer de. ‖ Sur; *he hadn't a shirt to his back*, il n'avait pas de chemise sur le dos; *to start to one's feet*, se dresser sur ses jambes. ‖ Avec; *a suspicious resemblance to*, une ressemblance suspecte avec; *to make oneself amiable to*, faire l'aimable avec. ‖ Pour; *easy to him*, facile pour lui; *s.o. to protect her*, qqn pour la protéger. ‖ A part; *to one's self*, à part soi. ‖ Contre; *to bet ten to one*, parier dix contre un. ‖ Selon; *he acted up to his principles*, il a agi selon ses principes; *to all appearances*, selon toute apparence; ‖ A l'égard de, pour; *as to him*, quant à lui; *what is this to you?*, qu'est-ce que cela peut vous faire? ‖ (Infinitive); *to be or not to be*, être ou ne pas être.
— adv. Dans l'état normal; *to come to*, revenir à soi; *to leave the door to*, laisser la porte fermée; *to turn to it*, s'y mettre. ‖ **To and fro,** de long en large; *to go to and fro*, aller et venir; *to-and-fro movement*, mouvement de va-et-vient.
toad [tóud] n. Zool. Crapaud *m*. ‖ Fam. Sale bougre *m*.
toadstone [-stoun] n. Crapaudine *f*.
toadstool [-stu:l] n. Bot. Champignon vénéneux *m*.
toady ['toudi] n. Flagorneur *s*.
— v. intr. **To toady to,** flagorner, lécher les bottes à.
toadyism [-izm̩] n. Flagornerie *f*.
toast [toust] n. Rôtie *f.*; toast *m*. (bread). ‖ Toast *m*. (drink); personne (*f*.) à laquelle on porte un toast. ‖ Fam. *To have s.o. on toast*, tenir qqn. ‖ **Toast-rack,** n. Porte-rôties *m*.
— v. tr. Griller (bread); porter un toast à (s.o.).
toaster [-ə*] n. Grille-pain *m*.
tobacco [tə'bækou] n. Tabac *m*. ‖ **Tobacco-jar,** n. Pot à tabac *m*. ‖ **Tobacco-pouch,** n. Blague (*f*.) à tabac. ‖ **Tobacco-stopper,** n. Bourre-pipe *m*.
tobacconist [-ənist] n. Marchand (or) débitant de tabac *m*.
toboggan [tə'bɔgən] n. Sports. Toboggan *m*. ‖ **Toboggan-run,** n. Piste (*f*.) de toboggan.
— v. intr. Sports. Faire du toboggan. ‖ U. S. Fam. Dégringoler (prices).

tobogganer [-ə*], **tobogganist** [-ist] n. Sports. Tobogganniste *s*.
toby ['toubi] n. Pot (*m*.) à bière en forme de poussah.
tocsin ['tɔksin] n. Tocsin *m*.
tod [tɔd] n. Pop. *On one's tod*, seulâbre, tout seul.
to-day, today [tə'dei] adv., n. Aujourd'hui *m*.
toddle ['tɔdl̩] v. intr. Trottiner, avancer à pas chancelants (child). ‖ Fam. *To toddle along*, avancer en flânochant; *to toddle off*, se trotter.
— n. Trottinement *m.;* démarche chancelante *f*.
toddler [-ə*] n. Enfant (*m*.) faisant ses premiers pas; château branlant *m*. (fam.). ‖ Pl. Tout-petits *m. pl*.
toddy ['tɔdi] n. Grog au whisky *m*. ‖ Toddy, alcool (*m*.) de palme.
to-do [tə'du:] n. Remue-ménage *m*. (stir). ‖ Façons, cérémonies *f. pl.;* chichis *m. pl*. (fuss).
toe [tou] n. Med. Orteil *m*. ‖ Techn. Talon, patin *m*. (of G cramp); pince *f*. (of horseshoe); bout *m*. (of shoes). ‖ Archit. Eperon *m*. ‖ Arts. *To dance on one's toes*, faire des pointes. ‖ Fam. *To turn up one's toes*, passer l'arme à gauche. ‖ **Toe-cap,** n. Bout (*m*.) de chaussure. ‖ **Toe-clip,** n. Cale-pied *m*. ‖ **Toe-dancing,** n. Pointes *f. pl*. ‖ **Toe-nail,** n. Ongle (*m*.) de pied.
— v. tr. Mettre un bout à (a shoe); refaire le bout de (a sock). ‖ Sports. Botter (at football); frapper du bout du club (at golf). ‖ Fam. Botter (s.o.); *to make s.o. toe the line*, dresser qqn, mettre qqn au pas; *to toe the line*, se mettre au pas, s'aligner.
— v. intr. *To toe in, out*, tourner les pieds en dedans, en dehors.
toehold [-hould] n. Prise de possession *f.; to get a toehold on the island*, prendre pied sur l'île.
toff [tɔf] n. Gommeux *m*.
toffee, toffy ['tɔfi] n. Caramel *m*. ‖ **Toffee-apple,** n. Sucette à la pomme *f*.
toft [tɔft] n. Agric. Petite ferme *f*.
tog [tɔg] v. tr. *To tog out* (or) *up*, accoutrer, attifer; ficeler (fam.).
toga ['tougə] n. Toge *f.; toga'd, togaed*, en toge.
together [tə'geðə*] adv. Ensemble; *to gather together*, rassembler; *to live together*, cohabiter, vivre ensemble. ‖ Ensemble, en même temps; *all together*, tous ensemble; *to speak together*, parler tous à la fois. ‖ De suite, d'affilée; *for months together*, des mois durant. ‖ En même temps (*with, que*).
toggle ['tɔgl̩] n. Naut. Cabillot *m*.
Togo ['tougou] n. Geogr. Togo *m*.
togs [tɔgz] n. pl. Fam. Nippes, frusques, fringues *f. pl*.
toil [tɔil] v. intr. Peiner, travailler dur; trimer (fam.). ‖ Avoir du mal, s'épuiser (*at*, à); *to toil along*, avancer péniblement, se traîner; *to toil up*, gravir avec peine.
— n. Labeur, dur travail *m.;* peine *f*. ‖ **Toil-worn,** adj. Usé par le travail.
toiler [-ə*] n. Travailleur; trimeur *s*. (fam.).
toilet ['tɔilit] n. Toilette *f*. (action, dress). ‖ Toilette, coiffeuse, table (*f*.) à toilette (table). ‖ Toilettes *f. pl*. (w.-c.). ‖ **Toilet-accessories,** n. pl. Objets (*m. pl*.) de toilette. ‖ **Toilet-paper,** n. Papier hygiénique *m*. ‖ **Toilet-set,** n. Nécessaire (*m*.) [or] garniture (*f*.) de toilette. ‖ **Toilet-table,** n. Coiffeuse *f*.
toiletry [-ri] n. Article (*m*.) de toilette.
toilette [tɔi'let] n. Toilette *f*. (action, dress).
toilsome ['tɔilsəm] adj. Laborieux, pénible, dur, ardu, fatigant.
toilsomeness [-nis] n. Difficulté *f.;* caractère ardu *m*.
toing [tu:iŋ] n. *Toing and froing*, va-et-vient, allées et venues.
token ['toukən] n. Témoignage, gage, signe *m.;* marque *f*. (symbol); *as a token of*, en témoignage

de. ‖ Signe *m.*; marque *f.* (mark). ‖ Souvenir *m.* (keepsake). ‖ Jeton *m.* (for telephone). ‖ FIN. *Token payment,* paiement symbolique. ‖ LOC. *By this token,* à telle enseigne que, la preuve en est que; *by the same token,* de plus.
— adj. Symbolique (payment, raid, resistance). ‖ D'avertissement (gesture, strike); *token one day strike,* grève symbolique d'un jour. ‖ FIN. Fiduciaire (money). ‖ COMM. Echantillonnaire (import).
told [tould] pret., p. p. See TELL.
Toledo [tə'li:dou] n. GEOGR., COMM. Tolède *m.*
tolerable ['tɔlərəbl] adj. Tolérable, supportable. ‖ Passable, assez bon; potable (fam.).
tolerably [-bli] adv. Tolérablement. ‖ Passablement, pas mal. ‖ A peu près, assez (fairly).
tolerance ['tɔlərəns] n. Tolérance, patience *f.* ‖ Endurance, résistance *f.* (of, à). ‖ FIN., MED., TECHN., ECCLES. Tolérance *f.*
tolerant [-ənt] adj. Tolérant, patient. ‖ Endurant, résistant.
tolerantly [-əntli] adv. Avec tolérance.
tolerate [-eit] v. tr. Agir avec tolérance à l'égard de (s.o.); admettre, tolérer (sth.). ‖ Tolérer, supporter, souffrir, endurer (to bear). ‖ Tolérer, supporter (to permit). ‖ MED. Tolérer.
toleration [,tɔlə'reiʃən] n. ECCLES. Tolérance *f.*
toll [toul] n. Droit de passage, péage *m.*; *town toll,* octroi. ‖ Droit (*m.*) de place (market). ‖ Droit (*m.*) de mouture (miller's). ‖ FIG. Prélèvement *m.*; *to take heavy toll of the enemy,* décimer les rangs de l'ennemi, infliger de grosses pertes à l'ennemi; *the toll of the roads,* la mortalité sur routes. ‖ **Toll-bridge,** n. Pont à péage *m.* ‖ **Toll-call,** n. Communication (*f.*) avec la grande banlieue (on the phone). ‖ **Toll-gate,** n. Barrière (*f.*) à péage. ‖ **Toll-line,** n. Ligne téléphonique de grande banlieue *f.*
— v. intr. Prélever (or) payer le péage.
toll v. tr. Tinter (a bell); sonner (the hour). ‖ Sonner le glas pour (a death); *for whom the bell tolls,* pour qui sonne le glas.
— v. intr. Tinter, sonner, sonner le glas.
— n. Tintement *m.*
tolu [tɔ'lju:] n. MED. Baume de Tolu *m.*
toluene ['tɔlju,i:n] n. CHIM. Toluène *m.*
Tom [tɔm] n. Tom, Thomas *m.* ‖ FAM. *Any Tom, Dick or Harry,* le premier (or) dernier venu; Pierre, Jacques et Paul. ‖ **Tom-cat,** n. ZOOL. Matou *m.*
tomahawk ['tɔməhɔ:k] n. Tomahawk *m.* ‖ LOC. *To bury the tomahawk,* enterrer la hache de guerre.
tomato [tə'mɑ:tou] n. AGRIC. Tomate *f.*
tomb [tu:m] n. Tombe *f.*; tombeau *m.*
— v. tr. Mettre au tombeau.
tombac ['tɔmbæk] n. Tombac *m.*
tombola [tɔm'boulə] n. Loterie, tombola *f.*
tomboy [tɔmbɔi] n. Garçon manqué *m.*
tombstone ['tu:m,stoun] n. Pierre tombale *f.*
tome [toum] n. Gros volume *m.* ‖ Tome *m.*
tomfool ['tɔm'fu:l] n. FAM. Cornichon, bêta, serin *m.*
— adj. Idiot, bêta.
— v. intr. Faire l'imbécile.
tomfoolery [-əri] n. Bêtise, sottise *f.*
Tommy ['tɔmi] n. Thomas, Tommy *m.* ‖ MILIT., FAM. *British Tommy,* soldat anglais. ‖ **Tommy-gun,** n. MILIT. Mitraillette *f.* ‖ **Tommy-rot,** n. FAM. Niaiseries *f. pl.*
tomorrow [tɔ'mɔrou] n. Lendemain *m.*
— adv. Demain.
tomtit ['tɔm'tit] n. ZOOL. Mésange bleue *f.*
tomtom ['tɔmtɔm] n. Tam-tam *m.*
ton [tʌn] n. Tonne *f.* ‖ NAUT. Tonneau *m.* ‖ FAM. Tonne *f.*; *to have tons of money,* remuer l'argent à la pelle.
ton [tɔ̃] n. Ton *m.*; mode *f.*
tonal ['toun] adj. MUS. Tonal.
tonality [to'næliti] n. MUS., ARTS. Tonalité *f.*
tone [toun] n. Ton, timbre *m.* (of a sound, voice).

‖ Ton *m.*; expression *f.* ‖ GRAMM. Accent, ton *m.* ‖ MED. Tonus, ton *m.*; *to lose tone,* se déprimer; *want of tone,* atonie. ‖ ARTS. Ton *m.*; nuance, tonalité *f.* ‖ MUS. Ton *m.* ‖ FIG. Ton, caractère *m.*; allure *f.* ‖ **Tone-colour,** n. MUS. Timbre *m.* ‖ **Tone-control,** n. RADIO. Bouton (*m.*) d'intensité.
— v. tr. MUS. Accorder; régler la tonalité. ‖ ARTS. Adoucir les tons. ‖ MED. Tonifier. ‖ TECHN. Virer (in photogr.). ‖ **To tone down,** atténuer. ‖ **To tone up,** aviver; MED. Tonifier.
— v. intr. S'harmoniser (with, avec). ‖ TECHN. Virer. ‖ **To tone down,** s'atténuer. ‖ **To tone up,** MED. Se tonifier.
toneless [-lis] adj. Sans éclat (colour); blanche, sans timbre (voice).
tonelessness [-lisnis] n. Atonie *f.*
Tonga ['tɔŋgə] n. GEOGR. Iles (*f. pl.*) Tonga.
tongs [tɔŋz] n. pl. Pincettes *f. pl.* (for fire). ‖ TECHN. Pinces, tenailles *f. pl.* ‖ CULIN. Pince *f.*
tongue [tʌŋ] n. MED., CULIN. Langue *f.* ‖ Langue *f.* (gift of the gab); *to have a quick tongue,* ne pas avoir la langue dans sa poche. ‖ Bonne langue *f.* (person); *smooth tongue,* beau parleur. ‖ Langue *f.*; langage *m.* (language); *slip of the tongue,* lapsus. ‖ Aiguille *f.* (of balance); ardillon *m.* (of buckle); langue *f.* (of flame, land, metal); soie *f.* (of knife); languette *f.* (of shoe). ‖ CH. DE F. Aiguille *f.* ‖ MUS. Languette *f.* ‖ SPORTS. *To give tongue,* donner de la voix (hound). ‖ FAM. *To put out one's tongue,* tirer la langue; *to speak with one's tongue in one's cheek,* parler avec une ironie voilée. ‖ **Tongue-depressor,** n. MED. Abaisse-langue *m.* ‖ **Tongue-rail,** n. CH. DE F. Aiguille *f.* ‖ **Tongue-tied,** adj. MED. Qui a le filet; FAM. Muet, à la langue liée. ‖ **Tongue-traction,** n. MED. Traction de la langue *f.* ‖ **Tongue-twister,** n. Phrase (*f.*) à décrocher la mâchoire; mot imprononçable *m.*
— v. tr. TECHN., ARCHIT. Langueter. ‖ MUS. Détacher les notes de. ‖ SPORTS. Donner de la voix.
tongueless [-lis] adj. Sans langue. ‖ FAM. Muet.
tonguelet [-lit] n. Languette *f.*
tonic ['tɔnik] adj. MUS., GRAMM., MED., FIG. Tonique.
— n. MUS., GRAMM. Tonique *f.* ‖ MED. Tonique *m.*
tonicity [to'nisiti] n. Tonicité *f.*
to(-)night [tə'nait] adv., n. Ce soir; cette nuit.
tonish ['touniʃ] adj. Dans le ton.
tonite ['tounait] n. Tonite *f.*
tonnage ['tʌnidʒ] n. Tonnage *m.*
tonne [tʌn] n. Tonne *f.* (metric ton).
tonometer [tou'nɔmitə*] n. MUS. Diapason *m.* ‖ MED. Tonomètre *m.* (for measuring eyeball tension); tensiomètre *m.* (for measuring blood pressure). ‖ PHYS. Tensiomètre *m.*
tonsil ['tɔnsl] n. MED. Amygdale *f.*
tonsillectomy [,tɔnsi'lektəmi] n. MED. Amygdalotomie *f.*
tonsillitis [,tɔn'silaitis] n. MED. Amygdalite *f.*
tonsorial [tɔn'sɔ:riəl] adj. Capillaire (artist).
tonsure ['tɔnʃə*] n. ECCLES. Tonsure *f.*
— v. tr. ECCLES. Tonsurer.
tontine [tɔn'ti:n] n. Tontine *f.*
too [tu:] adv. Trop; *too far,* trop loin; *I know it only too well,* je ne le sais que trop; *I'm not too sure,* je n'en sais trop rien; *it's going too far,* c'en est trop; *it's too kind of you,* vous êtes trop aimable; *none too clever,* pas trop intelligent; *to drink too heavily,* boire trop; *to talk too much,* trop parler; *to work too hard,* trop travailler; *too well known,* trop connu. ‖ Aussi; également; *the clergyman too was married,* le pasteur aussi était marié. ‖ De plus, encore, en outre; *the clergyman was married too,* le pasteur d'ailleurs était marié. ‖ FAM. Très; *it was just too delicious,* c'était tout simplement délicieux. ‖ U. S. FAM. *She is too much!,* elle y va fort!, c'est un drôle de corps!
took [tuk] pret. See TAKE.

tool [tu:l] n. TECHN. Outil *m.; woodworker's tools*, outils pour le bois. ‖ FIG. Instrument; homme (*m.*) de paille. ‖ **Tool-box**, n. Coffre (*m.*) [or] boîte (*f.*) à outils. ‖ **Tool-making**, n. Outillerie *f.* ‖ **Tool-outfit**, n. Jeu (*m.*) d'outils; outillage *m.* ‖ **Tool-roll**, U. S. **tool kit**, n. AUTOM. Trousse (*f.*) à outils. ‖ **Tool-shed**, n. Resserre (*f.*) à outils.
— v. tr. Travailler, usiner. ‖ ARTS. Ciseler. ‖ FAM. AUTOM. Conduire.
— v. intr. **To tool along**, FAM., AUTOM. Rouler.
tooling [-iŋ] n. Outillage *m.* ‖ TECHN. Usinage *m.* ‖ ARTS. Ciselage *m.; ciselure f.*
toot [tu:t] v. tr. MUS. Sonner (a horn). ‖ AUTOM. *To toot the horn*, klaxonner, corner.
— v. intr. MUS. Sonner du cor (or) de la trompette (person); trompeter (trumpet). ‖ AUTOM. Klaxonner. ‖ NAUT. Hurler (hooter).
— n. MUS. Son du cor *m.* ‖ AUTOM. Coup de klaxon *m.* ‖ NAUT. Hurlement (or) appel (*m.*) de sirène.
tooth [tu:θ] (pl. **teeth** [ti:θ]) n. MED., TECHN. Dent *f.* ‖ ARCHIT. Harpe *f.* ‖ FAM. *In the teeth of*, à la tête (or) figure de (s.o.); malgré, en dépit de (sth.); *to be long in the tooth*, ne plus être de la première jeunesse, avoir de la bouteille; *tooth and nail*, avec acharnement (or) bec et ongles. ‖ U. S. FAM. *Dressed to the teeth*, tiré à quatre épingles. ‖ **Tooth-brush**, n. Brosse (*f.*) à dents. ‖ **Tooth-comb**, n. Peigne fin *m.* ‖ **Tooth-paste**, n. Pâte dentifrice *f.*
— v. tr. TECHN. Denter, endenter.
— v. intr. TECHN. S'engrener.
toothache [-eik] n. MED. Mal (*m.*) de dents.
toothful [-ful] n. FAM. Goutte *f.; hardly a toothful*, juste de quoi remplir une dent creuse.
toothing [-iŋ] n. TECHN. Denture *f.; crénelage m.* ‖ ARCHIT. Harpes *f. pl.*
toothless [-lis] adj. Edenté, démeublé (mouth); édenté (person).
toothpick [-pik] n. Cure-dent *m.*
toothsome [-səm] adj. Savoureux, succulent.
toothy [-i] adj. Tout en dents.
tootle ['tu:tl] v. intr. MUS. Seriner un petit air.
tootsy ['tu:tsi] n. FAM. Peton *m.*
top [tɔp] n. Haut *m.* (in general); tranche *f.* (of a book); couvercle *m.* (of a box); revers *m.* (of boots, stockings); impériale *f.* (of a bus); haut, sommet *m.* (of the head); tête *f.* (of a map, page); cime *f.*, sommet *m.* (of a mountain); dessus *m.* (of a shoe); haut, bout *m.* (of the street); haut bout *m.* (of the table); faîte, cime *f.* (of a tree). ‖ BOT. Pl. Fanes *f. pl.* (of carrots). ‖ AUTOM. *To climb a hill in top*, monter une côte en prise. ‖ NAUT. Hune *f.* (mast); haut *m.* (of the flood); *fore top*, hune de misaine. ‖ THEATR. *Big top*, chapiteau de cirque. ‖ FAM. Faîte, sommet *m.; at the top of one's form*, en pleine forme; *on top of the world*, au sommet de l'échelle; *to shout at the top of one's voice*, élever le diapason, crier à tue-tête; U. S. *to blow one's top*, sortir de ses gonds (anger); perdre la boule (insanity). ‖ **Top-boots**, n. Bottes (*f. pl.*) à revers. ‖ **Top-drawer**, adj. FAM. De premier plan (or) ordre. ‖ **Top-dress**, v. tr. AGRIC. Fumer en surface. ‖ **Top-flight**, adj. U. S. FAM. De haute volée. ‖ **Top-hat**, n. Haut-de-forme *m.* ‖ **Top-heavy**, adj. Trop lourd en haut. ‖ **Top-hole**, adj. FAM. Chic, épatant. ‖ **Top-lantern**, n. NAUT. Œuvres mortes *f. pl.* ‖ **Top-soil**, n. AGRIC. Couche arable *f.*
— adj. De dessus, d'en haut, le plus haut. ‖ FAM. *At top speed*, à une vitesse grand V; *top dog*, coq, vainqueur.
— v. tr. (1). Couronner, surmonter, coiffer (*with*, de). ‖ Monter au sommet de (a hill). ‖ Dépasser (*in*, en) [height, weight, wit]. ‖ AGRIC. Ecimer, étêter. ‖ NAUT. Apiquer. ‖ SPORTS. Topper. ‖ FAM. Mesurer (three feet). ‖ **To top off**, parachever, couronner. ‖ **To top up**, remplir; AVIAT. Renflouer.
top n. Toupie *f.*

topaz ['toupæz] n. Topaze *f.*
topcoat ['tɔp.kout] n. Pardessus *m.* (See OVER-COAT.) ‖ Dernière couche *f.* (of paint).
tope [toup] v. intr. FAM. Siroter.
topee ['toupi] n. Casque colonial *m.*
toper ['toupə*] n. FAM. Soiffard *m.*
topgallant [-'gælənt] n. NAUT. Perroquet *m.*
topiary ['toupiəri] adj. Topiaire.
— n. Topiaire *f.*, taille (*f.*) ornementale des arbres.
topic ['tɔpik] n. Sujet (*m.*) de discussion (or) de conversation. ‖ PHILOS. Topique *m.*
topical [-əl] adj. Se rapportant au sujet. ‖ D'actualité, d'intérêt courant (or) local. ‖ MED. Topique.
topicality [tɔpi'kæliti] n. Actualité *f.*
topknot ['tɔpnɔt] n. Aigrette *f.* (of feathers); nœud *m.* (of ribbons). ‖ Toupet *m.* (hair). ‖ ZOOL. Huppe *f.* (tuft).
topless [-lis] adj. Aux seins nus (woman); sans haut (garment); *topless swim-suit*, monokini.
topman [-mən] (pl. **topmen**) n. Scieur (*m.*) de long. ‖ NAUT. Gabier *m.*
topmast [-mɑ:st] n. NAUT. Mât (*m.*) de hune.
topmost [-moust] adj. Le plus haut.
topnotch [-nɔtʃ] adj. U. S. FAM. Sélect, de la haute, du gratin.
topographer [tə'pɔgrəfə*] n. Topographe *m.*
topography [-i] n. Topographie *f.*
toponymy [tə'pɔnimi] n. Toponymie *f.*
topper ['tɔpə*] n. Haut-de-forme *m.* (hat). ‖ U. S. Surtout, manteau court *m.* (woman's). ‖ FAM. Type (or) truc formidable *m.*
topping [-iŋ] adj. FAM. A la hauteur, formidable, de première classe.
— n. AGRIC. Etêtage *m.* ‖ NAUT. Apiquage *m.* ‖ CULIN. Glaçage *m.;* crème glacée *f.* (on a cake).
topple ['tɔpl] v. intr. Culbuter, tomber; dégringoler (fam.).
— v. tr. Faire tomber, renverser.
topsail ['tɔpsl] n. NAUT. Hunier *m.*
topsy-turvy ['tɔpsi'tə:vi] adv. Sens dessus dessous, à l'envers.
— adj. Bouleversé, à l'envers, retourné; chamboulé (fam.).
— n. Bouleversement; chamboulement *m.* (fam.).
topsy-turvydom [-dəm] n. FAM. Le monde à l'envers *m.*
toque [touk] n. Toque *f.*
tor [tɔ:*] n. Pic rocheux *m.*
torch [tɔ:tʃ] n. Torche *f.* ‖ ELECTR. Lampe-torche de poche *f.* ‖ **Torch-bearer**, n. Porte-flambeau *m.* ‖ **Torch-light**, n. Lumière (*f.*) des torches; adj. Aux flambeaux (procession). ‖ **Torch-race**, n. Course (*f.*) aux flambeaux. ‖ **Torch-song**, n. U. S. Chanson sentimentale *f.*
tore [tɔ:*] pret. See TEAR.
tore n. ARCHIT. Tore *m.*
toreador [,tɔriə'dɔ:*] n. Toréador *m.*
torero [tɔ'rɛərou] n. Torero, toréador *m.*
toric ['tɔrik] adj. MATH., ARCHIT. Torique.
torment ['tɔ:ment] n. Supplice *m.;* torture *f.* ‖ Source (*f.*) de soucis; bête (*f.*) à chagrin (fam.). ‖ FIG. Pl. Affres *f. pl.; tourments m. pl.*
— [tɔ:'ment] v. tr. Torturer, tourmenter.
tormentor [tɔ:'mentə*] n. Bourreau, tourmenteur *m.* ‖ AGRIC. Scarificateur *m.*
tormina ['tɔ:minə] n. pl. MED. Tranchées *f. pl.*
torn [tɔ:n] p. p. See TEAR.
tornado [tɔ:'neidou] n. Tornade *f.*
torous ['tɔ:rəs] adj. BOT. Noueux.
torpedo [tɔ:'pi:dou] n. NAUT., MILIT., AVIAT., ZOOL. Torpille *f.* ‖ CH. DE F. Pétard *m.* ‖ **Torpedo-boat**, n. NAUT. Torpilleur *m.* ‖ **Torpedo-body**, n. AUTOM. Torpédo *f.* ‖ **Torpedo-tube**, n. NAUT. Lance-torpilles *m.*
— v. tr., intr. MILIT., AVIAT., NAUT. Torpiller.
torpid ['tɔ:pid] adj. Torpide, engourdi, léthargique.

|| MED. Paresseux (liver). || FAM. Endormi, apathique, engourdi.

torpidity [tɔː'piditi] n. Torpeur *f.*; engourdissement *m.* || FIG. Apathie *f.*

torpify ['tɔːpifai] v. tr. (2). Engourdir.

torpor ['tɔːpə*] n. Torpeur *f.*

torque [tɔːk] n. † Torque *f.* || TECHN. Couple *m.*; torsion *f.*

torr [tɔː*] n. PHYS. Torr *m.*

torrefaction [,tɔri'fæk ʃən] n. Torréfaction *f.*

torrefy ['tɔrifai] v. tr. (2). Torréfier.

torrent ['tɔrənt] n. Torrent *m.* (lit. and fig.).

torrential [tɔ'ren ʃəl] adj. Torrentiel (rain); torrentueux (stream).

torrid ['tɔrid] adj. Torride.

torridity [tɔ'riditi] n. Torridité *f.*

torsion ['tɔː ʃən] n. Torsion *f.* || **Torsion-bar,** n. AUTOM. Barre de torsion *f.*

torsional [-l̩] adj. De torsion.

torsk [tɔːsk] n. ZOOL. Cabillaud *m.*

torso ['tɔːsou] n. ARTS. Torse *m.*

tort [tɔːt] n. JUR. Acte dommageable *m.*

torticollis [,tɔːti'kɔlis] n. MED. Torticolis *m.*

tortilla [tɔː'tiːə] n. CULIN. Tortilla *f.*, galette (*f.*) de maïs.

tortious ['tɔː ʃəs] adj. JUR. Dommageable.

tortoise ['tɔːtəs] n. ZOOL., MILIT. † Tortue *f.* || **Tortoise-shell,** n. Ecaille *f.*; adj. Comme en écaille; ZOOL. Moucheté (cat).

tortuosity [,tɔːtju'ɔsiti] n. Tortuosité *f.*

tortuous ['tɔːtjuəs] adj. Tortueux.

tortuously [-li] adv. Tortueusement.

torture ['tɔːtʃə*] n. Torture *f.*; supplice *m.*
— v. tr. Torturer, supplicier (lit. and fig.). || FAM. Dénaturer, déformer.

torturer [-rə*] n. Bourreau *m.*

torus ['tɔːrəs] (pl. **tori** [-ai]) n. ARCHIT. Tore *m.* || BOT. Réceptacle *m.*

Tory ['tɔːri] adj., n. Tory, conservateur *m.*

Toryism [-izm̩] n. Torysme *m.*

tosh [tɔ ʃ] n. FAM. Foutaise *f.*, sottises *f. pl.*

toss [tɔs] v. tr. Lancer, projeter en l'air. || Ballotter, secouer. || Jouer à pile ou face avec (a coin). || Relever dédaigneusement (one's head). || SPORTS. *To toss its head,* encenser (horse). || NAUT. Mater (the oars). || **To toss about,** jeter de-ci de-là; *to toss money about,* jeter son argent par les fenêtres. || *To toss away,* jeter, rejeter. || **To toss off,** sabler (champagne); entonner (wine); expédier (work). || **To toss up,** lancer en l'air.
— v. intr. Jouer à pile ou face. || S'agiter, se démener, se tourner et retourner (person). || S'agiter, se secouer, ballotter (thing). || NAUT. Etre ballotté.
— n. Lancée *f.*; lancement en l'air *m.* || Jeu (or) coup (*m.*) de pile ou face. || Mouvement dédaigneux (*m.*) de la tête. || SPORTS. Chute (*f.*) de cheval. || **Toss-up,** n. Coup (*m.*) de pile ou face (lit. and fig.).

tot [tɔt] n. Bambin, gamin *m.* (see TODDLER); *tiny tots' class,* classe des tout petits. || FAM. Goutte *f.* (of whisky).

tot n. Colonne (*f.*) de chiffres; total (*m.*) à faire.
— v. tr. (1). **To tot up,** additionner.
— v. intr. **To tot up,** s'additionner.

total ['toutl̩] adj., n. Total *m.*
— v. tr. (1). Totaliser, faire le total de (to find the total of). || Se monter à (to equal a total of).

totalitarian [,toutæli'tɛəriən] adj. Totalitaire.

totalitarianism [-izm̩] n. Totalitarisme *m.*

totality [tou'tæliti] n. Totalité *f.*

totalizator ['toutəlai,zeitə*] n., **totalizer** [-aizə*] n. SPORTS. Totalisateur *m.*; *totalizator system,* pari mutuel.

totalize [-aiz] v. tr. Totaliser.

totally [-i] adv. Totalement.

tote [tout] n. FAM. Totalisateur *m.*

tote v. tr. U. S. FAM. Porter.

totem ['toutəm] n. Totem *m.*

totemism ['toutəmizm̩] n. Totémisme *m.*

totter ['tɔtə*] v. intr. Chanceler, branler (building); tituber (drunkard); chanceler (person).

tottering [-riŋ] adj. Chancelant.

totteringly [-riŋli] adv. En chancelant.

toucan [tu:'kɑːn] n. ZOOL. Toucan *m.*

touch [tʌtʃ] v. tr. Toucher; *to touch one's hat,* porter la main à son chapeau. || Toucher, atteindre (to reach). || Toucher, effleurer (to strike lightly). || Toucher à, manier; tripoter (fam.) [to handle]. || Molester (to mishandle). || Toucher à, goûter (to taste). || Toucher à, s'approprier (to misappropriate). || Toucher, prendre contact avec (to contact). || Eprouver (to test). || Endommager (to injure). || Toucher à, se rapporter à (to concern). || Toucher à, se référer à (to mention). || Egaler, se comparer à, approcher de (to rival). || Toucher, émouvoir, remuer (to move). || Toucher, piquer, blesser, froisser (to vex). || Teinter, toucher (*with,* de). || NAUT. Toucher, toucher à. || MATH. Etre tangent à. || MUS. Jouer (an air); toucher (or) jouer de (an instrument); toucher (the strings). || FAM. Taper (*for,* de) [s.o.]. || FAM. *To touch the spot,* mettre le doigt dessus, taper dans le mille. || **To touch down,** AVIAT. Faire escale; se poser, toucher terre. || **To touch in,** ARTS. Esquisser, ébaucher, dessiner. || **To touch off,** déclencher; † MILIT. Décharger. || **To touch up,** toucher du fouet (a horse); ARTS. Rehausser (a colour); retoucher (photograph, text).
— v. intr. Se toucher, être en contact. || NAUT. Toucher, faire escale (at a port); être en ralingue (sail); talonner (ship). || FAM. *Touched,* un peu timbré. || **To touch on,** toucher à, traiter de, effleurer (a topic).
— n. Attouchement *m.*; action (*f.*) de toucher (action). || Contact *m.* (result); *to get into touch with,* prendre contact avec, se mettre en rapport avec. || MED. Toucher, tact *m.* (sense). || ARTS. Touche *f.*; *to put the finishing touches to,* mettre la dernière main (or) touche à, fignoler, lécher. || MUS. Toucher, doigté *m.* || TECHN. Frappe *f.* (in typewriting). || ELECTR., SPORTS. Touche *f.* || † Pierre de touche *f.* || FIG. Trait *m.*; *a touch of nature,* un trait naturel, le cri du cœur. || FAM. Pointe *f.*; soupçon *m.*; *at the least touch of cold,* pour peu qu'il fasse froid; *a touch of fever,* un brin de fièvre. || **Touch-and-go,** adj. Hasardeux, risqué; n. situation hasardeuse *f.*; *it was touch-and-go with him,* c'était moins cinq pour lui. || **Touch-hole,** n. MILIT. Lumière *f.* || **Touch-line,** n. SPORTS. Ligne de touche *f.* || **Touch-needle,** Toucheau *m.* || **Touch-paper,** n. Papier (*m.*) d'amorce. || **Touch-typist,** n. Bonne dactylo *f.*

touchable [-əbl̩] adj. Tangible, palpable.

touchdown [-daun] n. U. S. SPORTS. But, score (in American football).

touché [tu:'ʃei] interj. SPORTS. Touché! (in fencing). || FIG. Ça c'est vrai!, très juste!

touched [-t] adj. FAM. Toqué. (See CRACKED.)

toucher [-ə*] n. SPORTS. Boule (*f.*) qui touche le cochonnet. || FAM. *It was a toucher for him,* il a passé près.

touchily [-ili] adv. Maussadement, rudement.

touchiness [-inis] n. Irascibilité, humeur *f.*

touching [-iŋ] adj. Touchant, émouvant.
— prep. Touchant, au sujet de. (See CONCERNING.)

touchingly [-iŋli] adv. De façon touchante.

touchstone [-stoun] n. Pierre de touche *f.*

touchwood [-wud] n. Amadou *m.* || FAM. *Like touchwood,* à cran, comme un crin.

touchy [-i] adj. Chatouilleux, irritable, coléreux, emporté, vif.

tough [tʌf] adj. Résistant, solide, costaud (person). || CULIN. Dur, coriace (meat). || FIG. Dur à cuire (person); tenace, entêté, obstiné (temper); coriace (truth); rude, dur, pénible (work); *tough guy,* las-

car ; *tough luck*, déveine. ‖ Fam. *They've been tough on him*, on l'a salé.
— n. U. S. Fam. Dur *m*.

toughen [-ŋ] v. tr. Durcir. ‖ Fig. Endurcir.
— v. intr. Se durcir. ‖ Fig. S'endurcir.

toughish [-iʃ] adj. Culin. Duret, plutôt coriace (meat). ‖ Fig. Quelque peu entêté (person) ; pas commode (person, work) ; coriace (fam.).

toughness [-nis] n. Dureté *f*. ‖ Endurcissement *m*. ‖ Obstination *f*. ; entêtement *m*. ‖ Caractère grincheux *m*. (of a person) ; difficulté (of work).

toupee [tu:'pi:] n. Faux toupet *m*.

tour [tuə*] n. Voyage *m*. ; *conducted tour*, voyage organisé ; *motor tour*, randonnée. ‖ Tour *m*. ; promenade, excursion *f*. ‖ Tournée *f*. (for inspection).
— v. intr. Voyager ; *to tour through Switzerland*, faire un circuit en Suisse.
— v. tr. Visiter ; *to tour France*, parcourir la France.

touring [-riŋ] n. Tourisme *m*. ‖ **Touring-car**, n. Voiture (*f*.) de tourisme.
— adj. En randonnée. ‖ Theatr. En tournée.

tourism [-rizm] n. Tourisme *m*.

tourist [-rist] n. Touriste *s*.
— adj. Pour touristes, touristique ; *tourist class*, classe touriste ; *the tourist industry*, le tourisme ; *tourist office*, syndicat d'initiative ; *tourist trap*, piège à touristes.

tourmalin(e) ['tuəməlin] n. Tourmaline *f*.

tournament ['tuənəmənt] n. † Tournoi *m*. ‖ Milit. Carrousel *m*. ‖ Sports. Match *m*.

tourney ['tuəni] n. Tournoi *m*.

tourniquet ['tə:nikei] n. Med. Garrot *m*.

tousle ['tauzl] v. tr. Ebouriffer (hair). ‖ Chiffonner (a dress) ; bousculer, houspiller (s.o.).

tousled [-d] adj. Ebouriffé, échevelé.

tout [taut] v. intr. Racoler. ‖ Sports. Espionner les entraîneurs. ‖ U. S. *To tout for*, solliciter.
— n. Rabatteur, racoleur *m*. ‖ Comm. Démarcheur, placier *m*. ‖ Sports. Tout *m*.

tow [tou] n. Naut. Remorquer, haler, touer. ‖ Fig. Remorquer.
— n. Remorque *f*. ; convoi poussé *m*. ‖ Fam. *She always has her children in tow*, elle traîne toujours toute sa smala. ‖ **Tow-boat**, n. Naut. Pousseur *m*. ‖ **Tow-net**, n. Senne *f*. ‖ **Tow-path**, n. Chemin de halage *m*. ‖ **Tow-rope**, n. Remorque *f*.

tow n. Etoupe *f*. ‖ **Tow-coloured**, adj. Filasse (hair).

towage [-idʒ] n. Remorquage *m*. ‖ Droits (*m. pl.*) de remorquage (charge).

toward(s) [tɔ:d(z)] [tə'wɔ:d(z)] prep. Vers ; *towards the city, the end of the summer*, vers la ville, la fin de l'été. ‖ Envers ; *his attitude towards everybody*, son attitude à l'égard de tout le monde. ‖ En vue de, pour ; *I was saving towards a new car*, j'économisais pour acheter une nouvelle voiture.
— adv. A venir, prêt à arriver.

towel ['tauəl] n. Serviette de toilette *f*. (for face) ; essuie-mains *m*. (for hands) ; *sanitary towel*, serviette hygiénique. ‖ **Towel-hook**, Accroche-essuie-main *m*. ‖ **Towel-horse** (or) **-rail** (or) **-roller**, U. S. **towel rack**, n. Porte-serviettes *m*.
— v. tr. (1). Essuyer avec une serviette. ‖ Fam. Donner une frottée à.

towelling [-iŋ] n. Tissu-éponge *m*. ; toile (*f*.) à essuie-main. ‖ Fam. Frottée *f*.

tower ['tauə*] n. Archit. Tour *f*. ‖ Aviat. *Control tower*, tour de contrôle. ‖ Techn. *Water tower*, château d'eau. ‖ Loc. *Tower of strength*, puissant soutien.
— v. intr. S'élever, monter. ‖ Zool. Planer (eagle). ‖ *To tower above*, s'élever au-dessus de, dominer.

towered [-d] adj. Archit. Flanqué de tours.

towering [-riŋ] adj. Elevé, dominant. ‖ Fam. Violent ; *towering rage*, rage folle.

town [taun] n. Ville *f*. (city, people) ; *market town*, bourg. ‖ Londres *m*. (in England). ‖ U. S. Centre

commercial (*m*.) d'une ville. ‖ Fam. *To paint the town red*, faire la nouba. ‖ **Town-cheque**, n. Fin. Chèque (*m*.) sur place. ‖ **Town-clerk**, n. Secrétaire (*m*.) de mairie. ‖ **Town-council**, n. Conseil municipal *m*. ‖ **Town-crier**, n. Crieur public ; tambour (*m*.) de ville. ‖ **Town-hall**, n. Mairie *f*. ; hôtel (*m*.) de ville. ‖ **Town-planning**, n. Urbanification *f*. ; urbanisme *m*. ‖ **Town-suit**, n. Costume (*m*.) de ville. ‖ **Town-talk**, n. Sujet du jour *m*. ; fable (*f*.) du pays.

townee [tau'ni:], U. S. **townie, towny** ['tauni] n. Fam. Citadin *s*.

townlet ['taunlit] n. Petite ville, bourgade *f*.

townsfolk [-zfouk] n. Citadins *m. pl.*

township [-ʃip] n. Commune *f*.

townsman [-zmən] n. (pl. **townsmen**) n. Citadin *m*.

toxaemia, U. S. **toxemia** [tɔk'si:miə] n. Med. Toxémie *f*. (blood-poisoning) ; toxémie gravidique *f*. (disease of pregnancy).

toxic ['tɔksik] adj. Med. Toxique.

toxicological [,tɔksikə'lɔdʒikel] adj. Med. Toxicologique.

toxicologist [,tɔksi'kɔlədʒist] n. Toxicologue *m*.

toxicology [-dʒi] n. Toxicologie *f*.

toxin ['tɔksin] n. Med. Toxine *f*.

toxophilite [tɔk'sɔfilait] n. Sports. Tireur à l'arc *m*.

toy [tɔi] n. Jouet *m*. ‖ Fig. Jouet *m*. ; *to make a toy of*, se jouer de.
— adj. D'enfant (trumpet). ‖ Petit, minuscule ; *toy dog*, chien de manchon.
— v. intr. Jouer, s'amuser (with, avec). ‖ Fig. Badiner (with, avec) ; *to toy with one's food*, chipoter.

toying [-iŋ] n. Badinage, jeu *m*.

toyman [-mən] n. (pl. **toymen**) n. Marchand (*m*.) de jouets.

toyshop [-ʃɔp] n. Magasin (*m*.) de jouets.

trabeation ['treibi'eiʃən] n. Entablement *m*.

trace [treis] m. Trait *m*. (harness).

trace v. tr. Tracer (letters, plan). ‖ Suivre le tracé de ; *to trace the line with one's finger*, suivre la ligne imprimée avec le doigt. ‖ Suivre à la trace, pister (s.o.). ‖ Longer, suivre (a way). ‖ Fig. Retrouver les traces de (an influence). ‖ *To trace back*, faire remonter (*to*, à). ‖ *To trace out*, tracer (a plan) ; découvrir, dépister (a thief) ; Fig. Déterminer (a date, an origin). ‖ *To trace over*, calquer.
— n. Trace, empreinte *f*. (footprint). ‖ Trace, marque *f*. (mark) ; trace *f*. ; vestige *m*. (remnant). ‖ Culin. Nuage *m*. (of milk) ; brin *m*. (of salt). ‖ Med. Trace *f*. (of albumen). ‖ Fig. Ombre *f*. (of anger).

traceable [-əbl] adj. Retraçable.

tracer [-ə*] n. Traçoir *m*. (device) ; traceur *m*. (person). ‖ Calqueur *m*. ‖ **Tracer-bullet**, n. Milit. Balle traçante *f*. ‖ **Tracer-element**, n. Chim. Elément radio-actif décelable *m*. ‖ **Tracer-shell**, n. Milit. Traçant *m*.

tracery [-əri] n. Archit. Découpures *f. pl.*

trachea [trə'ki:ə] n. Med. Trachée-artère *f*. ‖ Bot., Zool. Trachée *f*.
— N. B. Deux pluriels : *tracheas, tracheae*.

tracheal [-əl] adj. Med. Trachéen.

tracheitis [-'aitis] n. Med. Trachéite *f*.

tracheotomy [,træki'ɔtəmi] n. Med. Trachéotomie *f*.

trachoma [træ'koumə] n. Med. Trachome *m*.

trachyte ['trækait] n. Trachyte *m*.

tracing ['treisiŋ] n. Traçage ; tracé *m*. ‖ Calquage ; calque *m*. ‖ **Tracing-paper**, n. Papier-calque *m*. ‖ **Tracing-wheel**, n. Roulette (*f*.) à patrons.

track [træk] n. Trace, piste *f*. (of an animal, a person) ; trace *f*. (of a car). ‖ Pl. Traces, empreintes *f. pl.* (footprints). ‖ Chemin tracé *m*. ; route *f*. (road). ‖ Chemin, sentier *m*. (path) ; *cart track*, chemin de terre. ‖ Sports. Piste *f*. ; *motor-racing track*, autodrome. ‖ Naut. Sillage *m*. ‖ Astron.

Cours *m.* (of a comet). ‖ CH. DE F. Voie *f.; to go off the track,* dérailler. ‖ AUTOM. Chenille *f.* ‖ TECHN. Guidages *m. pl.* ‖ FIG. Piste, trace *f.; on the right track,* sur la bonne voie ; *to keep track of,* suivre la marche de, prendre note de. ‖ **Track-gauge,** n. CH. DE F. Gabarit d'écartement (*m.*) des voies. ‖ **Track man,** n. U. S. SPORTS. Athlète (*m.*) sur piste. ‖ **Track-suit,** n. Chemisier-tricot *m.* — v. tr. Traquer, suivre à la piste (an animal, s.o.) ; suivre (a track). ‖ Laisser des traces de ; *to track dirt over the floor,* laisser des empreintes boueuses sur le plancher. ‖ NAUT. Remorquer. (See TOW.) ‖ **To track down,** dépister, capturer (a thief). ‖ **To track out,** découvrir en pistant, retrouver les traces de.

trackage [-idʒ] n. Remorquage *m.* ‖ CH. DE F. Longueur (*f.*) du réseau.

tracked [-t] adj. AUTOM., MILIT. A chenille. ‖ Traqué.

tracker [-ə*] n. Traqueur *m.*

trackless [-lis] adj. Sans traces. ‖ Sans chemin.

tract [trækt] n. Etendue, région *f.* (area). ‖ Tract *m.* (leaflet) ; opuscule *m.* (pamphlet). ‖ ECCLES. Trait *m.* ‖ MED. Appareil *m.; voies f. pl.* ‖ † Espace *m.* (of time).

tractability [,træktə'biliti] n. Docilité *f.*

tractable ['træktəbl] adj. Docile, traitable, gouvernable (character, person) ; maniable (device) ; facile à travailler (material).

traction ['trækʃən] n. Traction *f.* — adj. Tracteur, moteur. ‖ **Traction-engine,** n. Remorqueuse, locomotive routière *f.;* locotracteur *m.*

tractive [-tiv] adj. De traction.

tractor [-tə*] n. Tracteur *m.* ‖ **Tractor-drawn,** adj. MILIT. Tracté. ‖ **Tractor-propeller,** n. AVIAT. Hélice tractive *f.*

trade [treid] n. Métier *m.* (craft). ‖ Commerce *m.;* affaires *f. pl.* (bargain, business) ; commerce, négoce *m.* (buying and selling). ‖ Commerce *m.;* commerçants *m. pl.* (tradespeople). ‖ U. S. Clientèle *f.* (customers). ‖ **Trade-company,** n. Corps de métier *m.* ‖ **Trade-disputes,** n. pl. Conflits (*m. pl.*) du travail. ‖ **Trade-mark,** n. Marque de fabrique *f.* ‖ **Trade-name,** n. Appellation commerciale, marque déposée *f.* ‖ **Trade-show,** n. CINEM. Présentation (*f.*) d'un film. ‖ **Trade-union,** n. Syndicat ouvrier *m.; member of a trade-union,* syndiqué. ‖ **Trade-unionism,** n. Syndicalisme *m.* ‖ **Trade-unionist,** n. Syndiqué ; syndicaliste *m.* ‖ **Trade-wind,** n. NAUT. Alizé *m.* — v. tr. Echanger, troquer (*for,* contre). ‖ FAM. Trafiquer de. — v. intr. Faire du commerce, commercer (*with,* avec). ‖ **To trade in,** trafiquer de (commodities) ; U. S. donner en reprise (a used car). ‖ **To trade on,** exploiter, tabler (or) spéculer sur (s.o.'s ignorance).

trader [-ə*] n. Commerçant, négociant *s.* ‖ NAUT. Navire marchand *m.*

tradescantia [,trædes'kænʃiə] n. BOT. Tradescantia *m.,* misère *f.*

tradesman [-zmən] (pl. **tradesmen**) n. Marchand *m.; tradesmen's entrance,* entrée des fournisseurs.

tradespeople ['treidz,pi:pl] n. Commerçants *m. pl.*

trading ['treidiŋ] n. Commerce *m.; trading concern,* entreprise commerciale. ‖ FIN. *Trading year,* exercice. ‖ U. S. *Trading in,* reprise en compte, vente en reprise ; *trading stamp,* bon-prime.

tradition [trə'diʃən] n. Tradition *f.*

traditional [-əl] adj. Traditionnel.

traditionalism [-əlizm] n. Traditionalisme *m.*

traditionalist [-əlist] n. Traditionaliste *s.*

traditionally [-əli] adv. Traditionnellement.

traditor ['træditə*] (pl. **traditor(e)s** [,trædi'to:ri:z]) n. ECCLES. Traditeur *s.*

traduce [trə'dju:s] v. tr. Diffamer, calomnier.

traducement [-mənt] n. Diffamation, calomnie *f.*

traducer [-ə*] n. Diffamateur, calomniateur *m.;* diffamatrice, calomniatrice *f.*

traffic ['træfik] v. intr. COMM. Faire du commerce (*with,* avec). ‖ Trafiquer (*in,* de). — v. tr. COMM. Vendre. ‖ FIG. *To traffic away,* vendre (one's honour). — n. COMM. Commerce, négoce *m.* ‖ Trafic *m.* (pej.) ; *white slave traffic,* traite des blanches. ‖ CH. DE F. Mouvement, trafic *m.* ‖ AUTOM. Trafic *m.;* circulation *f.* (cars, movement, people). ‖ **Traffic island,** n. Refuge *m.* (for pedestrians). ‖ **Traffic-jam,** n. Embouteillage, encombrement *m.* ‖ **Traffic-light,** n. Feu *m.* (at crossings). ‖ **Traffic warden,** n. Contractuel *s.*

trafficator [-eitə*] n. AUTOM. Clignotant *m.*

trafficker [-ə*] n. Trafiquant, trafiqueur *m.*

tragedian [trə'dʒi:diən] n. Tragique *m.* (writer). ‖ THEATR. Tragédien *s.* (actor).

tragedienne [trə,dʒi:di'en] n. THEATR. Tragédienne *f.*

tragedy ['trædʒidi] n. THEATR., FIG. Tragédie *f.*

tragic(al) [-ik(əl)] adj. THEATR. Tragique. ‖ FIG. Tragique, dramatique ; *don't be so tragic about it,* ne prenez pas cela tellement au tragique ; *tragic occurrence,* drame.

tragically [-ikəli] adv. Tragiquement.

tragicomedy ['trædgi'kɔmədi] n. THEATR. Tragicomédie *f.*

tragicomic [-'kɔmik] adj. Tragi-comique.

trail [treil] n. Traînée *f.* (of blood, light, smoke). ‖ Trace *f.* (of snail). ‖ Piste *f.; chemin m.* (path). ‖ SPORTS. Piste, voie *f.* (of game). ‖ MILIT. Crosse *f.* ‖ ASTRON. Queue *f.* (of a meteor). ‖ FIG. *On the trail, of,* sur la piste de. ‖ **Trail-blazer,** n. Pionnier *m.* ‖ **Trail-net,** n. Chalut *m.* — v. tr. Traîner. ‖ Tracer un chemin dans. ‖ SPORTS. Suivre à la trace. ‖ MILIT. Tenir à bout de bras (arms). ‖ FIG. Pister, filer (s.o.). — v. intr. Traîner (*on,* sur). ‖ Pendre. ‖ BOT. Ramper, grimper (plant). ‖ FAM. Traîner, être à la traîne. ‖ **To trail along,** se traîner, marcher d'un pas traînant.

trailer [-ə*] n. Remorque *f.* (lorry, U. S. truck). ‖ AUTOM. Roulotte, roulotte-remorque, caravane *f.* ‖ BOT. Plante grimpante (or) rampante *f.* ‖ CINEM. Film-annonce *m.* ‖ FAM. Traînard *s.* ‖ **Trailer-caravan,** n. Roulotte-remorque *f.*

train [trein] v. tr. Dresser (an animal) ; élever (a child) ; discipliner, dresser (s.o.). ‖ Entraîner, former, instruire, exercer. ‖ SPORTS. Entraîner. ‖ BOT. Faire grimper (a plant). ‖ MILIT. Pointer (a gun). ‖ CH. DE F., FAM. *To train it,* faire le voyage par le train. — v. intr. SPORTS. S'entraîner. ‖ FAM. Voyager par le train (*from,* de ; *to,* à). ‖ MILIT. Faire l'exercice. — n. Traîne *f.* (of a dress). ‖ Escorte, suite *f.;* cortège *m.* (of attendants) ; *war with all that follows in its train,* la guerre et son train. ‖ File, théorie *f.* (procession) ; train *m.* (of animals) ; file *f.* (of persons). ‖ Traînée *f.* (of gunpowder). ‖ NAUT. Train, convoi (of ships). ‖ MILIT. Train *m.* ‖ TECHN. Train d'engrenage *m.;* rouages *m. pl.* ‖ RADIO. Train *m.* (of waves). ‖ ZOOL. Longue queue *f.* (of bird). ‖ ASTRON. Queue *f.* (of comet). ‖ CH. DE F. Train *m.; slow train,* omnibus. ‖ FIG. Suite, série *f.* (of difficulties) ; série, succession *f.* (of facts) ; chaîne *f.* (of ideas) ; cours normal *m.* (of things). ‖ **Train-bearer,** n. Porte-queue *m.;* ECCLES. Caudataire *m.* ‖ **Train-dress,** n. Robe à traîne *f.* ‖ **Train-sickness,** n. MED. Mal (*m.*) des transports. ‖ **Train-work,** n. Mouvement (*m.*) d'horlogerie.

trainable ['treinəbl] adj. Dressable ; éducable. ‖ SPORTS. Entraînable.

trainee [trei'ni:] n. SPORTS. Poulain *m.* ‖ COMM. Stagiaire *m.*

trainer ['treinə*] n. Dresseur *m.* ‖ SPORTS. Entraîneur *m.* ‖ **Trainer-plane,** n. AVIAT. Avion-école *m.*

training [-iŋ] n. Dressage *m.* (of animal); éducation, instruction, formation *f.* (of s.o.); *further training*, perfectionnement. ‖ SPORTS. Entraînement *m.* ‖ MILIT. Pointage *m.* (of gun); entraînement *m.* (of troops). ‖ **Training-college** (or) **-school**, n. école normale *f.* ‖ **Training-ship**, n. NAUT. Bateauécole *m.*

trainless [-lis] adj. Sans traîne. ‖ CH. DE F. Sans réseau ferroviaire, sans train.

train-oil ['trein,ɔil] n. Huile de baleine *f.*

traipse [treips] v. intr. FAM. Se balader.

trait [treit] n. FIG. Trait *m.*

traitor ['treitə*] n. Traître *m.*

traitorous [-rəs] adj. Traître.

traitorously [-rəsli] adv. Traîtreusement.

traitorousness [-rəsnis] n. Traîtrise *f.*

traitress [-ris] n. Traîtresse *f.*

trajectory ['trædʒiktəri] n. Trajectoire *f.*

tram [træm] n. FAM. Tram, tramway *m.* ‖ **Tramline,** n. Ligne (*f.*) de tramway.
— v. tr., intr. (1). FAM. Faire le trajet en tramway.

tram n. Trame *f.*

trammel ['træməl] n. SPORTS. Trémail *m.* (net). ‖ ARTS. Compas elliptique *m.* ‖ ARCHIT. Crémaillère *f.* ‖ FIG. Pl. Entraves *f. pl.*
— v. tr. (1). FIG. Entraver.

tramontana [,træmɔn'tɑ:nə] n. Tramontane *f.*

tramontane [træ'montein] adj. Ultramontain.

tramp [træmp] v. intr. Marcher lourdement (or) d'un pas pesant. ‖ Marcher, cheminer, faire un trajet à pied. ‖ Trimarder, être chemineau.
— v. tr. Parcourir à pied ; *to tramp up and down,* arpenter.
— n. Bruit (*m.*) de pas lourds ; marche pesante *f.* ; piétinement sourd *m.* (noise). ‖ Marche (*f.*) à pied : *to be on the tramp,* courir les routes. ‖ NAUT. Tramp *m.* ‖ FAM. Chemineau, vagabond, trimardeur *m.* ‖ U. S. POP. Traînée *f.* (prostitute); souillon *f.* (slattern).

trample ['træmpl] v. tr. Piétiner, fouler aux pieds, écraser (lit. and fig.).
— v. intr. Marcher d'un pas lourd (*on*, sur). ‖ Piétiner. ‖ **To trample on,** FIG. Ecraser (s.o.); fouler aux pieds (s.o.'s feelings).
— n. Piétinement, bruit (*m.*) de pas.

trampoline ['træmpəlin] n. SPORTS. Trampoline *m.*
— v. intr. SPORTS. Faire du trampoline.

tramway ['træmwei] n. Tramway *m.*

trance [trɑ:ns] n. Transe *f.* ; *to fall into a trance,* entrer en transe. ‖ MED. Catalepsie *f.* ‖ ECCLES., FIG. Extase *f.*
— v. tr. FIG. Transporter, ravir. (See ENTRANCE.)

tranny ['træni] n. FAM. Transistor *m.* (radio set).

tranquil ['træŋkwil] adj. Tranquille.

tranquillity [træŋ'kwiliti] n. Tranquillité *f.*

tranquillize ['træŋkwilaiz] v. tr. Tranquilliser.

tranquillizer [-aizə*] n. MED. Tranquillisant *m.*

tranquilly [-i] adv. Tranquillement.

trans- [trænz] pref. Trans-. ‖ **Trans-Caucasian,** adj. Tanscaucasien. ‖ **Trans-ship,** v. tr. (1). NAUT. Transborder. ‖ **Trans-shipment,** n. NAUT. Transbordement *m.* ‖ **Trans-Siberian,** adj. Transsibérien.

transact [træn'zækt] v. tr. Traiter (business).
— v. intr. Faire des affaires (*with*, avec).

transaction [træn'zækʃən] n. COMM. Transaction, affaire *f.* (business); gestion *f.* (of business). ‖ Pl. Actes *m. pl.* (of a society). ‖ JUR. Transaction *f.*

transactor [-tə*] n. Négociateur *m.* ; négociatrice *f.*

transalpine ['trænz'ælpain] adj., n. Transalpin *m.*

transatlantic [,trænzət'læntik] adj. Transatlantique.

transceiver [træn'si:və*] n. RADIO. Emetteurrécepteur *m.*

transcend [træn'send] v. tr. Transcender, dépasser. ‖ Surpasser.

transcendence [-əns] n. Transcendance *f.*

transcendent [-ənt] adj. ECCLES., FIG. Transcendant.

transcendental [,trænsen'dentl] adj. PHILOS. Transcendantal. ‖ MATH. Transcendant.

transcendentalism [-ə,lizm] n. PHILOS. Transcendantalisme *m.*

transcendentally [-əli] adv. Transcendantalement.

transcontinental [,trænzkɔnti'nentl] adj. Transcontinental.

transcribe [træns'kraib] v. tr. Transcrire.

transcript ['trænskript] n. Transcription *f.* ‖ U. S. Copie (*f.*) d'un dossier universitaire.

transcription [træns'kripʃən] n. Transcription *f.* ‖ RADIO. Emission différée *f.*

transect [træn'sekt] v. tr. Couper transversalement.

transection [træn'sekʃən] n. Coupe transversale *f.*

transept ['trænsept] n. ARCHIT. Transept *m.*

transfer [træns'fə:*] v. tr. (1). Transférer, transporter (from one place to another). ‖ Transmettre, transférer (from one person to another). ‖ ARTS. Reporter, décalquer. ‖ MILIT. Déplacer (troops).
— v. intr. Etre muté (employee); se déplacer (*to,* à) [company]; *to transfer to another university,* changer d'université. ‖ CH. DE F. Changer, transiter.
— ['trænsfə*] n. Transfert, transport *m.* ‖ Transmission *f.* ; transfert *m.* ‖ Changement *m.* (of class). ‖ ARTS. Report, décalque *m.* ‖ JUR. Cession *f.* (of lease); déplacement *m.* (of an official); mutation *f.* (of property). ‖ FIN. Virement *m.* (of funds). ‖ **Transfer-book,** n. COMM. Registre (*m.*) des transferts. ‖ **Transfer-ink,** n. Encre autographique *f.* ‖ **Transfer-paper,** n. Papier (*m.*) à report (or) à décalquer. ‖ **Transfer-tax,** n. JUR. Droits (*m. pl.*) de mutation.

transferable [-rəbl] adj. Transportable. ‖ Transmissible. ‖ JUR. Transférable, cessible (right). ‖ FIN. Négociable (securities). ‖ CH. DE F. *Not transferable,* strictement personnel (ticket).

transferee [,trænsfə'ri:] n. JUR. Cessionnaire *s.*

transference ['trænsfərəns] n. Transfèrement *m.* ‖ PSYCH. Transfert *m.*

transferrer [træns'fə:rə*] n. JUR. Cédant *s.*

transfiguration [,trænsfigju'reiʃən] n. Transfiguration *f.*

transfigure [træns'figə*] v. tr. Transfigurer.

transfix [træns'fiks] v. tr. Transpercer. ‖ FIG. Pétrifier.

transfixion [-ʃən] n. Transpercement *m.* ‖ MED. Transfixion *f.*

transform [træns'fɔ:m] v. tr. TECHN., MATH., CHIM. Convertir. ‖ ELECTR., FIG. Transformer.
— [træns,fɔ:m] n. MATH., GRAMM. Transformée *f.*

transformable [-əbl] adj. Transformable.

transformation [,trænsfə'meiʃən] n. MATH. Conversion *f.* ‖ CHIM. † Transmutation *f.* ‖ ZOOL. Métamorphose *f.* ‖ ELECTR., GRAMM., FIG. Transformation *f.* ‖ **Transformation-scene,** n. THEATR. Changement (*m.*) à vue.

transformer [træns'fɔ:mə*] n. ELECTR., FIG. Transformateur *m.*

transformism [-mizm] n. Transformisme *m.*

transformist [-mist] n. Transformiste *s.*

transfuse [træns'fju:z] v. tr. Transvaser. ‖ MED. Transfuser (blood); injecter (a solution). ‖ FIG. Transfuser.

transfusion [-ʒən] n. Transvasement *m.* ‖ MED., FIG. Transfusion *f.*

transfusionist [-ʒənist] n. Transfuseur *m.*

transfusive [-siv] adj. De transfusion.

transgress [træns'gres] v. tr. Transgresser. (See CONTRAVERSE.)
— v. intr. ECCLES. Pécher. ‖ FIG. Violer la loi.

transgression [træns'greʃən] n. Transgression *f.*

transience ['trænziəns] n. Nature éphémère, brève durée *f.*

transient [-ənt] adj. Ephémère, passager, transitoire, peu durable. ‖ Hâtif. ‖ De passage (guest, lodger). ‖ Mus. De liaison.
— n. Client de passage *s.* (visitor); travailleur itinérant *s.* (worker). ‖ Phys. Transitoire *m.*, phénomène transitoire *m.*

transiently [-əntli] adv. Transitoirement, passagèrement.

transire [træn'saiəri] n. Comm. Passavant *m.*

transistor [træn'zistə*] n. Electr. Transistor *m.* (device); *transistor, transistor radio,* transistor.

transistorize [-ə,raiz] v. tr. Electr. Transistoriser.

transit ['trænsit] n. Traversée *f.;* passage *m.* (action). ‖ Transport, parcours *m.; in transit,* en cours de route. ‖ Comm. Transport, transit *m.; goods in transit,* marchandises en transit. ‖ Astron. Passage *m.* ‖ Aviat. *Air transit,* parcours aérien *m.* ‖ **Transit-circle,** n. Astron. Cercle méridien *m.* ‖ **Transit-duty,** n. Comm. Droit de transit *m.* ‖ **Transit-instrument,** n. Astron. Lunette méridienne *f.*
— v. tr. Astron. Passer sur.

transition [træn'siʃən] n. Transition *f.* (*from,* de; *to,* à). ‖ Ch. de F. Raccordement *m.*

transitional [-l] adj. De transition.

transitive ['træ:nsitiv] adj. Gramm. Transitif.
— n. Gramm. Verbe transitif *m.*

transitively [-li] adv. Transitivement.

transitorily ['trænsitərili] adv. Transitoirement.

transitoriness [-ərinis] n. Nature transitoire *f.*

transitory [-əri] adj. Transitoire.

translatable [træns'leitəbl] adj. Traduisible.

translate [-leit] v. tr. Transporter. ‖ Eccles. Transférer (a bishop, a saint's body); ravir au paradis (a living saint). ‖ Gramm. Traduire (*as,* par; *into* en). ‖ Fig. Traduire, interpréter (*as,* comme); faire passer (*into,* dans); reproduire (*into,* en).

translation [-ʃən] n. Transport *m.;* translation *f.* ‖ Eccles., Techn. Translation *f.* ‖ Gramm. Traduction, version *f.*

translational [-ʃnəl] adj. De translation.

translator [-tə*] n. Gramm. Traducteur *m.;* traductrice *f.* ‖ Radio. Translateur *m.*

transliterate [træns'litəreit] v. tr. Transcrire.

transliteration [,trænslitə'reiʃən] n. Transcription *f.*

translocation [,trænslə'keiʃən:] n. Déplacement *m.* ‖ Jur. *Police translocation,* relégation.

translucence n. Translucidité *f.*

translucent [-ənt] adj. Diaphane, translucide.

transmarine [,trænsmə'ri:n] adj. D'outre-mer.

transmigrate ['trænsmigreit] v. intr. Emigrer (person); transmigrer (soul).

transmigration [,trænsmai'greiʃən] n. Emigration *f.* ‖ Transmigration *f.*

transmigrator ['trænsmigreitə*] n. Emigrant *s.*

transmigratory [-əri] adj. Migrateur *m.;* migratrice *f.*

transmissibility [træns,misi'biliti] n. Transmissibilité *f.*

transmissible [træns'misibl] adj. Transmissible.

transmission [-ʃən] n. Transmission *f.*

transmissive [-siv] adj. Transmetteur (person); transmissible (thing).

transmit [trænz'mit] v. tr. (1). Transmettre (*to,* à). [See forward.]
— v. intr. Radio. Emettre.

transmittable [-əb] adj. Transmissible.

transmittal [-l] n. Transmission *f.*

transmitter [-ə*] n. Transmetteur *m.* ‖ Radio. Emetteur *m.;* station émettrice *f.* ‖ Manipulateur *m.* (telegraph); parleur *m.* (telephone).

transmutable [trænz'mju:təbl] adj. Transmuable, transmutable (*into,* en).

transmutation [,trænzmju:'teiʃən] n. Transmutation *f.* ‖ Math., Med. Transformation *f.*

transmute [trænz'mju:t] v. tr. Transmuer.

transoceanic ['trænz,ouʃi'ænik] adj. Transocéanique, transocéanien.

transom ['trænsəm] n. Archit. Linteau *m.;* imposte *f.* ‖ U. S. Vasistas *m.;* imposte *f.* ‖ Naut. Arcasse *f.;* tableau arrière *m.* ‖ Milit., Aviat. Entretoise *f.*

transonic [træn'sɔnic] adj. Aviat. Transsonique.

transparence [træns'pɛərəns] n. Transparence *f.*

transparency [-ənsi] n. Transparence *f.* (quality). ‖ Transparent *m.* (material). ‖ Diapositif *m.* (in photography).

transparent [-ənt] adj. Transparent, limpide. ‖ Fig. Limpide, clair, transparent, évident.

transparently [-əntli] adv. De façon transparente.

transpierce [træns'piəs] v. tr. Transpercer.

transpiration [,trænspaiə'reiʃən] n. Transpiration *f.* (See sweat.)

transpire [træns'paiə*] v. intr. Med., Bot., Fig. Transpirer. ‖ Fam. Se produire; se passer, arriver (event).
— v. intr. Med., Bot., Fig. Transpirer.

transplant [træns'plɑ:nt] v. tr. Med. Greffer. ‖ Bot., Fig. Transplanter.
— ['træns,plɑ:nt] n. Med. Greffe, transplantation *f.* (operation); greffe *f.,* greffon *m.,* transplant *m.* (organ transplanted).

transplantation [,trænsplɑ:n'teiʃən] n. Bot., Fig. Transplantation *f.*

transplanter [træns'plɑ:ntə*] n. Transplanteur *s.* (person); transplantoir *m.* (tool).

transpontine ['træns'pɔntain] adj. Transpontin; de la rive droite de la Tamise. ‖ Fam. Mélodramatique.

transport [træns'pɔ:t] v. tr. Transporter (goods, persons). ‖ Jur. Déporter. ‖ Fig. Transporter, ravir, enthousiasmer.
— ['trænspɔ:t] n. Transport *m.* (action). ‖ Moyens (*m. pl.*) de transport. ‖ Naut. Transport *m.* ‖ Jur. Déporté *m.* ‖ Fig. Transport *m.* ‖ **Transport-plane,** n. Aviat. Avion-cargo *m.*

transportability [træns'pɔ:tə'biliti] n. Possibilité (*f.*) de transport.

transportable [træns'pɔ:təbl] adj. Transportable.

transportation [,trænspɔ:'teiʃən] n. Transport *m.* ‖ Jur. Déportation *f.* ‖ U. S. Titre de transport *m.* (ticket).

transporter [træns'pɔ:tə*] adj., n. Transporteur *m.*

transporting [-iŋ] adj. Ravissant, transportant.

transposable [træns'pouzəbl] adj. Transposable.

transpose [-pou:z] v. tr. Mus., Math., Fig. Transposer.

transposition [,trænspə'ziʃən] n. Transposition *f.*

transpositive [træns'pɔzitiv] adj. Transpositif.

transsonic [-'sɔnik] adj. Transsonique.

transubstantiate [,trænsəb'stænʃieit] v. tr. Eccles. Transsubstantier.

transubstantiation ['trænsəb,stænʃi'eiʃən] n. Eccles. Transsubstantiation *f.*

transudation [,trænsju'deiʃən] n. Transsudation *f.*

transudatory [træn'sju:dətəri] adj. De transsudation.

transude [træn'sju:d] v. tr. Transsuder.

transuranic [,trænzju'rænik] adj. Chim. Transuranien *adj. m.*

transversal [trænz'və:səl] adj. Transversal.
— n. Math. Transversale *f.* ‖ Med. Transverse *m.*

transversally [-əli], **transversely** [-li] adv. Transversalement.

transverse ['trænzvə:s] adj. Transversal. ‖ Med. Transverse.
— n. Med. Transverse *m.*

transvestism [trænz'vestizṃ] n. Travestisme, transvestisme *m.*

transvestite [-'vestait] n. Travesti *m.*

tranter ['træntə*] n. Colporteur *m.*

trap [træp] n. Piège *m.* (in general) ; trappe ; chausse-trape *f.* (for big game). || TECHN. Siphon *m.* || JUR. *Police trap,* souricière (for gangsters) ; zone de contrôle de vitesse (for motorists). || SPORTS. Ball-trap *m.* || FIG. Piège, panneau *m.* || POP. *Shut your trap!,* ta gueule ! || **Trap-door,** n. Trappe *f.* (in a floor) ; TECHN. Porte (*f.*) d'aérage.
— SYN. : PITFALL, SNARE.
— v. tr. (1). Prendre au piège (game) ; tendre des pièges dans (a wood). || Mettre un siphon dans (a drain). || SPORTS. Bloquer (the ball).

trap v. tr. (1). Caparaçonner.

trapes [treips] v. intr. FAM. Se balader.

trapeze [trə'pi:z] n. MATH., SPORTS. Trapèze *m.* ; *trapeze acrobatics,* jeux icariens ; *trapeze artist,* trapéziste.

trapeziform [-ifɔ:m] adj. Trapéziforme.

trapezium [-jəm] n. MATH. Trapèze *m.*
— N. B. Deux pluriels : *trapezium, trapezia.*

trapezoid ['træpizɔid] adj., n. Trapézoïde *m.*

trapper ['træpə*] n. Trappeur *m.* || TECHN. Portier *m.*

trappings [-iŋz] n. Harnachement *m.* (of horse). || FIG. Atours *m. pl.*

Trappist [-ist] n. ECCLES. Trappiste *m.; Trappist monastery,* Trappe.

Trappistine [-istin] n. ECCLES. Trappistine *f.*

trash [træʃ] n. Bagasse *f.* (cane-trash). || Rebut *m.;* débris, déchets *m. pl.* || Camelote ; gnognote *f.* (fam.). || AGRIC. Emondes *f. pl.* || FAM. Ineptie, balourdise *f.* || FAM. Racaille *f.; white trash,* petits blancs. || **Trash-can,** n. U. S. Poubelle, boîte (*f.*) à ordures.
— v. tr. AGRIC. Emonder. || FAM. Malmener (s.o.) ; mettre au rebut (sth.).

trashiness [-inis] n. Médiocrité *f.*

trashy [-i] adj. De pacotille, de camelote.

trass [træs] n. GEOL. Trass *m.*

trauma ['trɔ:mə] n. MED. Trauma *m.* (wound) ; traumatisme *m.* (condition).
— N. B. Deux pluriels : *traumata, traumas.*

traumatic [trɔ:'mætik] adj. MED Traumatique.

traumatism [trɔ:'mætizṃ] n. Traumatisme *m.*

travail ['træveil] n. MED. Travail *m.*
— v. intr. MED. Etre en travail.

travel ['trævl] v. intr. (1). Voyager, faire un voyage. || COMM. Voyager. || TECHN. Voyager, courir (*on,* sur). || SPORTS. Se déplacer (big game). || FIG. Se promener (eye) ; parcourir, passer en revue (mind) ; circuler (news).
— v. tr. Voyager en, parcourir (a country). || Parcourir (a distance). || Faire voyager (cattle).
— n. Voyage *m.* || TECHN. Course *f.* (of piston). || **Travel agency,** n. Agence (*f.*) de voyages. || **Travel agent,** n. Personne (*f.*) travaillant dans une agence de voyages ; *ask your travel agent,* renseignez-vous auprès de votre agence de voyages. || **Travel-sick,** adj. Qui a le mal des transports. || **Travel-sickness,** n. Mal (*m.*) des transports.

travelled [-d] adj. Qui a beaucoup voyagé.

traveller [-ə*] n. Voyageur *s.* || COMM. Voyageur de commerce, commis voyageur *m.* || FIN. *Traveller's cheque,* chèque de voyage. || TECHN. Curseur *m.* (see CURSOR) ; pont roulant, chariot *m.* || NAUT. Rocambeau *m.*

travelling [-iŋ] adj. Ambulant (person) ; mobile (thing). || De voyage (bag, companion, expenses). || U.S. COMM. *Travelling salesman,* commis voyageur. || TECHN. *Travelling crane, platform, staircase,* pont, trottoir, escalier roulant.
— n. Voyage *m.* || Déplacement *m.* || CINEM. Travelling *m.*

travelogue ['trævəlɔg] n. U. S. Conférence (*f.*) sur un voyage avec projections. || U. S. CINEM. Documentaire (*m.*) sur un voyage (or) une expédition.

traversable ['trævə:səbḷ] adj. Traversable. || JUR. Contestable.

traverse ['trævə:s] n. Traversée *f.* (of a forest). || TECHN. Translation *f.;* chariotage *m.* || MILIT. Pointage *m.* || MATH. Transversale *f.* || NAUT. Route sinueuse *f.* || ARCHIT. Traverse *f.* || CH. DE F. Chariot transbordeur *m.;* plate-forme roulante *f.* || SPORTS. Traversée *f.* (in mountaineering).
— v. tr. Traverser (a forest). || Parcourir (a distance) ; suivre (a street). || JUR. Nier, s'élever contre. || MILIT. Pointer. || ARCHIT. Traverser. || CH. DE F. Transborder. || FIG. Examiner de fond en comble, passer au crible (a question). || FAM. Contrarier, s'opposer à (an opinion, s.o.).
— v. intr. NAUT. Pivoter (compass-needle). || SPORTS. Prendre une traverse. || JUR. Opposer une dénégation.

traverser [-ə*] n. CH. DE F. Chariot roulant *m.*

travesty ['trævisti] v. tr. (2). FIG. Travestir, parodier.
— n. Travestissement *m.;* parodie *f.*

trawl [trɔ:l] v. tr. Traîner (a net).
— v. intr. SPORTS. Chaluter.
— n. Chalut *m.* (net).

trawler [-ə*] n. NAUT. Chalutier *m.* (boat, person).

tray [trei] n. Plateau *m.* || Casier, compartiment *m.* (of trunk) ; *wicker tray,* clayon.

treacherous ['tretʃrəs] adj. Déloyal (blow) ; traître, déloyal, perfide (action, person) ; infidèle (memory).

treacherously [-li] adv. Traîtreusement.

treacherousness [-nis] n. Traîtrise *f.*

treachery ['tretʃəri] n. Trahison *f.* (act).

treacle ['tri:kḷ] n. Mélasse *f.*

tread [tred] v. intr. (182). Marcher, poser le pied sur, appuyer (*on,* sur). || Se poser (foot). || ZOOL. Côcher. || FIG. Avancer, marcher (person) ; *to tread on air,* être transporté de joie ; *to tread on the heels of,* suivre de près.
— v. tr. Marcher sur, piétiner, fouler. || Faire (steps). || ZOOL. Côcher. || SPORTS. *To tread water,* nager debout. || THEATR. *To tread the boards,* monter sur les planches. || **To tread down,** piétiner, fouler aux pieds (lit. and fig.). || **To tread in,** enfoncer en marchant. || **To tread out,** étouffer (fire, revolt).
— n. Pas *m.;* démarche, allure *f.* (gait). || Bruit de pas *m.* (noise). || Giron *m.* (of a stair). || Semelle *f.* (of a shoe). || AUTOM., CH. DE F. Ecartement *m.* || AUTOM. Chape *f.* (of tyre) ; portant *m.* (of wheel). || ZOOL. Accouplement *m.* (of a male bird) ; germe *m.* (of an egg).

treadle ['tredḷ] n. Pédale *f.* (of grindstone, lathe). || **Treadle-type,** adj. A pédale.
— v. intr. Actionner la pédale.

treadmill ['tredmil] n. † Moulin (*m.*) de discipline. || Trépigneuse *f.*

treason ['tri:zṇ] n. Trahison *f.* || JUR. *High treason,* lèse-majesté. || **Treason-felony,** n. JUR. Attentat (*m.*) contre la sûreté de l'Etat.

treasonable [-əbḷ] adj. De trahison (act) ; perfide (libel) ; traître (person).

treasure ['treʒə*] n. Trésor *m.* (lit. and fig.). || **Treasure-hunt,** n. Chasse (*f.*) au trésor. || **Treasure-ship,** n. NAUT. † Galion *m.* || **Treasure-trove,** n. Trésor (*m.*) découvert par hasard.
— v. tr. Priser, garder précieusement. || **To treasure up,** thésauriser, amasser.

treasurer [-rə*] n. Trésorier *s.*

treasurership [-rəʃip] n. Trésorerie *f.*

treasury ['treʒəri] n. Trésor *m.* (place). || FIN. Ministère (*m.*) des Finances (department) ; Trésor (funds) ; trésorerie *f.* (place).

treat [tri:t] v. tr. Traiter, agir envers (s.o.) ; traiter,

considérer, envisager (*as,* comme) [sth.]. ‖ Traiter, recevoir, régaler (a guest); *to treat s.o. to a good dinner,* offrir un bon dîner à qqn. ‖ CHIM., TECHN., FIG. Traiter. ‖ MED. Traiter, soigner; *to be treated,* recevoir des soins (at a clinic).
— v. intr. Traiter (*of,* de; *with,* avec).
— n. Régal, banquet, festin *m.* (meal). ‖ Fête, réjouissance *f.* (delight).

treater [-ə*] n. Négociateur *m.;* négociatrice *f.* ‖ Hôte *m.* ‖ Personne (*f.*) qui traite un sujet.

treating [-iŋ] n. Action (*f.*) de régaler. ‖ Traitement *m.* (act).

treatise ['tri:tis] n. Traité *m.*

treatment ['tri:tmənt] n. CHIM., ARTS, MED., FIG. Traitement *m.* ‖ CINEM. Adaptation *f.*

treaty ['tri:ti] n. Traité *m.* (between nations). ‖ Accord *m.* (agreement); *treaty obligations,* obligations conventionnelles. ‖ **Treaty-port,** n. NAUT. COMM. Port ouvert au commerce étranger *m.*

treble ['trebl] adj. Triple. ‖ MUS. De sol (clef); aigu, de soprano (voice).
— n. Triple *m.* ‖ MUS. Soprano *m.* ‖ RADIO. Aigu *m.*
— v. tr. Tripler.

trebly [-i] adv. Triplement.

trebuchet ['trebjuʃit] n. Trébuchet *m.*

trecento [trei'tʃentou] n. Quatorzième siècle italien *m.*

tree [tri:] n. BOT., FIG. Arbre *m.* ‖ ECCLES. Gibet, arbre (*m.*) de la croix; croix *f.* ‖ ARCHIT. Poutre *f.* ‖ TECHN. Embauchoir *m.* (boot-tree). ‖ FIG. *Family tree,* arbre généalogique. ‖ FAM. *At the top of the tree,* au sommet de l'échelle; *to be up a tree,* être coincé (or) aux abois. ‖ **Tree-dwelling,** adj. Arboricole. ‖ **Tree-fern,** n. BOT. Fougère arborescente *f.* ‖ **Tree-frog** (or) **-toad,** n. ZOOL. Rainette *f.* ‖ **Tree-top,** n. Cime (*f.*) d'un arbre. ‖ **Tree-trunk,** n. Tronc d'arbre *m.*
— v. tr. Forcer à s'abriter dans un arbre. ‖ TECHN. Mettre sur un embauchoir. ‖ FAM. Réduire a quia (s.o.).

treeless [-lis] adj. Sans arbres, déboisé.

trefoil ['tri:fɔil] n. BOT., ARCHIT. Trèfle *m.*

trek [trek] v. intr. (1). Voyager en char à bœufs. ‖ Emigrer. ‖ FAM. Faire route.
— n. Migration *f.* ‖ FAM. Voyage pénible *m.,* sacrée balade *f.*

trellis ['trelis] n. Treillis, treillage *m.* (lattice). ‖ Treille *f.* (arbour).
— v. tr. Treillisser (a wall). ‖ Echalasser (a vine).

tremble ['trembl] v. intr. Trembler, frissonner, frémir (person, thing).
— n. Tremblement *m.*

tremblement [-mənt] n. MUS. Trémolo *m.*

trembler [-ə*] n. Trembleur, froussard *s.* ‖ ELECTR. Trembleur *m.*

trembling [-iŋ] adj. Tremblant.
— n. Tremblement *m.*

tremendous [tri'mendəs] adj. Effrayant, terrifiant, affreux, terrible. ‖ FAM. Enorme; *to take tremendous trouble to,* prendre toute la peine du monde pour, se démener pour.

tremendously [-li] adv. Terriblement.

tremendousness [-nis] n. Nature terrible *f.;* aspect terrifiant *m.* ‖ FAM. Enormité *f.*

tremolant ['treməlant] n. MUS. Tremblant *m.*

tremolo ['treməˌlou] n. MUS. Trémolo *m.* (tremulous effect). ‖ MUS. Tremblant *m.* (device in organ).

tremor ['tremə*] n. Tremblement, frisson, frémissement *m.* (lit. and fig.). ‖ Trépidation *f.; earth tremor,* tremblement de terre. ‖ Tremblotement *m.* (of the voice). ‖ MED. Tremblement *m.*

tremulous ['tremjuləs] adj. Fébrile, fiévreux (excitement); tremblant, hésitant (smile); tremblotant (voice); tremblé (writing).

tremulously [-li] adv. En tremblant.

tremulousness [-nis] n. Tremblement *m.*

trench [trentʃ] n. AGRIC. Fossé *m.; rigole *f.* (drain). ‖ MILIT. Tranchée *f.; communication trench,* boyau. ‖ **Trench-coat,** n. Trench-coat *m.* ‖ **Trench-foot,** n. MED. Pied gelé *m.* ‖ **Trench-mortar,** n. MILIT. Mortier, lance-bombes *m.* ‖ **Trench-mouth,** n. U. S. MED. Angine (*f.*) de Vincent.
— v. tr. AGRIC. Creuser un fossé (or) une rigole dans (a meadow); défoncer (a piece of ground). ‖ ARCHIT. Rainer (a board).
— v. intr. **To trench upon,** empiéter sur (s.o.'s land, rights).

trenchancy ['trentʃnsi] n. FIG. Causticité *f.*

trenchant [-ənt] adj. FIG. Energique, vigoureux (argument); mordant, tranchant, caustique (words).

trenchantly [-əntli] adv. De façon énergique (or) tranchante.

trencher ['trentʃə*] n. AGRIC., MILIT. Faiseur (*m.*) de fossés (or) de tranchées. ‖ CULIN. Tranchoir *m.*

trencherman [-mən] (pl. **trenchermen**) n. Mangeur *m.* (eater); écornifleur (sponger).

trend [trend] v. intr. Se diriger (*towards,* vers). ‖ Etre orienté, tendre (*towards,* vers).
— n. Direction. ‖ FIG. Tendance, orientation *f.;* mode, vogue *f.* (fashion). ‖ **Trend-setter,** n. Personne (*f.*) qui lance une mode.

trendy [-i] adj. FAM. Dans le vent, in.

trental ['trentl] n. ECCLES. Trentain *m.*

trepan [tri'pæn] v. tr. (1). Enlever par surprise (*from,* de). ‖ Entraîner, amener (*into,* à).

trepan n. MED. † Trépan *m.* ‖ TECHN. Foreuse *f.*
— v. tr. (1). MED. Trépaner.

trepanation [ˌtrepə'neiʃən] n. MED. Trépanation *f.*

trephine [tri'fi:n] n. MED. Tréphine *f.,* trépan *m.*

trepidation [ˌtrepi'deiʃən] n. Trépidation *f.* ‖ FIG. Agitation *f.* ‖ FAM. Trac *m.*

treponema [trepə'ni:mə] n. MED. Tréponème *m.*

trespass ['trespəs] v. intr. Entrer sans permission. ‖ *To trespass against,* enfreindre (a law); léser (right); offenser (s.o.). ‖ *To trespass on,* empiéter sur (s.o.'s rights); abuser de (s.o.'s time). ‖ FAM. *To trespass on s.o.'s preserves,* empiéter sur les plates-bandes de qqn.
— n. JUR. Délit *m.; trespass to land,* violation de propriété. ‖ ECCLES. Offense *f.* ‖ FAM. Abus *m.* (upon, de); [s.o.'s patience].

trespasser [-ə*] n. JUR. Délinquant *s.;* intrus *s.* (on another's land); *trespassers will be prosecuted,* défense d'entrer sous peine d'amende. ‖ ECCLES. Pécheur, transgresseur *m.*

tress [tres] n. Tresse *f.* (of hair). ‖ Pl. Chevelure *f.*
— v. tr. Tresser.

trestle ['tresl] n. Tréteau *m.* ‖ ARCHIT. Chevalet *m.* (of bridge).

trews [tru:z] n. pl. Pantalon écossais *m.*

trey [trei] n. Trois *m.* (at cards, dice).

triable ['traiəbl] adj. Tentable. ‖ JUR. Jugeable.

triad ['traiəd] n. Triade *f.* ‖ CHIM. Elément trivalent *m.* ‖ MUS. Accord (*m.*) en tierce. ‖ ECCLES. Unité (*f.*) en trois personnes.

trial ['traiəl] n. Essai *m.;* expérience *f.; on trial,* à l'essai; *to give sth. a trial,* faire l'essai de; *to make the trial,* tenter l'expérience; *to proceed by trial and error,* procéder par tâtonnements. ‖ JUR. Procès, jugement *m.; civil trial,* action civile; *famous trials,* causes célèbres; *to bring to trial,* faire passer en jugement. ‖ FIN. *Trial balance,* balance de vérification. ‖ AVIAT., FIG. *Trial balloon,* ballon d'essai. ‖ FIG. Epreuve *f.* (to, pour).
— adj. D'essai (speed, trip). ‖ FIN. De vérification (balance).

triangle ['traiæŋgl] n. MATH., NAUT., MUS., ASTRON. Triangle *m.* ‖ ARTS. Equerre (*f.*) à dessin.

triangular [trai'æŋgjulə*] adj. Triangulaire.

triangularly [-ləli] adv. En triangle.

triangulate [-leit] v. tr. Trianguler.
— adj. A triangles.

triatomic [traiə'tɔmik] adj. Phys. Triatomique.

tribal ['traibəl] adj. Tribal.

tribalism ['traibə,lizm] n. Tribalisme m.

tribasic [trai'beisik] adj. Chim. Tribasique.

tribe [traib] n. Tribu f. ‖ Zool., Bot. Famille f. ‖ Fig. Gent f.

tribesman [-zmən] (pl. **tribesmen**) n. Membre (m.) d'une (or) de la tribu.

triblet ['triblit] n. Techn. Triboulet m.

tribometer [tri'bɔmitə*] n. Phys. Tribomètre m.

tribrach [,tribræk] n. Tribraque m.

tribulation [,tribju'leiʃən] n. Tribulation, épreuve, affliction f.

tribunal [trai'bju:nḷ] n. Jur. Tribunal m. (court); siège de magistrat m. (seat).

tribunate ['tribjunət] n. † Tribunat m.

tribune ['tribju:n] n. Tribun m.

tribune n. Tribune f. ‖ Eccles. Trône m.

tributary ['tribjutəri] adj. Tributaire.
— n. Tributaire m. ‖ Geogr. Affluent m.

tribute ['tribju:t] n. Tribut m. (to, à) [money, obligation, tax]. ‖ Fig. Tribut m.; to pay tribute to, rendre hommage à.

tricar ['traikɑ:*] n. Tricar, tricycle m.

trice [trais] n. Instant m.; in a trice, en une seconde.

trice v. tr. Naut. Hisser (a sail).

triceps ['traiseps] adj., n. Med. Triceps m.

trichina [tri'kainə] (pl. **trichinae** [-ni:]) n. Med. Trichine f.

trichologist [tri'kɔlədʒist] n. Med. Spécialiste (m.) du cuir chevelu.

trichromatic [,traikrə'mætik] adj. Trichrome.

trick [trik] n. Tour m.; ruse, astuce, attrape, supercherie f.; to play a trick on, jouer un tour à. ‖ Tour m.; farce, blague f.; to be up to one's old tricks again, faire encore des siennes. ‖ Tour, tour (m.) de main; truc m. (fam.); the tricks of the trade, les astuces du métier, les ficelles. ‖ Tour, tour (m.) d'adresse; card trick, tour de cartès. ‖ Tic m.; manie f.; it's a trick of his, c'est une manie chez lui; he has a trick of, il a le chic pour. ‖ Levée f. (at cards). ‖ Naut. Tour m. (at the wheel). ‖ Fam. The whole bag of tricks, tout le bataclan. ‖ **Trick-shot**, n. Cinem. Truquage m.
— v. tr. Tromper, attraper; refaire, avoir (fam.); to trick s.o. into, amener par ruse qqn à; to trick s.o. out of sth., carotter qqch. à qqn. ‖ To trick out (or) up, Fam. Attifer.
— v. intr. Jouer des tours.

trickery [-əri] n. Tromperie; roublardise f.; piece of trickery, supercherie.

trickiness [-inis] n. Fourberie, rouerie f. ‖ Fam. Complication f. (of a machine).

trickish [-iʃ] adj. Rusé, fourbe.

trickle ['trikḷ] v. intr. Dégoutter, couler goutte à goutte, suinter; dégouliner (fam.). ‖ Fig. Se faire jour, transpirer (truth). ‖ To trickle in, s'infiltrer; Fig. Pénétrer peu à peu (news); arriver par petits groupes (refugees).
— v. tr. Faire couler goutte à goutte. ‖ Sports. Faire rouler (the ball).
— n. Filet m. (of water). ‖ **Trickle-charger**, n. Electr. Chargeur par filtrage m.

tricklet [-lit] n. Petit filet m.

trickster ['trikstə*] n. Fourbe s. ‖ Escroc m.; confidence trickster, voleur à l'américaine.

tricksy [-si] adj. Espiègle.

trick-track ['triktræk] n. Trictrac m.

tricky ['triki] adj. Rusé, astucieux, malin (person); compliqué (problem); délicat (work).

tricolo(u)r ['trikələ*] adj. Tricolore.
— n. Milit. Drapeau tricolore m.; les trois couleurs f. pl.

tricorn ['traikɔ:n] adj., n. Tricorne m.

tricycle ['traisikḷ] n. Tricycle m.
— v. intr. Faire du tricycle.
— v. tr. Porter en tricycle.

tridactyl [trai'dæktil] adj. Zool. Tridactyle.

trident ['traidənt] n. Trident m.

tridimensional [,traidi'menʃənḷ] adj. A trois dimensions, tridimensionnel.

triduum ['tridjuəm] n. Eccles. Triduum m.

tried [traid] adj. Eprouvé. (See try.)

triennial [trai'enjəl] adj. Triennal.
— n. Bot. Plante triennale f.

trier ['traiə*] n. Juge; arbitre m. ‖ Fam. Personne (f.) qui tente l'expérience; he's a trier, il ne s'avoue jamais vaincu. ‖ **Trier-on**, n. Comm. Essayeur s.

trifacial [trai'feiʃiəl] adj., n. Med. Trijumeau m.

trifid ['traifid] adj. Bot. Trifide.

trifle ['traifḷ] n. Bagatelle, broutille, vétille f.; rien m. ‖ Petite somme f. (money). ‖ Etain m. (pewter). ‖ Culin. Charlotte (f.) au xérès, aux amandes et à la crème fouettée. ‖ Fam. Brin m.
— v. intr. Agir (or) parler avec légèreté. ‖ Badiner, marivauder (with, avec) [s.o.]; jouer (with, avec) [sth.]. ‖ Chipoter (with, sur) [one's food].
— v. tr. To trifle away, gaspiller (or) gâcher sottement (one's money, time).

trifler [-ə*] n. Baguenaudier, marivaudeur m. ‖ Fantaisiste s.

trifling [-iŋ] adj. Léger, frivole, fantaisiste (person); insignifiant, négligeable, sans importance (thing).
— n. Légèreté, frivolité f.

triflingly [-iŋli] adv. En badinant.

trifocal [trai'foukḷ] adj. A triple foyer.

trifocals [-z] n. pl. Lunettes (f. pl.) à triple foyer.

trifoliate [trai'foulieit] adj. Bot. Trifolié.

triforium [trai'fɔ:riəm] n. Archit. Triforium m.

trig [trig] adj. Soigné, pimpant (person); net, bien tenu (room).

trig v. tr. (1). Caler.
— n. Cale f. (See wedge.)

trigamist ['trigəmist] n. Trigame s.

trigamous [-əs] adj. Trigame.

trigamy [-i] n. Trigamie f.

trigeminal [trai'dʒeminḷ] adj., n. Med. Trijumeau m. (See trifacial.)

trigger ['trigə*] n. Déclenchement, déclic m. ‖ Milit. Gâchette, détente f. ‖ **Trigger-happy**, adj. Fam. A la gâchette facile.
— v. tr. Presser la détente de (gun). ‖ To trigger off, déclencher, entraîner, provoquer.

trigonal [-ḷ] adj. Math., Bot., Zool. Trigone.

trigonometric [,trigənə'metrik] adj. Math. Trigonométrique.

trigonometry [,trigə'nɔmitri] n. Math. Trigonométrie f.

trihedral [trai'hi:drəl] adj. Math. Trièdre.

trihedron [-ən] n. Math. Trièdre m.
— N. B. Deux pluriels : trihedra, trihedrons.

trike [traik] n. Fam. Tricycle m.

trilateral [trai'lætərəl] adj. Trilatéral.

trilby ['trilbi] n. Feutre, chapeau mou m.

trilingual [trai'liŋwəl] adj. Trilingue.

trilith ['triliθ], **trilithon** [-ɔn] n. Trilithe m.

trill [tril] v. intr. Mus., Zool. Faire des trilles. ‖ Fig. Perler (laugh). ‖ Fam. Chevroter.
— v. tr. Mus. Triller. ‖ Fam. Chevroter.
— n. Mus. Trille m. ‖ Gramm. Consonne roulée f. ‖ Fam. Chevrotement m.

trilling [-iŋ] n. Mus. Trilles m. pl. ‖ Gramm. Roulement (m.) de consonne.

triling [-iŋ] n. Triplet m.

trillion ['triljən] n. Math. Trillion m. (10^{18}); U. S. billion m. (10^{12}).

trilobate [trai'loubeit] adj. Trilobé.
trilogy ['trilədʒi] n. Trilogie *f.*
trim [trim] adj. Net, soigné, bien tenu, coquet, pimpant. ‖ Bien fait (or) tourné. ‖ NAUT. Etarque (sail).
— n. Etat, ordre *m.* (of sth.) ; *in perfect trim,* en parfait état, parfaitement tenu. ‖ Etat, aplomb *m.* (of s.o.) ; *in good trim,* en bon état, d'aplomb, de bonne humeur. ‖ Coupe *f.* (in hairdressing) ; *to give just a trim to,* rafraîchir (hair-cut). ‖ Tenue *f.* (equipment). ‖ NAUT. Orientation *f.* (of sails) ; arrimage *m.* (of ship). ‖ AVIAT. Equilibrage *m.* ‖ SPORTS. Forme *f.*
— v. tr. (1). Arranger, mettre en état (or) en ordre (sth.). ‖ Moucher (a candle) ; préparer, arranger (fire). ‖ Rafraîchir, couper (hair). ‖ Garnir (a dress, hat). ‖ AGRIC. Emonder (branches) ; tailler (hedge). ‖ TECHN. Raboter, dégrossir (wood). ‖ NAUT. Orienter (sails) ; dresser (a ship). ‖ FAM. Tondre, plumer (to fleece) ; corriger (to thrash) ; attraper (to tick off). ‖ **To trim away** (or) **off,** enlever ce qui dépasse ; TECHN. Ebarber. ‖ **To trim·up,** regarnir (a hat) ; *to trim oneself up,* se pomponner, se mettre en tenue.
— v. intr. Louvoyer, nager entre deux eaux.
trimaran ['traimə,ræn] n. NAUT. Trimaran *m.*
trimensual [trai'mensjuəl], **trimestrial** [-mestriəl] adj. Trimestriel.
trimester [trai'mestə*] n. Trimestre *m.*
trimly ['trimli] adv. Nettement, proprement, coquettement.
trimmer ['trimə*] n. Garnisseur *s.* (of hats). ‖ TECHN. Pareur *m.* (person) ; massicot *m.* (tool). ‖ ARCHIT. Chevêtre *f.* ‖ NAUT. Arrimeur *m.* ‖ AVIAT. Flettner, compensateur, volet *m.* ‖ FAM. Opportuniste *s.*
trimming [-iŋ] n. Arrangement *m.;* mise (*f.*) en ordre. ‖ Garniture *f.* (of hats) ; pl. Passementerie *f.* ‖ AGRIC. Taille *f.* (of hedges). ‖ TECHN. Débordage, ébarbage *m.* (of sheet-iron) ; dégrossissage *m.* (of wood). ‖ NAUT. Orientation *f.* (of sails) ; arrimage *m.* (of ship). ‖ CULIN. Pl. Garniture *f.* ‖ FAM. Raclée *f.* ‖ FAM. Louvoyage, opportunisme *m.* ‖ **Trimming-axe,** n. AGRIC. Emondoir *m.* ‖ **Trimming-machine,** n. TECHN. Ebarbeuse *f.* ‖ **Trimming-tab,** n. AVIAT. Flettner *m.*
trimness [-nis] n. Netteté, apparence soignée *f.;* aspect coquet *m.*
trinary ['trainəri] adj. Trinaire.
trine [train] adj. Triple. ‖ ASTRON. Trin.
tringle ['triŋgḷ] n. Tringle *f.*
Trinidad ['trinidæd] n. GEOGR. Ile de la Trinité *f.*
trinitarian [,trini'tɛəriən] n. Trinitaire *m.*
trinitrotoluene [trai,naitrou'tɔlju,iːn], **trinitrotoluol** [-'tɔlju,ɔl] n. CHIM. Trinitrotoluène *m.*
trinity ['triniti] n. ECCLES., FIG. Trinité *f.*
trinket ['triŋkit] n. Colifichet *m.* (jewelry) ; babiole, broutille *f.* (trifle).
trinketry [-ri] n. Colifichets *m. pl.*
trinomial [trai'noumjəl] adj., n. MATH. Trinôme *m.*
trio ['triːou] n. MUS., FAM. Trio *m.*
triode ['traioud] n. ELECTR. Triode *f.*
triolet ['triolit] n. Triolet *m.* (poem).
trioxide [trai'ɔksaid] n. CHIM. Trioxyde *m.*
trip [trip] v. intr. (1). Aller d'un pas léger, trotter menu ; *to trip up,* grimper lestement. ‖ Broncher (horse) ; trébucher, faire un faux pas (person). ‖ TECHN. Se déclencher. ‖ FIG. Faire une erreur (or) une bévue (person) ; fourcher (tongue). ‖ **To trip up,** trébucher ; FIG. Faire une gaffe.
— v. tr. Faire trébucher, donner un croc-en-jambe à (s.o.). ‖ NAUT. Déraper (the anchor). ‖ TECHN. Déclencher. ‖ FAM. Prendre en défaut, pincer (s.o.). ‖ **To trip in,** TECHN. Embrayer. ‖ **To trip up,** faire trébucher (to make stumble) ; prendre en faute (to catch in error).

— n. Excursion, randonnée *f.; honeymoon trip,* voyage de noces. ‖ Démarche légère *f.* (tread). ‖ Croc-en-jambe *m.* ‖ Faux pas *m.* (stumble). ‖ NAUT. Traversée *f.; maiden trip,* premier voyage ; *round trip,* croisière. ‖ FAM. Faux pas *m.* (error). ‖ POP. Trip, voyage *m.* (on drugs). ‖ **Trip-recorder,** n. AUTOM. Compteur kilométrique *m.* ‖ **Trip-wire,** n. Fil (*m.*) déclenchant un mécanisme lorsque l'on trébuche dessus.
tripartite ['trai'pɑːtait] adj. Tripartite (thing, treaty). ‖ En trois exemplaires (copy). ‖ BOT. Triparti.
tripe [traip] n. ZOOL., CULIN. Tripe(s) *f. (pl.)* ‖ FAM. Gnognote, foutaise *f.; navet m.* ‖ **Tripe-dealer,** n. COMM. Tripier *s.* ‖ **Tripe-shop,** n. COMM. Triperie *f.*
tripeman [-mən] (pl. **tripemen**) n. COMM. Tripier *m.*
tripersonal [trai'pəːsnḷ] adj. ECCLES. En trois personnes.
tripery ['traipəri] n. COMM. Triperie *f.*
triphase ['traifeiz] adj. ELECTR. Triphasé.
triphthong ['trifθɔŋ] n. GRAMM. Triphtongue *f.*
triplane ['trai,plein] n. AVIAT. Triplan *m.*
triple ['tripḷ] adj. Triple. ‖ MUS. A trois temps.
— v. tr., intr. Tripler. (See TREBLE.)
triplet [-it] n. Trio *m.* (of persons, things). ‖ MED. Triplet *s.* ‖ GRAMM. Tercet *m.* ‖ MUS. Triolet *m.*
triplex ['tripleks] adj. TECHN. Triplex.
— n. MUS. Mesure (*f.*) à trois temps.
triplicate ['triplikit] adj. Triple. ‖ En trois exemplaires.
— n. Triple exemplaire *m.*
— [-keit] v. tr. Tripler. ‖ Faire en trois exemplaires.
tripod ['traipɔd] n. Trépied *m.*
tripodal [-ḷ] adj. A trois pieds.
tripos ['traipɔs] n. Examen du B. A. à Cambridge
tripper ['tripə*] n. Excursionniste, touriste *s.*
trippingly [-iŋli] adv. D'un pas léger. ‖ FIG. Lestement.
triptych ['triptik] n. ARTS. Triptyque *m.*
triptyque [trip'tiːk] n. AUTOM. Triptyque *m.*
trireme ['traiəriːm] n. NAUT. Trirème *f.*
trisect [trai'sekt] v. tr. Diviser en trois parties égales, couper en trois.
trisection [-sekʃən] n. Trisection *f.*
trismus ['trismǝs] n. MED. Trismus *m.*
trisyllabic [traisi'læbik] adj. Trisyllabique.
trisyllable [trai'siləbḷ] n. Trisyllabe *m.*
trite [trait] adj. Rebattu, usé, banal.
tritely [-li] adv. Banalement.
triteness [-nis] n. Banalité *f.*
tritium ['tritiəm] n. PHYS. Tritium *m.*
Triton ['traitṇ] n. ZOOL. † Triton *m.*
triton ['traitɔn] n. PHYS. Triton *m.*
tritone ['trai,toun] n. MUS. Triton *m.,* quarte augmentée *f.*
triturable ['tritjuərəbḷ] adj. Triturable.
triturate [-reit] v. tr. Triturer.
trituration [,tritju'reiʃən] n. Trituration *f.*
triumph ['traiəmf] n. Triomphe *m.* (act, spectacle). ‖ Jubilation *f.* (joy).
— v. intr. Triompher (*over,* de) [an enemy]. ‖ Chanter victoire, jubiler, exulter.
triumphal [trai'ʌmfəl] adj. De triomphe (arch) ; triomphal (progress).
triumphant [-ənt] adj. Triomphant.
triumphantly [-əntli] adv. Triomphalement.
triumpher [-ə*] n. Triomphateur *m.;* triomphatrice *f.*
triumvir [trai'ʌmvə:*] n. Triumvir *m.*
triumvirate [-virit] n. Triumvirat *m.*
triune ['traiˈjuːn] adj. ECCLES. Trine.
trivalent [trai'veilənt] adj. CHIM. Trivalent.
trivet ['trivit] n. Trépied *m.*

trivia ['triviə] n. pl. Broutilles, vétilles, bêtises *f. pl.*
trivial ['triviəl] adj. Banal, ordinaire, monotone (commonplace). ‖ Frivole, léger. ‖ Insignifiant, sans importance (person). ‖ GRAMM. Vulgaire.
triviality [‚trivi'æliti] n. Insignifiance *f.* ‖ Pl. Banalités *f. pl.*
triweekly [trai'wi:kli] adj. Trihebdomadaire, qui paraît trois fois par semaine. ‖ Qui a lieu (or) paraît toutes les trois semaines.
troat [trout] v. intr. ZOOL. Bramer.
— n. ZOOL. Bramement *m.*
trocar ['troukə*] n. MED. Trocart *m.*
trochaic [tro'keiik] adj. GRAMM. Trochaïque.
trochanter [tro'kæntə*] n. MED. Trochanter *m.*
trochee ['trouki:] n. GRAMM. Trochée *m.*
trochoid ['troukɔid] adj. MATH. Cycloïdal. ‖ ZOOL., MED. Trochoïde.
— n. MATH. Cycloïde *m.* ‖ ZOOL., MED. Trochoïde *m.*
trod [trod] pret., p. p., **trodden** [-n̩] p. p. See TREAD.
troglodyte ['troglədait] n. ZOOL., † Troglodyte *m.*
troglodytic [‚troglə'ditik] adj. Troglodytique.
Trojan ['troudʒən] adj. GEOGR. De Troie (horse, war); Troyen (person).
— n. GEOGR. Troyen *s.* ‖ FAM. *To work like a Trojan*, travailler comme un nègre.
troll [troul] v. intr., tr. SPORTS. Pêcher à la cuiller. ‖ MUS. Chantonner.
— n. SPORTS. Cuiller *f.* (lure); moulinet *m.* (tool). ‖ MUS. Canon *m.*
troll n. Troll *m.*
trolley ['troli] n. CH. DE F. Chariot *m.* (four-wheeled); diable *m.* (two-wheeled). ‖ COMM. Petite voiture *f.* ‖ TECHN. Trolley *m.* ‖ AUTOM. Patin transbordeur *m.* ‖ CULIN. *Dinner trolley*, table roulante, serveuse. ‖ **Trolley-bus**, n. Trolleybus *m.* ‖ **Trolley-pole**, n. Perche *f.*
trollop ['troləp] n. Souillon *f.* (or) *m.* (slattern); traînée *f.* (prostitute).
trombone [trom'boun] n. MUS. Trombone *m.*
trombonist [-ist] n. MUS. Tromboniste *m.*
troop [tru:p] n. Bande, troupe *f.* ‖ Troupe *f.* (of Boy Scouts). ‖ MILIT. Troupe *f.* (body); peloton *m.* (company); *three thousand troops*, trois mille hommes. ‖ **Troop-carrier** (or) **-ship**, n. NAUT., AVIAT. Transport (*m.*) de troupes. ‖ **Troop-horse**, n. Cheval (*m.*) de troupe.
— v. intr. S'attrouper, s'assembler (*around*, autour de). ‖ Marcher en troupe (or) à la file. ‖ **To troop away** (or) **off**, s'en aller en troupe (or) en bande. ‖ **To troop together**, s'attrouper. ‖ **To troop up**, arriver en foule.
— v. tr. MILIT. *To troop the colours*, présenter les couleurs.
trooper [-ə*] n. MILIT. Cavalier *m.* ‖ FAM. *Old trooper*; vieux routier.
trooping [-iŋ] n. Attroupement *m.* ‖ MILIT. *Trooping the colours*, salut au drapeau.
trope [troup] n. Trope *m.*
trophy ['troufi] n. †, MILIT., FIG. Trophée *m.* ‖ Panoplie *f.* (wall-weapons). ‖ SPORTS. Coupe *f.*
tropic ['tropik] n. GEOGR. Tropique.
— adj. Tropical.
tropical [-əl] adj. GEOGR. Tropical. ‖ FAM. Ardent, dévorant (passion).
tropism ['troupizm] n. BOT., ZOOL. Tropisme *m.*
tropology [tro'polədʒi] n. Tropologie *f.*
troposphere ['tropə‚sfiə*] n. Troposphère *f.*
trot [trot] v. intr. (1). Trotter. ‖ FAM. Courir, trotter, filer.
— v. tr. Faire trotter (a horse). ‖ Faire au trot (two miles). ‖ **To trot out**, faire parader (a horse); FAM. Exhiber (s.o., sth.).
— n. Trot *m.* ‖ FAM. *To keep s.o. on the trot*, faire trotter qqn. ‖ U. S. FAM. Traduction juxtalinéaire.

troth [trouθ] n. † Foi, parole *f.*
Trotskyist ['trotskiist], **Trotskyite** [-ait] n. Trotskiste *m.*
trotter ['trotə*] n. Trotteur *m.* (horse). ‖ CULIN. Pl. Pieds *m. pl.* ‖ FAM. Peton *m.*
troubadour ['tru:bə‚duə*] n. Troubadour *m.*
trouble ['trʌbl] v. tr. Troubler (water). ‖ Déranger, embarrasser, gêner; *may I trouble you for the mustard?*, puis-je vous demander la moutarde?; *to trouble s.o. with*, importuner qqn avec. ‖ Affliger, tourmenter; inquiéter, préoccuper; *to be troubled about*, se tourmenter au sujet de, être soucieux à cause de.
— v. intr. Se déranger; *don't trouble to answer*, ne vous donnez pas la peine de répondre. ‖ S'inquiéter, se tourmenter (*about*, de).
— n. Dérangement *m.*; peine *f.*; *to put oneself to great trouble*, se mettre en quatre. ‖ Ennui *m.*; difficulté *f.*; *to have trouble in doing*, avoir des difficultés à faire; *to have trouble with*, avoir des désagréments avec (s.o.). ‖ Souci, ennui *m.*; *the trouble it gave me!*, ce que ça m'a coûté d'ennuis!; *to be in trouble*, avoir des ennuis. ‖ Peine *f.*; chagrin, tourment *m.*; *to be in trouble*, être dans l'adversité. ‖ Pl. Désordres, troubles *m. pl.* ‖ MED. Trouble *m.* ‖ POP. *My trouble and strife*, ma légitime, mon gouvernement. ‖ **Trouble-maker**, n. Fomenteur (*m.*) de troubles; factieux, FAM. Trublion *m.* ‖ **Trouble-shooter**, n. Expert *m.* ‖ **Trouble-spot**, n. Point chaud *m.*
troublesome [-səm] adj. Fatigant, agaçant, importun (person); gênant, encombrant, ennuyeux (thing); pénible (work).
troublesomeness [-səmnis] n. Caractère fatigant (or) ennuyeux; tintouin *m.* (fam.).
trough [trof] n. Abreuvoir *m.* (drinking); auge *f.* (feeding); auget *m.* (in a bird-cage). ‖ Pétrin *m.* (kneading). ‖ CHIM. Cuve *f.* ‖ PHYS. Creux *m.* (of a wave). ‖ NAUT. *Trough of the sea*, creux de la lame. ‖ ASTRON. Zone de dépression *f.* ‖ ARCHIT. Chéneau *m.*
trounce [trauns] v. tr. FAM. Rosser.
trouncing [-iŋ] n. FAM. Raclée *f.* (See DRUBBING.)
troupe [tru:p] n. THEATR. Troupe *f.*
trousers [trauzəz] n. pl. Pantalon *m.*; *skiing trousers*, pantalon de ski, fuseaux. ‖ FAM. *To wear the trousers*, porter la culotte (woman). ‖ **Trouser-clip**, n. Pince (*f.*) à pantalon. ‖ **Trouser-stretcher**, n. Tendeur de pantalon *m.*
trousse [tru:s] n. MED. Trousse *f.*
trousseau ['tru:sou] n. Trousseau *m.*
trout [traut] n. invar. ZOOL. Truite *f.* ‖ FAM. *Old trout*, vieille toupie.
— v. intr. SPORTS. Pêcher la truite.
troutlet [-lit] n. ZOOL. Truiton *m.*
trove [trouv]. See TREASURE-TROVE.
trowel ['trauəl] n. ARCHIT. Truelle *f.* ‖ AGRIC. Déplantoir *m.*
— v. tr. (1). ARCHIT. Etaler à la truelle.
troy(weight) ['trɔi(‚weit)] n. COMM. Troy, troy-weight *m.*
truancy ['truənsi] n. Habitude (*f.*) de manquer l'école; absentéisme scolaire *m.*
truant [-ənt] n. † Truand *m.* ‖ Elève (*s.*) qui manque l'école, absentéiste scolaire *s.*; *to play truant*, faire l'école buissonnière.
— adj. Vagabond.
— v. tr. Vagabonder. ‖ Faire l'école buissonnière.
truce [tru:s] n. MILIT., FIG. Trêve *f.* ‖ **Truce-bearer**, n. MILIT. Parlementaire *m.*
truceless [-lis] adj. Sans trêve.
truck [trʌk] v. intr. Faire le commerce (*in*, de); troquer (*with*, avec).
— v. tr. Troquer (*for*, contre).
— n. Troc, échange *m.* (see BARTER); *truck system*, système du paiement en nature (or) en produits manufacturés. ‖ Articles divers, menus objets *m. pl.*

‖ U. S. Produits maraîchers *m. pl.; truck garden,* jardin maraîcher; *truck gardener,* maraîcher. ‖ Camelote, pacotille *f.* ‖ FAM. Rapports *m. pl. (with,* avec).
truck n. AUTOM. Camion *m.* ‖ CH. DE F. Wagon-tombereau, truc *m;* plate-forme *f.;* bogie *m.* ‖ NAUT. Pomme *f.* (of mast). ‖ **Truck-load,** n. Plein wagon; tombereau *m.*
— v. tr. Camionner.
truckage [-idʒ] n. Camionnage *m.* ‖ CH. DE F. Roulage *m.*
trucker [-ə*] n. U. S. Camionneur, routier *m.* (truck-driver).
trucker n. U. S. Maraîcher *s.* (market-gardener).
truckle [-l] v. intr. Ramper, s'aplatir *(to,* devant).
— n. † Lit *(m.)* à roulettes (trundle-bed). ‖ Lit *(m.)* de fortune (bed). ‖ Poulie *f.*
truckler [-ə*] n. Flagorneur *s.*
truculence ['trʌkjuləns] n. Férocité, sauvagerie *f.* ‖ Violence *f.* (in style).
truculent [-t] adj. Batailleur, belliqueux, agressif (pugnacious); virulent, au vitriol (scathing); féroce, sauvage (cruel).
truculently [-tli] adv. Agressivement, de manière belliqueuse (pugnaciously); avec virulence (scathingly); férocement, sauvagement (cruelly).
trudge [trʌdʒ] v. intr. Traîner la jambe.
— v. tr. Parcourir en se traînant.
— n. Marche pénible *f.;* cheminement *m.*
true [tru:] adj. Vrai, exact; to come true, se réaliser, se vérifier. ‖ Vrai, véritable (diamond, hour). ‖ Véritable, bien compris (interest). ‖ Sincère, fidèle (description); fidèle, loyal *(to,* à) [person]. ‖ MUS. Juste (voice). ‖ TECHN. Rectiligne, conforme, centré, droit; *out of true,* décentré (wheel). ‖ **True-blue,** adj. FAM. Bon teint, sûr. ‖ **True-born,** adj. Vrai. ‖ **True-bred,** adj. De bonne race. ‖ **True-hearted,** adj. Au cœur sincère. ‖ **True-love,** n. Bien-aimé *s.; true-love knot,* lacs d'amour.
— adv. Vrai, juste.
— v. tr. TECHN. Ajuster; dégauchir.
trueness [-nis] n. Fidélité; vérité *f. (of,* de). ‖ MUS. Justesse *f.*
truffle ['trʌfl] n. BOT. Truffe *f.* ‖ **Truffle-bed,** n. Truffière *f.* ‖ **Truffle-growing** n. Trufficulture *f.*
trug [trʌg] n. Panier de jardinage *m.*
truism ['tru:izm] n. Truisme *m.;* lapalissade *f.*
truly ['tru:li] adv. Vraiment, réellement, en vérité (really). ‖ Vraiment, sincèrement (sincerely). ‖ Fidèlement, loyalement (faithfully); *yours truly,* salutations distinguées.
trump [trʌmp] n. † Trompette *f.*
trump n. Atout *m.* (lit. and fig.).
— v. tr. Couper (a card). ‖ **To trump up,** se créer, forger (an excuse).
— v. intr. Jouer atout.
trumpery ['trʌmpəri] n. Pacotille, camelote *f.* ‖ Sottises, balivernes, fadaises *f. pl.*
— adj. En toc, de clinquant, de pacotille. ‖ FIG. Spécieux (argument).
trumpet ['trʌmpit] n. MUS. Trompette *f.* (instrument); fanfare *f.* (music); trompette *m.* (musician). ‖ MED. Cornet acoustique *m.* ‖ FAM. *To blow one's own trumpet,* s'envoyer des fleurs, se faire mousser. ‖ **Trumpet-call,** n. MUS. Sonnerie de trompette *f.;* FIG. Rappel *m.* ‖ **Trumpet-major,** n. MILIT. Trompette-major *m.* ‖ **Trumpet-player,** n. MUS. Trompettiste *m.*
— v. tr. Publier à son de trompe.
— v. intr. Trompeter, sonner de la trompette. ‖ ZOOL. Barrir.
trumpeter [-ə*] n. MUS., ZOOL. Trompette *m.*
truncal ['trʌŋkl] adj. MED. Du tronc.
truncate [-eit] v. tr. Tronquer.
— [-it] adj. Tronqué.
truncheon [trʌnʃən] n. Matraque *f.* (cudgel). ‖ Bâton *m.* (policeman's).

trundle ['trʌndl] n. Roulette *f.* (wheel). ‖ Fardier, camion bas *m.* (cart). ‖ Lit *(m.)* à roulettes (bed). ‖ TECHN. Lanterne *f.*
— v. tr. Faire rouler (a hoop). ‖ Pousser (a barrow). ‖ SPORTS. Bôler.
— v. intr. Rouler (hoop).
trunk [trʌŋk] n. MED., BOT., FIG. Tronc *m.* ‖ Inter, interurbain *m.* (telephone). ‖ COMM. Malle *f.* ‖ ZOOL. Trompe *f.* (of elephant). ‖ CH. DE F. Grande ligne *f.* ‖ TECHN. Fourreau *m.* ‖ Pl. Slip *m.* ‖ U. S. AUTOM. Coffre arrière *m.* (boot). ‖ **Trunk-call,** n. Communication interurbaine *f.* ‖ **Trunk-hose,** n. † Haut-de-chausses *m.* ‖ **Trunk-line,** n. Ligne interurbaine *f.* (telephone); U. S. CH. DE F. Grande ligne *f.* ‖ **Trunk rack,** n. U. S. Porte-bagages *m.* ‖ **Trunk-road,** n. Route nationale *f.* ‖ **Trunk-sleeve,** n. Manche bouffante *f.*
trunkful [-ful] n. Malle, pleine malle *f.*
trunnion ['trʌnjən] n. MILIT., TECHN. Tourillon *m.*
truss [trʌs] v. tr. AGRIC. Botteler. ‖ ARCHIT. Armer, renforcer. ‖ SPORTS. † Saisir. ‖ CULIN. Trousser. ‖ FAM. Ligoter.
— n. AGRIC. Botte *f.* ‖ BOT. Touffe *f.* ‖ ARCHIT. Cintre *m.;* armature, ferme *f.* ‖ NAUT. Drosse *f.* ‖ MED. Bandage herniaire *m.* ‖ **Truss-maker,** n. MED. Bandagiste *m.*
trust [trʌst] n. Confiance *f. (in,* en); *to take on trust,* prendre de confiance. ‖ Espérance *f.;* espoir *m.* (hope). ‖ Charge *f.* (duty); dépôt *m.* (person, thing). ‖ JUR. Fidéicommis *m.;* fiducie *f.* ‖ COMM., FIN. Trust *m.; investment trust,* trust de placement. ‖ COMM. Crédit *m.; on trust,* à crédit. ‖ **Trust-buster,** n. U. S. FAM. Fonctionnaire *(m.)* chargé de la lutte contre les trusts.
— v. tr. Se fier à, avoir confiance en (s.o.'s honesty, s.o.). ‖ Se fier à, ajouter foi à (s.o.'s word). ‖ Confier *(with,* à) [sth.]. ‖ Laisser sans surveillance; *he doesn't trust you out of his sight,* il ne vous perd pas de vue. ‖ COMM. Faire crédit à.
— v. intr. Espérer, compter fermement. ‖ Compter *(in,* sur); se fier *(in,* à). ‖ Se fier, se confier, s'en remettre, faire confiance *(to,* à).
trustee [trʌs'ti:] n. Dépositaire, mandataire *m.* ‖ Administrateur *m.* (of a fund); syndic *m.* (in bankruptcy). ‖ Curateur; fidéicommissaire *m.*
trusteeship [-ʃip] n. Administration *f.* ‖ Curatelle *f.;* fidéicommis *m.* ‖ Syndicat *(m.)* de faillite. ‖ Tutelle *f.* (in politics).
trustful ['trʌstful] adj. Confiant.
trustfully [-i] adv. Avec confiance.
trustfulness [-nis] n. Confiance *f.*
trustification [,trʌstifi'keiʃən] n. Groupement *(m.)* d'industries; formation *(f.)* de trusts.
trustily ['trʌstili] adv. Loyalement.
trusting [-iŋ] adj. Confiant.
trustworthiness [-,wə:ðinis] n. Loyauté, fidélité *f.* (of s.o.). ‖ Véracité, crédibilité *f.* (of a statement).
trustworthy [-,wə:ði] adj. Digne de confiance (person); digne de foi (statement).
trusty [-i] adj. Sûr, loyal.
— n. FAM. Forçat privilégié *m.*
truth [tru:θ] n. Vérité, exactitude, véracité *f.* (of a statement). ‖ Sincérité, loyauté, honnêteté *f.* (of s.o.). ‖ Vérité *f.* (in general); *strong in the strength of truth,* fort de la vérité; *to tell s.o. a few home truths,* dire à qqn ses quatre vérités (or) quelques bonnes vérités. ‖ TECHN. Aplomb *m.*
truthful [-ful] adj. Véridique, sincère (person); vrai, véridique (witness). ‖ ARTS. Fidèle (portrait).
truthfully [-fuli] adv. Véridiquement; sincèrement.
truthfulness [-fulnis] n. Sincérité *f.* (of s.o.); véracité *f.* (of a statement). ‖ ARTS. Fidélité *f.*
truthless [-lis] adj. Faux, fourbe (person); faux, mensonger (statement).
truthlessness [-lisnis] n. Fausseté *f.*
try [trai] v tr. (2). Essayer, expérimenter, éprouver

(sth.) ; *to try one's hand at*, s'essayer à. ‖ Tenter (an experience) ; *to be willing to try anything once*, se prêter à toutes les expériences. ‖ Essayer, tenter (*to*, de) ; *to try one's best*, faire tous ses efforts. ‖ Eprouver, exercer, mettre à l'épreuve (s.o.'s patience). ‖ Fatiguer, user (one's eyes). ‖ Techn., Chim. Affiner (gold). ‖ Jur. Juger, mettre en jugement. ‖ **To try on**, essayer (a coat) ; Fam. *To try it on with s.o.*, essayer de monter le coup à qqn. ‖ **To try out**, essayer à fond, soumettre à un essai concluant ; Techn. Epurer. ‖ **To try up**, Archit. Varloper.
— v. intr. *To try and see*, chercher à constater, essayer de voir. ‖ **To try back**, Sports, Fig. Revenir en arrière. ‖ **To try for**, essayer (or) tenter (or) tâcher d'obtenir (or) d'avoir.
— n. Essai *m.* ; tentative *f.* ‖ Sports. Essai *m.* ‖ **Try-on**, n. Fam. Tentative (*f.*) de bluff ; ballon d'essai *m.* ‖ **Try-out**, n. Essai à fond *m.* ; Theatr. Audition *f.* ‖ **Try-your-strength-machine**, n. Tête (*f.*) de Turc (at fairs).
trying [-iŋ] adj. Pénible, critique, éprouvant (situation). ‖ Fatigant (light). ‖ Agaçant, pénible, insupportable (person). ‖ Contrariant, ennuyeux (event). ‖ **Trying-plane**, n. Techn. Varlope *f.*
trysail ['traiseil] n. Naut. Voile goélette *f.*
tryst [trist] n. † Rendez-vous *m.*
— v. tr. Donner rendez-vous à.
tsar [za:*] n. Tsar *m.*
tsarevitch ['za:rəvitʃ] n. Tsarévitch *m.*
tsarina [za:'ri:nə] n. Tsarine *f.*
tsetse ['tsetsi] n. Zool. Mouche tsé-tsé *f.*
tub [tʌb] n. Baquet, cuvier *m.* (for washing). ‖ Tine *f.* (butt) ; tonneau *m.* (cask). ‖ Tub *m.* (bath, bathtub). ‖ Agric. Caisse *f.* ‖ Techn. Berline *f.* ‖ Naut. Canot lourd ; rafiot *m.* ‖ Fam. *A tale of a tub*, un conte fantastique. ‖ **Tub-chair**, n. Fauteuil crapaud *m.* ‖ **Tub-thumper**, n. Fam. Laïusseur, déclamateur, orateur de carrefour *m.*
— v. tr. (1). Donner un tub à. ‖ Agric. Mettre en caisse. ‖ Naut. Entraîner.
— v. intr. Prendre un tub. ‖ Naut. Ramer.
tuba ['tju:bə] n. Mus. Tuba, bombardon *m.* (in band) ; trompette *f.* (organ).
tubal ['tjubəl] adj. De tube. ‖ Med. Tubaire.
tubar ['tjubə*] adj. Tubaire.
tubbish ['tʌbiʃ], **tubby** [-i] adj. Fam. Rondelet ; *tubby little man*, pot à tabac.
tube [tju:b] n. Tube *m.* (of toothpaste). ‖ Tuyau *m.* (pipe). ‖ Med. Canal *m.* ; trompe *f.* ‖ Naut., Phys. Tube *m.* ‖ Milit. Etoupille *f.* ‖ Autom. Chambre (*f.*) à air. ‖ Ch. de f. Métro *m.* ‖ U. S. Radio. Lampe *f.* (valve). ‖ **Tube-colour**, n. Couleur (*f.*) en tube. ‖ **Tube-fed**, adj. Med. Alimenté à la sonde. ‖ **Tube-skirt**, n. Jupe-fourreau *m.* ‖ **Tube-station**, n. Ch. de f. Station (*f.*) de métro. ‖ **Tube-traveller** (or) **-user**, n. Usager du métro *m.*
— v. tr. Techn. Tuber. ‖ Med. Intuber.
tubeless [-lis] adj. Autom. Sans chambre à air (tyre).
tuber [-ə*] n. Bot. Tubercule *m.* ; truffe *f.* ‖ Med. Tubérosité *f.*
tubercle ['tju:bə:k]] n. Bot., Med. Tubercule *m.* ‖ **Tubercle-bacillus**, n. Med. Bacille de Koch *m.*
tubercular [tju'bə:kjulə*] adj. Bot., Med. Tuberculeux.
tuberculin [tju:'bə:kjulin] n. Med. Tuberculine *f.*
tuberculization [tju,bə:kjulai'zeiʃən] n. Tuberculisation *f.*
tuberculize [tju'bə:kjulaiz] v. tr. Med. Tuberculiser.
tuberculosis [tju,bə:kju'lousis] n. Med. Tuberculose *f.*
tuberculous [tju'bə:kjuləs] adj. Med. Tuberculeux.

tuberiferous [,tju:bə'rifərəs] adj. Tubérifère.
tuberiform ['tju:berifɔ:m] adj. Tubériforme.
tuberose ['tju:bərous] n. Bot. Tubéreuse *f.*
tuberous ['tju:bərəs] adj. Tubéreux.
tubful [tʌbful] n. Plein baquet *m.* ; cuvée *f.*
tubing ['tju:biŋ] n. Tube *m.* ‖ Tuyauterie *f.* ‖ Med., Techn. Tubage *m.*
tubular ['tju:bjulə*] adj. Tubulaire. ‖ Med. Tubaire (breathing).
tubulate [-lit] adj. Tubulé.
tubulure [-juə*] n. Tubulure *f.*
T.U.C. [,ti:ju:'si:] abbr. *Trades Union Congress*, confédération des syndicats britanniques.
tuck [tʌk] v. tr. Plisser (a garment) ; replier (a napkin). ‖ Border (s.o.) [in bed]. ‖ Enfoncer, fourrer (fam.) [to cram]. ‖ **To tuck away**, reléguer, écarter. ‖ **To tuck in**, rentrer (a hem) ; border (s.o.). ‖ **To tuck up**, resserrer (gathers) ; replier (one's legs) ; border (s.o.) ; relever, retrousser (one's sleeves).
— v. intr. Se placer ; se fourrer (fam.). ‖ **To tuck in**, Fam. Becqueter, bouffer, se caler les côtes, s'en mettre jusque-là.
— n. Pli, *m.* ‖ Naut. Cul *m.* ‖ Fam. Mangeaille *f.* ; sucreries *f. pl.* ‖ **Tuck-in**, n. Fam. Bâfrée *f.* ; gueuleton *m.* ‖ **Tuck-shop**, n. Fam. Pâtisserie, confiserie *f.*
tucker [-ə*] n. † Fichu *m.* ‖ Guide (*m.*) à plisser (of a sewing-machine). ‖ Fam. Boustifaille *f.*
tucker [-ə*] v. tr. U. S. *To tucker out*, fatiguer.
Tuesday ['tju:zdi] n. Mardi *m.*
tufa [tju:fə], **tuff** [tʌf] n. Tuf *m.*
tuft [tʌft] n. Touffe *f.* (of feathers, hair, grass) ; houppe *f.* (of silk). ‖ Impériale *f.* (beard) ; toupet *m.* (hair). ‖ Pompon *m.* (on a hat). ‖ Zool. Huppe, aigrette.
— v. tr. Garnir de touffes (or) de groupes. ‖ Capitonner (a quilt). ‖ Fig. Piquer, parsemer.
— v. intr. Former une touffe (or) un groupe.
tufted [-id] adj. En touffes. ‖ Zool. Huppé.
tufty [-i] adj. En touffe. ‖ Couvert de touffes.
tug [tʌg] v. tr. (1). Tirer fort, traîner. ‖ Naut. Remorquer. ‖ **To tug in**, Fig. Introduire de force.
— v. intr. Tirer fort. ‖ **To tug at**, tirer sur.
— n. Traction, saccade *f.* ; *to give a good tug*, donner un bon coup de collier (horse) ; tirer violemment (person). ‖ Trait *m.* (of harness). ‖ Naut. Remorqueur *m.* ‖ Fig. Effort, déchirement *m.* ‖ **Tug-of-war**, n. Sports. Lutte à la corde de traction *f.*
tugboat [-bout] n. Naut. Remorqueur *m.*
tuition [tju'iʃən] n. Enseignement *m.* ; *private tuition*, leçons particulières ; *postal tuition*, enseignement par correspondance. ‖ U. S. Frais (*m.*) d'inscription.
tuitional [-]] adj. De leçons, d'enseignement.
tulip ['tju:lip] n. Bot. Tulipe *f.* ‖ **Tulip-tree**, n. Bot. Tulipier *m.* ‖ **Tulip-wood**, n. Tulipier ; bois (*m.*) de rose.
tulle [tju:l] n. Tulle *m.*
tumble ['tʌmbl] v. intr. Tomber, culbuter, dégringoler (fam.). ‖ Se hâter, se précipiter ; *to tumble down*, descendre en vitesse. ‖ Rencontrer ; tomber (fam.) [*upon*, sur]. ‖ Sports. Faire des culbutes (or) des sauts périlleux. ‖ Naut. Déferler (waves). ‖ Med. S'agiter, se retourner dans son lit. ‖ **To tumble out**, Fam. Piger, saisir.
— v. tr. Bouleverser, mettre sens dessus dessous. ‖ Défaire (a bed) ; chiffonner (s.o.'s dress) ; ébouriffer, décoiffer (s.o.'s hair). ‖ Jeter, renverser, culbuter (*into*, dans). ‖ **To tumble down**, renverser ; flanquer par terre (fam.) ; Sports. Descendre (a bird).
— n. Chute *f.* ‖ Sports. Culbute *f.* ‖ **Tumble-down**, adj. Croulant, délabré (house). ‖ **Tumble-drier**, n. Sèche-linge *m.*, machine (*f.*) à sécher le linge.
tumbler [-ə*] n. Verre, gobelet *m.* ‖ Sports. Acrobate *m.* ‖ Zool. Pigeon culbutant *m.* ‖ Milit.

Gâchette *f.* ‖ TECHN. Culbuteur *m.* ‖ **Tumbler-drier,** n. Sèche-linge *m.*, machine (*f.*) à sécher le linge. ‖ **Tumbler-switch,** n. ELECTR. Commutateur (*m.*) à bascule.

tumblerful [-əful] n. Plein gobelet *m.*

tumbling [-iŋ] n. Chute *f.* (action). ‖ SPORTS. Acrobatie *f.* ‖ **Tumbling-shaft,** n. TECHN. Arbre (*m.*) à cames.

tumbrel [-tʌmbrəl] n. Tombereau *m.*

tumefaction [,tju:mi'fækʃən] n. MED. Tuméfaction *f.*

tumefy [tju:mifai] v. tr. (2). MED. Tuméfier. — v. intr. Se tuméfier.

tumescence [tju'mesn̩s] n. Tumescence *f.*

tumescent [-n̩t] adj. Tumescent.

tumid ['tju:mid] adj. MED. Enflé. ‖ FIG. Ampoulé.

tumidity [tju:'miditi] n. MED. Enflure *f.* ‖ FIG. Boursouflure *f.*

tummy ['tʌmi] n. FAM. Estomac, ventre *m.* (See BELLY.)

tumo(u)r ['tju'mə*] n. MED. Tumeur *f.*

tumular ['tju:mjulə*] adj. Tumulaire.

tumult ['tju:mʌlt] n. Tumulte *m.* ‖ FIG. Emoi *m.*; agitation *f.*

tumultuous [tju'mʌltjuəs] adj. Tumultueux.

tumultuously [-li] adv. Tumultueusement.

tumulus ['tju:mjuləs] (pl. **tumuli** [-ai]) n. Tumulus *m. invar.*

tun [tʌn] n. Tonne *f.* ‖ Cuve *f.* (in brewing). — v. tr. (1). Entonner, mettre en fût.

tuna (fish) ['tu:nɑ(fiʃ] n. U. S. ZOOL. Thon *m.*

tunable ['tju:nəb] adj. MUS. Accordable.

tundra ['tʌndrə] n. GEOGR. Toundra *f.*

tune [tju:n] n. MUS. Air *m.* (melody); justesse (*f.*) d'accord; *in tune,* juste; *out of tune,* faux. ‖ RADIO. Accord *m.* ‖ FAM. Humeur *f.; to change one's tune,* baisser le caquet, changer de ton; *to sing another tune,* chanter une autre antienne; *to the tune of five millions,* pour la petite somme de cinq millions. ‖ Tune-up, n. U. S. Réglage *m.* — v. tr. MUS. Accorder. ‖ RADIO. Syntoniser; « *you are tuned in to»,* « vous êtes à l'écoute de ». ‖ TECHN. Régler (an engine). ‖ FIG. Accorder (*with,* à); harmoniser (*with,* avec). — v. intr. **To tune in,** RADIO. Se brancher (*to,* sur), être à l'écoute (*to,* de). ‖ **To tune up,** MUS. S'accorder (band); FAM. Se mettre à chanter (singer); *all tuned up,* fin prêt; U. S. TECHN. Régler. ‖ **To tune with,** être en harmonie avec.

tuneful [-ful] adj. Harmonieux, mélodieux.

tunefully [-fuli] adv. Harmonieusement.

tuneless [-lis] adj. Discordant. ‖. Muet.

tuner [-ə*] n. MUS. Accordeur *m.* ‖ RADIO. Tuner *m.*

tungstate ['tʌŋsteit] n. CHIM. Tungstate *m.*

tungsten [-stən] n. CHIM. Tungstène *m.*

tungstic [-stik] adj. CHIM. Tungstique.

tunic ['tju:nik] n. Blouse, chemisette *f.* ‖ † MED., BOT. Tunique *f.* ‖ MILIT. Veste, tunique *f.*

tunicle [-l] n. ECCLES., BOT., ZOOL. Tunique *f.*

tuning [-iŋ] n. MUS. Accordage *m.* ‖ RADIO. Réglage *m.;* syntonisation *f.* ‖ **Tuning-fork,** n. MUS. Diapason *m.* ‖ **Tuning-hammer,** n. MUS. Accordoir *m.*

Tunisia [tju:'niziə] n. GEOGR. Tunisie *f.*

tunnel ['tʌn!] n. CH. DE F. Tunnel *m.* ‖ TECHN., ZOOL. Galerie *f.* ‖ **Tunnel-vault,** n. Voûte (*f.*) en berceau. — v. tr. (1). Percer un tunnel dans; *to tunnel one's way through,* se creuser un chemin à travers. — v. intr. Creuser un tunnel.

tunny ['tʌni] n. ZOOL. Thon *m.*

tup [tʌp] n. ZOOL. Bélier *m.* ‖ TECHN. Mouton *m.* — v. tr. Flécher (a ewe).

tuppence ['tʌpəns] n. pl. See TWOPENCE.

tuppenny ['tʌpəni] adj. See TWOPENNY.

turban ['tə:bən] n. Turban *m.* ‖ ZOOL. Turbo *m.*

turbaned [-d] adj. Turbané; à turban.

turbary ['tə:bəri] n. Tourbière *f.*

turbid ['tə:bid] adj. Trouble (liquid). ‖ U. S. Epais, dense (smoke). ‖ FIG. Confus (mind, utterance).

turbidity [tə:'biditi], **turbidness** ['tə:bidnis] n. Turbidité *f.; aspect trouble *m.*

turbinate ['tə:binit] adj. Turbiné.

turbine ['tə:bin] n. Turbine *f.* ‖ **Turbine-pump,** n. Turbopompe *f.*

turbit ['tə:bit] n. ZOOL. Pigeon cravaté *m.*

turbo ['tə:bɔ] pref. Turbo-. ‖ **Turbo-alternator,** n. ELECTR. Turbo-alternateur *m.* ‖ **Turbo-blower,** n. TECHN. Turbosouffleuse *f.* ‖ **Turbo-compressor** (or) **supercharger,** n. TECHN. Turbocompresseur *m.* ‖ **Turbo-dynamo,** n. ELECTR. Turbodynamo *f.* ‖ **Turbo-generator,** n. Turbogénérateur *m.* ‖ **Turbo-jet engine,** n. Turboréacteur *m.* ‖ **Turbo-motor,** n. Turbomoteur *m.* ‖ **Turbo-prop,** adj. A turbopropulseur. ‖ **Turbo-pump,** n. Turbopompe *f.* ‖ **Turbo-reaction,** n. Turboréaction *f.*

turbot ['tə:bət] n. ZOOL. Turbot *m.*

turbulence ['tə:bjuləns] n. Turbulence, agitation *f.* ‖ Trouble *m.;* effervescence *f.* ‖ Indiscipline *f.*

turbulent [-ənt] adj. Turbulent (child). ‖ Agité (sea). ‖ Indiscipliné.

turd [tə:d] n. ARG. Merde *f.,* étron *m.* (excrement). ‖ ARG. Fumier, salaud *m.;* salope, ordure *f.*

tureen [tju'ri:n] n. Saucière *f.* (for sauce); soupière *f.* (for soup).

turf [tə:f] n. Gazon *m.* ‖ Motte (*f.*) de gazon. ‖ Tourbe *f.* (peat). ‖ SPORTS. Turf *m.* ‖ **Turf-accountant,** n. Bookmaker *m.* ‖ **Turf-man,** n. Turfiste *s.* — v. tr. Gazonner. ‖ **To' turf out,** FAM. Vider, balancer.

turfite [-ait] n. Turfiste *m.*

turfy [-i] adj. Gazonné, couvert de gazon. ‖ Tourbeux. ‖ SPORTS. Du turf, des courses.

turgescence [tə:'dʒesn̩s] adj. MED. Turgescence *f.* ‖ FIG. Boursouflure *f.*

turgescent [-n̩t] adj. MED. Turgescent. ‖ FIG. Ampoulé.

turgid ['tə:dʒid] adj. Enflé. ‖ FIG. Boursouflé.

turgidity [tə:'dʒiditi] n. MED. Enflure, turgescence *f.* ‖ FIG. Boursouflure *f.*

Turk [tə:k] n. GEOGR. Turc *m.; Turque *f.* ‖ ECCLES. Musulman *s.* ‖ FAM. Enfant terrible *m.* (child); tyran *m.* (person). ‖ **Turk's head,** n. NAUT. Tête (*f.*) de Maure; FAM. Tête-de-loup *f.* (broom).

Turkey ['tə:ki] n. GEOGR. Turquie *f.* — adj. De Turquie (carpet); d'Andrinople (red).

turkey n. ZOOL. Dindon *m.; young turkey,* dindonneau. ‖ CULIN. Dinde *f.* ‖ FAM. Dindon *m.* ‖ U. S. FAM. Four, fiasco *m.* ‖ **Turkey-buzzard,** n. U. S. ZOOL. Urubu *m.* ‖ **Turkey-hen,** n. ZOOL. Dinde *f.*

Turkish ['tə:kiʃ] adj. n. Turc *m.* ‖ **Turkish-towel,** n. Serviette éponge *f.*

Turkoman [-mən] n. Turcoman *m.*

turmeric ['tə:mərik] n. BOT., CULIN. Curcuma *m.* ‖ CHIM. *Turmeric paper,* papier de curcuma.

turmoil ['tə:mɔil] n. Agitation, effervescence *f.;* trouble, remous *m.*

turn [tə:n] v. tr. Tourner (in general); *to turn the pages,* tourner les pages. ‖ Tourner, faire tourner (a key, wheel). ‖ Faire en tournant (a somersault). ‖ Retourner (a coat, bag). ‖ Tourner (a corner). ‖ Tourner, diriger (*on, to,* vers) [one's eyes, face]. ‖ Détourner (*from,* de) [a blow, the conversation, s.o.]. ‖ Traduire, rendre (*into,* en) [a text]. ‖ Tourner (fine phrases, a letter). ‖ Changer, transformer (*into,* en) [to change]. ‖ Changer, échanger, troquer (*into,* contre) [to barter]. ‖ Dépasser (a certain age, an amount). ‖ Rendre, faire, devenir (sick). ‖ Tourner, diriger, orienter (*to,* vers) [one's thoughts]; *it turns my thoughts in another direction,* cela me change les idées. ‖ Appliquer (*to,* à) [one's knowledge]. ‖ Tourner, éluder (a difficulty). ‖ Tourner, monter (*against,* contre) [s.o.]. ‖ Tourner, troubler (s.o.'s head). ‖ MILIT. Repousser (an attack);

tourner (the enemy's flank); pointer (*on*, sur) [a gun]. ‖ TECHN. Tourner (in a lathe). ‖ AGRIC. Retourner (ground). ‖ CULIN. Faire tourner (cream, milk). ‖ MED. Soulever (s.o.'s stomach). ‖ FIN. Maintenir en circulation (money). ‖ FAM. *To turn tail and run*, détaler comme un lapin. ‖ LOC. *To turn the tables on s.o.*, retourner un argument contre quelqu'un; retourner la situation. ‖ **To turn about**, faire faire demi-tour à (s.o); tourner dans le sens opposé (sth.). ‖ **To turn away**, détourner (one's head, s.o.'s curiosity); congédier, renvoyer (s.o.). ‖ **To turn back**, rabattre (collar); retrousser (one's sleeves); faire retourner (s.o.). ‖ **To turn down**, retourner (a card); rabattre (a collar); baisser (the gas); corner (a page); repousser (a proposition); écarter (a suitor); FAM. Recaler (a candidate). ‖ **To turn in**, dénoncer, livrer (a criminal); replier, rentrer (a hem); tourner en dedans (one's toes). ‖ **To turn off**, fermer (gas, tap, wireless); couper (steam, water); CH. DE F. Garer; FAM. Mettre dehors (s.o.). ‖ **To turn on**, préparer (a bath); allumer (electricity); ouvrir (gas); FAM. *To turn on the waterworks*, ouvrir les écluses (to cry). ‖ **To turn out**, faire confectionner (a dress); vider (a drawer); fermer (the gas); éteindre (the light); trier (papers); pondre (a piece of writing); retourner (one's pockets); mettre dehors; envoyer dinguer, vider (fam.) [s.o.]; expulser (a tenant); AGRIC. Mettre au vert (cattle); MILIT. Alerter (troops); CULIN. Démouler (cake); FAM. *To turn out one's toes*, marcher en dehors. ‖ **To turn over**, rabattre (the edges); tourner (the pages); retourner (an object); remettre (*to*, à) [sth.]; AGRIC. Retourner (the soil); FIN. S'élever à (an amount); FIG. Retourner, agiter (*in*, dans) [an idea, a subject]. ‖ **To turn up**, retourner (a card); relever (one's collar); allumer (the gas); retrousser (one's sleeves); trouver (*in*, dans) [a word]; FAM. *To turn up one's eyes*, faire des yeux blancs; *to turn up one's nose at*, faire le méprisant à l'égard de, ne pas daigner envisager; cracher sur (pop.).
— v. intr. Tourner (key, top, wheel). ‖ Tourner (*to*, à); *to turn sharply*, tourner court. ‖ Se tourner (*towards*, vers) [s.o.]; se diriger (*towards*, vers) [a place]. ‖ Tourner, changer (luck, wind). ‖ Se changer, se transformer, se convertir (*into*, en). ‖ Devenir (mad, pale, sick); se faire (soldier). ‖ Se changer (*to*, en) [sth. else]. ‖ Dépendre (*on*, de) [circumstances]. ‖ Se retourner (*against*, *on*, contre); *to turn against eggs*, se dégoûter des œufs. ‖ Se reporter, se référer (*to*, à) [a document]. ‖ Avoir recours (*to*, à); se tourner (*to*, vers) [s.o.]. ‖ Rouler, porter (*on*, sur) [a subject]. ‖ Se mettre (*to*, à) [work]. ‖ CULIN. Tourner (milk). ‖ TECHN. Se tourner (wood). ‖ MED. Tourner (head); se soulever (stomach). ‖ NAUT. *To turn upside down*, chavirer. ‖ AUTOM. Capoter. ‖ **To turn about**, se tourner, se retourner, s'agiter. ‖ **To turn around**, se retourner. ‖ **To turn away**, se détourner (*from*, de). ‖ **To turn back**, tourner bride (horseman); se retourner (person); s'en retourner, rebrousser chemin (walker). ‖ **To turn down**, se rabattre, se replier. ‖ **To turn in**, tourner en dedans; FAM. Aller au pieu. ‖ **To turn off**, se détourner; tourner (*to*, à) [person]; bifurquer (road). ‖ **To turn out**, sortir (*to*, pour); devenir (rainy, sad); tourner, se présenter (things) [bad, well]; tourner en dehors (toes); se mettre en grève (workmen); FAM. Sortir du lit; LOC. *He turned out to be mad*, il se trouva être fou; *it turns out that*, il se trouve que; *that will turn out all right*, ça s'arrangera. ‖ **To turn over**, se retourner (*on*, sur), AVIAT., AUTOM. Capoter; FAM. Tourner casaque. ‖ **To turn round**, se retourner (*on*, contre; *to*, vers) [person]; FAM. Tourner (head); tourner casaque, virer de bord (person). ‖ **To turn to**, FAM. S'y mettre. ‖ **To turn up**, se relever, se redres-

ser (branch); sortir (card); s'émousser (edge of tool); se retrousser (tail); FIG. Arriver, survenir (event); arriver, se présenter; rappliquer (fam.) [person]; FAM. *His nose turned up*, il fit le nez.
— n. Tour *m.* (of handle, key, wheel); *in the turn of a hand*, en un tournemain. ‖ Tour *m.*; spire *f.* (coil). ‖ Coude, tournant *m.* (of the road). ‖ Détour *m.* (*to*, vers) [on the road]. ‖ Tour *m.*; promenade *f.* (*on*, sur) [walk]. ‖ Contour, galbe *m.* (of the arm). ‖ Tour *m.*; *by turns*, tour à tour; *it's your turn to*, c'est votre tour de, c'est à vous de; *turn and turn about*, à tour de rôle. ‖ Tournure, orientation *f.* (of affairs, discussion, things). ‖ Penchant *m.*; disposition, aptitude *f.* (*for*, pour). ‖ Tournure, disposition *f.* (of mind). ‖ Intention *f.*; but, dessein *m.*; *to serve s.o.'s turn*, faire l'affaire de qqn. ‖ Procédé *m.*; *bad turn*, mauvais tour; *to do s.o. a good turn*, rendre un service à qqn. ‖ Changement *m.* (in circumstances); tournant *m.* (in events); fin *f.* (of the century). ‖ Instant *m.*; *at every turn*, à tout bout de champ. ‖ MILIT. *Right-about turn*, demi-tour à droite. ‖ AUTOM., AVIAT. Virage *m.*; *a good turn of speed*, bonne allure. ‖ NAUT. Giration *f.* (of the ship); changement *m.* (of the tide); saute *f.* (of wind). ‖ MED. Tournure *f.* (of illness). ‖ GRAMM. Tournure *f.* (of a sentence). ‖ MUS. Grupetto *m.* ‖ THEATR. *Music-hall turn*, numéro. ‖ FAM. Choc, coup *m.*; *it gave me a turn*, ça m'a donné un coup (or) une émotion. ‖ FAM. Ombre *f.*; brin *m.*; *not to do a turn of work*, ne pas en ficher une ramée. ‖ LOC. Done to a turn, à point. ‖ **Turn-away**, n. NAUT. Dérobement *m.* ‖ **Turn-cap**, n. ARCHIT. Capuchon *m.* (of chimney). ‖ **Turn-down**, adj. Rabattu (collar). ‖ **Turn-in**, n. Rentré *m.* ‖ **Turn-indicator**, n. U. S. AUTOM. Flèche *f.*; clignotant *m.* ‖ **Turn-out**, n. Foule, assemblée *f.* (crowd); grève *f.* (strike); attelage *m.* (team); CH. DE F. Aiguillage *m.*; voie (*f.*) d'évitement; U. S. AUTOM. Garage *m.* (in a road). ‖ **Turn-screw**, n. Tournevis *m.* ‖ **Turn-table**, CH. DE F. Plaque tournante *f.*; MILIT. Plate-forme tournante *f.*; ARTS. Sellette *f.*; MUS. Tourne-disques. ‖ **Turn-up**, n. Pliant *m.* (bed); retourne *f.* (at cards); revers *m.* (of trousers); FAM. Bagarre *f.* (quarrel).

turnbuckle [-,bʌkl] n. Tourniquet *m.* (for shutters). ‖ TECHN. Lanterne (*f.*) de serrage. ‖ AVIAT. Tendeur *m.* ‖ NAUT. Ridoir *m.*

turncoat [-kout] n. Renégat, transfuge, paillasse *m.*; girouette *f.* (fam.).

turner ['tə:nə*] n. TECHN. Tourneur *m.*

turnery [-ri] n. TECHN. Tournage *m.* (art, work); objets tournés *m. pl.* (product); tournerie *f.* (workshop).

turning [-iŋ] n. Action (*f.*) de tourner. ‖ Tournant *m.* (of the road). ‖ Rue (*f.*) qui croise (street). ‖ AUTOM., AVIAT. Virage *m.* ‖ TECHN. Tournage *m.* ‖ **Turning-point**, n. Moment décisif, tournant *m.*

turnip [tə:nip] n. BOT. Navet *m.* ‖ **Turnip-top**, n. Fanes (*f. pl.*) de navet. ‖ **Turnip-watch**, n. Oignon *m.* (watch).

turnkey ['tə:nki:] n. Geôlier, gardien (*m.*) de prison; guichetier, porte-clefs *m.*

turnover [-ouvə*] n. Renversement *m.* ‖ Retour *m.* (of a sheet). ‖ Revers *m.* (of stockings). ‖ Texte (*m.*) chevauchant sur deux pages (text). ‖ COMM. Chiffre (*m.*) d'affaires. ‖ CULIN. Chausson *m.*

turnpike [-paik] n. † Barrière (*f.*) route (*f.*) de péage. ‖ MILIT. Chevaux (*m. pl.*) de frise. ‖ U. S. Autoroute *f.*

turnsole [-soul] n. BOT. Tournesol *m.*

turnspit [-spit] n. CULIN. Tournebroche *m.*

turnstile [-stail] n. Tourniquet *m.* (at entrance).

turpentine ['tə:pəntain] n. CHIM. Térébenthine *f.*

turpitude ['tə:pitju:d] n. Turpitude *f.*

turps [tə:ps] n. sg. FAM. Térébenthine *f.*

turquoise ['tə:kwɔiz] n. Turquoise *f.* ‖ **Turquoise-blue**, adj. Bleu turquoise.

turret ['tʌrit] n. Tourelle f.
— v. tr. Garnir de tourelles.
turriculate [tə'rikjuleit] adj. Zool. Turriculé.
turtle ['tə:tl] n. Zool. Tortue de mer f. ‖ Loc.
To turn turtle, capoter (car, plane); chavirer (ship).
‖ **Turtle-neck**, adj. U. S. Roulé (collar). ‖ **Turtle-shell**, n. Ecaille de tortue f. ‖ **Turtle-soup**, n.
Culin. Potage (m.) à la tortue.
turtle-dove [-dʌv] n. Zool. Tourterelle f. ‖ Fam.
Tourtereau m.
turtler [-ə*] n. Pêcheur (m.) de tortues.
Tuscan ['tʌskən] adj., n. Geogr. Toscan s.
Tuscany [-i] n. Geogr. Toscane f.
tush [tʌʃ] n. Zool. Canine f. (of horse).
tush interj. Peuh!
tusk [tʌsk] n. Zool. Broche f. (of boar); défense
f. (of elephant). ‖ Agric. Dent f. ‖ Techn. Mordâne m.
— v. tr. Blesser d'un coup de défense.
tusker [-ə*] n. Zool. Eléphant adulte m.
tussle ['tʌsl] n. Bagarre f.; verbal tussle, prise de
bec.
— v. intr. Se bagarrer; se flanquer une peignée,
se crêper le chignon (fam.).
tussock ['tʌsək] n. Agric. Touffe d'herbe f.
tussore ['tʌsɔ:*] n. Tussor m.
tut [tʌt] interj. Ta ta ta!; tu tu!; flûte!
— v. intr. (1). Dire (or) émettre des ta ta ta,
exprimer sa désapprobation.
tutelage ['tju:tilidʒ] n. Tutelle f. (function,
period).
tutelary ['tju:tiləri] adj. Tutélaire.
tutenag ['tju:tinæg] n. Maillechort m.
tutor ['tju:tə*] n. Précepteur, répétiteur m. (in a
family); professeur-moniteur m. (in a university).
‖ Jur. Tuteur m.
— v. tr. Servir de répétiteur (or) de moniteur à.
‖ Jur. Etre tuteur de.
tutorage [-ridʒ] n. Jur. Tutelle f. (charge, duties).
tutoress [-ris] n. Institutrice, répétitrice; monitrice
f. ‖ Jur. Tutrice f.
tutorial [tju'tɔ:riəl] adj. De précepteur; de moniteur; tutorial system, système du monitorat par
répétiteurs-professeurs.
— n. Travaux pratiques m. pl.
tutorship ['tju:təʃip] n. Fonctions (f. pl.) de moniteur. ‖ Jur. Tutelle f.
tut-tut ['tʌt'tʌt] See tut.
tutu ['tu:tu:] n. Theatr. Tutu m.
tu-whoo [tu'hwu:] n. Ululement m.
— v. intr. Ululer.
tuxedo [tʌk'si:dɔ] n. U. S. Smoking m.
tuyere [twi:'jɛə*] n. Techn. Tuyère f.
T. V. [,ti:'vi:] abbr. television, télévision, télé.
twaddle ['twɔdl] n. Fariboles, niaiseries f. pl.;
verbiage m.
— v. intr. Jacasser, débiter des fariboles.
twaddler [-ə*] n. Débiteur (m.) de niaiseries.
twain [twein] adj. † Deux.
twang [twæŋ] v. intr. Mus. Résonner, frémir (harp,
string); to twang on, gratter de (a guitar). ‖ Fam.
Nasiller (person).
— v. tr. Mus. Gratter de (a guitar); faire vibrer
(a string). ‖ Fam. Dire en nasillant.
— n. Mus. Son vibrant m. ‖ Fam. Parler nasillard m.
twat [twæt] n. Arg. Con m. (female genitals).
‖ Con s. (stupid person).
tweak [twi:k] v. tr. Pincer en tordant; to tweak
s.o.'s nose, moucher qqn.
— n. Pinçon m.; torsion f.
twee [twi:] adj. Fam. Cucul adj. invar., chichiteux.
tweed [twi:d] n. Geogr., Comm. Tweed m.
tweedle ['twi:dl] v. intr. Mus. Seriner (or) racler
un air.
— v. tr. Fam. Entortiller (s.o.).

Tweedledum [-dʌm] loc. Fam. It's Tweedledum
and Tweedledee, c'est toujours la même chanson
(or) du pareil au même.
tween-decks ['twi:n'deks] n. Naut. Entrepont m.
tweeny ['twi:ni] n. Fam. Cigarillo m. (cigar);
petite aide de maison f. (servant).
tweet [twi:t] v. intr. Zool. Pépier.
— n. Pépiement m.
tweezers ['twi:zəz] n. pl. Techn. Pince f. (tool);
pince à épiler.
— v. tr. Enlever à la pince.
twelfth [twelfθ] adj. Douzième. ‖ Douze (chapter,
date, king). ‖ **Twelfth-cake**, n. Culin. Galette (f.)
des Rois. ‖ **Twelfth-day**, n. Jour (m.) des Rois,
Epiphanie f. ‖ **Twelfth-night**, n. Veille (f.) des
Rois.
— n. Douzième s.
twelfthly [-li] adv. Douzièmement.
twelve [twelv] adj., n. Douze m.
twelvemo [-mou] adj., n. In-douze m.
twelvemonth [-mʌnθ] n. Année f.; this day twelvemonth, dans un an aujourd'hui (future); il y a un
an aujourd'hui (past).
twentieth ['twentiiθ] adj., n. Vingtième s.
twenty ['twenti] adj., n. Vingt m.
twerp [twə:p] n. Fam. Andouille f., couillon m.
twice [twais] adv. Deux fois; twice as tall, plus
grand du double; twice as many planes, deux fois
plus d'avions. ‖ **Twice-told tale**, n. Fam. Du
réchauffé m.
twiddle ['twidl] v. tr. Tortiller (one's hat); to
twiddle one's thumbs, se tourner les pouces.
— v. intr. Jouer (with, avec).
— n. Tortillement m.
twig [twig] n. Bot. Brindille, ramille f. ‖ Baguette
f. (dowser's).
twig v. tr. Fam. Saisir, piger.
twilight ['twailait] n. Crépuscule m. (See dusk.)
‖ Arts. Demi-jour m. ‖ Fig. Crépuscule m.
— adj. Crépusculaire. ‖ Obscurci, assombri; twilight effect, demi-jour. ‖ Med. Crépusculaire, demi-conscient.
twill [twil] n. Twill, croisé m.
— v. tr. Croiser.
twin [twin] adj. Med. Jumeau m.; jumelle f. ‖
Techn. Jumelé. ‖ Naut. Frère, jumeau. ‖ Bot.
Double. ‖ **Twin-beds**, n. pl. Lits jumeaux m. pl.
‖ **Twin-boom**, n. Aviat. Bipoutre f. ‖ **Twin-engine**, adj. Aviat. Bimoteur. ‖ **Twin-track**, adj.
Ch. de F. A deux voies. ‖ **Twin-wire**, n. Electr.
Fil torsadé m.
— n. Med. Jumeau m.; jumelle f.; Siamese twins,
frères siamois. ‖ Astron. Pl. Gémeaux m. pl.
— v. intr. Med. Avoir des jumeaux. ‖ Fig. S'apparier (with, à).
twine [twain] n. Ficelle f.; fil retors m. ‖ Enchevêtrement, entrelacement m. ‖ Méandre m. (of a
river); repli m. (of a snake).
— v. tr. Tordre, tortiller (threads). ‖ Tresser, entrelacer (wreath); to twine about (or) around, enrouler
autour de; to twine one's arms round s.o., entourer
qqn de ses bras, enlacer qqn.
— v. intr. S'entrelacer. ‖ Serpenter (road). ‖ S'enrouler (about, round, autour de).
twiner [-ə*] n. Techn. Retordoir m. ‖ Bot. Plante
volubile f.
twinge [twindʒ] v. intr. Med. Elancer. ‖ Fig. Lanciner, tourmenter.
— n. Med. Elancement m. ‖ Fig. Lancinement m.;
brûlure f. (of remorse).
twining ['twainiŋ] adj. Med., Fig. Lancinant.
twining [-iŋ] adj. Sinueux (river, road). ‖ Bot.
Volubile.
twinkle ['twiŋkl] v. intr. Scintiller, étinceler (star).
‖ Fig. Pétiller (with, de).
— v. tr. Faire étinceler (light). ‖ Faire clignoter
(eyes).

— n. Scintillement *m.* (of light); lueur clignotante *f.* (light). ‖ Clin d'œil *m.; in a twinkle,* en une seconde. ‖ Fig. Pétillement *m.* (of the eyes).

twinkling [-iŋ] n. Scintillement *m.* (of stars). ‖ Clignement, clignotement *m.* (of eyelids); pétillement *m.* (of eyes). ‖ Fam. *In the twinkling of an eye,* en un clin d'œil.

— adj. Scintillant; clignotant. ‖ Fig. Pétillant.

twirl [twə:l] v. tr. Faire tournoyer (a wheel). ‖ Tortiller, friser (one's moustache); *to twirl one's thumbs,* se tourner les pouces.

— v. intr. Tournoyer.

— n. Tournoiement *m.;* rotation *f.* ‖ Fioriture *f.* (in writing). ‖ Volute *f.* (of smoke). ‖ Archit. Volute *f.* ‖ Arts. Pirouette *f.* (of dancers). ‖ Sports. Moulinet *m.* (in fencing).

twirp [twə:p] n. See TWERP.

twist [twist] n. Torsion *f.* (of thread). ‖ Cordonnet *m.* (thread). ‖ Torsade *f.* (of hair); cornet, tortillon *m.* (of paper); carotte *f.,* boudin *m.* (of tobacco). ‖ Tournant, coude *m.* (of the road). ‖ Contorsion *f.* (of the face). ‖ Med. Entorse, foulure *f.; to give one's ankle a twist,* se fouler la cheville. ‖ Sports. Effet *m.* (on the ball); *twist of the wrist,* tour de poignet. ‖ Techn. Gondolage *m.* ‖ Culin. Fam. Feuilleté torsadé *m.* (pastry). ‖ Gramm. Déformation *f.* ‖ Fig. Entorse *f.* (to the truth). ‖ Fig. Perversion *f.; criminal twist,* tendances criminelles; *mental twist,* déformation mentale. ‖ **Twist-drill,** n. Techn. Foret hélicoïdal *m.*

— v. tr. Tordre, cordonner (thread). ‖ Tresser, entrelacer (a garland); torsader (hair); tire-bouchonner (one's handkerchief); torquer (tobacco). ‖ Entrelacer (*with,* de); entortiller (*round,* autour de). ‖ Tordre, déformer, contorsionner (s.o.'s face). ‖ Med. Fouler (one's ankle); déboîter (one's knee). ‖ Sports. Donner de l'effet à (a ball). ‖ Gramm., Fig. Déformer, dénaturer (meaning, truth). ‖ Fam. *You can twist him round your little finger,* on en fait ce qu'on veut, on l'entortille facilement. ‖ **To twist off,** arracher en tordant. ‖ **To twist up,** tordre en spirale (or) en cornet.

— v. intr. Se tordre, s'enrouler, s'entortiller (thread). ‖ Se tordre en spirale (paper). ‖ Serpenter (road). ‖ Se tordre, se tortiller, se contorsionner (person). ‖ Se faufiler, se glisser (*through,* à travers). ‖ Bot. Vriller, vrillonner. ‖ Zool. Se tortiller (worm).

twister [-ə*] n. Tordeur, retordeur *m.* (person); retordoir *m.* (tool). ‖ Sports. Balle (*f.*) qui a de l'effet. ‖ U. S. Tornade *f.* ‖ Fam. *That's a twister for him,* ça lui donnera du fil à retordre.

twit [twit] v. tr. (1). Rappeler une faute à; *to twit s.o. with sth.,* reprocher qqch. à qqn.

twit n. Fam. Cloche *f.,* cornichon *m.*

twitch [twitʃ] n. Bot. Chiendent *m.*

twitch n. Saccade *f.;* coup sec *m.* ‖ Crispation *f.* (of hands); tiraillements *m. pl.* (in the stomach); *facial twitch,* tic.

— v. intr. Se crisper, se contracter.

— v. tr. Tirer d'un coup sec. ‖ **To twitch off,** arracher d'une secousse.

twite [twait] n. Zool. Linotte *f.*

twitter ['twitə*] n. Zool. Gazouillement, gazouillis *m.* ‖ Fam. Agitation *f.*

— v. intr., tr. Zool., Fam. Gazouiller.

twittingly [-iŋli] adv. D'un ton de reproche.

two [tu:] adj., n. Deux *m.; in two,* en deux; *to have two of everything,* avoir tout en double; *to go two and two,* aller deux à deux; *to put two and two together,* faire un rapprochement et tirer des conclusions. ‖ **Two-bladed,** adj. Aviat. Bipale. ‖ **Two-cleft,** adj. Bot. Bifide. ‖ **Two-dimensional,** adj. A deux dimensions; incomplet. ‖ **Two-edged,** adj. A deux tranchants (lit. and fig.). ‖ **Two-engined,** adj. Aviat. Bimoteur; *two-engined jet plane,* biréacteur. ‖ **Two-faced,** adj. A double face

(lit. and fig.). ‖ **Two-handed,** adj. A deux mains; *two-handed sword,* espadon. ‖ **Two legged,** adj. Bipède. ‖ **Two-master,** n. Naut. Deux-mâts *m.* ‖ **Two-phase,** adj. Electr. Diphasé. ‖ **Two-piece,** adj. En deux pièces; *two-piece bathing-suit,* maillot deux-pièces. ‖ **Two-ply,** adj. Double, redoublé. ‖ **Two-seater,** n. Autom., Aviat. Biplace *m.* ‖ **Two-sided,** adj. Bilatéral; Fig. A deux aspects. ‖ **Two-speed,** n. A deux vitesses. ‖ **Two-step,** n. Mus. Two-step *m.* ‖ **Two-stroke,** adj. Techn. A deux temps. ‖ **Two-time,** v. tr. U. S. Fam. Cocufier (one's husband, wife). ‖ **Two-timer,** n. U. S. Fam. Faux jeton, fourbe *m.* ‖ **Two-way,** adj. A deux sens (street); à deux arrivées (tap); Electr. Va-et-vient; Radio. Emetteur-récepteur.

twofold [-fould] adj. Double.

— adv. Doublement; deux fois plus.

twopence ['tʌpəns] n. pl. Deux pence *m. pl.* ‖ Fam. *Not care twopence,* s'en ficher.

twopenny [-pəni] adj. De deux pence. ‖ Fam. De quatre sous.

twosome ['tu:səm] n. Danse (*f.*) par couple. ‖ U. S. Couple *m.*

tycoon [tai'ku:n] n. Fam. Magnat (*m.*) de la finance; brasseur (*m.*) d'affaires.

tye [tai] n. Naut. Itague *f.*

tying [-iŋ]. See TIE.

tyke [taik] n. Fam. Cabot *m.* (dog). ‖ Fam. Natif (*m.*) du Yorkshire. ‖ U. S. Fam. Gosse *m.* (kid).

tympan ['timpən] n. Med., Archit., Techn. Tympan *m.*

tympanic [tim'pænik] adj. Med. Tympanique.

tympanist ['timpənist] n. Mus. Timbalier *m.*

tympanum ['timpənəm] n. Med., Archit., Techn. Tympan *m.*

typal ['taipəl] adj. Typique. ‖ Techn. Typographique.

type [taip] n. Type, spécimen, exemple *m.* ‖ Type, genre *m.;* sorte *f.* (kind). ‖ Chim., Arts. Type *m.* ‖ Techn. Caractère (*m.*) d'imprimerie. ‖ **Type-area,** n. Techn. Justification *f.* ‖ **Type-cast,** v. tr. (32). Theatr. Attribuer toujours le même rôle à; *he's typecast as a murderer,* on lui fait toujours jouer les meurtriers. ‖ **Type-script,** n. Texte dactylographié *m.* ‖ **Type-setter,** n. Techn. Compositeur *m.* ‖ **Type-setting,** n. Techn. Composition *f.*

— v. tr. Représenter le type de; typer (fam.). ‖ Dactylographier, taper. ‖ Med. Chercher le groupe sanguin sur (a blood sample).

typewrite [-rait] v. tr. (195). Dactylographier, taper.

typewriter [-raitə*] n. Machine (*f.*) à écrire. ‖ Dactylographe s. (person).

typewriting [-raitiŋ] n. Dactylographie *f.*

typewritten [-ritn] adj. Dactylographié.

typhlitis [ti'flaitis] n. Med. Typhlite *f.*

typhoid ['taifɔid] adj., n. Med. Typhoïde *f.*

typhoidal [tai'fɔidl] adj. Med. Typhoïdique.

typhoon [tai'fu:n] n. Typhon *m.*

typhous ['taifəs] adj. Med. Typhique.

typhus ['taifəs] n. Med. Typhus *m.*

typical ['tipikəl] adj. Typique, caractéristique.

typically ['tipikəli] adv. Typiquement; *he is typically English,* c'est le type de l'Anglais (or) l'Anglais type.

typification [,tipifi'keiʃən] n. Représentation, figuration *f.* ‖ Type, spécimen *m.*

typify ['tipifai] v. tr. (2). Figurer, représenter, symboliser; être le type de.

typing ['taipiŋ] n. Dactylographie *f.* (act).

typist [-ist] n. Dactylographe, dactylo s. ‖ **Typist-invoice-clerk,** n. Dactylo-facturière *f.* ‖ **Typist-stenographer,** n. U. S. Sténo-dactylo s.

typographer [tai'pɔgrəfə*] n. Typographe; typo *m.* (fam.).

typographic(al) [,taipo'græfik(əl)] adj. Typogra-

phique; *typographical error,* coquille. ‖ U. S. Fam. De frappe, de dactylographie (error).
typography [tai'pɔgrəfi] n. Typographie *f.*
typological [ˌtaipə'lɔdʒikl̩] adj. Typologique.
typology [tai'pɔlədʒi] n. Typologie *f.*
tyrannical [ti'rænikəl] adj. Tyrannique.
tyrannically [-i] adv. Tyranniquement.
tyrannicide [ti'rænisaid] n. Tyrannicide *m.*
tyrannize ['tirənaiz] v. intr. Agir en tyran (*over,* envers); exercer la tyrannie (*over,* contre).
— v. tr. Tyranniser.
tyrannous [-nəs] adj. Tyrannique.
tyranny [-ni] n. Tyrannie *f.* (act, despotism).

tyrant ['taiərənt] n. Tyran *m.*
tyre ['taiə*] n. Autom. Pneu *m.* ‖ **Tyre-lever,** n. Démonte-pneu *m.*
Tyrian ['tiriən] adj. De Tyr (purple).
— n. Geogr. Tyrien *s.*
tyro ['tairo] n. Fam. Novice, néophyte, blanc-bec *m.*
Tyrol ['tirəl] n. Geogr. Tyrol *m.*
Tyrolese ['tirə'li:z] adj., n. Geogr. Tyrolien *s.*
tyrolienne [ti,rouli'en] n. Mus. Tyrolienne *f.*
Tyrrhenian [ti'ri:njən] adj. Geogr. Tyrrhénien (Sea).
tzar [tzɑ*]. See CZAR.
tzigane [tzi'gɑ:n] adj., n. Tzigane *s.* (See GYPSY.)

U

u [ju:] n. U, u *m.; U-shaped,* en U. ‖ **U-boat,** n. Naut. Sous-marin allemand *m.* ‖ **U-turn,**, n. Autom. Demi-tour *m.;* Fig. Volte-face *f. invar.,* revirement *m.*
— adj. Qui se fait, distingué, bien.
ubiquitous [ju'bikwitəs] adj. Doué d'ubiquité. ‖ Eccles. Omniprésent.
ubiquity [-ti] n. Ubiquité *f.* ‖ Eccles. Omniprésence *f.*
udder [ʌdə*] n. Mamelle *f.;* pis *m.*
udometer [ju'dɔmitə*] n. Techn. Udomètre, pluviomètre *m.*
U.F.O. ['ju:fou] abbr. *unidentified flying object,* objet volant non identifié, ovni.
Uganda [ju:'gændə] n. Geogr. Ouganda *m.*
ugh [uh] interj. Pouah!
uglification ['ʌglifi'keiʃən] n. Enlaidissement *m.*
uglify ['ʌglifai] v. tr. (2). Enlaidir.
uglily [-li] adv. Laidement.
ugliness [-nis] n. Laideur *f.*
ugly ['ʌgli] adj. Laid (person); *as ugly as sin,* laid comme le péché; *to grow ugly,* enlaidir. ‖ Dangereux (dangerous); vilain (unpleasant); *an ugly customer,* un sale type; un individu dangereux; *to look ugly,* avoir vilain aspect (person); prendre mauvaise tournure (situation).
U.H.F. [ˌju:eitʃ'ef] abbr. *Ultrahigh frequency,* ultra-haute fréquence, U. H. F.
uhlan ['u:lən] n. Milit. Uhlan *m.*
U.K. [ˌju:'kei] abbr. *United Kingdom,* Royaume-Uni.
ukase [ju:'keiz] n. Ukase *m.*
ukulele [ˌju:kə'leili] n. Mus. Ukulélé *m.*
ulcer ['ʌlsə*] n. Med. Ulcère *m.*
ulcerate [-reit] v. tr. Med. Ulcérer.
— v. intr. Med. S'ulcérer.
ulcerated [-reitid] adj. Med. Ulcéré, ulcéreux.
ulceration [ˌʌlsə'reiʃən] n. Med. Ulcération *f.*
ulcered ['ʌlsəd] adj. Med. Ulcéré, ulcéreux.
ulcerous ['ʌlsərəs] adj. Med. Ulcéreux.
ullage ['ʌlidʒ] n. Vidange *f.* (dry); *filling up of the ullage,* ouillage. ‖ Fam. Lie, lavasse *f.* (dregs).
— v. tr. Ouiller (to fill); tirer du liquide de (to draw liquid from).
ullaged [-d] adj. En vidange.
ulmin ['ʌlmin] n. Chim. Ulmine *f.*
ulna ['ʌlnə] n. Med. Cubitus *m.*

ulnar [-ə*] adj. Med. Ulnaire, cubital.
Ulster ['ʌlstə*] n. Geogr., Comm. Ulster *m.*
ult [ʌlt], **ultimo** [-imo] adv. Comm. Du mois dernier.
ulterior [ʌl'tiariə*] adj. Ultérieur. ‖ Inavoué, secret (motive).
ulteriorly [-li] adv. Ultérieurement.
ultimate ['ʌltimit] n. Absolu *m.*
— adj. Ultime, dernier (see FINAL); définitif; extrême. ‖ Fondamental (cause); élémentaire (truth).
ultimately [-li] adv. A la fin; en fin de compte; finalement, en dernier lieu; *he ultimately accepted it,* il finit par l'accepter.
ultimatum [ˌʌlti'meitəm] n. Ultimatum *m.*
ultimo ['ʌlti,mou] adv. See ULT.
Ultonian [ʌl'touniən] adj. Geogr. Ulstérien *s.*
ultra ['ʌltrə] n., adj. Ultra *m.*
ultra– préfixe. Ultra-. ‖ **Ultra-critical,** adj. Hypercritique. ‖ **Ultra-fashionable,** adj. A la dernière mode, ultra-chic. ‖ **Ultra-liberal,** n., adj. Ultra-libéral *s.* ‖ **Ultra-modern,** adj. Ultra-moderne. ‖ **Ultra-rapid,** adj. Ultra-rapide. ‖ **Ultra-rich,** adj. Richissime. ‖ **Ultra-royalist,** n., adj. Ultra-royaliste *s.* ‖ **Ultra-short,** adj. Phys. Ultra-court. ‖ **Ultra-sound,** n. Phys. Ultra-son *m.* ‖ **Ultra-violet,** adj. Phys. Ultraviolet. ‖ **Ultra-virtuous,** adj. Prude.
ultracentrifuge [ˌʌltrə'sentri,fju:dʒ] n. Techn. Ultracentrifugeuse *f.*
ultrahigh ['ʌltrə,hai] adj. Radio. *Ultrahigh frequency,* ultra-haute fréquence.
ultraist [-ist] n., adj. Ultra *m.*
ultramarine [ˌʌltrəmə'ri:n] adj. D'outre-mer.
— n. Outremer, bleu d'outremer *m.* (colour).
ultramicroscope [ˌʌltrə'maikrə,skoup] n. Ultramicroscope *m.*
ultramicroscopic [-,maikrə'skɔpik] adj. Ultramicroscopique.
ultramontane [ˌʌltrə'mɔntein] adj., n. Ultramontain *s.*
ultramundain [ˌʌltrə'mʌndein] adj. Ultramondain.
ultrasonic [-'sɔnik] adj. Ultrasonore, supersonique.
ultrastructure ['ʌltrə,strʌktʃə*] n. Ultrastructure *f.*

ultra vires [ˈʌltrə ˈvairiːz] adv. JUR. *To act ultra vires*, commettre un abus de pouvoir. — adj. JUR. Au-delà des pouvoirs.

ululate [ˈjuːljuleit] v. intr. Ululer. ‖ Hurler.

ululation [ˌjuːljuˈleiʃən] n. Ululement *m.* ‖ Hurlement *m.*

Ulysses [juˈlisiːz] n. Ulysse *m.*

umbel [ˈʌmbəl] n. BOT. Ombelle *f.*

umbellate [ˈʌmbeleit] adj. BOT. Ombellé.

umbelliferous [ˌʌmbeˈlifərəs] adj. BOT. Ombellifère.

umbelliform [ʌmˈbelifɔːm] adj. BOT. Ombelliforme.

umber [ˈʌmbə*] adj. ARTS. Couleur d'ombre. — n. ARTS. Ombre, terre d'ombre *f.*

umbilical [ʌmˈbilikəl] adj. MED. Ombilical. ‖ FAM. Du côté maternel, par les femmes (relationship).

umbilicate [-keit] adj. Ombiliqué.

umbilicus [-kəs] n. MED. Ombilic *m.* (See NAVEL.)

umbra [ˈʌmbrə] (pl. umbrae [-briː]) n. Ombre *f.*

umbrage [-bridʒ] n. Ombrage *m.* (in poetry). ‖ Ombrage *m.; to take umbrage at*, prendre ombrage de, se froisser de.

umbrageous [ʌmˈbreidʒəs] adj. Ombragé (place). ‖ FIG. Ombrageux (person).

umbrella [ʌmˈbrelə] n. Parapluie *m.; beach umbrella*, parasol. ‖ AVIAT. *Air umbrella*, écran (or) rideau de protection (*f.*) aérienne. ‖ FIG. Protection *f.* (in politics). ‖ ZOOL. Ombrelle *f.* (of jelly-fish). ‖ **Umbrella-shaped**, adj. En forme de parasol. ‖ **Umbrella-stand**, n. Porte-parapluies *m. invar.* ‖ **Umbrella-tree**, n. BOT. Magnolier parasol *m.*

umlaut [ˈumlaut] n. GRAMM. Umlaut *m.;* métaphonie *f.* (See MUTATION.)

umpirage [ˈʌmpaiəridʒ] n. Arbitrage *m.*

umpire [-paiə*] n. Arbitre *m.* — v. tr., intr. Arbitrer.

umpiring [-paiəriŋ] n. Arbitrage *m.*

umpteen [ʌmpˈtiːn] adj. FAM. Je ne sais combien, trente-six.

umpteenth [-θ] adj. FAM. Trente-sixième (time).

'un [ʌn] pron. FAM. *A bad'un*, un vilain coco; *a little'un*, un petiot; *a rum'un*, un drôle de numéro.

un- pref. A-, anti-, dé-, in-, non-, peu, sans (before a noun); dé-, dés- (before a verb).

U.N. [ˌjuːˈen] abbr. *United Nations,* Nations unies, O. N. U.

unabashed [ˌʌnəˈbæʃt] adj. Imperturbable; sans se décontenancer.

unabated [-ˈbeitid] adj. Nom diminué (undiminished); sans répit (without respite); *with unabated interest*, avec un intérêt non diminué.

unabating [-ˈbeitiŋ].adj. Soutenu.

unabbreviated [ˌʌnəˈbriːvieitid] adj. Non abrégé.

unabetted [-ˈbetid] adj. Sans aide; sans complices.

unabiding [-ˈbaidiŋ] adj. Passager, éphémère.

unable [ʌˈneibl] adj. Incapable; *to be unable to do sth.*, ne pouvoir faire qqch.; être dans l'impossibilité de faire qqch.; ne pas être en mesure de faire qqch. ‖ Incompétent (person).

unabridged [ˌʌnəˈbridʒd] adj. Non abrégé; intégral; total.

unabsorbant [ˌʌnəbˈsɔːbənt] adj. Hydrofuge.

unaccented [ˌʌnækˈsentid] adj. Non accentué.

unaccentuated [-jueitid] adj. Non accentué.

unacceptable [ˌʌnækˈseptəbl] adj. Inacceptable; irrecevable; désagréable.

unaccepted [-id] adj. Inaccepté, non accepté.

unacclimatized [ˌʌnəˈklaimətaizd] adj. Mal acclimaté; inacclimaté.

unaccommodating [-ˈkɔmədeitiŋ] adj. Peu accommodant; de mauvaise composition.

unaccompanied [-ˈkʌmpənid] adj. Non accompagné. ‖ MUS. Seul.

unaccomplished [-ˈkɔmpliʃt] adj. Inachevé (unfinished); non réalisé (unrealized). ‖ Sans talents.

unaccountable [ˌʌnəˈkauntəbl] adj. Inexplicable,

étrange, bizarre. ‖ Qui ne doit de comptes à personne (*for*, au sujet de).

unaccountableness [-əblnis] n. Nature inexplicable *f.;* étrangeté, bizarrerie *f.* ‖ Irresponsabilité *f.*

unaccountably [-əbli] adv. Inexplicablement.

unaccounted [-id] adj. *Unaccounted for*, dont on est sans nouvelles (person); inexpliqué (phenomenon). ‖ COMM. Ne figurant pas au bilan. ‖ AVIAT. Manquant, qui n'est pas rentré, disparu.

unaccredited [ˌʌnəˈkreditid] adj. Non accrédité (person). ‖ Sans aucun crédit (source).

unaccustomed [-ˈkʌstəmd] adj. Inaccoutumé, non habituel. ‖ Inaccoutumé, peu habitué (*to*, à).

unachievable [-ˈtʃiːvəbl] adj. Irréalisable.

unacknowledged [ˌʌnəkˈnɔlidʒd] adj. Non reconnu, non avoué. ‖ Resté sans réponse (letter).

unacquaintance [ˌʌnəˈkweintəns] n. Manque (*m.*) de familiarité (*with*, avec).

unacquainted [-id] adj. Ignorant, qui n'est pas au courant (*with*, de) [sth.]. ‖ *Unacquainted with s.o.*, qui ne connaît pas qqn; qui n'a pas fait la connaissance de qqn; qui n'est pas en relation avec qqn.

unacquired [ˌʌnəˈkwaiəd] adj. Naturel, inné.

unadaptable [ˌʌnəˈdæptəbl] adj. Qui ne sait pas s'adapter.

unadapted [-id] adj. Mal adapté, inadapté.

unadmired [ˌʌnədˈmaiəd] adj. Sans admirateurs.

unadmiring [-riŋ] adj. Peu admiratif.

unadmitted [ˌʌnədˈmitid] adj. Inavoué. ‖ Non admis.

unadopted [ˌʌnəˈdɔptid] adj. Non adopté (resolution). ‖ Non entretenu par la municipalité (road).

unadorned [-ˈdɔːnd] adj. Sans ornements, sans parure; naturel. ‖ FIG. Sans fard.

unadulterated [-ˈdʌltəreitid] adj. Non falsifié, non frelaté. ‖ FIG. Pur, sans mélange.

unadvisable [ˌʌnədˈvaizəbl] adj. Imprudent; à déconseiller (action); rebelle à tout avis, opiniâtre (person).

unadvisableness [-nis] n. Imprudence *f.*

unadvised [ˌʌnədˈvaizd] adj. Imprudent, irréfléchi. ‖ Sans avoir pris conseil.

unadvisedly [-li] adv. Imprudemment.

unaffected [ˌʌnəˈfektid] adj. Insensible (*by*, à) [person]; qui résiste (*by*, à) [thing]. ‖ Naturel, sans affectation. ‖ Sincère, véritable. ‖ MED. Indemne, non atteint.

unaffectedly [-li] adv. Sans affectation. ‖ Simplement. ‖ Sincèrement.

unaffectedness [-nis] n. Absence d'affectation *f.* ‖ Simplicité *f.* ‖ Sincérité *f.*

unaffiliated [ˌʌnəˈfilieitid] adj. Non affilié (*to*, à).

unafraid [ˌʌnəˈfraid] adj. Sans peur, sans crainte.

unaggressive [-ˈgresiv] adj. Peu agressif.

unaided [ʌnˈeidid] adj. Seul, sans aide.

unalarmed [ˌʌnəˈlɑːmd] adj. Sans inquiétude.

unalienable [ʌnˈeiljənəbl] adj. Inaliénable.

unallayed [ˌʌnəˈleid] adj. Inapaisé (grief).

unalleviated [-ˈliːvieitid] adj. Qui n'est pas soulagé; sans soulagement.

unallotted [-ˈlɔtid] adj. Disponible (free). ‖ Non réparti (not divided up).

unallowable [ˌʌnəˈlauəbl̩] adj. Inadmissible.

unallowed [-ˈlaud] adj. Interdit, défendu, non permis, illicite.

unalloyed [-ˈlɔid] adj. Sans alliage, pur. ‖ FIG. Sans mélange, pur.

unalterable [ʌnˈɔːltərəbl] adj. Immuable.

unalterableness [-əblnis] n. Invariabilité *f.*

unalterably [-əbli] adv. Immuablement.

unaltered [ʌnˈɔːltəd] adj. Inchangé, sans changement, non modifié.

unambiguous [ˌʌnæmˈbigjuəs] adj. Sans ambiguïté, non équivoque.

unambitious [-ˈbiʃəs] adj. Peu ambitieux. ‖ Modeste, sans prétention.

unamenable [‚ʌnə'miːnəbl̩] adj. Réfractaire (*to*, à). ‖ Peu commode, difficile (awkward).

un-American [‚ʌnə'merikən] adj. Anti-américain, antipatriotique.

unamiable [ʌn'eimjəbl̩] adj. Peu aimable.

unanimated [ʌn'ænimeitid] adj. Sans animation.

unanimity [‚juːnə'nimiti], **unanimousness** [juː'næniməsnis] n. Unanimité *f*.

unanimous [juː'næniməs] adj. Unanime.

unanimously [-li] adv. Unanimement, à l'unanimité ; d'un commun accord.

unannounced [‚ʌnə'naunst] adj. Sans être annoncé.

unanswerable [ʌn'ɑːnsərəbl̩] adj. Sans réplique, incontestable, irréfutable.

unanswered [-əd] adj. Resté sans réponse. ‖ Irréfuté (charge). ‖ Non payé de retour (love).

unanticipated [‚ʌnæn'tisipeitid] adj. Imprévu.

unappalled [‚ʌnə'pɔːld] adj. Impassible ; peu ému.

unapparent [-'pærənt] adj. Inapparent.

unappealing [-'piːliŋ] adj. Peu attirant (or) attrayant. ‖ Peu sympathique (person).

unappeasable [-'piːzəbl̩] adj. Inapaisable.

unappeased [-'piːzd] adj. Inapaisé.

unappetizing [ʌn'æpitaiziŋ] adj. Peu appétissant.

unapplied [‚ʌnə'plaid] adj. Inappliqué.

unappreciated [‚ʌnə'priːʃieitid] adj. Inapprécié ; méconnu ; incompris.

unappreciative [-ʃiətiv] adj. Insensible ; peu favorable.

unapprehensive [ʌn‚æpri'hensiv] adj. Sans appréhension ; insouciant (of danger). ‖ Lourd, sans vivacité (mind).

unapprised [‚ʌnə'praizd] adj. Ignorant.

unapproachable [-'prəutʃəbl̩] adj. Inabordable.

unappropriated [-'prouprieitid] adj. Libre, disponible. ‖ Sans destination précise.

unapproved [-'pruːvd] adj. *Unapproved of*, inapprouvé.

unapproving [-'pruːviŋ] adj. Désapprobateur *m*.; désapprobatrice *f*.

unapt [ʌn'æpt] adj. Inapte, incapable ; *unapt for*, inapte à. ‖ Impropre, inapproprié ; hors de propos (remark).

unaptness [-nis] n. Inaptitude *f*. (*for*, à). ‖ Impropriété *f*. ‖ Manque d'à-propos *m*.

unarm [ʌn'ɑːm] v. tr. Désarmer.

unarmed [-d] adj. Sans armes, désarmé. ‖ Bot., Zool. Inerme.

unartistic ['ʌnɑː'tistik] adj. Non artistique.

unascertained [‚ʌnæsə'teind] adj. Non vérifié.

unashamed [‚ʌnə'ʃeimd] adj. Sans honte, sans pudeur, sans vergogne.

unashamedly [-idli] adv. Carrément ; sans rougir.

unasked [ʌn'ɑːskt] adj. Non invité (guests). ‖ Sans y avoir été invité ; spontanément ; *never give advice unasked*, ne donnez jamais un avis qu'on ne vous demande pas. ‖ *Unasked for*, spontané ; immérité (undeserved).

unassailable [‚ʌnə'seiləbl̩] adj. Inattaquable.

unasserted [-'sə:tid] adj. Non affirmé.

unassertive [-'sə:tiv] adj. Timide, modeste.

unassignable [-'sainəbl̩] adj. Inassignable. ‖ Jur. Inaliénable.

unassimilated [-'simileitid] adj. Inassimilé. ‖ Fig. Mal assimilé.

unassisted [-'sistid] adj. Sans aide. (See UNAIDED.)

unassuming [-'sjuːmiŋ] adj. Modeste, simple, sans prétentions.

unattached [‚ʌnə'tætʃt] adj. Non attaché. ‖ Disponible (free for other duties) ; libre (without other commitments). ‖ Seul (alone). ‖ Indépendant.

unattackable [-'tækəbl̩] adj. Inattaquable.

unattainable [-'teinəbl̩] adj. Inaccessible (*by*, à).

unattended [-'tendid] adj. Seul, sans escorte ; non accompagné ; *unattended by*, non suivi de ; *unattended to*, négligé.

unattested [-'testid] adj. Non attesté.

unattired [-'taiəd] adj. Sans vêtements (undressed). ‖ Sans parure (unadorned).

unattractive [-'træktiv] adj. Peu attrayant, peu séduisant. ‖ Peu sympathique.

unauthentic [‚ʌnɔː'θentik] adj. Inauthentique.

unauthenticated [-eitid] adj. Non authentifié. ‖ D'auteur inconnu. ‖ Jur. Non légalisé.

unauthorized [ʌn'ɔːθəraizd] adj. Non autorisé, sans autorisation. ‖ Injustifié, abusif.

unavailability [‚ʌnəveilə'biliti] n. Indisponibilité *f*. ‖ Invalidité *f*.

unavailable [‚ʌnə'veiləbl̩] adj. Non disponible ; indisponible ; inutilisable.

unavailing [-'veiliŋ] adj. Vain, inutile, inefficace, infructueux.

unavenged [-'vendʒd] adj. Invengé.

unavoidable [‚ʌnə'vɔidəbl̩] adj. Inévitable.

unavoidableness [-bl̩nis] n. Inévitabilité *f*.

unavoidably [-bli] adv. Inévitablement.

unavowable [‚ʌnə'vauəbl̩] adj. Inavouable.

unavowed [-'vaud] adj. Inavoué.

unaware [‚ʌnə'wɛə*] adj. Ignorant, non informé (*of*, de ; *that*, que).

unawareness [-nis] n. Ignorance *f*.

unawares [-z] adv. Au dépourvu, à l'improviste (off one's guard). ‖ Par mégarde, par inadvertance (unintentionally), through carelessness).

unbacked [ʌn'bækt] adj. Sans appui, non épaulé (or) soutenu (candidate). ‖ Sports. Sur lequel on n'a pas parié (horse).

unbaked [ʌn'beikt] adj. Techn. Cru (brick).

unbalance [ʌn'bæləns] v. tr. Déséquilibrer.
— n. Manque d'équilibre *m*.

unbalanced [-t] adj. Mal (or) non équilibré. ‖ Fin. Non soldé (account). ‖ Fig. Déséquilibré, déplombé, désaxé (mind).

unballast [ʌn'bæləst] v. tr. Naut. Délester.

unbandage [ʌn'bændidʒ] v. tr. Méd. Débander.

unbaptized [‚ʌnbæp'taizd] adj. Non baptisé.

unbar [ʌn'bɑː*] v. tr. (1). Enlever la barre de, débarrer. ‖ Fig. Ouvrir.

unbarred [ʌn'bɑːd] adj. Débarré, ouvert. ‖ Mus. Non divisé en mesures.

unbarricade [‚ʌnbæri'keid] v. tr. Débarricader.

unbearable [ʌn'bɛərəbl̩] adj. Insupportable, intolérable ; atroce (agony).

unbearably [-bli] adv. Insupportablement.

unbearded [ʌn'biədid] adj. Imberbe.

unbeatable [ʌn'biːtəbl̩] adj. Invincible.

unbeaten [-n̩] adj. Invaincu. ‖ Non battu, inexploré (untrodden).

unbecoming [‚ʌnbi'kʌmiŋ] adj. Déplacé ; malséant ; inconvenant. ‖ Peu seyant (clothes).

unbecomingly [-li] adv. D'une manière déplacée (or) inconvenante (or) peu seyante.

unbecomingness [-nis] n. Manque (*m*.) de bienséance. ‖ Effet malheureux *m*. (of a dress).

unbefitting [‚ʌnbi'fitiŋ] adj. Qui ne sied pas, qui ne convient guère.

unbegotten [-'gɔtn̩] adj. Eccles. Non engendré.

unbeknown [-'noun] adj. Inconnu (*to*, de).
— adv. A l'insu (*to*, de).

unbelief [-'liːf] n. Incrédulité *f*.; scepticisme *m*.

unbelievable [‚ʌnbi'liːvəbl̩] adj. Incroyable.

unbeliever [-ə*] n. Incrédule *s*. ‖ Eccles. Incroyant *s*.

unbelieving [-iŋ] adj. Incrédule. ‖ Eccles. Incroyant.

unbeloved [‚ʌnbi'lʌvd] adj. Peu (or) non aimé.

unbend [ʌn'bend] v. intr. (16). Se mettre droit, se redresser. ‖ Se détendre, se déraidir, s'assouplir ; se dégeler (fam.) [person].
— v. tr. Redresser, détordre (to straighten). ‖ Débander (a bow). ‖ Fig. Détendre.

unbending [-iŋ] n. Redressement *m*. ‖ Fig. Affabilité *f*.
— adj. Inflexible, raide, ferme, rigide.

unbeneficial [,ʌnbene'fiʃəl] adj. Peu avantageux (or) profitable. ‖ Inefficace, peu salutaire (unsuccessful).

unbenefited [ʌn'benifitid] adj. Qui n'a pas tiré profit (*by*, de).

unbias(s)ed [-'baist] adj. SPORTS. Qui n'a pas de fort (bowl). ‖ FIG. Impartial, sans préjugé, sans parti pris, non prévenu.

unbidden [-'bidn̩] adj. Spontané. ‖ Non invité, intrus.

unbigoted [-'bigətid] adj. Sans esprit de parti, sans fanatisme.

unbind [ʌn'baind] v. tr. (21). Délier (to free); détacher, dénouer (to untie). ‖ MED. Débander (to unbandage).

unblamable [-'bleiməbl̩] adj. Irréprochable.

unbleached [-'bli:tʃt] adj. Non blanchi, écru; U. S. *unbleached muslin*, calico.

unblemished [-'blemiʃt] adj. Sans tache.

unblest [ʌn'blest] adj. ECCLES. Non béni. ‖ FIG. Infortuné.

unblindfold [-'blaindfould] v. tr. Débander les yeux à. ‖ FIG. Ouvrir les yeux à.

unblinking [-'bliŋkiŋ] adj. Qui ne cligne pas des yeux. ‖ FIG. Sans un battement de cils (or) de paupières, impénétrable, impassible.

unblock [ʌn'blɔk] v. tr. Dégager. ‖ Décaler (to unchock).

unblown [-'bloun] adj. BOT. Non épanoui.

unblushing [ʌn'blʌʃiŋ] adj. Qui ne rougit pas. ‖ FIG. Ehonté, sans vergogne.

unbolted [ʌn'boultid] adj. Déverrouillé. ‖ TECHN. Déboulonné.

unbolted adj. AGRIC. Non bluté (flour).

unbooted [-'bu:tid] adj. Débotté, déchaussé.

unborn [ʌn'bɔ:n] adj. A naître, futur.

unbosom [ʌn'buzəm] v. tr. Confier, découvrir; révéler. ‖ *To unbosom oneself*, s'épancher, ouvrir son cœur; se débonder, se déboutonner (fam.).

unbound [ʌn'baund] adj. Délié, détaché. ‖ Broché (book). ‖ FIG. Libre.

unbounded [-id] adj. Illimité, démesuré, sans bornes (or) limites.

unbrace [ʌn'breis] v. tr. Détendre, débander, relâcher. ‖ Affaiblir, énerver.

unbreakable [ʌn'breikəbl̩] adj. Incassable.

unbreathable [-'bri:ðəbl̩] adj. Irrespirable.

unbred [-'bred] adj. Mal élevé.

unbribable [ʌn'braibəbl̩] adj. Incorruptible.

unbribed [-d] adj. Qui ne s'est pas laissé acheter.

unbridle [ʌn'braidl̩] v. tr. Débrider. ‖ FIG. Donner libre cours à, débrider, déchaîner.

unbridled [-d] adj. Débridé, sans bride. ‖ FIG. Effréné, déchaîné, débridé.

unbroached [-'broutʃt] adj. Non entamé (barrel). ‖ FIG. Non abordé (question).

unbroken [ʌn'broukn̩] adj. Intact, non brisé. ‖ AGRIC. Non labouré (ground). ‖ SPORTS. Non dressé (horse); toujours imbattu (record). ‖ MILIT. Inentamé (front). ‖ JUR. Inviolé (rule). ‖ FIG. Ininterrompu (silence); jamais abattu (spirit).

unbrotherly [-'brɔðəli] adj. Indigne d'un frère.

unbuckle [-'bʌkl̩] v. tr. Défaire la boucle de, déboucler.

unbuilt [-'bilt] adj. Non encore construit. ‖ Unbuilt-on, adj. Vague (ground).

unbung [-'bʌŋ] v. tr. Débonder.

unburden [ʌn'bə:dn̩], **unburthen** [-ðən] v. tr. Décharger. ‖ FIG. Soulager; *to unburden oneself*, s'épancher; se débonder (fam.); *to unburden oneself to*, confier ses soucis à, se confier à (s.o.).

unburied [ʌn'berid] adj. Sans sépulture.

unbusinesslike [-'biznislaik] adj. Qui manque de méthode, fantaisiste. ‖ COMM. Peu commerçant, dépourvu de sens commercial (person).

unbutton [ʌn'bʌtn̩] v. tr. Déboutonner.

unbuttoned [-d] adj. Détaché (coat); *all unbuttoned*, dépoitraillé, débraillé.

uncalled [ʌn'kɔ:ld] adj. Sans être appelé (or) invité. ‖ *Uncalled for*, déplacé; injustifié.

uncannily [ʌn'kænili] adv. Mystérieusement.

uncanny [-i] adj. Mystérieux, inquiétant. ‖ Surnaturel. (See WEIRD.)

uncap [ʌn'kæp] v. tr. (1). Décoiffer. ‖ Décapsuler (a bottle).
— v. intr. Se découvrir (*to*, devant).

uncared-for [ʌn'kɛədfɔ:] adj. Peu soigné; négligé (appearance); abandonné, livré à lui-même (child).

uncarpeted [-'kɑ:pitid] adj. Sans tapis.

uncaught [-'kɔ:t] adj. Qui n'a pas été attrapé.

unceasing [ʌn'si:siŋ] adj. Incessant, continu, continuel. (See CEASELESS.)

unceasingly [-li] adv. Continuellement, sans arrêt, sans cesse, sans trêve.

uncensored [ʌn'sensəd] adj. Non soumis à la censure (letter). ‖ Non expurgé (passage).

uncensured [-ʃəd] adj. Non censuré.

unceremonious ['ʌn,seri'mounjəs] adj. Peu cérémonieux; sans façons, sans gêne (person).

unceremoniously [-li] adv. Sans cérémonie.

uncertain [ʌn'sə:tn̩] adj. Incertain, douteux (indefinite, temporary); indéterminé (not calculated). ‖ Incertain, irrésolu, vacillant, hésitant (hesitant). ‖ Incertain, variable (changeable). ‖ Peu sûr (unreliable).

uncertainly [-li] adv. D'une façon incertaine.

uncertainty [-ti] n. Incertitude *f.*

uncertificated [ʌnsə'tifikeitid] adj. Non diplômé.

uncertified [-'sə:tifaid] adj. Non certifié (or) authentifié.

unchain [ʌn'tʃein] v. tr. Déchaîner.

unchallengeable [ʌn'tʃælindʒəbl̩] adj. Indiscutable (statement).

unchallenged [-dʒd] adj. Incontesté, indisputé; *to pass unchallenged*, passer sans soulever d'objection. ‖ Non interpellé (or) contredit; non contré (fam.) [speaker]. ‖ MILIT. Non sommé de s'arrêter. ‖ JUR. Non récusé (witness).

unchangeable [ʌn'tʃeindʒəbl̩] adj. Immuable, invariable.

unchangeableness [-dʒəblnis] n. Immutabilité *f.*

unchanged [-dʒd] adj. Inchangé.

unchanging [-dʒiŋ] adj. Invariable, immuable.

uncharged [ʌn'tʃɑ:dʒd] adj. Non chargé. ‖ JUR. Non accusé. ‖ COMM. *Uncharged for*, gratuit.

uncharitable [ʌn'tʃæritəbl̩] adj. Peu charitable.

uncharitableness [-blnis] n. Manque (*m.*) de charité. ‖ Manque (*m.*) d'indulgence.

uncharitably [-bli] adj. Peu charitablement.

uncharted [ʌn'tʃɑ:tid] adj. Inexploré. ‖ GEOGR. Non mentionné sur la carte.

unchaste [ʌn'tʃeist] adj. Impudique.

unchastened [ʌn'tʃeisnd] adj. Qui n'a pas rabattu son caquet, toujours aussi revendicateur.

unchastised ['ʌntʃəs'taizd] adj. Impuni.

unchastity [ʌn'tʃæstiti] n. Impudicité *f.* (in general); infidélité *f.* (of a wife).

unchecked [-'tʃekt] adj. Sans opposition (advance). ‖ Non maîtrisé; non contenu, non réprimé (feelings). ‖ FIN. Non vérifié.

unchivalrous [-'ʃivəlrəs] adj. Peu galant (or) chevaleresque, discourtois.

unchristened [ʌn'krisnd] adj. ECCLES. Non baptisé.

unchristian [-'kristjən] adj. ECCLES. Infidèle. ‖ Peu chrétien. ‖ FAM. Indu (hour).

uncial ['ʌnsiəl] adj. Oncial.
— n. Onciale *f.*

uncircumcised [-'sə:kəmsaizd] adj. ECCLES. Incirconcis.

uncivil [ʌn'sivil] adj. Incivil, impoli. (See RUDE.)

uncivilized [-aizd] adj. Incivilisé, barbare.

uncivilly [-i] adv. Impoliment.
unclad [ʌn'klæd] adj. Nu, dévêtu.
unclaimed [ʌn'kleimd] adj. Non réclamé. ‖ Jur. Non revendiqué.
unclasp [ʌn'klɑ:sp] v. tr. Dégrafer, défaire (a bracelet). ‖ Desserrer (one's hand).
unclassical [ʌn'klæsikəl] adj. Contraire à l'esprit classique.
unclassifiable [-faiəbl̩] adj. Inclassifiable.
unclassified [-faid] adj. Non classé. ‖ U. S. Contractuel, non titularisé.
uncle ['ʌŋkl] n. Oncle m.; to talk to s.o. like a Dutch uncle, faire un sermon en trois points à qqn; Uncle Sam, l'Oncle Sam. ‖ Pop. At my uncle's, chez ma tante, au clou (in pawn).
unclean [ʌn'kli:n] adj. Sale, malpropre (dirty). ‖ Eccles. Impur, immonde.
uncleanable [-əbl̩] adj. Indécrottable.
uncleanly [ʌn'klenli] adj. Malpropre. ‖ Impur. — adv. Malproprement.
uncleanness [ʌn'kli:nnis] n. Malpropreté f. ‖ Impureté f.
uncleansed [ʌn'klenzd] adj. Malpropre. ‖ Fig. Non purifié.
unclear [ʌn'kli:ə*] adj. Peu clair. ‖ Fig. Peu certain.
uncleared [-d] adj. Non débarrassé; non desservi (table). ‖ Non déblayé (ground). ‖ Jur. Non innocenté. ‖ Comm. Non passé en douane (goods). ‖ Fin. Non acquitté (debt). ‖ Fig. Non éclairci; non dissipé (doubt).
unclench [ʌn'klentʃ] v. tr. Desserrer.
unclimbable [ʌn'klaiməbl̩] adj. Dont l'ascension est impossible, impraticable.
uncloak [-'klouk] v. tr. Oter le manteau de. ‖ Fig. Démasquer.
unclothe [ʌn'klouð] v. intr. Se déshabiller. — v. tr. Déshabiller; mettre à nu.
unclothed [-d] adj. Déshabillé; nu.
unclouded [ʌn'klaudid] adj. Sans nuages. ‖ Fig. Pur, clair; serein.
uncock [ʌn'kɔk] v. tr. Désarmer (a rifle).
uncoil [ʌn'kɔil] v. tr. Dérouler. — v. intr. Se dérouler.
uncoiled [-d] adj. Déroulé. ‖ Non roulé.
uncollected ['ʌnkə'lektid] adj. Non réuni, non rassemblé. ‖ Agité, troublé (person). ‖ Jur. Non perçu (taxes).
uncoloured [ʌn'kʌləd] adj. Non coloré, incolore. ‖ Fig. Incolore; impartial.
uncombed [ʌn'koumd] adj. Non peigné; ébouriffé, échevelé.
uncome-at-able [,ʌnkəm'ætəbl̩] adj. Fam. Inaccessible.
uncomeliness [ʌn'kʌmlinis] n. Manque (m.) de grâce.
uncomely [-li] adj. † Peu seyant. ‖ Disgracieux.
uncomfortable [ʌn'kʌmfətəbl̩] adj. Incommode; peu confortable (thing); to make things incomfortable for, faire des ennuis à. ‖ Gêné, mal à l'aise; inquiet (person).
uncomfortableness [-nis] n. Manque (m.) de confort. ‖ Gêne f.; inquiétude f.
uncomfortably [-i] adv. Peu confortablement. ‖ Anxieusement. ‖ Désagréablement, fâcheusement.
uncommercial [,ʌnkə'mə:ʃəl] adj. Peu commercial. ‖ Peu commerçant (town).
uncommissioned [,ʌnkə'miʃənd] adj. Non commissionné. ‖ Naut. Désarmé (ship).
uncommitted [-'mitid] adj. Non commis (action). ‖ Non compromis; non engagé (person).
uncommon [ʌn'kɔmən] adj. Rare, peu commun. (See exceptional.) ‖ Singulier, extraordinaire. — adj. Fam. Remarquablement, singulièrement.
uncommonly [-li] adv. Remarquablement, singulièrement, extraordinairement. ‖ Loc. Not uncommonly, assez souvent.

uncommonness [-nis] n. Rareté f. ‖ Singularité f.
uncommunicative [,ʌnkə'mju:nikətiv] adj. Renfermé. (See undemonstrative.)
uncompanionable [,ʌnkəm'pænjənəbl̩] adj. Peu sociable, insociable.
uncomplaining [,ʌnkəm'pleiniŋ] adj. Qui ne se plaint pas; résigné.
uncomplainingly [-li] adv. Sans se plaindre.
uncompleted [,ʌnkəm'pli:tid] adj. Inachevé.
uncomplicated [ʌn'kɔmpli,keitid] adj. Simple, peu compliqué.
uncomplimentary ['ʌnkɔmpli'mentəri] adj. Peu flatteur.
uncomplying [,ʌnkəm'plaiiŋ] adj. Inflexible.
uncomprehensive ['ʌn,kɔmpri'hensiv] adj. Incomplet.
uncompromising [,ʌn'kɔmprəmaiziŋ] adj. Intransigeant, inflexible. ‖ Absolu (measure).
unconcealed [,ʌnkən'si:ld] adj. Non dissimulé (or) caché.
unconcern [,ʌnkən'sə:n] n. Indifférence, insouciance f.; détachement m.
unconcerned [-d] adj. Impartial. ‖ Indifférent, impassible, détaché. ‖ Sans inquiétude.
unconcernedly [-idli] adv. Avec indifférence (or) insouciance.
unconditional [,ʌnkən'diʃənl̩] adj. Inconditionnel, sans condition, sans réserve. ‖ Catégorique, définitif (refusal).
unconditionally [-li] adv. Sans conditions, inconditionnellement.
unconfessed [,ʌnkən'fest] adj. Inavoué (crime); inconfessé (person).
unconfined [-'faind] adj. Libre (free). ‖ Illimité, sans bornes (boundless).
unconfirmed [-'fə:md] adj. Eccles., Fig. Non confirmé.
unconformable [-'fɔ:məbl̩] adj. Incompatible (to, avec). ‖ Réfractaire (person).
unconformity [-'fɔ:miti] n. Inconformité.
uncongealable [-'dʒi:ləbl̩] adj. Incongelable.
uncongenial [-'dʒi:njəl] adj. Peu sympathique, antipathique (person); peu agréable (work).
unconnected [-'nektid] adj. Sans rapport, sans liaison. ‖ Sans suite, décousu (ideas).
unconquerable [ʌn'kɔŋkərəbl̩] adj. Ihvincible. ‖ Fig. Invincible; insurmontable; incorrigible.
unconquered [-kəd] adj. Invaincu.
unconscientious ['ʌnkɔnʃi'enʃəs] adj. Peu consciencieux.
unconscionable [ʌn'kɔnʃənəbl̩] adj. † Peu scrupuleux (person). ‖ Excessif, exorbitant.
unconscious [ʌn'kɔnʃəs] n. Med. Inconscient m. — adj. Inconscient; to be unconscious of, ne pas avoir conscience de, ne pas s'apercevoir de (sth.). ‖ Med. Sans connaissance, inanimé, évanoui; to become unconscious, perdre connaissance.
unconsciously [-li] adv. Inconsciemment; sans s'en rendre compte; à son insu.
unconsciousness [-nis] n. Inconscience, ignorance f. ‖ Med. Evanouissement m.; perte de connaissance f.; état (m.) d'inconscience.
unconsenting [,ʌnkən'sentiŋ] adj. Non consentant, n'étant pas d'accord.
unconsidered [,ʌnkən'sidəd] adj. Inconsidéré, irréfléchi.
unconsolable [-'souləbl̩] adj. Inconsolable.
unconsoled [-'sould] adj. Inconsolé.
unconsolidated [-'sɔlideitid] adj. Non consolidé.
unconstitutional [,ʌnkɔnsti'tju:ʃnl̩] adj. Inconstitutionnel, anticonstitutionnel.
unconstrained [,ʌnkən'streind] adj. Sans contrainte, non contraint; libre.
unconstraint [-'streint] n. Absence de contrainte; franchise, liberté f.
unconstricted [-'striktid] adj. Libre; sans restriction. ‖ A l'aise (person).

unconsumed [-'sju:md] adj. Inconsumé. ‖ Inconsommé (food).

uncontainable [‚ʌnkən'teinəbl̩] adj. Irrépressible.

uncontaminated [-‚tæmineitid] adj. Non contaminé (by, par).

uncontemplated [ʌn'kɔntempleitid] adj. Fig. Imprévu, inattendu.

uncontested [‚ʌnkən'testid] adj. Incontesté.

uncontinuous [-'tinjuəs] adj. Non continu, discontinu.

uncontradictable [‚ʌnkɔntrə'diktəbl̩] adj. Incontestable; irréfutable, indiscutable.

uncontradicted [-id] adj. Non contredit.

uncontrite [ʌn'kɔntrait] adj. Impénitent.

uncontrollable [‚ʌnkən'trouləbl̩] adj. Irrésistible; indomptable. ‖ Indiscipliné (child).

uncontrollably [-əbli] adv. Irrésistiblement.

uncontrolled [-d] adj. Effréné, sans frein. ‖ Irresponsable (person).

uncontroversial [‚ʌnkɔntrə'və:ʃəl] adj. Non controversé, sur lequel tout le monde est d'accord.

uncontroverted [ʌn'kɔntrəvə:tid] adj. Incontesté.

uncontrovertible [ʌn'kɔntrə'və:tibl̩] adj. Incontroversable, incontesté, indiscutable.

uncontrovertibly [-bli] adv. Incontestablement.

unconventional [‚ʌnkən'venʃn̩l̩] adj. Peu conventionnel, original.

unconventionality [‚ʌnkənvenʃə'næliti] n. Originalité f.

unconversant [‚ʌnkən'və:sənt] adj. Peu familier (with, avec); peu au courant (with, de) [a fact].

unconverted [-tid] adj. Non converti.

unconvertible [-tibl̩] adj. Inconvertible (into, en).

unconvicted [‚ʌnkən'viktid] adj. Non condamné.

unconvinced [‚ʌnkən'vinst] adj. Inconvaincu, sceptique.

unconvincing [-iŋ] adj. Peu convaincant.

uncooked [ʌn'kukt] adj. Culin. Non cuit, cru.

unco-operative [‚ʌnkou'ɔpərətiv] adj. Peu coopératif.

unco-ordinated [‚ʌnkou'ɔ:dineitid] adj. Non coordonné.

uncork [ʌn'kɔ:k] v. tr. Déboucher.

uncorking [-iŋ] n. Débouchage m.

uncorrected [‚ʌnkə'rektid] adj. Non corrigé.

uncorroborated [-'rɔbəreitid] adj. Non corroboré, sans confirmation.

uncorrupted [-'rʌptid] adj. Incorrompu.

uncountable [ʌn'kountəbl̩] adj. Incomptable, incalculable, innombrable.

uncouple [ʌn'kʌpl̩] v. intr., tr. Mus., Techn. Découpler. ‖ Ch. de f. Dételer.

uncourteous [ʌn'kə:tjəs] adj. Peu courtois, impoli, incivil.

uncourteously [-li] adv. Impoliment.

uncourteousness [-nis] n. Manque (m.) de courtoisie; impolitesse f.

uncourtly [ʌn'kɔ:tli] adj. Peu courtois; inélégant.

uncouth [ʌn'ku:θ] adj. † Bizarre, baroque, étrange. ‖ Sauvage (country); grossier (language); gauche, maladroit, lourd (person).

uncouthly [-li] adj. † Bizarrement. ‖ Gauchement. ‖ Grossièrement.

uncouthness [-nis] n. † Bizarrerie f. ‖ Gaucherie f. (of s.o.). ‖ Grossièreté f. (of language).

uncover [ʌn'kʌvə*] v. intr. Se découvrir.
— v. tr. Découvrir, mettre à découvert. ‖ Détendre (a seat). ‖ Déshabiller (to undress). ‖ Techn. Débâcher. ‖ Fig. Dévoiler (a secret).

uncovered [-d] adj. Découvert; mis à découvert. ‖ Nu (naked); tête nue (bare-headed).

uncreasable [ʌn'kri:səbl̩] adj. Infroissable.

uncreated ['ʌnkri'eitid] adj. Incréé, non encore créé.

uncritical ['ʌn'kritikəl] adj. Dépourvu de sens critique. ‖ Peu porté à critiquer. ‖ Non conforme aux règles de la critique.

uncropped [-'krɔpt] adj. Agric. Non coupé; non moissonné (corn).

uncross [ʌn'krɔs] v. tr. Décroiser.

uncrossable [-əbl̩] adj. Infranchissable.

uncrossed [-t] adj. Non croisé. ‖ Décroisé (legs). ‖ Non encore franchi (desert). ‖ Fin. Non barré (cheque).

uncrowded [ʌn'kraudid] adj. Peu encombré (street). ‖ Non serré (people).

uncrown [ʌn'kraun] v. tr. Découronner.

uncrowned [-d] adj. Non couronné (not yet crowned); sans couronne (without a title). ‖ Fig. Uncrowned king, queen, roi, reine incontesté(e).

uncrushable [ʌn'krʌʃəbl̩] adj. Infroissable (dress).

unction ['ʌnkʃən] n. Onguent, baume m. (balm). ‖ Eccles. Onction m.; extreme unction, extrême-onction. ‖ Fam. Onction f. (affectation); délectation, saveur f. (relish).

unctuosity [‚ʌŋktju'ɔsiti], **unctuousness** ['ʌŋktjuəsnis] n. Onctuosité f.

unctuous [-əs] adj. Onctueux. ‖ Fig. Onctueux, mielleux.

uncultivated [ʌn'kʌltiveitid] adj. Inculte, non cultivé, en friche (land). ‖ Fig. Sans culture.

uncultured [-'kʌltʃə:d] adj. Inculte; sans culture.

uncurbed [ʌn'kə:bd] adj. Sans gourmette (horse). ‖ Déchaîné (unrepressed); libre (unrestricted).

uncured [-'kjuə:d] adj. Culin. Frais (fish). ‖ Med. Non guéri.

uncurl [-'kə:l] v. tr. Dérouler. ‖ Déboucler (hair).
— v. intr. Se dérouler. ‖ Se déboucler, se défriser (hair).

uncurtailed [‚ʌnkə:'teild] adj. Sans restriction (authority). ‖ Non abrégé (account).

uncurtained [ʌn'kə:tn̩d] adj. Sans rideaux.

uncustomary [ʌn'kʌstəməri] adj. Inaccoutumé. (See uncommon, unusual.)

uncut [ʌn'kʌt] adj. Non coupé.

undamaged [-'dæmid3d] adj. Non endommagé; indemne; en bon état.

undamped [-'dæmpt] adj. Non mouillé (clothes). ‖ Non étouffé (sounds). ‖ Fig. Tout neuf, non encore refroidi (enthusiasm).

undated [-'deitid] adj. Non daté, sans date.

undauntable [ʌn'dɔ:ntəbl̩] adj. Impossible à décourager, indomptable.

undaunted [-id] adj. Intrépide. ‖ Non effrayé, non intimidé; inébranlé (by, par).

undauntedly [-idli] adj. Intrépidement.

undebarred [‚ʌndi'bɑ:d] adj. Non exclu (from, de). ‖ Non empêché (from, de).

undebatable [‚ʌndi'beitəbl̩] adj. Indiscutable.

undebated [-id] adj. Indiscuté; non encore discuté.

undecagon [ʌn'dekəgən] n. Math. Hendécagone m.

undecaying [‚ʌndi'keiiŋ] adj. Impérissable.

undeceive [‚ʌndi'si:v] v. tr. Désabuser, détromper.

undeceived [-d] adj. Désabusé, détrompé (disabused). ‖ Non attrapé, qui ne s'est pas laissé prendre (not taken in).

undecennial [‚ʌndi'senjəl] adj. Undécennal.

undecided [-'saidid] adj. Indécis; irrésolu; incertain, douteux; vacillant, hésitant.

undecipherable [-'saifərəbl̩] adj. Indéchiffrable.

undeciphered [-'saifəd] adj. Indéchiffré.

undecked [ʌn'dekt] adj. Sans parure; Naut. Non ponté.

undeclared [‚ʌndi'klɛəd] adj. Non déclaré.

undeclinable [‚ʌndi'klainəbl̩] adj. Gramm. Indéclinable.

undefaced [-'feist] adj. Non dégradé. ‖ Non enlaidi. ‖ Non oblitéré (stamp).

undefeated [-'fi:tid] adj. Invaincu.

undefended [-'fendid] adj. Sans défense; non défendu. ‖ Jur. Sans défenseur (prisoner); non défendu (suit).

undefensible [-'fensəbl] adj. Indéfendable.

undefiled [-'faild] adj. Pur, sans tache, sans souillure, immaculé.

undefinable [ˌʌndi'fainəbl] adj. Indéfinissable. ‖ Indéterminable.

undefined [-d] adj. Non défini. ‖ Indéterminé.

undeliverable [ˌʌndi'livərəbl] adj. Non livrable.

undelivered [-əd] adj. Non délivré. ‖ Non livré (goods); non encore remise au destinataire (letter). ‖ Non prononcé (speech). ‖ MED. Non délivré (woman). ‖ JUR. Non rendu (judgment).

undemanding [ˌʌndi'mɑ:ndiŋ] adj. Peu exigeant.

undemocratic [ˌʌndemə'krætik] adj. Peu démocratique.

undemonstrable [ˌʌndi'mɒnstrəbl] adj. Indémontrable, impossible à démontrer.

undemonstrated [ʌn'demənstreitid] adj. Non démontré.

undemonstrative [ˌʌndi'mɒnstrətiv] adj. Réservé, peu expansif. (See UNCOMMUNICATIVE.)

undeniable [ˌʌndi'naiəbl] adj. Indéniable, incontestable; irréfutable.

undeniably [-bli] adv. Incontestablement.

undenominational [ˌʌndinɒmi'neiʃənəl] adj. Non confessionnel; laïque (school).

undependable [ˌʌndi'pendəbl] adj. Peu sûr.

under ['ʌndə*] prep. Sous; *under the bed,* sous le lit; *under key,* sous clef; *under my raincoat,* sous mon imperméable. ‖ Sous, au-dessous de; *under age,* mineur; *under £ 200,* au-dessous de 200 livres; *those under us,* nos subordonnés; *to speak under one's breath,* parler dans un souffle. ‖ Sous, sous l'influence de; *under penalty of,* sous peine de; *under a vow,* lié par un vœu; *to prosper under a king,* prospérer sous le gouvernement d'un roi. ‖ Sous, au temps de; *under Charles I,* sous Charles Iᵉʳ. ‖ En; *a few acres under wheat,* quelques acres semés en blé; *under examination,* à l'examen, en cours d'examen; *under repair,* en réparation; *under the circumstances,* dans ces (or) vu les circonstances. ‖ Dans, parmi; *to be classified under,* être classé parmi.
— adv. Dessous, au-dessous, en-dessous; *as under,* comme ci-dessous; *from under,* de dessous.
— adj. De dessous, inférieur; *under jaw,* mâchoire inférieure. ‖ Inférieur, subalterne; *under servants,* basse domesticité. ‖ Insuffisant (food).
— pref. Sous-. ‖ **Under-agent,** n. Sous-agent *m.* ‖ **Under-frame,** n. TECHN. Infrastructure *f.* ‖ **Under-part,** n. Dessous, ventre *m;* THEATR. Rôle subalterne (or) secondaire *m.* ‖ **Under-sexed,** adj. Qui a une faible libido, qui a peu de besoins sexuels; peu porté sur la chose (fam.). ‖ **Under-voltage,** n. ELECTR. Sous-voltage *m.*

underachieve [ˌʌndərə't ʃi:v] v. intr. Obtenir des résultats en deçà de ses possibilités.

underact [ˌʌndər'ækt] v. tr., intr. THEATR. Jouer un ton au-dessous, jouer en retrait.

underarm ['ʌndər,ɑ:m] adj., adv. SPORTS. Par en dessous.

underbelly ['ʌndə,beli] n. ZOOL., AVIAT. Ventre *m.* ‖ FIG. Ventre mou, point faible *m.*

underbid [-'bid] v. tr. (20). Faire une offre inférieure à celle de (s.o.).

underbrush [-brʌʃ] n. Broussailles *f. pl.*

underbuy [-'bai] v. tr. (31). Acheter à vil prix.

undercarriage [-kærid ʒ] n. AVIAT. Train d'atterrissage, atterrisseur *m.*

undercharge [-'t ʃɑ:d ʒ] v. tr. COMM. Demander moins cher à (*for,* pour) [s.o.]. ‖ MILIT. Sous-charger (a gun).

underclothes [-klouðz] n. pl. Sous-vêtements *m. pl.;* linge de corps *m.; set of underclothing,* parure.

undercoat [-kout] n. TECHN. Sous-couche, couche (*f.*) de fond. ‖ ZOOL. Sous-poil *m.*

undercover [ˌʌndə'kʌvə*] adj. Secret, subreptice. ‖ Secret (agent); clandestin (operation).

undercroft [-krɔft] n. ARCHIT. Crypte *f.*

undercurrent [-,kʌrənt] n. Courant inférieur *m.* (in atmosphere); courant sous-marin *m.* (in sea). ‖ FIG. Courant, fond *m.;* vague (*f.*) de fond.

undercut [-'kʌt] v. tr. (43). ARTS. Fouiller, sculpter en relief. ‖ COMM. Prendre moins cher que. ‖ SPORTS. Lifter.
— [-kʌt] n. CULIN. Filet *m.;* U. S. Macreuse *f.* (of beef). ‖ TECHN. Encoche (*f.*) à un arbre.

underdevelop ['ʌndədi'veləp] v. tr. Développer insuffisamment, sous-développer.

underdeveloped [-t] adj. Peu développé (intelligence, muscle); sous-développé (country). ‖ TECHN. Sous-développé (photograph).

underdo ['ʌndə'du:] v. tr. (47). Sous-effectuer, ne pas faire assez. ‖ CULIN. Ne pas faire cuire suffisamment.

underdog ['ʌndə,dɔg] n. SPORTS. Vaincu, perdant *s.* (loser); sans-grade *m. invar.* (outsider). ‖ FIG. Victime *f.,* opprimé *s.;* sous-fifre *m.*

underdone [-d ʌn] adj. CULIN. Pas assez cuit (food); saignant (meat).

underdress [-dres] v. tr. Se négliger, ne pas s'habiller avec assez de chic.

underemployed [ˌʌndərim'plɔid] adj. Sous-employé.

underemployment [-'plɔimənt] n. Sous-emploi *m.*

underestimate ['ʌndə'restimeit] v. tr. Sous-estimer.
— [-mit] n. Sous-estimation *f.*

underestimation ['ʌndə,resti'meiʃən] n. Sous-estimation *f.*

underexpose [ˌʌndərik'spouz] v. tr. Sous-exposer (a photograph).

underexposure [-'spouʒə*] n. Sous-exposition *f.* (in photography).

underfeed ['ʌndə'fi:d] v. tr. (55). Sous-alimenter.

underfelt [-,felt] n. Thibaude *f.*

underfloor [-,flɔ:*] adj. *Underfloor heating,* chauffage par le sol. ·

underfoot [-'fut] adv. En dessous, sous les pieds.

undergarment [-,gɑ:mənt] n. Sous-vêtement *m.*

undergo [-'gou] v. tr. (72). Subir (a change, an operation); supporter, subir (trials).

undergraduate [-'grædjuit] n. Etudiant non diplômé *s.*

underground [ˌʌndə'graund] adv. Sous terre.
— ['ʌndəgraund] adj. Souterrain, sous terre. ‖ CH. DE F. *Underground railway,* métro. ‖ MILIT. De la Résistance (movement). ‖ FIG. Souterrain, secret, occulte.
— n. CH. DE F. Métropolitain, métro *m.* ‖ MILIT. Résistance *f.*

undergrown ['ʌndə'groun] adj. Embroussaillé (forest-land). ‖ BOT. Rabougri (plant). ‖ MED. Chétif, insuffisamment développé, rabougri (child).

undergrowth [-grouθ] n. Broussailles *f. pl.* ‖ MED. Croissance insuffisante *f.*

underhand [-hænd] adj. Clandestin, fait en sous-main (or) en dessous (act); sournois (person).
— adv. En sous-main, en dessous, sournoisement.

underhanded [-'hændid] adj., adv. See UNDERHAND.

underhung [-'hʌŋ] adj. Coulissant (door). ‖ MED. Prognathe.

underlay [-'lei] v. tr. (89). Placer en dessous. ‖ Soutenir, appuyer, étayer.
— [-,lei] n. Thibaude *f.* (for carpet). ‖ TECHN. Hausse *f.* (in printing).

underlet [-'let] v. tr. (96). Sous-louer (to sublet). ‖ Louer à trop bas prix.

underlie [-'lai] v. tr. (97). Etre sous (or) en-dessous de. ‖ FIG. Etre le fondement de (or) à la base de.

underline [-'lain] v. tr. Souligner. (See UNDERSCORE.) ‖ FIG. Souligner, mettre l'accent sur.

— ['ʌndəlain] n. Trait (m.) qui souligne. ‖ Pl. Transparent m.

underlinen ['ʌndə,linen] n. Linge de corps m.

underling [-ʌndəliŋ] n. Sous-ordre; sous-verge (fam.) m.

underlying [,ʌndə'laiiŋ] adj. Sous-jacent. ‖ Fig. Fondamental, de base, profond.

undermanned [-'mænd] adj. A court d'équipage, avec un équipage insuffisant (ship); à court (or) qui manque de personnel (factory, hospital).

undermentioned [-'men,ʃənd] adj. Ci-dessous mentionné.

undermine [-'main] v. tr. Miner, saper.

undermost ['ʌndəmoust] adj. Inférieur, le plus en dessous, le plus bas. ‖ Le dernier (in a pile).

underneath [,ʌndə'ni:θ] adv. En dessous.
— prep. Sous.
— adj. Inférieur, de dessous.
— n. Dessous m.

underpants ['ʌndəpænts] n. pl. Caleçon, slip m.

underpass [-pɑ:s] n. U. S. Passage (m.) souterrain (or) sous un pont.

underpay ['ʌndə'pei] v. tr. (105). Payer trop peu, mal rétribuer.

underpeopled [-'pi:pl̩d] adj. Sous-peuplé.

underpin [-'pin] v. tr. ARCHIT., FIG. Etayer.

underplot [-plɔt] n. THEATR. Intrigue secondaire f.

underprivileged [-'privilidʒd] adj., n. Déshérité m.

underproduction [-prə'dʌkʃən] n. Sous-production f.

underprop [-'prɔp] v. tr. (1). Etayer en sous-œuvre.

underrate [-'reit] v. tr. Sous-estimer, sous-évaluer.

underripe [-'raip] adj. Insuffisamment mûr.

underscore [-'skɔ:*] v. tr. Souligner.

undersea [-,si:] adj. Sous-marin.
— adv. Sous l'eau, sous la mer.

underseal [-,si:l] v. tr. AUTOM. Passer à l'antirouille le châssis de.

undersell [-'sel] v. tr. (120). COMM. Vendre moins cher que.

underset [-'set] v. tr. (122). ARCHIT. Etayer en sous-œuvre.

undershirt [-ʃə:t] n. Gilet de corps m.

undershoot [-'ʃu:t] v. tr. (128). AVIAT. Atterrir avant (a runway). ‖ MILIT. Tirer en deçà de, ne pas atteindre (a target).

undershorts [-,ʃɔ:ts] n. pl. U. S. Caleçon, slip m.

undershot [-,ʃɔt] adj. MED. Prognathe. ‖ TECHN. *Undershot water wheel,* roue par-dessous.

underside [-said] n. Côté du dessous m.

undersign [-'saiŋ] v. tr. Signer sous, signer.

undersigned [-'saind] adj. Soussigné.

undersized [-'saizd] adj. Rabougri, de taille insuffisante.

underskirt ['ʌndə,skə:t] n. Jupon, fond (m.) de robe.

underslung [,ʌndə'slʌŋ] adj. AUTOM. Surbaissé.

understaffed [-'stɑːft] adj. A court (or) qui manque de personnel.

understand [,ʌndə'stænd] v. tr. (183). Comprendre, concevoir, saisir (to grasp mentally). ‖ Comprendre (a language, s.o.); se rendre compte, conclure (to infer); *these things work, I understand, on the principle that,* tout cela s'appuie, si j'ai bien compris, sur le principe que. ‖ S'entendre à, savoir, être versé dans (to know how to). ‖ Comprendre, convenir; *it must be understood that,* il doit être entendu que. ‖ GRAMM. Sous-entendre.
— v. intr. Comprendre.

understanding [-iŋ] n. Compréhension f. (act). ‖ Intelligence, compréhension, perception f.; entendement m. (faculty); *it's beyond understanding,* c'est à n'y rien comprendre. ‖ Interprétation f.; *in my understanding of the matter,* selon ma manière de concevoir cette affaire. ‖ Entente, bonne intelligence f. (between, entre, with, avec).

‖ Accord, arrangement m.; convention f. (agreement); convention tacite f. ‖ Condition f.; *on this understanding,* à cette condition.
— adj. Compréhensif, pénétrant.

understate ['ʌndə'steit] v. tr. Atténuer (or) minimiser en exposant.

understatement [-steitmənt] n. Atténuation f. (or) amoindrissement (m.) des faits; exposé (m.) en dessous de la vérité. ‖ Fait (m.) de demeurer en dessous de la réalité. ‖ Euphémisme m.

understeer [-,stiə] n. AUTOM. Sous-virage m.
— v. intr. AUTOM. Sous-virer.

understock [-'stɔk] v. tr. COMM. Pourvoir d'un stock insuffisant.

understrapper [-stræpə*] n. Subalterne s.

understratum [-'streitəm] n. GEOL. Sous-sol m.

understroke [-'strouk] v. tr. Souligner.

understudy [-,stʌdi] n. THEATR. Doublure f.
— v. tr. THEATR. Doubler.

undertake [-'teik] v. tr. (174). Entreprendre (a journey, task). ‖ Promettre, se charger (to, de); s'engager (to, à). ‖ Garantir, affirmer, assurer (that, que).
— v. intr. † Se faire fort (for, pour). ‖ FAM. Etre entrepreneur de pompes funèbres.

undertaker ['ʌndəteikə*] n. Entrepreneur (m.) de pompes funèbres. ‖ Personne (f.) qui entreprend.

undertaking [-'teikiŋ] n. Entreprise f. ‖ Entreprise (f.) de pompes funèbres.

undertenancy [-'tenənsi] n. Sous-location f.

undertenant [-'tenənt] n. Sous-locataire s.

undertone ['ʌndətoun] n. Ton atténué m. (colour, sound). ‖ FIG. Fond obscur m.

undertow [-tou] n. NAUT. Courant sous-marin; ressac m.; contre-marée f.

undervaluation ['ʌndə,vælju'eiʃən] n. Sous-estimation f.

undervalue ['ʌndə'vælju:] v. tr. Sous-estimer, sous-évaluer (sth.). ‖ Déprécier, mésestimer (s.o.).

undervest ['ʌndəvest] n. Tricot (m.) de corps (or) de peau.

underwater ['ʌndə'wɔ:tə*] adj. Sous l'eau, sous-marin.
— adv. Sous l'eau.

underwear ['ʌndəwɛə*] n. Sous-vêtements, dessous m. pl.

underweight [-'weit] adj. Trop maigre (person); qui ne fait pas le poids (goods).

underwood [-wud] n. Sous-bois m.; broussailles f. pl.

underworld [-wə:ld] n. Monde infernal, enfer m. (Hades). ‖ Milieu m.; bas-fonds m. pl.; pègre f.

underwrite [-rait] v. tr. (195). FIN. Souscrire (bonds, policy). ‖ † Souscrire, inscrire en suscription (one's name).

underwriter [-raitə*] n. Assureur m.

underwriting [-raitiŋ] n. Assurance f.

undescribable [,ʌndis'kraibəbl̩] adj. Indescriptible, impossible à décrire.

undeserved [,ʌndi'zə:vd] adj. Immérité.

undeservedly [-zə:vidli] adv. A tort, injustement.

undeserving [-'zə:viŋ] adj. Peu méritant (person); peu méritoire (thing); indigne (of, de).

undesigned [,-zaind] adj. Involontaire, non prémédité (act); imprévu (result).

undesigning [-'zainiŋ] adj. Candide, sans malice.

undesirable [-'zaiərəbl̩] adj., n. Indésirable s.

undetected [-'tektid] adj. Non décelé; *to go undetected,* passer inaperçu.

undetermined [-'tə:mind] adj. Indéterminé (date, quantity, question); irrésolu (person).

undeterred [-'tə:d] adj. Non ébranlé (or) retenu (by, par).

undeveloped [-'veləpt] adj. Non développé. ‖ AGRIC. Inexploité. ‖ FIG. Sous-développé (country); inculte (mind).

undeviating [ʌn'di:vieitiŋ] adj. Direct, sans déviation (road). ‖ Fɪɢ. Sans faiblesse, rigoureux, qui ne se dément pas.

undid [ʌn'did] pret. See UNDO.

undies ['ʌndiz] n. pl.ᐧ Fᴀᴍ. Dessous *m. pl.*

undigested ['ʌndi'dʒestid] adj. Mᴇᴅ. Non digéré. ‖ Fɪɢ. Mal digéré.

undignified [ʌn'dignifaid] adj. Peu digne ; sans tenue (or) dignité.

undiluted ['ʌndai'lju:tid] adj. Non dilué.·

undiminished [ˌʌndi'miniʃt] adj. Qui n'a pas faibli (or) fléchi, qui ne s'est pas démenti.

undimmed [ʌn'dimd] adj. Encore net (or) clair, non terni.

undine ['ʌndi:n] n. Ondine *f.*

undiplomatic [ˌʌndiplə'mætik] adj. Peu diplomatique, qui manque de tact, maladroit.

undiscernible [ˌʌndi'sə:nibl̩] adj. Indiscernable, imperceptible.

undiscerning [-'sə:niŋ] adj. Sans discernement.

undischarged [ˌʌndis'tʃɑ:dʒd] adj. Mɪʟɪᴛ. Non déchargé (rifle) ; non libéré (soldier). ‖ Jᴜʀ. Non réhabilité (bankrupt) ; non acquitté (debt). ‖ Fɪɢ. Inaccompli (duty) ; non libéré (person).

undisciplined [ʌn'disiplind] adj. Indiscipliné.

undisclosed [ˌʌndis'klouzd] adj. Non divulgué, resté secret.

undiscoverable [ˌʌndis'kʌvərəbl̩] adj. Introuvable, indécouvrable.

undiscovered [-'kʌvəd] adj. Non découvert (crime) ; introuvable (criminal) ; inconnu (place).

undiscriminating [ˌʌndis'krimineitiŋ] adj. Sans discernement, peu judicieux.

undisguised ['ʌndis'gaizd] adj. Non déguisé (or) dissimulé.

undismayed [ˌʌndis'meid] adj. Impavide, inébranlé, sans peur.

undisposed [-pouzd] adj. *Undisposed of,* dont on n'a pas disposé ; Cᴏᴍᴍ. Invendu.

undisputed [-'pju:tid] adj. Incontesté.

undisseverable ['ʌndi'sevərəbl̩] adj. Inséparable, indivisible.

undissolvable [-'zɔlvəbl̩] adj. Indissoluble.

undissolved ['zɔlvd] adj. Non dissous.

undistinguishable [-'tingwiʃəbl̩] adj. Indistinct.

undistinguished [-'tingwiʃt] adj. Indistingué (from, de). ‖ Médiocre, sans intérêt.

undisturbed [-'tə:bd] adj. Non dérangé (papers) ; non troublé (peace, sleep) ; paisible, sans inquiétude (person).

undiversified [-'və:sifaid] adj. Uniforme, monotone.

undivided [-'vaidid] adj. Indivisé. ‖ Fɪɢ. Entier.

undo [ʌn'du] v. tr. (184). Détruire, annuler, défaire (to annul). ‖ Défaire, dénouer (a fastening) ; défaire (knitting). ‖ Ouvrir (a door) ; défaire, déficeler, ouvrir (a parcel). ‖ Déboutonner, dégrafer (one's dress). ‖ Ruiner (s.o.).

undoing [-'du:iŋ] n. Action (*f.*) de défaire. ‖ Perte, ruine *f.*

undone [-'dʌn] adj. Inachevé, non effectué, inaccompli (work). ‖ Déboutonné (button) ; dégrafé (dress) ; défait (knot) ; dénoué (hair) ; déficelé, défait, ouvert (parcel) ; délacé (shoe) ; *to come undone,* se délacer (shoe). ‖ Perdu (person) ; fichu (fam.).

undoubted ['ʌn'dautid] adj. Indubitable, indiscutable, certain.

undoubtedly [-idli] adv. Indubitablement. (See DOUBTLESS.)

undoubting [-iŋ] adj. Convaincu, sûr.

undraw [ʌn'drɔ:] v. tr. (48). Tirer (curtain).

undreamed [ʌn'dri:md], **undreamt** [-'dremt] adj. Inimaginé, insoupçonné ; *an undreamed-of happening,* un événement qui dépasse l'imagination.

undress [ʌn'dres] v. tr. Déshabiller. (See DISROBE.) ‖ Mᴇᴅ. Défaire le pansement de.
— v. intr. Se déshabiller.
— n. Déshabillé, négligé *m.*
— ['ʌndres] n. Mɪʟɪᴛ. Petite tenue *f.*

undressed [ʌn'drest] adj. Déshabillé, dévêtu. ‖ En négligé (or) déshabillé. ‖ Tᴇᴄʜɴ., Aɢʀɪᴄ. Non taillé.

undrinkable [-drinkəbl̩] adj. Imbuvable.

undue [ʌn'dju:] adj. Exagéré, indu, excessif (haste). ‖ Injuste (exaction) ; injustifié, immérité (reward). ‖ Fɪɴ. Non exigible, non échu. ‖ Jᴜʀ. Illégitime, indû.

undulate ['ʌndjuleit] v. intr. Onduler.
— [-lit] adj. Ondulé, onduleux.

undulating [-leitiŋ] adj. Ondulé. ‖ Vallonné, accidenté (country). ‖ Aɢʀɪᴄ. Ondoyant (corn).

undulation [ˌʌndju'leiʃən] n. Ondulation *f.*

undulatory ['ʌndjuleitəri] adj. Onduleux. ‖ Pʜʏs. Ondulatoire.

unduly [ʌn'dju:li] adv. Indûment ; excessivement.

undying [-'daiiŋ] adj. Immortel.

unearned [ʌn'ə:nd] adj. Non gagné ; *unearned increment,* plus-value. ‖ Immérité (reward).

unearth [ʌn'ə:θ] v. tr. Déterrer. ‖ Sᴘᴏʀᴛs. Faire bouquer (a fox). ‖ Fᴀᴍ. Dénicher, déterrer, dégoter.

unearthly [-li] adj. Qui n'est pas de la terre, surnaturel. ‖ Fantomatique, sinistre. ‖ Fᴀᴍ. Fantastique, infernal (din) ; indu (hour).

unease [ʌn'i:z] n. Gêne *f.,* malaise, embarras *m.* (embarrassment) ; appréhension, inquiétude *f.* (anxiety).

uneasily [ʌn'i:zili] adv. Sans aisance. ‖ Avec inquiétude. ‖ Difficilement.

uneasiness [-nis] n. Gêne *f. ;* malaise *f.* ‖ Anxiété *f. ; to feel some uneasiness,* avoir quelque inquiétude. ‖ † Difficulté *f.*

uneasy [ʌn'i:zi] adj. Mal à l'aise, gêné, embarrassé. ‖ Inquiet, tourmenté. ‖ Gênant, incommode (situation). ‖ Mᴇᴅ. Agité (patient, sleep). ‖ † Difficile, malaisé.

uneatable [-'i:təbl̩] adj. Immangeable.

uneaten [-'i:tn̩] adj. Qui n'a pas été mangé (or) touché.

uneconomic [ʌn,i:kə'nɔmik] adj. Non rémunérateur (work). ‖ Peu économique (method).

unedifying [ʌn'edifaiiŋ] adj. Peu édifiant.

unedited [-'editid] adj. Non revu (manuscript) ; non monté (film, tape). ‖ Non édité (unpublished).

uneducated [ʌn'edjukeitid] adj. Sans éducation, inculte. (See UNLEARNED.)

uneffected [ʌni'fektid] adj. Ineffectué (work). ‖ Irréalisé (project).

unembodied [ʌnem'bɔdid] adj. Incorporel.

unemotional [ˌʌni'mouʃn̩l̩] adj. Peu émotif (or) impressionnable.

unemployable [ˌʌnim'plɔiəbl̩] adj. Inapte à travailler.

unemployed [ˌʌnim'plɔid] adj. Inemployé (thing). ‖ Sans emploi (or) travail (person).
— n. *The unemployed,* les chômeurs.

unemployment [-mənt] n. Chômage *m. ; unemployment compensation,* indemnité de chômage.

unencumbered [ˌʌnin'kʌmbəd] adj. Peu encombré ; sans enfants (or) attaches familiales. ‖ Jᴜʀ. Dégrevé, franc d'hypothèques.

unending [ʌn'endiŋ] adj. Incessant, interminable, sempiternel. (See ENDLESS.)

unendurable [ˌʌnin'djuərəbl̩] adj. Intolérable.

unengaged [-'geidʒd] adj. Libre (person, room, seat).

un-English [ˌʌn'iŋgliʃ] adj. Peu anglais.

unenjoyed [-'dʒɔid] adj. Dont on n'a pas joui.

unenlightened [-'laitənd] adj. Non éclairé.

unenterprising [ʌn'entəpraiziŋ] adj. Peu entreprenant ; peu dynamique.

unentertaining [ʌnentə'teiniŋ] adj. Peu distrayant ; plutôt ennuyeux.

unenthusiastic [,ʌnin,θju:zi'æstik] adj. Peu enthousiaste, tiède, indifférent (lukewarm) ; peu optimiste (not optimistic).

unenviable [-'enviəbl] adj. Peu enviable.

unenvied [-'envid] adj. Peu envié.

unequal ['ʌn'i:kwəl] adj. Inégal. ‖ MED. Irrégulier (pulse). ‖ FIG. Inférieur (to a task) ; *to be unequal to doing,* n'être pas de taille à faire.

unequalled [-d] adj. Inégalé.

unequivocal [ʌni'kwivəkl] adj. Sans (or) non équivoque.

unerring [ʌn'ə:riŋ] adj. Sûr, infaillible.

UNESCO [ju:'neskou] abbr. *United Nations Educational, Scientific and Cultural Organization,* Organisation des Nations unies pour l'éducation, la science et la culture, Unesco.

unessential [,ʌni'senʃəl] adj. Non essentiel.
— n. Accessoire, secondaire *m.*

unestimable ['ʌn'estiməbl] adj. Inestimable.

unethical [ʌn'eθikl] adj. Immoral. ‖ Contraire à la déontologie (against professional ethics).

uneven [ʌn'i:vn] adj. Inégal. ‖ Accidenté (ground). ‖ MATH. Impair. ‖ FIG. Inégal, irrégulier.

unevenness [-nis] n. Inégalité *f.*

uneventful [ʌni'ventful] adj. Uni, peu mouvementé, sans incidents.

unexampled [ʌnig'zɑ:mpld] adj. Sans exemple (or) précédent, exceptionnel.

unexceptionable ['ʌnik'sepʃənəbl] adj. Irréprochable. ‖ JUR. Irrécusable.

unexceptional [-'sepʃənəl] adj. Ordinaire, banal, qui n'a rien d'exceptionnel.

unexciting [-'saitiŋ] adj. Peu palpitant (or) passionnant.

unexecuted [ʌn'eksikju:tid] adj. Inexécuté.

unexpected [,ʌnəks'pektid] adj. Inattendu.

unexpectedly [-li] adv. A l'improviste, inopinément, de façon inattendue.

unexperienced [,ʌniks'pi:riənst] adj. Inéprouvé, inexpérimenté.

unexpired [-'paiəd] adj. Non périmé (passport, ticket) ; qui n'est pas arrivé à expiration (lease, term of office).

unexplained [-'pleind] adj. Inexpliqué.

unexploited [-'plɔitid] adj. Inexploité.

unexplored [-'plɔ:d] adj. Inexploré. ‖ MED. Non sondé.

unexposed [-'pouzd] adj. Non exposé. ‖ FIG. Non démasqué (crime).

unexpressed [-'prest] adj. Inexprimé. ‖ GRAMM. Sous-entendu.

unexpurgated [ʌn'ekspə,geitid] adj. Non expurgé.

unextinguishable [-'tiŋgwiʃəbl] adj. Inextinguible.

unfading [ʌn'feidiŋ] adj. Non fané. ‖ COMM. Bon teint. ‖ FIG. Impérissable, ineffaçable.

unfailing [-'feiliŋ] adj. Inépuisable, intarissable. ‖ FIG. Infaillible, non démenti.

unfair [-'fɛə*] adj. Injuste, partial (person). ‖ Déloyal (competition, play). ‖ Exorbitant (price) ; inéquitable (wage).

unfairly [-'fɛəli] adv. Injustement. ‖ Déloyalement.

unfairness [-'fɛənis] n. Injustice *f.* ‖ Déloyauté *f.*

unfaithful [ʌn'feiθful] adj. Infidèle (to, à) ; déloyal (to, envers).

unfaithfulness [-nis] n. Infidélité *f.*

unfaltering [ʌn'fɔltəriŋ] adj. Ferme, sans défaillance.

unfamiliar [ʌnfə'miljə*] adj. Peu familier, étranger ; *to become unfamiliar with Latin,* se désaccoutumer du latin.

unfashionable [ʌn'fæʃnəbl] adj. Démodé.

unfasten [-'fɑ:sn] v. tr. Dégrafer (one's dress). ‖ Ouvrir (a door). ‖ Détacher, délier (*from,* de).

unfathered [-'fɑ:ðəd] adj. Sans père. ‖ FIG. De source inconnue (news) ; d'auteur inconnu (theory).

unfathomable [-'fæðəməbl] adj. Insondable.

unfathomed [-'fæðəmd] adj. Insondé.

unfavourable [-'feivərəbl] adj. Défavorable.

unfeeling [-'fi:liŋ] adj. Insensible. ‖ FIG. Insensible, impitoyable, inhumain.

unfeigned [-'feind] adj. Non simulé, sincère.

unfelt [-'felt] adj. Insensible, non perçu (or) ressenti.

unfeminine [-'feminin] adj. Peu féminin.

unfermented ['ʌnfə'mentid] adj. Azyme (bread) ; non fermenté (liquor).

unfetter [ʌn'fetə*] v. tr. Briser les fers (or) entraves de. ‖ FIG. Libérer.

unfettered [-d] adj. Sans entraves, libre.

unfilial [-'filjəl] adj. Indigne d'un fils.

unfilmed [-'filmd] adj. Non porté à l'écran.

unfinished [-'finiʃt] adj. Inachevé, incomplet, imparfait. ‖ Manquant de fini.

unfit [ʌn'fit] adj. Incapable (*to,* de) ; inapte (*to,* à) [person]. ‖ Impropre (*to,* à) [thing]. ‖ MED. Peu dispos, souffrant.
— v. tr. (1). Rendre inapte (or) impropre (*for,* à).

unfitness [-nis] n. Incapacité, inaptitude *f.* (*for, to,* à). ‖ Inopportunité *f. ;* inappropriation *f.* ‖ MED. Faiblesse de constitution *f.*

unfitted [-id] adj. Inapte, impropre (*for,* à). ‖ Non équipé (*with,* de).

unfitting [-iŋ] adj. Peu approprié (or) convenable. ‖ Inopportun, inapproprié, mal à propos.

unfix [ʌn'fiks] v. tr. Détacher, enlever (to unfasten). ‖ Déranger, ébranler (to unsettle).

unfixed [ʌn'fikst] adj. Détaché. ‖ Non fixé, indéterminé (date) ; irrésolu, indécis, instable (person).

unflagging [-'flægiŋ] adj. Infatigable, inlassable, non démenti. (See UNFAILING.)

unflappable [-'flæpəbl] adj. FAM. Flegmatique, imperturbable.

unflattering [-'flætəriŋ] adj. Peu flatteur (*to,* pour).

unfledged [-'fledʒd] adj. ZOOL. Sans plumes. ‖ FIG. Inexpérimenté, novice.

unflinching [-'flinʃiŋ] adj. Sans défaillance, impassible ; qui ne bronche pas. ‖ Inébranlé, inhésitant, stoïque.

unfold [-'fould] v. tr. Déplier, ouvrir (to open). ‖ Déployer, dérouler (to show). ‖ FIG. Dévoiler, révéler, exposer (to reveal).
— v. intr. Se dérouler, se déployer, se développer. ‖ Se dévoiler.

unforbidden [,ʌnfə'bidn] adj. Permis.

unforced [ʌn'fɔ:st] adj. Libre, non forcé. ‖ Spontané, franc.

unfordable [-'fɔ:dəbl] adj. Inguéable.

unforeseeing [,ʌnfɔ:'si:iŋ] adj. Imprévoyant.

unforeseen [-'si:n] adj. Imprévu.

unforgettable [-'getəbl] adj. Inoubliable.

unforgivable [-'givəbl] adj. Impardonnable.

unforgiven [-'givn] adj. Non pardonné.

unforgiving [-'giviŋ] adj. Implacable.

unforgotten [-'gɔtn] adj. Inoublié.

unformed [-'fɔmd] adj. Informe.

unforthcoming [,ʌnfɔ:θ'kʌmiŋ] adj. Réticent.

unfortified [-'fɔ:tifaid] adj. MILIT. Non fortifié ; *unfortified town,* ville ouverte.

unfortunate [ʌn'fɔ:tʃənit] adj. Fâcheux, malencontreux (event) ; infortuné, malheureux (person).
— n. Infortuné *s.*

unfortunately [-li] adv. Malheureusement, par malheur.

unfounded [ʌn'faundid] adj. Non fondé, sans fondement (or) consistance.

unfreeze [-'fri:z] v. intr. (67). Dégeler (river, ground) ; fondre (ice).
— v. tr. Dégeler, décongeler (frozen food). ‖ FIN. Débloquer, dégeler (prices, goods).

unfrequent [-'fri:kwənt] adj. Peu fréquent.

unfrequented ['ʌnfri'kwentid] adj. Peu fréquenté.

unfriendliness [ʌn'frendlinis] n. Hostilité, inimitié *f*. (*towards*, envers).

unfriendly [-li] adj. Inamical. ‖ Hostile (*towards*, à). ‖ Défavorable (circumstance).

unfrock [ʌn'frɔk] v. tr. Défroquer.

unfruitful [ʌn'fru:tful] adj. AGRIC. Infertile, stérile. ‖ FIG. Stérile, improductif.

unfruitfulness [-nis] n. Stérilité *f*.

unfulfilled [,ʌnful'fild] adj. Non rempli (condition); inaccompli (desire, duty); irréalisé (prophecy); inachevé (task); inexaucé (wish).

unfunny [ʌn'fʌni] adj. Pas drôle, qui ne fait pas rire personne.

unfurl [ʌ'fə:l] v. tr. Déployer. ‖ NAUT. Larguer, déferler.
— v. intr. Se déployer.

unfurnished [-'fə:niʃd] adj. Démeublé, dénudé, dégarni, non meublé, vide (room). ‖ FIG. Dépourvu (*with*, de).

ungainliness [-'geinlinis] n. Gaucherie; dégaine *f*. (fam.).

ungainly [-'geinli] adj. Gauche; empoté (fam.). ‖ Dégingandé.

ungallant [-'gælənt] adj. Peu galant, discourtois.

ungarnished [-'gɑ:niʃt] adj. Sans ornements, nu.

ungear [-'giə*] v. tr. TECHN. Débrayer, désengrener.

ungenerous [-'dʒenərəs] adj. Peu généreux (selfish); injuste (unfair).

ungenteel [,ʌndʒen'ti:l] adj. Peu convenable.

ungentle [ʌn'dʒentl] adj. Rude, peu aimable.

ungentlemanlike [-mənlaik], **ungentlemanly** [-mənli] adj. Indigne d'un homme correct. ‖ Impoli, mal élevé.

unget-at-able [,ʌnget'ætəbl] adj. FAM. Inaccessible.

ungird [ʌn'gə:d] v. tr. Détacher, dénouer; déceindre.

unglazed [ʌn'gleizd] adj. Non vitré (window). ‖ Non glacé, mat (paper). ‖ ARTS. Non vernissé.

unglove [-'glʌv] v. tr. Déganter.

unglue [-'glu:] v. tr. Décoller.

ungodliness [ʌn'gɔdlinis] n. Impiété *f*.

ungodly [-li] adj. Impie.

ungovernable [ʌn'gʌvənəbl] adj. Ingouvernable (country, person). ‖ Effréné, irrépressible (desire); indompté (passion).

ungoverned [-'gʌvənd] adj. Non gouverné. ‖ Effréné, déréglé, désordonné.

ungraceful [-'greisful] adj. Disgracieux, inélégant.

ungracious [-'greiʃəs] adj. Déplaisant, peu aimable, peu gracieux.

ungrammatical [,ʌngrə'mætikəl] adj. Incorrect, contraire à la grammaire.

ungrantable [ʌn'grɑ:ntəbl] adj. Inaccordable (privilege). ‖ A quoi l'on ne peut souscrire, irrecevable (demand).

ungrateful [ʌn'greitful] adj. Ingrat, peu reconnaissant (*to*, envers). ‖ Ingrat, déplaisant (work).

ungratefulness [-nis] n. Ingratitude *f*.

ungratified [ʌn'grætifaid] adj. Insatisfait.

ungrounded [-'graundid] adj. Non fondé. (See UNFOUNDED.)

ungrudging [-'grʌdʒiŋ] adj. Accordé de bon cœur (gift); généreux, large (person).

ungual [ʌŋgwəl] adj. ZOOL. Unguéal, ongulé.

unguarded [ʌn'gɑ:did] adj. Non gardé (or) protégé. ‖ D'inadvertance (moment); qui ne se tient pas sur ses gardes (person); inconsidéré, incontrôlé, irréfléchi (speech).

unguent ['ʌŋgwənt] n. Onguent *m*.

unguided [-'gaidid] adj. Sans guide.

unguiform ['ʌŋgwifɔ:m] adj. ZOOL. Onguiforme.

ungula ['ʌŋgjulə] n. ZOOL. Onglon *m*. ‖ MATH. Onglet *m*.

ungulate [-leit] adj., n. ZOOL. Ongulé *m*.

unhackneyed [ʌn'hæknid] adj. Non rebattu, neuf.

unhallowed [-'hæloud] adj. Profane, non consacré. ‖ Impie.

unhampered [-'hæmpəd] adj. Non entravé, libre.

unhand [-'hænd] v. tr. Lâcher.

unhandsome [-'hænsəm] adj. Vilain, sans beauté (plain). ‖ Laid, indélicat (rude). ‖ Mesquin, peu généreux (stingy).

unhandy [-'hændi] adj. Maladroit, malhabile (person); peu maniable, incommode (tool).

unhang [-'hæŋ] v. intr. (75). Dépendre. ‖ Enlever les tentures de.

unhappily [ʌn'hæpili] adv. Malheureusement.

unhappiness [-inis] n. Malheur *m*.

unhappy [-i] adj. Malheureux (event, person).

unharmed [ʌn'hɑ:md] adj. Indemne, sain et sauf (person); intact (thing).

unharness [-'hɑ:nis] v. tr. Dételer, déharnacher (a horse). ‖ Désarmer, dévêtir (a knight).

unhealthful [ʌn'helθful] adj. Insalubre.

unhealthiness [-inis] n. Insalubrité *f*. ‖ MED. Mauvaise santé *f*. ‖ FIG. Morbidité *f*.

unhealthy [-i] adj. Insalubre, malsain. ‖ MED. Maladif. ‖ FIG. Malsain, morbide.

unheard [ʌn'hə:d] adj. Non entendu; *unheard-of*, inouï, sans précédent.

unheeded [ʌn'hi:did] adj. Inaperçu, non remarqué, auquel on ne prête pas attention.

unheeding [-iŋ] adj. Inattentif (*of*, à); insouciant (*of*, de).

unhelpful [ʌn'helpful] adj. Peu secourable, vain, inutile, sans effet.

unheralded [ʌn'herəldid] adj. Inattendu, imprévu, inopiné.

unhesitating [ʌn'heziteitiŋ] adj. Immédiat (answer); décidé, non hésitant (person).

unhesitatingly [-li] adv. Sans hésitation.

unhinge [ʌn'hindʒ] v. tr. Démonter, enlever de ses gonds (a door). ‖ FAM. Déséquilibrer, détraquer, déplomber; déboussoler (fam.) [mind].

unhistoric(al) [,ʌnhis'tɔrik(l)] adj. Peu historique. ‖ Insignifiant, peu important.

unhitch [-'hitʃ] v. tr. Décrocher (sth.). ‖ Dételer (a horse).

unholiness [ʌn'houlinis] n. Caractère profane *m*. ‖ Impiété *f*.

unholy [-i] adj. Impie (person); profane (thing). ‖ FAM. Infernal.

unhonoured [ʌn'ɔnəd] adj. Non honoré, dédaigné.

unhook [-'huk] v. tr. Dégrafer (dress); décrocher (sth.); *to become unhooked*, se dégrafer (dress).

unhoped [ʌn'houpt] adj. *Unhoped-for*, inespéré, inattendu.

unhopeful [-ful] adj. Désespérant.

unhorse [ʌn'hɔ:s] v. tr. Désarçonner.

unhouse [-'hauz] v. tr. Déloger.

unhurried [-'hʌrid] adj. Lent, nonchalant (pace); qui prend son temps (person); mûr, long (consideration).

unhurriedly [-'hʌridli] adv. Sans se presser, en prenant son temps.

unhurt [-'hə:t] adj. Indemne, sain et sauf.

unicameral [,ju:ni'kæmərəl] adj. JUR. Comportant une seule chambre législative.

UNICEF ['ju:ni,sef] abbr. *United Nations Children's Fund*, Fonds des Nations unies pour l'enfance, UNICEF.

unicellular [,ju:ni'seljulə] adj. BOT., ZOOL. Unicellulaire.

unicorn ['ju:nikɔ:n] n. ZOOL., ASTRON. Licorne *f*.

unidentified [,ʌnai'dentifaid] adj. Non identifié. ‖ *Unidentified flying object (U. F. O.)*, objet volant non identifié (ovni).

unidirectional [,ju:nidi'rekʃənl] adj. Unidirectionnel.

unification [,ju:nifi'keiʃən] n. Unification *f*.

uniflorous [,ju:ni'flɔ:rəs] adj. BOT. Uniflore.

uniform ['ju:nifɔ:m] adj., n. Uniforme *m*.
— v. tr. MILIT. Vêtir d'un uniforme.

uniformed [-d] adj. En uniforme.
uniformity [,ju:ni'fɔ:miti] n. Uniformité f.
uniformly ['ju:ni,fɔ:mli] adv. Uniformément.
unify ['ju:nifai] v. tr. (2). Unifier.
unilateral ['ju:ni'lætərəl] adj. Unilatéral.
unilluminated [ʌn'ilju:mineitid] adj. Non illuminé (or) éclairé.
unimaginable [ʌni'mædʒinəbl̩] adj. Inimaginable.
unimaginative [-'mædʒinətiv] adj. Dépourvu d'imagination.
unimpaired ['ʌnim'pɛəd] adj. Non détérioré; inentamé; intact.
unimpassioned [-'pæʃənd] adj. Sans passion, imperturbable, froid.
unimpeachable [-'pi:tʃəbl̩] adj. Inattaquable; incontestable; irréprochable.
unimpeached [-'pi:tʃt] adj. Inattaqué; incontesté.
unimpeded [-'pi:did] adj. Que rien n'arrête, sans obstacle.
unimportance [-'pɔ:təns] n. Insignifiance f.
unimportant [-'pɔ:tənt] adj. Peu important, insignifiant.
unimposing [-'pouziŋ] adj. Peu imposant.
unimpressed [-'prest] adj. Non frappé (medal). ‖ Fɪɢ Non impressionné (person).
unimpressionable [-'preʃnəbl̩] adj. Peu impressionnable.
unimpressive [-'presiv] adj. Peu émouvant (or) frappant; peu impressionnant.
unimproved [-'pru:vd] adj. Non amélioré (or) amendé. ‖ Inutilisé. ‖ Aɢʀɪᴄ., Fɪɢ. Inculte.
unimpugned [-'pju:nd] adj. Non combattu, incontesté.
uninflated [-'fleitid] adj. Aᴜᴛᴏᴍ. A plat, non gonflé (tyre).
uninfluenced [ʌn'influənst] adj. Non influencé.
uninfluential ['ʌninflu'enʃəl] adj. Peu influent, sans influence.
uninformed [-'ʌnin'fɔ:md] adj. Non informé (or) averti. ‖ Ignorant, inculte.
uninhabitable [,ʌnin'hæbitəbl̩] adj. Inhabitable.
uninhabited [-id] adj. Inhabité.
uninhibited [,ʌnin'hibitid] adj. Sans complexes (or) inhibitions (person); débridé (party).
uninitiated [,ʌnin'iʃieitid] adj. Non initié.
uninjured [-'indʒəd] adj. Indemne (person); non endommagé (thing). ‖ Non lésé.
uninominal ['ju:ni'nɔminəl] adj. Uninominal.
uninspired [,ʌnin'spaiəd] adj. Dépourvu d'inspiration, terne, morne.
uninspiring [-'spaiəriŋ] adj. Peu inspirant.
uninstructed [,ʌnin'strʌktid] adj. Sans instruction, non instruit. ‖ Qui n'a pas reçu d'instruction.
uninstructive [-'strʌktiv] adj. Peu instructif.
uninsured [-'ʃuəd] adj. Non assuré.
unintelligent [-'telidʒənt] adj. Inintelligent.
unintelligibility [ʌnin,telidʒi'biliti] n. Inintelligibilité f.
unintelligible [,ʌnin'telidʒibl̩] adj. Inintelligible.
unintelligibly [-i] adv. Inintelligiblement.
unintentional [,ʌnin'tenʃn̩l] adj. Non intentionnel, involontaire.
uninterested [ʌn'intristid] adj. Non intéressé, indifférent. ‖ Désintéressé.
uninteresting [-iŋ] adj. Sans intérêt, inintéressant.
unintermitting [,ʌnintə'mitiŋ] adj. Ininterrompu, non intermittent.
uninterrupted [-'rʌptid] adj. Ininterrompu, continu, sans interruption.
uninterruptedly [-'rʌptidli] adv. Sans interruption, de façon continue.
uninured [,ʌnin'juəd] adj. Non habitué (or) aguerri.
uninventive [-'ventiv] adj. Peu inventif.
uninvited [-'vaitid] adj. Non invité.
uninviting [-'vaitiŋ] adj. Peu attirant (or) engageant. ‖ Cᴜʟɪɴ. Peu appétissant.

union ['ju:njən] n. Union f. (act, result). ‖ Union f.; mariage m.; *very successful union*, mariage très réussi. ‖ Syndicat m. (trade union). ‖ Jᴜʀ., Mᴀᴛʜ. Union f. ‖ Gᴇᴏɢʀ. *Union of Soviet Socialist Republics*, Union des républiques socialistes soviétiques. ‖ Fɪɢ. Union, concorde, harmonie f. ‖ **Union-elbow**, n. Tᴇᴄʜɴ. Coude de raccord m. ‖ **Union Jack**, n. Union Jack, drapeau britannique m.
unionism ['ju:njə,nizm̩] n. Unionisme m. (in politics). ‖ Syndicalisme m. (trade unionism).
unionist ['ju:njənist] n. Unioniste s. (in politics). ‖ Syndicaliste s. (trade unionist).
unionize ['ju:njə,naiz] v. tr. Syndiquer.
— v. intr. Se syndiquer.
unionized [-d] adj. Syndiqué.
uniparous [ju:'nipərəs] adj. Mᴇᴅ., Zᴏᴏʟ. Unipare.
unipetalous [,ju:ni'petələs] adj. Bᴏᴛ. Unipétale.
unipolar [-'poulə*] adj. Pʜʏs. Unipolaire.
unique [ju:'ni:k] adj., n. Unique; exceptionnel.
uniquely [-li] adv. Uniquement.
uniqueness [-nis] n. Caractère unique m.
uniserial [,ju:ni'siəriəl] adj. En une série.
unisex ['ju:ni,seks] adj. Unisexe.
— n. Mode unisexe f.
unison ['ju:nizn̩] n. Mᴜs. Unisson m.; *in unison*, à l'unisson. ‖ Fɪɢ. Unisson m.
unit ['ju:nit] n. Unité f. ‖ *Kitchen unit*, bloc-cuisine; *motor-unit*, bloc-moteur.
Unitarian [,ju:ni'tɛəriən] adj., n. Eᴄᴄʟᴇs. Unitarien m. ‖ Jᴜʀ. Unitaire m.
unitary ['ju:nitəri] adj. Unitaire.
unite [ju'nait] v. tr. Unir, réunir.
— v. intr. S'unir, se réunir. ‖ S'unir, s'allier. ‖ S'unir, s'entendre, s'associer (*in*, pour).
united [-id] adj. Uni; réuni; *United Nations Organization (U. N. O.)*, Organisation des nations unies (O. N. U.); *United Arab Emirates*, Emirats arabes unis; *United Kingdom*, Royaume-Uni; *United States of America*, Etats-Unis.
unitedly [-idli] adv. En union, ensemble.
unity ['ju:niti] n. Unité. ‖ Mᴀᴛʜ. Unité f. ‖ Fɪɢ. Union, harmonie f.
univalent [ju'nivələnt] adj. Cʜɪᴍ. Univalent, monovalent.
universal [,ju:ni'və:səl] adj., n. Universel m.
universalism [-izm̩] n. Universalisme m.
universalist [-ist] n. Universaliste m.
universality [,ju:nivə'sæliti] n. Universalité f.
universalization [,ju:nivə:səlai'zeiʃən] n. Universalisation f.
universalize [-'və:səlaiz] v. tr. Universaliser.
universally [-'və:səli] adv. Universellement.
universe ['ju:nivə:s] n. Univers m.
university [,ju:ni'və:siti] n. Université f.
— adj. D'université; de faculté; universitaire.
unjust [ʌn'dʒʌst] adj. Injuste (*to*, envers).
unjustifiable [-ifaiəbl̩] adj. Injustifiable.
unjustified [-ifaid] adj. Injustifié.
unjustly [-li] adv. Injustement.
unkempt [ʌn'kempt] adj. Dépeigné, mal peigné, ébouriffé, hirsute. ‖ Aɢʀɪᴄ. Mal tenu, embroussaillé.
unkind [ʌn'kaind] adj. Peu aimable. ‖ Dur, sans bonté.
unkindliness [-linis], **unkindness** [-nis] n. Manque (m.) d'amabilité. ‖ Dureté f.
unkindly [-li] adj. Peu aimable; dur.
— adv. Sans amabilité; durement.
unknot [ʌn'nɔt] v. tr. Dénouer, défaire.
unknowable [ʌn'nouəbl̩] adj. Inconnaissable.
unknowing [-iŋ] adj. Ignorant (*of*, de).
unknowingly [-iŋli] adv. Sans le savoir, inconsciemment.
unknown [ʌn'noun] adj. Inconnu.
— n. Pʜɪʟᴏs. Inconnu m. ‖ Mᴀᴛʜ. Inconnue f.
— adv. A l'insu (*to*, de).
unlaboured [-'leibəd] adj. Non travaillé, facile, coulant (style).

unlace [-'leis] v. tr. Délacer.

unladderable [-lædərəbl] adj. Indémaillable.

unlade [-'leid] v. tr. (88). Décharger.

unladen [-'leidn] adj. A vide.

unladylike [-'leidilaik] adj. Indigne d'une femme distinguée.

unlamented ['ʌnlə'mentid] adj. Non regretté.

unlash [ʌn'læʃ] v. tr. NAUT. Démarrer.

unlatch [-'lætʃ] v. tr. Lever le loquet de (a door).

unlawful [ʌn'lɔ:ful] adj. Illégitime (child) ; illicite (means). ‖ JUR. Illégal.

unlawfully [-i] Illégalement.

unlawfulness [-nis] n. Illégitimité f. ‖ JUR. Illégalité f.

unleaded [ʌn'ledid] adj. Non plombé. ‖ TECHN. Sans interlignes, compact (in printing).

unlearn [ʌn'lə:n] v. tr. Désapprendre. ‖ Se défaire de (a habit) ; chasser (an idea).

unlearned [-id] adj. Ignorant.

— [-d] adj. Peu versé (in, dans). ‖ Inappris.

unlearnt [-t] adj. Inappris.

unleash [ʌn'li:ʃ] v. tr. Lâcher, détacher.

unleavened [-'levnd] adj. Azyme, sans levain (bread). ‖ FIG. Non adouci (with, par).

unless [ʌn'les] conj. A moins que.

— prep. Sauf, excepté, sinon.

unlettered [-'letəd] adj. Illettré.

unlicensed [-'laisənst] adj. Illicite, non permis. ‖ Sans licence (or) brevet.

unlicked [-'likt] adj. Mal léché.

unlike [ʌn'laik] adj. Différent ; peu ressemblant.

— conj. Autrement que.

unlikelihood [-lihud], **unlikeliness** [-linis] n. Invraisemblance f.

unlikely [-li] adj. Invraisemblable, improbable ; *it is unlikely that,* il y a peu de chances que. ‖ Peu prometteur. ‖ Auquel on penserait le moins (to, pour).

unlikeness [-nis] n. Dissemblance, différence f.

unlimited [ʌn'limitid] adj. Illimité.

unlined [-'laind] adj. Sans doublure, non doublé (garment).

unlined adj. Non réglé (paper). ‖ Lisse, sans rides (face).

unlink [-'liŋk] v. tr. Dénouer, détacher. ‖ Enlever les anneaux de.

unlisted [-'listid] adj. Qui ne figure pas sur une liste. ‖ Qui ne figure pas dans l'annuaire téléphonique. ‖ FIN. Non inscrit (or) admis à la cote officielle.

unlit [-'lit] adj. Non allumé (fire, lamp) ; sans éclairage (car, street).

unliv(e)able [-livəbl] adj. Intenable, intolérable.

unload [-loud] v. tr. Décharger. ‖ FIG. Décharger, alléger, soulager.

unlock [-'lɔk] v. intr. Ouvrir (a door). ‖ FIG. Dévoiler (a secret).

unlooked [-'lukt] adj. *Unlooked-for,* imprévu, inattendu, inopiné.

unloose [-'lu:s] v. tr. Dénouer, délier, détacher.

unlovable [-'lʌvəbl] adj. Peu attachant, antipathique.

unlovely [-'lʌvli] adj. Peu aimable. ‖ Peu joli (or) attrayant ; sans charme.

unloving [-'lʌviŋ] adj. Peu aimant (or) affectueux.

unlucky [-'lʌki] adj. Malchanceux ; *to be unlucky,* avoir de la déveine. ‖ Malheureux. ‖ Malencontreux. ‖ Maléfique, portant malheur ; *unlucky omen,* funeste présage.

unmade [-'meid] adj. Défait, non fait (bed) ; non goudronné (road).

unmaidenly [-'meidənli] adj. Indigne d'une jeune fille.

unmake [-'meik] v. tr. (100). Défaire, démolir.

unman [-'mæn] v. tr. Amollir. ‖ NAUT. Désarmer (a ship). ‖ TECHN. *Unmanned capsule,* capsule-robot. ‖ FIG. Décourager, déprimer, démoraliser.

unmanageable [-'mænidʒəbl] adj. Ingouvernable, intenable, indocile. ‖ Peu maniable. ‖ Intraitable.

unmanly [-'mænli] adj. Indigne d'un homme. ‖ Efféminé, peu viril.

unmannerly [-'mænəli] adj. Sans éducation (or) savoir-vivre, mal élevé, impoli.

unmarked [-'mɑ:kt] adj. Non marqué, sans marques. ‖ Banalisé (police car). ‖ Non corrigé (exercise). ‖ Peu marqué, insensible, indifférent (untouched). ‖ Inaperçu (unobserved). ‖ SPORTS. Démarqué.

unmarketable [-'mɑ:kitəbl] adj. COMM. Invendable.

unmarriageable [ʌn'mæridʒəbl] adj. Non mariable. ‖ Non encore nubile.

unmarried [-'mærid] adj. Non marié, célibataire.

unmask [-'mɑ:sk] v. tr. Démasquer.

— v. intr. Se démasquer.

unmatched [-'mætʃt] adj. Désassorti, dépareillé. ‖ FIG. Inégalé, sans rival (or) pareil.

unmeaning [-'mi:niŋ] adj. Dépourvu de sens.

unmeant [-'ment] adj. Involontaire.

unmeasurable [-'meʒərəbl] adj. Incommensurable.

unmeasured [-'meʒəd] adj. Non mesuré. ‖ Incommensurable, immense.

unmendable [-'mendəbl] adj. Irréparable ; non raccommodable.

unmentionable [ʌn'menʃnəbl] adj. Dont il ne convient pas de parler ; innommable (fam.).

— n. pl. FAM. Culotte f.

unmerciful [-'mə:siful] adj. Impitoyable.

unmerited [-'meritid] adj. Immérité.

unmetalled [-'metld] adj. Non revêtu (road).

unmethodical [-mi'θɔdikl] adj. Peu méthodique, brouillon, désordonné.

unmindful [-'maindful] adj. Inattentif, négligent. ‖ Insoucieux (of, de) ; indifférent (of, à).

unmistakable [ˌʌnmis'teikəbl] adj. Qui ne prête pas à erreur, sans équivoque.

unmitigated [ʌn'mitigeitid] adj. Non mitigé. ‖ FAM. Total, parfait, pur, avéré, fieffé. (See ARRANT.)

unmixed [-'mikst] adj. Sans mélange, pur.

unmolested [ˌʌnmo'lestid] adj. Non molesté, tranquille ; en paix.

unmoor [ʌn'muə*] v. tr. NAUT. Désaffourcher.

— v. intr. NAUT. Démarrer, désamarrer.

unmotived [-'moutivd], **unmotivated** [-'moutiveitid] adj. Immotivé.

unmounted [-'mauntid] adj. MILIT., TECHN. Non monté.

unmourned [-'mɔ:nd] adj. Pas du tout regretté, peu pleuré.

unmoved [-'mu:vd] adj. Qui n'a pas remué, non déplacé. ‖ FIG. Inébranlable ; impassible ; insensible (by, à) ; non ému (by, par).

unmuffle [-'mʌfl] v. tr. Désemmitoufler (s.o., sth.). ‖ Oter le voile de (a bell).

— v. intr. Se désemmitoufler.

unmusical [-'mju:zikəl] adj. Peu musical (ear) ; inharmonieux (sound) ; n'aimant pas la musique, peu amateur de musique (person).

unmuzzle [-'mʌzl] v. tr. Démuseler.

unnameable [ʌn'neiməbl] adj. Innommable.

unnamed [-d] adj. Innommé. ‖ Anonyme.

unnatural [ʌn'nætʃrəl] adj. Anormal, monstrueux ; contre nature (vice). ‖ Dénaturé (son). ‖ Forcé, peu naturel (laugh, style).

unnecessarily [ʌn'nesisərili] adj. Inutilement, sans nécessité.

unnecessary [-ri] adj. Inutile, non nécessaire ; superflu.

— n. pl. Inutilité f. (thing).

unneighbourly [ʌn'neibəli] adj. Indigne d'un bon voisin, de mauvais voisinage.

unnerve [-'nə:v] v. tr. † Enerver, amollir. ‖ FIG. Décourager, abattre.

unnoticed [-'noutist] adj. Inaperçu, non remarqué, inobservé. ‖ Négligé, traité comme quantité négligeable.

unnumbered [-'nʌmbəd] adj. Non dénombré (ou) numéroté. ‖ Innombrable.

U. N. O. ['ju:nou] abbr. *United Nations Organization*, Organisation des Nations unies, O. N. U.

unobjectionable [,ʌnəb'dʒekʃənəbl] adj. Ne soulevant pas d'objections, irréprochable.

unobservant [-'zə:vənt] adj. Peu observateur. ‖ *Unobservant of*, ne tenant pas compte de, n'observant pas.

unobserved [-'zə:vd] adj. Non observé (or) remarqué, inaperçu.

unobstructed [-'strʌktid] adj. Non obstrué. ‖ Non encombré, sans obstacle. ‖ AUTOM. Découvert (turning).

unobtrusive [-'tru:siv] adj. Modeste, réservé, effacé. ‖ Discret.

unoccupied [ʌn'ɔkjupaid] adj. Inoccupé.

unoffending [,ʌno'fendiŋ] adj. Innocent.

unofficial [-'fiʃəl] adj. Non officiel, officieux.

unopened [-'oupənd] adj. Non ouvert; non décacheté (letter); non déplié (paper).

unopposed [-'pouzd] adj. Sans opposition.

unordinary [ʌn'ɔ:dinəri] adj. Peu ordinaire.

unorganized [ʌn'ɔ:gə,naizd] adj. Inorganisé.

unoriginal [,ʌnə'ridʒənl] adj. Dépourvu d'originalité, banal.

unorthodox [ʌn'ɔ:θə,dɔks] adj. Peu orthodoxe. ‖ ECCLES. Hétérodoxe.

unostentatious ['ʌn,ɔsten'teiʃəs] adj. Sans ostentation, simple.

unoxidizable [,ʌnɔksi'daizəbl] adj. Inoxydable.

unpack [ʌn'pæk] v. tr. Dépaqueter, défaire.

unpaid [-'peid] adj. FIN. Impayé (bill); non versé (capital); non rétribué (or) payé (person).

unpaired [-'pɛəd] adj. Dépareillé.

unpalatable [-'pælətəbl] adj. Peu agréable au goût. ‖ FAM. Peu goûté; difficile à avaler, dur à digérer (fam.).

unparalleled [-'pærələld] adj. Sans égal, incomparable. ‖ Sans précédent (action).

unpardonable [-'pɑ:dnəbl] adj. Impardonnable.

unparliamentary ['ʌn,pɑ:lə'mentəri] adj. Antiparlementaire. ‖ FAM. Grossier.

unpatented [ʌn'peitəntid] adj. Non breveté.

unpatriotic [-pætri'ɔtik] adj. Peu patriotique, antipatriotique (action); peu patriote (person).

unpaved [ʌn'peivd] adj. Non pavé; dépavé.

unpeople [ʌn'pi:pl] v. tr. Dépeupler.

unperceivable [,ʌnpə'si:vəbl] adj. Imperceptible.

unperceived [-'si:vd] adj. Inaperçu.

unperformed [-'fɔ:md] adj. Inaccompli, inexécuté, inachevé. ‖ THEATR. Non joué.

unperson ['ʌnpə:sn] n. Non-entité *f.*; *to become an unperson*, être jeté aux oubliettes, être rayé des cadres (fig.).

unpersuasive [-'sweisiv] adj. Non convaincant.

unperturbed [-tə:bd] adj. Imperturbable.

unperverted [-və:tid] adj. Non perverti.

unphilosophical ['ʌn,filə'sɔfikəl] adj. Peu philosophique.

unpick [ʌn'pik] v. tr. Découdre, défaire (seam).

unpin [ʌn'pin] v. tr. (1). Désépingler. ‖ TECHN. Dégoupiller.

unpitying [-'pitiiŋ] adj. Impitoyable.

unplaced [-'pleist] adj. Sans emploi (person). ‖ Non classé (candidate). ‖ SPORTS. Non placé (horse).

unplanned [-'plænd] adj. Imprévu, fortuit (event); non prévu (child); non planifié (economy).

unplayable [-'pleiəbl] adj. Injouable. ‖ Impraticable. ‖ MUS. Inexécutable.

unpleasant [ʌn'pleznt] adj. Déplaisant, désagréable. ‖ Mauvais, vilain (weather).

unpleasantness [-nis] n. Caractère déplaisant *m.* ‖ Brouille, mésentente *f.*

unpleasing [ʌn'pli:ziŋ] adj. Déplaisant, désagréable.

unpliable [ʌn'plaiəbl] adj. Peu souple. ‖ FIG. Raide; sans souplesse.

unploughed [-'plaud] adj. AGRIC. Non labouré.

unplug [-'plʌg] v. tr. (1). Débrancher (an electrical appliance). ‖ Déboucher (a hole, a tube).

unplumbed [-'plʌmbd] adj. Insondé. ‖ FIG. Non dévoilé (mystery).

unpoetical [,ʌnpo'etikəl] adj. Peu poétique, prosaïque, terre à terre.

unpolished [ʌn'poliʃt] adj. Non poli, brut. ‖ Non ciré (boots); non verni (furniture). ‖ FIG. Fruste, non policé.

unpolite ['ʌnpo'lait] adj. Impoli.

unpolluted [-'lju:tid] adj. Impollué, pur.

unpopular [ʌn'pɔpjulə*] adj. Impopulaire.

unpopularity ['ʌn,pɔpju'læriti] n. Impopularité *f.*

unpractical [ʌn'præktikəl] adj. Peu pratique.

unpractised [-'præktist] adj. Non pratiqué. ‖ Inhabile, inexpert (*in*, dans).

unprecedented [-'presidentid] adj. Sans précédent, inédit (fact).

unpredictable [,ʌnpri'diktəbl] adj. Imprévisible.

unprejudiced [ʌn'predʒudist] adj. Sans préjugés. ‖ Impartial.

unpremeditated [,ʌnpri'mediteitid] adj. Non prémédité. ‖ Impromptu (speech).

unprepared [-'pɛəd] adj. Non préparé. ‖ Improvisé (speech).

unprepossessing [,ʌnpri:pə'zesiŋ] adj. Peu attirant (or) engageant, rébarbatif.

unpresentable [-'zentəbl] adj. Peu présentable.

unpreservable [-'zə:vəbl] adj. Inconservable.

unpresuming [-'zju:miŋ] adj. Modeste, sans présomption.

unpretending [-'tendiŋ], **unpretentious** [-'tenʃəs] adj. Sans prétention.

unpriced [ʌn'praist] adj. Dont le prix n'est pas affiché (or) fixé. ‖ Sans prix, inestimable (priceless).

unprincipled [ʌn'prinsipld] adj. Sans principes (or) scrupule.

unprintable [-'printəbl] adj. Impubliable.

unprivileged [-'privilidʒd] adj. Déshérité, défavorisé.

unprized [-'praizd] adj. Peu prisé, peu estimé.

unprocurable ['ʌnprə'kjuərəbl] adj. Impossible à obtenir, introuvable.

unproductive [-'dʌktiv] adj. Improductif.

unprofessional [-'feʃənl] adj. Contraire aux règles (or) aux habitudes de la profession. ‖ SPORTS. Amateur, non professionnel.

unprofitable [ʌn'prɔfitəbl] adj. Peu profitable (or) lucratif. ‖ ECCLES., FIG. Inutile (servants).

unprogressive [,ʌnpro'gresiv] adj. Routinier, sans esprit de progrès.

unpromising [ʌn'promisiŋ] adj. Peu prometteur.

unprompted [-'promtid] adj. Spontané.

unpronounceable [,ʌnpro'naunsəbl] adj. Imprononçable.

unprosperous [ʌn'prɔspərəs] adj. Peu florissant. ‖ Peu propice.

unprotected [,ʌnpro'tektid] adj. Sans protection.

unprovable [ʌn'pru:vəbl] adj. Indémontrable; *to be unprovable*, ne pas se démontrer (or) se prouver.

unproved [-'pru:vd], **unproven** [-ən] adj. Non prouvé (accusation). ‖ Inéprouvé (fidelity).

unprovided [,ʌnpro'vaidid] adj. Dépourvu, démuni (*with*, de). ‖ Sans moyens (*against*, contre); *unprovided for*, sans ressources. ‖ Imprévu, non prévu (*by*, for).

unprovoked [-'voukt] adj. Non provoqué (act); calme, non irrité (person).

unpublished [ʌn'pʌbliʃt] adj. Inédit, non publié (book). ‖ FIG. Non rendu public.

unpunctual [-'pʌŋktjuəl] adj. Inexact, non ponctuel.

unpuncturable [-'pʌŋktjurəbḷ] adj. Autom. Increvable (tyre).
unpunished [-'pʌniʃt] adj. Impuni.
unqualifiable [-'kwɔlifaiəbḷ] adj. Inqualifiable.
unqualified [-'kwɔlifaid] adj. Incompétent (to, pour); inapte (to, à). ‖ Sans réserve, absolu.
unquenchable [-'kwentʃəbḷ] adj. Inextinguible.
unquenched [-'kwentʃt] adj. Non éteint (fire). ‖ Fig. Inassouvi.
unquestionable [ʌn'kwestʃənəbḷ] adj. Indiscutable; hors de doute.
unquestioned [-d] adj. Non questionné (person). ‖ Indiscuté, incontesté (right, statement).
unquestioning [-iŋ] adj. Aveugle, qui ne questionne pas, qui croit sur parole.
unquiet [ʌn'kwaiət] adj. Inquiet, troublé. ‖ Bruyant.
unquietness [-nis] adj. Inquiétude f. ‖ Bruit, manque de calme m.
unquote [ʌn'kwout] v. intr. Fermer les guillemets.
— interj. Fin de citation, fermez les guillemets.
unquoted [ʌn'kwoutid] adj. Non cité. ‖ Fin. Non coté (securities).
unrationed [-'ræʃṇd] adj. Comm. En vente libre, non rationné.
unravel [-'rævəl] v. tr. (1). Effilocher. ‖ Démêler, détortiller. ‖ Fig. Dénouer, tirer au clair, débrouiller.
— v. intr. S'effiler, se démêler. ‖ Fig. Se débrouiller.
unread [-'red] adj. Non lu, qu'on ne lit pas (book). ‖ Non instruit (person).
unreadable [-'ri:dəbḷ] adj. Illisible.
unready [-'redi] adj. Non prêt; pas disposé (for, to, à).
unreal [-'riəl] adj. Irréel.
unrealistic [,ʌnriə'listik] adj. Irréaliste.
unrealizable [ʌn'riəlaizəbḷ] adj. Irréalisable.
unrealized [-'riəlaizd] adj. Irréalisé, inaccompli (unaccomplished); insoupçonné (unexpected). ‖ Fin. Non réalisé.
unreason [ʌn'rizṇ] n. Déraison f.
unreasonable [-əbḷ] adj. Déraisonnable.
unreasoning [-iŋ] adj. Irraisonné.
unreceipted [,ʌnri'si:tid] adj. Fin. Non acquitté.
unreclaimed [,ʌnri'kleimd] adj. Non défriché (land); non asséché (marsh). ‖ Impénitent, non repenti (sinner).
unrecognizable [ʌn'rekɔgnaizəbḷ] adj. Méconnaissable.
unrecognized [-naizd] adj. Méconnu. ‖ Non reconnu (by, par).
unrecorded ['ʌnri'kɔ:did] adj. Non enregistré.
unredeemed [-'di:md] adj. Non racheté (or) compensé (by, par). ‖ Inaccompli (promise). ‖ Non dégagé (pawned article). ‖ Fin. Non remboursé (or) amortissable.
unreel [ʌn'ri:l] v. tr. Dérouler.
unrefined [,ʌnri'faind] adj. Techn. Non raffiné, brut. ‖ Fig. Peu raffiné, fruste.
unreflecting [-'flektiŋ] adj. Irréfléchi.
unreformed [-'fɔ:md] adj. Impénitent, non amendé. ‖ Eccles. Non réformé (church).
unregarded [-gɑ:did] adj. Peu considéré, négligé.
unregardful [-gɑ:dful] adj. Peu attentif (of, à); peu soigneux (of, de).
unregistered [ʌn'redʒistəd] adj. Non enregistré (luggage). ‖ Sans immatriculation (car). ‖ Non inscrit (candidate). ‖ Non inscrit sur la liste électorale (voter). ‖ Non déposé (trade mark). ‖ Non déclaré (birth).
unregretted [,ʌnri'gretid] adj. Peu regretté.
unrehearsed [-'hə:st] adj. Non préparé, inapprêté. ‖ Theatr. Non répété.
unrelated [-'leitid] adj. Non rapporté (fact). ‖ Sans lien de parenté (person).
unrelenting [-'lentiŋ] adj. Implacable.
unreliable [-'laiəbḷ] adj. Instable, inconstant (cha-

racter); sujet à caution, auquel on ne peut se fier, douteux (information, person).
unrelieved [-'li:vd] adj. Non soulagé (pain); non secouru (person). ‖ Monotone, plat (landscape).
unreligious [-lidʒəs] adj. Non religieux. ‖ U. S. Irréligieux.
unremarkable [-'mɑ:kəbḷ] adj. Peu remarquable, quelconque, ordinaire.
unremembered [-'membəd] adj. Oublié.
unremitting [-'mitiŋ] adj. Incessant, soutenu (effort); assidu, constant, infatigable (person).
unremunerative [-'mju:nərətiv] adj. Peu rémunérateur (or) lucratif (badly paid). ‖ Fig. Qui n'apporte rien, peu fructueux.
unrepaid [-'paid] adj. Non vengé (insult); non récompensé (person); non rendu (service). ‖ Fin. Non remboursé.
unrepealed [-'pi:ld] adj. Jur. Non abrogé.
unrepented [-'pentid] adj. Non regretté (sin).
unrepentent [-'pentənt] adj. Impénitent.
unrepresentative [,ʌnrepri'zentətiv] adj. Peu représentatif (of, de).
unrepresented [-'zentid] adj. Non représenté.
unrepressed [-'prest] adj. Irréprimé.
unrequested [-'kwestid] adj. Non demandé (or) sollicité; spontané.
unrequired [-'kwaiəd] adj. Non exigé. ‖ Inutile, peu nécessaire.
unrequited [-'kwaitid] adj. Non partagé (love); non récompensé (service).
unresented [-'zentid] adj. Accepté sans rancune.
unresentful [-'zentful] adj. Sans rancune.
unreserved [-'zə:vd] adj. Non réservé (seat). ‖ Entier, total, sans réserve (or) restriction (approval). ‖ Ouvert, expansif, extérieur (person).
unresisting [-'zistiŋ] adj. Souple, docile, qui ne résiste pas.
unresolved [-'zɔlvd] adj. Non résolu (problem). ‖ Irrésolu, indécis (person).
unresponsive [,ʌnris'pɔnsiv] adj. Indifférent, insensible (person, public); mou (car).
unrest [ʌn'rest] adj. Agitation f.; trouble m.; public unrest, remous populaire.
unrestrained [,ʌnri'streind] adj. Sans contrainte; non réprimé (or) retenu.
unrestricted [-'striktid] adj. Sans restriction.
unretentive [-'tentiv] adj. Peu fidèle.
unrevealed [-'vi:ld] adj. Non révélé (or) divulgué.
unrewarded [-'wɔ:did] adj. Non récompensé.
unriddle [ʌn'ridḷ] v. tr. Expliquer (a dream); donner la clef de, résoudre (a mystery).
unrig [-'rig] v. tr. (1). Naut. Dégréer.
unrighteous [-'raitʃəs] adj. Inique, injuste; peu honnête.
unripe [-'raip] adj. Vert, pas mûr. ‖ Fig. Sans maturité, insuffisamment mûr.
unrivalled [-'raivəld] adj. Sans rival (or) égal, incomparable.
unrobe [-'roub] v. tr. Dévêtir.
— v. intr. Se dévêtir.
unroll [-'roul] v. tr. Dérouler.
— v. intr. Se dérouler.
unruffled [-'rʌfḷd] adj. Lisse (hair); sans ride, calme (water). ‖ Serein, calme (person, temper).
unruled [-'ru:ld] adj. Non réglé (paper). ‖ Non gouverné (people). ‖ Non maîtrisé (passion).
unruly [-'ru:li] adj. Turbulent, indiscipliné (child); fougueux (horse). ‖ Déchaîné, incontrôlé (passions).
unsaddle [-'sædḷ] v. tr. Desseller (a horse); désarçonner (a horseman).
unsafe [ʌn'seif] adj. Dangereux.
unsaid [ʌn'sed] adj. Inexprimé.
unsalaried [-'sælərid] adj. Non rémunéré.
unsal(e)able [-'seiləbḷ] adj. Invendable.
unsanitary [-'sænitəri] adj. Non hygiénique (or) sanitaire; peu salubre.

unsatisfactory [-təri] adj. Peu satisfaisant, médiocre.

unsatisfied [ʌn'sætisfaid] adj. Peu satisfait, insatisfait (*with*, de). ‖ Non convaincu, doutant (*about*, de). ‖ Inassouvi (appetite).

unsatisfying [-'sætisfaiiŋ] adj. Peu satisfaisant.

unsaturated [-'sætʃə,reitid] adj. Qui n'est pas saturé. ‖ CHIM. Non saturé, insaturé.

unsaved [-'seivd] adj. ECCLES., TECHN. Perdu.

unsavoury [-'seivəri] adj. Désagréable, nauséabond (smell, taste). ‖ FIG. Equivoque, douteux, déplaisant, louche.

unsay ['ʌn'sei] v. tr. (116). Rétracter, revenir sur, se dédire de; *to leave unsaid*, passer sous silence.

unscathed [-'skeiðd] adj. Indemne; *not to come off unscathed*, y laisser des plumes.

unscholarly [ʌn'skɔləli] adj. Peu érudit. ‖ Indigne d'un savant.

unschooled [-'skuːld] adj. Sans instruction (person). ‖ Non maîtrisé (or) éduqué (feeling).

unscientific [ʌn,saiən'tifik] adj. Peu scientifique.

unscramble [ʌn'skræmbl̩] v. tr. Démêler, débrouiller. ‖ Décoder, déchiffrer (a scrambled message).

unscreened [-'skriːnd] adj. Sans écran. ‖ Non abrité (place). ‖ Non criblé (coal). ‖ FIG. Non interrogé (refugees).

unscrew [-'skruː] v. tr. Dévisser.

unscripted [-'skriptid] adj. Improvisé (speech, discussion).

unscrupulous [-'skruːpjuləs] adj. Sans scrupules.

unseal [-'siːl] v. tr. Desceller. ‖ Décacheter (a letter). ‖ FIG. Dessiller (eyes).

unsearchable [-'səːtʃəbl̩] adj. Impénétrable.

unseasonable [-'siːzənəbl̩] adj. Hors de saison (fruit, weather). ‖ Inopportun, intempestif, mal à propos (act).

unseasoned [-'siːznd] adj. Vert (timber). ‖ CULIN. Non assaisonné. ‖ MILIT. Inaguerri. ‖ FIG. Inexpérimenté, non habitué.

unseat [-'siːt] v. tr. Renverser, faire choir. ‖ Désarçonner (a horseman). ‖ JUR. Invalider.

unseaworthy [-'siːwəːði] adj. Incapable de prendre (or) tenir la mer.

unseconded [-'sekəndid] adj. Non soutenu (motion); non secondé (person).

unsecured [ʌnsi'kjuəːd] adj. Mal assujetti. ‖ FIN. Non garanti.

unseeing [ʌn'siːiŋ] adj. Aveugle.

unseemliness [ʌn'siːmlinis] adj. Inconvenance *f.*

unseemly [-li] adj. Inconvenant, malséant, incongru. ‖ Qui ne sied pas (*in*, à).

unseen [ʌn'siːn] adj. Inaperçu, non entrevu. ‖ Invisible. ‖ A livre ouvert (translation). — n. Traduction (or) version (*f.*) à livre ouvert. ‖ Invisible, au-delà *m.*

unselfconscious [,ʌnself'kɔnʃəs] adj. Naturel, qui se sent à l'aise.

unselfish [-'selfiʃ] adj. Sans égoïsme, dévoué.

unsensational [,ʌnsen'seiʃənl̩] adj. Sobre (unemotional). ‖ Anodin, insignifiant (trivial).

unsentimental [,ʌnsenti'mentl̩] adj. Peu sentimental.

unserviceable [-'səːvisəbl̩] adj. Inutilisable, hors de service (thing). ‖ Peu serviable (person).

unset ['ʌn'set] v. tr. (122). Desservir.

unsettle [-'setl̩] v. tr. Déranger; ébranler.

unsettled [-'setld] adj. Variable, détraqué (weather), agité, troublé (mind, nation). ‖ JUR. Non colonisé (country); sans domicile fixe (person). ‖ FIN. Non réglé (bill). ‖ FIG. Irrésolu, indécis (person); irrésolu (question).

unsew [-'sou] v. tr. Découdre.

unsex [-'seks] v. tr. Déviriliser, émasculer (man); faire perdre de sa féminité à (woman).

unshackle [-'ʃækl̩] v. tr. Désentraver (a horse); briser les fers de (a prisoner).

unshaded [-'ʃeidid] adj. Non ombragé, découvert (place). ‖ Sans abat-jour (lamp). ‖ ARTS. Sans ombres; au trait (drawing).

unshak(e)able [-'ʃeikəbl̩] adj. Inébranlable.

unshaken [-ʃeikən] adj. Inébranlé.

unshaped [ʌn'ʃeipt] adj. Non formé.

unshapely [-li] adj. Difforme, informe.

unshapen [-n] adj. Difforme.

unshaven [ʌn'ʃeivn] adj. Pas rasé.

unsheathe [ʌn'ʃiːð] v. tr. Dégainer.

unsheltered [-'ʃeltəd] adj. Non abrité. ‖ Sans soutien; non protégé (*from*, contre).

unship [-'ʃip] v. tr. (1). NAUT. Débarquer (goods); enlever (masts); rentrer (oars).

unshod [-'ʃɔd] adj. Déferré (horse); déchaussé, nu-pieds (person).

unshorn [-ʃɔːn] adj. Non tondu.

unshrinkable [-'ʃriŋkəbl̩] adj. Irrétrécissable.

unshroud [-'ʃraud] v. tr. Désensevelir.

unsighted [ʌn'saitid] adj. Non en vue. ‖ MILIT. Sans mire (gun).

unsightly [-li] adj. Laid, disgracieux.

unsigned [ʌn'saind] adj. Non signé, sans signature.

unsized [-'saizd] adj. Sans colle.

unskilful [-'skilful] adj. Maladroit (*at*, *in*, à).

unskilled [-'skild] adj. Inexpert (*in*, dans); inhabile (*in*, à). ‖ Non spécialisé, de manœuvre (labour); non qualifié (workman).

unskimmed [-'skimd] adj. Non écrémé, entier (milk).

unslaked [-'sleikt] adj. Non étanché (thirst). ‖ CHIM. Vif (chalk).

unsling [-'sliŋ] v. tr. NAUT. Dégréer.

unsmiling [-'smailiŋ] adj. Peu souriant.

unsmooth [-'smuːð] adj. Malaisé (road); non poli, rugueux (surface).

unsociable [-'souʃəbl̩] adj. Insociable, sauvage. (See DISSOCIAL.)

unsocial [,ʌn'souʃəl] adj. Asocial. ‖ *Unsocial hours*, horaires peu commodes (or) incompatibles avec la vie de famille.

unsold [-'sould] adj. COMM. Invendu; *unsold copies*, bouillon, invendus.

unsoldierly [-'souldʒəli] adj. Indigne d'un soldat (conduct); peu martial (look).

unsolicited [,ʌnsə'lisitid] adj. Non sollicité, spontané. (See UNREQUESTED.)

unsolicitous [-'lisitəs] adj. Peu soucieux, peu désireux (*about*, de).

unsolvable [ʌn'sɔlvəbl̩] adj. Insoluble.

unsolved [-'sɔlvd] adj. Impénétré (mystery); non résolu (problem).

unsophisticated [,ʌnse'fisti,keitid] adj. Simple, peu sophistiqué, naturel.

unsought [ʌn'sɔːt] adj. Non recherché. ‖ Spontané (unsolicited).

unsound [-'saund] adj. CULIN. Avarié, gâté. ‖ NAUT. En mauvais état (ship). ‖ MED. Malade. ‖ COMM. Peu sain (business); défectueux (goods). ‖ FIG. Faux, malsain.

unsparing [-'spɛəriŋ] adj. Prodigue (*of*, de). ‖ Impitoyable (*of*, pour).

unspeakable [-'spiːkəbl̩] adj. Inexprimable. (See INEFFABLE.)

unspecified [-'spesifaid] adj. Non spécifié.

unspent [-'spent] adj. Non dépensé.

unspoiled [-'spɔild], **unspoilt** [-'spɔilt] adj. En parfait état (not damaged); préservé, non défiguré (or) gâché (not marred). ‖ Bien élevé; *unspoiled by fame*, à qui la gloire n'est pas montée à la tête.

unspoken [-'spoukən] adj. Non prononcé, sous-entendu (word); *the theatre of the unspoken*, le théâtre du silence. ‖ Tacite (consent).

unsporting [-'spɔːtiŋ], **unsportsmanlike**

[-'spɔ:tsmən,laik] adj. Déloyal, antisportif, peu fair-play.
unspotted [-'spɔtid] adj. Sans tache. ‖ Fɪɢ. Immaculé, pur, sans souillure.
unstable [-'steibl] adj. Instable (equilibrium, position). ‖ Fɪɢ. Instable, inconstant.
unstained [-'steind] adj. Sans tache.
unstamped [-stæmpt] adj. Non frappé (coin); non estampillé (document); non poinçonné (gold); non timbré (letter).
unstatesmanlike [-'steitsmən,laik] adj. Indigne d'un homme d'Etat.
unsteadiness [ʌn'stedinis] adj. Instabilité *f. ;* mauvais équilibre *m.* ‖ Fɪɴ. Variabilité *f.* (of prices). ‖ Fɪɢ. Irrésolution, indécision (of mind); dissipation *f.* (of a young man).
unsteady [-'stedi] adj. Peu stable, chancelant (thing). ‖ Mal assuré (hand, position); vacillant, tremblant (light). ‖ Variable (barometer); changeant (wind). ‖ Fɪɴ. Agité (market). ‖ Fɪɢ. Inconstant (affection); dissipé, peu rangé (conduct); indécis, fluctuant (mind).
unstick [-'stik] v. tr. (160). Décoller; *to come unstuck,* se décoller. ‖ Loc FAM. *To come unstuck,* tomber à l'eau, foirer.
unstinted [ʌn'stintid] adj. Sans bornes.
unstintedly [-li] adv. FAM. Dans les grandes largeurs, sans restriction.
unstinting [ʌn'stintiŋ] adj. Sans restriction (or) réserve (support, praise); généreux, prodigue (person, aid).
unstitch [-'stitʃ] v. tr. Défaire, découdre.
unstop [ʌn'stɔp] v. tr. Déboucher.
unstoppable [-'stɔpəbl] adj. Qu'on ne peut arrêter (or) maîtriser, irrésistible.
unstressed [-'strest] adj. Inaccentué, atone.
unstring [-'striŋ] v. tr. Déficeler. ‖ Débander (bow). ‖ Désenfiler (pearls). ‖ Mus. Détendre les cordes de. ‖ Fɪɢ. Ebranler (s.o.'s nerves).
unstuck [-'stʌk] pret., p. p. See UNSTICK.
unstudied [-'stʌdid] adj. Non étudié (subject); naturel, spontané (style). ‖ Ignorant (*in,* de).
unsubdued [,ʌnsəb'dju:d] adj. Indompté (country); constant (faith, passion).
unsubmissive [,ʌnsəb'misiv] adj. Insoumis.
unsubstantial [-stænʃəl] adj. Immatériel. ‖ Sans consistance.
unsubstantiated [-'stænʃi,eitid] adj. Sans fondement, non fondé.
unsuccess [,ʌnsək'ses] n. Insuccès *m.*
unsuccessful [-ful] adj. Sans succès, infructueux, raté (attempt); ajourné, malheureux (candidate); victime d'un échec (person); *to be unsuccessful,* échouer, n'avoir pas de succès.
unsuitable [ʌn'sju:təbl] adj. Mal assorti (marriage); inopportun, inconvenant (remark). ‖ Inapte (person); non approprié (or) adapté (thing) [*for, to,* à].
unsuited [-id] adj. Inapte, impropre (*for, to,* à). ‖ Qui n'a pas trouvé son affaire (person).
unsullied [ʌn'sʌlid] adj. Sans souillure.
unsung [ʌn'sʌŋ] adj. Méconnu.
unsupported [,ʌnsə'pɔ:tid] adj. Sans support. ‖ Fɪɢ. Non appuyé (or) soutenu.
unsuppressed [-'prest] adj. Non supprimé. ‖ Fɪɢ. Non contenu.
unsure [-'ʃuə*] adj. Qui manque d'assurance (lacking assurance). ‖ Incertain; *I am unsure of her agreement,* je ne suis pas sûr qu'elle accepte. ‖ Peu sûr, dangereux (unsafe). ‖ Sur lequel on ne peut compter (untrustworthy). ‖ Incertain, vacillant (unsteady).
unsurpassable [-sə'pɑ:səbl] adj. Insurpassable.
unsurpassed [-'pɑ:st] adj. Non surpassé, inégalé.
unsuspected [,ʌnsəs'pektid] adj. Insoupçonné.
unsuspecting [-iŋ] adj. Sans soupçons, insoupçonneux, confiant.
unswaddle [ʌn'swɔdl] adj. Démailloter.

unsweetened [-'swi:tənd] adj. CULIN. Non sucré.
unswerving [-'swə:viŋ] adj. Inébranlable, qui ne s'écarte pas du but, qui suit son chemin.
unsymmetrical [ʌnsi'metrikəl] adj. Asymétrique.
unsympathetic [ʌn,simpə'θetik] adj. Peu compatissant, sec.
unsystematic [ʌn,sisti'mætik] adj. Non systématique, sans méthode.
untainted [ʌn'teintid] adj. CULIN. Frais, non gâté. ‖ Fɪɢ. Sans tache.
untamable [-'teiməbl] adj. Inapprivoisable. ‖ Fɪɢ. Indomptable.
untamed [-'teimd] adj. Indompté, farouche (unsubdued); sauvage (wild).
untangle [-'tæŋgl] v. tr. Démêler, débrouiller.
untanned [-'tænd] adj. Non tanné (leather). ‖ Non bronzé (person).
untapped [-'tæpt] adj. Inexploité (ressources).
untarnished [-'tɑ:niʃt] adj. Non terni. ‖ Fɪɢ. Sans ternissure, non entaché.
untasted [-'teistid] adj. Non goûté.
untaught [-'tɔ:t] adj. Non instruit (person); non enseigné (thing).
untaxed [-'tækst] adj. Non imposé, exempt d'impôts.
unteachable [-'ti:tʃəbl] adj. A qui on ne peut rien enseigner, indocile (child). ‖ Intransmissible, qui ne peut être enseigné (skill).
untempered [-'tempəd] adj. Non tempéré (or) adouci. ‖ TECHN. Non trempé (steel).
untenable [-'tenəbl] adj. Intenable (position); insoutenable (theory).
untenanted [-'tenəntid] adj. Vide, sans locataire.
untested [-'testid] adj. Non éprouvé.
unthankful [-'θæŋkful] adj. Ingrat. (See THANKLESS.)
unthinkable [ʌn'θiŋkəbl] adj. Inimaginable. (See INCONCEIVABLE.)
unthinking [-iŋ] adj. Irréfléchi.
unthought [ʌn'θɔ:t] adj. *Unthought-of,* inimaginable, imprévu.
unthread [-'θred] v. tr. Désenfiler.
unthrifty [-'θrifti] adj. Dépensier; prodigue (*of,* de). ‖ Aɢʀɪc. Malvenant.
untidy [-'taidi] adj. Négligé (dress); ébouriffé (hair); en désordre, mal tenu (room); sans soin, négligé (person).
untie [-'tai] v. tr. (3). Détacher (a dog); délier (a knot); déficeler (a parcel).
until [ʌn'til] prep. Jusqu'à; avant. (See TILL.) — conj. Jusqu'à ce que; avant que.
untilled [-'tild] adj. Aɢʀɪc. Inculte.
untimely [-'taimli] adj. Prématuré (death); indu (hour). ‖ Inopportun, mal venu (question). ‖ Aɢʀɪc. Précoce (fruit). — adv. Prématurément. ‖ Inopportunément.
untiring [-'taiəriŋ] adj. Infatigable.
unto ['ʌntu] prep. A; vers; jusqu'à. ‖ Envers.
untold [ʌn'tould] adj. Non relaté (story). ‖ Incalculable (wealth).
untouchable [-'tʌtʃəbl] adj. Intouchable, intangible. — n. Intouchable *s.,* paria *m.*
untouched [-'tʌtʃt] adj. Non touché, intact (thing). ‖ Inentamé (question, reputation). ‖ Insensible, indifférent (*by,* à) [person].
untoward [ʌn'touəd], [ʌn'tɔ:d] adj. Malséant; incongru (behaviour); fâcheux (event); indocile; pervers (person); peu commode (thing); peu propice (weather); *with nothing untoward taking place,* en tout bien tout honneur.
untowardness [-nis] n. Caractère fâcheux *m.* ‖ Indocilité *f.*
untraceable [-'treisəbl] adj. Indécouvrable.
untrained [-'treind] adj. Non dressé (animal); inexpérimenté (person). ‖ Spoʀts. Non entraîné.

untrammelled [-'træməld] adj. Sans entraves; dégagé (*by*, de).

untransferable [ˌʌntræns'fərəbḷ] adj. Intransférable. ‖ Personnel, non communicable. ‖ JUR. Inaliénable.

untranslatable [-'leitəbḷ] adj. Intraduisible.

untransportable [-'pɔːtəbḷ] adj. Intransportable.

untravelled [ʌn'trævəld] adj. Inexploré (country); qui n'a pas voyagé (person).

untried [-'traid] adj. Non tenté, inessayé. ‖ Non éprouvé. ‖ JUR. Non jugé.

untrimmed [-'trimd] adj. Non garni (hat). ‖ AGRIC. Mal tenu (garden); non taillé (hedge). ‖ TECHN. Brut (stone). ‖ CULIN. Non paré (meat).

untrodden [-'trɔdən] adj. Inexploré (country); vierge (forest); non foulé (snow); non frayé, impratiqué (track).

untroubled [-'trʌbld] adj. Non troublé. ‖ FIG. Calme, paisible.

untrue [-'truː] adj. Faux, mensonger. ‖ Erroné, inexact (statement). ‖ Déloyal (*to*, envers); infidèle (*to*, à). ‖ TECHN. Gauchi; faux.

untrussed [-'trʌst] adj. ARCHIT. Délié (bridge). ‖ CULIN. Non troussé.

untrustworthy [ʌn'trʌst,wəːði] adj. Sujet à caution, douteux, sur lequel on ne peut compter. (See UNRELIABLE.)

untruth [ʌn'truːθ] n. Contre-vérité *f.* (lie). ‖ Fausseté *f.* (falsity).

untruthful [-'truːθful] adj. Menteur (person); mensonger, trompeur (statement).

untruthfully [-'truːθfuli] adv. Mensongèrement, trompeusement.

untruthfulness [-'truːθfulnis] n. Fausseté *f.*

untune [-'tjuːn] v. tr. MUS. Désaccorder.

untuneful [-'tjuːnful] adj. Discordant, dissonant.

unturned [-'təːnd] adj. Non retourné. ‖ FIG. *To leave no stone unturned*, ne rien négliger.

untutored [-'tjuːtəd] adj. Non instruit, non formé. ‖ Inhabile (*in*, dans).

untwine ['-twain] v. tr. Démêler, détortiller. — v. intr. Se démêler, se détortiller.

untwist [-'twist] v. tr. Détordre, détortiller. — v. intr. Se détordre.

unused [-juːzd] adj. Inutilisé, non employé. ‖ Neuf (new). ‖ GRAMM. Inusité (word). — [-juːst] adj. Inaccoutumé, inhabitué (*to*, à).

unusual [-'juːʒuəl] adj. Inhabituel, peu commun (or) banal; inaccoutumé. ‖ GRAMM. Inusité, rare (word).

unutterable [-'ʌtərəbḷ] adj. Inexprimable. (See INEFFABLE.)

unvalued [ʌn'væljuːd] adj. FIN. Non évalué. ‖ FIG. Peu apprécié.

unvanquished [-'væŋkwiʃt] adj. Invaincu.

unvaried [-'vɛərid] adj. Peu varié; monotone.

unvarnished [-'vɑːniʃt] adj. Non verni. ‖ FIG. Sans fard, nu (truth).

unvarying [-'vɛəriiŋ] adj. Invariable.

unveil [-'veil] v. tr. Dévoiler (a secret); inaugurer (a statue). — v. intr. Se dévoiler.

unverifiable [-'verifaiəbḷ] adj. Invérifiable.

unversed [-'vəːst] adj. Peu versé (*in*, dans).

unviolated [-'vaiəleitid] adj. Inviolé.

unvoiced [-'vɔist] adj. Non exprimé. ‖ GRAMM. Sourd; muet.

unvouched [-'vautʃt] adj. *Unvouched for*, non garanti (or) confirmé.

unwaked [ʌn'weikt] adj. Non éveillé.

unwanted [-'wɔːntid] adj. Non souhaité. ‖ Superflu, inutile.

unwariness [-'wɛərinis] adj. Etourderie, irréflexion; imprévoyance *f.*

unwarlike [-'wɔː,laik] adj. Pacifique, paisible.

unwarned [-'wɔːnd] adj. Inaverti.

unwarped [-wɔːpt] adj. Non gauchi (wood). ‖ FIG. Non dévié (mind).

unwarrantable [ʌn'wɔrəntəbḷ] adj. Injustifiable.

unwarranted [-id] adj. Injustifié. ‖ Sans garantie.

unwary [ʌn'wɛəri] adj. Imprudent; irréfléchi.

unwashed [-'wɔʃt] adj. Non lavé, sale. ‖ FAM. *The Great Unwashed*, les pouilleux.

unwatered [-'wɔːtəd] adj. Sans eau (country); non arrosé (garden). ‖ Non abreuvé (cattle). ‖ Non dilué (or) baptisé (wine). ‖ Non moiré (silk).

unwavering [-'weivəriŋ] adj. Non chancelant. ‖ Non démenti, ferme, inébranlable.

unweaned [-'wiːnd] adj. Non sevré.

unwearable [-'wɛərɛbḷ] adj. Non mettable.

unwearied [ʌn'wiərid] adj. Dispos, sans fatigue. ‖ FIG. Jamais lassé.

unwearying [-iŋ] adj. Infatigable, inlassable.

unwelcome [-'welkəm] adj. Fâcheux, désagréable (news); mal venu, importun (visitor).

unwell [-'wel] adj. MED. Souffrant, indisposé.

unwholesome [-houlsəm] adj. Malsain.

unwieldy [-wiːldi] adj. Peu maniable (tool). ‖ Lourd, pesant (person).

unwilling [ʌn'wiliŋ] adj. Rétif, de mauvaise volonté; non disposé (*to*, à); *to be unwilling that*, ne pas vouloir que.

unwillingly [-li] adv. A contrecœur, de mauvaise grâce, à regret.

unwind [ʌn'waind] v. tr. (190). Dérouler; dévider. — v. intr. Se dérouler, se dévider.

unwinking [-'wiŋkiŋ] adj. Fixe (attention); qui ne cligne pas (eye).

unwisdom [-'wizdəm] n. Imprudence *f.*

unwise [-'waiz] adj. Imprudent, peu sage; malavisé. ‖ Peu sage, contraire au bon sens (action).

unwished [-'wiʃt] adj. *Unwished-for*, non désiré (or) souhaité.

unwitting [ʌn'witiŋ] adj. Inconscient (*of*, de).

unwittingly [-li] adv. Sans le vouloir, inconsciemment, involontairement.

unwomanly [ʌn'wumənli] adj. Indigne d'une femme; peu convenable de la part d'une femme.

unwonted [-'wountid] adj. Inhabituel, insolite.

unwordable [-'wəːdəbḷ] adj. Inexprimable.

unworkable [-'wəːkəbḷ] adj. TECHN. Inexploitable. ‖ FIG. Inexécutable.

unworldly [-'wəːldli] adj. Ingénu, naïf (unsophisticated). ‖ Indifférent aux choses de ce monde (not materially minded). ‖ Surnaturel, céleste (unearthly).

unworn [-'wɔːn] adj. Non usé (or) usagé; neuf.

unworthily [ʌn'wəːðili] adv. Indignement.

unworthiness [-inis] n. Indignité *f.* ‖ Défaut de mérite *m.*

unworthy [-i] adj. Indigne (*of*, de). ‖ Sans mérite, peu méritoire. ‖ Méprisable, peu digne.

unwounded [ʌn'wuːndid] adj. Non blessé, sans blessure.

unwrap [-'ræp] v. tr. (1). Déballer, déplier, dépaqueter, développer.

unwritten [-'ritṇ] adj. Non écrit. ‖ Oral (tradition). ‖ Vierge, blanc (paper). ‖ JUR. *Unwritten law*, droit coutumier, loi morale.

unyielding [ʌn'jiːldiŋ] adj Ferme, solide. ‖ FIG. Inflexible, inébranlable.

unyoke [-jouk] v. tr., intr. Dételer (lit. and fig.).

unzip ['-zip] v. tr. (1). Baisser (or) défaire la fermeture Eclair de. — v. intr. S'ouvrir, se défaire.

up [ʌp] adv. En haut; *an egg beaten up*, un œuf monté au fouet; *to dig up*, déterrer; *to row up*, remonter à force de rames; *to show s.o. up*, faire monter qqn en haut (or) au premier; *to walk up*, gravir à pied; *up in the air*, haut dans l'air. ‖ Debout; *to sit up*, se mettre sur son séant; *to stand up*, se tenir debout; *to stay up all night with a sick man*, passer la nuit à (or) veiller un malade. ‖ Complètement; *to fill up a glass*, remplir un verre; *to give up the ghost*, rendre l'âme. ‖ NAUT. *To put up the helm*, mettre la barre au vent.

— prep. Vers le haut, en haut de; *up and down the room*, en long et en large dans la pièce; *up hill and down dale*, par monts et par vaux; *up the hill*, en haut de la colline. ‖ Au fond de; *up the yard*, au bout de la cour. ‖ **Up-stream**, adj. D'amont; adv. En amont. ‖ **Up to**, jusqu'à; *up to now*, jusqu'ici; *up to what age?*, jusqu'à quel âge? ‖ *Up to*, au niveau de, à la hauteur de; *to live up to his promises*, tenir ses promesses; *to praise s.o. up to the skies*, porter qqn aux nues; *up to sample*, conforme à l'échantillon. ‖ *Up to*, capable de; *to be up to anything*, être capable de tout; *to be up to one's work*, connaître son affaire. ‖ *Up to*, occupé à; *to be up to something*, avoir qqch. en tête. ‖ *Up to*, dévolu à; *it is up to us to*, il nous appartient de, c'est à nous de. ‖ **Up with**; *it's all up with him*, son affaire est faite; *what's up with him?*, qu'est-ce qui lui prend?
— adj. Montant; *up train*, train montant. ‖ Debout; *he is up at seven*, il est levé à sept heures; *the house is up*, la Chambre en siège pas. ‖ Monté; *the glass is up*, le thermomètre a monté. ‖ Soulevé, excité; *my blood is up*, je bous; *to be up in arms*, être soulevé; être indigné (or) monté (*against*, contre). ‖ Achevé; *the game is up*, tout est perdu; *time is up*, le temps est expiré; *to be hard up*, être fauché. ‖ Fort, compétent; *to be well up in English*, être calé en anglais. ‖ En question; *what's up?*, de quoi s'agit-il?
— n. *Ups and downs*, vicissitudes, hauts et bas, cahots.
upbear [ʌp'bɛə*] v. tr. (9). Soutenir, supporter.
upbeat ['ʌp,biːt] adj. FAM. Optimiste.
upbraid [ʌp'breid] v. tr. Réprimander, semoncer; *to upbraid s.o. for* (or) *with sth.*, reprocher vivement qqch. à qqn.
upbraiding [-iŋ] n. Reproches m. pl.
upbringing ['ʌp,briŋiŋ] n. Education f.
upcast ['ʌpkɑːst] n. Rejet (m.) en haut. ‖ TECHN. Courant d'air ascendant m. (air-current); puits (m.) de sortie d'air (shaft).
— [ʌp'kɑːst] v. intr. (32). Jeter en l'air (sth.). ‖ Lever au ciel (eyes).
update [ʌp'deit] v. tr. Mettre à jour (to bring up to date); moderniser, mettre au goût du jour (to modernize).
updrawn ['ʌpdrɔːn] adj. Haussé, relevé.
up-end [ʌp'end] v. tr. Renverser, retourner (to set on end); renverser (to knock over). ‖ FIG. Bouleverser, retourner.
upgrade [ʌp'greid] v. tr. Faire monter en grade, donner de l'avancement à (an employee); revaloriser (a job); améliorer, perfectionner (a product); rénover (a neighbourhood).
— ['ʌp,greid] n. U. S. Pente, côte f. (upward slope). ‖ LOC. *To be on the upgrade*, aller en augmentant (or) en s'améliorant.
upheaped [ʌp'hiːpt] adj. Entassé.
upheaval [-'hiːvəl] n. Soulèvement m. (lit. and fig.).
upheave [-hiːv] v. tr. Soulever.
— v. intr. Se soulever.
uphill ['ʌp'hil] adv. En côte, en montant.
— adj. Montant. ‖ FIG. Ardu, fatigant.
— ['ʌphil] n. Côte, montée f.
uphold [ʌp'hould] v. tr. (82). Soutenir, supporter, étayer. ‖ FIG. Soutenir (a position); soutenir, encourager, épauler (s.o.).
upholder [-ə*] n. Soutien, appui m. (lit. and fig.).
upholster [ʌp'houlstə] v. tr. Capitonner; tapisser (in, with, de).
upholsterer [-rə*] n. Tapissier m.
upholstery [-ri] n. Tapisserie, garniture f. ‖ Capitonnage m.
upkeep ['ʌpkiːp] n. Entretien m.
upland ['ʌplənd] adj. Montagneux, haut, des montagnes.
— n. pl. Hautes terres f. pl.; plateaux m. pl.

uplander [-ə*] n. Montagnard s.
uplift [ʌp'lift] v. tr. Soulever.
— adj. *Uplift brassiere*, soutien-gorge qui met la poitrine en valeur.
— ['ʌplift] n. Elévation f.
upmost ['ʌp,moust] adj., adv. See UPPERMOST.
upon [ə'pɔn] prep. Sur; *lying upon a divan*, étendu sur son divan; *upon the wide sea*, sur la vaste mer. ‖ Au moment de; *upon the heavy middle of the night*, en plein milieu de la nuit. ‖ Au cours de; *upon a long voyage*, au cours d'un long voyage. ‖ Contre; *to draw one's sword upon s.o.*, tirer l'épée contre qqn.
upper ['ʌpə*] adj. Supérieur, en dessus de, de dessus, d'en haut; *upper branches, forms*, hautes branches, classes; *upper jaw*, mâchoire supérieure. ‖ GEOGR. *Upper Egypt*, Haute-Egypte; *Upper Volta*, Haute-Volta. ‖ MUS. Aigu. ‖ FIG. Supérieur; *to get the upper hand*, prendre le dessus. ‖ FAM. *Upper crust*, gratin.
— n. pl. Tiges f. pl.; empeigne f. (of boot). ‖ U. S. Guêtres f. pl. ‖ FAM. *On one's uppers*, dans la dèche (or) débine.
uppercut ['ʌpəkʌt] n. SPORTS. Uppercut m.
uppermost [-moust] adj. Le plus haut.
— adv. Sur le dessus. ‖ FIG. A la surface, au premier rang.
uppish ['ʌpiʃ] adj. Suffisant, arrogant, monté sur ses ergots; merdeux (pop.).
uppishness [-nis] n. Grands airs m. pl.; présomption f.
uppity ['ʌpiti] adj. Arrogant, prétentieux (snobbish). ‖ Indocile, peu maniable (or) malléable (uncontrollable).
upright ['ʌprait] adj. Debout (person); droit (mur). ‖ MATH. Vertical, perpendiculaire. ‖ FIG. Droit, intègre, probe.
— adv. Droit.
— n. TECHN. Montant, jambage m.
uprightly [-li] adv. Droit, d'aplomb. ‖ Verticalement. ‖ FIG. Honnêtement.
uprightness [-nis] n. Aplomb m.; verticalité f. ‖ FIG. Droiture, rectitude, intégrité f.
uprise [ʌp'raiz] v. intr. (113). Se lever, s'élever. ‖ FIG. Se soulever, se rebeller, se révolter.
uprising [-iŋ] n. Lever m. ‖ FIG. Soulèvement m.; rébellion, révolte, émeute f.
uproar ['ʌprɔː*] n. Tumulte, vacarme m. (din). ‖ Bouleversement, tumulte m. (disturbance).
uproarious [ʌp'rɔːriəs] adj. Tapageur, tumultueux. ‖ Bruyant (laughter).
uproot [ʌp'ruːt] v. tr. Déraciner.
upset [ʌp'set] v. tr. (185). Renverser (a bottle); faire verser (a car); culbuter, renverser (s.o.). ‖ Bouleverser (a room). ‖ NAUT. Faire chavirer (a boat). ‖ MED. Rendre malade; déranger. ‖ TECHN. Refouler. ‖ FIG. Détraquer, déranger, bouleverser (to disturb); bouleverser, émouvoir, retourner (to distress); *upset at*, contrarié de; *the least things upset him*, un rien l'émeut.
— v. intr. Verser.
— ['ʌpset] adj. FIN. *Upset price*, mise à prix.
— n. Renversement m. ‖ Bouleversement m.
upshot ['ʌpʃət] n. Résultat m.; *on the upshot*, au bout du compte.
upside-down ['ʌpsaid'daun] adj. Renversé, à l'envers. ‖ FIG. Biscornu, bizarre, baroque.
— adv. Sens dessus dessous.
upstage ['ʌp'steidʒ] adv. THEATR. Au fond de la scène.
— adj. FIG. Hautain, prétentieux, crâneur.
— v. tr. THEATR. Obliger à tourner le dos aux spectateurs. ‖ FIG. Eclipser, voler la vedette à.
upstairs ['ʌp'stɛəz] adv. En haut, à l'étage supérieur.
— ['ʌpstɛəz] adj. D'en haut, du dessus.

upstanding [ʌp'stændiŋ] adj. Hérissé, dressé (hair); debout, droit (person, thing). ‖ Fin. Fixe (wages).

upstart [['ʌpstɑ:t] n. Nouveau riche *m.* ‖ U.S. Opposant *m.*

upstroke [-strouk] n. Délié *m.* (in handwriting).

upsurge [-sə:dʒ] n. Poussée *f.* (economic).

upswept ['ʌpswept] adj. Incurvé vers le haut; ramené sur le dessus de la tête (hair).

upswing ['ʌp,swiŋ] n. Essor *m.*, croissance *f.*

uptake [-teik] n. Compréhension; comprenotte *f.* (fam.); *to be quick on the uptake*, saisir à demi-mot. ‖ Techn. Colonne d'aération *f.*

upthrow [ʌp'θrou] v. tr. (180). Rejeter en haut.

upthrust ['ʌpθrʌst] n. Geol. Soulèvement *m.*

uptight [ʌp'tait] adj. Fam. Tendu, crispé (nervous); irrité, en rogne (angry). ‖ Fauché, dans la débine (broke).

uptown ['ʌp'taun] adj. U.S. Résidentiel, loin du centre.
— adv. U.S. Dans les quartiers résidentiels, loin du centre.
— n. U.S. Quartiers résidentiels *m. pl.*

upturn [ʌp'tə:n] v. tr. Lever, tourner vers le haut (eyes). ‖ Agric. Retourner (ground).
— ['ʌp,tə:n] n. Bouleversement, chambardement *m.* (upheaval). ‖ Amélioration, reprise *f.* (upswing).

upward ['ʌpwəd] adj. Montant, ascendant, ascentionnel. ‖ Fin. De hausse.
— adv. Vers le haut. ‖ En amont. ‖ Au-dessus (*of*, de).

upwind [ʌp'wind] adj. Au vent.
— adv. Contre le vent, face au vent.

ur(a)emia [juə'ri:miə] n. Med. Urémie *f.*

ur(a)emic [-mik] adj. Med. Urémique.

uranic [juə'rænik] adj. Chim. Uranique.

uranium [-'reiniəm] n. Chim. Uranium *m.*

uranography [,juərə'nɔgrəfi] n. Uranographie *f.*

uranometry [-mitri] n. Uranométrie *f.*

urban ['ə:bn] adj. Urbain. ‖ **Urban renewal,** n. Rénovation urbaine *f.*

urbane [ə:'bein] adj. Courtois.

urbanely [-li] adv. Avec urbanité.

urbanity [ə:'bæniti] n. Urbanité *f.*

urbanization [,ə:bənai'zeiʃən] n. Urbanisation *f.*

urbanize ['ə:bə,naiz] v. tr. Urbaniser.

urchin ['ə:tʃin] n. Gosse, gamin; garnement *m.* ‖ Zool. Oursin *m.*

urea ['juəriə] n. Med. Urée *f.*

ureter [juə'ri:tə*] n. Med. Uretère *m.*

urethane ['juəri,θein] n. Chim. Uréthanne *m.*

urethra [juə'ri:θrə] n. Med. Urètre *m.*

urethral [-θrəl] adj. Med. Urétral.

urge [ə:dʒ] v. tr. Faire avancer, pousser, presser. ‖ Exhorter, engager vivement (*to*, à) [to entreat]. ‖ Pousser, inciter (*to*, à) [to incite]. ‖ Préconiser, soutenir, proposer avec vigueur (to advocate). ‖ Faire valoir, mettre en avant (to allege).
— n. Incitation, poussée, force déterminante *f.*

urgency [-ənsi] n. Urgence *f.* ‖ Instance *f. pl.* (insistence).

urgent [-ənt] adj. Urgent, pressant (matter). ‖ Pressant, insistant (person); *to be urgent with*, insister auprès de.

uric ['juərik] adj. Med. Urique.

urinal ['juərinḷ] n. Urinoir *m.; street urinal,* vespasienne.

urinalysis [,juəri'nælisis] (pl. **urinalyses** [-,si:z]) n. Med. Analyse d'urine *f.*

urinary [-əri] adj. Med. Urinaire; *urinary system,* voies urinaires.
— n. Agric. Fosse (*f.*) à purin.

urinate [-eit] v. intr. Med. Uriner.

urine ['juərin] n. Med. Urine *f.*

urinous [-əs] adj. Med. Urineux.

urn [ə:n] n. Urne *f.* ‖ Culin. Samovar *m.* ‖ Fig. Tombeau *m.*
— v. tr. Mettre dans une urne.

urogenital [,juərou'dʒenitḷ] adj. Med. Urogénital, génito-urinaire.

urologic(al) [,juərə'lɔdʒik(ḷ)] adj. Med. Urologique.

urologist [ju'rɔlədʒist] n. Med. Urologue *s.*

urology [juə'rɔlədʒi] n. Med. Urologie *f.*

ursine ['ə:sain] adj. Zool. Ursin.

Ursuline ['ə:sjulain] n. Eccles. Ursuline *f.*

urtica ['ə:tikə] n. Bot. Ortie *f.*

urticaria [,ə:ti'kɛəriə] n. Med. Urticaire *f.*

urticate ['ə:tikeit] v. tr. Ortier; piquer comme une ortie.

urtication [,ə:ti'keiʃən] n. Urtication *f.*

urubu ['u:rubu:] n. Zool. Urubu *m.*

Uruguay ['juərə,gwai] n. Geogr. Uruguay *m.*

urus ['juərəs] n. Zool. Aurochs *m.*

us [ʌs] pr. pers. Nous (objective case).

U.S. [,ju:'es] abbr. *United States,* Etats-Unis, U.S.

U.S.A. [,ju:es'ei] abbr. *United States of America,* Etats-Unis d'Amérique, U.S.A.

usable ['ju:zəbḷ] adj. Utilisable.

usage [-idʒ] n. Usage *m.;* coutume *f.* ‖ Traitement *m.;* manière (*f.*) de procéder; *ill usage,* traitement brutal. ‖ Gramm. Usage *m.*

usance [-əns] n Comm. Usance *f.*

use [ju:s] n. Usage, emploi *m.; in common use,* d'usage (or) d'emploi courant; *out of use,* inusité, désuet; hors de service; *to continue in use,* demeurer en usage. ‖ Usage, droit (*m.*) d'utiliser; *to have the use of the bathroom,* pouvoir utiliser la salle de bains. ‖ Usage *m.;* possession *f.; to have the full use of one's faculties,* jouir de toutes ses facultés. ‖ Usage *m.;* coutume, habitude *f.* (custom). ‖ Utilité *f.; to be of use for,* être utile à, servir à; *what's the use of?,* à quoi sert; à quoi bon?; *to have no use for,* n'avoir que faire de, n'avoir pas besoin de (to have no need of); ne pas pouvoir souffrir (to dislike). ‖ Eccles. Rite *m.* ‖ Jur. Usufruit *m.*
— [ju:z] v. tr. Employer, user de, se servir de (sth.); *to be used for,* servir à. ‖ User de, avoir recours à; *to use every means,* épuiser tous les moyens. ‖ Utiliser, se servir de, profiter de; *he's only using you,* il profite de vous simplement; *to use one's opportunities,* profiter des occasions. ‖ Consommer (gas, goods, power). ‖ En user avec, traiter (s.o.); *to use s.o. roughly,* maltraiter qqn. ‖ **To use up,** épuiser.

used [ju:zd] adj. D'occasion.

used [ju:st] v. tr. *We used to go swimming,* avant, nous allions à la piscine; *they don't eat as much as they used to,* ils ne mangent plus autant qu'avant; *I used to live there when I was young,* j'habitais là lorsque j'étais enfant.
— N.B. La négation de *he used to* est soit *he did not use to,* soit *he used not to.* L'interrogation est soit *did he use to,* soit *used he to.*

used adj. Habitué, accoutumé (*to,* à); *to be used to doing sth.,* avoir l'habitude de faire qqch.

useful ['ju:sful] adj. Utile. ‖ Fam. Honorable (attempt); habile, dégourdi (person); *to be pretty useful with one's fists,* savoir se servir de ses poings.

usefully [-i] adv. Utilement.

usefulness [-nis] n. Utilité *f.*

useless ['ju:slis] adj. Inutile. ‖ Fam. Patraque.

uselessly [-li] adv. Inutilement.

uselessness [-nis] n. Inutilité *f.*

user ['ju:zə*] n. Usager *m.* ‖ Jur. Usage *m.*

usher ['ʌʃə*] n. Jur. Huissier *m.*
— v. tr. Introduire (*in,* dans); *to usher out,* reconduire.

usherette [ʌʃə'ret] n. Cinem. Ouvreuse *f.*

usquebaugh ['ʌskwibɔ:] n. Whisky *m.*

U.S.S.R. [,ju:eses'ɑ:*] abbr. *Union of Soviet Socialist Republics,* Union des républiques socialistes soviétiques, U.R.S.S.

usual ['juːʒuəl] adj. Usuel, habituel, coutumier; *as usual,* comme d'habitude.

usually [-i] adv. Usuellement, ordinairement, d'habitude.

usualness [-nis] n. Caractère habituel (or) fréquent *m.;* fréquence *f.*

usufruct ['juːzjufrʌkt] n. JUR. Usufruit *m.*

usufructuary [ˌjuːzju'frʌktjuəri] adj., n. JUR. Usufruitier *m.*

usurer ['juːʒərə*] n. Usurier *m.*

usurious [juː'zuəriəs] adj. Usuraire.

usurp [juː'zəːp] v. tr. Usurper.
— v. intr. Empiéter *(upon,* sur). [See ENCROACH.]

usurpation [ˌjuːzə'peiʃən] n. Usurpation *f.*

usurper [juː'zəːpə*] n. Usurpateur *m.;* usurpatrice *f.*

usurpingly ['-zəːpiŋli] adv. Par usurpation.

usury ['juːʒuri] n. Usure *f.*

ut [ut] n. Mus. Ut, do *m.*

utensil [juː'tensl̩] n. CULIN. Ustensile *f.* ‖ TECHN. Outil, instrument *m.*

uterine ['juːtərain] adj. MED., JUR. Utérin.

uterus [-rəs] (pl. **uteri** [-rai]) n. MED. Utérus *m.;* matrice *f.*

utilitarian ['juːtili'tɛəriən] adj., n. Utilitaire *s.*

utilitarianism [-izm̩] n. Utilitarisme *m.*

utility [juː'tiliti] n. Utilité *f.; utility goods,* articles utilitaires; *utility room,* buanderie, cellier. ‖ MILIT. *Utility footwear,* chaussure nationale. ‖ Utilitarisme *m.* ‖ THEATR. Utilité *f.* ‖ U. S. *Public utility,* entreprise de service public.

utilizable ['juːtilaizəbl̩] adj. Utilisable.

utilization [ˌjuːtilai'zeiʃən] n. Utilisation *f.* ‖ FIN. Réalisation *f.*

utilize ['juːtilaiz] v. tr. Utiliser, employer. (See USE.) ‖ Tirer parti de.

utmost ['ʌtmoust] adj. Le plus éloigné, extrême (farthest). ‖ Le plus grand, extrême (greatest).
— n. Maximum *m.; at the utmost,* en mettant les choses au mieux; *to do one's utmost,* faire tout son possible.

utopia [juː'toupjə] n. Utopie *f.*

utopian [-jən] adj. Utopique.
— n. Utopiste *s.*

utopianism [-jənizm̩] n. Utopisme *m.*

utricle ['juːtrik] n. BOT., MED. Utricule *m.*

utter ['ʌtə*] adj. Complet, total, absolu.

utter v. tr. Pousser (a cry, sigh); dire, faire (a lie); prononcer, proférer, dire (a word). ‖ Emettre (counterfeit money, sounds); publier (a libel). ‖ Exprimer (one's feelings).

utterance [-rəns] n. Expression *f.; to give utterance to,* exprimer. ‖ Elocution, articulation *f.; defective utterance,* défaut de prononciation. ‖ Pl. Propos *m. pl.*

utterly [-li] adv. Complètement, totalement.

uttermost [-moust]. See UTMOST.

uvula ['juːvjulə] n. MED. Luette *f.*

uvular [-ə*] adj. MED. Uvulaire.

uxorious [ʌk'sɔːriəs] adj. FAM. Enjuponné, mené par sa femme. (See HENPECKED.)

uxoriousness [-nis] n. FAM. Soumission (*m.*) à sa femme.

v [viː] n. V, v *m.* ‖ Cinq *m.* (Roman numeral). ‖ MILIT. Cran *m.* (of backsight). ‖ TECHN. En V. ‖ COMM. *V-decolletage, V-neck,* décolletage en pointe. ‖ AVIAT. *V1, V2,* V1, V2 (robot bomb).

vac [væk] n. FAM. Vacances *f. pl.*

vacancy ['veikənsi] n. Vide *m.;* vacuité *f.* ‖ Lacune *f.;* espace vide *m.* (gap). ‖ Vide *m.* (mental); absence (*f.*) d'idées. ‖ Disponibilité *f.* (lodging).

vacant [-ənt] adj. Vacant, vide (see EMPTY); de loisirs (hours); inoccupé (room); libre, disponible (seat). ‖ Vague, distrait, atone (expression); vide (mind); *with a vacant stare,* le regard perdu. ‖ JUR. Vacant (succession). ‖ COMM. Vacant, libre (post); *to be vacant,* vaquer.

vacantly [-əntli] adv. D'un air vague; d'un œil terne; avec un regard perdu.

vacate [və'keit] v. tr. Quitter (a post). ‖ Evacuer (a flat); quitter (a room); laisser libre (a seat); *to vacate the premises,* vider les lieux. ‖ JUR. Annuler (a law).

vacation [və'keiʃən] n. Vacances *f. pl.* ‖ JUR. Vacations *f. pl.*
— v. intr. U. S. Prendre des vacances.

vacationist [-ist] n. U. S. Villégiaturiste, estivant *s.,* vacancier *m.* (See HOLIDAY-MAKER.)

vaccinal ['væksinəl] adj. MED. Vaccinal.

vaccinate [-neit] v. tr. MED. Vacciner; *to be vaccinated,* se faire vacciner.

vaccination [ˌvæksi'neiʃən] n. MED. Vaccination *f.*

vaccinator ['væksineitə*] n. MED. Vaccinateur *m.*

vaccine [-siːn] n. MED. Vaccin *m.*
— adj. MED. Vaccinal, vaccinique. ‖ AGRIC. De vache.

vaccinia ['væk'siniə] n. MED. Vaccine *f.*

vacillate ['væsileit] v. intr. Vaciller. ‖ FIG. Vaciller, fluctuer. (See HESITATE.)

vacillating [-iŋ] n. Vacillation *f.*
— adj. Vacillant. ‖ FIG. Vacillant, irrésolu.

vacillation [ˌvæsi'leiʃən] n. Vacillation *f.;* hésitation *f.*

vacillatory ['væsilitəri] adj. Vacillatoire.

vacuity [væ'kjuiti], **vacuousness** ['vækjuəsnis] n. Vide *m.;* vacuité *f.*

vacuous ['vækjuəs] adj. Vide. (See EMPTY.) ‖ Vide d'expression; vague, absent (look); hébété, stupide (person).

vacuum ['vækjuəm] n. PHYS. Vide, vacuum *m.; to make a vacuum,* faire le vide. ‖ **Vacuum-bottle** (or) **-flask,** n. Bouteille Thermos *f.* ‖ **Vacuum-cleaner,** n. Aspirateur *m.* ‖ **Vacuum-cleaning,** n. Dépoussiérage *m.* ‖ **Vacuum-packed,** adj. Empaqueté sous vide. ‖ **Vacuum-pump,** n. TECHN. Pompe (*f.*) à vide. ‖ **Vacuum-tube,** n. TECHN. Tube à vide *m.*
— N. B. Deux pluriels : *vacua, vacuums.*
— v. intr. FAM. Passer l'aspirateur.
— v. tr. Passer l'aspirateur sur, aspirer.

vade-mecum ['veidi'miːkəm] n. Vade-mecum *m.*

vagabond ['vægəbənd] adj. Vagabond, errant. (See VAGRANT.)
— n. Vagabond s.; chemineau m.
— v. intr. Vagabonder.
vagabondage ['vægəbɔndidʒ] n. Vagabondage m.
vagabondize [-aiz] v. intr. Vagabonder.
vagary ['veigəri] n. Caprice m.; fantaisie, lubie f.
vagina [və'dʒainə] n. MED. Vagin m. ‖ BOT. Gaine f.
vaginal [-əl] adj. MED. Vaginal.
vaginitis [,vædʒi'naitis] n. MED. Vaginite f.
vagrancy ['veigrənsi] n. Vagabondage m.
vagrant [-grənt] n. Vagabond s.
— adj. Vagabond, errant. ‖ MUS. Ambulant.
vague [veig] n. FAM. Vague m.; to be completely in the vague about, n'avoir pas la plus vague (or) la moindre idée de, être complètement dans le brouillard en ce qui concerne.
— adj. Vague; indécis, indéterminé (colour); imprécis (memory); estompé (shape).
vaguely [-li] adv. Vaguement.
vagueness [-nis] n. Vague m.; imprécision f.
vagus [-əs] n. MED. Vague m.
vain [vein] adj. Vain (hope, promise). ‖ Vain (pointless, unavailing). ‖ Futile, inutile, infructueux (futile, otiose). ‖ Vain, vaniteux (conceited).
— loc. adv. In vain, en vain.
vainglorious [vein'glɔ:riəs] adj. Vaniteux, glorieux.
vaingloriously [-li] adv. Vaniteusement.
vaingloriousness [-nis] n. Vanité f.
vainglory ['vein'glɔ:ri] n. Vaine gloire, gloriole f. ‖ Vanité f.
vainly ['veinli] adv. En vain, vainement, inutilement (in vain). ‖ Avec vanité, vaniteusement (conceitedly).
vainness [-nis] n. Vanité f. ‖ Inutilité, futilité f.
vair [vɛə*] n. BLAS. Vair m.
vairy [-ri] adj. BLAS. Vairé.
valance ['væləns] n. † Cantonnière f.; lambrequin m. ‖ Frange (f.) de lit.
valanced [-d] adj. Orné d'une frange.
vale [veil] n. Vallon m.; vallée f.
valediction [,væli'dikʃən] n. Adieu m.
valedictorian [,vælidik'tɔ:riən] n. U.S. Elève (m.) qui prononce le discours d'adieu.
valedictory [,væli'diktəri] adj. D'adieu.
— n. U.S. Discours d'adieu m.
valence ['veiləns], **valency** [-i] n. CHIM. Valence f.
Valencia [və'lenʃjə] n. GEOGR. Valence f. ‖ COMM. Valencia orange, valence.
Valenciennes [,vælənsi'en] n. GEOGR. Valenciennes f. ‖ COMM. Valenciennes lace, valenciennes.
valency ['veilensi] n. See VALENCE.
Valentine ['væləntain] n. Valentin m.; Valentine f. (names); St. Valentine's Day, la Saint-Valentin. ‖ Carte (f.) pour la Saint-Valentin (card). ‖ Valentine f.; Valentin m. (sweetheart).
valerate ['væləreit] n. CHIM. Valérianate m.
valerian [və'liəriən] n. BOT. Valériane f.
valet ['vælit] n. Valet (m.) de chambre.
— v. tr. Etre le valet de chambre de. ‖ COMM. Remettre en état (clothing).
valetudinarian ['væli,tju:di'nɛəriən] n., adj. MED. Valétudinaire s.
valetudinary ['væli'tju:dinəri] adj. MED. Valétudinaire.
valiant ['væljənt] adj. Vaillant, valeureux, courageux. (See BRAVE.)
valiantly [-li] adv. Vaillamment.
valid ['vælid] adj. Solide, irréfutable (argument). ‖ JUR. Valide, valable (documents); régulier (passport). ‖ CH. DE F. Valable (ticket); no longer valid, périmé.
validate [-deit] v. tr. Valider.
validation [,væli'deiʃən] n. Validation f.

validity [væ'liditi] n. Valeur, justesse, force f. (of an argument). ‖ JUR. Validité f.
valine ['veili:n] n. CHIM. Valine f.
valise [və'li:z] n. Valise f. ‖ MILIT. Portemanteau m.
Valkyrie [væl'ki:ri] n. Walkyrie f.
valley ['væli] n. GEOGR. Vallée f.; vallon m. (small). ‖ ARCHIT. Cornière f. (between two roofs); noue f. (valley-tile).
valorization [vælərai'zeiʃən] n. COMM. Valorisation f.
valorize ['væləraiz] v. tr. COMM. Valoriser.
valorous ['vælərəs] adj. Valeureux, vaillant, brave.
valorously [-li] adv. Valeureusement.
valo(u)r ['vælə *] n. Valeur, vaillance f.
valuable ['væljuəbḷ] adj. Evaluable. ‖ De valeur, précieux (of great value). ‖ JUR. For a valuable consideration, à titre onéreux.
— n. pl. Objets (m. pl.) de valeur.
valuation [vælju'eiʃən] n. Evaluation, estimation, appréciation, expertise f. (valuing). ‖ Valeur f.; prix estimé m.; to take s.o. at his own valuation, estimer qqn à la cote qu'il se donne.
valuator ['væljueitə*] n. Expert; estimateur m.
value ['vælju:] v. tr. Priser, estimer, faire cas de, tenir à, attacher du prix à; to value one's life, tenir à la vie; to value oneself, se flatter, tirer vanité (on, de). ‖ FIN. Valoriser (cheques). ‖ COMM. Evaluer, estimer, expertiser.
— v. intr. COMM. Tirer (upon, sur).
— n. Valeur f.; prix m. (lit. and fig.); to be of value, avoir de la valeur; of no value, sans valeur; to set a value on, évaluer; to set too much value on, surestimer, attacher trop de prix à. ‖ PHILOS., MUS., GRAMM., MATH. Valeur f. ‖ FIN. Valeur f.; to lose value, se dévaloriser; loss in value, tare. ‖ COMM. Valeur f.; decrease, increase in value, moins-value, plus-value; market value, valeur marchande; this article is good value, cet article est avantageux; to get good value for one's money, en avoir pour son argent. ‖ **Value-added tax**, n. Taxe (f.) à la valeur ajoutée. ‖ **Value-judgement**, n. Jugement (m.) de valeur.
valued [-d] adj. Précieux, estimé. ‖ COMM. Evalué.
valueless [-lis] adj. Sans valeur.
valuer [-ə*] n. Estimateur, appréciateur, expert m.; official valuer, commissaire-priseur.
valuing [-iŋ] n. Evaluation, estimation f. ‖ FIN. Valorisation f.
valve [vælv] n. TECHN. Soupape f.; clapet m. (of a pump); water valve, vanne à eau. ‖ AUTOM. Valve f. (of tyre); butterfly valve, volet. ‖ MED. Valvule f. (of the heart). ‖ RADIO. Lampe f.; valve set, poste à lampes. ‖ ELECTR. Tube électronique m. ‖ BOT. Valve f. ‖ **Valve-cap**, n. AUTOM. Chapeau, bouchon m. ‖ **Valve-gear**, n. TECHN. Organes (m. pl.) de distribution. ‖ **Valve-holder**, n. RADIO. Douille f. ‖ **Valve-rocker**, n. TECHN. Culbuteur m. ‖ **Valve-rod**, n. TECHN. Tige de soupape f.
valved [-d] adj. TECHN. A soupapes. ‖ BOT. A valves.
valveless [-lis] adj. Sans soupapes, sans valves.
valvula ['vælvjulə] (pl. **valvulae** [-li:]) n. Valvule f.
valvular [vælvjulə*], **valvulate** [-leit] adj. MED. Valvulaire.
vamoose [və'mu:s] v. intr. U.S. POP. Décaniller, mettre les bouts.
vamp [væmp] n. TECHN. Empeigne f. (in shoemaking). ‖ MUS., FAM. Accompagnement improvisé m.
— v. intr. MUS., FAM. Tapoter du piano.
— v. tr. Remettre une empeigne à (a shoe). ‖ MUS., FAM. Improviser un accompagnement pour. ‖ To vamp up, FAM. Rafistoler; monter de bric et de broc.
vamp n. FAM. Femme fatale, vamp f.; allumeuse f. (fam.).

— v. intr. Fam. Flirter outrageusement. ‖ Mus. Improviser un accompagnement.
— v. tr. Fam. Provoquer; vamper (pop.).
vamper [-ə*] n. Fam. Rafistoleur *s.* ‖ Mus., Fam. Accompagnateur-improvisateur *m.;* accompagnatrice-improvisatrice *f.*
vampire ['væmpaiə*] n. Vampire *m.* (lit. and fig.). ‖ Theatr. Trappe *f.* ‖ Fam. Vamp *f.* ‖ **Vampire-bat**, n. Zool. Vampire *m.*
vampiric [væm'pirik] adj. Vampirique.
vampirism ['væmpaiərism] n. Vampirisme *m.*
van [væn] n. Techn. Van *m.*
— v. tr. Techn. Vanner.
van n. Milit. Front *m.;* avant-garde *f.* ‖ Fig. Avant-garde *f.; in the van of*, à l'avant-garde de.
van v. tr. (1). Comm. Transporter dans une voiture de livraison.
— n. Autom. Fourgon automobile, camion *m.; delivery van*, voiture de livraison, camionnette; *prison van*, voiture cellulaire. ‖ Ch. de f. Fourgon *m.; guard's van*, fourgon aux bagages. ‖ **Van-man**, n. Livreur *m.*
van n. Sports. *Van in, out,* avantage (*m.*) dedans, dehors.
vanadium [və'neidiəm] n. Chim. Vanadium *m.*
Vandal ['vændəl] n. Vandale *s.*
vandalism [-izm] n. Vandalisme *m.*
Vandyke [væn'daik] adj. A la Van Dyck (beard, cape, collar).
vane [vein] n. Girouette *f.* (weather-vane). ‖ Bras *m.* (of a windmill). ‖ Techn. Aube, ailette, lamette, pale, palette *f.* ‖ Techn. Viseur *m.* (of an alidade); voyant *m.* (slide-vane).
vanguard ['væŋɑ:d] n. Milit., Fig. Avant-garde *f.*
vanilla [və'nilə] n. Vanille *f.; vanilla ice* (or) U. S. *ice cream*, glace à la vanille. ‖ **Vanilla-flavoured**, adj. Culin. Vanillé. ‖ **Vanilla-plant**, n. Bot. Vanillier *m.* ‖ **Vanilla-plantation**, n. Vanillerie *f.*
vanillin [-in] n. Chim. Vanilline *f.*
vanish ['væniʃ] v. intr. Disparaître; se perdre; s'éclipser (fam.); *to vanish from sight*, disparaître ‖ Math. Tendre vers zéro. ‖ Fig. Se dissiper, s'évanouir. (See Evanesce.)
— n. Gramm. Elément fugitif (*m.*) d'une diphtongue.
vanishing [-iŋ] adj. Qui disparaît. ‖ Med. De jour (cream). ‖ Arts. D'horizon (line); de fuite (point).
— n. Disparition *f.*
vanity ['væniti] n. Vanité; chose vaine; futilité *f.; all is vanity*, tout est vanité; *Vanity Fair*, la foire aux vanités. ‖ Vanité, prétention *f.; out of vanity*, par vanité. ‖ U. S. Coiffeuse *f.; vanity bag*, sac de dame; *vanity case*, pochette-poudrier.
vanner ['vænə*] n. Agric., Techn. Vanneur *m.*
vanquish ['væŋkwiʃ] v. intr., tr. Vaincre.
vanquishable [-əbl̩] adj. Dont on peut triompher.
vanquished [-t] n. pl. Vaincus *m. pl.*
vanquisher [-ə*] n. Vainqueur *m.*
vanquishing [-iŋ] n. Conquête *f.*
— adj. Vainqueur.
vantage ['vɑ:ntidʒ] n. Avantage *m.; place* (or) *point of vantage*, position avantageuse. ‖ Sports. Avantage *m.* (in tennis). ‖ **Vantage-ground**, n. Terrain favorable *m.; situation avantageuse *f.*
vapid ['væpid] adj. Insipide, fade. (See Insipid.)
vapidity [væ'piditi], **vapidness** ['væpidnis] n. Insipidité, fadeur *f.*
vaporization [,veipərai'zeiʃən] n. Vaporisation *f.*
vaporize ['veipəraiz] v. tr. Vaporiser.
— v. intr. Se vaporiser. ‖ Se volatiliser (nose cone). ‖ Autom. Carburer.
vaporizer [-ə*] n. Vaporisateur *m.*
vaporizing [-iŋ] n. Vaporisation *f.*
— adj. De vaporisation.
vaporous ['veipərəs] adj. Vaporeux.
vaporously [-li] adv. Vaporeusement.

vapo(u)r ['veipə*] v. intr. Se vaporiser (water). ‖ Fam. Fanfaronner (to brag); débiter des fadaises (to drivel).
— n. Vapeur *f.* ‖ † Med. Pl. Vapeurs *f. pl.* ‖ **Vapour-bath**, n. Med. Bain (*m.*) de vapeur. ‖ **Vapour-trail**, n. Aviat. Sillage (*m.*) de fumée.
vapourer [-rə*] n. Fam. Fanfaron *s.* (braggart); radoteur *s.* (driveller).
vapouring [-riŋ] n. Fam. Fanfaronnades *f. pl.* (bragging); fadaises *f. pl.* (drivel).
— adj. Fam. Fanfaron (bragging); débiteur de fadaises (drivelling).
vapourish [-riʃ], **vapoury** [-ri] adj. Vaporeux.
varec(h) ['værek] n. Comm. Soude (*f.*) du varech.
variability [,vɛəriə'biliti], **variableness** ['vɛəriəbl̩nis] n. Variabilité, inconstance *f.*
variable ['vɛəriəbl̩] n. Naut. Vent variable *m.* ‖ Math. Variable *f.*
— adj. Bot., Zool., Math., Techn. Variable. ‖ U. S. Geogr. Tempéré (zone). ‖ Fig. Inconstant, changeant, capricieux.
variably [-bli] adv. Variablement; capricieusement.
variance ['vɛəriəns] n. Désaccord, différend *m.;* discorde *f.* (controversy); *at variance*, en désaccord, en contradiction (*with*, avec). ‖ Variation *f.* ‖ Jur. Divergence *f.*
variant [-ənt] n. Variante *f.*
— adj. † Variable. ‖ Différent; *variant reading*, variante. ‖ Bot., Zool. Aberrant.
variate ['vɛəriit] n. Math. Variable aléatoire *f.* (in statistics).
variation [,vɛəri'eiʃən] n. Variation *f.;* changement *m.* ‖ Ecart *m.;* différence *f.* ‖ Mus. Variation *f.* (*on*, sur). ‖ Bot., Zool. Variation, déviation *f.* ‖ Electr. Fluctuation *f.* ‖ Techn. Variation *f.; magnetic variation*, déclinaison magnétique.
varicated ['værikeitid] adj. Med. Variqueux.
varicella [,væri'selə] n. Med. Varicelle *f.*
varices ['værisi:z] n. pl. See Varix.
varicocele [-kəsi:l] n. Med. Varicocèle *f.*
varicolo(u)red ['vɛəri,kʌləd] adj. Multicolore, bariolé.
varicose [-kous] adj. Med. Variqueux; *varicose vein*, varice.
varicosity [,væri'kɔsiti] n. Med. Varice *f.* (vein); état variqueux *m.* (of vein).
varied ['vɛərid] adj. Varié; divers.
variegate ['vɛərigeit] v. tr. Diversifier. ‖ Barioler, bigarrer (colourfully).
variegated [-id] adj. Divers. ‖ Bariolé, bigarré, diapré, multicolore.
variegation [,vɛəri'geiʃən] n. Diversité (*f.*) de couleurs; bariolage *m.;* bigarrure *f.*
variety [və'raiəti] n. Variété, diversité *f.; for a variety of reasons*, pour des quantités de raisons. ‖ Bot. Variété *f.* ‖ Theatr. *Variety entertainment* (or) *show*, attractions, numéros de music-hall; *variety theatre*, théâtre de variétés, music-hall.
variform ['vɛərifɔ:m] adj. Diversiforme, hétéromorphe.
variola [və'raiələ] n. Med. Variole *f.*
variolous [-əs] adj. Med. Varioleux; variolique.
variometer [,vɛəri'ɔmitə*] n. Electr. Variomètre *m.*
various ['vɛəriəs] adj. Divers, différent (differing); varié (varied). ‖ Fam. Divers, plusieurs (several).
variously [-li] adj. Diversement.
varix ['vɛəriks] (pl. **varices** [-si:z]) n. Med. Varice *f.*
varlet ['vɑ:lit] n. † Page *m.* ‖ Fam. Coquin *m.*
varmint ['vɑ:mint] n. Pop. Vermine *f.*
varnish ['vɑ:niʃ] v. tr. Vernir. ‖ Arts. Vernisser (pottery). ‖ Fig. Embellir, enjoliver.
— n. Vernis *m.; nail varnish*, vernis à ongles. ‖ Arts. Vernissure *f.* (for pottery). ‖ Fig. Vernis *f.* ‖ **Varnish-remover**, n. Décapant pour vernis *m.* ‖ **Varnish-tree**, n. Bot. Vernis du Japon *m.*
varnisher [-ə*] n. Vernisseur *s.*

varnishing [-iŋ] n. Vernissage m. ‖ ARTS. Vernissure f. ‖ FIG. Enjolivement m. ‖ **Varnishing-day,** n. ARTS. Vernissage m.

varsity ['vɑ:siti] n. FAM. See UNIVERSITY. ‖ U. S. SPORTS. Equipe universitaire ou scolaire f.

varus ['vɛərəs] n. MED. Pied-bot m.

vary ['vɛəri] v. tr. (2). Varier, donner de la variété à ; diversifier. ‖ MUS. Faire des variations sur.
— v. intr. Varier, se modifier, changer (to change). ‖ Varier, différer, être différent (from, de) [to be different]. ‖ Différer, ne pas être d'accord, être en désaccord (to disagree). ‖ MATH. Varier.

vascular ['væskjulə*] adj. BOT., MED. Vasculaire.

vase [vɑ:z] n. Vase m. ‖ **Vase-shaped,** adj. En forme de vase, évasé.

vasectomy [væ'sektəmi] n. MED. Vasectomie f.

Vaseline ['væsəli:n] n. MED. Vaseline f.
— v. tr. MED. Vaseliner, enduire de vaseline.

vaso- ['vɑ:zo] pref. MED. Vaso-. ‖ **Vaso-constrictor,** n. MED. Vaso-constricteur m. ‖ **Vaso-dilator,** n. MED. Vaso-dilatateur m. ‖ **Vaso-motor,** n. MED. Vaso-moteur m.; adj. vaso-moteur m.; vaso-motrice f.

vassal ['væsəl] adj., n. Vassal s.

vassalage ['væsəlidʒ] n. Vasselage m.; vassalité f.

vast [vɑ:st] adj. Vaste, immense. ‖ Enorme (huge).

vastitude [-itju:d] n. Vastitude, amplitude, immensité f.

vastly [-li] adj. Vastement. ‖ Infiniment (amused); énormément (mistaken).

vastness [-nis] n. Immensité f. ‖ Importance f.

vat [væt] v. tr. TECHN. Encuver.
— n. TECHN. Cuve f.; bac m. (brewer's); fosse f. (tanner's).

V.A.T. [væt] abbr. value-added tax, taxe à la valeur ajoutée, T.V.A.

vatful [-ful] n. Cuvée f.

Vatican ['vætikən] n. Vatican m.; Vatican City, Cité du Vatican ; Vatican Library, Vaticane.

Vaticanism [-izm] n. Ultramontanisme m.

vaticinal [væ'tisinəl] adj. Vaticinateur m.; vaticinatrice f.

vaticinate [-neit] v. intr. Vaticiner.

vaticination [,vætisi'neiʃən] n. Vaticination f.

vaticinator [-tə*] n. Vaticinateur m.

vatting ['vætiŋ] n. Cuvage m. (of wine).

vaudeville ['voudəvil] s. THEATR. Vaudeville m. (play) ; variétés f. pl. (variety show).

vaudevillist [-ist] n. Vaudevilliste s.

vault [vɔ:lt] n. SPORTS. Saut m.
— v. tr., intr. SPORTS. Sauter.

vault v. tr. ARCHIT. Voûter. ‖ **To vault over,** voûter.
— v. intr. ARCHIT. Se voûter.
— n. Chambre forte f. (of a bank). ‖ Cave f.; cellier m. (for wine). ‖ ECCLES. Caveau m. ‖ ARCHIT., MED. Voûte f. ‖ FIG. Vault of heaven, voûte céleste.

vaulted [-id] adj. ARCHIT. Voûté.

vaulter [-ə*] n. SPORTS. Sauteur ; acrobate s.

vaulting [-iŋ] n. SPORTS. Exercice du saut m. ‖ **Vaulting-horse,** n. SPORTS. Cheval d'arçons m.

vaunt [vɔ:nt] n. Fanfaronnade f.
— v. intr. Se vanter, fanfaronner. (See BOAST.)
— v. tr. Vanter ; se vanter de, se faire gloire de.

vaunter [-ə*] n. Vantard s.

vavasour ['vævəsuə*] n. Vavasseur, vavassal m.

V.D. [,vi:'di:] abbr. venereal disease, maladie vénérienne.

veal [vi:l] n. CULIN. Veau m.

vector ['vektə*] n. MATH. Vecteur m. ‖ MED. Porteur m. (of a virus).
— v. tr. AVIAT. Diriger par radio (a plane).

vectorial [,vek'tɔ:riəl] adj. MATH. Vectoriel.

vedette [vi'det] n. MILIT., NAUT. Vedette f.

Veep [vi:p] n. U. S. FAM. Vice-président s.

veer [vi:ə*] n. Saute f. (of the wind). ‖ NAUT. Virage (m.) vent arrière (of a ship). ‖ FIG. Revirement m.
— v. tr. NAUT. Faire virer vent arrière (a ship); to veer away (or) out the cable, filer du câble.

— v. intr. Tourner (wind) ; to veer astern, culer (wind). ‖ NAUT. Virer. ‖ FIG. To veer round, changer d'avis ; donner un coup de barre (fam.) ; to veer round to, se ranger à (an opinion).

veg [vedʒ] n. FAM. Légume m.; meat and 2 veg, plat de viande garni de légumes.

vegan [vi:gən] adj., n. Partisan (s.) du végétalisme.

vegetable ['vedʒitəbl] adj. BOT. Végétal ; vegetable kingdom, règne végétal. ‖ COMM. Végétal. ‖ CULIN. Végétal (butter) ; vegetable soup, potage aux légumes.
— n. BOT. Végétal m.; plante f. ‖ CULIN. Légume m.; early vegetables, primeurs ; vegetable garden, potager. ‖ **Vegetable-dish,** n. Légumier m. ‖ **Vegetable-man,** n. U. S. COMM. Fruitier s. ‖ **Vegetable-slicer,** n. Taille-légumes m. invar.

vegetal [-itl] n., adj. BOT. Végétal m.

vegetarian [,vedʒi'tɛəriən] adj., n. Végétarien s.

vegetarianism [-izm] n. Végétarianisme, végétarisme m.

vegetate ['vedʒiteit] v. intr. Végéter.

vegetation [,vedʒi'teiʃən] n. Végétation f. ‖ MED. Excroissance f.

vegetative ['vedʒitətiv] adj. Végétatif.

vehemence ['vi:iməns] n. Véhémence ; violence f.

vehement [-ənt] adj. Véhément ; violent (attack, wind) ; ardent, passionné (defence, love).

vehemently [-əntli] adv. Véhémentement.

vehicle ['vi:ikl] n. Véhicule m.; voiture f. ‖ MILIT. Engin m. ‖ MED. Véhicule, agent vecteur m. (of disease); excipient m. (in pharmacy). ‖ FIG. Véhicule, vecteur, support m.

vehicular [,vi:'ikjulə*] adj. Véhiculaire, des voitures.

veil [veil] v. tr. Voiler (lit. and fig.).
— n. Voile m. ‖ Voilette f. (hat-veil). ‖ BOT., ZOOL., MED., ECCLES. Voile m. ‖ FIG. Voile, déguisement m.; beyond the veil, derrière le rideau de la vie ; to draw a veil over, jeter un voile sur.

veiled [-d] adj. Voilé. ‖ MED. Voilé (voice). ‖ FIG. Voilé, dissimulé, caché, déguisé.

veiling [-iŋ] n. Action (f.) de voiler.

vein [vein] v. tr. Veiner, marbrer.
— n. MED., BOT. Veine f. ‖ ZOOL. Nervure f. (of a wing). ‖ FIG. Veine, humeur, disposition f.; tour d'esprit m. (see MOOD) ; to be in the vein for doing sth., être en veine de faire qqch.; in the same vein, dans le même esprit. ‖ **Vein-gold,** n. GEOL. Or filonien m.

veined [-d] adj. Veiné, à veines.

veining [-iŋ] n. Veinage m.; marbrure f.

veinlet [-lit] n. Veinule f.

veinstone [-stoun] n. GEOL. Roche (f.) de filon.

veiny [-i] adj. Veineux. ‖ Veiné (marble).

velamen [ve'leimən] (pl. **velamina** [-minə]) n. BOT. Tégument m. ‖ MED. Membrane f.

velar ['vi:lə*] adj., n. GRAMM. Vélaire f.

velarize [-əraiz] v. tr. GRAMM. Vélariser.

veld, veldt [felt] n. GEOGR. Veld m.

velleity [ve'li:iti] n. Velléité f.

vellum ['veləm] adj., n. Vélin m.

velocipede [vi'lɔsipi:d] n. † Vélocipède m. ‖ Tricycle m.

velocity [vi'lɔsiti] n. Vélocité f.

velour(s) [və'luə*] n. COMM. Velours (m.) de laine (material); bichon m. (polishing-pad).

velum ['vi:ləm] (pl. **vela** [-ə]) n. MED. Voile m.; voile du palais m.

velutinous [ve'lju:tinəs] adj. Velouteux.

velvet ['velvit] n. COMM. Velours m. ‖ FAM. On velvet, sur le velours.
— adj. COMM. De velours, velouté. ‖ FIG. De velours (glove) ; with velvet tread, à pas feutrés. ‖ **Velvet-eyed,** adj. Au regard velouté. ‖ **Velvet-pile,** n. COMM. Moquette f.

velveteen [,velvi'ti:n] n. COMM. Velvet m.

velvetiness ['velvitinis] n. Velouté m.

velveting [-iŋ] n. pl. COMM. Velours *m. pl.*
velvety [-i] adj. Velouté, velouteux.
venal ['vi:nəl] adj. Vénal (bargain, person, services).
venality [vi:'næliti] n. Vénalité *f.*
venally ['vi:nəli] adv. Vénalement.
vend [vend] v. tr. Vendre. (See SELL.) ‖ JUR. Vendre. ‖ U. S. Publier (opinions).
— v. intr. U. S. Vendre; se vendre.
vendee [ven'di:] n. JUR. Acheteur, acquéreur *s.*
vendetta [ven'detə] n. Vendetta *f.*
vendibility [,vendi'biliti] n. COMM. Caractère vendable *m.*
vendible ['vendibl] adj. COMM. Vendable.
vendor [-ɔ:*] n. Vendeur *s.* ‖ FIN. *Vendor's shares,* actions de fondation (or) d'apport. ‖ U. S. Machine à vente automatique *f.*
veneer [və'niə*] v. tr. TECHN. Plaquer (wood). ‖ FIG. Cacher sous un vernis.
— n. TECHN. Placage *m.* (on furniture); bois de placage *m.* (wood). ‖ FIG. Vernis *m.; with a veneer of,* sous un vernis de.
veneerer [-rə*] n. TECHN. Plaqueur *m.*
veneering [-riŋ] n. TECHN. Placage *m.*
venepuncture ['veni,pʌŋktʃə*] n. MED. Ponction de veine *f.*
venerability [,venərə'biliti] n. Vénérabilité *f.*
venerable ['venərəbl] adj. Vénérable.
venerate [-eit] v. tr. Vénérer.
veneration [,venə'reiʃən] n. Vénération *f.* (*for,* pour); révérence *f.*
venerator ['venəreitə*] n. Vénérateur *m.;* véné-ratrice *f.*
venereal [vi'niːəriəl] adj. MED. Vénérien.
venereologist [vi,niəri'ɔlədʒist] n. MED. Spécialiste (*m.*) des maladies vénériennes.
venereology [vi,niəri'ɔlədʒi] n. MED. Vénéréologie, vénérologie *f.*
venery ['venəri] n. SPORTS. Vénerie *f.*
venery n. Pratique (*f.*) des plaisirs charnels.
venesection [,veni'sekʃən] n. MED. Saignée *f.*
Venetian [vi'ni:ʃən] n. GEOGR. Vénitien *s.* ‖ COMM. Jalousie *f.*
— adj. GEOGR., ARTS. Vénitien. ‖ COMM. De Venise (glass); vénitien (red); *Venetian blind,* jalousie; *Venetian shutter,* persienne.
Venezuela [,venez'weilə] n. GEOGR. Venezuela *m.*
Venezuelan [-ən] adj., n. GEOGR. Vénézuélien *s.*
vengeance ['vendʒəns] n. Vengeance *f.* (see REVENGE); *to cry for vengeance,* crier vengeance; *to take vengeance for,* tirer vengeance de, venger (sth.); *to take vengeance on,* se venger de (or) sur (s.o.). ‖ FAM. *With a vengeance,* furieusement, rageusement.
vengeful ['vendʒful] adj. Vindicatif *f.* (See VINDICTIVE.) ‖ FIG. Vengeur *m.;* vengeresse *f.*
vengefulness [-nis] n. Caractère vindicatif *m.;* esprit (*m.*) de vengeance.
venial ['vi:niəl] adj. Véniel, léger, excusable. ‖ ECCLES. Véniel.
veniality [,vi:ni'æliti] n. Caractère véniel *m.*
venially ['vi:niəli] adv. Véniellement.
Venice ['venis] n. GEOGR. Venise *f.*
venipuncture ['veni,pʌŋktʃə*] n. See VENEPUNCTURE.
venison ['venizn] n. CULIN. Venaison *f.*
venom ['venəm] n. Venin *m.* ‖ FIG. Venin, poison *m.*
venomous ['venəməs] adj. ZOOL. Venimeux. ‖ BOT. Vénéneux. ‖ FIG. Venimeux, empoisonné (criticism); *venomous tongue,* langue de vipère.
venomously [-li] adv. D'une manière venimeuse; haineusement.
venomousness [-nis] n. Venimosité *f.*
venosity [vi'nɔsiti] n. MED. Vénosité *f.*
venous ['vi:nəs] adj. MED. Veineux.

vent [vent] v. tr. TECHN. Donner vent à (a barrel). ‖ FIG. Décharger, laisser éclater (one's anger).
— v. intr. ZOOL. Remonter à la surface pour respirer (otter).
— n. Trou, orifice, passage *m.;* ouverture *f.* ‖ Trou de fausset *m.* (of a barrel); *to make a vent in,* donner vent à. ‖ MILIT. † Lumière *f.* (of a cannon). ‖ MUS. Trou *m.* (of a flute). ‖ GEOL. Cheminée *f.* (of a volcano). ‖ ZOOL. Ouverture anale *f.* (of an animal). ‖ ARCHIT. Tuyau *m.* (of a chimney). ‖ FIG. Issue *f.;* libre cours *m.; to give vent to,* laisser éclater (one's anger); manifester (one's discontent); décharger (one's ill humour); laisser échapper (a shout). ‖ **Vent-faucet** (or) **peg** (or) **plug,** n. Foret *m.* ‖ **Vent-hole,** n. Event *m.;* trou de fausset *m.* (of a barrel). ‖ **Vent-stack,** n. TECHN. Aspirateur (*m.*) de fumée.
vent n. COMM. Fente *f.* (in a coat).
ventage ['ventidʒ] n. Trou *m.* ‖ ELECTR. Trou (*m.*) d'aération.
ventail ['venteil] n. MILIT. † Ventail *m.;* ventaille *f.*
venter ['ventə*] n. MED. Ventre *m.* (abdomen); protubérance *f.* (of a muscle). ‖ JUR. Mère *f.; a son by another venter,* fils d'un autre lit.
ventilate ['ventileit] v. tr. Ventiler, aérer. ‖ MED. † Oxygéner (blood). ‖ FIG. Faire connaître (opinions); mettre en discussion (questions).
ventilating [-iŋ] adj. Aérateur *m.;* aératrice *f.*
— n. See VENTILATION. ‖ **Ventilating-cowl,** n. TECHN. Manche (*f.*) à air. ‖ **Ventilating-fan,** n. TECHN. Ventilateur *m.*
ventilation [,venti'leiʃən] n. Ventilation, aération *f.;* aérage *m.* ‖ MED. † Oxygénation *f.* ‖ FIG. Discussion publique *f.* ‖ **Ventilation-shaft,** n. TECHN. Puits d'aérage *m.*
ventilator ['ventileitə*] n. Ventilateur *m.* ‖ AUTOM. Volet (*m.*) d'aération; déflecteur *m.* ‖ NAUT. Manche (*f.*) à air. ‖ ARCHIT. Vasistas *m.*
Ventimiglia [venti'miljə] n. GEOGR. Vintimille *m.*
ventral ['ventrəl] adj. ZOOL., MED. Ventral.
— n. ZOOL. Nageoire ventrale *f.*
ventricle ['ventrikl] n. MED. Ventricule *m.*
ventricular [ven'trikjulə*] adj. MED. Ventriculaire.
ventriloquism [ven'triləkwizm], **ventriloquy** [-kwi] n. Ventriloquie *f.*
ventriloquist [-kwist] n. Ventriloque *s.*
ventriloquize [-kwaiz] v. intr. Etre ventriloque.
ventriloquous [-kwəs] adj. Ventriloque.
ventripotent [ven'tripɔtənt] adj. FAM. Ventripotent, bedonnant.
venture [-ventʃə*] n. Aventure, entreprise risquée *f.;* risque *m.; at a venture,* au hasard, à l'aventure. ‖ COMM. Aventure, spéculation *f.*
— v. tr. Risquer, hasarder (a guess, an opinion). ‖ Aventurer, risquer, hasarder (one's life). ‖ FIN., COMM. Aventurer.
— v. intr. Oser, se hasarder (to dare); *to venture to do sth.,* oser faire qqch. ‖ Se risquer, s'aventurer (to expose oneself to risks); *to venture abroad* (or) *out,* se risquer à sortir; *to venture on,* se risquer à faire (sth.).
venturesome ['ventʃəsəm] adj. Aventuré, risqué, hasardeux, imprudent (action); aventureux, entreprenant (person).
— SYN. : HAZARDOUS, RISKY, VENTUROUS.
venturesomely [-li] adv. Aventureusement.
venturesomeness [-nis] n. Esprit aventureux *m.*
venturi [ven'tjuəri] n. TECHN. Venturi, tube venturi *m.*
venturous ['ventʃurəs]. See VENTURESOME.
venue ['venju:] n. Rendez-vous *m.* ‖ JUR. Juridiction *f.;* lieu du procès *m.*
venule ['venjul] n. ZOOL., MED. Veinule *f.*
Venus ['vi:nəs] n. ARTS, ASTRON. Vénus *f.*
veracious [ve'reiʃəs] adj. Véridique.

veraciously [-li] adv. Véridiquement.
veraciousness [-nis], **veracity** [ve'ræsiti] n. Véracité *f*. (See TRUTHFULNESS.)
veranda(h) [və'rændə] n. Véranda *f*.
veratria [ve'rætriə], **veratrine** ['verətri:n] n. CHIM. Vératrine *f*.
verb [və:b] n. GRAMM. Verbe *m*.
verbal [-əl] adj. GRAMM. Verbal ; *verbal inhibitions*, mots tabous. ‖ Littéral, mot à mot (translation).
verbalism [-əlizm̩] n. Verbalisme *m*.
verbalist [-əlist] n. Fanatique (*s*.) du mot.
verbalization [ˌvə:bəlaiˈzeiʃən] n. Expression verbale, traduction en parole *f*. (of an idea). ‖ GRAMM. Emploi comme verbe *m*.
verbalize ['və:bəlaiz] v. intr. Etre verbeux.
— v. tr. Traduire en paroles, exprimer (an idea). ‖ GRAMM. Employer comme verbe.
verbally [-i] adv. Verbalement, oralement. ‖ Littéralement, mot à mot (word for word).
verbatim [və:ˈbeitim] adv. Textuellement, mot pour mot.
— adj. Textuel, mot pour mot.
verbena [və:ˈbi:nə] n. Verveine *f*.
verbiage ['və:biidʒ] n. Verbiage *m*.
verbose [və:ˈbous] n. Verbeux, prolixe.
verbosely [-li] adv. Avec verbosité.
verboseness [-nis], **verbosity** [və:ˈbɔsiti] n. Verbosité, prolixité *f*.
verdancy ['və:dənsi] n. Verdure *f*. ‖ FIG. Naïveté *f*.
verdant [-ənt] adj. Vert, verdoyant. (See GREEN.) ‖ FIG. Naïf (immature).
verdict ['və:dikt] n. Jugement, avis *m*. ; décision *f*. ‖ JUR. Verdict *m*.
verdigris ['və:digris] n. Vert-de-gris *m*.
verdigrised [-t] adj. Vert-de-grisé.
verdure ['və:dʒə:*] n. Verdure *f*. ‖ FIG. Vigueur, verdeur *f*. ‖ FIG. Jeunesse ; naïveté *f*.
verge [və:dʒ] n. Bordure *f*. (of grass) ; bord *m*. (of a road) ; orée *f*. (of a wood). ‖ Limite *f*. ; bord *m*. ; confins *m*. pl. ; *on the verge of*, sur le point de (doing sth.) ; à deux doigts de (ruin) ; *to be on the verge of forty*, friser la quarantaine. ‖ ECCLES. Verge *f*. ‖ TECHN. Tige, tringle *f*.
— v. intr. Approcher (*towards*, de) ; tendre (*towards*, vers). ‖ Descendre, baisser (*towards*, vers). ‖ **To verge on**, toucher à, être contigu à ; FIG. Friser (an age) ; tirer sur (a colour) ; confiner à (madness) ; *boredom verging on tears*, ennui voisin des larmes.
verger [-ə*] n. ECCLES. Suisse *m*.
Vergil ['və:dʒil] n. Virgile *m*.
Vergilian [və:ˈdʒiliən] adj. Virgilien.
veridical [veˈridikl̩] adj. Véridique.
verifiable ['verifaiəbl̩] adj. Vérifiable.
verification [ˌverifiˈkeiʃən] n. Vérification *f*., contrôle *m*.
verificatory [-təri] adj. Vérificatif.
verifier ['verifaiə*] n. Vérificateur *m*. ; vérificatrice *f*. ; contrôleur *s*.
verify [-fai] v. tr. (2). Vérifier, contrôler (to check) ; confirmer (to confirm). ‖ JUR. Prouver.
verily [-li] adv. † En vérité.
verisimilar [ˌveriˈsimilə*] adj. Vraisemblable.
verisimilitude [ˌverisiˈmilitju:d] n. Vraisemblance *f*.
veritable ['veritəbl̩] adj. Véritable, vrai.
veritably [-təbli] adv. Véritablement.
verity [-ti] n. Vérité *f*. (truth). ‖ Chose réelle *f*. ; fait *m*. (fact).
verjuice ['və:dʒu:s] n. Verjus *m*.
verjuiced [-t] adj. Verjuté. ‖ FIG. Aigre.
vermeil ['və:mil] n. Vermeil *m*. ‖ COMM. Grenat *m*.
vermicelli [ˌvə:miˈseli] n. CULIN. Vermicelle *m*.
vermicide ['və:miˌsaid] n. Vermicide *m*.

vermicular [və:ˈmikjulə*] adj. Vermiculaire, vermiforme. ‖ MED. Vermiculaire.
vermiculate [-lit] adj. ZOOL., ARCHIT. Vermiculé.
vermiculated [-leitid] adj. Vermiculé. ‖ Vermoulu (worm-eaten).
vermiculation [ˌvə:mikjuˈleiʃən] n. Vermiculation *f*. ‖ Vermoulure *f*.
vermiform ['və:mifɔ:m] adj. Vermiforme.
vermifuge |-fju:dʒ] adj., n. MED. Vermifuge *m*.
vermilion [və:ˈmiljən] n. Vermillon, cinabre *m*.
— adj. Vermeil, vermillon, de vermeil.
— v. tr. Vermillonner.
vermin ['və:min] n. ZOOL. Vermine ; bête nuisible *f*. ‖ FIG. Vermine *f*.
verminate [-eit] v. intr. Engendrer de la vermine. ‖ Grouiller de vermine.
vermination [ˌvə:miˈneiʃən] n. Vermination *f*.
verminous ['və:minəs] adj. Couvert de vermine. ‖ MED. Vermineux.
vermouth ['və:muθ] n. Vermouth *m*.
vernacular [və:ˈnækjulə*] n. Vernaculaire *m*. ; langue nationale *f*. (native language). ‖ Langage vulgaire *m*. (colloquial speech) ; jargon de métier *m*. (jargon).
— adj. Vernaculaire (language). ‖ Du pays (arts). ‖ MED. Endémique.
vernacularism [-rizm̩] n. Idiotisme *m*.
vernacularize [-raiz] v. tr. Acclimater, faire entrer dans la langue commune.
vernal ['və:nəl] adj. Printanier. ‖ ASTRON. De printemps (equinox). ‖ BOT. Vernal.
vernier ['və:niə*] n. MATH. Vernier *m*. ; *vernier caliper*, jauge micrométrique.
vernissage ['və:nisɑ:ʒ] n. ARTS. Vernissage *m*.
Verona [vəˈrounə] n. GEOGR. Vérone *f*.
Veronese [veroˈni:z] n., adj. GEOGR. Véronais *s*.
— [veroˈneizi] n. ARTS. Véronèse *m*.
veronica [viˈrɔnikə] n. BOT. Véronique *f*. ‖ ECCLES. Sainte Face *f*.
verruca [veˈru:kə] n. MED. Verrue *f*.
verrucose ['verukous] adj. MED. Verruqueux.
versant ['və:sənt] n. Pente *f*. (See SLOPE.) ‖ GEOGR. Versant *m*.
versatile ['və:sətail] adj. Aux talents variés ; universel (genius) ; souple (mind). ‖ † Inconstant. ‖ BOT., ZOOL. Versatile. ‖ TECHN. Souple.
versatility [ˌvə:səˈtiliti] n. Faculté d'adaptation, souplesse (*f*.) d'esprit. ‖ † Inconstance *f*. ‖ BOT., ZOOL. Versatilité *f*.
verse [və:s] v. intr. † Faire des vers ; versifier.
— v. tr. Mettre en vers.
— n. Vers *m*. (structure). ‖ Vers *m*. pl. ; poésie *f*. (poetry). ‖ Strophe, stance *f*. (stanza). ‖ ECCLES. Verset *m*. ‖ **Verse-maker**, n. Versificateur *m*. ; versificatrice *f*. ‖ **Verse-monger**, n. Rimailleur *s*.
versed [-t] adj. Versé (*in*, dans, en).
versed adj. MATH. *Versed sine*, sinus verse.
versicle ['və:sikl̩] n. Versiculet *m*. (verse). ‖ ECCLES. Verset *m*.
versicoloured ['və:siˌkʌləd] adj. Versicolore.
versification [ˌvə:sifiˈkeiʃən] n. Versification *f*.
versifier ['və:sifaiə*] n. Versificateur *m*. ; versificatrice *f*.
versify [-fai] v. tr. (2). Versifier, mettre en vers.
— v. intr. Versifier, faire des vers.
version ['və:ʃən] n. Version, traduction *f*. (See TRANSLATION.) ‖ Version, interprétation *f*. (point of view). ‖ Récit *m*. ; version *f*. (account). ‖ MED. Version *f*. (of fœtus).
verso ['və:sou] n. Verso *m*. (of a page). ‖ Envers *m*. (of a coin, medal).
versus ['və:səs] prep. Contre.
vertebra ['və:tibrə] (pl. **vertebrae** [-bri:]) n. MED. Vertèbre *f*.
vertebral [-brəl] adj. MED. Vertébral.
vertebrate [-brit] adj., n. ZOOL. Vertébré *m*.

vertex |'və:teks] (pl. **vertices** [-tisi:z]) n. Sommet. ‖ MED. Vertex m. ‖ ASTRON. Zénith m.

vertical ['və:tikəl] n. Verticale f.
— adj. Vertical. ‖ Situé au zénith. ‖ Du sommet de la tête. ‖ MATH. Opposé par le sommet (angle).

vertically [-i] adv. Verticalement.

vertiginous [,və:'tidʒinəs] adj. Vertigineux.

vertiginously [-li] adv. Vertigineusement.

vertigo ['və:tigou] n. MED. Vertige m.

vervain ['və:vein] n. BOT. Verveine f.

verve [və:v] n. Verve f. ‖ TECHN. Nerf m. (of an engine).

very ['veri] adj. Vrai, véritable, authentique ; *very God of very God*, vrai Dieu de vrai Dieu. ‖ Même ; seul ; justement, exactement ; *at the very back of the room*, tout au fond de la salle ; *he is the very man*, c'est exactement l'homme qu'il nous faut (or) l'homme de la situation ; *I tremble at the very thought*, je tremble rien que d'y penser ; *in the very middle*, au beau milieu ; *on that very day*, ce jour même.
— adv. Très ; bien ; fort ; absolument (absolutely) ; tout à fait, extrêmement (extremely) ; tellement (so) ; *are you hungry? Very*, avez-vous faim? Très. ‖ Exactement, précisément (exactly). ‖ Bien, beaucoup (with comparatives) ; *very much better*, bien (or) beaucoup mieux. ‖ Tout (emphatic use) ; *to do one's very best*, faire tout son possible ; *of the very best quality*, de toute première qualité ; *at the very latest*, au plus tard ; *at the very least*, tout au moins.

Very n. MILIT. *Very light*, fusée lumineuse, étoile éclairante ; *Very pistol*, pistolet à fusée.

vesica [ves'aikə] n. MED. Vessie f.

vesical ['vesikəl] adj. MED. Vésical.

vesicant ['vesikənt] adj., n. MED. Vésicant m.

vesicate [-keit] v. tr. MED. Produire des ampoules.
— v. intr. MED. S'ampouler.

vesicatory [,vesi'keitəri] adj., n. MED. Vésicatoire m.

vesicle ['vesikḷ] n. MED. Vésicule f.

vesicular [ve'sikjulə*] adj. MED. Vésiculaire.

vesiculose [-ous], **vesiculous** [-əs] adj. MED. Vésiculeux.

vesper ['vespə*] n. Soir m. (in poetry). ‖ ASTRON. Vesper m. ; étoile (f.) du soir. ‖ ECCLES. Pl. Vêpres f. pl.
— adj. Des vêpres, vespéral (bell).

vesperal [-rəl] n. ECCLES. Vespéral m.

vespertine [-tain] adj. Vespéral.

vespiary ['vespiəri] n. Guêpier m. ; nid (m.) de guêpes.

vessel ['vesḷ] n. Vase, récipient m. (for liquid). ‖ NAUT. Vaisseau, navire, bateau, bâtiment m. ‖ ECCLES. Vase m. ; *chosen vessel*, vase d'élection ; *vessel of wrath*, vaisseau de colère. ‖ MED., BOT. Vaisseau m. ‖ FIG. *Weaker vessels*, le sexe faible.

vest [vest] n. Gilet m. (undershirt, waistcoat). ‖ **Vest-pocket**, adj. De poche ; n. Poche (f.) du gilet.

vest v. intr. Etre dévolu, échoir (*in*, à).
— v. tr. † Vêtir, revêtir (to clad). ‖ Assigner, attribuer, confier (*in*, à). ‖ Investir, revêtir (*with*, de).

vesta ['vestə] n. Allumette-bougie f. ‖ ASTRON. Vesta f.

vestal ['vestḷ] n. Vestale f.
— adj. De Vesta ; de vestale ; *vestal virgin*, vestale.

vested ['vestid] adj. Acquis (interests) ; dévolu (right) ; *vested with power to*, investi de l'autorité de.

vestibule ['vestibju:l] n. Vestibule m. ‖ **Vestibule-car**, n. U. S. CH. DE F. Voiture à couloir m.

vestige |'vestidʒ] n. Vestige m. ; trace f.

vestimentary [vesti'mentəri] adj. Vestimentaire.

vestment ['vestmənt] n. Vêtement m. ‖ ECCLES.

Vêtement sacerdotal m. ; chasuble f. (garment) ; nappe (f.) d'autel (altar-cloth).

vestry ['vestri] n. ECCLES. Sacristie f. (in the church) ; salle (f.) d'œuvres (or) de réunion (for meetings) ; *common vestry*, membres de la fabrique. ‖ **Vestry-meeting**, n. ECCLES. Réunion (f.) du conseil curial.

vestryman [-mən] (pl. **vestrymen**) n. ECCLES. Marguillier m.

vesturer ['vestʃurə*] n. ECCLES. Sacristain m. (sexton) ; sous-trésorier m. (sub-treasurer).

Vesuvius [ve'sju:viəs] n. GEOGR. Vésuve m.

vet [vet] n. FAM., MED. Vétérinaire m.
— v. tr. FAM., MED. Examiner. ‖ FAM. Corriger, revoir (an article).

vetch [vetʃ] n. BOT. Vesce f.

veteran ['vetərən] n. MILIT. Vétéran m. ‖ U. S. MILIT. Ancien combattant m. ; *a young veteran*, un jeune homme ancien combattant. (See EX-SERVICE MAN.)
— adj. De vétéran ; expérimenté (experienced) ; vieux (old) ; *veteran soldier*, vétéran, vieux soldat ; *veteran troops*, troupes aguerries.

veterinarian [,vetəri'nɛəriən]. **veterinary** ['vetənri] adj., n. MED. Vétérinaire m.

veto ['vi:tou] (pl. **vetoes**) n. Veto m. ; *power* (or) *right of veto*, droit de veto ; *to put* (or) *set a veto on*, mettre son veto à.
— v. tr. Interdire ; mettre son veto à.

vetoist [-ist] n. Partisan (m.) du droit de veto.

vex [veks] v. tr. Vexer, contrarier, fâcher (to annoy). ‖ † Affliger (to afflict) ; tourmenter (to torment).

vexation [vek'seiʃən] n. Vexation f. ; tourment m. ; tracasseries f. pl. (harassing). ‖ Ennui m. ; irritation, contrariété f. (irritation). ‖ Cause d'irritation f. (source of annoyance).

vexatious [-ʃəs] adj. Vexant, contrariant, irritant. ‖ JUR. Vexatoire (measure).

vexed [vekst] adj. Vexé, contrarié. ‖ Fâché (*with*, contre) ; *to become vexed*, se vexer. ‖ Très débattu (question).

vexer [-ə*] n. Vexateur m. ; vexatrice f.

vexing [-iŋ] adj. Vexant, contrariant, ennuyeux.

V.H.F. [,vi:eitʃʃ'ef] abbr. *very high frequency*, très haute fréquence, VHF.

via ['vaiə] prep. Via, en direction de.

viability [,vaiə'biliti] n. Viabilité f.

viable ['vaiəbḷ] adj. Viable.

viaduct ['vaiədʌkt] n. Viaduc m.

vial ['vaiəl] n. Fiole f.

viands ['vaiəndz] n. pl. † Mets, aliments m. pl.

viaticum |vai'ætikəm] n. † ECCLES., FIG. Viatique m.

vibes [vaibz] n. pl. FAM. Vibrations f. pl. ; *good, bad vibes*, atmosphère relaxe, tendue. ‖ MUS. FAM. Vibraphone m.

vibex ['vaibeks] (pl. **vibices** [vai'baisi:z]) n. MED. Vergeture f.

vibrancy ['vaibrənsi] n. Qualité vibrante, résonance f.

vibrant [-brənt] adj. Vibrant. ‖ FAM. Energique (woman).

vibraphone ['vaibrə,foun] n. MUS. Vibraphone m.

vibrate [vai'breit] v. tr. Faire vibrer (or) osciller.
— v. intr. Vibrer. ‖ Résonner, retentir (*in, on*, à) [one's ear]. ‖ PHYS. Vibrer, osciller. ‖ FIG. Vibrer, frémir (*with*, de).

vibratile ['vaibrətail] adj. Vibratile.

vibrating [vai'breitiŋ] adj. Vibrant ; vibratoire.

vibration [-ʃən] n. Vibration f. ‖ Oscillation f. (of a pendulum). ‖ Vibration, trépidation f. ; tremblement m. (quiver).

vibrator [-tə*] n. ELECTR. Vibrateur, trembleur m. ‖ MED. Vibromasseur m. ‖ MUS. Anche f.

vibratory ['vaibrətəri] adj. Vibratoire.

vibrio ['vaibriou] n. MED. Vibrion m.

vibro-massage [-vaibro'mæsɑ:ʒ] n. MED. Massage vibratoire m.

vibroscope ['vaibrəskoup] n. ELECTR. Vibroscope m.

viburnum [vai'bə:nəm] n. BOT. Viorne f.

vicar ['vikə] n. ECCLES. Pasteur, curé m.; the vicar of Christ, le vicaire de Jésus-Christ. ‖ **Vicar apostolic**, vicaire apostolique. ‖ **Vicar general**, n. ECCLES. Grand vicaire, vicaire général m.

vicarage [-ridʒ] n. ECCLES. Cure f.; presbytère m.

vicarial [vai'kɛəriəl] adj. ECCLES. Vicarial.

vicariate [vi'kɛəriət] n. ECCLES. Vicariat; poste curial m.

vicarious [vai'kɛəriəs] adj. Substitut (agent); délégué (authority); partagé (pleasure); souffert pour autrui (punishment); ressenti par contrecoup (thrill); fait à la place d'un autre (work). ‖ ECCLES. Vicaire.

vicariously [-li] adv. Par délégation; à la place d'autrui.

vicarship ['vikə:ʃip] n. ECCLES. Fonctions curiales f. pl.; pastorat m.

vice ['vaisi] prep. A la place de; vice Mr. Brown resigned, aux lieu et place de M. Brown démissionnaire.

vice [vais] n. Vice m. (depravity); défaut m. (fault). ‖ Vice m. (of a horse). ‖ **Vice-squad**, n. JUR. Brigade (f.) des mœurs.

vice v. tr. TECHN. Serrer dans un étau.
— n. TECHN. Etau m. ‖ **Vice-clamp**, n. TECHN. Mordache f.

vice n. FAM. Vice-président m.

vice préfixe. Vice-. ‖ **Vice-admiral**, n. NAUT. Vice-amiral m. ‖ **Vice-admiralty**, n. NAUT. Vice-amirauté f. ‖ **Vice-chairman**, n. Vice-président m. ‖ **Vice-chairmanship**, n. Vice-présidence f. ‖ **Vice-chancellor**, n. Vice-chancelier m.; recteur m. (of a university). ‖ **Vice-consul**, n. Vice-consul m. ‖ **Vice-managership**, n. Vice-gérance f. ‖ **Vice-marshal**, n. AVIAT. Air vice-marshal, général (m.) de division. ‖ **Vice-presidency**, n. Vice-présidence f. ‖ **Vice-president**, n. Vice-président m. ‖ **Vice-principal**, n. Sous-principal m. ‖ **Vice-rector**, n. Vice-recteur m. ‖ **Vice-reine**, n. Vice-reine f.

vicegerent [vais'dʒi:ərənt] n. Représentant, délégué m.

vicenary ['visənəri] adj. MATH. Vicésimal.

vicennial [vi'senjəl] adj. Vicennal.

viceroy ['vaisrɔi] n. Vice-roi m.

viceroyalty [vais'rɔiəlti] n. Vice-royauté f.

vice versa ['vaisi'və:sə] adv. Vice versa.

Vichy ['viʃi] n. GEOGR. Vichy; the Vichy government, le gouvernement de Vichy. ‖ Vichy m.; eau (f.) de Vichy (Vichy water).
— adj. De Vichy (water).

vicinage ['visinidʒ] n. Voisinage m. (neighbourhood); voisins m. pl. (persons).

vicinal [-nəl] adj. Vicinal.

vicinity [vi'siniti] n. Voisinage m.; proximité f. ‖ Voisinage m.; environs, parages, alentours m. pl.

vicious ['viʃəs] adj. Vicieux, corrompu, dépravé (depraved). ‖ Haineux (ill-tempered); méchant (spiteful). ‖ Vicieux, rétif (restive) [horse]. ‖ Corrupteur, dépravant (debasing). ‖ FAM. Vicieux (circle).

viciously [-li] adv. Vicieusement (depravedly). ‖ Défectueusement, incorrectement. ‖ Rageusement, avec fureur (angrily); méchamment (spitefully).

viciousness [-nis] n. Nature vicieuse, dépravation f. ‖ Méchanceté, malignité f. (spitefulness).

vicissitude [vi'sisitju:d] n. Vicissitude f.

victim ['viktim] n. JUR., MILIT., MED. Victime f.; to fall a victim to, être victime de, succomber à. ‖ FIG. Dupe, victime f.

victimization [viktimai'zeiʃən] n. Tyrannisation f. ‖ Duperie f. (trickery).

victimize ['viktimaiz] v. tr. Prendre pour victime. ‖ Exercer des représailles contre. ‖ Duper (to trick).

victor ['viktə*] n. Vainqueur s.

victoria [vik'tɔ:riə] n. Victoria f. (carriage).

Victorian [-iən] n. Victorien s.
— adj. Victorien, de la période victorienne.

Victorianism [-iənizm] n. Esprit victorien m.

victorious [vik'tɔ:riəs] adj. Victorieux.

victoriously [-li] adv. Victorieusement.

victory ['viktəri] n. MILIT., FIG. Victoire f.; to gain a victory, être victorieux, remporter la victoire (over, sur); to win the victory, remporter la palme.

victress ['viktrəs] n. Triomphatrice f.

victual ['vitl] n. See VICTUALS.
— v. intr. Se ravitailler. ‖ Se restaurer (to eat).
— v. tr. Ravitailler, approvisionner.

victualler [-ə*] n. Approvisionneur; fournisseur m.; licensed victualler, débitant de boissons. ‖ NAUT. Bateau de ravitaillement m.

victualling [-iŋ] n. Approvisionnement, ravitaillement m. ‖ **Victualling-book**, n. NAUT. Rôle (m.) de rations. ‖ **Victualling-office**, n. NAUT. Bureau (m.) de subsistances.

victuals [-z] n. pl. Victuailles f. pl. (food); vivres m. pl. (provisions).

vide ['vaidi] v. tr. Voyez, voir; vide supra, voir plus haut.

videlicet [vi'di:li,set] adv. C'est-à-dire, à savoir (viz.).

video ['vidi,ou] n. TECHN. Vidéo f. ‖ U. S. FAM. Télévision f. ‖ **Video disc**, n. Vidéodisque m.
— adj. Vidéo adj. invar.

videophone ['vidiə,foun] n. Vidéophone m.

videotape ['vidiou,teip] n. TECHN. Bande vidéo (or) magnétoscopique f.; videotape recorder, magnétoscope.
— v. tr. Enregistrer au magnétoscope, magnétoscoper.

vie [vai] v. intr. (3). Rivaliser, lutter (with, avec); to vie in civilities with, faire assaut d'amabilités avec; to vie with each other, rivaliser d'efforts (or) d'émulation; vying with one another, à qui mieux mieux.

Vienna [vi'enə] n. GEOGR. Vienne f.

Viennese [vie'ni:z] adj., GEOGR. Viennois s.

Viet-nam ['vjet'næm] n. GEOGR. Viet-nam m.

Viet-namese [,vjetnə'mi:z] adj., n. GEOGR. Vietnamien s.

view [vju:] v. tr. Regarder, voir, examiner. ‖ Regarder, envisager, considérer.
— v. intr. RADIO. Avoir (or) regarder la télévision (to teleview).
— n. Vue, portée de la vue f.; hidden from view, caché aux regards; in view, en vue; to come into view, apparaître; to go out of view, disparaître. ‖ Vue, perspective f.; coup d'œil, panorama m. (see PROSPECT, VISTA); front view of a house, une maison vue de face; house with a good view, maison qui a une belle vue; point of view, point de vue; to get a side view of sth., voir qqch. de côté. ‖ Vue f.; aperçu, exposé m. (survey). ‖ Vue, inspection f.; coup d'œil, examen m.; to have a closer view of, voir de plus près; on view, exposé. ‖ Avis m.; vue, idée, opinion f.; in my view, à mon avis; what are your views on the subject?, qu'en pensez-vous?; to hold advanced, decided views, avoir des idées avancées, arrêtées; to share s.o.'s views, partager les sentiments de qqn. ‖ But m.; vue, intention f.; to have sth. in view, avoir qqch. en vue; avoir des projets; with a view to, dans l'intention de, en vue de; with this in view, à cette fin, dans ce dessein. ‖ ARTS. Vue f. (picture); private view, vernissage; avant-première. ‖ JUR. Descente (f.) sur les lieux. ‖ TECHN. Champ, champ visuel m. (field of vision). ‖ FIG. Vue f.; to keep sth. in view, ne pas perdre qqch. de vue; from the political point of view, sur le plan politique; point of view, point de vue,

opinion. ‖ Loc. *In view of,* vu, eu égard à, étant donné. ‖ **View-finder,** n. Viseur *m.* ‖ **View-halloo,** n. Sports. Vue *f.*

viewer [-ə*] n. Spectateur *m.; spectatrice f.* ‖ Inspecteur *m.* ‖ Radio. Téléspectateur *m.; téléspectatrice f.* ‖ Techn. Visionneuse *f.*

viewing [-iŋ] n. Examen *m.;* inspection *f.*

viewless [-lis] adj. Qui n'a pas de vue. ‖ Invisible. ‖ Fig. Sans opinion.

viewpoint [-pɔint] n. Point (*m.*) de vue; attitude mentale *f.*

viewy ['vju:i] adj. U. S. Fam. Visionnaire, aux théories baroques.

vigesimal [vi'dʒesiməl] adj. Math. Vicésimal.

vigil ['vidʒil] n. Veille *f.; to keep vigil,* veiller. ‖ Eccles. Vigile *f.*

vigilance [-əns] n. Vigilance *f.; Vigilance Committee,* comité de vigilance. ‖ Med. Insomnie *f.*

vigilant [-ənt] adj. Vigilant.

vigilante [,vidʒi'lænti] n. Membre (*m.*) d'un comité de vigilance.

vigilantly ['vidʒiləntli] adv. Avec vigilance.

vignette [vi'njet] v. tr. Dégrader (in photography). — n. Vignette *f.* ‖ Portrait (*m.*) en buste dégradé (in photography). ‖ Theatr. Sketch *m.;* saynète *f.* ‖ **Vignette-engraver,** n. Vignettiste *s.*

vignettist [-ist] n. Vignettiste *s.*

vigorous ['vigərəs] adj. Vigoureux, robuste.

vigorously [-li] adj. Vigoureusement.

vigo(u)r ['vigə*] n. Vigueur *f.;* vitalité, énergie *f.*

Viking ['vaikiŋ] n. Viking *m.*

vile ['vail] adj. Vil, sans valeur (metals). ‖ Fig. Vil, ignoble, infâme, abject. (See BASE.) ‖ Fam. Abominable, exécrable (cigar); infect (smell); sale, détestable (weather).

vilely [-li] adv. Vilement; bassement. ‖ Abominablement, affreusement.

vileness [-nis] n. Bassesse, abjection *f.* ‖ Fam. *The vileness of the weather,* cette abomination de temps.

vilification [,vilifi'keiʃən] n. Diffamation *f.;* dénigrement *m.* (of s.o.); avilissement (of sth.).

vilifier ['vilifaiə*] n. Diffamateur *m.;* diffamatrice *f.*

vilify [-fai] v. tr. (2). † Avilir. ‖ Diffamer, dénigrer. (See REVILE.)

vilipend ['vilipend] v. tr. Vilipender.

villa ['vilə] n. Maison de campagne *f.* (rural residence); villa *f.* (suburban residence).

village ['vilidʒ] n. Village *m.*

villager [-ə*] n. Villageois *s.*

villain ['vilən] n. † Vilain *m.* ‖ Bandit *m.;* scélérat *s.* ‖ Fam. Coquin *s.;* garnement *m.*

villainous [-əs] adj. De coquin, de scélérat (deed). ‖ Vil, infâme, ignoble; vilain (face). ‖ Fam. Abominable, exécrable; sale (weather).

villainy [-i] n. Vilenie *f.* (action); scélératesse, infamie *f.* (of an action).

villein ['vilən] n. † Vilain, serf *m.*

villosity [vi'lɔsiti] n. Med. Villosité *f.* ˉ

vim [vim] n. Fam. Vigueur, force, énergie *f.*

vinaceous [vi'neiʃəs] adj. Vineux (colour).

vinaigrette [,vinə'gret] n. Flacon (*m.*) de sels (for smelling-salts). ‖ Burette (*f.*) à vinaigre, vinaigrier *m.* (cruet). ‖ Culin. Vinaigrette *f.*

vindicable ['vindikəbl] adj. Justifiable.

vindicate [-keit] v. tr. Défendre, justifier, soutenir (an opinion, s.o.). ‖ Revendiquer, défendre (one's rights).

vindication [,vindi'keiʃən] n. Justification *f.*

vindicative ['vindikeitiv] adj. Justificatif.

vindicator [-keitə*] n. Défenseur *m.*

vindicatory [-kətəri] adj. Justificatif. ‖ Vindicatif (vindictive).

vindictive [vin'diktiv] adj. Vindicatif (person); vengeur *m.;* vengeresse *f.* (punishment).

vindictively [-li] adv. D'une manière vindicative.

vindictiveness [-nis] n. Caractère vindicatif, esprit rancunier *m.*

vine [vain] n. Bot. Vigne *f.* (grape-vine); tige *f.* (stem). ‖ U. S. Bot. Plante grimpante *f.* ‖ **Vine-bearing,** adj. Agric. Vinifère. ‖ **Vine-disease,** n. Agric. Maladie de la vigne *f.* ‖ **Vine-dresser,** n. Vigneron *m.* ‖ **Vine-grower,** n. Viticulteur *m.* ‖ **Vine-growing,** n. Agric. Viticulture *f.* ‖ **Vine-harvest,** n. Vendange *f.* ‖ **Vine-leaf,** n. Bot. Feuille de vigne *f.*

vinegar ['vinigə*] n. Vinaigre *m.; vinegar cruet,* burette à vinaigre, vinaigrier; *vinegar factory* (or) *trade,* vinaigrerie. ‖ Culin. *Vinegar sauce,* vinaigrette. ‖ **Vinegar-maker,** n. Vinaigrier *m.* ‖ **Vinegar-making,** n. Vinaigrerie *f.* — v. tr. Culin. Vinaigrer. — adj. Fam. Revêche; aigre.

vinegarish [-əriʃ], **vinegary** [-əri] adj. De vinaigre (flavour). ‖ Fam. Aigre, revêche.

vinery ['vainəri] n. Agric. Serre (*f.*) à raisins.

vineyard ['vinjɑ:d] n. Agric. Clos (*m.*) de vigne; vignoble, coteau *m.;* vigne *f.* ‖ Eccles. Vigne *f.* (Lord's).

vinic ['vainik] adj. Vinique.

vinicultural [,vinikʌltʃərəl] adj. Vinicole.

viniculture ['vinikʌltʃə*] n. Agric. Viniculture.

vinification [,vinifi'keiʃən] n. Vinification *f.*

vinous ['vainəs] adj. Vineux. (See VINACEOUS.) ‖ Aviné (drunk).

vint [vint] v. tr. Faire (wine).

vintage ['vintidʒ] n. Agric. Vendange *f.* (crop); vendanges *f. pl.* (grape-picking, season). ‖ Cru *m.* (wine). ‖ Fig. Epoque *f.* — adj. Grand, de grand cru (wine); grand (year). ‖ Autom. Construite entre 1917 et 1930 (car). ‖ Fig. Excellent, grand, du meilleur cru. — v. tr. Agric. Cueillir (grapes); faire (wine).

vintager [-ə*] n. Vendangeur *s.*

vintner ['vintnə*] n. Négociant (*m.*) en vins.

viny ['vaini] adj. Vinicole.

vinyl ['vainil] n. Chim. Vinyle *m.*

viol ['vaiəl] n. † Mus. Viole *f.; consort of viols,* jeu de violes; *viol d'amore, da gamba,* viole d'amour, de gambe. ‖ Mus. *Base viol,* violoncelle *m.*

viola ['vi'oulə] n. † Mus. Viole *f.* ‖ Mus. Alto *m.; viola player,* altiste.

viola ['vaiələ] n. Bot. Violette *f.*

violate ['vaiəleit] v. tr. Violer (an oath). ‖ Troubler (s.o.'s peace). ‖ Violer (a woman). ‖ Jur. Violer, enfreindre (a law). ‖ Eccles. Profaner (a sanctuary).

violation [,vaiə'leiʃən] n. Violation *f.* ‖ Intrusion *f.;* interruption *f.* ‖ Viol *m.* (rape). ‖ Jur. Infraction *f.; in violation of,* en violation de. ‖ Eccles. Profanation *f.* (of a sanctuary).

violator ['vaiəleitə*] n. Violateur *m.;* violatrice *f.*

violence ['vaiələns] n. Violence *f.; to do violence to,* violenter, faire violence à. ‖ Jur. *Acts of violence,* voies de fait.

violent [-lənt] adj. Violent; extrême; intense; vif, fort (strong). ‖ Eclatant; criard, voyant (colours). ‖ Jur. *To lay violent hands on oneself,* attenter à ses jours; *to lay violent hands on s.o.,* se porter à des voies de fait contre qqn. ‖ Fam. Carabiné (cold).

violently [-ləntli] adv. Violemment. ‖ Extrêmement; terriblement; follement; *to be violently sick,* vomir.

violet ['vaiəlit] adj. Violet (colour). — n. Violet *m.* (colour). ‖ Bot. Violette *f.* ‖ **Violet-wood,** Bot. Palissandre *m.*

violin [,vaiə'lin] n. Mus. Violon *m.* (See FIDDLE.)

violinist [,vaiə'linist] s. Mus. Violoniste *s.*

violist [,vaiəlist] n. Mus. † Violiste *s.* ‖ Mus. Altiste *s.*

violoncellist [,vaiələn'tʃelist] n. Mus. Violoncelliste *s.*

violoncello [-lou] n. Mus. Violoncelle *m.*

V.I.P. [ˌviːaiˈpiː] abbr. *very important person,* personnalité de marque, V.I.P.; *I got the* V.I.P. *treatment,* on m'a déroulé le tapis rouge.
viper [ˈvaipə*] n. ZOOL., FIG. Vipère *f.*
viperine [ˈvaipərain] adj. ZOOL. Vipérin; *viperine snake,* vipérine.
viperish [-iʃ] adj. Vipérin, de vipère (tongue).
virago [viˈreigou] n. Virago, mégère *f.;* dragon, gendarme *m.* (nagging woman). ‖ Grosse malabare (or) dondon *f.* (fam.) [strapping woman].
viral [ˈvairəl] adj. MED. Viral.
virelay [ˈvirəlei] n. Virelai *m.*
Virgil [ˈvəːdʒil] n. Virgile *m.*
Virgilian [-iən] adj. Virgilien.
virgin [ˈvəːdʒin] adj. Vierge (forest, snow). ‖ CULIN. Vierge (oil). ‖ FIG. Virginal (modesty); vierge (person).
— n. Vierge *f.* ‖ ECCLES. *The Blessed Virgin,* la Sainte Vierge.
virginal [-əl] adj. De vierge, virginal.
— n. MUS. *Virginal* (or) *virginals* (or) *pair of virginals,* virginal *m.*
virginalist [-əlist] n. MUS. Virginaliste *s.*
virginhood [-hud] n. Virginité *f.*
Virginia [vəˈdʒinjə] n. Virginie *f.* (name). ‖ GEOGR. Virginie *f.* ‖ BOT. *Virginia creeper,* vigne vierge. ‖ COMM. Tabac (*m.*) de Virginie.
Virginian [vəˈdʒinjən] adj. De Virginie.
virginity [vəːˈdʒiniti] n. Virginité *f.*
virgo [ˈvəːgou] n. ASTRON. Vierge *f.* ‖ MED. *Virgo intacta,* vierge.
viridescent [viriˈdesṇt] adj. Verdâtre.
virile [ˈvirail] adj. Viril, mâle (lit. and fig.). ‖ MED. Viril (member).
virility [viˈriliti] n. Virilité *f.*
virology [viˈrɔlədʒi] n. MED. Science (*f.*) des virus.
virtual [ˈvəːtjuəl] adj. Vrai, effectif, de fait (practical). ‖ Virtuel, quasi; qui équivaut à (what amounts to). ‖ TECHN., PHYS. Virtuel.
virtuality [ˌvəːtjuˈæliti] n. Virtualité *f.*
virtually [-i] adv. En fait; en pratique; effectivement. ‖ Presque; virtuellement.
virtue [ˈvəːtjuː] n. Vertu *f.* (in general); honnêteté *f.* (in woman); *woman of virtue, of easy virtue,* femme honnête, légère. ‖ Qualité *f.;* mérite, avantage *m.* ‖ MED. Vertu, efficacité *f.* (of drugs, plants). ‖ LOC. *By virtue of,* en vertu de, en raison de; *to make a virtue of necessity,* faire de nécessité vertu.
virtuosity [ˌvəːtjuˈɔsiti] n. Virtuosité *f.*
virtuoso [ˌvəːtjuˈousou] (pl. **virtuosi** [-si]) n. Virtuose *s.* (artist). ‖ Amateur, connaisseur *s.*
virtuous [ˈvəːtjuəs] adj. Vertueux.
virtuously [-li] adv. Vertueusement.
virtuousness [-nis] n. Vertu *f.*
virulence [ˈviruləns] n. Virulence *f.*
virulent [-lənt] adj. Virulent. ‖ FIG. Virulent, violent, venimeux.
virulently [-ləntli] adv. Avec virulence.
virus [ˈvaiərəs] n. MED. Virus *m.* ‖ FIG. Poison *m.*
visa [ˈviːzə] n. Visa *m.*
— v. tr. Viser, apposer un visa à.
visage [ˈvizidʒ] n. Visage *m.;* figure *f.* (See FACE.)
vis-a-vis [ˈvizəvi] n. Vis-à-vis *m.*
— adv. Vis-à-vis (*to, with,* de); face à face (*to, with,* avec).
viscera [ˈvisərə] n. pl. Viscères *m. pl.*
visceral [-əl] adj. Viscéral.
viscid [ˈvisid] adj. Poisseux, gluant, visqueux.
viscose [ˈviskous] n. Viscose *f.*
viscosity [visˈkɔsiti] n. Viscosité *f.*
viscount [ˈvaikaunt] n. Vicomte *m.*
viscountcy [-si], **viscountship** [-ʃip], **viscounty** [-i] n. Vicomté *f.*
viscountess [-is] n. Vicomtesse *f.*
viscous [ˈviskəs] adj. Visqueux, gluant.
vise [vais] v. tr., n. U. S. TECHN. See VICE.
Vishnu [ˈviʃnu] n. Vichnou *m.*

visibility [ˌviziˈbiliti] n. Visibilité *f.; low* (or) *poor visibility,* mauvaise visibilité.
visible [ˈvizibḷ] adj. Visible; *to become visible,* apparaître. ‖ Visible, apparent, manifeste, évident (obvious).
visibleness [-nis] n. Visibilité *f.* ‖ Fait (*m.*) d'être visible.
visibly [ˈvizibli] adv. Visiblement; manifestement.
Visigoth [ˈvizigɔθ] n. Wisigoth *m.*
Visigothic [ˌviziˈgɔθik] adj. Wisigoth, wisigothique.
vision [ˈviʒən] n. Vision, vue *f.; field of vision,* champ visuel; *within range of vision,* à portée de vue. ‖ Vision, apparition *f.;* fantôme, spectre *m.* (ghost). ‖ Vision (*f.*) de l'avenir; prévoyance; puissance d'anticipation (or) d'imagination *f.; man of vision,* homme d'une grande perspicacité.
visional [-əl] adj. De vision. ‖ Imaginaire; irréel.
visionary [-əri] n. Visionnaire *s.*
— adj. Visionnaire; rêveur (person). ‖ Fantastique, chimérique (idea); imaginaire.
visionist [-ist] n. Visionnaire *s.*
visit [ˈvizit] n. Visite *f.; to pay s.o. a visit,* rendre visite à qqn. ‖ Visite *f.* (call); séjour *m.* (stay); *visit to Russia,* voyage en Russie. ‖ Visite (or) tournée d'inspection *f.* ‖ MED. Visite *f.* ‖ JUR. *Right of visit,* droit de visite; *visit to the scene of the crime,* descente sur les lieux. ‖ FAM. *To pay a visit,* aller au petit coin. ‖ FAM. U. S. Causette *f.*
— v. intr. Faire des visites; être en visite. ‖ U. S. Rendre visite (*with,* à). ‖ FAM. U. S. Bavarder.
— v. tr. Visiter, aller voir (a place). ‖ Rendre visite à, aller voir (to call on); aller faire un séjour chez (to stay with). ‖ Visiter, inspecter. ‖ Atteindre, s'abattre sur (to assail). ‖ JUR. *To visit the scene of the crime,* faire une descente sur les lieux. ‖ ECCLES. Affliger (*with,* de); punir (punish); *to visit the sins of the fathers upon the children,* châtier les enfants des péchés de leurs pères.
visitable [-əbḷ] adj. Qui peut être visité.
visitant [-ənt] adj. Qui visite; en visite.
— n. † Visiteur *s.* ‖ ECCLES. Visitandine *f.* ‖ ZOOL. Oiseau de passage *m.*
visitation [ˌviziˈteiʃən] n. Visite (or) tournée d'inspection *f.* ‖ Apparition *f.* ‖ NAUT. Visite *f.* ‖ MED. *Visitation of the sick,* visites aux malades. ‖ ECCLES. Visitation *f.* (festival); *nuns of the Visitation,* Visitandines. ‖ ECCLES. Visite pastorale *f.* (of a bishop); *visitation of God,* épreuve, *f.* ‖ FIG. Calamité, épreuve *f.* ‖ FAM. Visite fâcheuse *f.*
visiting [ˈvizitiŋ] adj. En visite. ‖ SPORTS. *The visiting team,* les visiteurs.
— n. Visites *f. pl.; visiting hours,* heures de visite; *to be on visiting terms with,* être en relations de visites avec. ‖ *Visiting-card,* n. Carte de visite *f.*
visitor [-ə*] n. Visiteur *s.* (caller, guest). ‖ Voyageur, client *s.* (to a hotel); *visitors' book,* livre des voyageurs, registre des visiteurs. ‖ Inspecteur *m.;* inspectrice *f.*
visitorial [ˌviziˈtɔːriəl] adj. D'inspecteur; d'inspection.
vison [ˈvaizən] n. ZOOL. Vison *m.*
visor [ˈvaizə*] n. † Visière *f.* ‖ AUTOM. Pare-soleil, parasol *m.*
vista [ˈvistə] n. Perspective; échappée *f.;* panorama *m.* ‖ FIG. Perspective *f.;* horizon *m.*
visual [ˈvizjuəl] adj. MED. Visuel (field); optique (nerve). ‖ Visuel (aids); de visibilité (distance).
visualization [ˌvizjuəlaiˈzeiʃən] n. Evocation *f.*
visualize [ˈvizjuəlaiz] v. tr. Rendre visible. ‖ Se représenter, évoquer l'image de; visualiser (fam.).
— v. intr. Visualiser; former une image mentale.
visually [-i] adv. Visuellement.
vital [ˈvait] adj. Vital (principle). ‖ Fatal (mistake); mortel (wound). ‖ Vital, capital, essentiel, fondamental; *of vital importance,* d'une importance capitale (or) vitale; *vital discussion,* échange de

vues (or) entretien des plus importants. ‖ U. S. Plein de vie, énergique (personality). ‖ JUR. Démographique (statistics); *vital statistics*, état civil. ‖ FAM. *Vital statistics*, mesures du corps féminin.
— n. pl. MED. Organes vitaux *m. pl.* ‖ NAUT. Œuvres vives *f. pl.* ‖ FIG. Parties essentielles *f. pl.*
vitality [vai'tæliti] n. Vitalité *f.*; vigueur *f.*
vitalize ['vaitəlaiz] v. tr. Vitaliser. ‖ FIG. Donner de la vie à.
vitally [-i] adv. De façon vitale.
vitamin ['vaitəmin] n. MED. Vitamine *f.*
vitelline [vi'teli:n] adj. Vitellin.
vitiate ['vi∫ieit] adj. Vicier, pervertir, corrompre. ‖ JUR. Vicier.
vitiation ['vi∫i'ei∫ən] n. Viciation *f.*
viticultural [,viti'kʌlt∫ərəl] adj. Viticole.
viticulture ['vitikʌlt∫ə*] n. AGRIC. Viticulture *f.*
viticulturist [,viti'kʌlt∫ərist] n. Viticulteur *m.*
vitrage [vi'trɑ:ʒ] adj. *Vitrage-curtain* (or) *net*, vitrage.
vitreous ['vitriəs] adj. Vitreux. (See GLASSY.) ‖ MED., ELECTR. Vitré.
vitrifiable ['vitrifaiəbl̩] adj. Vitrifiable.
vitrification [,vitrifi'kei∫ən] n. Vitrification *f.*
vitrify ['vitrifai] v. tr. (2). Vitrifier.
— v. intr. Se vitrifier.
vitriol ['vitriəl] n. CHIM. Vitriol *m.*; *to throw vitriol at*, vitrioler. ‖ FIG. Vitriol *m.* ‖ **Vitriol-thrower**, n. Vitrioleur *s.* ‖ **Vitriol-throwing**, n. Vitriolage *m.*
— v. tr. (1). Vitrioler.
vitriolated ['vitriəleitid] adj. CHIM. Vitriolé; transformé en sulfate.
vitriolic [,vitri'ɔlik] adj. Vitriolique. ‖ FIG. Trempé dans du vitriol (pen).
vitriolize ['vitriəlaiz] v. tr. Vitrioler.
vituperate [vai'tju:pəreit] v. tr. Injurier, insulter, vilipender.
— v. intr. Déblatérer, vitupérer (*against*, contre).
vituperation [,vaitju:pə'rei∫ən] n. Injures *f. pl.*
vituperative [vai'tju:pərətiv] adj. Injurieux.
Vitus ['vaitəs] n. MED. *St. Vitus's dance*, danse de Saint-Guy.
viva ['vaivə] interj., n. Vivat *m.* ‖ FAM. Oral *m.*
vivacious [vi'vei∫əs] adj. Vif, animé, plein de verve (person). ‖ BOT. Vivace.
vivaciousness [-nis] n. Vivacité *f.*
vivacity [vi'væsiti] n. Vivacité *f.*
vivarium [vai'vɛəriəm] n. Vivarium *m.*
vivat ['vaivæt] interj., n. Vivat *m.*
viva voce ['vaivə'vousi] adv. Oralement; de vive voix.
— adj. Oral, verbal.
— n. Oral *m.* (examination); soutenance de thèse *f.* (on completion of a thesis).
vivid ['vivid] adj. Vif, éclatant (colour, light). ‖ Vivant (description); vif (imagination); net, précis (recollection).
vividly [-li] adv. Vivement; d'une manière frappante; avec éclat.
vividness [-nis] n. Vivacité *f.*; éclat *m.* ‖ FIG. Vigueur, force *f.*
vivify ['vivifai] v. tr. (2). Vivifier, animer.
viviparous [vi'vipərəs] adj. ZOOL. Vivipare.
vivisect ['vivisekt] v. intr. MED. Faire de la vivisection.
— v. tr. MED. Pratiquer la vivisection sur.
vivisection [,vivi'sek∫ən] n. MED. Vivisection *f.*
vivisectionist [-∫ənist] n. MED. Vivisecteur *m.* ‖ Partisan (*m.*) de la vivisection.
vivisector [-tə*] n. MED. Vivisecteur *m.*
vixen ['viksən] n. ZOOL. Renarde *f.* ‖ FIG. Mégère *f.*
viz. (usually read : ['neimli]) adv. C'est-à-dire, à savoir.
vizier [vi'ziə*] n. Vizir *m.*
vizor ['vaizə*] n. See VISOR.

vocable ['voukəbl̩] n. Vocable *m.*
vocabulary [vo'kæbjuləri] n. Vocabulaire; lexique *m.*
vocal ['voukəl] adj. MED. Vocal; oral. ‖ MUS. Vocal. ‖ FIG. Mélodieux, harmonieux. ‖ GRAMM. Sonore; vocalique. ‖ FAM. Braillard (person).
vocalic [vo'kælik] adj. GRAMM. Vocalique.
vocalism ['voukəlizm̩] n. GRAMM. Vocalisme *m.*
vocalist [-ist] n. MUS. Chanteur *s.*
vocalization [,voukəlai'zei∫ən] n. GRAMM. Vocalisation *f.*
vocalize ['voukəlaiz] v. tr. Articuler, prononcer. ‖ MUS. Chanter. ‖ GRAMM. Vocaliser, sonoriser.
— v. intr. MUS. Vocaliser, chanter. ‖ FAM. Gueuler.
vocally [-i] adv. Vocalement.
vocation [vo'kei∫ən] n. Vocation *f.* (to the ministry). ‖ Inclination *f.* ‖ Profession, carrière *f.*; métier *m.* (trade).
vocational [-əl] adj. Professionnel; *vocational guidance*, orientation professionnelle; U. S. *vocational schools*, cours techniques, écoles professionnelles.
vocationally [-əli] adj. Du point de vue professionnel.
vocative ['vɔkətiv] adj., n. GRAMM. Vocatif *m.*
vociferant [vo'sifərənt] adj. Vociférant.
vociferate [-eit] v. intr. Vociférer, crier.
vociferation [vo,sifə'rei∫ən] n. Vocifération *f.*
vociferator [vo'sifəreitə*] n. Vociférateur *m.*; vociératrice *f.*
vociferous [-əs] adj. Vociférant; criard, braillard (fam.). [See CLAMOROUS.]
vociferously [-əsli] adv. En vociférant.
vodka ['vɔdkə] n. Vodka *f.*
vogue [voug] n. Vogue, mode *f.* (see FASHION); *in vogue*, en vogue, à la mode.
voice [vɔis] v. tr. Exprimer, énoncer, formuler (an opinion). ‖ MUS. Harmoniser (an organ). ‖ GRAMM. Sonoriser (a consonant).
— n. Voix *f.*; *in a loud voice*, à haute voix; *in a low voice*, à voix basse; *to give voice to*, exprimer; *with one voice*, à l'unanimité. ‖ MUS. Voix *f.*; *in voice*, en voix; *voice part*, partie vocale. ‖ GRAMM. Voix, forme *f.* ‖ FIG. *The still, small voice*, la voix de la conscience. ‖ FAM. *To love the sound of one's own voice*, aimer à s'écouter parler. ‖ **Voice-over**, n. CINEM. Voix (*f.*) hors champ (or) off. ‖ **Voice-print**, n. Empreinte vocale *f.* ‖ **Voice-production**, n. Diction, élocution *f.*
voiced [-t] adj. GRAMM. Sonore.
voiceless [-lis] adj. Sans voix, muet. ‖ MED. Aphone. ‖ GRAMM. Sourd.
voicelessly [-lisli] adv. Silencieusement.
voicelessness [-lisnis] n. Silence *m.*
voicer [-ə*] n. MUS. Harmoniste *s.*
void [vɔid] n. Vide *m.*
— v. tr. JUR. Annuler. ‖ MED. Evacuer.
— n. Vacant (post). ‖ Vide (space). ‖ Inutile, vain. ‖ Dénué, dépourvu (*of*, de) [devoid]. ‖ JUR. Nul; *to make void*, annuler, frapper de nullité.
voidable [-əbl̩] adj. JUR. Annulable.
voidance [-əns] n. ECCLES. Expulsion *f.*; vacance *f.* ‖ JUR. Annulation *f.* ‖ MED. Evacuation *f.*
voidness [-nis] n. Vide *m.*; vacuité *f.* ‖ JUR. Nullité *f.*
voile [vɔil] n. Voile *m.* (material).
volar ['voulə*] adj. MED. Palmaire; plantaire.
volatile ['vɔlətail] adj. CHIM. Volatil. ‖ FIG. Volage, inconstant (fickle); vif, gai (merry).
volatileness [-nis] n. FIG. Inconstance *f.*
volatility [,vɔlə'tiliti] n. CHIM. Volatilité *f.* ‖ FIG. Inconstance, versatilité *f.*
volatilizable [vɔ,læti'laizəbl̩] adj. Volatilisable.
volatilization [vɔ,lætilai'zei∫ən] n. Volatilisation *f.*
volatilize [vɔ'lætilaiz] v. tr. Volatiliser.
— v. intr. Se volatiliser, s'évaporer.
vol-au-vent [vɔlo'vɑ̃] n. CULIN. Vol-au-vent *m.*

volcanic [vɔl'kænik] adj. Volcanique; *volcanic glass*, verre volcanique, obsidienne. ‖ FIG. Volcanique.

volcanism ['vɔlkənizm̩] n. Volcanisme *m.*

volcanize [-aiz] v. tr. Volcaniser.

volcano [vɔl'keinou] n. GEOL. Volcan *m.*

volcanological [,vɔlkənə'lɔdʒikḷ] adj. Volcanologique.

volcanologist [,vɔlkən'ɔlədʒist] n. Volcanologue, volcanologiste *s.*

volcanology [,vɔlkə'nɔlədʒi] n. Volcanologie *f.*

vole [voul] n. SPORTS. Vole *f.* (at cards).
— v. intr. SPORTS. Faire la vole (at cards).

vole n. ZOOL. Campagnol *m.; water vole*, rat d'eau.

volet ['vɔlei] n. ECCLES. Volet *m.*

volition [və'liʃən] n. Volition, volonté *f.; of one's own volition*, de son propre gré.

volitional [-əl], **volitive** ['vɔlitiv] adj. Volitif.

volley ['vɔli] v. tr. Lancer une volée de. ‖ SPORTS. Reprendre de volée (a ball). ‖ FIG. Lâcher une bordée de (abuse).
— v. intr. MILIT. Tirer par salves (guns). ‖ SPORTS. Renvoyer une volée.
— n. Volée *f.;* grêle *f.* (hail). ‖ MILIT. Salve *f.* (salvo). ‖ SPORTS. Volée *f.* ‖ FIG. Salve *f.* (of applause); volée, bordée *f.* (of oaths). ‖ **Volleyball,** n. SPORTS. Volley-ball, volley *m.*

volplane ['vɔlplein] v. intr. AVIAT. Planer; descendre en vol plané.
— n. U. S. AVIAT. Vol plané *m.*

volt [voult] n. ELECTR. Volt *m.* ‖ **Volt-rise,** n. ELECTR. Surtension *f.*

voltage [-idʒ] n. ELECTR. Tension *f.; voltage drop,* perte de charge; *high voltage,* haute tension.

voltaic [vɔl'teiik] adj. ELECTR. Voltaïque.

Voltairian [vɔl'tɛəriən] adj., n. Voltairien *s.*

Voltairianism [-izm̩] n. Voltairianisme *m.*

voltameter [vɔl'tæmitə*] n. ELECTR. Voltamètre *m.*

volte-face ['vɔlt'fæs] n. Volte-face *f.*

voltmeter ['voultmi:tə*] n. ELECTR. Voltmètre *m.*

volubility [,vɔlju'biliti] n. Volubilité *f.*

voluble [-bḷ] adj. Volubile (person); facile, rapide (speech). ‖ BOT. Volubile.

volubly [-bli] adv. Avec volubilité.

volume ['vɔljum] n. Volume *m.* (book).‖ Volume *m.* (of a sound); ampleur *f.* (of a voice). ‖ PHYS. Volume *m.* ‖ RADIO. Puissance *f.* ‖ Pl. Tourbillon *m.;* nuages *m. pl.* (of smoke); flots *m. pl.* (of water).

volumetric(al) [,vɔlju'metrik(əl)] adj. Volumétrique.

voluminous [vɔ'lju:minəs] adj. Volumineux. ‖ FAM. Fécond, abondant, prolifique (writer).

voluminously [-li] adj. Abondamment; en grande quantité.

voluntarily ['vɔləntərili] adv. Volontairement.

voluntariness [-rinis] n. Caractère volontaire *m.;* spontanéité *f.*

voluntary [-ri] n. Sujet facultatif *m.* (optional). ‖ ECCLES. Partisan (*m.*) de la séparation de l'Eglise et de l'Etat. ‖ MUS. Morceau (*m.*) d'orgue improvisé.
— adj. Volontaire (by choice); volontaire, librement consenti, spontané (willing). ‖ Libre (school). ‖ MILIT. De volontaires (army); franc (corps). ‖ MED. Volontaire (muscle). ‖ JUR. A titre gratuit (conveyance); volontaire (manslaughter); amiable (partition).

volunteer [,vɔlən'tiə*] n. MILIT., FIG. Volontaire *s.*
— adj. MILIT. Volontaire; de volontaires (army).
— v. intr. S'offrir; s'engager (*for,* pour). ‖ MILIT. S'engager comme volontaire.
— v. tr. Donner volontairement (information); offrir spontanément (or) volontairement (one's services); *to volunteer to do sth.,* s'offrir à faire qqch.; faire qqch. de plein gré.

volunteering [,vɔlən'tiəriŋ] n. Volontariat *m.*

voluptuary [və'lʌptjuəri] adj., n. Voluptueux; épicurien *s.*

voluptuosity [və,lʌptju'ɔsiti] n. Voluptuosité *f.*

voluptuous [və'lʌptjuəs] adj. Voluptueux.

voluptuously [-li] adv. Voluptueusement.

voluptuousness [və'lʌptjuəsnis] n. Voluptuosité, sensualité *f.*

volute [və'lju:t] n. Volute *f.*

voluted [-id] adj. Voluté; à volutes.

vomica ['vɔmikə] n. MED. Caverne pulmonaire *f.* (cavity); expectoration (*f.*) de pus (coughing up).

vomit ['vɔmit] n. MED. Vomissement *m.* (act); vomitif *m.* (agent); vomissure *f.* (matter).
— v. intr. MED. Vomir.
— v. tr. MED. Vomir, rendre. ‖ FIG. Vomir.

vomiting [-iŋ] n. MED. Vomissement *m.*

vomitive [-iv] adj. MED. Vomitif.

vomitory [-əri] n., adj. MED. Vomitif *m.*

voodoo ['vu:du:] n. Vaudou *m.*
— v. tr. Envoûter.

voodooism [-izm̩] n. Envoûtement *m.*

voracious [vɔ'reiʃəs] adj. Vorace.

voraciously [-li] adv. Voracement.

voraciousness [-nis], **voracity** [vɔ'ræsiti] n. Voracité *f.*

vortex ['vɔ:teks] n. Tourbillon *m.* (whirlpool, whirlwind). ‖ MED. Vortex *m.* ‖ PHYS. Tourbillon *m.; vortex ring,* vortex. ‖ FIG. Tourbillon *m.*
— N. B. Deux pluriels : *vortexes, vortices.*

vortiginous [vɔ:'tidʒinəs] adj. Tourbillonnant.

votaress ['voutəris] n. Adoratrice *f.*

votary [-i] n. Adorateur *m.;* adoratrice *f.;* fidèle, dévoué, dévot *s.* ‖ Partisan *m.;* amateur *s.*

vote [vout] v. intr. Voter, donner sa voix.
— v. tr. Voter. ‖ Décider, décréter (to decide). ‖ FAM. Déclarer, proclamer à l'unanimité (to proclaim); proposer (to suggest). ‖ **To vote down,** repousser. ‖ **To vote in,** élire. ‖ **To vote out,** battre aux élections.
— n. Vote, scrutin *m.* (action); *to take the vote,* procéder au scrutin. ‖ Motion, résolution *f.;* vote *m.* (decision). ‖ Vote, suffrage *m.* (choice); *cast votes,* suffrages exprimés; *to count the votes,* dépouiller le scrutin; *the floating vote,* les suffrages des sans-parti: *to give one's vote for,* donner sa voix à. ‖ Droit de vote *m.* (right to vote). ‖ FIN. Crédits votés *m. pl.*

voter [-ə*] n. Votant *s.* ‖ Electeur *m.;* électrice *f.*

voting [-iŋ] n. Vote, scrutin *m.; voting paper,* bulletin de vote.

votive [-tiv] adj. Votif; *votive tablet,* plaque commémorative. ‖ ECCLES. Votif.

vouch [vautʃ] v. tr. Affirmer; confirmer, prouver (statement). ‖ Citer en confirmation (authority).
— v. intr. To vouch for, répondre de (s.o.); se porter garant de (sth.); *to vouch for the truth of,* garantir la véracité de.

voucher [-ə*] n. JUR. Garant *s.* (person). ‖ FIN. Certificat *m.;* pièce justificative *f.* (or) à l'appui (or) de comptabilité. ‖ Reçu, récipissé *m.;* quittance *f.* (receipt). ‖ COMM. Bon *m.; cash voucher,* bon de caisse. ‖ THEATR. Contremarque *f.* ‖ LOC. *Luncheon voucher,* bon de repas à prix réduit.

vouchsafe [vautʃ'seif] v. tr. Daigner accorder.
— v. intr. *To vouchsafe to do sth.,* condescendre à (or) daigner faire qqch.

voussoir ['vu:swɑ:*] n. ARCHIT. Voussoir, vousseau *m.*

vow [vau] n. Vœu *m.* ‖ Serment *m.* ‖ ECCLES. Vœu *m.; to take one's vows,* prononcer ses vœux, entrer en religion. ‖ JUR. *Marriage vows,* les promesses du mariage.
— v. intr. † Jurer.
— v. tr. Vouer. ‖ Jurer; *to vow vengeance against,* jurer de se venger de. ‖ † Déclarer (to declare).

vowel ['vauəl] n. GRAMM. Voyelle *f.; vowel change, sound,* changement, son vocalique. ‖
Vowel-point, n. GRAMM. Point-voyelle *f.*
voyage ['vɔiədʒ] n. NAUT. Voyage *m.; to go on a voyage,* faire un voyage (*to,* à). ‖ U. S. AVIAT. Voyage par air *m.*
— v. tr. NAUT. Traverser.
— v. intr. NAUT. Voyager par mer. ‖ U. S. AVIAT. Voyager par air.
voyager [-ə*] n. NAUT. Voyageur, passager *s.;* navigateur *m.*
voyeur [vwæ'jəː*] n. Voyeur *m.*
vs. Written abbr. for *versus,* contre.
Vulcan ['vʌlkən] n. Vulcain *m.*
vulcanic [vʌlk'ænik] adj. See VOLCANIC.
vulcanite [-ait] n. Vulcanite *f.*
vulcanization [,vulkənai'zeiʃən] n. Vulcanisation *f.*
vulcanize ['vʌlkənaiz] v. tr. Vulcaniser.
— v. intr. Se vulcaniser.
vulcanizer [-ə*] n. TECHN. Vulcanisateur *m.*
vulcanological [,vʌlkənə'lɔdʒikl] adj. Vulcanologique.
vulcanologist [,vʌlkən'ɔlədʒist] n. Vulcanologue *s.*
vulcanology [,vʌlkə'nɔlədʒi] n. Vulcanologie *f.*
vulgar ['vʌlgə*] n. Vulgaire, peuple *m.;* masse *f.;* populo *m.* (fam.).
— adj. Vulgaire, commun, répandu (widespread). ‖ Vulgaire; commun, bas (cheap, coarse, low); de mauvais goût (profane); *vulgar expression,* expression triviale; *the vulgar herd,* le vulgum pecus. ‖ MATH. Ordinaire (fraction). ‖ LOC. *The vulgar era,* l'ère chrétienne.

vulgarian [vʌl'gɛəriən] n. Personne vulgaire *f.;* parvenu *s.*
vulgarism ['vʌlgərizm̩] n. GRAMM. Expression vulgaire *f.* ‖ FIG. Vulgarité, trivialité *f.*
vulgarity [vʌl'gæriti] n. Vulgarité, trivialité, grossièreté *f.;* vulgaire, trivial *m.*
vulgarization [,vʌlgərai'zeiʃən] n. Vulgarisation, popularisation *f.*
vulgarize ['vulgəraiz] v. tr. Vulgariser, banaliser. ‖ Vulgariser, populariser.
vulgarly [-li] adv. Vulgairement, trivialement (coarsely); grossièrement (rudely). ‖ Vulgairement, communément (generally).
Vulgate ['vulgit] n. ECCLES. Vulgate *f.*
vulnerability [,vʌlnərə'biliti] n. Vulnérabilité *f.*
vulnerable ['vʌlnərəbl] adj. Vulnérable; *vulnerable spot,* défaut de la cuirasse, talon d'Achille, point faible. ‖ MILIT. Vulnérable, perméable.
vulnerary ['vʌlnərəri] n., adj. MED. Vulnéraire *m.*
vulpine ['vʌlpain] adj. ZOOL. De renard. ‖ FIG. Rusé.
vulture ['vʌltʃə*] n. ZOOL. Vautour *m.*
vulturine [-tʃurain] adj. ZOOL. De vautour.
vulturish [-tʃəriʃ] adj. ZOOL., FIG. De vautour; rapace.
vulva ['vʌlvə] n. MED. Vulve *f.*
vulval [-əl], **vulvar** [-ə*] adj. MED. Vulvaire.
vulvitis [vʌl'vaitis] n. MED. Vulvite *f.*
vulvo-vaginitis ['vʌlvo,vædʒi'naitis] n. MED. Vulvo-vaginite *f.*
vying ['vaiiŋ]. See VIE.
— n. Rivalité *f.*

w ['dʌb]ju:] n. W, w *m.* (letter). ‖ GEOGR. Abbr. *West,* ouest, O.; abbr. *western,* de l'Ouest, occidental. ‖ ELECTR. W, watt *m.* ‖ CHIM. W, tungstène *m.*
wacky [-i] adj. U. S. FAM. Cinglé. (See CRAZY.)
wad [wɔd] n. Tampon *m.* (of cotton-wool); bouchon *m.* (of straw). ‖ Prise *f.* (of chewing tobacco). ‖ MILIT. Bourre *f.* (of cartridge, gun). ‖ U. S. FAM. Liasse *f.;* rouleau *m.* (of banknotes). ‖ U. S. POP. Pèze, fric *m.* (oof).
— v. tr. Presser, tasser (cotton); faire une boulette de (paper). ‖ Rembourrer (a coverlet); ouater (a garment); capitonner (a wall). ‖ Boucher (an aperture). ‖ MILIT. Bourrer (gun-barrel); enfoncer (powder).
wadding [-iŋ] n. Ouatage *m.* (of garment); capitonnage *m.* (of wall). ‖ Ouate *f.* (cotton-wool). ‖ MILIT. Bourre *f.*
waddle ['wɔdl] v. intr. Se dandiner, se dodeliner; *to waddle along,* se déhancher.
— n. Dandinement, déhanchement *m.*
waddling [-iŋ] adj. Dandinant, déhanché (gait).
waddlingly [-iŋli] adv. En canard, en se dandinant, en chaloupant.
waddy ['wɔdi] n. Assommoir *m.* (in Australia). ‖ U. S. Canne *f.* (walking stick).

wade [weid] v. intr. Avancer péniblement; patauger (fam.); *to wade in,* s'y mettre, s'y attaquer.
— v. tr. Passer à gué (a brook).
— n. Pataugeage *m.* (act).
wader [-ə*] n. Pataugeur *m.* ‖ Pl. Bottes (*f. pl.*) d'égoutier. ‖ ZOOL. Echassier *m.*
wadi ['wɔdi] n. Oued *m.*
wafer ['weifə*] n. CULIN. Gaufrette *f.* ‖ JUR. Cachet de papier *m.* (seal). ‖ Pain (*m.*) à cacheter. ‖ ECCLES. Pain (*m.*) d'hostie. ‖ MED. Cachet *m.* ‖ **Wafer-thin,** adj. Extrêmement mince, mince comme du papier à cigarettes.
— v. tr. Cacheter.
waffle ['wɔfl] n. CULIN. Gaufre *f.* ‖ **Waffle-iron,** n. CULIN. Gaufrier *m.*
waffle v. intr. FAM. Epiloguer (*about,* sur).
— n. FAM. Dissertation *f.;* discours *m.* (*about,* sur).
waft [wɔːft] v. tr. Porter (smells, sounds). ‖ † Envoyer (a kiss); tourner (the eyes).
— v. intr. Flotter (on the wind). ‖ Souffler (breeze). ‖ S'exhaler (*from,* de).
— n. Bouffée *f.* (of music, perfume, wind). ‖ Coup (*m.*) d'aile (of a bird). ‖. NAUT. *With a waft,* en berne (flag).
wag [wæg] v. tr. (1). Agiter, remuer; *to wag its*

tail, hocher la queue (bird); remuer la queue (dog); *to wag one's head*, hocher la tête.
— v. intr. Branler (head); s'agiter, remuer (tail). ‖ FAM. Marcher, aller; *to set tongues wagging*, faire causer, faire marcher les langues.
— n. Hochement *m.* (of the head, of a bird's tail); frétillement *m.* (of a dog's tail). ‖ Signe *m.* (of the finger).

wag n. FAM. Plaisantin, loustic *m.*

wage ⌊weidʒ⌋ n. Salaire *m.* (in general); gages *m. pl.* (of servants); paye *f.* (of workmen). ‖ FIG. Prix *m.* ‖ **Wage-earner**, n. Salarié *s.* ‖ **Wage-rise,** U. S. **wage hike,** n. Hausse (*f.*) des salaires. ‖ **Wage-scale,** n. Echelle (*f.*) des salaires. ‖ **Wage-sheet,** n. Feuille de paie *f.* ‖ **Wage-working,** adj. Salarié.
— v. tr. † Gagner (to bet); engager (to pledge). ‖ MILIT. Faire (war); *to wage war against,* guerroyer contre.

wager [-ə*] n. Gageure *f.;* pari *m.* (bet).
— v. tr. Gager, parier. (See BET.)

waggery ['wægəri] n. Facétie *f.*

waggish [-iʃ] adj. Facétieux, farceur (jocular). ‖ Badin, fait par jeu (playful).

waggishly [-iʃli] adv. Facétieusement, en badinant, par jeu.

waggishness [-iʃnis] n. Caractère facétieux, goût (*m.*) de la blague.

waggle ['wægl] v. intr. Frétiller (tail).
— v. tr. Agiter, remuer.
— n. Frétillement *m.*

wag(g)on ['wægən] n. † Chariot *m.;* charrette *f.* ‖ Roulage *m.* ‖ MILIT. Fourgon (load, transport); caisson *m.* (for ammunition). ‖ CH. DE F. Wagon *m.;* voiture *f.* ‖ TECHN. Wagonnet *m.* ‖ AUTOM. Camion *m.* ‖ U. S. FAM. Panier (*m.*) à salade (Black Maria). ‖ FAM. *To be on the water-waggon,* être buveur d'eau; *to hitch one's waggon to a star,* viser très haut. ‖ **Waggon-load,** n. Charretée *f.;* CH. DE F. Charge (*f.*) de wagon. ‖ **Waggon-train,** n. MILIT. Train (*m.*) des équipages.

wag(g)onage [-idʒ] n. U. S. Roulage, wagonnage *m.*

wag(g)oner [-ə*] n. Voiturier, roulier *m.*

wag(g)onette [,wægə'net] n. Wagonnette *f.*

wagtail ['wægteil] n. ZOOL. Bergeronnette *f.*

waif [weif] n. NAUT., FIG. Epave *f.* ‖ FIG. Enfant abandonné *m.* (child).

wail [weil] n. Vagissement *m.* (of a child); lamentation, plainte *f.;* gémissement *m.* (of the wind).
— v. intr. Se lamenter, gémir.
— v. tr. Pleurer, gémir sur.

wailful [-ful] adj. Plaintif.

wailing [-iŋ] adj. Vagissant (child); plaintif (cry); gémissant (person).

wain [wein] n. AGRIC. Charrette, gerbière *f.* ‖ ASTRON. *Charles's Wain,* le Chariot, la Grande Ourse.

wainscot ['weinskət] n. Lambris *m.*
— v. tr. Lambrisser.

wainscot(t)ing [-iŋ] n. Lambrissage *m.* (act); lambris *m.* (panel).

waist [weist] n. Taille *f.; up* (or) *down to the waist,* jusqu'à la ceinture; *waist measurement,* tour de taille. ‖ SPORTS. *To grip round the waist,* saisir à bras-le-corps (or) à mi-corps, ceinturer. ‖ TECHN. Etranglement *m.* ‖ NAUT. Embelle *f.* ‖ U. S. Chemisier *m.;* blouse *f.* ‖ **Waist-cincher,** n. U. S. Guêpière *f.* ‖ **Waist-deep,** adj. Jusqu'à la ceinture (in water). ‖ **Waist-high,** adj. Montant jusqu'à la taille.

waistband [-bænd] n. Ceinture *f.* (of skirt).

waistcoat [-kout] n. Gilet *m.*

wait [weit] v. intr. Attendre (*till, until,* que); *to wait for,* attendre (s.o.); *dinner is waiting for us,* le dîner nous attend (or) est prêt. ‖ Servir (at table). ‖ † Etre de service. ‖ **To wait on,** attendre encore

(to wait longer); servir (s.o. at table); présenter ses devoirs à, se présenter chez (to call on); découler de (sth.); SPORTS. Se réserver (absolutely); suivre de près (a competitor). ‖ **To wait up for,** FAM. Veiller pour attendre (s.o.).
— v. tr. Attendre (orders, one's turn). ‖ Différer, retarder (dinner). ‖ † Escorter, accompagner.
— n. Attente *f.* (act, time). ‖ Embuscade *f.; to lie in wait for,* être aux aguets pour (or) à l'affût de. ‖ Pl. MUS. Chanteurs (*m. pl.*) de noëls.

waiter [-ə*] n. Personne (*f.*) qui attend. ‖ Garçon *m.* (in a restaurant); *head waiter,* maître d'hôtel; *hired waiter,* extra. ‖ Plateau *m.* (tray).

waiting [-iŋ] adj. Qui attend. ‖ D'attente. ‖ De service. ‖ JUR. Attentiste (policy). ‖ **Waiting-list,** n. Liste d'attente *f.* ‖ **Waiting-maid,** n. Camériste *f.* ‖ **Waiting-room,** n. Salle d'attente *f.*
— n. Attente *f.* ‖ Service *m.; in waiting to,* de service auprès de (the monarch).

waitress [-ris] n. Servante *f.* (in an inn); serveuse *f.* (in a restaurant).

waive [weiv] v. tr. JUR. Se désister de (a claim); renoncer à, abandonner (privilege, right); déroger à (a requirement); ne pas insister sur (a rule).

waiver [-ə*] n. JUR. Renonciation; dérogation *f.;* désistement *m.*

wake [weik] n. NAUT., FIG. Sillage *m.*

wake v. intr. Etre éveillé, veiller, être à l'état de veille; *to wake up,* s'éveiller, se réveiller (*from,* de). ‖ FIG. S'éveiller; *to wake up,* se dégourdir; se déboucher (fam.).
— v. tr. Veiller (a dead person). ‖ **To wake up,** éveiller, réveiller (s.o.); FIG. Réveiller, ranimer.
— N. B. *To wake* fait *woke* ou *waked* au prét., *waked, woken* ou *woke* au p. p.
— n. † Etat (*m.*) de veille. ‖ Veillée mortuaire *f.* ‖ Fête votive *f.*

wakeful [-ful] adj. D'insomnie, blanc (night); éveillé, tenu éveillé (person). ‖ FIG. Vigilant, en alerte, sur ses gardes.

wakefully [-fuli] adv. Sans dormir. ‖ FIG. Avec vigilance.

wakefulness [-fulnis] n. Insomnie *f.* (sleeplessness). ‖ Etat (*m.*) de veille (not asleep). ‖ FIG. Vigilance *f.*

waken [-ən] v. tr. Eveiller, réveiller (s.o.).
— v. intr. S'éveiller, se réveiller.

wale [weil] n. Zébrure *f.* (mark). ‖ Côte *f.* (on corduroy). ‖ NAUT. Plat-bord *m.;* pl. préceintes *f. pl.* ‖ TECHN. Moise *f.*
— v. tr. Zébrer (the skin). ‖ Côteler (a cloth). ‖ TECHN. Moiser.

Wales [weilz] n. GEOGR. Pays (*m.*) de Galles; *North, South Wales,* Galles du Nord, du Sud.

walk [wɔ:k] v. intr. Marcher (in general). ‖ Se rendre à pied; *to walk home,* rentrer chez soi à pied; *to walk in procession,* suivre la procession. ‖ Se promener, faire une promenade (to stroll). ‖ Revenir, apparaître (ghost). ‖ † Vivre, agir; *to walk in peace,* vivre en paix. ‖ **To walk about,** se promener. ‖ **To walk along,** marcher, s'avancer, aller. ‖ **To walk away,** s'en aller; SPORTS, FAM. *To walk away from,* semer (a competitor). ‖ **To walk back,** revenir à pied. ‖ **To walk down,** descendre. ‖ **To walk in,** entrer. ‖ **To walk into,** entrer dans; FAM. Enguirlander (to abuse); tomber sur (to meet); rentrer dans (to thrash). ‖ **To walk off,** partir; FAM. Filer, décamper. ‖ **To walk on,** poursuivre sa marche; THEATR. Faire de la figuration. ‖ **To walk out,** sortir; FAM. *To walk out on,* plaquer (s.o.); laisser en plan (sth.); *to walk out with,* fréquenter, être bien avec (a young man); U. S. FAM. Se mettre en grève. ‖ **To walk over,** SPORTS. Gagner dans un fauteuil (easily); gagner d'office (without competitor). ‖ **To walk through,** parcourir; traverser. ‖ **To walk up,** monter; *to walk up to,* marcher vers, s'approcher de.
— v. tr. Parcourir, suivre en marchant; *to walk*

the streets, battre le pavé (person); faire le trottoir (prostitute). ‖ Faire à pied (a distance). ‖ Faire marcher (a horse, s.o.); *I walked him off his legs,* je l'ai tellement fait marcher qu'il ne tient plus debout. ‖ Dresser (a puppy). ‖ THEATR. *To walk the boards,* faire du théâtre. ‖ MILIT. *To walk one's beat,* faire sa faction. ‖ SPORTS. Faire de la marche à pied contre. ‖ NAUT. *To walk the plank,* passer à la planche. ‖ U. S. FAM. *To walk the plank,* être obligé de rendre son tablier. ‖ *To walk off, to walk off one's lunch,* aller se promener pour faire descendre son déjeuner. ‖ *To walk out,* sortir, promener; balader (fam.) [s.o.].
— Marche *f.* (act). ‖ Pas (pace); *to come at a walk,* venir au pas. ‖ Démarche *f.* (manner); *to know s.o. by his walk,* reconnaître qqn au pas. ‖ Trajet *m.* (distance); *to be an hour's walk from,* être à une heure de marche de. ‖ Promenade *f.* (stroll); *to go for a walk,* se promener, faire une promenade (or) un tour; *to take s.o. for a walk,* balader qqn. ‖ Promenade *f.* (route); *my usual walk is along the Seine,* je me promène habituellement le long de la Seine. ‖ Avenue, promenade *f.* (avenue); allée (*f.*) d'arbres (row). ‖ Tournée *f.* (of a hawker, postman). ‖ AGRIC. † Parquet, parcage *m.* ‖ ARCHIT. Ambulatoire *m.* ‖ SPORTS. Epreuve (*f.*) de marche. ‖ FIG. Orientation *f.; walk of life,* carrière (profession); condition sociale (status). ‖ **Walk-away,** n. SPORTS. Course (*f.*) sur le velours. U. S. FAM. Jeu d'enfant *m.* ‖ **Walk-out,** n. Grève improvisée *f.* ‖ **Walk-over,** n. SPORTS. Walk-over *m.;* FAM. Victoire (*f.*) dans un fauteuil; jeu d'enfant *m.* ‖ **Walk-up,** n. U. S. FAM. Appartement sans ascenseur *m.* ‖ **Walk-way,** n. Passerelle *f.* (in factory); allée *f.* (in garden).

walker [-ə*] n. Marcheur; promeneur *s.* ‖ **Walker-on,** n. THEATR. Figurant *s.*

walkie-talkie ['wɔ:ki'tɔ:ki] n. RADIO. Talkie-walkie *m.*

walking ['wɔ:kiŋ] n. Marche *f.* ‖ **Walking-boots,** n. pl. Chaussures (*f. pl.*) de sport (or) de fatigue. ‖ **Walking-on part,** n. THEATR. Rôle (*m.*) de figurant, utilité *f.* ‖ **Walking-pace,** n. Pas *m.; at a walking-pace,* au pas. ‖ **Walking-papers,** n. pl. FAM. Congédiement, largage *m.; to give s.o. his walking-papers,* larguer qqn. ‖ **Walking-stick,** n. Canne *f.*

wall [wɔ:l] n. Mur *m.* (in a room). ‖ Muraille *f.* (of a castle, a mountain). ‖ Mur, rempart *m.* (in a town). ‖ Haut du pavé *m.* (in a street); *to give the wall,* céder le haut du pavé *m.* ‖ AGRIC. Espalier *m.* ‖ GEOL. Eponte *f.* ‖ MED. Paroi *f.* ‖ U. S. FIN. *Wall Street,* quartier de la finance; marché américain; *Wall Streeter,* boursier. ‖ FAM. *To go to the wall,* être acculé (or) ruiné. ‖ **Wall-board** (or) tile, n. ARCHIT. Panneau, carreau de revêtement *m.* ‖ **Wall-clock,** n. Cartel *m.* ‖ **Wall-creeper,** n. ZOOL. Grimpereau *m.* ‖ **Wall-eye,** n. MED. Œil vairon *m.:* FAM. Œil rond *m.* ‖ **Wall-fitting,** n. ELECTR. Applique *f.* ‖ **Wall-fruit,** n. AGRIC. Fruit d'espalier *m.* ‖ **Wall-lizard,** n. ZOOL. Lézard gris *m.* ‖ **Wall-map,** n. Carte murale *f.* ‖ **Wall-newspaper,** n. Journal affiché *m.* ‖ **Wall-paper,** n. Papier peint *m.; U. S. POP. Faux billet (*m.*) de banque. ‖ **Wall-plate,** n. ARCHIT. Ligneul *m.; TECHN. Plaque murale *f.* ‖ **Wall-seat,** n. Banquette *f.* ‖ **Wall-walk,** n. Chemin (*m.*) de ronde.
— v. tr. Fortifier (a town); murailler (a wall). ‖ *To wall in,* clore de murs (a garden). ‖ *To wall off,* séparer par un mur (*from,* de). ‖ *To wall up,* murer (an aperture).

wallaby ['wɔləbi] n. ZOOL. Petit kangourou, wallaby *m.*

wallah ['wɔlə] n. FAM. Type *m.; the insurance wallah,* le type des assurances; *the navy wallahs,* les types de la marine.

wallet ['wɔlit] n. † Bissac *m.;* besace *f.* ‖ Portefeuille *m.* (notecase).

wallflower ['wɔ:l,flauə*] n. BOT. Ravenelle *f.* ‖ FAM. Personne (*f.*) qui fait tapisserie (at a dance).

Walloon [wɔ'lu:n] adj., n. GEOGR. Wallon *s.*

wallop ['wɔləp] v. tr. FAM. Flanquer une raclée à. — n. FAM. Gnon *m.* (blow); *with a wallop,* à grand fracas.

walloping [-iŋ] n. FAM. Raclée *f.* — adj. FAM. Enorme, formidable.

wallow ['wɔlou] v. intr. Se vautrer (animal); se plonger (person); *to wallow in vice,* croupir dans le vice; *to wallow in wealth,* être cousu d'or, nager dans l'opulence. — n. Bauge, souille *f.* (of a boar).

walnut ['wɔ:lnʌt] n. BOT. Noix *f.* (fruit); noyer *m.* (tree). ‖ COMM. Noyer *m.* (wood). — adj. En noyer.

walrus ['wɔ:lrəs] n. ZOOL. Morse *m.* — adj. FAM. A la gauloise (moustache).

waltz [wɔ:ls] n. MUS. Valse *f.* — v. intr. MUS. Valser.

waltzer [-ə*] n. MUS. Valseur *s.*

wampum ['wɔmpəm] n. Wampum *m.* ‖ FAM. Fric *m.* (oof).

wan [wɔn] adj. Blême, livide (complexion); blafard (light); pâle (smile). ‖ † Sombre.

wand [wɔnd] n. Baguette *f.* (magic rod); *divining wand,* baguette de sourcier. ‖ JUR. Verge *f.* ‖ MED. *Mercury's wand,* caducée. ‖ MUS. Baguette *f.*

wander ['wɔndə*] v. intr. Errer, vaguer (*about,* par, dans). ‖ Serpenter (river). ‖ MED., FIG. Divaguer, délirer. ‖ FIG. S'égarer, s'écarter (from a subject). — v. tr. Parcourir.

wanderer [-rə*] n. Errant *m.* ‖ Voyageur (*s.*) sans but. ‖ Vagabond *s.* (pej.). ‖ FIG. Brebis perdue *f.;* dévoyé *s.*

wandering [-riŋ] n. Errance *f.;* voyage (*m.*) à l'aventure. ‖ Vagabondage *m.* (pejoratively). ‖ MED., FIG. Délire *m.;* pl. divagations *f. pl.* ‖ FIG. Déviation *f.* (*from,* de). ‖ FIG. Rêverie, distraction *f.* — adj. Errant (Jew). ‖ Sinueux (river). ‖ Nomade (tribe). ‖ MED. Flottant (kidney); délirant (person). ‖ FIG. Distrait (attention, eyes); incohérent (speech).

wanderingly [-riŋli] adv. A l'aventure. ‖ FIG. De façon incohérente.

wane [wein] v. intr. ASTRON. Décroître. ‖ FIG. Diminuer, décliner. — n. ASTRON. Décours *m.* ‖ FIG. Déclin *m.* (See EBB.)

wangle ['wæŋgl] v. tr. FAM. Se débrouiller pour avoir, resquiller. — v. intr. FAM. Pratiquer le système D.

wangler [-ə*] n. FAM. Resquilleur *s.*

wangling [-iŋ] n. FAM. Resquille *f.;* système D *m.*

wanker ['wæŋkə*] n. ARG. Branleur *s.*

wanness ['wɔnnis] n. Pâleur *f.*

want [wɔnt] n. Manque, défaut *m.* (lack); *for want of asking, of sth. better,* faute de demander, de mieux; *in want of,* à court de. ‖ Besoin *m.* (need); *a man of few wants,* un homme qui a peu de besoins (or) qui sait se contenter de peu. ‖ Besoin *m.;* pauvreté *f.* (destitution); *to be in want,* vivre dans la gêne, être dans le besoin. ‖ Désir *m.* (wish); *I am in want of a dress,* il me faudrait bien (or) je voudrais bien une robe. ‖ U. S. FAM. *Want ad,* petite annonce. — v. tr. Manquer de, être à court de, ne pas avoir (to lack). ‖ Avoir besoin de (to need); *I have all I want,* j'ai tout ce qu'il me faut. ‖ Vouloir, désirer (to wish); *he wants to go with us,* il veut nous accompagner; *what else do you want?,* que désirez-vous d'autre ? ‖ Demander : *your father wants you,* votre père vous demande (or) veut vous voir. ‖

Rechercher ; *the man you want,* l'homme qu'il vous faut. ‖ Demander, réclamer, exiger (to require). — v. intr. Manquer, faire défaut (to lack). ‖ Etre dans la gêne ; *she does not want,* elle n'est pas dans le besoin. ‖ **To want for,** manquer de, avoir besoin de ; U. S. FAM. Désirer.

wanted [-id] adj. Demandé. ‖ JUR. Recherché par la police. ‖ COMM. *Wanted : cook-general,* on demande une bonne à tout faire.

wanting [-iŋ] adj. Manquant. ‖ Dépourvu (in, de). ‖ FAM. Déficient (idiot). — prep. Sans. ‖ † Sauf.

wanton ['wɔntən] adj. Espiègle, indiscipliné (child). ‖ Capricieux, folâtre (wind). ‖ Gratuit (cruelty, insult). ‖ Déréglé, licencieux (love) ; impudique, débauché (woman). ‖ AGRIC. Luxuriant (vegetation). ‖ FAM. Extravagant (dress, speech). — n. Femme légère *f.* — v. intr. Folâtrer.

wantonly [-li] adv. En folâtrant. ‖ Gratuitement. ‖ De gaieté de cœur.

wantonness [-nis] n. Etourderie, espièglerie *f.* ‖ Gratuité, gaieté (*f.*) de cœur. ‖ Libertinage *m.* ‖ AGRIC. Exubérance *f.*

wapiti ['wɔpiti] n. ZOOL. Wapiti, élan *m.*

wapperjaw ['wɔpə,dʒɔ:] n. U. S. FAM. Menton (*m.*) en galoche.

war [wɔ:*] n. MILIT. Guerre *f.* ; *the war to end all wars,* la der des ders ; *to declare war on,* déclarer la guerre à ; *to go to war,* se mettre en guerre ; *to go to the wars,* partir pour la guerre ; *war of nerves,* guerre des nerfs. ‖ FIG. Guerre, lutte *f.* ‖ **War-baby,** n. Enfant (*m.*) de la guerre (illegitimate child). ‖ **War-cloud,** n. FAM. Menace de guerre *f.* ‖ **War-correspondent,** n. Correspondant (*m.*) de guerre. ‖ **War-crime,** n. Crime (*m.*) de guerre. ‖ **War-cry** n. Cri (*m.*) de guerre ‖ **War-fever,** n. Psychose de guerre *f.* ‖ **War-game,** n. Jeu de stratégie, war-game *m.* ; MILIT. Kriegspiel *m.,* manœuvre *f.* ‖ **War-horse,** n. †, FAM. Cheval (*m.*) de bataille. ‖ **War-paint,** n. Peinture de guerre *f.* ; FAM. Tralala *m.* ; U. S. FAM. Maquillage *m.* ‖ **War-path,** n. Sentier (*m.*) de la guerre ; FAM. *To be on the war-path,* se faire agressif, être d'une humeur de dogue. ‖ **War-plane,** n. AVIAT. Avion (*m.*) de guerre. ‖ **War-ravaged,** adj. Déchiré par la guerre. ‖ **War-song,** n. Chant guerrier *m.* ‖ **War-time,** n. Temps (*m.*) de guerre. ‖ **War-widow,** n. Veuve (*f.*) de guerre. ‖ **War-zone,** n. Zone (*f.*) des armées. — v. intr (1). MILIT. Faire la guerre, guerroyer (*against,* contre). ‖ FIG. Etre en conflit (to contend). ‖ FIG. Batailler, lutter (*with,* contre).

warble ['wɔ:b] n. MÉD. Tumeur indurée ; œstridiose *f.* ‖ **Warble-fly,** n. ZOOL. Œstre *m.*

warble n. ZOOL. Gazouillement *m.* (of a bird). ‖ FAM. Gazouillis, roucoulement *m.* (of a person). — v. intr. ZOOL. Gazouiller. ‖ FAM. Roucouler. — v. tr. Gazouiller (a song).

warbler [-blə*] n. ZOOL. Fauvette *f.* ; oiseau chanteur *m.*

warbling [-bliŋ] adj. Gazouillant. — n. Gazouillis.

warcraft ['wɔ:krɑft] n. MILIT. Art (*m.*) de la guerre.

ward [wɔ:d] n. † Garde *f.,* guet *m.* (look-out). ‖ † SPORTS. Garde *f.* (in fencing). ‖ † Surveillance *f.* ‖ Quartier *m.* (in a prison, town) ; *electoral ward,* circonscription électorale. ‖ Pl. TECHN. Garde, bouterolle (of a key, lock). ‖ JUR. Tutelle *f.* (guardianship) ; pupille *s.* (person). ‖ MÉD. Salle *f.* ; service *m.* (in a hospital). — v. tr. † Garder. ‖ **To ward off,** parer (a blow) ; FIG. Détourner (a danger).

warden [-n] n. † Gardien *m.* ‖ MILIT. *Air-raid warden,* chef d'îlot. ‖ Directeur *m.* (of a hostel, prison) ; conservateur *m.* (of a park) ; gouverneur *m.* (of a town). ‖ Garde-chasse *m.* (game-warden).

wardenship [-n,ʃip] n. Charge (*f.*) de gardien (or) gouverneur.

warder [-ə*] n. JUR. Geôlier, gardien (*m.*) de prison.

wardress [-ris] n. JUR. Gardienne de prison, geôlière *f.*

wardrobe [-roub] n. Garde-robe *f.* (closet, clothes). ‖ **Wardrobe-keeper,** n. Costumier *m.*

wardroom [-rum] n. NAUT. Carré (*m.*) des officiers.

wardship [-ʃip] n. JUR. Tutelle *f.*

ware [wɛə*] adj. See AWARE. — interj. Attention (or) gare à.

ware n. ARTS. Faïence *f.* ; *China ware,* porcelaine. ‖ Pl. COMM. Marchandises *f. pl.* ; articles (*m. pl.*) de vente.

warehouse ['wɛəhaus] n. † Magasin *m.* ‖ Entrepôt, dépôt *m.* ; *furniture warehouse,* garde-meuble. — [-hauz] v. tr. Entreposer (goods). ‖ Mettre au garde-meuble (furniture).

warehouseman [-hausmən] (pl. **warehousemen**) n. Entrepositaire, magasinier *m.* ‖ JUR. Entreposeur *m.*

warehousing [-hauziŋ] n. Entreposage *m.*

warfare ['wɔ:fɛə*] n. MILIT. Guerre *f.* (action. conflict).

warhead [-hed] n. MILIT. Tête active (or) explosive, ogive *f.*

warily ['wɛərili] adv. Prudemment.

wariness [-nis] n. Circonspection *f.*

warlike ['wɔ:laik] n. Guerrier (feat) ; martial (humour) ; belliqueux (temper).

warlock ['wɔ:lɔk] n. Sorcier, magicien *s.* ; mage *m.*

warm [wɔ:m] adj. Chaud ; *to be warm,* avoir chaud (person) ; faire chaud (weather) ; *to grow warm,* se réchauffer. ‖ Réchauffant (exercise). ‖ ARTS. Chaud (colour). ‖ SPORTS. Chaud (scent). ‖ FIG. Ardent (admirer) ; chaud, animé (controversy) ; cordial, vif (encouragement) ; ardent, bouillant, enflammé (person) ; chaleureux (thanks, welcome) ; *warm with,* échauffé par. ‖ FAM. Qui brûle (in games). ‖ FAM. Où ça chauffe, dangereux (position) ; *to make it warm for,* en faire baver à. ‖ **Warm-blooded,** adj. ZOOL. A sang chaud ; FIG. Passionné, enflammé. ‖ **Warm-hearted,** adj. Généreux, plein de cœur. — v. tr. Chauffer (in general) ; bassiner (a bed) ; *to warm oneself,* se chauffer. ‖ CULIN. Faire chauffer (water) ; chambrer (wine). ‖ FIG. Echauffer (blood, s.o.) ; réchauffer (heart). ‖ FAM. Dérouiller, secouer (s.o.). ‖ **To warm up,** réchauffer (s.o.) ; CULIN. Faire réchauffer (meal). — v. intr. Se chauffer, se réchauffer. ‖ CULIN. Chauffer. ‖ FIG. S'échauffer, s'enflammer ; *to warm to,* se prendre de sympathie pour. ‖ **To warm up,** s'animer ; SPORTS. S'échauffer, se mettre en train. — n. Chauffe *f.* ; *to have, to give a warm,* prendre, donner un air de feu.

warmer [-ə*] n. CULIN. Réchaud *m.*

warming [-iŋ] n. Chauffage *m.* ‖ FAM. Dégelée *f.* ‖ **Warming-pan,** n. Bassinoire *f.* — adj. Chauffant, réchauffant. ‖ **Warming-up,** adj. D'assouplissement (exercices).

warmly [-li] adv. Chaudement, chaleureusement, avec feu.

warmonger ['wɔ:,mʌŋgə*] n. Belliciste *m.*

warmongering [-iŋ] n. Incitation à la guerre *f.*

warmth [wɔ:mθ] n. Chaleur *f.* (See HEAT.) ‖ ARTS. Chaleur *f.* (of colours). ‖ FIG. Ardeur, ferveur *f.* ; feu *m.* (of s.o.) ; chaleur *f.* (of a welcome).

warn [wɔ:n] v. tr. Prévenir, mettre en garde (*against,* contre) ; avertir (*of,* de) ; *he was warned against smoking,* on l'avait averti de ne pas fumer. ‖ **To warn off,** détourner, faire tenir à l'écart.

warner [-ə*] n. TECHN. Avertisseur *m.*

warning [-iŋ] n. Avertissement *m.* ; notification *f.* ; ‖ Leçon *f.* (lesson) ; avertissement *m.* ; semonce *f.* (to, pour) [scolding]. ‖ Préavis *m.* ; *without warning,* sans prévenir, à l'improviste, au débotté. ‖ Congé *m.* ; *to give one's employer warning* (or) *an*

employee warning, donner ses huit jours à son patron (or) à un employé. ‖ Autom. Pl. Signalisation *f.*
— adj. D'avertissement (letter). ‖ Autom. De signalisation. ‖ Naut. *Warning shot,* coup de semonce.
warningly [-iɳli] adv. Pour avertir, en guise d'avertissement.
warp [wɔːp] n. Techn., Archit., Aviat. Gauchissement *m.* ‖ Techn. Chaîne *f.* (of a cloth). ‖ Naut. Aussière *f.* ‖ Agric. Limon *m.* ‖ Fig. Déformation *f.* (of mind). ‖ **Warp-frame,** n. Ourdissoir *m.*
— v. tr. Techn., Archit. Gondoler, déjeter (a board); voiler (a wheel). ‖ Techn. Ourdir (in weaving). ‖ Aviat. Gauchir. ‖ Naut. Haler, touer. ‖ Agric. Colmater. ‖ Fig. Déformer, fausser, pervertir (s.o.'s mind).
— v. intr. Techn. Se gondoler, jouer, travailler (wood); se voiler (wheel). ‖ Naut. Se haler; *to warp out,* se déhaler.
warping ['wɔːpiɳ] n. Techn. Gondolage *m.* (of wood); voilure *f.* (of wheel). ‖ Techn. Ourdissage *m.* (of cloth). ‖ Aviat. Gauchissement *m.* ‖ Naut. Halage *m.* ‖ Agric. Colmatage *m.* ‖ Fig. Déformation, perversion *f.*
warrant ['wɔrənt] n. Autorisation *f.* (by a superior). ‖ Justification, raison valable *f.* (for an act, a statement). ‖ Garantie *f.*; garant *m.* (as an assurance). ‖ Jur. Mandat *m.*; *warrant of attorney,* pouvoir, procuration; *search warrant,* mandat de perquisition. ‖ Comm. Certificat *m.*; *dock* (or) *warehouse warrant,* certificat d'entrepôt, warrant; *to issue a warehouse warrant for,* warranter. ‖ Fin. Ordonnance *f.* (for payment). ‖ Milit. Brevet *m.* ‖ **Warrant-officer,** n. Milit. Sous-officier breveté *m.*; Naut. Premier maître *m.*
— v. tr. Garantir, assurer (to guarantee); justifier (to justify). ‖ Loc. *I'll warrant,* je parie.
warrantable [-əbl̦] adj. Justifiable, soutenable. ‖ Permis, légitime.
warrantee [,wɔrən'tiː] n. Personne (*f.*) munie d'une garantie. ‖ Jur. Personne (*f.*) sous le coup d'un mandat d'amener.
warranter ['wɔrəntə*] n. Jur. Garant, répondant *m.*
warranty [-i] n. Autorisation *f.*; droit *m.* (*for,* de). ‖ Jur. Garantie *f.*
warren ['wɔrən] n. Garenne *f.*
warrior ['wɔriə*] n. Milit. Guerrier *m.*
warship ['wɔːʃip] n. Naut. Navire (*m.*) de guerre.
wart [wɔːt] n. Med. Verrue *f.*
wartwort [-wəːt] n. Bot. Euphorbe *f.*
warty [-i] adj. Med. Verruqueux.
wary ['wɛəri] adj. Circonspect, avisé, prudent (see cautious); *to be wary of,* se méfier de, se garder de.
was [wɔz]. See be.
wash [wɔʃ] v. tr. Laver; *to wash one's hands,* se laver les mains. ‖ Laver, blanchir (sth.); *to wash one's linen,* faire sa lessive. ‖ Faire la lessive de, blanchir (s.o.). ‖ Baigner, arroser (the shore). ‖ Enlever; *to wash overboard,* emporter par-dessus bord; *to wash ashore,* rejeter sur le rivage. ‖ Tremper, mouiller, humecter (*with,* de). [to moisten]. ‖ Dorer (a metal); badigeonner (*with,* de) [walls]. ‖ Arts. Laver. ‖ Techn. Débourber. ‖ Fig. Laver, purifier. ‖ **To wash away,** enlever au lavage (a stain); affouiller (the shore); emporter dans les flots (sth.). ‖ **To wash down,** laver largement; Fam. *An excellent meal washed down with a very good Burgundy,* un excellent repas arrosé d'un très bon bourgogne. ‖ **To wash off,** enlever au lavage. ‖ **To wash out,** laver (a bottle); délaver (a colour); extraire en lavant (gold); enlever au lavage (a stain); Fig. Laver (an insult); Fam. Passer l'éponge sur. ‖ **To wash up,** laver; *to wash up the dishes,* faire la vaisselle; Naut. Rejeter (sth.).
— v. intr. Se laver, se débarbouiller, faire sa toilette (to wash oneself). ‖ Laver, faire la lessive; *to wash for s.o.,* blanchir qqn. ‖ Se laver (cloth). ‖ Naut. Baigner; *to wash over the deck,* balayer le pont. ‖ **To wash off,** partir au lavage. ‖ **To wash out,** se délaver, se décolorer, passer, déteindre (colour); partir au lavage (stain); Fam. *To feel washed out,* se sentir à plat; *to feel completely washed out,* être lessivé. ‖ **To wash up,** refluer (*on, sur*); U. S. Se laver, faire sa toilette; U. S. Fam. *To be washed up,* être mis au rancart.
— n. Toilette *f.*; bain *m.*; ablutions *f. pl.* (of person); *to have a wash,* faire un brin de toilette. ‖ Lavage *m.* (of sth.); *to give sth. a wash,* laver qqch. ‖ Blanchissage *m.*; *to send to the wash,* donner à blanchir; envoyer à la lessive. ‖ Lessive *f.*; linge blanchi *m.*; *to bring back the week's wash,* rapporter la lessive de la semaine. ‖ Couche légère *f.* (on a metal); badigeon *m.* (on a wall). ‖ Geol. Alluvion *f.* ‖ Arts. Lavis *m.* ‖ Med. Lotion *f.* ‖ Naut. Sillage *m.* (of a ship); remous, ressac *m.* (of waves); brisants *m. pl.* (waves). ‖ U. S. Fam. Lavasse *f.* (drink). ‖ **Wash-basin,** U. S. **Wash-bowl,** n. Cuvette (*f.*) de lavabo. ‖ **Wash-house,** n. Buanderie *f.* (at home); lavoir *m.* (public); U. S. Blanchisserie *f.* ‖ **Wash-leather,** n. Peau (*f.*) de chamois, ‖ **Wash-out,** n. Fam. Fiasco, four *m.* (failure); propre à rien, inadapté, fruit sec *m.* (person). ‖ **Wash-sale,** n. Fin. Lessivage *m.* ‖ **Wash-tub,** n. Baquet *m.*
washable [-əbl̦] adj. Lavable.
washboard [-bɔːd] n. Planche (*f.*) à laver. ‖ Naut. Fargue *f.*
washcloth [-klɔθ] n. U. S. Linge (*m.*) de toilette.
washday [-dei] n. U. S. Jour (*m.*) de lessive.
washer [-ə*] n. Lessiveuse *f.* (device); laveur *s.* (person). ‖ Lavette *f.* (wash-cloth). ‖ Techn. Rondelle *f.* ‖ **Washer-up,** n. Laveur (*s.*) de vaisselle (at home); plongeur *s.* (in restaurant).
washerman [-mən] (pl. **washermen**) n. Techn. Laveur *m.* (of ore).
washerwoman [-,wumən] (pl. **washerwomen** [-wimən]) n. Blanchisseuse; lavandière (†) *f.*
washily [-ili] adv. Mollement.
washiness [-inis] n. Culin. Fadeur, insipidité (of food); faiblesse *f.* (of wine). ‖ Fig. Fadeur, platitude *f.*
washing [-iɳ] n. Toilette *f.* (of a person); lavage *m.* (of a thing). [See lavation.] ‖ Blanchissage *m.* (act); lessive *f.* (clothes). ‖ **Washing-day,** n. Jour (*m.*) de lessive. ‖ **Washing-machine,** n. Machine (*f.*) à laver. ‖ **Washing-powder,** n. Lessive *f.* ‖ **Washing-up,** n. Vaisselle *f.*
washroom [-rum] n. U. S. Toilettes *f. pl.*
washwoman [-'wuːmən] n. U. S. Blanchisseuse *f.*
washy [-i] adj. Délavé, décoloré, passé (colour). ‖ Culin. Fade, insipide (food); faible, mouillé (wine). Fig. Fade, terne (feeling); délayé (style).
wasp [wɔsp] n. Zool. Guêpe *f.*; *wasp's nest,* guêpier. ‖ **Wasp-waist,** n. Taille de guêpe *f.* ‖ **Wasp-waisted,** adj. A la taille de guêpe.
W. A. S. P. [wɔsp] abbr. *White Anglo-Saxon Protestant,* Blanc protestant d'origine anglo-saxonne.
waspish [-iʃ] adj. Acerbe, irascible, piquant, mordant, acéré.
waspishly [-iʃli] adv. Méchamment, avec mordant.
waspishness [-iʃnis] n. Malignité *f.*
wassail ['wɔsl̦] n. † Santé *f.*; toast *m.* (salutation). ‖ Beuverie *f.* (drinking bout). ‖ Boisson épicée *f.* (ale).
— v. intr. Faire la fête.
wastage ['weistidʒ] n. Gaspillage, coulage *m.* ‖ Déperdition *f.* (loss).
waste [weist] v. tr. Dévaster, ravager (to destroy). ‖ User, consumer (to use up). ‖ Affaiblir, user, épuiser (to weaken). ‖ Gaspiller, dissiper (to squander); *to waste one's time,* perdre son temps. ‖ U. S.

Perdre, laisser passer (an opportunity). ‖ JUR. Détériorer, dégrader. ‖ MED. Amaigrir.
— v. intr. S'user (to be used up). ‖ S'épuiser, diminuer (to lessen). ‖ Passer (to be spent). ‖ Etre gaspillé, se perdre (to be squandered). ‖ MED. Dépérir, s'affaiblir. ‖ JUR. Se dégrader. ‖ **To waste away**, MED. S'affaiblir, languir, dépérir.
— adj. Désolé, désert (country). ‖ AGRIC. En friche, inculte, vague (ground). ‖ TECHN. Perdu (gas, heat, steam); de rebut (paper); de déchet (products); résiduaire (water). ‖ CULIN. Ménagère (water). ‖ **Waste-paper-basket**, n. Corbeille (f.) à papier.
— n. Désert m. (wilderness). ‖ AGRIC. Lande, friche f.; terrain vague m. ‖ CULIN. Ordures f. pl. ‖ TECHN. Déchets m. pl. (by-products); déperdition f. (of heat, steam). ‖ JUR. Dégradations f. pl.; dégâts m. pl. ‖ FIG. Gaspillage m.; it's a sheer waste of time, c'est en pure perte; to run to waste, se gaspiller. ‖ **Waste-cock**, n. Purgeur m. ‖ **Waste-heap**, n. Tas (m.) d'ordures. ‖ **Waste-pipe**, n. Trop-plein m.; vidange f.

wastebasket [-,bæskit] n. U. S. Corbeille (f.) à papier.

wasteful [-ful] adj. Ruineux (expenditure); de gaspillage (habits); gaspilleur, dissipateur, dilapidateur (person).

wastefully [-fuli] adv. En gaspillant.

wastefulness [-fulnis] n. Gaspillage m. ‖ Dissipation, prodigalité f.

waster [-ə*] n. Gaspilleur s. ‖ TECHN. Pièce manquée f.

wasting [-iŋ] adj. Dévastateur m.; dévastatrice f.; ravageur. ‖ MED. De langueur (disease); atrophié (limb); tabescent, qui dépérit (patient). ‖ FIG. Rongeur, dévorant (care).
— n. Dévastation f.; ravage m. ‖ MED. Atrophie f. (of a limb); dépérissement m. (of the body, a patient).

wastrel ['weistrəl] n. Gaspilleur s. (waster). ‖ Prodigue s. (spendthrift). ‖ TECHN. Pièce (f.) de rebut. ‖ FIG. Raté, bon à rien m. ‖ FAM. Gamin (m.) des rues.

watch [wɔtʃ] v. intr. Veiller, demeurer éveillé (to stay awake). ‖ Veiller, guetter (to be on the alert). ‖ U. S. Observer, remarquer (to observe). ‖ **To watch after**, suivre du regard. ‖ **To watch for**, guetter, épier (s.o., sth.). ‖ **To watch out**, faire attention, prendre garde. ‖ **To watch over**, surveiller, veiller sur (a child); garder (a flock).
— v. tr. Observer, suivre des yeux (to look at); to watch s.o. working (or) work, regarder travailler qqn. ‖ Surveiller, tenir à l'œil, épier (to spy). ‖ Guetter, attendre (to look for). ‖ Garder (to tend). ‖ FAM. To make s.o. watch his step, mettre qqn au pas.
— n. Veille f. (act, fact, period). ‖ Guet m.; aguets m. pl.; on the watch, aux aguets; to be on the watch for, guetter. ‖ Surveillance, garde f.; to keep a close watch over, surveiller attentivement. ‖ Veilleur, surveillant m. (person). ‖ Montre f.; the time by my watch, l'heure à ma montre. ‖ † MILIT. Guet m. ‖ NAUT. Bordée f. (crew on duty); quart m. (period of duty). ‖ **Watch-case**, n. Boîtier (m.) de montre. ‖ **Watch-chain**, n. Chaîne de montre, giletière f. ‖ **Watch-dog**, n. Chien (m.) de garde; adj. U. S. Watch-dog committee, comité de surveillance. ‖ **Watch-glass**, n. Verre (m.) de montre. ‖ **Watch-guard**, n. Montre-breloque f. ‖ **Watch-keeper**, n. NAUT. Homme de quart m. ‖ **Watch-maker**, n. Horloger m. ‖ **Watch-making**, n. Horlogerie f. ‖ **Watch-night**, n. U. S. Réveillon du jour de l'An m. ‖ **Watch-pocket**, n. Gousset m. (in a waistcoat). ‖ **Watch-stand**, n. Porte-montre m. ‖ **Watch-tower**, n. Tour (f.) de guet. ‖ **Watch-train**, n. Mouvement m.

watcher [-ə*] n. Veilleur s. ‖ Observateur m.; observatrice f.

watchful [-ful] adj. Vigilant, aux aguets, en alerte (on the look-out). ‖ De veille (night).

watchfulness [-fulnis] n. Vigilance f.

watchman [-mən] (pl. **watchmen**) n. Veilleur (m.) de nuit. ‖ MILIT. † Guetteur m. ‖ MILIT. Sentinelle f.

watchword [-wə:d] n. MILIT. Mot (m.) de passe. ‖ FIG. Mot d'ordre m.

water ['wɔ:tə*] n. Eau f. (for drinking). ‖ Eau f. (lake, river, sea); English waters, les eaux anglaises; by water, par eau, par mer; to cross the water, faire la traversée. ‖ NAUT. Fond m.; to draw six feet of water, avoir un tirant d'eau de six pieds; to make water, faire eau. ‖ NAUT. Marée f.; at high water, à marée haute. ‖ MED. Eau f.; mineral water, eau minérale; to make water, uriner; to take the waters at, aller aux eaux à, faire une cure thermale à; water on the knee, épanchement de synovie. ‖ Pl. Eaux f. pl. (in pregnancy). ‖ TECHN. Eau f. (of a diamond); lustre, moirage m. (on metal, silk). ‖ ARTS. Aquarelle f. (in painting). ‖ FAM. An artist of the first water, un artiste de premier plan; I am in low water, les fonds sont bas, je suis à sec (penniless); to be in hot water, avoir chaud, être dans une fichue position; to hold water, tenir debout (argument); to keep one's head above water, se maintenir à flot; to throw cold water on, refroidir. ‖ **Water-bailiff**, n. Garde-pêche m. ‖ **Water-bearer**, n. ASTRON. Verseau m. ‖ **Water-beetle**, n. ZOOL. Gyrin m. ‖ **Water-biscuit**, n. CULIN. Biscuit sans œuf m. ‖ **Water-boat**, n. NAUT. Bateau-citerne m. ‖ **Water-borne**, adj. NAUT. Transporté par eau (goods); flottant (ship). ‖ **Water-bottle**, n. Gourde f.; MILIT. Bidon m.; hot water bottle, bouillotte. ‖ **Water-brash**, n. MED. Pyrosis f. ‖ **Water-bus**, n. NAUT. Bateau-mouche m.; vedette f. ‖ **Water-carriage**, n. Transport (m.) par eau. ‖ **Water-carrier**, n. Porteur (s.) d'eau; ASTRON. Verseau m. ‖ **Water-cart**, n. Arroseuse f. ‖ **Water-clock**, n. Clepsydre f. ‖ **Water-closet**, n. W.-C., cabinets m. pl. ‖ **Water-colour**, n. ARTS. Couleur d'aquarelle f. (colour); aquarelle f. (painting). ‖ **Water-colourist**, n. ARTS. Aquarelliste s. ‖ **Water-company**, n. Compagnie (f.) des Eaux. ‖ **Water-cooler**, n. Alcarazas m. ‖ **Water-crane**, n. TECHN. Grue hydraulique f. ‖ **Water-cure**, n. MED. Hydrothérapie f. ‖ **Water-diviner**, n. Sourcier m. ‖ **Water-dog**, n. ZOOL. Chien (m.) qui aime l'eau; U. S. FAM. Loup (m.) de mer (sailor); bon nageur s. (swimmer). ‖ **Water-drinker**, n. Buveur (s.) d'eau. ‖ **Water-farming**, n. U. S. Culture (f.) de plantes aquatiques. ‖ **Water-fence**, n. U. S. Fossé (m.) de clôture. ‖ **Water-festival**, n. Fête aquatique f. ‖ **Water-finding**, n. Radiesthésie f. ‖ **Water-gate**, n. Vanne f. ‖ **Water-gauge**, n. Hydromètre m.; échelle (f.) d'étiage. ‖ **Water-glass**, n. Verre (m.) à eau; CHIM. Silicate (m.) de potasse. ‖ **Water-hammer**, n. TECHN. Coup de bélier m. (in a pipe). ‖ **Water-harden**, n. TECHN. Tremper (steel). ‖ **Water-haul**, n. U. S. FAM. Fiasco m. ‖ **Water-hen**, n. ZOOL. Sarcelle, poule d'eau f. ‖ **Water-heater**, n. U. S. Chauffe-eau m. ‖ **Water-ice**, n. CULIN. Sorbet m. ‖ **Water-intake**, n. Prise d'eau f. ‖ **Water-jug**, n. Pot (m.) à eau (pitcher); broc m. (for toilet). ‖ **Water-jump**, n. SPORTS. Brook m. ‖ **Water-level**, n. Niveau (m.) d'eau. ‖ **Water-lily**, n. BOT. Nénuphar m. ‖ **Water-line**, n. NAUT. Ligne de flottaison f. ‖ **Water-lined**, adj. Filigrané (paper). ‖ **Water-melon**, n. BOT. Pastèque f. ‖ **Water-mill**, n. Moulin (m.) à eau. ‖ **Water-motor**, n. TECHN. Moteur hydraulique m. ‖ **Water-nymph**, n. Naïade f. ‖ **Water-pipe**, n. Conduite d'eau f. ‖ **Water-plant**, n. BOT. Plante aquatique f. ‖ **Water-police boat**, n. NAUT. Patache f. ‖ **Water-polo**, n. SPORTS. Water-polo m. ‖ **Water-pot**, n. Pot à eau m. (pitcher); arrosoir m. (watering-pot). ‖ **Water-**

power, n. Energie hydraulique; houille blanche *f.* ‖ **Water-rat** (or) **-vole,** n. ZOOL. Rat (*m.*) d'eau. ‖ **Water-resisting,** adj. Hydrofuge. ‖ **Water-route,** n. Voie navigable *f.* ‖ **Water-shoot,** n. Gargouille *f.* ‖ **Water-sick,** adj. AGRIC. Trop arrosé. ‖ **Water-side,** adj. Riverain; n. Bord (*m.*) de l'eau. ‖ **Water-skiing,** n. SPORTS. Ski nautique *m.* ‖ **Water-softener,** n. Adoucisseur (*m.*) d'eau. ‖ **Water-soluble,** adj. Hydrosoluble. ‖ **Water-spaniel,** n. ZOOL. Epagneul *m.* ‖ **Water-spider,** n. ZOOL. Argyronète; araignée d'eau *f.* ‖ **Water-sprite,** n. Ondin *s.* ‖ **Water-stained,** adj. Taché d'humidité. ‖ **Water-strider,** n. U. S. ZOOL. Hydromètre, dystique *m.* ‖ **Water-supply,** n. Approvisionnement (*m.*) d'eau; *water-si·pply point,* point d'eau. ‖ **Water-system,** n. TECHN. Canalisation d'eau. ‖ **Water-tower,** n. TECHN. Château (*m.*) d'eau. ‖ **Water-vapour,** n. Vapeur d'eau *f.* ‖ **Water-wall,** n. Digue *f.* ‖ **Water-washable,** adj. MED. Hydrosoluble. ‖ **Water-wave,** v. tr. Mettre en plis (of hair); moirage *m.; * moirure *f.* (of silk). ‖ **Waterway,** n. NAUT. Voie navigable, passe *f.;* TECHN. Passage d'eau. ‖ **Water-weed,** n. BOT. Plante aquatique *f.* ‖ **Water-wheel,** n. Roue hydraulique *f.*
— v. tr. Arroser (*with*, de) [plants; streets]. ‖ Irriguer (country). ‖ Faire boire, donner à boire à (animals). ‖ Baptiser, mouiller, couper d'eau (milk, wine). ‖ TECHN. Alimenter en eau (an engine); moirer (silk). ‖ FIN. Diluer (capital, stocks). ‖ **To water down,** FIG. Atténuer, édulcorer; FAM. *To water down one's claims,* mettre de l'eau dans son vin.
— v. intr. Boire, s'abreuver, aller à l'abreuvoir (animals). ‖ Se mouiller, s'humecter, larmoyer (eyes). ‖ TECHN., NAUT., AUTOM. Faire de l'eau.

waterage [-ridʒ] n. Batelage, transport (*m.*) par eau; droits (*m. pl.*) de batelage.

watercourse [-kɔ:s] n. Cours (*m.*) d'eau (stream). ‖ Conduit *m.; * conduite *f.* (pipe).

watercress [-kres] n. BOT. Cresson (*m.*) de fontaine.

watered [-d] adj. Moire (silk); mouillé (wine).

waterfall [-fɔ:l] n. Chute d'eau, cascade *f.*

waterfowl [-faul] n. ZOOL. Gibier (*m.*) d'eau.

waterfront [-frʌnt] n. U. S. NAUT. Quai *m.* (part of a city); bord (*m.*) de l'eau, quai *m.* (wharf).

wateriness [-rinis] n. Humidité *f.* ‖ FIG. Insipidité, fadeur *f.*

watering [-riŋ] n. Arrosage *m.* (*with*, avec) [of flowers, streets]. ‖ Irrigation *f.* (of land). ‖ Abreuvage *m.* (of animals). ‖ Mouillage *m.* (of milk, wine). ‖ TECHN. Approvisionnement (*m.*) en eau (of an engine); moirage *m.* (of silk). ‖ FIN. Dilution *f.* (of capital). ‖ **Watering-can** (or) **-pot,** n. Arrosoir *m.* ‖ **Watering-place,** n. Abreuvoir *m.* (for animals); plage *f.* (seaside resort); ville d'eau, station thermale *f.* (spa). ‖ **Watering-trough,** n. Abreuvoir *m.*

waterlogged [-lɔgd] adj. Détrempé (wood). ‖ AGRIC. Aqueux, détrempé (land). ‖ NAUT. Engagé (ship).

waterman [-mən] (pl. **watermen**) n. NAUT. Batelier, marinier *m.* (ferryman); canotier *m.* (oarsman).

watermark [-mɑ:k] n. Filigrane *m.* (in paper). ‖ NAUT. Laisse *f.*

waterplane [-plein] n. AVIAT. Hydroplane, hydroglisseur *m.*

waterproof [-pru:f] adj., n. Imperméable *m.*
— v. tr. Imperméabiliser.

watershed [-ʃed] n. Ligne (*f.*) de partage des eaux (ridge). ‖ Bassin hydrographique *m.* (basin).

waterspout [-,spaut] n. ARCHIT. Gouttière *f.* ‖ NAUT. Trombe *f.;* siphon *m.*

watertight [-tait] adj. Etanche. ‖ FIG. Inattaquable (argument).

waterworks [-wə:ks] n. Pl. Canalisations (*f. pl.*)

d'eau (supply). ‖ Jeux (*m. pl.*) d'eau. ‖ FAM. *To turn on the waterworks,* ouvrir les écluses (to weep).

watery [-ri] adj. Aqueux, rempli d'eau. ‖ Humide, larmoyant, mouillé (eyes). ‖ Chargé de pluie (cloud); pluvieux (weather). ‖ Délavé, déteint (colour). ‖ Des eaux; *a watery grave,* les flots pour tombeau. ‖ CULIN. Insipide, fade, délavé (food); clair (soup). ‖ FIG. Délayé (style).

watt [wɔt] n. ELECTR. Watt *m.*

wattage ['wɔtidʒ] n. ELECTR. Puissance (*f.*) en watts.

wattle ['wɔtl] n. Clayonnage *m.* ‖ ZOOL. Barbes *f. pl.* (of cock); barbillon *m.* (of fish).
— v. tr. Tresser (twigs). ‖ Clayonner (roofs).

wattless ['wɔtlis] adj. ELECTR. Déwatté.

waul [wɔ:l] v. intr. Miauler.

wave [weiv] v. intr. Onduler (hair); onduler, ondoyer (fields of corn); flotter (flag). ‖ Faire signe de la main (person).
— v. tr. Faire flotter, déployer (a flag); agiter (a handkerchief); brandir (a sword). ‖ Onduler (hair); *to have one's hair waved,* se faire onduler. ‖ Exprimer par signe; *to wave s.o. aside, back,* écarter, faire revenir (or) reculer qqn d'un signe; *to wave sth. away,* refuser qqch. du geste.
— n. Ondulation *f.* (of hair); *permanent wave,* permanente, indéfrisable. ‖ Geste, signe *m.* (of the hand). ‖ Vague, lame *f.; * flot *m.* (of sea). ‖ RADIO. Onde *f.; long waves,* grandes ondes; *medium, short waves,* ondes moyennes, courtes. ‖ PHYS. Onde *f.; wave surface, train,* front, train d'ondes. ‖ MILIT. Vague *f.* (of assault). ‖ U. S. NAUT. *Wave,* femme marin. ‖ FIG. Vague *f.* (of anger, enthusiasm); flot *m.* (of bitterness); courant *m.* (of opinion). ‖ **Waveband,** n. RADIO. Gamme (*f.*) d'ondes. ‖ **Wave-detector,** n. PHYS. Détecteur (*m.*) d'ondes. ‖ **Wave-front,** n. PHYS. Onde enveloppe *f.* ‖ **Wave-length,** n. RADIO. Longueur d'onde *f.; * U. S. FAM. *To have s.o.'s wavelength,* connaître son bonhomme, savoir à quoi s'en tenir sur qqn.

waveless [-lis] adj. Sans vagues, calme.

wavelet [-lit] n. Ondulation, ride, petite vague *f.* (See RIPPLE.) ‖ Ondulation serrée *f.* (on hair).

waver [-ə*] v. intr. Vaciller, trembloter (flame); trembler, se troubler (voice). ‖ MILIT. Perdre pied, fléchir. ‖ FIG. Chanceler, défaillir (courage); hésiter, balancer, osciller (person).

waverer [-rə*] n. Indécis *s.*

wavering [-riŋ] adj. Vacillant, tremblotant (flame); troublé (voice). ‖ MILIT. Flottant; flanchant (fam.). ‖ FIG. Chancelant, défaillant (courage); hésitant, indécis, irrésolu (person).

wavily [-ili] adv. En ondulant.

waviness [-inis] n. Vague (or) ondulation naturelle *f.* (of s.o.'s hair).

wavy [-i] adj. Ondoyant (field); ondulé (hair); tremblé (line); onduleux (surface).

wax [wæks] v. intr. ASTRON. Croître, grossir (moon). ‖ † Devenir (to grow).

wax n. Cire *f.* ‖ FAM. Rogne *f.* (anger). ‖ U. S. FAM. Disque *m.* (record). ‖ **Wax-candle,** n. Bougie *f.;* ECCLES. Cierge *m.* ‖ **Wax-cloth,** n. Toile cirée *f.* ‖ **Wax-doll,** n. Poupée *f.* ‖ **Wax-end,** n. Fil poissé *m.* ‖ **Wax-paper,** n. Papier ciré *m.* ‖ **Wax-sheet,** n. Papier stencil *m.* ‖ **Wax-stencil,** n. Cliché *m.* ‖ **Wax-taper,** n. Rat (*m.*) de cave; ECCLES. Cierge *m.*
— v. tr. Cirer, encaustiquer (furniture). ‖ Poisser (thread).

waxen [-ən] adj. De (or) en cire. ‖ Cireux (complexion, pallor). ‖ FIG. Mou, impressionnable, modelable.

waxwork [-wə:k] n. Modelage *m.* (act); figure de cire *f.* (result). ‖ Pl. Musée Grévin *m.* (in Paris).

waxy [-i] adj. Cireux (complexion). ‖ MED. *Waxy liver,* amylose du foie. ‖ FIG. Mou, malléable (mind, person). ‖ FAM. A cran.

way [wei] n. Chemin m.; voie f.; way in, out, through, entrée, sortie, passage. ‖ Route f.; chemin m. (to, de, vers); on one's way to, en route pour; to be under way, être en route; to go one's way, passer son chemin; to lose one's way, se perdre, s'égarer; to make one's way to, prendre la direction de, partir pour. ‖ Voie f.; passage m.; to clear the way, dégager le passage; to give way, céder; to make way for, se ranger, livrer passage à; to pave the way for, ouvrir la voie à. ‖ Trajet, chemin m.; distance f.; it's a long way to, il y a loin jusqu'à. ‖ Côté m.; direction f.; the wrong way, le mauvais côté, l'envers; to go this way, aller de ce côté. ‖ Manière, façon f.; moyen m.; in no way, en aucune façon; to go the right way to, prendre le bon moyen pour; to go one's own way, faire à sa guise; to see one's way to, avoir le moyen de. ‖ Manière, façon, habitude f.; it is his way, il est comme ça, c'est son genre; in a friendly way, amicalement. ‖ Domaine m.; compétence f.; it's not in my way, ce n'est pas de mon rayon, mon affaire. ‖ Manière, guise f.; by way of compliment, en manière de compliment. ‖ Etat m.; to be in a bad way, filer un mauvais coton; to be in a fair way of (or) to, être en passe de. ‖ Mesure f.; in a way, dans une certaine mesure; in a small way, modestement, petitement. ‖ Point m.; in a way, en un certain sens; in many ways, à bien des égards; in every way, sous tous les rapports. ‖ Progrès m.; to make one's way, faire son chemin; to make way, avancer, progresser. ‖ Portée f.; to go a long way, aller loin. ‖ Jur. Cours m. (of the law). ‖ Comm. Way of business, genre d'affaires; to be in a large way of business, faire des affaires en grand. ‖ Naut. Erre f.; to gather way, prendre de l'erre; to get under way, appareiller; to make stern way, culer. ‖ U.S. Way ahead, back, down, off, up, en avant, en arrière, en bas, au loin, en haut. ‖ Loc. By the way, en passant, à ce sujet, à propos (incidentally); en chemin, en route (on the way); by way of, en guise de, à titre de (as); en passe de (in the condition of); par, en passant par (via); by a long way, de beaucoup. ‖ Way-bill, n. Comm. Lettre de voiture, feuille de route f. ‖ Way-leave, n. Droit de passage m.; Aviat. Droit de survol m. ‖ Way-out, adj. Fam. Avant-gardiste, non-conformiste (unconventional); formidable, du tonnerre (excellent). ‖ Way station, n. U.S. Ch. de F. Petite gare. ‖ Way train, n. U.S. Ch. de F. Omnibus f. ‖ Way-worn, adj. Exténué par la marche; I am way-worn, les jambes me rentrent dans le ventre (fam.).

wayfarer ['wei,fɛərə*] n. Voyageur (s.) à pied.

wayfaring [-iŋ] adj. Voyageant à pied, parcourant les routes.

waylay [wei'lei] v. tr. (89). Attirer dans une embuscade; to be waylaid, tomber dans un guet-apens. ‖ Fam. Accrocher au passage.

waylayer [-ə*] n. Dresseur de guet-apens m. ‖ Fam. Importun s.

wayside ['weisaid] n. Bord (m.) de route; bas-côté m.
— adj. Du bord de la route; de campagne.

wayward [-wəd] adj. Capricieux, fantasque (erratic). ‖ Entêté, opiniâtre (wilful).

waywardly [-wədli] adv. Capricieusement. ‖ Obstinément, avec opiniâtreté.

waywardness [-wədnis] n. Caprice m.; nature fantasque f. ‖ Obstination, opiniâtreté f.; entêtement m.

W.C. [,dʌbəlju:'si:] abbr. water-closet, water-closet, W.-C.

we [wi:] pron. pers. Nous; we two, nous les deux.

weak [wi:k] adj. Faible, sans force; weak moment, moment de défaillance. ‖ Faible, sans vigueur, sans énergie; weak character, faiblesse de caractère, manque d'énergie; weak decision, décision de faiblesse. ‖ Faible, déficient (point). ‖ Faible, sans valeur (in, dans) [a subject]. ‖ Milit., Mus., Gramm., Culin. Faible. ‖ Med. Débile, chétif, peu solide; to grow weak, s'affaiblir. ‖ Weak-eyed (or) -sighted, adj. A la vue faible. ‖ Weak-headed, adj. Faible d'esprit. ‖ Weak-minded, adj. D'esprit faible. ‖ Weak-spirited, adj. Mou, pusillanime.

weaken [-ən] v. tr. Affaiblir.
— v. intr. S'affaiblir.

weakening [-niŋ] n. Affaiblissement m.

weakish [-iʃ] adj. Fam. Faiblard.

weakling [-liŋ] n. Med. Personne chétive f. ‖ Fig. Personne influençable et faible; chiffe f. (fam.).

weakly [-li] adj. Med. Chétif, débile.
— adv. Faiblement.

weakness [-nis] n. Faiblesse f. ‖ Med. Faiblesse, débilité f. ‖ Fig. Faiblesse f. (of argument, character, mind); point faible m. (weak point). ‖ Fig. Faible m. (for, pour).

weal [wi:l] n. Zébrure f. (See WALE.)

weal n. Bien-être m.; prospérité f.; for weal or woe, pour la bonne et la mauvaise fortune; general weal, bien public.

weald [wi:ld] n. Région boisée f.

wealth [welθ] n. † Prospérité f. (weal). ‖ Richesse, opulence, fortune f.; man of wealth, homme riche. ‖ Abondance, profusion, richesse f. (of, de) [details, ideas]. ‖ Richesses f. pl., trésors m. pl. (of the oceans).

wealthily [-ili] adv. Très richement.

wealthiness [-inis] n. Opulence f.

wealthy [-i] adj. Riche, opulent, fortuné; wealthy parvenu, nouveau riche.

wean [wi:n] v. tr. Sevrer. ‖ Fig. Détacher, détourner (from, de).

weaning [-iŋ] n. Sevrage m.

weanling [-liŋ] n. Petit animal (or) nourrisson sevré m.

weapon ['wepən] n. Milit. Arme f.; engin meurtrier m. ‖ Fig. Arme f.

weaponless [-lis] adj. Désarmé, sans armes.

wear [wɛə*] v. tr., intr. (186). Naut. Virer lof pour lof; to wear round, donner un coup de barre.

wear v. tr. (186). Porter (a dress, a pistol, a ring); to wear black, porter du noir. ‖ Porter, avoir (a beard, glasses); to wear one's hair curled, avoir les cheveux bouclés. ‖ User (one's clothes); to wear one's coat to rags, user son veston jusqu'à la corde; to wear a hole in, trouer par usure, faire un trou à. ‖ Rendre à l'usage; to wear a pair of shoes comfortable, mettre des chaussures (or) faire ses chaussures à son pied en les portant. ‖ Fig. Porter (one's age, a famous name); avoir, arborer (an air, a smile). ‖ Fig. Ronger; worn with care, consumé par les soucis. ‖ To wear away, effacer (an inscription); ronger, effriter (the shore); Fig. User (one's life); effacer (s.o.'s memory). ‖ To wear down, user (lit. and fig.). ‖ To wear off, râper (one's clothes); effacer en frottant (an inscription). ‖ To wear out, user entièrement (one's clothes); Fig. Passer (one's life); épuiser (s.o.'s patience); to wear oneself out, s'épuiser; se décarcasser (fam.).
— v. intr. S'user (to become impaired). ‖ Faire de l'usage (to stand up to use). ‖ Se faire; to wear to one's feet, se faire aux pieds (new shoes). ‖ Fig. Devenir; her courage wore thin, son courage s'amenuisa peu à peu. ‖ Fig. Passer, s'écouler (time). ‖ Fig. Se conserver; she wears well, on ne lui donnerait pas son âge; their friendship has worn well, leur amitié a tenu bon. ‖ To wear away, user (clothes); s'effacer (inscription). ‖ Fig. S'atténuer (pain); se consumer, s'user (person); s'écouler (time). ‖ To wear down, user. ‖ To wear off, s'effacer, se dissiper (lit. and fig.). ‖ To wear on, se poursuivre (discussion); s'écouler (time). ‖ To wear out, s'user (material); Fig. Se traîner (time).
— n. Fait (m.) de porter, usage, port m.; for

autumn wear, pour porter à l'automne. ‖ Habits *m. pl.; evening wear*, vêtements de soirée; *men's wear*, articles d'habillement pour hommes. ‖ Usage *m.;* résistance à l'usure *f.; of never-ending wear*, inusable; *there's a lot of wear left in my dress*, ma robe est encore très mettable (or) portable. ‖ Usure *f.; the worse for wear*, usé, plus mettable (dress); *wear and tear*, usure, détérioration. ‖ Jur. *Wear and tear*, détérioration, dépréciation (of a building). ‖ Fam. *The worse for wear*, paf, pompette.

wearable [-rəbļ] adj. Mettable, portable.

wearer [-rə*] n. Personne (*f.*) qui porte (clothes).

wearied ['wiərid] adj. Fatigué.

weariless ['wiərilis] adj. Infatigable.

wearily [-li] adv. D'un air las, avec fatigue; péniblement.

weariness [-nis] n. Fatigue, lassitude *f.* ‖ Fig. Ennui *m.;* lassitude *f.*

wearisome [-səm] adj. Fatigant. ‖ Fig. Ennuyeux, lassant, fastidieux.

wearisomely [-səmli] adv. Fastidieusement.

wearisomeness [-səmnis] n. Nature fastidieuse *f.;* ennui *m.*

weary ['wiəri] adj. Fatigué, las, lassé (tired); fatigant, lassant, épuisant (tiring). ‖ Ennuyeux, fastidieux (tiresome); assommant, abrutissant, mortel (fam.).
— v. tr. (2). Fatiguer, lasser. ‖ Fig. Lasser, ennuyer, agacer.
— v. intr. Se fatiguer. ‖ Fig. Languir (*for*, de); se lasser (*of*, de).

weasel ['wi:zļ] n. Zool. Belette *f.* ‖ U. S. Fam. Mouchard *m.; weasel words*, remarques équivoques. ‖ Weasel-faced, adj. A figure de fouine.

weather ['weðə*] n. Temps *m.;* conditions atmosphériques *f. pl.; bad weather*, mauvais temps, intempéries; *in such weather*, par le temps qu'il fait. ‖ Bulletin météorologique *m.* (in the newspaper). ‖ Naut. *Heavy weather*, gros temps. ‖ Fam. *Under the weather*, patraque; U. S. désargenté, à court d'argent; *to keep one's weather eye open*, ouvrir l'œil et le bon. ‖ **Weather-beaten**, adj. Battu des vents (coast); hâlé (person); usé par les intempéries, dégradé (wall). ‖ **Weather-bound**, adj. Arrêté par le mauvais temps. ‖ **Weather-box**, n. Hygroscope *m.* ‖ **Weather-cloth**, n. Naut. Cagnard *m.* ‖ **Weather-glass**, n. Baromètre *m.* ‖ **Weather-map**, n. Carte météorologique *f.* ‖ **Weather-proof**, adj. Imperméable, étanche (clothes); résistant aux intempéries (wall). ‖ **Weather-strip**, n. Bourrelet *m.* (for windows). ‖ **Weather-wise**, adj. Qui sait prévoir le temps; U. S. Fig. Habile à prévoir les réactions et les fluctuations d'opinion. ‖ **Weather-worn**, adj. Usé par les intempéries.
— adj. Météorologique; *weather bureau, forecast, station*, office, bulletin, station météorologique; *weather prophet*, personne qui prédit le temps. ‖ Naut. Au vent; *weather board*, côté du vent; *weather helm*, barre au vent; *weather side*, bord du vent.
— v. tr. Geol. User par les intempéries. ‖ Naut. Doubler la voile (a headland); passer au vent de (a ship); étaler (a storm). ‖ Comm. Patiner (bronze). ‖Archit. Tailler en rejeteau. ‖ Fam. *To weather one's difficulties*, doubler le cap dangereux.
— v. intr. Geol. S'effriter, s'user. ‖ Comm. Se patiner. ‖ **To weather through**, Fam. S'en tirer, s'en sortir.

weathercock [-kɔk] n. Girouette *f.* (lit. and fig.).

weathering [-riŋ] n. Intempéries *f. pl.* ‖ Geol. Désagrégation *f.* ‖ Comm. Patine *f.* ‖ Archit. Rejeteau *m.*

weatherly [-li] adj. Naut. Fin (ship).

weatherman [-mæn] (pl. **weathermen**) n. U. S. Fam. Météorologue *m.*

weathermost [-moust] adj. Naut. Le plus au vent.

weave [wi:v] v. tr. (187). Tisser (a fabric, threads). ‖ Tresser (baskets, flowers, garlands). ‖ Zool. Faire (a web). ‖ Fig. Bâtir (an allegory); tramer (a plot); *to weave facts into a story*, introduire des faits dans un récit. ‖ U. S. Fam. *To weave one's way*, se frayer un chemin.
— N. B. Au sens familier américain, *to weave* est régulier.
— v. intr. Tisser. ‖ Aviat., Fam. Se défiler. ‖ U. S. Fam. Tituber, marcher en zigzaguant.
— n. Texture *f.* (of a cloth). ‖ Tissage *m.* (method, quality).

weaver [-ə*] n. Tisserand *m.* ‖ **Weaver-bird**, n. Zool. Tisserin *m.*

WEAVING — TISSAGE

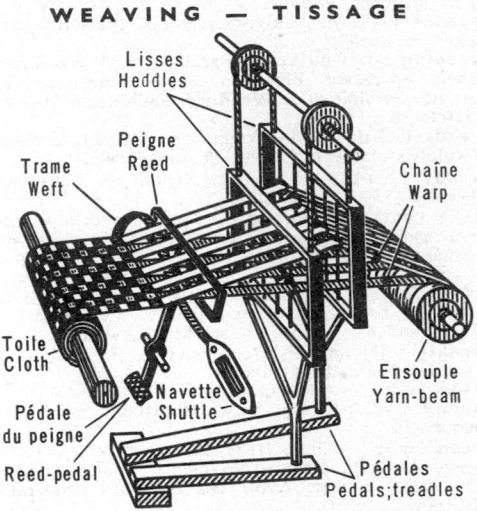

Lisses
Heddles

Peigne
Reed

Trame
Weft

Chaîne
Warp

Toile
Cloth

Ensouple
Yarn-beam

Navette
Shuttle

Pédale
du peigne

Reed-pedal

Pédales
Pedals;treadles

web [web] n. Tissu, rouleau (*m.*) d'étoffe (material). ‖ Rouleau de papier *m.; web paper*, papier continu. ‖ Zool. Toile d'araignée *f.* (cobweb); lame *f.* (of feather); palme *f.* (of swimming bird). ‖ Archit. Ame *f.* (of beam). ‖ Techn. Panneton *m.* (of key); lame *f.* (of saw). ‖ Ch. de f. Ame *f.* (of rail). ‖ Fig. Tissu *m.* (of lies); trame *f.* (of life). ‖ **Web-footed**, adj. Zool. Palmipède, aux pieds palmés. ‖ **Web-winged**, adj. Zool. Cheiroptère.

webbed [-d] adj. Zool. Palmé. ‖ Archit. Evidé.

webbing ['webiŋ] n. Toile de sangle *f.* (material); sangles *f. pl.* (strips).

wed [wed] v. tr. (1). Marier; épouser. ‖ Fig. Marier, unir (*to*, à).
— v. intr. Se marier.

wedded [-id] adj. Conjugal (bliss, life); *the wedded pair*, les mariés. ‖ Fig. Uni (*by*, par); attaché (*to*, à).

wedding [-iŋ] n. Mariage *m.;* noce *f.; village wedding*, noce de village. ‖ Noces *f. pl.; golden wedding*, noces d'or. ‖ Eccles. Mariage *m.;* bénédiction nuptiale *f.*
— adj. De mariage (day); *wedding card*, faire-part de mariage; *wedding dress*, robe de mariage; *wedding ring*, alliance. ‖ De noce (cake); *wedding breakfast*, repas de noce, lunch; *wedding party*, la noce, les invités; *wedding present*, cadeau de noce. ‖ Eccles. Nuptial (march); *wedding garment*, robe nuptiale.

wedge [wedʒ] n. Coin *m.* (to split wood). ‖ Cale *f.* (for casks). ‖ Culin. Part *f.* (of cake, cheese). ‖ Milit. Pointe *f.; to drive a wedge*, pousser une pointe. ‖ **Wedge-heeled**, adj. A semelles compensées (shoes). ‖ **Wedge-shaped**, adj. En forme de coin; Gramm. Cunéiforme.
— v. tr. Fendre au coin (to split). ‖ Coincer, caler

(to fix). ‖ Insérer, enclaver, caler (in, into, dans). ‖ **To wedge away** (or) **off**, écarter.

wedlock ['wedlɔk] n. JUR. Mariage m. (state); vie conjugale f.; born in wedlock, légitime (child).

Wednesday ['wenzdi] n. Mercredi m.

wee [wi:] adj. Tout petit, infime, minuscule.

wee n., v. See WEE(-WEE).

weed [wi:d] n. BOT., AGRIC. Mauvaise herbe f. ‖ FAM. Cigare m.; cigarette f.; tabac m. ‖ FAM. Rosse f. (jade). ‖ **Weed-grown**, adj. AGRIC. Envahi par les mauvaises herbes. ‖ **Weed-killer**, n. AGRIC. Herbicide m.
— v. tr. AGRIC. Sarcler (a garden); arracher (a weed). ‖ **To weed out**, AGRIC. Eclaircir; FIG. Extirper, arracher, éliminer.

weeder [-ə*] n. AGRIC. Sarcleur s. (person); sarcloir m. (tool).

weeding [-iŋ] n. AGRIC. Sarclage m. ‖ **Weeding-fork**, n. AGRIC. Binette f. ‖ **Weeding-hook**, n. AGRIC. Sarcloir m. ‖ **Weeding-machine**, n. AGRIC. Sarcleuse f.

weeds [wi:dz] n. Pl. Vêtements (m. pl.) de deuil (widow's clothes). ‖ Crêpe m. (on sleeve).

weedy ['wi:di] adj. AGRIC. Rempli de mauvaises herbes. ‖ FAM. Efflanqué.

week [wi:k] n. Semaine f.; a week from now, to-day week, d'aujourd'hui en huit; in the week, en semaine; yesterday week, il y a eu hier huit jours. ‖ ECCLES. Holy Week, semaine sainte. ‖ FAM. Week in week out, toute la sainte semaine. ‖ **Week-day**, n. Jour (m.) de semaine. ‖ **Week-end**, n. Week-end m.; v. intr. Passer le week-end.

weekly [-li] adj., n. Hebdomadaire m.
— adv. Toutes les semaines.

ween [wi:n] v. tr. † Imaginer.

weeny ['wi:ni] adj. FAM. Minuscule, microscopique.

weep [wi:p] v. intr. (188). Pleurer (over, sur); to weep for joy, pleurer de joie. ‖ Couler, suinter (to drip). ‖ BOT. Avoir des branches pendantes (willow).
— v. tr. Pleurer sur, déplorer. ‖ Verser, répandre (tears); to weep away the time, passer son temps à pleurer; to weep one's heart out, se consumer de chagrin. ‖ Suinter, couler (wall). ‖ MED. Couler (sore).
— n. Pleurs m. pl. ‖ **Weep-hole**, n. ARCHIT. Chantepleure f.

weeper [-ə*] n. Pleureur s. (at funeral). ‖ † Crêpe m. (band, veil). ‖ Pl. † Favoris m. pl.

weeping [-iŋ] adj. En pleurs (person). ‖ Suintant (rock, wall). ‖ MED. Humide, coulant. ‖ BOT. Pleureur (ash, willow).

weepy [-i] adj. FAM. Pleurnicheur, pleurnichard (whining); au bord des larmes (upset).
— n. FAM. Mélo m.

weever ['wi:və*] n. ZOOL. Vive f.

weevil ['wi:vil] n. ZOOL. Charançon m.

weevilled [-d] adj. Charançonné.

wee(-wee) ['wi:(wi:)] n. FAM. Pipi m.
— v. intr. FAM. Faire pipi.

weft [weft] n. Trame f.

weigh [wei] n. NAUT. Under weigh, en route.

weigh v. tr. Soupeser (in the hand); peser (on a scale). ‖ Peser, avoir un poids de (ten pounds). ‖ NAUT. Lever (anchor). ‖ FIG. Peser (consequences, words). ‖ **To weigh down**, surcharger, appesantir (branch); faire pencher (a scale); peser plus que (sth. else). ‖ FIG. L'emporter sur (an argument); accabler, écraser (s.o.). ‖ **To weigh on**, peser (in small amounts). ‖ **To weigh up**, soulever par contrepoids.
— v. intr. Peser, avoir du poids, être lourd (to have weight). ‖ Se peser (to be weighed). ‖ FIG. Peser, avoir du poids (argument); peser, être accablant (remorse); to weigh upon, peser sur. ‖ **To weigh**

in, SPORTS. Se faire peser; FIG. To weigh in with an argument, apporter un argument.
— n. Pesage m. ‖ **Weigh-beam**, n. Romaine f. (balance). ‖ **Weigh-bridge**, n. Pont-bascule m.

weighage [-idʒ] n. Droit de pesage m.

weight [weit] n. Poids m. (heaviness); to gain weight, prendre du poids; to try the weight of, soupeser. ‖ Poids m.; set of weights, série de poids; weights and measures, poids et mesures. ‖ Poids m. (in a clock). ‖ COMM. Poids m.; sold by the weight, vendu au poids; to give good weight, faire bon poids; to give short weight, tromper sur le poids. ‖ SPORTS. Poids m.; heavy-weight, poids lourd; to carry weight, être handicapé (horse); to putt the weight, lancer le poids. ‖ MED. Lourdeur f. (in the head); pesanteur f. (in the stomach). ‖ ARCHIT. Charge f. ‖ PHYS. Pesanteur f.; poids spécifique m. ‖ FIG. Poids, fardeau m. (of care). ‖ FIG. Poids m.; importance f.; man of weight, personnage influent; to carry weight, avoir du poids. ‖ FAM. To pull one's weight, donner un bon coup de collier, en faire sa part. ‖ **Weight-lifting**, n. SPORTS. Poids et haltères.
— v. tr. Lester, plomber (a net); plomber (a stick); alourdir (with, par). ‖ Charger (thread). ‖ FIG. Accabler.

weightily [-ili] adv. Pesamment. ‖ FIG. Avec poids (or) force.

weightiness [-inis] n. Pesanteur f.; poids m. ‖ FIG. Importance f.; poids m.

weightlessness [-lisnis] n. Non-pesanteur f.

weighty [-i] adj. Pesant, lourd (burden). ‖ FIG. Puissant, de poids (argument); important (business); important, influent (person); grave, sérieux (reason); solide (style).

weir [wiə*] n. (†) Barrage m. (See DAM.)

weird [wiə:d] n. Destinée f.
— adj. Du destin; Weird Sisters, les Parques (Fates); les sorcières (witches). ‖ Surnaturel, fantastique. ‖ FAM. Etrange.

weirdly [-li] adv. Etrangement.

welch [welʃ] v. intr. See WELSH.

welcome ['welkəm] adj. Bienvenu, bien accueilli (guest); to make s.o. welcome, faire bon accueil à qqn. ‖ Autorisé (to, à); libre (to, de) [person]; you are welcome to my car, ma voiture est à votre disposition. ‖ Agréable, plaisant (change, news, thing); to be most welcome, tomber fort à propos. ‖ FAM. You are welcome, de rien, je vous en prie, il n'y a pas de quoi (in response to thanks).
— interj. Bienvenue!; soyez le bienvenu! (to, à). ‖ FAM. Avec joie, volontiers.
— v. tr. Faire bon accueil à, souhaiter la bienvenue à (s.o.). ‖ Accueillir avec joie, recevoir avec plaisir (sth.); to welcome an opportunity, se réjouir d'une occasion (to, de).
— n. Bienvenue f.; to bid s.o. welcome, souhaiter la bienvenue à. ‖ Accueil m.; réception f. ‖ FAM. To wear out one's welcome, s'éterniser, s'incruster, lasser ses hôtes.

weld [weld] v. tr. TECHN. Corroyer, souder. ‖ FIG. Amalgamer, fondre.
— v. intr. TECHN. Se corroyer, se souder.
— n. TECHN. Corroyage m.; soudure f.

welfare ['welfεə*] n. Bien-être, bien, intérêt m.; public welfare, salut public; welfare state, Etat providence; welfare work, assistance sociale. ‖ MED. Child welfare centre, centre de protection infantile; child welfare, protection de l'enfance; infant welfare centre, consultation de nourrissons.

welk [welk] v. intr. † Se flétrir.

welkin ['welkin] n. Ciel, firmament m.; to make the welkin ring, ébranler la voûte céleste.

well [wel] n. Puits m.; dead well, puisard. ‖ Cage f. (for a staircase). ‖ Encrier m. (ink-well). ‖ SPORTS. Vivier m. (in a boat). ‖ NAUT. Plat-fond m. (of a canoe); archipompe f. (of a ship); cockpit m. (of

a yacht). ‖ Aviat. Carlingue *f.* ‖ Geol., Fig. Source *f.* ‖ **Well-boring,** n. Forage *m.* ‖ **Well-curb,** n. Margelle *f.* ‖ **Well-deck,** n. Naut. Coffre *m.* ‖ **Well-digger,** n. Puisatier *m.* ‖ **Well-head,** n. Source *f.* (lit. and fig.). ‖ **Well-hole,** n. Cage *f.* ‖ **Well-room,** n. Buvette *f.* (at a spa). ‖ **Well-seat,** n. Aviat. Baquet *m.* ‖ **Well-spring,** n. Source *f.* ‖ **Well-water,** n. Eau (*f.*) de puits.
— v. intr. Jaillir (blood, tears, liquid); sourdre (spring).

well adv. Bien, comme il faut; *to end well,* finir bien, favorablement, aimablement; *to be well disposed towards,* être dans de bonnes dispositions à l'égard de; *to treat s.o. well,* bien traiter qqn. ‖ Bien, habilement, avec art; *to sing well,* bien chanter. ‖ Bien, de manière appropriée; *well spoken,* bien dit. ‖ Bien, largement, confortablement; *I lived well in London,* je vivais bien à Londres; *to do well,* prospérer. ‖ Bien, à juste titre; *to do well to,* bien faire de, avoir raison de; *you may well ask,* vous pouvez bien demander. ‖ Bien, beaucoup; *to stir well,* bien remuer. ‖ Bien, intimement; *to know s.o. well,* bien connaître qqn; *to stand well with,* être en bons termes avec. ‖ Bien, en bonne part; *to take the news well,* bien prendre la nouvelle. ‖ Bien, largement; *to be well over forty,* avoir largement dépassé la quarantaine. ‖ Med. Bien, en bonne santé. ‖ Loc. *As well,* aussi; *as well as,* de même que, aussi bien que, comme, non moins que. ‖ **Well-appointed,** adj. Bien équipé (office). ‖ **Well-balanced,** adj. Bien équilibré. ‖ **Well-behaved,** adj. De bonne conduite; bien élevé. ‖ **Well-being,** n. Bien-être *m.* (of s.o.); bon état *m.* (of sth.). ‖ **Well-born,** adj. Bien né. ‖ **Well-bred,** adj. Racé (animal); bien élevé (person). ‖ **Well-built,** adj. Bien charpenté (person). ‖ **Well-disposed,** adj. Bien disposé. ‖ **Well-doer,** n. Personne (*f.*) de bien. ‖ **Well-doing,** n. Bien; acte (*m.*) de faire le bien. ‖ **Well-done,** adj. Bien fait; Culin. Bien cuit; interj. Bravo! ‖ **Well-fed,** adj. Bien nourri. ‖ **Well-fixed,** adj. U. S. Fam. Bien renté. ‖ **Well-found,** adj. Bien fourni (in, de); Naut. Bien équipé. ‖ **Well-groomed,** adj. Orné, paré, bien vêtu. ‖ **Well-grounded,** adj. Bien fondé. ‖ **Well-informed,** adj. Bien documenté (on, sur). ‖ **Well-knit,** adj. Charpenté, costaud, râblé. ‖ **Well-known,** adj. Bien connu. ‖ **Well-mannered,** adj. Bien élevé, courtois. ‖ **Well-matched,** adj. Bien assorti. ‖ **Well-meaning,** adj. Bien intentionné. ‖ **Well-meant,** adj. Fait (or) dit dans une bonne intention. ‖ **Well-off,** adj. Cossu, bien renté. ‖ **Well-preserved,** adj. Bien conservé. ‖ **Well-read,** adj. Cultivé (person). ‖ **Well-spoken,** adj. Qui s'exprime bien (or) courtoisement. ‖ **Well-thought-of,** adj. De bonne réputation. ‖ **Well-timed,** adj. Opportun. ‖ **Well-to-do,** adj. Aisé, cossu, argenté; rupin (fam.). ‖ **Well-up,** adj. Fam. Calé (in, en). ‖ **Well-wisher,** n. Partisan sincère *m.;* personne (*f.*) qui veut du bien à autrui. ‖ **Well-worn,** adj. Usé; Fig. Rebattu.
— interj. Bien!, soit! (resignation); *well, such is life,* enfin quoi, c'est la vie. ‖ Soit; bien (acquiescence). ‖ Eh bien, peut-être! (hesitation). ‖ Par exemple!, comment?, quoi!, pas possible! (surprise). ‖ Eh bien, voilà (result). ‖ Eh bien!, et alors? (interrogation). ‖ Alors, donc (summarizing). ‖ Allons!, voyons! (appeasement). ‖ C'est bon!, il suffit!, assez (expostulation).
— adj. Bien, en bonne condition; *things are well with you,* les événements vous réussissent, ça va bien pour vous. ‖ Bon, bien, opportun; *it is well that he has come,* c'est bien tombé qu'il soit venu. ‖ Bien, satisfaisant; *that's all very well,* tout cela est bel et bon. ‖ Med. Bien, en bonne santé, bien portant.
— N. B. *Well* a pour comparatif *better,* pour superlatif *best.*
— n. Bien *m.; to wish s.o. well,* vouloir du bien à. ‖ Med. Bien portants *m. pl.*

welladay ['welə'dei] interj. Hélas, las!
wellies ['weliz] n. pl. Fam. Bottes (*f. pl.*) en caoutchouc (wellingtons).
wellingtonia [,weliŋ'tounjə] n. Bot. Séquoia *m.*
wellingtons ['weliŋtʌnz] n. pl. Demi-bottes *f. pl.;* bottillons *m. pl.* ‖ Fam. Bottes (*f. pl.*) en caoutchouc.
welsh [welʃ] v. intr. Sports. Lever le pied (bookmaker). ‖ U. S. Manquer à ses obligations.
Welsh adj. Geogr. Gallois. ‖ Culin. *Welsh rabbit,* fondue sur canapé.
— n. Gallois *m.* (language).
welsher [-ə*] n. Sports. Bookmaker marron *m.*
Welshman [-mən] (pl. **Welshmen**) n. Geogr. Gallois *m.*
Welshwoman [-wumən] (pl. **Welshwomen** [-wimən]) n. Geogr. Galloise *f.*
welt [welt] n. Bordure *f.* (of glove); passepoil *m.* (on pocket); trépointe *f.* (of sole). ‖ Zébrure *f.*
— v. tr. Border (gloves); passepoiler (pockets); mettre une trépointe à (soles). ‖ Zébrer de coups.
welter ['weltə*] adj. Sports. Lourd. ‖ **Welterweight,** n. Sports. Poids mi-moyen *m.*
welter v. intr. Se vautrer. ‖ Bouillonner (sea). ‖ Fig. Baigner (in, dans).
— n. Désordre, embrouillamini *m.*
wen [wen] n. Med. Goitre *m.* (on the neck); verrue *f.* (on the nose); loupe *f.* (on the scalp). ‖ Fam. Ville surpeuplée *f.*
wench [wenʃ] n. Fille, gaillarde *f.* ‖ † Traînée *f.* (prostitute).
— v. intr. Courir la gueuse.
wend [wend] v. tr. Marcher vers; *to wend one's way,* diriger ses pas, s'acheminer (to, vers).
went [went] pret. See go.
wept [wept] pret., p. p. See weep.
were [wɛə*] pret. See be.
wer(e)wolf ['wə:wulf] n. Loup-garou *m.*
west [west] n. Ouest *m.* (direction, point). ‖ Occident *m.* (part of the earth). ‖ Vent d'ouest *m.* (wind). ‖ **West-north-west,** n., adv. Ouest-nord-ouest *m.*
— adv. A l'ouest (of, de); *east and west,* de l'est à l'ouest. ‖ Fam. *To go west,* passer l'arme à gauche.
— adj. D'ouest (wind). ‖ Geogr. Occidental (Africa); *West Indies,* Antilles.
— v. intr. Passer à l'ouest.
westbound [-,baund] adj. En direction de l'ouest.
wester [-ə*] v. intr. Astron. Passer à l'ouest (sun). ‖ Naut. Virer à l'ouest (wind).
westerly [-əli] adj. D'ouest, ouest.
— adv. Vers l'ouest.
— n. Vent d'ouest *m.*
western [-ən] adj. D'ouest, de l'ouest. ‖ Geogr. D'Occident (Empire); occidental (Europe, States). ‖ Eccles. Latine (Church).
— n. Cinem. Western *m.*
westerner [-ənə*] n. Occidental *s.* ‖ U. S. Américain (*s.*) de l'ouest.
westernize ['ənaiz] v. tr. Occidentaliser.
westing [-iŋ] n. Naut. Route (*f.*) vers l'ouest.
westward ['westwəd] adv., adj. En direction de l'ouest.
— n. Direction (*f.*) de l'ouest.
westwards [-z] adv., n. Direction ouest *f.*
wet [wet] adj. Mouillé; *wet as a drowned rat,* mouillé comme un rat; *wet through,* mouillé jusqu'aux os; *wringing wet,* trempé à tordre. ‖ De pluie, pluvieux (day, season, weather). ‖ Med. Sacrifié (cup); humide (pack). ‖ Arts. Non sèche, humide (paint). ‖ Fam. *Wet blanket,* rabat-joie. ‖ U. S. Antiprohibitionniste (person, town). ‖ U. S. Fam. *All wet,* faux. ‖ **Wet-brain,** n. Med. Méninge séreuse *f.* ‖ **Wet-nurse,** n. Nourrice *f.* ‖ **Wet suit,** n. Sports. Combinaison de plongée *f.*
— v. tr. (1). Mouiller, tremper; *to wet oneself,* se

mouiller. ‖ Servir de nourrice à. ‖ MED. Mouiller (one's bed). ‖ FAM. Humecter ; *to wet one's whistle*, se rincer la dalle. ‖ FAM. Arroser, fêter (an event). — n. Humidité *f.* (state). ‖ Pluie *f.* (rain) ; temps pluvieux *m.* (weather). ‖ FAM. Pot *m.* (drink). ‖ U. S. FAM. Antiprohibitionniste *s.*

wether ['weðə*] n. ZOOL. Mouton ; bélier châtré *m.*

wetness [['wetnis] n. Humidité *f.* (See DAMPNESS.)

wetting [-iŋ] n. Mouillage *m. ; to get a wetting*, se faire tremper.

wettish [-iʃ] adj. Plutôt humide, moite.

whack [(h)wæk] v. tr. FAM. Cogner. (See WHANG.) ‖ **To whack up,** POP. Partager.
— interj. Paf !, pan !
— n. Coup retentissant, claquement *m. ;* claque *f.* (blow). ‖ FAM. *To have a whack at*, tenter, essayer. ‖ POP. Part, contribution *f.* (share). ‖ U. S. LOC. *Out of whack*, détraqué, qui déraille.

whacked [-t] adj. FAM. Ereinté, crevé, lessivé.

whacker ['(h)wækə*] n. FAM. Gros tas, poussah, mastodonte *f.* (person) ; énormité *f.* (story, thing).

whacking [-iŋ] adj. FAM. Formidable.

whale [(h)weil] n. ZOOL. Cétacé *m.* (in general) ; baleine *f.* (right whale) ; *whale calf*, baleineau. ‖ U. S. *A whale of*, un exemplaire épatant ; *a whale of a city*, une ville du tonnerre ; *we had a whale of a time*, on s'est follement amusé. ‖ **Whale-boat,** n. NAUT. Baleinière *f.* ‖ **Whale-oil,** n. Huile de baleine *f.*
— v. intr. NAUT. Pêcher la baleine.

whalebone [-boun] n. Baleine *f.* (corset stay).

whaleman [-mən] (pl. **whalemen**) n. NAUT. Baleinier *m.* (man).

whaler [-ə*] n. NAUT. Baleinier *m.* (man, ship).

whaling [-iŋ] n. NAUT. Pêche à la baleine *f.* ‖ **Whaling-gun,** n. Fusil-harpon *m.* ‖ **Whaling-industry,** n. Industrie baleinière *f.* ‖ **Whaling-spade,** n. Louchet *m.*

wham [wæm] interj. Vlan !
— n. Coup violent *m.*
— v. tr. (1). Frapper.
— v. intr. (1). Cogner.

whang [wæŋ] v. tr. Cogner, flanquer un coup à. (See WHACK.)
— v. intr. Résonner.
— n. Coup retentissant *m.*

wharf [(h)wɑ:f] n. NAUT. Quai, appontement ; débarcadère, embarcadère *m.*
— N. B. *Wharf* a deux pluriels : *wharfs* commun en Angleterre et *wharves* commun en Amérique.
— v. tr. NAUT. Débarquer (goods) ; amarrer à quai (a ship).
— v. intr. NAUT. Venir à quai.

wharfage [-idʒ] n. Quayage *m.*

wharfinger [-indʒə*] n. Garde-quai *m.* (manager). ‖ Propriétaire de quai *m.* (owner).

what [(h)wɔt] pron. interrog. Que ? ; quoi ? ; qu'est-ce qui ? ; qu'est-ce que ? ; quel ? *m. ;* quelle ? *f. ;* quels ? *m. pl. ;* quelles ? *f. pl. ; what is he like ?*, comment est-il ? ; *what's the matter ?*, qu'est-ce qu'il y a ? ; *what's your name ?*, quel est votre nom ? ; comment vous appelez-vous ? ; *what will they say of our plan ?*, que diront-ils de notre projet ? ; *what would you say to a drink ?*, que diriez-vous de prendre un verre ? ; *what ?*, *what of it ?*, la belle affaire ! ; *you are rather late, what ?*, vous êtes plutôt en retard, hein ? ‖ **What about ?**, quelles nouvelles de ? (news) ; que pensez-vous de ? (proposition) ; *what about a cup of tea ?*, que diriez-vous d'une tasse de thé ? ; *what is it all about ?*, de quoi s'agit-il ? ‖ **What for ?**, pourquoi donc ? ; *what ever for ?*, mais pourquoi, grand Dieu ? ‖ **What if ?**, et si ?, si par hasard, à supposer que ; *what if he refuses to answer ?*, qu'arrivera-t-il s'il refuse de répondre ? ‖ **What not ?**, et que sais-je ? ; *his hat, his gloves and what not,* son chapeau, ses gants

et le reste ! ‖ **What of ?**, que faire au sujet de ? ; *what of that ?*, qu'est-ce que ça fait ? ‖ **What then ?**, et après ?, et alors ? ‖ **What though ?**, qu'importe que ?
— pron. exclam. Comment ! ; *what ! she is ill !* quoi ! elle est malade !
— pron. relat. Ce qui, ce que ; *he obtained what he needed*, il a obtenu ce qui lui manquait ; *what he did he did well*, ce qu'il faisait il le faisait bien. ‖ *I see what you are alluding to*, je vois ce à quoi vous faites allusion. ‖ Quoi ; *you know what he is busy with*, vous savez de quoi il s'occupe. ‖ Quoi, que ; *do what I may*, quoi que je fasse ; *happen what may*, advienne que pourra. ‖ FAM. *I know what*, je sais, ça vient ; *he'll tell you what*, il va vous expliquer ; *what's what*, ce dont il retourne. ‖ U. S. FAM. *And what have you*, et tout le saint-frusquin, et tutti quanti. ‖ **But what**, sauf ce que ; *not but what*, il se peut bien que. ‖ **What though**, quand bien même, même si. ‖ **What with**, par le fait de ; *what with... and what with*, étant donné d'une part... et d'autre part. ‖ **What-not,** n. Etagère *f.* (shelf). ‖ FAM. Que-sais-je *m.* ‖ **What's-his-name,** n. FAM. Truc, machin *m.* (person).
— adj. Interrog. Quel ; *of what use is it to learn Latin ?*, à quoi sert d'apprendre le latin ? ; *what use is this bag to you ?*, à quoi sert ce sac ?
— adj. exclam. Quel ; *what an intelligent man he is !*, comme (or) que cet homme est intelligent ! ; *what a queer idea !*, quelle idée bizarre !
— adj. relat. Le (or) la (or) les... que (or) qui ; *what little he said was interesting*, le peu qu'il a dit était intéressant. ‖ Quel ; *I know what books you will need*, je sais quels livres il vous faudra. ‖ Tout le... que ; *I shall incur what expenses will be necessary*, je ferai toutes les dépenses qu'il faudra.

whatever [-'evə*], **whatsoever** [,(h)wætsou-'evə*] pron. Tout ce qui (or) que ; *whatever you like*, tout ce qui vous plaira. ‖ Quoi que ; *whatever you see, keep mum !*, quoi que vous voyiez, motus !
— adj. Quel... que soit ; *whatever difficulties you may encounter*, quelles que soient les difficultés. ‖ Quelque... que ; *whatever doubt I may have*, quelque doute que je puisse avoir. ‖ Quelconque ; *there did not remain any doubt whatever in my mind*, il ne restait absolument aucun doute dans mon esprit ; *this will be no trouble whatever for us*, cela ne nous causera aucun dérangement.

wheal [(h)wi:l] n. MED. Papule *f.*

wheat [(h)wi:t] n. BOT. Froment *m. ;* U. S. blé *m.*

wheatear [-iə*] n. BOT. Epi de blé *m.*

wheatear [-i:ə*] n. ZOOL. Cul-blanc *m.*

wheaten [-ņ] adj. De froment, de blé.

wheedle ['(h)wi:d] v. tr. Cajoler (s.o.). ‖ Influencer par des cajoleries ; enjôler ; entortiller, embobeliner (fam.) ; *to wheedle s.o. into*, amener qqn en l'embobelinant à. ‖ Soutirer par des cajoleries (*out of*, à) [gift, money].

wheedler [-ə*] n. Enjôleur *s.*

wheedling [-iŋ] adj. Enjôleur, cajoleur.
— n. Cajolerie *f. ;* enjôlement ; embobelinage, entortillage *m.* (fam.).

wheel [(h)wi:l] n. Roue *f.* (of a vehicle). ‖ Roue *f.* (of torture) ; *to break on the wheel*, rouer. ‖ Rouet *m.* (spinning wheel). ‖ Rotation *f. ;* tournoiement *m.* (movement). ‖ TECHN. Tour (potter's) ; pl. rouages *m. pl.* ‖ AUTOM. Volant *m.* ‖ *To take the wheel*, prendre le volant. ‖ NAUT. Barre *f. ;* gouvernail *m. ; the man at the wheel*, le timonier. ‖ AVIAT. Pl. Train roulant *m.* (of a plane). ‖ MILIT. Conversion *f. ;* left wheel, conversion à gauche. ‖ FIG. Roue *f.* (of fortune) ; pl. rouages *m. pl.* (of government). ‖ U. S. FAM. Bécane *f.* (bike). ‖ FAM. *To go on wheels*, marcher sur des roulettes ; *wheels within wheels*, complications sur complications. ‖ U. S. FAM. *Big wheels*, grosses légumes, gros bonnets. ‖ **Wheel-base,** n. CH. DE F., AUTOM. Empat-

tement *m.* ‖ **Wheel-chair,** n. Fauteuil roulant *m.* ‖ **Wheel-clearance,** n. AUTOM. Débattement *m.* ‖ **Wheel-disc,** n. AUTOM. Enjoliveur *m.* ‖ **Wheel-horse,** n. ZOOL. Timonier *m.; U.* S. FAM. Bûcheur *s.;* cheval de labour *m.* ‖ **Wheel-house,** n. NAUT. Timonerie *f.* ‖ **Wheel-rope,** n. NAUT. Drosse (*f.*) du gouvernail. ‖ **Wheel-train,** n. Train (*m.*) de roues. ‖ **Wheel-window,** n. ARCHIT. Rosace *f.*
— v. tr. Rouler (a wheel-chair, a barrow). ‖ Pousser (a bicycle); faire pivoter (one's chair). ‖ Promener (s.o.); porter (sth.); *to wheel in a barrow,* brouetter. ‖ Rouer (a victim). ‖ TECHN. Marquer à la roulette (leather).
— v. intr. Tourner en rond, tournoyer. ‖ MILIT. Faire une conversion; *right wheel!,* par file à droite, droite! ‖ U. S. FAM. Rouler, faire du vélo. ‖ **To wheel about,** faire demi-tour (or) volte-face.

wheelbarrow [-bærou] n. Brouette *f.*
wheeled [-d] adj. A roues.
wheeler [-ə*] n. Timonier *m.* (horse). ‖ TECHN. Charron *m.* (man).
wheelwright [-rait] n. TECHN. Charron *m.; wheelwright's work,* charronnage.
wheeze [(h)wi:z] n. MED. Respiration sifflante *f.* ‖ THEATR. Gag *m.* ‖ FAM. Idée *f.*
— v. intr. MED. Corner (horse); respirer en asthmatique (person). ‖ FAM. Siffler (organ).
— v. tr. **To wheeze out,** dire d'une voix sifflante; *to wheeze out a tune,* s'essouffler à moudre un air (barrel-organ).
wheezily [-ili] adv. D'une façon poussive.
wheezing [-iɳ] n. MED. Cornage *m.* (of horse); essoufflement asthmatique *m.* (of s.o.).
wheezy [-i] adj. MED. Poussif, cornard (horse); asthmatique, poussif (fam.) [person].
whelk [(h)welk] n. ZOOL. Buccin *m.*
whelm [(h)welm] v. tr. Engloutir. ‖ FIG. Submerger.
whelp [(h)welp] n. ZOOL. Chiot, petit chien *s.* (puppy); petit *m.* (of leopard, tiger); lionceau *m.* (lion's); louveteau *m.* (wolf's). ‖ NAUT. Flasque *m.* ‖ FAM. Garnement *m.*
— v. tr., intr. ZOOL. Mettre bas.
when [(h)wen] adv. Quand; *she asked when she should come,* elle demanda quand elle devait venir; *when did that happen?,* quand est-ce arrivé?
— conj. Quand, à quel moment; *she told me when to sing,* elle m'a dit à quel moment je devrais chanter; *to say when,* dire : arrêtez (or) assez (or) ça suffit. ‖ Au moment où; *now is the time when you must work,* maintenant c'est l'heure où vous devez travailler; *on the day when you finally understand,* le jour où vous aurez enfin compris. ‖ Quand; *when I was a boy,* quand j'étais petit garçon; *you'll come when he arrives,* vous viendrez quand il arrivera. ‖ Dès que, aussitôt que; *we will have lunch when father comes,* nous mangerons dès que papa sera là. ‖ Alors que, bien que; *he is playing when he might be studying,* il joue au lieu d'étudier. ‖ Alors que, puisque, étant donné que; *how can I finish, when you won't help?,* comment finirai-je, si vous ne voulez pas m'aider?
— pron. Quand; *since when,* et depuis lors; *since when?,* depuis quand?; *till then,* et jusque-là; *till when?,* jusqu'à quand?
— n. Moment *m.; date f.* (of an event). ‖ LOC. *The when and the how,* la date et la manière; *the when and where,* le moment et le lieu.
whence [(h)wens] adv. D'où?
— pron. relat. D'où.
— n. Source *f.*
whencesoever [-sou'evə*] adv. D'où que ce soit.
whenever [(h)we'nevə*], **whensoever** [,(h)wen-sou'evə*] adv. A n'importe quel moment.
— conj. A quelque moment que.
where [(h)wɛə*] adv. Où?, en quel endroit (or)

lieu?; *where did you go?,* où êtes-vous allé?; *where are my gloves?,* où sont mes gants? ‖ Comment?, en quelle situation?, *where will you be if you lose?,* où aboutirez-vous si vous perdez? ‖ En quoi; *where do I come into it?,* en quoi suis-je impliqué dans l'affaire? ‖ D'où; *where did he get the information?,* d'où a-t-il tiré ce renseignement?
— conj. Où; *I know where John is,* je sais où est Jean. ‖ Où, là où; *that is where you are mistaken,* voilà où vous faites erreur; *the district where the fire occurred,* le quartier où a eu lieu l'incendie; *you are going where you aren't wanted,* vous allez là où l'on ne veut pas de vous.
— pron. Où; *from where?,* d'où?; *from where,* de l'endroit où, d'où; *to where,* à l'endroit où.
— n. Lieu, endroit *m.*
whereabout ['(h)wɛərəbaut] adv. A propos duquel (or) de quoi.
whereabouts [-s] adv. Où donc?; de quel côté?, en quel endroit?
— n. Endroit (*m.*) où se trouve (s.o., sth.).
whereas [(h)wɛə'ræz] conj. Tandis qu'au contraire. ‖ JUR. Attendu que, vu que, étant donné que, considérant que.
whereat [-'ræt] adv. A quoi? de quoi? pourquoi?
— conj. A quoi; sur quoi.
whereby [-'bai] adv. Par où?; par quoi.
wherefore ['(h)ɛəfɔ:*] adv. Pourquoi?
— conj. A cause de quoi, ce pour quoi.
— n. Raison, cause *f.;* pourquoi *m.*
wherefrom [(h)wɛə'frɔm] adv. D'où; de quoi; duquel.
wherein [-'rin] adv. D'où; en quoi; dans lequel.
whereof [-'rɔv] adv. Dont, de quoi, duquel.
whereon [-'rɔn] adv. Sur quoi?; sur quoi, sur lequel.
wheresoever [,(h)wɛɛsou'evə*]. See WHEREVER.)
whereto [(h)wɛə'tu:] adv. A quoi?, vers quoi?; à quoi, auquel; vers quoi, vers lequel.
whereupon [,(h)wɛərə'pɔn] adv. Sur quoi.
— conj. Sur quoi, sur lequel; sur ce.
wherever [,(h)wɛə'revə*] adv. Où donc?
— conj. N'importe où, où que ce soit, partout où; *wherever it comes from,* d'où que cela vienne.
wherewith [-'wiδ] adv. Avec quoi?; avec lequel.
— pron. De quoi; avec quoi; au moyen duquel.
wherewithal ['(h)wɛəwiδɔ:l] n. Moyens *m. pl.;* ressources nécessaires *f. pl.; to have the wherewithal to pay,* avoir de quoi payer.
wherry ['(h)weri] n. NAUT. Bachot *m.*
whet [(h)wet] v. tr. Aiguiser, affûter, affiler. ‖ FIG. Aiguiser (the appetite); stimuler (courage).
— n. Affûtage *m.* ‖ FAM. Apéro *m.*
whether ['(h)weδə*] conj. Si; *he asked whether it was true,* il a demandé si c'était vrai; *whether or not,* si oui ou non. ‖ *Whether... or,* soit... soit, ou...; *whether or... soit,* soit que... ou; *whether he drives or takes the train,* qu'il y aille en voiture ou par le train; *whether today or tomorrow,* soit aujourd'hui soit demain.
— pron. † Lequel des deux.
whetstone ['(h)wetstoun] n. Pierre (*f.*) à aiguiser, affiloire, meule *f.*
whew [hju:] interj. Oh, là là!; fichtre!
whey [(h)wei] n. Petit-lait *m.*
which [(h)witʃ] pron. interrog. Lequel?; *which do you want?,* lequel voulez-vous?
— pron. relat. Ce qui, ce que; *he lied, which I should have never believed,* il a menti, ce que je n'aurais jamais cru; *he refused to come, which did not surprise me,* il refusa de venir, ce qui ne m'étonna nullement. ‖ Que; *the table which I see,* la table que je vois. ‖ Lequel; *the state in which,* l'état où (or) dans lequel; *the work to which she devoted all her time,* le travail auquel elle consacrait tout son temps; *the table one leg of which is broken,* la table dont un pied est cassé. ‖ Quoi;

he thinks so, in which he is right, il le pense, en quoi il a raison ; *upon which she came out,* sur ce (or) quoi, elle sortit. ‖ **All which,** toutes choses qui (or) que.

— adj. Quel ? ; *which book do you choose?,* quel livre choisissez-vous ? ‖ N'importe lequel ; *try which method you please,* essayez la méthode que vous voudrez. ‖ Lequel ; *he announced a dearth, which forecast came true,* il annonça la disette, prédiction qui s'est réalisée ; *he stayed here six months, during which time,* il resta ici six mois, et pendant ce temps.

whichever [(h)wi't∫evə*], **whichsoever** [ˌ(h)wit∫sou'evə*] pron. N'importe lequel... qui (or) que, quelque... que ; *whichever party comes to power,* quel que soit le parti qui vienne au pouvoir.

whiff [hwif] n. Bouffée *f.* (of air, smoke, wind). ‖ NAUT. Skiff *m.* ‖ FAM. Cigarillo *m.*

— v. tr., intr. Emettre des bouffées.

whig [(h)wig] adj., n. Whig.

whiggery [-əri], **whiggism** [-izm̩] n. Whiggisme *m.*

whiggish [-i∫] adj. De whig.

while [(h)wail] n. Temps *m.;* *after a while,* quelque temps après ; *a long while,* pas mal de temps ; *all the while,* tout le temps ; *between whiles,* entretemps ; *for a while,* pour le moment ; *the while,* pendant ce temps, pendant que. ‖ Temps passé *m.;* *it's not worth your while,* cela ne vaut pas la peine que cela vous donne.

— v. tr. **To while away,** dissiper (cares) ; passer, tuer (the time).

— conj. Tandis que, pendant que ; *while you are about it,* pendant que vous y êtes. ‖ Tant que ; *never, while I live,* jamais, tant que je vivrai. ‖ Tout en ; *while he is not poor,* sans être pauvre. ‖ Alors que ; tandis que ; *the hat is red, while the shoes are black,* le chapeau est rouge, tandis que les souliers sont noirs.

whilom [ˈhwailəm] adv. Autrefois.

— adj. D'autrefois, de jadis.

whilst [(h)wailst] conj. See WHILE.

whim [(h)wim] n. Fantaisie *f.;* caprice *m.;* toquade, foucade *f.* (fam.). ‖ TECHN. Cabestan à cheval *m.*

whimbrel [(h)wimbril] n. ZOOL. Courlis *m.*

whimper [ˈ(h)wimpə*] v. intr. Pleurnicher, gémir ; chialer (fam.).

— v. tr. Dire en pleurnichant.

— n. Pleurnicherie *f.;* ton geignard *m.*

whimperer [-rə*] n. Pleurnicheur *s.*

whimpering [-riŋ] adj. Pleurnicheur, pleurard.

whimsical [ˈ(h)wimzikəl] adj. Fantasque, capricieux, lunatique (mind, person) ; bizarre, étrange (thing).

whimsicality [ˌ(h)wimzi'kæliti] n. Humeur fantasque ; bizarrerie *f.*

whimsically [ˈ(h)wimzikəli] adv. Capricieusement ; bizarrement.

whimsy [ˈ(h)wimzi] n. Caprice *f.*

whin [(h)win] n. BOT. Ajonc *m.*

whine [(h)wain] v. intr. Pleurnicher (child) ; gémir (dog) ; gémir, geindre (person).

— v. tr. Dire en geignant.

— n. Pleurnicherie *f.;* gémissement *m.* (See WHIMPER.)

whiner [-ə*] n. FAM. Pleurard, geignard *s.*

whining [ˈ(h)wainiŋ] adj. Pleurard, geignard.

whinny [ˈ(h)wini] v. intr. (2). Hennir. (See NEIGH.)

— n. Hennissement *m.*

whinny adj. Couvert d'ajoncs.

whip [hwip] v. intr. (1). Se jeter, s'élancer (behind, derrière) [person] ; *to whip down the stairs,* dévaler l'escalier. ‖ Fouetter (rain).

— v. tr. (1). Fouetter, donner le fouet à (a child) ; fouetter (a horse). ‖ Fouetter, cingler, battre (the windows). ‖ Surjeter (a seam). ‖ Remuer promptement ; *to whip a knife out of one's pocket,* sortir

brusquement un couteau de sa poche. ‖ CULIN. Fouetter (cream) ; battre (eggs). ‖ NAUT. Surlier (a rope). ‖ SPORTS. Fouetter (a stream). ‖ FAM. Enfoncer (s.o.) [to defeat]. ‖ **To whip in,** rassembler. ‖ **To whip out,** sortir busquement ; *to whip out one's sword,* dégainer promptement.

— n. Fouet *m.* (instrument). ‖ Cocher *m.* (coachman). ‖ SPORTS. Piqueur *m.* (whipper-in). ‖ JUR. Appel *m.* (call) ; chef (m.) de file et rabatteur (m.) de couloirs (official). ‖ NAUT. Cartahu *m.* ‖ **Whip-bucket,** n. Porte-fouet *m.* ‖ **Whip-hand,** n. Haute main *f.* (of, sur). ‖ **Whip-lash,** n. Mèche (f.) de fouet. ‖ **Whip-round,** n. Collecte *f.;* *to have a whip-round for,* faire une collecte pour. ‖ **Whipsaw,** n. TECHN. Scie (f.) à chantourner ; v. tr. Chantourner ; v. intr. U. S. FAM. Faire une spéculation malheureuse. ‖ **Whip-stitch,** n. Surjet *m.* ‖ **Whiptop,** n. Sabot *m.* (toy).

whipcord [-kɔ:d] n. Corde (f.) à fouet. ‖ Whipcord *m.* (cloth).

whipper [-ə*] n. Fouetteur *s.* ‖ **Whipper-in,** n. SPORTS. Piqueur *m.* ‖ **Whipper-snapper,** n. FAM. Freluquet ; merdeux *m.* (pop.).

whippet [-it] n. ZOOL. Whippet, lévrier (m.) de course. ‖ MILIT. Char léger *m.;* chenillette *f.*

whipping [-iŋ] n. Correction, fustigation, fouettée *f.* ‖ Fouettement *m.* (act). ‖ Surjet *m.* (of a seam). ‖ NAUT. Surliure *f.* ‖ **Whipping-boy,** n. † Enfant (m.) élevé avec un jeune prince et fouetté à sa place ; FAM. Bouc émissaire *m.*

whippoorwill [ˈ(h)wippuəwil] n. ZOOL. Engoulevent *m.*

whir [(h)wə:*] v. intr. (1). Ronfler (engine, propeller). ‖ Bruisser (wings). ‖ Grésiller (phone).

— n. Ronflement *m.* ‖ Bruissement *m.*

whirl [(h)wə:l] v. intr. Tournoyer, tourbillonner. ‖ Passer en tournoyant ; *to whirl along,* filer comme un dard ; *to whirl down,* descendre en tournoyant. ‖ MED. Tourner (head).

— v. tr. Faire tournoyer (or) tourbillonner. ‖ Entraîner à toute vitesse.

— n. Tournoiement, tourbillonnement *m.* (act). ‖ Tourbillon *m.* (of dust). ‖ FAM. Tourbillon *m.;* *to be in a whirl,* avoir la tête à l'envers. ‖ U. S. FAM. *To give sth. a whirl,* faire l'essai de qqch.

whirligig [-igig] n. Toton, tourniquet *m.* (toy). ‖ Manège *m.* (merry-go-round). ‖ ZOOL. Gyrin *m.* ‖ FIG. Tourbillon *m.*

whirling [-iŋ] adj. Tournoyant, tourbillonnant.

— n. See WHIRL.

whirlpool [-pul] n. Tourbillon, remous *m.* (of water).

whirlwind [-wind] n. Tourbillon *m.;* trombe *f.* (of wind).

whirr [(h)wə:*] v. intr., n. See WHIR.

whisk [(h)wisk] n. Effleurement rapide *m.* (motion). ‖ Epoussette *f.* (dusting-whisk). ‖ CULIN. Fouet *m.*

— v. tr. Fouetter (the air) ; agiter (its tail). ‖ CULIN. Battre, fouetter. ‖ **To whisk away,** chasser (a fly) ; escamoter (sth.) ; essuyer furtivement (a tear). ‖ **To whisk along,** entraîner à toute allure.

— v. intr. Passer à toute vitesse. ‖ **To whisk away,** filer comme un dard. ‖ **To whisk through,** traverser comme une flèche.

whiskered [ˈ(h)wiskəd] adj. Portant des favoris.

whiskers [ˈ(h)wiskəz] n. pl. Barbe *f.* (beard) ; favoris *m. pl.* ‖ Moustache *f.* (of a cat, rat). ‖ NAUT. Arc-boutant *m.* (of the bowsprit).

whisk(e)y [ˈ(h)wiski] n. Whisky *m.*

whisper [ˈ(h)wispə*] v. intr. Chuchoter, parler bas, susurrer (person). ‖ Murmurer, bruire (leaves, wind).

— v. tr. Chuchoter, murmurer à l'oreille (to, de). ‖ Faire courir (news).

— n. Chuchotement *m.* ‖ Murmure *m.* (of leaves, wind). ‖ FIG. Rumeur *f.*

winningly [-li] adv. De manière attachante, avec séduction.

winnow ['winou] v. tr. AGRIC. Vanner. ‖ Séparer (*from*, de). ‖ FIG. Battre (the air); agiter (wings). ‖ FIG. Trier, séparer (*from*, de).

winnower [-ə*] n. AGRIC. Vanneur *s.* (person). ‖ TECHN. Van *m.*

winnowing [-iŋ] n. AGRIC. Vannage *m.* ‖ FIG. Tri, triage *m.* ‖ **Winnowing-machine**, n. TECHN. Van, tarare *m.*

wino ['wainou] n. POP. Poivrot, pochard *s.*

winsome ['winsəm] adj. Séduisant, captivant, attirant, charmant.

winsomeness [-nis] n. Séduction *f.*; attrait, charme *m.*

winter ['wintə*] n. Hiver *m.* (lit. and fig.). ‖ **Winter-time**, n. Hiver *m.*
— adj. D'hiver, hivernal.
— v. intr. Hiverner.
— v. tr. Faire passer l'hiver à.

winterize [-təraiz] v. tr. Préparer pour l'utilisation en hiver.

wintry [-tri] adj. D'hiver. ‖ FIG. Glacial.

wipe [waip] v. tr. Essuyer; *to wipe one's face*, s'essuyer le visage. ‖ **To wipe away**, effacer (a stain); essuyer (one's tears). ‖ **To wipe off**, enlever en essuyant; FAM. Eteindre (a smile). ‖ **To wipe out**, essuyer; FIN. Amortir (a debt); FIG. Passer l'éponge sur, liquider (the past); FAM. Lessiver, nettoyer (s.o.).
— v. intr. **To wipe at**, FAM. Flanquer un gnon à.
— n. Coup de torchon *m.* ‖ Geste (*m.*) pour essuyer. ‖ FAM. Gnon *m.* (blow).

wiper [-ə*] n. Torchon, chiffon *m.* ‖ TECHN. Came *f.* ‖ AUTOM. Essuie-glace *m. invar.* ‖ ELECTR. Balai, frotteur *m.*

wire ['waiə*] n. Fil métallique *m.*; *gold wire*, fil d'or. ‖ Fil de fer *m.*; *barbed wire*, fil de fer barbelé. ‖ Fil télégraphique *m.*; *by wire*, par télégramme. ‖ Télégramme *m.*; *to send off a wire*, envoyer une dépêche. ‖ ELECTR. Fil électrique *m.* ‖ AVIAT. Câble *m.*; *landing wire*, hauban d'atterrissage. ‖ FIG. Pl. Ficelles *f. pl.*; *to pull the wires*, tirer les ficelles. ‖ FAM. *A live wire*, un dégourdi; *to be a live wire*, être très dynamique, péter du feu. ‖ **Wire-brush**, n. Brosse métallique *f.* ‖ **Wire-cloth**, n. Toile métallique *f.* ‖ **Wire-cutter**, n. Cisailles *f. pl.* ‖ **Wire-haired**, adj. ZOOL. A poil dur (dog). ‖ **Wire-mat**, n. Décrottoir, paillasson (*m.*) métallique (or) à grille. ‖ **Wire-netting**, n. Treillis *m.* ‖ **Wire-pull**, v. intr. FAM. Tirer les ficelles. ‖ **Wire-puller**, n. FAM. Intrigant, manœuvrier *s.* ‖ **Wire-pulling**, n. FAM. Intrigues, influences secrètes *f. pl.* ‖ **Wire-tapping**, n. Mise (*f.*) sur écoutes téléphoniques. ‖ **Wire-walker**, n. Fildefériste *s.* ‖ **Wire wool**, n. Laine (*f.*) d'aluminium; *wire wool pad*, tampon à récurer. ‖ **Wire-wove**, adj. Vergé (paper).
— v. tr. Monter sur fil métallique. ‖ Grillager (an opening). ‖ Télégraphier (news). ‖ SPORTS. Prendre au lacet (game). ‖ ELECTR. Equiper (a house).
— v. intr. FAM. Télégraphier, envoyer une dépêche. ‖ **To wire in**, FAM. Y aller de tout son long; *to wire into*, rentrer dans le chou à.

wiredraw [-drɔː] v. tr. (48). TECHN. Tréfiler.

wiredrawer [-ˌdrɔːə*] n. TECHN. Tréfileur *s.* (person); étireuse *f.* (tool).

wiredrawing [-ˌdrɔːiŋ] n. TECHN. Tréfilage *m.* ‖ FIG. Tarabiscotage *m.*

wireless [-lis] adj. RADIO. Radiophonique (association); sans fil (telegraphy); *wireless set*, appareil (or) poste de T. S. F. (or) radio; *wireless telephony*, radiotéléphonie. ‖ NAUT. *Wireless operator*, radio (man).
— n. RADIO. T. S. F. *f.*; *to give a talk on the wireless*, parler au micro (or) à la radio.
— v. tr. Radiotélégraphier.

— v. intr. Faire savoir par radio (*to*, à).

wiring ['waiəriŋ] n. TECHN., RADIO. Montage *m.* ‖ TECHN. Grillage *m.* ‖ ELECTR. Pose (*f.*) des fils. ‖ FAM. Envoi d'un télégramme *m.*

wiry [-i] adj. Raide (hair); métallique (sound). ‖ MED. Filiforme (pulse). ‖ FAM. Nerveux, en fil de fer, sec et vif.

wisdom ['wizdəm] n. Sagesse, sagacité, expérience *f.* ‖ Sagesse *f.* (of ages). ‖ MED. *Wisdom tooth*, dent de sagesse. ‖ ECCLES. *Wisdom of Solomon*, livre de la Sagesse.

wise [waiz] n. Guise, façon, manière *f.*; *in any wise*, en quelque manière que ce soit; *in no wise*, en aucune façon.

wise adj. Sage, sagace, expérimenté (person). ‖ Eclairé, informé; *none the wiser*, pas plus avancé. ‖ Judicieux, sage (action, saying); grave, sérieux (look). ‖ Savant, érudit (learned). ‖ Sage, prudent (cautious). ‖ † Sorcier. ‖ U. S. FAM. Au courant; *wise guy*, type plus malin que tout le monde; *to get wise to*, se mettre à la coule de.
— v. intr. **To wise up**, U. S. FAM. Se mettre à la page; se dessaler, se dégourdir; se détromper, se désabuser.

wiseacre ['wai,zeikə*] n. Pédant, sot prétentieux, imbécile instruit *s.*

wisecrack ['waiz,kræk] n. U. S. FAM. Bon mot *m.*
— v. intr. U. S. FAM. Faire de l'esprit.

wisely [-li] adv. Sagement.

wish [wiʃ] v. tr. Désirer, vouloir; *I wish to say a word to you*, je veux vous dire un mot; *I wish I were a hundred miles away*, je voudrais être à cent lieues d'ici; *I wish him to let me know when he comes*, je voudrais qu'il me prévienne de son arrivée; *I wish the month were over*, je voudrais que le mois fût fini; *I wish you could understand it*, je voudrais que vous puissiez le comprendre. ‖ Souhaiter; *to wish s.o. well*, vouloir du bien à qqn.
— v. intr. Souhaiter, exprimer un souhait. ‖ **To wish for**, souhaiter, désirer, avoir envie de.
— (pl. **wishes** [-iz]) n. Désir *m.*; envie *f.* (desire). ‖ Désir *m.*; volonté *f.* (behest). ‖ Chose souhaitée *f.*; *to have one's wish*, voir ses désirs réalisés. ‖ Pl. Souhaits, vœux *m. pl.* ‖ **Wish-bone**, n. CULIN. Fourchette *f.* (of fowl).

wisher [-ə*] n. Personne (*f.*) qui désire.

wishful [-ful] adj. D'envie (look). ‖ Désireux (*of*, de). ‖ FAM. *That's a piece of wishful thinking*, c'est prendre ses désirs pour des réalités.

wishing [-iŋ] n. Souhaits *m. pl.* (act; wishes).

wish-wash [-wɔʃ] n. FAM. Tisane, lavasse *f.*

wishy-washy ['wiʃi,wɔʃi] adj. CULIN. Délavé, fade. ‖ FAM. Fade, douceâtre (speech).

wisp [wisp] n. Bouchon, tortillon *m.* (of straw). ‖ Ruban *m.* (of smoke). ‖ ZOOL. Vol *m.* (of snipe). ‖ FAM. *Little* (or) *mere wisp of a man*, un homuncule, un Tom Pouce, un petit bouchon.

wistaria [wis'tɛəriə] n. BOT. Glycine *f.*

wistful ['wistful] adj. D'envie, de convoitise, de désir (covetous). ‖ Rêveur, pensif (dreamy). ‖ Désenchanté (unsatisfied).

wistfully [-i] adv. Avec envie. ‖ Pensivement.

wit [wit] v. tr., intr. † Savoir; *to wit*, à savoir.

wit n. Intelligence *f.*; esprit *m.*; *at one's wit's end*, à bout d'imagination; au bout de son rouleau (fam.). ‖ Pl. Esprits *m. pl.*; *out of one's wits*, la tête perdue; *to collect one's wits*, retrouver ses esprits; *to keep one's wits about one*, ne pas perdre la tête. ‖ Pl. Expédients *m. pl.*; *to live by one's wits*, vivre d'expédients. ‖ Esprit *m.* (humour); *flash of wit*, trait d'esprit. ‖ Homme d'esprit, bel esprit *m.* (person).

witch [witʃ] n. Sorcière *f.* (sorceress). ‖ Vieille sorcière, mégère *f.* (hag). ‖ FAM. Ensorceleuse *f.* ‖ **Witch-broom**, n. Balai (*m.*) de sorcière. ‖ **Witch-doctor**, n. Sorcier guérisseur *m.* ‖ **Witch-hunting**,

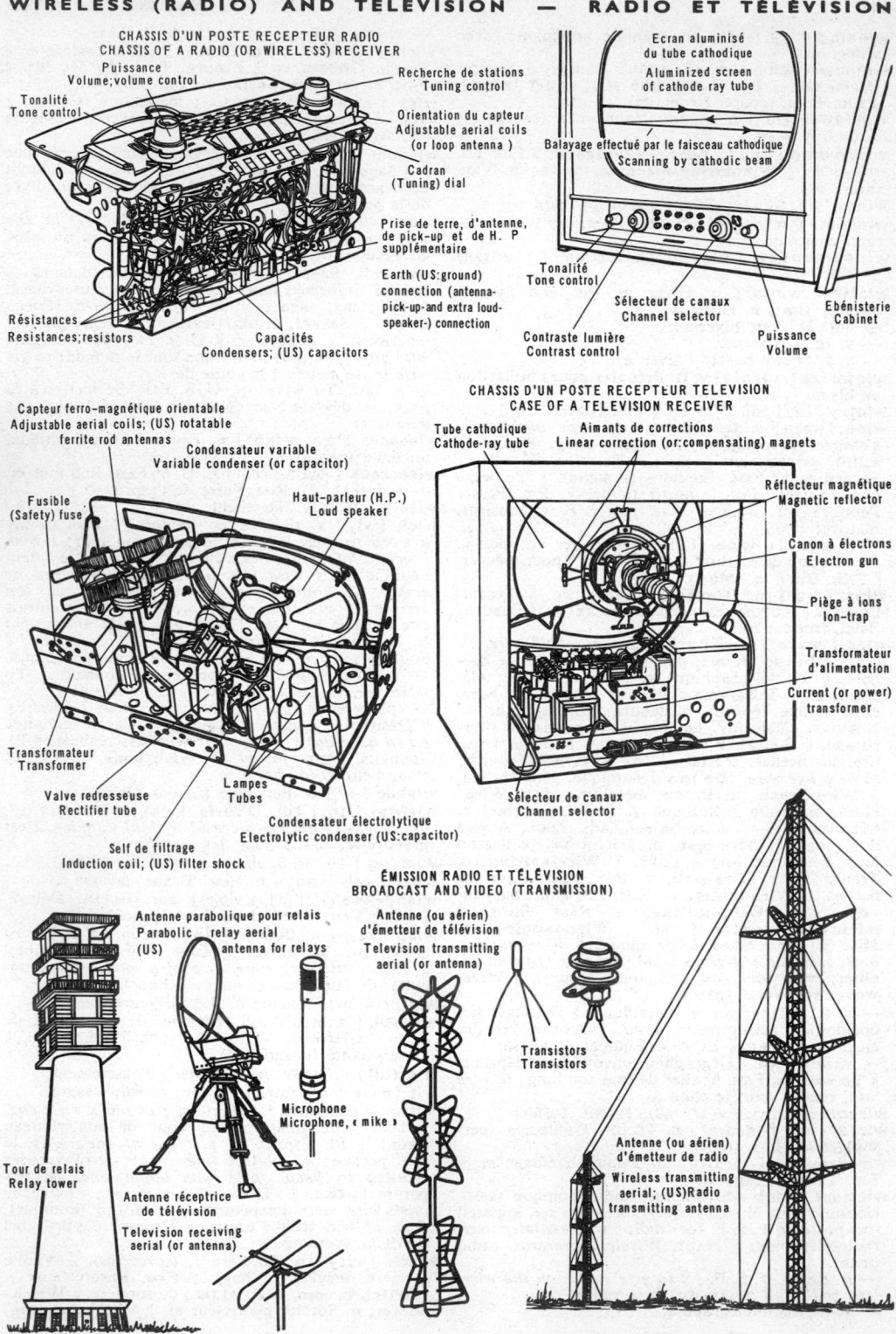

CHASSIS D'UN POSTE RECEPTEUR RADIO
CHASSIS OF A RADIO (OR WIRELESS) RECEIVER

Puissance
Volume; volume control

Tonalité
Tone control

Recherche de stations
Tuning control

Orientation du capteur
Adjustable aerial coils
(or loop antenna)

Cadran
(Tuning) dial

Prise de terre, d'antenne,
de pick-up et de H. P
supplémentaire

Earth (US:ground)
connection (antenna-
pick-up-and extra loud-
speaker-) connection

Résistances
Resistances; resistors

Capacités
Condensers; (US) capacitors

Ecran aluminisé
du tube cathodique
Aluminized screen
of cathode ray tube

Balayage effectué par le faisceau cathodique
Scanning by cathodic beam

Tonalité
Tone control

Sélecteur de canaux
Channel selector

Contraste lumière
Contrast control

Puissance
Volume

Ebénisterie
Cabinet

CHASSIS D'UN POSTE RECEPTEUR TELEVISION
CASE OF A TELEVISION RECEIVER

Capteur ferro-magnétique orientable
Adjustable aerial coils; (US) rotatable
ferrite rod antennas

Condensateur variable
Variable condenser (or capacitor)

Fusible
(Safety) fuse

Haut-parleur (H.P.)
Loud speaker

Transformateur
Transformer

Valve redresseuse
Rectifier tube

Lampes
Tubes

Condensateur électrolytique
Electrolytic condenser (US:capacitor)

Self de filtrage
Induction coil; (US) filter shock

Tube cathodique
Cathode-ray tube

Aimants de corrections
Linear correction (or:compensating) magnets

Réflecteur magnétique
Magnetic reflector

Canon à électrons
Electron gun

Piège à ions
Ion-trap

Transformateur
d'alimentation
Current (or power)
transformer

Sélecteur de canaux
Channel selector

ÉMISSION RADIO ET TÉLÉVISION
BROADCAST AND VIDEO (TRANSMISSION)

Antenne parabolique pour relais
Parabolic   relay aerial
(US)   antenna for relays

Antenne (ou aérien)
d'émetteur de télévision
Television transmitting
aerial (or antenna)

Transistors
Transistors

Microphone
Microphone, « mike »

Tour de relais
Relay tower

Antenne réceptrice
de télévision
Television receiving
aerial (or antenna)

Antenne (ou aérien)
d'émetteur de radio
Wireless transmitting
aerial; (US)Radio
transmitting antenna

n. Chasse (*f.*) aux sorcières (persécution des adversaires politiques).
— v. tr. Ensorceler.
witchcraft [-krɑːft] n. Sortilège *m.* (charm); sorcellerie *f.* (power).
witchery [-əri] n. FIG. Fascination *f.*; charme *m.*
witching [-iŋ] adj. Ensorcelant, fascinant, enchanteur (charming). ‖ Magique.
— n. Sorcellerie *f.*; ensorcellement *m.* ‖ Fascination *f.*
with [wiθ] prep. Avec; *a kettle with a lid*, une marmite avec couvercle; *to argue with s.o.*, discuter avec qqn; *to be with s.o. on a point*, être d'accord avec qqn sur un point. ‖ A; *the man with the long beard*, l'homme à la longue barbe; *to talk with*, parler à. ‖ Auprès; *to find credit with s.o.*, trouver crédit auprès de qqn. ‖ Contre; *furious with him*, furieux contre lui. ‖ Chez; *he lives with us*, il vit chez nous; *it's a habit with him*, chez lui c'est une habitude; *with Keats*, chez Keats. ‖ De; *he followed her out with his eyes*, il la suivit des yeux; *with all my might*, de toutes mes forces; *pleased, red, sick with*, content, rouge, malade de; *with an appetite*, de bon appétit. ‖ En; *with a jacket on*, en veston. ‖ Par; *to begin, to end with*, commencer, finir par. ‖ Pour; *it's the case with you*, c'est le cas pour vous. ‖ Sur; *to have a thimble with one*, avoir un dé sur soi. ‖ Alors que (elliptically); *what is to become of her, with both her parents gone?*, que va-t-il advenir d'elle, maintenant que son père et sa mère ne sont plus là? ‖ (Not translated); *to meet with s.o.*, rencontrer qqn; *with his hat on*, le chapeau sur la tête; *with tears in his eyes*, les larmes aux yeux. ‖ U. S. *To be with it*, être à la coule (or) dans le jeu.
withal [wiˈɔːl] adv. Aussi, de plus, en outre.
— prep. † Avec.
withdraw [wiðˈdrɔː] v. tr. (191). Retirer (*from*, de) [s.o., sth.]. ‖ Rétracter (a promise, statement); *to withdraw one's candidature*, se désister, retirer sa candidature.
— v. intr. Se retirer (in general); se dégager (*from*, de) [an enterprise]; se désolidariser (*from*, de) [a party].
withdrawal [-əl] n. Retraite *f.* (of s.o.); retrait *m.* (of sth.). ‖ JUR. Rappel *m.* (of a decree). ‖ FIN. Retrait *m.* (of money). ‖ MED. *Withdrawal symptom*, symptôme d'état de manque. ‖ FIG. Retrait *m.* (of a project); rétractation *f.* (of a statement).
withe [wiθ] n. See WITHY.
wither [ˈwiðə*] v. tr. BOT., FIG. Faner. ‖ FAM. Foudroyer (with a look).
— v. intr. BOT. Se flétrir, se faner. ‖ FIG. Languir.
withering [-riŋ] adj. Qui se fane (flower). ‖ Desséchant (wind). ‖ FIG. Foudroyant (look).
withers [ˈwiðəz] n. pl. Garrot *m.* (of horse).
withhold [wiðˈhould] v. tr. (82). Refuser de donner (*from*, à) [a document, one's help]. ‖ Dissimuler, taire (*from*, à) [a fact, the truth]. ‖ Empêcher, retenir (*from*, de) [s.o.]. ‖ JUR. Détenir; U. S. *withholding tax*, impôt retenu à la source.
within [wiˈðin] adv. A l'intérieur, chez soi, à la maison (at home). ‖ A l'intérieur; *from within*, de dedans. ‖ FIG. Dans son for intérieur, en dedans.
— prep. A l'intérieur de, dans; *within the castle*, dans le château. ‖ Au sein de; *within the Church*, au sein de l'Eglise. ‖ En moins de; *within a year*, en l'espace d'un an; *within three months*, dans un délai de trois mois; *within three miles*, à moins de trois milles. ‖ Dans les limites de; *within our jurisdiction*, dans notre compétence; *within his activities*, dans le cadre de ses activités (or) fonctions. ‖ A la différence de; *to agree to within twenty francs*, être d'accord à vingt francs près.
without [wiˈðaut] adv. Au-dehors, dehors, à l'extérieur, extérieurement; *from without*, de l'extérieur.
— prep. En dehors de, hors de (a place). ‖ Sans (s.o., sth.). ‖ FAM. *To do without*, se passer de.

withstand [wiðˈstænd] v. tr. (192). Résister à.
— v. intr. Résister.
withy [ˈwiði] n. Brin d'osier *m.*
witless [ˈwitlis] adj. Sot, stupide (action); inintelligent, faible d'esprit (person).
witloof [ˈwitlouf] n. BOT. Endive; chicorée (*f.*) de Bruxelles; witloof *f.*
witness [ˈwitnis] n. Témoignage *m.* (act); témoin *m.* (person); *witness box* (or) U. S. *stand*, banc des témoins, barre.
— v. tr. Témoigner, attester (to testify). ‖ Témoigner, prouver (to prove). ‖ Assister, être témoin de (to be present at). ‖ Signer (to sign).
— v. intr. Témoigner (*against, for*, contre, pour).
witted [-id] adj. D'esprit (in compounds).
witticism [-isizm] n. Mot d'esprit *m.*
wittily [-ili] adv. Avec esprit, spirituellement.
wittiness [-inis] n. Esprit, sel *m.* (of a remark).
witting [-iŋ] adj. Volontaire, délibéré.
wittingly [-iŋli] adv. Sciemment, de propos délibéré.
witty [ˈwiti] adj. Spirituel. (See HUMOROUS.)
wive [waiv] v. intr. Prendre femme.
wives [waivz]. See WIFE.
wiz [wiz] adj. FAM. Impec, au poil, super.
— n. FAM. Champion *s.*, as *m.*
wizard [ˈwizəd] n. Magicien, sorcier *m.* ‖ Prestidigitateur *m.* (conjurer). ‖ FAM. *I am no wizard*, je ne suis pas sorcier.
— interj. FAM. Epatant!, au poil!
wizardry [-ri] n. Sorcellerie *f.*
wizen(ed) [ˈwizn(d)] adj. Desséché, ratatiné, racorni. ‖ Parcheminé (face).
woad [woud] n. Guède *f.*
— v. tr. Guéder.
wobble [ˈwɔbl] v. intr. Zigzaguer, tituber (person); chevroter, trembloter (voice). ‖ Brimbaler, zigzaguer (car); branler (table); brimbaler (wheel). ‖ CULIN. Trembler (jelly). ‖ FIG. Hésiter, osciller, vaciller.
— n. Zigzag *m.* ‖ Tremblement, branlement *m.* ‖ Chevrotement *m.* (of the voice). ‖ FIG. Tergiversation *f.*
wobbler [ˈwɔblə*] n. Hésitant; tergiversateur *m.* ‖ TECHN. Branleur *m.*
wobbly [-i] adj. Zigzaguant, titubant (person); chevrotant (voice). ‖ Brimbalant (car, wheel); bancal (chair, table). ‖ FIG. Hésitant, fluctuant.
woe [wou] n. Malheur *m.*
woebegone [ˈwoubi,gɔn] adj. Abattu, navré, désolé; inconsolable.
woeful [ˈwouful] adj. Affligé, désolé, navré (person). ‖ Déplorable, lamentable (event); de malheur, de calamité (period).
woefully [-i] adv. Douloureusement, tristement (mournfully). ‖ Lamentablement (pitifully). ‖ FAM. Terriblement.
wog [wɔg] n. POP. Métèque *m.* (péj.).
wold [would] n. Région vallonnée *f.*
wolf [wulf] (pl. **wolves** [wulvz]) n. ZOOL. Loup *m.* ‖ FAM. *To keep the wolf from the door*, se mettre à l'abri du besoin. ‖ U. S. FAM. Tombeur, coureur (*m.*) de femmes. ‖ **Wolf-call**, n. U. S. FAM. Sifflement admiratif *m.* ‖ **Wolf-cub**, n. ZOOL., FIG. Louveteau *m.* ‖ **Wolf-dog**, n. ZOOL. Chien-loup *m.* ‖ **Wolf-fish**, n. ZOOL. Loup marin *m.* ‖ **Wolf-hunt**, n. SPORTS. Louveterie *f.* ‖ **Wolf-whistle**, n. FAM. Sifflement admiratif *m.*
— v. tr. Engloutir, dévorer; bâfrer (fam.).
— v. intr. S'empiffrer.
wolfish [-iʃ] adj. ZOOL. De loup. ‖ FIG. Cruel, dévorant. ‖ FAM. U. S. Affamé.
wolfram [ˈwulfrəm] n. Wolfram *m.*
wolverine [ˈwulvə,riːn] n. ZOOL. Carcajou *m.*
wolves [wulvz]. See WOLF.
woman [ˈwumən] (pl. **women** [ˈwimin]) n. Femme *f.* (person). ‖ Féminité *f.*; *it's the woman*

in her, c'est ce qu'il y a de féminin en elle. ‖ Fam. *There's a woman in it,* il y a une femme là-dessous, cherchez la femme. ‖ **Woman-hater,** n. Misogyne *m.*
— adj. Femme; *a woman artist,* une artiste; *a woman friend,* une amie; *woman suffrage,* suffrage des femmes.

womanhood [-hud] n. Féminité *f.* (characteristic). ‖ Maturité féminine *f.* (quality). ‖ Femmes *f. pl.* (collectively).

womanish [-iʃ] adj. Efféminé. (See effeminate.)

womanize [-aiz] v. tr. Efféminer.
— v. intr. Courir le jupon.

womanizing [-aiziŋ] n. Bonnes fortunes *f. pl.*

womankind ['wumən'kaind] n. Femmes *f. pl.* (women). ‖ Parentes *f. pl.* (relatives).

womanlike [-,laik] adj. De femme.
— adv. En femme.

womanliness [-linis] n. Féminité *f.*

womanly [-li] adj. De femme, féminin.

womb [wu:m] n. Med. Utérus, matrice *f.* ‖ Fig. Sein *m.; from the womb to the tomb,* du berceau à la tombe.

wombat ['wɔmbæt] n. Zool. Wombat *m.*

women ['wimin]. See woman.

womenfolk ['wimin,fouk] n. Fam. *My womenfolk,* mes femmes.

won [wʌn] pret., p. p. See win.

wonder ['wʌndə*] n. Merveille *f.;* prodige *m.* (marvel); *for a wonder,* par miracle. ‖ Étonnement *m.;* surprise *f.; no wonder that,* rien d'étonnant que (or) si, il n'est pas surprenant que. ‖ Emerveillement *m.;* admiration *f.; filled with wonder,* rempli d'étonnement (or) d'émerveillement. ‖ Fam. *No wonder,* bien entendu, c'est normal. ‖ **Wonderstruck,** adj. Emerveillé (admiring); stupéfait (surprised). ‖ **Wonder-worker,** n. Faiseur (*m.*) de miracles.
— v. intr. S'étonner (*at,* de; *that,* que); *I don't wonder at it,* cela ne me surprend pas. ‖ S'émerveiller (*at,* de); *that's not to be wondered at,* il n'y a pas de quoi se récrier d'admiration. ‖ Se demander (*why,* pourquoi); *I wonder why,* je voudrais bien savoir pourquoi. ‖ Fam. *Oh! I just wondered!,* je me posais la question seulement; pour rien!

wonderful [-ful] adj. Etonnant, surprenant (astonishing). ‖ Merveilleux, prodigieux, sensationnel (marvellous).

wonderfully [-fuli] adv. Etonnamment. ‖ Merveilleusement.

wondering [-riŋ] adj. Etonné, surpris. ‖ Emerveillé.

wonderingly [-riŋli] adv. Avec étonnement (or) émerveillement.

wonderland [-lænd] n. Pays (*m.*) des merveilles.

wonderment [-mənt] n. Etonnement, émerveillement *m.* ‖ Sujet d'étonnement *m.*

wondrous ['wʌndrəs] adj. Surprenant, étonnant (astonishing). ‖ Prodigieux, inimaginable, merveilleux (marvellous).
— adv. Prodigieusement.

wondrously [-li] adv. Etonnamment. ‖ A merveille.

wonky ['wɔŋki] adj. Fam. Bancal, boiteux (chair); patraque, vaseux (person).

won't [wount]. See will (N. B.).

wont adj. Habitué (*to,* à); *to be wont to,* avoir coutume de, avoir l'habitude de.
— n. Habitude *f.* (See habit.)

wonted [-id] adj. Accoutumé, coutumier, habituel.

woo [wu:] v. tr. Courtiser, faire la cour à (a woman). ‖ Fig. Solliciter (*to,* de) [s.o.]. ‖ Fig. Rechercher (danger, glory).
— v. intr. Faire sa cour.

wood [wud] n. Bois *m.;* forêt *f.* (forest). ‖ Bois *m.* (material); *white wood,* bois blanc. ‖ Fût *m.* (cask). ‖ Mus. Bois *m.* ‖ Fam. *He is wood from the neck*

up, il est bouché à l'émeri, il en a une couche; *out of the wood,* hors d'affaire, tiré du pétrin.
— adj. Des bois (flowers, folk). ‖ En bois, de bois (floor, pavement). ‖ **Wood-block,** n. Arts. Bois *m.;* planche *f.* ‖ **Wood-carver,** n. Arts. Sculpteur sur bois *m.* ‖ **Wood-carving,** n. Arts. Sculpture (*f.*) sur bois. ‖ **Wood-engraver,** n. Arts. Xylographe, graveur sur bois *m.* ‖ **Wood-engraving,** Arts. Xylographie, gravure (*f.*) sur bois. ‖ **Woodlouse,** n. Zool. Cloporte *m.* ‖ **Wood-nymph,** n. Dryade *f.* ‖ **Wood-pigeon,** n. Zool. Ramier *m.;* palombe *f.* ‖ **Wood-shed,** n. Bûcher *m.* ‖ **Woodvice,** n. Techn. Presse *f.* ‖ **Wood-wind,** n. Mus. Bois *m.* ‖ **Wood-worker,** n. Travailleur du bois *m.; wood-worker's tools,* outils pour le bois.

woodbine [-bain] n. Bot. Chèvrefeuille *m.* ‖ U. S. Bot. Vigne vierge *f.*

woodchuck [-t.ʃʌk] n. Zool. Marmotte *f.*

woodcock [-kɔk] n. Zool. Bécasse *f.*

woodcut [-kʌt] n. Arts. Gravure (*f.*) sur bois, bois *m.*

woodcutter [-kʌtə*] n. Bûcheron *m.* ‖ Arts. Graveur sur bois *m.*

wooded [-id] adj. Boisé. (See woody.)

wooden [-n] adj. De bois, en bois (object). ‖ Fam. De bois, inerte. ‖ **Wooden-headed,** adj. Fam. Obtus, stupide. ‖ **Wooden-headedness,** n. Fam. Stupidité *f.*

woodenness [-nnis] n. Stupidité, inertie *f.*

woodiness [-inis] n. Nature boisée *f.* (or) du bois.

woodland [-lənd] n. Région boisée *f.*

woodman [-mən] (pl. **woodmen**) n. Bûcheron *m.* ‖ Forestier *m.* (forester).

woodpecker [-,pekə*] n. Zool. Pic, pivert *m.*

woodsman [-zmən] (pl. **woodsmen**) n. Homme (*m.*) des bois.

woodsy [-si] adj. U. S. De bois, de forêt.

woodwork [-,wə:k] n. Menuiserie *f.* (craft); menuiserie, boiserie *f.* (object).

woody [-i] adj. Boisé (land); des bois (nook). ‖ Bot. Des bois (plant); sylvestre (path); ligneux (tissue). ‖ Fig. Mat (sound).

wooer ['wuə*] n. Soupirant *m.*

woof [wu:f] n. Trame *f.* (of a cloth).

woof [wuf] n. Aboiement, grondement *m.* (of a dog).
— v. intr. Aboyer, gronder.

woofer ['wu:fə*] n. Techn. Boomer, haut-parleur (*m.*) de basses.

wooing ['wu:iŋ] n. Cour *f.* (courting).
— adj. Qui fait sa cour, amoureux.

wool [wul] n. Laine *f.; ball of wool,* pelote de laine; *natural wool,* laine écrue. ‖ Laine *f.;* lainage *m.* (cloth). ‖ Substance laineuse *f.; mineral wool,* coton minéral. ‖ Fam. Tignasse crêpue *f.* ‖ **Wool-bearing,** adj. Lanifère. ‖ **Wool-clip,** n. U. S. Production annuelle de laine *f.* ‖ **Wool-combing,** n. Techn. Peignage (*m.*) de la laine. ‖ **Wool-fell,** n. Peau (*f.*) de mouton. ‖ **Wool-gathering,** n. Rêvasserie, distraction *f.;* adj. Distrait, rêveur. ‖ **Wool-grower,** n. Eleveur (*m.*) de moutons. ‖ **Wool-hall,** n. Comm., Fin. Marché (*m.*) [or] bourse (*f.*) aux laines. ‖ **Wool-sorter,** n. Trieur (*s.*) de laine. ‖ **Wool-stapler,** n. Comm. Marchand (*s.*) de laine.

woollen [-ən] adj. En (or) de laine (material). ‖ Comm. En drap (merchant); du drap (trade); *woollen draper,* drapier.
— n. Lainage *m.* (cloth).

woolliness [-nis] n. Fig. Flou, vague *m.;* imprécision *f.* (of style, thought).

woolly [-i] adj. Laineux, de laine. ‖ Crépu (hair). ‖ Bot. Cotonneux (fruit); lanigère (plant). ‖ Arts. Flou. ‖ Fam. Empâté, confus (style); vaseux (thought).
— n. Fam. Vêtement (*m.*) de laine; pull-over *m.*

woolsey ['wulzi] n. Comm. Tissu (*m.*) de laine et coton.

woozy ['wu:zi] adj. FAM. Eméché, pompette (drunk); chancelant, étourdi, dans les vapes (dizzy); brumeux, vaseux (vague).

word [wə:d] n. Mot, terme *m.; expression f.; in other words,* autrement dit, en d'autres termes; *in so many words,* en propres termes. ‖ Mot *m.;* parole *f.; by word of mouth,* de vive voix; *to be a man of few words,* ne pas prodiguer ses paroles; *put one's word in,* placer son mot. ‖ Expression *f.; beyond words,* au-delà de toute expression; *to have no words for,* manquer de mots pour, ne pouvoir exprimer; *too beautiful for words,* d'une indicible beauté. ‖ Entretien *m.; to have a word with s.o. about sth.,* dire un mot de qqch. à qqn. ‖ Nouvelle *f.; to leave word that,* faire dire que, prévenir que; *word came that,* on apprit que. ‖ Parole, promesse *f.; to be better than one's word,* tenir plus qu'on n'a promis; *to give one's word,* donner sa parole; *to keep one's word,* tenir parole (or) sa promesse. ‖ Mot d'ordre *m.; at a word,* sur-le-champ; *to pass the word round,* se donner le mot. ‖ Pl. Mots *m. pl.;* discussion, dispute *f.; to have words with,* se disputer avec; *they had words,* ils ont eu des mots. ‖ ECCLES. Verbe *m.* ‖ FAM. *To eat one's words,* revenir sur ce qu'on a dit; *to hang on s.o.'s words,* être suspendu aux paroles de qqn. ‖ **Word-book,** n. Vocabulaire *m.* ‖ **Word-order,** n. GRAMM. Ordre (*m.*) des mots. ‖ **Word-painting** (or) **-picture,** n. Description *f.* ‖ **Word-play,** n. Jeu (*m.*) de mots. ‖ **Word-square,** n. Mot carré *m.*
— v. tr. Exprimer (an idea); rédiger, libeller (a text).

wordily [-ili] adv. Verbeusement.

wordiness [-inis] n. Verbosité, prolixité *f.*

wording [-iŋ] n. Rédaction *f.;* libellé *m.* (act); termes *m. pl.* (words).

wordy [-i] adj. Verbeux, prolixe (person, speech). ‖ Oratoire, verbal (battle).

wore [wɔ:*] pret. See WEAR.

work [wə:k] n. Travail, labeur *m.* (action); *to cease* (or) *stop work,* cesser le travail. ‖ Travail *m.;* œuvre *f.* (action); *to set to work,* se mettre à l'œuvre. ‖ Travail *m.;* besogne, tâche *m.; to have plenty of work to do,* avoir beaucoup de besogne à faire; *avoir du pain sur la planche* (fam.). ‖ Ouvrage, travail *m.;* œuvre *f.; a work of genius,* une œuvre géniale; *the works of Milton,* les œuvres de Milton. ‖ Ouvrage, travail *m.;* emploi, métier *m.; out of work,* en chômage; *work-to-rules action,* grève du zèle. ‖ Motifs *m. pl.;* décoration *f.* (in needlework). ‖ TECHN. Pl. Mouvement *m.* (of clock); mécanisme *m.;* rouages *m. pl.* (of a machine); *at work,* en marche; *to be at work,* marcher, fonctionner. ‖ TECHN. Pl. Usine, fabrique *f.* (factory); « men at work », « work in progress », « chantier ». ‖ JUR. *Minister of Works,* ministre des Travaux publics; *Public Works,* Travaux publics; *Work Committee,* commission de la main-d'œuvre. ‖ MILIT. Ouvrages fortifiés *m. pl.* ‖ NAUT. Œuvres *f. pl.* ‖ PHYS. Travail *m.* ‖ GÉOL. Action *m.* ‖ LOC. *The Great Work,* le grand œuvre *m.* ‖ FIG. Œuvre, action *f.; good works,* bonnes œuvres. ‖ U. S. FAM. *To give s.o. the works,* passer qqn à tabac; *to shoot the works,* aller jusqu'au bout, tenter le coup. ‖ FAM. *To get through a lot of work,* en abattre. ‖ **Work-basket,** n. Corbeille (*f.*) à ouvrage. ‖ **Work-bench,** n. Etabli *m.* ‖ **Work-box,** n. Boîte (*f.*) à ouvrage. ‖ **Work-force,** n. Personnel *m.,* effectif *m.,* main-d'œuvre *f.* (of a company); population active *f.* (of a country). ‖ **Work-load,** n. Charge (*f.*) de travail; *to have a heavy work-load,* être surchargé de travail. ‖ **Work-out,** n. U. S. SPORTS. Séance (*f.*) d'entraînement; U. S. FAM. Essai *m.* ‖ **Work-room,** n. Ouvroir *m.* (for needlework); TECHN. Atelier *m.* ‖ **Work-shy,** adj. FAM. Flemmard.
— v. intr. (193). Travailler (*at,* à) [to labour]. ‖

Agir, opérer (to operate). ‖ Se travailler (to be manipulated). ‖ Fermenter, travailler (to ferment). ‖ Avancer, progresser (to move). ‖ TECHN. Fonctionner, marcher; *to work loose,* prendre du jeu, se desserrer. ‖ NAUT. Fatiguer; *to work to windward,* louvoyer. ‖ FIG. Se contracter, se crisper (face). ‖ FAM. *That won't work with me,* ça ne prend pas avec moi. ‖ **To work down,** descendre, tomber. ‖ **To work off,** se dissiper. ‖ **To work on,** continuer à travailler, poursuivre son travail; FAM. Travailler, monter la tête à (s.o.). ‖ **To work out,** aboutir, finir; MATH. Se monter (*at,* à). ‖ **To work round,** tourner, changer; prendre un détour. ‖ **To work up,** remonter (garment); avancer (person); TECHN. Faire.
— v. tr. (193). Faire travailler (s.o.); *to work oneself to death,* se tuer au travail. ‖ Faire fermenter (beer). ‖ Faire tricoter (a sweater); broder (to embroider). ‖ Faire entrer (*into,* dans) [sth.]. ‖ TECHN. Faire fonctionner, actionner, manœuvrer (a machine); exploiter (a mine); *to be worked by,* marcher à. ‖ COMM. Opérer dans (a region). ‖ Ouvrir; *to work one's way to,* se frayer un passage vers. ‖ AGRIC. Cultiver (soil). ‖ NAUT. Payer en travaillant (one's passage); manœuvrer (sails, ship). ‖ MATH. Résoudre (a problem). ‖ MÉD. Opérer (a cure, recovery). ‖ CULIN. Travailler, malaxer (the butter, dough). ‖ ARTS. Pétrir (clay); forger (iron); faire (a portrait); ouvrer, ouvrager, façonner (silver); sculpter (wood). ‖ FIG. Produire (an effect); causer (harm); exercer (influence); amener (ruin); exécuter (a scheme); accomplir, réaliser (wonders). ‖ FIG. Amener, pousser; *to work oneself into s.o.'s favour,* se mettre dans les bonnes grâces de qqn; *to work oneself into a rage,* se mettre en fureur. ‖ FAM. Manigancer, goupiller (sth.). ‖ **To work down,** descendre. ‖ **To work in,** faire entrer (or) introduire. ‖ **To work off,** se débarrasser de (sth.); *to work off one's bad temper on,* passer sa mauvaise humeur sur. ‖ **To work on,** agir sur, monter la tête à (s.o.); travailler sur (sth.). ‖ **To work out,** exécuter, mener à bien (an affair); développer (an idea); étudier (a project); MATH. Résoudre (a problem); FIN. S'acquitter de (a debt); établir (a price); TECHN. Epuiser (a mine); NAUT. Calculer (a bearing). ‖ **To work up,** TECHN., ARTS. Ouvrer; COMM. Se faire (a connection); FIG. Fomenter (disturbance); monter la tête à (s.o.); préparer (a speech); élaborer (a text); *to work oneself up,* s'échauffer, s'emballer; *to work oneself up to,* s'élever par son travail à; *to work s.o. up against s.o. else,* remonter la pendule à qqn contre qqn d'autre (fam.).

workable [-əbl] adj. Exécutable, praticable, faisable (feasible). ‖ ARTS. Ouvrable. ‖ TECHN. Manœuvrable; exploitable. ‖ FIG. Influençable, maniable (person).

workaday [-ədei] adj. De travail (clothes). ‖ FIG. Prosaïque, terre à terre (world).

workday [-dei] n. Jour ouvrable *m.;* journée (*f.*) de travail.

worker [-ə*] n. Travailleur *s.* (in general). ‖ TECHN. Ouvrier *s.* ‖ Pl. Classe ouvrière (or) laborieuse *f.* ‖ ZOOL. Ouvrière *f.* (bee).

workhouse [-haus] n. Asile, hospice *m.*

working [-iŋ] n. Travail *m.* (action). ‖ Fermentation *f.* (of beer, wine). ‖ TECHN. Fonctionnement *m.* (of a machine); exploitation *f.* (of a mine); pl. chantier *m.* ‖ NAUT. Manœuvre *f.* ‖ MÉD. Effet *m.* (of remedy). ‖ FIG. Crispation *f.* (of face). ‖ **Working-out,** FIN. Calcul (of interests); MATH. Résolution *f.* (of a problem); FIG. Elaboration, exécution *f.* (of a plan).
— adj. Laborieux, ouvrier, prolétaire (classes). ‖ De travail (clothes, party). ‖ Ouvrable (day). ‖ TECHN. De marche (order); en marche, en action (part). ‖ FIN., COMM. D'exploitation, de roulement

(capital, expenses); *working costs*, frais généraux. || Jur. De travail (agreement); suffisant (majority). || Fig. Admissible (theory). || **Working-man,** n. Travailleur *m.* (artisan, mechanic, labourer). || **Working-woman,** n. Ouvrière, travailleuse manuelle *f.*

workman [-mən] (pl. **workmen**) n. Ouvrier *m.*

workmanlike [-mənlaik] adj. Bon (manner); bien fait, fait de main d'ouvrier (work).

workmanship [-mənʃip] n. Habileté professionnelle *f.* (artistry). || Exécution habile *f.* || Fabrication *f.* || Travail de professionnel *m.* (work).

workshop [-ʃɔp] n. Atelier *m.*

workwoman [-,wumən] (pl. **workwomen** [-wimin]) n. Ouvrière *f.*

world [wə:ld] n. Monde *m.; in the next world,* dans l'autre monde; *in this world,* dans ce bas monde. || Monde, univers *m.; the beginning of the world,* le commencement du monde. || Monde *m.;* terre *f.; the New World,* le Nouveau Monde. || Monde *m.;* gens *m. pl.; all the world,* tout le monde. || Monde *m.;* vie *f.; a man of the world,* un homme qui a vécu; *as the world goes,* à notre époque, par les temps actuels; *to have the world before one,* avoir la vie devant soi. || Monde *m.;* vie sociale *f.; out of the world,* retiré du monde. || Monde *m.;* sphère *f.; the world of science,* le monde savant. || Eccles. Monde, siècle *m.* || Astron. Monde, astre *m.* || Fam. Monde *m.* (great deal); *a world of good,* un bien énorme (or) fou. || Fam. *Not for anything in the world,* pour rien au monde; *to give the world for,* donner tout l'or du monde pour; *out of this world,* extraordinaire, épatant. || **World-famous,** adj. De renommée mondiale, connu dans le monde entier. || **World-history,** n. Histoire universelle *f.* || **World-old,** adj. Vieux comme le monde. || **World-politics,** n. sg. Politique mondiale *f.* || **World-power,** n. Puissance mondiale *f.* || **World-war,** n. Milit. Guerre mondiale *f.* || **World-weary,** adj. Las de vivre. || **World-wide,** adj. Universel, mondial.

worldliness [-linis] n. Mondanité *f.;* goûts mondains *m. pl.* (See EARTHLINESS.)

worldling [-liŋ] n. Mondain *s.* (See EARTHLING.)

worldly [-li] adj. Terrestre. (See EARTHLY.) || Temporel, matériel. || Mondain. || Du monde, du siècle. || **Worldly-minded,** adj. Attaché aux biens terrestres.

worm [wə:m] n. Zool., Med. Ver *m.* || Techn. Filet *m.* (of screw). || Chim. Serpentin *m.* (of a still). || **Worm-eaten,** adj. Mangé aux vers; vermoulu. || **Worm-gear,** n. Techn. Engrenage (*m.*) à vis sans fin. || **Worm-hole,** n. Trou de ver *m.* || **Worm-like,** adj. Vermiculaire. || **Worm-powder,** n. Med. Vermifuge (*m.*) en poudre. || **Worm-wheel,** n. Roue hélicoïdale *f.*
— v. intr. Ramper. || Fig. S'insinuer.
— v. tr. Enlever les vers de. || Everrer (a dog). || Techn. Fileter (a screw). || Naut. Congréer. || Fig. Soutirer; *to worm a secret out of s.o.,* faire parler qqn, tirer les vers du nez à qqn. || Fig. Insinuer; *to worm one's way* (or) *oneself into,* se faufiler dans; *to worm oneself into,* s'insinuer dans.

wormling [-liŋ] n. Zool. Vermisseau *m.*

wormseed [-si:d] n. Bot. Semen-contra *m.*

wormwood [-wud] n. Bot. Absinthe *f.* || Fig. Fiel *m.;* amertume *f.*

wormy [-i] adj. Véreux.

worn [wɔ:n]. See WEAR.

worriment ['wʌrimənt] n. U. S. Ennui, empoisonnement, embêtement *m.* (fam.).

worry ['wari] v. tr. (2). Déchiqueter (a sheep); mordiller (an old shoe). || Agacer, harceler (to harass). || Ennuyer, importuner (to bother). || Tourmenter, tracasser, inquiéter (to distress); *to be dreadfully worried,* se tourmenter.
— v. intr. Se mordiller (dogs). || Se tracasser, s'in-

quiéter; s'en faire, se faire des cheveux (fam.); *to worry about,* se mettre en peine de.
— n. Mordillement *m.* || Souci *m.;* inquiétude *f.* (anxiety); *beside oneself with worry,* aux cent coups. || Souci, tracas *m.; the least of my worries,* le moindre (or) le cadet (fam.) de mes soucis.

worse [wə:s] adj. Pire, plus mauvais (more nasty). || Pire, plus méchant (more wicked). || Pire, plus grave (more serious). || Med. Plus malade. || Loc. *I was none the worse for it,* je ne m'en suis pas plus mal porté (or) trouvé; *to have the worse ground,* avoir le désavantage du terrain.
— N. B. *Worse* est le comparatif de *bad* et de *ill.*
— adv. Pis, plus mal; *so much the worse,* tant pis; *to grow worse and worse,* aller de mal en pis; *worse still,* pis encore. || Plus, davantage (more intensively).
— n. Pire *m.; he has been through worse,* il en a vu d'autres; *there was worse to come,* le pire était à venir; *to change for the worse,* se modifier dans le mauvais sens.

worsen [-ŋ] v. tr. Rendre pire. || Fam. Avoir le dessus sur.
— v. intr. Empirer.

worsening [-niŋ] n. Aggravation *f.*

worship ['wə:ʃip] n. Honneur *m.* (title). || Eccles., Fig. Culte *m.;* adoration *f.*
— v. tr. (1). Eccles. Adorer. || Fig. Adorer, avoir un culte pour.
— v. intr. Eccles. Faire acte d'adoration. || Fig. Adorer.

worshipful [-ful] adj. Honorable (title). || Vénérable (freemason).

worshipfully [-fuli] adv. Avec adoration.

worshipper [-ə*] n. Eccles., Fig. Adorateur *m.;* adoratrice *f.*

worst [wə:st] adj. Le pire, le plus mauvais, le plus méchant, le plus grave; *the two worst pupils,* les deux plus mauvais élèves. || Med. Plus malade.
— N. B. *Worst* est le superlatif de *bad* et de *ill.*
— adv. Le pis, le plus mal. || Le plus.
— n. Pire *m.; if (the) worst comes to (the) worst,* en mettant les choses au pire. || Le plus fort, le pire moment *m.; the worst is soon over,* le plus mauvais moment passe vite. || Désavantage *m.; to get the worst of it,* avoir le dessous.
— v. tr. Battre, l'emporter sur.

worsted ['wustid] n. Peigné *m.* (cloth); laine peignée *f.* (thread).
— adj. En laine peignée.

wort [wɔ:t] n. Moût *m.* (of beer). || Bot. Herbe *f.*

worth [wə:θ] adj. Valant; *for what it is worth,* pour ce que ça vaut; *it is not worth much,* ça ne vaut pas cher; *to be worth little,* valoir peu. || Méritant; *is it worth while?,* cela en vaut-il la peine (or) le coup (fam.)?; *not worth reading,* qui ne mérite pas d'être lu. || Possédant; *he is worth a million,* il est milliardaire. || Fam. *For all one is worth,* tant qu'on peut. || U. S. Fam. *To put in one's two cents' worth,* y mettre son grain de sel. || **Worth-while,** adj. De valeur, qui en vaut la peine.
— n. Valeur *f.;* prix (of sth.); *three pounds' worth of,* pour trois livres de; *to have one's money's worth,* en avoir pour son argent. || Fig. Valeur *f.;* mérite *m.*

worthily ['wə:ðili] adv. Dignement. || A juste titre.

worthiness [-inis] n. Mérite *m.*

worthless ['wə:θlis] adj. Sans valeur (argument, excuse). || Bon à rien, sans valeur, indigne (person); *worthless fellow,* vaurien.

worthlessness [-lisnis] n. Non-valeur, inutilité *f.* || Bassesse, vilenie *f.*

worthy ['wə:ði] adj. Estimable, digne, respectable (people, person). || Convenable, approprié, digne; *a worthy reward,* une juste récompense. || Digne (of, to, de); *worthy of death,* méritant la mort; *worthy of note,* digne de remarque.
— (pl. **worthies**) n. Notable *m.*

would [wud]. See WILL.
would–be ['wudbi:] adj. Soi-disant, prétendu (so called). || FAM. A la manque, à la noix (useless).
wound [waund] pret., p. p. See WIND.
wound [wu:nd] n. MED. Plaie, blessure *f*. || FIG. Blessure *f*. (*to*, à).
— v. tr. MED., FIG. Blesser.
woundable [-əbl̩] adj. Vulnérable.
wounded [-id] adj. MED., FIG. Blessé.
— n. MED. Blessés *m. pl.*
woundily [-ili] adv. FAM. Formidablement.
woundwort [-wə:t] n. BOT. Epiaire *f*.
wove [wouv], **woven** [-n]. See WEAVE.
wove [wouv] adj. Vergé (paper).
wow [wau] n. FAM. Succès formidable *m.*; *it's a wow of a show*, c'est un spectacle du tonnerre.
— v. tr. FAM. En mettre plein la vue à, éblouir.
— interj. FAM. Oh là là!, terrible!
wow n. TECHN. Pleurage *m*.
wrack [ræk] n. BOT. Varech *m*.
wraith [reiθ] n. Apparition *f.*; double *m*. (ghost).
wrangle ['ræŋgl̩] v. intr. Se quereller, se disputer.
— n. Querelle, dispute *f*.
wrangler [-ə*] n. Querelleur; disputailleur *s*. (fam.). || Etudiant (*s.*) de mathématiques à Cambridge. || U. S. Cow-boy *m*.
wrap [ræp] v. tr. (1). Envelopper (lit. and fig.); *to be wrapped up in*, être pris (or) absorbé par (to be absorbed); être lié à; dépendre de (to be involved). || **To wrap about** (or) **around**, enrouler autour de, entourer, envelopper.
— v. intr. **To wrap up**, s'envelopper.
— n. Fichu, châle *m*. (neckerchief). || Couverture *f*. (blanket); *quilted wrap*, douillette (of child). || *Evening wrap*, manteau (or) cape du soir.
wrappage [-idʒ] n. Enveloppement *m*. (act); enveloppe *f*. (thing). || COMM. Emballage, conditionnement *m*.
wrapper [-ə*] n. Couverture *f*. (of book); bande *f*. (of newspaper). || Robe *f*. (of a cigar). || COMM. Emballeur *s*. (person); toile (*f.*) d'emballage (thing).
wrapping [-iŋ] n. Mise sous bande *f*. (of a newspaper). || COMM. Emballage *m.; wrapping paper*, papier d'emballage.
wrath [rɔθ] n. Courroux *m.*, ire *f*. (See ANGER.)
wrathful [-ful] adj. Courroucé, furieux.
wreak [ri:k] v. tr. Assouvir (vengeance); *to wreak vengeance upon*, se venger de. || Donner libre cours à (one's anger, malice).
wreath [ri:θ] n. Couronne *f*. (for funeral). || Guirlande *f*. (garland). || Spirale *f.;* panache *m*. (of smoke).
wreathe [ri:ð] v. tr. Couvrir (to cover); enguirlander (to decorate); couronner (to encircle); entrelacer (to twist). || Enrouler (*round*, autour de).
— v. intr. S'enrouler (foliage, serpent). || S'élever en volutes, tourbillonner (smoke).
wreck [rek] n. Perdition, ruine, perte *f*. || Destruction, ruine *f*. || ARCHIT., CH. DE F. Décombres, débris *m. pl.* || NAUT. Epave *f*. (remains); naufrage *m*. (shipwreck). || FIG. Ruine *f*. (person).
— v. tr. Causer la perte de. || NAUT. Faire naufrager. || CH. DE F. Faire dérailler. || AUTOM. Démolir (a car). || FIG. Ruiner (hope); briser (a life); démolir (s.o.'s nerves); faire échouer (a plan); causer la ruine de (s.o.).
— v. intr. NAUT. Faire naufrage.
wreckage [-idʒ] n. NAUT. Epaves *f. pl.* || ARCHIT., CH. DE F. Décombres *m. pl.*
wrecker [-ə*] n. Destructeur *m.;* destructrice *f*. || NAUT. Naufrageur, pilleur (*m.*) d'épaves (pej.). || JUR., NAUT. Récupérateur (*m.*) d'épaves. || CH. DE F. Dérailleur (*m.*) de trains. || U. S. AUTOM. Dépanneur *m*.
wrecking [-iŋ] U. S. AUTOM. Dépannage; *wrecking truck*, dépanneuse.
wren [ren] n. ZOOL. Roitelet *m*. || MILIT. Wren, femme marin. || U. S. FAM. Donzelle *f*.

wrench [renʃ] n. Effort d'arrachement *m*. (pull); torsion *f*. (twist). || MED. Foulure *f.;* effort *m*. || TECHN. Clef *f*. || FIG. Arrachement *m*. (separation); entorse *f*. (*to*, à) [a meaning].
— v. tr. Tordre, tirer en tordant. || Arracher brutalement (*from*, de). || MED. Fouler. || FIG. Fausser, forcer (a meaning); altérer (a statement).
wrest [rest] n. MUS. Clef *f*. (for tuning). || † Torsion *f*. || **Wrest-pin**, n. MUS. Cheville *f*. (in a piano).
— v. tr. Arracher violemment (*from*, à). || FIG. Arracher (a confession); dénaturer, forcer (a meaning).
wrestle ['resl̩] v. intr. SPORTS. Lutter à main plate (or) corps à corps (*with*, avec). || FIG. S'attaquer (*with*, à) [a difficulty]; lutter (*with*, contre) [a habit].
— v. tr. SPORTS. Lutter avec.
— n. SPORTS. Lutte (*f.*) corps à corps. || FIG. Lutte *f*.
wrestler [-ə*] n. SPORTS. Lutteur *s*.
wrestling [-iŋ] n. SPORTS. Lutte *f*.
wretch [retʃ] n. Malheureux, infortuné *s*. (unhappy); *poor wretch*, pauvre hère. || Misérable *s*. (scoundrel). || FAM. Etre *m.; poor little wretch*, pauvre gosse!
wretched ['retʃid] adj. Malheureux, infortuné (unhappy). || Pitoyable, misérable, souffreteux, lamentable (pitiable). || Mauvais, détestable, piètre (unsatisfactory). || Pénible, mauvais; *to lead s.o. a wretched life*, mener la vie dure à qqn. || FAM. Sacré, satané (intensive).
wretchedly [-li] adv. Misérablement; lamentablement.
wretchedness [-nis] n. Malheur *m.;* infortune *f*. (unhappiness). || Médiocrité, pauvreté *f*. (poor quality). || Tristesse *f*. (sadness).
wrick [rik] v. tr. MED. Tordre; *to wrick one's back*, se donner un effort dans le dos; *to wrick one's neck*, se donner le torticolis.
— n. MED. Effort *m*. (in a muscle); torticolis *m*. (in the neck).
wriggle ['rigl̩] v. intr. Se tortiller, frétiller (fish, person, worm); *to wriggle through*, se faufiler à travers. || FIG. S'insinuer (*into*, dans); se retirer habilement (*out of*, de). || FAM. Tortiller.
— v. tr. Tortiller, agiter; *to wriggle one's way into*, se faufiler dans.
— n. Tortillement *m*.
wring [riŋ] v. tr. (194). Tordre (clothes); *to wring out water*, faire sortir l'eau en tordant. || Serrer fortement (s.o.'s hand); *to wring one's hands*, se tordre les mains. || FIG. Fendre, serrer (s.o.'s heart); *to wring money from* (or) *out of*, extorquer de l'argent à.
— n. Torsion *f*. || Forte poignée de main *m*. (handshake).
wringer [-ə*] n. Essoreuse *f*. (machine).
wrinkle ['riŋkl̩] n. FAM. Truc, tuyau *m*. || U. S. FAM. Nouveauté *f.; the latest wrinkle*, le dernier cri, la dernière mode.
wrinkle n. Ride *f*. (on the skin, on water). || Faux pli *m*. (on cloth). || GEOL. Plissement *m*.
— v. tr. Rider (skin, water); *to wrinkle one's brow*, froncer les sourcils. || Faire des faux plis à, chiffonner, froisser (a dress).
— v. intr. Se rider (skin, water). || Se froisser, faire des faux plis (dress).
wrinkled [-d] adj. Ridé.
wrinkling [-iŋ] n. Plissement, froncement *m*. (act); rides *f. pl.* (collectively). || TECHN. Réticulation *f*.
wrinkly [-i] adj. Ridé.
wrist [rist] n. MED. Poignet *m*. || SPORTS. Coup de poignet *m*. || **Wrist-pin**, n. TECHN. Maneton *m*. || **Wrist-watch**, n. Bracelet-montre *m*.
wristband [-bænd] n. Poignet *m.;* manchette *f*. (of shirt).

wristlet [-lit] n. Bracelet m. ‖ Pl. Fam. Bracelets m. pl.; menottes f. pl.

writ [rit] n. Jur. Acte judiciaire, mandat m.; assignation, ordonnance f.; to draw up a writ, dresser un exploit; writ of attachment, ordre de saisie-arrêt. ‖ Eccles. Ecriture f.
— v. tr. (1). Jur. Assigner.

write [rait] v. intr. (195). Ecrire; to write legibly, écrire lisiblement. ‖ Ecrire, correspondre (by letters). ‖ Ecrire, être écrivain (to write books). ‖ U. S. Etre employé aux écritures (to be a clerk, copyist). ‖ Fam. It's nothing to write home about, ça ne casse rien, il n'y a pas de quoi faire passer le tambour de ville. ‖ To write back, répondre à une lettre.
— v. tr. Ecrire (letters, words); to write a good hand, avoir une bonne écriture. ‖ Ecrire, rédiger (an account); écrire, composer (a novel). ‖ Remplir (a form). ‖ Fig. Inscrire; innocence is written on his face, l'innocence se lit sur son visage. ‖ To write down, noter, coucher par écrit. ‖ To write in, insérer. ‖ To write off, écrire au courant de la plume (or) d'un trait; Fin. Déduire, défalquer; Milit., Aviat. Rayer; two machines were written off, deux appareils ont été détruits. ‖ To write out, transcrire; Med. Rédiger; Fin. Etablir, faire (a cheque); Fig. To write oneself out, épuiser sa veine d'écrivain. ‖ To write up, rédiger (an account); faire un article sur (in a newspaper); Fin. Mettre à jour (bookkeeping); Fam. Prôner (s.o.). ‖ Write-off, n. Annulation (f.) par écrit (act); Fam. Non-valeur f. (person). ‖ Write-up, n. Fam. Battage m. (boosting); papier m. (in a newspaper).

writer [-ə*] n. Personne (f.) qui écrit; scripteur m.; scriptrice f. ‖ Ecrivain; auteur m. (of, de) [author]. ‖ Employé (s.) aux écritures; rédacteur m.; rédactrice f. (clerk).

writhe [raiδ] v. intr. (196). Se tordre de douleur. ‖ Fig. Frémir, se crisper.
— v. tr. Tordre, crisper, contracter.
— n. Contraction f.

writing ['raitiɳ] n. Ecriture f. (act, handwriting). ‖ Inscription f. ‖ Ecrit m. (document, letter). ‖ Ecrit, ouvrage m. (work). ‖ Métier d'écrivain m. (profession). ‖ Art (m.) d'écrire (art). ‖ Writing-block, n. Bloc-correspondance m. ‖ Writing-case, n. Nécessaire de bureau m. ‖ Writing-desk, n. Pupitre, bureau m. ‖ Writing-pad, n. Sous-main m. ‖ Writing-paper, n. Papier (m.) à lettres. ‖ Writing-tablet, n. Bloc-notes m.

written ['ritɳ] adj. Ecrit, fait par écrit. ‖ Written-off, adj. Aviat. Perdu, détruit.

wrong [rɔɳ] adj. Mal (not right); it is wrong to, c'est mal de. ‖ Dans son tort; to be wrong, avoir tort (to, de). ‖ Faux, erroné (idea); dans l'erreur (person); not to·be far wrong, ne pas se tromper de beaucoup. ‖ Mauvais, qu'il ne faut pas; in the wrong place, mal placé; in the wrong sense, à contresens; the wrong side, l'envers (of material); le mauvais côté (of a road); wrong side foremost, out, up, devant derrière, à l'envers, sens dessus dessous. ‖ Choisir par erreur; to take the wrong book, se tromper de livre, ne pas prendre le livre qu'il faut. ‖ Dérangé, détraqué, qui ne va pas; there is something wrong with him, il y a quelque chose qui ne va pas (or) qui cloche à son sujet. ‖ Sports. On the wrong foot, à contre-pied. ‖ Mus. Faux (note).
— n. Mal m.; to make wrong right, changer le mal en bien. ‖ Tort, préjudice m.; to do wrong to, faire du tort à, nuire à. ‖ Tort m.; erreur f.; to be in the wrong, avoir tort; to put s.o. in the wrong, mettre qqn dans son tort.
— adv. Mal; to go wrong, se tromper de chemin; Techn. Se déranger, se détraquer; Comm. Mal marcher; Med. Se détraquer; Fig. Tourner mal.
— v. tr. Nuire à, faire tort à, desservir (s.o.).

wrongdoer [-'duə*] n. Auteur d'un méfait m. ‖ Jur. Délinquant s.

wrongdoing [-'duiɳ] n. Méfaits m. pl.; mauvaises actions f. pl.; mal m. ‖ Jur. Infraction f.

wrongful ['rɔɳful] adj. Injuste, injustifié. ‖ Dommageable, préjudiciable. ‖ Jur. Illégal.

wrongfully [-fuli] adv. A tort, avec injustice.

wrongfulness [-fulnis] n. Injustice f.

wrongheaded ['rɔɳ'hedid] adj. Qui a mauvaise tête, obstiné.

wrongheadedly [-'hedidli] adv. Obstinément.

wrongheadedness [-'hedidnis] n. Mauvaise tête f.

wrongly ['rɔɳli] adv. Mal. ‖ Injustement. ‖ A tort.

wrote [rout] pret. See write.

wroth [rɔθ] adj. Courroucé, en courroux.

wrought [rɔːt] adj. Forgé (iron); soudé (steel).

wrung [rʌɳ] pret., p. p. See wring.

wry [rai] adj. Tordu; to pull a wry face, faire la grimace. ‖ Fig. Forcé (smile).

wryneck [-nek] n. Med. Torticolis m. ‖ Zool. Torcol, torcou m.

wunderkind ['wʌndə,kind] n. Enfant prodige s.

wynd [waind] n. Ruelle, venelle f. (in Scotland).

wyvern ['waivə:n] n. Vouivre f. ‖ Blas. Dragon m.

X

x [eks] n. X, x m. ‖ Math. Inconnue f.; dix m. (Roman numeral). ‖ Comm. Etoile f. ‖ Chim. Xenon m. ‖ U. S. See extension. ‖ X-ray, n. Phys. Rayon X; v. tr. Med. Radiographier; adj. Med. Radiologique, radiographique; X-ray dermatitis, radiodermite; x-ray photograph, radiographie, cliché radiographique; x-ray photographer, radiologiste; x-ray treatment, radiothérapie.

xanthein ['zænθiin] n. Chim. Xanthéine f.

xanthin ['zænθin] n. Chim. Xanthine f.

xanthous ['zænθəs] adj. Geogr. Mongoloïde.

xebec ['ziːbek] n. Naut. Chébec m.

xenon ['zenɔn] n. Chim. Xénon m.

xenophobe ['zenəfoub] adj., n. Xénophobe s.

xenophobia [,zenə'foubiə] n. Xénophobie f.

xenophobic [-'foubik] adj. Xénophobe.
Xmas Written abbr. for *Christmas*, Noël.
xylograph ['zailəgrɑ:f] n. ARTS. Xylographie, gravure (*f.*) sur bois.
xylographer [zai'lɔgrəfə*] n. ARTS. Xylographe *s.*

xylography [-i] n. ARTS. Xylographie *f.*
xylophone ['zailəfoun] n. MUS. Xylophone *m.*
xylophonist [zai'lɔfənist] n. MUS. Joueur (*m.*) de xylophone.
xyster ['zistə*] n. MED. Rugine *f.* ; xystre *m.*

y [wai] n. Y, y *m.* ‖ MATH. Y *m.* ‖ CHIM. Yttrium *m.* ‖ **Y-connection,** n. ELECTR. Montage (*m.*) en étoile. ‖ **Y-gun,** n. U. S. MILIT. Canon anti-sous-marin *m.* ‖ **Y-tube,** n. Tube en Y *m.*
yacht [jɔt] n. NAUT. Yacht *m.*
— v. intr. NAUT. Fœire du yachting.
yachting [-iŋ] n. NAUT. Yachting *m.*
yachtsman [-smən] (pl. **yachtsmen**) n. NAUT. Yachtman *m.*
yack(ety)-yack ['jæk(iti)'jæk] n. FAM. Papotage, jacassement *m.*
— v. intr. FAM. Papoter, jacasser.
yah [jɑ:] interj. FAM. Oh ! là là !, pouah !
yahoo [jɑ:'hu:] n. FAM. Brute *f.* ‖ U. S. FAM. Petzouille *m.*
Yahveh ['jɑ:vei] n. ECCLES. Jéhovah, Iahvé *m.*
yak [jæk] n. ZOOL. Yack *m.*
yak v. intr. (1). U. S. FAM. Jacasser.
yam [jæm] n. BOT. Igname *f.* ‖ U. S. Patate *f.*
yammer ['jæmə*] v. intr. FAM. Brailler.
yank [jæŋk] v. tr. FAM. Tirer brusquement ; *to yank out one's sword,* dégainer ; *to yank up,* faire monter d'un coup.
— n. Coup sec *m.* ; saccade *f.*
Yank n. FAM. Yankee *m.*
Yankee. ['jæŋki] n. Yankee *m.*
yankeeism [-izm] n. GRAMM. Américanisme *m.*
yap [jæp] n. U. S. POP. Gueule *f.* (mouth) ; petzouille, rustre *m.* (person).
yap v. intr. (1). ZOOL. Japper (dog) ; glapir (fox). ‖ U. S. FAM. Rouspéter, grommeler.
— n. ZOOL. Jappement *m.* ‖ U. S. FAM. Rouspétance *f.*
yarborough ['jɑ:bərə] n. Main (*f.*) qui ne comporte aucune carte au-dessus du 9 (at cards).
yard [jɑ:d] n. Yard *m.* (measure). ‖ NAUT. Vergue *f.* ‖ **Yard-arm,** n. NAUT. Bout (*m.*) de vergue. ‖ **Yard-stick,** n. Yard en bois *m.* ; FIG. Aune *f.* (standard of comparison).
yard n. Cour *f.* (of farm, house, prison) ; préau *m.* ; cour *f.* (of school). ‖ Dépôt *m.* ; *coal yard,* dépôt de charbon. ‖ NAUT. Chantier naval. ‖ CH. DE F. *Goods yard,* U. S. *freight yard,* dépôt de marchandises ; *marshalling yard,* centre de triage. ‖ **Yard-dog,** n. ZOOL. Chien (*m.*) de garde. ‖ **Yard-master,** n. CH. DE F. Chef de dépôt *m.*
yardage [-idʒ] n. Métrage *m.*
yardage n. Parcage *m.* ‖ Frais (*m. pl.*) de dépôt. ‖ CH. DE F. Manœuvres *f. pl.*
yard(s)man [-(z)mən] n. TECHN. Manœuvre *m.* ‖ AGRIC. Palefrenier *m.* ‖ CH. DE F. Homme (*m.*) d'équipe.
yarn [jɑ:n] n. Fil *m.* (of cotton, flax, nylon, silk, wool). ‖ NAUT. Fil de caret *m.* ; touée *f.* ‖ FAM.

Histoire (*f.*) à dormir debout. ‖ **Yarn-dyed,** adj. Teint avant tissage.
— v. intr. FAM. En débiter, raconter des histoires.
yarrow ['jærou] n. BOT. Achillée *f.*
yataghan ['jætəgən] n. Yatagan *m.*
yatter ['jætə*] v. intr. FAM. Bavarder ; jacasser.
yaw [jɔ:] v. intr. NAUT. Faire une embardée. ‖ AVIAT. Embarder.
— n. NAUT. Embardée *f.* ‖ AVIAT. Embardée, giration *f.*
yawl [jɔ:l] n. NAUT. Yole *f.* (rowing-boat) ; yawl, sloop *m.* (sailing-boat).
yawn [jɔ:n] v. intr. Bâiller (person) ; béer, être béant (thing).
— v. tr. Dire en bâillant. ‖ FAM. *To yawn one's head off,* bâiller à se décrocher la mâchoire.
— n. Bâillement *m.* ; gouffre béant *m.* ; large ouverture *f.*
yawning [-iŋ] adj. Bâillant (person) ; béant (thing).
— n. Bâillement *m.*
yawny ['jɔ:ni] adj. U. S. FAM. Rasoir, barbant (tedious).
yaws [jɔ:z] n. pl. MED. Pian *m.*
yclept [i'klept] adj. † Appelé.
ye [ji:] pron. pers. † Vous.
ye [ji:] art. def. † Le. (See THE.)
yea [jei] adv. Eh oui !, mais oui !, vraiment ! ‖ Voire !, que dis-je !
— n. Oui *m.*
yeah [jɛə] adv. FAM. Ouais, oui.
yean [ji:n] v. tr., intr. ZOOL. Chevreter (goat) ; agneler (sheep).
yeanling [-liŋ] n. ZOOL. Chevreau *m.* (kid) ; agnelet *m.* (lamb).
year [jə:*] n. An *m.* ; année *f.* ; *every year,* tous les ans ; *every other year,* tous les deux ans ; *year after year,* des années durant ; *year in year out,* d'un bout à l'autre de l'année ; bon an mal an. ‖ Année *f.* ; *school year,* année scolaire. ‖ Pl. Age *m.* ; *the weight of years,* le poids des ans ; *well on in years,* assez mûr (person). ‖ ECCLES. *Year's end mass,* bout de l'an. ‖ FAM. *Donkey's years,* de nombreuses années ; *it puts years on me,* ça me rase. ‖ **Year-book,** n. Annuaire *m.* ‖ **Year-long,** adj. Qui dure un an.
yearling [-liŋ] n. ZOOL. Animal d'un an *m.* (animal) ; brocard *m.* (roe-deer).
— adj. D'un an.
yearly [-li] adj. Annuel.
— adv. Annuellement.
yearn [jə:n] v. intr. Aspirer (*after, for,* à) ; soupirer (*after, for,* après) ; brûler, languir (*for,* de) ; avoir envie (*to,* de). [See LONG.] ‖ † S'apitoyer (*to, towards,* sur).
yearning [-iŋ] n. Aspiration *f.* ; élan *m.* (*after, for,*

vers). ‖ Vif désir *m.*; envie *f.* (*for*, de). ‖ Tendresse émue *f.* (sympathy).
— adj. Aspirant (*for*, à). ‖ Plein de désir, brûlant d'envie.

yearningly [-iŋli] adv. Avec envie (or) compassion.

yeast [ji:st] n. Levure *f.* (See LEAVEN.) ‖ FIG. Ferment *m.*

yeasty [-i] adj. De levure (taste). ‖ Ecumeux (frothy). ‖ FIG. En ébullition (in a ferment); superficiel, frivole (frivolous).

yegg [jeg] n. U. S. POP. Cambrioleur *m.*

yell [jel] v. intr. Hurler (*with*, de).
— v. tr. Hurler.
— n. Hurlement *m.*

yelling [-iŋ] n. Hurlements *m. pl.*

yellow ['jelou] adj. Jaune; *to become* (or) *grow* (or) *turn yellow*, jaunir; *yellow metal*, laiton; *yellow soap*, savon de Marseille. ‖ GEOGR. Jaune. ‖ Beurre (gloves); blond (hair). ‖ MED. Jaune (fever). ‖ NAUT. Jaune, de quarantaine (flag). ‖ FIG. Jaloux, envieux (look). ‖ FAM. A sensation (press). ‖ U. S. FAM. Froussard. ‖ **Yellow-belly**, n. U. S. FAM. Dégonflé, froussard *m.* ‖ **Yellow-band**, adj. FAM., AUTOM. A parcage interdit. ‖ **Yellow-dog**, adj. U. S. *Yellow-dog contract*, contrat de travail illégal *m.*; *yellow-dog fund*, caisse noire. ‖ **Yellow jacket**, n. U. S. ZOOL. Frelon *m.* ‖ **Yellow line**, n. AUTOM. Ligne (*f.*) jaune en bordure de route matérialisant des restrictions de stationnement.
— n. Jaune *m.* ‖ MED. Pl. Jaunisse *f.* ‖ CHIM. Jaune *m.*
— v. intr., tr. Jaunir.

yellowback [-,bæk] n. Livre broché *m.*

yellowish [-iʃ] adj. Jaunâtre.

yellowness [-nis] n. Couleur jaune *f.* ‖ MED. Teint jaune *m.*

yelp [jelp] v. intr. ZOOL. Japper (dog); glapir (fox); clabauder (hound).
— n. ZOOL. Jappement; clabaudement *m.*

Yemen ['jemən] n. GEOGR. Yémen *m.*

Yemeni [-i] adj., n. GEOGR. Yéménite, *adj., s.*

yen [jen] n. U. S. FAM. Désir *m.*; envie *f.*
— v. intr. (1). U. S. FAM. Languir (*for*, de).

yen n. FIN. Yen *m.*

yeoman ['joumən] (pl. **yeomen**) n. † Franc tenancier *m.* ‖ MILIT. Yeoman, hallebardier *m.* ‖ LOC. *To do yeoman service*, rendre des services inestimables.

yeomanly [-li] adj. † De franc tenancier. ‖ FIG. Hardi et franc.

yeomanry [-ri] n. † Classe (*f.*) des petits propriétaires. ‖ MILIT. Troupes territoriales montées (or) motorisées.

yep [jep] adv. FAM. Ouais, oui.

yes [jes] adv. Oui; *say yes or no*, dites oui ou non. ‖ Si; *you didn't see him?, yes I did*, vous ne l'avez pas vu?, mais si. ‖ **Yes-man**, n. FAM. Béni-oui-oui, sempiternel approbateur *m.*; *to be a yes-man*, dire toujours amen.
— (pl. **yeses** [-iz]) n. Oui *m.*

yesterday ['jestədi] adj., adv., n. Hier *m.*; *the day before yesterday*, avant-hier; *yesterday week*, il y a eu hier huit jours.

yestereve(n) [-,ri:v(ņ)] adv., n. Hier soir.

yestermorn(ing) [-,mɔ:n(iŋ)] adv., n. Hier matin.

yesternight [-,nait] adv., n. La nuit dernière; hier soir.

yesteryear [-,jəːʳ] n., adv. † L'année (*f.*) d'avant; antan *m.*

yet [jet] adv. Encore, jusqu'à présent (thus far); *as yet*, jusqu'ici, jusqu'alors; *she has not yet finished*, elle n'a pas encore fini. ‖ Maintenant, alors (now); *you can't leave just yet*, vous ne pouvez pas partir tout de suite. ‖ Encore maintenant (even now); *there is yet a chance*, il y a encore une chance. ‖ Encore, de plus, en outre (in addition);

yet once more, encore une fois de plus. ‖ Encore, davantage (even); *yet richer*, encore plus riche. ‖ Néanmoins, toutefois, pourtant (nevertheless); *beautiful, yet stupid*, belle mais idiote; *I'll do it yet*, j'y arriverai bien quand même. ‖ *Nor yet*, ni... non plus, ni même... ‖ U. S. D'ailleurs, du reste.
— conj. Toutefois, néanmoins, tout de même (nevertheless). ‖ Cependant, pourtant (however).

yew [ju:] n. BOT. If *m.* ‖ COMM. Bois d'if *m.*

Yid [jid] n. POP. Youpin *s.* (péj.).

Yiddish ['jidiʃ] adj., n. Yiddish *m.*

yield [ji:ld] v. tr. Exhaler, dégager (a scent). ‖ Concéder, accorder, donner (to grant). ‖ Céder, abandonner; *to yield ground*, céder du terrain. ‖ MILIT. Livrer. ‖ AGRIC., FIN. Produire, rapporter (crop, profit). ‖ **To yield up**, abandonner; *to yield oneself up to*, s'abandonner à, se livrer à; *to yield up the ghost*, rendre l'âme.
— v. intr. Céder, fléchir, s'affaisser (*under*, sous) [a weight]. ‖ Céder, accéder (*to*, à); *to yield to the necessities*, se plier aux nécessités. ‖ Etre inférieur (*to*, à); *to yield to nobody in courage*, ne le céder à personne en courage. ‖ AGRIC., FIN. Rapporter.
— n. Fléchissement, affaissement *m.* ‖ AGRIC. Rendement *m.* ‖ FIN. Rapport, rendement *m.* ‖ **Yield-capacity**, n. Productivité *f.* ‖ **Yield-point**, n. Limite de résistance *f.* ‖ **Yield-stress**, n. Résistance élastique *f.*

yielding [-iŋ] adj. Fléchissant, mou (*under*, sous). ‖ Souple, flexible, élastique. ‖ AGRIC., FIN. En plein rendement. ‖ FIG. Souple, accommodant.
— n. See YIELD.

yip [jip] n. U. S. FAM. Rouspétance *f.*
— v. intr. U. S. FAM. Rouspéter.

yippee [ji'pi:] interj. Hourra, hurrah!, youpi!

Y. M. C. A. [,waiemsi:'ei] abbr. *Young Men's Christian Association*, Union chrétienne de jeunes gens, Y. M. C. A.

yob [jɔb], **yobbo** ['jɔbou] (pl. **yobbos** [-z]) n. POP. Loubard, loub, vaurien *m.* (hooligan); rustre *m.* (lout).

yod [jɔd] n. GRAMM. Yod *m.*

yodel ['joudl] v. tr., intr. MUS. Iouler, yodler.
— n. MUS. Ioulement *m.* (act); tyrolienne *f.* (song).

yod(e)ler [-ə*] n. MUS. Chanteur (*s.*) de tyroliennes.

yoga ['jougə] n. Yoga *m.*

yog(h)urt ['jouguət] n. CULIN. Yogourt, yaourt *m.*

yogi ['jougi] n. Yogi *m.*

yo-heave-ho [,jouhi:v'hou] interj. NAUT. Oh! hisse!

yoicks [jɔiks] interj. SPORTS. Taïaut *m.*

yoke [jouk] n. Joug *m.* (frame). ‖ Couple *m.*, paire *f.* (of oxen). ‖ Sommier, mouton *m.* (of bell). ‖ Joug *m.*, palanche *f.* (for carrying pails). ‖ Support de timon *m.* (harness). ‖ Empiècement *m.* (in dressmaking). ‖ ARCHIT. Moise *f.* ‖ ELECTR. Culasse *f.* ‖ TECHN. Joug *m.* (cross-head); chape *f.* (for pipes). ‖ FIG. Joug *m.*; servitude *f.* ‖ **Yoke-elm**, n. BOT. Charme *m.* ‖ **Yoke-fellow**, n. FAM. Compagnon (*m.*) de misère.
— v. tr. Mettre (or) atteler au joug. ‖ TECHN., FIG. Accoupler, unir.
— v. intr. Etre accouplé (*with*, à); *to yoke together*, s'accoupler. ‖ FIG. S'entendre.

yokel ['joukl] n. FAM. Péquenot *m.*

yolk [jouk] n. Jaune d'œuf *m.* (in egg); suint *m.* (in sheep's wool).

yolky [-i] adj. De jaune d'œuf; de suint.

yon(der) ['jɔn(də*)] adv. Là-bas.
— adj. Qui est là-bas, de là-bas.

yonks [jɔŋks] n. pl. FAM. *For yonks*, depuis un bail.

yoo-hoo ['ju:,hu:] interj. Hep!, eh oh!

yore [jɔ:*] adv. *Of yore*, jadis.

you [ju:] pron. pers. Vous (subject and object; sg. and pl.); *with you*, avec vous; *you and I must stay here*, vous et moi devons rester ici. ‖ Tu (familiar form; sg.; subject); te, toi (object); *how are you?*, comment vas-tu? *with you*, avec toi. ‖ On (one); *you can never tell*, on ne sait jamais. ‖ Oh vous!, que vous êtes! (emphatically); *you naughty boy!*, Oh! méchant garçon!

young [jʌŋ] adj. Jeune; *young lady*, jeune fille; *young people*, jeunes gens, jeunes, jeunesse. ‖ Nouveau, commençant (year). ‖ FIG. De jeunesse (hope, love). ‖ FIG. Jeune, novice (immature). ‖ Jeune, vigoureux, plein d'allant (active). ‖ FAM. Petit; *young Smith*, le petit Smith. ‖ **Young-eyed**, adj. Enthousiaste, optimiste.
— n. ZOOL. Petit *m.* (of an animal); *with young*, pleine. ‖ *The young*, les jeunes, la jeunesse.

younger [gə*] adj. comp. See YOUNG. ‖ Cadet (brother). ‖ *The younger*, jeune (after a proper name).

youngish [-iʃ] adj. FAM. Jeunet.

youngling [-liŋ] n. Jeune *s.* ‖ ZOOL. Jeune animal *m.*

youngster [-stə*] n. Adolescent, jeune *m.*

your [jɔ:*,juə*] adj. poss. Votre (sg.); vos (pl.); *your mother*, votre mère; *your parents*, vos parents. ‖ Ton, ta, tes (familiar form); *it's your mother?*, c'est ta mère? ‖ (Ethic); *one of your reformers*, un de ces fameux réformateurs.

yours [jɔ:z,ju:z] pron. poss. Le vôtre, les vôtres (subject); le tien, la tienne, les tiens (familiar form); *yours are better*, ce sont les vôtres (or) les tiens qui sont les mieux. ‖ A vous (object); à toi (familiar form); *a friend of yours*, un de vos amis, un ami à vous, un de tes amis; *that book is yours*, ce livre est à vous (or) à toi. ‖ COMM. Votre honorée (letter). ‖ LOC. *Yours truly*, sincèrement vôtre.

yourself [jɔ:'self, juə'self] (pl. **yourselves**) pron. intensive. Vous-même; toi-même (sg.); vous-mêmes (pl.); *you yourself came*, vous êtes venu vous-même

(or) en personne; tu es venu toi-même. ‖ LOC. *By yourself*, seul.
— pron. reflexive : Vous; te; *you hurt yourself*, vous vous êtes blessé; tu t'es blessé.

youth [ju:θ] n. Jeunesse *f.* (period, quality, state). ‖ Jeune homme *m.* (young man). ‖ Jeunesse *f.*; jeunes *m. pl.* (young people). ‖ **Youth-hostel**, n. Auberge (*f.*) de la jeunesse. ‖ **Youth-hosteller**, n. Usager (*m.*) des auberges de la jeunesse.

youthful [-ful] adj. Jeune. (See YOUNG.) ‖ De jeunesse (of youth). ‖ Neuf, nouveau (new). ‖ Jeune, juvénile, vigoureux, actif (active).

youthfully [-fuli] adv. Comme un jeune, avec jeunesse.

youthfulness [-fulnis] n. Jeunesse *f.* (quality).

yowl [jaul] v. intr. Hurler (with alarm, pain, surprise).
— n. Hurlement *m.*

yo-yo ['jou'jou] n. Yo-yo *m.*

yperite ['i:pərait] n. CHIM., MILIT. Ypérite *f.*

ytterbium [i'tə:biəm] n. CHIM. Ytterbium *m.*

yttrium ['itriəm] n. CHIM. Yttrium *m.*

yucca ['jukə] n. BOT. Yucca *m.*

Yugoslav ['ju:gouslɑ:v] adj., n. GEOGR. Yougoslave *s.*

Yugoslavia ['ju:gou'slɑ:viə] n. GEOGR. Yougoslavie *f.*

yule [ju:l] n. Noël *m.* ‖ **Yule-log**, n. Bûche (*f.*) de Noël. ‖ **Yule-tide**, n. Epoque de Noël *f.*

yummy ['jʌmi] adj. FAM. Vachement bon, délicieux, fameux.

yum-yum [jʌm'jʌm] interj. FAM. Miam-miam!

Y.W.C.A. [,waidʌbelju:si'ei] abbr. *Young Women's Christian Association*, Union chrétienne de jeunes femmes, Y.W.C.A.

ywiss [iwis] adv. † Certainement.

Z

z [zed] U.S. [zi:] n. Z, z *m.*
— adj. TECHN. A z, en Z.

Zaire [zɑ:'iə*] n. GEOGR. Zaïre *m.* (country, river).

Zambezi [zæm'bi:zi] n. GEOGR. Zambèze *m.*

Zambia ['zæmbiə] n. GEOGR. Zambie *f.*

zambo ['zæmbou] n. Métis *m.* (See SAMBO.)

zany ['zeini] adj. Farfelu, cocasse, dingue.
— n. THEATR. Zan(n)i *m.* ‖ FIG. Gugusse, clown *m.*

Zanzibar [,zænzi'bɑ:*] n. GEOGR. Zanzibar *m.*

zap [zæp] v. tr. (1). POP. Assommer, mettre K.-O. (to hit); zigouiller (to kill).
— v. intr. Filer, foncer (to rush).
— interj. Vlan!, schlack!

zeal [zi:l] n. Zèle *m.*; ardeur *f.*; *to make a great show of zeal*, faire du zèle.

Zealand ['zi:lənd] n. GEOGR. Zélande *f.*

zealot ['zelət] n. ECCLES. Zélote *m.* ‖ FIG. Fanatique *s.*

zealotry [-ri] n. ECCLES. Zélotisme *m.* ‖ FIG. Fanatisme *m.*

zealous ['zeləs] adj. Zélé.

zealously [-li] adv. Avec zèle.

zebra ['zi:brə] ZOOL. Zèbre *m.* ‖ **Zebra-crossing**, n. AUTOM. Passage clouté *m.* ‖ **Zebra-marking**, n. Zébrure *f.*

zebu ['zi:bu] n. ZOOL. Zébu *m.*

zed [zed] n. Z *m.*

zee [zi:] n. U.S. Z *m.*

Zen [zen] n. ECCLES. Zen *m.*

zenana [ze'nɑ:nə] n. Harem *m.*

Zend [zend] n. Zend *m.*

zenith ['zeniθ] n. ASTRON. Zénith *m.* ‖ FIG. Comble *m.*
— adj. Zénithal (distance).

zenithal ['zeniθəl] adj. Zénithal.

zephyr ['zefə*] n. Zéphyr *m.* (wind). ‖ COMM. *Zephyr wool*, laine zéphire.

zeppelin ['zepəlin] n. AVIAT. Zeppelin *m.*

zero ['ziərou] n. Zéro *m.* ‖ AVIAT. Altitude zéro *f.*; *at zero level*, au ras du sol, en rase-mottes. ‖ MILIT., FIG. U.S. *Zero hour*, heure H.
— v. tr. *To zero in*, MILIT. U.S. Etre pointé sur.

zest [zest] n. † Zeste *m.* ‖ FIG. Piquant *m.*; *to give zest to*, assaisonner. ‖ FIG. Goût *m.* (for, pour).

Zeus [zju:s] n. Zeus, Jupiter *m.*

zigzag ['zigzəg] n. Zigzag *m.*
— adj., adv. En zigzag.
— v. intr. (1). Zigzaguer.
zillion ['ziljən] n. U. S. FAM. Million, milliard *m.* (fig.) ; masse *f.*
Zimbabwe [zim'bɑ:bwi] n. GEOGR. Zimbabwe *m.*
zinc [ziŋk] n. Zinc *m.* ‖ **Zinc-ointment,** n. MED. Pommade (*f.*) à l'oxyde de zinc. ‖ **Zinc-ware,** n. COMM. Zinguerie *f.* ‖ **Zinc-works,** n. TECHN. Zinguerie *f.* ‖ **Zinc-yellow,** n. CHIM. Chromate de zinc *m.*
— v. tr. Galvaniser (iron) ; zinguer (a roof).
zinciferous [ziŋ'kifərəs] adj. Zincifère.
zincograph ['ziŋkogrɑ:f] n. ARTS. Zincographie, zincogravure *f.* (plate, print).
— v. tr. ARTS. Graver sur zinc.
zincographer [ziŋ'kografə*] n. ARTS. Zincographe *s.*
zincography [-fi] n. ARTS. Zincographie *f.*
zing [ziŋ] n. Sifflement *m.* (of a bullet). ‖ FAM. Allant, punch *m.*
— v. intr. Passer en sifflant.
zingaro ['ziŋgərou] (pl. **zingari** [-ri:]) n. Bohémien *s.* (See GIPSY.)
zinnia ['zinjə] n. BOT. Zinnia *m.*
Zion ['zaiən] n. Sion *f.*
Zionism [-izm] n. Sionisme *m.*
Zionist [-ist] n. Sioniste *s.*
zip [zip] n. Sifflement *m.* (of a bullet) ; bruit de déchirement *m.* (of material). ‖ Fermeture à glissière *f.* ; fermeture Eclair *f.* (nom dép.). ‖ FAM. Allant, brio *m.* ; verve *f.* ‖ **Zip code,** n. U. S. Code postal *m.*
— v. intr. (1). Foncer (*through,* à travers). ‖ *To zip (up),* se fermer par une fermeture Eclair.
— v. tr. *To zip up,* remonter la fermeture Eclair de.
zipper [-ə] n. Fermeture à glissière *f.* ; fermeture Eclair *f.* (nom dép.).
zippy [-i] adj. FAM. Dynamique.
zircon ['zə:kən] n. Zircon *m.*
zirconium [zə'kounjəm] n. CHIM. Zirconium *m.*
zither(n) ['ziθə:(n)] n. MUS. Cithare *f.*
zodiac ['zoudiæk] n. Zodiaque *m.*
zodiacal [zo'daiəkəl] adj. Zodiacal.
zombi ['zombi] n. Zombi *m.* ‖ FAM. Crétin *m.*
zona ['zounə] n. MED. Zona *m.*
zonal [-əl] adj. Zonal.
zone ['zoun] n. † Ceinture *f.* ‖ Zone, région *f.* ‖

MILIT. Zone *f.* ; *battle zone,* zone avancée (or) de combat.
— v. tr. Répartir en zones ; *the town-planners have zoned this district for industry,* les urbanistes ont réservé cette zone à l'industrie.
zoning [-iŋ] adj. De zone.
zoo ['zu:] n. Zoo *m.*
zoochemistry [,zouə'kemistri] n. Zoochimie *f.*
zoographer [zou'ogrəfə*] n. Zoographe *m.*
zoography [-fi] n. Zoographie *f.*
zooid ['zouoid] adj., n. Zooïde *m.*
zoological [,zouə'lodʒikəl] adj. Zoologique.
zoologist [zou'olədʒist] n. Zoologue, zoologiste *s.*
zoology [-dʒi] n. Zoologie *f.*
zoom [zu:m] v. intr. Vrombir (motor). ‖ *To zoom past, off,* passer, partir en trombe. ‖ Grimper (prices). ‖ AVIAT. Monter en chandelle. ‖ CINEM. Faire un zoom.
— n. Vrombissement *m.* ‖ AVIAT. Chandelle *f.* ‖ TECHN. *Zoom lens,* zoom.
zoomorphism [,zouə'mo:fizm] n. Zoomorphisme *m.*
zoophyte ['zouəfait] n. Zoophyte *m.*
zooplankton [,zouə'plæŋktən] n. Zooplancton *m.*
zooplasty [,zouə'plæsti] n. MED. Zooplastie *f.*
zootomy [zou'otəmi] n. Zootomie *f.*
zoot-suit ['zout-'sju:t] n. Costume zazou *m.*
zoot-suiter [-ə*] n. U. S. Zazou *m.*
Zoroastrian [,zorou'æstriən] adj., n. Zoroastrien *s.*
Zoroastrianism [-izm] n. Zoroastrianisme *m.*
zouave [zwɑ:v] n. MILIT. Zouave *m.*
zounds [zu:nds] interj. Sacrebleu !
zucchini [tsu:'ki:ni] n. U. S. BOT., CULIN. Courgette *f.*
— N. B. Deux pluriels : zucchini, zucchinis.
Zulu ['zu:lu] adj., n. GEOGR. Zoulou *m.*
Zululand [-lænd] n. GEOGR. Zoulouland *m.*
Zwinglian ['zwiŋgliən] adj., n. Zwinglien *m.*
zygodactyl [,zaigo'dæktil] adj., n. ZOOL. Zygodactyle *m.*
zygoma [zai'goumə] (pl. **zygomata** [-ətə]) n. MED. Zygoma *m.*
zygomatic [,zaigo'mætik] adj. MED. Zygomatique.
zygote ['zaigout] n. MED. Zygote *m.*
zyme [zaim] n. Enzyme *m.* ; diastase *f.*
zymosis [zai'mousis] n. Fermentation *f.*
zymotic [zai'motik] adj. MED. Zymotique.

– Édition 1984 –
Imprimerie Berger-Levrault, Nancy. – N° 779242.
Dépôt légal : juillet 1981 – N° 12099.
Imprimé en France (Printed in France).
451201 C avril 1984.